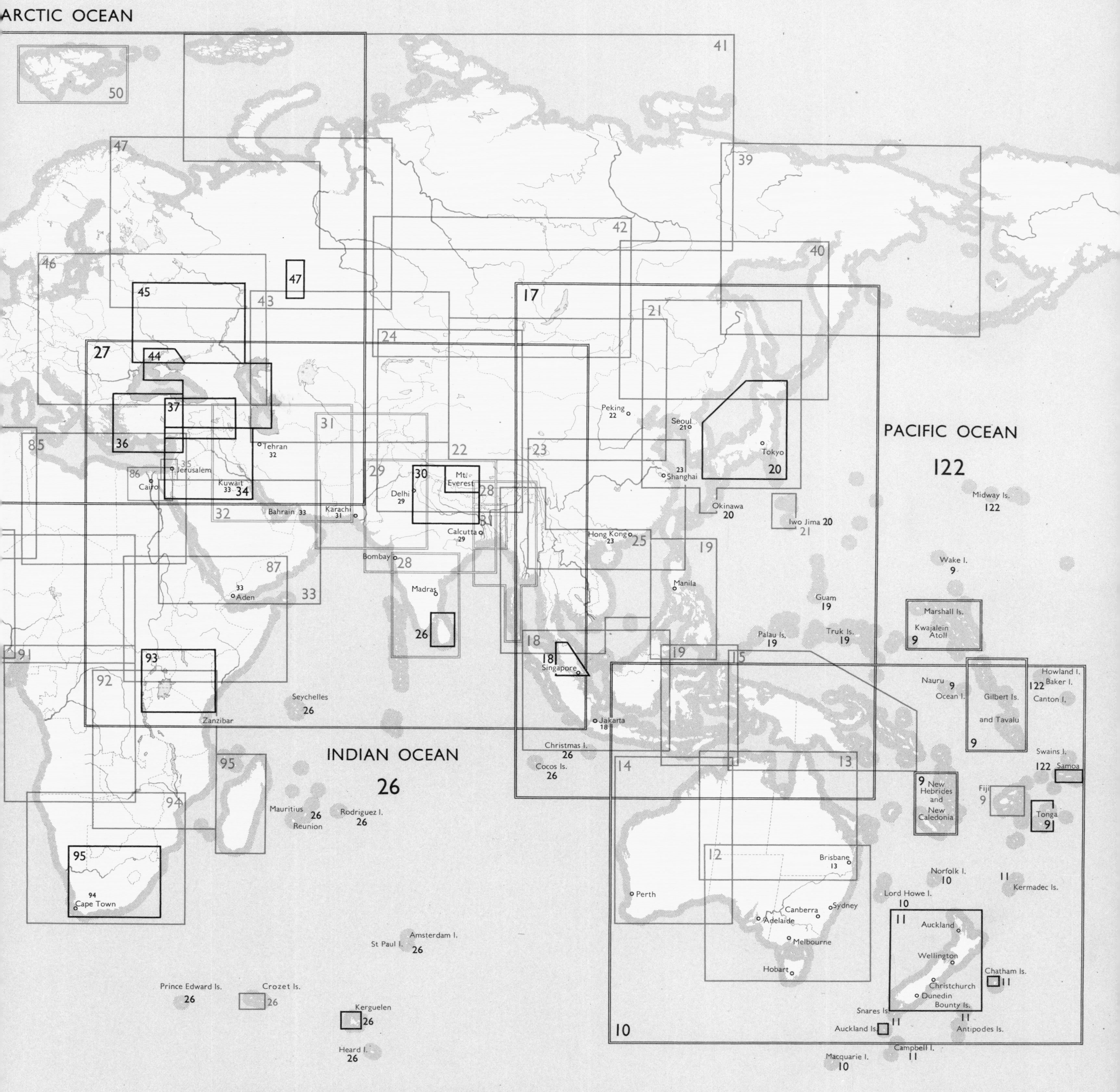

KEY TO MAP PLATES

excluding larger scales in North America and Europe (*see other end-paper*)

97 1 : 10 000 000 & smaller	30 1 : 2 500 000 1 : 2 000 000
94 1 : 5 500 000 1 : 5 000 000	35 1 : 1 250 000 & larger
28 1 : 4 000 000	Inset maps of islands, cities, etc. are named

GENERAL MAPS

Plate	
9	The Orient
16	Eurasia
38	U.S.S.R.
73	Mediterranean & Africa
114	The Americas
117	South America

WORLD MAPS

Plate	
2	Physiography
3	Oceanography
4	Climatology
5	Vegetation
6	Mankind
7	Political
8	Air Routes

Pages	
	Introductory Section
xviii	Minerals
xx	Energy
xxii	Food
xxiv	Climate & Food Potential

THE TIMES

ATLAS OF THE WORLD

COMPREHENSIVE EDITION

ATLAS OF

COMPREHENSIVE EDITION

THE TIMES

THE WORLD

TIMES BOOKS
LONDON
In collaboration with John Bartholomew & Son Limited

ACKNOWLEDGEMENTS

The publishers would like to express their particular gratitude to Mr John C. Bartholomew and to Mr H. A. G. Lewis, O.B.E., Geographical Consultant to *The Times*, for their valuable contributions to the preparation of this Atlas. Times Books Limited and John Bartholomew & Son Limited would also like to extend their grateful thanks to the following:

American Geographical Society, New York, U.S.A.
Professor D. H. K. Amiran, The Hebrew University, Jerusalem, Israel
Mr David L. Rex, Arabian American Oil Company, Ras Tanura, Saudi Arabia
Director of National Mapping, Department of National Development, Canberra, Australia
Dr Randall Baker, University of East Anglia, Norwich
Mr R. Beer, Institute of Offshore Engineering, Heriot-Watt University, Edinburgh
Institut Géographique Militaire, Brussels, Belgium
Instituto Brasileiro de Geografia, Rio de Janeiro, Brazil
The British Petroleum Company Ltd., London
Professor H. A. Brück, lately Astronomer Royal for Scotland, Edinburgh
Dr R. C. Burgess, University of Edinburgh
Surveys and Mapping Branch, Department of Energy, Mines and Resources, Ottawa, Canada
Ceskoslovenské Akademie Ved, Prague, Czechoslovakia
Dr C. M. Clapperton, University of Aberdeen
Mr L. S. Cobley, University of Edinburgh
Columbia University Press, New York, U.S.A.
Kongelig Dansk Geodætisk Institut, Copenhagen, Denmark
Mr John C. Dewdney, University of Durham
Professor P. McL. D. Duff, University of Strathclyde
Mr E. W. Entwhistle, University of Nottingham
Esselte Map Service, Stockholm, Sweden
Dr M. W. Feast, Director, South African Astronomical Observatory, Cape Town
Professor C. A. Fisher, School of Oriental & African Studies, University of London
Food & Agriculture Organisation of the United Nations, Rome, Italy
Le Directeur Général, Institut Géographique National, Paris, France
French Railways, London
Freytag-Berndt und Artaria, Vienna, Austria
Mr P. J. M. Geelan, and the Permanent Committee on Geographical Names, London
General Drafting Company Inc., Convent Station, New Jersey, U.S.A.
Institute of Geological Sciences, Herstmonceux, Sussex
Global Seismology Unit, Institute of Geological Sciences, Edinburgh
Dr R. Habel, VEB Hermann Haack, Geographisch-Kartographische Anstalt, Gotha, East Germany
E. Hausman, Carta, The Israel Map and Publishing Company Ltd., Jerusalem
Hunting Surveys Limited, Boreham Wood
The High Commission of India, London
Survey of India, Dehra Dun, Uttar Pradesh, India
Embassy of the Republic of Indonesia, London
International Atomic Energy Agency, Vienna, Austria
International Hydrographic Bureau, Monaco
International Road Federation, London
Iran National Geographic Organisation, Tehran
Iranian Embassy, London
Embassy of the Republic of Iraq, London
State of Israel Department of Surveys, Tel-Aviv, Israel
Survey of Kenya, Nairobi, Kenya
Ir. Salmon Kodijat, Directorate of City and Regional Planning, Jakarta, Indonesia
Mr P. Laffitte, Ecole des Mines, Paris, France
Dr R. I. Lawless, Centre for Middle Eastern & Islamic Studies, University of Durham
Dr D. H. McIntosh, University of Edinburgh
Dr D. N. McMaster, University of Edinburgh
The Mauritius Institute, Port Louis, Mauritius
Professor R. E. H. Mellor, University of Aberdeen
Dr W. H. Menard, Jr., Scripps Institution of Oceanography, La Jolla, California, U.S.A.
The Meteorological Office, Bracknell, Berkshire
Mexican Embassy, London
National Aeronautical and Space Administration, Washington, D.C., U.S.A.
National Geographic Society, Washington, D.C., U.S.A.
Department of Lands and Survey, Wellington, New Zealand
Nigerian Land and Survey Department, Lagos, Nigeria
Norges Geografiske Oppmåling, Oslo, Norway
Nuclear Engineering International, London
Dr R. H. Osborne, University of Nottingham
Office of the High Commission for Pakistan, London
Dr R. Passmore, University of Edinburgh
Dr John Paxton, Editor, *The Stateman's Year Book*, London
Instituto Geografico Militar, Lima, Peru
Ministerio de Transportes y Comunicaciones, Lima, Peru
Petroleum Information Bureau, London
Petroleum Press Service, London
Petroleum Publishing Co., Tulsa, Oklahoma, U.S.A.
Bureau of Coast and Geodetic Survey, Manila, Republic of the Philippines
S. R. Junta Antónoma de Estradas, Direcção dos Serviços de Exploração, Lisbon, Portugal
Centro de Geografia do Ultramar, Lisbon, Portugal
Instituto Geografico e Cadastral, Lisbon, Portugal
Surveyer General, Salisbury, Rhodesia
Dr B. B. Roberts, Antarctic Place-Names Committee, London
Dr C. J. Robertson, University of Edinburgh
Mr P. Rouveyrol, Bureau de Recherches Géologiques et Minières, Paris, France
Royal Geographic Society, London
Royal Scottish Geographical Society, Edinburgh
Mr John Sallnow, School of Environmental Sciences, Plymouth
Schmidt Unit, Royal Observatory, Edinburgh
Scientific American, New York
National Library of Scotland, Edinburgh
Scottish Development Department, Edinburgh
Mr Theodore Shabad, *The New York Times*
Survey Department, Singapore
Automobile Association of South Africa, Johannesburg, Republic of South Africa
The Trigonometrical Survey Office, Pretoria, Republic of South Africa
Instituto Geografico y Catastral, Madrid, Spain
Dr H. J. Störig, Lexikon-Redaktion, Munich
Surveys & Mapping Division, Dar-es-Salaam, United Republic of Tanzania
Professor P. H. Temple, University of Birmingham
The Information Service of Thailand, London
Touring Club Italiano and Dr S. Toniolo, Milan, Italy
General Directorate of Highways, Ankara, Turkey
Ministry of National Defence, Ankara, Turkey
Turkish Embassy, London
Survey, Lands and Mines Department, Entebbe, Uganda
Foreign and Commonwealth Office, London
Hydrographic Department, Ministry of Defence, London
Director-General, Ordnance Survey, Southampton
Directorate of Overseas Surveys, Tolworth, Surrey
The Controller, H. M. Stationery Office, London
Office of the Geographer, Department of State, Washington, D.C., U.S.A.
Defense Mapping Agency, Aerospace Center, St Louis, Missouri, U.S.A.
Defense Mapping Agency, Hydrographic Center, Washington, D.C., U.S.A.
Defense Mapping Agency, Topographic Center, Washington, D.C., U.S.A.
United States Board on Geographic Names, Washington, D.C., U.S.A.
The United States Geological Survey, Washington, D.C., U.S.A.
Academy of Sciences of the U.S.S.R. and the National Atlas Committee, Moscow, U.S.S.R.
Mr P.-E. Victor, Expéditions Polaires Françaises, Paris, France
Professor R. G. Ward, The Australian National University, Canberra Australia
Sir Maurice Yonge, Edinburgh
Surveyor General, Ministry of Lands and Natural Resources, Lusaka, Zambia

Maps prepared by
John Bartholomew & Son Limited, Edinburgh

Printed in Great Britain by
John Bartholomew & Son Limited, Edinburgh

Editorial direction
John C. Bartholomew
P. J. M. Geelan
H. A. G. Lewis OBE
Paul Middleton
Barry Winkleman

Index set by
Computaprint Limited, London

Index printed by
The Anchor Press Limited, Tiptree

Bound in
Holland

Published in Great Britain by
Times Books Limited
Times Books is the book publishing subsidiary of
Times Newspapers Limited, New Printing House Square,
Grays Inn Road, London WC1X 8EZ

Copyright © 1967, 1968, 1972, 1973, 1974, 1975, 1977, 1978, 1980 by
John Bartholomew & Son Limited and Times Books Limited

All rights reserved. No part of this publication
may be reproduced or transmitted in any form
or by any means without the permission
of the publisher.
Comprehensive Edition first published 1967
Second Edition 1968
Third Edition for U.S.A. only 1971
Fourth Edition 1972
Reprinted with corrections 1973
Reprinted 1974
Reprinted 1975
Fifth Edition 1975
Reprinted with revisions 1977
Reprinted 1978
Sixth Edition 1980

ISBN 0 7230 0235 5

British Library Cataloguing in Publication Data
'The Times' atlas of the world. – Comprehensive ed.
6th ed.
1. Atlases, British
912 G1019

CONTENTS

The Maps

Dedicated by gracious permission to
Her Majesty Queen Elizabeth II

FOREWORD

There is a measure of truth in the saying that map-making is older than agriculture. Orientation was as essential to the pre-historic hunter as was observation of the length of the day or a knowledge of the coming seasons. If the definition of a map embraces any depiction of terrain features, whether traced in sand or scratched on stone or bone, then cartography must be reckoned among the most ancient communications, preceding any system of writing by millennia.

Palaeolithic hunters with no written language nor a concept of numbers beyond two or three, may yet be adept at setting out the topographic features pertaining to their mode of life. Pacific islanders surrounded by open seas displayed their cartographic sense in charts made from ribs of palm leaves arranged in a lattice to indicate the direction of prevailing currents and winds, with islands indicated by sea-shells.

Considering that a map is so ancient a human creation, the cartographic historian could be expected to have at hand a rich legacy of material. This is far from the case. No map prepared by the Romans has survived. A single twelfth-century copy of a route map once the property of Charlemagne's counsellor, is the sole example of the type of map which served the Roman legions and the administration of this Empire. Except for the maps of Ptolemy, prepared in the second century AD, not a single Greek map has survived, in original or in copy. From the Carthaginians and Phoenicians not a vestige of a map remains.

The situation is similar in China, where surveying and mapping flourished at an early date. In the second century AD a thriving cartographic office worked to directives based on principles laid down four centuries earlier. Almost every major settlement had its maps, yet the oldest extant maps, until a few years ago, were engravings on stone prepared in AD 1137. Then the discovery of two maps of about 168 BC took history back 1,300 years to confirm the highly developed nature of Chinese cartography at that remote period.

Two maps which have survived from 1300 BC show the importance of mapping to Mesopotamia and Egypt where, as in China, astronomy, surveying and cartography were intimately associated with a highly developed agriculture. Almost three thousand years passed before comparable maps were prepared in western Europe. Maps are by nature utilitarian, part of the equipment of the tax-collector, the agricultural planner, the landowner, and as such are working documents which, like tools, are expendable. For this reason, perhaps, few medieval maritime charts have survived from the untold numbers which must have been drawn.

It is not until the time of the Greeks that we find any evidence of maps like the modern atlas, serving as a compendium of geographical knowledge, furthering the ends of scholarship as well as the purposes of administration.

For a brief period, mapping the world flourished as a science, but it was then removed from its eminence by the Romans, who abandoned it, together with science in general, in favour of the simpler basic needs of communication and administration. The theory of the flat Earth was reinstated, and was to remain as the vulgar companion of the spherical Earth, which was supported by only a select band of scholars, until the end of the fifteenth century.

Ptolemy's *Geography*, together with certain other Greek works, was carefully preserved by the devotees of the Nestorian church. Persecuted in the sixth century by the Byzantines, their fellow Christians, they migrated from western Asia to south-west Persia and formed a nucleus of learning which was to blossom into the centre of Islamic science. Their scholars later moved to Damascus and finally, in the ninth century, settled in Baghdad. By this tenuous route Ptolemy's *Geography* came through Islam into the hands of the Moorish rulers in Spain and so reached western Europe. It was translated into Latin in Florence in 1400, and in 1478 became the first of the classical Greek works to be printed.

For centuries maps had been drawn to represent the Earth as a disk with land arbitrarily disposed around the Mediterranean, the Black Sea, and the rivers Nile and Don. The twenty-seven maps which originally accompanied Ptolemy's *Geography* treated the Earth as a sphere. They furnished the great navigators with the geographic data for their great voyages of discovery. Vasco da Gama, Columbus, Cabot, Amerigo Vespucci, Magellan and Drake all owed much to the fortuitous chain of circumstances which had brought them this basic navigational aid. Their debt was repaid by the details of new lands and fresh discoveries with which they supplemented and corrected the maps passed on to their successors.

In 1507 the name America was added to a world map by Waldseemüller, in honour of Amerigo Vespucci. Doubt as to whether the newly discovered lands were part of Asia was finally resolved in 1522 by the handful of survivors of the proud fleet which three years before had set out under Magellan to circumnavigate the world.

The first modern atlas was published in 1570 under the title *Theatrum Orbis Terrarum* by Abraham Ortelius, a Fleming. Two years later, Lafreri in Rome published a set of maps adding the figure of Atlas the Titan holding up the world, a device repeated on the collection of maps by Mercator – whose vernacular name was Gerard Kremer – which were published posthumously in 1594. The word atlas thus came to be applied to a collection of maps.

For the next century cartography developed as fresh geographical knowledge was acquired. Picard in France made the first measurements of the Earth using a theodolite. His radius, 6,370 km (3,690 miles), about 8 km (5 miles) too small, was the value used by Sir Isaac Newton in his calculations of the flattening of the Earth at the poles.

The eighteenth century was a period of development in surveying techniques, reflecting a general advance in all the sciences, but the innovations had little effect on cartography until early in the following century. Principles then adopted remained essentially the same until the second world war.

Towards the end of the nineteenth century *The Times*, in its first major venture into the cartographic field, enlisted the aid of German cartographers and printers in the preparation of an atlas. It appeared in 1895, and remained a standard work of reference until the first world war, running to several impressions. Of its 117 map plates, half were devoted to Europe, still pre-eminent both politically and economically at that time.

With the advent of peace Lord Northcliffe, then the proprietor of *The Times*, set in train the preparation of a new atlas, remarking that 'a world re-made must be a world re-mapped'. On this occasion the cartography and printing of the maps were entrusted to the firm of John Bartholomew & Son, with whom *The Times* has collaborated ever since. Entitled *The Times Survey Atlas of the World*, the new atlas of 112 double-page maps apportioned one-third to Europe, an indication that the world was indeed being re-shaped. The Index-Gazetteer was widely acclaimed and became a standard and authoritative work of reference on place-names of the world.

Once more a world war re-cast the territories of the

world. A new atlas was required, but it was not until the turn of the mid-century that the third *Times Atlas* was initiated. This was the most splendid of the series, a five-volume work entitled the *Mid-Century Edition of The Times Atlas of the World*. Europe occupied a smaller proportion of space than in its forerunners; the colonial era was coming to an end; the number of member states of the United Nations was steadily augmented as the world took up its new shape.

This was also a period when new methods of surveying, coupled with the use of aerial photography, were returning a harvest of maps, of all scales and types, deployed in the service of reconstruction and development. The blank areas of the world were becoming filled. The face of the world was changing at a prodigious rate. Up-dating and publication of the five-volume atlas invoked complex problems which led to the decision to publish the same maps in a single-volume atlas to be called the *Comprehensive Edition*. The new work appeared in 1967. The present volume is the sixth revised version. The Atlas has been translated into a German edition (1970) and a Dutch edition (1978), and a Concise version was first published in 1972.

Before the last volume of the *Mid-Century Edition* was issued the Space Age had dawned. Within four years satellite observation showed the Earth to be flattened at the poles by 42·8 kilometres (26·6 miles). Ever since Newton's estimate in the eighteenth century a reliable figure had been sought. Next was the requirement to measure the equatorial diameter which had still to be determined. Here again, special satellites provided the answer. There had until then been no way of measuring accurately from continent to continent across the oceans.

Satellites now play a part in weather-reporting, communications and navigation. Their future potential for mapping was demonstrated by the Orbiter space-craft circling the Moon to send back photographs of the Near and the Far Side to enable the whole to be mapped to reveal details of the part we can never see from Earth.

Yet these were just the first tentative steps into space. With the deployment of Earth Resources Satellites there is an opportunity for cooperation in a global sense to help solve collectively the enormous problems which confront the human race, now in the early stages of a population explosion which is the most awesome challenge that has ever confronted mankind.

From the recent advances in astronomy, cosmology has received a new impetus. The history and destiny of the universe is gradually unfolding. Life itself may possibly be shown to originate in molecules formed in space. Black holes in space are the beginnings of a new universe for which the physical laws have yet to be found.

No less dramatic are the discoveries in geophysics, once thought of as an adjunct to geology mainly concerned with the quest for oil, but now sharing a golden age with astronomy. Plate tectonics have laid bare many secrets of the geological past, but of even greater importance is the disclosure of the processes by which minerals are being generated. Further studies on the quantities formed will define the rate of extraction permissible if succeeding generations are not to inherit a sadly depleted Earth.

An atlas is a series of compromises in the choice of area, scale and projection of the maps included in it. Rigid uniformity in scales and projections, though desirable in theory, can provide undesirable results. The bulk can be increased or decreased excessively; less populous areas may receive over-generous treatment at the expense of the densely populated.

While aiming at a standard range of scales for the maps in *The Times Atlas*, the publishers have departed from the principle where a special scale best suits a particular area. Similarly, a variety of projections has been used. The surface of a spherical Earth cannot be transferred to a flat sheet of paper without some modification of shape or direction any more than it is possible to remove the peel from an orange and lay it out flat and unbroken. The reverse is equally impossible: an orange cannot be wrapped in a flat sheet of paper without cuts or folds. Map projections are the means by which the round Earth is converted into a flat map.

In this atlas, as in those which have preceded it, the Index-Gazetteer is an important feature. It contains more than 200,000 names, stored on magnetic tape and subsequently up-dated by computer. Each entry is checked against the maps to verify spellings and coordinates. For reasons of economy it has long been the custom for atlases to dispense with coordinates of latitude and longitude, reference being given by plate number and a simplified grid system indicating where the name is to be located. *The Times Atlas* has a similar reference system but the latitudes and longitudes have been retained so that locations may be more precisely defined and also related to other maps or documents. 'Where is it?' is the question which most often prompts reference to an atlas. The latitudes and longitudes allow positions to be defined to within about half a mile.

Locating a place is often easier than spelling its name. Of the many problems associated with atlases few surpass the complexities of place-names. International standardisation has not yet resolved the manifold problems. The various ways in which the letters of the Latin alphabet are pronounced leads to a variety of spellings when non-Latin alphabet scripts are transcribed. An added difficulty is the widespread use of conventional names in one country for the names in another country.

Place-names have been turned into the Latin alphabet by systems agreed jointly by the British Permanent Committee on Geographical Names and the United States Board on Geographical Names. English conventional names of important places have been added throughout the Atlas where space permits.

In this edition names in Mainland China are given in their Pinyin spellings. For many years the question of Pinyin versus Wade-Giles has been kept under review. Since the *Times Atlas* contains more Chinese names than any other world atlas the decision to adopt Pinyin was not made without considering factors which included the quantity of reference material existing in both systems. The reader is referred to page 5 of the index section for further details.

In recent years much political significance has been attached to the manner in which international boundaries are depicted and the way names are spelled in atlases. The position of *The Times* as publishers of this and all other atlases has been stated repeatedly and unequivocally. To attempt to judge the rights and wrongs of territorial disputes is beyond the function of the publishers of an atlas. The portrayal of boundaries and spelling of place-names in such areas must not be taken as implying approval by *The Times* of the political status of the territories. Neither must it be inferred that *The Times* propagates the views of the government of the United Kingdom, the United States of America or any other nation. In its atlases *The Times* aims to show the territorial situation obtaining at the time of publication without regard to the *de jure* situation in contentious areas or the rival claims of contending parties. The aim has always been to inform, to strive for accuracy and to be as up to date as possible. To show on a map a situation which does not exist on the ground would be to render a disservice to those – the scholar, the traveller and the general reader – on whose shelves it is hoped this atlas will find a place.

STATES, TERRITORIES & PRINCIPAL ISLANDS OF THE WORLD

Name [Plate] and *Description*	Sq. km	Sq. miles	Population	
Abu Dhabi, *see United Arab Emirates*				
Afghanistan [31]	650,088	251,000	17,855,000	1978
Capital: Kabul				
Ajman, *see United Arab Emirates*				
Albania [83]	28,752	11,101	2,616,000	1977
Capital: Tirana				
Aleutian Islands [113]	17,666	6,821	6,011	1970
Territory of U.S.A.				
Algeria [88]	2,381,731	919,591	18,515,000	1978
Capital: Algiers				
American Samoa [10]	197	76	34,000	1977
Unincorporated Territory of U.S.A.				
Andorra [75]	453	175	29,000	1977
Capital: Andorra la Vella				
Angola [91]	1,246,694	481,351	6,761,000	1976
Capital: Luanda				
Anguilla [116]	91	35	6,600	1977
U.K. Associated State				
Antigua [116]	443	171	72,000	1977
U.K. Associated State				
Argentina [121]	2,776,643	1,072,067	26,393,000	1978
Capital: Buenos Aires				
Aruba [116]	189	73	62,288	1976
Self-governing Island of Netherlands Antilles				
Ascension [96]	88	34	996	1977
Island Dependency of St Helena				
Australia [10]	7,686,855	2,967,909	14,215,000	1978
Capital: Canberra				
Commonwealth Nation				
Australian Capital Territory (Canberra) [12]	2,432	939	197,622*	1976
Federal Territory				
New South Wales [12] *State*	801,428	309,433	4,777,103*	1976
Northern Territory [13] *Territory*	1,347,520	520,280	97,090*	1976
Queensland [13] *State*	1,727,523	667,000	2,037,197*	1976
South Australia [12] *State*	984,378	380,070	1,244,756*	1976
Tasmania [12] *State*	68,332	26,383	402,866*	1976
Victoria [12] *State*	227,619	87,884	3,646,981*	1976
Western Australia [14] *State*	2,527,623	975,920	1,144,857*	1976
Australian Antarctic Territory, The [123]	6,044,063	2,333,624	*No permanent population*	
Dependency of Australia				
Austria [65]	83,848	32,374	7,509,000	1978
Capital: Vienna (Wien)				
Burgenland [65] *Province*	3,966	1,531	266,500	1977
Kärnten (Carinthia) [65] *Province*	1,533	3,681	528,300	1977
Niederösterreich (Lower Austria) [65] *Prov.*	19,171	7,402	1,381,800	1977
Oberösterreich (Upper Austria) [65] *Prov.*	11,972	4,625	1,241,500	1977
Salzburg [65] *City with province status*	7,154	2,762	425,800	1977
Steiermark (Styria) [65] *Province*	16,386	6,327	1,189,800	1977
Tirol [65] *Province*	12.647	4,883	575,300	1977
Vorarlberg [65] *Province*	2,601	1,004	294,500	1977
Wien (Vienna) [65] *City with province status*	414	160	1,614,800	1977
Azores [88]	2,344	905	292,200*	1975
Island Districts of Portugal				
Bahamas [116]	11,406	4,404	225,000	1978
Capital: Nassau. Commonwealth Nation				
Bahrain [33]	598	231	267,000	1977
Capital: Manama				
Balearic Islands [77]	5,014	1,936	621,925	1976
Island Province of Spain				
Bangladesh [31]	142,776	55,126	84,655,000	1978
Capital: Dacca				
Commonwealth Nation				
Barbados [116]	430	166	254,000	1977
Capital: Bridgetown				
Commonwealth Nation				
Basutoland, *see Lesotho*				
Bear Island (Bjørnøya) [49]	176	68	*n/a*	
Island of Svalbard, Norway				
Bechuanaland, *see Botswana*				
Belgium [61]	30,512	11,781	9,837,000	1977
Capital: Brussels				
Belize [115]	22,965	8,867	149,000	1977
Capital: Belmopan				
Benin [89]	115,763	44,696	3,377,000	1978
Capital: Porto Novo				
Bermuda [96]	55	21	57,000	1977
Self-governing U.K. Dependent Territory				
Bhutan [29]	46,620	18,000	1,232,000	1977
Capital: Thimbu				
Bjørnøya, *see Bear Island*				
Bolivia [120]	1,098,575	424,162	6,113,000	1978
Capital: La Paz				
Bonaire [116]	288	111	8,845	1976
Self-governing Island of Netherlands Antilles				
Bonin Islands [122]	104	40	200	1970
Islands of Japan				
Bophuthatswana, *see South Africa*				
Borneo, *Island of East Indies, see Sabah, Sarawak, Brunei, Kalimantan*				
Botswana [94]	574,978	222,000	726,000	1978
Capital: Gaborone				
Commonwealth Nation				
Bougainville Island [15]	10,619	4,100	77,880*	1970
Part of Papua New Guinea				
Brazil [114]	8,511,968	3,286,487	115,397,000	1978
Capital: Brasília				
Acre [120] *State*	152,589	58,915	264,000	1977
Alagoas [117] *State*	27,731	10,707	1,872,700	1977
Amapá [117] *Federal Territory*	140,276	54,161	154,300	1977
Amazonas [119] *State*	1,564,445	604,035	1,151,600	1977
Bahia [118] *State*	561,025	216,613	8,849,500	1977
Ceará [117] *State*	148,015	57,149	5,409,000	1977
Distrito Federal [118] *Federal District*	5,815	2,245	*Population included with Goiás*	
Espírito Santo [118] *State*	45,597	17,605	1,776,500	1977
Fernando de Noronha [117]	26	10	1,241*	1970
Federal Territory				
Goiás [118] *State*	642,092	247,913	4,694,200	1977
Guanabara [118] *State*	1,357	524	4,251,918*	1970
Maranhão [117] *State*	328,662	126,897	3,470,500	1977
Mato Grosso[1] [118] *State*	1,231,551	475,504	2,190,900	1977
Minas Gerais [118] *State*	587,172	226,708	12,985,000	1977
Pará [117] *State*	1,248,044	481,872	2,710,900	1977
Paraíba [117] *State*	56,371	21,765	2,785,300	1977
Paraná [118] *State*	199,554	77,048	9,145,700	1977
Pernambuco [117] *State*	98,280	37,946	6,141,000	1977
Piauí [117] *State*	250,934	96,886	2,109,600	1977
Rio de Janeiro [118] *State*	42,911	16,568	11,019,200	1977
Rio Grande do Norte [117] *State*	53,015	20,469	1,972,900	1977
Rio Grande do Sul [121] *State*	282,182	108,951	7,794,500	1977
Rondônia [120] *Federal Territory*	243,045	93,840	153,100	1977
Roraima [119] *Federal Territory*	230,105	88,844	51,300	1977
Santa Catarina [118] *State*	95,985	37,060	3,553,400	1977
São Paulo [118] *State*	247,898	95,714	21,921,900	1977
Sergipe [118] *State*	21,994	8,492	1,031,300	1977
British Antarctic Territory [123]	1,553,994	600,000	*No permanent population*	
U.K. Dependent Territory				
British Guiana, *see Guyana*				
British Indian Ocean Territory [26]	60	23	*No permanent population*	
U.K. Dependent Territory				
British Virgin Islands [116]	153	59	12,000	1977
U.K. Dependent Territory				
Brunei [18]	5,765	2,226	190,000	1977
Commonwealth State				
Bulgaria [83]	110,911	42,823	8,814,000	1978
Capital: Sofia				
Burma [25]	678,031	261,789	32,205,000	1978
Capital: Rangoon				
Burundi [92]	27,731	10,707	3,966,000	1977
Capital: Bujumbura				
Cambodia [25]	181,035	69,898	8,606,000	1977
Capital: Phnom Penh				
Cameroon [90]	475,499	183,591	7,914,000	1977
Capital: Yaoundé				
Canada [97]	9,976,147	3,851,809	23,644,800	1979
Capital: Ottawa				
Commonwealth Nation				
Alberta [101] *Province*	661,186	255,285	1,950,300	1978
British Columbia [101] *Province*	948,597	366,255	2,530,200	1978
Manitoba [98] *Province*	651,901	251,700	1,032,400	1978
New Brunswick [98] *Province*	73,437	28,354	695,000	1978
Newfoundland [97] *Province*	404,518	156,185	568,900	1978
Northwest Territories [97] *Territory*	3,379,686	1,304,903	43,500	1978
Nova Scotia [98] *Province*	55,491	21,425	841,200	1978
Ontario [97] *Province*	1,068,583	412,582	8,443,800	1978
Prince Edward Island [98] *Province*	5,657	2,184	122,000	1978
Quebec [97] *Province*	1,540,681	594,860	6,285,000	1978
Saskatchewan [97] *Province*	651,901	251,700	947,100	1978
Yukon Territory [101] *Territory*	536,325	207,076	21,700	1978
Canal Zone, *see Panama*				
Canary Islands [96]	7,273	2,808	1,138,801*	1970
Island Provinces of Spain				
Cape Verde [89]	4,033	1,557	306,000	1977
Capital: Praia				
Caroline Islands, *see Pacific Islands, Trust Territory of the*				
Cayman Islands [116]	259	100	14,000	1976
U.K. Dependent Territory				
Celebes (Sulawesi) [19]	189,036	72,987	8,964,000	1974
Island Provinces of Indonesia				
Central African Republic [90]	622,996	240,540	2,610,000	1974
Capital: Bangui				
Ceylon, *see Sri Lanka*				
Chad [90]	1,270,994	490,733	4,309,000	1978
Capital: N'Djamena				
Channel Islands [56]	194	75	126,000	1977
British Crown Dependency				
Alderney	8	3	1,785	1975
Guernsey	65	25	54,256	1977
Jersey	116	45	74,382	1977
Sark	5	2	604	1976
Chile [114]	756,943	292,257	10,656,000	1977
Capital: Santiago				
China [17]	9,560,948	3,691,500	865,677,000	1977
Capital: Peking (Beijing)				
Anhui (Anhwei) [23] *Province*	139,911	54,020	45,000,000	1976
Beijing (Peking) [22] *Municipality*	8,770	3,386	8,000,000	1976
Fujian (Fukien) [23] *Province*	123,102	47,530	20,000,000	1976

[1] In 1979 a new state, Mato Grosso do Sul, was created with an estimated population of 1,200,000

n/a indicates that no reliable figure is available
An asterisk (*) indicates that the population figure relates to a census

Name [Plate] and *Description*	Sq. km	Sq. miles	Population	
Gansu (Kansu) [23] *Province*	366,484	141,500	18,000,000	1976
Guangdong (Kwangtung) [23] *Province*	231,390	89,340	53,000,000	1976
Guangxi (Kwangsi) [23] *Autonomous Region*	220,408	85,100	31,000,000	1976
Guizhou (Kweichow) [23] *Province*	173,996	67,180	24,000,000	1976
Hebei (Hopeh) [22] *Province*	202,693	78,260	47,000,000	1976
Heilongjiang (Heilungkiang) [21] *Province*	463,608	179,000	32,000,000	1976
Henan (Honan) [23] *Province*	167,026	64,489	60,000,000	1976
Hubei (Hupeh) [23] *Province*	187,515	72,400	40,000,000	1976
Hunan (Hunan) [23] *Province*	210,488	81,270	40,000,000	1976
Jiangsu (Kiangsu) [23] *Province*	102,201	39,460	55,000,000	1976
Jiangxi (Kiangsi) [23] *Province*	164,801	63,630	28,000,000	1976
Jilin (Kirin) [21] *Province*	186,997	72,200	23,000,000	1976
Liaoning (Liaoning) [22] *Province*	150,996	58,300	33,000,000	1976
Nei Monggol Zizhiqu (Inner Mongolia) [22] *Autonomous Region*	1,177,513	454,640	8,000,000	1976
Ningxia (Ningsia) [22] *Autonomous Region*	66,407	25,640	3,000,000	1976
Qinghai (Chinghai) [24] *Province*	721,001	278,380	3,000,000	1976
Shaanxi (Shensi) [22] *Province*	195,803	75,600	26,000,000	1976
Shandong (Shantung) [23] *Province*	153,302	59,190	68,000,000	1976
Shanghai (Shanghai) [23] *Municipality*	5,799	2,239	10,000,000	1976
Shanxi (Shansi) [22] *Province*	157,109	60,660	23,000,000	1976
Sichuan (Szechwan) [23] *Province*	568,995	219,690	80,000,000	1976
Tianjin (Tientsin) [22] *Municipality*	29,899	11,544	6,280,000	1974
Yunnan (Yunnan) [23] *Province*	436,206	168,420	28,000,000	1976
Xinjiang Uygur Zizhiqu (Sinkiang-Uighur) [24] *Autonomous Region*	1,646,793	635,830	10,000,000	1976
Xizang Zizhiqu (Tibet) [24] *Autonomous Region*	1,221,595	471,660	2,000,000	1976
Zhejiang (Chekiang) [23] *Province*	101,787	39,300	35,000,000	1976
China (Taiwan), *see Taiwan*				
Christmas Island [26] *External Territory of Australia*	140	54	3,000	1977
Cocos (Keeling) Islands [26] *External Territory of Australia*	16	6	460	1977
Colombia [119] *Capital: Bogotá*	1,138,907	439,734	25,048,000	1977
Comoros [95] *Capital: Moroni*	2,274	878	370,000	1977
Congo [91] *Capital: Brazzaville*	348,999	134,749	1,454,000	1978
Cook Islands [122] *Self-governing country in free association with New Zealand*	241	93	18,000	1977
Coral Sea Islands Territory [10] *External Territory of Australia*	22	8·5	3*	1971
Corsica (Corse) [67] *Island Region of France*	8,723	3,368	227,425*	1975
Costa Rica [115] *Capital: San José*	50,899	19,652	2,111,000	1978
Crete (Kriti) [84] *Island Province of Greece*	8,314	3,210	456,642*	1971
Cuba [116] *Capital: Havana (La Habana)*	114,524	44,218	9,464,000	1976
Curaçao [116] *Self-governing Island of Netherlands Antilles*	471	182	160,625	1976
Cyprus [84] *Capital: Nicosia* *Commonwealth Nation*	9,251	3,572	616,000	1978
Czechoslovakia [62] *Capital: Prague (Praha)*	127,870	49,371	15,178,000	1978
Dahomey, *see Benin*				
Denmark [53] *Capital: Copenhagen (København)*	43,030	16,614	5,111,000	1978
Djibouti [87] *Capital: Djibouti*	21,699	8,378	111,000	1977
Dominica [116] *Capital: Roseau* *Commonwealth Nation*	751	290	80,000	1977
Dominican Republic [116] *Capital: Santo Domingo*	48,441	18,703	5,124,000	1978
Dubai, *see United Arab Emirates*				
Ecuador [119] *Capital: Quito*	455,502	175,870	7,814,000	1978
Egypt [85] *Capital: Cairo*	1,000,250	386,198	39,939,000	1978
Eire, *see Irish Republic*				
Ellice Islands, *see Tuvalu*				
El Salvador [115] *Capital: San Salvador*	20,865	8,056	4,255,000	1977
Equatorial Guinea [91] *Capital: Malabo*	45,392	17,526	322,000	1977
Ethiopia [87] *Capital: Addis Ababa*	1,221,895	471,776	29,705,000	1978
Faeroe Islands [53] *Island Territory of Denmark*	1,373	530	41,000	1977
Falkland Islands [121] *U.K. Dependent Territory*	16,265	6,280	2,000	1977
Fernando Póo [91] *Island of Equatorial Guinea*	2,034	755	80,000	1968
Fiji [9] *Capital: Suva* *Commonwealth Nation*	18,272	7,055	596,000	1977
Finland [51] *Capital: Helsinki*	360,317	139,119	4,759,000	1978
Formosa, *see Taiwan*				
France [67] *Capital: Paris*	549,619	212,209	53,324,000	1978
Franz Josef Land [41] *Islands of U.S.S.R.*	16,576	6,400	*n/a*	
French Guiana [117] *Overseas Department of France*	90,000	34,749	59,000	1977
French Polynesia [122] *Overseas Territory of France*	4,198	1,621	137,382*	1977
French Southern and Antarctic Lands [123] *Overseas Territory of France*	439,405	169,655	*No permanent population*	
French Territory of the Afars and Issas, *see Djibouti*				
Fujairah, *see United Arab Emirates*				
Gabon [91] *Capital: Libreville*	265,000	102,317	534,000	1977
Galapagos Islands [119] *Territory of Ecuador*	8,006	3,091	4,057	1974
Gambia, The [89] *Capital: Banjul* *Commonwealth Nation*	10,368	4,003	569,000	1978
Germany, East [62] *Capital: Berlin* *German Democratic Republic*	107,860	41,645	16,765,000	1977
Germany, West [62] *Capital: Bonn* *German Federal Republic*	248,528	95,957	61,332,000	1978
Baden-Württemberg [64] *State*	35,750	13,803	9,121,000	1977
Bayern (Bavaria) [64] *State*	70,549	27,239	10,813,000	1977
Berlin (West) [63] *State*	479	185	1,938,000	1977
Bremen [63] *City with province status*	404	156	707,000	1977
Hamburg [63] *City with province status*	746	288	1,688,000	1977
Hessen [64] *State*	21,108	8,150	5,539,000	1977
Niedersachsen (Lower Saxony) [63] *State*	47,392	18,298	7,227,000	1977
Nordrhein-Westfalen [63] *State*	34,045	13,145	17,051,000	1977
Rheinland-Pfalz [64] *State*	19,832	7,657	3,645,000	1977
Saarland [64] *State*	2,567	991	1,085,000	1977
Schleswig-Holstein [63] *State*	15,659	6,046	2,586,000	1977
Ghana [89] *Capital: Accra* *Commonwealth Nation*	238,538	92,100	10,475,000	1977
Gibraltar [77] *U.K. Dependent Territory*	5·8	2·25	29,000	1978
Gilbert Islands, *see Kiribati*				
Great Britain, *see United Kingdom*				
Greece [83] *Capital: Athens*	131,955	50,948	9,284,000	1977
Greenland [97] *Self-governing Island* *Territory of Denmark*	2,175,592	840,000	56,000	1977
Grenada [116] *Capital: St George's* *Commonwealth Nation*	345	133	97,000	1977
Guadeloupe [116] *Overseas Department of France*	1,779	687	317,000	1978
Guam [19] *Unincorporated Territory of U.S.A.*	549	212	104,000	1977
Guatemala [115] *Capital: Guatemala*	108,888	42,042	6,621,000	1978
Guinea [89] *Capital: Conakry*	245,855	94,925	4,646,000	1977
Guinea-Bissau [89] *Capital: Bissau*	36,125	13,948	544,000	1977
Guyana [117] *Capital: Georgetown* *Commonwealth Nation*	214,969	83,000	819,000	1978
Haiti [116] *Capital: Port-au-Prince*	27,749	10,714	4,833,000	1978
Hawaiian Islands, *see U.S.A.*				
Heard and McDonald Islands [26] *External Territory of Australia*	370	143	*No permanent population*	
Hispaniola [116] *Island of the West Indies comprising Haiti and Dominican Republic*				
Hokkaido [20] *Island of Japan*	78,461	30,294	5,338,206*	1975
Honduras [115] *Capital: Tegucigalpa*	112,087	43,277	2,831,000	1976
Hong Kong (including **Kowloon** and the **New Territories**) [23] *U.K. Dependent Territory*	1,033	399	4,606,000	1978
Honshu [20] *Main Island of Japan*	230,455	88,979	89,101,702*	1975
Hungary [82] *Capital: Budapest*	93,030	35,919	10,699,000	1978
Iceland [50] *Capital: Reykjavik*	102,828	39,702	224,000	1978
India [27] *Capital: New Delhi* *Commonwealth Nation*	3,287,593	1,269,346	638,388,000	1978
Andaman and Nicobar Islands [27] *Union Territory*	8,327	3,215	120,000*	1971
Andhra Pradesh [28] *State*	274,539	106,000	43,390,000*	1971
Arunachal Pradesh [28] *Union Territory*	82,880	32,000	470,000*	1971
Assam [28] *State*	99,197	38,300	14,950,000*	1971
Bihar [29] *State*	173,529	67,000	56,350,000*	1971
Chandigarh [29] *Union Territory*	114	44	260,000*	1971

n/a indicates that no reliable figure is available
An asterisk (*) indicates that the population figure relates to a census

Name [Plate] and *Description*	Sq. km	Sq. miles	Population	
Dadra and Nagar Haveli [29]	490	189	70,000*	1971
Union Territory				
Delhi [29] *Union Territory*	1.484	573	4,070,000*	1971
Goa, Daman and Diu [28]	3,706	1,431	860,000*	1971
Union Territory				
Gujarat [29] *State*	186,479	72,000	26,700,000*	1971
Haryana [29] *State*	44,030	17,000	9,970,000*	1971
Himachal Pradesh [29] *State*	55,673	21,489	3,460,000*	1971
Jammu and Kashmir [31] *State*	221,962	85,700	4,620,000*	1971
(in dispute)				
Karnataka [28] *State*	191,659	74,000	29,300,000*	1971
Kerala [28] *State*	38,850	15,000	21,350,000*	1971
Laccadive, Minicoy and Amindivi Islands,				
see Lakshadweep				
Lakshadweep [27] *Union Territory*	29	11	30,000*	1971
Madhya Pradesh [29] *State*	442,888	171,000	41,650,000*	1971
Maharashtra [28] *State*	306,914	118,500	50,410,000*	1971
Manipur [28] *State*	22,274	8,600	1,070,000*	1971
Meghalaya [28] *State*	22,489	8,680	1,010,000*	1971
Mizoram [28] *Union Territory*	21,090	8,140	320,000*	1971
Nagaland [28] *State*	16,151	6,236	520,000*	1971
Orissa [29] *State*	155,399	60,000	21,940,000*	1971
Pondicherry [28] *Union Territory*	482	186	470,000*	1971
Punjab [29] *State*	50,376	19,445	13,550,000*	1971
Rajasthan [29] *State*	341,879	132,000	25,770,000*	1971
Sikkim [29] *State*	7,110	2,745	208,609*	1971
Tamil Nadu [28] *State*	129,500	50,000	41,200,000*	1971
Tripura [28] *State*	10,360	4,000	1,560,000*	1971
Uttar Pradesh [30] *State*	292,669	113,000	88,340,000*	1971
West Bengal [29] *State*	88,060	34,000	44,310,000*	1971
Indonesia [18–19]	1,919,263	741,031	143,282,000	1977
Capital: Jakarta				
Iran [32]	1,648,184	636,367	35,213,000	1978
Capital: Teheran				
Iraq [34]	433,999	167,568	12,171,480*	1977
Capital: Baghdad				
Irian Jaya [15]	412,782	159,376	1,007,000	1974
Province of Indonesia				
Irish Republic [59]	70,282	27,136	3,221,000	1978
Capital: Dublin				
Israel [35]	20,702	7,993	3,709,000	1978
Capital: Jerusalem				
Italy [78]	301,190	116,290	56,779,000	1978
Capital: Rome				
Ivory Coast [89]	319,820	123,483	5,152,000	1977
Capital: Abidjan				
Jamaica [116]	11,425	4,411	2,085,000	1977
Capital: Kingston				
Commonwealth Nation				
Jan Mayen [50]	373	144	*No permanent population*	
Island Territory of Norway				
Japan [20]	369,698	142,741	116,050,000	1979
Capital: Tokyo				
Java (Jawa) [18]	126,500	48,842	79,929,000	1975
Island of Indonesia				
Jordan [35]	97,739	37,737	2,779,000	1976
Capital: Amman				
Kalimantan [18]	538,718	208,000	5,574,000	1974
Indonesian Provinces of Borneo				
Kampuchea, *see Cambodia*				
Kenya [93]	582,644	224,960	15,322,000*	1979
Capital: Nairobi				
Commonwealth Nation				
Khmer Republic, *see Cambodia*				
Kiribati [122]	655	253	70,000	1977
Capital: Bairiki				
Commonwealth Nation				
(includes Banaba (Ocean) Island,				
Canton Island, Enderbury Island,				
Line Islands, Phoenix Islands)				
Korea, North [21]	121,248	46,814	16,651,000	1977
Capital: Pyongyang				
Korea, South [21]	99,590	38,452	37,019,000	1978
Capital: Seoul				
Kuril Islands [40]	15,540	6,000	*n/a*	
Islands of U.S.S.R.				
Kuwait [33]	20,150	7,780	1,199,000	1978
Capital: Kuwait				
Kyushu [20]	42,007	16,219	13,459,665*	1975
Island of Japan				
Laos [25]	236,798	91,428	3,427,000	1977
Capital: Vientiane				
Lebanon [34]	10,399	4,015	3,056,000	1977
Capital: Beirut				
Leeward Islands, *see Antigua, St Christopher-Nevis,*				
Anguilla and Montserrat				
Lesotho [95]	30,344	11,716	1,213,960*	1976
Capital: Maseru				
Commonwealth Nation				
Liberia [89]	111,370	43,000	1,684,000	1977
Capital: Monrovia				
Libya [85]	1,759,530	679,358	2,512,000	1976
Capital: Tripoli				
Liechtenstein [66]	161	62	25,000	1977
Capital: Vaduz				
Luxembourg [61]	2,587	999	356,000	1977
Capital: Luxembourg				
Macau (Macao) [23]	16	6	279,000	1977
Overseas Territory of Portugal				
Madagascar [95]	587,042	226,658	8,520,000	1977
Capital: Antananarive				
Madeira Islands [96]	798	308	265,000	1975
Province of Portugal				
Malagasy Republic, *see Madagascar*				
Malawi [92]	94,485	36,481	5,571,567*	1977
Capital: Lilongwe				
Commonwealth Nation				
Malaysia [18]	330,669	127,672	12,600,000	1977
Capital: Kuala Lumpur				
Commonwealth Nation				
Peninsular Malaysia [18] *State*	131,235	50,670	9,502,131	1973
Sabah [18] *State*	76,115	29,388	711,306	1971
Sarawak [18] *State*	124,967	48,250	1,060,434	1973
Maldives [27]	298	115	143,046*	1978
Capital: Malé				
Mali [89]	1,204,022	464,875	5,994,000	1977
Capital: Bamako				
Malta [84]	316	122	336,000	1978
Capital: Valletta				
Commonwealth Nation				
Man, Isle of [57]	575	222	61,000	1977
British Crown Dependency				
Mariana Islands, *see Marianas, Northern*				
Marianas, Northern	479	185	14,355	1974
Commonwealth. External Territory				
of U.S.A.				
Marquesas Islands, *see French Polynesia*				
Marshall Islands, *see Pacific Islands, Trust Territory of the*				
Martinique [116].	1,101	425	316,000	1978
Overseas Department of France				
Mauritania [89]	1,118,604	431,895	1,481,000*	1976
Capital: Nouakchott				
Mauritius [26]	1,865	720	909,000	1977
Capital: Port Louis				
Commonwealth Nation				
Mayotte [95]	376	145	40,000	1976
Administered by France since 1975.				
Claimed by Comoros				
Mbini [91]	26,017	10,043	290,000	1970
Part of Equatorial Guinea				
Mexico [115]	1,972,355	761,530	66,944,000	1978
Capital: Mexico City				
Moluccas [19]	73,815	28,500	1,187,000	1974
Island Group of Indonesia				
Monaco [67]	1·6	0·6	25,000	1977
Capital: Monaco				
Mongolia [22]	1,565,001	604,250	1,531,000	1977
Capital: Ulan Bator				
Montserrat [116]	98	38	13,000	1977
U.K. Dependent Territory				
Morocco [88]	622,012	240,160	18,245,000	1977
Capital: Rabat				
Mozambique [73]	784,961	303,075	9,678,000	1977
Capital: Maputo				
Namibia (S.W. Africa) [94]	824,293	318,261	852,000	1974
Capital: Windhoek				
United Nations Trust Territory – de facto				
administration by Republic of South Africa				
Nauru [9]	21	8	8,000	1977
Capital: Yaren				
"Special membership" of the Commonwealth				
Nepal [29]	141,414	54,600	13,421,000	1978
Capital: Kathmandu				
Netherlands [60]	36,174	13,967	13,971,000	1978
Capital: The Hague				
Netherlands Antilles [116]	1,020	394	245,000	1977
Self-governing part of Netherlands Realm				
New Britain [15]	36,674	14,160	189,000	1975
Island of Papua New Guinea				
New Caledonia [9]	19,104	7,376	136,000	1977
Overseas Territory of France				
New Guinea [15]	808,512	312,168	3,600,000	1973
Island comprising Irian Jaya (West Irian)				
and part of Papua New Guinea				
New Hebrides [9]	14,763	5,700	99,000	1977
Anglo-French Condominium				
New Zealand [11]	268,675	103,736	3,107,000	1978
Capital: Wellington				
Commonwealth Nation				
Nicaragua [115]	148,005	57,145	2,395,000	1978
Capital: Managua				
Niger [90]	1,188,994	459,073	4,994,000	1978
Capital: Niamey				
Nigeria [90]	923,769	356,669	66,628,000	1977
Capital: Lagos				
Commonwealth Nation				
Niue [122]	259	100	3,843*	1976
Self-governing country				
in free association				
with New Zealand				
Norfolk Island [10]	36	14	2,000	1977
External Territory of Australia				
North Yemen, *see Yemen*				
Norway [49]	324,218	125,181	4,059,000	1978
Capital: Oslo				

n/a indicates that no reliable figure is available
An asterisk (*) indicates that the population figure relates to a census

Name [Plate] and *Description*	Sq. km	Sq. miles	Population	
Novaya Zemlya [41]	82,621	31,900	*n/a*	
Islands of U.S.S.R.				
Okinawa [20]	1,176	454	1,042,572*	1975
Island Prefecture of Japan				
Oman [33]	212,379	82,000	817,000	1977
Capital: Muscat				
Pacific Islands, Trust Territory of the [9]	1,300	502	100,438	1974
United Nations Trust Territory administered by U.S.A.				
Caroline Islands [9] *Island Group*	1,119	432	75,394	1974
Marshall Islands [9] *Island Group*	181	70	25,044	1974
Pakistan [31]	803,941	310,403	75,278,000	1977
Capital: Islamabad				
Panama [115]	75,648	29,208	1,826,000	1978
Capital: Panama				
Panama Canal Zone [115]	1,432	553	38,000	1977
Territory under Panamanian sovereignty				
Papua New Guinea [15]	461,692	178,260	3,000,000	1978
Capital: Port Moresby				
Commonwealth Nation				
Paraguay [118]	406,750	157,047	2,888,000	1978
Capital: Asunción				
Peru [120]	1,285,215	496,224	16,819,000	1978
Capital: Lima				
Philippines [19]	299,765	115,740	46,351,000	1978
Capital: Quezon City				
Pitcairn Islands Group [122]	48	18·5	70	1977
U.K. Dependent Territory				
Poland [62]	311,700	120,348	35,040,000	1978
Capital: Warsaw				
Portugal [74]	91,971	35,510	9,798,000	1978
Capital: Lisbon				
Portuguese Guinea, *see Guinea-Bissau*				
Puerto Rico [105]	8,897	3,435	3,319,000	1977
Self-governing commonwealth associated with U.S.A.				
Qatar [33]	10,360	4,000	98,000	1977
Capital: Doha (Dawhah)				
Ras al Khaimah, *see United Arab Emirates*				
Réunion [26]	2,510	969	496,000	1978
Overseas Department of France				
Rhodesia, *see Zimbabwe*				
Río Muni, *see Mbini*				
Rodriguez [26]	104	40	26,000	1976
Dependency of Mauritius				
Romania [82]	237,500	91,699	21,559,416*	1977
Capital: Bucharest (București)				
Ross Dependency [123]	414,398	160,000	*No permanent population*	
Antarctic Territory of New Zealand				
Rwanda [93]	26,338	10,169	4,368,000	1977
Capital: Kigali				
Ryukyu Islands [17]	2,196	848	973,000	1969
Islands of Japan				
Sabah, *see Malaysia*				
St Christopher (St Kitts)-Nevis [116]	311	120	64,900	1977
U.K. Associated State				
St Helena [96]	122	47	5,000	1977
U.K. Dependent Territory				
St Lucia [116]	616	238	112,000	1977
Capital: Castries				
Commonwealth Nation				
St Pierre et Miquelon [98]	241	93	6,000	1977
Overseas Territory of France				
St Vincent [116]	389	150	113,000	1979
Capital: Kingstown				
Commonwealth Nation				
Sakhalin [21]	76,400	29,498	*n/a*	
Island of U.S.S.R.				
Samoa, *see American Samoa and Western Samoa*				
San Marino [79]	60	23	20,000	1977
Capital: San Marino				
São Tomé and Principe [91]	964	372	82,000	1977
Capital: São Tomé				
Sarawak, *see Malaysia*				
Sardinia (Sardegna) [81]	24,090	9,301	1,582,115	1977
Island Region of Italy				
Saudi Arabia [33]	2,263,579	873,972	7,012,642*	1974
Capital: Riyadh				
Senegal [89]	197,160	76,124	5,085,388*	1976
Capital: Dakar				
Seychelles [26]	443	171	62,000	1977
Capital: Victoria				
Commonwealth Nation				
Sharjah, *see United Arab Emirates*				
Shikoku [20]	18,754	7,241	4,040,070*	1975
Island Prefecture of Japan				
Sicily [81]	25,701	9,923	4,936,176	1977
Island Region of Italy				
Sierra Leone [89]	72,326	27,925	3,470,000	1977
Capital: Freetown				
Commonwealth Nation				
Sikkim, *see India*				
Singapore [18]	580	224	2,334,000	1978
Capital: Singapore				
Commonwealth Nation				
Society Islands, *see French Polynesia*				
Socotra [33]	3,108	1,200	*n/a*	
Island of South Yemen				
Solomon Islands [9]	29,785	11,500	213,000	1978
Capital: Honiara				
Commonwealth Nation				
Somalia [87]	637,539	246,155	3,354,000	1977
Capital: Mogadishu				
South Africa [94]	1,221,038	471,445	23,894,000	1978
Capital: Pretoria				
Bantu Homelands, The [95]	150,046	57,933	7,034,125*	1970
Self-governing Territories of S. Africa				
Bophuthatswana [95]	37,718	14,563	1,036,000	1976
Self-governing Republic within S. Africa				
Cape Province [95] *Province*	721,001	278,380	6,731,820*	1970
Natal [95] *Province*	86,967	33,578	4,236,770*	1970
Orange Free State [95] *Province*	129,152	49,866	1,716,350*	1970
Transkei, The [95]	43,188	16,675	1,751,142*	1970
Self-governing Republic within S. Africa				
Transvaal [94] *Province*	283,917	109,621	8,717,530*	1970
Venda [95]	2,579	6,670	301,000	1973
Self-governing Republic within S. Africa				
South Arabia, *see South Yemen*				
Southern Rhodesia, *see Zimbabwe*				
South Georgia [121]	4,144	1,600	22	1972
Dependency of Falkland Islands				
South West Africa, *see Namibia*				
South Yemen [33]	290,273	112,075	1,853,000	1978
Capital: Aden				
Spain [74]	504,745	194,883	37,109,000	1978
Capital: Madrid				
Spanish Sahara, *see Western Sahara*				
Spitsbergen [50]	61,230	23,641	*n/a*	
Main Island of Svalbard				
Sri Lanka [26]	65,610	25,332	13,971,000	1977
Capital: Colombo				
Commonwealth Nation				
Sudan [87]	2,505,792	967,491	16,953,000	1977
Capital: Khartoum				
Sumatra (Sumatera) [18]	473,606	182,860	22,658,000	1974
Island of Indonesia				
Suriname [117]	163,820	63,251	448,000	1977
Capital: Paramaribo				
Svalbard [50]	62,051	23,958	3,495	1976
Islands Territory of Norway				
Swaziland [94]	17,366	6,705	507,000	1977
Capital: Mbabane				
Commonwealth Nation				
Sweden [49]	449,791	173,665	8,285,000	1978
Capital: Stockholm				
Switzerland [66]	41,287	15,941	6,298,000	1978
Capital: Berne				
Syria [34]	185,179	71,498	8,103,000	1978
Capital: Damascus				
Tahiti [122]	1,041	402	84,552*	1970
Main Island of French Polynesia				
Taiwan (Formosa) [23]	35,980	13,892	16,813,127	1977
Capital: Taipei				
Tanzania [92]	939,762	362,844	16,553,000	1978
Capital: Dar es Salaam				
Commonwealth Nation				
Thailand [25]	513,517	198,270	45,100,000	1978
Capital: Bangkok (Krung Thep)				
Timor [19]	33,913	13,094	*n/a*	
Island of Indonesia				
Togo [89]	56,591	21,850	2,404,000	1978
Capital: Lomé				
Tokelau Islands [10]	10	4	2,000	1977
Island Territory of New Zealand				
Tonga [9]	699	270	91,000	1977
Capital: Nuku'alofa				
Commonwealth Nation				
Transkei, *see South Africa*				
Trinidad and Tobago [116]	5,128	1,980	1,133,000	1978
Capital: Port of Spain				
Commonwealth Nation				
Tristan da Cunha [96]	98	38	314	1977
Dependency of St Helena				
Tuamotu-Gambier Archipelago, *see French Polynesia*				
Tubuai Islands, *see French Polynesia*				
Tunisia [88]	164,148	63,378	6,216,000	1978
Capital: Tunis				
Turkey [36]	780,576	301,382	43,210,000	1978
Capital: Ankara				
Turks and Caicos Islands [116]	430	166	6,000	1977
U.K. Dependent Territory				
Tuvalu [9]	24·6	9·5	10,000	1976
Capital: Funafuti				
Commonwealth Nation				
Uganda [93]	236,036	91,134	12,780,000	1978
Capital: Kampala				
Commonwealth Nation				
Umm al Qaiwain, *see United Arab Emirates*				
Union of Soviet Socialist Republics (U.S.S.R.) [38]	22,272,000	8,599,341	260,020,000	1978
Capital: Moscow				
Armenia [44] *Union Republic*	29,759	11,490	2,950,000	1978
Azerbaydzhan [44] *Union Republic*	86,583	33,430	5,866,000	1978
Byelorussia [46] *Union Republic*	207,588	80,150	9,451,000	1978

n/a indicates that no reliable figure is available
An asterisk (*) indicates that the population figure relates to a census

Name [Plate] and *Description*	Sq. km	Sq. miles	Population	
Estonia [46] *Union Republic*	45,092	17,410	1,459,000	1978
Georgia [44] *Union Republic*	69,671	26,900	5,041,000	1978
Kazakhstan [43] *Union Republic*	2,714,387	1,048,030	14,654,000	1978
Kirghizia [43] *Union Republic*	198,652	76,700	3,512,000	1978
Latvia [46] *Union Republic*	66,278	25,590	2,530,000	1978
Lithuania [46] *Union Republic*	65,190	25,170	3,364,000	1978
Moldavia [46] *Union Republic*	33,799	13,050	3,915,000	1978
Russian Soviet Federated Socialist Republic (R.S.F.R.) [38] *Union Republic*	17,078,005	6,593,850	136,532,000	1978
Tadzhikistan [43] *Union Republic*	143,071	55,240	3,689,000	1978
Turkmenistan [43] *Union Republic*	487,954	188,400	2,722,000	1978
Ukraine [46] *Union Republic*	600,852	231,990	49,481,000	1978
Uzbekistan [43] *Union Republic*	449,482	173,546	14,854,000	1978
United Arab Emirates (U.A.E.) [33] *Capital: Abu Dhabi*	86,449	33,378	862,000	1977
Abu Dhabi [33] *State*	64,750	25,000	235,662*	1975
Ajman [33] *State*	259	100	21,566*	1975
Dubai [33] *State*	3,885	1,500	206,861*	1975
Fujairah [33] *State*	1,165	450	26,498*	1975
Ras al Khaimah [33] *State*	1,683	650	57,282*	1975
Sharjah [33] *State*	2,590	1,000	88,188*	1975
Umm al Qaiwain [33] *State*	777	300	16,879*	1975
United Kingdom of Great Britain and Northern Ireland (U.K.) [54] *Capital: London* *Commonwealth Nation*	244,754	94,500	55,836,000	1978
England [56] *Constituent Country*	130,362	50,333	46,352,000	1977
Northern Ireland [59] *Constituent Region*	14,147	5,462	1,537,000	1977
Scotland [58] *Constituent Country*	78,749	30,405	5,196,000	1977
Wales [56] *Principality*	20,761	8,016	2,768,000	1977
United States of America (U.S.A.) [102] *Capital: Washington*	9,363,132	3,615,123	219,530,000	1979
Alabama [107] *State*	133,667	51,609	3,665,000	1976
Alaska [113] *State*	1,518,801	586,412	382,000	1976
Arizona [111] *State*	295,023	113,909	2,270,000	1976
Arkansas [107] *State*	137,539	53,104	2,109,000	1976
California [111] *State*	411,013	158,693	21,520,000	1976
Colorado [109] *State*	269,999	104,247	2,583,000	1976
Connecticut [103] *State*	12,973	5,009	3,117,000	1976
Delaware [104] *State*	5,328	2,057	582,000	1976
District of Columbia [104] *Federal District*	174	67	702,000	1976
Florida [105] *State*	151,670	58,560	8,421,000	1976
Georgia [105] *State*	152,488	58,876	4,970,000	1976
Hawaii [114] *State*	16,705	6,450	887,000	1976
Idaho [110] *State*	216,412	83,557	831,000	1976
Illinois [102] *State*	146,075	56,400	11,229,000	1976
Indiana [102] *State*	93,993	36,291	5,302,000	1976
Iowa [102] *State*	145,791	56,290	2,870,000	1976
Kansas [109] *State*	213,063	82,264	2,310,000	1976
Kentucky [102] *State*	104,623	40,395	3,428,000	1976
Louisiana [107] *State*	125,674	48,523	3,841,000	1976
Maine [104] *State*	80,847	31,215	1,070,000	1976
Maryland [104] *State*	27,394	10,577	4,144,000	1976
Massachusetts [104] *State*	21,386	8,257	5,809,000	1976
Michigan [106] *State*	150,779	58,216	9,104,000	1976
Minnesota [108] *State*	217,735	84,068	3,965,000	1976
Mississippi [107] *State*	123,584	47,716	2,354,000	1976
Missouri [107] *State*	180,486	69,686	4,778,000	1976
Montana [102] *State*	381,086	147,138	753,000	1976
Nebraska [108] *State*	200,017	77,227	1,553,000	1976
Nevada [111] *State*	286,297	110,540	610,000	1976
New Hampshire [104] *State*	24,097	9,304	822,000	1976
New Jersey [103] *State*	20,295	7,836	7,336,000	1976
New Mexico [109] *State*	315,114	121,666	1,168,000	1976
New York [104] *State*	128,401	49,576	18,084,000	1976
North Carolina [105] *State*	136,197	52,586	5,469,000	1976
North Dakota [108] *State*	183,022	70,665	643,000	1976
Ohio [104] *State*	106,765	41,222	10,690,000	1976
Oklahoma [109] *State*	181,090	69,919	2,766,000	1976
Oregon [110] *State*	251,180	96,981	2,329,000	1976
Pennsylvania [104] *State*	117,412	45,333	11,862,000	1976
Rhode Island [103] *State*	3,144	1,214	927,000	1976
South Carolina [105] *State*	80,432	31,055	2,848,000	1976
South Dakota [108] *State*	199,551	77,047	686,000	1976
Tennessee [107] *State*	109,412	42,244	4,214,000	1976
Texas [112] *State*	678,924	262,134	12,487,000	1976
Utah [111] *State*	219,932	84,916	1,228,000	1976
Vermont [104] *State*	24,887	9,609	476,000	1976
Virginia [104] *State*	105,716	40,817	5,032,000	1976
Washington [110] *State*	176,617	68,192	3,612,000	1976
West Virginia [104] *State*	62,629	24,181	1,821,000	1976
Wisconsin [106] *State*	145,438	56,154	4,609,000	1976
Wyoming [102] *State*	253,596	97,914	390,000	1976
Upper Volta [89] *Capital: Ouagadougou*	274,122	105,839	6,319,000	1977
Uruguay [121] *Capital: Montevideo*	186,925	72,172	2,864,000	1978
Vatican City [80] *Ecclesiastical State*	0·44	0·17	723	1977
Venezuela [119] *Capital: Caracas*	912,047	352,143	13,122,000	1978
Vietnam [25] *Capital: Hanoi*	334,331	129,086	47,872,000	1977
Virgin Islands (U.K.), *see British Virgin Islands*				
Virgin Islands (U.S.A.) [105] *Unincorporated Territory of U.S.A.*	345	133	95,000	1976
Wallis and Futuna Islands [10] *Overseas Territory of France*	240	92·5	9,000	1977
Western Sahara [88] *Part of Mauritania and Morocco*	266,000	102,676	128,000	1976
Western Samoa [10] *Capital: Apia* *Commonwealth Nation*	2,841	1,097	153,000	1977
West Irian, *see Irian Jaya*				
Windward Islands, *see Dominica, Grenada, St Lucia, St Vincent*				
Wrangel Island (Vrangelya Ostrov) [39] *Island Territory of U.S.S.R.*	7,252	2,800	*No permanent population*	
Yemen [33] *Capital: Sana*	195,000	75,290	7,078,000	1977
Yemen, South, *see South Yemen*				
Yugoslavia [82] *Capital: Belgrade (Beograd)*	255,803	98,766	22,047,000	1978
Bosnia and Hercegovina [82] *Constituent Republic*	51,129	19,741	3,716,786*	1971
Croatia [82] *Constituent Republic*	56,537	21,829	4,346,376*	1971
Macedonia [82] *Constituent Republic*	25,713	9,928	1,611,069*	1971
Montenegro [82] *Constituent Republic*	13,812	5,333	531,213*	1971
Serbia [82] *Constituent Republic*	88,360	34,116	8,432,108*	1971
Slovenia [82] *Constituent Republic*	20,251	7,819	1,687,499*	1971
Zaire [73] *Capital: Kinshasa*	2,344,104	905,063	27,080,000	1978
Zambia [92] *Capital: Lusaka. Commonwealth Nation*	752,617	290,587	5,472,000	1978
Zimbabwe [92] *(also called Zimbabwe-Rhodesia) Capital: Salisbury*	389,361	150,333	6,930,000	1978

An asterisk (*) indicates that the population figure relates to a census

PLANETARY DATA

	Mercury	Venus	Earth	Mars	Jupiter	Saturn	Uranus	Neptune	Pluto
Equatorial diameter (km)	4,880	12,104	12,756	6,787	142,800	120,000	51,800	49,500	5,800
Mass (Earth = 1)	0·055	0·815	1	0·108	317·9	95·2	14·6	17·2	0·1?
Volume (Earth = 1)	0·06	0·88	1	0·15	1·316	755	67	57	0·1?
Density (Water = 1)	5·4	5·2	5·5	3·9	1·3	0·7	1·2	1·7	?
Polar flattening	0	0	0·003	0·009	0·06	0·1	0·06	0·02	?
Surface gravity (Earth = 1)	0·37	0·88	1	0·38	2·64	1·15	1·17	1·18	?
Number of satellites	0	0	1	2	14	11	5	2	1
Distance from Sun (max) Mkm	69·7	109	152·1	249·1	815·7	1,507	3,004	4,537	7,375
Distance from Sun (min) Mkm	45·9	107·4	147·1	206·7	740·9	1,347	2,735	4,456	4,425
Distance from Sun (mean) Mkm	57·9	108·2	149·6	227·9	778·3	1,427	2,869·6	4,496·6	5,900
Length of days (in Earth days)	58·65 days	243 days (retrograde)	23hrs 56mins 4secs	24hrs 37mins 23secs	9hrs 50mins 30secs	10hrs 14mins	11hrs (retrograde)	16hrs	6 days 9hrs
Length of year (in Earth days and years)	88 days	224·7 days	365·26 days	687 days	11·86 years	29·46 years	84·01 years	164·8 years	247·7 years
Orbital velocity (km/sec)	47·9	35	29·8	24·1	13·1	9·6	6·8	5·4	4·7
Inclination of axis	28°	3°	23° 27′	23° 59′	3° 05′	26° 44′	82° 5′	28° 48′	?
Inclination of orbit to ecliptic	7°	3·4°	0°	1·9°	1·3°	2·5°	0·8°	1·8°	17·2°

GEOGRAPHICAL COMPARISONS

LAKE AREAS

Areas are average and some are subject to seasonal variations

Sq. Km	Sq. Miles	
371,000	143,240	**Caspian** U.S.S.R.-Iran *(salt)*
83,270	32,150	**Superior** U.S.A.-Canada
68,800	26,560	**Victoria** Kenya-Uganda-Tanzania
65,500	25,300	**Aral** U.S.S.R. *(salt)*
60,700	23,430	**Huron** U.S.A.-Canada
58,020	22,400	**Michigan** U.S.A.
32,900	12,700	**Tanganyika** Tanzania-Zambia-Zaire-Burundi
31,790	12,270	**Great Bear** Canada
30,500	11,800	**Baykal** U.S.S.R.
28,440	10,980	**Great Slave,** Canada
25,680	9,910	**Erie** U.S.A.-Canada
24,510	9,460	**Winnipeg** Canada
22,490	8,680	**Nyasa** *(Malawi)* Malawi-Mozambique
19,230	7,430	**Ontario** U.S.A.-Canada
18,390	7,100	**Ladoga** U.S.S.R.
17,400	6,700	**Balkhash** U.S.S.R.
16,300	6,300	**Maracaibo** Venezuela
10–26,000	4–10,000	**Chad** Nigeria-Niger-Chad-Cameroon
9,600	3,710	**Onega** U.S.S.R.
0–8,900	0–3,430	**Eyre** Australia
8,340	3,220	**Titicaca** Peru-Bolivia
8,270	3,190	**Nicaragua** Nicaragua
6,410	2,470	**Rudolf** Kenya-Ethiopia
5,780	2,230	**Torrens** Australia *(salt)*
5,580	2,160	**Vänern** Sweden
4,710	1,820	**Manitoba** Canada
70	27	**Loch Lomond** Scotland
26	10	**Windermere** England

MOUNTAIN HEIGHTS

Metres	Feet	
8,848	29,028	**Everest** Nepal-Tibet
8,611	28,250	**K2** *(Godwin Austen)* Kashmir-Sinkiang
8,586	28,168	**Kangchenjunga** Nepal-India
8,475	27,805	**Makalu** Tibet-Nepal
8,172	26,810	**Dhaulagiri** Nepal
8,126	26,660	**Nanga Parbat** Kashmir
8,078	26,504	**Annapurna** Nepal
8,068	26,470	**Gasherbrum** Kashmir
8,013	26,291	**Xixabangma Feng** *(Gosainthan)* Tibet
7,817	25,645	**Nanda Devi** India
7,780	25,550	**Rakaposhi** Kashmir
7,756	25,447	**Kamet** India-Tibet
7,756	25,447	**Namcha Barwa** Tibet
7,728	25,355	**Gurla Mandhata** Tibet
7,723	25,338	**Muztag** *(Ulugh Muztagh)* Sinkiang
7,719	25,325	**Kongur Shan** *(Kungur)* Sinkiang
7,690	25,230	**Tirich Mir** Pakistan
7,590	24,903	**Gongga Shan** *(Minya Konka)* China
7,546	24,757	**Muztagata** *(Muztagh Ata)* Sinkiang
7,495	24,590	**Pik Kommunizma** U.S.S.R.
7,439	24,407	**Pik Pobedy** *(Sheng-li Feng)* U.S.S.R.-Sinkiang
7,313	23,993	**Chomo Lhari** Bhutan-Tibet
7,134	23,406	**Pik Lenina** U.S.S.R.
7,084	23,240	**Ojos del Salado** Chile-Argentina
7,014	23,012	**Ancohuma** Bolivia
6,960	22,834	**Aconcagua** Argentina
6,870	22,541	**Bonete** Argentina
6,800	22,310	**Tupungato** Argentina-Chile
6,770	22,211	**Mercedario** Argentina
6,768	22,205	**Huascarán** Peru
6,723	22,057	**Llullaillaco** Argentina-Chile
6,714	22,028	**Kangrinboqê Feng** *(Kailas)* Tibet
6,634	21,765	**Yerupaja** Peru
6,542	21,463	**Sajama** Bolivia
6,485	21,276	**Illampu** Bolivia
6,425	21,079	**Nudo Coropuna** Peru
6,402	21,004	**Illimani** Bolivia
6,310	20,702	**Chimborazo** Ecuador
6,194	20,320	**Mt. McKinley** U.S.A.
6,050	19,850	**Logan** Canada
5,895	19,340	**Kilimanjaro** Tanzania
5,700	18,700	**Citlaltepetl** Mexico
5,642	18,510	**El'bruz** U.S.S.R.
5,452	17,887	**Popocatepetl** Mexico
5,200	17,058	**Mt. Kenya** Kenya
5,165	16,946	**Mt. Ararat** Turkey
5,140	16,864	**Vinson Massif** Antarctica
5,110	16,763	**Stanley** Zaire/Uganda
5,030	16,500	**Jaya** *(Carstensz)* New Guinea
4,810	15,781	**Mont Blanc** France
4,477	14,688	**Matterhorn** Switzerland-Italy
2,963	9,721	**Zugspitze** Germany
1,343	4,406	**Ben Nevis** Scotland
1,085	3,560	**Snowdon** Wales
1,041	3,414	**Carrantuohill** Ireland
978	3,210	**Scafell Pike** England

RIVER LENGTHS

Km	Miles	
6,695	4,160	**Nile** Africa
6,570	4,080	**Amazon** South America
6,380	3,964	**Yangtze** Asia
6,020	3,740	**Mississippi-Missouri** North America
5,410	3,360	**Ob-Irtysh** Asia
4,840	3,010	**Huang He** *(Yellow River)* Asia
4,630	2,880	**Zaïre** *(Congo)* Africa
4,500	2,796	**Paraná** South America
4,440	2,760	**Irtysh** Asia
4,416	2,745	**Amur** Asia
4,400	2,730	**Lena** Asia
4,240	2,630	**Mackenzie** North America
4,180	2,600	**Mekong** Asia
4,100	2,550	**Niger** Africa
4,090	2,540	**Yenisey** Asia
3,969	2,466	**Missouri** North America
3,779	2,348	**Mississippi** North America
3,750	2,330	**Murray-Darling** Australia
3,688	2,292	**Volga** Europe
3,240	2,013	**Madeira** South America
3,180	1,980	**Indus** Asia
3,058	1,900	**St Lawrence** North America
3,030	1,880	**Rio Grande** North America
3,020	1,870	**Yukon** North America
2,960	1,840	**Brahmaputra** Asia
2,850	1,770	**Danube** Europe
2,820	1,750	**Salween** Asia
2,780	1,730	**São Francisco** South America
2,700	1,678	**Ganges** Asia
2,655	1,650	**Zambezi** Africa
2,570	1,600	**Nelson-Saskatchewan** North America
2,430	1,510	**Euphrates** Asia
2,330	1,450	**Arkansas** North America
2,330	1,450	**Colorado** North America
2,200	1,370	**Dnepr** Europe
2,090	1,300	**Irrawaddy** Asia
2,060	1,280	**Orinoco** South America
2,000	1,240	**Negro** South America
1,870	1,160	**Don** Europe
1,859	1,155	**Orange** Africa
1,799	1,118	**Pechora** Europe
1,609	1,000	**Marañón** South America
1,410	876	**Dnestr** Europe
1,320	820	**Rhine** Europe
1,183	735	**Donets** Europe
1,159	720	**Elbe** Europe
1,094	680	**Gambia** Africa
1,080	671	**Yellowstone** North America
1,014	630	**Vistula** Europe
1,006	625	**Tagus** Europe
909	565	**Oder** Europe
761	473	**Seine** Europe
336	209	**Thames** England
80	50	**Liffey** Ireland

OCEANS & SEAS

Areas and greatest depths

Sq. Km	Sq. Miles		Metres	Feet
165,384,000	63,855,000	**Pacific Ocean**	11,033	36,198
82,217,000	31,744,000	**Atlantic Ocean**	8,381	27,498
73,481,000	28,371,000	**Indian Ocean**	8,047	26,400
14,056,000	5,427,000	**Arctic Ocean**	5,450	17,880
2,505,000	967,000	**Mediterranean Sea**	4,846	15,900
2,318,000	895,000	**South China Sea**	5,514	18,090
2,269,000	876,000	**Bering Sea**	5,121	16,800
1,943,000	750,000	**Caribbean Sea**	7,492	24,580
1,544,000	596,000	**Gulf of Mexico**	4,377	14,360
1,528,000	590,000	**Sea of Okhotsk**	3,475	11,400
1,248,000	482,000	**East China Sea**	2,999	9,840
1,243,000	480,000	**Yellow Sea**	91	300
1,233,000	476,000	**Hudson Bay**	259	850
1,008,000	389,000	**Sea of Japan**	3,743	12,280
575,000	222,000	**North Sea**	661	2,170
461,000	178,000	**Black Sea**	2,243	7,360
438,000	169,000	**Red Sea**	2,246	7,370
422,000	163,000	**Baltic Sea**	439	1,440

AREAS

Sq. Km	Sq. Miles	
22,272,000	8,599,341	**U.S.S.R.**
9,976,147	3,851,809	**Canada**
9,560,948	3,691,500	**China**
9,363,132	3,615,123	**U.S.A.**
8,511,968	3,286,487	**Brazil**
7,686,855	2,967,909	**Australia**
3,287,593	1,269,346	**India**
2,776,643	1,072,067	**Argentina**
2,505,792	967,491	**Sudan**
2,381,731	919,591	**Algeria**
244,754	94,500	**U.K.**

POPULATIONS

865,677,000	**China**
625,818,000	**India**
260,020,000	**U.S.S.R.**
216,817,000	**U.S.A.**
143,282,000	**Indonesia**
115,397,000	**Brazil**
115,361,000	**Japan**
84,655,000	**Bangladesh**
75,278,000	**Pakistan**
66,944,000	**Mexico**
66,628,000	**Nigeria**
61,325,000	**West Germany**
56,636,000	**Italy**
55,852,000	**U.K.**
53,241,000	**France**
47,872,000	**Vietnam**
46,351,000	**Philippines**
45,100,000	**Thailand**
43,210,000	**Turkey**
39,711,000	**Egypt**
37,019,000	**South Korea**
36,672,000	**Spain**
35,040,000	**Poland**

POPULATIONS

(estimated) of selected metropolitan areas

17,180,500	**New York-N.E. New Jersey** U.S.A.
11,540,283	**Tokyo** Japan
11,339,774	**Mexico City** Mexico
11,308,800	**London** England
11,300,000	**Shanghai** China
10,041,132	**São Paulo** Brazil
9,863,400	**Paris** France
8,925,000	**Buenos Aires** Argentina
8,328,784	**Rio de Janeiro** Brazil
8,049,233	**Osaka** Japan
7,632,000	**Moscow** U.S.S.R.
7,570,000	**Beijing** *(Peking)* China
7,500,000	**Seoul** South Korea
7,031,000	**Calcutta** India
6,971,200	**Chicago** Illinois-N.W. Indiana U.S.A.
6,926,100	**Los Angeles-Long Beach** California U.S.A.
6,588,000	**Cairo** Egypt
5,970,575	**Bombay** India
5,849,000	**Jakarta** Indonesia
5,200,000	**Essen-Dortmund-Duisburg** W. Germany
4,809,900	**Philadelphia** Pennsylvania-New Jersey U.S.A.
4,545,608	**Bangkok** *(Krung Thep)* Thailand
4,444,000	**Hong Kong**
4,434,300	**Detroit** Michigan U.S.A.
4,311,000	**Leningrad** U.S.S.R.
4,280,000	**Tianjin** *(Tientsin)* China
4,025,000	**Berlin** W. Germany
4,000,799	**Santiago** Chile
4,000,000	**Manila** Philippines
3,918,400	**Boston** Massachusetts U.S.A.
3,864,493	**Istanbul** Turkey
3,647,000	**Delhi-New Delhi** India
3,600,000	**Shenyang** *(Mukden)* China
3,589,933	**Karachi** Pakistan
3,500,000	**Lima** Peru
3,146,071	**Madrid** Spain
3,135,900	**San Francisco-Oakland** California U.S.A.
3,015,300	**Washington D.C.** U.S.A.
2,923,000	**Sydney** Australia
2,856,309	**Rome** Italy
2,798,000	**Montreal** Canada
2,747,900	**Birmingham** England
2,741,000	**Toronto** Canada
2,687,000	**Manchester** England
2,661,400	**Melbourne** Australia
2,600,000	**Wuhan** China
2,530,000	**Athens-Piraeus** Greece
2,371,400	**St Louis** Missouri-Illinois U.S.A.
2,333,600	**Pittsburgh** Pennsylvania U.S.A.
2,300,000	**Hamburg** W. Germany
2,249,900	**Singapore**
2,065,000	**Budapest** Hungary
1,984,000	**Cleveland** Ohio U.S.A.
1,870,100	**Lisbon** Portugal
1,807,017	**Glasgow** Scotland
1,755,366	**Havana** Cuba
1,745,142	**Barcelona** Spain
1,732,451	**Milan** Italy
1,593,000	**Vienna** Austria
1,476,837	**Lagos** Nigeria
1,463,400	**Warsaw** Poland
1,432,643	**Johannesburg-Germiston** South Africa
1,364,175	**Stockholm** Sweden
1,327,940	**Copenhagen** Denmark
1,250,000	**Montevideo** Uruguay
1,170,000	**Prague** Czechoslovakia
1,050,787	**Brussels** Belgium
987,205	**Amsterdam** Netherlands

RESOURCES OF THE WORLD

People

In the period from 1975 to 1978 the population of the world increased by 230 millions. This increase was greater than in the 800 years before 1700. Awesome as this mighty three-year increase may seem, representing 1·9 per cent growth per annum, it was a decided reduction in the 2 per cent growth, which had continued for well over a decade before 1975. There are signs that the reduction is continuing. Nonetheless, the population in 1978 of 4,200 millions was more than double the population of 1930. Had the previous high rate continued, the world's population would have doubled every 35 years. At 1·9 per cent doubling takes 37 years.

For no accountable reason, falls in the birth rate have been astounding in Japan and very marked in India, China and Indonesia. In Europe, including the U.S.S.R., the trend is towards zero growth. West Germany's population is actually declining. If present trends continue. North America will achieve zero growth in less than 40 years.

Not all areas of the world are subject to this reversal of the increase in the rate of growth which has characterised the past two centuries. So it is unwise to extrapolate too far into the future. Nevertheless, it looks most unlikely that the world's population by the end of the century will be as great as was feared it might be in 1975. At that time the population was expected to rise to 8,000 million. Now a minimum of 5,800 million would appear to be certain, but the population could be as high as 6,600 million.

In the developing world there is a continuous movement of people away from a rural life to an urban life, and by AD 2000 it appears almost certain that one-third of the population will live in cities of 100,000 or more.

Land

Plate 6, like many another population map, shows how little land is densely settled and this sometimes leads to the supposition that there is ample scope to bring new lands under agriculture whenever population pressures become too great, in exactly the same way as was done throughout history. Yet the empty appearance of the map is misleading. In all there are only 14·9 billion hectares (approximately 57·5 million square miles) which comprise the total of all land on Earth; 4·3 billion hectares cannot be used for agriculture because the climate is too cold. A further 1·9 billion hectares are too arid and not capable of irrigation; desert and other soils not cultivable amount to a further 3·3 billion hectares. Mountainous terrain adds up to 2·6 billion hectares. When we subtract from the total land area all those areas which by reason of climate or terrain are unfavourable for agriculture only 3·2 billion hectares are left. This is less than 22 per cent of the land.

Considering that all the food in the world is produced from only 1·36 million hectares there would appear to be plenty of land capable of being brought under the plough, since only about three-sevenths of potential agricultural land is now in use. Many of the soils in the land potentially suitable for agriculture require lengthy and continuous chemical treatment and, in addition, are often deficient in water supply. The first of these would involve great cost over a long period of time. To remedy the second is likewise costly but would also impose heavy demands on manpower and construction resources to bring water from rivers or lakes far removed from the land to be developed. Some of the land, however, would be required for crops other than food. Finally there is as yet no way in which the humid tropical lands in certain areas can be turned into arable land.

Assuming that all the necessary steps could be taken to crop all the available land, the probable yield would be sufficient to feed eight or ten times the present population, but this presupposes that all the land can be brought successfully into use and the depredations of pests, diseases and weather are averted.

The lessons of soil conservation were learnt long ago when over-cropping led to impoverishment of the soil. Lakes, whether natural or man-made, and forests all play an important part. To remove trees wantonly could result in the irretrievable loss of many shallow soils. Equally important is the risk of pollution through the uncontrolled application of pesticides and fertilisers.

Very little of all this additional land happens to be in areas like south-east Asia, India and Africa where vast numbers of people are inadequately fed.

Water

Although 70 per cent of the Earth is covered in water, the resources of the oceans remain largely unexploited. Until the Law of the Sea permits responsibility to be defined, the riches of the ocean floor cannot be put to the service of mankind. For the past few years total landings of fish have been around 70 million tons. Overfishing of certain types of fish in the more accessible areas is reflected in a 5 per cent fall in the following year's catch. Unless present conservation measures are maintained the present tonnage cannot be assured.

Fresh water forms only 2 per cent of the water on Earth. Most of the rain which falls on land is carried off by rivers to run eventually into the ocean and seas without being used.

Water has been used for irrigation since the early founding of agricultural communities, yet there are now only 160 million hectares of land under irrigation. There is said to be twenty times as much water below ground in water-bearing strata (aquifers) as there is at the surface. This underground supply is tapped wherever the need and the capability to do so exist. However, the soils of the land most readily accessible for irrigation are all too frequently poorly suited for cultivation.

In the last 30 years, industrial use of water has outstripped the supply from rivers and subterranean sources. Throughout the industrialised world water storage projects have been undertaken in great number to meet both the needs of industry and the increasing concentration of people in urban communities, but the creation of dams and reservoirs has frequently led to a loss of fertile valley land. A glance at a map of western Russia, of southern Africa or of Spain will show how the face of the world is being changed by the construction of artificial lakes.

Water conservation has been a feature of industrial development of the last few decades and has led to recycling of water used for domestic purposes or by industry. This, in turn, has resulted in measures to guard against pollution either from industrial or domestic activities or from the use of pesticides and fertilisers in agriculture.

In arid regions desalination plants have come more and more into use in the last two decades, but the cost is high and the quantity of water produced is adequate for domestic use and only to a very small extent for industry or for cultivation purposes. The high cost of fossil fuels has led to experiments in using solar energy for the distillation processes, but these have yet to prove effective on a large scale. Desalination plants utilising freezing processes are in operation in the United States and an experimental plant exists in Britain.

Minerals

More than 7,000 years have passed since copper and tin were first used to make bronze. Sea travel and trade developed with the need to acquire new sources of metals as old mines were worked out. In those days metals were extracted from ores with a metal content of more than 15 per cent. By medieval times, copper had to be extracted from ores containing only 8 per cent metal whilst today the concentration has fallen to 0·65 per cent.

Industrialisation has brought into use almost all the elements present in the Earth. Tungsten, chromium, molybdenum and vanadium have, like nickel, become important steel-making metals. Phosphates are mined in increasing quantities to provide fertilisers. Other non-metallic minerals are used in the chemical industry. Gold and silver are now fundamental to the electronics industry. Uranium, once considered as of little practical importance is now an essential mineral for nuclear power. The widespread use of plastics and the increased use of aluminium have not reduced world demand for copper or other less plentiful metals.

A world with an expanding population committed to a constantly expanding economy and more extensive industrialisation has turned attention to the oceans as a potential source of metallic minerals. Metals are brought to the ocean crust by magma welling up where the ocean floor separates at the mid-ocean ridges.

Manganese nodules were first discovered on the sea floor more than a century ago. They were not considered commercially worthwhile since the concentrations of copper and nickel were so low. It is now thought that as much as 15 per cent of the ocean floor may contain nodules or encrustations which could be a source for copper and nickel and possibly cobalt, vanadium, molybdenum, zinc and lead apart from the basic manganese and iron which are the most abundant metals present. The richest concentrations of copper and nickel appear to be roughly equal to the content of the lowest grade ores exploited on land, but the question of how to recover the most coveted minerals from depths of around 4,000 metres and how to separate them far from land has yet to be answered.

Energy

Coal was the main source of power for the industrial revolution in Europe and North America and it remained the dominant fuel from 1760 to 1910. By the end of the third quarter of the 19th century oil had replaced coal as the primary source of energy, coal having fallen to 19 per cent of world energy consumption. Only in the U.S.S.R., China and Poland had the level of production of coal been maintained. The rest of the world preferred oil, although unlike coal it is consumed for the most part far from its place of origin and had to be imported into the industrially developed world. In the twenty years preceding the 1979 oil price increases, consumption of oil by the non-communist world rose to three times the previous level. The great reduction of oil production in Iran plus the ten-fold increase in price over a period of less than six years brought full realisation of the western world's complete dependence on oil. With oil production estimated to fall short of demand after 1986 and the prospects that the U.S.S.R. may be obliged to import large quantities of oil, the need to develop new sources of energy becomes more pressing. Some countries are already taking up this challenge.

The promise of abundant cheap energy from nuclear power has yet to be fulfilled because of opposition from conservationists and anti-nuclear lobbies. France alone has proceeded with its large programme undeterred. Even at the present slow rate of development of nuclear energy, a shortfall in the supply of uranium could occur from the middle of the 1980's. Coal alone offers an immediate answer. It is the only fossil fuel capable of meeting world energy demands beyond the 21st century when oil and natural gas will fail to match demand with supply and in the period when possible new sources of energy are being developed. Burning very large quantities of coal, however, imposes a further threat to the environment. More efficient means of extracting energy from coal and ways of making use of waste products are under active study. In the past extraction of energy from coal has been of very low efficiency.

Processes involving the direct extraction of energy from coal are being developed but the research is slow and costly, and a satisfactory outcome to present research is not expected until the last decade of the century and the question of application of the processes will depend on the price of the liquid fuel, gas or unit of energy produced.

Solar power, hydro power, wind or tidal power are not likely to make a significant contribution to the energy requirement in the next twenty years. Nuclear power stations of the fission type need to be built now. Perhaps by the end of the century fusion power may offer a solution to the fuel problems of an expanding population bent on increased industrialisation and perpetual economic growth. Existing nuclear technology offers the only feasible alternative to coal in the period before some such revolutionary source of energy is developed. How far fission power can be extended depends ultimately on uranium production.

Food

Since 1961, when the developing world as a whole produced a surplus of food, the increase in production has failed to keep pace with the expansion of the population. Emphasis has tended to be on the development of industry rather than agriculture. Half a century ago western Europe alone in the world imported grain. The U.S.S.R. and a large part of the developing world were able to export to western Europe. Today, apart from a small quantity exported from Latin America, only North America, Australia and New Zealand have achieved sufficient production to make good the deficiencies of the rest of the world. In spite of the development of special strains which has made Mexico self-sufficient and has produced increases in output in India, Indonesia and elsewhere, the developing world fails by an ever-increasing margin to feed itself from its own resources. Unless agricultural production can be dramatically increased, exports from North America will become a dominant factor.

Somehow world production of food will need to rise by 57 per cent to meet the dietary aims for the world in AD 2000. This is not a particularly difficult target to meet if all the resources of the world could be brought to bear but there are economic and political factors which may prevent the development of agriculture at the desired rate. Increased yield from the land necessitates the application of fertilisers and pesticides on a scale approaching that used in the developed world. For large parts of the developing world yield per acre is between one-fourth and one-fifth of the yield currently being achieved in New Zealand. For a great deal of the rest of the developing world production is less than half that of New Zealand and only just over half the yield per acre achieved in North America.

With 12 per cent of the world's population undernourished in the very areas where production is failing to keep pace with population growth there is no simple way to remedy this situation. Production of the chemicals required, the construction of food processing and packaging plants and the need to transport products efficiently make enormous demands on finance and energy. Since 1973, energy costs have been responsible to an appreciable extent for agricultural production in the developing world not rising as rapidly as it otherwise might have done. Further increases in the cost of energy since 1978 will certainly have grave consequences in the future.

MAIN SOURCES OF ECONOMIC MINERALS

(excluding Fuel Minerals,—see page xx—WORLD ENERGY)

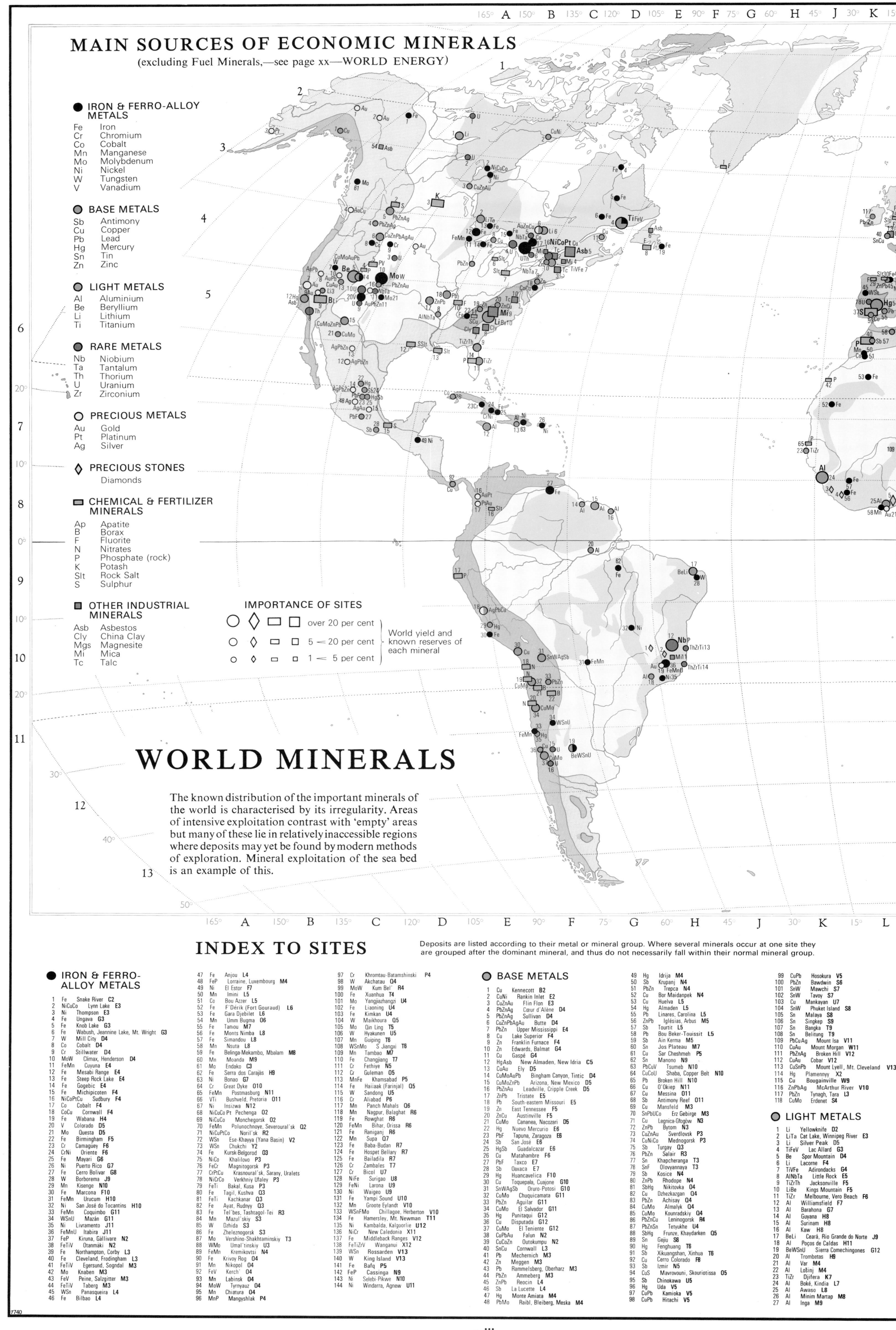

● IRON & FERRO-ALLOY METALS

Fe	Iron
Cr	Chromium
Co	Cobalt
Mn	Manganese
Mo	Molybdenum
Ni	Nickel
W	Tungsten
V	Vanadium

BASE METALS

Sb	Antimony
Cu	Copper
Pb	Lead
Hg	Mercury
Sn	Tin
Zn	Zinc

LIGHT METALS

Al	Aluminium
Be	Beryllium
Li	Lithium
Ti	Titanium

RARE METALS

Nb	Niobium
Ta	Tantalum
Th	Thorium
U	Uranium
Zr	Zirconium

○ PRECIOUS METALS

Au	Gold
Pt	Platinum
Ag	Silver

◊ PRECIOUS STONES

Diamonds

CHEMICAL & FERTILIZER MINERALS

Ap	Apatite
B	Borax
F	Fluorite
N	Nitrates
P	Phosphate (rock)
K	Potash
Slt	Rock Salt
S	Sulphur

■ OTHER INDUSTRIAL MINERALS

Asb	Asbestos
Cly	China Clay
Mgs	Magnesite
Mi	Mica
Tc	Talc

IMPORTANCE OF SITES

over 20 per cent
5 — 20 per cent
1 — 5 per cent

World yield and known reserves of each mineral

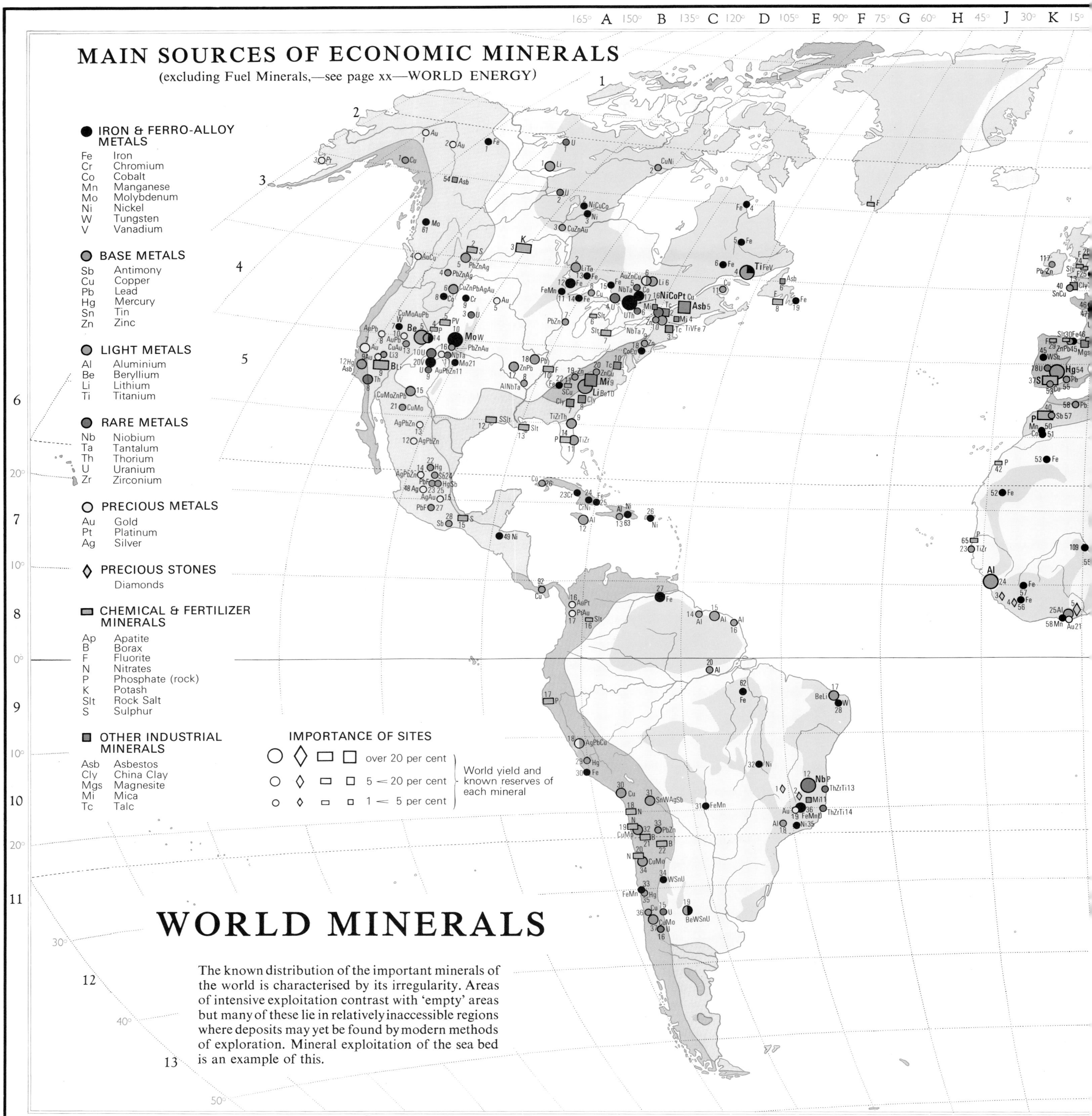

WORLD MINERALS

The known distribution of the important minerals of the world is characterised by its irregularity. Areas of intensive exploitation contrast with 'empty' areas but many of these lie in relatively inaccessible regions where deposits may yet be found by modern methods of exploration. Mineral exploitation of the sea bed is an example of this.

INDEX TO SITES

Deposits are listed according to their metal or mineral group. Where several minerals occur at one site they are grouped after the dominant mineral, and thus do not necessarily fall within their normal mineral group.

● IRON & FERRO-ALLOY METALS

1 Fe Snake River **C2**
2 NiCuCo Lynn Lake **E3**
3 Ni Thompson **E3**
4 Fe Ungava **G3**
5 Fe Knob Lake **G3**
6 Fe Wabush, Jeannine Lake, Mt. Wright **G3**
7 W Mill City **D4**
8 Co Cobalt **D4**
9 Cr Stillwater **D4**
10 MoW Climax, Henderson **D4**
11 FeMn Cuyuna **E4**
12 Fe Mesabi Range **E4**
13 Fe Steep Rock Lake **E4**
14 Fe Gogebic **E4**
15 Fe Michipicoten **F4**
16 NiCoPtCu Sudbury **F4**
17 Co Cobalt **F4**
18 CoCu Cornwall **F4**
19 Fe Wabana **H4**
20 V Colorado **D5**
21 Mo Questa **D5**
22 Fe Birmingham **F5**
23 Cr Camagüey **F6**
24 CrNi Oriente **F6**
25 Fe Mayari **G6**
26 Ni Puerto Rico **G7**
27 Fe Cerro Bolivar **G8**
28 W Borborema **J9**
29 Mn Kisenge **N10**
30 Fe Marcona **F10**
31 FeMn Urucum **H10**
32 Ni San José do Tocantins **H10**
33 FeMn Coquimbo **G11**
34 WSnU Mazán **G11**
35 Ni Livramento **J11**
36 FeMnU Itabira **J11**
37 FeP Kiruna, Gällivare **N2**
38 FeTiV Otanmäki **N2**
39 Fe Northampton, Corby **L3**
40 Fe Cleveland, Frodingham **L3**
41 FeTiV Egersund, Sogndal **M3**
42 Mo Knaben **M3**
43 FeV Peine, Salzgitter **M3**
44 FeTiV Taberg **M3**
45 WSn Panasqueira **L4**
46 Fe Bilbao **L4**
47 Fe Anjou **L4**
48 FeP Lorraine, Luxembourg **M4**
49 Ni El Estor **F7**
50 Mn Imini **L5**
51 Co Bou Azzer **L5**
52 Fe F'Dérik (Fort Gouraud) **L6**
53 Fe Gara Djebilet **L6**
54 Mn Umm Bugma **O6**
55 Fe Tamou **M7**
56 Fe Monts Nimba **L8**
57 Fe Simandou **L8**
58 Mn Nsuta **L8**
59 Fe Belinga-Mekambo, Mbalam **M8**
60 Mn Moanda **M9**
61 Mo Endako **C3**
62 Fe Serra dos Carajás **H9**
63 Ni Bonao **G7**
64 Cr Great Dyke **O10**
65 FeMn Postmasburg **N11**
66 VTi Bushveld, Pretoria **O11**
67 Ni Insizwa **N12**
68 NiCuCo Pt Pechenga **O2**
69 NiCuCo Monchegorsk **O2**
70 FeMn Polunochnoye, Severoural'sk **Q2**
71 NiCuPtCo Noril'sk **R2**
72 WSn Ese-Khayya (Yana Basin) **V2**
73 WSn Chukchi **Y2**
74 Fe Kursk-Belgorod **O3**
75 NiCo Khalilovo **P3**
76 FeCr Magnitogorsk **P3**
77 CrPtCu Krasnoural'sk, Sarany, Uralets
78 NiCrCo Verkhniy Ufaley **P3**
79 FeTi Bakal, Kusa **P3**
80 Fe Tagil, Kushva **Q3**
81 FeTi Kachkanar **Q3**
82 Fe Ayat, Rudnyy **Q3**
83 Fe Tel'bes, Tashtagol-Tei **R3**
84 Mn Mazul'skiy **S3**
85 W Dzhida **S3**
86 Fe Zheleznogorsk **S3**
87 Mo Vershino-Shakhtaminskiy **T3**
88 WMo Umal'tinskiy **U3**
89 FeMn Kremikovtsi **N4**
90 Fe Krivoy Rog **O4**
91 Mn Nikopol **O4**
92 FeV Kerch' **O4**
93 Mn Labinsk **O4**
94 MoW Tyrnyauz **O4**
95 Mn Chiatura **O4**
96 MnP Mangyshlak **P4**
97 Cr Khromtau-Batamshinski **P4**
98 W Akchatau **Q4**
99 MoW Kum Bel' **R4**
100 Fe Xuanhua **T4**
101 Mo Yangjiazhangzi **U4**
102 Fe Liaoning **U4**
103 Fe Kimkan **U4**
104 W Maikhoura **Q5**
105 Mo Qin Ling **T5**
106 W Hyakunen **U5**
107 Mn Guiping **T6**
108 WSnMo S Jiangxi **T6**
109 Mn Tambao **M7**
110 Fe Changjiang **T7**
111 Cr Fethiye **N5**
112 Cr Guleman **O5**
113 MnFe Khamsabad **P5**
114 Fe Haiiaak (Farinjal) **Q5**
115 W Sandong **U5**
116 Cr Aliabad **P6**
117 Mn Panch Mahals **Q6**
118 Mn Nagpur, Balaghat **R6**
119 Fe Rowghat **R6**
120 FeMn Bihar, Orissa **R6**
121 Fe Raniganj **R6**
122 Mn Supa **Q7**
123 Fe Baba-Budan **R7**
124 Fe Hospet Bellary **R7**
125 Fe Bailadila **R7**
126 Cr Zambales **T7**
127 Cr Bicol **U7**
128 NiFe Surigao **U8**
129 FeNi Larona **U9**
130 Ni Waigeo **U9**
131 Fe Yampi Sound **U10**
132 Mn Groote Eylandt **V10**
133 WSnFMo Chillagoe, Herberton **V10**
134 Fe Hamersley, Mt. Newman **T11**
135 Ni Kambalda, Kalgoorlie **U12**
136 NiCr New Caledonia **X11**
137 Fe Middleback Ranges **V12**
138 FeTiZrV Wanganui **X12**
139 WSn Rossarden **V13**
140 W King Island **V13**
141 Fe Bafq **P5**
142 FeP Cassinga **N9**
143 Ni Selebi-Pikwe **N10**
144 Ni Windarra, Agnew **U11**

BASE METALS

1 Cu Kennecott **B2**
2 CuNi Rankin Inlet **E2**
3 CuZnAu Flin Flon **E3**
4 PbZnAg Cœur d'Alène **D4**
5 PbZnAg Sullivan **D4**
6 CuZnPbAgAu Butte **D4**
7 PbZn Upper Mississippi **E4**
8 Cu Lake Superior **F4**
9 Zn Franklin Furnace **F4**
10 Zn Edwards, Balmat **G4**
11 Cu Gaspé **G4**
12 HgAsb New Almaden, New Idria **C5**
13 CuAu Ely **D5**
14 CuMoAuPb Bingham Canyon, Tintic **D4**
15 CuMoZnPb Arizona, New Mexico **D5**
16 PbZnAu Leadville, Cripple Creek **D5**
17 ZnPb Tristate **E5**
18 Pb South-eastern Missouri **E5**
19 Zn East Tennessee **F5**
20 ZnCu Austinville **F5**
21 CuMo Cananea, Nacozari **D5**
22 Hg Nuevo Mercurio **E6**
23 PbF Tapuna, Zaragoza **E6**
24 Sb San José **E6**
25 HgSb Guadalcazar **E6**
26 Cu Matahambre **F6**
27 PbF Taxco **E7**
28 Sb Oaxaca **E7**
29 Hg Huancavelica **F10**
30 Cu Toquepala, Cuajone **G10**
31 SnWAgSb Oruro-Potosi **G10**
32 CuMo Chuquicamata **G11**
33 PbZn Aguilar **G11**
34 CuMo El Salvador **G11**
35 Hg Punitaqui **G12**
36 Cu Disputada **G12**
37 CuMo El Teniente **G12**
38 CuPbAu Falun **N2**
39 CuCoZn Outokumpu **N2**
40 SnCu Cornwall **L3**
41 Pb Mechernich **M3**
42 Zn Meggen **M3**
43 Pb Rammelsberg, Oberharz **M3**
44 PbZn Ammeberg **M3**
45 ZnPb Reocin **L4**
46 Sb La Lucette **L4**
47 Hg Monte Amiata **M4**
48 PbMo Raibl, Bleiberg, Meska **M4**
49 Hg Idrija **M4**
50 Sb Krupanj **N4**
51 PbZn Trepca **N4**
52 Cu Bor Maidanpek **N4**
53 Cu Huelva **L5**
54 Hg Almaden **L5**
55 Pb Linares, Carolina **L5**
56 ZnPb Iglésias, Arbus **M5**
57 Sb Tourtit **L5**
58 Pb Bou Beker-Touissit **L5**
59 Sb Aïn Kerma **M5**
60 Sn Jos Plateau **M7**
61 Cu Sar Cheshmeh **P5**
62 Sn Manono **N9**
63 PbCuV Tsumeb **N10**
64 CuCoU Shaba, Copper Belt **N10**
65 Pb Broken Hill **N10**
66 Cu O'Okiep **N11**
67 Cu Messina **O11**
68 Sb Antimony Reef **O11**
69 Cu Mansfeld **M3**
70 SnPbUCo Erz Gebirge **M3**
71 Cu Legnica-Głogów **N3**
72 ZnPb Bytom **N3**
73 CuZnAu Sverdlovsk **P3**
74 CuNiCo Mednogorsk **P3**
75 Sb Turgay **Q3**
76 PbZn Salair **R3**
77 Sn Khapcheranga **T3**
78 SnF Olovyannaya **T3**
79 Sb Kosice **N4**
80 ZnPb Rhodope **N4**
81 SbHg Nikitovka **O4**
82 Cu Dzhezkazgan **Q4**
83 PbZn Achisay **Q4**
84 CuMo Almalyk **Q4**
85 CuMo Kounradskiy **Q4**
86 PbZnCu Leninogorsk **R4**
87 PbZnSn Tetyukhe **U4**
88 SbHg Frunze, Khaydarken **Q5**
89 Sn Gejiu **S6**
90 Hg Fenghuang **T6**
91 Sb Xikuangshan, Xinhua **T6**
92 Cu Cerro Colorado **F8**
93 Sb Izmir **N5**
94 CuS Mavrovouni, Skouriotissa **O5**
95 Sb Chinokawa **U5**
96 Hg Uda **V5**
97 CuPb Kamioka **V5**
98 CuPb Hitachi **V5**
99 CuPb Hosokura **V5**
100 PbZn Bawdwin **S6**
101 SnW Mawchi **S7**
102 SnW Tavoy **S7**
103 Cu Mankayan **U7**
104 SnW Phuket Island **S8**
105 Sn Malaya **S8**
106 Sn Singkep **S9**
107 Sn Bangka **T9**
108 Sn Belitung **T9**
109 PbCuAg Mount Isa **V11**
110 CuAu Mount Morgan **W11**
111 PbZnAg Broken Hill **V12**
112 CuAu Cobar **V12**
113 CuSnPb Mount Lyell, Mt. Cleveland **V13**
114 Hg Plamennyy **X2**
115 Cu Bougainville **W9**
116 ZnPbAg McArthur River **V10**
117 PbZn Tynagh, Tara **L3**
118 CuMo Erdenet **S4**

LIGHT METALS

1 Li Yellowknife **D2**
2 LiTa Cat Lake, Winnipeg River **E3**
3 Li Silver Peak **D5**
4 TiFeV Lac Allard **G3**
5 Be Spor Mountain **D4**
6 Li Lacorne **F4**
7 TiVFe Adirondacks **G4**
8 AlNbTa Little Rock **E5**
9 TiZrTh Jacksonville **F5**
10 LiBe Kings Mountain **F5**
11 TiZr Melbourne, Vero Beach **F6**
12 Al Williamsfield **F7**
13 Al Barahona **G7**
14 Al Guyana **H8**
15 Al Surinam **H8**
16 Al Kaw **H8**
17 BeLi Ceará, Rio Grande do Norte **J9**
18 Al Poços de Caldas **H11**
19 BeWSnU Sierra Comechingones **G12**
20 Al Trombetas **H9**
21 Al Var **M4**
22 Al Lošinj **M4**
23 TiZr Djifera **K7**
24 Al Boké, Kindia **L7**
25 Al Awaso **L8**
26 Al Minim Martap **M8**
27 Al Inga **M9**

7740

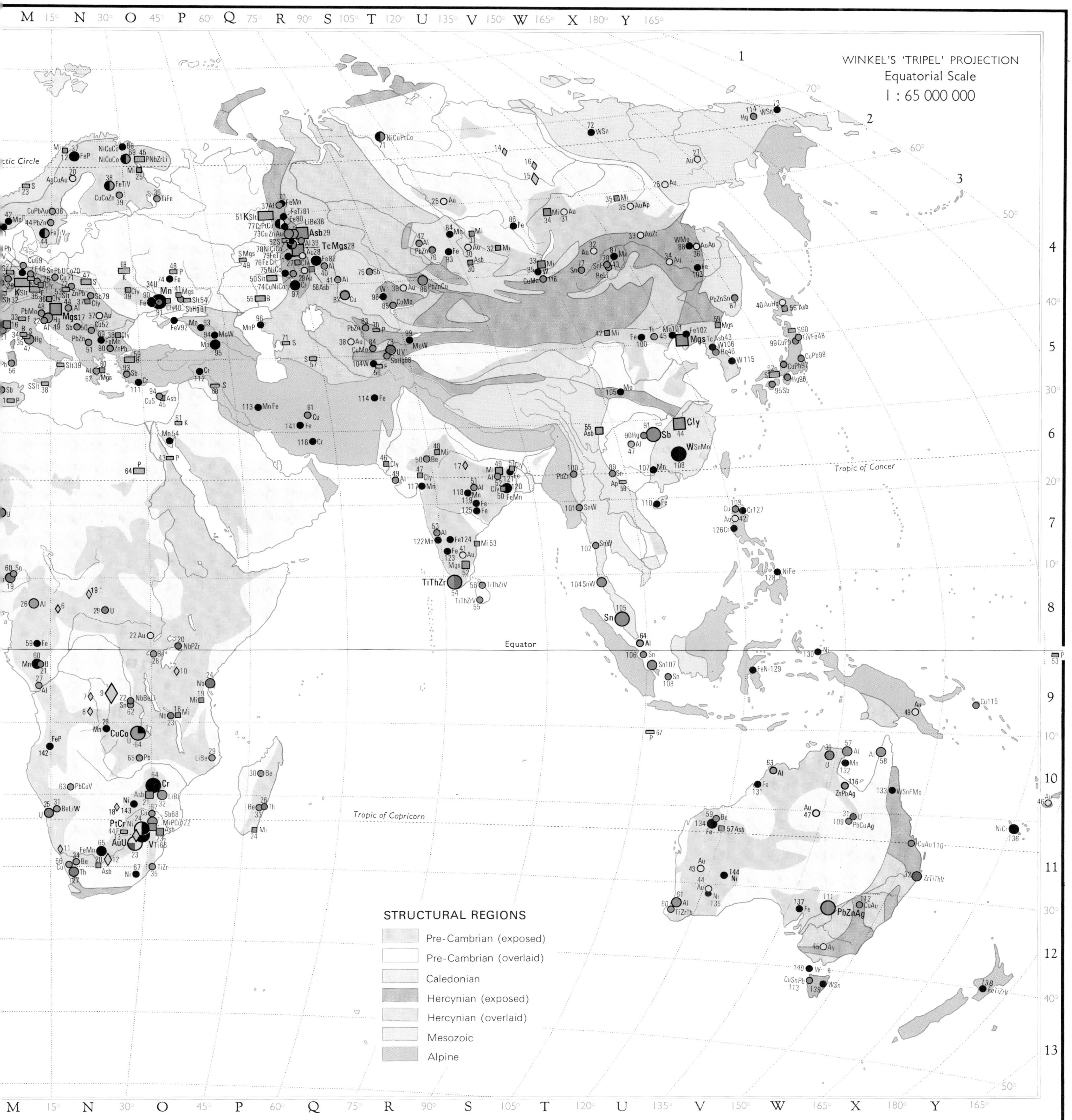

28 Be Ankole O9
29 LiBe Alto Ligonha O10
30 Be Maevatanana P10
31 BeLiW Omaruru, Karibib N11
32 LiBe Bikita O11
33 Be Fianarantsoa P11
34 Be Namaqualand N11
35 TiZr Umgababa O12
36 TiFe Pudozhgora O2
37 Al Krasnaya-Shapochka P2
38 LiBe Izumrod Q3
39 Al Kamensk-Ural'skiy Q3
40 Al Ubagan Q3
41 Al Arkalyk Q3
42 Al Salair R3
43 BeLi Sherlovaya Gora T3
44 Al Bakony N4
45 Ti Liaoning T4
46 Be Hyakunen U5
47 Al Guizhou T6
48 TiVFe Kamaishi, Unjo V5
49 Al Bhuj Q6
50 Be Ajmer, Merwara Q5
51 Al Madhya Pradesh R6
52 Al Ranchi R6
53 Al Maharashtra Q7
54 TiThZrV Travancore R8
55 TiThZrV S.W. Sri Lanka R8
56 TiThZrV Pulmoddai R8
57 Al Gove Peninsula V10
58 Al Weipa V10
59 Be Pilbara T11
60 TiZrTh Capel T12
61 Al Darling Ranges T12
62 Al Parnassos, Giona N5
63 Al Mitchell Plateau U10
64 Al Tanjung Ramunia S8

RARE METALS

1 U Port Radium D2
2 U Uranium City D3
3 U Gas Hills D4
4 U Elliot Lake F4
5 NbTa Lakner Lake F4
6 UTh Bancroft F4
7 NbTa Oka F4
8 Th Mountain Pass D5
9 U Grants D5
10 U Colorado Plateau D5
11 NbTa Powderhorn D5
12 NbP Araxá J10
13 ThZrTi Caravelas J10
14 ThZrTi Espírito Santo J11
15 U Mendoza G12
16 U Malargüe G12
17 U Limousin M4
18 U Montauchez L5
19 Nb Jos, Bukuru M8
20 NbPZr Sukulu O8
21 U Mounana M9
22 NbBeLi Manono N9
23 Nb Mbeya O9
24 Nb Mrima O9
25 U Rossing M11
26 Th Ambatofotsy P11
27 Th Nieuwe Rust N12
28 UV Fergana Q4
29 U Bakouma N8
30 U Jabiluka Ranger U10
31 U Mary Kathleen V11
32 ZiTiThV Queensland, N.S.W. W11
33 U Arlit M7
34 U Zheltyye Vody O4

PRECIOUS METALS

1 Au Fairbanks, Yukon B2
2 Au Klondike B2
3 Pt Goodnews Bay A3
4 AuCu Britannia C4
5 Au Black Hills E4
6 AuZnCu Porcupine, Kirkland Lake, Noranda F4
7 Au Mother Lode C5
8 AuPb Comstock Lode D5
9 Au Goldfield, Tonopah D5
10 AuPb Eureka D5
11 AuPbZn San Juan Telluride D5
12 AgPbZn San Francisco del Oro D6
13 AgPbZn Aquiles Serdán D6
14 AgPbZn Fresnillo E6
15 AgAu Pachuca E6
16 AuPt Titiribi F8
17 PtAu Chaco F8
18 AgPbCu Cerro de Pasco F10
19 Au Morro Velho J11
20 AgCuAu Skellefte, Boliden N2
21 Au Tarkwa L8
22 Au Kilo Moto N8
23 AuU Rand N11
24 PtCrNi Bushveld N11
25 Au Severo-Yeniseyskiy S2
26 Au Allakh-Yun' V2
27 Au Kolyma W2
28 Au Plast Q3
29 Au Kumak Q3
30 Au Minusinsk S3
31 Au Bodaybo, Vitim T3
32 Au Vershino-Darasunskiy T3
33 AuZr Zeya, Urkan U3
34 Au Kheykhe U3
35 AuAp Aldan U3
36 Au Kerbi U3
37 Au Baia Mare N4
38 Au Kyzylkum Q4
39 Au Khr. Chingiz-Tau R4
40 AuHg Konomai-Omenai V4
41 Au Kolar R7
42 Au Baguio U7
43 Au Mount Magnet T11
44 Au Kalgoorlie, Norseman U12
45 Au Bendigo, Ballarat V12
46 Au Fiji X10
47 Au Tennant Creek U10
48 Ag Guanajuato E6
49 Au Wau V9

DIAMONDS

1 Paracatu H10
2 Diamantina J10
3 Kono L8
4 Sanokole L8
5 Akwatia L8
6 Berbérati N8
7 Tshikapa N9
8 Verissimo Sarmento N9
9 Bakwanga N9
10 Shinyanga O9
11 Oranjemund N11
12 Kimberley N11
13 Premier N11
14 Daldyn T2
15 Mirnyy T2
16 Markha, Vilyuy T2
17 Panna R6
18 Orapa, Jwaneng N11
19 Bria N8

CHEMICAL & FERTILIZER MINERALS

1 F Ivigtut H2
2 S Alberta D3
3 K Saskatchewan D3
4 P Utah D4
5 PV Conda, Wyoming D4
6 Slt Manistee F4
7 Slt Windsor F4
8 F St Lawrence H4
9 BLi Searles Lake D5
10 F Rosiclare F5
11 SCu Ducktown F5
12 SSlt Texas, Louisiana E6
13 Slt Grand Isle F6
14 P Mulberry F6
15 S Isthmus of Tehuantepec E7
16 Slt Zipaquirá G8
17 P Sechura F9
18 N Tarapacá G10
19 N Maria Elena G11
20 N Taltal G11
21 B Atacamá G11
22 B Los Andes G11
23 S Lökken, Joma M2
24 Slt Meadowbrook L3
25 F Derbyshire L3
26 F Durham L3
27 S Meggen M3
28 KSlt Strassfurt, Werra M3
29 F Oviedo L4
30 Slt Polanco L4
31 S Lacq L4
32 Slt Lorraine M4
33 F Torgola M4
34 B Larderello M4
35 S Grosseto M4
36 F Nabburg M4
37 S Huelva L5
38 SSlt Caltanissetta, Agrigento M5
39 Slt Lungro N5
40 P Khouribga, Youssoufia L5
41 P Gafsa, Djebel Onk M5
42 P Bu Craa L6
43 P Quseir, Safâga O6
44 F Zeerust N11
45 PNbZrLi Kirovsk, Lovozero O2
46 F Vogtland M3
47 S Tarnobrzeg N3
48 P Shchigry O3
49 SMgs Kuybyshev P3
50 Slt Sol'Iletsk P3
51 KSlt Solikamsk P3
52 S Degtyarsk, Polevskoy P3
53 Slt Rybnik N4
54 Slt Artemovsk O4
55 B Inderborskiy P4
56 F Takob Q5
57 S Sernyy-Zavod P5
58 Ap Lao Cai S6
59 B Balikesir N4
60 S Matsuo V4
61 K Dead Sea O5
62 S Yanahara U5
63 P Nauru X9
64 P Abu Tartur N6
65 P Taiba K7
66 P Ganavé M8
67 P Christmas I. T10
68 S Mosul O5
69 K Soligorsk N3
70 P Kara Tau Q4
71 S Kara-Bogaz Gol P4

OTHER INDUSTRIAL MINERALS

1 Mi Cantley F4
2 Tc Talcville G4
3 Tc Chester G4
4 Mi Grafton G4
5 Asb Thetford Mines, Asbestos G4
6 Asb Baie Verte H4
7 Cly Dry Branch, McIntyre F5
8 Cly Aiken Co. F5
9 Mi Blue Ridge F5
10 Tc Schuyler F5
11 Mi Pecanha J10
12 Mi Nordland N2
13 Cly St Austell L3
14 Mgs Navarra L4
15 Tc Luzenac M4
16 AsbTc San Vittore, Pinerolo M4
17 Mgs Veitsch, Sunk N4
18 Mi Mbeya O9
19 Mi Morogoro O9
20 Asb Prieska N11
21 Asb Shabani, Mashaba N11
22 MiPCu Phalaborwa O11
23 Asb Transvaal, Swaziland O11
24 Mi Taolañaro P11
25 Mi Chupa O2
26 Cly Zettlitz M3
27 Cly S. Urals P3
28 TcMgs Satka, Miass Q3
29 Asb Asbest Q3
30 Asb Chadan S3
31 Mi Barga S3
32 Mi Biryusa S3
33 Mi Slyudyanka S3
34 Mi Mama T3
35 Mi Tommot U3
36 Cly Schwertberg M4
37 Cly Zempléni-hory N4
38 Cly Vetovo N4
39 Cly Berdichev N4
40 Cly Pologi O4
41 Mgs Yama O4
42 Mi Togrog Ul T4
43 MgsTcAsb Kaiping, Haicheng, Dandong U4
44 Cly Boyang T6
45 Asb Amiandos O5
46 Cly Hyderabad Q6
47 Cly Gujarat, Rajasthan Q6
48 Mi Jaipur R6
49 Mi Hazaribagh R6
50 Cly Bihar, Orissa R6
51 Cly Uttar Pradesh R6
52 Mgs Salem R7
53 Mi Nellore R7
54 Asb Cassiar C3
55 Asb Shimian S6
56 Asb Yamabe V4
57 Asb Wittenoom Gorge U10
58 Asb Dzhetygara Q3
59 Mgs Ch'ongjin U4
60 Mgs Euboea N5

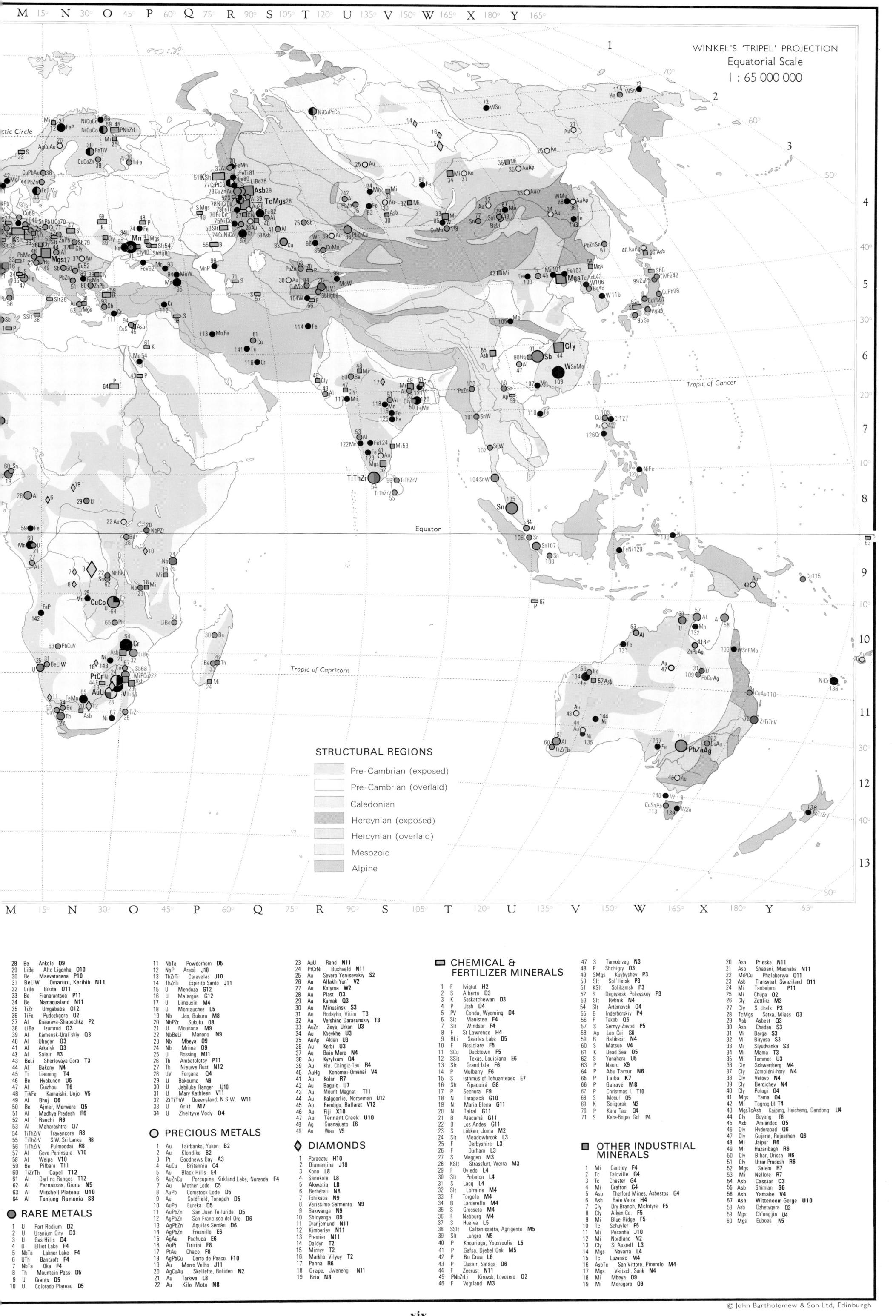

© John Bartholomew & Son Ltd, Edinburgh

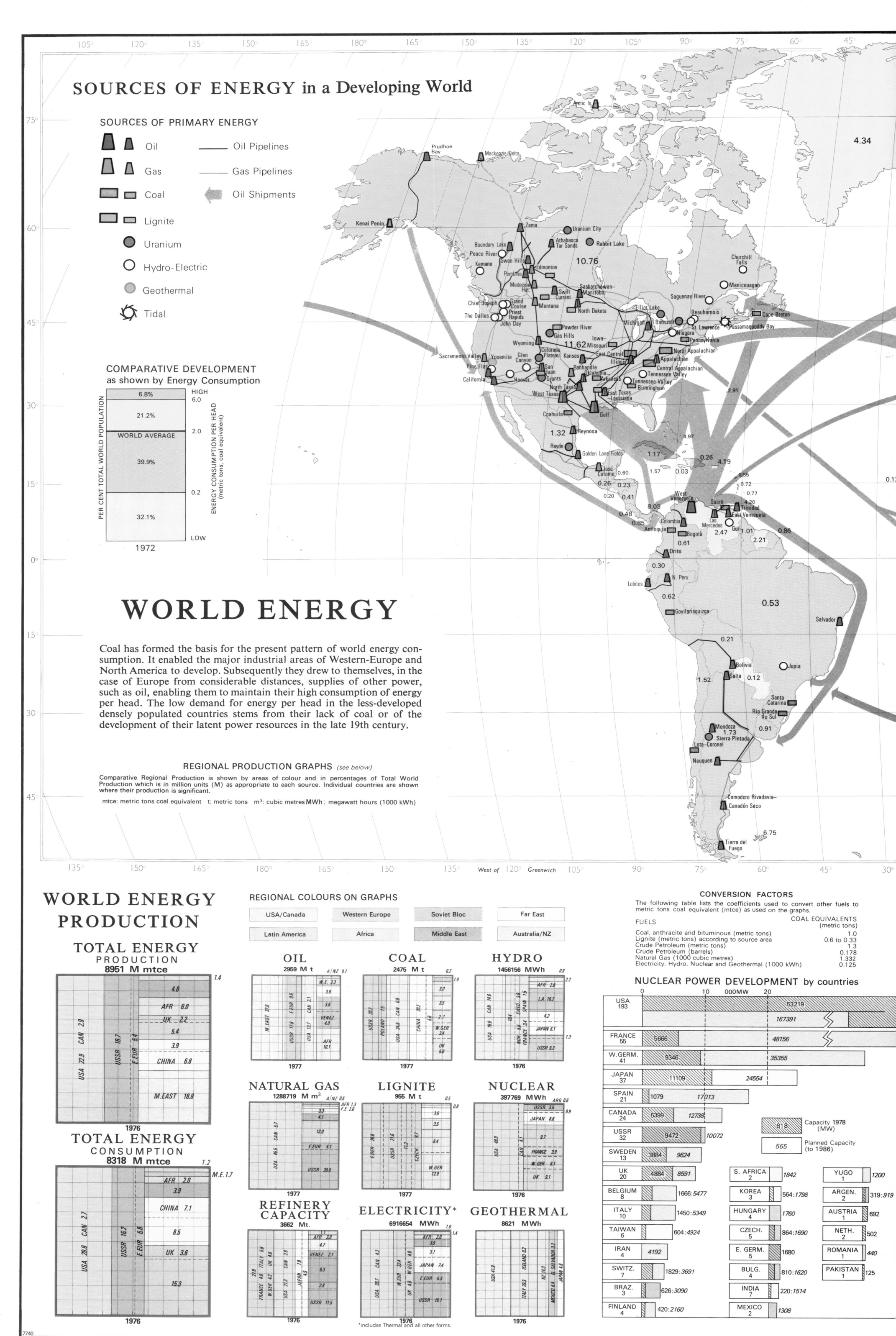

SOURCES OF ENERGY in a Developing World

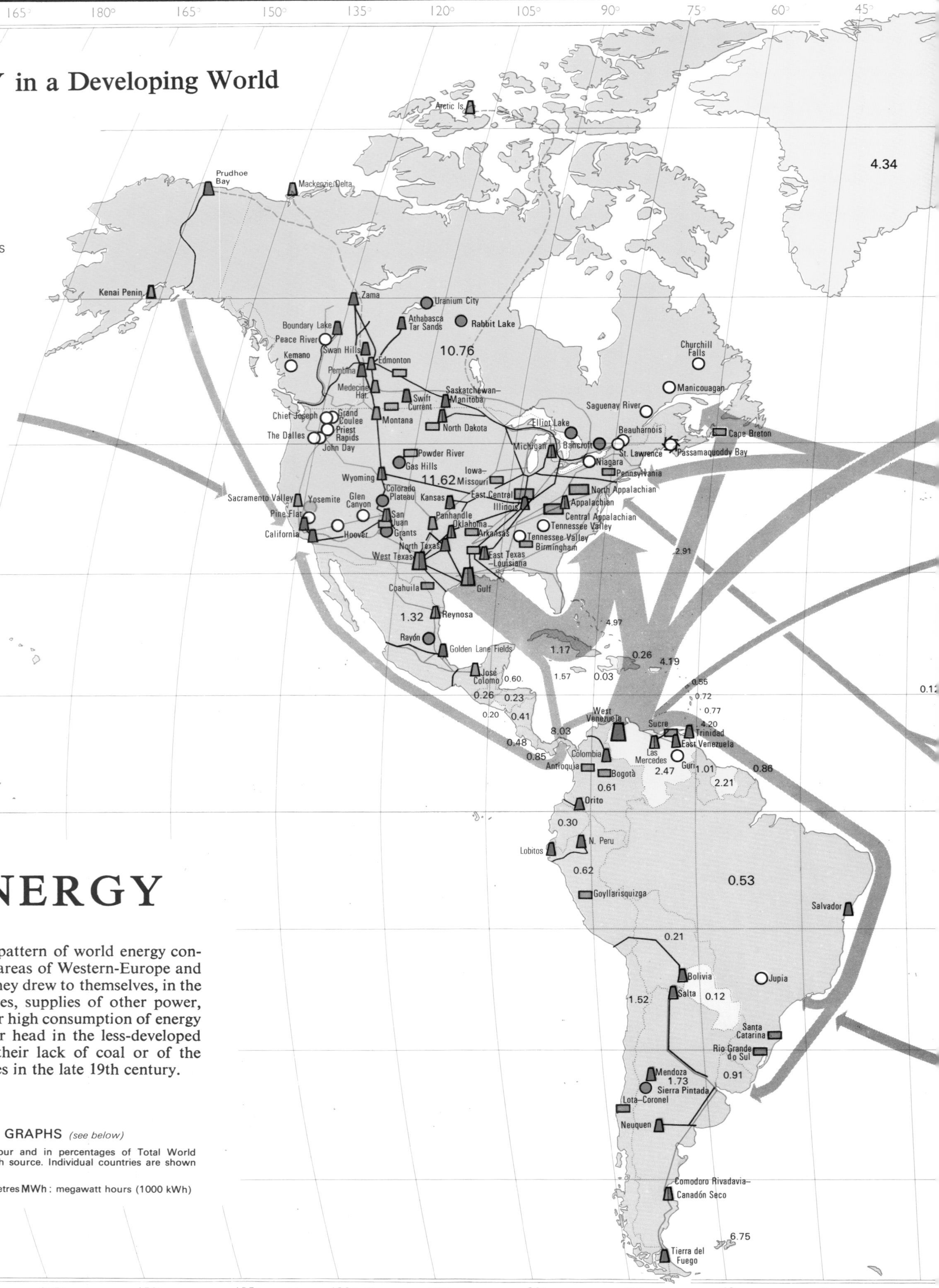

COMPARATIVE DEVELOPMENT as shown by Energy Consumption

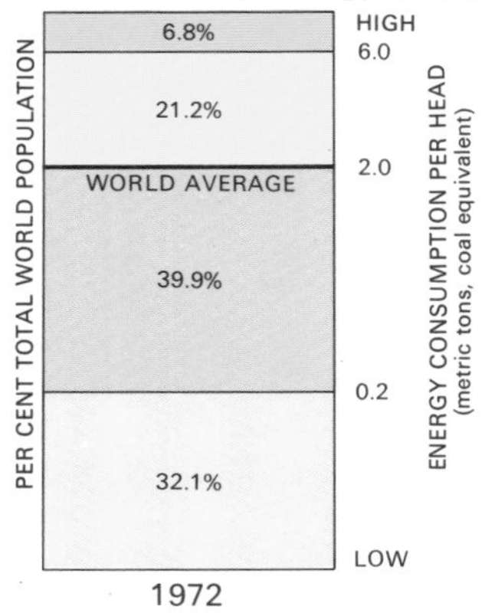

WORLD ENERGY

Coal has formed the basis for the present pattern of world energy consumption. It enabled the major industrial areas of Western-Europe and North America to develop. Subsequently they drew to themselves, in the case of Europe from considerable distances, supplies of other power, such as oil, enabling them to maintain their high consumption of energy per head. The low demand for energy per head in the less-developed densely populated countries stems from their lack of coal or of the development of their latent power resources in the late 19th century.

REGIONAL PRODUCTION GRAPHS *(see below)*

Comparative Regional Production is shown by areas of colour and in percentages of Total World Production which is in million units (M) as appropriate to each source. Individual countries are shown where their production is significant.

mtce: metric tons coal equivalent t: metric tons m³: cubic metres MWh: megawatt hours (1000 kWh)

WORLD ENERGY PRODUCTION

TOTAL ENERGY PRODUCTION
8951 M mtce

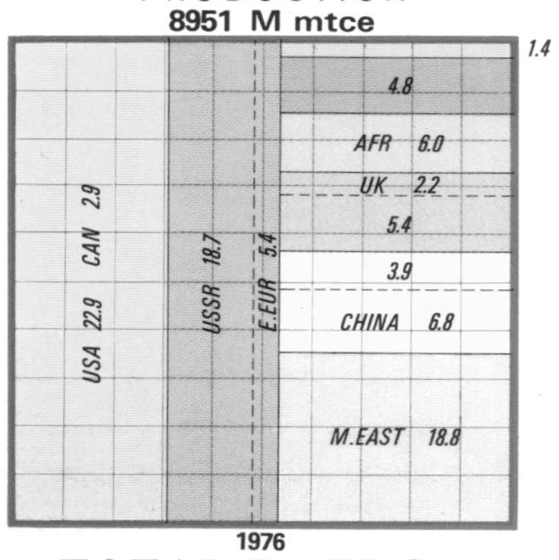

TOTAL ENERGY CONSUMPTION
8318 M mtce

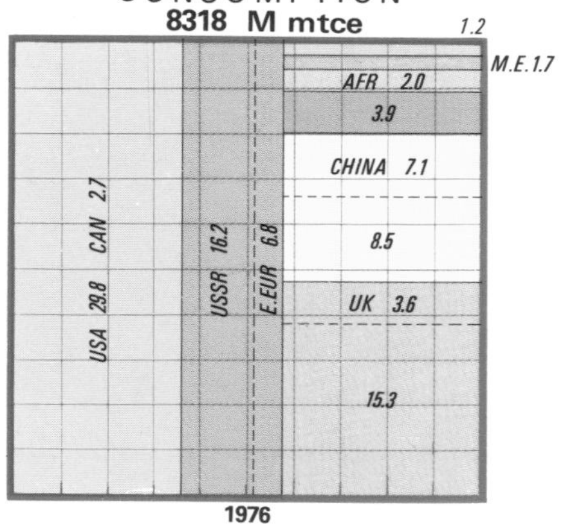

REGIONAL COLOURS ON GRAPHS

USA/Canada	Western Europe	Soviet Bloc	Far East
Latin America	Africa	Middle East	Australia/NZ

OIL
2959 M t

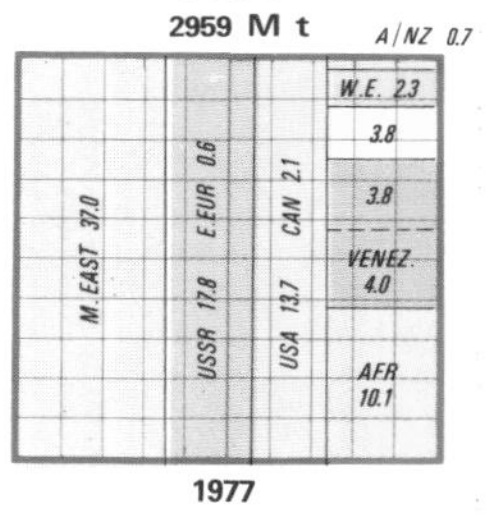

COAL
2475 M t

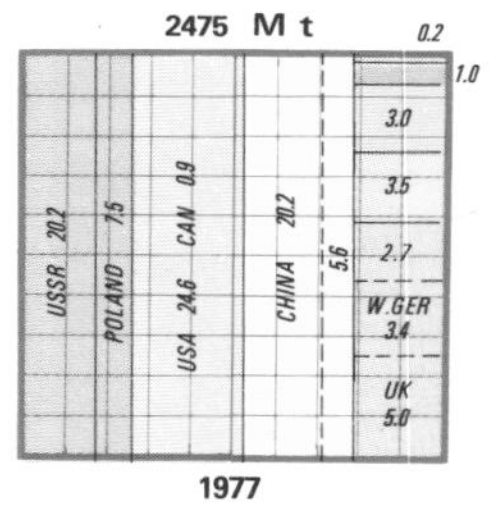

HYDRO
1456156 MWh

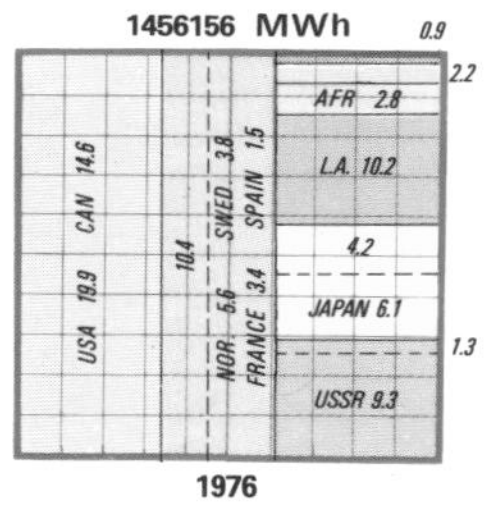

NATURAL GAS
1288719 M m³

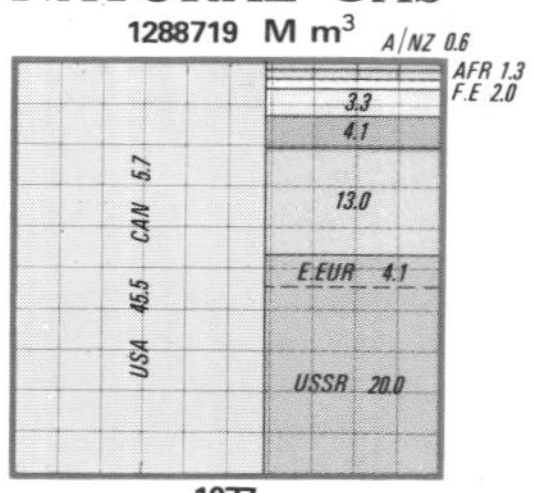

LIGNITE
955 M t

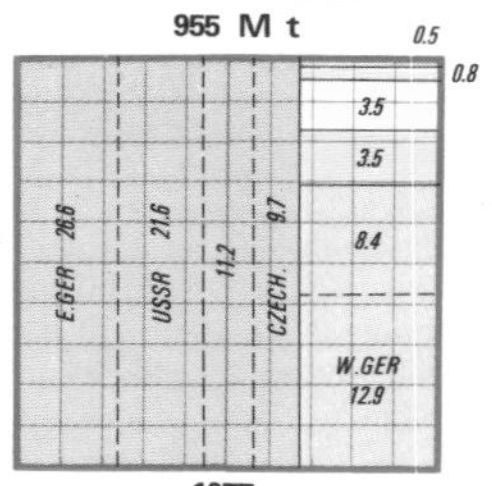

NUCLEAR
397769 MWh

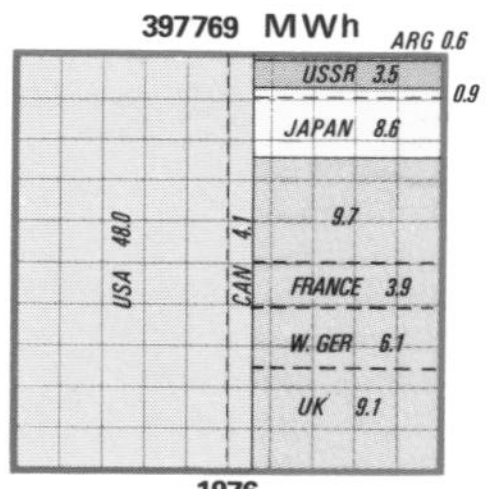

REFINERY CAPACITY
3662 Mt.

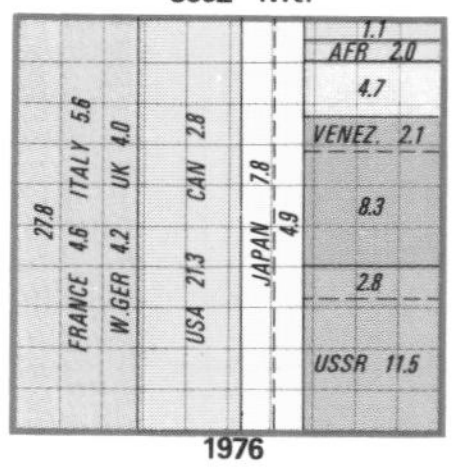

ELECTRICITY*
6916654 MWh

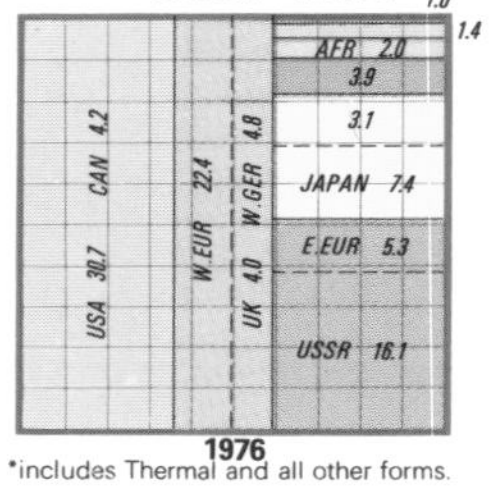

*includes Thermal and all other forms.

GEOTHERMAL
8621 MWh

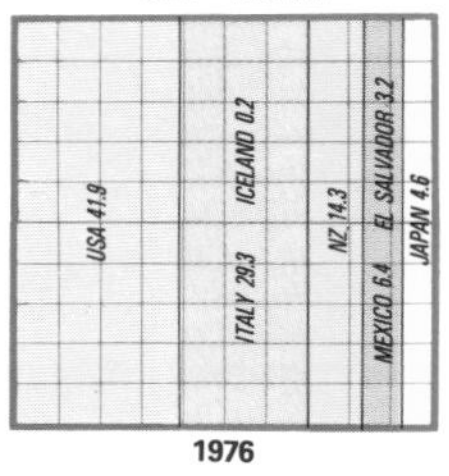

CONVERSION FACTORS

The following table lists the coefficients used to convert other fuels to metric tons coal equivalent (mtce) as used on the graphs.

FUELS	COAL EQUIVALENTS (metric tons)
Coal, anthracite and bituminous (metric tons)	1.0
Lignite (metric tons) according to source area	0.6 to 0.33
Crude Petroleum (metric tons)	1.3
Crude Petroleum (barrels)	0.178
Natural Gas (1000 cubic metres)	1.332
Electricity: Hydro, Nuclear and Geothermal (1000 kWh)	0.125

NUCLEAR POWER DEVELOPMENT by countries

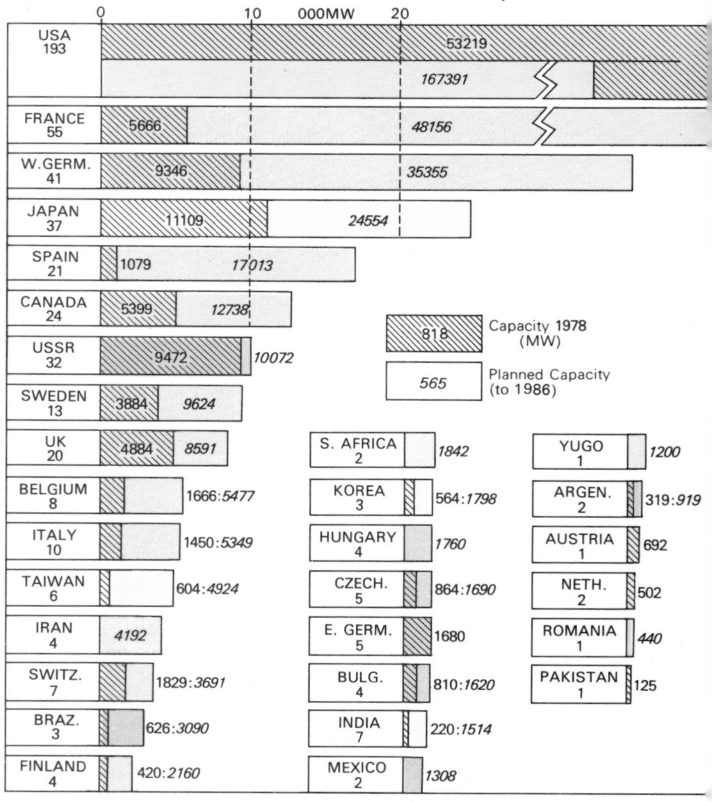

7740

EUROPE—Energy Consumption per head (mtce)

Czech.	6.84	Poland	4.56	Bulgaria	4.13
E. Germany	5.99	Neth.	5.71	Ireland	3.30
U.K.	5.40	France	4.15	Rumania	3.15
Belgium	6.47	Hungary	3.28	Yugoslavia	1.61
W. Germany	5.40	Austria	3.61	Spain	1.77
Denmark	5.57	Switz.	3.62	Albania	0.67

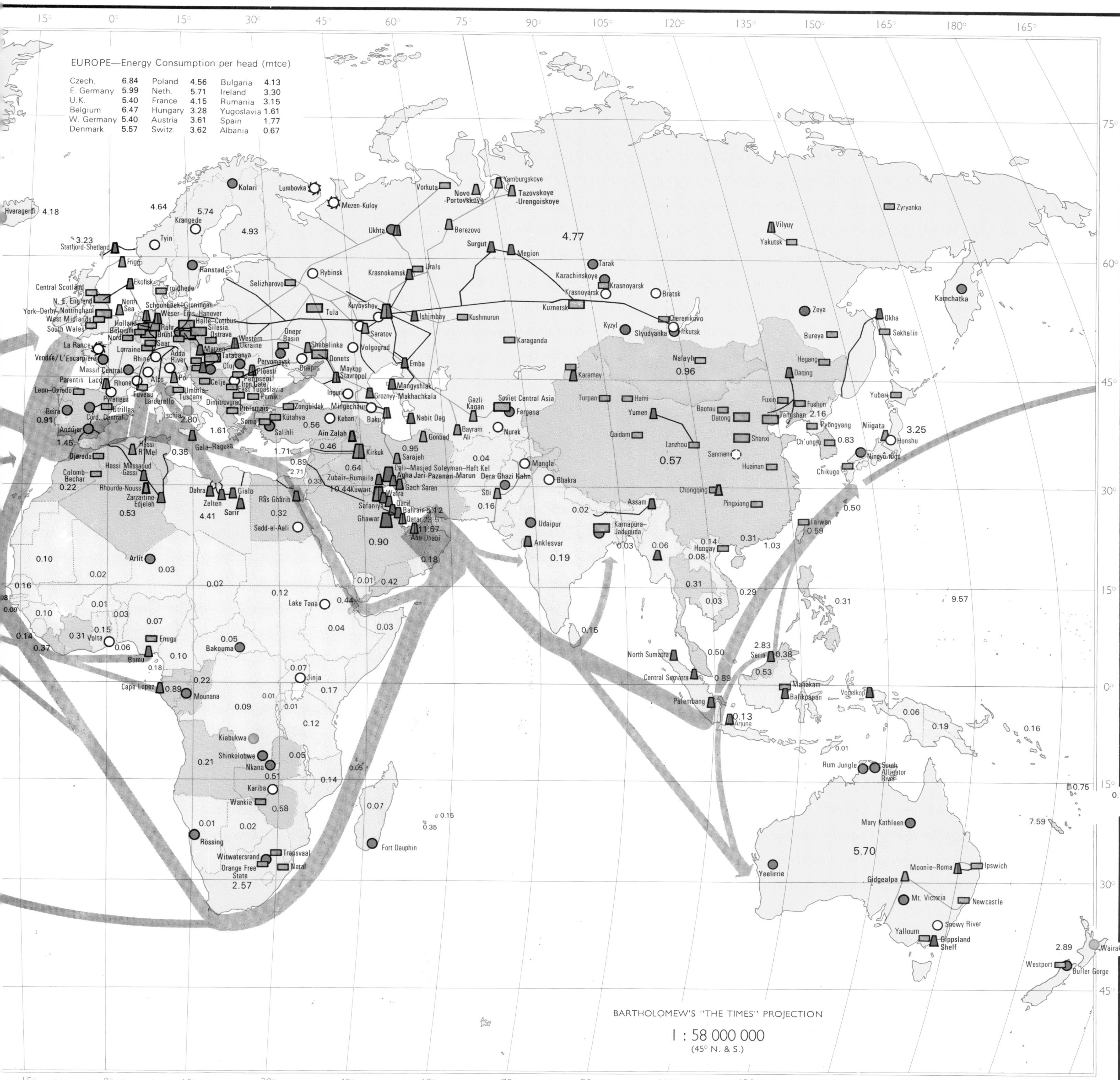

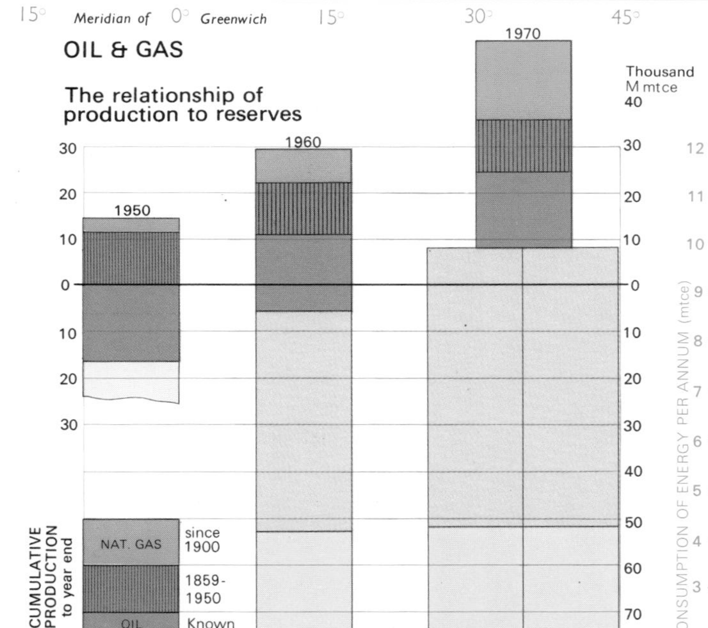

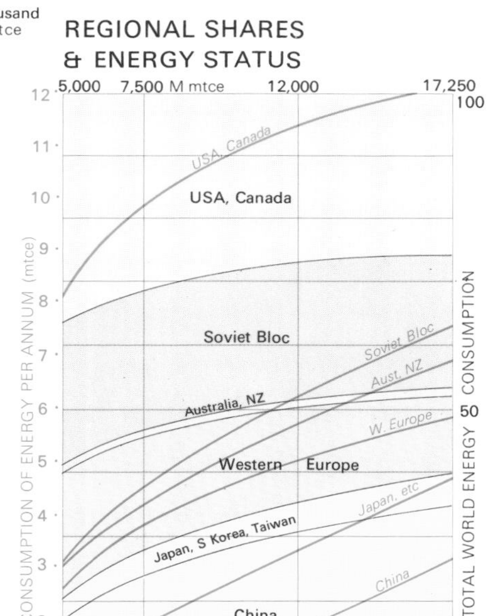

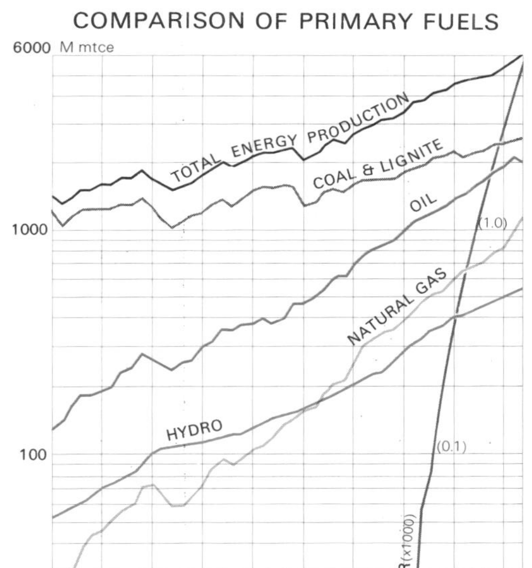

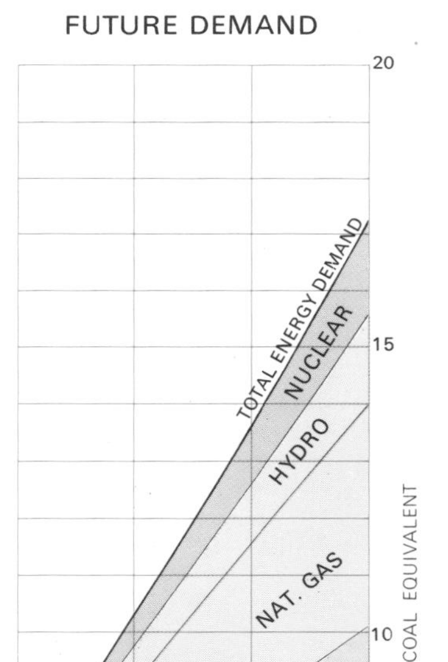

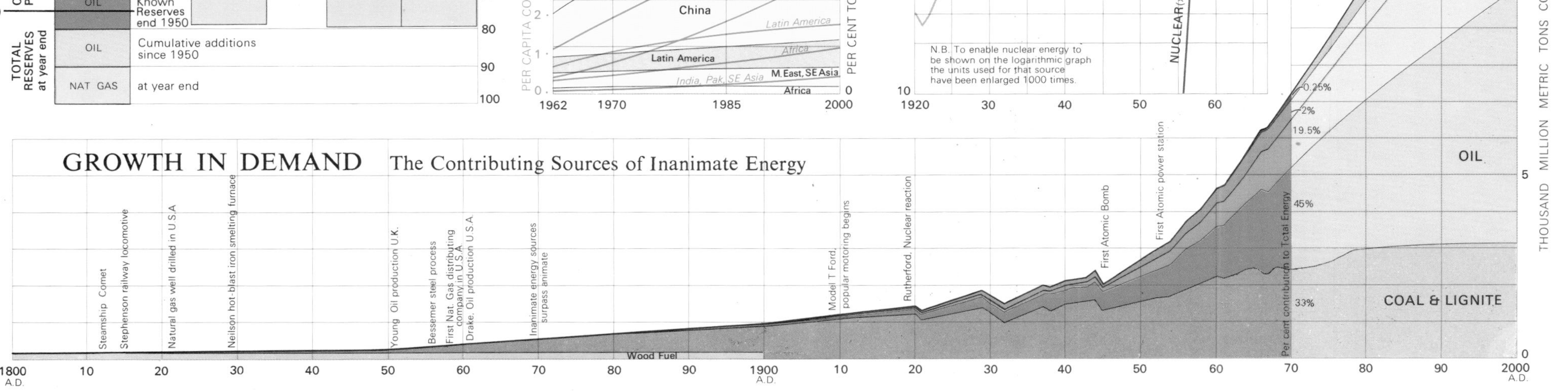

Printed in U.K.

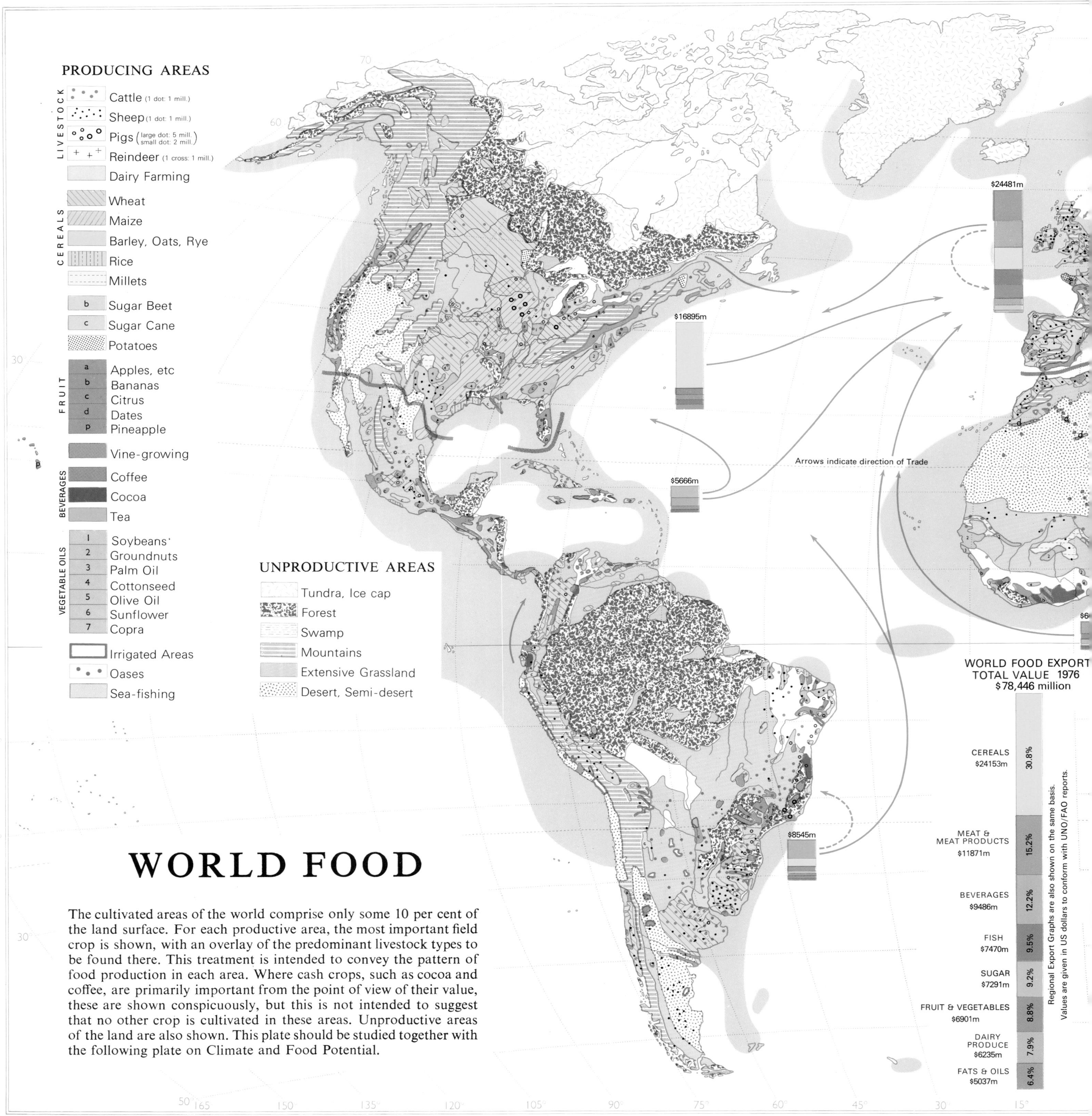
PRODUCING AREAS
LIVESTOCK
Cattle (1 dot: 1 mill.)
Sheep (1 dot: 1 mill.)
Pigs (large dot: 5 mill. small dot: 2 mill.)
Reindeer (1 cross: 1 mill.)
Dairy Farming
CEREALS
Wheat
Maize
Barley, Oats, Rye
Rice
Millets
Sugar Beet
Sugar Cane
Potatoes
FRUIT
Apples, etc
Bananas
Citrus
Dates
Pineapple
Vine-growing
BEVERAGES
Coffee
Cocoa
Tea
VEGETABLE OILS
Soybeans
Groundnuts
Palm Oil
Cottonseed
Olive Oil
Sunflower
Copra
Irrigated Areas
Oases
Sea-fishing
UNPRODUCTIVE AREAS
Tundra, Ice cap
Forest
Swamp
Mountains
Extensive Grassland
Desert, Semi-desert
Arrows indicate direction of Trade
$24481m
$16895m
$5666m
$8545m
WORLD FOOD EXPORTS
TOTAL VALUE 1976
$78,446 million
CEREALS $24153m 30.8%
MEAT & MEAT PRODUCTS $11871m 15.2%
BEVERAGES $9486m 12.2%
FISH $7470m 9.5%
SUGAR $7291m 9.2%
FRUIT & VEGETABLES $6901m 8.8%
DAIRY PRODUCE $6235m 7.9%
FATS & OILS $5037m 6.4%
Regional Export Graphs are also shown on the same basis.
Values are given in US dollars to conform with UNO/FAO reports.

WORLD FOOD

The cultivated areas of the world comprise only some 10 per cent of the land surface. For each productive area, the most important field crop is shown, with an overlay of the predominant livestock types to be found there. This treatment is intended to convey the pattern of food production in each area. Where cash crops, such as cocoa and coffee, are primarily important from the point of view of their value, these are shown conspicuously, but this is not intended to suggest that no other crop is cultivated in these areas. Unproductive areas of the land are also shown. This plate should be studied together with the following plate on Climate and Food Potential.

WORLD FOOD PRODUCTION AND TRADE by Regions

Boundaries of Regions on main map

REGIONAL PRODUCTION GRAPHS

Comparative Regional Production is shown by areas of colour and in percentages (3-year averages) of Total World Production which is in million metric tons (M) for a given year. Individual countries are only shown where their production is significant.

Each unit square equals one per cent World production.

REGIONAL TRADE GRAPHS

The balance of World Trade is shown by regions for main meats and cereals. Each coloured unit square equals 10 per cent of World Trade for the particular commodity (3-year average). Totals of World Exports and Imports are in million metric tons (M) for a given year.

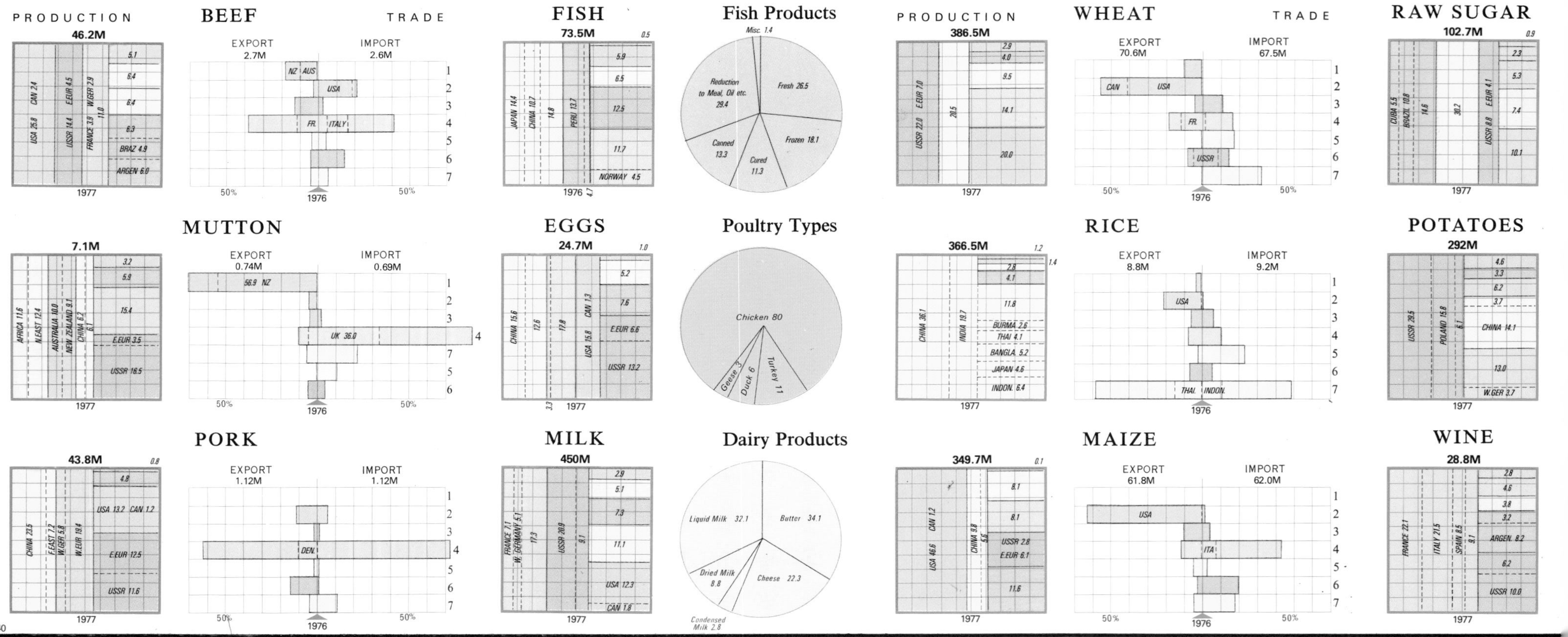
PRODUCTION
BEEF
TRADE
46.2M
EXPORT 2.7M
IMPORT 2.6M
FISH
73.5M
Fish Products
WHEAT
386.5M
EXPORT 70.6M
IMPORT 67.5M
RAW SUGAR
102.7M
MUTTON
7.1M
EXPORT 0.74M
IMPORT 0.69M
EGGS
24.7M
Poultry Types
Chicken 80
RICE
366.5M
EXPORT 8.8M
IMPORT 9.2M
POTATOES
292M
PORK
43.8M
EXPORT 1.12M
IMPORT 1.12M
MILK
450M
Dairy Products
Liquid Milk 32.1
Butter 34.1
Cheese 22.3
MAIZE
349.7M
EXPORT 61.8M
IMPORT 62.0M
WINE
28.8M
1977
1976

7740

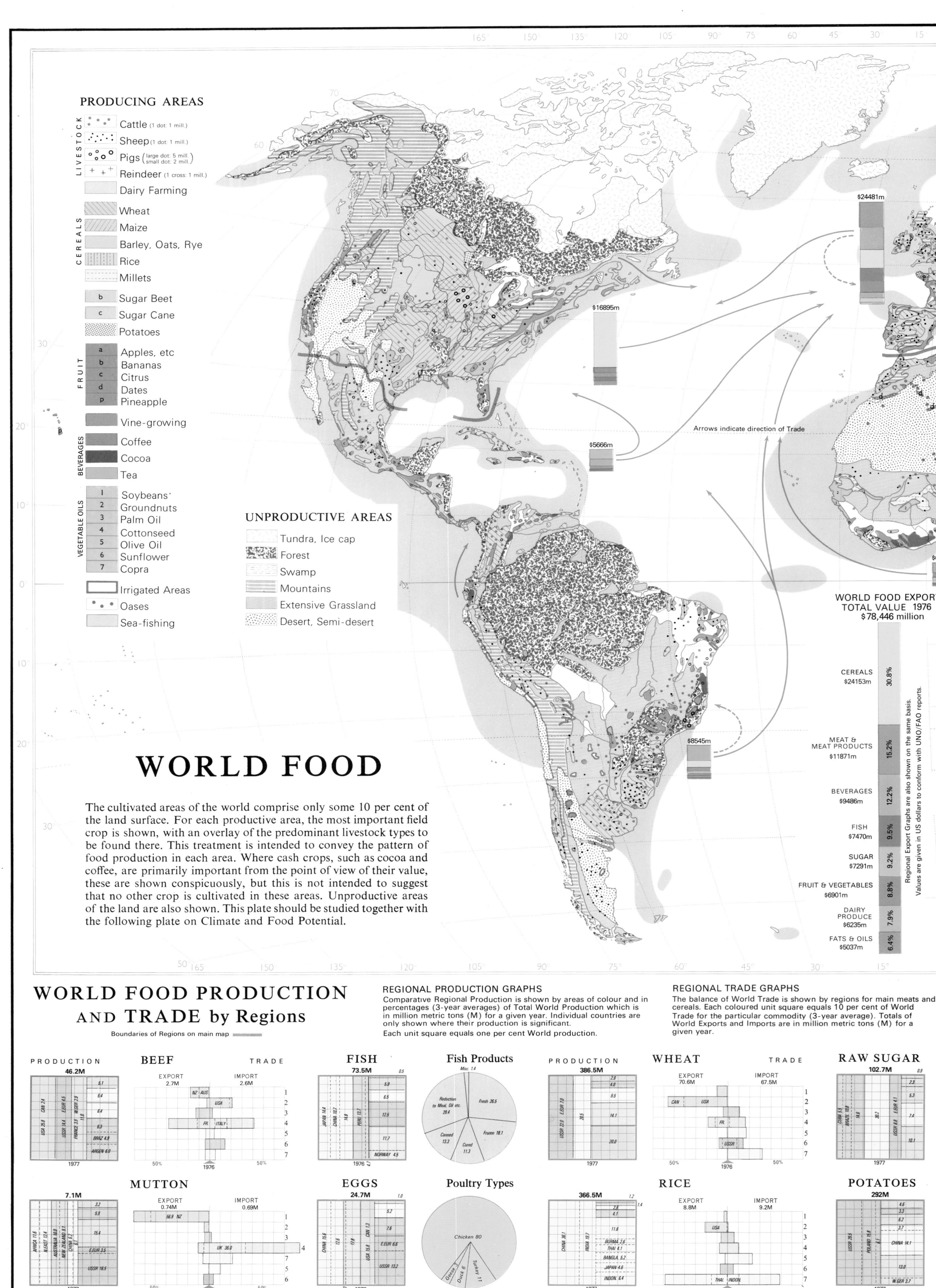

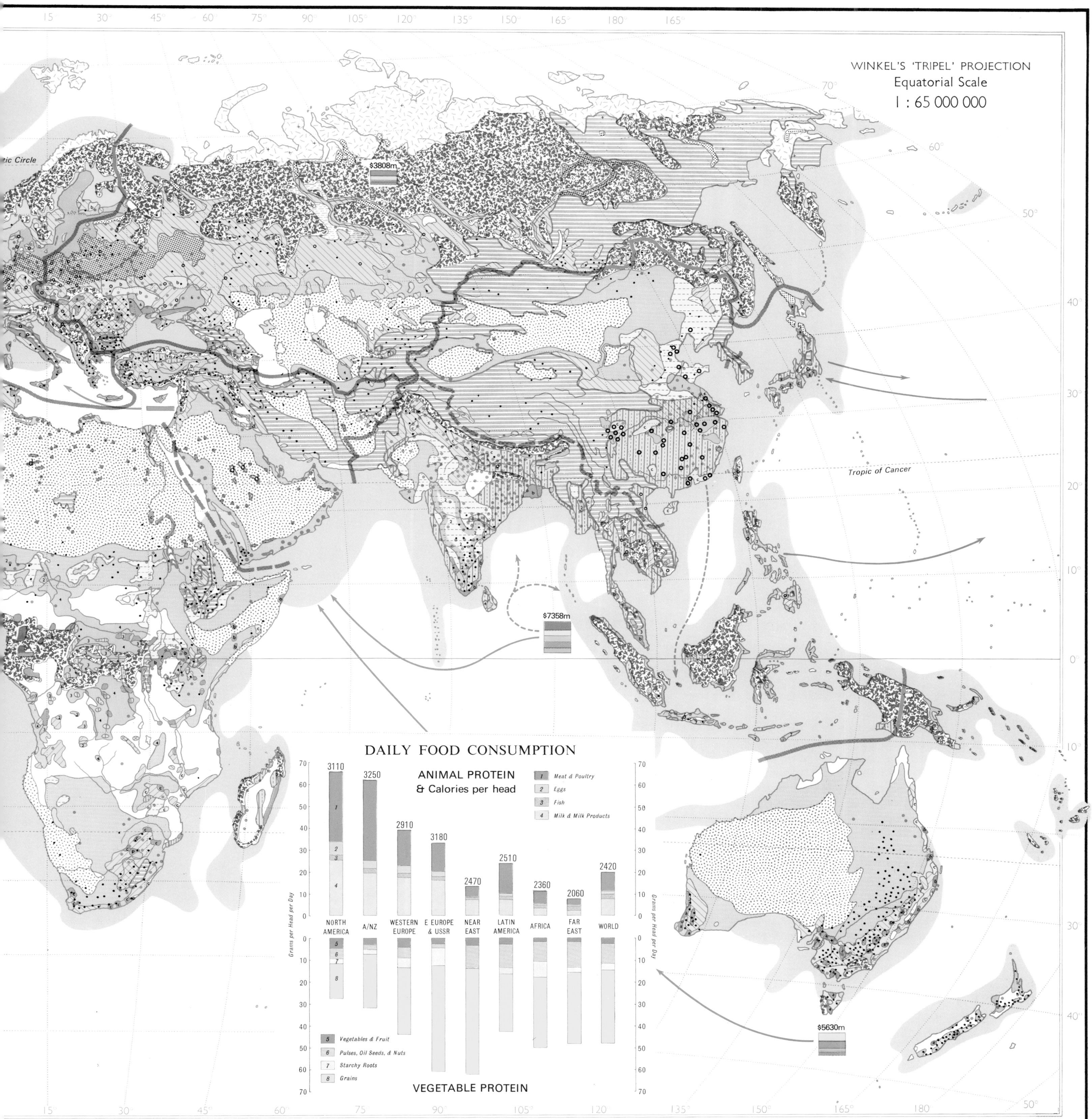
WINKEL'S 'TRIPEL' PROJECTION
Equatorial Scale
1 : 65 000 000
Tropic of Cancer
$3808m
$7358m
$5630m
DAILY FOOD CONSUMPTION
ANIMAL PROTEIN
& Calories per head
1 Meat & Poultry
2 Eggs
3 Fish
4 Milk & Milk Products
3110
3250
2910
3180
2470
2510
2360
2060
2420
NORTH AMERICA
A/NZ
WESTERN EUROPE
E EUROPE & USSR
NEAR EAST
LATIN AMERICA
AFRICA
FAR EAST
WORLD
Grams per Head per Day
5 Vegetables & Fruit
6 Pulses, Oil Seeds, & Nuts
7 Starchy Roots
8 Grains
VEGETABLE PROTEIN

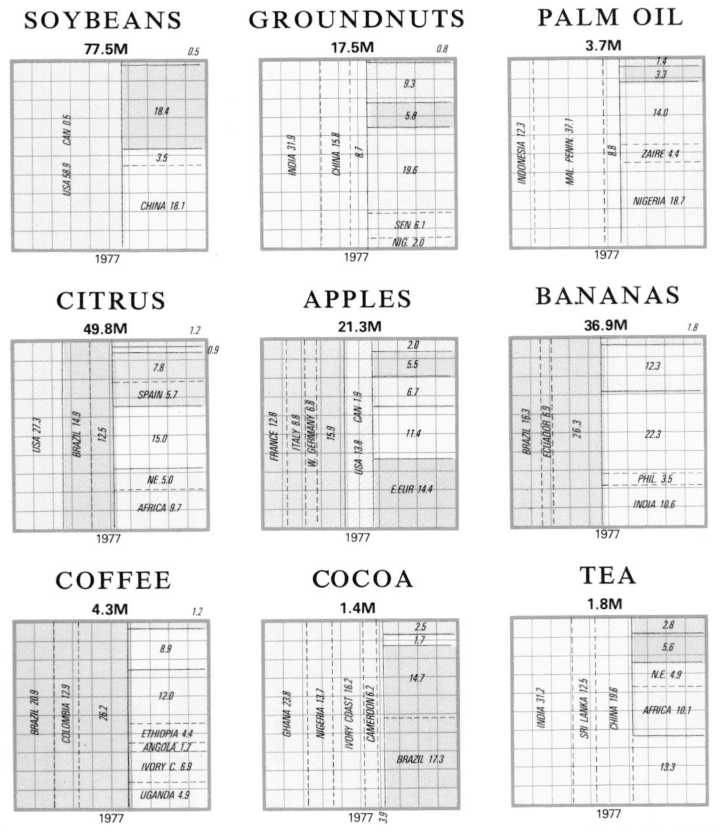
REGIONAL COLOURS ON GRAPHS
1 Australia/N.Z.
2 U.S.A./Canada
3 Latin America
4 W. Europe
5 Africa/Near East
6 Soviet Bloc
7 Far East
Others
SOYBEANS
77.5M
USA 58.9
CAN 0.5
18.4
3.5
CHINA 18.1
1977
GROUNDNUTS
17.5M
INDIA 31.9
CHINA 15.8
8.7
9.3
5.8
19.6
SEN 6.1
NIG. 2.0
1977
PALM OIL
3.7M
INDONESIA 12.3
MAL. PENIN. 37.1
8.8
1.4
3.3
14.0
ZAIRE 4.4
NIGERIA 18.7
1977
CITRUS
49.8M
USA 27.3
BRAZIL 14.9
12.5
1.2
0.9
7.8
SPAIN 5.7
15.0
NE 5.0
AFRICA 9.7
1977
APPLES
21.3M
FRANCE 12.8
ITALY 8.8
W. GERMANY 6.8
15.9
USA 13.8
CAN 1.9
2.0
5.5
6.7
11.4
E.EUR 14.4
1977
BANANAS
36.9M
BRAZIL 16.3
ECUADOR 6.9
26.3
1.8
12.3
22.3
PHIL. 3.5
INDIA 10.6
1977
COFFEE
4.3M
BRAZIL 20.9
COLOMBIA 12.9
26.2
1.2
8.9
12.0
ETHIOPIA 4.4
ANGOLA 1.7
IVORY C. 6.9
UGANDA 4.9
1977
COCOA
1.4M
GHANA 23.8
NIGERIA 13.7
IVORY COAST 16.2
CAMEROON 6.2
2.5
1.7
14.7
BRAZIL 17.3
1977
3.9
TEA
1.8M
INDIA 31.2
SRI LANKA 12.5
CHINA 19.6
2.8
5.6
N.E. 4.9
AFRICA 10.1
13.3
1977

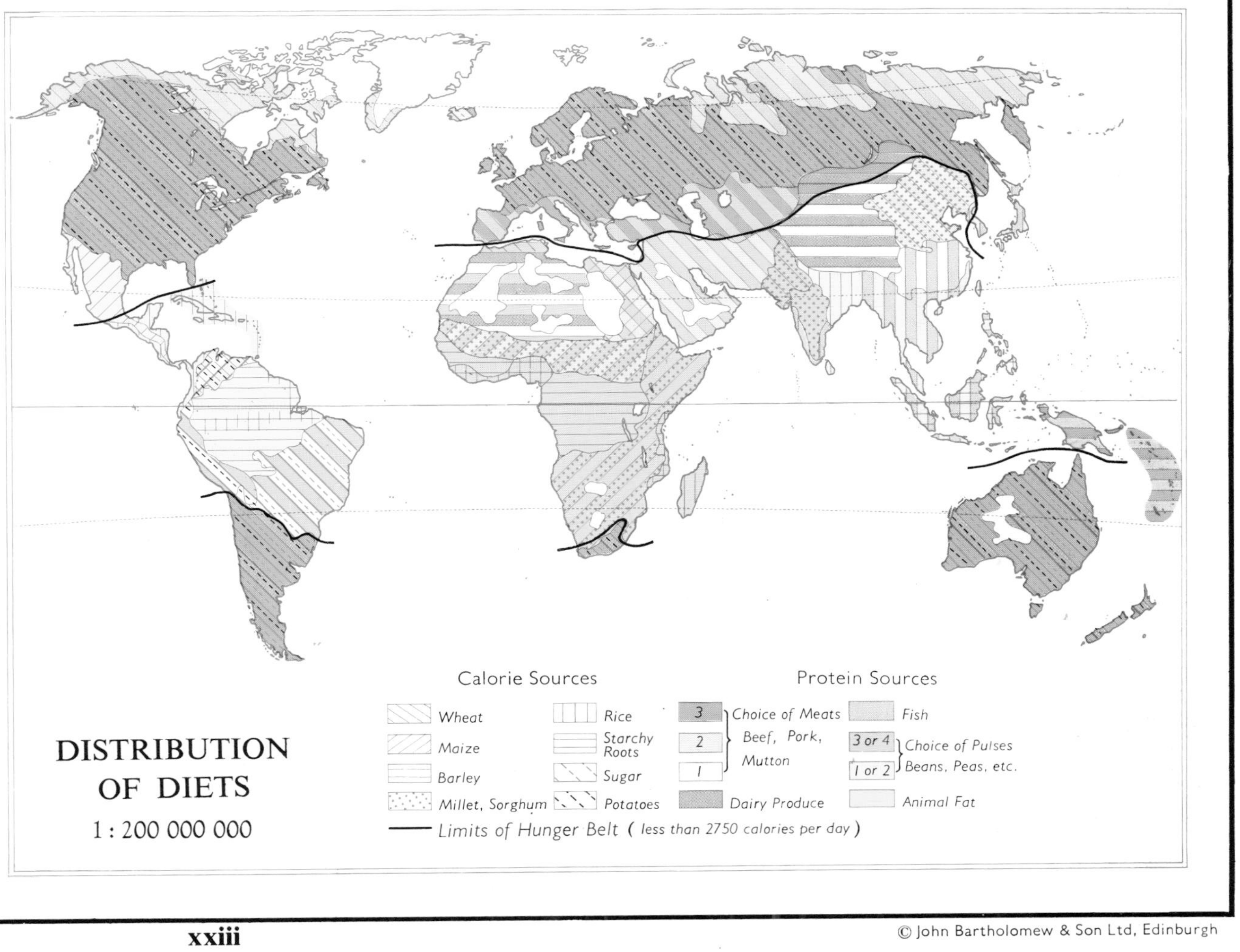
DISTRIBUTION OF DIETS
1 : 200 000 000
Calorie Sources
Wheat
Maize
Barley
Millet, Sorghum
Rice
Starchy Roots
Sugar
Potatoes
Protein Sources
3
2
1
Choice of Meats Beef, Pork, Mutton
Dairy Produce
Fish
3 or 4
1 or 2
Choice of Pulses Beans, Peas, etc.
Animal Fat
Limits of Hunger Belt (less than 2750 calories per day)

WORLD CLIMATE
and Food Potential

		APPROPRIATE SYSTEMS & FOOD PRODUCTS	AREAS OF UNEXPLOITED POTENTIAL	MEASURES REQUIRED
POLAR	EF Ice cap	*NIL*	NIL	
	ET Tundra	*Reindeer (Nomadic)*		
COOLER HUMID	Dc Dd Subarctic	*Barley, Oats, Rye,* *Cattle, Forage crops*	*Canada, Siberia: Northern river valleys	*D, F, C* *Stone removal* *Quick growing strains*
	Db Continental Cool Summer	*Dairy Cattle, Forage Crops, Barley, Oats, Rye, Spring Wheat, Potatoes*	**N. Canadian prairie **Central European Russia	
	Da Continental Warm Summer	*Wheat, Millet, Maize, Soybeans, Forage Crops, Cattle, Sheep*	*Manchuria	*P, F, Flood control* *Improved husbandry*
WARMER HUMID	Cb Cc Marine West Coast	*Dairy Cattle, Sheep, Fodder Crops, Horticulture, Wheat, Barley, Oats*	***New Zealand ***S.E. Australia	*D, F, P* *More intensive farming*
	Ca Humid Subtropical	*Cattle Ranching, Wheat, Maize, Rice, Truck Farming*	***Uruguay ***Australia: E. coast plains	*A, E, F, P* *Selective breeding*
	Cs Mediterranean	*Horticulture, Viticulture, Citrus, Wheat, Sheep, Goats*	***S. Australia ***S. Africa **Mediterranean littoral	*I, E, F, M, A* *Restoration and preservation of pasture*
DRY	BS Steppe	*Cattle, Sheep, Fodder Crops, Wheat, Maize, Millet*	***USSR: Steppe ***China: Northern loess ***Queensland (NSW) **N. American prairies	*I, F, P* *Selective breeding*
	BW Desert	*Sheep, Goats, Millet, Wheat, Date Palms*	***Great American desert ***Soviet Central Asia ***Upper Egypt **S.W. Asia: River basins *Sahara NW & SE (aquifers)	*Provision of water* *Prevention of salinity* *I, F, M*
TROPICAL HUMID	Aw As Savanna	*Cattle, Pigs, Poultry Millet, Maize, Padi Rice, Vegetable Oils, Sugar Cane* *Padi Rice, Fish Farming*	**Ethiopia, W. Madagascar *African savanna *Llanos and campos *Northern Australia **S.E. Asia: Great river basins	*Water conservation* *Fire control* *Disease control* *Selective breeding* *E, F, C* *Soil and water conservation* *A, F*
	Af Am Rain forest	*Rice, Vegetable Oils, Citrus, Bananas, Coffee, Tea, Cocoa, Fish Farming, Pigs, Poultry*	**Malaysia **Guinea Coast *Amazon basin *Indonesia *Congo *Central America	*Penetration, C* *Maintenance of fertility, F* *Mixed cropping, Bush fallowing* *Water and Erosion control* *Disease and Weed control*
		NOTES Ease of exploitation: ***Most practical **Possible *Difficult	A Agrarian reform C Communications D Drainage E Erosion control F Fertilizers I Irrigation	M Mechanization P Pasture improvement: Controlled grazing, Selected species; Rotation with fodder crops

The main factors of environment which determine plant development and distribution are those provided by climate and the soil. Climate thus imposes limits to agricultural systems according to the varying conditions of temperature, moisture and light. This plate shows the seasonal variation of these factors classified according to the Köppen system (as modified by Trewartha). The table above provides a simple guide to areas of unexploited food-growing potential, but it should be emphasised that the most effective short-term solution to the problems of food supply can be achieved by the application of modern agricultural methods in existing areas of cultivation to attain a two- or three-fold increase of yield particularly in those countries with severe population problems.

See also related plates:

pp. xxii–iii : Food Production.
Plate 4: Precipitation, Evaporation and Air Circulation.
Plate 5: Natural Vegetation, Temperature, Soil Groups.

1 Nome
ET
Dcf
3 Edmonton
11 Victoria
Cbf
Dcf
Dbf
6 Minneapolis
4 Ottawa
BSk
Daf
38 Denver
20 San Francisco
BWh
7 New York
30 Washington
21 Los Angeles
47 Yuma
Caf
29 New Orleans
67 Miami
BSh
Ca
14 Mexico City
56 Veracruz
Aw
Am
Af
BS
57 Caracas
Am
Aw
16 Bogotá
Cb
Aw
68 Belém
Af
BS
48 Lima
Aw
58 Goiás
Af
69 Rio de Janeiro
ET
BWn
BS
45 Tucuman
Cb
Caf
26 Santiago
36 Buenos Aires
BW
49 Sarmiento
Cb
Cc

CLIMATE GRAPHS

These graphs relate by number, name and colour to selected stations on the map and present mean temperature and rainfall values for each month. Curves show temperatures in degrees centigrade and fahrenheit. Vertical blue columns depict rainfall in millimetres and inches with the total of the mean annual rainfall shown in millimetres. The altitude of each station above sea level is given in metres.

The letter symbols constitute a short description of the chief characteristics of a climate. These are defined on the opposite page.

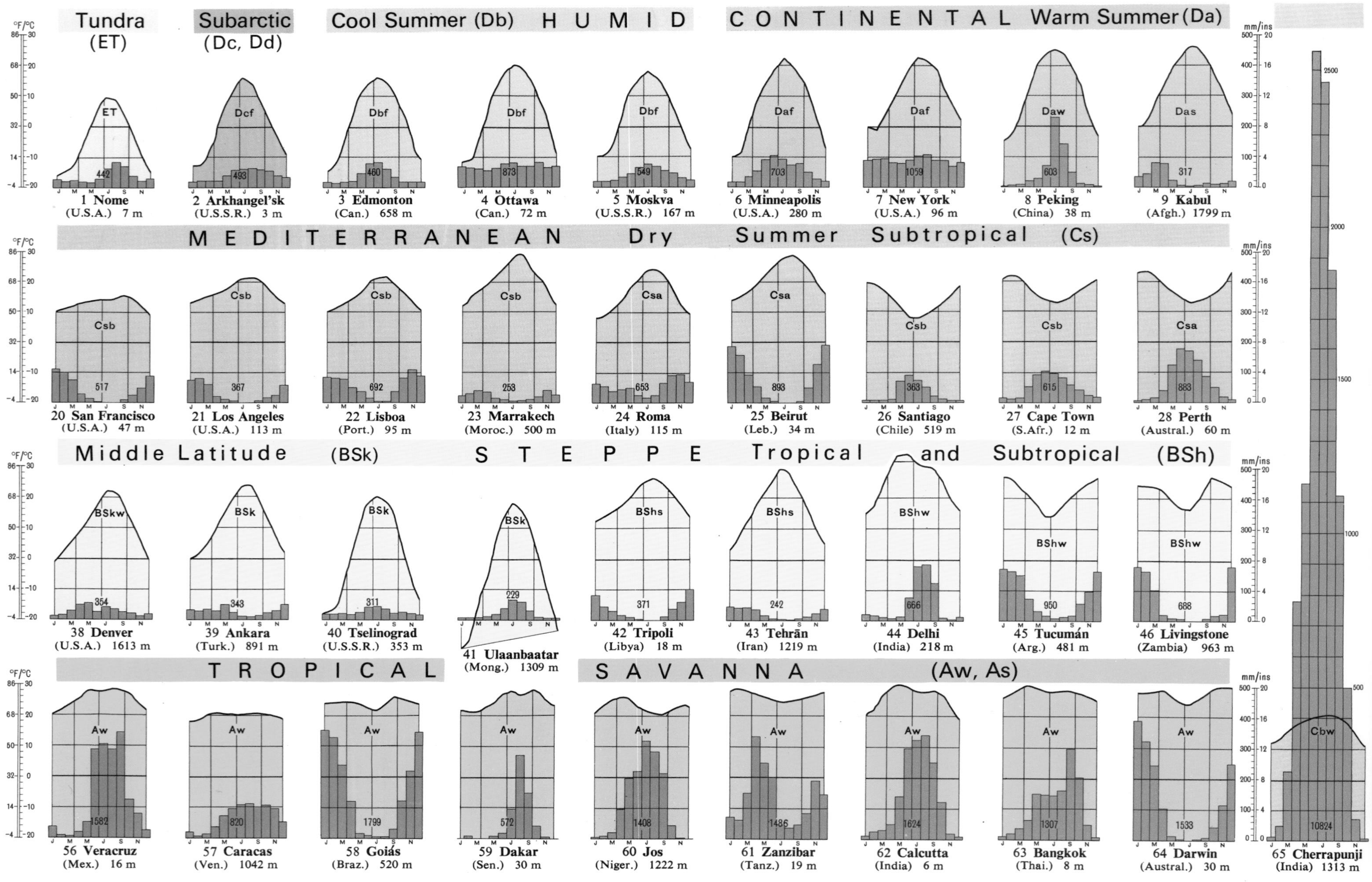
Tundra (ET)
Subarctic (Dc, Dd)
Cool Summer (Db) H U M I D C O N T I N E N T A L Warm Summer (Da)
1 Nome (U.S.A.) 7 m
2 Arkhangel'sk (U.S.S.R.) 3 m
3 Edmonton (Can.) 658 m
4 Ottawa (Can.) 72 m
5 Moskva (U.S.S.R.) 167 m
6 Minneapolis (U.S.A.) 280 m
7 New York (U.S.A.) 96 m
8 Peking (China) 38 m
9 Kabul (Afgh.) 1799 m
M E D I T E R R A N E A N Dry Summer Subtropical (Cs)
20 San Francisco (U.S.A.) 47 m
21 Los Angeles (U.S.A.) 113 m
22 Lisboa (Port.) 95 m
23 Marrakech (Moroc.) 500 m
24 Roma (Italy) 115 m
25 Beirut (Leb.) 34 m
26 Santiago (Chile) 519 m
27 Cape Town (S.Afr.) 12 m
28 Perth (Austral.) 60 m
Middle Latitude (BSk) S T E P P E Tropical and Subtropical (BSh)
38 Denver (U.S.A.) 1613 m
39 Ankara (Turk.) 891 m
40 Tselinograd (U.S.S.R.) 353 m
41 Ulaanbaatar (Mong.) 1309 m
42 Tripoli (Libya) 18 m
43 Tehrān (Iran) 1219 m
44 Delhi (India) 218 m
45 Tucumán (Arg.) 481 m
46 Livingstone (Zambia) 963 m
T R O P I C A L S A V A N N A (Aw, As)
56 Veracruz (Mex.) 16 m
57 Caracas (Ven.) 1042 m
58 Goiás (Braz.) 520 m
59 Dakar (Sen.) 30 m
60 Jos (Niger.) 1222 m
61 Zanzibar (Tanz.) 19 m
62 Calcutta (India) 6 m
63 Bangkok (Thai.) 8 m
64 Darwin (Austral.) 30 m
65 Cherrapunji (India) 1313 m

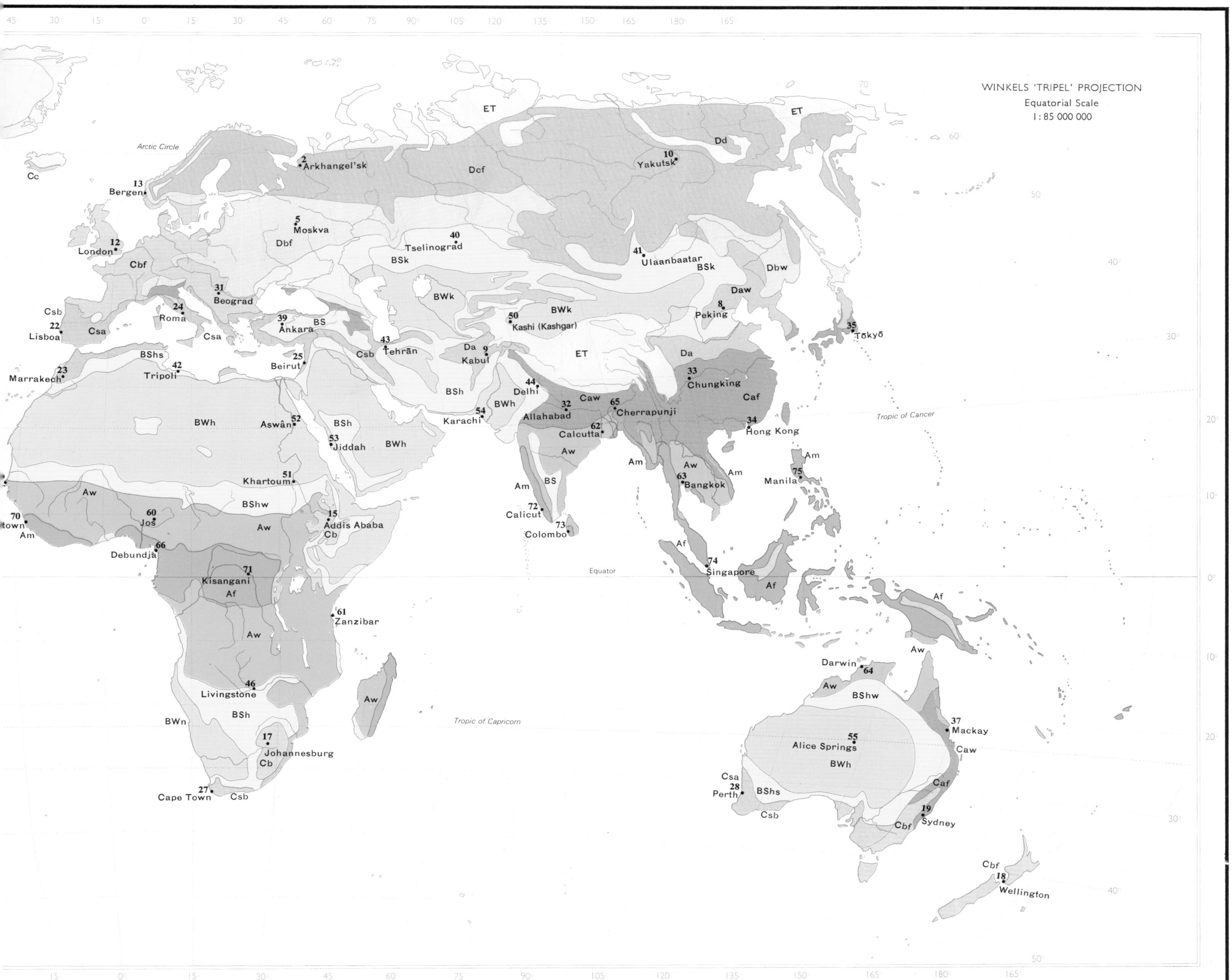
WINKELS 'TRIPEL' PROJECTION
Equatorial Scale
1 : 85 000 000
Arctic Circle
Tropic of Cancer
Equator
Tropic of Capricorn
ET
Dd
Dcf
Dbf
Dbw
Daw
Da
BSk
BWk
BWh
BSh
BShs
BShw
BWn
Cc
Cbf
Csb
Csa
Caw
Caf
Cb
Aw
Am
Af
BS
2 Arkhangel'sk
10 Yakutsk
13 Bergen
5 Moskva
40 Tselinograd
12 London
41 Ulaanbaatar
31 Beograd
8 Peking
24 Roma
39 Ankara
50 Kashi (Kashgar)
35 Tōkyō
22 Lisboa
43 Tehrān
9 Kabul
25 Beirut
42 Tripoli
23 Marrakech
44 Delhi
33 Chungking
32 Allahabad
65 Cherrapunji
54 Karachi
52 Aswân
34 Hong Kong
62 Calcutta
53 Jiddah
51 Khartoum
63 Bangkok
75 Manila
72 Calicut
60 Jos
15 Addis Ababa
73 Colombo
70 Freetown
66 Debundja
74 Singapore
71 Kisangani
61 Zanzibar
64 Darwin
46 Livingstone
37 Mackay
55 Alice Springs
17 Johannesburg
28 Perth
27 Cape Town
19 Sydney
18 Wellington

Definitions of MAJOR CLIMATIC REGIONS and SUB-TYPES

A Rainy climate with no winter: coolest month above 18°C (64.4°F).

B Dry climates; limits are defined by formulae based on rainfall effectiveness:
- BS Steppe or semi-arid climate.
- BW Desert (German: Wüste) or arid climate.

*C Rainy climates with mild winters: coolest month above 0° C (32° F), but below 18°C (64.4°F); warmest month above 10°C (50°F).

*D Rainy climates with severe winters: coldest month below 0°C (32°F); warmest month above 10°C (50°F).

E Polar climates with no warm season: warmest month below 10°C (50°F).
- ET Tundra climate: warmest month below 10°C (50°F) but above 0°C (32°F).
- EF Perpetual frost: all months below 0°C (32°F).

a Warmest month above 22°C (71.6°F).
b Warmest month below 22°C (71.6°F).
c Less than four months over 10°C (50°F).
d As 'c', but with severe cold: coldest month below −38°C (−36.4°F).

f Constantly moist: rainfall of the driest month is at least 60 mm. (2.4 ins.).
*h Warmer dry: all months above 0°C (32°F).
*k Cooler dry: at least one month below 0°C (32°F).

m Monsoon rain: short dry season, but is compensated by heavy rains during rest of the year.
n Frequent fog.
s Dry season in summer.
w Dry season in winter.

*Modification of Köppen definition.

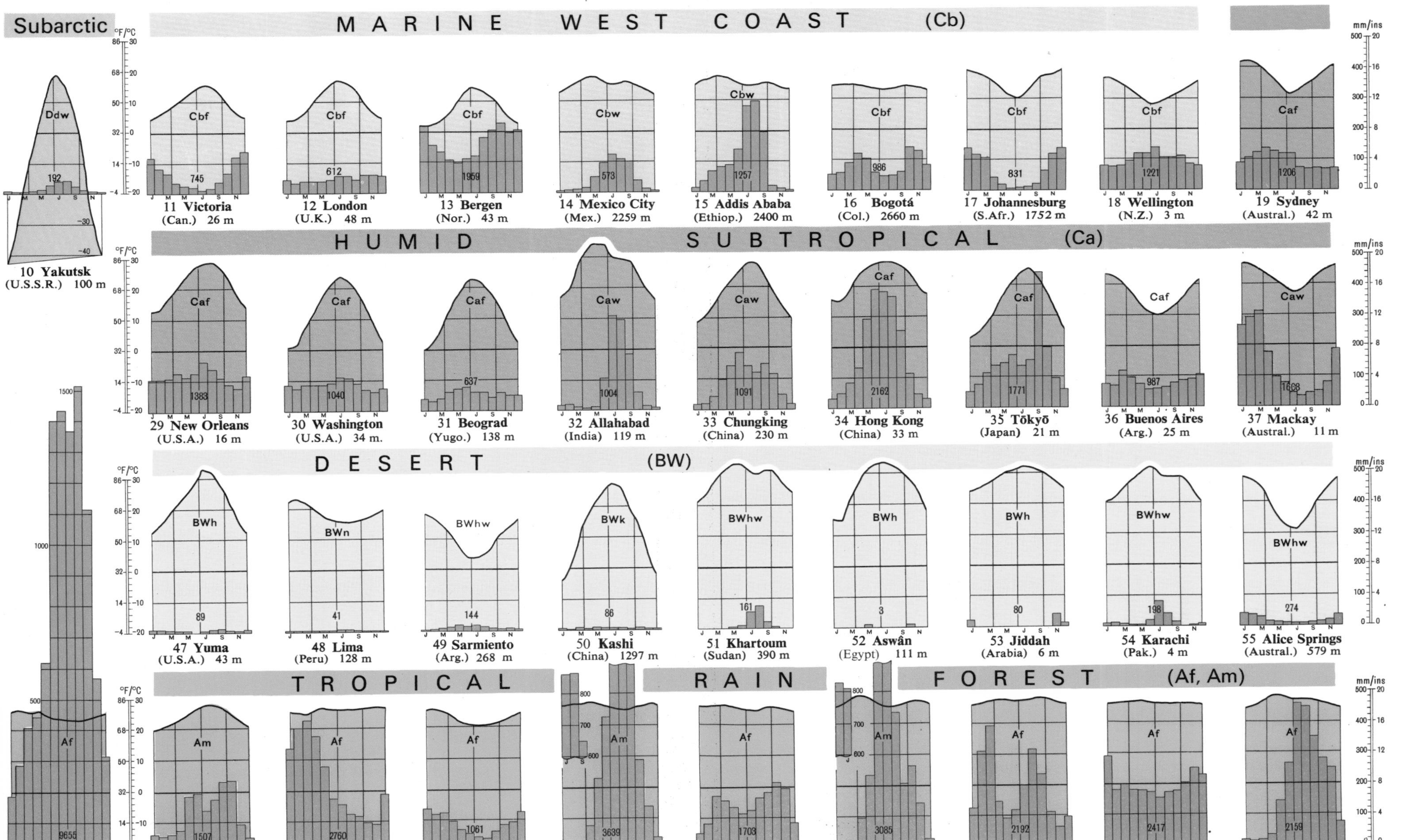
Subarctic
MARINE WEST COAST (Cb)
HUMID SUBTROPICAL (Ca)
DESERT (BW)
TROPICAL RAIN FOREST (Af, Am)
°F/°C
mm/ins
10 Yakutsk (U.S.S.R.) 100 m
11 Victoria (Can.) 26 m
12 London (U.K.) 48 m
13 Bergen (Nor.) 43 m
14 Mexico City (Mex.) 2259 m
15 Addis Ababa (Ethiop.) 2400 m
16 Bogotá (Col.) 2660 m
17 Johannesburg (S.Afr.) 1752 m
18 Wellington (N.Z.) 3 m
19 Sydney (Austral.) 42 m
29 New Orleans (U.S.A.) 16 m
30 Washington (U.S.A.) 34 m.
31 Beograd (Yugo.) 138 m
32 Allahabad (India) 119 m
33 Chungking (China) 230 m
34 Hong Kong (China) 33 m
35 Tōkyō (Japan) 21 m
36 Buenos Aires (Arg.) 25 m
37 Mackay (Austral.) 11 m
47 Yuma (U.S.A.) 43 m
48 Lima (Peru) 128 m
49 Sarmiento (Arg.) 268 m
50 Kashi (China) 1297 m
51 Khartoum (Sudan) 390 m
52 Aswân (Egypt) 111 m
53 Jiddah (Arabia) 6 m
54 Karachi (Pak.) 4 m
55 Alice Springs (Austral.) 579 m
66 Debundja (Cameroun) 5 m
67 Miami (U.S.A.) 25 m
68 Belém (Braz.) 24 m
69 Rio de Janeiro (Braz.) 60 m
70 Freetown (Sa. Leone) 68 m
71 Kisangani (Zaire) 415 m
72 Calicut (India) 8 m
73 Colombo (Sri Lanka) 7 m
74 Singapore 5 m
75 Manila (Philip.) 14 m

THE UNIVERSE

The Sun is one of some hundred thousand million stars in our Galaxy, the Milky Way, itself one of billions of galaxies of which 10,000 million are within range of our largest optical telescopes. Apart from stars and planets the galaxies contain clouds of gas and dust.

The majority of galaxies exhibit spiral structure, in which arms wind more or less closely round their central regions. No spiral arms are found in what are called elliptical galaxies which show large numbers of stars arranged in rotationally symmetric clusters. A third type of galaxy is irregular in shape and structure.

Our own Galaxy is a spiral galaxy. Most of its stars and nearly all its diffuse material are situated in a flat disk, thicker at the centre than the edge, and surrounded by a spherical halo composed of old red stars and of some 200 globular star clusters containing from 100,000 to a few million stars.

The dust in the interstellar medium prevents us from actually observing visually or photographically the centre of the Galaxy, which is in the direction of the constellation Sagittarius. Infra-red and radio observations, however, can penetrate the dust and reach the central regions where large numbers of stars are found concentrated. There are several thousand times as many stars near the galactic centre as there are in an equal volume of space near the Sun. Radio observations of the galactic centre have also discovered the existence there of clouds of various highly complex molecules with stars in the early stages of formation in their midst.

Observations of stellar motions have shown that the stars of the galactic disk revolve round the galactic centre with speeds which depend on their position in the Galaxy. The sun and neighbouring stars take about 225 million years to complete a revolution: since the carboniferous age they have travelled once round the galactic system. The theory of stellar structure and stellar evolution makes it possible to attach ages to different types of stars and to different regions of the Galaxy. The theory is based on the recognition that the stars are kept shining for long periods of time by the energy released in nuclear reactions in their hot interiors and that the gradual exhaustion of their nuclear energy sources leads to changes in their internal structure and to corresponding changes in their observable external appearance. It is thus found that the oldest stars which are members of the globular star clusters in the galactic halo date back to some ten thousand million years, whereas the youngest stars which are found in or near the clouds of gas and dust in the spiral arms of the Galaxy have ages of only a few million or less years. The ages of the stars of the galactic disk lie between these two extremes; the Sun, a disk star, is between four and five thousand million years old.

The stars are formed out of the diffuse clouds of the interstellar medium, and their chemical composition at the time of their formation can therefore be assumed to be the same as that of the interstellar matter. This is made up principally of hydrogen and helium atoms in the ratio of ten to one, but there are also some atoms of heavier elements. The numbers of such atoms will increase with time if, as is widely assumed, they have been formed through nucleo-synthesis in the interiors of massive stars and returned into the interstellar medium in the course of explosions of such stars. Young stars formed out of the present interstellar medium should therefore contain a slightly greater abundance of heavy elements than old stars formed out of earlier material. This is in fact what one observes if one compares the chemical composition of old stars in the galactic halo with that of young stars in the spiral arms.

The final stages in the evolution of stars depend largely on their mass. Stars may collapse into dense white dwarfs with diameters comparable to those of planets, or, if they are appreciably more massive than the Sun, into extremely dense neutron stars with diameters of the order of only 20 kilometres. The existence of such rapidly spinning neutron stars has been discovered through the observation of the fast radio pulses of the so-called pulsars. Theoretical considerations indicate that if a star is sufficiently massive, it may eventually collapse into a 'black hole' with a circumference of only a few kilometres. According to the theory of general relativity no light or radiation of any sort can escape from such a black hole, whose existence can only be inferred indirectly from its possible influence on its surroundings.

Distances involved in stellar and galactic astronomy are too large to be expressed in kilometres. Light, travelling at a speed of 300,000 kilometres per second (186,000 miles per second), takes 8 minutes to cover the distance between the Sun and Earth (150 million kilometres). Distances within the planetary system can, therefore, be reckoned in light hours. Light takes more than four years to reach us from the nearest star, and it is in light years that distances between the stars in our galaxy are measured. The Sun's distance from the centre of the galaxy is about 30,000 light years and the diameter of the galactic disk is about 100,000 light years. In early 1979 a spiral galaxy, 250 million light years away was found to be six times the diameter of ours.

Our own galaxy is one of a local group, numbering about 20, all within about 3 million light years of each other and all linked by an envelope of hydrogen gas. The group includes the spiral galaxy in Andromeda at a distance of 2·2 million light years – it is in every respect similar to the Milky Way Galaxy, but larger – and two irregular galaxies, the large and small Magellanic clouds at about 160,000 light years, which are our nearest galactic neighbours.

Black holes were predicted before evidence was obtained of their possible existence. Matter drawn towards a black hole from a companion star probably accretes onto a kind of disk before passing into the black hole and out of the Universe. The black hole continues to exert intense gravitational attraction and its mass will increase as it absorbs new matter. The black hole has no linear dimensions, only extraordinary density

In astronomy the brightness of stars and other objects is usually expressed in 'magnitudes'. Hipparchus in the second century BC classed the brightest stars as being of first magnitude and the faintest of sixth magnitude. The principle remains in use today but in the 19th century a logarithmic scale was adopted so that a difference of five magnitudes corresponded to a ratio of 100 to 1 in brightness. A difference of one magnitude makes one star $\sqrt[5]{100}$ (or 2·512) times brighter than the other. Because of the fixing of the zero point in the scale certain very bright stars have negative magnitudes. Arcturus has a magnitude of 0·10; that of Sirius is −1·47. The magnitude difference between Sirius, the brightest star, and the faintest star discernible in telescopes today is 25 (a brightness ratio of 10,000 million to 1).

Within the local group, establishment of distances depends on the comparison of the measured brightness of stars with their intrinsic luminosity. Certain stars vary in brightness either periodically or irregularly. In some cases this is due to a binary star eclipsing its companion. True intrinsic variables are of many types. They include pulsating variables and of these the classical Cepheids, called after the star Delta Cephei, with periods of light variations between one and seventy days, are of particular interest. They are readily recognisable and being highly luminous – a thousand and more times as luminous as the Sun – are visible from great distances. Because their intrinsic luminosity is closely related to their period of variation distances can be measured with considerable precision.

Beyond the local group the Cepheids cannot serve in this way but individual objects of exceptional luminosity, such as Novae, can still be observed at distances of from 10 to 20 million light years. From then on the individual stars are no longer visible and distances are determined from the luminosity of whole galaxies.

Galaxies are too remote to show movement visually but their motion can be measured by means of the Doppler principle. The light from galaxies (as well as stars) moving away from the observer becomes redder and when approaching there is a similar shift towards the blue end of the spectrum. Except for nearby galaxies whose apparent motion is affected by our own galactic rotation, all galaxies show a red shift which means they are all moving away; the greater the distance the faster the recession, ultimately approaching the speed of light. The universe is thus observed to be expanding.

Possibly half the galaxies in the Universe are members of a cluster. Our local group is sparsely inhabited. 'Rich' clusters, on the other hand, occupying a sphere of no more than 3 million light years radius may contain as many as 1,000 galaxies, more densely packed towards the centre where a super-giant celestial galaxy may be found. Study of the gravitational forces in such galaxies is of great importance in astrophysics.

Expansion of the realm of galaxies points to a catastrophic beginning of the Universe. Because of the problems of measuring very distant objects the time of this event can be placed at 10,000 million years or 20,000 million years. Which figure is accepted depends on which value of a coefficient is adopted in the formula expressing Hubble's Law. If the Big Bang occurred 20,000 million years ago, the oldest of the stars observed are three times older than our Sun. Quasars have been observed out to 18,000 million light years.

There have been indications that the expansion is slowing down, but this is not certain. The initial Big Bang, however, has been confirmed by the detection of a very weak thermal radiation received from the whole sky; the last faint trace of the initial fireball.

The cluster of galaxies in Virgo comprises more than 1,000 members, of which only a few are shown here. From left to right the photograph covers 4 million light years. The pin-point size objects are stars in our own galaxy. At lower centre is the bright spiral galaxy M87. A black hole may exist at its centre. An unusual feature of this galaxy is a jet of material some 6,000 light years long, which can be seen emerging on the right hand side.

Galaxy NGC 1365 in the constellation Fornax is a fine example of a barred spiral galaxy. The bright central bar from which the spiral arms extend is 45,000 light years in length. NGC 1365 is the third brightest galaxy in Fornax. It is also one of the most luminous of the barred spirals. A supernova was detected in 1957.

THE SOLAR SYSTEM

Of the many theories for the origin of the Solar System two modern contending versions visualise the planets condensing and growing by accretion either in a nebular disk around the Sun or in a plume of material drawn out of a large protoplanet by the Sun. In either event the planets and all the smaller bodies of the Solar System were formed from primordial gas and dust.

In the process of accretion the planets swept up most of the solid matter and the Sun in a period of mass-shedding caused all the gas in interplanetary space to be carried away.

The Sun accounts for 99·866 per cent of all the matter in the Solar System. Jupiter accounts for two-thirds of the remainder leaving less than one-twentieth of one per cent for the rest. In diameter, 1,392,000 km (864,960 miles), the Sun is almost large enough to contain the whole lunar orbit twice over. Yet its density is only 1·409, the density of water being 1. Its main constituent is hydrogen but all the chemical elements are present.

The Sun rotates once in 27 days around an axis inclined at 7° 15′ to the plane of the ecliptic, but the rate varies considerably and may be as slow as 30 days or as fast as 23½ days. Away from the equator the rate of rotation is slower.

At the photosphere, the Sun's visible surface, temperature is 5,600° Kelvin but in the corona the Sun's tenuous outer atmosphere it is in excess of one million degrees. The corona is continuously expanding outwards creating the solar wind of charged particles which travels at 300 to 600 kms per second through space.

How the Sun yields its energy is not fully understood. Like other stars, the Sun loses energy by converting hydrogen to helium in nuclear reactions and in the process 4 million tons of matter are lost every second. Much of the interior activity and nature of the interior of the Sun remains unknown. External activity, sun spots, solar flares and prominences are known to be associated with gas flowing in magnetic fields but the magnitude of the activity cannot be repeated experimentally in laboratories. Thus the reason for the eleven-year cycle of sun spot activity, the long periods when there were little or no sun spots have yet to be explained.

Mercury has a particularly large core of about 1,800 km radius – more than 74 per cent of the planet's radius, compared with Earth's outer core of 54 per cent of its own radius. The heavily cratered surface of Mercury could be mistaken for the Moon in appearance showing the bombardment to which the planets were subjected in their early existence, but the surface temperature varies from 700°K at perihelian on the sunlit side to 100°K on the other side. The weak magnetic field was probably induced externally by the solar wind.

The rate of rotation which makes three days equal two years is due to tidal interaction with the Sun.

Venus has often been called Earth's twin but apart from size there is little similarity. Venus has a rocky core but it is smaller than the Earth's and no magnetic field is generated. Its very slow retrograde rotation is also unlike the Earth's rotation. The whole planetary surface is covered in yellowish clouds which completely conceal the level but cratered surface. The atmosphere is predominantly carbon dioxide. Only 2 per cent of sunlight reaches the surface. Most of the heat is trapped by the greenhouse effect of the atmosphere and the 40 km-thick clouds which extend to 70 km above the surface. Temperature is about constant by day or night at 730°K (467°C). Winds up to 100 m/s, known as 4-day winds because they circle the world in 4 days, drive the clouds. From the top cloud level where sulphur dioxide and sulphur trioxide are present, droplets of concentrated sulphuric acid slowly descend.

Mars is the planet most likely to be explored by a manned mission before the year AD 2000. Precession caused the Martian equator to migrate from 25° N to 25° S, or perhaps even more, over a period of many hundreds of millennia. The rugged southern hemisphere is divided from the smoother northern hemisphere by a line inclined at about 30° to the equator. Carbon dioxide makes up most of the very thin atmosphere. Even strong winds up to 17 m/s can only transport very fine materials. Spacecraft have resolved the question of the polar ice caps. They are composed of ice perhaps from 1 m to 1 km thick with a great deal of dust incorporated. Water is present in the regolith (the top layer of loose surface material) and below. In Spring and Summer the water is released to the atmosphere.

Jupiter is two and a half times as massive as all the other planets put together, yet its density is only 1·33 indicating that it is composed mainly of hydrogen. This factor plus its high rate of rotation causes flattening of 4,400 km at each of the poles. There is possibly a small rocky core but the bulk of the planet is composed of liquid metallic hydrogen out to 57,120 km from the centre and then liquid molecular hydrogen extends out to the base of the atmosphere which is the equivalent of a surface. From there to the top of the clouds 1,490 km above this layer are proceeding upwards droplets and ice crystals; ammonia hydrosulphide particles; ammonia crystals which form the top of the clouds; and beyond the clouds gaseous hydrogen.

Jupiter can be seen to have 7 or 8 bright cloud bands (zones) and alternating dark bands (belts). Zones represent upward movements and belts downward movements. The nature of the Great Red Spot is not known but it has remained as a feature for more than three centuries wandering from side to side about 1° every 90 days but remaining fixed in latitude. Jupiter transmits about twice as much heat as it receives. Of the 14 known satellites Amalthea, the nearest, appears to be on the point of being torn apart. Of the four Galilean satellites, Io is the most curious. At least seven active volcanoes have been observed.

Four known thin rings surround the planet at distances of 1·68, 1·7, 1·785 and 1·8 times the planet's radius.

Saturn the second largest planet rotates only slightly less rapidly than Jupiter. Since it is the only planet less dense than water (0·7) it is even more flattened at the poles, the polar radius being 6,000 km less than the equatorial. Like Jupiter it exhibits cloud bands parallel to the equator but less colourful. A central rocky core much larger than Jupiter's is enclosed by a shell of ice, then liquid metallic hydrogen and finally molecular hydrogen.

Saturn's rings are its most striking feature. They are composed of ice crystals probably coated with frost. Just outside the visible rings Pioneer XI identified a new planet 200–300 km diameter and two further rings beyond the five already designated ABCDE. Ring F is at 2·35 Saturn radii, the 'G' ring is further out still.

Uranus and **Neptune** are probably of similar composition. A rocky core is surrounded by a shell of ice, another of liquid metallic hydrogen and finally by one of liquid molecular hydrogen. Hydrogen is the most abundant gas. Methane is the main constituent of their atmosphere. Uranus is now known to have at least five rings, four of no more than 10 km width, the fifth and outer being probably 50 to 100 km wide. Uranus rotates in a retrograde fashion and its five satellites orbit in the equatorial plane as though the whole system had been displaced together. Of Neptune's two planets, Triton with a diameter of about 6,000 km may be the biggest.

Pluto the outermost planet moves in an orbit which is exceptional in two ways. It is inclined at 17·2° to the plane of the ecliptic and its great eccentricity brings the planet in 1983 within the orbit of Neptune. Little is known of Pluto. It is now known to have a small satellite moving in synchronous orbit.

Minor bodies

Between Mars and Jupiter where Bode's Law would expect a planet to be located lies the broad **asteroid belt**. Small gaps in the belt known as Kirkwood Gaps are attributed to the gravitational effects of Jupiter. There are estimated to be more than 400,000 asteroids of diameter greater than 1 km. The largest, Ceres, measures 955 km. Two small separate groups of asteroids, The Trojans, remain fixed in the orbit of Jupiter at exactly 60° ahead and 60° behind the planet.

The asteroid belt may be the result of the fragmentation of a planet or the result of failure of the material to coalesce to form a planet.

Meteorites abound in the Solar System and often collide with the Earth but most burn up in the atmosphere. Under the influence of planetary gravity asteroid orbits precess, that is the major axis rotates through 360°. Those with very elongated orbits will thus intrude into the orbit of the Earth. Such asteroids belong to a group known as Apollo objects, so called after one of its members. Fortunately the Earth is rarely in that part of its orbit at the same time but it is inevitable that there will be occasions when collision occurs. Present estimates imply a possible encounter a few times every million years.

Comets, usually described as "dirty snowballs" are only visible when they approach the Sun and vaporisation produces the corona by which they are recognised. It has been suggested that they inhabit a region far beyond the orbit of Pluto and only acquire their very elongated elliptical orbits when displaced from their original orbits under the influence of planetary gravitational forces.

Jupiter as photographed by Voyager 1 with Io over the Great Red Spot and Europa nearby. Jupiter's rapid rotation and lack of a solid surface are responsible for the banding of the clouds. Dark bands are known as belts and light bands as zones. Swirls and eddies in the cloud pattern are induced by winds of different velocities or winds blowing in opposing directions. From time to time coloured or white spots appear and disappear, but the Great Red Spot measuring about 25,000 by 11,000 km remains as a permanent feature.

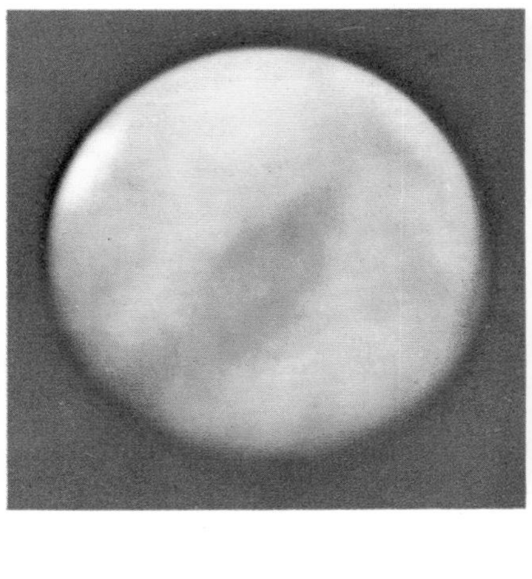

Mars in spite of its smooth appearance in the photograph is heavily cratered as are also Mercury and Venus and the two tiny satellites of Mars. Dust storms raised by very powerful winds cover the planet from time to time.

Saturn is conspicuous by its rings, but other planets too have rings, though they are not so prominent. Saturn's rings are made up of small fragments of material which in certain circumstances might have accreted to form satellites.

Jupiter The existence of a ring system was discovered by Voyager I in 1979. Four closely spaced narrow rings have been identified, the thickest being from 50 to 100 km wide.

STAR CHARTS

NORTHERN SKY

PISCES
PEGASUS
CETUS
EQUULEUS
ARIES
DELPHINUS
TRIANGULUM
ANDROMEDA
LACERTA
AQUILA
CYGNUS
CASSIOPEIA
PERSEUS
TAURUS
CEPHEUS
LYRA
ORION
AURIGA
CAMELOPARDALIS
DRACO
URSA MINOR
HERCULES
OPHIUCHUS
LYNX
GEMINI
CORONA BOREALIS
CANIS MINOR
URSA MAJOR
SERPENS CAPUT
CANES VENATICI
CANCER
BOOTES
LEO MINOR
HYDRA
COMA BERENICES
LEO
SEXTANS
VIRGO
MONOCEROS

Markab, Enif, Scheat, Alpheratz, Menkar, Hamal, Mirach, M31, Almach, Altair, Pleiades, Algol, Schedar, Hyades, Deneb, Caph, Ruchbah, Mirfak, Aldebaran, Bellatrix, Vega, Elnath, Capella, Betelgeuse, Eltanin, Polaris, M35, Rasalhague, M92, Kochab, M13, Castor, Dubhe, Pollux, Mizar, Merak, Procyon, Alkaid, Alioth, Phecda, Alphecca, M44, M3, M5, Arcturus, N. Galactic Pole, Regulus, Denebola

Ecliptic
Equator
Galactic Equator

STAR MAGNITUDE
0
1
2
3
4
5

Each unit of magnitude indicates a difference in brightness of 2.512 times. The brightest star is Sirius (mag.–1.43).

Link Line
Variable Star
Open Star Cluster
Globular Star Cluster

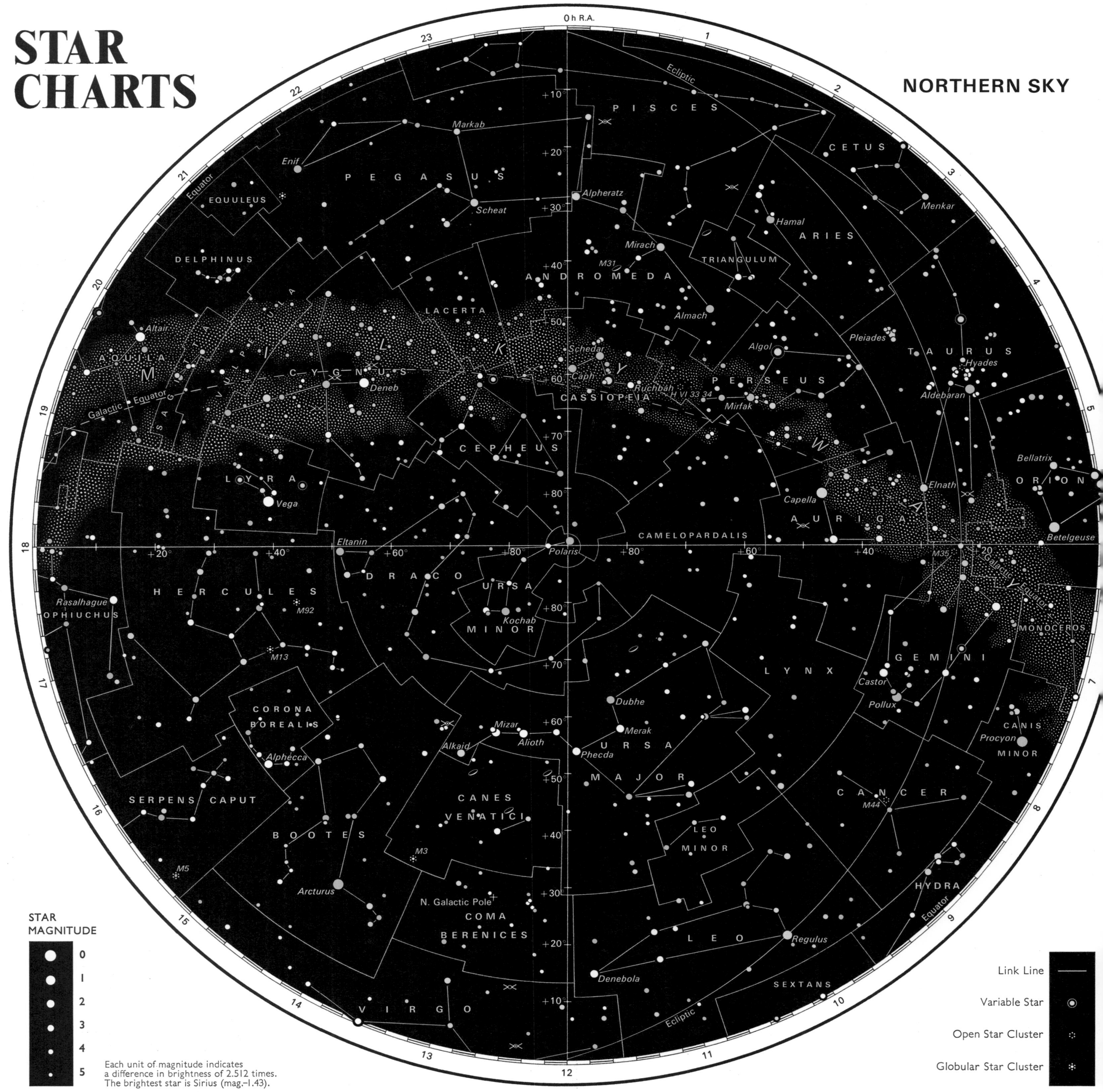

EQUATORIAL ZONE

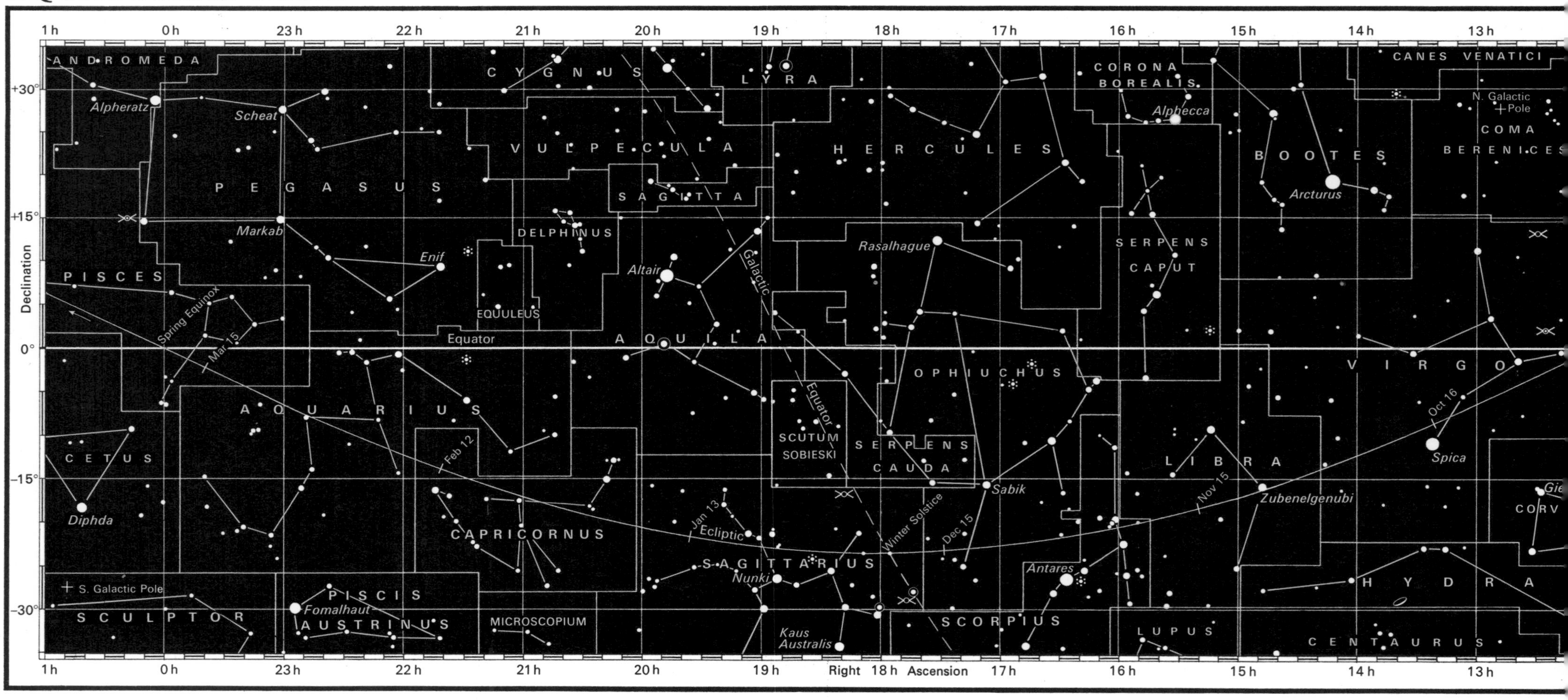

SOUTHERN SKY

Galaxy

Quasar

Radio Source

Constellation Boundary

STAR COLOURS
SPECTRAL TYPES

* Temp. in 000° C	Type
50.0—25.0	O-B
11.0	A
7.5	F
6.0	G
5.0	K
3.5	M

* The surface temperature of a star is indicated both by its colour and its spectrum.

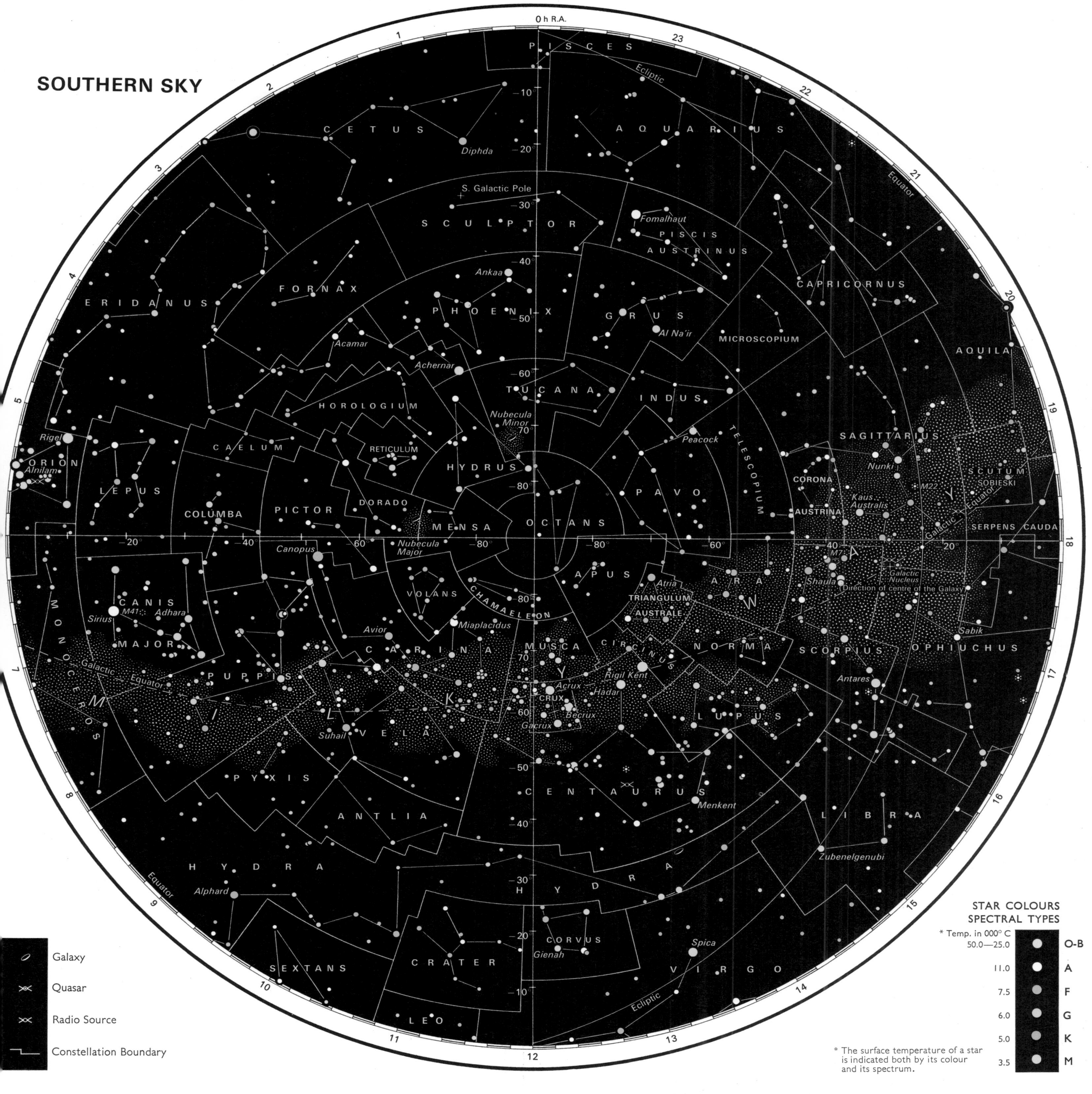

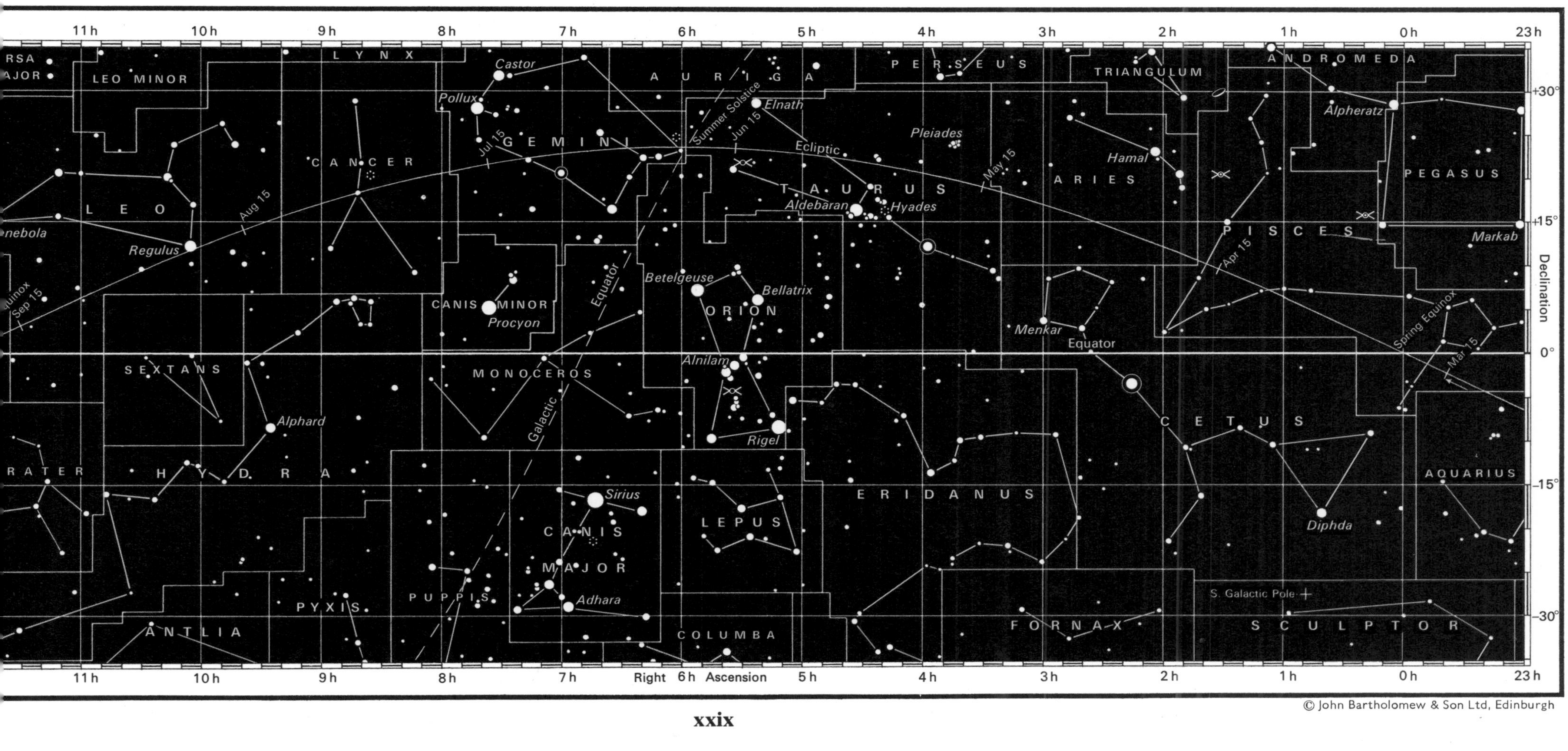

THE EARTH

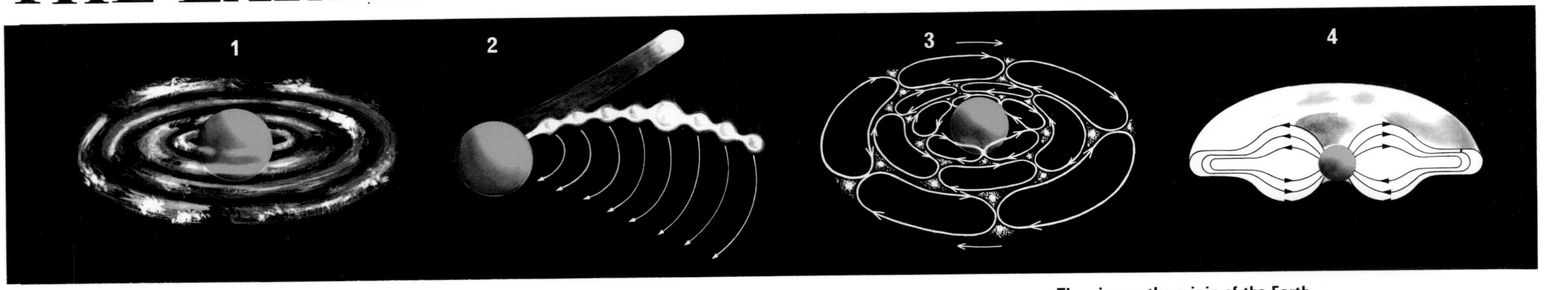
1
2
3
4

Theories on the origin of the Earth
1 *NEBULAR THEORY* The sun formed at the centre of a rotating cloud of gas and dust. Planets consolidated in the surrounding rings.
2 *TIDAL THEORY* A passing star drew a long filament out of the Sun within which nodules of gas and dust formed into planets.
3 *VON WEIZSACKER (1944)* The Sun captured a large cloud of gas and dust and planets were formed in the spaces between eddies.
4 *HOYLE (1960)* A disk of gas around which the Sun's lines of magnetic force spiralled: gases being forced outwards and heavier planetesimals inwards.

The origin of the Earth

As far as the Earth is concerned it is easier to forecast the future than to recount the past. The Earth's future is the future of the Solar System, whose end, like its beginning, depends upon the Sun.

The Sun began life not much before the Earth was formed. It condensed from a cloud of hot electrified gas into a sphere fifty times its present size. Gravitational forces from this immense body were sufficient to generate heat to an incandescence 500 times brighter than the Sun we see today. Its rate of rotation was rapid enough for the outer layers of material to be thrown off. A great amount of matter was lost through radiation of light and heat. Helped by the strong magnetic forces of the original gas cloud wrapped round it as spiral filaments, the Sun contracted to its present size and relatively slow rate of rotation.

In shrinking to one-fiftieth of its former size in a short period of time gravitational forces caused reheating of the centre so that nuclear fusion began. Once started, the fusion process has continued for 4,600 million years or so, consuming hydrogen at the rate of 500 million tons per second.

For another 1,500 million years the Sun will continue much as it is now, but by then the hydrogen at the centre will become exhausted, having been converted into helium. Burning will then spread outwards and proceed more rapidly. Outward pressure of radiation will reduce the inward pull of gravity and the Sun will begin to expand. Expansion for 4,000 million years will make the Sun three times its present size, emitting four times as much heat and light. From then on expansion will accelerate. In a few hundreds of millions of years it will be fifty times its present size. Then the helium at the centre will ignite. The Sun will collapse and perhaps in the space of a few hours will shrink to only ten times the size it is now. Almost at once a fresh expansion will begin. Mercury, Venus, Earth and Mars will be swallowed up as the Sun increases its size by a factor of forty. It will then shine 10,000 times as brightly as at present.

At the age of 20,000 million years there will be no fuels left to burn and radiation will decline and finally cease altogether. Gravitational forces will then predominate and the giant Sun will rapidly shrink to the size of the Earth. Heat generated by the collapse will cause the Sun to glow as a white dwarf, but only for a paltry 50,000 to 60,000 years, by which time the final supply of heat will have been dissipated and our magnificent Sun will end its days as a black dwarf.

The life course of the Sun, and therefore of the Solar System, can be predicted with confidence because at each step more questions are resolved than are created. Reconstruction of the history of the Solar System and with it the past life of the Earth appeared to raise many irreconcilable issues in the past.

Radio-active elements gradually lose their radioactivity, and since this loss is at a constant rate the measurement of the stage of the decay is an indication of the age of the rocks in which they are found. Measurement of the age of the rocks in the Earth by this method shows that the oldest rocks solidified about 3,900 million years ago, and that the age of the Earth is about 4,600 million years.

Examination of Moon rocks and meteorites shows them to be of similar age. Since both the Moon and the meteorites originated in space, we have extra-terrestrial evidence for the age of at least parts of the Solar System. The similarity in age lends weight to the supposition that the Solar System came into being as part of a single system. Added weight is lent by the study of the chemical composition of Moon rocks and of meteorites, particularly the latter.

Meteorites provide us with specimens of the original rocky substance of the universe. Chemically, the composition of meteorites bears a great similarity to the inferred composition of the Earth. Rocks formed at the surface can be examined but, unlike the meteorites, by the time they arrive at the surface they have been heated and reheated, and have changed physically and chemically from their original form.

A thin shell of light rocky material of only 25 miles average thickness under the continents, and much thinner under the oceans, formed the solid exterior of the planet. These are the rocks most readily accessible to us, and it is obvious that they must in various degrees represent all the materials that are present in the Earth. We find that silica and alumina make up more than 74 per cent of the composition. Silica and alumina are the oxides of silicon and aluminium. Below the crust are the rocks of the upper mantle, appreciably denser and consisting primarily of oxides of magnesium and silicon with an addition of 10 per cent ferrous oxide. This combination of chemicals makes up the rocks known as olivine and pyroxene.

The mantle is divided into two parts separated by a transition zone. The lower mantle is composed of rocks denser than those found in the upper mantle. The core, likewise, is divided into two parts. The inner core is solid, and appears to have a density equal to that of nickel-iron at the same pressure. Surrounding this inner core is an outer core of liquid iron, lighter than one would expect, suggesting the presence of either silicon or sulphur. Majority opinion nowadays leans towards the presence of sulphur. Until just before the first world war the layered nature of the interior of the Earth was unknown; then the study of seismic waves revealed anomalies in the manner of their transmission through the body of the Earth. From the epicentre of an earthquake the primary waves pass through the Earth and are refracted by the change of density in passing from layer to layer of the Earth's interior. Short (S) waves vibrate at right-angles to the primary waves, and while they are transmitted readily through solid rock they cannot pass through the liquid or semi-liquid outer core. From the refraction and spread of the waves the thickness of the layers can be determined. From the velocity of the waves the density of the layers can be adduced.

Early in the last century scientists had observed that gravity was less than the theoretical amount near large mountain ranges. Since the material of which the mountains are composed is lighter in density than the underlying rocks, the mountains had far less gravitational pull than their volume would suggest. It was discovered that the light material of which they were composed must extend a long way below the crust. This gave birth to the principle of isostasy. Below mountain ranges, the continental material dips deeply down into the mantle, rather like an iceberg, with about one-tenth of its matter above the surface and nine-tenths below. In this condition the continents with their mountain masses are said to be in 'flotational equilibrium'.

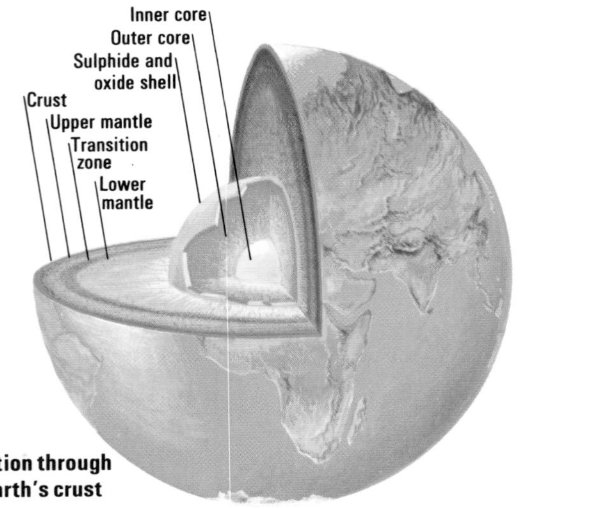
Inner core
Outer core
Sulphide and oxide shell
Crust
Upper mantle
Transition zone
Lower mantle

A section through the Earth's crust

Just as gravity is anomalous over most of the surface of the Earth, so terrestrial magnetism shows departures from the expected theoretical measurement. The Earth acts as a huge bar magnet running north and south but not coincident with the Earth's axis of rotation.

The magnetic poles 'migrate' over a period of time. The rate can be measured and therefore the theoretical direction and intensity of the magnetism can be predicted for any place on Earth. Indeed, the fact that the needle of a magnet points to the north has been an essential part of navigation since the twelfth century AD. All that is required for improved accuracy is knowledge of the amount by which magnetic north departs from true north and its annual rate of change.

Since metal-bearing rocks originated deep inside the Earth, they contain crystals of ferro-magnetic materials and reveal their presence by producing anomalous local magnetism. Magnetometers are used to measure magnetic anomalies in prospecting for metallic minerals.

The Earth's behaviour as a magnet arises from the presence of a large quantity of iron at its centre. Any surface rock containing ferro-magnetic material, such as basaltic lavas, will be magnetised by the Earth's magnetic field. As rocks cool and solidify, the magnetised molecules are aligned like small magnets in the direction of the magnetic poles, thus preserving as 'frozen magnetism' a permanent record of the magnetism at the place and time of their solidification. Such a record tells us not only the original alignment of the rock but also the geographic latitude of its place of origin, always provided there has been no drastic change in the alignment of the Earth's magnetic axis.

Study of the palaeomagnetism of rock specimens in the laboratory, where the local magnetism can be precisely set out, allows the deduction of the original orientation and location of the rock specimens. From such examination a long-suspected theory has been proved that the Earth's magnetic poles have on a number of occasions in the past reversed their positions: the north magnetic pole coming to the south polar region and the south magnetic pole moving to the northern hemisphere. About 15 million years ago the poles repeatedly reversed themselves over a period of about one thousand years. Until 1969, it had been assumed that the last transposition of the magnetic poles occurred about 70,000 years ago, but evidence was then found of a reversal of magnetism as recently as 30,000 years ago. Reversed magnetism in rocks had been observed almost from the beginning of this century, but it was at first assumed that the rocks somehow reversed the polarity of their magnetism rather than that the reversal occurred within the whole Earth as a single, sudden event.

Geology

The word 'geology' means, literally, the study of the Earth, but the science of geology is specifically concerned with elucidating the history of the Earth by the study of its rocks and by identifying changes which have taken place or are occurring now.

In the geological sense rock means any of the materials which make up the Earth's crust: sand and mud are classed as rock equally with granite or limestone.

Geology has several branches. Stratigraphy is concerned with the composition, sequence and correlation of the stratified rocks of the crust and with the geographical and climatic conditions at the time of their deposition.

Palaeontology is the study of fossils preserved in rocks and the conditions prevailing at the time the fossilised creatures and plants inhabited the Earth.

Petrology is the branch of geology which deals with the origins of rocks, their present conditions, alterations and decay, and their systematic description.

Structural geology (of which tectonics forms part) is concerned with the causes and effects of rock movement and the structures (e.g. folds and faults) resulting from crustal deformations.

Physical geology is that branch concerned with all the terrestrial agents of denudation and processes of change, and the forms they bring about. It embraces all land and rock formations and applies this knowledge to an understanding of past geological environments.

Geology has important practical applications: engineering geology concerns itself with factors which affect design and operation of man-made works such as dams, bridges, harbours, etc. Mining geology and petroleum geology are other applied aspects of the subject.

The rocks of the Earth's crust are classified according to origin into igneous, sedimentary and metamorphic. Igneous rocks solidify from molten magma, which originates below the crust in the upper mantle. Their physical appearance depends upon the rate of cooling:

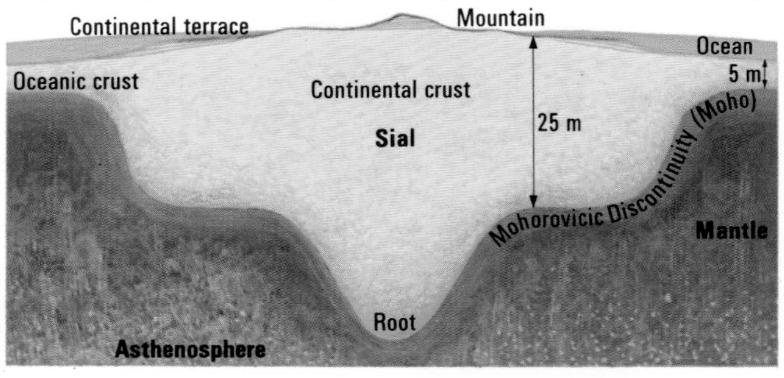
Continental terrace
Mountain
Ocean
5 m
Oceanic crust
Continental crust
Sial
25 m
Mohorovicic Discontinuity (Moho)
Mantle
Root
Asthenosphere

The continents with their mountains remain in flotational equilibrium.

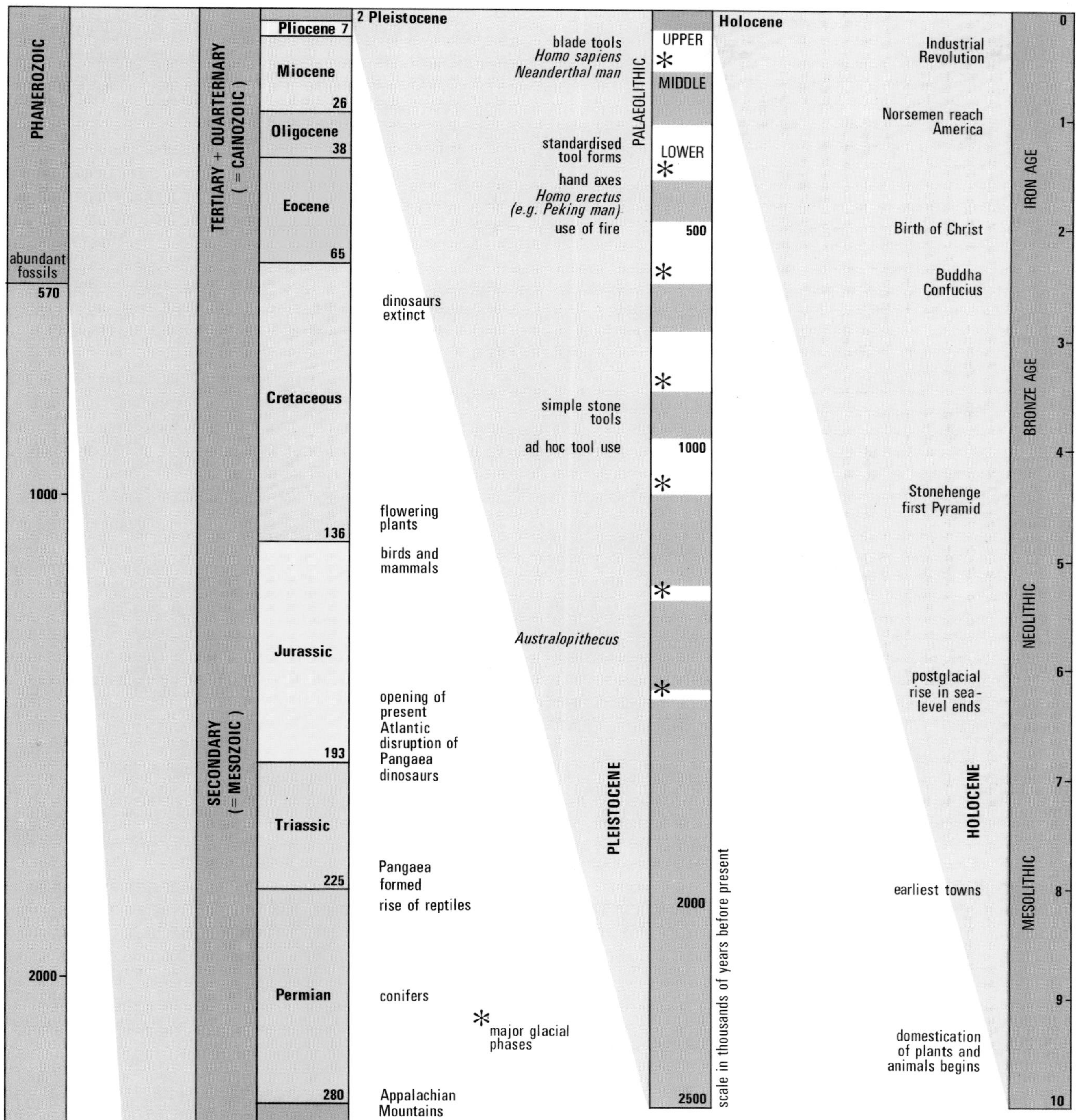
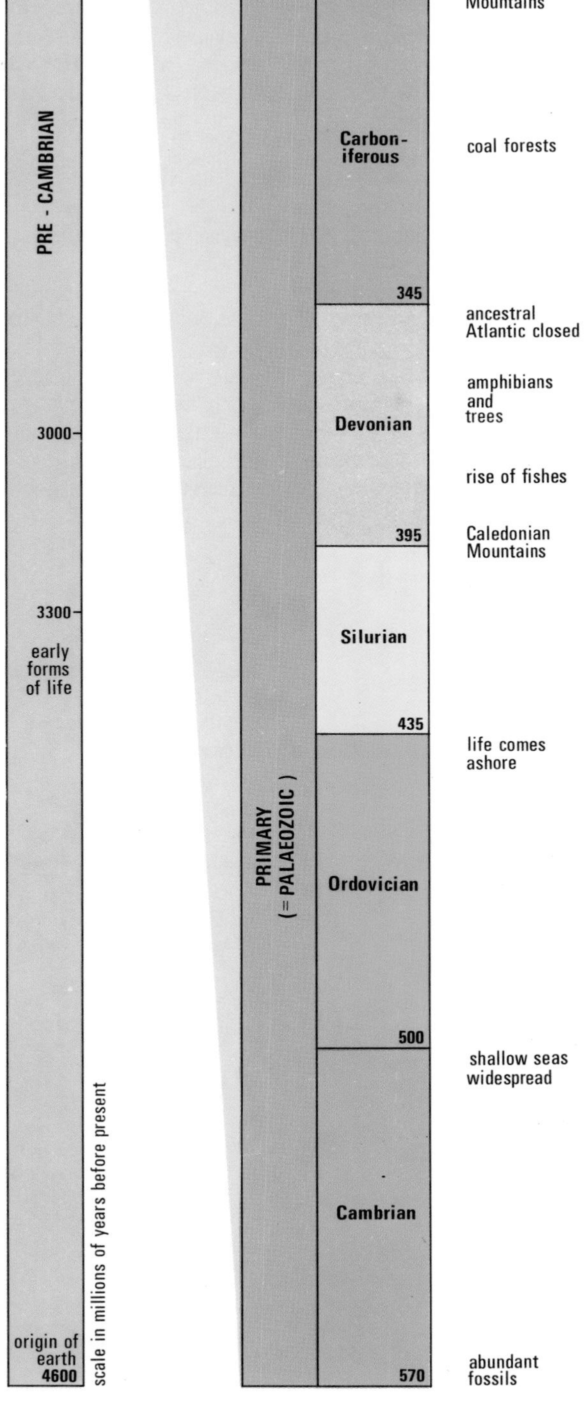

PHANEROZOIC
abundant fossils
570
1000
2000
3000
3300
early forms of life
PRE - CAMBRIAN
origin of earth 4600
scale in millions of years before present
TERTIARY + QUARTERNARY (= CAINOZOIC)
SECONDARY (= MESOZOIC)
PRIMARY (= PALAEOZOIC)
Pliocene 7
Miocene
26
Oligocene
38
Eocene
65
Cretaceous
136
Jurassic
193
Triassic
225
Permian
280
Carbon-iferous
345
Devonian
395
Silurian
435
Ordovician
500
Cambrian
570
2 Pleistocene
dinosaurs extinct
flowering plants
birds and mammals
opening of present Atlantic
disruption of Pangaea
dinosaurs
Pangaea formed
rise of reptiles
conifers
* major glacial phases
Appalachian Mountains
coal forests
ancestral Atlantic closed
amphibians and trees
rise of fishes
Caledonian Mountains
life comes ashore
shallow seas widespread
abundant fossils
blade tools
Homo sapiens
Neanderthal man
standardised tool forms
hand axes
Homo erectus (e.g. Peking man)
use of fire
simple stone tools
ad hoc tool use
Australopithecus
PALAEOLITHIC
UPPER
MIDDLE
LOWER
500
1000
2000
2500
PLEISTOCENE
scale in thousands of years before present
Holocene
Industrial Revolution
Norsemen reach America
Birth of Christ
Buddha Confucius
Stonehenge first Pyramid
postglacial rise in sea-level ends
earliest towns
domestication of plants and animals begins
HOLOCENE
IRON AGE
BRONZE AGE
NEOLITHIC
MESOLITHIC
0
1
2
3
4
5
6
7
8
9
10

Geological periods and the emergence of Man
Using a complex variety of analytical techniques, it is now possible to reconstruct at least some aspects of the earth's climate as far back as 3,000 million years, early in the Pre-Cambrian era. The chart sets out the main geological periods, the climatic conditions prevailing at the time, the evolution of species of flora and fauna, ending with the history of Man.

slow cooling forms large crystals (e.g. granite); very rapid cooling produces non-crystalline volcanic glass (e.g. obsidian). Slow cooling occurs when the molten rock does not reach the Earth's surface but intrudes into rock strata, forcing them apart. These are the intrusive igneous rocks, which range from the enormous plutonic granite batholiths to small dykes and sills. When the magma forces its way to the surface rapid cooling ensues, forming the finely crystalline extrusive volcanic rocks or lava, building either volcanoes or great lava sheets.

Sedimentary rocks result from external forces on the Earth's crust. They are formed of particles deposited by rivers, glaciers, the winds, the sea or by chemical deposition from lakes or ocean. These rocks are usually laid down as horizontal beds, the individual layers or strata being separated by bedding planes which, when deformed, help us to recognise folds and faults. Sandstone is a common sedimentary rock, often used as a building stone, and is frequently made up of grains of quartz cemented by calcite. It is clearly a second-hand rock, being derived from the break-up of an existing rock, e.g. a granite. Another popular building stone is limestone, which is a sedimentary rock made up of the skeletons of marine animals, or it may be a chemical precipitate. Sedimentary rocks also provide a record of the past. Fossil remains reveal much information on the changing pattern of plant and animal life throughout the ages and have enabled geologists to construct the divisions of geological time.

Metamorphic rocks are those that have been so altered by heat, pressure and the passage of chemically active hot gases and liquids that they have lost their original character and have often been recrystallised into new types of rock. One result is that originally dull rock may be transformed into an attractive, bright crystalline stone. Gneisses and schists are metamorphic: gneiss forming from large-grained material, and schist from material of fine grain. A metamorphosed and recrystallised limestone is known as marble as, for example, the renowned statuary marble from Carrara, Italy. The fine quality roofing slates from north Wales are metamorphosed mudstones and shales. Internal pressure has forced the flaky minerals into parallel layers so that the slate easily splits, or cleaves, into thin slabs.

Almost all the rock-forming minerals are silicates, or compounds of silica combined with metallic oxides. Silica makes up from 40 per cent to 80 per cent of the chemical composition of most rocks. Since it plays the part of an acid while the metallic oxides serve as bases, rocks with more than 65 per cent content of silica are classified as acid rocks, those with 55 per cent to 65 per cent as intermediate rocks and those containing 45 per cent to 55 per cent as basic rocks.

The discovery of radioactivity at the end of the last century offered a new method of dating geological time by the isoptic or radiometric methods. Radioactive elements spontaneously decay at a steady rate into a radiogenic end-product – uranium to lead, for example. Hence the proportion of radioactive element to daughter element changes progressively with the passage of time, and provided that the rate of decay is known this ratio can be used for dating the rock. The period over which half a given quantity of a radioactive rock has decayed into its daughter element is described as its half-life.

Continental drift

Study of the fossils preserved in rocks over the past two hundred million years reveals climatic changes inexplicable without changes in latitude. Two hundred million years ago the climate of the British Isles and north-west Europe was subtropical. Certain equatorial regions were ice-covered at that time. Had both occupied their present relative positions, the equatorial regions could not possibly have been colder than those at, say, latitude 45° to 55°. It must be assumed that they were not always at their present latitudes.

Palaeomagnetism has contributed to modern acceptance of the theory of continental drift and sea floor spreading. Magma flowing out onto the sea floor in the central rift valley of an ocean ridge preserves in its magnetic rock material, the polarity in which it solidified.

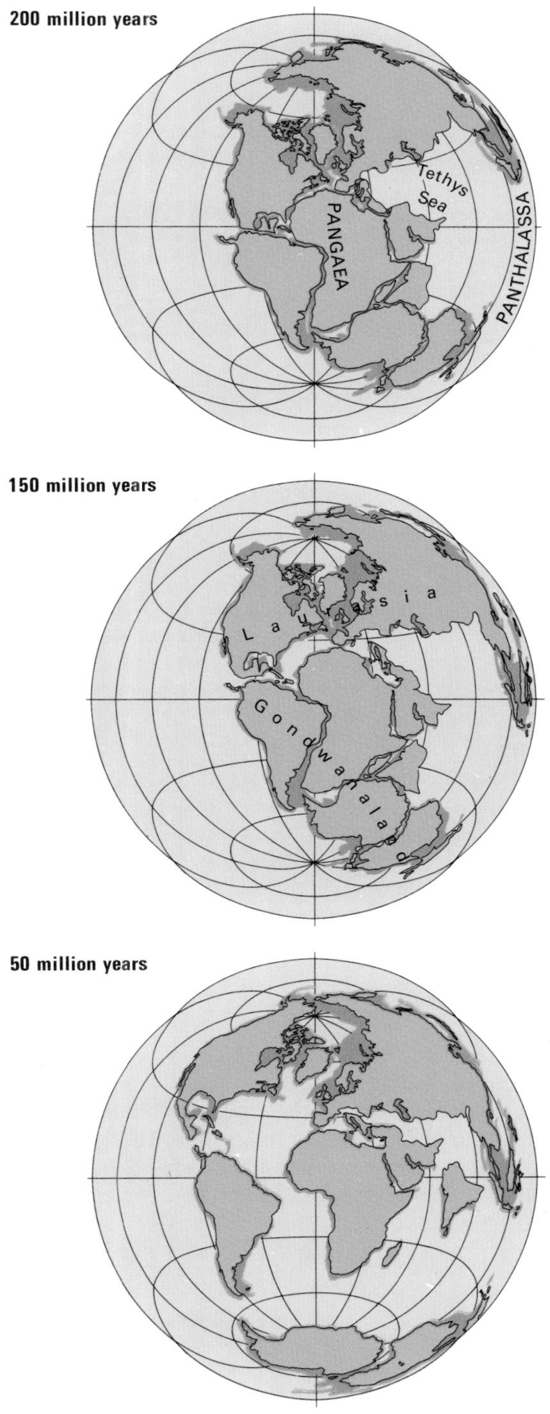

200 million years
Tethys Sea
PANGAEA
PANTHALASSA
150 million years
Laurasia
Gondwanaland
50 million years

Continental drift is the name of the theory which led to the discovery of plate tectonics. Palaeomagnetism preserved in the rocks of the ocean floor provided the evidence that there was once a single continent, Pangaea, surrounded by a single ocean, Panthalassa. Rather more than 200 million years ago Pangaea began to separate into two continents, Laurasia and Gondwanaland separated by the Tethys Sea. Subsequent break up and collisions produced the present disposition of land and sea. Australia and India separated from Antarctica. India drifted north to impinge on the Eurasian continent and caused the buckling which is now the Himalaya range. Drifting did not just begin 200 million years ago. It has probably been going on for 2,500 million years.

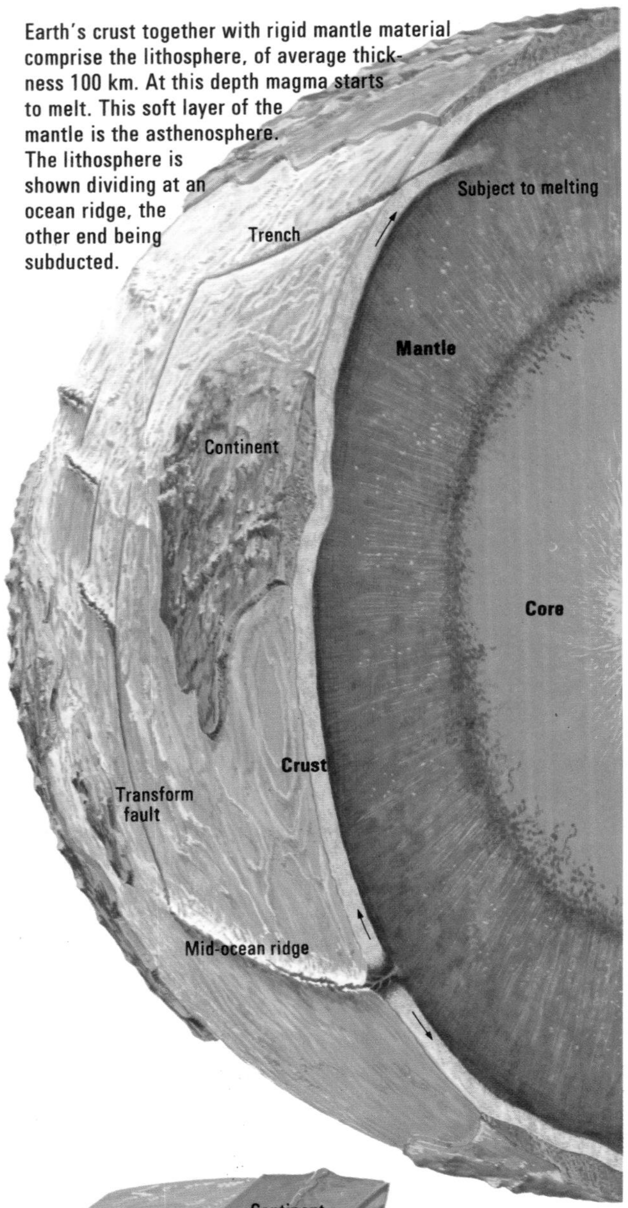

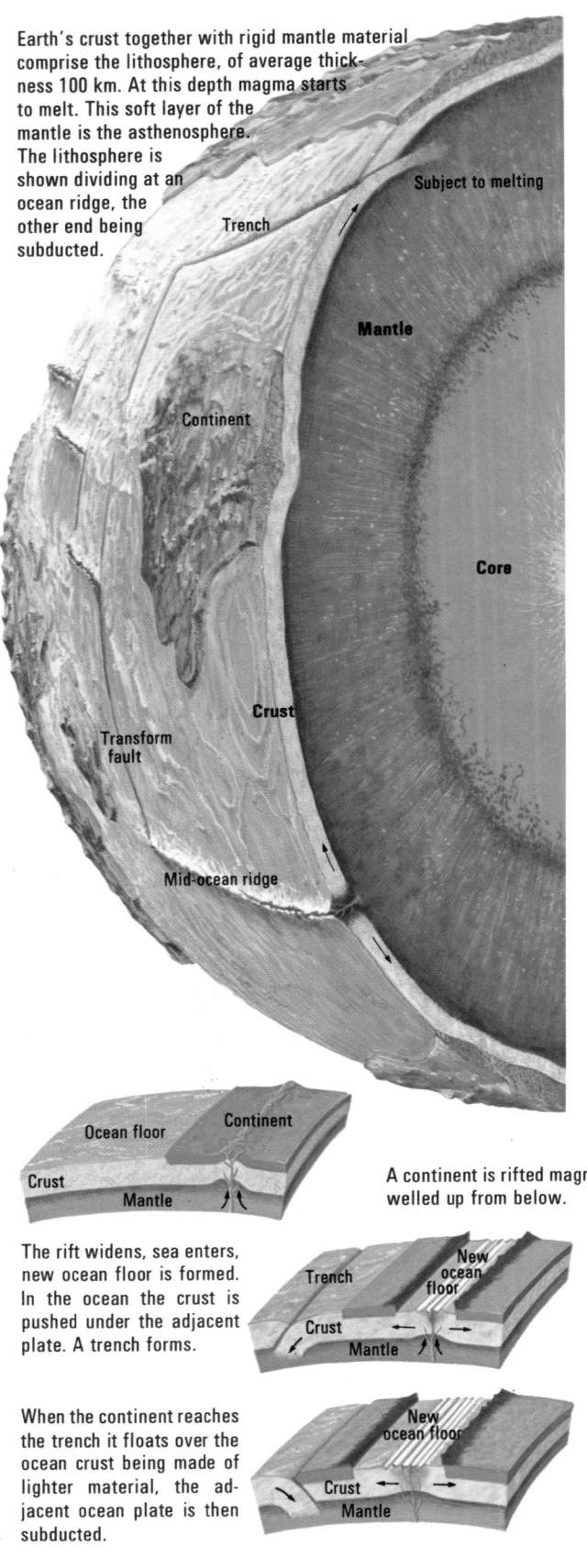

Earth's crust together with rigid mantle material comprise the lithosphere, of average thickness 100 km. At this depth magma starts to melt. This soft layer of the mantle is the asthenosphere. The lithosphere is shown dividing at an ocean ridge, the other end being subducted.

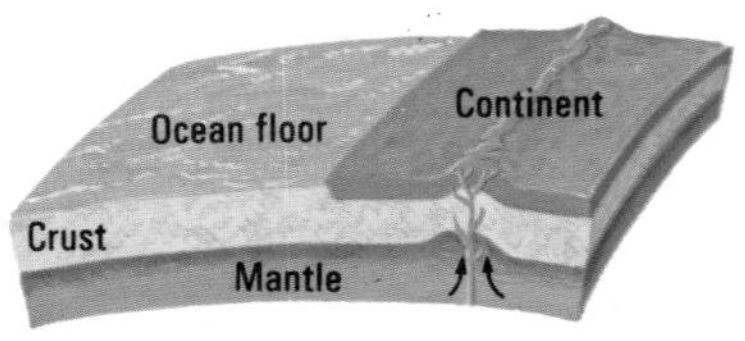

A continent is rifted magma welled up from below.

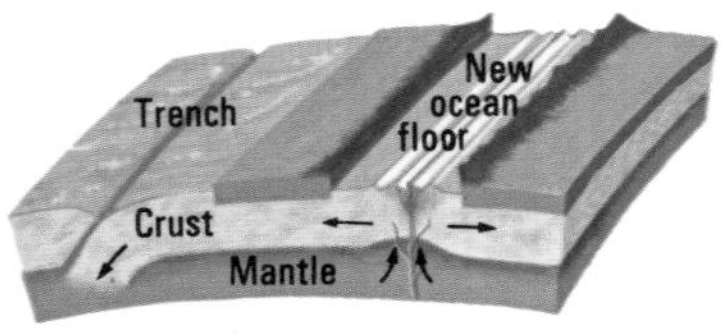

The rift widens, sea enters, new ocean floor is formed. In the ocean the crust is pushed under the adjacent plate. A trench forms.

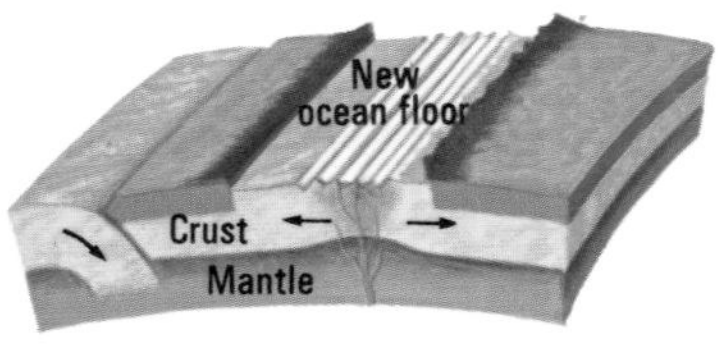

When the continent reaches the trench it floats over the ocean crust being made of lighter material, the adjacent ocean plate is then subducted.

Since the Earth's magnetism periodically changes its polarity, the alternating bands of north and south polarity give an indication of the stages and rate of extrusion on to the sea floor, and the original orientation of the molecules within the magma with respect to the magnetic poles.

Continental drift is explained today by plate tectonics. The lithosphere is divided into six or seven major plates and some five or six minor ones which wander over the Earth impelled by convection currents in the asthenosphere, a layer of the mantle, close to melting point, lying immediately below the lithosphere. The continents are carried on the plates.

When tensional forces rupture the mid-ocean floor, magma wells up from the asthenosphere and is deposited on the ocean floor. As the tensional forces continue to widen the rift, the bounding ridges, formed of magma material, are pushed further apart. The mid-Atlantic ridge is just such a formation. It is part of an almost unbroken system running through all the oceans and measuring 64,000 km (40,000 miles) in length.

Where plates diverge the boundary is known as 'extensional'. They converge at 'compressional boundaries' and slide past each other at 'transform faults'.

When two plates collide and one rides over the other, the upper plate will be crumpled at its edge by compression and a mountain range or string of islands may result. In addition, fractures appear in the plates (particularly the lower plate) because of differential resistance of the various parts of the plates to sliding. The Pacific Ocean possesses a number of fracture zones to the west of North America, and these can be attributed to the continent riding over the ocean plate.

In such a case the continental plate, being very thick, is deep enough for the material at its base to be heated to the point where it offers less resistance to sliding. The ocean plate is bent down into the magma of the asthenosphere, a trench being formed at the continental edge. This trench then becomes the repository of the sediments from the continents. The submerged part of the plate may descend 700 km (430 miles) into the mantle before it finally melts, the lighter material floating up to build up the base of the continent and to form volcanoes at the surface. Heavier material sinks into the magma. Thus the continents acquire additional material both by collision and by accretion from below.

Convergent ocean plates produce volcanic island arcs bounded by a trench where the descending plate is subducted. Melting of the subducted plate causes a string of volcanoes in the overriding plate. Island arcs divide the ocean into small basins which, like the trenches, form efficient traps for the sediments and organic matter emanating from the continents and the oceans. Such traps are a potential source of petroleum.

In order for petroleum to be formed, the area must be a poor environment for living beings which would feed on the organic matter. There must also be a deficiency of oxygen or the organic matter would decompose. In the quiet basins of the island arcs circulation of water is limited and oxygen consumed by decaying matter is less likely to be replaced. A favourable condition is thus achieved. In an ocean trench the accumulation of sediments and the tectonic conditions are conducive to the formation of petroleum.

When continents separate through rifting, a small sea is formed, of which the Red Sea is an example. Here, too, conditions may be favourable for the accumulation of petroleum. There is the same restriction of circulation of sea water, and the bottom of the narrow, enclosed sea is an effective trap for both organic matter and sediments. The geology and tectonics are likewise favourable. It therefore appears most likely that whether they be divergent or convergent, oil is likely to be found where plates meet.

Most of the rich metallic ore deposits found on the continents have been precipitated from solutions and are known as hydrothermal deposits. Of particular importance are the sulphide deposits with which the metal ores, in combination with sulphur, exist. Deposits of this kind are found at plate boundaries or where such boundaries have existed in the past.

When the end of a descending plate is consumed by the hot magma, hot mineralising solutions are created from which minerals are deposited to become part of an advancing continent, as is the case in the Andes which were formed by the advancing edge of the American plate.

Sulphide deposits are, therefore, associated with the movement of plates but the exact process by which the mineral-rich solutions are formed is not fully understood.

Ore deposits are likewise left behind on the ocean floor as divergent plates move apart. These are likewise sulphide deposits.

Both convergent and divergent plates thus provide a mechanism for the replacement of metallic ores. In time it will be possible to assess the rate at which ore deposits accrue and so arrive at the permissible rate of consumption of metals by the human race.

The present phase of continental drifting appears to have begun about 200 million years ago. At that time there was one ocean – Panthalassa – and the previously separate continents had coalesced to form a single continent – Pangaea – which broke initially into two parts, Laurasia and Gondwana. The date of the initial break-up is known from the age of the oldest basaltic rocks along the margins of the oceans.

The appearance of great rifts in Pangaea caused Africa and South America to move northwestwards, split off from the rest of Gondwana. India also split off and moved rapidly northwards to impinge violently on the Asian part of the continent Laurasia. The impact of the Indian plate with the Asian mainland brought the Himalayas into being. This colossal mountain range is, therefore, the result of the folding of the crust under the tremendous compressional forces engendered by the collision.

Further rifting brought about the separation of the continents into those existing today. Australia splitting off from Antarctica and North America from Eurasia. Collision between plates caused the linking up of North and South America.

The present coastlines do not fit together very well when brought back together. Since the oceans have an average depth of 4,000 m (13,000 ft), the 2,000 m line being half-way down the continental slope gives a much more convincing fit.

Continents have drifted around the world for at least 2,500 million years and possibly as long as 3,500 million years. Pangaea itself was formed piecemeal. The first stage, 480 million years ago, was the collision between North America and Europe which resulted in the mountain-building of the Caledonian system, ending in the huge mountain range running through Norway and Scotland.

The second stage was when the African plate collided with the North American-European continent 280 million years ago. This was the great mountain-building period known as the Hercynian Period. The resulting mountain range ran through central Europe, westwards to North America to form part of the Appalachians.

Volcanoes

Volcanoes occur at plate margins and are the manifestation of plate tectonics. About 500 are active. Volcanic activity occurs at the mid-ocean ridges and where a plate passing under another generates so much heat by friction that melting occurs and volcanic activity begins.

Volcanoes are formed by the eruption of magma, extruded from the mantle to solidify and build a conical mountain with a crater. In eruption great quantities of steam, stones, ashes and dust are ejected and lava may flow from the crater down the side of the cone. Hot magma from the mantle supplies the volcanic material which issues from the main crater or from fissures in the sides of the cone.

Cinder cones are structurally the simplest of all types of volcano, rarely exceeding 1 km in diameter. Only fragmental material is ejected and this falls in a ring about the pipe from which it issues. In time, the ring is built into a hill with a conical crater leading down to the mouth of the vent.

Hornitos – a term which originated in Mexico (meaning 'a little furnace') – are volcanoes with sides formed of large pieces of lava not hot enough to flow. They are small and steep-sided.

Shield volcano Shield volcanoes form by the slow deposition of large quantities of liquid or viscous lava. Their sides slope very gently, usually between 2 degrees and 10 degrees. The shields build up gradually layer upon layer and may result in volcanoes with a base diameter of at least 30 km (20 miles). The finest example of a shield volcano is Mauna Loa in Hawaii, 100 km wide at base and 10,000 metres high.

Silhouette structures of volcanoes and a cross-section through a composite volcano

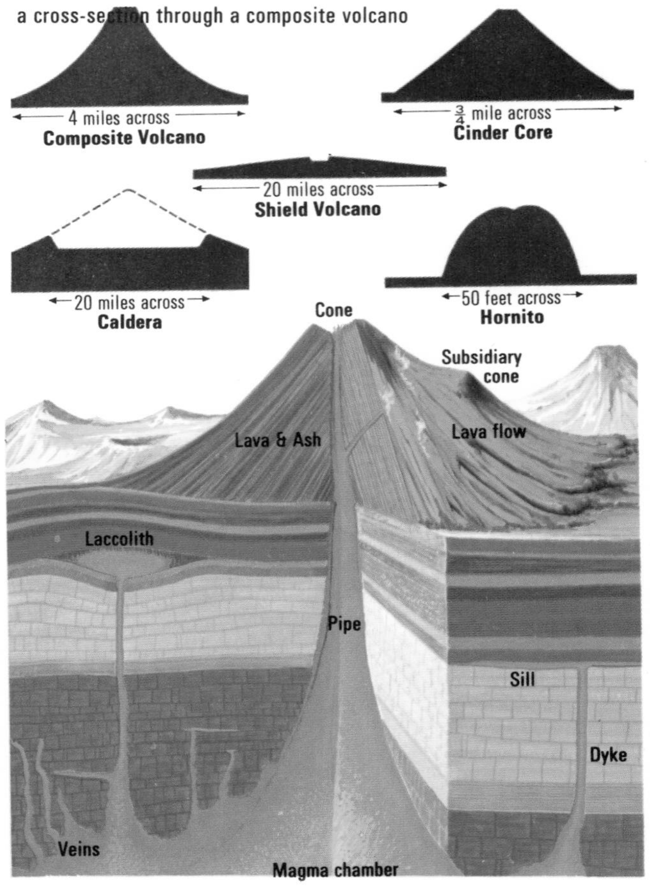

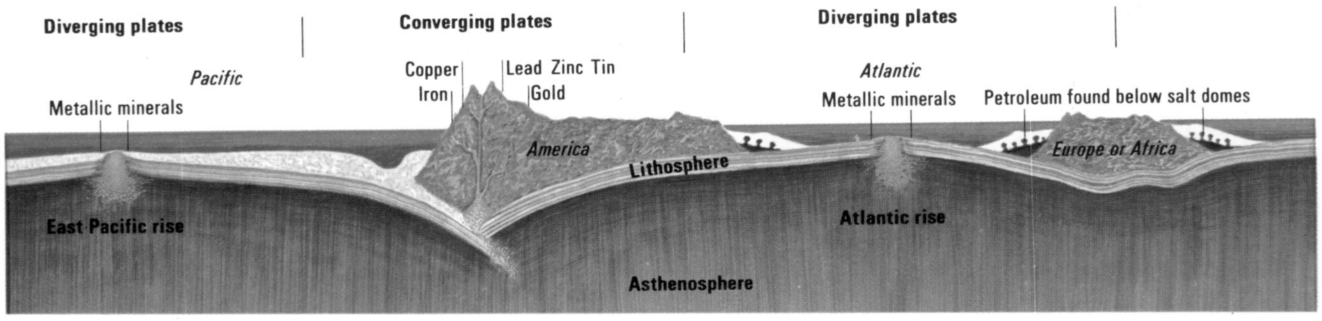

Minerals are deposited as part of the process of plate tectonics. At ocean ridges contact between hot magma and sea water leads to deposition of metallic minerals on the ocean floor. Where a plate is subducted melting adds igneous material, rich in minerals, to the continents. Oil forms in deep ocean areas where oxygen is lacking and organic matter is not destroyed.

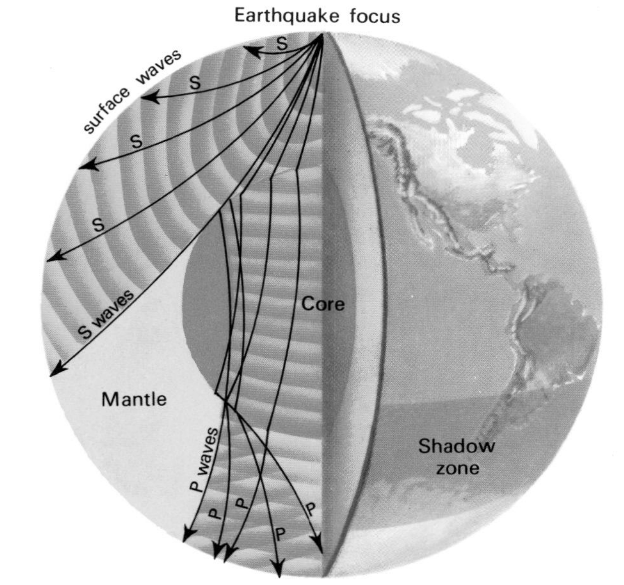

Earthquakes cause the particles of the Earth to vibrate, producing seismic waves running longitudinally in the direction of travel and transversely, known respectively as P and S waves. S waves do not travel through fluids; P waves travel about twice as fast as S waves and are refracted in passing through the layers of the Earth's interior. Because S waves cannot pass through fluids, most P and S waves fail to reach the surface at angles of 105° to 142° from the earthquake. This area is called the "shadow zone".
Magnitude of earthquakes is determined from the amplitude of the waves. The slow S waves cause the violent surface tremors.

Calderas are formed as the result of paroxysmal eruptions when the upper part of the volcanic cone is destroyed, or by the collapse of the unsupported rim following the ejection of large quantities of lava. In either event the cone is reduced in height but greatly increased in circumference. 'Collapse' volcanoes are very common. Collapse of the floor occurs when the reservoir of molten metal issues through a side fissure instead of through the central vent. The floor of the crater, having lost its underlying support, caves in. The surrounding crater walls slump so widening the crater. Crater Lake, Oregon, an example of a caldera, measures 6·4–9·6 km (4 to 6 miles) in diameter. 'Explosive' calderas occur when the mouth of the caldera becomes plugged by infalling material or rapid cooling by sea water. Trapped gases and molten rock become heated and erupt violently.

The solfatara stage In the periods between eruptions volcanoes give off steam and various gases. As they approach extinction steam and gases are emitted instead of lava and ashes only in very small quantities. The quantity produced is insufficient to build up the pressure which causes violent fracture of the lava crust. This stage in the life of a volcano is known as the solfatara stage, named after the large crater near Naples. Among the gases emitted are hydrochloric acid, sulphuretted hydrogen, sulphur dioxide, ammonium chloride, carbon dioxide, etc. The surrounding lavas and ashes are greatly altered from contact with the emission and crumble to a white powdery mass.

Fumaroles and mofettes The term solfatara is applied to volcanoes giving off a combination of acid gases. Fumaroles give off chiefly steam. Those emitting mainly carbon dioxide are named mofettes.

The Valley of Ten Thousand Smokes, near the volcano Katmai in Alaska, is the most famous fumarole area.

Geysers and mud volcanoes In certain parts of the world volcanic eruption expresses itself by the ejection of hot water. Geysers throw out clear water. Mud volcanoes eject water with a high solid content which comes from the surrounding rocks and is carried in suspension.

Geysers and mud volcanoes mark the terminal phase of volcanic activity. Water heated deep in the Earth achieves a temperature much higher than boiling point at the surface. Heating continues until steam is formed. Pressure increases until the water above is ejected violently. Hot water and steam are thrown into the air.

Earthquakes

Earthquakes are the surface manifestation of plate tectonics and the instability of the Earth's crust. They occur either as the result of volcanic eruption or from parts of the Earth's crust sliding one past another, either vertically or horizontally. Most earthquakes occur in narrow zones at the boundaries of tectonic plates, the interior of the plate being a rigid zone generally free of earthquakes. There are four types of zone: the mid-ocean ridges, with shallow earthquakes associated with vulcanicity; non-volcanic regions; areas of deep ocean trenches and volcanic islands; and shallow earthquake areas associated with crustal compression.

Major earthquakes are caused by movements, often very slight – a few inches – of parts of the Earth's crust. The effect of this movement between two faces which had been in a state of relative equilibrium is the release of the stress or strain energy which had kept them together, so producing the shock waves which cause earth tremors.

Interaction between the North American plate and the Pacific plate, for example, causes the horizontal movements along the San Andreas fault. A network of faults from southern California to the Aleutians is responsible for the earth tremors and earthquakes associated with the region like those of 1906, 1952 and 1971.

The focus, or point of origin, of an earthquake can be as deep as 700 km below the surface. The epicentre is the place on the Earth's surface vertically above the focus where the shock waves first strike the surface.

There are many ways of expressing the magnitude and intensity of earthquakes. For scientists the amount and direction of movement of fault faces, the energy involved, speed of movement and so on are important. Seismic instruments give magnitude according to the Richter scale which is based on the amplitude of the vibrations as measured along a record trace drawn by a torsion seismometer.

A scale better suited to the needs of the general public is the Modified Mercalli Intensity Scale which grades shocks according to the degree of disturbance felt by ordinary citizens. The scale defines categories ranging from the mildest tremor to total destruction.

In order to predict earthquakes fault movements are recorded. Ground acceleration is measured by accelerometers designed to trace an immediate record.

Modified Mercalli Earth Intensity Scale

1	Shock only felt by a few people
11	Shock felt by people at rest. Suspended objects swing.
111	Shock felt noticeably indoors. Stationary cars rock.
1V	Shock felt generally. People awakened, windows rattle.
V	Shock felt outdoors. Some plaster falls, dishes and windows break, pendulum clocks stop.
V1	Shock felt by all. Many frightened, chimneys and plaster damaged, furniture moves and objects upset.
V11	Shock felt in moving cars. Damage to buildings.
V111	General alarm, shock very destructive. Damage to weak structures. Furniture overturned.
1X	Panic. Total destruction of weak structures, foundations damaged, ground fissures and cracks.
X	Panic. All but strongest buildings destroyed, foundations ruined, rails bend, water slops over river banks.
X1	Panic. Few buildings survive, broad fissures form, underground pipes out of service.
X11	Panic. Total destruction, waves seen in ground.

The Earth's atmosphere

Besides providing the gases essential to support life, the atmosphere acts as a shield against a perpetual bombardment from space. Harmful rays and charged particles are absorbed or reflected back into space. Almost all meteorites burn up in the upper atmosphere.

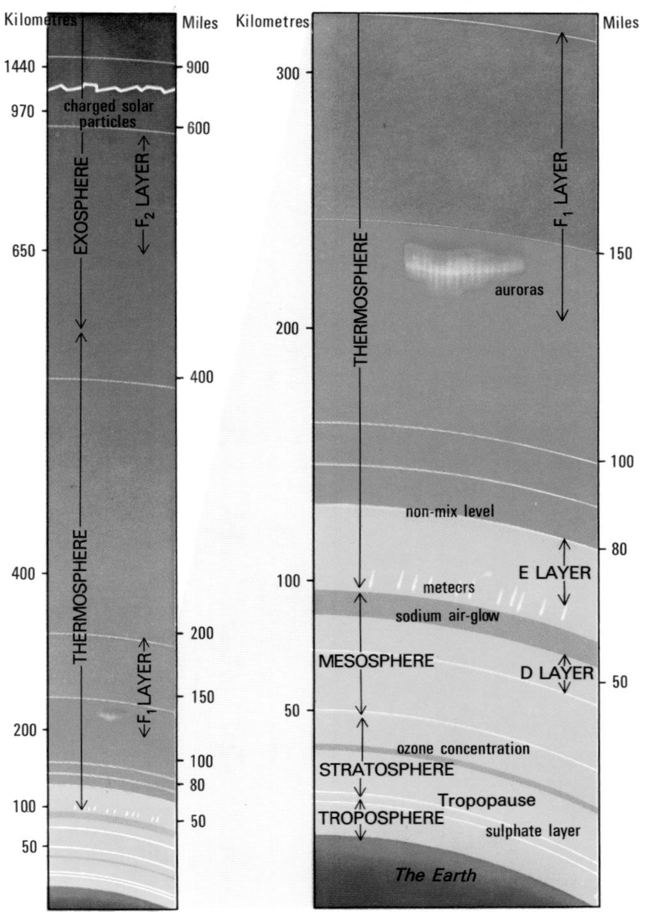

The layers of the Earth's atmosphere

For the first fifty miles or so, the composition of the atmosphere remains constant, with approximately 21 per cent oxygen and 78 per cent nitrogen, together with nearly 1 per cent argon and small quantities of carbon dioxide and other gases. The density of the atmosphere decreases with height, so that at ten miles it is one-tenth of the density at sea level; at twenty miles the density is one-tenth of the density at ten miles, and so on. Although the density decreases, the molecules of nitrogen and oxygen remain associated with each other in the mixture which we call air.

Above an altitude of eighty kilometres, the oxygen and nitrogen molecules are less able to remain associated and tend to separate from each other under the influence of the Earth's gravitational attraction. Thus the heavier nitrogen molecules tend to sink to the lower portions of this region, and oxygen in the atomic form becomes increasingly predominant as altitude increases until oxygen has completely replaced nitrogen. Higher still, at about 965 kilometres (600 miles), helium and hydrogen, both of which are present in very small quantities at sea level, become the predominating gases, replacing oxygen until finally hydrogen replaces helium. The hydrogen layer, which extends out into space from about 2,400 kilometres above the Earth's surface, becomes more and more attenuated, until some 9,700 kilometres out it becomes indistinguishable from interplanetary gas.

In the diagram of the layers of the atmosphere the major subdivisions have been classified as the troposphere, stratosphere, mesosphere, thermosphere and exosphere. Other names are also commonly used, for example the chemosphere is often used for the upper stratosphere and mesosphere. The ionosphere is a region of electrification extending from the upper limit of the stratosphere and encompassing the mesosphere and thermosphere. This electrification is caused by the penetration into the atmosphere of x-rays and ultra-violet radiation, resulting in distinct layers which are identified as D, E, F1 and F2. These important layers, which reflect radio waves back to Earth, can now be studied from above as well as from below. The lower part of the F2 layer and the upper part of the F1 layer are regions of intense concentration of charged particles, caused by the effects of ultra-violet radiation in this region. At night the F layers combine to make a single layer. The belts of electrification do not stay fixed at particular altitudes: they vary with night and day conditions and other physical factors.

Plate tectonics
Tectonic plates are all in motion. There are about a dozen major and a number of minor plates. At plate junctions they diverge or converge. The arrows and figures denote the direction and relative rates of plate motions. Where plates separate as at ocean ridges new crust is formed. The other end of the plate descends and is destroyed. Continental material being relatively light floats over descending plates. In the process new continental material is added to the continent and mountain ranges may also form as the edge of the continental material is buckled and forced upwards. The Himalayas, Alps and Andes are examples of this orogenic process.

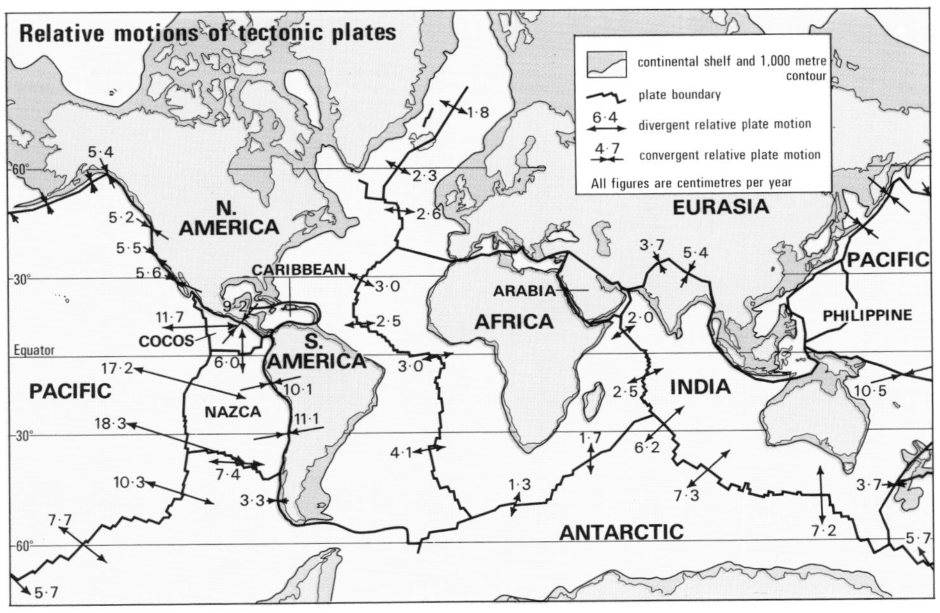

Volcanic activity and earthquakes are associated with plate tectonics. At A, an extensional boundary, magma from the upper mantle forms two parallel ridges. The rift between them broadens and new ridges are formed. At compressional plate boundary, B, the ocean crust descends to perhaps 700 km and melting takes place.

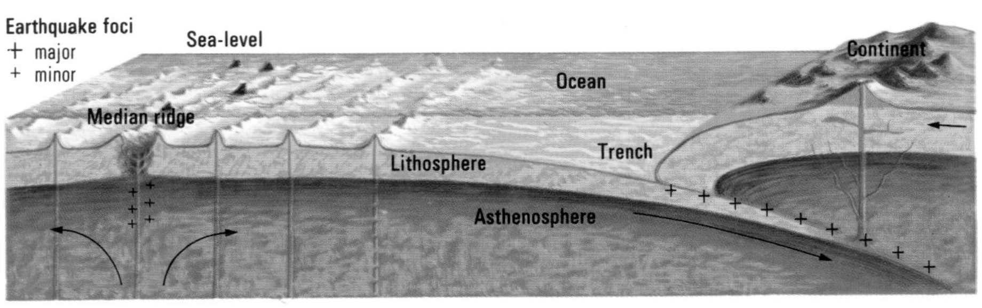

SPACE FLIGHT AND SATELLITES

Principles of flight

Popular literature has never abandoned entirely the legend of Newton and the apple. A falling apple may have been used by Newton as an illustration of the way gravity operates, but it most surely did not inspire him to an awareness that objects would fall towards the centre of the Earth unless prevented from doing so. The phenomenon of falling objects, of 'what goes up must come down' unquestionably exercised the burgeoning mind of man in remotest antiquity. Greek and Roman philosophers wrote on the subject but they were simply reverting to an intriguing topic of earlier societies seeking an explanation of natural phenomena.

It would be almost truer to say that Newton's great contribution to science was to explain why bodies did *not* fall rather than why they fell. The real question to be resolved was if the apple fell to Earth, why should the Moon revolving round the Earth remain aloft? Newton's work, added to Kepler's, provided an explanation of this riddle of the Moon and the planets, all of which rotate around the Sun without coming closer to it.

Newton proved that gravity decreases with distance: the higher above the Earth's surface the less the strength of the Earth's gravitational pull. Launched from the top of a mountain in a horizontal direction, a stone will fall some distance away from the summit having followed a curved path dictated by the combined forces of the thrower and of Earth's gravity.

Newton showed that the faster an object is projected from a mountain the further it will travel round the Earth. If launched fast enough it will orbit the Earth

Increasing the velocity will eventually bring the stone to rest at the foot of the mountain after completing a circuit of the Earth. A final extra speed of launch will cause the stone to orbit the Earth. In this condition the stone still falls towards Earth and continues to do so, but the amount it falls due to gravity is always exactly equal to the amount the curvature of the circular path has departed from a straight line.

If, from the summit of Newton's mountain, a projectile is launched with a velocity of 8 km per second (17,900 miles per hour) parallel to the Earth's surface at the moment of launch, it will orbit the Earth.

If the velocity of launch is increased above eight kilometres per second the stone or other body will assume an elliptical orbit, the ellipse becoming more elongated with each increase in the velocity of its launching. At 11 km per second (24,600 miles per hour) the elliptical orbit becomes parabolic, and the body will not come back to complete its orbit but will disappear into space.

At this velocity the projectile is moving at too great a speed for gravity to constrain it, and it escapes into space. If the velocity is increased further the parabola becomes a hyperbola. A hyperbola is similar to a parabola, but the arms are not parallel but divergent.

At the surface of the Earth the velocity required for a circular orbit is 7,912 metres per second. At 250 kilometres altitude it is 7,759 metres per second and at 500 kilometres becomes 7,617 metres per second. Velocity reduces with height until at an altitude of 35,870 kilometres (22,300 miles) the satellite will orbit at 3,072 metres per second, which is exactly equal, at that altitude, to the rate of rotation of the Earth. If its orbit is in the plane of the Equator, it will thus appear to remain always on the same spot. The satellite is then in a geosynchronous orbit.

Velocity is reduced by air resistance. This reduces the height of perigee but also the height of apogee (the point furthest from Earth in an elliptical orbit). The result is that the orbit becomes ever more nearly circular but the height of perigee continues to decrease until the satellite is burned up in the denser layers of the atmosphere or falls to Earth.

High-altitude orbits are affected to a very minor degree by the attenuated atmosphere through which they pass. Low-altitude satellites, on the other hand, have a short life. At 250 km (155 miles) altitude a satellite in circular orbit will orbit for only four days. At 300 km (186 miles) the life would be twenty days, and at 500 km (312 miles) almost three years.

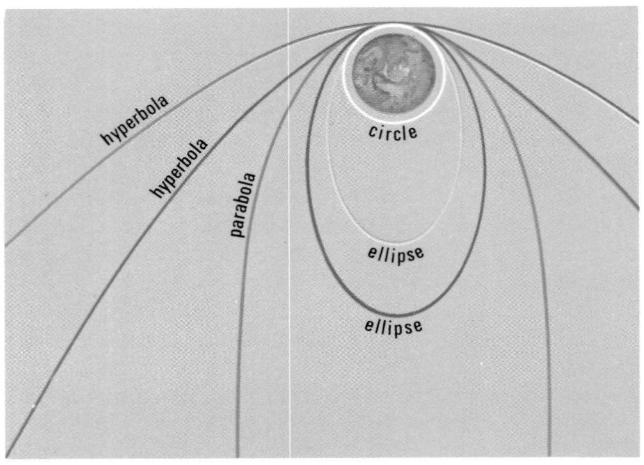

An elliptical orbit of 200 km (124 miles) perigee and apogee of 1,000 km (620 miles) will last thirty-seven days in orbit. If perigee and apogee are increased to 260 km (162 miles) and 1,300 km (808 miles) respectively, the life would be extended to 370 days, ten times as long.

Many satellites launched into low altitude for a specific purpose remain in orbit only a short time. Others already launched will still be orbiting the Earth in 100,000 years.

Flight to the Moon

In a flight to the Moon, escape velocity must first be attained either by direct launching from Earth – a method not yet used because of the enormous rockets required – or else by launching from an orbit around the Earth. Whichever method is used, and irrespective of whether the lunar spacecraft is assembled in orbit, a special orbit must be acquired from which translunar injection (TLI) takes place. Two revolutions at 7·8 kilometres per second (17,400 miles per hour), are normally required to stabilise the orbit so that TLI occurs at the right place. This is at a point behind the Earth, exactly opposite where the Moon will be when the spacecraft goes into orbit round it.

At TLI the spacecraft is accelerated until velocity is 10·9 kilometres per second (24,400 miles per hour), an operation requiring split-second timing for the start and finish of the rocket burst. From then on the spacecraft 'coasts' to the Moon – the translunar coast – steadily slowed down by the Earth's gravitational pull. Mid-course corrections are made as necessary.

At the final approach to the Moon, when the spacecraft has been slowed down to only 1·2 kilometres per second (2,700 miles per hour), the Moon's gravity accelerates the spacecraft to double its approach velocity. It must be slowed down to avoid being flung back towards Earth after swinging round the Far Side.

For the return to Earth the spacecraft must once more go into lunar orbit. This cannot be the same orbit as that from which descent was made because the Moon will have rotated on its axis and moved appreciably in its orbit around the Earth during the time the space vehicle was on the Moon. In the Apollo missions changes in the inclination of the orbit to accommodate these factors were made by the command module. Without them, rendezvous with the lunar module would have been difficult, even impossible.

Flight to other planets

Minimum energy flights to other planets make use of the gravitational attraction of the Sun and basically consist of unshackling the spacecraft from the Earth's gravitational field while at the same time retaining the Earth's orbital velocity around the Sun. From then on the principle is simply one of interlocking orbits. Having left Earth's orbit, the spacecraft follows an orbit which will intersect the other planet's orbit at exactly the time when the planet itself arrives there.

In the case of an outer planet like Mars the procedure would be to orbit the Earth long enough to allow the spacecraft to be positioned at a previously calculated orbital launch point and then to launch it from orbit with the extra velocity needed to achieve escape from Earth. The launch would take place in the direction of revolution of the Earth around the Sun. This would launch the spacecraft from Earth orbit at a velocity equal to the velocity of the Earth in orbit, 30 kilometres per second (18 miles per second) plus the velocity added by its launch from orbit. This increased velocity will cause the spacecraft to move outwards from the Earth into an orbit bigger in radius than the Earth's orbit. A number of course corrections are necessary, but most of the flight is made inertially, i.e. with no forces used except those of nature. On reaching Mars, the spacecraft must take up an orbit around the planet before a descent to the surface can be made if the aim is to arrive at a pre-selected site.

The return flight from Mars is a separate orbital problem. The Earth will have moved on some distance in its orbit. In order to intersect the Earth's orbit at a point where the Earth will be when the spacecraft arrives, an orbit around the Sun is chosen. For this orbit to intersect the Earth's orbit at the right time, launching from Mars is made in the direction opposite to its direction of travel round the Sun. This is exactly the same procedure as that followed in a landing on Venus, whose orbit is nearer to the Sun than is the Earth's.

In a flight to Venus the orbits are opposite in kind to those of a flight to Mars. Because the orbit of Venus is nearer the Sun, launching from the Earth takes place in the direction opposite to the direction in which the Earth is revolving round the Sun. The spacecraft will thus have a velocity of 30 kilometres per second (the velocity of the Earth around the Sun) less the velocity of launch. Spacecraft velocity will therefore be less than the Earth's velocity, by its gravitational attraction the Sun will draw the spacecraft towards itself. With the appropriate course corrections, the spacecraft will arrive

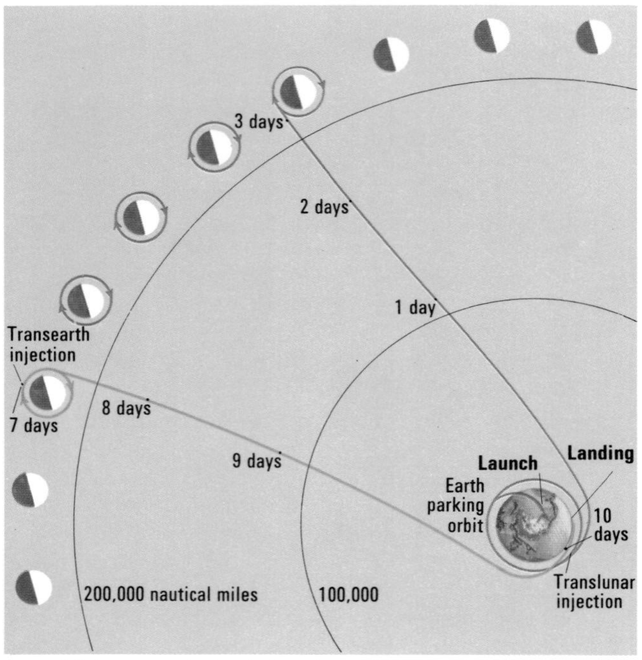

Lunar flight Launch date is five days after New Moon so that the Sun will be at a low angle and behind the astronauts on landing. By monitoring from Earth, course, velocity and direction are all accurately calculated

at Venus and descend to the surface from an orbit around the planet.

Beyond Mars are Jupiter, Saturn, Uranus and Pluto. Once, in almost two centuries, these outer planets are more or less in line so that planetary gravitational forces can be used to propel a spacecraft from one planet to the next beyond. Fortunately such an alignment occurring in the late 1970s gave US space agencies the opportunity to put theory into practice, reconnoitring Jupiter and the planets beyond. Jupiter's gravitational pull had been used by Pioneer 10 which, in 1972, was the first spacecraft to use a gravity-assisted trajectory to leave the solar system.

Escape from the solar system is but a short step along the space road. It requires a velocity of 16 km per second, but it would take 250,000 years at that speed to reach the nearest star. Until speeds approaching half the speed of light can be attained interstellar travel cannot seriously be contemplated.

The electro-magnetic spectrum

It is frequently said that we live at the bottom of the atmosphere like creatures on the floor of the ocean, and satellites act as a kind of periscope showing what exists above our atmospheric environment. Another analogy is to liken the atmosphere to a greenhouse which provides a comfortable habitat for life which could not exist in the

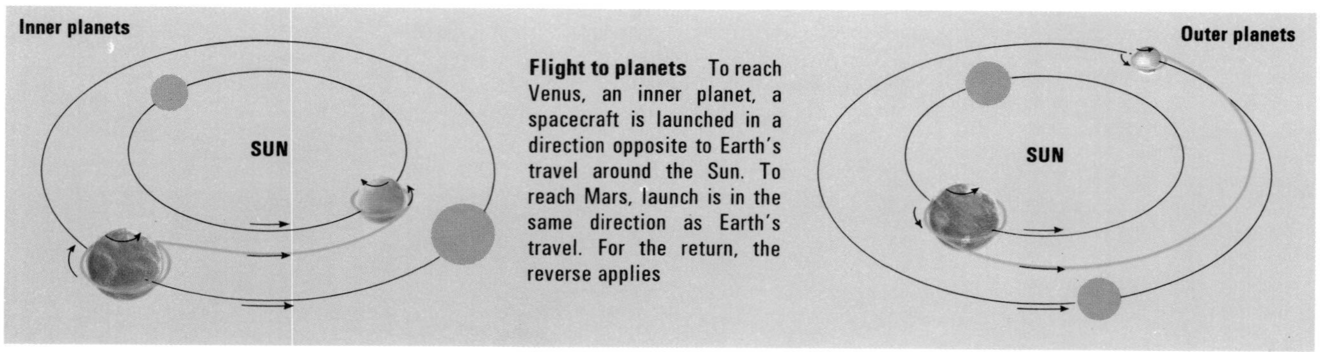

Flight to planets To reach Venus, an inner planet, a spacecraft is launched in a direction opposite to Earth's travel around the Sun. To reach Mars, launch is in the same direction as Earth's travel. For the return, the reverse applies

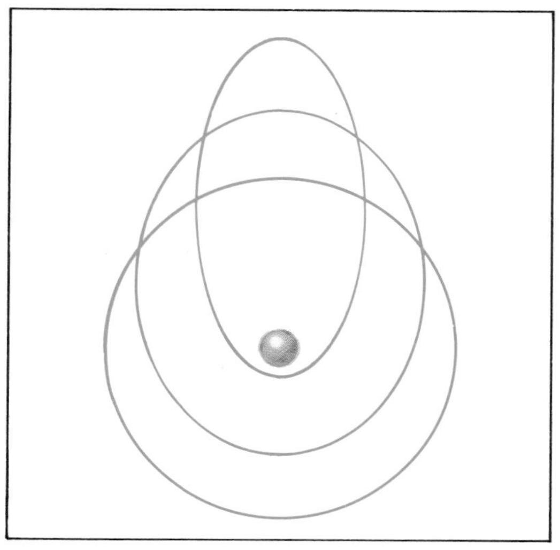

Types of equivalent orbit (left) A spacecraft in any of the three orbits, all of which have the same major axis, will orbit the Earth in exactly the same period. At perigee in the less elongated orbit velocity is double that in the circular orbit which remains constant throughout. At apogee it is half the circular velocity.
Orbital links without loss of energy (right) If two spacecraft are launched from places 90° apart, at the point where their orbits cross they will be travelling at equal velocities. If they link up they will take up a circular orbit without loss of energy

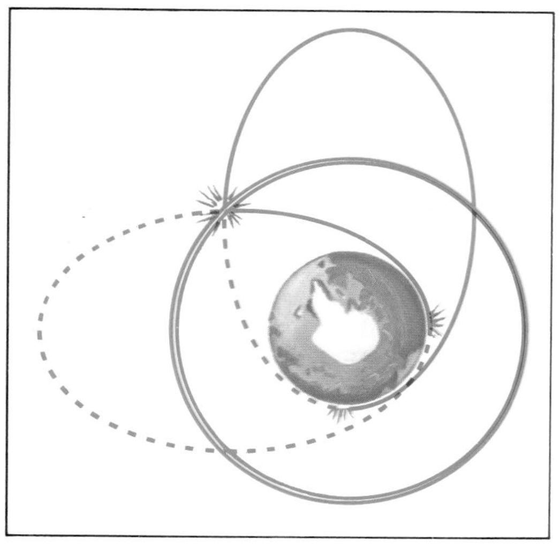

hostile environment outside.

If our greenhouse keeps out all kinds of unpleasant rays and solid objects it also prevents us from looking out at least as efficiently as we could were it not there. Outside the atmosphere the stars would not twinkle. Our view upwards is limited by water vapour, dust particles and atmospheric turbulence. Observing the heavens through a telescope shows that the glass of our greenhouse is misty, dirty and constantly vibrating. Because of the scattering of sunlight in the upper atmosphere, observations can be made by optical telescopes only for a few hours at night, and even then a clear view is rarely obtained, and is for the most part confined to a few locations. So poor is the telescopic image that magnification more than 300 to 400 times is impossible: the detail of the image breaks down.

All energy is transmitted through space in the form of electro-magnetic waves which are collectively known as the electro-magnetic spectrum. The part of the spectrum which contains the light waves by which we see is known as the optical part of the spectrum. It is a very narrow band in a broad spectrum. It encompasses a range of wavelengths with violet light at the short-wave end and red light at the other. Since the human eye cannot separate these wavelengths, the whole range from violet to red is combined to form white light. Objects appear in a particular colour because they absorb all other colours.

On either side of the optical spectrum are a whole range of energy emissions ranging from millions of times shorter in wavelength to millions of times longer. Almost all these are excluded by the atmosphere. It is just as if our greenhouse were opaque except for two small areas which allowed light in, with here and there some scratches which allowed a small amount of light to filter through. One reasonably clear area is the optical part of the spectrum; the other is the radio spectrum. These are the main atmospheric windows.

Wavelength is the distance between the crests of a wave. This distance is extremely short in electro-magnetic waves so a special unit is used, equal to one ten-millionth of a centimetre and called the Ångstrom. Visible light is a band from 4000 to 7000 Ångstrom units. Below 4000Å is the ultra-violet band, and below that again the gamma rays. Both gamma rays and ultra-violet are almost completely absorbed by the ozone layer in the atmosphere. From 7000Å upwards we move into the infra-red zone. Most of the infra-red radiations are absorbed by the interlocking bands of carbon dioxide and water vapour. Beyond the infra-red radiations are the radio wavelengths. Extremely long radio waves are reflected back from the ionosphere, which leaves a radio window extending between one-tenth of a millimetre and one hundred centimetres in wavelength (300 to 300,000 megacycles frequency). Radio astronomy is confined to these limits unless we observe from outside the atmosphere.

By the use of special films the optical window can be extended to provide a photographic spectrum stretching beyond the visible spectrum in both directions – into the ultra-violet and into the infra-red – enlarging the window's limits to 2900Å and 12,500Å. Below the lower limit the ultra-violet radiations are absorbed to almost total extinction by the ozone layer. At 14,000Å even the small quantity of water vapour present in the gelatine of the film coating is sufficient to absorb the radiations entirely.

To give some idea of how effectively the ozone layer absorbs ultra-violet rays, at 40°N when the Sun is highest in the sky the intensity of the Sun's radiation reaching the Earth at 2898Å is only one-millionth of the radiation at 3142Å. The absolute upper and lower limits are, therefore, 14,000Å and 2900Å. This means that photography from the Earth or of the Earth from space is not possible beyond these limits. Yet this is only a small portion of the total electro-magnetic spectrum; most of the information transmitted through space can never be received on Earth. It is for this reason that satellites are so important in the study of the universe and for examining the Earth from above the greenhouse roof.

Satellites provide the means of improving visual exploration of space and, more particularly, the use of the whole range of the spectrum. The high-energy part of the spectrum, the ultra-violet and gamma rays, are likely to return the greatest rewards. Mapping of the short-wave sky by satellites acting as space platforms is the means of studying the pulsars, quasars, black holes in space and other high-energy phenomena.

Remote sensing

Sensing an object is examining it by the use of any of the five senses, but particularly by touch. Remote sensing is examining the same object but not making physical contact with it.

Our eyes are remote sensors by virtue of their ability to collect information on something within optical range. The photographic camera is one of the means we have of preserving sensing by the eyes. Radio waves are also methods of sensing, and their recording on discs or tape as electro-magnetic signals fulfils the same role for the ears as the photograph does for the eyes. Videotapes record television transmissions, thus providing both a visual and an aural record for future use.

In everyday life, therefore, photography, radio and television have extended our remote-sensing capabilities. Not so well known are the methods of sensing in parts of the spectrum beyond optical range, that is at wavelengths which the eye cannot record, or in parts of the spectrum which neither eyes nor ears are capable of receiving. Magnetism, radio-activity, gravity, micro-wave emissions which have super-high frequencies, infra-red and ultra-violet sensing all extend the range of perception far beyond the physiological potential of human beings. It is this aspect of remote sensing, the ability of our current technology to exploit areas far beyond the normal audio-visual sphere, which imparts a special significance to air-borne and, more especially, satellite-borne remote sensors.

An important addition to the aircraft and camera was the development of radar. This allowed obstacles to normal optical viewing to be removed to some degree. Cloud and fog, which were a barrier to vision, could now be penetrated, and what was on the other side of the barrier could be seen or photographed as a radar photograph. This was the first airborne application of remote sensing in the specialised way in which the term is used in satellite operations.

A second wartime development in the field of remote sensing was infra-red photography. Special film sensitive to infra-red wavelengths was developed for the purpose of penetrating camouflage. Originally the films were in black and white or, more correctly, shades of grey. After the war infra-red sensitive colour film was produced, increasing the potential of photography in the infra-red region of the spectrum.

Three airborne sensors which were to prove invaluable as a means of surveying and exploration were the magnetometer, the electro-magnetometer and the radiation detector, also known as the scintillation-counter, which added a new type of sensing. Whereas all the others were concerned with the electro-magnetic spectrum in its infra-red, visual and radio regions, these new instruments sensed the Earth's natural magnetism and radiation, phenomena quite distinct from the electro-magnetic spectrum.

The magnetometer records variations in the Earth's overall magnetic field. The electro-magnetometer records the conductivity of the ground immediately below an aircraft. Radiation detectors record variations in the intensity of radiation of the terrain below the aircraft. All three are important geophysical tools. Uranium, thorium, radium and other radioactive minerals are identified by the radiation counter. Magnetometers recording the variation of the general magnetic field of the Earth disclose the presence of magnetic ores, iron, titanium and pyrrhotite. Skilled interpretation of the magnetic intensity record can also, however, lead to the identification of many other minerals: gold, platinum, diamond, asbestos, copper, nickel and so on. Ore bodies which act as good conductors compared with the surrounding rock are detected by the electro-magnetometer.

Of particular importance in the application of these instruments to prospecting is the search for oil. Oil-bearing structures are by no means always accompanied by a particular terrain feature. Locating oil-bearing structures involves an unavoidable exploration of areas at considerable depths below ground. However the search is conducted, it is inevitably expensive. When oil is sought in areas of jungle or in remote deserts, airborne magnetometers are a valuable tool. Properly interpreted, the instrumental records can show the depth to the oil-bearing rocks, the thickness of the sedimentary rocks above the oil, the shape of the structure, the nature of the surrounding rocks and any odd intrusions of extraneous rocks. All three instruments are often used together for the whole area being surveyed, a photographic survey being conducted separately.

These techniques of aerial photography and airborne geophysical instruments allow vast areas of territory to be covered in a short period of time unless unfavourable weather conditions hinder the acquisition of photographs. To accomplish the same coverage of terrain by old-fashioned field methods could take years, and where terrain conditions are bad, as in the equatorial rain forests or the polar regions, they may prove beyond the capabilities of field teams. By using airborne methods the general reconnaissance of the area can be completed without the time and effort of using men on the ground.

An airborne gravimeter was also developed, and though it proved to be of little importance for normal geophysical work, it was valuable as a means of studying the general gravity field of the Earth. A final addition to remote sensing devices was the introduction of ultra-violet photography. Ultra-violet, all the other sensing systems and the use of ordinary colour in photography, are the means by which data on the Earth and its resources can be obtained from an orbiting platform, the artificial Earth satellite.

Radar can be used to penetrate cloud and the resulting radar imagery (radar photography) has much the appearance of an ordinary photograph except that closer examination will show surprising differences in the features which appear prominently and those which appear inconspicuous or are absent altogether. Radar waves are reflected with greater or less intensity according to the angle of incidence of the ray which is, of course, dependent on the configuration of the ground, and by the electrical properties of the material from which it is reflected. Resolution of detail depends upon wavelength – the shorter the wavelength the greater the detail in the imagery. Radar waves are very long compared to optical wavelengths and there is consequently a smaller capability of picking up fine detail.

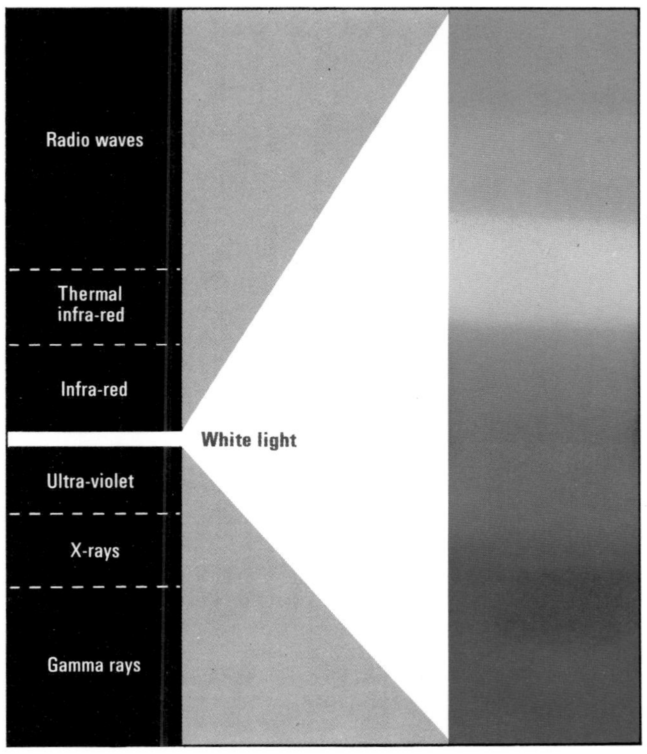

Electro-magnetic spectrum All waves are absorbed in the atmosphere or reflected back into space except for a narrow window admitting visible light and a broader window which lets in radio waves

Conventional photography, whether in black and white or in colour, is a record of the way in which the objects photographed reflect the Sun's energy acting on them in the form of light. It is, therefore, the energy reflected in the 4000 to 9000 Ångstrom unit range. This band of the spectrum comprises four principal bands of wavelength: blue, green, red and near infra-red. Photographic film can be made sensitive to each spectral band, all others being excluded by filters. Separately recording each band is known as multi-spectral photography. To this range of multi-spectral photography may be added the ultra-violet, the long infra-red and also micro-wave sensing.

Sensing in several bands discloses characteristics not discernible in conventional photography. Infra-red sensing is the sensing of thermal properties and can, like radar, be used by day or at night to reveal heat sources, such as power stations, in the form of a thermal map. Ideally, several infra-red channels should be used at the same time, since the longer wavelength seems to depict more thermal emission while the shorter infra-red wavelength portrays the differences between temperatures.

Astronomical satellites

Astronomical satellites are one of the types of space-oriented satellites designed to explore the universe from Earth orbit, as opposed to the Earth-oriented satellites whose mission is study of the Earth and its phenomena. In some way linking the two are the geophysical satellites, equipped to observe the composition, temperature and electrical properties of the upper atmosphere. Their elliptical orbits take them through the layers of the atmosphere out to the edge of inter-planetary space. Other geophysical satellites measure the electro-magnetic, gravitational and particle fields of the ionosphere.

Communications satellites

Intercontinental communication was one of the first benefits which artificial satellites conferred upon mankind. Were it not for the ionosphere the range of radio transmission would be strictly limited to 'line-of-sight'. The transmitted waves would not follow the curvature of the Earth but would continue to the horizon and on out into space. All transmitters would, therefore, have only a short range, no matter how elevated the ground on which they were built. Fortunately, the ionosphere reflects the waves back to Earth, thus extending the range far beyond the visible horizon. The curvature of the Earth imposes an absolute limit on the range, which also varies with the movements of the reflecting layers of the ionosphere – movements which are very marked in transition from day to night.

Communications satellites are the means by which radio signals can be received anywhere on Earth. Placed in orbit above the Equator at 35,870 km (22,300 miles) above the Earth's surface, the satellite's period of revolution is exactly twenty-four hours. It thus remains permanently above the same point on the Earth. Placed in mid-Atlantic, a direct radio link is established between America and Europe and Africa.

A minimum of three satellites can provide a complete radio, telephone and television chain over the whole Earth. Eight satellites are maintained to give a greater capacity. Each satellite can handle thousands of simultaneous telephone calls or a large number of colour television broadcasts.

Navigation satellites

From the days that the first sailors put out to sea, a means of navigation in all weathers has been every mariner's dream. Until radio techniques were used the only means of navigating over great distances was by

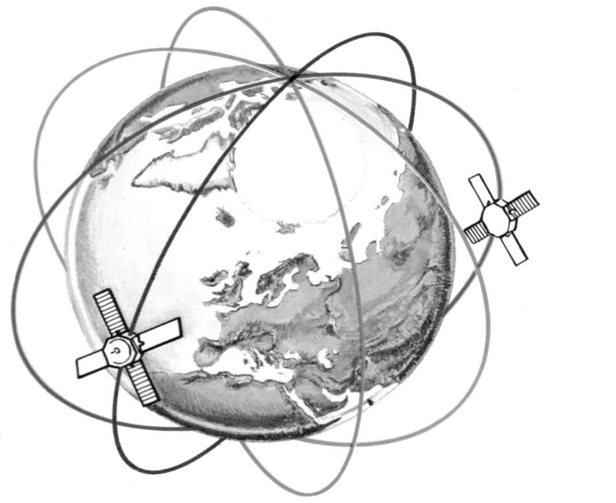

Navigational satellites at an altitude of 700 miles (1130 km) form a 'birdcage' of orbits. Three satellites allow a ship to fix its position every 2 hours and four satellites every 1½ hours

periodic checks of position by observation of the Sun or the stars. When the sky is cloud-covered the observations cannot be made.

Radio techniques of various kinds now help the sailor or aviator to obtain an estimate of his position. The more refined systems afford him the means of an accurate fix, but these depend on a network of transmitting stations. The potential of satellite navigation was anticipated long before a satellite was put into orbit.

The principle is quite simple. If a satellite is placed in polar orbit and its orbit can be tracked and plotted accurately, it would be possible at any given instant of time to say exactly where the satellite is in latitude and longitude and how high it is. All that is then required is a means of obtaining the slant range from ship to satellite to be able to say where the ship is or, likewise, the position of an aircraft as long as its height above sea level is known.

Slant range to satellite is obtained by means of the Doppler principle: that electro-magnetic waves (like sound waves) are modified by the motion of the source. As the satellite approaches the ship, its motion – which is very rapid – shortens the wavelength of the signals. More waves thus reach the ship per second than would be received from a stationary source. Wavelength is lengthened as the satellite moves away from the ship and fewer waves per second are received. From the change in the number of signals received during the transit of the satellite, slant range can be calculated.

In the case of a ship which is moving, the position is fixed from one or two passes of the satellite. If the ship is stationary, fixes could be made over a long period of time involving a great number of satellite passes. This method of fixing can be applied to oil rigs or other off-shore installations which are out of sight of land. Such fixes, which are far more accurate than the fix of a moving ship, are called geodetic fixes. A small pack of Doppler equipment carried by a man allows him to fix his position in a desert or other isolated place to an accuracy of less than ten metres using only the satellite transmissions – as long, of course, as the necessary calculations can be made.

Geodetic satellites

Geodesy is the science of measuring the Earth, and satellites have become a valuable tool for this purpose.

The Earth can be loosely described as an ellipsoid, that is to say a body whose form is created by rotating an ellipse about its axis. More specifically, the Earth is sometimes called an oblate spheroid. This means simply that the spheroid is flattened at its poles. In fact the Earth is not a regular geometrical figure at all. Its centre of mass is not precisely located at the geometrical centre and the materials which constitute the Earth's crust are not evenly distributed. The effect of these irregularities is that the actual form of the Earth cannot be accurately deduced by observation and extrapolation. The whole surface has to be measured. This is at present an impossible task as more than seven-tenths of the Earth's surface is covered in water. Even if the three-tenths of the surface which is land had all been accurately surveyed, the ocean areas could still not be defined in shape and size.

In order to determine the distance apart of places widely separated on the Earth's surface, scientists in the United States used satellite observations. Three systems were employed. A satellite with a flashing light was photographed against the background of stars, and from measurements of the photographic plates the position of the observing station on the ground was calculated. A second method involved measurement of radio ranges to the satellite by sending signals from three stations, the geographical position of two of which was known. The third system, employing the Doppler principle used in the navigation satellite, was the one adopted for all purposes of position fixing, including navigation.

An accurate knowledge of the flattening of the Earth, its equatorial diameter and the nature of its irregularities in shape are essential for the accurate operation of satellites for purposes such as navigation. Equally important is a knowledge of the Earth's gravitational field. All satellites orbit the Earth under the influence of gravity; the perturbations of the orbit reflect undulations in the Earth's surface carried to a higher altitude. Knowledge of the deformations of the Earth's surface due to gravity variations helps to refine the calculations of satellite orbits. Equally, monitoring the perturbations in the satellite orbit helps to identify the undulations of the Earth's mean sea level surface. From such observations we know that the Earth is slightly pear-shaped, being wider south of the Equator; that the South Pole is in a hollow and that there are several depressions and elevations in the oceans and on the continents. These deformations are quite separate from the elevations and depressions of the mountains and valleys. They would still exist if the Earth were liquid provided the gravity field remained as it is now.

Meteorological satellites

Satellites which are employed to observe the Earth form a category known as observation satellites. Apart from military satellites, about which no official information is available, the first photographic satellites and the first

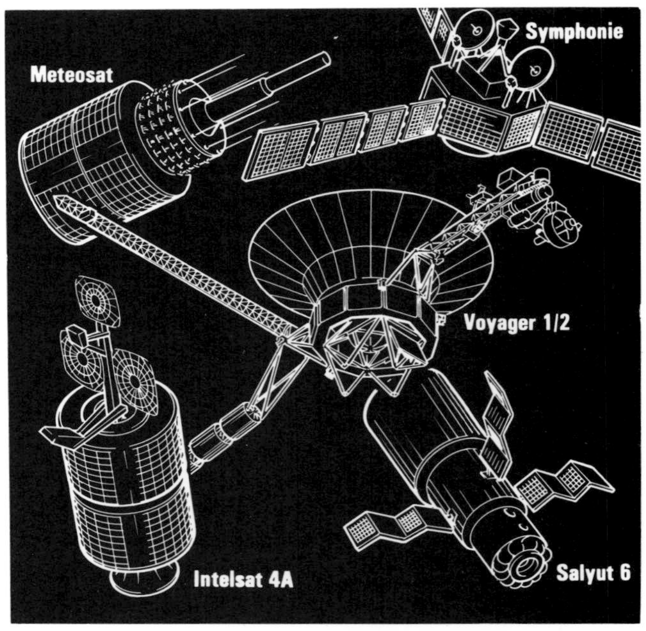

to make use of remote sensing other than ordinary photography were the meteorological satellites. Sensing outside the photographic range is carried out by special detectors (radiometers) which measure electro-magnetic energy and convert it into electrical energy which can be stored on magnetic tape or used to produce an image – not a photograph – by means of a cathode ray tube. If several radiometers are used, each sensing a different part of the spectrum, we call the result multi-spectral sensing. A typical multi-spectral scanning operation would show: the total reflected solar radiation; the total thermal radiation; the amount of energy absorbed by the carbon dioxide layer; the amount absorbed by water vapour; the Earth surface temperature – where the clouds can be penetrated – and the height of the clouds. Each of these five measurements would be made in its own spectral band.

A knowledge of global weather patterns is a great boon to long-term weather forecasting and study of possible changes in the climate of the world as a whole.

Meteorology was the first science to profit from space techniques. Most of the weather changes could not be observed from the surface of the Earth: there were not enough observing stations, and in any case seven-tenths of the weather patterns originated over the oceans. Of the land surface large areas are uninhabited or lack meteorological stations and reporting systems necessary to obtain a global view.

Meteorological satellites are either geosynchronous or polar-orbiting. A geosynchronous satellite can photograph the whole of one hemisphere every twenty-four minutes, so monitoring the movement of large air masses and keeping track of the changing weather patterns indicated by the cloud formations. Hurricanes can be detected and advance warning of their course and magnitude given to the areas threatened.

The Earth's atmosphere is subjected to the daily switching on and off of the energy of the Sun as night follows day: to the rotation of the Earth and to the increase and decrease of water vapour by evaporation of the oceans or condensation in the form of rain. Changes occur, generally, too rapidly to allow a world picture to be built up quickly from ground reporting. Meteorological satellites provide a world picture that is being constantly updated.

Monitoring weather patterns, the sea temperature, the atmospheric jet streams are essential if man is ever to control his environment or to understand why drought, flood, frost and winds, etc., occasionally reach disaster proportions.

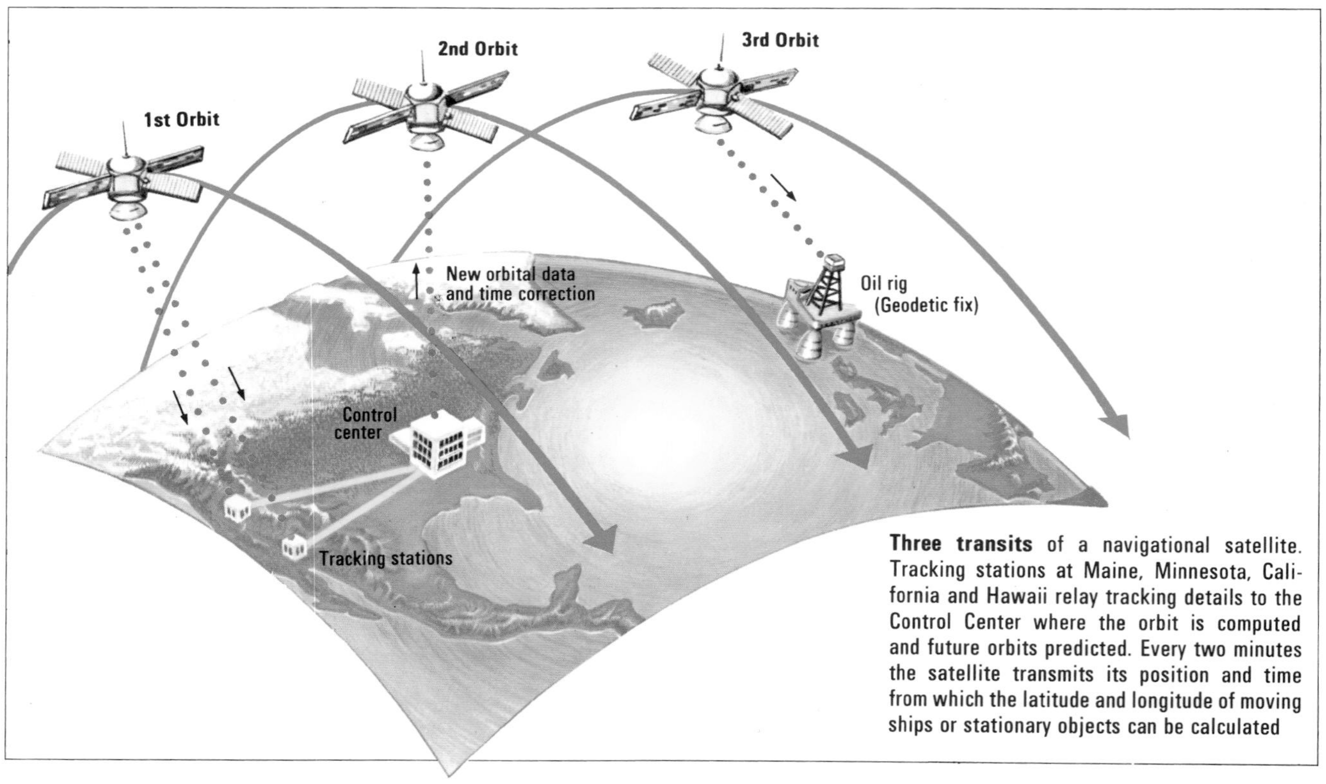

Three transits of a navigational satellite. Tracking stations at Maine, Minnesota, California and Hawaii relay tracking details to the Control Center where the orbit is computed and future orbits predicted. Every two minutes the satellite transmits its position and time from which the latitude and longitude of moving ships or stationary objects can be calculated

Constant surveillance of the Earth by satellite will help to predict long-term climatic changes. The extension of polar ice and the rate of advance pose an ominous threat to the future of the human race. Such terrifying possibilities must be predicted if unimaginable suffering is to be avoided. Meteorological satellites are now an everyday tool in short- and long-term weather forecasting; the monitoring of long-term climatic changes may ultimately yield the most beneficial returns of all.

Polar-orbiting satellites operate at relatively low altitudes – about 1,200 km (750 miles) – circling the Earth every two hours. Global coverage is obtained in twelve orbital passes. These satellites are Sun-synchronous. Half of their orbit is always in sunlight; continuous photographic cover can be obtained by using cameras whose photographs cover 30° of latitude at the Equator. One half of the orbit can be used for photography, the other for sensors, which are not restricted to daylight.

An important requirement is the measurement of the total amount of solar energy reflected back into space by the Earth, and particularly by its cloud cover. For this purpose a waveband width of 0·2 to 4·0 microns is used. A micron is equal to one-thousandth of a millimetre. A band width of 5 to 30 microns will reveal the total radiation energy emitted by the Earth. Water vapour absorbed is handled by the band covering 6·4 to 6·9 microns, and carbon dioxide absorption by the 14 to 16 micron band. At 10 to 11 microns there is an atmospheric 'window' which permits the surface of the Earth to be examined in this part of the spectrum.

From the first two sensors, the Earth's radiation balance is given. Temperature in the lower stratosphere is controlled by the carbon dioxide content of the atmosphere. The 14 to 16 micron band maps out the temperature field in this region of the atmosphere. Water vapour measurements give the moisture content of the upper part of the troposphere. Surface temperatures and cloud heights are observed through the 'window'.

From the scanning instruments a strip of imagery for each band covering the same region of the Earth allows comparisons to be made. An interesting characteristic of the pictures is the contrast between energy emissions and reflections. Radiations of low intensity from clouds, cold or moist areas appear as light areas while high intensities, warm or dry, show up as dark areas. This is exactly the opposite of the imagery sensitive to reflection, as in the 0·2 to 4·0 microns.

Earth Resources Satellites

By chance artificial Earth satellites were developed just when concern for the ravages of our environment was becoming widespread. Almost as soon as the first satellites were in orbit the question of their suitability as platforms for photographic cameras began to be discussed. A large body of opinion dismissed this possibility with scorn on the grounds that the scale of photography from so great an altitude would be useless. Then rumours about the results obtained from military satellites invoked second thoughts among the sceptics. The Apollo programmes included photography of Earth from orbit and pointed the way to the future of space photography of Earth.

The first and most obvious application of satellite photography is to the production and revision of maps, particularly small-scale maps and atlases. Sensing in bands other than the visible part of the spectrum was also possible; thus emerged the prospect of a satellite devoted exclusively to monitoring Earth resources and assessing the degree of pollution and contamination by the use of sensing devices.

For long periods of its life the Earth has been in the grip of ice ages which in the remote geological past have occupied a greater span of time than the ice-free periods. We are still emerging from the last glaciation. Contaminants ejected into the atmosphere could expedite the return of the next ice age.

Timely warning of this possibility is one of the tasks of Earth Resources Satellites, helped by meteorological satellites, in their study of the atmosphere, air movements and climate as part of our resources. The realisation that a modest increase in the quantity of dust particles could reduce the mean world temperature by some 11°C (20°F) alerted conservationists to the current danger. Further study showed that the quantity of contaminants was less serious than the fact that they could not be extricated from the atmosphere once they were there. Pollution of rivers, lakes and inland seas by effluent; the destruction of life by the use of large quantities of insecticide; the rate at which erosion was taking place through inefficient agriculture or mining operations, were all topics which the Earth Resources Satellites were to embrace.

Smog is a local problem caused by pollutants and sunlight acting together; the effect on the atmosphere and the climate of carbon dioxide, nitrous oxides, hydrocarbons and lead are global problems and monitoring is therefore required. The change in the ozone content of the atmosphere, particularly, could be disastrous. Pollution of the oceans can only be monitored effectively from space, supplemented by observations in the oceans themselves. Food resources on land and in the oceans, crop and tree diseases detectable by infra-red colour photography; agricultural census; the nature of settlement by human beings; the elimination rate of forests with a consequent inevitable prospect of soil erosion; the rate of advance or retreat of glaciers; all these were considered as capable of assessment and evaluation by the imagery from the satellites. New sources of minerals or agricultural products might also be discovered.

This stupendously ambitious list of tasks, as well as others, was allotted to Earth Resources Satellites, now called Landsat. A vast amount of imagery has been obtained. Its exploitation will take a very long time, but it is to be hoped that the process of exploitation will show the direction in which future monitoring by satellites should move.

The satellite has a life of one year. It is Sun-synchronous, all imagery being taken on the descending part of the orbit, which is the part of the orbit always in daylight. A single orbit of the Earth takes 103·267 minutes (about 1 hour and 43 minutes), passing over latitude 81°N on its downward path from north to south and over 81°S in its passage northwards on the night-side of its circuit. The polar regions are therefore not covered. To every observer on the Equator the satellite passes overhead at 9.42 a.m., and to the satellite the time is always 9.42 a.m. when it crosses the Equator. At that time of day the Sun is not very high in the sky, so fairly long shadows are thrown and the detail of ground relief brought out. If the satellite crossed the Equator just before or just after noon the lack of pronounced shadows would give the ground a very flat appearance on the imagery.

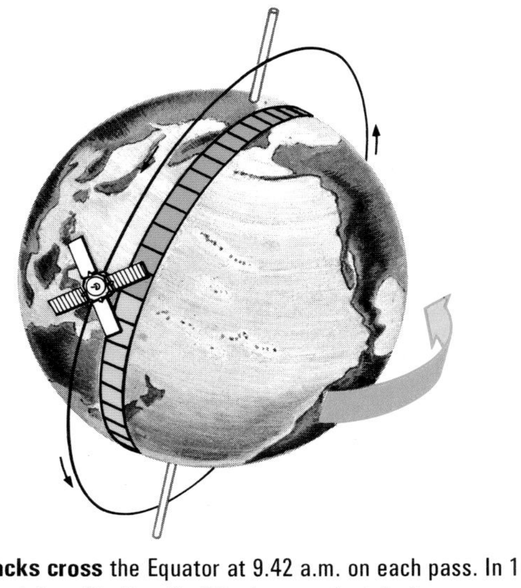

Landsat tracks cross the Equator at 9.42 a.m. on each pass. In 18 days the whole Earth from 81° N to 81° S is photographed. Each exposure covers 100 nautical miles (185 km) square

A complete cycle of orbits takes eighteen days, at the end of which the satellite begins a new cycle, passing over exactly the same track on the Earth's surface as it covered in its first pass in the first cycle. Imagery of an identical area is thus produced by the satellite every eighteen days. Each satellite track is 159·38 km (99·6 miles) from those on either side at the Equator. Since the imagery is 185 km square, there is a slight but essential overlap.

The satellite is equipped with vidicon cameras and a multi-spectral scanner for remote sensing. Vidicon (television-type) cameras operate in three separate wavelength bands, blue-green, red and near infra-red. The multi-spectral scanner is an optical scanning system furnishing imagery on four wavelength bands in the visible part of the spectrum and in the near infra-red. Each image is about 100 nautical miles wide, 185 kilometres square.

Ground sensors installed at certain points transmit data to the satellite from stream gauges, vegetation and soil temperature recorders, seismometers and tiltmeters recording slopes of terrain. All this data is sent back by the satellite to the collection centre where it is used to correlate and assess the satellite imagery in comparison with known ground conditions.

The results of the multi-spectral scanner are relayed to ground receiving stations where the electronic signals can be converted into their pictorial form. Finally, imagery is available on 70 mm film; an enlargement of 3·369 times makes its scale exactly 1:1,000,000.

Future Earth resources satellite systems will undoubtedly make good many of the deficiencies of the present experimental version. Uniformity of coverage is an asset, but the small scale will not suit all purposes. A larger scale of imagery is not only possible, it is a pressing demand if the whole range of Earth resources monitoring is to be effective. However, large-scale imagery obtained continuously, year in and year out, would result in an unmanageable quantity of material and legions of experts engaged in the examination and interpretation of the information obtained.

There are other practical considerations. There are only two ways of obtaining large-scale imagery on a worldwide basis. One is to increase the focal length (or equivalent focal length) of the sensing system. This poses many problems of design because the present satellite orbit was selected to give coverage at the scale now in use. An alternative is to reduce the height of the orbit. If the height is reduced by a large amount, which would be necessary if the scale of the present sensing system were to be appreciably increased, the life of the satellite would be shortened. Three times as large a scale would mean the altitude of the circular orbit would be only 155 miles (250 km). The life of the satellite would then be only four days. Yet the scale of 1:300,000 would still be too small for many purposes. The answer must lie in the direction of new sensing systems capable of larger-scale imagery.

In spite of all these problems, space methods for achieving imagery are the methods to use in the future. There is no other way of obtaining global information; the answer must lie in finding a solution to the problems of space technology rather than avoiding them as too difficult to solve.

The mantle of cloud enveloping the Earth is an irksome obstacle to any form of photography of the Earth. Radar is useful, but its potential to resolve small detail is limited. Areas almost permanently covered in cloud can only be photographed on those rare occasions when the air is clear after a storm and a camera happens to be passing overhead at just that moment. So periodic monitoring of terrain features from orbiting platforms is not possible, and ground methods may prove to be the only way out of this difficulty.

For the rest of the world, with a 55 per cent chance of being covered by cloud, satellite imagery is at no greater disadvantage than aircraft. Indeed, satellite imagery operates with an advantage over aircraft. Satellites can cover the same area countless times, certain of eventual success in acquiring cloud-free cover. Above all, the satellite imagery is obtained by a uniform system. It is computer-controlled. It is stored and can be selected for use by computer; the proportion of cloud cover can be defined by computer; statistical data can be selected from the imagery or keyed to it, also using computers. Satellite imagery, therefore, is a means – and the only means – of setting up a world data bank of terrestrial reconnaissance linked to resources inventories, assessments or commentaries or any other special terrestrial study based on or plotted on imagery. For indexing Earth studies the present system has much to commend it. Though improved systems will evolve real progress will come with the next generation of space vehicles. In June 1978 an oceanographic research satellite, Seasat, heralded this advance. It was launched to monitor the microwave features of the ocean surface. It orbited the Earth every 100 minutes at an altitude of 800 km but failed in October 1978 after providing valuable data to shipping, fishing fleets and off-shore drilling operations. The Synthetic Aperture Radar Sensor, a special feature of Seasat, was used for experimental terrain imagery covering a 100 km swath.

The need to find a substitute for the wasteful operation of sending a vehicle into orbit by means of a rocket became obvious before the first orbit was ever achieved by a satellite. Today thousands of pieces of space debris are in orbit around the Earth occasionally plunging back to Earth as in the case of Skylab on south-west Australia in 1979. Rockets built at stupendous cost are used once; satellites, equally expensive, are sent into orbit to remain there or be burned up in the atmosphere. The space shuttle, a combination of spacecraft and aircraft, is the first creation designed to orbit the Earth and return again to be re-used for further missions.

Re-usable satellites based on this principle may well be the answer to future Earth resources questions. Operating as an aircraft, the satellite could bring back its imagery rather than having to signal it back to be re-assembled from electronic recordings. An immediate effect would be a marked enhancement of the quality of imagery. Operations at a variety of altitudes and orbits would put Earth resources studies into a new setting. Perhaps a combination of both fixed geosynchronous and variable orbit vehicles is the ideal. Skylab photographs taken from a manned satellite may be seen in the future as the first step towards a manned Earth Resources Satellite.

Skylab photograph of Montevideo, Uruguay, showing the Santa Lucia River carrying sediment into the Rio de la Plata – the large expanse of water. White beaches and sand dune areas are conspicuous. Roads, urban areas, farmland, and an airport east of Montevideo are all visible. The island where the rivers meet is Isla del Tigra. Landsat photographs are similar, but their format makes them less suitable as illustrations

LUNAR CHARTS

NORTH POLAR REGION

POLAR STEREOGRAPHIC PROJECTION
1:16 000 000 at the Poles

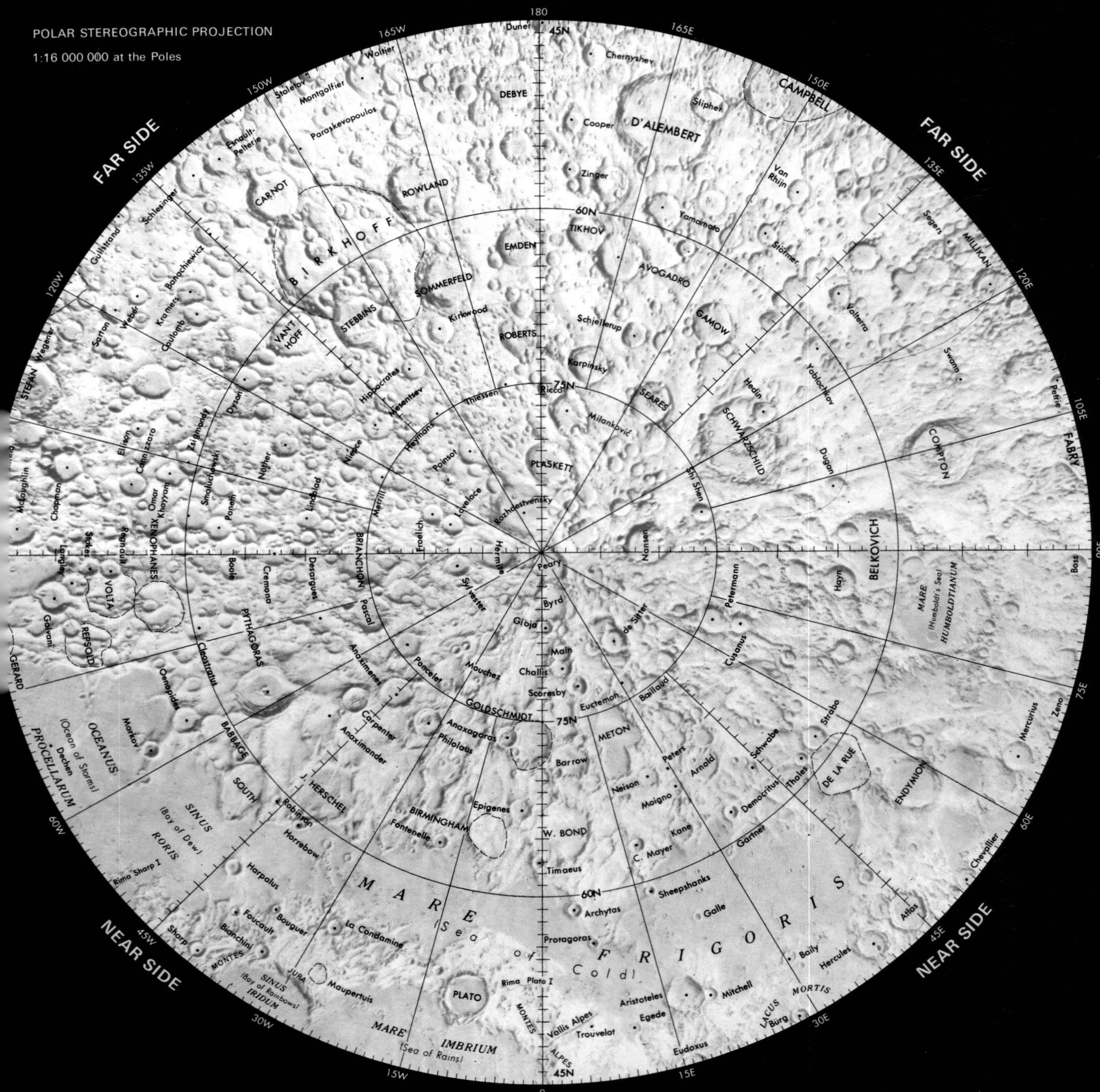

LUNAR DATA

Earth/Moon Mass Ratio	M_e/M_m 81.3015
Density (mean)	3.34g/cm^3
Synodic Month (new Moon to new Moon)	29.530 588d
Sidereal Month (fixed star to fixed star)	27.321 661d
Inclination of Lunar orbit to ecliptic	5°8′43″
Inclination of equator to ecliptic	1°40′32″
Inclination of Lunar orbit to Earth's equator	18°.5 to 28°.5
Distance from Moon to Earth (mean)	384.400 km (238.328 mi)
Optical libration in longitude	±7°.6
Optical libration in latitude	±6°.7
Magnitude (mean of full Moon)	−12.7
Temperature	120°K to 407°K (−244°F to +273°F)
Escape velocity	2.38 km/sec (1.48 mi/sec)
Diameter of Moon	3476 km (2160 mi)
Surface gravity	162.2 cm/sec^2
Orbital velocity	1.024 km/sec (Moon) 0.64 mi/sec
Temperature	29.6 km/sec (Earth) 18.5 mi/sec
Kelvin is the number of Celcius degrees above absolute zero (−273°)	

◀ FAR SIDE | NEAR SIDE ▶

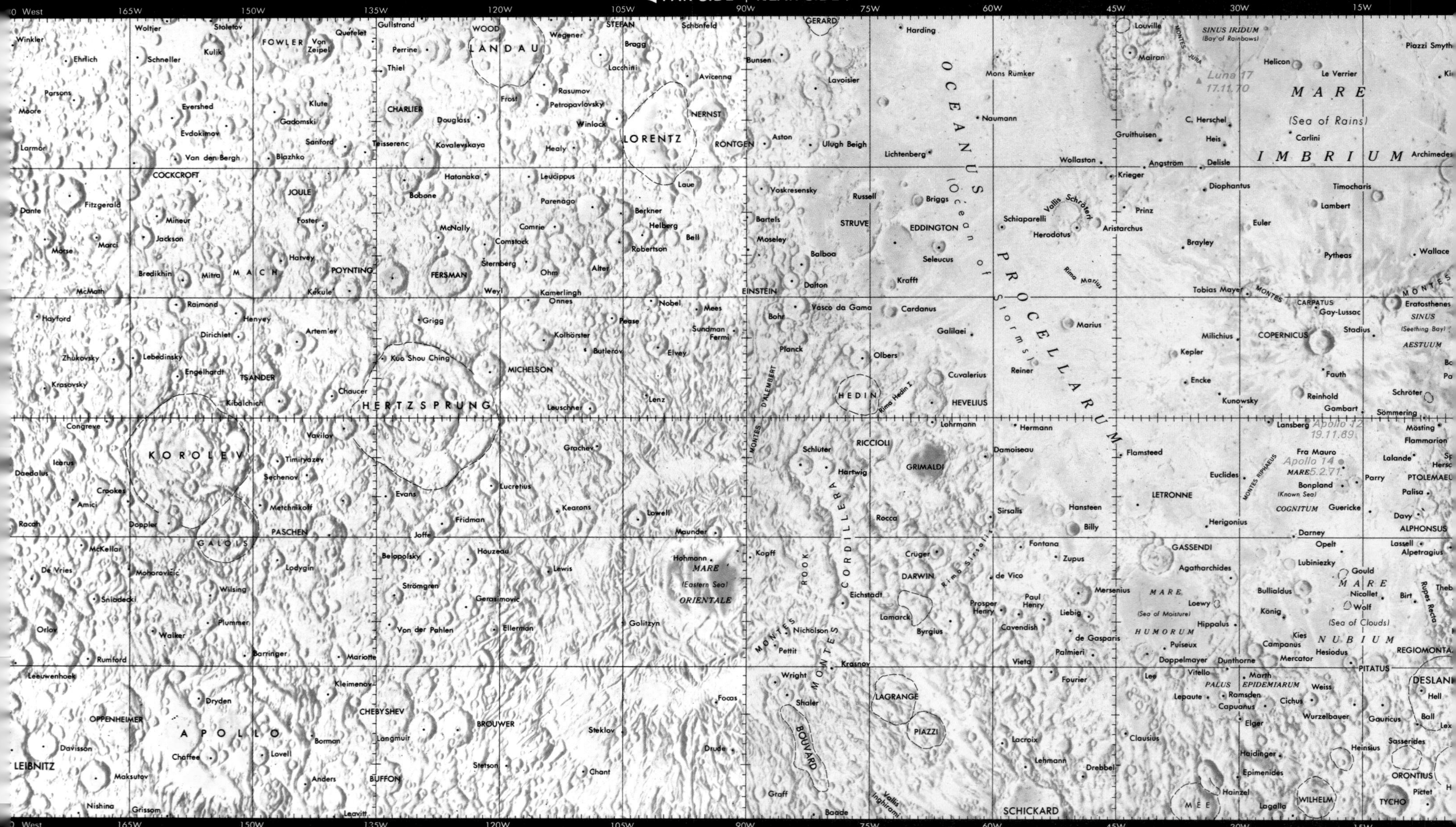

◀ FAR SIDE | NEAR SIDE ▶

This chart of the Moon is based upon the photography obtained by Lunar Orbiter Missions I, II, III, IV &V. The positions of lunar features are based on the ACIC Positional Reference System, 1969. Names of lunar features are those approved by the International Astronomical Union in 1935, 1961, 1964 and 1970.

MERCATOR PROJECTION
1:16 000 000 at 34°N and S

PHASES OF THE MOON

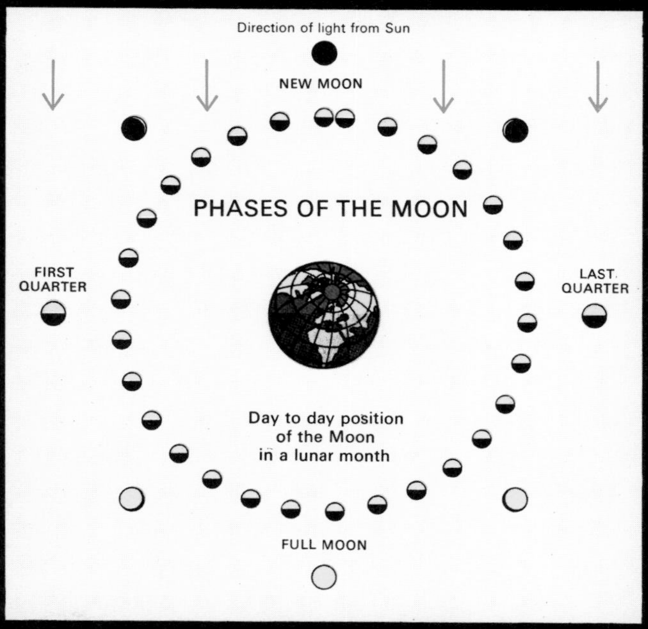

SOUTH POLAR REGION

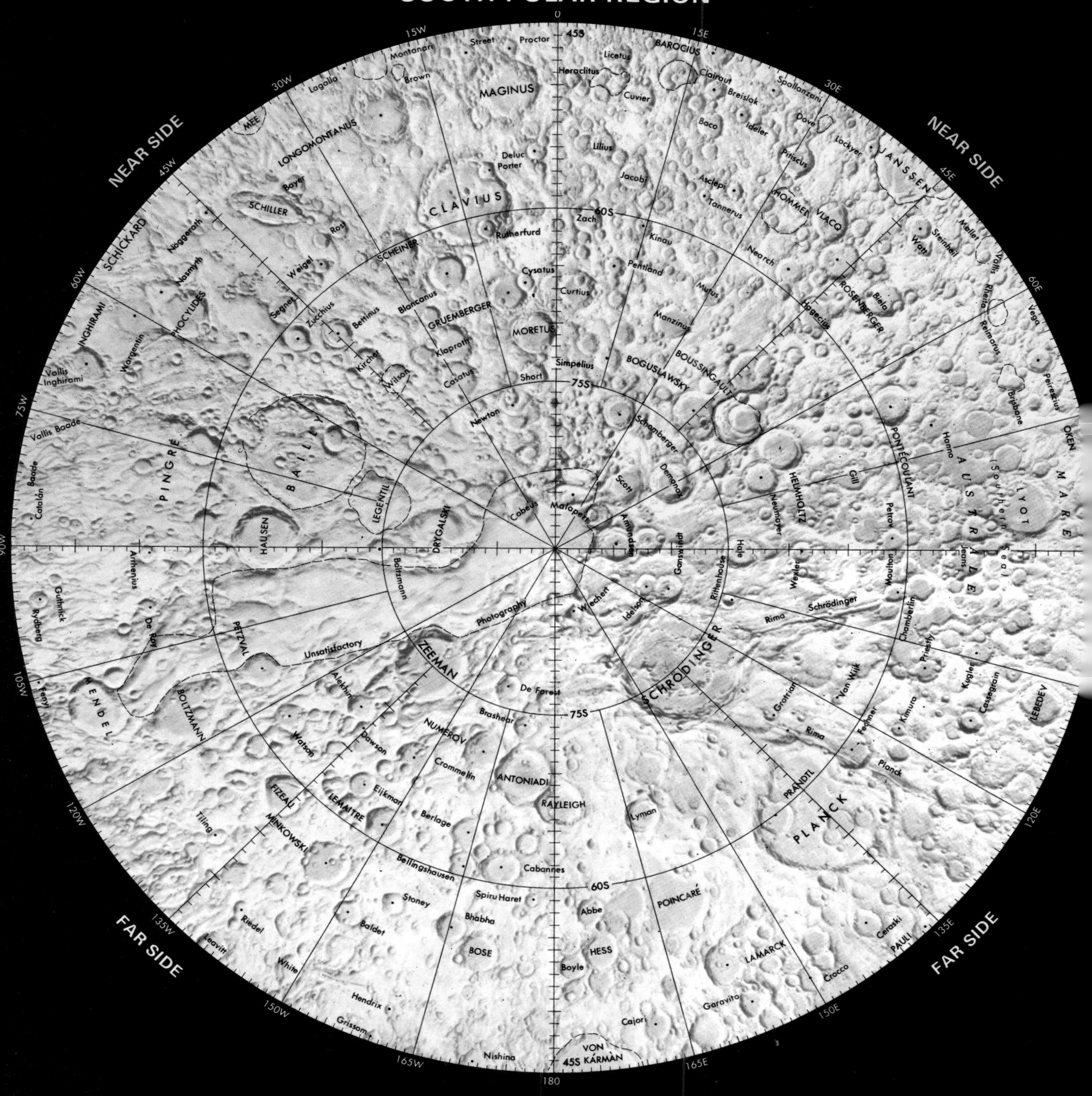

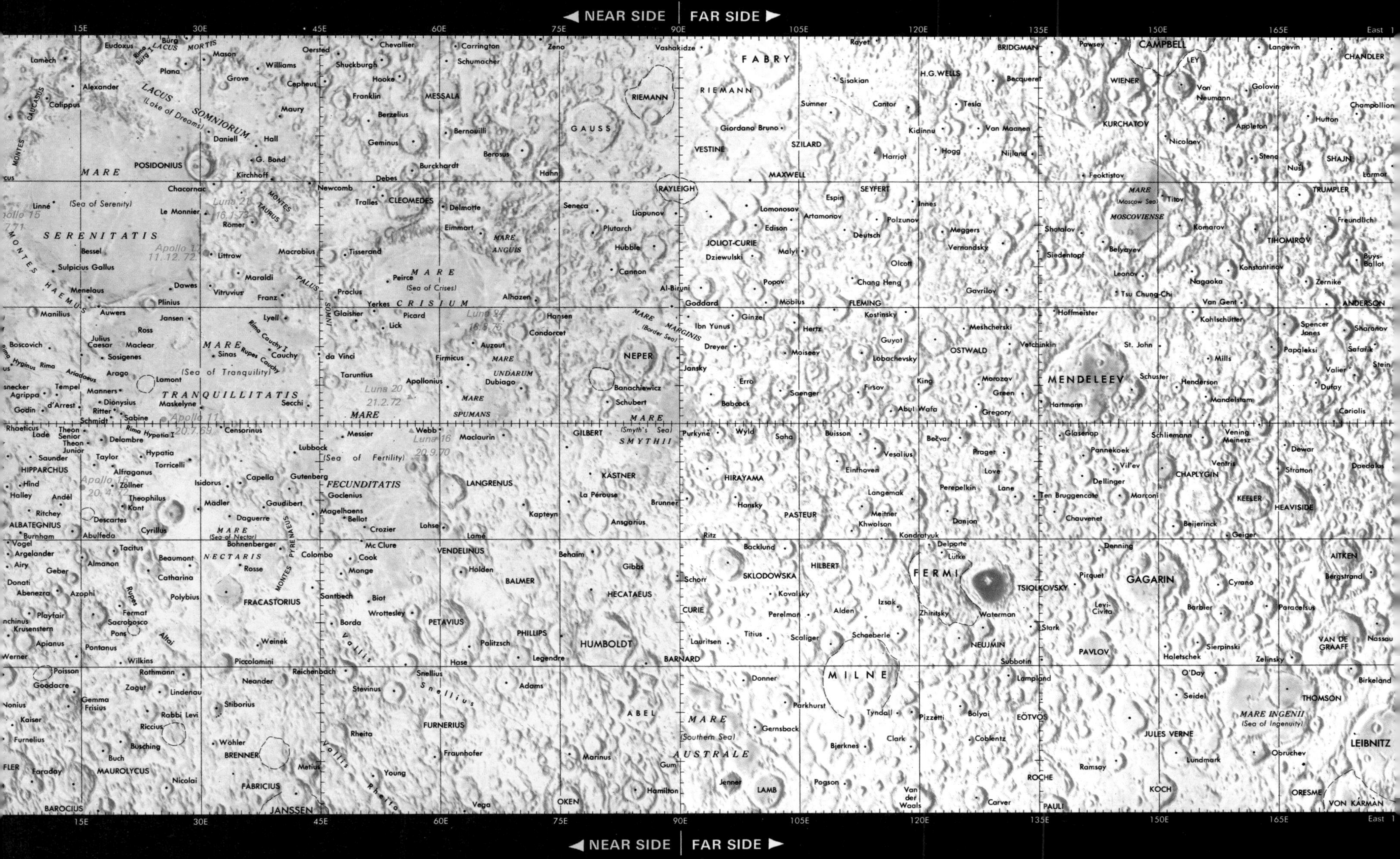

● Manned Spacecraft landing site
▲ Landing site of Soviet moon vehicle "Lunokhod"

Based with permission on LUNAR CHART (1:10,000,000) by the Aeronautical Chart and Information Centre, United States Air Force.

(c) Copyright in this form - H.A.G. Lewis, Es

THE MOON

It is customary to regard the Moon as a satellite of the Earth; its size is so great compared with that of its parent planet that the two may be described as a double-planet system. Loosely, the Moon may be said to revolve around the Earth. In fact the Earth and the Moon revolve around a common centre of gravity, the Moon attracting the Earth and the Earth in turn attracting the Moon. However, because the mass of the Earth is some eighty-one times greater than the mass of the Moon, the common centre of gravity actually falls within the Earth itself at a point 1,700 km (1,062 miles) in from the surface.

The Moon's orbit is elliptical, with a mean radius of approximately 384,400 km (239,000 miles) and is inclined to the plane of the Earth's orbit. The Moon's diameter is approximately 3,476 km (2,172 miles). Gravitational attraction at the surface is only about one-sixth of that of the Earth.

Temperature at midday on the lunar equator is approximately 407°K (273°F), but at night it falls to 120°K (−244°F). There is virtually no atmosphere and the Moon is completely devoid of surface water.

The lunar day – the period of rotation of the Moon about its own axis – is exactly equal to the lunar year – the period of revolution around the Earth. The Moon thus presents the same face towards the Earth at all times, the reverse side remaining invisible.

From earliest times men have noted the dark patches on the Moon, which from the seventeenth century have been designated seas (maria). The bright regions of the Moon are full of densely packed topographical features whose surfaces reflect a considerable amount of sunlight. When examined under even small magnification the bright regions are seen to consist of mountains, peaks, cliffs, valleys and other features. Innumerable craters spatter every type of landscape. The southern hemisphere has the most magnificent relief, with the greatest mountain ranges, the most impressive valleys and the largest and deepest craters.

While the greatest mountain masses are located in the southern hemisphere, with the Leibnitz Range attaining more than 8,000 m. (25,000 feet), the most conspicuous mountain ranges are to be found in the northern hemisphere. At the south-eastern boundary of Mare Imbrium, the magnificent Apennine Range, some 605 km (400 miles) in extent, rises from the mare floor to heights of 3,500 m. to 5,500 m. (12,000 to 18,000 feet). The highland areas abound with mountain peaks. By far the most impressive examples are those which occur in the maria where, as seen from Earth, they rise majestically from the mare floor, many with multiple summits. Their apparent steepness is, however, illusory and results from the contrast between intensely bright slopes and deep shadows.

Lunar valleys are also plentiful in the highland regions. In the more central areas of the highland masses, many broad valleys are to be seen. While 'valleys' is the term used in the highland areas, elongated depressions in the maria are known as 'rilles'.

The lunar Far Side is in many respects like the Near Side, but there is one important difference. The maria which are such conspicuous features of the Near Side are almost completely lacking. Almost all the mare material has been formed on the Near Side, and as a result many craters which on the Near Side would be filled are on the Far Side empty or only partly filled.

By its proximity, the Moon is favourably placed for observation from Earth, yet questions about its surface, its internal temperature, composition, magnetism and so on were unresolved until the acquisition of photographs from lunar probes and orbiting satellites, followed by study of the actual lunar rocks and interpretation of data gathered by instruments left on the Moon to record lunar phenomena. That the Earth and the Moon are very different worlds is beyond doubt, but how they evolved so differently is still a matter for conjecture.

Lunar rocks, all of basaltic type, vary in age from 4,000 million years to 3,200 million years. Their magnetism has decayed with time. The origin of the Moon's magnetic field, only one-thousandth of our own is not known. It may have been induced by movements of a small iron core or by some external action.

Unlike the Earth, which gets steadily hotter towards its centre the Moon is relatively cool, with an internal temperature of only some 800°K to 1,000°K. The crust is about 60 km thick and a rigid mantle extends for 1,000 km below the crust. For this reason the Moon exhibits great strength and rigidity. Moonquakes occur daily and are of great duration compared with similar shocks on Earth, where the nature of the interior produces a dampening effect. These daily quakes are mostly feeble, but each month when the Moon is nearest to Earth (i.e. at perigee) stronger quakes occur on the Near Side, the Earth's gravitational attraction being sufficient to cause a tidal effect within the Moon.

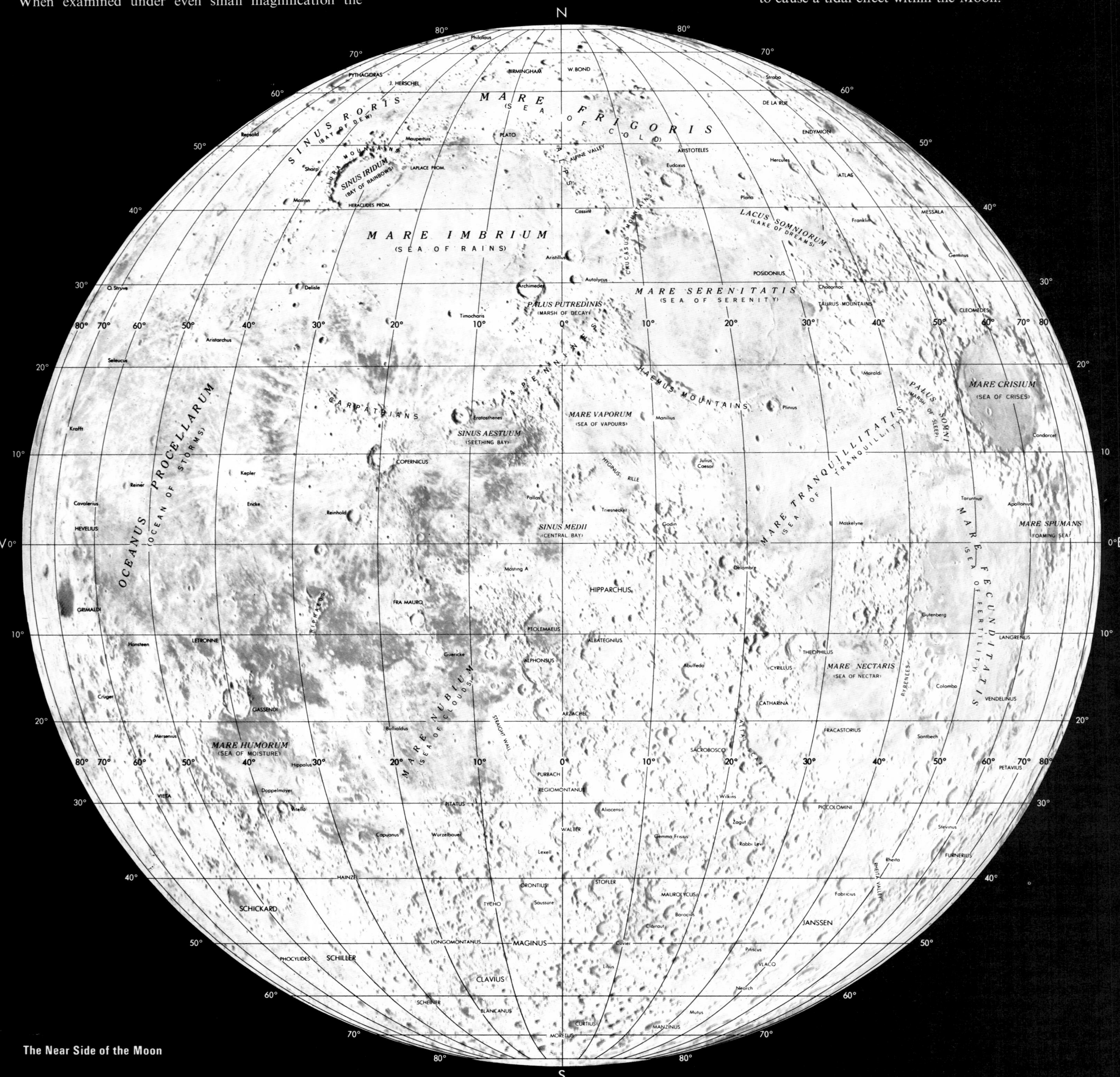

The Near Side of the Moon

SYMBOLS & ABBREVIATIONS

BOUNDARIES

- International
- International, Undefined or Alignment Uncertain
- Limits of Sovereignty across Water Areas
- Autonomous, Federal State
- Main Administrative
- Other Administrative
- Offshore Administrative
- Armistice, Cease-Fire Line
- Demilitarised Zone
- National Park
- Reserve, Reservation

COMMUNICATIONS

- Main Railways
- Other Railway
- Light Railway
- Projected Railways
- Railway Tunnels
- Road Tunnel
- Projected — Special Highway
- Projected — Main Road
- Projected — Other Road
- Tracks
- Car Ferries
- Rail Ferries
- Locks — Navigable Canals
- Projected or Disused Canal
- Drainage or Irrigation Canal
- Canal Tunnel
- Tunnel Aqueduct

LAKE TYPES

- Fresh-water
- Dam — Reservoir
- Seasonal Fresh
- Seasonal Brackish
- Salt-lake, Lagoon
- Perennial Salt-lake
- Seasonal Salt-lake
- Saline Mud-flat
- Salt-flat

LANDSCAPE FEATURES

- Ice-field and Glaciers
- Ice-cap, Ice-sheet
- Lava-fields (33-35)
- Lava-fields (50, 109)
- Sand Desert, Dunes
- Saline Marsh, Salt Desert
- Marsh, Swamp
- Swamp, Flood-area
- Mangrove Swamp
- Tidal Area
- Atoll

OTHER FEATURES

- River, Stream
- Seasonal Watercourses
- Seasonal Flood-plain
- Undefined Course of River
- Pass; Gorges
- Waterfalls, Rapids
- Dam, Barrage
- Escarpments
- Flood Dyke
- Limits of Ice-shelf
- Reefs
- Rocks
- · 9650 Spot Depth
- Lighthouse
- Lightship; Beacon
- Waterhole, Well
- Active Volcano
- Summit, Peak
- Oil Wells
- Oil or Natural Gas Pipeline
- Mine
- Site of Battle
- Historic Site
- Historic Ruin
- Ancient Walls
- Mosque, Sheikh's Tomb
- + Cathedral, Monastery, Church
- International or Main Airport
- Airport, Airfield

CITY INSET MAPS

- City Limits
- City-County Boundaries
- County, Department Boundary
- London Borough Boundary
- Station — Main Railways
- Bridge — Other Railways
- Projected Railways
- Station — Underground Railway
- Aerial Cableway, Funicular
- Projected — Main Road
- Projected — Secondary Road
- Other Road, Street
- Track
- Road Tunnel
- Bridge; Flyover
- Locks — Seaway
- Canals
- Drainage Canal
- Waterfalls, Rapids
- Historic Walls
- Airport Runways
- Racecourses
- Stadium
- Cemetery; Churches
- Woodland, Park
- Built-up Area

STYLES OF LETTERING

- T O G O — Country Name
- A L B E R T A — Major Administrative Divisions
- KENT CHER — Other Administrative Divisions
- PARIS Bern — National Capitals
- Omsk, Denver, Krakow — Administrative Centres
- GANDER Gatwick — Airports
- *M O A B* — Historic Region
- D E C C A N, *S I N A I*, *Mato Grosso* — Physical Regions
- *ATLAS Nile*, *Mt Blanc Thames* — Physical Features
- *BASIN Ridge* — Ocean Bottom Features
- *M A S A I* — Tribal Name

PRINCIPAL MAP ABBREVIATIONS

A.	1. Alp, Alpen, Alpi. 2. Alt
Abb^{e}	Abbaye
A.C.T.	Australian Capital Territory
Aig.	Aiguille
Akr.	Ákra, Akrotírion
Anch.	Anchorage
A.O.	Avtonómnaya Oblast'
App^{no}	Appennino
Aqued.	Aqueduct
Ar.	Arroyo
Arch.	Archipel, Archipelago, Archipiélago
Arr.	Arrecife
A.S.S.R.	Avtonómnaya Sovétskaya Sotsialistícheskaya Respúblika
Ay.	Ayía, Áyioi, Áyion, Ayios
B.	1. Baai, Bahía, Baía, Baie, Baja, Bay, Bucht, Bukhta, Bukt. 2. Bad, 3. Ban. 4. Barazh, Barrage, Barragem 5. Bayou. 6. Bír. 7. Bonto. 8. Bulu
B^{c}	Banc
B^{ca}	Boca
Bel.	Belgium, Belgian
Bg.	Berg
Bgt.	Bight, Bugt
B^{i}	Bani, Beni
B^{j}	Burj
B^{k}	Bank
Bk.	Buku
B^{n}	Basin
Bol.	Bol'shoy
Bos.	Bosanski
Br.	1. Branch. 2. Bredning. 3. Bridge, Brücke. 4. Britain, British. 5. Burun
Bt.	Bukit
Bü.	Büyük
Bukh.	Bukhta
C.	1. Cabo, Cap, Cape. 2. Cay. 3. Česká, -é, -y. 4. Col.
Cab^{o}	Cabeço, (Azores)
Cach.	Cachoeira, -o
Can.	1. Canal. 2. Canale. 3. Canavese. 4. Cañon, Canyon
Cas.	Castle
Cat.	1. Cataract. 2. Catena (Sardinia)
Cath.	Cathedral
C^{d}	Ciudad
Cerv.	Cervená, -é, -ȳ
Ch.	1. Chapel, Chapelle, Church. 2. Chaung. 3. Chott.
Chan.	Channel
Ch^{au}	Château
Ch^{e}	Chaine
Ch^{lle}	Chapelle
C^{ma}	Cima
C^{no}	Corno
C^{o}	Cerro
Const^{n}	Construction
Cord.	Cordillera
Cr.	Creek
Cuch.	Cuchilla
Cuc^{ru}	Cuccuru (Sardinia)
Cy.	City
Czo.	Cozzo
D.	1. Da, Dag, Dagh, Dağı, Dağları. 2. Danau. 3. Darreh. 4. Daryācheh
-d.	dake
D.C.	District of Columbia
Den.	Denmark
Dists.	Districts
Div.	Division
Dj.	Djebel
Dns.	Downs
Dz.	Dzong
E.	East
E.D.	Existence doubtful
Eil.	Eiland, Eilanden
Escarp.	Escarpment
Est.	Estacion
E^{tg}	Étang
F.	Firth
F.D.	Federal District
Fj.	1. Fjell. 2. Fjord, Fjörður
F^{k}	Fork
Fl.	Fleuve
Fr.	France, French
Ft.	Fort
F^{te}	Fonte
Fy.	Ferry
G.	1. Gawa. 2. Gebel. 3. Ghedir. 4. Göl, Gölü, Gōl. 5. Golfe, Golfo, Gulf. 6. Gompa. 7. Gora, Gory. 8. Guba. 9. Gunung
G^{a}	Gara
G^{d}	Grand
G^{de}	Grande
Geb.	Gebergte, Gebirge
Geog^{l}	Geographical
Gez.	Gezira
Ghub.	Ghubba
Gl.	1. Gamle, Gammel. 2. Glacier
Gp.	Group
Gr.	1. Graben. 2. Gross, -e
G^{r}	Gasr
Gr^{tes}	Grottes
Gt.	Great, Groot, -e
H.	1. Hawr. 2. Hill. 3. Hoch. 4. Hora, Hory
Halv.	Halvøy
Har.	Harbour
H^{d}	Head
H.E.P.	Hydro-Electric Power
H^{g}	Hegység
H^{gts}	Heights
H^{i}	Hasi, Hasy
Hist.	Historic
H^{n}	Horn
Hosp.	1. Hospice, Hospiz 2. Hospital
Ht.	Haut
Hte.	Haute
H^{ter}	Hinter
H^{y}	Highway
I.	Île, Ilha, Insel, Isla, Island, Isle, Isola, Isole
IJ.	IJssel
im.	imeni
In.	1. Inder, Indre, Inner, Inre. 2. Inlet
IND.	India
Inf.	Inferior, -e, Inférieure
Int.	International
I^{s}	Îles, Ilhas, Islands, Islas, Isles
ISR.	Israel
Isth.	Isthmus
J.	1. Jabal, Jebel, Jibāl. 2. Järvi, Jaure, Jazira, Jezero, Jezíoro. 3. Jökull
Jap.	Japan, Japanese
Jct.	Junction
K.	1. Kaap, Kap, Kapp. 2. Kaikyo. 3. Kato. 4. Kerang, Kering. 5. Kiang. 6. Kirke. 7. Ko. 8. Koh, Kūh, Kūhha. 9. Kolpos. 10. Kopf. 11. Kuala. 12. Kyst
Kan.	Kanal, Kanaal
Kap.	Kapelle
Kep.	Kepulauan
Kg.	Kampong, Kompong, Kong
Kh.	1. Khawr. 2. Khirbet, Khīābān, -e. 3. Khowr
Khr.	Khrebet
Kl.	1. Kechil. 2. Klein, -e
Kör.	Körfez, -i
Kr.	Kangar
Kü.	Küçük
L.	1. Lac, Lago, Lagôa, Lake, Liman, Limni, Liqen, Loch, Lough. 2. Lam
Lag.	Lagoon, Laguna, -e
L^{d}	Land
Ldg.	Landing
L.H.	Light House
Lit.	Little
Ll.	Lille
M.	1. Mae, Me. 2. Meer. 3. Muang. 4. Muntil 5. Muong. 6. Mys
m	metre/s
Mal.	Malyy
Mem.	Memorial
Mex.	Mexico, Mexican
M^{f}	Massif
M^{gna}	Montagna
M^{gne}	Montagne
Mkt.	Markt
Mon.	Monasterio, Monastery
Mont.	Monument
Mt.	Mont, Mount, Mountain
Mte.	Monte
M^{tes}	Montes
Mti.	Monti, Munti
Mts.	Monts, Mountains
N.	1. Nam. 2. Neu, Ny. 3. Nevado, Nudo, 4. Noord, Nord, Nörre, Nørre, North. 5. Nos
N^{a}	Nuestra
Nat.	National
Nats. Okr.	Natsionalnyy Okrug
N.D.	Notre Dame
N^{dr}	Neder, Nieder
N.E.	North East
Neth.	Netherlands
Nizh.	Nizhne, Nizhniy
Nizm.	Nizmennost
N.O.	Noord Oost, Nord Ost
Nor.	Norway, Norwegian
N^{os}	Nudos
Nov.	Novyy
N^{r}	Nether
N.T.	Neutral Territory
N.W.	North West
N.Z.	New Zealand
O.	1. Old. 2. Oost, Ost. 3. Ostrov
Ö.	1. Östre. 2. Öy
Ø.	1. Østre. 2. Øy
Ob.	Ober
O^{de}	Oude
O^{et}	Oguilet
Ogl.	Oglat
O.L.V.	Onze Lieve Vrouw
Or.	Ori, Oros
Orm.	Ormos
Ot.	Olet
Öv.	Över, Övre
O^{va}	Ostrova
Oz.	Ozero
P.	1. Pass. 2. Pic, Pico, Piz. 3. Pulau
Pal.	Palace, Palacio, Palais
Pass.	Passage
Peg.	Pegunungan
Pen.	Peninsula, Penisola
Per.	Pereval
P^{gio}	Poggio
Pk.	1. Park. 2. Peak, Pik
Pkwy.	Parkway
Pl.	1. Planina, Planinski. 2. Plei
P^{la}	Playa
Plat.	Plateau
Plosk.	Ploskogor'ye
P^{no}	Pantano
P^{nte}	Pointe
Por.	Porog
Port.	Portugal Portuguese
P^{ov}	Poluostrov
Pr.	1. Proliv. 2. Przyladek 3. Prince
Prom^{y}	Promontory
Prop.	Proposed
PROT.	Protectorate
PROV.	Provincial
P^{so}	Passo
Pt.	1. Point. 2. Pont
P^{t}	1. Petit. 2. Point. 3. Pont
P^{ta}	1. Ponta, Punta. 2. Puerta
P^{te}	1. Pointe. 2. Ponte, Puente
P^{to}	1. Porto, Puerto. 2. Ponto, Punto
P^{zo}	Pizzo
Q.	1. Qala, Qara, Qarn. 2. Quang
R.	1. Reka, Río, River, Rivière, Rud, Rzeka. 2. Ria
Ra.	Range
Rap.	Rapids
R^{ca}	Rocca
R^{d}	Road
REC.	Recreation
Res.	Reservoir
R^{f}	Reef
R^{ge}	Ridge
Rib^{a}	Ribeira
R^{k}	Rock
Rly.	Railway
R.S.F.S.R.	Rossíyskaya Sovétskaya Federatívnaya Sotsialistícheskaya Respúblika
R^{te}	Route
Rom.	Romania, Romanian
S.	1. Salar, Salina. 2. San. 3. Saw. 4. See. 5. Seto. 6. Sjö. 7. Sör, South, Syd. 8. Sung. 9. sur
S^{a}	Serra, Sierra
Sab.	Sabkhat
Sc.	Scoglio (Sardinia)
S^{d}	Sound, Sund
S.E.	South East
Seb.	Sebjet, Sebkhat, Sebkra
Sev.	Sever, Severnaya
S^{gno}	Stagno (Sardinia)
Sh.	1. Sh'aīb. 2. Sharif. 3. Shatt. 4. Shima
S^{i}	Sidi
S^{knoll}	Seaknoll
S^{kt}	Sankt
Sl.	Slieve
S^{mt}	Seamount
Snr^{a}	Senhora
Snr^{o}	Senhoro
Sp.	1. Spain, Spanish 2. Spitze
S^{pk}	Seapeak
Spr.	Spring
S^{r}	Sönder, Sønder
Sr.	Sredniy
S.S.R.	Sovétskaya Sotsialístícheskaya Respúblika
S^{t}	Saint, Sint, Staryy
St.	1. State. 2. Stor, Store
Sta	Santa
Sta.	Station
Stby.	Staby, Statsjonsby
S^{te}	Sainte
Ste.	Store
Sten.	Stenon, Stenos
S^{to}	Santo
Str.	Strait
S^{tu}	Stuvina (Sardinia)
Sv.	Svaty, Sveti
S.W.	South West
T.	1. Tal. 2. Tal, Tall, Tell. 3. Tepe, Tepesi
Talsp.	Talsperre
Tel.	Teluk
Terr.	Terrace
Terr^{y}	Territory
Tg.	Tanjung
Thwy.	Throughway, Thruway
Tk.	Teluk
T^{mt}	Tablemount
T^{o}	Tando
Tpk.	Turnpike
Tr.	Trench, Trough
T^{re}	Torre
Tun.	Tunnel
U.	Uad
U.A.E.	United Arab Emirates
Ug.	Udjung
U.K.	United Kingdom
Unt.	Unter
Up^{r}	Upper
U.S.A.	United States of America
U.S.S.R.	Union of Soviet Socialist Republics
V.	1. Val, Valle, 2. Väster, Vest, Vester. 3. Vatn. 4. Ville. 5. Vorder
V^{a}	Vila
Vdkhr.	Vodokhranilishche
Vel.	Velikiy
Ven.	Venezuela, Venezuelan
Verkh.	Verkhniy
Vol.	Volcán, Volcano, Vulkán
Vost.	Vostochnyy
Vozv.	Vozvyshennost'
W.	1. Wadi. 2. Wald. 3. Wan. 4. Water. 5. Well. 6. West
W^{r}	Wester
Y.	Yama
Y^{t}	Ytre, Ytter, Ytri
Yuzh.	Yuzhnaya, Yuzhno, Yuzhnyy
Z.	Zaliv
Zal.	Zaliv
Zap.	Zapadnyy, -aya, -o, -oye
Zem.	Zemlya

7740

Printed in U.K.

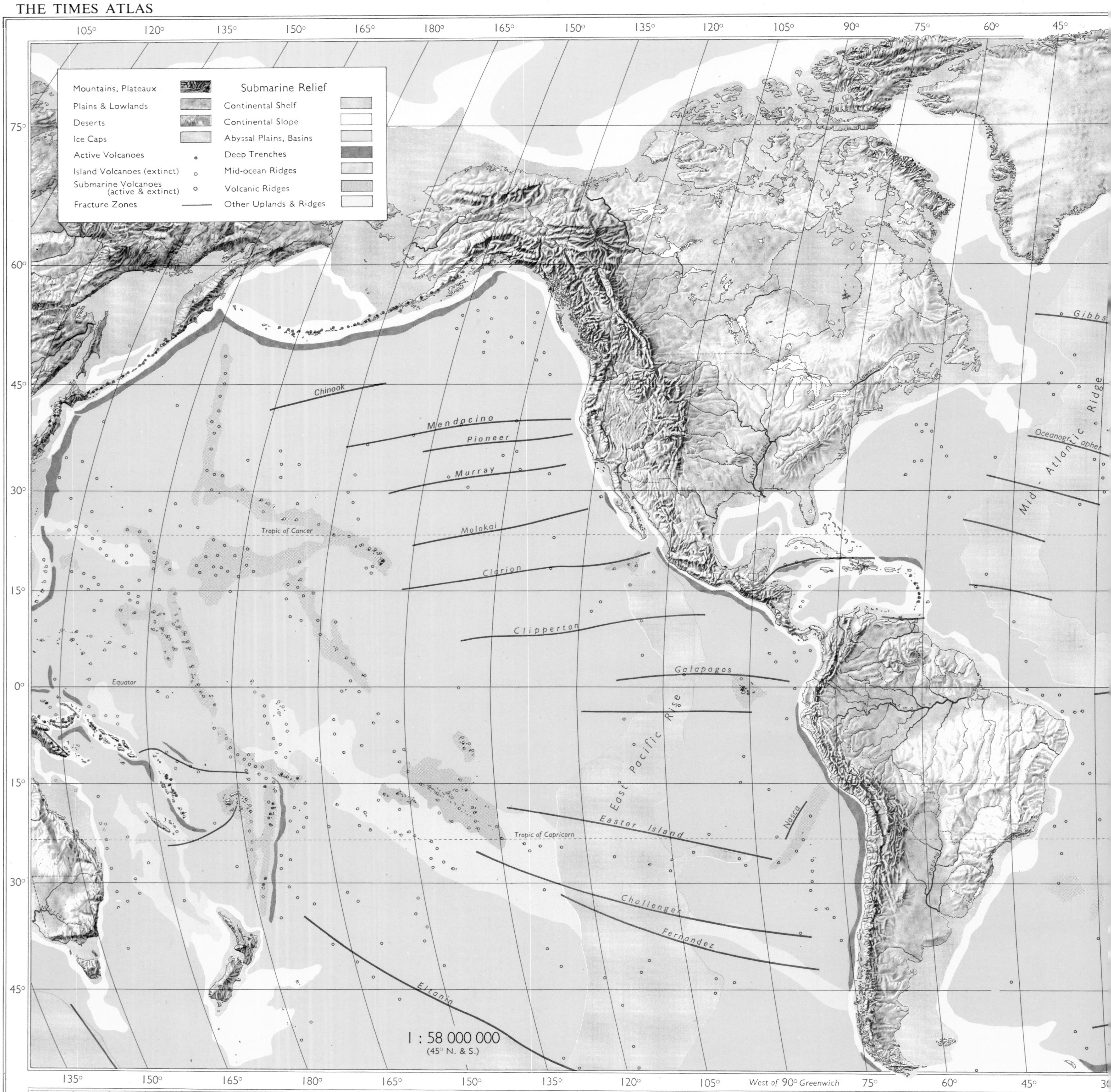
Mountains, Plateaux
Plains & Lowlands
Deserts
Ice Caps
Active Volcanoes
Island Volcanoes (extinct)
Submarine Volcanoes (active & extinct)
Fracture Zones
Submarine Relief
Continental Shelf
Continental Slope
Abyssal Plains, Basins
Deep Trenches
Mid-ocean Ridges
Volcanic Ridges
Other Uplands & Ridges
Chinook
Mendocino
Pioneer
Murray
Molokai
Clarion
Clipperton
Galapagos
East Pacific Rise
Easter Island
Challenger
Fernandez
Eltanin
Nasca
Gibbs
Oceanographer
Mid-Atlantic Ridge
Tropic of Cancer
Tropic of Capricorn
Equator
1 : 58 000 000
(45° N. & S.)
West of 90° Greenwich

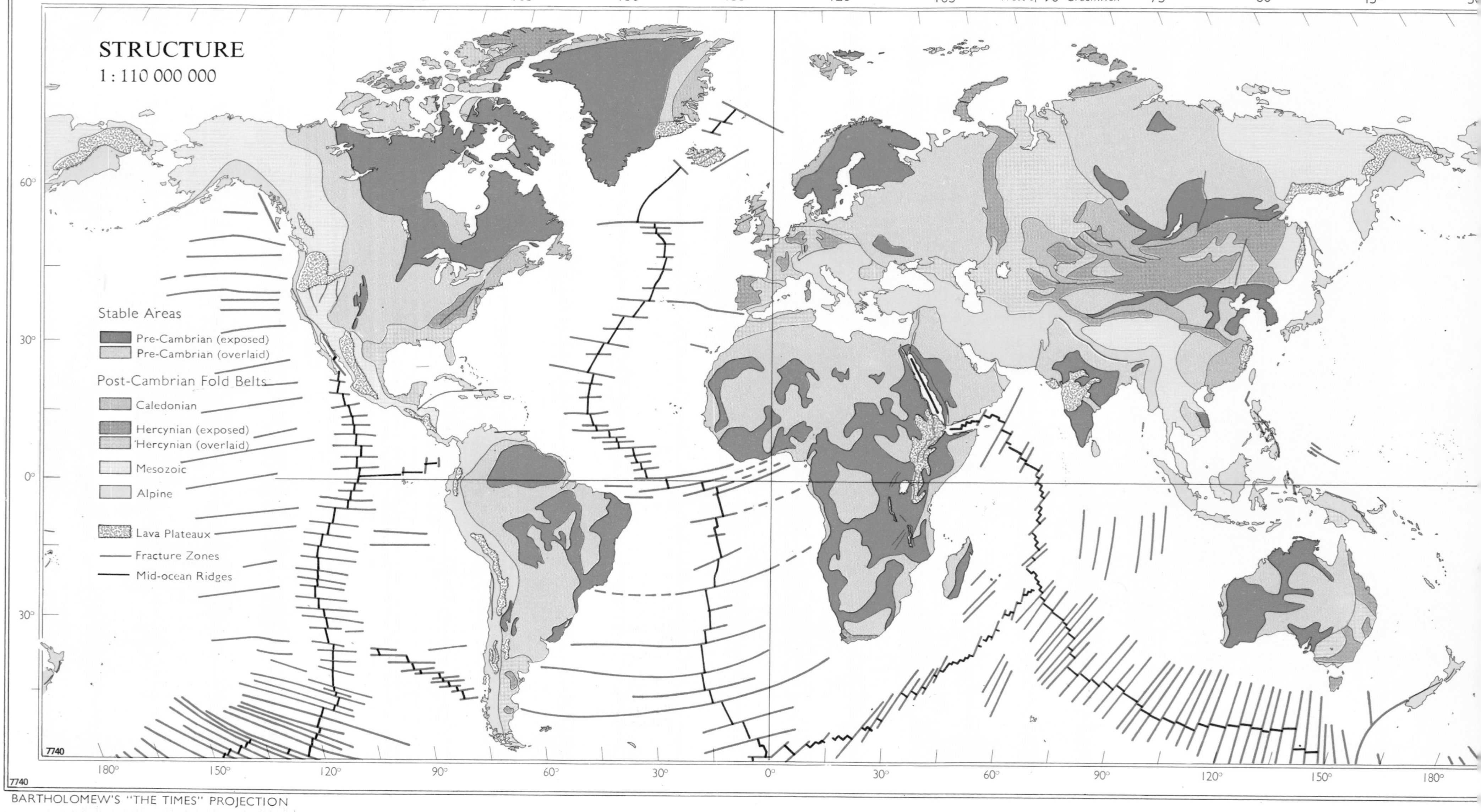
STRUCTURE
1 : 110 000 000
Stable Areas
Pre-Cambrian (exposed)
Pre-Cambrian (overlaid)
Post-Cambrian Fold Belts
Caledonian
Hercynian (exposed)
Hercynian (overlaid)
Mesozoic
Alpine
Lava Plateaux
Fracture Zones
Mid-ocean Ridges
7740

Greenland
Jan Mayen
Congo
Owen
Chagos
Vema
Mid
Indian
Rodrigues
Malagasy
Mocambique
Prince Edward
Amsterdam
Rise
Diamantina
Tropic of Cancer
Tropic of Capricorn
Equator
Ridge
Meridian of 0° Greenwich
East of 90° Greenwich

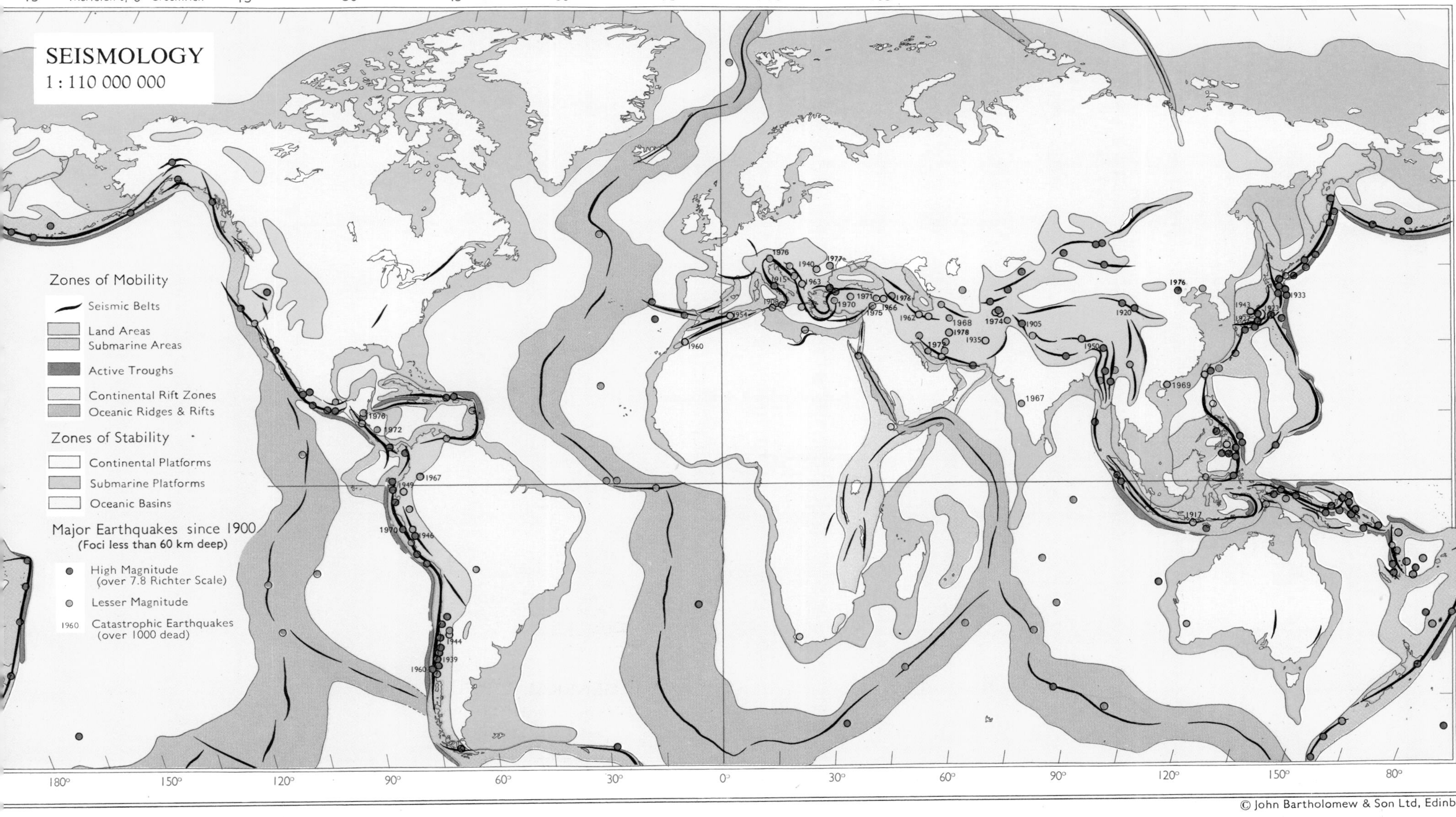
SEISMOLOGY
1 : 110 000 000
Zones of Mobility
Seismic Belts
Land Areas
Submarine Areas
Active Troughs
Continental Rift Zones
Oceanic Ridges & Rifts
Zones of Stability
Continental Platforms
Submarine Platforms
Oceanic Basins
Major Earthquakes since 1900
(Foci less than 60 km deep)
High Magnitude
(over 7.8 Richter Scale)
Lesser Magnitude
1960 Catastrophic Earthquakes
(over 1000 dead)

© John Bartholomew & Son Ltd, Edinburgh

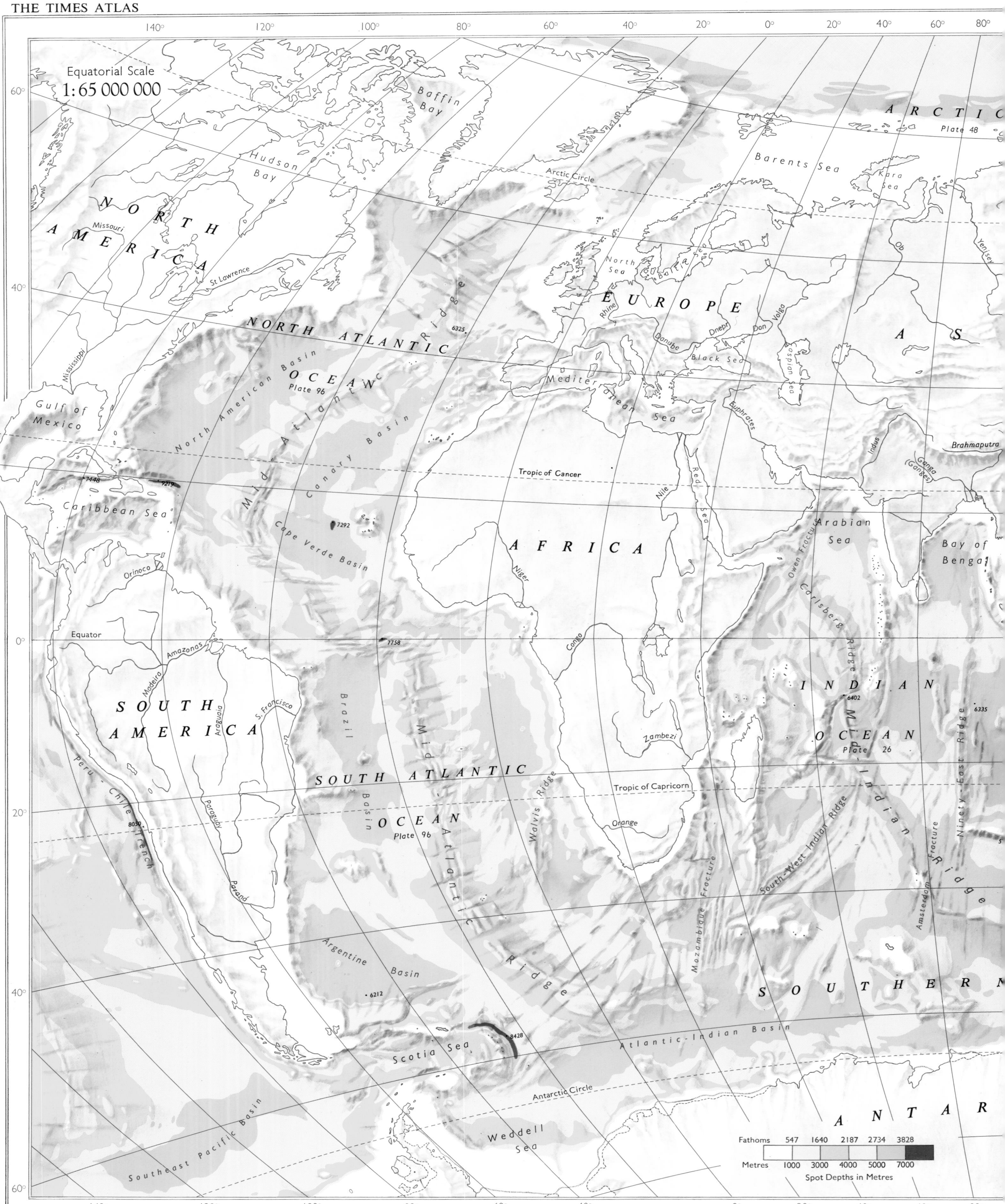
Equatorial Scale
1:65 000 000
140° 120° 100° 80° 60° 40° 20° 0° 20° 40° 60° 80°
60° 40° 0° 20° 40° 60°
Baffin Bay
Hudson Bay
A R C T I C
Plate 48
Barents Sea
Kara Sea
Arctic Circle
NORTH AMERICA
Missouri
St Lawrence
Mississippi
Gulf of Mexico
NORTH ATLANTIC OCEAN
Plate 96
North American Basin
Mid-Atlantic Ridge
Canary Basin
Cape Verde Basin
Caribbean Sea
North Sea
Baltic Sea
Ob
Yenisey
E U R O P E
Rhine
Danube
Dnepr
Don
Volga
Black Sea
Caspian Sea
A S
Mediterranean Sea
Euphrates
Indus
Brahmaputra
Ganga (Ganges)
Tropic of Cancer
Nile
Red Sea
A F R I C A
Niger
Congo
Zambezi
Orange
Arabian Sea
Bay of Bengal
Owen Fracture
Carlsberg Ridge
I N D I A N O C E A N
Plate 26
Mid-Indian Ridge
Ninety-East Ridge
Orinoco
Equator
Amazonas
Madeira
Araguaia
S. Francisco
SOUTH AMERICA
Peru-Chile Trench
Paraguay
Paraná
Brazil Basin
SOUTH ATLANTIC OCEAN
Plate 96
Walvis Ridge
Tropic of Capricorn
Mozambique Fracture
South-West Indian Ridge
Amsterdam Fracture
Argentine Basin
Scotia Sea
Atlantic-Indian Basin
S O U T H E R N
Antarctic Circle
Weddell Sea
Southeast Pacific Basin
A N T A R
7440
9219
7292
6325
7758
8050
6402
6335
6212
8428
Fathoms 547 1640 2187 2734 3828
Metres 1000 3000 4000 5000 7000
Spot Depths in Metres

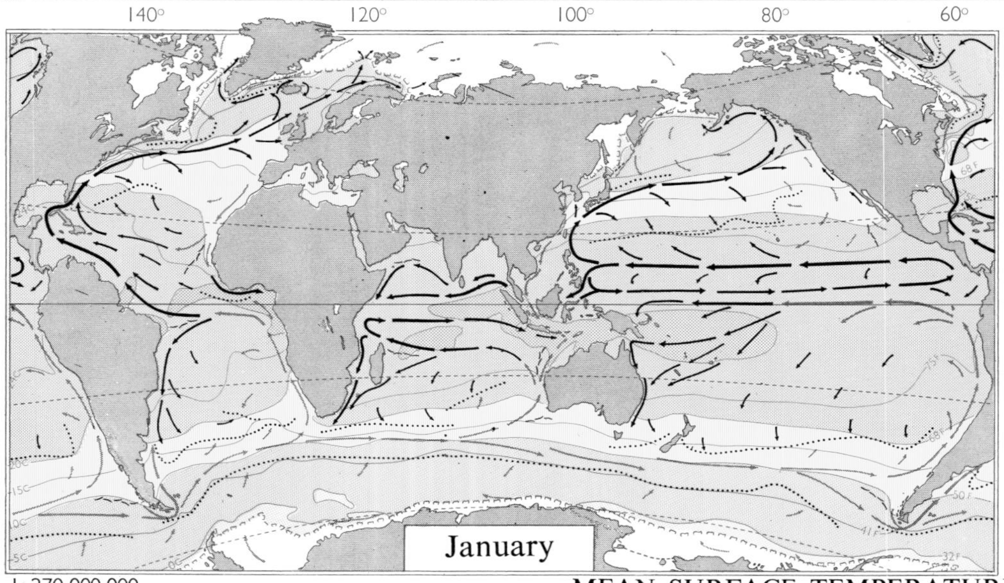
January

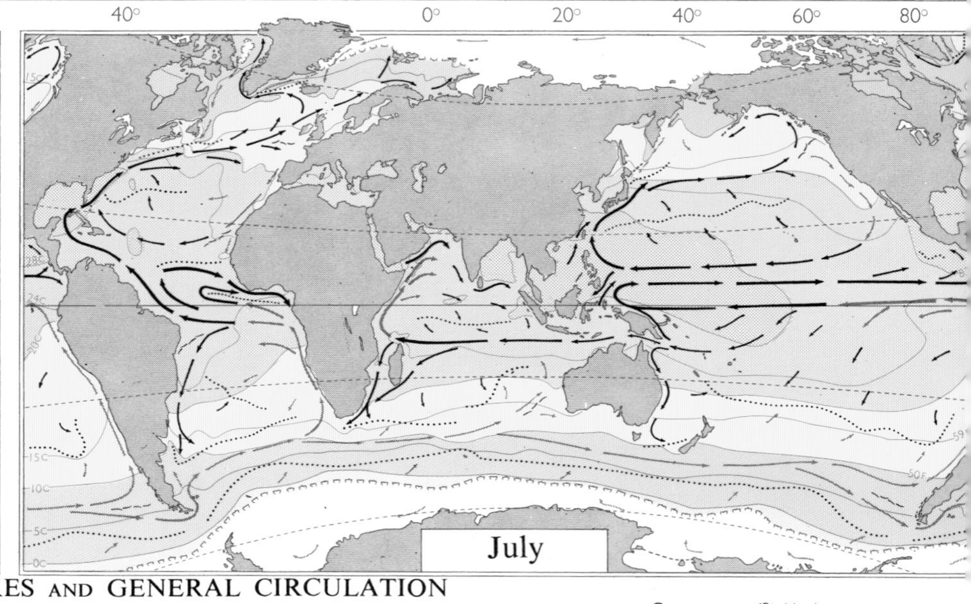
July

1: 270 000 000

MEAN SURFACE TEMPERATURES AND GENERAL CIRCULATION

Warmer Currents
Colder Currents

The thickness of the arrows is an indication of the relative flow of respective currents, which can exceed 3 knots.

Temperature in Degrees Centigrade
0 5 10 15 20 24 28

Convergence *(Sinking)*
Divergence *(Up-welling)*
Limit of Drift Ice

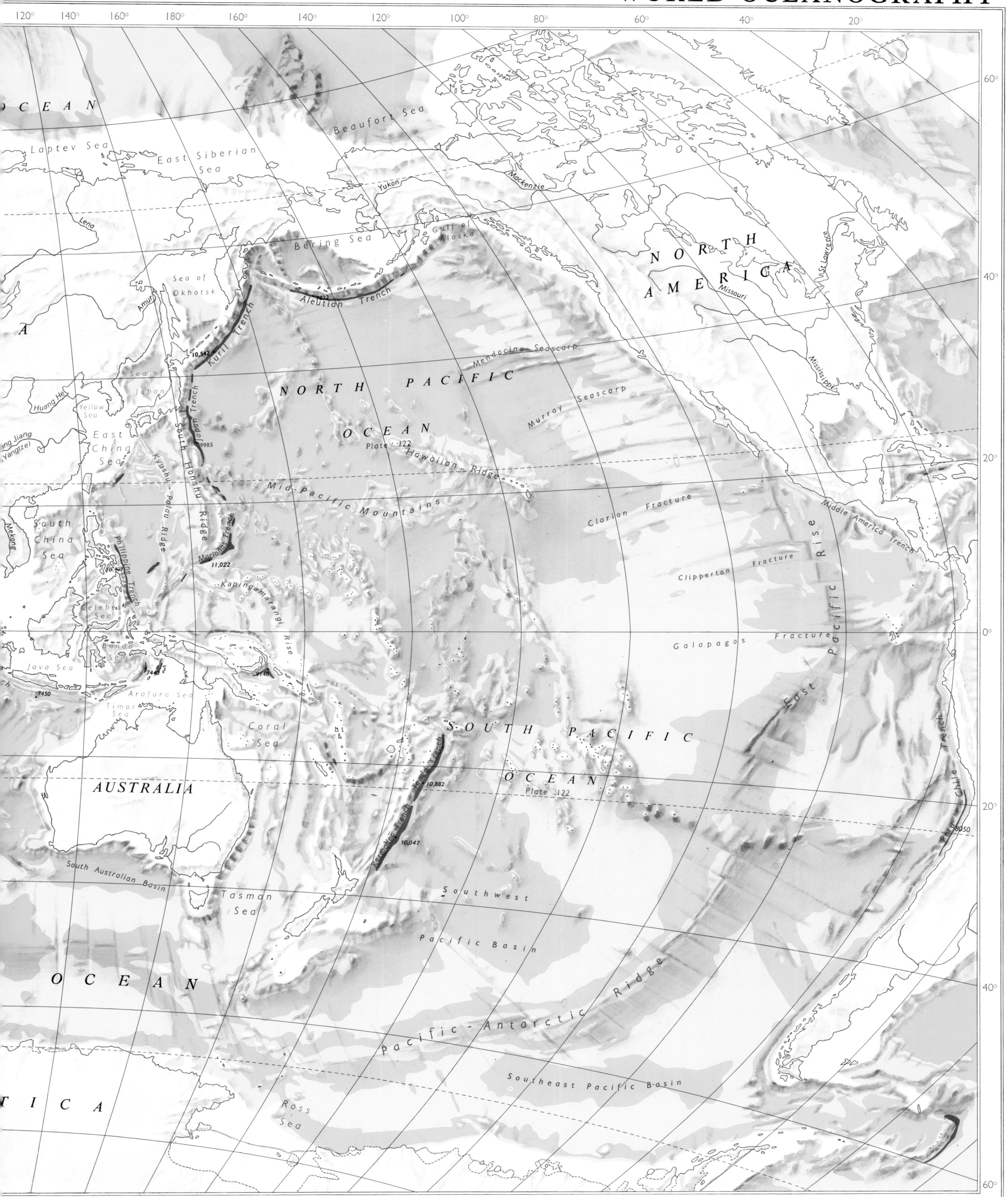

OCEAN
Laptev Sea
East Siberian Sea
Beaufort Sea
Yukon
Mackenzie
Lena
Bering Sea
Gulf of Alaska
Sea of Okhotsk
Amur
Aleutian Trench
Kuril Trench
10,542
NORTH AMERICA
Missouri
St Lawrence
Mississippi
Mendocino Seascarp
Murray Seascarp
NORTH PACIFIC OCEAN
Plate 122
Hawaiian Ridge
Mid-Pacific Mountains
Sea of Japan
Huang He
Yellow Sea
Chang Jiang (Yangtze)
East China Sea
Japan Trench
South Honshu Ridge
Kyushu-Palau Ridge
9985
South China Sea
Mekong
Philippine Trench
Mariana Trench
11,022
Clarion Fracture
Clipperton Fracture
Galapagos Fracture
Middle America Trench
East Pacific Rise
Kapingamarangi Rise
Celebes Sea
Banda Sea
Java Sea
Arafura Sea
Timor Sea
7440
7450
9140
Coral Sea
AUSTRALIA
SOUTH PACIFIC OCEAN
Plate 122
Tonga Trench
10,882
Kermadec Trench
10,047
Peru-Chile Trench
8050
South Australian Basin
Tasman Sea
Southwest Pacific Basin
OCEAN
Pacific-Antarctic Ridge
Southeast Pacific Basin
Ross Sea
TICA

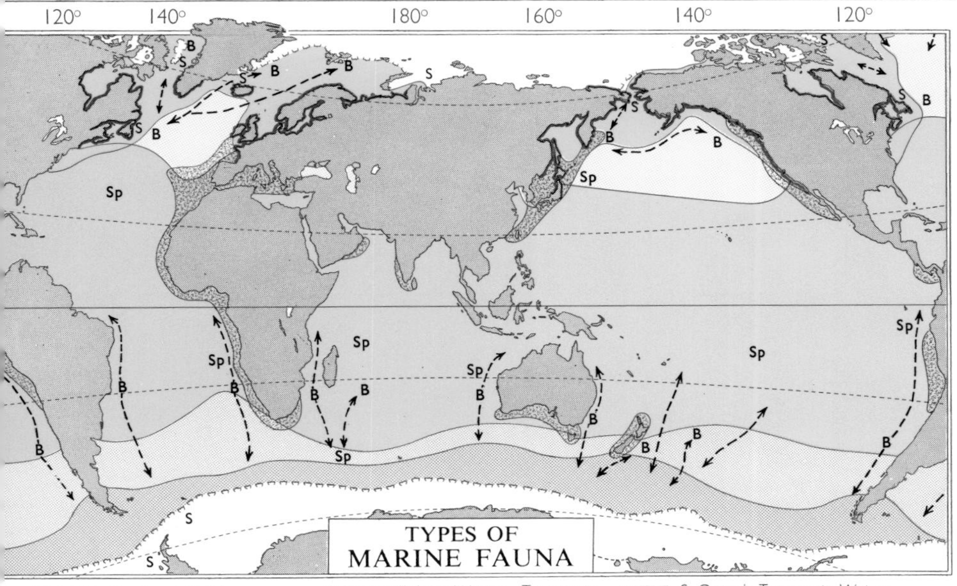

TYPES OF MARINE FAUNA

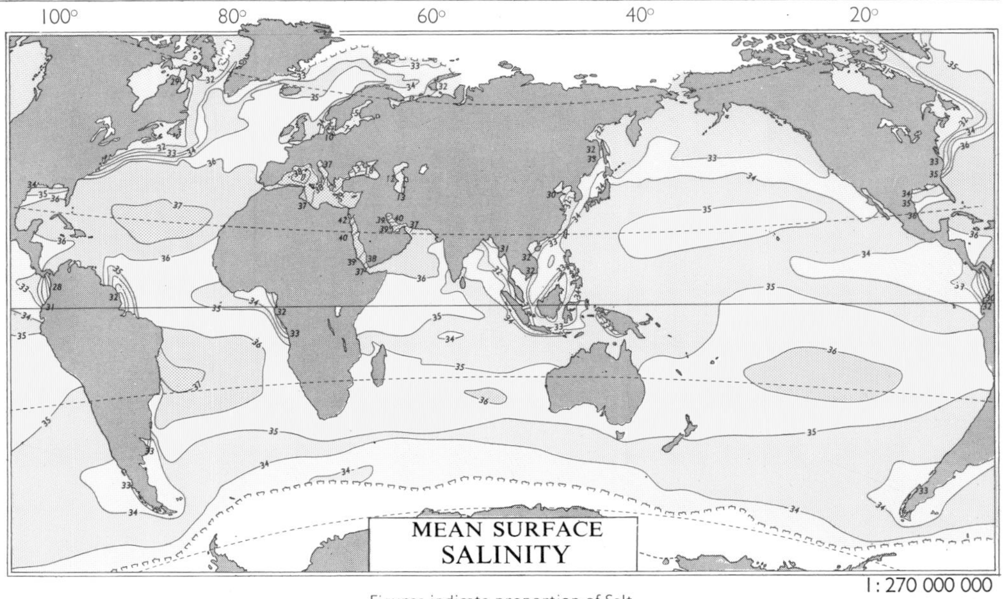

MEAN SURFACE SALINITY

- N. Continental Waters — Cod, Haddock, Flatfish, Herring, Walruses
- N. Oceanic Temperate Waters — Relatively few fish; Dolphins, etc.
- Off-shore Waters—Temperate — Mackerel, Pilchards, Sardines
- Tropical Waters — Flying Fish, Sharks, Sword-fish, Tuna, etc.
- S. Oceanic Temperate Waters — Barracouta, Hake, Sharks, etc.
- Antarctic Waters — Whales, Notothenia, Penguins, Seals, etc.

B ←--→ Baleen Whale Migration
S Seal Breeding Grounds
Sp Sperm Whales
Salmon-frequented Coasts

1 : 270 000 000

Figures indicate proportion of Salt in 1000 parts of Sea-water

32 33 34 35 36 37

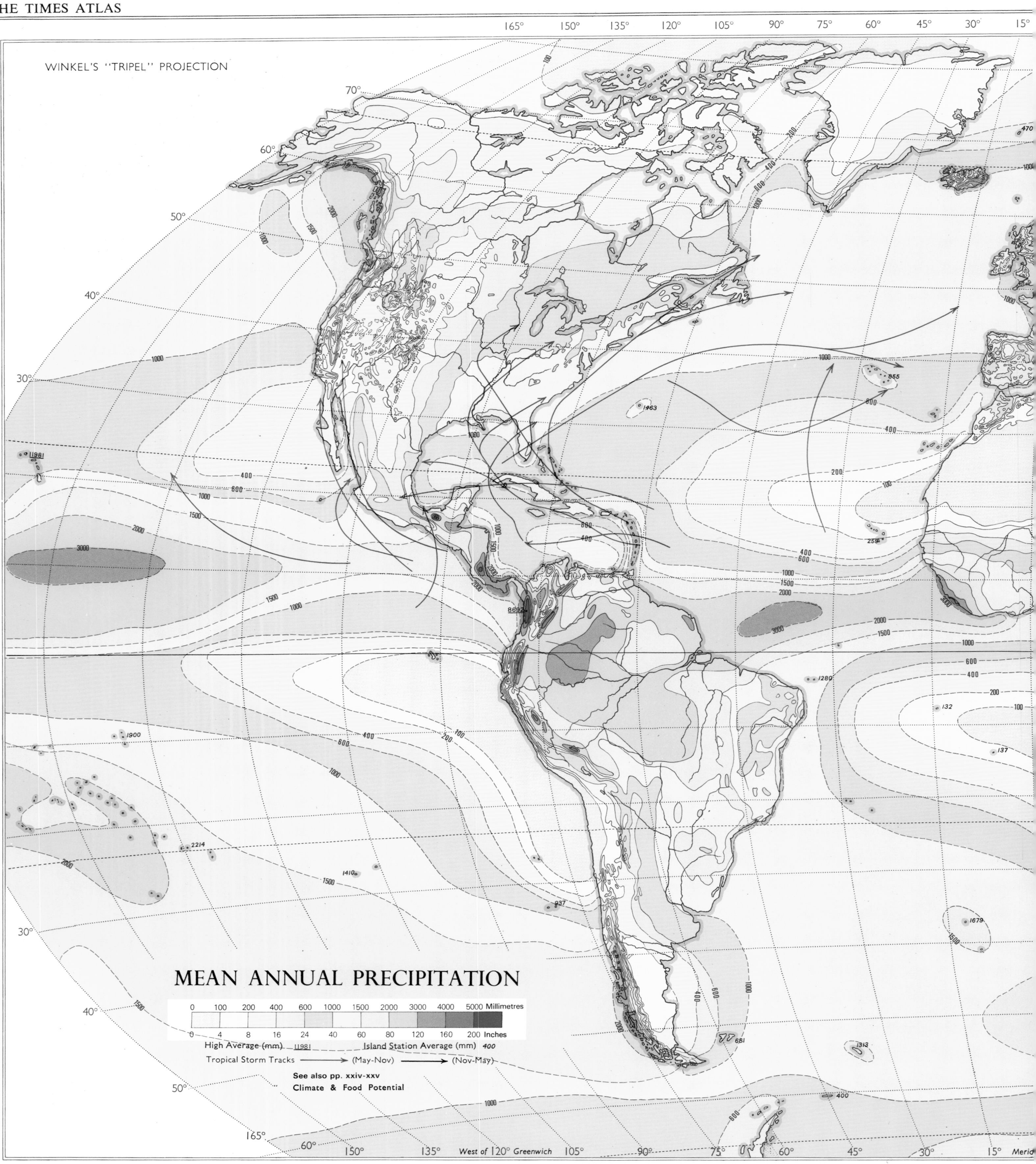
WINKEL'S "TRIPEL" PROJECTION
0 100 200 400 600 1000 1500 2000 3000 4000 5000 Millimetres
0 4 8 16 24 40 60 80 120 160 200 Inches
High Average (mm) 11981
Island Station Average (mm) 400
Tropical Storm Tracks (May-Nov) (Nov-May)
See also pp. xxiv-xxv
Climate & Food Potential
West of 120° Greenwich

MEAN ANNUAL PRECIPITATION

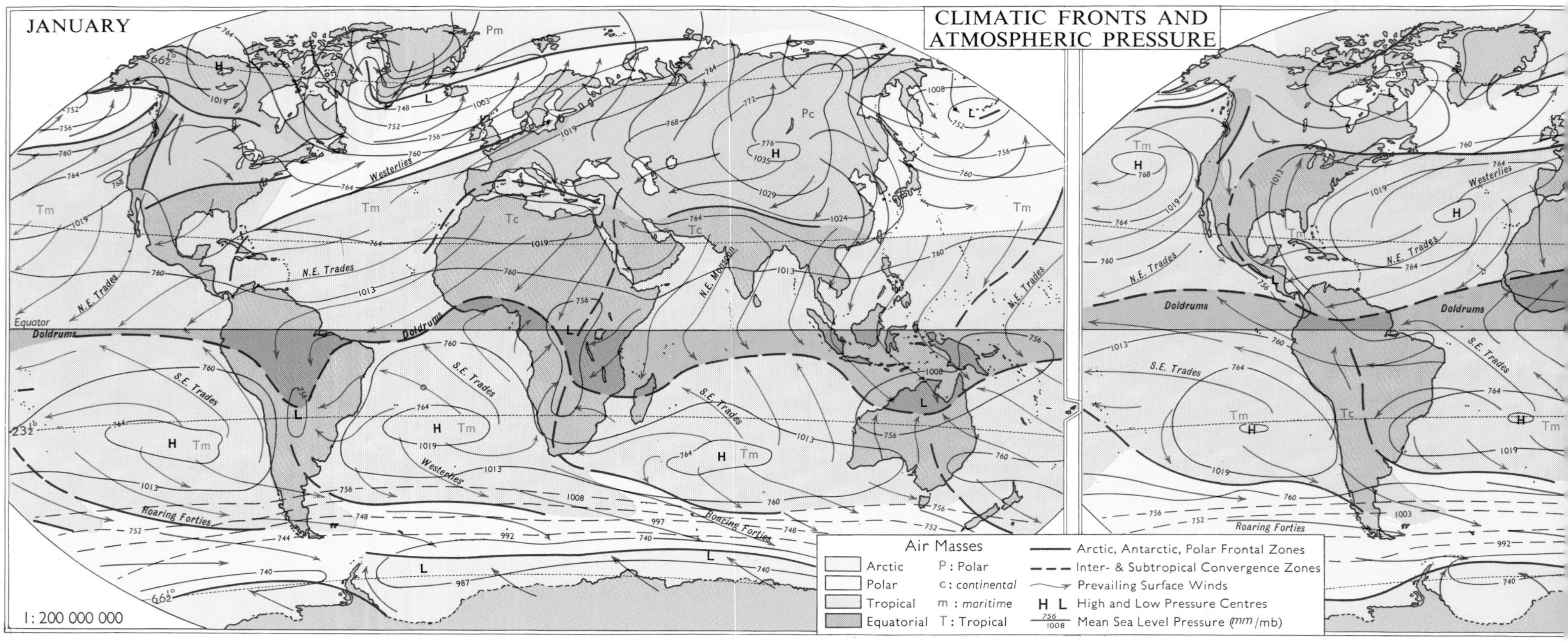
JANUARY
Westerlies
N.E. Trades
S.E. Trades
Doldrums
Roaring Forties
Equator
Air Masses
Arctic
Polar
Tropical
Equatorial
P : Polar
c : continental
m : maritime
T : Tropical
Arctic, Antarctic, Polar Frontal Zones
Inter- & Subtropical Convergence Zones
Prevailing Surface Winds
H L High and Low Pressure Centres
Mean Sea Level Pressure (mm/mb)
1: 200 000 000

CLIMATIC FRONTS AND ATMOSPHERIC PRESSURE

Equatorial Scale
1: 65 000 000
Tropic of Cancer
Equator
Tropic of Capricorn
Antarctic Circle
East of 150° Greenwich
10,800
8100
5812
3129
1613
3960
2273
6566
6655
2350
2665
1986
9355
12558
852
1379
1062
855
JULY
S.W. Monsoon
S.E. Trades
S.E. Monsoon
Roaring Forties
MEAN ANNUAL
EVAPORATION
0 200 400 600 800 1000 1500 2000 3000
Millimetres per year
1: 200 000 000

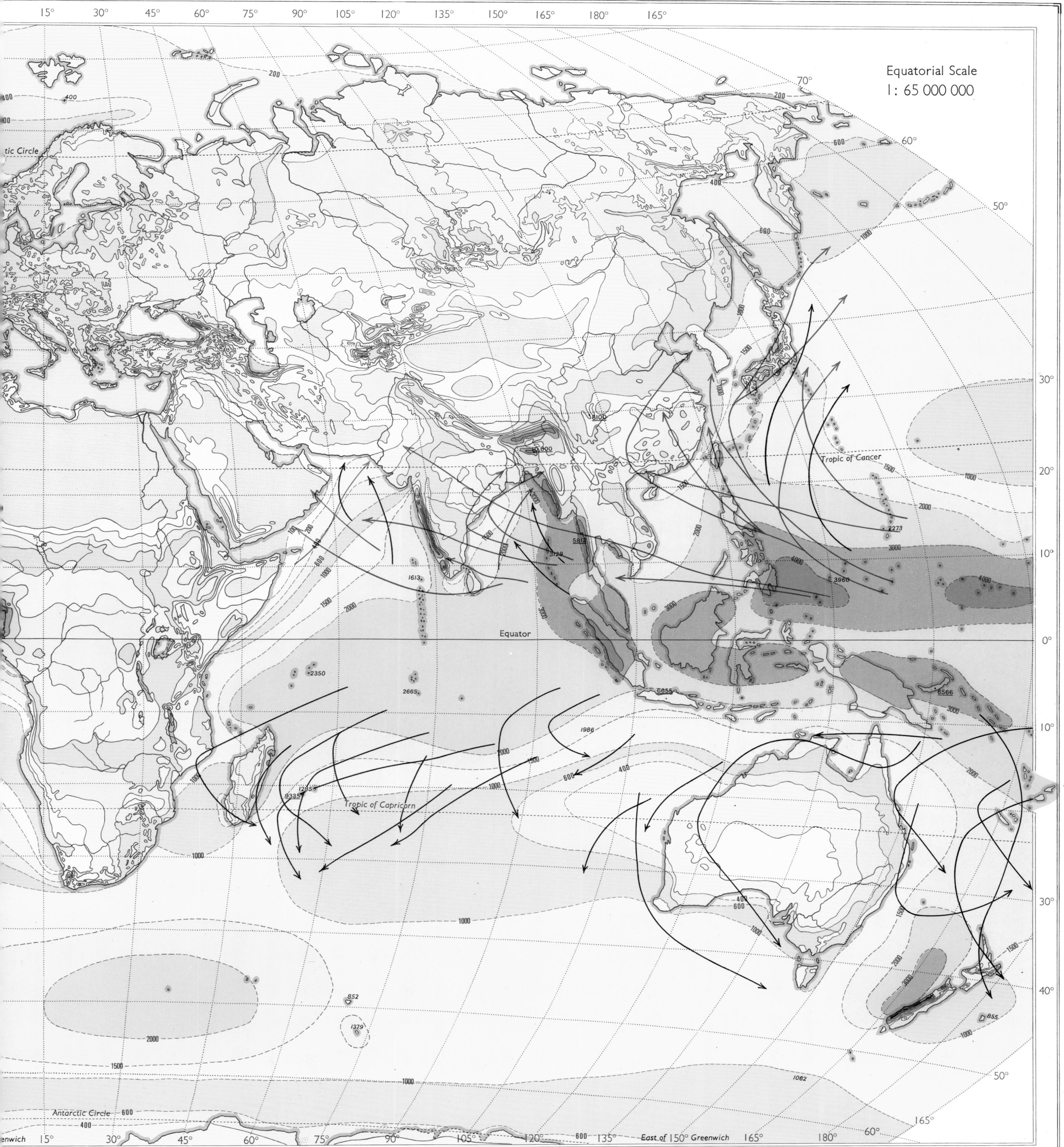

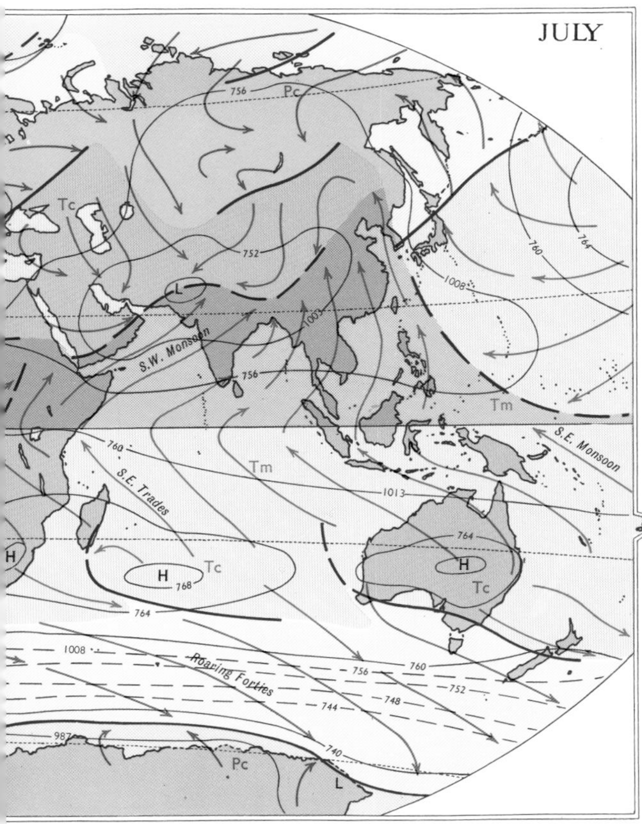

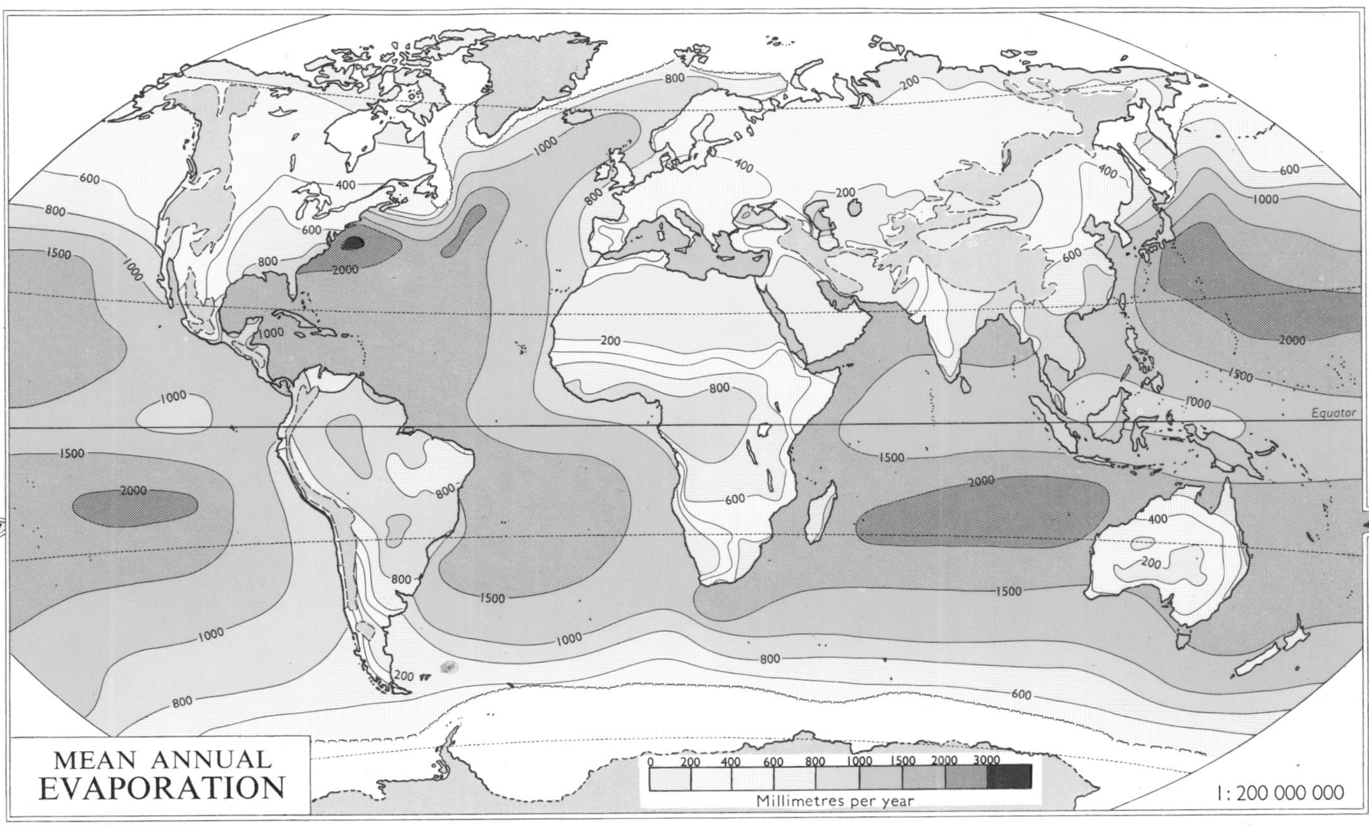

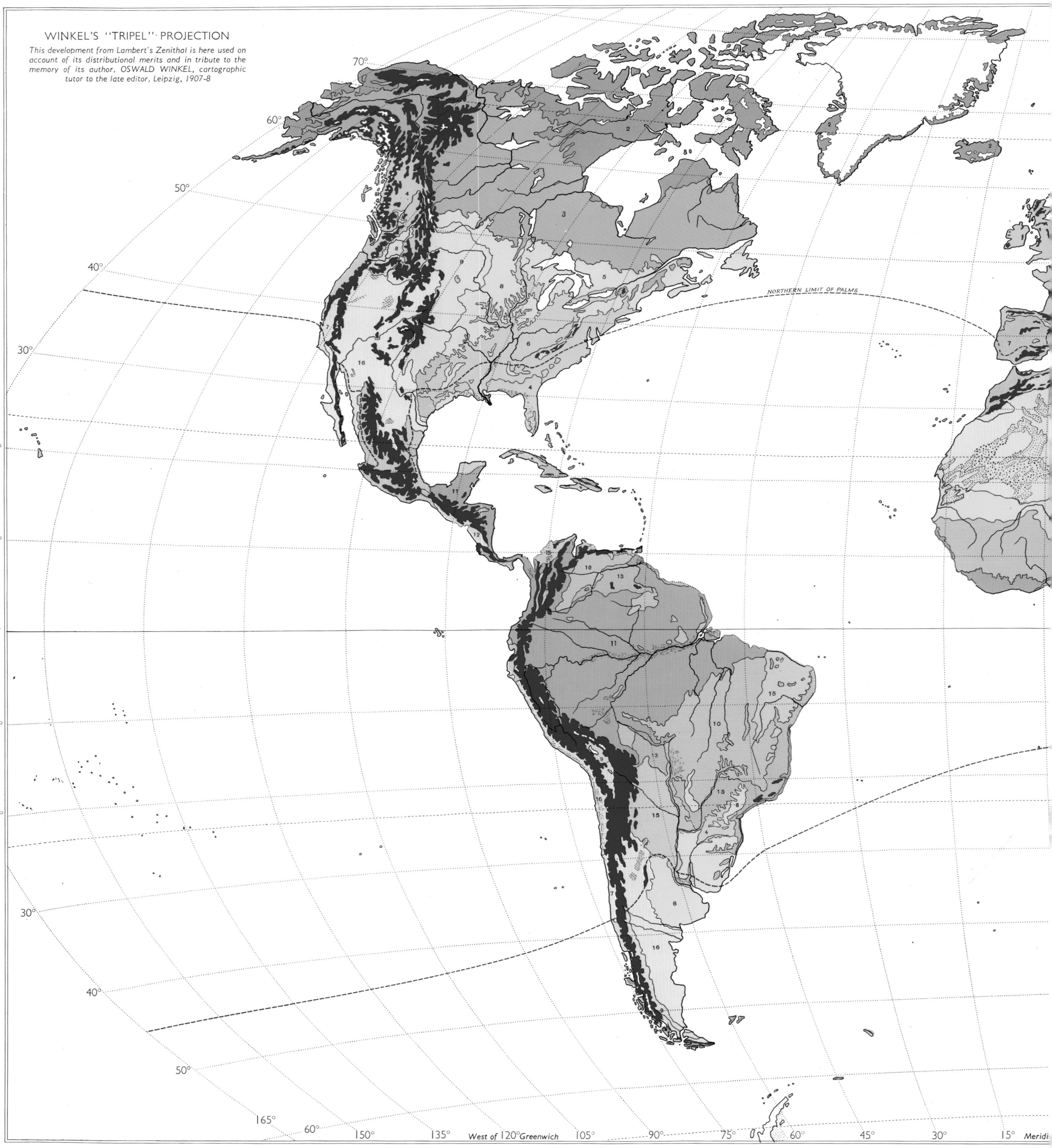
WINKEL'S "TRIPEL" PROJECTION
This development from Lambert's Zenithal is here used on account of its distributional merits and in tribute to the memory of its author, OSWALD WINKEL, cartographic tutor to the late editor, Leipzig, 1907-8
NORTHERN LIMIT OF PALMS
165° 150° 135° 120° 105° 90° 75° 60° 45° 30° 15°
70° 60° 50° 40° 30° 20° 10° 0° 10° 20° 30° 40° 50°
West of 120° Greenwich
Meridi

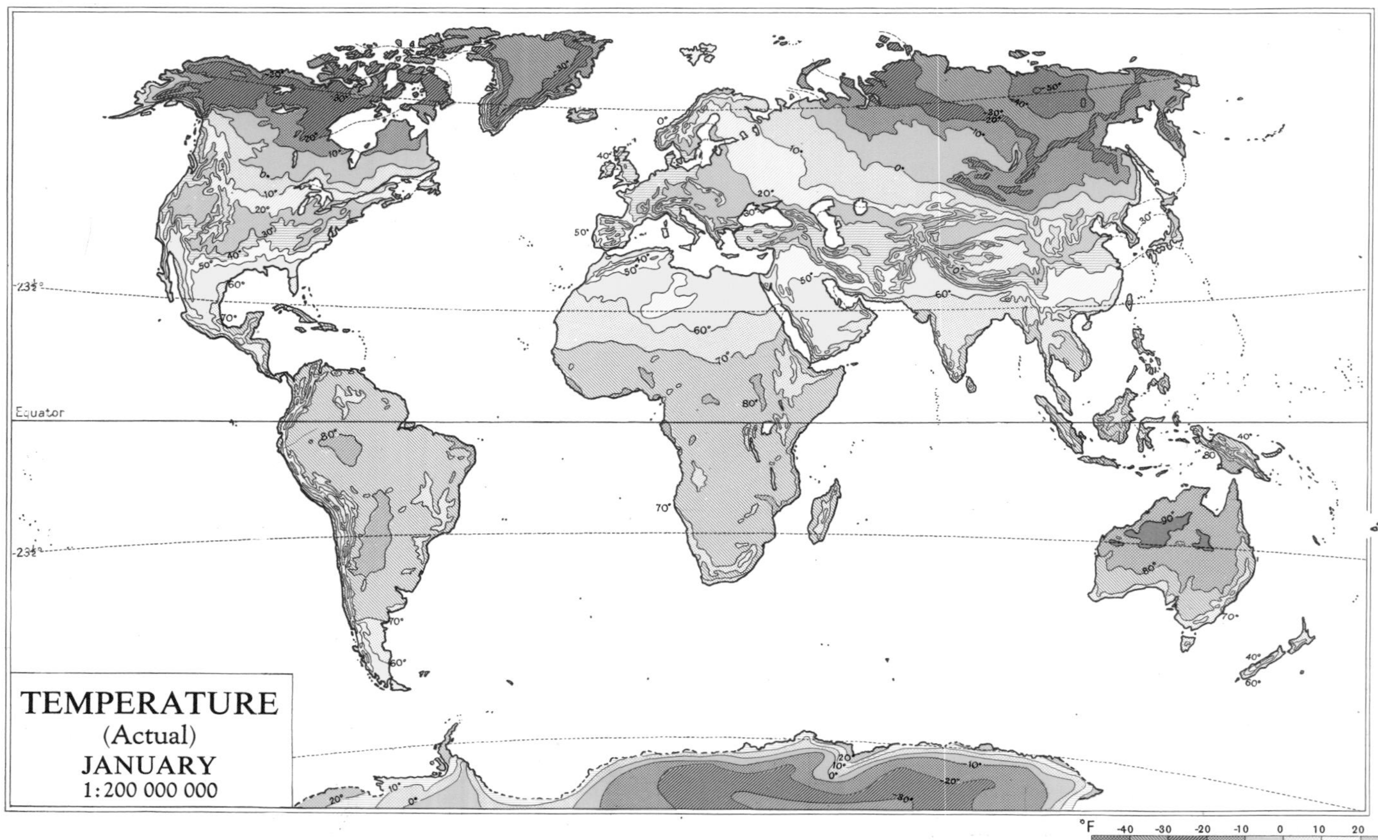
Equator
23½°
TEMPERATURE
(Actual)
JANUARY
1:200 000 000

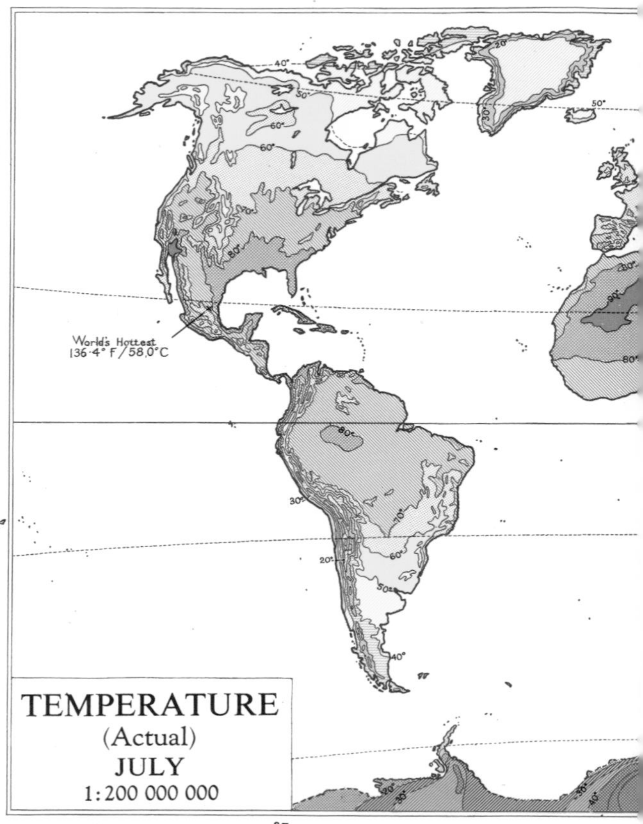
World's Hottest
136·4° F/58.0°C
TEMPERATURE
(Actual)
JULY
1:200 000 000

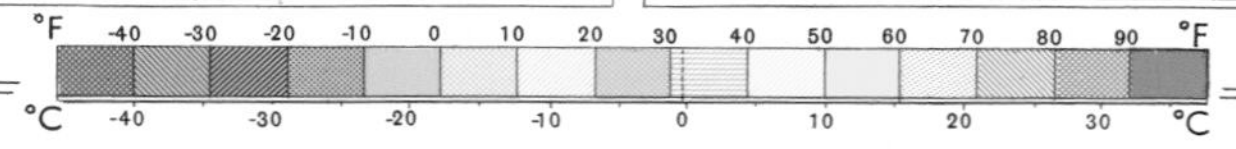
°F -40 -30 -20 -10 0 10 20 30 40 50 60 70 80 90 °F
°C -40 -30 -20 -10 0 10 20 30 °C

WORLD VEGETATION

Plate 5

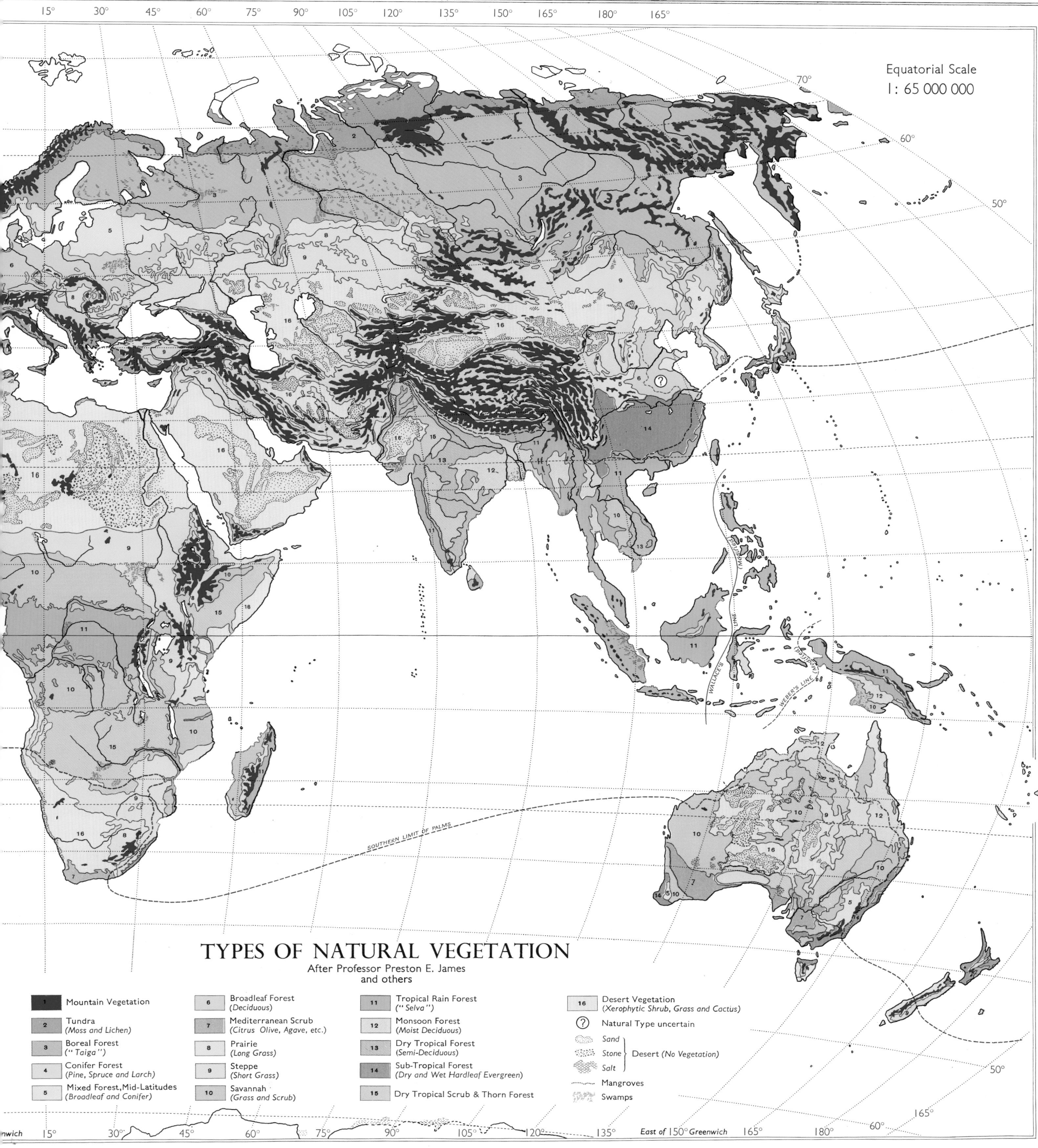

Equatorial Scale
1: 65 000 000
SOUTHERN LIMIT OF PALMS
WALLACE'S LINE
WEBER'S LINE
TYPES OF NATURAL VEGETATION
After Professor Preston E. James
and others
1 Mountain Vegetation
2 Tundra (Moss and Lichen)
3 Boreal Forest ("Taiga")
4 Conifer Forest (Pine, Spruce and Larch)
5 Mixed Forest, Mid-Latitudes (Broadleaf and Conifer)
6 Broadleaf Forest (Deciduous)
7 Mediterranean Scrub (Citrus Olive, Agave, etc.)
8 Prairie (Long Grass)
9 Steppe (Short Grass)
10 Savannah (Grass and Scrub)
11 Tropical Rain Forest ("Selva")
12 Monsoon Forest (Moist Deciduous)
13 Dry Tropical Forest (Semi-Deciduous)
14 Sub-Tropical Forest (Dry and Wet Hardleaf Evergreen)
15 Dry Tropical Scrub & Thorn Forest
16 Desert Vegetation (Xerophytic Shrub, Grass and Cactus)
? Natural Type uncertain
Sand, Stone, Salt — Desert (No Vegetation)
Mangroves
Swamps
East of 150° Greenwich

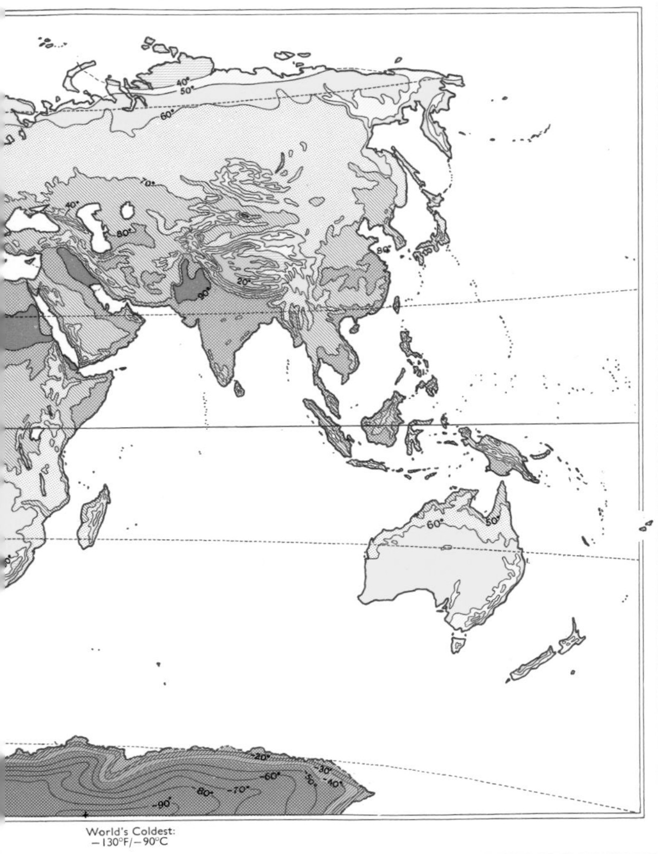

World's Coldest
−130°F/−90°C

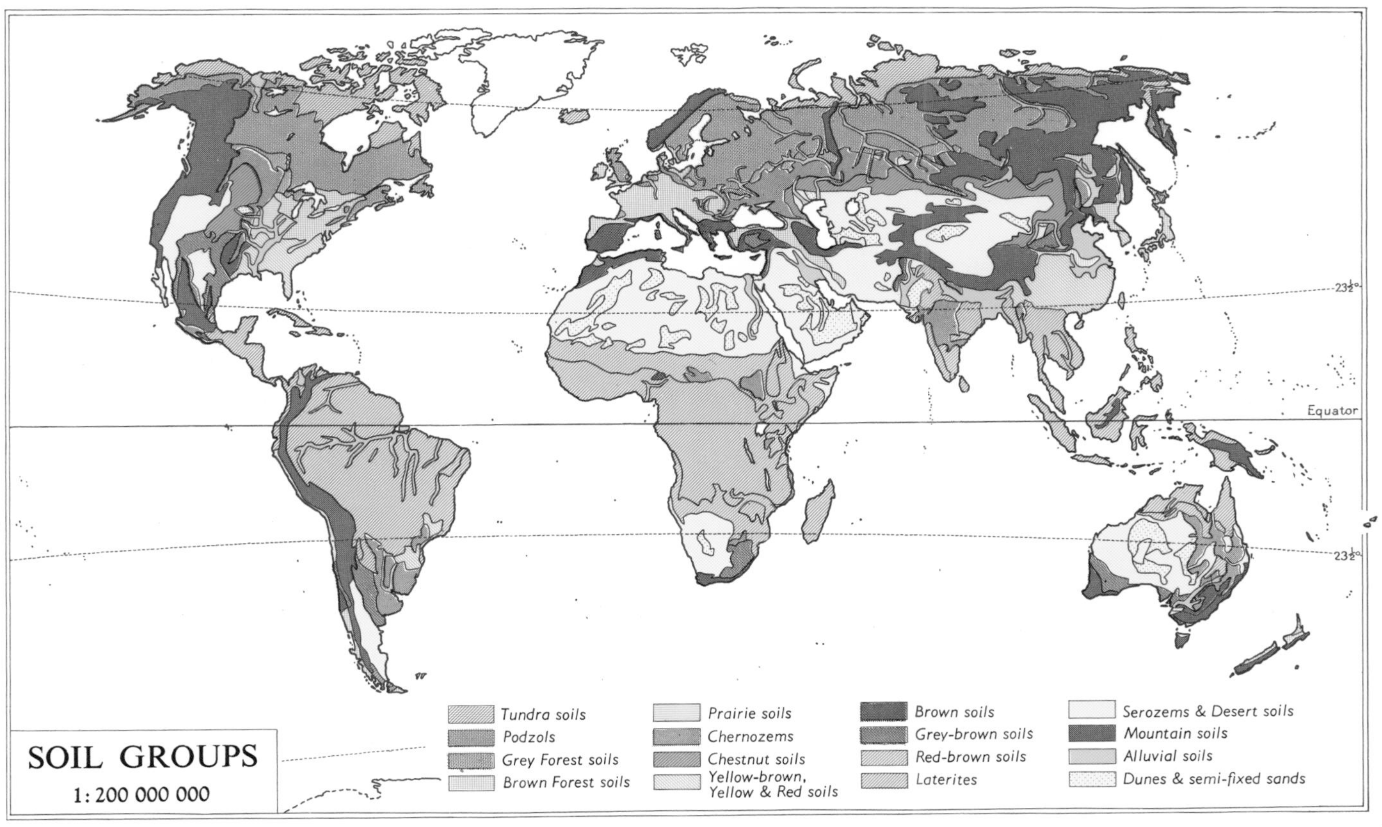

SOIL GROUPS
1: 200 000 000
Equator
Tundra soils
Podzols
Grey Forest soils
Brown Forest soils
Prairie soils
Chernozems
Chestnut soils
Yellow-brown, Yellow & Red soils
Brown soils
Grey-brown soils
Red-brown soils
Laterites
Serozems & Desert soils
Mountain soils
Alluvial soils
Dunes & semi-fixed sands

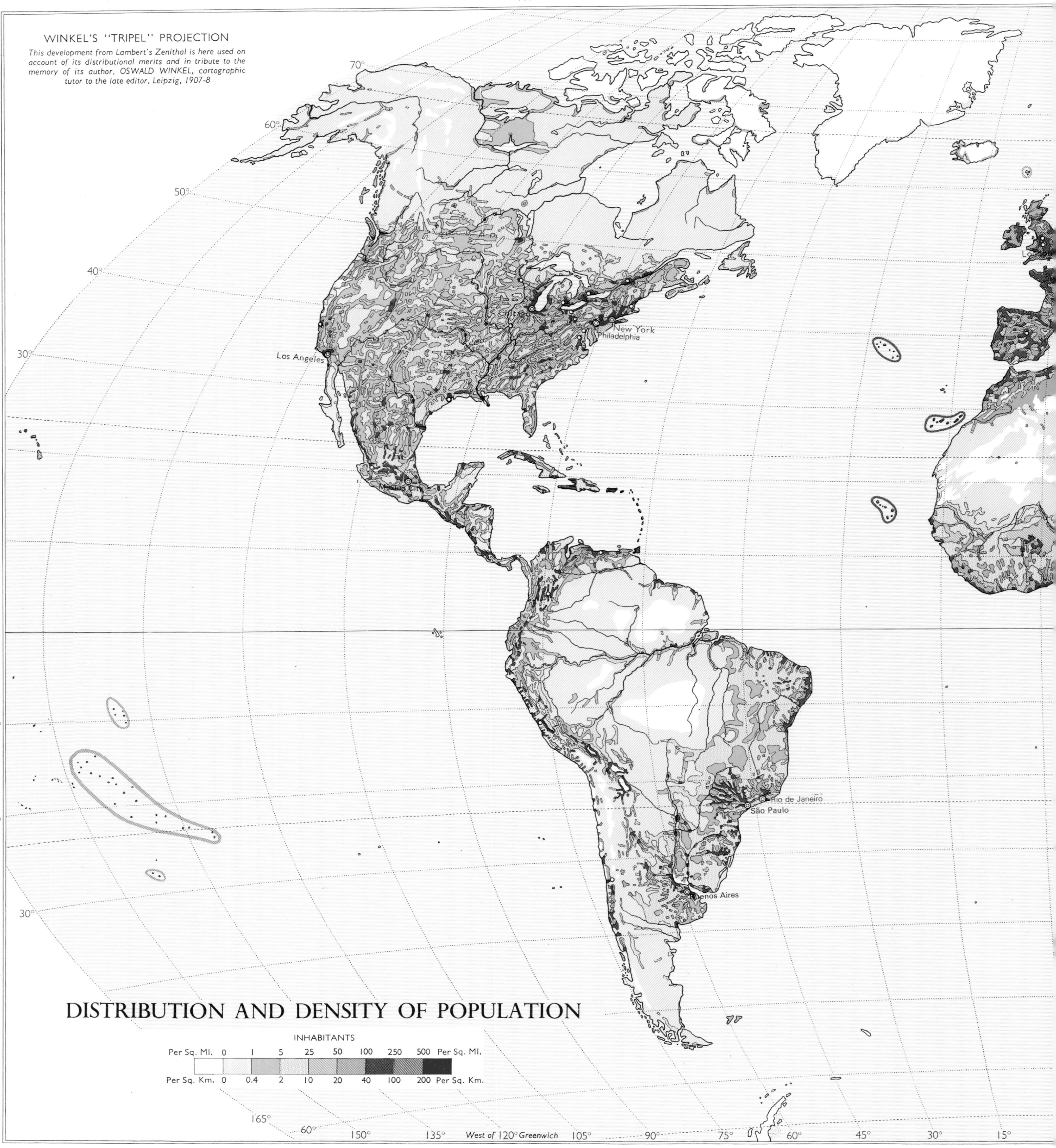
WINKEL'S "TRIPEL" PROJECTION
This development from Lambert's Zenithal is here used on account of its distributional merits and in tribute to the memory of its author, OSWALD WINKEL, cartographic tutor to the late editor, Leipzig, 1907-8
Los Angeles
New York
Philadelphia
Rio de Janeiro
São Paulo
Buenos Aires
INHABITANTS
Per Sq. Ml. 0 1 5 25 50 100 250 500 Per Sq. Ml.
Per Sq. Km. 0 0.4 2 10 20 40 100 200 Per Sq. Km.
West of 120° Greenwich

DISTRIBUTION AND DENSITY OF POPULATION

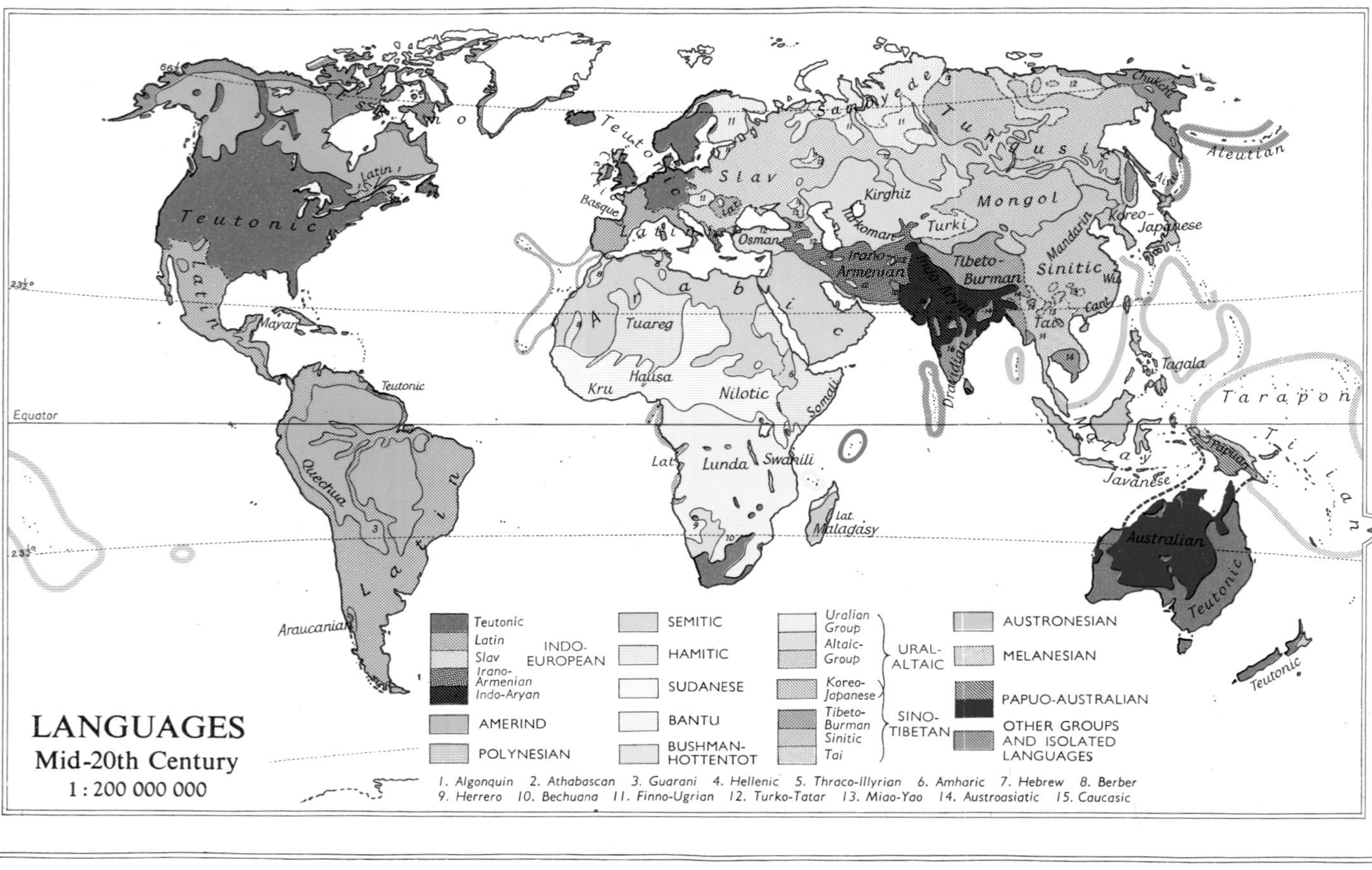
Teutonic
Latin
Slav
Mongol
Turki
Sinitic
Tibeto-Burman
Irano-Armenian
Osmanli
Tuareg
Hausa
Kru
Nilotic
Lunda
Swahili
Malagasy
Javanese
Australian
Tagala
Quechua
Araucanian
Mayan
Aleutian
Japanese
Teutonic
Latin
Slav
Irano-Armenian
Indo-Aryan
INDO-EUROPEAN
AMERIND
POLYNESIAN
SEMITIC
HAMITIC
SUDANESE
BANTU
BUSHMAN-HOTTENTOT
Uralian Group
Altaic-Group
URAL-ALTAIC
Koreo-Japanese
Tibeto-Burman
Sinitic
Tai
SINO-TIBETAN
AUSTRONESIAN
MELANESIAN
PAPUO-AUSTRALIAN
OTHER GROUPS AND ISOLATED LANGUAGES
1. Algonquin 2. Athabascan 3. Guarani 4. Hellenic 5. Thraco-Illyrian 6. Amharic 7. Hebrew 8. Berber
9. Herrero 10. Bechuana 11. Finno-Ugrian 12. Turko-Tatar 13. Miao-Yao 14. Austroasiatic 15. Caucasic

LANGUAGES
Mid-20th Century
1 : 200 000 000

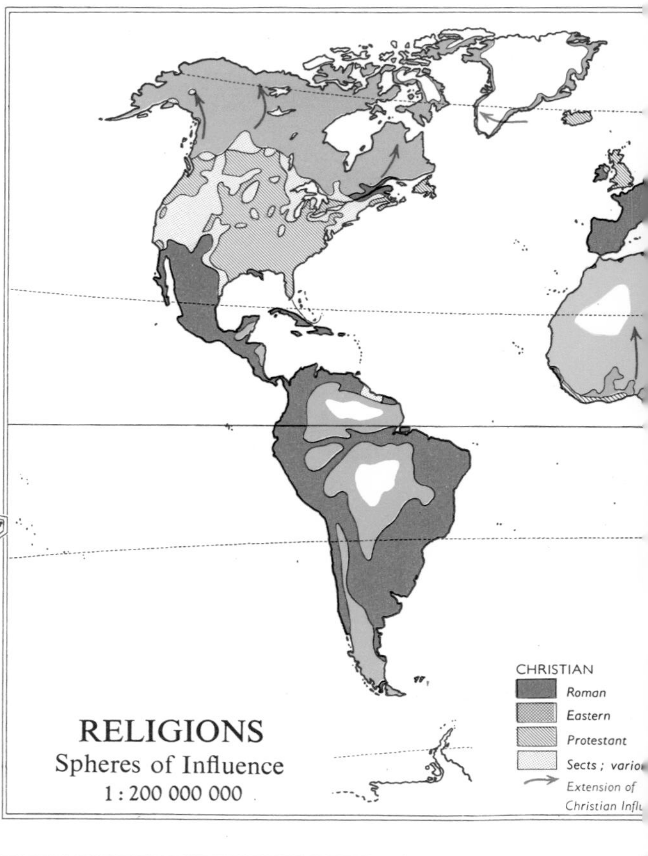
CHRISTIAN
Roman
Eastern
Protestant

RELIGIONS
Spheres of Influence
1 : 200 000 000

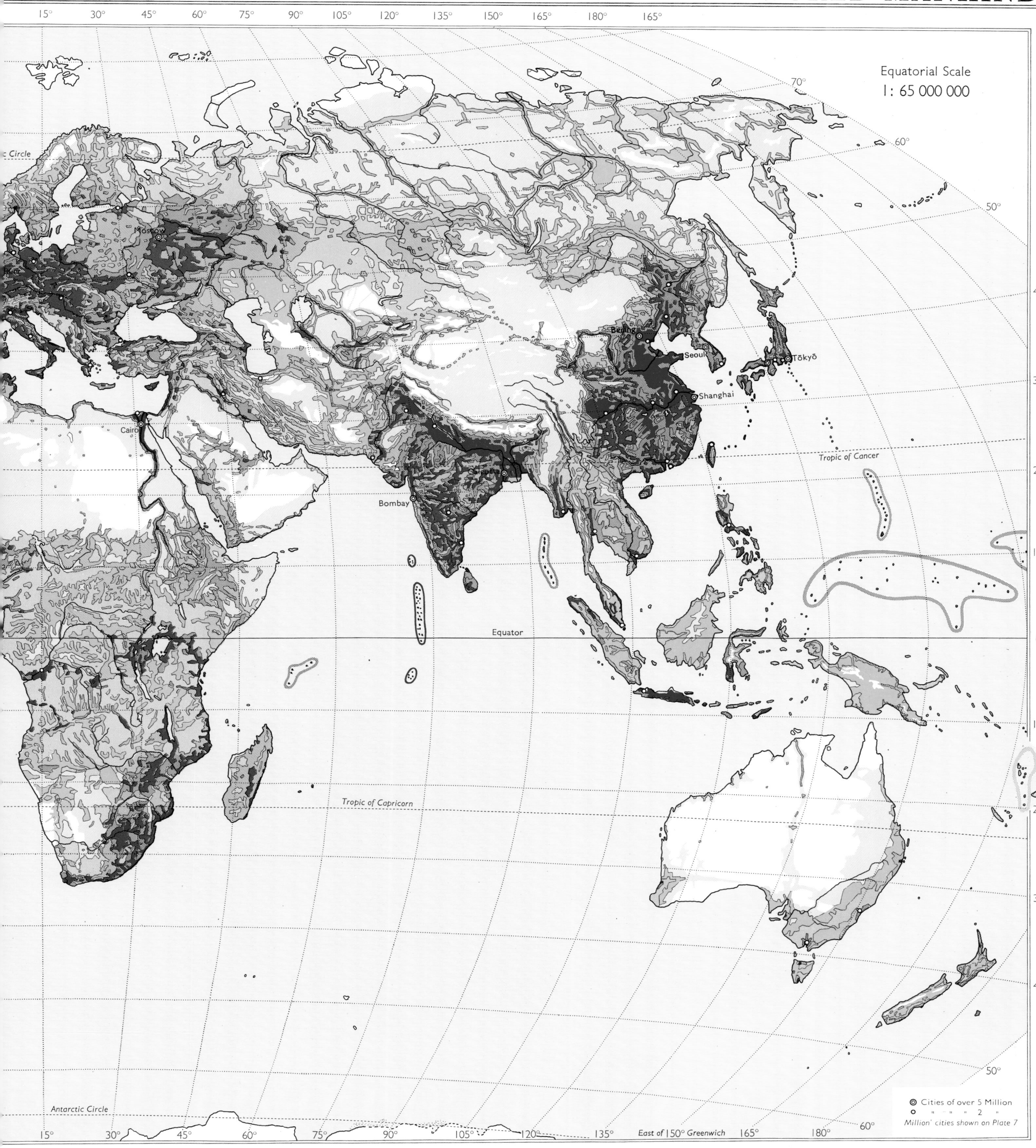
Equatorial Scale
1: 65 000 000
Arctic Circle
Moscow
Cairo
Bombay
Beijing
Seoul
Tōkyō
Shanghai
Tropic of Cancer
Equator
Tropic of Capricorn
Antarctic Circle
East of 150° Greenwich
Cities of over 5 Million
" " " 2 "
Million' cities shown on Plate 7

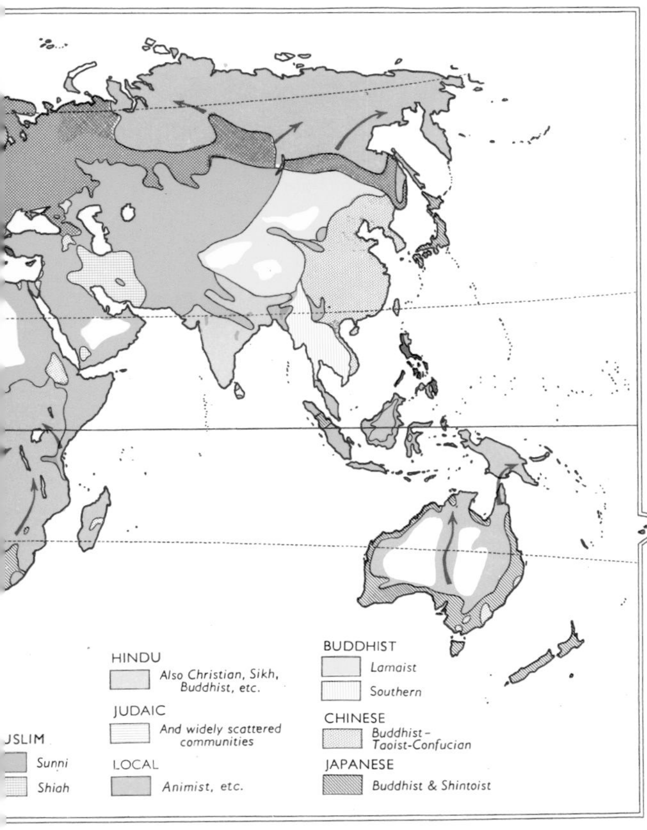
HINDU
Also Christian, Sikh, Buddhist, etc.
JUDAIC
And widely scattered communities
LOCAL
Animist, etc.
BUDDHIST
Lamaist
Southern
CHINESE
Buddhist–Taoist–Confucian
JAPANESE
Buddhist & Shintoist
USLIM
Sunni
Shiah

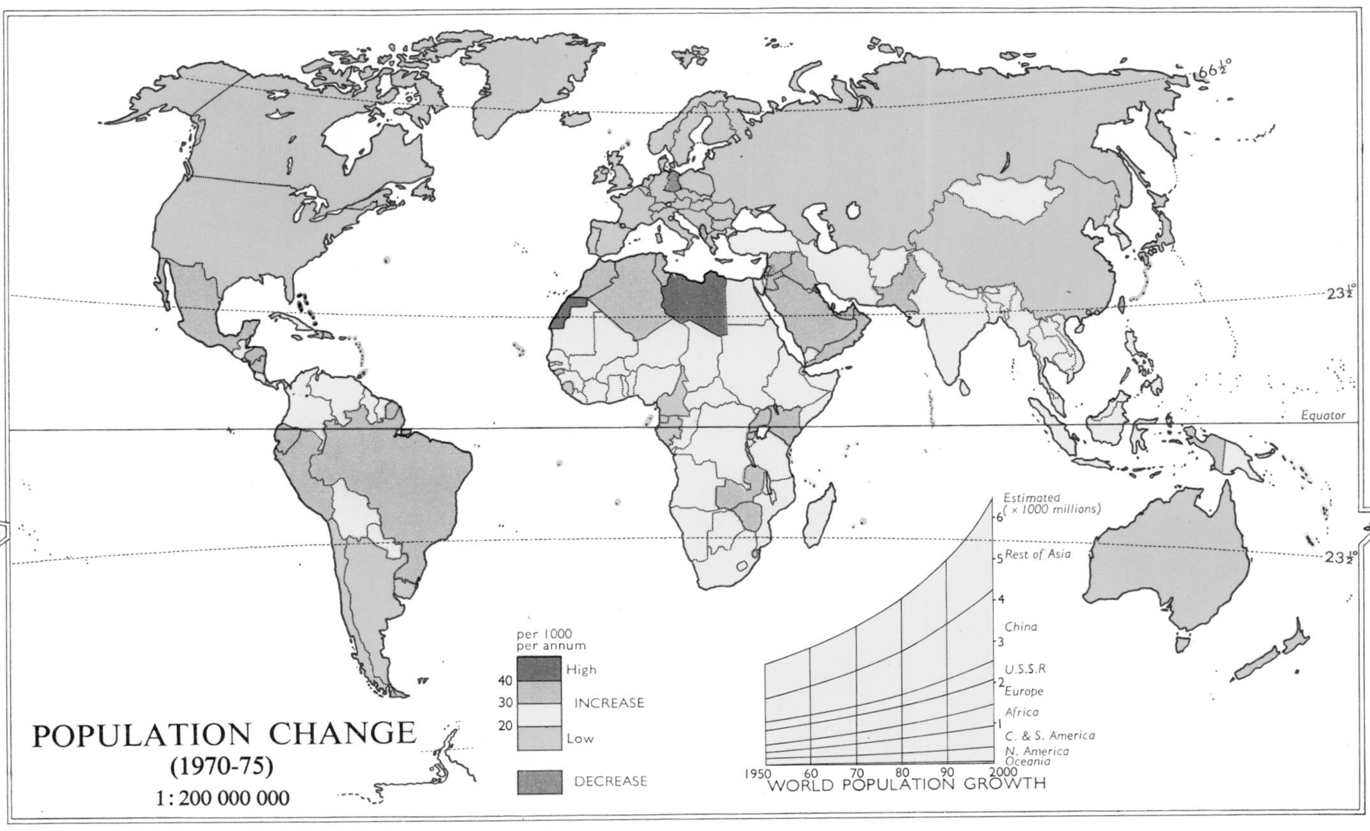
Equator
23½°
66½°
per 1000 per annum
40
30
20
High
INCREASE
Low
DECREASE
Estimated (× 1000 millions)
Rest of Asia
China
U.S.S.R.
Europe
Africa
C. & S. America
N. America
Oceania
1950 60 70 80 90 2000
WORLD POPULATION GROWTH

POPULATION CHANGE
(1970-75)
1: 200 000 000

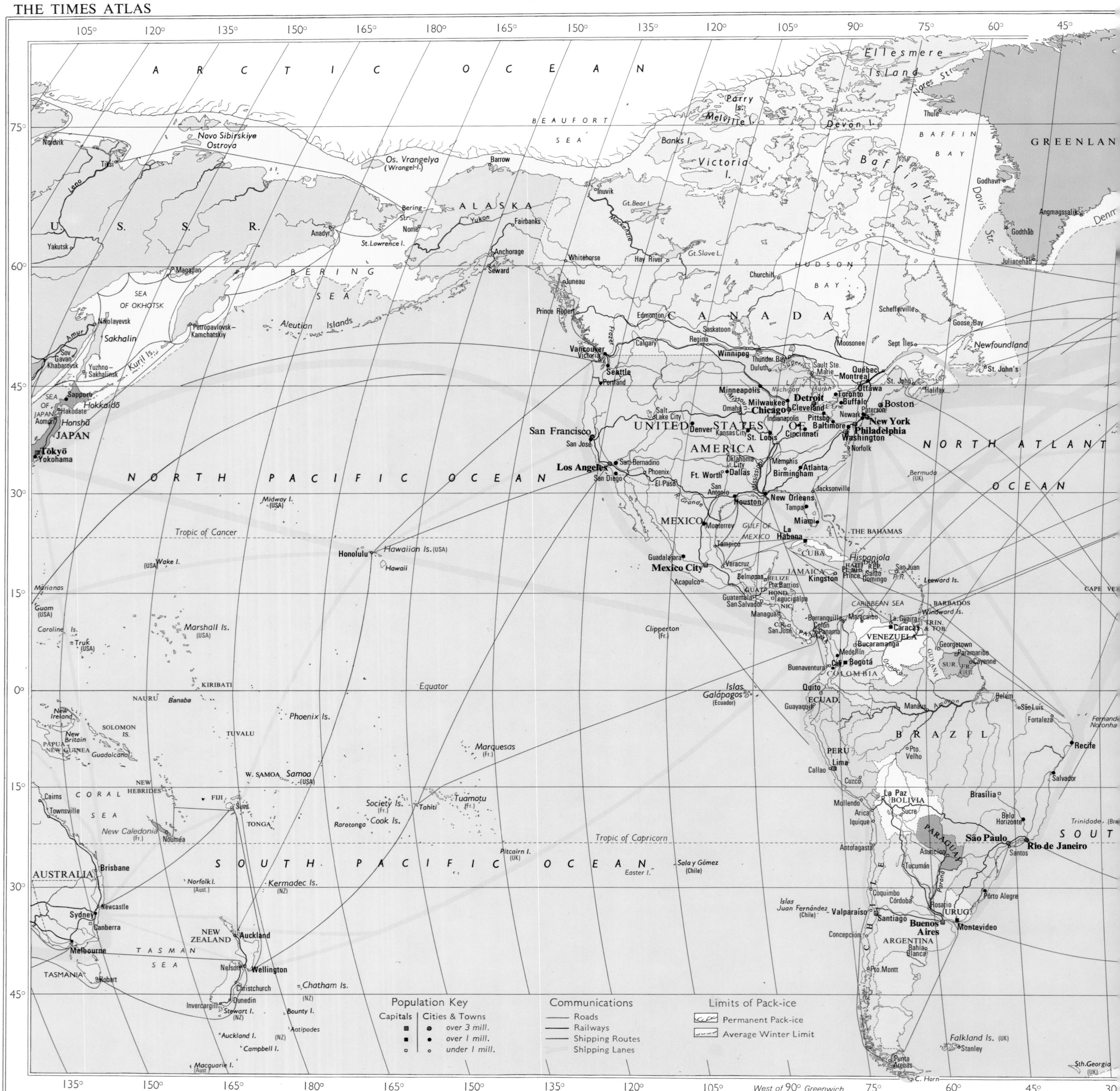
ARCTIC OCEAN
Ellesmere Island
Parry Is.
Melville I.
Devon I.
BEAUFORT SEA
Banks I.
Victoria I.
BAFFIN BAY
Baffin I.
GREENLAND
Novo Sibirskiye Ostrova
Os. Vrangelya (Wrangel I.)
Barrow
ALASKA
Bering Str.
Nome
Fairbanks
Anchorage
Seward
Yakutsk
U.S.S.R.
Magadan
SEA OF OKHOTSK
BERING SEA
Aleutian Islands
Petropavlovsk-Kamchatskiy
Sakhalin
Kuril Is.
Khabarovsk
Hokkaidō
Honshū
JAPAN
Tokyō
Yokohama
CANADA
HUDSON BAY
Churchill
Edmonton
Calgary
Vancouver
Victoria
Seattle
Portland
Winnipeg
Quebec
Montreal
Ottawa
Toronto
Newfoundland
St. John's
Halifax
UNITED STATES OF AMERICA
San Francisco
Los Angeles
San Diego
Minneapolis
Chicago
Detroit
Cleveland
Boston
New York
Philadelphia
Washington
Denver
St. Louis
Cincinnati
Dallas
Houston
New Orleans
Atlanta
Miami
NORTH PACIFIC OCEAN
NORTH ATLANTIC OCEAN
Tropic of Cancer
Honolulu
Hawaiian Is. (USA)
Midway I. (USA)
Wake I. (USA)
MEXICO
Mexico City
GULF OF MEXICO
La Habana
CUBA
THE BAHAMAS
Hispaniola
Kingston
CARIBBEAN SEA
Caracas
VENEZUELA
Bogotá
COLOMBIA
Quito
ECUAD.
Equator
Islas Galápagos (Ecuador)
Marshall Is. (USA)
KIRIBATI
NAURU
TUVALU
Phoenix Is.
Marquesas (Fr.)
W. SAMOA
Samoa (USA)
FIJI
Tahiti
Tuamotu
CORAL SEA
New Caledonia (Fr.)
AUSTRALIA
Brisbane
Sydney
Canberra
Melbourne
TASMANIA
TASMAN SEA
NEW ZEALAND
Auckland
Wellington
Christchurch
Dunedin
Chatham Is.
SOUTH PACIFIC OCEAN
Tropic of Capricorn
Easter I.
BRAZIL
Manaus
Recife
Salvador
Brasília
São Paulo
Rio de Janeiro
PERU
Lima
BOLIVIA
La Paz
PARAGUAY
Asunción
CHILE
Santiago
Valparaíso
ARGENTINA
Buenos Aires
URUG.
Montevideo
Falkland Is. (UK)
C. Horn
Population Key
Capitals | Cities & Towns
over 3 mill.
over 1 mill.
under 1 mill.
Communications
Roads
Railways
Shipping Routes
Shipping Lanes
Limits of Pack-ice
Permanent Pack-ice
Average Winter Limit
West of 90° Greenwich

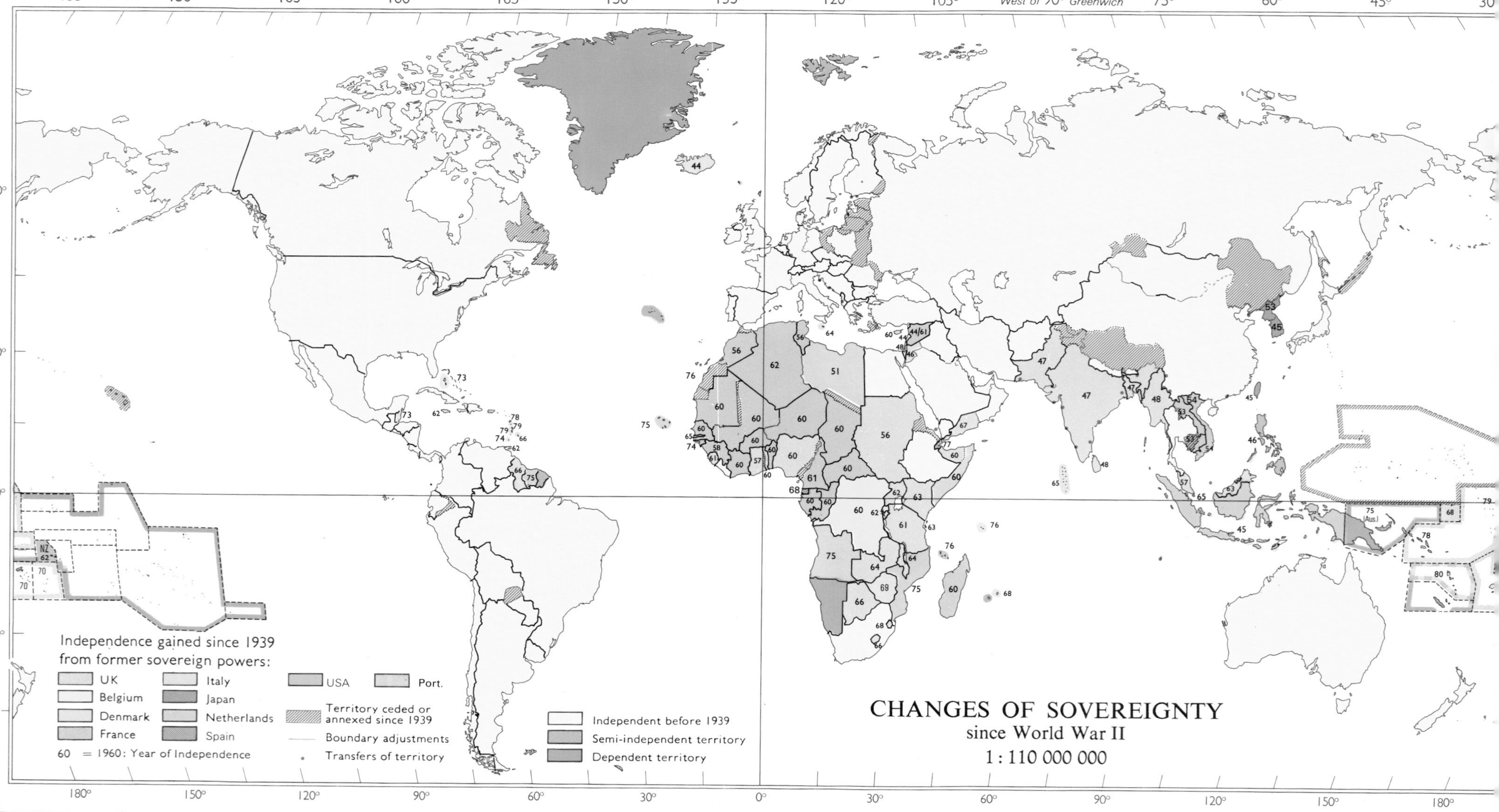
Independence gained since 1939
from former sovereign powers:
UK
Belgium
Denmark
France
Italy
Japan
Netherlands
Spain
USA
Port.
Territory ceded or annexed since 1939
Boundary adjustments
Transfers of territory
60 = 1960: Year of Independence
Independent before 1939
Semi-independent territory
Dependent territory

CHANGES OF SOVEREIGNTY
since World War II
1 : 110 000 000

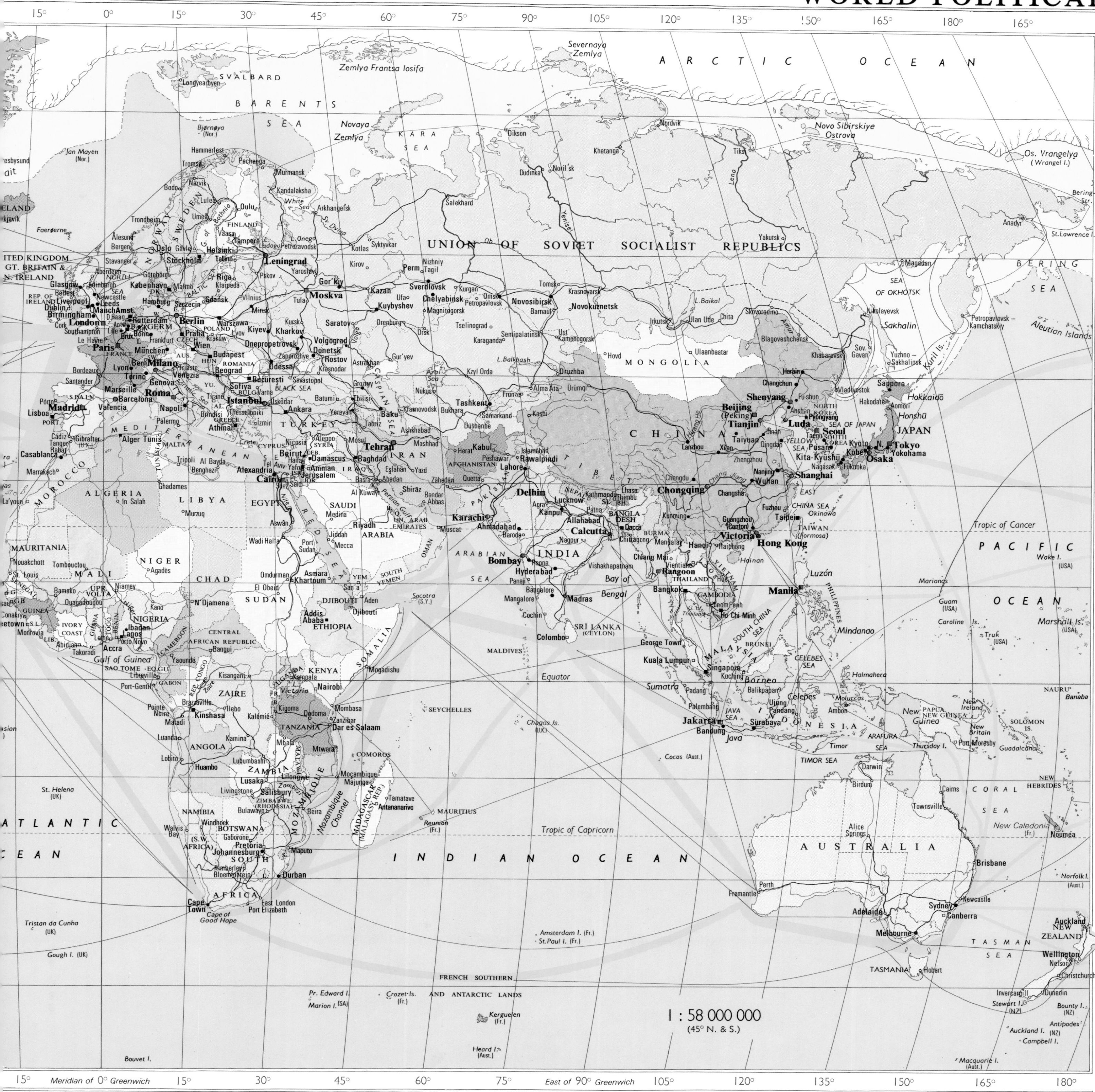

ARCTIC OCEAN
BARENTS SEA
KARA SEA
UNION OF SOVIET SOCIALIST REPUBLICS
MONGOLIA
CHINA
JAPAN
INDIA
TIBET
AFGHANISTAN
IRAN
TURKEY
SAUDI ARABIA
EGYPT
LIBYA
ALGERIA
MOROCCO
MAURITANIA
MALI
NIGER
CHAD
SUDAN
ETHIOPIA
SOMALIA
KENYA
ZAIRE
TANZANIA
ANGOLA
ZAMBIA
NAMIBIA
BOTSWANA
MOZAMBIQUE
MADAGASCAR
SOUTH AFRICA
NIGERIA
INDONESIA
AUSTRALIA
NEW ZEALAND
PHILIPPINES
PACIFIC OCEAN
INDIAN OCEAN
ATLANTIC OCEAN
BERING SEA
SEA OF OKHOTSK
CORAL SEA
TASMAN SEA
ARABIAN SEA
Bay of Bengal
SOUTH CHINA SEA
EAST CHINA SEA
Tropic of Cancer
Equator
Tropic of Capricorn
FRENCH SOUTHERN AND ANTARCTIC LANDS
Leningrad
Moskva
Berlin
Paris
London
Roma
Istanbul
Tehran
Karachi
Delhi
Bombay
Calcutta
Madras
Beijing (Peking)
Shanghai
Tianjin
Shenyang
Chongqing
Wuhan
Hong Kong
Seoul
Tokyo
Osaka
Manila
Jakarta
Singapore
Cairo
Kinshasa
Dar es Salaam
Sydney
Melbourne
Adelaide
Brisbane
Perth
Auckland
Wellington
Meridian of 0° Greenwich
East of 90° Greenwich
1 : 58 000 000
(45° N. & S.)

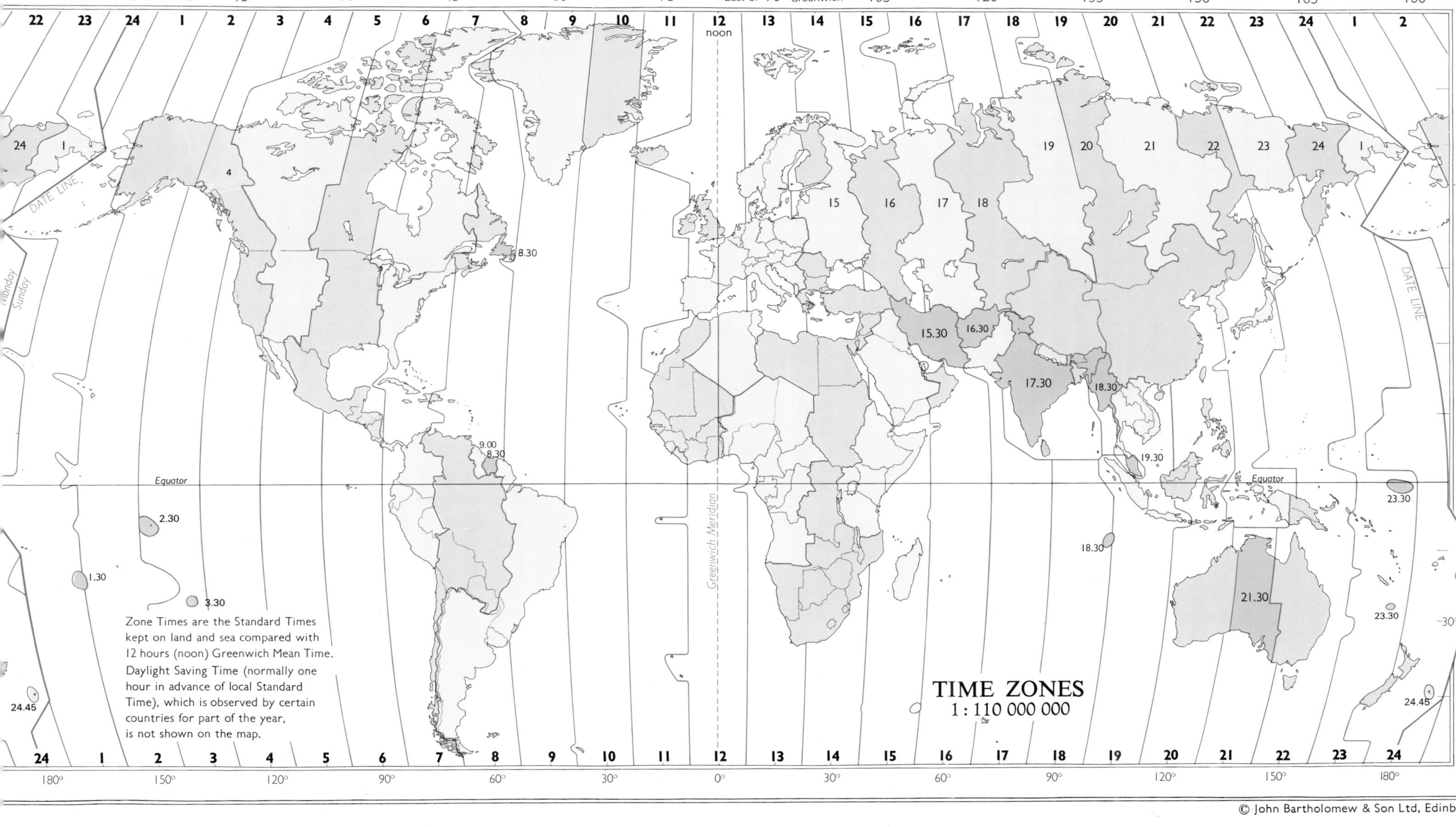

TIME ZONES
1 : 110 000 000
Zone Times are the Standard Times kept on land and sea compared with 12 hours (noon) Greenwich Mean Time. Daylight Saving Time (normally one hour in advance of local Standard Time), which is observed by certain countries for part of the year, is not shown on the map.
12 noon
Greenwich Meridian
DATE LINE
Monday
Sunday
Equator

NORDIC ' PROJECTION

By John Bartholomew, M.C., LL.D.

An Oblique Area-true Projection designed to give optimum representation to Europe and to routes in the Atlantic, Arctic and Indian Oceans. Major Axis, a Great Circle touching 45° N. Lesser Axis, Meridian of Greenwich.

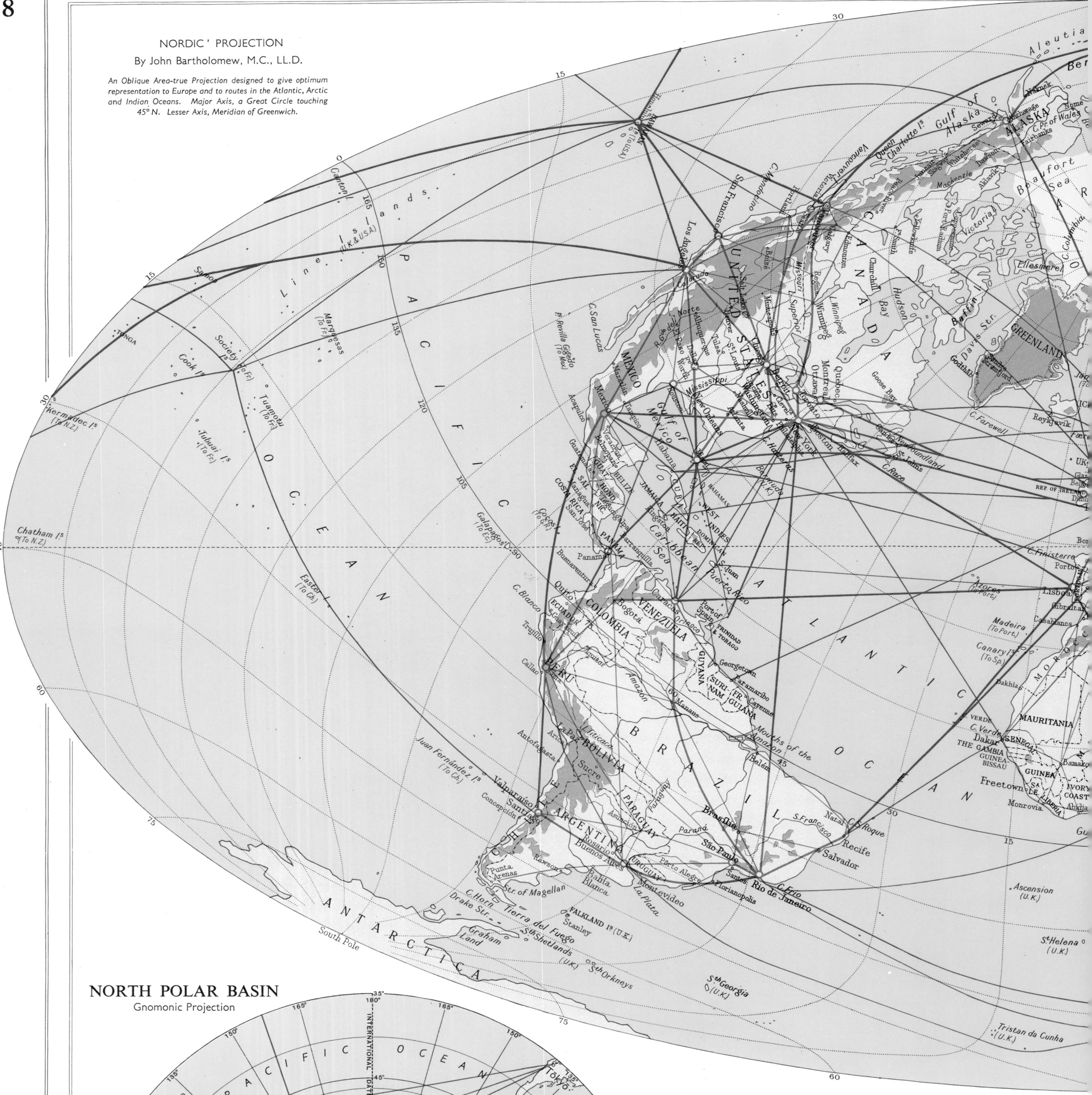

NORTH POLAR BASIN

Gnomonic Projection

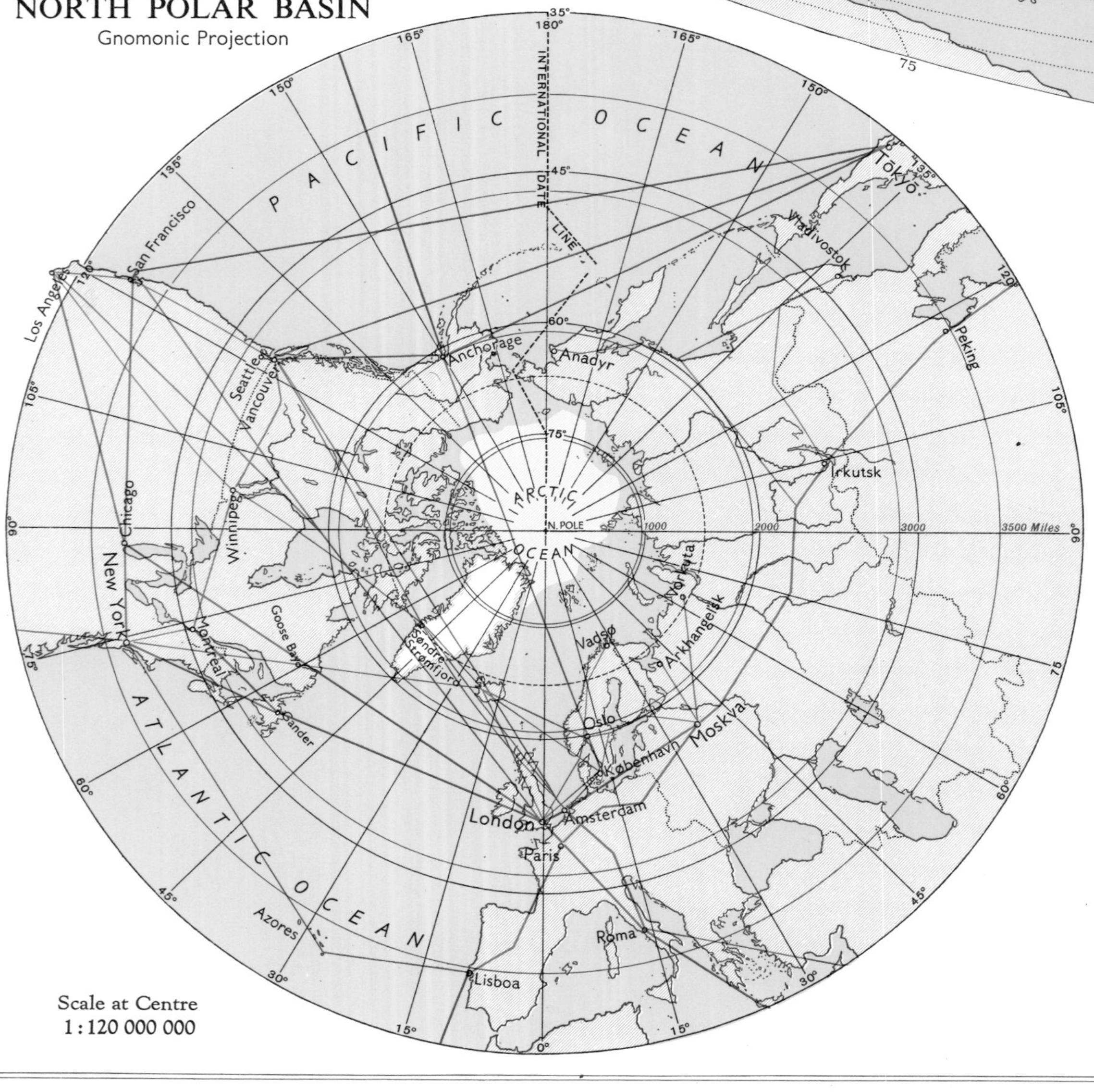

Scale at Centre
1 : 120 000 000

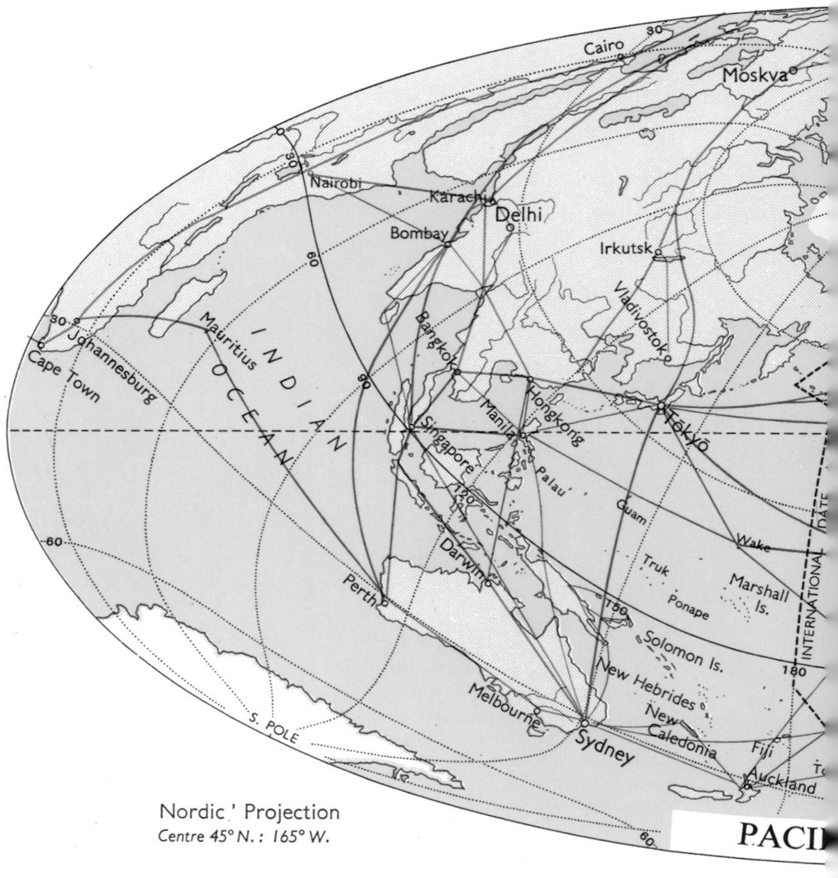

Nordic ' Projection
Centre 45° N. : 165° W.

Scale 1: 60 000 000

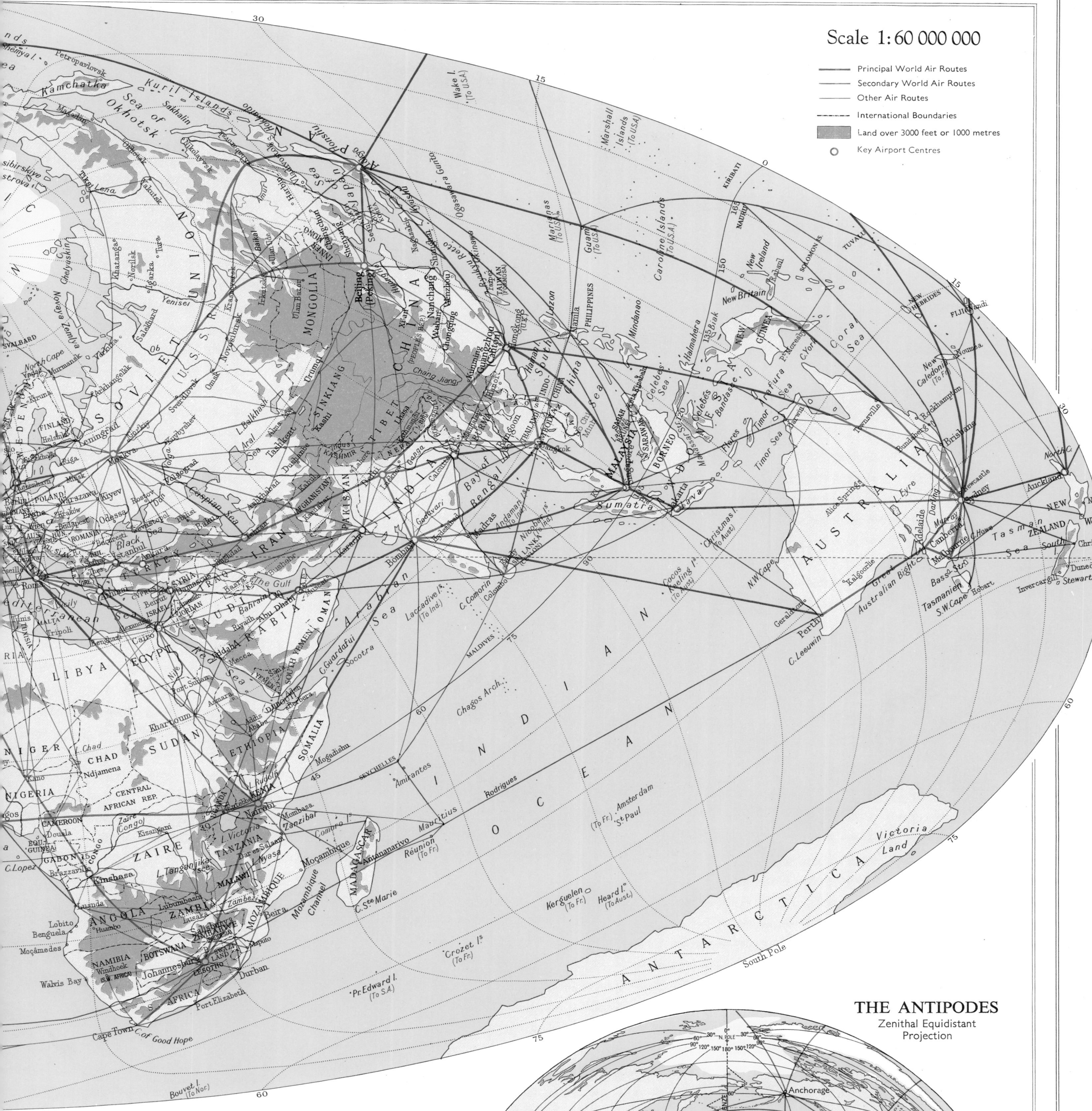

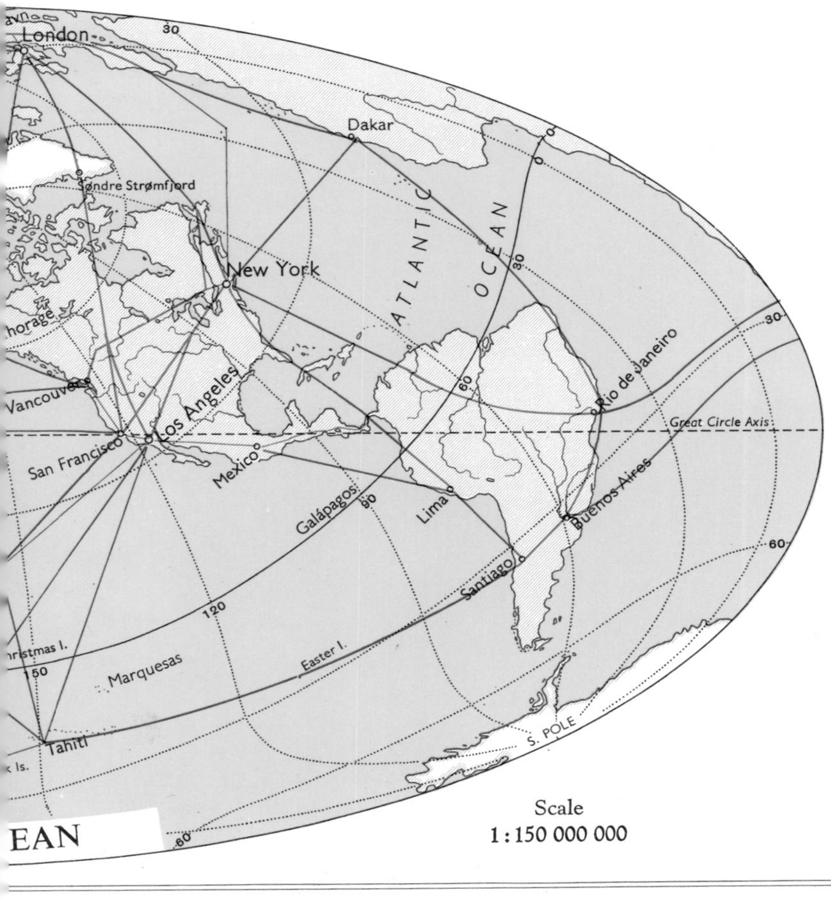

Scale
1 : 150 000 000

THE ANTIPODES

Zenithal Equidistant
Projection

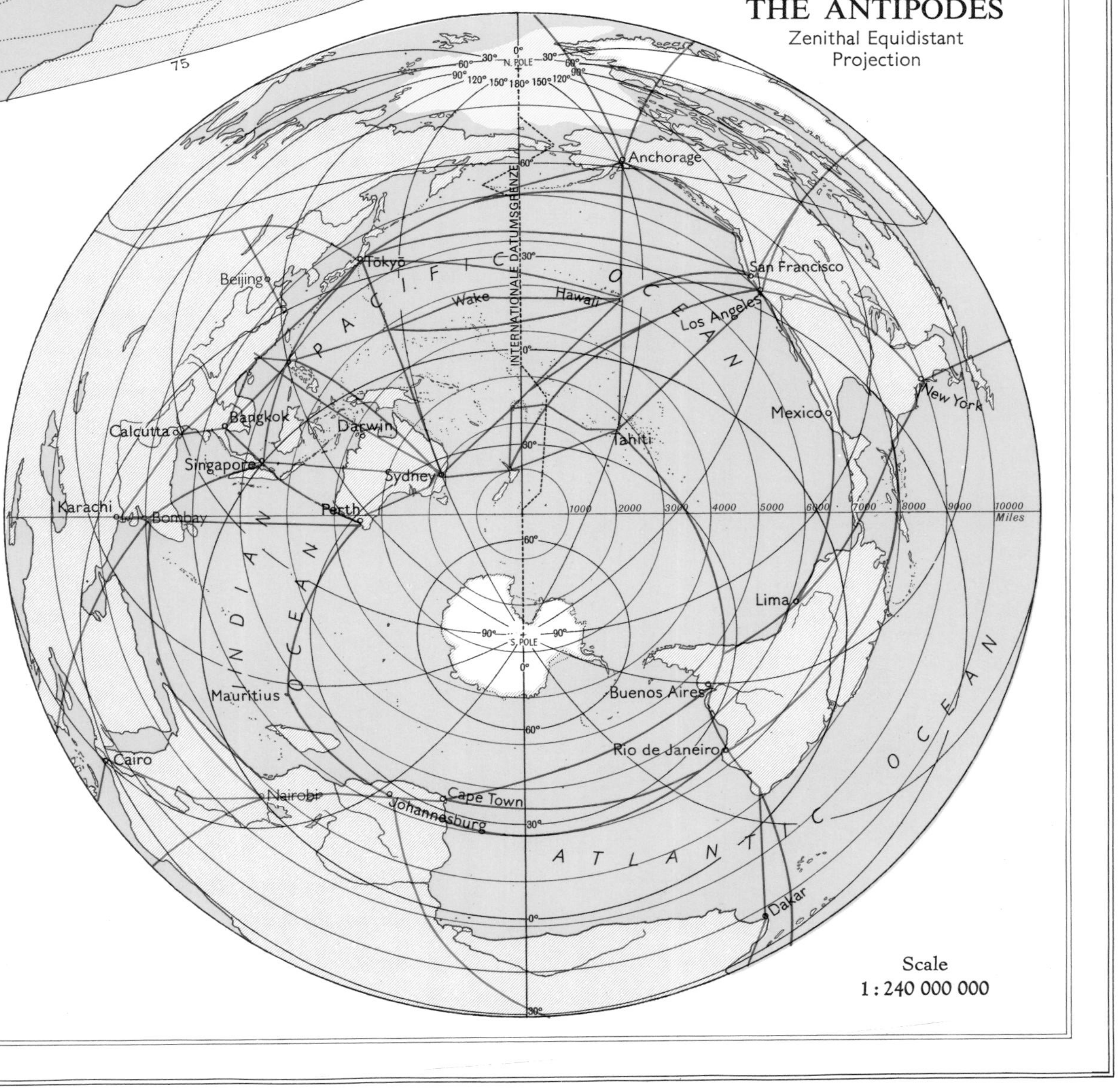

Scale
1 : 240 000 000

MARSHALL ISLANDS
(U.S.A. Trust Territory)
1:10 000 000
Ralik Chain
Ratak Chain
Eniwetok
Bikini
Rongelap
Rongerik
Utirik
Ailinginae
Wotho
Kwajalein
Wotje
Maloelap
Majuro
Arno
Jaluit
Mili
Ebon
KWAJALEIN ATOLL
(U.S.A. Trust Territory)
1:2 500 000
BANABA
(Ocean I.)
1:250,000
KIRIBATI
(GILBERT ISLANDS)
Kingsmill Group
Makin
(Butaritari)
Marakei
Abaiang
Tarawa
Maiana
Abemama
Nonouti
Tabiteuea
Onotoa
WAKE ISLAND
(To U.S.A.)
1:250 000
Peale Island
Wilkes Island
Wake I.
NAURU
1:250 000
TUVALU
(Ellice Is.)
1:10 000 000
Nanumea Is.
Vaitupu
Nukufetau
Funafuti
Nukulaelae
0 20 40 80 120 Statute Miles
0 100 200 Kilometres
NEW HEBRIDES AND
NEW CALEDONIA
1:7 500 000
0 30 60 20 Statute Miles
0 30 60 120 180 Kilometres
Torres Islands
Banks Islands
Espíritu Santo I.
(I. Marina)
Malekula
(Mallicolo)
Ambrim (Ambrym)
Pentecost I. (Raga)
Efate
Vila (Fila)
Eromanga
(Erromango)
Tana
(Tanna)
Aneityum
(Anatom)
CORAL SEA
NEW HEBRIDES
Récifs d'Entrecasteaux
Grand Récif de Cook
Îs. Loyauté
(Loyalty Is.)
(to France)
Lifou
Maré
NOUVELLE
CALÉDONIE
(to France)
Nouméa
I. des Pins
Grand Récif du Sud
MEDITERRANEAN SEA
Cairo
Jerusalem
Beirut
Damascus
Baghdad
SYRIA
IRAQ
TURKEY
Ankara
Istanbul
BLACK SEA
CASPIAN SEA
IRAN
(PERSIA)
Tehran
SOVIET UNION
Moskva
Leningrad
Kiyev
AFGHANISTAN
PAKISTAN
Karachi
Lahore
Islamabad
INDIA
Delhi
Bombay
Calcutta
Madras
Hyderabad
BAY OF BENGAL
SRI LANKA
(CEYLON)
Colombo
CHINA
TIBET
MONGOLIA
Beijing
(Peking)
Shanghai
Nanjing
Chongqing
Guangzhou
(Canton)
TAIWAN
(FORMOSA)
Hong Kong
BURMA
THAILAND
(SIAM)
Bangkok
VIETNAM
Hanoi
Ho Chi Minh
(Saigon)
Manila
Luzon
SOUTH CHINA SEA
MALAYSIA
Kuala Lumpur
Singapore
BORNEO
SUMATRA
INDONESIA
JAVA
Jakarta
EQUATOR
Christmas I.
(to Aust.)
Cocos or Keeling Is.
(to Aust.)
AUST
SOUTHERN OCEAN
FRENCH SOUTHERN & ANTARCTIC LANDS
Is. de Kerguelen
I. Amsterdam
(to Fr.)
Is. Crozet
(to Fr.)
ANTARC
N. ATLANTIC OCEAN
ICELAND
Reykjavik
London
Berlin
Warszawa
Wien
Budapest
Beograd
Helsinki
Stockholm
Oslo
Edinburgh
Scale
according to vertical grid
g f e d c b a
Feet
Metres

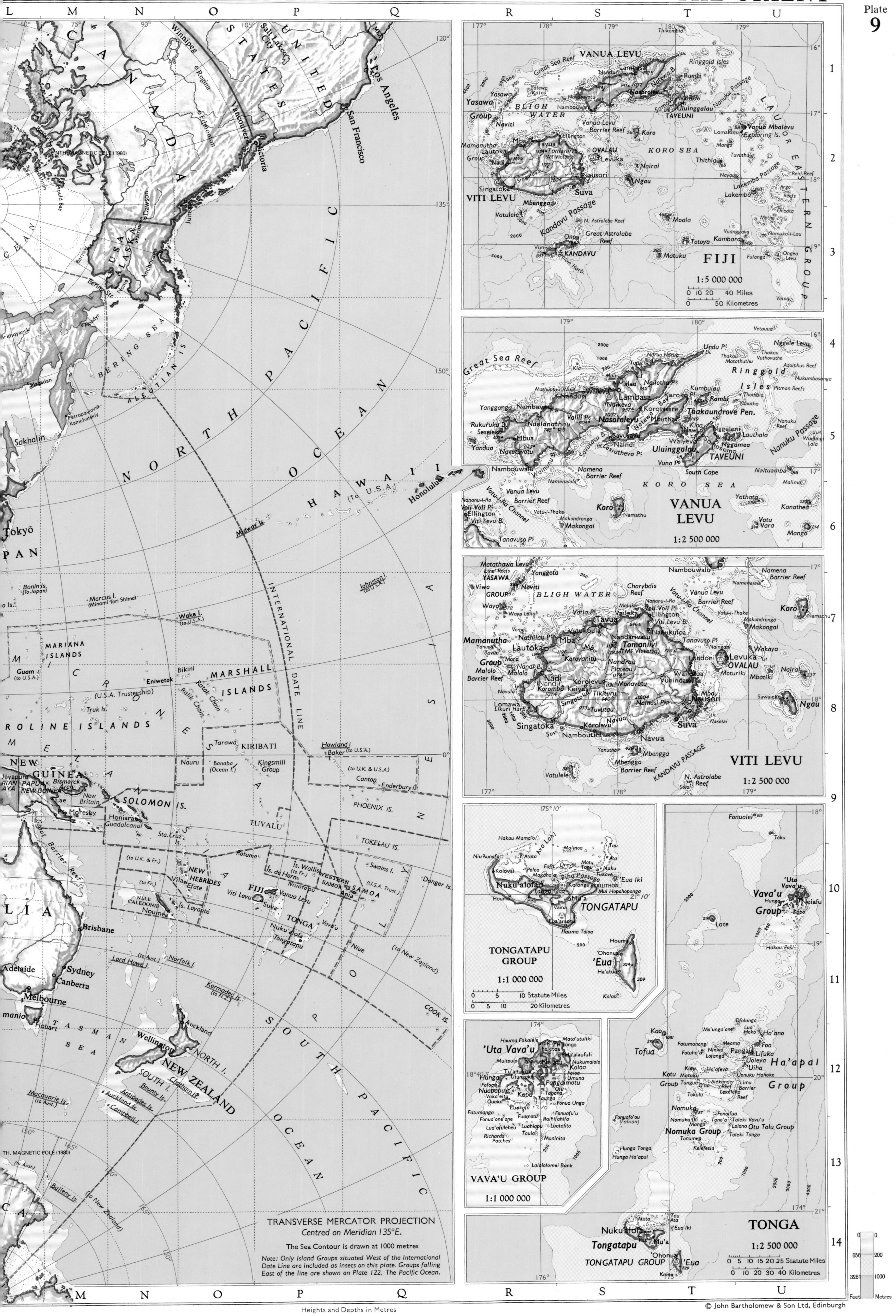
TRANSVERSE MERCATOR PROJECTION
Centred on Meridian 135°E.
The Sea Contour is drawn at 1000 metres
Note: Only Island Groups situated West of the International Date Line are included as insets on this plate. Groups falling East of the line are shown on Plate 122, The Pacific Ocean.
NORTH PACIFIC OCEAN
SOUTH PACIFIC OCEAN
INTERNATIONAL DATE LINE
HAWAII (To U.S.A.)
Honolulu
CANADA
UNITED STATES
ALASKA (U.S.A.)
BERING SEA
ALEUTIAN IS.
MARSHALL ISLANDS
MARIANA ISLANDS
CAROLINE ISLANDS
KIRIBATI
TUVALU
PHOENIX IS.
TOKELAU IS.
SOLOMON IS.
NEW HEBRIDES
FIJI
TONGA
WESTERN SAMOA
NEW ZEALAND
TASMAN SEA
FIJI
1:5 000 000
VANUA LEVU
1:2 500 000
VITI LEVU
1:2 500 000
TONGATAPU GROUP
1:1 000 000
VAVA'U GROUP
1:1 000 000
TONGA
1:2 500 000

Heights and Depths in Metres

© John Bartholomew & Son Ltd, Edinburgh

BORNEO
SULAWESI (Celebes)
MOLUCCAS
Halmahera
CERAM SEA
BANDA SEA
FLORES SEA
TIMOR
INDONESIA
IRIAN JAYA
NEW GUINEA
PAPUA NEW GUINEA
BISMARCK SEA
ARAFURA SEA
TIMOR SEA
Gulf of Carpentaria
INDIAN OCEAN
CORAL SEA ISLANDS
Coral Sea
NORTHERN TERRITORY
QUEENSLAND
WESTERN AUSTRALIA
SOUTH AUSTRALIA
NEW SOUTH WALES
VICTORIA
TASMANIA
AUSTRALIA
Great Sandy Desert
Gibson Desert
Great Victoria Desert
Simpson Desert
Nullarbor Plain
Great Australian Bight
GREAT DIVIDING RANGE
SOUTH AUSTRALIAN BASIN
Bass Strait
Darwin
Perth
Adelaide
Melbourne
Sydney
CANBERRA A.C.T.
Brisbane
Hobart
Alice Springs
Kalgoorlie
Port Moresby
MACQUARIE I.
(To Australia)
1 : 500 000
LORD HOWE I.
(To Australia)
1 : 500 000

BONNE PROJECTION

1: 15 000 000

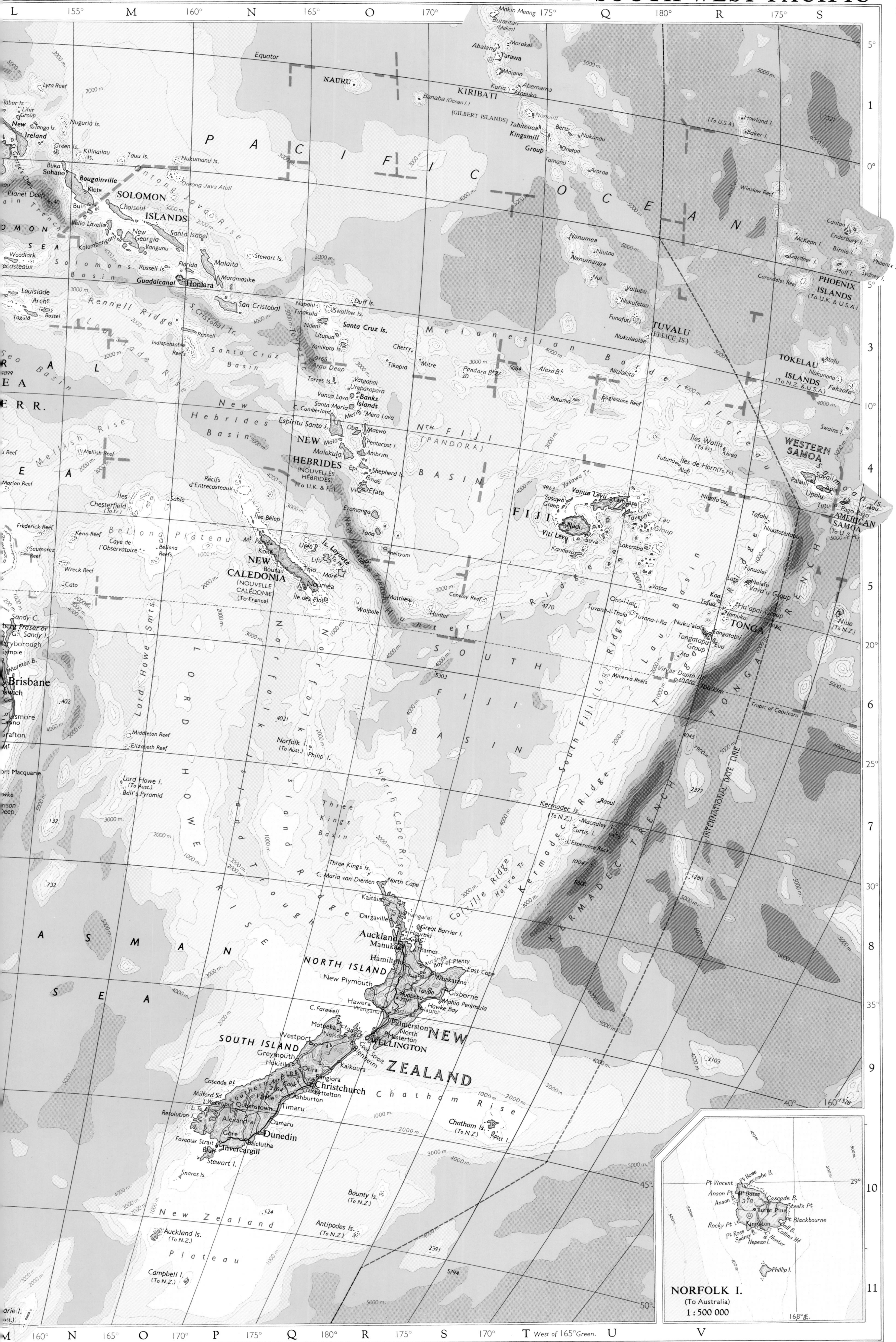
PACIFIC OCEAN
NAURU
KIRIBATI
(GILBERT ISLANDS)
Equator
SOLOMON ISLANDS
Bougainville
Guadalcanal
Honiara
San Cristobal
Santa Cruz Is.
TUVALU
(ELLICE IS.)
Funafuti
PHOENIX ISLANDS
(To U.K. & U.S.A.)
TOKELAU ISLANDS
(To N.Z. & U.S.A.)
WESTERN SAMOA
AMERICAN SAMOA
(To U.S.A.)
NEW HEBRIDES
(NOUVELLES HEBRIDES)
(To U.K. & Fr.)
Espiritu Santo I.
Efate
NTH FIJI (PANDORA) BASIN
FIJI
Vanua Levu
Viti Levu
Suva
Lau Group
Îles Wallis (To Fr.)
Îles de Horn (To Fr.)
Niuafo'ou
TONGA
Vava'u Group
Ha'apai Group
Nuku'alofa
Tongatapu Group
Niue (To N.Z.)
Tropic of Capricorn
NEW CALEDONIA
(NOUVELLE CALÉDONIE)
(To France)
Nouméa
Îs. Loyauté
Chesterfield (To Fr.)
Bellona Plateau
SOUTH FIJI BASIN
New Hebrides Trench
Lord Howe Smts.
LORD HOWE RISE
Norfolk Island Ridge
Norfolk I. (To Aust.)
Lord Howe I. (To Aust.)
Ball's Pyramid
Three Kings Basin
North Cape Rise
Kermadec Is. (To N.Z.)
Raoul
Kermadec Ridge
KERMADEC TRENCH
TONGA TRENCH
INTERNATIONAL DATE LINE
South Fiji Ridge
Colville Ridge
Havre Tr.
TASMAN SEA
Brisbane
Ipswich
Lismore
NEW ZEALAND
NORTH ISLAND
Auckland
Hamilton
New Plymouth
Gisborne
Palmerston North
WELLINGTON
SOUTH ISLAND
Christchurch
Dunedin
Invercargill
Stewart I.
Chatham Rise
Chatham Is. (To N.Z.)
Bounty Is. (To N.Z.)
Antipodes Is. (To N.Z.)
Snares Is.
New Zealand Plateau
Auckland Is. (To N.Z.)
Campbell I. (To N.Z.)
NORFOLK I.
(To Australia)
1 : 500 000
Kingston
Phillip I.
West of 165° Green.

200 150 100 50 0 100 200 400 600 800 1000 Kilometres   Heights in Metres   Depths in Metres

© John Bartholomew & Son Ltd, Edinburgh

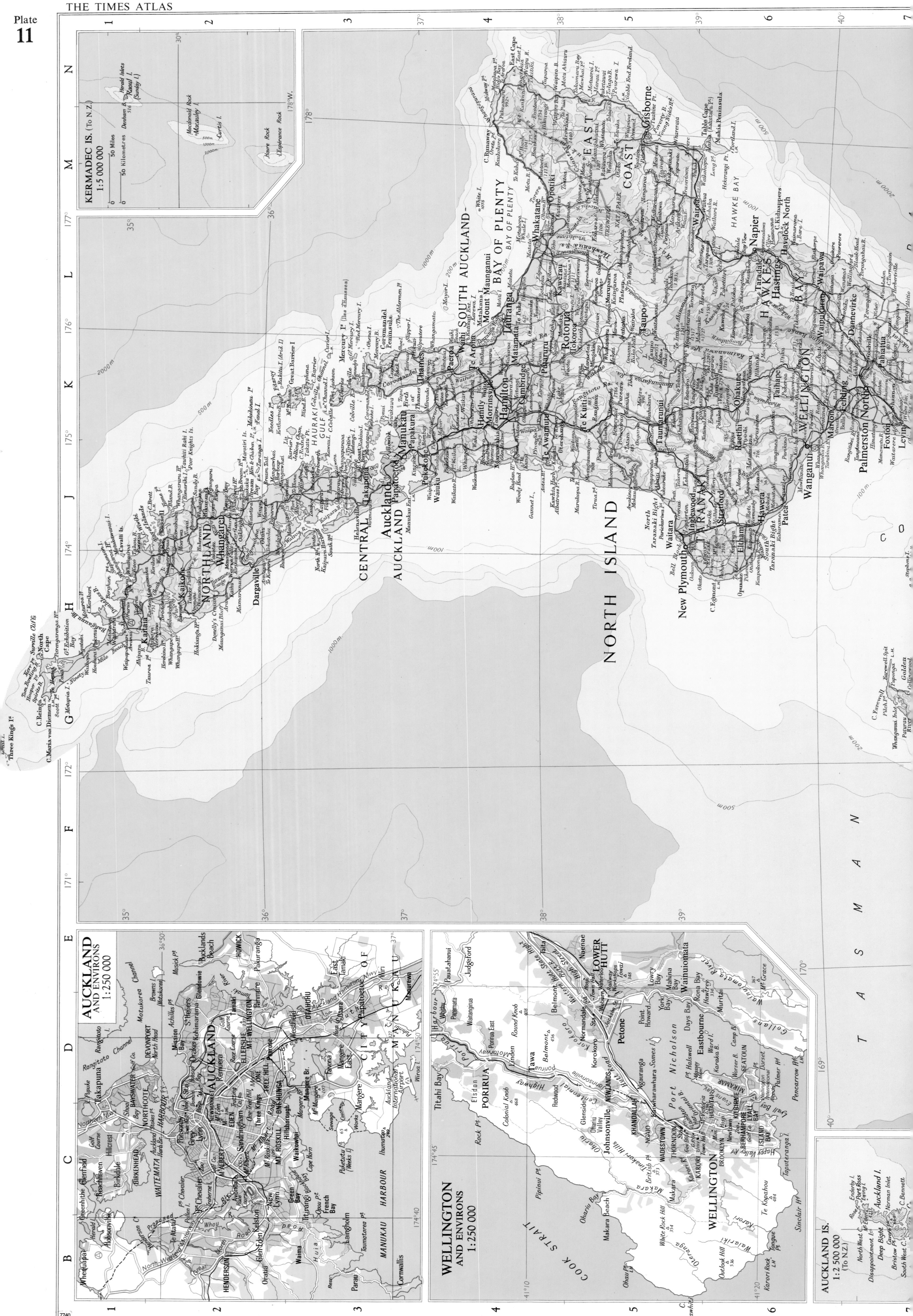
KERMADEC IS. (To N.Z.)
1:5 000 000
AUCKLAND
AND ENVIRONS
1:250 000
WELLINGTON
AND ENVIRONS
1:250 000
AUCKLAND IS.
1:2 500 000
(To N.Z.)
NORTH ISLAND
NORTHLAND
CENTRAL AUCKLAND
SOUTH AUCKLAND-BAY OF PLENTY
EAST COAST
HAWKE'S BAY
TARANAKI
WELLINGTON
T A S M A N
COOK STRAIT
Auckland
Wellington
Hamilton
Gisborne
Napier
Hastings
New Plymouth
Wanganui
Palmerston North
Rotorua
Taupo
HAURAKI GULF
BAY OF PLENTY
HAWKE BAY

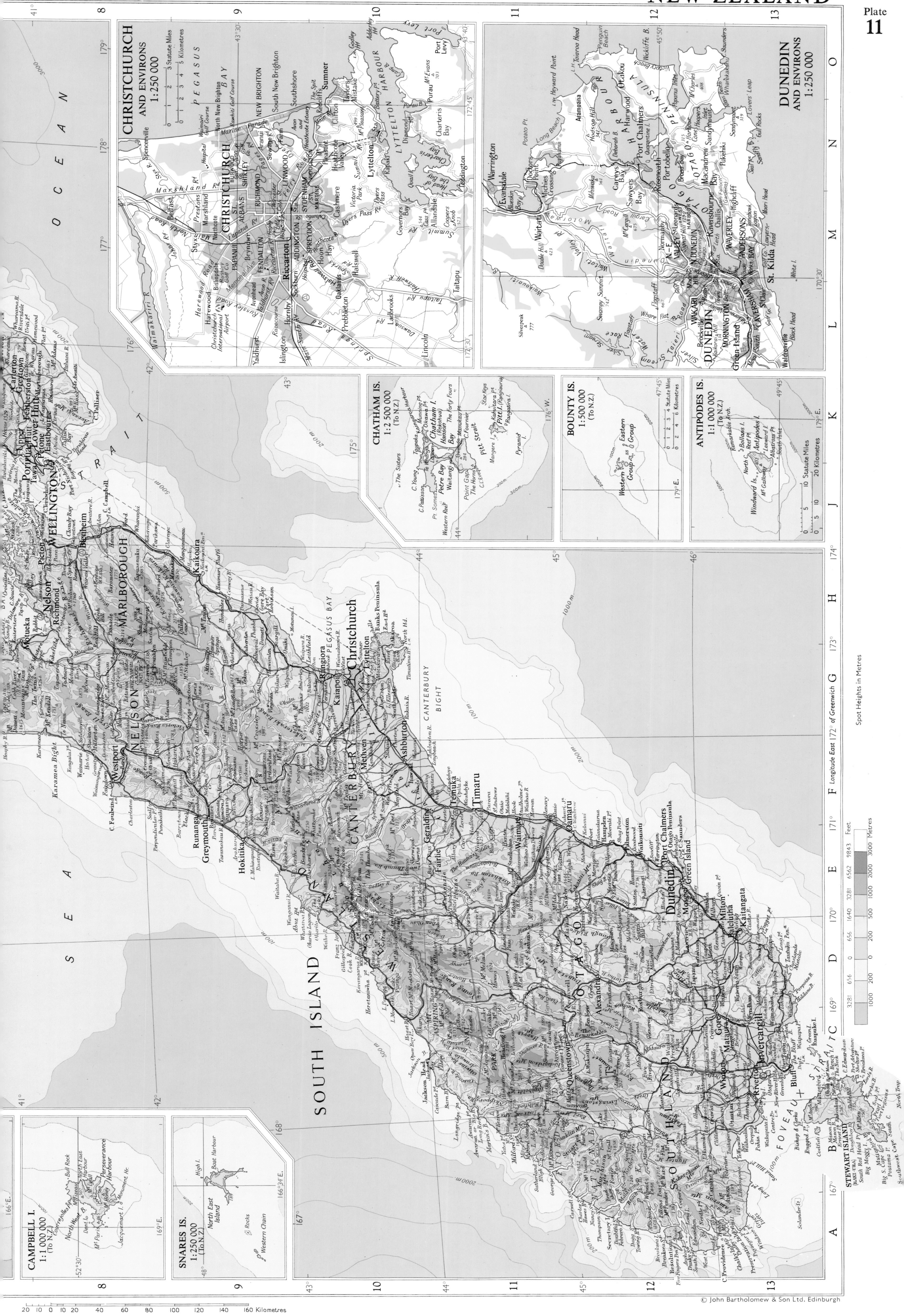
CHRISTCHURCH AND ENVIRONS 1:250 000
DUNEDIN AND ENVIRONS 1:250 000
CHATHAM IS. 1:2 500 000 (To N.Z.)
BOUNTY IS. 1:500 000 (To N.Z.)
ANTIPODES IS. 1:1 000 000 (To N.Z.)
CAMPBELL I. 1:1 000 000 (To N.Z.)
SNARES IS. 1:250 000 (To N.Z.)
SOUTH ISLAND
STEWART ISLAND
Spot Heights in Metres
Longitude East 172° of Greenwich
20 10 0 10 20 40 60 80 100 120 140 160 Kilometres

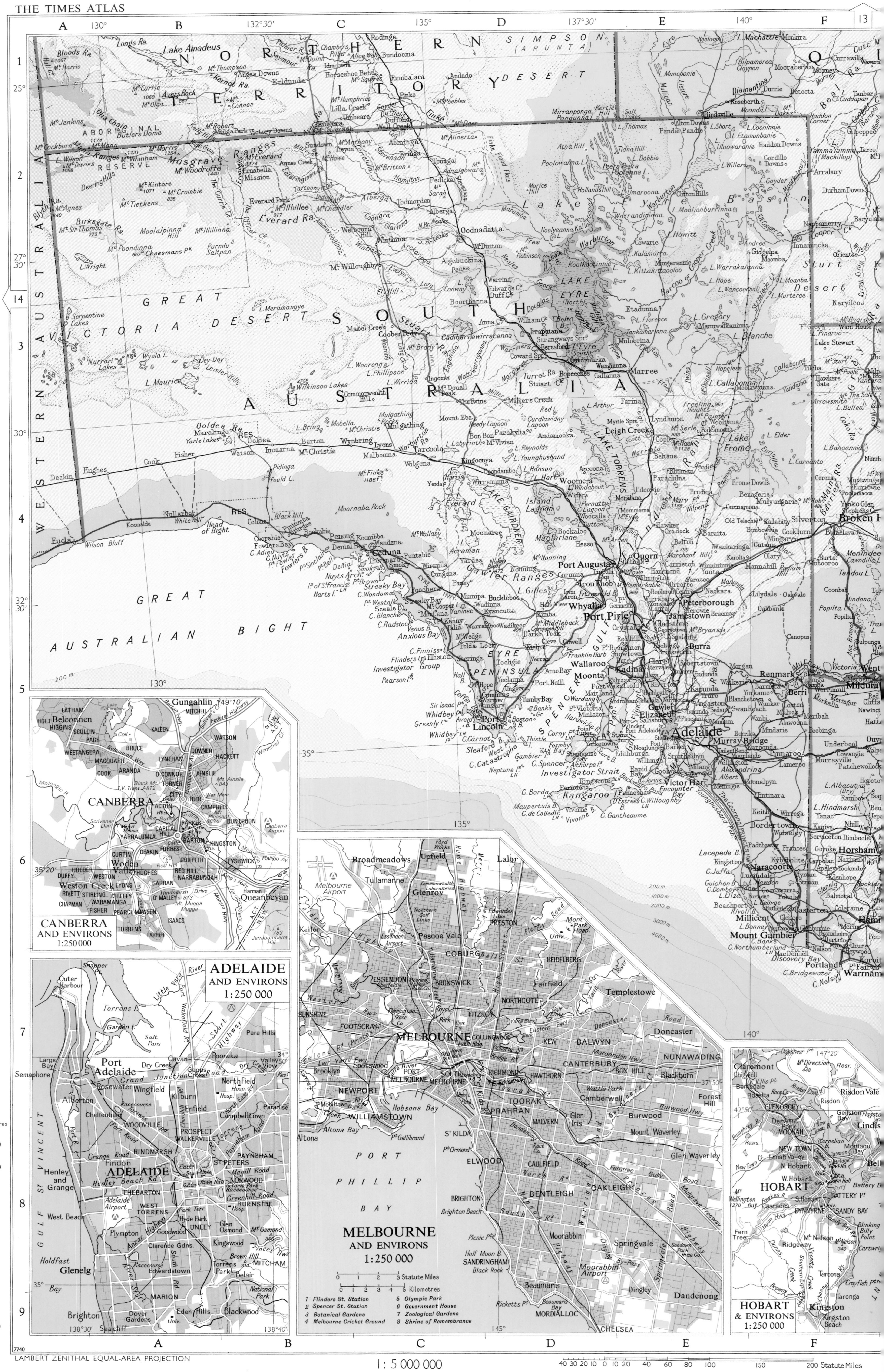
NORTHERN TERRITORY
SIMPSON (ARUNTA) DESERT
SOUTH AUSTRALIA
WESTERN AUSTRALIA
GREAT VICTORIA DESERT
GREAT AUSTRALIAN BIGHT
EYRE PENINSULA
Lake Eyre
Lake Torrens
Lake Gairdner
Lake Frome
Gawler Ranges
Musgrave Ranges
Spencer Gulf
Gulf St Vincent
Kangaroo I.
Investigator Strait
Sturt Desert
Oodnadatta
Coober Pedy
Port Augusta
Whyalla
Port Pirie
Port Lincoln
Ceduna
Adelaide
Murray Bridge
Renmark
Mildura
Broken Hill
Mount Gambier
Naracoorte
Horsham
Portland
Peterborough
Leigh Creek
Marree
Tarcoola
Kadina
Moonta
Wallaroo
Victor Har.
Birdsville
CANBERRA AND ENVIRONS 1:250 000
CANBERRA
Queanbeyan
ADELAIDE AND ENVIRONS 1:250 000
ADELAIDE
Port Adelaide
Glenelg
MELBOURNE AND ENVIRONS 1:250 000
MELBOURNE
PORT PHILLIP BAY
1 Flinders St. Station
2 Spencer St. Station
3 Botanical Gardens
4 Melbourne Cricket Ground
5 Olympic Park
6 Government House
7 Zoological Gardens
8 Shrine of Remembrance
HOBART & ENVIRONS 1:250 000
HOBART
Kingston

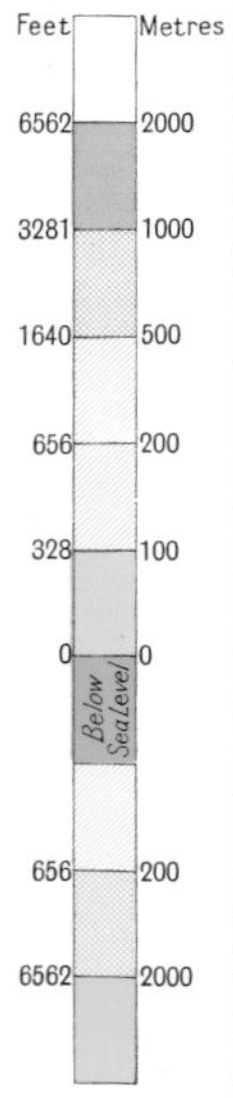
Feet
Metres
6562
2000
3281
1000
1640
500
656
200
328
100
0
Below Sea Level
656
200
6562
2000

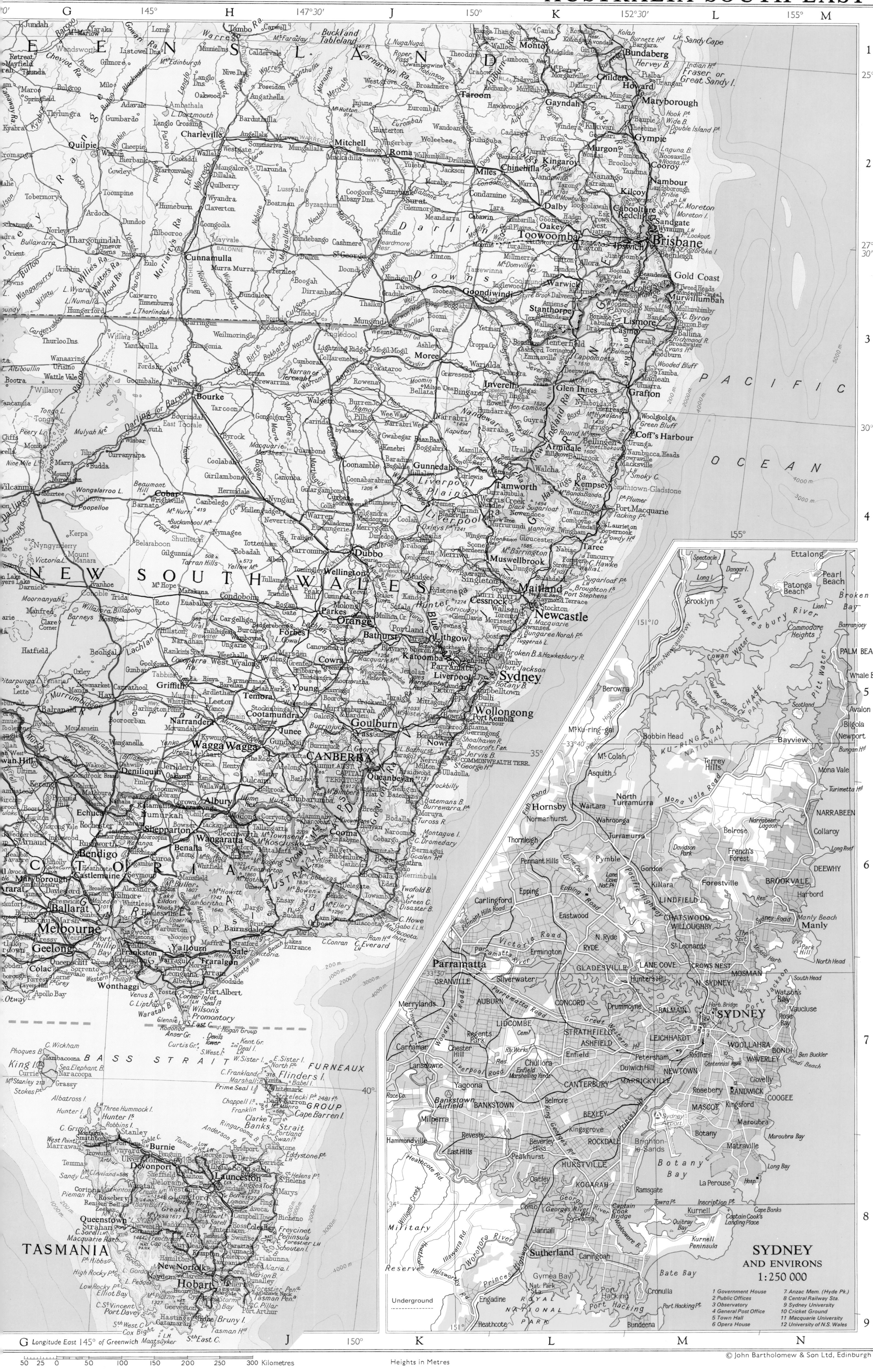
QUEENSLAND
NEW SOUTH WALES
VICTORIA
TASMANIA
BASS STRAIT
PACIFIC OCEAN
Brisbane
Sydney
Melbourne
CANBERRA
Hobart
Newcastle
Wollongong
Gold Coast
Launceston
Geelong
Toowoomba
Bundaberg
Maryborough
Rockhampton
Grafton
Coff's Harbour
Port Macquarie
Tamworth
Armidale
Dubbo
Orange
Bathurst
Goulburn
Wagga Wagga
Albury
Bendigo
Ballarat
Charleville
Bourke
Cunnamulla
Roma
Dalby
Lismore
Maitland
Cessnock
Katoomba
Lithgow
Parramatta
Liverpool
Griffith
Narrandera
Deniliquin
Shepparton
Wangaratta
Sale
Bairnsdale
Cooma
Devonport
Burnie
Queenstown
New Norfolk
FURNEAUX GROUP
Flinders I.
King I.
Darling Downs
Liverpool Plains
SYDNEY AND ENVIRONS 1:250 000
1 Government House
2 Public Offices
3 Observatory
4 General Post Office
5 Town Hall
6 Opera House
7 Anzac Mem. (Hyde Pk.)
8 Central Railway Sta.
9 Sydney University
10 Cricket Ground
11 Macquarie University
12 University of N.S. Wales
Underground
Botany Bay
Port Jackson
Manly
Hornsby
Bankstown
Sutherland
Longitude East 145° of Greenwich
Kilometres
Heights in Metres

© John Bartholomew & Son Ltd, Edinburgh

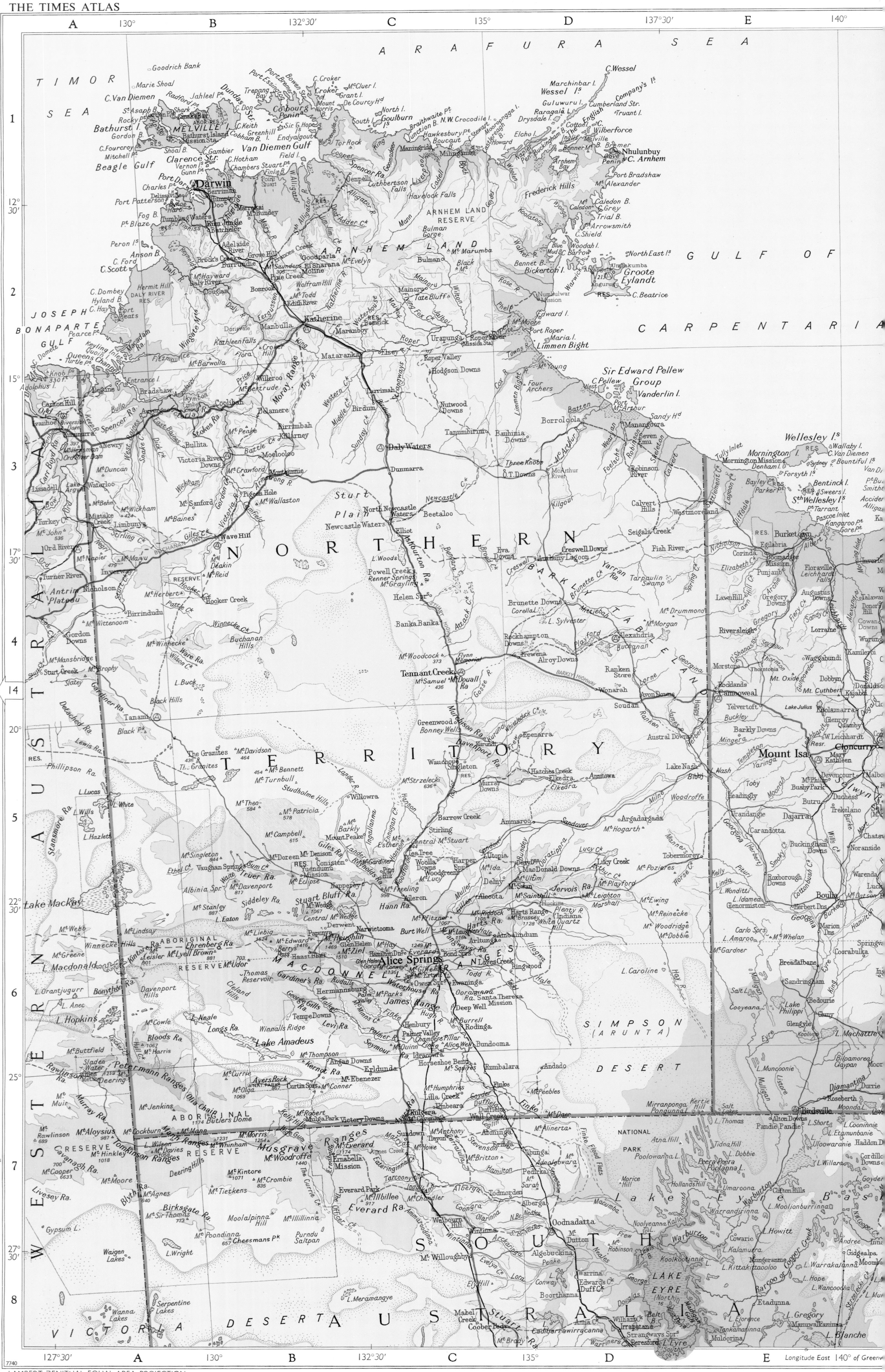
A R A F U R A   S E A
T I M O R   S E A
J O S E P H   B O N A P A R T E   G U L F
G U L F   O F   C A R P E N T A R I A
N O R T H E R N   T E R R I T O R Y
W E S T E R N   A U S T R A L I A
S O U T H   A U S T R A L I A
S I M P S O N (A R U N T A) D E S E R T
V I C T O R I A   D E S E R T
ARNHEM LAND
ARNHEM LAND RESERVE
BARKLY TABLELAND
Sturt Plain
M A C D O N N E L L   R A N G E S
ABORIGINAL RESERVE
Lake Eyre Basin
LAKE EYRE (North)
Darwin
Katherine
Daly Waters
Tennant Creek
Alice Springs
Oodnadatta
Mount Isa
Cloncurry
Birdsville
Nhulunbuy
Groote Eylandt
MELVILLE I.
Bathurst I.
Wessel Is
Sir Edward Pellew Group
Wellesley Is
Mornington I.
Lake Amadeus
Lake Mackay
Musgrave Ranges
Everard Ra.
Petermann Ranges
Ayers Rock
Feet
Metres
3281
1000
1640
500
656
200
328
100
0
0
Below Sea level
656
200
6562
2000
130°
132°30'
135°
137°30'
140°
127°30'
12° 30'
15°
17° 30'
20°
22° 30'
25°
27° 30'
Longitude East 140° of Greenwich

BRISBANE
1:250 000
Statute Miles
Kilometres
CORAL SEA
GREAT BARRIER REEF
GREAT DIVIDING RANGE
QUEENSLAND
NEW SOUTH WALES
CAPE YORK PENINSULA
Torres Strait
Gulf of Carpentaria
Cooktown
Cairns
Innisfail
Townsville
Bowen
Mackay
Rockhampton
Gladstone
Bundaberg
Maryborough
Gympie
Toowoomba
Ipswich
Brisbane
Gold Coast
Charters Towers
Hughenden
Longreach
Barcaldine
Emerald
Winton
Charleville
Roma
Cunnamulla
Goondiwindi
Warwick
Dalby
Tropic of Capricorn
Capricorn Channel
Heights in Metres
Kilometres

© John Bartholomew & Son Ltd, Edinburgh

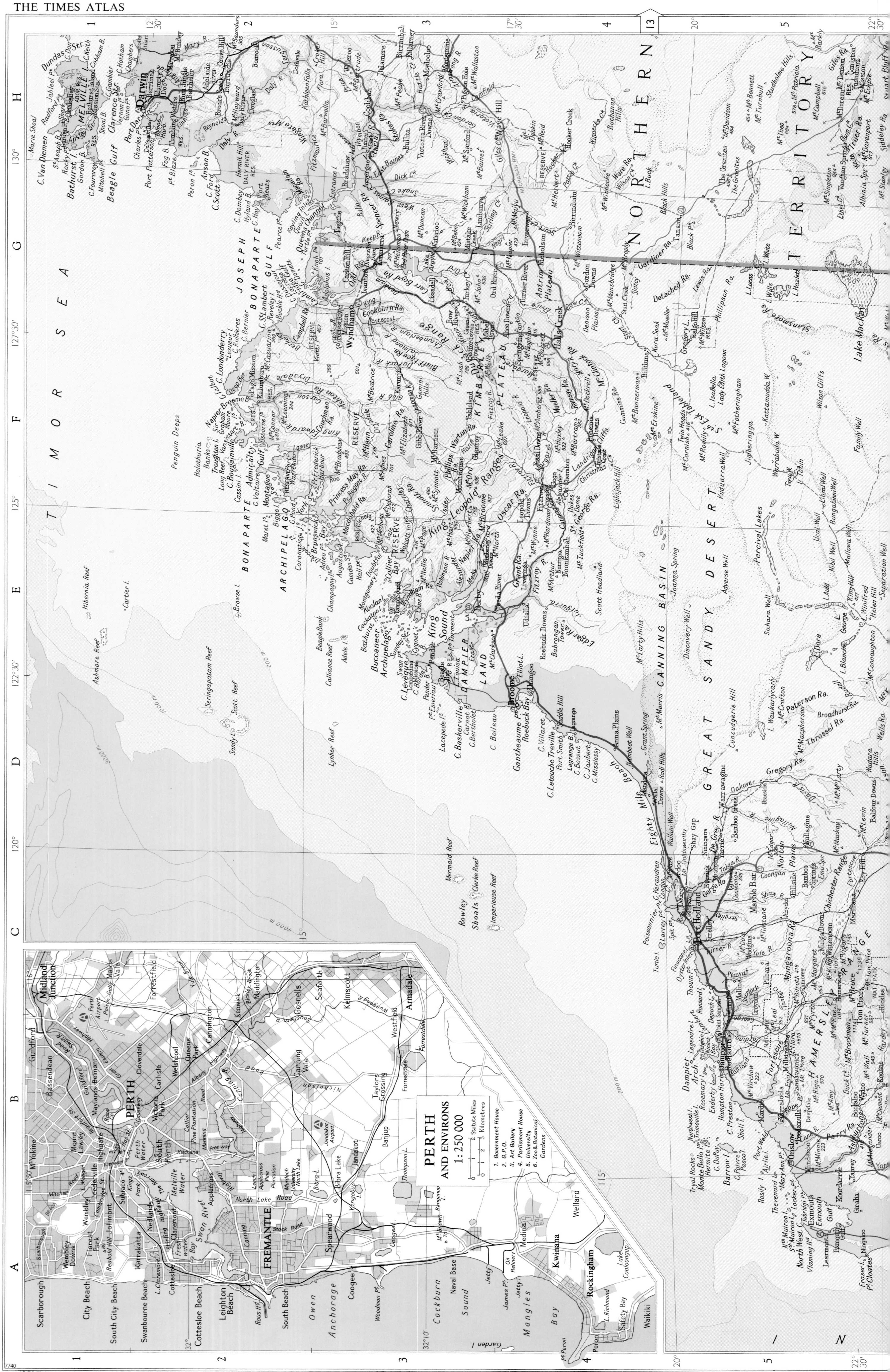
TIMOR SEA
BONAPARTE ARCHIPELAGO
JOSEPH BONAPARTE GULF
KIMBERLEY PLATEAU
KING LEOPOLD RANGES
DAMPIER LAND
King Sound
CANNING BASIN
GREAT SANDY DESERT
Eighty Mile Beach
HAMERSLEY RANGE
NORTHERN TERRITORY
Darwin
Wyndham
Derby
Broome
Port Hedland
Onslow
Exmouth
Lake Mackay
PERTH
AND ENVIRONS
1: 250 000
Statute Miles
Kilometres
1. Government House
2. G.P.O.
3. Art Gallery
4. Parliament House
5. University
6. Zoo & Botanical Gardens
PERTH
FREMANTLE
Midland Junction
Guildford
Armadale
Kwinana
Rockingham
Cockburn Sound
Mangles Bay

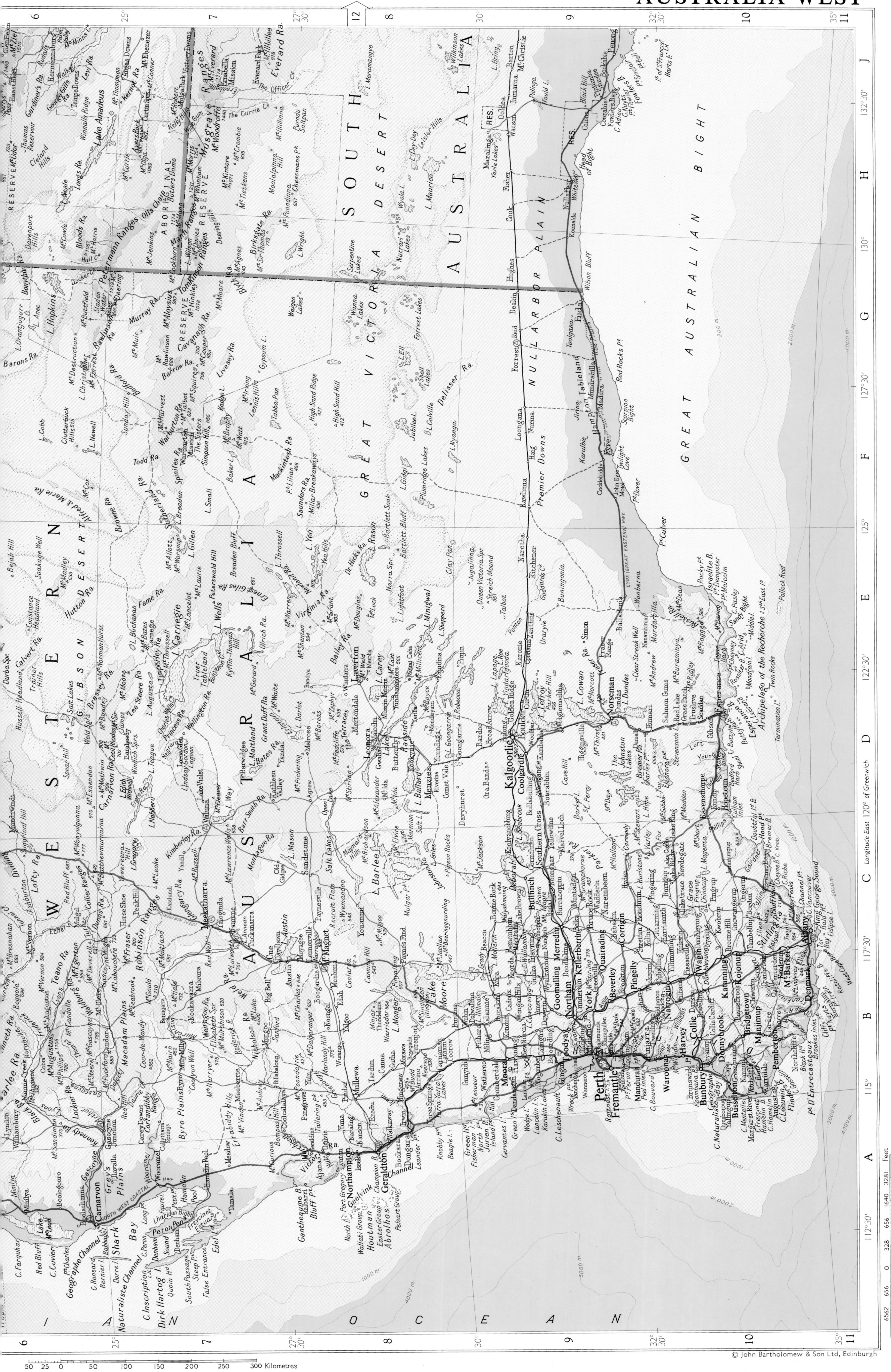
WESTERN AUSTRALIA
SOUTH AUSTRALIA
GREAT VICTORIA DESERT
GIBSON DESERT
NULLARBOR PLAIN
GREAT AUSTRALIAN BIGHT
INDIAN OCEAN
Perth
Fremantle
Kalgoorlie
Coolgardie
Geraldton
Carnarvon
Albany
Esperance
Norseman
Bunbury
Meekatharra
Wiluna
Menzies
Leonora
Laverton
Northam
York
Southern Cross
Shark Bay
Lake Moore
Lake Barlee
Lake Carnegie
Lake Amadeus
Petermann Ranges
Musgrave Ranges
Robinson Ranges
Archipelago of the Recherche
Houtman Abrolhos
Longitude East 120° of Greenwich
50 25 0 50 100 150 200 250 300 Kilometres
Feet 6562 656 0 328 656 1640 3281
Metres 2000 200 0 100 200 500 1000

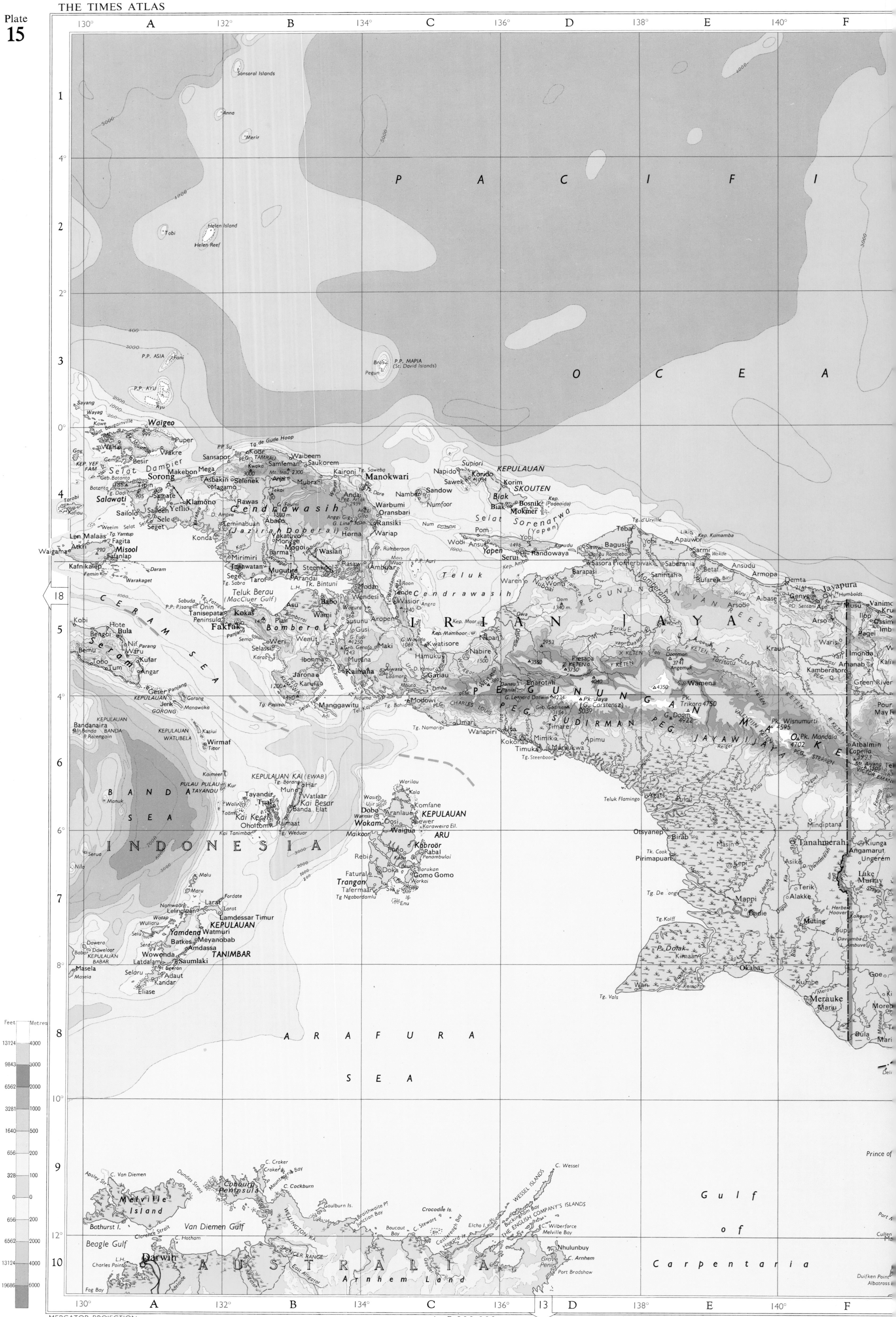
P A C I F I C
O C E A N
Sonsorol Islands
Anna
Merir
Tobi
Helen Island
Helen Reef
P.P. ASIA
P.P. AYU
P.P. MAPIA
(St. David Islands)
Waigeo
Sorong
Salawati
Misool
Selat Dampier
Manokwari
Biak
KEPULAUAN
SKOUTEN
Yapen
Selat Sorenarwa
Cendrawasih
Teluk Cendrawasih
Teluk Berau
(MacCluer Gulf)
Fakfak
Kaimana
Bomberai
CERAM SEA
Seram
Bula
Ambon
Nabire
Enarotali
Pk. Jaya
(G. Carstensz)
5039
PEGUNUNGAN MAOKE
PEG. SUDIRMAN
PEG. JAYAWIJAYA
Pk. Trikora 4750
Wamena
Pk. Mandala
4702
IRIAN JAYA
PEGUNUNGAN VAN REES
Mamberamo
Jayapura
Sarmi
Teluk Flamingo
Tanahmerah
Lake Murray
Mappi
P. Dolak
Okaba
Merauke
Mindiptana
BANDA SEA
INDONESIA
KEPULAUAN KAI (EWAB)
Kai Besar
Tual
KEPULAUAN ARU
Dobo
Wokam
Trangan
KEPULAUAN TANIMBAR
Yamdena
Saumlaki
Selaru
A R A F U R A
S E A
Melville Island
Bathurst I.
Van Diemen Gulf
Beagle Gulf
Darwin
Cobourg Peninsula
Arnhem Land
A U S T R A L I A
WESSEL ISLANDS
THE ENGLISH COMPANY'S ISLANDS
Nhulunbuy
C. Arnhem
Gulf
of
Carpentaria
Prince of
Feet
Metres
13124
4000
9843
3000
6562
2000
3281
1000
1640
500
656
200
328
100
0
0
656
200
6562
2000
13124
4000
19686
6000
40 30 20 10 0 10 20 40 60 80 100 150 200 Statute Miles

MERCATOR PROJECTION

1: 5 000 000

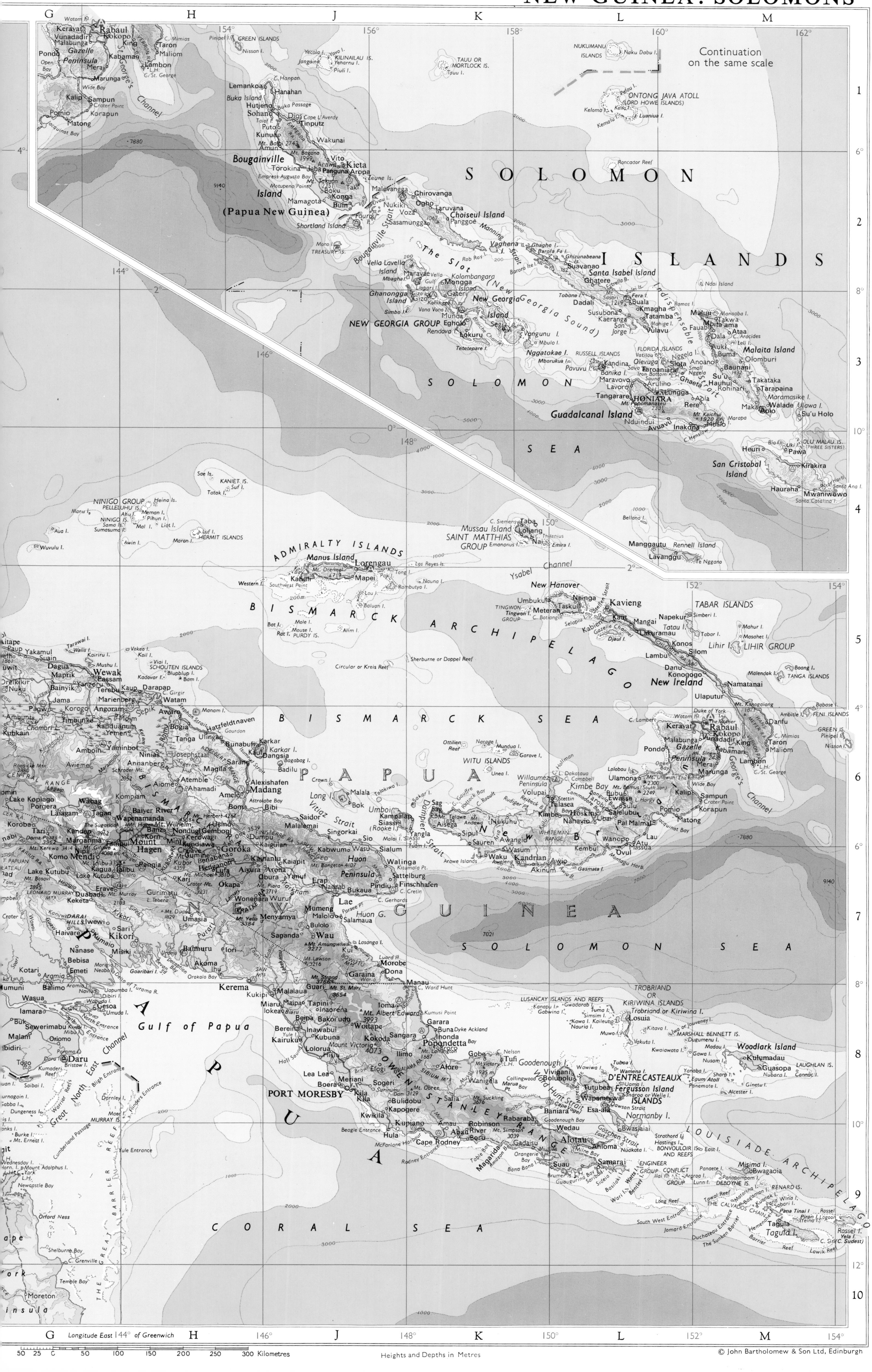
Continuation
on the same scale
SOLOMON ISLANDS
SOLOMON SEA
Bougainville
Island
(Papua New Guinea)
Choiseul Island
Santa Isabel Island
NEW GEORGIA GROUP
New Georgia
Malaita Island
Guadalcanal Island
HONIARA
San Cristobal
Island
ONTONG JAVA ATOLL
(LORD HOWE ISLANDS)
Rennell Island
The Slot (New Georgia Sound)
Indispensable Strait
Bougainville Strait
ADMIRALTY ISLANDS
Manus Island
Lorengau
SAINT MATTHIAS GROUP
BISMARCK ARCHIPELAGO
BISMARCK SEA
New Hanover
Kavieng
New Ireland
TABAR ISLANDS
LIHIR GROUP
New Britain
Rabaul
Kokopo
Gazelle Peninsula
St. George's Channel
PAPUA NEW GUINEA
Wewak
Madang
Mount Hagen
Goroka
Lae
Huon Peninsula
Wau
Gulf of Papua
PORT MORESBY
OWEN STANLEY RANGE
Daru
Popondetta
Alotau
Samarai
D'ENTRECASTEAUX ISLANDS
Goodenough I.
Fergusson Island
Normanby I.
TROBRIAND OR KIRIWINA ISLANDS
Woodlark Island
LOUISIADE ARCHIPELAGO
Misima I.
Tagula
Rossel I.
CORAL SEA
GREAT BARRIER REEF
Longitude East 144° of Greenwich
50 25 0 50 100 150 200 250 300 Kilometres
Heights and Depths in Metres

Plate
16

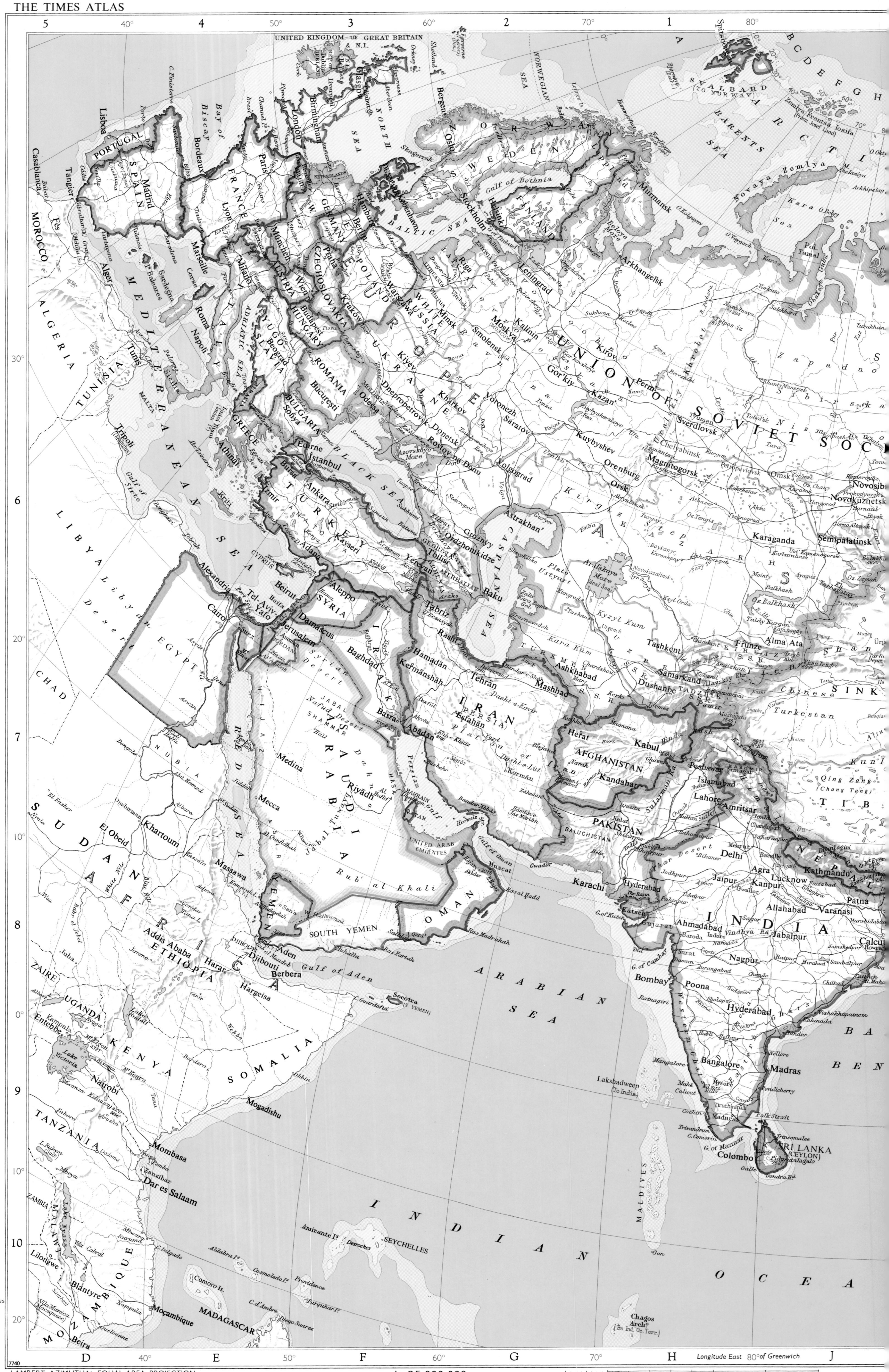

Feet | Metres
656 | 200
6562 | 2000

7740

LAMBERT AZIMUTHAL EQUAL-AREA PROJECTION

1: 25 000 000

200 100 50 0 50 100 200 300 400 500 750 1000 Statute Miles

NORTH PACIFIC OCEAN
BERING SEA
SEA OF OKHOTSK
SEA OF JAPAN
YELLOW SEA
EAST CHINA SEA
SOUTH CHINA SEA
SULU SEA
CELEBES SEA
BANDA SEA
JAVA SEA
ARAFURA SEA
CORAL SEA
East Siberian Sea
Laptev Sea
Bismarck Sea
Gulf of Carpentaria
Gulf of Thailand
Gulf of Tongking
Gulf of Papua
Luzon Strait
Bashi Chan.
Tropic of Cancer
Equator
Aleutian Is
Kuril'skiye Ostrova
Kamchatka
SAKHALIN
Caroline Islands
(U.S.A. Trust Territory)
Marianas or Ladrones Is
(U.S.A. Trust Territory)
Guam
Marcus I.
Ogasawara gunto (Bonin Is)
Kazan Retto (Volcano Is)
Okinawa gunto
Sakishima-shoto
Tokara-retto
Daito
Yap
Palau Is
Truk
Admiralty Is
Chukotskiy Khr.
Khr. Cherskogo
Verkhoyanskiy Khrebet
Sredne Sibirskoye Ploskogor'ye
Yablonovyy Khr.
Da Hinggan Ling
Qin Ling
Nan Ling
Qilian Shan
Gobi
Ordos
ALASKA (USA)
Bering Str.
Severnaya Zemlya
Novosibirskiye Ostrova
Yakutsk
Magadan
Okhotsk
Khabarovsk
Vladivostok
Krasnoyarsk
Irkutsk
Ulan Ude
Chita
Ulaanbaatar
MONGOLIA
INNER MONGOLIA
MANCHURIA
Harbin
Changchun
Shenyang
Luda
Beijing (Peking)
Tianjin (Tientsin)
Shijiazhuang
Taiyuan
Jinan
Lanzhou
Xi'an (Sian)
Zhengzhou
Nanjing (Nanking)
Shanghai
Hefei
Wuhan
Hangzhou
Chengdu
Chongqing
Changsha
Nanchang
Fuzhou
Guiyang
Kunming
Nanning
Guangzhou (Canton)
Hong-Kong (U.K.)
CHINA
PEOPLES REPUBLIC
TAIWAN (FORMOSA)
T'ai-pei
T'ai-nan
NORTH KOREA
SOUTH KOREA
Seoul
Inchon
Pusan
JAPAN
Hokkaido
Sapporo
Honshu
Tokyo
Yokohama
Nagoya
Osaka
Kyoto
Hiroshima
Shikoku
Kyushu
Nagasaki
BURMA
Mandalay
Rangoon
Moulmein
THAILAND (SIAM)
Bangkok (Krung Thep)
Vientiane
LAOS
Hanoi
Haiphong
Hue
VIETNAM
CAMBODIA
Phnom Penh
Ho-Chi-Minh
INDO-CHINA
Andaman Is
Nicobar Islands
MALAYSIA
PENINSULAR MALAYSIA
Kuala Lumpur
Singapore
SUMATRA
Padang
Palembang
Jakarta
JAVA
Surabaya
Yogyakarta
BORNEO
Kalimantan
Kuching
SARAWAK
SABAH
Banjarmasin
SULAWESI (CELEBES)
Ujung Pandang (Makassar)
INDONESIA
Timor
Flores
Sumba
PHILIPPINES
Luzon
Manila
Quezon City
Mindanao
Davao
Mindoro
Palawan
Iloilo
Samar
Halmahera
Seram
Buru
IRIAN JAYA
New Guinea
PAPUA NEW GUINEA
Port Moresby
Darwin
Arnhem Land
AUSTRALIA
Townsville
Cape York Peninsula
Torres Str.
250 125 0 250 500 750 1000 1250 1500 Kilometres

© John Bartholomew & Son Ltd, Edinburgh

1: 15 000 000

100 80 60 40 20 0 50 100 200 300 400 500 600 Statute Miles

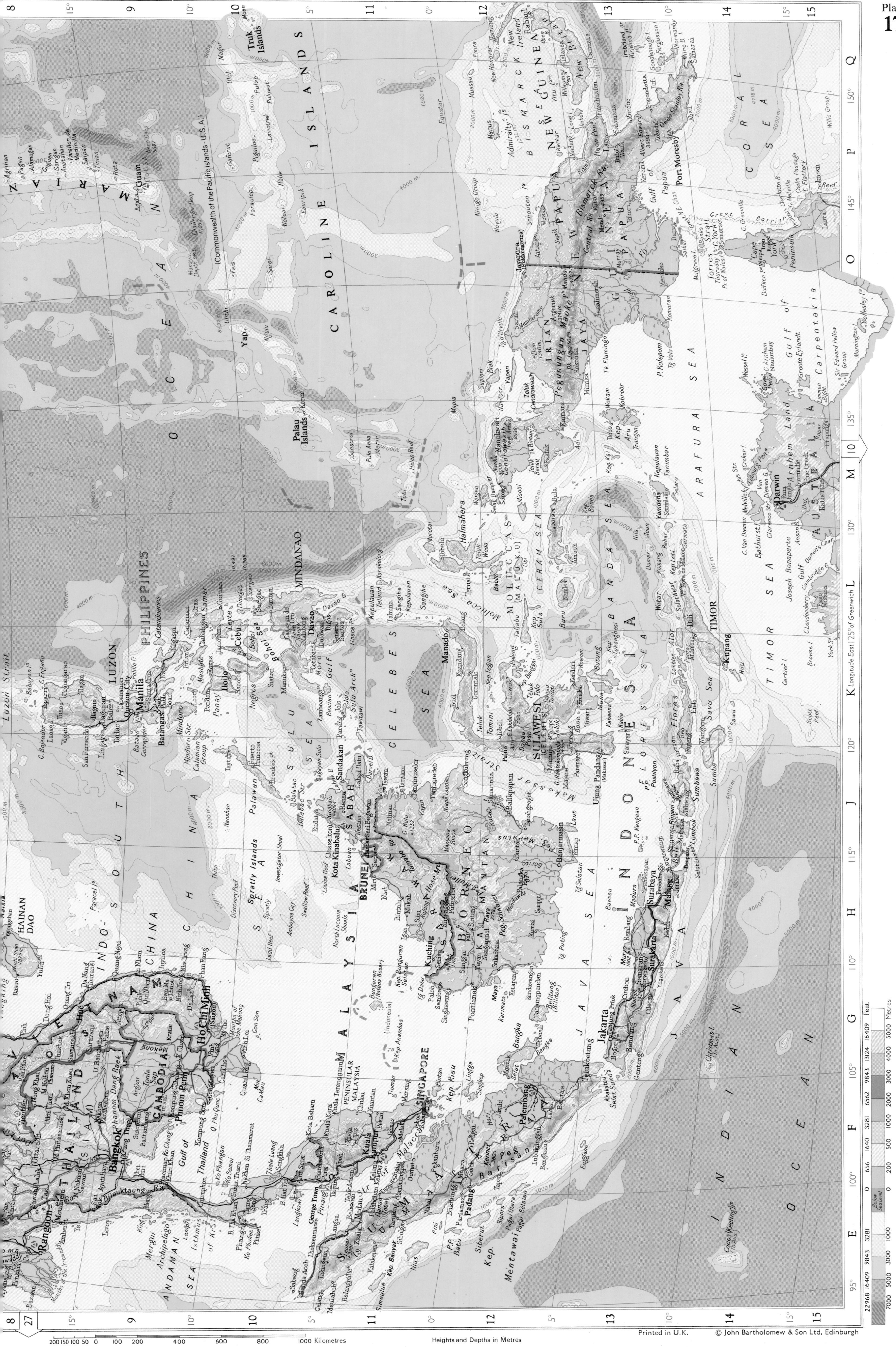
PHILIPPINES
LUZON
Manila
Quezon City
MINDANAO
Davao
CAROLINE ISLANDS
Palau Islands
Yap
Truk Islands
Guam
(Commonwealth of the Pacific Islands - U.S.A.)
MALAYSIA
SABAH
BRUNEI
SINGAPORE
PENINSULAR MALAYSIA
Kuala Lumpur
Kota Kinabalu
Kuching
Sandakan
BORNEO
KALIMANTAN
SARAWAK
INDONESIA
SULAWESI (CELEBES)
Jakarta
Surabaya
Ujung Pandang
Banjarmasin
Balikpapan
Manado
Padang
Palembang
Medan
JAVA
JAVA SEA
TIMOR
Kupang
TIMOR SEA
ARAFURA SEA
BANDA SEA
CERAM SEA
MOLUCCAS
CELEBES SEA
SULU SEA
SOUTH CHINA SEA
INDO-CHINA
VIETNAM
THAILAND
CAMBODIA
Bangkok
Phnom Penh
Ho Chi Minh
Rangoon
Gulf of Thailand
ANDAMAN SEA
HAINAN DAO
NEW GUINEA
PAPUA NEW GUINEA
IRIAN JAYA
Port Moresby
Jayapura
BISMARCK ARCHIPELAGO
New Britain
New Ireland
CORAL SEA
Gulf of Carpentaria
Darwin
AUSTRALIA
Arnhem Land
Torres Strait
INDIAN OCEAN
Christmas I.
Cocos (Keeling) Is
Equator
Longitude East 125° of Greenwich
Heights and Depths in Metres
Kilometres

Printed in U.K. © John Bartholomew & Son Ltd, Edinburgh

JAKARTA
1:300 000
Teluk Jakarta
Tanjung Priok
Grogol Hilir
Jatinegara
Kebayoran
Pasarminggu
Ragunan
Pasarrebo
ANDAMAN SEA
Gulf of Thailand
THAILAND (SIAM)
PENINSULAR MALAYSIA
KEDAH
PERAK
KELANTAN
TERENGGANU
PAHANG
SELANGOR
NEGERI SEMBILAN
MELAKA
JOHOR
SINGAPORE
George Town
Kuala Lumpur
Pelabohan Kelang
Kuala Terengganu
Kuantan
Johor Baharu
Strait of Malacca
Selat Mentawai
KEPULAUAN MENTAWAI
KEPULAUAN RIAU
KEPULAUAN LINGGA
ACEH
SUMATERA UTARA
SUMATERA BARAT
RIAU
JAMBI
SUMATERA SELATAN
BENGKULU
LAMPUNG
Medan
Padang
Palembang
Pekanbaru
Bengkulu
Bangka
Simeulue
Nias
Siberut
Enggano
PEGUNUNGAN BUKIT BARISAN
Selat Sunda
Christmas Island
SOUTH MALAYA
1: 2 500 000
Statute Miles
Kilometres
Feet
Metres

SINGAPORE
1:300 000
Statute Miles
Kilometres
Plantation
Jungle
JOHOR STRAIT
Johor Baharu
SINGAPORE
BRUNEI
BANDAR SERI BEGAWAN
SABAH
Kota Kinabalu
(Jesselton)
Sandakan
SARAWAK
Kuching
Sibu
Miri
Tawau
SULU SEA
CELEBES SEA
KALIMANTAN TIMUR
KALIMANTAN BARAT
KALIMANTAN TENGAH
KALIMANTAN SELATAN
BORNEO
Pontianak
Samarinda
Balikpapan
Banjarmasin
Palangkaraya
Tarakan
Belitung
(Billiton)
Selat Karimata
Makassar Strait
SULAWESI
(CELEBES)
Ujung Pandang
(Makassar)
Parepare
JAVA SEA
INDONESIA
MALAYSIA
Bandung
Cirebon
Semarang
Surakarta
(Solo)
Yogyakarta
Surabaya
Malang
Madura
BALI
Denpasar
Lombok
Mataram
SUMBAWA
SUMBA
NUSA TENGGARA
BALI SEA
JAWA (JAVA)
Longitude East 108° of Greenwich
Heights and Depths in Metres
300 Kilometres

SABAH
MINDANAO
SULU ARCHIPELAGO
TAWITAWI GROUP
C E L E B E S
S E A
MINAHASSA PENINSULA
Manado
KEPULAUAN SANGIHE
KEPULAUAN TALAUD
HALMAHERA
(JAILOLO GILOLO)
Ternate
Teluk Tomini
Gorontalo
Equator
Palu
Poso
SULAWESI
(CELEBES)
KEPULAUAN BANGGAI
KEPULAUAN SULA
Mangole
KEPULAUAN OBI
M O L U C C A S E A
Halmahera Sea
BURU
SERAM
(CERAM)
Ambon
(Amboina)
Kendari
I N D O N E S I A
Ujung Pandang
(Makassar)
Watampone
Butung
Baubau
B A N D A S E A
F L O R E S S E A
FLORES
Wetar
Dili
TIMOR
Kupang
Roti
SUMBA
Waingapu
SUMBAWA
Ende
N U S A T E N G G A R A
S A V U S E A
T I M O R S E A
Olongapo
Equatorial Scale 1: 5 000 000
Longitude East 126° of Greenwich

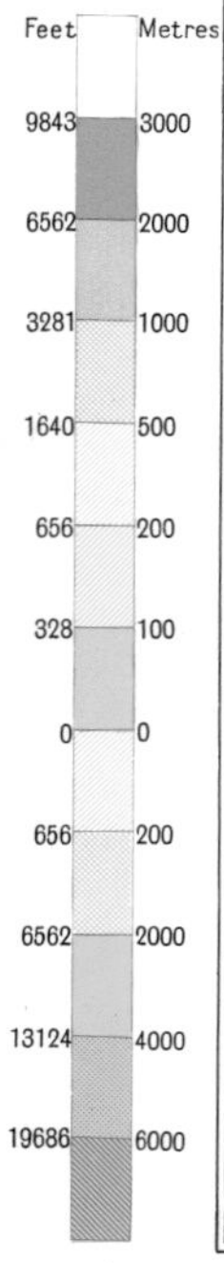
Feet Metres
9843 3000
6562 2000
3281 1000
1640 500
656 200
328 100
0 0
656 200
6562 2000
13124 4000
19686 6000

Equatorial Scale 1: 5 000 000

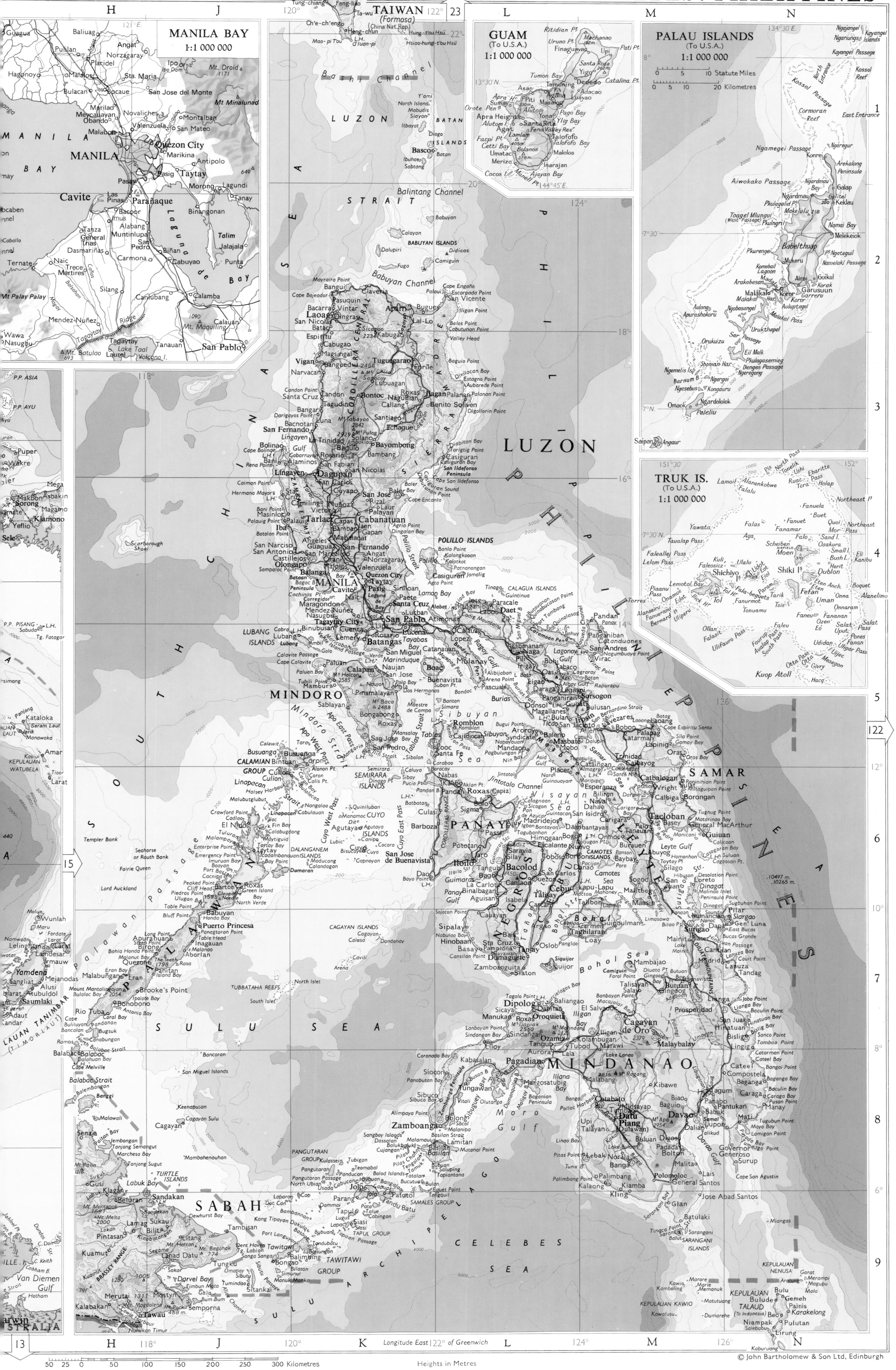
MANILA BAY
1:1 000 000
GUAM
(To U.S.A.)
1:1 000 000
PALAU ISLANDS
(To U.S.A.)
1:1 000 000
TRUK IS.
(To U.S.A.)
1:1 000 000
TAIWAN
(Formosa)
LUZON
MANILA
Quezon City
MINDORO
PANAY
SAMAR
LEYTE
NEGROS
CEBU
MINDANAO
SABAH
SOUTH CHINA SEA
LUZON STRAIT
SULU SEA
CELEBES SEA
PHILIPPINE SEA
Sibuyan Sea
Visayan Sea
Bohol Sea
Moro Gulf
SULU ARCHIPELAGO
Palawan Passage
PALAWAN
Balintang Channel
Babuyan Channel
Bashi Channel
Longitude East 122° of Greenwich

50 25 0 50 100 150 200 250 300 Kilometres

Heights in Metres

TŌKYŌ
1:300 000
TŌKYŌ-WAN
KANAGAWA-KEN
SAITAMA-KEN
CHIBA-KEN
TŌKYŌ-TO
SOUTH KOREA
KOREA STRAIT
SEA OF JAPAN
Feet
Metres
CONIC PROJECTION
1: 2 600 000
80 Statute Miles

JAPAN

Continuation
on the same scale
HOKKAIDO
Sapporo
Asahikawa
Otaru
Hakodate
Muroran
Obihiro
Aomori
Hachinohe
Hirosaki
Akita
Morioka
Sendai
Yamagata
Niigata
Fukushima
Kōriyama
Utsunomiya
Mito
Hitachi
TŌKYŌ
Yokohama
Kawasaki
Chiba
Nagano
Matsumoto
Kanazawa
Toyama
Fukui
Gifu
Nagoya
Shizuoka
Hamamatsu
Toyohashi
Tsu
Sado-shima
Izu-shotō
Hachijō-jima
P A C I F I C   O C E A N
IWO JIMA
1:250 000
Statute Miles
Kilometres
OKINAWA
1:1 000 000
Miles
Kilometres
Naha
East 136° of Greenwich
Kilometres
Heights in Metres

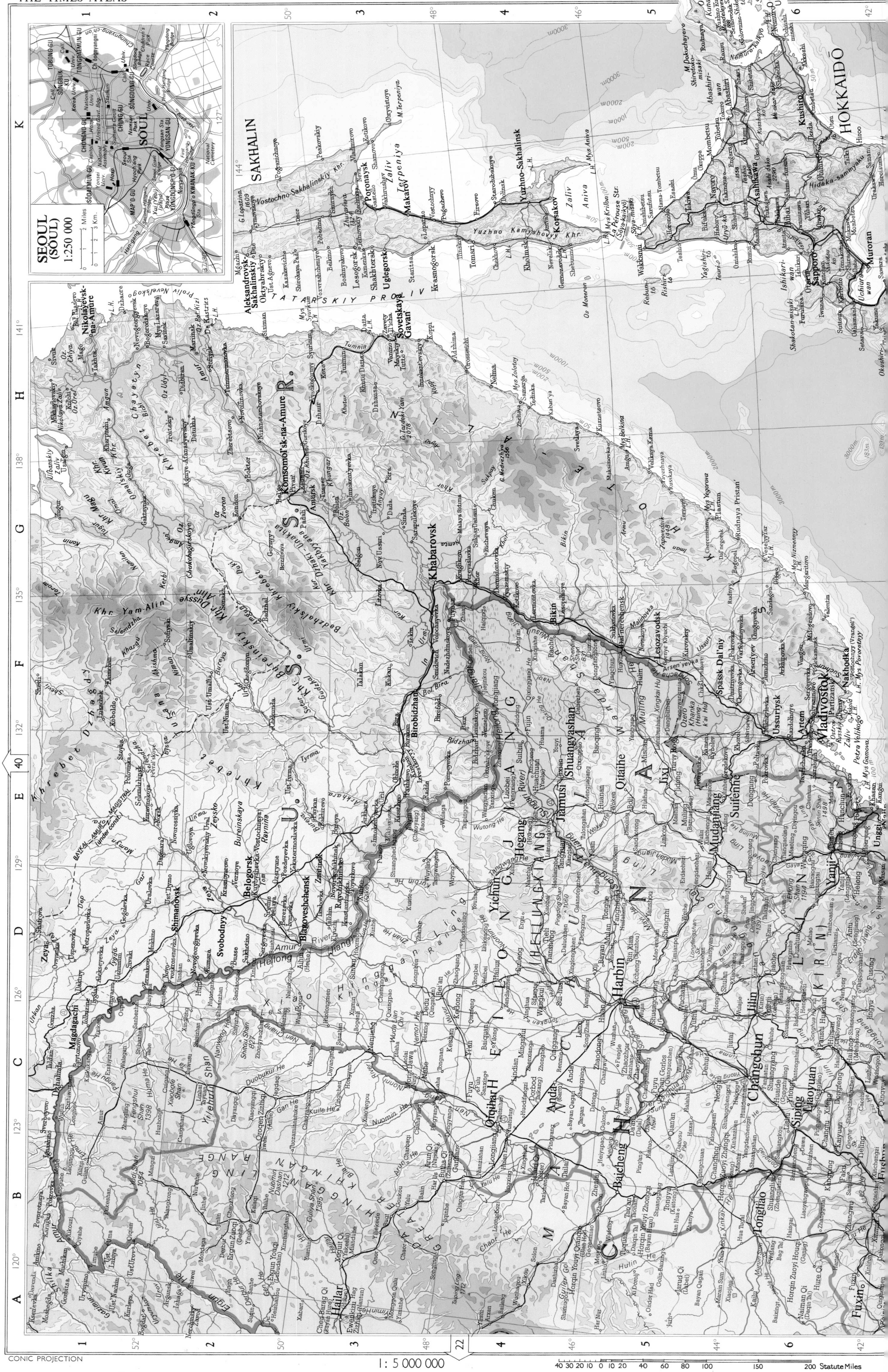
SEOUL (SŎUL)
1:250 000
SAKHALIN
HOKKAIDŌ
TATARSKIY PROLIV
Yuzhno-Sakhalinsk
Korsakov
Khabarovsk
Komsomol'sk-na-Amure
Nikolayevsk-na-Amure
Sovetskaya Gavan'
Vladivostok
Nakhodka
Ussuriysk
Birobidzhan
Blagoveshchensk
Svobodnyy
Belogorsk
Harbin
Qiqihar
Changchun
Jilin
Jiamusi
Mudanjiang
Hailar
Baicheng
Siping
Liaoyuan
Tongliao
Fuxin
Yanji
Sapporo
Asahikawa
Kushiro
Muroran
U. S. S. R.
HEILUNGKIANG
KIRIN
MANCHURIA
Amur
Khrebet Dzhagdy
Bureinskiy Khrebet
Sikhote-Alin'
Zaliv Terpeniya
Zaliv Aniva
La Pérouse Str.
Khanka (Hsing-k'ai Hu)
CONIC PROJECTION
1: 5 000 000
40 30 20 10 0 0 10 20 40 60 80 100 150 200 Statute Miles

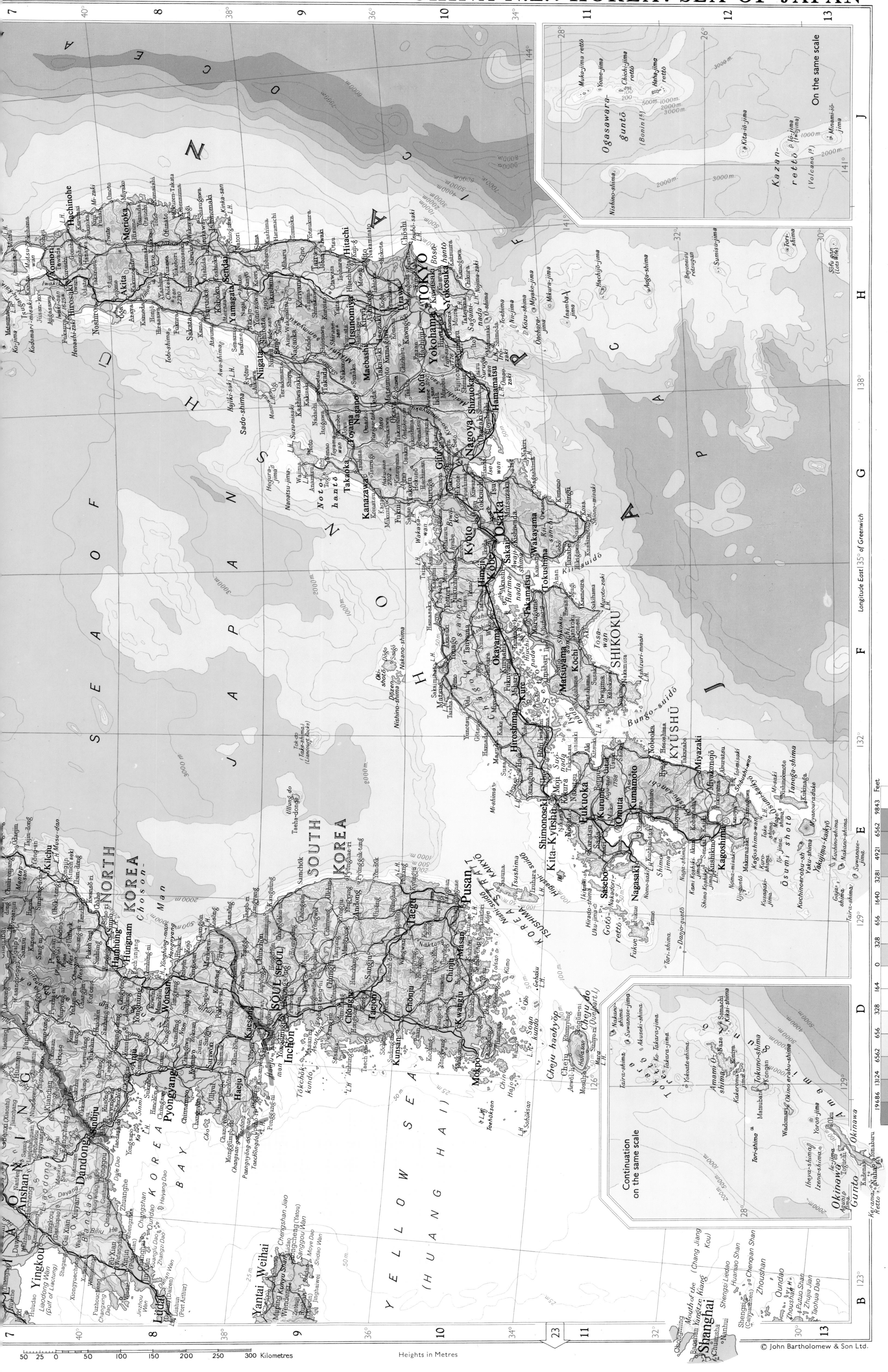
SEA OF JAPAN
NORTH KOREA
SOUTH KOREA
YELLOW SEA (HUANG HAI)
KOREA BAY
KOREA STRAIT
PACIFIC OCEAN
HONSHU
SHIKOKU
KYUSHU
TOKYO
Yokohama
Nagoya
Osaka
Kyoto
Kobe
Hiroshima
Fukuoka
Kagoshima
Sendai
Niigata
Kanazawa
SOUL (SEOUL)
Pusan
Taegu
Inchon
Pyongyang
Wonsan
Hamhung
Dandong
Anshan
Yingkou
Luda
Yantai
Weihai
Shanghai
Okinawa
Continuation on the same scale
On the same scale
Ogasawara-gunto (Bonin Is.)
Kazan-retto (Volcano Is.)
Longitude East 135° of Greenwich
Heights in Metres
Kilometres
50 25 0 50 100 150 200 250 300
Metres 3000 2000 1500 1000 500 200 100 50 0 50 100 200 2000 4000 6000
Feet 9843 6562 4921 3281 1640 656 328 164 0 164 328 656 6562 13124 19686

© John Bartholomew & Son Ltd.

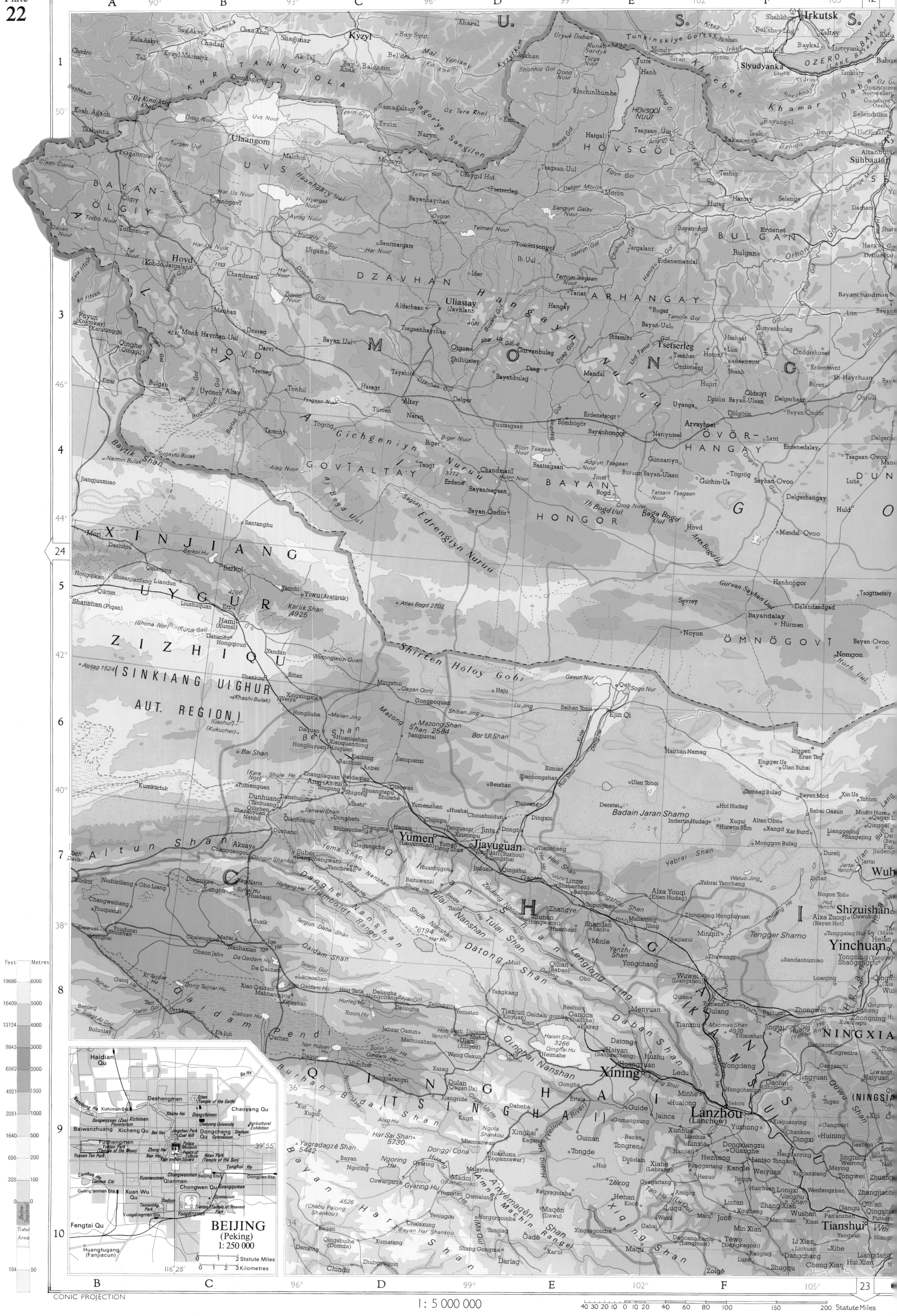
U. S. S. R.
Irkutsk
Kyzyl
KHR. TANNU OLA
Uvs Nuur
Ulaangom
Hövsgöl Nuur
HÖVSGÖL
UVS
BAYAN-ÖLGIY
Hovd
DZAVHAN
Uliastay (Javhlant)
ARHANGAY
Tsetserleg
HOVD
M O N G O L I A
Altay
GOVĬ-ALTAY
BAYAN-HONGOR
ÖVÖR-HANGAY
BULGAN
Erdenet
Sühbaatar
ÖMNÖGOVĬ
Dalandzadgad
Gurvan Sayhan Uul
Hangayn Nuruu
XINJIANG UYGUR ZIZHIQU (SINKIANG UIGHUR AUT. REGION)
Hami (Kumul)
Barkol
Shanshan (Piqan)
Bei Shan
Shirten Holoy Gobi
Ejin Qi
Badain Jaran Shamo
Altun Shan
Yumen (Laojunmiao)
Jiayuguan
Dunhuang
Qaidam Pendi
Qilian Shan
QINGHAI (TSINGHAI)
Xining
Qinghai Hu
Lanzhou (Lanchow)
GANSU (KANSU)
NINGXIA
Yinchuan
Shizuishan
Tengger Shamo
Wuwei (Liangzhou)
Tianshui
Bayan Har Shan
A'nyêmaqên Shan
HAIDIAN QU
Deshengmen
Chaoyang Qu
Xicheng Qu
Dongcheng Qu
Fuchengmen
Baiwanzhuang
Chongwen Qu
Xuan Wu Qu
Fengtai Qu
Huangtugang (Fanjiacun)
BEIJING
(Peking)
1: 250 000
Statute Miles
Kilometres
Feet
Metres
19686 6000
16409 5000
13124 4000
9843 3000
6562 2000
4921 1500
3281 1000
1640 500
656 200
328 100
0 0
Below Sea Level
Tidal Area
164 50
CONIC PROJECTION
1: 5 000 000
Statute Miles

42
24
23

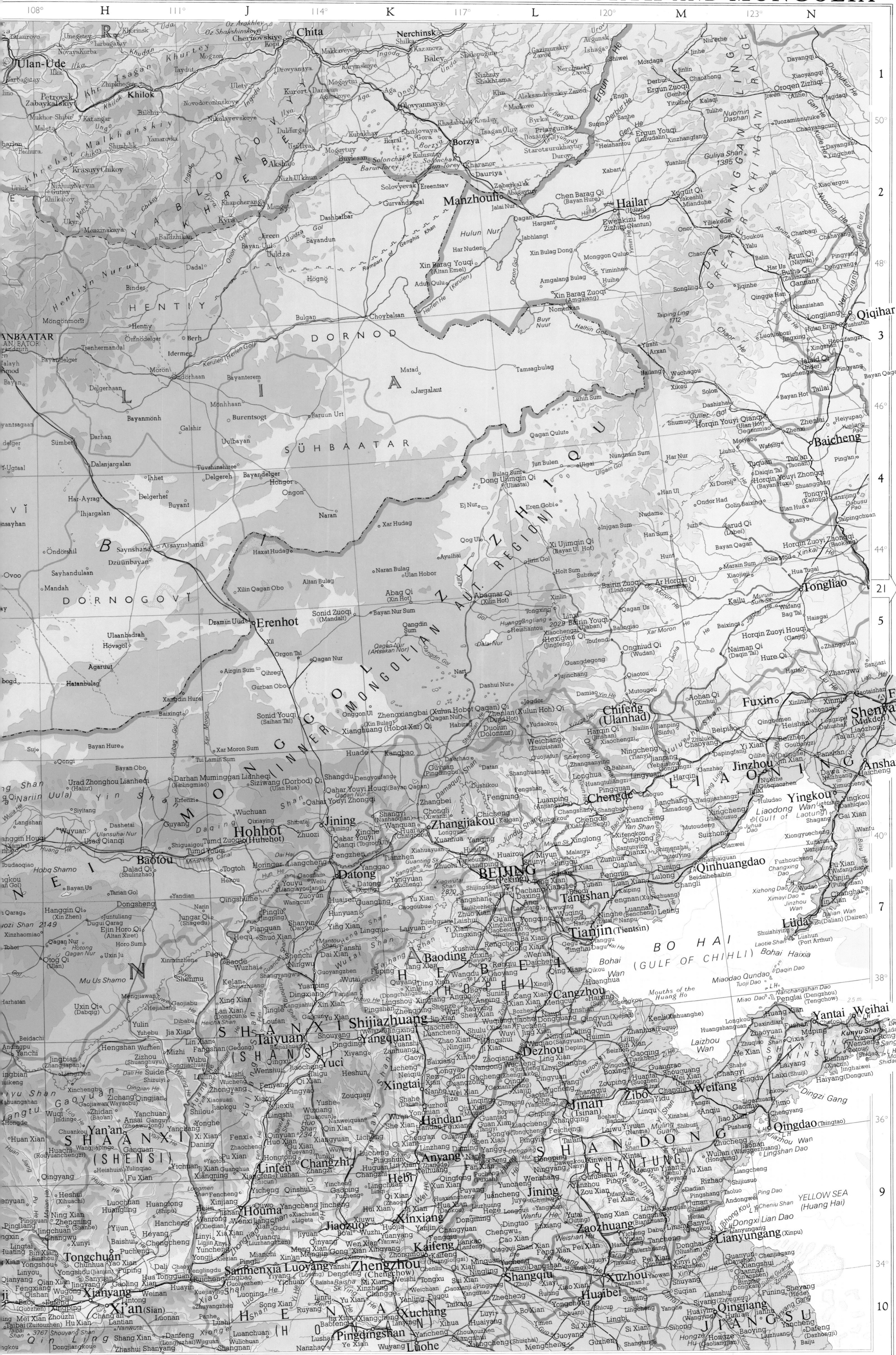

Heights in Metres
50 25 0 50 100 150 200 250 300

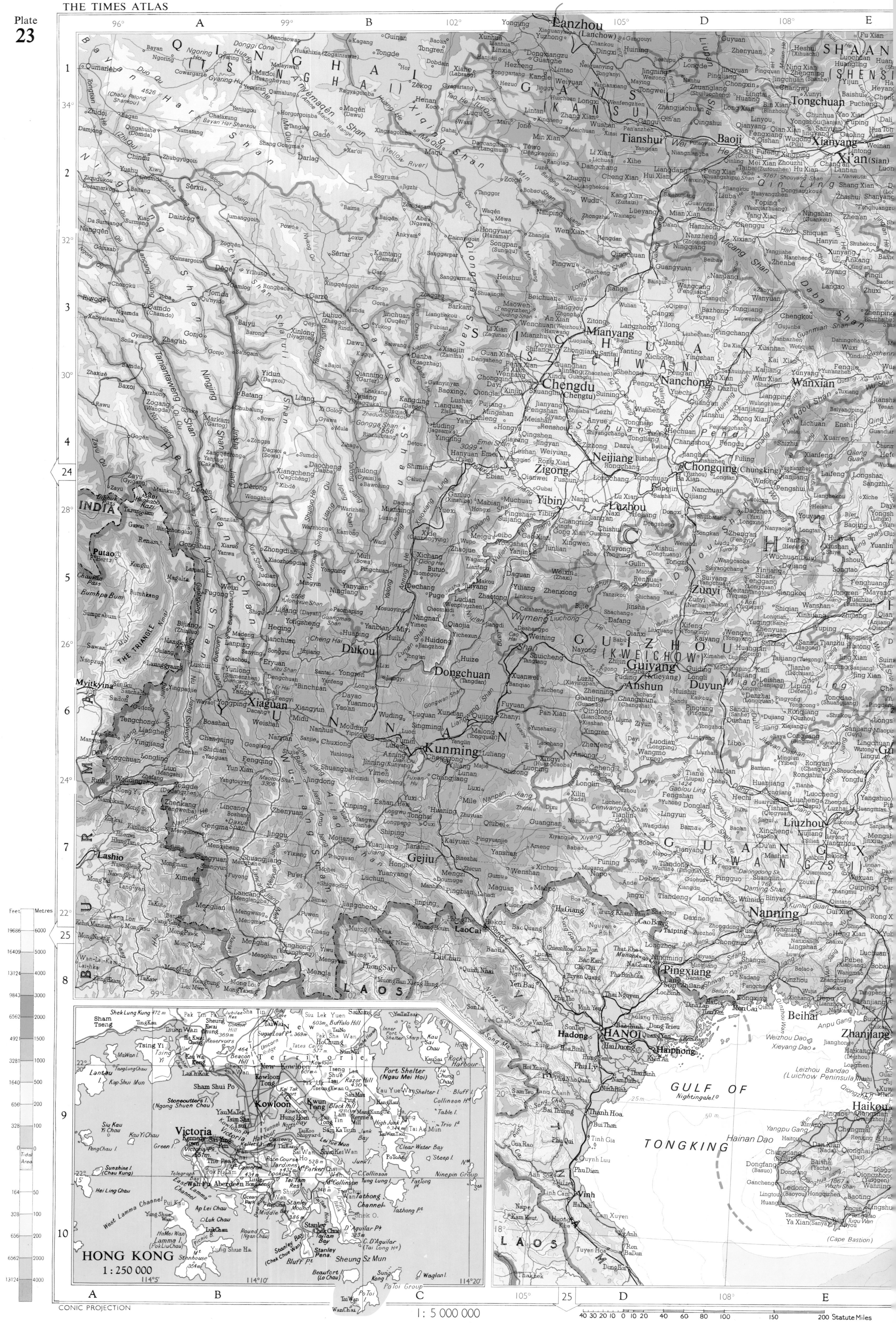
QINGHAI (TSINGHAI)
GANSU (KANSU)
SICHUAN (SZECHWAN)
YUNNAN
GUIZHOU (KWEICHOW)
GUANGXI (KWANGSI)
SHAANXI (SHENSI)
INDIA
BURMA
LAOS
GULF OF TONGKING
Lanzhou (Lanchow)
Tianshui
Baoji
Xianyang
Xi'an (Sian)
Chengdu (Chengtu)
Nanchong
Wanxian
Mianyang
Neijiang
Zigong
Yibin
Luzhou
Chongqing (Chungking)
Zunyi
Guiyang (Kueyang)
Anshun
Duyun
Dukou
Dongchuan
Kunming
Xiaguan
Gejiu
Nanning
Liuzhou
Pingxiang
Beihai
Zhanjiang
Haikou
Hainan Dao
HANOI
Haiphong
Myitkyina
Lashio
LaoCai
HONG KONG
1 : 250 000
Victoria
Kowloon
New Kowloon
Aberdeen
CONIC PROJECTION
1 : 5 000 000
Feet Metres
Statute Miles

SHANDONG (SHANTUNG)
Qingdao (Tsingtao)
YELLOW SEA
Jinan
Zaozhuang
Lianyungang
Xuzhou
Kaifeng
Zhengzhou
Luoyang
Sanmenxia
HENAN
Xuchang
Pingdingshan
Nanyang
JIANGSU (KIANGSU)
Qingjiang
Yangzhou
Taizhou
Nantong
Zhenjiang
Nanjing (Nanking)
Wuxi
Suzhou (Soochow)
Shanghai
ANHUI (ANHWEI)
Bengbu
Huainan
Hefei
Ma'anshan
Wuhu
Tongling
Anqing
Fuyang
Huaibei
HUBEI (HUPEH)
Xiangfan
Yichang
Wuhan
Huangshi
Shashi
ZHEJIANG (CHEKIANG)
Hangzhou (Hangchow)
Ningbo
Wenzhou
Jiujiang
Jingdezhen
Nanchang
Shangrao
Fuzhou
JIANGXI (KIANGSI)
Ji'an
Ganzhou
Yueyang
Changsha
Xiangtan
Zhuzhou
Lengshuijiang
Shaoyang
Hengyang
Pingxiang
HUNAN
Nanping
Sanming
FUJIAN (FUKIEN)
Fuzhou (Foochow)
Quanzhou
Zhangzhou
Xiamen (Amoy)
TAIWAN HAIXIA (FORMOSA STRAIT)
P'eng-hu Lieh-tao (Pescadores)
TAIWAN (China Nat. Rep.) (FORMOSA)
T'ai-pei
Chi-lung
Hsin-chu
T'ai-chung
Chang-hua
Chia-i
T'ai-nan
Kao-hsiung
P'ing-tung
Hua-lien
T'ai-tung
Yu Shan 3997
Sakishima guntō (Japan)
Senkaku guntō (Tiaoyu Tao)
GUANGDONG (KWANGTUNG)
Shaoguan
Guangzhou (Canton)
Foshan
Zhaoqing
Jiangmen
Huizhou
Shantou (Swatow)
Wuzhou
Maoming
Victoria
HONG KONG (To U.K.)
Tropic of Cancer
Dongsha Qundao (Pratas)
SOUTH CHINA SEA
HAINAN DAO
SHANGHAI 1:186,000
1 People's Square
2 1st. Natl. Congress
3 Seamen's Club
4 Cultural Square
5 Children's Palace
6 Industrial Exhibition
7 International Hotel
8 Tst. Department Store
9 Peace Hotel
10 Municipal Revolutionary Committee
Statute Miles
Kilometres
BOASHAN XIAN
Jiangwan
Wujiaochang
Dachang
Zhenru
JIADING XIAN
Zhabei
Hongkou
Yangpu
Putuo
Jing'an
Huangpu
Changning
Xuhui
Luwan
Nanshi
CHUANSHA XIAN
Longitude East 114° of Greenwich

U. S. S. R.
KAZAKHSTAN
KIRGIZIYA
MONGOLIA
DZUNGARIA
SINKIANG UIGHUR AUT. REGION
XINJIANG UYGUR ZIZHIQU
GANSU (KANSU)
QINGHAI
Taklimakan Shamo (Takla Makan)
Tarim Pendi (Tarim Basin)
Junggar Pendi (Dzungarian Basin)
Gurbantünggüt Shamo
Oz. Balkhash
Oz. Zaysan
Uvs Nuur
Altun Shan
Tian Shan
Bogda Shan
Kuruktag
Khr. Tarbagatay
Dzhungarskiy Alatau
Khr. Chingiz-Tau
Sary-Ishikotrau
Semipalatinsk
Ust-Kamenogorsk
Leninogorsk
Zyryanovsk
Karaganda
Balkhash
Ayaguz
Alma-Ata
Frunze
Tokmak
Przheval'sk
Ürümqi (Urumchi)
Karamay
Kuytun
Shihezi
Yining (Kuldja)
Turpan
Hami (Kumul)
Yumen
Kashi
Aksu
Ulaangom
Hovd
Ölgiy
Uliastay
Altay
Ulaanbaatar
CONIC PROJECTION
1: 5 000 000
200 Statute Miles

CHINA WEST AND TIBET

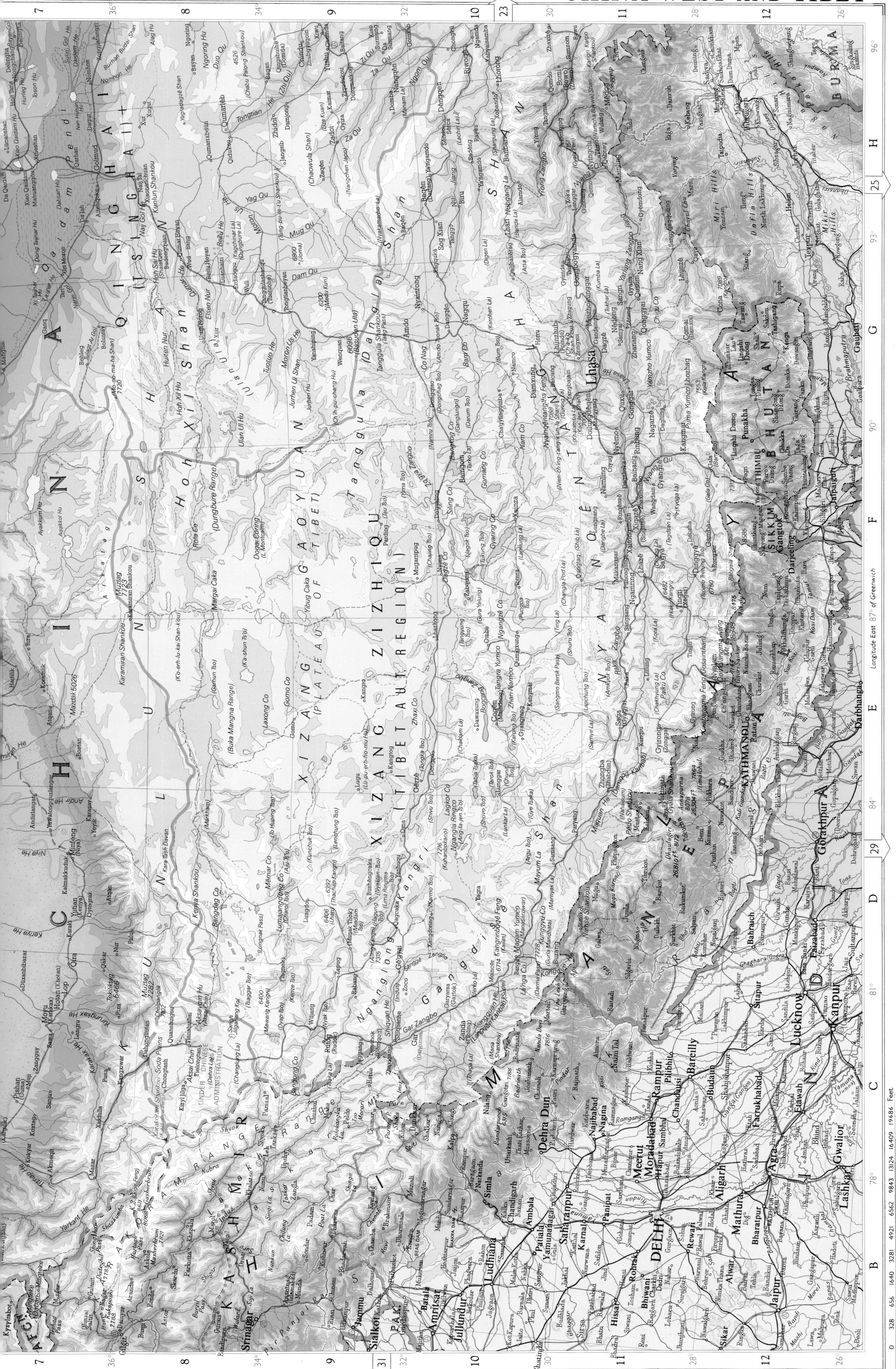

50 25 0 50 100 150 200 250 300 Kilometres

Heights in Metres

© John Bartholomew & Son Ltd, Edinburgh

MERCATOR PROJECTION

Equatorial Scale 1: 5 000 000

40 30 20 10 0 10 20 40 60 80 100 150 200 Statute Miles

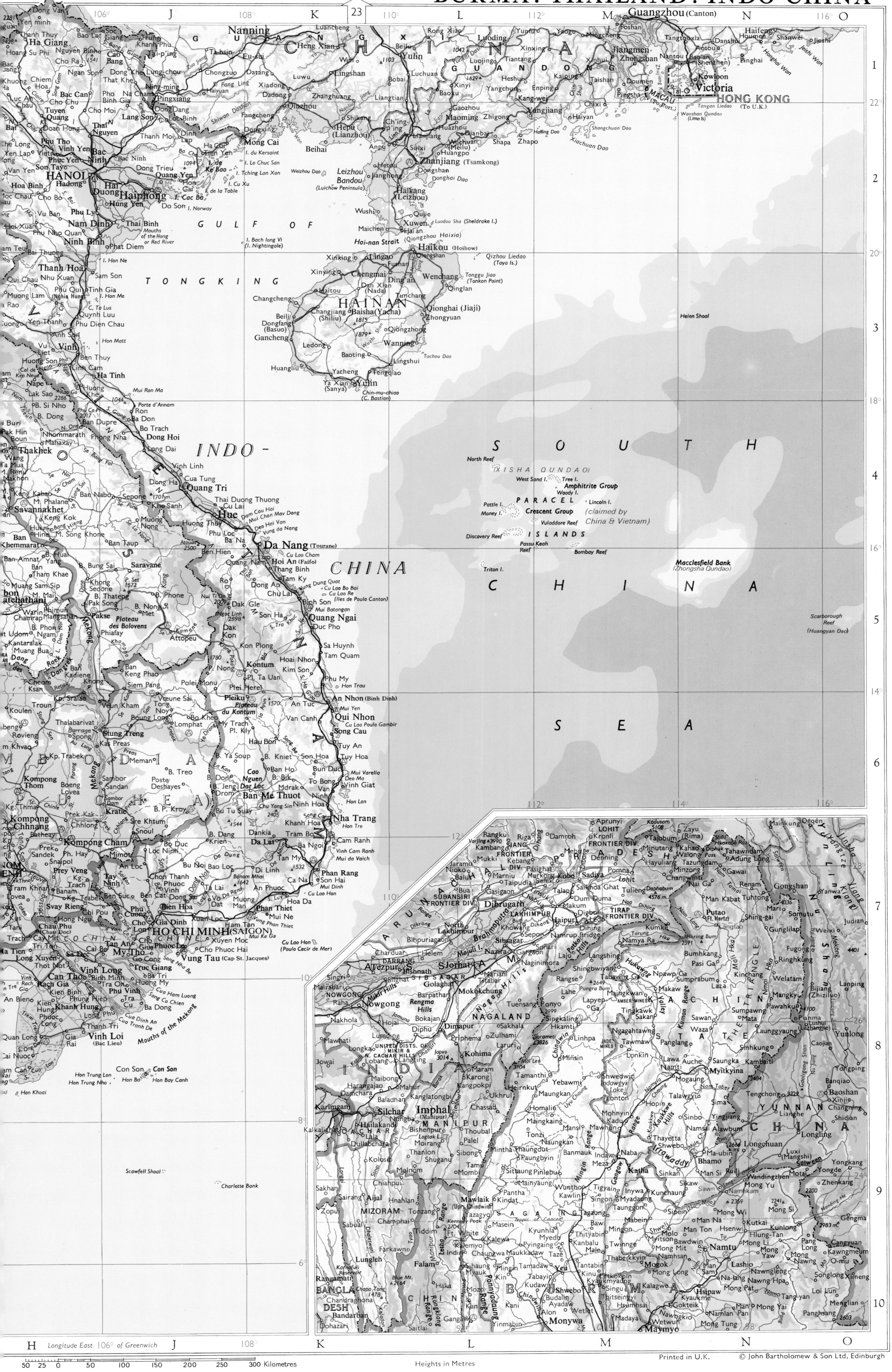

Heights in Metres

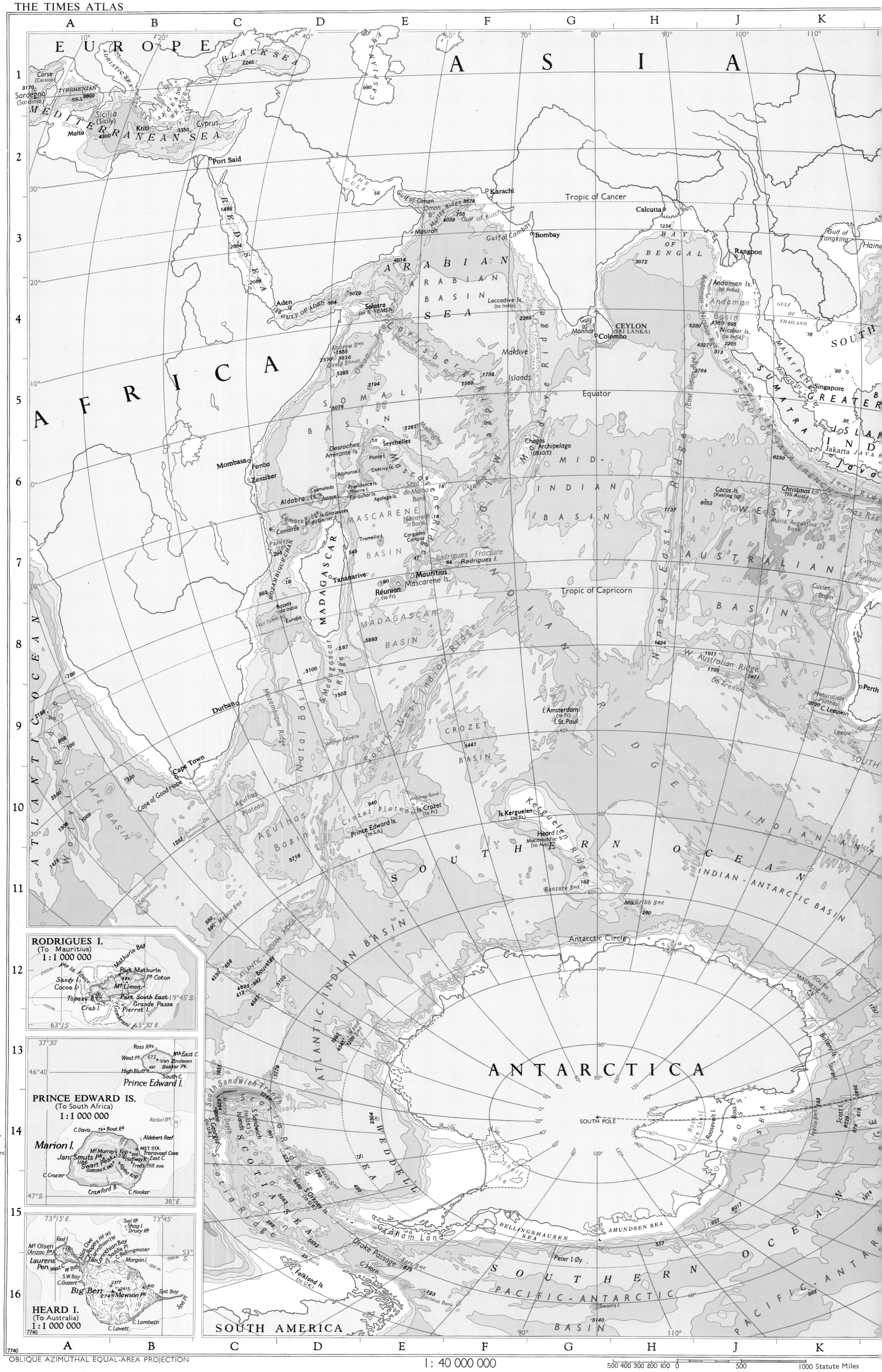
EUROPE
ASIA
AFRICA
ANTARCTICA
SOUTH AMERICA
ATLANTIC OCEAN
ARABIAN SEA
BAY OF BENGAL
MEDITERRANEAN SEA
BLACK SEA
CASPIAN SEA
RED SEA
GULF OF ADEN
THE GULF
Gulf of Oman
ARABIAN BASIN
SOMALI BASIN
MASCARENE BASIN
MADAGASCAR BASIN
MID-INDIAN BASIN
WEST AUSTRALIAN BASIN
CROZET BASIN
CAPE BASIN
ATLANTIC-INDIAN BASIN
INDIAN-ANTARCTIC BASIN
PACIFIC-ANTARCTIC BASIN
SOUTHERN OCEAN
SCOTIA SEA
WEDDELL SEA
ROSS SEA
AMUNDSEN SEA
BELLINGSHAUSEN SEA
Drake Passage
Graham Land
Antarctic Circle
Tropic of Cancer
Tropic of Capricorn
Equator
SOUTH POLE
Port Said
Aden
Karachi
Bombay
Calcutta
Rangoon
Singapore
Jakarta
Perth
Mombasa
Zanzibar
Durban
Cape Town
Cape of Good Hope
Tananarive
MADAGASCAR
CEYLON (SRI LANKA)
Colombo
Maldive Islands
Laccadive Is. (to India)
Chagos Archipelago (B.I.O.T.)
Seychelles
Mauritius
Réunion (to Fr.)
Rodrigues I.
Andaman Is. (to India)
Nicobar Is. (to India)
Cocos Is. (Keeling Is.)
Christmas I. (to Austr.)
I. Amsterdam (to Fr.)
I. St. Paul
Is. Kerguelen (to Fr.)
Heard I. Macdonald Is. (to Aus.)
Is. Crozet (to Fr.)
Prince Edward Is. (to S.A.)
Falkland Is. (to U.K.)
RODRIGUES I.
(To Mauritius)
1 : 1 000 000
Mathurin Bay
Port Mathurin
Sandy I.
Cocoa I.
Mt. Limon
Port South East
Grande Passe
Pierrot I.
Topaze B.
Crab I.
63°15′
63°30′ E.
19°45′ S.
PRINCE EDWARD IS.
(To South Africa)
1 : 1 000 000
Prince Edward I.
Marion I.
Jan Smuts Pk.
Swart Peak
Crawford B.
C. Hooker
C. Crozier
C. Davis
46°40′
47° S.
37°30′
38° E.
HEARD I.
(To Australia)
1 : 1 000 000
Big Ben
Mawson Pk.
Laurens Pen.
C. Lambeth
C. Lavett
Spit Bay
73°15′ E.
73°45′
53° S.
A B C D E F G H J K
1 2 3 4 5 6 7 8 9 10 11 12 13 14 15 16

Colour Note for Indian Ocean

Fathoms	Metres
547	1000
1094	2000
1640	3000
2187	4000
2734	5000
3281	6000
3828	7000
4374	8000

OBLIQUE AZIMUTHAL EQUAL-AREA PROJECTION

1: 40 000 000

500 400 300 200 100 0 500 1000 Statute Miles

INDIAN OCEAN : SRI LANKA (CEYLON)

Plate 26

SRI LANKA (CEYLON)
1 : 2 000 000
Statute Miles
Kilometres
LAMBERT CONFORMAL CONIC PROJECTION
INDIA
Palk Strait
Palk Bay
Gulf of Mannar
COLOMBO
Kandy
Jaffna
Trincomalee
Batticaloa
Galle
COCOS IS. (KEELING IS.) (To Australia)
1 : 1 000 000
CHRISTMAS I. (To Australia)
1 : 1 000 000
SEYCHELLES
1 : 2 500 000
MAURITIUS
1 : 1 000 000
Port Louis
MAHÉ (To U.K.)
1 : 1 000 000
KERGUELEN (To France)
1 : 2 500 000
RÉUNION (To France)
1 : 1 000 000
AMSTERDAM I. (To France)
1 : 250 000
ST PAUL I. (To France)
1 : 250 000
CROZET IS. (To France)
1 : 5 000 000
PACIFIC OCEAN
SEA OF JAPAN
PHILIPPINE SEA
NEW GUINEA
AUSTRALIA
TASMAN SEA
NEW ZEALAND
Colour Note for all Inset Maps
Feet
Metres

Heights and Depths in Metres

© John Bartholomew & Son Ltd, Edinburgh

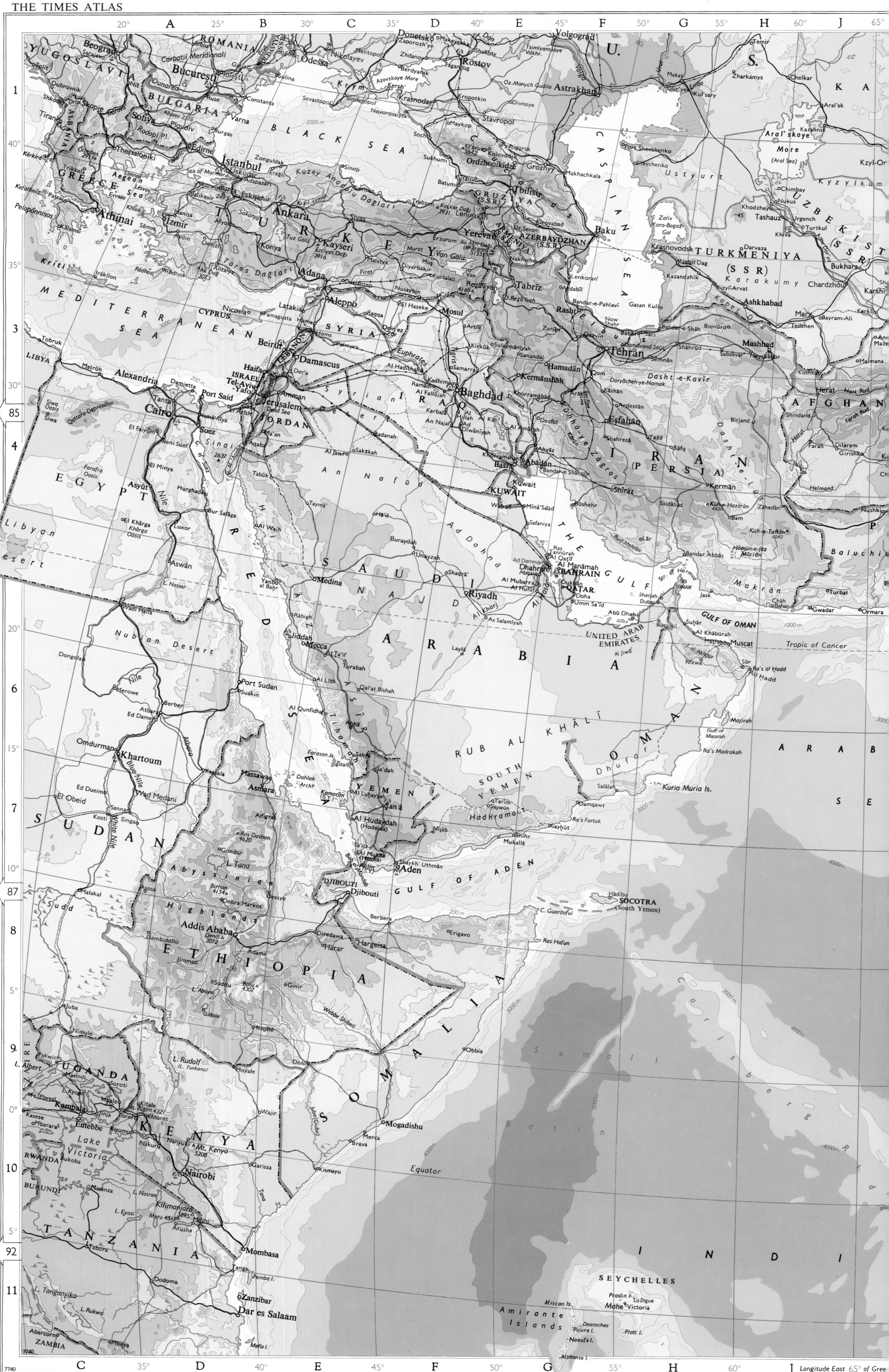
BLACK SEA
MEDITERRANEAN SEA
CASPIAN SEA
RED SEA
GULF OF ADEN
GULF OF OMAN
THE GULF
YUGOSLAVIA
ROMANIA
BULGARIA
ALBANIA
GREECE
TURKEY
CYPRUS
SYRIA
LEBANON
ISRAEL
JORDAN
IRAQ
IRAN (PERSIA)
KUWAIT
BAHRAIN
QATAR
UNITED ARAB EMIRATES
OMAN
SAUDI ARABIA
YEMEN
SOUTH YEMEN
EGYPT
LIBYA
SUDAN
ETHIOPIA
DJIBOUTI
SOMALIA
KENYA
UGANDA
RWANDA
BURUNDI
TANZANIA
ZAMBIA
AFGHANISTAN
GRUZIYA (S.S.R.)
ARMENIYA
AZERBAYDZHAN (S.S.R.)
TURKMENIYA (S S R)
UZBEKISTAN (SSR)
SOCOTRA (South Yemen)
SEYCHELLES
Amirante Islands
Beograd
Bucureşti
Sofiya
Istanbul
Ankara
Athinai
Izmir
Odessa
Rostov
Volgograd
Astrakhan'
Tbilisi
Baku
Yerevan
Tabrīz
Tehrān
Mashhad
Esfahān
Baghdad
Mosul
Basra
Aleppo
Damascus
Beirut
Amman
Jerusalem
Tel Aviv-Yafo
Cairo
Alexandria
Port Said
Suez
Medina
Mecca
Jiddah
Riyadh
Muscat
Aden
Şan'ā
Khartoum
Omdurman
Port Sudan
Asmara
Addis Ababa
Djibouti
Mogadishu
Nairobi
Kampala
Mombasa
Zanzibar
Dar es Salaam
Mt. Kenya 5200
Kilimanjaro 5895
Lake Victoria
L. Rudolf (L. Turkana)
L. Tana
Abyssinian Highlands
Nile
Blue Nile
White Nile
Euphrates
Tigris
Libyan Desert
Nubian Desert
Syrian Desert
An Nafūd
Ad Dahnā
Najd
Rub al Khālī
Dasht-e-Kavir
Kuhhā-ye Zāgros
Karakumy
Ustyurt
Aral'skoye More (Aral Sea)
Kuria Muria Is.
Tropic of Cancer
Equator
Somali Basin
Carlsberg Ridge
ARABIAN SEA
INDIAN OCEAN
Feet / Metres
16409 5000
13124 4000
9843 3000
6562 2000
3281 1000
1640 500
656 200
0 Sea Level
Below Sea Level
656 200
3281 1000
9843 3000
13124 4000
16409 5000
Longitude East 65° of Greenwich

BONNE PROJECTION

1: 15 000 000

100 80 60 40 20 0 50 100 200 300 400 500 600 Statute Miles

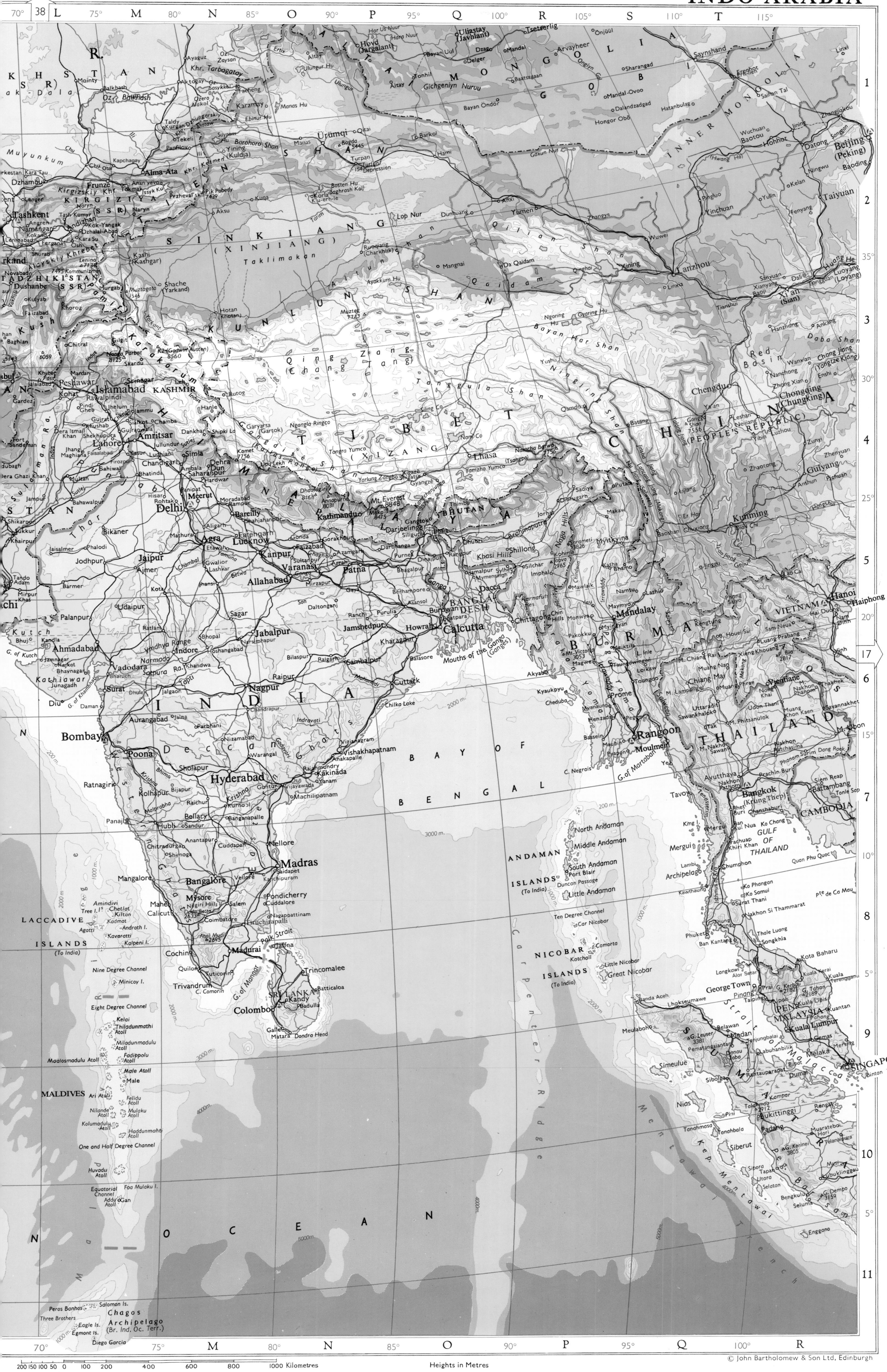

MONGOLIA
GOBI
INNER MONGOLIA
SINKIANG (XINJIANG)
Taklimakan
KUNLUN SHAN
TIBET (XIZANG)
Qing Zang (Chang Tang)
Tanggula Shan
Bayan Har Shan
CHINA (PEOPLE'S REPUBLIC)
Red Basin
Beijing (Peking)
Taiyuan
Lanzhou
Xi'an (Sian)
Chengdu
Chongqing (Chungking)
Kunming
Guiyang
Hanoi
Haiphong
VIETNAM
KIRGIZIYA (S.S.R.)
TADZHIKISTAN (S.S.R.)
Tashkent
Dushanbe
Frunze
Alma-Ata
Ürümqi
Kashi (Kashgar)
Islamabad
KASHMIR
Lahore
Amritsar
Delhi
Agra
Lucknow
Kanpur
Varanasi
Allahabad
Patna
Jaipur
Jodhpur
Ahmadabad
Vadodara
Indore
Jabalpur
Nagpur
Bombay
Poona
Hyderabad
Bangalore
Madras
Mysore
Madurai
Calcutta
Howrah
Jamshedpur
Cuttack
Vishakhapatnam
Kathmandu
Mt. Everest 8848
NEPAL
BHUTAN
BANGLADESH
Dacca
Chittagong
Lhasa
HIMALAYA
INDIA
Deccan
Thar
Kutch
Kathiawar
Mouths of the Ganga (Ganges)
BAY OF BENGAL
BURMA
Mandalay
Rangoon
Moulmein
THAILAND
Bangkok (Krung Thep)
Chiang Mai
Vientiane
CAMBODIA
GULF OF THAILAND
ANDAMAN ISLANDS (To India)
North Andaman
Middle Andaman
South Andaman
Port Blair
Little Andaman
Ten Degree Channel
Car Nicobar
NICOBAR ISLANDS (To India)
Great Nicobar
LACCADIVE ISLANDS (To India)
Nine Degree Channel
Minicoy I.
Eight Degree Channel
MALDIVES
Male
One and Half Degree Channel
Equatorial Channel
Chagos Archipelago (Br. Ind. Oc. Terr.)
Diego Garcia
SRI LANKA
Colombo
Trincomalee
Kandy
Galle
Palk Strait
G. of Mannar
C. Comorin
Trivandrum
Cochin
George Town
Kuala Lumpur
MALAYSIA
SINGAPORE
Strait of Malacca
SUMATRA
Medan
Padang
Simeulue
Nias
Siberut
Enggano
Mentawai Trench
Carpenter Ridge
INDIAN OCEAN
Heights in Metres
0 100 200 400 600 800 1000 Kilometres

MAHARASHTRA
INDIA
KARNATAKA
ANDHRA PRADESH
TAMIL NADU
ARABIAN SEA
BAY OF BENGAL
SRI LANKA
Bombay
Poona
Hyderabad
Bangalore
Madras
Mysore
Madurai
Colombo
LAKSHADWEEP
(Laccadive Islands)
Cannanore
Islands
GULF OF MANNAR
PALK STRAIT
Malabar Coast
Coromandel Coast
BOMBAY
1:200 000
MADRAS
1:200 000
Longitude East 80° of Greenwich

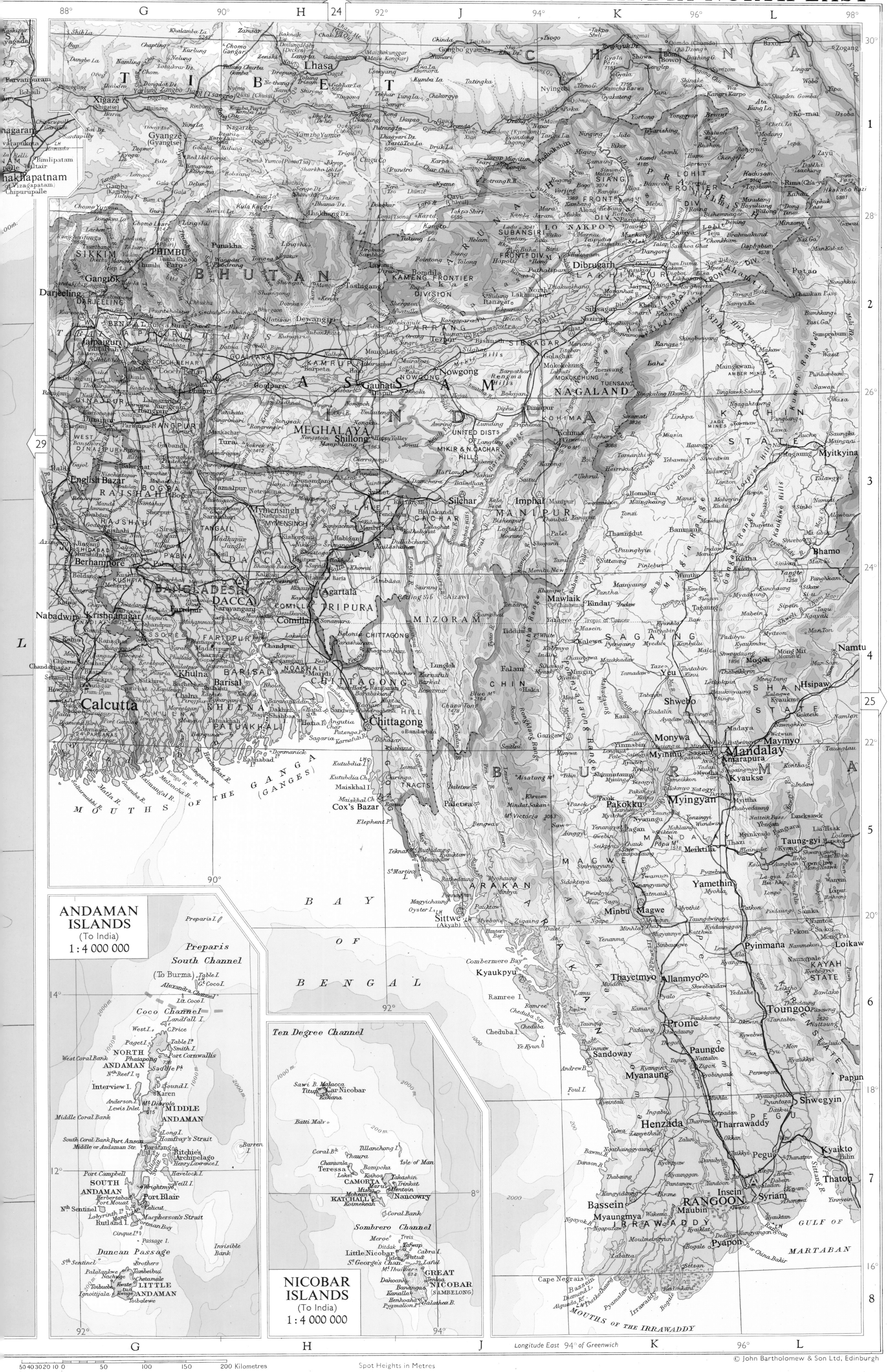

TIBET
CHINA
BHUTAN
ASSAM
MEGHALAYA
NAGALAND
MANIPUR
MIZORAM
TRIPURA
BANGLADESH
BURMA
KACHIN STATE
SHAN STATE
KAYAH STATE
KAREN STATE
SIKKIM
Lhasa
Xigaze
Gyangze
Gangtok
Darjeeling
Thimbu
Shillong
Gauhati
Dibrugarh
Kohima
Imphal
Silchar
Agartala
DACCA
Calcutta
Chittagong
Cox's Bazar
Sittwe (Akyab)
Mandalay
Myitkyina
Bhamo
Lashio
Hsipaw
Maymyo
Monywa
Shwebo
Myingyan
Pakokku
Meiktila
Magwe
Minbu
Yamethin
Pyinmana
Loikaw
Toungoo
Prome
Thayetmyo
Allanmyo
Henzada
Tharrawaddy
Pegu
Shwegyin
Kyaikto
Thaton
RANGOON
Syriam
Bassein
Maubin
Myaungmya
Pyapon
Sandoway
Kyaukpyu
Ramree I.
Cheduba I.
Myanaung
Vishakhapatnam
BAY OF BENGAL
MOUTHS OF THE GANGA (GANGES)
MOUTHS OF THE IRRAWADDY
GULF OF MARTABAN
ANDAMAN ISLANDS
(To India)
1 : 4 000 000
Preparis South Channel
Coco Channel
NORTH ANDAMAN
MIDDLE ANDAMAN
SOUTH ANDAMAN
LITTLE ANDAMAN
Ritchie's Archipelago
Port Blair
Duncan Passage
Ten Degree Channel
Car Nicobar
Sombrero Channel
GREAT NICOBAR
NICOBAR ISLANDS
(To India)
1 : 4 000 000
Longitude East 94° of Greenwich
Spot Heights in Metres
50 40 30 20 10 0 50 100 150 200 Kilometres
© John Bartholomew & Son Ltd, Edinburgh

DELHI
1:200 000
NEW DELHI
OLD CITY
PAKISTAN
RAJASTHAN
PUNJAB
HARYANA
HIMACHAL PRADESH
JAMMU AND KASHMIR
UTTAR PRADESH
MADHYA PRADESH
MAHARASHTRA
GUJARAT
INDIAN DESERT
GREAT RANN OF KUTCH
GULF OF KUTCH
GULF OF KHAMBHAT (CAMBAY)
ARABIAN SEA
Lahore
Amritsar
Jullundur
Ludhiana
Chandigarh
Simla
Dehra Dun
DELHI
Meerut
Agra
Gwalior
Jaipur
Ajmer
Jodhpur
Bikaner
Udaipur
Ahmadabad
Vadodara
Surat
Bombay
Poona
Nasik
Indore
Bhopal
Ujjain
Jhansi
Nagpur
Hyderabad
Sukkur
Bahawalpur
Multan
Faisalabad
Gujranwala
Sialkot
Jammu
Sargodha
Rajkot
Jamnagar
Bhavnagar
Porbandar
Aurangabad
Ahmadnagar
Jalgaon
Akola
Amravati
Tropic of Cancer

CONIC PROJECTION
1: 4 000 000

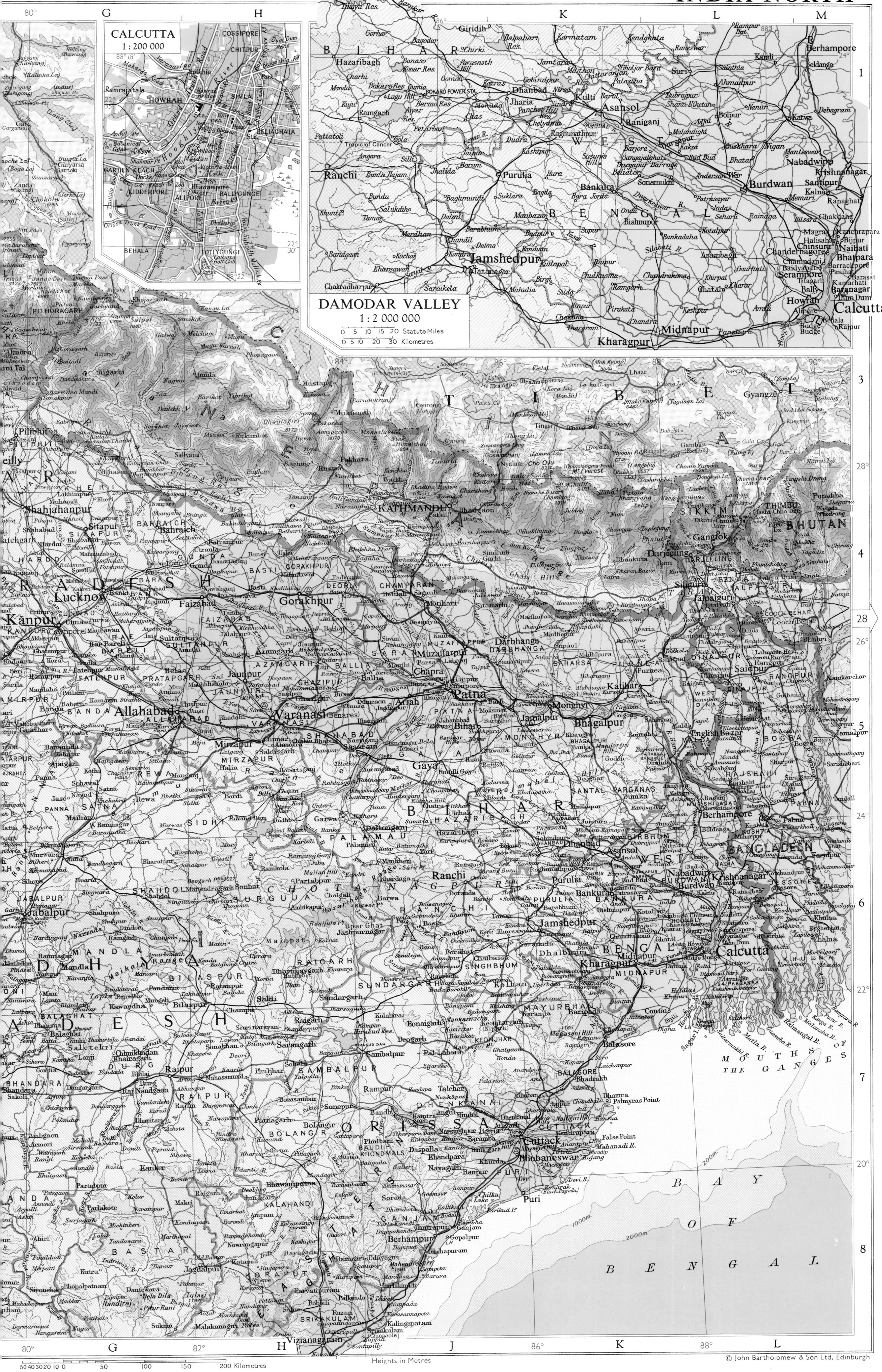

Heights in Metres

50 40 30 20 10 0 50 100 150 200 Kilometres

© John Bartholomew & Son Ltd, Edinburgh

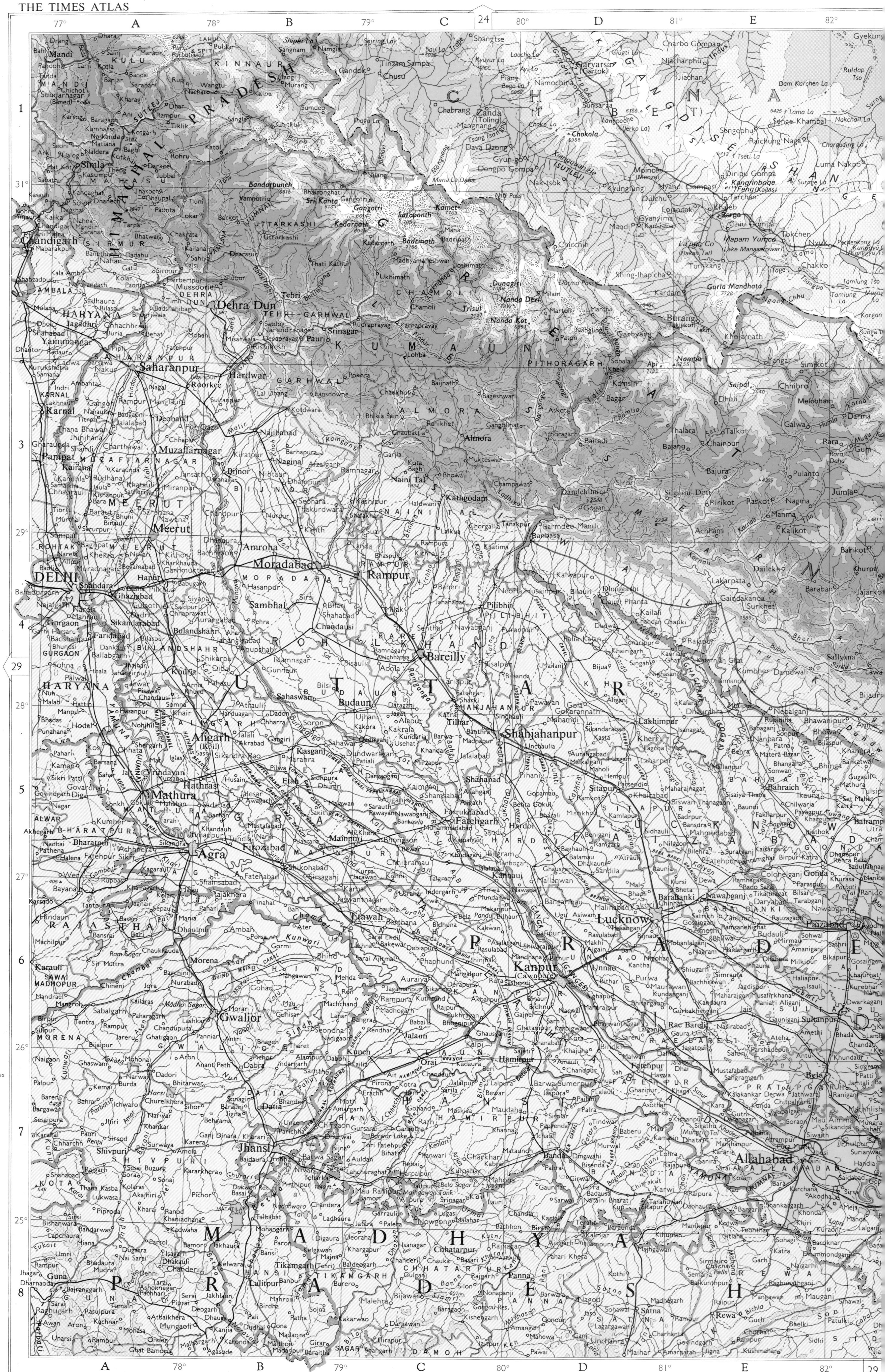
C H I N A
T I B E T
HIMACHAL PRADESH
UTTAR PRADESH
MADHYA PRADESH
HARYANA
RAJASTHAN
DELHI
Simla
Chandigarh
Dehra Dun
Saharanpur
Hardwar
Muzaffarnagar
Meerut
Moradabad
Rampur
Bareilly
Aligarh
Mathura
Agra
Firozabad
Shahjahanpur
Lucknow
Kanpur (Cawnpore)
Allahabad
Gwalior
Jhansi
Faizabad
Naini Tal
Almora
Nanda Devi
Kamet
Badrinath
Gurla Mandhata
Mapam Yumco
Kangrinboqe Feng (Kailas)
Bandarpunch
KUMAUN
GARHWAL
ROHILKHAND
BUNDELKHAND
GANGES
JUMNA
GHAGHARA
SUTLEJ
24
29

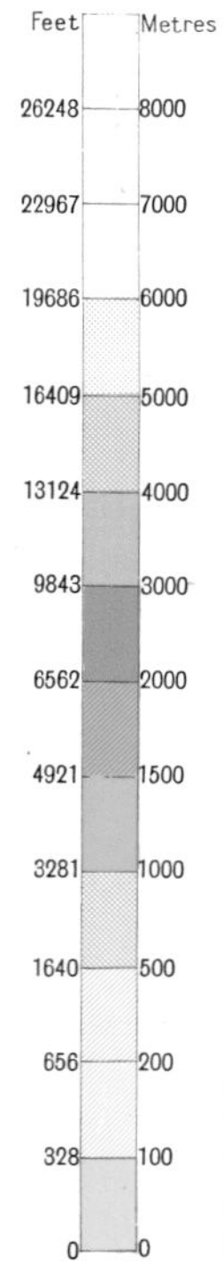
Feet
Metres
26248
8000
22967
7000
19686
6000
16409
5000
13124
4000
9843
3000
6562
2000
4921
1500
3281
1000
1640
500
656
200
328
100
0
0

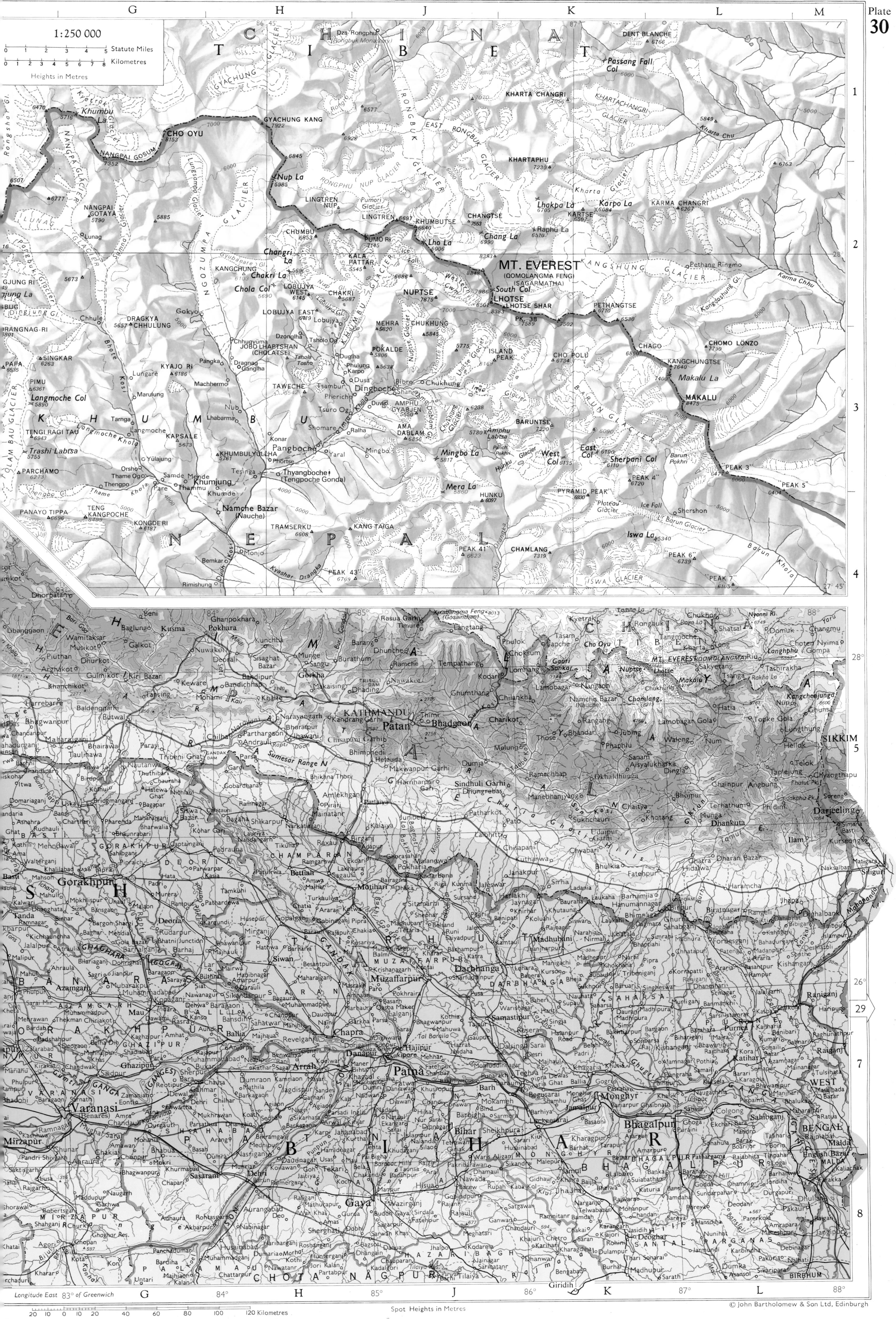
1:250 000
Statute Miles
Kilometres
Heights in Metres
T I B E T
C H I N A
MT. EVEREST
(QOMOLANGMA FENG)
(SAGARMATHA)
8848
CHO OYU
8153
GYACHUNG KANG
7922
LHOTSE
8501
LHOTSE SHAR
8383
NUPTSE
7879
MAKALU
8475
CHOMO LÖNZO
7790
KHARTA CHANGRI
7056
KHARTAPHU
7230
CHANGTSE
7553
PUMO RI
7145
AMA DABLAM
6856
BARUNTSE
7220
CHAMLANG
7319
KANGSHUNG GLACIER
BARUN GLACIER
RONGBUK GLACIER
NGOZUMPA GLACIER
KHUMBU GLACIER
South Col
Lho La
Chang La
Nup La
Makalu La
Namche Bazar
(Nauche)
Thyangboche
(Tengpoche Gonda)
Pangboche
Dingboche
K H U M B U
N E P A L
Peak 3
Peak 4
Peak 5
Peak 6
Peak 7
Peak 41
Peak 43
KATHMANDU
Patan
Bhadgaon
Pokhara
Gorkha
Darjeeling
SIKKIM
Gorakhpur
Varanasi
(Benares)
Mirzapur
Ghazipur
Ballia
Arrah
Chapra
Patna
Danapur
Hajipur
Muzaffarpur
Darbhanga
Samastipur
Madhubani
Motihari
Bettiah
Monghyr
Bhagalpur
Purnea
Katihar
Siliguri
Gaya
Bihar
Sasaram
Dehri
Deoghar
English Bazar
Malda
Raiganj
WEST BENGAL
B I H A R
H I M A L A Y A
GANGA
GANGES
GHAGHARA
GANDAK
KOSI
SON
CHOTA NAGPUR
SANTAL PARGANAS
BIRBHUM
29
Longitude East 83° of Greenwich
84°
85°
86°
87°
88°
26°
28°
27° 45'
Spot Heights in Metres
Kilometres
© John Bartholomew & Son Ltd, Edinburgh

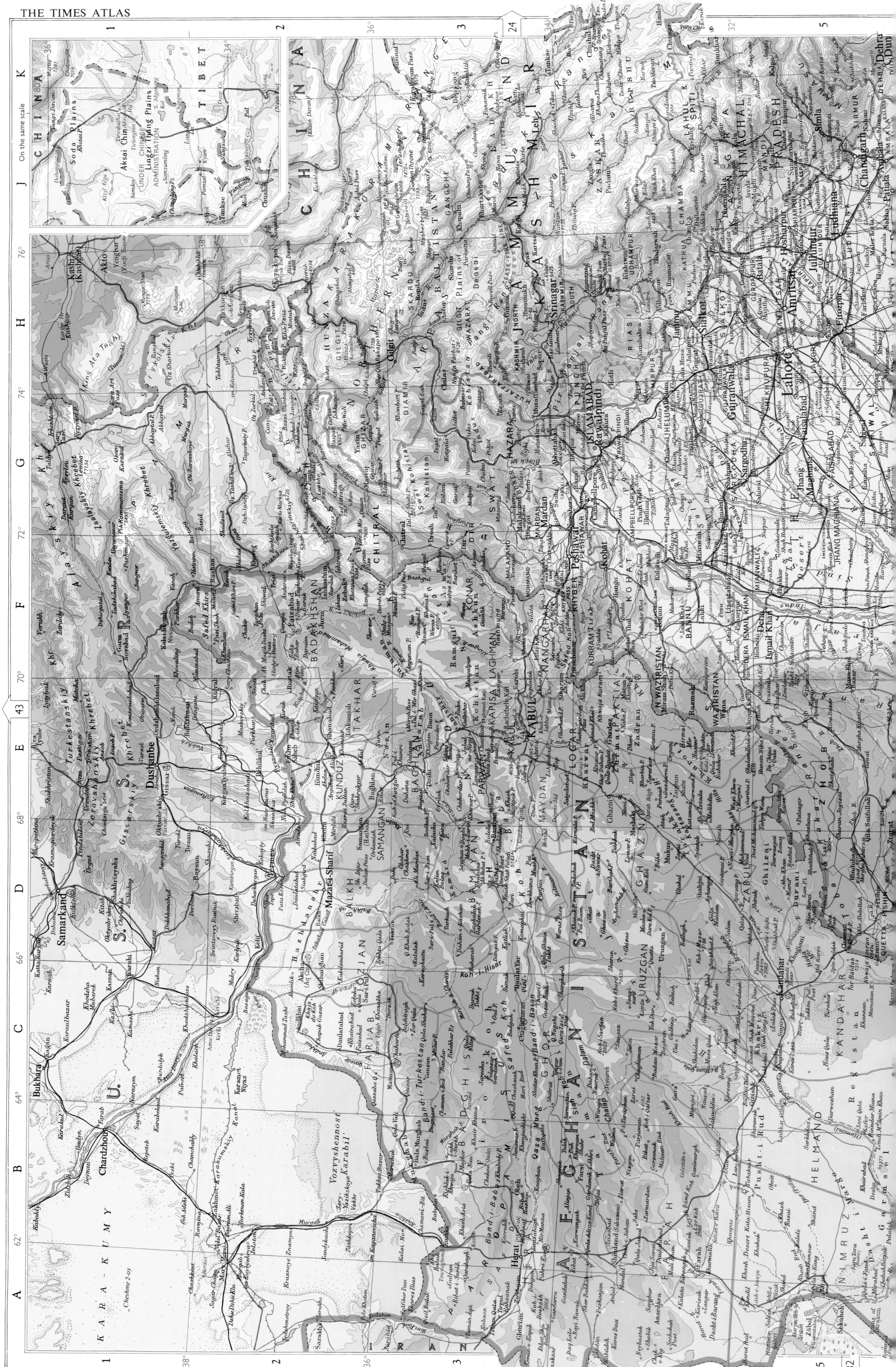
On the same scale
TIBET
AFGHANISTAN
KABUL
Samarkand
Dushanbe
Bukhara
Chardzhou
Mazar-i-Sharif
Herat
Kandahar
Peshawar
Rawalpindi
ISLAMABAD
Srinagar
Lahore
Amritsar
Jullundur
Ludhiana
Simla
Chandigarh
Sialkot
Gujranwala
Faisalabad
Sargodha
KASHMIR
HIMACHAL PRADESH
Gilgit
KABUL
Koh-i-Hisar
HELMAND
KANDAHAR
IRAN
KARA-KUMY

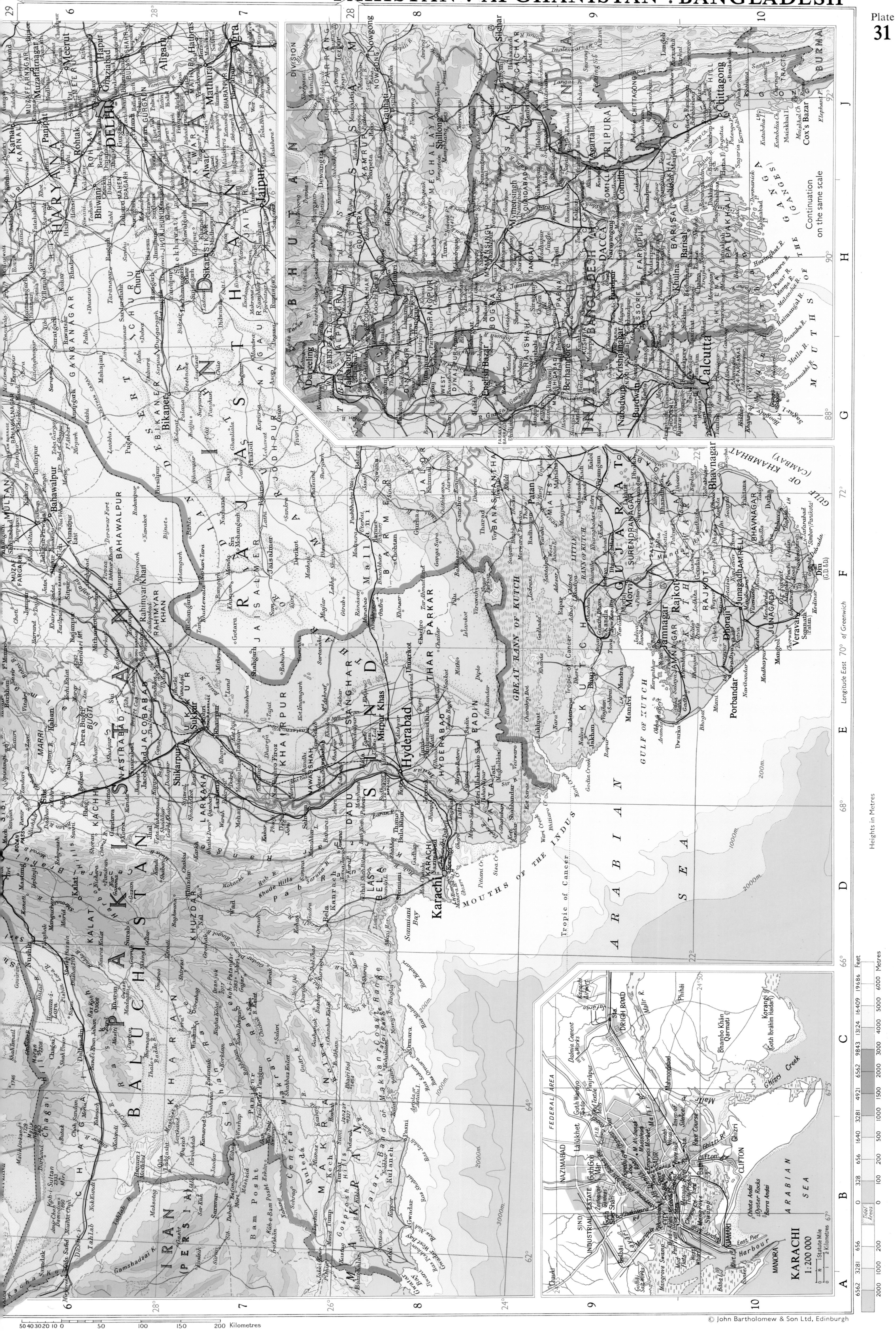
KARACHI
1:200 000
Continuation on the same scale
Heights in Metres
ARABIAN SEA
GULF OF KUTCH
GREAT RANN OF KUTCH
MOUTHS OF THE INDUS
Longitude East 70° of Greenwich
50 40 30 20 10 0 50 100 150 200 Kilometres

© John Bartholomew & Son Ltd, Edinburgh

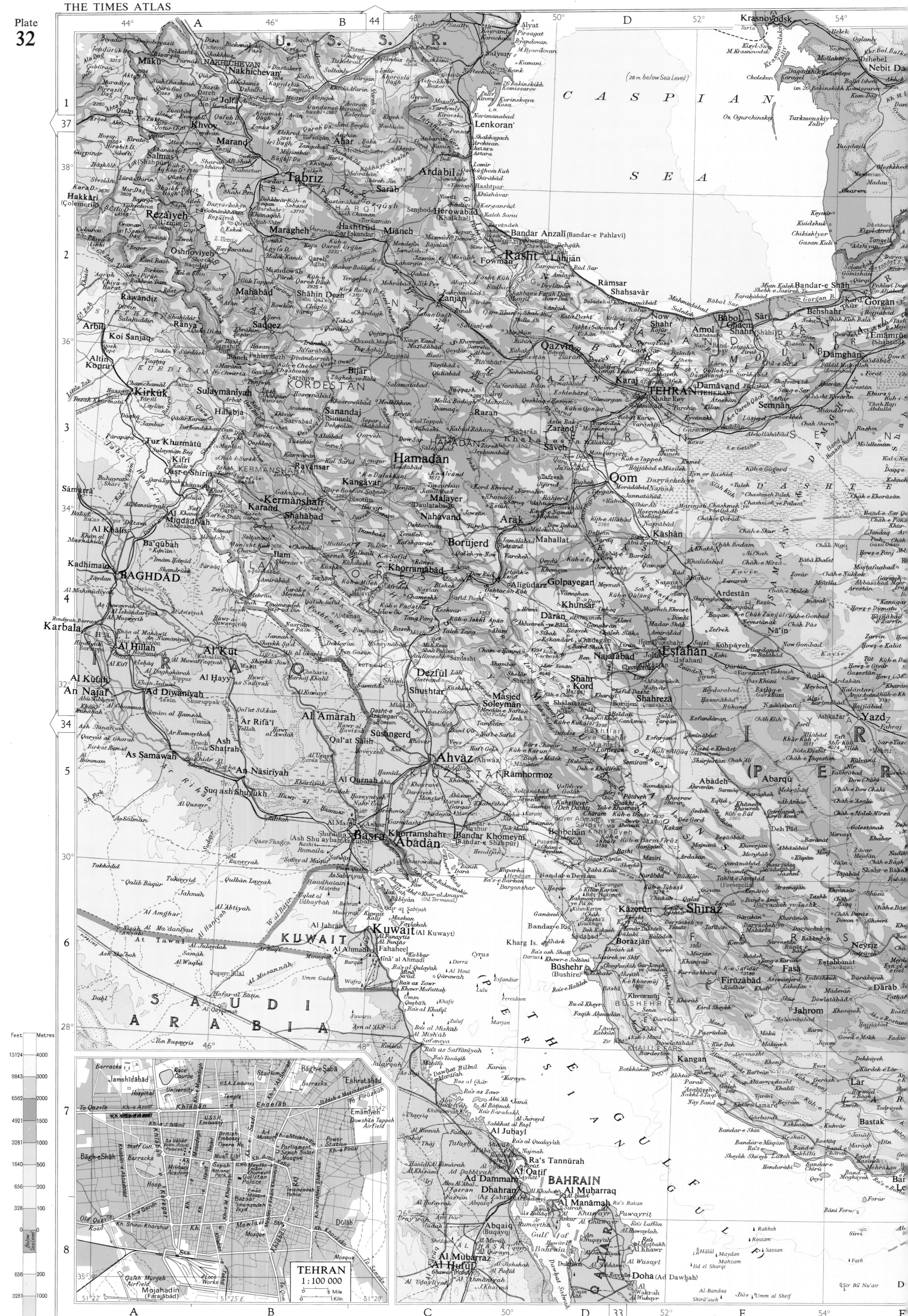
U. S. S. R.
CASPIAN SEA
(28 m. below Sea Level)
IRAQ
IRAN
KUWAIT
SAUDI ARABIA
BAHRAIN
QATAR
PERSIAN GULF
TEHRAN
BAGHDAD
Tabriz
Rasht
Qazvin
Hamadan
Kermanshah
Qom
Esfahan
Shiraz
Yazd
Ahvaz
Abadan
Basra
Kuwait (Al Kuwayt)
Dezful
Kirkuk
Karbala
Al Kut
An Nasiriyah
Al Amarah
Bushehr
Krasnovodsk
Nebit Dag
Gorgan
Semnan
Kashan
Arak
Borujerd
Khorramabad
Sanandaj
Zanjan
Ardabil
Rezaiyeh
Maragheh
Mahabad
Lenkoran'
Nakhichevan'
Al Jubayl
Ad Dammam
Dhahran
Al Hufuf
Al Manamah
Doha (Ad Dawhah)
Ras Tanurah
Kharg Is.
KHUZESTAN
KORDESTAN
FARS
TEHRAN
1:100 000
Feet
Metres
13124
4000
9843
3000
6562
2000
4921
1500
3281
1000
1640
500
656
200
328
100
0
Below Sea Level
656
200
3281
1000

IRAN (PERSIA)

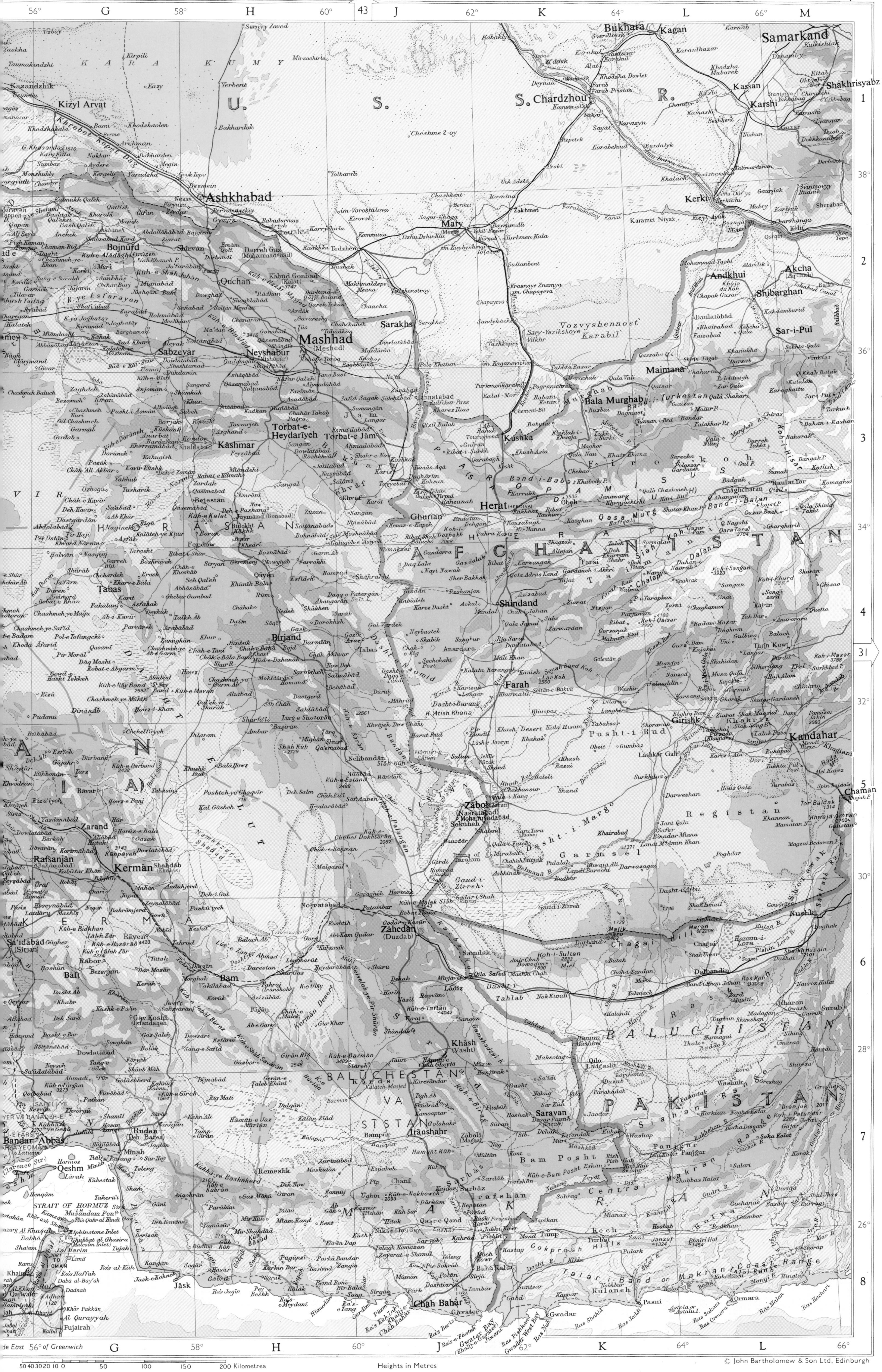
U. S. S. R.
AFGHANISTAN
PAKISTAN
IRAN
KARA KUMY
KHORĀSĀN
DASHT-E LUT
KERMĀN
BALUCHESTAN VA SISTAN
BALUCHISTAN
MAKRAN
Ashkhabad
Mashhad
(Meshed)
Bukhara
Samarkand
Chardzhou
Mary
Kerki
Karshi
Herat
Kushka
Maimana
Bala Murghab
Shibarghan
Sar-i-Pul
Andkhui
Akcha
Kandahar
Chaman
Girishk
Farah
Shindand
Birjand
Tabas
Kashmar
Torbat-e-Heydariyeh
Torbat-e Jām
Sabzevār
Neyshābūr
Quchan
Bojnurd
Kizyl Arvat
Sarakhs
Tedzhen
Zābol
Zāhedān
(Duzdab)
Kermān
Rafsanjan
Zarand
Bam
Khāsh
Iranshahr
Saravan
Bandar Abbās
Qeshm
Jāsk
Chāh Bahār
Gwadar
Pasni
Ormara
Dalbandin
Nushki
STRAIT OF HORMUZ
Hills
Registan
Garmsel
Dasht-i-Margo
Central Makran Range
Talar-i-Band or Makran Coast Range
Siahan Range
Chagai Hills
Koh-i-Sultan
Band-i-Turkestan
Paropamisus
Firoz koh
Kopet Dag
Vozvyshennost' Karabil
Amu-Dar'ya
Murghab
Hari Rud
Helmand R.
Khash Rud
Farah Rud
Hāmūn-i-Sāberi
Hāmūn-i-Māshkel
Kūh-e Bazmān
Kūh-e Taftān
Kūh-e Hazār
Heights in Metres
Kilometres
56° of Greenwich
© John Bartholomew & Son Ltd, Edinburgh

JORDAN
EGYPT
SINAI PENINSULA
ISRAEL
IRAQ
SAUDI ARABIA
SUDAN
ETHIOPIA
YEMEN
DJIBOUTI
RED SEA
AN NAFŪD
Ma'ān
Tabūk
Taymā'
Al Jawf
Sakākah
Ha'il
Buraydah
'Unayzah
Khaybar
Medina (Al Madīnah)
Yanbu' al Bahr
MECCA (MAKKAH)
(Jedda) Jiddah
At Ta'if
Turabah
Al Khurmah
Rābigh
Al Lith
Al Qunfidhah
Abhā
Najrān
Şabyā
Jīzān
Abū 'Arish
Al Hudaydah (Hodeida)
SAN'A'
Dhamār
Ibb
TA'IZZ
Al Mukhā (Mocha)
Lahej
Little Aden
ADEN
Shaykh 'Uthmān
Shuqra
Massawa
Port Sudan
Suakin
Hurghada (Al Ghardaqah)
Quseir
Al Wajh
Umm Lajj
Shaqra
Ad Dir'iyah
Tropic of Cancer
BAHRAIN
1:1 000 000
GULF OF BAHRAIN
Al Muharraq
AL MANAMAH
Dhahran (Az Zahrān)
Al Khubar (Khobar)
Ad Dammām
Al Qatif
Ra's Tannūrah
ADEN
1:250 000
Khormaksar Airport
Aden Harbour
Crater
Ma'alla
Tawahi
Little Aden
Bandar Tawahi
Feet
Metres
13124
4000
9843
3000
6562
2000
4921
1500
3281
1000
1640
500
656
200
328
100
0
Below Sea-level
Longitude East 46° of Greenwich
40 30 20 10 0 10 20 40 60 80 100 200 Statute Miles

ARABIAN PENINSULA

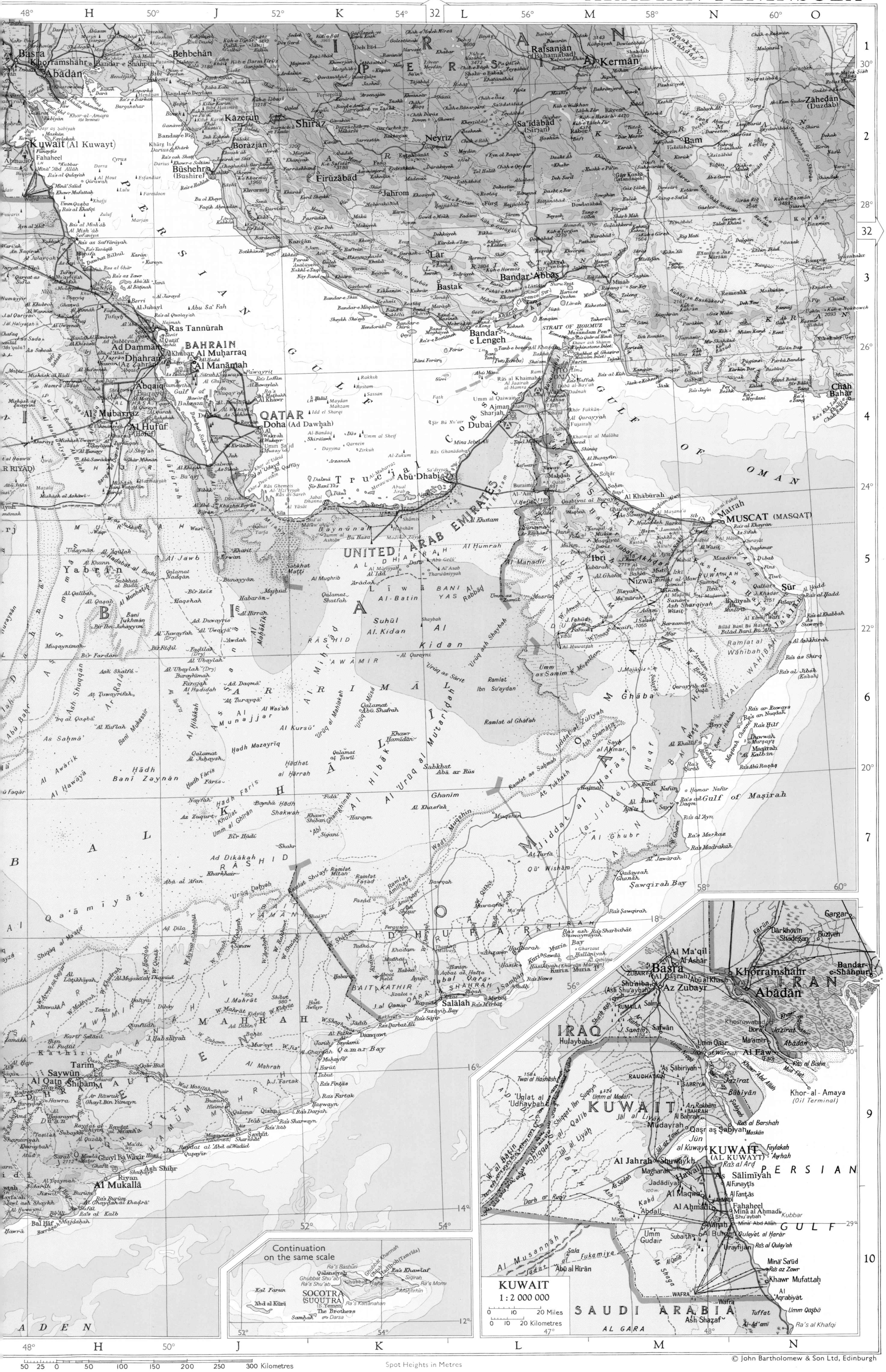

50 25 0 50 100 150 200 250 300 Kilometres

Spot Heights in Metres

© John Bartholomew & Son Ltd, Edinburgh

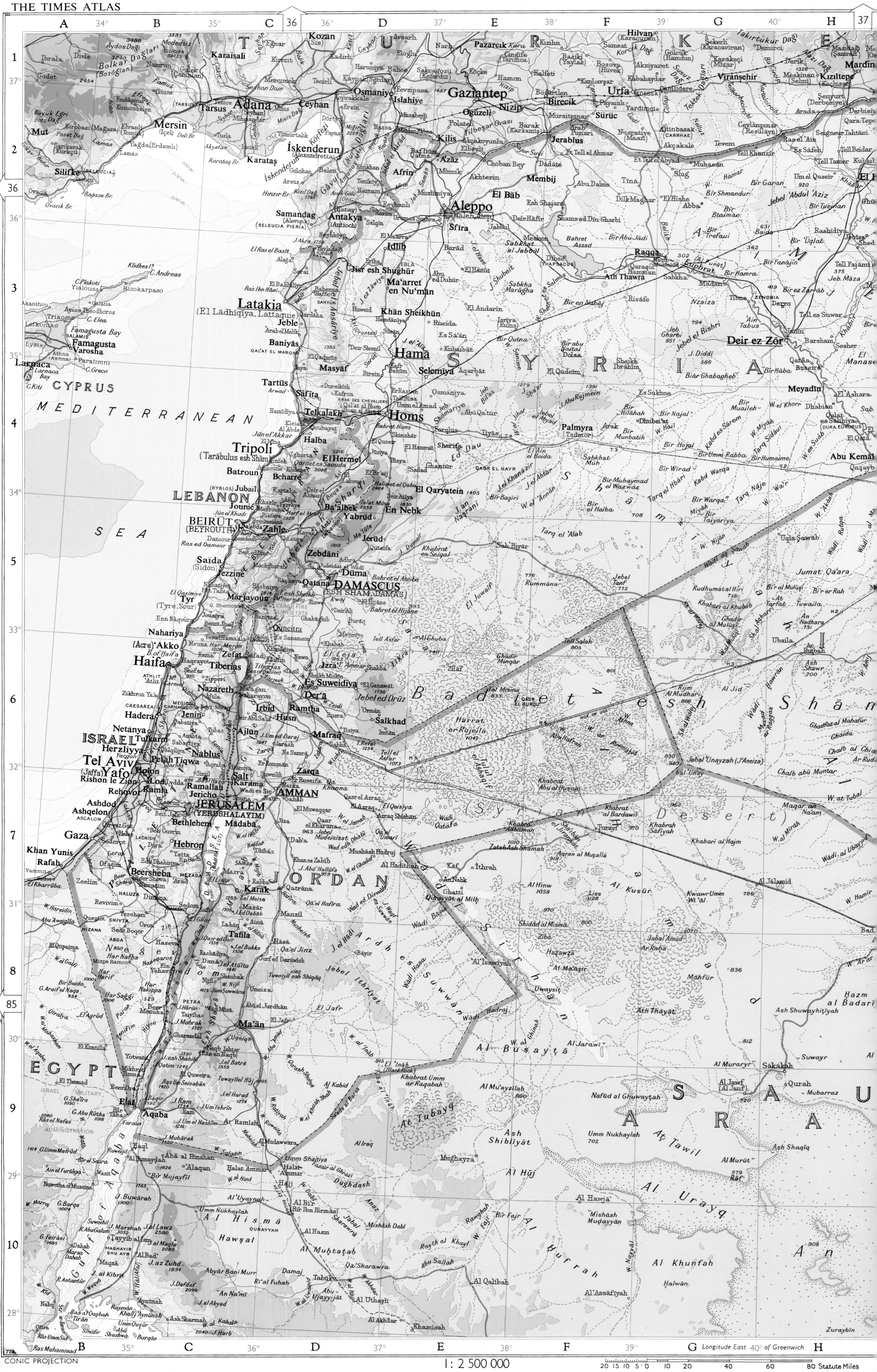
TURKEY
SYRIA
LEBANON
ISRAEL
JORDAN
EGYPT
CYPRUS
SAUDI ARABIA
MEDITERRANEAN SEA
Adana
Mersin
Tarsus
Ceyhan
İskenderun
Gaziantep
Kilis
Urfa
Birecik
Jerablus
Mardin
Aleppo
Antakya
Idlib
Latakia
Hama
Homs
Tartūs
Tripoli
Batroun
Jubail
BEIRUT
Zahle
Saïda
Tyr
Baniyās
Masyāf
Selemiya
Palmyra
Raqqa
Deir ez Zōr
Abu Kemāl
Meyadīn
El Qaryatein
DAMASCUS
Quneitra
Der'a
Es Suweidiya
Haifa
'Akko
Nazareth
Tiberias
Netanya
Tel Aviv Yafo
Herzliyya
Ramallah
Jericho
JERUSALEM
Bethlehem
Hebron
Ashdod
Ashqelon
Gaza
Khan Yunis
Rafah
Beersheba
AMMAN
Zarqa
Salt
Irbid
Mafraq
Mādabā
Karak
Tafila
Ma'ān
Aqaba
Elat
Famagusta
Larnaca
Badiet esh Shām
(Syrian Desert)
Wādi as Sirhān
Al Busaytā
An Nafūd
Gulf of Aqaba
Dead Sea
Al Hismā
Sakakah
Al Jawf

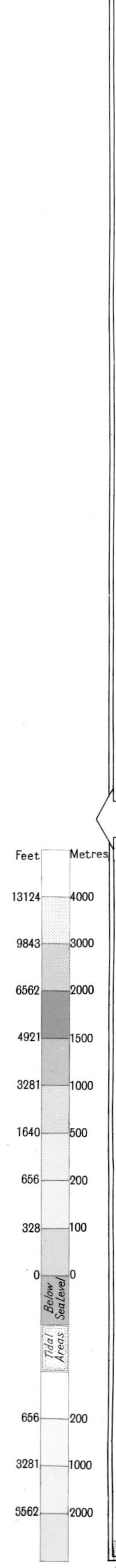
Feet
Metres
13124
4000
9843
3000
6562
2000
4921
1500
3281
1000
1640
500
656
200
328
100
0
0
Below Sea level
Tidal Areas
656
200
3281
1000
5562
2000

Mosul
Arbil
Kirkūk
Sulaymaniyah
Tikrīt
Sāmarrā'
Ba'qūbah
BAGHDAD
Ar Ramādī
Al Fallūjah
Karbalā'
Al Ḥillah
An Najaf
Ad Dīwānīyah
Al Kūt
Al 'Amārah
An Nāṣirīyah
As Samāwah
Basra
Khorramshahr
Abadan
Ahvāz
Kuwait
Kermānshāh
Hamadān
Sanandaj
Zanjān
Rezā'īyeh
Mahābād
Dahuk
Zākho
Sinjār
Tall 'Afar
Hīt
Anah
Al Ḥadīthah
Rafḥā
KURDISTAN
SOUTHERN
IRAQ
IRAN (PERSIA)
KUWAIT
LURISTAN
Ṣaḥrā al Ḥijārah
Al Bādiyah al Janūbīyah
Ad Dahnā
Euphrates
Tigris
J K L M N O P Q
42° 43° 44° 45° 46° 47° 48°
1 2 3 4 5 6 10
37° 36° 35° 34° 33° 32° 28°

LEBANON
SYRIA
Mt Hermon
2814
DEMILITARIZED ZONE
ISRAEL MILITARY ADMINISTRATION
CEASE FIRE LINES 1974
LAKE TIBERIAS
(YAM KINNERET)
(SEA OF GALILEE)
Tiberias
Haifa
Cape Karmel
BAY OF HAIFA
'Akko
(Acre)
Nahariyya
Tyre
Zefat
(Safad)
Nazareth
'Afula
Jenin
Nablus
Tulkarm
Hadera
Netanya
Herzliyya
Tel Aviv
Qalqiliya
Irbid
Ramtha
Der'a
Jarash
'Ajlun
Mafraq
Quneitra
Sheikh Miskin
Nawa
Jordan
Oil Pipe Line (underground)
JERUSALEM
1:75 000
1 Statute Mile
2 Kilometres
WHOLE AREA OF INSET
UNDER ISRAEL CONTROL.
JUNE 1967.
Bethlehem
Beit Jala
Beit Sahur
OLD CITY
ISRAEL
JORDAN
Ramat Rahel
Ein Kerem
Sur Bahir

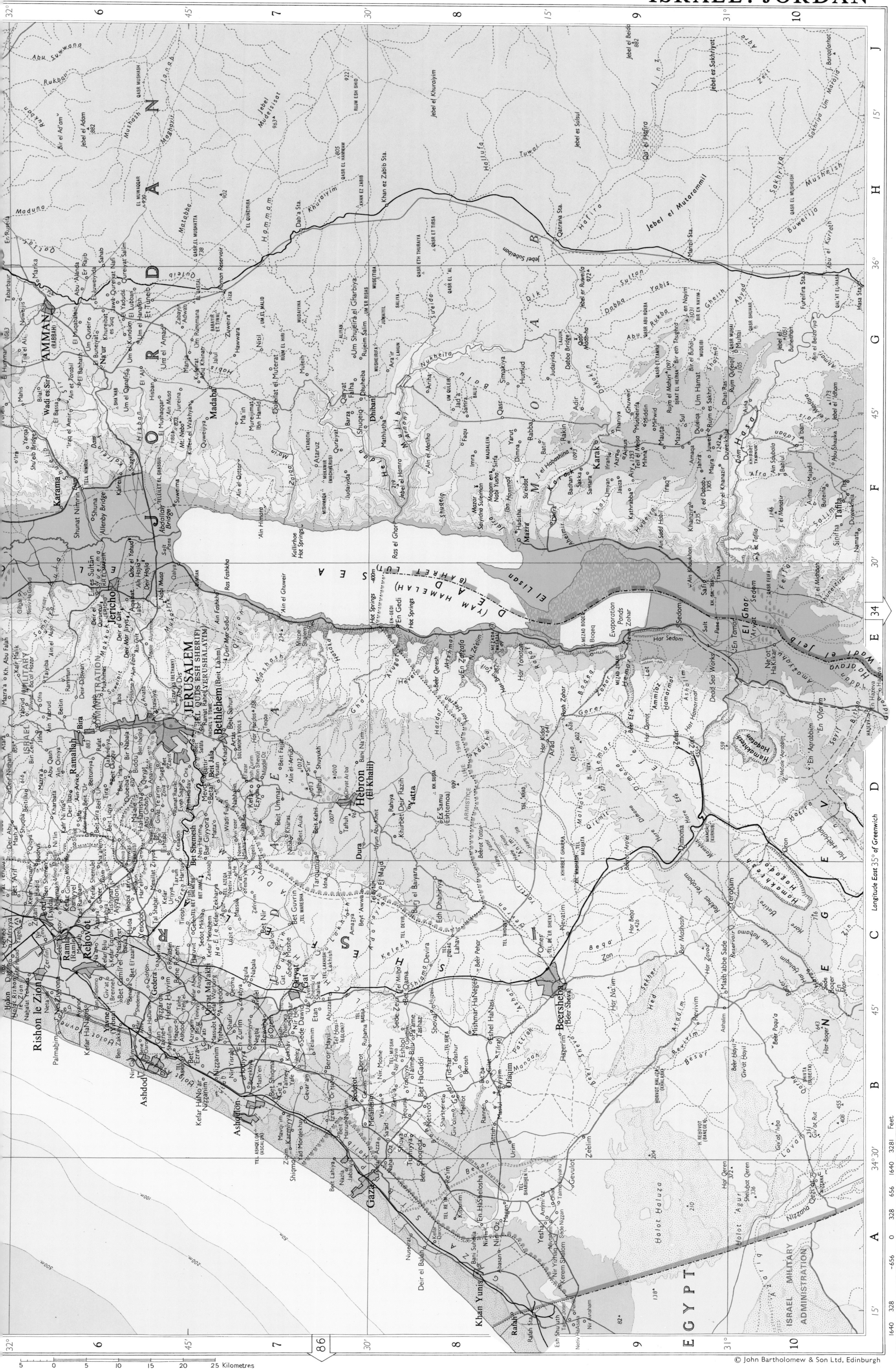
JORDAN
ISRAEL
EGYPT
AMMAN
JERUSALEM
Jericho
Bethlehem
Ramallah
Hebron (El Khalil)
Beersheba (Be'er Sheva)
Gaza
Ashdod
Ashqelon
Rishon le Zion
Rehovot
Ramla
Lod
Khan Yunis
Rafah
Madaba
Karak
Tafila
Dimona
Arad
Yatta
Dura
Dhiban
DEAD SEA (YAM HAMELAH) (BAHRET LUT)
El Lisan
Sedom
Longitude East 35° of Greenwich
Heights and Depths in Metres
Feet
Metres
Below Sea Level
Kilometres

CASPIAN SEA
SEA OF AZOV
AZOVSKOYE MORE
KASPIYSKOYE MORE
KAZAKHSTAN (S.S.R.)
KALMYTSKAYA A.S.S.R.
DAGESTAN A.S.S.R.
AZERBAYDZHAN S.S.R.
ARMENIYA S.S.R.
GRUZIYA (GEORGIA)
Rostov-na-Donu
Volgograd
Saratov
Astrakhan
Kazan
Gorkiy
Kuybyshev
MOSKVA
Kharkov
Donetsk
Voronezh
Krasnodar
Tbilisi
Baku
Groznyy
Ryn Peski
28 metres (92 feet) below sea level
Heights in Metres
300 Kilometres

BARENTSOVO MORE
(BARENTS SEA)
NORWAY
SWEDEN
FINLAND
MURMANSKIY POLUOSTROV
KOLSKIY POLUOSTROV
BELOYE MORE
(WHITE SEA)
KARELSKAYA A.S.S.R.
Ladozhskoye Ozero (Ladoga)
Onezhskoye Ozero
Murmansk
Kandalaksha
Kirovsk
Kemi
Oulu
Belomorsk
Kem'
Severodvinsk
Arkhangel'sk
Onega
Mezen'
Petrozavodsk
Leningrad
Vyborg
Kronshtadt
Volkhov
Kotlas
Syktyvkar
Vologda
Cherepovets
Rybinsk
Yaroslavl'
Kostroma
Kalinin
Ivanovo
MOSKVA
Gorkiy
Kirov
Kazan'
Izhevsk
Yoshkar Ola
Cheboksary
Ul'yanovsk
Saransk
Ryazan'
Tula
Kaluga
Orel
Bryansk
Michurinsk
Ostrov Kolguyev
Chëshskaya Guba
Rybinskoye Vodokhranilishche
Kuybyshevskoye Vodokhranilishche
Feet
Metres
4921
1500
3281
1000
1640
500
656
200
328
100
0
0
328
100
656
200
C 35° D 40° 46 E 45° F Longitude East 50° of Greenwich G
20° A 30° C 35° D 40° E 45° F 50° G

CONIC PROJECTION

1: 5 000 000

40 30 20 10 0 10 20 40 60 80 100 150 200 Statute Miles

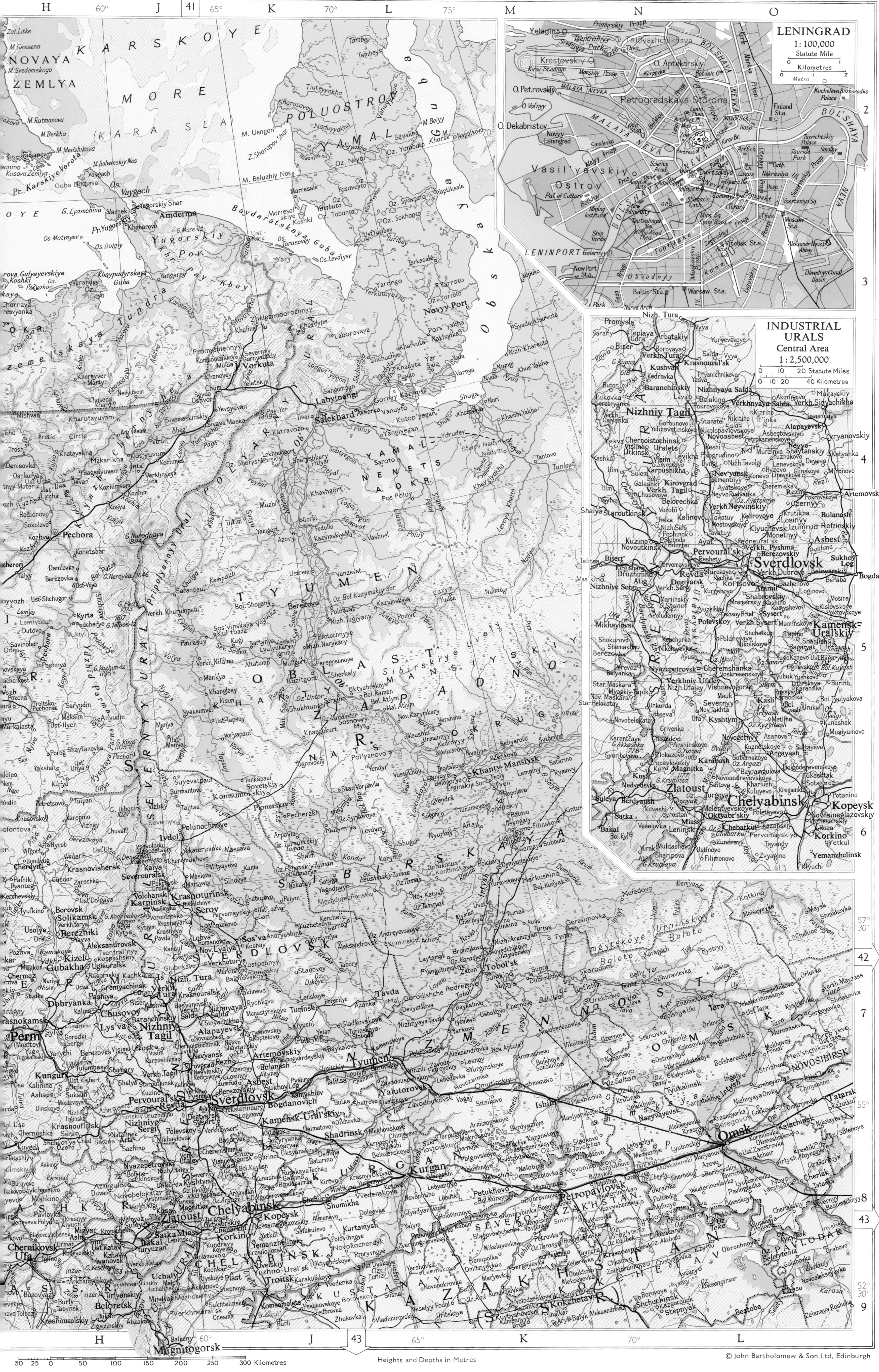
LENINGRAD
1: 100,000
Statute Mile
Kilometres
INDUSTRIAL URALS
Central Area
1 : 2,500,000
Statute Miles
Kilometres
KARSKOYE MORE
(KARA SEA)
NOVAYA ZEMLYA
POLUOSTROV YAMAL
Obskaya Guba
Baydaratskaya Guba
YAMAL - NENETS A.O.KR.
TYUMEN OBLAST'
KHANTY - MANSIYSKIY NATS. OKRUG
ZAPADNO - SIBIRSKAYA RAVNINA
POLYARNYY URAL
SEVERNYY URAL
Sibirskiye Uvaly
SVERDLOVSK
CHELYABINSK
KURGAN
OMSK
SEVERO-KAZAKHSTAN
KAZAKHSTAN
KOKCHETAV
KUSTANAY
PAVLODAR
NOVOSIBIRSK
Sverdlovsk
Chelyabinsk
Perm'
Nizhniy Tagil
Zlatoust
Magnitogorsk
Tyumen'
Kurgan
Omsk
Petropavlovsk
Tobol'sk
Khanty-Mansiysk
Salekhard
Labytnangi
Vorkuta
Pechora
Ufa
Kokchetav
Heights and Depths in Metres
Kilometres
© John Bartholomew & Son Ltd, Edinburgh

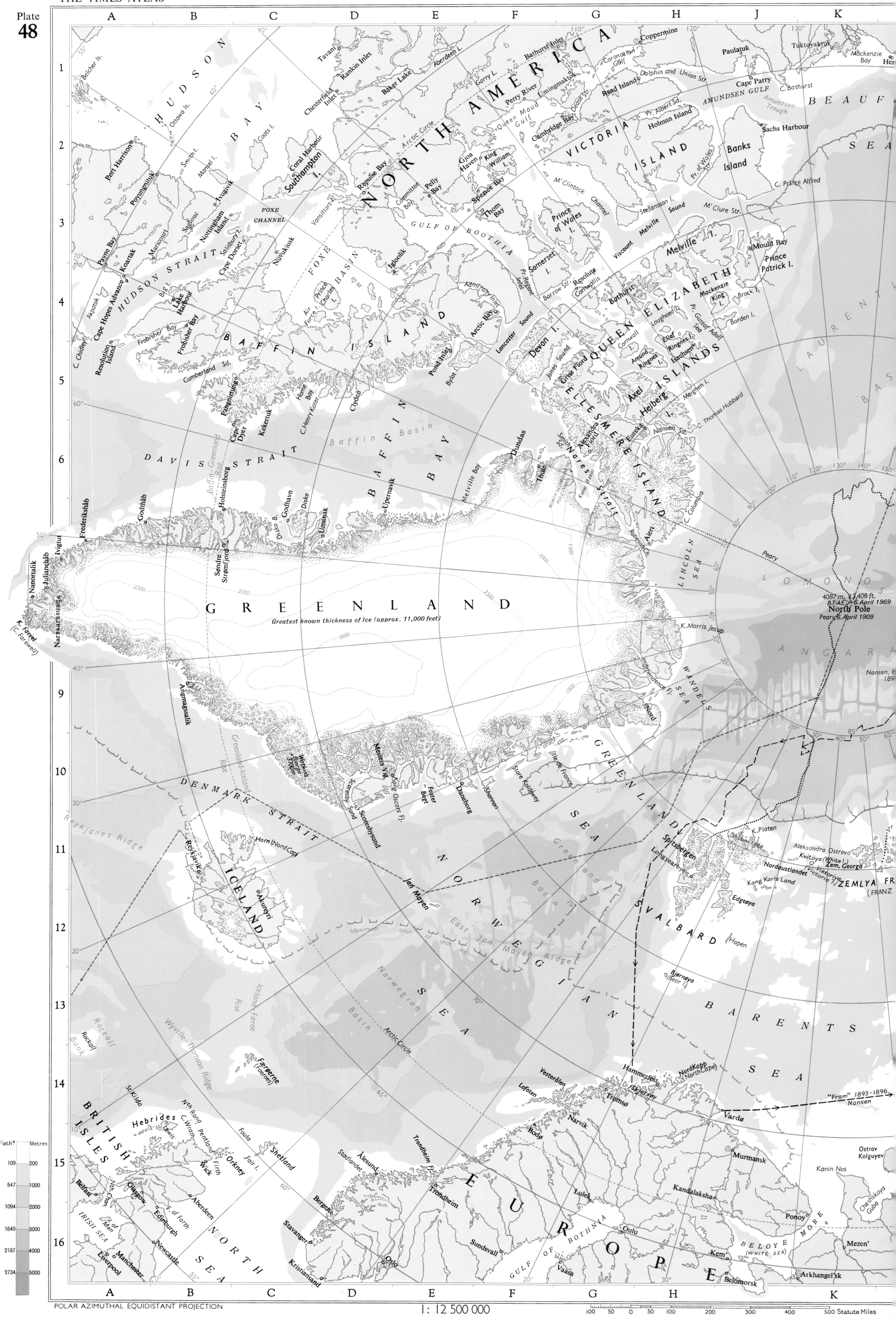
NORTH AMERICA
HUDSON BAY
HUDSON STRAIT
FOXE CHANNEL
FOXE BASIN
Southampton I.
Coral Harbour
Chesterfield Inlet
Rankin Inlet
Baker Lake
Tavani
Aberdeen L.
Bathurst Inlet
Coppermine
Coronation Gulf
Dolphin and Union Str.
Cambridge Bay
Queen Maud Gulf
Perry River
Gjoa Haven
King William I.
Spence Bay
Pelly Bay
Repulse Bay
Committee Bay
GULF OF BOOTHIA
Thom Bay
VICTORIA ISLAND
Holman Island
Pr. Albert Sd.
AMUNDSEN GULF
Cape Parry
Paulatuk
Tuktoyaktuk
Mackenzie Bay
C. Bathurst
Amundsen Trough
Banks Island
Sachs Harbour
C. Prince Alfred
BEAUFORT SEA
M'Clintock Channel
Prince of Wales I.
Stefansson I.
Viscount Melville Sound
M'Clure Str.
Melville I.
Mould Bay
Prince Patrick I.
Somerset I.
Barrow Str.
Resolute
Cornwallis
Bathurst I.
QUEEN ELIZABETH ISLANDS
Mackenzie King I.
Brock I.
Borden I.
Lougheed I.
Pr. Gustaf Adolf Sea
Ellef Ringnes I.
Amund Ringnes I.
Isachsen
Cornwall I.
Meighen I.
Axel Heiberg I.
Eureka
Nansen Sd.
C. Thomas Hubbard
ELLESMERE ISLAND
Grise Fiord
Jones Sound
Alexandra Fiord
Devon I.
Lancaster Sound
Admiralty Inlet
Arctic Bay
Pond Inlet
Bylot I.
BAFFIN ISLAND
Igloolik
Prince Charles I.
Air Force I.
Frobisher Bay
Lake Harbour
Cumberland Sd.
Pangnirtung
Cape Dyer
Kekertuk
Home Bay
C. Henry Kater
Clyde
Resolution Island
Cape Hopes Advance
Koartak
Payne Bay
Maricourt
Sugluk
Ivugivik
Nottingham Island
Salisbury I.
Cape Dorset
Nuvukjuak
Port Harrison
Povungnituk
Smith I.
Mansel I.
Coats I.
Ottawa Is.
Belcher Is.
Akpatok I.
C. Chidley
DAVIS STRAIT
BAFFIN BAY
Baffin Basin
Baffin-Greenland Rise
Melville Bay
Dundas
Thule
Smith Sd.
Nares Strait
Kane Basin
Robeson Ch.
Alert
C. Columbia
LINCOLN SEA
Peary
North Pole
Peary 6 April 1909
LOMONOSOV
ANGARA
Nansen
GREENLAND
Greatest known thickness of Ice (approx. 11,000 feet)
Upernavik
Umanak
Disko
Godhavn
Disko B.
Holsteinsborg
Godthåb
Fredrikshåb
Søndre Strømfjord
Ivigtut
Julianehåb
Nanortalik
Narssarssuaq
K. Farvel (C. Farewell)
Angmagssalik
Mesters Vig
Kong Oscars Fj.
Scoresby Sund
Scoresbysund
Foster Bugt
Daneborg
Shannon
Store Koldewey
Île de France
Nord
Independence Fj.
K. Morris Jesup
WANDELS SEA
GREENLAND SEA
Greenland Basin
DENMARK STRAIT
Greenland-Iceland Rise
Reykjanes Ridge
ICELAND
Reykjavík
Akureyri
Horn (Nord Cap)
Jan Mayen
East Jan Mayen Ridge
NORWEGIAN SEA
Norwegian Basin
Iceland-Faeroe Rise
Wyville-Thomson Ridge
Maximum limit of drift ice
Limit of permanent pack ice
Arctic Circle
Færøerne (Faeroes)
Rockall
Rockall Bank
SVALBARD
Spitsbergen
Longyearbyen
Nordaustlandet
Kong Karls Land
Edgeøya
Hopen
Bjørnøya (Bear I.)
K. Platen
Kvitøya (White I.)
Zem. Georga
O. Viktoriya (Victoria I.)
Aleksandra Ostrova
ZEMLYA FRANZ
BARENTS SEA
"Fram" 1893–1896 Nansen
Hammerfest
Nordkapp (North Cape)
Skjervøy
Tromsø
Vesterålen
Lofoten
Narvik
Bodø
Vardø
Murmansk
Kandalaksha
Kanin Nos
Ostrov Kolguyev
Cheshskaya Guba
Ponoy
Mezen'
BELOYE MORE (WHITE SEA)
Kem'
Belomorsk
Arkhangel'sk
Oulu
Luleå
GULF OF BOTHNIA
Vaasa
Sundsvall
Trondheim
Trondheim Fj.
Ålesund
Stadlandet
Bergen
Stavanger
Kristiansand
Oslo
EUROPE
Shetland
Fair I.
Foula
Orkney
Pentland Firth
Wick
C. Wrath
Nth Rona
Hebrides
Lewis
St. Kilda
BRITISH ISLES
Aberdeen
F. of Forth
Edinburgh
Glasgow
Belfast
Nth. Chan.
I. of Man
IRISH SEA
Newcastle
Liverpool
Manchester
NORTH SEA
Faths
Metres
109
200
547
1000
1094
2000
1640
3000
2187
4000
2734
5000
100 50 0 50 100 200 300 400 500 Statute Miles

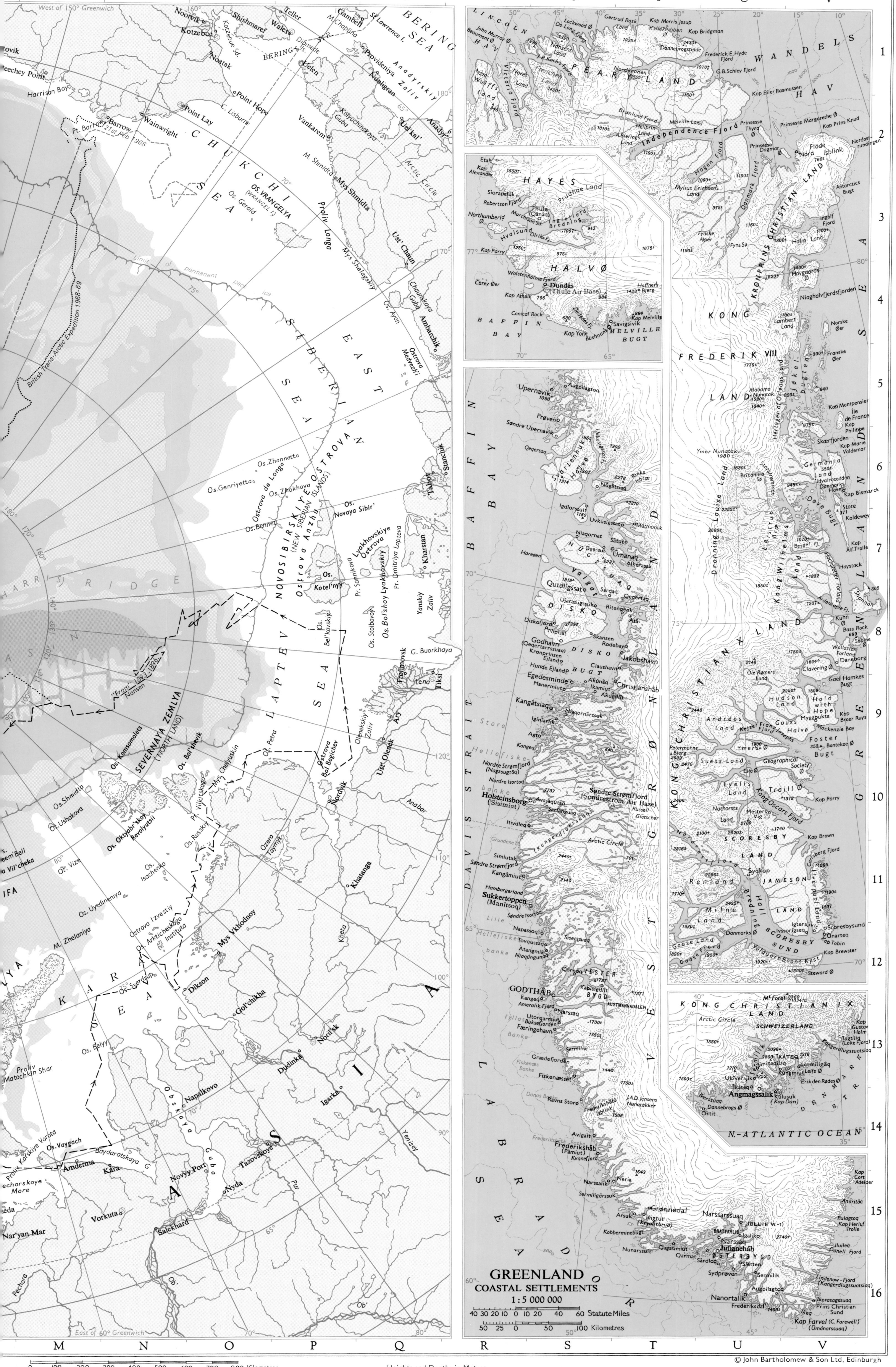

M N O P Q R S T U V
CHUKCHI SEA
BERING SEA
EAST SIBERIAN SEA
LAPTEV SEA
KARA SEA
NOVOSIBIRSKIYE OSTROVA (NEW SIBERIAN ISLANDS)
SEVERNAYA ZEMLYA (NORTH LAND)
OS. VRANGELYA (WRANGEL I.)
Limit of permanent pack ice
British Trans-Arctic Expedition 1968-69
"Fram" 1893-1896 Nansen
West of 150° Greenwich
East of 60° Greenwich
Arctic Circle
Barrow
Point Hope
Point Lay
Wainwright
Kotzebue
Noorvik
Shishmaref
Wales
Teller
Gambell
St Lawrence I.
Providenciya
Uelen
Anadyr'
Vankarem
Mys Shmidta
Proliv Longa
Ust' Chaun
Ambarchik
Os. Kotel'nyy
Yanskiy Zaliv
Tiksi
Os. Bol'shevik
Os. Komsomolets
Os. Oktyabr'skoy Revolyutsii
Mys Chelyuskin
Khatanga
Nordvik
Dikson
Mys Vkhodnoy
Noril'sk
Dudinka
Igarka
Napalkovo
Novyy Port
Tazovskoye
Nyda
Salekhard
Vorkuta
Nar'yan Mar
Amderma
Kara
Os. Vaygach
Yenisey
Ob'
Pechora
A S I A
ARCTIC OCEAN: GREENLAND
LINCOLN HAV
WANDELS HAV
PEARY LAND
Independence Fjord
Kap Morris Jesup
HAYES HALVØ
Thule (Qânâq)
Dundas (Thule Air Base)
BAFFIN BAY
MELVILLE BUGT
KRONPRINS CHRISTIAN LAND
KONG FREDERIK VIII LAND
Danmarkshavn
DRONNING LOUISE LAND
KONG CHRISTIAN X LAND
KONG CHRISTIAN IX LAND
SCORESBY LAND
JAMESON LAND
SCORESBY SUND
Angmagssalik
N.-ATLANTIC OCEAN
DAVIS STRAIT
LABRADOR SEA
GRØNLAND
VESTERBYGD
ØSTERBYGD
Upernavik
Umanaq
Disko
Godhavn (Qeqertarssuaq)
Jakobshavn
Egedesminde
Holsteinsborg (Sisimiut)
Søndre Strømfjord (Søndrestrom Air Base)
Sukkertoppen (Manitsoq)
GODTHÅB
Frederikshåb (Pâmiut)
Grønnedal
Ivigtut
Narssarssuaq (BLUIE W.-1)
Julianehåb
Nanortalik
Kap Farvel (C. Farewell)
GREENLAND COASTAL SETTLEMENTS
1:5 000 000
Statute Miles
Kilometres

© John Bartholomew & Son Ltd, Edinburgh

Plate
49

BONNE'S PROJECTION

Heights and Depths in Metres

1: 12 900 000

0 100 200 300 400 500 Statute Miles

EUROPE

BARENTS SEA
OCEAN
KARA SEA
Novaya Zemlya
Yamal
Obskaya Guba
Kol'skiy Poluostrov
Beloye More (White Sea)
FINLAND
Helsinki
Leningrad
ESTONIA
LATVIA
Riga
LITHUANIA
WHITE RUSSIA
Minsk
UKRAINE
Kiyev
Kharkov
Dnepropetrovsk
Donetsk
Odessa
Rostov
Volgograd
Astrakhan
Moskva
Yaroslavl'
Gor'kiy
Kazan
Kuybyshev
Saratov
Sverdlovsk
Magnitogorsk
Omsk
Novosibirsk
UNION OF SOVIET SOCIALIST REPUBLICS
KAZAKHSTAN
UZBEKISTAN
TURKMENISTAN
Aral'skoye More (Aral Sea)
CASPIAN SEA
BLACK SEA
Azovskoye More (Sea of Azov)
Krim (Crimea)
Sevastopol
MOLDAVIA
ROMANIA
București
BULGARIA
Sofiya
GEORGIA
Tbilisi
AZERBAIJAN
Baku
ARMENIA
Yerevan
TURKEY
Ankara
Istanbul
Izmir
GREECE
Athinai
Kriti (Crete)
CYPRUS
SYRIA
Aleppo
Damascus
Beirut
LEBANON
ISRAEL
Tel-Aviv-Yafo
Jerusalem
JORDAN
SAUDI ARABIA
IRAQ
Baghdad
Basra
KUWAIT
IRAN (PERSIA)
Tehrān
Tabriz
Esfahan
PERSIAN GULF
Alexandria
Cairo
EGYPT
Longitude East of Greenwich
0 100 200 300 400 500 600 700 800 Kilometres

Feet
Metres
4921
1500
3281
1000
1640
500
656
200
328
100
0
0
328
100
656
200
Arctic Circle
HÚNA-
FLÓI
BREIÐA
FJÖRÐUR
FAXA-
FLÓI
REYKJAVÍK
Akranes
Borgarnes
Keflavík
Hafnarfjörður
Kópavogur
Grindavík
Ísafjörður
Flateyri
Bolungavík
Patreksfjörður
Stykkishólmur
Ólafsvík
Hellissandur
Grundarfjörður
Blönduós
Höfðakaupstaður
(Skagaströnd)
Hveragerði
Selfoss
Eyrarbakki
Stokkseyri
Hella
Vestmannaeyjar
Surtsey
Reykjanestá
Eldey
LANGJÖKULL
Eiríks jökull
Hekla
Drangajökull
Snæfellsjökull
Glámá
GULLBRINGU SÝSLA
KJÓSAR SÝSLA
BORGARFJARÐAR SÝSLA
MÝRA SÝSLA
SNÆFELLSNES SÝSLA
DALA SÝSLA
BARÐASTRANDAR SÝSLA
VESTUR ÍSAFJARÐAR SÝSLA
STRANDA SÝSLA
HUNAVATNS SÝSLA
SKAGAFJARÐA
ÁRNES SÝSLA
RANGÁRVALLA SÝSLA
Jan Mayen
Nordkapp
Kapp Muyen
Beerenberg
NORD-JAN
SØR-JAN
Kapp Wien
Sørvestkapp
JAN MAYEN
(To Norway)
1 : 1 000 000
NOTE: SPECIAL ICELANDIC CHARACTERS
Þ, þ, (initial) equivalent to soft 'th' (as in thing).
Ð, ð, (never initial) equivalent to harder 'dh' (as in this).
Longitude West 20° of Greenwich
9° West
50 Statute Miles

ICELAND

0 5 10 20 30 40 50 60 70 80 Kilometres

Heights and Depths in Metres

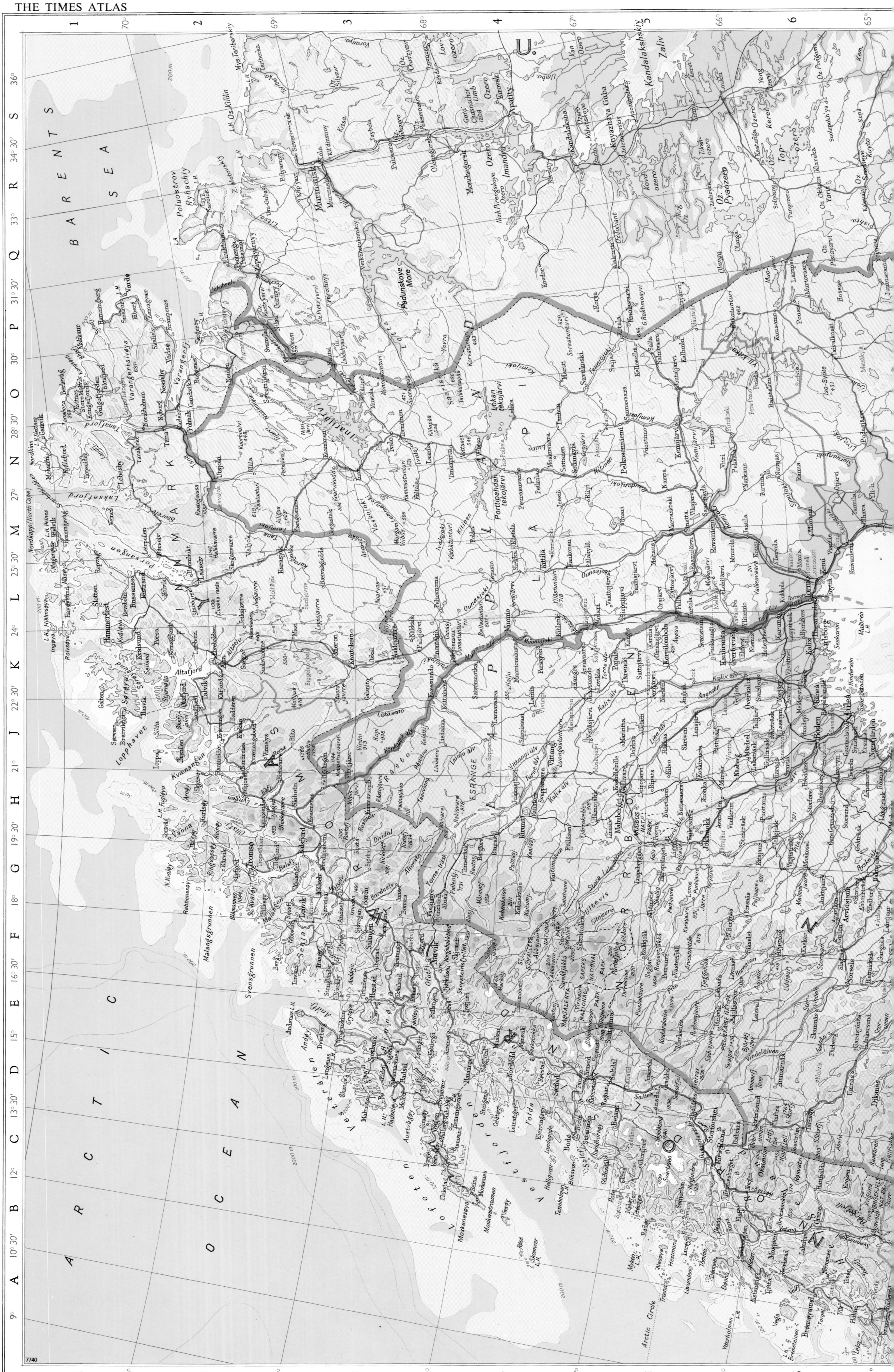

SIMPLE CONIC PROJECTION

1: 2 550 000

0 10 20 40 60 80 100 120 Statute Miles

FINLAND AND SCANDINAVIA NORTH

Plate 51

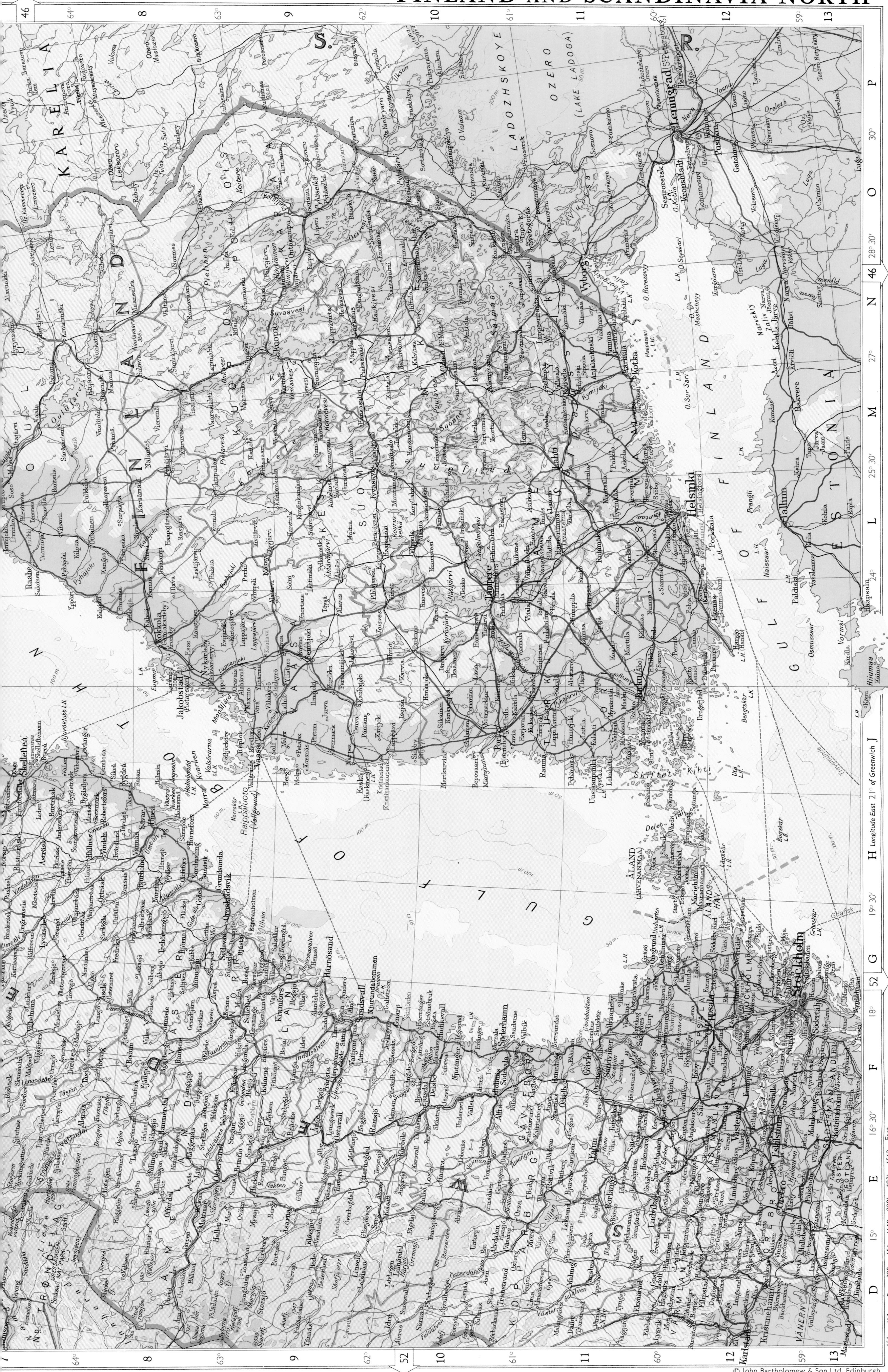

Heights and Depths in Metres
Metres 2000 1500 1000 500 200 100 50 0 50 200
Feet 6562 4921 3281 1640 656 328 164 0 164 656
0 10 20 40 60 80 100 120 140 160 180 200 Kilometres

SIMPLE CONIC PROJECTION

1: 2 550 000

0 10 20 40 60 80 100 120 Statute Miles

SCANDINAVIA SOUTH

Plate
52

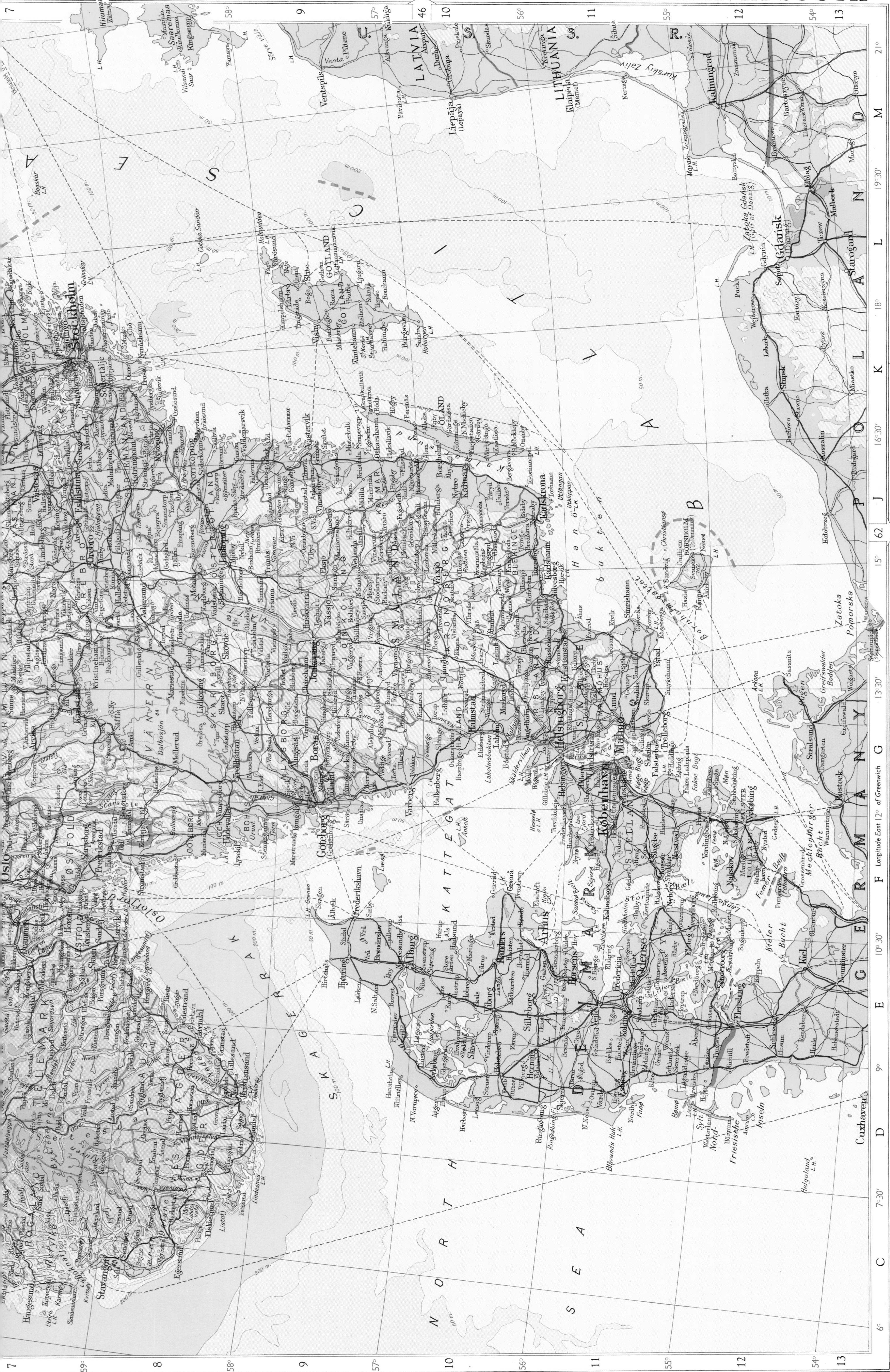

0 10 20 40 60 80 100 120 140 160 180 200 Kilometres

Metres	Feet
2000	6562
1500	4921
1000	3280
500	1640
200	656
100	328
0	0
Below Sea Level	
50	164
200	656

© John Bartholomew & Son Ltd, Edinburgh

SKAGERRAK
KATTEGAT
JYLLAND
DENMARK
FÆRØERNE
(FØROYAR)
(FAEROES)
(To Denmark)
For Ð and ð see note on Plate 50, Iceland.
SJÆLLAND
FYN
(FÜNEN)
LOLLAND
FALSTER
SØNDERJYLLAND
SCHLESWIG-HOLSTEIN
GERMANY
NORDFRIESISCHE INSELN
KIELER BUCHT
MECKLENBURGER BUCHT
STORE BÆLT
LILLE BÆLT
Fehmarn
Femer Bælt
Samsø Bælt
Ålborg
Århus
Odense
Esbjerg
Randers
Viborg
Vejle
Kolding
Horsens
Silkeborg
Herning
Holstebro
Frederikshavn
Hjørring
Skagen
Flensburg
Kiel
Schleswig
Rendsburg
Husum
Sylt
Helgoland
Læsø
Anholt
Limfjorden
Jammerbugten
Heights and Depths in Metres
Longitude East 11° of Greenwich

SECANT CONIC PROJECTION

Heights and Depths in Metres

1:1 000 000

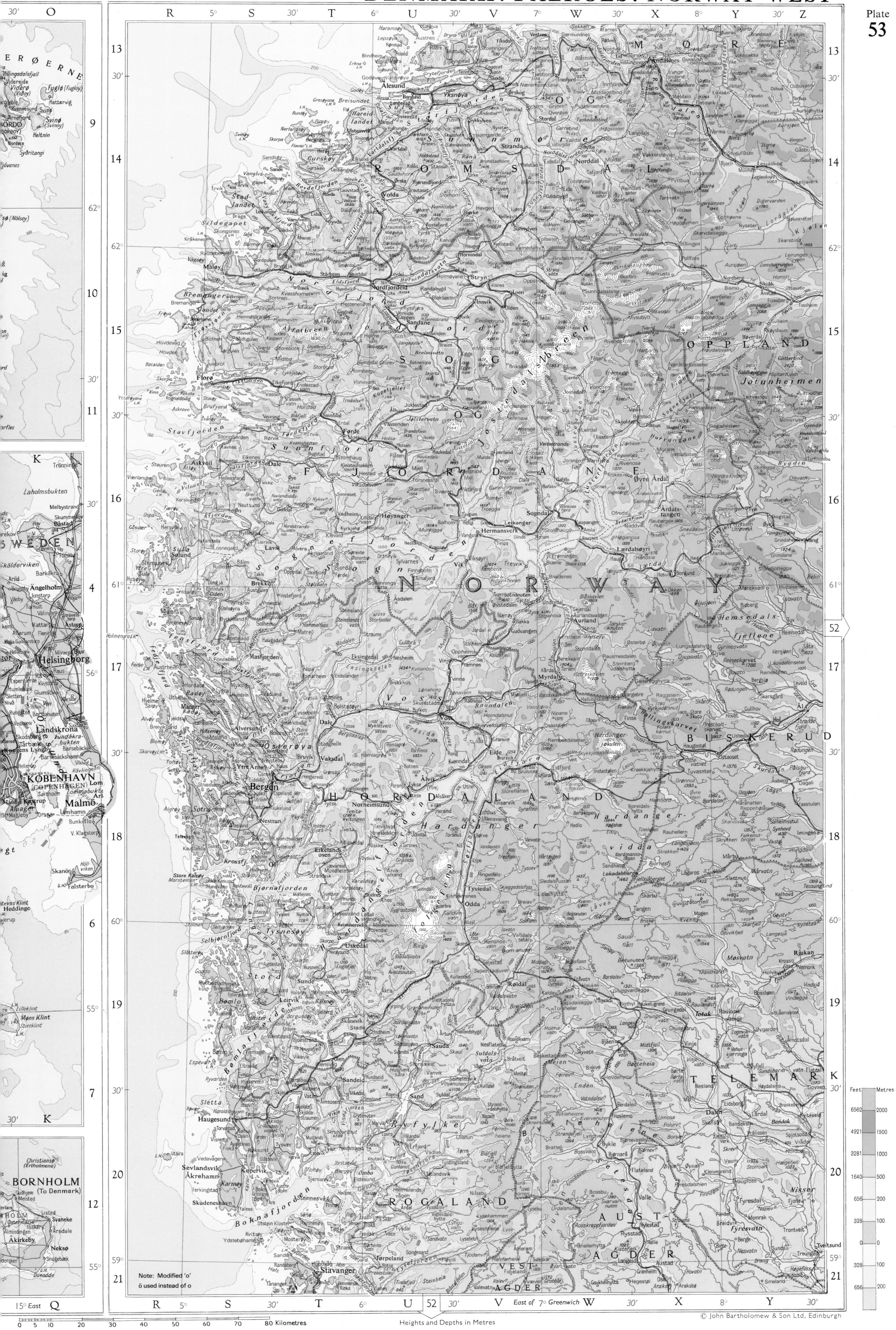

FÆRØERNE
BORNHOLM (To Denmark)
SWEDEN
Helsingborg
KØBENHAVN (COPENHAGEN)
Malmö
NORWAY
MØRE OG ROMSDAL
SOGN OG FJORDANE
HORDALAND
ROGALAND
OPPLAND
BUSKERUD
TELEMARK
AUST AGDER
VEST AGDER
Jotunheimen
Hardangervidda
Ålesund
Molde
Florø
Bergen
Haugesund
Stavanger
Sognefjorden
Hardangerfjorden
Nordfjord
Note: Modified 'o' ö used instead of ø
Heights and Depths in Metres
East of 7° Greenwich
Feet / Metres
80 Kilometres

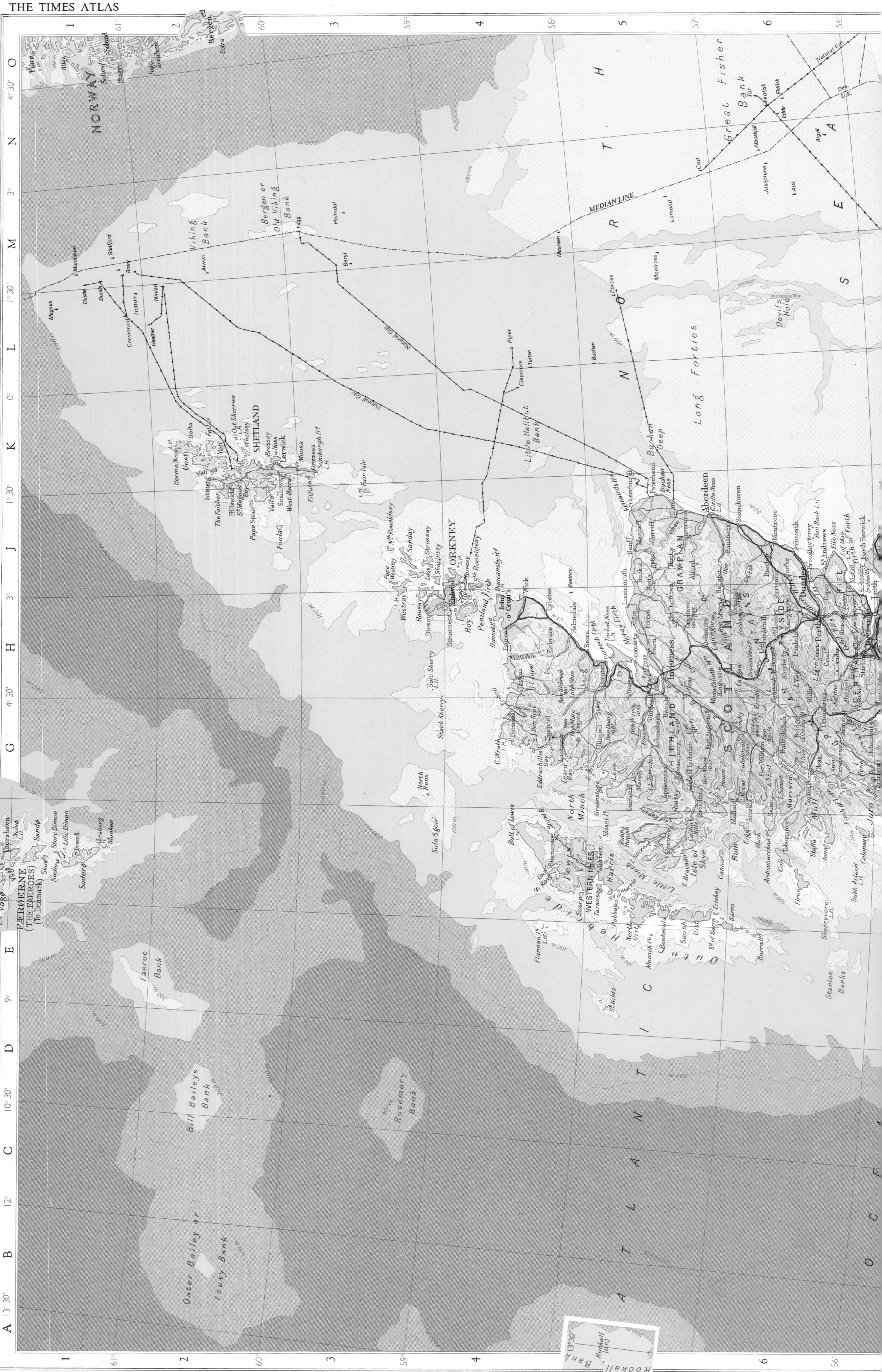

SECANT, CONIC PROJECTION

1: 2 500 000

0 10 20 40 60 80 100 120 Statute Miles

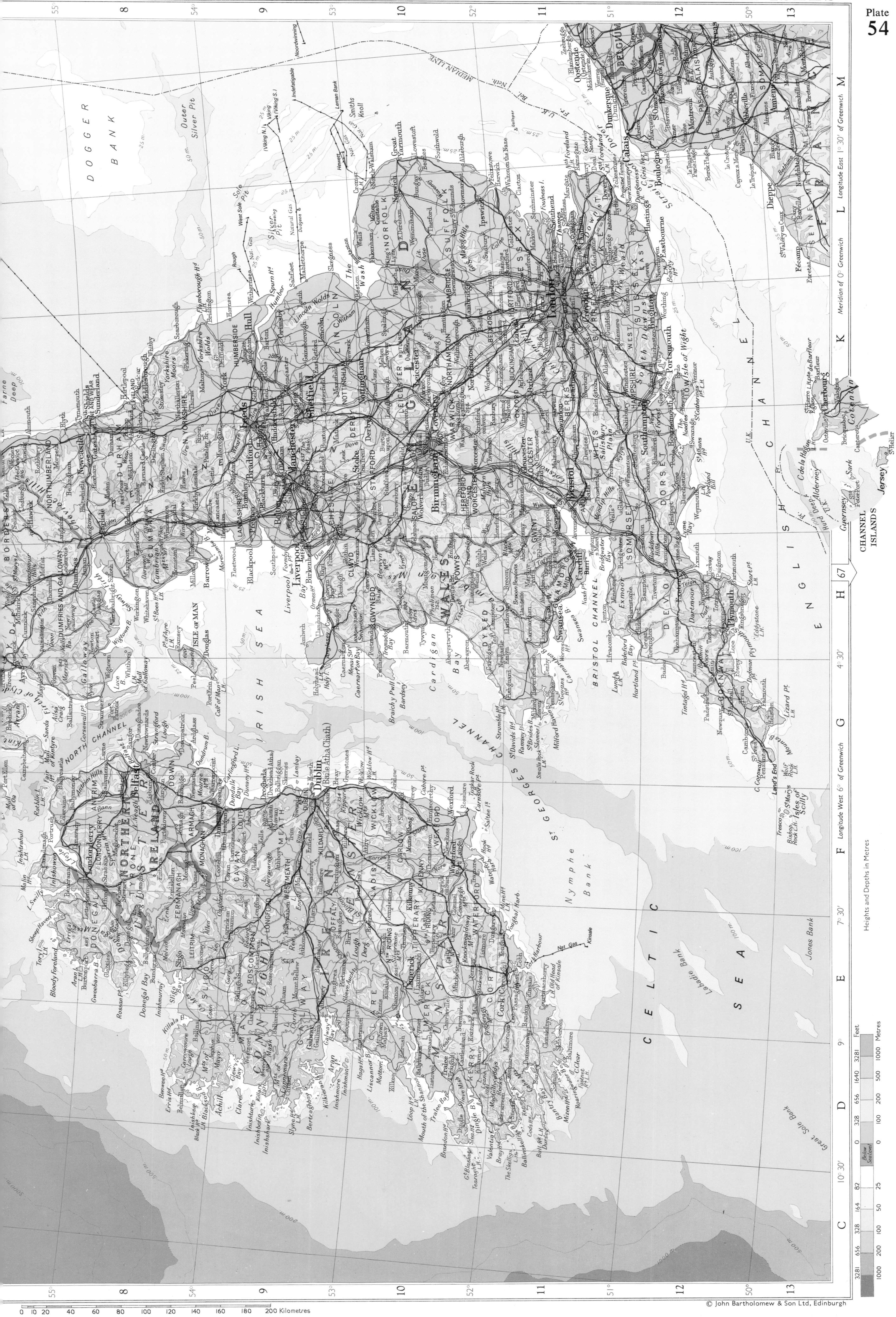
THE BRITISH ISLES
Heights and Depths in Metres
0 10 20 40 60 80 100 120 140 160 180 200 Kilometres

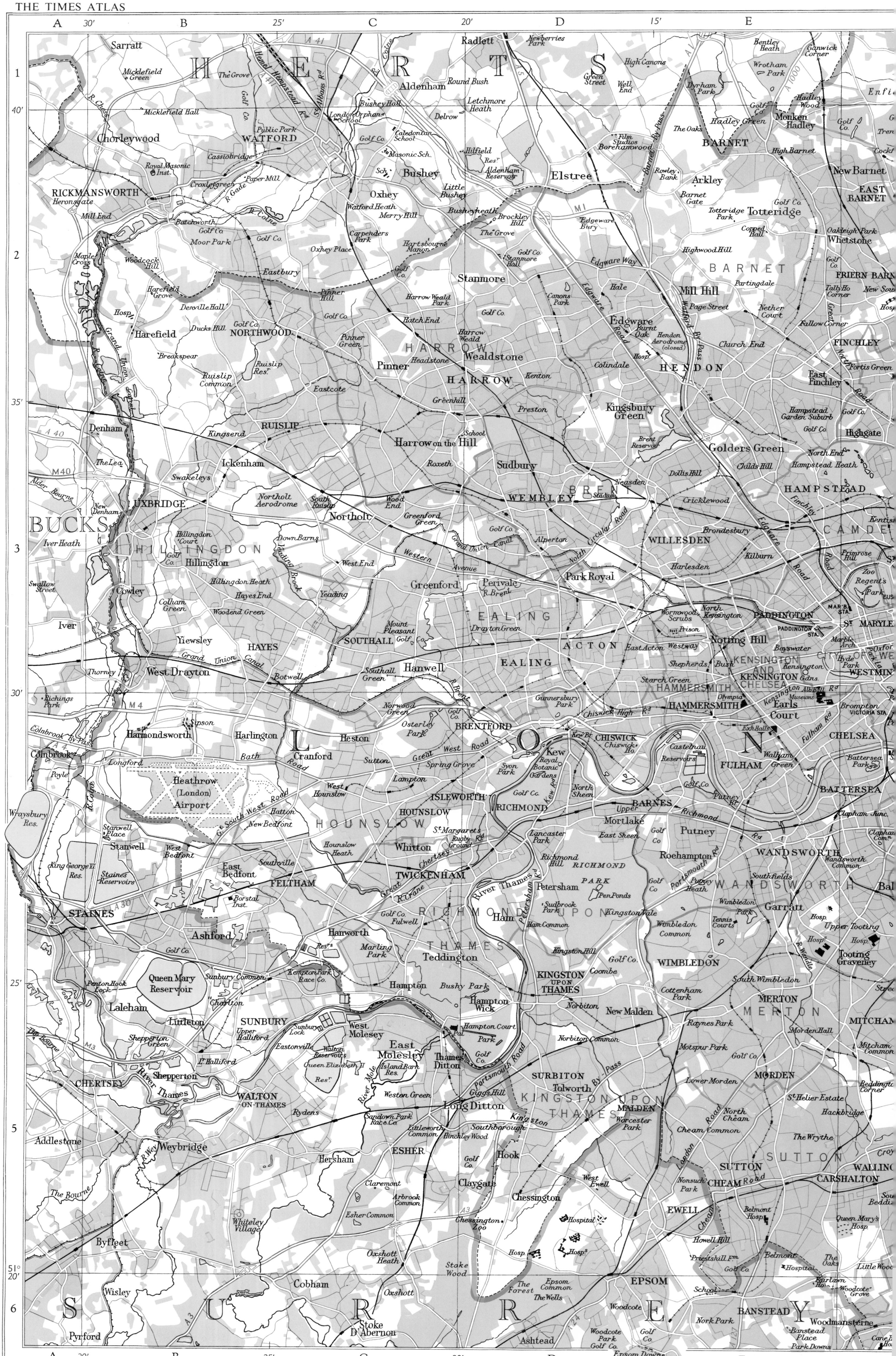
A
B
C
D
E
30'
25'
20'
15'
40'
35'
30'
25'
51° 20'
1
2
3
4
5
6
H
E
R
T
S
Sarratt
Micklefield Green
Micklefield Hall
The Grove
Chorleywood
WATFORD
Public Park
Cassiobridge
Royal Masonic Inst.
RICKMANSWORTH
Heronsgate
Mill End
Croxleygreen
Paper Mill
Batchworth
Moor Park
Maple Cross
Woodcock Hill
Eastbury
Harefield Grove
Deroville Hall
Hosp.
Harefield
Ducks Hill
NORTHWOOD
Breakspear
Ruislip Res.
Ruislip Common
Denham
The Lea
M40
A 40
Alder Bourne
New Denham
UXBRIDGE
BUCKS
Iver Heath
HILLINGDON
Hillingdon Court
Hillingdon
Hillingdon Heath
Hayes End
Swallow Street
Cowley
Colham Green
Woodend Green
Iver
Yiewsley
HAYES
Thorney
West Drayton
Grand Union Canal
Richings Park
M4
Colnbrook By Pass
Sipson
Harmondsworth
Harlington
Colnbrook
Poyle
Longford
Bath Road
Heathrow (London) Airport
Wraysbury Res.
Stanwell Place
Stanwell
West Bedfont
King George VI Res.
Staines Reservoirs
East Bedfont
STAINES
A 30
Ashford
Penton Hook Lock
Queen Mary Reservoir
Laleham
Littleton
Shepperton Green
Lr. Halliford
M3
CHERTSEY
Shepperton
River Thames
Addlestone
Weybridge
R. Wey
The Bourne
Byfleet
Wisley
Pyrford
S
U
R
R
E
Y
Radlett
Newberries Park
Aldenham
Round Bush
Bushey Hall
London Orphan School
Letchmore Heath
Delrow
Caledonian School
Masonic Sch.
Hilfield
Aldenham Reservoir
Bushey
Oxhey
Little Bushey
Watford Heath
Merry Hill
Bushey heath
Carpenders Park
Oxhey Place
Hartsbourne Manor
Brockley Hill
The Grove
Stanmore
Pinner Hill
Harrow Weald Park
Hatch End
Pinner Green
Harrow Weald
HARROW
Wealdstone
Pinner
Headstone
Eastcote
Kenton
Greenhill
Preston
Kingsend
RUISLIP
Ickenham
Swakeleys
Harrow on the Hill
Roxeth
Sudbury
Northolt Aerodrome
South Ruislip
Northolt
Wood End
Greenford Green
WEMBLEY
Down Barns
Yeading Brook
West End
Western Avenue
Greenford
Perivale
Yeading
Mount Pleasant
SOUTHALL
EALING
Hanwell
Botwell
Southall Green
Norwood Green
Osterley Park
Heston
BRENTFORD
Cranford
Sutton
Great West Road
Spring Grove
Lampton
West Hounslow
Hatton
New Bedfont
HOUNSLOW
ISLEWORTH
Hounslow Heath
Whitton
St. Margarets
Southville
TWICKENHAM
FELTHAM
Borstal Inst.
R. Crane
Fulwell
Hanworth
Marling Park
Teddington
Sunbury Common
Kempton Park Race Co.
Charlton
Hampton
Bushy Park
Hampton Wick
SUNBURY
Upper Halliford
Sunbury Lock
West Molesey
Hampton Court Pal.
Walton Reservoirs
East Molesey
Island Barn Res.
Queen Elizabeth II Res.
Thames Ditton
WALTON ON-THAMES
River Mole
Weston Green
Rydens
Giggs Hill
Long Ditton
Sandown Park Race Co.
Littleworth Common
Hinchley Wood
ESHER
Hersham
Claremont
Claygate
Arbrook Common
Esher Common
Whiteley Village
Oxshott Heath
Stake Wood
Cobham
Oxshott
Stoke D'Abernon
Elstree
Film Studios
Borehamwood
Green Street
High Canons
Well End
Edgware Bury
Edgware Way
M1
Stanmore Hall
Canons Park
Hale
Edgware
Burnt Oak
Hendon Aerodrome (closed)
Colindale
Kingsbury Green
Brent Reservoir
BRENT
Neasden
Stadium
Alperton
North Circular Road
Park Royal
ACTON
East Acton
Drayton Green
Gunnersbury Park
Chiswick High Rd.
CHISWICK
Kew
Royal Botanic Gardens
Kew Br.
Syon Park
RICHMOND
North Sheen
Mortlake
East Sheen
Lancaster Park
Richmond Hill
RICHMOND PARK
Pen Ponds
Petersham
Sudbrook Park
Ham
Ham Common
Kingston Vale
Kingston Hill
Coombe
KINGSTON UPON THAMES
Norbiton
New Malden
Norbiton Common
Portsmouth Road
SURBITON
Tolworth
Kingston By-Pass
MALDEN
Worcester Park
Southborough
Hook
West Ewell
Chessington
Chessington Zoo
Hospital
Hosp.
The Forest
Epsom Common
The Wells
EPSOM
Woodcote
Ashtead
Woodcote Park Golf Co.
Epsom Downs Race Course
Bentley Heath
Wrotham Park
Ganwick Corner
Dyrham Park
Hadley Green
Hadley Wood
Monken Hadley
The Oaks
BARNET
High Barnet
New Barnet
EAST BARNET
Rowley Bank
Arkley
Barnet Gate
Totteridge Park
Totteridge
Copped Hall
Oakleigh Park
Whetstone
Highwood Hill
BARNET
FRIERN BARNET
Mill Hill
Partingdale
Page Street
Nether Court
Tally Ho Corner
Fallow Corner
Watford By Pass
HENDON
Church End
FINCHLEY
East Finchley
Fortis Green
Hampstead Garden Suburb
Highgate
Golders Green
North End
Hampstead Heath
Dollis Hill
Childs Hill
HAMPSTEAD
Cricklewood
WILLESDEN
Brondesbury
Kilburn
Harlesden
Edgware Road
Primrose Hill
Zoo
Regents Park
Wormwood Scrubs
North Kensington
PADDINGTON
Notting Hill
Westway
Bayswater
Hyde Park
KENSINGTON AND CHELSEA
Shepherds Bush
Kensington Gdns.
Olympia
HAMMERSMITH
Starch Green
Earls Court
Brompton
CHELSEA
Castelnau Reservoirs
Exh. Halls
Fulham Rd
FULHAM
Walham Green
BARNES
Putney Br.
Battersea Park
BATTERSEA
Clapham Junc.
Putney
Roehampton
WANDSWORTH
Wandsworth Common
Southfields
Putney Heath
Wimbledon Park
Garratt
Upper Tooting
Tennis Courts
Wimbledon Common
WIMBLEDON
Tooting Graveney
South Wimbledon
Cottenham Park
MERTON
Morden Hall
MITCHAM
Mitcham Common
Raynes Park
Motspur Park
MORDEN
Lower Morden
Beddington Corner
St. Helier Estate
North Cheam
Hackbridge
Cheam Common
The Wrythe
SUTTON
CARSHALTON
CHEAM
Nonsuch Park
EWELL
Belmont Hosp.
Queen Mary's Hosp.
Howell Hill
Priestshill Fm.
Belmont
The Oaks
Burgh Heath
Nork Park
BANSTEAD
Banstead Place
Park Downs
Woodmansterne
Golf Co.
A
B
C
D
E
Longitude West 10' of Greenwich
1: 100 000
5 Statute Miles

LONDON AND ENVIRONS

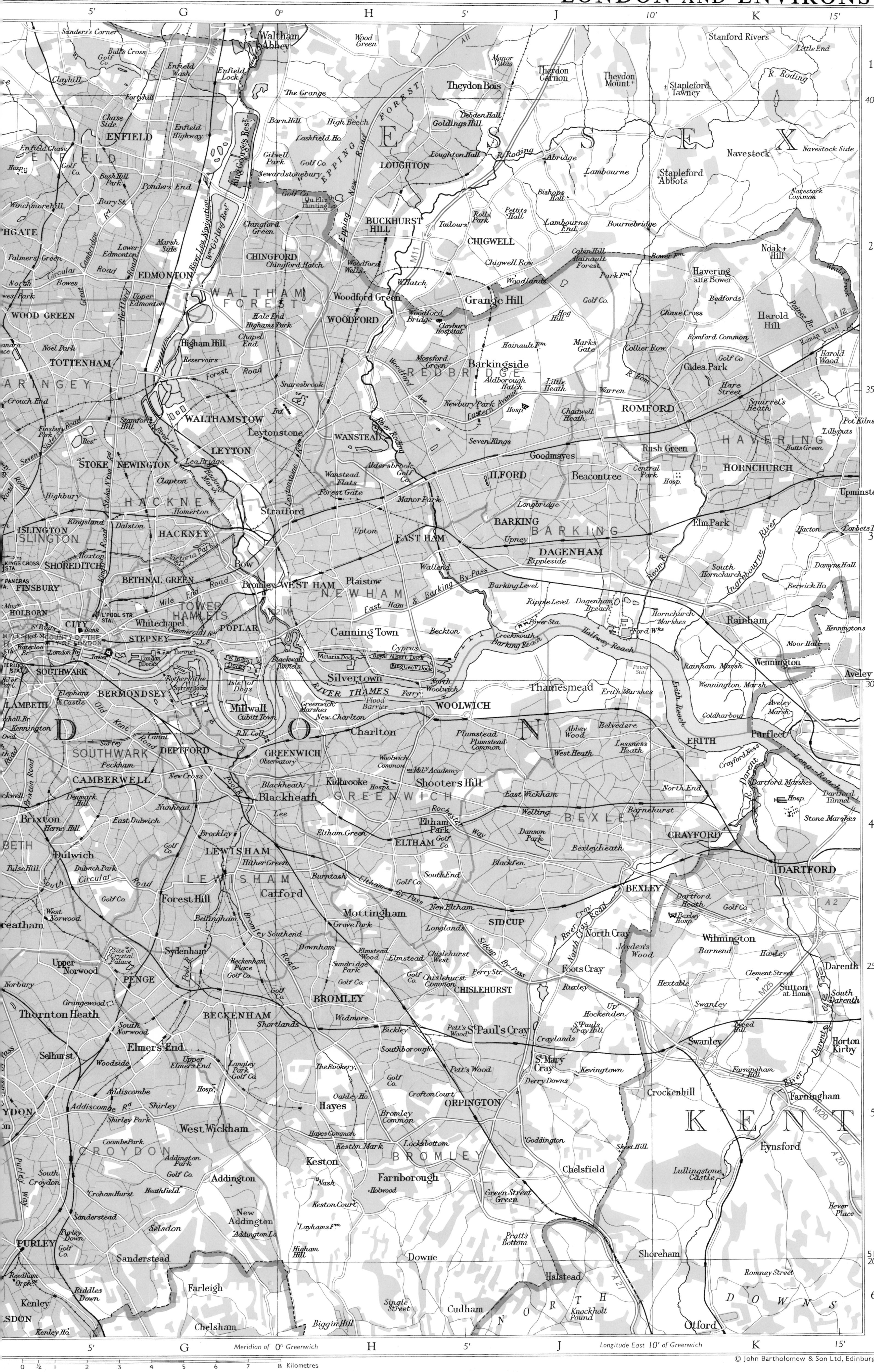

WALES
CARDIGAN BAY
BRISTOL CHANNEL
ENGLISH CHA
GWYNEDD
CLWYD
POWYS
DYFED
WEST GLAMORGAN
MID GLAMORGAN
SOUTH GLAMORGAN
GWENT
CHESHIRE
SALOP
HEREFORD AND WORCESTER
GLOUCESTER
AVON
SOMERSET
DEVON
CORNWALL
DORSET
CAMBRIAN MOUNTAINS
Anglesey (Môn)
Holyhead
Bangor
Caernarfon
Llandudno
Conwy
Colwyn Bay
Rhyl
Liverpool
Birkenhead
Wallasey
Chester
Wrexham
Stockport
Crewe
Stoke on Trent
Shrewsbury
Wolverhampton
Telford
Pwllheli
Dolgellau
Aberystwyth
Cardigan
Fishguard
Haverfordwest
Milford Haven
Pembroke
Tenby
Carmarthen
Swansea
Neath
Port Talbot
Merthyr Tydfil
Rhondda
Pontypridd
Caerphilly
Newport
Cardiff
Hereford
Worcester
Gloucester
Cheltenham
Bristol
Bath
Weston super Mare
Taunton
Yeovil
Ilfracombe
Barnstaple
Bideford
Lundy
Exeter
Torbay
Plymouth
Devonport
Truro
Newquay
Bodmin
Dartmoor
Exmoor
Weymouth
Dorchester
Lyme Bay
Carmarthen Bay
St Brides Bay
Caernarfon Bay
Tremadog Bay
Bridgwater Bay
Continued on Inset
Longitude West 2° of Greenw
Feet
Metres
3000
914
2000
609
1500
457
1000
304
500
152
250
76
0
0
150
46

SIMPLE CONIC PROJECTION

1: 850 000

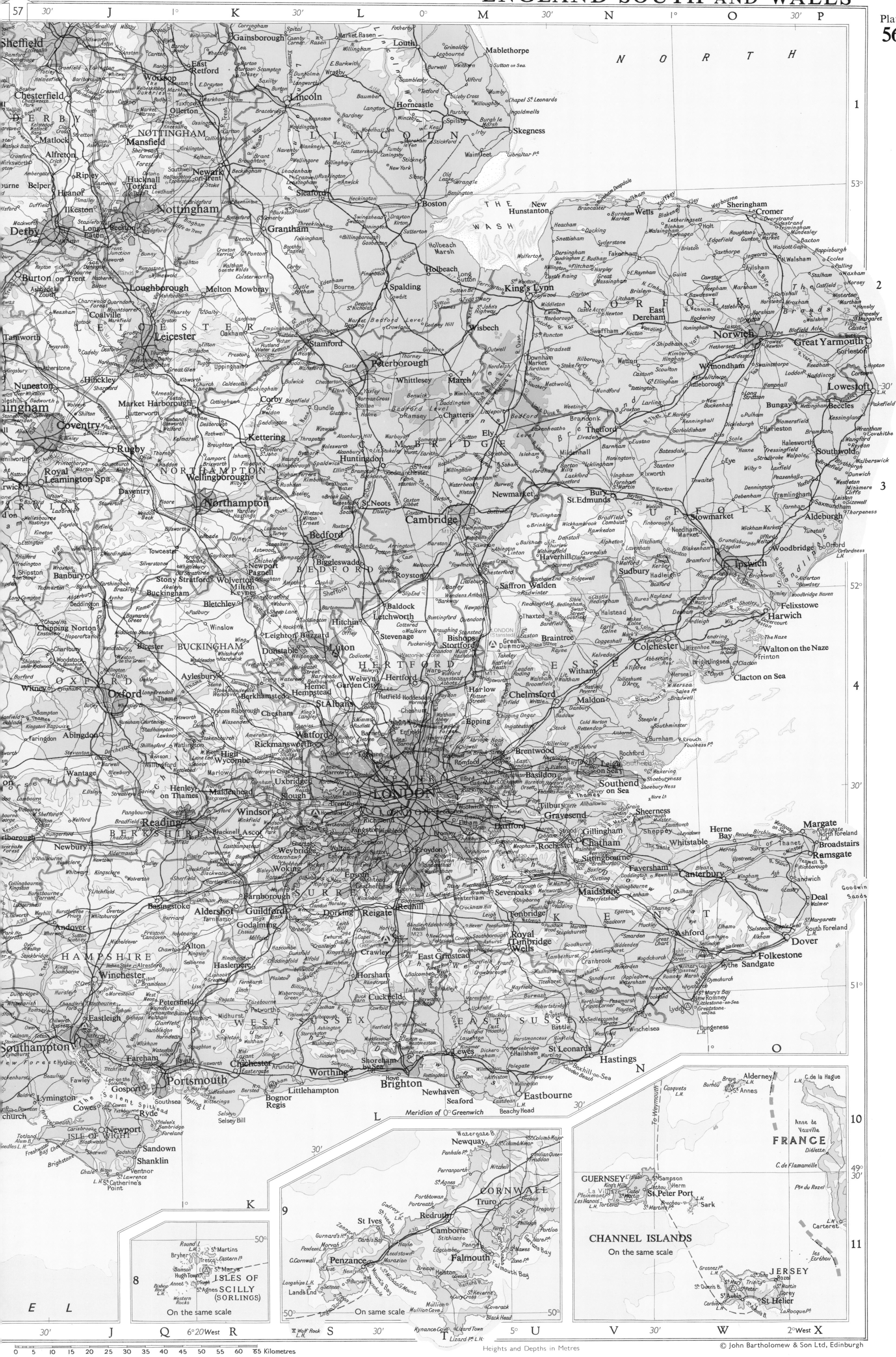
NORTH
THE WASH
LINCOLN
NORFOLK
SUFFOLK
CAMBRIDGE
NORTHAMPTON
NOTTINGHAM
DERBY
LEICESTER
BEDFORD
BUCKINGHAM
OXFORD
HERTFORD
ESSEX
BERKSHIRE
SURREY
KENT
HAMPSHIRE
WEST SUSSEX
EAST SUSSEX
ISLE OF WIGHT
CORNWALL
Sheffield
Chesterfield
Gainsborough
Lincoln
Louth
Mablethorpe
Skegness
Horncastle
Boston
Nottingham
Mansfield
Newark
Derby
Grantham
Sleaford
Hunstanton
Sheringham
Cromer
King's Lynn
Norwich
Great Yarmouth
Lowestoft
East Dereham
Thetford
Bury St.Edmunds
Stowmarket
Ipswich
Felixstowe
Harwich
Colchester
Clacton on Sea
Walton on the Naze
Leicester
Loughborough
Melton Mowbray
Stamford
Peterborough
Spalding
Wisbech
March
Ely
Cambridge
Huntingdon
Newmarket
Kettering
Corby
Coventry
Rugby
Royal Leamington Spa
Northampton
Wellingborough
Bedford
Luton
Oxford
Aylesbury
Chelmsford
Southend on Sea
Watford
St Albans
LONDON
Reading
Windsor
Slough
Guildford
Croydon
Maidstone
Canterbury
Margate
Ramsgate
Dover
Folkestone
Ashford
Hastings
Brighton
Eastbourne
Worthing
Portsmouth
Southampton
Winchester
Newport
Chichester
Meridian of 0° Greenwich
Newquay
Truro
Penzance
Falmouth
St Ives
ISLES OF SCILLY (SORLINGS)
On the same scale
CHANNEL ISLANDS
On the same scale
GUERNSEY
St Peter Port
Sark
JERSEY
St Helier
Alderney
FRANCE
On same scale

© John Bartholomew & Son Ltd, Edinburgh

SIMPLE CONIC PROJECTION

1: 850 000

0 5 10 15 20 25 30 35 40 Statute Miles

0 5 10 15 20 25 30 35 40 45 50 55 60 65 Kilometres

Heights and Depths in Metres

Printed in U.K.

ST KILDA
On the same scale
Boreray
Soay
Hirta
Levenish
Butt of Lewis
Stornoway
Lewis
Harris
North Uist
Benbecula
South Uist
Barra
Mingulay
Flannan Is or Seven Hunters
Monach Is
Taransay
Scarp
Lochmaddy
ATLANTIC OCEAN
Outer Hebrides
NORTH MINCH
LITTLE MINCH
SEA OF THE HEBRIDES
Sound of Shiant
Shiant Is
Skye
Portree
Dunvegan
Broadford
Raasay
Canna
Rum
Eigg
Muck
Cuillin Sound
Mallaig
Arisaig
Ardnamurchan
Coll
Tiree
Mull
Tobermory
Iona
Staffa
Oban
Colonsay
Oronsay
Jura
Islay
Port Ellen
Bowmore
Mull of Oa
Gigha
Arran
Cape Wrath
Ullapool
Lairg
Dingwall
Inverness
Fort William
Fort Augustus
Kingussie
Ben Nevis
Loch Ness
Glen More
HIGHLAND
GRAMPIAN
Inveraray
Dunoon
Greenock
Gourock
Port Glasgow
Dumbarton
Helensburgh
Clydebank
Glasgow
Paisley
Renfrew
Hamilton
East Kilbride
Rothesay
Largs
Ardrossan
Callander
Strathaven
Firth of Lorn
Firth of Clyde
Sound of Jura
Loch Linnhe
Sound of Mull
Inner Sound
Sound of Sleat
Loch Lomond
Kintyre
Cowal
Morvern
Sunart
Moidart
Knoydart
Rannoch Moor
Loch Shin
Loch Maree
Torridon
Gairloch
Applecross
Kyle of Lochalsh
Kinlochleven
Ballachulish
Crianlarich
Tyndrum
Killin
Dalwhinnie
Monadhliath Mountains

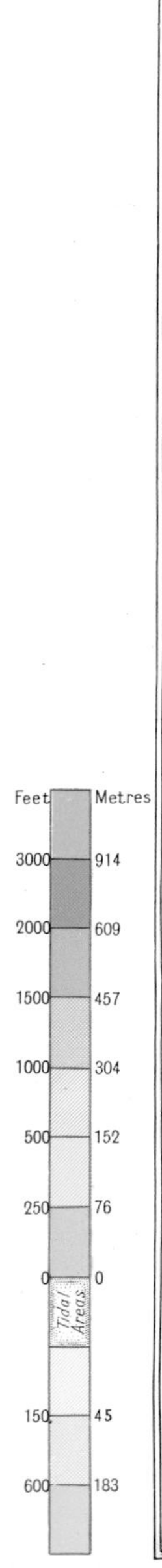
Feet
Metres
3000
914
2000
609
1500
457
1000
304
500
152
250
76
0
0
Tidal Areas
150
45
600
183

SCOTLAND NORTH

© John Bartholomew & Son Ltd, Edinburgh

NORTH CHANNEL
IRISH SEA
ATLANTIC
NORTHERN IRELAND
ULSTER
ANTRIM
LONDONDERRY
TYRONE
FERMANAGH
ARMAGH
DOWN
DONEGAL
MONAGHAN
CAVAN
LOUTH
MEATH
WESTMEATH
LONGFORD
LEITRIM
SLIGO
ROSCOMMON
MAYO
CONNACHT
Campbeltown
Belfast
Londonderry
Coleraine
Ballymena
Larne
Carrickfergus
Bangor
Newtownards
Lisburn
Portadown
Armagh
Newry
Dundalk
Drogheda
Enniskillen
Omagh
Strabane
Letterkenny
Donegal
Sligo
Ballina
Castlebar
Westport
Roscommon
Longford
Cavan
Monaghan
Mullingar
Lough Neagh
Lough Foyle
Lough Swilly
Lower Lough Erne
Donegal Bay
Sligo Bay
Clew Bay
Killala Bay
Tory Sound
Inishtrahull Sound
7740

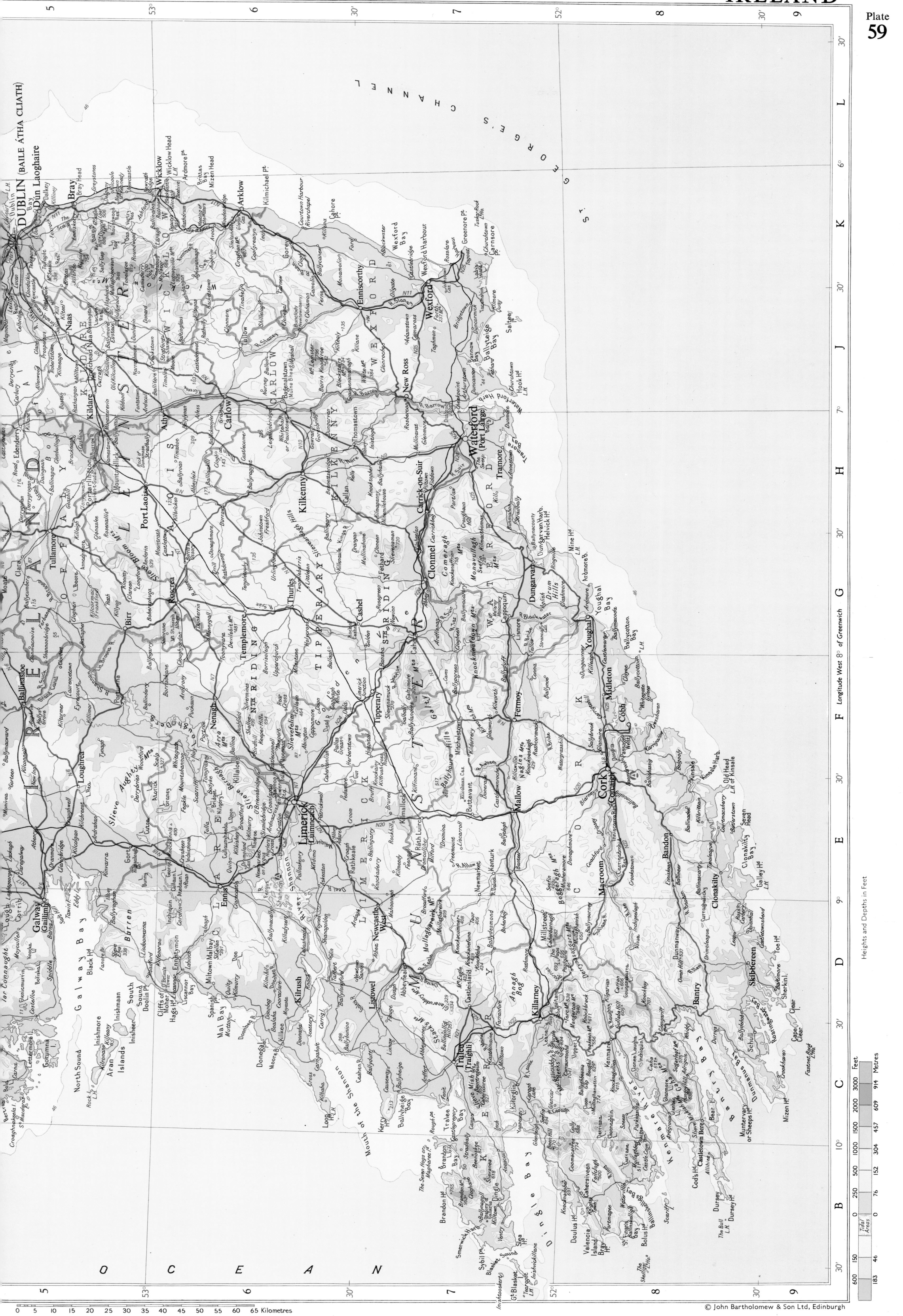
ST GEORGE'S CHANNEL
OCEAN
DUBLIN (BAILE ÁTHA CLIATH)
Dún Laoghaire
Bray
Wicklow
Arklow
Wexford
Waterford (Port Láirge)
Kilkenny
Carlow
Athy
Port Laoise
Tullamore
Birr
Roscrea
Thurles
Clonmel
Tipperary
Cashel
Limerick (Luimneach)
Ennis
Galway (Gaillimh)
Ballinasloe
Loughrea
Nenagh
Dungarvan
Youghal
Fermoy
Mallow
Cork (Corcaigh)
Cobh
Midleton
Bandon
Kinsale
Clonakilty
Skibbereen
Bantry
Macroom
Killarney
Tralee (Trá Lí)
Listowel
Kilrush
Dingle
Kenmare
Galway Bay
Dingle Bay
Bantry Bay
Mouth of the Shannon
Aran Islands
Heights and Depths in Feet
Longitude West 8° of Greenwich
Feet 3000 2000 1500 1000 500 250 0 Tidal Areas 150 600
Metres 914 609 457 304 152 76 0 46 183
0 5 10 15 20 25 30 35 40 45 50 55 60 65 Kilometres

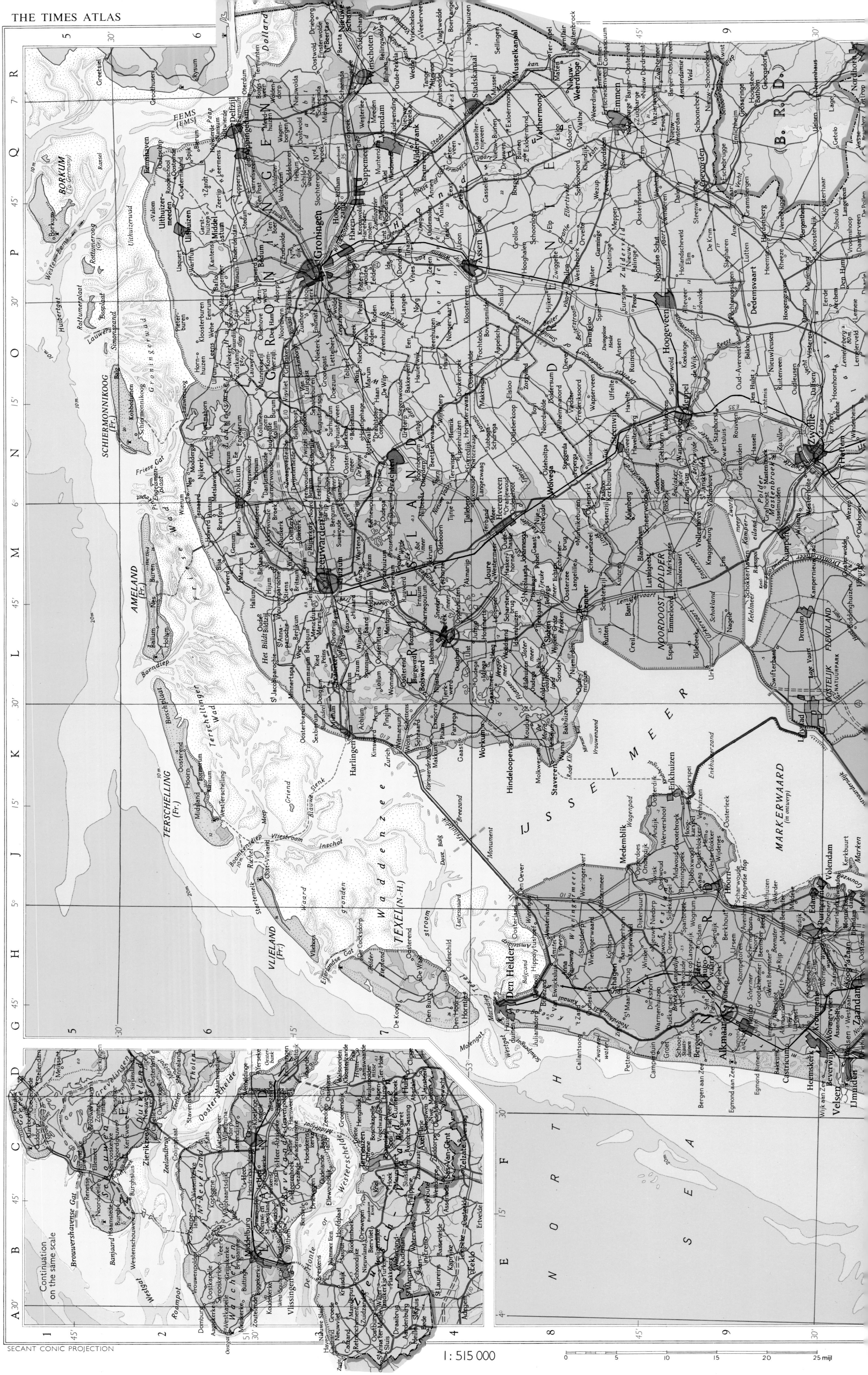
Groningen
Leeuwarden
Assen
Emmen
Zwolle
Hoogeveen
Meppel
Kampen
Lelystad
Harlingen
Den Helder
Alkmaar
Hoorn
Enkhuizen
Medemblik
Sneek
Drachten
Heerenveen
Dokkum
Delfzijl
Appingedam
Veendam
Stadskanaal
Musselkanaal
Coevorden
Steenwijk
Emmeloord
Dronten
Urk
Purmerend
Edam
Volendam
Zaandam
IJmuiden
Velsen
Beverwijk
Heemskerk
Castricum
Bergen
Schagen
Middelburg
Vlissingen
Zierikzee
Goes
Terneuzen
Sas-Van-Gent
Eeklo
Hulst
Breskens
Sluis
BORKUM (To Germany)
SCHIERMONNIKOOG
AMELAND (Fr.)
TERSCHELLING (Fr.)
VLIELAND (Fr.)
TEXEL (N.-H.)
Rottumeroog (Gr.)
Rottumerplaat
Boschplaat
Waddenzee
IJSSELMEER
NORTH SEA
NOORDOOST POLDER
OOSTELIJK FLEVOLAND
MARKERWAARD (in ontwerp)
Wieringermeer
EEMS (EMS)
Dollard
B. R. D.
Walcheren
Noord-Beveland
Zuid-Beveland
Schouwen
Duiveland
Tholen
Oosterschelde
Westerschelde
Brouwershavense Gat
Continuation on the same scale
E F

NETHERLANDS

© John Bartholomew & Son Ltd, Edinburgh

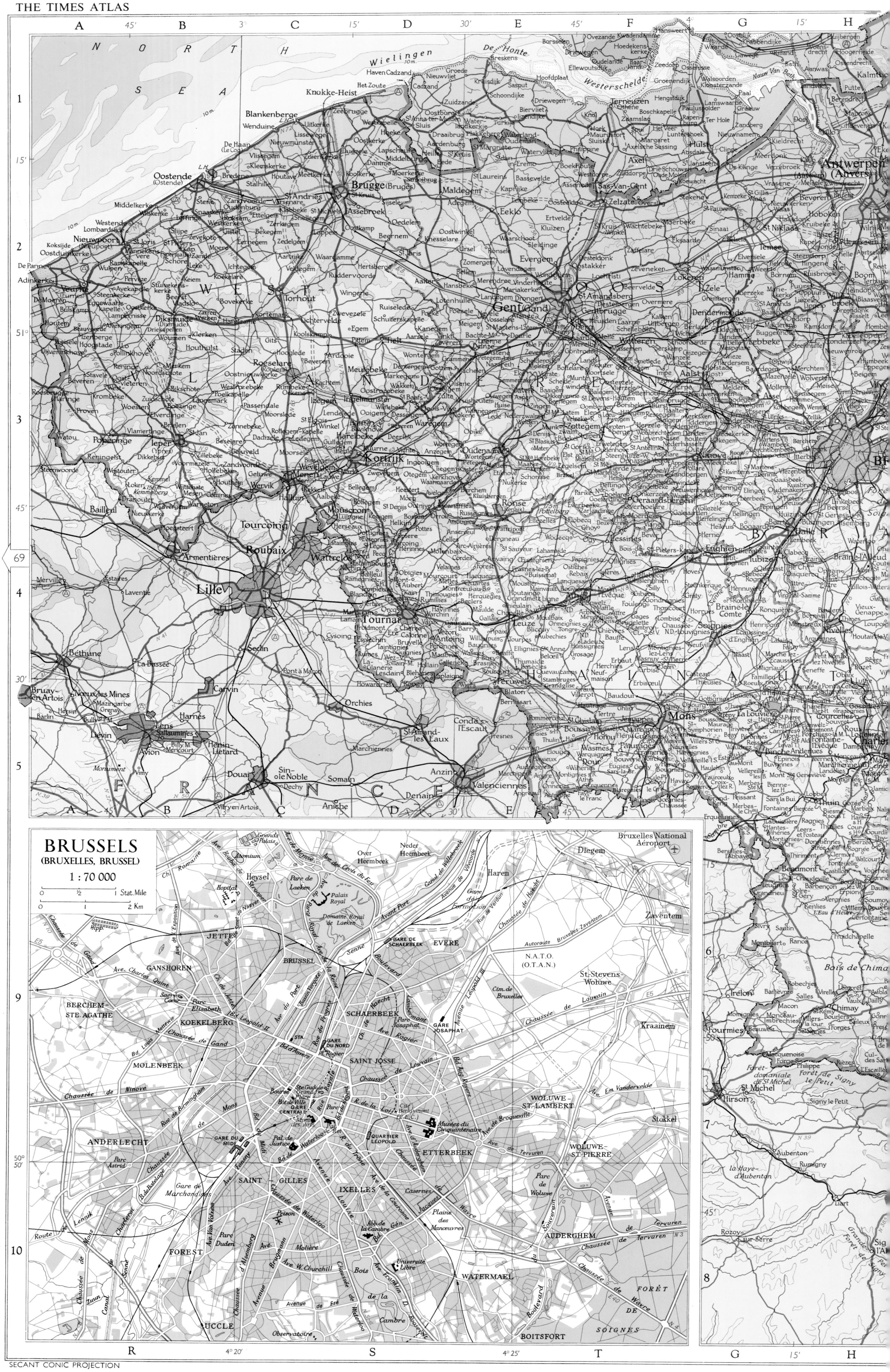

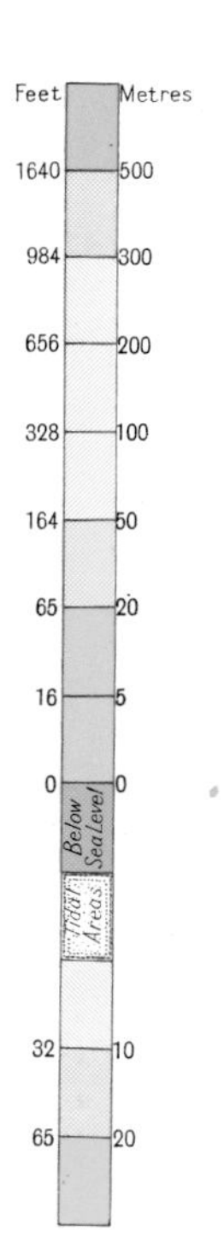

SECANT CONIC PROJECTION

1: 515 000

0 5 10 15 20 Statute Miles

BELGIUM AND LUXEMBOURG

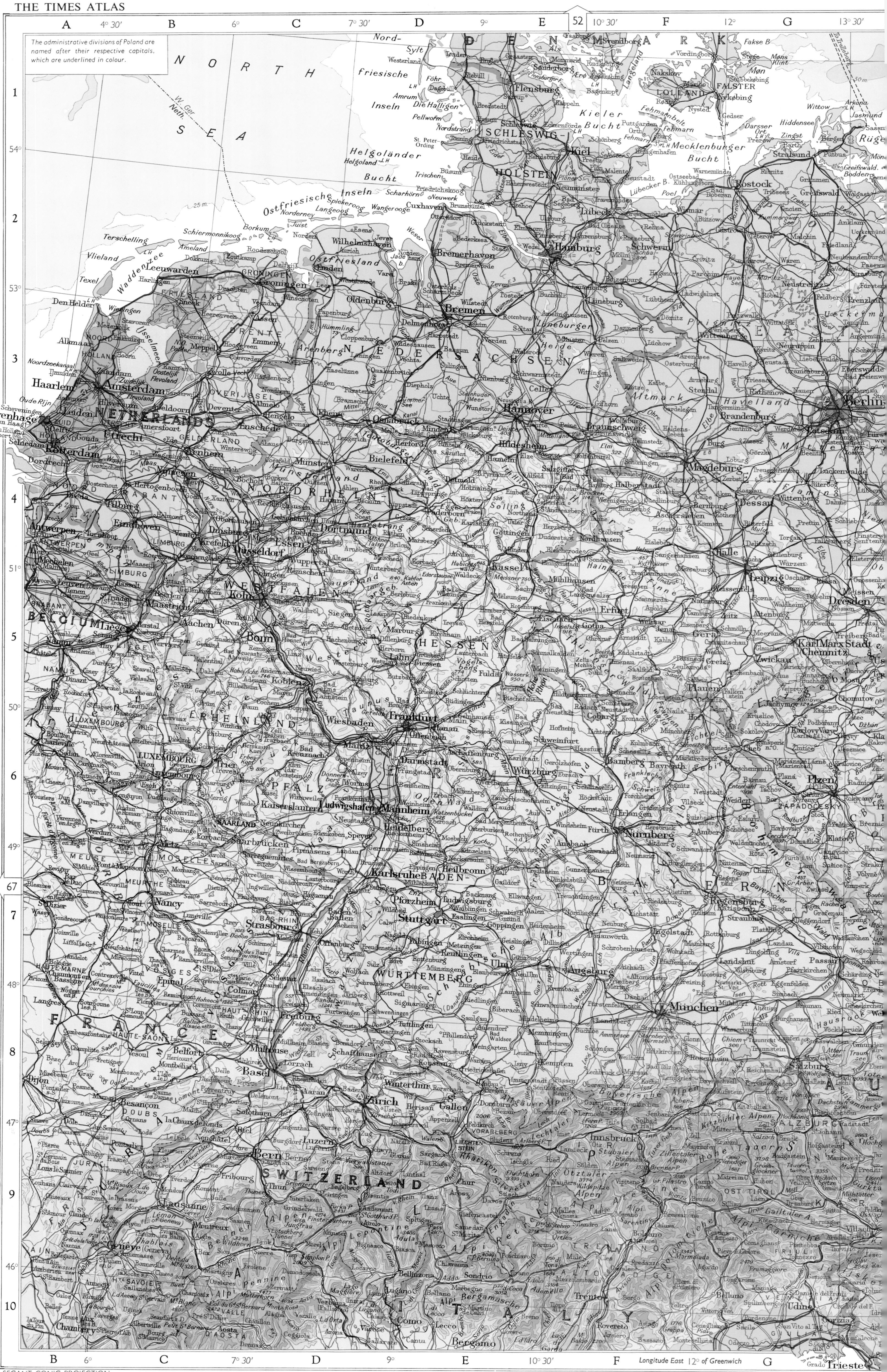
The administrative divisions of Poland are named after their respective capitals, which are underlined in colour.
NORTH SEA
Nordfriesische Inseln
Helgoländer Bucht
Ostfriesische Inseln
DENMARK
SCHLESWIG-HOLSTEIN
NIEDERSACHSEN
NETHERLANDS
NORDRHEIN-WESTFALEN
BELGIUM
LUXEMBOURG
HESSEN
RHEINLAND-PFALZ
SAARLAND
BADEN-WÜRTTEMBERG
BAYERN
FRANCE
SWITZERLAND
ITALY
Hamburg
Bremen
Hannover
Berlin
Amsterdam
Rotterdam
Düsseldorf
Köln
Frankfurt
Leipzig
Dresden
Nürnberg
Stuttgart
München
Zürich
Bern
Innsbruck
Strasbourg
Luxembourg
Karl Marx Stadt
Plzeň
Trieste
Longitude East 12° of Greenwich
0 10 20 40 60 80 100 120 Statute Miles

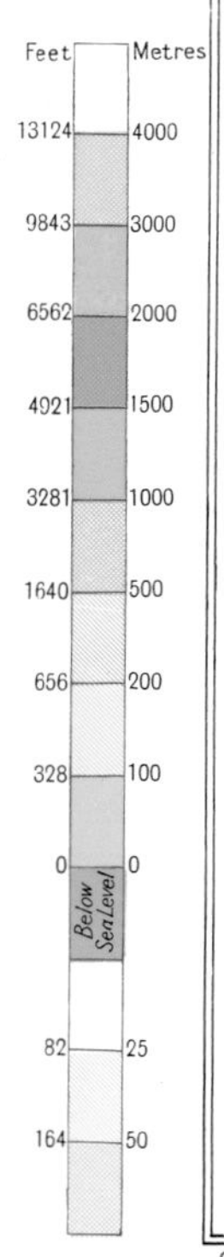
Feet
Metres
13124 4000
9843 3000
6562 2000
4921 1500
3281 1000
1640 500
656 200
328 100
0 0
Below Sea level
82 25
164 50

SECANT CONIC PROJECTION

1: 2 500 000

GERMANY: POLAND: CZECHOSLOVAKIA

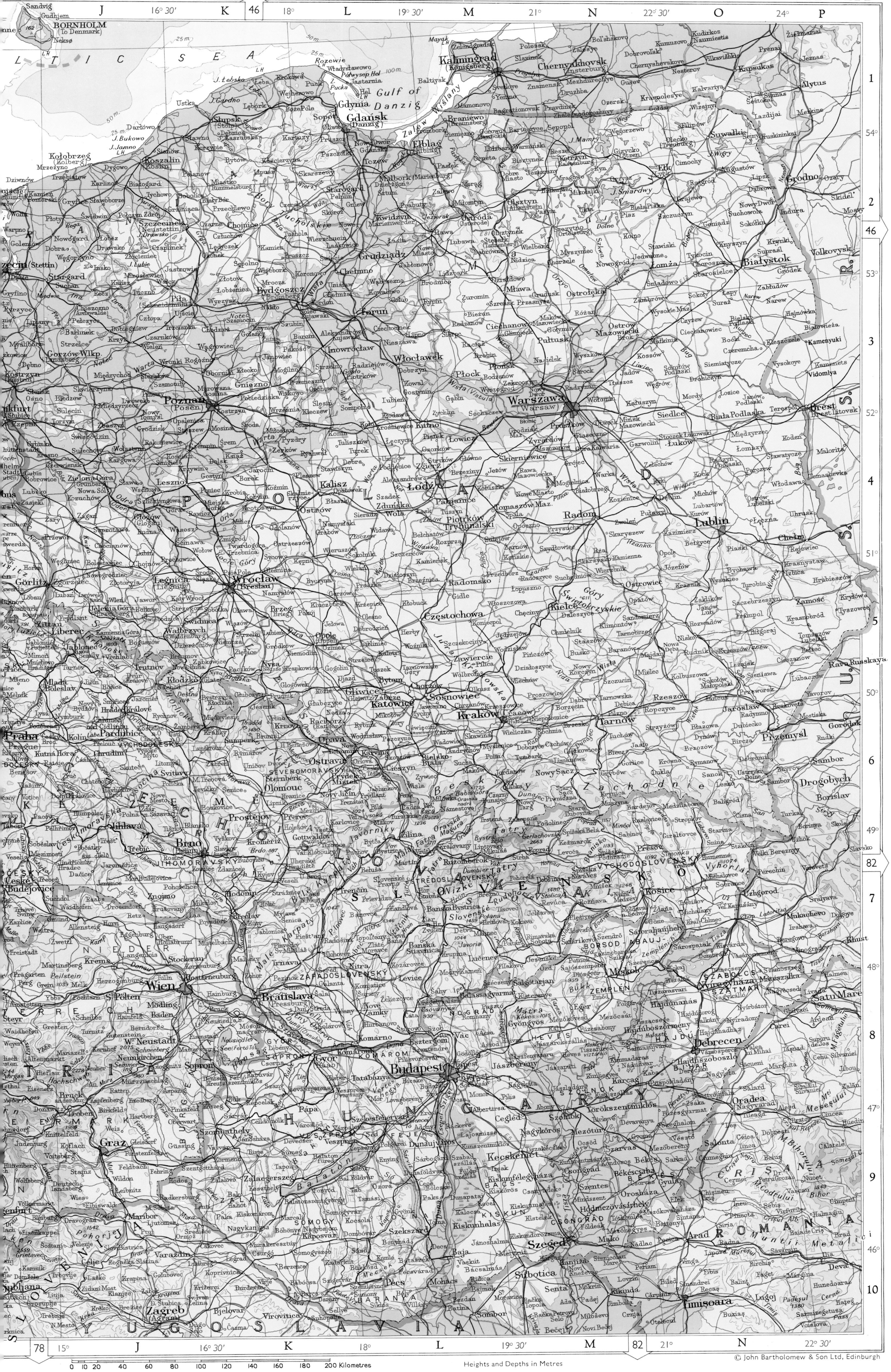

0 10 20 40 60 80 100 120 140 160 180 200 Kilometres

Heights and Depths in Metres

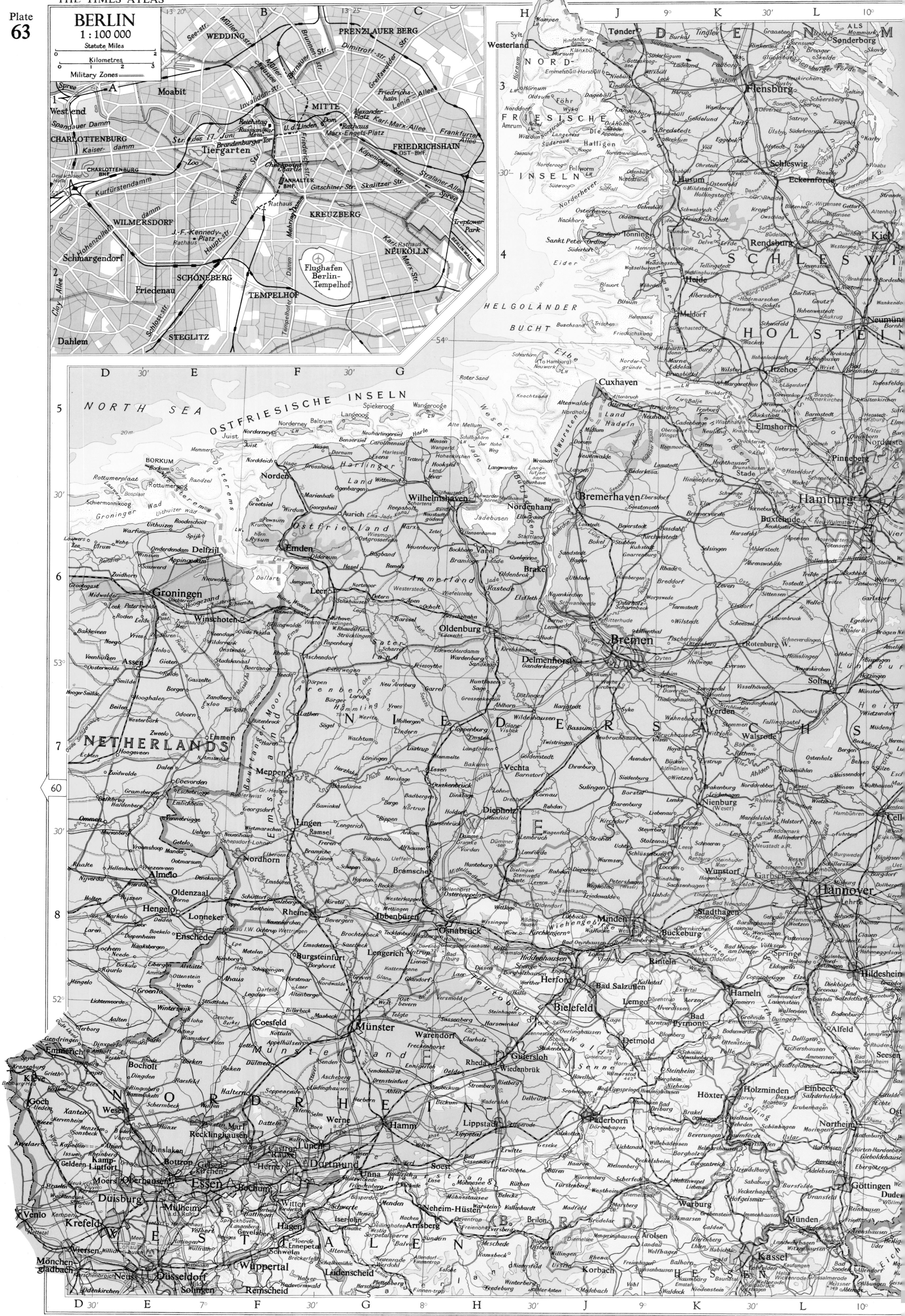
BERLIN
1 : 100 000
Statute Miles
Kilometres
Military Zones
WEDDING
PRENZLAUER BERG
Moabit
MITTE
West end
Spandauer Damm
CHARLOTTENBURG
Kaiserdamm
Tiergarten
FRIEDRICHSHAIN
OST-BHF.
Str. des 17. Juni
Reichstag
Brandenburger Tor
U.d. Linden
Alexander-Platz
Karl-Marx-Allee
Marx-Engels-Platz
Rathaus
Frankfurter Allee
CHARLOTTENBURG BHF.
Zoo
Checkpoint Charlie
ANHALTER BHF.
Kurfürstendamm
Gitschiner Str.
Skalitzer Str.
Stralauer Allee
Spree
WILMERSDORF
KREUZBERG
Treptower Park
J.-F.-Kennedy-Platz
Rathaus
NEUKÖLLN
BERLIN WALL
Hohenzollerndamm
Schmargendorf
Flughafen Berlin-Tempelhof
SCHÖNEBERG
Friedenau
TEMPELHOF
Dahlem
STEGLITZ
NORTH SEA
OSTFRIESISCHE INSELN
NORDFRIESISCHE INSELN
HELGOLÄNDER BUCHT
DENMARK
SCHLESWIG-HOLSTEIN
NIEDERSACHSEN
NETHERLANDS
NORDRHEIN-WESTFALEN
HESSEN
Tønder
Sønderborg
Westerland
Flensburg
Husum
Schleswig
Eckernförde
Kiel
Rendsburg
Heide
Neumünster
Itzehoe
Cuxhaven
Elmshorn
Pinneberg
Hamburg
Stade
Buxtehude
Bremerhaven
Nordenham
Wilhelmshaven
Emden
Aurich
Norden
Delfzijl
Groningen
Leer
Oldenburg
Bremen
Delmenhorst
Verden
Soltau
Celle
Hannover
Hildesheim
Assen
Emmen
Meppen
Lingen
Cloppenburg
Vechta
Diepholz
Nienburg
Minden
Osnabrück
Rheine
Nordhorn
Almelo
Hengelo
Enschede
Münster
Bielefeld
Herford
Detmold
Paderborn
Gütersloh
Hameln
Göttingen
Höxter
Kassel
Hamm
Dortmund
Recklinghausen
Essen
Bochum
Duisburg
Oberhausen
Krefeld
Düsseldorf
Mönchengladbach
Wuppertal
Hagen
Solingen
Remscheid
Lüdenscheid
Arnsberg
Soest
Lippstadt
Wesel
Kleve
Emmerich
Venlo
Bocholt
Coesfeld
Korbach
Warburg
Münden

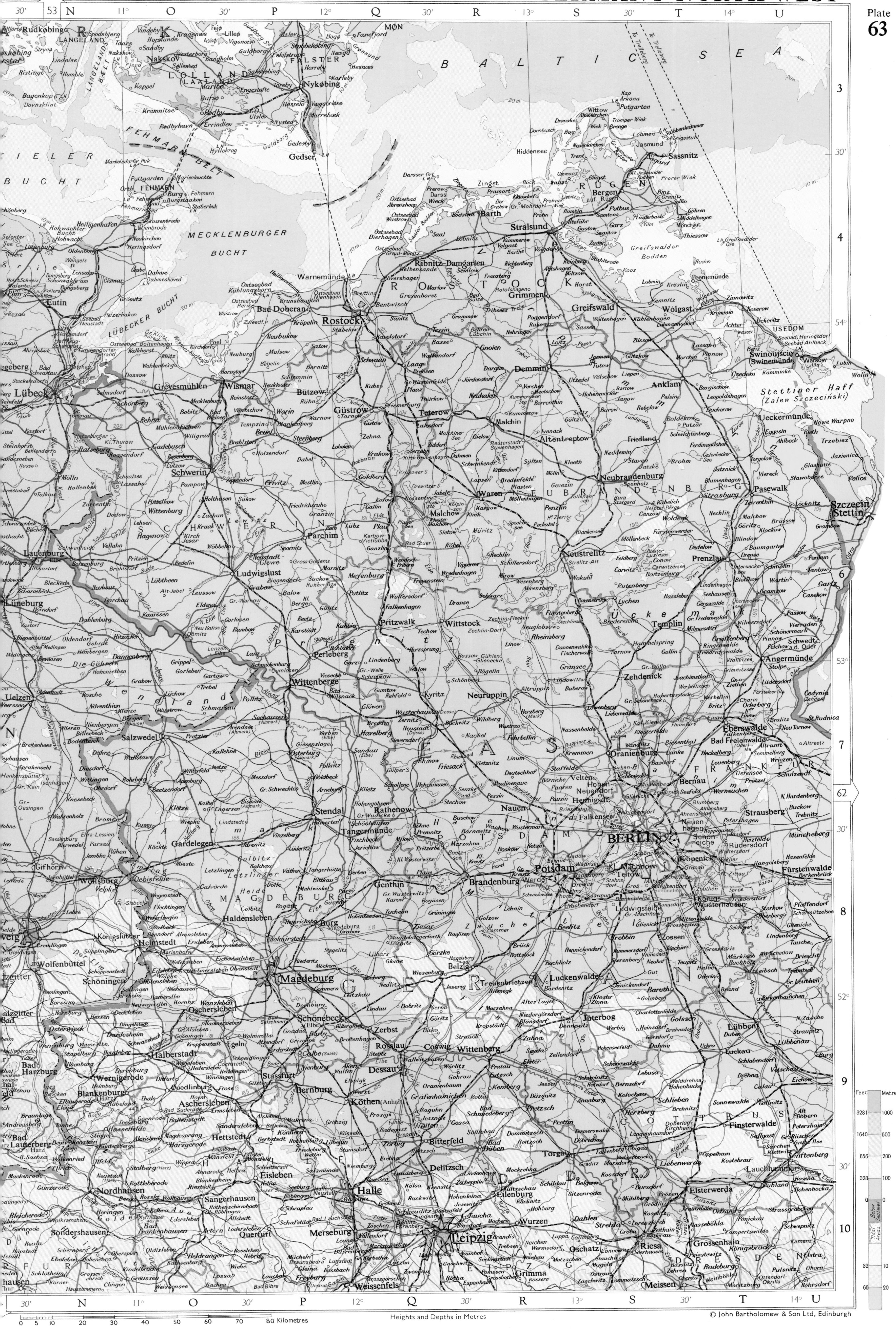
BALTIC SEA
MECKLENBURGER BUCHT
LÜBECKER BUCHT
KIELER BUCHT
FEHMARN BELT
LOLLAND
FALSTER
MØN
LANGELAND
RÜGEN
USEDOM
Stettiner Haff (Zalew Szczeciński)
Greifswalder Bodden
ROSTOCK
NEUBRANDENBURG
SCHWERIN
POTSDAM
FRANKFURT
MAGDEBURG
HALLE
LEIPZIG
DRESDEN
COTTBUS
ERFURT
BERLIN
Rostock
Stralsund
Greifswald
Wismar
Lübeck
Schwerin
Neubrandenburg
Szczecin (Stettin)
Potsdam
Brandenburg
Magdeburg
Halle
Leipzig
Dessau
Wittenberg
Stendal
Frankfurt
Eberswalde
Oranienburg
Neuruppin
Prenzlau
Pasewalk
Anklam
Demmin
Güstrow
Parchim
Ludwigslust
Wittenberge
Salzwedel
Lüneburg
Halberstadt
Merseburg
Riesa
Meissen
Torgau
Lübben
Finsterwalde
Heights and Depths in Metres
Feet Metres
3281 1000
1640 500
656 200
328 100
0 0
32 10
65 20
Below Sea level
Tidal Areas
0 5 10 20 30 40 50 60 70 80 Kilometres
© John Bartholomew & Son Ltd, Edinburgh

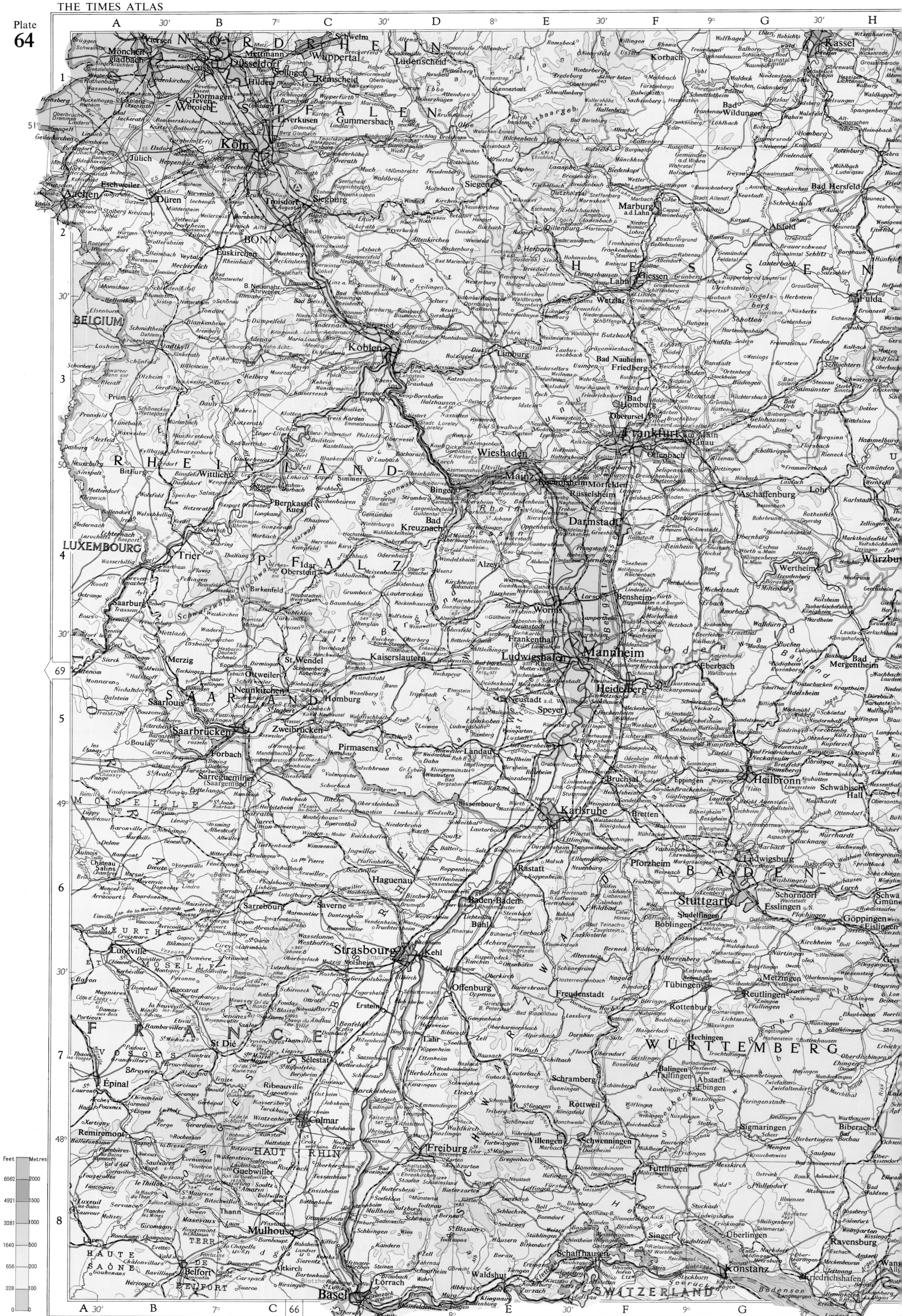
NORDRHEIN-WESTFALEN
RHEINLAND-PFALZ
SAARLAND
HESSEN
BADEN-WÜRTTEMBERG
BELGIUM
LUXEMBOURG
FRANCE
SWITZERLAND
MOSELLE
MEURTHE-ET-MOSELLE
VOSGES
HAUT-RHIN
BAS-RHIN
HAUTE-SAÔNE
TERR. DE BELFORT
SCHWARZWALD
ODENWALD
PFÄLZER BERGLAND
Köln
BONN
Düsseldorf
Wuppertal
Aachen
Koblenz
Frankfurt am Main
Wiesbaden
Mainz
Darmstadt
Mannheim
Ludwigshafen
Heidelberg
Karlsruhe
Stuttgart
Heilbronn
Saarbrücken
Trier
Kaiserslautern
Strasbourg
Colmar
Mulhouse
Freiburg
Basel
Konstanz
Kassel
Fulda
Würzburg
Épinal
Belfort
Lunéville
Bodensee
Feet
Metres
6562
2000
4921
1500
3281
1000
1640
500
656
200
328
100
0
0
A
B
C
D
E
F
G
H
1
2
3
4
5
6
7
8
51°
50°
49°
48°
7°
8°
9°
30'
69
66

SIMPLE CONIC PROJECTION

1: 1 000 000

0 5 10 20 30 40 50 Statute Miles

GERMANY SOUTH-WEST

Plate 64

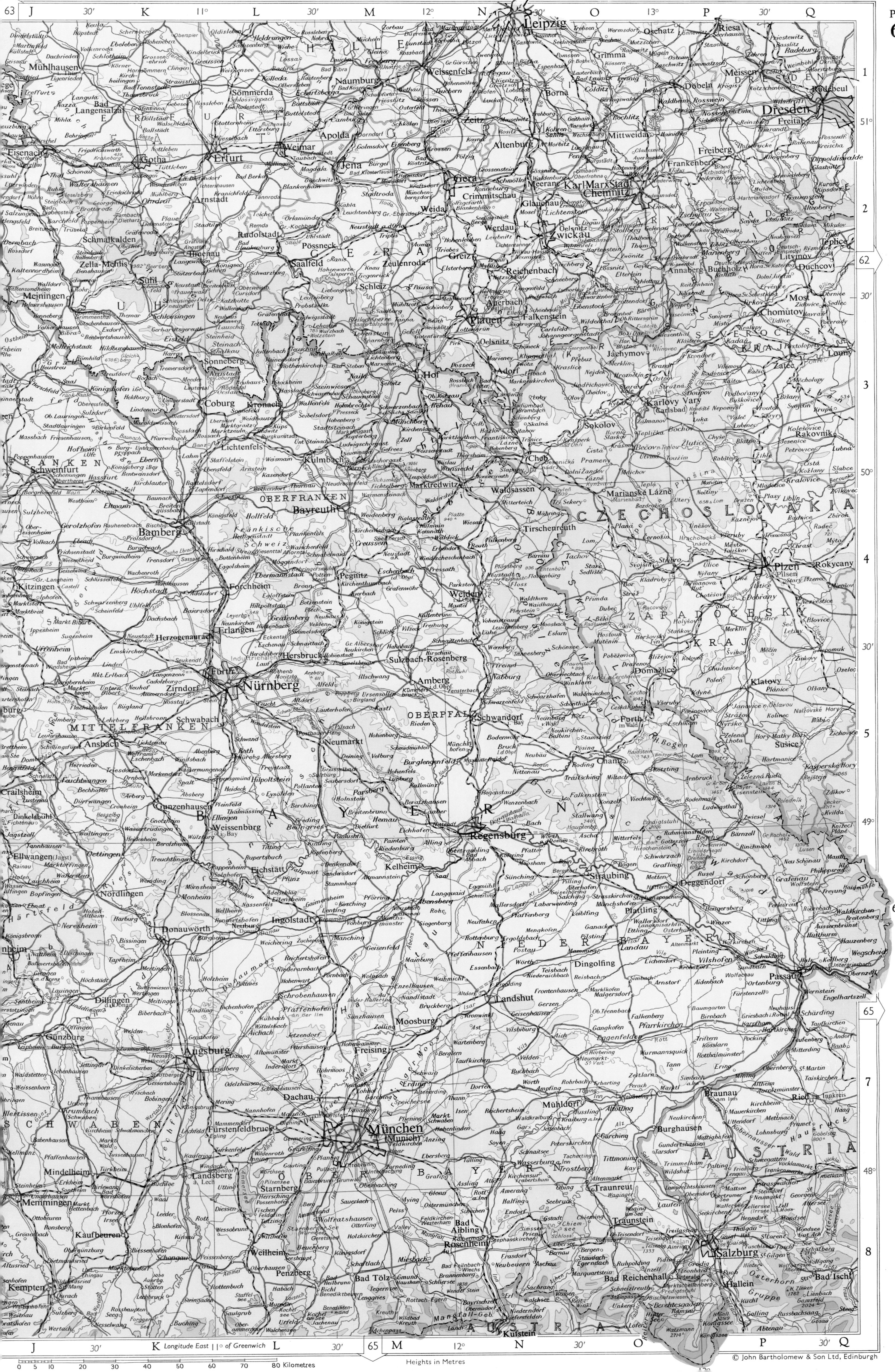

VIENNA
(WIEN)
1 : 20 000
Statute Mile
Kilometre
München (Munich)
Augsburg
Innsbruck
Salzburg
Bolzano (Bozen)
Merano (Meran)
SWITZERLAND
VORARLBERG
SIMPLE CONIC PROJECTION
1: 1 000 000
Longitude East 13° of Greenwich
Statute Miles

AUSTRIA

Plate 65

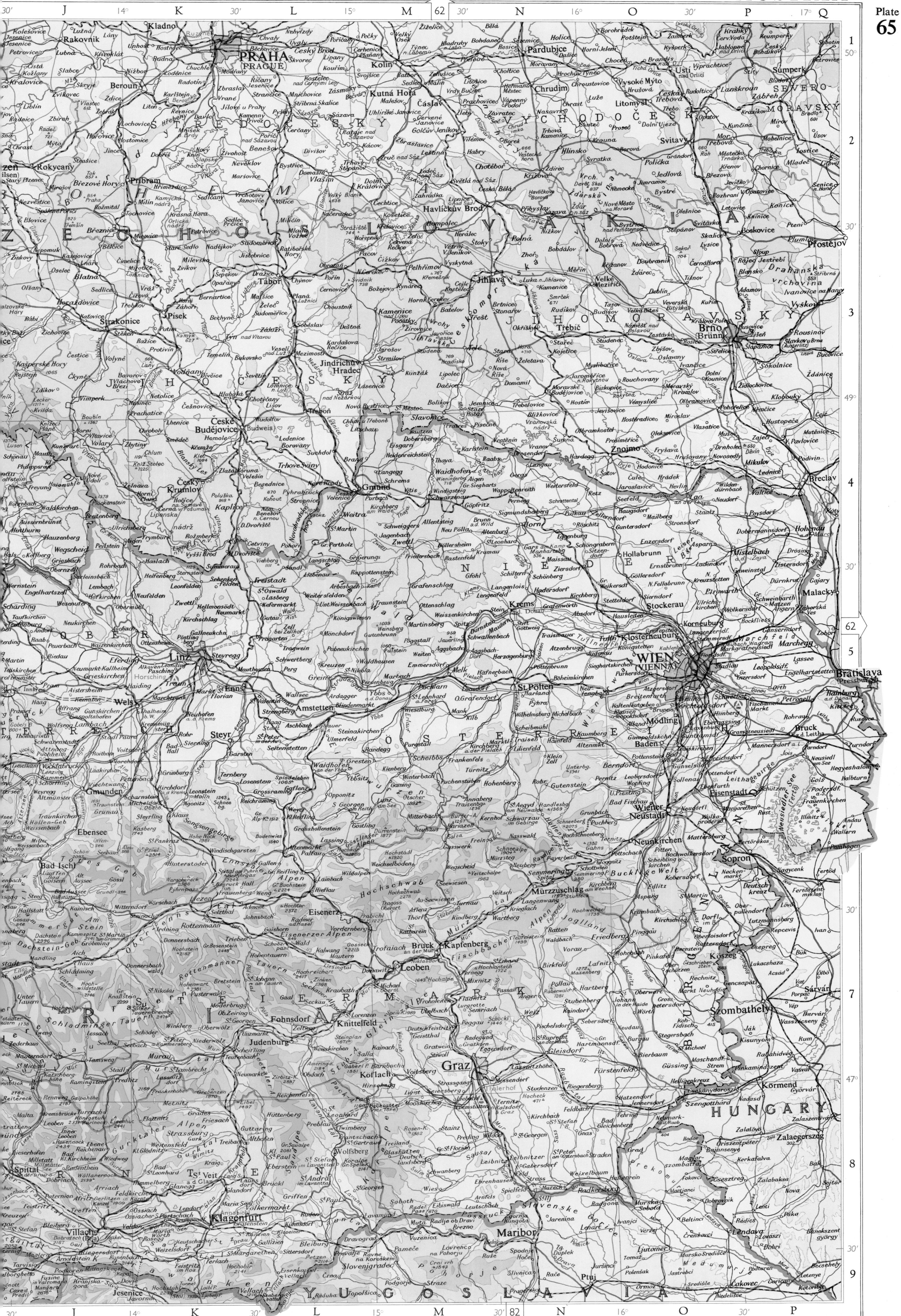

0 5 10 20 30 40 50 60 70 80 Kilometres

Heights in Metres

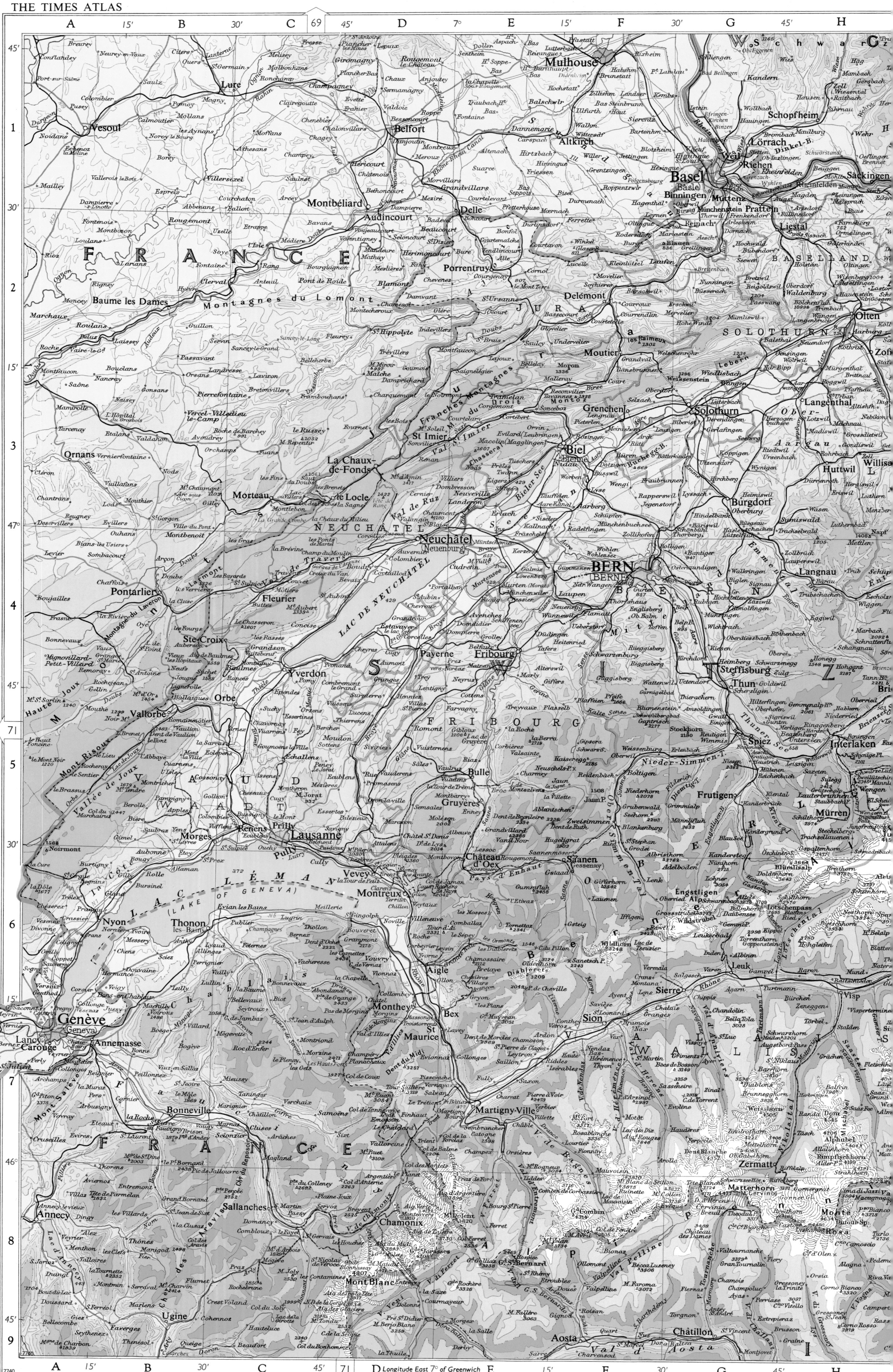
FRANCE
SWITZ
Mulhouse
Basel
Belfort
Vesoul
Lure
Montbéliard
Delle
Porrentruy
Delémont
Olten
Solothurn
Biel
La Chaux-de-Fonds
Le Locle
Neuchâtel
Pontarlier
Yverdon
Fribourg
BERN
Thun
Interlaken
Lausanne
Vevey
Montreux
Genève
Annecy
Chamonix
Mont Blanc
Martigny-Ville
Sion
Sierre
Zermatt
Matterhorn
Aosta
Châtillon
LAC LÉMAN (LAKE OF GENEVA)
LAC DE NEUCHÂTEL
JURA
VAUD
FRIBOURG
NEUCHÂTEL
SOLOTHURN
BASELLAND
WALLIS
Longitude East 7° of Greenwich
Feet / Metres
9843 3000
8202 2500
6562 2000
4921 1500
3281 1000
2624 800
1640 500
656 200

SWITZERLAND

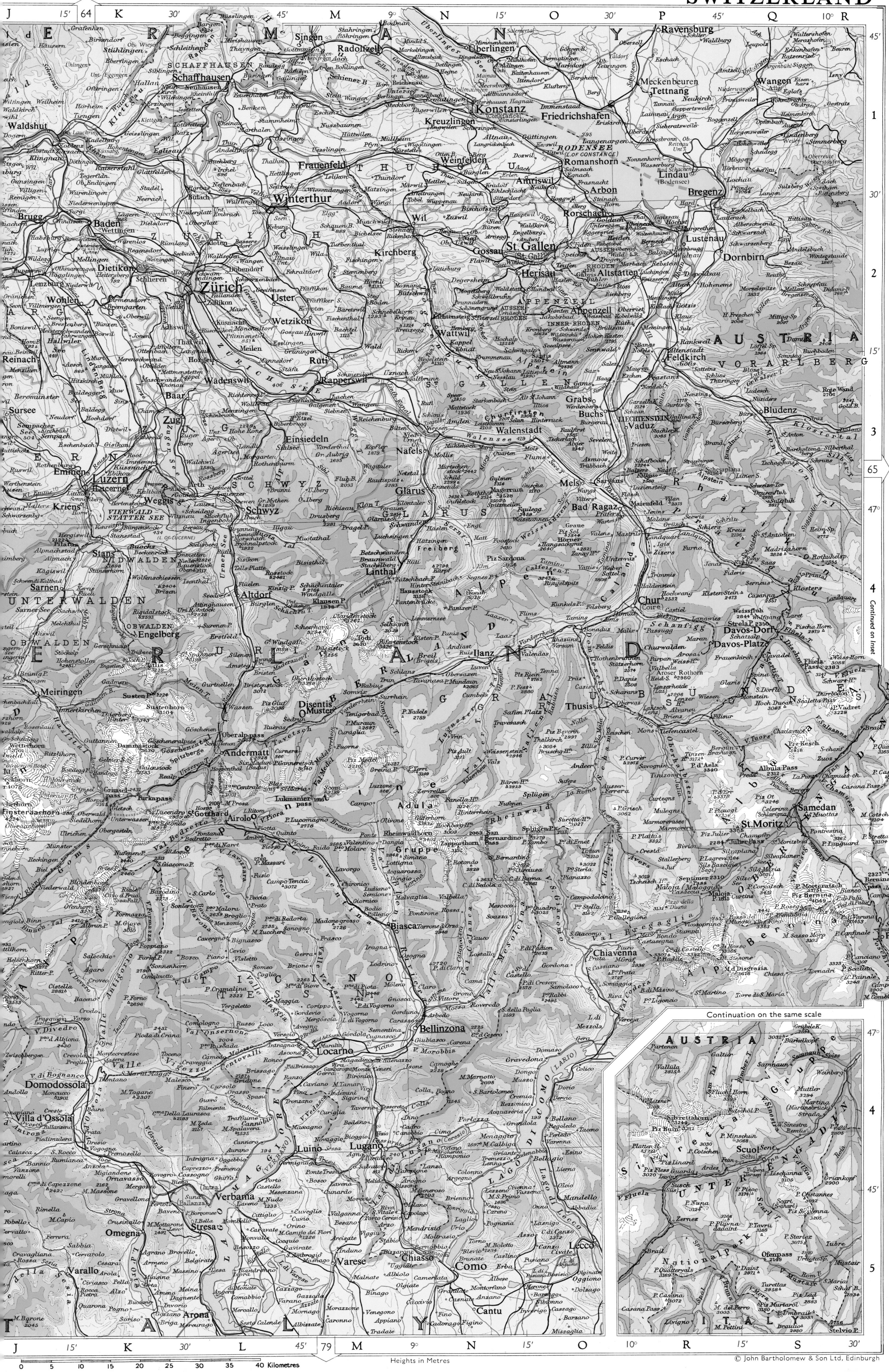

GERMANY
AUSTRIA
VORARLBERG
LIECHTENSTEIN
ITALY
SCHAFFHAUSEN
THURGAU
ZÜRICH
AARGAU
APPENZELL
ST. GALLEN
SCHWYZ
ZUG
LUZERN
GLARUS
NIDWALDEN
OBWALDEN
UNTERWALDEN
URI
GRAUBÜNDEN
TICINO (TESSIN)
BERN
BODENSEE (L. OF CONSTANCE)
ZÜRICHSEE
WALENSEE
VIERWALDSTÄTTER SEE (L. OF LUCERNE)
LAGO MAGGIORE
LAGO DI COMO (LARIO)
Lago di Lugano
Schaffhausen
Winterthur
Zürich
Baden
Brugg
Frauenfeld
Konstanz
Kreuzlingen
Friedrichshafen
Lindau
Bregenz
Dornbirn
Feldkirch
Bludenz
St. Gallen
Herisau
Appenzell
Rorschach
Arbon
Romanshorn
Wil
Rapperswil
Zug
Luzern (Lucerne)
Schwyz
Altdorf
Stans
Sarnen
Engelberg
Meiringen
Andermatt
Glarus
Chur (Coire)
Vaduz
Bad Ragaz
Davos-Dorf
Davos-Platz
Klosters
Thusis
Ilanz
Disentis/Muster
St. Moritz
Samedan
Poschiavo
Bellinzona
Locarno
Lugano
Chiasso
Como
Varese
Domodossola
Chiavenna
Lecco
Airolo
Biasca
St. Gotthard
Furkapass
Oberalp-pass
Lukmanier pass
Albula Pass
Bernina pass
Julier Pass
Maloja
Piz Bernina 4049
Finsteraarhorn 4274
Tödi 3620
Piz Kesch 3418
Säntis 2504
Continuation on the same scale
Scuol
Silvretta Gruppe
UNTER ENGADIN
Nationalpark
Ofenpass
Zernez
Continued on Inset
Heights in Metres
0 5 10 15 20 25 30 35 40 Kilometres

© John Bartholomew & Son Ltd, Edinburgh

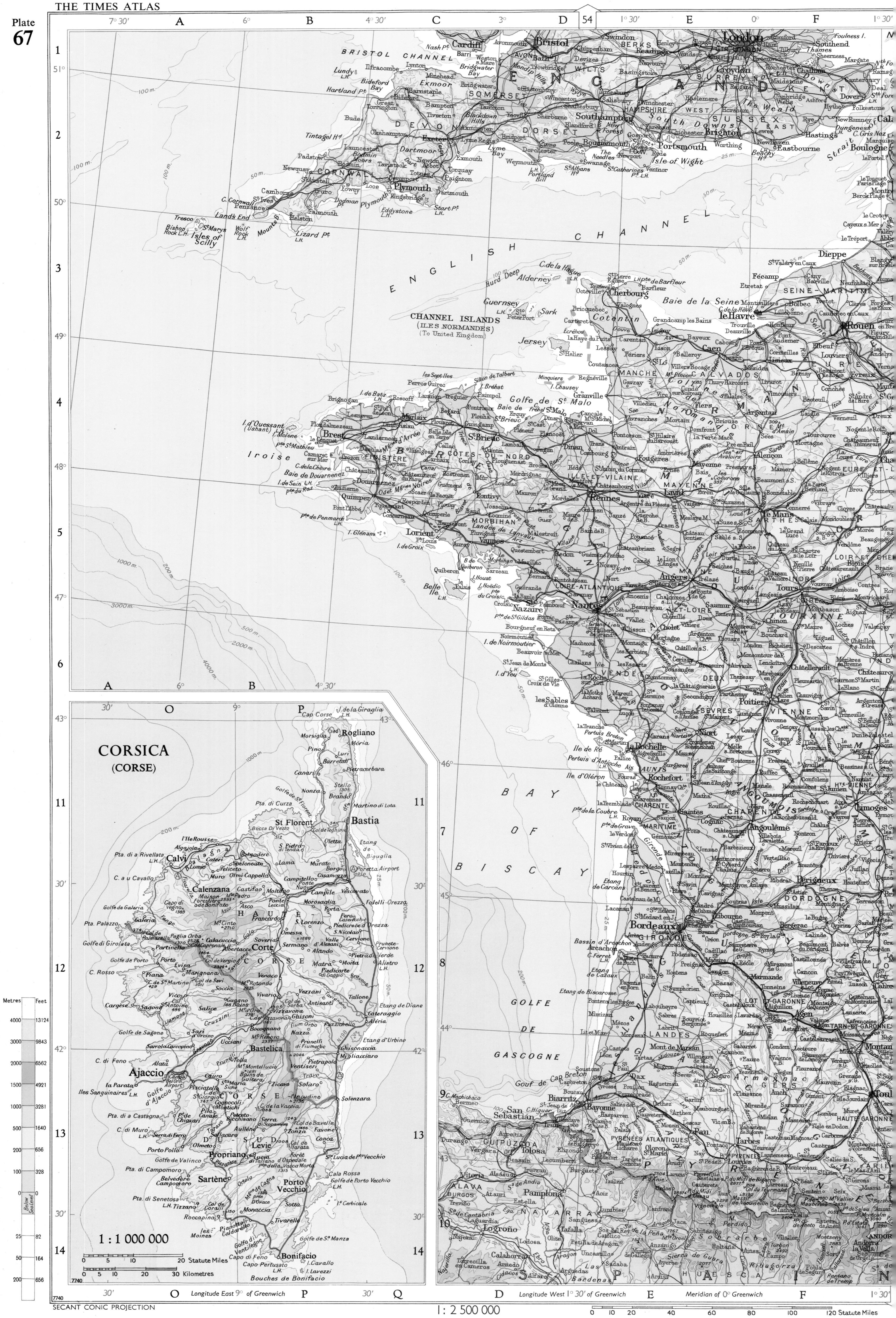

1: 2 500 000

0 10 20 40 60 80 100 120 Statute Miles

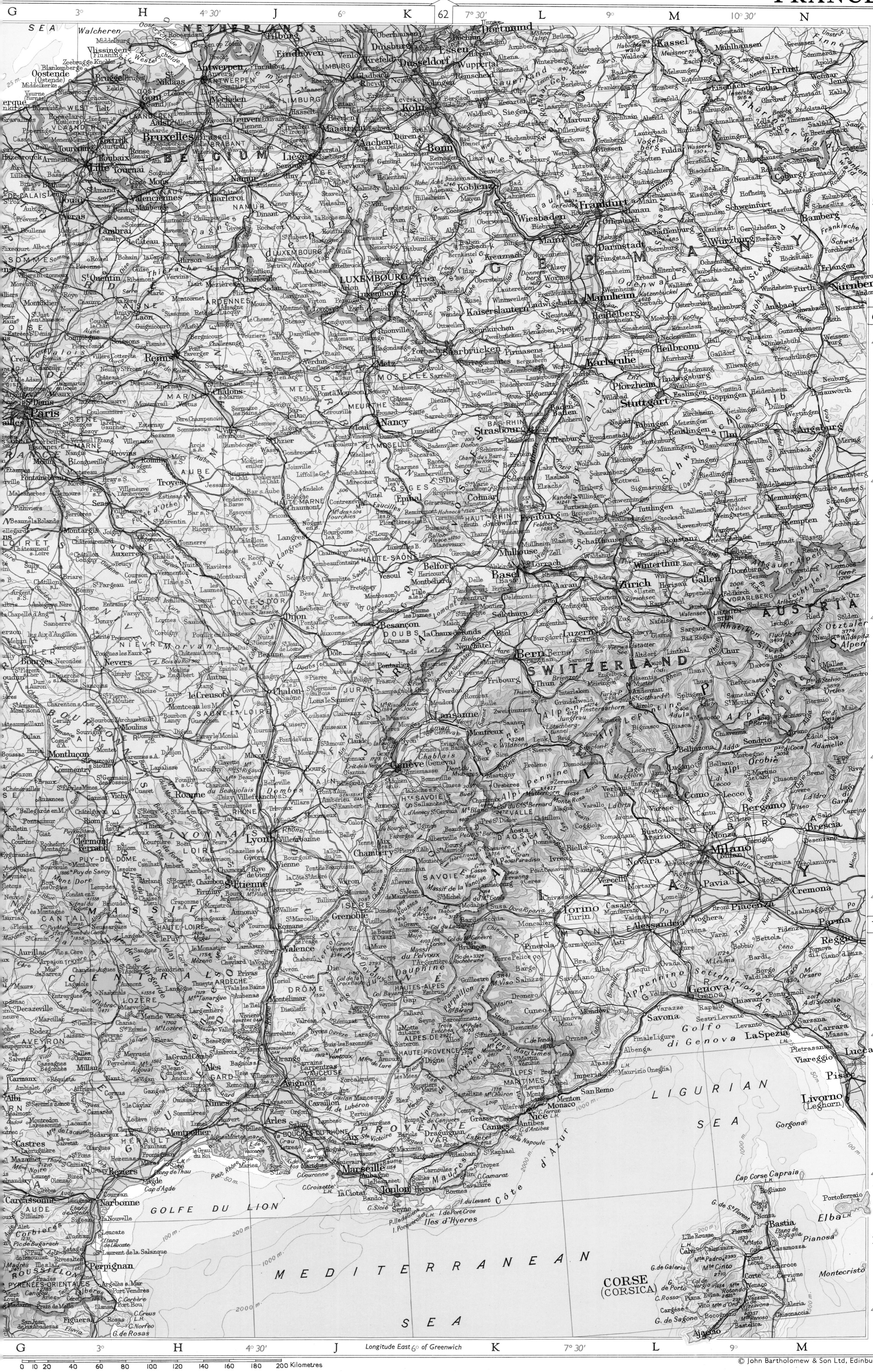
NETHERLANDS
BELGIUM
LUXEMBOURG
GERMANY
SWITZERLAND
AUSTRIA
ITALY
FRANCE
MASSIF CENTRAL
LIGURIAN SEA
MEDITERRANEAN SEA
GOLFE DU LION
CORSE (CORSICA)
Paris
Bruxelles
Lyon
Marseille
Genève
Milano
Torino
Genova
Longitude East of Greenwich
0 10 20 40 60 80 100 120 140 160 180 200 Kilometres

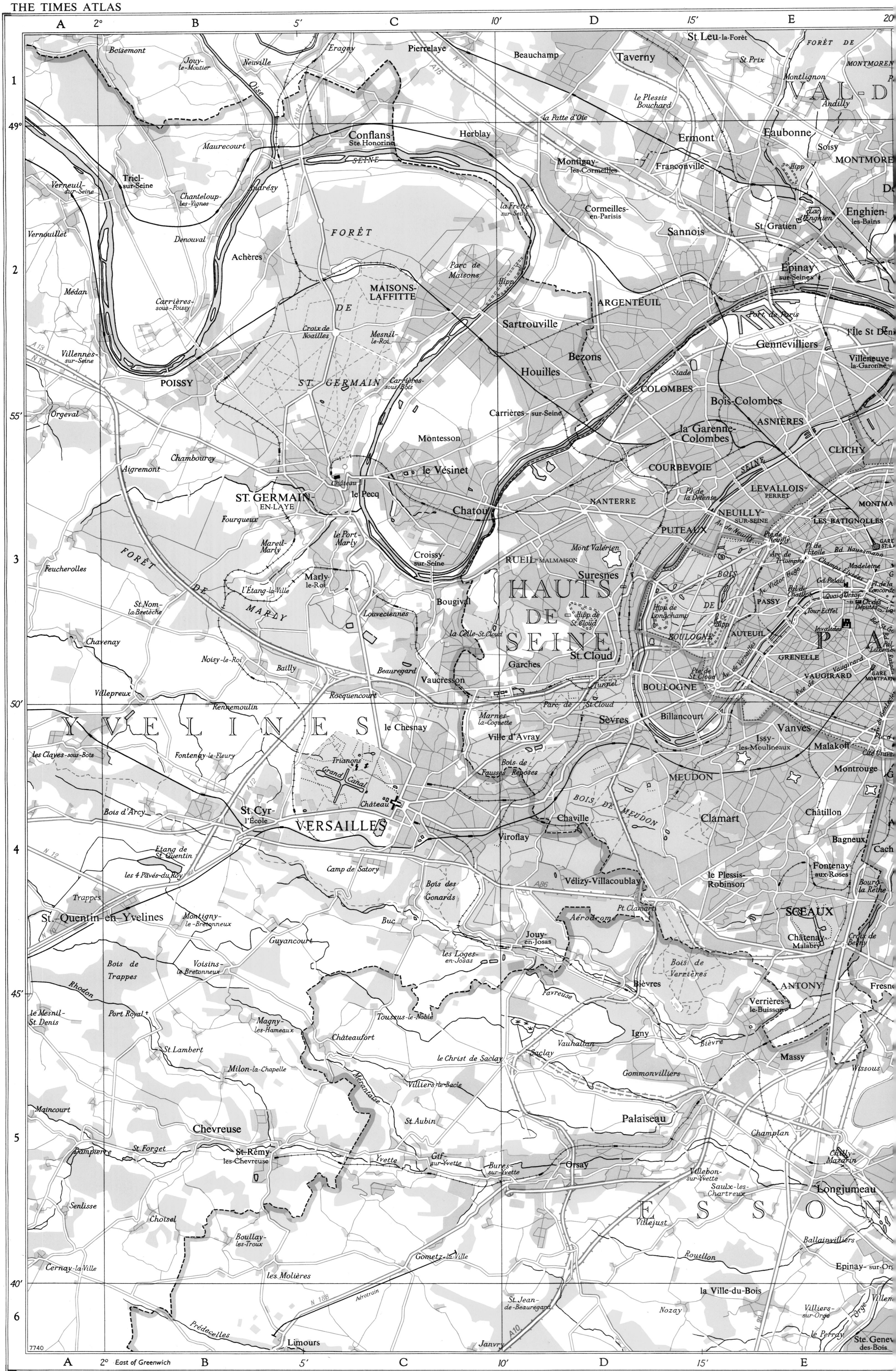
A
B
C
D
E
2°
5′
10′
15′
20′
49°
55′
50′
45′
40′
1
2
3
4
5
6
VAL-D
HAUTS DE SEINE
Y V E L I N E S
E S S O N
PA
FORÊT DE MONTMORENCY
FORÊT DE ST. GERMAIN
FORÊT DE MARLY
SEINE
Oise
Boisemont
Jouy-le-Moutier
Neuville
Eragny
Pierrelaye
Beauchamp
Taverny
St. Leu-la-Forêt
St. Prix
Montlignon
Andilly
le Plessis Bouchard
la Patte d'Oie
Herblay
Conflans-Ste. Honorine
Ermont
Eaubonne
Soisy
Maurecourt
Triel-sur-Seine
Verneuil-sur-Seine
Chanteloup-les-Vignes
Andrésy
Montigny-les-Cormeilles
Franconville
la Frette-sur-Seine
Cormeilles-en-Parisis
Sannois
St. Gratien
Lac d'Enghien
Enghien-les-Bains
Vernouillet
Denouval
Achères
Parc de Maisons
Epinay-sur-Seine
Médan
MAISONS-LAFFITTE
ARGENTEUIL
Port de Paris
Carrières-sous-Poissy
Croix de Noailles
Mesnil-le-Roi
Sartrouville
l'Île St. Denis
Gennevilliers
Villennes-sur-Seine
Bezons
Villeneuve-la-Garenne
POISSY
Carrières-sous-Bois
Houilles
Stade
COLOMBES
Orgeval
Carrières-sur-Seine
Bois-Colombes
ASNIÈRES
Montesson
la Garenne-Colombes
CLICHY
Chambourcy
le Vésinet
COURBEVOIE
Aigremont
Château
le Pecq
Pl. de la Défense
LEVALLOIS-PERRET
ST. GERMAIN-EN-LAYE
Chatou
NANTERRE
NEUILLY-SUR-SEINE
LES BATIGNOLLES
Fourqueux
le Port-Marly
PUTEAUX
Mareil-Marly
Croissy-sur-Seine
Mont Valérien
RUEIL-MALMAISON
Feucherolles
Marly-le-Roi
Suresnes
Arc de Triomphe
Champs Élysées
Madeleine
l'Étang-la-Ville
BOIS DE BOULOGNE
Bougival
Hipp. de Longchamp
Hipp. de St. Cloud
PASSY
St. Nom-la-Bretèche
Louveciennes
la Celle-St. Cloud
AUTEUIL
Invalides
Tour Eiffel
Chavenay
St. Cloud
GRENELLE
Noisy-le-Roi
Bailly
Beauregard
Vaucresson
Garches
VAUGIRARD
Villepreux
Rocquencourt
Tunnel
BOULOGNE
Rennemoulin
Parc de St. Cloud
Billancourt
le Chesnay
Marnes-la-Coquette
Sèvres
Vanves
Issy-les-Moulineaux
Malakoff
les Clayes-sous-Bois
Fontenay-le-Fleury
Ville d'Avray
Trianons
Grand Canal
Bois de Fausses Reposes
MEUDON
Montrouge
Bois d'Arcy
St. Cyr-l'École
VERSAILLES
BOIS DE MEUDON
Chaville
Clamart
Châtillon
Étang de St. Quentin
Viroflay
Bagneux
les 4 Pavés-du-Roy
Camp de Satory
Vélizy-Villacoublay
le Plessis-Robinson
Fontenay-aux-Roses
Trappes
Bois des Gonards
Pt. Clamart
Aérodrome
SCEAUX
St.-Quentin-en-Yvelines
Montigny-le-Bretonneux
Buc
Jouy-en-Josas
Châtenay-Malabry
Guyancourt
les Loges-en-Josas
Bois de Trappes
Voisins-le-Bretonneux
Bois de Verrières
Bièvres
ANTONY
Rhodon
Favreuse
Verrières-le-Buisson
le Mesnil-St. Denis
Port Royal
Magny-les-Hameaux
Toussus-le-Noble
Igny
Châteaufort
Vauhallan
Bièvre
St. Lambert
Saclay
le Christ de Saclay
Massy
Milon-la-Chapelle
Gommonvilliers
Villiers-le-Bacle
Mérantaise
Maincourt
Palaiseau
St. Aubin
Chevreuse
Champlan
Dampierre
St. Forget
St-Rémy-lès-Chevreuse
Yvette
Gif-sur-Yvette
Bures-sur-Yvette
Orsay
Villebon-sur-Yvette
Chilly-Mazarin
Saulx-les-Chartreux
Longjumeau
Senlisse
Choisel
Villejust
Boullay-les-Troux
Ballainvilliers
Roullon
Gometz-la-Ville
Cernay-la-Ville
Epinay-sur-Orge
les Molières
la Ville-du-Bois
Aérotrain
St. Jean-de-Beauregard
Nozay
Villiers-sur-Orge
Orge
Prédecelles
le Perray
Ste. Geneviève-des-Bois
Limours
Janvry
A15
N14
N184
A13
N13
N12
A12
A86
N10
N188
A10
7740
East of Greenwich
1: 100 000
0 ½ 1 2 3 4 5 Statute Miles

F
25′
G
30′
H
35′
J
40′
K
1
2
3
4
5
6
49°
55′
50′
45′
40′
Bouqueval
le Mesnil-Amelot
Écouen
Villiers-le-Bel
Goussainville
Aérogare
Aéroport de Paris - Charles de Gaulle
Roissy-en-France
Thieux
Juilly
St. Brice-sous-Forêt
le Thillay
Vaudherland
Nantouillet
Sarcelles
Compans
Gonesse
Mitry-Mory
Vineuil
Arnouville-lès-Gonesse
la Patte d'Oie
Tremblay-lès-Gonesse
St. Mesmes
Croult
Bonneuil
Pierrefitte-sur-Seine
Garges
Mory
Villepinte
Messy
Gressy
Aéroport de Paris - Le Bourget
Mitry-le-Neuf
Stains
Garonor
Dugny
Souilly
ST. DENIS
le Blanc-Mesnil
Sevran
Claye-Souilly
Parc de la Courneuve
Stade
le Bourget
Aulnay-sous-Bois
Canal de l'Ourcq
Villeparisis
la Courneuve
SEINE-ST. DENIS
Vaujours
DRANCY
les 4 Routes
AUBERVILLIERS
BOBIGNY
les Pavillons-sous-Bois
Livry-Gargan
Coubron
Courtry
Villevaudé
le Pin
Montjay
Clichy-sous-Bois
Pte de la Chapelle
Pte de la Villette
PANTIN
BONDY
le Raincy
Montfermeil
Carnetin
LA CHAPELLE
Pte de Pantin
Noisy-le-Sec
le Pré-St-Gervais
Villemomble
Chantereine
SEINE-
Thorigny-sur-Marne
GARE DE L'EST
BELLEVILLE
les Lilas
Brou-sur-Chantereine
Pomponne
Gagny
Lagny
Romainville
Rosny-sous-Bois
Chelles
MENILMONTANT
Pl. de la République
Vaires-sur-Marne
St. Thibault-des-Vignes
Bagnolet
Neuilly-Plaisance
Chelles
Gondoire
Gouvernes
CHARONNE
MONTREUIL
Marne
Canal
Gournay-sur-Marne
Neuilly-sur-Marne
Noisiel
Torcy
Guermantes
Hôt. de Ville
Pl. de la Bastille
Pl. de la Nation
Fontenay-sous-Bois
Noisy-le-Grand
Champs
Marne-la-Vallée
VINCENNES
Bussy-St. Martin
GARE DE LYON
REUILLY
Pte de Vincennes
St. Mandé
le Perreux-sur-Marne
Collégien
GARE D'AUSTERLITZ
Nogent-sur-Marne
Bry-sur-Marne
Lognes
ET-
BERCY
Villiers-sur-Marne
Croissy-Beaubourg
Pl. d'Italie
BOIS DE VINCENNES
Pte de la Gare
Charenton-le-Pont
Ferrières
St. Maurice
CHAMPIGNY SUR MARNE
Pte d'Italie
Alfort
Joinville-le-Pont
le Plessis-Trévise
Kremlin-Bicêtre
IVRY-SUR-SEINE
ST. MAUR-DES-FOSSÉS
Émerainville
Alfortville
Combault
Pontcarré
Maisons-Alfort
Pontault-Combault
Chennevières-sur-Marne
Pince-Vent
Vitry-sur-Seine
la Varenne-St. Hilaire
CRÉTEIL
Roissy
la Queue-en-Brie
VILLEJUIF
Ormesson-sur-Marne
Morbras
MARNE
FORÊT D'ARMAINVILLIERS
VAL-DE-MARNE
Choisy-le-Roi
Carrefour Pompadour
Noiseau
Chevilly-Larue
Bonneuil-sur-Marne
Ozoir-la Ferrière
Thiais
Sucy-en-Brie
Belle Croix
Rungis
la Belle Épine
BOIS NOTRE-DAME
Valenton
Boissy-St. Léger
Lésigny
Orly
Limeil-Brévannes
Villeneuve-le-Roi
Marolles-en-Brie
Férolles-Attilly
Aéroport de Paris-Orly
Ablon-sur-Seine
VILLENEUVE-ST. GEORGES
Réveillon
Santeny
Chevry-Cossigny
Crosne
Yerres
Villecresnes
Servon
Vieille-Poste
SEINE
Athis-Mons
Mandres
Vigneux-sur-Seine
Montgeron
Val d'Yerres
Brie-Comte-Robert
Juvisy-sur-Orge
Brunoy
Périgny
Epinay-sous-Sénart
Boussy-St. Antoine
Grisy-Suisnes
Draveil
Varennes-Jarcy
Yerres
Savigny-sur-Orge
FORÊT DE SÉNART
Coubert
Viry-Châtillon
Quincy-sous-Sénart
Grégy-sur-Yerres
Champrosay
Morsang-sur-Orge
Combs-la-Ville
Évry-les-Châteaux
Soignolles-en-Brie
Grigny
Soisy-sur-Seine
Ris-Orangis
N 3
N 4
N 6
N 19
A 4
0 ½ 1 2 3 4 5 6 7 8 Kilometres

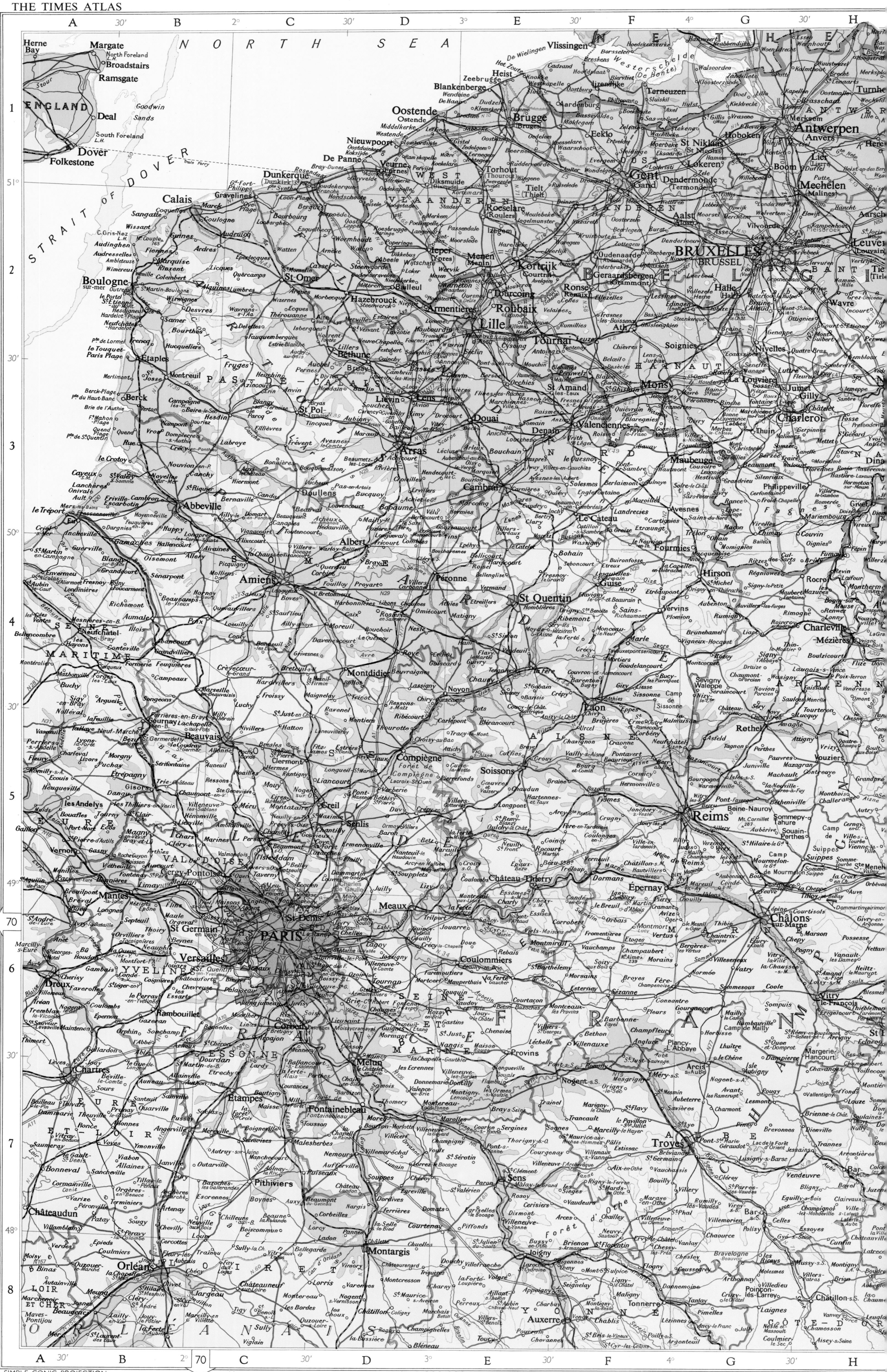
NORTH SEA
STRAIT OF DOVER
ENGLAND
NETHERLANDS
BELGIQUE
FRANCE
Margate
Broadstairs
Ramsgate
Deal
Dover
Folkestone
Vlissingen
Oostende
Brugge
Gent
Antwerpen
Dunkerque
Calais
Boulogne
Lille
Roubaix
Tourcoing
Kortrijk
Tournai
Mons
Charleroi
BRUXELLES
Mechelen
Arras
Douai
Cambrai
Valenciennes
Abbeville
Amiens
St Quentin
Péronne
Laon
Soissons
Reims
Compiègne
Beauvais
Senlis
Meaux
PARIS
Versailles
St Germain
Mantes
Chartres
Évreux
Melun
Fontainebleau
Étampes
Orléans
Montargis
Sens
Troyes
Auxerre
Épernay
Châlons-sur-Marne
Charleville-Mézières
Rethel
Vitry-le-François
Château-Thierry
Provins
Pithiviers
Châteaudun
Dreux
Rambouillet
PAS-DE-CALAIS
NORD
SOMME
AISNE
OISE
SEINE-MARITIME
EURE
EURE-ET-LOIR
YVELINES
ESSONNE
VAL-D'OISE
SEINE-ET-MARNE
MARNE
AUBE
YONNE
LOIRET
LOIR-ET-CHER
ARDENNES
HAINAUT
VLAANDEREN
ORLÉANAIS
70

Metres
Feet
1000
3281
500
1640
200
656
100
328
0
0
Below Sea Level
Tidal Areas
50
164

SIMPLE CONIC PROJECTION

1 : 1 000 000

0 5 10 20 30 40 50 Statute Miles

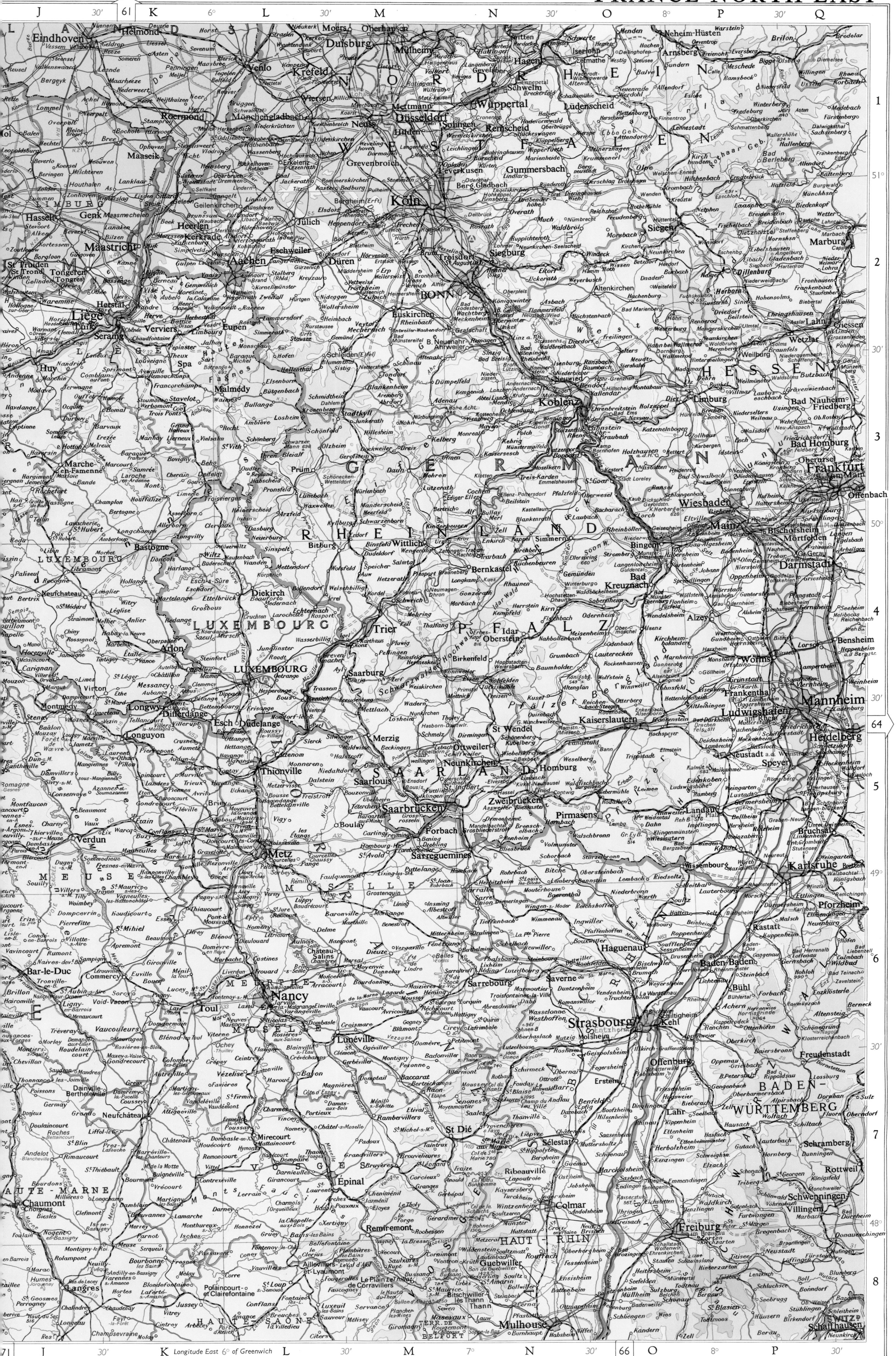

0 5 10 20 30 40 50 60 70 80 Kilometres

Heights and Depths in Metres

Plate
70

ENGLISH CHANNEL (LA MANCHE)
CHANNEL ISLANDS
(To United Kingdom)
(ILES NORMANDES)
GUERNSEY
JERSEY
Alderney
Passage de la Déroute
GOLFE DE ST MALO
BAY OF BISCAY
(GOLFE DE GASCOGNE)
FINISTÈRE
CÔTES DU NORD
MORBIHAN
ILLE-ET-VILAINE
LOIRE ATLANTIQUE
BRETAGNE
Cherbourg
Granville
St Malo
Dinan
Rennes
Brest
Morlaix
Lannion
Guingamp
St-Brieuc
Quimper
Douarnenez
Concarneau
Quimperlé
Lorient
Pontivy
Loudéac
Vannes
Auray
Quiberon
Redon
Ploërmel
St. Nazaire
Nantes
La Roche-sur-Yon
Châteaubriant
Belle Ile
I. d'Ouessant (Ushant)
I. d'Yeu
Noirmoutier
Iroise
Longitude West 3° of Greenwich

Metres
Feet
200
656
100
328
0
0
Tidal Areas
50
164
200
656

7740

SIMPLE CONIC PROJECTION

1: 1 000 000

0 5 10 20 30 40 50 Statute Miles

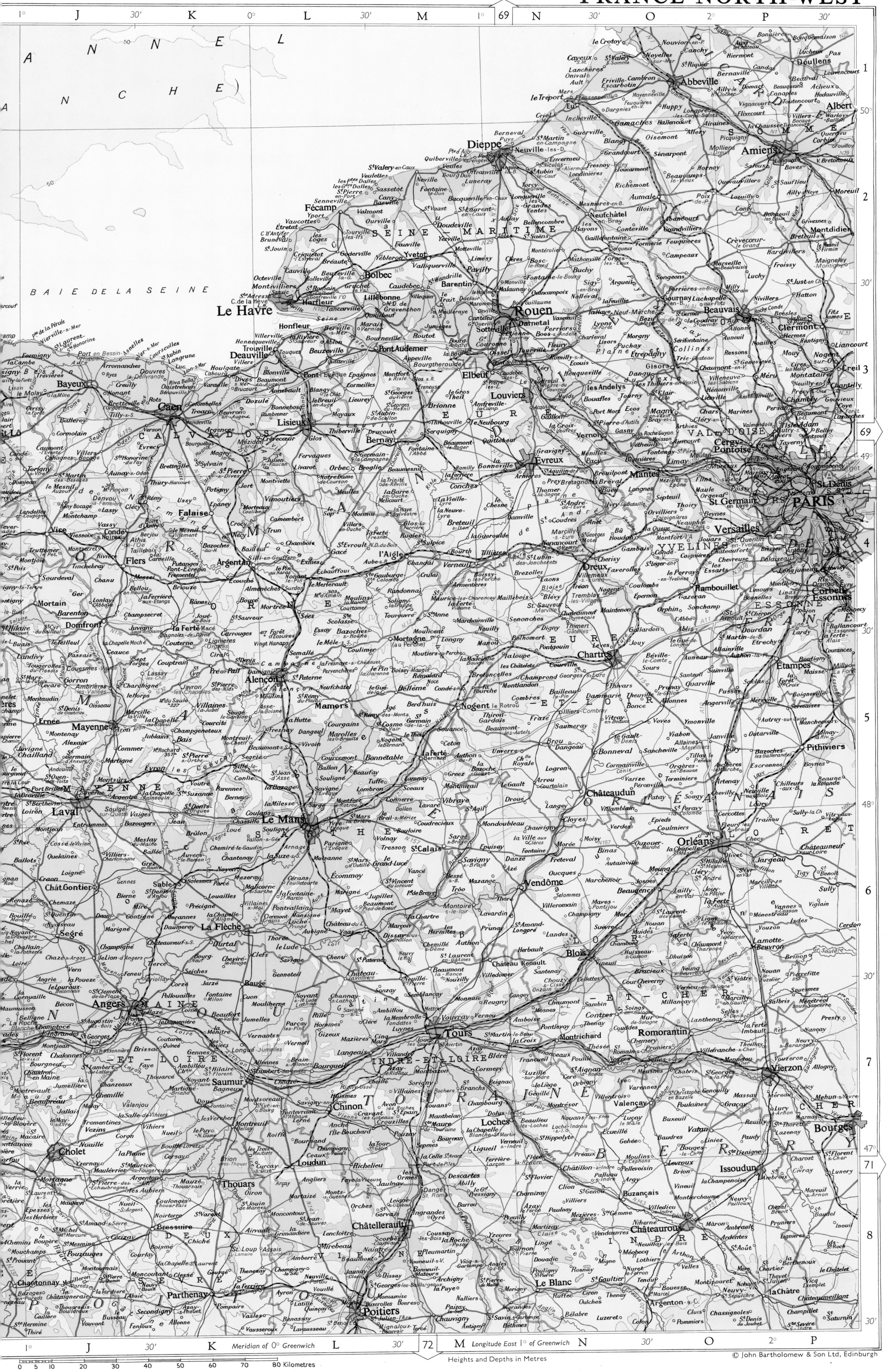

Manche
Baie de la Seine
Le Havre
Rouen
Dieppe
Abbeville
Amiens
Albert
Beauvais
Caen
Bayeux
Lisieux
Évreux
Alençon
Le Mans
Laval
Mayenne
Chartres
Dreux
Versailles
PARIS
St Denis
St Germain
Orléans
Blois
Tours
Angers
Saumur
Cholet
Chinon
Châtellerault
Poitiers
Châteauroux
Vierzon
Bourges
Issoudun
Vendôme
Châteaudun
Étampes
Rambouillet
Seine-Maritime
Calvados
Eure
Orne
Mayenne
Sarthe
Eure-et-Loir
Loir-et-Cher
Indre-et-Loire
Maine-et-Loire
Deux-Sèvres
Indre
Cher
Loiret
Essonne
Yvelines
Val d'Oise
Somme
Oise
Meridian of 0° Greenwich
Longitude East 1° of Greenwich
Heights and Depths in Metres
0 5 10 20 30 40 50 60 70 80 Kilometres
© John Bartholomew & Son Ltd, Edinburgh

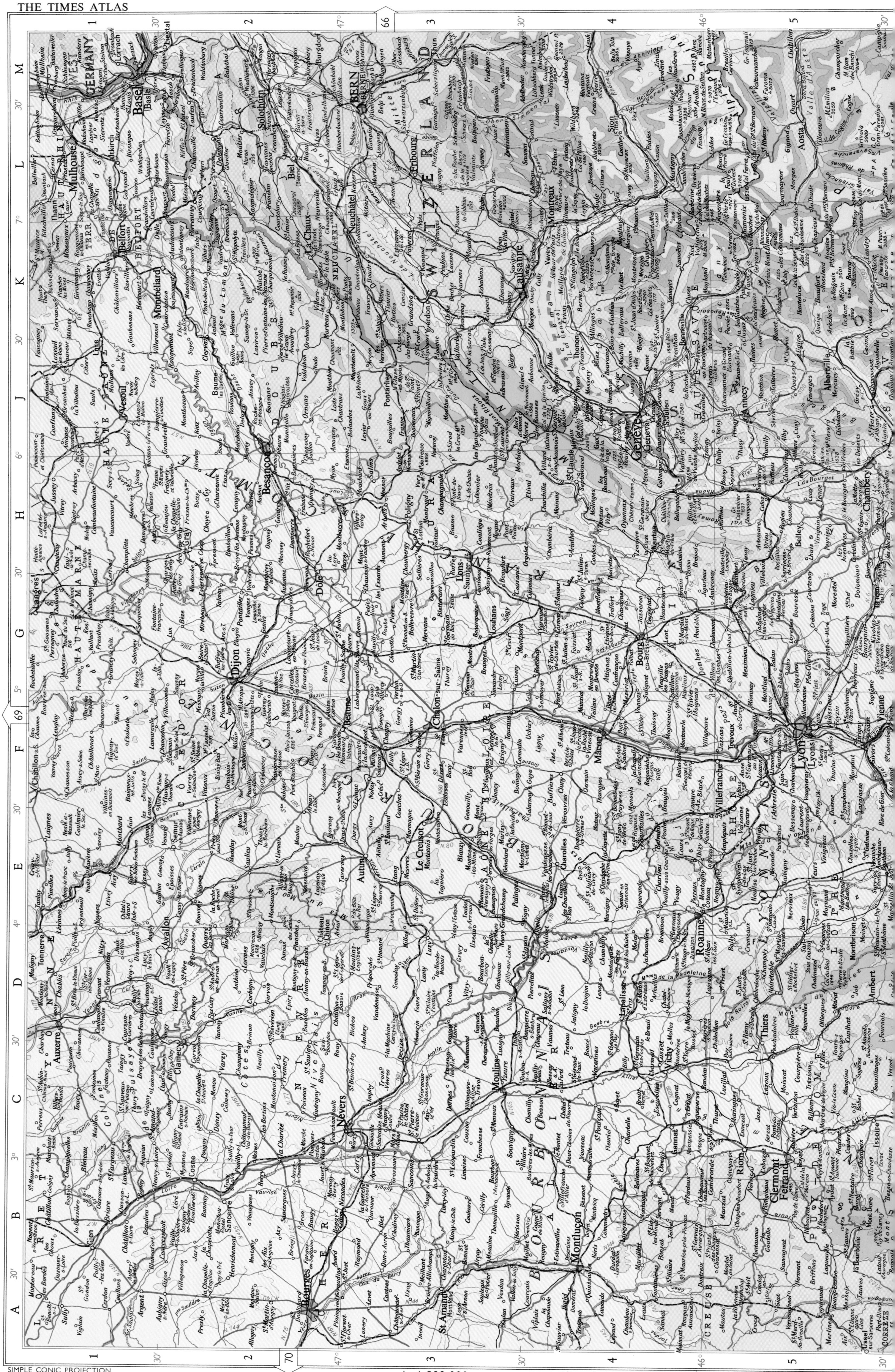

SIMPLE CONIC PROJECTION

1: 1 000 000

0 5 10 20 30 40 50 Statute Miles

FRANCE SOUTH-EAST

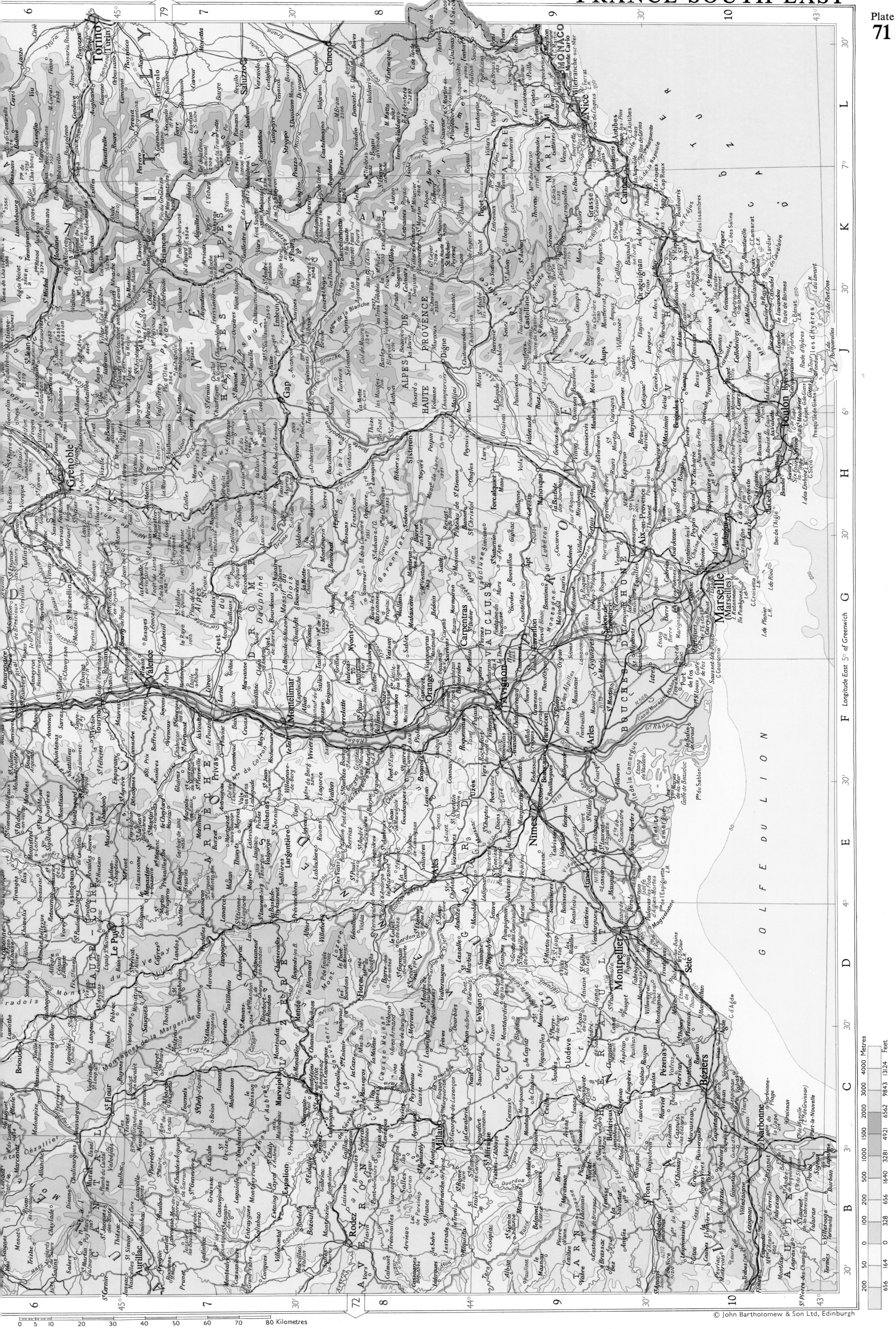

0 5 10 20 30 40 50 60 70 80 Kilometres

Valencia
Alicante
Murcia
Cartagena
Albacete
Almería
Granada
Motril
Lorca
Elche
Orihuela
Alcoy
Gandía
Játiva
Requena
Utiel
Almansa
Hellín
Villena
Cieza
Jumilla
Yecla
Ubeda
Baeza
Linares
Guadix
Baza
Huéscar
Aguilas
Valdepeñas
Manzanares
Tomelloso
Villarrobledo
La Roda
Socuéllamos
Alcázar de San Juan
Daimiel
Denia
Sagunto
G O L F O   D E   V A L E N C I A
C O S T A   B L A N C A
SIERRA NEVADA
Golfo de Almería
C. de Gata
Cabo de Palos
M E D I T E R R A N E A N   S E A
BALEARIC ISLANDS
(ISLAS BALEARES)
(To Spain)
1 : 1,250,000
MALLORCA
MENORCA
Palma
Mahón
Ciudadela
Manacor
Cabrera
GIBRALTAR
(To United Kingdom)
1 : 31 680
Neutral Zone
The British Lines
Airfield
Runway
North Mole
Gibraltar Harbour
Detached Mole
South Mole
Bahía de Algeciras
Moorish Castle (Ruins)
Reservoir
King's Bastion
Government Ho.
Grand Parade
Rock Hotel
Alameda Gd.
Casino
Mt. Misery
Queens Road
Dock Yard
Rosia
Rosia Bay
Camp Bay
Buena Vista
Little Bay
Windmill Hill Flats
Europa Flats
Europa Point
Catalan Bay (Caleta)
St. Abb's Head
Shirley Cove
Sandy Bay
Water Catchments
Signal Hill
Middle Hill
Cemetery
Eastern Beach
THE ROCK
Longitude East 3° of Greenwich
West of Green.
100 Kilometres

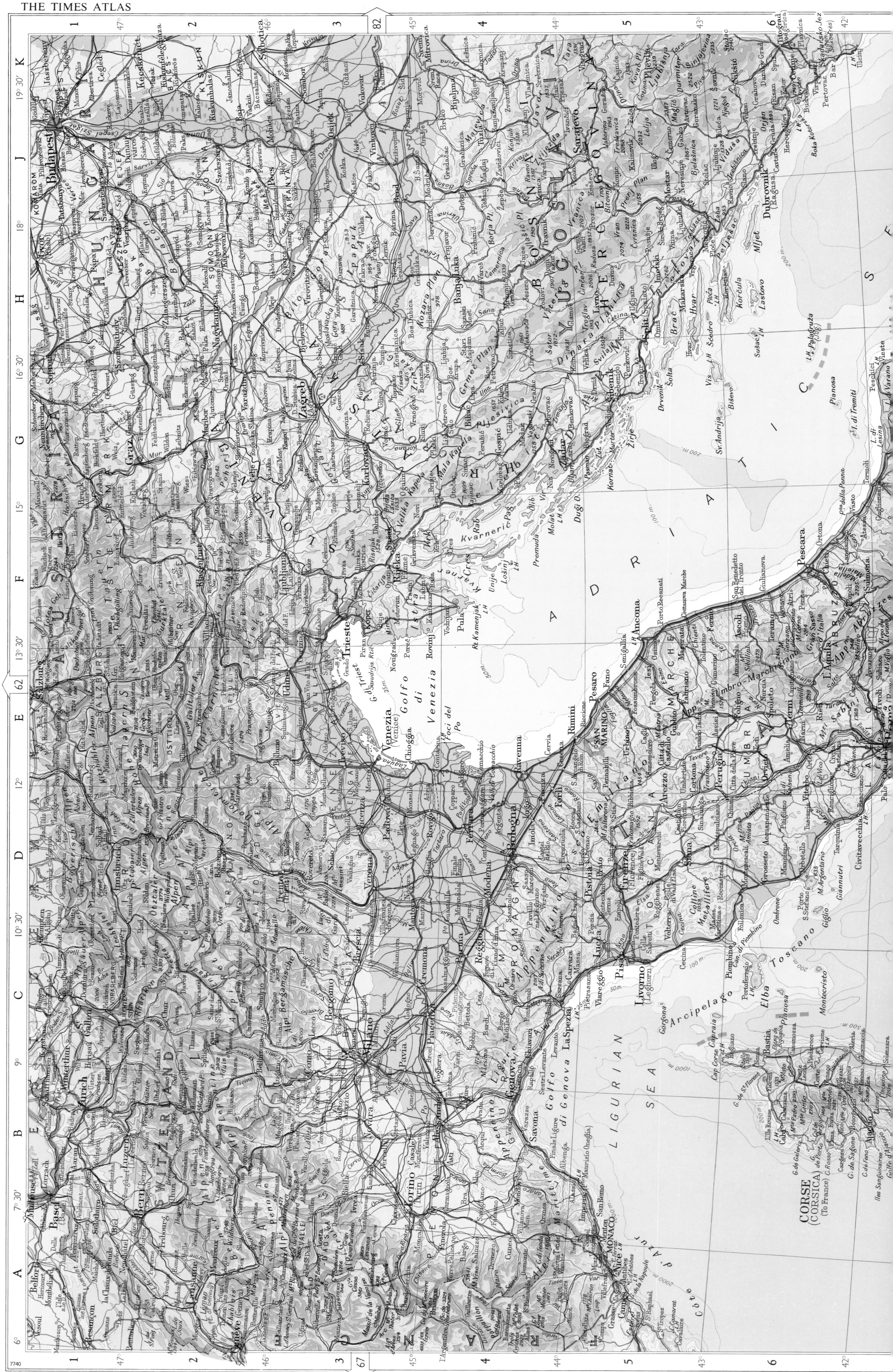

7740

SECANT CONIC PROJECTION

1: 2 500 000

0 10 20 40 60 80 100 120 Statute Miles

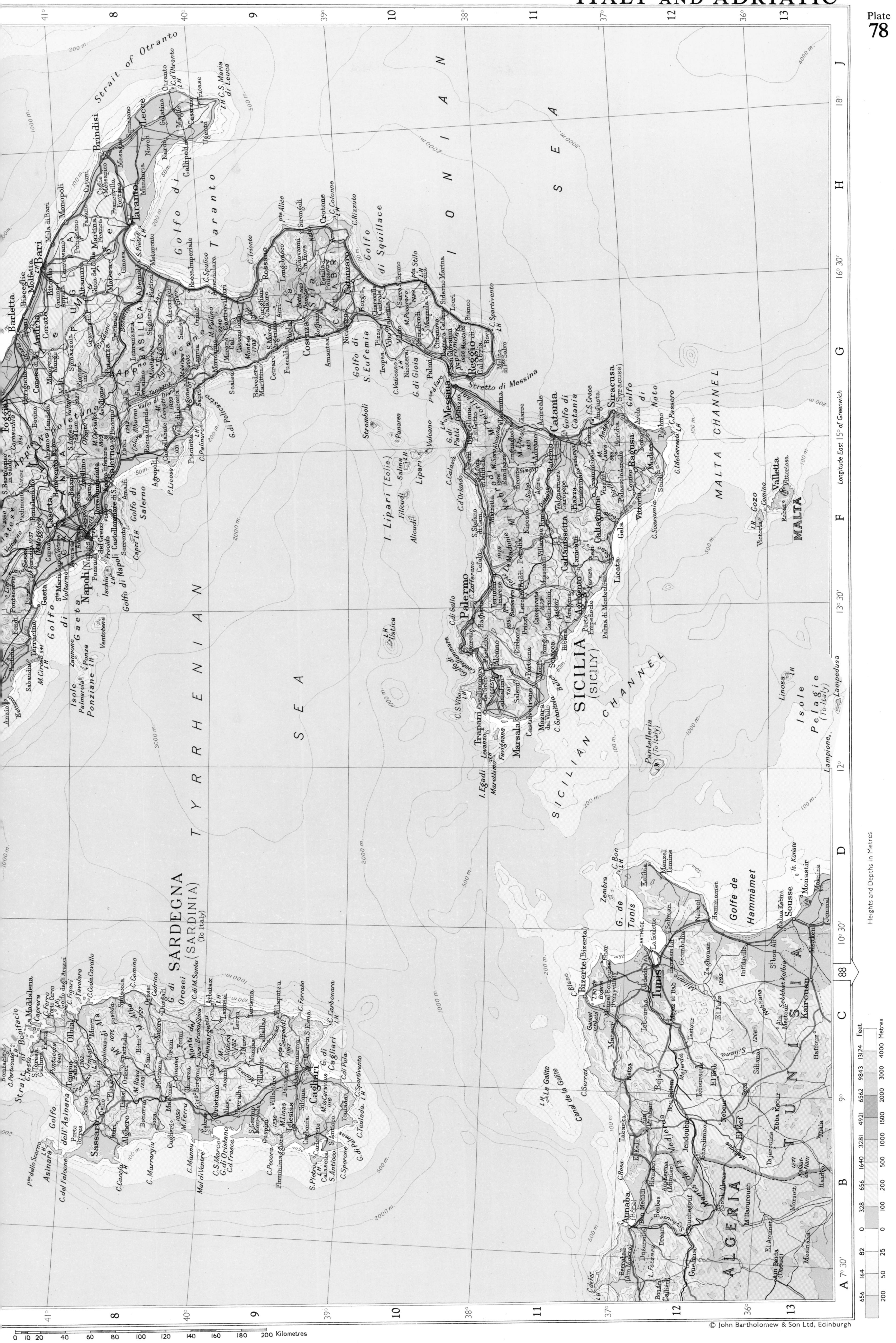
TYRRHENIAN SEA
IONIAN SEA
SARDEGNA (SARDINIA) (To Italy)
SICILIA (SICILY)
MALTA CHANNEL
SICILIAN CHANNEL
MALTA
TUNISIA
ALGERIA
Strait of Otranto
Golfo di Taranto
Stretto di Messina
I. Lipari (Eolie)
Isole Pelagie (To Italy)
Pantelleria (To Italy)
Longitude East 15° of Greenwich
Heights and Depths in Metres
0 10 20 40 60 80 100 120 140 160 180 200 Kilometres

66
71
SWITZERLAND
FRANCE
ITALIA
LIGURIAN SEA
GOLFO DI GENOVA
RIVIERA DI PONENTE
RIVIERA DI LEVANTE
CÔTE D'AZUR
BERN (BERNE)
Fribourg
Thun
Interlaken
Sion
Montreux
Vevey
Martigny-Ville
Chamonix
Mont Blanc
Aosta
Ivrea
Biella
Torino (Turin)
Novara
Vercelli
Milano (Milan)
Como
Varese
Lecco
Bergamo
Monza
Lodi
Pavia
Crema
Cremona
Piacenza
Alessandria
Asti
Cuneo
Savona
Genova (Genoa)
Rapallo
La Spezia
Sanremo
Imperia
Alassio
Albenga
Menton
Monte-Carlo
MONACO
Nice
Antibes
Cannes
Grasse
Lugano
Locarno
Bellinzona
Chur
Domodossola
Verbania
St. Moritz
Sondrio
Voghera
Tortona
Chiavari
MILAN (Milano)
1:250 000
Miles
Km
Feet
Metres
13124
4000
9843
3000
6562
2000
4921
1500
3281
1000
1640
500
656
200
328
100
0
0
164
50
656
200
Longitude East 10° of Greenwich
SECANT CONIC PROJECTION
1: 1 000 000
50 Statute Miles

ITALY NORTH

0 5 10 20 30 40 50 60 70 80 Kilometres

Heights and Depths in Metres

Firenze (Florence)
Pisa
Livorno (Leghorn)
Empoli
Pontedera
Volterra
Siena
Arezzo
Perugia
Cortona
Assisi
Foligno
Spoleto
Terni
Rieti
Orvieto
Viterbo
Grosseto
Piombino
Portoferràio
I. d'Elba
Orbetello
Porto S. Stéfano
Tarquinia
Civitavecchia
Tivoli
ROMA (ROME)
Frascati
Velletri
Latina
Anzio
Nettuno
Tuscania
Montepulciano
Massa Marittima
Follonica
Golfo di Follónica
Cecina
Urbino
Gubbio
Fabriano
Città di Castello
Sansepolcro
Lago Trasimeno
Lago di Bolsena
Lago di Bracciano
U M B R I A
T Y R R
Isole Ponziane
ROME
(ROMA)
1 : 21 000
CITTA DEL VATICANO
S. Pietro in Vaticano
Castel S. Angelo
VILLA BORGHESE
Colosseo
Foro Romano
Pantheon
Terme di Caracalla
Staz. di Termini
TEVERE (TIBER)
Feet
Metres
6562
2000
4921
1500
3281
1000
1640
500
656
200
328
100
0
0
164
50
656
200

ADRIATIC SEA
YUGOSLAVIA
Šibenik
Split (Spalato)
Ancona
Osimo
Recanati
Civitanova Marche
Macerata
Porto S Giórgio
Fermo
San Benedetto del Tronto
Ascoli Piceno
Giulianova
Teramo
GRAN SASSO D'ITALIA
Pescara
Chieti
Ortona
L'Aquila
Lanciano
Vasto
Sulmona
Avezzano
Termoli
Palagruža L.H (Yug.)
I.di Tremiti
Pianosa
Vis
Lastovo
Campobasso
Isernia
Sora
Frosinone
Cassino
Gaeta
Formia
Terracina
Mondragone
Caserta
Benevento
Napoli (Naples)
Pozzuoli
Torre del Greco
Torre Annunziata
Castellammare di Stabia
Sorrento
Amalfi
Salerno
Capri
L.d'Ischia
I. di Ventotene
Golfo di Gaeta
Golfo di Napoli
Golfo di Salerno
Avellino
Foggia
Lucera
San Severo
Manfredonia
Golfo di Manfredónia
Vieste
Barletta
Trani
Andria
Cerignola
Canosa di Puglia
Melfi
Potenza
Eboli
Battipaglia
Agropoli
Sapri
Lauria
Lagonegro
BASILICATA
Gravina in Puglia
Irsina
Tricarico
Grassano
Stigliano
Longitude East 14° of Greenwich
Heights and Depths in Metres
0 5 10 20 30 40 50 60 70 80 Kilometres

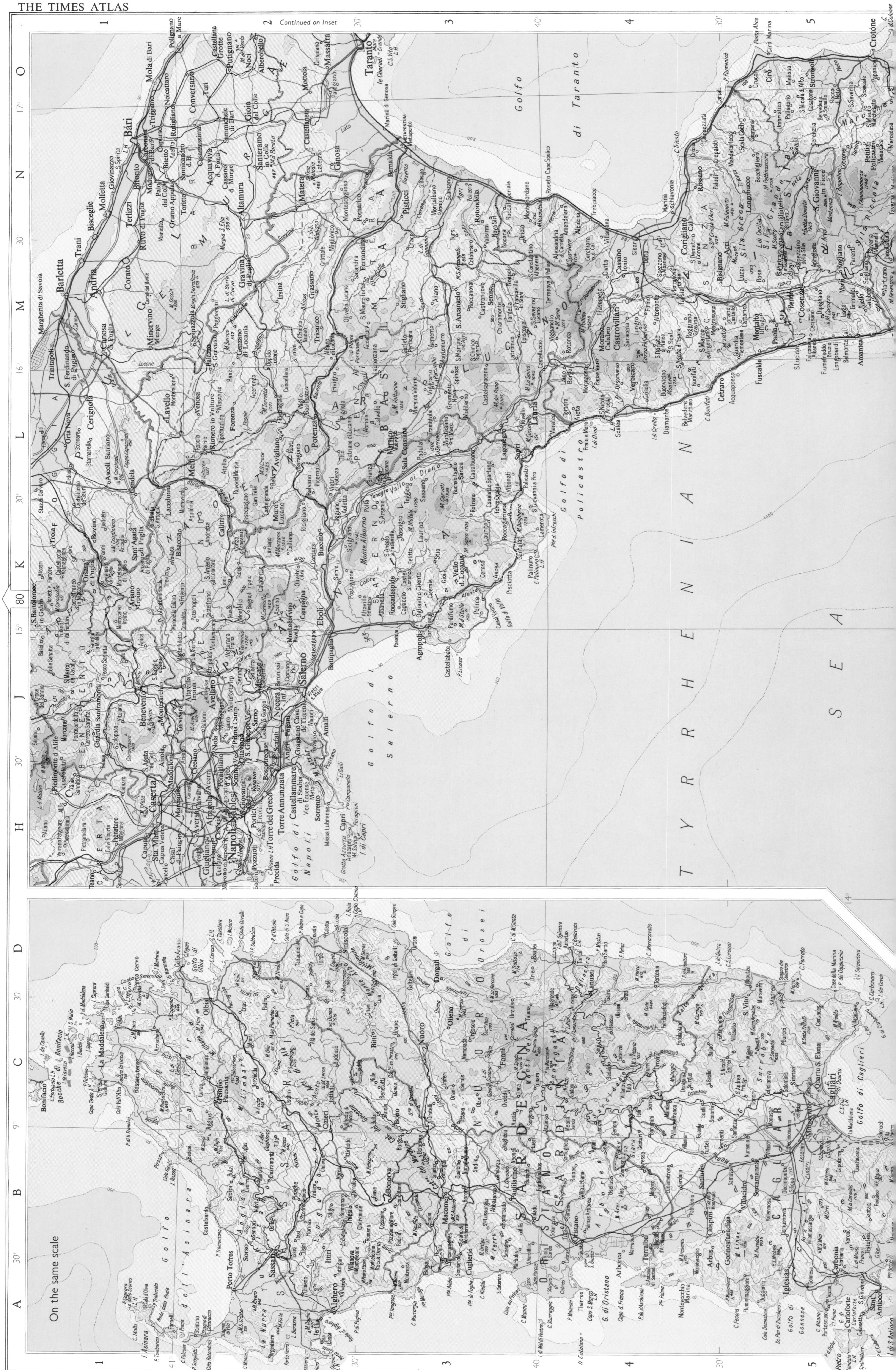

SECANT CONIC PROJECTION

1: 1 000 000

0 5 10 20 30 40 50 Statute Miles

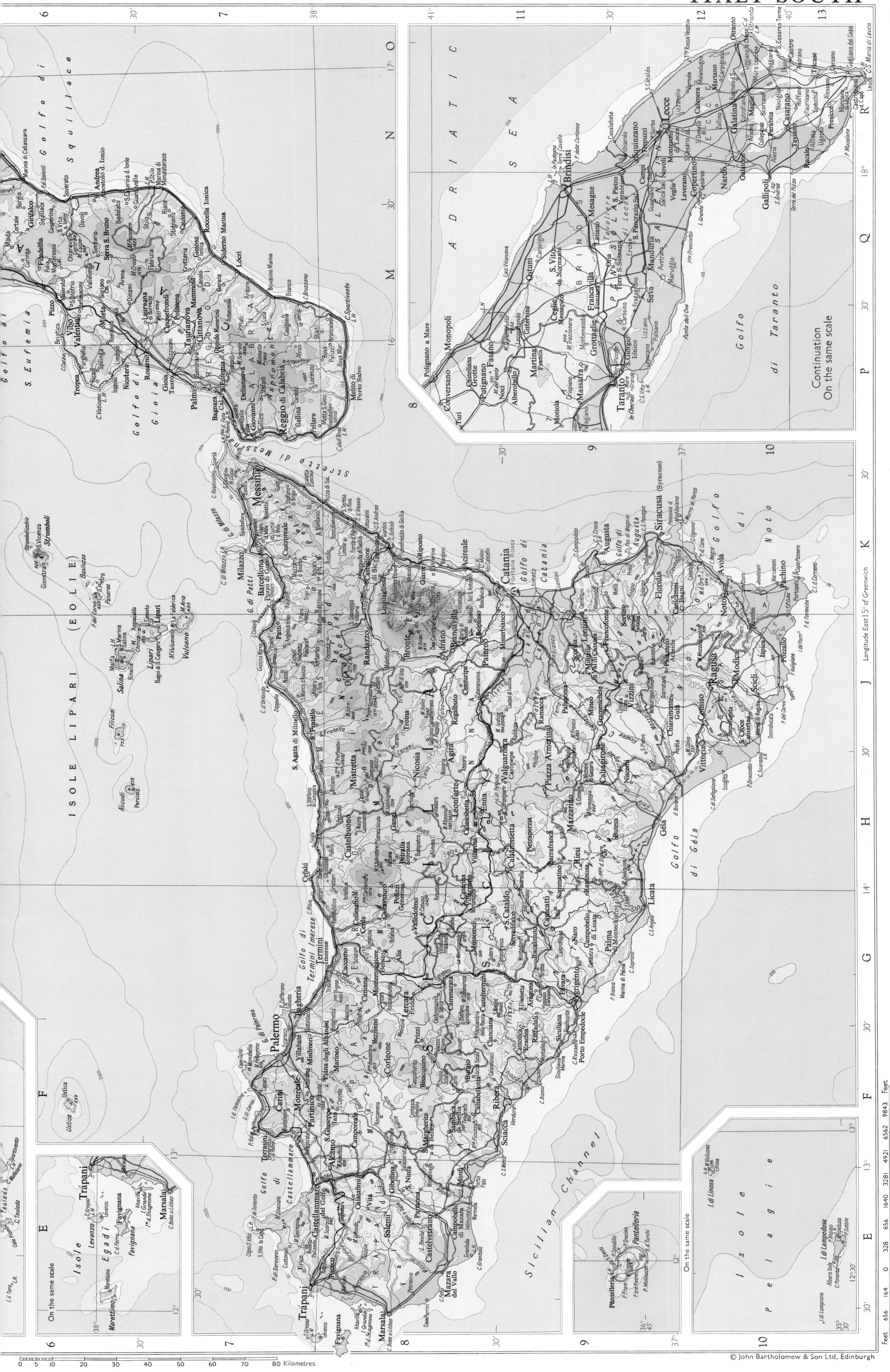
ISOLE LIPARI (EOLIE)
Stromboli
Lipari
Vulcano
Salina
Filicudi
Alicudi
Ustica
Messina
Catania
Siracusa (Syracuse)
Palermo
Trapani
Marsala
Agrigento
Caltanissetta
Enna
Ragusa
Gela
Licata
Sciacca
Reggio di Calabria
Golfo di Catania
Golfo di Noto
Golfo di Gela
Golfo di Castellammare
Golfo di Termini Imerese
Sicilian Channel
Stretto di Messina
Golfo di Squillace
Golfo di S. Eufemia
Golfo di Gioia
Golfo di Taranto
ADRIATIC SEA
Brindisi
Lecce
Taranto
Gallipoli
Otranto
Continuation
On the same scale
On the same scale
Isole Egadi
Isole Pelagie
Pantelleria
I. di Lampedusa
I. di Linosa
Longitude East 15° of Greenwich
Heights and Depths in Metres
0 5 10 20 30 40 50 60 70 80 Kilometres

© John Bartholomew & Son Ltd, Edinburgh

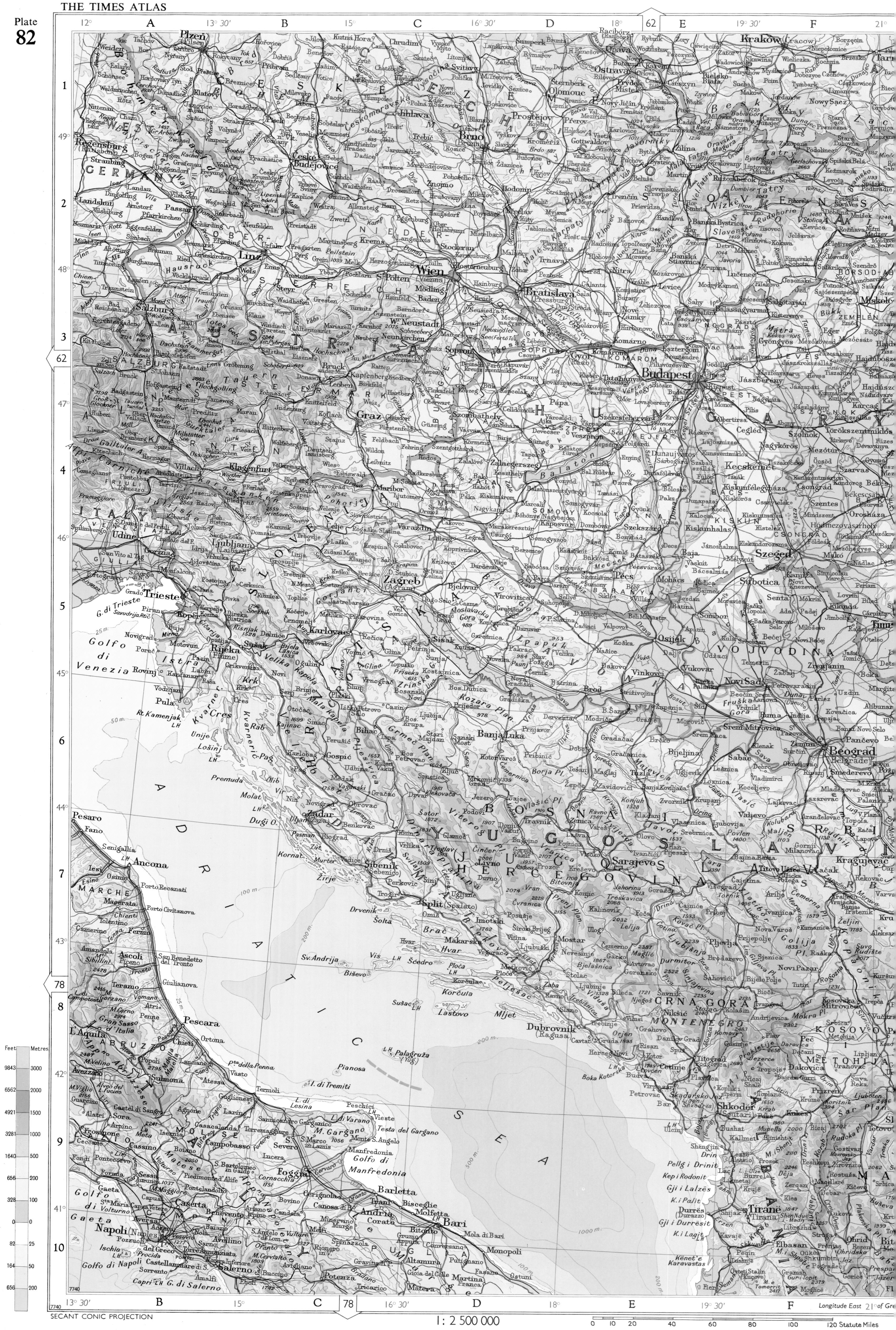

SECANT CONIC PROJECTION

1: 2 500 000

0 10 20 40 60 80 100 120 Statute Miles

HUNGARY ROMANIA AND YUGOSLAVIA

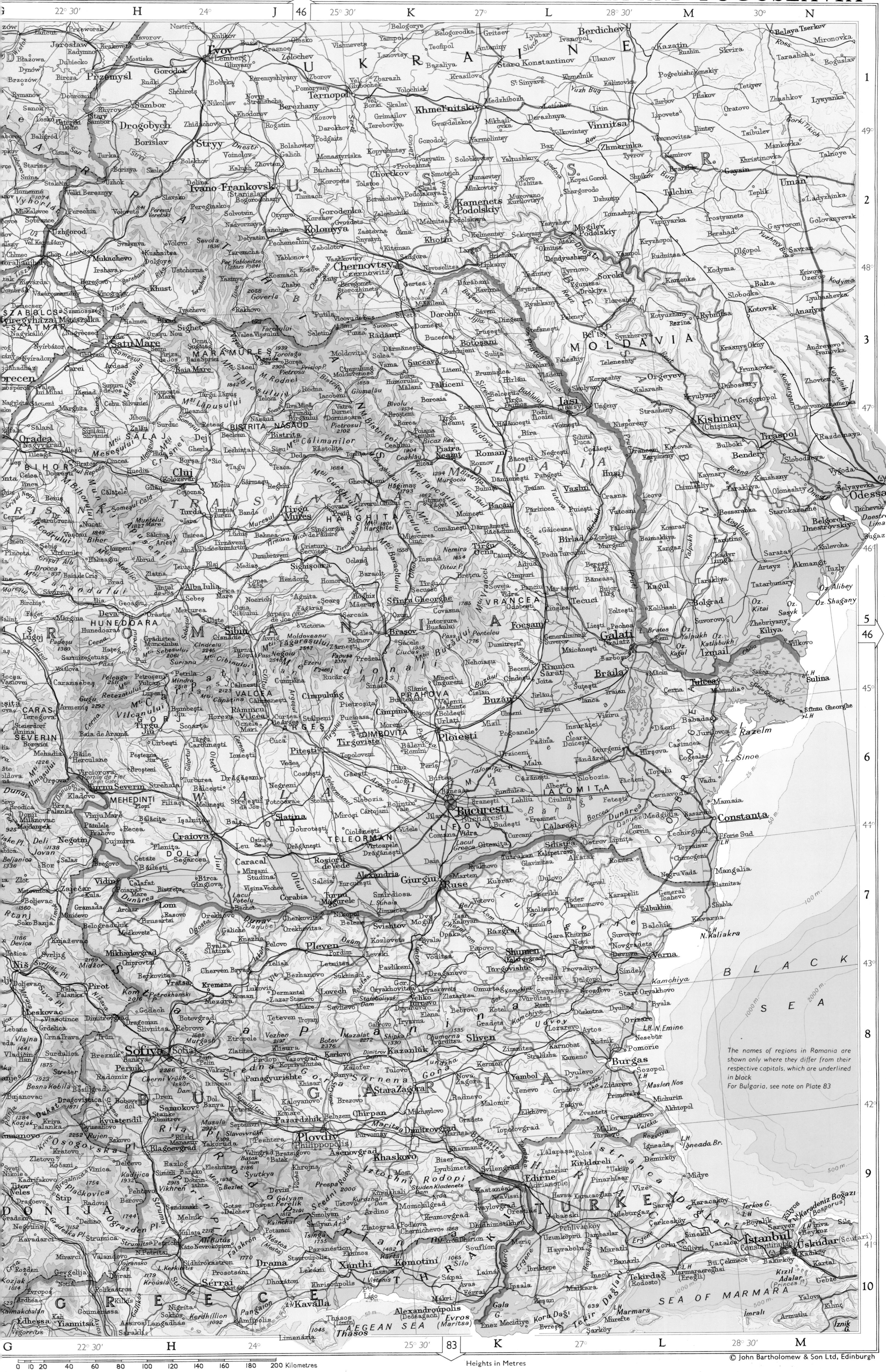

UKRAINE
MOLDAVIA
TRANSYLVANIA
ROMANIA
WALLACHIA
BULGARIA
GREECE
TURKEY
BLACK SEA
SEA OF MARMARA
AEGEAN SEA
The names of regions in Romania are shown only where they differ from their respective capitals, which are underlined in black
For Bulgaria, see note on Plate 83

0 10 20 40 60 80 100 120 140 160 180 200 Kilometres

Heights in Metres

© John Bartholomew & Son Ltd, Edinburgh

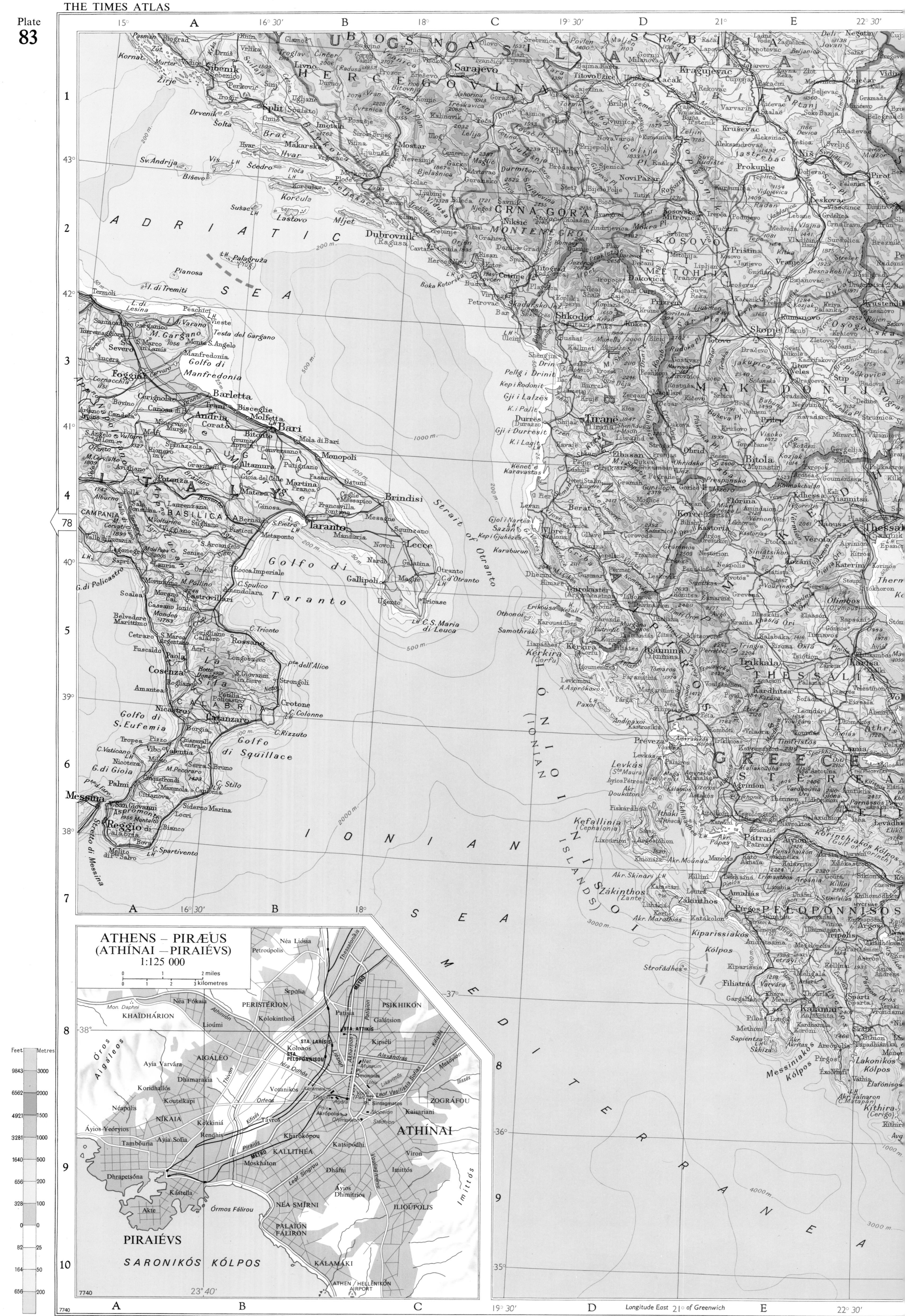
ATHENS – PIRÆUS
(ATHÍNAI – PIRAIÉVS)
1:125 000
ADRIATIC SEA
IONIAN SEA
MEDITERRANEAN SEA
IÓNIOI NÍSOI (IONIAN ISLANDS)
Golfo di Taranto
Golfo di Manfredonia
Golfo di Squillace
Strait of Otranto
ITALY
PUGLIA
BASILICATA
CALABRIA
CAMPANIA
CRNA GORA (MONTENEGRO)
BOSNA I HERCEGOVINA
SRBIJA
KOSOVO METOHIJA
MAKEDONIJA
ALBANIA
GREECE
THESSALIA
STEREA ELLAS
PELOPONNISOS
ÍPIROS
JUGOSLAVIA
Sarajevo
Dubrovnik (Ragusa)
Tiranë
Bari
Taranto
Brindisi
Lecce
Foggia
Messina
Reggio di Calabria
Kérkira (Corfu)
Pátrai
Skopje
Split (Spalato)
ATHÍNAI
PIRAIÉVS
SARONIKÓS KÓLPOS
Feet Metres
9843 3000
6562 2000
4921 1500
3281 1000
1640 500
656 200
328 100
0 0
82 25
164 50
656 200
Longitude East 21° of Greenwich

GREECE ÆGEAN AND BULGARIA

Plate
83

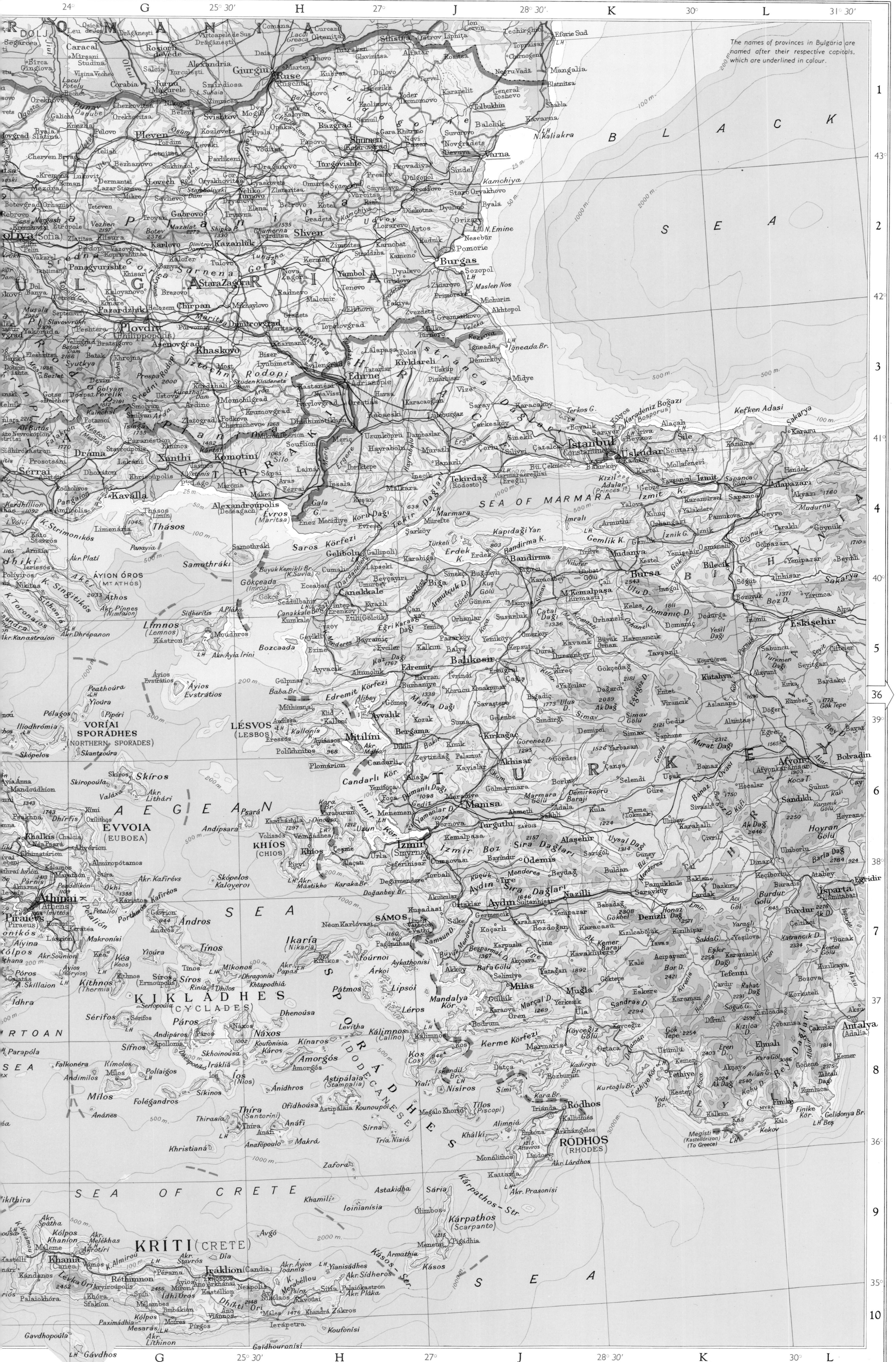

0 10 20 40 60 80 100 120 140 160 180 200 Kilometres

Heights in Metres

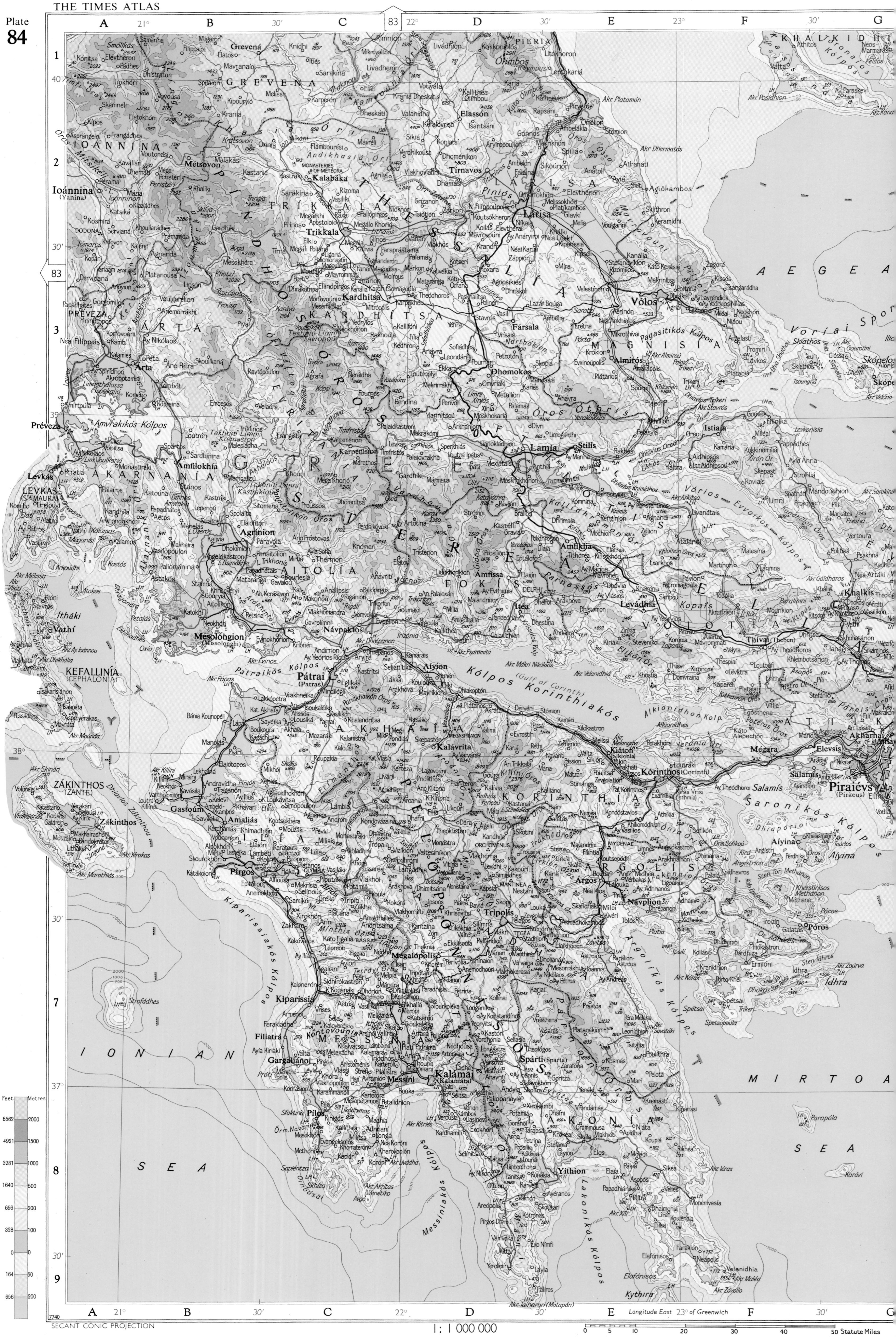
AEGEAN
IONIAN SEA
MIRTOAN SEA
GREECE
THESSALIA
PELOPONNISOS
STEREA ELLAS
IOÁNNINA
GREVENA
TRÍKKALA
KARDHÍTSA
LÁRISA
MAGNISÍA
ÁRTA
PREVEZA
AKARNANÍA
AITOLÍA
FOKIS
VOIOTÍA
ATTIKÍ
AKHAÏA
ILÍA
KORINTHÍA
ARGOLÍS
ARKADHÍA
MESSINÍA
LAKONÍA
KEFALLINÍA (CEPHALONIA)
ZÁKINTHOS (ZANTE)
LEVKAS (STA MAURA)
Ithákí
Ioánnina (Yanina)
Métsovon
Grevená
Kalabáka
Tríkkala
Kardhítsa
Lárisa
Tírnavos
Elassón
Vólos
Fársala
Almirós
Dhomokos
Lamía
Stilís
Árta
Préveza
Levkás
Amfilokhía
Agrínion
Karpenísion
Mesolóngion (Missolonghi)
Návpaktos
Ámfissa
Itéa
Levádhia
Thívai (Theben)
Khalkís
Elevsís
Megara
Piraiévs (Piraeus)
Salamís
Pátrai (Patras)
Aíyion
Kalávrita
Kórinthos (Corinth)
Kiáton
Árgos
Návplion
Trípolis
Pírgos
Amaliás
Gastoúni
Zákinthos
Kiparissía
Filiatrá
Gargaliánoi
Megalópolis
Kalámai (Kalamata)
Messíni
Pílos
Spárti (Sparta)
Yíthion
Monemvasía
Pindhos Óros
Ólimbos
Parnassós
Óthris Óros
Amvrakikós Kólpos
Patraikós Kólpos
Kólpos Korinthiakós (Gulf of Corinth)
Saronikós Kólpos
Argolikós Kólpos
Lakonikós Kólpos
Messiniakós Kólpos
Kiparissiakós Kólpos
Vórios Evvoikós Kólpos
Pagasitikós Kólpos
Alkionidhon Kolp.
Akr. Tainaron (Matapan)
Strofádhes
Kíthira
Ídhra
Póros
Aíyina
Feet Metres
6562 2000
4921 1500
3281 1000
1640 500
656 200
328 100
0 0
164 50
656 200
A B C D E F G
21° 30' 22° 30' 23° 30'
Longitude East 23° of Greenwich
SECANT CONIC PROJECTION
1: 1 000 000
0 5 10 20 30 40 50 Statute Miles

CRETE
(KRITI)
(To Greece)
1 : 1 000 000
SEA OF CRETE
MEDITERRANEAN SEA
Khania (Canea)
Kastélli
Réthimnon
Iráklion (Candia)
Áy. Nikólaos
Ierápetra
Sitía
Gávdhos
CYPRUS
1 : 1 000 000
S.B.A. U.K. Sovereign Base Area
Atilla Line
NICOSIA
Famagusta
Larnaca (Lárnax)
Limassol
Paphos
Kyrenia
Morphou Bay
Khrysokhou Bay
Famagusta Bay
Larnaca Bay
Episkopi Bay
Akrotiri Bay
MEDITERRANEAN SEA
Klidhes Islands
MALTA
AND GOZO
1 : 250 000
Statute Miles
Kilometres
GOZO
Victoria (Rabat)
Comino (Kemmuna)
MALTA
Valletta (Valletta)
Sliema
Mdina
Rabat
MEDITERRANEAN SEA
RHODES
(RÓDHOS)
(To Greece)
1 : 1 000 000
Ródhos
TURKEY
AEGEAN SEA
CORFU
(KÉRKIRA)
(To Greece)
1 : 1 000 000
Kérkira
ALBANIA
EVVOIA
(EUBOEA)
KIKLÁDHES
(CYCLADES)
Skíros
Kéa
Kíthnos
Sérifos
Mílos
Longitude East 25° of Greenwich
Longitude East 14° 30' of Greenwich
Kilometres

TUNIS
Kelibia
Nabeul
Hammamet
Kairouan
Sousse (Susa)
Monastir
Moknine
Mahdia
Ksour Essaf
Sfax
Iles Kerkenna
TUNISIA
G. de Gabès
Gabès
I. de Jerba
Zarzis
Medenine
Pantelleria
Lampedusa I.
Linosa I.
Vittoria
Ragusa
SICILIA (SICILY)
C. Passero
Malta Channel
Gozo
MALTA
Valletta
M E D I T E R R A N
Kalamai
Kithira
TRIPOLI (Tarābulus al Gharb)
Zuwārah
Az Zāwiyah
Al Khums (Homs)
Zlitan
Tarhūnah
Gharyān
Misrātah (Misurata)
Yefren
Bani Walid
Nālūt
Ghadāmis (Ghadames)
Khalīj Surt
(Gulf of Sirte)
Sirt (Sirte)
Benghāzī (Banghazi)
Al Baydā'
Darnah (Derna)
Al Marj (Barce)
Tūkrah (Tocra)
Ajdābiyah (Agedabia)
Marsá al Burayqah
Ra's Lanūf
T R I P O L I T A N I A
Ḥammādah al Ḥamrā'
Waddān (Uaddan)
Hūn
Al Jufrah Oasis
Sawknah (Socna)
Marādah
Awjilah (Augila)
Jalū Oasis (Jalo Oasis)
Calanscio
Calanscio Sand Sea
Calanscio Serir
C Y R E N A I C A
L I B Y A
Al Harūj al Aswad
Al Fuqahā'
Sabhā (Sebha)
Awbārī (Ubari)
Idehan Ubari
Murzuq (Murzuk)
F E Z Z A N
IDEHAN MARZŪQ
Ghāt (Gat)
Tāzerbo
Rebiana Sand Sea
Serir Nerastro
Al Kufrah (Cufra)
Rebiana
Tropic of Cancer
S A H A R A
Sarīr Tibesti
Plateau du Djado
Djado
Plateau du Tchigaï
TÉNÉRÉ DU TAFASSASSET
N I G E R
Grand Erg
Bilma
T I B E S T I
Emi Koussi
Tarso
Bardai
Zouar
C H A D
Faya-Largeau
B O R K O U
Ounianga Kebir
Erdi
Dépression de Mourdi
LAMBERT ZENITHAL EQUAL-AREA PROJECTION
1: 5 000 000
0 20 40 60 80 100 150 200 250 Statute Miles

Feet	Metres
9843	3000
6562	2000
4921	1500
3281	1000
1640	500
656	200
328	100
0	0
Below Sea Level	
656	200
3281	1000

LIBYA: 'Baladiyahs' are named after their ...

EGYPT AND LIBYA

Alexandria
CAIRO
Port Said
Suez
Dumyat
Rashid
Damanhur
Tanta
El Mansûra
Zagazig
Benha
Ismâ'iliya
Helwan
El Giza
El Faiyûm
Beni Suef
Biba
El Fashn
Maghâgha
Beni Mazâr
Samâlût
El Minya
Mallawi
Dairût
Manfalut
Asyût
Abu Tig
Tahta
Sohâg
Akhmîm
Girga
El Balyana
Dishna
Qena
Qus
Luxor
Isna
Idfu
Kom Ombo
Aswân
Hurghada
Bur Safâga
Quseir
Berenice
Halaib
Port Sudan
Suakin
Tokar
Atbara
Berber
Merowe
Karima
Korti
Ed Debba
Old Dongola
Dongola
Kerma
Argo I.
Delgo
Wadi Halfa
Abu Hamed
Siwa
Siwa Oasis
Matruh
Sidi Barrani
El 'Alamein
Bahariya Oasis
Farafra Oasis
Dakhla Oasis
El Khârga
The Great Oasis
El Wâhât el-Khârga
Qattara Depression
Libyan Plateau
Great Sand Sea
Gilf Kebir Plateau
Lake Nasser
Lake Nuba
Tropic of Cancer
E G Y P T
LOWER EGYPT
UPPER EGYPT
S I N A I
ISRAEL
JORDAN
SYRIA
LEBANON
SAUDI ARABIA
C Y P R U S
NICOSIA
Famagusta
Limassol
Larnaca
Iráklion (Candia)
Rhodos
Karpathos
Kasos
T U R K E Y
Antalya
Mersin
Adana
Iskenderun
Aleppo
Latakia
Hama
Homs
Tripoli
BEIRUT (BEYROUTH)
DAMASCUS (ESH SHAM, DAMAS)
Saida (Sidon)
Haifa
Nazareth
Tel-Aviv-Yafo
JERUSALEM
AMMAN
Gaza
Hebron
Beersheba
El 'Arish
Ma'an
Aqaba
Tabuk
Al Wajh
S E A
R E D S E A
Gulf of Suez
Gulf of Aqaba
NORTHERN SUDAN
NORTHERN DARFUR
Nubian Desert
BAYUDA DESERT
Batn el Hajar
Dar Sukkot
Dar Mahas
Selima Oasis
Bir Misâha
Bir Dibis
Bir Sahara
Abu Simbel Temple
Tadrart
H J K L M N O P
1 2 3 4 5 6 7 8 9 10 11
26° 28° 30° 32° 34° 36° 38°
36 34 33 87

Longitude East 26° of Greenwich

0 50 100 150 200 250 300 350 400 Kilometres

Spot Heights in Metres and Feet

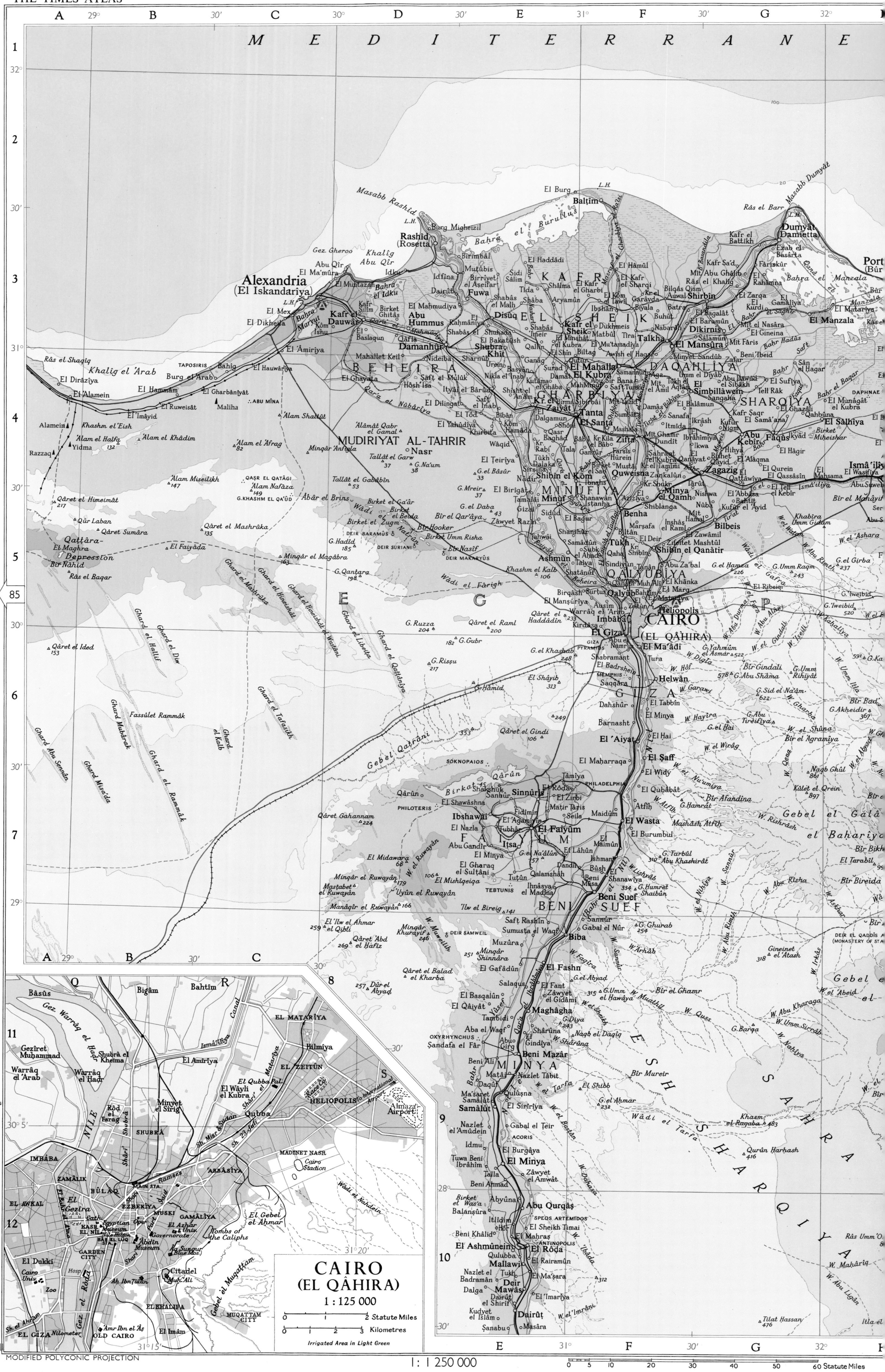
MEDITERRANEAN
Alexandria
(El Iskandarîya)
Rashîd
(Rosetta)
Dumyât
(Damietta)
Abu Qîr
Bahra el Burullus
Bahra el Manzala
Kafr el Dauwâr
Damanhûr
Abu Hummus
Disûq
Fuwa
Kafr el Sheik
El Mahalla el Kubra
Tanta
Shibîn el Kôm
Minûf
Zifta
Mit Ghamr
El Mansûra
Zagazig
Talkha
Shirbîn
El Manzala
Benha
Bilbeis
Qalyûb
Shibîn el Qanâtir
Ismâ'ilîya
Abu Kebir
Fâqûs
El Sâlhiya
BEHEIRA
GHARBIYA
KAFR EL SHEIK
DAQAHLIYA
SHARQIYA
MINUFIYA
QALYUBIYA
MUDIRIYAT AL-TAHRIR
Nasr
El 'Alamein
El Hammam
Burg el 'Arab
Khalig el 'Arab
El Dirâzîya
Qattâra Depression
Râs el Shaqiq
Râs el Baqar
Wâdi el Natrûn
Wâdi el Fârigh
CAIRO
(EL QÂHIRA)
Heliopolis
Imbâba
El Giza
GIZA PYRAMIDS
El Ma'âdi
Helwân
Saqqâra
MEMPHIS
Dahshûr
El 'Aiyat
El Saff
El Wasta
GIZA
Gebel Qatrâni
Birkat Qârûn
El Faiyûm
Sinnûris
Ibshawâi
Itsa
FAIYUM
Beni Suef
BENI SUEF
Biba
El Fashn
Maghâgha
Beni Mazâr
MINYA
Samâlût
El Minya
Abu Qurqâs
Mallawi
Deir Mawâs
Dairût
El Ashmûnein
El Rôda
Bahr Yûsef
Gebel el Galâla el Bahariya
ESH SHARQIYA
SAHRA
Wâdi el Tarfa
Port
CAIRO
(EL QÂHIRA)
1 : 125 000
2 Statute Miles
3 Kilometres
Irrigated Area in Light Green
NILE
SHUBRÂ
IMBÂBA
ZAMÂLIK
BÛLÂQ
EZBEKIYA
MUSKI
GAMÂLIYA
ABBÂSIYA
HELIOPOLIS
EL ZEITÛN
EL MATARÎYA
Almaza Airport
MADINET NASR
Cairo Stadium
Citadel
Tombs of the Caliphs
Gebel el Muqattam
MUQATTAM CITY
OLD CAIRO
EL GIZA
El Dukki
Cairo Univ.
Zoo
GARDEN CITY
Gezîra
EL KHALIFA
El Imâm
Nilometer
Amr Ibn el Âs
Ah Ibn Tûlûn
El Azhar Univ.
Governorate
Museum
'Âbdîn
Feet
Metres
6562
2000
4921
1500
3281
1000
1640
500
656
200
328
100
0
Below Sea-level
65
20
328
100
85

NILE DELTA AND SINAI

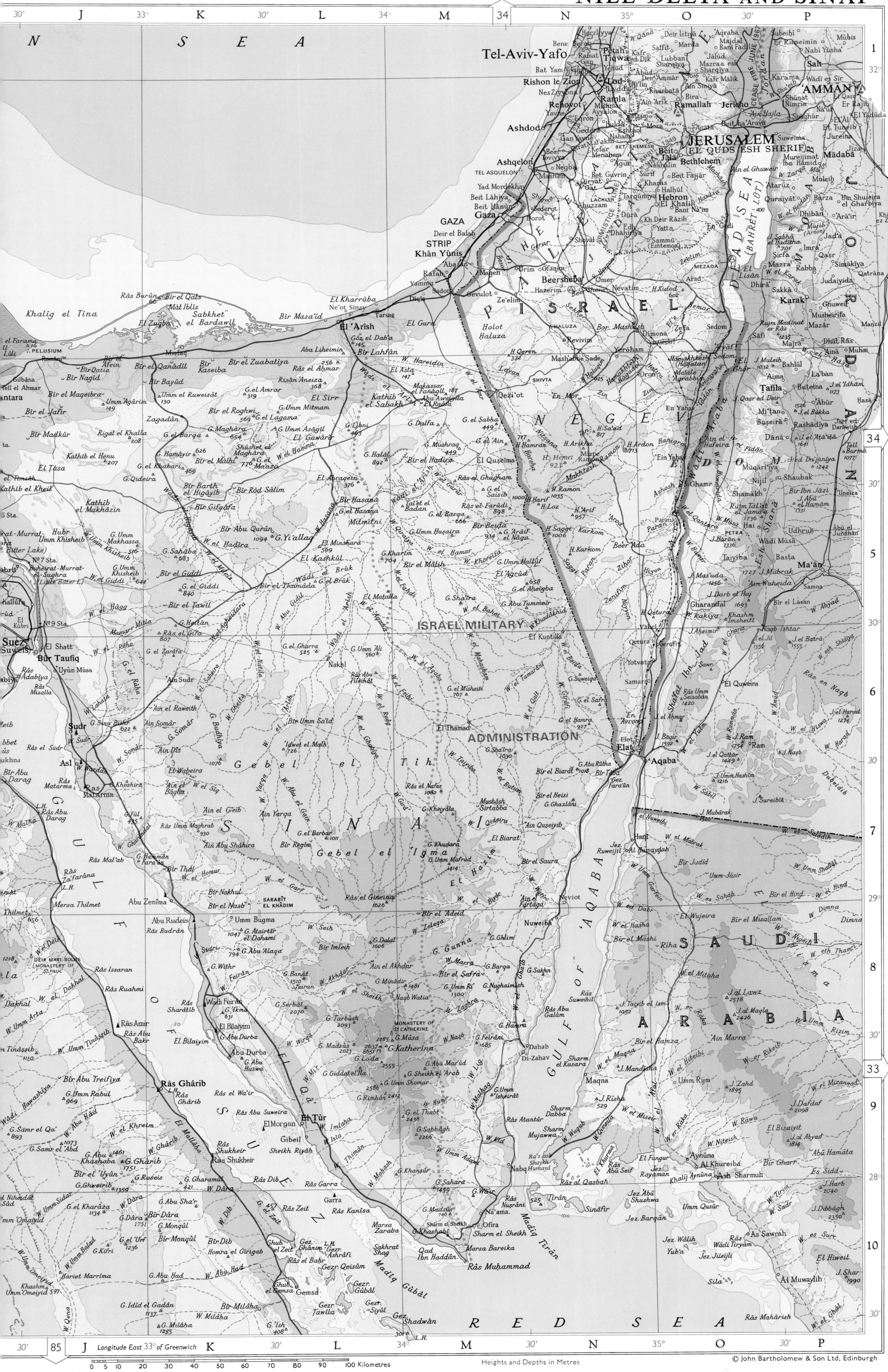
Tel-Aviv-Yafo
JERUSALEM
(EL QUDS ESH SHERIF)
'AMMAN
Gaza
GAZA STRIP
El 'Arîsh
ISRAEL
NEGEV
ISRAEL MILITARY
ADMINISTRATION
SINAI
Gebel el Tih
Gebel el 'Igma
GULF OF SUEZ
GULF OF 'AQABA
DEAD SEA
SAUDI ARABIA
JORDAN
EDOM
RED SEA
Suez
Bûr Taufiq
Elat
'Aqaba
Ma'ân
Karak
Hebron
Beersheba
El Tûr
Sharm el Sheikh
Râs Muhammad
G. Katherina
Longitude East 33° of Greenwich
Kilometres
Heights and Depths in Metres

THE TIMES ATLAS
LIBYAN DESERT
NORTHERN
NORTHERN DARFUR
SOUTHERN DARFUR
NORTHERN KORDOFAN
SOUTHERN KORDOFAN
SUDAN
KHARTOUM
KHARTOUM NORTH
Omdurman
Atbara
Ed Damer
Berber
Shendi
Merowe
Karima
Ed Debba
Korti
Old Dongola
Wad Medani
Sennar
Kosti
El Obeid
Umm Ruwaba
En Nahud
Dilling
Kadugli
Talodi
Gedaref
Kassala
KASSALA
Port Sudan
RED SEA
Tokar
Sinkat
Roseires
Singa
Gallabat
EL GEZIRA
WHITE NILE
BLUE NILE
UPPER NILE
Malakal
Kodok
Renk
Nasir
Akobo
Bor
JONGLEI
BAHR EL GHAZAL
Wau
Aweil
EL BUHEYRAT
Rumbek
WESTERN EQUATORIA
Yambio
Maridi
Tambura
EASTERN EQUATORIA
Juba
Torit
Kapoeta
Nimule
Malek
Terekeka
Mongalla
UGANDA
KAMPALA
Entebbe
Jinja-Bugembe
Masindi
Hoima
Ft. Portal
Soroti
Mbale
Tororo
Lira
Gulu
Arua
L. VICTORIA
L. ALBERT
L. Kyoga
HAUT-ZAÏRE
ZAÏRE
KIVU
Bunia
Isiro
Niangara
Watsa
KENYA
RIFT VALLEY
NYANZA
Kitale
Eldoret
Kakamega
L. RUDOLF
TURKANA
Lodwar
ETHIOPIA
ILUBABOR
KEFA
WELEGA
GEMU-GWEFA
BEGEMDIR
Gonder
Dabat
Dembī Dolo
Gore
Jima
Maji
Gambela
Asosa
Mojo
LAMBERT ZENITHAL EQUAL-AREA PROJECTION
1: 5 000 000
Longitude East 36° of Greenwich
250 Statute Miles
Feet
Metres
Below Sea-level

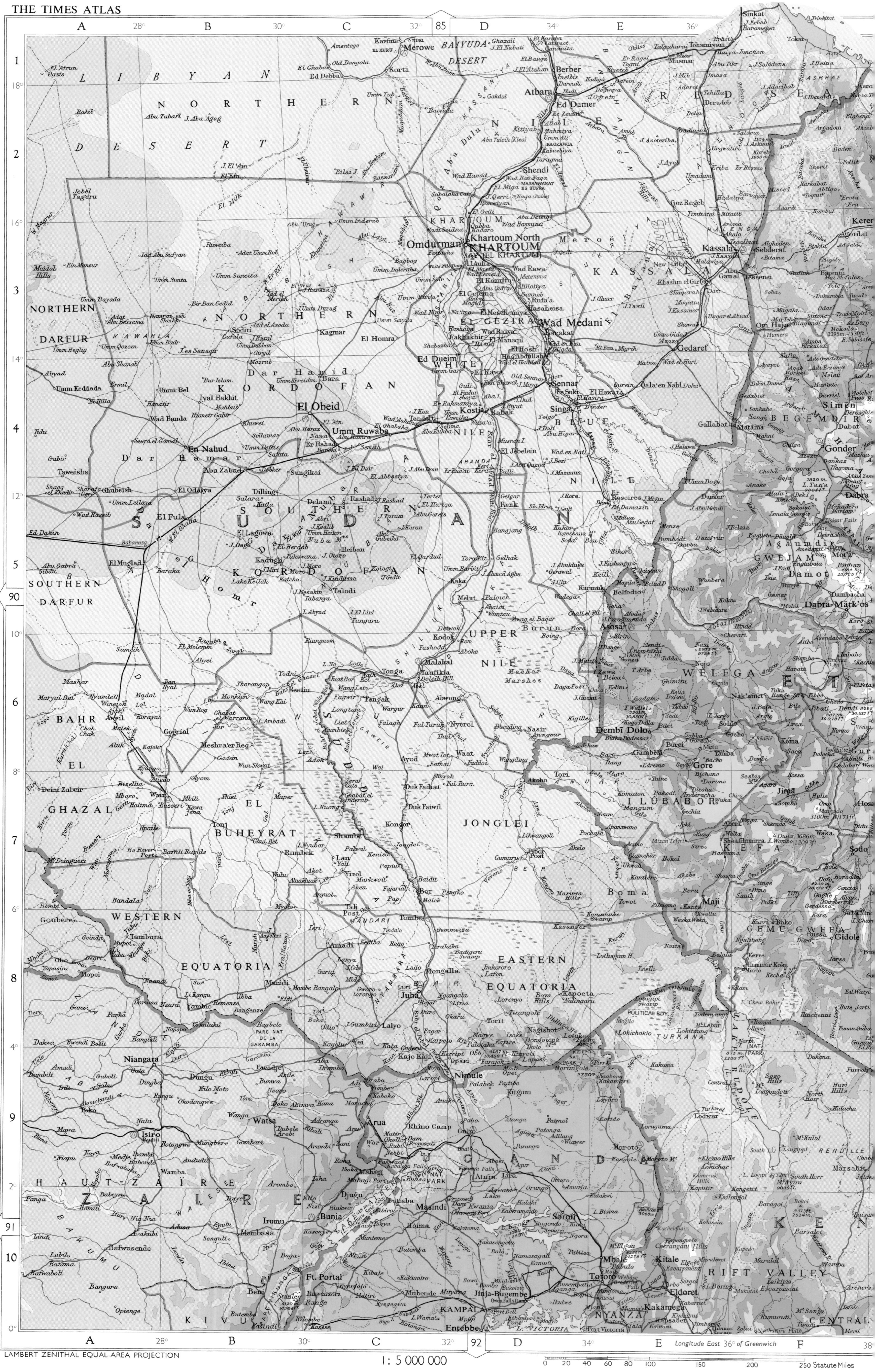

RED SEA
GULF OF ADEN
INDIAN OCEAN
YEMEN
SOUTH YEMEN
SAN'A'
Al Hudaydah (Hodeida)
TA'IZZ
ADEN
Shaykh 'Uthman
Mukalla
Shihr
DJIBOUTI
Zeila
Berbera
Erigavo
Borama
Hargeisa
Burao
Las Anod
Gardo
Bender Cassim
Dante (Hafun)
Dire Dawa
Harer
Jijiga
ADDIS ABABA
Dessie
Nagele
Galcaio
Obbia (Obiat) (Hobyo)
Belet Uen
Bulo Burti
Lugh Ganana
Iscia Baidoa
Bardera
MOGADISCIO (MOGADISHU) (MUQDISHO)
Merca
Brava
NORTH WEST
NORTH EAST
MIGIURTINIA
MUDUGH
HIRAN
ALTO GIUBA
BASSO GIUBA
BENADIR
WELO
ERITREA
HARERGE
Ogaden
BALE
SIDAMO
ARUSI
ETHIOPIA
SOMALIA
Continuation on the same scale
SOCOTRA (Suqutra) (S.Y.)
Abd-Al-Kuri
The Brothers
Chisimaio (Kismayu)
Lamu
Continuation on the same scale
400 Kilometres
Heights in Metres and Feet

© John Bartholomew & Son Ltd, Edinburgh

AZORES
(AÇÔRES)
Portugal)
1 : 5 000 000
Corvo
Flores
Santa Cruz
Graciosa
Terceira
São Jorge
Angra do Heroismo
Faial
Horta
Lajes do Pico
Pico
A T L A N T I C O C E A N
São Miguel
Ponta Delgada
Vila Franca do Campo
Ilheus das Formigas
Santa Maria
Vila do Porto
MADEIRA
Porto Santo
Funchal
Ilhas Selvagens
(Port.)
ISLAS CANARIAS
CANARY Is (TO SPAIN)
La Palma
Sta. Cruz de la Palma
La Laguna
Sta. Cruz de Tenerife
Tenerife
Gomera
Hierro
Valverde
Lanzarote
Arrecife
Fuerteventura
Las Palmas
Gran Canaria
Pto. Maspalomas
PORTUGAL
Huelva
Sevilla
Faro
C. de S. Vicente
Gulf of Cádiz
Jerez
Cádiz
Ronda
GIBRALTAR (U.K.)
Algeciras
Str. of Gibraltar
Tanger
Ceuta (Sp)
Tetouan
Asilah
Larache (El Araïch)
Chaouen (Xauen)
Ksar el Kebir
Ouezzane
Kenitra
Salé
RABAT
Sidi Kacem
Fès
Meknès
Sefrou
Mohammedia
Casablanca
(Dar el Beida)
El Jadida
Azemmour
Settat
Oued Zem
Khouribga
Azrou
Khenifra
Kasba Tadla
Beni Mellal
Safi
Youssoufia
Marrakech
(Marrakesh)
Demnate
Essaouira
Er-Rachida
Taroudannt
Agadir
Ouarzazate
Jbel Sarhro
Tiznit
Sidi Ifni
Tan-Tan
Tarfaya
Cabo Juby
(Villa Bens)
Tindouf
La'youn
Smara
Bojador
Dakhla
(Villa Cisneros)
Hamada du Dra
Hamada Tounassine
Erg Iguidi
Erg Chech
El Eglab
Fderik
(Fort Gouraud)
Zouerate
Atar
Chinguetti
Akjoujt
Adrar
Ouadane
Tichit
MAURITANIA
Taoudenni
Araouane
El Mreyer
Rall Amane
Hank
Majabat al Koubra
Aoukar
Azlef
Zarma
Route du Mauritanie
Longitude West 8° of Greenwich
250 Statute Miles

MOROCCO ALGERIA AND TUNISIA

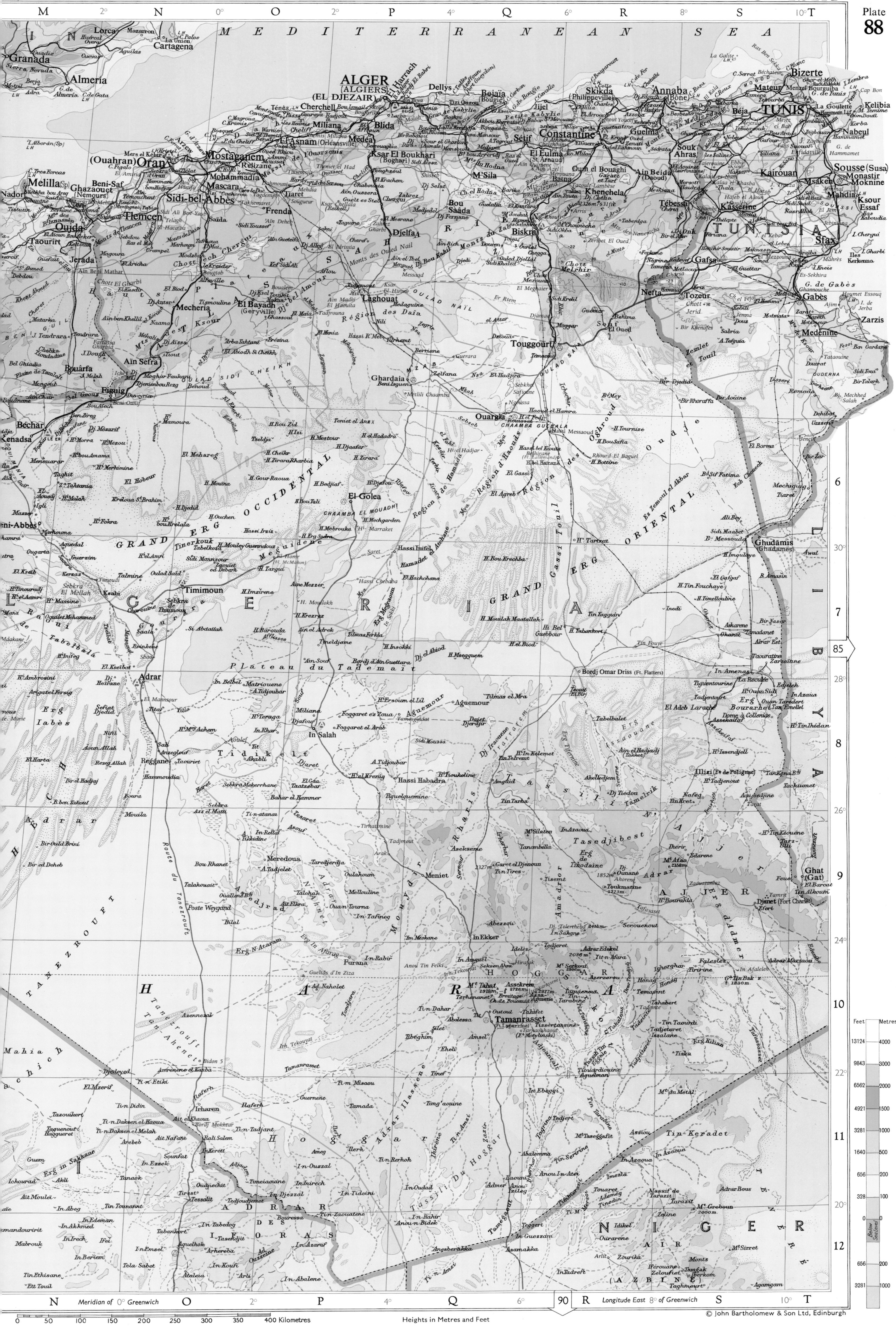

MEDITERRANEAN SEA
(EL DJEZAIR)
(ALGIERS)
Bizerte
Annaba
(Bône)
Skikda
(Philippeville)
Constantine
Sétif
Bejaia
(Bougie)
Blida
Médéa
Miliana
Cherchell
El Asnam
(Orléansville)
Mostaganem
Oran
(Ouahran)
Mascara
Sidi-bel-Abbès
Tlemcen
Oujda
Melilla
Nador
Ghazaouet
(Nemours)
Granada
Almeria
Lorca
Cartagena
Kairouan
Sousse (Susa)
Monastir
Mahdia
Sfax
Gabès
Gafsa
Tozeur
Nefta
Kasserine
Tébessa
Batna
Biskra
Touggourt
Ouargla
Ghardaia
Laghouat
Djelfa
El Golea
Tiaret
Saïda
Frenda
Mecheria
Aïn Sefra
Figuig
Bechar
Kenadsa
Beni-Abbes
Timimoun
Adrar
Reggane
In Salah
Tamanrasset
Djanet (Fort Charles)
Ghat (Gat)
Ghudamis (Ghadames)
In Amenas
Bordj Omar Driss (Ft. Flatters)
GRAND ERG OCCIDENTAL
GRAND ERG ORIENTAL
Plateau du Tademait
LIBYA
NIGER
HOGGAR
TANEZROUFT
ADRAR DES IFORAS
AJJER
Tassili N'Ajjer
Meridian of 0° Greenwich
Longitude East 8° of Greenwich
90
85
Heights in Metres and Feet
400 Kilometres
0 50 100 150 200 250 300 350
Feet
Metres
13124 4000
9843 3000
6562 2000
4921 1500
3281 1000
1640 500
656 200
328 100
0 0
Below Sea Level
656 200
3281 1000

LAMBERT ZENITHAL EQUAL-AREA PROJECTION

1: 5 000 000

0 20 40 60 80 100 150 200 250 Statute Miles

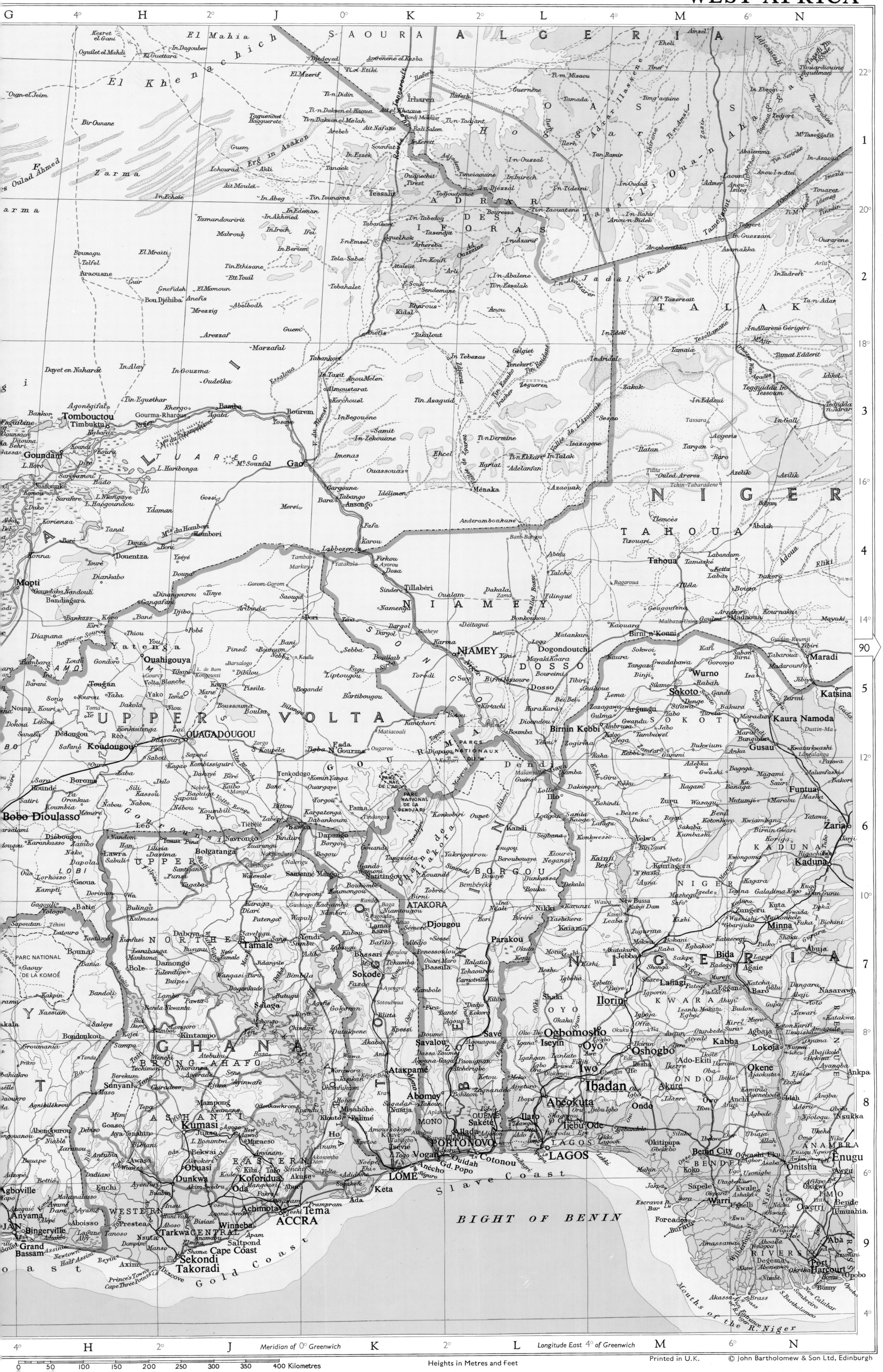

Heights in Metres and Feet

Printed in U.K.

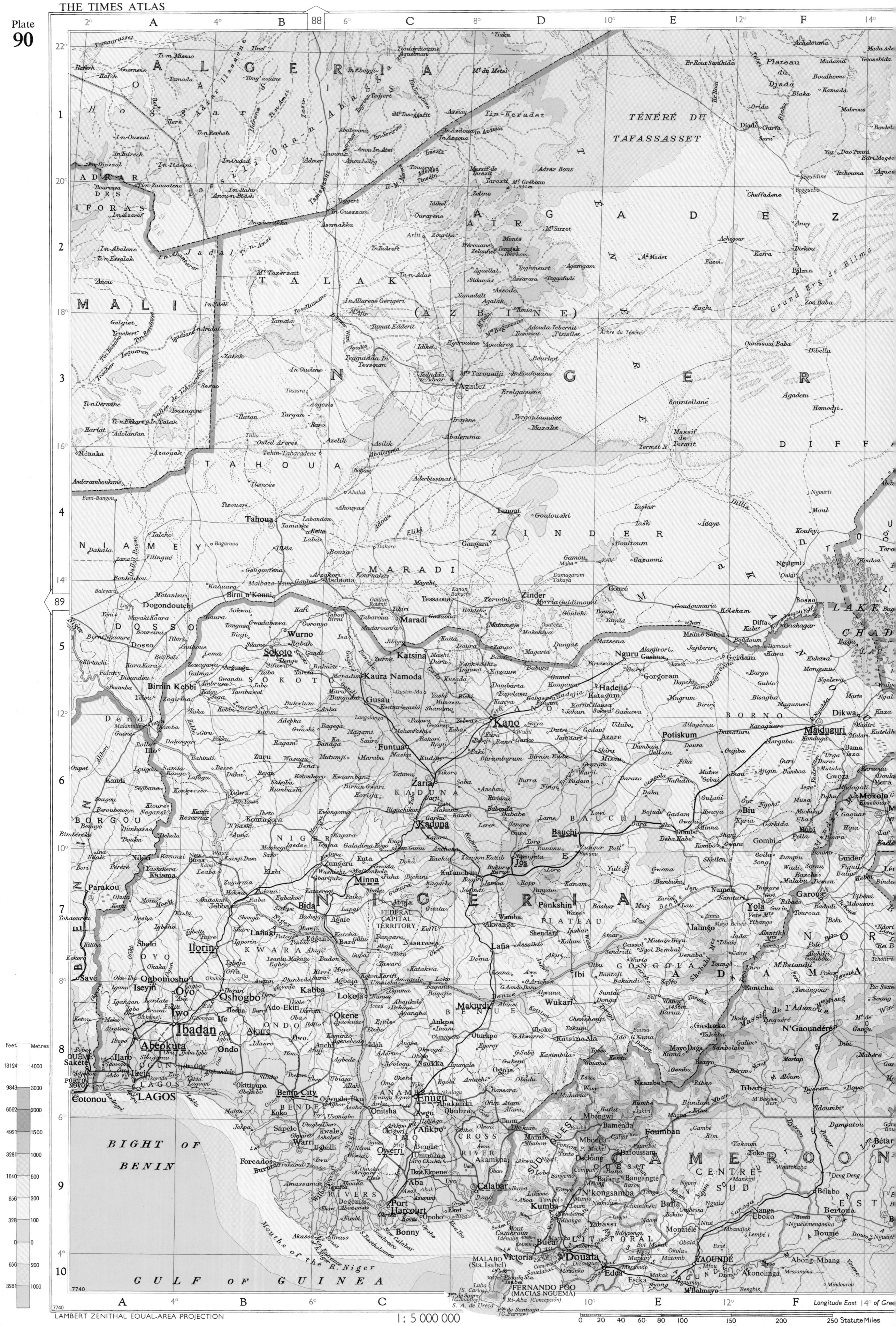

LAMBERT ZENITHAL EQUAL-AREA PROJECTION

1: 5 000 000

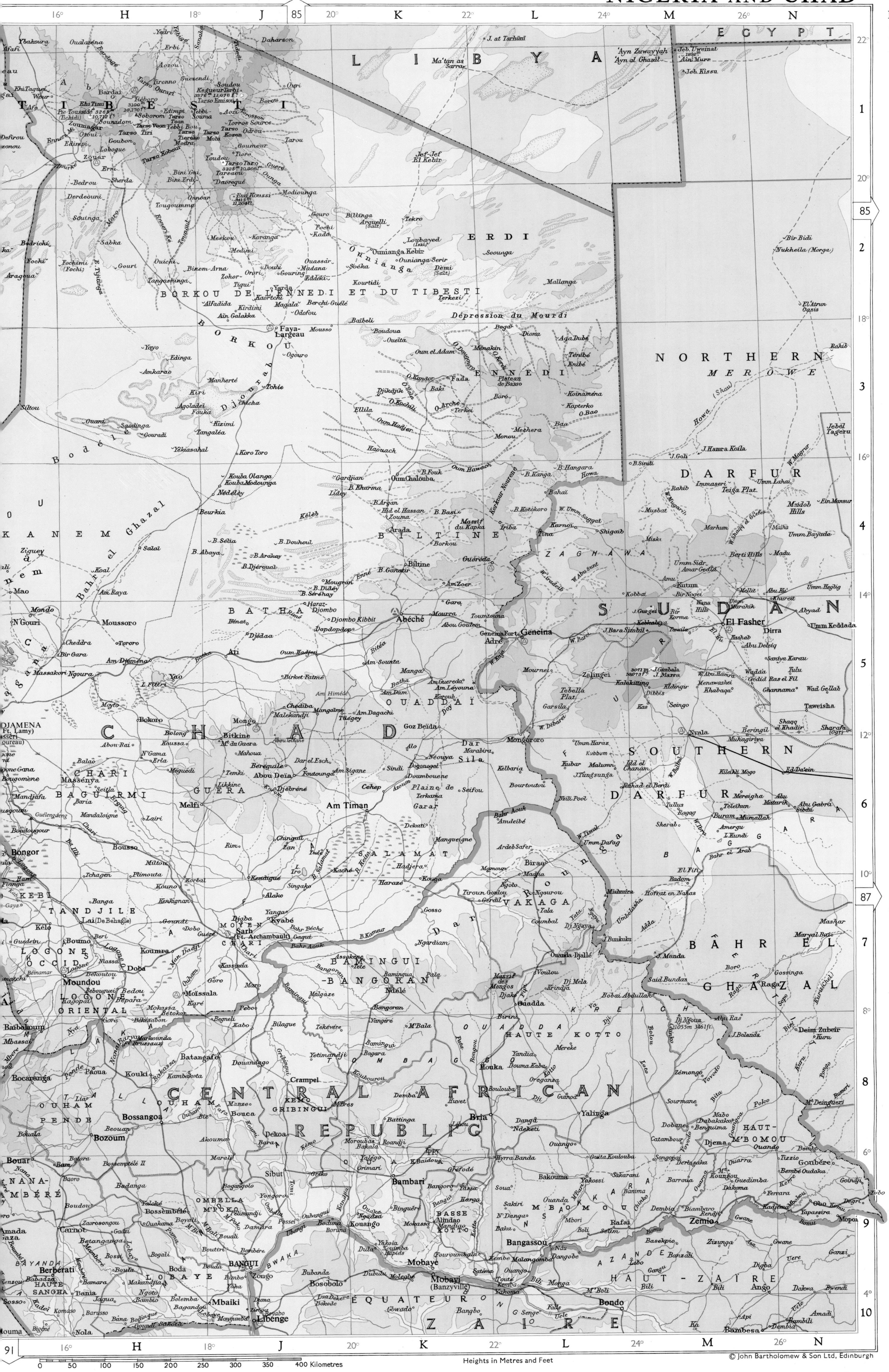
LIBYA
EGYPT
TIBESTI
ERDI
BORKOU DE L'ENNEDI ET DU TIBESTI
Dépression du Mourdi
BORKOU
ENNEDI
NORTHERN
MEROWE
DARFUR
BILTINE
ZAGHAWA
KANEM
Ghazal
Bahr el Ghazal
BATHA
SUDAN
OUADDAÏ
CHAD
GUERA
CHARI BAGUIRMI
SALAMAT
SOUTHERN DARFUR
TANDJILE
MOYEN CHARI
LOGONE OCCIDENTAL
LOGONE ORIENTAL
VAKAGA
BAMINGUI BANGORAN
BAHR EL GHAZAL
HAUTE KOTTO
OUHAM
OUHAM PENDE
NANA-MAMBÉRÉ
CENTRAL AFRICAN REPUBLIC
OMBELLA M'POKO
BASSE KOTTO
MBOMOU
HAUT-M'BOMOU
LOBAYE
HAUTE SANGHA
HAUT-ZAÏRE
ÉQUATEUR
ZAÏRE
Faya-Largeau
Abéché
Geneina
El Fasher
Nyala
NDJAMENA (Ft. Lamy)
Am Timan
Moundou
Sarh (Ft. Archambault)
Bangui
Bambari
Bangassou
Berbérati
Bossangoa
Bouar
Bozoum
Bria
Mobaye
Zemio
Bondo
Libenge
Mbaiki
Heights in Metres and Feet
0 50 100 150 200 250 300 350 400 Kilometres
© John Bartholomew & Son Ltd, Edinburgh

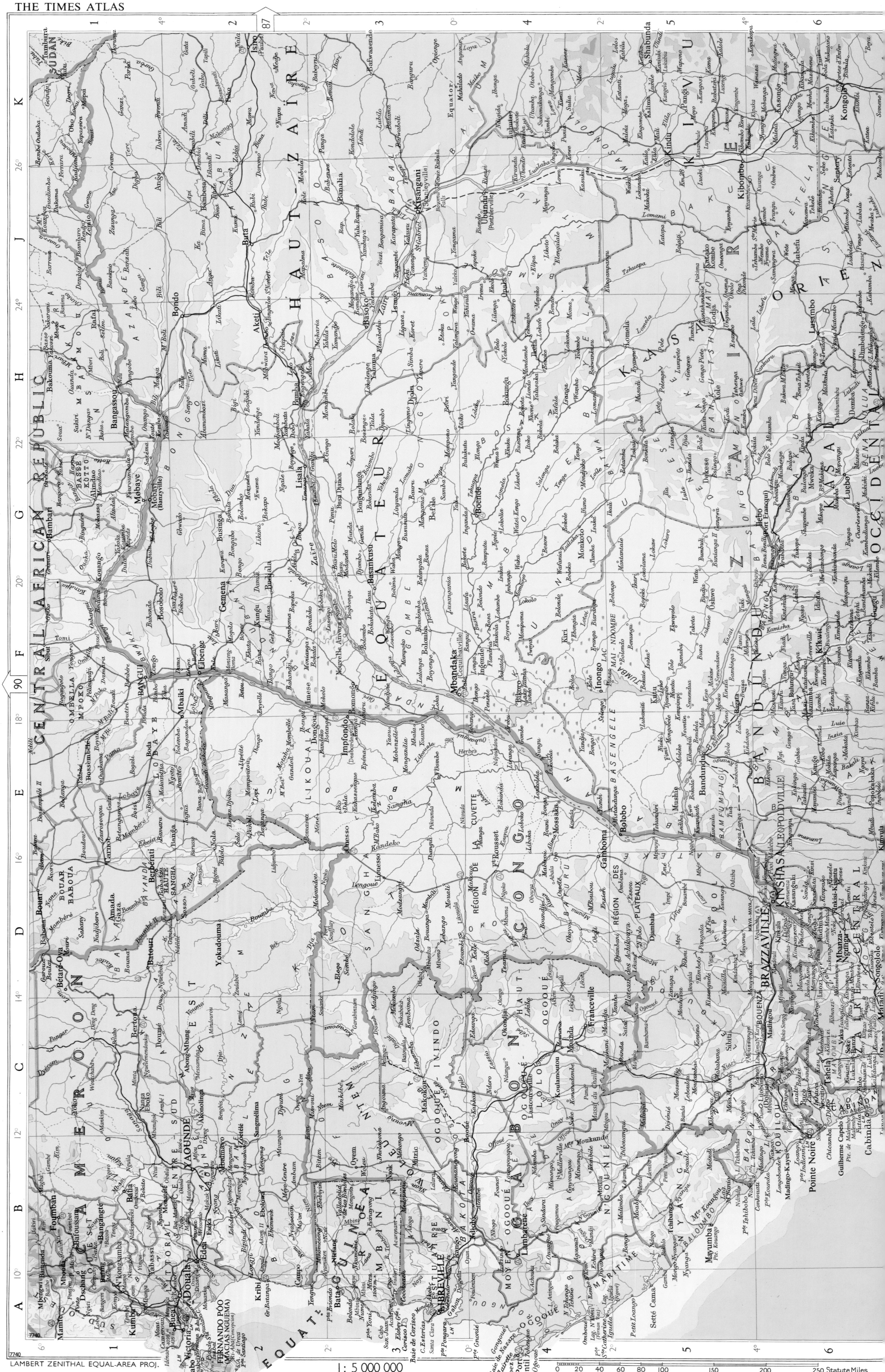

7740

LAMBERT ZENITHAL EQUAL-AREA PROJ.

1: 5 000 000

0 20 40 60 80 100 150 200 250 Statute Miles

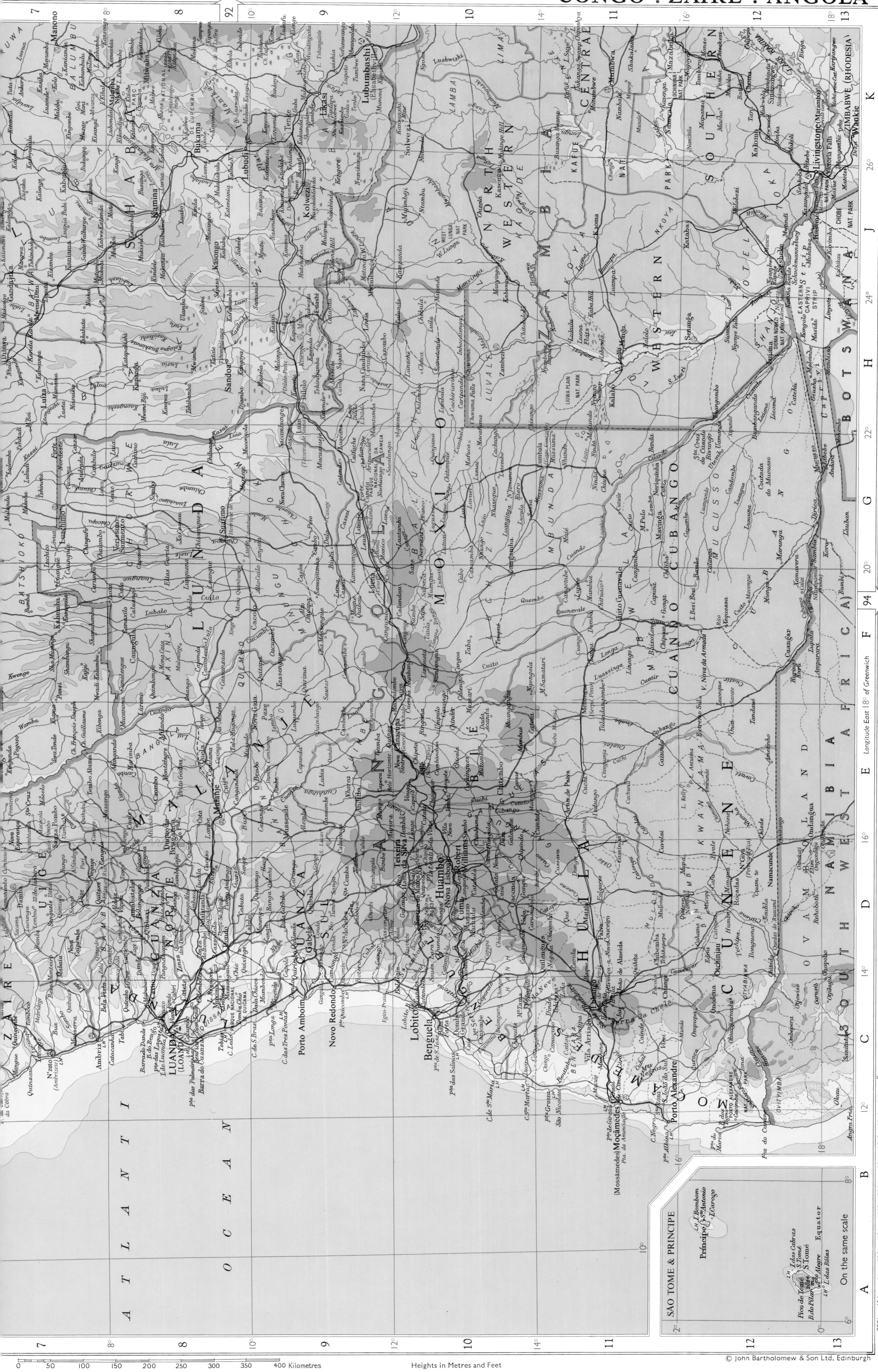
ATLANTIC OCEAN
SAO TOME & PRINCIPE
On the same scale
Longitude East 18° of Greenwich
Heights in Metres and Feet
0 50 100 150 200 250 300 350 400 Kilometres

1: 5 000 000

0 20 40 60 80 100 150 200 250 Statute Miles

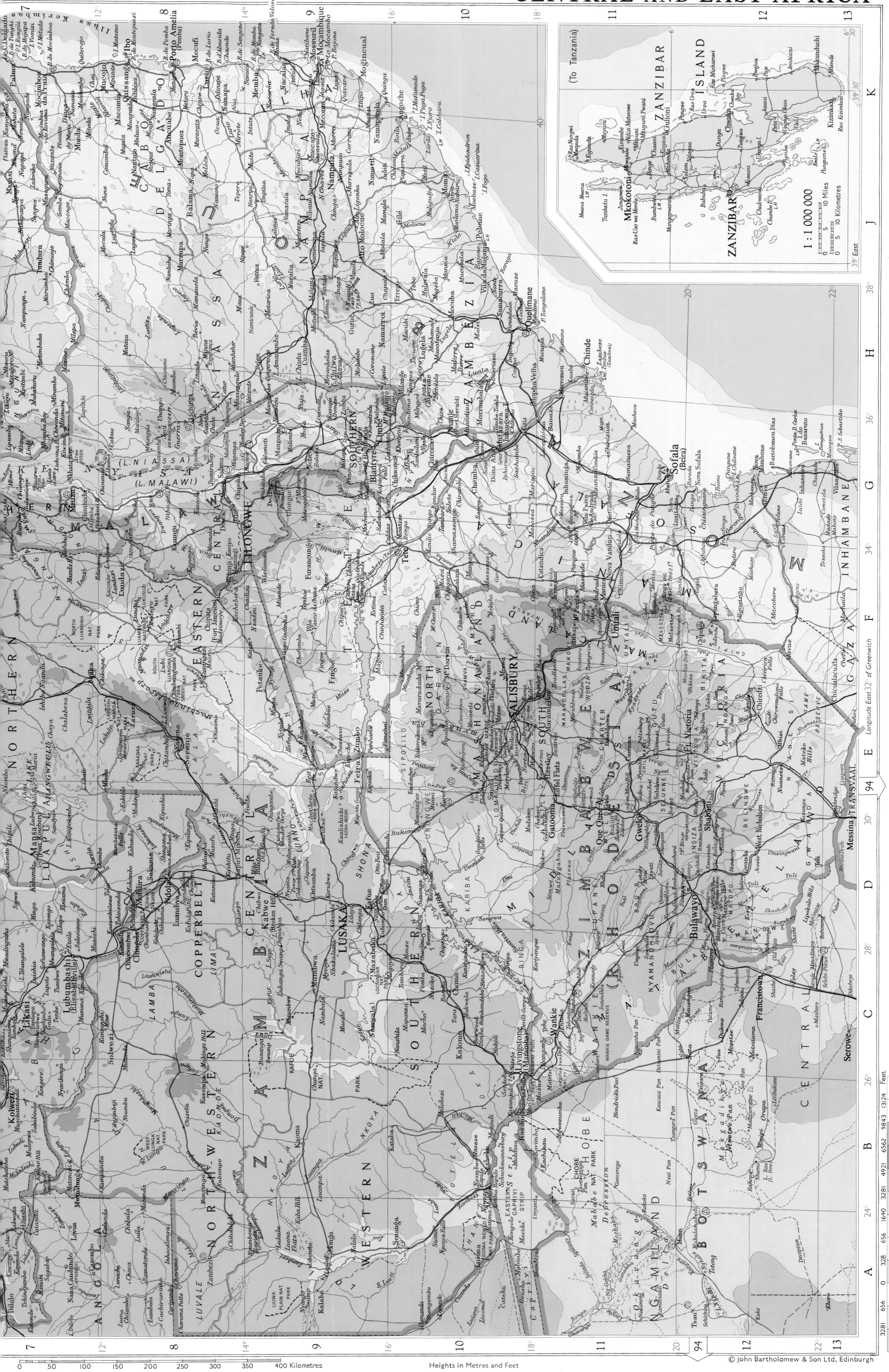
ZANZIBAR ISLAND
ZANZIBAR
Mkokotoni
(To Tanzania)
1:1 000 000
ZAMBIA
RHODESIA
MALAWI
MOZAMBIQUE
BOTSWANA
ANGOLA
SALISBURY
LUSAKA
Bulawayo
Blantyre
Lilongwe
Zomba
Beira
Sofala
Quelimane
Chinde
Tete
Umtali
Gwelo
Gatooma
Fort Victoria
Francistown
Serowe
Messina
Livingstone
Wankie
Kabwe (Broken Hill)
Ndola
Kitwe
Mufulira
Chingola
Lubumbashi (Elisabethville)
Likasi
Kolwezi
Mansa (Fort Rosebery)
Kasama
Porto Amelia (Pemba)
Nampula
Moçambique
Vila Cabral
Maun
Mongu
Kafue
Mazabuka
Kariba
Chipata (Fort Jameson)
COPPERBELT
NORTHERN
EASTERN
CENTRAL
SOUTHERN
WESTERN
NORTH WESTERN
LUAPULA
MASHONALAND
MATABELELAND
MANICA
VICTORIA
INHAMBANE
GAZA
CABO DELGADO
NIASSA
ZAMBEZIA
TRANSVAAL
Heights in Metres and Feet
Longitude East 32° of Greenwich
400 Kilometres
94

1: 2 500 000

0 10 20 40 60 80 100 120 Statute Miles

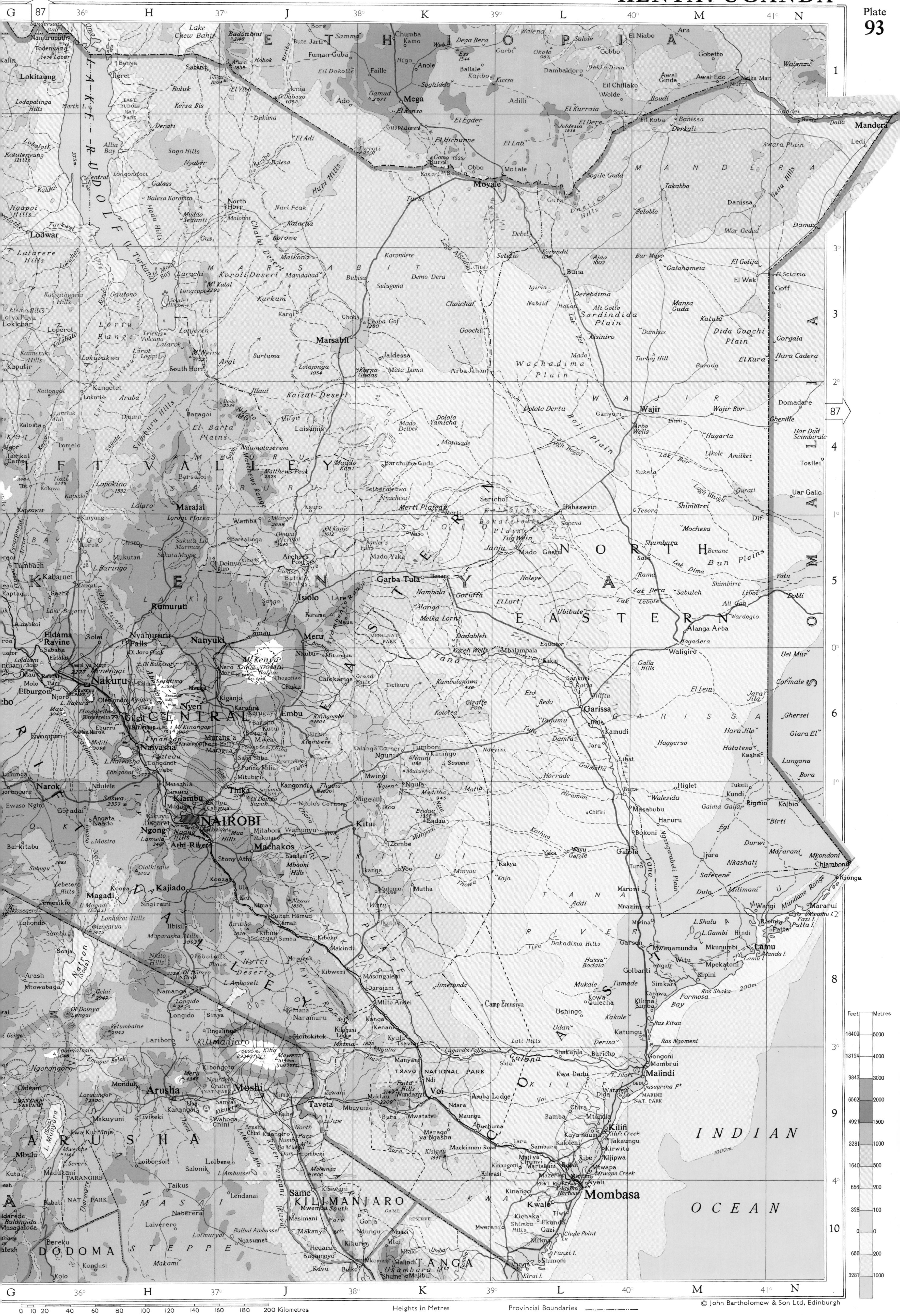
E T H I O P I A
Moyale
Mega
Mandera
Lake Chew Bahir
LAKE RUDOLF (L. Turkana)
Lokitaung
Lodwar
Lokichar
Koroli Desert
Chalbi Desert
Marsabit
Kaisut Desert
Maralal
Wajir
Dida Gochi Plain
Sardindida Plain
Wachadima Plain
Bojil Plain
RIFT VALLEY
EASTERN
NORTH EASTERN
CENTRAL
COAST
Garba Tula
Isiolo
Nanyuki
Meru
Mt. Kenya 5200m. (17058 ft)
Nyeri
Nakuru
Eldama Ravine
Elburgon
Naivasha
L. Naivasha
Thika
NAIROBI
Machakos
Kitui
Embu
Garissa
Athi River
Kajiado
Magadi
Narok
Ngong
Namanga
Kilimanjaro
Kibo 5895 m. (19340 ft.)
Mawenzi 5149m. (16893ft)
Arusha
Moshi
Taveta
Voi
TSAVO NATIONAL PARK
Malindi
Kilifi
Mombasa
Kwale
Lamu
Kiunga
Tana
Galana
ARUSHA
MASAI STEPPE
DODOMA
TANGA
KILIMANJARO GAME RESERVE
INDIAN OCEAN
S O M A L I A
36°
37°
38°
39°
40°
41°
G
H
J
K
L
M
N
87
0 10 20 40 60 80 100 120 140 160 180 200 Kilometres
Heights in Metres
Provincial Boundaries
Feet
Metres
16409 5000
13124 4000
9843 3000
6562 2000
4921 1500
3281 1000
1640 500
656 200
328 100
0 0
656 200
3281 1000

© John Bartholomew & Son Ltd, Edinburgh

A N G O L A
O V A M B O L A N D
ETOSHA GAME RESERVE
K A O K O V E L D
N A M I B I A (S. W. A F R I C A)
D A M A R A L A N D
N A M A Q U A L A N D
N A M I B D E S E R T
K A L A H A R I
K A L A H A R I D E S E R T
KGALAGADI
GEMSBOK NATIONAL PARK
KALAHARI GEMSBOK NATIONAL PARK
NGAMILAND
GHANZI
BOTSWANA
REPUBLIC OF SOUTH AFRICA
GRIQUALAND WEST
BOPHUTHATSWANA
Bushman Land
Great Karroo
CAPE PROVINCE
A T L A N T I C O C E A N
Tropic of Capricorn
WINDHOEK
Swakopmund
Walvis Bay
Lüderitz
Keetmanshoop
Mariental
Rehoboth
Okahandja
Karibib
Usakos
Omaruru
Otjiwarongo
Grootfontein
Tsumeb
Gobabis
Karasburg
Alexander Bay
Oranjemund
Port Nolloth
Springbok
Upington
Kuruman
Prieska
De Aar
Carnarvon
Calvinia
Victoria West
Beaufort West
Graaff Reinet
Aberdeen
Laingsburg
Oudtshoorn
Mosselbaai
George
Knysna
Swellendam
Worcester
Wellington
Paarl
Stellenbosch
Malmesbury
CAPE TOWN
Simonstown
Cape of Good Hope
Hermanus
C. Agulhas
Ghanzi
Maun
CAPE PENINSULA
1:500 000
Cape Town (Kaapstad)
Table Bay (Tafelbaai)
Robben Island
Bellville
Durbanville
Muizenberg
Simonstown (Simonstad)
FALSE BAY (VALSBAAI)
Cape of Good Hope (Kaap de Goeie Hoop)
Statute Miles
Kilometres
Feet
Metres
LAMBERT ZENITHAL EQUAL-AREA PROJECTION
1: 5 000 000
Longitude East 24° of Greenwich
250 Statute Miles

SOUTH AFRICA
ZIMBABWE (RHODESIA)
TRANSVAAL
ORANGE FREE STATE
NATAL
SWAZILAND
LESOTHO
(BASUTOLAND)
MOZAMBIQUE
INHAMBANE
GAZA
INDIAN OCEAN
Tropic of Capricorn
SALISBURY
Bulawayo
Livingstone
Victoria Falls
Wankie
Gatooma
Gwelo
Que Que
Umtali
Fort Victoria
Shabani
Francistown
Serowe
Mahalapye
Molepolole
Mochudi
GABORONE
Lobatse
Mafeking
Zeerust
Rustenburg
PRETORIA
Johannesburg
Krugersdorp
Germiston
Springs
Vereeniging
Heidelberg
Potchefstroom
Klerksdorp
Lichtenburg
Pietersburg
Potgietersrus
Thabazimbi
Louis Trichardt
Messina
Beitbridge
Lydenburg
Nelspruit
Barberton
Middelburg
Witbank
Ermelo
Standerton
Volksrust
Newcastle
Vryheid
Dundee
Ladysmith
Harrismith
Bethlehem
Kroonstad
Welkom
Heilbron
Ficksburg
Ladybrand
MASERU
Bloemfontein
Wepener
Zastron
Aliwal North
Burgersdorp
Sterkstroom
Queenstown
Stutterheim
King Williams Town
East London
Grahamstown
Port Alfred
Port Elizabeth
Fort Beaufort
Kokstad
Umtata
Port Shepstone
Durban
Pietermaritzburg
Estcourt
Stanger
Eshowe
MBABANE
Manzini
MAPUTO
Xai Xai
Chibuto
Inhambane
Vilanculos
Sofala
(Beira)
Chimoio
Quelimane
Chinde
Nsanje
Kruger National Park
WITWATERSRAND
1 : 500 000
Arterial Roads
Main Roads
Other Roads
Railways
Mineral Lines
Gold Mines
JOHANNESBURG
Krugersdorp
Roodepoort
Randfontein
Soweto
Germiston
Boksburg
Benoni
Brakpan
Springs
Alberton
Nigel
Westonaria
Kempton Park
Edenvale
Sandton
Randburg
Heights in Metres and Feet
0 50 100 150 200 250 300 350 400 Kilometres
© John Bartholomew & Son Ltd, Edinburgh

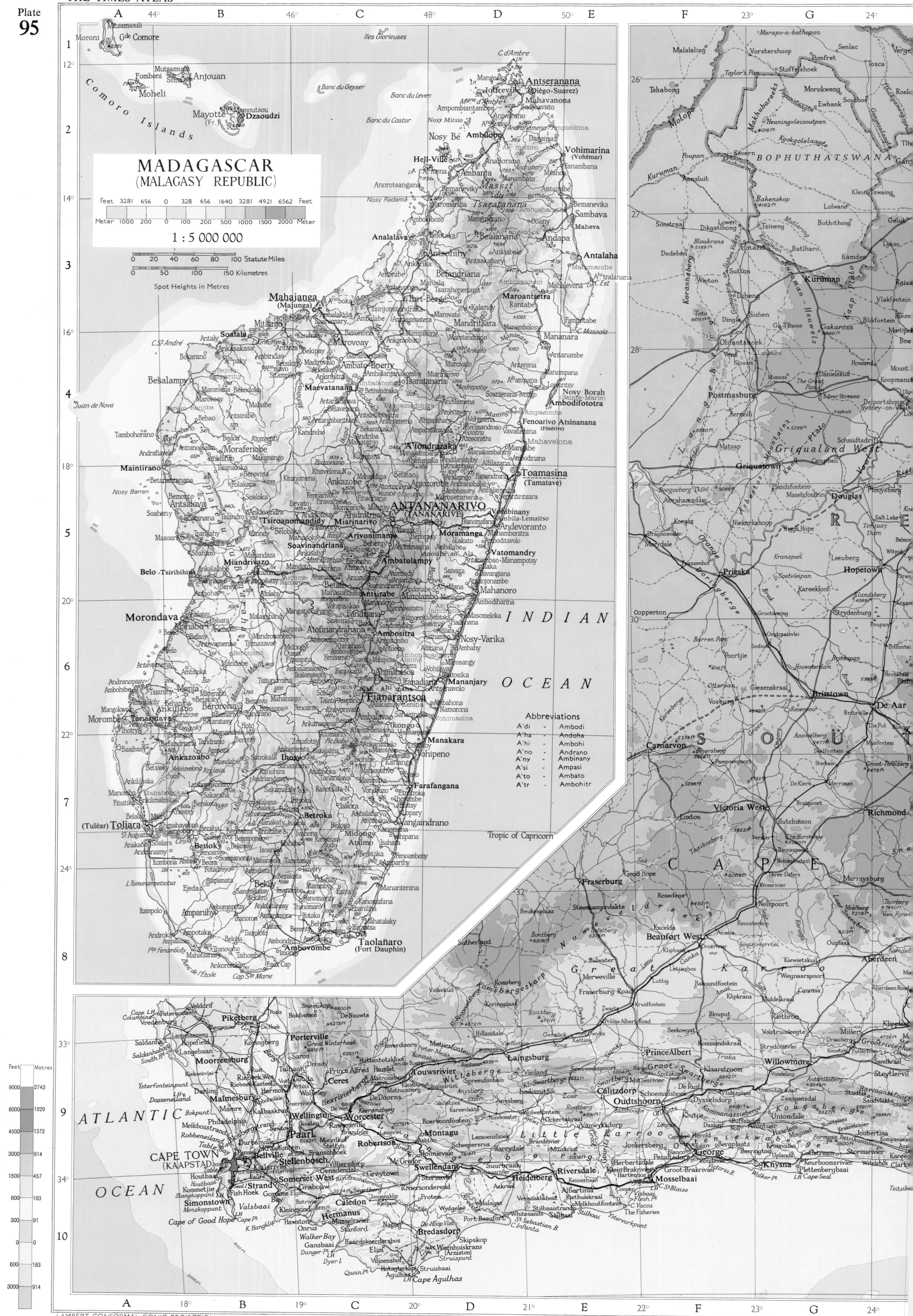
MADAGASCAR
(MALAGASY REPUBLIC)
Feet 3281 656 0 328 656 1640 3281 4921 6562 Feet
Meter 1000 200 0 100 200 500 1000 1500 2000 Meter
1 : 5 000 000
0 20 40 60 80 100 Statute Miles
0 50 100 150 Kilometres
Spot Heights in Metres
Abbreviations
A'di - Ambodi
A'ha - Andoha
A'hi - Ambohi
A'no - Andrano
A'ny - Ambinany
A'si - Ampasi
A'to - Ambato
A'tr - Ambohitr
Comoro Islands
INDIAN OCEAN
ANTANANARIVO (TANANARIVE)
ATLANTIC OCEAN
CAPE TOWN (KAAPSTAD)
BOPHUTHATSWANA
Griqualand West
Great Karroo
Little Karroo
CAPE
Tropic of Capricorn

LAMBERT CONFORMAL CONIC PROJECTION

1: 2 500 000

0 10 20 40 60 80 100 120 Statute Miles

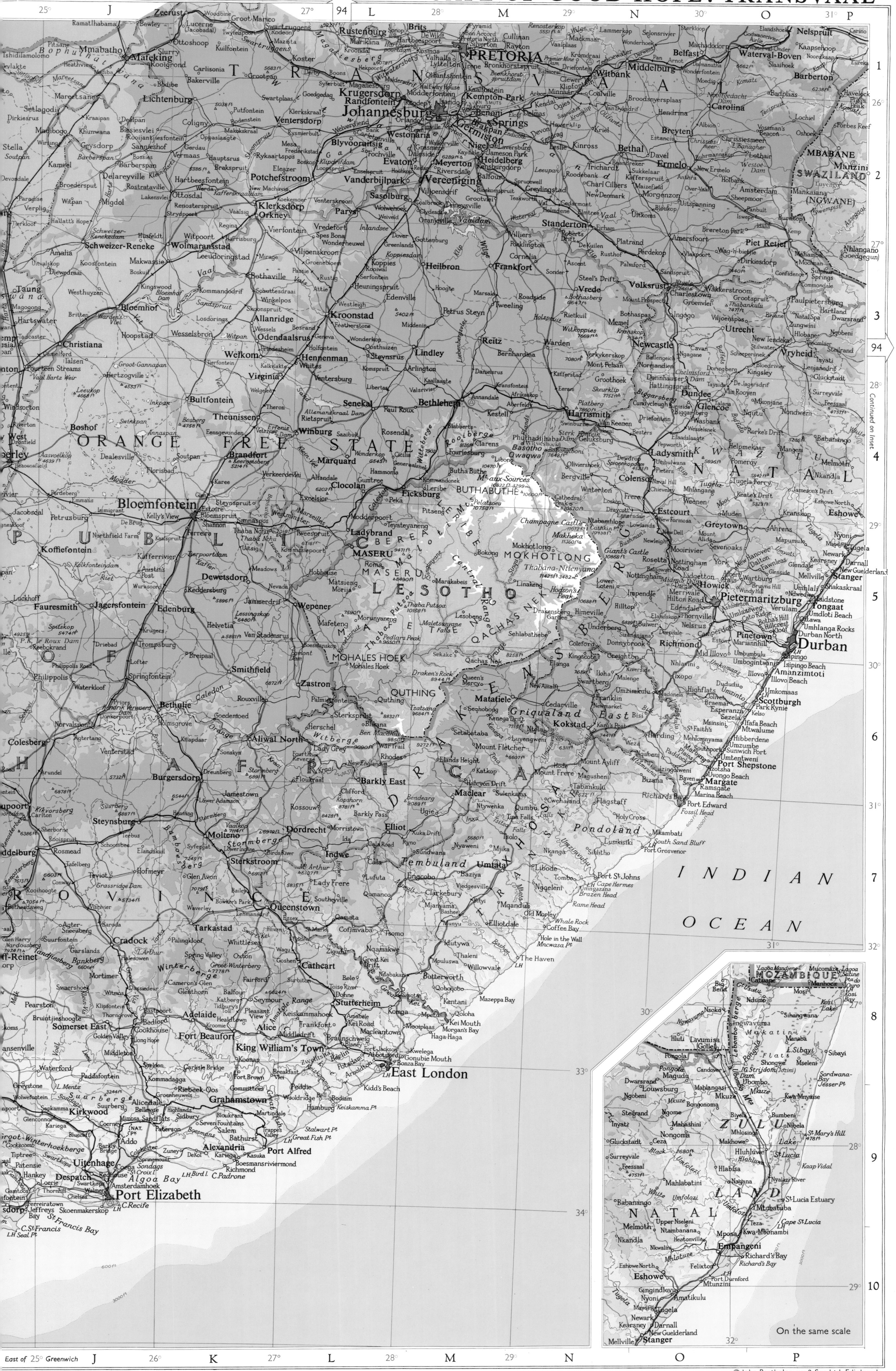
CAPE OF GOOD HOPE: TRANSVAAL
Plate
95
TRANSVAAL
ORANGE FREE STATE
LESOTHO
SWAZILAND
NATAL
KWAZULU
INDIAN OCEAN
PRETORIA
Johannesburg
Durban
Pietermaritzburg
Bloemfontein
Kimberley
MASERU
MBABANE
East London
Port Elizabeth
King William's Town
Grahamstown
Queenstown
Kokstad
Ladysmith
Newcastle
Vereeniging
Kroonstad
Welkom
Klerksdorp
Potchefstroom
Harrismith
Bethlehem
Ermelo
Piet Retief
Vryheid
Port Shepstone
Algoa Bay
MOZAMBIQUE
ZULULAND
On the same scale
Continued on Inset
East of 25° Greenwich
Spot Heights in Feet
0 10 20 40 60 80 100 120 140 160 180 200 Kilometres
© John Bartholomew & Son Ltd, Edinburgh

BERMUDA
(To U.K.)
1 : 350 000
Statute Miles
Kilometres
Murray's Anchorage
St George's Island
St George
St Catherine's Pt
The Narrows
St David's Island
Kindley (U.S. Air Force Base)
Castle Harbour
Nonsuch I.
The Crawl
Harrington Sound
Tucker's Town
Spittal Pond
Sue Wood Bay
Commissioner's Pt
Ireland Island
Daniel's Hd
Somerset Island
Hamilton
Hungry Bay
Great Sound
U.S. Naval Station
Elbow Bay
Little Sound
Evans Bay
Horseshoe Bay
Chaddock Bar
S.W. Breaker
NORTH AMERICA
Hudson Bay
Baffin Bay
GREENLAND
Davis Strait
Denmark Strait
Iceland
Greenland Basin
Jan Mayen
Norwegian Basin
Arctic Circle
BARENTS SEA
NORTH SEA
Baltic Sea
Rockall Bank
Porcupine Bank
Dogger Bk
London
Paris
Quebec
New York
Washington
Georges Bank
Sable I.
Grand Banks of Newfoundland
Flemish Cap
Newfoundland Basin
Newfoundland Rise
North Eastern Atlantic Basin
Azores
Azores-Cape St Vincent Ridge
Lisbon
Madeira
Canary Is.
Bermuda
Bermuda Rise
New England Seamount Chain
North American Basin
Nares Deep
SARGASSO SEA
Oceanographer Fr.
Atlantis Fr.
MID ATLANTIC RIDGE
Canary Basin
Tropic of Cancer
GULF OF MEXICO
Campeche Bk
Mexico
Yucatan Basin
Cayman Trench
Puerto Rico Trench
Milwaukee Depth
CARIBBEAN SEA
Colombian Basin
Venezuelan Basin
Aves Ridge
Cape Verde Fracture
Cape Verde Is.
Cape Verde Plateau
Cape Verde Basin
Dakar
Vema Fracture
Guyana Basin
Panama
Middle America Trench
Cocos I.
Cocos Ridge
Malpelo I.
Galapagos Is.
Carnegie Ridge
Sierra Leone Rise
Sierra Leone Basin
St Paul Rks
Romanche Gap
Guinea Basin
Rocas
Fernando de Noronha
Ascension
SOUTH AMERICA
Brazil Basin
MID-ATLANTIC RIDGE
St Helena
St Helena Fracture
Martin Vaz
Trinidade
Rio de Janeiro
Peru-Chile Trench
Bartholomew Deep
Richards Deep
Rio Grande Rise
Buenos Aires
Walvis Ridge
Tristan da Cunha
Gough I.
Argentine Basin
Falkland Is.
Scotia Ridge
S. Georgia
South Sandwich Trench
Meteor Depth
Burdwood Bk
SCOTIA SEA
Drake Passage
S. Orkney Is.
Atlantic-Indian Basin
Bouvet I.
Atlantic-Antarctic Basin
WEDDELL SEA
Shelf Ice
Pacific-Antarctic Basin
Antarctic Circle
Peter Ist I.
Vahsel Bay
ANTARCTICA
Maud Seamount
Discovery Tablemount
ASCENSION
(To U.K.)
1 : 350 000
Georgetown
English B.
North Pt
Porpoise Pt
Pyramid Pt
Lava Fields
NE. Bay
Clarence Bay
Catherine Pt
Sisters Pk
Boatswain-bird I.
White Hill
Green Mt
N.A.S.A. Tracking Sta.
SE. Head
SE. Bay
Unicorn Pt
White Rk
Pillar Bay
Mars Bay
South Pt
Portland Pt
S.W. Bay
Wideawake
Dampier Drip
ST HELENA
(To U.K.)
1 : 350 000
Sugar Loaf Pt
Flagstaff Bay
Barn Long Pt
Jamestown
Flagstaff Hill
The Barn
Turk's Cap
Prosperous Bay
Long Ledge
High Knoll
Cable Sta.
Longwood
Plantation Ho.
Napoleon's Tomb
Dry Gut Bay
Bennett's Pt
Egg I.
Mt Actaeon
Diana's Pk
Gill Pt
Stone Top Bay
George I.
Deep Valley Bay
High Pk
Sandy Bay
White Pt
Horse Pt
S.W. Pt
Lot's Wife
Powell Pt
Manati Bay
Speery I.
Castle Rock Pt
TRISTAN DA CUNHA
(To U.K.)
1 : 1 000 000
Rookery Pt
Settlement of Edinburgh
Queen Mary's Peak
Anchorstock Pt
Sandy Pt
Tristan da Cunha
Lyon Pt
Seal Bay
Stonyhill Pt
North Pt
West Pt
Inaccessible I.
East Pt
South Hill
Stoltenhoff I.
Middle I.
Nightingale I.
Fathoms
Metres

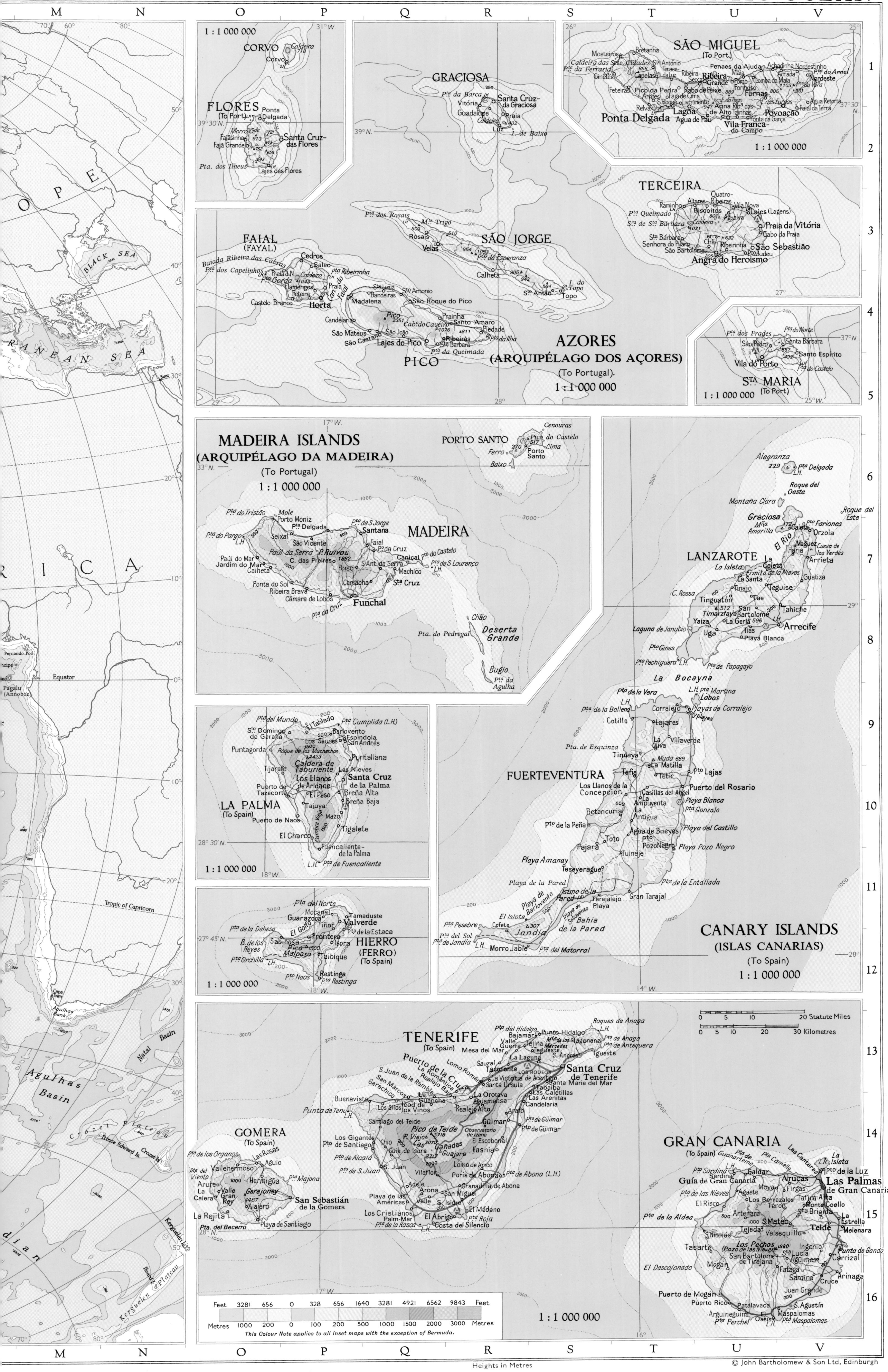
CORVO
FLORES
(To Port.)
Santa Cruz-das Flores
Lajes das Flores
GRACIOSA
Santa Cruz-da Graciosa
SÃO MIGUEL
(To Port.)
Ponta Delgada
Ribeira Grande
Vila Franca-do Campo
Povoação
Nordeste
TERCEIRA
Praia da Vitória
Angra do Heroismo
São Sebastião
FAIAL
(FAYAL)
Horta
SÃO JORGE
Velas
Calheta
PICO
Madalena
Lajes do Pico
AZORES
(ARQUIPÉLAGO DOS AÇORES)
(To Portugal).
STA. MARIA
(To Port.)
Vila do Porto
1 : 1 000 000
MADEIRA ISLANDS
(ARQUIPÉLAGO DA MADEIRA)
(To Portugal)
MADEIRA
PORTO SANTO
Funchal
Deserta Grande
LANZAROTE
Arrecife
Graciosa
Alegranza
FUERTEVENTURA
Puerto del Rosario
CANARY ISLANDS
(ISLAS CANARIAS)
(To Spain)
LA PALMA
(To Spain)
Santa Cruz de la Palma
HIERRO
(FERRO)
(To Spain)
Valverde
TENERIFE
(To Spain)
Santa Cruz de Tenerife
Pico de Teide
GOMERA
(To Spain)
San Sebastián de la Gomera
GRAN CANARIA
(To Spain)
Las Palmas de Gran Canaria
0 5 10 20 Statute Miles
0 5 10 20 30 Kilometres
Feet 3281 656 0 328 656 1640 3281 4921 6562 9843 Feet
Metres 1000 200 0 100 200 500 1000 1500 2000 3000 Metres
This Colour Note applies to all inset maps with the exception of Bermuda.
BLACK SEA
Equator
Tropic of Capricorn
Agulhas Basin
Natal Basin

© John Bartholomew & Son Ltd, Edinburgh

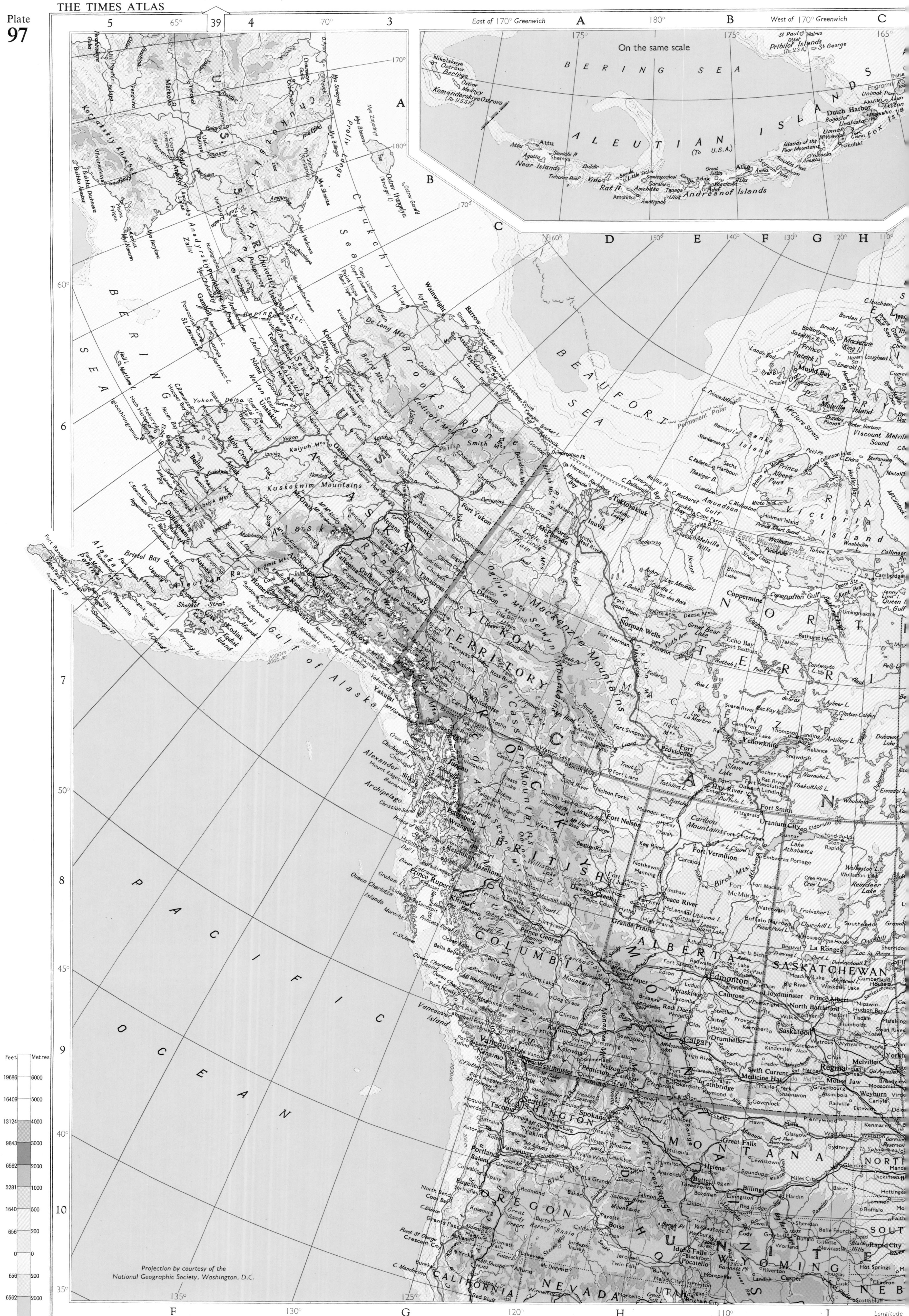
East of 170° Greenwich
West of 170° Greenwich
On the same scale
BERING SEA
ALEUTIAN ISLANDS
(To U.S.A.)
Pribilof Islands
Komandorskiye Ostrova
Attu
Near Islands
Rat Is
Andreanof Islands
Adak
Atka
Dutch Harbor
Unalaska
Fox Is
U.S.S.R.
Chukchi Sea
BERING SEA
BEAUFORT SEA
ALASKA
Brooks Range
Kuskokwim Mountains
Alaska Range
Gulf of Alaska
Fairbanks
Anchorage
Nome
Barrow
YUKON TERRITORY
Mackenzie Mountains
Dawson
Whitehorse
Juneau
Inuvik
Great Bear Lake
Great Slave Lake
Yellowknife
Victoria Island
Banks Island
NORTHWEST TERRITORIES
BRITISH COLUMBIA
ALBERTA
SASKATCHEWAN
Edmonton
Calgary
Vancouver
Victoria
Vancouver Island
Queen Charlotte Islands
Prince Rupert
Prince George
Seattle
Spokane
Portland
WASHINGTON
OREGON
IDAHO
MONTANA
WYOMING
NEVADA
UTAH
CALIFORNIA
PACIFIC OCEAN
ROCKY MOUNTAINS
Regina
Saskatoon
Lake Athabasca
Projection by courtesy of the National Geographic Society, Washington, D.C.
Feet
Metres
Longitude

Spot Heights in Feet

0 100 200 300 400 500 600 700 800 Kilometres

Printed in U.K.

© John Bartholomew & Son Ltd, Edinburgh

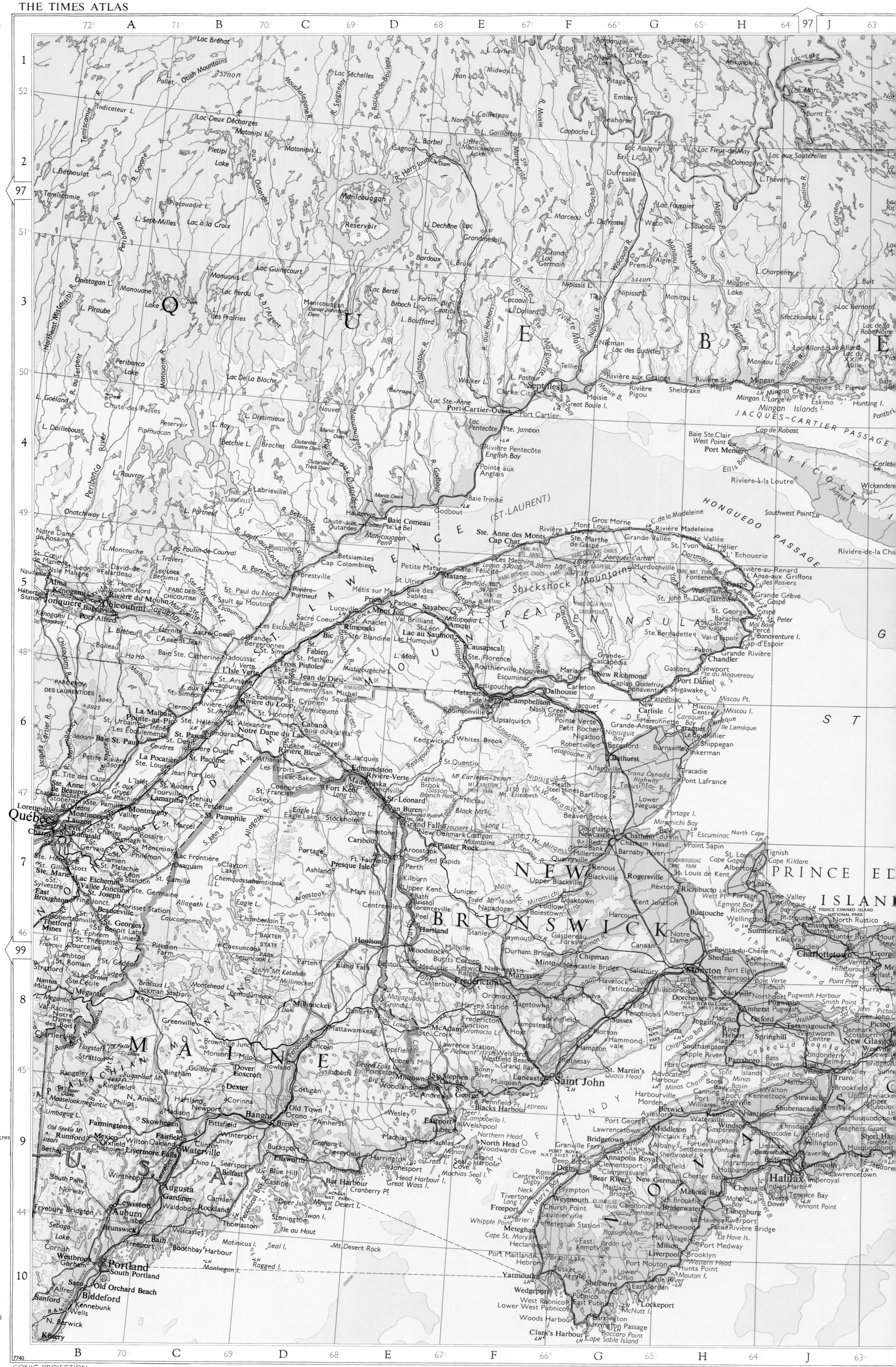
QUEBEC
NEW BRUNSWICK
MAINE
U.S.A.
NOVA SCOTIA
PRINCE EDWARD ISLAND
(ST-LAURENT)
GASPÉ PENINSULA
NOTRE DAME MOUNTAINS
HONGUEDO PASSAGE
JACQUES-CARTIER PASSAGE
ANTICOSTI
BAY OF FUNDY
Québec
Chicoutimi
Rimouski
Baie Comeau
Sept-Îles
Gaspé
Edmundston
Fredericton
Moncton
Saint John
Charlottetown
Halifax
Bangor
Augusta
Portland
Yarmouth
Manicouagan Reservoir
Shickshock Mountains
Anticosti

Feet / Metres
3000 914
1500 457
600 183
300 91
0 0
Tidal Areas
656 200
3281 1000

NEWFOUNDLAND
LABRADOR
ATLANTIC OCEAN
GULF OF ST. LAWRENCE
CABOT STRAIT
CAPE BRETON ISLAND
ÎLES DE LA MADELEINE (Magdalen Islands) (To Quebec)
SAINT-PIERRE & MIQUELON (To France)
LONG RANGE MOUNTAINS
SABLE ISLAND BANK
Sable Island
St. John's
Corner Brook
Gander
Grand Falls
Stephenville
Channel Port aux Basques
Port Hope Simpson
St. Anthony
Bonavista
Placentia
Sydney
Glace Bay
Louisburg
QUEBEC
1:100 000
Statute Miles
Kilometres
QUÉBEC
LÉVIS
Ste.-Foy
Sillery
Charlesbourg
Beauport
Vanier
St Laurent
West 62° of Greenwich
160 Kilometres

© John Bartholomew & Son Ltd, Edinburgh

LAKE SUPERIOR
LAKE MICHIGAN
LAKE HURON
GEORGIAN BAY
LAKE ERIE
LAKE NIPIGON
ONTARIO
MICHIGAN
Sault Ste. Marie
Detroit
Windsor
Sudbury
Thunder Bay
Flint
Lansing
Saginaw
London
Sarnia
Port Huron
Timmins
Cochrane
Moosonee
Marquette
OTTAWA
1: 200 000
TORONTO
1: 250 000
Feet
Metres
3000 914
1500 457
600 183
300 91
0 0
CONIC PROJECTION
0 10 20 40 60 80 100 Statute Miles
1: 2 500 000
Longitude West 81° of Greenwich
7740

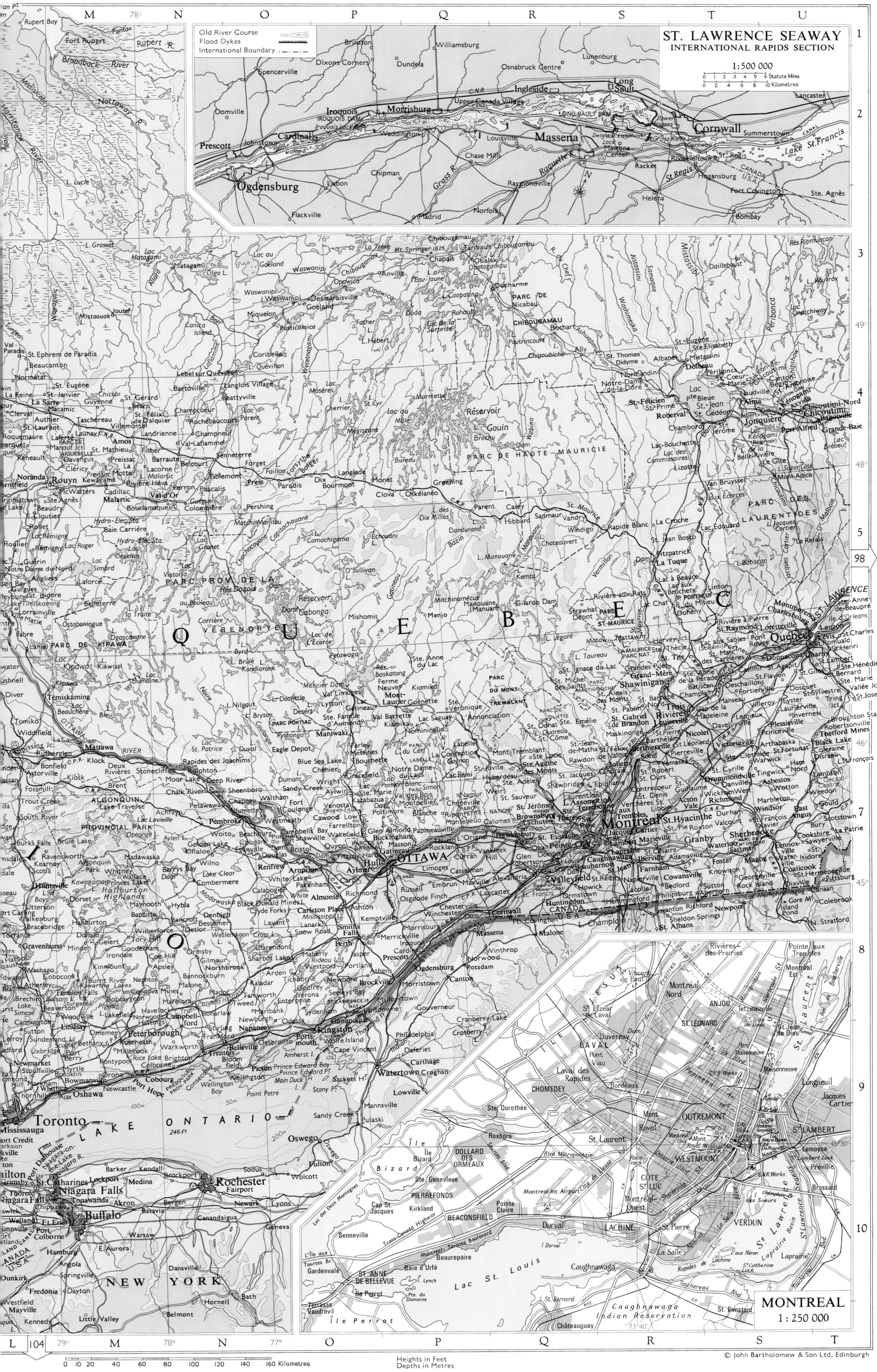
ST. LAWRENCE SEAWAY
INTERNATIONAL RAPIDS SECTION
1:500 000
Statute Miles
Kilometres
Old River Course
Flood Dykes
International Boundary
QUEBEC
LAKE ONTARIO
NEW YORK
MONTREAL
1:250 000
98
104

0 10 20 40 60 80 100 120 140 160 Kilometres

Heights in Feet
Depths in Metres

© John Bartholomew & Son Ltd, Edinburgh

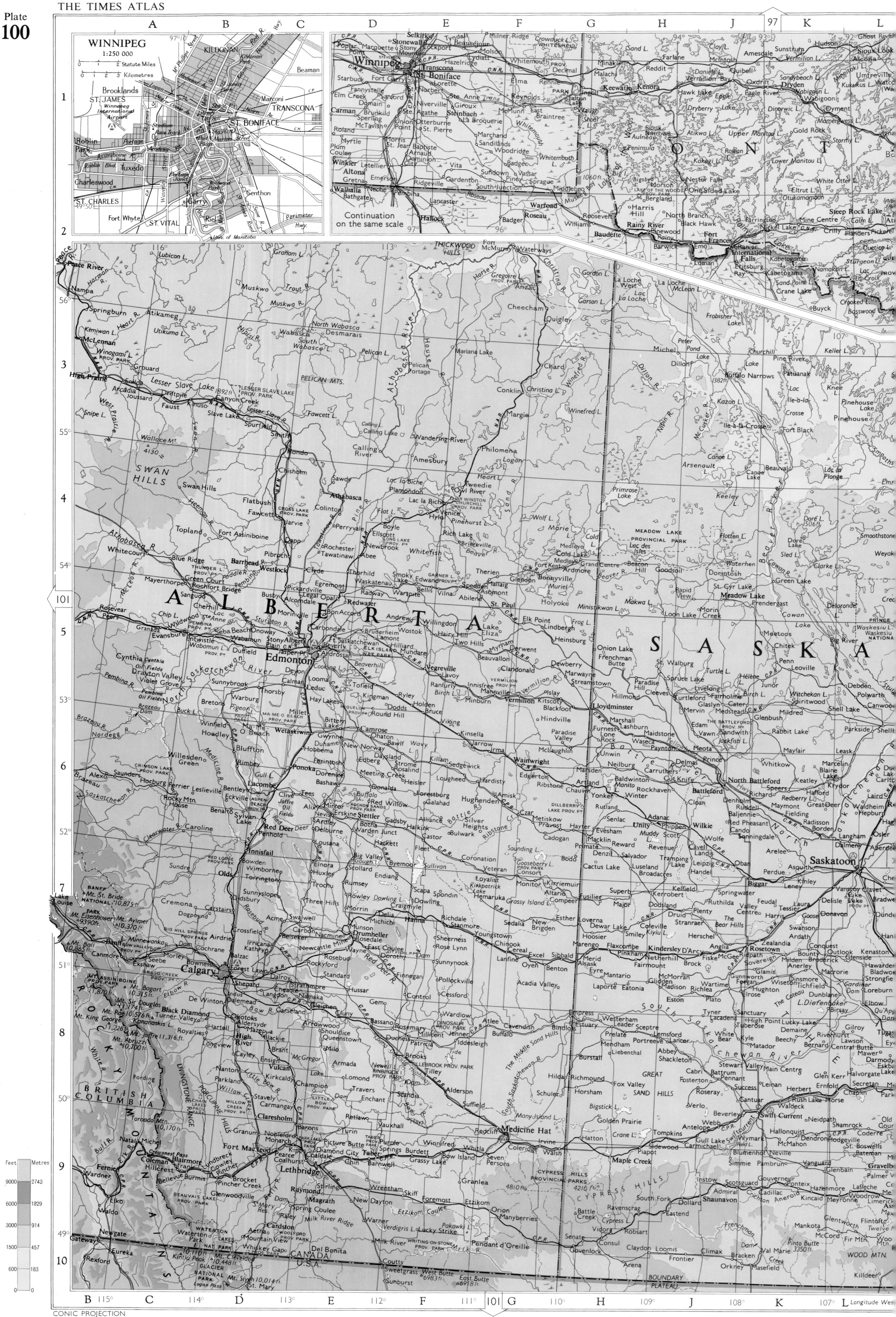
WINNIPEG
1:250 000
Statute Miles
Kilometres
Continuation on the same scale
ALBERTA
SASKA
ONT
BRITISH COLUMBIA
ROCKY MOUNTAINS
CANADA
U.S.A.
Winnipeg
St Boniface
Edmonton
Calgary
Lethbridge
Medicine Hat
Red Deer
Saskatoon
Swift Current
North Battleford
Lloydminster
Kenora
Fort Frances
Lesser Slave Lake
SWAN HILLS
CYPRESS HILLS
GREAT SAND HILLS
MEADOW LAKE PROVINCIAL PARK
BANFF NATIONAL PARK
LIVINGSTONE RANGE
PORCUPINE HILLS
BOUNDARY PLATEAU
Feet
Metres
9000 2743
6000 1829
3000 914
1500 457
600 183
0 0
Longitude West
CONIC PROJECTION
1: 2 550 000
0 10 20 40 60 80 100 Statute Miles

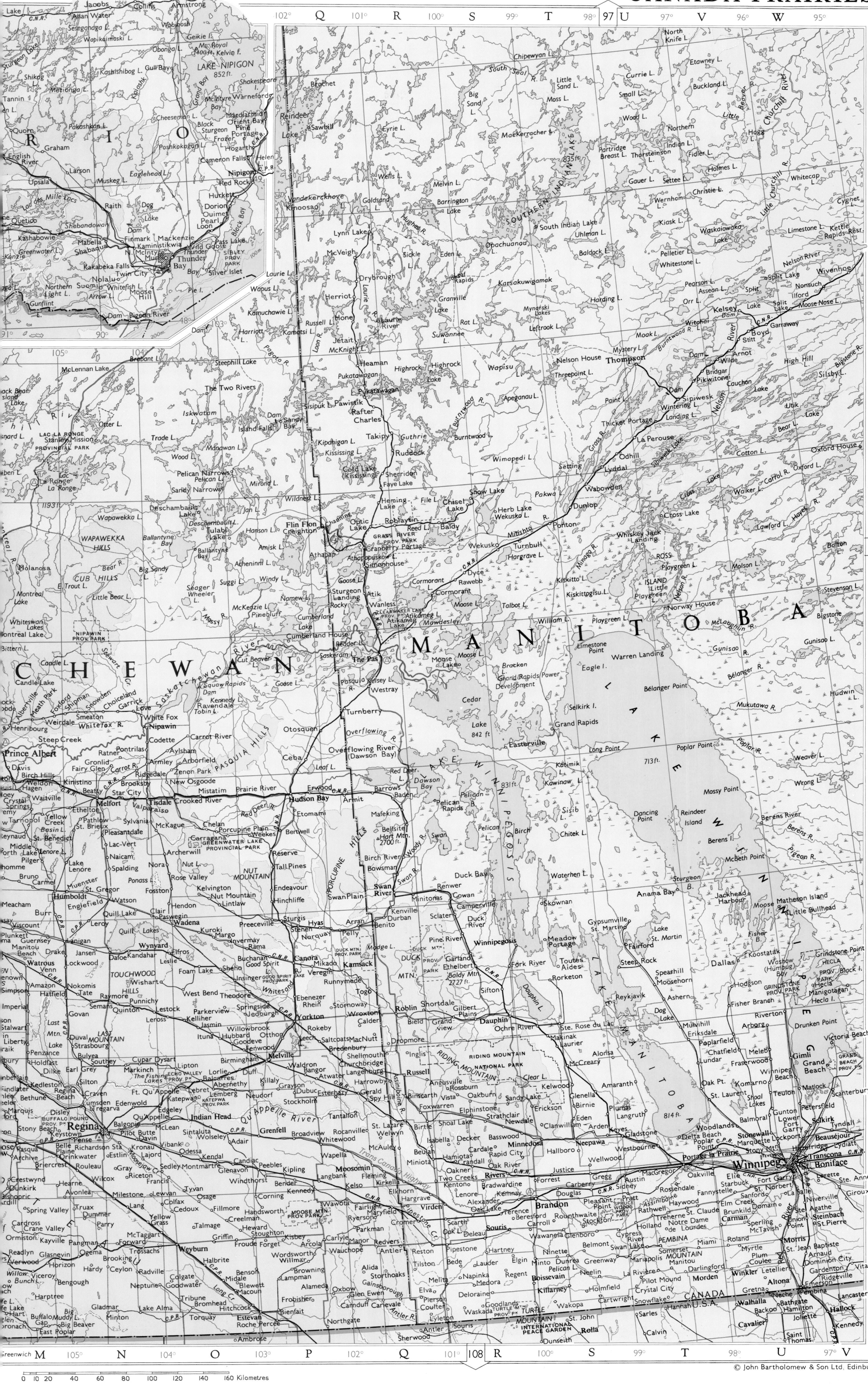
MANITOBA
LAKE WINNIPEG
LAKE MANITOBA
LAKE WINNIPEGOSIS
LAKE NIPIGON
852 ft.
713 ft.
814 ft.
831 ft.
842 ft.
835 ft.
SOUTHERN INDIAN LAKE
Cedar Lake
Winnipeg
St. Boniface
Regina
Brandon
Prince Albert
Melfort
Thompson
Flin Flon
The Pas
Dauphin
Yorkton
Portage la Prairie
Selkirk
Weyburn
Estevan
Moosomin
Virden
Souris
Lynn Lake
Churchill River
Nelson River
Saskatchewan River
Qu'Appelle River
Assiniboine R.
Red River
Winnipegosis
Swan River
Hudson Bay
Humboldt
Nipawin
Tisdale
Melville
Minnedosa
Neepawa
Gimli
Thunder Bay
Nipigon
RIDING MOUNTAIN NATIONAL PARK
GRASS RIVER PROV. PARK
DUCK MTN. PROV. PARK
MOOSE MTN. PROV. PARK
TURTLE MOUNTAIN PROV. PARK
INTERNATIONAL PEACE GARDEN
PORCUPINE HILLS
PASQUIA HILLS
WAPAWEKKA HILLS
CUB HILLS
TOUCHWOOD HILLS
LAST MOUNTAIN
NUT MOUNTAIN
Baldy Mtn. 2727 ft.
Hart Mtn. 2700 ft.
LAC LA RONGE PROVINCIAL PARK
NIPAWIN PROV. PARK
GREENWATER LAKE PROVINCIAL PARK
HECLA PROV. PARK
GRAND BEACH PROV. PK
CANADA
U.S.A.
Trans Canada Highway
C.N.R.
C.P.R.
Q R S T U V W
M N O P Q R S T U V
102° 101° 100° 99° 98° 97° 96° 95°
105° 104° 103° 102° 101° 100° 99° 98° 97°
57° 56° 55° 54° 53° 52° 51° 50° 49°
1 2 3 4 5 6 7 8 9 10
97
108
Greenwich
0 10 20 40 60 80 100 120 140 160 Kilometres

BEAUFORT SEA
Amundsen Gulf
VICTORIA ISLAND
Queen Maud Gulf
Coronation Gulf
DISTRICT OF KEEWATIN
DISTRICT OF FRANKLIN
DISTRICT OF MACKENZIE
NORTHWEST TERRITORIES
YUKON TERRITORY
ALASKA U.S.A.
GREAT BEAR LAKE
GREAT SLAVE LAKE
Coppermine
Yellowknife
Fort Resolution
Fort Smith
Uranium City
Hay River
Fort Providence
Fort Simpson
Fort Liard
Norman Wells
Fort Norman
Fort Good Hope
Inuvik
Aklavik
Fort McPherson
Tuktoyaktuk
Dawson
Mayo Landing
Carmacks
Whitehorse
Teslin
Carcross
Skagway
Haines
Tungsten
Mackenzie Mountains
Selwyn Mountains
Richardson Mountains
Franklin Mts
Ogilvie Mts
Pelly Mountains
Mackenzie River
CONIC PROJECTION
0 10 20 40 60 80 100 150 200 Statute Miles
1: 5 000 000

CANADA WEST AND NORTH-WEST

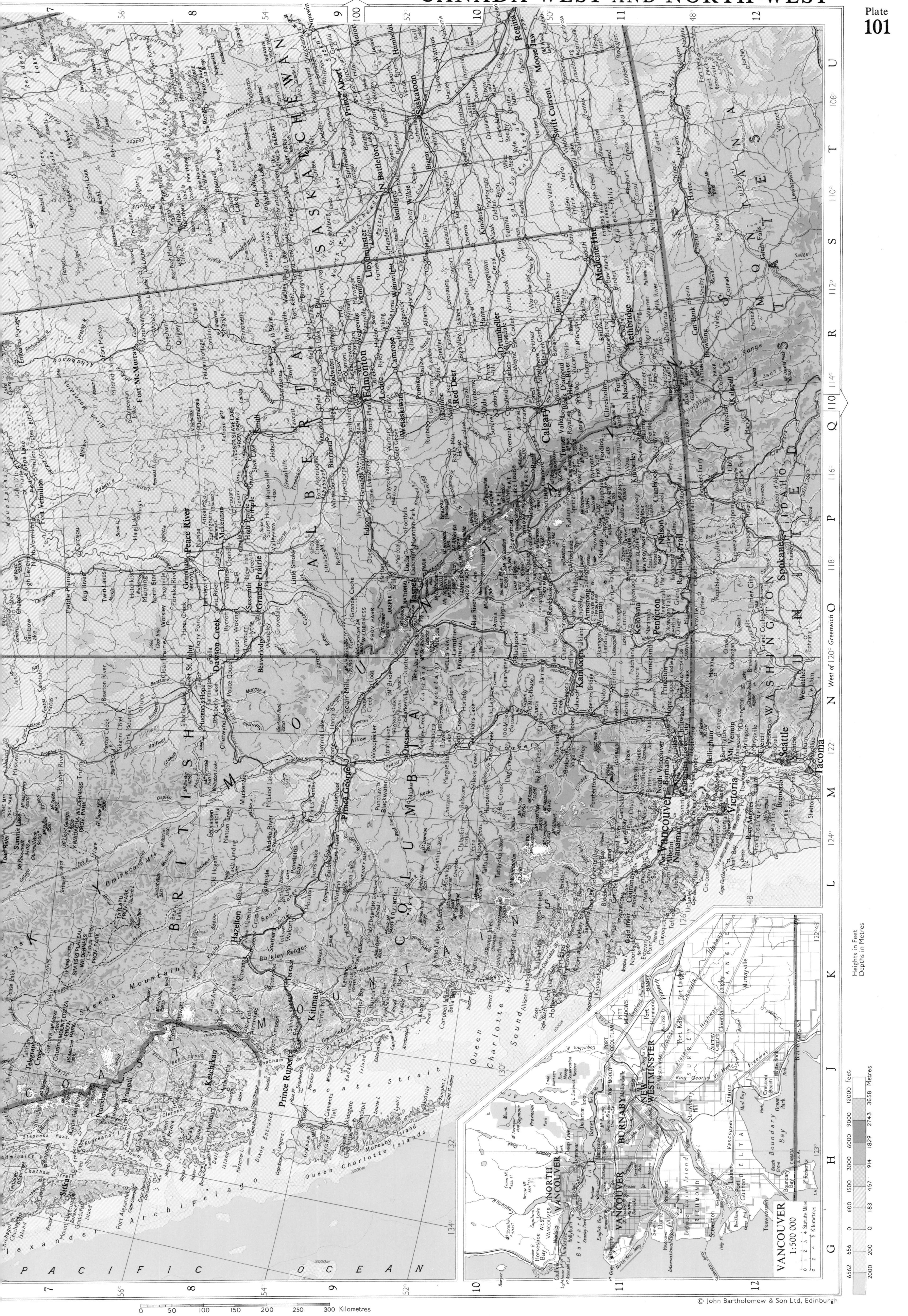

CHAMBERLIN TRIMETRIC PROJECTION

1: 12 500 000

0 100 200 300 400 500 Statute Miles

ATLANTIC OCEAN
CARIBBEAN SEA
WEST INDIES
GREATER ANTILLES
LESSER ANTILLES
LEEWARD ISLANDS
WINDWARD ISLANDS
THE BAHAMAS
HISPANIOLA
BERMUDA (To U.K.)
CUBA
HAITI
DOMINICAN REPUBLIC
PUERTO RICO (To U.S.A.)
JAMAICA
HONDURAS
NICARAGUA
COSTA RICA
PANAMA
BELIZE
COLOMBIA
VENEZUELA
BRAZIL
TRINIDAD AND TOBAGO
NETHERLANDS ANTILLES
BARBADOS
GRENADA
ST. LUCIA
ST. VINCENT
DOMINICA
NORTH CAROLINA
SOUTH CAROLINA
GEORGIA
ALABAMA
FLORIDA
VIRGINIA
WEST VIRGINIA
KENTUCKY
INDIANA
OHIO
PENNSYLVANIA
NEW YORK
MAINE
NEW BRUNSWICK
NOVA SCOTIA
PRINCE EDWARD I.
QUEBEC
ONTARIO
WASHINGTON
New York
Boston
Philadelphia
Baltimore
Montreal
OTTAWA
Toronto
Detroit
Cleveland
Pittsburgh
Buffalo
Quebec
Halifax
HABANA (HAVANA)
Kingston
Port au Prince
Santo Domingo
San Juan
Caracas
Bogotá
Panamá
Tropic of Cancer
Straits of Florida
Yucatán Channel
Gulf of Saint Lawrence
Golfo de Venezuela
Golfo de Panamá
0 100 200 300 400 500 600 700 800 Kilometres

© John Bartholomew & Son Ltd, Edinburgh

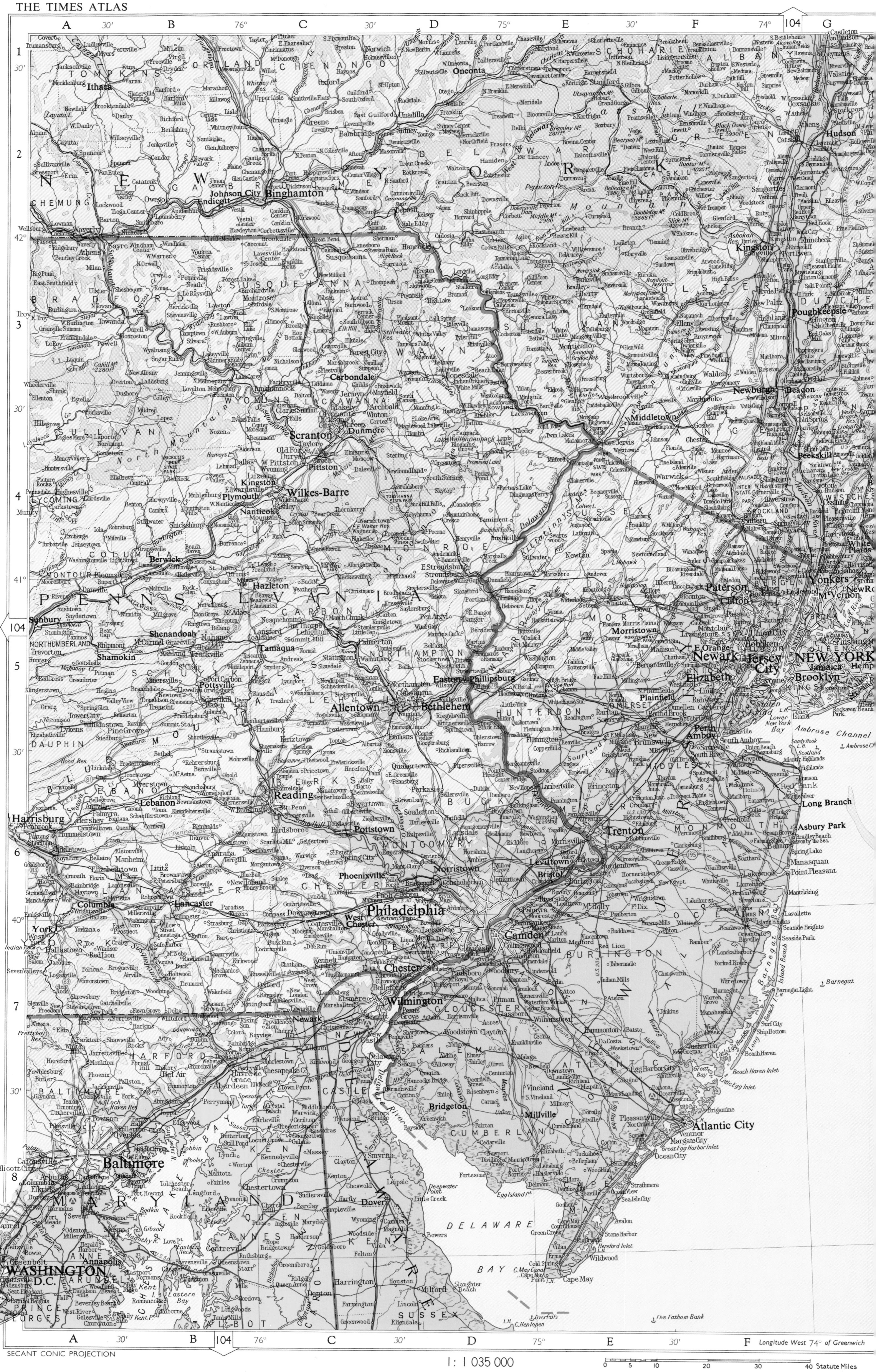
NEW YORK
PENNSYLVANIA
NEW JERSEY
MARYLAND
DELAWARE
Binghamton
Scranton
Wilkes-Barre
Allentown
Bethlehem
Reading
Harrisburg
Lancaster
Philadelphia
Camden
Chester
Wilmington
Trenton
Newark
Jersey City
NEW YORK
Brooklyn
Yonkers
Paterson
Elizabeth
Atlantic City
Baltimore
WASHINGTON D.C.
DELAWARE BAY
Ambrose Channel
Feet Metres
3000 914
1500 457
600 183
300 91
0 0
164 50
656 200
SECANT CONIC PROJECTION
1: 1 035 000
0 5 10 20 30 40 Statute Miles
Longitude West 74° of Greenwich

U.S.A. MIDDLE ATLANTIC SEABOARD
Plate
103
104
H
J
K
L
M
N
O
73°
30'
72°
71°
42°
41°
40°
MASSACHUSETTS
MASSACHUSETTS BAY
CAPE COD BAY
CAPE COD
NANTUCKET SOUND
Nantucket Island
Martha's Vineyard
Block Island Sound
LONG ISLAND SOUND
RHODE ISLAND
CONNECTICUT
Boston
Worcester
Springfield
Providence
Hartford
New Haven
Bridgeport
New London
Fall River
New Bedford
Newport
Waterbury
Plymouth
Brockton
Pittsfield
Holyoke
Northampton
New Britain
Taunton
Pawtucket
Cranston
Woonsocket
NEW YORK
AND ENVIRONS
1:250 000
Statute Miles
Kilometres
PATERSON
NEWARK
JERSEY CITY
HOBOKEN
BRONX
MANHATTAN
BROOKLYN
QUEENS
JAMAICA
FLUSHING
BAYONNE
ELIZABETH
YONKERS
NEW ROCHELLE
MOUNT VERNON
HEMPSTEAD
FREEPORT
LEVITTOWN
OYSTER BAY
Upper New York Bay
Lower New York Bay
Jamaica Bay
Rockaway Inlet
Ambrose Channel
Sandy Hook
John F. Kennedy Intern^l Airport
La Guardia Airport
Newark Airport
74°
73°45'
74°15'
0 5 10 20 30 40 50 60 Kilometres

LAMBERT CONFORMAL CONIC PROJECTION

1: 2 500 000

ATLANTIC OCEAN
Montreal
OTTAWA
Boston
New York
Philadelphia
Portland
Providence
Hartford
Springfield
Albany
Long Island Sound
Cape Cod
Nantucket Island
Marthas Vineyard
WASHINGTON
1 : 250 000
Statute Miles
Kilometres
BOSTON
1 : 250 000
0 10 20 40 60 80 100 120 140 160 Kilometres

© John Bartholomew & Son Ltd, Edinburgh

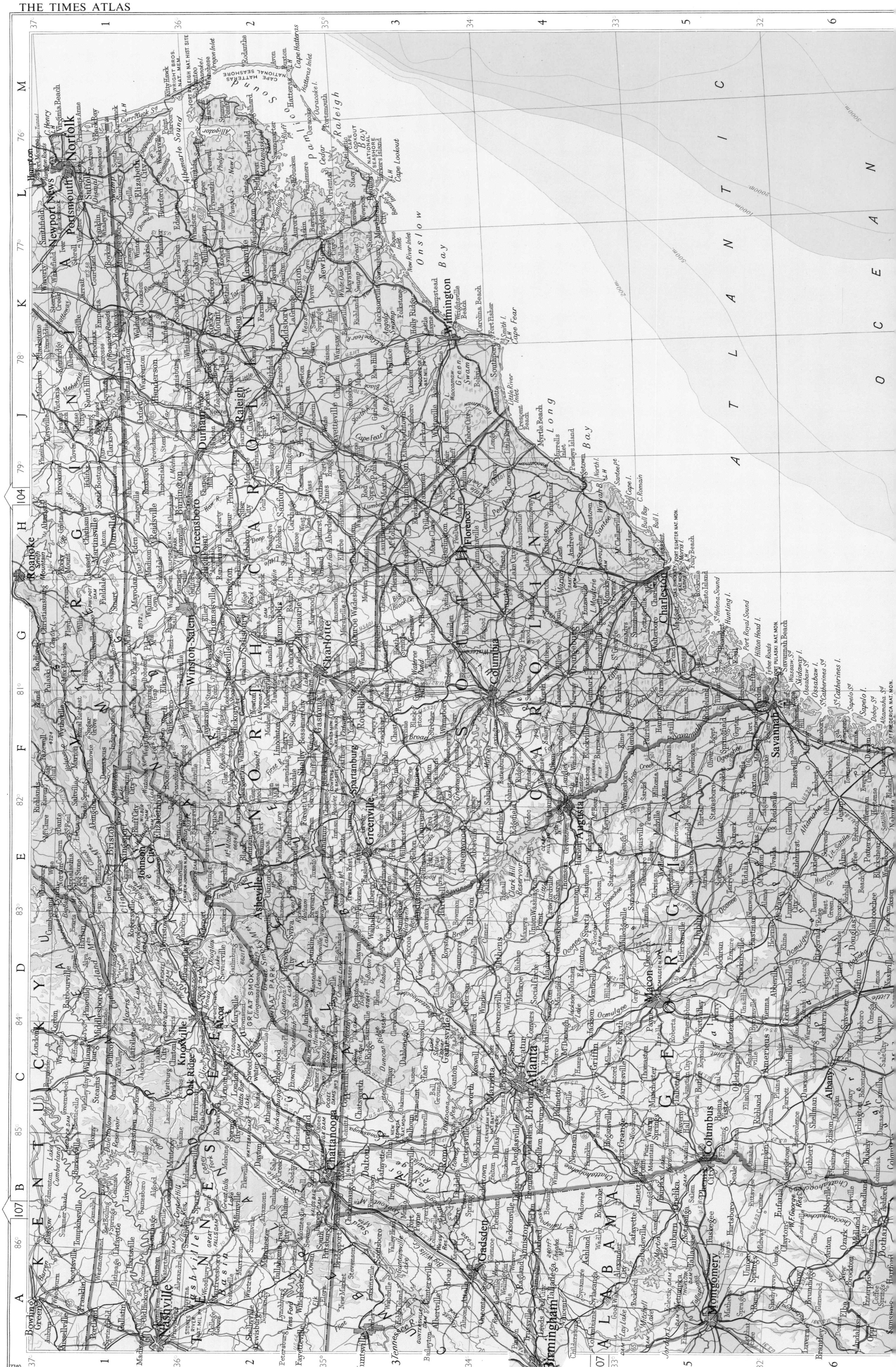

LAMBERT CONFORMAL CONIC PROJECTION

1: 2 500 000

0 10 20 40 60 80 100 Statute Miles

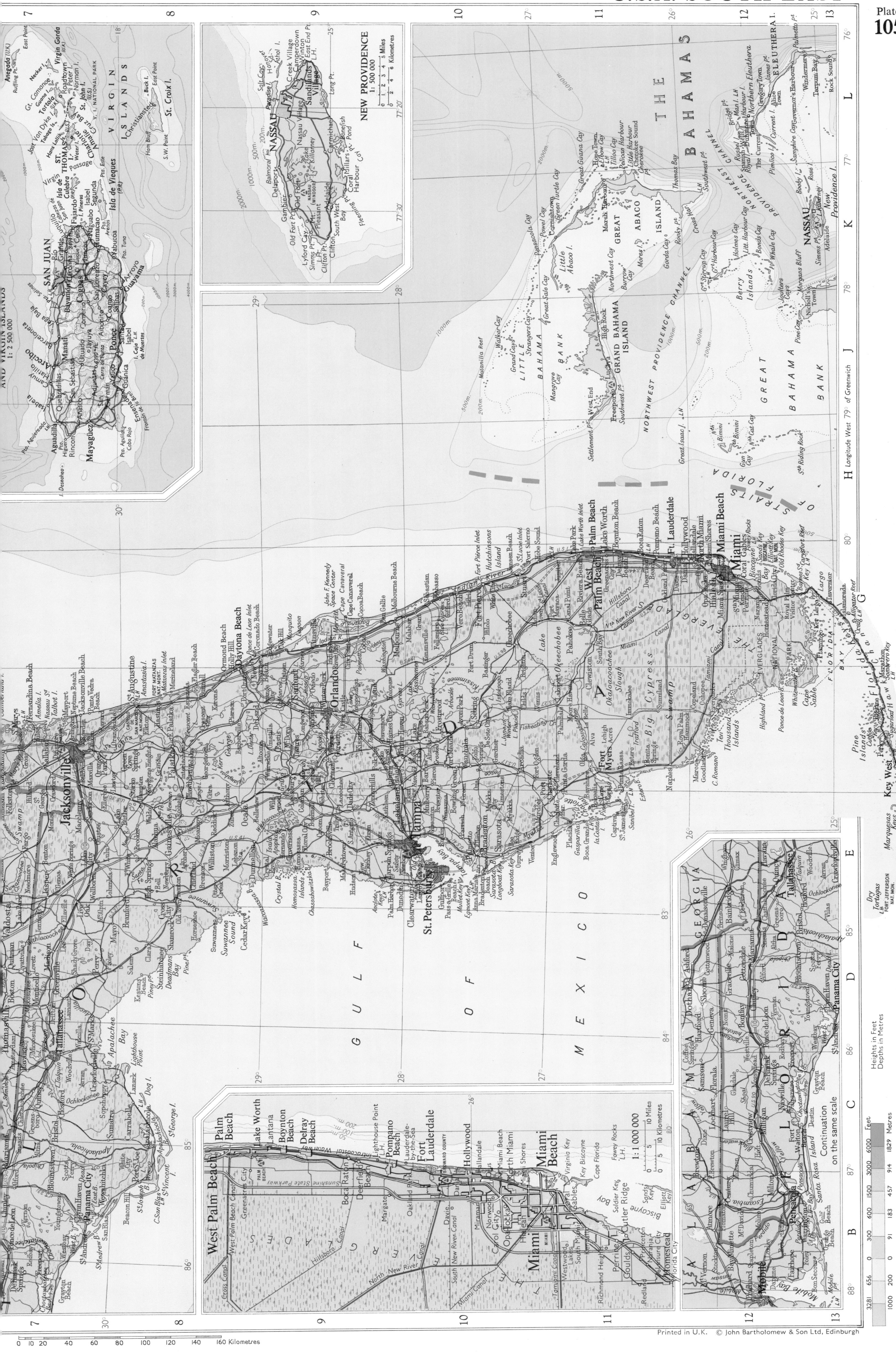
THE BAHAMAS
GULF OF MEXICO
NEW PROVIDENCE
1: 500 000
NASSAU
GRAND BAHAMA ISLAND
GREAT ABACO ISLAND
NORTHWEST PROVIDENCE CHANNEL
GREAT BAHAMA BANK
LITTLE BAHAMA BANK
STRAITS OF FLORIDA
ELEUTHERA I.
VIRGIN ISLANDS
SAN JUAN
Jacksonville
Orlando
Tampa
St. Petersburg
Miami
Miami Beach
West Palm Beach
Ft. Lauderdale
Key West
Tallahassee
Panama City
Pensacola
Mobile
Continuation on the same scale
1:1 000 000
Heights in Feet
Depths in Metres
160 Kilometres

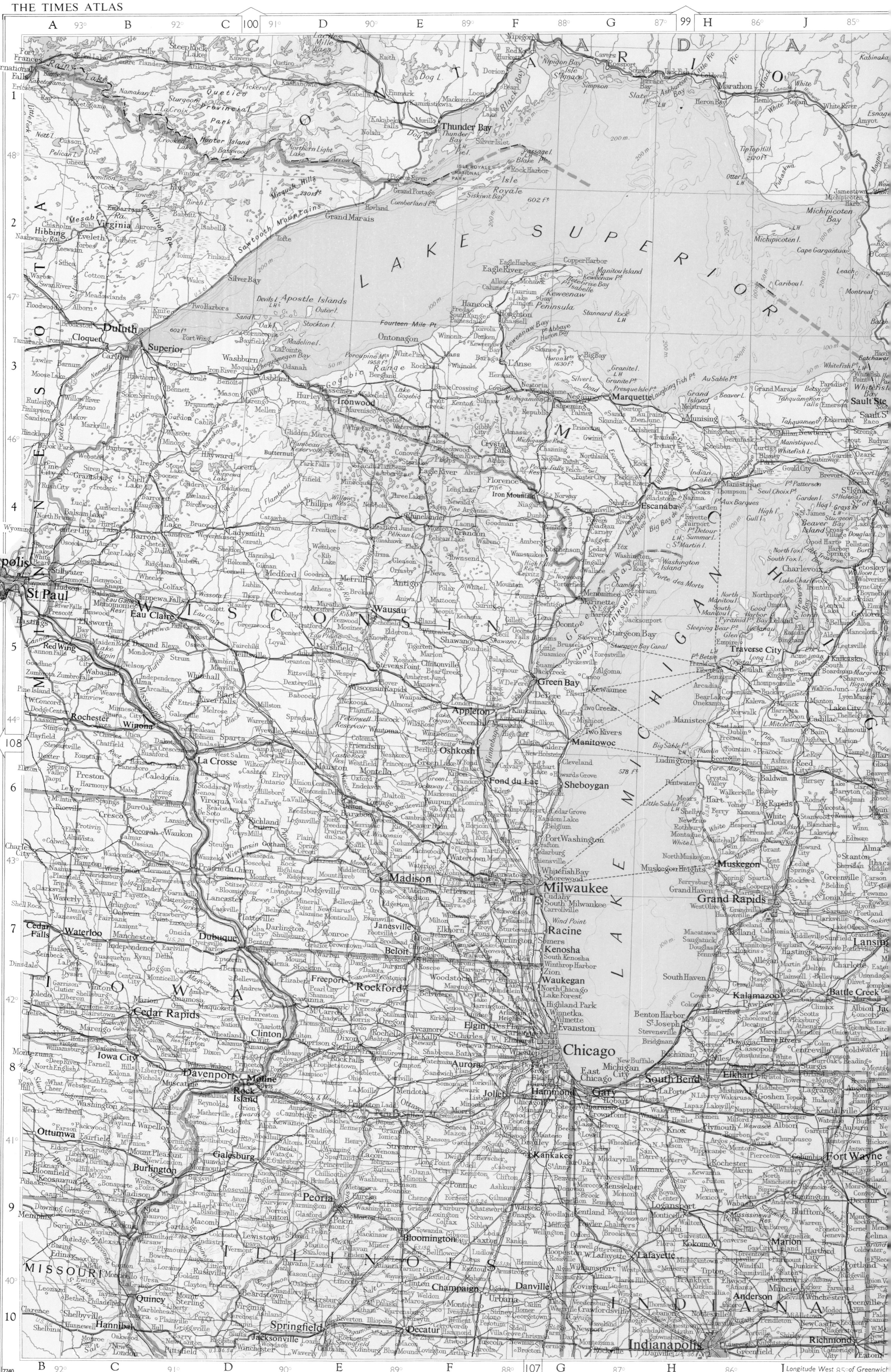
LAKE SUPERIOR
LAKE MICHIGAN
WISCONSIN
MINNESOTA
IOWA
ILLINOIS
INDIANA
MICHIGAN
MISSOURI
Minneapolis
St Paul
Duluth
Milwaukee
Chicago
Madison
Indianapolis
Thunder Bay

Feet | Metres
3000 | 914
1500 | 457
600 | 183
300 | 91
0 | 0

LAMBERT CONFORMAL CONIC PROJECTION

1: 2 500 000

0 10 20 40 60 80 100 Statute Miles

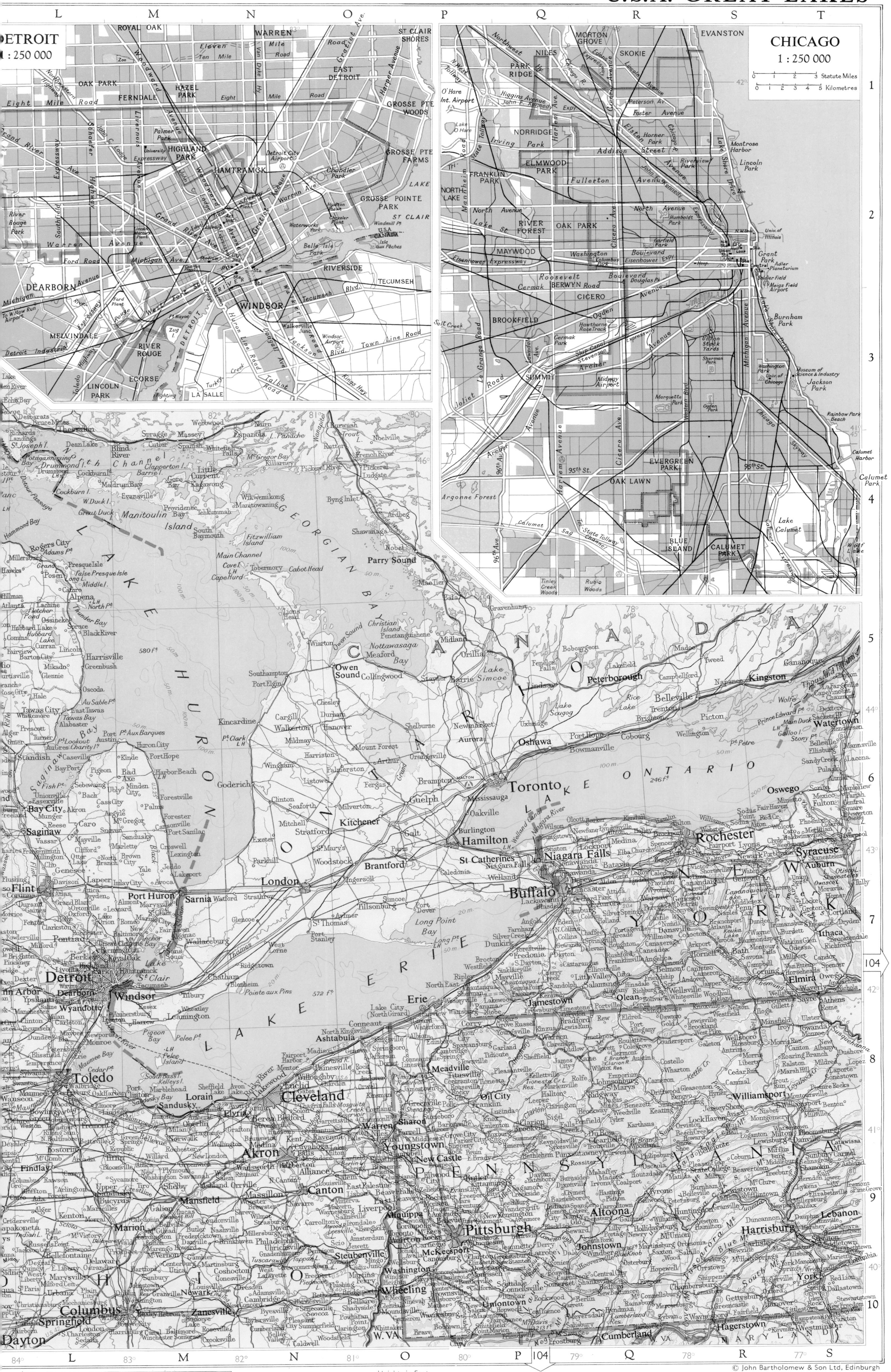
DETROIT
1 : 250 000
CHICAGO
1 : 250 000
Statute Miles
Kilometres
LAKE HURON
GEORGIAN BAY
LAKE ONTARIO
LAKE ERIE
CANADA
NEW YORK
PENNSYLVANIA
OHIO
MICHIGAN
Detroit
Windsor
Toledo
Cleveland
Akron
Canton
Youngstown
Pittsburgh
Columbus
Toronto
Hamilton
Kitchener
London
Buffalo
Niagara Falls
Rochester
Syracuse
Erie
Flint
Saginaw
Bay City
Port Huron
Sarnia
Kingston
Peterborough
Oshawa
Altoona
Johnstown
Harrisburg
Williamsport
Wheeling
Owen Sound
Parry Sound
Manitoulin Island
Heights in Feet
Depths in Metres
0 10 20 40 60 80 100 120 140 160 Kilometres
© John Bartholomew & Son Ltd, Edinburgh

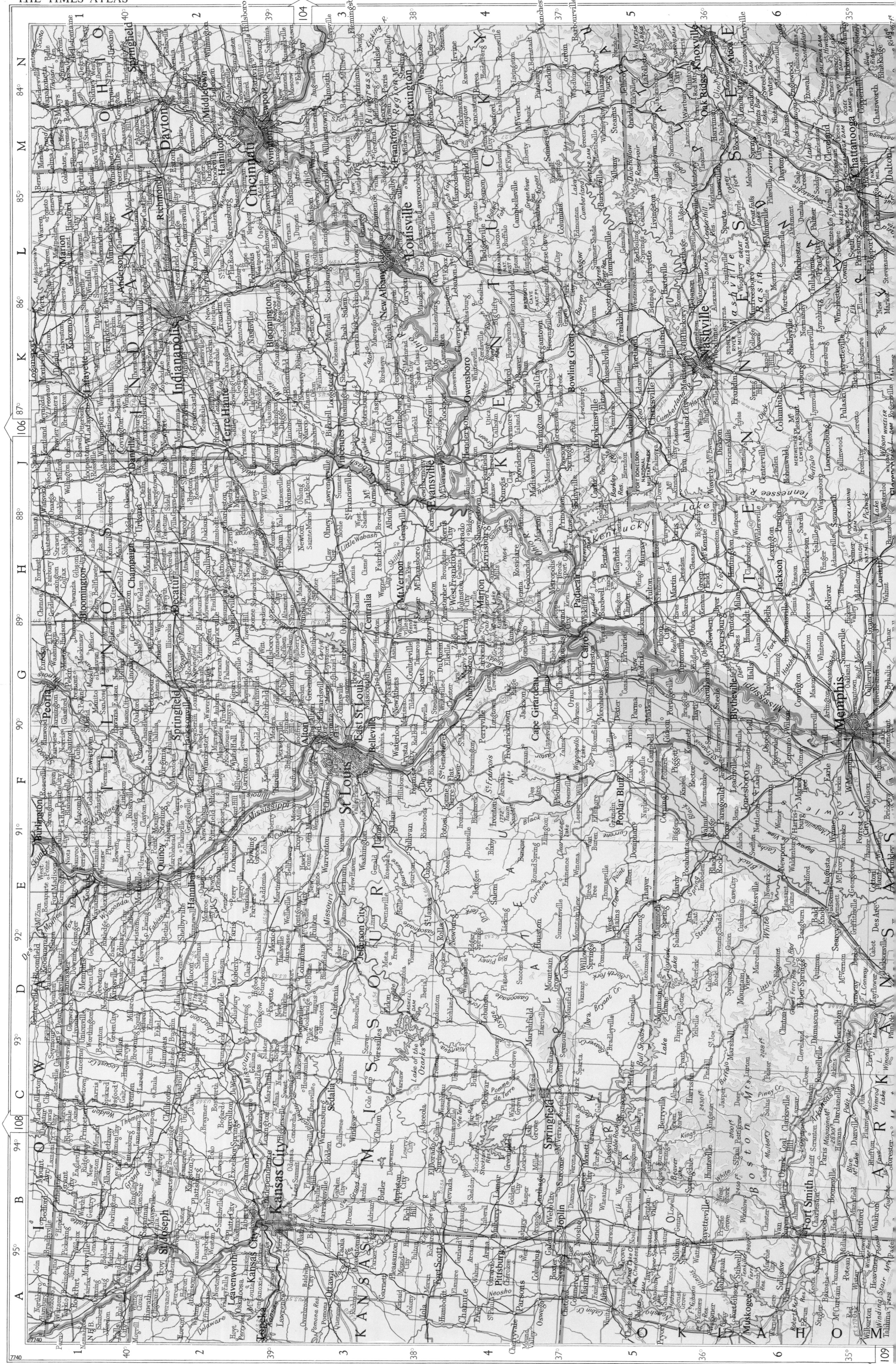

LAMBERT CONFORMAL CONIC PROJECTION

1: 2 500 000

0 10 20 40 60 80 100 Statute Miles

ST LOUIS
1 : 250 000
NEW ORLEANS
1 : 250 000
GULF OF MEXICO
ALABAMA
MISSISSIPPI
LOUISIANA
GEORGIA
FLORIDA
TEXAS
Longitude West 90° of Greenwich
Heights in Feet
Depths in Metres
0 10 20 40 60 80 100 120 140 160 Kilometres

© John Bartholomew & Son Ltd. Edinburgh

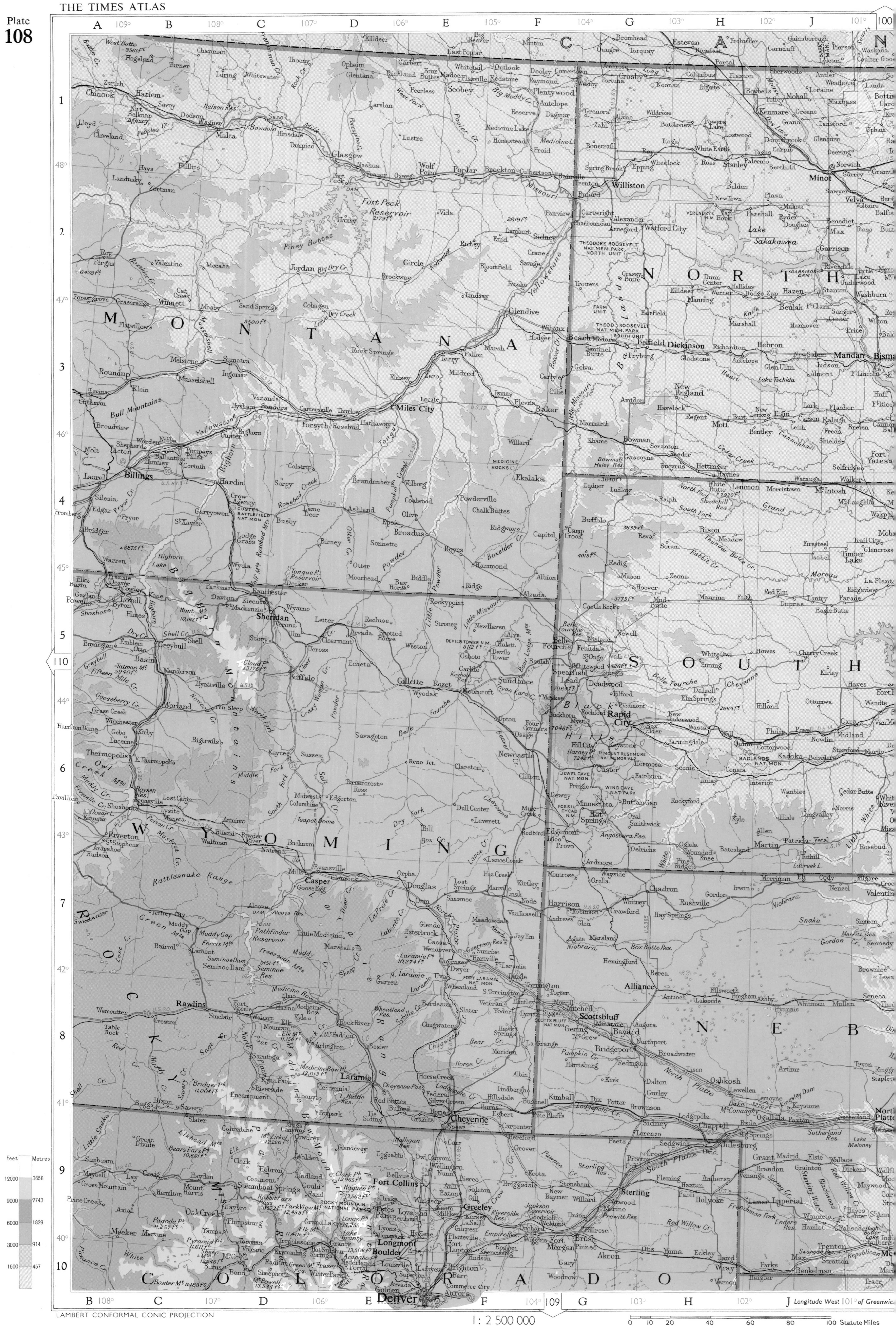

LAMBERT CONFORMAL CONIC PROJECTION

1: 2 500 000

0 10 20 40 60 80 100 Statute Miles

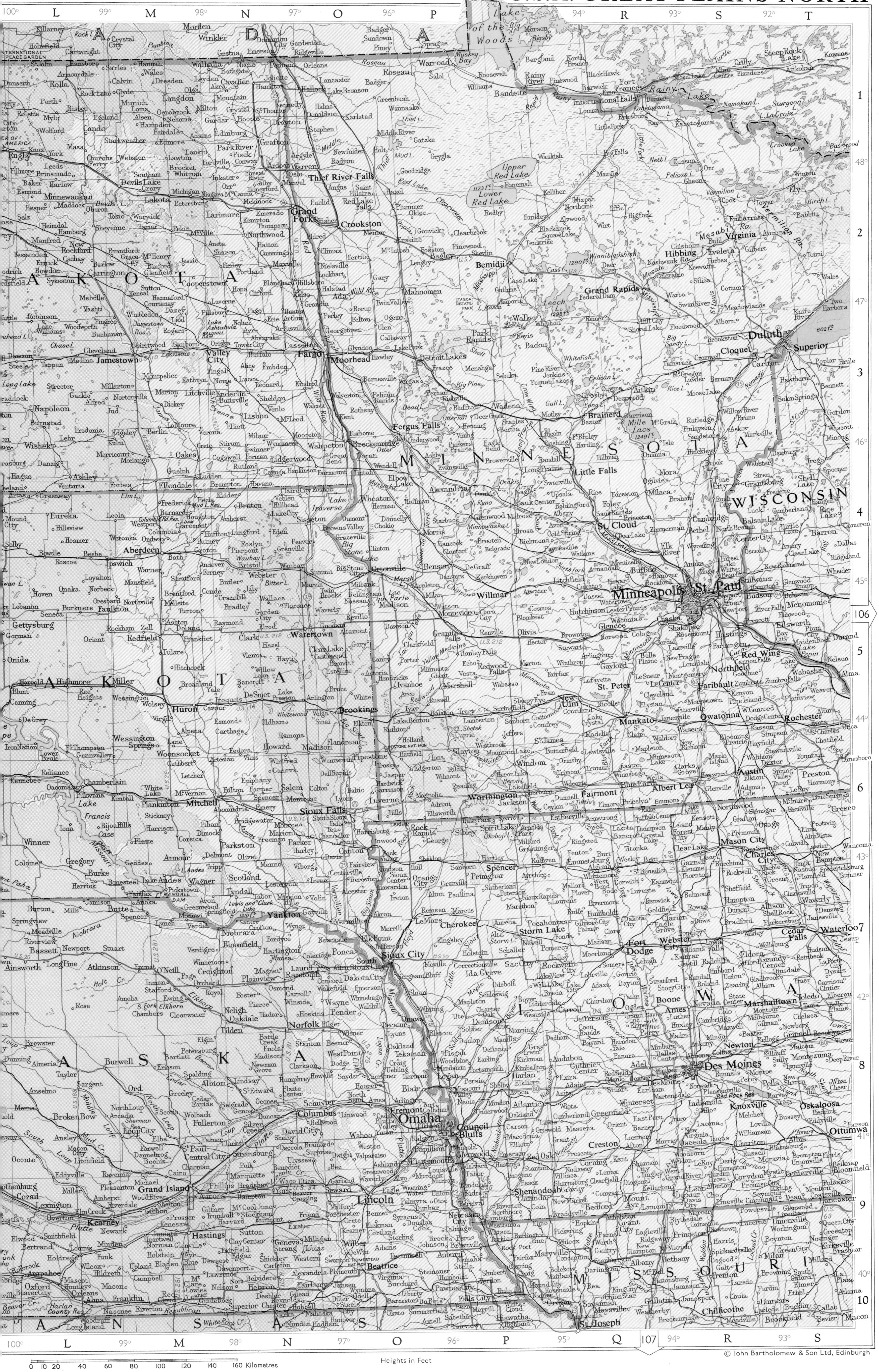

Heights in Feet

0 10 20 40 60 80 100 120 140 160 Kilometres

© John Bartholomew & Son Ltd, Edinburgh

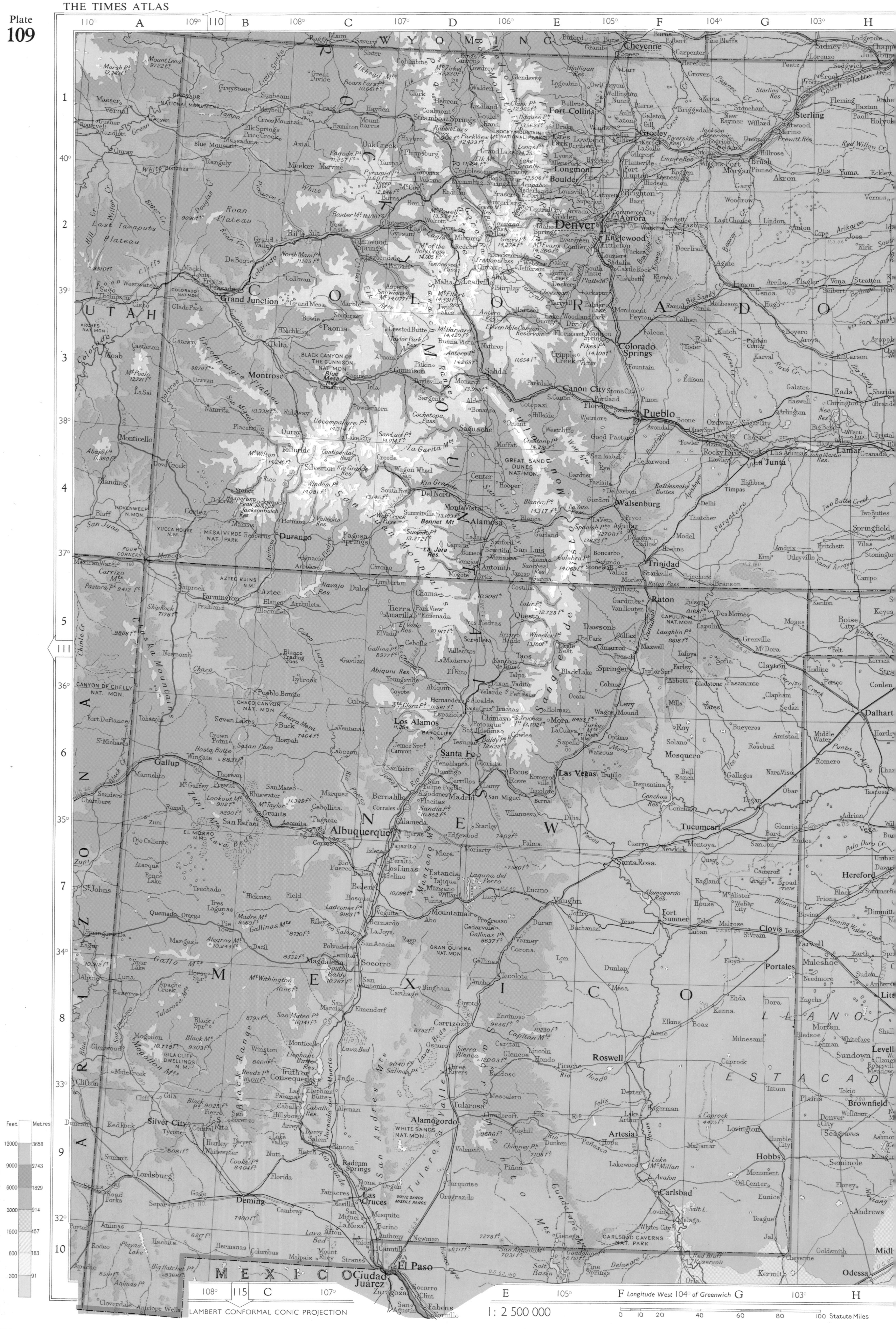
WYOMING
UTAH
COLORADO
NEW MEXICO
ARIZONA
MEXICO
ROCKY MOUNTAINS
LLANO ESTACADO
Denver
Cheyenne
Colorado Springs
Pueblo
Grand Junction
Santa Fe
Albuquerque
El Paso
Ciudad Juárez
Roswell
Amarillo
Lubbock
Feet
Metres
12000 3658
9000 2743
6000 1829
3000 914
1500 457
600 183
300 91
LAMBERT CONFORMAL CONIC PROJECTION
1: 2 500 000
Longitude West 104° of Greenwich
0 10 20 40 60 80 100 Statute Miles

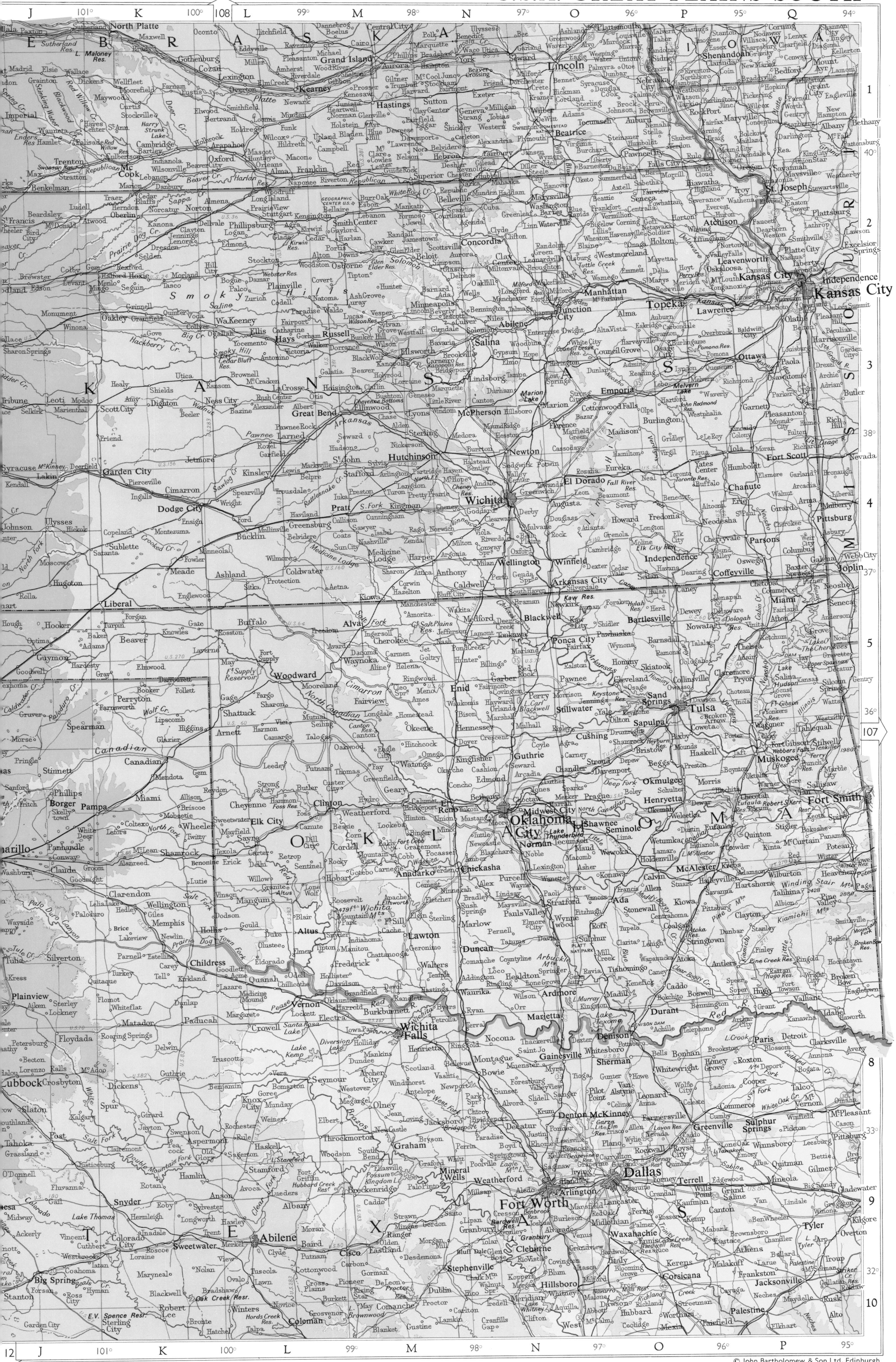

0 10 20 40 60 80 100 120 140 160 Kilometres

Heights in Feet

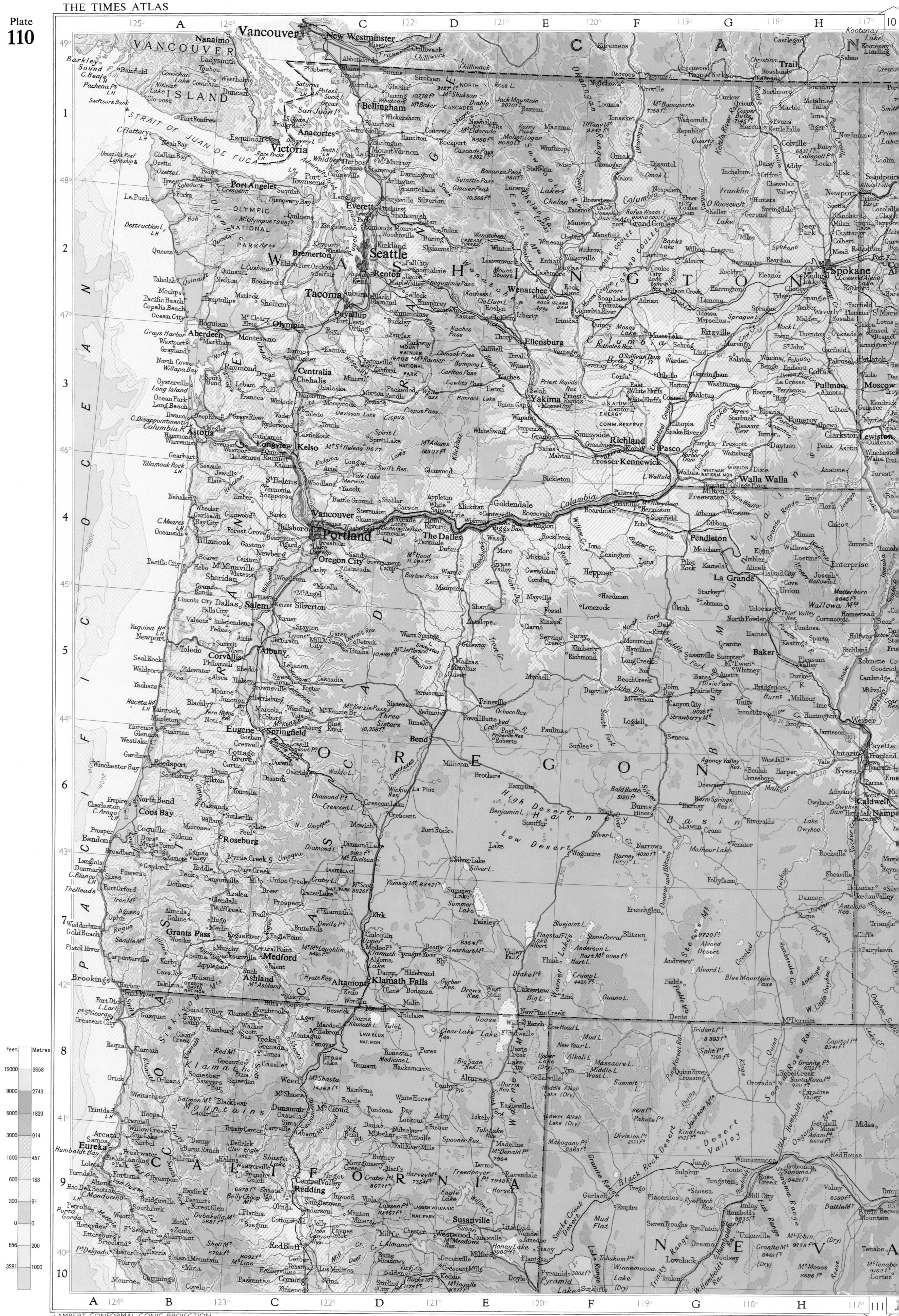

1: 2 500 000

0 10 20 40 60 80 100 Statute Miles

CANADA
WASHINGTON
OREGON
CALIFORNIA
NEVADA
PACIFIC OCEAN
VANCOUVER ISLAND
STRAIT OF JUAN DE FUCA
Vancouver
New Westminster
Nanaimo
Victoria
Bellingham
Everett
Seattle
Tacoma
Olympia
Bremerton
Aberdeen
Port Angeles
Spokane
Yakima
Wenatchee
Ellensburg
Richland
Pasco
Kennewick
Walla Walla
Portland
Salem
Eugene
Springfield
Corvallis
Albany
Astoria
Longview
The Dalles
Pendleton
La Grande
Baker
Bend
Medford
Grants Pass
Ashland
Roseburg
Coos Bay
Klamath Falls
Eureka
Redding
Susanville
Alturas
Winnemucca
Lewiston
Moscow
Pullman
Boise
Caldwell
Nampa
OLYMPIC NATIONAL PARK
MOUNT RAINIER NATIONAL PARK
CRATER LAKE NAT. PARK
LASSEN VOLCANIC NAT. PARK
LAVA BEDS NAT. MON.
CASCADE RANGE
Columbia
Snake
Deschutes
Willamette
Klamath Mountains
Blue Mountains
High Desert
Harney Basin
Black Rock Desert
Steens Mts
Mt Rainier 14,408
Mt Hood 11,245
Mt Shasta 14,162
Mt St Helens 9677
Mt Adams 12,307
Mt Jefferson 10,499
Three Sisters 10,358
Lassen P^k 10,457
Feet
Metres
12000 3658
9000 2743
6000 1829
3000 914
1500 457
600 183
300 91
656 200
3281 1000

U.S.A. PACIFIC COAST NORTH

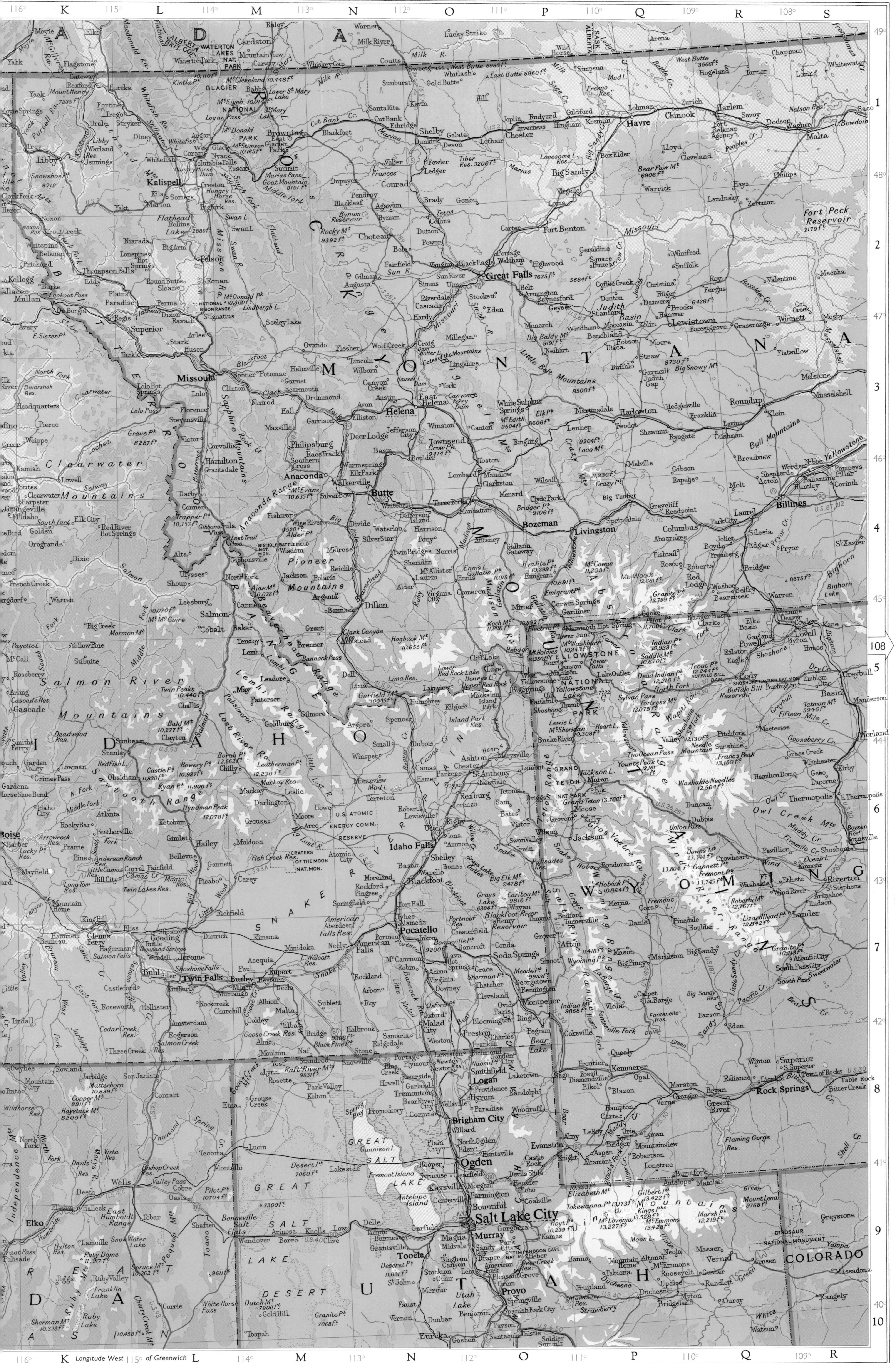

0 10 20 40 60 80 100 120 140 160 Kilometres

LAMBERT CONFORMAL CONIC PROJECTION

1: 2,500,000

0 10 20 40 60 80 100 Statute Miles

GLOSSARY AND ABBREVIATIONS

Language Abbreviations

Afr:	Afrikaans
Alb:	Albanian
Amh:	Amharic
Ar:	Arabic
Ber:	Berber
Bul:	Bulgarian
Bur:	Burmese
Ch:	Chinese
Cz:	Czechoslovakian (Czech and Slovak)
Dan:	Danish
Dut:	Dutch
Est:	Estonian
Fae:	Faeroese
Fin:	Finnish
Fle:	Flemish
Fr:	French
Gae:	Gaelic
Ger:	German
Gr:	Greek
Heb:	Hebrew
Hin:	Hindi
Hun:	Hungarian
I-C:	Indo-Chinese (Annamese, Romanized Thai (Laotian), Khmer)
Ice:	Icelandic
Ir:	Irish
It:	Italian
Jap:	Japanese
Kor:	Korean
Lat:	Latvian
Lit:	Lithuanian
Mal:	Malay
Man:	Manchurian
Mon:	Mongolian
Nor:	Norwegian
Per:	Persian
Pol:	Polish
Por:	Portuguese
Rom:	Romanian
Rus:	Russian*
S-C:	Serbo-Croat
Som:	Somali
Sp:	Spanish
Swe:	Swedish
Th:	Thai (Siamese)
Tib:	Tibetan
Tu:	Turkish
Ur:	Urdu

*Including terms from the Siberian etc. languages

International Glossary

A

á *(Ice)* on, at; river, stream
å *(Dan, Nor, Swe)* brook, river
a'ali *(Ar)* plural of a'lā
āb *(Per)* water
-abad *(Rus-Per)* -town
ābār, âbâr *(Ar)* plural of bīr
'abd *(Ar)* man, servant
aber *(Welsh)* junction (of rivers)
abiaḍ *(Ar)* white
ab/oû, -û, -ū *(Ar)* father of . . . , owner of . . .
abyad, abyadh *(Ar)* white
ada, -sı *(Tu)* island
adalar, -ı *(Tu)* islands
addis *(Amh)* new
adi *(Amh)* tribe, village
adrar *(Ar-Ber)* mountain, mountainous region
afsuitdijk *(Dut)* enclosing dam, barrage
ağaç *(Tu)* tree
ağil *(Tu)* (sheep) pen
agro *(It)* field, arable land
agua *(Por, Sp)* water
agulha *(Por)* needle
aḥmar *(Ar)* red
ahrāmāt *(Ar)* pyramids
aigue *(Fr)* water
aiguille *(Fr)* needle, peak
aïn, 'aïn, 'ain *(Ar)* source, spring
aing *(Bur)* lake
air *(Mal)* water, stream
aiz *(Lat)* behind
ak *(Tu)* white
akbar *(Ar)* great (est)
åker *(Swe)* field, arable land
akmens *(Lat)* stone
ákra, akrotírion *(Gr)* cape
ala- *(Fin)* under, nether
a'lā *(Ar)* upper, high (er), highest
Alb *(Ger)* mountain height
alb *(Rom)* white
alb/o, -a *(Sp)* white
alcalá *(Sp)* castle, fortress
alegre *(Por, Sp)* gay, lively
'ālī *(Ar)* high
alin *(Mon, Man)* mountain-range, mountain
Alm *(Ger)* mountain-pasture
almadén *(Sp)* mine
alt *(Ger)* old, ancient
alt *(Mon)* gold
alt/o, -a *(It, Por, Sp)* high
älv *(Swe)* river
an, am *(Ger)* on, upon
äng *(Swe)* meadow
áno *(Gr)* up, upper
anse *(Fr)* bay
ao *(Ch, Th)* bay, gulf
āq *(Per)* white
aqra' *(Ar)* bald; denuded
aral *(Mon)* island
arāẓi *(Per)* land-surface, lands
arc *(Fr)* arch
arco *(Por, Sp)* arch, ring
arêa, areia *(Por)* sand
arena *(Sp)* sand
arroio *(Pt)* **arroyo** *(Sp)* rivulet
asouad, aswad *(Ar)* black
assîf *(Ar-Ber)* river
asunción *(Sp)* assumption
asundus *(Est)* settlement
au *(Bur)* gulf
-au, Aue *(Ger)* water-meadow
auf *(Ger)* on, upon
aukko *(Fin)* an opening
aul *(Rus)* village
aust *(Nor)* east, eastern
austral *(Sp)* south, southern
austr, austur *(Ice)* east, eastern
áyios *(Gr)* saint, holy
azraq *(Ar)* blue

B

baai *(Afr, Dut)* bay
baatar *(Mon)* hero, heroic
bāb, bâb *(Ar)* gate
băc *(I-C)* north
Bach *(Ger)* brook, stream
bäck *(Swe)* brook, stream
backe *(Swe)* hill
Bad *(Ger)* bad *(Swe)* spa
bādiya, -t *(Ar)* steppe, desert
bæk *(Dan)* brook, stream
bælt *(Dan)* (great, little) belt; strait
bær *(Ice)* town
baga *(Mon)* small; junior
bagno *(Pol)* marsh
bagn/o: -i *(It)* bath; baths
bah/arī, -rī *(Ar)* by the sea; northern
baharu *(Mal)* new
bahçe *(Tu)* garden
bahía *(Sp)* bay
bahr, baḥr *(Ar)* sea; great lake; great river
bahra *(Ar)* lake; swamp
baia *(Por)* stall
baía *(Por)* bay
ba'id *(Ar)* far
baie *(Fr)* bay
bai/e: -a: băile *(Rom)* bath
baile *(Ir)* town, place
bain *(Fr)* bath
baixamar *(Por)* low tide
baix/o, -a *(Sp)* low
baj/o, -a *(Sp)* low
bakke *(Nor)* hill
bala *(Lit)* swamp, marsh
bālā *(Per)* up, upper, upwards
balka *(Rus)* ravine
balneario *(Sp)* bathing place
baltă *(Rom)* bog, pool
ban *(I-C)* village *(Ch)* half
bana *(Jap)* cape, headland
bañado *(Sp)* marshy land
banc *(Fr)* (sand-) bank
banco *(Sp)* (sand-) bank
banda *(It)* band
bandao *(Ch)* peninsula
bandar *(Ar, Mal)* port
bandar *(Per)* port, harbour
bando, (Kor) peninsula
bani *(Ar)* sons of; (plural of ibn)
banja *(S-C)* bath, spa
baño *(Sp)* bath, spa
bansk/ý,-á, -é *(Cz)* mountainous
banya *(Bul)* spa, bath
bara *(Ur)* large
baraj, -ı *(Tu)* dam
barat *(Mal)* west, western
bardhë *(Alb)* white
barra *(Por)* bar; sandbank
barracão *(Por)* weir, dam
baruun *(Mon)* west, right
bas, -se *(Fr)* lower, nether
bassin *(Fr)* basin
batang *(Mal)* river
bāṭin, batn *(Ar)* depression
batu *(Mal)* rock, stone
Baum *(Ger)* tree
bayan *(Mon)* rich
bazar, bāzār *(Rus, Tu, Per; etc.)* bazaar, market
Becken *(Ger)* basin
beek *(Dut)* brook, stream
bëer *(Heb)* well, cistern
bei *(Ger)* at, near *(Ch)* north; behind
beinn: ben *(Gae)* mountain
beit *(Heb)* house
bekasan *(Mal)* ruins
bel/aya, - o, -yy *(Rus)* white
belge *(Fr)* Belgian
bel/i, -a, -e *(S-C)* white
bell/o, -a *(It, Sp)* beautiful
belsö *(Hun)* inner
Belt *(Ger)* strait, belt
běl/y, -á, -é *(Cz)* white
ben *(Ar)* *see* ibn
bender *(Som)* harbour
benî, beni, 'benī *(Ar)* *see* banī
be/o, -a *(S-C)* white
bereg *(Rus)* bank, shore
berëza *(Rus)* birch-tree
berg *(Nor, Swe)* mountain, rock
Berg, -e *(Ger)* mountain, -s
bergskedja *(Swe)* mountain range
bergstopp *(Swe)* mountain
besar *(Mal)* big, great
bey: -ler *(Tu)* sir; lord
biał/y, -a, -o *(Pol)* white
bianc/o, -a *(It)* white
biel/y, -a, -e *(Cz)* white
biên hô *(I-C)* sea; boundary
bilo *(S-C)* ridge, crest
bíl/ý, -á, -é *(Cz)* white
bir, bîr, bîr, bír *(Ar)* well, cistern
birk/ah, -at, -et *(Ar)* lake, bay, marsh
bistrica *(S-C)* rapids
bjerg: -e *(Dan)* mountain; -s
bjeshk/-ë, -a, ët *(Alb)* mountain-range
blaauw *(Afr)* blue
blan/c, -che *(Fr)* white
blanc/o, -a *(Sp)* white
blau *(Ger)* blue
bo *(Swe)* dwelling
bô *(I-C)* mine, water-hole
bo/a, -m *(Por)* good
bobr *(Rus)* beaver
boca *(Por, Sp)* mouth
bocage *(Fr)* grove
boc/ca, -che (tta) *(It)* mouth
Bodden *(Ger)* bay, gulf
Boden *(Ger)* ground, soil
bogaz, -ı *(Tu)* strait
bogdo *(Mon)* elevated, holy
bogen *(Nor)* bay
bois *(Fr)* wood(s)
boloto *(Rus)* marsh, bog
bol'sh/aya, -oy, -oye *(Rus)* big
bo/m, -a *(Por)* good
bong *(Kor)* mountain
bor *(Mon)* grey
bor *(Rus)* pine-wood, pine-forest
bór *(Pol)* forest
Börde *(Ger)* flat, fertile tract of land
bor/dj, -g -j *(Ar)* *see* burj
boreal *(Sp)* north, northern
borg *(Dan, Nor, Swe)* castle
borgo *(It)* market-town, suburb
-born *(Ger)* spring, well
bos *(Afr, Dut)* bush, wood
bosank/i, -a *(S-C)* Bosnian
bosch *(Dut)* bush
bosquet *(Fr)* grove, thicket
botn *(Nor)* **botten** *(Swe)* valley floor
bou, bou *(Ar)* father
bouche *(Fr)* mouth, estuary
bouḥaira, -t, bouḥeir/a, -á, -et *(Ar)* *see* buḥayrah
bourg *(Fr)* town
boven *(Afr)* over, above
brae *(Nor)* *see* **bre**
brána *(Cz)* gate
branc/o, -a *(Por)* white
braţ *(Rom)* arm
bratt *(Nor)* steep, rugged
brav/o, -a *(Sp)* brave; intractable, savage
bre *(Nor)* glacer
bredning *(Dan)* bay
breg *(S-C)* hill
breit *(Ger)* broad
bro *(Dan, Nor, Swe)* bridge
brod *(Rus, Cz)* ford
bron *(Afr)* well, spring
brønn *(Nor)* well, spring
bru *(Nor)* **brú** *(Ice)* bridge
Bruch *(Ger)* cleft; peat water; quarry
Brücke *(Ger)* bridge
brug *(Afr)* bridge
brugge *(Fle)* bridge
bruk *(Nor, Swe)* factory, works
brunn *(Swe)* well, spring
brygga *(Swe)* wharf, quay, bridge
brygge *(Nor)* wharf, quay
bū, bü *(Ar)* short for abū, (father)
Buche *(Ger)* beech
Bucht *(Ger)* bay
buen/o, -a *(Sp)* good
bugor *(Rus)* mound, hill
bugt *(Dan)* bay
buḥayr/ah, at: buḥeir/a, -at *(Ar)* lake; marsh
Bühel, Bühl *(Ger)* wooden hill
bukhta *(Rus)* bay
bukit *(Mal)* hill, height
bukt *(Nor, Swe)* bay
buku *(Mal)* hill, mountain
bula/g: -k *(Mon, Rus)* spring
būr *(Ar)* port
burā *(Bur)* pagoda
bur'at *(Ar)* bay
burg *(Ar)* *see* burj
Burg *(Ger)* castle
burj *(Ar)* tower, fort; cliff; bluff
bur/un, -nu *(Tu)* nose; point
busk *(Nor)* bush
butte *(Fr)* knoll
büyük *(Tu)* big
by *(Dan, Nor, Swe)* town
bygd *(Nor, Swe)* parish

C

cabeço *(Por)* summit
cabeza *(Sp)* head; summit
cabo *(Por, Sp)* cape, headland
cachoeira *(Por)* waterfall, rapids
cald, -a *(Rom)* hot, warm
caliente *(Sp)* warm, hot; fiery
câmp *(Rom)* **campo** *(Por, Sp)* field
campagna *(It)* countryside, campaign
campagne *(Fr)* countryside, campaign
cañada *(Sp)* dell; ravine; cattle path
cañadón *(Sp)* deep gorge
cano *(Sp)* frosty, hoary
cañon *(Sp)* canyon
cao *(I-C)* high, great
cap *(Fr)* **capo** *(It)* cape, headland
cap, -ul *(Rom)* cape, headland
carrera *(Sp)* highroad; avenue; racetrack
carretera *(Sp)* highroad
casa *(It, Por, Sp)* house
castel, -lo *(It)* castle
cast/ello *(Por)* **-illo** *(Sp)* castle
castro *(Sp)* hill with ruined castle
çatal *(Tu)* fork
catarata *(Sp)* cataract, waterfall
çay, -ı *(Tu)* brook, stream, river
cayo *(Sp)* rock, islet
cerro *(Sp)* hill, peak
červen/ý, -á, -é *(Cz)* red
česk/ý, -á, -é *(Cz)* Czech
chaco *(Sp)* jungle region
chāī *(Per)* brook, stream
chaîne *(Fr)* chain
châm *(Ar)* north, northern
changcheng *(Ch)* great(long)wall
chapada *(Por)* high ground in the prairies
chatal *(Bul)* fork
chapelle *(Fr)* chapel
charqī *(Ar)* east, eastern
chaung *(Bur)* stream, river
chebir *(Ar)* big
chedo *(sor)* archipelago
chen *(Ch)* market town
chenal *(Fr)* channel (of a river)
cheng *(Ch)* wall, town
chërn/aya-, -oye, -yy *(Rus)* black
chernozem *(Rus)* black soil
chhe, -n *(Tib)* big
chhu, -bo *(Tib)* river
chhung *(Tib)* small
ch'i *(Ch)* *see* qi
chia *(Ch)* *see* jia
chiang *(Ch)* *see* jiang
chiang *(Th)* town
chiao *(Ch)* *see* jiao
ch'iao *(Ch)* *see* qiao
chien *(Ch)* *see* jian
ch'ien *(Ch)* *see* qian
ch'ih *(Ch)* *see* qi
chink *(Rus)* escarpment
ch'ŏn *(Kor)* river
chong *(Th)* bay
chott, choṭṭ *(Ar)* salt lake, swamp
chou *(Ch)* *see* zhou
chuang *(Ch)* *see* zhuang
chung *(Ch)* *see* zhong
ch'ün-tao *(Ch)* *see* qundao
chute (d'eau) *(Fr)* fall (waterfall)
ciems *(Lat)* village, hamlet
čiern/y, -a, -e *(Cz)* black
cima *(It)* **cime** *(Fr)* summit
cîmp *(Rom)* field
città *(It)* town, city
ciudad *(Sp)* town, city
clar/o, -a *(Sp, Por)* clear, light
col *(Fr)* high pass
col, -le *(It)* pass
collado *(Sp)* hill, saddle
collina *(It)* **colline** *(Fr)* hill
colorad/o, -a *(Sp)* red, coloured
combe *(Fr)* small valley
conca *(It)* hollow
cordillera *(Sp)* mountain chain
corne *(Fr)* peak
corno *(It)* peak
corte *(Sp)* courtyard
cort/o, -a *(It)* short
costa *(Sp)* coast, shore, beach
côte *(Fr)* coast; slope
coteau *(Fr)* small hill, slope
court, -e *(Fr)* short
coxilha *(Por)* mountain pasture
crkva *(S-C)* church
crn/i, -a, -o *(S-C)* black
croce *(It)* **croix** *(Fr)* cross
cruz *(Por)* cross
csatorna *(Hun)* canal, sewer
cu'a *(I-C)* gate; mouth (river)
cuchillas *(Sp)* chain of mountains
cuenca *(Sp)* deep valley; (river) basin
cuesta *(Sp)* rising ground; mesa
cueva *(Sp)* cave, grotto
cu lao *(I-C)* island; delta island
culme *(Rom)* ridge; crest
czarn/y, -a *(Pol)* black

D

da *(Ch)* great, greater
Dach *(Ger)* roof, ridge
dacha *(Rus)* country house
dağ, -ı: dağlar, -ı *(Tu)* mountain, mountain range
dāgh *(Per)* mountain
daḥr, -at *(Ar)* hill, island
dake *(Jap)* peak
dakhan *(Ur)* south, southern
dal *(Afr, Dan, Nor, Swe)* valley
dalay *(Mon)* sea, large lake; great
dalek/o, iy, etc. *(Rus)* far, distant
dalir: dalur *(Ice)* valley (-s)
dal'n/e, -iy etc. *(Rus)* far, distant
dan *(Kor)* cape
danau, dano *(Mal)* lake
danche *(Kor)* place
dao *(I-C)* island; *(Ch)* route; paddy
dar, dār, dâr *(Ar)* house; region
darreh *(Per)* valley
dar'yā *(Rus)* **daryā** *(Per)* sea, ocean, river
daryācheh *(Per)* lake, mere
dasht *(Per, Ur)* desert
date *(Jap)* palace, guest-house
daung *(Bur)* *see* taung
davaan *(Mon)* pass
davs *(Mon)* salt
dawb *(Ar)* well
dayr *(Ar)* monastery; depression; hill
deir *(Ar)* *see* dayr
deniz, -i *(Tu)* sea
dere, -si *(Tu)* valley, stream
derevo *(Rus)* tree, wood
dhar *(Ar)* house, region
diep *(Dut)* deep
dios *(Sp)* god
dīp *(Ur)* island
dizh *(Per)* fort, fortress
djebel *(Ar)* mountain
djezîr/a, -et: djezir *(Ar)* island; -s
djibâl *(Ar)* mountain range
dług/i, -a *(Pol)* long
do *(Kor)* island
dō *(Jap)* island
doi *(Th)* mountain
dolg/o, -iy, -aya *(Rus)* long
dolina *(Rus)* valley
doln/a, -i *(Bul)* lower
doln/í, -á, -é *(Cz)* **dolny** *(Pol)* **doln/ý, -á, -é** *(Cz)* lower, nether
dolok *(Mal)* mountain
domb *(Hun)* hill
domingo *(Sp)* Sunday
don *(Sp)* gentleman
dong *(Ch)* east, winter; cave, ravine
dong *(Kor)* village, town
dong *(Th)* deep jungle
dông *(I-C)* east, eastern
donj/i, -a, -e *(S-C)* lower, nether
Dorf *(Ger)* village
doroga *(Rus)* road
dorozhnyy *(Rus)* adj.-of the road
dorp *(Afr)* village
drif *(Afr)* ford
dronning *(Nor)* queen
dsong *(Tib)* castle, fort, mansion
dub *(Rus)* oak-tree
dug/i, -a, -o *(S-C)* long
dulaan *(Mon)* warm
dund *(Mon)* middle, central
duoddar *(Nor)* plateau
duwayr *(Ar)* hill
dvor *(Rus,* etc.*)* courtyard
dvorets *(Rus)* palace
dyb *(Dan)* deep

E

e *(Ch)* high, commanding
Ebene *(Ger)* plain
ed *(Swe)* tongue of land
edehin *(Ar-Ber)* sandy plain
ees- *(Est)* fore-
église *(Fr)* church
eid *(Nor)* isthmus
eiland, -en *(Afr, Dut)* island; -s
'ein *(Ar, Heb)* source
Eis *(Ger)* ice
Eisen *(Ger)* iron
Eisenbahn *(Ger)* railroad
Eisenhütte *(Ger)* iron foundry
elv *(Nor)* river
embalse *(Sp)* reservoir
embouchure *(Fr)* mouth, estuary
eparkhía *(Gr)* eparchy (admin.unit)
Erde *(Ger)* earth, soil
erdő *(Hun)* wood, forest
erípion *(Gr)* ruin
'erg *(Ar)* desert with dunes
Erz *(Ger)* ore
eşi k, -ği *(Tu)* threshold, sill
eski *(Tu)* old, ancient
español, -a *(Sp)* Spanish
estacada *(Sp)* stockade, palisade
estación *(Sp)* station
estado *(Por, Sp)* state
estero *(Sp)* inlet, estuary; swamp
estrada *(Por)* highway, street
estrecho *(Sp)* strait **estreito** *(Por)* strait
étang *(Fr)* pond
ey *(Ice)* island
eyri *(Ice)* sandy (shingly) bank
eystur *(Fae)* east, eastern
ežeras *(Lat)* lake
ezero *(Bul)* lake
ezers *(Lat)* lake

F

Fähre *(Ger)* ferry
farsh *(Ar)* plateau
fazenda *(Por)* farm
fehér *(Hun)* white
Fels *(Ger)* rock
felső *(Hun)* upper
feng *(Ch)* mountain peak
Festung *(Ger)* fortress
fier *(Rom)* iron
figueira *(Por)* fig-tree
fiume *(It)* river
fjall *(Ice)* mountain, hill
fjäll *(Swe)* mountain
fjärd *(Swe)* fjord
fjeld *(Dan)* mountain, hill, rock
fjeld, fjell *(Nor)* mountain, rock
fjoll *(Ice)* plural of fjall

Glossary—continued

fjord (Dan, Nor, Swe) fjord
fjördhur (Fae, Ice) fjord
fleuve (Fr) large river
fljót (Ice) large river
flod (Dan, Swe) river
flói (Ice) bay, marshy country
Fluss (Ger) river
fő- (Hun) main, head, chief
foce (It) mouth (of a river)
föld (Hun) earth, land
folyó (Hun) river, stream
fonn (Nor) glacier
fontaine (Fr) fountain, spring
fontein (Afr) fountain, spring
Förde (Ger) inlet, creek
forêt (Fr) forest
fors (Swe) waterfall
Forst (Ger) forest
fortín (Sp) small fort
fos, -s (Ice, Nor) waterfall
fossé (Fr) ditch
fourche (Fr) fork
foz (Por) mouth
fran c, -che (Fr) free
franc o, -a (Sp) free
frei (Ger) free
freixo (Por) ash-tree
frontera (Sp) frontier
frio (Por) cold
frío (Sp) cold
fu (Ch) palace, prefecture
fuente (Sp) source, well
fuerte (Sp) sort
fürdő (Hun) bath(s), spa
Fürst (Ger) prince
Furt, Fürth (Ger) ford
futuro (Por) future
fyr (Nor) fire; lighthouse

G

ganale (Amh) waterway, river
gang (Kor) river, bay
gang, gangri (Tib) glacier
gap (Kor) cape
gård (Nor, Swe) farm
gardaneh (Per) pass
Garten (Ger) garden
gata (Jap) bay, lake
Gau (Ger) district
gavan' (Rus) harbour
gave (Fr) torrent (in Pyrenees)
gawa (Jap) see kawa
gebel (Ar) mountain
gebergte (Afr, Dut) mountain range
Gebiet (Ger) district, region
Gebirge (Ger) mountains
geçit (Tu) pass
gedida (Ar) new
Gegend (Ger) region
gemeente (Afr) parish
Gemeinde (Ger) community, parish
gezâ'ir, gezir (Ar) islands
gezîra, -t, gezîret (Ar) island
ghubba, -t (Ar) bay, cove
ghur/d, -ud (Ar) dune, -s
giang (I-C) river
Gipfel (Ger) peak, summit
gji (Alb) bay
gjol (Alb) pond
gjytet (Alb) city, town
glavn/o, -yy (Rus) chief (adj.)
Gletscher (Ger) glacier
glina (Rus) clay
glubok/o, iy etc. (Rus) deep
gobi (Mon) desert
gol (Mon) river
göl (Swe) pond, pool
göl, -ü (Tu) lake
golfe (Fr) golfo (It, Sp) bay, gulf
golova (Rus) head
gora (Bul) forest
gora (Rus, S-C) mountain
gór/a: -ka (Pol) mountain; hill
gorica (S-C) hill
gorje (S-C) mountain range
gorn/o, -yy (Rus) mountain; -ous
gorod: -ok (Rus) town
-gorsk (Rus) mining town
gory (Rus) góry (Pol) mountains
gosudarstvo (Rus) state
goulet (Fr) narrow entrance
gouw, -en (Fle) district, province
Graben (Ger) trench, ditch
grad (Bul, Rus, S-C) town, castle
Grat (Ger) crest, ridge
greben' (Rus) mountain ridge; comb
grense (Nor) border, frontier
Grenze (Ger) border, frontier
gród (Pol) castle, town
grøn (Dan) green
groot (Afr) large
gross (Ger) great, big
gross o, -a (Por) big
Grube (Ger) pit, mine
grün (Ger) green
Grund (Ger) ground, valley
grunn, -e (Nor) ground; shallows, mud flat
Gruppe (Ger) group
gruppo (It) group
gruv/a (Swe) -e (Nor) pit, mine
gryada (Rus) ridge
gryaz (Rus) mud
guan (Ch) pass
guba (Rus) bay
guchi (Jap) strait, channel
gudār (Per) ford
gundo (Kor) island group
guntō (Jap) island group
gunung (Mal) mountain
gyaung (Bur) river; stream

H

ḥad, -d (Ar) peak
hadabat (Ar) plateau
haehyŏp (Kor) strait
Hafen (Ger) harbour, port
Haff (Ger) bay
hafn ar, -ir (Ice) see höfn
hai (I-C, Ch) sea
Hain (Ger) wood, coppice
Halbinsel (Ger) peninsula
hals (Dan, Nor) neck, isthmus
halv/ø (Dan) -øy (Nor) peninsula
hama (Jap) beach
ḥamād, hamada, hamád/a, -et, hammāda (Ar) stony desert
hamina (Swe) harbour, port
hammar: hammer (Swe, Dan, Nor) cliff
hamn (Nor, Swe) harbour
hāmūn (Per) plain, fenland
hang (Kor) harbour, port
hantō (Jap) peninsula
har (Mon) black
har (Heb) mountain (range)
Hardt (Ger) wooded hills
harju (Fin) ridge
has y, -i, ḥassî (Ar) waterhole
hát (Hun) ridge
haug (Nor) hill
haur, hawr (Ar) lake, marsh
Haus, -hausen (Ger) house
hav (Dan, Nor, Swe) sea
havn (Dan, Fae, Nor) harbour
havza, -si (Tu) basin
ház: háza (Hun) house
he (Ch) river
hed (Swe) heath
hede (Dan, Nor) heath
hegy/-ség (Hun) mountain; mountainous country
hei (Nor) heath, moor
Heide (Ger) heath, moor
heilig (Ger) holy
heim (Nor) -heim (Ger) homestead
hely (Hun) place
hem (Swe) home
her/ad, -red: -adh (Nor; Ice) district
hermos/o, -a (Sp) beautiful
hısar, hisar (Tu) castle
hka (Bur) river
ho (Kor) river (Ch) see he
hø (Nor) peak
hoch (Ger) high
hoë (Afr) high, height
hoek (Afr, Dut) cape
Hof, -hofen, -höfen (Ger) farm, court (yard)
höfdhi (Ice) headland
höfn (Ice) harbour, port
hög (Swe) high; height
høg: -d (Nor) high; height
höh (Mon) blue
Höhe, Hohen- (Ger) height
høj (Dan) high; height
holm (Dan) -e (Nor, Swe) islet
holt (Nor) wood, grove
Holz (Ger) wood
hon (I-C) island
hoog (Dut) high
hoorn (Afr) corner
hôpital (Fr) hospital
hōr (Ar) see haur, hawr
hora (Cz) mountain
Horn (Ger) peak, summit
horn (Nor, Swe) peak, summit
hornatina (Cz) mountainous country
horn/í, -ý (Cz) upper
hory (Cz) mountain; forest
hosu (Kor) lake
hot (Mon) town
hoved (Dan) head
høy (Nor) high
hoyno (Mon) north, northern
hrad (Cz) castle, fortress
hradiště (Cz) citadel, ft. town
hsi (Ch) see xi
hsia (Ch) see xia
hsiang (Ch) see xiang
hsiao (Ch) see xiao
hsien (Ch) see xian
hsü (Ch) see xu
hu (Ch) lake
huai (Th) small stream, creek; marsh
huang (Ch) yellow; imperial
hudag (Mon) well
Hügel (Ger) hill
huis (Dut) house
hükûmet (Tu) government
hult (Swe) copse
hüree (Mon) large monastery
hus (Dan, Ger, Nor, Swe) -husen (Ger) house
huta (Pol) foundry
hutag (Mon) happiness
hutagt (Mon) holy
Hutte (Ger) hut; foundry
huvud (Swe) head
huys (Afr) house
hver, -ar (Ice) hot spring(s)
hvid (Dan), hvita (Ice) white
hytta (Swe) foundry

I

i (Rus, etc.) and
ibn (Ar) son, descendant
idehan (Ar-Ber) sandy plain
igr/ós, -á, -ón (Gr) wet
île (Fr) island
ilha (Por) island
iméni (Rus) in the name of
in, im (Ger) in (Bur) lake
indre, inn/-, -er- (Nor) inner
inférieur, -e (Fr) lower, nether
Insel: -n (Ger) island; -s
insulă (Rom) island
ipsoma (Gr) high ground
ipsos (Gr) height; altitude
iqlīm (Ar) district
ırma/k, -gı (Tu) large river
'irq (Ar) sand-dune; dune area
is (Nor, Swe) is (Ice) ice
ishi (Jap) stone, rock
ishull (Alb) island
isla (Sp) isle (Fr) island
iso- (Fin) large-: great-
isola: -e (It) island; -s
issyk (Rus) warm
istoch/en, -ni, na, no (Bul) eastern
itä (Fin) east, eastern
iwa (Jap) mountain, island

J

ja (Fin) and
jabal (Ar, Per) mountain, mt. range
jang (Tib) north, northern
janūb (Ar) south, south wind
jard in (Fr) -ín (Sp) garden
jarn (Swe) iron
järv (Swe, Est) lake
jauns (Lat) new
jaure (Swe) lake
javrre (Nor) lake
jazero (Cz) lake
jaz/īra, -ā'ir (Ar) island; -s
jazir/eh, at (Per) island
jbel, jebel (Ar) mountain; -s
jedo (Kor) archipelago
jezero (S-C, Cz) jezioro (Pol) lake
jia (Ch) beautiful
jian (Ch) pointed; torrent
jiang (Ch) river
jiao (Ch) suburbs; reef; point
jib/āl, -âl (Ar) mountain range
jima (Jap) island, sandbank
jõgi (Est) river
jok (Nor) joki (Fin) river
jøkel (Nor) glacier
jökull (Ice) glacier
jomo (Tib) goddess
jord (Nor) earth
juoda (Lit) black
jūra (Lit) sea
jūŗas licis (Lat) bay, gulf
jūŗmala (Lat) beach, shore
južn/i, -a (S-C) south, southern

K

kâ, kâs (I-C) neck; island
kaap (Afr, Dut) cape
kabir (Ar) great, big
kafr (Ar) village, hamlet
kai (Jap) sea (Gr) and
kaikyō (Jap) strait
kajse (Swe) mountain range
kala (Fin) fish
kalan (Bur) mountain range
kale (Tu) fort
kali (Mal) large river, canal
kalli- (Gr) beautiful
kallio (Fin) rock, cliff
kaln as: -ynas (Lit) mountain; -s
kaln/s: -i (Lat) mountain; -s
kal ós, -í, -ón (Gr) good, well
kamen' (Rus) stone
kamenn o, -yy (Rus) stony
Kamm (Ger) crest, ridge
kampoeng, kampung (Mal) village
kamysh (Rus) reed
kanat (Rus) see qanat (Per)
kanava (Fin, Rus) canal
kang (Kor) river, bay
kangas (Fin) heath, moor
Kap (Ger) cape
Kapelle (Ger) chapel
kapp (Nor) cape
kar (Tib) white
kara (Rus, Tu) black, dark
karang (Mal) reef, coral reef
kari (Fin) rock-reef, shoal
kärr (Swe) morass
kastër (Alb) fortress
kástron (Gr) castle, fortress
kátō (Gr) lower, down
kaupstadhur (Ice) market-town
kaupunki (Fin) town
kavir (Per) salt desert
kawa (Japan) river, stream
kébir, keb/ir, -ir (Ar) great, big
kĕfar (Heb) village, hamlet
kënet/ë, -a (Alb) bog, marsh
kep, -i (Alb) cape, headland
kepulauan (Mal) archipelago
kerk (Fin) church
kero (Fin) gorge
keskus (Fin) middle, central
ketjil (Mal) small, little
kha (Tib) mouth, valley
khalā (Ar) empty land, desert
khal/idj, -ig, ig: -ij (Ar; Per) bay, gulf, river, canal
khamba (Tib) source, spring
khan (Per) inn; lord
khang (Tib) house, settlement
khao (Th) mountain, hill; rice
khar (Tib) castle
khashm (Ar) nose, cape, mouth
khaur, khawr (Ar) ravine, water-course; creek, inlet
khersónisos (Gr) peninsula
khetr (Th) boundary
khirb/a, -á, -ah, -at (Ar) ruin(s)
khlon (Th) mud, clay
khọ, khọt (Th) isthmus
khōr, khūr (Per) creek, estuary
khōr (Ar) see khaur, khawr
khóra (Gr) country, main town of an island
khrebet (Rus) mountain range
khutor (Rus) farm, farmhouse
kiang (Ch) see jian; jiang
Kirche: -kirchen (Ger) church
kirk (Tu) forty
kirke (Dan, Nor) kirkja (Ice) kirkko (Fin) church
kis (Hun) small
kivi (Fin) stone
kızıl (Tu) kizyl (Rus) red
Klamm (Ger) ravine
Klause (Ger) defile
klein (Afr, Ger) small
klint (Dan) cliff
klit (Dan) dune
klong (Th) canal, creek
kloof (Afr) gorge
Kloster (Ger) kloster (Dan, Swe) monastery
ko (Jap) lake, bay (Th) island
kō (Jap) high
Kofel, Kog(e)l (Ger) dome-shaped hill-top
koh (I-C) island
koinótis (Gr) commune
koivu (Fin) birch-tree
kok (Lat) tree
kokkyo (Jap) frontier, boundary
kol' (Rus) lake
kolodets (Rus) well
kólpos (Gr) gulf
kompong (I-C) river-bank, landing-place
komuni (Alb) place
kong (Dan, Nor) king
König (Ger) king
Koog (Ger) polder
kop (Afr) hill
Kopf (Ger) head
köping (Swe) market-town
koppar (Swe) copper
köprü (Tu) bridge
körfez, -i (Tu) gulf, bay
korpi (Fin) wilderness, fen
kosa (Rus) spit of land
koseki (Jap) ruins
koski (Fin) cataract, rapids
kosui (Jap) lake
kota, kotō, kuta (Mal) fortress, fortified town
kotlina (Pol, Cz) basin, depression
kou (Ch) pass; harbour, valley
köy (Tu) village
kraal (Afr) native village
kraj (Cz, Pol, S-C) border, region
králov/y, -á, -é (Cz) royal
krasn/o, -iy etc. (Rus) red
krásn/y, -á, -é (Cz) beautiful
kray (Rus) border, region
Kreis (Ger) circle, district
krepost' (Rus) fortress, citadel
Kreuz (Ger) cross
kriv/o, -oy (Rus) bent, curved
królewsk/i, -a (Pol) royal
kroon (Afr) crown
krug (Rus) circle
krut/o, -oy (Rus) steep
kuala (Mal) estuary, confluence
kuan (Ch) see guan
kubrā (Ar) see akbar
kubri (Ar) bridge, viaduct, ferry
küçük (Tu) small
kuduk (Rus) well, spring
kūh (Per) mountain
kul' (Rus) lake
küla (Est) village
kule (Tu) tower, peak
kulle (Swe) hill
külső (Hun) outer
kum (Tu) sand
kum (Rus) sandy desert
kundo (Kor) island group
Kuppe (Ger) hilltop
kurgan (Rus) mound, barrow
kuru (Fin) gorge
kuru (Tu) dry
kust (Dut) coast
Küste (Ger) coast
kutal (Per) col, steep hill
kuusi (Fin) spruce, fir
kuznets (Rus) blacksmith
kwe (Bur) bay
kyi (Bur) great, big
kylä (Fin) village
kyō (Jap) waterway
kyrka (Swe) church
kyrkje (Nor) church
kyûn: -myã, -zu (Bur) island; -s
kyzyl (Rus) red

L

laakso (Fin) valley
lääni (Fin) province
labuan (Mal) anchorage, harbour
lac (Fr) lake (Rom) lake
låg (Nor) lower
lago (It, Por, Sp) lake
lagoa (Por) lagoon
laguna (Sp) lagoon, lake
lágy (Hun) soft
laht (Est) lahti (Fij) bay, gulf
laja (Por) rock ledge
lakóhely (Hun) place
lakhti (Rus) see lahti (Fin)
lam (Mon) lama (Tib) road
lam (Th) river-bed
lampi (Fin) pond, pool
län (Swe) district
Land (Ger) land, province
lande (Fr) sandy moor, heath
landgewinning (Dut) reclaimed land
lang (Dan, Ger, Nor) long, far
länsi (Fin) west, western
las (Pol) wood, forest
latse (Tib) cairn
laut (Mal) sea; north
ledovityy (Rus) ice-covered
léja (Lat) valley
les (Rus, Cz) wood, forest
lès (Fr) near, beside
lesisty (Pol) -y (Rus) wooded
lesn/o, -oy etc. (Rus) adj. of a wood
leso- (Rus) wood-
lez (Fr) near
lha: -khang (Tib) god; temple
lho (Tib) south, southern
līcis (Lat) bay, gulf
lido (It) shore
liels (Lat) large
lieu (Fr) place
ligeni (Alb) see liqen, -i
lilla (Swe) small
lille (Dan, Nor) small
liman (Rus) bay, gulf
liman, -ı (Tu) harbour, port
límnı (Gr) lake, lagoon
ling (Tib) island; monastery
ling (Ch) ice; mountain range
linn, -ad (Est) town, city
lipa (Rus) lime-tree, linden
liqen, -i (Alb) lake
litla (Fae) small
llano (Sp) level, flat; prairie
loma (Sp) hill, knoll
lõuna (Est) south
löv: løv (Swe; Dan) foliage
lug (Rus) meadow
lugar (Sp) place
lule (Swe) east, eastern
lund (Dan, Nor, Swe) grove
luokte (Swe) bay, cove
luoto (Fin) crag, rocky islet
lyng (Dan) heath

M

maa (Est, Fin) land, earth, country
maanmittaus (Fin) surveying, geodesy
maantie (Fin) road, highway
machi (Jap) town
macizo (Sp) massif
madh, madhë (Alb) big, large, great
mad/ina, -ina, -îná, -înah (Ar) town, city
mae (Jap) front
mae nam (Th) river (mother of waters)
mäestik (Est) mountain range
magas (Hun) high; great
maggiore (It) greater
mägi (Est) mountain
magura (Cz) mountain
magyar (Hun) Hungarian
maḥaṭṭa-h: -t (Ar) railway station, police post
maidān (Ar, Per) square, open space
maior (Por) greater
maison (Fr) house
maíz (Sp) maize
maj/ë, -a (Alb) summit, peak
maja (Est) house
majrá (Ar) waterway
makhta (Ar) see maqta'
mäki (Fin) hill, hillside, slope
mal (Alb) mountain, -s
mal/o, -a (It, Sp) bad, evil
mal/i, -a, -o (S-C); -ý, -á, -é (Cz); -o, -yy etc. (Rus) small
mamarr (Ar) passage, ford, pass
man (Kor) bay
manāqir (Ar) hill
manastir (Bul, S-C) monastery
mansap (Tu) estuary
mänty (Fin) pine
mäntymesta (Fin) pine-forest
manzil (Ar) camping-place
maqām (Ar) place, hallowed place
maqta' (Ar) ford, ferry, quarry
mar, -e (Por, Sp, It) sea
mar (Tib) red
marais (Fr) swamp, marsh
marché (Fr) market
mare (Rom) large, old; sea
marina (It) coast, maritime
maritime (Fr) sea-coast
marittim/o, -a (It) maritime
marj (Ar) meadow
Mark (Ger) marches, borderland
mark (Dan, Nor, Swe) land
markaz (Ar) administrative district; centre
marrku (Fin-Swe) region
marsá (Ar) anchorage, fort
Marsch (Ger) marsh, fen
maru (Jap) mountain

Glossary–continued

más *(Sp)* more
maşabb *(Ar)* river mouth
mashra' *(Ar)* watering place; crossroads
mashriq *(Ar, Per)* the east
masīl *(Ar)* watercourse
masjid *(Ar)* (small) mosque
masna'a *(Ar)* cistern, reservoir
matla' *(Ar)* height, ascent; pass
matsu *(Jap)* pine; end
mayor *(Sp)* larger, higher; major
maža *(Lit)* small
mazār *(Per)* tomb, shrine
mazs *(Lat)* small
mdo *(Tib)* border region
mé *(I-C)* mother
mechra' *(Ar)* *see* mashra'
medved' *(Rus)* bear
medvezh/iy *(Rus)* of a bear (adj)
Meer *(Ger, Afr, Dut)* lake, sea
megál/o, os, -i *(Gr)* big, great
még/as, -áli, -a *(Gr)* big, great
meidān *(Ar, Per)* *see* maidān
men *(Ch)* door, gate
me nam *(I-C)* *see* mae nam
menor *(Por, Sp)* smaller, minor
menzel *(Ar)* *see* manzil
mer *(Fr)* sea
mercado *(Sp, Por)* market
merelaht *(Est)* bay, gulf
meri *(Fin, Est)* sea, ocean
merkez *(Tu)* administrative centre
mes/a, -eta *(Sp)* tableland, mesa
meshra' *(Ar)* *see* mashra'
més/os, -a, -on *(Gr)* middle
mesto *(Rus, S-C)* place
město *(Cz)* town
mets, -ad *(Est)* wood, forest
mezi *(Cz)* between
mezö *(Hun)* field, land, plain
mežs *(Lat)* forest, wood
mezzo *(It)* middle, mid-
mi *(Ch)* rice; secret
miao *(Ch)* temple, shrine; fair
miasto *(Pol)* town
mic *(Rum)* small
michi *(Jap)* way
midān *(Ar)* *see* maidān
midi *(Fr)* midday, the South
midori *(Jap)* green
miestas *(Lit)* city, town
mikr/ós, -á, -ón, -í *(Gr)* small
min *(Ch)* the people
minā *(Ar)* port, anchorage
minh *(Ar)* clear, bright; immense
misaki *(Jap)* cape
míti *(Gr)* nose, cape
Mittel-, Mitten- *(Ger)* middle, central
mjesto *(S-C)* place
mlad/ý, -á, -é *(Cz)* young
mlin *(C-S)* mill
mnam: m'nom *(I-C)* mountain
mo *(Nor, Swe)* heath
mocsár *(Hun)* marsh
moer *(Dut)* moss
mokh *(Rus)* moss
mokr/o, -yy *(Rus)* wet, moist
monasterio *(Sp)* monastery
monastyr' *(Rus)* monastery
mönh *(Mon)* eternal
moni *(Gr)* monastery
mont *(Fr)* mountain
montagna *(It)* mountain
montagne *(Fr)* mountain
monta/ña *(Sp)* mountain
montanha *(Por)* mountain
monte *(It, Por, Sp)* mountain
montée *(Fr)* an up-slope
Moor *(Ger)* bog, swamp, moor
Moos *(Ger)* moss, bog
more *(Bul, S-C, Rus)* sea
mori *(Jap)* wood, forest
mörk *(Ice)* forest
morne *(Fr)* hill; gloomy
mörön *(Mon)* river
morro *(Por)* hill, quarry
-morsk *(Rus)* by the sea
mort, -e *(Fr)* dead, standing water
morze *(Pol)* sea
mose *(Dan)* bog, moor
most *(Bul, Rus)* bridge
moto *(Jap)* source, beginning
mouillage *(Fr)* anchorage
moûlây *(Ar)* noble
moutaouassiţ *(Ar)* middle
moûtiers *(Fr)* monastery
moyen *(Fr)* middle, mid-
mu'addiya *(Ar)* ferry
muang *(Th)* kingdom, province, town
muang, muong *(I-C)* canal; town
mu'askar *(Ar)* military camp
muban *(Th)* place
mudīriya *(Ar)* province
muḥāfazat *(Ar)* governate
Mühle, -mühl *(Ger)* mill
mui *(Ar)* cape
munkhafaḍ *(Ar)* depression
munti: -i *(Rum)* mountain; -s
muotka *(Fin)* promontory
mur *(Fr)* wall
mura *(Jap)* village
murābit *(Ar)* saint's tomb
muro *(Sp)* wall
murr *(Ar)* bitter
must: -a *(Est, Fin)* black
mutawassiţ *(Ar)* middle
muthallat *(Ar)* rail junction
muttaḥida *(Ar)* united
myit *(Bur)* river
myitwanyā *(Bur)* mouths
myo, myong *(Bur)* town
myothit *(Bur)* new town
myr *(Nor, Swe)* **myri** *(Ice)* moor, swamp
mýri *(Ice)* bog
mys *(Rus)* cape

N

na *(Bul, Rus, S-C)* on
nabk, a *(Ar)* small dune
naberezhnaya *(Rus)* quay
nacional *(Por, Sp)* national
nad *(Pol, Cz, Rus)* over, above
nada *(Jap)* sea, bay, channel
naes *(Dan)* promontory
nafūd *(Ar)* sandy desert soil
nag *(Tib)* black
nagorn/o, -yy *(Rus)* upland, mountainous
nagor'ye *(Rus)* uplands, highland
nagy *(Hun, Rom)* big, tall; great
nahiya *(Ar)* environs, district
nahr *(Ar)* river, stream
naikai *(Jap)* sea
nakh/īl, -la, *(Ar)* date-palm (s)
nakhon *(Th)* town
nam *(I-C, Kor)* south, southern
nam *(Th)* river
nam *(Bur, I-C)* water
namakzār *(Per)* salt desert
nam mae *(Th)* river
nan *(Ch)* south, southern
nanbu *(Jap)* South
nao *(Ch)* mud
naqb *(Ar)* pass
nariyn *(Mon)* thin, narrow
narod *(Rus)* people
näs *(Swe)* promontory, cape
naşb *(Ar)* hill, mountain
Natsional'nyy *(Rus)* national
nau- *(Lit)* **nau** *(Ur)* new
nauja *(Lit)* new
nava *(Sp)* hollow, plain surrounded by mountains
naviglio *(It)* navigable canal
navolok *(Rus)* cape, headland
nawa *(Ur)* new
neam *(Rum)* tribe, clan
neder *(Dut, Swe)* lower
ned/er, -re, ner *(Nor)* lower, nether
neem *(Est)* cape, promontory
neft' *(Rus)* petroleum
negr/o, -a *(Por, Sp)* black
negri *(Mal)* state
negru *(Rom)* black
neh/ir, -ri *(Tu)* river
Nehrung *(Ger)* spit of land
nei *(Ch)* inner, within
nei-ao *(Ch)* inland port
ne/ós, -a, -on *(Gr)* new
neró *(Gr)* water
nes *(Ice, Nor)* promontory, cape
neu *(Ger)* new
neu/f, -ve *(Fr)* new
neva *(Fin)* treeless marsh or fen
nevad/o, -a *(Sp)* snowy
névé *(Fr)* half-solidified snow
nez *(Fr)* nose
nguyen *(I-C)* plain
ni *(Kor)* village, town
niang *(Ch)* lady, mother
Nieder- *(Ger)* Lower Nether
niemi *(Fin)* cape, point
nieu *(Afr, Fle)* new
nieuw *(Dut)* new
nij *(Dut)* new
nisáki *(Gr)* islet
nishi *(Jap)* west
nisi *(Gr)* island
nisis *(Gr)* islet
nisk/iy, etc. *(Rus)* low
nísos: nísoi *(Gr)* island; islands
niu *(Ch)* ox
niva *(Fin)* stream, waterfall
niva *(Bul, Cz, Rus)* cornfield, arable land
nizh/en, -ni *(Bul)* lower
nizhn/e, iy *(Rus)* lower
nižina *(Bul)* lowland
nížina *(Cz)* depression, lowland
nizmennost' *(Rus)* lowland
nižn/ý, -á, -é *(Cz)* lower, nether
njargga *(Nor)* peninsula
nodo *(It)* knot
nogueira *(Sp)* walnut tree
noir, -e *(Fr)* black
nōjō *(Jap)* farm
nojon *(Mon)* prince
nong *(Th)* swamp, lake
noor *(Fin-Swe)* north, northern
noord *(Dut)* north
noordelijk *(Dut)* northern
nord *(Dan, Fr)* north, northern
Nord(er)- *(Ger)* north, northern
nord, -er, -re *(Nor)* northern
nördlich *(Ger)* northern
nord-, norr, -a *(Swe)* north
norhur *(Fae, Ice)* northern
nordre, norre *(Dan)* north
norte *(Por, Sp)* north, northern
nos *(Bul, Rus)* cape
nót/ios, -ia, -ion *(Gr)* southern
nou *(Rom)* new
nouv/eau, -elle *(Fr)* new
nov/a, -i, -o *(It)* new
nov/i: -, -a, -o *(Bul, S-C)* new
nov/o, -a *(Por)* new
nov/o, yy *(Rus)* new
nov/ý, -á, -é *(Cz)* new
now o, -y, -a, -e *(Pol)* new
nü *(Ch)* women, female
nudo *(It, Sp)* naked; bare; (Sp) knot
nuev/o, -a *(Sp)* new
nui *(I-C)* mountain
num *(Rus)* upper
numa *(Jap)* lake, pond
numata *(Jap)* marsh land
nummi *(Fin)* moor
nuov/o, -a *(It)* new
nuruu *(Mon)* ridge, mountain range
nusa *(Mal)* island
nut *(Nor)* mountain summit
nuur *(Mon)* lake
nuwaybi' *(Ar)* spring
ny, nye, nyt *(Dan, Nor, Swe)* new
nyár *(Hun)* summer
nyugat *(Hun)* west

O

o *(Ch)* *see* e
ō *(Jap)* great
ö, öar *(Swe)* island;-s
o, ob *(Rus)* water
oba *(Tu)* felt tent *(Rus)* mound
Ober- *(Ger)* upper, higher
oblas, oblast; oblast' *(Cz; Bul, Rus)* province, region
öböl *(Hun)* bay
oboo *(Mon)* cairn
öbör *(Mon)* inner, bosom
obshtina *(Bul)* parish, commune
óbygdh *(Ice)* unpeopled track
och *(Swe)* and
odde *(Dan, Nor)* point, headland
öde *(Ger, Swe)* waste, deserted
og *(Dan, Nor)* and
ogla *(Ar)* *see* 'uqla
oja *(Est)* brook, stream
ojo *(Sp)* eye; spring
oka *(Jap)* land, coast
okean *(Rus)* ocean
oki *(Jap)* bay
okoliya *(Bul)* district, commune
okrug *(Rus)* district
oktyabr' *(Rus)* October
öls *(Mon)* sand
oltre *(It)* over, above
ömnö *(Mon)* south, southern
onder *(Dut)* under
öndör *(Mon)* high, tall
-oog *(Ger)* island
oord *(Dut)* place, region
oos *(Afr)* east, eastern
oost, -er, -elijk *(Dut)* east, eastern easterly
'oqlet *(Ar)* *see* 'uqla
or *(Fr)* gold
oraş *(Rom)* town
orekh *(Rus)* nut
óri *(Gr)* mountains
oriental, -e *(Rom, Sp, Fr)* east, eastern
orman *(Bul, Tu)* forest
órmos *(Gr)* bay
oro *(Sp)* gold
oron *(Mon)* country, region, tract
óros *(Gr)* mountain
ország *(Hun)* country, realm
Ort *(Ger)* place, settlement
ortolana *(It)* market-garden
oseaan *(Afr)* ocean
Ost- *(Ger)* east, eastern
öst, -er, -ra *(Swe)* **øst, -er, ra** *(Dan, Nor)* east, eastern
ostān *(Per)* province
östlich *(Ger)* eastern
ostrov; -a *(Bul, Cz, Rus)* island; -s
ostrów *(Pol)* island
otok *(S-C)* island
ouâdi, oued, ouèd *(Ar)* dry river-bed
ouden- *(Fle)* old
oûl/âd, -ed *(Ar)* tribe, children of-
oum *(Ar)* mother
ouzan *(Per)* river
ova, -sı *(Tu)* plain lowland
over *(Dut)* above, over, upper
over-, ov er, -re *(Nor)* upper
över-, övre *(Swe)* upper
oy: -ar *(Fae)* island; -s
øy: -er *(Nor)* island; -s
Ozean *(Ger)* ocean
ozek *(Rus)* stream
ozer o: -a *(Rus)* lake; -s

P

pää *(Fin)* head, chief-
-pää *(Fin)* head, point
padang *(Mal)* plain; moorland
padi *(Mal)* paddy
padina *(Bul)* slope, declivity
pădure *(Rom)* wood, forest
paese *(It)* country, village
paikka *(Fin)* place, locality
pais *(Por)* land
pal *(Hin)* dam, embankment
palai/ós, -á, -ón } *(Gr)* old
pali/ós, -á -ó }
palazzo *(It)* palace
palo *(Fin)* fire
pamyatnik *(Rus)* monument
pan *(Ch)* *see* ban
pandjang *(Mal)* length; long, tall
panstwo *(Pol)* state
pantai *(Mal)* beach, sea-shore
pantanal *(Por, Sp)* swampy ground
pantano *(Sp)* swamp; reservoir
pan tao *(Ch)* *see* bandao
parada *(Por, Sp)* **paradero** *(Sp)* stopping place, halt
parbat *(Ur)* mountain
parc *(Fr)* park
pardo *(Por)* grey
paroisse *(Fr)* parish
parque *(Sp)* park, zoo
pas *(Dan, Dut)* defile
pas *(Fr, Rom)* channel; defile
paşa *(Tu)* pasha, general
pasar *(Mal, Per)* market place
pasir *(Mal)* sand, sandbank
paso *(Sp)* pass, strait
Pass *(Ger)* pass
passage *(Fr)* ferry
passo *(It)* pass
pathar *(Hin)* plateau
pat/na, -tan a, -am *(Hin)* small village
pazar *(S-C, Tu)* market
pea- *(Est)* main
pedra *(Por)* stone
pei *(Ch)* *see* bei
pegunungan *(Mal)* mt. range
pélagos *(Gr)* sea
pellg *(Alb)* bay, swamp
peña *(Sp)* cliff, rock
penisola *(It)* peninsula
perä- *(Fin)* further
peralta *(Sp)* rise, bank
pereval *(Rus)* mountain pass
perevoz *(Rus)* ferry, crossing
pertuis *(Fr)* strait
perv/o, -yy *(Rus)* first
peščara *(S-C)* sandy ground, sandpit
peshchan/o, -yy *(Rus)* sandy
pes/ok: -ki *(Rus)* sand; -s
petit, -e *(Fr)* little
petra *(Gr)* rock, stone
Pforte *(Ger)* gate
phanom, phnom *(Th, I-C)* mountain
phnom *(I-C)* hill, mountain
phrobrang *(Tib)* mansion, palace
phu *(I-C)* prefecture; mountain
phum *(I-C)* settlement
phum *(Th)* bush
piatră *(Rom)* stone, rock
pic *(Fr, Sp)* peak, summit
picacho *(Sp)* sharp peak, summit
pico *(Sp)* peak, high mountain
pieni *(Fin)* small
pierre *(Fr)* stone
pieve *(It)* parish
pik *(Rus)* peak
pilis *(Lit)* castle
pilós *(Gr)* clay
pils *(Lat)* castle
pinar *(Tu)* running spring
ping *(Ch)* peace, tranquillity
pinggir *(Mal)* edge, boundary
pírgos *(Gr)* tower
pitäjä *(Fin)* parish
pitkä *(Fin)* long, large
pizzo *(It)* peak, summit
pla, plé, pleû, plo, plou, plu *(Fr)* village, parish
plaas *(Afr)* farm
plaat *(Dut)* sand-bank, shoal, flat
plaats *(Dut)* place
plage *(Fr)* beach
plaine *(Fr)* plain
plana *(S-C, Sp)* plain
planalto *(Por)* plateau
planicie *(Sp)* plain
planina *(Bul, S-C)* mountain; mountain-range
plass *(Nor)* place, spot
plateau *(Fr)* plateau
plat/ís, -ia, -i *(Gr)* broad
plato *(Afr, Bul, Rus)* plateau
Platte *(Ger)* plateau, ledge, plain
playa *(Sp)* beach
playí, playiá *(Gr)* side, slope
plaza *(Sp)* market-place, square
plošina *(Cz)* tableland
plosk/o, iy *(Rus)* flat
ploskogor'ye *(Rus)* plateau
po *(Ch)* white; hundred
poartă *(Rom)* gate
pochva *(Bul, Rus)* soil, earth
pod *(Rom)* bridge
pod *(Rus, Cz)* under, sub-
podiş, -ul *(Rom)* plateau
pogost *(Rus)* churchyard
pohja *(Fin)* base, ground; north
pohoří, pohorie *(Cz)* mountain range
pointe *(Fr)* promontory, point
pokhya *(Rus)* north, northern
pokrajina *(S-C)* admin. unit
Pol *(Ger)* pole
pol'ana *(Cz)* upland plain
pole *(Bul, Pol, Rus)* field
pólis *(Gr)* city, town
pol/ís, -lí, -í *(Gr)* many
politeia *(Gr)* state
poljana *(S-C)* fields, plain
polje *(S-C)* field
poluostrov *(Rus)* peninsula
pólwysep *(Pol)* peninsula
polyana *(Rus)* glade, clearing
polyarn/o: -yy, etc. *(Rus)* polar
pont *(Fr)* bridge
pont *(Dut)* ferry-boat, flying bridge
ponta *(Por)* point, cape
ponte *(I, Por)* bridge
póntos *(Gr)* sea
poolsaar *(Est)* peninsula
poort *(Afr)* passage gate,
pōōsa *(Est)* bush
porogi *(Rus)* rapids
póros *(Gr)* food
port *(Fr, Rus)* harbour
porte *(Fr)* gate
porthmíon, porthmós *(Gr)* narrows of strait; ferryboat
porţi/-le *(Rom)* gate, entrance
portillo *(Sp)* gap; *(S. America)* pass
porto *(I, Por, Sp)* port
posad *(Rus)* suburb
Posëlok *(Rus)* (worker's) settlement
potámi, potamós *(Gr)* river
potok *(Rus, Cz)* stream, current
poyas *(Rus)* belt, zone
pradesh *(Hin)* state
praia *(Por)* beach, shore
prairie *(Fr)* meadow, grassland
pré *(Fr)* meadow
prêk *(I-C)* river
près *(Fr)* near
presqu'île *(Fr)* peninsula
pri *(Rus)* near, **cis-** (opp. to trans-)
prigorod *(Rus)* suburb
prins: -esse *(Nor)* prince; princess
prinses *(Dut)* princess
pristan' *(Rus)* landing stage
prohod *(Bul)* pass
proseka *(Bul, Rus)* cutting through forest
provliv *(Rus)* strait
protok *(Bul)* strait, sound, narrow
průchod, průchody *(Cz)* passage, arcade
prud *(Rus)* pond
průsek, průseky *(Cz)* forest clearing
průsmyk *(Cz)* pass
przełęcz *(Pol)* pass
przesmyk *(Pol)* isthmus
przylądek *(Pol)* cape
psil/ós, -í, -ó; psíloma *(Gr)* high, tall; high ground
Pu *(Ch)* tributary, reach of a river; universal
pu *(I-C)* mountain
pueblo *(Sp)* town, village
puente *(Sp)* bridge
puerta *(Sp)* gate; narrow mountain pass
puerto *(Sp)* harbour
püha *(Est)* holy, sacred
puits *(Fr)* well
puk *(Kor)* north, northern
pulau *(Mal)* island
pulau-pulau *(Mal)* islands
puna *(Sp)* desert plateau (in the Andes)
pundjung *(Mal)* mountain
punta *(It, Sp)* point, promontory, cape
pura *(Bur)* town
pustynya *(Rus)* desert
puszcza *(Pol)* wilderness
puszta *(Hun)* desert; steppe; cattle farm
putih *(Mal)* white
putra *(Hin)* son
puu *(Fin)* tree, wood
puy *(Fr)* peak
pyhä *(Fin)* holy, sacred
pyinnei *(Bur)* state
pynt *(Nor)* promontory

Q

qafr *(Ar)* desert
qal/a', -'at *(Ar)* castle, fortress; prominent peak
qal'/ah-'ajāt *(Per)* castle, fortress
qanā, qanât, qanāt *(Ar)* canal
qanāt *(Per)* underground conduit
qāra *(Ar)* isolated mountain, small plateau(s)
qara *(Per)* black
qar'ā *(Ar)* *see* aqra'
qar'a *(Ar)* fertile depression
qārah, qarat *(Ar)* hill, mound
qasaba, qaşb/á, -ah *(Ar)* citadel
qarya *(Ar)* village
qaşr *(Ar, Per)* fort, castle
qattār/a *(Ar)* well with only trickle of water
qi *(Ch)* mountain, stream, pool; banner (admin. div., Inner Mongolia)
qian *(Ch)* thousand; black; heaven; male
qiao *(Ch)* bridge; lofty
qibl/a, -ī *(Ar)* towards Mecca
qirba, -t *(Ar)* ruin, ruins
qiryat *(Heb)* town
qizil *(Per)* red
qşar, qsoûr *(Ar)* palace, fortified settlement; hill
quai *(Fr)* quay
quan *(Ch)* stream
Quelle *(Ger)* spring, well
qūm *(Per)* sand
qundao *(Ch)* archipelago
quraiyāt *(Ar)* diminutive of qarya
qūrkāneh *(Per)* arsenal
qytet *(Alb)* city, town

R

rada *(It, Sp)* roadstead
rade *(Fr)* roadstead
radja *(Mal)* king, ruler
rags *(Lat)* cape, headland
rainha *(Por)* queen
raja *(Fin)* boundary
raja *(Mal)* magnificent; public
raml, ramla, -t *(Ar)* sand tract
ran, rann *(Hin)* swampy region
rancho *(Sp)* ranch
ranee, rani *(Hin)* queen
ranta *(Fin)* beach, shore, bank

Glossary—continued

rantja *(Mal)* marsh, swamp
rās, rás, râs, râss *(Per, Ar)* cape
rāṣhṭra *(Hin, Ur)* state
ras/o, -a *(Por)* flat
rata *(Mal)* flatness
ratna *(Hin)* jewel
raudha *(Ar)* meadow, garden
raunioalue *(Fin)* ruins
rauta *(Fin)* iron
ravan *(S-C)* plain
rayon *(Rus)* district, region
real *(Por, Sp)* royal
reale, regio *(It)* royal
rece *(Rom)* cold
rechnoy *(Rus)* of a river, riparian
reggio *(It)* royal
régi *(Hun)* old, ancient
região *(Por)* region
région *(Fr)* region
regiune *(Rom)* region
rei *(Por)* king
reich; Reich *(Ger)* rich; realm
reina *(Sp)* queen
reka *(Bul, Rus)* river
řeka *(S-C, Cz)* river
relangyā, reletkyā *(Bur)* strait
repede *(Rom)* dam
represa *(Por)* dam
Reservat *(Ger)* reserve
réservation *(Fr)* reserve
reshteh *(Per)* mountain (range)
respublika *(Rus)* republic
rét *(Hun)* meadow
rettō *(Jap)* group of islands
rev *(Nor, Swe)* reef, cliff
rey *(Sp)* king
ri *(Tib)* mountain
ri *(Kor)* village ,town
ria *(Por)* **ria** *(Sp)* mouth of river; drowned valley
ribeira *(Por)* meadow, low moist ground, *(Sp)* stream, river
ribeirão *(Por)* great river
ribeiro *(Por)* stream
ribo *(Tib)* mountain
ric/o, -a *(Por, Sp)* rich
Ried *(Ger)* reed, swampy ground
rijeka *(S-C)* river
rik, -e *(Nor)* rich, realm
ring *(Tib)* long
rio *(Por)* **río** *(Sp)* river
ripa *(It)* bank, shore
rîu *(Rom)* river
riva *(It)* bank
rivier *(Afr)* river
riviera *(It)* strip of land between hills and sea; river
rivière *(Fr)* river
rječica *(S-C)* small river
roc, rocher *(Fr)* rock, cliff
roca *(Por, Sp)* rock, cliff
rocca *(It)* rock; tower
rød *(Dan)* red
rodnik *(Rus)* spring of water
rog *(Rus)* horn
roi *(Fr)* king
roj/o, -a *(Sp)* red, reddish yellow
rong *(Tib)* valley, gorge
rosa *(It)* rose
roshcha *(Rus)* grove, copse
ross/o, -a *(It)* red
rouge *(Fr)* red
rov *(Rus)* ditch, trench
rova *(Fin)* brook
rovine *(It)* ruins
rreth *(Alb)* region; district
rt *(S-C)* cape, point, spur
ru *(Tib)* peak, summit
řubezh *(Rus)* border
Rücken *(Ger)* **ridge**
rūd *(Per)* river
ruda *(Rus)* ore
rūdkhāneh *(Per)* river-bed, river
rudohoři, rudohorie *(Cz)* ore-bearing mountains
ryba *(Rus)* fish
rybachiy *(Rus)* fishing; fisherman
rybnyy *(Rus)* fishing (adj.)
rynok *(Rus)* market
rzeka *(Pol)* river

S

sa *(Tib)* earth, land
saar *(Est)* island
saari *(Fin)* island
sabkha *(Ar)* salt flats
sable *(Fr)* sand
sad *(Rus)* garden
sadd *(Ar)* dam; mountain slope
sag *(Nor)* saw(mill)
såg *(Swe)* saw(mill)
sagar/a *(Hin, Ur)* lake
saghir *(Ar)* small
saha *(Fin)* saw
sahara *(Ar)* *see* sahra
sahel, sāhil *(Ar)* coastal plain
ṣaḥr/ā', -á, -â, *(Ar)* desert
said, sa'id, sa'īd, sa'id *(Ar)* Upper Egypt; highland
saivva *(Nor, Lappish)* fresh water (lake)
saiyidī *(Ar)* my lord
saki *(Jap)* cape
sala *(Lat, Lit)* island
salada *(Sp)* salt-lake
salar *(Sp)* salt-pan
salina *(Sp)* salt-pan
salmi *(Fin)* strait, sound
salt *(Dan, Nor, Swe)* salt
salto *(Por, Sp)* waterfall
Salz *(Ger)* salt
sammyaku *(Jap)* mountain range
samundar *(Hin)* sea
san *(Jap, Kor)* hill, mountain
san/to, -ta *(It, Sp, Por)* saint
Sankt *(Ger, Swe)* saint
sanmaek *(Kor)* mountain range
são *(Por)* saint
sap *(I-C)* (of water) sweet, fresh
sar *(Per)* head
sarai *(Per)* **sarāy,** *(Hin)* house, inn
saray *(Rus)* shed, barn
sărat *(Rom)* salty
ṣarh/īr, -rî *(Ar)* *see* saghīr
sasso *(It)* stone
sat/ -ul *(Rom)* village
säter *(Swe)* mountain pasture
sayhan *(Mon)* pretty, good
sayr *(Mon)* dry river-bed
Schloss *(Ger)* castle, mansion
Schlucht *(Ger)* gorge, ravine
schnee *(Ger)* snow
schön *(Ger)* beautiful
Schutzgebiet *(Ger)* reserve
schwarz *(Ger)* black
Schwelle *(Ger)* sill; shelf
scoglio *(It)* rock, reef
se *(Jap)* rapids; shallows
se; sé *(I-C)* river
seb/kha, -kra *(Ar)* salt-flats
sec/o, -a *(Sp)* dry
See *(Ger)* lake; sea
şehir *(Tu)* town
sela *(Mal)* pass
selat *(Mal)* strait
selatan *(Mal)* south, southern
selkä *(Fin)* back, ridge; open water
sélloma *(Gr)* saddle (mountain)
selo *(Rus, S-C)* village
selva *(Sp)* wood, forest
sembilan *(Mal)* mine
sen *(Jap)* mountain
Senke *(Ger)* depression
seno *(Sp)* hollow, bay
şerhir *(Ar)* *see* şaghir
serir *(Ar)* desert of small stones
serra *(Por)* mountain range
serra, sierra *(It)* mountain range
serran/ia *(Por)* **-ía** *(Sp)* mountain-range, mountainous, country
serrilhada *(Por)* serrated, jagged
seter *(Nor)* mountain pasture
sever/o, -nyy *(Rus)* north
sfânt, sfînt *(Rom)* saint, holy
sha *(Ch)* sand, gravel
shahr *(Per)* city, town
sha'ib *(Ar)* road; ravine
shamāl *(Ar)* north
shamo *(Ch)* desert
shan *(Ch)* hill, mountain, -range; -pass
shankou *(Ch)* mountain pass
shanmo *(Ch)* mountain range
shar *(Mon)* yellow
sharm *(Ar)* anchorage; bay
sharq *(Ar)* east
shaṭṭ *(Ar)* large river; bank
shën *(Alb)* Saint
shi *(Jap)* city
shibin *(Ar)* village, settlement
shih *(Ch)* market; stone, municipality
shima *(Jap)* island
shimāl/-iya *(Ar)* northern
shirok/o, -iy *(Rus)* broad, wide
shotō *(Jap)* group of islands
shū *(Jap)* administrative unit
shūr *(Per)* dried salt deposit
si *(Ch)* Buddhist temple; monastery
sidi, sīdi, sidî, sídi *(Ar)* *see* saiyidi
sierra *(Sp)* mountain range
síkság *(Hun)* plain, lowland
sindh *(Ur)* sea; river
sin/e, iy *(Rus)* (dark) blue
sin/gh, -h *(Hin)* lion
sinn *(Ar)* tooth, summit
sint *(Afr, Fle, Dut)* saint
situ *(Mal)* lake
sjø *(Nor)* *(Swe)* lake, sea
skaer *(Dan)* shelf, small rocky island, skerry
skag/-, -i *(Ice)* peninsula
skála, skály *(Cz)* rock, cliff
skála *(Gr)* quay; stairway
sker *(Ice)* rock
skíti *(Gr)* hermitage
skog *(Nor, Swe)* **skóg** *(Ice)* wood, forest
skov *(Dan)* wood, forest
slätt *(Swe)* plain
slava *(Rus)* fame, renown
slette *(Nor)* plain
sloboda *(Rus)* suburb, large village
slot, -t; -t *(Nor; Swe)* castle, mansion
små *(Dan, Swe)* small
smal *(Nor)* narrow
sne, snø *(Nor)* snow
sneeu *(Afr)* snow
snjór *(Ice)* snow
sø *(Dan, Nor)* lake
söd/er, -ra *(Swe)* south, southern
sogn *(Nor)* parish
sol' *(Rus)* salt
sola *(Fin)* pass
solonchak *(Rus)* salt lake; salt marsh
sommet *(Fr)* summit, peak
sønd/er, -re *(Dan)* southern
søndre, sør *(Nor)* south, southern
sông *(I-C)* river
sŏng *(Kor)* castle, mansion
soo *(Est)* swamp
sopka *(Rus)* mound, small volcano
sopra *(It)* upper
sør *(Nor)* south, southern
sort *(Nor)* black
sosna *(Rus)* pine
soto *(Sp)* grove, undergrowth
sotto *(It)* lower
sotsialisticheskiy *(Rus)* socialist
soûq *(Ar)* *see* sūq
sous *(Fr)* under
sovetskiy *(Rus)* soviet
soyuz *(Rus)* union
spång *(Swe)* landing-stage
spíti *(Gr)* house
Spitze *(Ger)* peak
spruit *(Afr)* stream, brook
srê *(I-C)* field
sredn/a *(Bul)* middle
sredn/e, iy *(Rus)* mid-; middle
śred/n/i, -e, -o *(Pol)* middle
sremot *(I-C)* sea
Staat *(Ger)* state
stad *(Afr, Nor, Swe)* town
stadhur *(Ice)* town
Stadt *(Ger)* town
stam *(Nor)* main
Stapi *(Ice)* cliff
star/o, -a *(Bul)* old
star/o, -yy *(Rus)* old
star/y, -a, -e: -ý, -á, -é *(Pol; Cz)* old
stat *(Dan, Nor, Swe)* **-o** *(It)* state
Stausee *(Ger)* reservoir
staw *(Pol)* pond
sted *(Dan, Nor)* place
Stein *(Ger, Nor, Swe)* stone
sten *(Swe)* cliff
stenón *(Gr)* pass, strait
step' *(Rus)* steppe
sti *(Nor)* path
štít *(Cz)* peak, signal
Stock *(Ger)* stick; massif
stöduvatn *(Ice)* lake
stok *(Pol)* slope
stóma *(Gr)* mouth
stor *(Dan, Nor, Swe)* large
stora *(Fae)* large
straat *(Dut)* street, road, region
straede *(Dan)* strait
strana *(Rus)* country
Strand *(Ger)* **strand** *(Dan, Nor, Swe)* beach
strandar *(Ice)* beach
Strasse *(Ger)* street, road
strede *(Nor)* straits, narrow passage
středohoří, stredohorie *(Cz)* uplands
stretto *(It)* strait
Strom *(Ger)* large river, ocean stream, current
strøm *(Nor)* **ström** *(Swe)* large river
strook *(Afr)* strip
stroom *(Afr)* large river
studen/ý, á-, -é *(Cz)* cold
stung *(I-C)* river, stream
su *(Tu)* water, stream
sū *(Per)* water
suak *(Mal)* indentation, a hollow
suando *(Fin)* pond
sud *(Fr)* south, southern
Süd(er)- *(Ger)* south, southern
sudhur *(Fae, Ice)* southern
südlich *(Ger)* southern
sudo *(Kor)* strait
suid *(Afr)* south-, southern
suidō *(Jap)* strait
sukh/o, -oy *(Rus)* dry
sul, -l' *(It)* on
sul *(Por)* **south, southern**
sum *(Mon)* village, soviet
süm *(Mon)* temple
Sumpf *(Ger)* swamp, bog
sûn *(Bur)* cape
Sund *(Ger)* sound
sund *(Dan, Ice, Nor, Swe)* sound
sung/ai, -ei *(Mal)* river, large stream
sunn *(Nor)* south, southern
suo *(Fin)* swamp, marsh, moor
suom/i, -en *(Fin)* Finnish
superior *(Sp)* higher, upper
sūq *(Ar)* market
sur *(Fr)* on
sur *(Sp)* south, southern
surau *(Mal)* chapel
suu *(Est, Fin)* estuary
suur-, *(Est)* large, big
svart *(Nor, Swe)* black
svarta *(Ice)* black
svat/ý; svät/ý; -á, -é *(Cz)* holy
svent/-, -asis *(Lit)* holy
svet *(Rus)* light, world
svet/i, -a *(S-C)* holy
swart *(Afr)* black
syn *(Rus)* son
syrk *(Rus)* mountain chain
syrt *(Rus)* ridge, watershed
syssel *(Dan)* district
sze *(Ch)* *see* si
szeg *(Hun)* bend in a river; corner
székes *(Hun)* residential
szent *(Hun)* saint, holy
sziget *(Hun)* island; island-town
szlachechki *(Pol)* noble

T

ta *(Ch)* pagoda
ta, t'ai *(Ch)* *see* da
taberna *(Sp)* tavern
tai *(Ch)* tower; great; prosperous, exalted
taing *(Bur)* province
take *(Jap)* mountain peak
Tal *(Ger)* valley
tal *(Mon)* plain, steppe
talang *(Mal)* ridge, hill
tall, tulūl *(Ar)* hill (s), hummoch (s)
talok *(I-C)* *see* tlok
tambon *(Th)* administrative unit
tan *(Kor)* cape
tandjung *(Mal)* cape
tang *(Ch)* hall; embankment; pool
tang *(Per)* strait, pass
tanjong *(Mal)* cape
tao *(Ch)* *see* dao
ṭarā *(Rom)* land
tårn *(Dan, Nor)* tower
taş *(Tu)* stone
tāsh *(Per)* stone
tashi *(Tib)* blessing
tassili *(Ar)* plateau
tau *(Rus)* mountain, -range
taung; daung *(Bur)* south; mountain, hill
taungya *(Bur)* shifting cultivation on hillside
tayga *(Rus)* taiga, Siberian forests
Teich *(Ger)* pond
teik *(Bur)* top, summit
tel *(Heb)* hill
telaga *(Mal)* lake
tělok, těluk *(Mal, I-C)* bay, bight, bend in river
ténéré *(Ar)* sandy plain
tengah *(M l)* middle
tengiz *(Rus)* lake
tengri *(Mon)* heaven, gods
tepe, -si *(Tu)* hill, peak
tepl/o, yy *(Rus)* warm
tepl/ý, -á, -é *(Cz)* warm
terra *(Sp)* earth, land
terre *(Fr)* earth, land
territorio *(Sp)* territory
testa *(It)* head
tête *(Fr)* head
thálassa *(Gr)* sea, lake
-thal *(Ger)* valley
thale *(Th)* sea
thale sap *(Th)* lake, pond
thamilah *(Ar)* water remaining in pools
thang *(Tib)* plain, steppe
thog *(Tib)* upper
thom *(I-C)* large
ti *(Ch)* the earth
tian *(Ch)* field; heaven, sky
Tief *(Ger)* deep, marine trench
tierra *(Sp)* earth, land, territory
timur *(Mal)* east, eastern
tind *(Nor)* **-ur** *(Fae)* peak
tinggi *(Mal)* high; height
tir'a *(Ar)* canal
tîrg *(Rom)* market
tizi, tîzi *(Ar)* pass
tjåkko *(Swe)* mountain
tjärro *(Swe)* plateau
tiji *(Mal)* water, stream, river
tjörn *(Ice)* tarn
tjuku *(Mal)* cape
tlŏk *(I-C)* swamp, pond
to *(Kor)* island; province
tó *(Hun)* lake
tō *(Jap)* island; tower; east, eastern
todo *(Sp)* all
tōge *(Jap)* pass
tohoy *(Mon)* bend in a river
tolgoy *(Mon)* summit, peak, head
toll *(Nor)* ferry, customs
tong *(Kor)* village, town
tonle *(I-C)* large river, lake
top, -pen *(Dut)* top, peak
topp *(Nor)* peak, top
torg *(Nor)* market
torn *(Swe)* **torni** *(Fin)* tower
torp *(Swe)* small hut
torre *(It, Por)* tower
torre *(Sp)* tower, fortress
torrente *(Sp)* torrent, rapids
tō-shō *(Jap)* island
tou *(Ch)* head, chief
tour *(Fr)* tower
tras- *(Por)* trans-
trás *(Por)* behind
träsk *(Swe)* swamp, marsh
travesía *(Sp)* crossing
tres- *(Por)* trans-
trud *(Rus)* work, labour
trung *(I-C)* mid-, middle
tsangpo *(Tib)* large river
tse *(Tib)* peak, summit
tshāidam *(Tib)* salt bog
tshā/ka, -kha *(Tib)* salt lake, salt pan
tsho *(Tib)* lake
tsu *(Ch)* *see* zu
tsu *(Jap)* entrance, bay
tsui *(Ch)* *see* zui
ts'un *(Ch)* *see* zun
tu *(Ch)* soil, earth; map plan
tumsyk *(Rus)* cape
tun *(Ch)* village, hamlet
tung *(Ch)* *see* dong
tunturi *(Fin)* treeless mountain
tur'a *(Ar)* canal
Turm *(Ger)* tower, look-out
turn *(Rom)* tower
tutul *(Ar)* tall, hummock (-s)
tuz *(Tu)* salt
tyube *(Rus)* hill

U

uad, uádí, uat *(Ar)* wadi
über *(Ger)* above
uchi umi *(Jap)* bay
udde *(Swe)* cape
udjung *(Mal)* point, extremity
ugla *(Ar)* *see* 'uqla
ugol' *(Rus)* coal
uit *(Dut)* outer
új *(Hun)* new
ulaa *(Mon)* relay station
ul/aan *(Mon)* red
uls *(Mon)* state, country, nation
ulya *(Tu)* largest
umi *(Jap)* sea
umm *(Ar)* mother
unter *(Ger)* under, nether, lower
upè *(Lat)* river
upė *(Lit)* river
'uqla *(Ar)* group of shallow wells or pools
ur *(Rus)* mountain
ura *(Jap)* bay, coast, lake
urd, -a *(Rus-Mon)* south, southern
us *(Mon)* water
ust', -yë *(Rus)* estuary
ustup *(Rus)* shelf, ledge, escarpment
utara *(Mal)* north, northern
uttar, -ī *(Hin, Ur)* northern
uuden, uusi *(Fin)* new
uul *(Mon, Rus)* mountain range
uval *(Rus)* rise, elevation
úval *(Cz)* valley basin
už *(Lit)* behind, beyond
uzboy *(Rus)* river-bed

V

v *(Rus, Cz, etc.)* in
va *(Per)* and
vaara *(Fin)* Arctic hill-country
väärtti *(Fin-Swe)* bay
vad *(Dan, Nor)* ford
vaer *(Nor)* fishing village
våg *(Nor)* bay
vágur *(Fae)* bay
vähä *(Fin)* small
väike *(Est)* small
väin *(Est)* strait, channel
val *(Afr)* drop, gradient
val *(Rom, Rus)* wall
val *(Sp)* valley
vale *(Por, Rom)* valley
valkea *(Fin)* white
vall *(Swe)* meadow; rampart, dam
valla *(Sp)* rampart, stockade
vall/e *(Sp)* valley
valle *(It)* valley
vallée *(Fr)* valley
vallon *(Fr)* small valley
valt/a, -io *(Fin)* state-, governmental, main-,
vand *(Dan)* water
vann *(Nor)* water, small lake
vár *(Hun)* castle, mansion
város *(Hun)* town
varre *(Nor)* mountain
vásár *(Hun)* market
väst/-, -er, -ra *(Swe)* west, western
vat *(Th)* monastery, temple
vatn *(Ice, Nor)* lake, small lake
vatn *(Ice)* water
vatten *(Swe)* lake
vaux *(Fr)* valleys
vecchio *(It)* old
vechi *(Rom)* old
vecs *(Lat)* old
veen *(Dut)* peat-bog
vej *(Dan)* path, road
veld *(Afr)* field
velh/o, -a *(Por)* old
vel/i, -a; velik/o, -i, -a, -e; velk/o, -a *(S-C)* large
velik/o, -iy *(Rus)* large
velk/ý, -á, -é; vel'k/ý, -á, -é *(Cz)* large
vêng *(I-C)* long; length
verde *(Por, Sp)* green
verk *(Swe)* works, factory
verkhn/e, -iy *(Rus)* upper
verkhov'ye *(Rus)* source, upper reaches of a river
vert, -e *(Fr)* green
Verwaltung *(Ger)* administration
ves *(Cz)* village
vesel/-, -o, -yy *(Rus)* merry
vesi *(Fin)* water
vest, -er *(Dan)* west, western
vest/-, -er, -re *(Nor)* west, western
vestur *(Ice)* west, western
via *(It)* road, way
vidda *(Nor)* plateau
viej/o, -a *(Sp)* old
viento *(Sp)* wind
vig *(Dan)* **vik** *(Nor, Swe)* **vik** *(Fae, Ice)* bay
vila *(Pt)* small town, villa
vilâyet *(Tu)* administrative unit
villa *(Sp)* country house, town
vill/a *(It)* country house
villaggio *(It)* village
ville *(Fr)* town
vinh *(I-C)* bay
virane *(Tu)* ruins
virf *(Rom)* peak, top
virgen *(Sp)* virgin
vista *(Sp)* vista, view
vit *(Swe)* white
víz *(Hun)* water

Glossary—continued

vladi- *(Rus)* commanding-
vlakte *(Dut)* plain
vlei *(Afr)* pond, pool
voda *(Rus, Vz)* water
vodokhranilishche *(Rus)* reservoir
vodopad *(Rus)* waterfall
volcán *(Sp)* volcano
vold *(Nor)* meadow
volk *(Ger)* people
voll *(Nor)* meadow
vor, Vorder- *(Ger)* before, near-
voron *(Rus)* raven
vorota *(Rus)* gate, gateway
voskreseniye *(Rus)* Sunday; resurrection
vostochn/o, yy etc. *(Rus)* eastern
vostok *(Rus)* east
vozvyshennost' *(Rus)* uplands
vpadina *(Rus)* hollow, depression
vrata *(Bul)* gate
vrch *(Cz)* mountain
vrchovina *(Cz)* mountainous country
vrchy *(Cz)* mountain range
vrh *(S-C)* ridge, summit
vruh *(Bul)* ridge, summit
vrukh *(Bul)* peak
vung *(I-C)* gulf
vuoma *(Fin)* marshland
vuopio *(Fin)* bay; marsh, stretch of
vuori; -sto *(Fin)* mountain; -range
vyshe *(Rus)* higher
vysok/o, -iy *(Rus)* high, upper
vysok/ý, -á, -é *(Cz)* high, upper
vyšší *(Cz)* higher

W

wad *(Dut)* flats
wāḩat, wâḩat, wáḩat: wāḩāt, wâḩât, wáhát *(Ar)* oasis
walad *(Ar)* tribe, descendents of-
Wald *(Ger)* wood, forest
wan *(Jap)* bay
wan *(Ch)* bay
Wand *(Ger)* steep cliff
Wasser *(Ger)* water
Weg *(Ger)* path, way
Weide *(Ger)* meadow
Weiher *(Ger)* pond
Weiler *(Ger)* hamlet
weiss *(Ger)* white
Werder *(Ger)* river-island
wes *(Afr)* west, western
westlich *(Ger)* western, westerly
wielk/i, -a, -ie, -o *(Pol)* large, great
wies *(Pol)* village
Wiese *(Ger)* meadow
wijk *(Dut)* district, quarter
woda *(Pol)* water
woestyn *(Afr)* desert
województwo *(Pol)* province
wold, woud *(Dut)* wood, forest
Wüste *(Ger)* desert
wysepka *(Pol)* islet
wysok/i, -a, -ie *(Pol)* high
wyspa *(Pol)* island
wyżyna *(Pol)* upland

X

xén/os, -i, -on *(Gr)* foreign, strange
xi *(Ch)* west; mountain; stream
xia *(Ch)* narrow; street; gorge
xian *(Ch)* provincial capital; district
xiang *(Ch)* village, town; rural district
xiao *(Ch)* small, lesser
xir/ós, -á, -ón, í, ó *(Gr)* dry
xu *(Ch)* islet; wasteland

Y

y *(Sp)* and
yam *(Heb)* sea
yama *(Rus)* pit, hole
yama *(Jap)* mountain
yan *(Ch)* cliff, precipice, cave
yang *(Ch)* ocean; poplar; sun; male
yar *(Rus)* steep bank
yarımada *(Tu)* peninsula
yaylâ *(Tu)* plateau
yel' *(Rus)* fir-tree
yeni *(Tu)* new
yeşil *(Tu)* green
ylä-, yli- *(Fin)* upper
yō *(Jap)* ocean
yok *(I-C)* mountain
yol *(Tu)* track
yōma *(Bur)* mountain range
yŏn *(Kor)* lake
yt/re -ter, tre; -tra *(Nor, Swe)* outer
yuan *(Ch)* spring; garden, park
yugo, yuzhn/o, aya, -oye, -yy *(Rus)* south
yul *(Tib)* land
yun *(Ch)* clouds; transport, revolve
yunhe *(Ch)* canel
ywa *(Bur)* village

Z

za *(Rus)* behind, beyond, trans-
zaki *(Jap)* cape, peninsula
zalew *(Pol)* swamp, lagoon
zaliv *(Bul, Rus, S-C)* bay
zan *(Jap)* mountain (range)
zand *(Dut)* sand
zapadn/o, -yy *(Rus)* west, western
zapovednik *(Rus)* forest preserve, nature conservancy
zatoka *(Pol)* bay, gulf
zavod *(Rus)* factory
zdrój *(Pol)* spring, well, source, spa
ze *(Jap)* sandbank, reef
zee *(Dut)* sea
zelën/o, -yy *(Rus)* green
železn/ý, -á, -é *(Cz)* iron-
Zell, -zell *(Ger)* cell
žeme-; zeme *(Lit; Lat)* land
zem; žemas *(Lat; Lit)* low
zemin *(Tu)* earth, ground
zemlya *(Rus)* land, earth
zen *(Jap)* mountain
zhelezo *(Rus)* iron
zheleznodoroga *(Rus)* railway
zheleznodorozhnyy *(Rus)* railway (adj.)
zhëlt o, -yy etc. *(Rus)* yellow
zhong *(Ch)* middle; central
zhou *(Ch)* district; islet
zhuang *(Ch)* farmstead; village
zhusa *(Tib)* place
zlato- etc. *(Rus)* gold, golden
zlat/ý, á, -é *(Cz)* gold, golden
zolot/o, -oy etc. *(Rus)* gold, golden
zona *(It, Por, Sp)* zone, area
Zone *(Ger)* zone, area
zu *(Ch)* ancestors
zui *(Ch)* point; spit
zuid *(Dut)* south, southern
żuława *(Pol)* marshland
zun *(Ch)* village; hamlet

ABBREVIATIONS USED IN THE INDEX

A.C.T. Australian Capital Territory
Aer. Aerodrome
Afghan. Afghanistan
Afr. Africa, African
Ala. Alabama, U.S.A.
Alta. Alberta, Canada
Amer. America, American
Anat. Anatolia
Anc. Ancient
And. Prad. Andhra Pradesh
Antarct. Antarctica
Arch. Archipelago, Archipel, Archipiélago
Arg. Argentine Republic, Argentina
Ariz. Arizona, U.S.A.
Ark. Arkansas, U.S.A.
Atl. Oc. Atlantic Ocean
A.S.S.R. Autonomous Soviet Socialist Republic
Aust. Australia
Aut. Autonomous
B. Bay, Baai, Baie, Bahia, Baía
Baluch. Baluchistan
B.C. British Columbia
Beds. Bedfordshire, England
Belg. Belgium
Berks. Berkshire, England
Bk. Bank
Bor. Borough
Br. British
Br. Col., Brit. Col. British Columbia
Bucks. Buckinghamshire, England
C. Cape, Cap, Cabo, Capo
Cal. California, U.S.A
Cambs. Cambridgeshire, England
Can. Canal, Canada
Cant. Canton
Cas. Castle
Cat Cataract(s)
Cent. Central
Cent. Afr. Central Africa(n)
Cent. Amer. Central America
Ch. Chaung
Chan. Channel
Co. County
Col. Colony
Colo. Colorado, U.S.A.
Conn. Connecticut, U.S.A.
Cont. Continent
Cord. Cordillera
Cr. Creek
Cst. Coast
Ct. Ho. Courthouse
Czech. Czechoslovakia
D.C. District of Columbia, U.S.A.
Del. Delaware, U.S.A.
Den. Denmark
Dep. Department
Derby, Derbys. Derbyshire, England
Des. Desert, Desierto
Devon. Devonshire, England
Dist. District
Div. Division
Dj. Djebel
Dom. Dominion
E. East, Eastern
Eil. Eilanden
Elect. Electric
Eng. England
Ent. Entrance
Equat. Equatorial
Escarp. Escarpment
Est. Estuary
Fd. Fjord
Fed. Federal, Federation
Fed. Dist. Federal District
Fla. Florida, U.S.A.
Fr. France, French
Ft. Fort
G. Gulf, Golfe, Golfo
Ga. Georgia, U.S.A.
Gd., Gde. Grand, Grande
Geb. Gebirge, Gebergte
Ger. Germany
Glam. Glamorgan, Wales
Gloucester, Glos. Gloucestershire, England
Gov. Government
Gr. Gross, Grosse, Grosser, Grosses
Grp. Group
Gt. Great
Guj. Gujarat
Hants. Hampshire, England
Harb. Harbour, Harbor
Hd. Head
H.E. Hydro-electric (station)
Herts. Hertfordshire, England
Him. Prad. Himachal Pradesh
Hist. Historical
Ho. House
Hond. Honduras
I., Isld. Island, Île, Îlet, Ȋsla, Ȋlha, Isola, Isle, Islet
Ia. Iowa, U.S.A.
Ida. Idaho, U.S.A.
Ill. Illinois, U.S.A.
im. iméni
In. Inner
Ind. India, Indian, Indiana, U.S.A.
Indon. Indonesia
Inter. International
Ire. Ireland
Is., Islds. Islands, Isles, Ilhas, Isole, Islas, Îles
Isth. Isthmus
Jap. Japan, Japanese
Jeb. Jebel
Junc. Junction
Kan. Kansas, U.S.A., Kanal
Kep. Kepulauan
King. Kingdom
Kl. Klein, Kleine, Kleiner
Ky. Kentucky, U.S.A.
L. Lake, Lough, Loch, Lac, Lago, Lagóa, Lagoon, Laguna
La. Louisiana, U.S.A.
Lancs. Lancashire, England
Ld. Land
Leics. Leicestershire, England
Lincs. Lincolnshire, England
Lit. Little
Lith. Lithuania
Lr. Lower
Lt. Ho. Light House
Lux. Luxembourg
Mad. Prad. Madhya Pradesh
Mah. Maharashtra
Man. Manitoba, Canada
Mass. Massachusetts, U.S.A.
Md. Maryland, U.S.A.
Me. Maine, U.S.A.
Med. Mediterranean
Met. Meteoric
Mem. Memorial
Mex. Mexico
Mich. Michigan, U.S.A.
Mil. Military
Minn. Minnesota, U.S.A.
Miss. Mississippi, U.S.A.
Mo. Missouri, U.S.A.
Mon. Monument
Mont. Montana, U.S.A.
Moz. Mozambique
Mt., Mte., Mtgne., Mti. Mountain, Mont. Monte, Montagne, Monti
Mth., Mths. Mouth, Mouths
Mts. Mountains, Monts
N. North, Northern, Norte
Nat. National
Nats. Natsional'nyy
N.B., New Bruns. New Brunswick
N.C., N. Car. North Carolina, U.S.A.
N.D., N. Dak. North Dakota, U.S.A.
Nebr. Nebraska, U.S.A.
Neth. Netherlands
Nev. Nevada, U.S.A.
Nfld. Newfoundland
N.H., New Hamps. New Hampshire, U.S.A.
Nic. Nicaragua
N.J. New Jersey, U.S.A.
N. Mex. New Mexico, U.S.A.
Nor. Norway
Norf. Norfolk, England
Northants. Northamptonshire, England
Northld., Northumb. Northumberland, England
Notts. Nottinghamshire, England
Nr. Near
N.S., N. Scotia Nova Scotia
N.S.W., New S. Wales New South Wales
N.W. Terr. North West Territories
N.Y. New York *State*, U.S.A.
N.Z. New Zealand
O., O-va. Ostrov, Ostrova
Oc. Ocean
O.F.S. Orange Free State
Okla. Oklahoma, U.S.A.
Ont. Ontario, Canada
Ore., Oreg. Oregon, U.S.A.
Oxford., Oxon. Oxfordshire, England
Oz. Ozero
P. Poelau, Pulau
Pa., Penn. Pennsylvania, U.S.A.
Pac. Pacific
Pak. Pakistan
Par. Parish
Para. Paraguay
Pass. Passage
P.E.I. Prince Edward Island
Pen. Peninsula, Peninsular
Philipp. Philippines
Pk. Peak, Park
Plat. Plateau
Port. Portugal, Portuguese
P-ov. Poluostrov
Prad. Pradesh
Prefect. Prefecture
Prom. Promontory
Prot. Protectorate
Prov. Province, Provincial
Pt., Pte. Point, Pointe, Punt
Pta. Ponta, Punta
Pto. Pôrto, Puerto, Porto, Portillo
Que. Quebec, Canada
Qnsld. Queensland, Australia
R. River, Rivière, Rio
Ra. Range
Raj. Rajasthan
Rd. Road
Rec. Recreational
Reg. Region
Rep. Republic
Res. Reservoir, Reservoirs, Reserve, Reservation
R.I. Rhode Island, U.S.A.
Rly. Sta. Railway Station
R.S.F.S.R. Russian Soviet Federated Socialist Republic
S. South, Southern ,São
Sa. Sierra, Serra, Serrania
Salop, Shrops. Shropshire, England
Sask. Saskatchewan
S. Austral. South Australia
S.C., S. Car. South Carolina, U.S.A.
Scot. Scotland
Sd. Sound, Sund
S. Dak. South Dakota, U.S.A.
Som. Somerset, England
Span. Spanish
S.S.R. Soviet Socialist Republic
St., Ste., Sta. Saint, Sainte, Santa
Sta. Station, Santa
Staffs. Staffordshire, England
Stat. Statistical
Str. Strait, Straat
Sub. Suburb
Suff. Suffolk, England
Switz. Switzerland
Tas. Tasmania
Tenn. Tennessee, U.S.A.
Terr. Territory
Tex. Texas, U.S.A.
T.F.A.I. Territoire Français des Afars et des Issas
Tg. Tandjoeng, Tanjung, Tanjong
Tk. Teloek, Teluk
U.A.E. United Arab Emirates
U.K. United Kingdom
U.S.A., U.S. United States of America
U.S.S.R. Union of Soviet Socialist Republics
Uttar Prad. Uttar Pradesh
V. Valley, Val, Valle
Va. Virginia, U.S.A.
Vdkhr. Vodokhranilishche
Venez. Venezuela
Vill. Village
Vol. Volcano, Volcan
Vt. Vermont, U.S.A.
W. West, Western
Warwicks, Warwickshire, Eng.
Wash. Washington, U.S.A.
W. Austral. West Australia
W.I. West Indies
Wilts. Wiltshire, England
Wis. Wisconsin, U.S.A.
W. Va West Virginia, U.S.A.
Wyo. Wyoming, U.S.A.
Yorks, N , W., S. Yorkshire North, West, South, England

THE TRANSCRIPTION OF CHINESE PLACE-NAMES

Chinese is written in Han characters, a system of writing which has remained in use for more than 3,000 years. Its most conspicuous features are the large number of characters and the complexity of most of them. It is impossible to say how many characters there may be. All told, there cannot be fewer than 50,000. Of these, perhaps 11,000 may be encountered in bibliographic or similar research. Up to 3,000 characters are used in everyday written communication.

Han characters are ideographs but since the language is a spoken language and not just written, each character can be represented by a syllable – a vowel or a vowel with one or more consonants. Because the spoken language evolves with time and pronunciation varies with dialect many different readings of a character are possible.

Compared with English and other European languages, Chinese has few syllables, in Modern Standard Chinese only 404. With thousands of characters in use, many characters are equated with the same syllable. The syllable **nü** is represented by only one character. In contrast **yi** can be expressed by over 240. Tone (the modulation of the voice) helps to distinguish meaning, but generally context alone determines what is meant.

So complex a system of writing is not well suited to a modern industrial society but rather to a peasant community where the literate few have unlimited time to study. Printing is a formidable matter compared with European languages. Learning to read and write involves mastery of a large number of characters, imposing a great demand on memory and requiring a considerable amount of time.

There are many romanization systems for Chinese. Four are widely used in English. Of these the Wade-Giles system is most familiar. All British and American official maps have used the system exclusively since 1942, and millions of references exist in Wade-Giles romanizations. The system was first published in 1859 by Sir Thomas Wade and it was the basis, slightly modified, for the Chinese-English Dictionary of H. A. Giles published in 1912.

Of all the dialects of China, Northern Chinese (formerly called Mandarin Chinese) is most widespread. Wade-Giles and all systems since have used the educated Peking dialect of Northern Chinese as the standard language and the preferred readings of characters are given in that dialect which has become the model for Modern Standard Chinese.

Chinese, as distinct from European, interest in romanization was stimulated by the desire to promote a national language as well as to assist in learning to read the characters. Romanization would also serve as a means of writing the non-Chinese languages spoken within China and to help to write them in Chinese. A further aim was to encourage foreigners to learn Chinese.

As a first step towards these goals the most commonly used characters were simplified. Much discussion has centred around the replacement of Han characters by an alphabet, but this can only happen in the very remote future. Romanized Chinese may increasingly exist side-by-side with the characters but that does not mean that the Han characters are about to be dropped from use.

In 1958, the Chinese government approved the system called **Pinyin zimu** (phonetic alphabet) for the romanization of Chinese. Teachers of Chinese prefer Pinyin to Wade-Giles. It is a better source for up-to-date idiom and vocabulary but a great amount of material is not yet available in Pinyin. Students of Chinese, therefore, have to deal with other systems of romanization. For geographical names almost nothing existed in Pinyin for many years. Everything worth considering was in Wade-Giles. Yet in spite of the fact that the letters **c**, **q** and **x** were used in a way totally alien to English usage, Pinyin was neater than Wade-Giles which, for example, produces **Wu-lu-mu-chi** for English Conventional **Urumchi** where Pinyin gives **Urumqi**. **Harbin** is so spelled in Pinyin but becomes **Ha-erh-pin** in Wade-Giles.

Ever since Pinyin was launched in 1958, the publishers of *The Times Atlas* have considered but, until now, rejected, the adoption of Pinyin for the map plates covering China. Among the factors considered were the availability of sources for Pinyin names, the extent to which Pinyin was used in China and the acceptance and use of Pinyin outside China, particularly for geographical names. In spite of a State Council directive of 1975 that Pinyin would be used as the standard and sole romanization system for geographical and personal names, little was done in China to follow the directive until 1977. Early in 1979 Pinyin was accepted by most nations of the world as the system to be employed officially for romanized Chinese names. Times Books of London, the publishers of the Atlas, therefore, decided to adopt Pinyin, in place of Wade-Giles for the names of Mainland China and the map plates in this atlas now contain Pinyin names in place of Wade-Giles.

In Taiwan, where Pinyin is not used, Wade-Giles has been retained to conform to local practice. In Hong Kong a romanization based on Cantonese is used. Pinyin would be in conflict with official practice in Hong Kong.

In order to facilitate reference to Wade-Giles names, the relationship of consonants and vowels in the two systems is shown on this page.

No attempt has been made in this atlas to fabricate Pinyin names by conversion from Wade-Giles or by other methods: all Pinyin names have been taken from official Chinese sources. There are several reasons why fabrication would be inadmissible. The name itself may have changed; the administrative status of the place may not be known; there may be errors in the Wade-Giles transcription; the reading of the Han character may have changed. In areas where the people are not Chinese, e.g. Sinkiang, Tibet, Inner Mongolia, guessing at the Pinyin spelling could produce nonsensical names. For example, the character **shen** in Chinese is used to produce **xain** in **xainza** but **sên** in **Sêndo**. Likewise, to convert **Pa-yen-wu-la** from Wade-Giles would give **Bayan Wula** for the place in Inner Mongolia which is shown on Plate 23 as **Xi Ujimqin Qi (Bayan Ul Hot)**. From the Pinyin name we know that the local name for the centre of administration in West Ujimqin Banner is **Bayan Ul Hot**.

The reader will, no doubt, be curious as to why the same name often occurs twice in the same area. For example, to the south-west of Shanghai there is, apparently, a smaller place with the same name. This smaller place is the centre of Shanghai county which falls within the municipality of Shanghai. This explanation may then raise the question as to why administrative names are given in preference to other names. The answer lies in the organisation of China as a closely-knit community with a hierarchical structure designed to bond society into a single entity as well as for administering to the needs of the people. Where we would talk of a Town Hall or a City Hall as an inanimate and rather remote unit of administration, the Chinese talk of the Workers' revolutionary committee whether the place in question be Shanghai City or the smallest village where such a committee may exist. Thus, it does not seem odd to the Chinese that a street plan of a city should reflect the administrative elements where one might expect corresponding 'geographical' elements. Rail and bus maps also refer to places by their administrative title distinguishing in a particular area a city under its administrative title, a county, perhaps of the same name, and a station designed to serve both places if it should happen to be separate from both.

Most of Mainland China is divided into provinces (**sheng**) but in areas inhabited by national minorities the **sheng** is replaced by the autonomous region (**zizhiqu**). There are five autonomous regions – Inner Mongolia, Sinkiang, Tibet, Ningxia and Guangxi. In this atlas the word **sheng** has been omitted from the province names and the description 'autonomous region' has been omitted from Ningxia and Guangxi partly for reasons of space but also because Ningxia (Ningsia) and Guangxi (Kwangsi) are more familiar as entities of province status in China. Beijing (Peking), Shanghai and Tianjin (Tientsin) and their surrounding areas have been constituted as municipalities of province status (**zhixiashi** – city under direct control).

The provinces are subdivided into regions (**diqu**) or municipalities (**shi** – a region taking the title of a city). Where the population is non-Chinese this level of administration is often named **zizhizhou** which means autonomous area. In the case of Inner Mongolia the tribal tradition is preserved in the name **meng** (league) for this second level of administration. Hainan Island which is part of Quangdong Sheng has the unique title of **xingshengqu** – administrative zone.

At the next level down are the counties (**xian** – Wade-Giles etc. **hsien**). In non-Chinese ethnic areas the **xian** is often autonomous – **zizhixian**. Inner Mongolia's leagues (**meng**) are divided into banners (**qi**) and the name **Qi** will be found as part of certain names on the appropriate map plates. In Tibet the county becomes a **dzong**.

Below the county level is the town (**zhen**), the commune (**gonghe**) and the village (**cunzhen**).

Within cities the districts (or quarters) are named '**qu**'.

On Plates 21 to 24 administrative divisions below the province (**sheng**) level have not been shown. Yet the selection of places has been made with administrative status in mind. The full administrative name of **Jianghua Yaozu Zizhixian** (which means **Jianghua Yao** people's autonomous county) can hardly be shown as such and the name **Jianghua** alone is given since this name is descriptive enough.

For continuity of reference, the commonly used English conventional name for the provinces and cities and other well-known names, e.g. in Tibet, have been added in brackets where necessary. Wade-Giles names have been replaced by Pinyin names. The Wade-Giles equivalent (not always the same as the Wade-Giles name) of the Pinyin name can be obtained by conversion of the letters. Where it has been felt necessary to retain a Wade-Giles name, it has been enclosed in brackets.

Two additional categories of name are also given in brackets, namely, the local name of an administrative centre, e.g. **Zhizuishan (Dawukuo)** and, in certain areas, a non-Chinese name which has equal standing with the Chinese name.

COMPARATIVE TABLE OF PINYIN AND WADE-GILES

CONSONANTS

Wade-Giles	Pinyin	Approximate pronunciation	Pinyin	Wade-Giles
ch (except when followed by i or ü)	**zh**	**j** as in **j**ump	**b**	p
			c	ts'
ch' (except when followed by i or ü)	**ch**	**ch** as in **ch**urch	**ci**	tz'u
			chi	ch'ih
chi; chü	**ji; ju**	**j** as in **j**am	**ch**	ch'
ch'i; ch'ü	**qi; qu**	**ch** as in **ch**urch	**d**	t
chih	**zhi**		**g**	k
ch'ih	**chi**		**j**	ch (when followed by i or u)
hs	**x**	**sh** as in **sh**oe		
j	**r**	**r** as in **r**ed or **z** as in a**z**ure	**k**	k'
k	**g**	**g** as in **g**ood	**p**	p
k'	**k**	**k** as in **k**in	**q**	ch' (when followed by i or u)
p	**b**	**b** as in **b**at		
p'	**p**	**p** as in **p**at	**r**	j
ssu (sze)	**si**	**si** as in **si**erra	**si**	ssu (sze)
t	**d**	**d** as in **d**og	**t**	t'
t'	**t**	**t** as in **t**ot	**x**	hs
ts	**z**	**z** as in **z**ulu	**yi**	i
ts'	**c**	**ts** as in si**ts**	**you**	yu
tzu	**zi**	**ze** as in **ze**ro	**z**	ts
tz'u	**ci**	**tsy** as in Be**tsy**	**zi**	tzu
			zh	ch
			zhi	chih

VOWELS

Wade-Giles	Pinyin	Approximate pronunciation	Pinyin	Wade-Giles
eh	**e**	**e** as in m**e**t	**e** (after h, g, k)	o
erh	**er**	**er** as in h**er**	**e** (after i, u, y)	eh
i (when initial or standing alone)	**yi**	**yea** as in **yea**st	**er**	erh
			i (after j, q, r, sh)	ih
ieh	**ie**	**ie** as in f**ie**sta	**ian**	ien
ien	**ian**	**ean** as in m**ean**der	**ie**	ieh
ih	**i**	**e** as in h**e**r	**ong**	ung
o (standing alone or after h, k, k')	**e**	**e** as in h**e**r	**ou** (after y)	u
			u (after j, q, x, y)	ü
o (after f, m, p, p', w)	**o**	**o** as in c**o**rn	**ü** (after l, n)	ü
o (after other consonants)	**uo**	**uo** as in d**uo**	**ui** (after g, k')	uei
			uo (after g, h, k, sh)	uo
u (after y)	**ou**	**ou** as in y**ou**	**uo** (otherwise)	o
ü (after l, n)	**ü**	**u** as in t**u** (French) or **ü** as in d**ü**nn (German)	**yan**	yen
			yi	i
ü	**u**	**o** as in d**o**		
uei (occurs only after k, k')	**ui**	**uai** as in q**uai**nt		
ung	**ong**	**ung** as in j**ung** (German)		

Note
In both panels the first column gives the Wade-Giles in alphabetical order; the second gives the Pinyin equivalent; the third, the pronunciation. The fourth and fifth columns give the same information as the first and second, but in Pinyin alphabetical order, to enable the reader to refer back from Pinyin. Unless otherwise stated, consonants are pronounced as in English and vowels as in Italian.

53 T15 Å town Norway 61.43N 5.56E
69 C2 Aa R France
63 G8 Aa R Niedersachsen W Germany
63 E9 Aa R Nordrhein-Westfalen W Germany
66 J2 Aa R Switzerland
Aabd-el-Aaziz,Jebel mt see 'Abdul 'Aziz,Jebel
66 Q1 Aach Austria 47.31N 9.58E
64 F8 Aach W Germany 47.50N 8.52E
66 M1 Aach R W Germany
Aachâra,El see 'Ashara,El
Aache see 'Ashan watercourse
64 A2 Aachen W Germany 50.46N 6.06E
A Adama see Nazaret
88 G10 Aadam Aagueilet Anayin reg Morocco
88 G9 Aadam Bu Deira reg Morocco
88 F10 Aadam Meselut reg Mauritania
88 F9 Aadam Uerg reg Morocco
35 F1 Aadeissé, El Lebanon 33.15N 35.33E
88 J8 Aadme Rich Morocco 27.09N 8.48E
66 M2 Aadorf Switzerland 47.30N 8.54E
60 P10 Aadorp Netherlands 52.22N 6.37E
Aadra see Adhra
Aafrine see Afrin
88 G9 Aagued Edhacha reg Morocco
61 F3 Aaigem Belgium 50.53N 3.56E
77 E9 Aakba Amra Morocco 35.36N 5.55W
61 C3 Aalbeke Belgium 50.47N 3.14E
60 J12 Aalburg Netherlands 51.45N 5.08E
64 J6 Aalen W Germany 48.50N 10.07E
35 D1 Aalma ech Chaab Lebanon 33.06N 35.11E
60 G10 Aalsmeer Netherlands 52.16N 4.45E
61 L3 Aalst Limburg Belgium 50.47N 5.12E
60 J12 Aalst Netherlands 51.47N 5.08E
60 K14 Aalst Noord-Brabant Netherlands 51.23N 5.29E
61 G3 Aalst Oost Vlaanderen Belgium 50.57N 4.03E
60 P12 Aalten Gelderland Netherlands 51.56N 6.35E
61 D2 Aalter Belgium 51.05N 3.27E
35 E1 Aamel,Jebel mts Lebanon
Aâmoudiyé see Amudiye
51 M9 Äänekoski Finland 62.38N 25.40E
Aannâne,Ouâdi el watercourse see 'Annân, Wâdî el
95 F2 Aansluit S Africa 26.44S 22.28E
60 F14 Aanwas Netherlands 51.24N 4.18E
51 N4 Aapajärvi Finland 67.15N 27.20E
51 K5 Aapua mt Sweden 66.48N 23.27E
60 G11 Aar R Netherlands
Aarab Pennar see 'Arab Punari
66 J2 Aarau Switzerland 47.24N 8.04E
66 F3 Aarberg Switzerland 47.03N 7.17E
64 E3 Aarbergen W Germany 50.13N 8.04E
69 P3 Aarbergen W Germany 50.14N 8.04E
66 H2 Aarburg Switzerland 47.19N 7.54E
60 A3 Aardenburg Netherlands 51.17N 3.26E
66 J1 Aare R Switzerland
66 E3 Aare-Kanal Switzerland
66 J2 Aargau canton Switzerland
66 H3 Aargau, Ober reg Switzerland
88 F10 Aargub Mauritania 23.37N 15.50W
60 L13 Aarle Rixtel Netherlands 51.30N 5.39E
61 K3 Aarschot Belgium 50.59N 4.50E
61 D2 Aarsele Belgium 51.00N 3.25E
61 C2 Aartrijke Belgium 51.07N 3.05E
61 H2 Aartselaar Belgium 51.08N 4.23E
66 H3 Aarwangen Switzerland 47.15N 7.46E
Aâssi R see 'Asi R
95 G6 Aasvoëlberg mt S Africa 30.55S 23.38E
95 J4 Aasvoëlkop mt S Africa 28.44S 25.00E
Aateîbe, Bahr el L see Ateibe, Bahret el, L
88 F10 Aatf, El reg Mauritania/Morocco
51 K5 Aavasaksa Finland 66.24N 02.343
Aayouûn Hadîd see 'Uyun Hadid
74 E9 Aazanèn Morocco 35.12N 3.09W
90 C9 Aba Nigeria 5.06N 7.21E
23 B2 Aba Sichuan China 32.56N 101.58E
33 F3 Abā ad Dūd Saudi Arabia 27.02N 44.01E
33 H3 'Abā,Al Saudi Arabia 26.45N 49.46E
33 H3 Abā al 'Abal Saudi Arabia 26.21N 49.34E
33 J7 Abā al 'Afan Saudi Arabia 18.51N 50.38E
34 C9 Abā al Hinshan Saudi Arabia 29.13N 35.12E
34 J8 Abā al Qūr, Wādī watercourse Saudi Arabia
18 E7 Abab Sumatra Indon 3.18S 103.50E
91 J2 Ababua tribe Zaïre
75 J6 Ababuj Spain 40.33N 0.49W
117 A7 Abacaxis,R Brazil
105 K11 Abaco I.,Great Bahamas
105 K11 Abaco I.,Little Bahamas
Abad see Yukuriawat
Abad see Awat
85 N10 Abadab,Jebel mt Sudan 18.54N 35.56E
32 C5 Ābādān Iran 30.20N 48.15E
32 C5 Ābādān, Jazīreh isld Iran
120 B3 Abad, Boquerón gorge Peru 8.51S 75.36W
32 E5 Ābādeh Fārs Iran 31.06N 52.40E
32 E6 Ābādeh Fārs Iran 29.08N 52.50E
32 F2 Abaden Tappeh Iran 37.25N 55.11E
76 L7 Abades Spain 40.55N 4.15W
76 H8 Abadia Spain 40.16N 5.58W
118 F6 Abadia dos Dourados Brazil 18.27S 47.22W
75 E1 Abadiano Spain 43.09N 2.36W
76 E2 Abadín Spain 43.21N 7.29W
88 M6 Abadla Algeria 31.01N 2.45W
44 C3 Abadzekhskaya U.S.S.R. 44.24N 40.14E
86 E8 Aba el Waqf Egypt 28.36N 30.45E
50 G4 Âbær Iceland 65.18N 18.53W
118 F6 Abaeté Brazil 19.10S 45.24W
118 F6 Abaeté R Brazil
117 D5 Abaetetuba Brazil 1.45S 48.54W
40 F1 Abaga U.S.S.R. 61.02N 132.13E
42 K7 Abagaytuy U.S.S.R. 49.35N 117.55E
22 K5 Abagnar Qi Nei Monggol Zizhiqu China 43.56N 116.11E
22 K4 Abag Qi Nei Monggol Zizhiqu China 43.53N 114.33E
118 C9 Abai Paraguay 25.58S 55.54W
87 D4 Aba I Sudan 13.20N 32.38E
9 B4 Abaiang atoll Kiribati, Pacific Oc 1.43N 173.00E
87 D5 Abaiat Sudan 10.21N 32.31E
90 C7 Abaji Nigeria 8.30N 6.54E
90 C8 Abajikolo Nigeria 7.46N 7.33E
111 P4 Abajo Pk Utah 37.50N 109.29W
90 C9 Abak Nigeria 4.59N 8.32E
90 D8 Abakaliki Nigeria 6.17N 8.04E
42 E5 Abakan U.S.S.R. 53.43N 91.25E
42 D6 Abakan R U.S.S.R.
42 D6 Abakanskiy Khrebet mts U.S.S.R.
91 D4 Abala Congo 1.17S 15.35E
89 L4 Abala Niger 14.56N 3.22E
89 N4 Abalak Niger 15.22N 6.21E
42 E3 Abalakova U.S.S.R. 58.08N 92.44E
88 Q11 Abalemma Algeria 20.51N 5.59E
90 C3 Abalemma Niger 16.11N 7.45E
90 C4 Abalemma watercourse Niger
88 Q10 Abalessa Algeria 22.55N 4.52E
87 F6 Abalti Ethiopia 8.10N 37.36E
Ab Ambar see Āb Anbār
42 F4 Aban U.S.S.R. 56.42N 96.02E
36 G1 Abana Turkey 41.58N 34.03E
75 F6 Abánades Spain 40.54N 2.30W
32 E5 Āb Anbār Iran 30.55N 53.20E
120 C5 Abancay Peru 13.37S 72.52W
69 B4 Abancourt France 49.42N 1.46E
18 L10 Abang mt Bali Indon 8.17S 115.20E
91 B3 Abanga R Gabon
77 O4 Abanilla Spain 38.12N 1.02W
19 C3 Abapi Celebes Indon 0.55N 122.22E
120 F8 Abapó Bolivia 18.48S 63.25W
87 A9 Abara tribe Zaïre
77 O4 Abarán Spain 38.12N 1.23W
86 D5 Âb'âr el Brins Egypt 30.29N 30.05E
85 J4 Abâr el Kanâyis Egypt 30.59N 27.18E
87 L8 Abar Irir Somalia 4.50N 46.10E
91 C12 Abaro Ferreira, Sa mts Angola
32 E5 Abarqū Iran 31.09N 53.18E
Abarquh see Abarqū
75 F2 Abarzuza Spain 42.44N 2.01W

86 M3 Abasân Gaza Strip 31.19N 34.21E
Abā-Sa'ūd see Najran
44 E5 Abasha Georgia U.S.S.R. 42.13N 42.12E
21 K5 Abashiri Japan 44.02N 144.17E
21 K5 Abashiri-wan B Japan
15 B4 Abaso Irian Jaya 1.21S 132.39E
115 K5 Abasolo Tamaulipas Mexico 24.02N 98.22W
44 E6 Abastumani Georgia U.S.S.R. 41.44N 42.51E
47 L7 Abatskiy U.S.S.R. 56.19N 70.29E
88 H8 Abattih Morocco 27.11N 11.27W
15 K9 Abau Papua New Guinea 10.04S 148.34E
Abauro see Ubauro
43 L3 Abay Kazakhstan U.S.S.R. 49.40N 72.47E
87 F7 Abaya,L Ethiopia
42 E5 Abaza U.S.S.R. 52.44N 90.12E
34 G2 Abba oil bore Syria 36.20N 39.24E
66 O8 Abbadia Italy 45.54N 9.22E
80 E3 Abbadia San Salvatore Italy 42.53N 11.40E
87 E5 Abbai,R Ethiopia
35 G5 'Abbara, El anc site Jordan 32.14N 35.54E
70 G6 Abbaretz France 47.33N 1.32W
32 F4 Abbasabad Esfahān Iran 33.54N 55.03E
32 F4 Abbāsābād Esfahān Iran 33.33N 54.19E
32 E5 Abbāsābād Fārs Iran 30.25N 53.20E
32 H4 Abbāsābād Khorāsān Iran 33.31N 58.20E
32 G2 'Abbāsābād Semnān Iran 36.21N 56.25E
86 G4 'Abbâsa,El Egypt 30.32N 31.43E
81 B3 Abbasanta Sardinia 40.13N 8.49E
86 R12 'Abbâsîya Cairo Egypt
87 C4 Abbasiya,El Sudan 12.12N 31.19E
66 B5 Abbaye,l' Switzerland 46.39N 6.20E
106 F3 Abbaye Pt Michigan 46.57N 88.07W
87 H5 Abbe,L Ethiopia/Djibouti
69 B6 Abbé,l' France 48.33N 1.50E
66 B1 Abbenans France 47.30N 6.27E
60 E12 Abbenbroek Netherlands 51.51N 4.15E
60 G11 Abbenes Netherlands 52.14N 4.36E
56 N4 Abberton Essex Eng 51.50N 0.55E
107 L10 Abbeville Alabama 31.35N 85.16W
69 B3 Abbeville France 50.06N 1.51E
105 D6 Abbeville Georgia 31.59N 83.19W
107 D12 Abbeville Louisiana 29.58N 92.08W
105 E3 Abbeville S Carolina 34.10N 82.23W
100 J8 Abbey Saskatchewan 50.44N 108.45W
59 G7 Abbey Tipperary Irish Rep 52.21N 7.45W
59 C7 Abbeydorney Kerry Irish Rep 52.20N 9.40W
59 D7 Abbeyfeale Limerick Irish Rep 52.24N 9.18W
59 H4 Abbeylara Longford Irish Rep 53.46N 7.27W
59 H6 Abbeyleix Leix Irish Rep 52.55N 7.20W
13 G2 Abbey Pk Queensland 14.11S 144.30E
58 M7 Abbey St.Bathans Borders Scotland 55.51N 2.23W
57 G3 Abbey Town Cumbria England 54.50N 3.17W
79 F4 Abbiategrasso Italy 45.24N 9.05E
51 G6 Abborrträsk Sweden 65.28N 19.25E
13 J4 Abbot B Queensland
123 H12 Abbot Ice Shelf Antarctica
13 J5 Abbot,Mt Queensland 20.08S 147.40E
56 H2 Abbots Bromley Staffs Eng 52.49N 1.52W
56 F6 Abbotsbury Dorset England 50.40N 2.36W
95 B9 Abbotsdale S Africa 33.29S 18.41E
57 H1 Abbotsford Borders Scotland 55.36N 2.47W
101 M11 Abbotsford Br Columbia 49.02N 122.18W
95 L8 Abbotsford S Africa 32.57S 27.55E
106 D5 Abbotsford Wisconsin 44.57N 90.20W
58 H7 Abbotsinch airport Strathclyde Scotland 55.52N 4.26W
109 F5 Abbott New Mexico 36.18N 104.17W
112 K4 Abbott Texas 31.53N 97.06W
31 G3 Abbottabad Pakistan 34.12N 73.15E
60 H10 Abcoude Netherlands 51.17N 4.59E
74 H9 Abd R Algeria
34 B8 Abda anc site Israel 30.48N 34.47E
88 J5 Abda reg Morocco
'Abdah,Al see 'Abde, Al
33 J4 Abd,Al Saudi Arabia 24.09N 50.51E
77 G7 Abdalagís, Sierra de mts Spain
33 M10 'Abdalī Kuwait 29.03N 47.44E
33 J10 'Abd al Kūrī isld Indian Ocean
87 J7 Abdalla tribe Ethiopia
35 F6 Abdallah Bridge Jordan 31.47N 35.52E
87 J5 Abdal Qadr Somalia 10.26N 43.02E
31 E2 Abdan Afghanistan 36.41N 68.32E
34 P6 Ābdānān Iran 32.57N 47.27E
34 C4 'Abde, Al Lebanon 34.33N 35.58E
87 D3 Abd el Magid Sudan 14.42N 32.42E
85 H8 Abd el Malik watercourse Egypt
45 W1 Abdi U.S.S.R. 55.53N 50.46E
32 G3 Abdolabād Iran 34.14N 56.30E
32 G2 Abdollāhābād Iran 37.34N 57.27E
32 E3 Abdollāhābād Semnān Iran 35.17N 52.46E
Abdulabad see Abdolabād
34 H2 'Abdul 'Aziz, Jebel mts Syria
90 G4 Abdulfeta Niger 15.35N 14.14E
46 R3 Abdulino U.S.S.R. 53.40N 53.38E
Abdullahabad see Abdollāhābād
30 A2 Abdullahpur Haryana India 30.07N 77.17E
34 P4 Ab-e-Bad Āvar R Iran
90 K5 Abéché Chad 13.49N 20.49E
Abécher see Abéché
100 E4 Abee Alberta 54.19N 112.59W
61 M5 Abée Belgium 50.28N 5.22E
69 D2 Abeele Belgium 50.48N 2.40E
32 H6 Āb-e Garm Iran 28.30N 59.00E
76 C2 Abegondo Spain 43.13N 8.18W
86 H8 'Abeid, Wâdî el watercourse Egypt
75 E4 Abéjar Spain 41.48N 2.47W
119 C5 Abejorral Colombia 5.48N 75.28W
75 J8 Abejuela Spain 39.55N 0.54W
87 C6 Abel Sudan 9.17N 31.30E
76 B12 Abela Portugal 38.01N 8.34W
89 J2 Abelbodh Mali 18.31N 1.18W
50 W13 Abeløya isld Spitsbergen Arctic Ocean 79.00N 30.15E
11 G7 Abel Tasman Nat. Pk New Zealand
51 D6 Abelvatten L Sweden 65.31N 14.50E
9 B5 Abemama atoll Kiribati, Pacific Oc 0.20N 173.50E
64 K5 Abenberg W Germany 49.15N 10.59E
77 N2 Abengibre Spain 39.13N 1.33W
89 H8 Abengourou Ivory Coast 6.42N 3.27W
77 H3 Abenójar Spain 38.53N 4.21W
77 H3 Abenojar R Spain
53 C6 Åbenrå Denmark 55.03N 9.26E
53 C6 Åbenrå Fjord inlet Denmark 55.02N 9.30E
Åbenra-Sønderborg co see Sønderjylland
64 M6 Abens R W Germany
64 M6 Abensberg W Germany 48.49N 11.52E
90 A8 Abeokuta Nigeria 7.10N 3.26E
57 E6 Aber Gwynedd Wales 53.14N 4.01W
87 E7 Abera Ethiopia 7.11N 35.54E
56 C3 Aberaeron Dyfed Wales 52.15N 4.15W
58 K6 Aberargie Tayside Scotland 56.20N 3.23W
56 C3 Aberarth Dyfed Wales 52.15N 4.14W
56 D4 Aberavon W Glam Wales 51.37N 3.47W
70 A4 Aber-Benoit R France
56 E4 Abercarn Gwent Wales 51.39N 3.08W
58 L3 Aberchirder Grampian Scotland 57.33N 2.38W
99 S7 Abercorn Quebec 45.03N 72.40W
Abercorn Zambia see Mbala
12 J5 Abercrombie R New S Wales
56 E4 Aberdare Mid Glam Wales 51.43N 3.27W
93 H6 Aberdare Nat. Park Kenya
93 H6 Aberdare Range Kenya
56 B2 Aberdaron Gwynedd Wales 52.49N 4.43W
111 F5 Aberdeen California 36.59N 118.12W
58 M4 Aberdeen Grampian Scotland 57.10N 2.04W
23 B9 Aberdeen Hong Kong E. Asia 22.14N 114.09E
110 N7 Aberdeen Idaho 42.57N 112.50W
103 B7 Aberdeen Maryland 39.31N 76.10W
107 H8 Aberdeen Mississippi 33.49N 88.34W
105 H2 Aberdeen N Carolina 35.08N 79.26W
12 K4 Aberdeen New S Wales 32.09S 150.53E
95 H8 Aberdeen S Africa 32.29S 24.04E
100 L6 Aberdeen Saskatchewan 52.20N 106.16W

108 M4 Aberdeen S Dakota 45.28N 98.30W
110 B3 Aberdeen Washington 46.58N 123.49W
Aberdeen co see Grampian reg
23 B10 Aberdeen I Hong Kong 22.12N 114.09E
101 Y3 Aberdeen L N W Terr
95 H8 Aberdeen Road S Africa 32.45S 24.19E
58 K6 Aberdour Fife Scotland 56.03N 3.18W
56 C2 Aberdovey Gwynedd Wales 52.33N 4.02W
56 E3 Aberedw Powys Wales 52.08N 3.21W
56 E4 Aber-fan Mid Glam Wales 51.42N 3.21W
95 M4 Aberfeldy S Africa 28.14S 28.52E
58 J5 Aberfeldy Tayside Scotland 56.37N 3.54W
57 E6 Aberffraw Gwynedd Wales 53.12N 4.28W
57 L5 Aberford W Yorks England 53.51N 1.20W
58 H6 Aberfoyle Central Scotland 56.11N 4.23W
13 H5 Aberfoyle Queensland 21.40S 145.17E
56 F4 Abergavenny Gwent Wales 51.50N 3.00W
57 F6 Abergele Clwyd Wales 53.17N 3.34W
56 D3 Abergwesyn Powys Wales 52.10N 3.40W
56 D4 Abergwynfi W Glam Wales 51.40N 3.35W
58 L6 Aberlady Lothian Scotland 56.01N 2.51W
56 D2 Aberllefenni Gwynedd Wales 52.40N 3.49W
58 K4 Aberlour Grampian Scotland 57.28N 3.14W
112 F2 Abernathy Texas 33.50N 101.52W
100 O8 Abernethy Saskatchewan 50.45N 103.25W
58 K6 Abernethy Tayside Scotland 56.20N 3.19W
Abersee see St. Wolfgangsee lake
56 B2 Abersoch Gwynedd Wales 52.50N 4.31W
56 E4 Abersychan Gwent Wales 51.44N 3.04W
56 E5 Aberthaw S Glam Wales 51.24N 3.23W
56 E4 Abertillery Gwent Wales 51.45N 3.09W
76 H10 Abertura Spain 39.15N 5.49W
58 J6 Aberuthven Tayside Scotland 56.19N 3.40W
70 A4 Aber Wrach,L' France 48.36N 4.35W
56 C3 Aberystwyth Dyfed Wales 52.25N 4.05W
87 H10 Abessali Somalia 1.33N 41.52E
79 J6 Abetone Italy 44.07N 10.43E
47 J3 Abez' U.S.S.R. 66.33N 61.51E
88 Q9 Abezzou Algeria 24.17N 5.22E
65 G8 Abfaltersbach Austria 46.46N 12.32E
32 H7 Āb Gāh Iran 26.25N 59.50E
87 K9 Abgal tribe Somalia
45 Q8 Abganerovo U.S.S.R. 48.05N 44.12E
33 E7 Abhā Saudi Arabia 18.14N 42.31E
33 D4 Abhā,Jabal mts Saudi Arabia
29 G7 Abhanpur Madhya Prad India 21.05N 81.46E
32 C2 Abhar Iran 36.05N 49.18E
32 C2 Abhar Rud R Iran
87 G4 Abi Addi Ethiopia 13.39N 39.03E
75 F7 Abia de Obispalía Spain 40.01N 2.25W
Abiak see Ābyek
32 D4 Ab-i Bazuft R Iran
119 C4 Abibe,Sa.de mts Colombia
88 K5 Abid, el R Morocco
35 G2 'Abidin Syria 32.47N 35.49E
Ab-i Diz see Dez R
89 G9 Abidjan Ivory Coast 5.19N 4.01W
75 K3 Abiego Spain 42.07N 0.05W
Ab-i-Garm see Āb-e Garm
31 E4 Ab-i-Istada L Afghanistan
32 J6 Ab-i-Kam Gudar pass Iran 29.30N 60.08E
32 G4 Ab-i-Kavir salt waste Iran
Ab-i-Kham see Ab-i-kam Gudar, pass
53 B4 Abild Ringkøbing Denmark 56.07N 8.39E
53 B7 Abild Sønderjylland Denmark 54.59N 8.52E
Abil el Qamh see Tel Avel bet Ma'akha anc site
100 F4 Abilene Alberta 54.05N 111.26W
109 N3 Abilene Kansas 38.55N 97.14W
112 H3 Abilene Texas 32.27N 99.45W
104 G9 Abilene Virginia 37.09N 78.35W
72 F2 Abilly France 46.57N 0.45E
87 B9 Abimva Zaïre 3.08N 29.50E
106 D9 Abingdon Illinois 40.48N 90.25W
103 B8 Abingdon Maryland 39.26N 76.18W
56 J4 Abingdon Oxon Eng 51.41N 1.17W
104 D10 Abingdon Virginia 36.42N 81.59W
13 G4 Abingdon Downs Queensland 17.35S 143.10E
Abingdon I see Pinta, I
13 J4 Abingdon Reef Gt Barrier Reef Australia 18.00S 149.35E
56 M3 Abington Cambs England 52.07N 0.15E
59 F6 Abington Irish Rep 52.38N 8.25W
103 N2 Abington Massachusetts 42.07N 70.55W
57 F2 Abington Strathclyde Scotland 55.29N 3.42W
90 D8 Abinsi Nigeria 7.45N 8.52E
44 B3 Abinsk U.S.S.R. 44.52N 38.11E
88 Q7 Abiod,Djebel el mts Algeria
88 R4 Abiod, el R Algeria
88 O5 Abiodh Sidi Cheikh,El Algeria 32.54N 0.35E
31 G2 Ab-i-Panja R Afghanistan
109 D5 Abiquiu New Mexico 36.12N 106.20W
109 D5 Abiquiu Res New Mexico
31 A3 Ab-i-Rahuk Afghanistan 35.23N 62.00E
31 C2 Ab-i-Safed R Afghanistan
51 G3 Abisko Sweden 68.21N 18.50E
101 U5 Abitau L N W Terr 60.25N 107.10W
99 K3 Abitibi Ontario 49.03N 80.52W
99 J3 Abitibi Canyon Dam Ontario 49.54N 81.36W
99 K4 Abitibi, L Ontario
99 J2 Abitibi R Ontario
76 B9 Abiul Portugal 39.52N 8.32W
44 D4 Abkhazskaya A.S.S.R U.S.S.R.
39 F3 Abkit U.S.S.R. 64.10N 157.27E
31 E2 Ab Kul Afghanistan 36.19N 68.45E
77 L6 Abla Spain 37.09N 2.46W
43 P2 Ablaketka U.S.S.R. 49.55N 82.44E
66 F5 Ablantschen Switzerland 46.34N 7.17E
42 J6 Ablatukan U.S.S.R. 51.16N 112.08E
87 F2 Abligo Ethiopia 16.17N 37.59E
69 B6 Ablis France 48.31N 1.50E
75 G4 Ablitas Spain 41.58N 1.39W
70 L3 Ablon France 49.23N 0.17E
68 G5 Ablon-sur-Seine France 48.44N 2.26E
43 M7 Ablyk Tadzhikistan U.S.S.R. 40.59N 70.03E
12 C2 Abminga S Australia 26.08S 134.50E
85 L6 Abnub Egypt 27.14N 31.06E
Åbo see Turku
109 D7 Abo New Mexico 34.27N 106.21W
90 H1 Abo mountain reg Chad
90 D9 Aboa Cameroon 4.49N 8.56E
75 H2 Abodi, Sierra de mts Spain
29 D2 Abohar India 30.11N 74.14E
88 J10 Aboïliga reg Mauritania
76 C5 Aboim Portugal 41.55N 8.27W
89 H9 Aboisso Ivory Coast 5.26N 3.13W
87 D6 Aboke Sudan 9.42N 32.11E
93 D3 Aboki Uganda 2.22N 32.42E
89 K8 Abomey Benin 7.14N 2.00E
96 R14 Abona,Pta.de Tenerife Canary Is 28.09N 16.26W
71 K4 Abondance France 46.17N 6.44E
90 C9 Abonema Nigeria 4.41N 6.49E
18 B3 Abongabong,Gunung mt Sumatra Indonesia 4.20N 96.45E
90 F10 Abong-Mbang Cameroon 3.58N 13.10E
62 M8 Abony Hungary 47.10N 20.00E
33 K8 Aboot Field Oman 17.24N 53.21E
19 J7 Aborlan Philippines 9.25N 118.32E
28 K2 Abors tribe Assam India
106 E4 Abor Vitae Wisconsin 45.55N 89.40W
52 K3 Åbosjö Sweden 63.44N 17.45E
89 J9 Aboso Ghana 5.23N 1.57W
35 D1 Abou Châch Lebanon 33.08N 35.13E
Abou Daame see Abu Da'me
90 J6 Abou Deïa Chad 11.30N 19.18E
Abou ed Douhour see Abu ed Duhūr
Abou Fije,Ouâdi see Abu Fīje, Wādī watercourse
90 K5 Abou Goulem Chad 13.41N 21.40E
Abou-Kemâl see Abu Kemāl
117 B2 Abounamy R Fr Guiana S America
90 H6 Abou-Rai Chad 11.56N 17.00E
Abou Rejmeïne,Jebel see Abu Rujmein, Jebel Mts
90 J5 Abou Telfane mt Chad 12.03N 19.00E
44 F7 Abovyan Armenia U.S.S.R. 40.17N 44.36E

58 L4 Aboyne Grampian Scotland 57.04N 2.48W
33 H4 Abqaiq Saudi Arabia 25.56N 49.40E
33 H3 Abqaiq oil well Saudi Arabia 26.08N 49.45E
120 E9 Abra Chile 21.55S 68.50W
121 J9 Abra, Canal str Chile
33 F9 Abrād,Wādī watercourse Yemen
76 C6 Abragão Portugal 41.09N 8.14W
113 L9 Abraham B Aleutian Is Pacific Oc
77 H2 Abraham, Embalse de T res Spain 39.25N 4.15W
107 L4 Abraham Lincoln Nat.Hist.Park Kentucky
98 R9 Abraham,Plains of Quebec 46.48N 71.13W
116 H3 Abraham's Bay Mayaguana Bahamas 22.23N 72.58W
95 F5 Abrahamsdam S Africa 29.09S 22.37E
44 G8 Abrakunis Nakhichevan' U.S.S.R. 39.08N 45.36E
121 D8 Abra,L.del Argentina
57 H5 Abram Greater Manchester England 53.31N 2.36W
45 N5 Abramovka U.S.S.R. 51.12N 41.02E
47 E3 Abramov,Mys C U.S.S.R. 66.24N 43.12E
106 F5 Abrams Wisconsin 44.46N 88.04W
45 J1 Abramtsevo U.S.S.R. 56.14N 37.58E
76 C10 Abrantes Portugal 39.28N 8.12W
120 F10 Abra Pampa Argentina 22.47S 65.41W
86 L4 Abraquein, El hill Egypt 30.33N 33.52E
44 B3 Abrau Dyurso U.S.S.R. 44.42N 37.37E
76 D7 Abraveses Portugal 40.41N 7.55W
87 K8 Abred,El Ethiopia 5.37N 45.12E
119 D3 Abrego Colombia 8.08N 73.14W
115 C4 Abreojos, Pta C Mexico 26.44N 113.40W
75 O4 Abrera Spain 41.31N 1.55E
69 N6 Abreschviller France 48.39N 7.06E
71 H5 Abrets,les France 45.32N 5.35E
85 L9 'Abri Sudan 20.46N 30.21E
87 C5 Abri Sudan 11.41N 30.26E
56 M4 Abridge Essex England 51.40N 0.08E
71 K7 Abriès France 44.48N 6.56E
76 A10 Abrigada Portugal 39.08N 9.01W
80 N7 Abriola Italy 40.31N 15.49E
37 J8 Abrīsham mt Iran 37.16N 45.11E
118 J5 Abrolhos,Arquipélago dos arch Brazil
41 A3 Abrosimova R Novaya Zemlya U.S.S.R.
77 L6 Abrucena Spain 37.08N 2.47W
82 H4 Abrud Romania 46.16N 23.05E
46 E1 Abruka isld Estonia U.S.S.R. 58.05N 22.30E
76 D7 Abrunhosa Portugal 40.32N 7.45W
76 D7 Abrunhosa Velha Portugal 40.35N 7.40W
80 H4 Abruzzese,Appennino mts Italy
100 B8 Abruzzi, Mt Br Columbia 50.28N 115.09W
80 J4 Abruzzo prov Italy
108 N3 Absaraka N Dakota 46.59N 97.24W
110 P4 Absaroka Ra Montana/Wyoming
110 Q4 Absarokee Montana 45.31N 109.26W
64 K5 Absberg W Germany 49.09N 10.53E
65 N5 Absdorf Austria 48.24N 15.59E
103 F8 Absecon New Jersey 39.26N 74.30W
72 C2 Absie,l' France 46.38N 0.34W
34 F4 Abtar, Jebel el mts Syria
65 H6 Abtenau Austria 47.34N 13.21E
64 H1 Abterode W Germany 51.13N 9.55E
34 N9 'Abtīyah, Al Iraq 29.30N 45.58E
64 J6 Abtsgmünd W Germany 48.54N 10.01E
63 S4 Abtshagen E Germany 54.12N 13.02E
89 B6 Abu Guinea-Bissau 11.26N 15.58W
29 C5 Abu India 24.41N 72.50E
87 B2 Abu 'Agag,Jeb. mt Sudan 17.32N 28.59E
35 G6 Abu 'Alanda Jordan 31.54N 35.58E
86 K8 Abu 'Alaqa, Gebel hill Egypt 28.52N 33.22E
86 G5 Abu Alâwi, Wâdî watercourse Egypt
34 P10 Abū al Hīrān Saudi Arabia 28.45N 47.02E
34 F6 Abu al Husain, Khabrat salt marsh Jordan
33 H3 Abū 'Alī isld Saudi Arabia 27.22N 49.35E
33 K4 Abu al Jirab isld U.A.E.
34 P8 Abū al Khasīb Iraq 30.26N 48.00E
34 K4 Abu al Kufa Iraq 34.21N 42.51E
34 D8 Abu 'Amūd, Wādī watercourse Jordan
85 M9 Abu Araja, Wadi watercourse Sudan
Abu Araji see Abu Arāzi
34 J4 Abu Arāzi Iraq 34.58N 41.48E
33 E8 Abū 'Arīsh Saudi Arabia 16.59N 42.49E
34 J8 Abu ar Ruwath,Sha'ib watercourse Saudi Arabia
86 M4 Abu 'Aweigîla Egypt 30.50N 34.07E
33 G6 Abū Bahr gravel plain Saudi Arabia
85 J7 Abu Ballâs mt Egypt 24.26N 27.36E
19 G1 Abucay Luzon Philippines 14.43N 120.33E
86 O1 'Ābūd Jordan 32.01N 35.03E
33 F8 Abū Dā'ir dist Yemen
34 F2 Abu Da'me Syria 36.27N 38.16E
33 A6 Abu Daweim,Jabal mt Sudan 20.51N 34.55E
86 G4 Abu Dawûd el Sibâkh Egypt 30.55N 31.34E
90 M5 Abu Deleiq Darfur Sudan 13.17N 25.37E
87 D3 Abu Deleiq Khartoum Sudan 15.57N 33.48E
33 L4 Abū Dhabi U.A.E. 24.28N 54.25E
33 C5 Abū Ḍībā' Saudi Arabia 23.14N 39.34E
35 E6 Abu Dis Jordan 31.46N 35.16E
85 M10 Abu Dis Sudan 19.06N 33.35E
85 N7 Abu Diyâb, Gebel mt Egypt 25.13N 34.12E
87 C4 Abu Dom,Jeb mt Sudan 12.22N 31.31E
87 D1 Abu Dom,Wadi Sudan
Abū Dubā see Abū Ḍībā'
85 M6 Abu Dukhan,Gebel mt Egypt 27.10N 33.15E
86 K9 Abu Durba Egypt 28.29N 33.20E
86 K8 Abu Durba, Gebel hill Egypt 28.33N 33.20E
86 G5 Abu Durma, Wâdî watercourse Egypt
85 N9 Abu Duweim, Jebel mt Sudan 20.47N 34.53E
34 E3 Abu ed Duhūr Syria 35.45N 37.02E
86 L7 Abu el Gain, Wâdî watercourse Egypt
86 P5 Abū el Ḥamām, Jebel mt Jordan 30.26N 35.38E
34 K5 Abu el Jir Iraq 33.16N 42.53E
34 C8 Abū el Jurdhān Jordan 30.20N 35.46E
35 H10 Abu el Kurrath watercourse Jordan
86 F6 Abu el Namrus Egypt 29.57N 31.13E
35 F4 Abu el Qein Jordan 32.28N 35.40E
120 G1 Abufari Brazil 5.10S 62.59W
Abū Fījah,Wadi see Abu Fīje,Wādī, watercourse
34 H2 Abu Fīje, Wādī watercourse Syria
35 F2 Abu Fulah Syria 32.59N 35.39E
34 K5 Abū Furūkh watercourse Iraq
87 A5 Abu Gabra Sudan 11.02N 26.50E
87 F3 Abu Gamal Sudan 15.09N 36.26E
86 E7 Abu Gandîr Egypt 29.14N 30.41E
87 E5 Abu Gedaf Sudan 11.30N 34.50E
33 L5 Abū Gedū' oil field U.A.E. 23.17N 54.08E
34 J6 Abū Ghar watercourse Iraq
34 O8 Abū Ghar, Sha'ib watercourse Iraq
Abu Ghīrab see Abū Ghurāb
85 M10 Abu Ghirban Sudan 19.10N 32.19E
35 D6 Abū Ghōsh Israel 31.48N 35.06E
34 P6 Abū Ghurāb Iraq 32.23N 47.22E
86 L5 Abu Gidil, Wâdi watercourse Egypt
86 E8 Abu Girg Egypt 28.32N 30.47E
87 C5 Abu Gubeiha Sudan 11.29N 31.14E
85 N7 Abu Gurdi, Gebel mt Egypt 24.00N 35.04E
87 C5 Abu Gureis Sudan 11.41N 31.38E
87 C4 Abu Habl watercourse Sudan
86 K10 Abu Ḥad, Gebel hill Egypt 27.41N 33.03E
33 H3 Abū Ḥadrīyah oil field Saudi Arabia 27.18N 49.01E
86 J9 Abu Ḥâd, Wâdi watercourse Egypt
34 F6 Abu Ḥafrah, Wādī watercourse Jordan
85 J4 Abu Haggag Egypt 31.10N 27.49E
34 D7 Abū Hallūfa, Jebel mt Jordan 31.23N 36.18E
33 A4 Abu Hamamid,Gebel mt Egypt 24.10N 34.46E
86 P9 Abū Hamāta Saudi Arabia 28.06N 35.37E
85 M10 Abu Hamed Sudan 19.32N 33.20E
87 C4 Abu Hamra Sudan 12.47N 31.02E
90 M5 Abu Hamra, Wadi watercourse Sudan
85 M10 Abu Haraz Sudan 19.03N 32.08E
87 B4 Abu Haraz Sudan 13.00N 29.52E
85 J4 Abu Hashaifa B Egypt

85 M10 Abu Hashim Sudan 18.58N 33.33E
87 C2 Abu Hashim watercourse Sudan
34 K5 Abū Ḥaşwah Iraq 33.37N 42.54E
87 D4 Abu Higar Sudan 12.50N 33.59E
86 D3 Abu Hummus Egypt 31.06N 30.19E
86 K9 Abu Huswa,Gebel hill Egypt 28.29N 33.23E
87 C3 Abu Hut watercourse Sudan
87 G5 Abuia Mieda Ethiopia 10.30N 39.49E
90 C7 Abuja Nigeria 9.10N 7.06E
35 H1 Abu Jaj watercourse Syria
33 G4 Abū Jifān oil field Saudi Arabia 24.29N 47.47E
Abu Jir oil bore see Abu el Jir
87 A4 Abu Kabisa Sudan 13.06N 27.20E
Abu Kamāl see Abu Kemāl
86 G4 Abu Kebîr Egypt 30.44N 31.40E
34 H4 Abu Kemāl Syria 34.29N 40.56E
31 D5 Abu Khan Afghanistan 31.36N 67.16E
86 G8 Abu Kharaga, Wâdî watercourse Egypt
86 J9 Abu Khashaba, Gebel hill Egypt 28.08N 32.51E
90 M4 Abu Ku' Sudan 14.02N 25.59E
20 O4 Abukuma-gawa R Japan
20 O5 Abukuma-kōchi hills Japan
87 C3 Abu La'ot watercourse Sudan
33 D7 Abū Latt I Saudi Arabia 19.57N 40.07E
87 D5 Abulduga,Jeb. mt Sudan 11.00N 33.55E
Abul Hiran see Abū al Hīrān
86 H10 Abu Ligân, Wâdî watercourse Egypt
86 L3 Abu Liheimin hill Egypt 31.01N 33.49E
Abul Khasib see Abū al Khasīb
33 B4 Abū Madd,Ra's C Saudi Arabia 24.50N 37.12E
34 J6 Abū Masajid hill Iraq 32.45N 41.11E
86 M9 Abu Mas'ûd, Gebel hill Egypt 28.26N 34.06E
90 N6 Abu Matarik Sudan 10.59N 26.15E
87 E5 Abu Mendi,Jeb. hills Ethiopia
86 C4 Abu Mîna ruins Egypt 30.50N 29.41E
91 H2 Abumombozi Zaïre 3.34N 22.03E
32 F8 Abū Mūsá isld Iran 25.52N 55.00E
120 F3 Abunã Brazil 9.41S 65.20W
34 L4 Abu Nahla, Wādī watercourse Iraq
119 F8 Abunai Brazil 1.54S 66.35W
33 D4 Abū Namasah Saudi Arabia 24.50N 40.14E
120 E3 Abunã, R Bolivia/Brazil
35 G5 Abu Nuseir Jordan 32.05N 35.49E
35 G3 Abu Qantarah Syria 32.40N 35.59E
35 D6 Abu Qash Jordan 31.57N 35.10E
86 D3 Abu Qîr Egypt 31.19N 30.04E
33 B10 Abū Qīyāmah,Ra's C S Yemen 12.43N 44.54E
86 E10 Abu Qurqâs Egypt 27.56N 30.50E
87 D4 Abu Qurud,Jeb mt Sudan 12.30N 33.19E
87 D3 Abu Qut'a Sudan 14.55N 32.41E
86 P4 'Ābūr Jordan 30.48N 35.44E
33 B3 Abū Rāqah Saudi Arabia 27.06N 37.08E
90 M8 Abu Ras Sudan 7.59N 25.31E
33 N6 Abū Raşāş,Ra's C Oman 20.10N 58.38E
20 E10 Aburatsu Japan 31.35N 131.23E
89 J9 Aburi Ghana 5.53N 0.09W
86 G5 Aburimth Wâdî watercourse Egypt
86 G8 Abu Rimth, Wâdi watercourse Egypt
86 G7 Abu Rîsha, Wâdî watercourse Egypt
89 B3 Aburo mt Zaïre 2.01N 30.50E
29 C5 Abu Road India 24.30N 72.59E
33 C5 Abū Rubayq Saudi Arabia 23.45N 39.44E
86 K8 Abu Rudeis oil well Egypt 28.58N 33.11E
Abu Rujmayn,Jebel see Abu Rujmein,Jebel
34 F4 Abu Rujmein, Jebel mts Syria
87 C4 Abu Rukba Sudan 12.57N 31.59E
35 G9 Abu Rukba watercourse Jordan
86 N7 Abu Rûtha,Gebel hill Egypt 29.30N 34.44E
33 D6 Abū Şādi, Jabal mt Saudi Arabia 20.27N 40.02E
Abū Sād,Jabal see Abū Şādi, Jabal mt
33 J3 Abu Sa 'Fah oil well The Gulf 26.58N 50.30E
34 E10 Abu Sallah watercourse Saudi Arabia
33 H4 Abū Sawādah Saudi Arabia 24.50N 48.52E
34 M5 Abū Şaydah Saghīrah Iraq 33.56N 44.48E
33 B6 Abu Shagara,Ras C Sudan 21.06N 37.19E
86 G6 Abu Shâma, Gebel hill Egypt 29.52N 31.37E
87 A4 Abu Shanab Sudan 13.58N 27.49E
86 K10 Abu Sha'r, Gebel hill Egypt 27.57N 33.11E
35 F10 Abu Shauka Jordan 30.51N 35.40E
33 C6 Abū Shidād, Jabal mt Saudi Arabia 20.53N 39.33E
35 E5 Abu Sidra watercourse Jordan
85 L8 Abu Simbel Temple ruins Egypt 22.19N 31.38E
86 F4 Abu Sîr Bana Egypt 30.55N 31.15E
33 A3 Abu Soma,Ras C Egypt 26.50N 34.00E
34 M7 Abū Şukhayr Iraq 31.54N 44.27E
86 H5 Abu Şultân Egypt 30.24N 32.21E
90 L4 Abu Sunt, Wadi watercourse Sudan
86 H4 Abu Suweir Egypt 30.34N 32.09E
35 J6 Abu Suwwana watercourse Jordan
20 K2 Abuta Japan 42.34N 140.46E
87 B2 Abu Tabari Sudan 17.32N 28.32E
33 B3 Abū Ţāqah Saudi Arabia 27.00N 37.50E
85 K7 Abu Ṭartûr, Gebel Egypt
11 E10 Abut Hd New Zealand 43.05S 170.15E
85 L6 Abu Tig Egypt 27.06N 31.17E
87 F1 Abu Tikr Sudan 18.08N 36.17E
86 G6 Abu Tireifîya,Gebel hill Egypt 29.42N 31.48E
85 N7 Abû Tiyûr,Gebel mt Egypt 25.48N 34.23E
87 D2 Abu Tuleih battlefield Sudan 17.10N 33.05E
86 N5 Abu Tummeir,Gebel hill Egypt 30.05N 34.33E
34 D10 Abu Ujayyijāt Saudi Arabia 28.20N 36.40E
33 A8 Abū Urayqiţ,Ra's C Saudi Arabia 26.02N 50.07E
87 C3 Abu 'Urug Sudan 15.52N 30.25E
115 F5 Abuya Mexico 24.16N 107.01W
Abuya Myeda see Abuia Mieda
19 M6 Abuyog Philippines 10.44N 125.01E
87 B4 Abu Zabad Sudan 12.21N 29.16E
86 F5 Abu Za'bal Egypt 30.15N 31.21E
Abuzaidabad see Abū Zeydābād
32 C5 Abūzam Iran 30.58N 49.01E
86 K7 Abu Zenîma Egypt 29.03N 33.06E
32 D4 Abū Zeydābād Iran 33.54N 51.42E
87 D6 Abwong Sudan 9.05N 32.12E
52 J10 Åby Kalmar Sweden 56.46N 16.20E
52 J8 Åby Østergotland Sweden 58.40N 16.10E
87 A4 Abyad Sudan 13.47N 26.24E
35 G10 Abyad watercourse Jordan
85 C6 Abyaḍ, al Libya 26.49N 14.01E
33 C5 Abyaḍ,Ar Ra's al C Saudi Arabia 23.33N 38.32E
86 F8 Abyad, Gebel el hill Egypt 28.46N 31.01E
33 A2 Abyaḍ,Jabal al mt Saudi Arabia 28.10N 35.33E
85 K10 Abyad, Jebel mt Sudan
34 F4 Abyad, Jebel el mts Syria
87 B5 Abyad,L Sudan 10.17N 29.59E
86 P5 Abyaḍ, Wādī watercourse Jordan
86 H6 Abyad, Wâdî el watercourse Egypt
51 H6 Åby älv R Sweden
33 F10 Abyān dist S Yemen
85 F3 Abyār,Al Libya 32.13N 20.33E
33 C4 Abyār, 'Alī Saudi Arabia 24.22N 39.32E
34 C10 Abyār Banī Murr Saudi Arabia 28.23N 35.45E
53 D2 Åbybro Denmark 57.09N 9.45E
14 C5 Abydos W Australia 21.25S 118.56E
37 C3 Abydus anc site Turkey 40.12N 26.25E
87 B6 Abyei Sudan 9.35N 28.28E
32 D2 Ābyek Iran 36.01N 50.35E
89 H9 Aby,L Ivory Coast 5.15N 3.10W
116 N3 Abymes Guadeloupe W I 16.16N 61.31W
51 J6 Åbyn Sweden 65.03N 21.20E
86 E10 Abyûna Egypt 27.58N 30.49E
39 D1 Abyy U.S.S.R. 68.30N 145.10E
72 F3 Abzac France 46.06N 0.42E
43 E1 Abzakovo Bashkir U.S.S.R. 53.49N 58.35E
43 D2 Abzanovo Bashkir U.S.S.R. 51.51N 56.45E

87 J10 Acaca Somalia 1.30N 42.23E
95 F8 Acacia S Africa 32.18S 22.40E
13 K2 Acacia Ridge dist Brisbane, Qnsld
119 D6 Acacias Colombia 3.59N 73.46W
Academy of Sciences Range see Akademii Nauk, Khrebet Ra
104 R2 Acadia Nat.Park Maine
100 G7 Acadia Valley Alberta 51.10N 110.10W
118 E8 Açaí Brazil 23.29S 50.45W
118 J2 Acajutiba Brazil 11.40S 38.00W
115 P11 Acajutla El Salvador 13.34N 89.50W
115 N9 Acala Mexico 16.35N 92.46W
112 B4 Acala Texas 31.20N 105.56W
91 A3 Acalayong Equat Guinea 1.06N 9.39E
115 J7 Acámbaro Mexico 20.01N 100.42W
115 K8 Acambay Mexico 19.56N 99.52W
115 P7 Acancéh Mexico 20.49N 89.29W
119 C3 Acandí Colombia 8.32N 77.20W
115 G6 Acaponeta Mexico 22.30N 105.25W
115 K9 Acapulco Mexico 16.51N 99.56W
117 C5 Acapuzal,Sa.do mts Brazil
117 D5 Acará Brazil 2.00S 48.15W
119 F8 Acarabu, I Brazil 0.25S 66.25W
117 C6 Acarai R Brazil
119 H9 Acará,L Amazonas Brazil 3.37S 62.38W
120 G2 Acará,L Amazonas Brazil 6.23S 62.28W
117 D6 Acará Miri, R Brazil
117 D6 Acará,R Brazil
117 G6 Acaraú Brazil 2.56S 40.08W
117 G6 Acaraú R Brazil
118 C9 Acaray,R Paraguay
120 C6 Acari Peru 15.25S 74.37W
117 H8 Acarí Rio Grande do Norte Brazil 6.23S 36.35W
119 E3 Acarigua Venezuela 9.35N 69.12W
117 A8 Acari, R Brazil
120 C6 Acari,R.de Peru
117 A4 Acari,Sa. mts Brazil/Guyana
81 H9 Acate Sicily 37.02N 14.30E
115 K8 Acatlán Mexico 18.12N 98.02W
115 L8 Acatlán de Pérez Figueroa Mexico 18.32N 96.36W
115 L8 Acatzingo Mexico 18.59N 97.49W
120 E11 Acay,Nev. de pk Argentina 24.25S 66.08W
115 M9 Acayucán Mexico 17.59N 94.58W
80 M6 Accadia Italy 41.10N 15.20E
79 A6 Accéglio Italy 44.28N 6.59E
81 D4 Accettori,Pta s' Sardinia 39.36N 9.38E
81 M3 Accettura Italy 40.29N 16.10E
80 J4 Acciano Italy 42.10N 13.44E
13 F3 Accident Inlet Queensland
104 K9 Accomac Virginia 37.43N 75.41W
103 N2 Accord Massachusetts 42.11N 70.53W
103 F3 Accord New York 41.47N 74.14W
72 C10 Accous France 42.58N 0.36W
104 D9 Accoville W Virginia 37.46N 81.51W
89 J9 Accra Ghana 5.33N 0.15W
57 J5 Accrington Lancs England 53.46N 2.21W
80 H3 Accúmoli Italy 42.42N 13.15E
76 F8 Acebo Spain 40.13N 6.43W
77 E2 Acedera Spain 39.04N 5.34W
121 G3 Acegua Uruguay 31.54S 54.07W
18 B3 Aceh prov Sumatra Indonesia
76 F9 Acehuche Spain 39.48N 6.39W
110 M7 Acequia Idaho 42.40N 113.36W
77 M2 Acequion, Laguna Spain 39.02N 2.02W
75 G5 Acered Spain 41.10N 1.37W
80 N7 Acerenza Italy 40.48N 15.56E
80 M7 Acerno Italy 40.44N 15.04E
80 K7 Acerra Italy 40.56N 14.22E
77 D3 Aceuchal Spain 38.39N 6.30W
121 E4 Acevedo Argentina 33.46S 60.22W
64 G8 Ach R W Germany
120 E7 Achacachi Bolivia 16.01S 68.44W
96 V1 Achada Azores Atlantic Ocean 37.36N 25.16W
96 U1 Achadinha Azores 37.36N 25.17W
119 F4 Achaguas Venezuela 7.46N 68.06W
47 L8 Achair U.S.S.R. 54.40N 73.54E
30 C6 Achalda Uttar Prad India 26.44N 79.24E
29 E7 Achalpur Maharashtra India 21.19N 77.30E
44 F4 Achaluki U.S.S.R. 43.40N 44.41E
28 D2 Achampet Andhra Prad India 16.30N 78.38E
58 G3 Achanalt Highland Scotland 57.36N 4.55W
28 E2 Achanta Andhra Prad India 16.37N 81.55E
121 A9 Achao Chile 42.30S 73.30W
121 G4 Achar Uruguay 32.20S 56.15W
58 E5 Acharacle Highland Scotland 56.45N 5.48W
58 H5 Acharn Tayside Scotland 56.34N 4.02W
58 K2 Achavanich Highland Scotland 58.22N 3.24W
39 J4 Achayvayam U.S.S.R. 61.00N 170.16E
39 J4 Achayvayam R U.S.S.R.
Achchan see Bostan
Achchik Köl L see Aqqikkol Hu
41 O7 Achchygyy-Aly U.S.S.R. 67.29N 130.31E
65 E7 Ache R Austria
65 F7 Ache R Austria
90 E2 Achegour Niger 19.10N 11.54E
61 M2 Achel Belgium 51.15N 5.29E
90 F1 Achelouma Niger 22.12N 12.50E
89 F3 Achemine Mauritania 16.45N 6.53W
64 N8 Achen R W Germany
61 L5 Achêne Belgium 50.16N 5.03E
21 D5 Acheng Heilongjiang China 45.33N 127.00E
100 P4 Acheninni L Saskatchewan 54.30N 103.00W
65 E6 Achenkirch Austria 47.33N 11.43E
39 L3 Achen,Mys C U.S.S.R. 64.46N 175.31W
64 M8 Achenpass W Germany 47.36N 11.39E
65 E7 Achensee L Austria 47.26N 11.45E
65 E6 Achen-tal V Austria
65 E6 Achenwald Austria 47.34N 11.41E
68 B2 Achères France 48.58N 2.04E
64 E6 Achern W Germany 48.38N 8.05E
11 H9 Acheron R New Zealand
61 L5 Achet Belgium 50.20N 5.10E
76 B10 Achete Portugal 39.20N 8.42W
69 D3 Acheux-en-Amienois France 50.05N 2.32E
58 G2 Achfarry Highland Scotland 58.18N 4.55W
30 E3 Achham Nepal 29.02N 81.18E
30 A5 Achhnera Uttar Prad India 27.10N 77.45E
43 O7 Achi Kirgiziya U.S.S.R. 41.10N 73.02E
69 D3 Achicourt France 50.16N 2.45E
69 D3 Achiet-le-Grand France 50.08N 2.48E
99 F6 Achigan Ontario 46.53N 84.11W
91 D5 Achikouya,Plat.des Gabon/Congo
44 F3 Achikulak U.S.S.R. 44.34N 44.51E
59 C4 Achill Irish Rep 53.56N 9.54W
59 C4 Achillbeg I Irish Rep 53.52N 9.57W
109 O8 Achille Oklahoma 33.51N 96.24W
11 D2 Achilles Pt Auckland New Zealand 36.51S 174.52E
59 B4 Achill Hd Irish Rep 53.59N 10.13W
59 B4 Achill I Irish Rep 54.00N 10.00W
58 F2 Achiltibuie Highland Scotland 58.01N 5.25W
63 K6 Achim W Germany 53.01N 9.02E
89 J9 Achimota Ghana 5.35N 0.15W
42 B2 Achimovy 2-ye U.S.S.R. 60.08N 75.02E
31 F3 Achin Afghanistan 34.04N 70.41E
42 E4 Achinsk U.S.S.R. 56.20N 90.33E
121 D4 Achiras Argentina 33.10S 64.58W
120 B2 Achiras Peru 7.48S 77.06W
47 K6 Achiry U.S.S.R. 58.49N 67.12E
43 J5 Achisay Kazakhstan U.S.S.R. 43.15N 68.53E
44 H5 Achisu U.S.S.R. 42.39N 47.40E
47 H7 Achit U.S.S.R. 56.48N 57.50E
22 B2 Achit Nuur L Mongolia
120 B1 Achiyacu R Peru
44 G4 Achkhoy-Martan U.S.S.R. 43.12N 45.16E
60 K7 Achlum Netherlands 53.09N 5.29E
58 E4 Achmore Highland Scotland 57.20N 5.35W
58 F3 Achnasheen Highland Scotland 57.34N 5.05W
58 F4 Achnashellach Highland Scotland 57.28N 5.20W
29 G7 Achota India 20.40N 81.39E
89 B3 Achoueir Mauritania 17.59N 14.18W
91 A4 Achouka Gabon 0.54S 9.44E
99 N7 Achray Ontario 45.52N 77.45W
58 H6 Achray, L Central Scotland 56.14N 4.24W
60 K14 Acht Netherlands 51.28N 5.25E
60 K11 Achterveld Netherlands 52.08N 5.30E
63 T4 Achter-wasser L E Germany
60 G14 Achtmaal Netherlands 51.27N 4.35E
120 D12 Achura,Pta. C Chile 26.17S 70.45W
44 B2 Achuyevo U.S.S.R. 45.42N 37.46E
93 E3 Achwa Uganda 2.06N 33.50E
93 D2 Achwa R Uganda
Achzib see Tel Akhziv
37 D6 Acı R Turkey
81 K8 Aci Castello Sicily 37.33N 15.09E
103 D3 Acidalia New York 41.54N 75.03W
70 G5 Acigne France 48.08N 1.31W
36 H4 Acıgöl Turkey 38.33N 34.31E
36 D5 Acıgöl L Turkey
89 E4 Acil Barké Mali 15.01N 9.09W
87 E7 Acioio Ethiopia 6.58N 34.28E
36 D5 Acıpayam Turkey 37.28N 29.22E
81 K8 Acireale Sicily 37.36N 15.10E
81 K8 Aci Sant' Antonio Sicily 37.37N 15.08E
37 D6 Acısu R Turkey
36 F4 Acıtuz Gölü L Turkey
112 F3 Ackerly Texas 32.32N 101.47W
107 G8 Ackerman Mississippi 33.19N 89.11W
107 H7 Ackia Battleground Nat.Mon Mississippi 34.15N 88.49W
108 R7 Ackley Iowa 42.34N 93.02W
57 K2 Acklington Northumb England 55.18N 1.38W
116 G3 Acklins, Bight of Bahamas 22.30N 74.10W
116 G3 AcklinsI Bahamas
57 L5 Ackworth W Yorks England 53.39N 1.20W
59 E3 Aclare Irish Rep 54.02N 8.54W
56 P2 Acle Norfolk Eng 52.38N 1.33E
118 G10 Aclimacao dist São Paulo Brazil
100 D7 Acme Alberta 51.32N 113.28W
107 E10 Acme Louisiana 31.17N 91.49W
106 J5 Acme Michigan 44.46N 85.30W
105 J3 Acme N Carolina 34.20N 78.11W
109 F8 Acme New Mexico 33.36N 104.20W
112 H1 Acme Texas 34.20N 99.51W
120 C5 Acobamba Huancavelica Peru 12.46S 74.36W
120 C4 Acobamba Junín Peru 11.40S 74.43W
71 C3 Acolin R France
120 D5 Acomayo Cuzco Peru 13.50S 71.39W
120 B3 Acomayo Huánuco Peru 9.46S 76.05W
57 L5 Acomb N Yorks England 53.57N 1.08W
109 C6 Acomita New Mexico 35.04N 107.34W
121 B4 Aconcagua prov Chile
121 B4 Aconcagua, Cerro pk Argentina 32.40S 70.02W
121 B4 Aconcagua, R Chile
120 E12 Aconquija,Nev.de mts Argentina
117 G8 Acopiara Brazil 6.08S 39.30W
76 D8 Acor mt Portugal 40.14N 7.46W
120 D6 Acora Peru 15.59S 69.48W
96 H4 Açôres,Ilhas dos Atlantic Oc 38.30N 28.00W
86 E9 Acoris ruins Egypt 28.11N 30.46E
94 L5 Acorn Hoek S Africa 24.37S 31.02E
61 L4 Acosse Belgium 50.36N 5.03E
120 B5 Acostambo Peru 12.22S 75.06W
115 M4 Acoyapa Nicaragua 11.55N 85.05W
61 J5 Acoz Belgium 50.22N 4.32E
81 J6 Acquacalda Lipari Is Italy 38.32N 14.58E
79 N7 Acqualagna Italy 43.37N 12.40E
79 G4 Acquanegra Cremonese Italy 45.10N 9.53E
80 E3 Acquapendente Italy 42.44N 11.52E
81 L5 Acquappesa Italy 39.29N 15.58E
66 M6 Acquarossa Switzerland 46.27N 8.58E
80 H3 Acquasanta Italy 42.46N 13.25E
66 O7 Acquaséria Italy 46.04N 9.16E
80 G3 Acquasparta Italy 42.41N 12.33E
81 N2 Acquaviva delle Fonti Italy 40.54N 16.50E
80 J3 Acquaviva Picena Italy 42.57N 13.49E
79 D5 Acqui Italy 44.41N 8.28E
70 N3 Acquigny France 49.11N 1.11E
103 F2 Acra New York 42.18N 74.03W
12 D4 Acraman, L S Australia
88 P9 Acrar N'Ahnet reg Algeria
Acre Israel see 'Akko
120 D4 Acre R Brazil
120 D3 Acre state Brazil
103 D7 Acres New Jersey 39.41N 75.07W
81 M5 Acri Italy 39.29N 16.23E
75 F3 Acrijos Spain 42.03N 2.10W
62 K8 Acs Hungary 47.42N 18.00E
62 L8 Acsa Hungary 47.46N 19.21E
65 P7 Acsád Hungary 47.20N 16.44E
122 N10 Actaeon Group atolls Pacific Oc 22.00S 136.00W
96 B14 Actæon, Mt St Helena Atlantic Ocean 15.58S 5.42W
111 F7 Acton California 34.27N 118.11W
55 D3 Acton London Eng 51.31N 0.17W
110 R4 Acton Montana 45.57N 108.40W
99 K9 Acton Ontario 43.38N 80.04W
12 A6 Acton dist Canberra Australia
56 G4 Acton Turville Avon Eng 51.32N 2.17W
99 S7 Acton Vale Quebec 45.39N 72.34W
115 K7 Actopán Mexico 20.19N 98.59W
117 H7 Açu Brazil 5.35S 36.57W
120 F2 Açuã,R Amazonas Brazil
117 H8 Açude Oiticica res Brazil
117 F6 Açu, L Brazil
121 F2 Acuña Argentina 29.51S 57.55W
115 J3 Acuña,Ciudad Mexico 29.19N 100.58W
118 E9 Acungui Brazil 24.55S 49.25W
91 B3 Acurenam Equat Guinea 1.04N 10.46E
118 C4 Açurizal Brazil 15.14S 56.21W
103 N3 Acushnet Massachusetts 41.42N 70.54W
80 H5 Acuto Italy 41.47N 13.11E
81 C2 Acuto,Mte Sardinia 40.47N 9.07E
105 C3 Acworth Georgia 34.03N 84.40W
89 K9 Ada Ghana 5.47N 0.42E
109 N2 Ada Kansas 39.10N 97.54W
106 J7 Ada Michigan 42.58N 85.29W
108 O2 Ada Minnesota 47.19N 96.41W
104 B6 Ada Ohio 40.46N 83.49W
20 Q8 Ada Okinawa Japan 26.46N 128.18E
109 O7 Ada Oklahoma 34.47N 96.41W
82 F5 Ada Yugoslavia 45.49N 20.09E
87 G7 Adaba Ethiopia 7.01N 39.25E
37 G7 Adabağ Turkey 38.37N 42.27E
87 G6 Adabai,R Ethiopia
86 H6 Adabîya Egypt 29.52N 32.30E
19 M1 Adacao Guam Pacific Oc 13.29N 144.51E
20 E2 Adachi dist Tōkyō Japan
87 L6 Adad Somalia 9.23N 46.49E
87 K6 Adadle Somalia 9.47N 44.42E
89 E2 Adafer reg Mauritania
36 C4 Adagide Turkey 38.04N 28.01E
44 B2 Adagum R U.S.S.R.
75 K3 Adahuesca Spain 42.09N 0.01W
87 H3 Adailo Ethiopia 14.29N 40.50E
108 Q8 Adair Iowa 41.30N 94.38W
109 P5 Adair Oklahoma 36.27N 95.17W
100 O8 Adair Saskatchewan 50.22N 103.16W
111 L10 Adair, B. de Mexico
105 C3 Adairsville Georgia 34.22N 84.57W
34 K2 Adaiyah oil bore Iraq 36.10N 42.46E
76 K6 Adaja R Spain
113 Q10 Adak Aleutian Is 51.52N 176.40W
51 G6 Adakgruvan Sweden 65.23N 18.35E
113 Q10 Adak I Aleutian Is 51.50N 176.40W
44 L5 Ada,Kosa sand spit U.S.S.R.
113 Q10 Adak Str Aleutian Is
11 B11 Ada, L New Zealand 44.44S 167.51E
36 C4 Adala Turkey 38.35N 28.19E
87 K9 Adalei Somalia 2.27N 45.10E
87 J4 Adali tribe Djibouti
Adalia see Antalya
52 E6 Ådals-Elva R Norway
52 K3 Ådalsliden Sweden 63.30N 17.00E
33 M5 Adam Oman 22.22N 57.30E
Adamah see Damiya
111 P7 Adamana Arizona 34.59N 109.50W
118 D7 Adamantina Brazil 21.41S 51.04W
101 P10 Adamant Mt Br Columbia 51.44N 117.55W
90 E7 Adamawa reg Nigeria
79 J2 Adamello mts Italy
33 N10 Ad'ami,Al salt marsh Saudi Arabia
12 J6 Adaminaby New S Wales 36.08S 148.36E
35 D1 Adamit Israel 33.05N 35.28E
87 G7 Adamitullo Ethiopia 7.53N 38.41E
35 H6 Adam, Jebel el mt Jordan 31.54N 36.14E
121 E9 Adam, Mt Falkland Is Atlantic Ocean 51.36S 60.00W
65 P3 Adamov Czechoslovakia 49.19N 16.39E
43 E2 Adamovka U.S.S.R. 51.32N 59.55E
42 H5 Adamovo U.S.S.R. 53.28N 109.13E
110 H8 Adam Pk Nevada 41.10N 117.14W
111 B3 Adams California 38.50N 122.44W
104 M4 Adams Massachusetts 42.38N 73.08W
108 S6 Adams Minnesota 43.34N 92.42W
108 M1 Adams N Dakota 48.27N 98.06W
108 O9 Adams Nebraska 40.25N 96.30W
104 J3 Adams New York 43.50N 76.02W
109 J5 Adams Oklahoma 36.44N 101.06W
107 J5 Adams Tennessee 36.34N 87.03W
106 E6 Adams Wisconsin 43.56N 89.49W
110 D3 Adams mt Washington 46.13N 121.29W
28 D6 Adam's Bridge Sri Lanka/India
Adams Glacier see John Quincy Adams Glacier
11 B7 Adams I Auckland Is Pacific Oc
101 O10 Adams L Br Col
11 K8 Adams, Mt New Zealand 41.19S 175.40E
109 P7 Adamson Oklahoma 34.57N 95.33W
26 R8 Adam's Peak Sri Lanka 6.49N 80.30E
111 D2 Adams Pk California 39.55N 120.07W
106 L4 Adam's Pt Michigan 45.25N 83.42W
122 V10 Adam's Rock Pitcairn I Pacific Oc 25.04S 130.05W
59 J7 Adamstown Irish Rep 52.23N 6.43W
103 B6 Adamstown Pennsylvania 40.15N 76.03W
122 V10 Adamstown Pitcairn I Pacific Oc 25.04S 130.05W
107 K8 Adamsville Alabama 33.35N 86.58W
104 D6 Adamsville Ohio 40.04N 81.54W
99 S7 Adamsville Quebec 45.17N 72.46W
103 M3 Adamsville Rhode I 41.34N 71.08W
107 H6 Adamsville Tennessee 35.13N 88.25W
112 J4 Adamsville Texas 31.19N 98.11W
111 M3 Adamsville Utah 38.17N 112.46W
77 G4 Adamuz Spain 38.02N 4.32W
36 H5 Adana Turkey 37.00N 35.19E
100 H6 Adanac Saskatchewan Canada 52.29N 109.06W
'Adan as Sughra see Little Aden
76 K7 Adanero Spain 40.56N 4.36W
18 M6 Adang,Teluk B Kalimantan Indon
Adaouâne see Adwan
36 E2 Adapazarı Turkey 40.45N 30.23E
30 H6 Adapur Bihar India 26.57N 84.57E
87 D6 Adar watercourse Sudan
33 F10 Adaran,Jabal mt S Yemen 13.47N 45.09E
87 F2 Adardi Ethiopia 16.04N 37.06E
59 E6 Adare Irish Rep 52.34N 8.48W
123 K6 Adare, C Antarctica 71.30S 170.24E
87 F2 Adaribab,Jeb. mt Sudan 17.43N 37.18E
85 N9 Adarmo, Khor watercourse Sudan
85 O11 Adarot Sudan 17.47N 36.06E
35 D8 Adasha watercourse Israel/Jordan
87 A3 Adat Abu Bessema Sudan 14.31N 27.21E
87 B3 Adat Umm Rob Sudan 15.31N 29.16E
15 A8 Adaut Moluccas Indonesia 8.10S 131.09E
13 G7 Adavale Queensland 25.54S 144.35E
111 J3 Adaven Nevada 38.04N 115.32W
76 E3 Aday Spain 42.59N 7.23W
108 Q7 Adaza Iowa 42.14N 94.30W
29 H7 Adbhar India 21.57N 83.04E
87 H4 Adbidora Ethiopia 12.58N 41.17E
79 F4 Adda R Italy
90 M7 Adda watercourse Sudan
44 G5 Addala Shukhgelmezr mt U.S.S.R. 42.20N 46.14E
28 D3 Addanki Andhra Prad India 15.50N 80.00E
28 F2 Addatigala Andhra Prad India 17.31N 82.03E
56 J3 Adderbury Oxon Eng 52.01N 1.19W
35 C7 Adderet Israel 31.39N 34.59E
11 O10 Adderley Hd New Zealand 43.36S 172.49E
93 L7 Addi Kenya 1.58S 39.35E
112 M6 Addicks Texas 29.48N 95.40W
57 K5 Addingham W Yorks England 53.57N 1.53W
55 G5 Addington London England 51.22N 0.02W
109 N7 Addington Oklahoma 34.12N 97.58W
11 M10 Addington dist Christchurch New Zealand
107 E11 Addis Louisiana 30.20N 91.18W
87 G6 Addis Ababa Ethiopia 9.03N 38.42E
Addis Alam see Adis 'Alem
Addis Derra see Adis Dera
107 J7 Addison Alabama 34.12N 87.12W
104 S2 Addison Maine 44.38N 67.46W
104 H4 Addison New York 42.07N 77.16W
112 O8 Addison Texas 32.56N 96.50W
104 M2 Addison Vermont 44.05N 73.19W
104 E8 Addison W Virginia 38.30N 80.24W
87 F4 Addis Zemen Ethiopia 12.10N 37.45E
55 A5 Addlestone Surrey England 51.22N 0.31W
95 J9 Addo S Africa 33.33S 25.41E
27 L10 Addu Atoll Maldives, Ind Oc 0.42S 73.10E
110 H1 Addy Washington 48.22N 117.50W
90 B6 Adebka Nigeria 11.54N 5.33E
88 S8 Adeb Larache, El Algeria 27.32N 8.48E
29 F6 Adegaon India 22.37N 79.32E
61 D2 Adegem Belgium 51.12N 3.29E
32 A2 Adeh Iran 37.38N 45.08E
96 Q15 Adeje Tenerife Canary Is 28.08N 16.44W
105 D6 Adel Georgia 31.07N 83.27W
108 Q8 Adel Iowa 41.38N 94.02W
110 F7 Adel Oregon 42.10N 119.55W
12 E5 Adelaide Australia 34.56S 138.36E
105 K9 Adelaide New Providence I 25.00N 77.29W
95 K8 Adelaide S Africa 32.42S 26.17E
13 B2 Adelaide R N Terr Australia
123 F13 Adelaide U.K. Base Antarctica 67.46S 68.54W
123 F14 Adelaide I Antarctica
101 Y1 Adelaide Pen N W Terr
13 B2 Adelaide River N Terr Aust 13.14S 131.08E
89 L3 Adelanfan Mali 16.13N 2.50E
111 G7 Adelanto California 34.34N 117.24W
15 H6 Adelbert Ra Papua New Guinea
66 G6 Adelboden Switzerland 46.29N 7.34E
63 L9 Adelebsen W Germany 51.35N 9.45E
11 H7 Adele I New Zealand 41.00S 173.03E
14 E3 Adele I W Australia 15.33S 123.11E
87 H5 Adel-Esa reg Ethiopia
81 N1 Adelfia Italy 41.01N 16.52E
Adelie Coast see Terre Adélie
109 D7 Adelino New Mexico 34.45N 106.46W
64 J6 Adelmannsfelden W Germany 48.57N 10.02E
12 J6 Adelong Australia 35.21S 148.04E
116 H1 Adelphi Jamaica, W I 18.27N 77.48W
84 R15 Adelphi mt Cyprus 34.56N 33.00E
103 F6 Adelphia New Jersey 40.13N 74.15W
64 L6 Adelschlag W Germany 48.50N 11.15E
64 K4 Adelsdorf W Germany 49.43N 10.55E
64 G5 Adelsheim W Germany 49.23N 9.23E
88 R11 Ademeg watercourse Niger
85 G4 Adem,El Libya 31.52N 23.59E
75 H7 Ademuz Spain 40.04N 1.17W
75 H7 Ademuz R Spain
75 H7 Ademuz, Rincón de reg Spain
33 F10 Aden S Yemen 12.47N 45.03E
64 B3 Adenau W Germany 50.23N 6.57E
95 H8 Adendorp S Africa 32.20S 24.33E
27 F7 Aden,G of S Yemen/Somali Rep
33 C9 Aden Harb S Yemen
90 C4 Aderbissinat Niger 15.34N 7.54E
29 B6 Adesar Gujarat India 23.36N 70.58E
19 M7 Adgaoan R Mindanao Philippines
22 E4 Adgiyn Tsagaan Nuur L Mongolia
Adhaim Shatt-al R see 'Uzaym, Nahr al R
50 B2 Adhalvík inlet Iceland
Adhaman az Zaur,Wadi see Damin az Zawr, Wādī watercourse
34 F7 Adhaman, Khabra salt L Saudi Arabia
84 H8 Adhámas Greece 36.43N 24.27E
Adhamiya see Azamiyah, Al
33 F9 Adhanah,Wādī watercourse Yemen
33 M4 Adhan, Jabal mt U.A.E. 25.26N 56.14E
30 G8 Adhaura Bihar India 24.43N 83.37E
84 G3 Adhélfi isld Greece 39.07N 23.58E
53 V20 Adheram Norway 59.02N 6.55E
84 F7 Adhéres, Óros mt Greece 37.28N 23.26E
33 D2 'Adhfā' Saudi Arabia 29.09N 41.29E
84 F6 Adhíami Greece 37.35N 23.04E
31 F4 Adhi Kot Pakistan 32.10N 72.55E
Adhlam Wadi see Azlam, Wādī watercourse
29 B6 Adhoi Gujarat India 23.25N 70.32E
34 D5 Adhra Syria 33.37N 36.31E
84 C8 Adhrianí Greece 36.53N 21.52E
15 B6 Adi isld Irian Jaya
89 H9 Adiaké Ivory Coast 5.15N 3.18W
87 F4 Adi Arkai Ethiopia 13.35N 37.57E
89 K7 Adibo Ghana 9.15N 0.02E
87 G3 Adi Caieh Ethiopia 14.51N 39.22E
76 E13 Adica, Sa da mts Portugal
119 E2 Adícora Venezuela 11.57N 69.50W
89 K8 Adidome Ghana 6.06N 0.38E
93 J2 Adi,El Kenya 3.50N 37.34E
87 F4 Adi Erzanye Ethiopia 13.43N 37.21E
12 B4 Adieu,C S Australia 32.00S 132.08E
14 E3 Adieu Pt W Australia 15.15S 124.34E
79 L4 Adige R Italy
87 F4 Adi Gemtela Ethiopia 13.55N 37.20E
87 G3 Adigrät Ethiopia 14.20N 39.29E
Adi Kaie see Adi Caieh
29 F8 Adilabad Andhra Prad India 19.40N 78.31E
28 D1 Adilabad dist Andhra Prad India
93 E3 Adilang Uganda 2.44N 33.28E
37 G7 Adilcevaz Turkey 38.47N 42.42E
93 L1 Adilli Ethiopia 4.06N 39.15E
75 H1 Adi,Mte Spain 43.01N 1.26W
110 E8 Adin California 41.12N 120.56W
61 A2 Adinkerke Belgium 51.04N 2.36E
87 G3 Adi Quala Ethiopia 14.35N 38.50E
35 G9 Adir Jordan 31.12N 35.45E
37 G7 Adir isld Turkey 38.52N 43.16E
104 L2 Adirondack Mts New York
87 G6 Adis 'Alem Ethiopia 9.01N 38.21E
87 G5 Adis Dera Ethiopia 10.12N 38.46E
87 G4 Adisha Ethiopia 12.30N 38.10E
87 G3 Adi Ugri Ethiopia 14.47N 38.50E
37 D8 Adıyaman Turkey 37.46N 38.15E
88 O11 Adjadem watercourse Algeria
29 L2 Adjai R W Bengal India
89 L8 Adjara Benin 6.27N 2.13E
88 R10 Adjoantali reg Algeria
89 L8 Adjohon Benin 6.41N 2.32E
82 L4 Adjud Romania 46.07N 27.10E
105 J7 Adjuntas Puerto Rico Caribbean Sea 18.10N 66.42W
115 K6 Adjuntas, Presa de las res Mexico
97 O7 Adlavik Is Labrador, Nfld
44 C4 Adler U.S.S.R. 43.26N 35.59E
66 L2 Adliswil Switzerland 47.19N 8.32E
36 F5 Admağan Dağ mt Turkey 37.54N 32.59E
88 Q11 Admer Algeria 20.24N 5.27E
100 J9 Admiral Saskatchewan 49.44N 108.00W
41 B2 Admiralteystva, P-ov pen Novaya Zemlya U.S.S.R.
113 K1 Admiralty B Alaska
11 H7 Admiralty B New Zealand
14 F2 Admiralty G W Australia
113 U8 Admiralty I Alaska
101 X1 Admiralty I N W Terr 69.35N 101.12W
97 L3 Admiralty Inlet N W Terr
110 C1 Admiralty Inlet Washington
15 J5 Admiralty Is Bismarck Arch Pacific Ocean
10 E10 Admiralty Is Lord Howe I Pac Oc 31.30S 159.05E
123 K6 Admiralty Mts Antarctica
109 O3 Admire Kansas 38.38N 96.06W
65 K6 Admont Austria 47.35N 14.28E
12 D2 Adnalgowara, Mt S Australia 26.40S 135.50E
93 J1 Ado Ethiopia 4.04N 37.58E
90 A8 Ado Nigeria 6.38N 3.00E
90 B8 Ado Ekiti Nigeria 7.40N 5.16E
87 C6 Adok Sudan 8.10N 30.20E
Adola see Kibre Mengist
Adolfo Alsina see Carhué
51 F5 Adolfsström Sweden 66.18N 16.40E
14 G3 Adolphus I W Australia 15.22S 128.15E
9 U4 Adolphus Reef Fiji 16.17S 179.21W
19 C8 Adonara isld Indonesia
28 C3 Adoni Andhra Prad India 15.38N 77.16E
62 L8 Adony Hungary 47.10N 18.47E
77 Q3 Adór Spain 38.55N 0.14W
35 C8 Adorayim watercourse Israel
64 N3 Adorf E Germany 50.19N 12.15E
63 J10 Adorf W Germany 51.21N 8.48E
60 P6 Adorp Netherlands 53.16N 6.32E
90 C8 Adoru Nigeria 6.58N 7.11E
87 J7 Adot Ethiopia 6.02N 42.25E
89 N4 Adoua watercourse Niger
90 D3 Adouda Tebernit Niger 17.48N 8.57E
90 F7 Adoumri Cameroon 9.13N 13.45E
72 E9 Adour R France
77 K7 Adra Spain 36.45N 3.01W
29 K6 Adra W Bengal India 23.31N 86.43E
77 K7 Adra R Spain
75 F5 Adradas Spain 41.20N 2.28W
76 L6 Adrados Spain 41.22N 4.06W
Adrah see Adhra
93 B3 Adranga Zaïre 2.55N 30.26E
81 J8 Adrano Sicily 37.40N 14.50E
88 N8 Adrar Algeria 27.51N 0.19W
88 R9 Adrar mts Algeria
88 N9 Adrar reg Algeria
89 C1 Adrar reg Mauritania
88 S11 Adrar Bous reg Niger
90 A1 Adrar des Iforas reg Algeria/Mali
88 R10 Adrar Edekel mt Algeria 23.53N 6.49E
88 P11 Adrar Ilassene reg Algeria
90 E2 Adrar Madet mt Niger 18.54N 10.35E
88 S10 Adrar Mariaou mts Algeria
88 P10 Adrar Nahalet mt Algeria 23.18N 2.45E
89 B1 Adrar Soutouf reg Mauritania
88 P10 Adrar Tideridjaouine mts Algeria
36 E6 Adrasan Burun C Turkey 36.21N 30.32E
36 G6 Adras Dağı mt Turkey
31 B4 Adraskand R Afghanistan
43 J6 Adrasman Tadzhikistan U.S.S.R. 41.10N 70.00E
90 L5 Adré Chad 13.26N 22.14E
71 K9 Adrets-de-l'Esterel, les France 43.32N 6.49E
85 B6 Adri Libya 27.32N 13.14E
79 M4 Adria Italy 45.03N 12.04E
105 E5 Adrian Georgia 32.33N 82.36W
106 K8 Adrian Michigan 41.55N 84.01W
108 P6 Adrian Minnesota 43.38N 95.58W
107 B3 Adrian Missouri 38.22N 94.21W
110 H6 Adrian Oregon 43.45N 117.05W
112 B8 Adrian Texas 35.16N 102.40W
110 F2 Adrian Washington 47.23N 119.25W
104 E8 Adrian W Virginia 38.55N 80.16W
Adrianople see Edirne
42 J6 Adrianovka U.S.S.R. 51.35N 114.38E
78 F4 Adriatic Sea S Europe
72 F3 Adriers France 46.16N 0.48E
59 C8 Adrigole Cork Irish Rep 51.44N 9.42W
79 G3 Adro Italy 45.37N 9.57E
87 G3 Ad Sald Ethiopia 15.28N 38.12E
53 D7 Adsbøl Denmark 54.56N 9.39E
111 N10 Aduana del Sasabe Mexico 31.29N 111.32W
60 O6 Aduard Netherlands 53.15N 6.28E
93 D3 Aduku Uganda 2.03N 32.45E
66 N5 Adula Gruppe mts Switzerland
35 C7 'Adullam reg Israel
53 B5 Ådum Denmark 55.53N 8.36E
25 N7 Adung Long Burma 28.08N 97.43E
22 K2 Adun Qulu Nei Monggol Zizhiqu China 48.25N 116.11E
28 C6 Adur Kerala India 9.10N 76.46E
87 M8 Adur Somalia 5.41N 48.44E
56 L6 Adur, R W Sussex Eng
92 D1 Adusa Zaïre 1.25N 28.05E
Aduwa see Ådwa
107 G4 Advance Missouri 37.04N 89.58W
94 F8 Advance S Africa 31.11S 21.29E
121 A10 Adventure, B Chile
121 E10 Adventure Sd Falkland Is
14 E5 Adverse Well W Australia 20.52S 123.55E
98 H8 Advocate Harbour Nova Scotia 45.21N 64.45W
87 G3 Ådwa Ethiopia 14.12N 38.56E
35 G2 Adwan' Syria 32.49N 36.00E
103 B7 Ady Maryland 39.39N 76.19W
112 B8 Ady Texas 35.28N 102.09W
41 G6 Adyakit, Gora mt U.S.S.R. 69.48N 97.03E
39 B1 Adycha R U.S.S.R.
39 D3 Adygalakh U.S.S.R. 62.55N 146.29E
44 D3 Adyge-Khabl' U.S.S.R. 44.24N 41.59E
44 C3 Adygeyskaya Aut.Oblast' U.S.S.R.
44 G2 Adyk U.S.S.R. 45.48N 45.40E
75 K7 Adzaneta Spain 40.13N 0.11W
45 D8 Adzhamka U.S.S.R. 48.33N 32.32E
44 E6 Adzharis Tskali R U.S.S.R.
44 E6 Adzharo-Imeretinskiy Khrebet mts U.S.S.R.
44 D6 Adzharskaya A.S.S.R U.S.S.R.
43 E5 Adzhibay, Zaliv B Uzbekistan U.S.S.R.
44 J8 Adzhikabul, Ozero L U.S.S.R. 39.59N 48.57E
44 G7 Adzhikend Azerbaydzhan U.S.S.R. 40.30N 46.19E
21 H3 Adzhima U.S.S.R. 48.09N 139.40E
44 H6 Adzhinour, Ozero L U.S.S.R.
44 J5 Adzhi Ozero L U.S.S.R. 42.19N 48.05E
41 Q5 Adzhirgaydakh U.S.S.R. 72.29N 140.38E
43 C7 Adzhiyap Turkmeniya U.S.S.R. 37.30N 54.12E
89 H8 Adzopé Ivory Coast 6.07N 3.49W
47 H3 Adz'va U.S.S.R. 66.36N 59.30E
47 J2 Adz'va R U.S.S.R.
53 E5 Æbelø isld Denmark 55.38N 10.12E
21 D8 Aechang N Korea 39.48N 127.00E
50 C5 Ædharvatn Iceland 64.33N 22.12W
50 C2 Ædhey isld Iceland 66.06N 22.38W
49 J9 Ægean Sea S Europe
Aegina isld see Aíyina isld
66 P5 Aela, Piz d' Switzerland 46.37N 9.43E
53 U18 Ænes Norway 60.05N 6.08E
30 A7 Aer R Madhya Prad India
60 G10 Aerdenhout Netherlands 52.22N 4.35E
Aerhshunkuolo Ho R see Wu-erh-hsün Ho
84 E3 Aërinón Greece 39.20N 22.46E
50 J2 Ærlækur Iceland 66.05N 16.25W
53 E7 Ærø isld Denmark 54.52N 10.20E
53 E7 Ærøskøbing Denmark 54.54N 10.25E
41 M4 Aeros'yemki, Ostrov isld U.S.S.R. 74.00N 123.04E
63 K8 Aerzen W Germany 52.03N 9.16E
66 G2 Aesch Baselland Switzerland 47.28N 7.36E
66 J3 Aesch Luzern Switzerland 47.15N 8.15E
66 P1 Aeschach W Germany 47.33N 9.41E
66 G5 Aeschi Switzerland 46.40N 7.41E
100 D9 Aetna Alberta 49.10N 113.16W
109 M4 Aetna Kansas 37.06N 98.57W
84 B4 Aëtós Greece 38.42N 21.05E
84 C7 Aëtós Greece 37.15N 21.50E
57 F2 Ae, Water of R Dumfries & Galloway Scot
21 D11 Aewŏl-li S Korea 33.29N 126.15E
122 C12 Afaahiti Tahiti Pacific Ocean 17.43S 149.18W
87 G2 Af Abed Ethiopia 16.18N 38.51E
87 J7 Afadda Ethiopia 7.54N 42.35E
90 G5 Afade Cameroon 12.16N 14.33E
87 L5 Afaf Hills Somalia
90 G1 Afafi Chad 22.08N 15.14E
34 N6 'Afak Iraq 32.04N 45.17E
'Afal, Wādī al watercourse see 'Ifal, Wādī al
32 A2 Afan Iran 36.32N 45.35E
47 G6 Afanas'evo U.S.S.R. 58.52N 53.14E
84 V17 Afándou Rhodes 36.17N 28.10E
88 S9 Afao mt Algeria 25.09N 8.08E
33 M5 Afar Oman 22.08N 57.44E
90 D8 Afara Nigeria 6.08N 9.01E
122 A11 Afareaitu Society Is Pacific Oc 17.33S 149.47W
53 W13 Afarnes Norway 62.40N 7.31E
73 J4 Afars and Issas, French Territory of N E Africa see Djibouti
Afcheh see Afjeh
87 H6 Afdam mt Ethiopia 9.30N 40.48E
87 J7 Afdega Ethiopia 6.01N 43.30E
87 H6 Afdem Ethiopia 9.27N 40.58E
35 D2 Afeq Israel 32.51N 35.07E
70 F6 Aff R France
50 E7 Affall R Iceland
87 H5 Affambo,L Ethiopia 11.23N 41.39E
66 N1 Affeltrangen Switzerland 47.32N 9.02E
60 L12 Afferden Gelderland Netherlands 51.53N 5.38E
60 N13 Afferden Limburg Netherlands 51.38N 6.01E
88 O7 Afflisses watercourse Algeria
117 B2 Affobakka Surinam 5.01N 55.05W
66 K2 Affoltern Switzerland 47.17N 8.27E
79 E7 Affori dist Milan Italy
65 J5 Affrang Austria 48.09N 13.13E
58 F4 Affric, Loch Highland Scotland
58 F4 Affric Lodge Highland Scotland 57.15N 5.00W
58 F4 Affric, R Highland Scotland
88 P3 Affroun, El Algeria 36.29N 2.36E
27 J3 Afghanistan rep S Asia
87 K9 Afgoi Somalia 2.07N 45.02E
33 M5 Afi Oman 23.27N 57.48E
18 B5 Afia Indonesia 1.25N 97.30E
84 G5 Afídhnai Greece 38.12N 23.50E
33 E5 Afif Saudi Arabia 23.53N 42.59E
76 B5 Afife Portugal 41.46N 8.52W
90 C9 Afikpo Nigeria 5.53N 7.54E
90 C9 Afikpo Road Nigeria 5.52N 7.27E
46 L7 Afips R U.S.S.R.
44 B3 Afipskiy U.S.S.R. 44.56N 38.50E
35 F2 Afiq Syria 32.46N 35.43E
35 F3 Afiqim Israel 32.40N 35.34E
32 D3 Afjeh Iran 35.51N 51.42E
32 E3 Åfjord Norway 63.57N 10.12E
53 S16 Åfjorden inlet Norway 61.13N 5.08E
33 G5 Aflāj, Al oasis Saudi Arabia
65 M6 Aflenz Austria 47.33N 15.15E
88 P4 Aflou Algeria 34.08N 2.03E
87 J10 Afmadù Somalia 0.27N 42.05E
90 G1 Afo Chad 21.12N 15.34E
87 E5 Afodu Ethiopia 10.18N 34.49E
117 H8 Afogados da Ingazeira Brazil 7.45S 37.36W
113 L7 Afognak Alaska 58.00N 152.50W
113 L7 Afognak I Alaska 58.10N 152.50W
89 D3 Afollé reg Mauritania
56 D2 Afon Mawddach R Gwynedd Wales
118 C4 Afonso Brazil 14.30S 57.00W
118 H7 Afonso Cláudio Brazil 20.05S 41.06W
15 K8 Afore Papua New Guinea 9.10S 148.30E
34 C4 Afqa Lebanon 34.05N 35.54E
35 F10 'Afra watercourse Jordan
80 K7 Afragola Italy 40.55N 14.18E
117 G9 Afrânio Brazil 8.32S 40.54W
34 O3 Afrāsiāb Iran 35.39N 46.57E
84 G5 Afráti Greece 38.27N 23.41E
Afrera L see Giuletti
50 L5 Afrettartindur pk Iceland 64.32N 14.50W
27 G10 African Is Amirante Is Seychelles, Ind Oc 5.00S 53.16E
81 L7 Africo Italy 38.04N 15.59E
39 G6 Afrika Mys C U.S.S.R. 56.13N 163.21E
47 C3 Afrikanda U.S.S.R. 67.27N 32.48E
95 M4 Afrikaskop S Africa 28.12S 28.42E
34 D2 Afrin Syria 36.31N 36.51E
34 D2 Afrin R Syria
32 B4 Afrīneh Iran 33.20N 47.56E
71 F2 Afrique, Mt France 47.18N 4.55E
65 J8 Afritz Austria 46.44N 13.49E
36 J4 Afşin Turkey 38.14N 36.54E
61 E2 Afsnee Belgium 51.02N 3.40E
74 E10 Afsó Morocco 34.51N 3.10W
32 E3 Aftar Iran 35.40N 53.08E
108 Q8 Afton Iowa 41.02N 94.12W
108 S5 Afton Minnesota 44.56N 92.48W
109 D9 Afton New Mexico 32.03N 106.57W
103 C2 Afton New York 42.14N 75.33W
109 Q5 Afton Oklahoma 36.41N 94.58W
106 E7 Afton Wisconsin 42.36N 89.04W
110 P7 Afton Wyoming 42.44N 110.55W
57 E2 Afton Bridgend Strathclyde Scotland 55.23N 4.12W
88 M8 Aftout tribe Algeria
89 B2 Aftout de Faye reg Mauritania
89 B1 Aftout de Tassaret reg Mauritania
117 D5 Afuá Brazil 0.10S 50.22W
88 F11 Afuidich Mauritania 21.25N 15.35W
90 C8 Afuji Nigeria 6.58N 6.04E
35 E3 'Afula Israel 32.36N 35.17E
35 E3 'Afula 'Illit Israel 32.38N 35.19E
93 J1 Afurr, G mt Ethiopia/Kenya 4.24N 37.04E
92 F6 Afwa tribe Tanzania
60 J13 Afwateringskanaal canal Netherlands
87 L6 Afwein, El Somalia 9.54N 47.07E
36 E4 Afyon Turkey 38.46N 30.32E
Afyonkarahısar see Afyon
30 B3 Afzalgarh Uttar Prad India 29.24N 78.41E
86 F4 Aga Egypt 30.57N 31.17E
53 V18 Aga Norway 60.18N 6.36E
42 K6 Aga U.S.S.R. 51.12N 115.10E
19 N4 Aga isld Truk Is Pacific Oc 7.29N 151.44E
42 K6 Aga R U.S.S.R.
87 F4 Agab Workei Ethiopia 13.40N 37.00E
36 D1 Ağaçli Turkey 41.17N 28.48E
89 B1 Agada Mauritania 21.11N 15.05W
90 F3 Agadem Niger 16.50N 13.11E
90 C3 Agadès Niger 17.00N 7.56E
90 C2 Agadez reg Niger
88 J6 Agadir Morocco 30.30N 9.40W
90 L3 Aga Dubé Chad 17.49N 23.09E
43 L3 Agadyr' Kazakhstan U.S.S.R. 48.15N 72.55E
96 U15 Agaete Gran Canaria Canary Is 28.07N 15.42W
45 T6 Agafonovka U.S.S.R. 50.37N 47.29E
34 P4 Agāh Kolyā'ī Iran 34.55N 47.22E
90 C7 Agaie Nigeria 9.01N 6.18E
88 F10 Agailás Mauritania 22.28N 14.28W
99 L2 Again R Quebec
99 F5 Agaiva Ontario 47.41N 84.30W
119 D2 Agaja, C.de la Colombia 11.20N 74.12W
122 R15 Aga-Kauitai I Gambier Is Pacific Oc 23.10S 135.01W
90 D2 Agalak Niger 18.12N 8.37E
26 R9 Agalawatta Sri Lanka 6.33N 80.09E
26 E6 Agalega Is Seychelles, Ind Oc
84 C7 Agalianí Greece 37.21N 21.44E
87 E4 Agaliyin,el R Sudan
115 M2 Agalta, Sa. de ra Honduras
90 D2 Agamgam Niger 18.48N 9.30E
86 E7 'Agamîyîn, El Egypt 29.20N 30.43E
89 B3 Agamoun Mauritania 17.11N 16.01W
42 A2 Agan R U.S.S.R.
19 L1 Agana Guam Pacific Oc 13.28N 144.45E
20 N4 Agano Japan 37.59N 139.05E
20 N4 Agano-gawa R Japan
41 J6 Aganyli R U.S.S.R.
41 E5 Agapa U.S.S.R. 71.29N 89.06E
41 E5 Agapa R U.S.S.R.
41 E5 Agapa, Verkhov'ye R U.S.S.R.
41 E6 Agapitovo U.S.S.R. 67.59N 86.32E
43 E1 Agapovka U.S.S.R. 53.16N 59.09E
29 E6 Agar Madhya Prad India 23.44N 76.01E
108 K5 Agar S Dakota 44.50N 100.05W
44 F5 Agara Georgia U.S.S.R. 42.01N 43.53E
53 C5 Ågård Denmark 55.36N 9.27E
66 G6 Agarn Switzerland 46.18N 7.40E
87 F7 Agaro Ethiopia 7.50N 36.38E
66 K6 Agaro Italy 46.18N 8.18E
28 H4 Agartala Tripura India 23.49N 91.15E
22 H5 Agaruut Mongolia 43.15N 109.20E
29 C8 Agashi Maharashtra India 19.30N 72.50E
121 J8 Agasiz, Cerro pk Arg/Chile 50.05S 73.30W
30 B8 Agasode Madhya Prad India 24.17N 78.10E
88 J8 Agassel reg Morocco
101 N11 Agassiz Br Col 49.14N 121.52W
19 L1 Agat Guam Pacific Oc 13.24N 144.38E
89 J3 Agata Mali 17.01N 1.31W
41 F7 Agata U.S.S.R. 66.59N 93.33E
41 F7 Agata, Ozero L U.S.S.R.
109 G2 Agate Colorado 39.27N 103.56W
108 G7 Agate Nebraska 42.28N 103.48W
43 J4 Agat, Gora mt Kazakhstan U.S.S.R. 46.52N 69.13E
15 E6 Agats Irian Jaya 5.30S 138.03E
27 L7 Agatti isld Laccadive Is Ind Oc 10.59N 72.14E
113 L9 Agattu I Aleutian Is 52.25N 173.30E
113 L9 Agattu Str Aleutian Is
87 F5 Agaumdir reg Ethiopia
99 F5 Agawa Ontario 47.22N 84.37W
99 F5 Agawa R Ontario
103 J2 Agawam Massachusetts 42.04N 72.36W
110 N2 Agawam Montana 47.59N 112.10W
71 K10 Agay France 43.26N 6.51E
39 C3 Agayakan R U.S.S.R.
79 G5 Agazzano Italy 44.57N 9.31E
90 C8 Agbaja Nigeria 7.59N 6.35E
90 C8 Agbede Nigeria 6.52N 6.15E
90 C8 Agbor Nigeria 6.12N 6.10E
89 G9 Agboville Ivory Coast 5.55N 4.15W
36 J3 Ağcakışla Turkey 39.34N 36.22E
44 H8 Agdam Azerbaydzhan U.S.S.R. 39.59N 48.57E
44 H7 Agdash Azerbaydzhan U.S.S.R. 40.38N 47.29E
71 C10 Agde France 43.19N 3.29E
71 D10 Agde, C.d' France 43.16N 3.31E
53 T19 Agdestein Norway 59.52N 5.33E
88 K6 Agdz Morocco 30.43N 6.28W
44 H7 Agdzhabedi Azerbaydzhan U.S.S.R. 40.05N 47.27E
Agedabia see Ajdābiyah
85 A3 Agedir, Ras C Tunisia 33.13N 11.29E
53 E6 Agedrup Denmark 55.26N 10.30E
20 L6 Agematsu Japan 35.46N 137.41E
72 F7 Agen France 44.12N 0.38E
110 G6 Agency Valley Res Oregon 43.55N 118.10W
109 N2 Agenda Kansas 39.43N 97.26W
90 C8 Agenebode Nigeria 7.05N 6.41E
44 D4 Agepsta mt U.S.S.R. 43.34N 40.13E
110 C8 Ager California 41.53N 122.28W
75 M4 Ager Spain 42.00N 0.45E
65 J5 Ager R Austria
53 B5 Agerbæk Denmark 55.36N 8.48E
66 L3 Ägerisee L Switzerland 47.08N 8.37E
53 E5 Agernæs C Denmark 55.35N 10.18E
53 B3 Agerø isld Denmark 56.43N 8.35E
53 C6 Agerskov Denmark 55.08N 9.08E
53 G6 Agersø Denmark 55.13N 11.13E
53 G6 Agersø isld Denmark 55.13N 11.13E
53 G6 Agersø Sund str Denmark 55.13N 11.14E
53 E2 Agersted Denmark 57.12N 10.23E
53 H5 Agerup Denmark 55.40N 11.47E
53 A3 Agger Denmark 56.47N 8.15E
64 C2 Agger R W Germany
53 C3 Aggersborg Denmark 57.00N 9.16E
53 C2 Aggersund Denmark 57.01N 9.17E
53 A3 Agger Tange pen Denmark 56.45N 8.15E
87 J8 Aggherar Somalia 4.05N 42.39E
81 C2 Aggius Sardinia 40.56N 9.04E
65 M5 Aggsbach Austria 48.19N 15.25E
65 M5 Aggsbach-Dorf Austria 48.18N 15.26E
59 J1 Aghadowey Londonderry N Ireland 55.02N 6.39W
32 C5 Agha Jārī oil field Iran 30.45N 49.47E
59 K2 Aghalee Antrim N Ireland 54.32N 6.16W
31 D4 Aghangai Afghanistan 32.24N 67.18E
34 G5 Agharri, Sha'ib al watercourse Iraq
59 K6 Aghavannagh Wicklow Irish Rep 52.55N 6.25W
Aghda see 'Aqdā
34 Q1 Āgh Dāgh mt Iran 37.24N 48.35E
86 K5 Agheidara, Wâdi el watercourse Egypt
Agheila, El see 'Uqaylah, Al
84 L11 Aghia Triadha ruins Crete 35.03N 24.47E
31 J2 Aghil Pass Kashmir 36.13N 76.27E
113 J8 Aghiyuk I Alaska 56.10N 156.50W
44 H9 Aghiz pass Iran 38.52N 47.50E
59 F2 Aghla Mt Donegal Irish Rep 54.50N 8.10W
89 F1 Aghouavil reg Mauritania
88 G11 Aghrejit Mauritania 21.55N 12.10W
115 E4 Agiabampo Mexico 26.20N 109.09W
30 H7 Agiaon Shahabad, Bihar India 25.19N 84.21E
87 G5 Agibar Ethiopia 10.35N 38.36E
61 K6 Agimont Belgium 50.10N 4.47E
87 M6 Agin Somalia 8.28N 49.51E
37 D7 Agin Turkey 38.57N 38.43E
42 J6 Aginskiy Buryat Nats. Okr dist U.S.S.R.
42 J6 Aginskoye Chita U.S.S.R. 51.10N 114.32E
42 E4 Aginskoye Krasnoyarsk U.S.S.R. 55.15N 94.59E
84 E2 Agiókambos Greece 39.41N 22.53E
81 J8 Agira Sicily 37.39N 14.32E
87 E2 Agirwat Hills Sudan
87 G4 Agiza Ethiopia 12.04N 38.22E
36 D5 Ağla Turkey 37.02N 28.45E
79 C4 Agliè Italy 45.22N 7.46E
59 G7 Aglish Waterford Irish Rep 52.04N 7.50W
103 E3 Agloe New York 41.58N 74.55W
72 K10 Agly R France
88 H9 Agmar Mauritania 25.18N 10.50W
88 F11 Agmumuit Mauritania 21.50N 15.31W
79 L4 Agna Italy 45.10N 11.58E
84 B3 Agnanda Greece 39.28N 21.05E
84 C6 Ágnanda Greece 37.48N 21.40E
84 C3 Agnanderón Greece 39.28N 21.51E
84 E4 Ágnandi Greece 38.43N 22.53E

89 A2 **Agneitir** *reg* Mauritania
71 K8 **Agneliers, les** France 44.20N 6.35E
12 C2 **Agnes Creek** S Australia 26.25S 133.15E
100 L2 **Agnes L** Ontario 48.15N 91.10W
14 F3 **Agnes, Mt** W Australia 16.00S 125.51E
14 G7 **Agnes, Mt** W Australia 26.51S 128.57E
110 A7 **Agness** Oregon 42.35N 124.05W
14 D8 **Agnew** W Australia 28.01S 120.31E
121 B9 **Agnia, Pámpa de** *plain* Argentina
89 H8 **Agnibilékrou** Ivory Coast 7.10N 3.11W
82 J5 **Agnita** Romania 45.59N 24.40E
40 H6 **Agniye-Afanas'yevskiy** U.S.S.R. 51.58N 138.45E
66 M8 **Agno** Switzerland 45.59N 8.54E
79 K3 **Agno** *R* Italy
80 K5 **Agnone** Italy 41.48N 14.23E
89 K7 **Agofie** Ghana 8.26N 0.16E
79 E4 **Agogna** *R* Italy
89 J8 **Agogo** Ghana 6.47N 1.04W
89 D3 **Agohéni** Mauritania 17.00N 10.51W
85 L9 **Ago, Jebel** *mt* Sudan 21.07N 30.57E
76 B10 **Agolada** Portugal 39.00N 8.33W
90 H3 **Agoladeï** Chad 16.50N 17.40E
70 G3 **Agon** France 49.02N 1.34W
72 F5 **Agonac** France 45.18N 0.44E
89 J9 **Agona Swedru** Ghana 5.31N 0.42W
75 F3 **Agoncillo** Spain 42.27N 2.17W
89 H3 **Agonégifal** Mali 17.05N 2.59W
23 D5 **Agong** Guizhou China 26.28N 105.32E
18 C7 **Agong** *hill* Pen Malaysia Malaysia 4.14N 102.16E
65 K6 **Agonitz** Austria 47.53N 14.13E
87 F3 **Agordat** Ethiopia 15.35N 37.55E
79 M2 **Agordo** Italy 46.17N 12.02E
30 F8 **Agori khas** Uttar Prad India 24.33N 82.57E
93 E2 **Agoro** Uganda 3.46N 33.02E
77 P4 **Agost** Spain 38.26N 0.38W
80 H5 **Agosta** Italy 41.58N 13.03E
120 E3 **Agostinho** Brazil 9.54S 68.36W
72 D9 **Agos Vidalos** France 43.02N 0.04W
53 Y13 **Ågottind** *mt* Norway 62.30N 8.13E
89 L7 **Agoua** Benin 8.19N 2.01E
89 L8 **Agouagou** Benin 7.59N 2.21E
89 K7 **Agoulou** Togo 9.07N 1.19E
91 B4 **Agouma** Gabon 1.33S 10.08E
89 K8 **Agouna-Gaga** Benin 7.39N 1.47E
88 L5 **Agouraï** Morocco 33.38N 5.34W
72 H8 **Agout** *R* France
109 L2 **Agra** Kansas 39.45N 99.07W
109 O6 **Agra** Oklahoma 35.55N 96.54W
30 B5 **Agra** Uttar Prad India 27.09N 78.00E
30 A5 **Agra** *dist* Uttar Prad India
30 B5 **Agra** *div* Uttar Prad India
30 A5 **Agra Canal** India
121 F4 **Agraciada** Uruguay 33.47S 58.18W
119 C6 **Agrado** Colombia 2.16N 75.46W
84 C3 **Agrafa** Greece 39.08N 21.39E
84 C3 **Agrafiótis** *R* Greece
44 H4 **Agrakhanskiy Poluostrov** *pen* U.S.S.R.
Agram *see* **Zagreb**
77 N4 **Agramón** Spain 38.26N 1.38W
31 F2 **Agram Pass** Afghan/Pakistan 36.21N 71.30E
75 N4 **Agramunt** Spain 41.48N 1.06E
66 K8 **Agrano** Italy 45.51N 8.25E
84 C6 **Agrapidhokhóri** Greece 37.53N 21.32E
88 Q6 **Agreb, El** Algeria 30.42N 5.30E
75 G4 **Agreda** Spain 41.51N 1.55W
77 P3 **Agres** Spain 38.47N 0.31W
53 F4 **Agri** Denmark 56.14N 10.32E
37 G6 **Ağri** Turkey 39.44N 43.04E
81 N3 **Agri** *R* Italy
84 F3 **Agriá** Greece 39.20N 23.01E
19 K4 **Agria Pt** Luzon Philippines 15.22N 121.25E
44 H6 **Agrichay** *R* Azerbaydzhan U.S.S.R.
107 H11 **Agricola** Mississippi 30.48N 88.31W
37 H6 **Ağrı Dağı, Büyük** *mt* Turkey 39.44N 44.15E
37 H6 **Ağrı Dağı, Küçük** *mt* Turkey 39.40N 44.23E
84 C6 **Agrídhion** Greece 37.53N 21.59E
81 G9 **Agrigento** Sicily 37.19N 13.35E
81 F8 **Agrigento** *prov* Sicily
17 P8 **Agrihan** *isld* Marianas Pacific Oc 18.44N 145.39E
84 C2 **Agrilia** Greece 39.43N 21.55E
84 B4 **Agrinion** Greece 38.38N 21.25E
121 B7 **Agrio R** Argentina
84 D3 **Agriosikies** Greece 39.25N 22.25E
72 E4 **Agris** France 45.46N 0.21E
77 J6 **Agrón** Spain 37.02N 3.49W
81 J3 **Agropoli** Italy 40.21N 14.59E
80 G5 **Agro Pontino** *plain* Italy
84 W22 **Agrós** Corfu 39.44N 19.43E
89 C1 **Agrour Sfaya** Mauritania 20.15N 13.31W
86 H5 **'Agrûd, El** Egypt 30.04N 32.23E
86 M5 **'Agrûd, El** Egypt 30.11N 34.25E
46 R2 **Agryz** U.S.S.R. 56.30N 53.00E
19 K4 **Agta Pt** Philippines 14.38N 121.55E
95 H7 **Agter-Renosterberg** *mts* S Africa
95 J8 **Agter-Sneeuberg** S Africa 32.02S 25.12E
95 J6 **Agtertang** S Africa 30.41S 25.18E
48 S9 **Agto** Greenland 68.00N 53.35W
53 D6 **Agtrup** Denmark 55.28N 9.33E
77 N7 **Agua Amarga** Spain 36.56N 1.55W
121 B2 **Agua Amargo** Chile 28.45S 70.47W
121 D6 **Agua Blanca** Argentina 37.55S 65.25W
119 H7 **Agua Boa do Univini, R** Brazil
115 G6 **Agua Brava, L** Mexico
111 L9 **Agua Caliente** Arizona 32.59N 113.19W
120 G6 **Agua Caliente, R** Bolivia
77 P5 **Agua, C. del** Spain 37.33N 0.54W
118 D7 **Água Clara** Brazil 20.20S 52.54W
119 D5 **Aguaclara** Colombia 4.45N 73.01W
115 O8 **Aguada** Mexico 18.50N 91.20W
121 C8 **Aguada de Guerra** Argentina 41.03S 68.23W
119 E2 **Aguada Grande** Venezuela 10.38N 69.29W
119 C5 **Aguadas** Colombia 5.36N 75.30W
96 U2 **Agua de Atto** Azores 37.28N 25.28W
96 T10 **Agua de Bueyes** Fuerteventura Canary Is 28.20N 14.02W
115 J9 **Agua de Correra** Mexico 17.36N 101.30W
119 D5 **Agua de Dios** Colombia 4.22N 74.38W
96 U2 **Agua de Pau** Azores 37.28N 25.31W
105 J7 **Aguadilla** Puerto Rico 18.27N 67.08W
121 D8 **Aguado Cecillo** Argentina 40.50S 65.49W
115 O5 **Aguadulce** Panama 8.16N 80.31W
77 G6 **Aguadulce** Spain 37.15N 4.59W
112 K8 **Agua Dulce** Texas 27.47N 97.56W
111 M7 **Agua Fria** *R* Arizona
111 H9 **Agua Hechicera** Mexico 32.27N 116.14W
118 J8 **Agua, I. d'** Brazil 22.49S 43.10W
112 H9 **Agualeguas** Mexico 26.19N 99.32W
96 U3 **Agualva** Azores 38.47N 27.12W
96 R14 **Aguamansa** Tenerife Canary Is 28.22N 16.30W
76 E13 **Agua Negra** *mt* Portugal 37.47N 7.27W
111 H8 **Aguanga** California 33.29N 116.52W
98 K3 **Aguanish** Quebec 50.14N 62.02W
115 Q11 **Aguanqueterique** Honduras 13.55N 87.36W
115 F5 **Agua Nueva** Sinaloa Mexico 24.08N 106.51W
112 J9 **Agua Nueva** Texas 26.55N 98.37W
98 K3 **Aguanus R** Quebec
118 B5 **Aguapeí** Brazil 16.12S 59.40W
118 E7 **Aguapeí** *R* São Paulo Brazil
118 B4 **Aguapeí, R** Mato Grosso Brazil
118 B5 **Aguapeí, Serra** *mts* Brazil
121 G2 **Aguapey** *R* Argentina
115 E2 **Agua Prieta** Mexico 31.20N 109.32W
120 F9 **Aguaragüe, Cord. de** *mts* Bolivia
120 F10 **Aguaray** Argentina 22.14S 63.45W
118 C8 **Aguaray Guazú, R** Amambay/San Pedro Paraguay
118 B9 **Aguaray-Guazu, R** Presidente Hayes Paraguay
96 V1 **Agua Retorta** Azores 37.31N 25.10W
119 C8 **Aguarico, R** Ecuador
75 H5 **Aguarón** Spain 41.20N 1.15W
75 K3 **Aguas** Spain 42.13N 0.13W
75 J5 **Aguas** *R* Spain
99 C4 **Aguasabon Dam** Ontario 48.48N 87.08W
112 E6 **Agua Salada** Mexico 29.22N 102.36W
117 H9 **Águas Belas** Brazil 8.58S 37.02W
76 C9 **Aguas Belas** Portugal 39.43N 8.18W
120 D11 **Aguas Blancas** Chile 24.13S 69.50W
115 H7 **Aguascalientes** Mexico 21.51N 102.18W
115 H7 **Aguascalientes** *state* Mexico
120 E11 **Aguas Calientes, Sa. de** *mts* Argentina
120 E10 **Aguas Calientes, Salar de** *salt pan* Chile
77 Q3 **Aguas de Busot** Spain 38.30N 0.21W
76 B11 **Aguas de Moura** Portugal 38.35N 8.42W
118 H5 **Águas Formosas** Brazil 17.05S 40.58W
77 N6 **Aguas, R. de** Spain
118 C3 **Água Verde, R** Brazil
75 K6 **Aguaviva** Spain 40.49N 0.13W
75 F5 **Aguaviva de la Vega** Spain 41.17N 2.23W
115 O10 **Agua, Vol. de** *pk* Guatemala 14.28N 90.54W
120 B3 **Aguaytia, R** Peru
119 D5 **Aguazul** Colombia 5.12N 72.34W
'Agubba, Al *see* **'Aqabah, Al**
77 G3 **Agudo** Spain 38.59N 4.52W
118 E8 **Agudos** Brazil 22.27S 49.03W
76 C7 **Agueda** Portugal 40.34N 8.27W
76 C7 **Agueda** *R* Portugal
76 F7 **Agueda** *R* Spain
76 G8 **Agueda, Embalse del** *res* Spain 40.30N 6.30W
88 N7 **Aguedal** Algeria 29.49N 1.48W
89 K2 **Aguelhok** Mali 19.29N 0.52E
90 D2 **Aguellal** Niger 18.45N 8.06E
88 H10 **Aguelt el Adham** Mauritania 23.34N 11.59W
88 K8 **Aguelt el Bechera** Algeria 27.46N 7.43W
88 J10 **Aguelt el Melha** Mauritania 23.03N 8.28W
89 B2 **Aguelt en Naaje** Mauritania 19.22N 14.12W
88 K10 **Aguelt Hammada** Mauritania 23.36N 7.48W
88 H10 **Aguelt Lebouarin** *dry lake* Mauritania
88 J10 **Aguelt Nebka** Mauritania 23.16N 8.10W
89 D2 **Aguelt Némadi** Mauritania 19.48N 10.59W
88 J10 **Aguelt Sbara** Mauritania 23.09N 8.18W
89 B2 **Aguelt Sidi** Mauritania 19.50N 14.35W
88 H10 **Aguelt Sidi Haiba** Mauritania 23.18N 11.39W
91 G10 **Aguema** Angola 12.03S 21.52E
88 Q8 **Aguemour** Algeria 27.40N 4.40E
88 Q8 **Aguemour** *reg* Algeria
88 G10 **Aguenit** Mauritania 22.12N 13.08W
76 G2 **Agüera** Spain 43.13N 6.16W
75 D1 **Aguera** *R* Spain
88 K10 **Agueraktem** Mauritania 23.10N 6.21W
88 E10 **Aguerguer** *reg* Mauritania/Morocco
75 J3 **Agüero** Spain 42.22N 0.47W
72 L7 **Aguessac** France 44.10N 3.05E
90 G1 **Aguezi Tigu** Niger 20.15N 14.08E
93 E3 **Aguga** *R* Uganda
79 O7 **Agugliano** Italy 43.32N 13.23E
76 D12 **Aguiar** Portugal 38.23N 7.58W
76 F7 **Aguiar** *R* Portugal
76 D7 **Aguiar da Beira** Portugal 40.49N 7.33W
112 F8 **Aguijita** Mexico 27.53N 101.10W
111 L8 **Aguila** Arizona 33.58N 113.10W
75 G6 **Aguila** *mt* Spain 40.52N 1.47W
77 F5 **Aguila, El** Spain 37.51N 5.24W
76 L6 **Aguilafuente** Spain 41.13N 4.07W
89 B2 **Aguilal Faye** Mauritania 18.29N 14.44W
105 H8 **Aguila, Pta** *pt* Puerto Rico 17.56N 67.12W
109 F4 **Aguilar** Colorado 37.25N 104.40W
75 D2 **Aguilar de Bureba** Spain 42.35N 3.20W
76 L3 **Aguilar de Campóo** Spain 42.47N 4.15W
75 B2 **Aguilar de Campóo, Embalse de** *res* Spain
77 G5 **Aguilar de la Frontera** Spain 37.31N 4.40W
75 F4 **Aguilar de Rio Alhama** Spain 41.57N 2.00W
121 D1 **Aguilares** Argentina 27.20S 65.38W
112 H8 **Aguilares** Texas 27.27N 99.06W
120 F10 **Aguilar, Sa. del** *mts* Argentina
77 N6 **Aguilas** Spain 37.25N 1.35W
75 C4 **Aguilera, La** Spain 41.44N 3.47W
115 H8 **Aguililla** Mexico 18.45N 102.42W
76 D1 **Aguillones, C. de los** Spain 43.46N 7.51W
96 V16 **Agüimes** Gran Canaria Canary Is 27.54N 15.27W
22 F7 **Aguin Sum** Gansu China 39.38N 103.00E
121 M10 **Aguirre** *B* Argentina
19 L6 **Aguisan** Philippines 10.10N 122.53E
121 B9 **Aguja, Cerro** *pk* Chile 42.11S 71.54W
119 A10 **Aguja, Pta** *pt* Peru 5.52S 81.06W
105 H7 **Agujereado, Pta** *pt* Puerto Rico 18.30N 67.10W
42 F4 **Agul** *R* U.S.S.R.
87 G4 **Agula** Ethiopia 13.40N 39.40E
96 R8 **Agulha, Pta. da** *pt* Madeira Atlantic Ocean 32.23N 16.28W
95 D10 **Agulhas** S Africa 34.49S 20.01E
96 M12 **Agulhas Bank** Atlantic Oc
26 C10 **Agulhas Basin** Indian Ocean
95 D10 **Agulhas, Cape** S Africa 34.50S 20.00E
118 G8 **Agulhas Negras** *pk* Brazil 22.20S 44.43W
26 C10 **Agulhas Plateau** Indian Oc
75 Q3 **Agullana** Spain 42.24N 2.51E
96 O14 **Agulo** Gomera Canary Is 28.12N 17.11W
28 B4 **Agumbe** Karnataka India 13.30N 75.02E
Agumbi *see* **Agumbe**
18 L10 **Agung, Gunung** *mt* Bali Indonesia 8.25S 115.28E
21 C13 **Agunijima** *isld* Japan 26.35N 127.13E
35 C7 **'Agur** Israel 31.42N 34.55E
93 D3 **Agur** Uganda 2.26N 32.56E
35 A10 **'Agur, Holot** *sand dunes* Israel
19 M7 **Agusan** *R* Mindanao Philippines
19 K6 **Agutaya** Philippines 11.09N 120.58E
19 K6 **Agutaya** *isld* Philippines 11.09N 120.59E
37 H1 **Ağva** Turkey 41.08N 29.51E
44 G5 **Agvali** U.S.S.R. 42.31N 46.08E
37 D5 **Ağvanis** Turkey 40.04N 38.34E
93 D4 **Agwata** Uganda 1.59N 32.58E
87 D7 **Agwei** *watercourse* Sudan
20 Q8 **Aha** Okinawa Japan 26.45N 128.17E
32 G4 **Ahābād** Iran 32.32N 57.28E
94 F2 **Aha Hills** Botswana
15 H6 **Ahamadi** Papua New Guinea 5.11S 144.54E
87 D4 **Ahamda** *tribe* Sudan
26 R10 **Ahangama** Sri Lanka 6.00N 80.21E
32 B1 **Ahar** Iran 38.25N 47.07E
29 C5 **Ahar** Rajasthan India 24.33N 73.48E
30 B4 **Ahar** Uttar Prad India 28.29N 78.13E
44 H9 **Ahar** *R* Iran
59 F5 **Ahascragh** Galway Irish Rep 53.24N 8.20W
11 F9 **Ahaura** New Zealand 42.21S 171.33E
11 F9 **Ahaura, R** New Zealand
63 F8 **Ahaus** W Germany 52.04N 7.01E
122 C14 **Ahé** *atoll* Tuamotu Is Pacific Oc 14.30S 146.19W
86 N5 **Aheigba, Gebel el** *hill* Egypt 30.10N 34.33E
53 T14 **Aheim** Norway 62.02N 5.33E
35 F9 **Aheimir** *watercourse* Jordan
86 O6 **Aheimir, Jeb** *mt* Jordan 30.00N 35.19E
88 R8 **Ahelledjem** Algeria 26.33N 5.58E
59 F7 **Aherlow,R** Tipperary Irish Rep
88 L5 **Ahermoumou** Morocco 33.48N 4.26W
88 M4 **Ahfir** Morocco 35.04N 2.12W
30 C4 **Ahichhattra** Uttar Prad India 28.21N 79.08E
37 G3 **Ahi Dağ** *mt* Turkey
76 G8 **Ahigal** Spain 40.11N 6.12W
76 F7 **Ahigal de los Aceiteros** Spain 40.52N 6.45W
35 D2 **Ahihud** Israel 32.54N 35.10E
77 H5 **Ahillo** *mt* Spain 37.36N 4.02W
77 E4 **Ahillones** Spain 38.16N 5.52W
11 L5 **Ahimanawa Ra** New Zealand
15 L9 **Ahioma** Papua New Guinea 10.20S 150.35E
11 H2 **Ahipara** New Zealand 35.12S 173.10E
11 H2 **Ahipara B** New Zealand
37 C8 **Ahır Dağ** *mt* Turkey
29 G8 **Ahiri** Maharashtra India 19.26N 80.04E
36 F5 **Ahırlı** Turkey 37.17N 32.05E
35 C6 **Ahisamakh** Israel 31.56N 34.55E
11 J5 **Ahititi** New Zealand 38.50S 174.36E
37 G7 **Ahkis** *R* Turkey
113 G7 **Ahklun Mts** Alaska
51 J10 **Ahlainen** Finland 61.41N 21.35E
37 G7 **Ahlât** Turkey 38.45N 42.28E
Ahlbeck *see* **Seebad Ahlbeck**
63 U5 **Ahlbeck** Neubrandenburg E Germany 53.41N 14.14E
63 L7 **Ahlden** W Germany 52.46N 9.34E
63 G9 **Ahlen** W Germany 51.46N 7.53E
63 K6 **Ahlerstedt** W Germany 53.25N 9.27E
63 H7 **Ahlhorn** W Germany 52.54N 8.15E
88 J7 **Ahl Mader** Morocco 29.48N 9.40W
87 M5 **Ahl Mescat** *reg* Somalia
34 P2 **Ahmadābād** Āzarbāījan-e Bākhtarī Iran 36.38N 47.10E
29 C6 **Ahmadabad** Gujarat India 23.03N 72.40E
32 H3 **Ahmadābād** Khorāsān Iran 35.51N 59.36E
32 J3 **Ahmadābād** Khorāsān Iran 35.07N 60.40E
32 G7 **Ahmadī** Iran 27.57N 56.42E
33 M10 **Ahmadī** *oil field* Kuwait
33 M10 **Ahmadī, Al** Kuwait 29.05N 48.04E
35 G1 **Ahmadiye** Syria 33.09N 35.50E
31 E4 **Ahmad Khel** Afghanistan 33.46N 69.37E
29 D8 **Ahmadnagar** Maharashtra India 19.08N 74.48E
29 D8 **Ahmadnagar** *dist* Maharashtra India
28 C1 **Ahmadpur** Maharashtra India 18.40N 76.57E
29 L1 **Ahmadpur** W Bengal India 23.50N 87.41E
31 F6 **Ahmadpur East** Pakistan 29.06N 71.14E
31 F5 **Ahmadpur Sial** Pakistan 30.40N 71.52E
35 G10 **Ahmar** *watercourse* Jordan
86 R12 **Ahmar, El Gebel el** *hills* Cairo Egypt
86 F9 **Ahmar, Gebel el** *hill* Egypt 28.19N 31.07E
86 O6 **Ahmar, Jebel El** *mt* Jordan 29.40N 35.09E
87 H6 **Ahmar Mts** Ethiopia
29 B6 **Ahmedabad** *dist* Gujarat India
87 D5 **Ahmed Agha,Jeb** *mt* Sudan 10.54N 32.35E
88 K10 **Ahmed Degna** Mauritania 23.44N 6.41W
36 C4 **Ahmetli** Turkey 38.31N 27.56E
89 B1 **Ahmeyim** Mauritania 20.51N 14.25W
90 C9 **Ahoada** Nigeria 5.06N 6.40E
59 K2 **Ahoghill** Antrim N Ireland 54.51N 6.22W
115 E5 **Ahome** Mexico 25.55N 109.10W
77 S12 **Ahorcados** *isld* Balearic Is Mediterranean Sea 38.49N 1.25E
88 R9 **Ahorene** Algeria 24.55N 7.35E
64 L4 **Ahorntal** W Germany 49.50N 11.23E
105 L1 **Ahoskie** N Carolina 36.18N 77.00W
64 B3 **Ahr** *R* W Germany
32 D6 **Ahram** Iran 28.52N 51.18E
30 F6 **Ahraula** Uttar Prad India 26.12N 82.55E
30 G7 **Ahraura** Uttar Prad India 25.01N 83.02E
32 E5 **Āhravān** Iran 31.02N 52.10E
84 Y20 **Ahrax Pt** Malta 36.00N 14.22E
64 B3 **Ahrdorf** W Germany 50.23N 6.46E
95 O5 **Ahrens** S Africa 29.04S 30.46E
63 S6 **Ahrensberg** E Germany 53.16N 13.03E
63 N4 **Ahrensbök** W Germany 54.00N 10.34E
63 M5 **Ahrensburg** W Germany 53.41N 10.14E
63 T7 **Ahrensfelde** E Germany 52.35N 13.35E
63 K6 **Ahrenswohlde** W Germany 53.22N 9.25E
Ahrvan *see* **Āhravān**
Ahrweiler *see* **Bad Neuenahr-Ahrweiler**
63 H9 **Ahse** *R* W Germany
37 H7 **Ahta Dağ** *mt* Turkey 38.43N 43.48E
51 L9 **Ähtäri** Finland 62.34N 24.08E
51 L9 **Ähtärinjärvi** *L* Finland
25 C4 **Ahtaung** Burma 17.18N 95.20E
32 C5 **Āhū** Iran 31.04N 48.15E
115 G7 **Ahuacatlán** Mexico 21.02N 104.30W
115 P11 **Ahuachapán** El Salvador 13.57N 89.49W
115 H7 **Ahualulco** Jalisco Mexico 20.41N 103.55W
115 J6 **Ahualulco** San Luis Potosí Mexico 22.24N 101.11W
Ahuan *see* **Āhuvān**
115 K8 **Ahuatempan** Mexico 18.26N 98.01W
15 H4 **Ahu I** Bismarck Arch 1.19S 144.11E
90 C7 **Ahuji** Nigeria 8.31N 6.09E
114 B7 **Ahumoa** *mt* Hawaiian Is Pacific Ocean 19.48N 155.37W
72 J3 **Ahun** France 46.05N 2.02E
26 R9 **Ahungalla** Sri Lanka 6.19N 80.03E
122 E16 **Ahunui** *atoll* Tuamotu Is Pacific Oc 19.35S 140.28W
11 D11 **Ahuriri R** New Zealand
52 H11 **Åhus** Sweden 55.55N 14.20E
32 E3 **Āhuvān** Iran 35.47N 53.45E
35 C7 **Ahuzzam** Israel 31.33N 34.46E
32 C5 **Ahvāz** Iran 31.17N 48.43E
Ahvenanmaa *islds see* **Åland** *Is*
Ahvenjärvi *see* **Kuusajoki**
29 C7 **Ahwa** Gujarat India 20.44N 73.41E
33 G10 **Ahwar** S Yemen 13.33N 46.44E
Ahwāz *see* **Ahvāz**
19 F6 **Ai** *isld* Moluccas Indonesia 4.32S 129.46E
113 K8 **Aiaktalik I** Alaska 56.44N 154.05W
94 D2 **Aiams** Namibia 19.43S 17.00E
84 F6 **Aiándion** Greece 37.55N 23.28E
77 E4 **Aianís** Spain 38.03N 5.42W
120 G1 **Aiapuá** Brazil 4.29S 62.02W
120 G1 **Aiapuá, L** Brazil 4.24S 62.09W
119 F7 **Aiari R** Brazil
22 H5 **Aibag Gol** *R* Nei Monggol Zizhiqu China
75 H2 **Aibar** Spain 42.35N 1.21W
15 E5 **Aibase** Irian Jaya 2.39S 139.58E
88 J9 **Aï ben Tili** Mauritania 25.59N 9.30W
20 M1 **Aibetsu** Japan 43.56N 142.38E
105 J7 **Aibonito** Puerto Rico 18.10N 66.13W
65 J7 **Aich** Austria 47.26N 13.48E
64 N7 **Aich** W Germany 48.25N 12.25E
64 L7 **Aïchach** W Germany 48.26N 11.08E
20 L6 **Aichi** *prefect* Japan
113 Q2 **Aichilik** *R* Alaska
Aïchîyé *see* **'Ayshiye**
64 J8 **Aichstetten** W Germany 47.54N 10.05E
88 H8 **Aidar** *reg* Morocco
51 K3 **Aiddejavrre** Norway 68.45N 23.15E
64 P6 **Aidenbach** W Germany 48.34N 13.07E
84 F4 **Aidhipsós** Greece 38.53N 23.03E
32 F1 **Aidin** Turkmeniya U.S.S.R. 39.20N 54.50E
81 H9 **Aidone** Sicily 37.25N 14.27E
15 C5 **Aiduma, Pulau** *isld* Irian Jaya 3.59S 134.05E
35 G3 **Aidun** Jordan 32.31N 35.51E
35 H4 **Aidun** Jordan 32.18N 36.11E
114 B5 **Aiea** Hawaiian Is 21.23N 157.56W
81 M5 **Aiello in Cálabro** Italy 39.07N 16.10E
15 G7 **Aiema** *R* Papua New Guinea
81 L4 **Aieta** Italy 39.56N 15.50E
Aifur, Al *see* **Ajfar, Al**
84 G5 **Aigáleos Óros** *hills* Greece
65 M4 **Aigen** Nieder-Österreich Austria 48.49N 15.30E
65 J4 **Aigen** Ober-Österreich Austria 48.39N 13.59E
66 D6 **Aigle** Switzerland 46.20N 6.58E
72 J5 **Aigle, Barrage de l'** France 45.17N 2.15E
70 M4 **Aigle, l'** France 48.46N 0.38E
98 G2 **Aigle, L. à l'** Quebec
72 E8 **Aignan** France 43.42N 0.06E
71 F1 **Aignay-le-Duc** France 47.41N 4.43E
71 D8 **Aigoual, Montagne de l'** France 44.08N 3.35E
72 E4 **Aigre** France 45.53N 0.01E
72 C3 **Aigrefeuille d'Aunis** France 46.08N 0.56W
72 B1 **Aigrefeuille-sur-Maine** France 47.04N 1.24W
26 V13 **Aigrettes, I. aux** Mauritius, Indian Oc 20.25S 57.43E
26 T15 **Aigrettes, Pte. des** Réunion Ind Oc 21.02S 55.14E
121 G5 **Aigua** Uruguay 34.13S 54.46W
75 R4 **Aigua Blava** Spain 41.56N 3.14E
75 N5 **Aiguamurcia** Spain 41.20N 1.21E
71 H5 **Aiguebelette, Lac d'** France 45.33N 5.47E
71 H5 **Aiguebelette-le-Lac** France 45.32N 5.48E
71 J5 **Aiguebelle** France 45.33N 6.18E
99 M4 **Aiguebelle, Parc de** Quebec
71 K6 **Aigueblanche** France 45.30N 6.31E
71 C4 **Aigueperse** France 46.01N 3.12E
71 E9 **Aigues-Mortes** France 43.34N 4.11E
71 E9 **Aigues-Mortes, G. d'** France 43.32N 4.05E
72 H10 **Aigues Vives** Ariège France 42.59N 1.52E
71 B10 **Aigues-Vives** Hérault France 43.20N 2.50E
71 G7 **Aiguille** *mt* France 44.50N 5.30E
66 E8 **Aiguille d' Argentières** *mt* France/Switz 45.58N 7.02E
66 B4 **Aiguille de Baulmes** *mt* Switzerland 46.48N 6.28E
71 K7 **Aiguille de Chambeyron** *mt* France 44.33N 6.52E
71 K6 **Aiguille de Péclet** *mt* France 45.18N 6.36E
71 K6 **Aiguille de Scolette** *mt* France 45.10N 6.47E
66 D8 **Aiguille des Glaciers** *mt* France/Italy 45.47N 6.48E
66 D8 **Aiguille de Talefre** *mt* France/Italy 45.54N 7.00E
66 D8 **Aiguille de Tre-la-Tête** *mt* France/Italy 45.48N 6.48E
71 K5 **Aiguille du Midi** *mt* France 45.52N 6.53E
71 K7 **Aiguilles** France 44.39N 6.40E
71 J6 **Aiguilles d'Arves** *mt* France 45.07N 6.18E
66 F7 **Aiguilles Rouges** *mt* Switzerland 46.04N 7.27E
71 K5 **Aiguille Verte** *mt* France 45.57N 6.59E
72 E7 **Aiguillon** France 44.18N 0.21E
26 P14 **Aiguillon, C. d'** Kerguelen Ind Oc 48.49S 68.50E
72 B3 **Aiguillon, Pte. de l'** France 46.16N 1.13W
72 B3 **Aiguillon-sur-mer, l'** France 46.20N 1.18W
72 B3 **Aigullon, Anse de l'** France 46.17N 1.12W
72 H3 **Aigurande** France 46.26N 1.50E
20 A3 **Aihara** Kanagawa Japan
21 C7 **Ai He** *R* Liaoning China
Aihsien *see* **Yacheng**
21 D2 **Aihui** Heilongjiang China 50.16N 127.25E
120 B3 **Aija** Peru 9.50S 77.37W
29 G5 **Aijaigarh** Madhya Prad India
20 M3 **Aikawa** Japan 38.03N 138.16E
105 F4 **Aiken** S Carolina 33.34N 81.44W
112 F1 **Aiken** Texas 34.08N 101.33W
80 K6 **Ailano** Italy 41.23N 14.13E
23 B7 **Ailao Shan** *mt ra* Yunnan China
71 J7 **Ailefroide** France 44.52N 6.27E
13 C6 **Aileron** N Terr Australia 22.40S 133.20E
87 G3 **Ailet** Ethiopia 15.34N 39.10E
69 E5 **Ailette** *R* France
119 B3 **Ailigandi** Panama 9.15N 78.05W
51 M2 **Ailigas** *mt* Finland 69.25N 26.05E
9 B1 **Ailinginae** *atoll* Marshall Is Pacific Oc 11.10N 166.28E
9 C3 **Ailinglapalap** *atoll* Marshall Is Pacific Oc 7.30N 168.40E
69 E8 **Aillant-sur-Tholon** France 47.53N 3.21E
72 D7 **Aillas** France 44.29N 0.04W
71 J10 **Aille** *R* France
59 D4 **Aille R** Mayo Irish Rep
69 L8 **Aillevillers-et-Lyaumont** France 47.55N 6.20E
69 C3 **Ailly-le-Haut-Clocher** France 50.05N 2.00E
70 M2 **Ailly, Pte, d'** France 49.55N 0.58E
69 C4 **Ailly-sur-Noye** France 49.45N 2.22E
58 E5 **Ailort, L** Highland Scotland 56.51N 5.45W
99 J9 **Ailsa Craig** Ontario 43.08N 81.34W
57 C2 **Ailsa Craig** *isld* Strathclyde Scotland 55.16N 5.07W
9 D1 **Ailuk** *atoll* Marshall Is Pacific Oc 10.35N 169.53E
40 F2 **Aim** U.S.S.R. 58.50N 134.15E
43 O8 **Aim** Uzbekistan U.S.S.R. 40.51N 72.45E
40 F2 **Aim** *R* U.S.S.R.
35 F10 **'Aima** Jordan 30.53N 35.36E
28 C3 **Aimangala** Karnataka India 14.09N 76.30E
71 E9 **Aimargues** France 43.42N 4.12E
43 N8 **Aimchakakyr** Uzbekistan U.S.S.R. 40.21N 70.48E
71 K5 **Aime** France 45.33N 6.40E
69 F6 **Aime, Mt** France 48.50N 3.51E
19 B8 **Aimere** Indonesia 8.50S 120.55E
121 C2 **Aimogasta** Argentina 28.33S 66.50W
118 H6 **Aimorés** Brazil 19.30S 41.05W
118 H6 **Aimorés, Serra dos** Brazil
67 J6 **Ain** *dept* France
71 G5 **Ain** *R* France
86 P4 **'Ainā** Jordan 30.58N 35.46E
91 C2 **Aïna** *R* Cameroon/Gabon
93 G5 **Ainabkoi** Kenya 0.09N 35.32E
87 L6 **Ainabo** Somalia 8.57N 46.23E
86 K7 **'Ain Abu Shâhira** Egypt 29.16N 33.14E
114 B5 **Aina Haina** Hawaiian Is 21.17N 157.46W
33 L4 **'Ain, Al** U.A.E. 24.14N 55.46E
Ain al Hufayrah *see* **Hufayyirah, Al**
85 L7 **'Aîn 'Amûr** Egypt 25.39N 30.00E
Ain an Naft *oil bore see* **'Ayn an Naft**
114 C8 **Ainapo** Hawaiian Is 19.20N 155.24W
86 O2 **'Ain 'Arīk** Jordan 31.55N 35.08E
88 H10 **Ain Athil** Mauritania 22.21N 10.36W
72 K2 **Ainay-le Château** France 46.43N 2.41E
88 Q4 **'Aïn Azel** Algeria 35.46N 5.33E
46 E1 **Ainaži** Latvia U.S.S.R. 57.50N 24.29E
35 E1 **Ain Baâl** Lebanon 33.14N 35.16E
88 R4 **Aïn Beïda** Algeria 35.44N 7.22E
88 M4 **Ain Beni Mathar** Morocco 34.03N 2.02W
88 N5 **Aïn ben Khellil** Algeria 33.19N 0.50W
74 K8 **Aïn Bessem** Algeria 36.18N 3.41E
88 M5 **Aïn Chaïr** Morocco 32.10N 2.29W
35 D1 **'Aïn Chamaa** *watercourse* Lebanon
69 B5 **Aincourt** France 49.04N 1.46E
85 L7 **'Aîn Dakhâkhin** Egypt 24.45N 30.40E
85 J6 **'Aîn Dalla** Egypt 27.20N 27.23E
Ain Dar *oil field see* **'Ayn Dār**
88 O4 **'Aïn Deheb** Algeria 34.49N 1.33E
57 L4 **Ainderby Steeple** N Yorks Eng 54.19N 1.29W
35 G2 **'Ain Dhakar** Syria 32.52N 35.54E
86 K6 **'Ain Dîs** Egypt 29.37N 33.03E
34 K1 **'Ain Divar** Syria 37.17N 42.10E
64 K6 **Aindling** W Germany 48.30N 10.58E
88 S3 **Aïn Draham** Tunisia 36.48N 8.40E
35 E1 **Aïn Ebel** Lebanon 33.07N 35.24E
87 G2 **Ain, El** Ethiopia 16.04N 39.02E
87 C4 **'Ain, El** Sudan 13.00N 30.20E
88 P7 **Ain el Adrek** Algeria 28.38N 2.10E
86 L8 **'Ain el Akhdar** Egypt 28.49N 33.54E
35 D7 **'Ain el 'Arrub** Jordan 31.37N 35.08E
35 E6 **'Ain el 'Auja** Jordan 31.57N 35.23E
86 K7 **'Ain el Bâgha** Egypt 29.29N 33.05E
88 K8 **Aïn el Barka** Algeria 27.30N 6.50W
35 G5 **'Ain el Basha** Jordan 32.04N 35.50E
34 E4 **'Ain el Beida, El** Syria 34.33N 37.58E
35 G10 **'Ain el Beiza'iya** Jordan 30.53N 35.55E
86 N7 **'Ain el Furtâga** Egypt 29.03N 34.34E
86 K7 **'Ain el G'eib** Egypt 29.21N 33.14E
35 G3 **'Ain el Ghazal** Jordan 32.40N 35.53E
35 E7 **'Ain el Ghuweir** Jordan 31.37N 35.24E
88 R8 **Ain el Hadjadj** Algeria 26.55N 7.25E
74 H10 **Aïn el Hadjar** Algeria 34.45N 0.10E
74 K9 **Aïn el Hadjel** Algeria 35.40N 3.54E
35 G1 **Ain el Hajal** Syria 33.10N 35.46E
35 F5 **Ain el Hawari** Jordan 32.03N 35.40E
86 O4 **'Ain el Hufeira** Jordan 30.40N 35.16E
88 P4 **Aïn-el-Ibel** Algeria 34.20N 3.25E
89 C2 **Ain el Khadra** Mauritania 18.42N 12.18W
85 J6 **'Aîn el Khaleifa** Egypt 26.44N 27.48E
35 F8 **'Ain el Maliha** Jordan 31.25N 35.39E
Aïn el Ouardé *see* **'Ain el Wardah**
85 H5 **'Ain el Qaseibafya** Libya 29.36N 24.49E
35 F7 **'Ain el Qattar** Jordan 31.41N 35.40E
86 K6 **'Ain el Raweith** Egypt 29.45N 33.02E
85 H5 **'Aîn el Shifa** Egypt 29.09N 23.35E
85 K6 **Aîn el Wadi** Egypt 27.26N 28.17E
35 G1 **'Ain el Wardah** Syria 33.02N 35.47E
88 P7 **Aine Mezzer** Algeria 29.19N 2.30E
35 G3 **'Ain esh Shilaq** Jordan 32.35N 35.56E
35 G6 **'Ain et Tarabil** Jordan 31.55N 35.46E
35 G4 **'Ain et Teis** Jordan 32.21N 35.45E
35 E6 **'Ain Fara** Jordan 31.50N 35.18E
35 E4 **'Ain Fari'a** Jordan 32.17N 35.20E
35 E7 **'Ain Fashka** Jordan 31.43N 35.27E
34 J2 **Ain Fathi** Iraq 36.14N 41.56E
35 F1 **'Ain Fit** Syria 33.13N 35.42E
90 J2 **Aïn Galakka** Chad 18.04N 18.24E
86 M4 **'Ain, Gebel el** *hill* Egypt 30.40N 34.28E
25 C2 **Ainggyi** Burma 21.04N 94.22E
88 O4 **Aïn Gueteïfa** Algeria 34.38N 1.11E
35 F6 **'Ain Hajla** Jordan 31.49N 35.30E
35 H5 **Ain Hasu** Jordan 32.09N 36.05E
35 F7 **'Ain Himara** Jordan 31.39N 35.35E
72 B9 **Aïnhoa** France 43.18N 1.29W
Aïn Houeïzîye *see* **'Ain Hweiziya**
34 J2 **'Ain Hweiziya** Syria 36.12N 41.03E
35 G4 **'Ain Janna** Jordan 32.20N 35.46E
87 B2 **'Ain, Jebel el** *mt* Sudan
88 S3 **Aïn Kerma** Algeria 36.38N 8.10E
35 E9 **'Ain Khaukhan** Jordan 31.03N 35.28E
74 K9 **Aïn Khermane** Algeria 35.27N 4.08E
88 P5 **Ain Madhi El Haouita** Algeria 33.46N 2.28E
86 O9 **'Ain Marra** Saudi Arabia 28.30N 35.14E
74 K10 **Aïn Melah** Algeria 34.51N 4.10E
78 C13 **Aïn Mestour** Tunisia 35.54N 9.37E
88 R3 **Aïn M'lila** Algeria 36.02N 6.30E
Aïn Mokra *see* **Berrahall**
85 H9 **'Aîn Murr** Sudan 21.50N 25.09E
35 F6 **'Ain Musa** Jordan 31.47N 35.44E
35 D6 **'Ain Oiniya** Jordan 31.56N 35.09E
88 Q4 **Aïn Oulmene** Algeria 35.50N 5.18E
88 K6 **Aïn Ourir** Morocco 31.33N 7.38W
88 P4 **Aïn Oussera** Algeria 35.24N 2.54E
35 E6 **'Ain Qilt** Jordan 31.50N 35.23E
86 N7 **'Ain Quseiyib** Egypt 29.17N 34.40E
35 G4 **'Ain Rasun** Jordan 32.23N 35.46E
88 Q4 **Aïn Rich** Algeria 34.40N 4.04E
64 O8 **Ainring** W Germany 47.48N 12.57E
75 L3 **Ainsa** Spain 42.25N 0.08E
35 F9 **'Ain Sadd Habil** Jordan 31.06N 35.35E
85 H5 **'Aîn Sâfi** Egypt 29.04N 25.44E
89 C2 **Ain Safra** Mauritania 19.27N 12.02W
35 F10 **'Ain Saubala** Jordan 30.56N 35.39E
57 G5 **Ainsdale** Merseyside Eng 53.37N 3.03W
88 N5 **Aïn Sefra** Algeria 32.45N 0.35W
Ain Sifni *see* **'Ayn Sifnī**
86 O2 **'Ain Sīniya** Jordan 31.58N 35.14E
12 B6 **Ainslie** *dist* Canberra Australia
98 L7 **Ainslie, L** C Breton I, Nova Scotia
12 B6 **Ainslie, Mt** A.C.Terr Australia 35.17S 149.10E
85 M5 **Ain Sokhana** Egypt 29.35N 32.18E
86 K6 **'Ain Somâr** Egypt 29.40N 33.05E
88 P7 **Aïn Souf** Algeria 28.13N 2.15E
86 K6 **'Ain Sudr** Egypt 29.50N 33.07E
86 H6 **'Ain Sukhna** Egypt 29.35N 32.21E
106 C8 **Ainsworth** Iowa 41.18N 91.36W
108 L7 **Ainsworth** Nebraska 42.33N 99.51W
Aïn Taboûs *see* **'Ain Tabus**
34 G3 **'Ain Tabus** Syria 35.27N 39.55E
88 O9 **Aïn Tadjelet** Algeria 25.08N 1.45E
88 Q3 **Aïn Tagrout** Algeria 36.10N 5.04E
88 P3 **Aïn Taya** Algeria 36.51N 3.18E
74 H9 **Aïn Tédelès** Algeria 36.00N 0.15E
88 S5 **Aïn Tefguia** Tunisia 33.14N 8.45E
88 N4 **Aïn Témouchent** Algeria 35.18N 1.09W
85 J5 **'Aîn Tibaghbagh** Egypt 29.05N 26.25E
88 O8 **Aïn Tidjoubar** Algeria 27.44N 1.25E
88 P8 **Aïn Tidjoubar** Algeria 26.40N 3.34E
88 O9 **Aïn Tikkidine** Algeria 25.33N 1.24E
85 J5 **'Aîn Timeira** Egypt 29.17N 26.08E
88 Q4 **Aïn Touta** Algeria 35.26N 5.53E
57 H6 **Aintree** Merseyside Eng 53.29N 2.57W
35 F9 **Ainun** Jordan 31.09N 35.41E
87 L6 **Ain Valley** *reg* Somalia
'Ain, Wādī al *see* **'Ayn Wādī al** *watercourse*
86 P5 **'Ain Wuheida** Jordan 30.10N 35.36E
35 D6 **'Ain Yabrud** Jordan 31.57N 35.15E
86 K7 **'Ain Yarqa** Egypt 29.20N 33.28E
'Ain Zalah *oil field see* **'Ayn Zālah**
85 H5 **'Aîn Zeitun** Egypt 29.09N 25.49E
20 H7 **Aioi** Japan 34.48N 134.28E
20 J2 **Aioi** Japan 43.33N 143.59E
122 T15 **Aioia** *isld* Gambier Is Pacific Oc 23.08S 134.50W
15 H6 **Aiome** Papua New Guinea 5.08S 144.45E
88 K9 **Aïoun Abd el Malek** Mauritania 24.54N 7.25W
88 M4 **Aïoun, El** Morocco 34.39N 2.29W
89 E3 **Aioun el Atrouss** Mauritania 16.43N 9.30W
119 C6 **Aipe** Colombia 3.15N 75.17W
120 F8 **Aiquile** Bolivia 18.10S 65.10W
18 G4 **Airabu** *isld* Indonesia
19 N2 **Airai** Palau Is Pacific Oc 7.22N 134.34E
69 B4 **Airaines** France 49.58N 1.56E
119 H8 **Airão** Brazil 2.00S 61.20W
79 B5 **Airasca** Italy 44.55N 7.29E
90 D2 **Aïr (Azbine)** *mt reg* Niger
18 C5 **Airbangis** Sumatra Indon 0.09N 99.25E
58 B4 **Aird** Benbecula, W Isles Scotland 57.28N 7.25W
100 C7 **Airdrie** Alberta 51.20N 114.00W
58 J7 **Airdrie** Strathclyde Scotland 55.52N 3.59W
58 H4 **Aird, The, dist** Highland Scotland
69 J5 **Aire** *R* France
77 Y14 **Aire, I. del** Balearic Is 39.48N 4.16E
70 H3 **Airel** France 49.13N 1.05W
57 J4 **Aire, R** N Yorks Eng
76 B9 **Aire, Sa do** *mts* Portugal
72 D8 **Aire sur l'Adour** France 43.42N 0.15W
69 C2 **Aire-sur-la-Lys** France 50.38N 2.24E
97 M4 **Air Force I** N W Terr 68.00N 74.00W
22 J5 **Airgin Sum** Nei Monggol Zizhiqu China 43.12N 111.26E
18 J7 **Airhitam, R** Borneo Indon
18 J7 **Airhitam, Teluk** *B* Borneo Indon
110 B5 **Airlie** Oregon 44.45N 123.20W
95 O1 **Airlie** S Africa 25.38S 30.30E
14 B5 **Airlie I** W Australia 21.22S 115.05E
80 L6 **Airola** Italy 41.03N 14.33E
79 C7 **Airole** Italy 43.53N 7.33E
66 L5 **Airolo** Switzerland 46.32N 8.37E
57 G6 **Air, Pt. of** Clwyd Wales 53.22N 3.19W
58 J6 **Airth** Central Scotland 56.04N 3.47W
57 J4 **Airton** N Yorks Eng 54.02N 2.09W
72 D2 **Airvault** France 46.50N 0.08W
103 B7 **Airville** Pennsylvania 39.50N 76.24W
30 C6 **Airwa** Uttar Prad India 26.54N 79.25E
33 J9 **Ais** S Yemen 15.14N 51.05E
87 H5 **Aisaita** Ethiopia 11.35N 41.23E
20 C4 **Aisawa** Kanagawa Japan
64 K4 **Aisch** *R* W Germany
61 K4 **Aische-en-Refail** Belgium 50.36N 4.50E
87 J5 **Aiscia** Ethiopia 10.50N 42.36E
15 K6 **Aisega** New Britain Papua New Guinea 5.44S 148.22E
61 J5 **Aisemont** Belgium 50.25N 4.39E
121 J6 **Aisen** *prov* Chile
71 F1 **Aisey-sur-Seine** France 47.45N 4.35E
119 J6 **Aishalton** Guyana 2.33N 59.16W
22 M8 **Ai Shan** *mt* Shandong China 37.20N 120.45E
101 E5 **Aishihik** Yukon Terr 61.34N 137.31W
101 E5 **Aishihik L** Yukon Terr
51 F5 **Aisjaur** *L* Sweden 66.05N 17.30E
67 H3 **Aisne** *dept* France
69 F5 **Aisne** *R* France
79 B6 **Aisone** Italy 44.18N 7.12E
88 N5 **Aïssa Djebel** *mt* Algeria 32.56N 0.38W
71 J2 **Aissey** France 47.16N 6.20E
65 J5 **Aistersheim** Austria 48.12N 13.45E
30 K5 **Aisyalukharka** Nepal 27.21N 86.45E
71 E1 **Aisy-sur-Armançon** France 47.40N 4.13E
30 C7 **Ait** Uttar Prad India 25.54N 79.14E
35 E1 **Aïta ech Chaab** Lebanon 33.06N 35.20E
35 E1 **Aita ez Zoutt** Lebanon 33.10N 35.24E
77 Q3 **Aitana** *mt* Spain 38.39N 0.16W
15 G5 **Aitape** Papua New Guinea 3.10S 142.17E
35 E1 **Aïtaroûn** Lebanon 33.07N 35.28E
88 O11 **Ait el Khaoua** Algeria 21.21N 0.50E
88 P9 **Aït Elkra** Algeria 24.32N 2.31E
64 O6 **Aiterhofen** W Germany 48.50N 12.38E
88 M4 **Aït Fritissa** Morocco 34.07N 3.14W
58 T11 **Aith** Orkney Scotland 59.07N 2.37W
58 Q9 **Aith** Shetland Scotland 60.17N 1.23W
88 L6 **Aït Hani** Morocco 31.48N 5.30W
11 A13 **Aitken, Mt** New Zealand 46.10S 167.00E
108 R3 **Aitkin** Minnesota 46.38N 93.40W
88 J6 **Aït Melloul** Morocco 30.21N 9.31W
89 J1 **Ait Mouleï** Mali 20.14N 1.00W
89 K1 **Ait Nafane** Mali 21.09N 0.49E
84 C4 **Aitolía** *prov* Greece
84 B5 **Aitolikón** Greece 38.26N 21.21E
43 C1 **Aitova** U.S.S.R. 53.36N 54.14E
88 M5 **Aït Serhouchene** *tribe* Morocco
88 L6 **Aït Slilo** Morocco 30.54N 5.55W
122 L10 **Aitutaki** *isld* Cook Is Pacific Oc 18.52S 159.46W
88 L5 **Ait Youssi** *tribe* Morocco
75 F2 **Aitzgorri, Mte** Spain 42.57N 2.19W
82 H4 **Aiud** Romania 46.19N 23.43E
Aiún *see* **Aaiún, El**
Aivan-i Khaif *see* **Eyvānaki**
46 F2 **Aiviekste** *R* Latvia U.S.S.R.
15 C5 **Aiwasa** *L* Irian Jaya 3.37S 134.17E
19 N1 **Aiwokako Pass** Palau Is Pacific Oc
72 J4 **Aix** France 45.37N 2.22E
72 K1 **Aix d'Angillon, les** France 47.12N 2.34E
69 F7 **Aix-en-Othe** France 48.14N 3.45E
71 G9 **Aix-en-Provence** France 43.31N 5.27E
72 G4 **Aixe-sur-Vienne** France 45.47N 1.08E
72 B3 **Aix, Ile d'** France 46.02N 1.10W
Aix-la-Chapelle *see* **Aachen**
71 H5 **Aix-les-Bains** France 45.41N 5.55E
35 F9 **Aiy** Jordan 31.08N 35.38E
Aiyadh *see* **Ayādh**
15 F6 **Aiyang** *mt* Papua New Guinea 4.15S 141.18E
101 J8 **Aiyansh** Br Columbia 55.15N 129.05W
29 J1 **Aiyar Res** Bihar India
86 F6 **'Aiyat, El** Egypt 29.37N 31.15E
90 B8 **Aiyede** Nigeria 7.55N 5.24E
89 J8 **Aiyerade** Ghana 7.30N 1.40W
90 A8 **Aiyetoro** Nigeria 7.16N 3.05E
84 F6 **Aíyina** Greece 37.45N 23.26E
84 F6 **Aíyina** *isld* Greece
83 F4 **Aiyínion** Greece 40.31N 22.32E
84 D5 **Aíyion** Greece 38.15N 22.05E
Aiyun *see* **Ayun**
15 H7 **Aiyura** Papua New Guinea 6.20S 145.54E
28 J4 **Aizawl** Mizoram India 23.45N 92.45E
94 E3 **Aizeb** *watercourse* Namibia
72 A2 **Aizenay** France 46.44N 1.36W
75 G2 **Aizpun** Spain 42.50N 1.53W
46 D2 **Aizpute** Latvia U.S.S.R. 56.42N 21.32E
20 N4 **Aizu-Takada** Japan 37.27N 139.49E
20 N4 **Aizu-Wakamatsu** Japan 37.30N 139.58E
32 A2 **'Ajab Shir** Iran 37.28N 45.58E
67 O13 **Ajaccio** Corsica 41.55N 8.43E
67 O13 **Ajaccio, G. d'** Corsica 41.51N 8.43E
30 D8 **Ajaigarh** Madhya Prad India 24.52N 80.16E
33 M7 **'Ajā'iz** Oman 19.36N 57.08E
33 D3 **Ajā, Jabal** *mts* Saudi Arabia
'Ajājira, El *see* **Massu'a** Jordan
119 D7 **Ajajú** *R* Colombia
87 A6 **Ajak** Sudan 8.56N 27.30E
115 L8 **Ajalpán** Mexico 18.26N 97.20W
33 H3 **Ajām, Al** Saudi Arabia 26.34N 49.59E
35 G3 **'Ajami** Syria 32.44N 35.59E
75 F3 **Ajamil** Spain 42.10N 2.29W
14 A8 **Ajana** W Australia 27.59S 114.34E
29 D7 **Ajanta** Maharashtra India 20.30N 75.48E
Ajanta Range *see* **Sahyadriparvat Ra**
93 L3 **Ajao** *mt* Kenya 2.57N 39.43E
90 C8 **Ajaokuta** Nigeria 7.26N 6.43E
72 G5 **Ajat** France 45.10N 1.01E
99 L9 **Ajax** Ontario 43.48N 79.00W
110 M4 **Ajax Mt** Idaho 45.20N 113.44W
11 G9 **Ajax, Mt** New Zealand 42.34S 172.06E
19 L1 **Ajayan B** Guam Pacific Oc
22 C4 **Aj Bogd Uul** *mts* Mongolia
85 F4 **Ajdābiyah** Libya 30.48N 20.15E
82 B5 **Ajdovščina** Yugoslavia 45.54N 13.54E
90 B8 **Ajebandele** Nigeria 6.43N 4.24E
33 E3 **Ajfar, Al** Saudi Arabia 27.29N 43.01E
30 D6 **Ajgain** Uttar Prad India 26.37N 80.37E
35 J5 **'Ajib** *watercourse* Jordan
20 O1 **Ajigasawa** Japan 40.46N 140.12E
90 F6 **Ajigin** Nigeria 11.11N 12.25E
119 C6 **Ají, I** Colombia 3.20N 77.30W
88 T5 **Ajim** Tunisia 33.48N 10.44E
34 O2 **Ajirlū** *R* Iran
89 N2 **Ajir, Mt** Niger 18.05N 6.25E
20 N6 **Ajiro** Japan 35.03N 139.04E
20 P3 **Aji-shima** *islds* Japan
35 D4 **Ajja** Jordan 32.22N 35.12E
88 S9 **Ajjer** *reg* Algeria
'Ajjūr *see* **'Agur**
82 D3 **Ajka** Hungary 47.18N 17.32E
35 G4 **Ajlun** Jordan 32.20N 35.45E
33 L4 **Ajmān** U.A.E. 25.23N 55.26E
29 D4 **Ajmer** Rajasthan India 26.29N 74.40E
29 D4 **Ajmer** *dist* Rajasthan India
29 D2 **Ajnala** Punjab India 31.50N 74.48E
111 M9 **Ajo** Arizona 32.24N 112.51W
75 C1 **Ajo, C** Spain 43.30N 3.35W
Ajodhya *see* **Ayodhya**
75 C8 **Ajofrín** Spain 39.43N 3.59W
66 E2 **Ajoie** *reg* Switzerland
76 G2 **Ajo, L** Spain 43.03N 6.09W
111 M9 **Ajo, Mt** Arizona 32.02N 112.38W
28 B2 **Ajra** Maharashtra India 16.08N 74.17E
Aju *see* **Ayu**
119 G8 **Ajuana, R** Brazil
115 J8 **Ajuchitlán** Mexico 18.09N 100.30W
76 D16 **Ajuda** Portugal 38.42N 9.12W
76 E11 **Ajuda** Portugal 38.47N 7.10W
93 C2 **Ajumani** Uganda 3.22N 31.48E
87 D6 **Ajungmir** Sudan 8.29N 33.12E
120 E2 **Ajuricaba** Brazil 7.36S 66.37W
24 D8 **A-ju Ts'o** *L* Xizang Zizhiqu China 34.00N 82.25E
19 L6 **Ajuy** Philippines 11.10N 122.59E
36 C5 **Ak** *R* Turkey
93 A1 **Aka** *R* Zaïre
90 E8 **Aka** *tribe* Nigeria
89 K8 **Akaba** Togo 7.59N 1.12E
88 O8 **Akabli** Algeria 26.44N 1.25E
40 H1 **Akachan** *R* U.S.S.R.
42 C5 **Akademgorodok** U.S.S.R. 54.48N 83.06E
43 K7 **Akademii Nauk, Khr** *ra* Tadzhikistan U.S.S.R.
40 G4 **Akademii Zaliv** *B* U.S.S.R.
20 M4 **Akadomari** Japan 37.52N 138.25E
20 N3 **Aka-gawa** *R* Japan
15 J8 **Akaifu** *R* Papua New Guinea
20 M6 **Akaishi-dake** *pk* Japan 35.29N 138.07E
30 A7 **Akajhiri** Madhya Prad India 25.07N 77.51E
84 R14 **Akaki** Cyprus 35.07N 33.08E
87 F3 **Akala** Sudan 15.39N 36.13E
28 C2 **Akalkot** Maharashtra India 17.31N 76.14E
93 D3 **Akalu** Uganda 2.10N 32.52E
122 S16 **Aka-Maru** *isld* Gambier Is Pacific Oc 23.12S 134.54W
90 D9 **Akamkpa** Nigeria 5.18N 8.21E
84 S14 **Akanthou** Cyprus 35.22N 33.45E
93 A8 **Akanyaru** *R* Rwanda/Burundi
20 G8 **Akaoka** Japan 33.32N 133.42E
36 E4 **Akar** *R* Turkey
84 A4 **Akarnanía** *prov* Greece
84 B4 **Akarnaniká, Ori** *mts* Greece
11 G10 **Akaroa** New Zealand 43.50S 172.59E
11 G10 **Akaroa Harb** *inlet* New Zealand
28 J2 **Akas** *reg* Assam India
20 E2 **Akasaka** *dist* Tōkyō Japan
20 G6 **Akasaki** Japan 35.31N 133.40E
85 L9 **Akasha** Sudan 21.04N 30.45E
20 H7 **Akashi** Japan 34.39N 135.00E
34 H4 **'Akāsh, Wādī** *watercourse* Iraq
51 K4 **Akasjoensuu** Finland 67.28N 23.47E
51 K4 **Äkäsjoki** *R* Finland
51 K4 **Äkäsjokisuu** Finland 67.28N 23.44E
108 K4 **Akaska** S Dakota 45.19N 100.06W
90 C9 **Akassa** Nigeria 4.19N 6.02E
43 M7 **Akata** Uzbekistan U.S.S.R. 40.53N 70.01E
20 N4 **Akatani** Japan 37.49N 139.28E
20 D3 **Akatsutsumi** *dist* Tōkyō Japan
37 G5 **Akbaba Dağları** *mts* Turkey
35 F2 **'Akbara** Israel 32.56N 35.30E
31 E3 **Akbar Khel** Afghanistan 34.20N 69.45E
30 G8 **Akbarpur** Bihar India 24.39N 83.58E
30 F6 **Akbarpur** Faizabad, Uttar Prad India 26.25N 82.32E
30 C6 **Akbarpur** Kanpur, Uttar Prad Ind 26.21N 79.57E
24 A1 **Akbaur** Kazakhstan U.S.S.R. 49.02N 74.10E
43 L3 **Akbavro** Kazakhstan U.S.S.R. 49.15N 74.00E
31 G1 **Akbaytal** Tadzhikistan U.S.S.R. 38.30N 73.50E
43 L7 **Akbaytal, Pereval** *pass* Tadzhikistan U.S.S.R. 38.40N 73.45E
43 K2 **Akbent** Kazakhstan U.S.S.R. 51.38N 70.02E
88 Q3 **Akbou** Algeria 36.29N 4.32E
43 D2 **Akbulak** U.S.S.R. 51.00N 55.40E
43 O8 **Akbura** *R* Kirgiziya U.S.S.R.
37 E4 **Akçaabat** Turkey 41.03N 39.34E
37 D9 **Akçakale** Turkey 36.44N 38.59E
36 E1 **Akçakoca** Turkey 41.05N 31.08E
37 D9 **Akçakoyunlu** Turkey 36.44N 37.39E
37 F7 **Akçan** Turkey 38.54N 41.33E
36 C5 **Akçaova** Aydın Turkey 37.30N 28.02E
37 H1 **Akçaova** Kocaeli Turkey 41.02N 29.57E
37 F7 **Akçasır** Turkey 38.29N 41.17E
37 F3 **Akcasusığırlığı** Turkey 40.18N 28.26E
36 D6 **Akçay** Turkey 36.36N 29.46E
44 G4 **Akcay, R** U.S.S.R.
31 D2 **Akcha** Afghanistan 36.57N 66.06E
43 E6 **Akchakaya, Vpadina** *depression* Turkmeniya U.S.S.R.
89 B2 **Akchar** *reg* Mauritania
89 B1 **Akchar, Dunes de l'** *sand ridge* Mauritania
43 L3 **Akchatau** Kazakhstan U.S.S.R. 47.59N 73.45E
Akche *see* **Akqi**

43 M5 Akchi Kazakhstan U.S.S.R. 44.04N 76.22E
83 J7 Akçoava Turkey 37.31N 28.02E
36 H2 Akdağ Turkey 40.42N 35.59E
36 D6 Ak Dağ mt Antalya Turkey 36.32N 29.33E
36 F5 Ak Dağ mt Antalya Turkey
36 H2 Ak Dağ mt Çorum Turkey 40.49N 35.56E
36 D4 Ak Dağ mt Denizli Turkey 38.19N 29.57E
37 F5 Ak Dağ mt Erzurum Turkey 40.35N 41.46E
36 E5 Ak Dağ mt Isparta, etc Turkey 37.41N 30.34E
36 H3 Ak Dağ mt Kayseri Turkey 39.15N 35.43E
36 D3 Ak Dağ mt Kütahya Turkey 39.16N 28.48E
36 J3 Ak Dağ mt Sivas Turkey
37 F6 Ak Dağ mt Turkey
36 H3 Akdağmadeni Turkey 39.40N 35.52E
42 E6 Ak Dovurak U.S.S.R. 51.20N 90.40E
43 O8 Akdzhar Kirgiziya U.S.S.R. 40.32N 73.03E
20 L6 Akechi Japan 35.19N 137.22E
91 H5 Akela tribe Zaïre
19 F3 Akelamo Halmahera Indon 1.29N 128.39E
56 K3 Akeley Bucks Eng 52.02N 0.59W
108 Q2 Akeley Minnesota 47.00N 94.45W
87 D7 Akelo Sudan 6.59N 33.43E
56 K4 Akeman Street hist route Eng
63 Q9 Aken E Germany 51.51N 12.02E
44 H8 Akera R Azerbaydzhan U.S.S.R.
52 D8 Åkernes Norway 58.45N 7.32E
52 L7 Åkersberga Sweden 59.28N 18.19E
52 F7 Akershus co Norway
52 H3 Åkerskön Sweden 63.45N 14.10E
60 G9 Akersloot Netherlands 52.33N 4.44E
52 K7 Åkers-Styckebruk L Sweden 59.07N 17.15E
89 D3 Akerteyé Mauritania 17.05N 11.02W
19 E3 Akeselaka Halmahera Indon 1.00N 127.59E
43 F4 Akespe Kazakhstan U.S.S.R. 46.45N 60.31E
91 H2 Aketi Zaïre 2.42N 23.51E
87 C7 Akeu Sudan 6.20N 30.39E
24 E6 Akfaz Xinjiang Uygur Zizhiqu China 38.50N 86.45E
32 C2 Akgaduk Pass Iran 36.51N 48.46E
36 F4 Ak Göl L Turkey
36 G5 Ak Göl Sazlık marsh Turkey
37 H7 Ak Gölü L Turkey
44 H7 Akgyel, Ozero L Azerbaydzhan U.S.S.R. 40.01N 47.40E
84 C5 Akhaïa prov Akhaïa Greece
44 E6 Akhalkalaki Gruziya U.S.S.R. 41.25N 43.29E
44 D4 Akhalsheni Georgia U.S.S.R. 43.08N 41.02E
44 E6 Akhaltsikhe Georgia U.S.S.R. 41.37N 42.59E
84 G5 Akharnai Greece 38.05N 23.44E
31 J9 Akhaura Bangladesh 23.50N 91.10E
'Akhbera see 'Akbara
32 F1 Akhchaguyma Turkmeniya U.S.S.R. 39.20N 55.07E
33 B2 Akhdar,Al Saudi Arabia 28.06N 37.06E
33 M5 Akhdar, Jabal mt Oman 23.15N 57.16E
85 F3 Akhdar, Jabal al mts Libya
86 L8 Akhdar, Wâdî watercourse Egypt
34 D10 Akhdar, Wādī watercourse Saudi Arabia
30 A5 Akhegarh Rajasthan India 27.14N 77.04E
86 H6 Akheidir, Gebel hill Egypt 29.45N 32.11E
84 P15 Akhelia Cyprus 34.44N 32.28E
84 M12 Akhendriá Crete 35.00N 25.13E
84 E4 Akhíllion Greece 39.00N 22.58E
42 H5 Akhiny U.S.S.R. 53.15N 105.00E
113 K8 Akhiok Alaska 56.58N 154.18W
36 C4 Akhisar Turkey 38.54N 27.50E
84 H5 Akhladherí Greece 38.28N 24.10E
84 C6 Akhladhiní Greece 37.43N 21.47E
84 E6 Akhladhókambos Greece 37.31N 22.35E
45 R5 Akhmat U.S.S.R. 51.04N 45.54E
44 G5 Akhmeta Georgia U.S.S.R. 42.01N 45.12E
44 D3 Akhmetovskaya U.S.S.R. 44.11N 41.04E
85 L6 Akhmîm Egypt 26.35N 31.48E
Akhna see Athna
31 H4 Akhnur Kashmir 32.53N 74.46E
44 J7 Akhsu Azerbaydzhan U.S.S.R. 40.35N 48.24E
44 F7 Akhta Armenia U.S.S.R. 40.29N 44.45E
44 F6 Akhtala Armenia U.S.S.R. 41.10N 44.47E
32 E7 Akhtar Iran 27.45N 52.15E
41 K8 Akhtaranda R U.S.S.R.
34 E2 Akhterin Syria 36.31N 37.19E
82 L8 Akhtopol Bulgaria 42.06N 27.56E
45 Q5 Akhtuba U.S.S.R. 51.38N 44.24E
45 S9 Akhtuba R U.S.S.R.
45 S8 Akhtubinsk U.S.S.R. 48.20N 46.10E
44 H6 Akhty U.S.S.R. 41.27N 47.45E
45 F6 Akhtyrka Ukraine U.S.S.R. 50.19N 34.54E
47 H8 Akhunovo U.S.S.R. 54.13N 59.41E
44 F7 Akhuryan Armenia U.S.S.R. 40.47N 43.55E
32 D4 Akhvoreh Iran 32.54N 50.07E
21 E11 Aki Kyūshū Japan 33.27N 131.42E
20 G8 Aki Shikoku Japan 33.30N 133.53E
113 G6 Akiachak Alaska 60.55N 161.30W
113 G6 Akiak Alaska 60.51N 161.13W
122 F15 Akiaki atoll Tuamotu Is Pacific Oc 18.28S 139.12W
91 C4 Akiéni Gabon 1.12S 13.58E
91 C4 Akiéni Gabon 1.10S 13.52E
47 G4 Akim U.S.S.R. 63.45N 53.40E
42 K5 Akima U.S.S.R. 53.06N 115.45E
97 L7 Akimiski I James B, N W Terr 53.00N 81.00W
44 D8 Akimovka Ukraine U.S.S.R. 46.42N 35.09E
89 J9 Akim Swedru Ghana 5.55N 1.01W
20 F7 Aki-nada sea Japan
36 C5 Akıncılar Turkey 37.56N 27.25E
47 N3 Akinfiyevo U.S.S.R. 58.03N 61.02E
15 K7 Akinum New Britain 6.15S 149.45E
90 D7 Akiri Nigeria 8.22N 9.21E
53 P12 Åkirkeby Bornholm Denmark 55.04N 14.56E
20 A2 Akishima Tōkyō Japan
40 F5 Akishma R U.S.S.R.
20 O2 Akita Japan 39.44N 140.05E
20 O2 Akita prefect Japan
11 L7 Akitio New Zealand 40.35S 176.26E
42 H4 Akitkan, Khrebet mts U.S.S.R.
89 B2 Akjoujt Mauritania 19.44N 14.20W
89 G4 Akka Mali 15.24N 4.11W
88 J7 Akka Morocco 29.22N 8.14W
35 G4 'Akka anc site Jordan 32.15N 35.53E
43 F3 Akkabak Kazakhstan U.S.S.R. 49.53N 62.28E
51 F4 Akkajaure L Sweden 67.40N 17.30E
43 E5 Akkala, Mys C Uzbekistan U.S.S.R. 43.47N 59.31E
39 M2 Akkani U.S.S.R. 65.30N 171.17W
26 U7 Akkaraipattu Sri Lanka 7.13N 81.51E
43 F2 Akkarga Kazakhstan U.S.S.R. 51.32N 61.05E
34 C4 'Akkar, Jūn el B Lebanon
47 L5 Akkashka, Gora mt U.S.S.R. 55.32N 59.20E
51 F4 Akkavarre mt Sweden 67.36N 17.25E
36 G1 Akkaya Turkey 41.12N 33.59E
42 D6 Akkem U.S.S.R. 50.09N 86.40E
60 M6 Akkerwoude Netherlands 53.17N 5.58E
21 K6 Akkeshi Japan 43.02N 144.52E
36 J3 Akkışla Turkey 39.01N 36.10E
35 D2 'Akko Israel 32.55N 35.04E
43 M4 Akkol' Kazakhstan U.S.S.R. 45.04N 75.39E
36 C5 Akköy Aydın Turkey 37.28N 27.18E
37 G2 Akkoy Bursa Turkey 40.31N 29.41E
43 C3 Akkozinskiy Kazakhstan U.S.S.R. 49.30N 53.35E
60 M7 Akkrum Netherlands 53.03N 5.50E
43 K5 Akkul' Kazakhstan U.S.S.R.
43 L6 Ak-Kul' Kirgiziya U.S.S.R. 41.41N 74.15E
37 C5 Akkuş Turkey 40.45N 37.01E
43 C6 Akkyr, Gory mts Turkmeniya U.S.S.R.
19 L6 Aklan Pt Philippines 11.55N 122.23E
101 F1 Aklavik N W Terr 68.15N 135.02W
89 F2 Aklé Aouana reg Mauritania
29 E5 Aklera Rajasthan India 24.26N 76.32E
89 J1 Akli Mali 20.29N 1.05W
33 E7 Aklub tribe Saudi Arabia
82 M5 Akmangit U.S.S.R. 45.55N 29.15E
60 M7 Akmarijp Netherlands 53.00N 5.47E
41 H2 Akmatova, Zaliv gulf U.S.S.R.
46 E2 Akmene Lithuania U.S.S.R. 56.14N 22.44E
24 B7 Akmeqit Xinjiang Uygur Zizhiqu China 37.07N 77.12E
43 M6 Akmoyun Kirgiziya U.S.S.R. 41.14N 76.01E
46 F2 Akniste Latvia U.S.S.R. 56.09N 25.45E
88 M4 Aknoul Morocco 34.43N 3.49W
20 H7 Ako Japan 34.44N 134.22E
90 E6 Ako Nigeria 10.20N 11.01E
87 D7 Akobo Sudan 7.50N 33.05E
87 E7 Akobo watercourse Ethiopia
87 D7 Akobo,R Sudan/Ethiopia
30 E7 Akodha Uttar Prad India 25.14N 81.53E
29 E6 Akodia Madhya Prad India 23.20N 76.38E
91 B3 Akoga Gabon 0.55N 10.39E
91 A3 Akok Gabon 0.30N 9.40E
114 B6 Akokoa Pt Hawaiian Is 20.18N 155.43W
93 D4 Akokoro Uganda 1.43N 32.24E
29 D8 Akola Ahmadnagar, Maharashtra India 19.32N 74.03E
29 E7 Akola Akola, Maharashtra India 20.40N 77.05E
29 E7 Akola dist Maharashtra India
113 F6 Akolmint Alaska 61.00N 162.43W
91 B2 Akom Cameroon 2.51N 10.54E
15 H7 Akoma Papua New Guinea 7.50S 145.02E
94 D2 Akomas Namibia 18.59S 16.29E
90 F10 Akonolinga Cameroon 3.46N 12.17E
89 F4 Akor Mali 14.59N 6.58W
89 F4 Akor Tegdawich Mali 15.27N 6.48W
29 E7 Akot Maharashtra India 21.06N 77.08E
87 C7 Akot Sudan 6.31N 30.09E
117 B4 Akotipa Brazil 1.58N 55.31W
90 J8 Akouma Cent Afr Rep 6.11N 18.19E
117 C3 Akouménaye Fr Guiana 2.58N 52.22W
84 D7 Ákovos Greece 37.12N 22.10E
42 D6 Ak-Oyuk, Gora mt U.S.S.R. 50.41N 89.53E
97 N5 Akpatok I N W Terr 60.30N 68.00W
37 D8 Akpınar Adıyaman Turkey 37.34N 38.13E
37 C6 Akpınar Sivas Turkey 39.05N 37.01E
24 C5 Akqi Xinjiang Uygur Zizhiqu China 40.52N 78.10E
53 U19 Åkra Hordaland Norway 59.47N 6.05E
108 N1 Akra N Dakota 48.47N 97.44W
84 C8 Ákra Akrítas C Greece 36.43N 21.52E
37 A2 Ákra Akrotiri C Samothráki Greece 40.28N 25.28E
84 E3 Ákra Almiroú C Greece 39.11N 22.54E
84 F4 Ákra Arkítsa C Greece 38.45N 23.02E
84 W23 Ákra Asprókavos C Corfu 39.22N 20.07E
83 G5 Ákra Ayía Iríni C Greece 39.46N 25.23E
84 W22 Ákra Áyios Aikateríni C Corfu 39.50N 19.50E
84 H7 Ákra Áyios Dhimítrios C Greece 37.18N 24.22E
84 N11 Ákra Ayios Ioánnis C Crete Mediterranean Sea 35.20N 25.46E
84 A5 Ákra Ayioú Ioánnou C Greece 38.18N 20.46E
30 B5 Akrabad Uttar Prad India 27.49N 78.16E
53 N11 Akraberg C Faeroes Norwegian Sea 61.24N 6.40W
84 E2 Ákra Dhermatás C Greece 39.48N 22.51E
84 A5 Ákra Dhikhália C Greece 38.16N 20.40E
84 W22 Ákra Dhráhstis C Corfu 39.48N 19.40E
84 K11 Ákra Dhrápanon C Crete 35.29N 24.15E
84 C5 Ákra Dhrépanon C Akhaïa Greece 38.20N 21.51E
83 F5 Ákra Dhrépanon C Sithoniá Greece 39.57N 23.59E
34 D2 Akrād, Jebel el mts Syria
83 D6 Ákra Doukáton C Greece 38.34N 20.30E
84 B5 Ákra Évinos C Greece 38.17N 21.29E
84 O11 Ákra Faneroméni C Crete 35.14N 26.04E
50 D6 Akrafjall mt Iceland 64.21N 21.54W
53 U19 Åkrafjorden inlet Norway 59.47N 6.14E
84 O12 Ákra Goúdhora C Crete 35.00N 26.06E
84 G3 Ákra Gouroúni C Greece 39.13N 23.37E
84 F8 Ákra Iérax C Greece 36.47N 23.06E
84 F5 Akraífnion Greece 38.27N 23.13E
36 H7 Akra, Jebel mt Turkey 35.57N 35.59E
84 H5 Ákra Kafirévs C Greece 38.10N 24.35E
84 G2 Ákra Kanastraion C Greece 39.55N 23.45E
84 H4 Ákra Kártsino C Greece 38.59N 24.29E
84 H7 Ákra Kéfalos C Greece 37.29N 24.25E
84 M11 Ákra Khersónisos C Crete 35.20N 25.23E
84 H7 Ákra Kíklops C Greece 37.07N 24.25E
84 B6 Ákra Killíni C Greece 37.56N 21.08E
84 D8 Ákra Kitriés C Greece 36.55N 22.07E
84 F7 Ákra Kórax C Greece 37.21N 23.04E
84 J11 Ákra Koútoulos C Crete 35.23N 23.31E
84 J11 Ákra Kriós C Crete 35.13N 23.35E
84 V17 Ákra Lárdhos C Rhodes Mediterranean Sea 36.03N 28.05E
83 G6 Ákra Lithári C Greece 38.46N 24.42E
84 L12 Ákra Lithinon C Crete 34.55N 24.44E
84 C8 Ákra Livádha C Greece 36.48N 21.57E
84 E5 Ákra Mákri Nikólaos C Greece 38.17N 22.33E
84 F9 Ákra Maléa C Greece 36.27N 23.12E
83 H5 Ákra Maléa C Turkey 39.02N 26.47E
84 A6 Ákra Marathiás C Greece 37.38N 20.50E
83 H6 Ákra Mástikho C Greece 38.07N 26.01E
84 E5 Ákra Melangávi C Greece 38.02N 22.51E
84 L11 Ákra Mélissa C Crete 35.06N 24.33E
84 A4 Ákra Mélissa C Greece 38.30N 29.39E
84 A5 Ákra Moúnda C Greece 38.03N 20.47E
50 C6 Akranes Iceland 64.19N 22.05W
50 C5 Akraós B Iceland
84 B5 Ákra Pápas C Akhaïa Greece 38.13N 21.22E
83 H7 Ákra Papas C Ikaría Greece 37.32N 25.58E
83 G4 Ákra Pínnes C Greece 40.05N 24.17E
84 O11 Ákra Pláka C Crete 35.12N 26.18E
83 G4 Ákra Pláka C Greece 40.03N 25.27E
83 G4 Ákra Platí C Greece 40.26N 24.00E
84 F2 Ákra Posídhion C Greece 39.57N 23.22E
84 H8 Ákra Psális C Greece 36.39N 24.19E
84 D5 Ákra Psaromita C Greece 38.18N 22.11E
50 C5 Akrar Iceland 64.38N 22.23W
84 G4 Ákra Sarakínikon C Greece 38.46N 23.42E
84 E7 Ákra Savatáki C Greece 37.11N 22.54E
84 O11 Ákra Sídheros C Crete 35.19N 26.18E
83 F7 Ákra Skíllaion C Greece 37.25N 23.31E
84 A6 Ákra Skinári C Greece 37.56N 20.42E
84 J10 Ákra Spátha C Greece 35.42N 23.43E
84 H7 Ákra Spathí C Greece 37.07N 24.29E
84 L11 Ákra Stavros C Crete 35.26N 24.58E
84 F3 Ákra Stavrós C Greece 39.02N 23.04E
84 D5 Akráta Greece 38.09N 22.19E
84 D9 Ákra Taínaron C Greece 36.23N 22.29E
84 H6 Ákra Tamélos C Greece 37.31N 24.16E
84 G6 Ákra Toúrlos C Greece 37.46N 23.34E
84 H8 Ákra Váni C Greece 36.45N 24.21E
84 E5 Ákra Velanidhiá Greece 38.14N 22.46E
84 G3 Ákra Velóna C Greece 39.04N 24.43E
84 A5 Ákra Vlióti C Greece 38.28N 20.34E
84 E8 Ákra Xíli C Greece 36.40N 22.49E
84 G3 Ákra Yérakas C Voríai Sporádhes Greece 39.17N 23.57E
84 A6 Ákra Yérakas C Zákinthos Greece 37.42N 20.59E
84 G7 Ákra Zoúrva C Greece 37.22N 23.35E
84 F9 Ákra Zóvollo C Greece 36.26N 23.07E
Akrê see 'Aqrah
53 S20 Åkrehamn Norway 59.15N 5.13E
89 B2 Akreïdil Mauritania 18.31N 15.32W
89 E2 Akreïjit Mauritania 18.19N 9.11W
53 T16 Åkrestrard Norway 61.07N 5.47E
84 G4 Akr. Gáïdharos C Greece 38.31N 23.32E
31 D3 Ak Robat Pass Afghanistan 34.59N 67.40E
53 D6 Åkrog Bugt B Denmark 55.10N 9.55E
89 J8 Akrokeri Ghana 6.20N 1.35W
107 J9 Akron Alabama 32.52N 87.45W
109 G1 Akron Colorado 40.09N 103.13W
106 H8 Akron Indiana 41.03N 86.02W
108 O7 Akron Iowa 42.50N 96.32W
106 L6 Akron Michigan 43.34N 83.30W
104 G3 Akron New York 43.02N 78.30W
104 D5 Akron Ohio 41.04N 81.31W
99 F4 Akron Ontario 48.55N 84.08W
103 B6 Akron Pennsylvania 40.09N 76.12W
84 B3 Akropotamia Greece 39.06N 21.01E
84 H6 Akros Angálistros C Greece 37.38N 24.06E
84 Q15 Akrotiri Cyprus 34.35N 32.57E
84 R15 Akrotiri B Cyprus
84 Q15 Akrotiri (Sovereign Base Area) Cyprus
84 E2 Akr. Platamón C Greece 39.55N 22.42E
31 J1 Aksai Chin dist Kashmir
Aksai Chin L see Aksayqin Hit
31 J1 Aksai Chin L Kashmir 35.08N 79.45E
37 E3 Aksakal Turkey 40.09N 28.07E
46 R3 Aksakovo U.S.S.R. 54.00N 54.14E
37 C8 Aksaray Maraş Turkey 37.44N 37.24E
36 G4 Aksaray Niğde Turkey 38.22N 34.02E
47 K3 Aksarka U.S.S.R. 66.31N 67.50E
37 D2 Aksas Turkey 40.26N 27.10E
43 B2 Aksay Kazakhstan U.S.S.R. 51.24N 52.11E
43 C2 Aksay Kazakhstan U.S.S.R. 51.11N 53.00E
43 K5 Aksay Kazakhstan U.S.S.R. 43.19N 70.10E
45 L9 Aksay Rostov U.S.S.R. 47.18N 39.53E
45 P9 Aksay Volgograd U.S.S.R. 47.58N 43.59E
43 M6 Aksay R Kirgiziya U.S.S.R.
22 C7 Aksay Kazakzu Zizhixian Gansu China 39.28N 94.15E
24 C8 Aksayqin Hu L Xinjiang Uygur Zizhiqu China
53 S20 Aksdal Norway 59.25N 5.27E
53 S20 Aksdal Rogaland Norway 59.25N 5.27E
53 S20 Aksdalsvatnet L Norway 59.24N 5.26E
36 E4 Akşehir Turkey 38.22N 31.24E
36 E4 Akşehir Gölü L Turkey
36 F5 Akseki Turkey 37.03N 31.46E
43 C1 Aksenovo Bashkir A.S.S.R. U.S.S.R. 53.53N 54.36E
42 G3 Aksenovo Krasnoyarsk U.S.S.R. 58.52N 101.45E
42 K5 Aksenovo-Zilovskoye U.S.S.R. 53.05N 117.35E
32 F6 Aks-e-Rostam R Iran
42 J6 Aksha U.S.S.R. 50.18N 113.15E
44 M3 Akshimrau Kazakhstan U.S.S.R. 44.50N 52.51E
43 G3 Akshiy Kazakhstan U.S.S.R. 49.21N 62.55E
44 G6 Akstafa Azerbaydzhan U.S.S.R. 41.07N 45.27E
43 C2 Aksu Kazakhstan U.S.S.R. 50.53N 53.11E
43 K2 Aksu Kazakhstan U.S.S.R. 52.31N 72.00E
43 N4 Aksu Kazakhstan U.S.S.R. 45.37N 79.29E
44 M5 Aksu Kazakhstan U.S.S.R. 42.33N 52.44E
36 E6 Aksu Turkey 36.58N 30.48E
24 C5 Aksu Xinjiang Uygur Zizhiqu China 41.10N 80.20E
Ak Su R see Aksu He
43 N4 Aksu R Kazakhstan U.S.S.R.
43 N8 Aksu R Kirgiziya U.S.S.R.
36 E5 Aksu R Turkey
37 C8 Aksu R Turkey
43 G2 Aksuat Kazakhstan U.S.S.R. 50.28N 64.12E
43 P3 Aksuat Semipalatinsk, Kazakhstan U.S.S.R. 47.48N 82.51E
43 G2 Aksuat, Ozero L Kazakhstan U.S.S.R.
43 L3 Aksu-Ayuly Kazakhstan U.S.S.R. 48.48N 73.41E
46 Q3 Aksubayevo U.S.S.R. 54.45N 50.40E
24 C5 Aksu He R Xinjiang Uygur Zizhiqu China
Aksu Kona Shahr see Wensu
87 G3 Aksum Ethiopia 14.10N 38.45E
43 J5 Aksumbe Kazakhstan U.S.S.R. 44.23N 69.33E
24 D3 Aksüme Xinjiang Uygur Zizhiqu China 45.04N 81.15E
Aksu Yangi Shahr see Aksu
42 E6 Ak-Tal U.S.S.R. 51.15N 93.22E
46 R2 Aktanysh U.S.S.R. 55.42N 54.00E
43 H3 Aktas Kazakhstan U.S.S.R. 48.04N 66.15E
44 F8 Aktas Dâgh mt Iran/Turkey 39.10N 44.13E
42 D6 Aktash U.S.S.R. 50.18N 87.55E
43 H7 Aktash Uzbekistan U.S.S.R. 39.54N 65.55E
24 D3 Ak-Tasi Davan mt pass Xinjiang Uygur Zizhiqu China
24 D3 Ak-Tasi Davan pass Xinjiang Uygur Zizhiqu China 44.05N 82.55E
43 F2 Aktasty Kazakhstan U.S.S.R. 50.15N 61.45E
43 L2 Aktau Kazakhstan U.S.S.R. 50.16N 73.03E
24 E6 Aktaz Xinjiang Uygur Zizhiqu China 38.45N 86.30E
Akterine see Akhterin
83 G4 Aktí pen Greece
24 B6 Akto Xinjiang Uygur Zizhiqu China 39.07N 75.39E
43 C5 Aktobe Kazakhstan U.S.S.R. 43.58N 52.54E
43 F3 Aktogay Aktyubinsk, Kazakhstan U.S.S.R. 48.49N 60.12E
43 M5 Aktogay Alma-Ata, Kazakhstan U.S.S.R. 44.24N 76.40E
43 L3 Aktogay Karaganda, Kazakhstan U.S.S.R. 48.17N 74.58E
43 N4 Aktogay Semipalatinsk, Kazakhstan U.S.S.R. 46.57N 79.40E
43 H3 Aktuma Kazakhstan U.S.S.R. 48.09N 67.17E
43 D4 Aktumsyk Kazakhstan U.S.S.R. 46.38N 57.15E
43 E5 Aktumsyk, Mys C Uzbekistan U.S.S.R. 44.40N 58.18E
43 D2 Aktyubinsk Kazakhstan U.S.S.R. 50.16N 57.13E
43 M5 Aktyuz Kirgiziya U.S.S.R. 42.49N 76.05E
48 T9 Akugdlît Greenland 68.40N 51.10W
91 G2 Akula Zaïre 2.21N 20.16E
45 E3 Akulichi U.S.S.R. 53.10N 33.15E
48 S9 Akúnâq Greenland 68.45N 52.20W
20 D9 Akune Japan 32.00N 130.12E
113 E9 Akun I Aleutian Is 54.15N 165.30W
90 B8 Akure Nigeria 7.14N 5.08E
26 R10 Akuressa Sri Lanka 6.05N 80.29E
50 E7 Akurey Iceland 63.40N 20.23W
50 C4 Akureyjar islds Iceland 65.22N 22.17W
50 G3 Akureyri Iceland 65.41N 18.04W
89 K8 Akuse Ghana 6.04N 0.12E
21 D11 Akusekishima isld Japan 29.27N 129.37E
44 H5 Akusha U.S.S.R. 42.15N 47.22E
90 B7 Akutakuri Nigeria 9.15N 4.16E
113 E9 Akutan Aleutian Is 54.10N 165.50W
113 D9 Akutan I Aleutian Is 54.10N 166.00W
113 D9 Akutan Pass Aleutian Is
42 C6 Akutikha U.S.S.R. 52.29N 84.29E
36 F5 Akviran Turkey 37.27N 32.21E
90 D8 Akwana Nigeria 7.50N 9.19E
90 D7 Akwanga Nigeria 8.55N 8.26E
90 D9 Akwu Cameroon 5.21N 8.56E
Akyab see Sittwe
25 B2 Akyab Burma 20.09N 92.55E
43 E2 Ak'yar Bashkir U.S.S.R. 51.52N 58.13E
36 H6 Akyatan L Turkey
36 E2 Akyazı Turkey 40.41N 30.37E
43 L3 Akzhal Kazakhstan U.S.S.R. 47.45N 74.02E
43 O3 Akzhal Kazakhstan U.S.S.R. 49.15N 81.27E
43 K5 Akzhar Dzhambul, Kazakhstan U.S.S.R. 43.07N 71.40E
43 P3 Akzhar Kazakhstan U.S.S.R. 47.36N 83.38E
43 J5 Akzhaykyn, Ozero L Kazakhstan U.S.S.R.
37 D8 Akziyaret Turkey 37.20N 38.45E
44 J6 Akzybir, Liman lagoon Azerbaydzhan U.S.S.R.
53 Z17 Ål Norway 60.38N 8.33E
79 K3 Ala Italy 45.46N 11.01E
93 C3 Ala R Uganda
102 J4 Alabama state U.S.A.
48 U5 Alabama Nunatak pk Greenland 78.15N 23.45W
107 J10 Alabama R Alabama
Alaband, Kuh-i see Aliābād, Kūh-e mt
19 H2 Alabang Luzon Philippines 14.25N 121.02E
106 L5 Alabaster Michigan 44.12N 83.34W
11 C11 Alabaster, L New Zealand
19 L4 Alabat isld Luzon Philippines 14.07N 122.00E
47 L8 Alabota, Oz L Kokchetav, Kazakhstan U.S.S.R. 53.45N 70.55E
43 H1 Alabota, Ozero L Kustanay, Kazakhstan U.S.S.R. 52.46N 65.25E
43 K6 Ala-Buka Kirgiziya U.S.S.R. 41.22N 71.29E
36 H2 Alaca Turkey 40.10N 34.52E
37 E5 Alaca Dağ mt Gümüşane Turkey 40.48N 39.10E
36 F5 Alaca Dağ mt Konya Turkey 37.29N 32.07E
37 G5 Alaca Dağı mt Turkey 40.31N 43.25E
37 D6 Alacahan Turkey 39.07N 37.34E
37 G1 Alaçali Turkey 41.06N 29.30E
36 G6 Alaçam Içel Turkey 36.41N 33.15E
36 H1 Alaçam Samsun Turkey 41.36N 35.35E
36 B4 Alaçatı Turkey 38.16N 26.24E
40 G3 Alachakh U.S.S.R. 57.53N 137.25E
39 F4 Alachevo U.S.S.R. 62.09N 158.46E
105 E8 Alachua Florida 29.47N 82.30W
36 F5 Aladağ Turkey 37.02N 32.39E
37 G5 Ala Dağ mt Kars Turkey 40.11N 42.49E
36 F5 Ala Dağ mt Konya Turkey 37.58N 32.05E
37 G6 Ala Dağ mt Van Turkey
36 F2 Aladağ R Turkey
32 G2 Alādāgh, Kūh-e mts Iran
36 H5 Ala Dağları mts Turkey
81 C2 Alà dei Sardi Sardinia 40.39N 9.20E
79 B4 Alà di Stura Italy 45.19N 7.18E
Alado see Alamdo
76 J6 Alaejos Spain 41.18N 5.13W
84 U17 Alaérma Rhodes 36.09N 27.56E
87 F5 Alafa Ethiopia 11.55N 36.55E
50 D6 Alafoss Iceland 64.11N 21.41W
119 H6 Alagadiço Brazil 3.22N 60.39W
113 P6 Alaganik Alaska 60.27N 145.12W
28 D5 Alagapuram Tamil Nadu India 11.54N 78.53E
44 F7 Alagez Armenia U.S.S.R. 40.40N 44.15E
Alagez mt see Aragats mt
22 D9 Alag Hu L Qinghai China
44 F4 Alagir U.S.S.R. 43.01N 44.16E
113 J7 Alagnak R Alaska
79 C3 Alagna Valsesia Italy 45.51N 7.56E
72 L5 Alagnon R France
22 C4 Alag Nuur L Mongolia
76 D10 Alagôa Portugal 39.22N 7.33W
117 J8 Alagoa Grande Brazil 7.01S 35.32W
117 H9 Alagoas state Brazil
118 J3 Alagoinhas Brazil 12.09S 38.21W
75 H4 Alagón Spain 41.46N 1.07W
76 H7 Alagón R Spain
24 F4 Ala Gou R Xinjiang Uygur Zizhiqu China
Alaguy R see Ala Gou
44 G8 Alagyel, Oz L Azerbaydzhan U.S.S.R. 40.00N 45.40E
19 M8 Alah R Mindanao Philippines
18 D6 Alahanpanjang Sumatra Indon 1.03S 100.48E
51 K8 Alahärmä Finland 63.15N 22.50E
90 F7 Alahdji Galibou Cameroon 8.24N 13.31E
40 N6 Alaid Kuril Is U.S.S.R. 50.51N 155.39E
Alaid isld see Atlasova, Ostrov
113 L9 Alaid I Aleutian Is 52.46N 173.52E
72 J9 Alaigne France 43.05N 2.05E
81 E10 Alaimo, Pta Lampedusa, I di Italy 35.37N 12.37E
87 H4 Alaita,Mt Ethiopia 13.07N 40.52E
34 C3 Alaja Syria 35.50N 35.49E
77 C5 Alajar Spain 37.52N 6.40W
51 K8 Alajärvi Finland 63.00N 23.50E
34 D3 'Ala, Jebel el mts Syria
96 O15 Alajero Gomera Canary Is 28.04N 17.14W
115 M4 Alajuela Costa Rica 10.00N 84.12W
32 B1 Alajujeh Iran 38.56N 46.38E
114 E3 Alakai Swamp Hawaiian Is
95 C6 Alak-Ambohimaha Madagascar 21.19S 47.14E
95 C6 Alakamisy-Itenina Madagascar 21.38S 47.10E
113 E5 Alakanuk Alaska 62.39N 164.48W
44 C4 Alakhadzy Georgia U.S.S.R. 43.14N 40.20E
37 D6 Alakilise Turkey 39.56N 38.36E
36 E6 Alakır R Turkey
41 K7 Alakit R U.S.S.R.
15 F7 Alakke Irian Jaya 7.00S 140.07E
30 C2 Alaknanda R Uttar Prad India
90 J7 Alako Chad 9.47N 18.53E
43 O4 Alakol', Oz L Kazakhstan U.S.S.R.
113 K1 Alaktak Alaska 70.49N 155.15W
47 C3 Alakurtti U.S.S.R. 67.00N 30.23E
51 L4 Alakylä Finland 67.24N 24.55E
35 G3 'Al 'Al Jordan 32.38N 35.54E
114 E6 Alalakeiki Chan Hawaiian Is
44 J10 Ālālān Iran 37.45N 49.01E
119 H8 Alalaú, R Brazil
17 P8 Alamagan isld Marianas Pacific Oc 17.35N 145.50E
32 E7 Alāmarvdasht Iran 27.39N 52.59E
32 E7 Alāmarvdasht R Iran
86 D4 'Alâmât Qabr el Gamal hill Egypt 30.44N 30.17E
24 H10 Alamdo Xizang Zizhiqu China 30.39N 94.18E
111 B9 Alameda California 37.46N 122.15W
110 N7 Alameda Idaho 42.55N 112.26W
109 D6 Alameda New Mexico 35.11N 106.38W
100 P9 Alameda Saskatchewan 49.18N 102.16W
77 G6 Alameda Spain 37.12N 4.39W
77 K2 Alameda de Cervera Spain 39.16N 3.08W
76 F7 Alameda de Gardon, La Spain 40.39N 6.46W
77 K5 Alamedilla Spain 37.35N 3.14W
76 K7 Alamedilla del Berrocal, La Spain 40.42N 4.46W
76 F8 Alamedilla, La Spain 40.29N 6.49W
86 A4 Alamein oil well Egypt 30.43N 28.57E
86 A4 'Alamein, El Egypt 30.50N 28.57E
86 C4 'Alam el 'Afrag hill Egypt 30.40N 29.37E
86 B4 'Alam el Halfa hill Egypt 30.40N 29.09E
86 B4 'Alam el Khâdim hill Egypt 30.41N 29.14E
85 K5 Alam el Kûz mt Egypt 28.47N 28.50E
115 M3 Alamicamba Nicaragua 13.26N 84.09W
77 G3 Alamillo Spain 38.41N 4.48W
19 J3 Alaminos Luzon Philippines 16.11N 119.58E
75 E6 Alaminos Spain 40.51N 2.43W
112 C6 Alamito Cr Texas
115 H4 Alamítos, Sa. de los ra Mexico
31 C2 Alamlik Afghanistan 37.01N 65.55E
86 B4 'Alam Miseilikh hill Egypt 30.32N 29.22E
86 C4 'Alam Nafâza hill Egypt 30.30N 29.41E
30 K7 Alamnagar Bihar India 25.34N 86.54E
105 E5 Alamo Georgia 32.09N 82.49W
108 G1 Alamo N Dakota 48.36N 103.30W
111 J4 Alamo Nevada 37.23N 115.10W
107 G6 Alamo Tennessee 35.47N 89.09W
112 J9 Alamo Texas 26.12N 98.07W
111 J9 Alamo R California
112 H9 Alamo R Mexico
76 E12 Alamo R Portugal
75 C7 Alamo, El Spain 40.14N 4.00W
77 D5 Álamo, El Spain 37.39N 6.27W
109 E9 Alamogordo New Mexico 32.54N 105.57W
109 F7 Alamogordo Res New Mexico
Alamon see Zap Turkey
81 C2 Alà, Monti di Sardinia
119 B10 Alamor Ecuador 4.02S 80.02W
77 E8 Alamo, R. de Spain
111 L7 Alamo Res Arizona
115 D3 Alamos Sonora Mexico 29.12N 110.09W
115 E4 Alamos Sonora Mexico 27.01N 108.58W
109 E4 Alamosa Colorado 37.28N 105.54W
115 F2 Alamos de Peña Mexico 30.21N 106.43W
28 D3 Alampur Andhra Prad India 15.55N 78.06E
30 B7 Alampur Madhya Prad India 26.00N 78.46E
32 A1 'Alam Sarāy Iran 38.20N 45.07E
86 C4 'Alam Shaltût hill Egypt 30.47N 29.48E
52 J2 Alanäs Sweden 64.09N 15.40E
50 K2 Áland Iceland 66.14N 15.30W
28 C2 Aland Karnataka India 17.35N 76.38E
51 H11 Åland islds Finland
63 P7 Aland R E Germany
32 A1 Aland R Iran
67 P12 Alando Corsica 42.18N 9.17E
76 E11 Alandroal Portugal 38.41N 7.24W
52 K4 Ålandsbro Sweden 62.40N 17.50E
52 K7 Ålandsdal Sweden 59.54N 17.20E
51 G12 Ålands Hav Sweden/Finland
19 N4 Alanelimo isld Truk Is Pacific Oc 7.20N 152.02E
19 N4 Alanenkobwe isld Truk Is Pacific Oc 7.40N 151.42E
93 M5 Alanga Arba Kenya 0.06N 40.24E
18 M7 Alangalang, Tanjung C Kalimantan Indon 3.44S 116.22E
18 A9 Alang Besar isld Sumatra Indon 2.15N 100.40E
77 D3 Alange Spain 38.47N 6.15W
18 F6 Alanggantang isld Sumatra Indon
93 K5 Alango Kenya 0.19N 38.27E
28 D5 Alangudi Tamil Nadu India 10.22N 78.59E
51 L6 Alaniemi Finland 65.50N 25.19E
115 N5 Alanje Panama 8.26N 82.33W
90 E5 Alanjirori Nigeria 13.00N 11.10E
80 J4 Alanno Italy 42.18N 13.58E
79 L3 Alano di Piave Italy 45.54N 11.55E
112 D8 Alanreed Texas 35.14N 100.45W
19 M4 Alanseiru isld Truk Is Pacific Oc 7.18N 151.29E
Alanskoye see Psedakh
90 F7 Alantika mts Cameroon
36 F6 Alanya Turkey 36.32N 32.02E
95 D4 Alaotra, L Madagascar 17.30S 48.30E
105 D6 Alapaha R Georgia
28 D5 Alapakam Tamil Nadu India 11.36N 79.44E
47 N4 Alapayevsk U.S.S.R. 57.55N 61.42E
36 E1 Alaplı Turkey 41.12N 31.25E
80 C3 Ala, Pta Italy 42.48N 10.43E
30 C5 Alapur Uttar Prad India 27.57N 79.16E
35 G2 'Alaq watercourse Syria
34 C9 'Alaqan Saudi Arabia 29.13N 35.21E
32 F2 Alāqel, Darya-ye salt L Iran
86 G4 'Alâqma, El Egypt 30.38N 31.38E
50 E7 Álar R Iceland
36 F6 Alara R Turkey
76 J7 Alaraz Spain 40.45N 5.17W
75 F8 Alarcón Spain 39.32N 2.05W
75 F8 Alarcón, Embalse de L Spain 39.40N 2.15W
76 L3 Alar del Rey Spain 42.39N 4.19W
75 D6 Alarilla Spain 40.51N 3.06W
77 V14 Alaró Balearic Is 39.42N 2.47E
95 C6 Alarobia-Befeta Madagascar 21.12S 47.03E
95 C6 Alarobia-Vohiposa Madagascar 21.00S 47.10E
19 C4 Alasan Indonesia 1.45S 123.19E
36 D4 Alaşehir Turkey 38.22N 28.32E
42 D6 Alash R U.S.S.R.
Ala Shan see Helan Shan
24 D3 A-la Shan-k'ou pass Kazakhstan/Xinjiang Uygur Zizhiqu 45.08N 82.27E
42 E6 Alash, Plato tableland U.S.S.R.
97 C4 Alaska state U.S.A.
113 P7 Alaska, G. of Alaska
101 M7 Alaska Highway Alaska/Canada
113 G9 Alaska Pen Alaska
113 L6 Alaska Ra Alaska
18 M10 Alas, Selat str Indonesia
79 D6 Alassio Italy 44.01N 8.10E
89 F4 Alasso Mali 15.01N 7.58W
51 K11 Alastaro Finland 60.57N 22.50E
43 G7 Alat Uzbekistan U.S.S.R. 39.25N 63.45E
67 O13 Alata Corsica 41.58N 8.43E
36 G6 Alata R Turkey
24 D3 Alataw Shankou pass Xinjiang Uygur Zizhiqu China 45.12N 82.36E
113 L3 Alatna Alaska 66.33N 152.49W
113 L3 Alatna R Alaska
77 O2 Alatoz Spain 39.06N 1.22W
80 H5 Alatri Italy 41.44N 13.21E
84 A4 Álatro Greece 38.41N 20.40E
45 S2 Alatyr' U.S.S.R. 54.51N 46.35E
45 R2 Alatyr' R U.S.S.R.
114 F6 Alau I Hawaiian Is
51 Q10 Alauksu Karelia U.S.S.R. 61.32N 31.36E
119 B9 Alausí Ecuador 2.11S 78.52W
74 F2 Álava prov Spain
44 F6 Alaverdi Armenia U.S.S.R. 41.08N 44.40E
32 D4 'Alavī Iran 33.03N 51.04E
32 E4 'Alavi Iran 32.06N 53.38E
26 R8 Alavi Sri Lanka 6.38N 80.15E
51 O7 Alavuokki Finland 64.44N 29.26E
51 K9 Alavus Finland 62.35N 23.35E
29 D2 Alawalpur Punjab India 31.28N 75.42E
25 N9 Alawbum Burma 24.33N 97.36E
12 F5 Alawoona S Australia 34.44S 140.33E
57 E6 Alaw Res Gwynedd Wales 53.21N 4.26W
43 L6 Alaykel' Kirgiziya U.S.S.R. 40.17N 74.29E
77 Y14 Alayor Balearic Is 39.56N 4.08E
43 K7 Alayskiy Khrebet mts U.S.S.R.
36 E3 Alayunt Turkey 39.24N 30.06E
33 D7 'Alayyah, Al Saudi Arabia 19.43N 41.55E
112 K8 Alazan B Texas
44 G5 Alazani R Georgia U.S.S.R.
39 E1 Alazevo R U.S.S.R.
39 D1 Alazeya R U.S.S.R.
39 D2 Alazeyskoye Ploskogor'ye tableland U.S.S.R.
64 E8 Alb R W Germany
79 D5 Alba Italy 44.42N 8.02E
106 K5 Alba Michigan 44.59N 84.07W
75 H6 Alba Spain 40.37N 1.21W
112 M3 Alba Texas 32.48N 95.37W
77 N2 Albacete Spain 39.00N 1.52W
74 F6 Albacete prov Spain
12 F6 Albacutya, L Victoria
76 H7 Alba de Tormes Spain 40.50N 5.30W
53 E1 Ålbæk Denmark 57.36N 10.26E
53 F1 Ålbæk Bugt B Denmark
42 D6 Albagan, Gora mt U.S.S.R. 51.20N 86.50E
75 M5 Albagés Spain 41.27N 0.45E
77 B5 Albahacar R Spain
77 P3 Albaida Spain 38.51N 0.31W
82 H4 Alba Iulia Romania 46.04N 23.33E
28 E1 Albaka Andhra Prad India 18.15N 80.43E
77 L3 Albaladejo Spain 38.38N 2.49W
76 G10 Albalá del Caudillo Spain 39.15N 6.12W
75 L4 Albalate de Cinca Spain 41.44N 0.09E
75 J5 Albalate del Arzobispo Spain 41.06N 0.31W
75 E7 Albalate de Zorita Spain 40.18N 2.51W
75 K4 Albalatillo Spain 41.44N 0.09W
11 C11 Alba, Mt New Zealand 44.11S 168.59E
72 J8 Alban France 43.53N 2.27E
75 Q3 Albana Spain 42.19N 2.43E
77 M6 Albánchez Spain 37.17N 2.10W
77 K5 Albanchez de Ubeda Spain 37.47N 3.28W
32 E8 Al-Bandag oil well The Gulf 25.08N 52.43E
99 S4 Albanel Quebec 48.53N 72.27W
81 K3 Albanella Italy 40.28N 15.07E
49 J8 Albania rep S Europe
80 G5 Albani, Colli hills Italy
117 A6 Albano Brazil 2.28S 57.29W
81 M2 Albano di Lucania Italy 40.36N 16.03E
80 G5 Albano, Lago di Italy
80 G5 Albano Laziale Italy 41.44N 12.40E
79 J7 Albano, Monte mts Italy
79 L4 Albano Terme Italy 45.22N 11.47E
79 D4 Albano Vercellese Italy 45.26N 8.23E
111 B8 Albany California 37.53N 122.18W
105 C6 Albany Georgia 31.37N 84.10W
106 D8 Albany Illinois 41.46N 90.13W
106 J9 Albany Indiana 40.19N 85.13W
116 L1 Albany Jamaica, W I 18.17N 76.53W
107 L5 Albany Kentucky 36.42N 85.08W
107 F11 Albany Louisiana 30.31N 90.35W
108 Q4 Albany Minnesota 45.38N 94.35W
107 B1 Albany Missouri 40.15N 94.20W
104 M4 Albany New York 42.40N 73.49W
98 G9 Albany Nova Scotia 44.47N 65.05W
104 C7 Albany Ohio 39.14N 82.12W
110 B5 Albany Oregon 44.38N 123.07W
112 H3 Albany Texas 32.44N 99.18W
104 N2 Albany Vermont 44.42N 72.26W
14 C10 Albany W Australia 34.57S 117.54E
108 D8 Albany Wyoming 41.10N 106.09W
13 J7 Albany Downs Queensland 27.12S 148.02E
99 F2 Albany R Ontario
121 C3 Albardón Argentina 31.25S 68.32W
79 K4 Albaredo d'Adige Italy 45.19N 11.16E
75 D7 Albares Spain 40.19N 3.01W
76 G3 Albares de la Ribera Spain 42.36N 6.21W
71 C7 Albaret-le-Comtal France 44.52N 3.07E
79 G6 Albareto Italy 44.27N 9.42E
71 C7 Albaret-Ste. Marie France 44.54N 3.16E
71 G5 Albarine R France
71 E9 Albaron France 43.37N 4.28E
75 H7 Albarracín Spain 40.25N 1.26W
75 G6 Albarracín, Sierra de mts Spain
76 F10 Albarragena R Spain
76 C15 Albarraque Portugal 38.46N 9.21W
76 K2 Alba, Sierra de mts Spain
77 N3 Albatana Spain 38.35N 1.31W
77 P4 Albatera Spain 38.11N 0.51W
116 G6 Albatross Bank Caribbean Sea
13 F1 Albatross Bay Queensland
121 G8 Albatross I S Georgia S Atlantic Ocean 54.05S 37.28W
12 G8 Albatross I Tasmania 40.24S 144.40E
11 K13 Albatross Pt Antipodes Is Pacific Oc 49.44S 178.49E
11 J5 Albatross Pt New Zealand 38.06S 174.41E
63 K9 Albaxen W Germany 51.48N 9.23E
19 L5 Albay G Luzon Philippines
64 E8 Albbruck W Germany 47.35N 8.08E
80 D3 Albegna R Italy
75 K3 Albella y Janovas Spain 42.29N 0.16W
Albemarle I see Isabela, I
119 A5 Albemarle, Pta pt Galápagos Is Pacific Ocean 0.07N 91.20W
71 G6 Albenc, l' France 45.14N 5.27E
75 F7 Albendea Spain 40.29N 2.25W
77 H5 Albendín Spain 37.40N 4.15W
79 D6 Albenga Italy 44.03N 8.13E
110 J1 Albeni Falls Dam Idaho 48.11N 116.59W
79 G3 Alben, Monte Italy 45.53N 9.46E
71 H5 Albens France 45.47N 5.57E
75 J7 Albentosa Spain 40.06N 0.47W
75 F8 Alberca de Záncara, La Spain 39.30N 2.30W
76 G8 Alberca, La Spain 40.29N 6.06W
121 E5 Alberdi Buenos Aires Arg 34.27S 61.46W
118 B10 Alberdi Paraguay 26.10S 58.09W
121 E4 Alberdi Santa Fé Arg 32.55S 60.44W
80 D3 Alberese Italy 42.40N 11.07E
72 K11 Alberes, Mts France
12 D3 Alberga S Australia 27.10S 135.22E
12 C2 Alberga R S Australia
76 C5 Albergaria Portugal 41.47N 8.10W
76 C7 Albergaria-a-Nova Portugal 40.45N 8.29W
76 C7 Albergaria-a-Velha Portugal 40.42N 8.28W
76 B9 Albergaria dos Doze Portugal 39.48N 8.35W
60 Q10 Albergen Netherlands 52.23N 6.46E
79 A4 Albergian, Monte Italy 45.00N 6.59E
77 P2 Alberique Spain 39.07N 0.31W
75 F3 Alberite Spain 42.25N 2.25W
105 G2 Albermarle N Carolina 35.21N 80.12W
105 L1 Albermarle Sd N Carolina
101 L11 Alberni Vancouver I, Br Col 49.12N 124.51W
76 D13 Albernoa Portugal 37.51N 7.57W
81 O2 Alberobello Italy 40.46N 17.15E
80 M6 Alberona Italy 41.26N 15.08E
81 E10 Albero Sole mt Lampedusa, I di Italy 35.32N 12.33E
66 Q2 Alberschwende Austria 47.28N 9.50E
63 K4 Albersdorf W Germany 54.09N 9.17E
69 D3 Albert France 50.00N 2.40E
109 L3 Albert Kansas 38.26N 99.01W
98 H8 Albert New Brunswick 45.45N 64.47W
12 J4 Albert New S Wales 32.21S 147.33E
13 E4 Albert R Queensland
107 J9 Alberta Alabama 32.14N 87.23W
104 H10 Alberta Virginia 36.52N 77.53W
97 H7 Alberta prov Canada
67 O12 Albertacce Corsica 42.19N 8.58E
101 P9 Alberta, Mt Alberta 52.21N 117.28W
15 J8 Albert Edward, Mt Papua New Guinea 8.23S 147.20E
95 O5 Albert Falls S Africa 29.26S 30.26E
121 E5 Alberti Argentina 35.03S 60.15W
50 S13 Albert I Land Spitsbergen
95 E10 Albertinia S Africa 34.13S 21.35E
62 M8 Albertirsa Hungary 47.15N 19.36E
61 K2 Albertkanaal canal Belgium
110 E7 Albert, L Oregon 42.34N 120.14W
12 E6 Albert, L S Australia
108 R6 Albert Lea Minnesota 43.38N 93.16W
93 B4 Albert (Mobutu), L Uganda/Zaïre
11 C2 Albert, Mt hill Auckland New Zealand 36.54S 174.43E
93 C2 Albert Nile R Uganda
98 H7 Alberton Prince Edward I 46.50N 64.08W
94 T14 Alberton S Africa 26.16S 28.07E
95 M2 Alberton S Africa 26.16S 28.08E
12 H7 Alberton Victoria 38.37S 146.40E
12 A7 Alberton dist Adelaide, S Aust
Albert, Parc Nat see Virunga, Parc
116 J1 Albert Town Jamaica, W I 18.17N 77.33W
116 G3 Albert Town Long Cay Bahamas 22.36N 74.21W
107 K7 Albertville Alabama 34.15N 86.12W
71 J5 Albertville France 45.40N 6.24E
100 M5 Albertville Saskatchewan 53.25N 105.32W
Albertville Zaïresee Kalémié
75 M4 Albesa Spain 41.45N 0.39E
66 N8 Albese Italy 45.48N 9.11E
82 L6 Albeşti Romania 44.31N 27.11E
69 M6 Albestroff France 48.56N 6.52E
79 L4 Albettone Italy 45.22N 11.36E
66 E5 Albeuve Switzerland 46.32N 7.03E
72 J8 Albi France 43.56N 2.08E
108 S8 Albia Iowa 41.02N 92.48W
81 M4 Albidona Italy 39.55N 16.29E
108 F8 Albin Wyoming 41.26N 104.08W
117 B2 Albina Surinam 5.29N 54.08W
75 N5 Albiñana Spain 41.15N 1.29E
91 C11 Albina, Pta Angola 15.52S 11.44E
79 J5 Albinea Italy 44.37N 10.35E
66 G6 Albinen Switzerland 46.21N 7.39E
13 B5 Albinia Spring N Terr Australia 22.25S 130.39E
79 G3 Albino Italy 45.46N 9.47E
66 M8 Albiolo Italy 45.48N 8.57E
111 A2 Albion California 39.15N 123.45W
110 M7 Albion Idaho 42.25N 113.35W
107 H3 Albion Illinois 38.22N 88.04W
106 J8 Albion Indiana 41.23N 85.26W
108 S7 Albion Iowa 42.08N 92.59W
106 K7 Albion Michigan 42.14N 84.45W
108 F4 Albion Montana 45.11N 104.15W
108 M8 Albion Nebraska 41.41N 98.00W
104 G3 Albion New York 43.14N 78.12W
109 P7 Albion Oklahoma 34.40N 95.06W
104 E5 Albion Pennsylvania 41.54N 80.22W
95 O2 Albion S Africa 26.13S 30.02E
66 J7 Albiona, Pizzo d' mt Italy 46.11N 8.15E
77 O3 Albir, Pta. del Spain 38.34N 0.03W
79 D6 Albissola Marina Italy 44.19N 8.30E
66 M9 Albizzate Italy 45.43N 8.48E
60 G12 Alblasserdam Netherlands 51.52N 4.40E
75 L7 Albocácer Spain 40.21N 0.01E
52 K10 Alböke Sweden 56.57N 16.45E
32 G3 Albolāgh Iran 35.32N 57.55E
77 L6 Alboloduy Spain 37.03N 2.36W
77 J6 Albolote Spain 37.14N 3.39W
81 D2 Albo, Monte Sardinia
77 K7 Albondón Spain 36.50N 3.12W
74 E9 Alborán, I. de Spain 35.57N 3.05W
75 K9 Alboraya Spain 39.30N 0.22W
77 O2 Alborea Spain 39.17N 1.24W
53 D2 Ålborg Denmark 57.03N 9.56E
Ålborg co see Nordjylland
53 F3 Ålborg Bugt B Denmark
108 S3 Alborn Minnesota 46.58N 92.34W
79 G2 Albosággia Italy 46.09N 9.51E
77 M6 Albox Spain 37.23N 2.08W
101 O9 Albreda Br Columbia 52.38N 119.09W
56 G2 Albrighton Shropshire Eng 52.38N 2.16W
103 C4 Albrightsville Pennsylvania 41.02N 75.38W
66 F6 Albristhorn mt Switzerland 46.30N 7.30E
13 H6 Albro Queensland 22.42S 146.35E
66 K6 Albrun Pass Italy/Switz 46.22N 8.18E
85 C4 Al Bu'ayrāt Libya 31.23N 15.46E
77 O4 Albudeite Spain 38.01N 1.23W
53 F7 Albuen pen Denmark 54.50N 10.58E
77 C3 Albuera, La Spain 38.43N 6.49W
76 C14 Albufeira Portugal 37.05N 8.15W
76 A11 Albufeira, L. de Portugal
77 Q2 Albufera, La L Spain 39.20N 0.22W
77 W14 Albufera, La marsh Balearic Is
77 O5 Albujón Spain 37.44N 1.03W
66 P5 Albula R Switzerland
66 Q5 Albula Alpen mts Switzerland
66 Q5 Albula Pass Switzerland 46.35N 9.51E
66 Q5 Albula Tunnel Switzerland
64 J1 Albungen W Germany 51.14N 10.00E
77 K7 Albuñol Spain 36.48N 3.11W
77 J7 Albuñuelas Spain 36.56N 3.38W
118 B6 Albuquerque Brazil 19.24S 57.25W
109 D6 Albuquerque New Mexico 35.05N 106.38W
115 O3 Albuquerque, Cayos de islds Caribbean Sea
104 M2 Alburg Vermont 44.58N 73.19W
80 M7 Alburno, Monte Italy 40.32N 15.20E
76 F10 Alburquerque Spain 39.13N 6.59W
76 E9 Alburrel R Spain
103 C5 Alburtis Pennsylvania 40.31N 75.36W
12 H6 Albury New S Wales 36.03S 146.53E
11 E11 Albury New Zealand 44.13S 170.52E

56 K5 Albury Surrey Eng 51.13N 0.30W
52 J4 Alby Sweden 62.30N 15.25E
71 J5 Alby-sur-Chévan France 45.49N 6.02E
120 C6 Alca Peru 15.03S 72.40W
76 A11 Alcabideche Portugal 38.44N 9.25W
76 B12 Alcácer do Sal Portugal 38.22N 8.30W
76 C12 Alcáçovas Portugal 38.23N 8.09W
76 C12 Alcáçovas R Portugal
77 N3 Alcadozo Spain 38.40N 2.00W
76 E9 Alcafozes Portugal 39.58N 7.07W
76 E8 Alcaide Portugal 40.08N 7.26W
75 J6 Alcaine Spain 40.57N 0.44W
76 E9 Alcains Portugal 39.55N 7.27W
120 F8 Alcalá Bolivia 19.24S 64.28W
77 B5 Alcalaboza R Spain
75 L7 Alcalá de Chivert Spain 40.19N 0.13E
75 H4 Alcalá de Ebro Spain 41.48N 1.11W
77 E6 Alcalá de Guadaira Spain 37.20N 5.50W
75 D7 Alcalá de Henares Spain 40.28N 3.22W
75 J7 Alcalá de la Selva Spain 40.22N 0.43W
77 O2 Alcalá del Júcar Spain 39.12N 1.25W
77 E8 Alcalá de los Gazules Spain 36.29N 5.43W
77 E5 Alcalá del Río Spain 37.31N 5.59W
77 F7 Alcalá del Valle Spain 36.54N 5.10W
77 J6 Alcalá la Real Spain 37.28N 3.55W
96 Q14 Alcalá, Pto. de Tenerife Canary Is 28.13N 16.50W
109 D5 Alcalde New Mexico 36.05N 106.03W
121 B2 Alcalde, Pta C Chile 28.40S 71.20W
81 E8 Alcamo Sicily 37.58N 12.58E
75 L4 Alcampel Spain 41.55N 0.26E
75 F3 Alcanadre Spain 42.24N 2.07W
75 K4 Alcanadre R Spain
75 L6 Alcanar Spain 40.33N 0.28E
76 B10 Alcanede Portugal 39.25N 8.49W
76 B10 Alcanena Portugal 39.27N 8.40W
76 B10 Alcanhões Portugal 39.17N 8.40W
76 G5 Alcañices Spain 41.41N 6.21W
75 K5 Alcañiz Spain 41.03N 0.09W
117 F6 Alcantara Brazil 2.25S 44.28W
76 D16 Alcantara Portugal 38.42N 9.10W
76 F9 Alcántara Spain 39.44N 6.53W
81 K8 Alcantara R Sicily
76 G9 Alcántara, Embalse de res Spain
101 T5 Alcantara L N W Terr
76 C14 Alcantarilha Portugal 37.07N 8.21W
77 O5 Alcantarilla Spain 37.59N 1.12W
118 D5 Alcantilado Brazil 16.21S 53.30W
75 F6 Alcantud Spain 40.33N 2.20W
77 G4 Alcaracejos Spain 38.24N 4.58W
81 J7 Alcara li Fusi Sicily 38.02N 14.12E
77 M3 Alcaraz Spain 38.40N 2.29W
77 M3 Alcaraz, Sierra de mts Spain
76 D8 Alcaria Portugal 40.11N 7.31W
76 D14 Alcaria do Cume mt Portugal 37.14N 7.44W
76 D13 Alcaria Ruiva mt Portugal 37.42N 7.46W
76 E12 Alcarrache R Portugal
75 M4 Alcarrás Spain 41.34N 0.31E
75 E6 Alcarria, La tableland Spain
111 B8 Alcatraz I California
77 H7 Alcaucín Spain 36.54N 4.06W
77 H5 Alcaudete Spain 37.35N 4.05W
76 K9 Alcaudete de la Jara Spain 39.48N 4.52W
72 C9 Alçay-Alçabehety-Sunharette France 43.05N 0.54W
76 B2 Alcayán, L Spain 43.07N 8.44W
77 C3 Alcazaba R Spain
77 K2 Alcázar de San Juan Spain 39.24N 3.12W
76 K6 Alcazarén Spain 41.22N 4.40W
Alcazarquivir see Ksar-el-Kebir
75 C1 Alceda Spain 43.12N 3.54W
108 O6 Alcester S Dakota 43.01N 96.36W
56 H3 Alcester Warwicks Eng 52.13N 1.52W
15 M8 Alcester I Papua New Guinea 9.34S 152.25E
77 Q2 Alcira Spain 39.10N 0.27W
107 C10 Alco Louisiana 31.20N 93.05W
105 D2 Alcoa Tennessee 35.47N 84.00W
76 L10 Alcoba Spain 39.16N 4.28W
118 H5 Alcobaça Brazil 17.31S 39.14W
76 B9 Alcobaça Portugal 39.32N 8.59W
75 C6 Alcobendas Spain 40.32N 3.38W
76 B10 Alcobertas Portugal 39.25N 8.54W
76 L10 Alcobilla R Spain
75 L7 Alcocebre Spain 40.15N 0.16E
75 E7 Alcocer Spain 40.28N 2.36W
75 D3 Alcocero de Mola Spain 42.28N 3.21W
76 B11 Alcochete Portugal 38.45N 8.57W
76 B10 Alcoentre Portugal 39.12N 8.58W
76 C7 Alcofra Portugal 40.38N 8.11W
75 E7 Alcohujate Spain 40.25N 2.37W
77 L7 Alcolea Almería Spain 36.58N 2.57W
77 G5 Alcolea Cordoba Spain 37.56N 4.40W
77 H3 Alcolea de Calatrava Spain 38.59N 4.07W
75 L4 Alcolea de Cinca Spain 41.43N 0.07E
75 F5 Alcolea del Pinar Spain 41.02N 2.28W
77 E5 Alcolea del Río Spain 37.37N 5.40W
75 M4 Alcoletge Spain 41.39N 0.42E
76 H10 Alcollarín Spain 39.15N 5.44W
77 E2 Alcollarin R Spain
105 G4 Alcolu S Carolina 33.46N 80.14W
100 D5 Alcomdale Alberta 53.56N 113.50W
100 L1 Alcona Ontario 50.00N 91.40W
56 L3 Alconbury Cambs Eng 52.22N 0.16W
56 L3 Alconbury Hill Cambs Eng 52.24N 0.16W
77 B3 Alconchel Spain 38.31N 7.04W
77 B3 Alconchel R Spain
77 D4 Alconera Spain 38.24N 6.28W
77 L6 Alcóntar Spain 37.20N 2.35W
13 C6 Alcoota N Terr Australia 22.45S 134.25E
75 K7 Alcora Spain 40.05N 0.14W
75 K6 Alcorisa Spain 40.53N 0.23W
75 D5 Alcorlo Spain 41.01N 3.02W
76 E10 Alcorneo R Spain
77 D5 Alcornocosa, La Spain 37.45N 6.18W
75 G6 Alcoroches Spain 40.37N 1.45W
76 B10 Alcorouchel Portugal 39.25N 8.35W
121 E4 Alcorta Argentina 33.35S 61.14W
76 E14 Alcoutim Portugal 37.28N 7.29W
108 D7 Alcova Wyoming 42.35N 106.44W
108 D7 Alcova Reservoir Wyoming
75 N5 Alcover Spain 41.16N 1.10E
103 G1 Alcove Res New York
77 Q3 Alcoy Spain 38.42N 0.29W
75 K4 Alcubierre Spain 41.49N 0.28W
75 K4 Alcubierre, Sierra de mts Spain
75 D4 Alcubilla de Avellaneda Spain 41.43N 3.19W
77 K3 Alcubillas Spain 38.46N 3.08W
75 J8 Alcublas Spain 39.48N 0.43W
77 W14 Alcudia Balearic Is 39.51N 3.06E
77 G3 Alcudia R Spain
77 W14 Alcudia, B. de Balearic Is
77 P2 Alcudia de Carlet Spain 39.12N 0.30W
77 K6 Alcudia de Guadix Spain 37.16N 3.05W
77 G3 Alcudia, Valle de Spain
76 G10 Alcuéscar Spain 39.11N 6.14W
75 E5 Alcuneza Spain 41.07N 2.36W
26 D6 Aldabra Is Seychelles, Ind Oc
26 D6 Aldabra Ridge Indian Ocean
115 G3 Aldama Chihuahua Mexico 28.50N 105.52W
115 K6 Aldama Tamaulipas Mexico 22.54N 98.05W
40 C2 Aldan U.S.S.R. 58.44N 125.22E
41 O8 Aldan R U.S.S.R.
40 D3 Aldano Uchurskiy Khrebet mts U.S.S.R.
40 C3 Aldanskoye Nagor'ye highland U.S.S.R.
22 D3 Aldarhaan Mongolia 47.32N 96.34E
77 Q2 Aldaya Spain 39.28N 0.28W
56 H5 Aldbourne Wilts Eng 51.30N 1.37W
57 N5 Aldbrough Humberside Eng 53.50N 0.06W
57 K4 Aldbrough Yorks Eng 54.30N 1.41W
75 M6 Aldea Spain 40.45N 0.37E
76 H9 Aldeacentenera Spain 39.32N 5.38W
76 F6 Aldeadávila de la Ribera Spain 41.13N 6.38W
76 F6 Aldeadávila, Embalse de Spain
75 H8 Aldea de la Torre Spain 39.40N 1.16W
76 G10 Aldea del Cano Spain 39.17N 6.20W
76 L8 Aldea del Fresno Spain 40.19N 4.13W
76 F7 Aldea del Obispo Spain 40.43N 6.48W
77 J3 Aldea del Rey Spain 38.44N 3.50W
76 K7 Aldea del Rey Niño Spain 40.35N 4.45W
76 H9 Aldea de Trujillo Spain 39.34N 5.55W
75 F4 Aldealpozo Spain 41.46N 2.12W
76 K5 Aldeamayor de San Martin Spain 41.30N 4.39W
76 J9 Aldeanueva de Barbarroya Spain 39.46N 5.01W
75 G3 Aldeanueva de Ebro Spain 42.14N 1.53W
76 H6 Aldeanueva de Figueroa Spain 41.09N 5.31W
76 H8 Aldeanueva de la Vera Spain 40.08N 5.41W
76 J9 Aldeanueva de San Bartolomé Spain 39.39N 5.06W
96 U15 Aldea, Pta. de la Gran Canaria Canary Is 28.02N 15.49W
77 K4 Aldeaquemada Spain 38.25N 3.22W
76 H6 Aldearrodrigo Spain 41.06N 5.49W
76 L7 Aldeavieja Spain 40.44N 4.29W
26 B14 Aldebert Reef Marion I Ind Oc 46.51S 37.52E
56 P3 Aldeburgh Suffolk Eng 52.09N 1.35E
75 H7 Aldehuela Spain 40.16N 1.04W
76 G7 Aldehuela de la Bóveda Spain 40.50N 6.02W
76 G8 Aldehuela del Jerte Spain 40.00N 6.14W
76 G7 Aldehuela de Yeltes Spain 40.40N 6.15W
76 J8 Aldehuela, La Spain 40.24N 5.25W
118 J9 Aldeia Campista Brazil 22.56S 43.14W
76 D15 Aldeia da Beja Portugal 38.47N 9.14W
76 D10 Aldeia da Mata Portugal 39.18N 7.45W
76 F8 Aldeia da Ponte Portugal 40.25N 6.51W
76 E8 Aldeia de João Pires Portugal 40.06N 7.09W
76 C13 Aldeia dos Delbas Portugal 37.48N 8.17W
76 C13 Aldeia dos Fernandes Portugal 37.34N 8.10W
76 C13 Aldeia dos Palheiros Portugal 37.36N 8.15W
76 E13 Aldeia Nova de São Bento Portugal 37.55N 7.24W
117 D9 Aldeia Velha Pará Brazil 8.20S 50.18W
91 D8 Aldeia-Viçosa Angola 8.06S 14.57E
77 K6 Aldeire Spain 37.10N 3.03W
109 M3 Alden Kansas 38.14N 98.18W
106 J5 Alden Michigan 44.53N 85.16W
104 G4 Alden New York 42.54N 78.30W
53 R16 Alden isld Norway 61.19N 4.46E
55 C1 Aldenham Herts Eng 51.40N 0.22W
55 D2 Aldenham Res Herts England 51.39N 0.19W
64 A2 Aldenhoven W Germany 50.54N 6.17E
79 K3 Aldeno Italy 45.59N 11.06E
103 D3 Aldenville Pennsylvania 41.38N 75.22W
109 D3 Alder Colorado 38.21N 106.02W
110 N4 Alder Montana 45.20N 112.06W
55 A3 Alder Bourne R Bucks England
59 K2 Aldergrove Antrim N Ireland 54.38N 6.09W
110 C3 Alder L Washington 46.46N 122.15W
57 J6 Alderley Edge Cheshire Eng 53.18N 2.15W
11 L3 Alderman Is, The New Zealand
56 J5 Aldermaston Berks Eng 51.23N 1.09W
56 H3 Alderminster Warwicks Eng 52.08N 1.39W
70 F2 Alderney isld Channel Is 49.43N 2.12W
66 H7 Alder Pass Switzerland 46.02N 7.53E
110 M4 Alder Pk Montana 45.45N 113.10W
111 C6 Alder Pk mt California 35.55N 121.24W
110 B9 Alderpoint California 40.11N 123.37W
56 K5 Aldershot Hants Eng 51.15N 0.47W
53 D4 Alderslyst Denmark 56.11N 9.35E
100 F8 Alderson Alberta 50.20N 111.25W
103 B4 Alderson Pennsylvania 41.22N 76.02W
104 E9 Alderson W Virginia 37.43N 80.39W
100 D8 Aldersyde Alberta 50.44N 113.53W
56 O3 Alderton Suffolk Eng 52.02N 1.25E
57 H6 Aldford Cheshire Eng 53.08N 2.53W
87 H7 Aldie Ethiopia 6.55N 41.02E
103 D7 Aldine New Jersey 39.35N 75.17W
64 F7 Aldingen W Germany 48.07N 8.42E
40 H3 Aldoma U.S.S.R. 56.50N 138.21E
75 L6 Aldover Spain 40.53N 0.30E
56 H4 Aldsworth Glos Eng 51.48N 1.46W
72 B9 Aldudes France 43.06N 1.25W
53 D5 Åle Denmark 55.53N 9.34E
93 E3 Alebtong Uganda 2.17N 33.14E
89 K7 Aledjo Benin 9.23N 1.31E
106 D8 Aledo Illinois 41.12N 90.45W
77 N5 Aledo Spain 37.48N 1.34W
112 K3 Aledo Texas 32.43N 97.36W
75 H8 Aledua, Sierra de mts Spain
89 C3 Aleg Mauritania 17.02N 13.58W
89 B3 Aleg, Lac d' Mauritania 17.10N 14.00W
96 V6 Alegranza isld Canary Is 29.24N 13.32W
118 H7 Alegre Espírito Santo Brazil 20.44S 41.30W
118 F6 Alegre Minas Gerais Brazil 18.15S 47.05W
117 D6 Alegre Pará Brazil 2.13S 48.28W
118 B5 Alegre R Brazil
117 B5 Alegre Mte pk Brazil 1.50S 54.10W
91 A12 Alegre, Pto S Tomé São Tomé & Principe, Gulf Of Guinea 0.01N 6.30E
118 B4 Alegre, R Brazil
76 E10 Alegrete Portugal 39.14N 7.20W
75 F2 Alegria Spain 42.50N 2.29W
109 B7 Alegros Mt New Mexico 34.08N 108.12W
Alehdag, Kuh-i see Ālādāgh, Kūh-e mts
120 F5 Alejandria Bolivia 12.05S 65.06W
121 D4 Alejandro Roca Argentina 33.25S 63.45W
120 A12 Alejandro Selkirk isld Juan Fernández Is Pacific Oc 33.45S 80.45W
121 E4 Alejo Ledesma Argentina 33.39S 62.40W
84 Q15 Alekhtora Cyprus 34.42N 32.41E
113 H7 Aleknagik Alaska 59.15N 158.40W
113 H7 Aleknagik, L Alaska 59.20N 158.50W
40 H4 Aleksandra Mys C U.S.S.R. 54.16N 139.47E
48 K11 Aleksandra Ostrova isld U.S.S.R.
44 L4 Aleksandrbay, Zaliv B Kazakhstan U.S.S.R.
45 E8 Aleksandriya Ukraine U.S.S.R. 48.41N 33.05E
44 H4 Aleksandriyskaya U.S.S.R. 43.55N 47.09E
44 H4 Aleksandro Nevskaya U.S.S.R. 43.55N 46.35E
45 M3 Aleksandro-Nevskiy U.S.S.R. 53.28N 40.14E
45 K1 Aleksandrov U.S.S.R. 56.23N 38.45E
82 G6 Aleksandrovac Yugoslavia 44.28N 21.13E
82 G7 Aleksandrovac Yugoslavia 43.28N 21.03E
45 U6 Aleksandrov-Gay U.S.S.R. 50.08N 48.34E
43 D1 Aleksandrovka Bashkir U.S.S.R. 53.04N 56.14E
45 H8 Aleksandrovka Donetsk, Ukraine U.S.S.R. 48.43N 36.55E
47 K8 Aleksandrovka Kazakhstan U.S.S.R. 53.06N 69.54E
45 D8 Aleksandrovka Kirovograd, Ukraine U.S.S.R. 48.58N 32.14E
45 D5 Aleksandrovka Kiyev, Ukraine U.S.S.R. 51.38N 32.10E
44 B1 Aleksandrovka Krasnodar U.S.S.R. 46.46N 38.59E
45 L8 Aleksandrovka Lugansk, Ukraine U.S.S.R. 48.35N 39.11E
45 C9 Aleksandrovka Nikolayev, Ukraine U.S.S.R. 47.40N 31.16E
43 C1 Aleksandrovka Orenburg U.S.S.R. 52.44N 54.24E
45 S5 Aleksandrovka Saratov U.S.S.R. 51.16N 46.52E
47 K7 Aleksandrovka Tyumen U.S.S.R. 57.10N 66.55E
Aleksandrovsk see Zaporozh'ye
47 H6 Aleksandrovsk Perm U.S.S.R. 59.10N 57.32E
47 J6 Aleksandrovsk Sverdlovsk U.S.S.R. 58.58N 64.30E
45 H5 Aleksandrovskiy U.S.S.R. 51.03N 36.45E
42 D3 Aleksandrovskiy Shlyuz U.S.S.R. 59.27N 89.15E
42 K6 Aleksandrovskiy Zavod U.S.S.R. 50.58N 118.00E
44 E3 Aleksandrovskoye Stavropol' U.S.S.R. 44.45N 42.59E
42 B2 Aleksandrovskoye Tomsk U.S.S.R. 60.29N 77.45E
42 D4 Aleksandrovskoye Tomsk U.S.S.R. 56.48N 85.19E
40 J6 Aleksandrovsk-Sakhalinskiy Sakhalin U.S.S.R. 50.55N 142.12E
62 L4 Aleksandrów Poland 51.49N 19.13E
62 L3 Aleksandrów Kujawski Poland 52.52N 18.40E
41 M2 Aleksandry, Zemlya isld Franz Josef Land U.S.S.R.
39 D1 Aleksayevo U.S.S.R. 70.16N 147.32E
43 K2 Alekseyevka Akmolinsk, Kazakhstan U.S.S.R. 52.03N 70.29E
40 D5 Alekseyevka Amur U.S.S.R. 53.00N 126.43E
45 K6 Alekseyevka Belgorod U.S.S.R. 50.38N 38.43E
43 J1 Alekseyevka Kazakhstan U.S.S.R. 53.33N 69.32E
43 Q3 Alekseyevka Kazakhstan U.S.S.R. 48.57N 85.45E
43 B1 Alekseyevka Kuybyshev U.S.S.R. 53.14N 50.31E
46 Q3 Alekseyevka Kuybyshev U.S.S.R. 52.35N 51.19E
47 L7 Alekseyevka Omsk U.S.S.R. 55.20N 72.01E
43 M2 Alekseyevka Pavlodar, Kazakhstan U.S.S.R. 50.43N 75.05E
45 P5 Alekseyevka Saratov U.S.S.R. 51.50N 43.58E
45 U4 Alekseyevka Saratov U.S.S.R. 52.19N 48.01E
45 J6 Alekseyevka U.S.S.R. 50.46N 37.02E
42 L2 Alekseyevka Yakutsk U.S.S.R. 60.25N 124.10E
45 J8 Alekseyevo-Druzhkovka Ukraine U.S.S.R. 48.34N 37.37E
45 M7 Alekseyevo-Lozovskoye U.S.S.R. 49.24N 40.38E
42 H3 Alekseyevsk U.S.S.R. 57.50N 108.20E
45 O6 Alekseyevskaya U.S.S.R. 50.20N 42.10E
45 F1 Alekseyevskoye Smolensk U.S.S.R. 55.09N 34.20E
45 W1 Alekseyevskoye Tatar A.S.S.R. U.S.S.R. 55.20N 50.04E
46 M4 Aleksikovo U.S.S.R. 50.56N 42.20E
45 J2 Aleksin U.S.S.R. 54.31N 37.07E
82 G7 Aleksinac Yugoslavia 43.31N 21.42E
52 G9 Älekulla Sweden 57.20N 12.43E
35 G6 'Al, El Jordan 31.49N 35.50E
60 K12 Alem Netherlands 51.47N 5.21E
52 J10 Ålem Sweden 56.57N 16.25E
109 C9 Aleman New Mexico 33.00N 107.02W
115 K4 Alemán, Ciudad Miguel Mexico 26.26N 99.00W
115 L8 Alemán, General M Mexico 18.11N 96.06W
120 F11 Alemania Argentina 25.37S 65.36W
91 E9 Alemba Angola 10.48S 16.30E
91 B4 Alembe Gabon 0.03S 10.57E
37 G1 Alemdağ Turkey 41.03N 29.14E
37 G1 Alemdağ Ormanı forest Turkey
Alemlı see Salanda
118 G7 Além Paraíba Brazil 21.49S 42.36W
117 G8 Alencar Brazil 6.23S 39.09W
70 L5 Alençon France 48.25N 0.05E
70 L5 Alençon, Campagne d' plain France
71 D3 Alène R France
117 B5 Alenquer Brazil 1.58S 54.45W
76 A10 Alenquer Portugal 39.03N 9.00W
76 C11 Alentejo hist reg Portugal
81 K3 Alento R Italy
114 E7 Alenuihaha Chan Hawaiian Is
72 K10 Alénya France 42.39N 2.59E
Alenz see Ridvan
Alep see Aleppo
89 H9 Alépé Ivory Coast 5.29N 3.40W
34 E2 Aleppo Syria 36.14N 37.10E
67 Q12 Aléria Corsica 42.05N 9.30E
28 D2 Aler R Andhra Prad India
75 K3 Alerre Spain 42.10N 0.28W
97 N1 Alert N W Terr 82.30N 62.00W
120 D4 Alerta Peru 10.47S 71.48W
101 K10 Alert Bay Br Columbia 50.34N 126.58W
71 E8 Alès France 44.08N 4.05E
81 B4 Ales Sardinia 39.47N 8.49E
82 G3 Aleşd Romania 47.03N 22.22E
47 F3 Alëshki U.S.S.R. 65.42N 48.27E
42 G3 Aleshkino U.S.S.R. 58.38N 100.32E
103 A7 Alesia Maryland 39.42N 76.49W
51 G3 Alesjaure L Sweden 68.10N 18.30E
Aleşkirt see Eleşkirt
75 E3 Alesón Spain 42.24N 2.41W
79 E5 Alessándria Italy 44.55N 8.37E
79 D4 Alessándria prov Italy
81 M4 Alessandria del Carretto Italy 39.57N 16.23E
81 F8 Alessandria della Rocca Sicily 37.34N 13.27E
81 R13 Alessano Italy 39.53N 18.20E
Alessio see Lezhë
53 D3 Ålestrup Denmark 56.42N 9.31E
53 U14 Ålesund Norway 62.28N 6.11E
84 R15 Alethriko Cyprus 34.50N 33.30E
72 J10 Alet-les-Bains France 42.59N 2.16E
66 J6 Aletsch Gletscher, Gr glacier Switzerland
66 H6 Aletschhorn mt Switzerland 46.28N 8.00E
42 K5 Aleur U.S.S.R. 52.40N 117.10E
122 J2 Aleutian Basin Bering Sea
113 N9 Aleutian Is Bering Sea
113 H8 Aleutian Ra Alaska
122 J2 Aleutian Ridge Bering Sea
122 J3 Aleutian Trench Pacific Oc
39 E5 Alevina Mys C U.S.S.R. 58.50N 151.18E
Alevışık see Samandağ
66 A8 Alex France 45.54N 6.14E
109 N7 Alex Oklahoma 34.55N 97.48W
10 Q4 Alexa Bank sea feature Pacific Oc 11.32S 175.25W
70 J5 Alexain France 48.14N 0.46W
109 L3 Alexander Kansas 38.27N 99.34W
100 R9 Alexander Manitoba 49.50N 100.20W
108 G2 Alexander N Dakota 47.50N 103.39W
35 C4 Alexander R Israel
14 E3 Alexander R W Australia
113 T8 Alexander Archipelago Alaska
94 D7 Alexander Bay S Africa 28.40S 16.30E
123 E14 Alexander, C Antarctica 66.50S 62.15W
101 U1 Alexander, C N W Terr 68.57N 106.12W
107 L9 Alexander City Alabama 32.57N 86.00W
14 F4 Alexander I W Australia 18.30S 126.20E
123 F12 Alexander Island Antarctica
48 R2 Alexander, Kap C Greenland 78.10N 73.00W
13 D2 Alexander, Mt N Terr Australia 12.41S 136.38E
13 G5 Alexander,Mt Queensland 21.12S 144.28E
14 B6 Alexander, Mt W Australia 22.44S 115.31E
14 D8 Alexander, Mt W Australia 28.58S 120.13E
9 T12 Alexander Reef Tonga, Pacific Oc
32 F2 Alexander's Wall Iran
11 D12 Alexandra New Zealand 45.14S 169.26E
94 T13 Alexandra S Africa 26.07S 28.06E
12 H6 Alexandra Victoria 37.12S 145.14E
13 F4 Alexandra R Queensland
121 G8 Alexandra, C S Georgia 54.05S 37.58W
28 G6 Alexandra Chan Andaman Is Indian Ocean
101 P5 Alexandra Falls N W Terr 60.30N 116.17W
Alexandra Land see Aleksandry, Zemlya
Alexandretta see İskenderun
101 M9 Alexandria Br Columbia 52.41N 122.29W
86 C3 Alexandria Egypt 31.13N 29.55E
106 J9 Alexandria Indiana 40.16N 85.40W
116 J1 Alexandria Jamaica, W I 18.18N 77.21W
107 M3 Alexandria Kentucky 38.59N 84.22W
107 D10 Alexandria Louisiana 31.19N 92.29W
108 P4 Alexandria Minnesota 45.52N 95.22W
107 E1 Alexandria Missouri 40.20N 91.29W
108 N9 Alexandria Nebraska 40.16N 97.24W
13 D4 Alexandria N Terr 19.00S 136.42E
99 Q7 Alexandria Ontario 45.18N 74.39W
82 J7 Alexandria Romania 43.59N 25.19E
95 K9 Alexandria S Africa 33.39S 26.25E
108 N6 Alexandria S Dakota 43.39N 97.46W
58 G7 Alexandria Strathclyde Scotland 55.59N 4.36W
104 H8 Alexandria Virginia 38.49N 77.06W
Alexandria Ad Issum anc site see İskenderun
104 K2 Alexandria Bay New York 44.20N 75.55W
11 E10 Alexandrina, L New Zealand
12 E6 Alexandrina, L S Australia
35 E5 Alexandrium anc site Jordan 32.06N 35.28E
83 H4 Alexandroúpolis Greece 40.51N 25.53E
106 D8 Alexis Illinois 41.03N 90.34W
97 O7 Alexis B Labrador, Nfld
63 O9 Alexisbad E Germany 51.40N 11.06E
101 M9 Alexis Creek Br Col 52.05N 123.12W
15 H6 Alexishafen Papua New Guinea 5.08S 145.49E
98 P1 Alexis R Labrador, Nfld
100 B6 Alexo Alberta 52.29N 115.45W
34 C5 'Aley Lebanon 33.48N 35.37E
42 C5 Aley R U.S.S.R.
32 G2 Aleyak Iran 36.24N 57.50E
42 C5 Aleysk U.S.S.R. 52.32N 82.45E
93 B3 Aleza mt Zaïre 2.30N 30.35E
81 R12 Alezio Italy 40.03N 18.03E
64 C3 Alf W Germany 50.03N 7.08E
64 B3 Alf R W Germany
77 V14 Alfabia, Sierra de mts Balearic Is
77 J6 Alfacar Spain 37.15N 3.34W
90 J2 Alfadida Chad 18.20N 18.05E
75 J4 Alfajarín Spain 41.37N 0.42W
76 B14 Alfambra Portugal 37.15N 8.49W
75 H6 Alfambra Spain 40.33N 1.03W
75 J6 Alfambra R Spain
75 H5 Alfamén Spain 41.27N 1.15W
91 D7 Alfândega Angola 7.42S 15.53E
76 F6 Alfândega da Fé Portugal 41.20N 6.59W
75 M6 Alfaques, Pto. de los harb Spain
75 L6 Alfara Spain 40.52N 0.24E
76 H6 Alfaraz Spain 41.14N 5.59W
76 D6 Alfarela de Jales Portugal 41.26N 7.35W
76 B8 Alfarelos Portugal 40.08N 8.39W
77 H6 Alfarnate Spain 37.00N 4.15W
Alfaro see Duran
119 B9 Alfaro Ecuador 2.10S 79.51W
75 G3 Alfaro Spain 42.11N 1.45W
75 M4 Alfarrás Spain 41.50N 0.34E
82 L7 Alfatar Bulgaria 43.56N 27.18E
118 J10 Alfavaca, I. da Brazil 23.02S 43.18W
88 O5 Alfaville Algeria 33.53N 0.19E
77 Q3 Alfaz del Pi Spain 38.35N 0.07W
80 K5 Alfedena Italy 41.44N 14.02E
76 A10 Alfeizerão Portugal 39.30N 9.05W
64 M5 Alfeld Bayern W Germany 49.26N 11.33E
63 L9 Alfeld Niedersachsen W Germany 51.59N 9.51E
118 F7 Alfenas Brazil 21.28S 45.58W
123 E10 Alférez de Navio Sobral Arg Base Antarctica 81.04S 40.36W
43 M1 Alferovka U.S.S.R. 54.05N 76.33E
63 G8 Alfhausen W Germany 52.29N 7.57E
84 C6 Alfiós R Greece
84 C6 Alfioúsa Greece 37.38N 21.32E
53 T19 Alfjorden inlet Norway 59.35N 5.33E
56 K5 Alfold Surrey Eng 51.06N 0.31W
79 M5 Alfonsine Italy 44.30N 12.03E
105 B7 Alford Florida 30.41N 85.25W
58 L4 Alford Grampian Scotland 57.14N 2.42W
57 O6 Alford Lincs Eng 53.17N 0.11E
103 H2 Alford Massachusetts 42.14N 73.25W
103 C3 Alford Pennsylvania 41.47N 75.46W
75 M5 Alforja Spain 41.12N 0.58E
53 S19 Ålforø isld Norway 59.53N 5.15E
68 G4 Alfortville France 48.48N 2.25E
53 T15 Ålfotbreen glacier Norway 61.45N 5.40E
53 T15 Ålfoten Norway 61.50N 5.40E
76 E1 Alfoz Spain 43.31N 7.24W
104 P3 Alfred Maine 43.29N 70.44W
108 L3 Alfred N Dakota 46.36N 99.01W
14 F6 Alfred and Marie Ra W Australia
118 H7 Alfredo Chaves Brazil 20.34S 40.44W
26 O16 Alfred, Pt.- Crozet Is Indian Ocean 46.01S 51.55E
11 K7 Alfredton New Zealand 40.41S 175.52E
57 L6 Alfreton Derbys Eng 53.06N 1.23W
56 M6 Alfriston E Sussex Eng 50.48N 0.10E
76 D9 Alfrivida Portugal 39.44N 7.31W
50 E8 Álfsey isld Iceland 63.24N 20.21W
52 J5 Alfta Sweden 61.20N 16.05E
50 C5 Álftá R Iceland
50 K4 Álftadálsfjall mt Iceland 65.01N 15.50W
50 C2 Álftafjördhur B Ísafjardharsýsla, Nordhur Iceland
50 L5 Álftafjördhur B Múlasýsla, Sudhur Iceland
50 C4 Álftafjördhur B Snæfellsnessýsla Iceland
50 B3 Álftamýri Iceland 65.47N 23.40W
50 C6 Álftanes Gullbringusýsla Iceland 64.07N 22.02W
50 C6 Álftanes Mýrasýsla Iceland 64.28N 22.09W
50 C5 Álftártúnga Iceland 64.40N 22.01W
50 E6 Álftavatn L Iceland 64.01N 20.59W
50 L4 Álftavatn L Iceland 65.14N 14.51W
50 G7 Álftaver dist Iceland
64 C2 Alfter W Germany 50.45N 7.00E
48 V7 Alf Trolle, Kap C Greenland 75.58N 18.40W
76 C12 Alfundão Portugal 38.07N 8.04W
43 D3 Alga Kazakhstan U.S.S.R. 49.49N 57.16E
77 D6 Algaba, La Spain 37.27N 6.01W
43 B2 Algabas Kazakhstan U.S.S.R. 50.43N 52.09E
42 K6 Algachi U.S.S.R. 50.45N 117.52E
77 V14 Algaida Balearic Is 39.34N 2.53E
75 H5 Algairen, Sierra de mts Spain
67 O11 Algajola Corsica 42.37N 8.51E
76 E10 Algale Portugal 39.02N 7.22W
40 E3 Algama U.S.S.R. 56.25N 129.48E
40 E3 Algama R U.S.S.R.
77 F6 Algamitas Spain 37.02N 5.09W
72 H8 Algans France 43.34N 1.53E
39 J3 Alganskaya U.S.S.R. 64.15N 172.06E
77 E7 Algar Cadiz Spain 36.40N 5.39W
77 P5 Algar Murcia Spain 37.39N 0.51W
75 K8 Algar de Palancia Spain 39.46N 0.22W
77 H6 Algarinejo Spain 37.19N 4.09W
75 H7 Algarra Spain 40.00N 1.26W
121 B2 Algarrobal Chile 28.14S 70.37W
121 B2 Algarrobito Chile 29.56S 71.09W
121 B1 Algarrobo Atacamá Chile 27.05S 70.35W
77 H7 Algarrobo Spain 36.46N 4.03W
121 B4 Algarrobo Valparaiso Chile 33.24S 71.40W
77 O5 Algarrobo mt Spain 37.39N 1.16W
121 C6 Algarrobo del Aguila Argentina 36.26S 67.09W
76 B14 Algarve hist reg Portugal
74 B7 Algarve prov Portugal
75 L6 Algas R Spain
45 N3 Algasovo U.S.S.R. 53.41N 41.41E
42 F4 Algasy U.S.S.R. 56.03N 96.08E
43 K5 Algatart Kazakhstan U.S.S.R. 44.25N 72.18E
77 F7 Algatocin Spain 36.35N 5.16W
76 C9 Alge R Portugal
12 D3 Algebuckina S Australia 27.53S 135.50E
77 F8 Algeciras Spain 36.08N 5.27W
77 F8 Algeciras, B de Spain
77 Q2 Algemesí Spain 39.11N 0.27W
88 P3 Alger Algeria 36.50N 3.00E
106 K5 Alger Michigan 44.09N 84.07W
104 B6 Alger Ohio 40.42N 83.51W
88 P3 Alger, B d' Algeria
73 D3 Algeria rep N Africa
76 D16 Alges Portugal 38.42N 9.14W
75 D6 Algete Spain 40.35N 3.30W
87 G8 Alghe Ethiopia 5.40N 38.11E
87 G8 Alghe Ethiopia 5.13N 39.20E
87 F3 Algheden Ethiopia 15.29N 37.08E
81 A2 Alghero Sardinia 40.34N 8.19E
81 A2 Alghero, Rada d' B Sardinia
52 J9 Älghult Sweden 57.00N 15.35E
76 C14 Algibre R Portugal
Algiers see Alger
107 J13 Algiers dist New Orleans, Louisiana
77 Q2 Alginet Spain 39.16N 0.28W
95 J9 Algoa B S Africa
117 H9 Algodões Brazil 8.20S 37.15W
77 F7 Algodonales Spain 36.54N 5.24W
77 F7 Algodonales, Sierra de mts Spain
109 D6 Algodones New Mexico 35.23N 106.28W
119 D9 Algodón, R Peru
76 D13 Algodor Portugal 37.45N 7.47W
75 C8 Algodor R Spain
110 D7 Algoma Oregon 42.21N 121.49W
106 G5 Algoma Wisconsin 44.36N 87.27W
99 H6 Algoma Mills Ontario 46.12N 82.49W
108 Q6 Algona Iowa 43.04N 94.11W
106 M7 Algonac Michigan 42.38N 82.33W
99 M7 Algonquin Park Ontario 45.34N 78.36W
99 M7 Algonquin Prov Park Ontario
107 L5 Algood Tennessee 36.11N 85.28W
75 E6 Algora Spain 40.58N 2.40W
75 E1 Algorta Spain 43.20N 3.00W
121 F4 Algorta Uruguay 32.26S 57.18W
76 F6 Algoso Portugal 41.28N 6.34W
76 C14 Algoz Portugal 37.10N 8.18W
69 L5 Algrange France 49.22N 6.03E
53 R18 Algrøy isld Norway 60.20N 4.57E
52 K2 Älgsj Sweden 64.13N 17.30E
25 C5 Alguada Reef Burma 15.41N 94.12E
75 M4 Alguaire Spain 41.44N 0.35E
77 O4 Alguazas Spain 38.03N 1.14W
94 M3 Algueirão Mozambique 20.41S 32.47E
76 C15 Algueirão Portugal 38.48N 9.20W
77 O4 Algueña Spain 38.22N 1.01W
77 L7 Alhabia Spain 37.00N 2.35W
76 B8 Alhadas Portugal 40.11N 8.47W
34 K4 Al Hadīthah Iraq 34.09N 42.22E
75 G3 Alhama R Spain
77 L7 Alhama de Almería Spain 36.57N 2.34W
75 G5 Alhama de Aragón Spain 41.18N 1.54W
77 J6 Alhama de Granada Spain 37.00N 3.59W
77 O5 Alhama de Murcia Spain 37.51N 1.25W
77 H7 Alhama, Sierra de mts Spain
77 K3 Alhambra Spain 38.54N 3.04W
77 K3 Alhambra, Sierra de mts Spain
77 M6 Alhamilla, Sierra mts Spain
76 A11 Alhandra Portugal 38.56N 9.00W
57 E2 Alhang Strathclyde/Dumfries & Gall Scotland 55.17N 4.09W
85 O7 Al Hasânî I Saudi Arabia 25.00N 37.01E
77 G7 Alhaurin de la Torre Spain 36.40N 4.34W
77 G7 Alhaurin el Grande Spain 36.39N 4.41W
88 J9 Alhel, el watercourse Mauritania
77 J6 Alhendin Spain 37.06N 3.38W
87 M5 Al Hills Somalia
74 E9 Al Hoceima Morocco 35.14N 3.56W
88 M4 Al-Hoceima, B. d' Morocco
75 E6 Alhóndiga Spain 40.31N 2.50W
32 C6 Al Hout oil well The Gulf 28.55N 49.02E
121 E1 Alhuampa Argentina 27.07S 62.33W
53 U15 Ålhus Norway 61.32N 6.13E
33 B8 'Alī Bahrain, The Gulf 26.10N 50.32E
34 N6 'Alī Iraq 32.46N 45.21E
81 K7 Alì Sicily 38.02N 15.25E
81 G8 Alia Sicily 37.47N 13.48E
76 J10 Alia Spain 39.27N 5.13W
87 D2 'Aliab Sudan 17.20N 33.44E
31 E2 Aliabad Afghanistan 36.36N 68.55E
32 F6 Aliabad Banāder va Jazāyer-e Bahr-e Oman Iran 28.35N 55.50E
32 E5 'Alīābād Esfahān Iran 31.40N 53.50E
32 G5 'Alīābād Kermān Iran 30.42N 56.45E
32 H4 'Alīābād Khorāsān Iran 32.17N 58.54E
32 J5 'Alīābād Khorāsān Iran 31.21N 60.24E
32 B3 'Alīābād Kordestān Iran 35.02N 46.58E
32 F2 'Alīābād Māzandarān Iran 36.55N 54.33E
32 D3 'Alīābād Tehrān Iran 35.02N 50.48E
32 D3 'Alīābād, Kūh-e mt Iran 34.10N 50.48E
75 J6 Aliaga Spain 40.40N 0.42W
36 B4 Aliağa Turkey 38.49N 26.59E
Aliak see Aleyak
83 E4 Aliákmon R Greece 40.30N 22.40E
34 O6 'Alī al Gharbī Iraq 32.28N 46.42E
34 L5 Ali an Noman Iraq 33.28N 43.26E
81 M3 Aliano Italy 40.18N 16.14E
84 F5 Alíartos Greece 38.22N 23.06E
77 N6 Alias R Spain
34 O6 Alī ash Sharqī Iraq 32.08N 46.46E
28 A1 Alibag Maharashtra India 18.38N 72.55E
41 O6 Ali-Bagata U.S.S.R. 68.24N 132.05E
31 E8 Ali Bandar Pakistan 24.24N 69.06E
Alibardak see Mermer
44 J8 Ali Bayramly Azerbaydzhan U.S.S.R. 39.56N 48.55E
88 S6 Ali Bey Algeria 30.23N 9.10E
36 B3 Alibey isld Turkey
37 F1 Alibey R Turkey
37 J1 Alibeyköy Turkey 41.05N 28.53E
82 M5 Alibey, Oz L U.S.S.R.
19 L5 Alibijaban isld Luzon Philippines 13.20N 122.43E
87 F6 Alibo Ethiopia 9.52N 37.05E
89 L6 Alibori R Benin
82 F5 Alibunar Yugoslavia 45.05N 20.57E
82 H9 Alí Butús mt Bulgaria 41.24N 23.39E
77 Q4 Alicante Spain 38.21N 0.29W
74 G6 Alicante prov Spain
77 Q4 Alicante, B. de Spain
108 N3 Alice N Dakota 46.48N 97.33W
13 H6 Alice Queensland 23.32S 145.50E
95 K8 Alice S Africa 32.47S 26.50E
112 J8 Alice Texas 27.45N 98.06W
15 F6 Alice R Papua New Guinea
13 F3 Alice R Queensland
13 H6 Alice R Queensland
101 J8 Alice Arm Br Columbia 55.29N 129.31W
79 D5 Alice Bel Colle Italy 44.43N 8.27E
79 D4 Alice Castello Italy 45.22N 8.04E
19 J9 Alice Chan Philippines
95 K9 Alicedale S Africa 33.19S 26.05E
14 G4 Alice Downs W Australia 17.43S 127.57E
110 H4 Alicel Oregon 45.25N 117.59W
81 O5 Alice, Punta Italy 39.24N 17.09E
13 C6 Alice Springs N Terr Aust 23.42S 133.52E
107 H8 Aliceville Alabama 33.08N 88.10W
13 C6 Alice Well N Terr Australia 24.55S 134.16E
43 L7 Alichur Tadzhikistan U.S.S.R. 37.47N 73.31E
31 G2 Alichur R Tadzhikistan U.S.S.R.
107 E6 Alicia Arkansas 35.54N 91.06W
19 L8 Alicia Mindanao Philippines 7.30N 122.58E
13 F5 Alick R Queensland
117 C3 Alicoto Fr Guiana 3.07N 52.20W
81 H6 Alicudi isld Lipari Is Italy 38.33N 14.22E
77 K5 Alicún de Ortega Spain 37.36N 3.08W
100 Q9 Alida Saskatchewan 49.24N 101.51W
87 K8 Ali, El Somalia 4.11N 44.59E
80 K6 Alife Italy 41.20N 14.20E
93 M5 Ali Gab Kenya 0.18N 40.51E
29 B2 Aliganj Delhi India 28.34N 77.14E
30 C5 Aliganj Hardoi, Uttar Prad India 27.30N 79.10E
30 D4 Aliganj Kheri, Uttar Prad India 28.07N 80.36E
30 B5 Aligarh Aligarh, Uttar Prad India 27.54N 78.04E
30 C5 Aligarh Hardoi, Uttar Prad India 27.29N 79.41E
29 E5 Aligarh Rajasthan India 25.58N 76.09E
30 A5 Aligarh dist Uttar Prad India
93 L3 Ali Gollo hill Kenya 2.35N 39.54E
Ali Gudar see Alīgūdarz
32 C4 Alīgūdarz Iran 33.24N 49.19E
Alihe see Oroqen Zizhiqi
76 H4 Alija del Infantado Spain 42.09N 5.50W
76 E6 Alijó Portugal 41.16N 7.27W
32 D5 'Alījūq, Kūh-e mt Iran 31.28N 51.44E
31 E4 Ali Khel Afghanistan 33.55N 69.46E
28 C2 Alikher Karnataka India 17.47N 77.16E
30 C5 Ali Khera Uttar Prad India 27.18N 79.10E
84 J11 Alikianoú Crete 35.27N 23.55E
45 S1 Alikovo U.S.S.R. 55.44N 46.45E
91 D4 Alima R Congo
85 H7 Alima, Jabal mt Libya 24.41N 24.20E
31 D3 Ali Mardan Afghanistan 35.40N 67.09E
81 H8 Alimena Sicily 37.42N 14.07E
15 J5 Alim I Bismarck Arch 2.52S 147.05E
81 G8 Aliminusa Sicily 37.52N 13.47E
84 U17 Alimnía isld Rhodes 36.16N 27.43E
19 K8 Alimpaya Pt Mindanao Philippines 7.05N 121.55E
90 K9 Alindao Cent Afr Rep 5.01N 21.11E
19 A4 Alindau Celebes Indonesia 0.20S 119.49E
109 M5 Aline Oklahoma 36.32N 98.27W
12 D2 Alinerta, Mt S Australia 26.09S 135.46E
31 F3 Alingar R Afghanistan
24 D9 Aling Kangri mt pk Xizang Zizhiqu China 32.51N 81.03E
52 G9 Alingsås Sweden 57.55N 12.30E
31 B4 Alinjan Afghanistan 33.50N 64.28E
41 E8 Alinskoye U.S.S.R. 63.17N 87.36E
87 H8 Alintale Ethiopia 5.14N 41.21E
18 M3 Alipaga Borneo Indon 4.12N 116.08E
42 D3 Alipka U.S.S.R. 58.41N 86.08E
29 M3 Alipore W Bengal India 22.32N 88.20E
29 G2 Alipore dist Calcutta, W Bengal
29 F7 Alipur Maharashtra India 20.32N 78.41E
31 F6 Alipur Pakistan 29.22N 70.59E
30 C7 Alipura Madhya Prad India 25.10N 79.20E
29 L4 Alipur Duar W Bengal India 26.29N 89.38E
104 E6 Aliquippa Pennsylvania 40.38N 80.16W
87 J5 Ali-Sabieh Djibouti 11.10N 42.44E
111 C5 Alisal California 36.39N 121.35W
76 F10 Aliseda Spain 39.25N 6.42W
71 F1 Alise Ste. Reine France 47.33N 4.30E
44 G9 Ali Shah Iran 38.10N 45.50E
39 H1 Aliskerovo U.S.S.R. 67.53N 167.30E
115 D2 Alisos R Mexico
83 F3 Alistáti Greece 41.03N 23.58E
76 G5 Aliste R Spain
67 Q12 Alistro Corsica 42.16N 9.33E
113 K8 Alitak B Alaska
84 H5 Alivérion Greece 38.24N 24.02E
29 D2 Aliwal Punjab India 30.57N 75.38E
95 K6 Aliwal North S Africa 30.42S 26.43E
100 D6 Alix Alberta 52.25N 113.11W
71 G7 Alixan France 44.58N 5.01E
33 C10 'Aliyah isld S Yemen 12.48N 45.00E
35 G7 Aliyan anc site Jordan 31.32N 35.53E
74 E9 Ali-Youssef-ou-Ali Morocco 35.10N 3.22W
31 F4 Alizai Pakistan 33.32N 70.26E
77 D6 Aljarafe, El reg Spain
77 B6 Aljaraque Spain 37.16N 7.01W
32 F2 Alj Beyk Iran 37.34N 55.40E
76 B14 Aljezur Portugal 37.18N 8.49W
77 E7 Aljibe mt Spain 36.31N 5.36W
77 O5 Aljorra Spain 37.41N 1.04W
76 B9 Aljubarrota Portugal 39.34N 8.55W
77 D2 Aljucén Spain 39.02N 6.20W
77 D2 Aljucén R Spain
76 C13 Aljustrel Portugal 37.52N 8.10W
110 F8 Alkali L Nevada 41.40N 119.50W
61 M3 Alken Belgium 50.52N 5.19E
44 E6 Alkhalkalaki Georgia U.S.S.R. 41.26N 43.29E
56 O5 Alkham Kent Eng 51.08N 1.13E
84 E5 Alkionídhes islds Greece 38.07N 22.59E
84 E5 Alkionídhon Kólpos gulf Greece
60 G9 Alkmaar Netherlands 52.38N 4.44E
60 G9 Alkmaarden Meer L Netherlands
103 F2 Allaben New York 42.07N 74.22W
66 K6 All Acqua Switzerland 46.30N 8.29E
89 L8 Allada Benin 6.41N 2.10E
28 D3 Allagadda Andhra Prad India 15.08N 78.30E
104 Q6 Allagash Maine 47.04N 69.03W
104 P7 Allagash R Maine
104 P7 Allagash L Maine 46.19N 69.32W
90 E6 Allagernu Nigeria 11.57N 11.39E
90 C8 Allah Nigeria 6.26N 6.39E
32 F4 Allahabad Iran 32.44N 55.22E
31 F6 Allahabad Pakistan 28.57N 70.58E
30 E7 Allahabad Uttar Prad India 25.27N 81.50E
30 C6 Allahabad div Uttar Prad India
30 E7 Allahabad dist Uttar Prad India
30 C5 Allahganj Uttar Prad India 27.33N 79.41E
37 G5 Allahüekber Dağları mts Turkey
70 O5 Allaines-Mervilliers France 48.12N 1.50E
70 O5 Allainville France 48.27N 1.54E
70 F6 Allaire France 47.38N 2.10W
26 T5 Allai Tank Sri Lanka
113 L3 Allakaket Alaska 66.30N 152.45W
39 B4 Allakh-Yun' U.S.S.R. 61.10N 138.09E
40 G1 Allakh-Yun' R U.S.S.R.
66 H7 Allalinhorn mt Switzerland 46.03N 7.54E
66 B6 Allaman Switzerland 46.29N 6.24E
111 J9 All American Can California
112 C4 Allamoore Texas 31.04N 105.01W
103 E5 Allamuchy New Jersey 40.56N 74.49W
71 F8 Allan France 44.29N 4.48E
35 F5 Allan Jordan 32.07N 35.45E
100 L7 Allan Saskatchewan 51.54N 106.02W
35 G2 'Allan R Syria
72 K5 Allanche France 45.14N 2.56E
65 O5 Alland Austria 48.04N 16.06E
95 L4 Allandale S Africa 28.50S 27.08E
25 C3 Allanmyo Burma 19.25N 95.13E
26 V3 Allan Pt Christmas I Indian Oc 10.27S 105.45E
58 J6 Allan, R Tayside Scotland
95 K3 Allanridge S Africa 27.45S 26.40E
11 N13 Allans Beach New Zealand
100 N1 Allan Water Ontario 50.15N 90.14W
85 M8 'Allaqi, W watercourse Egypt
99 N3 Allard R Quebec
98 J3 Allard, L Quebec
98 G6 Allardville New Brunswick 47.29N 65.32W
76 D4 Allariz Spain 42.11N 7.48W
69 N7 Allarmont France 48.29N 7.01E
72 G5 Allassac France 45.16N 1.28E
87 G7 Allata Ethiopia 6.38N 38.25E
105 C3 Allatoona Res Georgia 34.08N 84.40W
71 G10 Allauch France 43.20N 5.28E
39 D1 Allaykha R U.S.S.R.
94 K4 Alldays Transvaal S Africa 22.40S 29.06E
61 K7 Alle Belgium 49.51N 4.58E
66 E2 Alle Switzerland 47.26N 7.08E
106 J7 Allegan Michigan 42.32N 85.51W
104 G4 Allegany New York 42.06N 78.30W
88 O4 Alleg, Djebel mt Algeria 34.29N 1.55E
79 M2 Alleghe Italy 46.24N 12.01E
104 F6 Allegheny R Pennsylvania
102 K3 Allegheny Mts U.S.A.
71 D6 Allegre France 45.13N 3.43E
116 M3 Allegre, Pte pt Guadeloupe W I 16.22N 61.44W
71 G9 Alleins France 43.42N 5.09E
107 F12 Allemands Louisiana 29.49N 90.29W
107 F12 Allemands, L. des Louisiana
95 L4 Allemanskraal Dam res S Africa 28.18S 27.15E
71 J6 Allemond France 45.08N 6.02E
104 C9 Allen Kentucky 37.36N 82.44W
108 O7 Allen Nebraska 42.28N 96.49W
109 O7 Allen Oklahoma 34.53N 96.24W
19 M5 Allen Philippines 12.31N 124.17E
108 J6 Allen S Dakota 43.16N 101.57W
112 L2 Allen Texas 33.07N 96.40W
113 Q5 Allen mt Alaska 62.15N 142.20W
59 H5 Allen, Bog of Irish Rep
35 F6 Allenby Bridge Jordan 31.52N 35.32E
103 F4 Allendale New Jersey 41.02N 74.08W
105 F4 Allendale S Carolina 33.01N 81.19W
57 J3 Allendale Town Northumb Eng 54.54N 2.15W
115 J3 Allende Coahuila Mexico 28.22N 100.50W
115 J5 Allende Nuevo León Mexico 25.20N 100.01W
64 F1 Allendorf Hessen W Germany 51.02N 8.41E
64 F2 Allendorf Hessen W Germany 50.40N 8.50E
64 H1 Allendorf Hessen W Germany 51.16N 9.59E
64 D1 Allendorf Westfalen W Germany 51.17N 7.58E
99 J8 Allenford Ontario 44.32N 81.10W
57 J3 Allenheads Northumb Eng 54.48N 2.13W
100 M7 Allen Hills Saskatchewan
59 F3 Allen,L Leitrim Irish Rep 54.08N 8.03W
11 B13 Allen, Mt Stewart I New Zealand 47.07S 167.50E
66 N1 Allensbach W Germany 47.43N 9.04E
109 E1 Allens Park Colorado 40.13N 105.31W
Allenstein see Olsztyn
104 O3 Allenstown New Hampshire 43.10N 71.26W
107 J5 Allensville Kentucky 36.43N 87.04W
103 M3 Allenton Rhode I 41.33N 71.28W
103 E6 Allentown New Jersey 40.11N 74.36W
103 C5 Allentown Pennsylvania 40.37N 75.30W
89 C7 Allen Town Sierra Leone 8.27N 13.13W
65 M4 Allentsteig Austria 48.42N 15.20E
59 J5 Allenwood Kildare Irish Rep 53.17N 6.53W
28 C6 Alleppey Kerala India 9.30N 76.22E
28 C6 Alleppey dist Kerala India
75 J7 Allepuz Spain 40.29N 0.44W
Aller see Cabañaquinta
76 H2 Aller R Spain
63 K7 Aller R W Germany
71 F3 Allerey-sur-Saône France 46.55N 4.59E
64 E6 Allerheiligen W Germany 48.32N 8.13E
80 E3 Allerona Italy 42.48N 11.58E
64 L5 Allersberg W Germany 49.15N 11.15E
53 J6 Allerslev Denmark 55.06N 12.03E
57 M4 Allerston N Yorks Eng 54.14N 0.39W
108 R9 Allerton Iowa 40.42N 93.21W
53 K4 Allerum Sweden 56.07N 12.42E
69 B4 Allery France 49.58N 1.53E
Alles see Peñamellera Alta
56 H3 Allesley W Midlands Eng 52.26N 1.33W
61 N4 Alleur Belgium 50.40N 5.30E
71 J6 Allevard France 45.23N 6.05E
112 L6 Alleyton Texas 29.43N 96.31W
65 A6 Allgau reg W Germany

65 B7 Allgäuer Alpen mts Austria
57 J6 Allgreave Cheshire Eng 53.12N 2.03W
56 N5 Allhallows Kent Eng 51.29N 0.39E
81 N6 Alli R Italy
93 H2 Allia B Kenya
100 F6 Alliance Alberta 52.24N 111.41W
108 H7 Alliance Nebraska 42.08N 102.54W
104 D6 Alliance Ohio 40.56N 81.06W
117 B2 Alliance Surinam 5.53N 54.52W
67 H6 Allier dept France
71 C4 Allier R France
11 J7 Alligator Hd New Zealand 40.58S 174.10E
116 J2 Alligator Pond Jamaica, W I 17.52N 77.34W
116 J2 Alligator Pond Bay Jamaica, W I
105 L2 Alligator R N Carolina
13 C2 Alligator R., E N Terr Australia
105 G13 Alligator Reef Florida 24.52N 80.37W
13 B2 Alligator, R., S N Terr Australia
71 C2 Alligny-Cosne France 47.28N 3.03E
71 E2 Alligny-en-Morvan France 47.12N 4.10E
59 B8 Allihies Cork Irish Rep 51.38N 10.03W
28 C1 Allikher Karnataka India 18.10N 77.14E
53 D4 Alling Denmark 56.06N 9.45E
64 M6 Alling W Germany 48.59N 11.59E
53 E4 Alling Å R Denmark
53 E4 Allingåbro Denmark 56.28N 10.20E
53 P12 Allinge Bornholm Denmark 55.18N 14.49E
71 J4 Allinges France 46.20N 6.27E
56 H5 Allington Wilts Eng 51.22N 1.54W
108 S7 Allison Iowa 42.45N 92.48W
112 D8 Allison Texas 35.37N 100.06W
101 K10 Allison Harbour Br Columbia 51.02N 127.31W
81 R13 Alliste Italy 39.56N 18.05E
99 L8 Alliston Ontario 44.09N 79.51W
66 N1 Allmannsdorf W Germany 47.41N 9.12E
75 F2 Allo Spain 42.34N 2.01W
58 J6 Alloa Central Scotland 56.07N 3.49W
72 J1 Allogny France 47.14N 2.18E
57 G3 Allonby Cumbria Eng 54.46N 3.25W
57 G3 Allonby B Cumbria Eng
76 B2 Allones, R. de Spain
35 D3 Allonim Israel 32.43N 35.08E
35 D3 Allonim Aba Israel 32.44N 35.10E
72 D2 Allonne Deux Sèvres France 46.35N 0.22W
69 C5 Allonne Oise France 49.24N 2.07E
70 O5 Allonnes Eure-et-Loir France 48.19N 1.40E
72 E1 Allonnes Maine-et-Loire France 47.18N 0.02E
72 D7 Allons France 44.12N 0.02W
13 K8 Allora Queensland 28.00S 151.56E
71 K8 Allos France 44.14N 6.38E
71 K8 Allos, Col d' France 44.18N 6.35E
14 E7 Allott, Mt W Australia 26.00S 124.50E
72 F3 Alloué France 46.01N 0.31E
106 F2 Allouez Michigan 47.18N 88.24W
103 D7 Alloway New Jersey 39.33N 75.22W
57 D2 Alloway Strathclyde Scot 55.25N 4.40W
103 D7 Alloway's Cr New Jersey
59 E7 Allow,R Cork Irish Rep
75 J6 Alloza Spain 40.58N 0.32W
75 G2 Alloz, Embalse de res Spain 42.43N 1.56W
30 A4 Allpur Delhi India 28.48N 77.06E
63 O10 Allstedt E Germany 51.25N 11.25E
59 D8 Allua,L Cork Irish Rep 51.50N 9.10W
99 N7 Allumette I Quebec
80 E4 Allumiere Italy 42.09N 11.55E
28 E3 Allur Andhra Prad India 14.40N 80.04E
28 E3 Alluru Kottapatnam Andhra Prad India 15.24N 80.07E
99 R3 Ally Quebec 49.00N 73.21W
65 G7 Alm Austria 47.25N 12.55E
65 J6 Alm R Austria
107 B6 Alma Arkansas 35.28N 94.16W
109 D2 Alma Colorado 39.17N 106.03W
105 E6 Alma Georgia 31.33N 82.29W
35 E1 'Alma Israel 33.03N 35.29E
109 O2 Alma Kansas 39.01N 96.18W
106 K6 Alma Michigan 43.23N 84.40W
107 C2 Alma Missouri 39.04N 93.32W
108 L9 Alma Nebraska 40.06N 99.22W
98 H8 Alma New Brunswick 45.36N 64.58W
99 T4 Alma Quebec 48.32N 71.41W
35 H3 Alma Syria 32.45N 36.15E
106 C5 Alma Wisconsin 44.21N 91.54W
44 C10 Al'ma R Ukraine U.S.S.R.
43 M5 Alma-Ata Kazakhstan U.S.S.R. 43.19N 76.55E
76 D8 Almaceda Portugal 40.01N 7.40W
75 L4 Almacellas Spain 41.44N 0.26E
77 H7 Almachar Spain 36.49N 4.14W
77 M5 Almáciles Spain 37.59N 2.20W
76 A11 Almada Portugal 38.40N 9.09W
76 D11 Almadafe R Portugal
13 G3 Almaden Queensland 17.18S 144.45E
77 G3 Almadén Spain 38.47N 4.50W
77 D5 Almadén de la Plata Spain 37.52N 6.05W
77 G3 Almadenejos Spain 38.45N 4.43W
77 G3 Almadén, Sierra de mts Spain
75 E6 Almadrones Spain 40.54N 2.46W
Almafigiya see Muwaffaqiyah,Al
Almagell see Saas-Almagell
35 F2 Almagor Israel 32.55N 35.36E
77 J3 Almagro Spain 38.54N 3.43W
19 M6 Almagro isld Philippines 11.58N 124.17E
77 N6 Almagro, Sierra mts Spain
32 B6 Al Magwa oil well Kuwait 29.10N 47.56E
75 F4 Almajano Spain 41.51N 2.20W
39 E1 Alma Kyuyel',Oz L U.S.S.R. 68.42N 151.27E
75 F5 Almaluez Spain 41.17N 2.15W
44 H6 Almaly Azerbaydzhan U.S.S.R. 41.20N 46.44E
43 J6 Almalyk Uzbekistan U.S.S.R. 40.50N 69.40E
50 D6 Almannagjá rift Iceland
110 D9 Almanor, L California 40.15N 121.10W
77 O3 Almansa Spain 38.52N 1.06W
77 P3 Almansa, Pto. de pass Spain 38.50N 0.55W
76 C14 Almansil Portugal 37.05N 8.02W
75 G5 Almantes, Sierra de mts Spain
76 J3 Almanza Spain 42.39N 5.03W
77 N6 Almanzora R Spain
76 J8 Almanzor, Pico de mt Spain 40.15N 5.18W
101 K7 Alma Pk Br Columbia 56.48N 127.31W
76 J7 Almar R Spain
76 H9 Almaraz Spain 39.50N 5.40W
76 H6 Almaraz de Duero Spain 41.28N 5.54W
75 F8 Almarcha, La Spain 39.41N 2.23W
76 C15 Almargem Portugal 38.51N 9.16W
77 F6 Almargen Spain 37.00N 5.01W
75 F4 Almarza Spain 41.57N 2.28W
118 F2 Almas Brazil 11.31S 47.09W
43 N7 Almas Uzbekistan U.S.S.R. 41.01N 71.07E
118 E3 Almas R Brazil
37 G7 Almaşat Turkey 38.35N 43.13E
118 E4 Almas, R. das Brazil
82 H3 Almasul R Romania
82 G6 Almasului, Munştii mts Romania
75 L5 Almatret Spain 41.19N 0.25E
86 S11 Almaza Airport Cairo Egypt
75 E5 Almazán Spain 41.29N 2.31W
42 J2 Almazny U.S.S.R. 62.30N 113.35E
75 K8 Almazora Spain 39.57N 0.04W
75 F4 Almazul Spain 41.35N 2.10W
52 J7 Almby Sweden 59.15N 15.14E
63 J9 Alme R W Germany
52 J10 Almeboda Sweden 56.35N 15.15E
110 B7 Almeda Oregon 42.37N 123.37W
112 F9 Almeda Texas 29.34N 95.26W
103 B4 Almedia Pennsylvania 41.01N 76.23W
77 L3 Almedina Spain 38.38N 2.57W
77 H6 Almedinilla Spain 37.27N 4.05W
77 K7 Almegijar Spain 36.54N 3.17W
76 F7 Almeida Portugal 40.43N 6.53W
76 G6 Almeida Spain 41.16N 6.05W
92 K8 Almeida, B. d' Mozambique
117 C5 Almeirim Brazil 1.30S 52.35W
76 B10 Almeirim Portugal 39.12N 8.37W
76 C13 Almeirim Portugal 37.44N 8.08W
117 C5 Almeirim, Sa. do mts Brazil
60 P10 Almelo Netherlands 52.21N 6.40E
60 Q10 Almelo Nordhorn Kanaal canal Netherlands
109 L2 Almena Kansas 39.54N 99.43W
76 K2 Almenada, I Spain 43.26N 4.48W
75 M4 Almenar Spain 41.47N 0.34E
118 H5 Almenara Brazil 16.13S 40.44W
75 K8 Almenara Spain 39.46N 0.14W
77 M3 Almenara mt Spain 38.33N 2.27W
76 H6 Almenara de Tormes Spain 41.05N 5.50W
77 O5 Almenara, Sierra de mts Spain
75 F4 Almenar de Soria Spain 41.41N 2.12W
76 E7 Almendra Portugal 41.00N 7.03W
76 G6 Almendra Spain 41.13N 6.20W
76 G6 Almendra, Embalse de res Spain
77 C3 Almendral Spain 38.36N 6.49W
77 D3 Almendralejo Spain 38.41N 6.25W
77 N6 Almendricos Spain 37.29N 1.46W
77 B5 Almendro, El Spain 37.30N 7.15W
75 E8 Almendros Spain 39.55N 2.54W
70 L4 Alménêches France 48.41N 0.06E
47 J8 Al'menevo U.S.S.R. 55.00N 63.30E
50 K3 Almenningsárvötn lakes Iceland
79 G3 Almenno San Salvatore Italy 45.45N 9.35E
56 G6 Almer Dorset Eng 50.47N 2.09W
60 J10 Almere Netherlands 52.41N 5.12E
108 L8 Almeria Nebraska 41.50N 99.32W
77 M7 Almería Spain 36.50N 2.26W
74 F7 Almería prov Spain
77 M7 Almería R Spain
77 M7 Almería, Golfo de Spain
79 B4 Almese Italy 45.08N 7.24E
46 Q3 Al'met'yevsk U.S.S.R. 54.50N 52.22E
52 H10 Älmhult Sweden 56.32N 14.10E
77 J7 Almijara, Sierra de mts Spain
77 F9 Almina, Pta Spain 35.54N 5.17W
53 C5 Almind Vejle Denmark 55.34N 9.30E
53 C4 Almind Viborg Denmark 56.23N 9.25E
53 P12 Almindingen Bornholm Denmark 55.07N 14.56E
110 G2 Almira Washington 47.42N 118.56W
121 K10 Almirantazgo, Seno del gulf Chile
115 N5 Almirante Panama 9.20N 82.22W
123 E14 Almirante Brown Arg Base Antarctica 64.53S 62.53W
121 B2 Almirante Latorre Chile 29.38S 70.51W
121 J8 Almirante Montt. G Chile
118 E9 Almirante Tamandaré Brazil 25.16S 49.20W
84 H5 Almiropótamos Greece 38.16N 24.11E
84 E3 Almirós Greece 39.11N 22.45E
84 K11 Almiroú, Kólpos gulf Crete
60 H12 Almkerk Netherlands 51.47N 4.57E
53 T15 Almklov Norway 62.00N 5.40E
110 M7 Almo Idaho 42.06N 113.38W
76 B15 Almocageme Portugal 38.47N 9.28W
76 C13 Almodôvar Portugal 37.31N 8.03W
77 E8 Almodovar R Spain
77 H3 Almodóvar del Campo Spain 38.43N 4.10W
75 G8 Almodóvar del Pinar Spain 39.44N 1.55W
77 F5 Almodóvar del Río Spain 37.49N 5.01W
76 D7 Almofala Portugal 40.57N 7.48W
77 G7 Almogia Spain 36.50N 4.32W
75 E7 Almoguera Spain 40.18N 2.59W
75 H6 Almohajá Spain 40.36N 1.26W
76 G10 Almoharín Spain 39.11N 6.03W
75 K4 Almolda, La Spain 41.32N 0.12W
115 J8 Almoloya Mexico 18.22N 100.12W
75 H5 Almonacid de la Sierra Spain 41.24N 1.20W
75 E8 Almonacid del Marquesado Spain 39.49N 2.46W
77 C5 Almonaster la Real Spain 37.52N 6.48W
104 H4 Almond New York 42.18N 77.44W
106 E5 Almond Wisconsin 44.17N 89.26W
58 K7 Almond R Lothian Scotland
58 J6 Almond, R Tayside Scotland
56 F4 Almondsbury Avon Eng 51.34N 2.34W
109 D3 Almont Colorado 38.40N 106.52W
106 L7 Almont Michigan 42.55N 83.02W
108 J3 Almont N Dakota 46.44N 101.30W
77 L5 Almontaras, Las Spain 37.46N 2.45W
99 O7 Almonte Ontario 45.13N 76.12W
77 C6 Almonte Spain 37.16N 6.31W
76 G9 Almonte R Spain
30 C3 Almora Uttar Prad India 29.36N 79.40E
30 C3 Almora dist Uttar Prad India
77 P4 Almoradí Spain 38.07N 0.46W
77 F3 Almorchón Spain 38.42N 5.17W
76 L8 Almorox Spain 40.14N 4.24W
76 B10 Almoster Portugal 39.15N 8.47W
110 H3 Almota Washington 46.43N 117.28W
89 K3 Almoustarat Mali 17.21N 0.08E
65 J6 Alm-see L Austria 47.45N 13.58E
75 J3 Almudébar Spain 42.03N 0.34W
52 H10 Almundsryd Sweden 56.25N 14.40E
77 J7 Almuñécar Spain 36.44N 3.41W
75 H5 Almunia de Doña Godina, La Spain 41.28N 1.23W
75 K4 Almuniente Spain 41.57N 0.24W
77 K3 Almuradiel Spain 38.31N 3.29W
76 E11 Almuro R Portugal
36 J2 Almus Turkey 40.22N 36.54E
77 Q2 Almusafes Spain 39.18N 0.25W
36 J2 Almus Barajı dam Turkey 40.23N 36.56E
52 J9 Almvik Sweden 57.49N 16.30E
110 O8 Almy Wyoming 41.20N 111.01W
42 D3 Al'myakovo U.S.S.R. 57.43N 85.34E
107 E7 Almyra Arkansas 34.24N 91.26W
58 H3 Alness Highland Scotland 57.42N 4.15W
58 H3 Alness, R Highland Scotland
39 F6 Alney, Gora mt U.S.S.R. 56.44N 159.34E
57 J2 Alnham Northumb Eng 55.24N 2.00W
88 L6 Alnif Morocco 31.07N 5.11W
57 K2 Alnmouth Northumb Eng 55.23N 1.36W
57 K2 Alnmouth B Northumb Eng 55.22N 1.35W
52 K4 Alnö Sweden 62.46N 17.30E
57 K2 Aln, R Northumb Eng
57 K2 Alnwick Northumb Eng 55.25N 1.42W
90 K6 Alo Chad 11.50N 20.52E
75 H7 Alobras Spain 40.11N 1.24W
75 E6 Alocén Spain 40.34N 2.45W
10 R4 Alofi isld Iles de Horn Pacific Oc 14.27S 178.05W
106 K4 Aloha Michigan 45.32N 84.26W
93 E3 Aloi Uganda 2.17N 33.10E
87 G4 Alomata Ethiopia 12.27N 39.35E
93 B2 Alomo Zaïre 3.11N 30.19E
25 C1 Alon Burma 22.11N 95.10E
84 R15 Alona Cyprus 34.55N 33.03E
28 K1 Along Assam India 28.10N 94.46E
Alonim see Allonim
84 G3 Alonissos Greece 39.09N 23.50E
84 D6 Alonístaina Greece 37.37N 22.13E
19 K6 Alonon Pt Philippines 12.00N 120.21E
100 T8 Alonsa Manitoba 50.48N 98.58W
19 D8 Alor isld Indonesia
77 B3 Alor mt Spain 38.37N 7.04W
77 G7 Alora Spain 36.50N 4.43W
18 C9 Alor Gajah Pen Malaysia 2.20N 102.12E
19 D7 Alor, Kep islds Indonesia
93 D3 Aloro Uganda 2.14N 32.34E
19 C8 Alor, Selat str Indonesia
18 D2 Alor Setar Pen Malaysia 6.06N 100.23E
Alos see Yoğun
75 N2 Alós Spain 42.43N 1.05E
77 B5 Alosno Spain 37.33N 7.07W
Alost see Aalst Oost Vlanderen Belgium
29 D6 Alot Madhya Prad India 23.56N 75.40E
120 E9 Alota Bolivia 21.25S 67.34W
15 L9 Alotau Papua New Guinea 10.20S 150.23E
85 A3 Alouet el Gounna Tunisia 33.13N 11.25E
88 K6 Alougoum Morocco 30.29N 6.48W
90 F8 Aloum Cameroon 6.40N 12.55E
75 D6 Alovera Spain 40.35N 3.15W
71 F2 Aloxe-Corton France 47.04N 4.53E
14 G7 Aloysius, Mt W Australia 25.58S 128.41E
77 G7 Alozaina Spain 36.44N 4.51W
47 C3 Alozero U.S.S.R. 65.02N 31.10E
75 O3 Alp Spain 42.23N 1.53E
121 D6 Alpachiri Argentina 37.24S 63.48W
76 D10 Alpalhão Portugal 39.24N 7.37W
77 F7 Alpandeire Spain 36.39N 5.12W
75 E5 Alpanseque Spain 41.15N 2.40W
75 H5 Alpartir Spain 41.25N 1.23W
111 E6 Alpaugh California 35.54N 119.29W
65 E7 Alpbach Austria 47.24N 11.58E
79 L2 Alpi Dolomitiche mts Italy
71 J6 Alpe-d'Huez France 45.05N 6.05E
76 E8 Alpedrinha Portugal 40.06N 7.27W
76 B9 Alpedriz Portugal 39.38N 8.57W
75 E5 Alpedroches Spain 41.14N 2.55W
63 E9 Alpen W Germany 51.34N 6.32E
107 C5 Alpena Arkansas 36.18N 93.19W
106 L4 Alpena Michigan 45.04N 83.27W
108 M5 Alpena S Dakota 44.11N 98.21W
104 F8 Alpena W Virginia 38.55N 79.39W
75 P3 Alpéns Spain 42.08N 2.06E
77 O3 Alpera Spain 38.57N 1.14W
77 O2 Alpera, Cueva de Spain 39.02N 1.15W
117 F8 Alpercatas, R Brazil
117 F7 Alpercatas, Sa. das mts Brazil
67 K8 Alpes-de-Haute-Provence dept France
67 K9 Alpes-Maritimes dept France
71 L9 Alpes, Route des France
82 F8 Alpet mts Albania
79 C6 Alpet, Monte Italy 44.15N 7.52E
106 D8 Alpha Illinois 41.12N 90.22W
106 F3 Alpha Michigan 46.02N 88.26W
103 D5 Alpha New Jersey 40.40N 75.11W
13 H6 Alpha Queensland 23.37S 146.37E
104 G9 Alpha Virginia 37.37N 78.25W
13 H6 Alpha R Queensland
26 B14 Alpha Kop hill Marion I Ind Oc 46.55S 37.47E
60 K12 Alphen Gelderland Netherlands 51.49N 5.29E
60 H14 Alphen Noord-Brabant Netherlands 51.28N 4.57E
60 G11 Alphen aan den Rijn Netherlands 52.08N 4.40E
56 N3 Alpheton Suffolk Eng 52.07N 0.45E
27 G11 Alphonse I Amirante Is Seychelles, Ind Oc 7.05S 52.50E
66 H7 Alphubel mt Switzerland 46.04N 7.53E
76 B10 Alpiarça Portugal 39.15N 8.35W
76 C10 Alpiarça R Portugal
66 P6 Alpi Bernina mts Switz/Italy
71 F9 Alpilles, Chaine des France
111 P8 Alpine Arizona 33.52N 109.08W
103 A2 Alpine New York 42.18N 76.44W
112 D5 Alpine Texas 30.22N 103.40W
79 B3 Alpi Pennine mts Italy
64 E7 Alpirsbach W Germany 48.20N 8.25E
66 K4 Alpnach Switzerland 46.57N 8.17E
66 K4 Alpnachstad Switzerland 46.58N 8.17E
84 B6 Alpokhóri Greece 37.44N 21.23E
76 D14 Alportel R Portugal
110 H3 Alpowa Washington 46.27N 117.19W
65 B6 Alp See L W Germany 47.35N 10.12E
66 O3 Alpstein mts Switzerland
49 F7 Alps, The Cent Europe
66 L3 Alp-Tal V Switzerland
36 E3 Alpu Turkey 39.46N 30.58E
75 H8 Alpuente Spain 39.53N 1.01W
35 J1 Alqin Syria 33.14N 36.16E
76 D12 Alqueva Portugal 38.13N 7.32W
75 L3 Alquézar Spain 42.10N 0.01E
77 M7 Alquián, El Spain 36.51N 2.20W
69 B2 Alquines France 50.44N 1.59E
72 K7 Alrance France 44.08N 2.39E
88 S7 Alrar Est Algeria 28.40N 9.43E
56 J5 Alresford Hants Eng 51.06N 1.10W
56 H2 Alrewas Staffs Eng 52.45N 1.43W
98 L6 Alright Is Madeleine Is, Que 47.27N 61.45W
53 E5 Alrø Denmark 55.52N 10.04E
53 E5 Alrø isld Denmark 55.52N 10.04E
13 D4 Alroy Downs N Terr Australia 19.19S 136.02E
53 E3 Als Denmark 56.46N 10.18E
53 E7 Als isld Denmark
67 K5 Alsace prov France
53 U18 Alsaker Norway 60.23N 6.30E
100 H7 Alsask Saskatchewan 51.22N 110.00W
75 F2 Alsasua Spain 42.54N 2.10W
61 P7 Alscheid Luxembourg 49.58N 6.00E
64 A2 Alsdorf W Germany 50.53N 6.10E
110 B5 Alsea Oregon 44.24N 123.35W
110 B5 Alsea R Oregon
101 E6 Alsek R Br Columbia
61 H4 Alsemberg Belgium 50.45N 4.20E
108 M1 Alsen N Dakota 48.39N 98.41W
103 G2 Alsen New York 42.11N 73.55W
69 O4 Alsenbrück-Langmeil W Germany 49.34N 7.54E
79 G5 Alseno Italy 44.53N 9.57E
64 D4 Alsenz W Germany 49.43N 7.49E
64 D4 Alsenz R W Germany
107 F2 Alsey Illinois 39.33N 90.28W
64 G2 Alsfeld W Germany 50.45N 9.17E
53 D6 Als Fjord inlet Denmark 55.02N 9.40E
45 Q4 Al'shanka U.S.S.R. 52.12N 44.31E
64 E4 Alsheim W Germany 49.46N 8.20E
58 E4 Alsh, L Highland Scotland 57.15N 5.36W
121 K4 Alsina Buenos Aires Arg 34.40S 58.25W
40 G4 Al'skiy Khrebet U.S.S.R.
63 P9 Alsleben E Germany 51.43N 11.40E
53 A5 Alslev Denmark 55.35N 8.25E
53 C6 Alslev Kro Denmark 55.03N 9.03E
53 W16 Alsmo Norway 61.29N 7.16E
53 F4 Alsø Denmark 56.23N 10.52E
53 D7 Als Sund inlet Denmark 54.54N 9.47E
51 C6 Alstahaug Norway 65.55N 12.25E
63 E8 Alstätte W Germany 52.07N 6.56E
104 N3 Alstead New Hampshire 43.10N 72.24W
53 B3 Alsted Denmark 56.51N 8.51E
51 C6 Alsten isld Norway 65.55N 12.35E
63 M5 Alster R W Germany
57 J3 Alston Cumbria Eng 54.49N 2.26W
12 L3 Alstonville New S Wales 28.49S 153.25E
108 P7 Alta Iowa 42.40N 95.20W
110 L4 Alta Montana 45.37N 114.18W
47 A1 Alta Norway 70.00N 23.15E
75 D2 Altable Spain 42.36N 3.05W
66 P2 Altach Austria 47.22N 9.39E
51 K2 Altaelv R Norway 69.50N 23.30E
51 K1 Altafjord inlet Norway 70.10N 23.00E
121 D3 Alta Gracia Argentina 31.42S 64.25W
115 M4 Alta Gracia Nicaragua 11.35N 85.38W
119 E2 Altagracia Venezuela 10.44N 71.30W
119 F3 Altagracía de Orituco Venezuela 9.54N 66.24W
24 F1 Altai mt ra China/Mongolia
112 L6 Altair Texas 29.34N 96.30W
39 B5 Altakan, Gora mt U.S.S.R. 59.50N 139.58E
120 E7 Altamachi Bolivia 17.00S 66.26W
120 E7 Altamachi R Bolivia
105 E6 Altamaha R Georgia
105 F6 Altamaha Sd Georgia 31.18N 81.18W
105 H1 Altamahaw N Carolina 36.11N 79.31W
119 F7 Altamira Amazonas Brazil 1.41N 67.15W
120 D11 Altamira Chile 25.30S 69.50W
119 C6 Altamira Colombia 2.04N 75.47W
115 L6 Altamíra Mexico 22.25N 97.55W
117 C6 Altamira Pará Brazil 3.13S 52.15W
76 L2 Altamira caves Spain 43.23N 4.08W
121 F5 Altamirano Argentina 35.23S 58.10W
115 N9 Altamirano Chiapas Mexico 16.48N 92.02W
115 J8 Altamirano, Ciudad Mexico 18.20N 100.40W
76 J10 Altamira, Sierra de mts Spain
111 C4 Altamont California 37.44N 121.40W
107 H2 Altamont Illinois 39.03N 88.45W
110 D7 Altamont Oregon 42.12N 121.47W
108 O5 Altamont S Dakota 44.50N 96.41W
107 L6 Altamont Tennessee 35.28N 85.42W
110 P8 Altamont Wyoming 41.11N 110.47W
11 D11 Alta, Mt New Zealand 44.30S 169.00E
81 N2 Altamura Italy 40.49N 16.34E
42 H7 Altan Chita U.S.S.R. 49.55N 109.05E
42 J7 Altan Chita U.S.S.R. 49.32N 111.35E
Altan Bulag see Altanbulag
22 G1 Altanbulag Mongolia 50.20N 106.26E
22 J4 Altan Bulag Nei Monggol Zizhiqu China 44.18N 113.20E
Altan Emel see Xin Barag Yquqi
22 K2 Altan Emel Nei Monggol Zizhiqu China 48.45N 116.55E
22 F6 Altan Obo Nei Monggol Zizhiqu China 40.21N 104.14E
81 A5 Altano, C Sardinia 39.14N 8.22E
Altan Xiret see Ejin Horo Qi
119 G3 Altapirire Venezuela 8.30N 64.25W
72 F10 Alta, Pta mt Spain 42.36N 0.54E
115 D2 Altar Mexico 30.41N 111.53W
79 D6 Altare Italy 44.20N 8.20E
75 F8 Altarejos Spain 39.54N 2.22W
96 U3 Altares Azores 38.48N 27.18W
100 G7 Altario Alberta 51.56N 110.21W
76 C11 Alta, Sa mt Portugal 38.32N 8.21W
75 G7 Alta, Sierra mt Spain 40.29N 1.36W
58 G3 Altass Highland Scotland 57.57N 4.32W
42 E3 Altat Krasnoyarsk U.S.S.R. 57.31N 91.24E
115 F5 Altata Mexico 24.40N 107.54W
45 U5 Altata U.S.S.R. 51.07N 48.44E
47 J4 Altatump U.S.S.R. 63.10N 63.40E
65 J6 Alt Aussee Austria 47.38N 13.46E
81 E8 Altavilla Sicily 37.53N 12.27E
80 L6 Altavilla Irpina Italy 41.00N 14.47E
80 M7 Altavilla Silentina Italy 40.32N 15.07E
108 S6 Alta Vista Iowa 43.12N 92.22W
109 O3 Alta Vista Kansas 38.52N 96.30W
104 F9 Altavista Virginia 37.07N 79.18W
22 D3 Altay Govĭaltay Mongolia 46.18N 96.16E
22 B3 Altay Hovd Mongolia 46.14N 92.35E
42 E5 Altay Khakass U.S.S.R. 53.27N 91.52E
47 K5 Altay Tyumen U.S.S.R. 60.15N 69.01E
24 F2 Altay Xinjiang Uygur Zizhiqu China 47.48N 88.07E
42 D6 Altay ra U.S.S.R.
Altay Kray see Altayskiy Kray terr
38 H3 Altayskiy Kray terr U.S.S.R.
42 D6 Altayskoye U.S.S.R. 52.00N 85.18E
72 H10 Alt del Grio mt Andorra 42.31N 1.39E
63 U9 Alt Döbern E Germany 51.39N 14.03E
64 L5 Altdorf Mittelfranken, Bayern W Germany 49.23N 11.22E
66 L4 Altdorf Switzerland 46.53N 8.38E
64 N6 Altdorf W Germany 48.32N 12.09E
76 C14 Alte Portugal 37.13N 8.10W
77 Q3 Altea Spain 38.37N 0.03W
63 O6 Alte Elde R E Germany
63 S4 Altefähr E Germany 54.20N 13.09E
76 D6 Altei Portugal 41.27N 7.55W
66 G6 Altels mt Switzerland 46.27N 7.41E
63 H5 Alte Mellum W Germany 53.45N 8.10E
64 D1 Altena W Germany 51.18N 7.40E
66 E1 Altenach France 47.37N 7.07E
64 B2 Altenahr W Germany 50.31N 7.00E
63 M9 Altenau W Germany 51.48N 10.25E
63 J9 Altenbeken W Germany 51.46N 8.56E
64 Q2 Altenberg E Germany 50.46N 13.46E
63 F8 Altenberge W Germany 52.02N 7.29E
63 J5 Altenbruch W Germany 53.50N 8.46E
65 N4 Altenburg Austria 48.39N 15.37E
64 N2 Altenburg E Germany 50.59N 12.27E
64 M7 Altenerding W Germany 48.15N 11.56E
64 C4 Altenglan W Germany 49.33N 7.28E
63 M4 Altenholz W Germany 54.26N 10.06E
63 S3 Altenkirchen E Germany 54.38N 13.22E
64 D2 Altenkirchen W Germany 50.41N 7.40E
65 N5 Altenmarkt Nieder-Österreich Austria 48.02N 16.00E
65 H7 Altenmarkt Salzburg Austria 47.23N 13.26E
65 L6 Altenmarkt Steiermark Austria 47.44N 14.39E
64 O7 Altenmarkt W Germany 48.00N 12.33E
64 P6 Altenmarkt W Germany 48.35N 13.01E
63 N6 Alten Medingen W Germany 53.08N 10.36E
24 H7 Altenqoke Qinghai China 36.27N 94.45E
66 P2 Altenstadt Austria 47.16N 9.37E
64 H6 Altenstadt Baden-Württemberg W Germany 48.38N 9.49E
64 F3 Altenstadt Hessen W Ger 50.17N 8.56E
64 F6 Altensteig W Germany 48.35N 8.36E
63 S5 Altentreptow E Germany 53.42N 13.15E
64 C1 Altenvörde W Germany 51.18N 7.23E
63 J5 Altenwalde W Germany 53.49N 8.40E
117 B6 Alter do Chão Brazil 2.30S 54.58W
76 D10 Alter do Chão Portugal 39.12N 7.40W
53 Y14 Alterhø mt Norway 62.18N 8.01E
66 F4 Alterswil Switzerland 46.48N 7.16E
81 H8 Altesina Mte Sicily 37.40N 14.17E
63 R8 Altes Lager E Germany 52.02N 12.58E
51 G3 Altevatn L Norway 68.35N 19.20E
60 O9 Alteveer Netherlands 52.41N 6.28E
60 L12 Altforst Netherlands 51.51N 5.34E
105 B7 Altha Florida 30.33N 85.09W
65 H5 Altheim Austria 48.15N 13.14E
64 J6 Altheim W Germany 48.34N 10.02E
107 E7 Altheimer Arkansas 34.19N 91.51W
65 K8 Althofen Austria 46.53N 14.29E
56 N4 Althorne Essex Eng 51.40N 0.45E
57 M5 Althorpe Humberside Eng 53.35N 0.45W
12 D6 Althorpe Is S Australia 35.13S 136.12E
37 E9 Altibasak Turkey 36.51N 39.01E
12 G3 Altiboullin, L New S Wales 29.50S 142.50E
71 D8 Altier France 44.28N 3.51E
72 H6 Altillac France 44.59N 1.51E
31 E4 Altimur Pass Afghanistan 33.44N 69.11E
37 G8 Altındağ Silsilesi mts Turkey
34 M3 Altin Köprü Iraq 35.45N 44.09E
79 M3 Altino Italy 45.33N 12.24E
36 B3 Altınoluk Turkey 39.37N 26.43E
36 B3 Altınova Turkey 39.12N 26.47E
36 J6 Altınözü Turkey 36.04N 36.15E
37 C1 Altıntaş Edirne Turkey 41.01N 26.42E
36 E3 Altıntaş Kütahya Turkey 39.05N 30.07E
120 D7 Alti Plano plat Peru/Bolivia
66 H3 Altishofen Switzerland 47.13N 7.58E
79 K1 Altissima, l' mt Italy 46.47N 11.02E
63 O6 Alt-Jabel E Germany 53.16N 11.10E
63 T6 Alt Käbelich E Germany 53.30N 13.30E
71 L1 Altkirch France 47.38N 7.15E
63 T7 Altlandsberg E Germany 52.34N 13.45E
64 E5 Altleiningen W Germany 49.30N 8.05E
66 O3 Altmann mt Switzerland 47.15N 9.23E
64 M6 Altmannstein W Germany 48.54N 11.40E
104 J3 Altmar New York 43.31N 76.02W
63 O7 Altmark reg E Germany
64 H1 Altmorschen W Germany 51.04N 9.37E
64 K5 Altmühl R W Germany
63 K7 Altmühlen W Germany 52.45N 9.04E
65 J6 Altmünster Austria 47.53N 13.46E
58 G2 Altnacealgach Highland Scotland 58.03N 4.56W
58 H2 Altnaharra Highland Scotland 58.16N 4.26W
66 O1 Altnau Switzerland 47.37N 9.16E
112 M4 Alto Texas 31.40N 95.08W
79 J3 Alto Adige reg Italy
74 B6 Alto Alentejo prov Portugal
118 D5 Alto Araguaia Brazil 17.19S 53.10W
116 G4 Alto Cedro Cuba 20.33N 75.58W
120 D4 Alto Chandless R Peru
91 F9 Alto Chicapa Angola 10.52S 19.17E
118 C4 Alto Coité Brazil 15.44S 54.15W
75 F4 Alto Cruz mt Spain 41.30N 2.03W
115 O10 Alto Cuchumatanes ra Guatemala
91 F9 Alto Cuilo Angola 10.04S 19.36E
118 J10 Alto da Bôa Vista Brazil 22.58S 43.17W
118 G10 Alto da Moóca dist São Paulo Brazil
76 L7 Alto de los Leones hill Spain 40.41N 4.08W
121 C4 Alto de Pencoso mts Argentina
76 C3 Alto de Santo Domingo pass Spain 42.34N 8.01W
81 C4 Alto di Flumendosa, L Sardinia 39.57N 9.28E
81 F7 Altofonte Sicily 38.03N 13.18E
118 D5 Alto Garças Brazil 16.57S 53.30W
87 J9 Alto Giuba prov Somalia
91 D10 Alto Hama Angola 12.11S 15.32E
92 J9 Alto Ligonha Mozambique 15.31S 38.14E
117 F7 Alto Longa Brazil 5.16S 42.15W
75 E7 Altomira, Sierra de mts Spain
92 H9 Alto Molocue Mozambique 15.38S 37.42E
79 D6 Alto, Monte Italy 44.16N 8.19E
81 M4 Altomonte Italy 39.42N 16.09E
64 L7 Altomünster W Germany 48.22N 11.15E
110 A9 Alton California 40.34N 124.08W
56 K5 Alton Hants Eng 51.09N 0.59W
107 F3 Alton Illinois 38.55N 90.10W
108 P7 Alton Iowa 42.59N 96.00W
109 M2 Alton Kansas 39.29N 98.56W
107 E5 Alton Missouri 36.41N 91.25W
104 O3 Alton New Hampshire 43.29N 71.14W
104 J3 Alton New York 43.13N 76.59W
111 M4 Alton Utah 37.27N 112.29W
106 D8 Altona Illinois 41.07N 90.10W
100 U9 Altona Manitoba 49.06N 97.35W
104 M2 Altona New York 44.54N 73.40W
Altona W Germany see Hamburg
12 B8 Altona dist Melbourne, Vic
12 B8 Altona B Victoria Australia
110 P9 Altonah Utah 40.26N 110.17W
12 E2 Alton Downs S Australia 26.04S 138.51E
121 A10 Alto Nevado mt Chile 44.30S 72.18W
107 K7 Altoona Alabama 34.02N 86.20W
105 F9 Altoona Florida 29.00N 81.39W
108 R8 Altoona Iowa 41.38N 93.26W
109 P4 Altoona Kansas 37.32N 95.40W
104 G6 Altoona Pennsylvania 40.32N 78.23W
117 D6 Alto Pacajá, R Brazil
118 B7 Alto Paraguay dept Paraguay
118 C9 Alto Paraná dept Paraguay
117 E9 Alto Parnaiba Brazil 9.08S 45.56W
79 J7 Altopascio Italy 43.48N 10.41E
87 M6 Altopiano del Shol reg Somalia
120 D4 Alto Purús, R Peru
76 C5 Alto Rabagro, Barragem do res Portugal 41.35N 8.07W
121 K5 Alto Río Senguerr Argentina 45.01S 70.55W
75 L4 Altorricón Spain 41.48N 0.24E
117 F7 Altos Brazil 5.03S 42.28W
120 D8 Altos de Chacaya Chile 18.48S 69.45W
77 N3 Altos de Chinchilla hills Spain
118 D6 Alto Sucuriú Brazil 19.23S 52.39W
75 C2 Altoteiro mt Spain 42.41N 3.31W
115 L8 Altotonga Mexico 19.46N 97.14W
64 O7 Altötting W Germany 48.13N 12.41E
121 G1 Alto Uruguai Brazil 27.20S 54.05W
116 A1 Alto Vista mt Aruba W I 12.34N 70.02W
120 D4 Alto Yaco R Peru
63 U7 Altranft E Germany 52.46N 14.06E
63 U7 Altreetz E Germany 52.45N 14.10E
57 J6 Altrincham Greater Manchester Eng 53.24N 2.21W
63 R7 Altruppin E Germany 52.58N 12.52E
66 O3 Alt St. Johann Switzerland 47.12N 9.17E
63 T8 Alt-Schadow E Germany 52.08N 13.58E
64 H8 Altshausen W Germany 47.55N 9.33E
66 P2 Altstatten Switzerland 47.22N 9.33E
75 E1 Altube R Spain
45 F4 Altukhovo U.S.S.R. 52.40N 34.20E
121 L6 Altuna Argentina 46.15S 67.47W
115 P9 Altun Ha hist site Belize 17.46N 88.22W
24 G6 Altun Shan mt pk Xinjiang Uygur Zizhiqu China
106 C5 Altura Minnesota 44.04N 91.56W
75 J8 Altura Spain 39.51N 0.32W
110 E8 Alturas California 41.30N 120.34W
105 F10 Alturas Florida 27.53N 81.44W
76 D5 Alturas de Barroso Portugal 41.42N 7.50W
76 D5 Alturas, Sa. de Portugal
109 L7 Altus Oklahoma 34.39N 99.21W
109 L7 Altus Res Oklahoma
64 J8 Altusried W Germany 47.49N 10.12E
69 M6 Altwiller France 48.56N 6.59E
44 J7 Altyagach Azerbaydzhan U.S.S.R. 40.50N 48.54E
43 N8 Alty-Aryk Uzbekistan U.S.S.R. 40.26N 71.29E
43 G4 Altynasar ruins Kazakhstan U.S.S.R. 45.11N 63.06E
47 J7 Altynay U.S.S.R. 57.10N 61.54E
43 O7 Altynkul' Uzbekistan U.S.S.R. 40.49N 72.12E
43 J6 Altyn-Topkan Tadzhikistan U.S.S.R. 40.38N 69.40E
45 S2 Altyshevo U.S.S.R. 54.54N 46.44E
92 J8 Alua Mozambique 13.56S 39.55E
87 C7 Aluakluak Sudan 6.29N 30.11E
39 H2 Aluchina R U.S.S.R.
37 D5 Alucra Turkey 40.20N 38.43E
87 A6 Aluk Sudan 8.25N 27.30E
35 G5 'Aluk, El Jordan 32.10N 35.55E
46 F2 Alūksne Latvia U.S.S.R. 57.22N 27.00E
87 N5 Alūla Somalia 11.59N 50.48E
53 D4 Ålum Denmark 56.56N 9.51E
32 C4 Alūm Iran 32.50N 49.25E
56 H6 Alum B I of Wight Eng 50.40N 1.34W
121 B7 Aluminé Argentina 39.15S 71.00W
121 B7 Aluminé, L Argentina 38.55S 71.10W
121 B7 Aluminé, R Argentina
51 J6 Ålund Sweden 65.09N 21.00E
52 L6 Alunda Sweden 60.04N 18.05E
111 K6 Alunite Nevada 35.58N 114.55W
44 C10 Alupka Ukraine U.S.S.R. 44.26N 34.02E
28 C3 Alur Andhra Prad India 15.24N 77.15E
93 E3 Alur mt Uganda 2.42N 33.43E
Aluri see 'Alavi
87 E7 Aluro watercourse Ethiopia
44 C10 Alushta Ukraine U.S.S.R. 44.41N 34.24E
75 G6 Alustante Spain 40.36N 1.40W
34 N3 Alūt Iran 36.00N 45.35E
37 D8 Alut Turkey 37.57N 38.39E
26 Q9 Alutgama Sri Lanka 6.26N 80.00E
19 L1 Alutom mt Guam Pacific Oc 13.26N 144.43E
19 L1 Alutom I Guam Pacific Oc 13.23N 144.38E
26 S5 Alut Oya Sri Lanka 8.13N 80.52E
85 D4 Al 'Uwayjah Libya 30.55N 17.50E
58 J6 Alva Central Scotland 56.09N 3.49W
105 F11 Alva Florida 26.43N 81.37W
105 D1 Alva Kentucky 36.45N 83.25W
109 M5 Alva Oklahoma 36.48N 98.40W
76 D7 Alva Portugal 40.52N 7.57W
108 F5 Alva Wyoming 44.40N 104.25W
76 C8 Alva R Portugal
76 B9 Alvados Portugal 39.33N 8.46W
76 C9 Alvaiázere Portugal 39.49N 8.23W
76 C13 Alvalade Portugal 37.56N 8.24W
76 D16 Alvalade Portugal 38.44N 9.09W
32 C3 Alvand, Kūh-e mt Iran 34.40N 48.32E
66 P5 Alvaneu Switzerland 46.41N 9.39E
57 H6 Alvanley Cheshire Eng 53.16N 2.45W
76 D6 Alvão, Sa. do mts Portugal
115 M8 Alvarado Mexico 18.47N 95.45W
112 K3 Alvarado Texas 32.25N 97.14W
121 B5 Alvarado, Paso de pass Arg/Chile 34.05S 69.56W
119 G9 Alvarães Brazil 3.14S 64.51W
76 B5 Alvarães Portugal 41.38N 8.45W
76 C8 Alvares Portugal 40.03N 8.07W
121 E4 Alvarez Argentina 33.10S 60.48W
Alvarez, Ciudad Doctor Hernández see San Felipe
76 D9 Alvaro Portugal 39.58N 7.58W
81 A2 Alvaro, Mte Sardinia 40.47N 8.20E
56 J2 Alvaston Derbys Eng 52.54N 1.25W
52 F4 Alvdal Norway 62.06N 10.42E
52 H5 Älvdalen Sweden 61.14N 14.05E
121 G2 Alvear Argentina 29.05S 56.35W
56 H3 Alvechurch Hereford & Worcs Eng 52.21N 1.57W
76 C10 Alvega Portugal 39.28N 8.03W
100 L6 Alvena Saskatchewan 52.32N 106.01W
63 O8 Alvensleben E Germany 52.16N 11.21E
53 T16 Alvera Norway 61.07N 5.34E
76 A11 Alverca Portugal 38.56N 9.01W
63 K8 Alverdissen W Germany 52.03N 9.07E
61 A2 Alveringem Belgium 51.01N 2.43E
60 M12 Alverna Netherlands 51.48N 5.45E
101 D5 Alverstone, Mt Yukon/Alaska 60.23N 139.00W
53 S17 Alversund Norway 60.35N 5.14E
58 K3 Alves Grampian Scotland 57.38N 3.28W
52 H10 Alvesta Sweden 56.54N 14.35E
56 F4 Alveston Avon Eng 51.36N 2.32W
52 H5 Älvho Sweden 61.30N 14.45E
50 G8 Alvidhruhamrar coast Iceland
76 B10 Alviella, Canal de Portugal
66 O3 Alvier mt Switzerland 47.07N 9.25E
72 H6 Alvignac-les-Eaux France 44.50N 1.40E
53 U18 Ålvik, Indre Norway 60.26N 6.26E
53 U18 Ålvik, Ytre Norway 60.25N 6.21E
106 G9 Alvin Illinois 40.19N 87.37W
112 M6 Alvin Texas 29.25N 95.16W
106 F4 Alvin Wisconsin 46.00N 88.47W
99 J10 Alvinston Ontario 42.48N 81.52W
76 J4 Alvires Spain 42.14N 5.15W
80 J5 Alvito Italy 41.41N 13.45E
76 D12 Alvito Portugal 38.15N 8.00W
76 D9 Alvito R Portugal
52 K6 Älvkarleby Sweden 60.35N 17.30E
108 O9 Alvo Nebraska 40.55N 96.22W
76 B14 Alvor Portugal 37.08N 8.35W
121 J1 Alvorado isld Brazil
112 K2 Alvord Texas 33.22N 97.43W
110 G7 Alvord Des Oregon
110 G7 Alvord L Oregon 42.24N 118.36W
118 E10 Alvoredo Lt. Ho. Brazil 27.15S 48.23W
53 S18 Alvøy Norway 60.21N 5.13E
53 R17 Alvøy isld Norway 60.37N 4.50E
52 H4 Älvros Jämtland Sweden 62.03N 14.40E
52 G5 Älvros Kopparberg Sweden 61.50N 12.55E
52 G9 Älvsborg dist Sweden
51 J6 Älvsbyn Sweden 65.41N 21.00E
52 G9 Älvsered Sweden 57.15N 12.52E
108 Q2 Alvwood Minnesota 47.43N 94.16W
34 N4 Alwand R Iran/Iraq
Alwand, Kūh-i- see Alvand, Kūh-e mt
29 E4 Alwar Rajasthan India 27.32N 76.35E
29 E4 Alwar dist Rajasthan India
28 C6 Alwar Tirunagari Tamil Nadu India 8.36N 77.57E
28 C5 Alwaye Kerala India 10.06N 76.23E
57 F6 Alwen Res Clwyd Wales 53.05N 3.35W
57 J2 Alwinton Northumb Eng 55.21N 2.07W
54 M2 Alwyn oil field North Sea 60.33N 1.36E
22 E7 Alxa Youqi Nei Monggol Zizhiqu China 39.12N 101.40E
22 G7 Alxa Zuoqi Nei Monggol Zizhiqu China 38.58N 105.35E
107 C7 Aly Arkansas 34.48N 93.28W
33 C5 'Alyā Saudi Arabia 23.47N 38.56E
43 N7 Alyame Uzbekistan U.S.S.R. 40.47N 71.10E
37 F8 Alyan Turkey 37.11N 41.48E
13 D2 Alyangula N Terr Aust 13.38S 136.26E
39 C3 Alyaskitovyy U.S.S.R. 64.45N 141.34E
44 J8 Alyat Azerbaydzhan U.S.S.R. 39.57N 49.25E
46 P8 Alyat Azerbaydzhan U.S.S.R. 39.59N 49.20E
42 F5 Alygdzher U.S.S.R. 53.40N 98.15E
47 K6 Alymka R U.S.S.R.
39 A1 Alysardakh Yakutsk U.S.S.R. 67.45N 134.41E
39 B4 Alysardakh Yakutsk U.S.S.R. 61.18N 138.08E
41 O7 Alysardakh Yakutsk U.S.S.R. 65.58N 131.29E
39 B2 Alys-Khaya U.S.S.R. 65.50N 135.28E
39 C1 Alysy-Garakh U.S.S.R. 68.11N 142.05E
58 K5 Alyth Tayside Scotland 56.38N 3.14W
46 E3 Alytus Lithuania U.S.S.R. 54.24N 24.03E
39 E2 Aly-Yuryakh R U.S.S.R.
64 O7 Alz R W Germany
108 F4 Alzada Montana 45.01N 104.26W
121 F6 Alzaga Argentina 37.50S 59.59W
42 F4 Alzamay U.S.S.R. 55.33N 98.40E
79 G3 Alzano Lombardo Italy 45.44N 9.43E
89 A1 Alzas Mauritania 20.22N 16.18W
79 F3 Alzate Italy 45.46N 9.11E
64 G3 Alzenau W Germany 50.05N 9.05E
61 P8 Alzette R Luxembourg
64 E4 Alzey W Germany 49.44N 8.07E
66 K8 Alzo Italy 45.47N 8.23E
75 F1 Alzola Spain 43.15N 2.22W
71 C9 Alzon France 43.58N 3.27E
72 J9 Alzonne France 43.15N 2.11E
30 F6 Ama Uttar Prad India 26.53N 82.39E
39 K3 Amaama U.S.S.R. 62.35N 179.26E
20 J4 Amaariki Chiba Japan
87 E2 Amab watercourse Sudan
95 L8 Amabele S Africa 32.40S 27.32E
90 D8 Amachi Nigeria 6.37N 8.32E
120 A2 Amachonga, Cerros de hills Peru
119 H3 Amacuro, R Venez/Guyana
30 J3 Ama Dablam mt Nepal 27.52N 86.52E
30 J3 Ama Dablam Glacier Nepal
90 G9 Amada Gaza Cent African Rep 4.46N 15.09E
13 B6 Amadeus,L N Terr Australia
87 C8 Amadi Sudan 5.32N 30.20E
87 A9 Amadi Zaïre 3.38N 26.46E
37 G8 Amādiyah Iraq 37.06N 43.29E
97 M4 Amadjuak L N W Terr 65.00N 71.00W
76 A11 Amadora Portugal 38.45N 9.13W
121 D2 Amadores Argentina 28.16S 65.36W
88 R9 Amadror reg Algeria
119 C4 Amaga Colombia 6.02N 75.43W
103 K5 Amagansett Long I, N Y 40.58N 72.07W
20 J7 Amagasaki Japan 34.42N 135.23E
90 C7 Amagede Nigeria 8.00N 7.35E
53 K5 Amager isld Denmark 55.35N 12.35E
20 D8 Amagi Japan 33.28N 130.37E
20 M7 Amagi-san mts Japan
69 H4 Amagne France 49.31N 4.30E
19 F5 Amahai Moluccas Indon 3.19S 128.56E
119 J5 Amaila Falls Guyana 5.25N 59.36W
70 L4 Amain, Mt. d' France 48.40N 0.20E
33 E6 Amā'ir Saudi Arabia 21.20N 43.00E
39 D5 Amakhtonskiy Zaliv B U.S.S.R.
113 F9 Amak I Alaska 55.25N 163.10W
41 K5 Amakinskiy 70.60N 114.07E
20 C9 Amakusa-nada sea Japan
20 D9 Amakusa-shotō islds Japan
52 G7 Åmål Sweden 59.04N 12.41E
28 F2 Amalapuram Andhra Prad India 16.36N 82.03E
42 J5 Amalat R U.S.S.R.
119 C4 Amalfi Colombia 6.54N 75.04W
80 L7 Amalfi Italy 40.37N 14.36E
95 J3 Amalia S Africa 27.15S 25.04E
84 E3 Amaliápolis Greece 39.10N 22.54E
84 B6 Amaliás Greece 37.48N 21.21E
85 F5 Amal Nafoora Libya 29.25N 21.10E
28 B1 Amalner Bir, Maharashtra India 18.57N 75.24E
29 D7 Amalner Jalgaon, Maharashtra India 21.01N 75.09E
93 A4 Amalutu Zaïre 1.02N 29.12E
119 B10 Amaluza Ecuador 4.37S 79.27W
118 C8 Amambaí Brazil 23.03S 55.16W
118 C8 Amambaí, R Brazil
118 C8 Amambaí, Serra de mts Brazil/Paraguay
118 C8 Amambay dept Paraguay
21 C13 Amami Guntō arch Japan
21 D12 Amami Ō shima isld Japan
92 C2 Amamula Zaïre 0.17S 27.49E
121 C3 Amana Argentina 30.02S 67.29W
119 G3 Amana R Venezuela
15 F5 Amanab Papua New Guinea 3.38S 141.16E
119 G9 Amanã L Brazil
69 L8 Amance France 47.48N 6.04E
71 J2 Amancey France 47.02N 6.05E
104 C7 Amanda Ohio 39.38N 82.44W
92 E10 Amandas Zimbabwe 17.24S 31.00E
80 H3 Amandola Italy 42.58N 13.22E
30 D8 Amanganj Madhya Prad India 24.25N 80.02E
43 H2 Amangel'dy Kazakhstan U.S.S.R. 50.12N 65.11E
92 J4 Amani Tanzania 5.09S 38.36E
30 E6 Amaniganj Uttar Prad India 26.40N 81.46E
39 F5 Amanino U.S.S.R. 58.07N 158.45E
43 G2 Amankaragay Kazakhstan U.S.S.R. 52.28N 64.04E
20 J6 Amano-hashidate sand bar Japan
43 F4 Amanotkel' Kazakhstan U.S.S.R. 46.05N 61.30E
81 M5 Amantea Italy 39.08N 16.05E
122 E15 Amanu atoll Tuamotu Is Pacific Oc 17.48S 140.44W
Amanus Mts see Gâvur Dağları
69 L5 Amanvillers France 49.10N 6.03E
95 O6 Amanzimtoti S Africa 30.03S 30.53E
117 D3 Amapá Brazil 2.00N 50.50W
120 D4 Amapa Brazil 10.20S 69.35W
117 C4 Amapá state Brazil
115 Q11 Amapala Honduras 13.16N 87.39W
117 C4 Amapari R Brazil
35 F9 'Amaqa Jordan 31.03N 35.42E
19 G6 Amar Moluccas Indonesia 4.30S 131.39E
90 E7 Amar Nigeria 8.43N 10.26E
30 A7 Amar R Madhya Prad India
87 E3 Amara Abu Sin Sudan 15.20N 34.49E
34 P7 'Amārah, Al Iraq 31.51N 47.10E
33 B8 'Amar, Al Bahrain, The Gulf 25.59N 50.33E
33 F4 'Amār, Al Saudi Arabia 25.35N 44.25E
121 H3 Amaral Ferrador Brazil 30.47S 52.16W
92 G9 Amaramba, L Mozambique 14.25S 35.55E
117 F8 Amarante Brazil 6.14S 42.51W
76 C6 Amarante Portugal 41.16N 8.05W
117 E7 Amarante do Maranhão Brazil 5.35S 46.50W
100 T8 Amaranth Manitoba 50.36N 98.43W
25 D2 Amarapura Burma 21.54N 96.01E
85 N10 Amarâr tribe Sudan
28 E2 Amaravati Andhra Prad Ind 16.35N 80.20E
28 C5 Amaravati R Tamil Nadu India
85 L9 Amara West Sudan 20.50N 30.29E
76 E12 Amareleja Portugal 38.12N 7.13W
76 C5 Amares Portugal 41.37N 8.22W

30 B7 **Amargarh** Uttar Prad India 25.42N 78.54E
90 M4 **Amar Gedid** Sudan 14.27N 25.13E
118 H3 **Amargosa** Brazil 13.01S 39.37W
111 H6 **Amargosa** *R* California
111 H5 **Amargosa Des** Nevada
111 H5 **Amargosa Ra** California
77 K2 **Amarguillo** *R* Spain
96 U7 **Amarilla, Montaña** Graciosa Canary Is 29.13N 13.33W
112 C8 **Amarillo** Texas 35.14N 101.50W
121 B4 **Amarillo, Cerro** *pk* Argentina 32.05S 70.02W
84 G5 **Amárinthos** Greece 38.23N 23.53E
29 G6 **Amarkantak** Madhya Prad Ind 22.40N 81.48E
79 O2 **Amaro** Italy 46.23N 13.06E
118 E3 **Amaro Leite** Goiás Brazil 13.54S 49.12W
117 E9 **Amaro Leite** Maranhão Brazil 8.55S 46.49W
80 K4 **Amaro, Monte** Italy 42.05N 14.06E
13 E6 **Amaroo,L** Queensland 23.30S 138.40E
84 G5 **Amaroúsion** Greece 38.03N 23.48E
30 D8 **Amarpatan** Madhya Prad Ind 24.18N 80.59E
30 K7 **Amarpur** Bhagalpur, Bihar India 25.02N 86.55E
30 H6 **Amarpur** Saran, Bihar India 26.06N 84.06E
87 H3 **Amarti** Ethiopia 14.18N 41.12E
15 B4 **Amaru, Danau** *L* Irian Jaya 1.17S 132.12E
20 N3 **Amarume** Japan 38.50N 139.55E
29 F6 **Amarwara** Madhya Prad Ind 22.20N 79.12E
30 H8 **Amas** Bihar India 24.38N 84.39E
106 F3 **Amasa** Michigan 46.15N 88.26W
80 H6 **Amaseno** Italy 41.28N 13.20E
44 F7 **Amasiya** Armenia U.S.S.R. 40.56N 43.45E
36 F1 **Amasra** Turkey 41.44N 32.24E
90 C9 **Amassama** Nigeria 5.02N 6.07E
36 H2 **Amasya** Turkey 40.37N 35.50E
115 N9 **Amatán** Mexico 17.22N 92.49W
119 J9 **Amatari** Brazil 3.15S 58.54W
119 F9 **Amataurá** Brazil 3.20S 68.06W
115 N9 **Amatenango** Mexico 16.30N 92.26W
84 R15 **Amathus** Cyprus 34.42N 33.09E
113 P10 **Amatignak I** Aleutian Is 51.19N 179.10W
95 O10 **Amatikulu** S Africa 29.03S 31.33E
115 P9 **Amatique, B. de** Hond/Guatemala/Belize
115 H7 **Amatitán** Mexico 20.50N 103.40W
115 L8 **Amatlán** Mexico 18.50N 96.54W
115 G7 **Amatlán de Cañas** Mexico 20.50N 104.25W
95 K8 **Amatole Ra** S Africa
80 H3 **Amatrice** Italy 42.38N 13.17E
28 J2 **Amatulla** Assam India 26.59N 92.06E
15 K9 **Amau** Papua New Guinea 10.02S 148.40E
117 C4 **Amauerapucú** *R* Brazil
30 D6 **Amauli** Uttar Prad India 26.01N 80.18E
103 G4 **Amawalk** New York 41.18N 73.45W
30 G7 **Amawan** Bihar India 25.06N 83.27E
61 M4 **Amay** Belgium 50.33N 5.19E
76 L3 **Amaya** *mt* Spain 42.39N 4.09W
40 B5 **Amazar** U.S.S.R. 53.51N 120.46E
40 B5 **Amazar** *R* U.S.S.R.
100 M7 **Amazon** Saskatchewan 51.31N 105.28W
Amazon *R see* **Amazonas** *R*
120 A1 **Amazonas** *dept* Peru
119 E8 **Amazonas** *div* Colombia
117 C5 **Amazonas** *R* Brazil etc
119 F10 **Amazonas** *state* Brazil
119 F6 **Amazonas** *state* Venezuela
15 K9 **Amazon B** Papua New Guinea 10.20S 149.25E
107 B2 **Amazonia** Missouri 39.54N 94.53W
117 D4 **Amazon, Mouths of the** Brazil
120 B4 **Amazon, Source of the** Peru 10.27S 76.43W
35 C7 **Amazya** Israel 31.32N 34.54E
35 E10 **Amazyahu** *watercourse* Israel
31 G3 **Amb** Pakistan 34.20N 72.52E
42 C4 **Amba** U.S.S.R. 55.22N 82.46E
87 G4 **Amba Alagi** *mt* Ethiopia 12.59N 39.40E
87 F3 **Amba Birkutan** *mt* Ethiopia 14.09N 37.20E
91 D8 **Ambaca** Angola 9.15S 15.15E
29 D8 **Ambad** Maharashtra India 19.38N 75.50E
87 B6 **Ambadi,L** Sudan 8.42N 29.22E
87 G5 **Amba Farit** *mt* Ethiopia 10.55N 38.50E
30 B6 **Ambah** Madhya Prad India 26.43N 78.13E
95 A6 **Ambahikily** Madagascar 21.37S 43.40E
95 B8 **Ambahita** Madagascar 24.00S 45.15E
95 D6 **Ambahona** Madagascar 21.34S 48.06E
30 A3 **Ambahta** Uttar Prad India 29.51N 77.20E
95 D6 **Ambahy** Madagascar 20.45S 48.30E
15 D4 **Ambai, Pulau Pulau** *islds* Irian Jaya 1.55S 136.22E
28 C1 **Ambajogai** Maharashtra India 18.44N 76.23E
87 F2 **Ambakta** *watercourse* Ethiopia
30 A2 **Ambala** Haryana India 30.19N 76.49E
30 A2 **Ambala** *dist* Haryana India
95 C3 **Ambalabe** Madagascar 15.45S 46.58E
95 D5 **Ambalabe** Madagascar 19.15S 48.37E
95 C7 **Ambalafary** Madagascar 23.14S 47.25E
95 C3 **Ambalakida** Madagascar 15.41S 46.31E
95 C6 **Ambalamalemy** Madagascar 21.03S 46.30E
26 R9 **Ambalangoda** Sri Lanka 6.14N 80.03E
95 C4 **Ambalanjanakomby** Madagascar 16.40S 47.05E
26 T9 **Ambalantota** Sri Lanka 6.07N 81.01E
95 D5 **Ambalarondra** Madagascar 18.27S 49.00E
95 C6 **Ambalavao** Madagascar 21.50S 46.56E
119 D5 **Ambalema** Colombia 4.49N 74.48W
13 C6 **Ambalindum** N Terr Aust 23.10S 134.54E
91 B2 **Ambam** Cameroon 2.23N 11.17E
26 S6 **Amban Ganga** *R* Sri Lanka
95 D2 **Ambanja** Madagascar 13.40S 48.27E
26 R6 **Ambanpola** Sri Lanka 7.54N 80.15E
32 H5 **Ambar** Iran 31.54N 58.46E
120 B4 **Ambar** Peru 10.45S 77.14W
41 F6 **Ambar** U.S.S.R. 68.24N 90.43E
95 C7 **Ambararata** Madagascar 22.20S 46.14E
18 J9 **Ambarawa** Java Indonesia 7.12S 110.30E
42 F4 **Ambarchik** Krasnoyarsk U.S.S.R. 55.08N 95.51E
39 G1 **Ambarchik** Yakutsk U.S.S.R. 69.39N 162.27E
39 G1 **Ambarchik, Bukhta** *gulf* U.S.S.R.
41 P4 **Ambardakh** U.S.S.R. 74.50N 139.40E
72 C6 **Ambarès-et-Lagrave** France 44.57N 0.30W
47 C3 **Ambarnyy** U.S.S.R. 65.59N 33.53E
28 H4 **Ambāsa** Tripura India 23.56N 91.52E
28 C6 **Ambasamudram** Tamil Nadu India 8.45N 77.27E
18 D9 **Ambat** *R* Pen Malaysia
13 H7 **Ambathala** Queensland 26.00S 145.20E
119 B8 **Ambato** Ecuador 1.18S 78.39W
95 C4 **Ambato-Boény** Madagascar 16.26S 46.43E
95 C6 **Ambatofinandrahana** Madagascar 20.33S 46.48E
95 B5 **Ambatolahy** Madagascar 20.00S 45.30E
95 C5 **Ambatolampy** Madagascar 19.21S 47.27E
95 C6 **Ambatomainty** Fianarantsoa Madagascar 21.59S 46.47E
95 B4 **Ambatomainty** Majunga Madagascar 17.40S 45.39E
95 C5 **Ambatomanoina** Madagascar 18.18S 47.37E
95 C5 **Ambatomiady** Madagascar 19.40S 47.25E
95 D4 **Ambatondrazaka** Madagascar 17.49S 48.28E
121 C2 **Ambato, Sa** *ra* Argentina
95 D4 **Ambatosoratra** Madagascar 17.34S 48.32E
95 B7 **Ambatry** Madagascar 23.50S 44.24E
28 C5 **Ambatturai** Tamil Nadu India 10.18N 77.57E
72 G4 **Ambazac** France 45.57N 1.22E
31 G3 **Ambela** Pakistan 34.26N 72.32E
84 G6 **Ambeláki** Greece 37.57N 23.31E
84 E2 **Ambelákia** Greece 39.51N 22.33E
19 E5 **Ambelau** *isld* Moluccas Indon 3.50S 127.13E
84 E3 **Ambélia** Greece 39.19N 22.30E
84 B6 **Ambelókambos** Greece 37.50N 21.19E
84 D2 **Ambelón** Greece 39.45N 22.22E
84 K12 **Ambelos** Crete 34.50N 24.03E
26 R7 **Ambepussa** Sri Lanka 7.14N 80.14E
106 C7 **Amber** Iowa 42.07N 91.06W
109 N6 **Amber** Oklahoma 35.10N 97.53W
29 D4 **Amber** Rajasthan India 27.00N 75.51E
110 H2 **Amber** Washington 47.22N 117.42W
113 J8 **Amber B** Alaska
106 G4 **Amberg** Wisconsin 45.31N 87.59W
57 L6 **Ambergate** Derbys Eng 53.03N 1.29W
64 M5 **Amberg in der Oberpfalz** W Germany 49.26N 11.52E
115 Q8 **Ambergris Cay** *isld* Belize
116 J4 **Ambergris Cays** *islds* Bahamas 21.20N 71.40W
71 G5 **Ambérieu-en-Bugey** France 45.57N 5.21E
11 G10 **Amberley** New Zealand 43.09S 172.46E
99 J8 **Amberley** Ontario 44.02N 81.44W
61 N6 **Amberloup** Belgium 50.02N 5.32E
25 M8 **Amber Mines** Burma
72 E2 **Amberre** France 46.46N 0.11E
71 D5 **Ambert** France 45.33N 3.45E
72 C5 **Ambès** France 45.01N 0.32W
31 G3 **Ambesh** Kashmir 35.56N 72.45E
95 C3 **Ambevongo** Madagascar 15.27S 47.27E
29 G7 **Ambgaon** Maharashtra India 20.38N 80.00E
72 J8 **Ambialet** France 43.57N 2.22E
89 D4 **Ambidédi** Mali 14.35N 11.47W
71 D4 **Ambierle** France 46.07N 3.54E
29 H6 **Ambikapur** Madhya Prad India 23.09N 83.12E
29 C7 **Ambika R** Gujarat India
25 L9 **Ambikol** Sudan 21.20N 30.50E
19 K5 **Ambil** *isld* Philippines 13.49N 120.16E
95 D5 **Ambila-Lemaitso** Madagascar 18.49S 49.09E
70 L7 **Ambillou** France 47.27N 0.27E
95 D2 **Ambilobe** Madagascar 13.10S 49.03E
95 D6 **Ambinanindrano** Madagascar 20.04S 48.25E
95 D3 **Ambinanitelo** Madagascar 15.20S 49.35E
95 D5 **Ambinanydilana** Madagascar 19.53S 48.28E
95 B4 **Ambinda** Madagascar 16.22S 45.50E
71 K6 **Ambin, Mt. d'** France 45.09N 6.53E
101 H7 **Ambition, Mount** Br Columbia 57.03N 131.32W
15 M6 **Ambitle I** Bismarck Arch 4.05S 153.32E
95 B6 **Ambitoka** Madagascar 21.01S 44.20E
71 G5 **Amblagnieu** France 45.50N 5.24E
69 C5 **Amblainville** France 49.12N 2.07E
57 K2 **Amble** Northumb Eng 55.20N 1.34W
103 D6 **Ambler** Pennsylvania 40.09N 75.13W
113 J3 **Ambler** *R* Alaska
57 H4 **Ambleside** Cumbria Eng 54.26N 2.58W
69 B2 **Ambleteuse** France 50.48N 1.38E
61 P5 **Amblève** Belgium 50.21N 6.10E
61 N5 **Amblève** *R* Belgium
61 M6 **Ambly** Belgium 50.08N 5.19E
29 K7 **Ambo** Orissa India 21.08N 86.16E
120 B4 **Ambo** Peru 10.05S 76.07W
13 G6 **Ambo** Queensland 22.47S 144.30E
95 D3 **Amboahangibe** Madagascar 14.07S 49.49E
95 D5 **Amboasary** Tamatave Madagascar 18.25S 48.17E
95 C8 **Amboasary** Tuléar Madagascar 25.01S 46.23E
95 D4 **Amboavory** Madagascar 17.17S 48.30E
95 D4 **Ambodiampana** Madagascar 16.48S 49.35E
95 D3 **Ambodiangezoka** Madagascar 14.34S 49.30E
95 D4 **Ambodifototra** Madagascar 16.59S 49.51E
95 D6 **Ambodiharina** Madagascar 20.00S 48.46E
95 D6 **Ambodilafa** Madagascar 20.30S 48.10E
95 D5 **Ambodilazana** Madagascar 18.03S 49.10E
95 D2 **Ambodimodiro** Madagascar 13.13S 49.10E
95 C6 **Ambodinonoka** Madagascar 20.21S 47.49E
95 D4 **Ambodiriana** Madagascar 17.55S 49.18E
95 D6 **Ambodiriana** Madagascar 20.50S 48.20E
95 D5 **Amboditavolo** Madagascar 19.10S 48.52E
95 C5 **Ambohibary** Madagascar 19.36S 47.09E
95 A6 **Ambohibe** Madagascar 21.21S 43.30E
95 C5 **Ambohidratrimo** Madagascar 18.48S 47.26E
95 D4 **Ambohijanahary** Madagascar 17.21S 48.23E
95 C6 **Ambohimahamasina** Madagascar 21.56S 47.11E
95 C6 **Ambohimahasoa** Madagascar 21.07S 47.13E
95 A7 **Ambohimahavelona** Madagascar 23.25S 43.55E
95 C6 **Ambohimahazo** Madagascar 20.40S 47.04E
95 D6 **Ambohimanarivo** Madagascar 21.45S 48.09E
95 C6 **Ambohimanga Atsimo** Madagascar 20.51S 47.36E
95 C5 **Ambohimanjaka** Madagascar 18.02S 47.49E
95 C5 **Ambohimasina** Madagascar 19.40S 46.42E
95 C6 **Ambohimiera** Madagascar 21.02S 47.30E
95 C6 **Ambohimitombo** Madagascar 20.41S 47.26E
95 B4 **Ambohipaky** Madagascar 16.23S 45.00E
95 E3 **Ambohitralanana** Madagascar 15.13S 50.28E
15 G6 **Amboin** Papua New Guinea 4.37S 143.42E
Amboina *see* **Ambon** Moluccas
70 N7 **Amboise** France 47.25N 1.00E
91 D9 **Amboiva** Angola 11.33S 14.43E
95 C3 **Ambolobozo** Madagascar 14.23S 47.50E
70 E6 **Ambon** France 47.34N 2.32W
19 F5 **Ambon** Moluccas Indon 3.41S 128.10E
19 E5 **Ambon** *isld* Moluccas Indon
95 B8 **Ambondro** Madagascar 25.10S 45.50E
69 G5 **Ambonnay** France 49.05N 4.10E
95 C6 **Amborompotsy** Fianarantsoa Madagascar 20.35S 46.14E
95 B8 **Amborompotsy** Tuléar Madagascar 24.40S 44.58E
93 J8 **Amboseli, L** Kenya
95 C6 **Ambositra** Madagascar 20.31S 47.15E
95 C6 **Ambovombe** Madagascar 20.48S 47.05E
95 C8 **Ambovombe** Madagascar 25.10S 46.06E
95 C6 **Ambovony** Madagascar 21.15S 46.42E
111 J7 **Amboy** California 34.33N 115.44W
106 E8 **Amboy** Illinois 41.43N 89.21W
17 H10 **Amboyna Cay** *I* S China Sea 7.50N 112.50E
72 H2 **Ambrault** France 46.48N 1.57E
95 D1 **Ambre, C. d'** Madagascar 11.58S 49.14E
26 V11 **Ambre, I. d'** Mauritius, Indian Oc 20.02S 57.41E
95 D2 **Ambre, Montagne d'** Madagascar
61 L4 **Ambresin** Belgium 50.38N 5.03E
66 L5 **Ambri** Switzerland 46.31N 8.42E
104 E6 **Ambridge** Pennsylvania 40.35N 80.15W
70 J5 **Ambrières-les-Vallées** France 48.24N 0.38W
9 C11 **Ambrim** *isld* New Hebrides Pacific Ocean
91 C7 **Ambriz** Angola 7.50S 13.09E
Ambrizete *see* **N 'Zeto**
44 E5 **Ambrolauri** Georgia U.S.S.R. 42.32N 43.12E
71 G4 **Ambronay** France 46.00N 5.22E
105 D6 **Ambrose** Georgia 31.33N 83.02W
108 G1 **Ambrose** N Dakota 48.58N 103.30W
103 G5 **Ambrose Chan** New Jersey/New York
103 G6 **Ambrose Chan. Lt. Ship** New Jersey/New York 40.27N 73.55W
119 F9 **Ambrosio** Brazil 2.54S 68.20W
90 B5 **Ambrusa** Nigeria 12.31N 4.20E
Ambrym *isld see* **Ambrim** *isld*
15 C5 **Ambuar** Irian Jaya 2.06S 134.05E
30 J3 **Ambu Gyabjen** *mt* Nepal 27.54N 86.52E
19 K3 **Ambuklao Dam** Luzon Philippines 16.29N 120.45E
30 J3 **Ambu Lapcha** *pass* Nepal 27.52N 86.55E
30 J3 **Ambu Lapcha Glacier** Nepal
19 B8 **Ambulombo** *vol* Indonesia 8.48S 121.12E
18 K10 **Ambulu** Java Indon 8.16S 113.36E
18 K9 **Ambunten** Indonesia 6.55S 113.45E
15 G6 **Ambunti** Papua New Guinea 4.12S 142.49E
28 D4 **Ambur** Tamil Nadu India 12.48N 78.44E
93 J9 **Ambussel, L** Tanzania 3.56S 37.16E
15 F7 **Ambuve** *L* Papua New Guinea
13 J7 **Amby** Queensland 26.33S 148.11E
88 K10 **Amchamiat, El** *watercourse* Mauritania
113 O10 **Amchitka I** Aleutian Is 51.30N 179.00E
113 O10 **Amchitka Pass** Aleutian Is
33 G9 **'Amd** S Yemen 15.23N 47.58E
90 K5 **Am Dagachi** Chad 12.22N 20.10E
53 Y20 **Åmdalsverk** Norway 59.23N 8.02E
90 K5 **Am Dam** Chad 12.41N 20.30E
15 A7 **Amdassa** Yamdena I Indon 7.48S 131.30E
90 L6 **Amdeibé** Cent Afr Rep 10.50N 22.09E
66 N3 **Amden** Switzerland 47.09N 9.08E
47 J2 **Amderma** U.S.S.R. 69.44N 61.35E
90 H5 **Am Djemena** Chad 13.10N 17.20E
24 G9 **Amdo** Xizang Zizhiqu China 32.22N 91.07E
Amdo Tsonak Tso *L see* **Co Nag**
33 H9 **'Amd, Wādī** *watercourse* S Yemen
115 J7 **Amealco** Mexico 20.12N 100.09W
115 G7 **Ameca** Mexico 20.34N 104.03W
115 K8 **Amecameca** Mexico 19.08N 98.48W
87 F5 **Amedamit** *mt* Ethiopia 11.10N 37.28E
110 E9 **Amedee** California 40.20N 120.11W
Amēdi *see* **Amādiyah**
40 C3 **Amedichi** *R* U.S.S.R.
88 P11 **Ameg** Algeria 20.55N 2.55E
121 E5 **Ameghino** Argentina 34.51S 62.28W
79 G6 **Ameglia** Italy 44.04N 9.57E
60 H12 **Ameide** Netherlands 51.58N 4.58E
76 D14 **Ameixial** Algarve Portugal 37.22N 7.58W
76 D11 **Ameixial** Alto Alentejo Portugal 38.54N 7.40W
60 M6 **Ameland** *isld* Netherlands
15 H6 **Amele** Papua New Guinea 5.16S 145.40E
80 F3 **Amelia** Italy 42.33N 12.25E
108 M7 **Amelia** Nebraska 42.14N 98.55W
104 H9 **Amelia** Virginia 37.20N 77.59W
105 F7 **Amelia I** Florida 30.36N 81.26W
80 G3 **Amelia, Passo d'** Italy 42.36N 12.33E
72 B5 **Amélie, l'** France 45.29N 1.09W
72 K11 **Amélie-les-Bains-Palalda** France
63 M6 **Amelinghausen** W Germany 53.08N 10.12E
64 J7 **Amendingen** W Germany 48.00N 10.13E
76 C9 **Amêndoa** Portugal 39.40N 8.04W
81 N4 **Amendolara** Italy 39.57N 16.35E
81 L7 **Amendolea** *R* Italy
23 C7 **Ameng** Yunnan China 23.47N 104.25E
103 G3 **Amenia** New York 41.51N 73.33W
66 K8 **Ameno** Italy 45.48N 8.27E
87 C1 **Amentego** Sudan 18.27N 30.43E
75 Q3 **Amer** Spain 42.01N 2.36E
60 G13 **Amer** *R* Netherlands
48 S13 **Ameralik Fd** Greenland
64 N8 **Amerang** W Germany 47.59N 12.19E
90 M6 **Amergu** Sudan 10.39N 25.13E
60 M14 **America** Netherlands 51.27N 5.59E
118 F8 **Americana** Brazil 22.44S 47.19W
110 N7 **American Falls** Idaho 42.47N 112.50W
110 N7 **American Falls Res** Idaho 43.00N 112.40W
110 O9 **American Fork** Utah 40.24N 111.48W
122 E1 **American Samoa** *islds* Pacific Oc
105 F13 **American Shoal** Florida 24.31N 81.31W
117 G9 **Américo Alves** Brazil 9.45S 41.37W
105 C5 **Americus** Georgia 32.04N 84.14W
65 L7 **Amering Kogel** *mt* Austria 47.05N 14.48E
60 N15 **Amern** W Germany 51.13N 6.14E
60 K11 **Amerongen** Netherlands 52.00N 5.27E
77 W14 **Amer, Pta. de** Balearic Is 39.35N 3.24E
60 K11 **Amersfoort** Netherlands 52.09N 5.23E
95 N3 **Amersfoort** S Africa 27.00S 29.52E
56 K4 **Amersham** Bucks Eng 51.40N 0.38W
14 B9 **Amery** W Australia 31.11S 117.03E
106 B4 **Amery** Wisconsin 45.18N 92.21W
123 C4 **Amery Ice Shelf** Antarctica
108 R7 **Ames** Iowa 42.02N 93.39W
108 O8 **Ames** Nebraska 41.28N 96.39W
109 M5 **Ames** Oklahoma 36.15N 98.13W
76 B3 **Ames** Spain 42.55N 8.39W
100 E3 **Amesbury** Alberta 55.05N 112.26W
104 P4 **Amesbury** Massachusetts 42.50N 70.56W
56 H5 **Amesbury** Wilts Eng 51.10N 1.47W
100 J1 **Amesdale** Ontario 50.02N 92.55W
88 J6 **Ameskhoud** Morocco 30.31N 9.21W
99 F3 **Ameson** Ontario 49.49N 84.34W
104 D7 **Amesville** Ohio 39.24N 81.57W
29 C5 **Amet** Rajasthan India 25.18N 73.59E
30 E6 **Amethi** Bara Banki, Uttar Prad India 26.51N 81.08E
30 E6 **Amethi** Sultanpur, Uttar Prad Ind 26.09N 81.48E
91 E12 **Ametinho** Angola 17.20S 17.10E
75 M6 **Ametlla de Mar** Spain 40.54N 0.48E
98 J8 **Amet Sd** Nova Scotia
75 D2 **Ameyugo** Spain 42.39N 3.04W
75 E2 **Amézaga** Spain 42.58N 2.51W
84 D7 **Amfia** Greece 37.07N 22.04E
84 E4 **Amfíklia** Greece 38.38N 22.35E
87 H3 **Amfile B** Ethiopia
84 B4 **Amfilokhía** Greece 38.52N 21.09E
83 F4 **Amfípolis** Greece 40.48N 23.52E
84 D4 **Amfissa** Greece 38.32N 22.22E
70 H3 **Amfreville** France 49.24N 1.24W
70 M3 **Amfreville-la-Campagne** France 49.12N 0.55E
40 E1 **Amga** U.S.S.R. 60.51N 131.59E
40 F1 **Amga** *R* U.S.S.R.
Amgalang *see* **Xin Barag Zuoqi**
42 K7 **Amgalang** Nei Monggol Zizhiqu China 48.15N 118.12E
22 L2 **Amgalang Bulag** Nei Monggol Zizhiqu China 48.14N 118.12E
93 F3 **Amgamwa** Uganda 2.51N 34.13E
34 K8 **Amghar, Al** Saudi Arabia 30.58N 42.11E
40 E1 **Amginskiy** U.S.S.R. 60.45N 131.41E
88 G8 **Amgriou, Playa de** Morocco 27.42N 13.08E
40 G9 **Amgu** U.S.S.R. 45.48N 137.36E
39 L2 **Amguema** U.S.S.R. 66.59N 179.02W
90 K5 **Am Guereda** Chad 12.53N 21.14E
88 Q8 **Amguid** Algeria 26.28N 5.21E
40 H5 **Amgun'** *R* U.S.S.R.
94 D2 **Amgurungunju** Namibia 18.20S 16.26E
39 L1 **Amguyema** *R* U.S.S.R.
87 F4 **Amhara** *reg* Ethiopia
30 G7 **Amhat** Uttar Prad India 25.47N 83.48E
Amherst Burma *see* **Kyaikkami**
109 H1 **Amherst** Colorado 40.41N 102.11W
104 R2 **Amherst** Maine 44.51N 68.21W
103 J2 **Amherst** Massachusetts 42.23N 72.31W
108 L9 **Amherst** Nebraska 40.50N 99.16W
104 O4 **Amherst** New Hampshire 42.52N 71.36W
98 H8 **Amherst** Nova Scotia 45.50N 64.14W
104 C5 **Amherst** Ohio 41.24N 82.14W
108 N4 **Amherst** S Dakota 45.44N 97.53W
112 E1 **Amherst** Texas 34.02N 102.26W
104 F9 **Amherst** Virginia 37.35N 79.04W
99 G10 **Amherstburg** Ontario 42.06N 83.06W
104 D9 **Amherstdale** W Virginia 37.48N 81.49W
98 L6 **Amherst I** Madeleine Is, Que 47.15N 61.55W
99 O8 **Amherst I** Ontario 44.09N 76.45W
106 E5 **Amherst Junc** Wisconsin 44.28N 89.19W
14 F4 **Amherst, Mt** W Australia 18.13S 126.56E
90 J5 **Am Himédé** Chad 12.36N 19.48E
Amia, Al *see* **Birkat al 'Amyā'**
84 Q15 **Amiandos** Cyprus 34.55N 32.55E
80 E3 **Amiata, Monte** Italy 42.53N 11.57E
88 R5 **Amiche** Algeria 33.18N 6.56E
108 G3 **Amidon** N Dakota 46.29N 103.19W
76 D10 **Amieira** Portugal 39.30N 7.49W
76 D12 **Amieira** Portugal 38.17N 7.34W
69 C4 **Amiens** France 49.54N 2.18E
13 K8 **Amiens** Queensland 28.35S 151.46E
76 E6 **Amiero** Portugal 41.17N 7.23W
76 J2 **Amieva** Spain 43.16N 5.08W
84 D5 **Amigdhaliá** Fokís Greece 38.25N 22.13E
84 C6 **Amigdhaliés** Greece 37.31N 21.51E
34 J5 **Amij, Wādī** *watercourse* Iraq
36 J6 **Amik Gölü** *L* Turkey
30 F5 **Amile** Nepal 27.59N 82.12E
33 K7 **Amilhayt, Wādī al** *watercourse* Oman
93 M4 **Amilkei** Kenya 1.24N 40.53E
32 E5 **'Amīnābād** Iran 31.40N 52.04E
83 E4 **Amíndaion** Greece 40.42N 21.42E
27 L7 **Amindivi Is** Laccadive Is Ind Oc 11.30N 72.58E
121 C2 **Aminga** Argentina 28.50S 66.55W
66 D3 **Amin, Mont d'** Switzerland 47.05N 6.55E
87 H8 **Amino** Ethiopia 4.25N 41.52E
20 J6 **Amino** Japan 35.43N 135.02E
94 E4 **Aminuis** Namibia 23.43S 19.21E
34 C4 **Amioune** Lebanon 34.19N 35.48E
35 F1 **'Amir** Israel 33.11N 35.37E
32 D4 **Amīrābād** Esfahān Iran 32.53N 51.35E
32 B4 **Amīrābād** Kermānshāh Iran 33.20N 46.19E
Amirabad Semnān Iran *see* **Fūlād Maḩalleh**
27 G11 **Amirante Is** Seychelles, Ind Oc
31 B6 **Amir Chah** Pakistan 29.14N 62.29E
35 E2 **Amirim** Israel 32.56N 35.28E
86 C3 **'Āmirîya, El** Beheira Egypt 31.01N 29.48E
86 R11 **Amîrîya, El** Cairo Egypt
35 F4 **'Amiriya, El** Jordan 32.18N 35.42E
100 F6 **Amisk** Alberta 52.36N 111.04W
100 P4 **Amisk L** Saskatchewan
109 G6 **Amistad** New Mexico 35.55N 103.10W
112 F6 **Amistad Res** Mexico/Texas
Amisus *anc site see* **Samsun**
85 O10 **Amit** Sudan 18.45N 36.30E
107 F11 **Amite** Louisiana 30.42N 90.30W
107 F11 **Amite** *R* Louisiana
107 C7 **Amity** Arkansas 34.14N 93.29W
103 H5 **Amityville** Long I, N Y 40.40N 73.25W
88 J6 **Amizmiz** Morocco 31.14N 8.14W
29 D6 **Amjhera** Madhya Prad India 22.30N 75.09E
39 C5 **Amka** U.S.S.R. 59.02N 141.01E
90 H3 **Amkarao** Chad 17.21N 17.10E
29 F7 **Amla** Madhya Prad India 21.53N 78.10E
53 W16 **Amla** Norway 61.10N 7.16E
33 E6 **Amlah, Al** Saudi Arabia 21.14N 42.44E
33 E7 **Amlah, Jabal al** *mt* Saudi Arabia 18.50N 43.44E
32 D2 **Amlash** Iran 37.04N 50.10E
30 H5 **Amlekhganj** Nepal 27.17N 85.00E
90 K5 **Am Léyouna** Chad 12.49N 21.50E
52 D8 **Åmli** Norway 58.45N 8.32E
113 S9 **Amlia I** Aleutian Is 52.05N 173.30W
Amlish *see* **Amlash**
57 E6 **Amlwch** Gwynedd Wales 53.25N 4.20W
35 G6 **'Amman** Jordan 31.57N 35.56E
56 D4 **Ammanford** Dyfed Wales 51.48N 3.59W
32 F1 **Ammannazar** Turkmeniya U.S.S.R. 38.53N 55.30E
51 O7 **Ämmänsaari** Finland 64.51N 28.48E
33 F9 **'Ammār** *tribe* Yemen
51 E5 **Ammarfjället** *mt* Sweden 66.06N 15.40E
33 G4 **'Ammārīyah, Al** Saudi Arabia 24.49N 46.26E
51 E6 **Ammarnäs** Sweden 65.58N 16.10E
13 D5 **Ammaroo** N Terr Australia 21.45S 135.17E
12 C2 **Ammaroodinna** *R* S Australia
34 D6 **'Ammar, Tel** *mt* Syria 32.54N 36.27E
53 E4 **Ammelhede** Denmark 56.26N 10.14E
60 Q11 **Ammelohe** W Germany 52.05N 6.47E
63 P10 **Ammendorf** E Germany 51.26N 11.59E
63 L9 **Ammensen** W Germany 51.54N 9.52E
64 L8 **Ammer** *R* W Germany
65 C6 **Ammer Gebirge** *mts* W Germany
64 L8 **Ammerland** W Germany 47.55N 11.02E
63 G6 **Ammerland** *reg* W Germany
113 R2 **Ammerman Mt** Yukon Terr 68.30N 140.59E
64 K5 **Ammerndorf** W Germany 49.25N 10.52E
64 L7 **Ammersee** *L* W Germany 48.00N 11.07E
60 J12 **Ammerzoden** Netherlands 51.45N 5.14E
35 F2 **'Ammia'd** Israel 32.56N 35.32E
35 E9 **'Ammi'az** *watercourse* Israel
88 O4 **Ammi Moussa** Algeria 35.50N 1.04E
35 D6 **Amminadav** Israel 31.46N 35.08E
35 A8 **Ammi'oz** Israel 31.15N 34.24E
35 D3 **Ammiqam** Israel 32.34N 35.00E
110 O6 **Ammon** Idaho 43.29N 111.57W
85 J7 **Ammonite Scarp** *dist* Egypt
35 E2 **'Ammud** *R* Israel
84 L11 **Amnátos** Crete 35.20N 24.37E
30 H7 **Amnaur** Bihar India 25.59N 84.56E
Amne Machin Range *see* **A'nyêmaqên Shan**
23 B1 **Amne Machin Range** Qinghai China
31 G8 **Amnura** Bangladesh 24.40N 88.26E
47 K4 **Amnya** *R* U.S.S.R.
41 H8 **Amo** U.S.S.R. 63.40N 104.00E
29 C7 **Amod** Gujarat India 21.59N 72.54E
76 D4 **Amoeiro** Spain 42.25N 7.58W
23 B7 **Amo Jiang** *R* Yunnan China
32 E2 **Amol** Iran 36.26N 52.24E
30 A7 **Amola** Madhya Prad India 25.25N 77.56E
118 B6 **Amolar** Brazil 18.01S 57.29W
45 F5 **Amon'** U.S.S.R. 51.48N 34.31E
64 F2 **Amöneburg** W Germany 50.48N 8.56E
117 G6 **Amontada** Brazil 3.20S 39.51W
76 L9 **Amor** *mt* Spain 39.35N 4.09W
64 G4 **Amorbach** W Germany 49.38N 9.14E
75 E1 **Amorebieta** Spain 43.13N 2.44W
76 A10 **Amoreira** Portugal 39.20N 9.12W
121 F2 **Amores** *R* Argentina
83 H8 **Amorgós** Greece 36.49N 25.54E
83 H8 **Amorgós** *isld* Greece 36.49N 25.54E
109 M5 **Amorita** Oklahoma 36.55N 98.17W
107 H8 **Amory** Mississippi 34.00N 88.30W
111 J8 **Amos** California 33.07N 115.14W
99 M4 **Amos** Quebec 48.34N 78.08W
95 F8 **Amos** *R* S Africa
53 G5 **Åmose Å** *R* Denmark
39 E3 **Amosova** U.S.S.R. 62.30N 153.21E
52 F5 **Åmot** Hedmark Norway 61.08N 11.20E
53 T15 **Åmot** Sogn og Fjordane Norway 61.35N 5.48E
53 V15 **Åmot** Sogn og Fjordane Norway 61.37N 6.44E
52 J6 **Åmot** Sweden 60.59N 16.30E
53 Y19 **Åmot** Telemark Norway 59.35N 7.59E
87 J4 **Amotahale** Djibouti 12.27N 42.49E
119 A10 **Amotape** Peru 4.55S 81.01W
119 B10 **Amotape ó de la Brea, Cerros** *mts* Peru
53 Y19 **Åmotsdal** Norway 59.38N 8.23E
72 C8 **Amou** France 43.35N 0.44W
61 E4 **Amougies** Belgium 50.44N 3.31E
89 B2 **Amoukrouz** *reg* Mauritania
122 F1 **Amouli** Amer Samoa Pacific Oc 14.16S 169.30W
88 O5 **Amour,Djebel** *mts* Algeria
89 K8 **Amoussokopé** Togo 6.41N 0.58E
Amoy *see* **Xiamen**
53 T20 **Åmøy** *isld* Norway 59.03N 5.46E
95 B8 **Ampalaza** Madagascar 25.07S 44.18E
29 H8 **Ampam** Orissa India 19.37N 82.40E
95 B8 **Ampamata** Madagascar 24.16S 44.37E
19 B4 **Ampana** Celebes Indon 0.54S 121.35E
18 B9 **Ampang** Pen Malaysia 3.08N 101.47E
95 B8 **Ampanihy** Madagascar 24.40S 44.45E
95 D4 **Amparafaravola** Madagascar 17.33S 48.13E
26 U7 **Amparai** Sri Lanka 7.17N 81.41E
94 E1 **Amparara** Namibia 17.59S 18.24E
95 C7 **Amparihy** Fianarantsoa Madagascar 23.57S 47.21E
118 F8 **Amparo** Brazil 22.44S 46.44W
95 C3 **Ampasimatera** Madagascar 15.55S 47.43E
95 D4 **Ampasimbe** Madagascar 17.10S 49.26E
95 D2 **Ampasimena** Madagascar 13.34S 48.03E
95 D6 **Ampasinambo** Madagascar 20.30S 48.00E
95 C7 **Ampataka** Madagascar 23.20S 47.29E
120 D6 **Ampato, Nev. de** *pk* Peru 15.52S 71.54W
18 M10 **Ampenan** Indonesia 8.35S 116.05E
64 M7 **Amper** *R* W Germany
79 N2 **Ampezzo** Italy 46.25N 12.48E
64 N7 **Ampfing** W Germany 48.15N 12.26E
111 O9 **Amphitheater** Arizona 32.17N 110.58W
12 G6 **Amphitheatre** Victoria 37.12S 143.25E
25 M4 **Amphitrite Group** *islds* Paracel Islands S China Sea
95 D2 **Ampisikina** Madagascar 12.55S 49.48E
57 L4 **Ampleforth** N Yorks Eng 54.12N 1.06W
71 E5 **Amplepuis** France 45.58N 4.20E
75 M6 **Ampolla, La** Spain 40.49N 0.42E
81 N5 **Ampollino** *L* Italy
95 D2 **Ampombiantambo** Madagascar 12.41S 48.58E
75 M6 **Amposta** Spain 40.43N 0.34E
95 B8 **Ampotaka** Madagascar 25.02S 44.40E
95 B7 **Ampoza** Madagascar 22.20S 44.42E
61 M4 **Ampsin** Belgium 50.32N 5.17E
56 K3 **Ampthill** Beds Eng 52.02N 0.30W
76 K5 **Ampudia** Spain 41.55N 4.48W
75 D1 **Ampuero** Spain 43.20N 3.24W
71 F6 **Ampuis** France 45.30N 4.48E
75 Q3 **Ampurdán,El** *reg* Spain
75 R3 **Ampurias** *anc site* Spain 42.08N 3.03E
71 J9 **Ampus** France 43.36N 6.23E
35 D2 **'Amqa** Israel 32.58N 35.10E
23 C1 **Amqog** Gansu China 34.38N 102.36E
98 E5 **Amqui** Quebec 48.28N 67.27W
30 G7 **Amra** Uttar Prad India 25.20N 83.27E
28 D2 **Amrabad** Andhra Prad India 16.22N 78.53E
33 E4 **'Amrah,Jabal** *mts* Saudi Arabia
33 E9 **Amrān** Yemen 15.42N 43.55E
Amrani *see* **'Emrâni**
30 L8 **Amrapara** Bihar India 24.33N 87.34E
29 B7 **Amrapur** Gujarat India 21.45N 70.02E
86 K4 **Amrar,Gebel el** *hill* Egypt 30.52N 33.25E
Amra Tala *see* **Amatulla**
29 E7 **Amravati** Maharashtra India 20.58N 77.50E
29 E7 **Amravati** *dist* Maharashtra India
35 G3 **Amrawa** Jordan 32.41N 35.56E
29 F6 **Amrawad** Madhya Prad India 23.00N 78.08E
90 H4 **Am Raya** Chad 14.11N 16.30E
29 B7 **Amreli** Gujarat India 21.36N 71.20E
29 B7 **Amreli** *dist* Gujarat India
88 O10 **Amrenene el Kasba** Algeria 22.04N 0.24E
31 E7 **Amri** Pakistan 26.09N 68.02E
74 G9 **Amria, El** Algeria 35.26N 1.04W
28 J3 **Amring** Assam India 25.43N 92.54E
66 O1 **Amriswil** Switzerland 47.33N 9.18E
29 D2 **Amritsar** Punjab India 31.35N 74.56E
29 D2 **Amritsar** *dist* Punjab India
30 B4 **Amroha** Uttar Prad India 28.54N 78.29E
63 H3 **Amrum** *isld* W Germany
86 M4 **'Amr,Wâdi el** *V* Egypt
88 Q10 **Amsel** Algeria 22.38N 5.26E
52 L2 **Åmsele** Sweden 64.30N 19.20E
90 J6 **Am Sigane** Chad 11.32N 19.50E
66 G5 **Amsoldingen** Switzerland 46.44N 7.35E
53 T20 **Åmsosen** Norway 59.28N 5.45E
90 K5 **Am-Sounta** Chad 13.05N 20.16E
66 L4 **Amsteg** Switzerland 46.47N 8.41E
65 J6 **Am Stein** *mts* Austria
60 H10 **Amstel** *R* Netherlands
60 H8 **Amstelmeer** *L* Netherlands 52.53N 4.55E
60 H10 **Amstelveen** Netherlands 52.18N 4.50E
60 T17 **Amstenrade** Netherlands 50.57N 5.55E
105 C7 **Amsterdam** Georgia 30.44N 84.26W
110 L7 **Amsterdam** Idaho 42.19N 114.35W
60 H10 **Amsterdam** Netherlands 52.21N 4.54E
104 L4 **Amsterdam** New York 42.56N 74.12W
104 E6 **Amsterdam** Ohio 40.29N 80.56W
95 O2 **Amsterdam** S Africa 26.38S 30.40E
95 J9 **Amsterdamhoek** S Africa 33.51S 25.38E
26 G9 **Amsterdam I** Indian Oc 37.55S 77.40E
60 J10 **Amsterdam Rijn Kanaal** Netherlands
65 L5 **Amstetten** Austria 48.08N 14.52E
103 K3 **Amston** Connecticut 41.37N 72.20W
29 L3 **Amta** W Bengal India 22.35N 88.01E
90 K6 **Am Timan** Chad 10.59N 20.18E
44 D4 **Amtkeli** Georgia U.S.S.R. 43.04N 41.21E
53 B2 **Amtoft** Denmark 57.01N 8.57E
64 H8 **Amtzell** W Germany 47.43N 9.45E
90 M4 **Amu** Sudan 14.16N 24.29E
119 D7 **Amú** *R* Colombia
119 E2 **Amuay** Venezuela 11.47N 70.15W
Amūd *R see* **'Ammud** *R*
93 F3 **Amuda** Uganda 2.13N 34.38E
43 F6 **Amu-Dar'ya** *R* U.S.S.R.
93 F4 **Amudat** Uganda 1.58N 34.58E
34 H1 **Amūde** Syria 37.07N 40.55E
35 F1 **Amudiye** Syria 33.00N 35.42E
34 G8 **Amūd,Jabal** *mt* Saudi Arabia 30.58N 39.21E
86 P6 **'Amūd, Wādī** *watercourse* Jordan
113 T9 **Amukta I** Aleutian Is 52.29N 171.18W
113 S9 **Amukta Pass** Aleutian Is
117 A4 **Amuku Mts** Guyana
Amul *see* **Amol**
29 E7 **Amulla** Madhya Prad India 21.24N 76.42E
58 J5 **Amulree** Tayside Scotland 56.30N 3.49W
15 J1 **Amun** Bougainville I Papua New Guinea 5.58S 154.45E
31 G2 **Amunat** Pakistan 36.38N 72.50E
97 K2 **Amund Ringnes I** N W Terr 78.00N 96.00W
123 A5 **Amundsen B** Antarctica
123 G8 **Amundsen Glacier** Antarctica
101 L1 **Amundsen Gulf** N W Terr
123 E3 **Amundsen Mt** Antarctica 67.14S 100.00E
123 F8 **Amundsen-Scott** *U.S.A. Base* Antarctica 90.00S
123 J12 **Amundsen Sea** Antarctica
48 J2 **Amundsen Trough** Arctic Oc
52 J5 **Amungen** *L* Sweden 61.10N 15.35E
15 J7 **Amungwiwa, Mt** Papua New Guinea 7.29S 146.39E
18 L7 **Amuntai** Borneo Indon 2.24S 115.14E
21 C1 **Amur** Heilongjiang China 52.50N 123.12E
85 N10 **'Amur** *watercourse* Sudan
19 D3 **Amurang** Celebes Indon 1.12N 124.37E
19 D3 **Amurang,Teluk** *B* Celebes Indon 1.15N 124.33E
31 F1 **Amurd** Afghanistan 38.11N 71.18E
93 E3 **Amuria** Uganda 2.04N 33.38E
11 G9 **Amuri Pass** New Zealand 42.32S 172.12E
42 B3 **Amurka** U.S.S.R. 58.02N 79.00E
75 D1 **Amurrio** Spain 43.03N 3.00W
21 D2 **Amur River** China/U.S.S.R.
40 G6 **Amursk** U.S.S.R. 50.16N 136.55E
38 M3 **Amurskaya Oblast'** *prov* U.S.S.R.
43 E1 **Amurskiy** U.S.S.R. 52.34N 59.36E
40 J5 **Amurskiy Liman** *B* U.S.S.R.
76 L4 **Amusco** Spain 42.10N 4.28W
84 A4 **Amvrakikós Kólpos** *gulf* Greece
45 K9 **Amvrosiyevka** Ukraine U.S.S.R. 47.46N 38.30E
30 H6 **Amwa Majhar** Bihar India 26.45N 84.36E
109 K3 **Amy** Kansas 38.28N 100.36W
42 E5 **Amyl** *R* U.S.S.R.
14 B5 **Amy, Mt** W Australia 22.17S 115.54E
99 F4 **Amyot** Ontario 48.30N 84.59W
41 L7 **Amysakh** U.S.S.R. 65.09N 119.52E
42 D5 **Amzas** U.S.S.R. 53.40N 88.58E
90 K4 **Am Zoer** Chad 14.13N 21.23E
74 E9 **Amzoughen-Khemis-Mrapten** Morocco 35.08N 3.48W
25 C3 **An** Burma 19.50N 94.03E
75 N4 **Aña** Spain 41.56N 1.07E
37 D1 **Ana** *R* Turkey
122 C15 **Anaa** *atoll* Tuamotu Is Pacific Oc 17.25S 145.30W
9 B8 **Anabar** Nauru, Pacific Oc 0.30S 166.57E
41 K4 **Anabar** *R* U.S.S.R.
41 K4 **Anabarskiy Zaliv** *B* U.S.S.R.
95 D2 **Anaborano** Madagascar 13.32S 48.50E
12 F5 **Ana Branch** *R* New S Wales
35 D4 **Anabta** Jordan 32.18N 35.07E
111 E8 **Anacapa Is** California
80 K7 **Anacapri** Italy 40.33N 14.31E
119 G3 **Anaco** Venezuela 9.30N 64.28W
107 C10 **Anacoco** Louisiana 31.13N 93.20W
107 C10 **Anacoco L** Louisiana 31.06N 93.25W
110 N3 **Anaconda** Montana 46.09N 112.56W
110 M4 **Anaconda Ra** Montana
110 C1 **Anacortes** Washington 48.30N 122.42W
104 N9 **Anacostia** Washington D C 38.52N 77.00W
33 F10 **'Anad,Al** S Yemen 13.13N 44.46E
109 M6 **Anadarko** Oklahoma 35.04N 98.16W
117 H9 **Anadia** Brazil 9.38S 36.16W
76 C8 **Anadia** Portugal 40.26N 8.27W
37 G1 **Anadolufeneri** Turkey 41.13N 29.09E
37 F1 **Anadoluhısarı** Turkey 41.06N 29.04E
39 J3 **Anadyr'** *R* U.S.S.R.
39 K2 **Anadyrskaya Nizmennost'** *lowland* U.S.S.R.
Anadyrskiy Khrebet *mts see* **Chukotskiy Khrebet**
39 K3 **Anadyrskiy Liman** *lagoon* U.S.S.R.
39 L3 **Anadyrskiy Zaliv** *gulf* U.S.S.R.
39 H2 **Anadyrskoye Ploskogor'ye** *tableland* U.S.S.R.
37 B3 **Anafarta Liman** *B* Turkey
83 H8 **Anáfi** Greece 36.23N 25.44E
83 H8 **Anáfi** *isld* Greece 36.23N 25.44E
52 G4 **Anåfjället** *mt* Sweden 62.35N 12.50E
83 H8 **Anafópoulo** *isld* Greece 36.15N 25.49E
96 S13 **Anaga, Pta. de** Tenerife Canary Is 28.33N 16.07W
96 S13 **Anaga, Roques de** *rocks* Tenerife Canary Is 28.35N 16.09W
118 H4 **Anagé** Brazil 14.45S 41.11W
87 G2 **Anaghit** Ethiopia 16.22N 38.41E
80 H5 **Anagni** Italy 41.44N 13.10E
34 J4 **'Anah** Iraq 34.29N 41.57E
34 J4 **Anah** *oil bore* Iraq 34.19N 41.27E
Anahadgarh *see* **Barnala**
111 G8 **Anaheim** California 33.50N 117.56W
111 E10 **Anaheim B** California
101 L9 **Anahim Lake** Br Col 52.30N 125.20W
114 F3 **Anahola** Hawaiian Is 22.09N 159.19W
114 F3 **Anahola** *B* Hawaiian Is
115 J4 **Anáhuac** Mexico 27.20N 100.01W
112 N6 **Anahuac** Texas 29.44N 94.41W
114 A4 **Anahulu** *R* Hawaiian Is
85 A7 **Anaï** Libya 24.12N 11.32E
28 C5 **Anaimalai Hills** Kerala/Tamil Nadu India
28 C5 **Anai Mudi Pk** Kerala India 10.14N 77.07E
85 A7 **Anaï, Tehi N** *pass* Libya 24.16N 11.34E
26 Q6 **Anaivilundawa** Sri Lanka 7.43N 79.50E
Anaize *see* **'Unayzah**
117 D5 **Anajás** Brazil 1.00S 49.54W
117 D5 **Anajás, I** Brazil
117 F6 **Anajatuba** Brazil 3.16S 44.40W
93 C3 **Anaka** Uganda 2.34N 31.52E
95 A7 **Anakao** Madagascar 23.40S 43.40E
28 F2 **Anakapalle** Andhra Prad India 17.42N 83.06E
13 J6 **Anakie** Queensland 23.33S 147.45E
44 D5 **Anaklia** Georgia U.S.S.R. 42.24N 41.34E
87 F4 **Anako** Ethiopia 12.03N 36.21E
Anak Reng *see* **Noring, Gunong**
113 M2 **Anaktuvuk** *R* Alaska
113 M2 **Anaktuvuk Pass** Alaska 68.10N 152.00W
26 Q2 **Analaitivu** *isld* Sri Lanka 9.41N 79.45E
95 B6 **Analaivo** Madagascar 20.19S 44.26E
95 C3 **Analalava** Madagascar 14.38S 47.46E
95 B7 **Analavelona** *mt* Madagascar 22.35S 44.10E
95 C7 **Analavoka** Madagascar 22.31S 46.30E
95 C5 **Analavory** Madagascar 18.57S 46.41E
87 H10 **Anale** Somalia 0.52S 41.53E
84 C5 **Análipsis** Aitolía Greece 38.29N 21.42E
84 C7 **Análipsis** Messinía Greece 37.01N 21.58E
103 D4 **Analomink** Pennsylvania 41.03N 75.13W
119 H9 **Anamã** Brazil 3.34S 61.22W
119 H9 **Anamã** *L* Brazil 3.31S 61.35W
100 T7 **Anama Bay** Manitoba 51.56N 98.05W
26 Q6 **Anamaduwa** Sri Lanka 7.52N 80.01E
41 F6 **Anama,Ozero** *L* U.S.S.R.
116 E4 **Ana Maria,Cayos de** *islds* Cuba
36 E5 **Anamas** Turkey 37.47N 31.09E
36 E5 **Anamas Dağları** *mts* Turkey
18 F4 **Anambas,Kep** *islds* Indonesia
20 K4 **Anamizu** Japan 37.14N 136.56E
108 K2 **Anamoose** N Dakota 47.54N 100.14W
106 C7 **Anamosa** Iowa 42.07N 91.16W
117 B4 **Anamu, R** Brazil
36 F6 **Anamur** Turkey 36.06N 32.49E
36 F6 **Anamur Burun** *C* Turkey 36.07N 32.47E
20 H8 **Anan** Japan 33.54N 134.40E
29 C6 **Anand** Gujarat India 22.34N 73.01E
28 B3 **Anandapuram** Karnataka India 14.04N 75.07E
29 J6 **Anandpur** Bihar India 22.29N 85.15E
29 B6 **Anandpur** Gujarat India 22.16N 70.53E
29 E2 **Anandpur** Himachal Prad India 31.13N 76.34E
29 K7 **Anandpur** Orissa India 21.14N 86.10E
29 K6 **Anandpur R** W Bengal India
84 H8 **Anánes** *islds* Greece 36.33N 24.08E
39 G5 **Anangravnen,Sopka** *vol* U.S.S.R. 59.16N 161.45E
117 D5 **Ananindeua** Brazil 1.22S 48.20W
41 E6 **Anan'inskiy** U.S.S.R. 69.46N 85.33E
19 D6 **Anano** *isld* Indonesia 5.18S 124.19E
120 D6 **Ananta, L** Peru 15.23S 70.51W
28 C3 **Anantapur** Andhra Prad India 14.42N 77.05E
28 C3 **Anantapur** *dist* Andhra Prad India
31 H4 **Anantnag** Kashmir 33.44N 75.11E
30 B7 **Anant Peth** Madhya Prad India 25.57N 78.16E
29 K7 **Anantpur** Orissa India 20.17N 86.34E
44 F5 **Ananuri** Georgia U.S.S.R. 42.10N 44.43E
46 G5 **Anan'yev** Ukraine U.S.S.R. 47.40N 30.00E
43 N5 **Anan'yevo** Kirgiziya U.S.S.R. 42.45N 77.42E
44 A3 **Anapa** U.S.S.R. 44.54N 37.20E
39 G5 **Anapka** U.S.S.R. 59.58N 163.40E
39 G5 **Anapka, Zaliv** *B* U.S.S.R.
84 W23 **Anapládhes** Corfu 39.25N 20.03E
81 K9 **Anapo** *R* Sicily
84 M12 **Anapodháris** *R* Crete
118 E5 **Anápolis** Brazil 16.19S 48.58W
117 C6 **Anapú, R** Brazil
32 F5 **Anār** Iran 30.55N 55.15E
32 E4 **Anārak** Iran 33.20N 53.44E
39 H4 **Anara Zaliv** *B* U.S.S.R. 60.01N 170.00E
32 D3 **Anarbar** *R* Iran
32 G3 **Anarbat** Iran 35.15N 57.49E
75 G1 **Añarbe, Embalse de** *res* Spain
31 A4 **Anardara** Afghanistan 32.45N 61.38E
52 G3 **Anarisfjällen** *mt* Sweden 63.04N 13.10E
51 L3 **Anarjokka** *R* Norway/Finland
31 C4 **Anarorara** Afghanistan 32.58N 65.41E
59 B7 **Anascaul** Kerry Irish Rep 52.09N 10.04W
105 J7 **Añasco** Puerto Rico 18.19N 67.11W
59 B5 **Anaserd** *L* Galway Irish Rep 53.26N 10.06W
51 J7 **Änäset** Sweden 64.17N 21.25E
42 E5 **Anash** U.S.S.R. 54.57N 91.00E
50 E4 **Anastadhir** Iceland 65.29N 20.59W
105 F8 **Anastasia I** Florida 29.50N 81.17W
39 J4 **Anastasii, Bukhta** *gulf* U.S.S.R.
45 K9 **Anastasiyevka** U.S.S.R. 47.34N 38.33E
35 E6 **Anata** Jordan 31.49N 35.16E
17 P8 **Anatahan** *isld* Marianas Pacific Oc 16.22N 145.38E
84 E2 **Anatolí** Greece 39.45N 22.42E
36 D4 **Anatolia** *reg* Turkey
78 D2 **Anatolin** *reg* Turkey
Anatom *isld see* **Aneityum** *isld*
110 H3 **Anatone** Washington 46.08N 117.09W
51 O7 **Änättijärvi** *L* Finland 64.28N 29.55E
121 E2 **Añatuya** Argentina 28.26S 62.48W
119 H7 **Anauá, R** Brazil
39 F6 **Anaun,Gora** *mt* U.S.S.R. 56.21N 158.48E
50 K4 **Anavatn** *L* Iceland 65.14N 15.32W
119 H9 **Anavilhanas,Arch.das** Brazil
84 G6 **Anávissos** Greece 37.43N 23.56E
84 D3 **Anávra** Kardhítsa Greece 39.11N 22.05E
84 E3 **Anávra** Magnisía Greece 39.04N 22.33E
84 C4 **Anavrití** Aitolía Greece 38.32N 21.54E
84 D7 **Anavrití** Lakonía Greece 37.02N 22.22E
76 J7 **Anaya de Alba** Spain 40.43N 5.29W
Anaypazarı *see* **Gülnar**
34 D10 **Anaz** *hills* Saudi Arabia
37 E7 **Anbar** *R* Turkey
32 C1 **'Anbarān** Iran 38.29N 48.27E
22 D6 **Anbei** Gansu China 40.26N 96.12E
25 H8 **An Bien** Vietnam 9.44N 105.00E
32 D2 **Anbūh** Iran 36.40N 50.00E
32 F7 **Anbūr-e Kālārī** Iran 27.45N 55.09E
21 D8 **Anbyŏn** N Korea 39.01N 127.35E
76 B8 **Ançã** Portugal 40.16N 8.31W
80 J3 **Ancarano** Italy 42.50N 13.45E
120 A4 **Ancash** *dept* Peru
57 M7 **Ancaster** Lincs Eng 52.59N 0.32W
121 D2 **Ancasti** Argentina 28.46S 65.32W
121 D2 **Ancasti, Sa** *ra* Argentina
71 D6 **Ance** *R* France
76 C6 **Ancede** Portugal 41.07N 8.03W
71 J7 **Ancelle** France 44.38N 6.11E
110 O4 **Anceney** Montana 45.39N 111.21W
70 H7 **Ancenis** France 47.23N 1.10W
69 J6 **Ancerville** France 48.38N 5.01E
39 B4 **Ancha** U.S.S.R. 61.03N 138.45E
39 B4 **Ancha** *R* U.S.S.R.
121 C9 **Anchán** Argentina 42.14S 66.05W
90 D6 **Anchau** Nigeria 10.55N 8.21E
72 E1 **Anché** France 47.08N 0.20E
118 H7 **Anchieta** Espírito Santo Brazil 20.45S 40.39W
118 H8 **Anchieta** Rio de Janeiro Brazil 22.50S 43.25W
109 E8 **Ancho** New Mexico 33.58N 105.46W
121 J8 **Ancho,Canal** *str* Chile
120 E6 **Anchodaya** Bolivia 14.03S 68.54W
90 D7 **Anchona** Nigeria 10.00N 8.05E
113 N6 **Anchorage** Alaska 61.10N 150.00W
107 L3 **Anchorage** Kentucky 38.20N 85.33W
106 M7 **Anchor B** Michigan

11 A12 Anchor I New Zealand
113 M7 Anchor Point Alaska 59.46N 151.54W
96 B15 Anchorstock Pt Tristan da Cunha Atlantic Ocean 37.07S 12.21W
116 H1 Anchovy Jamaica, W I 18.24N 77.55W
76 K10 Anchuras Spain 39.29N 4.50W
22 K7 Anci Hebei China 37.59N 116.40E
99 T6 Ancienne Lorette airport Quebec 46.47N 71.29W
75 F2 Ancín Spain 42.39N 2.10W
77 V15 Anciola,pta Balearic Is 39.07N 2.55E
116 E4 Anclitas,Cayo isld Cuba 20.49N 78.55W
105 E9 Anclote Keys islds Florida 28.11N 82.51W
120 E6 Ancohuma,Nev.de pk Bolivia 15.54S 68.30W
121 E5 Ancón Argentina 35.35S 61.46W
115 G10 Ancon Panama Canal Zone 8.57N 79.33W
120 B4 Ancón Peru 11.45N 77.08W
79 P7 Ancona Italy 43.37N 13.31E
80 G2 Ancona prov Italy
119 B7 Ancón de Sardinas,B.de Ecuador
103 G2 Ancram New York 42.03N 73.37W
69 D4 Ancre R France
58 M7 Ancroft Northumb Eng 55.42N 2.00W
92 J8 Ancuabe Mozambique 13.00S 39.50E
120 E8 Ancuaque Chile 19.27S 68.40W
92 G10 Ancuaze Mozambique 16.48S 34.45E
121 A8 Ancud Chile 41.53S 73.50W
121 A9 Ancud, G.de Chile
Ancyra anc site see Ankara
21 C4 Anda Heilongjiang China 46 25 125.20E
21 C4 Anda Heilongjiang China 46.37N 124.59E
72 K8 Andabre France 43.50N 2.54E
121 B6 Andacollo Argentina 37.10S 70.42W
121 B3 Andacollo Chile 30.15S 71.10W
33 D9 Andadda, Ras C Ethiopia 15.01N 40.34E
13 D7 Andado N Terr Australia 25.12S 135.20E
120 C6 Andahua R Peru
120 C5 Andahuaylas Peru 13.39S 73.24W
15 B4 Andai Irian Jaya 0.58S 133.59E
95 D5 Andaingo Madagascar 18.11S 48.17E
29 K6 Andal W Bengal Ind 23.35N 87.14E
95 B8 Andalatanosy Madagascar 24.40S 45.36E
109 N4 Andale Kansas 37.48N 97.38W
121 C1 Andalgalá Argentina 27.33S 66.18W
53 X13 Andalsnes Norway 62.33N 7.43E
74 C7 Andalucia reg Spain
107 K10 Andalusia Alabama 31.20N 86.30W
106 D8 Andalusia Illinois 41.25N 90.42W
Andalusia S Africa see Jan Kemp
26 J4 Andaman Basin Indian Ocean
27 P7 Andaman Is Bay of Bengal
26 J4 Andaman-Nicobar Ridge Bay of Bengal
17 E9 Andaman Sea Bay of Bengal
28 G7 Andaman Str Andaman Is
120 E8 Andamarca Bolivia 18.46S 67.31W
120 C4 Andamarca Peru 11.45S 74.45W
31 H2 Andamin Pass Afghan/U.S.S.R. 37.25N 74.15E
12 D4 Andamooka S Australia 30.29S 137.07E
33 N6 'Andām, Wādī Oman
71 F6 Andance France 45.15N 4.48E
47 F6 Andanga U.S.S.R. 59.11N 45.44E
95 D3 Andapa Madagascar 14.39S 49.40E
94 F2 Andara Namibia 18.04S 21.29E
31 E3 Andarab reg Afghanistan
118 H3 Andaraí Brazil 12.49S 41.22W
77 L7 Andarax R Spain
34 E3 Andarīn,El Syria 35.32N 37.20E
65 Q6 Andau Austria 47.47N 17.02E
76 H5 Andavias Spain 41.36N 5.51W
23 D7 Ande Guangxi China 23.16N 106.04E
66 O5 Andeer Switzerland 46.37N 9.27E
53 N9 Andefjord Faeroes 62.17N 6.51W
47 G2 Andeg U.S.S.R. 67.55N 53.10E
66 L1 Andelfingen Switzerland 47.36N 8.41E
70 N3 Andelle R France
69 J7 Andelot-Blanchville France 48.15N 5.17E
71 H3 Andelot-en-Montagne France 46.51N 5.56E
66 Q2 Andelsbuch Austria 47.25N 9.54E
60 L12 Andelst Netherlands 51.54N 5.44E
70 N3 Andelys,les France 49.15N 1.26E
95 C7 Andemaka Madagascar 22.19S 47.45E
51 E2 Andenes Norway 69.18N 16.10E
61 L5 Andenne Belgium 50.29N 5.06E
89 L4 Anderamboukane Mali 15.28N 3.02E
59 G5 Anderin mt Leix Irish Rep 53.02N 7.38W
61 R9 Anderlecht dist Bruxelles Belgium
61 H5 Anderlues Belgium 50.24N 4.16E
66 L5 Andermatt Switzerland 46.38N 8.36E
64 C3 Andernach W Germany 50.26N 7.24E
64 C3 Andernach-Land W Germany 50.23N 7.20E
72 B6 Andernos-les-Bains France 44.45N 1.06W
43 K8 Anderov Tadzhikistan U.S.S.R. 37.15N 71.29E
52 M2 Andersfors Sweden 64.30N 20.30E
121 E5 Anderson Argentina 35.16S 60.13W
110 C9 Anderson California 40.28N 122.18W
106 J9 Anderson Indiana 40.05N 85.41W
107 B5 Anderson Missouri 36.41N 94.27W
105 E3 Anderson S Carolina 34.30N 82.39W
101 J1 Anderson R N W Terr
101 V1 Anderson B N W Terr
12 H8 Anderson B Tasmania
28 G6 Anderson I Andaman Is
110 F7 Anderson L Oregon 42.32N 119.50W
14 A6 Anderson, Pt W Australia 23.21S 113.00E
110 K6 Anderson Ranch Res Idaho 43.25N 115.20W
11 M13 Andersons Bay dist Dunedin New Zealand
105 C5 Andersonville Georgia 32.11N 84.14W
107 L2 Andersonville Indiana 39.30N 85.16W
29 L2 Anderson Weir W Bengal India 23.18N 87.33E
52 H9 Anderstorp Sweden 57.17N 13.47E
119 C5 Andes Colombia 5.40N 75.56W
103 E2 Andes New York 42.12N 74.47W
117 G4 Andes,Cord.de los mts S America
108 M6 Andes, L S Dakota 43.10N 98.27W
53 V14 Andestadvatn L Norway 62.25N 6.40E
77 B5 Andévalo,Sierra de mts Spain
95 D5 Andevoranto Madagascar 18.56S 49.07E
15 K6 Andewa, Mt New Britain 5.35S 148.56E
51 E2 Andfjord inlet Norway
Andgird see Andūhjerd
Andhaur see Anzawr
28 A1 Andhra L Maharashtra India 18.55N 73.35E
28 D2 Andhra Pradesh state India
44 G5 Andi U.S.S.R. 42.47N 46.17E
75 G2 Andía, Sierra de mts Spain
66 N4 Andiast Switzerland 46.47N 9.07E
26 Q6 Andigama Sri Lanka 7.47N 79.57E
60 J9 Andijk Netherlands 52.44N 5.12E
84 C2 Andikhasiá Óri mts Greece
84 E5 Andíkira Greece 38.22N 22.38E
83 F9 Andikíthira isld Greece 35.52N 25.18E
95 D4 Andilamena Madagascar 17.00S 48.35E
95 D4 Andilanatoby Madagascar 17.56S 48.15E
75 J8 Andilla Spain 39.49N 0.49W
72 B3 Andilly France 46.16N 1.02W
69 K8 Andilly-en-Bassigny France 47.55N 5.31E
32 C4 Andīmeshk Iran 32.30N 48.26E
84 H8 Andimilos isld Greece 36.47N 24.14E
Andiminshk see Andīmeshk
22 G8 Andingpu Ningxia China 37.55N 107.12E
83 G7 Andipáros isld Greece
83 D5 Andípaxoi isld Greece 39.09N 20.13E
83 H6 Andípsara isld Greece 38.33N 25.31E
120 E3 Andirá R Brazil
24 D7 Andir He R Xinjiang Uygur Zizhiqu China
36 J5 Andirin Turkey 37.33N 36.18E
24 D7 Andirlangar Xinjiang Uygur Zizhiqu China 37.34N 83.51E
84 C5 Andírrion Greece 38.20N 21.46E
36 B3 Ándissa Lésvos Greece 39.15N 26.00E
44 G5 Andiyskiy Khrebet mts U.S.S.R.
44 G5 Andiyskoye Koysu R U.S.S.R.
28 C5 Andiyur Tamil Nadu India 11.36N 77.37E
43 O8 Andizhan Tadzhikistan U.S.S.R. 40.40N 72.12E
43 K6 Andizhan Uzbekistan U.S.S.R. 40.48N 72.23E
43 O7 Andizhan II Uzbekistan U.S.S.R. 40.50N 72.22E
31 C2 Andkhui Afghanistan 36.56N 65.05E
31 C2 Andkhui R Afghanistan
69 N7 Andlau France 48.24N 7.25E
75 F1 Andoain Spain 43.13N 2.01W
119 C9 Andoas Peru 2.53S 76.26W
119 C9 Andoas Nuevo Ecuador 2.36S 76.39W
47 D6 Andoga R U.S.S.R.
28 D2 Andol Andhra Prad India 17.49N 78.03E
28 C2 Andola Karnataka India 16.55N 76.47E
66 J7 Andolla,Passo d' Switz/Italy 46.07N 8.05E
95 C5 Andolofotsy Madagascar 18.43S 46.39E
69 N7 Andolsheim France 48.04N 7.26E
47 D5 Andomskiy Pogost U.S.S.R. 61.14N 36.41E
95 D5 Andonabe-Sud Madagascar 19.55S 48.11E
21 D9 Andong S Korea 36.37N 128.44E
23 H1 Andongwei Shandong China 35.08N 119.25E
13 F1 Andoom Queensland 12.25S 141.53E
79 D7 Andora Italy 43.58N 8.08E
65 J5 Andorf Austria 48.23N 13.35E
51 F3 Andørja isld Norway 68.51N 17.15E
79 D3 Andorno Micca Italy 45.37N 8.03E
75 K6 Andorra Spain 40.59N 0.27W
75 N2 Andorra rep Pyrénées France/Spain
75 O2 Andorra la Vella Andorra 42.30N 1.30E
Andorra la Vieja see Andorra la Vella
75 G3 Andosilla Spain 42.23N 1.56W
70 J5 Andouille France 48.11N 0.47W
72 J7 Andouque France 44.02N 2.18E
103 K3 Andover Connecticut 41.44N 72.23W
56 J5 Andover Hants Eng 51.13N 1.28W
98 E7 Andover New Brunswick 46.48N 67.43W
104 O3 Andover New Hampshire 43.26N 71.51W
103 E5 Andover New Jersey 40.58N 74.45W
104 H4 Andover New York 42.10N 77.49W
104 E5 Andover Ohio 41.35N 80.34W
108 N4 Andover S Dakota 45.23N 97.52W
56 H4 Andoversford Glos England 51.53N 1.56W
51 E2 Andøy isld Norway 69.05N 15.40E
91 G7 Andrada Angola 7.41S 21.22E
118 D7 Andradina Brazil 20.54S 51.19W
95 D2 Andrafiamena mt Madagascar 12.54S 49.20E
95 B4 Andrafiavelo Madagascar 17.47S 44.11E
95 D2 Andrahary mt Madagascar 13.37S 49.16E
77 U14 Andraitx Balearic Is 39.35N 2.25E
95 C5 Andramasina Madagascar 19.10S 47.35E
95 B7 Andranamy Madagascar 23.45S 44.03E
81 R13 Andrano Italy 39.59N 18.24E
95 C3 Andranoboka Madagascar 15.38S 46.53E
95 D5 Andranobolahy Madagascar 18.19S 49.01E
95 D2 Andranofotsy Madagascar 13.00S 48.58E
95 D5 Andranokabaka Madagascar 18.03S 48.16E
95 B7 Andranolava Madagascar 22.38S 44.40E
95 B4 Andranomavo Madagascar 16.32S 45.34E
95 A6 Andranopasy Madagascar 21.18S 43.44E
95 C5 Andranovelona Nord Madagascar 18.10S 46.50E
95 C6 Andranovorivato Madagascar 21.38S 47.00E
95 B7 Andranovory Madagascar 23.08S 44.10E
27 L7 Andrath I Laccadive Is Indian Ocean 11.00N 73.10E
30 H5 Andrauli Nepal 27.35N 84.11E
84 B6 Andravidha Greece 37.54N 21.16E
113 F5 Andreafsky Alaska 62.04N 163.20W
113 F5 Andreafsky R Alaska
113 Q10 Andreanof Is Aleutian Is
46 H2 Andreapol' U.S.S.R. 56.38N 32.21E
57 E4 Andreas Isle of Man U.K. 54.22N 4.26W
103 C5 Andreas Pennsylvania 40.45N 75.48W
50 S13 Andrée Land Spitsbergen
48 U9 Andrées Land Greenland
118 G7 Andrelândia Brazil 21.45S 44.22W
95 D4 Andrepatsy mt Madagascar 16.50S 48.28E
72 E9 Andrest France 43.18N 0.04E
80 M7 Andretta Italy 40.56N 15.20E
100 E5 Andrew Alberta 53.52N 112.14W
106 D7 Andrew Iowa 42.11N 90.37W
25 C3 Andrew B Burma
14 E10 Andrew, Mt W Australia 32.53S 122.51E
106 J9 Andrews Indiana 40.52N 85.36W
105 D2 Andrews N Carolina 35.13N 83.49W
108 G7 Andrews Nebraska 42.38N 103.44W
110 G7 Andrews Oregon 42.27N 118.37W
105 H4 Andrews S Carolina 33.27N 79.35W
112 E3 Andrews Texas 32.19N 102.34W
26 D4 Andrew Seamount Indian Oc 6.45N 50.29E
45 J9 Andreyevka Donetsk, Ukraine U.S.S.R. 47.29N 37.42E
43 J1 Andreyevka Kazakhstan U.S.S.R. 52.35N 67.32E
43 O4 Andreyevka Kazakhstan U.S.S.R. 45.50N 80.34E
45 H7 Andreyevka Khar'kov, Ukraine U.S.S.R. 49.34N 36.38E
46 Q4 Andreyevka Orenburg U.S.S.R. 52.21N 51.58E
45 H9 Andreyevka Zaporozh'ye, Ukraine U.S.S.R. 47.05N 36.35E
45 N1 Andreyevo U.S.S.R. 55.55N 41.09E
46 H6 Andreyevo-Ivanovka Ukraine U.S.S.R. 47.28N 30.29E
42 J3 Andreyevsk U.S.S.R. 58.08N 114.15E
42 J3 Andreyevskiy U.S.S.R. 59.32N 114.55E
47 K6 Andreyevskoye,Oz L U.S.S.R. 58.58N 67.00E
45 D4 Andreykovichi U.S.S.R. 52.16N 32.58E
39 E1 Andrey-Kyuyel' U.S.S.R. 68.45N 151.28E
39 C2 Andrey-Tas,Gory mts U.S.S.R.
71 E5 Andrézieux-Bouthéon France 45.32N 4.22E
80 O6 Andria Italy 41.14N 16.18E
95 C4 Andriamena Madagascar 17.25S 47.30E
95 B7 Andriandampy Madagascar 22.45S 45.40E
95 C4 Andriba Madagascar 17.33S 46.55E
95 H9 Andrieskraal S Africa 33.46S 24.40E
82 F8 Andrijevica Yugoslavia 42.45N 19.48E
95 C7 Andringitra mts Madagascar
84 C7 Andritsaina Greece 37.29N 21.54E
109 G4 Andrix Colorado 37.17N 103.13W
84 C6 Andróni Greece 37.48N 21.43E
84 H4 Andronianoi Greece 38.37N 24.04E
113 G9 Andronica I Alaska 55.20N 160.06W
51 Q7 Andronova Gora Karelia U.S.S.R. 64.04N 32.20E
47 C5 Andronovskoye U.S.S.R. 60.33N 34.25E
83 G7 Ándros Greece 37.49N 24.54E
83 G7 Ándros I Greece 37.49N 24.54E
116 E2 Andros isld Bahamas
104 O2 Androscoggin R New Hampshire/Maine
45 V4 Androsovka U.S.S.R. 52.44N 49.34E
116 F2 Andros Town Andros Bahamas 24.45N 77.50W
28 A5 Androth isld Laccadive Is Ind Oc 10.51N 73.41E
46 G4 Andrushevka Ukraine U.S.S.R. 50.00N 28.59E
62 L6 Andrychów Poland 49.51N 19.18E
47 J6 Andryushino U.S.S.R. 59.12N 63.00E
39 E1 Andryushka U.S.S.R. 69.30N 153.27E
51 G2 Andselv Norway 69.04N 18.35E
53 C6 Andst Denmark 55.29N 9.14E
87 B9 Andudu Zaïre 2.26N 28.39E
77 H4 Andújar Spain 38.02N 4.03W
32 G5 Andūjerd Iran 30.11N 57.47E
91 E9 Andulo Angola 11.29S 16.43E
71 D8 Anduze France 44.03N 3.59E
66 O2 Andwil Switzerland 47.27N 9.17E
41 L7 Andyngda U.S.S.R. 65.04N 115.30E
44 E3 Andzhiyevskiy U.S.S.R. 44.15N 43.05E
60 P9 Ane Netherlands 52.37N 6.39E
52 H9 Aneby Sweden 57.50N 14.45E
89 K8 Anécho Togo 6.17N 1.40E
14 G6 Anec, L W Australia 23.58S 128.03E
121 B8 Anecón Grande pk Argentina 41.27S 70.15W
89 H2 Anefis Mali 18.39N 2.01W
89 K2 Anéfis Mali 18.04N 0.39E
105 M7 Anegada isld Virgin Is Caribbean Sea 18.46N 64.24W
121 E8 Anegada, Bahía B Argentina
116 N5 Anegada Passage Leeward Is W I
119 A4 Anegada, Pta C Panama 7.19N 81.37W
20 H4 Anegasaki Chiba Japan 35.28N 140.02E
9 D13 Aneityum isld New Hebrides
'Aneiza, Jabal mt see 'Unayzah, Jabal mt
28 C4 Anekal Karnataka India 12.44N 77.41E
81 C3 Anela Sardinia 40.27N 9.04E
9 D13 Anelgauhat New Hebrides 20.14S 169.51E
121 C7 Anelo Argentina 38.22S 68.48W
84 D7 Anemodhoúri Greece 37.22N 22.13E
84 C6 Anemokhóri Greece 37.36N 21.33E
84 B3 Anemorrákhi Greece 39.19N 21.05E
94 D7 Anenous S Africa 29.17S 17.34E
88 K6 Anergane Morocco 31.00N 7.10W
100 K7 Anerley Saskatchewan 51.23N 107.18W
100 K9 Aneroid Saskatchewan 49.43N 107.20W
88 Q12 Anesberakka Algeria 19.26N 4.42E
70 N4 Anet France 48.51N 1.26E
108 N2 Aneta N Dakota 47.40N 97.59W
75 M2 Aneto,Pico de mt Spain 42.37N 0.40E
90 F2 Aney Niger 19.29N 12.53E
88 K5 Anfa airport Morocco 33.25N 8.20W
79 H3 Anfo Italy 45.46N 10.29E
23 G5 Anfu Jiangxi China 27.15N 114.42E
42 H5 Anga U.S.S.R. 54.00N 106.15E
28 C5 Angadipuram Kerala India 10.58N 76.15E
13 B3 Angalarri R N Terr Australia
91 B2 Angalé Cameroon 2.51N 10.13E
15 F7 Angamarut Papua New Guinea 6.22S 141.00E
26 S6 Angamedilla Sri Lanka 7.52N 80.55E
121 H7 Angamos isld Chile 49.10S 75.00W
120 D10 Angamos,Pta C Chile 23.00S 70.27W
87 G7 Angana,L Ethiopia
Angangki see Yushutun
115 J8 Angangueo Mexico 19.36N 100.18W
19 G5 Angar Moluccas Indon 3.40S 130.46E
29 J2 Angara Bihar India 23.24N 85.30E
42 E3 Angara R U.S.S.R.
48 K9 Angara Basin Arctic Oc
87 F4 Angareb watercourse Ethiopia
39 G2 Angarka R U.S.S.R.
87 F6 Angar,R Ethiopia
42 G5 Angarsk U.S.S.R. 52.31N 103.55E
13 B7 Angas Downs N Terr Aust 25.00S 132.02E
14 G6 Angas Ra W Australia
12 E5 Angaston S Australia 34.30S 139.03E
19 K4 Angat Luzon Philippines 14.55N 121.01E
19 H1 Angat R Luzon Philippines
93 H7 Angata Naado Kenya 1.17S 36.05E
118 E8 Angatuba Brazil 23.28S 48.28W
42 G5 Angaul U.S.S.R. 53.50N 100.25E
19 M3 Angaur isld Palau Is Pacific Oc 6.55N 134.09E
90 C8 Angba Nigeria 7.05N 7.11E
30 L5 Angbung Nepal 27.21N 87.44E
52 J4 Ånge Sweden 62.31N 15.40E
52 J5 Angebo Sweden 61.59N 16.25E
71 H10 Ange,Col de l' France 43.16N 5.40E
53 T16 Angedalen V Norway 61.30N 6.00E
76 B7 Angeja Portugal 40.41N 8.33W
44 G8 Angekhakot Armenia U.S.S.R. 39.34N 45.55E
115 C3 Angel de la Guarda isld Mexico
87 B8 Angeleri,Jeb mt Sudan 5.36N 29.30E
19 K4 Angeles Luzon Philippines 15.09N 120.33E
Angel Fall see Salto del Angel
52 G10 Ängelholm Sweden 56.15N 12.50E
53 K4 Angelholm Sweden 56.15N 12.51E
111 A8 Angel I California
104 G4 Angelica New York 42.18N 78.02W
112 N4 Angelina R Texas
13 H7 Angellala Queensland 26.25S 146.55E
63 L3 Angeln reg W Germany
84 B4 Angelókastron Aitolía Greece 38.34N 21.18E
84 E6 Angelókastron Korinthía Greece 37.45N 23.00E
14 C6 Angelo R W Australia
52 J7 Angelsberg Sweden 59.57N 16.02E
111 D3 Angels Camp California 38.05N 120.34W
71 E1 Angély France 47.33N 4.01E
15 E5 Angemuk mt Irian Jaya 3.29S 138.36E
65 N7 Anger Austria 47.17N 15.42E
79 E3 Angera Italy 45.47N 8.34E
52 K3 Änger,anälven R Sweden
60 M12 Angeren Netherlands 51.55N 5.57E
60 N12 Angerlo Netherlands 52.00N 6.09E
52 L4 Ångermanälven isld Sweden 62.45N 18.00E
63 E10 Angermund W Germany 51.20N 6.47E
63 U6 Angermünde E Germany 53.01N 14.01E
65 P5 Angern Austria 48.23N 16.50E
70 J7 Angers France 47.29N 0.32W
52 H5 Angersjö Sweden 61.59N 14.50E
69 B7 Angerville France 48.19N 2.00E
51 J5 Ängesä Sweden 66.43N 22.20E
51 K5 Ängesån R Sweden
52 M3 Ängesön isld Sweden 63.45N 20.55E
19 B6 Anggowala,Bukit mt Celebes Indon 4.15S 121.45E
79 M7 Anghiari Italy 43.32N 12.03E
118 G2 Angical Brazil 11.59S 44.40W
117 H7 Angicos Brazil 5.45S 36.32W
105 J2 Angier N Carolina 35.30N 78.45W
101 X4 Angikuni L N W Terr
84 F6 Angistri Greece 37.42N 23.20E
84 F6 Angistrion isld Greece
25 G6 Angkor anc site Cambodia 13.26N 103.50E
72 C5 Anglade France 45.12N 0.38W
98 E4 Anglais, Pointe aux Quebec 49.38N 67.15W
Ang-la-jen Ts'o L see Ngangla Ringco
72 J5 Anglards-de-Salers France 45.13N 2.26E
56 A4 Angle Dyfed Wales 51.41N 5.06W
11 B13 Anglem, Mt Stewart I New Zealand 46.45S 167.55E
99 D4 Angler Ontario 48.46N 86.24W
75 Q4 Anglés Spain 41.57N 2.38E
72 K8 Anglès Tarn France 43.34N 2.34E
72 B3 Angles Vendée France 46.25N 1.24W
Anglesey co see Gwynedd co
75 N4 Anglesola Spain 41.40N 1.05E
72 F2 Angles sur-l'Anglin France 46.42N 0.53E
72 A9 Anglet airport France 43.29N 1.30W
112 M6 Angleton Texas 29.10N 95.27W
61 N4 Angleur Belgium 50.37N 5.36E
100 J7 Anglia Saskatchewan 51.33N 108.10W
72 E2 Angliers France 46.58N 0.08E
99 L5 Angliers Quebec 47.33N 79.14W
72 G2 Anglin R France
81 B2 Anglona reg Sardinia
69 F6 Anglure France 48.35N 3.49E
48 U14 Angmagssalik Greenland 65.35N 38.00W
18 J3 Ang Mo Kio dist Singapore
91 J1 Ango Zaïre 4.01N 25.52E
92 J10 Angoche Mozambique 16.10S 39.58E
32 G7 Angohrān Iran 26.35N 57.55E
72 G5 Angoisse France 45.26N 1.09E
121 A6 Angol Chile 37.47S 72.45W
106 J8 Angola Indiana 41.38N 85.01W
104 F4 Angola New York 42.39N 79.02W
73 F7 Angola state Africa
96 K11 Angola Basin Atlantic Oc
105 K3 Angola Swamp N Carolina
113 U8 Angoon Alaska 57.30N 134.35W
108 G8 Angora Nebraska 41.52N 103.08W
15 H6 Angoram Papua New Guinea 4.04S 144.04E
115 J6 Angostura San Luis Potosí Mexico 22.12N 100.10W
115 E5 Angostura Sinaloa Mexico 25.22N 108.11W
121 C1 Angostura R Argentina
115 E2 Angostura,Presa de la res Mexico
108 G6 Angostura Res S Dakota
119 D6 Angostura 2,Salto de cat Colombia 2.37N 72.57W
119 D6 Angostura, Salto de cat Colombia 2.14N 73.56W
119 E6 Angostura 3, Salto de cat Colombia 2.41N 71.00W
Angoteros see San Martín
72 E4 Angoulême France 45.40N 0.10E
72 B3 Angoulins France 46.07N 1.07W
91 C3 Angouma Gabon 1.08N 12.20E
67 F7 Angoumois prov France
15 C5 Angra isld Irian Jaya 2.43S 134.48E
88 F9 Angra de los Ruivos B Morocco
96 U3 Angra do Heroismo Azores 38.40N 27.14W
118 G8 Angra dos Reis Brazil 22.59S 44.17W
94 B2 Angra Fria Namibia
94 C6 Angra Pequena Harb Namibia
61 E5 Angre Belgium 50.22N 3.42E
61 E5 Angreau Belgium 50.21N 3.41E
43 K6 Angren Uzbekistan U.S.S.R. 41.01N 70.10E
80 L7 Angri Italy 40.43N 14.34E
70 J6 Angrie France 47.35N 0.56W
64 L2 Angstedt-Gräfinau E Germany 50.42N 11.01E
25 F5 Ang Thong Thailand 14.35N 100.25E
91 J2 Angu Zaïre 3.23N 24.30E
121 B3 Angualasto Argentina 30.01S 69.15W
76 F5 Angueira R Portugal
75 K3 Angüés Spain 42.07N 0.10W
75 E3 Anguiano Spain 42.16N 2.46W
121 D6 Anguil Argentina 36.32S 64.00W
116 E3 Anguila Is Bahamas 23.34N 79.33W
116 N5 Anguilla isld Leeward Is W I 18.14N 63.05W
80 F4 Anguillara Sabazia Italy 42.05N 12.16E
79 L4 Anguillara Veneta Italy 45.08N 11.54E
98 N6 Anguille, C Newfoundland 47.55N 59.25W
98 N6 Anguille Mtns Newfoundland
75 E7 Anguix Spain 40.25N 2.49W
29 J7 Angul Orissa India 20.48N 85.04E
91 K4 Angumu Zaïre 0.10S 27.42E
22 K7 Anguo Hebei China 38.27N 115.20E
Angūran see Angohrān
13 D2 Angurugu Groote Eylandt, N Terr Australia 13.59S 136.30E
108 O1 Angus Minnesota 48.07N 96.41W
99 L8 Angus Ontario 44.19N 79.53W
94 T14 Angus S Africa 26.22S 28.07E
Angus co see Tayside reg
120 G3 Angustura Rondônia Brazil 8.52S 62.21W
100 Q8 Angusville Manitoba 50.44N 101.02W
31 J10 Angutia Char isld Bangladesh 22.20N 91.22E
41 E7 Angutikha U.S.S.R. 66.07N 87.15E
92 E10 Angwa R Zimbabwe
20 C1 Angyō Japan 35.52N 139.45E
76 B5 Anha Portugal 41.41N 8.48W
23 H6 Anhai Fujian China 24.39N 118.29E
61 K5 Anhee Belgium 50.18N 4.53E
53 H3 Anholt Denmark 56.43N 11.34E
63 D9 Anholt W Germany 51.51N 6.26E
53 H3 Anholt isld Denmark 56.43N 11.34E
25 H3 Anh Son Vietnam 18.55N 105.19E
23 F4 Anhua Hunan China 29.34N 120.06E
23 G2 Anhui prov China
118 C5 Anhumas Brazil 16.58S 54.43W
21 D9 Anhŭng S Korea 36.45N 126.09E
Anhwei prov China see Anhui
30 A1 Ani Himachal Prad India 31.25N 77.24E
20 O2 Ani Japan 40.00N 140.26E
113 H6 Aniak Alaska 61.32N 159.40W
113 H6 Aniak R Alaska
113 H8 Aniakchak Vol.Crater Alaska 56.53N 158.10W
71 D9 Aniane France 43.41N 3.35E
94 E4 Anias Namibia 23.28S 18.09E
121 J9 Aníbal Pinto L Chile 52.05S 72.25W
9 B9 Anibare B Nauru, Pacific Oc
69 E3 Aniche France 50.20N 3.15E
118 E5 Anicuns Brazil 16.30S 49.54W
83 H8 Ánidhros isld Greece 36.38N 25.43E
89 K8 Anie Togo 7.49N 1.17E
80 G5 Aniene R Italy
72 C10 Anie, Pic d' mt France 42.57N 0.43W
84 E6 Anifí Greece 37.40N 22.47E
33 A7 Anik Saudi Arabia 26.32N 50.02E
43 F2 Anikhovka U.S.S.R. 51.28N 60.15E
40 B5 Anikino U.S.S.R. 53.27N 120.15E
47 E6 Anikovo U.S.S.R. 59.23N 43.50E
118 H10 Anil Brazil 22.58S 43.20W
118 H10 Anil, R. do Brazil
35 D8 'Anim watercourse Israel
109 B10 Animas New Mexico 31.57N 108.48W
109 C4 Animas R Colorado
109 B10 Animas Pk New Mexico 31.35N 108.46W
35 D8 'Anim, Hare hills Israel
25 D5 Anin Burma 15.40N 97.45E
35 D4 Anin Jordan 32.30N 35.10E
82 G5 Anina Romania 45.05N 21.51E
91 A4 Aningué, L Gabon 1.03S 9.30E
75 G5 Aniñón Spain 41.27N 1.43W
44 F7 Anipemza Armenia U.S.S.R. 40.26N 43.37E
Ani,Ras see 'Ayn, Ra's al cape
42 C5 Anisimovo U.S.S.R. 54.03N 82.45E
41 P3 Anisiy, Mys C U.S.S.R. 76.14N 139.18E
111 M6 Anita Arizona 35.51N 112.14W
108 Q8 Anita Iowa 41.28N 94.49W
19 M6 Anitaguipan Pt Philippines 11.40N 125.29E
121 J1 Anitápolis Brazil 27.53S 49.10W
113 J2 Aniuk R Alaska
40 J8 Aniva Sakhalin U.S.S.R. 46.41N 142.31E
40 J8 Aniva,Mys C Sakhalin U.S.S.R. 46.03N 143.30E
40 J8 Aniva,Zaliv B Sakhalin U.S.S.R.
95 D2 Anivorano Madagascar 12.42S 49.12E
106 E4 Aniwa Wisconsin 45.02N 89.12W
9 D12 Aniwa isld New Hebrides 18.17S 169.36E
69 E4 Anizy-le-Château France 49.31N 3.28E
15 B4 Anjai Irian Jaya 1.56S 132.57E
95 C5 Anjamanga Madagascar 19.45S 47.30E
29 E7 Anjangaon Maharashtra India 21.11N 77.21E
28 A2 Anjanwel Maharashtra India 17.36N 73.10E
29 B6 Anjar Gujarat India 23.06N 70.05E
35 G4 'Anjara Jordan 32.18N 35.45E
28 C6 Anjengo Kerala India 8.40N 76.47E
23 H3 Anji Jiangsu China 30.46N 119.40E
29 F7 Anji Maharashtra India 20.52N 78.34E
21 D5 Anjia Heilongjiang China 45.04N 127.02E
Anjiang see Qianyang
Anjiangying see Luanping
22 L6 Anjiangying Hebei China 40.55N 117.17E
28 B3 Anjidiv isld Karnataka India 14.46N 74.07E
Anjirak see Anjir Avand
32 F4 Anjir Avand Iran 32.10N 54.28E
34 O4 Anjīrek Iran 34.06N 46.50E
20 L7 Anjō Japan 34.56N 137.05E
32 G3 Anjoman Iran 35.49N 57.47E
95 B5 Anjoma-Ramartina Madagascar 19.39S 45.58E
30 H7 Anjorpur Uttar Prad India 25.43N 84.03E
99 S8 Anjou Quebec 45.36N 73.36W
67 E5 Anjou prov France
95 B2 Anjouan isld Comoros, Indian Oc
66 D1 Anjoutey France 47.43N 6.56E
95 C5 Anjozorobe Madagascar 18.22S 47.52E
21 C8 Anjŭ N Korea 39.36N 125.42E
60 N6 Anjum Netherlands 53.22N 6.08E
Anjuman Iran see Anjoman
31 F3 Anjuman reg Afghanistan
31 F3 Anjuman Pass Afghanistan 35.50N 70.07E
34 J4 Anka Iraq 34.24N 41.04E
90 B5 Anka Nigeria 12.07N 5.59E
41 J8 Ankacho U.S.S.R. 63.15N 108.05E
95 B5 Ankalalobe Madagascar 19.38S 44.57E
23 E2 Ankang Shaanxi China 32.40N 109.12E
36 F3 Ankara Turkey 39.55N 32.50E
36 F3 Ankara R Turkey
95 C6 Ankaramena Madagascar 21.57S 46.39E
95 C4 Ankaraobato Madagascar 16.12S 47.34E
95 C5 Ankaratra mts Madagascar
52 H2 Ankarede Sweden 64.49N 14.15E
95 C7 Ankarimbelo Madagascar 22.08S 47.20E
52 J9 Ankarsrum Sweden 57.41N 16.20E
51 F6 Ankarsund Sweden 65.22N 16.30E
95 B4 Ankasakasa Madagascar 16.20S 44.51E
95 B5 Ankavandra Madagascar 18.43S 45.18E
95 B7 Ankazoabo Madagascar 22.18S 44.30E
95 C5 Ankazobe Madagascar 18.20S 47.07E
95 B5 Ankazomanga Madagascar 19.39S 45.20E
108 R8 Ankeny Iowa 41.44N 93.36W
95 C3 Ankerika Madagascar 14.58S 47.51E
95 D3 Ankiabelo Madagascar 14.50S 48.57E
95 A6 Ankiliabo Madagascar 21.41S 43.53E
95 B4 Ankilifito Madagascar 17.50S 44.43E
95 A7 Ankililoaka Madagascar 22.47S 43.37E
95 A7 Ankilimalinika Madagascar 22.57S 43.35E
95 B6 Ankilizato Madagascar 20.25S 45.02E
95 C4 Ankirihitra Madagascar 16.44S 46.26E
95 C5 Ankisabe Madagascar 19.18S 46.29E
63 T5 Anklam E Germany 53.52N 13.42E
29 C7 Anklesvar Gujarat India 21.38N 73.02E
87 G6 Ankober Ethiopia 9.32N 39.43E
89 H9 Ankobra R Ghana
74 D10 Ankod Morocco 34.56N 4.58W
95 D4 Ankofa mt Madagascar 16.20S 48.35E
65 H7 Ankogel Austria 47.03N 13.16E
28 B3 Ankola Karnataka India 14.40N 74.18E
91 K7 Ankoro Zaïre 6.47S 26.56E
95 B8 Ankororoka Madagascar 25.29S 45.10E
95 B5 Ankotrofotsy Madagascar 19.49S 45.32E
46 L2 An'kovo U.S.S.R. 56.51N 39.54E
90 C8 Ankpa Nigeria 7.20N 7.44E
95 B8 Ankroka Madagascar 25.00S 44.05E
63 G7 Ankum W Germany 52.33N 7.52E
90 D7 Ankwe R Nigeria
23 B2 Ankyam Sichuan China 32.43N 101.52E
57 N5 Anlaby Humberside Eng 53.45N 0.27W
23 G5 Anle Fujian China 27.54N 116.49E
76 F2 Anleo Spain 43.30N 6.41W
71 D3 Anlezy France 46.57N 3.30E
61 N7 Anlier Belgium 49.47N 5.37E
60 P7 Anlo Netherlands 53.02N 6.42E
25 J7 An Loc Vietnam 11.40N 106.35E
23 D6 Anlong Guizhou China 25.05N 105.30E
25 H5 Anlong Veng Cambodia 14.16N 104.08E
61 L7 Anloy Belgium 49.57N 5.13E
23 F3 Anlu Hubei China 31.18N 113.40E
52 G3 Ånn Sweden 63.20N 12.35E
52 G3 Ånn L Sweden 63.15N 12.35E
107 G4 Anna Illinois 37.29N 89.16W
9 A8 Anna Nauru, Pacific Oc 0.30S 166.56E
104 A6 Anna Ohio 40.23N 84.11W
77 P2 Anna Spain 39.02N 0.39W
112 L2 Anna Texas 33.20N 96.33W
45 M5 Anna U.S.S.R. 51.30N 40.28E
15 A1 Anna isld Caroline Is Pacific Oc 3.19N 131.59E
88 R3 'Annaba Algeria 36.55N 7.47E
65 M6 Annaberg Nieder-Österreich Austria 47.53N 15.24E
65 H6 Annaberg Salzburg Austria 47.31N 13.27E
64 P2 Annaberg-Buchholz E Germany 50.35N 13.01E
65 K8 Annabichl Austria 46.40N 14.21E
63 S9 Annaburg E Germany 51.45N 13.02E
101 H11 Annacis I Br Col 49.10N 122.58W
12 D3 Anna Creek S Australia 28.50S 136.07E
59 K4 Annagassan Lough Irish Rep 53.53N 6.20W
59 D7 Annagh Bog Kerry Irish Rep
59 C4 Annagh I Mayo Irish Rep 53.59N 9.52W
59 G5 Annaghmore L Offaly Irish Rep 53.11N 7.32W
59 F4 Annaghmore L Roscommon Irish Rep 53.48N 8.09W
59 H3 Annagh R Cavan Irish Rep
119 J6 Annai Guyana 3.57N 59.06W
Anna Jacoba see Sluis
20 M5 Annaka Japan 36.20N 138.54E
59 L3 Annalong Down N Ireland 54.06N 5.55W
25 H3 Annam reg Vietnam
105 E10 Anna Maria Florida 27.31N 82.43W
57 G3 Annan Dumfries & Galloway Scotland 54.59N 3.16W
15 H6 Annanberg Papua New Guinea 4.55S 144.39E
108 Q4 Annandale Minnesota 45.16N 94.05W
13 J5 Annandale Queensland 21.57S 148.18E
95 M4 Annandale S Africa 28.11S 28.23E
57 G2 Annandale V Dumfries & Galloway Scotland
57 G2 Annan, R Dumfries & Galloway Scotland
34 F4 'Annān,Wādī el watercourse Syria
60 H8 Anna Paulowna Netherlands 52.52N 4.50E
121 J5 Anna Pink, B Chile
14 D4 Anna Plains W Australia 19.18S 121.34E
103 B9 Annapolis Maryland 38.59N 76.30W
98 G9 Annapolis R Nova Scotia
98 G9 Annapolis Royal Nova Scotia 44.44N 65.32W
29 H3 Annapurna mt Nepal 28.34N 83.50E
106 L7 Ann Arbor Michigan 42.18N 83.43W
119 J4 Anna Regina Guyana 7.15N 58.31W
63 O9 Annarode E Germany 51.33N 11.24E
95 J4 Annaspan salt pan S Africa 28.32S 25.48E
58 F6 Annat Strathclyde Scotland 56.21N 5.11W
106 E8 Annawan Illinois 41.23N 89.54W
123 G12 Annawan, C Antarctica 72.30S 95.00W
57 D2 Annbank Strathclyde Scotland 55.28N 4.30W
123 A5 Ann, C Antarctica 66.13S 51.10E
103 A8 Anne co Maryland
14 C7 Annean, L W Australia 27.00S 118.10E
70 L3 Annebault France 49.15N 0.03E
71 J5 Annecy France 45.54N 6.07E
71 J5 Annecy,L.d' France 45.52N 6.10E
66 A8 Annecy le vieux France 45.55N 6.08E
71 J4 Annemasse France 46.11N 6.14E
60 P7 Annen Netherlands 52.03N 6.44E
121 G8 Annenkov I S Georgia 54.29S 37.10W
45 S3 Annenkovo U.S.S.R. 53.01N 46.24E
47 D5 Annenskiy-Most U.S.S.R. 60.49N 37.00E
13 K2 Annerley dist Brisbane, Qnsld
104 E1 Anneslie Maryland 39.23N 76.36W
59 H7 Annestown Waterford Irish Rep 52.08N 7.16W
56 Q8 Annet isld Is of Scilly Eng 49.54N 6.22W
113 W9 Annette Alaska 55.02N 131.36W
101 H8 Annette I Alaska
70 G3 Anneville-sur-Mer France 49.07N 1.35W
61 K5 Annevoie-Rouillon Belgium 50.21N 4.51E
71 F6 Anneyron France 45.16N 4.53E
25 K6 An Nhon Vietnam 13.53N 109.07E
13 G2 Annie R Queensland
98 P5 Annieopsquotch Mtns Newfoundland
96 C1 Annie's B Bermuda Atlantic Ocean 32.22N 64.40W
Annie Vale see Kyong Queensland
23 C6 Anning Yunnan China 24.55N 102.29E
23 C5 Anning He R Sichuan China
94 D7 Annis Fontein S Africa 28.25S 16.52E
53 J5 Annisse Denmark 55.59N 12.12E
107 L8 Anniston Alabama 33.38N 85.50W
13 D5 Annitowa N Terr Australia 21.08S 136.10E
66 G7 Anniviers,Val d' Switzerland
96 L9 Annobón isld Equat Guinea 1.24S 5.37E
69 D2 Annœullin France 50.32N 2.56E
112 N2 Annona Texas 33.35N 94.56W
71 F6 Annonay France 45.15N 4.40E
79 F3 Annone,Lago di Italy
79 N3 Annone Véneto Italy 45.48N 12.41E
71 K9 Annôt France 43.58N 6.42E
116 L1 Annotto Bay Jamaica, W I 18.16N 76.47W
45 E8 Annovka Ukraine U.S.S.R. 48.14N 33.30E
12 G5 Annuello Victoria 34.52S 142.54E
39 E4 Annushka U.S.S.R. 62.12N 152.36E
103 A6 Annville Pennsylvania 40.19N 76.32W
64 D5 Annweiler W Germany 49.12N 7.58E
84 C5 Áno Akhaïa Greece 38.06N 21.34E
84 C5 Ano Alissós Greece 38.08N 21.35E
15 M3 Anoano Malaita I Solomon Is 9.00S 160.46E
84 M11 Ano Arkhánai Crete 35.15N 25.09E
108 R4 Anoka Minnesota 45.11N 93.20W
108 M7 Anoka Nebraska 42.57N 98.50W
84 B5 Áno Kerásovon Greece 38.29N 21.27E
84 D6 Áno Klitoría Greece 37.53N 22.05E
84 W22 Ano Korakiána Corfu 39.43N 19.47E
93 K1 Anole Ethiopia 4.20N 38.26E
87 J9 Anole Somalia 2.02N 42.17E
84 G5 Áno Liósia Greece 38.05N 23.42E
89 J9 Anomabu Ghana 5.11N 1.08W
84 C5 Áno Makrinoú Greece 38.28N 21.37E
75 G4 Añón Spain 41.47N 1.43W
121 K10 Año Nuevo,Seno gulf Chile
84 D5 Áno Palaioxári Greece 38.29N 22.03E
84 B3 Áno Pétra Greece 39.10N 21.07E
45 M1 Anopino U.S.S.R. 55.43N 40.40E
84 C4 Áno Próstovas Greece 38.38N 21.38E
69 G4 Anor France 49.59N 4.06E
77 G4 Añora Spain 38.25N 4.54W
119 H9 Anori Brazil 3.48S 61.37W
48 V15 Anoritôq fjord Greenland
95 C2 Anorotsangana Madagascar 13.53S 47.56E
84 D8 Ano Sélitsa Greece 37.00N 22.11E
41 N4 Anoshkinsk U.S.S.R. 73.00N 129.08E
95 D5 Anosibe An 'Ala Madagascar 19.24S 48.11E
95 C4 Anosikely Madagascar 16.32S 46.40E
45 R1 Anosovo U.S.S.R. 55.05N 45.15E
117 C3 Anotaie R Brazil
84 D6 Áno Tríkkala Greece 37.59N 22.28E
89 L2 Anou Mali 18.30N 2.28E
88 M5 Anoual Morocco 32.40N 3.04W
88 R11 Anou I-n-Ateï Algeria 20.32N 6.10E
88 R11 Anou Izileg Algeria 20.28N 6.04E
69 M7 Anould France 48.11N 6.56E
89 G8 Anoumaba Ivory Coast 6.23N 4.38W
89 K3 Anou Melen Mali 17.29N 0.33E
88 Q12 Anou-n-Bidek Algeria 19.51N 4.07E
88 Q10 Anou Tin Felki Algeria 23.38N 4.43E
84 G5 Áno Váthia Greece 38.24N 23.55E
75 C8 Añover de Tajo Spain 39.59N 3.45W
84 M11 Ano Viánnos Crete 35.03N 25.25E
84 W22 Ano Virón Corfu 39.35N 19.53E
84 L11 Anóyia Crete 35.17N 24.53E
84 D7 Anóyia Greece 37.00N 22.26E
84 A3 Anóyion Greece 39.22N 20.56E
84 Q15 Anoyira Cyprus 34.44N 32.45E
25 K7 An Phuoc Vietnam 11.15N 108.31E
22 K7 Anping Hebei China 38.15N 115.30E
23 J7 An-p'ing Taiwan 23.01N 120.08E
23 E8 Anpu Guangdong China 31.30N 110.03E
23 E8 Anpu Gang inlet Guangdong China
23 H3 Anqing Anhui China 30.46N 119.40E
22 L8 Anqiu Shandong China 36.26N 119.12E
75 G6 Anquela del Pedregal Spain 40.44N 1.45W
63 D10 Anrath W Germany 51.17N 6.26E
23 F5 Anren Hunan China 26.45N 113.09E
63 H9 Anröchte W Germany 51.33N 8.19E
61 N4 Ans Belgium 50.39N 5.32E
53 D4 Ans Denmark 56.49N 9.36E
Anşāb see Nişāb
72 F4 Ansac-sur-Vienne France 45.59N 0.38E
53 B5 Ansager Denmark 55.43N 8.45E
22 H8 Ansai Shaanxi China 36.51N 109.18E
34 D3 Ansārīye, Jebel el mt Syria
64 K5 Ansbach W Germany 49.18N 10.36E
71 F5 Anse France 45.56N 4.43E
116 H5 Anse-à-Galets Haiti 18.49N 72.50W
98 Q2 Anse-Amour, L' Labrador, Nfld 51.28N 56.52W
116 J5 Anse-à-Pitre Haiti 18.03N 71.44W
98 Q2 Anse au Loup,L' Labrador, Nfld 51.32N 56.50W
26 S14 Anse Aux Pins B Mahé I Seychelles, Ind Oc
116 H5 Anse-à-Veau Haiti 18.30N 73.20W
87 G2 Anseba watercourse Ethiopia
116 N3 Anse Bertrand Guadeloupe W I 16.28N 61.31W
26 S14 Anse Boileau Mahé I Seychelles, Ind Oc 4.43S 55.29E
56 X10 Anse de Vauville B France
116 G5 Anse d'Hainault Haiti 18.30N 74.29W
80 D4 Ansedonia Italy 42.25N 11.17E
108 L8 Anselmo Nebraska 41.38N 99.52W
60 O8 Ansen Netherlands 52.47N 6.20E
61 K6 Anseremme Belgium 50.14N 4.54E
12 H7 Anser Group islds Tasmania 39.18S 146.30E
119 C5 Anserma Colombia 5.15N 75.47W
61 E4 Anserœul Belgium 50.43N 3.32E
26 S14 Anse Royal Mahé I Seychelles, Ind Oc 4.44S 55.31E
98 B5 Anse St Jean, L' Quebec 48.14N 70.10W
21 B7 Anshan Liaoning China 41.05N 122.58E
23 D5 Anshun Guizhou China 26.15N 105.51E
76 C9 Ansião Portugal 39.55N 8.26W
79 M1 Ansiei R Italy
121 B3 Ansilta pk Argentina 31.36S 69.50W
121 B3 Ansilta, C. de mts Argentina
121 G3 Ansina Uruguay 31.58S 55.28W
107 D9 Ansley Louisiana 32.29N 92.40W
108 L8 Ansley Nebraska 41.19N 99.22W
75 J2 Ansó Spain 42.45N 0.49W
112 H3 Anson Texas 32.45N 99.55W
10 U10 Anson B Norfolk I Pacific Oc 29.02S 167.55E
13 B2 Anson B N Terr Australia
89 K4 Ansongo Mali 15.40N 0.29E
103 H4 Ansonia Connecticut 41.21N 73.05W
104 A6 Ansonia Ohio 40.13N 84.38W
10 U10 Anson Pt Norfolk I Pacific Oc 29.01S 167.55E
105 G2 Ansonville N Carolina 35.05N 80.08W
99 K4 Ansonville Ontario 48.46N 80.43W
75 J2 Ansó,Valle de Spain
69 Q3 Anspach W Germany 50.18N 8.31E
53 Y15 Ånstad Norway 61.53N 8.24E
104 D8 Ansted W Virginia 38.07N 81.06W
57 L6 Anston S Yorks Eng 53.22N 1.13W
58 L6 Anstruther Fife Scotland 56.14N 2.42W
15 E5 Ansudu Irian Jaya 2.10S 139.19E
15 C4 Ansus Yapen I, Irian Jaya 1.45S 135.50E
An-ta see Anda
120 C5 Anta Peru 13.30S 72.08W
120 C6 Antabamba Peru 14.23S 72.54W
36 J6 Antakya Turkey 36.12N 36.10E
95 E3 Antalaha Madagascar 14.53S 50.16E
87 G4 Antalo Ethiopia 13.18N 39.31E
95 B4 Antaly Madagascar 16.10S 44.55E
36 E6 Antalya Turkey 36.53N 30.42E
36 E6 Antalya Körfezi B Turkey
95 D5 Antanambao-Manampotsy Madagascar 19.30S 48.36E
95 D4 Antanambe Madagascar 16.26S 49.50E
95 C5 Antananarivo Madagascar 18.52S 47.30E
95 C4 Antanandava Madagascar 17.00S 46.43E
95 C5 Antanifotsy Madagascar 19.40S 47.20E
95 C4 Antanimbaritsara Madagascar 17.24S 46.31E
95 B8 Antanimora Madagascar 24.49S 45.40E
95 D5 Antanjonambo Madagascar 19.47S 48.40E
123 E13 Antarctic Pen Antarctica
48 V3 Antarctics Bugt B Greenland
88 N5 Antar,Djebel mt Algeria 33.35N 0.20W
26 E10 Antares Bank Indian Ocean
33 A4 Antar,Wâdi watercourse Egypt
118 J2 Antas Brazil 10.20S 38.20W
77 N6 Antas Spain 37.15N 1.55W
77 N6 Antas R Spain
76 D3 Antas de Ulla Spain 42.46N 7.53W
121 J2 Antas,R.das Rio Grande do Sul Brazil
118 D10 Antas, R. das Santa Catarina Brazil
95 B7 Antatabe Madagascar 23.30S 45.50E
58 F3 An Teallach mt Highland Scotland 57.48N 5.16W
79 G4 Antegnate Italy 45.29N 9.47E
76 D4 Antela,L.de Spain 42.07N 7.41W
79 M2 Antelao mt Italy 46.28N 12.17E
85 F4 Antelāt Libya 31.09N 20.42E
108 F1 Antelope Montana 48.42N 104.28W
108 H3 Antelope N Dakota 46.52N 102.11W
110 E5 Antelope Oregon 44.56N 120.44W
100 J8 Antelope Saskatchewan 50.07N 108.23W
112 J2 Antelope Texas 33.27N 98.24W
110 Q9 Antelope Utah 40.59N 109.50W
110 H7 Antelope Cr Oregon
110 N9 Antelope I Utah 41.00N 112.14W
111 H2 Antelope Ra Nevada
110 H7 Antelope Res Oregon 42.54N 117.13W
109 B10 Antelope Wells New Mexico 31.22N 108.30W
95 D4 Antenina Madagascar 16.34S 49.15E
117 H8 Antenor Navarro Brazil 6.40S 38.26W
120 E8 Antequera Bolivia 18.28S 66.50W
77 G6 Antequera Spain 37.01N 4.34W
96 S13 Antequera,Pta.de Tenerife Canary Is 28.32N 16.07W
66 D8 Anterne, Col d' pass France 45.59N 6.48E
109 D3 Antero Pk Colorado 38.41N 106.16W
109 E3 Antero Res Colorado 38.59N 105.55W
79 M1 Anterselva Italy 46.52N 12.07E
71 K2 Anteuil France 47.23N 6.33E
95 B6 Antevamena Madagascar 20.40S 45.06E
95 B6 Antevamena Madagascar 21.00S 44.08E
79 C3 Antey St. André Italy 45.48N 7.36E
61 K6 Anthée Belgium 50.14N 4.46E
61 L4 Antheit Belgium 50.33N 5.14E
71 D2 Anthien France 47.18N 3.43E
84 D4 Anthili Greece 38.51N 22.29E
61 N5 Anthisnes Belgium 50.29N 5.31E
105 E8 Anthony Florida 29.17N 82.06W
109 M4 Anthony Kansas 37.10N 98.02W
109 D9 Anthony New Mexico 32.00N 106.36W
103 L3 Anthony Rhode I 41.42N 71.33W
12 C2 Anthony, Mt S Australia 26.11S 133.59E

95 O2 Anthra S Africa 26.34S 30.03E
66 B6 Anthy France 46.22N 6.26E
88 J7 Anti Atlas mts Morocco
71 L9 Antibes France 43.35N 7.07E
71 L9 Antibes,C.d' France 43.33N 7.08E
119 H2 Antica, I Venezuela 10.23N 62.40W
80 G4 Anticoli Corrado Italy 42.01N 12.59E
98 J4 Anticosti I Quebec
70 L2 Antifer,C.d' France 49.42N 0.10E
72 F10 Antignac France 42.50N 0.36E
80 B2 Antignano Italy 43.29N 10.18E
72 F2 Antigny France 46.32N 0.51E
106 E4 Antigo Wisconsin 45.10N 89.10W
98 K8 Antigonish Nova Scotia 45.39N 62.00W
66 K7 Antigorio,Valle Italy
115 O10 Antigua Guatemala 14.33N 90.42W
116 P4 Antigua isld Leeward Is Caribbean Sea 17.09N 61.49W
121 C3 Antigua,Salina La salt pan Arg
76 L5 Antigüedad Spain 41.56N 4.07W
116 N3 Antigues,Pte d' Guadeloupe W I 16.27N 61.32W
115 K6 Antiguo-Morelos Mexico 22.35N 99.08W
Anti Lebanon mts see Sharqi, Jebel esh
121 A7 Antilhue Chile 39.45S 73.00W
120 F12 Antilla Argentina 26.05S 64.36W
116 G4 Antilla Cuba 20.53N 75.46W
116 M6 Antilles, Lesser islds West Indies
81 K8 Antillo Sicily 37.58N 15.15E
120 E3 Antimari, R Brazil
111 N3 Antimony Utah 38.08N 111.59W
86 E10 Antinopolis ruins Egypt 27.49N 30.53E
111 C3 Antioch California 38.01N 121.49W
106 F7 Antioch Illinois 42.28N 88.06W
108 H7 Antioch Nebraska 42.04N 102.36W
Antioch Turkey see Antakya
72 B3 Antioche, Pertuis d' str France
122 K10 Antiope Reef Pacific Oc 18.10S 168.40W
119 C4 Antioquia Colombia 6.36N 75.53W
119 C4 Antioquia div Colombia
35 C5 Antipatris anc site Israel 32.06N 34.56E
41 C6 Antipayuta U.S.S.R. 69.03N 76.20E
84 S14 Antiphonitis Monastery Cyprus 35.19N 33.36E
45 E1 Antipino U.S.S.R. 55.54N 33.17E
41 N4 Antipinskiy U.S.S.R. 73.14N 128.32E
11 K13 Antipodes I Antipodes Is Pacific Oc 49.42S 178.49E
9 N12 Antipodes Is S Pacific Oc 49.42S 178.50E
19 J1 Antipolo Luzon Philippines 14.36N 121.11E
45 R7 Antipovka U.S.S.R. 49.49N 45.16E
45 D1 Antipovo U.S.S.R. 56.04N 32.49E
119 B8 Antisana,Cerro vol Ecuador 0.30S 78.09W
67 P12 Antisanti Corsica 42.10N 9.20E
108 J1 Antler N Dakota 48.58N 101.18W
100 Q9 Antler Saskatchewan 49.34N 101.27W
100 Q9 Antler R Man/Sask
109 P7 Antlers Oklahoma 34.15N 95.38W
95 C6 Antoetra Madagascar 20.46S 47.20E
120 D10 Antofagasta Chile 23.40S 70.23W
120 D10 Antofagasta prov Chile
120 E12 Antofagasta de la Sierra Argentina 26.06S 67.22W
120 E11 Antofalla vol Argentina 25.36S 67.55W
120 E11 Antofalla,Salina de salt pan Argentina
107 C7 Antoine Arkansas 34.02N 93.24W
61 D4 Antoing Belgium 50.34N 3.27E
79 F5 Antola,Monte Italy 44.34N 9.08E
109 G2 Anton Colorado 39.44N 103.13W
115 O5 Antón Panama 8.23N 80.15W
112 E2 Anton Texas 33.51N 102.12W
75 F2 Antonaña Spain 42.42N 2.24W
95 C3 Antonibe Madagascar 15.07S 47.23E
95 G9 Antoniesberg mt S Africa 33.28S 23.27E
81 M7 Antonimina Italy 38.16N 16.09E
118 E9 Antonina Brazil 25.36S 48.46W
109 L3 Antonino Kansas 38.49N 99.27W
42 D5 Antoninovka U.S.S.R. 54.15N 88.50E
82 K1 Antoniny U.S.S.R. 49.49N 26.57E
118 H4 Antônio R Brazil
118 G7 Antônio Carlos Brazil 21.18S 43.48W
121 L6 Antonio de Biedma Argentina 47.29S 66.30W
118 G6 Antônio Dias Brazil 19.39S 42.50W
118 C8 Antônio João Brazil 23.16S 55.31W
117 D5 Antônio Lemos Brazil 1.21S 50.48W
121 J8 Antonio Varas Pen Chile
109 D4 Antonito Colorado 37.04N 106.01W
46 Q5 Antonovo Kazakhstan U.S.S.R. 49.20N 51.54E
116 D3 Antón Recio Cuba 22.10N 80.36W
68 E4 Antony France 48.45N 2.17E
13 D4 Antony Lagoon N Terr Australia 17.56S 135.29E
120 F8 Antora Bolivia 19.05S 65.58W
76 E7 Antos Portugal 40.56N 7.24W
71 E7 Antraigues France 44.43N 4.22E
70 H5 Antrain France 48.28N 1.29W
95 B4 Antranogoaika Madagascar 17.50S 44.36E
45 L8 Antratsit U.S.S.R. 48.07N 39.05E
47 B5 Antrea U.S.S.R. 60.51N 29.12E
64 G5 Antrefftal W Germany 49.27N 9.05E
30 B6 Antri Madhya Prad India 26.03N 78.13E
59 K2 Antrim Antrim N Ireland 54.43N 6.13W
104 O3 Antrim New Hampshire 43.02N 71.57W
104 H5 Antrim Pennsylvania 41.37N 77.16W
59 K2 Antrim co N Ireland
59 K1 Antrim mts Antrim N Ireland
14 G4 Antrim Plat W Australia
80 H4 Antrodoco Italy 42.25N 13.05E
66 J7 Antrona Pass Switz/Italy 46.03N 8.02E
79 D2 Antronapiana Italy 46.04N 8.07E
66 J7 Antrona, V. d' Italy
46 N1 Antropovo Kostroma U.S.S.R. 58.22N 42.50E
42 E4 Antropovo Krasnoyarsk U.S.S.R. 55.50N 90.07E
95 D3 Antsakabary Madagascar 15.01S 48.57E
95 B5 Antsalova Madagascar 18.40S 44.37E
95 D6 Antsenavolo Madagascar 21.22S 48.03E
95 D2 Antseranana Madagascar 12.19S 49.17E
95 B4 Antseza Madagascar 16.11S 45.51E
95 C4 Antsiafabositra Madagascar 17.18S 46.57E
42 E3 Antsiferovo Krasnoyarsk U.S.S.R. 58.54N 91.50E
46 J1 Antsiferovo Novgorod U.S.S.R. 58.59N 34.00E
40 N6 Antsiferovo,O isld Kuril Is U.S.S.R. 50.12N 154.50E
95 B4 Antsirabe Madagascar 17.11S 45.01E
95 C5 Antsirabe Madagascar 19.51S 47.01E
95 D2 Antsirabe Madagascar 13.59S 49.59E
46 F1 Antsla Estonia U.S.S.R. 57.48N 26.30E
95 B5 Antsoha Madagascar 19.55S 44.50E
95 C3 Antsohihy Madagascar 14.50S 47.58E
51 N10 Anttola Finland 61.35N 27.40E
An-t'u see Antu
21 D6 Antu Jilin China 42.30N 128.20E
30 E6 Antu Uttar Prad India 26.03N 81.54E
89 H8 Antubia Ghana 6.21N 2.50W
25 K6 An Tuc Vietnam 13.55N 108.38E
121 B6 Antuco Chile 37.20S 71.44W
120 F4 Antuerpia Brazil 10.35S 63.14W
33 E9 Antufush isld Yemen 15.45N 42.26E
91 E12 Antuima, L Angola 16.10S 16.54E
33 C10 Antuk,Ra's C S Yemen 12.45N 45.01E
71 E3 Antully France 46.55N 4.24E
23 J7 An-tung Taiwan 23.13N 121.17E
29 D7 Antur Maharashtra India 20.26N 75.18E
Antwerp Belgium see Antwerpen
104 K2 Antwerp New York 44.13N 75.38W
106 K8 Antwerp Ohio 41.15N 84.45W
61 H2 Antwerpen Belgium 51.13N 4.25E
61 J1 Antwerpen prov Belgium
61 J1 Antwerpen à Turnhout,Can.d' Belgium
40 G4 Antykan U.S.S.R. 54.51N 135.03E
59 J4 An Uaimh Meath Irish Rep 53.39N 6.41W
87 D7 Anuak tribe Ethiopia
122 D16 Anuanu Raro atoll Tuamotu Is Pacific Oc 20.25S 143.30W
122 D16 Anuanu Runga atoll Tuamotu Is Pacific Oc 20.39S 143.14W
41 H2 Anuchina,Mys C U.S.S.R. 79.12N 100.29E
40 F10 Anuchino U.S.S.R. 43.59N 133.01E
121 B8 Anueque,Sierra ra Argentina
21 D10 Anŭi S Korea 35.36N 127.50E
89 K8 Anum Ghana 6.29N 0.12E
91 C11 Anunciação, Pta. da pt Angola 15.11S 12.02E
52 L3 Anundsjö Sweden 63.28N 18.05E
29 C3 Anupgarh Rajasthan India 29.10N 73.14E
29 G6 Anuppur Madhya Prad Ind 23.05N 81.45E
30 B4 Anupshahr Uttar Prad India 28.22N 78.15E
26 R5 Anuradhapura Sri Lanka 8.20N 80.25E
59 F2 Anure,L Donegal Irish Rep 55.00N 8.17W
61 E4 Anvaing Belgium 50.41N 3.34E
32 F7 Anveh Iran 27.25N 54.12E
117 E5 Anvera Brazil 1.11S 47.11W
Anvers see Antwerpen
80 J5 Anversa Degli Abruzzi Italy 42.00N 13.44E
123 E14 Anvers Island Antarctica 64.50S 64.00W
113 G5 Anvik Alaska 62.38N 160.20W
113 G5 Anvik R Alaska
99 P3 Anvilla Quebec 49.42N 75.24W
113 O10 Anvil Pk Aleutian Is 51.58N 179.30E
56 H6 Anvil Pt Dorset Eng 50.35N 1.59W
69 C3 Anvin France 50.27N 2.16E
57 N6 Anwick Lincs Eng 53.02N 0.21W
23 H6 Anxi Fujian China 25.03N 118.13E
22 C6 Anxi Gansu China 40.32N 95.57E
23 C3 An Xian Sichuan China 31.40N 104.25E
23 F4 Anxiang Hunan China 29.23N 112.09E
22 K7 Anxin Hebei China 38.55N 115.58E
12 C5 Anxious B S Australia
89 G9 Anyama Ivory Coast 5.29N 4.04W
23 G1 Anyang Henan China 36.04N 114.20E
93 D3 Anyeke Uganda 2.24N 32.31E
23 B1 A'nyêmaqên Shan mt ra Qinghai China
18 F9 Anyer Lor Java Indon 6.02S 105.57E
23 G4 Anyi Jiangxi China 28.54N 115.38E
23 F1 Anyi Shanxi China 35.08N 111.03E
89 J8 Anyinam Ghana 6.24N 0.37W
23 E9 Anyou Guangdong China 18.13N 109.30E
101 J8 Anyox Br Col 55.26N 129.50W
95 D9 Anysberg S Africa 33.31S 20.46E
95 D9 Anysberg mt S Africa 33.30S 20.36E
23 G6 Anyuan Jiangxi China 25.02N 115.01E
47 H4 An'yudin U.S.S.R. 62.31N 58.12E
23 D3 Anyue Sichuan China 30.06N 105.19E
87 C7 Anyuol Sudan 6.11N 30.29E
40 G7 Anyuy R U.S.S.R.
39 G1 Anyuysk U.S.S.R. 68.18N 161.36E
119 C4 Anzá Colombia 6.18N 75.54W
35 D4 Anza Jordan 32.22N 35.13E
79 D3 Anza R Italy
100 F2 Anzac Alberta 56.30N 111.01W
37 C3 Anzac Cove Turkey 40.12N 26.16E
Anzac Pk see Olsen,Mt
75 J3 Anzánigo Spain 42.24N 0.39W
66 N8 Anzano Italy 45.46N 9.12E
80 M6 Anzano di Puglia Italy 41.07N 15.17E
66 H8 Anzasca,Valle Italy
71 C6 Anzat-le-Luguet France 45.20N 3.02E
33 L8 Anẓawr Oman 17.39N 54.42E
33 L7 Anẓawr watercourse Oman
22 J8 Anze Shanxi China 36.11N 112.16E
81 B5 Anzeddu,Mte Sardinia 39.24N 8.38E
61 D3 Anzegem Belgium 50.50N 3.29E
88 O8 Anzeglouf Algeria 26.50N 0.03E
72 H3 Anzème France 46.16N 1.50E
42 D4 Anzhero-Sudzhensk U.S.S.R. 56.10N 86.01E
41 R3 Anzhu,Ostrova islds U.S.S.R.
80 N7 Anzi Italy 40.31N 15.56E
69 F3 Anzin France 50.22N 3.30E
64 M7 Anzing W Germany 48.08N 11.53E
80 G6 Anzio Italy 41.27N 12.38E
119 G3 Anzoátegui state Venezuela
31 E1 Anzob Tadzhikistan U.S.S.R. 39.10N 68.50E
31 E1 Anzob P Tadzhikistan U.S.S.R. 39.03N 68.51E
79 K5 Anzola dell'Emila Italy 44.33N 11.10E
75 F1 Anzuola Spain 43.06N 2.22W
77 G6 Anzur R Spain
Aoba isld see Oba isld
21 H11 Aoga-shima I Japan 32.26N 139.45E
89 M3 Aogesis Niger 16.39N 5.46E
22 L5 Aohan Qi Nei Monggol Zizhiqu China 42.17N 119.57E
75 H2 Aoíz Spain 42.47N 1.22W
31 A4 Aokal Afghanistan 33.16N 61.51E
15 L3 Aola Guadalcanal I Solomon Is 9.31S 160.30E
20 O1 Aomori Japan 40.50N 140.43E
20 O1 Aomori prefect Japan
20 O1 Aomori-wan B Japan
58 F5 Aonach Eagach mt Highland Scotland 56.41N 5.02W
30 C4 Aonla Uttar Prad India 28.17N 79.09E
122 C12 Aorai pk Tahiti Pacific Oc 17.36S 149.29W
11 K8 Aorangi Mts New Zealand
11 G7 Aorere R New Zealand
75 H2 Aos Spain 42.45N 1.23W
79 B3 Aosta Italy 45.43N 7.19E
Aosta, Valle d' aut reg see Valle d'Aosta
79 B3 Aosta, Valle d' V Italy
71 H5 Aoste France 45.35N 5.37E
11 J5 Aotea Harb inlet New Zealand
25 N1 Aotou Guangdong China 22.43N 114.31E
90 D3 Aoudéras Niger 17.38N 8.20E
88 M6 Aouedj,El Algeria 30.40N 2.08W
88 L6 Aoufouss Morocco 31.40N 4.10W
88 K8 Aouhinet Bel Egra Algeria 26.50N 6.49W
88 R4 Aouinet,El Algeria 35.50N 7.51E
89 C1 Aouinet N'cher Mauritania 20.13N 12.20W
89 C2 Aouinet Telleski Mauritania 19.01N 12.19W
88 M10 Aouker reg Mali
89 D3 Aouker reg Mauritania
88 O8 Aoulef Algeria 27.00N 1.04E
88 J6 Aoulime,Jbel mt Morocco 30.50N 8.48W
88 J6 Aoulouz Morocco 30.40N 8.10W
88 N8 Aoun Allah Algeria 26.55N 1.07W
88 S8 Aoussedjine Algeria 26.17N 9.20E
71 G7 Aouste-sur-Sye France 44.42N 5.06E
23 D5 Aoxi Guizhou China 27.37N 107.43E
20 G6 Aoya Japan 35.32N 133.59E
20 H4 Aoyagi Chiba Japan
90 J1 Aozi Chad 21.05N 18.21E
90 H1 Aozou Chad 21.45N 17.28E
119 H5 Apácara, R Venezuela
39 F7 Apacha U.S.S.R. 52.56N 157.03E
111 P10 Apache Arizona 31.41N 109.06W
109 M7 Apache Oklahoma 34.54N 98.22W
109 B8 Apache Creek New Mexico 33.51N 108.38W
111 N8 Apache Junction Arizona 33.26N 111.32W
111 N8 Apache L Arizona 33.38N 111.15W
111 O10 Apache Pk mt Arizona 31.50N 110.26W
120 E10 Apagado vol Bolivia/Chile 22.06S 67.58W
120 B1 Apaga R Peru
105 C7 Apalachee B Florida
105 C2 Apalachia Dam N Carolina 35.11N 84.18W
105 B8 Apalachicola Florida 29.43N 85.01W
105 C8 Apalachicola B Florida
105 B7 Apalachicola R Florida
103 B2 Apalachin New York 42.05N 76.08W
89 J9 Apam Ghana 5.19N 0.42W
Apamea anc site see Dinar
115 K8 Apan Mexico 19.48N 98.25W
87 E7 Apanawane Ethiopia 7.11N 34.12E
90 A8 Apapa Nigeria 6.27N 3.22E
119 E8 Apaporis, R Colombia
118 C8 Apa, R Brazil/Paraguay
44 F7 Aparan Armenia U.S.S.R. 40.35N 44.22E
118 D7 Aparecida do Tabuado Brazil 20.04S 51.07W
121 E7 Aparico Argentina 38.38S 60.54W
11 C13 Aparima R New Zealand
19 K2 Aparri Luzon Philippines 18.22N 121.40E
18 M7 Apar,Teluk B Kalimantan Indon
119 H5 Aparurén Venezuela 5.05N 62.07W
121 C8 Apas, Sierra ra Argentina
45 U1 Apastovo U.S.S.R. 55.14N 48.30E
122 C14 Apataki atoll Tuamotu Is Pacific Oc 15.30S 146.20W
75 E1 Apatamonasterio Spain 43.07N 2.35W
82 E5 Apatin Yugoslavia 45.40N 19.00E
51 R4 Apatity U.S.S.R. 67.32N 33.21E
117 B2 Apatou Fr Guiana 5.10N 54.22W
115 H8 Apatzingán Mexico 19.05N 102.20W
15 E4 Apauwor Irian Jaya 1.46S 138.26E
15 E4 Apauwor R Irian Jaya
50 E6 Apavatn L Iceland 64.10N 20.40W
113 C5 Apavawook C St Lawrence I, Bering Sea 63.10N 168.50W
115 K8 Apaxtla Mexico 18.09N 99.57W
46 F1 Ape Latvia U.S.S.R. 57.31N 26.40E
79 M7 Apecchio Italy 43.34N 12.25E
120 G5 Apediá, R Brazil
100 S3 Apeganau L Manitoba
76 E15 Apelação Portugal 38.49N 9.08W
60 M11 Apeldoorn Netherlands 52.13N 5.57E
60 N11 Apeldoornsch Kanaal canal Netherlands
75 F2 Apellániz Spain 42.44N 2.29W
63 G6 Apen W Germany 53.13N 7.48E
63 O7 Apenburg E Germany 52.43N 11.13E
44 G6 Apeni Georgia U.S.S.R. 41.48N 46.04E
63 L6 Apensen W Germany 53.27N 9.37E
120 F6 Apere, R Bolivia
105 J2 Apex N Carolina 35.45N 78.52W
103 D2 Apex New York 42.04N 75.16W
94 U13 Apex S Africa 26.13S 28.20E
64 H7 Apfingen W Germany 48.09N 9.51E
Aphek anc site see Antipatris
113 E6 Aphrewn R Alaska
91 J2 Api Zaïre 3.40N 25.26E
30 D2 Api mt Nepal 30.00N 80.56E
119 C5 Apia Colombia 5.08N 75.59W
122 C1 Apia W Samoa, Pacific Oc 13.48S 171.45W
118 B2 Apiacá, R Brazil
118 C2 Apiacas,Sa.dos mts Brazil
118 E9 Apiaí Brazil 24.29S 48.51W
18 K3 Api Api R Singapore
18 C10 Api Api, Tanjong C Pen Malaysia 1.46N 102.54E
119 H6 Apiaú, R Brazil
119 H6 Apiaú,Sa.do ra Brazil
80 L6 Apice Italy 41.07N 14.57E
84 E8 Apidhiá Greece 36.53N 22.47E
19 A8 Api,Gunung vol Indonesia 8.12S 119.05E
15 D6 Apimu Irian Jaya 4.45S 137.10E
118 E2 Apinagé Brazil 11.24S 48.21W
15 M3 Apio Malaita I Solomon Is 9.40S 161.27E
121 G1 Apipé Grande, I Argentina 27.30S 56.55W
115 K8 Apipilulco Mexico 18.11N 99.40W
80 H2 Apiro Italy 43.23N 13.08E
109 F4 Apishapa R Colorado
19 B4 Api, Tanjung C Celebes Indon 0.48S 121.39E
18 H5 Api, Tanjung C Kalimantan Indon 1.56N 109.18E
11 K6 Apiti New Zealand 39.59S 175.54E
115 K8 Apizaco Mexico 19.26N 98.09W
115 H5 Apizolaya Mexico 24.50N 102.19W
89 K8 Aplahoué Benin 6.58N 1.48E
Ap Lai Chau see Aberdeen I
120 C7 Aplao Peru 16.03S 72.30W
42 G3 Aplinskiy Porog falls U.S.S.R. 58.28N 100.30E
117 H7 Apodi Brazil 5.38S 37.51W
117 H7 Apodi,Chapada do plat Brazil
117 H7 Apodi, R Brazil
19 K5 Apo East Pass Philippines
117 A2 Apoera Surinam 5.12N 57.13W
84 U17 Apolakkiá Rhodes 36.04N 27.48E
53 V18 Apold Norway 60.09N 6.33E
64 M1 Apolda E Germany 51.02N 11.31E
122 B1 Apolima isld W Samoa, Pacific Oc 13.48S 172.06W
12 G7 Apollo Bay Victoria 38.46S 143.44E
Apollonia see Marsá Súsah
83 G8 Apollonía Greece 36.59N 24.43E
120 E6 Apolo Bolivia 14.48S 68.31W
120 D6 Apolobamba, Nudo de pks Peru
Apolonia anc site see Tel Arshaf
37 F3 Apolyont Gölü L Turkey
122 C12 Apomaoro Tahiti Pacific Oc 17.45S 149.27W
19 M8 Apo, Mt Mindanao Philippines 6.58N 125.17E
119 H5 Aponguao, R Venezuela
105 F9 Apopka Florida 28.41N 81.31W
105 F9 Apopka L Florida 28.37N 81.38W
117 D4 Aporema Brazil 1.08N 50.50W
118 D6 Aporé, R Brazil
106 D2 Apostle Is Wisconsin
121 G1 Apóstoles Argentina 27.54S 55.45W
84 C2 Apóstoli Tríkkala Greece 39.35N 21.43E
45 E9 Apostolovo Ukraine U.S.S.R. 47.40N 33.45E
117 A2 Apoteri Guyana 4.00N 58.35W
26 N16 Apôtres, Is. des Crozet Is Ind Oc 45.59S 50.22E
19 K5 Apo West Pass Philippines
31 E5 Apozai Pakistan 31.20N 69.30E
104 C10 Appalachia Virginia 36.54N 82.48W
102 K3 Appalachian Mts U.S.A.
52 H6 Äppelbo Sweden 60.30N 14.00E
63 F9 Appelhülsen W Germany 51.54N 7.25E
61 G2 Appels Belgium 51.02N 4.03E
60 O8 Appelscha Netherlands 52.57N 6.20E
60 L12 Appeltern Netherlands 51.50N 5.36E
61 F3 Appelterre-Eichen Belgium 50.49N 3.58E
78 E6 Appennino Abruzzese mts Italy
81 L2 Appennino Lucano mts Italy
78 G7 Appennino Napoletano mts Italy
64 D6 Appenweier W Germany 48.32N 7.59E
66 O2 Appenzell Switzerland 47.20N 9.25E
66 O2 Appenzell canton Switzerland
70 M3 Appeville France 49.19N 0.38E
66 M9 Appiano Italy 45.44N 8.59E
79 E3 Appiano Gentile Italy 45.43N 8.58E
79 D6 Appiano Ligure reg Italy
79 K2 Appiano San Michele Italy 46.28N 11.16E
79 G6 Appiano Tosco Emiliano reg Italy
80 H2 Appignano Italy 43.21N 13.20E
12 K5 Appin New S Wales 34.13S 150.47E
58 F5 Appin Strathclyde Scotland 56.34N 5.22W
58 F5 Appin dist Highland/Strathclyde Scotland
60 Q6 Appingedam Netherlands 53.18N 6.52E
57 J3 Appleby Cumbria Eng 54.36N 2.29W
112 N4 Appleby Texas 31.42N 94.38W
58 E4 Applecross Highland Scotland 57.26N 5.49W
14 A2 Applecross dist Perth, W Aust
56 C5 Appledore Devon Eng 51.03N 4.12W
56 N5 Appledore Kent Eng 51.02N 0.47E
111 D3 Applegate California 39.00N 120.59W
110 B7 Applegate Oregon 42.16N 123.10W
110 B7 Applegate R Oregon
98 H8 Apple River Nova Scotia 45.28N 64.49W
66 B5 Apples Switzerland 46.34N 6.27E
112 N4 Apple Springs Texas 31.15N 94.59W
104 Q2 Appleton Maine 44.19N 69.16W
108 P4 Appleton Minnesota 45.10N 96.00W
110 D4 Appleton Washington 45.49N 121.16W
106 F5 Appleton Wisconsin 44.17N 88.24W
107 B3 Appleton City Missouri 38.10N 94.03W
69 F8 Appoigny France 47.53N 3.31E
104 G9 Appomattox Virginia 37.21N 78.51W
117 C3 Approuague R Fr Guiana
19 L1 Apra Harb Guam Pacific Oc 13.27N 144.38E
19 L1 Apra Heights Guam Pacific Oc 13.24N 144.41E
45 J1 Aprelevka U.S.S.R. 55.32N 37.05E
42 J3 Aprel'sk U.S.S.R. 58.10N 114.35E
40 D5 Aprel'skiy U.S.S.R. 53.30N 126.12E
44 H7 Aprelya,28 Azerbaydzhan U.S.S.R. 40.37N 46.58E
72 L2 Apremont Cher France 46.55N 3.03E
69 H5 Apremont France 49.16N 5.00E
71 H2 Apremont Haute-Saône France 47.24N 5.32E
69 K6 Apremont Meuse France 48.52N 5.39E
72 A2 Apremont Vendée France 46.45N 1.43W
79 H2 Aprica,Passo d' pass Italy 46.09N 10.09E
80 M5 Apricena Italy 41.47N 15.27E
81 M5 Aprigliano Italy 39.14N 16.21E
15 G6 April R Papua New Guinea
80 G5 Aprilia Italy 41.35N 12.39E
87 H9 Aproni Somalia 2.29N 41.32E
28 K1 Aprunyi Assam India 28.35N 95.50E
36 G2 Apsarı* Turkey 40.42N 33.31E
44 C3 Apsheronsk U.S.S.R. 44.26N 39.45E
44 K7 Apsheronskiy P-ov pen Azerbaydzhan U.S.S.R.
99 M8 Apsley Ontario 44.45N 78.06W
12 F6 Apsley Victoria 36.58S 141.08E
13 B1 Apsley Str N Terr Australia
71 G9 Apt France 43.52N 5.23E
47 N1 Aptekarskiy,Ostrov isld Leningrad U.S.S.R.
19 E5 Apu R Buru I, Moluccas Indon
79 H6 Apuane Alpi mts Italy
114 C8 Apua Pt Hawaiian Is 19.15N 155.12W
118 D8 Apucarana Brazil 23.34S 51.28W
118 D8 Apucarana,Serra da mts Brazil
39 J4 Apuka R U.S.S.R.
39 J4 Apuka Chukotskaya U.S.S.R. 61.20N 170.29E
115 K7 Apulco Mexico 20.20N 98.20W
83 K4 Apulyont Gölü L Turkey
19 J7 Apurahuan Philippines 9.35N 118.22E
19 M2 Apurashokoru isld Palau Is Pacific Oc 7.17N 134.19E
119 E4 Apure state Venezuela
119 F3 Apure, R Venezuela
120 C6 Apurimac dept Peru
120 C5 Apurimac, R Peru
119 F4 Apurito Venezuela 7.54N 68.30W
119 F4 Apurito, R Venezuela
82 H4 Apuseni, Munţii mts Romania
44 F9 Āq R Iran
86 O6 'Aqaba Jordan 29.32N 35.00E
33 A2 'Aqaba,G.of Red Sea
34 K5 Aqabah Iraq 33.32N 42.57E
34 L8 'Aqabah Al Iraq 30.08N 43.40E
35 E6 'Aqabat Jabr Jordan 31.50N 35.26E
86 L5 'Aqaba,Wâdi el watercourse Egypt
85 L6 'Aqabet el Ramilîya Egypt 26.02N 30.41E
24 C5 Aqal Xinjiang Uygur Zizhiqu China 40.30N 79.36E
34 E3 'Aqarbāt Syria 35.02N 37.28E
32 F2 Aqband Iran 37.38N 55.10E
33 L8 Aqbat al Hatta pass Oman 17.25N 54.00E
34 Q3 Aq Bolāgh-e Āqdāq Iran 35.35N 48.28E
Aq Chah see Akcha
32 A1 Aq Chai R Iran
32 E4 'Aqdā Iran 32.24N 53.39E
32 B2 Āqdoghmish R Iran
33 G5 'Aqīmī, Sha'īb al watercourse Saudi Arabia
87 G1 Aqiq Sudan 18.13N 38.11E
33 D6 'Aqīq,Al Saudi Arabia 20.47N 41.27E
33 D4 Aqīq,Wādī Saudi Arabia
'Aqir see Kefar 'Eqron
24 G5 Aqitag mt pk Xinjiang Uygur Zizhiqu China 41.49N 90.38E
32 A1 Aq Kān Dagh, Kūh-e mt Iran 38.03N 44.57E
33 B4 Aqla Saudi Arabia 25.37N 37.45E
'Aqlat as Suqūr see 'Uqlat aş Şuqūr
35 E4 Aqqaba Jordan 32.21N 35.21E
24 F7 Aqqikkol Hu L Xinjiang Uygur Zizhiqu China
35 J10 Aqra watercourse Jordan
35 E5 'Aqraba Jordan 32.08N 35.21E
35 G3 'Aqraba Jordan 32.43N 35.48E
35 H1 'Aqrabab Syria 33.07N 36.07E
35 H1 'Aqraba Syria 33.06N 36.01E
33 A9 Aqrabi dist S Yemen
33 N10 'Aqrabīyāt,Al Saudi Arabia 28.32N 48.23E
34 L2 'Aqrah Iraq 36.46N 43.52E
34 M4 Aq Su R Iraq
111 L7 Aquarius Mts Arizona
111 N4 Aquarius Plat Utah
103 J5 Aquebogue Long I, N Y 40.57N 72.37W
118 B8 Aquidabán, R Paraguay
118 C7 Aquidauana Brazil 20.27S 55.45W
118 C6 Aquidauana, R Brazil
115 H8 Aquila Mexico 18.35N 103.30W
80 H4 Aquila,L' Italy 42.22N 13.24E
80 H4 Aquila, L' dist Italy
79 O3 Aquilèia Italy 45.47N 13.22E
115 G3 Aquiles Serdán Mexico 28.37N 105.54W
112 K4 Aquilla Texas 31.51N 97.14W
80 M7 Aquilónia Italy 40.59N 15.30E
75 K3 Aquilué Spain 42.23N 0.29W
116 H5 Aquin Haiti 18.29N 73.23W
80 J6 Aquino Italy 41.27N 13.42E
119 F6 Aquio, R Colombia
117 H6 Aquiraz Brazil 3.53S 38.28W
115 K7 Aquismón Mexico 21.40N 99.01W
119 D5 Aquitania Colombia 5.32N 72.52W
33 H5 'Āqūlah,Al Saudi Arabia 23.28N 49.10E
93 M1 Ara Ethiopia 4.36N 40.20E
35 D3 'Ara Israel 32.30N 35.05E
75 K3 Ara R Spain
35 F3 Arab R Jordan
87 E2 Arab watercourse Sudan
32 G4 'Arabābād Iran 33.03N 57.41E
34 N6 Arab Abdulla Iraq 32.31N 45.40E
33 J8 'Arabah, Wādī watercourse S Yemen
44 D9 Arabatskaya Strelka spit Ukraine U.S.S.R.
44 D9 Arabatskiy Zaliv B Ukraine U.S.S.R.
34 C8 'Araba,Wādi V Israel/Jordan
86 H7 'Araba, Wâdi watercourse Egypt
79 L2 Arabba Italy 46.30N 11.53E
35 E3 'Arabbuna Jordan 32.31N 35.22E
44 F8 'Arab-e Dizebsi Iran 39.19N 44.11E
87 L9 Arabei Dalon Somalia 3.30N 46.20E
88 R4 Arab,el R Algeria
34 C3 'Arab el Melik Syria 35.17N 35.55E
Arab el Meulk see 'Arab el Melik
119 G5 Arabelo Venezuela 4.55N 64.15W
105 D6 Arabi Georgia 31.50N 83.45W
107 K12 Arabi dist New Orleans, Louisiana
27 E5 Arabia pen W Asia
26 E4 Arabian Basin Arabian Sea
Arabian Gulf see The Gulf
98 N3 Arabian L Quebec
27 J6 Arabian Sea Indian Oc
77 T12 Arabi, Pta Balearic Is 38.59N 1.35E
33 J3 'Arabiyah, Al isld The Gulf 27.40N 50.21E
32 D7 'Arabīyeh, Al isld The Gulf 27.41N 50.20E
119 H5 Arabopó Venezuela 5.06N 60.45W
119 H5 Arabopó, R Venezuela
34 F2 'Arab Punari Syria 36.54N 38.22E
36 G1 Araç Turkey 41.14N 33.20E
36 G1 Araç R Turkey
118 J2 Aracaju Brazil 10.54S 37.07W
119 G7 Aracamuni,Cerro mts Venezuela
118 C9 Aracanguy, Mts. de Paraguay
119 G7 Araça, R Brazil
119 D2 Aracataca Colombia 10.38N 74.09W
117 H7 Aracati Brazil 4.32S 37.45W
118 H4 Aracatu Brazil 14.22S 41.25W
118 E7 Araçatuba Brazil 21.12S 50.24W
77 C5 Aracena Spain 37.54N 6.33W
77 D5 Aracena, Embalse de res Spain
121 K10 Aracena, I Chile
77 C5 Aracena, Sierra de mt Spain
66 C7 Arâches France 46.03N 6.38E
118 J2 Araci Brazil 11.22S 38.53W
15 M3 Aracides, C Malaita I Solomon Is 8.37S 161.01E
117 H7 Aracoiaba Brazil 4.20S 38.50W
118 H6 Aracruz Brazil 19.55S 40.16W
118 G5 Araçuaí Brazil 16.52S 42.03W
118 G5 Araçuaí, R Brazil
33 B7 Arad Bahrain, The Gulf 26.15N 50.38E
35 D7 'Arad Israel 31.16N 35.09E
82 G4 Arad Romania 46.10N 21.19E
90 K4 Arada Chad 15.00N 20.38E
37 E8 Arada Turkey 37.01N 40.23E
33 G1 Aradah Iraq 30.58N 47.20E
33 K5 'Arādah U.A.E. 23.00N 53.20E
32 E3 Arādān Iran 35.15N 52.30E
42 E5 Aradanskiy Khrebet mts U.S.S.R.
76 C14 Arade R Portugal
76 C14 Arade, Barragem de res Portugal 37.15N 8.24W
90 L4 Aradeib, Wadi watercourse Sudan
81 R12 Aradeo Italy 40.07N 18.08E
84 S15 Aradhippou Cyprus 34.56N 33.36E
85 M6 'Aradiya,Gebel mt Egypt 26.19N 33.27E
87 G3 Arafali Ethiopia 15.03N 39.43E
33 D6 Arafāt, Jabal mts Saudi Arabia
96 R14 Arafo Tenerife 28.20N 16.25W
17 M13 Arafura Sea Aust/Indon
118 D4 Aragarças Brazil 15.55S 52.12W
44 F7 Aragats Armenia U.S.S.R. 40.18N 43.40E
44 F7 Aragats mt Armenia U.S.S.R. 40.32N 44.11E
20 M5 Ara-gawa R Japan
85 J5 'Arag, el oasis Egypt
72 E10 Aragnouet France 42.47N 0.12E
110 A6 Arago, C Oregon 43.20N 124.23W
75 J2 Aragón R Spain
74 G4 Aragón reg Spain
81 G9 Aragona Sicily 37.25N 13.37E
75 F6 Aragoncillo Spain 40.56N 2.03W
75 F6 Aragoncillo mt Spain 40.58N 2.02W
75 L4 Aragón y Cataluña, Can. de Spain
90 G2 Aragoua Chad 18.46N 15.43E
119 F3 Aragua state Venezuela
117 D9 Araguacema Brazil 8.48S 49.31W
118 E3 Araguaçu Brazil 12.47S 49.54W
119 G3 Aragua de Barcelona Venezuela 9.30N 64.51W
119 G3 Aragua de Maturín Venezuela 9.58N 63.30W
117 D9 Araguaia,Arroios do R Brazil
118 D4 Araguaiana Brazil 15.41S 51.41W
118 D5 Araguaia, R Brazil
117 D8 Araguaína Brazil 7.16S 48.18W
117 D8 Araguanã Brazil 6.36S 48.39W
119 H3 Araguao,Caño R Venezuela
119 H3 Araguapiche, Pta Venezuela 9.31N 60.55W
118 E6 Araguari Brazil 18.38S 48.13W
117 D4 Araguari R Amapá Brazil
118 E6 Araguari R Minas Gerais Brazil
117 D7 Araguatins Brazil 5.38S 48.07W
44 F6 Aragvi R Georgia U.S.S.R.
77 E6 Arahal,El Spain 37.15N 5.33W
33 E10 'Arah,Ra's C S Yemen 12.38N 43.57E
11 F9 Arahura New Zealand 42.40S 171.01E
33 L7 'Arah,Wādī watercourse Oman
30 J8 Arai Bihar India 24.57N 85.21E
118 F3 Araí Brazil 13.31S 47.43W
20 L7 Arai Japan 34.40N 137.36E
20 M4 Arai Japan 37.02N 138.17E
Arâich, El see Larache
86 M5 'Arâif el Nâqa,Gebel hill Egypt 30.21N 34.26E
117 G6 Araiosos Brazil 2.54S 41.58W
86 P3 'Arā'ir Jordan 31.29N 35.50E
'Arai'ra see Uray'irah
87 H4 Araiu Ethiopia 13.43N 41.46E
33 A10 A'raja,R'as al C S Yemen 12.45N 44.51E
Ara Jirgalanta see Jargalant
88 P9 Arak Algeria 25.20N 3.46E
32 C3 Arāk Iran 34.05N 49.42E
34 F4 Arak Syria 34.40N 38.33E
90 G2 Araka Niger 19.09N 15.20E
19 N2 Arakabesan isld Palau Is Pacific Oc 7.22N 134.28E
20 N4 Arakai-yama mt Japan 37.02N 139.38E
119 H4 Arakaka Guyana 7.35N 60.07W
39 M3 Arakamchechen,Ostrov isld U.S.S.R.
25 B2 Arakan reg Burma
25 C2 Arakan Yoma ra Burma
20 Q8 Arakawa Okinawa Japan 26.40N 128.15E
20 E2 Arakawa dist Tōkyō Japan
20 E2 Arakawa-hōsuiro R Japan
84 B5 Arákhintos mts Greece
42 J6 Arakhley,Ozero L U.S.S.R. 52.15N 112.55E
84 E6 Arakhnaínon Greece 37.41N 22.57E
84 E6 Arakhnaíon Óros mts Greece
84 C5 Arákhova Akhaïa Greece 38.11N 21.58E
84 C6 Arákhova Arkadhía Greece 37.36N 21.59E
84 E5 Arákhova Voiotía Greece 38.28N 22.35E
84 B3 Árakhthos R Greece
44 H8 Araks R U.S.S.R.
53 X21 Araksbø Norway 58.56N 7.45E
53 X21 Araksfjord L Norway 58.56N 7.44E
99 C2 Ara L Ontario
24 D5 Aral Xinjiang Uygur Zizhiqu China 40.36N 81.24E
75 F2 Aralar,Sierra de mts Spain
44 K3 Araldy Kazakhstan U.S.S.R. 44.19N 50.23E
37 H6 Aralık Turkey 39.54N 44.28E
24 F6 Aralqi Xinjiang Uygur Zizhiqu China 38.10N 87.28E
Aral Sea see Aral'skoye More
43 F4 Aral'sk Kazakhstan U.S.S.R. 46.56N 61.43E
43 E5 Aral'skoye More sea U.S.S.R.
45 U8 Aralsor,Oz L Kazakhstan U.S.S.R.
43 F4 Aralsul'fat Kazakhstan U.S.S.R. 46.48N 61.58E
53 S14 Åram Norway 62.11N 5.30E
35 H2 'Aram watercourse Syria
13 H6 Aramac Queensland 22.54S 145.10E
13 G6 Aramac R Queensland
120 D1 Aramaçá, I Brazil 4.20S 69.53W
33 G4 Aramah plat Saudi Arabia
71 F9 Araman France 43.54N 4.42E
29 L2 Arambagh W Bengal India 22.54N 87.47E
115 K5 Aramberri Mexico 24.05N 99.50W
29 A6 Aramda Bombay India 22.28N 69.08E
115 L3 Aramecina Honduras 13.44N 87.41W
15 G8 Aramia isld Papua New Guinea 8.00S 143.30E
15 G7 Aramia R Papua New Guinea
47 M4 Aramil' U.S.S.R. 56.43N 60.50E
72 C9 Aramits France 43.07N 0.43W
76 H2 Aramo,El mts Spain
75 F2 Aranarache Spain 42.47N 2.13W
87 J6 Aran Areh Ethiopia 9.00N 43.58E
75 F2 Aranaz Spain 42.54N 2.04W
75 G1 Aranaz Spain 43.11N 1.44W
121 C3 Arancibia Argentina 30.59S 68.40W
81 D1 Aranci, G Sardinia 41.01N 9.38E
75 G4 Aranda R Spain
75 C4 Aranda de Duero Spain 41.40N 3.41W
75 G4 Aranda de Moncayo Spain 41.34N 1.47W
15 B5 Arandai Irian Jaya 2.10S 133.00E
32 B3 Arandān Iran 35.20N 46.58E
82 F6 Arandelovac Yugoslavia 44.19N 20.35E
75 D4 Arandilla R Spain
75 F6 Arandilla del Arroyo Spain 40.30N 2.23W
75 D4 Arandillo Spain 41.43N 3.27W
94 C4 Arandis Namibia 22.24S 15.00E
56 D2 Aran Fawddwy mt Gwynedd Wales 52.47N 3.41W
30 H7 Arang Bihar India 25.10N 84.05E
29 H7 Arang Madhya Prad India 21.14N 82.02E
11 H2 Aranga New Zealand 35.43S 173.39E
76 C2 Aranga Spain 43.14N 8.01W
39 D4 Arangas U.S.S.R. 60.42N 149.40E
39 E2 Arangastakh R U.S.S.R.
41 N4 Arangastakh, Zaliv B U.S.S.R.
120 F7 Arani Bolivia 17.34S 65.45W
59 E1 Aran I Donegal Irish Rep 55.00N 8.30W
59 C5 Aran Is Galway Irish Rep
75 C7 Aranjuez Spain 40.02N 3.37W
43 F5 Arankurgan Kazakhstan U.S.S.R. 44.48N 61.09E
15 C6 Aranlau Moluccas Indon 5.48S 134.42E
121 D6 Arano Argentina 37.06S 63.15W
75 G1 Arano Spain 43.12N 1.54W
94 E5 Aranos Namibia 24.10S 19.08E
29 E7 Aran R Maharashtra India
112 K8 Aransas B Texas
112 K8 Aransas Pass Texas 27.55N 97.10W
28 D5 Arantangi Tamil Nadu India 10.11N 79.00E
118 E6 Arantes, R Brazil
11 N9 Aranui dist Christchurch New Zealand
9 B5 Aranuka atoll Kiribati, Pacific Oc 0.10N 173.35E
75 M2 Arán, Valle de Spain
119 C5 Aranzazu Colombia 5.17N 75.31W
75 E1 Aránzazu Spain 43.09N 2.47W
75 F2 Aránzazu, Convento de hist ruin Spain 42.58N 2.22W
75 D7 Aranzueque Spain 40.30N 3.05W
20 D9 Arao Japan 32.58N 130.26E
89 H2 Araouane Mali 18.53N 3.31W
109 E1 Arapaho mt Colorado 40.02N 105.38W
109 H3 Arapahoe Colorado 38.52N 102.12W
108 L9 Arapahoe Nebraska 40.19N 99.52W
108 B7 Arapahoe Wyoming 42.58N 108.29W
93 E4 Arapai Uganda 1.45N 33.38E
120 D6 Arapa, L Peru 15.09S 70.00W
117 B5 Arapari Brazil 1.47S 54.25W
119 H7 Arapari, R Brazil
11 J8 Arapawa I New Zealand
121 F3 Arapey Uruguay 30.58S 57.33W
121 F3 Arapey Grande R Uruguay
119 C8 Arapicos Ecuador 1.54S 77.54W
76 H7 Arapiles Spain 40.54N 5.39W
117 H9 Arapiraca Brazil 9.45S 36.40W
117 B6 Arapiri, I Brazil
84 G6 Arápis Greece 37.58N 23.31E
117 B6 Arapiuns, R Brazil
37 D6 Arapkir Turkey 39.03N 38.29E
37 E1 Araplı R Turkey
118 D8 Arapongas Brazil 23.25S 51.25W
36 H4 Arapsun Turkey 38.45N 34.37E
113 F6 Arapuk L Alaska
11 K5 Arapuni New Zealand 38.07S 175.41E
11 K5 Arapuni L New Zealand
35 D4 'Araqa Jordan 32.28N 35.12E
117 B4 Araqua Brazil 1.33N 54.50W
118 E10 Araquari Brazil 26.23S 48.46W
34 J8 Ar'ar Saudi Arabia 30.58N 41.03E
35 D4 'Ar'ara Israel 32.29N 35.06E
119 D8 Araracuara Colombia 0.28S 72.13W
119 D7 Araracuara, Cerros de mts Colombia
30 H6 Araraj Bihar India 26.33N 84.40E
120 E9 Araral,Cerro pk Bolivia/Chile 21.35S 68.10W
121 J2 Araranguá Brazil 28.56S 49.30W
118 E7 Araraquara Brazil 21.46S 48.08W
119 G8 Arara, R Brazil
120 E3 Araras Amazonas Brazil 9.02S 68.06W
117 B8 Araras Brazil 6.08S 54.24W
120 F3 Ararás Rondônia Brazil 9.58S 65.16W
118 F8 Araras São Paulo Brazil 22.20S 47.23W
117 G7 Araras,Açude res Brazil
117 E8 Araras,Sa.das mts Piauí Brazil
118 D6 Araras,Serra das mts Mato Grosso do Sul Brazil
118 D9 Araras,Serra das mts Paraná Brazil
44 F8 Ararat Armenia U.S.S.R. 39.47N 44.46E
103 C3 Ararat Pennsylvania 41.48N 75.32W
12 G6 Ararat Victoria 37.20S 143.00E
Ararat, Little Mount see Ağrı Dağı, Küçük
Ararat, Mt see Ağrı Dağı, Büyük
87 G8 Arare Ethiopia 4.48N 38.50E
87 M8 Arar,El Somalia 4.47N 48.05E
117 F6 Arari Brazil 3.28S 44.44W
30 L6 Araria Bihar India 26.09N 87.31E
30 L6 Araria Bihar India 26.08N 87.24E
72 K9 Araric,Mtgne.d' France 43.08N 2.36E
117 D5 Arari, L Brazil
117 G8 Araripe Brazil 7.08S 40.10W
117 G8 Araripe,Chapada do mts Brazil
117 G8 Araripina Brazil 7.31S 40.35W
118 G8 Araruama, L. de Brazil 22.50S 42.10W
34 J7 'Ar'ar, Wādī watercourse Arabia/Iraq
Aras Iran see Ars
75 F2 Aras Spain 42.34N 2.21W
37 G6 Aras Turkey 39.59N 42.18E
37 F6 Aras R Turkey
32 F3 Arāsavān Iran 34.06N 55.02E
75 H8 Aras de Alpuente Spain 39.55N 1.09W
93 G8 Arash Tanzania 2.30S 35.37E
116 A1 Arasji Aruba W I 12.38N 70.03W
75 P3 Aras, Pto. de pass Spain/France 42.22N 2.26E
44 G9 Aras,R Iran etc
Arasun see Arâsavân
118 H4 Arataca Brazil 15.16S 39.27W
89 E2 Aratane Mauritania 18.24N 8.32W
11 H3 Aratapu New Zealand 36.01S 173.55E
117 D6 Arataú, R Brazil
11 L5 Aratiatia New Zealand 38.36S 176.10E
117 D5 Araticu Brazil 1.56S 49.52W
122 C14 Aratika atoll Tuamotu Is Pacific Oc 15.30S 145.30W
20 O3 Arato Japan 38.13N 140.04E
Aratürük see Yiwu
18 D2 Arau Pen Malaysia 6.25N 100.15E
120 F3 Arauá Brazil
120 F1 Arauá, R Brazil
120 G2 Arauá, R Brazil
119 E4 Arauca Colombia 7.04N 70.41W
119 E4 Arauca div Colombia
119 E4 Arauca, R Venez/Colombia
118 E9 Araucária Brazil 25.34S 49.30W
121 A6 Arauco Chile 37.15S 73.22W
121 A6 Arauco prov Chile
121 A6 Arauco, G. de Chile
30 D6 Araul Uttar Prad India 26.55N 80.02E
71 E6 Araules France 45.06N 4.10E
119 E4 Arauquita Colombia 6.57N 71.19W
119 E3 Araure Venezuela 9.36N 69.15W
86 O5 'Arava watercourse Israel
29 C5 Aravalli Ra Rajasthan Ind
43 O8 Aravan Kirgiziya U.S.S.R. 40.31N 72.30E
43 O8 Aravan R Kirgiziya U.S.S.R.
76 E9 Aravil R Portugal
66 B8 Aravis, Chaine des mts France
71 J5 Aravis,Col des France 45.53N 6.28E
15 J2 Arawa Bougainville I Papua New Guinea 6.15S 155.35E
11 C11 Arawata R New Zealand
15 K7 Arawe Is New Britain 6.10S 148.56E
118 F6 Araxá Brazil 19.37S 46.50W
75 H2 Araxa Mendi mt Spain 42.50N 1.10W
Araxes R Iran see Aras R
20 P1 Araya Japan 40.06N 141.02E
75 F2 Araya Spain 42.54N 2.19W
76 F9 Araya R Spain
119 G2 Araya,Pen.de Venezuela
119 G2 Araya, Pta de Venezuela 10.36N 64.18W
85 D8 Arayé watercourse Chad
36 F3 Arayit Dağ mt Turkey 39.18N 31.44E
33 G9 Arayn mt S Yemen 15.36N 46.29E
20 P10 Ara-zaki C Okinawa Japan 26.00N 127.40E
76 B8 Arazede Portugal 40.17N 8.39W
75 F2 Araz,Mte Spain 42.56N 2.17W
75 H4 Arba R Spain
50 E7 Arbær Iceland 63.52N 20.21W
42 K6 Arbagar U.S.S.R. 52.00N 116.20E
93 K3 Arba Jahan Kenya 2.05N 38.58E
87 F7 Arba Minch Ethiopia 6.02N 37.36E
74 D10 Arbaoua Morocco 34.53N 5.55W
72 F9 Arbas France 43.01N 0.55E
34 N3 Arbat Iraq 35.24N 45.36E
88 O5 Arba Tahtani Algeria 33.03N 0.38E
81 D4 Arbatax Sardinia 39.56N 9.44E
34 O1 Arbat Dāgh mt Iran 37.02N 46.48E
47 M3 Arbatskiy U.S.S.R. 58.28N 59.38E
87 E6 Arba,Tulu mt Ethiopia 9.22N 34.50E
Arbay Here see Arvayheer
46 P1 Arbazh U.S.S.R. 57.42N 48.20E
75 M4 Arbeca Spain 41.33N 0.56E
69 K8 Arbecey France 47.45N 5.56E
66 N7 Arbedo Switzerland 46.13N 9.03E
119 D5 Arbeláez Colombia 4.13N 74.33W
72 D9 Arbéost France 43.00N 0.17W
64 K5 Arberg W Germany 49.08N 10.38E
65 L5 Arbesbach Austria 48.30N 14.59E
Arbet see Arbat
75 F6 Arbeteta Spain 40.40N 2.24W
80 D2 Arbia R Italy
34 M2 Arbil Iraq 36.12N 44.01E
76 C4 Arbo Spain 42.07N 8.20W
52 J7 Arboga Sweden 59.24N 15.51E
52 J7 Arbogaån R Sweden
71 H3 Arbois France 46.55N 5.47E
71 K5 Arbois,Mt.d' France 45.51N 6.40E
77 M6 Arboleas Spain 37.21N 2.04W
109 C4 Arboles Colorado 37.03N 107.28W
119 C3 Arboletas,Pta Colombia 8.54N 76.28W
110 N7 Arbon Idaho 42.28N 112.36W
66 O1 Arbon Switzerland 47.31N 9.27E
76 F2 Arbón, Embalse de res Spain
107 D9 Arbonne,L.d' Louisiana
95 M2 Arbor S Africa 26.04S 28.52E
81 B4 Arborea Sardinia 39.47N 8.34E
81 B4 Arborea reg Sardinia
100 O5 Arborfield Saskatchewan 53.06N 103.39W
100 U8 Arborg Manitoba 50.55N 97.12W
79 D4 Arborio Italy 45.30N 8.23E
75 O5 Arbós Spain 41.16N 1.36E
93 M4 Arbo Wells Kenya 1.42N 40.02E
52 J5 Arbrå Sweden 61.29N 16.25E
50 E6 Árbrandsá R Iceland
61 F4 Arbre Hainaut Belgium 50.37N 3.49E
61 K5 Arbre Namur Belgium 50.22N 4.49E
90 E3 Arbre du Ténéré Niger 17.50N 10.04E
61 O5 Arbrefontaine Belgium 50.18N 5.50E
71 F5 Arbresle,l' France 45.50N 4.37E
58 L5 Arbroath Tayside Scotland 56.34N 2.35W
75 Q4 Arbucias Spain 41.49N 2.31E
111 B2 Arbuckle California 39.02N 122.04W
105 F10 Arbuckle L Florida 27.42N 81.23W
109 N7 Arbuckle Mts Oklahoma
72 D9 Arbus France 43.20N 0.30W
81 B4 Arbus Sardinia 39.32N 8.36E
66 A7 Arbusigny France 46.06N 6.13E
103 A8 Arbutus Maryland 39.15N 76.41W
45 C9 Arbuzinka Ukraine U.S.S.R. 47.55N 31.19E
41 N8 Arbyn U.S.S.R. 63.25N 129.40E
107 F5 Arbyrd Missouri 36.03N 90.17W
71 H2 Arc France 47.02N 5.46E

71 G9 **Arc** *R* Bouches-du-Rhône France
71 J6 **Arc** *R* Savoie France
72 B6 **Arcachon** France 44.40N 1.11W
72 B6 **Arcachon, Bassin d'** France
72 B6 **Arcachon, Pte. d'** France 44.33N 11.15W
37 D7 **Arçadağ** Turkey 38.22N 37.58E
104 G4 **Arcade** New York 42.32N 78.25W
100 A3 **Arcadia** Alberta 55.24N 116.02W
105 F10 **Arcadia** Florida 27.12N 81.52W
106 H9 **Arcadia** Indiana 40.11N 86.02W
109 Q4 **Arcadia** Kansas 37.37N 94.38W
107 D9 **Arcadia** Louisiana 32.33N 92.56W
106 H5 **Arcadia** Michigan 44.30N 86.13W
107 F4 **Arcadia** Missouri 37.35N 90.39W
108 L8 **Arcadia** Nebraska 41.27N 99.08W
104 B5 **Arcadia** Ohio 41.06N 83.30W
109 N6 **Arcadia** Oklahoma 35.42N 97.21W
103 L3 **Arcadia** Rhode I 41.34N 71.41W
106 C5 **Arcadia** Wisconsin 44.16N 91.30W
116 H5 **Arcahaie, L'** Haiti 18.50N 72.30W
61 E4 **Arc-Ainières** Belgium 50.42N 3.33E
72 C3 **Arçais** France 46.19N 0.40W
72 G7 **Arcambal** France 44.27N 1.30E
104 A7 **Arcanum** Ohio 39.59N 84.33W
75 F8 **Arcas** Spain 39.59N 2.06W
115 O7 **Arcas, Cayos** *reefs* G of Mexico 20.14N 91.59W
110 A9 **Arcata** California 40.54N 124.05W
72 E2 **Arçay** France 46.59N 0.02E
111 G3 **Arc Dome** *mt* Nevada 38.50N 117.20W
80 J5 **Arce** Italy 41.35N 13.35E
69 G7 **Arce** *R* France
115 J8 **Arcelia** Mexico 18.20N 100.16W
60 N14 **Arcen** Netherlands 51.28N 6.11E
69 J8 **Arc-en-Barrois** France 47.57N 5.01E
75 D1 **Arceniega** Spain 43.07N 3.08W
72 C4 **Arces** Charente-Maritime France 45.34N 0.52W
69 F7 **Arces** Yonne France 48.05N 3.36E
79 N7 **Arcevia** Italy 43.30N 12.56E
66 C1 **Arcey** France 47.32N 6.39E
66 F3 **Arch** Switzerland 47.10N 7.26E
66 A7 **Archamps** France 46.08N 6.09E
82 H7 **Archar** Bulgaria 43.49N 22.55E
103 C4 **Archbald** Pennsylvania 41.29N 75.33W
104 A5 **Archbold** Ohio 41.32N 84.19W
105 H2 **Archdale** N Carolina 35.57N 79.58W
77 O4 **Archena** Spain 38.07N 1.17W
61 J3 **Archennes** Belgium 50.45N 4.40E
105 E8 **Archer** Florida 29.32N 88.32W
13 F2 **Archer** *R* Queensland
112 J2 **Archer City** Texas 33.36N 98.37W
13 K2 **Archerfield Airfield** Brisbane, Qnsld 27.33S 153.01E
13 H3 **Archer Pt** Queensland 15.32S 145.20E
13 F2 **Archer R** Queensland
93 J5 **Archer's Post** Kenya 0.39N 37.40E
100 O6 **Archerwill** Saskatchewan 52.30N 103.52W
69 M7 **Arches** France 48.06N 6.32E
111 P3 **Arches Nat.Mon** Utah 38.40N 109.30W
80 K4 **Archi** Italy 42.05N 14.24E
72 D4 **Archiac** France 45.31N 0.18W
87 G3 **Archico** Ethiopia 15.32N 39.28E
77 H6 **Archidona** Spain 37.06N 4.23W
107 B3 **Archie** Missouri 38.28N 94.22W
13 E4 **Archie** *R* Queensland
58 K4 **Archiestown** Grampian Scotland 57.29N 3.18W
72 F2 **Archigny** France 46.41N 0.39E
75 E6 **Archilla** Spain 40.41N 2.55W
44 G5 **Archilo** Georgia U.S.S.R. 42.30N 45.14E
77 M4 **Archival** Spain 38.04N 2.00W
44 J9 **Archivan** Azerbaydzhan U.S.S.R. 38.32N 48.49E
100 M8 **Archive** Saskatchewan 50.18N 105.39W
43 D7 **Archman** Turkmeniya U.S.S.R. 38.33N 57.12E
109 C5 **Archuleta** New Mexico 36.46N 107.42W
80 E3 **Arcidosso** Italy 42.52N 11.32E
81 B4 **Arci, Mte** Sardinia 39.47N 8.44E
79 E3 **Arcisate** Italy 45.52N 8.51E
69 G6 **Arcis-sur-Aube** France 48.32N 4.09E
12 C3 **Arckaringa** *R* S Australia
71 H2 **Arc-lès-Gray** France 47.28N 5.35E
110 M6 **Arco** Idaho 43.38N 113.18W
79 J3 **Arco** Italy 45.55N 10.53E
108 O5 **Arco** Minnesota 44.23N 96.10W
76 G9 **Arco** Spain 39.48N 6.25W
76 D6 **Arco de Baulhe** Portugal 41.29N 7.58W
107 H2 **Arcola** Illinois 39.42N 88.18W
107 F8 **Arcola** Mississippi 33.16N 90.56W
100 P9 **Arcola** Saskatchewan 49.38N 102.26W
112 M6 **Arcola** Texas 29.29N 95.29W
79 K4 **Arcole** Italy 45.22N 11.17E
71 J3 **Arçon** France 46.55N 6.22E
71 E4 **Arconce** *R* France
12 D4 **Arcoona** S Australia 31.06S 137.19E
Arcoordaby *see* **Yerda**
121 B7 **Arco,Paso de** *pass* Arg/Chile 38.45S 71.08W
79 F3 **Arcore** Italy 45.38N 9.19E
118 F7 **Arcos** Brazil 20.19S 45.30W
76 E11 **Arcos** Portugal 38.50N 7.30W
75 C3 **Arcos** Spain 42.16N 3.45W
75 F5 **Arcos de Jalón** Spain 41.12N 2.16W
77 E7 **Arcos de la Frontera** Spain 36.45N 5.49W
75 H8 **Arcos de las Salinas** Spain 40.00N 1.03W
76 C5 **Arcos de Valdevez** Portugal 41.51N 8.25W
75 J5 **Arcos,Sierra de** *mts* Spain
81 B5 **Arcosu,Mte** Sardinia 39.12N 8.52E
28 D4 **Arcot** Tamil Nadu India 12.54N 79.20E
28 D4 **Arcot,North** *dist* Tamil Nadu India
28 D5 **Arcot,South** *dist* Tamil Nadu India
70 D4 **Arcouest,l'** France 48.49N 3.01W
117 H9 **Arcoverde** Brazil 8.23S 37.00W
76 C7 **Arcozelo das Maias** Portugal 40.44N 8.17W
71 E8 **Arc,Pont d'** France 44.23N 4.24E
71 J10 **Arcs, les** France 43.28N 6.28E
66 B3 **Arc sous Cicon** France 47.03N 6.24E
71 G2 **Arc-sur-Tille** France 47.21N 5.12E
97 L3 **Arctic Bay** N W Terr 73.05N 85.20W
113 D3 **Arctic Lagoon** Alaska
16 D1 **Arctic Ocean**
101 G2 **Arctic Red** *R* N W Terr
101 G2 **Arctic Red River** N W Terr 67.24N 133.40W
113 P2 **Arctic Village** Alaska 68.05N 145.47W
68 F4 **Arcueil** France 48.48N 2.20E
81 B4 **Arcuentu,Mte** Sardinia 39.36N 8.32E
79 L3 **Arcugnano** Italy 45.30N 11.32E
75 L3 **Arcusa** Spain 42.19N 0.04E
61 E4 **Arc-Wattripont** Belgium 50.43N 3.33E
69 D5 **Arcy-en-Multien** France 49.06N 2.57E
69 E5 **Arcy-Ste.Restitue** France 49.15N 3.28E
71 D1 **Arcy-sur-Cure** France 47.46N 3.45E
82 J9 **Arda** *R* Bulgaria
79 G5 **Arda** *R* Italy
76 C7 **Arda** *R* Portugal
32 C1 **Ardabil** Iran 38.15N 48.18E
65 L5 **Ardagger** Austria 48.11N 14.50E
59 D7 **Ardagh** Limerick Irish Rep 52.28N 9.04W
37 G4 **Ardahan** Turkey 41.08N 42.41E
32 H2 **Ardāk** Iran 36.42N 59.23E
32 E4 **Ardakān** Esfahān Iran 32.20N 53.59E
32 E5 **Ardakān** Fārs Iran 30.16N 52.00E
32 D5 **Ardal** Iran 31.59N 50.40E
53 U20 **Ardal** Rogaland Norway 59.09N 6.13E
77 G7 **Ardales** Spain 36.53N 4.51W
58 N4 **Ardallie** Grampian Scotland 57.27N 2.00W
53 U20 **Ardalsfjord** *inlet* Rogaland Norway 59.08N 6.03E
53 X16 **Ardalsfjord** *inlet* Sogn og Fjordane Norway 61.12N 7.32E
53 X16 **Ardalstangen** Sogn og Fjordane Norway 61.14N 7.45E
53 X16 **Ardalsvatn** *L* Norway 61.17N 7.46E
75 H2 **Ardanaz** Spain 42.45N 1.25W
58 A3 **Ard an Runair** *prom* N Uist, W Isles Scotland 57.37N 7.33W
37 G4 **Ardanuç** Turkey 41.07N 42.04E
59 F2 **Ardara** Donegal Irish Rep 54.46N 8.25W
81 B2 **Ardara** Sardinia 40.37N 8.49E
Ardasa *see* **Torut**
100 K7 **Ardath** Saskatchewan 51.36N 107.15W
45 P1 **Ardatov** Gor'kiy U.S.S.R. 55.14N 43.05E
45 S2 **Ardatov** Mordovian A.S.S.R. U.S.S.R. 54.51N 46.15E
58 D7 **Ardbeg** Islay, Strathclyde Scotland 55.39N 6.07W
99 K7 **Ardbeg** Ontario 45.38N 80.05W
58 F3 **Ardcharnich** Highland Scotland 57.50N 5.05W
59 F6 **Ardcrony** Tipperary Irish Rep 52.56N 8.10W
80 G5 **Ardea** Italy 41.36N 12.33E
82 H3 **Ardead** Romania 47.37N 22.52E
59 K4 **Ardeath** Meath Irish Rep 53.36N 6.23W
Ardebil *see* **Ardabīl**
90 L6 **Ardeb Safer** Cent Afr Rep 10.22N 22.35E
67 H8 **Ardèche** *dept* France
71 E8 **Ardèche,Gorges de l'** France
59 J4 **Ardee** Louth Irish Rep 53.52N 6.33W
100 S8 **Arden** Manitoba 50.25N 99.15W
111 J5 **Arden** Nevada 36.02N 115.14W
103 F4 **Arden** New York 41.16N 74.10W
99 O8 **Arden** Ontario 44.43N 76.56W
48 V8 **Ardencaple Fd** Greenland
56 H3 **Arden, Forest of** Warwicks Eng
12 E4 **Arden, Mt** S Australia 32.09S 138.00E
61 O6 **Ardenne, Plat. de l'** Belgium
67 H3 **Ardennes** *dept* France
79 G2 **Ardenno** Italy 46.10N 9.39E
72 H2 **Ardentes** France 46.45N 1.50E
58 G6 **Ardentinny** Strathclyde Scotland 56.03N 4.55W
79 H7 **Ardenza** Italy 43.31N 10.18E
58 H6 **Ardeonaig** Central Scotland 56.29N 4.10W
58 H3 **Ardersier** Highland Scotland 57.34N 4.02W
71 C6 **Ardes** France 45.24N 3.07E
37 F4 **Ardesen** Turkey 41.14N 41.00E
32 E4 **Ardestān** Iran 33.21N 52.23E
66 R4 **Ardez** Switzerland 46.47N 10.13E
59 C7 **Ardfert** Kerry Irish Rep 52.20N 9.47W
59 G7 **Ardfinnan** Tipperary Irish Rep 52.19N 7.53W
58 H3 **Ardgay** Highland Scotland 57.52N 4.22W
59 L3 **Ardglass** Down N Ireland 54.16N 5.37W
58 F5 **Ardgour** Highland Scotland 56.44N 5.16W
59 C8 **Ardgroom** Cork Irish Rep 51.44N 9.53W
58 C3 **Ardhasig** Harris, W Isles Scotland 57.55N 6.50W
83 E4 **Ardhéa** Greece 40.58N 22.03E
34 D8 **Ardh es Suwwān** *plain* Jordan
87 G5 **Ardibbo,L** Ethiopia 11.12N 39.46E
77 C4 **Ardila** *R* Spain/Portugal
100 M9 **Ardill** Saskatchewan 49.57N 105.50W
115 H6 **Ardilla,Cerro La** *pk* Mexico 22.22N 102.26W
72 C3 **Ardin** France 46.29N 0.33W
82 J9 **Ardino** Bulgaria 41.34N 25.09E
75 J3 **Ardisa** Spain 42.12N 0.46W
75 J3 **Ardisa, Embalse de** *res* Spain 42.14N 0.45W
Ardistan *see* **Ardestān**
58 B4 **Ardivachar Pt** S Uist, W Isles Scotland 57.23N 7.26W
59 L3 **Ardkeen** Down N Ireland 54.26N 5.32W
11 M5 **Ardkeen** New Zealand 38.57S 177.18E
58 H6 **Ard, L** Central Scotland 56.11N 4.28W
58 F7 **Ardlamont Pt** Strathclyde Scotland 55.50N 5.13W
56 N4 **Ardleigh** Essex Eng 51.56N 0.59E
58 J5 **Ardle, R** Tayside Scotland
12 H5 **Ardlethan** New S Wales 34.20S 146.53E
100 D6 **Ardley** Alberta 52.18N 113.13W
58 G6 **Ardlui** Strathclyde Scotland 56.18N 4.44W
58 E6 **Ardlussa** Strathclyde Scotland 56.02N 5.47W
58 F3 **Ardmair** Highland Scotland 57.55N 5.11W
58 E7 **Ardminish** Gigha I Scotland 55.42N 5.44W
12 H6 **Ardmona** Victoria 36.25S 145.17E
100 G4 **Ardmore** Alberta 54.20N 110.27W
109 N7 **Ardmore** Oklahoma 34.11N 97.08W
103 D6 **Ardmore** Pennsylvania 40.01N 75.18W
108 G6 **Ardmore** S Dakota 43.02N 103.35W
107 K6 **Ardmore** Tennessee 35.01N 86.50W
59 G8 **Ardmore** Waterford Irish Rep 51.57N 7.43W
59 G8 **Ardmore B** Waterford Irish Rep 51.57N 7.42W
59 K6 **Ardmore Pt** Wicklow Irish Rep 52.56N 6.01W
59 E6 **Ardnacrusha** Clare Irish Rep 52.42N 8.37W
58 D5 **Ardnamurchan** *dist* Highland Scotland
58 D5 **Ardnamurchan Pt** Highland Scotland 56.44N 6.14W
108 N1 **Ardoch** N Dakota 48.13N 97.10W
13 G7 **Ardoch** Queensland 27.28S 144.05E
71 F8 **Ardoise l'** France 44.05N 4.42E
66 F7 **Ardon** Switzerland 46.13N 7.16E
44 F4 **Ardon** U.S.S.R. 43.12N 44.19E
44 F5 **Ardon** *R* U.S.S.R.
76 F2 **Ardon, Emb. de** *res* Spain
61 C3 **Ardooie** Belgium 50.58N 3.13E
81 M7 **Ardore** Italy 38.12N 16.10E
59 E5 **Ardrahan** Galway Irish Rep 53.09N 8.48W
33 N9 **Ard, Ra's al** *C* Kuwait 29.22N 48.05E
69 B2 **Ardres** France 50.51N 1.59E
58 F6 **Ardrishaig** Strathclyde Scotland 56.00N 5.27W
100 D5 **Ardrossan** Alberta 53.34N 113.08W
12 E5 **Ardrossan** S Australia 34.25S 137.54E
58 G7 **Ardrossan** Strathclyde Scotland 55.39N 4.49W
59 J5 **Ardscull** Kildare Irish Rep 53.01N 6.55W
103 G5 **Ardsley** New York 41.00N 73.42W
57 L5 **Ardsley** S Yorks Eng 53.33N 1.25W
58 D7 **Ardtalla** Islay, Strathclyde Scotland 55.44N 6.02W
85 L10 **Arduan I** Sudan 19.54N 30.20E
37 F7 **Ardusin** Turkey 38.48N 41.02E
58 E4 **Ardvasar** Skye, Highland Scotland 57.03N 5.55W
58 K4 **Ardwell** Grampian Scotland 57.22N 3.02W
46 N3 **Ardym** U.S.S.R. 52.56N 44.45E
53 S20 **Are** Norway 59.10N 5.28E
52 G3 **Åre** Sweden 63.25N 13.05E
117 D7 **Areão** Brazil 4.26S 49.35W
51 K4 **Areavaara** Sweden 67.27N 23.30E
89 J1 **Arebeb** Mali 21.07N 0.06W
93 A3 **Arebi** Zaïre 2.47N 29.35E
53 S15 **Årebrot** Norway 61.39N 5.02E
71 K5 **Arèches** France 45.40N 6.35E
105 J7 **Arecibo** Puerto Rico 18.29N 66.44W
121 F5 **Areco** *R* Argentina
76 E16 **Areeiro** Portugal 38.44N 9.08W
42 E4 **Aref'yevo** U.S.S.R. 57.00N 90.44E
117 H7 **Areia Branca** Brazil 4.56S 37.10W
76 B16 **Areias** Portugal 38.43N 9.28W
76 C9 **Areias** Portugal 39.44N 8.21W
19 N1 **Arekalong Pen** Palau Is Pacific Oc
100 K6 **Arelee** Saskatchewan 52.16N 107.32W
52 F7 **Aremark** Norway 59.15N 11.41E
64 B3 **Aremberg** W Germany 50.25N 6.48E
75 M3 **Arén** Spain 42.16N 0.43E
81 M6 **Arena** Italy 38.34N 16.13E
103 E2 **Arena** New York 42.07N 74.43W
100 H9 **Arena** Saskatchewan 49.09N 109.17W
19 K7 **Arena** *isld* Philippines 9.14N 120.47E
115 L2 **Arenal** Honduras 15.22N 86.50W
120 E12 **Arenal,Campo del** *plain* Argentina
77 Y13 **Arenal d'en Castell** Balearic Is
77 V15 **Arenal,El** Balearic Is 39.30N 2.45E
76 J8 **Arenal,El** Spain 40.16N 5.05W
121 J6 **Arenales,Cerro** *pk* Chile 47.13S 73.36W
81 E8 **Arena o Delia** *R* Sicily
118 C4 **Arenápolis** Brazil 14.26S 56.55W
111 A3 **Arena, Pt** California 38.58N 123.44W
19 L5 **Arena Pt** Luzon Philippines 13.14N 122.43E
115 E6 **Arena,Pta** Mexico 23.35N 109.26W
77 H7 **Arenas** Spain 36.49N 4.03W
76 L2 **Arenas de Iguña** Spain 43.12N 4.04W
77 J7 **Arenas del Rey** Spain 36.57N 3.54W
77 K2 **Arenas de San Juan** Spain 39.14N 3.30W
76 J8 **Arenas de San Pedro** Spain 40.12N 5.05W
77 C6 **Arenas Gordas** *reg* Spain
120 D9 **Arenas, Pta** Chile 21.42S 70.08W
119 G2 **Arenas,Pta** Venezuela 11.00N 64.25W
105 K7 **Arenas,Pta** *C* Puerto Rico 18.08N 65.37W
121 L9 **Arenas, Pta de** Argentina 53.10S 68.15W
121 E5 **Arenaza** Argentina 34.55S 61.45W
63 F7 **Arenberg** *reg* W Germany
52 D8 **Arendal** Norway 58.27N 8.56E
61 L1 **Arendonk** Belgium 51.19N 5.05E
63 P7 **Arendsee (Altmark)** E Germany 52.54N 11.30E
72 C7 **Arengosse** France 44.00N 0.47W
44 G8 **Areni** Armenia U.S.S.R. 39.43N 45.12E
56 D2 **Arenig Fawr** *mt* Gwynedd Wales 52.55N 3.45W
75 C2 **Arenillas de Villadiego** Spain 42.32N 3.59W
77 H4 **Arenosillo** *R* Spain
77 H4 **Arenoso** *R* Spain
63 L10 **Arenshausen** E Germany 51.23N 9.58E
71 J4 **Arenthon** France 46.06N 6.20E
53 D2 **Arentsminde** Denmark 57.08N 9.38E
75 Q4 **Arenys de Mar** Spain 41.35N 2.33E
75 Q4 **Arenys de Munt** Spain 41.37N 2.33E
79 E6 **Arenzano** Italy 44.24N 8.40E
72 G10 **Areo** Spain 42.36N 1.16E
84 D8 **Areópolis** Greece 36.40N 22.22E
76 B5 **Areosa** Portugal 41.42N 8.52W
76 B6 **Areosa** Portugal 41.11N 8.36W
120 D7 **Arequipa** Peru 16.25S 71.32W
120 C6 **Arequipa** *dept* Peru
79 G3 **Arera,Pizzo** *mt* Italy 45.56N 9.49E
117 C5 **Arere** Brazil 0.15S 53.46W
87 L8 **Areri Mallim Uarfai** Somalia 4.31N 47.19E
72 B6 **Arès** France 44.47N 1.08W
76 C2 **Ares** Spain 43.25N 8.15W
75 K7 **Ares** *mt* Spain 40.29N 0.08W
75 K7 **Ares del Maestre** Spain 40.28N 0.08W
32 F4 **Arestān** Iran 33.22N 54.08E
75 E1 **Areta** Spain 43.08N 2.56W
72 C9 **Arette** France 43.05N 0.42W
66 C4 **Areuse, Gorges de l'** Switz
76 J7 **Arevalillo** Spain 40.34N 5.22W
76 K6 **Arévalo** Spain 41.04N 4.44W
76 D10 **Arez** Portugal 39.29N 7.43W
89 J2 **Arezzaf** Mali 18.04N 1.42W
80 E2 **Arezzo** Italy 43.28N 11.53E
79 L7 **Arezzo** *prov* Italy
33 C2 **'Arfajah** Saudi Arabia 29.59N 38.41E
15 C4 **Arfak Peg** *mt* Irian Jaya 1.14S 134.01E
84 D7 **Arfará** Greece 37.10N 22.03E
71 D4 **Arfeuilles** France 46.10N 3.43E
72 J9 **Arfons** France 43.26N 2.10E
39 D2 **Arga** U.S.S.R. 66.31N 149.45E
75 G2 **Arga** *R* Spain
42 J5 **Argada** U.S.S.R. 54.12N 110.42E
13 D5 **Argadargada** N Terr Australia 21.43S 136.40E
87 F2 **Argadom** *mt* Ethiopia 17.06N 37.47E
39 C1 **Arga-Emneke, Gora** *mt* U.S.S.R. 69.40N 141.15E
Argaeus Mt *see* **Erciyas Daği**
84 P14 **Argaka** Cyprus 35.03N 32.29E
84 F3 **Argalastí** Greece 39.13N 23.13E
35 F5 **Argaman** Jordan 32.10N 35.31E
77 K2 **Argamasilla de Alba** Spain 39.08N 3.05W
77 H3 **Argamasilla de Calatrava** Spain 38.44N 4.05W
77 M3 **Argamasón** Spain 38.52N 2.02W
24 F5 **Argan** Xinjiang Uygur Zizhiqu China 40.08N 88.21E
88 J6 **Argana** Morocco 30.38N 9.14W
31 E2 **Argana Pass** Afghanistan 36.41N 68.20E
75 D7 **Arganda** Spain 40.19N 3.26W
76 C8 **Arganil** Portugal 40.13N 8.03W
76 F3 **Arganza** Spain 42.38N 6.41W
76 F2 **Arganza** *R* Spain
75 O9 **Arganzuela-Villaverde** *dist* Madrid Spain
19 L7 **Argao** Philippines 9.47N 123.35E
29 E7 **Argaon** Maharashtra India 21.10N 77.04E
110 M1 **Argar** Montana 48.32N 113.59W
41 J6 **Arga-Sala** *R* U.S.S.R.
45 S3 **Argash** U.S.S.R. 53.58N 46.14E
80 J5 **Argatone,Monte** Italy 41.54N 13.49E
41 L7 **Arga Tyung** *R* U.S.S.R.
47 M5 **Argayash** U.S.S.R. 55.30N 60.51E
41 O6 **Arga-Yuryakh** *R* U.S.S.R.
47 M5 **Argazi,Oz** *L* U.S.S.R. 55.25N 60.20E
79 F3 **Argegno** Italy 45.57N 9.07E
72 D9 **Argelès Gazost** France 43.00N 0.06W
72 L10 **Argelès-sur-Mer** France 42.33N 3.02E
72 K9 **Argeliers** France 43.18N 2.54E
75 K7 **Argelita** Spain 40.04N 0.21W
66 Q2 **Argen** *R* Austria
64 H8 **Argen** *R* W Germany
66 Q1 **Argenbühl** W Germany 47.40N 9.54E
70 K3 **Argences** France 49.07N 0.10W
71 J10 **Argens** *R* France
101 P10 **Argenta** Br Col 50.11N 116.56W
79 L5 **Argenta** Italy 44.37N 11.50E
110 N4 **Argenta** Montana 45.18N 112.53W
70 K4 **Argentan** France 48.45N 0.01W
80 D4 **Argentario,Monte** Italy 42.23N 11.11E
72 H5 **Argentat** France 45.06N 1.56E
75 H6 **Argente** Spain 40.41N 1.10W
61 N4 **Argenteau** Belgium 50.42N 5.41E
79 A6 **Argentera** Italy 44.23N 6.56E
79 B6 **Argentera** *mt* Italy 44.10N 7.18E
69 C6 **Argenteuil** Seine-et-Oise France 48.57N 2.15E
68 D2 **Argenteuil** Val d'Oise France 48.57N 2.13E
69 G8 **Argenteuil-sur-Armançon** Yonne France 47.46N 4.06E
98 S6 **Argentia** Newfoundland 47.18N 54.00W
81 A2 **Argentiera** Sardinia 40.44N 8.14E
66 D8 **Argentière** France 45.58N 6.55E
71 K7 **Argentière,l'** France 44.47N 6.33E
71 E7 **Argentière-l'Eglise, L'** France 44.33N 4.18E
66 D8 **Argentières, Glacier d'** France
121 E2 **Argentina** Argentina 29.32S 62.15W
119 D7 **Argentina** Colombia 0.35N 74.15W
79 C7 **Argentina** *R* Italy
117 G4 **Argentina** *rep* S America
71 J5 **Argentine** France 45.30N 6.20E
96 F13 **Argentine Basin** Atlantic Oc
123 E14 **Argentine Islands** *U.K. Base* Graham Land Antarctica 65.15S 64.16W
121 J8 **Argentino, L** Argentina
70 A4 **Argenton** France 48.32N 4.45W
72 D1 **Argenton** *R* France
75 P4 **Argentona** Spain 41.33N 2.25E
72 D2 **Argenton-Château** France 46.59N 0.26W
72 H2 **Argenton-sur-Creuse** France 46.36N 1.30E
98 C3 **Argent,R.à l'** Quebec
70 J5 **Argentre** France 48.05N 0.38W
70 H5 **Argentré-du-Plessis** France 48.03N 1.08W
71 A1 **Argent-sur-Sauldre** France 47.33N 2.26E
77 M5 **Argerin** *mt* Spain 37.38N 2.24W
76 L9 **Argés** Spain 39.49N 4.03W
82 J5 **Argeş** *div* Romania
82 J5 **Argeşul** *R* Romania
24 F4 **Arghai Bulak Davan** *pass* Xinjiang Uygur Zizhiqu China 42.23N 88.32E
30 G4 **Arghakot** Nepal 28.02N 83.06E
31 C5 **Arghandab R** Afghanistan
31 D4 **Arghandab R** Afghanistan
87 J8 **Argheile** Ethiopia 5.19N 42.04E
93 J3 **Argi** Kenya 2.07N 37.02E
40 E4 **Argi** *R* U.S.S.R.
87 F6 **Argio** Ethiopia 8.43N 36.30E
36 F4 **Argıthanı** Turkey 38.18N 31.43E
85 L10 **Argo** Sudan 19.28N 30.20E
10 O4 **Argo Deep** Pacific Oc 12.30S 165.40E
85 L10 **Argo I** Sudan 19.25N 30.20E
70 B5 **Argol** France 48.15N 4.20W
84 E7 **Argolikós Kólpos** *gulf* Greece
84 E6 **Argolís** *prov* Greece
109 N4 **Argonia** Kansas 37.17N 97.46W
106 F4 **Argonne** Wisconsin 45.40N 88.49W
69 J5 **Argonne** *reg* France
69 H5 **Argonne,Forêt d'** *Argonne, Forêt d'* France
18 K9 **Argopuro,Gunung** *mt* Java Indon 7.58S 113.33E
110 N5 **Argora** Idaho 44.23N 112.36W
9 U2 **Argo Reefs** Fiji 18.10S 178.29W
84 E6 **Árgos** Greece 37.38N 22.43E
106 H8 **Argos** Indiana 41.14N 86.14W
77 N4 **Argos** *R* Spain
83 E4 **Argos Orestikón** Greece 40.27N 21.26E
83 D6 **Argostólion** Greece 38.13N 20.29E
70 H4 **Argouges** France 48.30N 1.24W
75 G3 **Arguedas** Spain 42.11N 1.36W
70 O2 **Argueil** France 49.33N 1.32E
77 M4 **Arguellite** Spain 38.20N 2.25W
111 D7 **Arguello, Pt** California 34.35N 120.38W
70 F5 **Arguenon** *R* France
89 A1 **Arguin,B.d'** Mauritania 20.31N 16.28W
89 A1 **Arguin,C.d'** Mauritania 20.30N 16.32W
96 U16 **Arguineguin** Gran Canaria Canary Is 27.45N 15.39W
75 K3 **Arguis** Spain 42.19N 0.25W
75 K3 **Arguis,Embalse de** *res* Spain 42.19N 0.26W
75 G8 **Arguisuelas** Spain 39.50N 1.50W
44 G4 **Argun** U.S.S.R. 43.17N 45.52E
Argun *R* *see* **Ergun He** China
38 L3 **Argun** *R* Nei Monggol Zizhiqu/U.S.S.R.
44 G5 **Argun** *R* U.S.S.R.
90 B5 **Argungu** Nigeria 12.44N 4.33E
15 B5 **Arguni, Teluk** *B* Irian Jaya
42 K6 **Argunsk** U.S.S.R. 51.32N 120.00E
42 K7 **Argunskiy Khrebet** *mts* U.S.S.R.
111 G6 **Argus Ra** California
108 O2 **Argusville** N Dakota 47.03N 96.58W
42 D7 **Argut** U.S.S.R. 49.51N 87.00E
24 D10 **Argu Tso** *L* Xizang Zizhiqu China 30.45N 82.50E
37 D7 **Arguvan** Turkey 38.46N 38.18E
72 G2 **Argy** France 46.56N 1.26E
106 M6 **Argyle** Michigan 43.35N 82.57W
108 O1 **Argyle** Minnesota 48.10N 96.50W
98 G10 **Argyle** Nova Scotia 43.50N 65.51W
106 E7 **Argyle** Wisconsin 42.42N 89.51W
54 M6 **Argyle** *oil field* North Sea 56.15N 2.41E
10 F5 **Argyle, L** W Australia
Argyll *co see* **Strathclyde and Highland** *regions*
58 F6 **Argyll** *dist* Strathclyde Scotland
58 G6 **Argyll's Bowling Green** *mts* Strathclyde Scotland
Argyrokastron *see* **Gjirokastër**
33 F9 **Arhab** *tribe* Yemen
86 F8 **'Arhâb, Wâdi** *watercourse* Egypt
22 E2 **Arhangay** *prov* Mongolia
37 F4 **Arhavi** Turkey 41.24N 41.15E
88 L5 **Arhbala** Morocco 32.29N 5.39W
89 K2 **Arhereba** Mali 19.28N 1.18E
51 G12 **Arholma** Sweden 59.51N 19.01E
22 M5 **Ar Horqin Qi** Nei Monggol Zizhiqu China 43.45N 120.00E
53 E4 **Århus** Denmark 56.10N 10.13E
53 E4 **Århus** *co* Denmark
53 E4 **Århus Bugt** *B* Denmark 56.09N 10.15E
11 J5 **Aria** New Zealand 38.32S 175.00E
15 K6 **Aria** *R* New Britain
87 F3 **Aria** *tribe* Ethiopia
12 H5 **Ariah Park** New S Wales 34.20S 147.10E
20 D9 **Ariake-kai** *sea* Japan
Ariake wan *B see* **Shibushi-wan** *bay*
94 E7 **Ariamsvlei** Namibia 28.08S 19.50E
81 J7 **Aria,Mte** Lipari Is Italy 38.23N 15.00E
79 M5 **Ariano,I.d'** *isld* Italy
80 M6 **Ariano Irpina** Italy 41.09N 15.05E
79 M5 **Ariano nel Polésine** Italy 44.57N 12.08E
119 D6 **Ariari, R** Colombia
121 E4 **Arias** Argentina 33.41S 62.22W
27 L9 **Ari Atoll** Maldives, Ind Oc 3.30N 72.45E
117 A6 **Ariaú** Brazil 3.08S 57.15W
89 J4 **Aribinda** Upper Volta 14.17N 0.52W
119 G3 **Aribí, R** Venezuela
37 C3 **Arı Burun** *C* Turkey 40.13N 26.16E
120 D8 **Arica** Chile 18.30S 70.20W
119 E9 **Arica** Colombia 2.07S 71.46W
119 C8 **Arica** Peru 1.43S 75.13W
119 E3 **Aricagua** Venezuela 8.14N 71.08W
80 G5 **Ariccia** Italy 41.43N 12.41E
88 N4 **Aricha,El** Algeria 34.12N 1.18W
98 M8 **Arichat** C Breton I, Nova Scotia 45.31N 61.00W
120 D6 **Aricoma,Nev** *pks* Peru
20 J7 **Arida** Honshu Japan 34.05N 135.04E
20 J7 **Arida-gawa** *R* Japan
35 G2 **Aridah** Syria 32.47N 35.49E
33 E8 **'Aridah,Al** Saudi Arabia 17.04N 43.07E
88 G9 **Aridal** Morocco 25.59N 13.54W
14 E10 **Arid, C** W Australia 33.58S 123.05E
26 Q12 **Aride I** Seychelles, Ind Oc 4.13S 55.40E
Arid I *see* **Rakitu I**
67 F9 **Ariège** *dept* France
72 H9 **Ariège** *R* France
121 F6 **Ariel** Argentina 36.31S 59.57W
110 C4 **Ariel** Washington 45.59N 122.34W
80 L6 **Arienzo** Italy 41.02N 14.30E
82 H4 **Arieşul** *R* Romania
31 G5 **Arifwala** Pakistan 30.15N 73.08E
88 M8 **Arigatel Fersig** Algeria 27.35N 2.07W
22 E1 **Arigiyn Gol** *R* Mongolia
119 D3 **Ariguaní** 9.51N 74.15W
Arihā *see* **Jericho** Jordan
35 G8 **Ariha** Jordan 31.25N 35.47E
34 L2 **Arīj** Iraq 36.10N 43.10E
75 C2 **Arija** Spain 42.59N 3.58W
9 A8 **Arijejen** Nauru, Pacific Oc 0.31S 166.55E
109 H2 **Arikaree** *R* Colorado
20 C9 **Arikawa** Japan 33.00N 129.08E
36 F5 **Arikören** Turkey 37.27N 32.55E
30 C4 **Aril** *R* Uttar Prad India
53 K4 **Arild** Sweden 56.17N 12.35E
82 F7 **Arilje** Yugoslavia 43.44N 20.07E
120 F1 **Arimã** Brazil 5.48S 63.38W
20 J7 **Arima** Japan 34.49N 135.13E
116 O1 **Arima** Trinidad & Tobago 10.38N 61.17W
110 N7 **Arimo** Idaho 42.35N 112.10W
119 J4 **Arimu Mine** Guyana 6.31N 59.10W
96 V16 **Arinaga** Gran Canaria Canary Is 27.50N 15.20W
58 C5 **Arinagour** Coll, Strathclyde Scotland 56.38N 6.31W
28 D1 **Arinda** Andhra Prad India 18.47N 79.48E
87 N6 **Arinder** Somalia 9.45N 50.53E
75 E2 **Ariñez** Spain 42.50N 2.45W
80 H3 **Aringo** Italy 42.34N 13.16E
37 G7 **Arin Gölü** *L* Turkey 38.47N 42.55E
84 C7 **Aríni** Greece 37.30N 21.42E
75 J5 **Ariño** Spain 41.01N 0.36W
118 C4 **Arinos** Brazil 14.17S 55.50W
118 F4 **Arinos** Brazil 15.53S 46.01W
110 M9 **Arinosa** Utah 40.44N 113.41W
118 B2 **Arinos, R** Brazil
71 H4 **Arinthod** France 46.24N 5.33E
33 E7 **'Arīn, Wādi** *watercourse* Saudi Arabia
115 J8 **Ario de Rosáles** Mexico 19.12N 101.42W
108 P8 **Arion** Iowa 41.58N 95.28W
116 O1 **Aripo, Mt** Trinidad & Tobago 10.43N 61.15W
119 E4 **Ariporo, R** Colombia
120 G3 **Aripuanã** Brazil 9.10S 60.40W
120 G2 **Aripuanã, R** Brazil
91 G9 **Aripucula** Angola 11.38S 21.48E
120 F3 **Ariquemes** Brazil 9.55S 63.06W
118 D5 **Ariranha** *R* Brazil
84 D7 **Aris** Greece 37.06N 22.00E
94 D4 **Aris** Namibia 22.48S 17.10E
58 E5 **Arisaig** Highland Scotland 56.55N 5.51W
58 E5 **Arisaig, Sound of** Highland Scotland
80 H4 **Arischia** Italy 42.25N 13.21E
66 H1 **Arisdorf** Switzerland 47.31N 7.46E
86 L3 **'Arîsh,El** Egypt 31.08N 33.48E
Arishk *see* **Eresk**
86 M4 **'Arîsh,Wâdi el** *watercourse* Egypt
119 F3 **Arismendi** Venezuela 8.30N 68.30W
87 H5 **Arissa** Ethiopia 11.10N 41.35E
121 D8 **Arista** Argentina 41.16S 65.50W
Aristan *see* **Arestān**
101 J9 **Aristazabal I** Br Col
121 L5 **Aristizábal, C** Argentina 45.13S 66.30W
84 C7 **Aristoménis** Greece 37.05N 21.05E
36 F1 **Arıt** Turkey 41.41N 32.37E
20 C8 **Arita** Japan 33.12N 129.52E
20 J7 **Arita** Japan 34.04N 135.04E
107 L10 **Ariton** Alabama 31.35N 85.45W
81 C4 **Aritzo** Sardinia 39.58N 9.13E
111 N10 **Arivaca** Arizona 31.37S 111.22W
75 H2 **Arive** Spain 42.56N 1.15W
95 C5 **Arivonimamo** Madagascar 19.00S 47.11E
Arixang *see* **Wenquan**
28 D5 **Ariyalur** Tamil Nadu India 11.11N 79.04E
75 F5 **Ariza** Spain 41.19N 2.03W
75 G2 **Arizala** Spain 42.44N 2.00W
120 E11 **Arizaro,Salina de** *salt marsh* Argentina
121 D5 **Arizona** Argentina 35.44S 65.16W
102 D4 **Arizona** *state* U.S.A.
115 D2 **Arizpe** Mexico 30.20N 110.11W
33 F4 **'Arjah** Saudi Arabia 24.41N 44.19E
52 G7 **Årjang** Sweden 59.24N 12.09E
18 L9 **Arjasa** Indonesia 6.51S 115.16E
34 N8 **Arjawi,Sha'ib al** *watercourse* Iraq
34 L6 **'Arjāwi, Wādi al** *watercourse* Iraq
51 F5 **Arjeplog** Sweden 66.04N 18.00E
119 C2 **Arjona** Colombia 10.14N 75.22W
77 H5 **Arjona** Spain 37.56N 4.04W
77 H5 **Arjonilla** Spain 37.59N 4.06W
30 C7 **Arjun** *R* Uttar Prad India
18 K9 **Arjuna, Gunung** *mt* Java Indon 7.45S 112.32E
29 G7 **Arjuni** Maharashtra India 21.04N 80.15E
72 C7 **Arjuzanx** France 44.01N 0.51W
39 C4 **Arka** U.S.S.R. 60.04N 142.16E
107 F7 **Arkabutla Res** Mississippi 34.45N 90.05W
45 P5 **Arkadak** U.S.S.R. 51.58N 43.30E
107 C7 **Arkadelphia** Arkansas 34.07N 93.06W
84 D6 **Arkadhía** *prov* Greece
39 D3 **Arkagala** U.S.S.R. 63.08N 147.01E
58 F5 **Arkaig, L** Highland Scotland
28 C4 **Arkalgud** Karnataka India 12.47N 76.03E
43 H2 **Arkalyk** Kazakhstan U.S.S.R. 50.17N 66.51E
102 H3 **Arkansas** *R* U.S.A.
102 H4 **Arkansas** *state* U.S.A.
107 E8 **Arkansas City** Arkansas 33.35N 91.13W
109 N4 **Arkansas City** Kansas 37.03N 97.02W
24 F7 **Arkatag** *mts* Xinjiang Uygur Zizhiqu China
Arka Tagh *ra see* **Arkatag**
60 H12 **Arkel** Netherlands 51.51N 5.00E
101 F5 **Arkell, Mt** Yukon Terr 60.34N 135.39W
52 H10 **Arkelstorp** Sweden 56.11N 14.15E
85 H8 **Arkenu, Jabal** *mt* Libya 22.20N 24.48E
84 V17 **Arkhángelos** Rhodes Greece 36.13N 28.07E
47 E4 **Arkhangel'sk** U.S.S.R. 64.32N 40.40E
44 C2 **Arkhangel'skaya** U.S.S.R. 45.41N 40.16E
41 B2 **Arkhangel'skaya Guba** Novaya Zemlya U.S.S.R. 75.55N 59.08E
38 D2 **Arkhangel'skaya Oblast'** *prov* U.S.S.R.
47 H8 **Arkhangel'skoye** Bashkir U.S.S.R. 54.26N 56.45E
44 F3 **Arkhangel'skoye** Stavropol' U.S.S.R. 44.37N 44.06E
45 J3 **Arkhangel'skoye** Tula U.S.S.R. 53.15N 37.44E
45 E9 **Arkhangel'skoye** Ukraine U.S.S.R. 47.26N 33.25E
45 M5 **Arkhangel'skoye** Voronezh U.S.S.R. 51.29N 40.56E
84 D4 **Arkhanion** Greece 38.58N 22.10E
40 E7 **Arkhara** U.S.S.R. 49.28N 130.02E
40 E7 **Arkhara** *R* U.S.S.R.
44 B3 **Arkhipo Osipovka** U.S.S.R. 44.22N 38.35E
40 F10 **Arkhipovka** Primor'ye U.S.S.R. 43.45N 133.51E
46 H3 **Arkhipovka** Smolensk U.S.S.R. 54.49N 31.32E
84 B4 **Arkhondokhóri** Greece 38.42N 21.02E
44 F4 **Arkhonskaya** U.S.S.R. 43.05N 44.32E
44 D4 **Arkhyz** U.S.S.R. 43.35N 41.20E
30 A1 **Arki** Himachal Prad India 31.09N 66.57E
46 J3 **Arkino** U.S.S.R. 52.30N 34.32E
58 G6 **Arklet, L** Central Scotland 56.14N 4.37W
55 E2 **Arkley** Herts Eng 51.39N 0.14W
59 K6 **Arklow** Wicklow Irish Rep 52.48N 6.09W
83 H7 **Árkoi** *isld* Greece 37.24N 26.44E
99 J9 **Arkona** Ontario 43.05N 81.51W
28 D4 **Arkonam** Tamil Nadu India 13.05N 79.40E
52 K8 **Arkösund** Sweden 58.28N 16.55E
84 A4 **Arkoúdhi** *isld* Greece 38.33N 20.43E
104 H4 **Arkport** New York 42.23N 77.42W
41 D3 **Arkticheskogo Instituta,Ostrova** *islds* U.S.S.R.
46 Q2 **Arkul'** U.S.S.R. 57.18N 50.02E
103 E2 **Arkville** New York 42.08N 74.38W
52 K7 **Ärla** Sweden 59.05N 16.37E
71 D6 **Arlanc** France 45.25N 3.43E
52 K7 **Arlanda** *airport* Sweden 59.42N 17.57E
75 C3 **Arlanza** *R* Spain
75 D3 **Arlanzón** Spain 42.19N 3.27W
75 C3 **Arlanzón** *R* Spain
75 D3 **Arlanzón, Embalse de** *res* Spain 42.15N 3.20W
75 E7 **Arlas** *R* Spain
65 B7 **Arlberg** *pass* Austria 47.09N 10.12E
110 L2 **Arlee** Montana 47.10N 114.05W
66 M1 **Arlen** W Germany 47.43N 8.50E
71 F9 **Arles** Bouches-du-Rhône France 43.41N 4.38E
66 G2 **Arlesheim** Switzerland 47.30N 7.37E
59 H6 **Arless** Leix Irish Rep 52.54N 7.01W
72 K11 **Arles-sur-Tech** France 42.27N 2.37E
71 E2 **Arleuf** France 47.03N 4.01E
69 E3 **Arleux** France 50.16N 3.07E
56 G3 **Arley** Hereford & Worcs Eng 52.26N 2.20W
88 O12 **Arli** Mali 19.04N 1.45E
89 K2 **Arli** Mali 19.05N 1.47E
37 E6 **Arlık** Turkey 39.39N 40.26E
110 J5 **Arling** Idaho 44.39N 116.05W
56 G4 **Arlingham** Glos Eng 51.49N 2.25W
111 M8 **Arlington** Arizona 33.20N 112.46W
111 G8 **Arlington** California 33.55N 117.28W
109 G3 **Arlington** Colorado 38.20N 103.19W
105 F7 **Arlington** Florida 30.20N 81.38W
105 C6 **Arlington** Georgia 31.25N 84.43W
106 C7 **Arlington** Iowa 42.44N 91.40W
109 M4 **Arlington** Kansas 37.54N 98.13W
107 G5 **Arlington** Kentucky 36.46N 89.01W
108 Q5 **Arlington** Minnesota 44.36N 94.06W
108 O8 **Arlington** Nebraska 41.33N 96.20W
103 G3 **Arlington** New York 41.42N 73.53W
104 B6 **Arlington** Ohio 40.53N 83.38W
110 E4 **Arlington** Oregon 45.43N 120.11W
95 L4 **Arlington** S Africa 28.02S 27.52E
108 N5 **Arlington** S Dakota 44.25N 97.09W
107 G6 **Arlington** Tennessee 35.18N 89.40W
112 N9 **Arlington** Texas 32.44N 97.05W
104 M3 **Arlington** Vermont 43.04N 73.09W
110 C1 **Arlington** Washington 48.12N 122.09W
108 D8 **Arlington** Wyoming 41.35N 106.12W
104 D1 **Arlington** *dist* Baltimore, Md
104 P8 **Arlington** *dist* Boston, Mass
104 L9 **Arlington** *dist* Virginia
106 G7 **Arlington Heights** Illinois 42.06N 88.00W
112 M9 **Arlington, L** Texas
88 R12 **Arlit** Niger 19.16N 7.19E
89 N2 **Arlit** Niger 19.15N 7.36E
90 C2 **Arlit** Niger 19.00N 7.30E
61 O8 **Arlon** Belgium 49.41N 5.49E
53 K5 **Arlöv** Sweden 55.38N 13.05E
13 C6 **Arltunga** N Terr Aust 23.15S 134.50E
66 C8 **Arly** *R* France
89 K6 **Arly,Parc Nat.de l'** Upper Volta
109 Q4 **Arma** Kansas 37.31N 94.44W
118 K9 **Armação** Brazil 22.53S 43.07W
76 C14 **Armação de Pêra** Portugal 37.06N 8.22W
118 K9 **Armação, Pta.d'** Brazil 22.54S 43.08W
100 E8 **Armada** Alberta 50.28N 112.42W
58 H1 **Armadale** Highland Scotland 58.33N 4.06W
58 J7 **Armadale** Lothian Scotland 55.54N 3.42W
14 B9 **Armadale** W Australia 32.10S 115.57E
115 J6 **Armadillo** Mexico 22.15N 100.41W
Armageddon *anc site see* **Tel Megiddo**
59 J3 **Armagh** Armagh N Ireland 54.21N 6.39W
98 B7 **Armagh** Quebec 46.45N 70.39W
59 J3 **Armagh** *co* N Ireland
72 D8 **Armagnac** *reg* France
28 E4 **Armagon** Andhra Prad India 13.55N 80.14E
33 J8 **Armah,Wādi** *watercourse* S Yemen
68 K4 **Armainvilliers,Forêt d'** France
75 F6 **Armallones** Spain 40.44N 2.18W
76 D6 **Armamar** Portugal 41.06N 7.42W
39 E4 **Arman'** Magadan U.S.S.R. 60.45N 150.39E
39 E5 **Arman'** Magadan U.S.S.R. 59.46N 150.10E
39 E5 **Arman'** *R* U.S.S.R.
69 F7 **Armance** *R* France
71 E2 **Armançon** *R* France
15 D6 **Armandville** *R* Irian Jaya
50 D6 **Ármannsfell** *mt* Iceland 64.20N 21.02W
85 M7 **Armant** Egypt 25.36N 32.30E
39 E1 **Armantsy** U.S.S.R. 68.19N 151.52E
101 X2 **Armark L** N W Terr 66.30N 100.50W
83 H9 **Armathia** *isld* Greece 35.25N 26.52E
57 H3 **Armathwaite** Cumbria Eng 54.50N 2.45W
44 D3 **Armavir** U.S.S.R. 44.59N 41.10E
72 B9 **Armendarits** France 43.18N 1.10W
Armenia *see* **Armeniya S.S.R**
119 C5 **Armenia** Colombia 4.32N 75.40W
37 E6 **Armenia** *hist reg* Turkey
82 G5 **Armeniş** Romania 45.14N 22.18E
44 F7 **Armeniya** *reg* U.S.S.R.
44 F7 **Armeniya** *S.S.R.* U.S.S.R.
66 K8 **Armeno** Italy 45.49N 8.27E
84 K11 **Arménoi** Crete 35.26N 24.09E
84 C7 **Arménoi** Greece 37.13N 21.40E
75 R3 **Armentera** Spain 42.10N 3.05E
70 M4 **Armentières** Eure France 48.41N 0.49E
69 D2 **Armentières** Nord France 50.41N 2.53E
81 M3 **Armento** Italy 40.18N 16.04E
115 H8 **Armeria** Mexico 18.55N 103.59W
119 D5 **Armero** Colombia 4.59N 74.55W
81 L8 **Armi,C.dell'** Italy 37.57N 15.40E
12 K4 **Armidale** New S Wales 30.32S 151.40E
115 Q5 **Armila** Panama 8.40N 77.23W
77 J6 **Armilla** Spain 37.09N 3.37W
75 J6 **Armillas** Spain 40.54N 0.54W
110 P2 **Armington** Montana 47.20N 110.55W
75 E2 **Armiñón** Spain 42.44N 2.52W
108 C6 **Arminto** Wyoming 43.11N 107.18W
100 Q6 **Armit** Saskatchewan 52.50N 101.51W
47 K7 **Armizonskoye** U.S.S.R. 56.00N 67.41E
100 N5 **Armley** Saskatchewan 53.06N 104.01W
103 G4 **Armonk** New York 41.08N 73.43W
15 E5 **Armopa** Irian Jaya 2.18S 139.37E
29 G7 **Armori** Maharashtra India 20.30N 80.01E
108 M6 **Armour** S Dakota 43.19N 98.20W
108 L1 **Armourdale** N Dakota 48.54N 99.23W
59 K1 **Armoy** Antrim N Ireland 55.07N 6.20W
99 D3 **Arms** Ontario 49.34N 86.01W
64 E4 **Armsheim** W Germany 49.48N 8.06E
110 N5 **Armstead** Montana 44.58N 112.53W
121 E4 **Armstrong** Argentina 32.46S 61.39W
101 O10 **Armstrong** Br Col 50.27N 119.14W
106 G9 **Armstrong** Illinois 40.18N 87.54W
108 Q6 **Armstrong** Iowa 43.25N 94.29W
107 D2 **Armstrong** Missouri 39.17N 92.40W
100 O1 **Armstrong** Ontario 50.20N 89.02W
112 K9 **Armstrong** Texas 26.56N 97.48W
13 B3 **Armstrong** *R* N Terr Australia
40 G9 **Armu** *R* U.S.S.R.137.50E
37 D6 **Armudan** Turkey 39.35N 38.26E
50 C2 **Ármúli** Iceland 66.07N 22.26W
76 L6 **Armuña** Spain 41.05N 4.19W
81 C4 **Armungia** Sardinia 39.31N 9.32E
28 D1 **Armur** Andhra Prad India 18.49N 78.15E
37 D3 **Armutçuk Dağları** *mts* Turkey
36 J5 **Armut Dağı** *mt* Turkey 37.56N 36.32E
37 F2 **Armutlu** Turkey 40.32N 28.49E
36 B3 **Armutova** Turkey 39.22N 26.48E
44 C8 **Armyansk** Ukraine U.S.S.R. 46.05N 33.43E
38 D4 **Armyanskaya S.S.R** U.S.S.R.
72 J8 **Arn** *R* France
84 D8 **Árna** Greece 36.53N 22.25E
53 S18 **Arna** Norway 60.25N 5.28E
53 B7 **Arnå** *R* Denmark
72 G5 **Arnac-Pompadour** France 45.24N 1.23E
53 M9 **Árnafjall** *mt* Faeroes 62.08N 7.26W
53 U16 **Arnafjord** Norway 61.01N 6.23E
70 L6 **Arnage** France 47.56N 0.11E
53 P12 **Arnager** Bornholm Denmark 55.03N 14.47E
83 F4 **Arnaía** Greece 40.30N 23.36E
87 F2 **Arnait** *watercourse* Ethiopia
50 G5 **Arnarfell hidh litla** *mt* Iceland 64.43N 18.40W
50 G5 **Arnarfellsjökull** *ice cap* Iceland 64.42N 18.50W
50 B3 **Arnarfjördhur** *B* Iceland
Arnarstadhir *see* **Dadhastadhir**
50 B5 **Arnarstapi** Iceland 64.46N 23.38W
50 E5 **Arnarvatn** *L* Iceland 64.58N 20.20W
50 E5 **Arnarvatnshædhir** *mt* Iceland
100 U9 **Arnaud** Manitoba 49.15N 97.08W
97 M6 **Arnaud** *R* Quebec
84 P14 **Arnauti** *C* Cyprus 35.07N 32.17E
69 L5 **Arnaville** France 49.01N 6.03E
37 F2 **Arnavut Burun** *C* Turkey 40.24N 28.52E
37 K1 **Arnavutköy** Turkey 41.04N 29.06E
31 F3 **Arnawai** Pakistan 35.17N 71.38E
71 E2 **Arnay-le-Duc** France 47.08N 4.30E
79 C3 **Arnaz** Italy 45.38N 7.44E
53 B4 **Arnborg** Denmark 56.01N 8.59E
64 P5 **Arnbruck** W Germany 49.08N 13.01E
57 J4 **Arncliffe** N Yorks Eng 54.09N 2.05W
63 Q7 **Arneburg** E Germany 52.42N 12.01E
75 F3 **Arnedillo** Spain 42.14N 2.15W
75 F3 **Arnedo** Spain 42.14N 2.05W
53 O9 **Arnefjord** Faeroes 62.16N 6.30W
108 G2 **Arnegard** N Dakota 47.49N 103.29W
66 O2 **Arnegg** Switzerland 47.28N 9.16E
76 C3 **Arnégo** *R* Spain
72 B9 **Arnéguy** France 43.06N 1.16W
117 G8 **Arneiroz** Brazil 6.21S 40.08W
69 C2 **Arnèke** France 50.50N 2.25E
88 D2 **Arnel, Pta do** *pt* Azores 37.50N 25.09W
51 J6 **Arnemark** Sweden 65.30N 21.15E
60 B3 **Arnemuiden** Netherlands 51.30N 3.40E
50 D2 **Arnes** Iceland 66.00N 21.29W
52 F6 **Årnes** Norway 60.07N 11.28E
75 L6 **Arnés** Spain 40.54N 0.16E
56 J2 **Arnesby** Leics Eng 52.31N 1.05W
50 D7 **Árnessýsla** *co* Iceland
109 L5 **Arnett** Oklahoma 36.08N 99.46W
104 D9 **Arnett** W Virginia 37.51N 81.27W
66 C5 **Arnex** Switzerland 46.42N 6.32E
65 M8 **Arnfels** Austria 46.41N 15.25E
50 C3 **Arngerdhareyri** Iceland 65.54N 22.20W
60 M12 **Arnhem** Netherlands 52.00N 5.53E
13 D1 **Arnhem Bay** N Terr Aust
13 D1 **Arnhem,C** N Terr Aust 12.18S 137.00E
13 C2 **Arnhem Land** *reg* N Terr Aust
13 C2 **Arnhem Land Res** N Terr Aust
28 D4 **Arni** Tamil Nadu India 12.41N 79.17E
30 A4 **Arnia Khurd** Uttar Prad India 28.08N 77.55E
70 N4 **Arnières** France 49.00N 1.07E
58 E4 **Arnisdale** Highland Scot 57.08N 5.34W
Arniston *see* **Waenhuiskrans**
112 D4 **Arno** Texas 31.39N 103.39W
9 D3 **Arno** *atoll* Marshall Is Pacific Oc 7.02N 171.40E
79 H7 **Arno** *R* Italy
12 D5 **Arno Bay** S Australia 33.53S 136.31E
53 J6 **Arnøje** Denmark 55.19N 12.18E
58 C2 **Arnol** Lewis, W Isles Scot 58.21N 6.36W
111 D3 **Arnold** California 38.15N 120.20W
108 K8 **Arnold** Nebraska 41.16N 100.11W
104 F6 **Arnold** Pennsylvania 40.36N 79.46W
79 H2 **Arno,L.d'** *L* Italy 46.03N 10.26E
104 D8 **Arnoldsburg** W Virginia 38.48N 81.09W
108 Q6 **Arnolds Park** Iowa 43.18N 94.52W
65 J8 **Arnoldstein** Austria 46.34N 13.43E
95 L8 **Arnoldton** S Africa 32.58S 27.47E
Arnon *R* *see* **Mujib** *R*
72 J1 **Arnon** *R* France 47.02N 2.04E
35 B2 **Arnona** *dist* Jerusalem
100 V3 **Arnot** Manitoba 55.46N 96.42W
95 N1 **Arnot** S Africa 25.48S 29.47E
68 F2 **Arnouville-les-Gonesse** France 48.59N 2.25E
51 H1 **Arnøy** *isld* Norway 70.10N 20.30E
76 C4 **Arnoya** Spain 42.15N 8.09W
76 D4 **Arnoya** *R* Spain
58 H6 **Arnprior** Central Scot 56.08N 4.15W
99 O7 **Arnprior** Ontario 45.26N 76.24W
63 H10 **Arnsberg** W Germany 51.23N 8.03E
57 H4 **Arnside** Cumbria Eng 54.12N 2.50W
64 K2 **Arnstadt** E Germany 50.50N 10.57E
64 L3 **Arnstein** Oberfranken, Bayern W Germany 50.03N 11.13E
99 L7 **Arnstein** Ontario 45.56N 79.55W
64 H4 **Arnstein** Unterfranken, Bayern W Ger 49.59N 9.59E
64 O6 **Arnstorf** W Germany 48.34N 12.50E
Arnswalde *see* **Choszczno**
99 L4 **Arntfield** Quebec 48.13N 79.16W
75 C1 **Arnuero** Spain 43.28N 3.33W
53 B6 **Arnum** Denmark 55.15N 8.59E
53 D6 **Årø** Denmark 55.16N 9.44E
53 D6 **Årø** *isld* Denmark 55.16N 9.45E
119 F2 **Aroa** Venezuela 10.31N 68.55W
94 E6 **Aroab** Namibia 26.47S 19.40E
84 D6 **Aroanía** Greece 37.52N 22.01E
84 D6 **Aroánia Óri** *mts* Greece
122 B11 **Aroa, Pt** Society Is Pacific Oc 17.27S 149.45W
115 H4 **Arocha** Mexico 27.08N 102.49W
93 D4 **Arocha** *R* Uganda
77 C5 **Aroche** Spain 37.56N 6.57W
77 C4 **Aroche, Picos de** *mts* Spain
90 C9 **Aro Chuku** Nigeria 5.21N 7.54E

86 N5 'Arod watercourse Israel
118 C7 Aroeira Brazil 21.38S 54.23W
76 C7 Arões Portugal 40.48N 8.18W
66 M8 Arogno Switzerland 45.58N 8.59E
75 F2 Arokiu Spain 42.55N 2.02W
66 K8 Arola Italy 45.49N 8.22E
87 L9 Arole Somalia 3.01N 46.37E
66 F7 Arolla Switzerland 46.02N 7.29E
63 K10 Arolsen W Germany 51.22N 9.01E
87 F3 Aroma Sudan 15.45N 36.13E
47 K7 Aromashevo U.S.S.R. 56.55N 68.39E
76 B3 Aro,Mte Spain 42.58N 8.57W
70 J5 Aron France 48.17N 0.34W
30 A8 Aron Guna, Madhya Prad India 24.23N 77.19E
30 A7 Aron Gwalior, Madhya Prad India 25.57N 77.56E
70 J5 Aron R Mayenne France
71 D3 Aron R Nièvre France
79 E3 Arona Italy 45.46N 8.33E
15 J7 Arona Papua New Guinea 6.20S 146.00E
96 O15 Arona Tenerife Canary Is 28.07N 16.42W
98 F7 Aroostook New Brunswick 46.50N 67.43W
104 Q7 Aroostook R Maine
15 J2 Aropa Papua New Guinea 6.22S 155.48E
15 C5 Aropen Irian Jaya 2.51S 134.30E
75 D1 Aro, Pico de mt Spain 43.02N 3.08W
119 G4 Aro, R Venezuela
9 C6 Arorae / Kiribati, Pacific Oc 2.39S 176.54E
122 A10 Arorangi Rarotonga Pacific Oc 21.13S 159.49W
15 L9 Arorow I Louisiade Arch Coral Sea 10.45S 151.45E
19 L5 Aroroy Philippines 12.30N 123.25E
76 C5 Arosa Portugal 41.33N 8.13W
66 P4 Arosa Switzerland 46.47N 9.41E
76 B3 Arosa, I Spain 42.33N 8.52W
76 B4 Arosa, Ria de B Spain
66 P5 Aroser Roth-Horn mt Switzerland 46.44N 9.37E
53 D6 Arøsund Denmark 55.14N 9.44E
76 C7 Arouca Portugal 40.56N 8.15W
116 O1 Arouca Trinidad & Tobago 10.38N 61.20W
90 K2 Aroueli Chad 19.27N 20.44E
88 B1 Aroueyite Mauritania 21.18N 15.05W
11 M5 Arowhana New Zealand 30.06S 177.54E
109 G3 Aroya Colorado 38.52N 103.07W
112 M3 Arp Texas 32.14N 95.03W
43 L6 Arpa Kirgiziya U.S.S.R. 40.47N 74.16E
58 H5 Arpa R Turkey/U.S.S.R.
44 G8 Arpa R U.S.S.R.
37 G5 Arpaçay Turkey 40.51N 43.20E
34 P2 Arpa Cha'i Iran 36.48N 47.06E
69 C6 Arpajon France 48.35N 2.15E
72 J6 Arpajon-sur-Cère France 44.54N 2.27E
29 F8 Arpalli Maharashtra India 19.45N 79.58E
37 G2 Arpanı Dere R Turkey
47 J5 Arpavla U.S.S.R. 60.34N 63.49E
82 J5 Arpaşu de Jos Romania 45.47N 24.39E
47 F4 Arpilik,Oz L Armenia U.S.S.R. 41.03N 43.45E
99 K4 Arpin Ontario 48.56N 80.43W
80 J5 Arpino Italy 41.38N 13.37E
118 J10 Arpoador, Pta. do Brazil 23.00S 43.12W
79 L4 Arquà Petrarca Italy 45.16N 11.44E
79 L4 Arquà Polèsine Italy 45.01N 11.44E
80 H3 Arquata del Tronto Italy 42.46N 13.17E
79 E5 Arquata Scrivia Italy 44.42N 8.53E
120 E7 Arque Bolivia 17.46S 66.23W
61 H4 Arquennes Belgium 50.34N 4.17E
72 J10 Arques Aude France 42.57N 2.21E
69 C2 Arques Pas de Calais France 50.44N 2.17E
70 N2 Arques R France
70 N2 Arques-la-Bataille France 49.53N 1.08E
71 B1 Arquiar France 47.33N 2.59E
77 K4 Arquillos Spain 38.11N 3.26W
35 E2 'Arrâba Israel 32.51N 35.20E
35 D4 'Arrāba Jordan 32.24N 35.12E
76 H4 Arrabalde Spain 42.07N 5.53W
76 A12 Arrábida, Sa da mts Portugal
13 F7 Arrabury Queensland 26.45S 141.00E
69 M6 Arracourt France 48.44N 6.31E
75 J2 Arraco, Venta de Spain 42.56N 0.52W
70 E6 Arradon France 47.38N 2.49W
121 D2 Arraga Argentina 28.05S 64.14W
76 F8 Arrago R Spain
30 H7 Arrah Bihar India 25.34N 84.40E
118 F3 Arraias Brazil 12.55S 46.55W
118 F3 Arraias, R Brazil
118 F3 Arraias,Serra de mts Brazil
115 F10 Arraiján Panama 8.56N 79.36W
76 D11 Arraiolos Portugal 38.44N 7.59W
75 G1 Arraiz-Orquin Spain 43.00N 1.39W
35 H1 'Arram watercourse Syria
59 F6 Arra Mts Tipperary Irish Rep
105 C7 Arran Florida 30.13N 84.24W
100 Q7 Arran Saskatchewan 51.52N 101.41W
57 C1 Arran / Strathclyde Scotland 55.35N 5.15W
35 F9 'Arrana Jordan 32.30N 35.19E
77 F7 Arrancacepas Spain 40.19N 2.22W
101 H8 Arrandale Br Col 54.55N 130.01W
31 C8 Arra R Pakistan
69 D3 Arras Pas de Calais France 50.17N 2.46E
72 D10 Arras-en-Lavedan France 42.59N 0.08W
72 F8 Arrats R France
72 B9 Arraute-Charritte France 43.24N 1.05W
75 F4 Arrazola Spain 43.05N 2.35W
55 B5 Arre Denmark 55.34N 8.40E
72 E10 Arreau France 42.55N 0.21E
118 F6 Arrecifal Colombia 3.38N 69.00W
96 V8 Arrecife Lanzarote Canary Is 28.57N 13.33W
115 P6 Arrecife Alacrán reefs Gulf of Mexico
115 N6 Arrecife Alargado islds Caribbean Sea
115 P4 Arrecife de la Media Luna islds Caribbean Sea
115 N2 Arrecife Edinburgh islds Caribbean Sea
121 E6 Arrecifes Argentina 34.06S 60.09W
75 C1 Arredondo Spain 43.16N 3.35W
70 C5 Arrée,Mtgne.d' France
72 D10 Arrens-Marsous France 42.57N 0.13W
69 H7 Arrentières France 48.16N 4.46E
87 G3 Arresa Ethiopia 14.54N 38.31E
65 E5 Arresø L Denmark 55.58N 12.08E
87 K2 Arrey New Mexico 32.50N 107.19W
65 J8 Arriach Austria 46.50N 13.52E
115 N9 Arriaga Chiapas Mexico 16.15N 93.52W
115 J7 Arriaga San Luis Potosí Mexico 21.55N 101.23W
77 F7 Arriate Spain 36.48N 5.09W
109 G2 Arriba Colorado 39.17N 103.16W
121 D5 Arribenos Argentina 34.14S 61.25W
96 V7 Arrieta Lanzarote Canary Is 29.08N 13.27W
76 E7 Arrifana Portugal 40.35N 7.12W
96 T1 Arrifes Azores 37.31N 25.43W
69 H6 Arrigny France 48.37N 4.43E
75 E1 Arrigorriaga Spain 43.11N 2.54W
12 G6 Arrilalah Queensland 23.42S 143.52E
53 B6 Arrild Denmark 55.09N 8.58E
56 L5 Arrington Cambs Eng 52.08N 0.05W
13 F8 Arrino W Australia 29.28S 115.36E
76 J2 Arriondas Spain 43.23N 5.11W
88 R4 Arris Algeria 35.13N 6.28E
76 K10 Arroba Spain 39.10N 4.32W
58 G6 Arrochar Strathclyde Scot 56.12N 4.45W
120 G5 Arroio do Só Brazil 29.52S 53.35W
118 H10 Arroio Fundo R Brazil
121 G2 Arroio Grande Brazil 32.14S 53.09W
118 H9 Arroio Pavuna R Brazil
118 J8 Arrojado, R Brazil
70 J3 Arromanches France 49.20N 0.38W
76 E10 Arronches Portugal 39.08N 7.16W
69 F5 Arronville France
80 E3 Arrone R Italy
80 H4 Arrone Italy 42.35N 12.46E
75 F2 Arróniz Spain 42.35N 2.05W
73 G5 Arrone R Kenya
72 F9 Arros France 43.12N 0.17W
72 E9 Arros R France
79 D6 Arroscia R Italy
70 N5 Arrou France 48.06N 1.08E
87 R3 Arrouch,El Algeria 36.39N 6.50E
72 F5 Arrouck R France
113 C10 Arrow Cr Montana
101 P10 Arrowhead Br Col 50.43N 117.57W
110 D7 Arrow L Ontario 48.12N 90.15W
59 F3 Arrow,L Sligo Irish Rep 54.03N 8.20W
101 P10 Arrow Park Br Col 50.06N 117.58W
102 D2 Arrow Rock Missouri 39.04N 92.58W
110 K6 Arrowrock Res Idaho 43.34N 115.50W
12 F4 Arrowsmith, Mt New S Wales 30.06S 141.40E
11 E10 Arrowsmith, Mt New Zealand 43.23S 170.58E
13 D2 Arrowsmith Pt N Terr Aust 13.10S 136.25E
11 C11 Arrowtown New Zealand 44.57S 168.51E
100 D8 Arrowwood Alberta 50.45N 113.07W
75 C3 Arroyal Spain 42.25N 3.44W
115 K8 Arroyo Puerto Rico 17.59N 66.03W
76 J6 Arroyo de Cuéllar Spain 41.20N 4.22W
76 F10 Arroyo de la Luz Spain 39.28N 6.36W
112 F6 Arroyo de la Zorra R Mexico
77 D3 Arroyo de San Serván Spain 38.51N 6.28W
115 J6 Arroyo, Dr Mexico 23.42N 100.15W
111 D6 Arroyo Grande California 35.08N 120.34W
121 F2 Arroyo Grande R Argentina
109 E5 Arroyo Hondo New Mexico 36.31N 105.42W
77 D4 Arroyomolinos de León Spain 38.01N 6.25W
77 D2 Arroyomolinos de Montánchez Spain 39.11N 6.10W
121 F4 Arroyo Negro R Uruguay
121 E4 Arroyo Seco Argentina 33.08S 60.30W
115 K7 Arroyo Seco Mexico 21.30N 99.41W
111 J8 Arroyo Seco R California
121 F5 Arroyos,L de los Bolivia 12.37S 65.00W
118 B9 Arroyos-y Esteros Paraguay 25.07S 57.05W
121 D9 Arroyo Verde Argentina 42.05S 65.14W
118 C4 Arruda Brazil 15.00S 56.01W
76 A11 Arruda dos Vinhos Portugal 38.59N 9.04W
69 L6 Arry France 49.00N 6.04E
53 D3 Ars Denmark 56.49N 9.32E
32 B2 Ars Iran 37.06N 47.45E
72 C6 Arsac France 45.00N 0.43W
53 Q12 Årsdale Bornholm Denmark 55.07N 15.10E
61 O7 Arsdorf Luxembourg 49.52N 5.51E
32 E6 Arsenajān Iran 29.58N 53.19E
77 D8 Arsenal de la Carraca Spain 36.29N 6.11W
100 J3 Arsenault L Saskatchewan
101 Q3 Arseno L N W Terr 64.30N 115.41W
72 A3 Ars-en-Ré France 46.13N 1.31W
40 F9 Arsen'yevka R U.S.S.R.
45 H3 Arsen'yevo U.S.S.R. 53.44N 36.44E
42 G6 Arshan Buryat U.S.S.R. 51.55N 102.30E
42 F5 Arshan Irkutsk U.S.S.R. 53.56N 99.53E
47 M5 Arshinskoye U.S.S.R. 55.32N 59.42E
84 G6 Arsidha isld Greece 37.42N 23.54E
79 L3 Arsiè Italy 45.59N 11.46E
79 K3 Arsiero Italy 45.48N 11.22E
28 C4 Arsikere Karnataka India 13.20N 76.13E
61 J5 Arsimont Belgium 50.26N 4.38E
Arsinjan see Arsenajān
84 C7 Arsinoi Greece 37.10N 21.55E
46 P2 Arsk U.S.S.R. 56.10N 49.58E
52 K4 Årskogen Sweden 62.08N 17.20E
50 G3 Arskogssandur Iceland 65.57N 18.19W
43 L6 Arslanbob Kirgiziya U.S.S.R. 41.17N 72.59E
36 G5 Arslanköy Turkey 37.05N 34.17E
53 U14 Årsnes Norway 62.20N 6.24E
15 E5 Arso Irian Jaya 3.05S 140.58E
80 H4 Arsoli Italy 42.03N 13.02E
84 Q15 Arsos Cyprus 34.50N 32.46E
84 S14 Arsos Cyprus 35.05N 33.40E
69 L5 Ars-sur-Moselle France 49.05N 6.04E
48 T15 Arsuk Greenland 61.15N 48.30W
52 K6 Årsunda Sweden 60.31N 16.45E
36 H6 Arsuz Turkey 36.26N 35.51E
69 D5 Arsy France 49.24N 2.41E
77 W14 Artá Balearic Is 39.42N 3.20E
84 A3 Arta Greece 39.10N 20.59E
79 O2 Arta Italy 46.28N 13.02E
84 B3 Arta prov Greece
37 E6 Artabil Gediği pass Turkey 40.23N 39.02E
75 G2 Artajona Spain 42.35N 1.46W
77 M7 Artal R Spain
75 H8 Artana Spain 39.54N 0.16W
66 F8 Artanavaz R Italy
35 D7 Artas Jordan 31.41N 35.11E
108 L4 Artas S Dakota 45.56N 99.48W
48 F10 Artashat Armenia U.S.S.R. 39.58N 44.34E
77 W14 Artá,Sierra de mts Balearic Is
33 F4 Artāwi, Al Saudi Arabia 25.24N 44.30E
33 F3 Artāwiyah, Al Saudi Arabia 26.31N 45.21E
75 G2 Artazu Spain 42.42N 1.51W
115 J5 Arteaga Coahuila Mexico 25.30N 100.52W
115 H8 Arteaga Michoacan Mexico 18.22N 102.18W
75 E1 Arteaga Spain 43.21N 2.39W
79 O2 Artegna Italy 46.14N 13.09E
76 C2 Arteijo Spain 43.19N 8.29W
44 C10 Artek Ukraine U.S.S.R. 44.34N 34.20E
40 F10 Artem U.S.S.R. 43.23N 132.08E
45 J8 Artema,im Ukraine U.S.S.R. 48.20N 37.55E
71 H5 Artemare France 45.52N 5.42E
116 C3 Artemisa Cuba 22.49N 82.47W
84 F7 Artemisia Greece 37.06N 22.13E
84 E6 Artemision Óros mt Greece 37.37N 22.31E
44 K7 Artem Ostrov / Azerbaydzhan U.S.S.R. 40.28N 50.20E
89 C4 Artémou Mauritania 15.38N 12.16W
45 G7 Artemovka Ukraine U.S.S.R. 49.46N 35.06E
45 J8 Artemovsk Ukraine U.S.S.R. 48.35N 38.00E
42 E5 Artemovsk U.S.S.R. 54.20N 93.27E
42 J3 Artemovskiy Irkutsk U.S.S.R. 58.12N 114.45E
45 M9 Artemovskiy Rostov U.S.S.R. 47.45N 40.16E
47 N4 Artemovskiy Sverdlovsk U.S.S.R. 57.25N 61.50E
79 L2 Arten Italy 46.01N 11.50E
80 G5 Artena Italy 41.44N 12.55E
96 U15 Artenara Gran Canaria Canary Is 28.01N 15.41W
69 B7 Artenay France 48.05N 1.53E
63 O10 Artern E Germany 51.23N 11.17E
75 J3 Artés Spain 41.48N 1.57E
75 N4 Artesa de Segre Spain 41.54N 1.03E
Artesia Botswana see Mosomane
107 H8 Artesia Mississippi 33.25N 88.39W
109 F9 Artesia New Mexico 32.51N 104.24W
108 N5 Artesian S Dakota 44.01N 97.55W
112 H7 Artesia Wells Texas 28.18N 99.19W
52 K4 Artfjället mt Sweden 65.56N 14.40E
66 L3 Arth Switzerland 47.03N 8.32E
99 T6 Arthabaska Quebec 46.03N 71.55W
72 J8 Arthes France 43.57N 2.12E
72 C9 Arthez France 43.28N 0.36W
72 D9 Arthez-d'Asson France 43.04N 0.14W
69 B5 Arthies France 49.06N 1.48E
57 E4 Arthog Gwynedd Wales 52.42N 4.00W
69 D8 Arthon France 46.42N 1.42E
72 A1 Arthon-en-Retz France 47.07N 1.56W
69 G8 Arthonnay France 47.56N 4.15E
107 H6 Arthur Illinois 39.43N 88.28W
108 L2 Arthur N Dakota 47.07N 97.12W
108 J8 Arthur Nebraska 41.35N 101.42W
99 K8 Arthur Ontario 43.50N 80.32W
95 L7 Arthur mt S Africa 31.39S 27.08E
12 H8 Arthur R Tasmania
112 M2 Arthur City Texas 33.52N 95.32W
13 D5 Arthur Cr N Terr Aust
Arthur I see Artura,Ostrov
103 H9 Arthur Kill R New York/New Jersey
107 D11 Arthur, L Louisiana 30.03N 92.40W
95 J4 Arthur, L S Africa 32.12S 25.59E
12 C4 Arthur, L S Australia 30.10S 137.21E
12 H8 Arthur Lakes Tasmania
11 H9 Arthur, Mt New Zealand 41.13S 172.42E
14 E4 Arthur, Mt W Australia 18.28S 124.11E
12 F4 Arthur Pt Queensland 22.00S 150.05E
15 J4 Arthur, R W Australia
14 B6 Arthursburg New York 41.37N 73.46W
103 G9 Arthur's Pass New Zealand 42.55S 171.34E
11 F9 Arthur's Pass Nat. Pk New Zealand
116 G2 Arthur's Town Cat I Bahamas 24.40N 75.41W
59 J7 Arthurstown Wexford Irish Rep 52.15N 6.57W
47 H7 Arti U.S.S.R. 56.26N 58.31E
59 J1 Articlave Londonderry N Ireland 55.08N 6.46W
75 J2 Artieda Spain 42.35N 0.59W
75 M2 Arties Spain 42.41N 0.52E
121 G3 Artigas Uruguay 30.25S 56.28W
121 F2 Artigas dept Uruguay
72 G9 Artigat France 43.08N 1.26E
72 F7 Artik Armenia U.S.S.R. 40.38N 44.03E
101 T4 Artillery L N W Terr
69 B7 Artins France 47.45N 0.45E
51 M11 Artjärvi Finland 60.46N 26.05E
101 H6 Artland Saskatchewan 52.44N 109.54W
64 M6 Artlenburg W Germany 53.23N 10.28E
111 B2 Artois California 39.39N 122.11W
95 C9 Artois S Africa 33.22S 19.10E
69 G2 Artois prov France
69 H4 Artois, Collines de l' France
71 C4 Artonne France 46.01N 3.08E
37 D3 Artos Dağ mt Turkey 38.14N 43.06E
84 F4 Artotina Greece 38.42N 22.02E
36 J2 Artova Turkey 40.04N 36.17E
77 X14 Artrutx, d' Balearic Is 39.55N 3.49E
Artsakan Nor see Qagan Nur
22 F4 Arts Bogd Uul mts Mongolia
45 M7 Artsyz U.S.S.R. 45.59N 29.26E
71 K9 Artuby R France
44 Q4 Artugan Turkey
42 F5 Artur U.S.S.R. 55.40N 102.10E
41 Q2 Artura, Ostrov / Franz Josef Land U.S.S.R.
91 E11 Artur de Paiva Angola 14.27S 16.20E
Artush see Artux
24 B6 Artux Xinjiang Uygur Zizhiu China 39.40N 75.49E
37 F4 Artvin Turkey 41.12N 41.48E
32 B4 Artyabash U.S.S.R. 51.52N 87.16E
43 E7 Artyk Turkmeniya U.S.S.R. 37.36N 59.16E
43 J8 Artyk Yakutsk U.S.S.R. 64.10N 145.13E
39 D3 Artyk R U.S.S.R.
93 B8 Aru Zaire 2.53N 30.50E
93 E4 Arua Uganda 3.02N 30.56E
117 B2 Aruana Brazil
120 E1 Arujá Brazil 5.04S 66.50W
93 H4 Aruba Kenya 1.54N 36.27E
116 E8 Aruba isld Lesser Antilles 12.30N 70.00W
Arubaland see 'Arabābad
116 E8 Aruba Lodge Kenya 3.20S 38.50E
96 V15 Arucas Gran Canaria Canary Is 28.08N 15.32W
72 D9 Arudy France 43.06N 0.25W
122 C11 Arué Tahiti Pacific Oc 17.30S 149.28W
10 J8 Arugam B Sri Lanka
Arugot watercourse Israel/Jordan
15 C6 Aru, Kepulauan islds Moluccas Indonesia
28 F1 Aruku Andhra Prad India 18.15N 82.56E
15 L3 Aruliho Guadalcanal I Solomon Is 9.20S 159.57E
60 K7 Arum Netherlands 53.08N 5.28E
120 G1 Arumā Brazil 4.43S 62.07W
121 F5 Arumanduba Brazil 1.26S 52.25W
20 B8 Arume Okinawa Japan 26.36N 128.08E
20 Q8 Arume-wan B Okinawa Japan
93 G3 Arumpo Zaire 2.34N 30.02E
29 J2 Arunachal Pradesh terr India
11 F10 Arundel New Zealand 43.58S 171.18E
95 J6 Arundel S Africa 30.57S 25.02E
56 K6 Arundel W Sussex Eng 50.51N 0.34W
103 A9 Arundel co Maryland
21 B3 Arun He R Nei Monggol Zizhiqu China
21 C3 Arun Qi Nei Monggol Zizhiqu China 48.10N 123.31E
56 K6 Arun, R W Sussex Eng
Arunta Des. see Simpson Des.
53 E6 Årup Denmark 55.23N 10.03E
28 D6 Aruppukkottai Tamil Nadu India 9.31N 78.03E
35 D5 'Arura Jordan 32.02N 35.10E
117 D7 Arurandéau, R Brazil
96 O15 Arure Gomera Canary Is 28.08N 17.19W
93 H9 Arusha Tanzania 3.23S 36.40E
93 G9 Arusha reg Tanzania
93 J9 Arusha Chini Tanzania 3.36S 37.20E
87 G7 Arusi prov Ethiopia
19 B3 Arus, Tanjung C Celebes Indon 1.20N 120.50E
18 M7 Aru, Tanjung C Kalimantan Indon 2.11S 116.35E
119 F8 Aruti Brazil 0.20S 66.03W
18 J6 Arut R Kalimantan Indon
122 C14 Arutua atoll Tuamotu Is Pacific Oc 15.15S 146.45W
26 Q4 Aruvi Aru R Sri Lanka
91 J3 Aruwimi R Zaire
75 G2 Aruye R Spain
109 E2 Arvada Colorado 39.47N 105.07W
108 D5 Arvada Wyoming 44.39N 106.05W
59 G4 Arvagh Cavan Irish Rep 53.55N 7.35W
52 L2 Arvån Sweden 64.32N 19.00E
71 C6 Arvant France 45.22N 3.18E
35 E10 'Arvat Sedom swamp Israel/Jordan
22 F3 Arvayheer Mongolia 46.15N 102.46E
71 J4 Arve R France
72 B4 Arvert France 45.45N 1.08W
51 G5 Arvestuottar mt Sweden 66.37N 18.05E
71 J5 Arveyres et Caillau France 44.53N 0.16W
29 F7 Arvi Maharashtra India 21.00N 78.18E
75 F4 Arviana R Spain
98 A5 Arvida Quebec 48.25N 71.08W
52 K3 Arvidsjaur Sweden 65.37N 19.10E
72 K7 Arvieu France 44.11N 2.38E
71 K7 Arvieux France 44.46N 6.45E
53 S14 Arvik Norway 62.12N 5.10E
52 G5 Arvika Sweden 59.41N 12.38E
53 U18 Arvikstrand Norway 60.10N 6.07E
61 M6 Arville Belgium 50.02N 5.19E
111 F6 Arvin California 35.11N 118.50W
81 N5 Arvo R Italy
81 M5 Arvo L Italy 39.14N 16.30E
104 G9 Arvonia Virginia 37.42N 78.21W
55 F4 Arwa' Saudi Arabia 23.57N 44.44E
34 C4 Arwad isld Syria 34.52N 35.51E
30 H7 Arwal Bihar India 25.16N 84.41E
19 E7 Arwala Indon 7.41S 126.49E
21 A4 Arxan Nei Monggol Zizhiqu China 47.11N 119.58E
24 E4 Arxang Xinjiang Uygur Zizhiqu China 43.06N 84.40E
41 M4 Ary U.S.S.R. 72.59N 122.33E
Aryam,Jabal see Arayn, mt
86 E3 Aryamūn Egypt 31.31N 30.54E
84 C5 Aryirá Greece 38.17N 21.52E
84 W23 Aryirádhes Corfu 39.27N 19.58E
84 D2 Aryiropoúlion Greece 39.50N 22.19E
43 J1 Aryk-Balyk Kazakhstan U.S.S.R. 53.00N 68.11E
41 M4 Ary-Kuba, Zaliv B U.S.S.R.
41 L8 Arylakh U.S.S.R. 64.35N 119.50E
41 L8 Arylakh U.S.S.R. 62.40N 117.32E
41 J4 Arylakh, Ozero L U.S.S.R.
43 J6 Arys' Kazakhstan U.S.S.R. 42.26N 68.49E
43 H5 Arys' R Kazakhstan U.S.S.R.
43 J5 Aryskannyg-Aryg U.S.S.R. 51.25N 90.36E
43 H4 Arys', Ozero L Kazakhstan U.S.S.R.
41 N8 Aryta U.S.S.R. 64.23N 126.32E
72 F5 Arz R France
81 C1 Arzachena Sardinia 41.05N 9.24E
81 C1 Arzachena,G,di Sardinia
71 E7 Arzaco-Arraziguet France 43.33N 0.24W
89 M4 Arzakori Niger 14.08N 5.52E
70 F6 Arzal, Barrage d' dam France 47.30N 2.22W
44 M3 Arzamas U.S.S.R. 55.24N 43.48E
81 P1 Arzana Sardinia 39.55N 9.33E
33 K4 Arzanah / The Gulf 24.45N 52.37E
32 F5 Arzaneh Iran 39.04N 47.50E
76 D6 Arzano France 47.54N 3.27W
33 L8 Arzat Oman 17.00N 54.18E
63 N3 Arzberg W Germany 50.03N 12.12E
62 P4 Arzberg mt W Germany 49.27N 11.26E
88 N4 Arzew Algeria 35.50N 0.19W
88 N4 Arzew,G.d' gulf Algeria
64 A3 Arzfeld W Germany 50.05N 6.16E
44 J2 Arzgir U.S.S.R. 45.24N 44.04E
72 F6 Arzhan U.S.S.R. 51.34N 98.01E
72 F6 Arzhan-Tarys U.S.S.R. 50.23N 98.12E
79 L3 Arzignano Italy 45.32N 11.20E
66 F7 Arzinol, Pic d' mt Switzerland 46.07N 7.26E
65 C7 Arzl Austria 47.12N 10.41E
66 M8 Arzo Switzerland 45.53N 8.57E
70 D5 Arzon France 47.33N 2.54W
76 C3 Arzúa Spain 42.55N 8.10W
75 E2 Arzubiaga Spain 42.53N 2.37W
61 M6 Ås Belgium 51.01N 5.35E
83 N3 Aš Czechoslovakia 50.18N 12.12E
50 L4 Ås Mulasýsla, Nordhur Iceland 65.13N 14.36W
52 F7 Ås Norway 59.40N 10.50E
50 J2 Ás Thingeyjarsýsla, Nordhur Iceland 66.01N 16.28W
53 H2 Aså Denmark 57.09N 10.25E
90 C9 Asa Nigeria 4.57N 7.17E
52 G9 Åsa Sweden 57.22N 12.10E
91 J1 Asa R Zaire
94 E5 Asab Namibia 25.29S 17.59E
90 C8 Asaba Nigeria 6.11N 6.43E
33 K5 'Asab, Al oil field U.A.E. 23.14N 54.12E
33 K5 'Asab'ah, Al Libya 32.03N 12.59E
33 H6 Asābi', Al Saudi Arabia 30.04N 40.53E
33 H5 Asadābad Hamadān Iran 34.45N 48.08E
32 H3 Asadābad Khorāsān Iran 35.39N 59.21E
20 D2 Asagai Japan 40.45N 141.23E
20 G4 Asagaya dist Tōkyō Japan
33 G2 Aşagıhanik Turkey 37.43N 40.03E
37 G2 Aşagı Söloz Turkey 40.24N 29.25E
36 G6 Aşagı Tefen Turkey 38.44N 28.46E
18 C9 Asahan Pen Malaysia 2.22N 102.32E
18 C4 Asahan R Sumatra Indon
20 D6 Asahi Japan 35.43N 140.38E
20 G6 Asahi dist Yokohama Japan
20 M1 Asahi-dake mt Japan 43.42N 142.54E
20 M1 Asahi-dake mt Japan 38.18N 139.56E
Asahigawa see Asahikawa
20 G6 Asahi-gawa R Japan
20 M1 Asahikawa Japan 43.46N 142.23E
20 C1 Asaka Japan 35.48N 139.37E
20 C6 Asakaigaonj Uttar Prad India 26.41N 79.53E
32 E2 'Asalūyeh Iran 27.30N 52.36E
89 M4 Asamakka Niger 19.25N 5.44E
20 M6 Asama-yama vol Japan 36.26N 138.30E
15 B7 Asan Guam Pacific Oc 13.28N 144.43E
30 D9 Asan R Madhya Prad India
53 E4 Asane Norway 60.28N 5.17E
30 A6 Asan R Madhya Prad India
21 P2 Asansol Japan 36.19N 136.19E
53 S18 Asane Norway 60.28N 5.17E
33 E8 Asan Man B S Korea
23 E8 Asanovo U.S.S.R. 56.59N 61.10E
47 M5 Asanovo U.S.S.R. 57.03N 95.38E
21 O9 Asansol W Bengal India 23.40N 86.59E
57 G6 Asaph, St Clwyd Wales 53.15N 3.27W
29 J6 Asar Iceland 63.41N 18.25W
57 G6 Asaph, St Clwyd Wales 53.15N 3.27W
119 G4 Asa, R Venezuela
36 F5 Asarcık Turkey 40.26N 38.24E
30 G7 Asarganj Bihar India 25.09N 86.44E
53 G4 Asarna Sweden 62.39N 14.20E
31 G5 Asarur Pakistan 31.37N 73.32E
72 D8 Asasp-Arros France 43.07N 0.36W
122 A1 Asau W Samoa, Pacific Oc 13.26S 172.35W
64 C2 Asbach W Germany 50.40N 7.26E
15 E6 Asbakin Irian Jaya 0.45S 131.43E
Asbe Teferi see Asba Tefari
53 Y18 Asberg Norway 60.25N 8.25E
47 N4 Asbest U.S.S.R. 57.05N 61.30E
99 T7 Asbestos Quebec 45.46N 71.56W
95 F5 Asbestos Mts S Africa
44 N5 Asbestovskiy U.S.S.R. 57.47N 61.24E
87 H6 Asbe Teferi Ethiopia 9.04N 40.49E
50 J2 Asbjarnarstadir mt Iceland 65.00N 18.53W
Asbjarnarvötn lakes Iceland
107 F3 Asbury Iowa 42.31N 90.44W
102 G4 Asbury Kansas 37.17N 94.38W
103 D5 Asbury New Jersey 40.42N 75.01W
103 D5 Asbury Park New Jersey 40.14N 74.00W
72 A9 Asbyrgi fault cliff Iceland
72 D9 Ascain France 43.21N 1.36W
Ascalon anc site see Tel Ashqelon
81 H3 Ascea Italy 40.08N 15.12E
120 E7 Ascensión Bolivia 15.41S 63.04W
120 F6 Ascensión Chihuahua Mexico 31.07N 107.59W
116 B1 Ascension Curaçao W I 12.21N 69.04W
115 H2 Ascension Nuevo León Mexico 24.21N 99.55W
96 A12 Ascension isld Atlantic Oc 7.57S 14.22W
115 Q8 Ascensión, B. de la Mexico
80 H3 Ascensione,Monte Italy 42.56N 13.34E
95 N3 Ascent S Africa 27.14S 28.24E
64 G3 Ascha W Germany 49.00N 12.39E
65 K6 Aschach Austria 48.23N 14.02E
64 H5 Aschaffenburg W Germany 49.58N 9.10E
64 L5 Aschbach W Germany 49.47N 10.45E
65 L5 Aschbach Austria 48.05N 14.45E
64 M1 Ascheberg Nordrhein-Westfalen W Germany 51.47N 7.37E
63 M4 Ascheberg Schleswig Holstein W Germany 54.08N 10.20E
63 F6 Aschendorf W Germany 53.03N 7.20E
69 B7 Aschères-le-Marché France 48.07N 2.00E
63 F6 Aschersleben E Germany 51.46N 11.28E
81 A4 Aschivoni, Pta. de s' Sardinia 39.43N 8.26E
80 E2 Asciano Italy 43.13N 11.33E
87 N5 Ascirà Somalia 10.22N 50.56E
67 P12 Asco Corsica 42.27N 9.01E
75 M5 Ascó Spain 41.10N 0.34E
67 O12 Asco R Corsica
87 G2 Asco Pass Ethiopia 17.30N 38.18E
58 F7 Ascog Strathclyde Scot 55.49N 5.02W
80 J3 Ascoli Piceno Italy 42.52N 13.35E
80 H3 Ascoli Piceno prov Italy
81 N8 Ascoli Satriano Italy 41.13N 15.34E
66 M7 Ascona Switzerland 46.09N 8.47E
120 A8 Ascope Peru 7.46S 79.08W
56 K5 Ascot Berks Eng 51.25N 0.41W
13 K1 Ascot dist Brisbane, Qnsld
120 E9 Ascotán Chile 21.45S 68.17W
120 E9 Ascotán,Salar de salt pan Chile
72 H10 Ascou France 42.43N 1.50E
Ascq see Villeneuve d'Ascq
53 U17 Åsdalen Norway 60.57N 6.10E
15 F5 Ase Irian Jaya 2.38S 140.37E
52 J9 Åseda Sweden 57.10N 15.20E
88 O9 Asedjrad hills Algeria
46 R3 Asekeyevo U.S.S.R. 53.32N 53.00E
88 Q9 Asekseme Algeria 25.28N 4.44E
87 G7 Asela Ethiopia 7.58N 39.04E
Aselle see Asela
32 E6 Asemānjerd Iran 28.54N 53.19E
93 F6 Asembo Kenya 0.11S 34.24E
52 F3 Åsen Norway 63.36N 11.35E
52 H5 Åsen Sweden 61.18N 13.50E
87 F6 Asendabo Ethiopia 9.49N 37.36E
63 G8 Asendorf W Germany 52.47N 9.01E
82 J9 Asenovgrad Bulgaria 42.00N 24.53E
52 C8 Åseral Norway 58.37N 7.25E
53 X15 Åsetvatn L Norway 61.34N 7.35E
52 A4 Asfahak Iran 33.19N 57.19E
32 G3 Aşfak Iran 34.05N 57.06E
34 D6 Asfar, Tell el mt Jordan 32.11N 36.52E
69 G5 Asfeld France 49.28N 4.06E
85 M7 Asfûn el Mata'na Egypt 25.21N 32.30E
50 D4 Asgardhur Iceland 65.13N 23.10W
52 E7 Åsgårdstrand Norway 59.22N 10.27E
84 Q13 Asgata Cyprus 34.46N 33.16E
56 O5 Ash Kent Eng 51.17N 1.16E
99 F2 Ash R Ontario
89 M4 Asha Cyprus 35.08N 33.37E
84 S14 Asha U.S.S.R. 55.01N 57.18E
87 G8 Ashabo Argasa Ethiopia 4.42N 38.07E
44 H6 Ashagy Geynyuk Azerbaydzhan U.S.S.R. 41.18N 47.02E
35 G2 'Ashah Syria 32.58N 35.52E
Ashaira see 'Ushayrah
90 C9 Ashaka Nigeria 9.45N 6.21E
86 N5 Ashalim watercourse Israel
34 N8 Ash'ali, Sha'ib al watercourse Iraq
47 N5 Ashan U.S.S.R. 57.37N 55.19E
35 D8 Ashan watercourse Israel
89 J8 Ashanti reg Ghana
47 H7 Ashap U.S.S.R. 57.10N 56.30E
34 E6 Ashaqif, Tulul el hills Jordan
34 F1 'Ashara, El Syria 34.57N 40.34E
34 P8 Ashar, Al Iraq 30.31N 47.52E
87 K5 Ashararet Ra Somalia
86 H5 'Ashara, Wâdi el watercourse Egypt
33 H5 Ash'ariyah Saudi Arabia 24.14N 43.00E
103 H5 Ashaway Rhode I 41.25N 71.37W
56 J4 Ashbourne Derbys Eng 53.01N 1.43W
59 K4 Ashbourne Meath Irish Rep 53.31N 6.24W
105 D6 Ashburn Georgia 31.42N 83.41W
56 D6 Ashburton Devon Eng 50.31N 3.45W
11 F10 Ashburton New Zealand 43.54S 171.46E
95 M3 Ashburton S Africa 29.40S 30.28E
14 C6 Ashburton R W Australia
11 F11 Ashburton R New Zealand
56 J4 Ashbury Oxon Eng 51.34N 1.37W
57 H5 Ashby Humberside Eng 53.34N 0.39W
108 P3 Ashby Minnesota 46.06N 95.49W
108 J7 Ashby Nebraska 42.03N 101.56W
56 J4 Ashby-de-la-Zouch Leics Eng 52.46N 1.28W
43 H4 Ashchikol', Ozero L Kazakhstan U.S.S.R. 45.05N 67.20E
43 K5 Ashchikol', Ozero L Kazakhstan U.S.S.R. 43.49N 70.37E
45 T7 Ashchiozek R Kazakhstan U.S.S.R.
43 G3 Ashchitastysor, Oz L Kazakhstan U.S.S.R. 49.19N 63.55E
101 N10 Ashcroft Br Columbia 50.41N 121.17W
35 B6 Ashdod Israel 31.48N 34.38E
35 B6 Ashdod, Holot sand dunes Israel
35 B6 Ashdot Ya'akov Israel 32.39N 35.35E
107 B8 Ashdown Arkansas 33.40N 94.09W
107 N6 Asheboro N Carolina 35.42N 79.50W
50 J3 Ashelhi heath Iceland
107 B6 Asher Oklahoma 34.59N 96.56W
100 T7 Ashern Manitoba 51.10N 98.20W
112 H7 Asherton Texas 28.27N 99.46W
105 E2 Asheville N Carolina 35.35N 82.35W
12 L7 Ashfield dist Sydney, N S W
107 E7 Ash Flat Arkansas 36.12N 91.38W
107 L10 Ashford Alabama 31.10N 85.15W
103 F5 Ashford Connecticut 41.52N 72.07W
56 N5 Ashford Kent Eng 51.09N 0.53E
12 K3 Ashford New S Wales 29.15S 151.07E
55 B4 Ashford Surrey Eng 51.26N 0.27W
110 L3 Ashford Washington 46.46N 122.02W
59 K6 Ashford Wicklow Irish Rep 53.01N 6.05W
111 P2 Ashford Airport Kent Eng 51.06N 0.57E
56 K2 Ashfordby Leics Eng 52.46N 0.57W
111 M6 Ash Fork Arizona 35.13N 112.29W
47 G4 Ash Grove Kansas 39.12N 98.22W
107 C4 Ash Grove Missouri 37.19N 93.35W
13 K1 Ashgrove dist Brisbane, Qnsld
11 E11 Ashhurst New Zealand 40.15S 175.45E
20 M1 Ashibetsu Japan 43.29N 142.14E
61 J6 Ashiga Nigeria 11.55N 9.05E
21 O6 Ashikaga Japan 36.21N 139.26E
59 J8 Ashill Somerset Eng 50.57N 2.59W
56 O1 Ashing Mozambique 4.34N 139.54W
55 K5 Ashington Northumb Eng 55.11N 1.34W
21 O6 Ashington W Sussex Eng 50.56N 0.24W
46 J6 Ashio Japan 36.39N 139.27E
20 J7 Ashit Japan 29.27E
20 J9 Ashiya Japan 34.42N 135.16E
20 G5 Ashizuri-misaki C Japan 32.42N 133.00E
46 A7 Ashkadar R U.S.S.R.
46 O3 Ashkadar R U.S.S.R.
43 C5 Ashkatau Kazakhstan U.S.S.R. 49.19N 54.32E
32 F5 Ashkazar Iran 31.56N 54.16E
43 E5 Ashkhabad Turkmeniya U.S.S.R. 37.58N 58.24E
32 G2 Ashkhaneh Iran 37.26N 56.55E
33 M6 Ashkhirah, Al Oman 21.52N 59.33E
31 B5 Ashkhara Afghanistan 30.15N 62.13E
57 H2 Ashkirk Borders Scotland 55.29N 2.50W
32 F5 Ashkum reg Afghanistan
107 L8 Ashland Alabama 33.15N 85.50W
110 K8 Ashland Illinois 39.53N 90.01W
102 B6 Ashland Kansas 37.12N 99.46W
104 C8 Ashland Kentucky 38.28N 82.40W
104 Q7 Ashland Maine 46.38N 68.24W
104 Q7 Ashland Massachusetts 42.16N 71.27W
108 B3 Ashland Montana 45.36N 106.14W
108 P9 Ashland Nebraska 41.03N 96.21W
103 J4 Ashland New Hampshire 43.42N 71.38W
103 J4 Ashland New York 42.18N 74.22W
104 D7 Ashland Ohio 40.52N 82.19W
110 B4 Ashland Oregon 42.14N 122.43W
104 J7 Ashland Pennsylvania 40.46N 76.21W
104 H9 Ashland Virginia 37.44N 77.29W
105 L7 Ashland Wisconsin 46.34N 90.54W
110 G3 Ashland City Tennessee 36.16N 87.05W
104 K3 Ashland, Mt Oregon 42.06N 122.43W
107 G3 Ashley Illinois 38.20N 89.10W
107 J3 Ashley Indiana 41.32N 85.05W
104 E6 Ashley Michigan 43.12N 84.28W
108 L3 Ashley N Dakota 46.03N 99.22W
12 J3 Ashley New S Wales 29.19S 149.52E
11 G10 Ashley New Zealand 43.17S 172.42E
103 D2 Ashley Pennsylvania 41.12N 75.54W
104 J8 Ashley Falls Massachusetts 42.03N 73.20W
99 K4 Ashley Mine Ontario 48.01N 80.53W
11 G10 Ashley, R New Zealand
47 K7 Ashlyk R U.S.S.R.
100 J7 Ashmont Alberta 54.07N 111.29W
103 A1 Ashmore Illinois 39.32N 88.01W
14 D2 Ashmore Reef Timor Sea
86 E6 Ashmûn Egypt 30.18N 30.59E
86 E10 Ashmûnein, El Egypt 27.47N 30.47E
103 F2 Ashokan New York 41.58N 74.12W
103 F2 Ashokan Res New York
30 A8 Ashoknagar Madhya Prad India 24.36N 77.43E
20 J4 Ashoro Japan 43.14N 143.35E
86 O4 Ashoro watercourse Israel
53 E5 As Hoved C Denmark 55.44N 10.11E
56 H5 Ashperton Hereford & Worcs Eng 52.05N 2.31W
35 B7 Ashqelon Israel 31.40N 34.35E
87 F6 Ashraf tribe Sudan
Ash Sha'b see Mainat ash Sha'b
86 O9 Ash Sharmuh Saudi Arabia 28.01N 35.14E
33 J5 Ash Shibliyat area Saudi Arabia
43 E8 Ashl Tadzhikistan U.S.S.R. 40.38N 70.20E
29 F7 Ashta Balaghat, Madhya Prad Ind 21.57N 79.56E
28 B2 Ashta Maharashtra India 17.03N 74.34E
30 B9 Ashta Sehore, Madhya Prad India 23.00N 76.47E
104 E5 Ashtabula Ohio 41.53N 80.47W
108 N3 Ashtabula, L N Dakota
28 C4 Ashtagram reg Karnataka India
44 E8 Ashtarak Armenia U.S.S.R. 40.19N 44.23E
55 D6 Ashtead Surrey Eng 51.19N 0.18W
84 E8 Ashti Chanda, Maharashtra India 19.52N 79.52E
29 F7 Ashti Wardha, Maharashtra India 21.13N 78.25E
32 C3 Ashtiān Iran 34.23N 49.55E
110 O5 Ashton Idaho 44.04N 111.29W
106 E8 Ashton Illinois 41.52N 89.14W
106 J6 Ashton Michigan 43.59N 85.32W
99 O7 Ashton Ontario 45.09N 76.03W
103 M3 Ashton Rhode I 41.56N 71.26W
95 D9 Ashton S Africa 33.50S 20.05E
108 M5 Ashton S Dakota 44.59N 98.29W
57 H6 Ashton-in-Makerfield Greater Manchester Eng 53.29N 2.39W
14 F3 Ashton Ra W Australia
57 J6 Ashton under Lyne Greater Manchester Eng 53.29N 2.06W
44 H6 Ashty U.S.S.R. 41.57N 47.30E
98 F1 Ashuanipi,L Labrador, Nfld
99 R3 Ashuapmuchuan R Quebec
45 L6 Ashukino U.S.S.R. 56.09N 37.59E
45 J1 Ashur anc site Iraq 35.29N 43.14E
34 L3 'Ashūriyah, Al Iraq 31.04N 43.04E
34 L7 Ashurst Kent Eng 51.08N 0.10E
56 M5 Ashville Alabama 33.49N 86.16W
107 K8 Ashwell Herts Eng 52.03N 0.09W
56 L5 Ashwellthorpe Norfolk Eng 52.31N 1.10E
56 O2 'Asi R Syria etc
34 D3 Asia Philippines see Hinobaan
Asia Bak Iran 35.19N 50.30E
32 D3 Asiabeg see Asiā Bak
Asiago Italy 45.53N 11.31E
79 L3 Asia, I. de Peru 12.47S 76.33W
120 B5 Asia, Pulau Pulau islds Irian Jaya
15 A5 Asid G Philippines
19 L5 Asientos Mexico 22.18N 102.05W
115 H6 Asifabad Andhra Prad India 19.22N 79.21E
28 D1 Asigliano Veneto Italy 45.19N 11.27E
79 K4 Asigliano Vercellese Italy 45.15N 8.25E
79 D4 Asike Irian Jaya 6.31S 140.20E
15 F7 Asikkala Finland 61.14N 25.30E
51 L10 Asilah Morocco 35.32N 6.04W
88 K4 Asilik Niger 16.05N 6.45E
89 N3 Asillo Peru 14.48S 70.23W
120 D6 'Asim Syria 32.57N 36.20E
35 J2 Asimi Crete 35.02N 25.05E
84 M11 Asimiro Halmahera Indon 2.00N 127.46E
19 E2 Asin Spain 42.17N 1.03W
75 H3 Asinara, G. dell' Sardinia
81 B2 Asinara, I. Sardinia
81 A1 Asind Rajasthan India 25.42N 74.21E
29 D5 Asino U.S.S.R. 57.05N 86.10E
42 D4 Asir see Asirgarh
Asir Iran 27.45N 52.40E
32 E7 Asira ash Shamaliya Jordan 32.15N 35.16E
35 E4
35 D5 Asira el Qibliya Jordan 32.11N 35.14E
29 E7 Asirgarh Madhya Prad Ind 21.31N 76.22E
33 C7 Asir, Ras C Sudan 18.25N 38.06E
36 D4 Asi Tepesi mt Turkey 38.56N 28.39E
30 D6 Asiwan Uttar Prad India 26.48N 80.26E
53 S18 Ask Norway 60.29N 5.11E
29 J8 Aska Orissa India 19.38N 84.41E
37 F6 Aşkale Turkey 39.57N 40.42E
Askan see Eskān
44 C8 Askaniya Nova Ukraine U.S.S.R. 46.27N 33.53E
37 F7 Askar R Turkey
88 S7 Askarene Algeria 18.46N 8.59E
43 E1 Askarovo Bashkir U.S.S.R. 53.22N 58.30E
59 E6 Askeaton Limerick Irish Rep 52.36N 8.59W
87 F2 Askeinib,Jeb mt Ethiopia 17.04N 37.05E
53 S17 Askeland Norway 60.39N 5.06E
52 E7 Asker Norway 59.50N 10.26E
57 L5 Askern S Yorks Eng 53.37N 1.09W
52 H8 Askersund Sweden 58.55N 14.55E
57 F3 Askham Cumbria Eng 54.37N 2.45W
86 H7 Askhar, Wâdi watercourse Egypt
52 K2 Askilje Sweden 64.55N 17.05E
57 F5 Askim Norway 59.15N 11.10E
Aski Mosul see Eski Mosul
105 K2 Askin N Carolina 35.10N 77.05W
47 H7 Askino U.S.S.R. 56.03N 56.30E
58 D5 Askival mt Rum, Highland Scotland 56.58N 6.18W
42 E5 Askiz U.S.S.R. 53.12N 90.31E
50 J3 Askja vol Iceland 65.04N 16.50W
53 H7 Asko isld Denmark 54.54N 11.30E
51 M11 Askola Finland 60.31N 25.36E
40 F10 Askol'd isld U.S.S.R.
31 H3 Askole Kashmir 35.39N 75.50E
30 D3 Askot Uttar Prad India 29.44N 80.20E
53 G8 Askov Denmark 55.29N 9.07E
108 S3 Askov Minnesota 46.10N 92.52W
53 S18 Askøy isld Norway 60.24N 5.10E
53 S18 Askøy isld Norway 60.27N 5.08E
95 D10 Askraal S Africa 34.10S 20.52E
57 J4 Askrigg N Yorks Eng 54.19N 2.04W
53 R15 Askrova isld Norway 61.31N 4.57E
53 S16 Askvoll Norway 61.21N 5.04E
44 H8 Askyaran Azerbaydzhan U.S.S.R. 39.53N 46.47E
86 J6 Asl Egypt 29.33N 32.44E
34 F4 Asla, El hill Egypt 30.56N 34.06E
33 F5 Aslam, Wâdi watercourse Saudi Arabia
36 D3 Aslanapa Turkey 39.13N 29.52E
32 B1 Aslānduz Iran 39.27N 47.25E
89 B3 Aslat Mauritania 16.51N 14.05W
Asmangird see Asemānjerd
31 F3 Asmar Afghanistan 35.03N 71.29E
31 F3 Asmar reg Afghanistan
33 E7 Asmar tribe Saudi Arabia
Asmara see Asmera
33 D3 Asmarah, Jibal oil well Saudi Arabia 26.23N 41.06E
87 G3 Asmera Ethiopia 15.20N 38.58E
53 F5 Asmindrup Denmark 55.58N 12.25E
50 K1 Asmundarstadhir Iceland 66.30N 15.55W
30 G7 Asna Uttar Prad India 25.21N 83.31E
55 F5 Asnæs Denmark 55.49N 11.30E
53 F5 Asnæs pen Denmark 55.38N 10.57E
29 F8 Asnai Bahar Uttar Prad India 27.06N 82.41E
88 O3 Asnam, El Algeria 36.11N 1.21E
70 J3 Asnelles France 49.20N 0.34W
52 H10 Asnen L Sweden 56.40N 14.40E
52 F6 Åsnes Norway 60.37N 11.36E
76 C7 Asnes R Portugal
86 K2 Asni Morocco 31.14N 7.55W
69 E6 Asnières France 48.55N 2.17E
72 C4 Asnières-la-Giraud France 45.54N 0.31W
77 N4 Asno, Cabeza del hill Spain 38.20N 1.32W
80 J2 Aso R Italy
117 B4 Asoenangka Brazil 1.50N 56.22W
79 L4 Asola Italy 45.13N 10.25E
51 K10 Asölfskali Iceland 63.34N 19.49W
50 J1 Asólfsstadhir Iceland 64.06N 20.00W
79 L3 Asolo Italy 45.48N 11.55E
77 N2 Asomadilla mt Spain 39.15N 1.39W
75 C1 Asón Spain 43.20N 3.36W
Aso Nat. Park Japan
28 K1 Asoni Assam India 28.44N 95.35E
29 D4 Asop Rajasthan India 26.48N 73.41E
84 E8 Asopós Greece 36.44N 22.51E
84 F5 Asopós R Greece
87 E5 Asosa Ethiopia 10.03N 34.31E
20 J5 Aso-san vol Japan 32.55N 131.02E
33 B6 Asoteriba, Jebel mt Sudan 21.55N 36.37E
86 E6 Asoteriba,Jeb mt Sudan 17.01N 35.22E
85 O9 Asoteriba, Jebel mt Sudan 21.55N 36.37E
107 P6 Asothar Uttar Prad India 25.45N 80.54E
110 H3 Asotin Washington 46.20N 117.02W
85 O10 Asotriba Sudan 19.33N 37.01E
80 F9 Asouf watercourse Algeria
88 D4 Aso-wan B Japan 34.22N 129.15E
96 G4 Aspach W Germany 49.58N 9.25E
66 E1 Aspach-le-Bas France 47.46N 7.16E
66 E1 Aspach-le-Haut France 47.46N 7.08E
Aspak see Asfahak
Aspak see Aşfak
65 O6 Aspang Austria 47.34N 16.06E
32 C2 Aspar Iran 37.32N 48.44E
43 G5 Aspara Kazakhstan U.S.S.R. 43.23N 73.36E
76 H5 Asparegos Spain 41.40N 5.35W
43 H5 Asparegos Spain 41.40N 5.35W
53 G4 Asparn Austria 48.36N 16.30E
50 G5 Asparvik Iceland 65.49N 21.18W
52 H5 Aspås Sweden 63.22N 14.30E
56 F3 Aspatria Cumbria Eng 54.46N 3.20W
77 P4 Aspe Spain 38.21N 0.45W
52 F3 Aspeå Sweden 63.23N 17.35E
61 F3 Aspelare Belgium 50.50N 3.58E
61 P8 Aspelt Luxembourg 49.32N 6.14E
89 B7 Aspen Colorado 39.12N 106.50W
109 D2 Aspen Colorado 39.12N 106.50W
110 P8 Aspen Wyoming 41.13N 110.45W
100 D6 Aspen Beach Prov. Park Alberta
Aspendos see Belkis anc site
61 E3 Asper Belgium 50.55N 3.39E
60 J12 Asperen Netherlands 51.53N 5.07E
64 G6 Asperg W Germany 48.54N 9.09E
112 J7 Aspermont Texas 33.08N 100.14W
53 D6 Asperup Denmark 55.29N 9.55E
72 F9 Aspet France 43.01N 0.48E
113 D10 Aspid mt Aleutian Is 53.24N 167.26W
44 E4 Aspindza Georgia U.S.S.R. 41.35N 43.15E
71 C9 Aspiran France 43.34N 3.26E
11 C11 Aspiring, Mt New Zealand 44.23S 168.46E
Aspish see Esfich
80 G3 Aspra, Monte Italy 42.38N 12.55E
84 A2 Asprángeloi Greece 39.49N 20.44E
71 H8 Aspremont France 44.24N 4.44E
71 H7 Aspres-sur-Buech France 44.31N 5.45E
72 J6 Asprières France 44.33N 2.08E
84 Q15 Asprókremmos Cyprus 34.38N 32.42E
81 P8 Aspromonte mts Italy
84 G4 Aspropirgos Attiki Greece 38.03N 23.35E
84 B3 Aspropótamos R Greece
84 B5 Asprovrekas Greece 38.07N 20.46E
84 B4 Aspróyerakata Greece 39.59N 24.05E
98 M7 Aspy B C Breton I, Nova Scotia
88 M2 Asqueimat Morocco 24.30N 15.06W
100 K6 Asquith Saskatchewan 52.09N 107.14W
12 K3 Asquith New S Wales 33.42S 151.41E
34 D6 Assa Morocco 28.34N 9.27W
88 R10 Assa-Aguiene mt Algeria 23.18N 6.10E
Assab see Aseb
87 J4 Assab Ethiopia 13.01N 42.47E
88 R8 Assabot mt Ethiopia 9.18N 40.32E
52 C2 'Assāfiyah, Al Saudi Arabia 28.16N 38.59E
85 A3 'Assah, Al Libya 32.51N 11.36E
87 H4 Assahara Ethiopia 14.00N 40.32E

90 D7 **Assaikio** Nigeria 8.34N 8.55E
72 D2 **Assais-les-Jumeaux** France 46.49N 0.03W
43 D6 **Assake-Audan, Vpadina** *depression* Uzbekistan U.S.S.R.
90 K7 **Assakène** Cent Afr Rep 8.49N 20.14E
Assale *see* **Dalul**
87 H3 **Assale,L** Ethiopia
87 J5 **Assal,L** Djibouti 11.40N 42.26E
28 H2 **Assam** *state* India
43 J7 **Assana** Uzbekistan U.S.S.R. 38.10N 67.56E
91 D9 **Assango** Angola 11.02S 14.26E
87 K6 **Assa Ra** Somalia
90 D2 **Assarara** Niger 18.38N 8.40E
117 G8 **Assaré** Brazil 6.47S 39.54W
104 K8 **Assateague I** Maryland
104 K8 **Assateague I.Nat Seashore** Maryland
44 H4 **Assaul** U.S.S.R. 43.26N 47.22E
103 N3 **Assawompset Pond** *L* Massachusetts
86 O10 **As Sawrah** Saudi Arabia 27.48N 35.20E
29 D7 **Assaye** Maharashtra India 20.15N 75.59E
61 G3 **Asse** Belgium 50.55N 4.12E
71 J9 **Asse** *R* France
100 V2 **Assean L** Manitoba
61 D2 **Assebroek** Belgium 51.12N 3.16E
76 D14 **Asseca** *R* Portugal
95 P2 **Assegaai** *R* Swaziland
95 H9 **Assegaaibos** S Africa 33.56S 24.19E
87 L5 **Asseh Hills** Somalia
88 S8 **Assekaifaf** Algeria 27.22N 8.41E
88 S8 **Assékeifaf** *watercourse* Algeria
88 Q10 **Assekrem** *mt* Algeria 23.18N 5.41E
63 K5 **Assel** W Germany 53.41N 9.26E
70 K5 **Asse la Boisne** France 48.19N 0.01W
61 O6 **Asselborn** Luxembourg 50.06N 5.58E
81 B5 **Assemini** Sardinia 39.18N 9.00E
60 P8 **Assen** Netherlands 53.00N 6.34E
60 G10 **Assendelft** Netherlands 52.28N 4.45E
61 F2 **Assenede** Belgium 51.13N 3.46E
64 F3 **Assenheim** W Germany 50.18N 8.50E
61 M7 **Assenois** Belgium 49.48N 5.28E
53 E3 **Assens** Århus Denmark 56.41N 10.05E
53 D6 **Assens** Fyn Denmark 55.16N 9.54E
66 C5 **Assens** Switzerland 46.37N 6.38E
61 L3 **Assent** Belgium 50.57N 5.01E
70 F7 **Asserac** France 47.26N 2.23W
80 J4 **Assergi** Italy 42.25N 13.31E
61 L5 **Assesse** Belgium 50.22N 5.02E
29 K7 **Assia Hills** Orissa India
72 H6 **Assier** France 44.40N 1.52E
98 G2 **Assigny, L** Quebec
53 B4 **Assing** Denmark 56.01N 8.52E
100 L9 **Assiniboia** Saskatchewan 49.39N 105.59W
101 Q10 **Assiniboine, Mt** Br Col/Alberta 50.51N 115.39W
100 Q8 **Assiniboine R** Manitoba/Sask
89 H9 **Assinie** Ivory Coast 5.08N 3.15W
88 R11 **Assiou** Algeria 21.07N 7.36E
83 F4 **Ássiros** Greece 40.49N 23.02E
118 E8 **Assis** Brazil 22.37S 50.25W
80 G2 **Assisi** Italy 43.04N 12.37E
69 Q2 **Asslar** W Germany 50.35N 8.27E
64 N7 **Assling** W Germany 48.00N 12.00E
64 D3 **Assmannshausen** W Germany 50.02N 7.52E
79 F3 **Asso** Italy 45.52N 9.16E
90 D2 **Assode** Niger 18.25N 8.26E
72 D9 **Asson** France 43.08N 0.15W
103 M3 **Assonet** Massachusetts 41.48N 71.04W
81 H8 **Assoro** Sicily 37.38N 14.26E
84 E6 **Ássos** Korinthía Greece 37.56N 22.50E
76 E10 **Assumar** Portugal 39.08N 7.24W
107 G2 **Assumption** Illinois 39.31N 89.02W
29 G8 **Assundi** Maharashtra India 19.52N 80.20E
64 C5 **Assweiler** Saarland W Germany 49.13N 7.11E
58 F2 **Assynt, L** Highland Scotland 58.10N 5.02W
64 N7 **Ast** W Germany 48.27N 12.05E
52 F5 **Åsta** *R* Norway
79 L2 **Asta, Cima d'** *mt* Italy 46.11N 11.38E
72 F7 **Astaffort** France 44.04N 0.39E
39 B2 **Astakh** U.S.S.R. 66.16N 136.40E
83 H9 **Astakidha** *isld* Greece 35.53N 26.50E
84 B4 **Astakós** Greece 38.32N 21.04E
31 B8 **Astalu** *isld* Pakistan 25.08N 63.52E
32 C2 **Astaneh** Iran 37.16N 49.58E
44 K10 **Āstāneh** Iran 37.17N 49.58E
44 J9 **Astara** Azerbaydzhan U.S.S.R. 38.27N 49.00E
32 C1 **Astara** Iran 38.25N 48.50E
115 M10 **Astata, Santiago** Mexico 16.00N 95.42W
53 E2 **Åsted** Nordjylland Denmark 57.27N 10.25E
53 B3 **Åsted** Viborg Denmark 56.47N 9.00E
60 L14 **Asten** Netherlands 51.24N 5.45E
61 E3 **Astene** Belgium 50.59N 3.34E
Asterabad *see* **Gorgān**
32 F2 **Asterabad** *reg* Iran
84 M12 **Asteroúsia** *mt* Crete 34.57N 25.05E
79 D5 **Asti** Italy 44.54N 8.13E
79 C5 **Asti** *prov* Italy
121 C3 **Astica** Argentina 30.55S 67.20W
120 D5 **Astillero** Peru 13.22S 69.38W
75 C1 **Astillero** Spain 43.24N 3.49W
Astin Tagh *mt ra see* **Altun Shan**
83 H8 **Astipálaia** Greece 36.32N 26.22E
83 H8 **Astipálaia** *isld* Greece 36.32N 26.22E
57 J5 **Astley Bridge** Greater Manchester Eng 53.37N 2.26W
31 B8 **Astola I** Pakistan 25.08N 63.53E
57 L6 **Aston** S Yorks Eng 53.22N 1.18W
56 G4 **Aston Cross** Glos Eng 52.00N 2.05W
31 H3 **Astor** Kashmir 35.21N 74.52E
31 H3 **Astor** *R* Kashmir
76 G4 **Astorga** Spain 42.27N 6.04W
106 D9 **Astoria** Illinois 40.14N 90.23W
110 B3 **Astoria** Oregon 46.12N 123.50W
108 O5 **Astoria** S Dakota 44.33N 96.32W
53 K4 **Åstorp** Sweden 56.09N 12.57E
99 L6 **Astorville** Ontario 46.12N 79.18W
26 D6 **Astove** *isld* Seychelles, Ind Oc 10.05S 47.40E
121 L5 **Astra** Argentina 45.45S 67.50W
45 T2 **Astradamovka** U.S.S.R. 54.32N 47.10E
75 G2 **Astrain** Spain 42.45N 1.45W
46 P6 **Astrakhan'** U.S.S.R. 46.22N 48.04E
44 J8 **Astrakhan Bazar** Azerbaydzhan U.S.S.R. 39.14N 48.30E
44 J7 **Astrakhanka** Azerbaydzhan U.S.S.R. 40.45N 48.44E
43 J2 **Astrakhanka** Kazakhstan U.S.S.R. 51.32N 69.46E
45 G10 **Astrakhanka** Ukraine U.S.S.R. 46.57N 35.40E
46 O5 **Astrakhanskaya Oblast'** *prov* U.S.S.R.
52 M2 **Åsträsk** Sweden 64.38N 20.00E
Astrida *see* **Butare**
15 H6 **Astrolabe B** Papua New Guinea
9 B13 **Astrolabe, Récifs de L'** *reefs* Loyalty Is Pacific Oc
84 E7 **Ástros** Greece 37.24N 22.43E
53 D3 **Åstrup** Nordjylland Denmark 56.47N 9.59E
53 B5 **Åstrup** Ribe Denmark 55.34N 8.50E
53 D6 **Åstrup** Sønderjylland Denmark 55.16N 9.33E
53 J7 **Åstrup** Storstrøm Denmark 54.15N 12.07E
53 E6 **Åstrup** Svendborg Denmark 55.05N 10.22E
53 D5 **Åstrup** Vejle Denmark 55.57N 9.38E
41 H3 **Astrupa, Gora** *mt* U.S.S.R. 77.28N 103.05E
76 L4 **Astudillo** Spain 42.12N 4.17W
80 G6 **Astura** *R* Italy
76 G4 **Asturianos** Spain 42.03N 6.29W
121 E6 **Asturias** Argentina 36.13S 61.52W
74 C1 **Asturias** *reg* Spain
56 K3 **Astwood** Bucks Eng 52.07N 0.37W
15 B5 **Asu** Irian Jaya 2.44S 132.53E
43 P3 **Asubulak** Kazakhstan U.S.S.R. 49.34N 83.01E
122 A1 **Asuisui, C** W Samoa, Pacific Oc 13.44S 172.29W
20 L6 **Asuke** Japan 35.08N 137.19E
53 E6 **Åsum** Denmark 55.24N 10.28E
120 E4 **Asunción** Bolivia 11.52S 67.53W
118 B9 **Asunción** Paraguay 25.15S 57.40W
17 P8 **Asuncion** *isld* Marianas Pacific Oc 19.34N 145.24E
115 P10 **Asunción Mita** Guatemala 14.20N 89.42W
81 B4 **Asuni** Sardinia 39.52N 8.57E
52 J9 **Asurden** *L* Sweden 58.00N 15.50E
87 G3 **Asus** Ethiopia 15.39N 39.07E
37 D6 **Aşutka** Turkey 39.09N 38.33E
53 E5 **As Vig** *B* Denmark 55.45N 10.04E
93 C3 **Aswa** *watercourse* Uganda
33 M4 **Aswad** Oman 24.54N 56.20E
33 C6 **Aswad, Ar Ra's al** *C* Saudi Arabia 21.23N 39.04E
33 M5 **Aswad, Wādī** *watercourse* Oman
85 M7 **Aswân** Egypt 24.05N 32.56E
85 M7 **Aswân Dam** Egypt 24.00N 32.58E
85 M8 **Aswân High Dam** Egypt 23.54N 32.52E
85 L6 **Asyût** Egypt 27.14N 31.07E
62 L8 **Aszod** Hungary 47.40N 19.27E
48 T8 **Atâ** Greenland 69.48N 51.00W
9 S10 **Ata** *isld* Tonga, Pacific Oc 21.03S 175.00W
10 R6 **Ata** *isld* Tongatupa Pacific Oc 22.35S 176.10W
15 M3 **Ataa** Malaita I Solomon Is 8.32S 161.00E
32 H3 **'Atāābād** Iran 35.37N 58.35E
87 G4 **Ataba** Ethiopia 13.30N 38.25E
119 F6 **Atabapo, R** Venez/Colombia
43 J5 **Atabay** Kazakhstan U.S.S.R. 43.27N 68.22E
36 E5 **Atabey** Turkey 37.58N 30.37E
121 B1 **Atacamá** *prov* Chile
120 D10 **Atacama, Des de** Chile
120 E10 **Atacamá, Salar de** *salt pan* Chile
119 B7 **Atacames** Ecuador 0.51N 79.48W
119 F6 **Atacavi, Lagunas** Venezuela 3.15N 66.58W
119 C6 **Ataco** Colombia 3.36N 75.23W
35 B9 **Atadim** *watercourse* Israel
10 S3 **Atafu** *isld* Tokelau Is Pacific Oc 8.40S 172.40W
75 H8 **Ataiaya** *mt* Spain 39.40N 1.04W
86 K8 **Atairtir el Dahami, Gebel** *hill* Egypt 28.56N 33.23E
86 P4 **'Aṭā'iṭā, Jabal el** *mt* Jordan 30.40N 35.39E
34 C8 **Atā'ita, Jebel el** *mt* Jordan 30.40N 35.39E
122 C12 **Ataiti** Tahiti Pacific Oc 17.45S 149.22W
31 E4 **Atak** Afghanistan 33.01N 68.01E
42 K2 **Atakh-Yuryakh** U.S.S.R. 61.05N 119.05E
82 L2 **Ataki** U.S.S.R. 48.25N 27.48E
89 K6 **Atakora, Chaine de l'** *mts* Benin
89 K8 **Atakpamé** Togo 7.34N 1.14E
117 J9 **Atalaia** Brazil 9.27S 36.00W
118 J2 **Ataláia** Brazil 11.31S 37.14W
76 E7 **Atalaia** Portugal 40.40N 7.02W
76 B12 **Atalaia** *mt* Portugal 38.10N 8.39W
120 D1 **Atalaia do Norte** Brazil 4.22S 70.10W
76 E12 **Atalaia Gordo** *mt* Portugal 38.06N 7.27W
76 B14 **Atalaia, Pta de** Portugal 37.18N 8.53W
84 F4 **Atalándi** Greece 38.39N 23.00E
120 D5 **Atalaya** Cuzco Peru 12.53S 71.15W
120 C4 **Atalaya** Loreto Peru 10.45S 73.51W
115 O5 **Atalaya** Panama 8.03N 80.55W
77 D4 **Atalaya** Spain 38.20N 6.28W
75 F8 **Atalaya del Canavate** Spain 39.30N 2.15W
77 S12 **Atalayasa** *mt* Balearic Is 38.53N 1.16E
75 L7 **Atalayas de Alcalá** *reg* Spain
87 L9 **Atalèh** Somalia 2.45N 46.20E
118 H6 **Ataléia** Brazil 18.06S 41.03W
89 K2 **Ataleïa** Mali 19.08N 0.59E
76 B11 **Atalho** Portugal 38.41N 8.36W
93 F1 **Ataloma Hills** Sudan
35 H3 **Ataman** Syria 32.40N 36.07E
19 D8 **Atambua** Timor Indon 9.06S 124.55E
20 N6 **Atami** Japan 35.07N 139.04E
121 D2 **Atamisqui** Argentina 28.31S 63.50W
93 D2 **Atanga** Uganda 3.02N 32.44E
48 S12 **Atangmik** Greenland 64.38N 52.00W
113 H1 **Atanik** Alaska 70.50N 159.38W
Ataniya *anc site see* **Adana**
43 K1 **Atansor, Ozero** *L* Kazakhstan U.S.S.R. 52.45N 71.32E
19 D8 **Atapupu** Timor Indon 9.02S 124.53E
33 G9 **'Ataq** S Yemen 14.31N 46.48E
86 H6 **'Ataqa, Gebel** *hill* Egypt 29.59N 32.22E
76 K6 **Ataquines** Spain 41.10N 4.48W
89 C1 **Atar** Mauritania 20.32N 13.08W
87 C6 **'Atar** Sudan 9.16N 31.23E
35 D5 **'Atara** Jordan 32.01N 35.12E
25 D4 **Ataran** *R* Burma
77 J6 **Atarfe** Spain 37.13N 3.40W
31 G5 **Atari** Pakistan 30.30N 74.00E
35 F7 **Ataroth** *anc site* Jordan 31.35N 35.41E
109 B7 **Atarque** New Mexico 34.44N 108.43W
30 D7 **Atarra** Uttar Prad India 25.17N 80.34E
35 F7 **Ataruz** Jordan 31.34N 35.40E
Atas *isld see* **South I**
111 D6 **Atascadero** California 35.29N 120.40W
112 J6 **Atascosa** *R* Texas
43 K3 **Atasu** Kazakhstan U.S.S.R. 48.42N 71.38E
9 R10 **Atata** *isld* Tonga, Pacific Oc 21.03S 175.16W
19 D8 **Atauro** *isld* Indonesia 8.15S 125.35E
75 D4 **Atauta** Spain 41.31N 3.13W
47 M8 **Atayech'ye, Oz** *L* U.S.S.R.
87 H5 **Ataye,R** Ethiopia
75 C6 **Atazar, Embalse del** *res* Spain
30 A8 **Atbaikhera** Madhya Prad India 24.26N 77.48E
15 F6 **Atbalmin** Papua New Guinea 4.48S 141.00E
87 D2 **Atbara** Sudan 17.42N 34.00E
87 E2 **Atbara,R** Sudan
43 J2 **Atbasar** Kazakhstan U.S.S.R. 51.49N 68.18E
43 M6 **At-Bashi** Kirgiziya U.S.S.R. 41.09N 75.46E
107 E12 **Atchafalaya** *area* Louisiana
107 E11 **Atchafalaya** *R* Louisiana
107 E12 **Atchafalaya B** Louisiana
56 F2 **Atcham** Shropshire Eng 52.41N 2.40W
88 M5 **Atchana** Morocco 32.15N 3.50W
89 L8 **Atchérigbe** Benin 7.37N 2.11E
109 P2 **Atchison** Kansas 39.33N 95.19W
113 G5 **Atchueelinguk** *R* Alaska
105 C3 **Atco** Georgia 34.10N 84.50W
103 E7 **Atco** New Jersey 39.46N 74.53W
103 D3 **Atco** Pennsylvania 41.37N 75.05W
75 G5 **Atea** Spain 41.09N 1.33W
89 J8 **Atebubu** Ghana 7.47N 1.00W
75 G5 **Ateca** Spain 41.20N 1.49W
59 D6 **Atedaun L** Clare Irish Rep 52.57N 9.03W
30 E6 **Ateha** Uttar Prad India 26.06N 81.38E
34 D5 **Ateibe, Bahret el** *L* Syria
80 K5 **Ateleta** Italy 41.51N 14.12E
80 N7 **Atella** Italy 40.53N 15.39E
15 H6 **Atemble** Papua New Guinea 5.03S 144.47E
120 E6 **Aten** Bolivia 14.54S 68.22W
81 L3 **Atena Lucana** Italy 40.27N 15.33E
115 G7 **Atenguillo** Mexico 20.26N 104.30W
93 D2 **Ateppi** *R* Sudan
30 B6 **Ater** Madhya Prad India 26.45N 78.39E
20 O3 **Aterazawa** Japan 38.23N 140.10E
78 F6 **Aterno** *R* Italy
117 E7 **Aterrado** Brazil 4.20S 45.35W
32 E3 **Ateshān** Iran 35.35N 52.40E
78 D2 **Atesine, Alpi** Italy
80 K4 **Atessa** Italy 42.04N 14.26E
33 F8 **'Aṭfayn, Wādī** *watercourse* Yemen
86 F7 **Atfîh** Egypt 29.25N 31.15E
86 F7 **Atfîh, Wâdi** *watercourse* Egypt
103 C7 **Atglen** Pennsylvania 39.58N 75.58W
61 F4 **Ath** Belgium 50.38N 3.47E
100 D4 **Athabasca** Alberta 54.44N 113.15W
101 S7 **Athabasca** *R* Alberta
101 S6 **Athabasca, L** Alberta/Sask
34 L8 **'Athāmin, Al** *hill* Arabia/Iraq 30.21N 43.40E
84 E2 **Athanáti** Greece 39.45N 22.48E
100 Q4 **Athapap** Manitoba 54.36N 101.40W
100 Q4 **Athapapuskow L** Manitoba
31 G5 **Atharan Hazari** Pakistan 31.13N 72.11E
59 J4 **Athboy** Meath Irish Rep 53.37N 6.55W
59 D7 **Athea** Limerick Irish Rep 52.28N 9.17W
108 Q9 **Athelstan** Iowa 40.37N 94.30W
110 G4 **Athena** Oregon 45.48N 118.29W
59 E5 **Athenry** Galway Irish Rep 53.18N 8.45W
107 K7 **Athens** Alabama 34.50N 86.59W
105 D4 **Athens** Georgia 33.57N 83.24W
Athens Greece *see* **Athínai**
107 G2 **Athens** Illinois 39.57N 89.44W
107 C9 **Athens** Louisiana 32.40N 93.01W
104 Q2 **Athens** Maine 44.56N 69.40W
106 J7 **Athens** Michigan 42.04N 85.14W
103 G2 **Athens** New York 42.15N 73.49W
104 C7 **Athens** Ohio 39.20N 82.06W
99 P8 **Athens** Ontario 44.37N 75.57W
103 A3 **Athens** Pennsylvania 41.58N 76.32W
107 M6 **Athens** Tennessee 35.27N 84.38W
112 M3 **Athens** Texas 32.12N 95.51W
106 D4 **Athens** Wisconsin 45.03N 90.03W
99 L8 **Atherley** Ontario 44.36N 79.21W
56 H2 **Atherstone** Warwicks Eng 52.35N 1.31W
111 C10 **Atherton** California 37.28N 122.11W
57 H5 **Atherton** Greater Manchester Eng 53.31N 2.31W
13 H3 **Atherton** Queensland 17.05S 145.40E
13 H3 **Atherton Plateau** Queensland
66 C1 **Athesans** France 47.36N 6.30E
29 J7 **Athgarh** Orissa India 20.31N 85.41E
93 J7 **Athi** *R* Kenya
89 K8 **Athiémé** Benin 6.38N 1.45E
84 S14 **Athienou** Cyprus 35.03N 33.33E
69 D4 **Athies** Somme France 49.51N 3.00E
69 F4 **Athies-sous-Laon** Aisne France 49.35N 3.41E
84 E6 **Athíkia** Greece 37.49N 22.55E
84 G5 **Athínai** Greece 38.00N 23.44E
84 D7 **Athínaion** Greece 37.24N 22.15E
93 H7 **Athi River** Kenya 1.28S 36.59E
61 F5 **Athis** Belgium 50.22N 3.47E
70 K4 **Athis-de-l'Orne** France 48.48N 0.29W
69 C6 **Athis-Mons** Essonne France 48.43N 2.23E
84 F1 **Athitos** Greece 40.06N 23.26E
59 F4 **Athleague** Roscommon Irish Rep 53.34N 8.15W
94 Q11 **Athlone** Cape Town S Africa 33.58S 18.31E
59 G5 **Athlone** W Meath Irish Rep 53.25N 7.56W
84 S14 **Athna** Cyprus 35.02N 33.48E
34 F6 **Athna, Wādī** *watercourse* Jordan
28 B2 **Athni** Karnataka India 16.44N 75.07E
110 J2 **Athol** Idaho 47.56N 116.45W
104 N4 **Athol** Massachusetts 42.36N 72.14W
11 C12 **Athol** New Zealand 45.32S 168.36E
103 C6 **Athol** Pennsylvania 40.17N 75.44W
105 L9 **Athol I** New Providence I 25.05N 77.16W
58 H5 **Atholl, Forest of** Tayside Scotland
48 S4 **Atholl, Kap** *C* Greenland 76.20N 69.30W
98 F6 **Atholville** New Brunswick 47.58N 66.45W
83 G4 **Áthos** *mt* Greece 40.10N 24.19E
30 D3 **Athpali** Nepal 29.39N 80.48E
85 A6 **'Athshān** Libya 27.20N 10.25E
61 O8 **Athus** Belgium 49.34N 5.50E
59 J6 **Athy** Kildare Irish Rep 52.59N 6.59W
90 J5 **Ati** Chad 13.11N 18.20E
93 D2 **Atiak** Uganda 3.14N 32.05E
11 L5 **Atiamuri** New Zealand 38.23S 176.03E
118 F8 **Atibaia** Brazil 23.08S 46.35W
120 C7 **Atico** Peru 16.14S 73.40W
98 N2 **Aticonipi L** Quebec
120 C7 **Atico, Pta** Peru 16.14S 73.40W
87 A7 **Atiedo** Sudan 7.55N 27.52E
75 E5 **Atienza** Spain 41.12N 2.52W
47 M4 **Atig** U.S.S.R. 56.42N 59.24E
113 N2 **Atigun Pass** Alaska 68.05N 149.30W
100 Q4 **Atik** Manitoba 54.16N 101.24W
100 B3 **Atikameg** Alberta 55.55N 115.39W
100 R4 **Atikameg L** Manitoba 54.00N 101.00W
100 R4 **Atikameg Lake** Manitoba 54.00N 100.56W
100 L2 **Atikokan** Ontario 48.45N 91.38W
98 H1 **Atikonak L** Labrador, Nfld
100 J1 **Atikwa L** Ontario 49.25N 93.35W
122 C12 **Atimaono** Tahiti Pacific Oc 17.47S 149.27W
19 K4 **Atimonan** Luzon Philippines 14.00N 121.55E
80 J5 **Atina** Italy 41.37N 13.48E
31 F2 **Atin Jilao** Afghanistan 36.57N 70.08E
115 P11 **Atiquizaya** El Salvador 13.59N 89.45W
28 D5 **Atirampattinam** Tamil Nadu India 10.21N 79.24E
85 L9 **Atiri, Jebel** *mt* Sudan 21.18N 31.00E
115 O10 **Atitlán** *L* Guatemala
115 O10 **Atitlán, Vol** *pk* Guatemala 14.38N 91.10W
122 S15 **Atituiti** Mangaréva Pacific Oc 23.08S 134.58W
122 L10 **Atiu** *isld* Cook Is Pacific Oc 20.00S 158.07W
Atjeh *prov see* **Aceh** *prov*
113 R9 **Atka** Aleutian Is 52.14N 174.15W
39 E4 **Atka** U.S.S.R. 60.50N 151.45E
113 R9 **Atka I** Aleutian Is 52.05N 174.40W
45 Q5 **Atkarsk** U.S.S.R. 51.55N 45.00E
113 J1 **Atkasuk** Alaska 70.30N 157.20W
Atkerio *see* **Atkri**
107 D6 **Atkins** Arkansas 35.13N 92.55W
106 D8 **Atkinson** Illinois 41.24N 90.01W
105 J3 **Atkinson** N Carolina 34.33N 78.12W
108 M7 **Atkinson** Nebraska 42.32N 98.59W
Atkinson Field *airfield see* **Timehri**
101 H1 **Atkinson Point** N W Terr 69.57N 131.30W
101 F11 **Atkinson, Pt** Br Col 49.20N 123.16W
15 A4 **Atkri** Misoöl I, Irian Jaya 1.45S 130.04E
33 G4 **'Atk, Wādī al** *watercourse* Saudi Arabia
115 K8 **Atlacomulco** Mexico 19.49N 99.54W
105 C4 **Atlanta** Georgia 33.45N 84.23W
110 K6 **Atlanta** Idaho 43.48N 115.07W
106 E9 **Atlanta** Illinois 40.16N 89.15W
106 H9 **Atlanta** Indiana 40.13N 86.02W
109 O4 **Atlanta** Kansas 37.27N 96.46W
106 K4 **Atlanta** Michigan 45.01N 84.07W
107 D2 **Atlanta** Missouri 39.54N 92.28W
104 H4 **Atlanta** New York 42.33N 77.30W
112 N2 **Atlanta** Texas 33.08N 94.10W
108 P8 **Atlantic** Iowa 41.24N 95.01W
105 L3 **Atlantic** N Carolina 34.54N 76.23W
103 E7 **Atlantic** *co* New Jersey
26 C12 **Atlantic-Antarctic Ridge** S Atlantic Oc
103 N8 **Atlantic Beach** New York 40.35N 73.44W
103 F8 **Atlantic City** New Jersey 39.23N 74.27W
110 R7 **Atlantic City** Wyoming 42.30N 108.45W
103 F6 **Atlantic Highlands** New Jersey 40.25N 74.03W
26 D13 **Atlantic-Indian-Antarctic Basin** Southern Oc
Atlantic Indian Ridge S Atlantic Oc *see* **Atlantic-Antarctic Ridge**
119 C2 **Atlántico** *div* Colombia
96 **Atlantic Ocean**
96 G5 **Atlantis Fracture** Atlantic Oc
106 L7 **Atlas** Michigan 42.57N 83.34W
103 B5 **Atlas** Pennsylvania 40.48N 76.25W
24 J4 **Atlas Bogd** *mt pk* Xinjiang Uygur Zizhiqu China
26 A16 **Atlas Cove** Heard I Antarctica
40 N6 **Atlasova, O** *isld* Kuril Is U.S.S.R. 50.53N 155.28E
50 C2 **Atlastadhir** Iceland 66.27N 22.55W
115 K8 **Atlatlah** Mexico 19.10N 99.32W
100 G8 **Atlee** Alberta 50.51N 110.58W
101 G6 **Atlin** Br Columbia 59.31N 133.41W
101 G6 **Atlin, L** Yukon/Br Col
35 C3 **'Atlit** Israel 32.42N 34.57E
35 C3 **Atlit** *anc site* Israel 32.42N 34.56E
115 K8 **Atlixco** Mexico 18.55N 98.26W
53 R16 **Atløy** *isld* Norway 61.21N 4.57E
28 D3 **Atmakur** Kurnool, Andhra Prad India 15.56N 78.43E
28 D3 **Atmakur** Nellore, Andhra Prad India 14.39N 79.43E
107 J10 **Atmore** Alabama 31.02N 87.30W
52 F5 **Atna** *R* Norway
12 D2 **Atna Hill** S Australia 26.22S 137.29E
101 L9 **Atnarko** Br Columbia 52.24N 125.42W
52 E5 **Atnasjø** *L* Norway 61.54N 10.10E
29 E7 **Atner** Madhya Prad India 21.40N 77.59E
47 K6 **Atnis** U.S.S.R. 58.45N 69.40E
28 C2 **Atnur** Karnataka India 17.16N 76.27E
87 J8 **Ato** Somalia 4.40N 43.19E
120 E9 **Atocha** Bolivia 20.55S 66.14W
75 P9 **Atocha** *dist* Madrid Spain
109 O7 **Atoka** Oklahoma 34.22N 96.08W
109 O7 **Atoka Res** Oklahoma 34.30N 96.05W
84 A5 **Atokos** *isld* Greece 38.28N 20.49E
24 F4 **At Ölgan Dawan** *pass* Xinjiang Uygur Zizhiqu China 42.17N 89.12E
111 G6 **Atolia** California 35.19N 117.36W
91 D9 **Atome** Angola 11.54S 14.38E
110 N6 **Atomic City** Idaho 43.26N 112.48W
59 E5 **Atorick,L** Clare Irish Rep 53.01N 8.33W
115 H7 **Atotonilco el Alto** Mexico 20.35N 102.30W
25 J4 **Atouat** *mt* Laos/Vietnam 16.03N 107.17E
76 A10 **Atouguia da Baleia** Portugal 39.20N 9.20W
89 B1 **Atoui** *watercourse* Mauritania
115 J9 **Atoyac de Alvarez** Mexico 17.12N 100.28W
28 B2 **Atpadi** Maharashtra India 17.28N 75.02E
24 D7 **Atqan** Xinjiang Uygur Zizhiqu China 36.29N 81.47E
24 E7 **Atqan** Xinjiang Uygur Zizhiqu China 37.20N 85.20E
29 L5 **Atrai R** Bangladesh/India
32 F2 **Atrak, Rūd-e** *R* Iran
30 E7 **Atrampur** Uttar Prad India 25.34N 81.45E
52 G9 **Atran** Sweden 57.07N 12.55E
52 G9 **Ätran** *R* Sweden
52 M2 **Åträsk** Sweden 64.19N 20.15E
119 C4 **Atrato** *R* Colombia
30 B4 **Atrauli** Aligarh, Uttar Prad India 28.02N 78.16E
30 D5 **Atrauli** Faizabad, Uttar Prad Ind 27.10N 80.40E
30 J5 **Atrauli** Nepal 27.07N 85.38E
30 F6 **Atraulia** Uttar Prad India 26.20N 82.57E
43 C7 **Atrek** *R* Turkmeniya U.S.S.R.
80 J3 **Atri** Italy 42.35N 13.59E
80 L7 **Atripalda** Italy 40.55N 14.50E
87 A1 **'Atrun, el** Sudan 18.11N 26.40E
85 J10 **'Atrun Oasis, el** Sudan 18.12N 26.40E
37 G9 **Atrush** Iraq 36.50N 43.20E
24 H10 **Atsa Tso** *L* Xizang Zizhiqu China 30.40N 93.15E
87 D1 **'Atshan, Jeb. el** *mt* Sudan 18.09N 33.49E
34 M7 **'Atshān, Shatt al** *R* Iraq
42 H5 **Atsikak** U.S.S.R. 54.12N 106.20E
103 E7 **Atsion** New Jersey 39.45N 74.43W
44 E6 **Atskuri** Georgia U.S.S.R. 41.42N 43.11E
40 L9 **Atsonupuri** *vol* Kuril Is U.S.S.R. 44.49N 147.08E
20 N6 **Atsugi** Japan 35.28N 139.22E
20 N3 **Atsumi** Japan 38.36N 139.37E
20 L7 **Atsumi-hantō** *pen* Japan
20 K7 **Atsumi-wan** *B* Japan
21 J6 **Atsunai** Japan 42.48N 143.48E
20 L1 **Atsuta** Japan 43.25N 141.24E
20 P9 **Atsuta** Okinawa Japan 26.30N 127.52E
20 P9 **Atsuta** Okinawa Japan 26.14N 127.49E
13 C4 **Attack Cr** N Terr Australia
33 L5 **Attaf** *des area* U.A.E.
Attalea *anc site see* **Antalya**
66 D5 **Attalens** Switzerland 46.31N 6.51E
107 K7 **Attalla** Alabama 34.00N 86.08W
29 E6 **Attar** Madhya Prad India 22.01N 76.14E
84 Y20 **Attard** Malta 35.53N 14.27E
88 Q5 **Attar el** *watercourse* Algeria
84 U17 **Attáviros** *mt* Rhodes 36.12N 27.52E
97 L7 **Attawapiskat** Ontario 53.00N 82.30W
97 L7 **Attawapiskat** *R* Ontario
64 N7 **Attel** W Germany 48.01N 12.11E
64 D1 **Attendorn** W Germany 51.08N 7.55E
53 E8 **Attenholz** W Germany 54.23N 10.07E
61 L3 **Attenhoven** Belgium 50.46N 5.05E
61 K3 **Attenrode** Belgium 50.52N 4.55E
65 J6 **Attersee** Austria 47.56N 13.33E
65 J6 **Attersee** *L* Austria
61 O7 **Attert** Belgium 49.45N 5.47E
61 O7 **Attert** *R* Luxembourg
106 G9 **Attica** Indiana 40.17N 87.15W
109 M4 **Attica** Kansas 37.13N 98.13W
106 L6 **Attica** Michigan 43.02N 83.10W
104 G4 **Attica** New York 42.52N 78.16W
104 C5 **Attica** Ohio 41.03N 82.53W
Attica *hist reg* Greece *see* **Attikí** *prov*
69 E5 **Attichy** France 49.25N 3.03E
95 L3 **Attie** S Africa 27.28S 27.15E
80 F3 **Attigliano** Italy 42.31N 12.17E
71 G4 **Attignat** France 46.17N 5.09E
69 K7 **Attignéville** France 48.23N 5.49E
69 H5 **Attigny** France 49.28N 4.35E
84 F5 **Attikí** *prov* Greece
35 D4 **Attil** Jordan 32.22N 35.04E
79 O2 **Attimis** Italy 46.11N 13.19E
28 C6 **Attingal** Kerala India 8.42N 76.51E
66 L4 **Attinghausen** Switzerland 46.52N 8.38E
103 M3 **Attleboro** Massachusetts 41.57N 71.16W
56 O2 **Attleborough** Norfolk Eng 52.31N 1.01E
56 O2 **Attlebridge** Norfolk Eng 52.42N 1.09E
52 K4 **Attmar** Sweden 62.20N 17.05E
65 J5 **Attnang-Puchheim** Austria 48.01N 13.44E
31 G4 **Attock** Pakistan 33.52N 72.20E
Attock *dist see* **Campbellpore**
25 J5 **Attopeu** Laos 14.51N 106.56E
112 N4 **Attoyac Bayou** *R* Texas
61 F4 **Attre** Belgium 50.37N 3.50E
113 L9 **Attu** Aleutian Is 52.55N 173.11E
113 L9 **Attu I** Aleutian Is 52.55N 173.00E
12 K4 **Attunga** New S Wales 30.59S 150.22E
28 C5 **Attur** Madura, Madras India 10.19N 77.52E
15 L6 **Atu** New Britain 5.58S 151.11E
120 E3 **Atucatiquini** *R* Brazil
121 F4 **Atucha** Argentina 33.59S 59.17W
33 H9 **Atūd** S Yemen 14.52N 48.08E
85 N7 **'Atûd, Gebel** *mt* Egypt 25.03N 34.21E
121 C6 **Atuel, Banados del** *swamps* Argentina
121 B5 **Atuel,R** Argentina
121 C5 **Atue, R** Argentina
88 J8 **Atuila** Morocco 26.34N 9.35W
119 B7 **Atuntaqui** Ecuador 0.21N 78.10W
122 V14 **Atuona** Marquesas Is Pacific Oc 9.47S 139.03W
28 D5 **Atur** Salem, Tamil Nadu India 11.36N 78.35E
93 D3 **Atura** Uganda 2.09N 32.22E
Atürük *see* **Yiwu**
42 C4 **Atuz** U.S.S.R. 56.11N 82.40E
52 J8 **Åtvidaberg** Sweden 58.13N 16.05E
33 E2 **Aṭwā', Al** Saudi Arabia 28.25N 42.10E
111 D4 **Atwater** California 37.20N 120.37W
108 Q4 **Atwater** Minnesota 45.08N 94.47W
100 P8 **Atwater** Saskatchewan 50.48N 102.17W
57 N5 **Atwick** Humberside Eng 53.57N 0.11W
109 G1 **Atwood** Colorado 40.32N 103.17W
107 H2 **Atwood** Illinois 39.48N 88.27W
109 J2 **Atwood** Kansas 39.48N 101.03W
103 F3 **Atwood** New York 41.53N 74.12W
99 J9 **Atwood** Ontario 43.40N 81.01W
106 N9 **Atwood Res** Ohio 40.32N 81.15W
56 G5 **Atworth** Wilts Eng 51.24N 2.12W
45 S2 **Atyashevo** U.S.S.R. 54.35N 46.05E
40 C4 **Atychan** *mt* U.S.S.R. 55.31N 125.55E
39 A2 **Atyr-Meyite** U.S.S.R. 67.15N 132.14E
39 B1 **At-Yuryakh** U.S.S.R. 69.24N 139.27E
45 P2 **Atyury'evo** U.S.S.R. 54.20N 43.21E
81 C4 **Atzara** Sardinia 39.59N 9.05E
65 N5 **Atzenbrugg** Austria 48.18N 15.55E
63 P9 **Atzendorf** E Germany 51.56N 11.36E
65 O5 **Atzgersdorf** Austria 48.10N 16.19E
65 A7 **Au** Austria 47.20N 9.59E
64 M8 **Au** Ober-Bayern W Germany 47.48N 11.59E
66 P2 **Au** Switzerland 47.27N 9.38E
88 G11 **Auadi** Mauritania 21.50N 13.13W
15 G4 **Aua, I** Bismarck Arch 1.29S 143.05E
19 N5 **Aualap Pass** Truk Is Pacific Oc 7.14N 151.48E
87 K6 **Auareh** Ethiopia 8.16N 44.11E
94 D4 **Auas Mts** Namibia
119 F9 **Auati-Paraná, R** Brazil
87 H7 **Auatu,Mt** Ethiopia 7.02N 41.03E
114 D6 **Auau Chan** Hawaiian Is
64 J4 **Aub** W Germany 49.33N 10.05E
71 H10 **Aubagne** France 43.17N 5.35E
61 O8 **Aubange** Belgium 49.34N 5.48E
19 L3 **Aubarede Pt** Luzon Philippines 17.15N 122.26E
87 K6 **Aubarkhadleh** Somalia 9.40N 44.20E
72 H5 **Aubazines** France 45.10N 1.39E
92 J10 **Aube** Mozambique 16.21S 39.45E
67 H4 **Aube** *dept* France
69 F6 **Aube** *R* France
61 E4 **Aubechies** Belgium 50.34N 3.41E
61 O4 **Aubel** Belgium 50.42N 5.51E
71 E7 **Aubenas** France 44.37N 4.24E
69 E3 **Aubencheul-au-Bac** France 50.15N 3.10E
69 G4 **Aubenton** France 49.51N 4.12E
69 H8 **Aubepierre-sur-Aube** France 47.55N 4.56E
69 J8 **Auberive** Haute-Marne France 47.47N 5.03E
69 G5 **Aubérive** Marne France 49.12N 4.25E
71 F6 **Auberives-sur-Varèze** France 45.25N 4.49E
98 R10 **Auberivière** Quebec 46.46N 71.12W
66 B4 **Auberson** Switzerland 46.49N 6.28E
26 P14 **Aubert C** Kerguelen Ind Oc 48.40S 68.56E
66 C4 **Aubert, Mt** Switzerland 46.53N 6.38E
68 F2 **Aubervilliers** France 48.55N 2.24E
70 M4 **Aube-sur-Rille** France 48.44N 0.33E
69 G7 **Aubeterre** Aube France 48.26N 4.07E
72 E5 **Aubeterre-sur-Dronne** Charente France 45.16N 0.10E
69 E6 **Aubetin** *R* France
72 D5 **Aubie et Espessas** France 45.02N 0.23W
71 C5 **Aubière** France 45.45N 3.07E
72 C2 **Aubiers, les** France 46.57N 0.35W
72 F8 **Aubiet** France 43.39N 0.48E
72 D3 **Aubigné** Deux Sèvres France 46.04N 0.09W
70 L6 **Aubigné** Sarthe France 47.41N 0.16E
72 B2 **Aubigny** Vendée France 46.36N 1.27W
69 D3 **Aubigny-en-Artois** Pas de Calais France 50.21N 2.36E
71 A2 **Aubigny-sur-Nère** France 47.29N 2.26E
72 J6 **Aubin** France 44.32N 2.14E
72 D10 **Aubisque, Col d'** France 42.58N 0.20W
61 H6 **Aublain** Belgium 50.04N 4.25E
72 K2 **Aubois** *R* France
66 B6 **Aubonne** Switzerland 46.30N 6.24E
69 K5 **Auboué** France 49.13N 5.58E
71 C7 **Aubrac, Mtgne. d'** France
111 M6 **Aubrey Cliffs** *ra* Arizona
14 B7 **Aubrey, Mt** W Australia 27.16S 115.48E
101 K2 **Aubry L** N W Terr
107 L9 **Auburn** Alabama 32.38N 85.30W
111 C3 **Auburn** California 38.53N 121.04W
107 G2 **Auburn** Illinois 39.35N 89.45W
106 J8 **Auburn** Indiana 41.22N 85.02W
109 P3 **Auburn** Kansas 38.55N 95.51W
107 K5 **Auburn** Kentucky 36.52N 86.41W
104 P2 **Auburn** Maine 44.04N 70.15W
103 L2 **Auburn** Massachusetts 42.13N 71.50W
106 K6 **Auburn** Michigan 43.36N 84.04W
108 P9 **Auburn** Nebraska 40.22N 95.41W
103 D7 **Auburn** New Jersey 39.42N 75.21W
104 J4 **Auburn** New York 42.57N 76.34W
103 B5 **Auburn** Pennsylvania 40.37N 76.06W
12 E5 **Auburn** S Australia 34.05S 138.43E
110 C2 **Auburn** Washington 47.19N 122.14W
12 K7 **Auburn** *dist* Sydney, N S W
13 K7 **Auburn** *R* Queensland
103 B3 **Auburn Center** Pennsylvania 41.40N 76.02W
105 F9 **Auburndale** Florida 28.02N 81.50W
106 E5 **Auburndale** Wisconsin 44.37N 89.59W
13 K7 **Auburn Ra** Queensland
72 J4 **Aubusson** France 45.58N 2.10E
61 L7 **Auby-sur-Semois** Belgium 49.49N 5.11E
121 C6 **Auca Mahuida** *pk* Argentina 37.43S 68.56W
72 G8 **Aucamville** Haute-Garonne France 43.39N 1.26E
72 G8 **Aucamville** Tarn-et-Garonne France 43.49N 1.13E
77 W14 **Aucanada** *isld* Balearic Is 39.50N 3.10E
120 E9 **Aucanquilcha, Cerro** *pk* Chile 21.13S 68.26W
120 B3 **Aucayacu** Peru 8.50S 76.05W
46 E2 **Auce** Latvia U.S.S.R. 56.29N 22.50E
72 F8 **Auch** France 43.40N 0.36E
58 K5 **Auchallater** Grampian Scotland 56.58N 3.24W
25 N8 **Auche** Burma 25.32N 97.05E
69 C2 **Auchel** France 50.30N 2.29E
57 F3 **Auchencairn** Dumfries & Galloway Scotland 54.51N 3.53W
57 F3 **Auchencairn B** Dumfries & Galloway Scotland 54.50N 3.53W
58 J7 **Auchengray** Strathclyde Scotland 55.46N 3.37W
57 D3 **Auchenmalg** Dumfries & Galloway Scotland 54.50N 4.45W
90 C8 **Auchi** Nigeria 7.01N 6.16E
58 M5 **Auchinblae** Grampian Scotland 56.53N 2.28W
58 K4 **Auchindown** Grampian Scotland 57.27N 3.05W
57 E2 **Auchinleck** Strathclyde Scotland 55.28N 4.17W
57 D2 **Auchinoruive** Strathclyde Scotland 55.29N 4.33W
58 J6 **Auchterarder** Tayside Scotland 56.18N 3.43W
58 K6 **Auchtermuchty** Fife Scotland 56.17N 3.15W
69 C2 **Auchy-au-Bois** France 50.33N 2.22E
105 D7 **Aucilla** *R* Florida
58 K1 **Auckingill** Highland Scotland 58.34N 3.06W
11 J3 **Auckland** New Zealand 36.55S 174.47E
25 E6 **Auckland B** Burma
11 B7 **Auckland I** Pacific Oc
11 B7 **Auckland Is** S Pacific Oc 50.35S 166.00E
72 D10 **Aucun** France 42.58N 0.12W
Auda *see* **'Awdah**
'Auda *see* **'Awdah, Al**
Auda, Haur *see* **'Awdah, Hawr al** *L*
88 G10 **Audarat** *reg* Morocco
67 G9 **Aude** *dept* France
72 J9 **Aude** *R* France
87 K10 **Audeghle** Somalia 1.58N 44.49E
99 C2 **Auden** Ontario 50.14N 87.54W
72 B6 **Audenge** France 44.42N 1.01W
103 C5 **Audenried** Pennsylvania 40.55N 75.59W
61 T10 **Auderghem** *dist* Bruxelles Belgium
70 G2 **Auderville** France 49.43N 1.56W
71 H2 **Audeux** France 47.15N 5.53E
66 B2 **Audeux** *R* France
50 E3 **Audhkúla** Iceland 65.30N 20.02W
70 A5 **Audierne** France 48.01N 4.33W
70 B6 **Audierne, B. d'** France
26 Q16 **Audierne, B. d'** Kerguelen Ind Oc
71 K2 **Audincourt** France 47.29N 6.50E
69 B2 **Audinghen** France 50.50N 1.36E
87 J9 **Auditnle** Somalia 3.08N 43.22E
79 N7 **Auditore** Italy 43.48N 12.34E
57 H7 **Audlem** Cheshire Eng 52.59N 2.31W
72 C8 **Audon** France 43.48N 0.49W
87 H7 **Audo Ra** Ethiopia
61 E5 **Audregnies** Belgium 50.23N 3.43E
69 B2 **Audresselles** France 50.49N 1.37E
69 C2 **Audruicq** France 50.52N 2.05E
108 Q8 **Audubon** Iowa 41.42N 94.56W
103 D7 **Audubon** New Jersey 39.53N 75.03W
69 K5 **Audun-le-Roman** France 49.22N 5.54E
64 O2 **Aue** E Germany 50.35N 12.42E
63 G6 **Aue** *R* W Germany
63 J7 **Aue** *R* W Germany
63 M7 **Aue** *R* W Germany
66 J2 **Auenstein** Switzerland 47.26N 8.08E
64 G5 **Auenstein** W Germany 49.03N 9.18E
64 M4 **Auerbach** Bayern W Germany 49.41N 11.39E
64 N2 **Auerbach** E Germany 50.30N 12.24E
64 F4 **Auerbach** Hessen W Germany 49.42N 8.37E
64 K8 **Auerberg** *mt* W Germany 47.45N 10.45E
66 Q1 **Auers** W Germany 47.37N 9.56E
64 O2 **Auerswaide** E Germany 50.55N 12.55E
43 O3 **Auezov** Kazakhstan U.S.S.R. 49.43N 81.35E
70 N2 **Auffay** France 49.43N 1.07E
69 D7 **Aufferville** France 48.13N 2.36E
64 K5 **Aufkirchen** W Germany 49.03N 10.32E
70 F6 **Augan** France 47.56N 2.17W
13 H7 **Augathella** Queensland 25.50S 146.32E
71 D5 **Augerolles** France 45.44N 3.36E
59 H3 **Augher** Tyrone N Ireland 54.26N 7.08W
59 J3 **Aughnacloy** Tyrone N Ireland 54.25N 6.59W
59 F5 **Aughrim** Galway Irish Rep 53.18N 8.19W
59 K6 **Aughrim** Wicklow Irish Rep 52.52N 6.20W
59 E3 **Aughris Hd** Sligo Irish Rep 54.17N 8.45W
57 H5 **Aughton** Lancs Eng 53.33N 2.55W
72 F4 **Augignac** France 45.34N 0.42E
Augila *see* **Awjilah**
48 S5 **Augpilagtoq** Greenland 72.47N 55.30W
48 U16 **Augpilagtoq** Greenland 60.12N 44.10W
106 L5 **Au Gres** Michigan 44.03N 83.40W
64 K7 **Augsburg** W Germany 48.21N 10.54E
66 G1 **Augst** Switzerland 47.32N 7.44E
66 H7 **Augstbord Pass** Switzerland 46.13N 7.46E
107 E6 **Augusta** Arkansas 35.16N 91.21W
105 E4 **Augusta** Georgia 33.29N 82.00W
106 D9 **Augusta** Illinois 40.14N 90.56W
109 O4 **Augusta** Kansas 37.41N 96.58W
107 M3 **Augusta** Kentucky 38.45N 84.00W
104 Q2 **Augusta** Maine 44.17N 69.48W
106 J7 **Augusta** Michigan 42.21N 85.22W
110 N2 **Augusta** Montana 47.29N 112.24W
103 E4 **Augusta** New Jersey 41.07N 74.44W
81 K9 **Augusta** Sicily 37.14N 15.14E
14 B10 **Augusta** W Australia 34.19S 115.09E
106 C5 **Augusta** Wisconsin 44.41N 91.08W
81 K9 **Augusta, G. di** Sicily
14 E7 **Augusta, L** W Australia 25.45S 122.33E
101 C5 **Augusta Mt** Yukon/Alaska 60.15N 140.29W
104 F8 **Augusta Springs** Virginia 38.06N 79.18W
120 D11 **Augusta Victoria** Chile 24.05S 69.22W
53 D7 **Augustenborg** Denmark 54.57N 9.53E
119 D2 **Augustin Codazzi** Colombia 10.17N 73.10W
113 L7 **Augustine I** Alaska 59.22N 153.30W
60 N7 **Augustinusga** Netherlands 53.13N 6.10E
118 G6 **Augusto de Lima** Brazil 18.06S 44.15W
117 H7 **Augusto Severo** Brazil 5.54S 37.16W
62 O2 **Augustów** Poland 53.51N 23.00E
13 E4 **Augustus Downs** Queensland 18.31S 139.50E
14 E3 **Augustus Island** W Australia
14 B6 **Augustus, Mt** W Australia 24.20S 116.49E
72 K2 **Augy-sur-Aubois** France 46.47N 2.50E
'Auha *isld see* **'Awhah**
64 M6 **Au in der Hallertau** W Germany 48.32N 11.45E
35 E6 **Auja** *watercourse* Jordan
69 J8 **Aujon** *R* France
54 M6 **Auk** *oil field* North Sea 56.26N 2.00E
87 H3 **Aukan I** Ethiopia 15.29N 40.50E
94 E2 **Aukas** Namibia 19.20S 18.10E
113 U7 **Auke Bay** Alaska 58.24N 134.40W
122 S15 **Au-Kéna** *isld* Gambier Is Pacific Oc 23.08S 134.54W
15 M3 **Auki** Malaita I Solomon Is 8.45S 160.44E
63 L4 **Aukrug** W Germany 54.05N 9.46E
51 G6 **Auktsjaur** Sweden 65.46N 19.20E
29 K7 **Aul** Orissa India 20.40N 86.41E
105 K1 **Aulander** N Carolina 36.14N 77.09W
30 C7 **Auldan** Uttar Prad India 25.24N 79.02E
58 J3 **Auldearn** Highland Scotland 57.34N 3.48W
14 E5 **Auld, L** W Australia
64 H8 **Aulendorf** W Germany 47.57N 9.40E
80 M7 **Auletta** Italy 40.33N 15.26E
87 J8 **Aulihan** *tribe* Ethiopia
79 G6 **Aulla** Italy 44.12N 9.58E
67 P13 **Aullène** Corsica 41.46N 9.04E
72 D3 **Aulnay** France 46.01N 0.20W
69 C7 **Aulnay-la-Rivière** France 48.11N 2.23E
69 D6 **Aulnay-sous-Bois** France 48.57N 2.31E
70 B5 **Aulne** *R* France
100 H1 **Aulneau Pen** Ontario
61 F5 **Aulnois** Belgium 50.21N 3.55E
69 L6 **Aulnois-sur-Seille** France 48.52N 6.19E
69 F3 **Aulnoye-Aymeries** France 50.12N 3.50E
72 F9 **Aulon** France 43.12N 0.50E
19 M2 **Aulong** *isld* Palau Is Pacific Oc 7.17N 134.18E
25 H6 **Au Long** *R* Cambodia
109 F1 **Ault** Colorado 40.35N 104.44W
69 A3 **Ault** France 50.07N 1.28E
58 E3 **Aultbea** Highland Scotland 57.50N 5.35W
58 G3 **Aultguish** Highland Scotland 57.41N 4.46W
66 N5 **Ault, Piz** Switzerland 46.38N 9.08E
19 N2 **Auluptagel** *isld* Palau Is Pacific Oc 7.19N 134.30E
72 G10 **Aulus-les-Bains** France 42.48N 1.19E
45 F8 **Auly** Ukraine U.S.S.R. 48.32N 34.30E
64 M2 **Auma** E Germany 50.42N 11.55E
64 M2 **Auma** *R* E Germany
Aumale Algeria *see* **Sour el Ghozlane**
70 O2 **Aumale** France 49.46N 1.45E
72 K3 **Aumance** *R* France
69 K5 **Aumetz** France 49.25N 5.57E
43 G6 **Auminzatau, Gory** *mts* Uzbekistan U.S.S.R.
71 H3 **Aumont** Jura France 46.55N 5.38E
66 D4 **Aumont** Switzerland 46.48N 6.51E
71 C7 **Aumont-Aubrac** Lozère France 44.43N 3.17E
63 M5 **Aumühle** W Germany 53.32N 10.20E
90 B6 **Auna** Nigeria 10.13N 4.44E
71 D2 **Aunay-en-Bazois** France 47.07N 3.42E
70 J3 **Aunay-sur-Odon** France 49.01N 0.38W
28 B2 **Aundh** Maharashtra India 17.33N 74.16E
29 G7 **Aundhi** Madhya Prad India 20.13N 80.32E
30 G7 **Aundi** Uttar Prad India 25.48N 83.58E
70 L6 **Aune** *R* France
70 O5 **Auneau** France 48.27N 1.46E
69 C5 **Auneuil** France 49.22N 2.00E
93 B3 **Aungba** Zaïre 2.35N 30.29E
28 L5 **Aungban** Burma 20.40N 96.34E
53 E4 **Auning** Denmark 56.26N 10.23E
67 E6 **Aunis** *prov* France
75 E6 **Auñón** Spain 40.31N 2.48W
30 F7 **Aunrai** Uttar Prad India 25.16N 82.34E
122 E1 **Aunuu** *isld* Amer Samoa Pacific Oc 14.16S 170.35W
94 E5 **Auob** *watercourse* Namibia
19 D4 **Auponhia** Moluccas Indon 1.56S 125.30E
71 J9 **Aups** France 43.38N 6.13E
9 D2 **Aur** *atoll* Marshall Is Pacific Oc 8.16N 171.02E
18 E9 **Aur** *isld* Pen Malaysia
51 K11 **Aura** Finland 60.37N 22.35E
53 Y14 **Aura** *R* Norway 62.25N 8.27E
64 K4 **Aurach** *R* W Germany
28 C1 **Aurad** Karnataka India 18.17N 77.27E
72 G8 **Auradé** France 43.35N 1.04E
53 V20 **Aurahortaen** *mt* Norway 59.13N 6.53E
30 C6 **Auraiya** Uttar Prad India 26.27N 79.31E
51 K11 **Aurajoki** *R* Finland
25 H6 **Aural, Phnom** *mt* Cambodia 12.01N 104.14E
30 H8 **Aurangabad** Bihar India 24.46N 84.23E
30 A4 **Aurangabad** Bulandshahr, Uttar Prad India 28.30N 77.57E
29 D8 **Aurangābād** Maharashtra India 19.52N 75.22E
30 D5 **Aurangabad** Shahjahanpur, Uttar Prad India 27.47N 80.22E
29 D8 **Aurangabad** *dist* Maharashtra India
66 L7 **Aurano** Italy 46.01N 8.36E
65 F7 **Aurauch** Austria 47.26N 12.26E
70 E6 **Auray** France 47.40N 2.59W
52 E6 **Aurdal** Norway 60.55N 9.26E
52 D3 **Aure** Norway 63.16N 8.34E
70 J3 **Aure** *R* France
71 E6 **Aurec-sur-Loire** France 45.22N 4.13E
72 E9 **Aureilhan** France 43.15N 0.06E
72 B7 **Aureilhan, Lac d'** France 44.13N 1.12W
71 G7 **Aurel** Drôme France 44.42N 5.18E
71 G8 **Aurel** Vaucluse France 44.08N 5.26E
108 P7 **Aurelia** Iowa 42.44N 95.24W
72 D8 **Aurensan** France 43.37N 0.11W
88 R4 **Aurès** *mts* Algeria
72 J5 **Auriac** Corrèze France 45.12N 2.08E
72 H8 **Auriac-sur-Vendinelle** France 43.31N 1.49E
71 K9 **Auribeau** France 43.36N 6.55E
63 F6 **Aurich** W Germany 53.28N 7.29E
72 F9 **Aurignac** France 43.14N 0.53E
118 E5 **Aurilândia** Brazil 16.43S 50.30W
72 J6 **Aurillac** France 44.56N 2.26E
75 K2 **Aurín** *R* Spain
79 L1 **Aurino** *R* Italy
79 L1 **Aurino, Val** *V* Italy
71 H10 **Auriol** France 43.22N 5.38E
15 C5 **Auri, Pulau Pulau** *islds* Irian Jaya 2.03S 134.42E
79 P3 **Aurisina** Italy 45.45N 13.40E
53 W17 **Aurland** Norway 60.54N 7.12E
53 W17 **Aurlandselv** *R* Norway
53 W16 **Aurlandsfjorden** *inlet* Norway 61.00N 7.03E
53 W17 **Aurlandsvangen** Norway 60.55N 7.12E
65 H5 **Aurolzmünster** Austria 48.14N 13.27E
71 K8 **Auron** France 44.13N 6.57E
72 K2 **Auron** *R* France
79 M1 **Auronzo** Italy 46.34N 12.27E
91 E9 **Aurora** Angola 11.57S 16.01E
117 H8 **Aurora** Brazil 6.53S 38.55W
109 F2 **Aurora** Colorado 39.45N 104.50W
106 F8 **Aurora** Illinois 41.45N 88.20W
107 M2 **Aurora** Indiana 39.03N 84.55W
109 N2 **Aurora** Kansas 39.27N 97.32W

19 L8 **Aurora** Mindanao Philippines 7.59N 123.35E
108 S2 **Aurora** Minnesota 47.30N 92.14W
107 C5 **Aurora** Missouri 36.58N 93.42W
105 L2 **Aurora** N Carolina 35.18N 76.48W
108 M9 **Aurora** Nebraska 40.52N 98.01W
104 J4 **Aurora** New York 42.45N 76.43W
99 L9 **Aurora** Ontario 44.00N 79.30W
94 E9 **Aurora** S Africa 32.40S 18.26E
117 B2 **Aurora** Surinam 4.27N 55.27W
111 N3 **Aurora** Utah 38.54N 111.57W
Aurora *isld see* **Maewo**
10 B11 **Aurora Pt** Macquarie I Pacific Oc 54.36S 158.51E
72 D7 **Auros** France 44.29N 0.09W
71 D7 **Auroux** France 44.46N 3.43E
71 H7 **Aurouze, Mtgne.,d'** France
53 Y15 **Aursjøen** *L* Norway 61.56N 8.15E
53 Z14 **Aursjøen** *L* Norway 62.23N 8.36E
52 D4 **Aursjøen** *L* Opland Norway 62.25N 8.40E
53 Z14 **Aursjøhytta** Norway 62.24N 8.35E
52 F7 **Aursmoen** Norway 59.55N 11.27E
52 F4 **Aursunden** *L* Norway 62.37N 11.40E
13 F2 **Aurukun** Queensland 13.12S 141.47E
80 J6 **Aurunci, Monti** Italy
94 D6 **Aus** Namibia 26.40S 16.15E
28 C1 **Ausa** Maharashtra India 18.15N 76.34E
106 K5 **Au Sable** *R* Michigan
104 M2 **Ausable** *R* New York
104 M2 **Ausable Forks** New York 44.26N 73.42W
106 H3 **Au Sable Pt** Michigan 46.39N 86.10W
106 L5 **Au Sable Pt** Michigan 44.21N 83.20W
35 F4 **Ausara** Jordan 32.23N 35.41E
65 M6 **Au-Seewiesen** Austria 47.34N 15.20E
75 F3 **Ausejo** Spain 42.21N 2.10W
88 F10 **Ausert** Mauritania 22.38N 14.18W
Ausha ziya *see* **Awsajiyah, Al**
92 D7 **Aushi** *tribe* Zambia
86 F5 **Ausîm** Egypt 30.08N 31.07E
58 T11 **Auskerry** *isld* Orkney Scotland 59.02N 2.34W
58 T11 **Auskerry Sd** Orkney Scotland
80 H6 **Ausoni, Monti** Italy
66 O5 **Ausser-Ferrera** Switzerland 46.34N 9.27E
64 Q6 **Aussernbrünst** W Germany 48.43N 13.32E
71 K6 **Aussois** France 45.14N 6.45E
72 C9 **Aussurucq** France 43.08N 0.55W
56 F4 **Aust** Avon Eng 51.36N 2.37W
53 X21 **Austad** Norway 58.59N 7.37E
52 D8 **Aust Agder** *co* Norway
50 G4 **Austari Pollar** *L* Iceland 65.06N 18.25W
53 W15 **Austdalsvatn** *L* Norway 61.47N 7.24E
53 U14 **Austefjord** Norway 62.04N 6.20E
53 U14 **Austefjord** *inlet* Norway 62.05N 6.12E
105 C4 **Austel** Georgia 33.48N 84.39W
Austerlitz Czechoslovakia *see* **Slavkov**
103 H2 **Austerlitz** New York 42.18N 73.28W
53 S18 **Austevoll** Norway 60.06N 5.15E
53 S17 **Austfjorden** *inlet* Norway 60.45N 5.17E
50 U13 **Austfonna Glacier** Spitsbergen 79.50N 24.30E
53 S17 **Austgulen** Norway 60.59N 5.18E
107 L3 **Austin** Indiana 38.46N 85.48W
100 T9 **Austin** Manitoba 49.57N 98.56W
108 S6 **Austin** Minnesota 43.40N 92.58W
110 N3 **Austin** Montana 46.38N 112.14W
111 G2 **Austin** Nevada 39.30N 117.05W
110 G5 **Austin** Oregon 44.37N 118.26W
104 G5 **Austin** Pennsylvania 41.38N 78.06W
112 K5 **Austin** Texas 30.18N 97.47W
14 C8 **Austin** W Australia 27.39S 117.50E
14 C8 **Austin, L** W Australia 27.30S 118.00E
95 J5 **Austin's Post** S Africa 29.31S 25.48E
81 C3 **Austis** Sardinia 40.05N 9.04E
48 T13 **Austmannadalen** *settlement* Greenland 64.10N 50.00W
53 U13 **Austnes** Norway 62.39N 6.15E
112 M4 **Austonio** Texas 31.12N 95.39W
13 E5 **Austral Downs** N Terr Australia 20.31S 137.45E
9 J11 **Australia** *dominion* Australasia
26 R16 **Australia, I** Kerguelen Ind Oc 49.28S 69.51E
12 J6 **Australian Alps** New S Wales/Victoria
123 J5 **Australian Antarctic Territory** Antarctica
12 J6 **Australian Capital Terr** Australia
122 M10 **Austral Ridge** Pacific Oc
52 E3 **Austråt** Norway 63.43N 9.45E
53 S20 **Austre Bokn** *isld* Norway 59.14N 5.29E
53 R17 **Austrheim** Norway 60.46N 4.55E
49 G7 **Austria** *rep* Cent Europe
50 E4 **Austurá** *R* Iceland
50 C7 **Austurháls edha Sveifluháls** *ridge* Iceland
50 L6 **Austurhorn** *C* Iceland 64.25N 14.32W
50 E7 **Austur Landeyjar** *dist* Iceland 63.38N 20.10W
51 D3 **Austvågøy** *isld* Norway 68.20N 14.40E
112 L7 **Austwell** Texas 28.23N 96.53W
70 N6 **Autainville** France 47.52N 1.26E
119 F5 **Autana, R** Venezuela
79 A5 **Autaret, Col dell** *pass* Italy/France 44.35N 6.56E
119 J9 **Autazes** Brazil 3.37S 59.08W
61 O8 **Autelbas** Belgium 49.39N 5.52E
72 G9 **Auterive** France 43.22N 1.28E
71 H1 **Autet** France 47.33N 5.42E
68 E3 **Auteuil** Paris France 48.51N 2.16E
98 L3 **Auteuil, L d'** Quebec
69 C3 **Authie** *R* France
69 B3 **Authie, B. de l'** France 50.22N 1.32E
99 M4 **Authier** Quebec 48.44N 78.53W
70 K7 **Authion** *R* France
71 J8 **Authon** Alpes de Haute Provence France 44.15N 6.07E
70 M6 **Authon** Loir-et-Cher France 47.39N 0.54E
70 M5 **Authon-du-Perche** France 48.11N 0.55E
69 B7 **Authon-la-Plaine** France 48.27N 1.58E
71 L8 **Aution, l'** *mt* France 44.00N 7.27E
72 C3 **Autize** *R* France
115 G8 **Autlán** Mexico 19.48N 104.20W
75 F3 **Autol** Spain 42.14N 2.00W
80 H5 **Autore, Monte** Italy 41.57N 13.13E
75 K2 **Autoria** *mt* Spain 42.32N 0.16W
106 H3 **Au Train** Michigan 46.27N 86.50W
71 H6 **Autrans** France 45.09N 5.34E
61 K4 **Autre, Église** Belgium 50.40N 4.55E
61 E5 **Autreppe** Belgium 50.21N 3.45E
69 K7 **Autreville** France 48.29N 5.51E
71 G2 **Autrey-les-Gray** France 47.29N 5.30E
69 C7 **Autruy-sur-Juine** France 48.16N 2.05E
69 H5 **Autry** France 49.16N 4.50E
71 B1 **Autry-le-Châtel** France 47.35N 2.34E
71 E3 **Autun** France 46.58N 4.18E
75 H1 **Autza, Mte** Spain 43.09N 1.25W
69 H5 **Auve** France 49.02N 4.43E
61 J5 **Auvelais** Belgium 50.27N 4.38E
13 B3 **Auvergne** N Terr Australia 15.35S 130.02E
67 H7 **Auvergne** *prov* France
71 B6 **Auvergne, Mts. d'** France
66 D4 **Auvernier** Switzerland 46.59N 6.53E
70 K6 **Auvers-le-Hamon** France 47.54N 0.21W
69 C5 **Auvers-sur-Oise** France 49.05N 2.10E
72 G5 **Auvezère** *R* France
72 F7 **Auvillar** France 44.04N 0.54E
69 G4 **Auvillers-les-Forges** France 49.51N 4.21E
66 K3 **Auw** Switzerland 47.13N 8.22E
64 B4 **Auw** W Germany 49.54N 6.37E
72 E2 **Auxances** *R* France 46.37N 0.12E
106 H4 **Aux Barques Pt** Michigan 45.48N 86.21W
106 M5 **Aux Barques Pt** Michigan 44.06N 82.59W
69 F8 **Auxerre** France 47.48N 3.35E
69 C3 **Auxi-le-Château** France 50.14N 2.08E
71 G2 **Auxonne** France 47.12N 5.23E
107 E2 **Auxvasse** Missouri 39.02N 91.54W
69 C7 **Auxy** Loiret France 48.07N 2.28E
71 E3 **Auxy** Saône-et-Loire France 46.56N 4.25E
119 H5 **Auyan Tepuí** *mt* Venezuela 5.48N 62.41W
72 A2 **Auzance** *R* France
72 J3 **Auzances** France 46.02N 2.29E
120 D5 **Auzangate, Nev** *pk* Peru 13.49S 71.15W
72 G10 **Auzat** France 42.45N 1.27E
72 J5 **Auze** *R* France
72 J7 **Auzits** France 44.30N 2.18E
71 C6 **Auzon** France 45.23N 3.22E
71 D5 **Auzon** *R* France
25 C2 **Ava** Burma 21.49N 95.57E
107 G4 **Ava** Illinois 37.53N 89.29W
107 D5 **Ava** Missouri 36.57N 92.40W
39 F7 **Avacha** U.S.S.R. 53.07N 158.33E
39 F7 **Avacha** *R* U.S.S.R.
Avacha *vol see* **Avachinskaya, Sopka** *vol*
39 F7 **Avachinskaya Guba** *gulf* U.S.S.R.
39 F7 **Avachinskaya, Sopka** *vol* U.S.S.R. 53.15N 158.50E
51 J5 **Avafors** Sweden 66.02N 22.20E
51 J6 **Avaheden** Sweden 65.49N 21.35E
87 J10 **Avai** Somalia 1.10N 43.40E
72 F3 **Availles-Limouzine** France 46.07N 0.39E
43 N8 **Aval'** Uzbekistan U.S.S.R. 40.19N 71.51E
9 R10 **Ava Lahi** *channel* Tonga, Pacific Oc
53 S20 **Avaldsnes** Norway 59.21N 5.18E
53 U19 **Avaldsnuten** *mt* Norway 59.52N 6.14E
113 H1 **Avalik** *R* Alaska
71 D1 **Avallon** France 47.30N 3.54E
111 F8 **Avalon** California 33.21N 118.20W
107 F8 **Avalon** Mississippi 33.39N 90.04W
103 E8 **Avalon** New Jersey 39.06N 74.43W
12 M5 **Avalon** New S Wales 33.39S 151.20E
109 F9 **Avalon L** New Mexico 32.30N 104.15W
98 T6 **Avalon Pen** Newfoundland
115 J5 **Avalos** Mexico 24.47N 101.25W
121 F2 **Avalos** *R* Argentina
44 F4 **Avalov** U.S.S.R. 43.54N 44.45E
41 F5 **Avam** *R* U.S.S.R.
32 B1 **Avān** Iran 38.44N 46.20E
43 F4 **Avan** Kazakhstan U.S.S.R. 46.15N 60.08E
28 C5 **Avanashi** Tamil Nadu India 11.12N 77.15E
76 B7 **Avanca** Portugal 40.48N 8.34W
71 J7 **Avançon** France 44.31N 6.11E
66 E6 **Avançon** *R* Switzerland
28 E2 **Avanigadda** Andhra Prad India 16.03N 80.59E
36 H4 **Avanos** Turkey 38.45N 34.51E
69 G7 **Avant-les-Ramerupt** France 48.27N 4.17E
66 D6 **Avants, les** Switzerland 46.28N 6.57E
120 D11 **Avanzada** Chile 24.08S 69.43W
109 M5 **Avard** Oklahoma 36.41N 98.47W
118 E8 **Avaré** Brazil 23.06S 48.57W
32 B1 **Avārsin** Iran 38.58N 47.05E
44 G5 **Avarskoye Koysu** *R* U.S.S.R.
122 A10 **Avarua** Rarotonga Pacific Oc 21.12S 159.46W
83 H4 **Avas** Greece 40.57N 25.56E
113 E9 **Avatanak I** Aleutian Is 54.05N 165.20W
122 A10 **Avatiu** Rarotonga Pacific Oc 21.12S 159.46W
52 J2 **Avaträsk** Sweden 64.21N 16.20E
51 H5 **Avaudden** Sweden 66.29N 20.40E
51 G6 **Avaviken** Sweden 65.39N 18.40E
111 H6 **Avawatz Mts** California
'Avaz Fārs Iran *see* **Evaz**
32 J4 **Avaz** Iran 32.55N 60.20E
44 M8 **Avazy** Turkmeniya U.S.S.R. 39.56N 52.53E
44 F6 **Avchala** Georgia U.S.S.R. 41.47N 44.49E
37 G1 **Avcı Koru** *forest* Turkey
37 G2 **Avdan Dağları** *mts* Turkey
45 J8 **Avdeyevka** Ukraine U.S.S.R. 48.06N 37.46E
Avdeyevka Pervaya *see* **Avdeyevka**
84 M11 **Avdhoú** Crete 35.14N 25.25E
35 D1 **'Avdon** Israel 33.03N 35.10E
45 J9 **Avdot'ino** Ukraine U.S.S.R. 47.54N 37.52E
76 B6 **Ave** *R* Portugal
56 H5 **Avebury** Wilts Eng 51.27N 1.51W
61 L6 **Ave-et-Auffe** Belgium 50.07N 5.09E
66 M7 **Avegno** Switzerland 46.13N 8.45E
Āveh *see* **Āvej**
74 D4 **Aveinte** Spain 40.45N 4.50W
76 B10 **Aveiras de Cima** Portugal 39.08N 8.53W
117 B6 **Aveiro** Brazil 3.15S 55.10W
76 B7 **Aveiro** Portugal 40.38N 8.40W
76 B7 **Aveiro** *dist* Portugal
32 C3 **Āvej** Iran 35.35N 49.12E
61 A2 **Avekapelle** Belgium 51.04N 2.44E
39 G4 **Avekova** U.S.S.R. 61.54N 160.28E
76 C9 **Avelar** Portugal 39.55N 8.21W
76 C8 **Avelãs do Caminho** Portugal 40.29N 8.27W
76 F5 **Aveleda** Portugal 41.53N 6.42W
55 K3 **Aveley** Essex England 51.30N 0.15E
61 D3 **Avelgem** Belgium 50.46N 3.27E
104 E6 **Avella** Pennsylvania 40.17N 80.30W
80 L7 **Avella, Monte** Italy 40.58N 14.41E
121 D3 **Avellanada** Córdoba Argentina 30.33S 64.15W
121 F2 **Avellaneda** Argentina 29.00S 59.40W
121 F5 **Avellaneda** Buenos Aires Arg 34.40S 58.20W
75 M4 **Avellanes** Spain 41.55N 0.46E
80 L7 **Avellino** Italy 40.49N 14.47E
80 L7 **Avellino** *prov* Italy
111 D6 **Avenal** California 36.00N 120.10W
71 C8 **Aven Armand** *cave* France 44.14N 3.22E
66 E4 **Avenches** Switzerland 46.53N 70.03E
71 C9 **Avène** France 43.45N 3.06E
60 H9 **Avenhorn** Netherlands 52.37N 4.56E
71 H5 **Avenières, les** France 45.38N 5.34E
56 G4 **Avening** Glos Eng 51.42N 2.10W
61 L4 **Avennes** Belgium 50.37N 5.07E
80 D8 **Aventino, Monte** *hill* Roma Italy
61 K2 **Averbode** Belgium 51.02N 4.59E
121 E2 **Averías** Argentina 28.45S 62.25W
53 E6 **Avernak By** Denmark 55.02N 10.16E
53 E6 **Avernakø** *isld* Denmark 55.01N 10.17E
52 C3 **Averøya** *isld* Norway 63.00N 7.35E
66 P6 **Avers** *R* Switzerland
80 K7 **Aversa** Italy 40.58N 14.13E
66 O5 **Averserrhein** *R* Switzerland
110 K2 **Avery** Idaho 47.15N 115.50W
108 S8 **Avery** Iowa 41.04N 92.42W
112 N2 **Avery** Texas 33.33N 94.48W
107 E12 **Avery Island** Louisiana 29.52N 91.55W
116 N7 **Aves** *isld* Caribbean Sea 15.42N 63.38W
76 J2 **Ave, Sierra de** *mts* Spain
69 D3 **Avesnes-le-Comte** France 50.17N 2.33E
69 E3 **Avesnes-les-Aubert** France 50.12N 3.21E
69 F3 **Avesnes-sur-Helpe** France 50.08N 3.57E
96 D7 **Aves Ridge** Caribbean Sea
70 G6 **Avessac** France 47.40N 1.59W
52 J6 **Avesta** Sweden 60.09N 16.10E
81 Q12 **Avetrana** Italy 40.21N 17.43E
53 N9 **Avevig** Faeroes 62.05N 6.41W
67 G8 **Aveyron** *dept* France
72 H7 **Aveyron** *R* France
80 H4 **Avezzano** Italy 42.02N 13.26E
84 N10 **Avgó** *isld* Crete 35.37N 25.36E
83 F8 **Avgó** *isld* Greece 36.05N 23.00E
84 C8 **Avgó** *isld* Greece 36.41N 21.53E
84 B3 **Avgó** *mt* Greece 39.29N 21.23E
84 D8 **Avía** Greece 36.57N 22.10E
76 C4 **Avia** *R* Spain
79 N2 **Aviano** Italy 46.04N 12.35E
118 A10 **Aviá Terai** Argentina 26.36S 60.47W
122 V7 **Aviation I** Palmyra I Pacific Oc 5.53N 162.05W
58 F6 **Avich, L** Strathclyde Scotland 56.17N 5.20W
35 D3 **Avi'el** Israel 32.32N 35.01E
15 G6 **Avieme** Papua New Guinea 4.54S 143.34E
58 J4 **Aviemore** Highland Scotland 57.12N 3.50W
11 E11 **Aviemore Dam** New Zealand 44.39S 170.22E
66 A8 **Aviernoz** France 45.59N 6.14E
35 D7 **Avi'ezer** Israel 31.41N 35.02E
48 S14 **Avigait** Greenland 62.20N 49.59W
35 B7 **Avigedor** Israel 31.43N 34.44E
79 B4 **Avigliana** Italy 45.04N 7.23E
80 N7 **Avigliano** Italy 40.44N 15.44E
71 F9 **Avignon** France 43.56N 4.48E
72 H9 **Avignonet-Lauragais** France 43.21N 1.47E
35 C4 **Aviḥayil** Israel 32.21N 34.52E
76 K7 **Ávila** Spain 40.39N 4.42W
74 D4 **Avila** *prov* Spain
76 J7 **Avila, Sierra de** *mts* Spain
76 H1 **Avilés** Spain 43.33N 5.55W
76 H1 **Avilés, Ría de** Spain
71 J2 **Avilley** France 47.25N 6.16E
112 N3 **Avinger** Texas 32.54N 94.33W
13 H6 **Avington** Queensland 24.04S 145.00E
75 O4 **Avinyó** Spain 41.52N 1.59E
75 O5 **Avinyonet** Spain 41.22N 1.47E
79 J3 **Avio** Italy 45.44N 10.56E
69 D3 **Avion** France 50.23N 2.50E
76 C4 **Avion** Spain 42.23N 8.15W
26 T16 **Avirons, Les** Réunion Ind Oc 21.14S 55.20E
104 H5 **Avis** Pennsylvania 41.12N 77.20W
79 K2 **Avisio** *R* Italy
119 G7 **Avispa, Cerro** Venezuela 1.00N 65.50W
26 R8 **Avissawella** Sri Lanka 6.57N 80.13E
35 E3 **Avital** Israel 32.33N 35.19E
Av-i Taniero *R see* **Tānjarō** *R*
35 E1 **Avivim** Israel 33.05N 35.28E
76 D10 **Aviz** Portugal 39.03N 7.54W
76 D10 **Aviz** *R* Portugal
69 G6 **Avize** France 48.58N 4.00E
36 H1 **Avlağı** Turkey 41.07N 34.50E
37 B3 **Avlaka Burun** *C* Gökçeada Turkey 40.07N 25.40E
36 G6 **Avlama Dağ** *mts* Turkey
36 D6 **Avlan Gölü** *L* Turkey
84 W22 **Avliótes** Corfu 39.47N 19.40E
84 C7 **Avlon** Greece 37.20N 21.45E
84 G5 **Avlón** Greece 38.15N 23.41E
84 H4 **Avlonárion** Greece 38.31N 24.07E
53 B4 **Avlum** Denmark 56.16N 8.48E
53 H6 **Avnø Fjord** *inlet* Denmark
53 F6 **Avnslev** Denmark 55.21N 10.44E
76 D8 **Avo** Portugal 40.17N 7.54W
108 P8 **Avoca** Iowa 41.29N 95.20W
106 M6 **Avoca** Michigan 43.03N 82.41W
104 H4 **Avoca** New York 42.24N 77.26W
11 F10 **Avoca** New Zealand 43.10S 171.52E
103 C4 **Avoca** Pennsylvania 41.20N 75.45W
12 J8 **Avoca** Tasmania 41.45S 147.47E
112 H3 **Avoca** Texas 32.52N 99.43W
12 G6 **Avoca** Victoria 37.05S 143.31E
59 K6 **Avoca** Wicklow Irish Rep 52.52N 6.13W
12 G6 **Avoca** *R* Victoria
59 K6 **Avoca, Vale of** Wicklow Irish Rep
58 H3 **Avoch** Highland Scotland 57.33N 4.10W
12 D5 **Avoid B** S Australia
101 O10 **Avola** Br Col 51.47N 119.19W
81 K10 **Avola** Sicily 36.54N 15.08E
80 D4 **Avoltore, Pta** Italy 42.22N 11.12E
109 D2 **Avon** Colorado 39.38N 106.31W
106 D9 **Avon** Illinois 40.40N 90.26W
103 M2 **Avon** Massachusetts 42.09N 71.03W
108 Q4 **Avon** Minnesota 45.35N 94.30W
110 N3 **Avon** Montana 46.35N 112.35W
105 M2 **Avon** N Carolina 35.22N 75.30W
104 H4 **Avon** New York 42.55N 77.44W
104 C5 **Avon** Ohio 41.26N 82.04W
108 M7 **Avon** S Dakota 43.00N 98.04W
56 F5 **Avon** *co* Eng
11 N10 **Avon and Heathcote Est** New Zealand
59 K6 **Avonbeg R** Wicklow Irish Rep
103 F6 **Avon by the Sea** New Jersey 40.12N 74.01W
111 M8 **Avondale** Arizona 33.28N 112.22W
109 F3 **Avondale** Colorado 38.14N 104.22W
107 B2 **Avondale** Missouri 39.10N 94.31W
103 C7 **Avondale** Pennsylvania 39.50N 75.47W
13 K6 **Avondale** Queensland 24.42S 152.10E
112 L8 **Avondale** Texas 32.56N 97.24W
11 C2 **Avondale** *dist* Auckland New Zealand
13 D4 **Avon Downs** N Terr Australia 20.00S 137.30E
13 H5 **Avon Downs** Queensland 21.50S 147.12E
95 D9 **Avondrust** S Africa 33.27S 20.11E
11 L9 **Avonhead** New Zealand 43.31S 172.33E
58 J4 **Avon, L** Grampian Scotland 57.06N 3.37W
104 C5 **Avon Lake** Ohio 41.31N 82.01W
100 M8 **Avonlea** Saskatchewan 50.01N 105.03W
72 E1 **Avon-les-Roches** France 47.11N 0.27E
104 F6 **Avonmore** Pennsylvania 40.32N 79.29W
56 F4 **Avonmouth** Avon Eng 51.31N 2.42W
105 F10 **Avon Park** Florida 27.36N 81.30W
56 F5 **Avon, R** Avon etc Eng
58 J7 **Avon, R** Central/Lothian Scotland
11 M9 **Avon R** Christchurch New Zealand
56 D7 **Avon, R** Devon Eng
58 K4 **Avon, R** Grampian Scotland
56 H6 **Avon, R** Hants etc Eng
56 G3 **Avon, R** Warwicks etc Eng
14 B9 **Avon, R** W Australia
95 G9 **Avontuur** S Africa 33.45S 23.10E
58 H7 **Avon Water** *R* Strathclyde Scotland
72 K1 **Avord** France 47.02N 2.38E
71 J2 **Avoudrey** France 47.09N 6.26E
84 C7 **Avramió** Greece 37.02N 21.56E
70 H4 **Avranches** France 48.42N 1.21W
70 N4 **Avre** *R* Eure etc France
69 D4 **Avre** *R* Somme France
69 M6 **Avricourt** France 48.39N 6.48E
82 J5 **Avrig** Romania 45.43N 24.21E
69 K5 **Avril** France 49.17N 5.58E
72 B3 **Avrillé** France 46.28N 1.28W
66 F8 **Avril, Mt** Italy/Switz 45.55N 7.16E
44 C9 **Avrora** Ukraine U.S.S.R. 45.43N 33.14E
Avşar *I see* **Türkeli**
36 J5 **Avşarlı** Turkey 37.27N 96.42E
48 S10 **Avssaqutaq** Greenland 66.55N 53.28W
41 O2 **Avstriyskiy Proliv** *str* Franz Josef Land U.S.S.R.
39 K3 **Avtatkuyel** *R* U.S.S.R.
82 E7 **Avtovac** Yugoslavia 43.09N 18.35E
37 F3 **Avualı** *R* Turkey
15 L3 **Avuavu** Guadalcanal I Solomon Is 9.51S 160.08E
15 F7 **Avu, L** Papua New Guinea 7.28S 141.41E
35 F4 **Avuqa** Israel 32.28N 35.32E
20 P8 **Awa** Okinawa Japan 26.36N 127.53E
33 M5 **Awābī, 'Al** Oman 23.20N 57.35E
'Awad al Atroz *see* **'Awwād al 'Atrūz**
30 B5 **Awagarh** Uttar Prad India 27.26N 78.29E
87 D5 **'Awag el Baqar** Sudan 10.10N 33.10E
94 C3 **Awahuab** *watercourse* Namibia
90 D9 **Awai** Nigeria 5.40N 8.25E
33 M5 **Awaifi** Oman 22.15N 56.58E
Awai Saiyid Rahim *see* **Āwāy, Sayyid Raḥim**
34 D5 **A'waj** *R* Syria
20 H7 **Awaji-shima** *isld* Japan
11 J5 **Awakino** New Zealand 38.39S 174.38E
11 J5 **Awakino R** New Zealand
85 A5 **Āwāl** *watercourse* Libya
93 M1 **Awal Edo** Ethiopia 4.15N 40.37E
93 M1 **Awal Ginda** Ethiopia 4.14N 40.21E
33 J3 **Awālī** Bahrain, The Gulf 26.05N 50.31E
33 K6 **'Awāmir** *tribe* Saudi Arabia
33 H8 **'Awāmir** *tribe* S Yemen
85 N8 **Awamtîb, Gebel** *mt* Egypt 23.25N 34.23E
30 A8 **Awan** Madhya Prad India 24.24N 77.08E
18 M10 **Awang** Indonesia 8.54S 116.22E
15 K6 **Awangio** New Britain 5.59S 149.28E
94 B2 **Awanoas** Namibia 18.36S 12.54E
11 H2 **Awanui** New Zealand 35.03S 173.18E
29 D5 **Awar** Rajasthan India 24.06N 75.56E
93 N2 **Awara Plain** Kenya
18 J9 **Awarawar Tanjung** *C* Java Indon 6.45S 111.58E
Awareh *see* **Auareh**
33 H6 **Awārik, Al** *area* Saudi Arabia
15 H6 **Awaro** Papua New Guinea 4.10S 144.50E
35 E5 **Awarta** Jordan 32.10N 35.17E
Awarua Bay *see* **Big Bay**
11 C11 **Awarua, Pt** New Zealand 44.16S 168.06E
87 G7 **Awasa** Ethiopia 7.02N 38.28E
87 H6 **Awash** Ethiopia 9.01N 40.10E
20 N3 **Awa-shima** *isld* Japan
87 G6 **Awash,R** Ethiopia
94 C5 **Awasib Mts** Namibia
89 H8 **Awaso** Ghana 6.20N 2.22W
34 N3 **Āw-a-Spī** *R* Iraq
24 C5 **Awat** Xinjiang Uygur Zizhiqu China 40.40N 80.20E
87 G8 **Awata,R** Ethiopia
11 H8 **Awatere R** New Zealand
34 N4 **Āwāy Sayyid Raḥim** Iraq 34.50N 45.22E
85 B6 **Awbārī** Libya 26.35N 12.47E
59 F7 **Awbeg,R** Cork Irish Rep
33 F10 **Awd** *tribe* Yemen
33 J5 **'Awdah** Saudi Arabia 22.14N 51.00E
33 F4 **'Awdah, Al** Saudi Arabia 25.35N 45.44E
34 O7 **'Awdah,Hawr al** *L* Iraq
90 A8 **Awe** Nigeria 7.49N 3.58E
90 D7 **Awe** Nigeria 8.08N 9.09E
87 A6 **Aweil** Sudan 8.42N 27.20E
58 F6 **Awe, L** Strathclyde Scotland
15 K7 **Aweleng Is** New Britain 6.15S 149.30E
93 D4 **Awelo** Uganda 1.42N 32.47E
105 H4 **Awendaw** S Carolina 33.02N 79.40W
61 M6 **Awenne** Belgium 50.04N 5.18E
11 D11 **Awful, Mt** New Zealand 44.10S 169.07E
90 C8 **Awgu** Nigeria 6.05N 7.26E
33 N9 **'Awhah** *isld* Kuwait 29.23N 48.27E
15 H4 **Awin I** Bismarck Arch 1.40S 144.04E
15 L7 **Awio** New Britain 6.12S 150.07E
15 L7 **Awio B** New Britain
61 M4 **Awirs** Belgium 50.36N 5.24E
86 F3 **Awîsh el Hagar** Egypt 31.01N 31.19E
85 F5 **Awjilah** Libya 29.05N 21.12E
90 C8 **Awka** Nigeria 6.12N 7.05E
86 Q12 **Awkaf,El** *dist* Cairo Egypt
33 G10 **Awlaqi** *tribe* S Yemen
19 B5 **Awo** *R* Celebes Indon
103 F3 **Awosting** New York 41.42N 74.17W
101 Q4 **Awry L** N W Terr 62.59N 114.56W
33 F3 **Awsajiyah,Al** Saudi Arabia 26.03N 44.07E
33 G10 **'Aws, Al** S Yemen 13.27N 46.27E
33 D3 **Awshaziyah,Al** Saudi Arabia 26.46N 41.45E
90 B8 **Awtun** Nigeria 8.00N 5.14E
19 D2 **Awu** *vol* Indonesia 3.44N 125.28E
Awul *see* **Ovulwul**
113 J2 **Awuna** *R* Alaska
87 G7 **Awusa,L** Ethiopia
34 N5 **'Awwād al 'Atrūz** Iraq 33.32N 45.12E
50 J2 **Axarfjördhur** *B* Iceland
72 J10 **Axat** France 42.47N 2.14E
56 F5 **Axbridge** Somerset Eng 51.18N 2.49W
60 C3 **Axel** Netherlands 51.16N 3.55E
52 G9 **Axelfors** Sweden 57.27N 13.05E
123 G8 **Axel Heiberg Glacier** Antarctica
97 K1 **Axel Heiberg I** N W Terr 80.00N 90.00W
60 C3 **Axelsche Sassing** Netherlands 51.17N 3.52E
66 L4 **Axenstein** Switzerland 46.59N 8.38E
109 C1 **Axial** Colorado 40.17N 107.48W
89 H9 **Axim** Ghana 4.53N 2.14W
119 J10 **Axinim** Brazil 4.04S 59.25W
120 F2 **Axioma** Brazil 6.43S 64.36W
83 F4 **Axiós** *R* Greece
117 F6 **Axixa** Brazil 2.51S 44.05W
72 H10 **Ax-les-Thermes** France 42.43N 1.49E
56 E6 **Axminster** Devon Eng 50.47N 3.00W
75 E1 **Axpe** Spain 43.22N 2.42W
105 E6 **Axson** Georgia 31.15N 82.44W
109 O2 **Axtell** Kansas 39.51N 96.12W
104 F10 **Axton** Virginia 36.40N 79.43W
52 H8 **Axvall** Sweden 58.24N 13.35E
69 G5 **Ay** France 49.04N 4.00E
43 O4 **Ay** Kazakhstan U.S.S.R. 47.26N 80.34E
70 H3 **Ay** *R* France
47 H7 **Ay** *R* U.S.S.R.
119 B10 **Ayabaca** Peru 4.40S 79.45W
20 J6 **Ayabe** Japan 35.19N 135.16E
87 L6 **Aya Bentih** Ethiopia 8.03N 46.32E
88 L5 **Ayachi,Jbel** *mt* Morocco 32.30N 4.55W
121 F6 **Ayacucho** Argentina 37.09S 58.30W
120 F7 **Ayacucho** Bolivia 17.50S 63.18W
120 C5 **Ayacucho** Peru 13.10S 74.15W
120 C5 **Ayacucho** *dept* Peru
25 C1 **Ayadaw** Burma 22.16N 95.26E
33 G9 **Ayādh** S Yemen 14.59N 46.50E
Ayagh Arghan *see* **Argan**
43 O3 **Ayaguz** Kazakhstan U.S.S.R. 47.59N 80.27E
43 N3 **Ayaguz,R** Kazakhstan U.S.S.R.
43 G6 **Ayakagytma,Vpadina** *depression* Uzbekistan U.S.S.R.
41 N5 **Ayakit** U.S.S.R. 70.50N 127.26E
43 H6 **Ayakkuduk** Kazakhstan U.S.S.R. 41.14N 65.14E
24 F7 **Ayakkum Hu** *L* Xinjiang Uygur Zizhiqu China
Ayak Kum Köl *L see* **Ayakkum Hu**
41 G5 **Ayakli** *R* U.S.S.R.
39 B3 **Ayama** *R* U.S.S.R.
89 H9 **Ayamé** Ivory Coast 5.35N 3.09W
89 H9 **Ayamé Dam** Ivory Coast 5.33N 3.13W
91 B2 **Ayamiken** Equat Guinea 2.03N 10.01E
77 B6 **Ayamonte** Spain 37.13N 7.24W
18 E10 **Ayam,Tanjong** *C* Pen Malaysia 1.20N 104.13E
42 J5 **Ayan** Buryat U.S.S.R. 54.42N 110.59E
42 H2 **Ayan** Irkutsk U.S.S.R. 61.40N 108.05E
42 H3 **Ayan** Irkutsk U.S.S.R. 59.32N 106.25E
40 H3 **Ayan** Khabarovsk U.S.S.R. 56.29N 138.07E
42 H2 **Ayan** Krasnoyarsk U.S.S.R. 61.48N 105.45E
41 F6 **Ayan** *R* U.S.S.R.
36 H1 **Ayancık** Turkey 41.56N 34.35E
119 J5 **Ayanganna** *mt* Guyana 5.27N 59.52W
89 N8 **Ayangba** Nigeria 7.30N 7.18E
39 H3 **Ayanka** U.S.S.R. 63.47N 167.30E
39 H3 **Ayanka** *R* U.S.S.R.
35 C6 **Ayanot** Israel 31.55N 34.46E
41 F6 **Ayan,Ozero** *L* U.S.S.R.
120 D5 **Ayapato** Peru 13.53S 70.21W
119 C3 **Ayapel** Colombia 8.16N 75.10W
119 C3 **Ayapel,Ciénaga de** *marshy L* Colombia 8.20N 75.07W
119 C4 **Ayapel,Sa.de** *mts* Colombia
79 C3 **Ayas** Italy 45.49N 7.41E
36 F2 **Ayaş** Turkey 40.02N 32.21E
47 M4 **Ayat'** U.S.S.R. 57.03N 60.15E
47 M4 **Ayatskoye** U.S.S.R. 57.26N 60.42E
47 M4 **Ayatskoye,Oz** *L* U.S.S.R. 57.20N 60.30E
41 F4 **Ayaturku,Oz** *L* U.S.S.R.
42 G3 **Ayava** U.S.S.R. 59.38N 103.15E
120 D6 **Ayaviri** Peru 14.53S 70.35W
40 F1 **Ayaya** U.S.S.R. 60.04N 134.45E
87 F4 **Ayayei** Ethiopia 13.48N 36.37E
89 H8 **Aya-Yenahin** Ghana 6.43N 2.03W
43 A3 **Aybas** Kazakhstan U.S.S.R. 47.52N 49.28E
37 C5 **Aybasti** Turkey 40.41N 37.23E
57 K3 **Aycliffe** Durham Eng 54.36N 1.34W
43 J1 **Aydabul'** Kazakhstan U.S.S.R. 52.45N 68.59E
45 K6 **Aydar** U.S.S.R. 50.05N 38.55E
45 L8 **Aydar** *R* Ukraine U.S.S.R.
43 H5 **Aydarly** Kazakhstan U.S.S.R. 44.00N 66.00E
45 T6 **Aydarly** Kazakhstan U.S.S.R. 50.07N 47.32E
43 H6 **Aydar,Solonchak** *salt marsh* Kazakhstan U.S.S.R.
71 B5 **Aydat** France 45.40N 2.57E
105 K2 **Ayden** N Carolina 35.28N 77.25W
43 D7 **Aydere** Turkmeniya U.S.S.R. 38.25N 56.46E
33 K8 **'Aydim, Wādī** *watercourse* Oman
24 F4 **Aydingkol Hu** *L* Xinjiang Uygur Zizhiqu China
37 G2 **Aydınlı** Turkey 40.52N 29.20E
36 C5 **Aydın Sıra Dağları** *mts* Turkey
36 G5 **Aydos Dağı** *mt* Turkey 37.20N 34.23E
43 E2 **Aydyrlinskiy** U.S.S.R. 52.04N 59.50E
61 M6 **Aye** Belgium 50.13N 5.18E
75 F3 **Ayedo** *mt* Spain 42.05N 2.17W
84 D5 **Ay. Efthimía** Greece 38.29N 22.21E
77 P3 **Ayelo de Malferit** Spain 38.53N 0.35W
87 H5 **Ayelu** *mt* Ethiopia 10.05N 40.42E
72 G5 **Ayen** France 45.15N 1.20E
89 J9 **Ayenfuri** Ghana 5.58N 1.57W
89 K7 **Ayengré** Togo 8.42N 1.02E
66 F6 **Ayent** Switzerland 46.17N 7.25E
104 O4 **Ayer** Massachusetts 42.33N 71.34W
66 G7 **Ayer** Switzerland 46.12N 7.37E
84 E8 **Ayéranos** Greece 36.42N 22.31E
18 D10 **Ayer Baloi** Pen Malaysia 1.34N 103.21E
75 J3 **Ayerbe** Spain 42.16N 0.41W
18 H3 **Ayer Chawan,Pulau** *isld* Singapore
18 C9 **Ayer Hitam** Pen Malaysia 2.58N 102.23E
18 D10 **Ayer Hitam** Pen Malaysia 1.56N 103.11E
18 C9 **Ayer Kuning** Pen Malaysia 2.30N 102.29E
18 H4 **Ayer Merbau,Pulau** *isld* Singapore
18 D9 **Ayer Panas** Pen Malaysia 2.28N 103.02E
110 G3 **Ayers** Washington 46.35N 118.22W
13 C7 **Ayers Ra** N Terr Australia
13 B7 **Ayers Rock** *mt* N Terr Australia 25.18S 131.18E
42 E5 **Ayeshka** U.S.S.R. 54.58N 90.54E
47 L7 **Ayev** *R* U.S.S.R.
36 H4 **Aygörmez Dağı** *mt* Turkey
75 P4 **Ayguafreda** Spain 41.45N 2.17E
71 G8 **Aygues** *R* France
42 D6 **Aygulakskiy Khrebet** *mts* U.S.S.R.
39 F4 **Aygur** U.S.S.R. 62.21N 155.39E
44 E2 **Aygurka** *R* U.S.S.R.
43 O3 **Aygyrzhal** Kazakhstan U.S.S.R. 48.16N 80.30E
84 E2 **Ayía** Lárisa Greece 39.43N 22.45E
84 F4 **Ayía Ánna** Greece 38.52N 23.24E
84 A5 **Ayía Evfimía** Greece 38.18N 20.36E
36 A3 **Ayía Iríni, Ákra** *C* Límnos Greece 39.46N 25.22E
84 C7 **Ayía Kiriakí** Greece 37.07N 21.35E
84 E4 **Ayía Marína** Greece 38.54N 22.35E
84 E4 **Ayía Marína** Greece 38.34N 22.42E
84 T15 **Ayia Napa** Cyprus 34.58N 34.00E
84 G2 **Ayía Paraskeví** Greece 39.57N 23.38E
84 C4 **Ayía Sofía** Greece 38.35N 21.39E
83 H5 **Ayiássos** Greece 39.05N 26.23E
84 D5 **Ayía Varvára** Akhaïa Greece 38.00N 22.16E
84 M11 **Ayía Varvára** Crete 35.08N 25.00E
30 D1 **Ayi La** *pass* Xizang Zizhiqu 31.43N 80.00E
33 E8 **Ayinah** Saudi Arabia 18.00N 42.19E
64 M8 **Aying** W Germany 47.58N 11.47E
89 J8 **Ayinwafe** Ghana 7.28N 0.53W
84 D2 **Áyioi Anáryiroi** Greece 39.32N 22.22E
84 F6 **Áyioi Theódhori** Greece 37.55N 23.08E
83 G4 **Áyion Óros** *aut monastic dist* Greece
84 E6 **Áyios Adhrianós** Greece 37.36N 22.50E
84 E7 **Áyios Andréas** Arkadhía Greece 37.21N 22.45E
84 L11 **Áyios Dhéka** Crete 35.04N 24.57E
84 H5 **Áyios Dhimítrios** Évvoia Greece 38.07N 24.26E
84 R15 **Ayios Epiphanios** Cyprus 34.59N 33.08E
83 G5 **Áyios Evstrátios** Greece 39.34N 24.58E
83 G5 **Áyios Evstrátios** *isld* Greece 39.32N 25.05E
84 B6 **Áyios Ilías** Ilía Greece 37.53N 21.27E
84 C7 **Áyios Ilías** Ilía Greece 37.25N 21.40E
84 H6 **Áyios Ilías** *mt* Kéa Greece 37.37N 24.21E
84 E7 **Áyios Ioánnis** Arkadhía Greece 37.21N 22.38E
84 D7 **Áyios Ioánnis** Lakonía Greece 37.03N 22.24E
83 H7 **Áyios Kírikos** Greece 37.34N 26.15E
84 A6 **Áyios Kírix** Greece 37.47N 20.50E
84 D7 **Áyios Konstandinos** Greece 37.13N 22.16E
84 E4 **Áyios Konstantínos** Greece 38.45N 22.51E
84 F3 **Áyios Lavréndios** Greece 39.21N 23.04E
84 H5 **Áyios Loukás** Évvoia Greece 38.26N 24.01E
84 W22 **Áyios Matthaíos** Corfu 39.30N 19.52E
84 M11 **Áyios Míron** Crete 35.15N 25.01E
84 P15 **Ayios Neophitos** Cyprus 34.51N 32.27E
84 E7 **Áyios Nikólaos** Arkadhía Greece 37.22N 22.31E
84 B3 **Áyios Nikólaos** Arta Greece 39.14N 21.03E
84 N11 **Áyios Nikólaos** Crete 35.11N 25.43E
84 Q15 **Áyios Nikolaos** Cyprus 34.52N 32.45E
84 G5 **Áyios Nikólaos** Évvoia Greece 38.25N 23.39E
84 A4 **Áyios Nikólaos** Greece 38.52N 20.48E
84 D8 **Áyios Níkon** Greece 36.45N 22.20E
84 E7 **Áyios Pétros** Arkadhía Greece 37.20N 22.33E
84 A4 **Áyios Pétros** Levkás Greece 38.40N 20.37E
84 S14 **Ayios Seryios** Cyprus 35.12N 33.53E
84 A3 **Áyios Spirídhon** Greece 39.08N 20.52E
84 R15 **Ayios Theodhoros** Cyprus 34.53N 33.02E
84 T14 **Ayios Theodhoros** Cyprus 35.21N 34.02E
84 D3 **Áyios Theódhoros** Greece 39.22N 22.00E
84 F5 **Áyios Theódhoros** Greece 38.19N 23.20E
84 G5 **Áyios Thomás** Greece 38.16N 23.35E
84 E6 **Áyios Vasílios** Korinthía Greece 37.47N 22.48E
84 E5 **Áyios Vlásios** Greece 38.29N 22.48E
84 C5 **Áyios Yeórios Ríou** Greece 38.17N 21.47E
84 C3 **Áyios Yeóryios** Kardhítsa Greece 39.17N 21.51E
84 E5 **Áyios Yeóryios** Voiotía Greece 38.23N 22.55E
84 G7 **Áyios Yeóryios** *isld* Greece
84 F3 **Áyios Yeóryios Nilías** Greece 39.20N 23.05E
93 B2 **Ayivu** Uganda 3.04N 30.57E
113 L2 **Ayiyak** *R* Alaska
83 H7 **Aykathonísi** *isld* Greece 37.28N 26.58E
43 F2 **Ayke,Oz** *L* Kazakhstan U.S.S.R. 50.27N 61.33E
41 K7 **Aykhal** U.S.S.R. 66.00N 111.30E
47 F5 **Aykino** U.S.S.R. 62.15N 49.59E
64 B4 **Ayl** W Germany 49.38N 6.33E
99 N7 **Aylen L** Ontario 45.37N 77.52W
56 K4 **Aylesbury** Bucks England 51.50N 0.50W
11 G10 **Aylesbury** New Zealand 43.32S 172.18E
100 M8 **Aylesbury** Saskatchewan 50.57N 105.41W
98 H8 **Aylesford** Nova Scotia 45.02N 64.52W
56 J2 **Aylestone** Leics Eng 52.37N 1.08W
101 D6 **Aylesworth, Mt** Br Col/Alaska 59.33N 140.52W
104 H9 **Aylett** Virginia 37.47N 77.09W
75 D5 **Ayllón** Spain 41.25N 3.23W
75 D5 **Ayllón,Sierra de** *mts* Spain
99 K10 **Aylmer** Ontario 42.47N 80.58W
99 P7 **Aylmer** Quebec 45.23N 75.51W
101 T3 **Aylmer L** N W Terr
100 B7 **Aylmer, Mt** Alberta 51.22N 115.23W
56 O2 **Aylsham** Norfolk Eng 52.49N 1.15E
100 O5 **Aylsham** Saskatchewan 53.12N 103.48W
99 O7 **Aylwin** Quebec 45.59N 76.02W
79 B3 **Aymavilles** Italy 45.42N 7.15E
121 K9 **Aymond,Mte** Arg/Chile 52.08S 69.27W
120 C5 **Ayna** Peru 12.39S 73.55W
77 M3 **Ayna** Spain 38.34N 2.05W
43 N5 **Aynabulak** Kazakhstan U.S.S.R. 44.37N 77.59E
72 H6 **Aynac** France 44.46N 1.50E
85 G7 **'Ayn 'ā 'Ilat al Judayyid** Libya 24.23N 23.31E
33 M5 **'Ayn,Al** Oman 23.10N 57.33E
33 C4 **'Ayn,Al** Saudi Arabia 25.04N 38.04E
85 E5 **'Ayn al 'Abd** Libya 29.15N 19.01E
33 H2 **'Ayn al 'Abd** Saudi Arabia 28.13N 48.20E
33 G6 **'Ayn al 'Ajalīyah** Saudi Arabia 21.26N 46.12E
'Ayn al Bayda *see* **'Ain el Beida, el**
85 H9 **'Ayn al Ghazāl** Libya 21.50N 24.58E
85 G3 **'Ayn al Ghazalah** Libya 32.09N 23.20E
34 L10 **'Ayn al Ḥufayrah** Saudi Arabia 28.57N 43.46E
33 C4 **'Ayn al Mazr'ah** Saudi Arabia 24.12N 38.26E
34 L5 **'Ayn an Naft** *oil bore* Iraq 33.32N 43.04E
66 B1 **Aynans, les** France 47.38N 6.27E
33 H4 **Ayn Dār** Saudi Arabia 25.59N 49.22E
33 M7 **'Ayn Hindī** Oman 19.59N 57.25E
56 J4 **Aynho** Northants Eng 52.00N 1.15W
'Ayn Huwayzīyāh *see* **'Ain Hweiziya**
Aynı *see* **Lodi** Turkey
43 J7 **Ayni** Tadzhikistan U.S.S.R. 39.26N 68.36E
33 D6 **'Aynīn** Saudi Arabia 20.47N 41.38E
85 H5 **'Ayn Malfa** Egypt 29.48N 24.51E
105 H4 **Aynor** S Carolina 34.00N 79.12W
33 M7 **'Ayn,Ra's al** *C* Oman 19.25N 57.49E
'Ayn Sawfar *see* **Sofar**
85 F5 **'Ayn Sīdī Muḥammad** Libya 29.08N 20.11E
34 L2 **'Ayn Sifnī** Iraq 36.42N 43.20E
34 K3 **'Ayn Ṭarfāwī** Iraq 35.09N 42.28E
34 K4 **'Ayn Ūmm al Banāt** Iraq 34.58N 42.41E
34 C10 **'Aynūnah** Saudi Arabia 28.06N 35.08E
34 B10 **'Aynūnah, Khalīj** *B* Saudi Arabia
33 M5 **'Ayn,Wādī al** *watercourse* Oman
85 E5 **Ayn Zaggūt** Libya 29.07N 19.44E
34 K2 **'Ayn Zālah** Iraq 36.44N 42.34E
85 H9 **'Ayn Zuwayyah** Libya 21.53N 24.51E
87 E2 **Ayob,Jeb** *mt* Sudan 16.40N 35.21E
87 C6 **Ayod** Sudan 8.08N 31.24E
30 F6 **Ayodhya** Uttar Prad India 26.47N 82.12E
87 B7 **Ayom** Sudan 7.55N 28.25E
39 H1 **Ayon** U.S.S.R. 69.55N 168.10E
39 H1 **Ayon,Ostrov** *isld* U.S.S.R.
76 G4 **Ayoo de Vidriales** Spain 42.09N 6.05W
115 L9 **Ayoquezco** Mexico 16.40N 96.51W
77 O2 **Ayora** Spain 39.04N 1.04W
89 K4 **Ayorou** Niger 14.53N 1.00E
90 F10 **Ayos** Cameroon 3.53N 12.31E
37 B3 **Ayos Ilias** *mt* Gökçeada Turkey 40.11N 25.48E
44 C10 **Ay Petri** Ukraine U.S.S.R. 44.29N 34.02E
47 L5 **Ay-Pim** *R* U.S.S.R.
42 B3 **Aypolovo** U.S.S.R. 58.44N 76.35E
108 N2 **Ayr** N Dakota 47.04N 97.30W
108 M9 **Ayr** Nebraska 40.26N 98.26W
13 H4 **Ayr** Queensland 19.32S 147.25E
57 D2 **Ayr** Strathclyde Scotland 55.28N 4.38W
Ayr *co see* **Strathclyde** *reg*
57 D2 **Ayr** *R* Strathclyde Scotland
22 C2 **Ayrag Nuur** *L* Mongolia
36 G5 **Ayrancı** Turkey 37.21N 33.41E
36 G5 **Ayrancı Barajı** *dam* Turkey 37.18N 33.44E
57 E4 **Ayre,Pt. of** Isle of Man U.K. 54.25N 4.22W
58 T12 **Ayre,Pt. of** Orkney Scotland 58.55N 2.42W
57 D2 **Ayr,Heads of** *headland* Strathclyde Scotland 55.26N 4.43W
72 L9 **Ayrolle,Étang de l'** France 43.04N 3.03E
72 E2 **Ayron** France 46.40N 0.05E
108 Q6 **Ayrshire** Iowa 43.03N 94.50W
13 G5 **Ayrshire Downs** Queensland 21.56S 142.42E
43 K1 **Aysary** Kazakhstan U.S.S.R. 53.09N 71.12E
57 K4 **Aysgarth** N Yorks Eng 54.17N 2.00W
43 K3 **Ayshirak** Kazakhstan U.S.S.R. 47.42N 71.36E
35 G1 **Ayshiye** Syria 33.03N 35.50E
44 H9 **Aytākhli, Kūh-e** *mt* Iran 38.18N 46.41E
58 M7 **Ayton** Borders Scotland 55.51N 2.07W
13 H3 **Ayton** Queensland 15.52S 145.20E
75 L5 **Aytona** Spain 41.29N 0.28E
82 L8 **Aytos** Bulgaria 42.41N 27.15E
72 B3 **Aytré** France 46.08N 1.09W
43 G6 **Aytym** Uzbekistan U.S.S.R. 42.11N 63.31E
15 A3 **Ayu** *isld* Irian Jaya 0.23N 131.04E
76 G10 **Ayuela** *R* Spain
44 D10 **Ayukawahama** *mt* Ukraine U.S.S.R. 44.54N 34.44E
22 K4 **Ayulhai** Nei Monggol Zizhiqu China 44.32N 115.33E
20 O4 **Ayuma Yama** *mt* Japan 37.43N 140.12E
33 K8 **Ayun** Oman 17.19N 53.50E
15 A3 **Ayu, Pulau Pulau** *islds* Irian Jaya
47 M5 **Ayush** U.S.S.R. 56.12N 59.52E
22 K4 **Ayuthai** Nei Monggol Zizhiqu China 44.36N 115.36E
45 M9 **Ayutinskiy** U.S.S.R. 47.48N 40.10E
115 K9 **Ayutla** Guerrero Mexico 16.51N 99.16W
115 G7 **Ayutla** Jalisco Mexico 20.09N 104.26W
25 F5 **Ayutthaya** Thailand 14.20N 100.35E
119 C9 **Ayuy** Ecuador 2.07S 77.39W
36 B3 **Ayvacık** Çanakkale Turkey 39.35N 26.23E
36 J2 **Ayvacık** Samsun Turkey 40.59N 36.40E
37 D7 **Ayvalı** Turkey 38.46N 37.36E
37 H2 **Ayvali** *watercourse* Turkey
36 B3 **Ayvalık** Turkey 39.18N 26.42E
42 B1 **Ayvasedapur** *R* U.S.S.R.
61 N5 **Aywaille** Belgium 50.28N 5.40E
33 J8 **Aywat al Manāhil, Wādī** *watercourse* S Yemen
33 H8 **Aywat as Say'ar, Wādī** *watercourse* S Yemen
93 D3 **Ayweri Cwero** Uganda 2.57N 32.32E
35 F1 **Ayyelet HaShahar** Israel 33.01N 35.34E
76 F7 **Azaba** *R* Spain
39 G6 **Azabach'ye,Oz** *L* U.S.S.R.
115 L2 **Azacualpa** Honduras 14.31N 86.07W
29 A1 **Azādpur** Delhi India 28.42N 77.11E
75 G3 **Azagra** Spain 42.19N 1.54W
89 G9 **Azaguié** Ivory Coast 5.39N 4.07W
75 J5 **Azaila** Spain 41.17N 0.30W
Azair,Al *see* **'Uzayr,Al**
37 F7 **Azakpur** Turkey 38.55N 41.49E
110 B7 **Azalea** Oregon 42.49N 123.16W
20 P9 **Azama** Okinawa Japan 26.08N 127.48E
76 B10 **Azambuja** Portugal 39.04N 8.52W
76 D12 **Azambuje** *R* Portugal
30 G6 **Azamgarh** Uttar Prad India 26.03N 83.10E
30 G7 **Azamgarh** *dist* Uttar Prad India
34 M5 **Aẓamīyah, Al** Iraq 33.22N 44.23E
30 L7 **Azamnagar** Bihar India 25.33N 87.50E
120 E8 **Azanaque,Cerro** *pk* Bolivia 19.02S 66.40W
91 H1 **Azande** *tribe* Zaïre
120 D6 **Azangaro** Peru 14.52S 70.16W
47 H7 **Azangulovo** U.S.S.R. 55.43N 58.30E
47 J6 **Azanka** U.S.S.R. 58.05N 64.50E
69 J5 **Azannes-et-Soumazannes** France 49.18N 5.28E
75 E6 **Azañón** Spain 40.41N 2.33W
75 L4 **Azanuy** Spain 41.59N 0.19E
89 L4 **Azaouak** Mali 15.56N 3.25E
89 L3 **Azaouak, Vallée de l'** Mali/Niger
120 D8 **Azapa** Chile 18.30S 70.15W
120 D8 **Azapa** *R* Peru
121 G2 **Azara** Argentina 28.05S 55.40W
32 A2 **Āẕarbāījān-e Gharbī** *prov* Iran
32 A2 **Āẕarbāījān-e Sharqī** *prov* Iran
90 E6 **Azare** Nigeria 11.40N 10.08E
35 A10 **'Azariq** *watercourse* Egypt/Israel
76 D11 **Azaruja** Portugal 38.42N 7.47W
35 C6 **'Azarya** Israel 31.53N 34.55E
42 F5 **Azas** *R* U.S.S.R.
72 G3 **Azat-le-Riz** France 46.19N 1.04E
47 D6 **Azatskoye,Oz** *L* U.S.S.R. 59.50N 37.47E
117 B4 **Azauri** Brazil 0.35N 54.13W
72 G2 **Azay-le-Ferron** France 46.52N 1.04E
72 E1 **Azay-le-Rideau** France 47.16N 0.28E
70 M7 **Azay-sur-Cher** France 47.20N 0.50E
72 D2 **Azay-sur-Thouet** France 46.37N 0.21W
34 E2 **A'zāz** Syria 36.35N 37.03E
87 E3 **'Azaza** Sudan 14.10N 35.31E
74 K8 **Azazga** Algeria 36.45N 4.24E
87 G4 **Azbi** Ethiopia 13.52N 39.50E
Azbine *mt reg see* **Aïr ou Azbine** *mountainous reg*
115 B9 **Azcapotzalco** *dist* Mexico City Mexico
75 F1 **Azcoitia** Spain 43.11N 2.19W
87 G3 **Az Daro** Ethiopia 14.20N 38.12E
36 G1 **Azdavay** Turkey 41.39N 33.18E
70 N6 **Azé** Loire France 47.52N 1.00E
71 F4 **Azé** Saône-et-Loire France 46.26N 4.45E
89 B1 **Azéffal,Dunes de l'** *sand ridge* Mauritania
88 Q3 **Azeffoun** Algeria 36.55N 4.24E
79 C4 **Azeglio** Italy 45.25N 7.59E
89 M3 **Azelik** Niger 16.05N 5.59E
88 J5 **Azemmour** Morocco 33.20N 8.25W
76 D9 **Azenha de Cima** Portugal 39.53N 7.44W
76 B15 **Azenhas do Mar** Portugal 38.50N 9.28W
88 O10 **Azennezal** Algeria 22.58N 0.43E
72 G3 **Azerables** France 46.20N 1.28E
Azerbaijan S.S.R *see* **Azerbaydzhanskaya S.S.R**
44 H7 **Azerbaydzhan** *reg* U.S.S.R.
38 D4 **Azerbaydzhanskaya S.S.R** U.S.S.R.
76 C8 **Azere** Portugal 40.21N 8.07W
71 E4 **Azergues** *R* France
120 F8 **Azero, R** Bolivia
88 R10 **Azerzerou** Algeria 23.35N 6.56E
46 M3 **Azeyevo** U.S.S.R. 54.39N 42.00E
87 F4 **Āzezo** Ethiopia 12.30N 37.25E
32 B1 **Azghān** Iran 38.30N 46.59E
32 H3 **Azghand** Iran 35.20N 58.50E
45 T9 **Azgir** Kazakhstan U.S.S.R. 47.51N 47.54E
41 O7 **Azhargalakh** U.S.S.R. 67.22N 130.30E
43 M1 **Azhbulat,Oz** Kazakhstan U.S.S.R. 53.19N 77.27E
28 B5 **Azhikal** Kerala India 11.59N 75.21E
42 D6 **Azhu-Tayga,Gora** *mt* U.S.S.R. 51.34N 88.50E
88 K6 **Azilal** Morocco 31.59N 6.35W
93 A2 **Azile** Zaïre 3.32N 29.53E
72 K9 **Azille** France 43.17N 2.39E
29 L5 **Azimganj** W Bengal India 24.14N 88.14E
Aẓimiya *see* **Aẓamīyah, Al**
93 A2 **Azimogu** Zaïre 3.24N 29.18E
69 C3 **Azincourt** France 50.28N 2.07E
91 B4 **Azingo, L** Gabon 0.31S 10.02E
76 B10 **Azinhaga** Portugal 39.20N 8.32W
76 E14 **Azinhal** Portugal 37.17N 7.28W
76 C12 **Azinheira dos Barros** Portugal 38.04N 8.25W
104 P1 **Aziscoos L** Maine
31 B4 **Azizabad** Afghanistan 33.20N 62.20E
32 H6 **'Azīzābād** Kermān Iran 28.52N 58.45E
34 P4 **Azīzābād** Lorestān Iran 34.10N 47.58E
37 J6 **Azizbekov** Armenia U.S.S.R. 39.44N 45.29E
85 B3 **'Azīziah, Al** Libya 32.30N 13.01E
86 F4 **'Azîzîya,El** Egypt 30.30N 31.17E
34 N6 **'Azīzīyah,Al** Iraq 32.55N 45.03E
33 A8 **'Azīzīyah,Al** Saudi Arabia 26.11N 50.12E
35 F1 **Azīzīyat** Syria 33.12N 35.44E
Aziziye *see* **Pınarbaşı** Kayseri
Azkī *see* **Izkī**
33 B3 **Azlam, Wādī** *watercourse* Saudi Arabia
88 L9 **Azlef** *reg* Mali
35 E2 **'Azmon, Har** *mt* Israel 32.50N 35.17E
66 O3 **Azmoos** Switzerland 47.05N 9.29E
Azna *see* **Istgāh-e Eznā**
77 D6 **Aznalcazar** Spain 37.18N 6.15W
77 D5 **Aznalcóllar** Spain 37.31N 6.16W
119 B9 **Azogues** Ecuador 2.46S 78.56W
47 F3 **Azopol'ye** U.S.S.R. 65.15N 45.18E
96 S4 **Azores** *islds* Atlantic Oc 38.30N 28.00W

96 H5 **Azores-Cape St.Vincent Ridge** Atlantic Oc
37 F5 **Azort** Turkey 40.32N 41.35E
90 K6 **Azoum** *R* Chad
88 K6 **Azourki, Jbel** *mt* Morocco 31.45N 6.16W
45 L9 **Azov** U.S.S.R. 47.06N 39.26E
47 L8 **Azovo** U.S.S.R. 54.42N 73.00E
Azov,Sea of *see* **Azovskoye More**
45 L9 **Azovskiy Kanal** U.S.S.R.
44 D9 **Azovskoye** Ukraine U.S.S.R. 45.35N 34.34E
46 K6 **Azovskoye More** *sea* U.S.S.R.
47 J4 **Azovy** U.S.S.R. 64.56N 65.00E
Azozo *see* **Azezo**
75 F1 **Azpeitia** Spain 43.11N 2.15W
Azqand *see* **Azghand**
35 F9 **'Azra** Jordan 31.09N 35.41E
34 D7 **Azraq,El** Jordan 31.50N 36.47E
34 D7 **Azraq Shīshan** Jordan 31.49N 36.48E
35 B7 **'Azriqam** Israel 31.44N 34.42E
88 L5 **Azrou** Morocco 33.27N 5.14W
31 E3 **Azrow** Afghanistan 34.11N 69.39E
111 L9 **Aztec** Arizona 32.48N 113.26W
109 C5 **Aztec** New Mexico 36.49N 107.59W
109 B5 **Aztec Ruins Nat.Mon** New Mexico 36.52N 108.01W
116 J5 **Azua** Dominican Republic 18.29N 70.44W
77 E4 **Azuaga** Spain 38.16N 5.40W
75 J5 **Azuara** Spain 41.15N 0.53W
119 B9 **Azuay** *prov* Ecuador
120 D11 **Azucar** *R* Chile
121 F6 **Azucena** Argentina 37.32S 59.20W
75 F2 **Azuelo** Spain 42.36N 2.20W
77 K3 **Azuer** *R* Spain
115 O6 **Azuero,Pen.de** Panama
121 B3 **Azufre,Paso del** *pass* Arg/Chile 31.17S 70.34W
121 F6 **Azul** Argentina 36.46S 59.50W
121 B5 **Azul** *pk* Chile 35.35S 70.51W
115 P9 **Azul** *R* Mex/Guatemala
120 E12 **Azul,Cerro** *pk* Catamarca Arg 26.55S 67.31W
119 A6 **Azul,Cerro** *pk* Galápagos Is 0.54S 91.23W
121 B8 **Azul,Cerro** *pk* Neuquén Arg 40.15S 71.13W
120 B2 **Azul,Cerro** *pk* Peru 6.53S 75.23W
120 B3 **Azul, Cord** *mts* Peru
118 C4 **Azul,Sa** *mts* Mato Grosso Brazil
117 B5 **Azul,Sa** *mts* Pará Brazil
20 G5 **Azuma** Chiba Japan
90 C9 **Azumini** Nigeria 4.54N 7.31E
72 B8 **Azur** France 43.48N 1.17W
120 F9 **Azurduy** Bolivia 20.00S 64.29W
76 K9 **Azutan, Embalse de** *res* Spain 39.45N 5.00W
72 K1 **Azy** France 47.10N 2.41E
71 C3 **Azy-le-Vif** France 46.47N 3.13E
88 R3 **Azzaba** Algeria 36.43N 7.05E
33 G9 **'Azzān** S Yemen 14.19N 47.28E
79 N3 **Azzano Décimo** Italy 45.53N 12.43E
66 M8 **Azzate** Italy 45.46N 8.47E
87 J3 **Az Zaydiyah** Yemen 15.24N 43.02E
85 B4 **Az Zimmit** Libya 31.43N 13.05E
35 D5 **Azzun** Jordan 32.10N 35.03E

89 H8 **Ba** *R* Ghana/Ivory Coast
19 C9 **Baa** Indonesia 10.44S 123.06E
9 A13 **Baaba** *isld* New Caledonia Pacific Ocean 20.01S 163.58E
34 C5 **Ba'abda** Lebanon 33.50N 35.31E
65 B7 **Baad** Austria 47.19N 10.07E
19 B9 **Baäh** Indonesia 10.28S 121.59E
18 M5 **Baai** *R* Borneo Indon
61 E3 **Baaigem** Belgium 50.56N 3.43E
33 G5 **Ba'aija** Saudi Arabia 23.06N 46.31E
33 D3 **Ba'ā'ith,Al** Saudi Arabia 26.02N 41.48E
60 N11 **Baak** Netherlands 52.04N 6.14E
61 J3 **Baal** Belgium 50.59N 4.45E
64 A1 **Baal** W Germany 51.02N 6.17E
34 D4 **Ba'albek** Lebanon 34.00N 36.12E
35 E6 **Ba'al Hazor** *mt* Jordan 31.59N 35.17E
69 J5 **Baâlon** France 49.29N 5.15E
60 H10 **Baambrugge** Netherlands 52.15N 4.59E
76 D2 **Baamonde** Spain 43.10N 7.45W
12 J4 **Baan Baa** New S Wales 30.28S 149.58E
95 N2 **Baanbreker** S Africa 26.31S 29.23E
86 E8 **Baaqalûn, El** Egypt 28.42N 30.44E
66 L3 **Baar** Switzerland 47.12N 8.32E
60 L7 **Baard** Netherlands 53.08N 5.40E
61 G3 **Baardegem** Belgium 50.57N 4.09E
95 C10 **Baardskeerdersbos** S Africa 34.35S 19.33E
60 C3 **Baarland** Netherlands 51.24N 3.54E
61 K1 **Baarle-Hertog** *exclave* Belgium 51.26N 4.56E
60 H14 **Baarle Nassau** Netherlands 51.26N 4.55E
60 N14 **Baarlo** Limburg Netherlands 51.20N 6.07E
60 K11 **Baarn** Netherlands 52.13N 5.16E
33 A5 **Báâs,Râs** *C* Egypt 23.54N 35.48E
61 G2 **Baasrode** Belgium 51.02N 4.10E
22 E4 **Baatsagaan** Mongolia 45.34N 99.26E
90 E9 **Bab** Cameroon 4.26N 10.55E
119 B8 **Baba** Ecuador 1.50S 79.40W
20 D10 **Baba** Japan 31.13N 130.47E
31 A10 **Bāba** *isld* Pakistan 24.49N 66.58E
82 G9 **Baba** *mts* Yugoslavia
36 B3 **Baba Burun** *C* Çanakkale Turkey 39.28N 26.05E
37 F2 **Baba Burun** *C* İstanbul Turkey 40.59N 28.33E
36 E1 **Baba Burun** *C* Zonguldak Turkey 41.20N 31.22E
117 E8 **Babaçulândia** Brazil 7.10S 47.44W
82 M6 **Babadag** Romania 44.53N 28.47E
36 D5 **Babadağ** Turkey 37.49N 28.52E
44 J6 **Babadag** *mt* Azerbaydzhan U.S.S.R. 41.02N 48.07E
36 D6 **Baba Dağ** *mt* Turkey 36.32N 29.10E
36 F1 **Baba Dağları** *mts* Turkey
43 E7 **Babadurmaz** Turkmeniya U.S.S.R. 37.39N 59.09E
90 G9 **Babadza** Cent Afr Rep 4.18N 15.36E
36 C1 **Babaeski** Turkey 41.26N 27.06E
30 E5 **Babaganj** Uttar Prad India 27.57N 81.34E
34 M3 **Baba Gurgur** Iraq 35.32N 44.23E
119 B8 **Babahoyo** Ecuador 1.53S 79.31W
119 B8 **Babahoyo, R** Ecuador
29 E6 **Babai** Madhya Prad India 22.44N 77.59E
30 C6 **Babai** Uttar Prad India 26.10N 79.29E
22 F6 **Babai Gaxun** Nei Monggol Zizhiqu China 40.30N 104.46E
30 E4 **Babai Khola** *R* Nepal
32 B1 **Bābā Jān** Āzarbāījān-e Khāvarī Iran 38.26N 47.20E
34 O4 **Bābā Jān** Kermānshāh Iran 34.24N 46.59E
19 M8 **Babak** Philippines 7.07N 125.42E
32 D5 **Bābā Kalū** Iran 30.06N 50.50E
Baba Kelu *see* **Bābā Kalū**
32 E4 **Bābā Khal'at** Iran 33.41N 53.36E
14 C9 **Babakin** W Australia 32.11S 117.58E
31 D3 **Baba,Koh-i** *mts* Afghanistan
91 J3 **Babali** *tribe* Zaïre
87 J4 **Bab al Mandab** *str* Red Sea
33 E10 **Bāb al Mandab, C** S Yemen 12.41N 43.29E
95 P4 **Babanango** S Africa 28.23S 31.05E
95 N4 **Babangiboni** *mt* S Africa 28.35S 28.59E
46 H5 **Babanka** Ukraine U.S.S.R. 48.41N 30.30E
Babao *see* **Qilian**
23 D7 **Babao** Yunnan China 23.45N 105.26E
19 F7 **Babar** *isld* Indonesia
19 F8 **Babar,Kep** *islds* Indonesia
15 M6 **Babase I** Bismarck Arch 4.00S 153.40E
18 K9 **Babat** Java Indonesia 7.08S 112.08E
43 J7 **Babatag,Khrebet** *mts* Tadzhikistan U.S.S.R.
93 G10 **Babati** Tanzania 4.12S 35.45E
46 K1 **Babayevo** U.S.S.R. 59.24N 35.50E
35 G7 **Babayir et Tiwal** *anc site* Jordan 31.43N 35.55E
44 H4 **Babayurt** U.S.S.R. 43.38N 46.48E
110 M1 **Babb** Montana 48.52N 113.26W
56 E6 **Babbacombe B** Devon England
101 D1 **Babbage** *R* Yukon Terr
14 A6 **Babbage I** W Australia 24.50S 113.43E
60 N12 **Babberik** Netherlands 51.54N 6.07E
108 T2 **Babbitt** Minnesota 47.40N 91.51W
106 D5 **Babcock** Wisconsin 44.18N 90.06W
B'abda *see* **Ba'abda**
85 H8 **Babein, Gebel** *mt* Egypt 22.55N 25.00E
34 E2 **Bāb,El** Syria 36.24N 37.32E
35 F2 **Bab el Hawa** Syria 32.53N 35.42E
12 J7 **Babel I** Tasmania 39.57S 148.20E
63 P5 **Bäbelin** E Germany 53.56N 11.41E
85 K4 **Bab el Qa'ûd** Egypt 30.36N 28.03E
63 S8 **Babelsberg** E Germany 5.224 13.05E
19 N2 **Babelthuap I** Palau Is Pacific Oc
92 D6 **Babemba** *tribe* Zaïre
64 F4 **Babenhausen** Hessen W Germany 49.58N 8.57E
64 J7 **Babenhausen** Schwaben, Bayern W Germany 48.09N 10.15E
34 D3 **Babenna** Syria 35.36N 36.02E
92 B1 **Babenza** Zaïre 1.41N 25.40E
30 D7 **Baberu** Uttar Prad India 25.32N 80.42E
87 A10 **Babeyru** Zaïre 1.51N 27.30E
18 B4 **Babi** *isld* Indonesia
62 M6 **Babia Góra** *mt* Czech/Poland 49.34N 19.30E
23 B6 **Babian Jiang** *R* Yunnan China
18 D9 **Babi Besar** *isld* Malaysia
115 E3 **Babícora** Mexico 29.29N 108.03W
115 F3 **Babícora, L. de** Mexico
86 E4 **Bâbil** Egypt 30.41N 31.00E
76 J7 **Babilafuente** Spain 40.58N 5.25W
90 D6 **Babinda** Nigeria 10.36N 8.29E
13 H3 **Babinda** Queensland 17.10S 145.50E
101 K8 **Babine** Br Col 55.19N 126.37W
101 K8 **Babine** *R* Br Col
101 L8 **Babine L** Br Col
101 K8 **Babine Ra** Br Col
45 P1 **Babino** U.S.S.R. 56.14N 43.37E
15 B5 **Babo** Irian Jaya 2.33S 133.25E
62 K9 **Babócsa** Hungary 46.02N 17.20E
32 E2 **Bābol** Iran 36.32N 52.42E
32 E2 **Bābol Sar** Iran 36.41N 52.39E
120 E2 **Babonã, R** Brazil
87 A9 **Babonde** Zaïre 2.19N 27.35E
111 N10 **Baboquivari Pk** *mt* Arizona 31.47N 111.36W
88 Q3 **Babor,Djebel** *mt* Algeria 36.30N 5.24E
90 G9 **Baboua** Cent Afr Rep 5.49N 14.51E
14 E4 **Babrongan Tower** *mt* W Australia 18.35S 123.32E
105 F10 **Babson Park** Florida 27.50N 81.32W
64 G5 **Babstadt** W Germany 49.15N 9.05E
40 F7 **Babstovo** U.S.S.R. 48.10N 132.21E
74 D9 **Bab Taza** Morocco 35.04N 5.09W
23 D5 **Babu** Guizhou China 26.52N 105.48E
30 A4 **Babugarh** Uttar Prad India 28.43N 77.51E
29 A4 **Babuhri** Rajasthan India 26.43N 69.38E
Babul *see* **Bābol**
31 B3 **Babulai** Afghanistan 35.20N 62.55E
82 G9 **Babuna** *mts* Yugoslavia
90 D5 **Babura** Nigeria 12.48N 9.01E
31 H3 **Babusar Pass** Kashmir 35.10N 75.04E
42 H6 **Babushkin** Irkutsk U.S.S.R. 51.44N 105.55E
47 E6 **Babushkina, Imeni** U.S.S.R. 59.44N 43.27E
39 E5 **Babushkina Mys** *C* U.S.S.R. 59.05N 154.08E
39 E5 **Babushkina Zaliv** *B* U.S.S.R.
19 J7 **Babuyan** Philippines 9.59N 118.54E
19 K2 **Babuyan** *isld* Philippines 19.30N 121.57E
19 K2 **Babuyan Chan** Philippines
19 K2 **Babuyan Is** Philippines
92 D4 **Babuye** *tribe* Zaïre
103 H5 **Babylon** Long I, N Y 40.42N 73.20W
34 M6 **Babylon** *anc site* Iraq 32.33N 44.25E
45 G2 **Babynino** U.S.S.R. 54.25N 35.45E
115 E4 **Baca** Mexico 26.49N 108.28W
119 E9 **Bacaba** *R* Brazil
115 E4 **Bacabachi** Mexico 26.54N 109.25W
117 F7 **Bacabal** Maranhão Brazil 4.15S 44.45W
117 B7 **Bacabal** Pará Brazil 5.10S 56.51W
117 C6 **Bacajá, R** Brazil
115 P8 **Bacalar** Mexico 18.41N 88.28W
115 Q8 **Bacalar Chico,Boca** *channel* Mexico/Belize 18.12N 87.51W
19 E4 **Bacan** *isld* Moluccas Indon
72 F10 **Bacanère** *mt* France 42.52N 0.36E
115 E3 **Bacanora** Mexico 28.58N 109.22W
77 M6 **Bacares** Spain 37.16N 2.26W
19 K2 **Bacarra** Luzon Philippines 18.24N 120.37E
82 K4 **Bacău** Romania 46.33N 26.58E
69 M7 **Baccarat** France 48.27N 6.45E
98 G10 **Baccaro Pt** Nova Scotia 43.28N 65.28W
79 L4 **Bacchiglione** *R* Italy
12 G7 **Bacchus Marsh** Victoria 37.41S 144.30E
79 D2 **Baceno** Italy 46.16N 8.19E
82 L4 **Băceşti** Romania 46.50N 27.14E
65 B7 **Bach** Austria 47.17N 10.25E
106 L6 **Bach** Michigan 43.42N 83.22W
64 N5 **Bach** W Germany 49.02N 12.20E
119 E3 **Bachaquero** Venezuela 9.57N 71.09W
64 D3 **Bacharach** W Germany 50.04N 7.46E
Bachau *see* **Bhachau**
25 J2 **Ba Che** *R* Vietnam
97 M2 **Bache Pen** N W Terr
30 D7 **Bachhon** Madhya Prad India 25.00N 80.06E
30 B4 **Bachhraon** Uttar Prad India 28.54N 78.14E
115 F3 **Bachiniva** Mexico 28.52N 107.20W
25 J2 **Bach long Vi** *isld* Vietnam 20.09N 107.58E
87 E6 **Bacho** Ethiopia 8.11N 35.37E
18 D2 **Bacho** Thailand 6.37N 101.39E
64 L1 **Bachra** E Germany 51.12N 11.23E
66 M2 **Bachtel** *mt* Switzerland 47.18N 8.54E
61 E2 **Bachte-Maria-Leerne** Belgium 51.00N 3.35E
24 C6 **Bachu** Xinjiang Uygur Zizhiqu China 39.44N 78.34E
24 C6 **Bachu Liuchang** Xinjiang Uygur Zizhiqu China 39.58N 79.30E
24 C6 **Bachu Yichang** Xinjiang Uygur Zizhiqu China 40.00N 79.06E
58 D2 **Back** Lewis, W Isles Scotland 58.17N 6.18W
101 Z2 **Back** *R* N W Terr
13 G3 **Back** *R* Queensland
94 E6 **Back** *watercourse* Namibia
82 E5 **Backa** *reg* Yugoslavia
52 H9 **Bäckaby** Sweden 57.15N 14.55E
58 T11 **Backaland** Orkney Scotland 59.09N 2.46W
25 H1 **Bac Kan** Vietnam 22.09N 105.50E
82 E5 **Bačka Palanka** Yugoslavia 45.14N 19.24E
82 F5 **Bačka Petrovo Selo** Yugoslavia 45.41N 20.04E
82 F5 **Bačka Topola** Yugoslavia 45.49N 19.39E
28 A8 **Back Bay** Bombay India
104 J10 **Back Bay** Virginia 36.37N 76.04W
101 J4 **Backbone Ranges** N W Terr
52 G8 **Bäckefors** Sweden 58.49N 12.08E
52 H7 **Bäckhammar** Sweden 59.09N 14.13E
101 T4 **Back L** N W Terr
64 G6 **Backnang** W Germany 48.57N 9.26E
103 B8 **Back R** Maryland
104 K2 **Back River** New York 44.03N 75.45W
12 E6 **Backstairs Pass** S Australia
51 E6 **Bäckstrand** Sweden 65.07N 16.25E
108 Q3 **Backus** Minnesota 46.50N 94.30W
58 K5 **Backwater Res** Tayside Scotland 56.44N 3.12W
Bac Lieu *see* **Vinh Loi**
25 J2 **Bac Ninh** Vietnam 21.10N 106.04E
25 J2 **Bac Ninh** Vietnam 21.16N 106.14E
19 K3 **Bacnotan** Luzon Philippines 16.45N 120.21E
115 D2 **Bacoachi** Mexico 30.36N 110.00W
116 P5 **Bacolet** Grenada, W I 12.02N 61.41W
80 K7 **Bacoli** Italy 40.47N 14.05E
19 L6 **Bacolod** Philippines 10.38N 122.58E
19 K5 **Baco, Mt** Philippines 12.49N 121.11E
105 C6 **Baconton** Georgia 31.23N 84.10W
19 H2 **Bacoor** Luzon Philippines 14.27N 120.58E
25 H1 **Bac Quang** Vietnam 22.30N 104.52E
70 N2 **Bacqueville-en-Caux** France 49.47N 1.00E
62 L9 **Bácsalmás** Hungary 46.07N 19.20E
82 E4 **Bács-Kiskun** *co* Hungary
56 O2 **Bacton** Norfolk England 52.52N 1.28E
115 F5 **Bacubirito** Mexico 25.50N 107.52W
19 N8 **Baculin B** Mindanao Philippines 7.26N 126.31E
19 N7 **Baculin Point** Mindanao Philippines 8.32N 126.21E
57 J5 **Bacup** Lancs England 53.43N 2.12W
117 D6 **Bacuri,I.do** Brazil
32 E4 **Bād** Iran 33.35N 52.02E
106 K6 **Bad** *R* Michigan
108 K5 **Bad** *R* S Dakota
Bada *see* **Xilin**
42 H6 **Bada** Chita U.S.S.R. 51.25N 109.58E
25 E7 **Bada** *isld* Burma
29 J6 **Bada Barabil** Orissa India 22.09N 85.20E
64 N6 **Bad Abbach** W Germany 48.56N 12.04E
28 B5 **Badagara** Kerala India 11.36N 75.34E
90 A8 **Badagri** Nigeria 6.25N 2.58E
30 J8 **Badahpur** Bihar India 24.54N 85.07E
33 C3 **Badā'i, Al** Saudi Arabia 26.30N 38.04E
64 N8 **Bad Aibling** W Germany 47.51N 12.01E
93 J1 **Badaichini** *mt* Ethiopia 4.37N 37.05E
22 E6 **Badain Jaran Shamo** *sand dunes* Nei Monggol Zizhiqu China
119 H9 **Badajós** Amazonas Brazil 3.24S 62.38W
117 E6 **Badajós** Pará Brazil 2.30S 47.46W
119 H9 **Badajós, L** Brazil 3.16S 62.43W
77 C3 **Badajoz** Spain 38.53N 6.58W
74 C6 **Badajoz** *prov* Spain
31 F2 **Badakhshan** *prov* Afghanistan
34 C10 **Bad,Al** Saudi Arabia 28.29N 35.02E
75 P5 **Badalona** Spain 41.27N 2.15E
79 C7 **Badalucco** Italy 43.54N 7.50E
29 J7 **Badamgarh** Orissa India 21.50N 85.22E
28 B3 **Badami** Karnataka India 15.58N 75.45E
31 C4 **Badam Mazar** Afghanistan 33.00N 64.38E
29 K6 **Badampahar** Orissa India 22.04N 86.06E
34 J7 **Badanah** Saudi Arabia 31.00N 41.05E
42 F4 **Badan,Khrebet** *mts* U.S.S.R.
21 D6 **Badaohe** Jilin China 43.18N 126.32E
Badaojiang *see* **Hunjiang**
75 E3 **Badarán** Spain 42.21N 2.49W
85 L6 **Badari,El** Egypt 27.04N 31.25E
42 G3 **Badarma** U.S.S.R. 57.45N 102.32E
18 L3 **Badas** Brunei, Borneo S E Asia 4.36N 114.29E
18 G5 **Badas,Kep** *islds* Indonesia 0.37N 107.05E
30 D7 **Badausa** Uttar Prad India 25.14N 80.38E
65 J6 **Bad Aussee** Austria 47.37N 13.47E
106 M6 **Bad Axe** Michigan 43.49N 82.59W
66 G1 **Bad Bellingen** W Germany 47.44N 7.34E
63 G7 **Badbergen** W Germany 52.38N 7.59E
64 D5 **Bad Bergzabern** W Germany 49.06N 8.00E
64 L2 **Bad Berka** E Germany 50.53N 11.16E
64 E1 **Bad Berleburg** W Germany 51.03N 8.24E
64 M3 **Bad Berneck** W Germany 50.03N 11.40E
64 C3 **Bad Bertrich** W Germany 50.05N 7.03E
64 M1 **Bad Bibra** Halle E Germany 51.13N 11.35E
64 L2 **Bad Blankenburg** E Germany 50.41N 11.15E
64 J3 **Bad Bocklet** W Germany 50.16N 10.05E
63 L5 **Bad Bramstedt** W Germany 53.56N 9.53E
64 C2 **Bad Breisig** W Germany 50.30N 7.17E
64 H3 **Bad Brückenau** W Germany 50.18N 9.47E
64 H7 **Bad Buchau** W Germany 48.05N 9.39E
58 F2 **Badcall** Highland Scotland 58.19N 5.09W
64 G6 **Bad Cannstatt** W Germany 48.48N 9.14E
87 G7 **Badda** *mt* Ethiopia 7.55N 39.23E
58 H2 **Baddanloch, L** Highland Scotland 58.16N 4.06W
98 M7 **Baddeck** C Breton I, Nova Scotia 46.06N 60.45W
63 M8 **Baddeckenstedt** W Germany 52.05N 10.14E
26 R9 **Baddegama** Sri Lanka 6.10N 80.04E
51 J2 **Badderen** Norway 69.50N 22.00E
63 P4 **Bad Doberan** E Germany 54.06N 11.55E
31 C6 **Baddo R** Pakistan
63 K9 **Bad Driburg** W Germany 51.43N 9.01E
63 R9 **Bad Düben** E Germany 51.36N 12.35E
64 E5 **Bad Dürkheim** W Germany 49.28N 8.12E
64 N1 **Bad Dürrenberg** E Germany 51.18N 12.04E
64 F7 **Bad Dürrheim** W Germany 48.01N 8.32E
72 G5 **Badefols d'Ans** France 45.14N 1.12E
90 C7 **Badeggi** Nigeria 9.01N 6.08E
64 N3 **Bad Elster** E Germany 50.16N 12.14E
Bademli *see* **Aladağ**
64 D3 **Bad Ems** W Germany 50.20N 7.43E
65 O5 **Baden** Austria 48.01N 16.14E
87 F2 **Baden** Ethiopia 16.55N 37.59E
70 E6 **Baden** France 47.38N 2.55W
100 Q6 **Baden** Manitoba 52.47N 101.12W
104 E6 **Baden** Pennsylvania 40.39N 80.15W
66 K2 **Baden** Switzerland 47.28N 8.19E
75 H5 **Bádenas** Spain 41.05N 1.08W
64 E6 **Baden Baden** W Germany 48.45N 8.15E
64 E6 **Baden-Baden West** W Germany 48.47N 8.12E
58 H5 **Badenoch** *dist* Highland Scotland
64 D8 **Badenweiler** W Germany 47.48N 7.40E
62 E6 **Baden-Württemberg** *land* W Germany
79 P4 **Baderna** Yugoslavia 45.13N 13.45E
81 B2 **Badesi** Sardinia 40.58N 8.53E
66 D2 **Badevel** France 47.30N 6.56E
64 N8 **Bad Feilnbach** W Germany 47.45N 12.01E
65 O6 **Bad Fischau** Austria 47.50N 16.11E
63 O10 **Bad Frankenhausen** E Germany 51.22N 11.07E
63 U7 **Bad Freienwalde (Oder)** E Germany 52.46N 14.01E
64 G5 **Bad Friedrichshall** W Germany 49.14N 9.13E
31 C3 **Badgah** Afghanistan 34.34N 65.30E
63 M9 **Bad Gandersheim** W Germany 51.53N 10.02E
30 A3 **Badgaon** Uttar Prad India 29.42N 77.32E
65 H7 **Badgastein** Austria 47.07N 13.09E
111 E5 **Badger** California 36.37N 119.00W
100 F1 **Badger** Manitoba 49.13N 95.58W
108 O1 **Badger** Minnesota 48.49N 96.00W
98 Q5 **Badger** Newfoundland 49.00N 56.04W
110 Q5 **Badger Basin** Wyoming 44.58N 109.04W
31 B3 **Badghis** *prov* Afghanistan
65 N8 **Bad Gleichenberg** Austria 46.53N 15.55E
Badgley,C *see* **Sagre,Pta.de**
64 C2 **Bad Godesberg** W Germany 50.41N 7.09E
62 H5 **Bad Gottleuba** E Germany 50.52N 13.55E
69 P7 **Bad Griesbach** W Germany 48.26N 8.14E
63 M9 **Bad Grund** W Germany 51.49N 10.14E
65 K5 **Bad-Hall** Austria 48.03N 14.13E
35 F9 **Badhan** Jordan 31.13N 35.39E
63 N9 **Bad Harzburg** W Germany 51.53N 10.33E
64 L8 **Bad Heilbrunn** W Germany 47.45N 11.27E
64 E6 **Bad Herrenalb** W Germany 48.48N 8.26E
64 H2 **Bad Hersfeld** W Germany 50.53N 9.43E
60 H10 **Badhoevedorp** Netherlands 52.21N 4.46E
65 H7 **Bad Hofgastein** Austria 47.11N 13.07E
64 F3 **Bad Homburg** W Germany 50.13N 8.37E
64 C2 **Bad Honnef** W Germany 50.38N 7.14E
64 C2 **Bad Hönningen** W Germany 50.31N 7.19E
79 L1 **Badia** Italy 46.37N 11.55E
34 J3 **Badi Al** Iraq 35.57N 41.32E
33 G5 **Badī', Al** Saudi Arabia 22.02N 46.35E
79 K4 **Badia Polésine** Italy 45.06N 11.30E
79 M7 **Badia Tedalda** Italy 43.42N 12.11E
79 L1 **Badia,Val** *V* Italy
63 H8 **Bad Iburg** W Germany 52.09N 8.03E
15 E7 **Badie** Irian Jaya 6.56S 139.33E
34 E6 **Badiet esh Sham** *des* Jordan/Iraq
87 D8 **Badigeru Swamp** Sudan
66 P6 **Badile,Piz** *mt* Switzerland 46.18N 9.34E
119 D4 **Badillo** Colombia 7.59N 73.50W
15 J6 **Badilu** Papua New Guinea 4.51S 146.14E
105 G2 **Badin** N Carolina 35.24N 80.08W
31 E8 **Badin** Pakistan 24.38N 68.53E
31 E8 **Badin** *dist* Pakistan
91 F6 **Badinga** *tribe* Zaïre
105 G2 **Badin L** N Carolina 35.28N 80.06W
115 F5 **Badiraguato** Mexico 25.21N 107.31W
65 J6 **Bad Ischl** Austria 47.43N 13.38E
33 N5 **Badīyah** *dist* Oman
34 O8 **Bādiyah al Janūbīyah,Al** *des* Iraq
19 B8 **Badjawa** Indonesia 8.46S 120.59E
31 E3 **Badkak Pass** Afghanistan 35.38N 68.11E
64 J3 **Bad Kissingen** W Germany 50.12N 10.05E
63 O5 **Bad Kleinen** E Germany 53.47N 11.28E
65 J8 **Bad Klein Kirshheim** Austria 46.49N 13.49E
64 M2 **Bad Klosterlausnitz** E Germany 50.55N 11.52E
64 G4 **Bad König** W Germany 49.44N 9.01E
64 M1 **Bad Kösen** E Germany 51.08N 11.43E
64 N2 **Bad Köstritz** E Germany 50.55N 12.00E
64 D4 **Bad Kreuznach** W Germany 49.51N 7.52E
64 D8 **Bad Krozingen** W Germany 47.55N 7.42E
108 G3 **Bad Lands** *reg* N Dakota
108 H6 **Badlands Nat.Mon** S Dakota
64 K1 **Bad Langensalza** E Germany 51.07N 10.40E
30 F7 **Badlapur** Uttar Prad India 25.54N 82.27E
63 P10 **Bad Lauchstädt** E Germany 51.24N 11.53E
64 O1 **Bad Lausik** E Germany 51.09N 12.39E
63 M9 **Bad Lauterberg im Harz** W Germany 51.38N 10.28E
30 A4 **Badli** Delhi India 28.47N 77.06E
64 K2 **Bad Liebenstein** E Germany 50.46N 10.50E
64 F6 **Bad Liebenzell** W Germany 48.46N 8.44E
63 J9 **Bad Lippspringe** W Germany 51.47N 8.49E
69 O2 **Bad Marienberg** W Germany 50.39N 7.57E
63 J9 **Bad Meinberg** W Germany 51.52N 8.59E
64 H5 **Bad Mergentheim** W Germany 49.29N 9.46E
Bad Mingolsheim *see* **Bad Schönborn**
63 K8 **Bad Münder am Deister** W Germany 52.12N 9.28E
64 D4 **Bad Münster Ebernburg** W Germany 49.49N 7.51E
69 M2 **Bad Münstereifel** W Germany 50.34N 6.46E
64 F3 **Bad Nauheim** W Germany 50.21N 8.44E
29 D6 **Badnawar** Madhya Prad India 23.01N 75.16E
63 K8 **Bad Nenndorf** W Germany 52.20N 9.23E
29 E7 **Badnera** Maharashtra India 20.50N 77.47E
64 C2 **Bad Neuenahr-Ahrweiler** W Germany 50.32N 7.06E
64 J3 **Bad Neustadt an der Saale** Suhl E Germany 50.20N 10.12E
29 D5 **Badnor** Rajasthan India 25.47N 74.18E
Bado *R* *see* **Baddo R**
65 B6 **Bad Oberdorf** W Germany 47.30N 10.25E
63 J8 **Bad Oeynhausen** W Germany 52.12N 8.48E
89 H3 **Bado,L** Mali 16.08N 3.04W
81 N6 **Badolato** Italy 38.34N 16.32E
77 G6 **Badolatosa** Spain 37.19N 4.40W
63 M5 **Bad Oldesloe** W Germany 53.49N 10.22E
89 C5 **Badon** Senegal 12.58N 12.22W
25 J4 **Ba Don** Vietnam 17.45N 106.25E
91 B5 **Badondo** *tribe* Congo
23 E3 **Badong** Hubei China 31.03N 110.24E
25 J8 **Ba Dong** Vietnam 9.45N 106.40E
69 M6 **Badonviller** France 48.30N 6.54E
64 G3 **Bad Orb** W Germany 50.13N 9.21E
30 E5 **Bado Sarai** Uttar Prad India 27.01N 81.27E
22 L8 **Badou** Shandong China 36.26N 117.55E
89 E6 **Badougou** Mali 11.01N 8.07W
89 D5 **Badoumbé** Mali 13.42N 10.15W
64 J8 **Bad Oy** W Germany 47.39N 10.28E
64 E7 **Bad Peterstal** W Germany 48.25N 8.13E
95 O1 **Badplaas** S Africa 25.58S 30.34E
29 K2 **Badpur** W Bengal India 22.59N 86.43E
63 K9 **Bad Pyrmont** W Germany 51.59N 9.16E
33 E8 **Badr** Saudi Arabia 17.52N 43.43E
Badra *see* **Badrah**
66 O3 **Bad Ragaz** Switzerland 47.01N 9.30E
34 N5 **Badrah** Iraq 33.06N 45.58E
35 G5 **Badran** Jordan 32.05N 35.54E
64 G5 **Bad Rappenau** W Germany 49.13N 9.07E
63 K8 **Bad Rehberg** W Germany 52.28N 9.14E
64 O8 **Bad Reichenhall** W Germany 47.43N 12.53E
33 C5 **Badr Ḥunayn** Saudi Arabia 23.43N 38.50E
30 C2 **Badrinath** Uttar Prad India 30.44N 79.29E
30 C2 **Badrinath** *mt* Uttar Prad India 30.44N 79.16E
69 P7 **Bad Rippoldsau** W Germany 48.26N 8.20E
86 F6 **Badrshein,El** Egypt 29.51N 31.14E
63 N9 **Bad Sachsa** W Germany 51.36N 10.33E
65 K8 **Bad St.Leonhard** Austria 46.48N 14.03E
63 M8 **Bad Salzdetfurth** W Germany 52.03N 10.00E
63 P8 **Bad Salzelmen** E Germany 52.00N 11.43E
64 H2 **Bad Salzschlirf** W Germany 50.38N 9.30E
63 J8 **Bad Salzuflen** W Germany 52.06N 8.45E
64 J2 **Bad Salzungen** E Germany 50.49N 10.15E
63 H9 **Bad Sassendorf** W Germany 51.35N 8.09E
66 P1 **Bad Schachen** W Germany 47.33N 9.40E
63 R9 **Bad Schmiedeberg** E Germany 51.43N 12.45E
69 Q5 **Bad Schönborn** W Germany 49.13N 8.39E
64 H8 **Bad Schussenried** W Germany 48.00N 9.40E
64 E3 **Bad Schwalbach** W Germany 50.08N 8.05E
63 N5 **Bad Schwartau** W Germany 53.55N 10.41E
63 M5 **Bad Segeberg** W Germany 53.56N 10.17E
30 A2 **Badshahibagh** Uttar Prad India 30.18N 77.39E
30 A4 **Badshahpur** Haryana India 28.24N 77.03E
30 F7 **Badshahpur** Uttar Prad India 25.46N 82.49E
95 E9 **Badshoogte** S Africa 33.37S 21.48E
64 G3 **Bad Soden** W Germany 50.17N 9.22E
64 E3 **Bad Soden am Taunus** W Germany 50.08N 8.30E
64 H1 **Bad Sooden** W Germany 51.16N 9.58E
64 M3 **Bad Steben** W Germany 50.22N 11.39E
63 Q6 **Bad Stuer** E Germany 53.24N 12.20E
63 O9 **Bad Suderode** E Germany 51.45N 11.07E
64 M1 **Bad Sulza** E Germany 51.05N 11.37E
63 R4 **Bad Sülze** E Germany 54.07N 12.40E
64 F6 **Bad Teinach-Zavelstein** W Germany 48.42N 8.42E
64 K1 **Bad Tennstedt** E Germany 51.10N 10.52E
64 M8 **Bad Tölz** W Germany 47.45N 11.34E
90 F7 **Badudi** Cameroon 9.13N 13.20E
87 L7 **Baduen** Somalia 7.10N 47.30E
75 H5 **Badules** Spain 41.08N 1.16W
26 T8 **Badulla** Sri Lanka 6.59N 81.03E
26 R9 **Badureliya** Sri Lanka 6.31N 80.13E
Badus *mt* *see* **Six Madun**
34 K2 **Badush** Iraq 36.26N 42.57E
28 D3 **Badvel** Andhra Prad India 14.46N 79.02E
64 F3 **Bad Vilbel** W Germany 50.11N 8.45E
65 O6 **Bad Vöslau** Austria 47.58N 16.14E
86 H6 **Bad', Wâdi** *watercourse* Egypt
64 H8 **Bad Waldsee** W Germany 47.55N 9.45E
111 H5 **Badwater** *L* California 36.15N 116.50W
64 G1 **Bad Wildungen** W Germany 51.08N 9.09E
63 P7 **Bad Wilsnack** E Germany 52.58N 11.57E
64 G5 **Bad Wimpfen** W Germany 49.14N 9.08E
64 J4 **Bad Windsheim** W Germany 49.30N 10.27E
64 K7 **Bad Wörishofen** W Germany 48.00N 10.36E
64 H8 **Bad Wurzach** W Germany 47.54N 9.54E
47 G5 **Bad'ya** U.S.S.R. 60.27N 53.20E
39 D1 **Badyarikha** *R* U.S.S.R.
40 F6 **Badzhal** U.S.S.R. 51.00N 134.23E
40 F7 **Badzhal'skiy,Khrebet** *mts* U.S.S.R.
50 G3 **Bægisárjökull** *ice field* Iceland 65.36N 18.20W
50 C2 **Bæir** Iceland 66.06N 22.30W
53 C5 **Bække** Denmark 55.34N 9.08E
53 A4 **Bækmarksbro** Denmark 56.25N 8.20E
61 O4 **Baelen** Belgium 50.38N 5.58E
53 E3 **Bælum** Denmark 56.50N 10.08E
77 H5 **Baena** Spain 36.37N 4.20W
50 D4 **Bær** Iceland 65.17N 21.10W
12 K4 **Baerami** New S Wales 32.23S 150.30E
69 O6 **Baerenthal** France 48.59N 7.30E
Baerle-Duc *see* **Baarle-Hertog**
51 K2 **Bæskades** *mt* Norway 69.42N 23.40E
64 A2 **Baesweiler** W Germany 50.54N 6.12E
51 L2 **Bævasgiedde** Norway 69.12N 24.40E
60 M15 **Baexem** Netherlands 51.13N 5.53E
119 C8 **Baeza** Ecuador 0.30S 77.52W
77 K5 **Baeza** Spain 38.00N 3.28W
77 J4 **Baeza, Est** Spain 38.04N 3.35W
36 C5 **Bafa Gölü** *L* Turkey
90 E9 **Bafang** Cameroon 5.10N 10.05E
89 B5 **Bafatá** Guinea-Bissau 12.09N 14.38W
Bafatan *see* **Bepātān**
31 G3 **Baffa** Pakistan 34.30N 73.18E
97 M3 **Baffin B** Greenland/Canada
112 K8 **Baffin B** Texas
48 D6 **Baffin Basin** Arctic Oc
96 F2 **Baffin-Greenland Rise** Atlantic Oc
97 L3 **Baffin I** N W Terr
13 K6 **Baffle Creek** Queensland
89 E9 **Baffu Pt** Liberia 5.13N 9.15W
89 D7 **Bafi** *R* Sierra Leone
90 E9 **Bafia** Cameroon 4.49N 11.14E
89 K7 **Bafilo** Togo 9.23N 1.20E
89 E6 **Bafing** Guinea 11.15N 9.21W
89 D5 **Bafing** *R* Mali/Guinea
89 D5 **Bafing Makana** Mali 12.37N 10.32W
Baflioun *oil bore* *see* **Bafliūn**
34 E2 **Bafliūn** Syria 36.37N 37.03E
60 P6 **Baflo** Netherlands 53.22N 6.31E
89 D7 **Bafodia** Sierra Leone 9.43N 11.45W
89 D5 **Bafoulabé** Mali 13.49N 10.50W
90 E9 **Bafoussam** Cameroon 5.31N 10.25E
32 F5 **Bāfq** Iran 31.35N 55.21E
36 H1 **Bafra** Turkey 41.34N 35.56E
36 H1 **Bafra Burun** *C* Turkey 41.44N 35.57E
32 G6 **Bāft** Iran 29.12N 56.36E
91 D4 **Bafuru** *tribe* Congo
90 E8 **Bafut** Cameroon 6.06N 10.07E
87 A9 **Bafwabaka** Zaïre 2.10N 27.39E
91 K3 **Bafwaboli** Zaïre 0.45N 26.08E
92 C1 **Bafwasende** Zaïre 1.09N 27.12E
36 J2 **Bağ** *R* Turkey
90 F5 **Baga** Niger 13.05N 13.55E
75 O3 **Baga** Spain 42.15N 1.52E
89 K7 **Baga** Togo 9.53N 1.05E
15 J6 **Bagabag I** Papua New Guinea 4.50S 146.15E
22 E4 **Baga Bogd Uul** *mts* Mongolia
19 F1 **Bagac** Luzon Philippines 14.35N 120.25E
19 F1 **Bagac Bay** Luzon Philippines
115 M4 **Bagaces** Costa Rica 10.31N 85.18W
41 L8 **Bagadzha** Yakutsk U.S.S.R. 64.07N 120.00E
41 M8 **Bagadzha** Yakutsk U.S.S.R. 64.31N 120.32E
118 E4 **Bagagem** *R* Brazil
30 H5 **Bagaha** Bihar India 27.08N 84.04E
Bagaha Ghat *see* **Bagaha**
18 N3 **Bagahak** *mt* Sabah Malaysia 5.09N 118.46E
90 C8 **Bagaji** Nigeria 7.50N 7.57E
86 G3 **Bagalât,El** Egypt 31.11N 31.37E
28 B2 **Bagalkot** Karnataka India 16.14N 75.47E
89 N4 **Bagam** Niger 15.43N 6.35E
15 M9 **Bagaman I** Louisiade Arch 11.09S 152.40E
92 J5 **Bagamoyo** Tanzania 6.26S 38.55E
93 J10 **Bagamoyo** Tanzania 4.33S 37.52E
23 A2 **Bagan** Qinghai China 33.59N 96.24E
24 J9 **Bagan** Qinghai China 33.5 N 96.24E
43 N1 **Bagan** U.S.S.R. 54.08N 77.39E
90 C7 **Bagana** Nigeria 8.00N 7.40E
42 K2 **Baganalakh** U.S.S.R. 61.28N 118.38E
15 J2 **Bagana, Mt** Bougainville I Papua New Guinea 6.10S 155.11E
18 A8 **Bagan Datoh** Pen Malaysia 3.58N 100.47E
90 H10 **Bagandou** Cent Afr Rep 3.48N 17.51E
19 N8 **Baganga** Mindanao Philippines 7.32N 126.31E
19 N8 **Baganga B** Mindanao Philippines 7.33N 126.31E
19 L8 **Baganian Pen** Mindanao Philippines
Baga Nor *L* *see* **Jili Hu**
18 A6 **Bagan Serai** Pen Malaysia 5.00N 100.30E
18 A9 **Bagan Siapiapi** Sumatra Indon 2.07N 100.53E
14 A3 **Baganup L** W Australia 32.10S 115.49E
47 H3 **Bagan'yuvam** U.S.S.R. 66.05N 58.01E
79 H5 **Baganza** *R* Italy
30 G5 **Bagapar** Uttar Prad India 27.13N 83.31E
30 D3 **Bagar** Nepal 29.50N 80.34E
43 O3 **Bagar** *R* Kazakhstan U.S.S.R.
90 K8 **Bagara** Cent Afr Rep 7.26N 20.11E
43 J6 **Bagara** Kazakhstan U.S.S.R. 40.57N 68.23E
90 B4 **Bagaroua** Niger 14.38N 4.21E
47 N5 **Bagaryak** U.S.S.R. 56.14N 61.30E
36 G6 **Bağase Burun** *C* Turkey 36.12N 33.56E
90 G5 **Baga Sola** Chad 13.32N 14.19E
91 E5 **Bagata** Zaïre 3.47S 17.57E
30 H6 **Bagaura** Bihar India 26.02N 84.30E
45 M9 **Bagayevskiy** U.S.S.R. 47.20N 40.24E
119 D10 **Bagazán** Peru 4.44S 73.38W
111 J7 **Bagbad** California 34.35N 115.53W
87 C3 **Bagbag** Sudan 15.23N 31.30E
63 G6 **Bagband** W Germany 53.21N 7.37E
87 B8 **Bagbele** Zaïre 4.21N 29.17E
57 L4 **Bagby** N Yorks England 54.13N 1.18W
30 A6 **Bagchini** Madhya Prad India 26.29N 77.49E
111 L7 **Bagdad** Arizona 34.35N 113.11W
107 L3 **Bagdad** Kentucky 38.16N 85.03W
112 K10 **Bagdad** Mexico 25.55N 97.10W
42 J5 **Bagdarin** U.S.S.R. 54.28N 113.38E
31 G8 **Bagdogra** Bangladesh 26.05N 88.55E
121 G3 **Bagé** Brazil 31.22S 54.06W
90 B6 **Bagega** Nigeria 11.50N 5.59E
71 F4 **Bâgé le Châtel** France 46.18N 4.55E
Bagemder *prov* *see* **Begēmdir**
24 H9 **Bagên** Xizang Zizhiqu China 32.17N 93.31E
59 J6 **Bagenalstown** Carlow Irish Rep 52.42N 6.57W
53 F7 **Bagenkop** Denmark 54.45N 10.42E
Bagepali *see* **Bagepalli**
28 C4 **Bagepalli** Karnataka India 13.46N 77.48E
37 J9 **Bāgerdān** Iran 36.35N 45.32E
44 E9 **Bagerovo** Ukraine U.S.S.R. 45.23N 36.19E
72 K10 **Bages** France 42.37N 2.54E
72 K9 **Bages,Etang de** France 43.07N 3.00E
30 C3 **Bageshwar** Uttar Prad India 29.50N 79.46E
28 C2 **Bagevadi** Karnataka India 16.34N 76.04E
87 A5 **Baggara** *tribe* Sudan
79 E8 **Bággio** *dist* Milan Italy
108 C8 **Baggs** Wyoming 41.01N 107.40W
56 C5 **Baggy Pt** Devon England 51.09N 4.16W
31 G4 **Bagh** Kashmir 34.00N 73.49E
29 D6 **Bagh** Madhya Prad India 22.22N 74.49E
30 D7 **Baghain** *R* Uttar Prad India
31 C6 **Baghak** Pakistan 29.27N 65.58E
31 D3 **Baghalak Gardeneh** *pass* Afghanistan 35.00N 66.56E
30 G6 **Baghar** Uttar Prad India 26.25N 83.07E
30 D5 **Baghauli** Uttar Prad India 27.14N 80.18E
32 J2 **Baghbaghū** Iran 36.05N 60.32E
Bagh Baqu *see* **Baghbaghū**
34 M5 **Baghdād** Iraq 33.20N 44.26E
29 G5 **Baghelkand** *reg* Madhya Prad India
30 E5 **Baghel Tal** *L* Uttar Prad India 27.24N 81.44E
32 C5 **Bāgh-e Malek** Iran 31.26N 49.55E
31 H9 **Bagherhat** Bangladesh 22.40N 89.48E
81 G7 **Bagheria** Sicily 38.05N 13.31E
32 B7 **Bāgh-e Ṣabā** *sub* Tehrān Iran
32 A7 **Bāgh-e Shāh** *sub* Tehrān Iran
30 A1 **Baghi** Himachal Prad India 31.14N 77.33E
32 G5 **Bāghīn** Iran 30.13N 56.49E
35 G2 **Baghlah** Syria 32.55N 35.50E
31 E2 **Baghlan** Afghanistan 36.11N 68.44E
31 E3 **Baghlan** *reg* Afghanistan
32 B1 **Bāghlī Dagh** *mt* Iran 38.12N 46.16E
29 J2 **Baghmundi** W Bengal India 23.11N 86.04E
58 B4 **Bagh nam Faoileann** *channel* S Uist, W Isles Scotland
30 A4 **Baghpat** Uttar Prad India 28.56N 77.14E
31 C4 **Baghran** Afghanistan 32.55N 64.57E
Baghrash Köl *L* *see* **Bosten (Bagrax) Hu**
31 D7 **Baghwana** Pakistan 27.58N 66.41E
31 H10 **Bagi** Bangladesh 22.24N 90.25E
39 D1 **Bagil'** U.S.S.R. 70.40N 148.15E
87 H10 **Bagilaf** Somalia 1.02N 41.33E
56 J3 **Baginton** *airport* Warwicks Eng 52.21N 1.25W
37 E6 **Bağırpaşa Dağı** *mts* Turkey 39.29N 40.06E
103 B7 **Bagley** Maryland 39.30N 76.24W
108 P2 **Bagley** Minnesota 47.32N 95.24W
106 C7 **Bagley** Wisconsin 42.55N 91.06W
113 Q6 **Bagley Icefield** Alaska 60.39N 143.20W
72 B8 **Baglose-sur-l'Adour** France 43.47N 1.00W
36 F2 **Bağlum** Turkey 40.03N 32.50E
30 G4 **Baglung** Nepal 28.16N 83.35E
30 J5 **Bagmati** *R* Nepal
52 E6 **Bagn** Norway 60.50N 9.33E
79 L6 **Bagnacavallo** Italy 44.25N 11.58E
72 J6 **Bagnac-sur-Célé** France 44.40N 2.09E
80 F4 **Bagnaia** Italy 42.25N 12.09E
81 L7 **Bagnara Cálabra** Italy 38.17N 15.48E
79 O3 **Bagnaria Arsa** Italy 45.53N 13.17E
22 C7 **Bag Narin** Qinghai China 38.58N 94.19E
79 D6 **Bagnasco** Italy 44.18N 8.02E
107 D3 **Bagnell Dam** Missouri 38.13N 92.37W
72 E9 **Bagnères-de-Bigorre** France 43.04N 0.09E
72 F10 **Bagnères-de-Luchon** France 42.48N 0.35E
66 E7 **Bagnes,Val de** Switzerland
68 E4 **Bagneux** Hauts-de-Seine France 48.48N 2.19E
72 D1 **Bagneux** Maine-et-Loire France 47.14N 0.06W
79 J6 **Bagni di Lucca** Italy 44.01N 10.35E
66 P7 **Bagni di Másino** Italy 46.15N 9.37E
79 J2 **Bagni di Rabbi** Italy 46.24N 10.48E
81 J7 **Bagni di San Calogero** Lipari Is Italy 38.28N 14.55E
79 K7 **Bagno a Ripoli** Italy 43.45N 11.19E
79 L7 **Bagno di Romagna** Italy 43.50N 11.57E
70 K4 **Bagnoles-de-l'Orne** France 48.33N 0.25W
68 G3 **Bagnolet** France 48.52N 2.25E
80 K5 **Bagnoli del Trigno** Italy 41.42N 14.28E
79 L4 **Bagnoli di Sopra** Italy 45.11N 11.53E
80 M7 **Bagnoli Irpino** Italy 40.49N 15.04E
81 R12 **Bagnolo del Salento** Italy 40.09N 18.21E
79 L4 **Bagnolo di Po** Italy 45.01N 11.30E
79 J5 **Bagnolo in Piano** Italy 44.46N 10.40E
79 H4 **Bagnolo Mella** Italy 45.26N 10.11E
79 B5 **Bagnolo Piemonte** Italy 44.46N 7.18E
79 J4 **Bagnolo San Vito** Italy 45.06N 10.53E
71 B6 **Bagnols** France 45.30N 2.37E
71 K9 **Bagnols-en-Forêt** France 43.33N 6.43E
71 D7 **Bagnols-les-Bains** France 44.30N 3.40E
71 F8 **Bagnols-sur-Cèze** France 44.10N 4.36E
79 G6 **Bagnone** Italy 44.19N 9.59E
80 F3 **Bagnoregio** Italy 42.37N 12.05E
69 H4 **Bagny-sur-Meuse** France 49.52N 4.45E
19 L6 **Bago** Philippines 10.34N 122.50E
53 D6 **Bågø** *isld* Denmark 55.19N 9.49E
29 J1 **Bagodar** Bihar India 24.04N 85.50E
89 F5 **Bagoé** *R* Mali
79 H3 **Bagolino** Italy 45.49N 10.28E
Bagong *see* **Sansui**
29 D5 **Bagor** Rajasthan India 25.22N 74.03E
98 B5 **Bagotville** Quebec 48.22N 70.54W
89 E6 **Bagoué** Guinea 10.15N 9.44W
29 L4 **Bagra Kote** W Bengal India 26.53N 88.36E
31 E3 **Bagrāmē** Afghanistan 34.29N 69.16E
46 D3 **Bagrationovsk** U.S.S.R. 54.26N 20.38E
87 D2 **Bagrawia** *ruins* Sudan 16.59N 33.45E
Bagrax *see* **Bohu**
117 D5 **Bagre** Brazil 1.52S 50.13W
29 D4 **Bagru** Rajasthan India 26.49N 75.36E
34 O6 **Bagsaya** Iraq 32.53N 46.26E
56 K5 **Bagshot** Surrey England 51.22N 0.42W
30 H8 **Bagsoti** Bihar India 24.31N 84.54E
21 B6 **Bag Tal** Nei Monggol Zizhiqu China 43.15N 122.13E
119 B10 **Bagua** Peru 5.37S 78.36W
120 A1 **Bagua Grande** Peru 5.46S 78.31W
121 D5 **Bagual** Argentina 35.09S 65.32W
41 Q5 **Baguchal'y-Kyuel** *L* U.S.S.R. 70.46N 144.17E
89 H5 **Bagué** *R* Mali/Upper Volta
75 H5 **Báguena** Spain 41.02N 1.21W
90 D3 **Baguezane, Mts** Niger
19 E8 **Baguia** Indonesia 8.33S 126.52E
19 K3 **Baguio** Luzon Philippines 16.25N 120.37E
19 M8 **Baguio** Mindanao Philippines 7.12N 125.26E
19 L3 **Baguio Pt** Luzon Philippines 17.38N 122.13E
75 R4 **Bagur** Spain 41.57N 3.12E
75 R4 **Bagur,C** Spain 41.57N 3.14E
86 F5 **Bagur,El** Egypt 30.26N 31.02E
15 D4 **Bagusi** Irian Jaya 1.51S 137.49E
87 F5 **Bagusta** Ethiopia 11.20N 36.24E
43 O7 **Bagysh** Kirgiziya U.S.S.R. 41.02N 73.05E
30 B6 **Bah** Uttar Prad India 26.52N 78.36E
75 C4 **Bahabón de Esgueva** Spain 41.52N 3.43W
87 L8 **Bahado** Somalia 5.45N 47.15E
31 H8 **Bahadurabad Ghat** Bangladesh 25.11N 89.46E
30 L6 **Bahadurganj** Bihar India 26.17N 87.49E
30 F5 **Bahadurganj** Nepal 27.34N 82.51E
30 A4 **Bahadurgarh** Delhi India 28.41N 76.55E
29 E3 **Bahadurgarh** Haryana India 28.42N 76.54E
31 F4 **Bahadur Khel** Pakistan 33.12N 71.00E
29 E4 **Bahadurpur** Rajasthan India 27.41N 76.42E
90 L4 **Bahaï** Chad 15.31N 22.53E
87 L7 **Bahai,El** Ethiopia 7.23N 47.12E
29 K6 **Bahalda** Orissa India 22.22N 86.10E
Bahāmabād *see* **Rafsanjān**
105 J12 **Bahama Bank,Great** Bahamas
105 J10 **Bahama Bank,Little** Bahamas
116 F2 **Bahamas, The** *state, islds* West Indies
116 L4 **Baham, Pte** *C* Martinique W I 14.25N 60.51W
35 D4 **Bahan** Israel 32.21N 35.02E
Bahao Kalat *see* **Bāhū Kālāt**
34 Q4 **Bahār** Iran 34.52N 48.29E
31 D7 **Bahara** Pakistan 26.13N 67.45E
29 K6 **Baharagora** W Bengal India 22.04N 86.47E
31 D3 **Baharak** Afghanistan 35.04N 66.21E
87 J4 **Bahar-Assoli** Ethiopia 13.38N 42.08E
Bahar Dar *see* **Bahir Dar**
31 E8 **Bahardipur** Pakistan 24.24N 68.01E
88 O8 **Bahar el Hammer** *salt L* Algeria
85 K5 **Baharîya Oasis** Egypt
33 J8 **Bahāt** S Yemen 16.31N 51.19E
18 C9 **Bahau** Pen Malaysia 2.48N 102.26E
18 L4 **Bahau** *R* Borneo Indon
87 K7 **Ba Hawadle** *tribe* Ethiopia
31 G6 **Bahawalnagar** Pakistan 29.57N 73.23E
31 G6 **Bahawalnagar** *dist* Pakistan
31 F6 **Bahawalpur** Pakistan 29.24N 71.47E
31 F6 **Bahawalpur** *div* Pakistan
31 F6 **Bahawalpur** *dist* Pakistan
36 J5 **Bahçe** Turkey 37.14N 36.34E
37 H2 **Bahçecik** Turkey 40.41N 29.55E
19 C4 **Baheësiuna** Celebes Indon 0.44S 122.59E
86 M5 **Bahei, Wâdi el** *watercourse* Egypt
37 F7 **Bahemdan** Turkey 38.19N 41.17E
30 K6 **Bahera** Bihar India 26.05N 86.08E
30 K7 **Baheri** Bihar India 25.57N 86.03E
30 C4 **Baheri** Uttar Prad India 28.43N 79.30E
30 C4 **Bahgul** *R* Uttar Prad India
86 H5 **Bahhâra, Wâdi el** *watercourse* Egypt
35 G6 **Bahhath,El** Jordan 31.54N 35.48E
92 G4 **Bahi** Tanzania 6.00S 35.20E
Bahia *see* **Salvador** Brazil
118 G3 **Bahia** *state* Brazil
121 E7 **Bahía Blanca** Argentina 38.45S 62.15W
121 L5 **Bahía Bustamante** Argentina 45.08S 66.30W
119 B8 **Bahía de Caráquez** Ecuador 0.38S 80.24W
19 J7 **Bahia Honda Pt** Philippines 9.24N 118.07E
115 D3 **Bahía Kino** Mexico 28.48N 111.55W
121 L7 **Bahía Laura** Argentina 48.18S 66.30W
115 C5 **Bahía Magdalena** Mexico 24.39N 112.10W
118 B7 **Bahía Negra** Paraguay 20.13S 58.09W
121 A8 **Bahía Pargua** Chile 41.45S 73.29W
121 E8 **Bahía San Blas** Argentina 40.35S 62.15W
15 C6 **Bahia, Tg** *C* Irian Jaya 4.08S 134.38E
115 B4 **Bahía Tortugas** Mexico 27.40N 114.56W
86 C4 **Bahîg** Egypt 30.56N 29.35E
76 K4 **Bahillo** Spain 42.26N 4.35W
90 B6 **Bahindi** Nigeria 11.26N 4.08E
87 F5 **Bahir Dar** Ethiopia 11.33N 37.25E
85 A3 **Bahiret el Biban** *salt marsh* Tunisia
29 D3 **Bahl** Haryana India 28.35N 75.30E
30 A1 **Bahl** Himachal Prad India 31.46N 76.56E
33 M5 **Bahlā** Oman 22.58N 57.16E
29 B4 **Bāhla** Rajasthan India 27.45N 71.32E
Bahloulié *see* **Bahlūlīye, El**
82 L3 **Bahluiul** *R* Romania
35 F10 **Bahlul** Jordan 30.55N 35.39E
Bahlūlīyah *see* **Bahlūlīye,El**
34 C3 **Bahlūlīye, El** Syria 35.38N 35.57E
34 Q8 **Bahmanshīr,Khowr** *R* Iran
32 C5 **Bahmanshīr, Khowr-e** *estuary* Iran 30.02N 48.40E
Bahman Yari *see* **Bahmanyārīye Pā'īn**
32 D6 **Bahmanyārīye Pā'īn** Iran 29.45N 50.37E
85 L5 **Bahnasa,El** Egypt 28.32N 30.40E
82 J4 **Bahnea** Romania 46.22N 24.28E
92 D5 **Baholoholo** *tribe* Zaïre

59 G3 **Ballyconnell** Cavan Irish Rep 54.07N 7.35W
59 F8 **Ballycotton** Cork Irish Rep 51.50N 8.01W
59 G8 **Ballycotton B** Cork Irish Rep 51.51N 7.57W
59 C3 **Ballycroy** Mayo Irish Rep 54.02N 9.49W
59 G5 **Ballycumber** Offaly Irish Rep 53.20N 7.41W
59 D8 **Ballydehob** Cork Irish Rep 51.34N 9.28W
59 D7 **Ballydesmond** Cork Irish Rep 52.10N 9.13W
59 C7 **Ballyduff** Kerry Irish Rep 52.27N 9.40W
59 F7 **Ballyduff** Waterford Irish Rep 52.09N 8.03W
59 F3 **Ballyfarnan** Roscommon Irish Rep 54.05N 8.12W
59 F5 **Ballyforan** Roscommon Irish Rep 53.28N 8.16W
59 L2 **Ballygally Hd** Antrim N Ireland 54.54N 5.51W
59 F4 **Ballygar** Galway Irish Rep 53.32N 8.19W
59 H3 **Ballygawley** Tyrone N Ireland 54.28N 7.02W
59 L2 **Ballygowan** Down N Ireland 54.30N 5.47W
58 D7 **Ballygrant** Islay, Strathclyde Scotland 55.49N 6.10W
29 H2 **Ballygunge** *dist* Calcutta, W Bengal
59 H3 **Ballyhaise** Cavan Irish Rep 54.03N 7.19W
59 M2 **Ballyhalbert** Down N Ireland 54.30N 5.28W
59 H7 **Ballyhale** Kilkenny Irish Rep 52.28N 7.12W
59 E4 **Ballyhaunis** Mayo Irish Rep 53.46N 8.46W
59 C7 **Ballyheige** Kerry Irish Rep 52.24N 9.50W
59 C7 **Ballyheige B** Kerry Irish Rep 52.23N 9.52W
59 J4 **Ballyhoe L** Meath Irish Rep 53.54N 6.43W
59 E7 **Ballyhoura Hills** Cork, etc Irish Rep
59 H4 **Ballyjamesduff** Cavan Irish Rep 53.52N 7.12W
59 H7 **Bally L** Waterford Irish Rep 52.12N 7.02W
59 F7 **Ballylanders** Limerick Irish Rep 52.23N 8.21W
59 D6 **Ballylongford** Kerry Irish Rep 52.33N 9.28W
59 H6 **Ballylynan** Leix Irish Rep 52.57N 7.02W
59 G7 **Ballymacarbry** Waterford Irish Rep 52.16N 7.12W
59 G8 **Ballymacoda** Cork Irish Rep 51.57N 7.54W
59 F5 **Ballymacward** Galway Irish Rep 52.23N 8.29W
59 G4 **Ballymahon** Longford Irish Rep 53.34N 7.45W
59 K2 **Ballymena** Antrim N Ireland 54.52N 6.17W
59 F4 **Ballymoe** Galway Irish Rep 53.42N 8.28W
59 J1 **Ballymoney** Londonderry N Ireland 55.10N 6.30W
59 G5 **Ballymore** W Meath Irish Rep 53.29N 7.40W
59 J5 **Ballymore Eustace** Kildare Irish Rep 53.08N 6.36W
59 E3 **Ballymote** Sligo Irish Rep 54.06N 8.31W
59 D6 **Ballynacally** Clare Irish Rep 52.43N 9.04W
59 G4 **Ballynacarrigy** W Meath Irish Rep 53.35N 7.32W
59 B7 **Ballynagall** Kerry Irish Rep 52.11N 10.21W
59 H5 **Ballynagore** W Meath Irish Rep 53.24N 7.27W
59 L3 **Ballynahinch** Down N Ireland 54.24N 5.54W
59 C5 **Ballynahinch Castle** Galway Irish Rep 55.20N 9.53W
59 B4 **Ballynakill Harb** Galway Irish Rep 53.35N 10.05W
59 E8 **Ballyneer** Cork Irish Rep 51.44N 8.57W
59 F7 **Ballynoe** Cork Irish Rep 52.03N 8.05W
59 L2 **Ballynure** Antrim N Ireland 54.47N 5.57W
59 F7 **Ballyporeen** Tipperary Irish Rep 52.16N 8.05W
59 L3 **Ballyquintin Pt** Down N Ireland 54.20N 5.30W
59 H6 **Ballyragget** Kilkenny Irish Rep 52.47N 7.20W
59 H6 **Ballyroan** Leix Irish Rep 52.57N 7.18W
59 J2 **Ballyronan** Londonderry N Ireland 54.43N 6.32W
59 K3 **Ballyroney** Down N Ireland 54.16N 6.10W
59 E3 **Ballysadare** Sligo Irish Rep 54.13N 8.30W
59 F2 **Ballyshannon** Donegal Irish Rep 54.30N 8.11W
59 J7 **Ballyteige B** Wexford Irish Rep 52.12N 6.45W
59 D5 **Ballyvaghan** Clare Irish Rep 53.11N 9.10W
59 D8 **Ballyvourney** Cork Irish Rep 51.55N 9.10W
59 K1 **Ballyvoy** Antrim N Ireland 55.12N 6.12W
59 M2 **Ballywalter** Down N Ireland 54.33N 5.30W
59 K3 **Ballyward** Down N Ireland 54.17N 6.02W
58 E4 **Balmacara** Highland Scotland 57.17N 5.38W
121 K5 **Balmaceda** Aisén Chile 45.52S 72.43W
120 D11 **Balmaceda** Antofagasta Chile 24.56S 69.45W
121 J8 **Balmaceda, L** Chile
121 K9 **Balmaceda,Sa** *mts* Chile
57 E2 **Balmaclellan** Dumfries & Galloway Scotland 55.05N 4.07W
58 G6 **Balmaha** Central Scotland 56.06N 4.33W
12 L7 **Balmain** *dist* Sydney, N S W
42 B4 **Balman** U.S.S.R. 55.50N 79.31E
104 K2 **Balmat** New York 44.16N 75.24W
62 N8 **Balmazújváros** Hungary 47.36N 21.18E
79 B4 **Balme** Italy 45.18N 7.12E
66 D7 **Balme,Col de** *pass* France/Switz 46.02N 6.58E
58 M4 **Balmedie** Grampian Scotland 57.15N 2.04W
71 G5 **Balme-les-Grottes,la** France 45.51N 5.20E
Balmer *see* **Barmer**
58 K6 **Balmerino** Fife Scotland 56.25N 3.02W
66 G6 **Balmhorn** *mt* Switzerland 46.26N 7.42E
100 U8 **Balmoral** Manitoba 50.16N 97.20W
11 G9 **Balmoral** New Zealand 42.50S 172.44E
95 M1 **Balmoral** S Africa 25.52S 28.58E
12 F6 **Balmoral** Victoria 37.17S 141.50E
13 K1 **Balmoral** *dist* Brisbane, Qnsld
58 K4 **Balmoral Castle** Grampian Scotland 57.02N 3.15W
105 L9 **Balmoral I** Bahamas 25.06N 77.26W
112 D5 **Balmorhea** Texas 31.00N 103.46W
79 D3 **Balmuccia** Italy 45.49N 8.08E
58 L6 **Balmullo** Fife Scotland 56.23N 2.56W
121 E3 **Balnearia** Argentina 30.59S 62.41W
77 H4 **Balneario de Arenosillo** Spain 38.04N 4.24W
29 G7 **Balod** Madhya Prad India 20.43N 81.13E
29 H6 **Baloda** Madhya Prad India 22.09N 82.31E
29 H7 **Baloda Bazar** Madhya Prad India 21.41N 82.13E
18 G7 **Balok Teluk** *B* Indonesia
91 D10 **Balombo** *R* Angola
13 J8 **Balonne R** Queensland
19 D2 **Balontohe** *isld* Indonesia 3.49N 125.47E
47 J6 **Balotovskoye** U.S.S.R. 58.35N 62.28E
29 C5 **Balotra** Rajasthan India 25.50N 72.21E
91 B5 **Baloumbo** *tribe* Gabon
Balovale Zambia *see* **Zambezi**
63 P6 **Balow** E Germany 53.16N 11.43E
29 K5 **Balpahari Res** Bihar India
58 H6 **Balquhidder** Central Scotland 56.21N 4.23W
30 F5 **Balrampur** Uttar Prad India 27.25N 82.10E
12 G5 **Balranald** New S Wales 34.37S 143.37E
59 K4 **Balrothery** Dublin Irish Rep 53.35N 6.11W
82 J6 **Balş** Romania 44.20N 24.06E
77 O2 **Balsa de Ves** Spain 39.16N 1.11W
19 H2 **Balsahan R** Luzon Philippines
106 B4 **Balsam Lake** Wisconsin
120 B1 **Balsapuerto** Peru 5.48S 76.33W
75 O4 **Balsareny** Spain 41.51N 1.52E
117 E8 **Balsas** Brazil 7.30S 46.00W
115 K8 **Balsas** Mexico 18.00N 99.44W
120 B2 **Balsas** Peru 6.51S 77.59W
115 H8 **Balsas** *R* Mexico
118 F2 **Balsas, R. das** Goiás Brazil
117 E8 **Balsas, R. das** Maranhão Brazil
66 E1 **Balschwiller** France 47.40N 7.10E
51 G2 **Balsfjord** Norway 69.20N 19.20E
51 G2 **Balsfjord** *inlet* Norway
56 M3 **Balsham** Cambs Eng 52.08N 0.20E
77 P5 **Balsicas** Spain 37.49N 0.57W
71 C8 **Balsièges** France 44.29N 3.28E
80 J5 **Balsorano** Italy 41.48N 13.35E
66 G2 **Balsthal** Switzerland 47.18N 7.42E
108 K1 **Balta** N Dakota 48.11N 100.02W
46 G5 **Balta** Ukraine U.S.S.R. 47.58N 29.39E
30 D3 **Baltadi** Nepal 29.33N 80.25E
76 L5 **Baltanás** Spain 41.56N 4.14W
76 D5 **Baltar** Spain 41.57N 7.43W
119 A4 **Baltasar,Pta** Panama 7.36N 81.46W
46 Q2 **Baltasi** U.S.S.R. 56.21N 50.12E
58 R8 **Baltasound** Shetland Scotland 60.45N 0.52W
45 S4 **Baltay** U.S.S.R. 52.27N 46.38E
103 K3 **Baltic** Connecticut 41.36N 72.08W
108 O6 **Baltic** S Dakota 43.47N 96.43W
49 H5 **Baltic Sea** N Europe
86 F2 **Balţîm** Egypt 31.34N 31.05E
59 D9 **Baltimore** Cork Irish Rep 51.29N 9.22W
103 A8 **Baltimore** Maryland 39.18N 76.38W
104 C7 **Baltimore** Ohio 39.51N 82.37W
94 K4 **Baltimore** S Africa 23.15S 28.20E
103 A8 **Baltimore** *co* Maryland
59 J6 **Baltinglass** Wicklow Irish Rep 52.57N 6.42W
31 H3 **Baltistan** *reg* Kashmir
46 C3 **Baltiysk** U.S.S.R. 54.41N 19.59E
31 J3 **Baltoro Glacier** Kashmir
119 B5 **Baltra, I** Galápagos Is 0.27S 90.15W
63 F5 **Baltrum** W Germany 53.44N 7.23E
66 H6 **Baltschieder** Switzerland 46.19N 7.52E
42 F4 **Balturino** U.S.S.R. 56.11N 99.13E
28 J2 **Balu** Assam India 27.51N 93.56E
35 G8 **Balu** *anc site* Jordan 31.22N 35.47E
35 G8 **Balu** *watercourse* Jordan
15 J5 **Baluan I** Admiralty Is Pacific Ocean 2.33S 147.22E
91 J7 **Baluba** *tribe* Zaïre
31 C4 **Baluch** Afghanistan 32.46N 65.52E
32 H6 **Baluch Ab** Iran 29.32N 59.00E
32 H7 **Balūchestān va Sīstān** *prov* Iran
31 B6 **Baluchistan** *prov* Pakistan
31 B6 **Baluchistan** *reg* Pakistan
91 G10 **Baluena** *tribe* Angola
76 B5 **Balugães** Portugal 41.38N 8.38W
18 K4 **Balui** *R* Sarawak Malaysia
19 K8 **Balukbaluk** *isld* Philippines 6.39N 121.42E
29 J6 **Balumath** Bihar India 23.50N 84.54E
91 K7 **Balumbu** *tribe* Zaïre
91 H7 **Balunda** *tribe* Zaïre
29 L5 **Balurghat** W Bengal India 25.12N 88.50E
19 M9 **Balut** *isld* Philippines 5.25N 125.23E
80 N7 **Balvano** Italy 40.38N 15.31E
63 G10 **Balve** W Germany 51.20N 7.52E
46 F2 **Balvi** Latvia U.S.S.R. 57.10N 27.20E
12 D7 **Balwyn** *dist* Melbourne, Vic
36 C3 **Balya** Turkey 39.45N 27.35E
42 H6 **Balyaga** U.S.S.R. 51.10N 108.52E
85 L6 **Balyana, El** Egypt 26.11N 32.00E
39 E3 **Balygychan** U.S.S.R. 63.55N 154.12E
39 E3 **Balygychan** *R* U.S.S.R.
43 N7 **Balykchi** Uzbekistan U.S.S.R. 40.54N 71.49E
46 Q3 **Balykla** U.S.S.R. 54.00N 52.10E
42 D5 **Balyksa** U.S.S.R. 53.24N 89.10E
43 B4 **Balykshi** Kazakhstan U.S.S.R. 47.04N 51.55E
42 F6 **Balyktyg Khem** *R* U.S.S.R.
39 E1 **Balyma,Ozero** *L* U.S.S.R. 67.50N 151.45E
100 D7 **Balzac** Alberta 51.15N 114.00W
84 Y20 **Balzan** Malta 35.53N 14.28E
119 B8 **Balzar** Ecuador 1.25S 79.54W
66 P3 **Balzers** Liechtenstein 47.04N 9.32E
42 J6 **Bal'zino** U.S.S.R. 51.05N 113.40E
90 G9 **Bam** Cent Afr Rep 5.51N 15.52E
32 G2 **Bām** Iran 36.57N 57.56E
32 H6 **Bam** Kermān Iran 29.07N 58.20E
40 C4 **Bam** U.S.S.R. 54.09N 123.51E
23 D6 **Bama** Guangxi China 24.04N 107.10E
90 F6 **Bama** Nigeria 11.31N 13.41E
91 F5 **Bamaba** Zaïre 3.04S 18.40E
13 F1 **Bamaga** Queensland 10.50S 142.25E
89 E5 **Bamako** Mali 12.40N 7.59W
29 K6 **Bamanghati** Orissa India 22.13N 86.15E
Bamani *see* **Bāmarnī**
29 E4 **Bamanwas** Rajasthan India 26.33N 76.24E
90 H9 **Bamara** Cent Afr Rep 4.11N 16.14E
34 L1 **Bāmarnī** Iraq 37.08N 43.16E
89 D7 **Bamba** Guinea 9.00N 10.17W
93 L9 **Bamba** Kenya 3.33S 39.33E
89 J3 **Bamba** Mali 17.05N 1.23W
89 C4 **Bamba** Senegal 14.07N 12.56W
91 F6 **Bamba** Zaïre 5.42S 18.20E
91 D7 **Bamba** *tribe* Angola
89 D6 **Bambafouga** Guinea 10.11N 11.51W
91 E6 **Bambala** *tribe* Zaïre
91 C5 **Bambama** Congo 2.55S 13.13E
120 A2 **Bambamarca** Peru 6.43S 78.34W
91 C6 **Bamba, Mts** Congo/Angola
19 K4 **Bamban** Luzon Philippines 15.22N 120.35E
19 K3 **Bambang** Luzon Philippines 16.24N 121.07E
91 G12 **Bambangando** Angola 17.06S 21.59E
19 K9 **Bambannan** *isld* Philippines 5.37N 120.16E
89 G5 **Bambara** Mali 13.26N 4.03W
90 K9 **Bambari** Cent Afr Rep 5.40N 20.37E
13 H4 **Bambaroo** Queensland 18.50S 146.15E
69 L7 **Bambasle-en-Xaintois** France 48.18N 6.00E
89 C6 **Bambaya** Guinea 10.55N 13.38W
91 F12 **Bambe** Angola 16.17S 19.50E
18 B4 **Bambel** Sumatra Indon 3.30N 97.47E
103 F7 **Bamber** New Jersey 39.55N 74.20W
57 H5 **Bamber Bridge** Lancs Eng 53.44N 2.40W
105 F4 **Bamberg** S Carolina 33.16N 81.02W
64 K4 **Bamberg** W Germany 49.54N 10.54E
91 J2 **Bambesa** Zaïre 3.25N 25.43E
89 A4 **Bambey** Senegal 14.40N 16.28W
91 D11 **Bambi** Angola 14.02S 15.31E
91 K2 **Bambili** Zaïre 3.34N 26.07E
91 F5 **Bambinga** Zaïre 3.43S 18.53E
90 H10 **Bambio** Cent Afr Rep 3.55N 16.57E
52 E8 **Bamble** Norway 58.59N 9.38E
95 K7 **Bamboesberg** *mts* S Africa
89 H7 **Bamboi** Ghana 8.13N 2.01W
91 J4 **Bambole** *tribe* Zaïre
14 D5 **Bamboo Creek** W Australia 21.00S 120.12E
14 C5 **Bamboo Springs** W Australia 22.00S 119.25E
89 D4 **Bambouk** *reg* Mali
26 V12 **Bambou Mts** Mauritius, Indian Oc
26 T12 **Bambous** Mauritius, Indian Oc 20.16S 57.23E
61 F3 **Bambrugge** Belgium 50.55N 3.56E
118 F7 **Bambuí** Brazil 20.01S 45.59W
90 E7 **Bambuka** Nigeria 9.30N 11.22E
57 K1 **Bamburgh** Northumb Eng 55.36N 1.42W
42 K4 **Bambuyka** U.S.S.R. 55.48N 115.45E
24 G10 **Bam Co** *L* Xizang Zizhiqu China 31.30N 91.10E
23 A3 **Bamda** Xizang Zizhiqu China 30.12N 97.25E
30 K8 **Bamdah** Bihar India 24.37N 86.25E
32 C5 **Bāmdezh** Iran 31.43N 48.38E
90 E9 **Bamenda** Cameroon 5.55N 10.09E
57 K6 **Bamford** Derbys Eng 53.21N 1.40W
91 E5 **Bamfumungu** *tribe* Zaïre
30 F7 **Bamhniaon** Uttar Prad India 25.33N 82.19E
15 H5 **Bam I** Papua New Guinea 3.38S 144.50E
43 D7 **Bami** Turkmeniya U.S.S.R. 38.44N 56.50E
23 E6 **Bamian** Guangxi China 25.06N 108.23E
21 C6 **Bamiancheng** Liaoning China 43.15N 124.05E
Bamiantong *see* **Muling**
90 K7 **Bamingua** Cent Afr Rep 8.32N 20.55E
90 J7 **Bamingui** *R* Cent Afr Rep
90 K7 **Bamingui-Bangoran** *dist* Cent Afr Rep
31 D3 **Bamiyan** *anc site* Afghanistan 34.52N 67.45E
31 D3 **Bamiyan** *prov* Afghanistan
89 J5 **Bam, L. de** Upper Volta 13.20N 1.35W
25 H6 **Bam Nak** Cambodia 12.19N 104.10E
25 F5 **Bamnet Narong** Thailand 15.24N 101.38E
31 H9 **Bamni R** Bangladesh
115 E5 **Bamoa** Mexico 25.41N 108.23W
30 B8 **Bamor** Madhya Prad India 24.52N 78.09E
29 F6 **Bamori** Raisen, Madhya Prad India 23.12N 78.20E
30 C7 **Bamori** Tikamgarh, Madhya Prad India 25.08N 79.05E
32 K7 **Bam Posht** *reg* Iran
32 K7 **Bam Posht,Kūh-e** *mts* Iran
57 H3 **Bampton** Cumbria Eng 54.34N 2.45W
56 E6 **Bampton** Devon Eng 51.00N 3.29W
56 H4 **Bampton** Oxon Eng 51.44N 1.33W
32 J7 **Bampūr** Iran 27.13N 60.28E
32 J7 **Bampūr** *R* Iran
32 J4 **Bamrūd** Iran 33.39N 60.05E
Bam Tso *L* *see* **Bam Co** *L*
15 L6 **Bamus, Mt** New Britain 5.14S 151.15E
30 B4 **Ban** *R* Uttar Prad India
90 E9 **Bana** Cameroon 5.12N 10.12E
90 H10 **Bana** Cent Afr Rep 3.36N 16.50E
25 J4 **Ba Na** Vietnam 16.02N 107.59E
9 C4 **Banaba** *isld* Kiribati, Pacific Oc
117 H7 **Banabuiu** *R* Brazil
117 G7 **Banabuiu,Açude** *res* Brazil
119 E4 **Banadia** Colombia 6.53N 71.46W
120 G8 **Bañados del Izozog** *marsh* Bolivia
118 B6 **Bañados de Otuquis** *marsh* Bolivia
90 B6 **Banaga** Nigeria 11.40N 5.59E
59 G5 **Banagher** Offaly Irish Rep 53.11N 7.59W
95 O2 **Banagher, L** S Africa 26.20S 30.18E
93 F8 **Banagi** Tanzania 2.16N 34.51E
19 K4 **Banahao, Mt** Luzon Philippines 14.05N 121.31E
Banaivan *see* **Bunayyān**
76 B3 **Baña,La** Spain 42.57N 8.45W
77 V14 **Bañalbufar** Balearic Is 39.41N 2.30E
76 F4 **Baña,L.de la** Spain 42.17N 6.44W
91 J3 **Banalia** Zaïre 1.33N 25.23E
25 H7 **Banam** Cambodia 11.20N 105.17E
89 F5 **Banamba** Mali 13.29N 7.22W
115 D2 **Banámichi** Mexico 30.00N 110.14W
25 H5 **Ban Amnat** Thailand 15.54N 104.30E
34 M3 **Bānamōrt** Iraq 35.56N 44.20E
Banamurd *see* **Bānamōrt**
13 K6 **Banana** Queensland 24.30S 150.08E
91 C6 **Banana** Zaïre 5.58S 12.27E
89 C7 **Banana Is** Sierra Leone 8.07N 13.15W
118 E2 **Bananal, I.do** Brazil
105 G9 **Banana R** Florida
117 J8 **Bananeiras** Brazil 6.41S 35.35W
28 J8 **Bananga** Nicobar Is Indian Ocean 6.50N 93.50E
91 E9 **Banano** *tribe* Angola
75 M6 **Baña,Pta.de la** *pt* Spain 40.33N 0.39E
25 G6 **Ban Aranyaphrathet** Thailand 13.43N 102.31E
30 F6 **Banaras Gorakhpur** *div* Uttar Prad India
75 E3 **Bañares** Spain 42.28N 1.55W
37 D1 **Banarlı** Turkey 41.06N 27.20E
37 D1 **Banarlı** *R* Turkey
25 G3 **Ba Na Sabaeng** Thailand 18.07N 103.49E
29 B5 **Banas Kantha** *dist* Gujarat India
29 J1 **Banaso** Bihar India 23.59N 85.47E
29 E4 **Banas R** Rajasthan India
71 C8 **Banassac** France 44.27N 3.12E
86 L8 **Banât,Gebel** *hill* Egypt 28.45N 33.38E
82 F6 **Banat Novo Selo** Yugoslavia 44.59N 20.49E
33 F10 **Banā, Wādī** *R* S Yemen
19 A7 **Banawaya** *isld* Indonesia 6.49S 119.15E
36 D4 **Banaz** Turkey 38.47N 29.46E
36 D4 **Banaz Ovasl** *plat* Turkey
25 G3 **Ban Ban** Laos 19.38N 103.32E
25 F4 **Ban Bang Mun Nak** Thailand 16.03N 100.22E
25 E4 **Ban Bang Rakam** Thailand 16.42N 100.07E
24 H10 **Banbar** Xizang Zizhiqu China 30.50N 95.00E
30 D3 **Banbasa** Nepal 29.01N 80.08E
19 M7 **Banbayan Pt** Mindanao Philippines 8.45N 124.46E
25 F10 **Ban Betong** Thailand 5.52N 100.02E
25 K6 **Ban Bik** Vietnam 12.48N 108.39E
59 K3 **Banbridge** Down N Ireland 54.21N 6.16W
25 F5 **Ban Bua Chum** Thailand 15.18N 101.14E
25 G5 **Ban Bua Yai** Thailand 15.35N 102.25E
25 F5 **Ban Bu Khanum** Thailand 14.29N 101.40E
25 J5 **Ban Bung Sai** Laos 15.40N 106.13E
56 J3 **Banbury** Oxon Eng 52.04N 1.20W
72 B9 **Banca** France 43.08N 1.22W
19 H7 **Bancalan** *isld* Philippines 8.14N 117.07E
12 F4 **Bancannia, L** New S Wales 30.49S 142.58E
25 H4 **Ban Chai Buri** Thailand 17.38N 104.28E
25 E3 **Ban Chang Khoeng** Thailand 18.30N 98.24E
25 G4 **Ban Channabot** Thailand 16.03N 102.25E
25 E3 **Ban Chiang Dao** Thailand 19.22N 98.59E
58 M4 **Banchory** Grampian Scotland 57.03N 2.30W
25 G4 **Ban Chum Phae** Thailand 16.34N 102.03E
115 Q8 **Banco Chinchorro** *islds* Mexico
115 N2 **Banco Gorda** *bank* Caribbean Sea
19 J8 **Bancoran** *isld* Philippines 7.59N 118.45E
110 O7 **Bancroft** Idaho 42.44N 111.54W
108 Q6 **Bancroft** Iowa 43.18N 94.11W
99 N7 **Bancroft** Ontario 45.03N 77.52W
108 N5 **Bancroft** S Dakota 44.29N 97.46W
Bancroft Zambia *see* **Chilabombwe**
82 J4 **Band** Romania 46.34N 24.20E
91 C5 **Banda** Congo 3.00S 12.05E
29 F5 **Banda** Madhya Prad India 24.01N 78.59E
30 D7 **Banda** Uttar Prad India 25.28N 80.20E
30 D7 **Banda** *dist* Uttar Prad India
19 F6 **Banda** *isld* Moluccas Indon 4.33S 129.55E
18 A3 **Banda Aceh** Sumatra Indon 5.30N 95.20E
12 K4 **Banda Banda, Mt** New S Wales 31.10S 152.26E
31 F4 **Banda Daud Shah** Pakistan 33.16N 71.12E
15 B6 **Banda Elat** Moluccas Indon 5.39S 132.59E
25 G5 **Ban Daeng Mut** Thailand 14.29N 103.25E
89 C5 **Bandafassi** Senegal 12.25N 12.15W
18 B4 **Bandahara,Gunung** *mt* Sumatra Indon 3.46N 97.47E
87 J9 **Bandai** Somalia 3.57N 43.10E
20 N3 **Bandai-Asahi Nat Park** Japan
20 O4 **Bandai-san** *mt* Japan 37.36N 140.04E
89 D8 **Bandajuma** Sierra Leone 7.35N 11.38W
53 Y20 **Bandak** *L* Norway 59.25N 8.20E
91 C6 **Banda Kani** Zaïre 4.48S 13.52E
19 F6 **Banda Kep** *islds* Moluccas Indon
53 Y20 **Bandaksli** Norway 59.24N 8.11E
30 A1 **Bandal** Himachal Prad India 31.38N 77.27E
87 A7 **Bandala** Sudan 6.09N 27.41E
24 H10 **Banda La** *pass* Xizang Zizhiqu China 30.45N 93.22E
90 E8 **Bandam** Cameroon 6.10N 11.26E
89 G9 **Bandama'** *R* Ivory Coast
89 G8 **Bandama Blanc** *R* Ivory Coast
Bandamir *see* **Band-e Amīr**
28 F2 **Bandamurlanka** Andhra Prad Ind 16.28N 82.03E
32 J5 **Bandān** Iran 31.22N 60.45E
19 F6 **Bandanaira** Moluccas Indon 4.31S 129.50E
25 J7 **Ban Dang Krien** Vietnam 11.59N 107.29E
32 J5 **Bandān Kūh** *mts* Iran
89 H7 **Banda Nkwanta** Ghana 8.28N 2.06W
111 H10 **Banda, Pta** *C* Mexico 31.43N 116.43W
33 K4 **Bandaq, Al** *oil field* The Gulf
31 C3 **Bandar** Afghanistan 35.21N 64.35E
Bandar Andhra Prad *see* **Machilipatnam**
29 B6 **Bandar** Gujarat India 22.50N 70.20E
29 C7 **Bandar** Gujarat India 21.48N 72.14E
92 G10 **Bandar** Mozambique 16.38S 34.09E
18 B9 **Bandar** Pen Malaysia 2.53N 101.24E
32 G7 **Bandar'Abbās** Iran 27.12N 56.15E
32 C2 **Bandar Anzalī** Iran 37.26N 49.29E
Bandar Asalu *see* **'Asalūyeh**
26 T8 **Bandarawela** Sri Lanka 6.50N 81.00E
18 A6 **Bandar Baharu** Pen Malaysia 5.06N 100.29E
31 J10 **Bandarban** Bangladesh 22.13N 92.13E
Bandar Dilām *see* **Bandar-e Deylam**
32 E7 **Bandar-e Chīrū** Iran 26.44N 53.44E
32 D5 **Bandar-e Deylam** Iran 30.04N 50.08E
32 F7 **Bandar-e Khoemir** Iran 26.56N 55.34E
32 F7 **Bandar-e Lengeh** Iran 26.34N 54.52E
32 E7 **Bandar-e Māqām** Iran 26.56N 53.30E
32 C5 **Bandar-e Ma'shūr** Iran 30.34N 49.10E
Bandar-e Pahlavī *see* **Bandar Anzalī**
32 D6 **Bandar-e Rīg** Iran 29.27N 50.39E
32 F2 **Bandar-e Shāh** Iran 36.55N 54.05E
Bandar-e Shāhpūr *see* **Bandar Khomeynī**
32 E7 **Bandar-e Shīū** Iran 27.04N 53.08E
32 C5 **Bandar Khomeynī** Iran 30.25N 49.02E
Bandar Ma'shur *see* **Bandar-e Ma'shūr**
Bandar Muqam *see* **Bandar-e Māqām**
Bandar Penggatam *see* **Batu Pahat**
30 B1 **Bandarpunch** *mt* Uttar Prad Ind 31.00N 78.33E
Bandar Rig *see* **Bandar-e Rīg**
18 L3 **Bandar Seri Begawan** Brunei 4.56N 114.58E
Bandar Shah *see* **Bandar-e Shāh**
Bandar Shahpur *see* **Bandar-e Shāhpūr**
Bandar Tank *see* **Tang** Iran
33 B10 **Bandar Tawahi** *B* S Yemen
30 A8 **Bandarwas** Madhya Prad India 24.57N 77.34E
17 L13 **Banda Sea** Indonesia
18 M2 **Bandau** Sabah Malaysia 6.33N 116.47E
30 A6 **Band Bareta** Rajasthan India 26.55N 77.23E
32 H8 **Band Bonī** Iran 25.33N 59.30E
61 M6 **Bande** Belgium 50.10N 5.25E
76 D4 **Bande** Spain 42.01N 7.59W
32 E6 **Band-e Amīr** Iran 29.48N 52.52E
32 F7 **Band-e Chārak** Iran 26.45N 54.15E
32 F7 **Band-e Hasīneh** Iran 26.41N 54.22E
118 H4 **Bandeira** Brazil 15.52S 40.30W
76 C3 **Bandeira** Spain 42.44N 8.18W
118 H7 **Bandeira** *mt* Brazil 20.25S 41.45W
118 E3 **Bandeirante** Brazil 13.46S 50.48W
118 E8 **Bandeirantes** Brazil 23.06S 50.24W
118 D8 **Bandeirantes, I. dos** Brazil 23.20S 53.50W
96 Q4 **Bandeiras** Azores 38.33N 28.28W
91 C11 **Bandeira, Sá da** *mts* Angola
91 E3 **Bandéko** Congo 1.56N 17.25E
32 F7 **Band-e Kong** Iran 26.37N 54.58E
109 D6 **Bandelier Nat.Mon** New Mexico
32 F7 **Band-e Moghūyeh** Iran 26.36N 54.35E
32 E7 **Band-e Nakhīlū** Iran 26.50N 53.34E
32 E2 **Band-e Pay** Iran 36.08N 52.32E
87 H8 **Bander** Ethiopia 5.04N 41.27E
121 E2 **Bandera** Argentina 28.53S 62.15W
112 H6 **Bandera** Texas 29.44N 99.06W
115 G2 **Banderas** Mexico 31.00N 105.33W
115 G7 **Banderas, B. de** Mexico
32 F3 **Band-e Sar Qom** Iran 34.16N 55.03E
29 J6 **Bandgaon** Bihar India 22.52N 85.24E
31 E7 **Bandhi** Pakistan 26.28N 68.22E
29 G6 **Bandhogarh** Madhya Prad India 23.40N 81.02E
53 G7 **Bandholm** Denmark 54.50N 11.30E
89 H4 **Bandiagara** Mali 14.25N 3.37W
31 D3 **Band-i-Āmir** *R* Afghanistan
29 G8 **Bandia R** Maharashtra India
72 E4 **Bandiat** *R* France
31 B3 **Band-i-Baba** *mts* Afghanistan
31 C3 **Band-i-Baian** *mts* Afghanistan
30 H5 **Bandichhap** Nepal 27.55N 84.04E
32 E3 **Band-i-Husain Nun** *mts* Iran
31 C6 **Band-i-Khan Jahan** Pakistan 28.52N 64.30E
29 E4 **Bandikui** Rajasthan India 27.01N 76.33E
Bandini *see* **Band Bonī**
30 H5 **Bandipur** Nepal 27.56N 84.24E
Band-i-Qir *see* **Band Qīr**
29 C5 **Bandi R** Rajasthan India
37 E2 **Bandirma** Turkey 40.21N 27.58E
37 E2 **Bandırma Körfezi** *gulf* Turkey
Band-i-Sar-i-Qum *see* **Band-e Sar Qom**
31 C3 **Band-i-Turkestan** *mts* Afghanistan
71 H10 **Bandol** France 43.08N 5.45E
89 H7 **Bandoli** Ivory Coast 8.39N 3.38W
94 K4 **Bandolier Kop** S Africa 23.20S 29.43E
59 E8 **Bandon** Cork Irish Rep 51.44N 8.44W
110 A6 **Bandon** Oregon 43.06N 124.26W
Ban Don Thailand *see* **Surat Thani**
25 J6 **Ban Don** Vietnam 12.54N 107.49E
25 E8 **Ban Don,Ao** *B* Thailand
25 H4 **Ban Dong** Laos 17.49N 105.04E
25 G4 **Ban Don Khi** Thailand 17.12N 102.25E
59 E8 **Bandon,R** Cork Irish Rep
32 C5 **Band Qīr** Iran 31.40N 48.54E
28 A7 **Bandra** Maharashtra India 19.04N 72.58E
28 A7 **Bandra Pt** Maharashtra India 19.03N 72.50E
29 K2 **Banduan** W Bengal Ind 22.52N 86.31E
91 E5 **Bandundu** Zaïre 3.20S 17.24E
91 E6 **Bandundu** *prov* Zaïre
18 G9 **Bandung** Java Indon 6.57S 107.34E
18 E5 **Bandung** Sumatra Indonesia 0.31N 103.15E
25 H4 **Ban Dupre** Laos 17.39N 105.45E
104 D9 **Bandy** Virginia 37.09N 81.42W
14 D8 **Bandya** W Australia 27.59S 122.22E
91 D6 **Bandza-Ndounga** Congo 4.31S 15.01E
89 H4 **Bané** Upper Volta 14.01N 2.27W
89 J6 **Bané** Upper Volta 11.42N 0.15W
91 B2 **Bane** *tribe* Cameroon
82 K6 **Băneasa** Romania 44.30N 26.05E
82 L5 **Băneasa** Romania 45.56N 27.55E
Baned *see* **Sundarnagar**
Banegev *see* **Horvot Rehovot**
32 A3 **Bāneh** Iran 35.58N 45.54E
59 H4 **Bane,L** W Meath Irish Rep 53.41N 7.10W
19 F3 **Banemo** Halmahera Indon 0.21N 128.35E
29 D5 **Banera** Rajasthan India 25.32N 74.42E
77 P3 **Bañeras** Spain 38.44N 0.39W
116 G4 **Banes** Cuba 20.59N 75.34W
30 A2 **Banethi** Himachal Prad India 30.38N 77.15E
76 H4 **Bañeza,La** Spain 42.18N 5.54W
101 Q10 **Banff** Alberta 51.10N 115.34W
58 L3 **Banff** Grampian Scotland 57.40N 2.31W
Banff *co see* **Grampian** *reg*
101 P10 **Banff Nat.Park** Alberta
89 G6 **Banfora** Upper Volta 10.36N 4.45W
91 D8 **Banga** Angola 8.43S 15.13E
91 D9 **Banga** Angola 10.15S 14.58E
90 H7 **Banga** Chad 9.40N 16.22E
91 F4 **Banga** Zaïre 0.03S 19.11E
91 G6 **Banga** Zaïre 5.25S 20.28E
19 M8 **Banga** *R* Mindanao Philippines
19 L8 **Bangaan** Mindanao Philippines 7.30N 122.24E
87 A8 **Bangadi** Zaïre 4.10N 27.51E
89 G5 **Bangadina** Mali 12.41N 4.38W
19 N8 **Bangai Pt** Mindanao Philippines 7.45N 126.35E
91 E8 **Bangala** *tribe* Angola
19 K8 **Bangalao** *isld* Philippines 6.00N 121.31E
103 G3 **Bangall** New York 41.53N 73.40W
13 G5 **Bangall** *R* Queensland
87 C8 **Bangalo** Sudan 4.50N 30.20E
28 C4 **Bangalore** Karnataka India 12.58N 77.35E
28 C4 **Bangalore** *dist* Karnataka India
12 L3 **Bangalow** New S Wales 28.38S 153.39E
28 D3 **Banganapalle** Andhra Prad India 15.21N 78.12E
29 E4 **Banganga R** Rajasthan Ind
91 B1 **Bangangté** Cameroon 5.09N 10.29E
29 L6 **Bangaon** W Bengal Ind 23.01N 88.50E
19 K3 **Bangar** Luzon Philippines 16.55N 120.26E
18 L3 **Bangar** Sarawak Malaysia 4.44N 115.01E
28 D4 **Bangarapet** Karnataka India 12.59N 78.11E
31 H10 **Bangara R** Bangladesh
30 D6 **Bangarmau** Uttar Prad India 26.54N 80.12E
90 L9 **Bangassou** Cent Afr Rep 4.41N 22.48E
52 J7 **Bångbro** Sweden 59.52N 15.03E
24 D8 **Bangdag Co** *L* Xizang Zizhiqu China 35.00N 81.40E
87 E6 **Bange,Jeb** *mt* Ethiopia 9.41N 34.20E
90 A9 **Bangem** Chad 5.06N 9.47E
Bangemall *see* **Cobra**
87 B8 **Bangenze** *mt* Sudan 4.30N 29.00E
123 E2 **Banger Hills** Antarctica
107 E4 **Bangert** Missouri 37.45N 91.32W
15 J7 **Bangeta, Mt** Papua New Guinea 6.17S 147.05E
25 H4 **Bang Fay, Se** *R* Laos
19 C4 **Banggai** Indonesia 1.34S 123.33E
19 C4 **Banggai** *isld* Indonesia 1.46S 123.31E
19 C4 **Banggai, Kepulauan** *islds* Indonesia
18 M2 **Banggi** *isld* Sabah Malaysia
18 K5 **Bang,Gunung** *mt* Borneo Indon 0.03N 112.07E
Banghāzi *see* **Benghāzī**
25 J4 **Bang Hieng,Se** *R* Laos
18 K9 **Bangil** Java Indon 7.34S 112.47E
87 D5 **Bangjang** Sudan 11.24N 32.40E
19 D3 **Bangka** *isld* Celebes Indon 1.48N 125.11E
18 G7 **Bangka** *isld* Sumatra Indon
18 K7 **Bangkal** Borneo Indon 2.44S 112.25E
19 A6 **Bangkala** Celebes Indon 5.33S 119.35E
18 K9 **Bangkalan** Indonesia 7.05S 112.44E
19 C4 **Bangkalan** *isld* Indonesia 1.13S 123.18E
18 B4 **Bangkaru** *isld* Indonesia
19 D3 **Bangka,Selat** *str* Celebes Indon
18 F7 **Bangka,Selat** *str* Sumatra Indon
19 B3 **Bangkir** Celebes Indon 0.47N 120.14E
18 E7 **Bangko** Sumatra Indon 2.05S 102.20E
24 F10 **Bangkog Co** *L* Xizang Zizhiqu China 31.45N 89.30E
25 F6 **Bangkok** Thailand 13.44N 100.30E
25 F6 **Bangkok,Bight of** Thailand
19 C4 **Bangkulu** *isld* Indonesia 1.49S 123.08E
27 O5 **Bangladesh** *rep* Asia
25 F6 **Bang Lamung** Thailand 12.56N 100.53E
92 C4 **Bango-Bango** *tribe* Zaïre
25 K7 **Ba Ngoi** Vietnam 11.56N 109.07E
24 C9 **Bangong Co** *L* Xizang Zizhiqu China
57 H6 **Bangor** Clwyd Wales 53.00N 2.55W
59 L2 **Bangor** Down N Ireland 54.40N 5.40W
70 B7 **Bangor** France 47.19N 3.10W
57 E6 **Bangor** Gwynedd Wales 53.13N 4.08W
104 R2 **Bangor** Maine 44.49N 68.47W
59 C3 **Bangor** Mayo Irish Rep 54.09N 9.44W
106 H7 **Bangor** Michigan 42.19N 86.07W
103 D5 **Bangor** Pennsylvania 40.52N 75.12W
100 P8 **Bangor** Saskatchewan 50.50N 102.24W
90 K7 **Bangoran** Cent Afr Rep 8.05N 20.21E
90 J7 **Bangoran** *R* Cent Afr Rep
90 K9 **Bangoro** Cent Afr Rep 5.28N 21.25E
30 C6 **Bangra** Uttar Prad India 26.12N 79.10E
Bang Rakam *see* **Ban Bang Rakam**
29 K6 **Bangriposi** Orissa India 22.10N 86.37E
66 P2 **Bangs** Austria 47.17N 9.33E
112 H4 **Bangs** Texas 31.44N 99.08W
18 M6 **Bangsalsembera** Borneo Indon 0.19S 117.16E
25 E7 **Bang Saphan Yai** Thailand 11.10N 99.33E
53 F2 **Bangsbostrand** Denmark 57.25N 10.32E
111 L5 **Bangs, Mt** Arizona 36.48N 113.48W
52 F2 **Bangsund** Norway 64.24N 11.24E
118 G9 **Bangú** Brazil 22.53S 43.27W
19 M8 **Bangu** Mindanao Philippines 6.28N 124.43E
19 K3 **Bangued** Luzon Philippines 17.36N 120.37E
90 J9 **Bangui** Cent Afr Rep 4.23N 18.37E
19 K2 **Bangui** Luzon Philippines 18.33N 120.45E
90 K9 **Bangui** *R* Cent Afr Rep
15 L6 **Bangula B** New Britain
18 C4 **Bangunpurba** Sumatra Indon 3.25N 98.52E
92 C1 **Banguru** Zaïre 0.30N 27.10E
92 D7 **Bangweulu, Lake** Zambia 11.15S 29.45E
25 G3 **Ban Hai** Laos 18.08N 103.04E
25 E4 **Ban Hat Sao** Thailand 17.36N 99.39E
25 F9 **Ban Hat Yai** Thailand 7.00N 100.28E
25 G3 **Ban Hin Heup** Laos 18.38N 102.21E
25 K6 **Ban Ho** Vietnam 12.58N 108.19E
25 F6 **Ban Hua Hin** Thailand 12.56N 100.02E
25 G3 **Ban Huai Kho** Thailand 18.10N 102.05E
25 E7 **Ban Huai Yang** Thailand 11.38N 98.45E
25 H5 **Ban Huai Yang** Thailand 15.53N 105.12E
113 L7 **Ban I** Alaska 58.20N 152.54W
116 J5 **Baní** Dominican Republic 18.19N 70.21W
19 J3 **Bani** Luzon Philippines 16.12N 119.52E
89 J5 **Bani** Upper Volta 13.39N 0.09W
30 D6 **Bani** Uttar Prad India 26.39N 80.48E
89 G5 **Bani** *R* Mali
90 H9 **Bania** Cent Afr Rep 4.01N 16.07E
89 H7 **Bania** Ivory Coast 9.05N 3.05W
33 E9 **Banī 'Abīd** Yemen 15.56N 43.57E
84 B5 **Bánia Kounopéli** Greece 38.06N 21.21E
15 K8 **Baniara** Papua New Guinea 9.46S 149.51E
Banias *see* **Baniyās**
33 B2 **Bani Atiyah** *tribe* Saudi Arabia
90 A4 **Bani-Bangou** Niger 15.03N 2.42E
116 J5 **Bánica** Dominican Republic 19.07N 71.35W
62 H2 **Banie** Poland 53.04N 14.40E
32 F7 **Bānī Forur** *isld* Iran 26.06N 54.25E
31 H4 **Banihal Pass** Kashmir 33.30N 75.18E
33 D7 **Banī 'Īsá** Saudi Arabia 19.15N 41.25E
88 K7 **Bani,Jbel** *mts* Morocco
15 L3 **Banika I** Solomon Is 9.10S 159.10E
33 F7 **Banī Khaṭmah** *des area* Saudi Arabia
33 F7 **Banī Khurb** *ridge* Saudi Arabia
33 G6 **Banī Labab** *area* Saudi Arabia
91 H1 **Banima** Cent Afr Rep 5.30N 23.50E
33 F7 **Banī Ma'āriḍ** *des area* Saudi Arabia
33 E7 **Banī Mālik** Saudi Arabia 18.25N 42.36E
33 H6 **Banī Mukassir** *des area* Saudi Arabia
85 F3 **Banīnah** Libya 32.06N 20.12E
35 D7 **Bani Na'im** Jordan 31.31N 35.10E
19 J4 **Bani Pt** Luzon Philippines 15.35N 119.53E
34 M5 **Banī Sa'd** Iraq 33.34N 44.32E
93 M2 **Banissa** Kenya 3.58N 40.19E
104 F10 **Banister** *R* Virginia
35 A8 **Bani Suheila** Gaza Strip 31.21N 34.19E
33 E7 **Banī Thawr** Saudi Arabia 18.36N 42.40E
33 H5 **Banī Tukhmān** *area* Saudi Arabia
32 F7 **Banī Tunb** *isld* Iran 26.14N 55.07E
85 C4 **Banī Walīd** Libya 31.43N 14.01E
85 B4 **Banī Walīd** *tribe* Libya
31 J9 **Baniyachung** Bangladesh 24.30N 91.21E
34 C3 **Baniyās** Syria 35.12N 35.57E
35 F1 **Bāniyās** Syria 33.14N 35.42E
33 L5 **Bani Yas** *tribe* U.A.E.
82 E6 **Banja Koviljača** Yugoslavia 44.30N 19.07E
82 D6 **Banja Luka** Yugoslavia 44.47N 17.11E
30 A1 **Banjar** Himachal Prad India 31.40N 77.20E
18 H9 **Banjar** Java Indon 7.21S 108.39E
18 L7 **Banjarmasin** Borneo Indon 3.22S 114.33E
25 J6 **Ban Jeng Drom** Vietnam 12.38N 107.32E
23 B7 **Banjia** Yunnan China 22.09N 99.14E
89 A5 **Banjul** The Gambia 13.28N 16.39W
14 B3 **Banjup** *dist* Perth, W Aust
44 J8 **Bank** Azerbaydzhan U.S.S.R. 39.26N 49.15E
94 R14 **Bank** S Africa 26.18S 27.31E
95 L2 **Bank** S Africa 26.18S 27.31E
30 K8 **Banka** Bihar India 24.53N 86.56E
13 C4 **Banka Banka** N Terr Aust 18.46S 134.02E
29 L2 **Bankadaha** W Bengal India 22.59N 87.23E
25 H5 **Ban Kadiene** Laos 14.27N 105.42E
25 F4 **Ban Kaeng** Thailand 17.24N 100.07E
25 E9 **Ban Kantang** Thailand 7.25N 99.30E
28 B3 **Bankapur** Karnataka India 14.55N 75.23E
89 H5 **Bankass** Mali 13.59N 3.24W
30 F5 **Bankatwa** Uttar Prad India 27.42N 82.14E
95 J8 **Bankberg** *mt* S Africa 32.19S 25.20E
57 F2 **Bankend** Dumfries & Galloway Scotland 55.00N 3.32W
25 J5 **Ban Keng Phao** Cambodia 14.16N 106.18E
25 G2 **Ban Keo Lom** Vietnam 21.15N 103.14E
92 E10 **Banket** Zimbabwe 17.22S 30.29E
58 J5 **Bankfoot** Tayside Scotland 56.30N 3.32W
25 F6 **Ban Khai** Thailand 12.46N 101.18E
25 G1 **Ban Khang Kha** Vietnam 22.44N 102.30E
25 E6 **Ban Khao Yoi** Thailand 13.15N 99.53E
107 J8 **Bankhead Lake** Alabama
25 H4 **Ban Khemmarat** Thailand 16.04N 105.10E
29 F6 **Bankheri** Madhya Prad India 22.47N 78.37E
25 F3 **Ban Khing** Laos 19.46N 100.49E
25 G7 **Ban Khlong Makham** Thailand 11.42N 102.54E
25 G6 **Ban Khlung** Thailand 12.27N 102.12E
25 E8 **Ban Khok Kloi** Thailand 8.15N 98.18E
25 E9 **Ban Khuan Mao** Thailand 7.59N 99.30E
25 F3 **Ban Khun Ban Hai** Thailand 18.54N 100.48E
25 G5 **Ban Khu Noi** Thailand 15.06N 102.53E
25 D3 **Ban Khun Yuam** Thailand 18.54N 97.54E
29 J7 **Bankigarh** Orissa India 20.20N 85.35E
30 J7 **Bankipore** Bihar India 25.36N 86.07E
25 K6 **Ban Kniet** Vietnam 13.06N 108.13E
89 D6 **Banko** Guinea 10.41N 10.47W
18 M8 **Bankobankoang** *isld* Indonesia 5.12S 117.52E
25 E3 **Ban Ko Kha** Thailand 18.14N 99.24E
89 H3 **Bankor** Mali 16.56N 3.50W
28 A2 **Bankot** Maharashtra India 17.57N 73.04E
25 E4 **Ban Krai** Thailand 16.53N 99.53E
107 D8 **Banks** Arkansas 33.34N 92.16W
110 J5 **Banks** Idaho 44.03N 116.09W
107 F7 **Banks** Mississippi 34.51N 90.13W
110 B4 **Banks** Oregon 45.38N 123.07W
119 A5 **Banks, B** Galápagos Is
12 M8 **Banks, C** New S Wales 34.00S 151.15E
12 F7 **Banks, C** S Australia 37.58S 140.24E
12 D5 **Bank's Group** *islds* S Australia
101 H9 **Banks I** Br Columbia
97 G3 **Banks I** N W Terr
13 F1 **Banks I** Queensland
9 C10 **Banks Is** New Hebrides
110 F2 **Banks L** Washington
11 H10 **Banks Pen** New Zealand
12 J8 **Banks Strait** Tasmania
12 K8 **Bankstown** *dist* Sydney, N S W
12 K7 **Bankstown Airfield** Sydney, N S W
25 E6 **Ban Kui Nua** Thailand 12.04N 99.52E
91 D12 **Bankumbi** *tribe* Angola
29 K2 **Bankura** W Bengal Ind 23.14N 87.05E
29 K6 **Bankura** *dist* W Bengal Ind
25 H4 **Ban Kut Hae** Thailand 16.15N 104.32E
91 H5 **Bankutshu** *tribe* Zaïre
82 H8 **Bankya** Bulgaria 42.40N 23.07E
25 H5 **Ban Lamduan** Thailand 14.37N 103.39E
19 L4 **Banla Pt** Philippines 15.00N 122.04E
25 E5 **Ban Le Kathe** Thailand 15.49N 98.49E
25 F5 **Ban Len** Thailand 14.15N 100.34E
25 D3 **Ban Mae La Luang** Thailand 18.28N 97.55E
25 E3 **Ban Mae Mo** Thailand 18.18N 99.46E
25 E4 **Ban Mae Ramat** Thailand 16.59N 98.36E
25 D3 **Ban Mae Sariang** Thailand 18.09N 97.57E
25 E4 **Ban Mae Sot** Thailand 16.44N 98.32E
25 E3 **Ban Mae Suai** Thailand 19.43N 99.30E
25 E3 **Ban Mae Thalop** Thailand 19.44N 99.11E
89 F5 **Banmana** *tribe* Mali
30 L7 **Banmankhi** Bihar India 25.53N 87.11E
25 M9 **Banmauk** Burma 24.26N 95.54E
25 K6 **Ban Me Thuot** Vietnam 12.41N 108.02E
25 E3 **Ban Mong Pong** Thailand 19.02N 98.15E
25 F3 **Ban Muang** Thailand 19.08N 100.21E
25 G6 **Ban Muang** Thailand 13.46N 102.16E
25 G5 **Ban Muang Phon** Thailand 15.50N 102.35E
69 O5 **Bann** W Germany 49.23N 7.37E
59 J1 **Bann** *R* Londonderry N Ireland
Banna *see* **Espiritu** Luzon **Philippines**
25 E8 **Ban Na** Thailand 8.58N 99.18E
25 G4 **Ban Na Baek** Thailand 17.07N 103.02E
25 J4 **Ban Nabo** Laos 16.42N 106.11E
110 N4 **Bannack** Montana 45.10N 112.59W
87 K7 **Bannahan** Ethiopia 7.16N 44.37E
25 H4 **Ban Na Kae** Thailand 16.59N 104.30E
25 F3 **Ban Na Kon** Thailand 19.24N 101.07E
70 C6 **Bannalec** France 47.56N 3.42W
25 F2 **Ban Na Mo** Laos 21.03N 101.48E
25 F4 **Ban Nam Pong** Thailand 16.53N 101.40E
25 G1 **Ban Nam Sau** Vietnam 22.43N 102.36E
25 F3 **Ban Na Noi** Thailand 18.20N 100.41E
25 G3 **Ban Naphong** Laos 18.18N 102.39E
25 F9 **Ban Na Thawi** Thailand 6.48N 100.04E
71 B2 **Bannay** France 47.23N 2.52E
42 H4 **Bannaya** U.S.S.R. 57.05N 108.10E
30 C8 **Banne** *R* Madhya Prad India
72 K2 **Bannegon** France 46.48N 2.42E
14 F4 **Bannerman, Mt** W Australia 19.29S 127.18E
116 F2 **Bannerman Town** Eleuthera I Bahamas 24.41N 76.09W
25 G4 **Ban Ngon** Thailand 17.28N 103.23E
111 H8 **Banning** California 33.56N 116.52W
Banningville *see* **Bandundu**
79 D3 **Bannio** Italy 45.59N 8.08E
58 J6 **Bannockburn** Central Scotland 56.05N 3.56W
11 D12 **Bannockburn** New Zealand 45.05S 169.11E
99 N8 **Bannockburn** Ontario 44.38N 77.33W
92 D12 **Bannockburn** Zimbabwe 20.16S 29.51E
110 M5 **Bannock Pass** Montana 44.50N 113.16W
110 N7 **Bannock Ra** Idaho
25 D4 **Ban Noi** Thailand 17.46N 97.48E
25 F2 **Ban Nong Kha** Laos 20.39N 100.28E
25 G5 **Ban Nong Makha** Thailand 15.08N 102.30E
25 J5 **Ban Nong Met** Laos 15.07N 106.32E
25 G5 **Ban Nong Waeng** Thailand 15.32N 103.36E
43 K6 **Bannovka** Kazakhstan U.S.S.R. 42.28N 70.29E
59 J7 **Bannow B** Wexford Irish Rep 52.13N 6.48W
59 K3 **Bann,R** Armagh N Ireland
59 K6 **Bann,R** Wexford Irish Rep
69 O5 **Bannstein** France 49.01N 7.30E
31 F4 **Bannu** Pakistan 33.00N 70.40E
31 F4 **Bannu** *dist* Pakistan
65 C6 **Bannwaldsee** *L* W Germany 47.37N 10.45E
29 J6 **Bano** Bihar India 22.38N 85.00E
76 F7 **Bañobárez** Spain 40.51N 6.36W
65 P8 **Banokszentgyörgy** Hungary 46.34N 16.48E
75 Q3 **Bañolas** Spain 42.06N 2.46E
71 H8 **Banon** France 44.02N 5.37E
115 H6 **Bañón** Mexico 23.11N 102.29W
75 H6 **Bañón** Spain 40.50N 1.12W
119 B8 **Baños** Ecuador 1.26S 78.24W
76 L5 **Baños de Cerrato** Spain 41.55N 4.29W
121 B8 **Baños de Chihuio** Chile 40.14S 71.59W
121 B6 **Baños de Copahue** Argentina 37.50S 71.07W
77 J4 **Baños de la Encina** Spain 38.10N 3.46W
76 D4 **Baños de Molgas** Spain 42.15N 7.40W
76 H8 **Baños de Montemayor** Spain 40.19N 5.51W
75 K2 **Baños de Panticosa** Spain 42.45N 0.14W
120 E10 **Baños de Puritama** Chile 22.45S 68.05W
77 W15 **Baños de San Juan** Balearic Is 39.22N 3.01E
77 M7 **Baños de Sierra Alhamilla** Spain 36.58N 2.23W
75 G6 **Baños de Tajo** Spain 40.43N 1.59W
75 C4 **Baños de Valdearados** Spain 41.46N 3.35W
121 B6 **Baños Maule** Chile 36.05S 70.39W
62 L7 **Bánovce** Czechoslovakia 48.43N 18.15E
25 G3 **Ban Pacpeup** Laos 18.40N 103.06E
25 E3 **Ban Pak Bong** Thailand 18.32N 98.57E
25 E7 **Ban Pak Chan** Thailand 10.32N 98.51E
25 E6 **Ban Pak Khlong** Thailand 12.34N 99.58E
25 E7 **Ban Pak Nam** Thailand 10.23N 99.15E
25 G6 **Ban Pak Nam** Thailand 12.28N 102.06E
25 F3 **Ban Pak Neun** Laos 19.14N 101.50E
25 F8 **Ban Pak Phanang** Thailand 8.20N 100.10E
25 G5 **Ban Pak Thong Chai** Thailand 14.41N 102.02E
25 F5 **Ban Phachi** Thailand 14.28N 100.41E
25 H4 **Ban Phaeng** Thailand 17.58N 104.12E
25 G4 **Ban Phai** Thailand 16.03N 102.45E
25 K6 **Ban Pha Kroy** Cambodia 12.19N 107.06E
25 F6 **Ban Phanat Nikhom** Thailand 13.25N 101.11E
25 J5 **Ban Phone** Laos 15.24N 106.43E
25 H5 **Ban Phon Ngam** Thailand 15.42N 105.02E
25 G4 **Ban Phon Thong** Thailand 16.08N 103.51E
25 E5 **Banphot Phisai** Thailand 15.52N 99.59E
25 E4 **Ban Phran Katai** Thailand 16.37N 99.36E
25 F5 **Ban Phrom Buri** Thailand 14.51N 100.24E
25 F4 **Ban Phrom Phirom** Thailand 17.02N 100.11E
25 G5 **Ban Phuttaisong** Thailand 15.28N 102.55E
Ban Pla Soi *see* **Chon Buri**
25 E6 **Ban Pong** Thailand 13.49N 99.53E
25 F3 **Ban Pua** Thailand 19.11N 100.56E
29 J8 **Banpur** Orissa India 19.50N 85.15E
30 B8 **Banpur** Uttar Prad India 24.42N 78.44E
22 E7 **Banqiao** Gansu China 39.10N 98.25E
23 C5 **Banqiao** Yunnan China 26.11N 103.56E
23 F2 **Banqiao Sk** *res* Henan China
23 H1 **Banquan** Shandong China 35.07N 118.42E
30 J6 **Banrapati** Nepal 26.51N 85.52E
25 F5 **Ban Ratcha Khram** Thailand 14.10N 100.27E
25 E4 **Ban Saen To** Thailand 16.20N 99.40E
25 F2 **Ban Sai** Laos 20.11N 100.35E
25 G5 **Ban Sai** Thailand 14.40N 103.13E
25 E5 **Ban Sai Yok** Thailand 14.09N 99.10E
37 G6 **Bansan** *watercourse* Turkey
25 F9 **Ban Sanam Chai** Thailand 7.32N 100.26E
25 G5 **Ban Sangae** Thailand 14.03N 102.53E
25 F5 **Ban Sao** Thailand 15.05N 100.33E
90 D8 **Bansara** Nigeria 6.29N 8.35E
25 E3 **Ban Saraphi** Thailand 18.45N 99.04E
25 F6 **Ban Sattahip** Thailand 12.36N 100.56E

25 E7 Ban Sawi Thailand 10.15N 99.06E
29 C7 Bansda Gujarat India 20.47N 73.25E
30 H7 Bansdih Uttar Prad India 25.54N 84.13E
30 G6 Bansgaon Uttar Prad India 26.32N 83.21E
59 F7 Bansha Tipperary Irish Rep 52.28N 8.04W
30 F5 Bansi Basti, Uttar Prad India 27.11N 82.47E
30 L8 Bansi Bihar India 24.49N 87.02E
30 B8 Bansi Jhansi, Uttar Prad India 24.51N 78.28E
29 D5 Bansi Rajasthan India 24.18N 74.32E
25 E8 Ban Sichon Thailand 9.00N 99.56E
29 L5 Bansihari W Bengal India 25.25N 88.30E
25 H4 Ban Si Nho Laos 17.57N 105.04E
25 F6 Ban Si Racha Thailand 13.09N 100.48E
62 L7 Banská Bystrica Czechoslovakia 48.44N 19.10E
62 L7 Banská Štiavnica Czechoslovakia 48.29N 18.50E
82 H9 Bansko Bulgaria 41.50N 23.30E
30 L8 Bansloi R Bihar India
25 H2 Ban Sop Bau Laos 20.48N 104.15E
25 E3 Ban Sop Huai Hai Thailand 19.33N 98.06E
25 E4 Ban Sop Prap Thailand 17.55N 99.20E
25 H3 Ban Sot Laos 18.08N 104.06E
29 J7 Banspani Orissa India 21.59N 85.25E
30 A6 Bansrai Rajasthan India 26.42N 77.23E
56 L5 Banstead Surrey Eng 51.19N 0.12W
29 E4 Bansur Rajasthan India 27.42N 76.20E
30 E5 Bansura Uttar Prad India 27.22N 81.15E
25 E4 Ban Sut Ta Thailand 17.10N 98.39E
28 C1 Banswada Andhra Prad India 18.20N 77.54E
29 D6 Banswara Rajasthan India 23.32N 74.28E
29 D6 Banswara dist Rajasthan India
60 L8 Bant Netherlands 52.47N 5.45E
19 A8 Banta isld Indonesia 8.27S 119.19E
19 A6 Bantaeng Celebes Indon 5.32S 119.58E
29 J2 Banta Hajam Bihar India 23.16N 85.50E
18 A10 Bantaian Sumatra Indonesia 1.55N 100.57E
90 E7 Bantaji Nigeria 8.06N 10.05E
25 F5 Ban Ta Khli Thailand 15.18N 100.21E
25 E8 Ban Takua Pa Thailand 8.55N 98.20E
18 D7 Bantal Sumatra Indonesia 2.41S 101.20E
26 V2 Bantam Cocos Is Ind Oc 12.07S 96.53E
103 H3 Bantam Connecticut 41.43N 73.14W
103 H3 Bantam L Connecticut
95 D9 Bantams S Africa 33.15S 20.31E
25 G5 Ban Tan Thailand 14.30N 103.41E
25 G6 Ban Ta Ruang Thailand 13.29N 102.09E
25 J4 Ban Taup Laos 16.23N 106.30E
25 G3 Ban Ta Viang Laos 19.02N 103.26E
19 L6 Bantayan isld Philippines 11.12N 123.45E
89 K7 Banté Benin 8.25N 1.58E
59 E7 Banteer Cork Irish Rep 52.08N 8.54W
63 L8 Banteln W Germany 52.04N 9.45E
18 G9 Banten Java Indon 6.00S 106.09E
18 G8 Banten, Teluk B Java Indon
25 E8 Ban Tha Chang Thailand 9.12N 99.13E
25 E2 Ban Tha Don Thailand 20.05N 99.21E
25 E8 Ban Thai Muang Thailand 8.24N 98.16E
25 E8 Ban Tha Kham Thailand 9.06N 99.14E
25 G4 Ban Tha Lat Thailand 16.55N 102.20E
25 F4 Ban Tha Li Thailand 17.37N 101.22E
25 H5 Ban Tham Khae Thailand 15.39N 105.01E
25 E5 Ban Thap Phung Thailand 15.00N 99.35E
25 E8 Ban Tha Sala Thailand 8.40N 99.58E
25 D4 Ban Tha Song Yang Thailand 17.33N 97.56E
25 F5 Ban Tha Tako Thailand 14.51N 100.28E
25 J5 Ban Thateng Laos 15.22N 106.23E
25 G5 Ban Tha Tum Thailand 15.16N 103.33E
25 H4 Ban Tha Uthen Thailand 17.32N 104.34E
25 F9 Ban Thepha Thailand 6.55N 101.00E
69 J5 Bantheville France 49.22N 5.06E
30 C5 Banthra Uttar Prad India 27.55N 79.49E
25 E6 Ban Thung Luang Thailand 12.40N 99.51E
66 G4 Bantiger mt Switzerland 46.59N 7.32E
18 B9 Banting Pen Malaysia 2.48N 101.29E
19 L5 Banton isld Philippines 12.56N 122.03E
25 J6 Ban Treo Cambodia 12.57N 106.54E
59 D8 Bantry Cork Irish Rep 51.41N 9.27W
108 K1 Bantry N Dakota 48.31N 100.36W
59 C8 Bantry B Cork Irish Rep
94 P11 Bantry Bay Cape Town S Africa 33.56S 18.26E
91 F6 Bantshamba Zaïre 5.35S 19.24E
18 J9 Bantul Java Indon 7.56S 110.21E
87 G6 Bantu Liben Ethiopia 8.37N 38.22E
29 B7 Bantva Gujarat India 23.31N 70.09E
28 B4 Bantval Karnataka India 12.54N 75.00E
69 O8 Bantzenheim France 47.50N 7.32E
31 E3 Banu Afghanistan 35.36N 69.18E
29 E2 Banur Punjab India 30.32N 76.42E
25 G4 Ban Waeng Noi Thailand 16.42N 103.39E
25 F4 Ban Wang Saphung Thailand 17.22N 101.41E
25 H4 Ban Wang Ta Mua Thailand 17.17N 104.27E
56 F5 Banwell Avon Eng 51.20N 2.52W
56 D2 Banw, R Powys Wales
82 J8 Banya Bulgaria 42.30N 24.50E
93 H1 Banya Kenya 4.24N 36.15E
18 B5 Banyak, Pulau Pulau islds Indonesia
25 G4 Ban Yang Talat Thailand 16.23N 103.21E
25 E6 Ban Yang Yong Thailand 13.00N 99.54E
25 J6 Ban Ya Soup Vietnam 13.05N 107.53E
90 E8 Banyo Cameroon 6.47N 11.50E
13 K1 Banyo dist Brisbane, Qnsld
77 X14 Banyos Balearic Is 40.00N 3.47E
18 F7 Banyuasin R Sumatra Indon
72 L11 Banyuls-sur-Mer France 42.29N 3.08E
18 H9 Banyumas Java Indon 7.30S 109.14E
18 L10 Banyuwangi Java Indon 8.12S 114.22E
15 H6 Banz Papua New Guinea 5.48S 144.39E
64 K3 Banz W Germany 50.08N 11.00E
91 G3 Banza Zaïre 0.28N 20.10E
91 F2 Banza tribe Zaïre
93 A10 Banza, C Zaïre 4.04S 29.14E
91 F6 Banza-Kifilu Zaïre 5.44S 18.07E
91 J1 Banzali Zaïre 4.35N 24.45E
91 C6 Banza Manteke Zaïre 5.24S 13.48E
123 G3 Banzare Coast Antarctica
26 G11 Banzare Seamount Southern Oc 59.20S 77.00E
80 O7 Banzi Italy 40.52N 16.02E
Banzyville see Mobayi
90 L3 Bao Chad 16.30N 23.01E
31 H4 Bao Kashmir 32.41N 74.55E
Bao'an see Zhidan
23 G7 Bao'an Guangdong China 22.31N 114.08E
23 D6 Bao'an Guangxi China 24.06N 107.51E
23 B1 Bao'an Qinghai China 35.38N 101.59E
22 J7 Baode Shanxi China 39.05N 111.10E
22 L7 Baodi Tianjin China 39.43N 117.20E
22 K7 Baoding Hebei China 38.54N 115.26E
76 E4 Bao, Emb. de res Spain
23 F2 Baofeng Henan China 33.52N 113.05E
23 E2 Baofeng Hubei China 32.15N 110.04E
25 H1 Bao Ha Vietnam 22.10N 104.22E
22 L6 Bao He R Hebei China
23 D1 Baoji Shaanxi China 34.23N 107.16E
23 D1 Baoji Shaanxi China 34.21N 107.23E
23 E4 Baojing Hunan China 28.45N 109.45E
Baokang see Horqin Zouyi Zhongqi
23 F3 Baokang Hubei China 31.58N 111.19E
25 H1 Bao Lac Vietnam 22.58N 105.40E
21 C6 Baolizhen Liaoning China 42.55N 123.51E
25 J7 Bao Loc Vietnam 11.33N 107.48E
21 F4 Baoqing Heilongjiang China 46.16N 132.10E
91 D1 Baoro Cent Afr Rep 5.40N 15.59E
21 B12 Baoshan Shanghai China 31.22N 121.28E
23 B6 Baoshan Yunnan China 25.07N 99.08E
22 G8 Baota Ningxia China 38.07N 106.49E
23 E9 Baoting Guangdong China 18.46N 109.44E
22 H6 Baotou Nei Monggol Zizhiqu China 40.38N 109.59E
89 J6 Baouiga Upper Volta 11.35N 1.39W
89 E5 Baoulé R Mali
21 E3 Baoxing Heilongjiang China 48.37N 130.30E
23 C3 Baoxing Sichuan China 30.24N 102.50E
25 L1 Baoxu Guangdong China 22.10N 110.40E
23 H2 Baoying Jiangsu China 33.14N 119.22E
Baoyou see Ledong
29 C4 Bap Rajasthan India 27.22N 72.23E
28 E3 Bapatla Andhra Prad India 15.56N 80.32E
69 D3 Bapaume France 50.07N 2.51E
111 N8 Bapchule Arizona 33.09N 111.51W
42 L1 Bappagay R U.S.S.R.
99 M7 Baptiste Ontario 45.05N 78.00W
Bapu see Liucheng
18 L7 Bapuyu Borneo Indon 3.18S 114.02E
33 E3 Baq'ā' depression Saudi Arabia
35 D4 Bāqa el Gharbiya Israel 32.25N 35.03E
32 E4 Baqam Iran 33.09N 52.19E
33 E5 Baqarah Saudi Arabia 23.00N 42.42E
24 H10 Baqên Xizang Zizhiqu China 31.56N 94.00E
34 P3 Bāqerābād Iran 35.42N 47.41E
33 G8 Bāqim S Yemen 16.08N 47.36E
34 C9 Bāqir, Jebel mt Jordan 29.36N 35.08E
33 D6 Baqrān Saudi Arabia 21.05N 40.41E
34 M5 Ba'qūbah Iraq 33.45N 44.40E
120 D10 Baquedano Chile 23.20S 69.50W
119 B6 Baquerizo Moreno Galápagos Is 0.54S 89.37W
35 F3 Baqura Jordan 32.39N 35.35E
46 G5 Bar Ukraine U.S.S.R. 49.05N 27.40E
42 H6 Bar U.S.S.R. 51.20N 107.40E
82 E8 Bar Yugoslavia 42.05N 19.06E
69 H4 Bar R France
30 F7 Bara Allahabad, Uttar Prad India 25.15N 81.42E
90 J8 Bara Cent Afr Rep 6.06N 18.45E
30 G7 Bara Ghazipur, Uttar Prad India 25.31N 83.52E
89 K4 Bara Mali 15.45N 0.24E
19 E5 Bara Moluccas Indon 3.08S 126.15E
90 E6 Bara Nigeria 10.20N 10.43E
87 C4 Bara Sudan 13.42N 30.21E
30 E7 Bara Uttar Prad India 25.15N 81.41E
47 N5 Baraba U.S.S.R. 56.46N 61.48E
18 L7 Barabai Borneo Indon 2.38S 115.22E
31 J10 Barabakund Bangladesh 22.36N 91.40E
30 F4 Baraban Nepal 28.44N 82.02E
30 E6 Bara Banki Uttar Prad India 26.56N 81.11E
30 E6 Bara Banki dist Uttar Prad India
30 J7 Barabar Hills Bihar India
40 E10 Barabash U.S.S.R. 43.11N 131.33E
29 K2 Barabhum W Bengal Ind 23.01N 86.20E
93 D3 Barabili Uganda 2.42N 32.22E
42 B4 Barabinsk U.S.S.R. 55.20N 78.18E
38 G3 Barabinskaya Step' U.S.S.R.
87 J8 Bar Abir Ethiopia 4.32N 42.20E
30 L7 Bara Boarijor Bihar India 25.04N 87.29E
13 G5 Barabon Queensland 20.50S 143.28E
106 E6 Baraboo Wisconsin 43.27N 89.45W
106 E6 Baraboo, R Wisconsin
118 D3 Baracaju, R Brazil
76 E7 Baraçal Portugal 40.41N 7.20W
75 E1 Baracaldo Spain 43.17N 2.59W
87 G3 Barachit Ethiopia 14.38N 39.28E
98 H5 Barachois Quebec 48.38N 64.17W
94 F4 Barachu Botswana 23.01S 21.49E
116 G4 Baracoa Cuba 20.23N 74.31W
115 Q10 Baracoa Honduras 15.46N 87.50W
34 E3 Barād Syria 35.56N 37.10E
94 N3 Barada Mozambique 20.01S 34.43E
34 D5 Barada R Syria
121 F4 Baradero Argentina 33.50S 59.30W
12 J4 Baradine New S Wales 30.56S 149.05E
12 J4 Baradine R New S Wales
36 E5 Baradis Turkey 37.55N 30.24E
106 F3 Baraga Michigan 46.48N 88.30W
82 K6 Bărăgan dist Romania
30 G6 Baragaon Azamgarh, Uttar Prad India 26.08N 83.33E
30 H7 Baragaon Ballia, Uttar Prad India 25.56N 84.09E
30 A1 Baragaon Himachal Prad India 31.20N 77.22E
30 C8 Baragaon Madhya Prad India 24.30N 79.35E
30 F7 Baragaon Varanasi, Uttar Prad Ind 25.26N 82.49E
80 N7 Baragiano Italy 40.41N 15.36E
93 H4 Baragoi Kenya 1.47N 36.48E
119 E2 Baragua Venezuela 10.38N 69.57W
119 E2 Baragua, Sa de mts Venezuela
94 S14 Baragwanath S Africa 26.16S 27.58E
31 H10 Barahanuddin Bangladesh 22.30N 90.41E
30 L7 Barahara Bihar India 25.47N 87.06E
30 L8 Barahat Bihar India 24.53N 87.01E
85 M7 Barâhma, El Egypt 25.59N 32.49E
116 J5 Barahona Dominican Rep 18.13N 71.07W
75 E5 Barahona Spain 41.17N 2.39W
30 J7 Baraila, Tal L Bihar India 25.46N 85.33E
28 J3 Barail Ra Assam/Nagaland India
30 B8 Baraitha Madhya Prad Ind 24.17N 78.56E
29 J6 Bara-Jamda Bihar India 22.12N 85.25E
75 C7 Barajas Spain 40.28N 3.35W
75 E7 Barajas de Melo Spain 40.07N 2.55W
29 K2 Bara Jorda W Bengal Ind 23.10N 86.51E
31 F2 Barak Afghanistan 36.58N 70.52E
37 D9 Barak Turkey 36.50N 37.59E
87 A5 Baraka Sudan 10.59N 27.59E
92 D4 Baraka Zaïre 4.09S 29.05E
87 F2 Baraka watercourse Ethiopia/Sudan
15 C7 Barakan isld Moluccas Indon 6.33S 134.47E
29 J1 Barakar R Bihar India
87 D3 Barakat Sudan 14.18N 33.32E
43 J2 Barakkul' Kazakhstan U.S.S.R. 52.10N 67.53E
29 J7 Barakot Orissa India 21.35N 85.05E
45 L2 Barakovo U.S.S.R. 54.38N 39.12E
28 J3 Barak R Manipur India
13 K7 Barakula Queensland 26.29S 150.30E
13 J6 Baralaba Queensland 24.10S 149.51E
29 E1 Bara Lacha Pass India 32.42N 77.30E
76 E3 Baralla Spain 42.53N 7.14W
35 E1 Bar'am Israel 33.04N 35.26E
18 L4 Baram R Sarawak Malaysia
119 J4 Barama R Guyana
89 E6 Baramana Guinea 10.09N 8.50W
119 J4 Baramanni Guyana 7.47N 59.10W
28 B1 Baramati Maharashtra India 18.12N 74.39E
29 J7 Baramba Orissa India 20.24N 85.22E
13 K7 Barambah R Queensland
75 E1 Barambio Spain 43.02N 2.55W
87 F1 Barameiya Sudan 18.39N 36.48E
18 K3 Baram, Tanjong C Sarawak Malaysia 4.35N 113.58E
31 H3 Baramula Kashmir 34.12N 74.24E
86 F3 Baramûn, El Egypt 31.08N 31.26E
45 B2 Baran' Belorussiya U.S.S.R. 54.28N 30.16E
29 E5 Baran Rajasthan India 25.08N 76.32E
87 L6 Baran Somalia 8.16N 47.15E
29 L6 Baranagar W Bengal India 22.38N 88.22E
42 C3 Baranakovo U.S.S.R. 58.10N 82.55E
34 N3 Barānān, Shākh i mts Iraq
47 M3 Baranchinskiy U.S.S.R. 58.14N 59.41E
37 H8 Barandūz R Iran
80 L5 Baranello Italy 41.32N 14.34E
30 J4 Barang Nepal 28.11N 85.06E
31 B4 Barangak Afghanistan 32.30N 62.13E
19 B7 Barangbarang Indonesia 6.30S 120.29E
72 J1 Barangeon R France
89 H5 Barani Upper Volta 13.09N 3.51W
30 A7 Barani R Madhya Prad India
39 H1 Baranikha U.S.S.R. 68.57N 168.12E
32 J5 Bārān, Kūh-e- mts Iran
43 H2 Barankul' Kazakhstan U.S.S.R. 51.10N 66.49E
119 D2 Baranoa Colombia 10.50N 74.55W
113 U8 Baranof Alaska 57.05N 134.50W
113 U8 Baranof I Alaska
46 F3 Baranovichi Belorussiya U.S.S.R. 53.09N 26.00E
45 T3 Baranovka Ul'yanovsk U.S.S.R. 53.02N 47.10E
45 S6 Baranovka Volgograd U.S.S.R. 50.00N 46.10E
62 N5 Baranów Poland 50.29N 21.29E
31 D8 Baran R Pakistan
40 L9 Baranskogo vol Kuril Is U.S.S.R. 45.06N 148.02E
82 E5 Baranya co Hungary
118 B3 Barão de Capanema Brazil 13.20S 57.52W
117 F8 Barão de Grajaú Brazil 6.43S 43.01W
118 C5 Barão de Melgaço Mato Grosso Brazil 16.14S 55.52W
120 G4 Barão de Melgaco Rondônia Brazil 11.15S 60.45W
76 B14 Barão de São Miguel Portugal 37.06N 8.47W
82 K4 Baraolt Romania 46.04N 25.36E
82 K4 Baraoltului, Munţii mts Romania
15 D5 Barapasi Irian Jaya 2.16S 137.02E
15 J2 Barapina Bougainville I Papua New Guinea 6.22S 155.35E
35 E3 Baraq Israel 32.32N 35.16E
61 N5 Baraque de Fraiture summit Belgium 50.15N 5.44E
61 P4 Baraque Michel summit Belgium 50.31N 6.04E
72 J7 Baraqueville Aveyron France 44.16N 2.25E
98 O5 Baraquois Pond Prov. Park Newfoundland
117 A9 Bararati, R Brazil
30 L7 Barari Bihar India 25.31N 87.23E
29 M2 Barasat W Bengal India 22.44N 88.31E
45 O2 Barashevo U.S.S.R. 54.31N 42.50E
46 G4 Barashi Ukraine U.S.S.R. 50.41N 27.59E
90 M5 Bara Simbil, Jebel mt Sudan 13.30N 24.19E
75 G2 Barasoain Spain 42.36N 1.39W
28 G7 Baratang I Andaman Is
107 F12 Barataria Louisiana 29.44N 90.09W
107 G12 Barataria B Louisiana 29.25N 89.50W
118 G9 Barata, Sa. do Brazil
19 E7 Barat Daya, Kep islds Indonesia
19 C8 Barate Timor Indon 9.56S 123.38E
44 B8 Baratovka Ukraine U.S.S.R. 46.56N 32.48E
12 E4 Baratta S Australia 32.01S 139.10E
66 H4 Bärau Switzerland 46.56N 7.49E
119 H7 Barauaná, Sa hills Brazil
30 H6 Barauli Bihar India 26.22N 84.36E
30 D7 Baraunda Madhya Prad India 25.02N 80.38E
29 G5 Baraundha Madhya Prad India 24.06N 81.10E
30 F8 Baraundha Uttar Prad India 24.57N 82.15E
30 J7 Barauni Bihar India 25.28N 85.59E
30 B7 Barauni Madhya Prad India 25.42N 78.23E
30 A3 Baraut Uttar Prad India 29.06N 77.15E
119 C6 Baraya Colombia 3.11N 75.04W
41 O8 Barayy R U.S.S.R.
34 M2 Barāzgir R Iraq
81 A2 Barazza, L Sardinia 40.42N 8.14E
119 C2 Barbacaos, B. de Colombia
118 G7 Barbacena Minas Gerais Brazil 21.13S 43.47W
117 C6 Barbacena Pará Brazil 2.46S 52.08W
76 E11 Barbacena Portugal 38.58N 7.17W
119 B7 Barbacoas Colombia 1.38N 78.08W
119 F3 Barbacoas Venezuela 9.31N 66.57W
76 D4 Barbadanes Spain 42.18N 7.53W
76 H7 Barbadillo Spain 40.56N 5.52W
75 D3 Barbadillo de Herreros Spain 42.09N 3.10W
75 D3 Barbadillo del Mercado Spain 42.03N 3.20W
75 D3 Barbadillo del Pez Spain 42.07N 3.14W
87 M7 Barbadle Somalia 7.48N 49.49E
118 B4 Barbado, R Mato Grosso Brazil
116 P6 Barbados isld Lesser Antilles
81 C3 Barbagia reg Sardinia
117 G8 Barbalha Brazil 7.15S 39.15W
75 F8 Barbalimpia Spain 39.59N 2.20W
44 G5 Barbalo mt Georgia U.S.S.R. 42.25N 45.13E
76 B3 Barbanza, Mtes. de Spain
Barbara Israel see Mavqi'im
79 O7 Barbara Italy 43.35N 13.02E
99 C3 Barbara L Ontario 49.20N 87.47W
79 L4 Barbarano Vicentino Italy 45.24N 11.33E
58 H3 Barbaraville Highland Scotland 57.43N 4.06W
86 L7 Barbar, Gebel el hill Egypt 29.16N 33.44E
79 H4 Barbariga Italy 45.24N 10.04E
36 B4 Barbaros İzmir Turkey 38.17N 26.34E
37 D2 Barbaros Tekirdağ Turkey 40.55N 27.28E
89 A1 Barbas, C Mauritania 22.20N 16.42W
72 E7 Barbaste France 44.10N 0.17E
75 L3 Barbastro Spain 42.02N 0.07E
77 E8 Barbate de Franco Spain 36.12N 5.55W
77 E8 Barbate, R. de Spain
70 F8 Barbâtre France 46.56N 2.10W
19 L6 Barbaza Philippines 11.14N 122.02E
72 F9 Barbazan France 43.02N 0.37E
98 D2 Barbel, L Quebec
61 H6 Barbençon Belgium 50.13N 4.17E
71 F9 Barbentane France 43.55N 4.45E
110 J6 Barber Idaho 43.34N 116.07W
77 S12 Barberia, Cabo de Balearic Is 38.39N 1.24E
71 K4 Barberine France 46.03N 6.57E
79 K6 Barberino di Mugello Italy 44.00N 11.14E
79 K7 Barberino di Val d'Elsa Italy 43.32N 11.11E
95 J2 Barberspan S Africa 26.37S 25.35E
95 J2 Barberspan salt pan S Africa 26.35S 25.35E
114 A5 Barbers Pt C Hawaiian Is 21.18N 158.07W
104 D5 Barberton Ohio 41.02N 81.37W
95 P1 Barberton S Africa 25.48S 31.03E
105 F8 Barberville Florida 29.11N 81.27W
72 D5 Barbezieux-St. Hilaire France 45.28N 0.09W
30 J7 Barbigha Bihar India 25.15N 85.42E
42 F5 Barbitay U.S.S.R. 53.40N 99.28E
69 D7 Barbizon France 48.26N 2.36E
79 J7 Barbona, Monte Italy 43.57N 10.36E
69 F6 Barbonne-Fayel France 48.39N 3.42E
119 D5 Barbosa Colombia 5.59N 73.38W
82 L5 Barboşi Romania 45.24N 28.00E
72 D8 Barbotan-les-Thermes France 43.57N 0.03W
104 G8 Barboursville Virginia 38.10N 78.17W
105 D1 Barbourville Kentucky 36.52N 83.54W
56 D5 Barbrook Devon Eng 51.13N 3.52W
116 O6 Barbuda isld Leeward Is W I 17.41N 61.48W
63 P9 Barby E Germany 51.58N 11.53E
75 E5 Barca Spain 41.27N 2.37W
76 F6 Barca d'Alva Portugal 41.01N 6.57W
116 A1 Barcadera Aruba W I 12.29N 69.59W
13 H6 Barcaldine Queensland 23.31S 145.15E
58 F5 Barcaldine Strathclyde Scotland 56.31N 5.19W
96 R1 Barca, Pta. da Azores 39.07N 28.04W
117 D5 Barcarena Brazil 1.30S 48.38W
76 C16 Barcarena Portugal 38.44N 9.17W
76 C16 Barcarena, R. de Portugal
72 L10 Barcarès, le France 42.47N 3.02E
77 C3 Barcarrota Spain 38.31N 6.51W
Barce see Marj, Al
81 K7 Barcellona Sicily 38.10N 15.15E
75 P5 Barcelona Spain 41.25N 2.10E
119 G2 Barcelona Venezuela 10.08N 64.43W
74 J3 Barcelona prov Spain
105 J7 Barceloneta Puerto Rico 18.17N 66.33W
72 D8 Barcelonne-du-Gers France 43.42N 0.14W
71 K8 Barcelonnette France 44.24N 6.40E
119 H8 Barcelos Brazil 0.59S 62.58W
76 B5 Barcelos Portugal 41.32N 8.37W
76 F2 Bárcena Spain 43.22N 6.30W
75 C1 Bárcena de Cicero Spain 43.25N 3.30W
76 L2 Bárcena de Pié de Concha Spain 43.08N 4.03W
76 G3 Bárcena, Embalse de res Spain 42.37N 6.30W
Barcham see Barsham
60 O11 Barchem Netherlands 52.08N 6.27E
77 Q2 Barcheta Spain 39.02N 0.25W
64 J2 Barchfeld E Germany 50.48N 10.19E
93 K4 Barchuma Guda Kenya 1.22N 38.13E
76 H5 Barcial del Barco Spain 41.56N 5.40W
76 L9 Barcience Spain 39.59N 4.14W
71 H8 Barcillonnette France 44.25N 5.55E
62 K3 Barcin Poland 52.51N 17.53E
79 N2 Barcis Italy 46.11N 12.34E
103 C8 Barclay Maryland 39.08N 75.52W
111 K4 Barclay Nevada 37.31N 114.17W
89 E9 Barclayville Liberia 4.48N 8.10W
105 L1 Barco N Carolina 36.24N 76.00W
76 D8 Barco Portugal 40.10N 7.36W
76 H8 Barco de Avila, El Spain 40.21N 5.31W
76 F4 Barco de Valdeorras, El Spain 42.24N 7.00W
75 E5 Barcones Spain 41.17N 2.49W
13 G6 Barcoo Cr Queensland/S Aust
119 D3 Barco Oilfields Colombia
13 H6 Barcoorah, L Queensland 22.32S 145.22E
62 K10 Barcs Hungary 45.58N 17.30E
72 C9 Barcus France 43.11N 0.46W
79 C3 Bard Italy 45.37N 7.45E
109 G6 Bard New Mexico 35.07N 103.14W
44 H7 Barda Azerbaydzhan U.S.S.R. 40.23N 47.08E
47 H7 Barda U.S.S.R. 56.58N 55.32E
121 C7 Barda del Medio Argentina 38.43S 68.13W
30 F7 Bardah Uttar Prad India 25.49N 82.51E
90 H1 Bardai Chad 21.21N 16.56E
36 E3 Bardakçi Turkey 39.20N 30.46E
34 K5 Bardasa Iraq 34.00N 42.28E
121 B5 Bardas Blancas Argentina 35.55S 69.47W
32 G3 Bardaskan Iran 35.11N 57.58E
34 F7 Bardawil, Khabrat al salt marsh Saudi Arabia
44 F10 Bardeh R Iran
37 H8 Bardeh Sūr R Iran
62 N6 Bardejov Czechoslovakia 49.18N 21.15E
66 L8 Bardello R Italy
75 H3 Bardenas, Can. de las Spain
61 P3 Bardenberg W Germany 50.50N 6.07E
63 R8 Bardenitz E Germany 52.05N 12.56E
87 J9 Bardera Somalia 2.18N 42.18E
32 D7 Bardestān Iran 27.55N 51.58E
50 F2 Bardh Iceland 66.03N 19.09W
50 H5 Bardharbunga ice cap Iceland 64.38N 17.34W
50 C3 Bardhastrandarsýsla, Austur co Iceland
50 B3 Bardhastrandarsýsla, Vestur co Iceland
58 Q9 Bard Hd Shetland Scotland 60.06N 1.05W
53 M9 Bardhidh headland Faeroes 62.07N 7.28W
50 M4 Bardhsneshorn C Iceland 65.11N 13.33W
50 C2 Bardhsvik inlet Iceland
79 G5 Bardi Italy 44.38N 9.43E
29 H5 Bardi Madhya Prad India 24.30N 82.28E
Bardia see Bardīyah
30 G8 Bardiha Bihar India 24.23N 83.43E
85 L6 Bardis Egypt 26.13N 31.59E
Bardistan see Bardestān
58 Q9 Bardister Shetland Scotland 60.29N 1.21W
85 H4 Bardīyah Libya 31.44N 25.08E
37 G5 Bardız Turkey 40.25N 42.20E
57 N6 Bardney Lincs Eng 53.12N 0.21W
14 D9 Bardoc W Australia 30.25S 121.19E
79 J3 Bardolino Italy 45.33N 10.43E
79 A4 Bardonecchia Italy 45.05N 6.42E
57 J3 Bardon Mill Northumb Eng 54.59N 2.20W
72 B9 Bardos France 43.28N 1.12W
98 E2 Bardoux, L Quebec
63 M6 Bardowick W Germany 53.18N 10.23E
57 G4 Bardsea Cumbria Eng 54.09N 3.05W
56 B2 Bardsey I Gwynedd Wales 52.46N 4.48W
32 D4 Bard Shah Iran 32.41N 50.30E
107 L4 Bardstown Kentucky 37.49N 85.29W
51 G3 Bardu Norway 68.54N 18.20E
51 G3 Barduelv R Norway 68.48N 18.22E
13 H7 Barduthulla Queensland 26.04S 146.25E
107 G5 Bardwell Kentucky 36.52N 89.01W
112 L3 Bardwell Texas 32.16N 96.43W
109 O9 Bardwell Reservoir Texas
47 M4 Bardym R U.S.S.R.
47 M4 Bardymskiy Khrebet mts U.S.S.R.
72 E10 Barèges France 42.53N 0.04E
11 M6 Bare I New Zealand 39.48S 177.03E
30 C4 Bareilly Uttar Prad India 28.20N 79.24E
30 C4 Bareilly dist Uttar Prad India
90 L5 Barei, Wadi watercourse Sudan
29 F6 Bareli Madhya Prad India 23.00N 78.18E
12 H5 Barellan New S Wales 34.17S 146.34E
63 J7 Barenburg W Germany 52.38N 8.48E
60 G12 Barendrecht Netherlands 51.52N 4.31E
28 H3 Barengapara Meghalaya India 25.16N 90.13E
66 N5 Bären Horn mt Switzerland 46.35N 9.14E
64 P3 Bärenstein E Germany 50.30N 13.02E
70 M2 Barentin France 49.33N 0.57E
70 J4 Barenton France 48.36N 0.50W
69 F4 Barenton-Bugny France 49.38N 3.40E
41 C2 Barentsa, Ostrova islds Novaya Zemlya U.S.S.R. 76.16N 61.00E
50 S14 Barentsburg Spitsbergen 78.03N 14.20E
Barentsovo More see Barents Sea
50 U14 Barentsøya isld Spitsbergen
38 C1 Barents Sea Arctic Oc
87 F3 Barentu Ethiopia 15.08N 37.36E
18 L4 Bareo Sarawak Malaysia 3.35N 115.22E
30 A7 Barer Madhya Prad India 25.42N 77.12E
81 B4 Baressa Sardinia 39.43N 8.53E
66 M2 Bäretswil Switzerland 47.21N 8.52E
103 B6 Bareville Pennsylvania 40.06N 76.10W
30 J8 Barew Bihar India 24.51N 85.33E
75 C1 Bareyo Spain 43.28N 3.35W
70 H2 Barfleur France 49.40N 1.16W
70 H2 Barfleur, Pte. de France 49.42N 1.16W
56 H3 Barford Warwicks Eng 52.15N 1.35W
56 H5 Barford Wilts Eng 51.05N 1.57W
79 H6 Barga Italy 44.04N 10.29E
24 D10 Barga Xizang Zizhiqu China 30.51N 81.20E
87 N5 Bargal Somalia 11.18N 51.03E
33 H2 Barganshar oil well Iran 29.54N 49.37E
30 K7 Bargaon Bihar India 25.45N 86.49E
13 K6 Bargara Queensland 24.49S 152.29E
29 H7 Bargarh Orissa India 21.25N 83.35E
30 E7 Bargarh Uttar Prad India 25.08N 81.26E
76 L9 Bargas Spain 39.56N 4.02W
30 A7 Bargawan Madhya Prad India 25.40N 77.03E
79 B5 Barge Italy 44.44N 7.19E
98 Q2 Barge Bay Labrador, Nfld 51.49N 56.11W
87 J8 Bargeilo Ethiopia 4.46N 42.37E
71 K9 Bargemon France 43.38N 6.33E
66 L1 Bargen Switzerland 47.46N 8.37E
60 Q9 Barger-Oosterveen Netherlands 52.43N 6.59E
60 Q8 Barger-Oosterveld Netherlands 52.46N 6.58E
32 G2 Barghamad Iran 36.30N 57.35E
79 H3 Barghe Italy 45.40N 10.24E
34 J4 Barghuth, Sabkhat el salt marsh Syria
Bargiri see Muradiye Van Turkey
63 T5 Bargischow E Germany 53.50N 13.46E
35 D7 Bar Giyyora Israel 31.43N 35.04E
56 E4 Bargoed Mid Glam Wales 51.43N 3.15W
30 G6 Bargon Shargi Uttar Prad India 26.30N 83.11E
57 D2 Bargrennan Dumfries & Galloway Scotland 55.04N 4.35W
63 M5 Bargteheide W Germany 53.44N 10.15E
72 G7 Barguelonne R France
31 H10 Barguna Bangladesh 22.09N 90.07E
28 C5 Bargur Tamil Nadu India 11.49N 77.33E
42 H5 Barguzin U.S.S.R. 53.40N 109.35E
42 H5 Barguzin R U.S.S.R.
42 H5 Barguzinskiy Khrebet mts U.S.S.R.
42 H5 Barguzinskiy Zaliv gulf U.S.S.R.
30 J7 Barh Bihar India 25.29N 85.43E
30 G6 Barhaj Uttar Prad India 26.16N 83.44E
30 G6 Barhalganj Uttar Prad India 26.17N 83.30E
30 K6 Barhamjia Nepal 26.38N 86.50E
30 J6 Barhampur Bihar India 26.18N 85.45E
30 B5 Barhan Uttar Prad India 27.21N 78.11E
30 B3 Barhapura Uttar Prad India 29.32N 78.32E
104 R2 Bar Harbor Maine 44.20N 68.14W
30 H6 Barharia Bihar India 26.19N 84.27E
57 E3 Barharrow Dumfries & Galloway Scotland 54.51N 4.10W
30 L8 Barharwa Bihar India 24.52N 87.47E
30 K7 Barhat Bihar India 25.02N 86.18E
18 E8 Barhau Indonesia 5.19S 102.10E
30 J8 Barhi Bihar India 24.19N 85.25E
30 K7 Barhiya Bihar India 25.18N 86.02E
30 F5 Barhni Uttar Prad India 27.29N 82.48E
Bar'hoûte, Sabkhet el see Barghuth, Sabkhat el
87 J8 Bar Hugn Ethiopia 5.10N 43.24E
81 N1 Bari Italy 41.07N 16.52E
30 A6 Bari Rajasthan Ind 26.39N 77.37E
91 F2 Bari Zaïre 3.20N 19.25E
81 N2 Bari prov Italy
87 C8 Bari tribe Sudan
90 H6 Baria Chad 11.05N 16.10E
Baria India see Devgad Baria
93 E8 Bariadi watercourse Tanzania
87 F2 Bariaiyat watercourse Sudan
30 K7 Bariarpur Bihar India 25.17N 86.35E
79 L5 Baricella Italy 44.39N 11.32E
93 L9 Baricho Kenya 3.05S 39.48E
33 B4 Baridī, Ra's C Saudi Arabia 24.17N 37.33E
31 G5 Bari Doab interfluve Pakistan
30 G4 Bari Gad R Nepal
79 G5 Barigazzo, Monte Italy 44.36N 9.49E
35 G3 Bariha, El Jordan 32.34N 35.49E
31 D4 Barihak Pass Afghanistan 33.34N 67.33E
88 Q4 Barika Algeria 35.23N 5.19E
88 Q4 Barika R Algeria
92 H6 Barikiwa Tanzania 9.30S 37.53E
31 F3 Barikot Afghanistan 35.18N 71.36E
30 F4 Barikot Nepal 28.58N 82.15E
80 N7 Barile Italy 40.56N 15.40E
15 J6 Barim Bismarck Arch 5.39S 147.52E
119 H3 Barima channel Venez/Guyana
119 J4 Barima R Guyana/Venez
119 E3 Barinas Venezuela 8.36N 70.15W
37 F7 Barınç Turkey 38.01N 41.08E
107 D1 Baring Missouri 40.15N 92.12W
110 D2 Baring Washington 47.46N 121.28W
101 P1 Baring, C Victoria I, N W Terr 69.57N 117.30W
14 B6 Baring Downs W Australia
11 J8 Baring Hd New Zealand 41.25S 174.52E
14 E10 Baring, Mt W Australia 33.45S 123.12E
93 G5 Baringo dist Kenya
93 H5 Baringo, L Kenya
53 D5 Båring Vig B Denmark 55.30N 9.55E
119 E3 Barinitas Venezuela 8.45N 70.26W
29 K7 Baripada Orissa India 21.52N 86.48E
35 G1 Bariqah Syria 33.02N 35.52E
19 E8 Barique Indonesia 8.51S 126.04E
118 E8 Bariri Brazil 22.04S 48.41W
85 L7 Bârîs Egypt 24.39N 30.35E
29 D5 Bari Sadri Rajasthan India 24.22N 74.45E
44 F5 Barisakho Georgia U.S.S.R. 42.28N 44.55E
31 H9 Barisal Bangladesh 22.41N 90.20E
31 H9 Barisal dist Bangladesh
81 D4 Bari Sardo Sardinia 39.51N 9.40E
80 J4 Barisciano Italy 42.20N 13.36E
93 J6 Barisho Kenya 0.35S 37.15E
69 E4 Barisis France 49.35N 3.20E
66 G3 Bäriswil Switzerland 47.02N 7.33E
34 K7 Barit, Al Iraq 31.15N 42.29E
18 L6 Barito R Kalimantan Indonesia
Bariya see Devgad Baria
71 E8 Barjac France 44.18N 4.21E
80 O2 Barjaki, Rtic pt Yugoslavia 43.03N 16.03E
71 J9 Barjaude mt France 43.40N 6.20E
71 J9 Barjols France 43.33N 6.01E
29 L2 Barjora W Bengal Ind 23.27N 87.18E
76 F3 Barjos Spain 42.37N 6.59W
85 B7 Barjuj watercourse Libya
33 M5 Barkā Oman 23.41N 57.58E
Barka Band see Parkā Bandar
30 H7 Barkagaon Bihar India 25.14N 84.26E
30 H7 Barkagaon Bihar India 25.27N 84.08E
53 K4 Barkåkra Sweden 56.18N 12.53E
31 J10 Barkal Bangladesh 22.45N 92.26E
23 C3 Barkam Sichuan China 31.42N 102.20E
32 C6 Barkan, Ra's-e C Iran 30.00N 49.35E
85 A7 Barkāt, Al Libya 24.51N 10.11E
52 J6 Barken, N Sweden 60.10N 15.35E
104 G3 Barker New York 43.20N 78.33W
14 D9 Barker L W Australia 31.49S 120.05E
101 N9 Barkerville Br Columbia 53.06N 121.35W
104 F5 Barkeyville Pennsylvania 41.12N 79.59W
Barkha see Barga
103 J3 Barkhamsted Res Connecticut
31 E6 Barkhan Pakistan 29.55N 69.34E
Barkhan Buddha Shan mts see Burhan Budai Shan
29 E6 Barkhera Madhya Prad India 22.54N 77.40E
55 J3 Barking London England 51.33N 0.06E
55 J3 Barking bor London England
55 J2 Barkingside London Eng 51.35N 0.06E
93 G7 Barkitabu Kenya 1.27S 35.37E
99 H6 Bark L Ontario
107 J5 Barkley Res Kentucky
110 A1 Barkley Sd Vancouver I, Br Col
95 J9 Barkly Bridge S Africa 33.37S 25.42E
13 E5 Barkly Downs Queensland 20.32S 138.25E
95 L6 Barkly East S Africa 30.58S 27.35E
13 D4 Barkly Highway rd N Terr Australia
13 B5 Barkly, Mt N Terr Australia 21.36S 132.30E
95 L7 Barkly Pass S Africa 31.11S 27.50E
13 D4 Barkly Tableland N Terr Australia
95 H4 Barkly West S Africa 28.32S 24.32E
Barköl see Barkol Hu
Bar Köl L see Barkol Hu
87 C2 Barkol watercourse Sudan
24 G4 Barkol Hu L Xinjiang Uygur Zizhiqu China 43.45N 92.50E
24 H4 Barkol Kazak Zizhixian Xinjiang Uygur Zizhiqu China 43.36N 93.02E
29 F2 Barkot Uttar Prad India 30.50N 78.12E
106 G4 Bark R Michigan 45.43N 87.18W
112 G6 Barksdale Texas 29.45N 100.04W
57 M7 Barkston Lincs Eng 52.58N 0.37W
32 G5 Barkūh Iran 30.39N 56.21E
56 M4 Barkway Herts Eng 52.00N 0.01E
36 E4 Barla Turkey 38.01N 30.45E
36 E4 Barla Dağ mt Turkey
57 D3 Barlae Dumfries & Galloway Scotland 54.55N 4.41W
24 G3 Barlag Gol R Mongolia
57 L6 Barlborough Derbys Eng 53.18N 1.16W
69 J6 Bar-le Duc France 48.46N 5.10E
14 C8 Barlee L W Australia
14 B6 Barlee Ra W Australia
71 J8 Barles France 44.15N 6.16E
80 O6 Barletta Italy 41.20N 16.17E
56 M3 Barley Herts Eng 52.01N 0.03E
57 G5 Bar Lightship Liverpool B England 53.33N 3.20W
69 D3 Barlin France 50.27N 2.37E
62 J3 Barlinek Poland 53.00N 15.11E
52 L9 Barlingbo Sweden 57.35N 18.27E
63 E9 Barlo W Germany 51.53N 6.41E
63 L4 Barlohe W Germany 54.09N 9.38E
89 C7 Barlo Pt Sierra Leone 8.53N 13.18W
96 P9 Barlovento La Palma Canary Is 28.49N 17.48W
108 L2 Barlow N Dakota 47.34N 99.09W
101 W4 Barlow L N W Terr
110 D4 Barlow Pass Oregon 45.18N 121.40W
42 G5 Barluk U.S.S.R. 54.30N 101.45E
43 P4 Barlyk, Khrebet mts Xinjiang Uygur Zizhiqu China
15 B4 Barma Irian Jaya 1.52S 132.59E
12 H6 Barmah Forest Victoria
44 E4 Barmamyt, mt U.S.S.R. 43.41N 42.29E
45 Q8 Barmantsak, Oz L U.S.S.R.
45 D9 Barmashovo Ukraine U.S.S.R. 47.05N 32.27E
57 M5 Barmby on the Moor Humberside Eng 53.56N 0.49W
30 D3 Barmdeo Mandi Nepal 29.06N 80.10E
12 H5 Barmedman New S Wales 34.08S 147.25E
Barmen W Germany see Wuppertal
53 S14 Barmen isld Norway
29 B5 Barmer Rajasthan India 25.43N 71.25E
29 B5 Barmer dist Rajasthan India
12 F5 Barmera S Australia 34.15S 140.31E
32 D5 Barm Fīrūz, Kūh-e mt Iran 30.25N 51.58E
56 C2 Barmouth Gwynedd Wales 52.43N 4.03W
63 L5 Barmstedt W Germany 53.47N 9.47E
59 D5 Barna Galway Irish Rep 53.15N 9.09W
98 G7 Barnaby River New Brunswick 46.54N 65.32W
66 O6 Barna, Cima di mt Switzerland 46.26N 9.17E
50 F3 Barnadalsfjall mt Iceland 65.56N 19.15W
59 E5 Barnaderg Galway Irish Rep 53.29N 8.43W
29 D6 Barnagar Madhya Prad India 23.01N 75.28E
29 D2 Barnala Punjab India 30.26N 75.33E
109 M2 Barnard Kansas 39.12N 98.02W
108 M4 Barnard S Dakota 45.43N 98.30W
57 K3 Barnard Castle Durham Eng 54.33N 1.55W
113 T7 Barnard, Mt Alaska/Br Col 59.06N 136.55W
86 F6 Barnasht Egypt 29.42N 31.15E
12 G4 Barnato New S Wales 31.38S 144.59E
64 N4 Bärnau W Germany 49.48N 12.27E
42 C5 Barnaul U.S.S.R. 53.21N 83.45E
42 C5 Barnaulka R U.S.S.R.
11 C11 Barn B New Zealand
12 H8 Barn Bluff mt Tasmania 41.44S 145.54E
57 L6 Barnby Moor Notts Eng 53.21N 1.00W
103 F7 Barnegat New Jersey 39.45N 74.14W
103 F7 Barnegat B New Jersey
103 F7 Barnegat Light New Jersey 39.46N 74.07W
103 G7 Barnegat Light Ship New Jersey
123 H7 Barne Inlet Antarctica
109 O2 Barnes Kansas 39.42N 96.54W
55 D4 Barnes London Eng 51.28N 0.15W
104 G6 Barnesboro Pennsylvania 40.40N 78.47W
59 G1 Barnes Gap V Donegal Irish Rep 55.04N 7.55W
29 L4 Barnes Ghat W Bengal India 26.30N 88.52E
97 M3 Barnes Icecap N W Terr 70.10N 74.00W
59 G2 Barnesmore Gap pass Donegal Irish Rep 54.43N 7.56W
105 G12 Barnes Sd Florida
108 O9 Barneston Nebraska 40.02N 96.33W
105 C4 Barnesville Georgia 33.04N 84.09W
108 O3 Barnesville Minnesota 46.40N 96.25W
104 D7 Barnesville Ohio 40.00N 81.11W
101 H11 Barnet Br Columbia 49.18N 122.57W
55 E2 Barnet London England 51.39N 0.12W
55 E2 Barnet bor London England
60 L11 Barneveld Netherlands 52.08N 5.35E
70 G3 Barneville France 49.23N 1.45W
63 R7 Barnewitz E Germany 52.34N 12.36E
108 Q8 Barney Iowa 41.09N 94.00W
12 G5 Barneys L New S Wales 33.16S 144.13E
111 N4 Barney Top mt Utah 37.46N 111.52W
60 R8 Barnflair Netherlands 52.51N 7.05E
56 N3 Barnham Suffolk Eng 52.22N 0.45E
112 F4 Barnhart Texas 31.09N 101.12W
99 S2 Barnhart I New York 44.59N 74.50W
63 S7 Barnim reg E Germany
96 B13 Barn Long Pt St Helena 15.55S 5.39W
98 F5 Barn Mt Quebec 48.55N 66.12W
70 E3 Barnouic / France 49.03N 2.50W
57 L5 Barnsdale Bar S Yorks Eng 53.37N 1.13W
109 O5 Barnsdall Oklahoma 36.35N 96.11W
56 H4 Barnsley Glos Eng 51.45N 1.54W
103 C7 Barnsley Pennsylvania 39.46N 75.59W
57 L5 Barnsley S Yorks Eng 53.34N 1.28W
103 O3 Barnstable Massachusetts 41.42N 70.17W
103 O3 Barnstable co Massachusetts
56 C5 Barnstaple Devon Eng 51.05N 4.04W
56 C5 Barnstaple B Devon Eng
56 D6 Barnstaple Cross Devon Eng 50.48N 3.43W
104 O3 Barnstead New Hampshire 43.21N 71.20W
101 J11 Barnston I Br Col 49.12N 122.44W
63 H7 Barnstorf W Germany 52.43N 8.30E
96 B13 Barn, The mt St Helena 15.55S 5.40W
63 K9 Barntrup W Germany 52.00N 9.06E
108 S3 Barnum Minnesota 46.30N 92.40W
19 M3 Barnum B Palau Is Pacific Oc
100 E9 Barnwell Alberta 49.47N 112.14W
105 F4 Barnwell S Carolina 33.14N 81.21W
64 P6 Bärnzell W Germany 48.59N 13.14E
89 E6 Baro Guinea 10.38N 9.39W
90 C7 Baro Nigeria 8.37N 6.19E
Baroda Gujarat see Vadodara
29 E5 Baroda Madhya Prad India 25.29N 76.42E
95 J8 Baroda S Africa 32.01S 25.31E
95 H9 Baroe S Africa 33.14S 24.34E
31 G2 Baroghil Pass Pakistan/Afghan 36.54N 73.22E
87 C4 Baroki Sudan 12.40N 30.36E
30 E8 Baroknar Uttar Prad India 24.54N 81.56E
11 H8 Barometer mt New Zealand 41.50S 173.39E
69 D5 Baron France 49.10N 2.45E
79 E8 Barona dist Milan Italy
Baroncourt see Dommary-Baroncourt
66 J9 Barone, Monte Italy 45.44N 8.10E
80 O5 Barone, Monte Italy 41.45N 16.10E
23 B3 Barong Sichuan China 31.03N 99.20E
80 L7 Baronissi Italy 40.44N 14.46E
71 G8 Baronnies, les dist France
100 D9 Barons Alberta 49.59N 113.03W
14 F6 Baron's Ra W Australia
61 K6 Baronville Belgium 50.08N 4.56E
69 M6 Baronville France 48.56N 6.36E
87 E6 Baro,R Ethiopia
15 K2 Barora Fa I Solomon Is 7.30S 158.16E
15 K2 Barora Ite I Solomon Is 7.35S 158.25E
76 D6 Barosa R Portugal
Barotse prov see Western prov Zambia
28 J2 Barpathar Assam India 26.16N 93.50E
28 H2 Barpeta Assam India 26.20N 91.02E
72 C6 Barp, le France 44.37N 0.46W
33 H4 Barqā ad Dumrān Saudi Arabia
33 F8 Barqā al Ashqar dist Yemen
35 J10 Barqafarhat, Jeb mt Jordan 30.51N 36.21E
86 G8 Barqa, Gebel hill Egypt 28.36N 31.43E
86 M8 Barqa, Gebel hill Egypt 28.46N 34.24E
86 K4 Barqa, Gebel el hill Egypt 30.43N 33.15E
86 M5 Barqa, Gebel el hill Egypt 30.25N 34.19E
85 M7 Barqa, Gebel el mt Egypt 24.24N 32.29E
35 D4 Barqay Israel 32.28N 35.01E
31 E4 Barqi Rajan Afghanistan 33.56N 68.54E
77 O5 Barqueros Spain 37.57N 1.22W
76 C10 Barquinha Portugal 39.27N 8.25W
119 E2 Barquisimeto Venezuela 10.03N 69.18W
109 F2 Barr Colorado 39.57N 104.47W
69 N7 Barr France 48.25N 7.27E
57 D2 Barr Strathclyde Scotland 55.13N 4.43W
118 G2 Barra Bahia Brazil 11.06S 43.15W
117 G6 Barra Piauí Brazil 3.46S 41.55W
76 B7 Barra Portugal 40.38N 8.45W
121 H4 Barra Rio Grande do Sul Brazil 32.10S 52.05W
58 B5 Barra isld W Isles Scotland
75 M8 Barra Alta, Placer de la sandbank Spain 39.49N 0.31E
31 B10 Barra Andai isld Pakistan 24.48N 67.00E
12 K4 Barraba New S Wales 30.24S 152.36E
118 E8 Barra Bonita Brazil 22.30S 48.35W
117 C5 Barraca da Bôca Brazil 0.32S 52.30W
117 A9 Barracão do Barreto Brazil 8.50S 58.17W
75 J7 Barracas Spain 40.01N 0.42W
121 K4 Barracas dist Buenos Aires Arg
75 H6 Barrachina Spain 40.54N 1.08W
29 L6 Barrackpore W Bengal India 22.45N 88.20E
76 K8 Barraco Spain 40.28N 4.39W
118 H3 Barra da Estiva Brazil 13.38S 41.20W
118 H10 Barra da Tijuca Brazil 23.01S 43.18W
118 J10 Barra da Tijuca pt Brazil 23.01S 43.17W
115 G8 Barra de Navidad Mexico 19.12N 104.41W
118 H8 Barra de São João Brazil 22.36S 41.59W
118 B4 Barra do Bugres Brazil 15.01S 57.11W
117 E7 Barra do Corda Brazil 5.30S 45.12W
91 C8 Barra do Cuanza Angola 9.18S 13.10E
118 H6 Barra do Cuieté Brazil 19.03S 41.31W
91 C8 Barra do Dande Angola 8.30S 13.22E
118 D4 Barra do Garças Brazil 15.54S 52.15W
118 G2 Barra do Mendes Brazil 11.35S 42.03W
118 F6 Barra do Paraopeba Brazil 18.51S 45.09W
118 G8 Barra do Piraí Brazil 22.30S 43.50W
121 F3 Barra do Quaraí Brazil 30.13S 57.30W
121 H3 Barra do Ribeiro Brazil 30.20S 51.15W
117 A8 Barra do São Manuel Brazil 7.17S 58.02W
118 E9 Barra do Turvo Brazil 24.52S 48.34W
94 N4 Barra Falsa, Pta Da Mozambique 22.51S 35.35E
81 H9 Barrafranca Sicily 37.23N 14.13E
118 F10 Barra Funda dist São Paulo Brazil
76 B13 Barragem de Campilhas res Portugal
33 F4 Barrah, Al Saudi Arabia 24.57N 45.50E
58 A5 Barra Head W Isles Scotland 56.47N 7.36W
115 N2 Barra Kruta Honduras 15.15N 83.24W
33 N6 Barr al Hikmān des Oman
118 G8 Barra Mansa Brazil 22.35S 44.12W
72 E8 Barran France 43.37N 0.28E
33 F9 Barrān Yemen 15.47N 44.34E
31 G5 Barrana Pakistan 31.45N 72.40E
120 B4 Barranca Lima Peru 10.46S 77.46W
120 B1 Barranca Loreto Peru 4.49S 76.38W
119 D3 Barranca Venezuela 9.07N 72.45W
119 D4 Barrancabermeja Colombia 7.06N 73.54W
119 E3 Barrancas Barinas Venez 8.47N 70.07W
119 D2 Barrancas Colombia 10.59N 72.46W
119 H3 Barrancas Monagas Venez 8.45N 62.13W
121 F9 Barrancas dist Santiago Chile
121 F3 Barrancas R Corrientes Arg
121 B6 Barrancas R Mendoza Arg
120 B10 Barranco dist Lima Peru
118 B7 Barranco Branco Brazil 21.05S 57.46W
76 C14 Barranco das Porcas Portugal 37.20N 8.18W
77 O3 Barranco de Jumilla R Spain

119 D3 **Barranco de Loba** Colombia 8.56N 74.07W
76 D14 **Barranco do Velho** Portugal 37.14N 7.56W
76 F12 **Barrancos** Portugal 38.08N 6.59W
12 M5 **Barranjoey** New S Wales 33.36S 151.20E
121 F1 **Barranqueras** Argentina 27.29S 58.54W
119 D2 **Barranquilla** Atlántico Colombia 11.10N 74.50W
119 D7 **Barranquilla** Vaupés Colombia 1.42N 72.17W
120 B1 **Barranquita** Peru 5.06S 76.53W
116 H10 **Barranquitas** Venezuela 9.58N 72.02W
33 H10 **Barrāqah** S Yemen 14.00N 48.28E
117 F7 **Barras** Brazil 4.16S 42.21W
119 D8 **Barras** Colombia 1.47S 73.12W
58 B4 **Barra, Sd. of** W Isles Scotland
99 N4 **Barraute** Quebec 48.26N 77.39W
71 H6 **Barraux** France 45.26N 5.59E
77 M2 **Barrax** Spain 39.04N 2.12W
103 K2 **Barre** Massachusetts 42.25N 72.07W
104 N2 **Barre** Vermont 44.13N 72.31W
121 C2 **Barreal** La Rioja Argentina 29.35S 66.10W
121 B3 **Barreal** San Juan Argentina 31.40S 69.27W
70 F8 **Barre-de-Monts, la** France 46.52N 2.07W
71 D8 **Barre-des-Cévennes** France 44.15N 3.38E
70 M4 **Barre-en-Ouche, la** France 48.57N 0.40E
103 K2 **Barre Falls Res** Massachusetts 42.24N 72.04W
118 G3 **Barreiras** Brazil 12.09S 44.58W
117 A6 **Barreirinha** Brazil 2.46S 57.02W
117 F6 **Barreirinhas** Brazil 2.46S 42.51W
76 A11 **Barreiro** Portugal 38.40N 9.05W
118 D4 **Barreiro** *R* Brazil
118 E2 **Barreiro do Nascimento** Brazil 11.56S 50.38W
117 J9 **Barreiros** Brazil 8.46S 35.08W
76 E1 **Barreiros** Spain 43.32N 7.14W
71 J9 **Barrême** France 43.57N 6.22E
107 K5 **Barren** *R* Kentucky
28 H7 **Barren I** Andaman Is 12.18N 93.49E
121 E10 **Barren I** Falkland Is 52.20S 59.40W
122 V7 **Barren I** Palmyra I Pacific Oc 5.53N 162.04W
113 L7 **Barren Is** Alaska
95 F6 **Barren Pan** *salt pan* S Africa 30.10S 22.47E
107 L5 **Barren River Res** Kentucky
103 K2 **Barre Plains** Massachusetts 42.23N 72.07W
77 M3 **Barreros** *mt* Spain 38.58N 2.29W
67 P11 **Barretali** Corsica 42.52N 9.20E
71 H8 **Barret-de-Lioure** France 44.11N 5.30E
118 K9 **Barreto** Brazil 22.53S 43.07W
118 E7 **Barretos** Brazil 20.40S 48.35W
111 H9 **Barrett L** California 32.40N 116.40W
14 F4 **Barrett, Mt** W Australia 18.11S 127.25E
100 C4 **Barrhead** Alberta 54.10N 114.22W
58 H7 **Barrhead** Strathclyde Scotland 55.48N 4.24W
57 D2 **Barrhill** Strathclyde Scotland 55.07N 4.46W
66 G7 **Barrhorn** *mt* Switzerland 46.10N 7.45E
87 H5 **Barri** Ethiopia 10.39N 41.02E
56 E5 **Barri** S Glam Wales 51.24N 3.18W
33 D8 **Barrī** *isld* Farasān Is Red Sea 16.18N 41.59E
99 L8 **Barrie** Ontario 44.22N 79.42W
99 H7 **Barrie I** Ontario 45.55N 82.38W
11 K3 **Barrier C** New Zealand 36.21S 175.32E
101 N10 **Barrière** Br Columbia 51.10N 120.07W
11 K3 **Barrier I, Gt** New Zealand
15 M9 **Barrier Reef** Louisiade Arch
9 U12 **Barrier Reef** Tonga, Pacific Oc
12 F6 **Barrika** S Australia 35.00S 140.02E
106 F7 **Barrington** Illinois 42.09N 88.08W
13 H8 **Barrington** New S Wales 29.02S 145.40E
98 G10 **Barrington** Nova Scotia 43.34N 65.35W
103 M3 **Barrington** Rhode I 41.45N 71.19W
95 F9 **Barrington** S Africa 33.55S 22.51E
Barrington I *see* **Santa Fé, I**
100 R1 **Barrington L** Manitoba
12 K4 **Barrington, Mt** New S Wales 32.03S 151.55E
98 G10 **Barrington Passage** Nova Scotia 43.32N 65.38W
12 H3 **Barringun** New S Wales 29.03S 145.44E
76 B3 **Barrio de la Maza, Embalse** *res* Spain 42.54N 8.45W
75 F4 **Barriomartín** Spain 42.00N 2.29W
120 B9 **Barrio Obrero Industrial** *dist* Lima Peru
76 H3 **Barrios de Luna, Emb. de los** *res* Spain 42.52N 5.55W
53 D5 **Barrit** Denmark 55.43N 9.53E
76 B3 **Barro** Spain 42.34N 8.38W
110 M9 **Barro** Utah 40.43N 113.30W
118 E4 **Barro Alto** Brazil 15.07S 48.53W
121 B9 **Barroa, Mte** Argentina 43.28S 70.17W
76 D8 **Barroca** Portugal 40.06N 7.43W
118 G5 **Barrocão** Brazil 16.22S 43.05W
115 E10 **Barro Colorado I** Panama Canal Zone
110 E1 **Barron** Washington 48.44N 120.43W
106 C4 **Barron** Wisconsin 45.24N 91.50W
106 C4 **Barronett** Wisconsin 45.38N 91.59W
13 H3 **Barron Falls & Gorge** Queensland 16.46S 145.38E
112 J8 **Barroso** Texas 27.04N 98.10W
115 J4 **Barroterán** Mexico 27.42N 101.20W
72 F2 **Barrou** France 46.53N 0.46E
90 M9 **Barroua** Cent Afr Rep 5.39N 24.45E
113 J1 **Barrow** Alaska 71.16N 156.50W
121 E7 **Barrow** Argentina 38.16S 60.14W
57 N5 **Barrow** Humberside Eng 53.41N 0.23W
Barrow, C *see* **Santiago, Pta. de**
13 D2 **Barrow, C** N Terr Australia 13.37S 136.00E
13 C5 **Barrow Creek** N Terr Australia 21.32S 133.53E
57 J5 **Barrowford** Lancs Eng 53.52N 2.13W
14 B5 **Barrow I** W Australia 21.00S 115.30E
57 G4 **Barrow in Furness** Cumbria Eng 54.07N 3.14W
113 J1 **Barrow, Point** Alaska
13 G2 **Barrow Pt** Queensland 14.19S 144.40E
59 J7 **Barrow,R** Wexford etc Irish Rep
14 F7 **Barrow Ra** W Australia
100 Q6 **Barrows** Manitoba 52.50N 101.26W
97 K3 **Barrow Str** N W Terr 73.50N 95.00W
33 B9 **Barr, Ra's al** *C* Bahrain, The Gulf 25.48N 50.35E
14 D7 **Barr Smith Ra** W Australia
76 F6 **Barruecopardo** Spain 41.04N 6.40W
76 L3 **Barruelo de Santullán** Spain 42.54N 4.17W
61 E4 **Barry** Belgium 50.35N 3.33E
107 E2 **Barry** Illinois 39.41N 91.01W
58 L5 **Barry** Tayside Scotland 56.30N 2.46W
95 D9 **Barrydale** S Africa 33.55S 20.44E
101 T2 **Barry I** N-W Terr
99 N7 **Barrys Bay** Ontario 45.30N 77.41W
106 J6 **Barryton** Michigan 43.45N 85.10W
103 G2 **Barrytown** New York 42.00N 73.55W
11 F9 **Barrytown** New Zealand 42.14S 171.19E
103 E4 **Barryville** New York 41.29N 74.55W
Bars *see* **Bārz Shovār**
72 D6 **Barsac** France 44.37N 0.19W
43 F4 **Barsa-Kel'mes, Ostrov** *isld* Kazakhstan U.S.S.R. 45.38N 60.00E
43 D5 **Barsa-Kel'mes, Shor** *salt marsh* Uzbekistan U.S.S.R.
93 J5 **Barsalinga** Kenya 0.46N 37.06E
89 J5 **Barsalogo** Upper Volta 13.26N 1.02W
93 H4 **Barsaloi** Kenya 1.19N 36.53E
30 A5 **Barsana** Uttar Prad India 27.38N 77.22E
66 F2 **Bärschwil** Switzerland 47.23N 7.29E
53 H6 **Bårse** Denmark 55.08N 11.58E
69 G7 **Barse** *R* France
53 K5 **Barsebäck** Sweden 55.47N 12.58E
53 K5 **Barsebäckshamn** Sweden 55.46N 12.56E
33 N9 **Barshah, Ra's al** *C* Kuwait 29.34N 48.12E
34 H3 **Barsham** Syria 35.22N 40.32E
28 B1 **Barsi** Maharashtra India 18.14N 75.48E
60 H8 **Barsingerhorn** Netherlands 52.47N 4.52E
63 K8 **Barsinghausen** W Germany 52.18N 9.28E
29 E7 **Barsi Takli** Maharashtra India 20.30N 77.06E
53 W16 **Barsnesfjord** *inlet* Norway 61.15N 7.07E
53 D6 **Barsø** Denmark 55.08N 9.35E
63 G6 **Barssel** W Germany 53.10N 7.45E
111 G7 **Barstow** California 34.55N 117.01W
112 D4 **Barstow** Texas 31.27N 103.24W
45 J2 **Barsuki** U.S.S.R. 54.15N 37.32E
28 E1 **Barsur** Madhya Prad India 19.06N 81.30E
69 H7 **Bar-sur-Aube** France 48.14N 4.43E
71 K9 **Bar-sur-Loup, le** France 43.42N 7.00E
69 G7 **Bar-sur-Seine** France 48.07N 4.23E
103 B7 **Bart** Pennsylvania 39.57N 76.05W
35 D4 **Barta'a** Jordan 32.16N 35.08E
34 L2 **Bartallah** Iraq 36.23N 43.22E
43 K7 **Bartang** Tadzhikistan U.S.S.R. 38.13N 71.54E
43 K7 **Bartang** *R* Tadzhikistan U.S.S.R.
93 H4 **Barta Plains, El** Kenya
30 H4 **Bartar** Nepal 28.09N 84.27E
85 M9 **Bartazuga, Jebel** *mt* Sudan 21.46N 33.36E
71 L1 **Bartenheim** France 47.38N 7.29E
64 H5 **Bartenstein** W Germany 49.22N 9.53E
113 Q1 **Barter I** Alaska 70.07N 143.40W
63 R4 **Barth** E Germany 54.23N 12.44E
30 C6 **Barthana** Uttar Prad India 26.47N 79.13E
123 B14 **Barth Bank** Antarctica
63 R4 **Barthe** *R* E Germany
72 E9 **Barthe-de-Neste, la** France 43.05N 0.23E
66 Q3 **Bartholomäberg** Austria 47.07N 9.55E
120 D10 **Bartholomew Deep** Pacific Oc
26 D14 **Barth Seamount** S Atlantic Oc 63.00S 41.00W
98 G6 **Bartibog** New Brunswick 47.17N 65.39W
89 K5 **Bartibougou** Upper Volta 13.00N 0.40E
117 A1 **Bartica** Guyana 6.24N 58.38W
36 F1 **Bartın** Turkey 41.37N 32.20E
110 D8 **Bartle** California 41.16N 121.49W
13 H3 **Bartle Frere,Mt** Queensland 17.20S 145.45E
111 O2 **Bartles, Mt** Utah 39.42N 110.24W
109 P5 **Bartlesville** Oklahoma 36.44N 95.59W
108 M8 **Bartlett** Nebraska 41.53N 98.33W
104 O2 **Bartlett** New Hampshire 44.04N 71.18W
112 K5 **Bartlett** Texas 30.49N 97.27W
14 E8 **Bartlett Bluff** W Australia 29.09S 124.36E
101 O4 **Bartlett L** N W Territory
111 N8 **Bartlett Res** Arizona 33.55N 111.36W
98 P3 **Bartlett's Harbour** Newfoundland 50.58N 57.00W
14 E8 **Bartlett Soak** *L* W Australia 29.02S 124.48E
108 K9 **Bartley** Nebraska 40.15N 100.18W
103 C6 **Barto** Pennsylvania 40.23N 75.37W
121 F5 **Bartolomé Bavio** Argentina 35.05S 57.43W
113 V9 **Bartolome C** Alaska 55.15N 133.39W
119 B5 **Bartolomé, I** Galápagos Is 0.18S 90.37W
94 N3 **Bartolomeu Dias** Mozambique 21.10S 35.09E
56 L4 **Barton** Beds Eng 51.58N 0.27W
57 N5 **Barton** Humberside Eng 53.41N 0.27W
57 H5 **Barton** Lancs Eng 53.50N 2.45W
108 K1 **Barton** N Dakota 48.31N 100.10W
103 B2 **Barton** New York 42.02N 76.28W
57 K4 **Barton** N Yorks Eng 54.28N 1.39W
19 J6 **Barton** Philippines 10.21N 119.10E
12 C4 **Barton** S Australia 30.30S 132.40E
104 N2 **Barton** Vermont 44.44N 72.12W
12 A6 **Barton** *dist* Canberra Australia
106 L5 **Barton City** Michigan 44.42N 83.36W
57 M4 **Barton Hill** N Yorks Eng 54.04N 0.55W
56 N3 **Barton Mills** Suffolk Eng 52.20N 0.31E
62 M1 **Bartoszyce** Poland 54.16N 20.49E
99 N4 **Bartoville** Quebec 48.56N 77.20W
63 S5 **Bartow** E Germany 53.50N 13.20E
105 F10 **Bartow** Florida 27.54N 81.51W
105 E5 **Bartow** Georgia 32.54N 82.28W
59 D3 **Bartragh** *isld* Mayo Irish Rep 54.13N 9.10W
90 E8 **Barua** Nigeria 7.38N 11.08E
30 K6 **Baruari** Bihar India 26.02N 86.36E
33 F4 **Barūd, Al** Saudi Arabia 25.04N 44.37E
119 C2 **Baru, I. de** Colombia 10.10N 75.36W
29 L6 **Baruipur** W Bengal India 22.22N 88.25E
42 G5 **Baruk-Gol** U.S.S.R. 52.50N 100.10E
29 K1 **Barul** W Bengal India 23.45N 87.06E
81 C4 **Barumini** Sardinia 39.43N 9.01E
30 H8 **Barun** Bihar India 24.53N 84.13E
42 G6 **Barun-Adag** U.S.S.R. 50.28N 104.15E
Barūn Bayan Ūla *see* **Buruun Bayan-Ulaan**
18 K10 **Barung** *isld* Java Indon
30 K3 **Barun Glacier** Nepal
30 L4 **Barun Glacier, Lr** Nepal
30 L4 **Barun Khola** *R* Nepal
30 L3 **Barun Pokhari** *L* Nepal
22 K1 **Barun-Torey, Solonchak** *salt marsh* Chita U.S.S.R.
30 K3 **Baruntse** *mt* Nepal 27.53N 86.59E
18 D5 **Barunum** *R* Sumatra Indonesia
Baruq *see* **Borun**
18 C4 **Barus** Sumatra Indon 2.02N 98.20E
63 T8 **Baruth** E Germany 52.03N 13.30E
22 J3 **Baruun Urt** Mongolia 46.42N 113.20E
42 J8 **Baruun Urta** Mongolia 46.48N 113.18E
29 J8 **Baruva** Andhra Prad India 18.54N 84.40E
50 K5 **Baruvatn** *L* Iceland 65.00N 15.55W
115 N5 **Barú, Volcán** Panama 8.49N 82.38W
58 C2 **Barvas** Lewis, W Isles Scotland 58.21N 6.31W
61 M5 **Barvaux** Belgium 50.21N 5.30E
61 M5 **Barvaux-Condroz** Belgium 50.20N 5.16E
45 J8 **Barvenkovo** Ukraine U.S.S.R. 48.55N 37.02E
29 J6 **Barwa** Bihar India 23.12N 84.18E
30 C5 **Barwa** Uttar Prad India 27.50N 79.33E
29 E6 **Barwah** Madhya Prad India 22.16N 76.03E
29 D3 **Barwala** Haryana India 29.20N 75.58E
29 D6 **Barwani** Madhya Prad India 22.02N 74.56E
30 D8 **Barwara** Madhya Prad India 24.36N 80.24E
30 C7 **Barwar L** Uttar Prad India 25.32N 79.08E
30 B7 **Barwa Sagar** Uttar Prad India 25.23N 78.42E
30 D7 **Barwa-Sumerpur** Uttar Prad India 25.50N 80.09E
63 N7 **Barwedel** W Germany 52.32N 10.47E
89 F5 **Barwéli** Mali 13.09N 6.50W
105 D7 **Barwick** Georgia 30.52N 83.45W
14 D7 **Barwidgee** W Australia 27.10S 121.00E
13 B2 **Barwolla, Mt** N Terr Australia 14.53S 131.00E
Barwon *R see* **Darling** *R*
45 F2 **Baryatino** U.S.S.R. 54.20N 34.30E
39 K3 **Barykova, Mys** *C* U.S.S.R. 63.07N 179.31E
41 O7 **Barylas** U.S.S.R. 65.50N 132.45E
40 E1 **Barylay** *R* U.S.S.R.
45 T3 **Barysh** U.S.S.R. 53.40N 47.09E
45 S2 **Barysh** *R* U.S.S.R.
13 F7 **Baryulah** Queensland 27.35S 141.37E
35 F7 **Barza** Jordan 31.32N 35.45E
66 O8 **Barzago** Italy 45.46N 9.20E
33 N5 **Barzamān** Oman 22.15N 58.04E
34 M2 **Barzan** Iraq 36.56N 44.04E
76 H2 **Barzana** Spain 43.10N 5.58W
66 O9 **Barzano** Italy 45.44N 9.20E
42 D4 **Barzas** U.S.S.R. 55.44N 86.18E
79 F3 **Barzio** Italy 45.57N 9.29E
32 D5 **Bārz Shovār** Iran 31.30N 50.25E
32 D4 **Barzūk** Iran 33.48N 51.11E
89 J8 **Basa** Ghana 7.47N 0.20W
91 F2 **Basa** Zaïre 2.47N 18.49E
30 G7 **Basah** Bihar India 25.08N 83.49E
30 B7 **Basai** Madhya Prad India 25.09N 78.24E
32 F7 **Basaidu** Iran 26.38N 55.19E
121 F1 **Basail** Argentina 27.54S 59.17W
31 G4 **Basal** Pakistan 33.35N 72.17E
75 L4 **Basal, El** *L* Spain 41.37N 0.09E
109 C2 **Basalt** Colorado 39.22N 107.01W
110 N6 **Basalt** Idaho 43.20N 112.10W
111 F3 **Basalt** Nevada 38.02N 118.18W
13 H4 **Basalt R** Queensland
79 E5 **Basaluzzo** Italy 44.46N 8.42E
45 H9 **Basan'** Ukraine U.S.S.R. 47.24N 36.10E
91 J9 **Basanga** *tribe* Zaïre
91 F3 **Basankusu** Zaïre 1.12N 19.50E
30 L6 **Basantpur** Bihar India 26.08N 87.28E
82 L6 **Basarabi** Romania 44.10N 28.26E
43 L4 **Basaral, Ostrov** *islds* Kazakhstan U.S.S.R. 45.30N 73.45E
30 J7 **Basarh** Bihar India 25.59N 85.04E
30 C8 **Basari** Madhya Prad India 24.49N 79.49E
91 J6 **Basase** Zaïre 5.48S 24.36E
30 K7 **Basauni** Bihar India 25.14N 86.23E
75 E1 **Basauri** Spain 43.13N 2.54W
121 F4 **Basavilbaso** Argentina 32.23S 58.55W
19 L7 **Basay** Negros Philippines 9.26N 122.37E
19 K9 **Basbas** *isld* Philippines 5.20N 120.14E
61 O6 **Basbellain** Luxembourg 50.09N 5.58E
37 F8 **Basbirin** Turkey 37.20N 41.33E
75 Q3 **Báscara** Spain 42.10N 2.54E
61 O8 **Bascharage** Luxembourg 49.34N 5.55E
90 F7 **Basche** Cameroon 9.39N 13.21E
80 F3 **Baschi** Italy 42.40N 12.12E
56 F2 **Baschurch** Shropshire Eng 52.48N 2.51W
19 K1 **Basco** Philippines 20.25N 122.00E
76 L3 **Basconcillos del Tozo** Spain 42.42N 4.00W
72 D8 **Bascons** France 43.50N 0.25W
72 E8 **Bascous** France 43.48N 0.09E
75 F7 **Bascuñana, Sierra de** *mts* Spain
121 B2 **Bascuñán, C** Chile 28.52S 71.35W
63 K6 **Basdahl** W Germany 53.27N 9.00E
63 S7 **Basdorf** E Germany 52.44N 13.27E
61 E4 **Basècles** Belgium 50.32N 3.39E
123 E13 **Base (de Ejercito) Primavera** *Arg. Base* Antarctica 64.09S 60.57W
91 J1 **Basekpio** Zaïre 4.43N 24.36E
66 G1 **Basel** Switzerland 47.33N 7.36E
80 L6 **Baselice** Italy 41.23N 14.58E
75 N3 **Basella** Spain 42.01N 1.17E
66 H2 **Baselland** *canton* Switzerland
71 E6 **Bas-en-Basse** France 45.19N 4.06E
91 E5 **Basengele** *tribe* Zaïre
81 M2 **Basentello** *R* Italy
81 N3 **Basento** *R* Italy
30 A6 **Baseri** Rajasthan India 26.45N 77.32E
37 H7 **Baset Dağları** *mts* Turkey
82 K2 **Başeul** *R* Romania
19 M6 **Basey** Samar Philippines 11.18N 125.08E
37 G5 **Başgedikler** Turkey 40.39N 43.29E
44 M5 **Başgurly, Vpadina** *depression* Kazakhstan U.S.S.R.
Bashagārd *see* **Bashākerd, Kūhhā-ye** *mts*
32 H7 **Bashākerd, Kūhhā-ye** *mts* Iran
90 E7 **Bashar** Nigeria 9.14N 10.07E
85 E4 **Bashar, M** Libya 30.19N 19.26E
100 E6 **Bashaw** Alberta 52.35N 112.58W
42 C6 **Bashchelakskiy Khrebet** *mts* U.S.S.R.
95 M7 **Bashee** S Africa 31.55S 28.27E
95 M8 **Bashee** *R* S Africa
66 F7 **Bas-Hérémence** Switz 46.11N 7.25E
31 F3 **Bashgul** *R* Afghanistan
32 D6 **Bāshī** Iran 28.40N 51.06E
19 K1 **Bashi Chan** Philippines/Taiwan
91 G7 **Bashilange** *tribe* Zaïre
87 G5 **Bashilo,R** Ethiopia
32 H8 **Bashind** Iran 25.48N 59.26E
Bashir Iraq *see* **Bushayrīyah**
43 G7 **Bashir** Turkmeniya U.S.S.R. 38.15N 64.45E
44 H7 **Bash Karvend** Azerbaydzhan U.S.S.R. 40.08N 47.03E
42 D6 **Bashkaus** *R* U.S.S.R.
44 G7 **Bashkend** Azerbaydzhan U.S.S.R. 40.39N 45.31E
38 E3 **Bashkirskaya A.S.S.R** U.S.S.R.
24 G6 **Bashkorgan** Xinjiang Uygur Zizhiqu China 39.05N 90.00E
47 M8 **Bashmachnyy** Kazakhstan U.S.S.R. 53.40N 75.10E
45 P3 **Bashmakovo** U.S.S.R. 53.14N 43.04E
32 G2 **Bash Qal'eh** Iran 37.41N 56.50E
32 D5 **Bāsht** Iran 30.24N 51.09E
45 D9 **Bashtanka** Ukraine U.S.S.R. 47.24N 32.26E
87 E7 **Bashuma** Ethiopia 6.48N 35.53E
33 K10 **Bashūri, Ra's** *pen* Socotra Ind Oc 12.43N 53.35E
29 E2 **Basi** Patiala, Punjab India 30.42N 76.29E
29 E2 **Basi** Patiala, Punjab India 30.10N 76.04E
29 J6 **Basia** Bihar India 22.52N 84.57E
89 C7 **Basia** Sierra Leone 9.18N 12.50W
19 L4 **Basiad B** Luzon Philippines
19 C4 **Basiano** Indonesia 1.18S 122.52E
95 A7 **Basibasy** Madagascar 22.10S 43.40E
31 G1 **Basid** Tadzhikistan U.S.S.R. 38.08N 72.05E
15 L9 **Basilaki I** Papua New Guinea 10.37S 151.00E
19 K8 **Basilan** Philippines 6.40N 121.59E
19 K8 **Basilan** *isld* Philippines
19 K8 **Basilan Str** Philippines
56 M4 **Basildon** Essex Eng 51.34N 0.25E
107 D11 **Basile** Louisiana 30.29N 92.38W
79 O2 **Basiliano** Italy 46.02N 13.07E
78 G8 **Basilicata** *reg* Italy
121 H3 **Basilio** Brazil 31.55S 52.58W
81 K6 **Basiluzzo** *isld* Lipari Is Italy 38.40N 15.07E
Basim *see* **Washim**
110 N3 **Basin** Montana 46.16N 112.16W
108 B5 **Basin** Wyoming 44.24N 108.02W
105 F10 **Basinger** Florida 27.24N 81.01W
56 J5 **Basingstoke** Hants Eng 51.16N 1.05W
100 M6 **Basin L** Saskatchewan
35 H1 **Basir** Syria 33.04N 36.14E
34 M3 **Bāsira** *R* Iraq
32 H5 **Başirān** Iran 31.57N 59.07E
29 L6 **Basirhat** W Bengal India 22.38N 88.52E
34 C3 **Basit, El Ras el** *C* Syria 35.52N 35.48E
104 S1 **Baskahegan L** Maine
37 H7 **Başkale** Turkey 38.03N 43.59E
37 F6 **Baskan** *R* Turkey
99 P6 **Baskatong, Rés** Quebec
14 D3 **Baskerville, C** W Australia 17.10S 122.15E
37 D7 **Baskil** Turkey 38.38N 38.47E
36 F5 **Başkışla** Turkey 37.08N 32.52E
43 N2 **Baskol'** Kazakhstan U.S.S.R. 50.38N 78.46E
37 E6 **Başköy** Turkey 39.54N 39.44E
45 S8 **Baskunchak, Oz** *L* U.S.S.R.
29 G7 **Basla** Madhya Prad India 20.16N 81.02E
86 D3 **Baslaqun, El** Egypt 31.05N 30.08E
37 D1 **Baslar** *R* Turkey
Basle *see* **Basel**
57 K6 **Baslow** Derbys Eng 53.16N 1.37W
36 E5 **Başmakçı** Turkey 37.53N 30.00E
29 E8 **Basmat** Maharashtra India 19.22N 77.10E
32 B2 **Bāsmenj** Iran 37.58N 46.28E
51 D5 **Båsmoen** Norway 66.20N 14.05E
53 G6 **Basnæs Nor** *inlet* Denmark 55.12N 11.22E
37 F7 **Başnik** Turkey 38.08N 40.42E
93 G10 **Basodesh** Tanzania 4.23S 35.05E
79 D2 **Basodino** *mt* Italy/Switz 46.25N 8.28E
61 L4 **Bas-Oha** Belgium 50.32N 5.12E
91 H3 **Basoko** Zaïre 1.14N 23.36E
91 J3 **Basoko** *tribe* Zaïre
31 H4 **Basoli** Kashmir 32.29N 75.51E
91 H6 **Basonge** *tribe* Zaïre
91 G6 **Basongo** Zaïre 4.23S 20.23E
91 G6 **Basongo-Meno** *tribe* Zaïre
116 A1 **Basora, Punt** *pt* Aruba W I 12.26N 69.53W
95 M4 **Basotho-Qwaqwa** *Bantu Homeland* Orange Free State S Africa
30 B1 **Baspa** *R* Himachal Prad India
37 D6 **Başpinar** Turkey 39.13N 38.41E
34 P8 **Basra** Iraq 30.30N 47.50E
Başrah, Al *see* **Basra**
67 K4 **Bas-Rhin** *dept* France
Bassa *see* **Shelomi**
90 D9 **Bassa** *tribe* Cameroon
81 C1 **Bassacutena** Sardinia 41.08N 9.16E
81 C1 **Bassacutena** *R* Sardinia
35 G6 **Bassa, El** Jordan 31.56N 35.46E
35 G2 **Bassah, El** Syria 32.55N 35.52E
100 E8 **Bassano** Alberta 50.48N 112.20W
79 L3 **Bassano del Grappa** Italy 45.46N 11.44E
89 K7 **Bassari** Togo 9.18N 0.53E
26 D8 **Bassas da India** *islds* Mozambique Chan
63 R5 **Basse** E Germany 53.59N 12.35E
61 O5 **Basse-Bodeux** Belgium 50.22N 5.50E
66 F2 **Bassecourt** Switzerland 47.20N 7.16E
69 D2 **Bassée, la** France 50.31N 2.49E
25 C4 **Bassein** Burma 16.46N 94.45E
29 C8 **Bassein** Maharashtra India 19.21N 72.52E
25 C5 **Bassein** *R* Burma
90 K9 **Basse Kotto** *dist* Cameroon
14 B1 **Bassendean** *dist* Perth, W Aust
61 N3 **Bassenge** Belgium 50.46N 5.37E
57 G3 **Bassenthwaite Lake** Cumbria Eng 54.40N 3.13W
116 L3 **Basse Pointe** Martinique W I 14.52N 61.07W
94 D3 **Bassermann** Namibia 21.33S 17.02E
66 L2 **Bassersdorf** Switzerland 47.27N 8.38E
89 B5 **Basse Santa Su** The Gambia 13.23N 14.15W
116 M4 **Basse Terre** Guadeloupe W I 16.00N 61.43W
116 P3 **Basseterre** St Kitts W I 17.17N 62.43W
116 O2 **Basse Terre** Trinidad & Tobago 10.08N 61.18W
116 M4 **Basse Terre** *I* Guadeloupe W I
56 J6 **Bassett** Hants Eng 50.57N 1.24W
108 L7 **Bassett** Nebraska 42.36N 99.31W
104 F10 **Bassett** Virginia 36.46N 80.00W
111 O9 **Bassett Pk** *mt* Arizona 32.31N 110.18W
56 H2 **Bassett's Pole** W Midlands Eng 52.36N 1.46W
61 E2 **Bassevelde** Belgium 51.13N 3.41E
107 G10 **Bassfield** Mississippi 31.30N 89.45W
43 N5 **Basshiy** Kazakhstan U.S.S.R. 44.09N 78.45E
89 G4 **Bassikounou** Mauritania 15.55N 5.59W
89 K7 **Bassila** Benin 9.01N 1.46E
61 F4 **Bassilly** Belgium 50.40N 3.56E
122 N11 **Bass, Ilots de** Tubuai Is Pacific Oc 27.55S 143.26W
Bassira *see* **Buseire**
111 E4 **Bass Lake** California 37.19N 119.32W
64 Q1 **Basslitz** E Germany 51.13N 13.33E
87 J10 **Basso Giuba** *prov* Somalia
90 L3 **Basso, Plat. de** Chad
72 E8 **Bassoues** France 43.35N 0.15E
98 J8 **Bass River** Nova Scotia 45.25N 63.48W
48 V8 **Bass Rock** Greenland 74.40N 18.30W
58 L6 **Bass Rock** *Lt Ho* Scotland 56.05N 2.38W
12 G7 **Bass Str** Tasmania/Victoria
63 J7 **Bassum** W Germany 52.52N 8.43E
100 R8 **Basswood** Manitoba 50.18N 100.02W
108 T1 **Basswood L** Minnesota/Ontario
71 H5 **Bassy** France 45.59N 5.50E
86 P5 **Basta** Jordan 30.14N 35.32E
52 G10 **Båstad** Sweden 56.25N 12.50E
32 F7 **Bastak** Iran 27.16N 54.26E
32 F2 **Bastam** Iran 36.30N 55.03E
32 B2 **Bastānābād** Iran 37.49N 46.54E
29 G8 **Bastar** *dist* Madhya Prad India
67 P12 **Bastelica** Corsica 42.00N 9.04E
61 P7 **Bastendorf** Luxembourg 49.53N 6.10E
72 C8 **Bastennes** France 43.40N 0.46W
30 F6 **Basti** Uttar Prad India 26.48N 82.44E
30 F5 **Basti** *dist* Uttar Prad India
67 P11 **Bastia** Corsica 42.41N 9.26E
80 G2 **Bastia** Italy 43.04N 12.34E
79 C6 **Bastia Mondovì** Italy 44.26N 7.54E
118 H3 **Bastião** Brazil 12.52S 41.45W
72 G9 **Bastide-de-Serou, la** France 43.01N 1.26E
71 H9 **Bastide-des-Jourdans,la** France 43.47N 5.38E
72 J7 **Bastide-l'Evêque,la** France 44.20N 2.08E
71 D7 **Bastide-Puylaurent,la** France 44.35N 3.54E
79 K5 **Bastiglia** Italy 44.43N 11.00E
98 L2 **Bastille,L** Quebec
119 A3 **Bastimentos** *isld* Panama 9.22N 82.10W
117 G8 **Bastioes, R** Brazil
Bastion, Cape *see* **Chin-mu Chiao**
61 N6 **Bastogne** Belgium 50.00N 5.43E
105 E4 **Bastonville** Georgia 33.19N 82.33W
107 E9 **Bastrop** Louisiana 32.49N 91.54W
112 K5 **Bastrop** Texas 30.07N 97.21W
52 M2 **Bastuträsk** Sweden 64.47N 20.00E
18 E6 **Basu** *isld* Sumatra Indon
24 G9 **Basudan Ula** *mt pk* Qinghai / Xizang Zizhiqu China
32 H7 **Bāsūd,Kūh** *mts* Iran
30 F7 **Basuhi** *R* Uttar Prad India
31 C8 **Basul** *R* Pakistan
37 E1 **Başulan** *R* Turkey
Basuo *see* **Dongfang**
86 E4 **Bâsûr,Gebel el** *hill* Egypt 30.35N 30.35E
86 Q11 **Bâsûs** Cairo Egypt
Basutoland *see* **Lesotho**
36 F1 **Başveren** Turkey 41.10N 31.41E
29 E4 **Baswa** Rajasthan India 27.06N 76.32E
44 H1 **Basy** U.S.S.R. 46.07N 47.07E
47 J6 **Bas'yanovskiy** U.S.S.R. 58.21N 60.45E
86 E4 **Basyûn** Egypt 30.57N 30.49E
91 D6 **Bas-Zaïre** *prov* Zaïre
91 A2 **Bata** Equat Guinea 1.51N 9.49E
91 F7 **Bata** Zaïre 6.00S 19.41E
19 G1 **Bataan** *pen* Luzon Philippines
116 C3 **Batabanó,G.de** Cuba
19 K2 **Batac** Luzon Philippines 18.03N 120.36E
115 E4 **Batacosa** Mexico 27.31N 109.24W
60 K14 **Batadorp** Netherlands 51.29N 5.24E
19 M5 **Batag** *isld* Philippines 12.39N 125.05E
42 G6 **Batagal** U.S.S.R. 52.28N 100.45E
39 A1 **Batagay** U.S.S.R. 67.40N 134.32E
41 O6 **Batagay-Alyta** U.S.S.R. 67.50N 130.28E
118 D7 **Bataguaçu** Brazil 21.40S 52.29W
33 L8 **Baţāhirah** *tribe* Oman
18 F8 **Batai,Gunung** *mt* Sumatra Indon 5.31S 105.07E
31 F4 **Batai Pass** Pakistan 33.22N 70.21E
82 J9 **Batak** Bulgaria 41.57N 24.12E
18 L8 **Batakan** Borneo Indon 4.03S 114.39E
18 M6 **Batakan** Borneo Indon 0.04S 116.22E
82 J9 **Batak Dam** Bulgaria 42.00N 24.11E
36 G5 **Bataklık Gölü** *L* Turkey
29 D2 **Batala** Punjab India 31.48N 75.17E
87 K5 **Batalaleh** Somalia 10.30N 45.10E
53 R15 **Batalden** *isld* Norway 61.39N 4.48E
117 F7 **Batalha** Brazil 4.02S 42.05W
76 B9 **Batalha** Portugal 39.40N 8.50W
18 E5 **Batam** *isld* Indonesia
42 G5 **Batama** U.S.S.R. 53.55N 101.38E
91 K3 **Batama** Zaïre 0.56N 26.37E
41 N8 **Batamay** Yakutsk U.S.S.R. 63.33N 129.32E
42 K2 **Batamayy** Yakutsk U.S.S.R. 60.50N 115.30E
43 E2 **Batamshinskiy** Kazakhstan U.S.S.R. 50.34N 58.14E
19 K1 **Batan** *isld* Philippines 20.25N 121.58E
19 M5 **Batan** *isld* Philippines 13.15N 124.00E
18 H9 **Batang** Java Indon 6.55S 109.42E
23 B3 **Batang** Sichuan China 30.02N 99.01E
90 J8 **Batangafo** Cent Afr Rep 7.27N 18.11E
19 K5 **Batangas** Luzon Philippines 13.46N 121.01E
18 B8 **Batang Berjuntai** Pen Malaysia 3.22N 101.25E
18 B8 **Batang Kali** Pen Malaysia 3.28N 101.37E
18 C9 **Batang Malaka** Pen Malaysia 2.27N 102.24E
19 G4 **Batangpele** *isld* Irian Jaya 0.20S 130.15E
18 J5 **Batangtarang** Borneo Indon 0.06N 110.00E
18 C5 **Batangtoru** Sumatra Indon 1.26N 99.02E
19 K1 **Batan Is** Philippines
34 L8 **Batan,Jal al** *ridge* Iraq/Arabia
15 A4 **Batanta** *isld* Irian Jaya 0.53S 130.37E
15 A4 **Batanta, Geb** *mts* Irian Jaya
90 H9 **Batara** Cent Afr Rep 5.55N 16.10E
62 L9 **Bátaszék** Hungary 46.10N 18.42E
118 F7 **Batatais** Brazil 20.54S 47.37W
121 D5 **Batavia** Argentina 34.46S 65.41W
106 F8 **Batavia** Illinois 41.51N 88.20W
Batavia Java *see* **Jakarta**
104 G3 **Batavia** New York 43.00N 78.11W
104 A7 **Batavia** Ohio 39.06N 84.11W
117 B2 **Batavia** Surinam 5.44N 55.54W
45 S8 **Batayevka** U.S.S.R. 48.08N 46.18E
45 L9 **Bataysk** U.S.S.R. 47.09N 39.46E
19 K6 **Batbatan** *isld* Philippines 11.30N 121.56E
99 F6 **Batchawana** Ontario 46.54N 84.37W
99 F5 **Batchawana** *R* Ontario
13 B2 **Batchelor** N Terr Australia 13.01S 131.00E
75 L5 **Batea** Spain 41.05N 0.19E
12 M8 **Bate B** New S Wales
18 A3 **Bateemucica, Gunung** *mt* Sumatra Indon 5.14N 95.32E
91 D5 **Bateké** *tribe* Congo
65 M3 **Batelov** Czechoslovakia 49.19N 15.25E
12 K5 **Batemans B** New S Wales
12 K6 **Batemans Bay** New S Wales 35.45S 150.09E
92 D6 **Batembo** *tribe* Zaïre
20 P10 **Baten** Okinawa Japan 26.06N 127.46E
60 L12 **Batenburg** Netherlands 51.50N 5.38E
42 E5 **Batenevskiy Kryazh** *ridge* U.S.S.R.
42 E5 **Bateni** U.S.S.R. 54.38N 90.59E
111 J9 **Bateques** Mexico 32.34N 115.02W
77 G3 **Baterno** Spain 38.57N 4.54W
110 O6 **Bates** Idaho 43.42N 111.14W
110 G5 **Bates** Oregon 44.37N 118.30W
105 F4 **Batesburg** S Carolina 33.56N 81.33W
108 H6 **Batesland** S Dakota 43.08N 102.08W
10 U10 **Bates,Mt** Norfolk I Pacific Oc 29.02S 167.56E
14 E7 **Bates,Mt** W Australia 25.39S 122.58E
14 D7 **Bates Ra** W Australia
107 E6 **Batesville** Arkansas 35.45N 91.39W
107 L2 **Batesville** Indiana 39.18N 85.12W
107 G7 **Batesville** Mississippi 34.18N 89.59W
112 H7 **Batesville** Texas 28.57N 99.39W
91 J6 **Batetela** *tribe* Zaïre
46 H1 **Batetskiy** U.S.S.R. 58.38N 30.31E
56 G5 **Bath** Avon Eng 51.23N 2.22W
106 D9 **Bath** Illinois 40.11N 90.08W
116 M2 **Bath** Jamaica, W I 17.57N 76.22W
104 Q3 **Bath** Maine 43.56N 69.50W
105 L2 **Bath** N Carolina 35.29N 76.48W
60 E14 **Bath** Netherlands 51.24N 4.13E
116 P4 **Bath** Nevis I W I 17.07N 62.37W
98 E7 **Bath** New Brunswick 46.30N 67.34W
104 H4 **Bath** New York 42.21N 77.19W
103 D5 **Bath** Pennsylvania 40.43N 75.24W
105 F4 **Bath** S Carolina 33.29N 81.54W
108 M4 **Bath** S Dakota 45.27N 98.19W
90 J5 **Batha** *div* Chad
90 H5 **Batha** *R* Chad
34 N7 **Baţhā', Al** Iraq 31.06N 45.54E
25 H7 **Batheay** Cambodia 11.59N 104.56E
56 G5 **Bathford** Avon Eng 51.24N 2.18W
58 J7 **Bathgate** Lothian Scotland 55.55N 3.39W
108 N1 **Bathgate** N Dakota 48.54N 97.29W
71 J5 **Bathie,la** France 45.38N 6.27E
31 B10 **Bath Island** Pakistan 24.50N 67.02E
95 G3 **Bathlaro** S Africa 27.17S 23.21E
60 O11 **Bathmen** Netherlands 52.15N 6.16E
30 L6 **Bathnaha** Bihar India 26.21N 87.14E
98 G6 **Bathurst** New Brunswick 47.37N 65.40W
12 J5 **Bathurst** New S Wales 33.27S 149.35E
95 K9 **Bathurst** S Africa 33.30S 26.50E
Bathurst The Gambia *see* **Banjul**
13 B1 **Bathurst** *isld* N Terr Australia
13 G2 **Bathurst Bay** Queensland
101 K1 **Bathurst,C** N W Terr 70.31N 128.00W
97 J2 **Bathurst I** N W Terr 76.00N 100.00W
101 T2 **Bathurst Inlet** N W Terr 66.49N 108.00W
101 U2 **Bathurst Inlet** N W Terr
14 E3 **Bathurst Is** W Australia 16.05S 123.33E
13 B1 **Bathurst Island Mission Sta** N Terr Australia 11.45S 130.41E
12 J6 **Bathurst,L** New S Wales 35.04S 149.12E
15 J5 **Bat I** Bismarck Arch 2.51S 146.12E
93 J6 **Batian** *mt* Kenya 0.10S 37.19E
66 E7 **Bâtiax, La** Switzerland 46.07N 7.04E
91 A1 **Batibo** Cameroon 5.56N 9.58E
87 H5 **Batie** Ethiopia 11.10N 40.00E
89 H7 **Batié** Upper Volta 9.53N 2.53W
71 J7 **Bâtie-Neuve,la** France 44.34N 6.12E
80 D3 **Batignano** Italy 42.52N 11.10E
68 E3 **Batignolles,Les** Paris France 48.53N 2.19E
29 H7 **Batiguda** Orissa India 20.12N 83.59E
19 B5 **Batikala,Tandjung** *C* Celebes Indon 2.48S 120.56E
34 J4 **Batikha,Wādī al** *watercourse* Iraq
82 E5 **Batina** Yugoslavia 45.50N 18.50E
33 H3 **Bāţinah,Al** *isld* Saudi Arabia 27.15N 49.32E
33 M4 **Bāţinah, Al** *plain* Oman
33 K5 **Batin, Al** *des area* U.A.E.
34 O10 **Bāţin, Wādī al** *watercourse* Iraq/Saudi Arabia
35 F8 **Batir** Jordan 31.16N 35.42E
99 S6 **Batiscan** Quebec 46.30N 72.16W
99 T5 **Batiscan, L** Quebec 47.22N 71.57W
118 H2 **Batista,Serra da** *mts* Bahia Brazil
117 G8 **Batista,Serra da** *mts* Piauí Brazil
89 C7 **Batkanu** Sierra Leone 9.07N 12.17W
43 N8 **Batken** Kirgiziya U.S.S.R. 40.04N 70.51E
15 A7 **Batkes** Moluccas Indon 7.41S 131.36E
32 E4 **Bāţlāq-e Gavkhūnī** *salt marsh* Iran
57 K5 **Batley** W Yorks Eng 53.44N 1.37W
12 J6 **Batlow** New S Wales 35.32S 148.10E
37 F8 **Batman** Turkey 37.52N 41.02E
37 F8 **Batman** *R* Turkey
88 R4 **Batna** Algeria 35.34N 6.10E
33 J5 **Batnaţ Tarfa** Saudi Arabia 23.50N 51.38E
85 L9 **Batn el Hajar** *dist* Sudan
92 C10 **Batoka** Zambia 16.46S 27.15E
19 L5 **Bato, L** Luzon Philippines 13.20N 123.21E
40 G3 **Batomga** U.S.S.R. 56.48N 135.59E
40 G3 **Batomga** *R* U.S.S.R.
90 F7 **Batondji, Mt** Cameroon 8.20N 13.15E
107 E11 **Baton Rouge** Louisiana 30.30N 91.10W
115 F4 **Batopilas** Mexico 27.00N 107.45W
90 G8 **Batou** Cameroon 7.23N 14.30E
91 C3 **Batouala** Gabon 0.50N 13.23E
90 G9 **Batouri** Cameroon 4.26N 14.27E
118 D4 **Batovi** Brazil 15.50S 53.12W
47 K5 **Batovo** U.S.S.R. 60.21N 69.58E
63 S8 **Batow** W Berlin 52.30N 13.11E
86 F3 **Batra** Egypt 31.11N 31.26E
33 B4 **Batrā,Jabal** *mts* Saudi Arabia
34 C9 **Batrā,Jebel el** *mt* Jordan 29.56N 35.34E
Batraki *see* **Oktyabr'sk**
25 J7 **Ba Tri** Vietnam 10.03N 106.36E
82 D5 **Batrina** Yugoslavia 45.11N 17.40E
34 C4 **Batroun** Lebanon 34.16N 35.40E
33 H3 **Batr Sabsab** *mts* Saudi Arabia
51 O1 **Båtsfjord** Norway 70.36N 29.40E
51 O1 **Båtsfjord** *inlet* Norway
91 G7 **Batshamba** Zaïre 6.18S 20.44E
35 D3 **Bat Shelomo** Israel 32.36N 35.00E
91 F7 **Batshioko** *tribe* Zaïre
103 E7 **Batsto** New Jersey 39.39N 74.40W
79 L4 **Battáglia Terme** Italy 45.17N 11.47E
25 G6 **Battambang** Cambodia 13.06N 103.13E
13 D3 **Batten** *R* N Terr Australia
64 F1 **Battenberg** W Germany 51.00N 8.40E
69 N8 **Battenheim** France 47.50N 7.25E
123 F12 **Batterbee Mts** Antarctica
66 G3 **Bätterkinden** Switzerland 47.08N 7.33E
55 E4 **Battersea** London Eng 51.28N 0.10W
12 F8 **Battery Bluff** Tasmania 42.54S 147.22E
12 F8 **Battery Point** *dist* Hobart, Tasmania
11 N10 **Battery Pt** New Zealand 43.36S 172.44E
59 K2 **Battery,The** Antrim N Ireland 54.50N 6.07W
14 C6 **Batthewmurnarna** *mt* W Australia 24.58S 119.21E
26 U6 **Batticaloa** Sri Lanka 7.43N 81.42E
61 O4 **Battice** Belgium 50.39N 5.50E
Battika,Wadi al *see* **Batikha, Wādī al** *watercourse*
28 H7 **Batti Malv** *isld* Nicobar Is 8.50N 92.49E
90 K8 **Battinga** Cent Afr Rep 6.30N 20.30E
80 L7 **Battipaglia** Italy 40.36N 14.59E
35 D7 **Battir** Jordan 31.44N 35.08E
56 M6 **Battle** E Sussex Eng 50.55N 0.29E
110 J7 **Battle Cr** Idaho
110 Q1 **Battle Cr** Montana
13 B3 **Battle Cr** N Terr Australia
106 J7 **Battle Creek** Michigan 42.20N 85.10W
108 N8 **Battle Creek** Nebraska 42.00N 97.35W
100 H9 **Battle Creek** Saskatchewan 49.29N 109.51W
56 F2 **Battlefield** Shropshire Eng 52.45N 2.43W
92 D11 **Battlefields** Zimbabwe 18.31S 29.52E
100 J6 **Battleford** Saskatchewan 52.45N 108.20W
110 C4 **Battle Ground** Washington 45.49N 122.30W
98 R1 **Battle Harbour** Labrador, Nfld 52.16N 55.36W
113 K7 **Battle L** Alaska 59.05N 154.55W
110 J9 **Battle Mountain** Nevada 40.39N 116.56W
110 H9 **Battle Mt** Nevada 40.41N 117.07W
100 F6 **Battle R** Alberta
108 H1 **Battleview** N Dakota 48.36N 102.46W
62 N9 **Battonya** Hungary 46.16N 21.00E
100 J8 **Battrum** Saskatchewan 50.34N 108.20W
87 G7 **Batu** *mt* Ethiopia 6.55N 39.49E
18 C9 **Batu Anam** Pen Malaysia 2.34N 102.43E
18 B8 **Batu Arang** Pen Malaysia 3.18N 101.27E
19 C7 **Batuata** *isld* Indonesia 6.14S 122.43E
18 L5 **Batuayau, Bukit** *mt* Borneo Indon 0.45N 114.50E
18 B7 **Batu Berinchang, Gunong** *mt* Pen Malaysia 4.29N 101.24E
18 G7 **Batubetumbang** Indonesia 2.48S 106.10E
18 L4 **Batu Bora,Bukit** *mt* Sarawak Malaysia 2.35N 114.52E
18 L5 **Batubrok,Bukit** *mt* Borneo Indon 1.05N 114.22E
18 B8 **Batu Caves** Pen Malaysia 3.16N 101.39E
19 B4 **Batudaka** *isld* Indonesia 0.28S 121.50E
18 K5 **Batuensambang,Bukit** *mt* Borneo Indon 0.15N 113.02E
18 B7 **Batu Gajah** Pen Malaysia 4.27N 101.02E
19 C4 **Batuhitam, Tanjung** *C* Celebes Indon 0.40S 122.43E
19 C4 **Batui** Celebes Indon 1.15S 122.34E
19 C9 **Batuidu** Indonesia 10.36S 123.24E
18 L10 **Batukau,Bukit** *mt* Bali Indon 8.17S 115.06E
18 L5 **Batukelau** Borneo Indon 0.50N 115.00E
19 M9 **Batulaki** Mindanao Philippines 5.35N 125.25E
18 M10 **Batulantee** *mt* Indonesia 8.39S 117.18E
19 G2 **Batulao, Mt** Luzon Philippines 14.03N 120.49E
18 B9 **Batu Laut** Pen Malaysia 2.40N 101.30E
18 L7 **Batulicin** Borneo Indon 3.26S 116.00E
18 L5 **Batulilangmebang, Gunung** *mt* Borneo Indon 0.23N 115.43E
Batum *see* **Batumi**
18 L4 **Batu Mabun,Bukit** *mt* Sarawak Malaysia 2.54N 114.34E
19 C8 **Batumanu, Tanjung** *C* Indonesia 8.27S 122.03E
44 D6 **Batumi** Georgia U.S.S.R. 41.37N 41.36E
18 C5 **Batumundam** Sumatra Indon 1.14N 98.50E
18 C10 **Batu Pahat** Pen Malaysia 1.50N 102.48E
18 B10 **Batupanjang** Sumatra Indon 1.42N 101.29E
18 C6 **Batu,Pulau Pulau** *islds* Indonesia
18 A7 **Batu Puteh, Gunong** *mt* Pen Malaysia 4.14N 101.28E
18 N5 **Batuputih** Borneo Indon 1.23N 117.30E
18 F8 **Baturaja** Sumatra Indon 4.10S 104.10E
18 J9 **Baturetno** Java Indon 7.54S 110.54E
45 D5 **Baturin** Ukraine U.S.S.R. 51.20N 32.52E
47 J7 **Baturino** Kurgan U.S.S.R. 55.55N 63.40E
46 J2 **Baturino** Smolensk U.S.S.R. 55.30N 32.47E
42 D3 **Baturino** Tomsk U.S.S.R. 57.45N 85.14E
44 C2 **Baturinskaya** U.S.S.R. 45.47N 39.22E
117 H7 **Baturité** Brazil 4.20S 38.56W
117 G7 **Baturite, Sa** *mts* Brazil
18 G7 **Baturusa** Indonesia 2.01S 106.08E
18 N4 **Batu, Tanjung** *C* Borneo Indon 2.16N 118.07E
18 B8 **Batu Tiga** Pen Malaysia 3.04N 101.33E
18 K6 **Batutinggi** Borneo Indonesia 1.54S 113.19E
92 D2 **Batwa** *tribe* Rwanda
91 G5 **Batwa** *tribe* Zaïre
35 B5 **Bat Yam** Israel 32.01N 34.45E
45 T1 **Batyrevo** U.S.S.R. 55.04N 47.37E
45 Q9 **Batyr Mala,Oz** *L* U.S.S.R.
70 F7 **Batz** France 47.17N 2.29W
70 B4 **Batz,I.,de** France 48.45N 4.00W
18 J5 **Bau** Sarawak Malaysia 1.25N 110.10E
87 E5 **Bau** Sudan 11.21N 34.05E
92 G11 **Bauaze** Mozambique 18.06S 35.43E
19 C6 **Baubau** Indonesia 5.30S 122.37E
90 D6 **Bauchi** Nigeria 10.16N 9.50E
81 G8 **Baucina** Sicily 37.56N 13.32E
70 D6 **Baud** France 47.53N 3.00W
Baud India *see* **Baudh**
108 Q1 **Baudette** Minnesota 48.42N 94.38W
29 J7 **Baudh** Orissa India 20.50N 84.25E
29 H7 **Baudh-Khondmals** *dist* Orissa India
119 C5 **Baudo,R** Colombia
119 C4 **Baudo,Sa.de** *mts* Colombia
Baudouinville *see* **Moba**
61 F5 **Baudour** Belgium 50.29N 3.50E
69 L6 **Baudrécourt** France 48.58N 6.27E
72 H1 **Baudres** France 47.04N 1.34E
71 J9 **Bauduen** France 43.44N 6.10E
66 L4 **Bauenstock,Nieder** *mt* Switz 46.57N 8.33E
66 L4 **Bauenstock,Ober** *mt* Switz 46.56N 8.32E
10 C10 **Bauer Bay** Macquarie I Pacific Oc
122 R10 **Bauer Deep** Pacific Oc 15.00S 98.00W
61 F4 **Bauffe** Belgium 50.34N 3.51E
87 D1 **Bauga,El** Sudan 18.18N 33.52E
70 K6 **Baugé** France 47.33N 0.06W
71 J5 **Bauges** *dist* France
61 E4 **Baugnies** Belgium 50.33N 3.33E
72 K1 **Baugy** France 47.05N 2.43E
13 D3 **Bauhinia Downs** N Terr Australia 16.10S 135.26E
13 J6 **Bauhinia Downs** Queensland 24.32S 149.15E
19 B6 **Baula** Celebes Indon 4.09S 121.39E
50 D5 **Baula** *mt* Iceland 64.50N 21.25W
30 C1 **Bau La** *pass* Xizang Zizhiqu 31.48N 79.22E
81 B3 **Bauladu** Sardinia 40.02N 8.41E
64 G5 **Bauland** *dist* W Germany
98 R2 **Bauld,C** Newfoundland 51.40N 55.25W
70 F7 **Baule,la** France 47.18N 2.23W
61 H4 **Baulers** Belgium 50.37N 4.21E
66 C4 **Baulmes** Switzerland 46.48N 6.32E
70 G6 **Baulon** France 47.59N 1.55W
66 M2 **Bauma** Switzerland 47.22N 8.52E
46 E7 **Bauman** *dist* U.S.S.R.
57 N6 **Baumber** Lincs Eng 53.15N 0.10W
64 B1 **Baumberg** W Germany 51.08N 6.53W
71 H3 **Baume** France 46.43N 5.38E
66 C6 **Baume, la** France 46.18N 6.36E
71 J2 **Baume-les-Dames** France 47.21N 6.21E
63 T6 **Baumgarten** E Germany 53.21N 13.58E
64 P7 **Baumgarten** W Germany 48.29N 12.59E
64 C4 **Baumholder** W Germany 49.37N 7.21E
35 F4 **Ba'un** Jordan 32.23N 35.44E
19 C9 **Baun** Timor Indon 10.19S 123.41E
15 C7 **Baun** *isld* Moluccas Indon
64 K4 **Baunach** W Germany 49.59N 10.51E
64 K3 **Baunach** *R* W Germany
15 M3 **Baunani** Malaita I Solomon Is 9.08S 160.32E
63 K10 **Baunatal** W Germany 51.25N 9.20E
29 D1 **Baundal** Himachal Prad India 32.48N 75.59E
30 E5 **Baundi** Uttar Prad India 27.27N 81.25E
81 D3 **Baunei** Sardinia 40.02N 9.41E
42 J4 **Baunt** U.S.S.R. 55.18N 113.10E
42 J4 **Baunt,Ozero** *L* U.S.S.R. 55.12N 113.00E
13 L7 **Bauple** Queensland 25.50S 152.35E
29 L4 **Baura** Bangladesh 26.20N 89.04E
30 K6 **Bauraha** Bihar India 26.34N 86.16E
90 D5 **Baure** Nigeria 12.52N 8.50E
120 F5 **Baures** Bolivia 13.35S 63.37W
120 F5 **Baures, R** Bolivia
59 C7 **Baurtregraum** *mt* Kerry Irish Rep 52.12N 9.50W
118 E8 **Bauru** Brazil 22.19S 49.07W
91 G3 **Bauru** Zaïre 0.38N 21.04E
118 D6 **Baús** Brazil 18.29S 53.05W
33 N5 **Baushar** Oman 23.32N 58.24E
31 H8 **Bausi** Bangladesh 24.49N 89.54E
46 E2 **Bauska** Latvia U.S.S.R. 56.22N 24.12E
81 K7 **Bauso** Sicily 38.13N 15.27E
44 K3 **Bautino** Kazakhstan U.S.S.R. 44.33N 50.14E
62 H4 **Bautzen** E Germany 51.11N 14.29E
71 F9 **Baux-de-Provence, les** France 43.45N 4.48E
107 D7 **Bauxite** Arkansas 34.33N 92.31W
89 C7 **Bauya** Sierra Leone 8.12N 12.38W
32 E5 **Bavānāt** Iran 30.29N 53.39E
115 P5 **Bavano, L** *res* Panama
66 C2 **Bavans** France 47.29N 6.42E
109 N3 **Bavaria** Kansas 38.49N 97.46W
Bavaria W Germany *see* **Bayern**
69 F3 **Bavay** France 50.18N 3.48E
28 A2 **Bavda** Maharashtra India 16.35N 73.55E
60 H13 **Bavel** Netherlands 51.34N 4.50E
67 P13 **Bavella, Col de** *pass* Corsica 41.47N 9.13E
52 K8 **Båven** *L* Sweden 59.00N 17.00E
79 D3 **Baveno** Italy 45.55N 8.30E
95 O6 **Baven on Sea** S Africa 30.53S 30.21E
95 D9 **Baviaan** S Africa 33.13S 20.45E
95 H9 **Baviaanskloofberge** *mts* S Africa
61 D3 **Bavikhove** Belgium 50.52N 3.19E
71 K1 **Bavilliers** France 47.37N 6.50E
115 E2 **Bavispe** Mexico 30.30N 108.58W
115 E3 **Bavispe** *R* Mexico
29 C6 **Bavliari** Gujarat India 22.02N 72.16E
46 R3 **Bavly** U.S.S.R. 54.23N 53.20E
66 L6 **Bavona** *R* Switzerland
66 L6 **Bavona, Val** Switzerland
65 K3 **Bavorov** Czechoslovakia 49.08N 14.05E
25 M9 **Baw** Burma 23.29N 95.48E
29 E3 **Bawal** Haryana India 28.05N 76.38E
18 J7 **Bawal** *isld* Borneo Indon
Bawanat *see* **Bavānāt**

18 H6 Bawang, Tanjung *C* Borneo Indon 1.51S 109.59E
33 G6 Bawāzim,Al *area* Saudi Arabia
56 O2 Bawdeswell Norfolk Eng 52.45N 1.01E
56 O3 Bawdsey Suffolk Eng 52.01N 1.25E
25 N9 Bawdwin Burma 23.06N 97.18E
18 K8 Bawean *isld* Indonesia
34 M2 Bāwīan Iraq 36.31N 44.24E
63 F7 Bawinkel W Germany 52.37N 7.25E
85 K5 Bawiti Egypt 28.21N 28.51E
99 D3 Bawk Ontario 49.58N 86.40W
89 J6 Bawku Ghana 11.05N 0.11W
25 D3 Bawlake Burma 19.10N 97.19E
100 E6 Bawlf Alberta 52.56N 112.27W
25 B2 Bawli Bazar Burma 21.08N 92.20E
25 C4 Bawmi Burma 17.20N 94.32E
25 C4 Bawmi B Burma
87 J5 Bawn Somalia 10.07N 43.07E
23 B4 Bawolung Sichuan China 28.51N 101.13E
Bawtaharah *see* Baṭāḥirah *tribe*
57 L6 Bawtry S Yorks Eng 53.26N 1.01W
25 G1 Ba Xat Vietnam 22.36N 102.48E
22 K7 Ba Xian Hebei China 39.05N 116.24E
23 D4 Ba Xian Sichuan China 31.22N 106.31E
24 G6 Baxkorgan Xinjiang Uygur Zizhiqu China 39.05N 90.00E
105 E6 Baxley Georgia 31.46N 82.22W
23 A3 Baxoi Xizang Zizhiqu China 30.03N 98.54E
108 R8 Baxter Iowa 41.49N 93.09W
108 Q3 Baxter Minnesota 46.20N 94.13W
109 C2 Baxter Mt Colorado 39.42N 107.19W
109 Q4 Baxter Springs Kansas 37.02N 94.45W
98 C7 Baxter State Park Maine
Bay *see* Baicheng
33 J4 Ba'yā U.A.E. 24.03N 51.45E
90 G9 Baya *tribe* Cameroon
35 E1 Bayada Lebanon 33.12N 35.19E
88 O5 Bayadh,El Algeria 33.40N 1.00E
91 E6 Bayaka *tribe* Zaïre
116 F4 Bayamo Cuba 20.23N 76.39W
105 K7 Bayamón Puerto Rico 18.24N 66.10W
44 G7 Bayan Azerbaydzhan U.S.S.R. 40.34N 46.09E
21 D4 Bayan Heilongjiang China 46.05N 127.24E
18 M10 Bayan Indonesia 8.16S 116.28E
22 G3 Bayan Mongolia 47.17N 107.44E
24 J8 Bayan Qinghai China 35.27N 96.30E
23 A1 Bayan *R* Qinghai China
30 A6 Bayana Rajasthan India 26.55N 77.18E
22 F2 Bayan-Agt Mongolia 49.02N 102.12E
43 M2 Bayan-Aul Kazakhstan U.S.S.R. 50.47N 75.39E
22 G3 Bayanbaraat Mongolia 46.50N 106.10E
22 D3 Bayanbulag Mongolia 46.50N 98.05E
24 E4 Bayanbulak Xinjiang Uygur Zizhiqu China 43.05N 84.05E
90 G9 Bayanda *tribe* Cent Afr Rep
42 H5 Bayanday U.S.S.R. 53.05N 105.40E
22 H3 Bayandelger Mongolia 47.40N 108.05E
22 J4 Bayandelger Mongolia 45.51N 112.15E
Bayan Dobo *see* Buyant Ovoo
22 J2 Bayandun Mongolia 49.12N 113.28E
22 G3 Bayandzürh Mongolia 47.48N 107.06E
91 E2 Bayanga Cent Afr Rep 2.52N 16.23E
Bayan Gol *see* Dengkou
22 D8 Bayan Gol *R* Qinghai China
18 J5 Bayang, Pegunungan *mts* Borneo Indon
23 A1 Bayan Har Shan *mts* Qinghai China 34.20N 97.00E
23 A1 Bayan Har Shankou *pass* Qinghai China 34.06N 97.38E
22 D2 Bayanhayrhan Mongolia 49.20N 96.21E
Bayan Hol *see* Alxa Zuoqi
22 E3 Bayanhongor Mongolia 46.07N 100.44E
22 E4 Bayanhongor *prov* Mongolia
Bayan Hot *see* Alxa Zuoqi
21 B4 Bayan Hot Nei Monggol Zizhiqu China 46.22N 122.22E
Bayan Hure *see* Chen Barag Qi
22 H5 Bayan Hure Nei Monggol Zizhiqu China 42.06N 109.02E
22 L2 Bayan Hure Nei Monggol Zizhiqu China 49.30N 119.31E
Bayan Huxu *see* Horqin Youyi Zhongqi
Bayan Kara Shan *mts see* Bayan Har Shan
42 E6 Bayan-Kol Tuvinsk U.S.S.R. 51.39N 93.37E
42 F7 Bayan-Kol Tuvinsk U.S.S.R. 49.58N 96.23E
18 A6 Bayan Lepas Pen Malaysia 5.18N 100.15E
22 F6 Bayan Mod Nei Monggol Zizhiqu China 40.49N 104.30E
22 H3 Bayanmönh Mongolia 46.50N 109.45E
22 K5 Bayan Nur Sum Nei Monggol Zizhiqu China 43.50N 114.12E
115 O6 Bayano Panama 7.40N 80.16W
Bayan Obō *see* Bayan-Ovoo
22 H6 Bayan Obo Nei Monggol Zizhiqu China 41.46N 109.58E
22 A2 Bayanölgiy *prov* Mongolia
22 D4 Bayan-Öndör Mongolia 44.45N 98.37E
22 F3 Bayan-Öndör Mongolia 46.27N 104.05E
22 G5 Bayan-Ovoo Mongolia 42.58N 106.03E
Bayan Qagan *see* Qahar Youyi Houqi
21 C4 Bayan Qagan Heilongjiang China 46.21N 124.03E
21 B5 Bayan Qagan Nei Monggol Zizhiqu China 44.20N 121.25E
22 J3 Bayanterem Mongolia 47.15N 112.21E
22 G7 Bayan Tohoi Nei Monggol Zizhiqu China 39.19N 106.55E
22 D4 Bayantsagaan Mongolia 45.02N 98.36E
22 G3 Bayantsagaan Mongolia 46.46N 107.04E
22 G3 Bayantsogt Mongolia 47.53N 106.12E
22 C3 Bayan Ula Mongolia 47.05N 95.10E
Bayan Ul Hot *see* Xi Ujimqin Qi
22 H6 Bayan Us Nei Monggol Zizhiqu China 40.10N 108.25E
22 E3 Bayan-Uul Mongolia 47.40N 101.46E
22 J2 Bayan-Uul Mongolia 49.09N 112.49E
91 E5 Bayanzi *tribe* Zaïre
77 L6 Bayárcal Spain 37.02N 2.59W
105 F7 Bayard Florida 30.10N 81.32W
108 Q8 Bayard Iowa 41.51N 94.35W
108 G8 Bayard Nebraska 41.46N 103.20W
104 F7 Bayard W Virginia 39.15N 79.24W
113 W8 Bayard *mt* Alaska/Br Col 56.10N 130.10W
71 J7 Bayard,Col *pass* France 44.36N 6.05E
75 E2 Bayas *R* Spain
Bayat Antalya Turkey *see* Akçay
36 E4 Bayat Turkey 38.58N 30.55E
36 G2 Bayat Turkey 40.34N 34.07E
19 L7 Bayawan Philippines 9.21N 122.47E
32 F5 Bayāz Iran 30.41N 55.29E
19 M6 Baybay Philippines 10.40N 124.54E
58 D2 Bayble Lewis, W Isles Scotland 58.11N 6.14W
105 L2 Bayboro N Carolina 35.08N 76.49W
98 T6 Bay Bulls Newfoundland 47.19N 52.50W
37 E5 Bayburt Turkey 40.15N 40.16E
25 J8 Bay Canh,Hon *islds* Vietnam
43 C4 Baychunas Kazakhstan U.S.S.R. 47.14N 53.00E
45 O5 Baychurovo U.S.S.R. 51.22N 42.42E
106 L6 Bay City Michigan 43.35N 83.52W
110 B4 Bay City Oregon 45.32N 123.52W
112 M7 Bay City Texas 28.59N 96.00W
106 B5 Bay City Wisconsin 44.36N 92.29W
85 F3 Baydā, Al Libya 32.49N 21.45E
33 F10 Baydā, Al Yemen 14.00N 45.39E
85 F4 Baydā'fumm Libya 31.14N 20.21E
33 C4 Baydā, Jabal al *mts* Saudi Arabia
47 J2 Baydaratskaya Guba *B* U.S.S.R.
47 F6 Baydarovo U.S.S.R. 59.41N 45.32E
98 T5 Bay de Verde Newfoundland 48.04N 52.55W
22 E3 Baydrag Gol *R* Mongolia
98 R6 Bay du Nord Newfoundland 47.43N 55.30W
43 J5 Baydzhansay Kazakhstan U.S.S.R. 43.10N 69.54E
32 D2 Bāyeh Iran 36.08N 50.00E
69 H7 Bayel France 48.12N 4.46E
34 O3 Bāyenchūb Iran 35.33N 46.59E
Bayenhot *see* Alxa Zuoqi
42 F4 Bayer U.S.S.R. 55.49N 99.30E
64 P5 Bayer-Eisenstein W Germany 49.07N 13.14E
65 D6 Bayerische Alpen *mts* W Germany
62 F6 Bayern *land* W Germany
72 L3 Bayet France 46.15N 3.15E
70 J3 Bayeux France 49.16N 0.42W
42 C5 Bayevo U.S.S.R. 53.18N 80.49E
111 B9 Bay Farm I California
99 J9 Bayfield Ontario 43.33N 81.41W
106 D3 Bayfield Wisconsin 46.49N 90.51W
98 O2 Bayfield I Quebec 51.15N 58.18W
98 F5 Bayfield Mt Quebec 48.48N 66.54W
43 H5 Baygakum Kazakhstan U.S.S.R. 44.17N 66.23E
43 G1 Baygara Kazakhstan U.S.S.R. 53.52N 63.20E
33 F9 Bayḥān al Qaṣāb S Yemen 14.52N 45.45E
108 E4 Bay Horse Montana 45.03N 105.32W
36 C4 Bayındır Turkey 38.12N 27.40E
34 D8 Bāyir Jordan 30.46N 36.40E
34 E7 Bāyīr, Wādī *watercourse* Jordan/Saudi Arabia
35 A1 Bayit V'gan *dist* Jerusalem
43 J5 Baykadam Kazakhstan U.S.S.R. 43.39N 69.56E
42 G6 Baykal U.S.S.R. 51.55N 104.40E
47 J7 Baykalovo Sverdlovsk U.S.S.R. 57.27N 63.45E
47 K6 Baykalovo Tyumen U.S.S.R. 57.47N 67.42E
41 G5 Baykalovskiy U.S.S.R. 71.43N 99.00E
42 H5 Baykal,Ozero *L* U.S.S.R.
42 G6 Baykal'sk U.S.S.R. 51.31N 104.08E
42 H5 Baykal'skiy Khrebet *mts* U.S.S.R.
42 H4 Baykal'skoye U.S.S.R. 55.23N 109.10E
40 J5 Baykal,Zaliv *gulf* Sakhalin U.S.S.R.
37 F7 Baykan Turkey 38.08N 41.43E
42 E6 Bay-khak U.S.S.R. 51.13N 94.28E
43 G4 Bay-Khozha Kazakhstan U.S.S.R. 45.46N 62.54E
47 H7 Baykibashevo U.S.S.R. 55.48N 56.30E
42 F2 Baykit U.S.S.R. 61.45N 96.22E
42 F2 Baykitskiy U.S.S.R. 62.07N 96.42E
43 H3 Baykonyr Kazakhstan U.S.S.R. 47.50N 66.03E
40 O6 Baykovo Kuril Is U.S.S.R. 50.40N 156.09E
24 B6 Baykurt Xinjiang Uygur Zizhiqu China 39.56N 75.33E
98 S6 Bay L'Argent Newfoundland 47.34N 54.52W
19 K4 Bay,L.de Luzon Philippines
13 E3 Bayley Pt Queensland 16.50S 139.00E
43 E1 Baymak Bashkir U.S.S.R. 52.36N 58.16E
107 J11 Bay Minette Alabama 30.52N 87.46W
56 J4 Baynards Green Oxon Eng 51.58N 1.11W
33 J7 Baynhā Saudi Arabia 19.54N 51.24E
33 K5 Baynūna'h *reg* U.A.E.
76 B2 Bayo Spain 43.09N 8.58W
19 K3 Bayombong Luzon Philippines 16.27N 121.10E
69 L7 Bayon France 48.29N 6.19E
76 B4 Bayona Spain 42.07N 8.51W
42 G6 Bayongol U.S.S.R. 50.42N 103.29E
Bayonnaise Rocks *see* Beyoneisu retsugan
72 B9 Bayonne France 43.30N 1.28W
103 K8 Bayonne New Jersey 40.39N 74.08W
19 K6 Bayo Pt Philippines 10.24N 121.57E
107 E7 Bayou Bartholomew *R* Arkansas
107 D11 Bayou Cocodrie *R* Louisiana
107 D9 Bayou d'Arbonne *R* Louisiana
107 E6 Bayou de View *R* Arkansas
107 H11 Bayou La Batre Alabama 30.24N 88.15W
107 F12 Bayou Lafourche *R* Louisiana
107 E9 Bayou Macon *R* Louisiana
107 E7 Bayou Meto *R* Arkansas
107 G4 Bayou Muddy *R* Illinois
107 F9 Bayou Pierre *R* Mississippi
119 A10 Bayóvar Peru 5.54S 81.01W
105 E9 Bayport Florida 28.33N 82.39W
106 L6 Bay Port Michigan 43.51N 83.22W
108 S4 Bayport Minnesota 45.00N 92.45W
101 K10 Bay Pt Br Col 51.21N 127.49W
19 J6 Bay Pt Philippines 10.40N 119.39E
117 B8 Bay, R Brazil
43 F7 Bayram-Ali Turkmeniya U.S.S.R. 37.44N 62.13E
47 M5 Bayramgulova U.S.S.R. 55.22N 60.31E
36 B3 Bayramiç Turkey 39.47N 26.37E
64 M4 Bayreuth W Germany 49.27N 11.35E
103 B9 Bay Ridge Maryland 38.56N 76.28W
103 J8 Bay Ridge New York 40.38N 74.02W
64 N5 Bayrischer Wald *mts* W Germany
64 N8 Bayrischzell W Germany 47.40N 12.02E
98 T6 Bay Roberts Newfoundland 47.35N 53.20W
37 E3 Bayrumiç Turkey 40.07N 27.49E
Bayrūt *see* Beirut
42 J5 Baysa U.S.S.R. 54.00N 113.31E
107 G11 Bay St.Louis Mississippi 30.20N 89.20W
105 F11 Bayshore Florida 26.42N 81.50W
103 H5 Bay Shore Long I, N Y 40.43N 73.15W
33 E8 Baysh,Wādī *watercourse* Saudi Arabia
103 D8 Bayside New Jersey 39.22N 75.24W
99 L7 Bays, L. of Ontario
105 E1 Bays Mts Tennessee
107 G10 Bay Springs Mississippi 31.59N 89.18W
43 H7 Baysun Uzbekistan U.S.S.R. 38.15N 67.12E
43 H7 Baysuntau,Gory *mts* Uzbekistan U.S.S.R.
11 D1 Bayswater New Zealand 36.49S 174.48E
42 F6 Bay-Syut U.S.S.R. 51.45N 95.30E
Bayt ad Dīn *see* Beit ed Dine
Baytag Bogdo *see* Baytik Shan
33 E9 Bayt al Faqīh Yemen 14.30N 43.17E
33 E9 Bayt Ḍamār Yemen 15.53N 43.06E
56 N3 Baythorn End Essex Eng 52.03N 0.30E
22 B4 Baytik Shan *mts* Xinjiang Uygur Zizhiqu China
24 G3 Baytik Shan *mt ra* Xinjiang Uygur Zizhiqu China
Bayt Jālā *see* Beit Jala
Bayt Laḥm *see* Bethlehem Jordan
112 N6 Baytown Texas 29.43N 94.59W
18 E6 Bayunglincir Sumatra Indon 2.00S 103.39E
110 J2 Bayview Idaho 47.58N 116.34W
103 C7 Bayview Maryland 39.39N 75.57W
11 L6 Bay View New Zealand 39.24S 176.52E
12 M5 Bayview *dist* Sydney, N S W
103 N6 Bayville Long I, N Y 40.55N 73.34W
103 F7 Bayville New Jersey 39.53N 74.10W
77 L5 Baza Spain 37.30N 2.45W
89 G8 Bazai Ivory Coast 6.45N 5.27W
46 F5 Bazaliya Ukraine U.S.S.R. 49.42N 26.29E
69 G5 Bazancourt France 49.22N 4.11E
42 K5 Bazar Chita U.S.S.R. 53.58N 116.08E
109 O3 Bazar Kansas 38.15N 96.33W
46 G4 Bazar Ukraine U.S.S.R. 51.02N 29.15E
77 L5 Baza,R.de Spain
44 H6 Bazar-Dyuzi *mt* Azerbaydzhan U.S.S.R. 41.14N 47.50E
32 C2 Bāzār-e Māsāl Iran 37.26N 49.08E
32 A1 Bāzargān Iran 39.22N 44.21E
43 H5 Bazarkol' Kazakhstan U.S.S.R. 44.46N 65.14E
43 L6 Bazar-Kurgan Kirgiziya U.S.S.R. 41.05N 72.47E
45 V2 Bazarnye Mataki U.S.S.R. 54.54N 49.56E
45 S4 Bazarnyy Karabulak U.S.S.R. 52.17N 46.24E
45 S3 Bazarnyy Syzgan U.S.S.R. 53.45N 46.45E
43 B3 Bazarshulan Kazakhstan U.S.S.R. 49.07N 52.00E
46 Q5 Bazartobe Kazakhstan U.S.S.R. 49.22N 51.58E
92 G12 Bazaruto,I.do Mozambique 21.40S 35.30E
72 D7 Bazas France 44.26N 0.12W
77 L6 Baza,Sierra de *mts* Spain
39 C5 Baza Urak U.S.S.R. 59.12N 142.29E
45 F9 Bazavluk *R* Ukraine U.S.S.R.
31 C7 Bazdar Pakistan 26.20N 65.12E
69 H4 Bazeilles France 49.41N 5.00E
61 H2 Bazel Belgium 51.09N 4.18E
21 C2 Bazhan Heilongjiang China 50.25N 125.38E
42 E3 Bazhenova U.S.S.R. 58.47N 92.00E
47 N5 Bazhenovo U.S.S.R. 56.45N 61.24E
44 G3 Bazhigan U.S.S.R. 44.33N 45.41E
23 D3 Bazhong Sichuan China 31.50N 106.49E
82 G6 Baziaş Romania 44.53N 21.25E
72 H9 Bazièges France 43.27N 1.36E
37 D8 Baziki Turkey 37.23N 38.22E
72 E9 Bazillac France 43.21N 0.07E
99 Q5 Bazin *R* Quebec
109 L3 Bazine Kansas 38.27N 99.43W
95 M7 Baziya S Africa 31.36S 28.25E
45 N7 Bazkovskaya U.S.S.R. 49.35N 41.45E
32 J7 Bazman Iran 27.50N 60.13E
32 J6 Bazmān,Kūh-e- *mt* Iran 28.05N 60.00E
70 M5 Bazoche-Gouet,la France 48.08N 0.59E
69 E6 Bazoches France 48.40N 3.19E
70 K4 Bazoches-au-Houlme France 48.48N 0.14W
69 C7 Bazoches-les Gallerandes France 48.10N 2.02E
70 L4 Bazoches-sur-Hoëne France 48.33N 0.28E
69 F5 Bazoches-sur-Vesle France 49.18N 3.38E
70 L5 Bazoge,la France 48.06N 0.09E
72 B2 Bazoges-en Paillers France 46.55N 1.07W
72 C2 Bazoges-en-Pareds France 46.40N 0.56W
71 D2 Bazolles France 47.08N 3.37E
91 B1 Bazou Cameroon 5.03N 10.28E
70 J5 Bazougers France 48.00N 0.35W
70 G5 Bazouges-la-Perouse France 48.26N 1.34W
42 C5 Bazovo U.S.S.R. 54.33N 81.14E
Bazqush,Kuh-i *see* Bozqūsh, Kūh-e- *mts*
75 G1 Baztán, El *V* Spain
79 K5 Bazzano Italy 44.30N 11.05E
34 D4 Bcharré Lebanon 34.15N 36.00E
105 E6 Beach Georgia 31.27N 82.32W
108 F3 Beach N Dakota 46.56N 104.01W
99 O7 Beachburg Ontario 45.43N 76.53W
101 H12 Beach Grove Br Col 49.02N 123.04W
103 F7 Beach Haven New Jersey 39.34N 74.14W
103 B4 Beach Haven Pennsylvania 41.04N 76.10W
103 F7 Beach Haven Inlet New Jersey
103 D3 Beach Lake Pennsylvania 41.36N 75.09W
56 F4 Beachley Glos Eng 51.37N 2.39W
103 F7 Beachwood New Jersey 39.57N 74.12W
56 M6 Beachy Head *prom* E Sussex Eng 50.44N 0.16E
103 G3 Beacon New York 41.31N 73.59W
14 C9 Beacon W Australia 30.27S 117.52E
103 H4 Beacon Falls Connecticut 41.26N 73.04W
105 B8 Beacon Hill Florida 29.55N 85.23W
23 B8 Beacon Hill Hong Kong 22.21N 114.09E
100 H4 Beacon Hill Saskatchewan 54.23N 109.40W
103 G4 Beacon, Mt New York 41.29N 73.56W
56 K4 Beaconsfield Bucks Eng 51.37N 0.39W
99 P10 Beaconsfield Quebec 45.26N 73.49W
95 H4 Beaconsfield S Africa 28.46S 24.48E
12 H8 Beaconsfield Tasmania 41.11S 146.46E
55 J3 Beacontree London Eng 51.34N 0.08E
76 C4 Beade Spain 42.20N 8.08W
57 K1 Beadnell Northumb Eng 55.33N 1.37W
57 K1 Beadnell B Northumb Eng 55.32N 1.35W
56 C6 Beaford Devon Eng 50.55N 4.03W
71 E7 Béage, le France 44.52N 4.08E
59 G1 Beagh,L Donegal Irish Rep 55.02N 7.59W
14 E3 Beagle Bank W Australia 15.08S 123.28E
14 E3 Beagle Bay W Australia 16.55S 122.33E
121 L10 Beagle,Canal *channel* Chile/Arg
15 J9 Beagle Ent Papua New Guinea 10.05S 147.35E
13 A1 Beagle G N Terr Australia
14 A8 Beagle I W Australia 29.49S 114.52E
58 N7 Beal Northumb Eng 55.40N 1.54W
59 C6 Bealaha Clare Irish Rep 52.43N 9.35W
95 D3 Bealanana Madagascar 14.33S 48.44E
71 D5 Béal,Col du *pass* France 45.41N 3.47E
101 L11 Beale,C Vancouver I, Br Col 48.46N 125.10W
29 C8 Beale, L Maharashtra India
104 H8 Bealeton Virginia 38.36N 77.47W
12 G6 Bealiba Victoria 36.45S 143.31E
13 F7 Beal Ra Queensland
112 F3 Beals Cr Texas
100 C1 Beaman Manitoba 49.56N 97.01W
56 F6 Beaminster Dorset Eng 50.49N 2.45W
95 C8 Beampingaratra *mts* Madagascar
95 B7 Beampombo Madagascar 23.35S 45.34E
55 K3 Beam R London England
99 L9 Beamsville Ontario 43.10N 79.31W
75 G7 Beamud Spain 40.11N 1.50W
110 J4 Bear Idaho 45.02N 116.40W
110 O7 Bear *R* Idaho
72 L10 Béar, Cap *C* France 42.31N 3.09E
110 R7 Bear Cr Wyoming
107 J7 Bear Creek Alabama
109 J4 Bear Creek Kansas
110 Q4 Bearcreek Montana 45.08N 109.10W
103 C4 Bear Creek Pennsylvania 41.11N 75.42W
106 F5 Bear Creek Wisconsin 44.31N 88.44W
108 F8 Bear Creek Wyoming
101 E5 Bear Creek Yukon Terr 60.46N 137.35W
103 C4 Bear Cr Res Pennsylvania
107 D8 Bearden Arkansas 33.43N 92.39W
107 M6 Bearden Tennessee 35.56N 84.01W
99 C3 Beardmore Ontario 49.36N 87.59W
123 G7 Beardmore Glacier Antarctica
13 J8 Beardmore Res Qnsld 27.33S 148.32E
111 M8 Beardsley Arizona 33.41N 112.21W
109 J2 Beardsley Kansas 39.49N 101.14W
106 D9 Beardstown Illinois 40.01N 90.26W
56 E6 Beare Devon Eng 50.49N 3.25W
103 F4 Bearfort Mt *ra* New Jersey/New York
103 A5 Bear Gap Pennsylvania 40.50N 76.30W
59 C8 Bear Haven Cork Irish Rep
98 K4 Bear Head Anticosti I, Que 49.34N 62.26W
100 J7 Bear Hills,The Saskatchewan
97 L7 Bear Is James B, N W Terr 54.20N 81.00W
Bear Is U.S.S.R. *see* Medvezh'i, Ostrova *Is*
123 H11 Bear Island Antarctica
59 C8 Bear Island Cork Irish Rep 51.38N 9.53W
99 K6 Bear Island Ontario 46.59N 80.05W
50 R11 Bear Island Spitsbergen 74.30N 19.00E
76 C4 Beariz Spain 42.28N 8.16W
110 O7 Bear L Idaho/Utah 42.00N 111.20W
101 K7 Bear Lake Br Col 56.12N 126.51W
100 V3 Bear Lake Manitoba
106 H5 Bear Lake Michigan 44.25N 86.10W
108 F5 Bear Lodge Mts Wyoming
29 F6 Bearma *R* Madhya Prad India
110 M3 Bearmouth Montana 46.43N 113.20W
103 F4 Bear Mt New York 41.18N 74.01W
99 M4 Béarn Quebec 48.47N 78.09W
67 E9 Béarn *prov* France
110 Q1 Bear Paw Mt Montana 48.09N 109.39W
103 E2 Bearpen Mt New York 42.16N 74.30W
100 N4 Bear R Saskatchewan
98 G9 Bear River Nova Scotia 44.34N 65.40W
110 N8 Bear River City Utah 41.37N 112.10W
58 H7 Bearsden Strathclyde Scotland 55.56N 4.20W
109 C1 Bears Ears Pk Colorado 40.46N 107.14W
97 K7 Bearskin Lake Ontario 53.58N 91.02W
77 C6 Beas Spain 37.25N 6.48W
30 A1 Beas *R* Himachal Prad India
75 F1 Beasain Spain 43.03N 2.11W
29 D2 Beas Dam Punjab India 31.57N 75.50E
77 L4 Beas de Segura Spain 38.15N 2.53W
29 E2 Beas R Himachal Prad India
116 J6 Beata,C Dominican Rep 17.41N 71.24W
116 J6 Beata, I Dominican Rep 17.38N 71.29W
66 H5 Beatenberg Switzerland 46.42N 7.48E
76 E16 Beato Portugal 38.44N 9.06W
101 P10 Beaton Br Col 50.44N 117.44W
107 J10 Beatrice Alabama 31.43N 87.12W
108 O9 Beatrice Nebraska 40.17N 96.45W
92 E11 Beatrice Zimbabwe 18.15S 30.55E
13 D2 Beatrice,C Groote Eylandt, N Terr Aust 14.12S 136.35E
14 F3 Beatrice,Mt W Australia 15.47S 127.15E
116 A1 Beatrix *airport* Aruba W I 12.31N 70.01W
109 O2 Beattie Kansas 39.51N 96.25W
57 G2 Beattock Dumfries & Galloway Scotland 55.18N 3.28W
57 F2 Beattock Summit *mt* Strathclyde/Borders Scotland 55.27N 3.33W
101 N7 Beatton R Br Col
101 N7 Beatton River Br Col 57.47N 121.19W
111 H5 Beatty Nevada 36.54N 116.45W
110 D7 Beatty Oregon 42.27N 121.15W
100 N6 Beatty Saskatchewan 52.55N 104.49W
104 B9 Beattyville Kentucky 37.33N 83.44W
99 N4 Beattyville Quebec 48.53N 77.10W
26 U12 Beau Bassin Mauritius, Indian Oc 20.13S 57.27E
71 F9 Beaucaire France 43.48N 4.37E
69 B4 Beaucamps-le-Vieux France 49.51N 1.47E
99 L3 Beaucanton Quebec 49.05N 79.15W
70 M6 Beauce *plain* France
72 D10 Beaucens France 42.58N 0.04W
98 B7 Beauceville Quebec 46.12N 70.45W
68 D1 Beauchamp France 49.01N 2.11E
70 H4 Beauchamps France 48.50N 1.21W
121 E10 Beauchene Is Falkland Is 52.55S 59.15W
99 M6 Beauchêne,L Quebec
66 D2 Beaucourt France 47.29N 6.55E
72 E9 Beaudéan France 43.02N 0.10E
13 L8 Beaudesert Queensland 28.00S 152.27E
99 L4 Beaudry Quebec 48.06N 79.10W
71 F10 Beauduc,G.de France 43.25N 4.33E
70 L5 Beaufay France 48.09N 0.23E
61 N4 Beaufays Belgium 50.33N 5.38E
71 G3 Beaufort Jura France 46.35N 5.26E
61 Q7 Beaufort Luxembourg 49.50N 6.17E
105 L3 Beaufort N Carolina 34.44N 76.41W
18 L3 Beaufort Sabah Malaysia 5.22N 115.42E
71 K5 Beaufort Savoie France 45.43N 6.35E
105 G5 Beaufort S Carolina 32.26N 80.40W
12 G6 Beaufort Victoria 37.28S 143.28E
58 H4 Beaufort Castle Highland Scotland 57.27N 4.30W
70 K7 Beaufort-en-Vallée France 47.27N 0.12W
123 J6 Beaufort I Antarctica 76.53S 167.00E
23 B10 Beaufort I Hong Kong 22.10N 114.14E
105 L3 Beaufort Inlet N Carolina
113 R2 Beaufort Lagoon Alaska
101 E1 Beaufort Sea Arctic Oc
95 F8 Beaufort West S Africa 32.21S 22.35E
70 O6 Beaugency France 47.47N 1.38E
99 R7 Beauharnois Quebec 45.18N 73.52W
99 Q7 Beauharnois Power Can Quebec
71 J8 Beaujeu Alpes de Haute Provence France 44.12N 6.22E
71 F4 Beaujeu Rhône France 46.09N 4.35E
71 H1 Beaujeu-St. Vallier-Pierrejux-et-Quitteur France 47.32N 5.41E
71 E4 Beaujolais,Mts.du France
104 P6 Beau L Maine/Quebec
72 D7 Beaulac France 44.22N 0.14W
71 L9 Beaulieu Alpes-Maritimes France 43.43N 7.20E
56 J6 Beaulieu Hants Eng 50.49N 1.27W
71 E9 Beaulieu Hérault France 43.43N 4.01E
71 B1 Beaulieu Loiret France 47.33N 2.48E
71 C6 Beaulieu Puy-de-Dôme France 45.26N 3.17E
72 H6 Beaulieu-sur-Dordogne France 44.59N 1.50E
72 E4 Beaulieu-sur-Sonnette France 45.56N 0.23E
71 D3 Beaulon France 46.36N 3.40E
58 H4 Beauly Highland Scotland 57.29N 4.29W
58 H4 Beauly Firth Highland Scotland
58 G4 Beauly R Highland Scotland
72 E8 Beaumarchés France 43.35N 0.06E
57 E6 Beaumaris Gwynedd Wales 53.16N 4.05W
12 D9 Beaumaris *dist* Melbourne, Vic
12 D9 Beaumaris B Victoria
71 G8 Beaumes-de-Venise France 44.07N 5.02E
70 M3 Beaumesnil France 49.01N 0.43E
69 D3 Beaumetz-lès-Loges France 50.15N 2.32E
61 G6 Beaumont Belgium 50.14N 4.14E
111 H8 Beaumont California 33.56N 117.00W
72 F6 Beaumont France 44.46N 0.47E
109 O4 Beaumont Kansas 37.40N 96.34W
69 K6 Beaumont Meurthe-et-Moselle France 48.51N 5.48E
107 H10 Beaumont Mississippi 31.10N 88.58W
98 R4 Beaumont Newfoundland 49.37N 55.41W
11 D12 Beaumont New Zealand 45.50S 169.34E
103 C4 Beaumont Pennsylvania 41.24N 75.59W
112 N5 Beaumont Texas 30.04N 94.06W
72 E2 Beaumont Vienne France 46.45N 0.25E
123 H7 Beaumont B Antarctica
72 F8 Beaumont-de-Lomagne France 43.53N 0.59E
69 C7 Beaumont-du-Gâtinais France 48.08N 2.29E
69 J4 Beaumont-en-Argonne France 49.32N 5.04E
70 L3 Beaumont-en-Auge France 49.16N 0.06E
69 E3 Beaumont-en-Cambrésis France 50.08N 3.27E
69 J5 Beaumont-en-Verdunois Meuse France 49.14N 5.25E
70 G2 Beaumont-Hague France 49.40N 1.51W
12 H4 Beaumont Hill New S Wales 31.33S 145.11E
70 M6 Beaumont-la-Ronce France 47.35N 0.41E
70 M3 Beaumont-le-Roger France 49.04N 0.47E
70 M5 Beaumont-les-Autels France 48.15N 0.57E
48 R1 Beaumont Ø *isld* Greenland 83.00N 51.00W
70 L6 Beaumont-Pied-de-Bœuf France 47.45N 0.24E
112 G8 Beaumont Place Texas 29.51N 95.11W
69 C5 Beaumont-sur-Oise France 49.09N 2.17E
70 L5 Beaumont-sur-Sarthe France 48.13N 0.07E
71 F2 Beaune France 47.02N 4.50E
69 C7 Beaune-la Rolande France 48.05N 2.25E
98 R7 Beauport Quebec 46.52N 71.12W
72 C1 Beaupréau France 47.12N 0.59W
69 C3 Beauquesne France 50.05N 2.23E
61 K6 Beauraing Belgium 50.07N 4.57E
99 P10 Beaurepaire Quebec 45.25N 73.49W
71 G6 Beaurepaire-d'Isère France 45.20N 5.03E
71 G3 Beaurepaire-en-Bresse France 46.40N 5.22E
71 H7 Beaurières France 44.34N 5.33E
69 F5 Beaurieux France 49.24N 3.44E
61 N6 Beausaint Belgium 50.10N 5.33E
100 V8 Beauséjour Manitoba 50.04N 96.30W
72 D3 Beaussais France 46.18N 0.08W
71 H10 Beausset,le France 43.10N 5.46E
9 B13 Beautemps-Beaupré *atoll* Loyalty Is Pacific Oc
72 D6 Beautiran France 44.34N 0.27W
69 C5 Beauvais France 49.26N 2.05E
100 C9 Beauvais Lake Prov.Park Alberta
72 D4 Beauvais-sous-Matha France 45.54N 0.10W
69 C3 Beauval France 50.07N 2.20E
100 K3 Beauval Saskatchewan 55.09N 107.35W
100 F5 Beauvallon Alberta 53.40N 111.25W
61 K3 Beauvechain Belgium 50.47N 4.47E
71 K8 Beauvezer France 44.09N 6.36E
72 F7 Beauville France 44.17N 0.54E
70 F8 Beauvoir-sur-Mer France 46.55N 2.02W
72 D3 Beauvoir-sur-Niort France 46.11N 0.28W
61 A2 Beauvoorde Belgium 51.01N 2.40E
61 G6 Beauwelz Belgium 50.01N 4.10E
71 E6 Beauzac France 45.15N 4.05E
113 O3 Beaver Alaska 66.22N 147.30W
109 M3 Beaver Kansas 38.38N 98.41W
109 K5 Beaver Oklahoma 36.48N 100.32W
110 B4 Beaver Oregon 45.18N 123.49W
104 E6 Beaver Pennsylvania 40.43N 80.20W
111 M3 Beaver Utah 38.18N 112.38W
111 L3 Beaver *R* Utah
101 L5 Beaver *R* Yukon Terr
98 J9 Beaverbank Nova Scotia 44.48N 63.41W
98 G6 Beaver Brook New Brunswick 47.09N 63.38W
103 E3 Beaver Brook New York 41.34N 74.55W
108 L9 Beaver City Nebraska 40.09N 99.50W
110 N5 Beaver Cr Idaho
113 O4 Beaver Creek Alaska
109 G2 Beaver Creek Colorado
109 J2 Beaver Creek Kansas
107 D5 Beaver Creek Missouri
108 F3 Beaver Creek Montana
108 K3 Beaver Creek N Dakota
108 L9 Beaver Creek Nebraska
108 M8 Beaver Creek Nebraska
108 F6 Beaver Creek Wyoming
101 C4 Beaver Creek Yukon Terr 62.20N 140.45W
109 J2 Beaver Creek,Lit Kansas
108 N9 Beaver Crossing Nebraska 40.47N 97.18W
107 K4 Beaver Dam Kentucky 37.24N 86.52W
106 F6 Beaver Dam Wisconsin 43.28N 88.50W
101 O11 Beaverdell Br Col 49.25N 119.09W
104 E6 Beaver Falls Pennsylvania 40.45N 80.21W
110 N4 Beaverhead *R* Montana
110 M4 Beaverhead Ra Montana
100 E5 Beaverhill L Alberta
101 V4 Beaverhill,L N W Terr
121 D10 Beaver I Falkland Is 51.50S 61.16W
106 J4 Beaver I Michigan
98 O2 Beaver Island L Quebec
103 E3 Beaver Kill New York 41.59N 74.50W
103 E3 Beaver Kill *R* New York
106 H3 Beaver L Michigan 46.34N 86.20W
101 N9 Beaver Lake Br Col 52.29N 121.52W
107 C5 Beaver Lake *res* Arkansas
101 O8 Beaverlodge Alberta 55.11N 119.29W
103 C5 Beaver Meadows Pennsylvania 40.57N 75.54W
101 P10 Beavermouth Br Col 51.30N 117.28W
113 J5 Beaver Mts Alaska
100 F4 Beaver R Alberta
100 K4 Beaver R Saskatchewan
104 K3 Beaver River Flow *L* New York
103 M4 Beaver Tail Lt.Ho Rhode I 41.27N 71.24W
106 K6 Beaverton Michigan 43.54N 84.30W
99 L8 Beaverton Ontario 44.25N 79.10W
110 C4 Beaverton Oregon 45.29N 122.49W
104 H6 Beavertown Pennsylvania 40.45N 77.11W
106 G9 Beaverville Illinois 40.58N 87.40W
29 D4 Beawar Rajasthan India 26.02N 74.20E
121 C4 Beazley Argentina 33.46S 66.42W
95 B4 Bebao Madagascar 17.20S 44.31E
18 D8 Bebar *R* Pen Malaysia
121 C4 Bebedero,Salina *salt pan* Argentina
118 E7 Bebedouro Brazil 20.54S 48.31W
90 D6 Bebeji Nigeria 11.40N 8.15E
37 K1 Bebek Turkey 41.05N 29.06E
64 G6 Bebenhausen W Germany 48.33N 9.05E
117 H7 Beberibe Brazil 4.10S 38.10W
15 G7 Bebisa Papua New Guinea 7.44S 143.16E
90 H7 Bebouguei Chad 8.23N 16.44E
64 H2 Bebra W Germany 50.59N 9.47E
82 K8 Bebrovo Bulgaria 42.57N 26.00E
76 D5 Beca *R* Portugal
77 V14 Beca,Pta *pt* Balearic Is 39.55N 2.56E
66 F8 Becca Luseney *mt* Italy 45.52N 7.27E
56 P3 Beccles Suffolk Eng 52.28N 1.34E
72 C5 Bec d'Ambes *pen* France
71 H10 Bec de l'Aigle *pt* France 43.10N 5.36E
75 L6 Beceite Spain 40.50N 0.11E
82 F5 Bečej Yugoslavia 45.36N 20.04E
82 K5 Beceni Romania 45.23N 26.48E
76 E3 Becerreá Spain 42.51N 7.10W
77 G6 Becerrero *mt* Spain 37.16N 4.52W
76 K4 Becerril de Campos Spain 42.06N 4.39W
116 C7 Becerro,Cayos *islds* Caribbean Sea 15.55N 83.27W
96 O15 Becerro, Pta del *pt* Gomera Canary Is 28.02N 17.15W
61 Q7 Bech Luxembourg 49.45N 6.22E
88 M6 Béchar Algeria 31.35N 2.17W
88 M6 Bechar *watercourse* Algeria
88 N6 Béchar,Djebel *mts* Algeria
113 J8 Becharof L Alaska 58.00N 156.30W
88 S3 Béchateur Tunisia 37.18N 9.44E
11 E10 Bêche,Mt.de la New Zealand 43.30S 170.15E
70 G5 Bécherel France 48.18N 1.56W
82 H7 Bechet Romania 43.45N 23.57E
113 F9 Bechevin B Alaska
64 K5 Bechhofen W Germany 49.10N 10.35E
75 K8 Bechi Spain 39.56N 0.13W
44 G5 Bechik U.S.S.R. 42.43N 45.32E
65 L1 Běchovice Czechoslovakia 50.06N 14.38E
103 C6 Bechtelsville Pennsylvania 40.22N 75.38W
Bechuanaland *see* Botswana
65 K3 Bechyně Czechoslovakia 49.17N 14.28E
76 J4 Becilla de Valderaduey Spain 42.06N 5.13W
63 M7 Beckedorf W Germany 52.48N 10.04E
55 G5 Beckenham London Eng 51.24N 0.01W
66 K4 Beckenried Switzerland 46.58N 8.29E
61 O8 Beckerich Luxembourg 49.44N 5.53E
103 H2 Becket Massachusetts 42.20N 73.05W
57 G3 Beckfoot Cumbria Eng 54.50N 3.25W
56 G3 Beckford Hereford & Worcs Eng 52.01N 2.02W
56 H5 Beckhampton Wilts Eng 51.26N 1.53W
64 B5 Beckingen W Germany 49.24N 6.42E
57 M6 Beckingham Lincs Eng 53.04N 0.41W
57 M6 Beckingham Notts Eng 53.24N 0.50W
56 G5 Beckington Somerset Eng 51.16N 2.18W
104 D9 Beckley W Virginia 37.46N 81.12W
11 D12 Becks New Zealand 45.02S 169.42E
60 P11 Beckum Netherlands 52.13N 6.45E
63 H9 Beckum W Germany 51.45N 8.02E
112 N3 Beckville Texas 32.13N 94.28W
111 D2 Beckwourth California 39.50N 120.23W
82 J3 Beclean Romania 47.10N 24.11E
61 E4 Beclers Belgium 50.37N 3.31E
76 C9 Beco Portugal 39.46N 8.17W
70 J6 Bécon France 47.30N 0.47W
71 G8 Béconne France 44.29N 5.03E
56 M4 Becontree London Eng 51.34N 0.10E
64 O3 Bečov nad Teplou Czechoslovakia 50.05N 12.51E
66 G7 Becs de Bosson *mt* Switzerland 46.10N 7.32E
65 P9 Becsehely Hungary 46.27N 16.50E
59 J4 Bective Meath Irish Rep 3.36N 6.42W
112 F2 Becton Texas 33.47N 101.38W
62 K6 Bečva *R* Czechoslovakia
65 M2 Bečváry Czechoslovakia 49.58N 15.05E
85 E5 Beda Libya 28.26N 19.00E
57 K4 Bedale N Yorks Eng 54.17N 1.35W
66 M7 Bedano Switzerland 46.03N 8.55E
77 N6 Bédar Spain 37.11N 1.59W
71 C9 Bédarieux France 43.37N 3.10E
71 F8 Bédarrides France 44.03N 4.54E
60 O13 Bedburg W Germany 51.44N 6.20E
64 B1 Bedburg W Germany 51.00N 6.35E
63 D9 Bedburg-Hau W Germany 51.44N 6.12E
57 E6 Beddgelert Gwynedd Wales 53.01N 4.06W
56 M6 Beddingham E Sussex Eng 50.51N 0.04E
55 F5 Beddington London Eng 51.22N 0.08W
104 R2 Beddington Maine 44.52N 68.03W
88 J5 Beddouza *C* Morocco 32.38N 9.19W
100 R9 Bede Manitoba 49.24N 100.49W
70 G5 Bédée France 48.10N 1.56W
87 F6 Bēdēlē Ethiopia 8.30N 36.20E
Bedelli *see* Bēdēlē
24 C5 Bedel Pass *pass* China/U.S.S.R. 41.21N 78.25E
43 N6 Bedel',Pereval *pass* U.S.S.R./China 41.21N 78.25E
72 D5 Bédenac France 45.09N 0.18W
53 E4 Beder Denmark 56.03N 10.13E
63 J5 Bederkesa W Germany 53.38N 8.51E
87 H6 Bedessa Ethiopia 8.57N 40.43E
87 K6 Bedewanak Somalia 9.33N 44.25E
47 H7 Bedeyeva Polyana U.S.S.R. 55.20N 56.28E
56 L3 Bedford Beds Eng 52.08N 0.29W
107 K3 Bedford Indiana 38.51N 86.30W
108 Q9 Bedford Iowa 40.39N 94.42W
107 L3 Bedford Kentucky 38.36N 85.18W
104 O4 Bedford New Hampshire 42.56N 71.33W
103 G4 Bedford New York 41.14N 73.37W
98 J9 Bedford Nova Scotia 44.44N 63.41W
104 D5 Bedford Ohio 41.23N 81.33W
104 G6 Bedford Pennsylvania 40.02N 78.31W
99 S7 Bedford Quebec 45.07N 72.59W
95 K8 Bedford S Africa 32.41S 26.05E
112 M9 Bedford Texas 32.49N 97.08W
104 F9 Bedford Virginia 37.20N 79.31W
110 P7 Bedford Wyoming 42.54N 110.56W
56 L3 Bedford *co* England
13 H3 Bedford C Queensland 15.12S 145.20E
14 F3 Bedford Downs W Australia 17.15S 127.22E
14 D10 Bedford Harb W Australia
103 G4 Bedford Hills New York 41.15N 73.41W
56 L2 Bedford Level *reg* Lincs etc Eng
116 P5 Bedford Point Grenada, W I 12.14N 61.36W
14 F7 Bedford Ra W Australia
12 J5 Bedgerebong New S Wales 33.22S 147.47E
29 B6 Bedi Gujarat India 22.32N 70.02E
18 G7 Bedinggong Indonesia 2.40S 106.10E
36 J6 Bedirge Turkey 36.22N 36.12E
29 C5 Bedla Rajasthan India 24.41N 73.47E
59 F1 Bedlam Donegal Irish Rep 55.07N 8.09W
57 K2 Bedlington Northumb Eng 55.08N 1.35W
47 C5 Bedlozero U.S.S.R. 61.30N 32.45E
77 K5 Bedmar Spain 37.50N 3.25W
31 E4 Bed Mashk Afghanistan 33.44N 68.23E
45 P3 Bednodem'yanovsk U.S.S.R. 53.56N 43.12E
95 B4 Bedoa Madagascar 17.39S 45.01E
42 F3 Bedoba U.S.S.R. 58.46N 97.18E
71 G8 Bédoin France 44.07N 5.10E
18 K3 Bedok Singapore 1.19N 103.57E
18 K3 Bedok *dist* Singapore 1.19N 103.57E
66 N6 Bedoletta, Cima di *mt* Switzerland 46.26N 9.10E
79 K2 Bedollo Italy 46.10N 11.18E
18 A6 Bedong Pen Malaysia 5.43N 100.31E
79 G5 Bedonia Italy 44.30N 9.38E
90 H7 Bedou Chad 8.19N 17.07E
13 E6 Bedourie Queensland 24.20S 139.17E
72 C9 Bedous France 43.00N 0.36W
14 C4 Bedout I W Australia 19.34S 119.03E
66 L5 Bedretto Switzerland 46.31N 8.31E
66 K6 Bedretto,Val Switzerland
90 H1 Bedrou Chad 20.04N 16.11E
56 A7 Bedruthan Steps Cornwall Eng 50.30N 5.02W
53 A3 Bedsted Denmark 56.49N 8.25E
53 C6 Bedsted Denmark 55.04N 9.07E
72 H6 Béduer France 44.34N 1.55E
34 L1 Bēdūh Iraq 37.16N 43.24E
60 P6 Bedum Netherlands 53.18N 6.36E
56 J3 Bedworth Warwicks Eng 52.29N 1.28W
108 N8 Bee Nebraska 41.01N 97.02W
12 G7 Beeac Victoria 38.12S 143.42E
107 E6 Beebe Arkansas 35.03N 91.54W
108 L4 Beebe S Dakota 45.26N 99.11W
13 H7 Beechal *R* Queensland
107 J4 Beech Creek Kentucky 37.09N 87.06W
110 F5 Beech Creek Oregon 44.35N 119.07W
104 H5 Beech Creek Pennsylvania 41.04N 77.37W
106 G8 Beecher Illinois 41.20N 87.39W
107 H2 Beecher City Illinois 39.11N 88.48W
101 U3 Beechey, L N W Terr
113 N1 Beechey Point Alaska 70.28N 149.18W
107 L4 Beech Fork *R* Kentucky
107 K2 Beech Grove Indiana 39.42N 86.06W
106 F3 Beechwood Michigan 46.10N 88.46W
98 E6 Beechwood Hydro-Electric Sta New Brunswick 47.04N 67.48W
12 H6 Beechworth Victoria 36.23S 146.42E
100 K8 Beechy Saskatchewan 50.53N 107.24W
12 K5 Beecroft Pen New S Wales 35.01S 150.49E
63 M7 Beedenbostel W Germany 52.38N 10.15E
60 M15 Beegden Netherlands 51.11N 5.55E
110 C9 Beegum California 40.21N 122.51W
59 K6 Beehive Wicklow Irish Rep 52.56N 6.05W
60 M12 Beek Gelderland Netherlands 51.50N 5.55E
60 N12 Beek Gelderland Netherlands 51.54N 6.12E
60 T17 Beek Limburg Netherlands 50.56N 5.47E
60 M11 Beekbergen Netherlands 52.10N 5.58E
60 L13 Beek-en-Donk Brabant Netherlands 51.34N 5.38E
107 E9 Beekman Louisiana 32.55N 91.53W
58 B4 Bee, L S Uist, W Isles Scotland 57.23N 7.22W
109 K3 Beeler Kansas 38.25N 100.12W
63 R8 Beelitz E Germany 52.15N 12.58E
108 O8 Beemer Nebraska 41.57N 96.48W
103 E4 Beemerville New Jersey 41.13N 74.41W
60 H9 Beemster *dist* Netherlands
63 O8 Beendorf E Germany 52.16N 11.05E
59 B7 Been Hill Kerry Irish Rep 52.01N 10.03W
13 L8 Beenleigh Queensland 27.43S 153.09E
59 B7 Beenoskee *mt* Kerry Irish Rep 52.13N 10.05W
56 E6 Beer Devon Eng 50.42N 3.06W
86 N5 Be'er 'Ada Israel 30.19N 34.54E
64 K2 Beerberg *mt* E Germany 50.40N 10.45E
35 D9 Be'er Ef'e Israel 31.09N 35.13E
50 O9 Beerenberg *vol* Jan Mayen I Arctic Ocean 71.05N 8.05W
64 F4 Beerfelden W Germany 49.33N 8.58E
35 B10 Be'er Hayil Israel 30.59N 34.42E
35 A8 Be'eri Israel 31.25N 34.29E
105 E10 Bee Ridge Florida 27.17N 82.29W
14 C8 Beeringgnurding, Mt W Australia 29.52S 117.51E
61 E3 Beerlegem Belgium 50.54N 3.43E
34 C8 Be'er Menuha Israel 30.18N 35.07E
61 D2 Beernem Belgium 51.08N 3.20E
34 B9 Be'er Ora Israel 29.43N 34.57E
35 C9 Be'erot 'Aro'er Israel 31.09N 34.59E
35 C4 Be'erotayim Israel 32.20N 34.59E
35 D8 Be'erot Yattir Israel 31.21N 35.01E
35 B10 Be'er Paqu'a Israel 30.56N 34.41E
35 C8 Be'er Pehar Israel 31.21N 34.49E
35 E8 Be'er Qeresh Israel 31.24N 35.17E
60 M13 Beers Noord-Brabant Netherlands 51.43N 5.50E
61 K1 Beerse Belgium 51.19N 4.51E
61 H3 Beersel Belgium 50.46N 4.19E
35 C9 Beersheba Israel 31.15N 34.47E
Be'er Sheva' *see* Beersheba
35 C9 Be'er Sheva' *anc site* Israel 31.15N 34.50E
35 B9 Be'er Sheva' *watercourse* Israel
61 B2 Beerst Belgium 51.03N 2.53E
103 D2 Beerston New York 42.08N 75.10W
61 G4 Be'ert Belgium 50.44N 4.11E
60 R7 Beerta Netherlands 53.11N 7.05E
35 B7 Be'er Toviyya Israel 31.44N 34.43E
61 F2 Beervelde Belgium 51.05N 3.52E
35 C6 Be'er Ya'aqov Israel 31.56N 34.50E
60 J14 Beerze *R* Netherlands
61 J2 Beerzel Belgium 51.04N 4.40E
60 J12 Beesd Netherlands 51.53N 5.12E
60 N14 Beesel Netherlands 51.16N 6.02E
62 H3 Beeskow E Germany 52.10N 14.15E
94 J5 Beestekraal S Africa 25.23S 27.38E
57 L7 Beeston Notts Eng 52.56N 1.12W
13 C3 Beetaloo N Terr Australia 17.10S 133.48E
60 L7 Beetgum Netherlands 53.14N 5.41E
123 F13 Beethoven Pen Antarctica
60 H9 Beets Noord-Holland Netherlands 52.35N 4.58E
60 N7 Beetsterzwaag Netherlands 53.03N 6.05E
63 O7 Beetzendorf E Germany 52.43N 11.06E
63 R8 Beetzsee *L* E Germany
112 K7 Beeville Texas 28.25N 97.47W
61 K5 Beez Belgium 50.28N 4.56E
91 G3 Befale Zaïre 0.25N 21.01E
95 A7 Befandriana Madagascar 22.06S 43.53E
95 D3 Befandriana Madagascar 15.14S 48.33E
95 B6 Befasy Madagascar 20.32S 44.21E
61 N6 Beffe Belgium 50.15N 5.32E
91 H3 Befori Zaïre 0.08N 22.22E
95 C7 Befotaka Madagascar 23.49S 47.00E
95 D3 Befotaka Madagascar 14.30S 48.00E
95 D6 Befotaka Madagascar 20.15S 48.22E
19 E5 Bega Moluccas Indonesia 2.22S 126.00E
12 J6 Bega New S Wales 36.41S 149.50E
72 C5 Bégadan France 45.22N 0.54W
30 A4 Begambad Uttar Prad India 28.49N 77.34E
31 J9 Begamganj Bangladesh 22.59N 91.04E
70 D4 Bégard France 43.38N 3.18W
88 H10 Begar,El Mauritania 22.11N 10.57W
31 E6 Begari Can Pakistan
56 B4 Begelly Dyfed Wales 51.45N 4.44W
87 F4 Begēmdir *prov* Ethiopia
116 P4 Beggars Pt Antigua W I 17.10N 61.48W
66 L1 Beggingen Switzerland 47.46N 8.32E
109 O6 Beggs Oklahoma 35.45N 96.05W
44 J8 Begh Iran 39.20N 48.20E
41 E4 Begichevskaya Kosa,Ostrov *isld* U.S.S.R.
41 M7 Begidzhyan *R* U.S.S.R.
77 J5 Begíjar Spain 37.59N 3.32W
61 K2 Begijnendijk Belgium 51.01N 4.46E
59 K2 Beg,L Irish Rep 54.48N 6.29W
72 C6 Bègles France 44.48N 0.32W
32 C1 Beglisavär Iran 39.20N 48.18E
70 C6 Beg-Meil France 47.52N 3.59W
52 E6 Begna *R* Norway
90 J8 Begneli Cent Afr Rep 7.57N 18.05W
66 B6 Begnins Switzerland 46.27N 6.16E
95 C7 Begogo Madagascar 23.29S 46.45E
46 G3 Begoml' Belorussiya U.S.S.R. 54.40N 28.06E
76 D2 Begonte Spain 43.10N 7.40W
37 H8 Begor Turkey 37.09N 44.20E
43 J6 Begovat Uzbekistan U.S.S.R. 40.14N 69.14E
53 E4 Begtrup Vig *inlet* Denmark 56.09N 10.28E
45 S4 Beguch U.S.S.R. 52.37N 46.11E
71 J9 Bégude-Blanche,la France 43.55N 6.08E

71 F7 Bégude-de-Mazenc, la France 44.33N 4.57E
29 D5 Begun Rajasthan India 24.57N 75.06E
39 F1 Begunovo U.S.S.R. 68.23N 157.40E
30 K7 Begusarai Bihar India 25.25N 86.08E
32 H4 Behābād Iran 32.23N 59.50E
Behagle,De see Lai Chad
117 C2 Béhague,Pte C Fr Guiana 4.38N 51.52W
29 M3 Behala W Bengal India 22.30N 88.20E
29 G2 Behala dist Calcutta, W Bengal
95 C8 Behara Madagascar 24.57S 46.23E
95 B6 Beharona Madagascar 21.30S 44.17E
30 A2 Behat Uttar Prad India 30.09N 77.36E
32 D5 Behbehān Iran 30.34N 50.18E
86 D4 Beheira div Egypt
95 C5 Behenjy Madagascar 19.11S 47.29E
87 J4 Beheta Ethiopia 13.29N 42.16E
30 B7 Behgama Madhya Prad India 25.38N 78.06E
88 R5 Behima Algeria 33.30N 6.59E
22 B8 Behleg Qinghai China 36.46N 91.42E
63 N5 Behlendorf W Germany 53.42N 10.40E
113 W9 Behm Canal Alaska
13 A3 Behn, Mt N Terr Australia 16.51S 129.02E
61 O6 Beho Belgium 50.13N 6.00E
72 A9 Béhobie France 43.20N 1.45W
30 E5 Behra Uttar Prad India 27.46N 81.23E
37 C7 Behramçalı mts Turkey
37 F8 Behramki Turkey 37.49N 40.45E
63 R4 Behren-Lübchin E Germany 54.02N 12.40E
64 L4 Behringersmühle W Germany 49.46N 11.20E
29 E4 Behror Rajasthan India 27.52N 76.20E
32 E2 Behshahr Iran 36.42N 53.36E
31 D3 Behsūd Afghanistan 34.21N 67.54E
88 K4 Beht R Morocco
30 D5 Behta Gokul Uttar Prad India 27.30N 80.02E
21 D3 Bei'an Heilongjiang China 48.16N 126.36E
51 D4 Beiarn Norway 67.02N 14.40E
23 D2 Beiba Shaanxi China 32.37N 107.08E
89 L5 Beï Beï Niger 12.52N 3.53E
23 D4 Beibei Sichuan China 29.50N 106.26E
87 E6 Beica Ethiopia 9.20N 34.30E
23 C6 Beicheng Yunnan China 24.16N 102.34E
23 C3 Beichuan Sichuan China 31.55N 104.39E
22 J8 Beichuan He R Shanxi China
22 G8 Beidachi Nei Monggol Zizhiqu China 38.00N 107.08E
22 D7 Beida He R Gansu China
22 D7 Beida He R Qinghai China
22 L7 Beidaihehaibin Hebei China 39.49N 119.30E
35 J9 Beida, Jeb.el mt Jordan 31.08N 36.22E
22 C6 Beidaqiao Gansu China 40.37N 95.45E
86 N6 Beiḍa, Wâdî el watercourse Egypt
Beidha,Al Libya see Bayḍā',Al
63 M10 Beienrode W Germany 51.28N 10.07E
64 O2 Beierfield E Germany 50.33N 12.48E
23 J5 Beigantang Dao isld Fujian China 26.14N 120.01E
61 H3 Beigem Belgium 50.57N 4.22E
79 E6 Beigua,Monte Italy 44.26N 8.34E
23 E8 Beihai Guangxi China 21.29N 109.10E
Beihan al Qasab see Bayḥān al Qaşāb
22 F9 Bei He R Gansu China
64 G6 Beihingen W Germany 48.56N 9.14E
22 D8 Bei Hulsan Hu L Qinghai China
60 F12 Beijerland isld Netherlands
22 K7 Beijing Beijing China 39.55N 116.26E
89 B2 Beila Mauritania 18.07N 15.56W
23 D4 Beilei Sichuan China 29.50N 106.26E
60 P8 Beilen Netherlands 52.51N 6.31E
60 O8 Beilerstroom R Netherlands
60 O8 Beiler vaart canal Netherlands
25 K3 Beili Hainan China 19.12N 108.42E
23 E7 Beiliu Guangxi China 22.50N 110.22E
72 C4 Beillant France 45.42N 0.32W
64 L5 Beilngries W Germany 49.02N 11.30E
64 G5 Beilstein Baden-Württemberg W Germany 49.03N 9.20E
64 E2 Beilstein Hessen W Germany 50.36N 8.14E
64 C3 Beilstein Rheinland Pfalz W Germany 50.06N 7.15E
24 H8 Beilu He R Qinghai China
24 G8 Beilu Heyan Qinghai China 34.58N 92.57E
87 J4 Beilul Ethiopia 13.11N 42.25E
23 D8 Beilun Ai pass Guangxi China 21.50N 107.48E
64 H7 Beimerstetten W Germany 48.29N 10.00E
50 L4 Beinageitarfjall mt Iceland 65.28N 14.02W
90 G7 Béinamar Chad 8.40N 15.23E
79 C4 Beinasco Italy 45.01N 7.35E
69 G5 Beine-Nauroy France 49.15N 4.14E
79 C6 Beinette Italy 44.22N 7.39E
69 P6 Beinheim France 48.52N 8.05E
58 E3 Beinn Alligin mt Highland Scotland 57.35N 5.35W
58 E4 Beinn Bhan mt Highland Scotland 57.26N 5.40W
58 G3 Beinn Dearg mt Highland Scotland 57.47N 4.55W
58 J5 Beinn Dearg mt Tayside Scotland 56.52N 3.54W
58 G5 Beinn Dorain Strathclyde Scotland 56.31N 4.44W
58 F3 Beinn Eighe mt Highland Scotland 57.35N 5.25W
58 C3 Beinn Mhor mt Lewis, W Isles Scotland 57.59N 6.40W
66 J2 Beinwil Switzerland 47.17N 8.12E
15 J8 Beipa Papua New Guinea 8.32S 146.30E
23 D6 Beipan Jiang R Guizhou China
21 B7 Beipiao Liaoning China 41.52N 120.40E
22 M6 Beipiao Liaoning China 41.52N 120.40E
87 D7 Beir tribe Sudan
94 N2 Beira Mozambique 19.49S 34.52E
74 B4 Beira Alta prov Portugal
74 B5 Beira Baixa prov Portugal
74 B4 Beira Litoral prov Portugal
75 G3 Beire Spain 42.28N 1.38W
71 G2 Beire-le-Châtel France 47.24N 5.13E
77 L6 Beires Spain 37.01N 2.47W
23 F1 Beiru He R Henan China
34 C5 Beirut Lebanon 33.52N 35.30E
100 D7 Beiseker Alberta 51.25N 113.30W
22 D6 Beishan Nei Monggol Zizhiqu China 40.45N 96.38E
22 C6 Bei Shan mts Gansu China
35 E5 Beita al Fauqa Jordan 32.08N 35.17E
21 C5 Beitaolaizhao Jilin China 44.54N 125.55E
35 G2 Beit Arrah Syria 32.45N 35.51E
35 D7 Beit Aula Jordan 31.36N 35.01E
92 E9 Beit Bridge Zambia 15.00S 30.15E
35 E5 Beit Dajan Jordan 32.12N 35.22E
35 D6 Beit Duqqu Jordan 31.52N 35.07E
34 C5 Beit ed Dine Lebanon 33.42N 35.34E
35 D7 Beit Fajjar Jordan 31.38N 35.09E
35 E5 Beit Furik Jordan 32.10N 35.20E
58 G7 Beith Strathclyde Scotland 55.45N 4.38W
35 A1 Beit Hakerem sub Jerusalem
35 B7 Beit Hanun Gaza Strip 31.33N 34.32E
35 F4 Beit Idis Jordan 32.26N 35.42E
35 D6 Beitillu Jordan 31.59N 35.07E
35 D6 Beitin Jordan 31.56N 35.15E
35 D6 Beit 'Inan Jordan 31.51N 35.06E
35 D7 Beit Jala Jordan 31.43N 35.11E
35 E2 Beit Jann Israel 32.58N 35.23E
35 D7 Beit Kahil Jordan 31.34N 35.04E
35 A7 Beit Lahiya Gaza Strip 31.33N 34.30E
Beit Lahm see Bethlehem Jordan
35 D6 Beit Liqya Jordan 31.52N 35.04E
35 E4 Beit Qad Jordan 32.28N 35.22E
35 G3 Beit Ras Jordan 32.36N 35.51E
92 D13 Beitridge Zimbabwe 22.10S 29.59E
35 D5 Beit Rima Jordan 32.02N 35.06E
35 D7 Beit Safâfa Jordan 31.45N 35.12E
35 D7 Beit Sahur Jordan 31.42N 35.13E
35 D3 Beit She'arim anc site Israel 32.42N 35.08E
35 D6 Beit Sira Jordan 31.53N 35.03E
52 F2 Beitstad Norway 64.07N 11.19E
52 F3 Beitstadfjord inlet Norway
35 D7 Beit Ummar Jordan 31.37N 35.06E
35 D4 Beit Umrin Jordan 32.17N 35.13E
24 F2 Beitun Xinjiang Uygur Zizhiqu China 47.19N 87.48E
35 D6 Beituniya Jordan 31.53N 35.10E
35 D6 Beit 'Ur el Fauqa Jordan 31.53N 35.07E
35 D6 Beit 'Ur et Tahta Jordan 31.54N 35.05E
35 G3 Beit Yafa Jordan 32.31N 35.47E
35 A1 Beit Zayit sub Jerusalem
35 A2 Beit Zefafa Jordan 31.45N 35.13E
119 F2 Beiuma Venezuela 10.15N 68.15W
82 G4 Beius Romania 46.40N 22.21E
21 C3 Beixing Heilongjiang China 48.30N 125.34E
23 J4 Beiyandang Shan Zhejiang China 28.22N 121.04E
21 B7 Beizhen Liaoning China 41.35N 121.50E
22 L8 Beizhen Shandong China 37.20N 117.51E
117 D5 Beja Brazil 1.34S 48.49W
76 D12 Beja Portugal 38.01N 7.52W
88 S3 Béja Tunisia 36.43N 9.13E
76 D12 Beja dist Portugal
14 E6 Bejah Hill W Australia 23.48S 124.06E
88 Q3 Bejaïa Algeria 36.49N 5.03E
95 B6 Bejangoa Madagascar 21.59S 44.10E
76 H8 Béjar Spain 40.24N 5.45W
32 H3 Bejestān Iran 34.32N 58.08E
31 E6 Beji R Pakistan
75 J8 Bejís Spain 39.54N 0.43W
95 B4 Bejofo-Amparihy Madagascar 16.37S 44.50E
14 B9 Bejoording W Australia 31.22S 116.30E
Bejsugskij Liman see Beysugskiy Liman gulf
115 J8 Bejucos Mexico 18.48N 100.18W
91 D2 Bek R Cameroon
43 N8 Bekabad Uzbekistan U.S.S.R. 40.38N 71.11E
91 F5 Bekaie Zaïre 2.29S 18.20E
28 B4 Bekal Kerala India 12.24N 75.04E
95 C4 Bekaratsaka Madagascar 17.26S 47.00E
18 G9 Bekasi Java Indon 6.12S 106.53E
45 H1 Bekasovo U.S.S.R. 55.24N 36.50E
43 C4 Bekboke Kazakhstan U.S.S.R. 47.26N 53.50E
43 C6 Bekdash Turkmeniya U.S.S.R. 41.32N 52.36E
41 L6 Beke R U.S.S.R.
61 C2 Bekegem Belgium 51.09N 3.03E
62 N9 Békés Hungary 46.45N 21.09E
82 F4 Békés co Hungary
90 H8 Békésabon Chad 7.57N 16.57E
62 N9 Békéscsaba Hungary 46.40N 21.05E
45 Q8 Beketovka U.S.S.R. 48.35N 44.25E
95 B8 Bekily Madagascar 24.12S 45.20E
95 C4 Bekipay Madagascar 16.17S 46.08E
95 B6 Bekisopa Madagascar 21.40S 45.51E
95 B8 Bekitro Madagascar 24.32S 45.19E
61 H3 Bekkerzeel Belgium 50.53N 4.15E
61 K3 Bekkevoort Belgium 50.57N 4.58E
53 S18 Bekkjarvik Norway 60.00N 5.13E
45 G2 Beklemishchevo U.S.S.R. 54.30N 35.14E
42 J6 Beklemishevo U.S.S.R. 52.12N 112.45E
95 B4 Bekodoka Madagascar 16.57S 45.06E
18 D9 Bekok Pen Malaysia 2.17N 103.05E
18 D9 Bekok hill Pen Malaysia 2.21N 103.08E
95 B5 Bekopaka Madagascar 19.07S 44.47E
95 B7 Bekopay Madagascar 23.44S 44.59E
90 H7 Bekoutou Chad 8.34N 16.40E
45 P4 Bekovo U.S.S.R. 52.29N 43.43E
88 L5 Bekrit Morocco 33.04N 5.16W
45 U3 Bektyashka-Russkaya U.S.S.R. 53.47N 48.51E
89 J8 Bekwai Ghana 6.28N 1.29W
Bela see Villach
30 H8 Bela Bihar India 24.58N 84.59E
65 N1 Bělá Czechoslovakia 50.07N 15.35E
31 D7 Bela Pakistan 26.12N 66.20E
30 C6 Bela Uttar Prad India 26.49N 79.40E
30 E7 Bela Uttar Prad India 25.55N 82.00E
93 A5 Bela Zaïre 0.38N 29.16E
31 D8 Bela dist Pakistan
90 D3 Bela mt Niger 17.55N 8.15E
87 E7 Bela watercourse Ethiopia
91 C1 Bélabo Cameroon 4.54N 13.10E
31 E6 Belab R Pakistan
72 G2 Bélâbre France 46.33N 1.10E
82 G6 Bela Crkva Yugoslavia 44.54N 21.25E
87 E5 Belad Deroz Ethiopia 10.42N 34.50E
28 E1 Bela Dila mt Madhya Prad India 18.46N 81.21E
18 K4 Belaga Sarawak Malaysia 2.45N 113.46E
43 O2 Bel'Agach Kazakhstan U.S.S.R. 50.47N 80.41E
30 K7 Belahi Bihar India 25.43N 86.24E
87 F5 Belaia,Jeb Ethiopia 11.25N 36.08E
70 F6 Bel-Air France 47.42N 2.26W
103 B7 Bel Air Maryland 39.33N 76.21W
12 B8 Belair dist Adelaide, S Aust
70 E5 Bel Air mt France 48.19N 2.35W
91 G4 Belaka Zaïre 1.18S 22.00E
95 A7 Belala Madagascar 23.17S 43.40E
77 F3 Belalcázar Spain 38.35N 5.10W
66 H6 Belalp Switzerland 46.23N 8.00E
30 J6 Bela Muchhpakauni Bihar India 26.49N 85.43E
30 E8 Belan R Uttar Prad etc India
64 O4 Bělá nad Radbuzou Czech 49.35N 12.43E
19 D3 Belang Celebes Indon 0.58N 124.46E
100 U5 Bélanger Pt Manitoba 53.25N 97.40W
100 U5 Bélanger R Manitoba
18 B4 Belangpidie Sumatra Indon 3.42N 96.52E
39 E3 Belan Noch' R U.S.S.R.
82 G7 Bela Palanka Yugoslavia 43.13N 22.17E
29 D8 Belapur Maharashtra India 19.36N 74.40E
12 H4 Belaraboon New S Wales 32.15S 145.03E
76 A11 Belas Portugal 38.46N 9.15W
30 C7 Bela Sagar L Uttar Prad India 25.16N 79.40E
95 C4 Belavenona Madagascar 17.12S 46.30E
119 F7 Bela Vista Amazonas Brazil 0.07N 67.53W
91 C7 Bela Vista Angola 7.52S 13.42E
91 E10 Bela Vista Angola 12.33S 16.18E
118 C8 Bela Vista Mato Grosso do Sul Brazil 22.04S 56.25W
94 M6 Bela Vista Mozambique 26.20S 32.40E
118 G10 Bela Vista dist São Paulo Brazil
118 E5 Bela Vista de Goiás Brazil 16.58S 48.59W
18 C4 Belawan Sumatra Indon 3.46N 98.44E
43 D1 Belaya R Bashkir U.S.S.R.
42 G5 Belaya R Irkutsk U.S.S.R.
39 H4 Belaya R Kamchatka U.S.S.R.
44 C3 Belaya R Krasnodar U.S.S.R.
39 J2 Belaya R Magadan U.S.S.R.
45 E4 Belaya-Berezka U.S.S.R. 52.25N 33.29E
45 C3 Belaya Dubrova Belorussiya U.S.S.R. 53.15N 31.58E
44 D1 Belaya Glina U.S.S.R. 46.04N 40.54E
39 J2 Belaya, Gora mt U.S.S.R. 65.59N 175.00E
45 M8 Belaya-Kalitva U.S.S.R. 48.10N 40.47E
46 Q1 Belaya Kholunitsa U.S.S.R. 58.49N 50.52E
18 L5 Belayan R Borneo Indon
18 L5 Belayan, Gunung mt Borneo Indon 1.26N 115.51E
46 H5 Belaya Tserkov' Ukraine U.S.S.R. 49.49N 30.10E
41 P1 Belaya Zemlya, Ostrova islds Franz Josef Land U.S.S.R.
79 D5 Belbo R Italy
72 H10 Belcaire France 42.49N 1.56E
72 J7 Belcastel France 44.24N 2.20E
82 L3 Belcești Romania 47.19N 27.07E
62 L4 Bełchatów Poland 51.23N 19.20E
64 D8 Belchen mt W Germany 47.50N 7.52E
23 B9 Belcher B Hong Kong
97 K2 Belcher Chan N W Terr
97 M6 Belcher Is.,North Hudson B, N W Terr
97 M6 Belcher, Les Iles Quebec
103 K2 Belchertown Massachusetts 42.17N 72.25W
31 C3 Belchiragh Afghanistan 35.50N 65.11E
75 J5 Belchite Spain 41.18N 0.45W
65 J2 Bělčice Czechoslovakia 49.31N 13.53E
36 J3 Belcik Turkey 39.47N 36.12E
59 E5 Belclare Galway Irish Rep 53.29N 8.55W
12 A5 Belconnen dist Canberra Australia
59 G3 Belcoo Fermanagh N Ireland 54.18N 7.52W
99 N4 Belcourt Quebec 48.24N 77.22W
29 L6 Beldanga W Bengal India 23.55N 88.15E
59 C3 Beldberg Harb Mayo Irish Rep 54.19N 9.33W
110 D9 Belden California 40.01N 121.15W
108 H1 Belden N Dakota 48.10N 102.21W
59 C3 Belderg Mayo Irish Rep 54.18N 9.33W
106 J6 Belding Michigan 43.06N 85.12W
41 G6 Bel'dunchana, Ozero L U.S.S.R.
41 G6 Bel'dunchan, Vozvyshennost' heights U.S.S.R.
46 H1 Belebelka U.S.S.R. 57.39N 30.49E
46 R3 Belebey U.S.S.R. 54.05N 54.07E
63 H10 Belecke W Germany 51.28N 8.20E
43 C7 Belek Turkmeniya U.S.S.R. 39.59N 53.20E
117 D5 Belém Brazil 1.27S 48.29W
92 G9 Belem Mozambique 14.11S 35.59E
76 A11 Belém Portugal 38.41N 9.12W
117 H9 Belém de São Francisco Brazil 8.44S 38.58W
121 H3 Belém Novo Brazil 30.14S 51.10W
121 C1 Belén Argentina 27.36S 67.00W
119 D4 Belén Boyaca Colombia 6.01N 72.55W
119 C7 Belén Caqueta Colombia 1.23N 75.50W
120 D8 Belen Chile 18.21S 69.31W
109 D7 Belen New Mexico 34.39N 106.48W
115 M4 Belén Nicaragua 11.30N 85.55W
118 B8 Belén Paraguay 23.25S 57.14W
36 J6 Belen Turkey 36.32N 36.11E
121 C1 Belen R Argentina
75 D6 Belena, Embalse de res Spain 40.57N 3.15W
121 G3 Belén, Cuchilla de mts Uruguay
115 H7 Belén del Refugio Mexico 21.32N 102.25W
82 J7 Belene Bulgaria 43.39N 25.10E
45 H6 Belenikhino U.S.S.R. 50.55N 36.44E
121 F3 Belén, Isla Uruguay
40 C4 Belen'kaya U.S.S.R. 54.50N 124.15E
45 U4 Belen'kaya, Gora hill U.S.S.R. 52.25N 48.01E
45 J8 Belenkoye Ukraine U.S.S.R. 48.45N 37.39E
121 D8 Belén, Prom Argentina 41.18S 65.30W
118 G10 Belenzinho dist São Paulo Brazil
95 B6 Beleo Madagascar 20.30S 44.17E
9 A12 Belep,Iles New Caledonia
76 D3 Belesar, Embalse de res Spain
87 H10 Beles Gogani Somalia 0.15N 41.40E
72 H10 Bélesta France 32.54N 1.55E
87 K8 Belet Uen Somalia 4.42N 45.12E
43 D5 Beleuli ruins Uzbekistan U.S.S.R. 44.30N 57.08E
43 H4 Beleutty R Kazakhstan U.S.S.R.
45 H3 Belev U.S.S.R. 53.50N 36.08E
88 Q4 Belezma, Mts de Algeria
110 C2 Belfair Washington 47.27N 122.51W
59 L2 Belfast Antrim N Ireland 54.35N 5.55W
104 Q2 Belfast Maine 44.26N 69.01W
11 G10 Belfast New Zealand 43.28S 172.40E
103 D5 Belfast Pennsylvania 40.47N 75.17W
98 K7 Belfast Prince Edward I 46.08N 62.53W
95 O1 Belfast S Africa 25.43S 30.03E
59 L2 Belfast L N Ireland 54.40N 5.50W
66 E4 Belfaux Switzerland 46.50N 7.07E
60 N14 Belfeld Netherlands 51.18N 6.06E
108 G3 Belfield N Dakota 46.55N 103.12W
87 E5 Belfodio Ethiopia 10.34N 34.49E
57 K1 Belford Northumb Eng 55.36N 1.49W
71 K1 Belfort France 47.38N 6.52E
72 H7 Belfort-du-Quercy France 44.17N 1.32E
71 K1 Belfort, Terr. de France
110 Q4 Belfry Montana 45.08N 109.01W
53 W18 Belganuten mt Norway 60.01N 7.08E
28 B3 Belgaum Karnataka India 15.54N 74.36E
28 B2 Belgaum dist Karnataka India
37 D6 Belgazi R Turkey
71 J10 Belgentier France 43.14N 6.01E
63 S10 Belgern E Germany 51.28N 13.08E
88 M5 Bel Ghiadia Morocco 32.40N 2.44W
123 B7 Belgicafjella ra Antarctica
79 F4 Belgiojoso Italy 45.10N 9.18E
66 L8 Belgirate Italy 45.50N 8.34E
106 G6 Belgium Wisconsin 43.30N 87.52W
49 E6 Belgium kingdom W Europe
40 G6 Bel'go U.S.S.R. 50.35N 137.00E
67 P11 Belgodere Corsica 42.35N 9.01E
59 F8 Belgooly Cork Irish Rep 51.44N 8.28W
45 H6 Belgorod U.S.S.R. 50.38N 36.36E
46 H6 Belgorod Dnestrovskiy Ukraine U.S.S.R. 46.10N 30.19E
46 K4 Belgorodskaya Oblast' prov U.S.S.R.
61 K5 Belgrade Belgium 50.28N 4.50E
108 P4 Belgrade Minnesota 45.27N 95.00W
108 M8 Belgrade Nebraska 41.29N 98.02W
Belgrade Yugoslavia see Beograd
121 K3 Belgrano dist Buenos Aires Argentina
121 K6 Belgrano, L Argentina
37 F1 Belgrat Ormanı forest Turkey
11 G8 Belgrove New Zealand 41.28S 172.59E
88 H9 Bel Guerdane Mauritania 25.23N 10.34W
72 C7 Belhade France 44.23N 0.40W
30 G7 Belha Dih Uttar Prad India 25.47N 83.13E
30 K8 Belhar Bihar India 24.58N 86.35E
59 F3 Belhavel L Leitrim Irish Rep 54.13N 8.11W
105 L2 Belhaven N Carolina 35.34N 76.36W
85 E5 Bel Hedan Libya 28.14N 19.10E
88 R6 Belhirane Algeria 31.20N 6.10E
70 N4 Belhomert France 48.31N 1.04E
29 H1 Beliaghata dist Calcutta, W Bengal
75 N4 Belianes Spain 41.34N 1.01E
29 K2 Beliator W Bengal India 23.18N 87.15E
81 E8 Belice R Sicily
81 F8 Belice destro R Sicily
81 F8 Belice sinistro R Sicily
39 D4 Beliche U.S.S.R. 62.24N 149.50E
45 B6 Belichi Ukraine U.S.S.R. 50.26N 30.20E
40 G4 Belichiy, Ostrov isld U.S.S.R. 54.30N 137.53E
81 G8 Belici R Sicily
82 F8 Beli Drim R Yugoslavia
44 J6 Belidzhi U.S.S.R. 41.54N 48.23E
72 C6 Beliet France 44.31N 0.47W
34 G2 Belikh R Syria
45 F7 Beliki Ukraine U.S.S.R. 49.15N 34.16E
82 K7 Beli Lom R Bulgaria
82 E5 Beli Manastir Yugoslavia 45.45N 18.36E
18 F8 Belimbing Sumatra Indon 5.56S 104.37E
72 C7 Belin France 44.29N 0.47W
75 D7 Belinchón Spain 40.03N 3.04W
91 C3 Belinga Gabon 1.09N 13.12E
104 F7 Belington W Virginia 39.02N 79.56W
92 D12 Belingwe Zimbabwe 20.30S 29.53E
92 D12 Belingwe dist Zimbabwe
45 P4 Belinskiy U.S.S.R. 52.58N 43.24E
18 F6 Belinyu Indonesia 1.37S 105.45E
18 D10 Belitong R Pen Malaysia
18 H7 Belitung isld Indonesia
91 C6 Belize Angola 4.34S 12.37E
115 P9 Belize Belize 17.29N 88.10W
115 P9 Belize Cent America
117 C2 Bélizon Fr Guiana 4.16N 52.40W
82 G6 Beljanića mt Yugoslavia 44.08N 21.43E
46 J4 Belka Ukraine U.S.S.R. 50.32N 34.58E
14 C9 Belka W Australia 31.45S 118.09E
40 E2 Bel'kachi U.S.S.R. 59.15N 131.50E
37 H2 Belkeris Turkey 40.29N 29.55E
40 G9 Belkina, Mys C U.S.S.R. 45.47N 137.43E
40 J7 Belkino Sakhalin U.S.S.R. 49.46N 142.12E
36 E6 Belkis anc site Turkey 36.59N 31.08E
106 B9 Belknap Iowa 40.49N 92.26W
110 K2 Belknap Montana 47.45N 115.30W
113 F9 Belkofski Alaska 55.06N 162.05E
41 P3 Bel'kovskiy, Ostrov isld U.S.S.R.
105 E8 Bell Florida 29.44N 82.53W
13 K7 Bell Queensland 26.56S 151.26E
95 L9 Bell S Africa 33.15S 27.20E
111 E9 Bell dist Los Angeles, California
12 J5 Bell R New S Wales
99 N3 Bell R Quebec
101 E2 Bell R Yukon Terr
80 N7 Bella Italy 40.46N 15.33E
101 J9 Bella Bella Br Col 52.07N 128.05W
72 G3 Bellac France 46.07N 1.04E
121 F4 Bellaco Uruguay 32.45S 57.48W
101 K9 Bella Coola Br Col 52.23N 126.46W
120 E4 Bella Flor Bolivia 11.07S 67.44W
59 J2 Bellaghy Londonderry N Ireland 54.58N 6.31W
79 F3 Bellagio Italy 45.59N 9.16E
59 E4 Bellahy Sligo Irish Rep 53.58N 8.48W
79 E3 Bella, I Italy 45.54N 8.31E
112 F9 Bellaire Houston, Texas 29.42N 95.27W
109 M2 Bellaire Kansas 39.48N 98.41W
106 J5 Bellaire Michigan 44.59N 85.12W
104 E6 Bellaire Ohio 40.02N 80.46W
103 A6 Bellaire Pennsylvania 40.12N 76.35W
13 G7 Bellalie Queensland 27.02S 142.56E
28 E2 Bellamkonda Andhra Prad India 16.35N 80.04E
59 H4 Bellananagh Cavan Irish Rep 53.56N 7.24W
79 F2 Bellano Italy 46.03N 9.18E
80 J3 Bellante Italy 42.45N 13.49E
84 R14 Bellapaise Abbey Cyprus 35.18N 33.21E
79 M6 Bellària Italy 44.09N 12.27E
28 C3 Bellary Karnataka India 15.11N 76.54E
28 B3 Bellary dist Karnataka India
75 O6 Bellas Vistas dist Madrid Spain
12 J3 Bellata New S Wales 29.55S 149.50E
66 G7 Bella Tola mt Switzerland 46.15N 7.40E
59 G5 Bellaugh Roscommon Irish Rep 53.25N 7.58W
121 F3 Bella Unión Uruguay 30.18S 57.35W
59 F4 Bellavagare Roscommon Irish Rep 53.51N 8.23W
59 D4 Bellavary Mayo Irish Rep 53.54N 9.09W
120 G6 Bella Vista Bolivia 15.46S 61.07W
119 B10 Bellavista Cajamarca Peru 5.43S 78.48W
121 F2 Bella Vista Corrientes Argentina 28.31S 59.00W
115 G10 Bella Vista Panama 8.58N 79.32W
118 C8 Bella Vista Paraguay 22.08S 56.20W
119 C8 Bellavista Peru 1.32S 75.32W
120 B2 Bellavista San Martín Peru 7.04S 76.35W
121 K8 Bella Vista Santa Cruz Arg 51.52S 70.35W
121 D1 Bella Vista Tucumán Argentina 27.05S 65.19W
120 A9 Bellavista dist Callao Peru
121 G10 Bellavista dist Santiago Chile
81 D4 Bellavista,C Sardinia 39.56N 9.44E
120 D9 Bella Vista,Salar de salt pan Chile
11 J6 Bell Block New Zealand 39.02S 174.07E
12 K4 Bellbrook New S Wales 30.48S 152.30E
98 P3 Bellburns Newfoundland 50.21N 57.32W
75 M4 Bellcaire de Urgel Spain 41.45N 0.55E
13 K5 Bell Cay / Gt Barrier Reef Aust 21.45S 151.10E
104 B6 Bell Centre Ohio 40.30N 83.45W
107 E3 Belle Missouri 38.16N 91.42W
104 D8 Belle W Virginia 38.15N 81.34W
103 E2 Belleayre Mt New York 42.07N 74.31W
98 R6 Belle B Newfoundland
63 P9 Belleben E Germany 51.41N 11.38E
66 A9 Bellecombe France 45.45N 6.09E
71 K6 Bellecote mt France 45.29N 6.48E
61 H5 Bellecourt Belgium 50.29N 4.15E
71 J6 Belledonne,Chaine de mts France
71 H6 Belledonne,Pic de mt France 45.11N 5.59E
59 K3 Belleek Armagh N Ire 54.11N 6.29W
59 F3 Belleek Fermanagh N Ire 54.29N 8.06W
61 M8 Bellefontaine Belgium 49.40N 5.30E
69 L7 Bellefontaine France 48.00N 6.29E
116 L4 Bellefontaine Martinique W I 14.41N 61.10W
104 B6 Bellefontaine Ohio 40.22N 83.45W
103 C7 Bellefonte Delaware 39.47N 75.30W
104 H6 Bellefonte Pennsylvania 40.55N 77.46W
108 G5 Belle Fourche S Dakota 44.40N 103.50W
108 E5 Belle Fourche R Wyoming
108 G5 Belle Fourche Res S Dakota
71 F9 Bellegarde Gard France 43.45N 4.30E
69 C8 Bellegarde Loiret France 48.00N 2.27E
72 J4 Bellegarde-en-Marche France 45.59N 2.17E
71 H4 Bellegarde-sur-Valserine France 46.06N 5.49E
61 D3 Bellegem Belgium 50.47N 3.17E
105 G11 Belle Glade Florida 26.41N 80.41W
103 A6 Bellegrove Pennsylvania 40.21N 76.33W
71 K2 Belleherbe France 47.16N 6.39E
70 D7 Belle Ile France 47.20N 3.10W
98 R2 Belle Isle Newfoundland
70 D4 Belle-Isle-en-Terre France 48.33N 3.23W
98 R2 Belle Isle Landing Belle Isle, Nfld 51.53N 55.22W
98 Q2 Belle Isle,Strait of Labrador, Nfld
66 E2 Bellelay Switzerland 47.16N 7.11E
61 D2 Bellem Belgium 51.06N 3.30E
70 M5 Bellême France 48.22N 0.34E
103 E6 Belle Mead New Jersey 40.28N 74.39W
107 K5 Belle Meade Tennessee 36.05N 86.55W
26 T15 Bellemene Réunion Indian Oc 21.01S 55.18E
111 N6 Bellemont Arizona 35.16N 111.49W
72 K3 Bellenaves France 46.12N 3.04E
70 N2 Bellencombre France 49.42N 1.14E
13 H3 Bellenden Ker Ra Queensland
69 E4 Bellenglise France 49.56N 3.15E
98 R6 Belleoram Newfoundland 47.32N 55.28W
103 E8 Belleplain New Jersey 39.16N 74.52W
100 M8 Belle Plain Saskatchewan 50.25N 105.09W
106 B8 Belle Plaine Iowa 41.53N 92.17W
109 N4 Belle Plaine Kansas 37.26N 97.17W
108 R5 Belle Plaine Minnesota 44.36N 93.45W
57 K4 Bellerby N Yorks Eng 54.20N 1.49W
107 H3 Belle Rive Illinois 38.14N 88.45W
12 H9 Bellerive Tasmania 42.52S 147.21E
72 L3 Bellerive-sur-Allier France 46.07N 3.27E
99 T4 Belle-Rivière,L.de la Quebec 48.15N 71.45W
69 M6 Belles-Forêts France 48.48N 6.54E
99 M5 Belleterre Quebec 47.25N 78.41W
104 D7 Belle Valley Ohio 39.47N 81.36W
61 L7 Bellevaux Belgium 49.51N 5.06E
71 K4 Bellevaux France 46.14N 6.31E
61 P5 Bellevaux-Ligneuville Belgium 50.23N 6.01E
71 G3 Bellevesvre France 46.50N 5.23E
105 E8 Belleview Florida 29.04N 82.04W
107 G3 Belleville Illinois 38.31N 89.59W
109 N2 Belleville Kansas 39.51N 97.38W
103 H7 Belleville New Jersey 40.47N 74.10W
104 J3 Belleville New York 43.47N 76.07W
99 N8 Belleville Ontario 44.10N 77.22W
68 F3 Belleville Paris France 48.53N 2.23E
104 H6 Belleville Pennsylvania 40.36N 77.36W
71 F4 Belleville Rhône France 46.06N 4.45E
106 E7 Belleville Wisconsin 42.52N 89.33W
104 D7 Belleville W Virginia 39.07N 81.44W
72 B2 Belleville sur Vie France 46.47N 1.26W
100 C9 Bellevue Alberta 49.33N 114.20W
110 L6 Bellevue Idaho 43.27N 114.16W
106 D7 Bellevue Iowa 42.16N 90.27W
106 J7 Bellevue Michigan 42.26N 85.01W
104 C5 Bellevue Ohio 41.16N 82.51W
104 E6 Bellevue Pennsylvania 40.32N 80.08W
13 G3 Bellevue Queensland 16.25S 144.19E
95 J9 Bellevue S Africa 33.22S 25.58E
112 J2 Bellevue Texas 33.38N 98.02W
15 G8 Belle Vue Is Torres Str, Qnsld 9.55S 142.10E
71 D6 Bellevue-la-Montagne France 45.13N 3.50E
71 H5 Belley France 45.46N 5.41E
89 D8 Belle Yella Liberia 7.24N 10.09W
106 F9 Bellflower Illinois 40.22N 88.31W
107 E2 Bellflower Missouri 39.00N 91.21W
111 E9 Bellflower dist Los Angeles, California
64 E5 Bellheim W Germany 49.11N 8.17E
69 E4 Bellicourt France 49.58N 3.10E
70 H7 Belligne France 47.28N 1.01W
97 M5 Bellin Quebec 60.00N 70.01W
Bellingen see Bad Bellingen
61 G4 Bellingen Belgium 50.45N 4.09E
12 L4 Bellingen New S Wales 30.28S 152.43E
103 M2 Bellingham Massachusetts 42.06N 71.28W
108 O4 Bellingham Minnesota 45.08N 96.18W
57 J2 Bellingham Northumb England 55.09N 2.16W
110 C1 Bellingham Washington 48.45N 122.29W
123 E15 Bellingshausen U.S.S.R. Base Antarctica 62.12S 58.56W
Bellingshausen Basin see Pacific-Antarctic Basin
121 A13 Bellingshausen I S Sandwich Is Atl Oc 59.25S 27.05W
123 G12 Bellingshausen Sea Antarctica
60 R7 Bellingwolde Netherlands 53.07N 7.11E
80 E3 Bellino,Monte Italy 42.31N 11.34E
79 E3 Bellinzago Novarese Italy 45.34N 8.38E
66 N7 Bellinzona Switzerland 46.12N 9.02E
100 E4 Bellis Alberta 54.07N 112.03W
113 W9 Bell Island Alaska 55.55N 131.40W
98 T6 Bell Island Conception Bay, Nfld
98 R3 Bell Island White B, Nfld
75 M4 Bell Lloch Spain 41.37N 0.47E
112 K4 Bellmead Texas 31.37N 97.02W
64 F2 Bellnhausen W Germany 50.42N 8.45E
119 C4 Bello Colombia 6.20N 75.41W
75 H6 Bello Spain 40.55N 1.30W
57 B1 Bellochantuy Strathclyde Scot 55.32N 5.41W
72 C8 Bellocq France 43.31N 0.55W
15 L4 Bellona I Solomon Is 11.20S 159.47E
10 M6 Bellona Plat Coral Sea
10 M6 Bellona Reefs Coral Sea
111 C3 Bellota California 38.04N 121.00W
70 K4 Bellou-en-Houlme France 48.41N 0.27W
104 N3 Bellows Falls Vermont 43.08N 72.28W
69 C5 Belloy-en-France France 49.05N 2.22E
31 E6 Bellpat Pakistan 29.00N 68.05E
97 L5 Bell Pen N W Terr 63.45N 81.30W
103 J5 Bellport Long I, N Y 40.46N 72.56W
12 C4 Bell,Pt S Australia 32.11S 133.08E
75 N4 Bellpuig Spain 41.37N 1.01E
109 F6 Bell Ranch New Mexico 35.33N 104.05W
77 Q3 Bellreguart Spain 38.57N 0.10W
Bell Rock Lt.Ho. see Inchcape Lt Ho
107 G6 Bells Tennessee 35.42N 89.06W
112 L2 Bells Texas 33.38N 96.24W
100 Q6 Bellsite Manitoba 52.35N 101.04W
50 S15 Bellsund sound Spitsbergen
75 N4 Belltall Spain 41.30N 1.11E
79 M2 Belluno Italy 46.08N 12.13E
79 L2 Belluno prov Italy
28 C4 Belluru Karnataka India 12.58N 76.44E
77 V14 Bellver Balearic Is 39.34N 2.37E
75 O3 Bellver de Cerdaña Spain 42.23N 1.46E
75 O5 Bellvey Spain 41.14N 1.35E
121 E4 Bell Ville Argentina 32.35S 62.41W
104 C6 Bellville Ohio 40.38N 82.31W
95 B9 Bellville S Africa 33.55S 18.38E
112 L6 Bellville Texas 29.57N 96.15W
75 M4 Bellvis Spain 41.40N 0.49E
109 E1 Bellvue Colorado 40.37N 105.12W
107 C10 Bellwood Louisiana 31.31N 93.11W
108 N8 Bellwood Nebraska 41.21N 97.15W
104 G6 Bellwood Pennsylvania 40.36N 78.21W
42 E5 Bellyk U.S.S.R. 54.30N 91.18E
100 D9 Belly R Alberta
47 L6 Belly Yar Omsk U.S.S.R. 57.36N 72.28E
103 F6 Belmar New Jersey 40.11N 74.01W
77 F4 Belmez Spain 38.16N 5.12W
77 K5 Belmez de la Moraleda Spain 37.44N 3.23W
42 E2 Bel'minskiye Porogi falls U.S.S.R. 61.59N 92.32E
108 R7 Belmond Iowa 42.50N 93.32W
111 B10 Belmont California 37.32N 122.18W
72 E8 Belmont Gers France 43.41N 0.15E
57 J5 Belmont Lancs Eng 53.39N 2.30W
100 S9 Belmont Manitoba 49.28N 99.30W
105 F2 Belmont N Carolina 35.13N 81.03W
111 H3 Belmont Nevada 38.35N 116.52W
104 O3 Belmont New Hampshire 43.27N 71.29W
104 G4 Belmont New York 42.14N 78.02W
11 D4 Belmont New Zealand 41.11S 174.55E
98 J8 Belmont Nova Scotia 45.26N 63.24W
99 J10 Belmont Ontario 42.52N 81.06W
95 H5 Belmont S Africa 29.25S 24.22E
58 R8 Belmont Shetland Scot 60.41N 0.58W
66 C5 Belmont Switzerland 46.32N 6.42E
112 K6 Belmont Texas 29.32N 97.43W
104 H8 Belmont Virginia 38.09N 77.52W
106 D7 Belmont Wisconsin 42.44N 90.21W
104 P9 Belmont dist Boston, Mass
14 B1 Belmont dist Perth, W Aust
11 D4 Belmont mt New Zealand 41.11S 174.52E
71 E4 Belmont-de-la-Loire France 46.10N 4.20E
118 J4 Belmonte Brazil 15.53S 38.54W
76 E8 Belmonte Portugal 40.21N 7.20W
75 E8 Belmonte Spain 39.34N 2.43W
81 M5 Belmonte Cálabro Italy 39.09N 16.05E
76 G2 Belmonte de Miranda Spain 43.16N 6.13W
75 F8 Belmontejo Spain 39.49N 2.21W
72 K8 Belmont-sur-Rance France 43.49N 2.45E
115 P9 Belmopan Belize 17.13N 88.48W
12 L7 Belmore dist Sydney, N S W
13 F4 Belmore R Queensland
12 L3 Belmore,Mt New S Wales 29.04S 152.16E
59 C3 Belmullet Mayo Irish Rep 54.14N 10.00W
95 B6 Belo Madagascar 20.44S 44.00E
91 G6 Belo Zaïre 4.19S 21.46E
91 H4 Belo Zaïre 0.32S 23.13E
95 B5 Belobaka Madagascar 18.59S 45.40E
93 M2 Beloble Kenya 3.18N 40.03E
118 H4 Belo Campo Brazil 15.05S 41.24W
61 E4 Belœil Belgium 50.33N 3.44E
42 C6 Beloglazovo U.S.S.R. 52.08N 82.33E
39 F6 Belogolovaya R U.S.S.R.
39 F6 Belogolovoye U.S.S.R. 56.43N 156.45E
42 D4 Belogorka U.S.S.R. 56.45N 89.13E
82 K1 Belogorodka U.S.S.R. 50.00N 26.37E
44 D9 Belogorsk Ukraine U.S.S.R. 45.04N 34.35E
40 D6 Belogorsk U.S.S.R. 50.55N 128.26E
42 D4 Belogorsk U.S.S.R. 55.01N 88.29E
43 P3 Belogorskiy Kazakhstan U.S.S.R. 49.30N 83.06E
82 K1 Belogorye Ukraine U.S.S.R. 50.00N 26.23E
45 M6 Belogorye U.S.S.R. 50.30N 40.00E
82 H7 Belogradchik Bulgaria 43.37N 22.40E
95 B8 Beloha Madagascar 25.09S 45.04E
119 F9 Belo Horizonte Amazonas Brazil 2.37S 67.30W
91 E9 Belo Horizonte Angola 11.52S 16.48E
118 G6 Belo Horizonte Minas Gerais Brazil 19.54S 43.54W
109 M2 Beloit Kansas 39.27N 98.06W
106 E7 Beloit Wisconsin 42.31N 89.04W
117 H9 Belo Jardim Brazil 8.22S 36.22W
44 G6 Belokany Azerbaydzhan U.S.S.R. 41.44N 46.24E
46 G4 Belokorovichi Ukraine U.S.S.R. 51.04N 28.00E
45 K7 Belokurakino Ukraine U.S.S.R. 49.33N 38.46E
42 C6 Belokurikha U.S.S.R. 52.00N 84.59E
45 L7 Belolutsk Ukraine U.S.S.R. 49.40N 39.01E
26 T13 Bel Ombre Mauritius, Indian Oc 20.30S 57.23E
45 J4 Belomestnaya U.S.S.R. 52.24N 37.35E
117 H9 Belo Monte Alagoas Brazil 9.47S 37.17W
117 C6 Belo Monte Pará Brazil 3.01S 51.45W
47 C4 Belomorsk U.S.S.R. 64.34N 34.45E
91 F4 Belondo Zaïre 1.23S 19.43E
91 F4 Belondo Zaïre 0.19S 19.31E
91 F5 Belonge Zaïre 2.07S 19.33E
31 J9 Belonia Tripura India 23.15N 91.25E
45 L2 Beloomut U.S.S.R. 54.55N 39.22E
45 F5 Belopol'ye Ukraine U.S.S.R. 51.09N 34.17E
45 T5 Belopol'ye U.S.S.R. 51.22N 47.01E
75 D3 Belorado Spain 42.25N 3.11W
44 C3 Belorechensk U.S.S.R. 44.46N 39.54E
Belorechenskaya see Belorechensk
47 M4 Belorechka U.S.S.R. 57.20N 60.01E
47 H8 Beloretsk U.S.S.R. 53.59N 58.20E
46 F3 Belorussiya S.S.R U.S.S.R.
Belorusskaya S.S.R see Belorussiya S.S.R
45 J10 Belosarayskaya Kosa sand spit Ukraine U.S.S.R.
44 F5 Beloti Georgia U.S.S.R. 42.18N 44.10E
101 K2 Belot, L N W Terr
95 B5 Belo-Tsiribihina Madagascar 19.40S 44.30E
84 A6 Beloúsi Greece 37.49N 20.50E
45 D7 Belousovka Cherkassy, Ukraine U.S.S.R. 49.58N 32.22E
43 P2 Belousovka Kazakhstan U.S.S.R. 50.08N 82.31E
45 C9 Belousovka Nikolayev, Ukraine U.S.S.R. 47.25N 31.32E
42 C5 Belovo Altay U.S.S.R. 52.58N 82.15E
42 D5 Belovo Kemerovo U.S.S.R. 54.27N 86.19E
45 L7 Belovodsk Ukraine U.S.S.R. 49.11N 39.34E
43 L5 Belovodskoye Kirgiziya U.S.S.R. 42.49N 74.07E
45 S2 Belovod'ye U.S.S.R. 54.15N 46.35E
40 D6 Beloyarovo U.S.S.R. 51.36N 128.46E
47 N4 Beloyarskiy U.S.S.R. 56.47N 61.28E
47 D4 Beloye Arkhangel'sk U.S.S.R. 64.19N 39.50E
45 G5 Beloye Kursk U.S.S.R. 51.04N 35.45E
47 D3 Beloye More sea U.S.S.R.
44 H2 Beloye Ozero U.S.S.R. 45.08N 46.50E
42 D4 Beloye,Ozero L Krasnoyarsk U.S.S.R. 55.38N 89.32E
47 D5 Beloye Ozero L Vologda U.S.S.R.
47 G6 Beloyevo U.S.S.R. 59.10N 54.27E
82 J8 Belozem Bulgaria 42.11N 25.00E
43 D1 Belozerka Bashkir U.S.S.R. 52.32N 55.03E
45 D10 Belozerka Ukraine U.S.S.R. 46.35N 32.08E
47 D6 Belozersk U.S.S.R. 60.00N 37.49E
47 K7 Belozerskoye U.S.S.R. 55.48N 65.31E
45 C7 Belozer'ye Ukraine U.S.S.R. 49.19N 31.59E
66 G4 Belp Switzerland 46.54N 7.31E
81 J8 Belpasso Sicily 37.35N 14.59E
66 G4 Belp Berg mt Switzerland 46.54N 7.32E
72 H9 Belpech France 43.11N 1.44E
57 L6 Belper Derbys Eng 53.01N 1.29W
29 G5 Belpora Madhya Prad India 24.05N 80.02E
109 L4 Belpre Kansas 37.57N 99.07W
104 D7 Belpre Ohio 39.17N 81.36W
12 M6 Belrose New S Wales 33.44S 151.13E
30 J6 Belsand Bihar India 26.27N 85.25E
57 K2 Belsay Northumberland Eng 55.06N 1.50W
61 G2 Belsele Belgium 51.09N 4.03E
63 L7 Belsen W Germany 52.47N 9.57E
42 E3 Bel'skoye Krasnoyarsk U.S.S.R. 57.50N 92.12E
45 M2 Bel'skoye Ryazan' U.S.S.R. 54.45N 40.22E
110 P2 Belt Montana 47.23N 110.56W
12 E4 Beltana S Australia 30.40S 138.27E
12 D3 Belt B S Australia
111 H4 Belted Ra Nevada
117 B6 Belterra Brazil 2.40S 54.53W
60 N9 Belterwijde L Netherlands
22 E1 Beltes Gol R Mongolia
65 O8 Beltinci Yugoslavia 46.37N 16.15E
56 J2 Belton Leics Eng 52.48N 1.18W
107 B3 Belton Missouri 38.48N 94.31W
12 E4 Belton S Australia 32.13S 138.45E
105 E3 Belton S Carolina 34.32N 82.30W
112 K4 Belton Texas 31.04N 97.30W
112 K4 Belton Res Texas
59 D4 Beltra Mayo Irish Rep 53.57N 9.24W
59 E3 Beltra Sligo Irish Rep 54.13N 8.37W
59 D4 Beltra,L Mayo Irish Rep 53.55N 9.25W
121 D1 Beltrán Argentina 27.50S 64.01W
121 E2 Beltrán, L Argentina
60 P11 Beltrum Netherlands 52.04N 6.33E
103 A8 Beltsville Maryland 39.02N 76.55W
46 G5 Belt'sy Moldavia U.S.S.R. 47.44N 27.41E
59 H3 Belturbet Cavan Irish Rep 54.06N 7.26W
113 M6 Beluga L Alaska 61.24N 151.40W
18 K5 Belui,Bukit mt Borneo Indon 1.07N 113.33E
42 D7 Belukha, Gora mt U.S.S.R. 49.50N 86.44E
18 B6 Belum R Pen Malaysia
18 D9 Belumut, Gunong mt Pen Malaysia 2.02N 103.31E
28 B4 Belur Karnataka India 13.08N 75.51E
18 M3 Beluran Sabah Malaysia 5.54N 117.34E
62 L6 Beluša Czechoslovakia 49.04N 18.15E
41 A4 Belush'ya Guba Novaya Zemlya U.S.S.R. 71.34N 52.28E
47 F3 Belush'ye U.S.S.R. 66.54N 47.37E
47 K1 Beluzhiy Nos,Mys C U.S.S.R. 70.04N 67.00E
79 O3 Belvedere Italy 45.44N 13.23E
81 K9 Belvedere Sicily 37.07N 15.13E
92 E10 Belvedere airport Zimbabwe 17.45S 31.05E
67 O13 Belvedere Campomoro Corsica 41.37N 8.48E
81 N5 Belvedere di Spinello Italy 39.13N 16.53E
81 L4 Belvedere Maríttimo Italy 39.37N 15.52E
79 O7 Belvedere Ostrense Italy 43.35N 13.10E
76 D10 Belver Portugal 39.30N 7.58W
75 L4 Belver Spain 41.41N 0.11E
37 D8 Belveran Turkey 37.40N 37.35E
76 J5 Belver de los Montes Spain 41.43N 5.28W
72 G6 Belvès France 44.46N 1.00E
72 J9 Belvèze-du-Razès France 43.08N 2.05E
106 F7 Belvidere Illinois 42.16N 88.50W
109 L4 Belvidere Kansas 37.27N 99.06W
105 L1 Belvidere N Carolina 36.15N 76.33W
108 N9 Belvidere Nebraska 40.16N 97.35W
103 D5 Belvidere New Jersey 40.50N 75.05W
108 J6 Belvidere S Dakota 43.50N 101.16W
36 F5 Belviran Turkey 37.12N 32.33E
76 K9 Belvis de la Jara Spain 39.45N 4.57W
35 F3 Belvoir anc site Israel 32.35N 35.31E
39 M2 Belyaka, Kosa sand spit U.S.S.R.
13 H5 Belyando R Queensland
47 L5 Belyanka U.S.S.R. 56.02N 59.13E
41 N8 Belyanka R U.S.S.R.
43 D2 Belyayevka Orenburg U.S.S.R. 51.23N 56.28E
46 H6 Belyayevka Ukraine U.S.S.R. 46.30N 30.12E
45 S6 Belyayevka Volgograd U.S.S.R. 50.18N 46.15E
45 F3 Bel'ye Berega U.S.S.R. 53.10N 34.39E
45 U3 Bel'ye Gory hills U.S.S.R.
45 Q6 Bel'ye-Prudy U.S.S.R. 50.35N 44.04E
45 J1 Bel'ye Stolby U.S.S.R. 55.20N 37.53E
43 J6 Bel'ye Vody Kazakhstan U.S.S.R. 42.24N 69.20E
45 A2 Belynichi Belorussiya U.S.S.R. 54.00N 29.42E
45 D3 Belynkovichi Belorussiya U.S.S.R. 53.14N 32.08E
45 D1 Belyy U.S.S.R. 55.49N 32.58E
42 D6 Belyy Bom U.S.S.R. 50.20N 87.03E
42 D5 Belyy Iyus U.S.S.R. 54.42N 89.45E
45 J6 Belyy Kolidez' Ukraine U.S.S.R. 50.11N 37.07E
41 B4 Belyy, Mys C Belyy, Ostrov U.S.S.R. 73.31N 70.48E
47 L1 Belyy, Mys C Tyumen U.S.S.R. 70.20N 72.44E
41 B4 Belyy, Ostrov isld U.S.S.R.
42 E5 Belyy Yar Khakass U.S.S.R. 53.36N 91.26E
42 D3 Belyy Yar U.S.S.R. 58.28N 85.03E
70 D6 Belz France 47.41N 3.09W
62 O5 Bełżec Poland 50.21N 23.28E
63 R8 Belzig E Germany 52.08N 12.35E
107 F8 Belzoni Mississippi 33.10N 90.30W
62 N4 Bełżyce Poland 51.10N 22.16E
95 E3 Bemanevika Madagascar 14.07S 50.09E
95 D2 Bemaneviky Madagascar 13.50S 48.30E
95 B5 Bemaraha, Plat. du Madagascar
95 B6 Bemarivo Madagascar 21.43S 44.44E
95 D3 Bemarivo R Madagascar
95 B6 Bemavo Madagascar 21.39S 45.22E
92 E7 Bemba tribe Zambia
18 C9 Bemban Pen Malaysia 2.14N 102.21E
91 D7 Bembe Angola 7.03S 14.25E
90 N9 Bembé Oudaka Cent Afr Rep 5.46N 26.03E
89 L6 Bembéréké Benin 10.10N 2.41E
77 F4 Bembézar R Spain
77 F5 Bembézar, Embalse del res Spain 37.57N 5.15W
92 D11 Bembezi Zimbabwe 20.00S 29.00E
76 G3 Bembibre Spain 42.37N 6.25W
91 E9 Bembo Angola 10.14S 16.55E
117 G9 Bem Bom Brazil 9.41S 41.46W
56 J6 Bembridge I of Wight Eng 50.41N 1.05W
60 T17 Bemelen Netherlands 50.50N 5.45E
107 H2 Bement Illinois 39.56N 88.34W
108 Q2 Bemidji Minnesota 47.29N 94.52W
107 H6 Bemis Tennessee 35.34N 88.50W
60 M12 Bemmel Netherlands 51.53N 5.54E
95 B5 Bemonto Madagascar 18.31S 44.23E
64 G6 Bempflingen W Germany 48.34N 9.17E
76 C10 Bemposta Portugal 39.21N 8.08W
76 G6 Bemposta Portugal 41.19N 6.30W
57 N4 Bempton Humberside Eng 54.08N 0.10W
77 A1 Bemquerença Portugal 39.47N 7.35W
19 F5 Bemu Moluccas Indon 3.37S 129.57E
104 F4 Bemus Point New York 42.11N 79.24W
92 D11 Bemzesi R Zimbabwe
32 D4 Ben Iran 32.31N 50.47E
90 B6 Bena Nigeria 11.16N 6.00E
92 G6 Bena tribe Tanzania
44 G9 Benāb Iran 38.26N 45.53E
75 L3 Benabarre Spain 42.06N 0.29E
15 H7 Benabena Papua New Guinea 6.09S 145.31E
91 G6 Bena Bendi Zaïre 4.16S 20.23E
77 D6 Benacazón Spain 37.21N 6.13W
58 F4 Ben Aden mt Highland Scot 57.01N 5.28W

91 H6 **Bena Dibele** Zaïre 4.04S 22.50E
87 J10 **Benadir** *reg* Somalia
76 C14 **Benafate** Portugal 37.22N 8.27W
75 K7 **Benafigos** Spain 40.16N 0.13W
76 C14 **Benafim** Portugal 37.13N 8.08W
77 H7 **Benagalbón** Spain 36.45N 4.15W
12 F4 **Benagerie** S Australia 31.30S 140.21E
75 J8 **Benaguacil** Spain 39.35N 0.35W
77 M7 **Benahadux** Spain 36.55N 2.26W
77 F7 **Benahavis** Spain 36.32N 5.03W
61 L4 **Ben-Ahin** Belgium 50.31N 5.11E
88 G8 **Ben Ahmadu** Morocco 26.37N 12.57W
88 K5 **Benahmed** Morocco 33.07N 7.17W
72 G3 **Benaixe** *R* France
77 F4 **Benajarafa** *R* Spain
18 E7 **Benakat** Sumatra Indon 3.19S 103.43E
77 F7 **Benalauria** Spain 36.36N 5.16W
58 H5 **Ben Alder** *mt* Highland Scot 56.49N 4.28W
12 H6 **Benalla** Victoria 36.35S 145.58E
100 C6 **Benalto** Alberta 52.20N 114.13W
77 K6 **Benalúa de Guadix** Spain 37.23N 3.09W
77 J6 **Benalúa de las Villas** Spain 37.25N 3.40W
91 G6 **Bena Lulua** *tribe* Zaïre
77 E8 **Benalup de Sidonia** Spain 36.21N 5.49W
91 G6 **Bena Makima** Zaïre 5.00S 21.07E
77 H7 **Benamargosa** Spain 36.50N 4.11W
77 L5 **Benamaurel** Spain 37.37N 2.41W
77 G6 **Benameji** Spain 37.16N 4.33W
89 C1 **Ben Amera** Mauritania 21.15N 13.41W
35 D1 **Ben 'Ammi** Israel 33.00N 35.06E
77 H7 **Benamocarra** Spain 36.48N 4.09W
93 K5 **Benane** Kenya 0.32N 38.38E
93 M5 **Benane** Kenya 0.42N 40.33E
77 F7 **Benaocaz** Spain 36.42N 5.25W
77 F7 **Benaoján** Spain 36.44N 5.15W
31 G9 **Benapol** Bangladesh 23.00N 89.55E
Benares India *see* **Varanasi**
26 U13 **Benares** Mauritius, Indian Oc 20.30S 57.35E
Benares *dist* India *see* **Varanasi** *Dist*
77 F7 **Benarraba** Spain 36.34N 5.16W
58 K6 **Benarty** *mt* Fife Scot 56.10N 3.22W
75 K7 **Benasal** Spain 40.23N 0.09W
75 M2 **Benasque** Spain 42.36N 0.31E
72 E2 **Benassay** France 46.34N 0.03E
77 L4 **Benatae** Spain 38.21N 2.39W
71 J10 **Bénat,C** France 43.05N 6.22E
95 B7 **Benato** Madagascar 23.05S 45.50E
91 H6 **Bena Tshadi** Zaïre 4.47S 22.52E
58 F4 **Ben Attow** *mt* Highland Scot 57.13N 5.18W
76 B11 **Benavente** Portugal 38.59N 8.49W
76 H4 **Benavente** Spain 42.00N 5.40W
120 E5 **Benavides** Bolivia 12.37S 67.19W
76 H4 **Benavides** Spain 42.30N 5.54W
112 J8 **Benavides** Texas 27.36N 98.26W
76 D10 **Benavila** Portugal 39.06N 7.52W
75 K8 **Benavites** Spain 39.45N 0.16W
58 K4 **Ben Avon** *mt* Grampian Scot 57.06N 3.27W
35 C6 **Benaya** Israel 31.50N 34.45E
72 G4 **Benayes** France 45.30N 1.28E
59 K1 **Benbane Hd** Antrim N Ire 55.15N 6.29W
58 D2 **Ben Barvas** *mt* Lewis, W Isles Scot 58.15N 6.30W
58 B4 **Benbecula** *isld* W Isles Scot
59 G3 **Benbrack** *mt* Cavan Irish Rep 54.09N 7.50W
112 L9 **Benbrook** Texas 32.41N 97.26W
112 L9 **Benbrook Dam** Texas 32.40N 97.27W
112 L9 **Benbrook Res** Texas
12 M7 **Ben Buckler** *C* New S Wales 33.54S 151.17E
59 F3 **Benbulbin** *mt* Sligo Irish Rep 54.22N 8.28W
59 C4 **Benbury** *mt* Mayo Irish Rep 53.39N 9.49W
25 J7 **Ben Cat** Vietnam 11.10N 106.36E
76 E11 **Bencatel** Portugal 38.45N 7.28W
Bencheng *see* **Luannan**
11 C13 **Bench I** New Zealand 46.54S 168.15E
110 P2 **Benchland** Montana 47.03N 110.02W
112 L5 **Benchley** Texas 30.45N 96.27W
58 J6 **Bencleuch** *mt* Central Scot 56.11N 3.47W
59 G3 **Bencroy** *mt* Leitrim Irish Rep 54.07N 7.56W
58 F6 **Ben Cruachan** *mt* Strathclyde Scot 56.26N 5.09W
14 C9 **Bencubbin** W Australia 30.49S 117.50E
110 D5 **Bend** Oregon 44.04N 121.20W
112 J4 **Bend** Texas 31.06N 98.32W
91 G11 **Benda** Angola 15.38S 21.39E
18 A6 **Bendahari** Pen Malaysia 5.34N 100.21E
89 D8 **Bendaja** Liberia 7.16N 11.13W
61 M5 **Bende** Belgium 50.25N 5.25E
90 C9 **Bende** Nigeria 5.32N 7.36E
92 E5 **Bende** *tribe* Tanzania
95 L7 **Bendearg** *mt* S Africa 31.06S 27.59E
91 E5 **Bendela** Zaïre 3.16S 17.36E
113 F4 **Bendeleben Mts** Alaska
12 K4 **Bendemeer** New S Wales 30.51S 151.09E
100 P8 **Bender** Saskatchewan 50.04N 102.33W
87 N6 **Bender Beila** Somalia 9.30N 50.50E
87 M5 **Bender Cassim** Somalia 11.18N 49.10E
58 F6 **Benderloch** Strathclyde Scot 56.29N 5.25W
87 N5 **Bender Merhagno** Somalia 11.41N 50.30E
46 G6 **Bendery** Moldavia U.S.S.R. 46.50N 29.29E
87 M5 **Bender Ziada** Somalia 11.15N 49.00E
12 E4 **Bendieuta** *R* S Australia
12 G6 **Bendigo** Victoria 36.48S 144.21E
37 H7 **Bendimahi** *R* Turkey
63 K7 **Bendingbostel** W Germany 52.57N 9.24E
12 J6 **Bendoc** Victoria 37.10S 148.55E
64 D3 **Bendorf** W Germany 50.25N 7.35E
89 D6 **Bendougou** Guinea 10.09N 10.39W
89 C8 **Bendu** Sierra Leone 7.29N 12.27W
89 D7 **Bendugu** Sierra Leone 9.34N 11.02W
92 F9 **Bene** Mozambique 15.05S 32.55E
35 C5 **Bene 'Atarot** Israel 32.02N 34.54E
Ben Eay *mt* *see* **Beinn Eighe**
35 C5 **Bene Beraq** Israel 32.05N 34.52E
35 E3 **Bene Berit** Israel 32.35N 35.27E
35 B6 **Bene Darom** Israel 31.49N 34.41E
109 P4 **Benedict** Kansas 37.37N 95.44W
104 J8 **Benedict** Maryland 38.32N 76.43W
108 J2 **Benedict** N Dakota 47.50N 101.05W
108 N8 **Benedict** Nebraska 41.01N 97.36W
64 L8 **Benediktbeuren** W Germany 47.44N 11.28E
64 L8 **Benediktenwand** *mt* W Germany 47.39N 11.29E
117 F7 **Beneditinos** Brazil 5.26S 42.22W
117 F8 **Benedito Leite** Brazil 7.09S 44.34W
56 K3 **Benefield** Northants England 52.29N 0.33W
76 H5 **Benegiles** Spain 41.37N 5.39W
77 P3 **Benejama** Spain 38.43N 0.46W
77 P4 **Benejúzar** Spain 38.05N 0.50W
95 B7 **Benenitra** Madagascar 23.25S 45.06E
57 D2 **Beneraird** *mt* Strathclyde Scotland 55.04N 4.55W
35 C6 **Bene Re'em** Israel 31.47N 34.48E
65 L2 **Benešov** Czechoslovakia 49.48N 14.41E
62 K6 **Benešov, H** Czechoslovakia 49.59N 17.39E
76 E8 **Benespera** Portugal 40.26N 7.17W
72 B8 **Benesse Maremne** France 43.38N 1.21W
72 E3 **Benest** France 46.02N 0.27E
69 M6 **Bénestroff** France 48.54N 6.46E
72 C3 **Benet** France 46.22N 0.36W
81 C3 **Benetutti** Sardinia 40.28N 9.11E
71 F1 **Beneuvre** France 47.42N 4.57E
79 C5 **Bene Vagienna** Italy 44.32N 7.50E
58 G4 **Beneveian,L** Highland Scotland 57.16N 4.55W
72 H3 **Bénévent l'Abbaye** France 46.07N 1.37E
80 L6 **Benevento** Italy 41.08N 14.46E
80 L6 **Benevento** *prov* Italy
105 C6 **Benevolence** Georgia 31.52N 84.45W
104 G5 **Benezett** Pennsylvania 41.21N 78.23W
35 C5 **Bene Ziyyon** Israel 32.13N 34.52E
69 O7 **Benfeld** France 48.23N 7.36E
77 P4 **Benferri** Spain 38.08N 0.58W
91 C8 **Benfica** Angola 9.12S 13.06E
76 B10 **Benfica** Portugal 39.09N 8.40W
76 D16 **Benfica** Portugal 38.45N 9.12W
92 F10 **Benga** Mozambique 16.10S 33.35E
30 K8 **Bengabad** Bihar India 24.19N 86.22E
27 O6 **Bengal,B.of** Indian Ocean
91 J3 **Bengamisa** Zaïre 0.58N 25.11E
18 M4 **Bengara** Borneo Indon 3.11N 117.15E
88 T5 **Ben Gardane** Tunisia 33.13N 11.13E
Bengasi *see* **Benghāzī**
91 C2 **Bengbis** Cameroon 3.27N 12.36E
23 H2 **Bengbu** Anhui China 32.56N 117.27E
110 G3 **Benge** Washington 46.56N 118.05W
85 F3 **Benghāzī** Libya 32.07N 20.05E
23 H1 **Beng He** *R* Shandong China
84 Z21 **Benghisa pt** Malta 35.49N 14.33E
18 C10 **Bengkalis** Sumatra Indon 1.27N 102.10E
18 C10 **Bengkalis** *isld* Sumatra Indon
18 H5 **Bengkayang** Borneo Indon 0.45N 109.28E
18 E7 **Bengkulu** Sumatra Indonesia 3.46S 102.16E
18 D7 **Bengkulu** *prov* Sumatra Indon
25 F2 **Beng, Nam** *R* Laos
91 D8 **Bengo** Angola 8.10S 15.53E
91 C8 **Bengo,B.do** Angola
19 G5 **Bengoi** Moluccas Indon 3.01S 130.10E
59 C4 **Bengorm** *mt* Mayo Irish Rep 53.38N 9.43W
100 M9 **Bengough** Saskatchewan 49.25N 105.10W
52 G7 **Bengtsfors** Sweden 59.03N 12.14E
51 J12 **Bengtskär Lt.Ho** Finland 59.43N 22.30E
91 C10 **Benguela** Angola 12.34S 13.24E
91 C10 **Benguela** *dist* Angola
88 K5 **Benguerir** Morocco 32.19N 7.59W
94 N3 **Benguérua, I** Mozambique 21.52S 35.30E
90 M8 **Benguima** Cent Afr Rep 6.20N 24.50E
72 K1 **Bengy-sur-Craon** France 47.01N 2.43E
86 F5 **Benha** Egypt 30.28N 31.11E
121 D7 **Benhamin Zorrillo** Argentina 39.03S 65.30W
25 J5 **Ben Hien** Vietnam 15.52N 107.49E
11 H8 **Benhope** *H E Station* New Zealand 41.40S 173.35E
58 G2 **Ben Hope** *mt* Highland Scotland 58.24N 4.36W
Beni India *see* **Bini**
30 G4 **Beni** Nepal 28.20N 83.32E
93 A5 **Beni** Zaïre 0.29N 29.29E
120 E5 **Beni** *dept* Bolivia
120 E5 **Beni** *R* Bolivia
88 M6 **Beni-Abbès** Algeria 30.11N 2.14W
85 L6 **Beni'Adi** Egypt 27.18N 30.52E
101 R4 **Beniah L** N W Terr
86 E9 **Beni Ahmad** Egypt 28.02N 30.45E
86 E9 **Beni 'Ali** Egypt 28.29N 30.43E
77 Q3 **Beniarda** Spain 38.42N 0.14W
77 Q3 **Beniarres** Spain 38.50N 0.22W
30 L7 **Benibari** Bihar India 25.45N 87.49E
75 L7 **Benicarló** Spain 40.25N 0.25E
75 L7 **Benicasim** Spain 40.03N 0.03E
77 Q3 **Benichembla** Spain 38.46N 0.07W
120 E5 **Benicito** *R* Bolivia
77 Q3 **Benidorm** Spain 38.33N 0.09W
77 Q3 **Benidorm,I.de** Spain 38.31N 0.09W
75 M6 **Benifallet** Spain 40.59N 0.31E
77 Q3 **Benifallim** Spain 38.40N 0.25W
77 Q2 **Benifayó** Spain 39.17N 0.26W
77 Q3 **Benigánim** Spain 38.56N 0.27W
30 D5 **Beniganj** Uttar Prad India 27.18N 80.27E
88 M5 **Beni Guil** *tribe* Morocco
85 L5 **Beni Hasan** Egypt 28.01N 30.51E
86 G3 **Beni 'Ibeid** Egypt 31.02N 31.39E
88 P5 **Beni Isguen** Algeria 32.25N 3.44E
74 F10 **Beni Iznassèn, Mts des** Morocco
86 E10 **Beni Khâlid** Egypt 27.51N 30.43E
77 Q3 **Benilloba** Spain 38.43N 0.24W
88 Q3 **Beni Mansour** Algeria 36.19N 4.22E
77 Q3 **Benimasot** Spain 38.45N 0.18W
86 E9 **Beni Mazâr** Egypt 28.29N 30.48E
88 K5 **Beni Mellal** Morocco 32.22N 6.29W
86 F7 **Beni Mûsa** Egypt 29.08N 31.03E
89 L8 **Benin** *rep* W Africa
77 K7 **Beninar** Spain 36.52N 3.01W
90 B8 **Benin City** Nigeria 6.19N 5.41E
69 M5 **Bening-lès-St.-Avold** France 49.08N 6.51E
57 O7 **Benington** Lincs England 53.00N 0.05E
77 Q3 **Beniopa** Spain 38.59N 0.12W
88 N5 **Beni Ounif** Algeria 32.03N 1.14W
30 J6 **Benipati** Bihar India 26.27N 85.54E
77 Q3 **Benipeixcar** Spain 38.58N 0.12W
77 R3 **Benisa** Spain 38.43N 0.03E
88 N4 **Beni-Saf** Algeria 35.28N 1.22W
75 M5 **Benisanet** Spain 41.04N 0.37E
75 J8 **Benisanó** Spain 39.37N 0.35W
74 K8 **Beni Sliman,Plaine des** Algeria
86 F7 **Beni Suef** Egypt 29.05N 31.05E
86 E7 **Beni Suef** *div* Egypt
77 R3 **Benitachell** Spain 38.44N 0.09E
88 M5 **Beni Tajjite** Morocco 32.15N 3.28W
28 C2 **Benithora R** Karnataka India
100 Q7 **Benito** Manitoba 51.55N 101.30W
115 B3 **Benito, Islas** Mexico
19 K3 **Benito Soliven** Luzon Philippines 17.01N 121.58E
77 M6 **Benizalon** Spain 37.13N 2.14W
119 E10 **Benjamim Constant** Brazil 4.23S 69.59W
112 H2 **Benjamin** Texas 33.35N 99.49W
110 O9 **Benjamin** Utah 40.06N 111.45W
115 D2 **Benjamín Hill** Mexico 30.13N 111.08W
110 E6 **Benjamin L** Oregon 43.30N 120.19W
30 H4 **Benkar** Nepal 27.47N 86.43E
20 J2 **Benkei-misaki** *C* Japan 42.51N 140.12E
108 J9 **Benkelman** Nebraska 40.02N 101.31W
66 L1 **Benken** Switzerland 47.39N 8.39E
58 H2 **Ben Klibreck** *mt* Highland Scotland 58.15N 4.22W
82 C6 **Benkovac** Yugoslavia 44.02N 15.39E
58 H5 **Ben Lawers** *mt* Tayside Scotland 56.33N 4.15W
58 H6 **Ben Ledi** *mt* Central Scotland 56.16N 4.20W
36 F2 **Benli Dağ** *mt* Turkey
13 G6 **Benlidi** Queensland 24.32S 144.51E
75 L7 **Benlloch** Spain 40.13N 0.01E
58 G6 **Ben Lomond** *mt* Central Scotland 56.12N 4.38W
12 K4 **Ben Lomond** *mt* New S Wales 30.04S 151.43E
12 J8 **Ben Lomond** *mt* Tasmania 41.36S 147.40E
58 H2 **Ben Loyal** *mt* Highland Scotland 58.24N 4.26W
58 G6 **Ben Lui** *mt* Central Scotland 56.23N 4.49W
58 J4 **Ben Macdhui** *mt* Grampian Scotland 57.04N 3.40W
95 L6 **Ben Macdhui** *mt* S Africa 30.39S 27.56E
78 B12 **Ben Mehidi** Algeria 36.46N 7.55E
58 G6 **Ben More** *mt* Central Scotland 56.23N 4.31W
58 D6 **Ben More** *mt* Mull, Strathclyde Scotland 56.25N 6.02W
58 B4 **Ben More** *mt* S Uist, W Isles Scotland 57.15N 7.18W
58 G2 **Ben More Assynt** *mt* Highland Scotland 58.07N 4.52W
11 E11 **Benmore Dam** New Zealand 44.34S 170.11E
11 E11 **Benmore Pk** *mt* New Zealand 44.25S 170.07E
Benna Beola *see* **Twelve Pins, The**
56 C6 **Bennacott** Cornwall England 50.42N 4.24W
60 G10 **Bennebroek** Netherlands 52.19N 4.35E
63 N9 **Benneckenstein** E Germany 51.40N 10.43E
60 L12 **Bennekom** Netherlands 52.00N 5.40E
108 O9 **Bennet** Nebraska 40.41N 96.30W
13 D2 **Bennet B** N Terr Australia
109 D4 **Bennet Mt** Colorado 37.29N 106.26W
101 F6 **Bennett** Br Col 59.49N 135.01W
109 F2 **Bennett** Colorado 39.45N 104.25W
106 D8 **Bennett** Iowa 41.44N 90.59W
106 C3 **Bennett** Wisconsin 46.26N 91.50W
41 R3 **Bennetta,Ostrov** *isld* U.S.S.R.
11 B7 **Bennett, C** Auckland Is Pacific Oc 50.49S 166.14E
101 F6 **Bennett, L** Br Col 59.55N 134.59W
13 B5 **Bennett,Mt** N Terr Aust 20.50S 131.22E
11 G10 **Bennetts** New Zealand 43.19S 172.19E
59 H6 **Bennettsbridge** Kilkenny Irish Rep 52.36N 7.12W
96 A13 **Bennett's Point** St Helena 15.58S 5.45W
103 D2 **Bennettsville** New York 42.15N 75.27W
105 H3 **Bennettsville** S Carolina 34.36N 79.40W
58 F5 **Ben Nevis** *mt* Highland Scotland 56.48N 5.00W
11 C12 **Ben Nevis** *mt* New Zealand 45.11S 168.52E
11 K5 **Benneydale** New Zealand 38.31S 175.23E
89 B2 **Bennichab** Mauritania 19.32N 15.12W
60 J9 **Benningbroek** Netherlands 52.42N 5.02E
110 O7 **Bennington** Idaho 42.25N 111.19W
109 N2 **Bennington** Kansas 39.04N 97.37W
104 O3 **Bennington** New Hampshire 43.01N 71.56W
109 O7 **Bennington** Oklahoma 34.01N 96.02W
104 M4 **Bennington** Vermont 42.54N 73.12W
35 E1 **Bennt Jbail** Lebanon 33.07N 35.26E
99 J6 **Benny** Ontario 46.47N 81.37W
91 E5 **Beno** Zaïre 3.41S 17.49E
18 L10 **Benoa** Bali Indon 8.47S 115.13E
70 B6 **Bénodet** France 47.53N 4.06W
70 B6 **Benodet,Anse de** *B* France
11 E11 **Ben Ohau Ra** New Zealand
106 C3 **Benoit** Wisconsin 46.31N 91.05W
18 C8 **Benom** *mt* Pen Malaysia 3.49N 102.04E
95 M2 **Benoni** S Africa 26.12S 28.18E
109 K6 **Benonine** Texas 35.13N 100.01W
88 O5 **Benoud** Algeria 32.23N 0.18E
90 F7 **Bénoué** *R* Cameroon
70 K3 **Bénouville** France 49.15N 0.17W
76 D9 **Benquerenca** Portugal 39.47N 7.37W
77 F3 **Benquerencia de la Serena** Spain 38.42N 5.29W
72 C8 **Benquet** France 43.50N 0.30W
64 B1 **Benrath** Nordrhein-Westfalen W Germany 51.10N 6.53E
58 K4 **Ben Rinnes** *mt* Grampian Scotland 57.24N 3.15W
76 B14 **Bensafrim** Portugal 37.09N 8.44W
122 J5 **Bensaleux Reef** Hawaiian Is 25.00N 178.00W
89 C6 **Bensané** Guinea 11.29N 13.57W
15 F8 **Bensbach** *R* Papua New Guinea
64 C2 **Bensberg** W Germany 50.58N 7.10E
60 H11 **Benschop** Netherlands 52.01N 4.59E
74 G9 **Bensekrane** Algeria 35.04N 1.13W
63 G5 **Bensersiel** W Germany 53.41N 7.35E
64 K2 **Benshausen** E Germany 50.38N 10.36E
64 F4 **Bensheim** W Germany 49.41N 8.38E
35 C6 **Ben Shemen** Israel 31.57N 34.56E
88 K5 **Ben Slimane** Morocco 33.40N 7.10W
111 O10 **Benson** Arizona 31.58N 110.19W
106 E9 **Benson** Illinois 40.52N 89.09W
107 C10 **Benson** Louisiana 31.52N 93.44W
108 P4 **Benson** Minnesota 45.19N 95.38W
105 J2 **Benson** N Carolina 35.24N 78.33W
56 J4 **Benson** Oxon England 51.38N 1.05W
100 O9 **Benson** Saskatchewan 49.27N 103.00W
58 G2 **Ben Stack** *mt* Highland Scotland 58.19N 4.57W
25 J7 **Ben Suc** Vietnam 11.10N 106.27E
32 H7 **Bent** Iran 26.16N 59.31E
58 B4 **Ben Tarbent** *mt* S Uist, W Isles Scotland 57.20N 7.20W
18 B7 **Benta Sebrang** Pen Malaysia 4.02N 101.56E
63 F8 **Bentheim** W Germany 52.18N 7.10E
60 G11 **Benthuizen** Netherlands 52.05N 4.32E
25 H3 **Ben Thuy** Vietnam 18.38N 105.43E
91 C11 **Bentiaba** *R* Angola
91 C11 **Bentiaba** *tribe* Angola
74 E9 **Ben Tib** Morocco 35.03N 3.28W
89 B6 **Bentimodia** Guinea 10.32N 14.28W
25 E7 **Bentinck I** Burma
13 E3 **Bentinck I** Queensland
87 B6 **Bentiu** Sudan 9.14N 29.49E
12 D8 **Bentleigh** *dist* Melbourne, Vic
100 C6 **Bentley** Alberta 52.29N 114.02W
109 N4 **Bentley** Kansas 37.54N 97.32W
108 H3 **Bentley** N Dakota 46.19N 102.06W
103 A3 **Bentley Creek** Pennsylvania 41.57N 76.43W
15 L9 **Bentley I** Louisiade Arch 10.44S 151.14E
104 E6 **Bentleyville** Pennsylvania 40.06N 80.02W
118 B5 **Bento Gomes,R** Brazil
121 H2 **Bento Gonçalves** Brazil 29.12S 51.34W
107 K9 **Benton** Alabama 32.19N 86.51W
100 G7 **Benton** Alberta 51.20N 110.22W
107 D7 **Benton** Arkansas 34.34N 92.35W
111 F4 **Benton** California 37.47N 118.33W
105 E7 **Benton** Florida 30.30N 82.40W
107 H3 **Benton** Illinois 38.01N 88.54W
107 H5 **Benton** Kentucky 36.51N 88.21W
107 C9 **Benton** Louisiana 32.41N 93.42W
107 G4 **Benton** Missouri 37.05N 89.34W
98 E7 **Benton** New Brunswick 46.00N 67.38W
103 B4 **Benton** Pennsylvania 41.12N 76.24W
106 D7 **Benton** Wisconsin 42.34N 90.23W
106 H7 **Benton Harbor** Michigan 42.07N 86.27W
107 F9 **Bentonia** Mississippi 32.40N 90.22W
107 B5 **Bentonville** Arkansas 36.23N 94.13W
118 H9 **Bento Ribeiro** Brazil 22.52S 43.22W
Bentota *see* **Beruwala**
26 R9 **Bentota Ganga** *R* Sri Lanka
25 J7 **Ben Tri** Vietnam 10.03N 106.36E
63 Q4 **Bentwisch** E Germany 54.07N 12.13E
89 C7 **Benty** Guinea 9.10N 13.14W
19 C6 **Benua** Celebes Indon 4.15S 122.09E
18 G5 **Benua** *isld* Indonesia 0.55N 107.28E
58 J2 **Ben Uarie** *mt* Highland Scotland 58.07N 3.49W
90 D8 **Benue** *R* Nigeria
90 D8 **Benue Plateau** *state* Nigeria
91 F5 **Benungu** Zaïre 2.18S 19.17E
18 D10 **Benut** Pen Malaysia 1.38N 103.15E
41 B5 **Benuyeua** *R* U.S.S.R.
76 F4 **Benuza** Spain 42.23N 6.43W
58 H6 **Ben Venue** *mt* Central Scotland 56.13N 4.29W
58 H6 **Ben Vorlich** *mt* Tayside Scotland 56.21N 4.13W
58 G6 **Ben Vrackie** *mt* Central Scotland 56.08N 4.33W
58 J5 **Ben Vrackie** *mt* Tayside Scotland 56.45N 3.45W
30 H7 **Benwaliya** Bihar India 25.38N 84.32E
59 C4 **Benwee** *mt* Mayo Irish Rep 53.37N 9.34W
59 C3 **Benwee Hd** Mayo Irish Rep 54.21N 9.48W
112 M3 **Ben Wheeler** Texas 32.26N 95.43W
56 L3 **Benwick** Cambs England 52.30N 0.01W
58 G3 **Ben Wyvis** *mt* Highland Scotland 57.40N 4.35W
21 C7 **Benxi** Liaoning China 41.20N 123.45E
21 C7 **Benxi** Liaoning China 41.21N 123.45E
35 E8 **Ben Yai'r Har** *hills* Israel
70 J4 **Bény Bocage,le** France 48.55N 0.50W
58 J5 **Ben-y-Gloe** *mt* Tayside Scotland 56.50N 3.44W
63 U5 **Benz** E Germany 53.57N 14.05E
91 C6 **Benza** Zaïre 4.49S 13.17E
35 B6 **Ben Zakkay** Israel 31.51N 34.43E
23 B4 **Benzilan** Sichuan China 28.06N 99.16E
88 N6 **Ben Zireg** Algeria 31.53N 1.51W
106 H5 **Benzonia** Michigan 44.35N 86.05W
77 F9 **Benzu** Spain 35.54N 5.23W
19 E1 **Beo** Indonesia 4.15N 126.50E
82 F5 **Beočin** Yugoslavia 45.12N 19.41E
82 F6 **Beograd** Yugoslavia 44.50N 20.30E
29 G5 **Beohari** Madhya Prad India 24.01N 81.25E
95 B7 **Beora** Madagascar 23.51S 44.40E
58 E5 **Beoraid, L** Highland Scotland 56.54N 5.35W
Beotia *see* **Voiotía**
90 H8 **Beouan** Cent Afr Rep 6.19N 16.51E
89 G8 **Beoumi** Ivory Coast 7.44N 5.23W
110 J9 **Beowawe** Nevada 40.36N 116.29W
18 E8 **Bepagut,Gunung** *mt* Sumatra Indon 4.20S 103.29E
23 D6 **Bepan Jiang** *R* Guizhou China
90 H7 **Bepara** Chad 8.17N 17.00E
95 D5 **Beparasy** Madagascar 19.09S 48.01E
32 J7 **Bepātān** Iran 26.27N 61.19E
20 E8 **Beppu** Japan 33.18N 131.30E
35 C9 **Beqa'** *watercourse* Israel
34 D4 **Beqa'a,El** *reg* Lebanon
35 C9 **Beqa',Har** *hill* Israel 31.07N 34.53E
35 C6 **Beqoa'** Israel 31.50N 34.56E
116 O8 **Bequia** *isld* Grenadines W I 13.00N 61.15W
117 F6 **Bequimão** Brazil 2.30S 44.45W
87 K6 **Ber** Somalia 9.20N 45.40E
31 H9 **Bera** Bangladesh 24.04N 89.38E
29 C3 **Bera** Rajasthan India 29.41N 73.39E
29 D5 **Berach R** Rajasthan India
59 H2 **Beragh** Tyrone N Ireland 54.33N 7.10W
15 D5 **Beraiwaro** *R* Irian Jaya
95 B7 **Beraketa** Madagascar 23.07S 44.25E
95 B8 **Beraketa** Madagascar 24.10S 45.40E
53 W18 **Berakopen** *mt* Norway 60.20N 7.15E
18 B9 **Beranang** Pen Malaysia 2.52N 101.51E
91 E2 **Beran Djoko** Congo 3.15N 17.00E
75 C1 **Beranga** Spain 43.25N 3.35W
75 E2 **Berantevilla** Spain 42.41N 2.50W
71 J7 **Bérarde,la** France 44.55N 6.17E
18 B7 **Beras** *mt* Pen Malaysia 4.43N 101.58E
29 E6 **Berasia** Madhya Prad India 23.40N 77.25E
18 C4 **Berastagi** Sumatra Indon 3.10N 98.30E
83 D4 **Berat** Albania 40.43N 19.46E
72 G9 **Bérat** France 43.25N 1.07E
18 C8 **Bera,Tasek** *L* Pen Malaysia
87 K6 **Berato** Somalia 9.16N 45.02E
64 M5 **Beratzhausen** W Germany 49.06N 11.49E
64 E8 **Berau** W Germany 47.41N 8.16E
18 M4 **Berau** *R* Borneo Indon
15 B5 **Berau, Teluk** *B* Irian Jaya
75 K4 **Berbegal** Spain 41.58N 0.01W
87 D1 **Berber** Sudan 18.01N 34.00E
87 K5 **Berbera** Somalia 10.28N 45.02E
75 D2 **Berberana** Spain 42.56N 3.02W
90 G9 **Berbérati** Cent Afr Rep 4.19N 15.51E
117 A2 **Berbice** *co* Guyana
117 A2 **Berbice** *R* Guyana
75 G2 **Berbinzana** Spain 42.31N 1.50W
61 L3 **Berbroek** Belgium 50.57N 5.12E
75 D1 **Bercedo** Spain 43.05N 3.28W
76 J5 **Bercero** Spain 41.35N 5.05W
79 G5 **Berceto** Italy 44.30N 9.59E
61 E3 **Berchem** Belgium 50.47N 3.31E
61 H3 **Berchem** Belgium 50.52N 4.18E
66 C5 **Bercher** Switzerland 46.43N 6.43E
81 C2 **Berchidda** Sardinia 40.48N 9.10E
90 J2 **Berchi-Guélé** Chad 18.15N 19.46E
64 L5 **Berching** W Germany 49.06N 11.28E
43 E3 **Berchogur** Kazakhstan U.S.S.R. 48.27N 58.43E
64 O8 **Berchtesgaden** W Germany 47.38N 13.00E
77 K7 **Bérchules** Spain 36.59N 3.11W
69 B3 **Berck** France 50.24N 1.35E
69 B3 **Berck-Plage** France 50.25N 1.34E
112 K7 **Berclair** Texas 28.32N 97.37W
68 F3 **Bercy** Paris France 48.50N 2.23E
44 G7 **Berd** Armenia U.S.S.R. 40.51N 45.21E
42 C5 **Berd'** *R* U.S.S.R.
44 E8 **Berda** *R* Ukraine U.S.S.R.
87 B5 **Berdab,El** Sudan 11.12N 29.40E
87 J9 **Berdale** Somalia 3.12N 43.11E
87 L7 **Berdale** Somalia 7.02N 47.49E
87 J8 **Berdaleh** Ethiopia 5.20N 43.32E
53 W20 **Berdalen** Norway 59.27N 7.26E
87 J8 **Berde,El** Somalia 4.50N 43.39E
76 A2 **Berdeogas** Spain 43.04N 9.05W
70 M5 **Berd'huis** France 48.21N 0.45E
46 G5 **Berdichev** Ukraine U.S.S.R. 49.54N 28.39E
37 D5 **Berdiga Dağları** *mts* Turkey
42 M2 **Berdigestyakh** U.S.S.R. 62.15N 127.10E
61 Q7 **Berdorf** Luxembourg 49.49N 6.21E
76 F2 **Berducedo** Spain 43.14N 6.45W
75 J2 **Berdún** Spain 42.36N 0.52W
45 H10 **Berdyansk** Ukraine U.S.S.R. 46.45N 36.47E
44 E8 **Berdyanskaya Kosa** *sand spit* Ukraine U.S.S.R.
44 E8 **Berdyanskiy Zaliv** *B* Ukraine U.S.S.R.
47 L5 **Berdyaush** U.S.S.R. 55.10N 59.08E
47 K7 **Berdyuzh'ye** U.S.S.R. 55.52N 68.20E
89 J6 **Béré** Upper Volta 11.50N 1.00W
107 M4 **Berea** Kentucky 37.34N 84.18W
108 H7 **Berea** Nebraska 42.14N 102.59W
104 D5 **Berea** Ohio 41.22N 81.51W
95 L5 **Berea** *dist* Lesotho
19 F2 **Berebere** Moluccas Indon 2.25N 128.41E
89 F9 **Béréby** Ivory Coast 4.37N 7.00W
87 N5 **Bereda** Somalia 11.52N 51.05E
82 J2 **Beregomet** Ukraine U.S.S.R. 48.11N 25.18E
82 H2 **Beregovo** U.S.S.R. 48.13N 22.39E
47 L7 **Beregovoy** U.S.S.R. 55.12N 73.13E
79 F4 **Bereguardo** Italy 45.16N 9.01E
90 J6 **Béréguile** Chad 11.38N 19.08E
15 J8 **Bereina** Papua New Guinea 8.29S 146.30E
37 C5 **Bereketli** Turkey 40.32N 37.16E
35 B7 **Berekhya** Israel 31.40N 34.37E
93 G10 **Bereku** Tanzania 4.27S 35.45E
89 H8 **Berekum** Ghana 7.30N 2.40W
53 W17 **Berekvam** Norway 60.47N 7.06E
43 Q3 **Berel'** Kazakhstan U.S.S.R. 49.25N 86.30E
39 D3 **Bërëlëkh** U.S.S.R. 62.48N 148.16E
39 D3 **Bërëlëkh** *R* U.S.S.R.
41 Q5 **Berelyëkh** *R* U.S.S.R.
18 D9 **Beremban,Gunong** *mt* Pen Malaysia 2.34N 103.15E
63 L8 **Berenbostel** W Germany 52.28N 9.32E
111 D4 **Berenda** California 37.02N 120.09W
61 H1 **Berendrecht** Belgium 51.20N 4.19E
120 D7 **Berenguela** Bolivia 17.15S 60.10W
85 N8 **Berenice** *ruins* Egypt 23.58N 35.22E
100 U6 **Berens I** Manitoba
100 V6 **Berens R** Manitoba
100 V6 **Berens River** Manitoba 52.22N 97.00W
95 B7 **Berenty** Madagascar 22.10S 45.06E
95 C8 **Berenty** Madagascar 25.00S 46.16E
56 G6 **Bere Regis** Dorset England 50.46N 2.14W
100 R9 **Beresford** Manitoba 49.43N 100.12W
98 G6 **Beresford** New Brunswick 47.41N 65.43W
12 D3 **Beresford** S Australia 29.10S 136.36E
108 O6 **Beresford** S Dakota 43.06N 96.45W
82 L4 **Bereşti Târg** Romania 46.05N 27.53E
45 G3 **Berestna** U.S.S.R. 53.37N 35.13E
62 N8 **Berettyó** *R* Romania/Hungary
62 N8 **Berettyóújfalu** Hungary 47.13N 21.31E
95 B5 **Berevo** Madagascar 19.45S 44.58E
95 B4 **Berevo-Ranobe** Madagascar 17.12S 44.17E
46 F3 **Bereza** Belorussiya U.S.S.R. 52.32N 25.00E
45 C6 **Berezan'** Ukraine U.S.S.R. 50.23N 31.32E
44 B8 **Berezanskiy Liman** *lagoon* Ukraine U.S.S.R.
46 F4 **Berezdov** Ukraine U.S.S.R. 50.30N 27.05E
41 Q3 **Berezhnykh, Mys** *C* U.S.S.R. 76.10N 141.30E
46 G3 **Berezina** *R* Belorussiya U.S.S.R.
46 G3 **Berezino** Belorussiya U.S.S.R. 54.52N 28.09E
45 U6 **Berezino** Kazakhstan U.S.S.R. 50.05N 48.54E
39 D1 **Berezkina** U.S.S.R. 70.09N 147.15E
45 C5 **Berezna** Ukraine U.S.S.R. 51.34N 31.46E
45 D9 **Bereznegovatoye** Ukraine U.S.S.R. 47.20N 32.51E
47 E4 **Bereznik** Arkhangel'sk U.S.S.R. 62.50N 42.39E
47 H6 **Berezniki** U.S.S.R. 59.26N 56.49E
46 F4 **Berezno** Ukraine U.S.S.R. 51.00N 26.41E
45 M6 **Bereznyagi** U.S.S.R. 50.04N 40.59E
47 H5 **Berezovaya** *R* Komi U.S.S.R.
39 J3 **Berezovaya** *R* Magadan U.S.S.R.
Berezovaya Sopka *vol see* **Karymskaya Sopka**
40 D6 **Berezovka** Amur U.S.S.R. 50.35N 127.53E
42 K3 **Berezovka** Irkutsk U.S.S.R. 57.48N 116.10E
47 H4 **Berezovka** Komi U.S.S.R. 64.32N 57.50E
42 E4 **Berezovka** Krasnoyarsk U.S.S.R. 56.03N 93.10E
45 K3 **Berezovka** Lipetsk U.S.S.R. 53.24N 38.53E
47 H6 **Berezovka** Perm U.S.S.R. 57.38N 57.21E
45 R4 **Berezovka** Saratov U.S.S.R. 52.07N 45.07E
47 L5 **Berezovka** Sverdlovsk U.S.S.R. 56.13N 58.50E
42 C3 **Berezovka** Tomsk U.S.S.R. 59.25N 82.38E
45 B9 **Berezovka** Ukraine U.S.S.R. 47.12N 30.56E
39 F2 **Berezovka** *R* U.S.S.R.
39 J3 **Berezovo** Magadan U.S.S.R. 63.28N 172.46E
45 U5 **Berezovo** Saratov U.S.S.R. 51.56N 48.26E
47 J4 **Berezovo** Tyumen U.S.S.R. 63.58N 65.00E
40 A2 **Berezovskaya** U.S.S.R. 59.41N 118.20E
45 Q6 **Berezovskaya** U.S.S.R. 50.15N 44.00E
43 E2 **Berezovskiy** Orenburg U.S.S.R. 52.25N 58.59E
47 M4 **Berezovskiy** Sverdlovsk U.S.S.R. 56.56N 60.50E
42 D4 **Berezovskiy** U.S.S.R. 55.38N 86.13E
42 D4 **Berezovskoye** U.S.S.R. 55.53N 89.33E
51 N11 **Berezovyy,Ostrov** *isld* U.S.S.R.
61 J3 **Berg** Belgium 50.56N 4.33E
60 T17 **Berg** Berg-en-Terblijt, Limburg Netherlands 50.52N 5.46E
61 P7 **Berg** Luxembourg 49.48N 6.05E
51 F2 **Berg** Norway 69.27N 17.15E
66 O2 **Berg** St Gallen Switzerland 47.29N 9.24E
52 H4 **Berg** Sweden 62.49N 14.30E
66 N1 **Berg** Thurgau Switzerland 47.35N 9.11E
60 T16 **Berg** Urmond, Limburg Netherlands 51.00N 5.46E
64 L8 **Berg** W Germany 47.57N 11.22E
66 O1 **Berg** W Germany 47.41N 9.28E
64 N2 **Berga** Gera E Germany 50.45N 12.10E
63 N10 **Berga** Halle E Germany 51.29N 11.00E
52 J9 **Berga** Kalmar Sweden 57.14N 16.03E
52 H10 **Berga** Kronoberg Sweden 56.55N 14.00E
75 O3 **Berga** Spain 42.06N 1.50E
85 N10 **Bergadem Jebel** *mt* Sudan 19.57N 34.48E
18 B7 **Bergading, Gunong** *mt* Pen Malaysia 4.03N 101.29E
36 C3 **Bergama** Turkey 39.08N 27.10E
78 C2 **Bergamasche,Alpi** Italy
60 H12 **Bergambacht** Netherlands 51.56N 4.47E
79 G3 **Bergamo** Italy 45.42N 9.40E
79 G3 **Bergamo** *prov* Italy
41 G1 **Berga, Mys** *C* U.S.S.R. 80.02N 99.29E
75 K6 **Bergantes** *R* Spain
75 M8 **Bergantin, I** Spain 39.50N 0.40E
79 K4 **Bergantino** Italy 45.04N 11.15E
76 B2 **Bergantiños** *V* Spain
75 F3 **Bergasa** Spain 42.15N 2.09W
53 Y19 **Berge** Norway 59.43N 8.03E
53 V16 **Berge** Sogn og Fjordane Norway 61.22N 6.46E
53 Y20 **Berge** Telemark Norway 59.04N 8.05E
63 G7 **Berge** W Germany 52.38N 7.44E
63 M6 **Bergedorf** Hamburg W Germany 53.29N 10.13E
64 B2 **Bergeim** W Germany 50.48N 6.38E
64 O8 **Bergen** Bayern W Germany 47.48N 12.36E
60 N13 **Bergen** Limburg Netherlands 51.36N 6.02E
108 K1 **Bergen** N Dakota 48.00N 100.42W
104 H3 **Bergen** New York 43.04N 77.58W
63 L7 **Bergen** Niedersachsen W Germany 52.48N 9.58E
60 G9 **Bergen** Noord-Holland Netherlands 52.40N 4.42E
53 S18 **Bergen** Norway 60.23N 5.20E
103 F5 **Bergen** *co* New Jersey
60 G9 **Bergen-aan-Zee** Netherlands 52.40N 4.37E
63 S4 **Bergen auf Rügen** E Germany 54.26N 13.27E
60 M12 **Berg-en-Dal** Netherlands 51.49N 5.55E
63 N7 **Bergen (Dumme)** Niedersachsen W Germany 52.53N 10.58E
64 F3 **Bergen-Enkheim** Hessen W Germany 50.10N 8.45E
103 L6 **Bergenfield** New Jersey 40.56N 74.01W
60 F14 **Bergen-op-Zoom** Netherlands 51.30N 4.17E
54 M2 **Bergen or Old Viking Bank** North Sea
60 P9 **Bergentheim** Netherlands 52.32N 6.36E
72 E6 **Bergerac** France 44.50N 0.29E
69 G6 **Bergères-les-Vertus** France 48.53N 4.00E
98 P8 **Berger,R.du** Quebec
98 P9 **Bergerville** Quebec 46.47N 71.16W
60 K14 **Bergeyk** Netherlands 51.19N 5.21E
51 H3 **Bergfors** Sweden 68.10N 19.46E
11 H1 **Berghan Pt** New Zealand 34.56S 173.34E
60 L12 **Bergharen** Netherlands 51.51N 5.40E
69 N7 **Bergheim** France 48.12N 7.22E
63 K9 **Bergheim** Nordrhein-Westfalen W Germany 51.49N 9.03E
66 O1 **Bergheim** W Germany 47.42N 9.25E
64 B2 **Bergheim (Erft)** W Germany 50.57N 6.38E
60 L12 **Berghem** Netherlands 51.46N 5.34E
104 E6 **Bergholz** Ohio 40.32N 80.54W
64 C2 **Bergisch Gladbach** W Germany 50.59N 7.10E
52 J10 **Bergkvara** Sweden 56.23N 16.05E
106 E3 **Bergland** Michigan 46.36N 89.33W
94 D4 **Bergland** Namibia 22.59S 17.10E
100 H2 **Bergland** Ontario 48.58N 94.22W
64 M7 **Berglern** W Germany 48.22N 11.56E
71 F8 **Berg,Mtgne.de** France 44.28N 4.31E
64 D1 **Bergneustadt** W Germany 51.02N 7.40E
51 J9 **Bergo** Finland 62.59N 21.10E
76 C2 **Bergondo** Spain 43.20N 8.14W
104 E8 **Bergoo** W Virginia 38.30N 80.18W
95 F9 **Bergplaats** S Africa 33.54S 22.40E
64 J3 **Bergrheinfeld** W Germany 50.00N 10.12E
95 B8 **Bergrivier** S Africa 32.56S 18.19E
60 H13 **Bergsche Maas** *R* Netherlands
60 F12 **Bergschenhoek** Netherlands 51.59N 4.30E
53 T17 **Bergsdalen** *V* Norway 60.34N 5.52E
52 L7 **Bergshamra** Sweden 59.38N 18.40E
53 Y17 **Bergsjø** Norway 60.43N 8.15E
52 K5 **Bergsjö** Sweden 62.00N 17.10E
53 T14 **Bergsøy** *isld* Norway 62.20N 5.37E
50 F4 **Bergsstadhir** Iceland 62.26N 19.44W
64 N6 **Bergstorf** W Germany 48.53N 12.29E
64 F4 **Bergstrasse** *dist* W Germany
64 J4 **Bergtheim** W Germany 49.54N 10.04E
75 D2 **Berguenda** Spain 42.46N 3.02W
69 C2 **Bergues** France 50.58N 2.26E
60 M7 **Bergum** Netherlands 53.12N 5.59E
60 N7 **Bergumer Meer** *L* Netherlands 53.12N 6.02E
66 P5 **Bergün Bravuogn** Switzerland 46.38N 9.45E
50 E4 **Bergvatn** *L* Iceland 65.15N 20.21W
95 N4 **Bergville** S Africa 28.44S 29.21E
18 F6 **Berhala,Selat** *str* Sumatra Indon
18 E9 **Berhala,Tanjong** *C* Pen Malaysia 2.43N 104.12E
29 L5 **Berhampore** W Bengal India 24.06N 88.18E
11 C6 **Berhampore** *dist* Wellington New Zealand
29 J8 **Berhampur** Orissa India 19.21N 84.51E
90 H7 **Beri** Chad 9.10N 16.24E
29 E3 **Beri** Haryana India 28.44N 76.37E
30 C7 **Beri** Uttar Prad India 25.54N 79.54E
75 G2 **Beriain** *mt* Spain 42.53N 2.00W
79 L4 **Berici,Monti** *mts* Italy
18 G2 **Berih** *R* Singapore
18 G7 **Berikat, Tandjung** *C* Indonesia 2.33S 106.50E
44 J5 **Berikey** U.S.S.R. 42.22N 48.06E
42 D4 **Berikul'skiy** U.S.S.R. 55.30N 88.03E
53 X14 **Berill** Norway 62.27N 7.30E
90 F8 **Bérim** Cameroon 6.41N 12.20E
39 L2 **Beringa,Mys** *C* U.S.S.R. 65.01N 175.55W
39 H6 **Beringa,Ostrov** *isld* U.S.S.R.
14 B7 **Beringarra** W Australia 25.57S 117.00E
76 D12 **Beringel** Portugal 38.03N 7.59W
61 L2 **Beringen** Belgium 51.03N 5.14E
60 M14 **Beringen** Netherlands 51.20N 5.56E
113 Q6 **Bering Glacier** Alaska 60.15N 143.40W
90 M5 **Beringil** Sudan 12.09N 25.40E
18 F7 **Beringin** Sumatra Indon 3.40S 104.15E
113 P6 **Bering L** Alaska 60.18N 144.19W
39 K3 **Beringovskiy** U.S.S.R. 63.08N 179.30E
38 R2 **Bering Str** U.S.S.R./Alaska
109 D9 **Berino** New Mexico 32.03N 106.37W
66 D8 **Berio Blanc,Monte** Italy 45.46N 6.54E
66 J6 **Berisal** Switzerland 46.18N 8.03E
87 L7 **Beri Siade** Ethiopia 7.20N 46.35E
45 E10 **Berislav** Ukraine U.S.S.R. 46.51N 33.26E
32 J8 **Beris, Ra's** *C* Iran 25.08N 61.09E
36 J4 **Berit Dağı** *mt* Turkey 38.01N 36.52E
26 U16 **Bérive** Réunion Indian Ocean 21.18S 55.33E
32 G7 **Berizak** Iran 26.09N 57.15E
77 L7 **Berja** Spain 36.51N 2.56W
70 K4 **Berjou** France 48.51N 0.28W
64 J2 **Berka an der Werta** E Germany 50.56N 10.05E
52 E4 **Berkåk** Norway 62.48N 10.03E
40 C3 **Berkakit** U.S.S.R. 56.36N 124.49E
88 M4 **Berkane** Morocco 34.59N 2.20W
60 F12 **Berkel** Netherlands 52.00N 4.29E
60 O11 **Berkel** *R* Netherlands
63 F9 **Berkel** *R* W Germany
111 B4 **Berkeley** California 37.53N 122.17W
56 G4 **Berkeley** Glos England 51.42N 2.27W
119 A5 **Berkeley,C** Galápagos Is 0.02N 91.38W
97 J3 **Berkeley,C** N W Terr 74.00N 100.30W
111 B8 **Berkeley Hills** California
14 G2 **Berkeley, R** W Australia
121 E10 **Berkeley Sound** Falkland Is
104 G7 **Berkeley Springs** W Virginia 39.38N 78.14W
63 U8 **Berkenbrück** E Germany 52.21N 14.10E
60 G12 **Berkenwoude** Netherlands 51.57N 4.43E
56 K4 **Berkhamsted** Herts England 51.46N 0.35W
47 H1 **Berkha,Mys** *C* Novaya Zemlya U.S.S.R. 70.58N 57.00E
60 H9 **Berkhout** Netherlands 52.38N 5.00E
103 M3 **Berkley** Massachusetts 41.51N 71.05W
106 L7 **Berkley** Michigan 42.31N 83.12W
123 E10 **Berkner I** Antarctica
82 H7 **Berkovitsa** Bulgaria 43.15N 23.05E
103 C6 **Berks** *co* Pennsylvania
103 H2 **Berkshire** Massachusetts 42.30N 73.12W
103 B2 **Berkshire** New York 42.17N 76.12W
56 J4 **Berkshire** *co* England
103 H2 **Berkshire** *co* Massachusetts
103 H2 **Berkshire Hills** Massachusetts
61 J2 **Berlaar** Belgium 51.07N 4.40E
69 F3 **Berlaimont** France 50.13N 3.49E
101 P8 **Berland** *R* Alberta
77 E4 **Berlanga** Spain 38.17N 5.50W
75 E5 **Berlanga de Duero** Spain 41.28N 2.51W
61 G2 **Berlare** Belgium 51.02N 4.01E
18 J4 **Berlayar,Tanjong** *C* Singapore 1.15N 103.49E
53 S15 **Berle** Norway 61.50N 5.05E
Berleburg *see* **Bad Berleburg**
76 A10 **Berlengo** *isld* Portugal 39.25N 9.30W
51 O1 **Berlevåg** Norway 70.50N 29.09E
60 K13 **Berlicum** Netherlands 51.42N 5.24E
60 L7 **Berlikum** Netherlands 53.15N 5.40E
63 S7 **Berlin** Germany 52.32N 13.25E
104 K8 **Berlin** Maryland 38.20N 75.13W
103 L2 **Berlin** Massachusetts 42.24N 71.39W
108 M3 **Berlin** N Dakota 46.23N 98.30W
104 O2 **Berlin** New Hampshire 44.27N 71.13W
103 E7 **Berlin** New Jersey 39.48N 74.56W
104 G7 **Berlin** Pennsylvania 39.56N 78.58W
95 L8 **Berlin** S Africa 32.53S 27.35E
106 F6 **Berlin** Wisconsin 43.58N 88.57W
61 M3 **Berlingen** Belgium 50.49N 5.19E
66 N1 **Berlingen** Switzerland 47.40N 9.02E
97 L3 **Berlinguet Inlet** N W Terr
104 D6 **Berlin Res** Ohio
11 F8 **Berlins** New Zealand 41.52S 171.52E
12 K6 **Bermagui** New S Wales 36.28S 150.03E
66 O1 **Bermatingen** W Germany 47.44N 9.21E
32 G1 **Berme** Turkmeniya U.S.S.R. 38.40N 56.52E
77 J7 **Bermejales,Embalse de los** *res* Spain 36.59N 3.51W
121 D8 **Bermeja,Pta** Argentina 41.08S 63.01W
77 F7 **Bermeja,Sierra** *mts* Spain
115 H5 **Bermejillo** Mexico 25.55N 103.39W
120 F10 **Bermejo** Bolivia 22.45S 63.23W
121 E7 **Bermejo, I** Argentina
118 B10 **Bermejo, R** Argentina
121 C2 **Bermejo, R** La Rioja Argentina
75 E1 **Bermeo** Spain 43.25N 2.44W
76 G6 **Bermillo de Sayago** Spain 41.22N 6.08W
95 F4 **Bermolli** S Africa 28.28S 22.50E
55 G4 **Bermondsey** London England 51.30N 0.04W
29 J1 **Bermo Res** Bihar India
96 B2 **Bermuda** *isld* Atlantic Oc
96 D5 **Bermuda Rise** Atlantic Oc
109 P2 **Bern** Kansas 39.57N 95.58W
66 F4 **Bern** Switzerland 46.57N 7.26E
66 F4 **Bern** *canton* Switzerland
72 E9 **Bernac-Dessus** France 43.09N 0.07E
109 E6 **Bernal** New Mexico 35.23N 105.19W
81 N3 **Bernalda** Italy 40.24N 16.44E
109 D6 **Bernalillo** New Mexico 35.18N 106.34W
18 B8 **Bernam** *R* Pen Malaysia
106 D7 **Bernard** Iowa 42.20N 90.50W
100 K8 **Bernard** Saskatchewan 50.50N 107.02W
97 G3 **Bernard I** N W Terr 73.30N 123.50W
111 P10 **Bernardino** Arizona 31.31N 109.17W
118 E8 **Bernardino de Campos** Brazil 23.01S 49.29W
19 M4 **Bernard Is** Truk Is Pacific Oc 7.18N 151.32E
98 J3 **Bernard,L** Quebec
109 D7 **Bernardo** New Mexico 34.26N 106.50W
118 D10 **Bernardo de Irigoyen** Misiones Argentina 26.14S 53.40W
121 E4 **Bernardo de Irigoyen** Santa Fé Argentina 32.12S 61.02W
76 L6 **Bernardos** Spain 41.08N 4.20W
103 E5 **Bernardsville** New Jersey 40.43N 74.35W
65 K3 **Bernartice** Czechoslovakia 49.22N 14.23E
121 D6 **Bernasconi** Argentina 37.55S 63.44W
64 E8 **Bernau** Baden-Württemberg W Germany 47.49N 8.02E
63 T7 **Bernau** E Germany 52.41N 13.36E
64 N8 **Bernau** Ober-Bayern W Germany 47.48N 12.23E
69 C3 **Bernaville** France 50.08N 2.10E
70 M3 **Bernay** Eure France 49.05N 0.36E
70 K5 **Bernay** Sarthe France 48.05N 0.04W
63 P9 **Bernburg** E Germany 51.49N 11.43E
65 O6 **Berndorf** Austria 47.58N 16.08E
106 K9 **Berne** Indiana 40.41N 84.57W
Berne Switzerland *see* **Bern**
63 H6 **Berne** W Germany 53.11N 8.29E
61 N4 **Berneau** Belgium 50.45N 5.45E
66 P2 **Berneck** Switzerland 47.26N 9.37E
64 F6 **Berneck** W Germany 48.37N 8.37E
58 C2 **Bernera, Gt** *isld* Lewis, W Isles Scotland 58.13N 6.50W
66 F6 **Berner Alpen** *mts* Switzerland
58 A5 **Berneray** *isld* W Isles Scotland 56.47N 7.38W
58 B3 **Berneray** *isld* W Isles Scotland 57.43N 7.11W
70 F7 **Bernerie la** France 47.05N 2.01W
76 H3 **Bernesga** *R* Spain
72 G3 **Berneuil** France 46.04N 1.06E
70 N2 **Berneval** France 49.58N 1.11E
71 K4 **Bernex** France 46.21N 6.40E
66 A7 **Bernex** Switzerland 46.11N 6.04E
79 B6 **Bernezzo** Italy 44.23N 7.26E
95 M3 **Bernhardina** S Africa 27.52S 28.40E
107 D9 **Bernice** Louisiana 32.50N 92.40W
107 G5 **Bernie** Missouri 36.40N 89.59W
97 L3 **Bernier Bay** N W Terr
14 G2 **Bernier,C** W Australia 14.05S 127.32E
14 A6 **Bernier I** W Australia 24.40S 113.00E
79 G2 **Bernina** *mts* Italy
66 R6 **Bernina Pass** Switzerland 46.25N 10.02E
79 G2 **Bernina,Pizzo** *mt* Italy/Switz 46.23N 9.54E
66 Q6 **Bernina,Val** Switzerland
75 E6 **Berninches** *mt* Spain 40.35N 2.49W
58 D4 **Bernisdale** Skye, Highland Scotland 57.27N 6.20W
61 E5 **Bernissart** Belgium 50.28N 3.39E
63 P5 **Bernitt** E Germany 53.56N 11.53E
64 C4 **Bernkastel-Kues** W Germany 49.55N 7.05E
63 S9 **Bernsdorf** E Germany 51.47N 13.13E
65 O7 **Bernstein** Austria 47.25N 16.15E
72 C11 **Bernüés** Spain 42.28N 0.36W
103 B6 **Bernville** Pennsylvania 40.55N 76.06W
66 B5 **Berolle** Switzerland 46.34N 6.21E
64 K6 **Berolzheim** W Germany 49.00N 10.53E
66 J3 **Beromünster** Switzerland 47.13N 8.12E
95 B6 **Beronono** Madagascar 20.50S 45.01E
95 C4 **Beronono** Madagascar 15.58S 47.10E
35 B7 **Beror Hayil** Israel 31.34N 34.39E
95 B6 **Béroroha** Madagascar 21.40S 45.10E
35 B8 **Berosh** Israel 31.22N 34.38E
89 L6 **Beroubouaye** Benin 10.34N 2.46E
65 K2 **Beroun** Czechoslovakia 49.58N 14.05E
65 K2 **Berounka** *R* Czechoslovakia
95 B5 **Berovina** Madagascar 18.10S 45.12E
82 H9 **Berovo** Yugoslavia 41.42N 22.51E
12 L5 **Berowra** New S Wales 33.38S 151.09E
12 K6 **Berowra Cr** New S Wales
79 L5 **Berra** Italy 44.59N 11.58E
78 A12 **Berrahall** Algeria 36.50N 7.28E
66 E5 **Berra,la** *mt* Switzerland 46.41N 7.12E
88 K5 **Berrechid** Morocco 33.17N 7.35W
71 G10 **Berre,Etang de** *lagoon* France 43.27N 5.05E
71 G10 **Berre-l'Etang** France 43.28N 5.10E
12 F5 **Berri** S Australia 34.17S 140.36E
33 H3 **Berri** *oil well* Saudi Arabia 27.07N 49.36E
88 P5 **Berriane** Algeria 32.55N 3.44E
71 E8 **Berrias** France 44.23N 4.12E
58 J2 **Berridale W** *R* Highland Scotland
58 J2 **Berriedale** Highland Scotland 58.11N 3.30W
70 C5 **Berrien** France 48.24N 3.45W
106 H8 **Berrien Springs** Michigan 41.57N 86.18W
12 H6 **Berrigan** New S Wales 35.41S 145.48E
87 J2 **Berri Is** Red Sea

13 B1 Berrimah N Terr Australia 12.28S 130.55E
75 E1 Bérriz Spain 43.10N 2.34W
77 C5 Berrocal Spain 37.37N 6.33W
76 G7 Berrocal de Huebra Spain 40.45N 6.05W
76 H2 Berrón, El Spain 43.23N 5.42W
88 P3 Berrouaghia Algeria 36.07N 2.52E
69 G5 Berru France 49.16N 4.09E
75 C6 Berrueco,El Spain 40.52N 3.34W
107 J8 Berry Alabama 33.39N 87.35W
107 M3 Berry Kentucky 38.31N 84.21W
12 K5 Berry New S Wales 34.48S 150.41E
67 G6 Berry prov France
69 F5 Berry-au-Bac France 49.24N 3.54E
116 L2 Berrydale Jamaica, W I 18.09N 76.29W
111 B3 Berryessa, L California
107 K5 Berry Field airport Tennessee 36.09N 86.40W
56 E7 Berry Hd Devon Eng 50.24N 3.29W
58 L3 Berryhillock Grampian Scotland 57.38N 2.50W
105 K12 Berry Is Bahamas
13 B6 Berrys Pass N Terr Australia 23.21S 131.20E
107 C5 Berryville Arkansas 36.22N 93.35W
104 H7 Berryville Virginia 39.08N 77.59W
72 G3 Bersac-sur-Rivalier France 46.04N 1.26E
94 D6 Berseba Namibia 26.00S 17.46E
69 E3 Bersée France 50.29N 3.09E
63 G7 Bersenbrück W Germany 52.34N 7.57E
53 W15 Berset Norway 61.39N 7.10E
79 A6 Bersezio Italy 44.23N 6.58E
46 G5 Bershad' Ukraine U.S.S.R. 48.20N 29.30E
61 G5 Bersillies'l'Abbaye Belgium 50.16N 4.09E
98 B5 Bersimis,Les Lacs Quebec 48.40N 70.35W
53 X17 Bersmulen mt Norway 60.30N 7.40E
58 T11 Berst Ness prom Orkney Scotland 59.16N 2.59W
43 F2 Bersuat Kazakhstan U.S.S.R. 52.11N 60.48E
37 F4 Berta Turkey 41.17N 42.00E
18 E3 Bertam Pen Malaysia 5.09N 102.01E
18 C8 Bertangga hill Pen Malaysia 3.16N 102.42E
98 D3 Berté,L Quebec
61 J3 Bertem Belgium 50.52N 4.38E
39 C1 Bertes U.S.S.R. 67.35N 143.11E
108 P3 Bertha Minnesota 46.17N 95.05W
69 N6 Berthelming France 48.49N 7.00E
Berthelot see Youb
72 J2 Berthenoux,la France 46.41N 2.03E
99 R6 Berthierville Quebec 46.05N 73.11W
108 J1 Berthold N Dakota 48.20N 101.44W
72 K7 Bertholène France 44.24N 2.46E
14 D3 Bertholet, C W Australia 17.20S 122.10E
109 E1 Berthoud Colorado 40.19N 105.05W
13 F1 Bertiehaugh Queensland 12.09S 142.36E
90 M4 Berti Hills Sudan
69 D3 Bertincourt France 50.05N 2.58E
117 D6 Bertinho Brazil 2.45S 50.22W
79 M6 Bertinoro Italy 44.09N 12.07E
71 C2 Bertins, les France 47.14N 3.06E
61 N6 Bertogne Belgium 50.05N 5.40E
117 F8 Bertolínia Brazil 7.32S 44.00W
90 F9 Bertoua Cameroon 4.34N 13.42E
59 C5 Bertraghboy Bay Galway Irish Rep
99 F3 Bertram Ontario 49.50N 84.26W
112 J5 Bertram Texas 30.45N 98.04W
14 F4 Bertram,Mt W Australia 18.40S 126.34E
108 L9 Bertrand Nebraska 40.32N 99.38W
121 J7 Bertrand,Cerro pk Arg/Chile 49.55S 73.29W
121 J6 Bertrand L Chile
61 P8 Bertrange Luxembourg 49.37N 6.03E
61 L4 Bertrée Belgium 50.42N 5.05E
69 M7 Bertrichamps France 48.26N 6.47E
61 L7 Bertrix Belgium 49.52N 5.15E
69 E3 Bertry France 50.05N 3.27E
100 P6 Bertwell Saskatchewan 52.35N 102.31W
87 E7 Beru Ethiopia 6.15N 35.16E
9 C6 Beru / Kiribati, Pacific Oc 1.15S 176.00E
18 A7 Beruas Pen Malaysia 4.29N 100.50E
18 A7 Beruas R Pen Malaysia
50 L5 Berufjördhur Iceland 64.48N 14.30W
50 C4 Berufjördhur B Bardhastrandarsýsla, Austur Iceland
50 L5 Berufjördhur B Múlasýsla, Sudhur Iceland
93 B3 Berunda Zaïre 2.17N 30.19E
50 L5 Berunes Iceland 64.43N 14.16W
53 X19 Berunuten mt Norway 59.52N 7.32E
119 H9 Beruri Brazil 3.54S 61.21W
40 K9 Berutaruve vol Kuril Is U.S.S.R. 44.28N 146.56E
50 B5 Beruvik inlet Iceland
26 Q9 Beruwala Sri Lanka 6.29N 79.59E
58 M5 Bervie Water R Grampian Scotland
70 L3 Berville-sur-Mer France 49.26N 0.22E
104 P3 Berwick Maine 43.17N 70.54W
98 H8 Berwick Nova Scotia 45.03N 64.44W
104 B5 Berwick Ohio 41.02N 83.18W
104 J5 Berwick Pennsylvania 41.04N 76.13W
12 H6 Berwick Victoria 38.02S 145.26E
Berwick co see Borders reg
58 N7 Berwick upon Tweed Northumberland England 55.46N 2.00W
101 P7 Berwyn Alberta 56.08N 117.45W
103 D6 Berwyn Pennsylvania 40.03N 75.26W
106 Q2 Berwyn dist Chicago, Illinois
111 L4 Beryl Utah 37.55N 113.40W
54 M3 Beryl oil field North Sea 59.36N 1.31E
61 H5 Berzée Belgium 50.17N 4.24E
71 F4 Berzé-le-Châtel France 46.24N 4.41E
62 K9 Berzence Hungary 46.11N 17.10E
76 J10 Berzocana Spain 39.27N 5.28W
36 E6 Beş isld Turkey 36.11N 30.25E
72 L6 Bès R France
95 B4 Besalampy Madagascar 16.43S 44.29E
75 Q3 Besalú Spain 42.12N 2.42E
71 J2 Besançon France 47.14N 6.02E
66 M8 Besano Italy 45.53N 8.53E
30 H6 Besantpur Bihar India 26.11N 84.40E
19 C8 Besar isld Indonesia 8.27S 122.23E
18 K8 Besar,Gunong mt Indonesia 5.51S 112.38E
18 B6 Besar,Gunong mt Pen Malaysia 5.12N 101.16E
18 D9 Besar,Gunong mt Pen Malaysia 2.30N 103.09E
18 L7 Besar,Gunung mt Borneo Indon 2.48S 115.45E
18 C9 Besar Hantu mt Pen Malaysia 3.13N 102.05E
76 L2 Besaya R Spain
71 G7 Besayes France 44.57N 5.04E
88 R3 Besbes Algeria 36.40N 7.49E
113 G4 Besboro I Alaska 64.10N 161.20W
71 D4 Besbre R France
75 Q4 Bescano Spain 41.58N 2.45E
46 H3 Besed' R U.S.S.R.
45 H5 Besedino U.S.S.R. 51.43N 36.28E
65 L4 Besednice Czechoslovakia 48.48N 14.34E
61 C3 Beselare Belgium 50.51N 3.02E
18 E4 Beserah Pen Malaysia 3.55N 103.15E
37 F3 Beşevler Turkey 40.13N 28.58E
43 O7 Beshbadam Kirgiziya U.S.S.R. 41.09N 72.54E
45 A1 Beshenkovichi Belorussiya U.S.S.R. 55.04N 29.26E
43 H7 Beshkent Uzbekistan U.S.S.R. 38.52N 65.39E
29 E6 Beshnagar Madhya Prad India 23.32N 77.49E
32 F6 Beshneh Iran 29.23N 54.50E
64 G5 Besigheim W Germany 49.01N 9.10E
19 D8 Besikama Timor Indon 9.38S 124.58E
37 F1 Beşiktaş Turkey 41.03N 29.01E
37 K2 Beşiktaş dist İstanbul Turkey 41.02N 29.01E
15 A4 Besir Irian Jaya 0.28S 130.40E
37 F8 Beşiri Turkey 37.56N 41.13E
62 L6 Beskidy Zachodnie mts Poland/Czech
36 E5 Beskonak Turkey 37.12N 31.16E
42 K3 Bes-Kyuyel' U.S.S.R. 59.30N 119.20E
44 F4 Beslan U.S.S.R. 43.02N 44.35E
82 G8 Besna Kobila mt Yugoslavia 42.31N 22.11E
100 M3 Besnard L Saskatchewan
37 D8 Besni Turkey 37.42N 37.53E
95 C6 Besoa Madagascar 21.55S 46.46E
43 L3 Besoba Kazakhstan U.S.S.R. 49.18N 74.29E
91 H4 Besoke Zaïre 1.12S 22.56E
45 H6 Besonovka U.S.S.R. 50.33N 36.20E
35 B9 Besor watercourse Israel
75 P4 Besós R Spain
46 J2 Besova U.S.S.R. 55.08N 34.31E
91 G4 Besow Zaïre 1.08S 20.18E
66 L8 Besozzo Italy 45.51N 8.39E
36 C5 Beşparmak Dağı mt Turkey 37.33N 27.35E
52 E2 Bessaker Norway 64.15N 10.21E
91 C7 Bessa Monteiro Angola 7.08S 13.44E
71 C10 Bessan France 43.22N 3.26E
71 K6 Bessans France 45.19N 7.00E
82 L2 Bessarabia old prov U.S.S.R.
82 M4 Bessarabka U.S.S.R. 46.20N 28.59E
50 D6 Bessastadhir Iceland 64.06N 22.00W
72 L3 Bessay-sur-Allier France 46.27N 3.21E
71 J6 Besse Isère France 45.04N 6.11E
90 B6 Besse Nigeria 11.14N 4.27E
71 B5 Besse-en-Chandesse France 45.30N 2.55E
71 E8 Bessèges France 44.16N 4.05E
48 V7 Bessel Fd Greenland
50 U14 Bessels,Kapp C Spitsbergen 78.33N 22.00E
107 J8 Bessemer Alabama 33.22N 87.00W
106 D3 Bessemer Michigan 46.28N 90.01W
99 N7 Bessemer Ontario 45.03N 77.38W
104 E6 Bessemer Pennsylvania 40.59N 80.31W
105 F2 Bessemer City N Carolina 35.17N 81.06W
71 F5 Bessenay France 45.47N 4.33E
64 G4 Bessenbach W Germany 49.57N 9.15E
53 F5 Besser Denmark 55.52N 10.38E
70 M6 Bessé-sur-Braye France 47.51N 0.45E
71 J10 Besse-sur-Issole France 43.21N 6.10E
44 M3 Besshoky mt Kazakhstan U.S.S.R. 44.05N 52.34E
109 M6 Bessie Oklahoma 35.23N 99.00W
72 H8 Bessières France 43.48N 1.35E
13 G6 Bessie's Castle Queensland 23.26S 143.08E
70 J3 Bessin reg France
72 G3 Bessines-sur-Gartempe France 46.07N 1.22E
44 D3 Besskorbnaya U.S.S.R. 44.39N 41.20E
72 L3 Besson France 46.29N 3.13E
66 D1 Bessoncourt France 47.39N 6.55E
45 R3 Bessonovka U.S.S.R. 53.20N 45.01E
72 J4 Bessou, Mont mt France 45.35N 2.05E
60 K13 Best Netherlands 51.31N 5.24E
112 F4 Best Texas 31.14N 101.38W
43 D3 Bestamak Kazakhstan U.S.S.R. 49.41N 55.05E
43 N3 Bestamak Kazakhstan U.S.S.R. 49.12N 78.20E
95 N4 Besters S Africa 28.26S 29.39E
76 B7 Bestida Portugal 40.46N 8.41W
43 L2 Bestobe Kazakhstan U.S.S.R. 52.32N 73.05E
47 E5 Bestuzhevo U.S.S.R. 61.40N 43.57E
41 L8 Bestyakh U.S.S.R. 64.41N 119.10E
41 N9 Bestyakh U.S.S.R. 61.15N 128.58E
41 M7 Bestyakh Yakutsk U.S.S.R. 65.15N 124.10E
41 O9 Bestyakh Yakutsk U.S.S.R. 61.56N 130.00E
110 C8 Beswick California 41.59N 122.12W
13 C2 Beswick N Terr Aust 14.32S 133.08E
41 N5 Bësyuke R U.S.S.R.
93 D6 Beta Uganda 0.18S 32.10E
15 E5 Betaf Irian Jaya 2.06S 139.12E
95 C5 Betafo Madagascar 19.50S 46.50E
35 E3 Bet Alfa Israel 32.32N 35.25E
91 G5 Betamba Zaïre 2.17S 21.24E
95 B5 Betanantanana Madagascar 18.10S 44.09E
96 T10 Betancuria Fuerteventura Canary Is 28.24N 14.05W
90 H9 Betanganga Cent Afr Rep 4.46N 16.50E
19 D8 Betano Indonesia 9.11S 125.42E
120 F8 Betanzos Bolivia 19.32S 65.24W
76 C2 Betanzos Spain 43.17N 8.13W
76 C2 Betanzos, Ría de B Spain
95 B6 Betaratasy Madagascar 21.48S 44.40E
90 G9 Bétaré-Oya Cameroon 5.34N 14.09E
35 C6 Bet 'Arif Israel 31.59N 34.56E
95 C5 Betatao Madagascar 18.11S 47.52E
18 B7 Betau R Pen Malaysia
98 C4 Betchie L Quebec
35 C5 Bet Dagan Israel 32.00N 34.50E
119 C4 Beté Colombia 6.01N 76.50W
Beted see Koppom
106 G2 Bete Grise B Michigan
61 K3 Betekom Belgium 50.59N 4.47E
35 C6 Bet El'azari Israel 31.49N 34.48E
75 F1 Betelu Spain 43.01N 2.00W
39 B1 Betenkes U.S.S.R. 67.42N 135.33E
75 K8 Betera Spain 39.35N 0.28W
75 F6 Beteta Spain 40.34N 2.04W
75 F6 Beteta,Embalse de res Spain 40.35N 2.05W
35 B7 Bet 'Ezra Israel 31.44N 34.39E
35 C6 Bet Gamli'el Israel 31.51N 34.46E
35 C7 Bet Guvrin Israel 31.37N 34.54E
35 D2 Bet Ha'Emeq Israel 32.57N 35.09E
35 B8 Bet HaGaddi Israel 31.26N 34.36E
95 N2 Bethal S Africa 26.27S 29.28E
35 C3 Bet Hananya Israel 32.32N 34.56E
94 D6 Bethanie Namibia 26.32S 17.11E
94 J5 Bethanie S Africa 25.30S 27.37E
94 C3 Bethanis Namibia 20.25S 14.22E
103 J4 Bethany Connecticut 41.26N 72.59W
Bethany Jordan see'Eizariya
107 B1 Bethany Missouri 40.16N 94.02W
109 N6 Bethany Oklahoma 35.33N 97.37W
99 M8 Bethany Ontario 44.11N 78.34W
103 D3 Bethany Pennsylvania 41.37N 75.18W
104 K8 Bethany Beach Delaware 38.31N 75.04W
35 E3 Bet HaShitta Israel 32.33N 35.26E
113 G6 Bethel Alaska 60.49N 161.49W
103 H4 Bethel Connecticut 41.25N 73.25W
104 K8 Bethel Delaware 38.33N 75.36W
104 P2 Bethel Maine 44.25N 70.47W
108 R4 Bethel Minnesota 45.27N 93.16W
107 D2 Bethel Missouri 39.52N 92.01W
105 K2 Bethel N Carolina 35.49N 77.24W
103 E3 Bethel New York 41.41N 74.52W
104 A8 Bethel Ohio 38.58N 84.04W
109 Q7 Bethel Oklahoma 34.22N 94.51W
103 B6 Bethel Pennsylvania 40.28N 76.17W
104 N3 Bethel Vermont 43.50N 72.38W
116 H1 Bethel Town Jamaica, W I 18.17N 77.58W
69 G5 Bétheniville France 49.17N 4.23E
57 E6 Bethesda Gwynedd Wales 53.11N 4.03W
104 H7 Bethesda Maryland 39.00N 77.05W
104 D6 Bethesda Ohio 40.02N 81.05W
95 H7 Bethesdaweg S Africa 31.55S 24.45E
35 F1 Bet Hillel Israel 33.13N 35.36E
72 F2 Béthines France 46.33N 0.59E
69 D5 Béthisy-St.Pierre France 49.17N 2.48E
103 H3 Bethlehem Connecticut 41.38N 73.12W
35 D7 Bethlehem Jordan 31.42N 35.12E
104 O2 Bethlehem New Hampshire 44.17N 71.42W
103 D5 Bethlehem Pennsylvania 40.36N 75.22W
95 M4 Bethlehem S Africa 28.15S 28.19E
55 G3 Bethnal Green London Eng 51.32N 0.03W
69 F6 Bethon France 48.37N 3.37E
66 D1 Bethoncourt France 47.32N 6.49E
87 G5 Bethor Ethiopia 11.38N 39.02E
98 A2 Béthoulat, L Quebec
107 K5 Bethpage Tennessee 36.30N 86.20W
103 H5 Bethpage Junc Long I, N Y 40.44N 73.29W
95 J6 Bethulie S Africa 30.30S 25.59E
109 H2 Bethune Colorado 39.17N 102.25W
69 D2 Béthune France 50.32N 2.38E
100 M8 Bethune Saskatchewan 50.44N 105.17W
105 G3 Bethune S Carolina 34.24N 80.22W
70 N2 Béthune R France
119 E3 Betijoque Venezuela 9.25N 70.45W
118 G6 Betim Brazil 19.56S 44.10W
95 B7 Betioky Madagascar 23.42S 44.22E
18 K10 Betiri Gunung mt Java Indon 8.19S 113.53E
35 C7 Bet Jimal Israel 31.44N 34.58E
Bet Ke'rem see Majd el Kurum
35 D3 Bet Leḥem HaGelilit Israel 32.44N 35.12E
28 J4 Betling Sib mt Mizoram India 23.47N 92.35E
45 E2 Betlitsa U.S.S.R. 54.00N 33.55E
45 S9 Betlyanka U.S.S.R. 47.39N 46.37E
35 D6 Bet Me'ir Israel 31.47N 35.02E
35 C7 Bet Nir Israel 31.39N 34.52E
90 H8 Bétokar Chad 7.59N 17.21E
69 E6 Beton France 48.39N 3.15E
18 J5 Betong Sarawak Malaysia 1.26N 111.30E
13 F7 Betoota Queensland 25.40S 140.40E
35 D3 Bet Oren Israel 32.44N 35.00E
91 F2 Betou Congo 3.02N 18.32E
43 K4 Bet-Pak-Dala Kazakhstan U.S.S.R. 46.03N 70.13E
43 J4 Betpak-Dala steppe Kazakhstan U.S.S.R.
35 C8 Bet Qama Israel 31.27N 34.45E
35 E3 Bet Qeshet Israel 32.43N 35.24E
95 C4 Betrandraka Madagascar 17.00S 47.33E
95 C7 Betroka Madagascar 23.15S 46.07E
66 N4 Betschwanden Switzerland 46.57N 9.02E
35 E3 Bet She'an Israel 32.30N 35.30E
35 C7 Bet Shemesh Israel 31.45N 34.59E
35 B7 Bet Shiqma Israel 31.38N 34.36E
98 D5 Betsiamites Quebec 48.56N 68.40W
98 C4 Betsiamites, R Quebec
95 C4 Betsiboka R Madagascar
106 H5 Betsie Pt Michigan 44.42N 86.14W
95 C4 Betsikiny Madagascar 16.27S 46.06E
95 A7 Betsioky Madagascar 22.26S 43.43E
95 B6 Betsioky Madagascar 21.30S 44.26E
106 J3 Betsy L Michigan 46.37N 85.16W
44 B3 Betta U.S.S.R. 44.24N 38.23E
61 O7 Bettborn Luxembourg 49.48N 5.56E
69 L5 Bettelainville France 49.14N 6.18E
65 E7 Bettelwurf-Spitze mt Austria 47.21N 11.32E
61 P8 Bettembourg Luxembourg 49.31N 6.06E
66 J6 Betten Switzerland 46.23N 8.04E
61 P7 Bettendorf Luxembourg 49.53N 6.13E
103 B8 Betterton Maryland 39.23N 76.04W
30 H6 Bettiah Bihar India 26.49N 84.30E
89 H8 Bettié Ivory Coast 6.01N 3.22W
112 N3 Bettie Texas 32.50N 94.59W
61 L4 Bettincourt Belgium 50.42N 5.15E
18 B7 Bettis R Pen Malaysia
113 M3 Bettles Alaska 66.53N 151.51W
66 J6 Bettlihorn Switzerland 46.20N 8.06E
52 K8 Bettna Sweden 58.53N 16.40E
79 G5 Béttola Italy 44.47N 9.36E
70 G5 Betton France 48.11N 1.38W
80 F2 Bettona Italy 43.01N 12.29E
57 F6 Bettws-y-Coed Gwynedd Wales 53.05N 3.48W
58 H1 Bettyhill Highland Scotland 58.30N 4.14W
29 E7 Betul Madhya Prad India 21.50N 77.59E
29 E6 Betul dist Madhya Prad India
19 D8 Betun Timor Indonesia 9.31S 124.59E
18 E6 Betung Sumatra Indon 1.48S 103.12E
18 K5 Betung,Gunung mt Borneo Indonesia 1.16N 112.29E
18 F8 Betung,Gunung mt Sumatra Indon 5.28S 105.10E
18 K6 Beturan,Gunung mt Borneo Indon 0.02S 112.28E
29 F5 Betwa R Madhya Prad etc India
35 C4 Bet Yannay Israel 32.23N 34.52E
35 C4 Bet Yizhaq Israel 32.20N 34.53E
35 F3 Bet Yosef Israel 32.34N 35.33E
69 D5 Betz France 49.09N 2.59E
35 D6 Bet Zayit Israel 31.47N 35.09E
61 Q8 Betzdorf Luxembourg 49.41N 6.21E
64 D2 Betzdorf W Germany 50.47N 7.54E
64 L4 Betzenstein W Germany 49.41N 11.25E
35 F3 Bet Zera Israel 32.41N 35.34E
91 D7 Béu Angola 6.15S 15.32E
64 C2 Beuel W Germany 50.44N 7.08E
64 L8 Beuerberg W Germany 47.50N 11.25E
60 M13 Beugen Netherlands 51.40N 5.56E
66 H1 Beuggen W Germany 47.35N 7.49E
71 K8 Beuil France 46.06N 7.00E
95 E8 Beukesplaas S Africa 32.07S 21.15E
100 Q8 Beulah Manitoba 50.16N 101.02W
106 H5 Beulah Michigan 44.36N 86.04W
108 J2 Beulah N Dakota 47.16N 101.49W
110 G6 Beulah Oregon 43.55N 118.08W
56 D3 Beulah Powys Wales 52.09N 3.35W
12 F6 Beulah Victoria 35.59S 142.26E
108 F5 Beulah Wyoming 44.32N 104.04W
60 N9 Beulakerwijde L Netherlands
105 K3 Beulaville N Carolina 34.57N 77.50W
60 M12 Beuningen Netherlands 51.52N 5.47E
79 D2 Beura Italy 46.04N 8.18E
71 J2 Beure France 47.12N 6.00E
66 R1 Beuren W Germany 47.44N 10.01E
64 B4 Beurig W Germany 49.36N 6.33E
90 H4 Beurkia Chad 15.20N 17.56E
90 D3 Beurkot Niger 17.22N 9.01E
72 C4 Beurlay France 45.52N 0.50W
64 F7 Beuron W Germany 48.03N 8.58E
69 H7 Beurville France 48.20N 4.51E
69 D4 Beuvraignes France 49.39N 2.46E
70 O6 Beuvron R France
70 K3 Beuvron-en-Auge France 49.11N 0.03W
70 A5 Beuzec-Cap-Sizun France 48.04N 4.30W
61 J4 Beuzet Belgium 50.32N 4.45E
70 L3 Beuzeville France 49.21N 0.21E
70 L2 Beuzeville-la-Grenier France 49.35N 0.26E
80 G3 Bevagna Italy 42.56N 12.37E
66 D4 Bevaix Switzerland 46.56N 6.49E
15 H7 Bevan Sd Papua New Guinea
95 C5 Bevato Madagascar 18.40S 46.15E
79 O3 Bevazzana Italy 45.40N 13.04E
61 J2 Bevel Belgium 51.08N 4.41E
63 N6 Bevensen W Germany 53.05N 10.34E
61 F4 Bever Belgium 50.43N 3.57E
63 G8 Bever R W Germany
61 P5 Bevercé Belgium 50.27N 6.03E
61 H2 Beveren Oost Vlaanderen Belgium 51.13N 4.15E
61 A3 Beveren West Vlaanderen Belgium 50.56N 2.38E
61 C3 Beveren West Vlaanderen Belgium 50.58N 3.10E
61 D3 Beveren West Vlaanderen Belgium 50.52N 3.20E
63 G8 Bevergern W Germany 52.17N 7.35E
122 K10 Beveridge Reef Pacific Oc 20.00S 168.00W
66 O5 Beverin,Piz mt Switzerland 46.39N 9.22E
57 N5 Beverley Humberside Eng 53.51N 0.26W
100 J8 Beverley Saskatchewan 50.16N 107.58W
110 F3 Beverley Washington 46.51N 119.56W
14 B9 Beverley W Australia 32.08S 116.54E
103 A9 Beverley Beach Maryland 38.53N 76.30W
13 J5 Beverley Grp islds Queensland
12 L8 Beverley Hills dist Sydney, New S Wales
113 H7 Beverley, L Alaska 59.40N 158.50W
61 L2 Beverlo Belgium 51.05N 5.13E
100 D5 Beverly Alberta 53.36N 113.21W
109 N2 Beverly Kansas 39.02N 97.57W
104 P4 Beverly Massachusetts 42.35N 70.52W
103 E6 Beverly New Jersey 40.04N 74.55W
104 D7 Beverly Ohio 39.34N 81.37W
104 F8 Beverly W Virginia 38.51N 79.53W
111 D8 Beverly Hills dist Los Angeles, California
101 X3 Beverly L N W Terr
110 C2 Beverly Park Washington 47.55N 122.13W
63 L9 Bevern W Germany 51.52N 9.30E
66 Q5 Bevers Switzerland 46.33N 9.53E
61 M3 Beverst Belgium 50.53N 5.28E
63 J6 Beverstedt W Germany 53.27N 8.50E
63 K9 Beverungen W Germany 51.39N 9.21E
60 G10 Beverwijk Netherlands 52.29N 4.40E
107 D2 Bevier Missouri 39.44N 92.33W
79 K4 Bevilacqua Boschi Italy 45.14N 11.24E
70 O5 Béville-le-Comte France 48.26N 1.43E
53 C6 Bevtoft Denmark 55.12N 9.13E
15 F5 Bewani R Irian Jaya
30 C7 Bewar Hamirpur, Uttar Prad India 25.46N 79.55E
30 C5 Bewar Mainpuri, Uttar Prad India 27.13N 79.18E
57 H2 Bewcastle Cumbria England 55.03N 2.42W
56 G3 Bewdley Hereford & Worcs Eng 52.22N 2.19W
95 J1 Bewley S Africa 25.38S 25.44E
66 E6 Bex Switzerland 46.16N 7.01E
69 N5 Bexbach W Germany 49.29N 7.16E
56 M6 Bexhill-on-Sea E Sussex Eng 50.50N 0.29E
55 J4 Bexley London England 51.27N 0.09E
11 G10 Bexley New Zealand 43.22S 172.04E
104 C7 Bexley Ohio 39.58N 82.55W
55 J4 Bexley bor London England
12 L8 Bexley dist Sydney, N S W
101 Q1 Bexley, C N W Terr 69.01N 115.58W
42 E5 Beya U.S.S.R. 52.58N 90.45E
91 K6 Beya Zaïre 5.40S 27.38E
85 C4 Bey al Kabir,Wadi watercourse Libya
32 B2 Beyānlū Iran 36.01N 47.50E
42 E5 Bey-Buluk U.S.S.R. 54.30N 90.33E
37 C3 Beyçayırı Turkey 40.16N 26.55E
Beyce Bursa Turkeysee Orhaneli
37 H3 Beyce Turkey 40.17N 29.55E
72 D6 Beychac France 44.53N 0.23W
36 F1 Beycuma Turkey 41.18N 31.59E
36 C4 Beydağ Turkey 38.05N 28.12E
37 D6 Bey Dağ mt Sivas Turkey 39.42N 37.51E
36 J4 Bey Dağı mt Seyhan Turkey 38.17N 36.02E
36 E4 Bey Dağı mt Turkey
36 E6 Bey Dağları mts Turkey
36 E2 Beydili Turkey 40.09N 30.57E
41 M5 Beyenchime R U.S.S.R.
37 C2 Beyendik Turkey 40.57N 26.34E
95 F6 Beyersberg mt S Africa 30.59S 22.30E
89 H9 Beyin Ghana 4.59N 2.33W
37 F1 Beykoz Turkey 41.09N 29.06E
89 E7 Beyla Guinea 8.42N 8.39W
37 K2 Beylerbeyi Turkey 41.02N 29.06E
37 C2 Beylik R Turkey
36 E3 Beylikahır Turkey 39.42N 31.10E
72 H5 Beynat France 45.08N 1.43E
69 B6 Beynes France 48.52N 1.53E
43 D4 Beyneu Kazakhstan U.S.S.R. 45.16N 55.04E
36 G3 Beyobası Turkey 39.52N 33.43E
37 J2 Beyoğlu İstanbul Turkey 41.03N 28.58E
21 H12 Beyoneisu retsugan rock Japan 31.54N 139.54E
36 F2 Beypazarı Turkey 40.10N 31.56E
37 D6 Beypınar Turkey 39.29N 37.43E
28 B5 Beypore Kerala India 11.11N 75.47E
32 E7 Beyram Iran 27.26N 53.35E
Beyrouth see Beirut
36 F5 Beyşehir Turkey 37.40N 31.43E
36 F5 Beyşehir Gölü L Turkey
46 L6 Beysug R U.S.S.R.
44 B1 Beysugskiy Liman gulf U.S.S.R.
44 C2 Beysuzhek Levyy R U.S.S.R.
29 A6 Beyt Gujarat India 22.27N 69.12E
37 G8 Beytişebap Turkey 37.35N 43.10E
56 N3 Beyton Suffolk Eng 52.14N 0.50E
40 C5 Beytonovo U.S.S.R. 53.14N 124.31E
Beytüşşebap see Beytişebap
44 H7 Běyuk Dakhna Azerbaydzhan U.S.S.R. 40.58N 47.07E
36 G5 Beyviran Turkey 37.53N 33.53E
95 B7 Bezaha Madagascar 23.30S 44.30E
32 G3 Bezameh Iran 35.43N 56.40E
75 H7 Bezas Spain 40.20N 1.19W
65 A7 Bezau Austria 47.24N 9.55E
82 E5 Bezdan Yugoslavia 45.50N 18.57E
64 O4 Bezdružice Czechoslovakia 49.55N 12.58E
71 G2 Bèze France 47.28N 5.16E
24 F4 Bezekuk Xinjiang Uygur Zizhiqu China 43.07N 89.52E
24 F4 Bezekuk anc site Xinjiang Uygur Zizhiqu China 43.01N 89.36E
45 V3 Bezenchuk U.S.S.R. 53.00N 49.27E
72 K3 Bézenet France 46.20N 2.50E
44 E4 Bezengi U.S.S.R. 43.12N 43.16E
32 G6 Bezenjān Iran 29.14N 56.45E
35 F4 Bezeq R Israel
35 D1 Bezet Israel 33.03N 35.08E
46 G2 Bezhanitsy U.S.S.R. 57.00N 29.55E
82 J7 Bezhanovo Bulgaria 43.13N 24.26E
45 U1 Bezhbatman U.S.S.R. 55.42N 48.26E
46 K1 Bezhetsk U.S.S.R. 57.49N 36.40E
45 H3 Bezhin Lug U.S.S.R. 53.28N 36.46E
45 F3 Bezhitsa U.S.S.R. 53.19N 34.17E
91 F12 Bezi Bezi, L Angola 16.16S 19.46E
71 C10 Béziers France 43.21N 3.13E
72 J8 Bez,le France 43.36N 2.28E
82 H9 Bezlet mt Bulgaria 41.46N 23.52E
45 H7 Bezlyudovka Ukraine U.S.S.R. 49.53N 36.17E
43 E7 Bezmein Turkmeniya U.S.S.R. 38.06N 58.14E
42 G5 Beznosova U.S.S.R. 54.08N 103.50E
72 J9 Bezole,la France 43.02N 2.06E
68 D2 Bezons France 48.56N 2.12E
44 D2 Bezopasnoye U.S.S.R. 45.39N 41.57E
70 O3 Bezu-la-Forêt France 49.25N 1.38E
69 E5 Bézu-St.Germain France 49.06N 3.25E
Bezwada see Vijayawada
45 P7 Bezymyanka U.S.S.R. 49.55N 43.16E
45 S5 Bezymyannaya U.S.S.R. 51.22N 46.25E
41 A3 Bezymyannaya,Guba gulf Novaya Zemlya U.S.S.R.
29 B5 Bhabhar Gujarat India 24.08N 71.42E
30 G7 Bhabua Bihar India 25.04N 83.39E
29 B6 Bhachau Gujarat India 23.12N 71.23E
29 B5 Bhachbhar Rajasthan India 25.40N 71.00E
30 F6 Bhada Uttar Prad India 26.11N 82.04E
29 B7 Bhadar R Gujarat India
31 H4 Bhadarwah Kashmir 32.56N 75.47E
30 A5 Bhadas Haryana India 27.55N 77.00E
29 D2 Bhadaur Punjab India 30.30N 75.22E
30 A8 Bhadaura Madhya Prad India 24.47N 77.24E
30 J5 Bhadgaon Nepal 27.41N 85.26E
30 F7 Bhadohi Uttar Prad India 25.24N 82.35E
28 B4 Bhadra Karnataka India 13.42N 75.08E
29 D3 Bhadra Rajasthan India 29.08N 75.14E
28 B4 Bhadra res Karnataka India
28 E2 Bhadrachalam Andhra Prad India 17.42N 80.59E
Bhadrachalam Road Sta see Kottagudem
29 C5 Bhadrajan Rajasthan India 25.36N 73.00E
29 K7 Bhadrakh Orissa India 21.05N 86.36E
28 B4 Bhadravati Karnataka India 13.54N 75.38E
31 D6 Bhag Pakistan 29.02N 67.52E
30 K7 Bhagalpur Bihar India 25.14N 86.59E
30 K8 Bhagalpur dist Bihar India
30 K8 Bhagalpur div Bihar India
29 E1 Bhaga R Himachal Prad India
30 H5 Bhagaura Nepal 27.27N 84.19E
30 B6 Bhageh Madhya Prad India 26.02N 78.26E
30 B2 Bhagirathi R Uttar Prad India
29 L6 Bhagirathi R W Bengal India
30 F5 Bhagwanpur Nepal 27.42N 82.57E
30 J7 Bhagwanpur Patna, Bihar India 25.51N 85.18E
30 G8 Bhagwanpur Shahabad, Bihar India 24.57N 83.36E
30 D6 Bhagwantnagar Uttar Prad India 26.13N 80.46E
28 C1 Bhainsa Andhra Prad India 19.08N 77.59E
29 E7 Bhainsdehi Madhya Prad India 21.40N 77.39E
29 D5 Bhainsror Rajasthan India 24.59N 75.40E
31 H9 Bhairab Bazar Bangladesh 24.04N 91.00E
29 H4 Bhairawa Nepal 27.20N 82.30E
30 G5 Bhairawa Nepal 27.32N 83.23E
31 C8 Bhairi Hol mt Pakistan 25.52N 64.10E
30 B1 Bhaironghati Uttar Prad India 31.01N 78.51E
Bhaisa see Bhainsa
31 F5 Bhakkar Pakistan 31.40N 71.08E
30 E5 Bhakla R Uttar Prad India
30 C3 Bhakra R Uttar Prad India
29 E2 Bhakra Dam Himachal Prad India 31.24N 76.28E
28 C1 Bhalki Karnataka India 18.04N 77.10E
30 L7 Bhaluka W Bengal India 25.17N 87.52E
29 L4 Bhalut Pk Nepal/Sikkim 27.16N 88.08E
31 G4 Bhalwal Pakistan 32.15N 72.59E
31 C10 Bhambo Khān Qarmati Pakistan 24.49N 67.08E
34 C5 Bhamdoun Lebanon 33.46N 35.37E
29 E7 Bhamgarh Madhya Prad India 21.50N 76.32E
25 N9 Bhamo Burma 24.15N 97.15E
29 F7 Bhandak Maharashtra India 20.08N 79.10E
30 K5 Bhandar Nepal 27.35N 86.20E
29 F7 Bhandara Maharashtra India 21.10N 79.41E
29 F7 Bhandara dist Maharashtra India
30 F5 Bhandaria Uttar Prad India 27.10N 82.33E
30 B7 Bhander Madhya Prad India 25.44N 78.44E
30 E5 Bhangaha Uttar Prad India 27.43N 81.51E
29 A6 Bhangor Gujarat India 22.03N 69.55E
29 J8 Bhanjanagar Orissa India 19.58N 84.40E
29 G7 Bhanpur Madhya Prad India 21.48N 80.36E
29 D5 Bhanpura Madhya Prad India 24.32N 75.50E
29 F6 Bhanrer Ra Madhya Prad India
30 K6 Bhaptiahi Bihar India 26.18N 86.44E
30 D5 Bharali Uttar Prad India 27.23N 80.17E
30 D7 Bharat Kup Uttar Prad India 25.13N 80.46E
29 G6 Bharatpur Madhya Prad India 23.42N 81.50E
30 H5 Bharatpur Nepal 27.39N 84.28E
30 A5 Bharatpur Rajasthan India 27.14N 77.29E
30 A5 Bharatpur dist Rajasthan India
28 J2 Bhareli R Assam India
31 B8 Bhari R Pakistan
29 C7 Bharuch Gujarat India 21.40N 73.02E
29 C7 Bharuch dist Gujarat India
29 E2 Bharwain Himachal Prad India 31.46N 76.07E
30 G5 Bharwalia Uttar Prad India 27.04N 83.43E
30 C4 Bhaspur Uttar Prad India 28.53N 79.16E
29 G7 Bhatapara Madhya Prad India 21.36N 81.56E
29 L2 Bhatar W Bengal India 23.25N 87.55E
28 A1 Bhatgar L Maharashtra India
31 H9 Bhatiapara Ghat Bangladesh 23.12N 89.41E
29 D2 Bhatinda Punjab India 30.10N 74.58E
29 D3 Bhatinda dist Punjab India
28 B4 Bhatkal Karnataka India 13.59N 74.34E
Bhatnair see Hanumangarh
30 G6 Bhatni Junction Uttar Prad India 26.23N 83.56E
29 L6 Bhatpara W Bengal India 22.51N 88.31E
30 A2 Bhatwar Himachal Prad India 30.42N 77.42E
30 D6 Bhauli Uttar Prad India 26.58N 80.52E
31 G4 Bhaun Pakistan 32.53N 72.48E
30 G5 Bhaunrabari Uttar Prad India 27.02N 83.20E
28 C5 Bhavani Tamil Nadu India 11.28N 77.41E
28 C5 Bhavani R Tamil Nadu India
28 C5 Bhavāni Sagar L Tamil Nadu India 11.50N 77.00E
29 C7 Bhavnagar Gujarat India 21.46N 72.14E
29 B7 Bhavnagar dist Gujarat India
31 G5 Bhawana Pakistan 31.34N 72.43E
29 H8 Bhawanipatna Orissa India 19.57N 83.10E
29 H1 Bhawanipore dist Calcutta
30 L7 Bhawanipur Bihar India 25.24N 87.30E
30 F5 Bhawanipur Nepal 27.59N 82.07E
30 H6 Bhawanipur Uttar Prad India 26.22N 84.10E
30 L7 Bhawanipur Rajdham Bihar India 25.39N 87.09E
30 K6 Bheja Bihar India 26.07N 86.24E
30 E8 Bhelki Madhya Prad India 24.26N 81.46E
30 K8 Bhelwa Bihar India 24.49N 86.37E
31 G4 Bhera Pakistan 32.28N 72.58E
Bheraghat see Marble Rocks
30 E4 Bheri R Nepal
30 E6 Bheta Uttar Prad India 26.59N 81.01E
30 H5 Bhikhna Thori Nepal 27.20N 84.38E
30 C3 Bhikia Sain Uttar Prad India 29.42N 79.16E
29 G7 Bhilai Madhya Prad India 21.12N 81.26E
29 C5 Bhildi Gujarat India 24.13N 72.04E
30 B2 Bhillunguna R Uttar Prad India
29 E6 Bhilsa dist Madhya Prad India
30 E6 Bhilwal Uttar Prad India 26.42N 81.16E
29 D5 Bhilwara Rajasthan India 25.23N 74.39E
29 D5 Bhilwara dist Rajasthan India
28 C2 Bhima R Maharashtra/Karnataka India
29 B4 Bhimar Rajasthan India 26.18N 71.30E
28 E2 Bhimavaram Andhra Prad India 16.34N 81.35E
31 H4 Bhimbar Kashmir 32.59N 74.06E
29 G6 Bhimlath Madhya Prad India 22.07N 80.48E
30 K6 Bhimnagar Bihar India 26.29N 86.57E
30 J5 Bhimphedi Nepal 27.32N 85.08E
30 B6 Bhind Madhya Prad India 26.33N 78.47E
30 B6 Bhind dist Madhya Prad India
29 D5 Bhindar Rajasthan India 24.30N 74.14E
30 E5 Bhinga Uttar Prad India 27.42N 81.55E
28 B1 Bhingar Maharashtra India 19.05N 74.53E
29 H7 Bhingeswar Madhya Prad India 20.58N 82.08E
29 C5 Bhinmal Rajasthan India 25.01N 72.22E
30 D6 Bhitargaon Uttar Prad India 26.18N 80.58E
31 G8 Bhitargarh Bangladesh 26.24N 88.40E
30 B7 Bhitarwar Madhya Prad India 25.48N 78.06E
31 B10 Bhit I Pakistan 24.49N 66.58E
31 E9 Bhitiaro Cr Pakistan
29 C8 Bhiwandi Maharashtra India 19.21N 73.08E
29 E3 Bhiwani Haryana India 28.50N 76.10E
28 H3 Bhogai R India/Bangladesh
29 A7 Bhogat Gujarat India 21.59N 69.16E
29 B6 Bhogava R Gujarat India
30 C6 Bhognipur Uttar Prad India 26.12N 79.48E
30 A2 Bhogriwala Haryana India 30.18N 77.32E
29 E6 Bhojpur Madhya Prad India 23.10N 77.41E
30 L5 Bhojpur Nepal 27.11N 87.03E
29 D7 Bhokardan Maharashtra India 20.18N 75.50E
31 H10 Bhola Bangladesh 22.40N 91.36E
30 E3 Bholi Nepal 29.20N 81.57E
30 C5 Bhongaon Uttar Prad India 27.15N 79.11E
24 F11 Bhong Chu R Xizang Zizhiqu
28 D2 Bhongir Andhra Prad India 17.33N 78.55E
29 D6 Bhongra Rajasthan India 23.41N 74.32E
29 E6 Bhopal Madhya Prad India 23.17N 77.28E
28 E1 Bhopalpatnam Madhya Prad India 18.50N 80.26E
28 A1 Bhor Maharashtra India 18.10N 73.55E
30 G3 Bhote Kosi R Nepal
25 F2 B. Houei Sai Laos 20.20N 100.30E
30 F5 Bhowa Nepal 27.55N 82.04E
30 C3 Bhowali Uttar Prad India 29.22N 79.31E
58 F3 Bhraoin, L.a' Highland Scotland 57.43N 5.07W
29 J7 Bhuban Orissa India 20.52N 85.51E
29 J7 Bhubaneswar Orissa India 20.13N 85.50E
28 J3 Bhuban Hills Assam India
29 A6 Bhuj Gujarat India 23.12N 69.54E
30 K6 Bhulkia Nepal 26.47N 86.42E
25 E4 Bhumiphol Dam Thailand 17.20N 98.42E
30 A4 Bhundsi Haryana India 28.21N 77.03E
30 A3 Bhuni Uttar Prad India 29.08N 77.34E
28 H2 Bhurgaon Bhutan 26.55N 90.30E
29 D7 Bhusawal Maharashtra India 21.01N 75.50E
28 G2 Bhutan state S Asia
29 B4 Bhuttewala Rajasthan India 27.42N 70.50E
28 D5 Bhuvanagiri Tamil Nadu India 11.28N 79.38E
89 H8 Bia R Ivory Coast/Ghana
32 G7 Biabān coastal reg Iran
Biabanak see Baiāzeh
89 A3 Biach Mauritania 16.34N 16.17W
31 H3 Biafo Glacier Kashmir
Biafra see
E.Central, S.Eastern and Rivers States Nigeria
87 F3 Biagundi Ethiopia 14.28N 37.11E
15 D4 Biak Biak I, Irian Jaya 1.10S 136.05E
19 C4 Biak Celebes Indon 0.54S 122.54E
15 C4 Biak isld Irian Jaya
93 A5 Biakatu Zaïre 0.52N 29.17E
62 N2 Biała Piska Poland 53.38N 22.08E
62 O3 Biała Podlaska Poland 52.03N 23.05E
62 M4 Białobrzegi Poland 51.40N 20.55E
62 J1 Białogard Poland 54.00N 16.00E
62 O3 Białowieża Poland 52.41N 23.50E
62 K2 Biały Bór Poland 53.53N 16.50E
62 O2 Białystok Poland 53.09N 23.10E
90 M9 Biambaro Cent Afr Rep 5.12N 24.40E
15 F7 Bian R Irian Jaya
81 G9 Bianca,Pta Sicily 37.12N 13.39E
79 G6 Bianca,Pta pt Italy 44.02N 9.58E
81 J8 Biancavilla Sicily 37.38N 14.52E
81 M7 Bianco Italy 38.05N 16.10E
79 L5 Bianco canal Italy
66 R6 Bianco L Switzerland 46.25N 10.02E
81 F9 Bianco,C Sicily 37.23N 13.17E
66 H8 Bianco,Corno mt Italy 45.49N 7.54E
79 K1 Bianco,Corno mt Italy 46.48N 10.24E
66 H8 Bianco, Pizzo mt Italy 45.57N 7.56E
79 D4 Biandrate Italy 45.28N 8.27E
66 L8 Biandronno Italy 45.48N 8.43E
41 G3 Bianki,Ostrov isld U.S.S.R. 76.18N 98.00E
89 F8 Biankouma Ivory Coast 7.50N 7.40W
21 C7 Bianmen Liaoning China 40.23N 124.05E
66 B4 Bians-lès Usiers France 46.58N 6.17E
Bianu see Beyānlū
79 D4 Bianzè Italy 45.18N 8.07E
Bianzhuang see Cangshan
19 M8 Biao Mindanao Philippines 7.18N 125.29E
25 G3 Bia,Pou mt Laos 18.59N 103.11E
120 E1 Biá, R Brazil
77 P3 Biar Spain 38.38N 0.46W
88 J10 Biar Aguelt Ould Moissate Mauritania 23.16N 8.20W
33 C5 Bi'ār,Al Saudi Arabia 22.39N 39.41E
88 J10 Biar Amran Mauritania 22.44N 8.44W
91 F4 Biaranga Zaïre 1.48S 19.30E
86 M7 Biarat, El Egypt 29.15N 34.21E
88 M10 Biar en Nahrat Mali 22.56N 3.37W
34 G3 Biār Ghabagheb Syria 35.07N 39.42E
32 F2 Biārjmand Iran 36.05N 55.50E
19 D2 Biaro isld Indonesia 2.06N 125.22E
29 E6 Biarora Madhya Prad India 23.56N 76.56E
Biâr Rhabârheb see Biār Ghabagheb
72 A9 Biarritz France 43.29N 1.33W
72 B8 Biarrotte France 43.34N 1.16W
33 F4 Bi'ār Tabrāk Saudi Arabia 24.23N 45.55E
15 J8 Biaru Papua New Guinea 8.31S 146.22E
72 B7 Bias France 44.08N 1.13W
Bias Bay see Daya Wan
66 M6 Biasca Switzerland 46.22N 8.58E
Biask see Pey Beshk
19 C3 Biau Celebes Indonesia 0.59N 122.16E
42 B4 Biaza U.S.S.R. 56.39N 78.21E
20 L1 Bibai Japan 43.21N 141.53E
86 E4 Bibân Egypt 30.47N 30.40E
91 H7 Bibanga Zaïre 6.17S 23.55E
12 J6 Bibbenluke New S Wales 36.31S 148.52E
79 H5 Bibbiano Italy 44.40N 10.28E
79 L7 Bibbiena Italy 43.42N 11.49E
80 C2 Bibbona Italy 43.16N 10.36E
13 E5 Bibby R N Terr Australia
90 F7 Bibémi Cameroon 9.17N 13.53E
66 M1 Biber R W Ger/Switz
64 E7 Biberach W Germany 48.21N 8.02E
64 H7 Biberach an der Riss W Germany 48.06N 9.48E
64 K6 Biberbach W Germany 48.30N 10.49E
66 L3 Biberbrugg Switzerland 47.09N 8.43E
66 G3 Biberist Switzerland 47.11N 7.34E
64 K5 Bibert R W Germany
65 C7 Biberwier Austria 47.23N 10.53E
76 E4 Bibey R Spain
15 J6 Bibi Papua New Guinea 5.32S 146.01E
89 H8 Bibiani Ghana 6.30N 2.08W
30 L6 Bibiganj Bihar India 26.22N 87.46E
32 D6 Bibi Hakimeh oil well Iran 29.50N 50.50E
33 J2 Bibi Hakimeh oil field Iran 30.10N 50.25E
26 T7 Bibile Sri Lanka 7.09N 81.14E
31 J9 Bibiyana R Bangladesh
119 B9 Biblián Ecuador 2.43S 78.53W
64 E4 Biblis W Germany 49.41N 8.27E
64 J3 Bibra Suhl E Germany 50.28N 10.27E
14 A3 Bibra Lake W Australia 32.06S 115.49E
14 A3 Bibra Lake dist Perth, W Aust
28 D1 Bibra R Andhra Prad India
30 J3 Bibre Nepal 27.55N 86.52E
56 H4 Bibury Glos Eng 51.47N 1.49W
98 D5 Bic Quebec 48.23N 68.43W
83 D3 Bicaj Albania 42.00N 20.25E
118 G7 Bicas Brazil 21.44S 43.04W
82 K4 Bicaz Romania 46.53N 26.05E
82 K3 Bicaz Res Romania
80 M6 Biccari Italy 41.23N 15.12E
36 F3 Biçer Turkey 39.42N 31.42E
56 J4 Bicester Oxon Eng 51.54N 1.09W
29 C5 Bichabhera Rajasthan India 24.17N 73.26E
87 E7 Bichano Ethiopia 7.55N 35.32E
116 P2 Biche Trinidad & Tobago 10.26N 61.07W
100 E4 Biche,L.la Alberta
66 M2 Bichelsee Switzerland 47.27N 8.57E
44 G8 Bichenakskiy Pereval pass Armenia U.S.S.R.
12 J8 Bicheno Tasmania 41.50S 148.17E
71 D2 Biches France 47.00N 3.38E
40 G8 Bichevaya U.S.S.R. 47.49N 135.40E
90 D5 Bichi Cameroon 12.17N 8.15E
40 H5 Bichi R U.S.S.R.
30 E8 Bichia R Madhya Prad India
90 C7 Bichini Nigeria 9.34N 7.20E
64 L8 Bichl W Germany 47.43N 11.26E
65 C7 Bichlbach Austria 47.26N 10.47E
28 A3 Bicholim Goa India 15.36N 73.57E
30 H5 Bichraltar Nepal 27.48N 84.57E
Bichri,Jebel el mts see Bishri,Jebel el
42 H6 Bichura U.S.S.R. 50.38N 107.35E
45 T2 Bichurga-Baishevo U.S.S.R. 54.46N 47.16E
98 D5 Bic,I.du Quebec 48.25N 68.51W
13 D2 Bickerton I N Terr Australia
87 H6 Bicket Ethiopia 9.33N 41.10E
56 D6 Bickington Devon Eng 50.32N 3.42W
56 E6 Bickleigh Devon Eng 50.52N 3.30W
110 E3 Bickleton Washington 46.00N 120.18W
57 H6 Bickley Cheshire Eng 53.02N 2.41W
14 B2 Bickley Brook Perth, W Aust
104 D8 Bickmore W Virginia 38.23N 81.08W
107 J3 Bicknell Indiana 38.47N 87.19W
111 N3 Bicknell Utah 38.21N 111.34W
76 B5 Bico Portugal 41.53N 8.32W
79 F7 Bicocca dist Milan Italy
19 F3 Bicoli Halmahera Indon 0.35N 128.30E
77 P2 Bicorp Spain 39.08N 0.48W
62 L8 Bicske Hungary 47.30N 18.36E
90 B7 Bida Nigeria 9.06N 5.59E
72 B9 Bidache France 43.29N 1.08W
18 N3 Bidadari,Tanjong C Sabah Malaysia 5.50N 118.21E
33 H4 Bidah, Al area Saudi Arabia
32 E5 Bida Khabit Iran 31.32N 53.55E
34 L10 Bid',Al Saudi Arabia 28.15N 43.15E
33 K5 Bid'al-Matāw'ah U.A.E. 23.47N 52.34E
28 C2 Bidar Karnataka India 17.56N 77.35E
28 C2 Bidar dist Karnataka India
72 B9 Bidarray France 43.17N 1.20W
72 A9 Bidart France 43.26N 1.35W
75 G1 Bidassoa R Spain
33 N5 Bidbid Oman 23.25N 58.08E
104 P3 Biddeford Maine 43.29N 70.27W
56 N5 Biddenden Kent Eng 51.07N 0.39E
60 L10 Biddinghuizen Netherlands 52.27N 5.40E
35 D5 Biddiya Jordan 32.07N 35.04E
108 E4 Biddle Montana 45.04N 105.20W
35 D6 Biddu Jordan 31.50N 35.09E
57 J6 Biddulph Staffs Eng 53.08N 2.10W
87 G8 Biddwara Ethiopia 5.11N 38.34E
Biddya see Biddiya
58 F5 Bidean nam Bian mt Highland Scotland 56.39N 5.02W
56 C5 Bideford Devon Eng 51.01N 4.13W
Bideford B see Barnstaple B
29 D4 Bidesir Rajasthan India 27.50N 74.25E
36 J2 Bidevi Turkey 40.38N 36.23E
56 H3 Bidford Warwicks Eng 52.10N 1.51W
30 D6 Bidhnu Uttar Prad India 26.19N 80.17E
30 C6 Bidhuna Uttar Prad India 26.48N 79.30E
87 J10 Bidi Somalia 0.56N 42.38E
81 B2 Bidighinzu, L Sardinia 40.33N 8.40E
32 G6 Bidkhan, Kūh-e mt Iran 29.38N 56.30E
26 B16 Bidlingmaier,C Heard I Antarctica 53.01S 73.32E
32 H3 Bidokht Iran 34.16N 58.44E
88 O10 Bidon Cinq Algeria 22.13N 1.00E
18 B7 Bidor Pen Malaysia 4.00N 101.19E
72 B9 Bidouze R France
104 C8 Bidwell Ohio 38.54N 82.18W
40 E8 Bidzhan U.S.S.R. 47.59N 131.54E
40 E7 Bidzhan R U.S.S.R.
Bié Angola see Silva Porto
91 E10 Bié Angola 12.25S 16.58E
90 J8 Bie Cent Afr Rep 6.33N 18.03E
91 E10 Bié dist Angola
110 D8 Bieber California 41.08N 121.08W
64 G3 Bieber W Germany 50.09N 9.20E
64 G3 Biebergemünd W Germany 50.11N 9.16E
64 F2 Biebertal W Germany 50.30N 8.37E
69 Q2 Biebertal W Germany 50.37N 7.36E
69 P4 Biebesheim W Germany 49.47N 8.28E
64 E3 Biebrich W Germany 50.02N 8.14E
62 O2 Biebrza R Poland
62 N6 Biecz Poland 49.45N 21.14E
64 F2 Biedenkopf W Germany 50.55N 8.33E
63 P8 Biederitz E Germany 52.10N 11.44E
20 M1 Biei Japan 43.36N 142.30E
20 M1 Biei-gawa R Japan
66 F3 Biel Bern Switzerland 47.09N 7.16E
75 J3 Biel Spain 42.23N 0.56W
66 J6 Biel Valais Switzerland 46.27N 8.13E
100 Q7 Bield Manitoba 51.13N 101.11W
75 J3 Biel, De R Spain

58 M4 **Bieldside** Grampian Scotland 57.07N 2.12W
63 J8 **Bielefeld** W Germany 52.02N 8.32E
65 B8 **Bielerhöhe** *pass* Austria 46.55N 10.07E
66 E3 **Bieler See** *L* Switzerland
79 D3 **Biella** Italy 45.34N 8.04E
72 D9 **Bielle** France 43.03N 0.26W
75 L2 **Bielsa** Spain 42.38N 0.13E
62 L6 **Bielsko-Biała** Poland 49.50N 19.00E
62 O3 **Bielsk Podlaski** Poland 52.47N 23.11E
Biendorf *see* **Zweedorf**
63 M6 **Bienenbüttel** W Germany 53.08N 10.28E
100 P9 **Bienfait** Saskatchewan 49.09N 102.48W
91 D6 **Bienga** Zaïre 4.32S 14.04E
25 J7 **Bien Hoa** Vietnam 10.58N 106.50E
Bienne *see* **Biel** Bern
71 H4 **Bienne** *R* France
61 G5 **Bienne-lez-Happart** Belgium 50.21N 4.13E
66 L8 **Bieno** Italy 45.58N 8.31E
77 L3 **Bienservida** Spain 38.31N 2.37W
79 J7 **Bientina** Italy 43.43N 10.37E
77 D4 **Bienvenida** Spain 38.18N 6.12W
117 C3 **Bienvenue** Fr Guiana 3.07N 52.38W
107 D9 **Bienville** Louisiana 32.21N 92.58W
98 S8 **Bienville** Quebec 46.49N 71.10W
97 M6 **Bienville, Lac** Quebec 55.00N 73.30W
91 D10 **Bié Plat** Angola
23 E4 **Bi'er** Hunan China
13 H7 **Bierbank** Queensland 26.45S 145.02E
65 O7 **Bierbaum** Austria 47.06N 16.05E
61 K3 **Bierbeek** Belgium 50.50N 4.46E
61 H5 **Biercée** Belgium 50.20N 4.16E
66 B5 **Bière** Switzerland 46.33N 6.21E
61 G4 **Bierghes** Belgium 50.42N 4.09E
64 F7 **Bieringen** W Germany 48.27N 8.51E
48 T2 **Bierings Land,A** Greenland
70 J6 **Bierne** France 47.49N 0.32W
71 E1 **Bierry-les-Belles-Fontaines** France 47.36N 4.11E
61 M4 **Bierset** Belgium 50.39N 5.26E
53 D2 **Biersted** Denmark 57.09N 9.51E
72 G10 **Biert** France 42.55N 1.19E
60 Q6 **Bierum** Netherlands 53.23N 6.52E
60 B3 **Biervliet** Netherlands 51.20N 3.41E
61 L4 **Bierwart** Belgium 50.33N 5.02E
76 G3 **Bierzo,El** *dist* Spain
60 H12 **Biesbos** *fenland* Netherlands
75 K2 **Biescas** Spain 42.37N 0.20W
63 P7 **Biese** *R* E Germany
63 T7 **Biesenthal** E Germany 52.46N 13.39E
95 G7 **Biesiespoort** S Africa 31.43S 23.11E
95 J2 **Biesiesvlei** S Africa 26.22S 25.54E
69 J7 **Biesles** France 48.06N 5.18E
61 J5 **Biesme** Belgium 50.20N 4.37E
61 J5 **Biesmerée** Belgium 50.18N 4.40E
61 H5 **Biesme-sous-Thuin** Belgium 50.19N 4.19E
64 K8 **Biessenhofen** W Germany 47.50N 10.38E
64 E6 **Bietigheim** W Germany 48.54N 8.15E
64 G6 **Bietigheim-Bissingen** W Germany 48.58N 9.08E
63 T6 **Bietikow** E Germany 53.16N 13.57E
66 H6 **Bietschhorn** *mt* Switzerland 46.24N 7.52E
61 L7 **Bièvre** Belgium 49.56N 5.01E
68 D4 **Bièvres** France 48.45N 2.13E
61 J4 **Biez** Belgium 50.43N 4.43E
60 C3 **Biezelinge** Netherlands 51.28N 3.58E
62 M3 **Bieżun** Poland 52.59N 19.42E
80 L5 **Biferno** *R* Italy
66 M4 **Bifertenstock** *mt* Switzerland 46.47N 8.58E
21 J5 **Bifuka** Japan 44.30N 142.24E
113 K5 **Big** *R* Alaska
111 A2 **Big** *R* California
37 D3 **Biğa** Turkey 40.13N 27.14E
36 C3 **Bigadiç** Turkey 39.24N 28.08E
37 E1 **Biğados** Turkey 41.04N 28.22E
86 Q11 **Bigâm** Cairo Egypt
72 C6 **Biganos** France 44.40N 0.59W
110 L2 **Big Arm** Montana 47.48N 114.17W
77 P4 **Bigastro** Spain 38.04N 0.54W
11 C11 **Big B** New Zealand
110 P3 **Big Baldy Mt** Montana 46.59N 110.36W
101 M10 **Big Bar Creek** Br Columbia 51.12N 122.08W
106 G3 **Big Bay** Michigan 46.49N 87.42W
111 H7 **Big Bear City** California 34.14N 116.53W
112 N9 **Big Bear Creek** Texas
111 H7 **Big Bear L** California 34.15N 116.58W
100 M9 **Big Beaver** Saskatchewan 49.05N 105.09W
99 H3 **Big Beaver Falls** Ontario 49.15N 82.32W
97 L7 **Big Beaver House** Ontario 52.59N 89.50W
14 C7 **Big Bell** W Australia 17.20S 117.35E
110 O3 **Big Belt Mts** Montana
26 A16 **Big Ben** *vol* Heard I Antarctica 53.05S 73.30E
110 D8 **Big Bend** California 41.01N 121.55W
109 H3 **Big Bend** Colorado 38.12N 102.46W
95 O8 **Big Bend** Swaziland 26.48S 31.56E
112 D6 **Big Bend Nat. Park** Texas
107 G8 **Big Black** *R* Mississippi
105 G3 **Big Black Cr** S Carolina
104 C10 **Big Black Mt** Virginia 36.53N 82.55W
109 O2 **Big Blue** *R* Kansas
56 D7 **Bigbury B** Devon Eng
56 D7 **Bigbury on Sea** Devon Eng 51.17N 3.53W
57 N5 **Bigby** Lincs Eng 53.34N 0.24W
112 E5 **Big Canyon** *R* Texas
98 E3 **Big Caotibi L** Quebec
111 M6 **Big Chino Wash** *crater* Arizona
107 K4 **Big Clifty** Kentucky 37.30N 86.10W
101 M10 **Big Creek** Br Columbia 51.42N 123.02W
110 K4 **Big Creek** Idaho 45.08N 115.20W
109 K3 **Big Creek** Kansas
104 C8 **Big Creek** W Virginia 38.01N 82.03W
105 F11 **Big Cypress Swamp** Florida
113 P4 **Big Delta** Alaska 64.10N 145.55W
108 D2 **Big Dry Cr** Montana
106 E5 **Big Eau Pleine Res** Wisconsin
9 B3 **Bigej** *islet* Marshall Is Pacific Ocean 8.52N 167.46E
110 O6 **Big Elk Mt** Idaho 43.14N 111.13W
109 O2 **Bigelow** Kansas 39.38N 96.30W
91 D2 **Bigéné** Cent Afr Rep 3.26N 15.34E
22 D4 **Biger** Mongolia 45.40N 97.11E
22 D4 **Biger Nuur** *L* Mongolia
108 R1 **Big Falls** Minnesota 48.12N 93.50W
108 R2 **Bigfork** Minnesota 47.44N 94.35W
110 L1 **Bigfork** Montana 48.05N 114.05W
112 M9 **Big Fossil Creek** Texas
100 K6 **Biggar** Saskatchewan 52.03N 107.59W
58 J7 **Biggar** Strathclyde Scotland 55.38N 3.32W
95 N4 **Biggarsberg** S Africa 28.15S 29.58E
95 N4 **Biggarsberg** *mts* S Africa
64 D1 **Bigge** *R* W Germany
14 F2 **Bigge I** W Australia 14.35S 125.14E
60 B3 **Biggekerke** Netherlands 51.30N 3.31E
51 K2 **Biggeluobbal** Norway 69.23N 23.25E
13 K7 **Biggenden** Queensland 25.30S 152.00E
63 H10 **Bigge-Olsberg** W Germany 51.22N 8.30E
101 E6 **Bigger,Mt** Br Columbia 59.21N 136.38W
107 F5 **Biggers** Arkansas 36.20N 90.49W
56 L3 **Biggleswade** Beds Eng 52.05N 0.17W
111 C2 **Biggs** California 39.27N 121.44W
110 E4 **Biggs** Oregon 45.40N 120.50W
106 D9 **Biggsville** Illinois 40.52N 90.52W
30 D6 **Bighapur** Uttar Prad India 26.20N 80.40E
109 B10 **Big Hatchet Pk** New Mexico 31.37N 108.23W
100 C7 **Big Hill Springs Prov. Park** Alberta
110 N4 **Big Hole** *R* Montana
110 M4 **Big Hole Battlefield Nat. Mon** Montana 45.39N 113.39W
108 C3 **Bighorn** Montana 46.09N 107.24W
108 C4 **Bighorn** *R* Montana/Wyoming
110 R4 **Bighorn Lake** *res* Montana/Wyoming
108 C5 **Bighorn Mts** Montana/Wyoming
89 L9 **Bight of Benin** W Africa
116 G2 **Bight,The** Cat I Bahamas 24.20N 75.25W
107 E8 **Big I** Arkansas 33.55N 91.05W
101 P5 **Big I** Gt Slave L, N W Terr 61.08N 116.42W
97 M5 **Big I** N W Terr 62.45N 70.30W
100 G1 **Big I** Ontario 49.10N 94.40W
91 H2 **Bigi** Zaïre 3.02N 22.25E
9 A3 **Bigi** *islet* Marshall Is Pacific Oc 9.17N 167.21E
103 F2 **Big Indian** New York 42.06N 74.27W
104 F9 **Big Island** Virginia 37.33N 79.24W
101 F4 **Big Kalzas L** Yukon Terr 63.10N 134.48W
113 H9 **Big Koniuji I** Alaska 55.10N 159.35W
110 E7 **Big L** Oregon 42.07N 120.01W
113 N3 **Big Lake** Alaska 67.30N 149.40W
104 S1 **Big Lake** Maine
101 R3 **Big Lake** N W Terr 64.54N 112.40W
99 H7 **Big Lake** Ontario 45.46N 82.05W
112 F4 **Big Lake** Texas 31.12N 101.29W
66 G4 **Biglen** Switzerland 46.56N 7.39E
104 H7 **Biglerville** Pennsylvania 39.56N 77.15W
110 M6 **Big Lost Rover** Idaho
11 B13 **Big Moggy I** New Zealand 47.09S 167.25E
104 L3 **Big Moose** New York 43.49N 74.57W
108 F1 **Big Muddy Cr** Montana
100 N9 **Big Muddy L** Saskatchewan
70 E6 **Bignan** France 47.53N 2.46W
66 L6 **Bignasco** Switzerland 46.21N 8.36E
89 A5 **Bignona** Senegal 12.48N 16.18W
79 C7 **Bignone,Monte** Italy 43.53N 7.44E
72 A1 **Bignon,le** France 47.07N 1.30W
93 C5 **Bigo** *hist site* Uganda 0.10N 31.19E
92 C4 **Bigobo** Zaïre 5.29S 27.36E
61 O7 **Bigonville** Luxembourg 49.52N 5.47E
76 D6 **Bigorne** Portugal 41.01N 7.53W
72 D9 **Bigorre** *reg* France
104 F9 **Big Otter** *R* Virginia
111 F4 **Big Pine** California 37.10N 118.18W
105 F13 **Big Pine** Florida 24.41N 81.21W
108 P3 **Big Pine L** Minnesota
111 E7 **Big Pine Pk** *mt* California 34.41N 119.39W
110 P7 **Big Piney** Wyoming 42.32N 110.06W
107 D4 **Big Piney** *R* Missouri
98 M8 **Big Pond** C Breton I, N S 45.54N 60.32W
103 A3 **Big Pond** Pennsylvania 41.54N 76.43W
106 J6 **Big Rapids** Michigan 43.42N 85.31W
106 E4 **Big Rib** *R* Wisconsin
100 K5 **Big River** Saskatchewan 53.50N 107.01W
110 E8 **Big Sage Res** California 41.36N 120.39W
101 F5 **Big Salmon** Yukon Terr 61.53N 134.55W
101 F5 **Big Salmon** *R* Yukon Terr
110 P1 **Big Sandy** Montana 48.11N 110.06W
107 H5 **Big Sandy** Tennessee 36.13N 88.07W
112 M3 **Big Sandy** Texas 32.36N 95.06W
110 Q7 **Big Sandy** Wyoming 42.37N 109.27W
111 L7 **Big Sandy** *R* Arizona
104 C8 **Big Sandy** *R* West Virginia/Kentucky
109 F2 **Big Sandy Cr** Colorado
110 P1 **Big Sandy Cr** Montana
108 R3 **Big Sandy L** Minnesota
100 N4 **Big Sandy L** Saskatchewan 54.27N 104.08W
110 Q7 **Big Sandy Res** Wyoming 42.15N 109.22W
100 H1 **Bigsby I** Ontario
108 O5 **Big Sioux** *R* S Dakota
111 G3 **Big Smoky Valley** Nevada
110 Q3 **Big Snowy Mt** Montana 46.46N 109.21W
11 B13 **Big South Cape I** Stewart I New Zealand 47.14S 167.24E
112 F3 **Big Spring** Texas 32.15N 101.30W
110 O5 **Big Springs** Idaho 44.31N 111.14W
108 H8 **Big Springs** Nebraska 41.04N 102.04W
100 H8 **Bigstick L** Saskatchewan 50.17N 109.20W
108 O4 **Big Stone City** S Dakota 45.17N 96.29W
104 C10 **Big Stone Gap** Virginia 36.52N 82.46W
100 W5 **Bigstone Lake** Manitoba
108 O4 **Big Stone Lake** S Dakota/Minnesota
100 W3 **Bigstone R** Manitoba
111 C5 **Big Sur** California 36.15N 121.47W
56 F4 **Bigsweir Bridge** Glos Eng 51.45N 2.40W
110 Q4 **Big Timber** Montana 45.50N 109.57W
108 C6 **Bigtrails** Wyoming 43.48N 107.19W
97 L7 **Big Trout L** Ontario 53.40N 90.00W
97 L7 **Big Trout Lake** Ontario 53.45N 90.00W
118 E10 **Biguaçú** Brazil 27.30S 48.50W
75 H2 **Biguezal** Spain 42.41N 1.10W
67 P11 **Biguglia, Etang de** *lagoon* Corsica 42.35N 9.28E
100 E6 **Big Valley** Alberta 52.03N 112.42W
92 J5 **Bigwa** Tanzania 7.12S 39.09E
112 H7 **Big Wells** Texas 28.34N 99.36W
111 M6 **Big Williams Mt** Arizona 35.12N 112.12W
107 L7 **Big Wills Cr** Alabama
99 K6 **Bigwood** Ontario 46.02N 80.36W
82 C6 **Bihac** Yugoslavia 44.49N 15.53E
61 O6 **Bihain** Belgium 50.14N 5.49E
93 B5 **Bihanga** Uganda 0.12N 30.36E
30 J7 **Bihar** Bihar India 25.13N 85.31E
29 J5 **Bihar** *state* India
93 C8 **Biharamulo** Tanzania 2.37S 31.20E
30 K7 **Bihariganj** Bihar India 25.44N 86.59E
30 C7 **Bihat** Uttar Prad India 25.26N 79.21E
87 M5 **Bihen** Somalia 10.36N 48.21E
87 M6 **Bihen** Somalia 8.21N 48.19E
87 K5 **Bihendula** Somalia 10.10N 45.10E
82 G4 **Bihor** *div* Romania
82 H4 **Bihor** *mt* Romania 46.26N 22.43E
21 K6 **Bihoro** Japan 43.50N 144.06E
82 G4 **Bihorului, Munţii** *mts* Romania
30 K7 **Bihpur** Bihar India 25.26N 86.57E
28 J2 **Bihpuriagaon** Assam India 27.03N 93.54E
30 H7 **Bihta** Bihar India 25.34N 84.51E
23 H4 **Bihu** Zhejiang China 28.22N 119.48E
64 F8 **Biisslingen** W Germany 47.47N 8.42E
29 D7 **Bijagarh** Madhya Prad India 21.39N 75.29E
89 A6 **Bijagós,Arquipélago Dos** Guinea-Bissau
28 E1 **Bijaipur** Bastar, Madhya Prad India 18.48N 80.55E
30 A6 **Bijaipur** Morena, Madhya Prad India 26.03N 77.22E
30 F7 **Bijaipur** Uttar Prad India 25.07N 82.23E
28 B2 **Bijapur** Karnataka India 16.47N 75.48E
28 B2 **Bijapur** *dist* Karnataka India
32 B3 **Bijār** Iran 35.52N 47.39E
29 J7 **Bijarakot** Orissa India 21.15N 85.08E
30 F4 **Bijauri** Nepal 28.07N 82.22E
30 C8 **Bijawar** Madhya Prad India 24.36N 79.30E
82 B5 **Bijela Lasica** *mt* Yugoslavia 45.15N 14.59E
82 E6 **Bijeljina** Yugoslavia 44.46N 19.14E
82 F7 **Bijelo Polje** Yugoslavia 43.03N 19.42E
29 G6 **Bijeraghogarh** Madhya Prad India 23.59N 80.41E
87 K5 **Biji** Somalia 10.15N 44.04E
23 A5 **Bijiang** Yunnan China 22.56N 113.15E
23 D5 **Bijie** Guizhou China 27.19N 105.22E
Bijistan *see* **Bejestān**
28 E1 **Bijji** Madhya Prad India 18.04N 81.26E
30 C7 **Bijna** Uttar Prad India 25.28N 79.02E
32 H7 **Bijnābād** Iran 27.57N 58.04E
30 D6 **Bijnaur** Uttar Prad India 26.44N 80.54E
28 H2 **Bijni** Assam India 26.30N 90.40E
30 B3 **Bijnor** Uttar Prad India 29.22N 78.09E
30 B3 **Bijnor** *dist* Uttar Prad India
31 F6 **Bijnot** Pakistan 28.04N 71.42E
29 D5 **Bijolia** Rajasthan India 25.08N 75.22E
108 L6 **Bijou Hills** S Dakota 43.30N 99.10W
29 M2 **Bijpur** W Bengal India 22.56N 88.27E
33 J4 **Bijrān** Saudi Arabia 24.04N 50.56E
30 D4 **Bijua** Uttar Prad India 28.17N 80.37E
30 F8 **Bijul** *R* Uttar Prad India
Bik *see* **Ban Bik**
29 C4 **Bikampur** Rajasthan India 27.43N 72.12E
29 C3 **Bikaner** Rajasthan India 28.01N 73.22E
29 C3 **Bikaner** *dist* Rajasthan India
30 F6 **Bikapur** Uttar Prad India 26.35N 82.09E
9 D1 **Bikar** *atoll* Marshall Is Pacific Oc 12.13N 170.05E
43 F4 **Bikbauli** Kazakhstan U.S.S.R. 45.57N 61.56E
34 C5 **Bikfaya** Lebanon 33.55N 35.40E
32 F7 **Bikhū** Iran 27.54N 55.11E
87 A8 **Biki** *watercourse* Sudan
40 F8 **Bikin** U.S.S.R. 46.52N 134.15E
9 B1 **Bikini** *atoll* Marshall Is Pacific Oc 11.35N 165.20E
92 E12 **Bikita** Zimbabwe 20.06S 31.41E
92 E12 **Bikita** *dist* Zimbabwe
93 C4 **Bikonzi** Uganda 1.35N 31.40E
87 E5 **Bikori** Sudan 11.06N 34.39E
91 F4 **Bikoro** Zaïre 0.45S 18.09E
91 D5 **Bikou** Congo 2.59S 14.23E
30 H7 **Bikramganj** Bihar India 25.13N 84.15E
61 B3 **Bikschote** Belgium 50.55N 2.52E
62 L6 **Bílá** Czechoslovakia 49.27N 18.25E
30 C8 **Bila** *R* Madhya Prad India
19 M7 **Bilaa Pt** Mindanao Philippines 9.45N 125.25E
Bilabad *see* **Balābād, Gardaneh-ye** *pass*
37 F3 **Bilada Yunus** Turkey 40.16N 29.06E
33 N5 **Bilād Banī Bū Hasan** Oman 22.02N 59.18E
33 D6 **Bilād Ghāmid** *dist* Saudi Arabia
33 D6 **Bilād Zahrān** *dist* Saudi Arabia
90 J8 **Bilague** Cent Afr Rep 7.48N 18.55E
21 B3 **Bila He** *R* Nei Monggol Zizhiqu China
29 H7 **Bilaigarh** Madhya Prad India 21.37N 82.47E
86 K8 **Bilaiyim,El** *inlet* Egypt 28.32N 33.17E
86 K8 **Bilaiyim,El** *oil well* Egypt 28.34N 33.18E
88 O9 **Bilal** Algeria 24.20N 1.13E
35 G6 **Bilal** Jordan 31.58N 35.48E
91 C6 **Bilala** Congo 4.26S 12.15E
89 J5 **Bilanga** Upper Volta 12.40N 0.01W
18 N4 **Bilangbilangan** *isld* Indonesia 1.57N 118.50E
31 J3 **Bilaphond Pass** Kashmir 35.26N 76.59E
29 C4 **Bilara** Rajasthan India 26.10N 73.48E
30 B4 **Bilari** Uttar Prad India 28.37N 78.48E
30 G6 **Bilariaganj** Uttar Prad India 26.13N 83.13E
34 E4 **Bil'as,Jebel** *mts* Syria
30 E5 **Bilaspur** Bahraich, Uttar Prad India 27.51N 82.00E
30 A4 **Bilaspur** Bulandshahr, Uttar Prad India 28.24N 77.37E
30 A2 **Bilaspur** Haryana India 30.18N 77.18E
29 E2 **Bilaspur** Himachal Prad India 31.18N 76.48E
29 H6 **Bilaspur** Madhya Prad India 22.03N 82.12E
29 E2 **Bilaspur** *dist* Himachal Prad India
29 G6 **Bilaspur** *dist* Madhya Prad India
19 J9 **Bilatan** *isld* Philippines 4.58N 120.00E
92 D2 **Bilati** Zaïre 0.34S 28.49E
19 C3 **Bilato** Celebes Indonesia 0.33N 122.40E
25 E5 **Bilauktaung Ra** Burma/Thailand
30 D4 **Bilauri** Nepal 28.41N 80.20E
75 E1 **Bilbao** Spain 43.15N 2.56W
86 G5 **Bilbeis** Egypt 30.25N 31.34E
58 K2 **Bilbster** Highland Scotland 58.27N 3.13W
42 J6 **Bil'chir** Chita U.S.S.R. 51.03N 110.40E
56 N3 **Bildeston** Suffolk Eng 52.06N 0.54E
50 B3 **Bildudalur** Iceland 65.41N 23.35W
82 E8 **Bileća** Yugoslavia 42.54N 18.24E
37 H3 **Bilecik** Turkey 40.10N 29.59E
82 G5 **Biled** Romania 45.51N 21.00E
30 E5 **Bilehra** Uttar Prad India 27.14N 81.16E
87 E6 **Bilei** Ethiopia 8.36N 34.59E
62 K7 **Bílé Karpaty** *mts* Czechoslovakia
12 M5 **Bilgola** *dist* Sydney, N S W 33.39S 151.19E
62 O5 **Biłgoraj** Poland 50.31N 22.41E
30 D5 **Bilgram** Uttar Prad India 27.10N 80.03E
29 G6 **Bilheri** Madhya Prad India 23.47N 80.18E
31 D4 **Bilhu** Afghanistan 33.02N 67.28E
91 J1 **Bili** Zaïre 4.08N 25.04E
91 H1 **Bili** *R* Zaïre
39 H1 **Bilibino** U.S.S.R. 68.02N 166.15E
92 K8 **Bilibiza** Mozambique 12.30S 40.20E
93 L6 **Biliftu** Kenya 0.25S 39.43E
47 M4 **Bilimbai** U.S.S.R. 56.58N 59.50E
25 D4 **Bilin** Burma 17.14N 97.12E
64 Q2 **Bílina** *R* Czechoslovakia
81 M2 **Bilioso** *R* Italy
41 O7 **Bilir** U.S.S.R. 65.33N 131.44E
40 F2 **Bilir** *R* Yakutsk U.S.S.R.
41 Q5 **Bilir** *R* Yakutsk U.S.S.R.
19 M6 **Biliran** *isld* Philippines
83 D4 **Bilisht** Albania 40.37N 20.59E
18 N3 **Bilit** Sabah Malaysia 5.25N 118.10E
21 B8 **Biliu He** *R* Liaoning China
108 E6 **Bill** Wyoming 43.16N 105.16W
14 B7 **Billabalong** W Australia 27.25S 115.48E
Billabong *R see* **Moulamein** *R*
68 D4 **Billancourt** France 48.50N 2.15E
87 G7 **Billate,R** Ethiopia
54 C2 **Bill Baileys Bank** N Atlantic Oc
Billē *see* **Zībār**
70 H5 **Billé** France 48.17N 1.15W
63 M5 **Bille** *R* W Germany
63 N7 **Billerbeck** Niedersachsen W Germany 52.52N 10.54E
63 F9 **Billerbeck** Nordrhein-Westfalen W Germany 51.59N 7.19E
56 M4 **Billericay** Essex Eng 51.38N 0.25E
56 K2 **Billesdon** Leics Eng 52.37N 0.55W
30 F8 **Billi** Uttar Prad India 24.30N 82.59E
71 H4 **Billiat** France 46.04N 5.48E
64 G5 **Billigheim** W Germany 49.21N 9.16E
14 G4 **Billiluna** W Australia 19.34S 127.10E
90 K2 **Billinga** *salt L* Chad 19.30N 20.10E
57 N7 **Billingborough** Lincs Eng 52.54N 0.20W
52 G11 **Billinge** Sweden 55.56N 13.20E
53 X14 **Billingen** Norway 62.01N 7.52E
57 L3 **Billingham** Cleveland Eng 54.36N 1.17W
57 N6 **Billinghay** Lincs Eng 53.05N 0.18W
110 R4 **Billings** Montana 45.47N 108.30W
103 G3 **Billings** New York 41.41N 73.45W
109 N5 **Billings** Oklahoma 36.32N 97.27W
39 K1 **Billingsa Mys** *C* U.S.S.R. 69.54N 176.13E
99 D9 **Billings Bridge** Ontario 45.24N 75.40W
56 L5 **Billingshurst** W Sussex Eng 51.01N 0.28W
56 G3 **Billingsley** Shropshire Eng 52.28N 2.26W
Billiton *isld see* **Belitung**
71 C5 **Billom** France 45.43N 3.20E
95 H9 **Billson** S Africa 34.00S 24.37E
53 A5 **Billum** Denmark 55.38N 8.20E
53 C5 **Billund** Denmark 55.44N 9.07E
111 L7 **Bill Williams** *R* Arizona
71 C4 **Billy** France 46.14N 3.26E
41 O7 **Billyakh** *R* U.S.S.R.
42 H2 **Billyakh Porog** *falls* U.S.S.R. 62.00N 109.50E
69 K5 **Billy-sous-Mangiennes** France 49.20N 5.35E
71 C2 **Billy-sur-Oisy** France 47.29N 3.24E
90 F2 **Bilma** Niger 18.46N 12.59E
87 F6 **Bilo** Ethiopia 8.52N 36.58E
13 K6 **Biloela** Queensland 24.21S 150.30E
82 D5 **Bilo Gora** *mts* Yugoslavia
117 A4 **Biloku** Guyana 1.47N 58.29W
28 C1 **Biloli** Maharashtra India 18.47N 77.42E
91 D2 **Bilolo** Cameroon 3.26N 15.53E
107 H11 **Biloxi** Mississippi 30.24N 88.55W
13 E7 **Bilpamorea Claypan** Queensland
86 F3 **Bilqâs Qism Auwal** Egypt 31.14N 31.22E
14 C5 **Bilroth,Mt** W Australia 21.47S 117.35E
30 C4 **Bilsanda** Uttar Prad India 28.14N 79.56E
30 E6 **Bilsar** Uttar Prad India 26.58N 81.54E
29 L2 **Bilsara** W Bengal India 23.05N 88.10E
58 M7 **Bilsdean** Lothian Scotland 55.57N 2.23W
30 B4 **Bilsi** Uttar Prad India 28.08N 78.52E
61 O4 **Bilstain** Belgium 50.37N 5.55E
64 E1 **Bilstein** W Germany 51.06N 8.01E
56 G2 **Bilston** W Midlands Eng 52.34N 2.04W
86 E3 **Biltag** Egypt 31.00N 31.00E
86 F5 **Biltân** Egypt 30.23N 31.10E
60 J11 **Bilt,de** Netherlands 52.06N 5.11E
66 N3 **Bilten** Switzerland 47.09N 9.02E
60 J11 **Bilthoven** Netherlands 52.07N 5.12E
30 G6 **Bilthra** Uttar Prad India 26.08N 83.53E
90 K4 **Biltine** Chad 14.30N 20.53E
90 K4 **Biltine** *div* Chad
51 J2 **Bilto** Norway 69.26N 21.35E
25 D4 **Bilugyun I** Burma
Biluk *see* **Bolūk**
115 N2 **Bilwascarma** Nicaragua 14.43N 83.51W
45 W2 **Bilyarsk** U.S.S.R. 54.59N 50.24E
61 N3 **Bilzen** Belgium 50.52N 5.31E
18 N10 **Bima** Indonesia 8.24S 118.44E
91 J2 **Bima** Zaïre 3.25N 25.13E
91 J2 **Bima** *R* Zaïre
18 N10 **Bima, Teluk** *B* Indonesia
85 M7 **Bimbân** Egypt 24.24N 32.54E
91 D9 **Bimbe** Angola 11.50S 15.50E
12 J6 **Bimberi, Mt** New S Wales 35.40S 148.48E
89 K7 **Bimbila** Ghana 8.54N 0.05E
90 J9 **Bimbo** Cent Afr Rep 4.15N 18.33E
12 F4 **Bimbowrie** S Australia 32.03S 140.15E
76 F2 **Bimeda** Spain 43.05N 6.32W
76 H2 **Bimenes** Spain 43.20N 5.34W
28 D1 **Bimgal** Andhra Prad India 18.44N 78.28E
105 H12 **Bimini,North** *isld* Bahamas 25.46N 79.14W
105 H12 **Bimini,South** *isld* Bahamas 25.43N 79.15W
28 F2 **Bimlipatam** Andhra Prad India 17.54N 83.31E
29 K6 **Bimpur** W Bengal India 22.36N 87.00E
35 E2 **Bi'na** Israel 32.56N 35.16E
29 F5 **Bina** Madhya Prad India 24.09N 78.10E
34 Q2 **Binab** Iran 36.34N 48.42E
75 L4 **Binaced** Spain 41.50N 0.12E
31 B5 **Binadar Miana** Afghanistan 30.15N 63.56E
66 M8 **Binago** Italy 45.47N 8.55E
33 J2 **Binak** *oil well* Iran 29.46N 50.28E
19 L6 **Binalbagan** Philippines 10.14N 122.54E
32 H2 **Bīnālūd, Kūh-e** *mts* Iran
19 J2 **Biñan** Luzon Philippines 14.21N 121.06E
19 J2 **Binangonan** Luzon Philippines 14.28N 121.11E
89 B5 **Binar** Guinea-Bissau 12.09N 15.42W
32 H3 **Binar** *pass* Iran 34.05N 58.39E
70 N6 **Binas** France 47.54N 1.28E
79 F4 **Binasco** Italy 45.20N 9.06E
18 J4 **Binatang** Sarawak Malaysia 2.09N 111.37E
30 A3 **Binauli** Uttar Prad India 29.06N 77.24E
30 D6 **Binaur** Uttar Prad India 26.23N 80.08E
13 J5 **Binbee** Queensland 20.20S 147.55E
36 J4 **Binboğa** *mt* Turkey 38.20N 36.30E
57 N6 **Binbrook** Lincs Eng 53.27N 0.10W
61 G5 **Binche** Belgium 50.25N 4.10E
23 B6 **Binchuan** Yunnan China 25.51N 100.34E
30 J7 **Bind** Bihar India 25.18N 85.42E
89 D5 **Binda** Mali 12.30N 10.32W
Bindaban *see* **Vrindavan**
13 J7 **Bindango** Queensland 26.30S 148.30E
53 C5 **Bindeballe** Denmark 55.40N 9.17E
90 G7 **Binder** Chad 9.56N 14.27E
22 H2 **Binder** Mongolia 48.35N 110.12E
90 G7 **Binder Nairi** Chad 9.36N 14.39E
61 L3 **Binderveld** Belgium 50.52N 5.10E
91 F5 **Bindja** Zaïre 3.23S 19.40E
30 D6 **Bindki** Uttar Prad India 26.02N 80.34E
13 J8 **Bindle** Queensland 27.40S 148.40E
Bindloe I *see* **Marchena, I**
100 G8 **Bindloss** Alberta 50.55N 110.13W
29 H7 **Bindra Nawagarh** Madhya Prad India 20.40N 82.12E
92 E10 **Bindura** Zimbabwe 17.20S 31.21E
92 E10 **Bindura** *dist* Zimbabwe
89 J6 **Binduri** Ghana 10.59N 0.16W
75 L4 **Binéfar** Spain 41.51N 0.17E
90 H2 **Binem-Arna** Chad 18.47N 17.49E
72 C9 **Binet** *mt* France 43.05N 0.30W
59 J1 **Binevenagh** *mt* Londonderry N Ireland 55.06N 6.55W
108 M2 **Binford** N Dakota 47.33N 98.21W
91 G2 **Binga** Zaïre 2.17N 20.33E
92 C10 **Binga** Zimbabwe 17.40S 27.22E
92 C10 **Binga** *dist* Zimbabwe
19 K3 **Binga Dam** Luzon Philippines 16.20N 120.43E
92 F11 **Binga Mt** Mozambique/Zimbabwe 19.47S 33.03E
12 K3 **Bingara** New S Wales 29.51S 150.38E
13 G8 **Bingara** Queensland 28.00S 144.52E
64 D4 **Bingen** W Germany 49.58N 7.55E
109 M6 **Binger** Oklahoma 35.20N 98.22W
89 H9 **Bingerville** Ivory Coast 5.20N 3.53W
71 G2 **Binges** France 47.20N 5.15E
104 Q1 **Bingham** Maine 45.03N 69.53W
106 J5 **Bingham** Michigan 44.53N 85.40W
108 H7 **Bingham** Nebraska 42.03N 102.06W
109 D8 **Bingham** New Mexico 33.54N 106.22W
57 M7 **Bingham** Notts Eng 52.57N 0.57W
110 N9 **Bingham Canyon** Utah 40.33N 112.09W
103 C2 **Binghamton** New York 42.06N 75.55W
85 C7 **Bin Ghunaymah, Jabal** *mts* Libya
92 D2 **Bingi** Zaïre 0.24S 29.02E
34 N3 **Bingird** Iraq 35.22N 45.48E
26 Q6 **Bingiriya** Sri Lanka 7.32N 79.54E
18 M3 **Bingkor** Sabah Malaysia 5.26N 116.15E
99 K4 **Bingle** Ontario 48.58N 80.23W
57 K5 **Bingley** W Yorks Eng 53.51N 1.50W
Bingmei *see* **Congjiang**
37 E7 **Bingöl** Turkey 38.54N 40.29E
37 F6 **Bingöl Dağları** *mts* Turkey
90 K9 **Binguéré** Cent Afr Rep 5.13N 20.35E
23 A5 **Bingzhongluo** Yunnan China 27.58N 98.31E
23 H2 **Binhai** Jiangsu China 34.00N 119.51E
56 N2 **Binham** Norfolk Eng 52.55N 0.56E
Binh Dinh *see* **An Nhon**
25 H7 **Binh Minh** Vietnam 10.02N 105.50E
25 K5 **Binh Son** Vietnam 15.18N 108.47E
28 K2 **Bini** Assam India 27.39N 94.08E
33 B3 **Binī, Al** Saudi Arabia 26.21N 36.49E
77 Y14 **Binibeca, C** Balearic Is 39.49N 4.14E
70 E4 **Binic** France 48.36N 2.50W
90 J1 **Bini Erdi** Chad 20.06N 18.01E
75 J2 **Biniés** Spain 42.38N 0.49W
90 J1 **Bini Gui** Chad 20.10N 18.04E
77 V14 **Binisalem** Balearic Is 39.41N 2.50E
18 C4 **Binjai** Sumatra Indon 3.37N 98.30E
90 B5 **Binji** Nigeria 13.10N 4.55E
29 H7 **Binka** Orissa India 21.02N 83.51E
61 K3 **Binkom** Belgium 50.52N 4.53E
56 J3 **Binley** W Midlands Eng 52.25N 1.26W
66 J6 **Binn** Switzerland 46.22N 8.12E
12 J4 **Binnaway** New S Wales 31.31S 148.51E
66 J6 **Binnen Tal** *V* Switzerland
66 G1 **Binningen** Switzerland 47.32N 7.35E
19 D6 **Binongko** *isld* Indonesia 5.58S 124.00E
29 K3 **Binpur** W Bengal India 22.35N 86.56E
91 D6 **Binsa** Zaïre 5.41S 15.27E
100 Q8 **Binscarth** Manitoba 50.38N 101.18W
11 F10 **Binser** *mt* New Zealand 43.02S 171.52E
64 B4 **Binsfeld** W Germany 49.58N 6.42E
Bint *see* **Bent**
18 F5 **Bintan** *isld* Indonesia
18 A6 **Bintang, Gunong** *mt* Pen Malaysia 5.25N 100.50E
19 C3 **Bintauna** Celebes Indon 0.55N 123.53E
19 K5 **Bintuan** Philippines 12.01N 120.04E
18 E8 **Bintuhan** Sumatra Indon 4.49S 103.22E
18 K4 **Bintulu** Sarawak Malaysia 3.12N 113.01E
15 B5 **Bintumi, Teluk** *B* Irian Jaya
19 K5 **Binubusan** Luzon Philippines 13.59N 120.37E
21 D5 **Bin Xian** Heilongjiang China 45.44N 127.28E
23 E1 **Bin Xian** Shaanxi China 35.00N 108.10E
22 L8 **Bin Xian** Shandong China 37.31N 117.58E
12 H5 **Binya** New S Wales 34.14S 146.22E
35 C3 **Binyamina** Israel 32.32N 34.57E
23 E7 **Binyang** Guangxi China 23.15N 108.40E
90 B6 **Bin Yauri** Nigeria 10.46N 4.45E
63 T4 **Binz** E Germany 54.24N 13.37E
66 G1 **Binzen** W Germany 47.38N 7.37E
Binzhou *see* **Bin Xian**
91 E3 **Bio** Congo 1.43N 16.39E
121 A6 **Bío-Bío** *prov* Chile
121 A6 **Bío-Bío** *R* Chile
82 F8 **Bioča** Yugoslavia 42.56N 19.51E
88 N5 **Biod, El** Algeria 33.49N 0.09W
88 K8 **Biodh,El** Algeria 26.05N 6.26W
66 M7 **Bioggio** Switzerland 46.02N 8.55E
79 D3 **Bioglio** Italy 45.37N 8.06E
82 C7 **Biograd** Yugoslavia 43.56N 15.29E
15 M4 **Bio I** Solomon Is 10.15S 161.44E
82 D7 **Biokova** *mts* Yugoslavia
71 G5 **Biol** France 45.30N 5.23E
111 D5 **Biola** California 36.46N 120.01W
87 K9 **Biolei** Somalia 3.55N 44.20E
71 H5 **Biolle,la** France 45.45N 5.56E
79 B3 **Bionaz** Italy 45.52N 7.26E
91 J4 **Biondo** Zaïre 0.22S 25.12E
71 K5 **Bionnassay** France 45.51N 6.55E
75 N4 **Biosca** Spain 41.50N 1.21E
71 L9 **Biot** France 43.38N 7.05E
75 H3 **Biota** Spain 42.16N 1.11W
71 K4 **Biot,le** France 46.15N 6.39E
88 J6 **Biougra** Morocco 30.14N 9.22W
61 K5 **Bioul** Belgium 50.20N 4.48E
91 B2 **Bipindi** Cameroon 3.06N 10.30E
63 G7 **Bippen** W Germany 52.35N 7.43E
106 J9 **Bippus** Indiana 40.57N 85.36W
35 E2 **Biq'at Bet Netofa** *flood plain* Israel
29 E1 **Bir** Himachal Prad India 32.02N 76.48E
Bir Iran *see* **Bīr Bālā**
29 E6 **Bir** Madhya Prad India 22.02N 76.32E
28 B1 **Bir** Maharashtra India 18.59N 75.50E
28 B1 **Bir** *dist* Maharashtra India
35 D6 **Bira** Jordan 31.54N 35.13E
40 G7 **Bira** Khabarovsk U.S.S.R. 49.12N 137.15E
30 D7 **Bira** Madhya Prad India 25.01N 80.15E
82 L3 **Bîra** Romania 47.02N 27.03E
40 F7 **Bira** Yevreysk U.S.S.R. 49.02N 132.25E
Bīra *R see* **Tavor** *R*
15 E7 **Birab** Irian Jaya 6.07S 138.25E
33 B3 **Bi'r Abā al'Ajjāj** Saudi Arabia 27.27N 36.07E
90 J4 **Bir Abaya** Chad 14.40N 18.18E
Bîr abou Neîtel *see* **Bîr abu Naîtal**
85 J4 **Bîr Abu Batta** Egypt 30.58N 27.21E
86 H7 **Bîr Abu Darag** Egypt 29.29N 32.26E
85 K4 **Bîr Abu Gharâdiq** Egypt 30.08N 28.08E
85 N8 **Bîr Abu Hashim** Egypt 23.42N 34.06E
85 N8 **Bîr Abu Hodeid** Egypt 22.22N 35.17E
85 K8 **Bîr Abu Husein** Egypt 22.57N 29.55E
34 F2 **Bīr Abu Jādi** Syria 36.07N 38.33E
85 J6 **Bîr Abu Minqâr** Egypt 26.33N 27.33E
34 F3 **Bīr abu Naîtal** Syria 35.20N 38.15E
Bir abu Naytal *see* **Bīr abu Naîtal**
86 L5 **Bîr Abu Qurûn** Egypt 30.22N 33.31E
86 J9 **Bîr Abu Treifiya** Egypt 28.25N 32.39E
85 G7 **Bi'r adh Dhikār** Libya 25.48N 22.35E
86 G7 **Bîr Afandîna** Egypt 29.26N 31.31E
85 H4 **Bir Afarid** Libya 31.56N 24.25E
32 J7 **Bīrag, Kūh-e** *mts* Iran
35 G2 **Birah, El** Syria 32.59N 35.46E
33 B9 **Bi'r Aḩmad** S Yemen 12.52N 44.54E
33 A9 **Bi'r Aḩmad Wells** S Yemen 12.52N 44.53E
35 G1 **Bir 'Ajam** Syria 33.03N 35.52E
40 E7 **Birakan** U.S.S.R. 49.00N 131.43E
34 M2 **Bira Kapra** Iraq 36.52N 44.02E
33 B2 **Bi'r, Al** Saudi Arabia 28.52N 36.15E
33 F4 **Bi'r, Al** Saudi Arabia 25.16N 45.59E
34 D10 **Bi'r,Al** Saudi Arabia 28.50N 36.16E
90 G4 **Bir Alali** Chad 14.26N 15.15E
33 C4 **Bi'r al Amīr** Saudi Arabia 25.11N 38.10E
33 C4 **Bi'r al Aṭbaq** Saudi Arabia 25.12N 39.30E
33 C5 **Bi'r al'Awādī** Saudi Arabia 22.38N 39.16E
85 C5 **Bi'r al Fatiyah** Libya 29.20N 14.07E
85 C5 **Bi'r al Ghaylānīyah** Libya 29.01N 14.19E
Bir al Halbā *see* **Bīr el Halba**
85 G7 **Bi'r al Harash** Libya 25.32N 22.05E
33 D4 **Bi'r al Ḩisw** Saudi Arabia 24.40N 41.44E
85 B4 **Bi'r Al Ḩumayrā** Libya 31.16N 12.30E
33 H9 **Bi'r 'Alī** S Yemen 14.00N 48.20E
85 G7 **Bi'r al Ikhwan** Libya 24.30N 23.18E
33 E6 **Bi'r al Jāhilīyah** Saudi Arabia 20.56N 42.51E
85 F4 **Bi'r Al Jarrārī** Libya 31.40N 21.48E
85 B4 **Bi'r Al Khawr** Libya 30.08N 12.49E
85 A4 **Bi'r 'Allāq** Libya 31.05N 11.55E
85 E4 **Bi'r al Marduma** Libya 30.25N 18.22E
33 C4 **Bi'r al Mashī** Saudi Arabia 24.06N 39.34E
85 C7 **Bi'r al Mastūtah** Libya 25.33N 14.29E
34 H5 **Bi'r al Mulūsī** Iraq 33.31N 40.06E
85 A4 **Bi'r Al Mushayqiq** Libya 30.57N 10.18E
85 C5 **Bi'r al Muzayri'āt** Libya 28.41N 15.29E
85 C5 **Bi'r al Qāf** Libya 28.14N 15.23E
85 D5 **Bi'r al Qaṭṭār** Libya 28.50N 17.53E
85 B6 **Bi'r Al Qawz** Libya 27.40N 12.50E
33 B3 **Bi'r al Qurr** Saudi Arabia 26.40N 36.55E
Bi'r al Wa'r *see* **Toummo**
88 S7 **Bir Amasin** Libya 29.37N 9.52E
Bir'Amiri *see* **Bi'r Haymir**
35 E1 **Biranit** Israel 33.03N 35.22E
Bīr an Nabâi *see* **Bīr en Nabāj**
85 A4 **Bi'r An Nāşirah** Libya 30.22N 11.35E
90 L6 **Birao** Cent Afr Rep 10.11N 22.49E
Bīr Aoglat *see* **Bir 'Uqlat**
88 S5 **Bir Aouine** Tunisia 32.22N 9.02E
90 J4 **Bir Arakay** Chad 14.40N 18.42E
90 K4 **Bir Argan** Chad 15.25N 20.24E
33 D4 **Bi'r 'Arja** Saudi Arabia 25.19N 41.01E
85 C5 **Bi'r ash Shuwayrif** Libya 29.59N 14.19E
33 E5 **Bi'r as Sakhā** Saudi Arabia 23.11N 43.39E
24 G5 **Biratar Bulak** *spring* Xinjiang Uygur Zizhiqu China 41.59N 90.18E
85 J4 **Bîr Atîya** Egypt 31.18N 26.39E
30 L6 **Biratnagar** Nepal 26.27N 87.17E
20 L2 **Biratori** Japan 42.36N 142.08E
85 H5 **Bi'r aṭ Ṭarfāwī** Libya 29.35N 24.04E
33 J5 **B'ir 'Azīz** Saudi Arabia 22.56N 50.26E
33 E7 **Bi'raz Zurq** Saudi Arabia 19.30N 43.48E
86 H6 **Bîr Bad'** Egypt 29.46N 32.14E
32 H8 **Bīr Bālā** Iran 25.29N 59.46E
87 B3 **Bir Ban Gedid** Sudan 14.47N 28.33E
86 K4 **Bîr Barth el Higâyib** Egypt 30.30N 33.11E
90 K4 **Bir Basi** Chad 15.25N 21.38E
34 E4 **Bīr Başīrī** Syria 34.08N 37.36E
Bîr Bassîri *see* **Bīr Başīrī**
33 B3 **Bi'r Baydā** Saudi Arabia 26.50N 36.54E
86 K4 **Bîr Bayûd** Egypt 30.55N 33.01E
86 M5 **Bîr Beida** Egypt 30.24N 34.28E
88 N8 **Bir ben Takoul** Algeria 26.04N 1.37W
29 K6 **Birbhum** dist W Bengal India
85 J10 **Bîr Bidi** Sudan 19.10N 26.30E
86 H7 **Bîr Bikheit** Egypt 29.14N 32.18E
87 E6 **Bir Bir** *watercourse* Ethiopia
86 H7 **Bîr Bireida** Egypt 29.09N 32.07E
34 G2 **Bīr Btaïman** Syria 36.13N 39.43E
33 C4 **Bi'r Budayy** Saudi Arabia 25.23N 38.15E
86 H8 **Bîr Buerât** Egypt 28.59N 32.10E
33 D6 **Bi'r Buraym** Saudi Arabia 21.55N 41.30E
82 H7 **Bîrca** Romania 43.59N 23.36E
88 L10 **Bir Chali** Mali 22.58N 4.58W
103 C3 **Birchardville** Pennsylvania 41.50N 76.00W
113 P3 **Birch Cr** Alaska
113 P3 **Birch Creek** Alaska 66.18N 145.59W
92 F11 **Birchenough Bridge** Zimbabwe 19.57S 32.20E
113 L4 **Birches** Alaska 65.09N 153.40W
11 H8 **Birch Hill** New Zealand 41.40S 173.17E
100 M5 **Birch Hills** Saskatchewan 53.00N 105.10W
100 S6 **Birch I** Manitoba
56 O5 **Birchington** Kent Eng 51.23N 1.19E
12 G6 **Birchip** Victoria 35.59S 142.59E
82 G5 **Birchiş** Romania 45.48N 22.10E
100 F5 **Birch L** Alberta 53.20N 111.35W
108 T2 **Birch L** Minnesota
101 P4 **Birch L** N W Terr 62.05N 116.34W
100 J5 **Birch L** Saskatchewan 53.28N 108.10W
94 T13 **Birchleigh** S Africa 26.04S 28.14E
Bîr Chmanndoûr *see* **Bîr Shmandur**
101 R7 **Birch Mts** Alberta
101 R6 **Birch R** Alberta
100 Q6 **Birch River** Manitoba 52.21N 101.08W
107 E5 **Birch Tree** Missouri 36.58N 91.31W
113 N6 **Birchwood** Alaska 61.15N 149.10W
11 B12 **Birchwood** New Zealand 45.57S 167.52E
106 C4 **Birchwood** Wisconsin 45.39N 91.32W
62 N6 **Bircza** Poland 49.42N 22.29E
97 K6 **Bird** Manitoba 56.45N 94.00W
60 M6 **Birdaard** Netherlands 53.18N 5.35E
85 J4 **Bîr Damdûm** Egypt 30.45N 27.31E
86 K10 **Bîr Dâra** Egypt 27.56N 33.00E
113 O10 **Bird C** Aleutian Is 51.40N 178.39E
109 J2 **Bird City** Kansas 39.45N 101.32W
98 Q2 **Bird Cove** Newfoundland 51.03N 56.53W
30 B8 **Birdha** Uttar Prad India 24.32N 78.24E
59 F6 **Birdhill** Tipperary Irish Rep 52.46N 8.26W
85 C4 **Bi'r Dhu'fān** Libya 31.58N 14.40E
Bird I *see* **Aves**
86 K10 **Bîr Dib** Egypt 27.50N 33.14E
85 K8 **Bîr Dibis** Egypt 22.12N 29.32E
85 K8 **Bîr Dibis (West)** Egypt 22.08N 29.27E
90 J4 **Bir Didey** Chad 14.10N 19.31E
85 K6 **Bîr Dikka** Egypt 26.04N 28.15E
85 H4 **Bîr Diqnâsh** Egypt 31.03N 25.23E
95 K9 **Bird Is** S Africa 33.49S 26.17E
113 H9 **Bird Island** Alaska 54.50N 159.45W
122 V7 **Bird Island** Palmyra I Pacific Oc 5.52N 162.04W
26 Q11 **Bird Island** Seychelles, Ind Oc 3.41S 55.13E
121 G8 **Bird Island** S Georgia 54.00S 38.00W
88 R5 **Bir Djedid** Algeria 32.37N 7.53E
90 J4 **Bir Djéroual** Chad 14.26N 18.50E
56 G4 **Birdlip** Glos Eng 51.51N 2.07W
90 J4 **Bir Douhoul** Chad 14.50N 19.01E
30 G5 **Birdpur** Uttar Prad India 27.23N 83.07E
98 L6 **Bird Rocks Lt.Ho** Madeleine Is, Que 47.50N 61.10W
103 C6 **Birdsboro** Pennsylvania 40.15N 75.48W
107 K3 **Birdseye** Indiana 38.19N 86.41W
95 K7 **Birds River** S Africa 31.30S 26.51E
13 E7 **Birdsville** Queensland 25.50S 139.20E
13 C3 **Birdum** N Terr Australia 15.38S 133.12E
13 C3 **Birdum** *R* N Terr Aust
37 D8 **Birecik** Turkey 37.03N 37.59E
88 N9 **Bir ed Deheb** Algeria 25.08N 1.57W
85 N8 **Bîr Eigat** Egypt 22.02N 35.00E
34 D3 **Birein** Syria 35.01N 36.40E
Bîr ej Jouaîf *see* **Bîr el Jueif**
41 L5 **Birekte** *R* U.S.S.R.
Bir,El *see* **Teouit**
88 K8 **Bir el Abbès** Algeria 26.08N 6.15W
86 J3 **Bîr el 'Abd** Egypt 31.01N 32.55E
35 H6 **Bîr el Ad'am** Jordan 31.56N 36.15E
86 M8 **Bîr el 'Adeid** Egypt 28.59N 34.05E
86 J3 **Bîr el 'Afein** Egypt 31.01N 32.55E
86 G6 **Bîr el 'Agramîya** Egypt 29.40N 31.50E
88 S4 **Bir el Ater** Algeria 34.45N 8.05E
85 H5 **Bîr el Basur** Egypt 29.51N 25.49E
86 N7 **Bîr el Biarât** Egypt 29.30N 34.43E
35 G9 **Bîr el Buhai** Jordan 31.03N 35.52E
86 H8 **Bîr el Dakhal** Egypt 28.40N 32.23E
89 A1 **Bir el Gareb** *well* Mauritania 20.33N 16.12W
86 F8 **Bîr el Ghamr** Egypt 28.43N 31.20E
86 K5 **Bîr el Giddi** Egypt 30.13N 33.04E
86 M4 **Bîr el Hadira** Egypt 30.38N 34.04E
88 N8 **Bir el Hadjaj** Algeria 26.26N 1.25W
85 M8 **Bîr el Haimur** Egypt 22.43N 33.48E
34 F4 **Bîr el Halba** Syria 34.05N 38.25E
86 N8 **Bîr el Hamza** Saudi Arabia 28.30N 34.57E
86 N7 **Bîr el Heisi** Egypt 29.23N 34.34E
Bîr el Helba *see* **Bîr el Halba**
86 P7 **Bîr el Hind** Saudi Arabia 29.02N 35.06E
85 J4 **Bîr el Istabl** Egypt 30.42N 26.37E
86 J4 **Bîr el Jafir** Egypt 30.50N 32.40E
34 H3 **Bîr el Jueif** Syria 35.29N 40.53E
85 H4 **Bîr el Khamsa** Egypt 30.58N 25.49E
88 K9 **Bir El Khzaim** Mauritania 24.24N 7.44W
86 P5 **Bîr el Lasan** Jordan 30.05N 35.31E
86 H7 **Bîr el Ma'in** Egypt 29.27N 32.15E
86 K4 **Bîr el Mâlhi** Egypt 30.39N 33.20E
86 M5 **Bîr el Malih** Egypt 30.14N 34.13E
86 H4 **Bîr el Manâyif** Egypt 30.31N 32.10E
86 J4 **Bîr el Maqeibra** Egypt 30.52N 32.50E
86 N8 **Bîr el Mâshi** Saudi Arabia 28.53N 34.50E
35 G4 **Bîr el Matwi** Jordan 32.19N 35.59E
86 O8 **Bîr el Misallam** Saudi Arabia 28.58N 35.27E
86 K7 **Bîr el Nasb** Egypt 29.02N 33.24E
85 H4 **Bîr el Nuss** Egypt 30.21N 15.43E
85 J6 **Bîr el Obeiyid** Egypt 27.19N 27.39E
86 K3 **Bîr el Qals** Egypt 31.14N 33.05E
86 K4 **Bîr el Qanâdîl** Egypt 30.59N 33.07E
86 E5 **Bîr el Qar'âya** Egypt 30.25N 30.38E
85 J4 **Bîr el Qatrâni** Egypt 30.53N 26.19E
85 H4 **Bîr el Râbia** Egypt 31.13N 25.42E
86 K4 **Bîr el Roghwi** Egypt 30.48N 33.28E
86 M8 **Bîr el Safra** Egypt 28.46N 34.20E
86 M7 **Bîr el Saura** Egypt 29.10N 34.29E
85 H4 **Bîr el Shaqqa** Egypt 30.54N 25.01E
85 N8 **Bîr el Sunta** Egypt 23.25N 34.50E
86 K5 **Bîr el Ṭawîl** Egypt 30.07N 33.05E
86 K5 **Bîr el Thamâda** Egypt 30.10N 33.27E
86 J9 **Bîr el 'Uyûn** Egypt 28.04N 32.54E
86 K3 **Bîr el Zuabatîya** Egypt 31.00N 33.25E
34 F3 **Bīr en Nabāj** Syria 35.34N 38.18E
35 G9 **Bir en Nayim** *anc site* Jordan 31.03N 35.54E
Bîr en Nbâj *see* **Bīr en Nabāj**
88 F10 **Bir Enzaran** Morocco 23.56N 14.33W
34 H5 **Bi'r er Rah** Iraq 33.32N 40.24E
Bir eth Thamila *see* **Be'er Hayil**
35 G9 **Bir eth Thughra** Jordan 31.04N 35.50E
18 B3 **Bireuën** Sumatra Indonesia 5.11N 96.40E
34 H3 **Bīr ez Zarrâb** Syria 35.41N 40.11E
33 H5 **Bi'r Fādil** Saudi Arabia 22.05N 49.52E
33 B9 **Bi'r Faḑl** S Yemen 12.52N 44.68E
33 A9 **Bi'r Faḑl** *well* S Yemen 12.53N 44.52E
34 E10 **Bi'r Fajr** Saudi Arabia 28.55N 37.52E
34 J4 **Bir Falloq** Iraq 34.47N 41.51E
34 G3 **Bīr Fanājīn** Syria 35.55N 39.54E
Bîr Fannâjîne *see* **Bīr Fanājīn**
33 H5 **Bi'r Fardān** Saudi Arabia 22.02N 48.47E
34 K4 **Bir Fatmah** Iraq 34.52N 42.15E
90 K4 **Bir Fouk** Chad 15.51N 21.05E
85 J4 **Bîr Fuâd** Egypt 30.35N 26.28E
33 A10 **Bi'r Fuqum** S Yemen 12.45N 44.50E
90 K4 **Bir Ganatir** Chad 14.30N 20.42E
89 A1 **Bir Gandus** *well* Mauritania 21.30N 16.30W
30 H5 **Birganj** Nepal 27.01N 84.54E
90 G5 **Bir Gara** Chad 13.13N 15.58E
34 H2 **Bīr Garan** Syria 36.28N 40.06E
85 H4 **Bi'r Ghabi** Libya 31.29N 24.00E
86 H9 **Bîr Ghalla** Egypt 28.22N 32.18E
58 M7 **Birgham** Borders Scotland 55.39N 2.19W
86 O9 **Bîr Gharr** Saudi Arabia 28.04N 35.26E
33 F5 **Bi'r Ghawdah** Saudi Arabia 22.58N 44.20E
36 C4 **Birgi** Turkey 38.15N 28.03E
29 K2 **Birgi** W Bengal India 22.41N 86.43E
85 C4 **Bi'r Giaafer** Libya 30.03N 14.22E
86 K5 **Bîr Gifgâfa** Egypt 30.28N 33.11E
86 G6 **Bîr Gindali** Egypt 29.55N 31.41E
64 M5 **Birgland** W Germany 49.25N 11.40E
65 B7 **Birgsau** W Germany 47.21N 10.17E
Birgu *see* **Vittoriosa**
34 G3 **Bīr Hāba** Syria 35.09N 39.56E
33 J7 **Bi'r Hādī** Saudi Arabia 19.26N 51.05E
Bîr Hajal *see* **Bīr Hojal**
34 G3 **Bīr Hamra** Syria 35.52N 29.46E
87 F5 **Birhan** *mt* Ethiopia 10.45N 37.55E
90 L4 **Bir Hangara** Chad 15.54N 23.01E
30 F6 **Birhar** Uttar Prad India 26.28N 82.57E
33 E5 **Bi'r Haraqī** Saudi Arabia 22.45N 42.59E
86 L5 **Bîr Hasana** Egypt 30.29N 33.47E
34 J3 **Bīr Ḩawīsīa** Iraq 35.38N 41.28E
33 C4 **Bi'r Ḩaymir** Saudi Arabia 24.44N 38.03E
33 C3 **Bi'r Ḩayzān** Saudi Arabia 27.43N 39.07E
34 L4 **Bir Ḩazim** Iraq 34.44N 43.28E
34 F4 **Bīr Hilāhah** Syria 34.48N 38.42E
Bîr Hlaté *see* **Bīr Hilāhah**
Bîr Hmaîmé *see* **Bīr Humaime**
34 G4 **Bīr Hojal** Syria 34.32N 39.06E
86 D5 **Bîr Hooker** Egypt 30.22N 30.21E
33 E5 **Bi'r Ḩudūf** Saudi Arabia 22.57N 42.10E
85 G4 **Bir Ḩukayyim** Libya 31.33N 23.31E
34 G4 **Bir Humaime** Syria 34.28N 39.50E
33 D4 **Bi'r Ḩuwaymidah** Saudi Arabia 25.39N 40.45E
52 F6 **Biri** Norway 60.57N 10.35E
19 M5 **Biri** *isld* Philippines 12.40N 124.22E
15 E5 **Biri** *R* Irian Jaya
92 E10 **Biri** *R* Zimbabwe
90 N8 **Biri** *watercourse* Sudan
85 C7 **Bir Iasco** Libya 24.33N 14.32E
33 B4 **Bi'r Ibn Ghunayn** Saudi Arabia 25.17N 37.15E
Bi'r Ibn Hirmas *see* **Bi'r,Al**
86 P5 **Bir ibn Jāzi** Jordan 30.29N 35.36E
Bir Ibn Juhaiyim *see* **Bi'r Ibn Juhayyim**
33 H5 **Bi'r Ibn Juhayyim** Saudi Arabia 22.27N 49.00E
33 E7 **Bi'r Ibn Sarrār** Saudi Arabia 19.30N 42.45E
33 F7 **Bi'r Īdīmah** Saudi Arabia 18.31N 44.11E
86 E4 **Birîgât, El** Egypt 30.31N 30.49E
89 B1 **Bir Igueni** *well* Mauritania 20.25N 14.50W
118 E7 **Birigüi** Brazil 21.18S 50.16W
42 D5 **Birikchul'** U.S.S.R. 53.20N 89.51E
42 E4 **Birilyussy** U.S.S.R. 57.11N 90.39E
89 J8 **Birim** *R* Ghana
86 E3 **Birimbâl** Egypt 31.22N 30.31E
13 H6 **Birimgan** Queensland 22.42S 147.27E
86 L8 **Bîr Imleih** Egypt 28.53N 33.41E
Birine *see* **Birein**
90 L8 **Birini** Cent Afr Rep 7.50N 22.13E
90 E5 **Biriri** Nigeria 12.10N 11.45E
Biriz *see* **Berīzak**
86 O7 **Bir Jadid** Saudi Arabia 29.08N 35.06E
32 H4 **Bīrjand** Iran 32.55N 59.10E
33 B3 **Bi'r Jaydah** Saudi Arabia 26.10N 37.24E
33 F9 **Bi'r Jifah** S Yemen 14.57N 45.58E
85 H4 **Bi'r Jubnī** Libya 31.18N 24.38E
33 E6 **Bi'r Jugjug** Saudi Arabia 21.20N 43.45E
33 D5 **Birkah,Al** Saudi Arabia 22.11N 40.49E
33 D7 **Birk,Al** Saudi Arabia 18.14N 41.33E
90 L4 **Bir Kanga** Chad 15.49N 22.34E
85 K6 **Bîr Karawein** Egypt 27.04N 28.37E
86 K4 **Bîr Kaseiba** Egypt 31.00N 33.17E
33 D4 **Birkat Abū Salīm** Saudi Arabia 24.41N 41.19E
34 L9 **Birkat al 'Āmyā'** Iraq 29.53N 43.38E
33 E1 **Birkat al 'Aqabah** Saudi Arabia 30.10N 43.38E
33 E2 **Birkat al Ḩamrā** Saudi Arabia 28.58N 43.22E
33 M5 **Birkat al Mawz** Oman 22.55N 57.39E
34 L9 **Birkat ash Shihīyāt** Saudi Arabia 29.07N 43.30E
33 E1 **Birkat'Athāmīn** Saudi Arabia 30.18N 43.40E
32 A5 **Birkat Hamad** Iraq 31.15N 44.10E
33 E2 **Birkat Zubālah** Saudi Arabia 29.25N 43.37E
11 C1 **Birkdale** New Zealand 36.47S 174.41E

52 D8 **Birkeland** Norway 58.18N 8.13E
53 B6 **Birkelev** Denmark 55.13N 8.49E
53 D2 **Birkelse** Denmark 57.09N 9.42E
64 F4 **Birkenau** W Germany 49.34N 8.44E
64 E8 **Birkendorf** W Germany 47.45N 8.19E
64 C4 **Birkenfeld** Rheinland-Pfalz W Germany 49.38N 7.10E
64 K3 **Birkenfield** Bayern W Germany 50.12N 10.37E
63 U8 **Birkenhainchen** E Germany 52.01N 14.04E
57 G6 **Birkenhead** Merseyside Eng 53.24N 3.02W
11 C1 **Birkenhead** New Zealand 36.49S 174.43E
63 S7 **Birkenwerder** E Germany 52.42N 13.17E
53 J5 **Birkerød** Denmark 55.52N 12.27E
64 A2 **Birkesdorf** W Germany 50.49N 6.28E
53 G7 **Birket** Denmark 54.54N 11.20E
86 D5 **Birket el Beida** *L* Egypt 30.26N 30.15E
86 D5 **Birket el Ga'âr** *L* Egypt 30.28N 30.10E
86 F4 **Birket el Sab'** Egypt 30.38N 31.05E
86 E10 **Birket el Was'a** *L* Egypt 27.57N 30.41E
86 D5 **Birket el Zugm** *L* Egypt 30.24N 30.18E
90 J5 **Birket-Fatmé** Chad 12.55N 19.07E
86 D3 **Birket Ghitâs** Egypt 31.08N 30.16E
86 G4 **Birket Miḥeishar** *L* Egypt 30.44N 31.57E
86 E7 **Birket Qârûn** *L* Egypt 29.30N 30.40E
86 D5 **Birket Umm Risha** *L* Egypt 30.20N 30.23E
65 N7 **Birkfeld** Austria 47.22N 15.42E
90 K4 **Bir Kharma** Chad 15.36N 20.05E
34 J3 **Bîr Khazrajiya** Iraq 35.57N 41.48E
88 S5 **Bir Khenafes** Tunisia 33.23N 8.04E
53 F7 **Birkholm** *isld* Denmark 54.56N 10.32E
33 B3 **Bi'r Khurbah** Saudi Arabia 26.07N 37.15E
33 D5 **Bi'r Khuwārah** Saudi Arabia 22.25N 41.30E
34 M2 **Birkim** Iraq 36.53N 44.46E
84 Y20 **Birkirkara** Malta 35.54N 14.29E
85 K8 **Bîr Kiseiba** Egypt 22.43N 29.55E
65 D7 **Birkkar-Spitze** *mt* Austria 47.25N 11.28E
90 M5 **Bir Korma** Sudan 13.50N 24.45E
30 G5 **Birkot** Nepal 27.51N 83.46E
90 L4 **Bir Kotokoro** Chad 15.17N 22.24E
12 A2 **Birksgate Ra** S Australia
85 K8 **Bîr Kurauîm** Egypt 22.28N 29.34E
82 L4 **Bîrlad** Romania 46.14N 27.40E
82 L4 **Bîrladul** *R* Romania
86 L3 **Bîr Lahfân** Egypt 31.01N 33.52E
88 J8 **Bir Lehlú** Morocco 26.23N 9.40W
88 H8 **Bir Lehmar** Morocco 26.03N 11.03W
43 J3 **Birlestik** Kazakhstan U.S.S.R. 48.00N 69.08E
88 J9 **Bir Lhassene-ould-Hassane** Mauritania 25.11N 8.25W
43 M4 **Birlik** Kazakhstan U.S.S.R. 45.05N 75.14E
86 E4 **Birma** Egypt 30.51N 30.54E
30 C7 **Birma** *R* Uttar Prad India
86 J4 **Bîr Madkûr** Egypt 30.43N 32.32E
31 E4 **Birmal** *reg* Afghanistan
33 E5 **B'ir Malīyah** Saudi Arabia 23.59N 44.00E
86 L3 **Bîr Masa'îd** Egypt 31.08N 33.45E
74 J8 **Bir Medfa** Algeria 36.22N 2.28E
66 K2 **Birmensdorf** Switzerland 47.22N 8.26E
66 J2 **Birmenstorf** Switzerland 47.28N 8.15E
86 K10 **Bîr Milâha** Egypt 27.35N 33.26E
107 K8 **Birmingham** Alabama 33.30N 86.55W
106 C9 **Birmingham** Iowa 40.52N 91.55W
106 L7 **Birmingham** Michigan 42.33N 83.12W
100 P8 **Birmingham** Saskatchewan 50.59N 102.54W
56 H3 **Birmingham** W Midlands Eng 52.30N 1.50W
56 D3 **Birmingham Corporation Reservoirs** Powys Wales
85 J8 **Bîr Misâha** Egypt 22.13N 27.59E
Bir Mlusi *see* **Bi'r al Mulūsī**
88 H9 **Bir Moghrein** Mauritania 25.10N 11.35E
Bîr Moheîmed el Ouezouez *see* **Bīr Muhaymad el Wazwaz**
86 K10 **Bîr Monqûl** Egypt 27.51N 33.03E
Bîr Mountbatch *see* **Bīr Munbatih**
34 G4 **Bīr Muaileh** Syria 34.52N 39.54E
33 C5 **Bi'r Mubayrīk** Saudi Arabia 23.17N 39.06E
34 F4 **Bīr Muhaymad El Wazwaz** Syria 30.15N 38.48E
34 J3 **Bîr Mujamma'a** Iraq 35.43N 41.32E
Bi'r Mujarimah *see* **Bi'r Mujayrimah**
34 C9 **Bi'r Mujayfil** Saudi Arabia 29.05N 35.06E
33 C6 **Bi'r Mujayrimah** Saudi Arabia 20.38N 39.40E
34 F4 **Bīr Munbatih** Syria 34.36N 38.48E
86 F9 **Bîr Mureir** Egypt 28.25N 31.15E
85 M8 **Bîr Murra** Egypt 22.32N 33.55E
33 A9 **Bi'r Na'ama** S Yemen 12.51N 44.53E
35 D6 **Bir Nabala** Jordan 31.51N 35.12E
33 B4 **Bi'r Nabt** Saudi Arabia 24.41N 37.31E
85 M8 **Bîr Nagîb** Egypt 22.53N 33.48E
86 J4 **Bîr Nagîd** Egypt 30.56N 32.40E
86 A5 **Bîr Nâhid** Egypt 30.14N 28.53E
34 G4 **Bīr Najal** Syria 34.49N 39.19E
34 K4 **Bīr Nakhili** Iraq 34.34N 42.24E
86 K7 **Bîr Nakhul** Egypt 29.04N 33.15E
58 J5 **Birnam** Tayside Scotland 56.33N 3.35W
88 S7 **Bir Nasar** Algeria 28.52N 9.42E
86 D5 **Bîr Nasîf** Egypt 30.19N 30.28E
33 C4 **Bi'r Nasīf** Saudi Arabia 24.52N 39.08E
29 J6 **Birnatrapur** Orissa India 22.24N 84.50E
64 P7 **Birnbach** W Germany 48.26N 13.06E
58 M4 **Birness** Grampian Scotland 57.24N 2.01W
108 D4 **Birney** Montana 45.19N 106.30W
89 K6 **Birni** Benin 10.01N 1.33E
100 S8 **Birnie** Manitoba 50.28N 99.26W
10 S2 **Birnie I** Phoenix Is Pacific Oc 3.40S 171.50W
89 L5 **Birni Ngaoure** Niger 13.09N 2.53E
90 C6 **Birnin Gwari** Nigeria 11.00N 6.50E
90 B5 **Birnin Kebbi** Nigeria 12.30N 4.11E
89 M5 **Birni n'Konni** Niger 13.49N 5.19E
90 D6 **Birnin Kudu** Nigeria 11.30N 9.31E
90 E5 **Birniwa** Nigeria 12.49N 10.19E
90 M4 **Bir Nogei** Sudan 14.02N 24.40E
50 K6 **Birnudalstindur** *pk* Iceland 64.16N 16.00W
40 F7 **Birobidzhan** U.S.S.R. 48.49N 132.54E
40 F7 **Birofeld** U.S.S.R. 48.29N 132.46E
19 J7 **Birong** Philippines 9.22N 118.08E
66 M7 **Birónico** Switzerland 46.07N 8.56E
Bîr Ouirad *see* **Bīr Wīrad**
88 N9 **Bir Ould Brini** Algeria 25.25N 1.45W
Bîr Oum Rabbah *see* **Bīr Umm Rabba**
89 H1 **Bir Ounane** Mali 21.18N 3.59W
Bîr Ouraqa *see* **Bīr Warqa**
30 K6 **Birpur** Bihar India 26.30N 86.59E
30 A6 **Birpur** Madhya Prad India 26.08N 77.08E
30 E5 **Birpur Katra** Uttar Prad India 27.12N 81.48E
Birq *see* **Birk,Al**
85 D5 **Bi'r Qaryās** Libya 29.47N 16.23E
86 F5 **Birqâsh** Egypt 30.10N 31.02E
85 J4 **Bîr Qasir el Sirr** Egypt 30.35N 26.45E
86 J4 **Bîr Qatia** Egypt 30.58N 32.45E
Bîr Qotné *see* **Bīr Qutna**
85 M7 **Bîr Quleib** Egypt 24.08N 33.37E
34 E3 **Bīr Qutnah** Syria 35.19N 37.56E
87 F5 **Bir,R** Ethiopia
59 G5 **Birr** Offaly Irish Rep 53.05N 7.54W
59 D4 **Birreencorragh** *mts* Mayo Irish Rep 53.50N 9.29W
86 L7 **Bîr Regîm** Egypt 29.15N 33.40E
88 S5 **Bir Rhoraffa** Algeria 32.18N 8.08E
12 H3 **Birrie** *R* New S Wales
13 B3 **Birrimbah** N Terr Australia 15.51S 132.00E
13 A4 **Birrindudu** N Terr Australia 18.24S 129.28E
86 E3 **Birrîyet el Aṣeifar** Egypt 31.18N 30.40E
88 P3 **Bir Robalou** Algeria 36.18N 3.34E
86 K4 **Bîr Rôd Sâlim** Egypt 30.32N 33.22E
33 B9 **Bi'r Rubāq** S Yemen 12.50N 44.55E
85 K8 **Bîr Safsaf** Egypt 22.45N 29.18E
85 K8 **Bîr Sahara** Egypt 22.54N 28.40E
Bir Samit *see* **Samīt,Al**
58 S11 **Birsay** Orkney Scotland 59.08N 3.18W
100 L7 **Birsay** Saskatchewan 51.04N 107.00W
66 F3 **Birse** *R* Switzerland
90 J4 **Bir Sélia** Chad 14.52N 18.09E
90 J4 **Bir Séréhay** Chad 14.09N 19.22E
66 G1 **Birsfelden** Switzerland 47.33N 7.37E
34 G2 **Bīr Shmandur** Syria 36.23N 39.25E
66 G1 **Birsig** *R* France/Switz
29 C3 **Birsilpur** Rajasthan India 28.12N 72.08E
90 M4 **Bir Sindi** Sudan 15.58N 24.06E
46 S2 **Birsk** U.S.S.R. 55.28N 55.31E
57 K5 **Birstall** W Yorks Eng 53.44N 1.40W
64 G3 **Birstein** W Germany 50.21N 9.19E
86 N7 **Bîr Tâba** Egypt 29.30N 34.55E
85 B6 **Bi'r Tabankurt** Libya 27.13N 12.38E
34 G4 **Bīr Taīyarīya** Syria 34.04N 39.26E
85 A6 **Bi'r Tajarhī** Libya 26.48N 10.18E
88 T7 **Bir Talarh** Tunisia 32.33N 11.20E
33 G5 **Bir Ṭalḥah** Saudi Arabia 23.11N 46.47E
33 H8 **Bi'r Tamīs** S Yemen 16.54N 48.55E
85 G4 **Bi'r Tanjadar** Libya 31.35N 22.16E
88 G8 **Bir Taoulekt** Morocco 27.56N 12.34W
85 K8 **Bîr Tarfâwi** Egypt 22.57N 28.55E
34 L5 **Bi'r Ṭarūfawī** Iraq 33.42N 43.38E
51 H2 **Birtavarre** Norway 69.32N 20.50E
85 M9 **Bir Tawil** Sudan 21.52N 33.42E
53 X20 **Birtevatn** *L* Norway 59.03N 7.57E
86 K7 **Bîr Thâl** Egypt 29.10N 33.04E
89 C1 **Bir Thaleb** Mauritania 21.28N 12.28W
13 G2 **Birthday Mt** Queensland 13.31S 143.06E
113 J2 **Birthday Pass** Alaska 69.25N 156.45W
93 N7 **Birti** Kenya 1.18S 41.01E
100 Q8 **Birtle** Manitoba 50.26N 101.04W
57 K3 **Birtley** Tyne and Wear Eng 54.54N 1.34W
Bîr Touaînâne *see* **Bīr Tueinan**
88 J10 **Bir Touevrest** Mauritania 22.42N 9.02W
Bîr Trefâoui *see* **Bīr Trefaui**
34 G2 **Bīr Trefaui** Syria 36.08N 39.24E
34 H2 **Bīr Tueinan** Syria 36.18N 40.32E
Bīr Tuwaynān *see* **Bīr Tueinan**
24 H10 **Biru** Xizang Zizhiqu China 31.30N 93.56E
86 H6 **Bîr Udeib** Egypt 29.42N 32.21E
85 M6 **Bîr Um el 'Abbas** Egypt 26.57N 32.35E
85 E4 **B'ir Umm al Gharānīq** Libya 30.20N 18.50E
85 C5 **Bi'r Umm al Khayl** Libya 29.56N 14.19E
85 M7 **Bîr Umm Fawâkhîr** Egypt 26.00N 33.33E
33 B4 **Bi'r Umm Missā** Saudi Arabia 24.30N 37.54E
86 H10 **Bîr Umm 'Omaiyid** Egypt 27.54N 32.30E
34 G4 **Bīr Umm Rabba** Syria 34.31N 39.22E
86 L6 **Bîr Umm Sa'îd** Egypt 29.41N 33.34E
85 M8 **Bîr Ungât** Egypt 22.08N 33.48E
43 F6 **Biruni** Uzbekistan U.S.S.R. 41.45N 60.10E
34 H2 **Bīr 'Uqlat** Syria 36.07N 40.18E
28 B4 **Birur** Karnataka India 13.38N 76.00E
33 G5 **Bi'r Usaylīlah** Saudi Arabia 22.24N 46.50E
34 G4 **Bīr Warqa** Syria 34.12N 39.39E
34 G4 **Bīr Wīrad** Syria 34.24N 39.22E
33 E6 **Bi'r Wurshah** Saudi Arabia 21.57N 43.26E
44 H4 **Biryuchek** U.S.S.R. 43.40N 47.26E
44 D8 **Biryuchiy,Poluostrov** *pen* Ukraine U.S.S.R.
42 K2 **Biryuk** *R* U.S.S.R.
45 J1 **Biryulevo** U.S.S.R. 55.33N 37.40E
42 H5 **Biryul'ka** U.S.S.R. 53.55N 106.25E
42 F4 **Biryusa** *R* U.S.S.R.
42 F4 **Biryusinsk** U.S.S.R. 55.56N 97.50E
46 E2 **Biržai** Lithuania U.S.S.R. 56.10N 24.48E
85 C6 **Bi'r Zallaf** Libya 27.23N 14.23E
85 A4 **B'ir Zār** Libya 31.28N 10.11E
84 Z21 **Birżebbuġa** Malta 35.49N 14.32E
35 D6 **Bir Zeit** Jordan 31.59N 35.12E
88 J10 **Bir Zreigat** Mauritania 22.29N 8.53W
28 K2 **Bisa** Assam India 27.27N 95.56E
19 E4 **Bisa** *isld* Moluccas Indon 1.13S 127.36E
92 E8 **Bisa** *tribe* Zambia
80 M6 **Bisaccia** Italy 41.02N 15.23E
81 F8 **Bisacquino** Sicily 37.43N 13.15E
90 F5 **Bisagua** Nigeria 12.20N 12.39E
20 K6 **Bisai** Japan 35.17N 136.43E
86 O9 **Bisaiyit, El** Saudi Arabia 28.12N 35.27E
30 C4 **Bisalpur** Pilibhit, Uttar Prad India 28.18N 79.48E
64 Q3 **Bišany** Czechoslovakia 50.13N 13.29E
30 B4 **Bisauli** Uttar Prad India 28.18N 78.55E
75 N5 **Bisbal del Panadés** Spain 41.17N 1.29E
75 R4 **Bisbal, La** Spain 41.58N 3.02E
111 P10 **Bisbee** Arizona 31.27N 109.55W
108 L1 **Bisbee** N Dakota 48.39N 99.22W
72 B7 **Biscarrosse** France 44.24N 1.10W
72 B7 **Biscarrosse-et-de-Parentis, Lac de** France 44.20N 1.10W
72 B7 **Biscarrosse Plage** France 44.26N 1.15W
75 J3 **Biscarrues** Spain 42.14N 0.45W
67 D7 **Biscay,B.of** France
105 G12 **Biscayne B** Florida
105 B11 **Biscayne,Key** *isld* Florida 25.53N 80.07W
105 G12 **Biscayne Nat. Mon.** Florida
81 N1 **Bisceglie** Italy 41.14N 16.31E
64 K4 **Bischberg** W Germany 49.55N 10.50E
64 H1 **Bischhausen** W Germany 51.09N 9.57E
69 O6 **Bischheim** France 48.36N 7.50E
64 M3 **Bischofsgrün** W Germany 50.03N 11.46E
64 E4 **Bischofsheim** Hessen W Germany 49.59N 8.22E
64 J3 **Bischofsheim an der Rhön** Bayern W Germany 50.24N 10.01E
65 H7 **Bischofshofen** Austria 47.25N 13.13E
62 H4 **Bischofswerda** E Germany 51.08N 14.13E
64 O8 **Bischofswiesen** W Germany 47.40N 12.48E
66 N2 **Bischofszell** Switzerland 47.30N 9.15E
69 O6 **Bischwiller** France 48.46N 7.53E
87 H10 **Bisciaba Uama Swamp** Somalia
105 H2 **Biscoe** N Carolina 35.22N 79.47W
123 F14 **Biscoe Is** Antarctica
96 U3 **Biscoitos** Azores 38.48N 27.16W
99 H5 **Biscotasing** Ontario 47.18N 82.07W
119 E3 **Biscucuy** Venezuela 9.17N 69.59W
20 P8 **Bise** Okinawa Japan 26.43N 127.52E
39 K3 **Bisekera** U.S.S.R. 64.20N 176.31E
66 E1 **Bisel** France 47.32N 7.14E
87 A7 **Bisellia** Sudan 7.47N 27.40E
30 D7 **Bisenda** Uttar Prad India 25.24N 80.37E
80 J3 **Bisenti** Italy 42.32N 13.48E
80 E3 **Bisentina** *isld* Italy 42.39N 11.54E
79 K7 **Bisenzio** *R* Italy
80 O3 **Biševo** *I* Yugoslavia
82 K9 **Biser** Bulgaria 41.52N 25.59E
47 M3 **Biser** U.S.S.R. 58.27N 58.58E
47 M4 **Bisert'** U.S.S.R. 56.55N 59.03E
47 H7 **Bisert'** *R* U.S.S.R.
80 O3 **Biševo** Yugoslavia 42.58N 16.01E
82 C8 **Biševo** *isld* Yugoslavia 42.59N 16.00E
80 N2 **Bisevski Kanal** Yugoslavia
20 P8 **Bise-zaki** *C* Okinawa Japan 26.44N 127.53E
23 C7 **Bisezhai** Yunnan China 23.28N 103.24E
Bisha *see* **Qal'at Bīshah**
33 E7 **Bishah** *oasis* Saudi Arabia
33 E6 **Bīshah Wādī** *watercourse* Saudi Arabia
23 D4 **Bishan** Sichuan China 29.36N 106.20E
33 N9 **Bisha, Ra's al** *C* Iraq 29.56N 48.34E
85 L10 **Bisharin** *dist* Sudan
85 N8 **Bisharin umm Ali** *dist* Egypt/Sudan
85 N10 **Bisharin umm Nagi** *dist* Sudan
32 C4 **Bisheh** Iran 33.18N 48.52E
28 L1 **Bishemnagar** Assam India 28.02N 96.01E
28 J3 **Bishenpur** Manipur India 24.40N 93.45E
86 G4 **Bîshet Qâyid** Egypt 30.39N 31.32E
45 F6 **Bishkin'** Ukraine U.S.S.R. 50.37N 34.38E
28 J2 **Bishnath** Assam India 26.37N 93.11E
Bishneh *see* **Beshneh**
29 K2 **Bishnupur** W Bengal India 23.05N 87.20E
Bishoftu *see* **Debre Zeyt**
111 F4 **Bishop** California 37.20N 118.24W
105 D4 **Bishop** Georgia 33.47N 83.27W
104 K8 **Bishop** Maryland 38.25N 75.14W
112 K8 **Bishop** Texas 27.36N 97.49W
11 B13 **Bishop and Clerks Is** New Zealand
57 K3 **Bishop Auckland** Durham Eng 54.40N 1.40W
11 L9 **Bishopdale** New Zealand 43.29S 172.34E
101 P3 **Bishop L** N W Terr 65.30N 116.10W
100 M8 **Bishopric** Saskatchewan 50.01N 105.48W
56 Q8 **Bishop Rock Lt.Ho** Is of Scilly England 49.52N 6.27W
56 F3 **Bishops Castle** Shropshire Eng 52.29N 3.00W
56 G6 **Bishop's Caundle** Dorset Eng 50.55N 2.26W
56 G4 **Bishop's Cleeve** Glos Eng 51.57N 2.04W
98 R4 **Bishop's Falls** Newfoundland 49.02N 55.29W
56 E5 **Bishops Lydeard** Somerset Eng 51.04N 3.12W
56 M4 **Bishop's Stortford** Herts Eng 51.53N 0.09E
56 C4 **Bishopston** W Glam Wales 51.35N 4.03W
56 J6 **Bishops Waltham** Hants Eng 50.58N 1.12W
58 G7 **Bishopton** Strathclyde Scotland 55.54N 4.31W
105 G3 **Bishopville** South Carolina 34.18N 80.15W
35 G3 **Bishra** Jordan 32.33N 35.53E
34 G3 **Bishri,Jebel el** *mts* Syria
95 N6 **Bisi** S Africa 30.25S 29.53E
95 N6 **Bisi** *R* S Africa
89 J9 **Bisiasi** Ghana 5.30N 1.10W
81 M4 **Bisignano** Italy 39.31N 16.17E
119 E5 **Bisinaca** Colombia 4.31N 69.40W
93 E4 **Bisina, L** Uganda
66 M4 **Bisisthal** Switzerland 46.56N 8.51E
Bisitun *see* **Bīsotūn**
87 F3 **Biskia** Ethiopia 15.30N 37.25E
30 F5 **Biskohar** Uttar Prad India 27.23N 82.34E
99 H5 **Biskotasi L** Ontario
88 Q4 **Biskra** Algeria 34.50N 5.41E
65 O3 **Biskupice** Czechoslovakia 49.03N 16.01E
62 M2 **Biskupiec** Poland 53.51N 20.58E
50 E6 **Biskupstungur** *dist* Iceland
53 D3 **Bislev** Denmark 56.57N 9.38E
56 K5 **Bisley** Surrey Eng 51.20N 0.39W
19 N7 **Bislig** Mindanao Philippines 8.10N 126.18E
19 N7 **Bislig B** Mindanao Philippines
107 C7 **Bismarck** Arkansas 34.19N 93.10W
106 G9 **Bismarck** Illinois 40.14N 87.37W
107 F4 **Bismarck** Missouri 37.45N 90.39W
108 K3 **Bismarck** N Dakota 46.50N 100.48W
15 J5 **Bismarck Arch** Papua New Guinea
15 H6 **Bismarck Ra** Papua New Guinea
123 E14 **Bismarck Str** Antarctica
63 P7 **Bismark (Altmark)** E Germany 53.40N 11.34E
37 F8 **Bismil** Turkey 37.53N 40.38E
53 Y15 **Bismo** Norway 61.54N 8.13E
53 C4 **Biso** Uganda 1.44N 31.26E
109 N5 **Bison** Oklahoma 36.12N 97.54W
108 H4 **Bison** S Dakota 45.31N 102.27W
93 B8 **Bisongou L** Tanzania 2.08S 30.58E
101 P7 **Bison L** Alberta 57.13N 116.10W
32 B3 **Bīsotūn** Iran 34.22N 47.29E
51 F8 **Bispfors** Sweden 63.00N 16.40E
63 L6 **Bispingen** W Germany 53.05N 9.59E
76 D15 **Bispo** *mt* Portugal 38.48N 9.13W
88 O3 **Bissa** *mt* Algeria 36.29N 1.33E
34 K8 **Bissah, Tulūl al** *hill* Saudi Arabia 30.31N 42.03E
29 H8 **Bissamcuttack** Orissa India 19.34N 83.32E
89 E7 **Bissandougou** Guinea 9.57N 9.09W
89 B6 **Bissau** Guinea-Bissau 11.52N 15.39W
29 D3 **Bissau** Rajasthan India 28.12N 75.08E
61 C3 **Bissegem** Belgium 50.49N 3.14E
61 P7 **Bissen** Luxembourg 49.47N 6.04E
97 K7 **Bissett** Manitoba 50.58N 95.10W
89 D6 **Bissikrima** Guinea 10.50N 10.58W
64 K6 **Bissingen** W Germany 48.42N 10.38E
66 M8 **Bissone** Switzerland 45.57N 8.58E
89 B5 **Bissorã** Guinea-Bissau 12.16N 15.35W
79 D5 **Bistagno** Italy 44.40N 8.22E
101 O6 **Bistcho L** Alberta
63 L4 **Bistensee** W Germany 54.24N 9.42E
107 C9 **Bistineau, L** Louisiana
82 H7 **Bistreţu** Romania 43.54N 23.29E
82 J3 **Bistriţa** Romania 47.08N 24.30E
82 J3 **Bistriţa** *R* Romania
82 J3 **Bistriţa-Năsăud** *div* Romania
82 K3 **Bistriţei, Munţii** *mts* Romania
48 U7 **Bistrup Bræ,L** *glacier* Greenland
19 K6 **Bisucay** *isld* Philippines 10.50N 120.59E
30 F5 **Bisuhi** *R* Uttar Prad India
30 F6 **Bisuhi** *R* Uttar Prad India
30 E5 **Biswan** Uttar Prad India 27.30N 81.00E
30 F6 **Biswi** *R* Uttar Prad India
33 M5 **Bisyah** Oman 22.43N 57.16E
62 M1 **Bisztynek** Poland 54.06N 20.53E
90 M8 **Bita** *R* Cent Afr Rep
93 A10 **Bitale** Tanzania 4.44S 29.37E
91 B2 **Bitam** Gabon 2.05N 11.30E
88 Q4 **Bitam** *R* Algeria
87 F3 **Bitama** Ethiopia 15.20N 36.47E
64 B4 **Bitburg** W Germany 49.58N 6.32E
87 G5 **Bitchana** Ethiopia 10.30N 38.12E
69 N5 **Bitche** France 49.03N 7.26E
53 X19 **Bitdalsvatn** *L* Norway 59.48N 7.55E
90 K5 **Bitéa** *R* Chad
106 J6 **Bitely** Michigan 43.46N 85.51W
81 N1 **Bitetto** Italy 41.02N 16.45E
35 B8 **Bit'ha** Israel 31.20N 34.38E
30 D6 **Bithar** Uttar Prad India 26.25N 80.34E
30 D6 **Bithur** Uttar Prad India 26.37N 80.16E
36 D2 **Bithynia** *hist reg* Turkey
43 B2 **Bitik** Kazakhstan U.S.S.R. 50.12N 50.30E
36 F2 **Bitik** Turkey 40.04N 32.35E
42 C5 **Bitki** U.S.S.R. 54.13N 82.18E
90 J5 **Bitkine** Chad 12.01N 18.16E
37 G7 **Bitlis** Turkey 38.23N 42.04E
82 G9 **Bitola** Yugoslavia 41.01N 21.21E
81 N1 **Bitonto** Italy 41.07N 16.41E
82 D7 **Bitovnja** *mt* Yugoslavia 43.48N 17.55E
33 F5 **Bitrān,Jabal** *mts* Saudi Arabia
35 D10 **Bitron** *watercourse* Israel
50 D4 **Bitrufjördhur** *B* Iceland
69 N8 **Bitschwiller-lès-Thann** France 47.50N 7.05E
56 C5 **Bittadon** Devon Eng 51.09N 4.05W
111 P2 **Bitter Cr** Utah
110 R8 **Bitter Cr** Wyoming
110 R8 **Bitter Creek** Wyoming 41.35N 108.31W
63 Q9 **Bitterfeld** E Germany 51.37N 12.20E
94 E8 **Bitterfontein** S Africa 31.03S 18.16E
108 N4 **Bitter L** S Dakota 45.16N 97.17W
Bitter L.,Gt *see* **Buheirat-Murrat-el-Kubra** *L*
Bitter L.,Lit *see* **Buheirat-Murrat-el-Sughra** *L*
56 J6 **Bitterne** Hants Eng 50.55N 1.21W
11 E11 **Bitterness,Mt** New Zealand 44.46S 170.19E
100 D5 **Bittern Lake** Alberta 53.00N 113.00W
100 M5 **Bittern Lake** Saskatchewan
110 L3 **Bitterroot** *R* Montana
110 K2 **Bitterroot Ra** Montana/Idaho
81 C3 **Bitti** Sardinia 40.29N 9.23E
87 D2 **Bittia** *watercourse* Sudan
63 P8 **Bittkau** E Germany 52.25N 11.57E
89 J6 **Bittou** Upper Volta 11.19N 0.17W
19 D3 **Bitung** Celebes Indon 1.28N 125.13E
117 G6 **Bitupitá** Brazil 2.53S 41.15W
95 M7 **Bityi** S Africa 31.48S 28.33E
46 M4 **Bityug** *R* U.S.S.R.
90 F6 **Biu** Nigeria 10.36N 12.11E
91 G9 **Biula** Angola 11.09S 20.13E
93 B7 **Biumba** Rwanda 1.36S 30.02E
75 G2 **Biurrún** Spain 42.41N 1.41W
95 O3 **Bivane** S Africa 27.31S 30.48E
81 H9 **Biviere, il** *L* Sicily 37.02N 14.20E
66 P6 **Bivio** Switzerland 46.28N 9.39E
82 L3 **Bivolari** Romania 47.30N 27.30E
82 K3 **Bivolu** *mt* Romania 47.16N 25.52E
81 F8 **Bivona** Sicily 37.37N 13.56E
Biwai Hills *see* **Darai Hills**
20 J6 **Biwa-ko** *L* Japan
61 Q8 **Biwer** Luxembourg 49.42N 6.23E
82 H3 **Bixad** Romania 47.57N 23.22E
107 E4 **Bixby** Missouri 37.39N 91.06W
109 P6 **Bixby** Oklahoma 35.56N 95.54W
58 Q9 **Bixter** Shetland Scotland 60.15N 1.24W
42 D5 **Biya** *R* U.S.S.R.
33 G6 **Biyāḍh, Al** *plain* Saudi Arabia
86 F3 **Biyala** Egypt 31.11N 31.13E
23 F2 **Biyang** Henan China 32.48N 113.24E
Biyār'Ar'ara *see* **Be'erot 'Aro'er**
86 M7 **Biyâr, Wâdî el** *watercourse* Egypt
95 O9 **Biyela** S Africa 27.48S 32.09E
41 O8 **Biyette** U.S.S.R. 62.58N 130.25E
43 K5 **Biylikol',Ozero** *L* Kazakhstan U.S.S.R.
87 J5 **Biyo Kaboba** Ethiopia 10.26N 42.38E
42 D5 **Biysk** U.S.S.R. 52.35N 85.16E
44 D9 **Biyuk Karasu** *R* U.S.S.R.
95 N6 **Bizana** S Africa 30.51S 29.52E
72 K9 **Bizanet** France 43.10N 2.52E
75 M2 **Bizberri** *mt* Spain 42.35N 0.49E
72 K9 **Bize-Minervois** France 43.19N 2.52E
Bizerta *see* **Bizerte**
88 S3 **Bizerte** Tunisia 37.18N 9.52E
78 C11 **Bizerte, Lac de** Tunisia 37.10N 9.50E
46 R3 **Bizhbulyak** U.S.S.R. 53.40N 54.17E
35 B6 **Bizzaron** Israel 31.48N 34.43E
66 M8 **Bizzarone** Italy 45.50N 8.56E
53 W19 **Bjåen** Norway 59.39N 7.26E
53 Y19 **Bjåenelva** *R* Norway 59.38N 8.23E
53 Y19 **Bjåenseter** Norway 59.43N 8.19E
53 J6 **Bjæverskov** Denmark 55.28N 12.02E
50 F6 **Bjallar** *lava field* Iceland
50 E4 **Bjarg** Iceland 65.17N 20.50W
50 A3 **Bjargtangar** *C* Iceland 65.30N 24.29W
52 J8 **Bjärka-Säby** Sweden 58.15N 15.45E
51 F2 **Bjarkøy** Norway 69.00N 16.35E
50 C2 **Bjarnanes** Ísafjardharsýsla, Nordhur Iceland 66.24N 22.20W
50 K6 **Bjarnanes** Skaftafellssýsla, Austur Iceland 64.19N 15.13W
50 E8 **Bjarnarey** *isld* Vestmannaeyjar Iceland 63.27N 20.11W
50 D2 **Bjarnarfjördhur** *B* Iceland
50 D3 **Bjarnarfjördhur** *B* Iceland
50 B4 **Bjarnarhöfn** Iceland 65.00N 22.56W
50 D3 **Bjarnarnes** Iceland 65.45N 21.20W
50 C4 **Bjarneyjar** *islds* Iceland 65.16N 22.51W
52 H10 **Bjärnum** Sweden 56.15N 13.45E
82 E7 **Bjelašnica** *mt* Yugoslavia 43.10N 18.21E
52 D8 **Bjelland** Norway 58.27N 7.47E
82 D5 **Bjelovar** Yugoslavia 45.54N 16.51E
53 E1 **Bjergby** Denmark 57.31N 10.03E
53 G5 **Bjerge** Denmark 55.36N 11.12E
53 T20 **Bjergøy** *isld* Norway 59.15N 5.52E
53 G5 **Bjergsted** Denmark 55.40N 11.21E
53 D4 **Bjerringbro** Denmark 56.23N 9.40E
51 F3 **Bjervik** Norway 68.34N 17.50E
53 Y17 **Bjøberg** Norway 60.56N 8.12E
53 T19 **Bjoestrand** Norway 59.40N 5.39E
53 Z14 **Bjøkneseter** Norway 62.06N 8.30E
50 L4 **Bjólfur** *mt* Iceland 65.16N 14.06W
51 D5 **Bjollånes** Norway 66.31N 14.59E
53 W18 **Bjonna** *R* Norway
52 H6 **Björbo** Sweden 60.26N 14.45E
53 T16 **Bjordal** Norway 61.04N 5.50E
53 Y18 **Bjordalsnuten** *mt* Norway 60.22N 8.03E
53 W18 **Bjoreia** *R* Norway
53 X18 **Bjoreidalshytta** Norway 60.20N 7.31E
53 V15 **Bjørga** *mt* Norway 61.33N 6.37E
62 E4 **Bjørgan** Norway 62.34N 10.20E
53 U20 **Bjørheimsvatn** *L* Norway 59.04N 6.00E
53 X15 **Bjørk** Sogn og Fjordane Norway 61.32N 7.45E
51 G3 **Bjørkas** Norway 68.51N 19.10E
51 F3 **Bjørkåsen** Norway 68.19N 16.45E
53 V14 **Bjørke** Möre og Romsdal Norway 62.06N 6.35E
51 F11 **Björke** Sweden 60.46N 17.15E
53 U14 **Bjørkedal** Norway 62.00N 6.03E
53 U14 **Bjørkedalsvatn** *L* Norway 62.01N 6.04E
52 F7 **Bjørkelangen** Norway 59.54N 11.33E
52 G9 **Björketorp** Sweden 57.40N 12.30E
51 E5 **Björkfjäll** *mt* Sweden 66.10N 16.15E
51 K6 **Björkfors** Sweden 65.55N 23.30E
51 G3 **Björkliden** Sweden 68.25N 18.40E
52 K6 **Björklinge** Sweden 60.03N 17.33E
51 J8 **Björköby** Finland 63.21N 21.20E
52 K3 **Björksele** Sweden 63.56N 17.10E
52 L2 **Björksele** Sweden 64.59N 18.30E
53 Y14 **Bjorli** Norway 62.16N 8.13E
52 L3 **Björna** Sweden 63.35N 18.35E
53 S18 **Bjørnafjorden** *inlet* Norway 60.05N 5.30E
53 V19 **Bjørnanuten** *mt* Norway 59.56N 6.48E
53 W20 **Bjørnarå** Norway 59.18N 7.25E
Björneborg Finland *see* **Pori**
52 H7 **Björneborg** Sweden 59.14N 14.15E
97 L2 **Bjorne Pen** N W Terr 77.30N 87.00W
53 X18 **Bjornesfjord** *L* Norway 60.10N 7.38E
53 X20 **Bjørnevasshytta** Norway 50.21N 7.33E
51 P2 **Bjørnevatn** Norway 69.38N 30.01E
53 W18 **Bjørnevatn** *L* Norway 60.02N 7.19E
53 X20 **Bjørnevatn** *L* Norway 59.20N 7.35E
50 H6 **Björninn** *ridge* Iceland
52 K7 **Björnlunda** Sweden 59.05N 17.11E
53 E6 **Bjørnø** *isld* Denmark 55.04N 10.16E
Bjørnøya *see* **Bear I** Arctic Oc
50 R11 **Bjørnøy Radio** Spitsbergen 74.31N 19.01E
53 C3 **Bjornsholm Å** *R* Denmark
51 E3 **Bjørnskinn** Norway 69.00N 15.40E
53 E5 **Bjørnsknude** *C* Denmark 55.42N 10.02E
53 S18 **Bjørøy** *isld* Norway 60.18N 5.12E
52 J8 **Björsäter** Sweden 58.20N 16.01E
53 T17 **Bjørsvik** Norway 60.38N 5.30E
52 K5 **Bjuråker** Sweden 61.51N 16.35E
52 L3 **Bjurholm** Sweden 63.56N 19.10E
35 G2 **Bjuriyeh** Syria 32.52N 35.47E
52 N2 **Bjuröklubb** *Lt Ho* Sweden 64.29N 21.32E
52 J6 **Bjursås** Sweden 60.44N 15.30E
52 H7 **Bjurtjärn** Sweden 59.26N 14.20E
52 M2 **Bjurträsk** Sweden 64.58N 19.45E
53 K4 **Bjuv** Sweden 56.05N 12.57E
25 F9 **B. Kam Phaeng Phet** Thailand 7.09N 100.16E
89 G5 **Bla** Mali 12.56N 5.47W
60 G12 **Blaak-Sedijk** Netherlands 51.49N 4.30E
61 H2 **Blaasveld** Belgium 51.04N 4.23E
94 F6 **Blaauwpan** *salt L* S Africa 27.50S 21.01E
53 A5 **Blåbjerg** *mt* Denmark 55.45N 8.15E
56 J2 **Blaby** Leics Eng 52.35N 1.09W
71 F4 **Blacé** France 46.02N 4.38E
98 C3 **Blache,L.de la** Quebec
110 B5 **Blachly** Oregon 44.13N 123.33W
113 E5 **Black** Alaska 62.19N 165.23W
112 E1 **Black** Texas 34.41N 102.36W
107 J8 **Black** *R* Alabama
113 Q3 **Black** *R* Alaska
111 P8 **Black** *R* Arizona
107 F5 **Black** *R* Arkansas
107 F4 **Black** *R* Ark/Missouri
107 E10 **Black** *R* Louisiana
106 M6 **Black** *R* Michigan
107 H11 **Black** *R* Mississippi
105 J3 **Black** *R* N Carolina
105 H4 **Black** *R* S Carolina
106 D5 **Black** *R* Wisconsin
58 M7 **Blackadder Water** *R* Borders Scotland
13 H6 **Blackall** Queensland 24.23S 145.27E
101 T6 **Black B** Athabasca, L, Sask
107 G12 **Black B** Louisiana 29.38N 89.34W
99 B4 **Black B** Ontario
11 F9 **Blackball** New Zealand 42.22S 171.23E
110 B8 **Blackbear** California 41.15N 123.12W
100 M3 **Black Bear Island L** Saskatchewan
107 H8 **Black Belt** *reg* Alabama/Miss
101 U7 **Black Birch L** Saskatchewan 56.55N 107.50W
10 V10 **Blackbourne,Pt** Norfolk I Pacific Oc 29.04S 167.59E
56 M6 **Blackboys** E Sussex Eng 50.58N 0.10E
57 J7 **Blackbrook** Staffs Eng 52.57N 2.21W
13 F4 **Blackbull** Queensland 17.56S 141.48E
58 M4 **Blackburn** Grampian Scotland 57.12N 2.17W
57 J5 **Blackburn** Lancs Eng 53.45N 2.29W
58 J7 **Blackburn** Lothian Scotland 55.53N 3.38W
12 E7 **Blackburn** *dist* Melbourne, Vic
113 Q6 **Blackburn, Mt** Alaska 61.44N 143.26W
111 B2 **Black Butte** *mt* California 39.45N 122.51W
111 K6 **Black Canyon** Nevada/Arizona
109 C3 **Black Canyon of the Gunnison Nat.Mon** Colorado
59 K6 **Black Castle** Wicklow Irish Rep 52.58N 6.03W
59 L2 **Blackcave Tunnel** Antrim N Ireland 54.52N 5.49W
123 E12 **Black Coast** Antarctica
111 P6 **Black Creek** Arizona/New Mexico
106 F5 **Black Creek** Wisconsin 44.29N 88.26W
100 C8 **Black Diamond** Alberta 50.45N 114.12W
110 C2 **Black Diamond** Washington 47.18N 122.01W
101 K9 **Black Dome** *pk* Br Columbia 53.17N 127.30W
103 F2 **Black Dome** *pk* New York 42.16N 74.07W
99 O7 **Black Donald Mines** Ontario 45.11N 76.54W
13 G3 **Blackdown** Queensland 17.01S 144.00E
56 E6 **Blackdown Hills** England
108 Q2 **Blackduck** Minnesota 47.40N 94.35W
110 O2 **Black Eagle** Montana 47.33N 111.14W
57 G2 **Black Esk** *R* Dumfries & Galloway Scotland
104 C9 **Blackey** Kentucky 37.06N 82.57W
100 G5 **Blackfoot** Alberta 53.18N 110.12W
110 N6 **Blackfoot** Idaho 43.13N 112.20W
110 N1 **Blackfoot** Montana 48.35N 112.52W
110 O6 **Blackfoot** *R* Idaho
110 M3 **Blackfoot** *R* Montana
110 O7 **Blackfoot River Res** Idaho 42.55N 111.35W
57 H3 **Blackford** Cumbria Eng 54.57N 2.56W
58 J6 **Blackford** Tayside Scotland 56.16N 3.48W
59 G2 **Black Gap** Donegal Irish Rep 54.33N 7.54W
100 H2 **Black Hawk** Ontario 48.49N 93.59W
59 D5 **Black Hd** Clare Irish Rep 53.09N 9.16W
56 T10 **Black Hd** Cornwall Eng 49.59N 5.05W
11 L7 **Black Hd** North I New Zealand 40.12S 176.48E
11 L13 **Black Hd** South I New Zealand 45.56S 170.26E
14 B10 **Black Hd** W Australia 34.40S 115.50E
98 T5 **Blackhead B** Newfoundland
94 Q11 **Blackheath** Cape Town S Africa 33.58S 18.42E
55 G4 **Blackheath** London Eng 51.28N 0.01E
12 K5 **Blackheath** New S Wales 33.37S 150.17E
57 K2 **Black Heddon** Northumb Eng 55.04N 1.53W
23 B9 **Black Hill** Hong Kong 22.18N 114.14E
12 B4 **Black Hill** S Australia 31.33S 132.08E
58 K3 **Blackhillock** Grampian Scotland 57.32N 3.05W
13 A4 **Black Hills** N Terr Australia
108 G5 **Black Hills** S Dakota
100 D8 **Blackie** Alberta 50.37N 113.32W
123 H6 **Black Island** Antarctica 78.10S 165.50E
100 V7 **Black Island** Manitoba
58 H3 **Black Isle** *pen* Highland Scotland
113 H8 **Black L** Alaska 56.29N 159.00W
57 D3 **Black L** Dumfries & Galloway Scotland 54.55N 4.56W
107 C10 **Black L** Louisiana 31.58N 93.08W
106 K4 **Black L** Michigan
105 J3 **Black L** N Carolina 34.40N 78.25W
104 K2 **Black L** New York
101 V6 **Black L** Saskatchewan
109 E5 **Black Lake** New Mexico 36.18N 105.14W
99 T6 **Black Lake** Quebec 46.03N 71.21W
110 N1 **Blackleaf** Montana 48.01N 112.39W
104 F6 **Black Lick** Pennsylvania 40.28N 79.13W
59 G3 **Blacklion** Cavan Irish Rep 54.18N 7.53W
116 P6 **Blackman's** Barbados 13.11N 59.33W
111 M6 **Black Mesa** *tableland* Arizona
111 O5 **Black Mesa** *tableland* Arizona
56 D5 **Blackmoor Gate** Devon Eng 51.11N 3.56W
58 G5 **Black Mount** *forest* Strathclyde Scotland
111 G6 **Black Mt** California 35.28N 117.51W
12 A6 **Black Mt** Canberra Australia 35.17S 149.06E
56 D4 **Black Mt** Dyfed Wales 51.54N 3.43W
105 E2 **Black Mt** N Carolina 35.38N 82.20W
109 B8 **Black Mt** New Mexico 33.23N 108.13W
13 C2 **Black Mt** N Terr Australia 13.45S 134.30E
31 G3 **Black Mt** *ra* Pakistan
111 K6 **Black Mts** Arizona
98 E6 **Black Mts** New Brunswick
56 E4 **Black Mts** Powys/Gwent Wales
58 J7 **Blackness** Central Scotland 56.00N 3.31W
Black Pagoda *see* **Kanarak**
56 C4 **Blackpill** W Glam Wales 51.36N 4.00W
110 M7 **Black Pine Pk** Idaho 42.07N 113.07W
101 N10 **Black Pines** Br Columbia 50.55N 120.15W
109 B9 **Black Pk** New Mexico 32.54N 108.10W
13 A5 **Black Pk** N Terr Australia 20.08S 129.36E
101 N10 **Blackpool** Br Columbia 51.33N 120.07W
57 G5 **Blackpool** Lancs Eng 53.50N 3.03W
113 Q3 **Black, R** Alaska
116 H2 **Black R** Jamaica, W I
26 T13 **Black R** Mauritius, Indian Oc
109 C9 **Black Ra** New Mexico
14 B6 **Black Ra** W Australia
113 P5 **Black Rapids** Alaska 63.30N 145.52W
116 H2 **Black River** Jamaica, W I 18.02N 77.52W
106 L5 **Black River** Michigan 44.51N 83.21W
106 D5 **Black River Falls** Wisconsin 44.18N 90.51W
113 Q3 **Black,R.,Lit** Alaska
107 E5 **Black Rock** Arkansas 36.05N 91.06W
111 M3 **Black Rock** Utah 38.41N 112.59W
12 D8 **Black Rock** Victoria 37.58S 145.01E
Black Rock *mt see* **'Inâb,El** *mt*
110 F9 **Black Rock Des** Nevada
59 B3 **Black Rock Lt.,Ho** Mayo Irish Rep 54.05N 10.20W
98 N3 **Black Rocks** Quebec 50.29N 59.29W
57 H5 **Blackrod** Greater Manchester Eng 53.36N 2.36W
105 F2 **Blacksburg** S Carolina 35.07N 81.32W
104 E9 **Blacksburg** Virginia 37.15N 80.25W
16 D4 **Black Sea** Turkey/U.S.S.R.
110 P8 **Blacks Fork** *R* Wyoming
98 F8 **Blacks Harbour** New Brunswick 45.03N 66.49W
105 E6 **Blackshear** Georgia 31.19N 82.16W
59 B3 **Blacksod B** Mayo Irish Rep 54.05N 10.02W
109 B8 **Black Springs** New Mexico 33.31N 108.09W
52 J9 **Blackstad** Sweden 57.47N 16.10E
59 J6 **Blackstairs Mt** Carlow Irish Rep 52.33N 6.49W
105 F3 **Blackstock** S Carolina 34.33N 81.08W
103 L2 **Blackstone** Massachusetts 42.01N 71.33W
104 G9 **Blackstone** Virginia 37.05N 78.02W
103 M3 **Blackstone** *R* Rhode I
101 E3 **Blackstone** *R* Yukon Terr
99 B3 **Black Sturgeon L** Ontario 49.20N 88.52W
12 K4 **Black Sugarloaf** *mt* New S Wales 31.24S 151.34E
104 E7 **Blacksville** W Virginia 39.42N 80.14W
95 O9 **Black Umfolozi** *R* S Africa
98 G7 **Blackville** New Brunswick 46.44N 65.51W
12 K4 **Blackville** New S Wales 31.34S 150.10E
105 F4 **Blackville** S Carolina 33.22N 81.17W
89 H7 **Black Volta** *R* W Africa
101 M9 **Black Water** Br Columbia 53.30N 123.13W
56 K5 **Blackwater** Hants Eng 51.20N 0.48W
56 J6 **Blackwater** I of Wight Eng 50.40N 1.16W
107 C3 **Blackwater** Missouri 38.58N 93.00W
13 J6 **Blackwater** Queensland 23.34S 148.51E
59 K7 **Blackwater** Wexford Irish Rep 52.26N 6.20W
107 K11 **Blackwater** *R* Florida/Ala
58 H2 **Black Water** *R* Highland Scotland
107 C3 **Blackwater** *R* Missouri
13 G7 **Blackwater** *R* Queensland
104 H9 **Blackwater** *R* Virginia
57 C1 **Blackwater Foot** Arran, Strathclyde Scotland 55.30N 5.19W
101 M3 **Blackwater L** N W Terr
59 J3 **Blackwater,R** Armagh etc N Ireland
56 N4 **Blackwater, R** Essex Eng
59 J4 **Blackwater,R** Meath etc Irish Rep
59 G7 **Blackwater,R** Waterford etc Irish Rep
58 G5 **Blackwater Res** Highland Scotland
109 N5 **Blackwell** Oklahoma 36.47N 97.18W
112 G3 **Blackwell** Texas 32.05N 100.19W
109 M3 **Black Wolf** Kansas 38.46N 98.22W
56 E4 **Blackwood** Gwent Wales 51.41N 3.13W
58 J7 **Blackwood** Strathclyde Scotland 55.41N 3.56W
12 B8 **Blackwood** *dist* Adelaide, S Aust
108 J9 **Blackwood Creek** Nebraska
14 B10 **Blackwood, R** W Australia
53 U19 **Blådalsvatn** *L* Norway 59.55N 6.10E
60 J14 **Bladel** Netherlands 51.22N 5.13E
105 F6 **Bladen** Georgia 31.14N 81.43W
108 M9 **Bladen** Nebraska 40.20N 98.35W
105 J3 **Bladenboro** N Carolina 34.32N 78.48W
103 A9 **Bladensburg** Maryland 38.56N 76.56W
94 E7 **Bladgrond** S Africa 28.55S 19.50E
57 E3 **Bladnoch** Dumfries & Galloway Scotland 54.51N 4.27W
57 D2 **Bladnoch** *R* Dumfries & Galloway Scotland
100 L7 **Bladworth** Saskatchewan 51.22N 106.09W
53 U19 **Blåelv** *R* Norway
57 F7 **Blaenau Ffestiniog** Gwynedd Wales 52.59N 3.56W
56 E4 **Blaenavon** Gwent Wales 51.48N 3.05W
56 D4 **Blaengarw** Mid Glam Wales 51.38N 3.35W
56 B3 **Blaenporth** Dyfed Wales 52.07N 4.33W
56 D4 **Blaenrhondda** Mid Glam Wales 51.42N 3.33W
53 D3 **Blære** Denmark 56.52N 9.32E
50 E5 **Bláfell** *mt* Iceland 64.59N 20.05W
50 F6 **Bláfell** *mt* Iceland 64.29N 19.51W
50 J4 **Bláfjall** *mt* Iceland 65.25N 16.50W
53 T15 **Blåfjell** *mt* Norway 61.31N 5.34E
53 V17 **Blåfjell** *mt* Norway 60.57N 6.40E
53 V20 **Blåfjell** *mt* Rogaland Norway 59.18N 6.41E
53 V20 **Blåfjellhytta** Norway 59.18N 6.45E
50 D7 **Blafjöll** *hills* Iceland 63.59N 21.36W
53 X14 **Blåfjord** *mt* Norway 62.17N 7.39E
56 F5 **Blagdon** Avon Eng 51.20N 2.43W
56 E6 **Blagdon** Somerset Eng 50.58N 3.09W
72 G8 **Blagnac** *airport* France 43.39N 1.23E
50 F5 **Blágnípa** *mt* Iceland 64.43N 19.11W
43 O4 **Blagodarnoye** Kazakhstan U.S.S.R. 47.01N 82.09E
44 E2 **Blagodarnyy** Stavropol' U.S.S.R. 45.06N 43.26E
43 L2 **Blagodatnoye** Kazakhstan U.S.S.R. 55.18N 72.46E
45 C9 **Blagodatnoye** Ukraine U.S.S.R. 47.59N 31.08E
40 G9 **Blagodatnyy** U.S.S.R. 45.30N 135.40E
82 H8 **Blagoevgrad** Bulgaria 42.01N 23.05E
41 C2 **Blagopoluchiya,Zaliv** *B* Novaya Zemlya U.S.S.R.
42 B5 **Blagoveshchenka** Altay U.S.S.R. 52.48N 79.47E
43 H1 **Blagoveshchenka** Kazakhstan U.S.S.R. 54.22N 66.59E
45 Q5 **Blagoveshchenka** Saratov U.S.S.R. 51.22N 44.02E
40 D6 **Blagoveshchensk** Amur U.S.S.R. 50.19N 127.30E
47 H7 **Blagoveshchensk** Bashkir U.S.S.R. 55.01N 56.00E
41 R3 **Blagoveshchenskiy Proliv** *str* U.S.S.R.
43 L5 **Blagoveshchenskoye** Kazakhstan U.S.S.R. 43.18N 74.13E
47 E5 **Blagoveshchenskoye** U.S.S.R. 61.29N 42.22E
44 A8 **Blagoyevo** Ukraine U.S.S.R. 46.56N 30.41E
53 V14 **Blåhorn** *mt* Norway 62.11N 6.58E
53 W14 **Blåhorn** *mt* Norway 62.04N 7.10E
61 K6 **Blaimont** Belgium 50.12N 4.50E
70 G7 **Blain** France 47.29N 1.45W
104 H6 **Blain** Pennsylvania 40.21N 77.32W
109 O2 **Blaine** Kansas 39.29N 96.24W
110 C1 **Blaine** Washington 49.00N 122.44W
104 F7 **Blaine** W Virginia 39.23N 79.13W
100 L6 **Blaine Lake** Saskatchewan 52.50N 106.54W
70 G3 **Blainville** France 49.04N 1.35W
69 L6 **Blainville-sur-l'Eau** France 48.33N 6.24E
108 O8 **Blair** Nebraska 41.32N 96.10W
109 L7 **Blair** Oklahoma 34.46N 99.21W
106 C5 **Blair** Wisconsin 44.19N 91.13W
104 D9 **Blair** W Virginia 37.53N 81.52W
13 H6 **Blair Athol** Queensland 22.41S 147.30E
58 J5 **Blair Atholl** Tayside Scotland 56.46N 3.51W
94 J5 **Blairbeth** S Africa 25.15S 26.08E
58 J5 **Blair Castle** Tayside Scotland 56.47N 3.53W
58 K5 **Blairgowrie** Tayside Scotland 56.36N 3.21W
111 G3 **Blair Junction** Nevada 38.00N 117.46W
100 C9 **Blairmore** Br Columbia 49.40N 114.28W
58 G6 **Blairmore** Strathclyde Scotland 56.00N 4.54W
14 B6 **Blair,Mt** W Australia 23.30S 117.09E
111 D2 **Blairsden** California 39.47N 120.38W
106 B8 **Blairstown** Iowa 41.54N 92.05W
103 E5 **Blairstown** New Jersey 40.59N 74.57W
105 D3 **Blairsville** Georgia 34.52N 83.52W
104 F6 **Blairsville** Pennsylvania 40.27N 79.17W
69 H7 **Blaise** France 48.16N 4.58E
70 N4 **Blaise** *R* Eure France
69 H6 **Blaise** *R* Haute-Marne France
71 F2 **Blaisy Bas** France 47.23N 4.44E
82 H4 **Blaj** Romania 46.10N 23.57E
72 F9 **Blajan** France 43.16N 0.38E
43 F2 **Blak** U.S.S.R. 51.18N 61.02E
90 F1 **Blaka** Niger 21.24N 12.49E
90 F1 **Blaka** *watercourse* Niger
18 J4 **Blakang Mati,Pulau** *isld* Singapore
105 C6 **Blakely** Georgia 31.22N 84.58W
103 C4 **Blakely** Pennsylvania 41.29N 73.35W
56 F3 **Blakemere** Hereford & Worcs Eng 52.04N 2.56W
56 G4 **Blakeney** Glos Eng 51.46N 2.29W
56 O2 **Blakeney** Norfolk Eng 52.58N 1.00E
106 F1 **Blake Pt** Michigan 48.12N 88.27W
108 S9 **Blakesburg** Iowa 40.59N 92.39W
103 C4 **Blakeslee** Pennsylvania 41.06N 75.35W
50 A3 **Blakknes** *C* Iceland 65.39N 24.18W
53 V15 **Bleksæter** Norway 61.52N 6.32E
105 D6 **Blakshear,L** Georgia 31.55N 83.57W
89 D8 **Blama** Sierra Leone 7.55N 11.22W
51 G2 **Blåmannen** *mt* Norway 69.45N 18.35E
51 E4 **Blåmannsisen** *mt* Norway 67.16N 16.05E
18 L10 **Blambangan, Semenanjung** *pen* Java Indon
66 D2 **Blamont** France 47.23N 6.51E
69 M6 **Blâmont** France 48.36N 6.50E
72 H8 **Blan** France 43.32N 2.00E
109 E4 **Blanca** Colorado 37.27N 105.32W
77 O4 **Blanca** Spain 38.10N 1.21W
121 E7 **Blanca, Bahía** Argentina
120 B3 **Blanca,Cord** *mts* Peru
109 G7 **Blanca Cr** New Mex/Texas
121 C7 **Blanca de la Totora, Sa** *ra* Argentina
71 B1 **Blancafort** France 47.32N 2.32E
121 D7 **Blanca Grande, L** Argentina
121 J5 **Blanca, L** Chile
121 K9 **Blanca, L** Chile
121 K5 **Blanca, L** Chubut Argentina 45.50S 71.15W
121 B7 **Blanca, L** Neuquén Argentina 39.02S 70.25W
121 E3 **Blanca, L** Santa Fé Argentina 30.15S 60.32W
109 E4 **Blanca Pk** Colorado 37.34N 105.29W
77 M2 **Blancares Viejos** *mt* Spain 39.05N 2.08W
75 H6 **Blancas** Spain 40.49N 1.29W
109 E8 **Blanca,Sa** *mt* New Mexico 33.23N 105.49W
112 B4 **Blanca,Sa** *mt* Texas 31.15N 105.27W
77 G7 **Blanca,Sierra** *mts* Spain
88 S3 **Blanc, C** Tunisia 37.20N 9.52E
66 F8 **Blanc de Seitlon, Mont** Switz 45.59N 7.25E
110 J1 **Blanchard** Idaho 48.01N 116.59W
106 J6 **Blanchard** Michigan 43.31N 85.05W
108 N2 **Blanchard** N Dakota 47.22N 97.14W
109 N6 **Blanchard** Oklahoma 35.08N 97.40W
110 C1 **Blanchard** Washington 48.36N 122.26W
99 E2 **Blanche** Ontario 50.05N 85.45W
99 P7 **Blanche** Quebec 45.44N 75.22W
71 J8 **Blanche** *R* France
12 C5 **Blanche,C** S Australia 33.04S 134.11E
15 K3 **Blanche Chan** Solomon Is
12 E3 **Blanche, L** S Australia
14 E5 **Blanche, L** W Australia 23.30S 123.18E
71 J8 **Blanche,Mtgne.de la** France
104 B7 **Blanchester** Ohio 39.16N 83.59W
12 E5 **Blanchetown** S Australia 34.21S 139.38E
116 O1 **Blanchisseuse** Trinidad & Tobago 10.47N 61.18W
57 J3 **Blanchland** Northumb Eng 54.51N 2.03W
72 G2 **Blanc,Le** France 46.38N 1.04E
68 G2 **Blanc-Mesnil,le** France 48.57N 2.28E
109 C5 **Blanco** New Mexico 36.43N 107.50W
95 F9 **Blanco** S Africa 33.56S 22.25E
112 J5 **Blanco** Texas 30.08N 98.30W
77 F6 **Blanco** *R* Spain
121 M6 **Blanco,C** Argentina 47.15S 65.46W
77 V15 **Blanco,C** Balearic Is 39.22N 2.47E
115 M5 **Blanco,C** Costa Rica 9.36N 85.06W
Blanco, C Morocco *see* **Jorf Lastar,El-.**
110 A7 **Blanco,C** Oregon 42.50N 124.32W
120 D11 **Blanco Encalada,Caleta** *B* Chile 24.25S 70.35W
120 E12 **Blanco, L** Argentina 26.36S 66.53W
115 G5 **Blanco, Peñón** *pk* Mexico 25.00N 104.02W
115 N5 **Blanco,Pico** *pk* Costa Rica 9.18N 83.01W
120 F6 **Blanco, R** Bolivia
121 J5 **Blanco, R** Chile
120 C1 **Blanco, R** Peru
76 D4 **Blancos** Spain 42.00N 7.45W
109 C5 **Blanco Trading Post** New Mexico 36.25N 107.46W
98 P2 **Blanc Sablon** Quebec 51.26N 57.08W
104 D9 **Bland** Virginia 37.06N 81.08W
12 J5 **Bland** *R* New S Wales

50 F4 Blandá R Iceland
61 D4 Blandain Belgium 50.37N 3.18E
78 B12 Blandan Algeria 36.47N 8.10E
71 D9 Blandas France 43.53N 3.31E
11 J2 Bland B New Zealand
61 J3 Blanden Belgium 50.50N 4.43E
56 G6 Blandford Dorset Eng 50.52N 2.11W
103 J2 Blandford Massachusetts 42.11N 72.56W
111 P4 Blanding Utah 37.37N 109.29W
106 D9 Blandinsville Illinois 40.34N 90.52W
103 C6 Blandon Pennsylvania 40.26N 75.53W
75 Q4 Blanes Spain 41.41N 2.48E
95 L8 Blaney S Africa 32.51S 27.31E
105 G3 Blaney S Carolina 34.10N 80.48W
106 J3 Blaney Park Michigan 46.06N 85.56W
87 H8 Blanga Ethiopia 4.45N 40.00E
18 B4 Blangkejeren Sumatra Indon 3.55N 97.27E
18 A3 Blangkuala Sumatra Indon 5.49N 95.22E
70 L3 Blangy-le-Château France 49.14N 0.17E
69 B4 Blangy-sur-Bresle France 49.56N 1.38E
69 C3 Blangy-sur-Ternoise France 50.25N 2.09E
65 K3 Blanice R Czechoslovakia
65 L2 Blanice R Czechoslovakia
63 P5 Blankenberg E Germany 53.47N 11.44E
61 C1 Blankenberge Belgium 51.19N 3.08E
66 F5 Blankenburg Switzerland 46.33N 7.24E
63 N9 Blankenburg (Harz) Magdeburg E Germany 51.48N 10.58E
63 S8 Blankenfelde E Germany 52.20N 13.24E
64 L2 Blankenhain Erfurt E Germany 50.51N 11.20E
64 N2 Blankenhain Gera E Germany 50.47N 12.16E
60 M8 Blankenham Netherlands 52.46N 5.53E
63 O9 Blankenheim E Germany 51.31N 11.26E
64 B3 Blankenheim W Germany 50.26N 6.39E
69 P5 Blankenloch W Germany 49.04N 8.28E
64 C3 Blankenrath W Germany 50.02N 7.18E
63 S6 Blankensee E Germany 53.26N 13.16E
64 M3 Blankenstein W Germany 50.23N 11.41E
112 J4 Blanket Texas 31.49N 98.48W
57 N6 Blankney Lincs Eng 53.07N 0.24W
72 C6 Blanquefort France 44.55N 0.37W
77 L4 Blanquilla mt Spain 38.05N 2.52W
116 M9 Blanquilla, Isla Lesser Antilles 11.53N 64.38W
77 E8 Blanquilla,Sierra mts Spain
121 G4 Blanquillo Uruguay 32.53S 55.37W
65 P3 Blansko Czechoslovakia 49.22N 16.39E
65 K4 Blanský,Les mts Czechoslovakia
92 G9 Blantyre Malawi 15.46S 35.00E
58 H7 Blantyre Strathclyde Scotland 55.47N 4.06W
72 E5 Blanzac-Porcheresse France 45.28N 0.02E
72 E3 Blanzay France 46.12N 0.14E
71 E3 Blanzy France 46.42N 4.23E
61 F5 Blaregnies Belgium 50.22N 3.54E
60 J10 Blaricum Netherlands 52.16N 5.15E
59 E8 Blarney Cork Irish Rep 51.56N 8.34W
66 L5 Blas mt Switzerland 46.35N 8.43E
104 G4 Blasdell New York 42.47N 78.50W
72 D6 Blasimon France 44.47N 0.04W
52 H2 Blåsjön L Sweden 64.45N 14.15E
53 W17 Blåskavlen mt Norway 60.57N 7.18E
59 B7 Blasket Sd Kerry Irish Rep
53 V21 Blåstøldalen V Norway 58.55N 6.30E
53 W13 Blåstolen mt Norway 62.33N 7.21E
62 L4 Błaszki Poland 51.40N 18.22E
84 Y20 Blata il-Bajda C Malta 35.57N 14.26E
65 J3 Blatná Czechoslovakia 49.26N 13.53E
82 M7 Blatnitsa Bulgaria 43.41N 28.32E
64 P3 Blatno Czechoslovakia 50.06N 13.24E
61 E4 Blaton Belgium 50.30N 3.40E
66 H6 Blatten Switzerland 46.22N 7.59E
66 H6 Blatten Switzerland 46.26N 7.47E
51 F6 Blattnicksele Sweden 65.22N 17.40E
69 M2 Blatzheim W Germany 50.51N 6.38E
64 H7 Blaubeuren W Germany 48.25N 9.47E
66 F2 Blauen mt Switzerland 47.28N 7.29E
64 H5 Blaufelden W Germany 49.18N 9.58E
63 J4 Blauort isld W Germany
66 G5 Blau See L Switzerland 46.32N 7.40E
50 G5 Blautakvísl R Iceland
60 K7 Blauwe Slenk channel Netherlands
53 A5 Blåvands Huk C Denmark 55.33N 8.03E
58 D4 Blaven mt Skye, Highland Scotland 57.13N 6.05W
70 D5 Blavet R France
57 M6 Blaxton S Yorks Eng 53.30N 0.59W
57 K3 Blaydon Tyne and Wear Eng 54.58N 1.42W
72 C5 Blaye France 45.08N 0.40W
71 J8 Blayeul mt France 44.15N 6.19E
12 J5 Blayney New S Wales 33.32S 149.19E
14 C5 Blaze,Mt W Australia 20.02S 119.39E
13 B2 Blaze Pt N Terr Australia 12.55S 130.10E
110 P8 Blazon Wyoming 41.40N 110.33W
62 N6 Błazowa Poland 49.54N 22.06E
77 F4 Blázques Spain 38.24N 5.26W
121 E10 Bleaker Island Falkland Is
112 O5 Bleakwood Texas 30.41N 93.49W
56 O5 Blean Kent Eng 51.19N 1.02E
63 N6 Bleckede W Germany 53.18N 10.44E
75 K3 Blecua Spain 42.04N 0.11W
82 B4 Bled Yugoslavia 46.22N 14.07E
41 D2 Blednaya,Gora mt Novaya Zemlya U.S.S.R. 76.23N 65.08E
112 E2 Bledsoe Texas 33.37N 103.01W
62 J3 Bledzew Poland 52.31N 15.23E
52 E7 Blefjell mt Norway 59.48N 9.12E
79 J2 Bleggio Italy 46.02N 10.50E
61 D4 Bleharies Belgium 50.31N 3.25E
53 W16 Bleia mt Norway 61.05N 7.14E
64 A3 Bleialf W Germany 50.14N 6.17E
65 J8 Bleiberg Austria 46.38N 13.42E
65 L8 Bleiburg Austria 46.35N 14.49E
63 N10 Bleicherode E Germany 51.27N 10.35E
61 N8 Bleid Belgium 49.34N 5.38E
50 H4 Bleiksmyrardalur V Iceland
64 M3 Bleilochsperre res E Germany 50.29N 11.43E
60 G11 Bleiswijk Netherlands 52.01N 4.32E
52 H10 Blekinge dist Sweden
108 O8 Blencoe Iowa 41.56N 96.06W
71 B1 Bléneau France 47.43N 2.56E
11 H8 Blenheim New Zealand 41.32S 173.58E
99 J10 Blenheim Ontario 42.20N 81.59W
56 J4 Blenheim Palace Oxon Eng 51.51N 1.21W
66 M6 Blenio Riviera, Val Switzerland
69 L6 Blénod-lès-Pont-à-Mousson France 48.53N 6.04E
69 K6 Blénod-les-Toul France 48.36N 5.50E
71 J8 Bléone R France
80 F4 Blera Italy 42.16N 12.02E
69 E4 Blérancourt France 49.31N 3.10E
69 J5 Blercourt France 49.07N 5.15E
70 M7 Bléré France 47.18N 1.00E
61 M4 Bleret Belgium 50.42N 5.17E
60 N14 Blerick Netherlands 51.22N 6.10E
75 J5 Blesa Spain 41.03N 0.54W
53 V19 Bleskestadmoen Norway 59.37N 7.00E
71 C6 Blesle France 45.20N 3.10E
95 H3 Blesmanspos S Africa 27.44S 24.11E
69 H6 Blesmes France 48.44N 4.47E
69 M2 Blessem W Germany 50.48N 6.47E
89 F6 Blessigué Ivory Coast 10.12N 6.27W
112 L7 Blessing Texas 28.52N 96.14W
59 J5 Blessington Kildare Irish Rep 53.10N 6.32W
72 K2 Blet France 46.54N 2.43E
56 K4 Bletchley Bucks Eng 52.00N 0.46W
56 K3 Bletsoe Beds Eng 52.13N 0.31W
71 G3 Bletterans France 46.45N 5.27E
18 B3 Bleuë Sumatra Indonesia 4.58N 96.16E
99 M6 Bleu,L Quebec
93 B4 Bleus,Mts Zaïre
107 C8 Blevins Arkansas 33.52N 93.35W
66 N8 Blevio Italy 45.51N 9.07E
70 N4 Blévy France 48.38N 1.12E
56 J4 Blewbury Oxon Eng 51.35N 1.15W
100 O9 Blewett Saskatchewan 49.23N 103.14W
112 G6 Blewett Texas 29.10N 100.02W
105 H2 Blewett Falls L N Carolina 35.01N 79.56W
63 J5 Blexen W Germany 53.32N 8.32E
63 J5 Blexen W Germany 53.32N 8.32E
71 D8 Bleymard,le France 44.29N 3.44E
61 E4 Blicquy Belgium 50.36N 3.41E
88 P3 Blida Algeria 36.30N 2.50E
35 F1 Blida Lebanon 33.08N 35.31E
52 L7 Blidö Sweden 59.37N 18.56E
52 G9 Blidsberg Sweden 57.56N 13.30E
89 F9 Bliéron Ivory Coast 4.25N 7.31W
64 C5 Blies R W Germany
69 N5 Bliesbrück France 49.07N 7.10E
64 C5 Blieskastel W Germany 49.14N 7.15E
15 G8 Bligh Ent Gt Barrier Reef Australia
113 O6 Bligh I Alaska 60.50N 146.49W
11 B11 Bligh Sd New Zealand
9 R1 Bligh Water Fiji
69 H7 Bligny France 48.11N 4.37E
71 F2 Bligny-sur-Ouche France 47.06N 4.40E
60 M6 Blija Netherlands 53.22N 5.51E
60 R7 Blijham Netherlands 53.06N 7.05E
50 J2 Blikalón Iceland 66.28N 16.14W
50 J2 Blikalonsdalur rift Iceland
95 L6 Blikana S Africa 30.35S 27.37E
95 G3 Blikfontein S Africa 27.50S 23.55E
51 D4 Bliksvær isld Norway 67.17N 14.00E
11 K3 Blind B New Zealand
57 G3 Blindcrake Cumbria Eng 54.42N 3.19W
79 D2 Blindenhorn mt Italy/Switz 46.26N 8.19E
65 L5 Blindenmarkt Austria 48.08N 14.59E
53 U13 Blindheim Norway 62.34N 6.04E
56 L5 Blindley Heath Surrey Eng 51.12N 0.04W
63 T6 Blindow E Germany 53.22N 13.55E
99 H6 Blind River Ontario 46.12N 82.59W
83 D3 Blinisht Albania 41.52N 20.01E
10 E11 Blinkenthorpe B Lord Howe I Pacific Oc
12 F8 Blinking Billy Pt Tasmania 42.55S 147.22E
12 E4 Blinman S Australia 31.05S 138.11E
45 O7 Blinovskiy U.S.S.R. 49.22N 42.18E
110 L7 Bliss Idaho 42.56N 114.57W
106 L8 Blissfield Michigan 41.49N 83.51W
53 J4 Blistrup Denmark 56.06N 12.13E
56 K3 Blisworth Northants Eng 52.11N 0.57W
18 K10 Blitar Java Indon 8.06S 112.12E
89 K7 Blitta Togo 8.23N 1.06E
60 N13 Blitterswijk Netherlands 51.31N 6.07E
110 F7 Blitzen Oregon 42.37N 119.05W
64 O5 Blížejov Czechoslovakia 49.30N 12.50E
65 N4 Blížkovice Czechoslovakia 48.59N 15.51E
45 H8 Bliznetsy Ukraine U.S.S.R. 48.53N 36.35E
123 J9 Block Bay Antarctica
11 C3 Blockhouse B Auckland New Zealand
103 L4 Block Island Rhode I 41.11N 71.34W
103 L4 Block Island Sd Rhode I
56 H3 Blockley Glos Eng 52.01N 1.45W
101 L10 Bloedel Vancouver I, Br Col 50.05N 125.21W
95 M2 Bloekomspruit S Africa 26.45S 28.21E
60 G10 Bloemendaal Netherlands 52.24N 4.37E
95 K5 Bloemfontein S Africa 29.07S 26.14E
95 J3 Bloemhof S Africa 27.39S 25.37E
95 J3 Bloemhof Dam S Africa 27.39S 25.40E
95 K5 Bloemspruit S Africa 29.08S 26.17E
56 O2 Blofield Norfolk Eng 52.38N 1.27E
70 N6 Blois France 47.36N 1.20E
53 D2 Blokhus Denmark 57.15N 9.36E
60 J9 Blokker Netherlands 52.40N 5.05E
60 M9 Blokzijl Netherlands 52.44N 5.57E
63 K9 Blomberg W Germany 51.57N 9.05E
108 Q5 Blomkest Minnesota 44.56N 95.00W
53 R17 Blomøy isld Norway 60.32N 4.52E
52 J10 Blomstermåla Sweden 56.58N 16.20E
66 D6 Blonay Switzerland 46.28N 6.54E
72 G3 Blond France 46.03N 1.01E
69 K8 Blondefontaine France 47.53N 5.52E
50 F4 Blöndudalur V Iceland
50 F3 Blöndu Hlidhar Fjöll mt Iceland 65.32N 19.00W
50 F5 Blóndukvíslar reg Iceland
50 E3 Blönduós Iceland 65.39N 20.18W
18 M10 Blongas Indonesia 8.52S 116.01E
64 K8 Blonhofen W Germany 47.54N 10.54E
62 M3 Błonie Poland 52.12N 20.24E
63 R9 Blönsdorf E Germany 51.57N 12.53E
70 L3 Blonville France 49.18N 0.03E
13 A6 Bloods Ra N Terr Australia
104 J8 Bloodsworth I Maryland
59 L3 Bloody Br Down N Ireland 54.09N 5.52W
59 F1 Bloody Foreland Donegal Irish Rep 55.09N 8.17W
106 C4 Bloomer Wisconsin 45.06N 91.29W
117 B8 Bloomesteinmeer, Prof. W.J.van res Surinam 5.30N 55.00W
103 J3 Bloomfield Connecticut 41.50N 72.45W
107 K2 Bloomfield Indiana 39.01N 86.58W
106 B9 Bloomfield Iowa 40.44N 92.25W
107 L4 Bloomfield Kentucky 37.55N 85.19W
107 G5 Bloomfield Missouri 36.54N 89.58W
108 F2 Bloomfield Montana 47.27N 104.56W
108 N7 Bloomfield Nebraska 42.37N 97.40W
103 K7 Bloomfield New Jersey 40.47N 74.11W
109 C5 Bloomfield New Mexico 36.43N 107.59W
99 N9 Bloomfield Ontario 44.00N 77.14W
104 O2 Bloomfield Vermont 44.46N 71.39W
103 F3 Bloomingburg New York 41.33N 74.27W
103 F5 Bloomingdale New Jersey 41.00N 74.20W
103 D4 Blooming Grove Pennsylvania 41.22N 75.08W
112 L3 Blooming Grove Texas 32.04N 96.43W
108 R6 Blooming Prairie Minnesota 43.53N 93.05W
110 O7 Bloomington Idaho 42.12N 111.24W
106 F9 Bloomington Illinois 40.29N 89.00W
107 K2 Bloomington Indiana 39.10N 86.31W
112 L7 Bloomington Texas 28.39N 96.55W
106 D7 Bloomington Wisconsin 42.54N 90.54W
103 B5 Bloomsburg Pennsylvania 40.59N 76.27W
103 D5 Bloomsbury New Jersey 40.38N 75.06W
13 J5 Bloomsbury Queensland 20.35S 148.40E
107 F3 Bloomsdale Missouri 38.01N 90.15W
103 E2 Bloomville New York 42.20N 74.48W
104 B5 Bloomville Ohio 41.02N 83.01W
18 J9 Blora Java Indon 6.55S 111.29E
104 H5 Blossburg Pennsylvania 41.41N 77.05W
64 K6 Blossenau W Germany 48.48N 10.56E
97 R4 Blosseville Kyst coast Greenland
112 M2 Blossom Texas 33.41N 95.24W
39 M1 Blossom,Mys C Vrangelya, Ostrov U.S.S.R. 70.46N 178.35E
66 F1 Blotzheim France 47.37N 7.30E
94 K4 Blouberg S Africa 23.08S 28.56E
94 K4 Blouberg mt S Africa 23.01S 28.59E
95 B9 Bloubergstrand S Africa 33.47S 18.28E
95 N2 Bloukop S Africa 26.50S 29.44E
95 K9 Bloukrans S Africa 33.21S 26.43E
95 F3 Bloukrans mt S Africa 27.15S 22.33E
105 B7 Blountstown Florida 30.27N 85.03W
95 F8 Blouput S Africa 32.58S 22.46E
72 E9 Blousson France 43.28N 0.12E
64 Q4 Blovice Czechoslovakia 49.35N 13.33E
101 E1 Blow R Yukon Terr
116 F6 Blower Rock Caribbean Sea
105 F1 Blowing Rock N Carolina 36.07N 81.42W
56 J3 Bloxham Oxon Eng 52.02N 1.22W
104 K9 Bloxom Virginia 37.51N 75.37W
56 H2 Bloxwich W Midlands Eng 52.37N 2.00W
57 K5 Blubberhouses N Yorks Eng 54.00N 1.45W
15 F6 Blucher Ra Papua New Guinea
65 A7 Bludenz Austria 47.10N 9.50E
65 P2 Bludov Czechoslovakia 49.57N 16.57E
111 P8 Blue R Arizona
109 D2 Blue R Colorado
109 O7 Blue R Oklahoma
103 B6 Blue Ball Pennsylvania 40.07N 76.03W
111 N3 Blue Bell Knoll mt Utah 38.10N 111.32W
101 N7 Blueberry R Br Columbia
95 J9 Bluecliff S Africa 33.30S 25.28E
11 E11 Blue Cliffs New Zealand 44.32S 170.58E
110 J7 Blue Cr Idaho
110 N8 Blue Creek Utah 41.54N 112.29W
105 G10 Blue Cypress L Florida 27.43N 80.46W
104 B9 Blue Diamond Kentucky 37.16N 83.14W
108 Q6 Blue Earth Minnesota 43.38N 94.06W
108 Q6 Blue Earth R Minnesota
107 C5 Blue Eye Missouri 36.30N 93.23W
104 D9 Bluefield W Virg/Virg 37.14N 81.17W
116 H1 Bluefields Jamaica, W I 18.10N 78.02W
115 N3 Bluefields Nicaragua 12.00N 83.49W
106 D8 Blue Grass Iowa 41.30N 90.45W
107 M3 Bluegrass Reg Kentucky
84 Y21 Blue Grotto B Malta 35.49N 14.28E
104 R2 Blue Hill Maine 44.24N 68.36W
108 M9 Blue Hill Nebraska 40.20N 98.26W
104 R2 Blue Hill B Maine
116 H4 Blue Hills Caicos Is W I 21.50N 72.20W
98 O6 Blue Hills of Couteau Newfoundland
106 G8 Blue I Illinois 41.40N 87.42W
106 R4 Blue Island dist Chicago, Illinois
110 F7 Bluejoint L Oregon 42.40N 119.40W
104 G6 Blue Knob mt Pennsylvania 40.16N 78.33W
111 M2 Blue L Utah 39.13N 112.37W
110 A9 Blue Lake California 40.55N 124.00W
109 C3 Blue Mesa Reservoir Colorado
104 H7 Bluemont Virginia 39.06N 77.51W
107 G2 Blue Mound Illinois 39.42N 89.06W
109 B1 Blue Mountain Colorado 40.15N 108.51W
107 G7 Blue Mountain Mississippi 34.40N 89.02W
107 C6 Blue Mountain L Arkansas 35.07N 93.45W
104 L3 Blue Mountain Lake New York 43.53N 74.26W
107 B7 Blue Mt Arkansas 34.40N 94.02W
28 J4 Blue Mt Mizoram India 22.35N 93.02E
104 H6 Blue Mt Pennsylvania
110 H7 Blue Mt.Pass Oregon 42.19N 117.50W
116 L2 Blue Mt Pk Jamaica, W I 18.03N 76.36W
98 B9 Blue Mts Maine
12 K5 Blue Mts New S Wales
11 D12 Blue Mts New Zealand
110 G5 Blue Mts Oregon/Wash
103 A6 Blue Mts Pennsylvania
116 L2 Blue Mts.,The Jamaica, W I
13 D2 Blue Mud B N Terr Australia
58 R8 Bluemull Sd Shetland Scotland 60.43N 0.59W
87 D4 Blue Nile prov Sudan
Blue Nile R Ethiopia see Abbai R
Blue Nile R Sudan see Bahr el Azraq R
101 O1 Bluenose L N W Terr
103 H5 Blue Point Long I, N Y 40.45N 73.02W
101 J6 Blue R Br Col
109 O2 Blue Rapids Kansas 39.41N 96.40W
100 B4 Blue Ridge Alberta 54.09N 115.20W
105 C3 Blue Ridge Georgia 34.51N 84.20W
102 K3 Blue Ridge mts U.S.A.
105 C3 Blue Ridge L Georgia 34.52N 84.16W
101 O9 Blue River Br Col 52.05N 119.09W
110 C5 Blue River Oregon 44.10N 122.21W
99 O6 Blue Sea Lake Quebec 46.10N 76.05W
11 M11 Blueskin B New Zealand
59 F2 Blue Stack Mts Donegal Irish Rep
104 E9 Bluestone Res W Virginia
109 C6 Bluewater New Mexico 35.16N 107.58W
11 C13 Bluff New Zealand 46.38S 168.21E
111 P4 Bluff Utah 37.18N 109.33W
109 N4 Bluff City Kansas 37.03N 97.54W
105 E1 Bluff City Tennessee 36.27N 82.28W
112 J3 Bluff Dale Texas 32.22N 98.03W
13 H4 Bluff Downs Queensland 19.40S 145.31E
14 F3 Bluff Face Ra W Australia
11 C13 Bluff Harb inlet New Zealand
23 C9 Bluff I Hong Kong
14 C10 Bluff Knoll mt W Australia 34.25S 118.15E
23 B10 Bluff Pt Hong Kong 22.11N 114.12E
105 L2 Bluff Pt N Carolina 35.20N 76.09W
19 J7 Bluff Pt Philippines 9.56N 118.36E
14 A8 Bluff Pt W Australia 27.50S 114.07E
107 F2 Bluffs Illinois 39.44N 90.31W
11 C13 Bluff, The pt New Zealand 46.38S 168.22E
100 C6 Bluffton Alberta 52.45N 114.17W
107 C7 Bluffton Arkansas 34.54N 93.37W
105 C6 Bluffton Georgia 31.31N 84.53W
106 J9 Bluffton Indiana 40.44N 85.11W
108 P3 Bluffton Minnesota 46.28N 95.14W
104 B6 Bluffton Ohio 40.53N 83.54W
105 G5 Bluffton S Carolina 32.14N 80.53W
48 U15 Bluie West One airport Greenland 61.10N 45.19W
93 B4 Blukwa Zaïre 1.45N 30.38E
112 K3 Blum Texas 32.09N 97.24W
63 T7 Blumberg E Germany 52.36N 13.38E
64 F8 Blumberg W Germany 47.51N 8.33E
15 D6 Blumen R Irian Jaya
118 E10 Blumenau Brazil 26.55N 49.07W
63 O8 Blumenberg E Germany 52.04N 11.28E
64 F8 Blumenfeld W Germany 47.49N 8.40E
63 T5 Blumenhagen E Germany 53.32N 13.53E
100 K8 Blumenhof Saskatchewan 50.01N 107.41W
66 G5 Blumenstein Switzerland 46.44N 7.32E
63 J6 Blumenthal Bremen W Germany 53.12N 8.34E
64 A2 Blumenthal Nordrhein-Westfalen W Germany 50.30N 6.28E
66 H6 Blümlisalp mt Switzerland 46.29N 7.46E
Blumut, Gunong mt see Belumut, Gunong mt
108 L5 Blunt S Dakota 44.30N 99.59W
15 H5 Blupblup I Papua New Guinea 3.30S 144.39E
110 D7 Bly Oregon 42.25N 121.04W
113 N7 Blying Sd Alaska
Bly-Khem R see Bol'shoy Yenisey R
57 L2 Blyth Northumb Eng 55.07N 1.30W
57 L6 Blyth Notts Eng 53.23N 1.03W
99 J9 Blyth Ontario 43.43N 81.26W
13 C1 Blyth R N Terr Australia
58 K7 Blyth Bridge Borders Scotland 55.42N 3.24W
56 P3 Blythburgh Suffolk Eng 52.19N 1.35E
111 K8 Blythe California 33.38N 114.35W
107 C1 Blythedale Missouri 40.29N 93.56W
57 K2 Blyth, R Northumb Eng
14 G7 Blyth Ra S Aust/W Aust
57 M6 Blyton Lincs Eng 53.27N 0.43W
42 B5 Blyudtsy U.S.S.R. 54.58N 76.58E
95 L2 Blyvooruitsig S Africa 26.25S 27.23E
53 M9 Bø Faeroes 62.06N 7.22W
51 D3 Bø Nordland Norway 68.38N 14.35E
20 A1 Bō Saitama Japan
89 D8 Bo Sierra Leone 7.58N 11.45W
53 S16 Bø Sogn og Fjordane Norway 61.08N 5.19E
52 J8 Bo Sweden 58.57N 15.30E
92 D7 Boa Zaïre 10.31S 28.04E
19 K5 Boac Philippines 13.26N 121.52E
115 M3 Boaco Nicaragua 12.28N 85.41W
76 G7 Boada Spain 40.49N 6.19W
75 Q3 Boadella, Embalse de res Spain
76 G7 Boadilla Spain 40.47N 6.14W
76 K4 Boadilla de Ríoseco Spain 42.10N 4.59W
120 G2 Bôa Esperança Amazonas Brazil 7.41S 62.53W
117 G8 Bôa Esperanca Brazil 7.20S 40.48W
119 H6 Boa Esperança Brazil 3.21N 61.23W
118 F7 Boa Esperança Minas Gerais Brazil 21.03S 45.37W
117 F8 Boa Esperança, Açude res Brazil 7.00S 44.00W
117 G8 Bôa Esperanca, R Brazil
120 C2 Boa Fé Brazil 7.17S 72.20W
76 C11 Bôa Fé Portugal 38.33N 8.05W
120 F4 Boa Hora Brazil 9.40S 65.08W
59 G2 Boa I Fermanagh N Ireland 54.30N 7.50W
23 F1 Bo'ai Henan China 35.10N 113.05E
23 F1 Bo'ai Henan China 32.57N 112.15E
99 K7 Boakview Ontario 45.34N 80.03W
76 F2 Boal Spain 43.25N 6.49W
76 C5 Boalhosa Portugal 41.44N 8.29W
95 C3 Boanamary Madagascar 15.48S 46.20E
94 M6 Boane Mozambique 26.02S 32.19E
15 M5 Boang I Bismarck Arch 3.25S 153.22E
19 E5 Boano isld Moluccas Indon 2.58S 127.56E
19 E5 Boano,Selat str Moluccas Indon
118 H4 Bôa Nova Brazil 14.22S 40.09W
23 F8 Bo'ao Guangdong China 19.11N 110.34E
79 L4 Boara Polésine Italy 45.07N 11.47E
110 F4 Boardman Oregon 45.50N 119.43W
106 J5 Boardman R Michigan
58 L6 Boarhills Fife Scotland 56.19N 2.43W
79 H3 Boario Terme Italy 45.53N 10.09E
40 J5 Boatasyn Sakhalin U.S.S.R. 52.05N 143.04E
11 B9 Boat Harb inlet Snares Is Pacific Oc
13 H7 Boatman Queensland 27.15S 146.56E
58 J4 Boat of Garten Highland Scotland 57.15N 3.45W
96 B11 Boatswain-bird I Ascension I Atlantic Ocean 7.57S 14.19W
116 D5 Boatswain Pt Grand Cayman I W I 19.26N 81.25W
117 G7 Boa Viagem Brazil 5.08S 39.46W
119 G8 Boa Vista Amazonas Brazil 0.24S 65.25W
120 C1 Boa Vista Amazonas Brazil 4.59S 72.23W
117 B6 Boa Vista Pará Brazil 3.23S 55.30W
119 H6 Boa Vista Roraima Brazil 2.51N 60.43W
89 P10 Boa Vista isld Cape Verde
119 E9 Boa Vista, Is Brazil 3.46S 69.23W
19 J6 Boayan isld Philippines 10.35N 119.10E
107 K7 Boaz Alabama 34.11N 86.10W
109 G8 Boaz New Mexico 33.44N 103.58W
96 B2 Boaz I Bermuda 32.18N 64.52W
12 H4 Bobadah New S Wales 32.18S 146.42E
77 G6 Bobadilla Spain 37.02N 4.44W
77 H5 Bobadilla Spain 37.40N 4.06W
76 J6 Bobadilla del Campo Spain 41.13N 5.01W
23 E7 Bobai Guangxi China 22.16N 110.02E
90 M7 Bobai Abdullah Cent Afr Rep 8.16N 24.18E
25 K5 Bo Bai,Cu Lao isld Vietnam 15.26N 109.05E
92 D2 Bobandana Zaïre 1.41S 29.00E
91 E4 Bobangi Zaïre 0.10S 17.45E
13 J4 Bobawaba Queensland 19.51S 147.35E
28 F1 Bobbili Andhra Prad India 18.32N 83.29E
12 L5 Bobbin Head dist Sydney, N S W 33.40S 151.09E
79 F5 Bobbio Italy 44.46N 9.23E
79 B5 Bobbio Pellice Italy 44.48N 7.07E
99 M8 Bobcaygeon Ontario 44.32N 78.33W
Böbekler see Sertaç
64 E4 Bobenheim-Roxheim W Germany 49.32N 8.23E
93 D3 Bobi Uganda 2.34N 32.22E
76 F2 Bobia,Sierra de la mts Spain
68 G3 Bobigny France 48.55N 2.27E
64 K7 Bobingen W Germany 48.15N 10.50E
63 O5 Bobitz E Germany 53.49N 11.22E
64 F6 Böblingen W Germany 48.41N 9.01E
19 E5 Bobo Moluccas Indon 3.36S 126.16E
89 G5 Bobo tribe Upper Volta
89 G6 Bobo Dioulasso Upper Volta 11.11N 4.18W
43 M7 Boboidorkhon Tadzhikistan U.S.S.R. 40.43N 70.16E
53 B6 Bobøl Denmark 55.26N 8.56E
89 G5 Bobola Mali 12.30N 5.20W
62 K2 Bobolice Poland 53.58N 16.35E
19 M5 Bobon Philippines 12.30N 124.33E
119 C9 Bobonaza, R Ecuador
94 K3 Bobonong Botswana 21.58S 28.26E
76 C4 Boboras Spain 42.26N 8.08W
82 H8 Bobovdol Bulgaria 42.21N 22.59E
46 G3 Bobr Belorussiya U.S.S.R. 54.19N 29.18E
62 J4 Bóbr R Poland
36 G3 Böbrek Dağı mt Turkey 39.43N 33.29E
45 C6 Bobrik Ukraine U.S.S.R. 50.38N 31.05E
45 D8 Bobrinets Ukraine U.S.S.R. 48.02N 32.10E
82 J1 Bobrka U.S.S.R. 49.40N 24.19E
113 Q10 Bobrof I Aleutian Is 51.55N 177.30W
45 M5 Bobrov U.S.S.R. 51.06N 40.01E
45 C6 Bobrovitsa Ukraine U.S.S.R. 50.45N 31.25E
45 J5 Bobrovo-Dvorskoye U.S.S.R. 51.10N 37.24E
62 J4 Bobrowice Poland 51.57N 15.05E
46 G3 Bobruysk Belorussiya U.S.S.R. 53.08N 29.10E
45 H5 Bobryshevo U.S.S.R. 51.11N 36.28E
23 C2 Bobso Sichuan China 33.28N 103.20E
104 E7 Bobtown Pennsylvania 39.46N 80.00W
119 E3 Bobures Venezuela 9.15N 71.10W
111 D2 Boca California 39.24N 120.05W
121 K4 Boca dist Buenos Aires Arg
119 H3 Boca Araguao river mth Venezuela
105 F13 Boca Chica Florida 24.34N 81.40W
112 K10 Boca Chica Texas 25.58N 97.10W
120 G1 Boca De Capanã Brazil 5.51S 61.41W
115 Q6 Boca de Cupe Panama 8.00N 77.32W
76 K3 Boca de Huérgano Spain 42.59N 4.56W
115 N5 Boca del Monte Panama 8.23N 82.09W
119 G3 Boca del Pao Venezuela 8.07N 64.20W
115 L8 Boca del Río Mexico 19.08N 96.08W
119 H3 Boca de Macareo Venezuela 8.55N 62.00W
119 H3 Boca de Uracoa Venezuela 9.08N 62.23W
120 E3 Bôca do Acre Brazil 8.45S 67.23W
120 F3 Bôca do Curuquetê Brazil 8.19S 65.40W
117 C5 Boca do Jari river mth Brazil 1.03S 51.56W
118 J9 Bôca do Mato Brazil 22.55S 43.17W
120 E2 Bôca do Moaco Brazil 7.39S 68.20W
70 J6 Bocages reg France
105 E11 Boca Grande Florida 26.44N 82.16W
119 H3 Boca Grande river mth Venezuela
116 N1 Boca Grande str Trinidad & Tobago
105 F13 Boca Grande Key isld Florida 24.32N 81.59W
77 P3 Bocairente Spain 38.46N 0.36W
118 G5 Bocaiúva Brazil 17.10S 43.50W
118 E9 Bocaiúva do Sul Brazil 25.09S 49.08W
118 C8 Bocajá Brazil 22.32S 55.25W
115 L5 Boca Jesús María channel Mexico 24.32N 97.40W
119 H3 Boca Lorán river mth Venezuela
119 G6 Boca Mavaca Venezuela 2.30N 65.13W
89 G8 Bocanda Ivory Coast 7.05N 4.31W
120 B9 Bocanegra dist Lima Peru
90 G8 Bocaranga Cent Afr Rep 7.01N 15.35E
105 G11 Boca Raton Florida 26.22N 80.05W
116 N1 Bocas del Dragón str Trinidad & Tobago
115 N5 Bocas del Toro Panama 9.20N 82.15W
115 N5 Bocas del Toro, Arch. de Panama
19 H1 Bocaue Luzon Philippines 14.48N 120.57E
115 M2 Bocay Nicaragua 14.20N 85.02W
96 T8 Bocayna, La str Canary Is
67 P11 Bocca di Vezzo pass Corsica 42.40N 9.09E
79 N5 Bocche del Po della Pila Italy
79 M5 Bocche del Po delle Tolle Italy
79 M5 Bocche del Po di Goro e di Gnocca Italy
81 N5 Bocchigliero Italy 39.25N 16.45E
79 G5 Boccolo dei Tassi Italy 44.40N 9.40E
75 C5 Boceguillas Spain 41.20N 3.39W
71 H8 Bochaine reg France
99 R3 Bochart Quebec 49.10N 73.34W
62 M6 Bochnia Poland 49.59N 20.25E
61 N2 Bocholt Belgium 51.10N 5.35E
63 E9 Bocholt W Germany 51.49N 6.37E
60 U17 Bocholtz Netherlands 50.48N 6.00E
64 P3 Bochov Czechoslovakia 50.09N 13.04E
63 F10 Bochum W Germany 51.28N 7.11E
75 D4 Bocigas Spain 41.40N 3.20W
66 H9 Bo, Cima di mt Italy 45.43N 8.00E
63 R4 Bock sand spit E Germany 54.26N 12.56E
64 O3 Bockau E Germany 50.32N 12.44E
63 M8 Bockenem W Germany 52.00N 10.08E
65 P5 Bockflüss Austria 48.23N 16.37E
63 H6 Bockhorn W Germany 53.24N 8.02E
62 O3 Boćki Poland 52.39N 23.00E
65 H7 Böckstein Austria 47.06N 13.07E
63 T10 Bockwitz E Germany 51.29N 13.46E
67 P12 Bocognano Corsica 42.05N 9.05E
119 E3 Boconó Venezuela 9.17N 70.17W
119 E3 Boconó, R Venezuela
75 C2 Bocos Spain 42.58N 3.32W
115 F4 Bocoyna Mexico 27.50N 107.32W
82 G5 Bocşa Vasiovei Romania 45.23N 21.47E
90 H9 Boda Cent Afr Rep 4.19N 17.26E
52 J5 Boda Kopparberg Sweden 61.00N 15.15E
52 K9 Böda Øland Sweden 57.16N 17.05E
52 K4 Boda Västernorrland Sweden 62.51N 16.40E
52 H9 Bodafors Sweden 57.30N 14.40E
53 W15 Bødal Norway 61.48N 7.00E
12 K6 Bodalla New S Wales 36.07S 150.02E
14 C9 Bodallin W Australia 31.24S 118.50E
90 H9 Bodanga Cent Afr Rep 5.30N 16.51E
87 J7 Bodawein Ethiopia 6.31N 43.20E
42 J3 Bodaybo U.S.S.R. 57.52N 114.05E
58 N4 Boddam Grampian Scotland 57.28N 1.48W
116 D5 Boddentown Grand Cayman I W I 19.20N 81.14W
14 B10 Boddington W Australia 32.48S 116.28E
108 Q7 Bode Iowa 42.55N 94.18W
63 O8 Bode R E Germany
111 A3 Bodega Hd California 38.19N 123.05W
60 H11 Bodegraven Netherlands 52.05N 4.45E
90 G3 Bodélé depression Chad
64 F7 Bodelhausen W Germany 48.24N 8.58E
29 C6 Bodeli Gujarat India 22.16N 73.42E
57 G6 Bodelwyddan Clwyd Wales 53.16N 3.29W
51 J6 Boden Sweden 65.50N 21.44E
66 M2 Boden Switzerland 47.21N 8.56E
63 L8 Bodenburg W Germany 52.02N 10.00E
56 F3 Bodenham Hereford & Worcs Eng 52.09N 2.41W
64 E4 Bodenheim W Germany 49.56N 8.19E
64 J3 Bodenlaube W Germany 50.12N 10.06E
64 P5 Bodenmais W Germany 49.05N 13.08E
64 G8 Bodensee L W Germany/Switzerland
95 K2 Bodenstein S Africa 26.20S 26.29E
63 N7 Bodenteich W Germany 52.50N 10.42E
63 K9 Bodenwerder W Germany 51.58N 9.30E
65 L6 Bodenwies mt Austria 47.46N 14.34E
64 N5 Bodenwöhr W Germany 49.16N 12.20E
59 F4 Boderg,L Roscommon Irish Rep 53.52N 8.00W
57 G6 Bodfari Clwyd Wales 53.13N 3.21W
111 F6 Bodfish California 35.36N 118.30W
28 C1 Bodhan Andhra Prad India 18.40N 77.51E
33 A2 Bodhiya,Gebel mts Egypt
19 B2 Bodi Celebes Indon 1.05N 121.47E
95 L9 Bodiam S Africa 33.15S 27.26E
95 J2 Bodibe S Africa 26.04S 25.52E
64 G5 Bödigheim W Germany 49.29N 9.20E
70 B4 Bodilis France 48.32N 4.07W
51 D4 Bodin Norway 67.18N 14.30E
Bodinayakanur see Bodinayakkanur
28 C5 Bodinayakkanur Tamil Nadu India 10.02N 77.18E
90 H10 Bodingue R Cent Afr Rep
66 M6 Bodio Switzerland 46.23N 8.55E
77 D4 Bodión R Spain
76 D7 Bodiosa Portugal 40.43N 7.59W
91 H2 Bodjoki Zaïre 2.55N 22.23E
103 B8 Bodkin Pt Maryland 39.08N 76.25W
87 J8 Bodleh Ethiopia 5.01N 42.48E
66 N1 Bodman W Germany 47.45N 9.02E
56 B7 Bodmin Cornwall Eng 50.29N 4.43W
56 B6 Bodmin Moor Cornwall Eng
100 G6 Bodo Alberta 52.11N 110.04W
51 D4 Bodø Norway 67.18N 14.26E
117 G8 Bodocó Brazil 7.45S 39.55W
77 C4 Bodonal de la Sierra Spain 38.09N 6.34W
22 B3 Bodonchiyn Gol R Mongolia
76 F8 Bodón, El Spain 40.29N 6.35W
118 C6 Bodoquena Brazil 19.53S 56.58W
118 B7 Bodoquena,Serra da mts Brazil
57 E6 Bodorgan Gwynedd Wales 53.12N 4.24W
90 G2 Bodrichí Chad 19.11N 15.54E
36 C5 Bodrum Turkey 37.03N 27.28E
52 H4 Bodsjö Sweden 62.50N 14.55E
63 R4 Bodstedt E Germany 54.23N 12.38E
25 J7 Bo Duc Vietnam 11.59N 106.49E
52 J3 Bodum Sweden 63.55N 16.20E
91 F1 Boduna Zaïre 5.05N 19.44E
62 M7 Bodva R Czech/Hungary
59 E6 Bodyke Clare Irish Rep 52.53N 8.36W
62 M3 Bodzanów Poland 52.30N 20.00E
61 J2 Boechout Belgium 51.09N 4.30E
76 K5 Boecillo Spain 41.33N 4.42W
76 L3 Boedo R Spain
71 J4 Boëge France 46.12N 6.25E
95 F5 Boegoeberg Dam res Cape Province S Africa 29.05S 22.13E
50 B4 Bœjarós inlet 65.25N 23.55W
50 H6 Bœjarstadharskogur wood Iceland
61 K2 Boekel Belgium 51.10N 4.54E
60 L13 Boekel Netherlands 51.37N 5.41E
60 Q11 Boekelo Netherlands 52.13N 6.47E
61 E1 Boekhoute Belgium 51.15N 3.43E
91 G2 Boela tribe Zaïre
15 E7 Boelaka R Irian Jaya
87 A8 Boeli Zaïre 4.05N 27.08E
108 M8 Boelus Nebraska 41.04N 98.42W
71 E5 Boën France 45.45N 4.00E
52 F7 Boen Norway 59.19N 11.40E
91 G4 Boende Zaïre 0.15S 20.51E
25 H6 Boeng Lovea Cambodia 12.33N 105.34E
25 H6 Boeng Me Alpa Cambodia 13.26N 104.14E
81 E8 Boeo o Lilibeo,C Sicily 37.48N 12.26E
15 J8 Boera Papua New Guinea 8.30S 147.05E
95 D9 Boerboonfontein S Africa 33.43S 20.31E
112 J6 Boerne Texas 29.47N 98.44W
60 R7 Boertange Netherlands 53.00N 7.10E
53 G6 Boeslunde Denmark 55.18N 11.17E
95 K9 Boesmans R S Africa
95 L6 Boesmanskop S Africa 30.02S 27.07E
95 K9 Boesmansriviermond S Africa 33.41S 26.40E
95 H3 Boetsap S Africa 27.58S 24.27E
107 E9 Boeuf R Ark/Louisiana
61 O6 Bœvange-Clervaux Luxembourg 50.03N 5.56E
61 P7 Bœvange-sur-Attert Luxembourg 49.47N 6.01E
76 G3 Boeza R Spain
61 B3 Boezinge Belgium 50.54N 2.51E
89 B6 Boffa Guinea 10.12N 14.02W
71 F7 Boffres France 44.55N 4.43E
59 G4 Bofin,L Roscommon Irish Rep 53.51N 7.56W
Bōfu see Hōfu
28 K1 Boga Assam India 28.25N 94.39E
92 D1 Boga Zaïre 1.04N 29.57E
93 A4 Boga Zaïre 1.03N 29.55E
61 G4 Bogaarden Belgium 50.44N 4.08E
39 G7 Bogachevka U.S.S.R. 54.50N 160.50E
25 C4 Bogale Burma 16.16N 95.21E
25 C5 Bogale R Burma
76 E7 Bogalhal Portugal 40.49N 7.07W
90 H9 Bogali Cent Afr Rep 4.34N 17.10E
107 G11 Bogalusa Louisiana 30.56N 89.53W
12 H4 Bogan R New S Wales
89 J5 Bogandé Upper Volta 13.02N 0.08W
12 J5 Bogan Gate New S Wales 33.08S 147.50E
90 J9 Bogangolo Cent Afr Rep 5.29N 18.13E
41 G5 Boganida R U.S.S.R.
13 H6 Bogantungan Queensland 23.40S 147.20E
90 L3 Bogar Chad 17.59N 22.29E
107 C2 Bogard Missouri 39.26N 93.31W
77 M3 Bogarra Spain 38.35N 2.13W
77 K6 Bogarre Spain 37.25N 3.23W
100 B8 Bogart, Mt Alberta 50.55N 115.10W
112 M2 Bogata Texas 33.28N 95.14W
46 Q3 Bogatoye U.S.S.R. 53.10N 51.19E
45 W1 Bogatye Saby U.S.S.R. 56.01N 50.28E
45 H9 Bogatyr' Ukraine U.S.S.R. 47.59N 36.58E
45 W3 Bogatyr' U.S.S.R. 53.25N 50.01E
45 U6 Bogatyrevo Kazakhstan U.S.S.R. 50.23N 48.45E
37 F2 Boğaz Turkey 40.24N 28.30E
36 C4 Boğazici Turkey 38.01N 27.32E
36 H3 Boğazlıyan Turkey 39.13N 35.17E
36 H2 Boğazkale Turkey 40.02N 34.37E
Boğazkoy see Boğazkale
91 F3 Bogbonga Zaïre 1.36N 19.24E
24 E10 Bogcang Zangbo R Xizang Zizhiqu China
22 E4 Bogd Mongolia 45.08N 100.44E
24 F4 Bogda Feng mt pk Xinjiang Uygur Zizhiqu China 43.45N 88.32E
47 N5 Bogdanovich U.S.S.R. 56.48N 62.00E
44 F6 Bogdanovka Georgia U.S.S.R. 41.14N 43.35E
43 C2 Bogdanovka U.S.S.R. 52.10N 52.34E
45 E2 Bogdanovo U.S.S.R. 54.15N 33.09E
24 F4 Bogda Shan mt ra Xinjiang Uygur Zizhiqu China
45 T2 Bogdashkino U.S.S.R. 54.38N 47.39E
Bogdo Ula ra see Bogda Shan
52 L9 Boge Sweden 57.40N 18.45E
43 K2 Bogembay Kazakhstan U.S.S.R. 52.30N 72.16E
51 F3 Bogen Norway 68.32N 17.02E
64 O6 Bogen W Germany 48.55N 12.42E
94 C6 Bogenfels Namibia 27.23S 15.22E
21 C3 Bogenli Heilongjiang China 49.25N 125.38E
53 E5 Bogense Denmark 55.34N 10.06E
45 T7 Boget Kazakhstan U.S.S.R. 49.40N 47.59E
43 F2 Bogetkol'skiy Kazakhstan U.S.S.R. 50.27N 60.30E
66 B7 Bogève France 46.12N 6.26E
12 K3 Boggabilla New S Wales 28.36S 150.21E
12 K4 Boggabri New S Wales 30.42S 150.01E
59 E7 Boggeragh Mts Cork Irish Rep
9 B3 Boggerik islet Marshall Is Pacific Oc 9.17N 167.21E
79 F2 Boggia R Italy
14 C6 Boggola mt W Australia 23.48S 117.41E
52 J3 Boggsjö Sweden 63.04N 15.25E
116 O4 Boggy Peak mt Antigua W I 17.03N 61.53W
34 H4 Bogham,El Syria 34.39N 40.54E
74 J9 Boghar Algeria 35.55N 2.42E
Boghari see Ksar El Boukhari
34 J4 Boghars,Sabkhat'al salt marsh Iraq
84 S14 Boghaz Cyprus 35.18N 33.57E
Boghé see Bogué
88 P3 Boghni Algeria 36.35N 4.00E
31 C5 Boghra Dam Afghanistan 31.54N 64.43E
15 H6 Bogia Papua New Guinea 4.16S 144.56E
58 L4 Bogie R Grampian Scotland
13 J5 Bogie R Queensland
Boglan see Solhan
79 D2 Bognanco Italy 46.08N 8.12E
66 J7 Bognanco,Valle di Italy
66 N7 Bogno Switzerland 46.06N 9.04E
56 K6 Bognor Regis W Sussex Eng 50.47N 0.41W
53 J7 Bogø Denmark 54.56N 12.04E
19 M6 Bogo Philippines 11.03N 124.02E
45 G6 Bogodukhov Ukraine U.S.S.R. 50.10N 35.32E
43 J1 Bogodukhovka Kazakhstan U.S.S.R. 54.04N 69.09E
87 H8 Bogol Manya Ethiopia 4.34N 41.29E
43 J1 Bogolyubovo Kazakhstan U.S.S.R. 54.37N 68.41E
45 D1 Bogolyubovo Smolensk U.S.S.R. 55.32N 32.57E
45 M1 Bogolyubovo Vladimir U.S.S.R. 56.14N 40.31E
12 H6 Bogong,Mt Victoria 36.45S 147.21E
40 G9 Bogopol U.S.S.R. 44.16N 135.25E
18 G9 Bogor Java Indon 6.34S 106.45E
93 H5 Bogoria, L Kenya 0.17N 36.04E
93 B4 Bogoro Zaïre 1.25N 30.15E
82 J2 Bogorodchany U.S.S.R. 48.48N 24.31E
45 K3 Bogoroditsk U.S.S.R. 53.45N 38.08E
45 G3 Bogoroditskoye U.S.S.R. 53.04N 35.21E
45 P1 Bogorodsk U.S.S.R. 56.06N 43.30E
47 G5 Bogorodsk U.S.S.R. 62.19N 52.30E
40 H5 Bogorodskoye U.S.S.R. 52.22N 140.23E
46 Q1 Bogorodskoye U.S.S.R. 57.50N 50.50E
113 C10 Bogoslof I Aleutian Is 53.57N 168.04W
42 D4 Bogoslovka U.S.S.R. 56.49N 86.45E
44 D3 Bogoslovskoye U.S.S.R. 44.46N 41.48E
44 G5 Bogosskiy Khrebet mts U.S.S.R.
119 D5 Bogotá Colombia 4.38N 74.05W
42 D4 Bogotol U.S.S.R. 56.13N 89.31E
89 K6 Bogou Togo 10.40N 0.12E
45 O3 Bogoyavlenskoye Penza U.S.S.R. 53.25N 42.21E
31 H8 Bogra Bangladesh 24.52N 89.28E
31 H8 Bogra dist Bangladesh
42 E5 Bograd U.S.S.R. 54.14N 90.54E
51 H12 Bogskär Lt Ho Finland 59.31N 20.20E
42 F3 Boguchany U.S.S.R. 58.24N 97.28E
45 M7 Boguchar U.S.S.R. 49.58N 40.34E
36 F4 Bögüdelik Turkey 38.49N 32.35E
109 L2 Bogue Kansas 39.22N 99.43W
89 B3 Bogué Mauritania 16.31N 14.17W
107 F10 Bogue Chitto Mississippi 31.29N 90.28W
107 F11 Bogue Chitto R Louisiana
105 K3 Bogue Inlet N Carolina
42 E4 Bogunay U.S.S.R. 56.12N 94.34E
37 D8 Böğürtlen Turkey 37.13N 38.04E
41 C2 Bogushevicha,Mys C Novaya Zemlya U.S.S.R. 74.52N 60.47E
45 B2 Bogushevsk Belorussiya U.S.S.R. 54.50N 30.13E
45 B7 Boguslav Ukraine U.S.S.R. 49.32N 30.52E
62 J5 Boguszów Poland 50.46N 16.12E
116 K2 Bog Walk Jamaica, W I 18.06N 77.01W
18 L5 Boh R Borneo Indonesia
22 L7 Bo Hai B Hebei China
22 M7 Bohai Haixia str China
69 E4 Bohain-en-Vermandois France 49.59N 3.28E
22 L7 Bohai Wan B Hebei China
61 K7 Bohan Belgium 49.52N 4.53E
100 M8 Boharm Saskatchewan 50.25N 105.42W
65 N3 Bohdálov Czechoslovakia 49.29N 15.53E
65 N1 Bohdaneč Czechoslovakia 50.05N 15.40E
65 N5 Böheimkirchen Austria 48.13N 15.47E
62 H6 Bohemia old prov Czechoslovakia
14 F4 Bohemia Downs W Australia 18.53S 126.12E
59 G5 Boheraphuca Offaly Irish Rep 53.01N 7.45W
59 D7 Boherboy Kerry Irish Rep 52.09N 9.04W
75 M2 Bohi,Caldas de res Spain
89 L8 Bohicon Benin 7.14N 2.10E
82 B4 Bohiniska Bistrica Yugoslavia 46.16N 13.59E
79 P2 Bohinjsko Jezero L Yugoslavia 46.17N 13.51E
64 N1 Böhlen W Germany 51.10N 12.23E
66 M1 Bohlingen W Germany 47.43N 8.54E
63 Q10 Böhlitz-Ehrenberg E Germany 51.22N 12.18E
63 K7 Böhme W Germany 52.48N 9.29E
63 L7 Böhme R W Germany
64 N4 Böhmer Wald mts W Germany
63 H8 Bohmte W Germany 52.24N 8.20E
32 H3 Bohnābād Iran 34.04N 59.54E
63 Q7 Böhne E Germany 52.34N 12.18E
19 M7 Bohol isld Philippines
19 L7 Bohol Sea Philippines
19 L7 Bohol Str Philippines
76 J9 Bohonal de Ibor Spain 38.47N 5.28W
62 K9 Böhönye Hungary 46.26N 17.25E
87 L6 Bohotleh Somalia 8.11N 46.20E
76 J8 Bohoyo Spain 40.19N 5.26W
66 M1 Böhringen W Germany 47.45N 8.56E
31 H2 Bohrt Kashmir 36.37N 74.05E
24 E5 Bohu Xinjiang Uygur Zizhiqu China 42.00N 86.40E
35 B8 Bohu watercourse Israel
119 H8 Boiaçu Brazil 0.27S 61.46W
80 K6 Boiano Italy 41.28N 14.20E
81 C5 Boi,C Sardinia 39.08N 9.27E
98 F7 Boiestown New Brunswick 46.28N 66.25W
61 J5 Boignée Belgium 50.30N 4.37E
69 C7 Boigneville France 48.20N 2.22E
15 G8 Boigu I Torres Str, Qnsld 9.15S 142.14E
92 J10 Boila Mozambique 16.09S 39.49E
98 B5 Boileau Quebec 48.07N 70.50W
14 D4 Boileau, C W Australia 17.40S 122.08E
117 B6 Boim Brazil 2.48S 55.11W
76 C2 Boimorto Spain 43.00N 8.08W
87 D6 Boing Sudan 9.56N 33.38E
118 J3 Boipeba, I Brazil 13.38S 38.55W
118 C9 Boi Preto,Serra de mts Brazil
118 F8 Boi,Pta.do C Brazil 23.59S 45.15W
61 N4 Boirs Belgium 50.45N 5.35E
25 G6 Boi Russey Cambodia 12.04N 103.29E
26 V15 Bois-Blanc Réunion Ind Oc 21.11S 55.49E
106 K4 Bois Blanc I Michigan
68 E2 Bois-Colombes France 48.55N 2.16E
69 C7 Boiscommun France 48.02N 2.23E
98 M7 Boisdale C Breton I, Nova Scotia 46.06N 60.30W
71 J3 Bois-d'Amont France/Switz 46.32N 6.09E
72 A2 Bois-de-Cené France 46.56N 1.54W
61 H6 Bois de Chimay woods Belgium
61 F4 Bois-de-Lessines Belgium 50.42N 3.53E
61 K5 Bois-de-Villers Belgium 50.23N 4.50E
61 G4 Bois-d'Haine Belgium 50.30N 4.13E
71 F5 Bois-d'Oingt, le France 45.55N 4.35E
71 E3 Bois-du-Roi,Pic du France 47.00N 4.02E
110 J6 Boise Idaho 43.38N 116.12W
110 J6 Boise R Idaho
109 H5 Boise City Oklahoma 36.44N 102.31W
110 K6 Boise Middle Fork R Idaho
110 K6 Boise N. Fork R Idaho
110 K6 Boise S. Fork R Idaho
61 M5 Bois-et-Borsu Belgium 50.24N 5.21E
70 F5 Boisgervilly France 48.10N 2.05W
70 N3 Bois Guillaume France 49.28N 1.06E
71 F2 Bois Janson mt France 47.10N 4.42E
101 L2 Bois,L.des N W Terr
66 D3 Bois,les Switzerland 47.11N 6.55E
72 D2 Boismé France 46.47N 0.25W
71 D5 Bois Noirs hills France
71 E8 Bois-Paiolive France 44.24N 4.11E
118 E6 Bois, R Brazil
71 E9 Boisseron France 43.45N 4.04E
72 J6 Boisset France 44.46N 2.14E
100 R9 Boissevain Manitoba 49.14N 100.02W
72 J8 Boissezon France 43.35N 2.22E
70 M4 Boissy-les-Perche France 48.41N 0.54E
70 M5 Boissy-Maugis France 48.27N 0.43E
68 H5 Boissy-St.Léger France 48.45N 2.31E
69 D6 Boissy-St.Léger France 48.45N 2.30E
79 M1 Boite R Italy
61 T10 Boitsfort dist Bruxelles Belgium
118 F8 Boituva Brazil 23.15S 47.41W
63 T6 Boitzenburg E Germany 53.16N 13.37E
75 M6 Boix,Sierra del mts Spain
63 N6 Boize R E Germany
63 N6 Boizenburg E Germany 53.23N 10.44E

15 E8 Bojake str Irian Jaya
83 C3 Bojana R Albania/Yugoslavia
75 L6 Bojar Spain 40.42N 0.06E
32 H4 Bojd Iran 32.54N 59.16E
53 E6 Bøjden Denmark 55.07N 10.07E
19 K2 Bojeador C Luzon Philippines 18.30N 120.36E
93 L4 Boji Plain Kenya
32 G2 Bojnūrd Iran 37.28N 57.20E
18 C6 Bojo isld Indonesia 0.35S 98.28E
18 J9 Bojonegoro Java Indonesia 7.06S 111.50E
90 E6 Bojude Nigeria 10.37N 11.05E
121 H3 Bojuru Brazil 31.35S 51.25W
15 J6 Bok Papua New Guinea 5.25S 147.13E
82 F5 Boka Yugoslavia 45.21N 20.50E
91 C3 Bokaboka Gabon 0.58N 13.31E
91 F3 Bokakata Zaïre 1.11N 19.34E
82 E8 Boka Kotorska B Yugoslavia 42.12N 18.35E
91 E5 Bokala Zaïre 3.08S 17.04E
91 F2 Bokala Zaïre 2.03N 19.03E
91 E4 Bokanda Congo 0.30S 16.38E
90 B7 Bokani Nigeria 9.28N 5.10E
91 G2 Bokapo Zaïre 2.43N 20.51E
95 B4 Bokarano Madagascar 16.20S 44.40E
29 J6 Bokaro Bihar India 23.46N 85.55E
29 J1 Bokaro Res Bihar India
91 F4 Bokatola Zaïre 0.37S 18.45E
89 B6 Boké Guinea 10.57N 14.13W
105 E11 Bokeelia Florida 26.43N 82.09W
63 J6 Bokel W Germany 53.24N 8.45E
91 G4 Bokela Zaïre 1.10S 21.59E
91 G4 Bokele Zaïre 1.30S 20.37E
63 K8 Bokeloh W Germany 52.25N 9.23E
91 G3 Bokenda Zaïre 1.16N 21.22E
95 C8 Bokfontein S Africa 32.50S 19.15E
39 E4 Bokhapcha U.S.S.R. 61.03N 150.26E
39 E4 Bokhapcha R U.S.S.R.
12 H3 Bokhara R New S Wales
25 J6 Bo Kheo Cambodia 13.39N 107.13E
90 F7 Boki Cameroon 8.59N 13.27E
90 F7 Boki R Cameroon
91 G6 Bokila Zaïre 4.04S 21.41E
90 E9 Bokito Cameroon 4.33N 11.05E
94 E8 Bokkeveld Berg mt S Africa 31.09S 18.58E
53 S20 Bokn Norway 59.13N 5.27E
53 S20 Bokn isld Norway 59.13N 5.27E
53 S20 Boknafjorden inlet Norway
91 D6 Boko Congo 4.51S 14.36E
43 O3 Boko Kazakhstan U.S.S.R. 49.06N 81.10E
91 D4 Boko tribe Congo
91 F2 Bokode Zaïre 3.55N 19.30E
87 E7 Bokol mts Ethiopia
93 J4 Bokol mt Kenya 1.50N 37.02E
91 B5 Bokolo Gabon 2.40S 10.12E
43 M6 Bokombayevskoye Kirgiziya U.S.S.R. 42.07N 77.00E
95 M5 Bokong Lesotho 29.20S 28.28E
19 D8 Bokong Timor Indon 9.59S 124.03E
93 M7 Bokoni Kenya 1.23S 40.02E
25 H7 Bokor Cambodia 10.33N 104.02E
90 H5 Bokoro Chad 12.17N 17.04E
109 Q6 Bokoshe Oklahoma 35.12N 94.42W
91 C6 Boko Songo Congo 4.27S 13.38E
91 H4 Bokota Zaïre 0.56S 22.24E
91 G4 Bokote Zaïre 0.06S 20.05E
45 N7 Bokovskaya U.S.S.R. 49.15N 41.50E
95 B9 Bokpunt pt S Africa 33.34S 18.19E
25 E7 Bokpyin Burma 11.14N 98.45E
95 M2 Boksburg S Africa 26.13S 28.15E
94 T13 Boksburg North S Africa 26.13S 28.15W
46 J1 Boksitogorsk U.S.S.R. 59.28N 33.49E
94 F6 Bokspits Botswana 26.53S 20.42E
40 G6 Boktor U.S.S.R. 51.06N 137.24E
15 J2 Boku Bougainville I Papua New Guinea 6.38S 155.20E
91 G2 Bokula Zaïre 3.09N 20.50E
91 H4 Bokungu Zaïre 0.44S 22.28E
91 H4 Bokwankusu Zaïre 1.54S 22.55E
25 D5 Bok Ye-gan isld Burma 14.16N 97.49E
90 G5 Bol Chad 13.27N 14.40E
91 G5 Bola Zaïre 3.18S 21.58E
19 C4 Bolaäng Celebes Indon 0.57S 122.06E
19 D3 Bolaang Celebes Indonesia 0.58N 124.10E
12 G6 Bolac, L Victoria 37.45S 142.55E
91 H3 Bolafa Zaïre 1.23N 22.06E
91 J5 Bolaiti Zaïre 3.06S 24.54E
87 F6 Bola,Jeb mt Ethiopia 8.50N 36.35E
59 C5 Bola L Galway Irish Rep 53.21N 9.51W
76 D4 Bola,La Spain 42.09N 7.55W
89 B6 Bolama Guinea-Bissau 11.35N 15.30W
37 D4 Bolaman Turkey 41.02N 37.34E
37 C5 Bolaman R Turkey
90 M8 Bolanda,Jebel mt Sudan 7.40N 25.21E
71 J2 Bolandoz France 47.01N 6.06E
29 H7 Bolangir Orissa India 20.41N 83.30E
29 H7 Bolangir dist Orissa India
115 H7 Bolaños Mexico 21.41N 103.46W
77 J3 Bolaños Spain 38.55N 3.39W
19 L1 Bolanos mt Guam Pacific Oc 13.18N 144.42E
31 D6 Bolan Pass Pakistan 29.41N 67.34E
31 D6 Bolan R Pakistan
23 E7 Bolao Guangxi China 22.07N 109.07E
75 E7 Bolarque, Pantano de L Spain 40.20N 2.49W
28 D2 Bolarum Andhra Prad India 17.32N 78.29E
46 P4 Bolat Kazakhstan U.S.S.R. 50.00N 48.00E
46 P2 Bolatnya U.S.S.R. 56.12N 49.29E
37 C2 Bolayır Turkey 40.33N 26.44E
77 P2 Bolbaite Spain 39.04N 0.41W
70 L2 Bolbec France 49.34N 0.28E
47 K6 Bolchary U.S.S.R. 59.48N 68.50E
66 H2 Bölchenfluh mt Switzerland 47.23N 7.48E
46 Q4 Bol. Chernigovka U.S.S.R. 52.10N 51.00E
107 B1 Bolckow Missouri 40.11N 94.50W
62 L9 Bölcske Hungary 46.43N 18.58E
44 J1 Bolda R U.S.S.R.
32 D5 Boldajī Iran 31.55N 51.04E
63 T5 Boldekow E Germany 53.44N 13.36E
53 C7 Bolderslev Denmark 54.59N 9.18E
82 K5 Boldeşti Romania 45.04N 26.02E
45 E2 Boldino U.S.S.R. 54.54N 33.31E
45 Q3 Boldovo U.S.S.R. 53.59N 44.36E
56 H6 Boldre Hants Eng 50.47N 1.33W
87 F7 Bole Ethiopia 6.36N 37.20E
89 H7 Bole Ghana 9.03N 2.23W
93 L6 Bole Kenya 0.35S 39.42E
89 F6 Bolé Mali 11.59N 6.54W
110 N2 Bole Montana 47.42N 112.00W
24 D3 Bole Xinjiang Uygur Zizhiqu China 44.52N 82.06E
75 J3 Bolea Spain 42.16N 0.33W
82 H1 Bolekhov U.S.S.R. 49.05N 23.50E
91 F4 Boleko Zaïre 1.33S 19.50E
90 H9 Bolemba Cent Afr Rep 4.00N 17.33E
40 G6 Bolen U.S.S.R. 51.26N 136.12E
19 C8 Boleng,Selat str Indonesia
77 L5 Bolera, Embalse de res Spain
110 J4 Boles Idaho 45.57N 116.33W
62 J4 Bolesławiec Poland 51.16N 15.34E
66 N8 Boletto,Monte mt Italy 45.51N 9.10E
109 O6 Boley Oklahoma 35.31N 96.30W
44 J8 Bolgar R U.S.S.R.
89 J6 Bolgatanga Ghana 10.44N 0.53W
99 O4 Bolger Quebec 48.15N 76.21W
46 G6 Bolgrad Ukraine U.S.S.R. 45.42N 28.35E
90 L9 Boli Cent Afr Rep 4.50N 23.20E
21 E5 Boli Heilongjiang China 45.47N 130.31E
92 C2 Boli Zaïre 0.10S 27.44E
91 F4 Bolia Zaïre 1.36S 18.22E
52 M2 Boliden Sweden 64.52N 20.20E
107 H9 Boligee Alabama 32.47N 88.01W
65 M3 Bolikov Czechoslovakia 49.01N 15.22E
91 F3 Bolima Zaïre 0.55N 19.54E
19 J3 Bolinao Luzon Philippines 16.24N 119.54E
19 J3 Bolinao,C Luzon Philippines 16.25N 119.50E
91 G5 Bolingo Zaïre 3.31S 21.43E
82 K6 Bolintin Vale Romania 44.27N 25.48E
19 C3 Boliohutu,Gunung mt Celebes Indon 0.51N 122.37E
76 C14 Boliqueime Portugal 37.07N 8.10W
45 T5 Bol. Irgiz R U.S.S.R.
59 D5 Boliska L Galway Irish Rep 53.17N 9.18W
119 C5 Bolívar Antioquia Colombia 5.52N 76.01W
121 E6 Bolívár Argentina 36.15S 61.07W
120 E5 Bolívar Bolivia 12.13S 67.22W
119 C7 Bolívar Cauca Colombia 1.52N 76.56W
107 C4 Bolivar Missouri 37.37N 93.25W
104 G4 Bolivar New York 42.03N 78.11W
120 B2 Bolívar Peru 7.16S 77.47W
107 H6 Bolivar Tennessee 35.17N 88.59W
119 D3 Bolívar div Colombia
119 B8 Bolívar prov Ecuador
119 F4 Bolívar state Venezuela
119 G4 Bolívar,Cerro mt Venezuela 7.27N 63.25W
112 N6 Bolivar Pen Texas
119 E3 Bolivar, Pico mt Venezuela 8.33N 71.03W
105 J3 Bolivia N Carolina 34.04N 78.10W
117 G3 Bolivia rep S America
82 G7 Boljevac Yugoslavia 43.50N 21.56E
36 G5 Bolkar Dağları mts Turkey
52 E7 Bolkesjø Norway 59.45N 9.16E
45 G3 Bolkhov U.S.S.R. 53.25N 36.00E
45 S8 Bolkhuny U.S.S.R. 48.00N 46.25E
99 G4 Bolkow Ontario 48.06N 83.55W
62 J5 Bolków Poland 50.56N 16.05E
64 E8 Boll W Germany 47.50N 8.22E
64 H6 Boll W Germany 48.40N 9.38E
61 O4 Bolland Belgium 50.40N 5.46E
11 K13 Bollans I Antipodes Is Pacific Oc 49.38S 178.51E
79 F3 Bollate Italy 45.32N 9.07E
88 H11 Bollé Mauritania 20.08N 11.40W
79 K7 Bolle, le Italy 43.38N 11.18E
64 A4 Bollendorf W Germany 49.51N 6.22E
71 F8 Bollène France 44.16N 4.45E
66 F4 Bolligen Switzerland 46.59N 7.30E
53 B5 Bølling Denmark 55.59N 8.33E
57 J6 Bollington Cheshire Eng 53.18N 2.06W
52 J5 Bollnäs Sweden 61.20N 16.25E
76 E4 Bollo,El Spain 42.18N 7.05W
13 H8 Bollon Queensland 28.02S 147.28E
87 G6 Bollo Selassie Ethiopia 8.51N 39.27E
69 D4 Bollot France 49.36N 2.39E
52 K4 Bollstabruk Sweden 62.58N 17.50E
77 D6 Bollullos de la Mitación Spain 37.20N 6.09W
77 C6 Bollullos par del Condado Spain 37.20N 6.32W
69 N8 Bollwiller France 47.52N 7.17E
52 H10 Bolmen L Sweden 56.55N 13.45E
56 L6 Bolney W Sussex Eng 51.00N 0.12W
44 F6 Bolnisi Georgia U.S.S.R. 41.28N 44.33E
19 L6 Bolo Philippines 11.31N 122.46E
95 L8 Bolo S Africa 32.23S 27.38E
91 E5 Bolo Zaïre 3.38S 17.23E
91 E5 Bolobo Zaïre 2.10S 16.17E
19 K8 Bolod Is Philippines 6.15N 121.35E
40 F6 Bolodzhak U.S.S.R. 51.22N 134.55E
79 K5 Bologna Italy 44.30N 11.20E
79 K5 Bologna prov Italy
69 J7 Bologne France 48.12N 5.08E
120 C2 Bolognesi Loreto Peru 6.35S 73.28W
120 C4 Bolognesi Loreto Peru 10.00S 74.03W
81 F8 Bolognetta Sicily 37.58N 13.27E
80 H3 Bolognola Italy 43.00N 13.24E
46 H2 Bologovo U.S.S.R. 56.51N 31.39E
46 J1 Bologoye U.S.S.R. 57.58N 34.00E
40 E1 Bologur U.S.S.R. 60.36N 131.28E
45 J2 Bolokhovo U.S.S.R. 54.05N 27.51E
93 G8 Bololedi watercourse Tanzania
91 F3 Bolomba Zaïre 0.27N 19.13E
91 F3 Bolombo Zaïre 1.24N 19.00E
91 G2 Bolombo Zaïre 2.57N 20.53E
91 G5 Bolombo Zaïre 4.00S 21.23E
91 G3 Bolombo R Zaïre
40 G7 Bolon' Khabarovsk U.S.S.R. 49.56N 136.05E
40 G7 Bolon' Khabarovsk U.S.S.R. 49.55N 136.35E
115 P8 Bolonchén de Rejón Mexico 20.00N 89.44W
91 A3 Bolondo Equat Guinea 1.40N 9.38E
91 F5 Bolondo Zaïre 2.12S 18.42E
90 H5 Bolong Chad 12.03N 17.45E
19 L8 Bolong Mindanao Philippines 7.05N 122.12E
91 D8 Bolongongo Angola 8.28S 15.16E
91 C10 Bolonguera Angola 13.32S 13.33E
40 G7 Bolon', Ozero L U.S.S.R.
19 L2 Bolos Pt Luzon Philippines 18.08N 122.13E
81 B3 Bolotana Sardinia 40.20N 8.58E
42 C4 Bolotnoye U.S.S.R. 55.40N 84.37E
45 N1 Bolotskiy U.S.S.R. 55.59N 41.07E
90 M8 Bolou R Cent Afr Rep
25 J5 Bolovens, Plat. des Laos
120 D4 Bolpebra Bolivia 10.59S 60.30W
29 L1 Bolpur W Bengal India 23.40N 87.41E
121 B2 Bolsa,Cerro pk Argentina 29.30S 69.05W
80 E3 Bolsena Italy 42.38N 11.59E
80 E3 Bolsena L di Italy
62 N1 Bol'shakovo U.S.S.R. 54.51N 21.40E
39 F7 Bol'shaya R Kamchatka U.S.S.R.
45 E9 Bol'shaya Aleksandrovka Ukraine U.S.S.R. 47.19N 33.18E
44 H3 Bol'shaya Areshevka U.S.S.R. 44.07N 46.54E
41 H4 Bol'shaya Balakhnya R U.S.S.R.
45 F9 Bol'shaya Belozerka Ukraine U.S.S.R. 47.16N 34.45E
40 F7 Bol'shaya Bira R U.S.S.R.
45 K4 Bol'shaya Boyevka U.S.S.R. 52.24N 38.31E
43 P3 Bol'shaya Bukon' Kazakhstan U.S.S.R. 48.53N 82.45E
43 B2 Bol'shaya Chernigovka U.S.S.R. 52.11N 50.51E
43 G1 Bol'shaya Churakovka Kazakhstan U.S.S.R. 53.04N 64.16E
39 F3 Bol'shaya Garmanda R U.S.S.R.
46 Q4 Bol'shaya Glushitsa U.S.S.R. 52.28N 50.30E
41 Q4 Bol'shaya,Guba gulf U.S.S.R.
42 E5 Bol'shaya Inya U.S.S.R. 53.50N 92.08E
39 G4 Bol'shaya Itkana U.S.S.R. 61.42N 163.17E
45 Q7 Bol'shaya Ivanovka U.S.S.R. 49.27N 44.20E
42 E3 Bol'shaya Ket' U.S.S.R. 57.41N 91.40E
45 J6 Bol'shaya Khalan U.S.S.R. 50.55N 37.29E
39 G6 Bol'shaya Khapitsa R U.S.S.R.
41 D6 Bol'shaya Kheta R U.S.S.R.
46 Q3 Bol'shaya Kinelyu R U.S.S.R.
45 E7 Bol'shaya Kokhnovka Ukraine U.S.S.R. 49.05N 33.29E
46 O2 Bol'shaya Kokshaga R U.S.S.R.
39 F1 Bol'shaya Kon'kovaya R U.S.S.R.
45 C10 Bol'shaya Korenikha Ukraine U.S.S.R. 46.56N 31.53E
41 J4 Bol'shaya Korga,Mys C U.S.S.R. 73.11N 106.20E
46 K3 Bol'shaya Kulikovka U.S.S.R. 52.53N 36.10E
Bol'shaya Kuonamka see Anabar R
39 F1 Bol'shaya Kuropatoch'ya R U.S.S.R.
45 E9 Bol'shaya Lepetikha Ukraine U.S.S.R. 47.09N 33.59E
45 N4 Bol'shaya Lipovitsa U.S.S.R. 52.34N 41.21E
45 N9 Bol'shaya Martynovka U.S.S.R. 47.19N 41.39E
42 E4 Bol'shaya Murta U.S.S.R. 56.54N 93.08E
47 M2 Bol'shaya Neva R Leningrad U.S.S.R.
45 H9 Bol'shaya Novoselka Ukraine U.S.S.R. 47.51N 36.51E
45 N9 Bol'shaya Orlovka U.S.S.R. 47.21N 41.17E
39 J2 Bol'shaya Osinovaya R U.S.S.R.
45 G6 Bol'shaya Pisarevka Ukraine U.S.S.R. 50.25N 35.30E
47 F4 Bol'shaya Pyssa U.S.S.R. 64.11N 48.44E
42 G6 Bol'shaya Rechka U.S.S.R. 52.00N 104.45E
47 J3 Bol'shaya Rogovaya R U.S.S.R.
41 D8 Bol'shaya Shirta R U.S.S.R.
47 H3 Bol'shaya Synya R U.S.S.R.
47 L7 Bol'shaya Tava R U.S.S.R.
45 V4 Bol'shaya Tavolozhka U.S.S.R. 52.07N 49.03E
47 M5 Bol'shaya Tyulyakova U.S.S.R. 55.51N 61.32E
47 H7 Bol'shaya Usa U.S.S.R. 56.48N 55.10E
40 G9 Bol'shaya Ussurka R U.S.S.R.
43 N2 Bol'shaya Vladimirovka Kazakhstan U.S.S.R. 50.53N 79.29E
46 H5 Bol'shaya Vradiyevka Ukraine U.S.S.R. 47.50N 30.40E
45 Q3 Bol'shaya Yelan U.S.S.R. 53.02N 44.41E
42 H2 Bol'shaya Yerema R U.S.S.R.
42 H5 Bol'shaya Zama U.S.S.R. 53.29N 107.32E
45 F9 Bol'shaya Znamenka Ukraine U.S.S.R. 47.26N 34.22E
45 L9 Bol'shekrepinskaya U.S.S.R. 47.36N 39.23E
47 G5 Bol'shelug U.S.S.R. 62.10N 52.29E
45 P8 Bol'shenabatovskiy U.S.S.R. 48.57N 43.36E
43 P3 Bol'shenarymskoye Kazakhstan U.S.S.R. 49.15N 84.30E
42 G4 Bol'sheokinskoye U.S.S.R. 55.48N 101.45E
47 L7 Bol'sherech'ye U.S.S.R. 56.07N 74.40E
39 F8 Bol'sheretsk U.S.S.R. 52.30N 156.16E
45 J6 Bol'shetroitskoye U.S.S.R. 50.32N 37.18E
47 H7 Bol'sheustikinskoye U.S.S.R. 55.58N 58.17E
45 B4 Bol'shevik Belorussiya U.S.S.R. 52.32N 30.52E
39 D3 Bol'shevik Magadan U.S.S.R. 62.43N 147.38E
43 E6 Bol'shevik Turkmeniya U.S.S.R. 42.18N 58.45E
41 A3 Bol'shevik,Mys C Novaya Zemlya U.S.S.R. 72.44N 52.31E
41 H2 Bol'shevik,Ostrov isld U.S.S.R.
47 G2 Bol'shezemel'skaya Tundra U.S.S.R.
45 N8 Bol'shinka U.S.S.R. 48.40N 41.08E
45 S1 Bol'shiye Algashi U.S.S.R. 55.22N 46.27E
43 E4 Bol'shiye Barsuki,Peski sand des Kazakhstan U.S.S.R.
45 R2 Bol'shiye Berezniki U.S.S.R. 54.10N 45.59E
47 M4 Bol'shiye Galashki U.S.S.R. 57.28N 59.30E
45 U1 Bol'shiye Kaybitsy U.S.S.R. 55.24N 48.10E
40 C3 Bol'shiye Khatymy U.S.S.R. 57.23N 124.55E
45 U2 Bol'shiye Klyuchishchi U.S.S.R. 54.07N 48.14E
42 E5 Bol'shiye Knyshi U.S.S.R. 54.14N 92.33E
44 C8 Bol'shiye Kopani Ukraine U.S.S.R. 46.26N 33.04E
45 R5 Bol'shiye Kopeny U.S.S.R. 51.11N 45.00E
47 D3 Bol'shiye Kozly U.S.S.R. 65.11N 40.00E
42 L5 Bol'shiye Kuli U.S.S.R. 54.18N 121.30E
42 C2 Bol'shiye Lar'yak U.S.S.R. 61.02N 80.45E
41 D1 Bol'shiye Oranskiye,Ostrova islds Novaya Zemlya U.S.S.R. 77.05N 67.30E
45 S4 Bol'shiye Ozerki U.S.S.R. 52.37N 46.32E
45 L9 Bol'shiye Saly U.S.S.R. 47.24N 39.46E
47 J4 Bol'shiye Shogany U.S.S.R. 63.58N 64.00E
45 U2 Bol'shiye Tarkhany U.S.S.R. 54.43N 48.31E
42 J3 Bol'shiye Ugli U.S.S.R. 57.48N 112.55E
47 L7 Bol'shiye Uki U.S.S.R. 56.59N 72.40E
42 C2 Bol'shoi Megtyg'yegan R U.S.S.R.
82 J1 Bolshovtsy U.S.S.R. 49.14N 24.46E
45 P6 Bol'shoy U.S.S.R. 50.13N 43.29E
44 F6 Bol'shoy Abul mt U.S.S.R. 41.28N 43.42E
40 F2 Bol'shoy Aim R U.S.S.R.
46 O6 Bol'shoy Altsyn,Oz L U.S.S.R.
39 G2 Bol'shoy Anyuy R U.S.S.R.
42 E4 Bol'shoy Arbay U.S.S.R. 55.10N 94.32E
47 K5 Bol'shoy Atlym U.S.S.R. 62.17N 66.30E
43 C7 Bol'shoy Balkhan,Khrebet mts Turkmeniya U.S.S.R.
42 A2 Bol'shoy Balyk R U.S.S.R.
39 G1 Bol'shoy Baranov,Mys C U.S.S.R. 69.44N 164.00E
41 K4 Bol'shoy Begichev, Ostrov isld U.S.S.R.
45 V2 Bol'shoy Cheremshan R U.S.S.R.
47 F4 Bol'shoy Chirk U.S.S.R. 63.46N 47.24E
42 J3 Bol'shoy Chuya R U.S.S.R.
44 E2 Bol'shoy Dzhalga U.S.S.R. 45.59N 42.45E
45 R2 Bol'shoye Boldino U.S.S.R. 55.00N 45.17E
45 K6 Bol'shoye Bykovo U.S.S.R. 50.52N 38.24E
42 H6 Bol'shoye Goloustnoye U.S.S.R. 52.05N 105.25E
45 J6 Bol'shoye Gorodishche Belgorod U.S.S.R. 50.38N 37.06E
45 R1 Bol'shoye Ignatovo U.S.S.R. 55.01N 45.31E
40 H6 Bol'shoye Kizi,Oz L U.S.S.R.
45 L2 Bol'shoye Korovino U.S.S.R. 54.30N 39.08E
45 P1 Bol'shoye Kozino U.S.S.R. 56.25N 43.45E
47 K8 Bol'shoye Kureynoye U.S.S.R. 54.56N 66.55E
45 Q1 Bol'shoye Mares'yevo U.S.S.R. 55.02N 44.56E
39 F1 Bol'shoye Morskoye,Oz L U.S.S.R.
45 Q1 Bol'shoye Murashkino U.S.S.R. 55.46N 44.46E
45 T2 Bol'shoye Nagatkino U.S.S.R. 54.30N 47.59E
47 H4 Bol'shoye Patok R U.S.S.R.
42 C3 Bol'shoye Pikovka U.S.S.R. 58.39N 82.32E
45 T1 Bol'shoye Podberez'ye U.S.S.R. 55.21N 47.59E
45 L4 Bol'shoye Popovo U.S.S.R. 52.54N 39.06E
45 O3 Bol'shoye Sheremetyevo U.S.S.R. 53.06N 42.16E
45 G5 Bol'shoye Soldatskoye U.S.S.R. 51.20N 35.32E
47 K7 Bol'shoye Sorokino U.S.S.R. 56.40N 69.50E
42 B2 Bol'shoye Tarkhovo U.S.S.R. 61.07N 77.05E
43 N1 Bol'shoye Topol'noye,Oz L U.S.S.R.
40 H5 Bol'shoye Vlas'evo U.S.S.R. 53.25N 140.55E
43 N1 Bol'shoye Yarovoye,Ozero L U.S.S.R.
42 J5 Bol'shoye Yeravnoye, Ozero L U.S.S.R. 52.35N 111.30E
41 R3 Bol'shoye Zimov'ye U.S.S.R. 75.04N 147.02E
43 N8 Bol'shoy Ferganskiy Kanal canal Uzbekistan U.S.S.R.
43 D2 Bol'shoy Ik R U.S.S.R.
46 P4 Bol'shoy Irgiz R U.S.S.R.
46 Q4 Bol'shoy Irgiz R U.S.S.R.
47 K5 Bol'shoy Kamen' U.S.S.R. 62.26N 66.19E
45 S2 Bol'shoy Kandarat' U.S.S.R. 54.25N 46.58E
42 D5 Bol'shoy Kanym, G mt U.S.S.R. 54.15N 88.27E
45 O5 Bol'shoy Karay U.S.S.R. 51.37N 42.40E
44 D4 Bol'shoy Kavkaz belt of mts U.S.S.R.
47 K4 Bol'shoy Kazymskiy Sor,Oz L U.S.S.R.
40 G2 Bol'shoy Khandyk U.S.S.R. 58.56N 135.05E
45 L4 Bol'shoy Khomutets U.S.S.R. 52.48N 39.50E
46 O2 Bol'shoy Kundysh R U.S.S.R.
47 L6 Bol'shoy Kun'yak U.S.S.R. 59.14N 71.02E
45 T2 Bol'shoy Kuvay U.S.S.R. 54.38N 47.05E
47 J7 Bol'shoy Kuyash U.S.S.R. 55.50N 61.08E
47 N5 Bol'shoy Kuyash,Oz L U.S.S.R. 56.06N 61.35E
47 L6 Bol'shoy Kyl U.S.S.R. 54.53N 59.12E
42 G6 Bol'shoy Lug U.S.S.R. 52.06N 104.08E
41 Q4 Bol'shoy Lyakhovskiy, Os isld U.S.S.R.
45 P6 Bol'shoy Lychak U.S.S.R. 50.07N 43.47E
45 P5 Bol'shoy Melik U.S.S.R. 51.40N 43.17E
42 E5 Bol'shoy Monok U.S.S.R. 52.54N 90.19E
45 N7 Bol'shoy Napolovskiy U.S.S.R. 49.27N 41.28E
40 C2 Bol'shoy Nimnyr U.S.S.R. 58.02N 125.22E
40 C2 Bol'shoy Nimnyr R U.S.S.R.
40 C4 Bol'shoy Ol'doy R U.S.S.R.
39 F1 Bol'shoy Oler, Ozero L U.S.S.R. 69.20N 156.15E
39 F2 Bol'shoy Oloy R U.S.S.R.
42 H5 Bol'shoy Onguren U.S.S.R. 53.40N 107.40E
41 J3 Bol'shoy,Ostrov isld U.S.S.R.
42 J3 Bol'shoy Patom U.S.S.R. 59.34N 114.12E
42 J2 Bol'shoy Patom R U.S.S.R.
39 H2 Bol'shoy Peledon R U.S.S.R.
42 E3 Bol'shoy Pit R U.S.S.R.
42 E5 Bol'shoy Porog U.S.S.R. 52.40N 92.17E
41 E7 Bol'shoy,Porog falls Krasnoyarsk U.S.S.R. 65.33N 89.59E
41 H5 Bol'shoy,Porog falls Krasnoyarsk U.S.S.R. 70.28N 103.20E
42 E2 Bol'shoy, Porogi falls U.S.S.R. 61.45N 93.35E
39 J1 Bol'shoy Rautan,Ostrova islds U.S.S.R. 69.45N 170.10E
47 L5 Bol'shoy Salym R U.S.S.R.
39 C3 Bol'shoy Selerikan R U.S.S.R.
39 F7 Bol'shoy Semlyachik vol Kamchatka U.S.S.R. 54.16N 159.59E
Bol'shoy Semyachik vol see Bol'shoy Semlyachik vol
40 G4 Bol'shoy Shantar Ostrov isld U.S.S.R.
47 K5 Bol'shoy Tap R U.S.S.R.
42 H5 Bol'shoy Tarel' U.S.S.R. 53.46N 106.45E
40 E3 Bol'shoy Toko,Oz L U.S.S.R. 56.12N 131.00E
45 T1 Bol'shoy Tsivil R U.S.S.R.
46 F1 Bol'shoy Tyuters,Ostrov isld U.S.S.R. 59.51N 27.15E
42 E4 Bol'shoy Uluy U.S.S.R. 56.41N 90.28E
46 R3 Bol'shoy Uran R U.S.S.R.
42 H5 Bol'shoy Ushkaniy, Ostrova islds Baykal, Oz U.S.S.R. 53.52N 108.35E
47 L6 Bol'shoy Uvat,Oz L U.S.S.R.
46 P4 Bol'shoy Uzen' R U.S.S.R.
45 R3 Bol'shoy V'yass U.S.S.R. 53.50N 45.30E
39 E2 Bol'shoy Yarkodon R U.S.S.R.
42 E6 Bol'shoy Yenisey R U.S.S.R.
42 A3 Bol'shoy Yugan R U.S.S.R.
46 O2 Bol'shoy Yugut U.S.S.R. 55.52N 46.20E
44 D3 Bol'shoy Zelenchuk R U.S.S.R.
115 M4 Bolson Costa Rica 10.20N 85.28W
115 G4 Bolsón de Mapimí des Mexico
53 X16 Bolstad Norway 61.30N 7.36E
53 T17 Bolstadfjord inlet Norway 60.38N 5.47E
50 F3 Bólstadharhlídh Iceland 65.31N 19.50W
50 G5 Bólstadhur Iceland 64.32N 18.49W
53 T17 Bolstadøyri Norway 60.38N 5.58E
60 L7 Bolsward Netherlands 53.04N 5.31E
75 L3 Boltaña Spain 42.27N 0.05E
Boltenhagen see Ostseebad Boltenhagen
56 D7 Bolt Hd Devon Eng 50.12N 3.47W
66 F5 Boltigen Switzerland 46.38N 7.24E
57 J5 Bolton Greater Manchester Eng 53.35N 2.26W
103 L2 Bolton Massachusetts 42.27N 71.37W
105 J3 Bolton N Carolina 34.20N 78.26W
99 L9 Bolton Ontario 43.53N 79.44W
57 K5 Bolton Bridge N Yorks Eng 53.58N 1.53W
100 W4 Bolton L Manitoba
57 H4 Bolton le Sands Lancs Eng 54.06N 2.47W
56 D7 Bolt Tail headland Devon Eng 50.14N 3.53W
40 F3 Bol Tyrhan R U.S.S.R.
36 F2 Bolu Turkey 40.45N 31.38E
15 L8 Bolubolu Papua New Guinea 9.22S 150.22E
37 D6 Bolucan Turkey 39.43N 37.44E
Boluch Ab see Baluch Ab
36 E2 Bolu Dağı mt Turkey
32 G6 Bolūk Iran 28.15N 57.35E
50 B2 Bolungavík Iceland 66.10N 23.13W
50 C2 Bolungavík inlet Iceland
22 B7 Boluntay Qinghai China 36.30N 92.11E
23 G7 Boluo Guangdong China 23.10N 114.17E
59 B8 Bolus Hd Kerry Irish Rep 51.47N 10.20W
45 V7 Bol. Uzen' R U.S.S.R.
45 F3 Bolva R U.S.S.R.
36 E4 Bolvadin Turkey 38.43N 31.02E
42 H3 Bolvaninka U.S.S.R. 58.58N 108.28E
47 H1 Bolvanskiy Nos,Mys C U.S.S.R. 70.28N 59.02E
56 B6 Bolventor Cornwall Eng 50.33N 4.34W
13 G4 Bolwarra Queensland 17.22S 144.11E
62 L10 Bóly Hungary 45.59N 18.30E
79 K1 Bolzano Italy 46.30N 11.22E
79 K1 Bolzano prov Italy
15 H6 Bom Papua New Guinea 5.30S 145.47E
91 G9 Boma Angola 11.48S 20.06E
91 C6 Boma Congo 4.03S 12.53E
91 C6 Boma Zaïre 5.50S 13.03E
87 E7 Boma tribe Sudan
12 K5 Bomaderry New S Wales 34.21S 150.34E
61 K4 Bomal Brabant Belgium 50.40N 4.52E
61 N5 Bomal Luxembourg 50.23N 5.32E
91 H3 Bomane Zaïre 1.19N 23.47E
112 H2 Bomarton Texas 33.31N 99.26W
80 F4 Bomarzo Italy 42.29N 12.15E
91 E2 Bomassa Congo 2.10N 16.10E
80 K4 Bomba Italy 42.02N 14.22E
12 J6 Bombala New S Wales 36.52S 149.23E
91 D6 Bombala Zaïre 4.02S 15.34E
88 F9 Bombarda.La Morocco 25.40N 14.42W
76 A10 Bombarral Portugal 39.15N 9.09W
87 E6 Bombashi,Jeb mt Ethiopia 9.45N 34.40E
Bombat see Cevizlik
28 A1 Bombay Maharashtra India 18.56N 72.51E
99 T3 Bombay New York 44.57N 74.35W
11 J4 Bombay New Zealand 37.12S 174.59E
61 N4 Bombaye Belgium 50.43N 5.45E
28 B7 Bombay Harb Maharashtra India
25 M5 Bombay Reef Paracel Islands S China Sea
15 B5 Bomberai pen Irian Jaya
15 B5 Bomberai R Irian Jaya
90 J9 Bombére Cent Afr Rep 4.35N 18.32E
90 N8 Bombi Cent Afr Rep 6.00N 26.31E
91 F3 Bombimba Zaïre 0.32N 19.31E
93 D5 Bombo Uganda 0.36N 32.33E
93 K10 Bombo R Tanzania
22 E3 Bömbögör Mongolia 46.14N 99.42E
91 G6 Bombo Kasanji Zaïre 5.51S 21.54E
89 C6 Bomboli Guinea 11.00N 12.14W
91 F2 Bomboma Zaïre 2.23N 19.03E
91 B12 Bombom, I São Tomé & Principe, Gulf of Guinea 1.43N 7.25E
120 F3 Bom Comércio Brazil 9.45S 65.55W
117 H9 Bom Conselho Brazil 9.03S 36.38W
Bomda see Bamda
118 F6 Bom Despacho Brazil 19.46S 45.15W
28 J2 Bomdila Assam India 27.20N 92.20E
52 K6 Bomhus Sweden 60.44N 17.19E
24 H11 Bomi Xizang Zizhiqu China 29.56N 95.45E
89 D8 Bomi Hills Liberia 7.00N 10.55W
92 C1 Bomili Zaïre 1.45N 27.08E
120 E3 Bom Jardim Amazonas Brazil 8.49S 66.09W
118 J3 Bom Jardim Bahia Brazil 12.15S 38.37W
117 C6 Bom Jardim Pará Brazil 2.21S 51.02W
117 J8 Bom Jardim Pernambuco Brazil 7.46S 35.35W
118 D5 Bom Jardim de Goiás Brazil 16.19S 52.03W
91 C8 Bom Jesus Angola 9.11S 13.34E
117 F9 Bom Jesus Piauí Brazil 9.03S 44.20W
121 J2 Bom Jesus Rio Grande do Sul Brazil 28.45S 50.16W
117 F9 Bom Jesus da Gurgueia,Sa.do mts Brazil
118 G3 Bom Jesus da Lapa Brazil 13.16S 43.23W
118 H7 Bom Jesus do Itabapoana Brazil 21.08S 41.44W
118 H7 Bom Jesus do Norte Brazil 21.07S 41.40W
53 S19 Bømlafjorden inlet Norway
53 S19 Bømlo Norway 59.37N 5.13E
53 S19 Bømlo isld Norway 59.45N 5.38E
40 D4 Bomnak U.S.S.R. 54.46N 128.55E
93 A3 Bomokandi R Zaïre
91 F3 Bomongo Zaïre 1.27N 18.21E
72 K10 Bompas France 42.44N 2.55E
14 B7 Bompas Hill W Australia 27.21S 115.21E
81 H8 Bompietro Sicily 37.45N 14.06E
28 H7 Bompoka isld Nicobar Is 8.16N 93.10E
91 G4 Bomputu Zaïre 0.12S 20.07E
121 J1 Bom Retiro Brazil 27.45S 49.31W
118 G10 Bom Retiro dist São Paulo Brazil
64 H8 Boms W Germany 47.58N 9.31E
118 G7 Bom Sucesso Brazil 21.00S 44.56W
90 C9 Bomu Nigeria 4.36N 7.21E
91 J1 Bomu R Zaïre/Cent Afr Rep
71 C2 Bona France 47.07N 3.24E
32 B2 Bonāb Iran 37.20N 46.03E
90 D9 Bonaberi Cameroon 4.05N 9.41E
15 K9 Bona Bona I Papua New Guinea 10.30S 149.50E
100 D5 Bon Accord Alberta 53.51N 113.21W
95 M1 Bon Accord S Africa 25.38S 28.13E
72 F10 Bonac-Irazein France 42.53N 0.59E
66 O4 Bonaduz Switzerland 46.49N 9.25E
29 J7 Bonaigarh Orissa India 21.47N 85.02E
72 F10 Bonaigua, Puerto de la pass Spain 42.41N 1.00E
104 H9 Bon Air Virginia 37.32N 77.34W
116 K9 Bonaire I Lesser Antilles 12.15N 68.27W
116 K9 Bonaire Trench Caribbean Sea
12 L3 Bonalbo New S Wales 28.45S 152.37E
113 R6 Bona,Mt Alaska 61.20N 141.50W
18 C5 Bonandolok Sumatra Indon 1.50N 98.48E
109 D3 Bonanza Colorado 38.17N 106.10W
115 M3 Bonanza Nicaragua 13.59N 84.30W
110 D7 Bonanza Oregon 42.11N 121.26W
77 D7 Bonanza Spain 36.49N 6.20W
109 A1 Bonanza Utah 40.00N 109.09W
110 E1 Bonanza Pk Washington 48.15N 120.52W
116 J5 Bonao Dominican Rep 18.55N 70.25W
106 C9 Bonaparte Iowa 40.43N 91.46W
14 E2 Bonaparte Arch W Australia
110 F1 Bonaparte,Mt Washington 48.48N 119.06W
76 J3 Boñar Spain 42.52N 5.19W
58 H3 Bonar Bridge Highland Scotland 57.53N 4.21W
81 B3 Bonarcado Sardinia 40.06N 8.39E
77 C6 Bonares Spain 37.19N 6.41W
99 N8 Bonarlaw Ontario 44.26N 77.37W
113 G5 Bonasila Dome mt Alaska 62.20N 160.34W
116 N2 Bonasse Trinidad & Tobago 10.05N 61.52W
79 G6 Bonassola Italy 44.11N 9.35E
98 G5 Bonaventure Quebec 48.03N 65.30W
98 H5 Bonaventure I Quebec 48.31N 64.11W
79 K4 Bonavigo Italy 45.16N 11.17E
98 T5 Bonavista Newfoundland 48.38N 53.08W
98 T5 Bonavista B Newfoundland
58 F6 Bonawe Strathclyde Scotland 56.26N 5.14W
71 H2 Bonboillon France 47.20N 5.42E
12 D4 Bon Bon S Australia 30.28S 135.15E
85 A1 Bon,C Tunisia 37.08N 11.00E
76 C9 Bonçã, Barragem do dam Portugal 39.49N 8.17W
109 F4 Boncarbo Colorado 37.13N 104.43W
56 B3 Boncath Dyfed Wales 52.01N 4.37W
70 O5 Bonce France 48.18N 1.32E
61 N4 Boncelles Belgium 50.35N 5.32E
57 H2 Bonchester Bridge Borders Scotland 55.25N 2.38W
66 E2 Boncourt Switzerland 47.30N 7.01E
109 D2 Bond Colorado 39.53N 106.41W
45 L7 Bondarevo U.S.S.R. 49.49N 39.29E
45 O4 Bondari U.S.S.R. 52.58N 42.02E
69 N8 Bon-de-Guebwiller mt France 47.54N 7.04E
63 L3 Bondenau R W Germany
79 K5 Bondeno Italy 44.53N 11.25E
53 U18 Bondhusbre glacier Norway 60.03N 6.20E
12 M7 Bondi dist Sydney, N S W
12 M7 Bondi Beach Sydney, N S W
66 P6 Bondo Switzerland 46.21N 9.34E
91 H2 Bondo Zaïre 3.47N 23.50E
91 H4 Bondo Zaïre 1.22S 23.54E
19 L5 Bondoc Pen Luzon Philippines
19 L5 Bondoc Pt Luzon Philippines 13.10N 122.38E
91 F2 Bondoko Zaïre 2.03N 19.12E
71 D8 Bondons,les France 44.23N 3.37E
64 F6 Bondorf W Germany 48.31N 8.49E
89 H7 Bondoukou Ivory Coast 8.03N 2.45W
18 K9 Bondowoso Java Indon 7.54S 113.50E
105 K12 Bonds Cay islds Bahamas 25.29N 77.42W
11 F10 Bonds Peak mt New Zealand 43.10S 171.01E
13 C6 Bond Springs N Terr Australia 23.30S 133.56E
103 K2 Bondsville Massachusetts 42.13N 72.20W
106 F5 Bonduel Wisconsin 44.44N 88.25W
110 P6 Bondurant Wyoming 43.14N 110.26W
68 G3 Bondy France 48.54N 2.29E
47 H5 Bondyug U.S.S.R. 60.30N 55.52E
Bône see 'Annaba
19 C6 Bone Butung I Indonesia 4.48S 122.53E
110 O6 Bone Idaho 43.18N 111.48W
19 C6 Bone Muna I Indonesia 5.10S 122.28E
105 L9 Bonefish Pond New Providence I
80 L5 Bonefro Italy 41.42N 14.56E
56 H2 Bonehill Staffs Eng 52.38N 1.42W
19 C6 Bonelipu Indonesia 4.49S 123.14E
19 B6 Bonelohe Indonesia 5.48S 120.28E
72 F7 Bon Encontrè France 44.11N 0.40E
25 H4 Boneng Laos 17.53N 104.36E
19 B7 Boneogeh Indonesia 7.18S 120.51E
19 B7 Bonerate isld Indonesia 7.22S 121.08E
58 J6 Bo'ness Central Scotland 56.01N 3.37W
108 M6 Bonesteel S Dakota 43.05N 98.55W
77 O3 Bonete Spain 38.53N 1.21W
121 C1 Bonete,Cerro pk Argentina 27.55S 68.41W
120 E9 Bonete,Cerro pk Bolivia 21.45S 66.30W
19 B6 Bone,Teluk B Celebes Indonesia
108 G1 Bonetraill N Dakota 48.26N 103.50W
99 L6 Bonfield Ontario 46.14N 79.10W
66 E2 Bonfol Switzerland 47.28N 7.09E
60 N14 Bong Netherlands 51.20N 6.05E
91 E4 Bonga Congo 1.10S 16.50E
87 F7 Bonga Ethiopia 7.15N 36.14E
91 G2 Bongabo Zaïre 3.07N 20.34E
19 K5 Bongabong Philippines 12.44N 121.30E
91 G3 Bongandanga Zaïre 1.28N 21.03E
19 J9 Bongao Philippines 5.01N 119.45E
19 B4 Bongka Celebes Indon 0.59S 121.25E
19 B4 Bongka R Celebes Indon
18 H9 Bongkok mt Java Indon 7.29S 108.21E
89 E8 Bong Mts Liberia 7.00N 10.00W
91 B5 Bongo Gabon 2.11S 10.12E
91 E4 Bongo Zaïre 1.47S 17.42E
91 G2 Bongo Zaïre 3.00N 20.01E
19 M8 Bongo isld Mindanao Philippines 7.19N 124.03E
91 G1 Bongo tribe Zaïre
95 O9 Bongonoma S Africa 27.43S 31.54E
90 G6 Bongor Chad 10.18N 15.20E
90 K8 Bongou R Cent Afr Rep
89 G8 Bongouanou Ivory Coast 6.44N 4.10W
112 L2 Bonham Texas 33.36N 96.12W
61 J2 Bonheiden Belgium 51.01N 4.33E
100 L1 Bonheur Ontario 49.20N 91.19W
58 G7 Bonhill Strathclyde Scotland 55.59N 4.34W
71 K5 Bonhomme,Col.du Savoie France 45.45N 6.45E
69 N7 Bonhomme,Col.du Vosges France 48.10N 7.05E
89 H4 Boni Mali 15.03N 2.10W
75 G8 Boniches Spain 39.59N 1.38W
89 G7 Boniérédougou Ivory Coast 8.20N 4.42W
67 P14 Bonifacio Corsica 41.23N 9.10E
78 C7 Bonifacio,Str.of Corsica/Sardinia
81 L4 Bonifati Italy 39.35N 15.54E
81 L4 Bonifati,C Italy 39.34N 15.53E
81 E8 Bonifato,Mt Sicily 37.57N 12.58E
105 B7 Bonifay Florida 30.49N 85.42W
80 H6 Bonifica Pontina marshland Italy
75 E7 Bonilla Spain 40.11N 2.33W
77 L3 Bonillo,El Spain 38.57N 2.32W
66 H5 Böningen Switzerland 46.41N 7.54E
Bonin Is see Ogaswara-guntō
61 K5 Boninne Belgium 50.30N 4.56E
66 J2 Boniswil Switzerland 47.18N 8.12E
111 P9 Bonita Arizona 32.35N 109.59W
107 E9 Bonita Louisiana 32.57N 91.40W
111 A8 Bonita, Pt California 37.48N 122.31E
105 F11 Bonita Springs Florida 26.19N 81.48W
118 G4 Bonito Bahia Brazil 15.17S 44.42W
118 C7 Bonito Mato Grosso do Sul Brazil 21.02S 56.23W
18 D6 Bonjol Sumatra Indon 0.00S 100.08E
91 G5 Bonkita Zaïre 2.33S 21.58E
89 L4 Bonkoukou Niger 14.00N 3.15E
61 J4 Bonlez Belgium 50.42N 4.41E
64 C2 Bonn W Germany 50.44N 7.06E
72 H9 Bonnac France 43.09N 1.34E
72 G4 Bonnac-la-Côte France 45.57N 1.17E
81 B2 Bonnanaro Sardinia 40.32N 8.46E
66 C8 Bonnant R France
72 H3 Bonnat France 46.19N 1.54E
58 E5 Bonnavoulin Highland Scotland 56.37N 5.58W
71 F3 Bonnay France 46.33N 4.36E
64 E8 Bonndorf W Germany 47.49N 8.21E
71 J4 Bonne France 46.10N 6.20E
98 O4 Bonne B Newfoundland
70 L3 Bonnebosq France 49.12N 0.04E
98 P2 Bonne Espérance Quebec 51.24N 57.40W
72 H4 Bonnefond France 45.32N 1.58E
72 E9 Bonnefont France 43.15N 0.21E
69 C6 Bonnelles France 48.37N 2.02E
70 G5 Bonnemain France 48.29N 1.48W
71 H7 Bonne,R France
110 M3 Bonner Montana 46.53N 113.50W
13 D1 Bonner Mt N Terr Australia 12.10S 136.26E
110 J1 Bonners Ferry Idaho 48.41N 116.20W
109 Q2 Bonner Springs Kansas 39.04N 94.54W
61 O8 Bonnert Belgium 49.43N 5.49E
51 G3 Bonnes Norway 68.39N 18.15E
53 A3 Bonnet Denmark 56.32N 8.14E
70 L5 Bonnétable France 48.10N 0.26E
107 F4 Bonne Terre Missouri 37.56N 90.33W
101 F3 Bonnet Plume R Yukon Terr
69 C4 Bonneuil-les-Eaux France 49.41N 2.14E
72 F2 Bonneuil-Matours France 46.41N 0.34E
70 N5 Bonneval Eure-et-Loir France 48.11N 1.24E
71 H7 Bonneval-en-Diois France 44.38N 5.35E
71 L6 Bonneval-sur-Arc France 45.22N 7.03E
66 C6 Bonnevaux France 46.18N 6.40E
71 J3 Bonnevaux France 46.49N 6.11E
71 J4 Bonneville France 46.05N 6.25E
110 D4 Bonneville Oregon 45.36N 121.59W
108 B6 Bonneville Wyoming 43.18N 108.03W
110 D4 Bonneville Dam Wash/Oregon 45.38N 121.59W
70 N3 Bonneville,la France 49.00N 1.04E
110 N7 Bonneville Pk Idaho 42.46N 112.07W
110 M9 Bonneville Salt Flats dry lake Utah 40.50N 113.50W
12 F7 Bonney,L S Australia 37.47S 140.23E
13 C5 Bonney Well N Terr Australia 20.21S 134.15E
69 C3 Bonnières Pas de Calais France 50.15N 2.16E
69 B5 Bonnières Seine-et-Oise France 49.02N 1.35E
14 C9 Bonnie Rock W Australia 30.33S 118.24E
71 G9 Bonnieux France 43.49N 5.18E
95 D9 Bonnievale S Africa 33.55S 20.05E
64 G5 Bönningheim W Germany 49.03N 9.06E
64 H3 Bonnland W Germany 55.03N 9.52E
72 C8 Bonnut France 43.33N 0.45W
90 C9 Bonny Nigeria 4.25N 7.10E
109 H2 Bonny Res Colorado
98 F8 Bonny River New Brunswick 45.14N 66.51W
71 B1 Bonny-sur-Loire France 47.34N 2.50E
100 G4 Bonnyville Alberta 54.16N 110.46W
107 F6 Bono Arkansas 35.55N 90.49W
70 E6 Bono France 47.39N 2.55W
81 C3 Bono Sardinia 40.25N 9.02E
19 H7 Bonobono Philippines 8.40N 117.32E
Bonoi see Bagusi
20 D10 Bōno-misaki C Japan 31.16N 130.13E
25 J7 Bonom Mhai mt Vietnam 11.20N 107.51E
81 B3 Bonorva Sardinia 40.25N 8.47E
72 F2 Bonres France 46.37N 0.35E
13 B2 Bonrook N Terr Australia 14.20S 131.40E
107 J11 Bon Secour Alabama 30.20N 87.44W
71 J4 Bons-en-Chablais France 46.15N 6.24E
12 K3 Bonshaw New S Wales 29.08S 150.53E
61 M5 Bonsin Belgium 50.22N 5.23E
18 M5 Bontang Borneo Indon 0.05N 117.31E
95 E8 Bontberg mt S Africa 32.21S 21.06E
48 V9 Bontekoe Ø isld Greenland 73.10N 21.15W
89 C8 Bonthe Sierra Leone 7.32N 12.30W
19 K3 Bontoc Luzon Philippines 17.07N 120.58E
19 A6 Bontosunggu Celebes Indonesia 5.42S 119.44E
Bön Tsagān Nūr L see Böön Tsagaan Nuur
56 E5 Bonvilston S Glam Wales 51.28N 3.23W
15 L9 Bonvouloir Is.&Reefs Louisiade Arch
94 J4 Bonwapitse Botswana 23.15S 26.46E
112 O5 Bon Wier Texas 30.43N 93.40W
62 L9 Bonyhád Hungary 46.20N 18.31E
14 E7 Bonython Cr Australia
14 G6 Bonython Ra N Terr/W Aust
95 L8 Bonza Bay S Africa 32.58S 27.58E
105 K12 Booby I Bahamas 25.09N 77.04W
13 F1 Booby I Queensland 10.38S 141.54E
26 Q12 Booby I Seychelles, Ind Oc 4.14S 55.41E
116 M2 Booby South Pt Jamaica, W I 17.58N 76.14W
69 O7 Boofzheim France 48.21N 7.42E
13 H8 Boogah Queensland 28.24S 147.25E
14 C8 Boogardie W Australia 28.03S 117.45E
61 K2 Booischot Belgium 51.03N 4.46E
12 C4 Bookabie S Australia 31.52S 132.40E
12 D4 Bookaloo S Australia 31.56S 137.21E
14 A8 Bookara W Australia 29.05S 114.52E
111 P2 Book Cliffs escarp Utah
91 H5 Booke Zaïre 2.34S 22.03E
112 D7 Booker Texas 36.27N 100.34W
89 E7 Boola Guinea 8.22N 8.41W
12 G5 Boolaboolka L New S Wales
14 B6 Boolaloo W Australia 22.30S 115.51E
14 A6 Boolathanna W Australia 24.35S 113.44E
12 E5 Booleroo Centre S Australia 32.52S 138.20E
12 G5 Booligal New S Wales 33.54S 144.54E
14 A6 Boologooro W Australia 24.21S 114.01E
61 H2 Boom Belgium 51.05N 4.22E
12 J3 Boomi New S Wales 28.45S 149.35E
60 J6 Boomkensdiep channel Netherlands
95 O3 Boomlaer S Africa 27.43S 30.58E
106 J5 Boon Michigan 44.17N 85.36W
13 L8 Boonah Queensland 28.00S 152.36E
109 F3 Boone Colorado 38.14N 104.16W
108 R7 Boone Iowa 42.04N 93.52W
105 F1 Boone N Carolina 36.13N 81.41W
104 F9 Boones Mill Virginia 37.07N 79.57W
107 C6 Booneville Arkansas 35.09N 93.57W
104 B9 Booneville Kentucky 37.26N 83.45W
107 H7 Booneville Mississippi 34.40N 88.35W
104 B9 Booneville Res Kentucky
13 H6 Boongoondoo Queensland 22.58S 145.54E
116 O4 Boon Pt Antigua W I 17.10N 61.50W
95 L1 Boons S Africa 25.58S 27.15E
104 H7 Boonsboro Maryland 39.31N 77.39W
103 F5 Boonton New Jersey 40.55N 74.24W
22 E4 Böön Tsagaan Nuur L Mongolia
111 A2 Boonville California 39.01N 123.21W
107 J3 Boonville Indiana 38.02N 87.16W
107 D3 Boonville Missouri 38.58N 92.43W
104 K3 Boonville New York 43.28N 75.20W
120 E6 Boopi, R Bolivia
19 F4 Boö Pulau Pulau islds Irian Jaya
14 D9 Boorabbin W Australia 31.14S 120.21E
59 G5 Boora L Offaly Irish Rep 53.13N 7.45W
12 H4 Boorindal New S Wales 30.23S 146.11E
60 N7 Boornbergum Netherlands 53.05N 6.03E
60 N7 Boorn of Konings diep R Netherlands
12 G5 Booroorban New S Wales 34.55S 144.50E
12 J5 Boorowa New S Wales 34.26S 148.48E
61 N3 Boorsem Belgium 50.57N 5.43E
12 G6 Boort Victoria 36.08S 143.46E
12 D3 Boorthanna S Australia 28.32S 135.52E
70 N3 Boos France 49.23N 1.12E
57 G4 Boot Cumbria Eng 54.24N 3.17W
57 M5 Booth Humberside Eng 53.44N 0.54W
104 Q3 Boothbay Harbor Maine 43.53N 69.40W
123 A5 Boothby,C Antarctica 67.50S 57.35E
56 K2 Boothby Pagnell Lincs Eng 52.52N 0.34W
97 L4 Boothia,G.of N W Terr
97 K3 Boothia Pen N W Terr
107 J8 Boothton Alabama 33.12N 87.00W
57 G4 Bootle Cumbria Eng 54.17N 3.23W
57 G6 Bootle Merseyside Eng 53.28N 3.00W
12 G3 Bootra New S Wales 30.00S 143.00E
26 A14 Boot Rock Marion I Ind Oc 46.49S 37.43E
91 B4 Booué Gabon 0.03S 11.58E
89 K8 Bopa Benin 6.36N 2.00E
12 E3 Bopeechee S Australia 29.38S 137.22E
91 F2 Bopeka Zaïre 2.17N 19.39E
64 J6 Bopfingen W Germany 48.52N 10.22E
95 G2 Bophuthatswana Bantu Homeland S Africa
22 K8 Boping Shandong China 36.39N 116.02E
51 M4 Bo-Poikela Finland 67.55N 26.50E
89 D8 Bopolu Liberia 7.03N 10.32W
64 D3 Boppard W Germany 50.13N 7.35E
Boqaâta see Buq'ata
35 E9 Boqeq watercourse Israel
35 C10 Boqer' watercourse Israel
35 B10 Boqer,Har hill Israel 30.52N 34.44E
70 E5 Boqueho France 48.30N 2.58W
76 C3 Boqueijon Spain 42.48N 8.25W
121 H3 Boqueirão Rio Grânde do Sul Brazil 31.20S 52.06W
118 J8 Boqueirão,I.do Brazil 22.47S 43.10W
121 G2 Boqueirão,Sa.,do mts Brazil
118 G2 Boqueirão,Serra do mts Bahia Brazil
116 G5 Boquerón Cuba 19.59N 75.07W
118 A8 Boquerón dept Paraguay

76 K7 Boquerón, Pto del pass Spain 40.35N 4.35W
19 N4 Boquet isld Truk Is Pacific Oc 7.22N 152.00E
Boquete see Bajo Panama
115 G4 Boquilla de Conchos Mexico 27.35N 105.21W
115 G4 Boquilla, Presa de la res Mexico
112 E6 Boquillas del Carmen Mexico 29.13N 102.55W
64 O4 Bor Czechoslovakia 49.42N 12.47E
87 C7 Bor Sudan 6.18N 31.34E
36 H5 Bor Turkey 37.53N 34.35E
45 Q1 Bor U.S.S.R. 56.22N 44.05E
82 G6 Bor Yugoslavia 44.05N 22.06E
93 N6 Bora Somalia 0.59S 41.14E
53 W19 Bora R Norway
122 A15 Bora-Bora isld Society Is Pacific Oc 16.30S 151.45W
110 M5 Borah Pk Idaho 44.09N 113.47W
29 G7 Borai Madhya Prad Ind 20.05N 81.58E
80 O1 Boraja Yugoslavia 43.38N 16.10E
41 O7 Boralakh R U.S.S.R.
29 J2 Boram W Bengal Ind 23.20N 86.08E
87 J6 Borama Somalia 9.56N 43.13E
87 G8 Boran tribe Ethiopia
15 B6 Borang,Tg C Moluccas Indon 5.17S 133.05E
52 G9 Borås Sweden 57.44N 12.55E
29 H7 Borasambar Orissa India 20.58N 83.00E
32 D6 Borāzjān Iran 29.15N 51.14E
119 J10 Borba Brazil 4.39S 59.35W
76 E11 Borba Portugal 38.48N 7.28W
53 B4 Borbjerg Denmark 56.24N 8.46E
76 F8 Borbollón, Embalse de res Spain 40.12N 6.35W
19 M6 Borbon Philippines 10.48N 124.01E
80 H3 Borbona Italy 42.32N 13.09E
117 H8 Borborema, Planalto da plat Brazil
82 K3 Borca Romania 47.09N 25.49E
79 M2 Borca di Cadore Italy 46.26N 12.14E
82 L6 Borcea R Romania
61 G3 Borchtlombeek Belgium 50.51N 4.09E
37 F4 Borçka Turkey 41.24N 41.38E
77 E9 Borck,El Morocco 35.41N 5.44W
60 P11 Borculo Netherlands 52.07N 6.31E
43 L7 Bordaba Kirgiziya U.S.S.R. 39.32N 73.14E
12 D6 Borda,C S Australia 35.45S 136.34E
14 E3 Borda,C W Australia 16.40S 122.43E
36 D5 Bor Dağı mt Turkey
75 F5 Bordalba Spain 41.25N 2.04W
53 U17 Bordalen V Norway 60.35N 6.28E
53 U19 Bordalen V Norway 59.50N 6.28E
53 W19 Bordalsvatn L Norway 59.50N 7.21E
72 C6 Bordeaux France 44.50N 0.34W
99 R9 Bordeaux Quebec 45.33N 73.41W
108 F8 Bordeaux Wyoming 41.57N 104.52W
72 C6 Bordeaux,Landes de reg France
75 E5 Bordecorex,Sierra de mts Spain
29 F6 Bordehi Madhya Prad India 22.02N 78.21E
76 B14 Bordeira Portugal 37.12N 8.52W
107 L3 Borden Indiana 38.28N 85.55W
98 J7 Borden Prince Edward I 46.16N 63.42W
100 K6 Borden Saskatchewan 52.24N 107.15W
14 C10 Borden W Australia 34.04S 118.12E
97 H2 Borden I N W Terr 78.30N 111.00W
97 L3 Borden Pen N W Terr
103 E6 Bordentown New Jersey 40.08N 74.43W
72 E10 Bordères-Louron France 42.53N 0.24E
72 E9 Bordères-sur-l'Echez France 43.16N 0.03E
58 K7 Borders reg Scotland
12 F6 Bordertown S Australia 36.18S 140.49E
72 E9 Bordes Hautes-Pyrénées France 43.12N 0.13E
72 D9 Bordes Pyrénées Atlantiques France 43.14N 0.16W
63 M4 Bordesholm W Germany 54.12N 10.02E
69 C8 Bordes,les France 47.49N 2.24E
72 G9 Bordes-sur-Arize,les France 43.08N 1.19E
50 D4 Bordheyri Iceland 65.12N 21.06W
Bordhoy see Bordø
79 C7 Bordighera Italy 43.47N 7.40E
75 Q3 Bordils Spain 42.02N 2.55E
53 C4 Bording Denmark 56.08N 9.18E
81 E8 Bordino R Sicily
88 Q3 Bordjbou Arrèridj Algeria 36.02N 4.49E
88 P7 Bordj d'Aïn Guettara Algeria 28.09N 3.06E
88 P3 Bordj El Bahri Algeria 36.51N 3.16E
88 M8 Bordj Flye Ste. Marie Algeria 27.19N 2.57W
88 S6 Bordj Messouda Algeria 30.10N 9.19E
88 R5 Bordj Mey Algeria 32.15N 6.51E
88 O11 Bordj Mokhtar Algeria 21.19N 1.02E
88 O11 Bordj Mokhtar Algeria
89 K1 Bordj-Moktor Algeria 21.10N 1.00E
88 R7 Bordj Omar Driss Algeria 28.04N 6.39E
88 S6 Bordj Sif Fatima Algeria 31.03N 8.39E
Bordj Welvert see Aïn el Hadjel
53 N9 Bordø isld Faeroes 62.15N 6.30W
75 K6 Bordón Spain 40.41N 0.20W
43 M5 Bordunskiy Kirgiziya U.S.S.R. 42.37N 75.35E
93 J1 Bore Ethiopia 4.39N 37.40E
79 G5 Bore Italy 44.43N 9.47E
89 H4 Boré Mali 15.09N 3.33W
14 D8 Boreas,Mt W Australia 28.03S 121.55E
65 N2 Borek Czechoslovakia 49.48N 15.38E
62 K4 Borek Poland 51.55N 17.10E
57 G2 Boreland Dumfries & Galloway Scotland 55.12N 3.19W
52 J8 Borensberg Sweden 58.33N 15.15E
58 A1 Boreray isld W Isles Scotland 57.53N 8.29W
58 B3 Boreray isld W Isles Scotland 57.43N 7.18W
Boresse-et-Martron see Martron
53 T14 Borevatn L Norway 62.08N 5.35E
66 B1 Borey France 47.35N 6.21E
50 E3 Borg Iceland 65.30N 20.35W
51 M11 Borgå Finland 60.24N 25.40E
52 J2 Borgafjäll Sweden 64.49N 15.05E
50 D5 Borgarfjardharsýsla Iceland
50 M3 Borgarfjördhur B Múlasýsla, Nordhur Iceland
50 C6 Borgarfjördhur B Mýrasýsla Iceland
50 K6 Borgarhöfn Iceland 64.13N 15.51W
50 D5 Borgarnes Iceland 64.33N 21.53W
51 D3 Borge Norway 68.15N 13.50E
51 D6 Børgefjell mts Norway
51 D6 Børgefjell Nat.Park Norway
63 K9 Borgentreich W Germany 51.34N 9.14E
60 Q8 Borger Netherlands 52.55N 6.46E
112 C8 Borger Texas 35.39N 101.24W
63 G7 Börger W Germany 52.54N 7.32E
60 S17 Borgharen Netherlands 50.53N 5.41E
79 J3 Borghetto Italy 45.42N 10.56E
79 G6 Borghetto di Vara Italy 44.13N 9.43E
79 F4 Borghetto Lodigiano Italy 45.13N 9.30E
52 K10 Borgholm Øland Sweden 56.50N 16.40E
63 K9 Borgholz W Germany 51.37N 9.15E
63 H8 Borgholzhausen W Germany 52.07N 8.19E
63 F8 Borghorst W Germany 52.08N 7.24E
81 N6 Bórgia Italy 38.49N 16.31E
58 H2 Borgie, R Highland Scotland 58.28N 4.18W
53 N10 Borgin mt Faeroes 61.39N 6.55W
61 M3 Borgloon Belgium 50.48N 5.21E
53 D2 Børglum Denmark 57.22N 9.51E
66 F7 Borgne R Switzerland
107 G12 Borgne, L Louisiana
67 P11 Borgo Corsica 42.33N 9.25E
53 U19 Borgo mt Norway 59.57N 6.17E
79 J7 Borgo a Mozzano Italy 43.59N 10.32E
79 D4 Borgo d'Ale Italy 45.21N 8.03E
79 J4 Borgoforte Italy 45.03N 10.45E
79 C3 Borgofranco d'Ivrea Italy 45.31N 7.52E
79 E4 Borgo Lavezzaro Italy 45.19N 8.42E
79 D3 Borgomanero Italy 45.42N 8.27E
79 C7 Borgomaro Italy 43.58N 7.57E
80 G5 Borgo Montello Italy 41.30N 12.46E
79 B4 Borgone Susa Italy 45.08N 7.14E
79 F4 Borgonovo Val Tidone Italy 45.01N 9.27E
79 M7 Borgo Pace Italy 43.39N 12.17E
79 K5 Borgo Panigale Italy 44.32N 11.16E
80 H4 Borgorose Italy 42.12N 13.14E
79 B6 Borgo San Dalmazzo Italy 44.20N 7.29E
79 K7 Borgo San Lorenzo Italy 43.57N 11.24E
79 D3 Borgosesia Italy 45.43N 8.16E
79 E3 Borgo Ticino Italy 45.42N 8.36E
89 K6 Borgou Togo 10.47N 0.39E
79 G6 Borgo Val di Taro Italy 44.29N 9.46E
79 K2 Borgo Valsugana Italy 46.03N 11.28E
79 D4 Borgo Vercelli Italy 45.22N 8.28E
52 J4 Borgsjö Sweden 62.32N 16.00E
52 G9 Borgstena Sweden 57.55N 13.00E
60 R6 Borgsweer Netherlands 53.18N 7.01E
57 E3 Borgue Dumfries & Galloway Scotland 54.49N 4.09W
58 K2 Borgue Highland Scotland 58.13N 3.29W
53 U14 Borgund Möre og Romsdal Norway 62.28N 6.15E
53 X16 Borgund Sogn og Fjordane Norway 61.02N 7.49E
53 T19 Børgundøy isld Norway 59.43N 5.40E
52 J3 Borgvattnet Sweden 63.25N 15.50E
Bor'ham,El see Bogham, El
37 J9 Borhān Iran 36.44N 45.57E
89 L7 Bori Benin 9.46N 2.35E
29 D6 Bori Madhya Prad India 22.32N 74.42E
29 F7 Bori Maharashtra India 20.52N 79.04E
42 K6 Bori U.S.S.R. 52.30N 118.02E
108 F8 Borie Wyoming 41.06N 104.59W
37 D8 Borik Dağı mt Turkey
25 G3 Borikhane Laos 18.35N 103.44E
46 K3 Borilovo U.S.S.R. 53.19N 35.58E
76 J2 Borines Spain 43.23N 5.19W
45 L4 Borinskoye U.S.S.R. 52.25N 39.21E
82 H1 Borinya U.S.S.R. 49.04N 22.58E
30 L7 Borio Bihar India 25.03N 87.35E
29 D7 Bori R Maharashtra India
Bori Sâfita see Sâfita
46 E5 Borislav Ukraine U.S.S.R. 49.18N 23.28E
45 O5 Borisoglebsk U.S.S.R. 51.23N 42.02E
46 G3 Borisov Belorussiya U.S.S.R. 54.09N 28.30E
41 B2 Borisova,Mys C Novaya Zemlya U.S.S.R. 74.46N 55.35E
40 G4 Borisova Mys C U.S.S.R. 55.56N 137.25E
45 H6 Borisovka Belgorod U.S.S.R. 50.36N 36.04E
43 J5 Borisovka Kazakhstan U.S.S.R. 43.15N 68.12E
47 D6 Borisovo Sudskoye U.S.S.R. 59.56N 36.00E
47 L8 Borisovskiy U.S.S.R. 54.37N 72.32E
45 B6 Borispol Ukraine U.S.S.R. 50.21N 30.59E
87 A7 Bo River Post Sudan 6.48N 27.55E
118 C9 Borja Paraguay 25.54S 56.28W
120 B1 Borja Peru 4.28S 77.35W
75 G4 Borja Spain 41.50N 1.32W
75 F4 Borjabad Spain 41.33N 2.22W
32 G3 Borjak Iran 35.25N 58.00E
82 D6 Borja Planina mts Yugoslavia
75 M4 Borjas Blancas Spain 41.31N 0.52E
35 D1 Borj Ech Chemâli Lebanon 33.16N 35.14E
32 D5 Borj-e Chin Iran 30.58N 50.59E
51 J6 Börjelslandet Sweden 65.46N 22.10E
88 T5 Borj Mechhed Salah Tunisia 32.20N 11.09E
35 D1 Borj Qibli Lebanon 33.15N 35.14E
63 F9 Bork W Germany 51.39N 7.28E
60 K14 Borkel Netherlands 51.18N 5.26E
64 G1 Borken Hessen W Germany 51.03N 9.18E
63 E9 Borken Nordrhein-Westfalen W Germany 51.50N 6.52E
87 H5 Borkenna,R Ethiopia
45 H7 Borki Khar'kov, Ukraine U.S.S.R. 49.40N 36.04E
45 K4 Borki Lipetsk U.S.S.R. 52.09N 38.07E
45 F6 Borki Poltava, Ukraine U.S.S.R. 50.06N 34.13E
46 M3 Borki Ryazan' U.S.S.R. 53.56N 41.50E
53 D5 Børkop Denmark 55.39N 9.40E
90 K4 Borkou Chad 14.49N 21.15E
90 H2 Borkou, Ennedi et Tibesti div Chad
46 G2 Borkovichi Belorussiya U.S.S.R. 55.39N 28.22E
47 F3 Borkovskaya U.S.S.R. 65.14N 49.31E
63 E5 Borkum W Germany 53.35N 6.40E
63 E5 Borkum isld W Germany
52 J6 Borlänge Sweden 60.29N 15.25E
61 L4 Borlez Belgium 50.38N 5.15E
61 L4 Borlo Belgium 50.44N 5.11E
61 M5 Borlon Belgium 50.23N 5.25E
36 C4 Borlu Turkey 38.45N 28.28E
88 S6 Borma,El Tunisia 31.35N 9.19E
35 C9 Bor Mashash Israel 31.04N 34.51E
71 J10 Bormes-les-Mimosas France 43.10N 6.21E
71 J10 Bormes,Rade de B France 43.07N 6.22E
79 D6 Bormida Italy 44.17N 8.14E
79 D5 Bórmida di Millésimo R Italy
79 D6 Bórmida di Spigno R Italy
79 H2 Bormio Italy 46.28N 10.22E
61 Q7 Born Luxembourg 49.46N 6.31E
60 T16 Born Netherlands 51.02N 5.48E
66 H2 Born mt Switzerland 47.19N 7.52E
64 O1 Borna E Germany 51.08N 12.30E
45 W2 Borna U.S.S.R. 54.02N 50.16E
60 L6 Borndiep channel Netherlands
60 Q10 Borne Netherlands 52.18N 6.45E
66 B8 Borne R France
61 G2 Bornem Belgium 51.06N 4.14E
17 H11 Borneo / East Indies
60 P10 Bornerbroek Netherlands 52.18N 6.40E
76 E6 Bornes Portugal 41.27N 7.00W
76 F6 Bornes,Sa.de mts Portugal
69 M2 Bornheim Alfter W Germany 50.46N 7.00E
53 P12 Bornholm co Denmark
53 P12 Bornholm isld Denmark
52 H11 Bornholmsgattet str Sweden
63 M4 Bornhöved W Germany 54.04N 10.14E
63 R7 Börnicke E Germany 52.41N 12.56E
63 R8 Bornim E Germany 52.26N 12.59E
61 H4 Bornival Belgium 50.36N 4.17E
79 H3 Borno Italy 45.57N 10.12E
75 D5 Bornoba R Spain
77 E7 Bornos Spain 36.50N 5.42W
77 E7 Bornos,Embalse de res Spain 36.50N 5.42W
36 C4 Bornova Turkey 38.28N 27.15E
90 L3 Boro Chad 16.58N 22.25E
94 G2 Boro R Botswana
90 M7 Boro watercourse Sudan
82 K3 Boroaia Romania 47.22N 26.21E
75 G4 Borobia Spain 41.40N 1.53W
18 J9 Borobudur ruins Java Indon 7.36S 110.08E
19 K6 Borocay isld Philippines 11.59N 121.56E
45 F8 Borodayevka Ukraine U.S.S.R. 48.45N 34.09E
87 F7 Borodda Ethiopia 6.27N 37.41E
42 D1 Borodina Krasnoyarsk U.S.S.R. 62.58N 88.06E
42 F4 Borodino Krasnoyarsk U.S.S.R. 55.51N 95.02E
Borodino Is see Daitō Is
46 G4 Borodyanka Ukraine U.S.S.R. 50.38N 29.59E
41 O8 Borogontsy U.S.S.R. 62.45N 131.15E
24 D4 Borohoro Shan mt ra Xinjiang Uygur Zizhiqu China
Boro Horo Ula mts see Borohoro Shan
65 O1 Borohrádek Czechoslovakia 50.07N 16.06E
19 C3 Boroko Celebes Indon 0.56N 123.16E
41 M7 Borolgustakh U.S.S.R. 65.20N 122.02E
45 F6 Boromlya Ukraine U.S.S.R. 50.38N 34.59E
89 H6 Boromo Upper Volta 11.47N 2.54W
111 G6 Boron California 35.01N 117.39W
89 G7 Boron Ivory Coast 8.41N 5.47W
29 H8 Borondi Orissa India 19.35N 82.20E
19 M6 Borongan Samar Philippines 11.38N 125.27E
39 B2 Borong,Khrebet mts U.S.S.R.
81 B3 Borore Sardinia 40.13N 8.48E
13 K6 Bororen Queensland 24.13S 151.30E
Borotala R see Bortala He
89 F7 Borotou Ivory Coast 8.46N 7.30W
90 J1 Borou watercourse Chad
57 L4 Boroughbridge N Yorks Eng 54.05N 1.24W
56 M5 Borough Green Kent Eng 51.17N 0.19E
88 K5 Borouj,El Morocco 32.30N 7.10W
Boro Uula see Bor Ul Shan
65 O2 Borová Czechoslovakia 49.45N 16.09E
65 L4 Borovany Czechoslovakia 48.54N 14.39E
45 J7 Borovaya Ukraine U.S.S.R. 49.22N 37.39E
47 M3 Borovaya U.S.S.R. 58.24N 59.50E
46 J1 Borovichi U.S.S.R. 58.22N 34.00E
42 C5 Borovikha U.S.S.R. 53.31N 83.54E
42 C5 Borovlyanka U.S.S.R. 52.38N 84.30E
42 D4 Borovoy U.S.S.R. 55.30N 86.05E
43 K1 Borovoye Kazakhstan U.S.S.R. 53.07N 70.20E
47 G4 Borovoye U.S.S.R. 62.40N 52.40E
45 H1 Borovsk Kaluga U.S.S.R. 55.12N 36.28E
47 H6 Borovsk Perm U.S.S.R. 59.45N 56.41E
47 K7 Borovskiy U.S.S.R. 57.04N 65.41E
43 G1 Borovskoy Kazakhstan U.S.S.R. 53.48N 64.09E
45 K8 Borovskoye Ukraine U.S.S.R. 48.52N 38.38E
75 C7 Borox Spain 40.05N 3.44W
81 E8 Borrania R Sicily
52 H11 Borrby Sweden 55.27N 14.10E
53 J7 Borre Denmark 54.59N 11.58E
63 R5 Borrenthin E Germany 53.49N 12.58E
76 F2 Borres Spain 43.20N 6.33W
72 G6 Borrèze France 44.57N 1.24E
75 K7 Borriol Spain 40.03N 0.05W
59 J6 Borris Carlow Irish Rep 52.36N 6.55W
53 B5 Borris Denmark 55.58N 8.39E
59 G6 Borris-in-Ossory Leix Irish Rep 52.57N 7.37W
59 F6 Borrisokane Tipperary Irish Rep 53.00N 8.08W
59 G6 Borrisoleigh Tipperary Irish Rep 52.45N 8.00W
13 D3 Borroloola N Terr Australia 16.00S 136.15E
66 L8 Borromee, I Italy 45.54N 8.31E
57 F3 Borron Pt Dumfries & Galloway Scotland 54.54N 3.34W
52 K8 Börrum Sweden 58.20N 16.40E
82 H4 Borşa Romania 46.56N 23.40E
82 J3 Borşa Romania 47.39N 24.40E
29 C6 Borsad Gujarat India 22.24N 72.59E
61 F3 Borsbeke Belgium 50.54N 3.53E
63 R10 Borsdorf E Germany 51.22N 12.32E
53 X20 Borsee L Norway 59.22N 7.48E
51 M1 Børselv Norway 70.20N 25.30E
82 H2 Borshava R U.S.S.R.
46 F5 Borshchev Ukraine U.S.S.R. 48.48N 26.00E
42 J7 Borshchovochnyy Khrebet mts U.S.S.R.
87 G6 Borshoto Ethiopia 8.48N 39.32E
34 M6 Borsippa anc site Iraq 32.23N 44.25E
46 Q3 Borskoye U.S.S.R. 53.05N 51.40E
82 F2 Borsod-Abaúj-Zemplén co Hungary
60 B3 Borsselen Netherlands 51.25N 3.45E
63 N8 Börssum W Germany 52.04N 10.37E
53 K5 Borstahusen Sweden 55.54N 12.50E
63 J7 Borstel W Germany 52.41N 8.58E
Bortala see Bole
24 D3 Bortala He R Xinjiang Uygur Zizhiqu China
53 X19 Børte Norway 59.34N 7.49E
53 X19 Børteheia moor Norway 59.36N 7.34E
53 X19 Børtevatn L Norway 59.32N 7.49E
56 C3 Borth Dyfed Wales 52.29N 4.03W
57 G2 Borthwick Water R Borders Scotland
81 B3 Bortigali Sardinia 40.17N 8.51E
52 H4 Börtnan Sweden 62.45N 13.50E
53 S15 Bortnen Norway 61.51N 5.24E
42 J5 Borto U.S.S.R. 53.38N 111.52E
15 K9 Boru Papua New Guinea 10.15S 148.50E
41 Q5 Boru U.S.S.R. 70.37N 142.43E
32 D5 Borūjen Iran 31.59N 51.16E
32 C4 Borūjerd Iran 33.55N 48.48E
Borujird see Borūjerd
22 D6 Bor Ul Shan mts Nei Monggol Zizhiqu China
53 E4 Borum Denmark 56.12N 10.02E
32 H3 Borun Iran 34.10N 58.10E
91 F1 Boruna Zaïre 4.58N 19.57E
53 H6 Borup Denmark 55.30N 11.59E
108 O2 Borup Minnesota 47.12N 96.30W
42 E5 Borus, Khrebet mts U.S.S.R.
58 D2 Borve Lewis, W Isles Scotland 58.25N 6.26W
53 V18 Børve Norway 60.16N 6.38E
58 A5 Borve W Isles Scotland 56.59N 7.31W
58 B3 Borvemore Harris, W Isles Scotland 57.50N 7.00W
62 K2 Bory Tucholskie forest Poland
41 L5 Bor-Yuryakh U.S.S.R. 71.17N 117.18E
62 M5 Borzęcin Poland 50.05N 20.40E
44 E6 Borzhomi Georgia U.S.S.R. 41.49N 43.23E
45 D5 Borzna Ukraine U.S.S.R. 51.15N 32.25E
79 F6 Borzonasca Italy 44.26N 9.23E
41 C2 Borzova,Zaliv B Novaya Zemlya U.S.S.R.
42 K6 Borzya U.S.S.R. 50.24N 116.35E
42 K6 Borzya R U.S.S.R.
81 A3 Bosa Sardinia 40.18N 8.30E
91 F4 Bosa Zaïre 0.24S 19.13E
43 L3 Bosaga Kazakhstan U.S.S.R. 47.53N 72.59E
43 H7 Bosaga Turkmeniya U.S.S.R. 37.33N 65.39E
91 H4 Bosaka tribe Zaïre
82 D5 Bosanska Dubica Yugoslavia 45.10N 16.50E
82 D5 Bosanska Gradiška Yugoslavia 45.09N 17.15E
82 C6 Bosanska Krupa Yugoslavia 44.53N 16.10E
82 C6 Bosanska Petrovac Yugoslavia 44.35N 16.21E
82 C5 Bosanski Novi Yugoslavia 45.02N 16.22E
82 E5 Bosanski Šamac Yugoslavia 45.03N 18.29E
Bosaso see Bender Cassim
63 M4 Bosau W Germany 54.07N 10.26E
15 G7 Bosavi, Mt Papua New Guinea 6.35S 142.50E
95 K4 Bosberg mt S Africa 28.28S 26.06E
117 B2 Boscamp Surinam 5.49N 55.55W
56 B6 Boscastle Cornwall Eng 50.41N 4.42W
104 O3 Boscawen New Hampshire 43.21N 71.40W
121 F6 Bosch Argentina 37.40S 58.12W
61 N2 Bosch Beek R Belgium
79 K4 Boschi Santa Anna Italy 45.13N 11.21E
60 C3 Boschkapelle Netherlands 51.20N 3.58E
Bosch, Tandjung van den C see Papesoi, Tg. C.
70 N2 Bosc-le-Hard France 49.37N 1.11E
66 M8 Bosco Italy 45.58N 8.47E
80 F2 Bosco Italy 43.08N 12.27E
107 D9 Bosco Louisiana 32.18N 92.04W
66 K6 Bosco Switzerland 46.19N 8.30E
106 D6 Boscobel Wisconsin 43.07N 90.42W
79 K3 Bosco Chiesanuova Italy 45.38N 11.02E
79 E5 Bosco Marengo Italy 44.49N 8.40E
56 H6 Boscombe Dorset Eng 50.44N 1.50W
79 C4 Bosconero Italy 45.16N 7.46E
80 K7 Boscotrecase Italy 40.46N 14.28E
23 D7 Bose Guangxi China 23.55N 106.32E
91 F5 Boseki Zaïre 2.34S 19.38E
91 H3 Bosenge Zaïre 1.18N 22.20E
22 L8 Boshan Shandong China 36.32N 117.47E
23 B7 Boshang Yunnan China 23.42N 100.01E
23 F2 Boshan Sk res Henan China 32.45N 113.37E
40 J7 Boshnyakovo Sakhalin U.S.S.R. 49.35N 142.12E
94 J5 Boshoek S Africa 25.30S 27.09E
95 J4 Boshof S Africa 28.32S 25.15E
32 G4 Boshruyeh Iran 33.54N 57.29E
82 G8 Bosiljgrad Yugoslavia 42.30N 22.27E
79 F3 Bosisio Italy 45.48N 9.17E
25 H4 Bo Si Song Khram Thailand 17.40N 104.12E
52 H7 Bosjön Sweden 59.46N 13.30E
60 G11 Boskoop Netherlands 52.04N 4.40E
95 L2 Boskop S Africa 26.34S 27.07E
65 P3 Boskovice Czechoslovakia 49.30N 16.39E
95 J3 Boskuil S Africa 27.25S 25.53E
117 B2 Boslanti Surinam 4.19N 55.49W
108 E8 Bosler Wyoming 41.35N 105.41W
57 J6 Bosley Cheshire Eng 53.11N 2.07W
82 D6 Bosna R Yugoslavia
82 D6 Bosna i Hercegovina rep Yugoslavia
15 D4 Bosnik Biak I, Irian Jaya 1.09S 136.14E
94 G5 Bosobogolo Pan Botswana 25.18S 22.12E
91 F1 Bosobolo Zaïre 4.11N 19.55E
20 O6 Bōsō-hantō pen Japan
94 J3 Bosoli Botswana 20.58S 27.39E
75 M2 Bosost Spain 42.46N 0.41E
63 G10 Bösperde W Germany 51.27N 7.47E
60 O5 Bosplaat isld Netherlands 53.32N 6.27E
Bosporus see Karadeniz Boğazı
109 D7 Bosque New Mexico 34.33N 106.49W
77 E7 Bosque,El Spain 36.46N 5.30W
88 O3 Bosquet Algeria 36.11N 0.22E
Bosra ech Châm see Busra
95 L3 Bosrand S Africa 27.45S 27.10E
Bosr el Hariri see Busra el Hariri
65 K6 Bosruck Tunnel tunnel Austria 47.38N 14.23E
90 H8 Bossangoa Cent Afr Rep 6.27N 17.21E
53 Y19 Bossbøen Norway 59.47N 8.15E
53 W20 Bossbu Norway 59.12N 7.17E
90 H9 Bossèmbélé Cent Afr Emp 5.10N 17.44E
90 H9 Bossemptélé II Cent Afr Rep 5.50N 16.39E
72 E6 Bosset France 44.56N 0.22E
90 H9 Bossi Cent Afr Rep 4.30N 16.48E
107 C9 Bossier City Louisiana 32.31N 93.44W
95 J2 Bossies S Africa 26.33S 25.42E
90 F5 Bosso Niger 13.43N 13.19E
79 D5 Bossolasco Italy 44.32N 8.03E
66 D8 Bossons, Glacier des France
117 G9 Bossoroca Brazil 9.28S 41.04W
61 D4 Bossuit Belgium 50.45N 3.25E
14 D4 Bossut, C W Australia 18.47S 121.40E
61 J3 Bossut-Gottechain Belgium 50.46N 4.42E
53 W20 Bossvatn L Norway 59.20N 7.10E
61 K3 Bost Belgium 50.47N 4.56E
Bostam see Bastam
32 B5 Bostan Iran 31.43N 47.55E
31 D5 Bostan Pakistan 30.23N 67.00E
24 D5 Bostan Xinjiang Uygur Zizhiqu China 41.20N 83.15E
24 E7 Bostan Xinjiang Uygur Zizhiqu China 37.00N 84.37E
44 H10 Bostānābād Iran 37.52N 46.51E
37 D3 Bostandere Turkey 40.06N 27.03E
43 A3 Bostandyk Kazakhstan U.S.S.R. 49.37N 48.42E
46 P5 Bostandyk Kazakhstan U.S.S.R. 49.37N 48.58E
32 F7 Bostāneh,Ra's-e C Iran 26.32N 54.35E
24 F5 Bosten (Bagrax) Hu L Xinjiang Uygur Zizhiqu China
105 D7 Boston Georgia 30.46N 83.47W
59 J5 Boston Kildare Irish Rep 53.14N 6.55W
57 N7 Boston Lincs Eng 52.59N 0.01W
103 M2 Boston Massachusetts 42.20N 71.05W
12 D5 Boston B S Australia
101 N11 Boston Bar Br Col 49.52N 121.25W
116 M2 Boston Bay Jamaica, W I 18.10N 76.22W
103 G2 Boston Corners New York 42.02N 73.30W
104 R9 Boston Harb Massachusetts
107 C6 Boston Mts Arkansas
53 F6 Bøstrup Fyn Denmark 55.03N 10.53E
53 D4 Bøstrup Viborg Denmark 56.19N 9.53E
89 J8 Bosumtwi,L Ghana 6.32N 1.20W
82 E5 Bosut R Yugoslavia
98 O5 Boswarlos Newfoundland 48.36N 58.50W
101 P11 Boswell Br Col 49.28N 116.46W
106 G9 Boswell Indiana 40.31N 87.25W
109 P7 Boswell Oklahoma 34.03N 95.53W
104 F6 Boswell Pennsylvania 40.10N 79.03W
66 K2 Boswil Switzerland 47.18N 8.19E
107 C2 Bosworth Missouri 39.28N 93.21W
75 L5 Bot Spain 41.01N 0.22E
29 B6 Botad Gujarat India 22.12N 71.44E
118 J9 Botafogo Rio de Janeiro Brazil 22.58S 43.12W
118 J9 Botafogo, Enseada de B Brazil
91 E3 Botanga Congo 1.55N 18.00E
12 M8 Botany dist Sydney, N S W
12 M8 Botany Bay Sydney, N S W
76 C8 Botâo Portugal 40.18N 8.24W
52 K3 Boteå Sweden 63.08N 17.45E
91 D9 Botera Angola 11.33S 14.16E
94 F8 Botersleegte S Africa 30.32S 21.18E
56 N3 Botesdale Suffolk Eng 52.21N 1.00E
82 J8 Botev mt Bulgaria 42.43N 24.55E
82 H8 Botevgrad Bulgaria 42.55N 23.47E
100 E6 Botha Alberta 52.20N 112.30W
95 N3 Bothasberg mt S Africa 27.29S 29.05E
95 O5 Botha's Hill S Africa 29.45S 30.45E
95 N3 Bothaspas S Africa 27.37S 29.45E
95 K3 Bothaville S Africa 27.24S 26.37E
57 G3 Bothel Cumbria Eng 54.45N 3.16W
61 J4 Bothey Belgium 50.32N 4.39E
95 G3 Bothithong S Africa 27.04S 23.50E
51 G11 Bothnia,Gulf of Sweden/Finland
99 J10 Bothwell Ontario 42.37N 81.53W
58 H7 Bothwell Strathclyde Scotland 55.48N 4.04W
12 H8 Bothwell Tasmania 42.20S 147.00E
87 M5 Botiala Somalia 11.30N 49.59E
15 L5 Botiangin,C Bismarck Arch 2.43S 150.08E
76 D5 Boticas Portugal 41.41N 7.40W
32 D7 Botkhāneh Iran 27.50N 51.45E
104 A6 Botkins Ohio 40.29N 84.11W
45 S8 Botkul, Oz L U.S.S.R.
94 H3 Botletle R Botswana
56 J6 Botley Hants Eng 50.55N 1.15W
56 J4 Botley Oxon Eng 51.46N 1.17W
44 G5 Botlikh U.S.S.R. 42.41N 46.14E
91 B1 Bot Makak Cameroon 4.02N 10.59E
60 M7 Botmeer L Netherlands
50 B3 Botn Iceland 65.32N 23.48W
82 M4 Botna R U.S.S.R.
50 G6 Botnafjöll mt Iceland 64.18N 18.43W
50 G7 Botnar Iceland 63.40N 18.17W
53 U21 Botne Norway 58.59N 6.06E
53 S15 Botnen Norway 61.44N 5.00E
53 U18 Botnen Norway 60.28N 6.13E
53 U15 Botnenipa mt Norway 61.40N 6.19E
52 E3 Botngård Norway 63.46N 9.48E
50 D6 Botnsheidhi heath Iceland
50 D6 Botnssulur mt Iceland 64.20N 21.09W
53 H7 Bøtø Denmark 54.42N 11.58E
19 J4 Botolan Pt Luzon Philippines 15.15N 120.00E
42 K1 Botomoyu R U.S.S.R.
87 B9 Botongwe Zaïre 2.34N 28.10E
117 B2 Boto-Pasi Surinam 4.15N 55.27W
87 G5 Boto,R Ethiopia
75 H4 Botorrita Spain 41.30N 1.01W
41 M7 Botor'una U.S.S.R. 66.20N 124.19E
82 K3 Botoşani Romania 47.44N 26.41E
89 K5 Botou Upper Volta 12.42N 1.59E
25 J4 Bo Trach Vietnam 17.34N 106.30E
61 P4 Botrange summit Belgium 50.30N 6.05E
95 C10 Botrivier S Africa 34.14S 19.12E
103 H4 Botsford Connecticut 41.22N 73.15W
84 D6 Bótsika mt Greece 37.38N 22.08E
52 M2 Botsmark Sweden 64.15N 20.15E
73 G8 Botswana rep Southern Africa
81 M5 Botte Donato mt Italy 39.17N 16.28E
61 F3 Bottelare Belgium 50.58N 3.45E
94 E8 Botter Kloof Pass S Africa 31.49S 19.18E
57 M7 Bottesford Leics Eng 52.56N 0.48W
80 D3 Bottigli,Monte Italy 42.42N 11.13E
108 K1 Bottineau N Dakota 48.50N 100.28W
56 M3 Bottisham Cambs Eng 52.13N 0.16E
116 H4 Bottle Creek Caicos Is W I 21.59N 72.01W
116 N6 Bottom Saba Lesser Antilles 17.42N 63.26W
79 M4 Bottrighe Italy 45.02N 12.05E
63 E9 Bottrop W Germany 51.31N 6.55E
118 E8 Botucatu Brazil 22.52S 48.30W
82 H7 Botunya R Bulgaria
118 G3 Botuporã Brazil 13.20S 42.32W
98 R4 Botwood Newfoundland 49.09N 55.22W
42 K5 Boty U.S.S.R. 52.26N 118.30E
89 G7 Bou R Ivory Coast
91 D4 Boua Congo 0.19S 15.36E
88 J6 Bouabout Morocco 31.15N 9.09W
78 A12 Bou Aci Algeria 36.36N 7.18E
89 G8 Bouaflé Ivory Coast 7.01N 5.47W
70 N3 Bouafles France 49.13N 1.24E
77 G10 Bou Ahmed Morocco 35.19N 4.58W
88 N5 Bou Aïech Algeria 32.02N 1.36W
89 G8 Bouaké Ivory Coast 7.42N 5.00W
90 G8 Bouala Cent Afr Rep 6.20N 15.30E
88 O5 Boualem Algeria 33.50N 1.35E
90 J9 Bouali Cent Afr Rep 4.47N 18.09E
91 B5 Bouali Gabon 3.04S 11.30E
91 D5 Bouambé Congo 2.59S 15.34E
88 M5 Bouânane Morocco 32.03N 3.03W
91 D3 Bouanga Congo 0.33N 15.10E
89 H8 Bouape Ivory Coast 6.18N 3.47W
90 G9 Bouar Cent Afr Rep 5.58N 15.35E
88 S3 Bou Arada Tunisia 36.21N 9.37E
34 J3 Bouara,Sabkhat salt marsh Iraq
88 N5 Bouârfa Morocco 32.30N 1.59W
89 L6 Bouaye Benin 10.23N 2.44E
72 A1 Bouaye France 47.09N 1.41W
88 K6 Bou Azzer Morocco 30.35N 6.45W
90 G7 Boubandjida reg Cameroon/Chad
89 E3 Bou Bata Mauritania 16.50N 8.58W
88 N4 Bou Beker Morocco 34.30N 1.48W
88 M8 Bou Bernous Algeria 27.22N 2.53W
65 J4 Boubín mt Czechoslovakia 48.59N 13.48E
72 K3 Bouble R France
88 L8 Boubout Algeria 27.26N 4.30W
90 J8 Bouca Cent Afr Rep 6.30N 18.21E
76 C9 Bouça, Barragem de res Portugal 39.47N 8.20W
72 B8 Boucau France 43.32N 1.29W
13 C1 Boucaut B N Terr Australia
71 C4 Boucé Allier France 46.20N 3.30E
70 K4 Boucé Orne France 48.38N 0.05W
69 E3 Bouchain France 50.17N 3.20E
72 E1 Bouchard, l'Île France 47.07N 0.26E
69 D4 Bouchavesnes-Bergen France 49.59N 2.55E
88 R3 Bouchegouf Algeria 36.30N 7.43E
98 N2 Boucher,L Quebec
99 T8 Boucherville, Isles de Quebec
67 P14 Bouches de Bonifacio str Corsica/Sardinia
99 P6 Bouchette Quebec 46.11N 75.59W
69 D4 Bouchoir France 49.45N 2.40E
71 H4 Bouchoux,les France 46.17N 5.50E
66 A3 Bouclans France 47.15N 6.15E
89 E5 Bouclé de Baoulé,Parc Nat.de la Mali
69 K6 Boucq France 48.45N 5.46E
90 J9 Bouda Cent Afr Rep 4.28N 18.10E
90 F1 Boudhema depression Niger
93 M1 Boudi Ethiopia 4.05N 40.08E
89 H2 Bou Djéhiba Mali 18.36N 2.36W
88 M6 Boudnib Morocco 31.57N 3.38W
90 K3 Boudoa Chad 17.55N 20.28E
89 E5 Boudofoni Mali 13.08N 9.30W
90 H9 Boudou Cent Afr Rep 5.17N 16.23E
90 G6 Boudougour Chad 10.38N 15.35E
90 F5 Boudoum Niger 13.12N 12.14E
107 G11 Boudreau,B Louisiana 30.00N 89.25W
69 H8 Boudreville France 47.56N 4.50E
66 D4 Boudry Switzerland 46.57N 6.51E
89 F1 Boué Boué,El Mauritania 22.11N 6.59W
70 G7 Bouée France 47.20N 1.55W
91 C6 Bouenza div Congo
72 E9 Bouès R France
72 H2 Bouesse France 46.37N 1.40E
70 H5 Bouexière, la France 48.10N 1.28W
88 P3 Boufarik Algeria 36.36N 2.54E
98 E3 Bouffard, L Quebec 50.40N 67.47W
61 J5 Bouffioulx Belgium 50.23N 4.31E
88 Q3 Bougaâ Algeria 36.24N 5.01E
88 Q3 Bougaa Algeria 36.23N 5.13E
76 B6 Bougado Portugal 41.20N 8.34W
14 F2 Bougainville, C W Australia 13.59S 126.05E
15 J2 Bougainville I Papua New Guinea
13 H3 Bougainville Reef Gt Barrier Reef Australia 15.31S 147.05E
15 A4 Bougainville,Selat str Irian Jaya
15 J2 Bougainville Str Papua New Guinea
89 D3 Bougara Mauritania 17.12N 11.39W
88 J8 Bou Garfa Algeria 27.24N 8.03W
88 R3 Bougaroun,C Algeria 37.10N 6.30E
61 K5 Bouge Belgium 50.28N 4.53E
72 H1 Bouges le-Château France 47.02N 1.40E
71 D8 Bougès, Mtgne du France 44.20N 3.44E
59 C8 Boughil mt Kerry Irish Rep 51.55N 9.40W
56 E3 Boughrood Powys Wales 52.03N 3.17W
88 P4 Boughzoul Algeria 35.42N 2.51E
Bougie see Bejaïa
88 Q3 Bougie,G.de Algeria
68 C3 Bougival France 48.52N 2.09E
72 E7 Bouglon France 44.24N 0.06E
61 F5 Bougnies Belgium 50.23N 3.57E
90 G6 Bougomène Chad 11.30N 15.13E
89 F6 Bougouni Mali 11.25N 7.28W
89 G5 Bougounso Mali 12.39N 5.09W
88 O4 Bougtob Algeria 34.02N 0.09E
88 O7 Bou Guema Algeria 28.47N 0.18E
72 A1 Bouguenais France 47.11N 1.37W
89 D1 Bou Guerba Mauritania 21.28N 11.42W
89 B2 Bou Guettara Mauritania 19.22N 15.35W
66 B6 Bougy Switzerland 46.29N 6.22E
88 L4 Bouhalf Souahel tribe Morocco
74 H8 Bouhalloufa Algeria 36.09N 0.17E
88 N4 Bou Hanifa el Hamamat Algeria 35.18N 0.08W
74 G9 Bou Hanifia, Barrage de res Algeria 35.16N 0.05W
71 C2 Bouhy France 47.29N 3.10E
72 G8 Bouillac France 43.51N 1.06E
116 M4 Bouillante Guadeloupe W I 16.08N 61.46W
71 E9 Bouillargues France 43.48N 4.25E
70 M3 Bouille,la France 49.21N 0.55E
72 D1 Bouillé Loretz France 47.05N 0.16W
70 J6 Bouillé-Ménard France 47.45N 0.57W
61 L7 Bouillon Belgium 49.47N 5.04E
69 F7 Bouilly France 48.11N 4.00E
70 G8 Bouin France 46.59N 2.00W
88 P3 Bouïra Algeria 36.22N 3.55E
74 K9 Bouira Sahari Algeria 35.22N 3.23E
89 B2 Bouir Diéri Mauritania 19.40N 15.50W
88 L9 Bouir Ikrlef Mali 24.50N 5.16W
88 P3 Bou Ismail Algeria 36.40N 2.42E
72 J10 Bouissé France 42.59N 2.27E
88 J7 Bou Izakarn Morocco 29.09N 9.44W
88 K5 Boujad Morocco 32.48N 6.26W
71 J3 Boujailles France 46.53N 6.05E
89 L6 Bouka Benin 10.11N 3.09E
84 C7 Boúka Greece 37.01N 21.59E
89 K6 Boukombé Benin 10.13N 1.09E
84 B5 Boúkoura Greece 38.04N 21.30E
90 H9 Boula Cent Afr Rep 4.21N 16.40E
88 L8 Bou Laber Algeria 27.48N 4.37W
61 O7 Boulaide Luxembourg 49.53N 5.49E
89 E4 Boulal Mali 15.08N 8.21W
89 A1 Boulanouar Mauritania 21.17N 16.29W
69 M5 Boulay-Moselle France 49.11N 6.30E
72 F5 Boulazac France 45.09N 0.48E
109 E1 Boulder Colorado 40.02N 105.16W
110 N3 Boulder Montana 46.14N 112.07W
111 N4 Boulder Utah 37.56N 111.25W
14 D9 Boulder W Australia 30.55S 121.32E
110 Q7 Boulder Wyoming 42.45N 109.44W
111 K5 Boulder Canyon gorge Nevada/Arizona
111 K6 Boulder City Nevada 35.59N 114.51W
110 J7 Boulder Cr Idaho
111 B4 Boulder Creek California 37.07N 122.09W
91 B2 Boulé tribe Cameroon
99 N5 Bouleau,L.au Quebec
90 G1 Boulelougou Niger 20.55N 14.05E
111 H9 Boulevard California 32.39N 116.17W
13 E6 Boulia Queensland 22.54S 139.53E
89 K5 Boulkab Niger 13.30N 1.28E
71 B2 Boulleret France 47.25N 2.52E
68 D3 Boulogne Seine-et-Oise France 48.50N 2.14E
72 B2 Boulogne R France
68 D3 Boulogne,Bois de park Paris France
72 F9 Boulogne-sur-Gesse France 43.18N 0.38E
69 B2 Boulogne-sur-Mer Pas de Calais France 50.43N 1.37E
70 M6 Bouloire France 47.58N 0.33E
90 L8 Boulouba Cent Afr Rep 6.52N 22.15E
72 K10 Boulou,le France 42.32N 2.50E
89 E4 Boulouli Mali 15.30N 9.25W
71 K10 Boulouris France 43.25N 6.49E
89 J5 Boulsa Upper Volta 12.41N 0.29W
71 J2 Boult France 47.22N 6.00E
69 H5 Boult-aux-Bois France 49.26N 4.50E
90 E4 Boultoum Niger 14.36N 10.18E
89 D4 Bouly Mauritania 15.22N 11.40W
69 H4 Boulzicourt France 49.42N 4.42E
90 G9 Bouma Cent Afr Rep 4.43N 14.42E
88 L6 Boumalne Morocco 31.20N 6.00W
89 E2 Bou Maya Mauritania 18.26N 8.06W
89 L5 Boumba Niger 12.25N 2.54E
91 D2 Boumba R Cameroon
90 G9 Boumbé I R Cent Afr Rep
90 G9 Boumbé II R Cent Afr Rep
88 L5 Boumia Morocco 32.37N 5.10W
90 H7 Boumo Chad 9.01N 16.24E
75 N3 Boumort,Sierra de mts Spain
89 H7 Bouna Ivory Coast 9.19N 2.53W
89 C2 Bou Naga Mauritania 19.01N 13.12W
89 H2 Bounagu Mali 19.15N 3.40W
89 D4 Bou Nas Mauritania 15.52N 10.42W
64 G1 Bounatal W Germany 51.15N 9.23E
101 C3 Boundary Alaska 64.03N 141.00W
110 H1 Boundary Washington 49.00N 117.38W
101 H12 Boundary Bay Br Col
101 H12 Boundary Bay Br Col 49.00N 123.02W
101 H12 Boundary Bay dist Vancouver I, Br Col
101 H12 Boundary Bay Airport Br Col 49.04N 123.00W
98 B8 Boundary Mts Maine/Quebec
111 F4 Boundary Pk mt Nevada 37.51N 118.23W
100 J9 Boundary Plat Mont/Sask
103 E5 Bound Brook New Jersey 40.33N 74.32W
89 F7 Boundiali Ivory Coast 9.30N 6.31W
91 D4 Boundji Congo 1.05S 15.18E
89 C4 Boundou reg Senegal
89 G4 Boundoubadi Mali 15.39N 5.19W
90 E5 Bouné Niger 13.33N 10.09E
91 E4 Bouni Congo 1.12S 16.19E
72 F6 Bouniagues France 44.46N 0.32E
25 F2 Boun Neua Laos 21.27N 101.54E
89 B4 Bounoum R Senegal
109 E4 Bountiful Colorado 37.14N 105.59W
110 O9 Bountiful Utah 40.54N 111.54W
13 E3 Bountiful Is Queensland
100 K7 Bounty Saskatchewan 51.33N 107.22W
122 V10 Bounty B Pitcairn I Pacific Oc 25.04S 130.05W
11 K12 Bounty Is Pacific Oc
72 C2 Boupère, le France 46.48N 0.55W
69 C3 Bouquemaison France 50.13N 2.20E
121 E4 Bouquet Argentina 32.26S 61.51W
88 N8 Boura Algeria 26.09N 0.28W
90 F6 Boura Cameroon 10.15N 13.31E
9 B13 Bourail New Caledonia 21.34S 165.29E
107 E3 Bourbeuse R Missouri
106 H8 Bourbon Indiana 41.17N 86.07W
107 E3 Bourbon Missouri 38.10N 91.13W
26 P16 Bourbon, C Kerguelen Ind Oc 49.45S 68.45E
71 D3 Bourbon-Lancy France 46.37N 3.46E
72 L2 Bourbon l'Archambault France 46.36N 3.03E
67 G6 Bourbonnais prov France
69 K8 Bourbonne-les-Bains France 47.58N 5.46E
71 B5 Bourboule,la France 45.35N 2.44E
69 C2 Bourbourg France 50.57N 2.12E
71 H5 Bourbre R France
70 D5 Bourbriac France 48.29N 3.11W
72 B4 Bourcefranc-le-Chapus France 45.50N 1.08W
71 G7 Bourdeaux France 44.35N 5.09E
72 F5 Bourdeilles France 45.19N 0.35E
69 M6 Bourdonnay France 48.43N 6.43E
71 C1 Bourdon,Res,de France 47.37N 3.05E
69 J7 Bourdons-sur-Rognon France 48.10N 5.21E
89 D5 Bouréa Mali 12.51N 10.40W
74 E10 Boured Morocco 34.45N 4.06W
88 K5 Bou Regreg R Morocco
89 L5 Boureimi Niger 13.15N 3.42E
89 J3 Bourem Mali 16.59N 0.20W
88 P12 Bouressa Mali 19.58N 2.20E
72 F3 Bouresse France 46.22N 0.36E
72 H4 Bourganeuf France 45.57N 1.44E
72 G3 Bourg-Archambault France 46.23N 1.01E
70 M3 Bourg-Archard France 49.21N 0.49E
71 F6 Bourg-Argental France 45.18N 4.33E
71 J7 Bourg d'Arud France 44.58N 6.08E
71 G6 Bourg-de-Péage France 45.02N 5.03E
70 G6 Bourg-des-Comptes France 47.56N 1.44W
72 F7 Bourg-de-Visa France 44.16N 0.58E
71 J6 Bourg-d'Oisans,le France 45.03N 6.02E
70 M2 Bourg Dun France 49.52N 0.54E
71 G4 Bourg-en-Bresse France 46.12N 5.13E
72 J1 Bourges France 47.05N 2.23E
69 F5 Bourg-et-Comin France 49.24N 3.40E
71 H5 Bourget-du-Lac, le France 45.38N 5.52E
71 H5 Bourget,L.du France 45.43N 5.50E
69 C6 Bourget,le Paris France 48.57N 2.27E
68 F2 Bourget, Le Seine-St Denis France 48.57N 2.25E
71 B5 Bourg-Lastic France 45.39N 2.33E
72 H6 Bourg,le Lot France 44.43N 1.53E
72 H11 Bourg-Madame France 42.26N 1.55E
70 K6 Bourg-Neuf France 47.37N 0.19W
70 F7 Bourgneuf,B.de France
72 C1 Bourgneuf-en-Mauges France 47.18N 0.50W
72 A1 Bourgneuf-en-Retz France 47.03N 1.56W
70 J5 Bourgneuf,le France 48.10N 0.58W
69 G5 Bourgogne France 49.20N 4.04E
67 J6 Bourgogne prov France
71 E1 Bourgogne R France
71 G5 Bourgoin-Jallieu France 45.34N 5.17E
71 F8 Bourg-St.Andéol France 44.22N 4.38E
72 H8 Bourg St. Bernard France 43.36N 1.42E
71 K5 Bourg-St.Maurice France 45.37N 6.47E
66 E8 Bourg St. Pierre Switzerland 45.58N 7.13E
72 C5 Bourg-sur-Gironde France 45.03N 0.34W
70 M3 Bourgtheroulde-Infreville France 49.18N 0.52E
70 K3 Bourguébus France 49.06N 0.17W
72 E1 Bourgueil France 47.18N 0.12E
66 D2 Bourguignon France 47.25N 6.46E
88 O9 Bou Rhanet Algeria 25.13N 1.18E
88 F12 Bou Rjeima Mauritania 19.04N 15.03W
12 H4 Bourke New S Wales 30.09S 145.59E
99 K4 Bourkes Ontario 48.17N 80.14W
99 N4 Bourlamaque Quebec 48.05N 77.47W
61 H6 Bourlers Belgium 50.02N 4.20E
84 C4 Bourlésia Greece 38.32N 21.33E
69 E3 Bourlon France 50.11N 3.08E
69 K7 Bourmont France 48.12N 5.36E
99 P4 Bourmont Quebec 48.12N 75.50W
72 F1 Bournan France 47.04N 0.44E
72 E1 Bournand France 47.05N 0.06E
56 L2 Bourne Lincs Eng 52.46N 0.23W
103 N3 Bourne Massachusetts 41.44N 70.36W
71 G6 Bourne R France
97 K1 Bourne,C N W Terr 81.35N 91.50W
56 H6 Bournemouth Dorset Eng 50.43N 1.54W
55 A5 Bourne, The R Surrey England
70 M3 Bourneville France 49.23N 0.38E
72 B2 Bournezeau France 46.38N 1.10W
84 G4 Boúrnos Greece 38.31N 23.46E
76 C5 Bouro Portugal 41.40N 8.17W
89 J5 Bouroum Upper Volta 13.38N 0.40W
72 E7 Bourran France 44.21N 0.25E
72 D7 Bourriot-Bergonce France 44.08N 0.13W
69 D7 Bourron-Marlotte France 48.20N 2.42E
61 P7 Bourscheid Luxembourg 49.55N 6.04E
61 K6 Bourseigne-Neuve Belgium 50.02N 4.51E
61 K6 Bourseigne-Vielle Belgium 50.02N 4.52E
63 F7 Bourtanger Moor W Germany
70 M4 Bourth France 48.46N 0.48E
69 B2 Bourthes France 50.36N 1.56E
90 L6 Bourtoutou Chad 11.21N 22.48E
61 Q8 Bous Luxembourg 49.33N 6.20E
74 Q4 Bou Saâda Algeria 35.10N 4.09E
78 B12 Bou Salem Tunisia 36.38N 8.56E
72 C6 Bouscat,le France 44.53N 0.32W
111 L8 Bouse Arizona 33.57N 114.00W
111 K8 Bouse Wash R Arizona
71 C9 Bousquet-d'Orb,le France 43.42N 3.10E
69 M5 Bous/Saar W Germany 49.17N 6.48E
72 J3 Boussac Creuse France 46.21N 2.12E
70 G4 Boussac,la France 48.30N 1.39W
72 B1 Boussay France 47.02N 1.11W
69 L5 Bousse France 49.17N 6.12E
71 H2 Boussières France 47.09N 5.54E
90 H6 Bousso Chad 10.32N 16.45E
61 G5 Boussoit Belgium 50.27N 4.05E
89 J5 Boussouma Upper Volta 12.52N 1.13W
89 C5 Boussoura Guinea 12.19N 13.02W
61 F5 Boussu Belgium 50.27N 3.48E
61 H6 Boussu-en-Fagne Belgium 50.05N 4.28E
61 H6 Boussu-lez-Walcourt Belgium 50.13N 4.23E
61 J4 Bousval Belgium 50.37N 4.31E
66 A8 Bout-du-Lac France 45.47N 6.13E
88 H11 Bou Telis Mauritania 21.00N 11.25W
61 K3 Boutersem Belgium 50.51N 4.50E
84 E6 Boútia Greece 37.39N 22.45E
69 C7 Boutigny France 48.26N 2.23E
89 B3 Boutilimit Mauritania 17.40N 14.46W
90 J9 Boutiri Cent Afr Rep 4.40N 18.16E
74 G9 Bou Tlélis Algeria 35.35N 0.55W
Boutmîyé see Butmiye
72 D3 Boutonne R France
Boutoum,Ouadi el see Butm watercourse
14 B10 Bouvard,C W Australia 32.40S 115.34E
66 D6 Bouveret Switzerland 46.23N 6.52E
71 G5 Bouvesse-Quirieu France 45.47N 5.25E
96 K14 Bouvet I S Atlantic Oc 54.26S 3.24E
26 C12 Bouvetøy isld S Atlantic Oc 54.26S 3.24E
71 G7 Bouvières France 44.31N 5.13E

61 K5 **Bouvignes** Namur Belgium 50.17N 4.53E
61 F4 **Bouvignies** Hainaut Belgium 50.38N 3.46E
70 G7 **Bouvron** France 47.26N 1.50W
61 K2 **Bouwel** Belgium 51.11N 4.45E
69 N6 **Bouxwiller** France 48.50N 7.28E
69 G5 **Bouy** France 49.05N 4.20E
91 C5 **Bouyala** Congo 3.07S 13.59E
89 N4 **Bouza** Niger 14.29N 6.02E
72 H2 **Bouzanne** *R* France
88 K5 **Bouznika** Morocco 33.49N 7.10W
69 M5 **Bouzonville** France 49.18N 6.32E
53 C7 **Bov** Denmark 54.51N 9.23E
81 L8 **Bova** Italy 38.00N 15.56E
81 M7 **Bovalino Marina** Italy 38.09N 16.10E
81 L8 **Bova Marina** Italy 37.56N 15.56E
79 P2 **Bovec** Yugoslavia 46.20N 13.33E
76 E3 **Bóveda** Spain 42.37N 7.29W
76 J6 **Bóveda de Toro,La** Spain 41.20N 5.25W
79 H3 **Bóvegno** Italy 45.47N 10.16E
61 B2 **Bovekerke** Belgium 51.03N 2.58E
61 M4 **Bovelingen** Belgium 50.45N 5.16E
63 L9 **Bovenden** W Germany 51.35N 9.55E
61 M4 **Bovenistier** Belgium 50.40N 5.17E
18 K5 **Boven Kapas** *mts* Sarawak Malaysia
60 K9 **Bovenkarspel** Netherlands 52.42N 5.15E
53 F6 **Bovense** Denmark 55.23N 10.44E
60 O8 **Bovensmilde** Netherlands 52.58N 6.30E
53 Y15 **Bøverdal** Norway 61.43N 8.21E
53 Y15 **Bøvertun** Norway 61.38N 8.01E
69 C4 **Boves** France 49.51N 2.23E
79 C6 **Boves** Italy 44.20N 7.33E
61 K4 **Bovesse** Belgium 50.32N 4.47E
56 D6 **Bovey Tracey** Devon Eng 50.36N 3.40W
61 O6 **Bovigny** Belgium 50.13N 5.55E
110 J3 **Bovill** Idaho 46.53N 116.24W
112 E1 **Bovina** Texas 34.31N 102.54W
103 E2 **Bovina Center** New York 42.16N 74.47W
56 G6 **Bovington** Dorset Eng 50.42N 2.15W
80 M6 **Bovino** Italy 41.15N 15.20E
32 D5 **Bovir Ahmadi** Iran 30.40N 51.32E
79 E7 **Bovisa** *dist* Milan Italy
98 L3 **Bovlain, L** Quebec
53 A4 **Bøvlingbjerg** Denmark 56.27N 8.13E
79 L4 **Bovolenta** Italy 45.16N 11.56E
79 K4 **Bovolone** Italy 45.16N 11.07E
53 Y15 **Bøvra** *R* Norway
121 F3 **Bovril** Argentina 31.24S 59.25W
56 D6 **Bow** Devon Eng 50.48N 3.49W
55 G3 **Bow** London Eng 51.32N 0.01W
14 G3 **Bow** *R* W Australia
Bowa *see* **Muli**
93 D5 **Bowa** Uganda 0.40N 32.28E
108 H1 **Bowbells** N Dakota 48.48N 102.14W
100 C7 **Bowden** Alberta 51.58N 114.01W
105 F7 **Bowden** Florida 30.14N 81.37W
116 M2 **Bowden** Jamaica, W I 17.53N 76.20W
108 L4 **Bowdle** S Dakota 45.28N 99.38W
110 S1 **Bowdoin,L** Montana 48.26N 107.40W
105 B4 **Bowdon** Georgia 33.32N 85.17W
108 L2 **Bowdon** N Dakota 47.28N 99.41W
14 B10 **Bowelling** W Australia 33.25S 116.27E
106 C9 **Bowen** Illinois 40.14N 91.04W
13 J5 **Bowen** Queensland 20.00S 148.10E
13 J5 **Bowen** *R* Queensland
13 J5 **Bowen** *R* Queensland
13 H5 **Bowen Downs** Queensland 22.28S 145.02E
101 M11 **Bowen I** Br Col 49.24N 123.24W
12 J6 **Bowen,Mt** Victoria 37.11S 148.34E
13 B1 **Bowen Str** N Terr Australia
103 D8 **Bowers** Delaware 39.04N 75.24W
122 J2 **Bowers Bank** Bering Sea
104 B7 **Bowersville** Ohio 39.34N 83.44W
110 L5 **Bowery Pk** Idaho 44.05N 114.23W
57 J3 **Bowes** Durham Eng 54.30N 2.01W
14 B8 **Bowgada** W Australia 29.18S 116.05E
58 T11 **Bow Hd** Orkney Scotland 59.22N 2.57W
111 P9 **Bowie** Arizona 32.20N 109.30W
109 C3 **Bowie** Colorado 38.55N 107.34W
103 A8 **Bowie** Maryland 39.01N 76.46W
13 H5 **Bowie** Queensland 21.47S 145.52E
112 K2 **Bowie** Texas 33.36N 97.52W
100 F9 **Bow Island** Alberta 49.53N 111.24W
32 B2 **Bowkān** Iran 36.31N 46.10E
95 K7 **Bowker's Park** S Africa 31.52S 26.45E
57 H4 **Bowland Bridge** Cumbria Eng 54.18N 2.54W
57 H4 **Bowland Fells** *hills* Lancs/N Yorks England
105 F10 **Bowling Green** Florida 27.39N 81.50W
107 J2 **Bowling Green** Indiana 39.24N 87.01W
107 K4 **Bowling Green** Kentucky 37.00N 86.29W
107 E2 **Bowling Green** Missouri 39.21N 91.11W
104 B5 **Bowling Green** Ohio 41.22N 83.40W
104 H8 **Bowling Green** Virginia 38.02N 77.22W
13 H4 **Bowling Green B** Queensland
13 H4 **Bowling Green,C** Queensland 19.20S 147.28E
105 D3 **Bowman** Georgia 34.12N 83.02W
108 G3 **Bowman** N Dakota 46.11N 103.26W
97 M4 **Bowman B** N W Terr
108 G3 **Bowman Haley Reservoir** North Dakota
123 E2 **Bowman I** Antarctica 65.30S 103.25E
103 B6 **Bowmansville** Pennsylvania 40.12N 76.01W
99 M9 **Bowmanville** Ontario 43.55N 78.43W
58 D7 **Bowmore** Islay, Strathclyde Scotland 55.45N 6.17W
100 C7 **Bowness** Alberta 51.08N 114.12W
57 H4 **Bowness** Cumbria Eng 54.22N 2.55W
Bowo *see* **Bomi**
23 B4 **Bowo** Sichuan China 29.42N 99.26E
100 D8 **Bow R** Alberta
12 K5 **Bowral** New S Wales 34.28S 150.52E
12 L4 **Bowraville** New S Wales 30.40S 152.53E
14 G3 **Bow River** W Australia 16.54S 128.05E
101 N9 **Bowron Lake Prov.Pk** Br Col
101 N9 **Bowron R** Br Col
12 H6 **Bowser** Victoria 36.19S 146.23E
101 J7 **Bowser L** Br Col 56.29N 129.40W
100 Q6 **Bowsman** Manitoba 52.15N 101.12W
56 C3 **Bow Street** Dyfed Wales 52.27N 4.01W
15 J7 **Bowutu Mts** Papua New Guinea
100 B7 **Bow Valley Prov.Park** Alberta
92 C10 **Bowwood** Zambia 17.09S 26.16E
101 F10 **Bowyer I** Br Col 49.26N 123.17W
56 G5 **Box** Wilts Eng 51.25N 2.15W
64 H5 **Boxberg** W Germany 49.29N 9.39E
108 G7 **Box Butte Res** Nebraska
108 E6 **Box Cr** Wyoming
110 P1 **Box Elder** Montana 48.20N 110.02W
108 G5 **Box Elder** S Dakota 44.07N 103.02W
109 F2 **Box Elder Cr** Colorado
110 R2 **Boxelder Cr** Montana
56 N3 **Boxford** Suffolk Eng 52.02N 0.51E
12 E7 **Box Hill** *dist* Melbourne, Victoria
52 J8 **Boxholm** Sweden 58.12N 15.05E
23 G2 **Bo Xian** Anhui China 33.55N 115.41E
22 L8 **Boxing** Shandong China 37.08N 118.05E
56 N5 **Boxley** Kent Eng 51.19N 0.33E
60 M13 **Boxmeer** Netherlands 51.39N 5.57E
12 F4 **Box Tank** New S Wales 32.13S 142.17E
60 K13 **Boxtel** Netherlands 51.36N 5.20E
60 L7 **Boxum** Netherlands 53.11N 5.44E
90 F8 **Boya** Cameroon 6.26N 13.43E
36 H1 **Boyabat** Turkey 41.27N 34.45E
91 F2 **Boyabo** Zaïre 3.40S 18.42E
119 D5 **Boyaca** *div* Colombia
87 D8 **Boya Hills** Sudan
90 H9 **Boyali** Cent Afr Rep 5.01N 17.51E
36 G1 **Boyalı** Turkey 41.04N 33.21E
37 G2 **Boyalıca** Turkey 40.30N 29.34E
Boyalık Kirşehir Turkey *see* **Çiçekdağı**
37 F1 **Boyalık** Turkey 41.10N 28.37E
23 G4 **Boyang** Jiangxi China 29.00N 116.38E
91 G2 **Boyange** Zaïre 2.19N 21.48E
14 B10 **Boyanup** W Australia 33.29S 115.40E
72 B4 **Boyardville** France 45.59N 1.14W
45 B6 **Boyarka** Ukraine U.S.S.R. 50.20N 30.26E
41 G5 **Boyarka** U.S.S.R. 70.48N 97.30E
42 H4 **Boyarsk** Irkutsk U.S.S.R. 56.20N 106.02E
107 D10 **Boyce** Louisiana 31.21N 92.41W
104 G7 **Boyce** Virginia 39.06N 78.06W
14 D8 **Boyce,Mt** W Australia 29.34S 122.02E
100 V3 **Boyd** Manitoba 55.54N 96.26W
110 Q4 **Boyd** Montana 45.28N 109.04W
112 K2 **Boyd** Texas 33.04N 97.35W
12 K4 **Boyd** *R* New S Wales
101 W5 **Boyd Lake** N W Terr
98 S4 **Boyd's Cove** Newfoundland 49.25N 54.40W
104 G10 **Boydton** Virginia 36.40N 78.26W
22 K7 **Boye** Hebei China 38.30N 115.28E
91 H4 **Boyela** *tribe* Zaïre
91 F3 **Boyenge** Zaïre 0.14N 18.55E
108 P7 **Boyer** Iowa 42.10N 95.12W
108 P7 **Boyer** *R* Iowa
91 F4 **Boyera** Zaïre 0.40S 19.23E
32 D5 **Boyer Ahmadi-ye Sardsir va Kohkīlūyeh** *prov* Iran
109 G3 **Boyero** Colorado 38.57N 103.16W
103 C6 **Boyertown** Pennsylvania 40.19N 75.39W
108 E4 **Boyes** Montana 45.19N 105.02W
104 H10 **Boykins** Virginia 36.35N 77.13W
44 B2 **Boykov Liman** *lagoon* U.S.S.R.
60 N8 **Boyl** Netherlands 52.54N 6.12E
100 E4 **Boyle** Alberta 54.35N 112.44W
107 F8 **Boyle** Mississippi 33.40N 90.46W
59 F4 **Boyle** Roscommon Irish Rep 53.58N 8.18W
103 L2 **Boylston** Massachusetts 42.22N 71.44W
98 L8 **Boylston** Nova Scotia 45.26N 61.30W
13 K6 **Boyne** *R* Queensland
106 K4 **Boyne City** Michigan 45.13N 85.00W
106 K4 **Boyne Falls** Michigan 45.11N 84.55W
59 K4 **Boyne,R** Louth etc Irish Rep
69 C7 **Boynes** France 48.08N 2.21E
26 P16 **Boynes, Îs** Kerguelen Ind Oc 50.00S 68.49E
107 C1 **Boynton** Missouri 40.17N 93.05W
109 P6 **Boynton** Oklahoma 35.40N 95.39W
105 G11 **Boynton Beach** Florida 26.32N 80.04W
91 J3 **Boyoma Falls** Zaïre 0.18N 25.30E
108 B6 **Boysen Res** Wyoming 43.20N 108.10W
120 F9 **Boyuibe** Bolivia 20.28S 63.18W
14 B10 **Boyup Brook** W Australia 33.50S 116.22E
43 N8 **Boz** Uzbekistan U.S.S.R. 40.42N 71.55E
36 C6 **Bozburun** Turkey 36.42N 28.07E
37 F2 **Boz Burun** *C* Bursa Turkey 40.32N 28.48E
37 C2 **Boz Burun** *C* Çanakkale Turkey 40.25N 26.55E
36 E5 **Bozburun Dağ** *mt* Turkey 37.19N 31.05E
36 B3 **Bozca** *isld* Turkey
36 B3 **Bozcaada** Turkey 39.49N 26.03E
83 H5 **Bozcaada** *isld* Turkey 39.49N 26.02E
36 C4 **Boz Dağ** *mt* İzmir Turkey 38.20N 28.08E
36 F4 **Boz Dağ** *mt* Turkey
36 G5 **Boz Dağ** *mt* Turkey 37.52N 33.10E
36 E3 **Boz Dağı** *mt* Turkey 39.56N 30.25E
37 G6 **Boz Dağı** *mt* Turkey
36 C5 **Bozdoğan** Turkey 37.40N 28.20E
65 M3 **Boz̆ejov** Czechoslovakia 49.22N 15.09E
71 K6 **Bozel** France 45.26N 6.40E
110 P4 **Bozeman** Montana 45.40N 111.00W
Bozen *see* **Bolzano**
91 F2 **Bozene** Zaïre 3.00N 19.21E
62 K1 **Boże Pole** Poland 54.33N 17.56E
39 G4 **Bozhedomova Mys** *C* U.S.S.R. 60.20N 161.50E
22 K7 **Bozhen** Hebei China 38.04N 116.34E
64 O3 **Boží Dar** Czechoslovakia 50.25N 12.55E
87 D4 **Bozi,Jeb** *mt* Sudan 12.30N 33.30E
66 F3 **Bözingen** Switzerland 47.10N 7.17E
36 F5 **Bozkır** Turkey 37.10N 32.15E
36 G2 **Bozkir Dağı** *mt* Turkey 40.21N 33.35E
43 F4 **Bozkol',Zaliv** *gulf* Kazakhstan U.S.S.R.
36 G1 **Bozkurt** Turkey 41.54N 34.03E
37 D3 **Bozlar** Turkey 40.20N 27.24E
32 H4 **Boznābād** Iran 33.57N 59.24E
45 F1 **Boznya** U.S.S.R. 55.11N 34.21E
Bozoğlak *see* **İhtik**
Bozoğlan Dağları *mts see* **Bolkar Dağları**
72 K7 **Bozouls** France 44.28N 2.43E
90 H8 **Bozoum** Cent Afr Rep 6.16N 16.22E
36 E5 **Bozova** Antalya Turkey 37.14N 30.17E
37 D8 **Bozova** Urfa Turkey 37.23N 38.33E
82 G6 **Bozovici** Romania 44.56N 22.00E
32 B2 **Bozqūsh, Kūh-e** *mts* Iran
43 L2 **Bozshakul'** Kazakhstan U.S.S.R. 51.50N 74.16E
36 C4 **Boz Sira Dağları** *mts* Turkey
60 L7 **Bozum** Netherlands 53.05N 5.42E
36 E3 **Bozüyük** Turkey 39.55N 30.03E
Bozyaka *see* **Beskonak**
79 H4 **Bozzolo** Italy 45.07N 10.29E
61 N5 **Bra** Belgium 50.20N 5.44E
79 C5 **Bra** Italy 44.42N 7.51E
60 B3 **Braakman** *polder* Netherlands
117 B1 **Braams Punt** *C* Surinam 6.00N 55.10W
61 G4 **Brabant** *prov* Belgium
91 G6 **Brabanta** Zaïre 4.26S 20.19E
123 E14 **Brabant I** Antarctica
100 O2 **Brabant L** Saskatchewan 56.00N 103.42W
77 M5 **Brabatas** *R* Spain
53 E4 **Brabrand** Denmark 56.09N 10.08E
53 H6 **Bråby** Denmark 55.18N 11.58E
82 D7 **Brač** *isld* Yugoslavia
58 D4 **Bracadale** Skye, Highland Scotland 57.22N 6.24W
58 C4 **Bracadale, L** Skye, Highland Scotland
81 H10 **Braccetto,Pta** Sicily 36.51N 14.28E
80 F4 **Bracciano** Italy 42.06N 12.11E
80 F4 **Bracciano,Lago di** Italy
57 M6 **Bracebridge** Lincs Eng 53.13N 0.33W
99 L7 **Bracebridge** Ontario 45.02N 79.19W
72 C5 **Brach** France 45.03N 0.57W
85 C6 **Brach** Libya 27.33N 14.17E
60 T16 **Brachterbeek** Netherlands 51.08N 5.55E
70 O6 **Bracieux** France 47.34N 1.33E
52 J4 **Bräcke** Sweden 62.44N 15.30E
100 J9 **Bracken** Saskatchewan 49.12N 108.02W
112 J6 **Bracken** Texas 29.37N 98.20W
94 Q11 **Brackenfell** Cape Town S Africa 33.53S 18.41E
64 G5 **Brackenheim** W Germany 49.05N 9.05E
100 S5 **Bracken L** Manitoba 53.40N 99.50W
112 G6 **Brackettville** Texas 29.19N 100.27W
56 J3 **Brackley** Northants Eng 52.02N 1.09W
59 G3 **Brackley L** Cavan Irish Rep 54.08N 7.42W
58 H6 **Bracklinn, Falls of** Central Scotland 56.15N 4.11W
59 H5 **Bracknagh** Offaly Irish Rep 53.13N 7.05W
56 K5 **Bracknell** Berks Eng 51.26N 0.46W
63 J9 **Brackwede** W Germany 51.59N 8.31E
58 J6 **Braco** Tayside Scotland 56.16N 3.54W
76 E16 **Braço de Prata** Portugal 38.44N 9.07W
118 E3 **Braço Menor do Rio Araguaia** *R* Brazil
117 B9 **Braço Norte,R** Brazil
82 H4 **Brad** Romania 46.07N 22.47E
81 M2 **Bradano,R** Italy
108 K3 **Braddock** N Dakota 46.36N 106.06W
104 F6 **Braddock** Pennsylvania 40.24N 79.53W
12 B6 **Braddon** *dist* Canberra Australia
108 Q9 **Braddyville** Iowa 40.36N 94.00W
105 E10 **Bradenton** Florida 27.29N 82.33W
105 E10 **Bradenton Beach** Florida 27.27N 82.42W
56 J5 **Bradfield** Berks Eng 51.28N 1.08W
56 N3 **Bradfield Combust** Suffolk Eng 52.11N 0.45E
107 E6 **Bradford** Arkansas 35.26N 91.28W
106 E8 **Bradford** Illinois 41.11N 89.40W
108 R7 **Bradford** Iowa 42.36N 93.12W
104 R1 **Bradford** Maine 45.03N 68.56W
104 O3 **Bradford** New Hampshire 43.17N 71.59W
104 A6 **Bradford** Ohio 40.07N 84.26W
99 L8 **Bradford** Ontario 44.07N 79.34W
104 G5 **Bradford** Pennsylvania 41.57N 78.39W
103 L4 **Bradford** Rhode I 41.24N 71.45W
104 N3 **Bradford** Vermont 43.59N 72.09W
56 G5 **Bradford** Wilts Eng 51.22N 2.15W
57 K5 **Bradford** W Yorks Eng 53.48N 1.45W
103 A3 **Bradford** *co* Pennsylvania
107 L4 **Bradfordsville** Kentucky 37.29N 85.10W
107 C8 **Bradley** Arkansas 33.05N 93.40W
111 D6 **Bradley** California 35.54N 120.48W
106 G8 **Bradley** Illinois 41.10N 87.51W
103 E3 **Bradley** New York 41.49N 74.44W
109 N7 **Bradley** Oklahoma 34.53N 97.44W
108 N4 **Bradley** S Dakota 45.07N 97.39W
103 F6 **Bradley Beach** New Jersey 40.12N 74.01W
103 J3 **Bradley Field** *airport* Connecticut 41.56N 72.41W
107 D5 **Bradleyville** Missouri 36.47N 92.55W
65 Q2 **Bradlo** *mt* Czechoslovakia 49.50N 17.03E
104 B5 **Bradner** Ohio 41.19N 83.27W
98 P2 **Bradore Bay** Quebec 51.28N 57.14W
98 P2 **Bradore Hills** Quebec
44 F10 **Bradost** *R* Iran
108 N9 **Bradshaw** Nebraska 40.55N 97.45W
13 B3 **Bradshaw** N Terr Australia 15.20S 130.16E
112 H3 **Bradshaw** Texas 32.05N 99.55W
14 F3 **Bradshaw,Mt** W Australia 15.27S 125.56E
11 B12 **Bradshaw Sd** New Zealand
100 R9 **Bradwardine** Manitoba 49.59N 100.30W
56 N4 **Bradwell** Essex Eng 51.44N 0.54E
100 L7 **Bradwell** Saskatchewan 51.58N 106.12W
110 O1 **Brady** Montana 48.01N 111.50W
108 K8 **Brady** Nebraska 41.02N 100.21W
112 H4 **Brady** Texas 31.08N 99.22W
113 T7 **Brady Glacier** Alaska 58.30N 136.50W
12 C3 **Brady,Mt** S Australia 29.05S 135.00E
58 Q9 **Brae** Shetland Scotland 60.24N 1.21W
50 E6 **Brædhratunga** Iceland 64.10N 20.24W
58 K5 **Braedownie** Tayside Scotland 56.52N 3.10W
53 D5 **Brædstrup** Denmark 55.58N 9.38E
58 K4 **Braemar** Grampian Scotland 57.01N 3.24W
95 O6 **Braemar** S Africa 30.19S 30.34E
12 E5 **Braemar** S Australia 33.15S 139.43E
58 K4 **Braemar** *dist* Grampian Scotland
81 H9 **Braemi** *R* Sicily
58 F3 **Braemore** Highland Scotland 57.45N 5.01W
58 J4 **Braeriach** *mt* Highland Scotland 57.05N 3.45W
14 D5 **Braeside** W Australia 21.10S 121.04E
58 T11 **Braeswick** Orkney Scotland 59.13N 2.41W
61 E4 **Braffe** Belgium 50.33N 3.35E
76 C5 **Braga** Portugal 41.32N 8.26W
76 C5 **Braga** *dist* Portugal
121 E5 **Bragado** Argentina 35.10S 60.29W
58 C2 **Bragair** Lewis, W Isles Scotland 58.20N 6.38W
117 E5 **Bragança** Pará Brazil 1.02S 46.46W
76 F5 **Bragança** Portugal 41.47N 6.46W
118 F8 **Bragança Paulista** Brazil 22.55S 46.34W
105 E6 **Braganza** Georgia 31.05N 82.16W
107 G5 **Bragg City** Missouri 36.17N 89.55W
100 C7 **Bragg Creek Prov.Park** Alberta
45 B5 **Bragin** Belorussiya U.S.S.R. 51.58N 30.20E
46 H4 **Bragin** Belorussiya U.S.S.R. 51.49N 30.16E
39 K3 **Bragina** U.S.S.R. 64.28N 177.29E
Bragman's Bluff *see* **Puerto Cabezas**
108 R4 **Braham** Minnesota 45.42N 93.10W
63 N6 **Brahlstorf** E Germany 53.22N 10.59E
63 P5 **Brahlstorf** E Germany 53.42N 11.34E
28 L2 **Brahmakund** Assam India 27.52N 96.23E
31 J9 **Brahman Baria** Bangladesh 23.58N 91.04E
Brahmaputra *R see* **Maquan He**
27 P4 **Brahmaputra** *R* Asia
29 E1 **Brahmaur** Himachal Prad India 32.25N 76.35E
63 L4 **Brahmsee** *L* W Germany
61 L5 **Braibant** Belgium 50.19N 5.04E
106 F8 **Braidwood** Illinois 41.15N 88.13W
12 J6 **Braidwood** New S Wales 35.27S 149.50E
79 M1 **Braies,L.di** *L* Italy 46.42N 12.05E
34 D4 **Br'aij,El** Syria 34.15N 36.46E
66 R5 **Brail** Switzerland 46.39N 10.02E
82 L5 **Brăila** Romania 45.17N 27.58E
57 K7 **Brailsford** Derbys Eng 52.59N 1.36W
108 N8 **Brainard** Nebraska 41.11N 97.01W
103 D5 **Brainards** New Jersey 40.46N 75.10W
103 H2 **Brainard Sta** New York 42.30N 73.30W
69 F5 **Braine** France 49.20N 3.32E
61 H4 **Braine-l'Alleud** Belgium 50.41N 4.22E
61 H4 **Braine-le-Château** Belgium 50.41N 4.16E
61 G4 **Braine-le-Comte** Belgium 50.37N 4.08E
108 Q3 **Brainerd** Minnesota 46.20N 94.10W
72 E1 **Brain-sur-Allonnes** France 47.20N 0.05E
56 N4 **Braintree** Essex Eng 51.53N 0.32E
103 M2 **Braintree** Massachusetts 42.14N 71.00W
107 G12 **Braithwaite** Louisiana 29.51N 89.57W
13 C1 **Braithwaite Pt** N Terr Australia 11.45S 133.56E
94 K4 **Brak** *R* S Africa
95 D9 **Brak** *R* S Africa
95 G5 **Brak** *R* S Africa
63 H6 **Brake** Niedersachsen W Germany 53.20N 8.28E
61 E3 **Brakel** Belgium 50.48N 3.45E
60 J12 **Brakel** Netherlands 51.49N 5.06E
63 K9 **Brakel** W Germany 51.43N 9.10E
89 B3 **Brakna** *reg* Mauritania
94 U13 **Brakpan** S Africa 26.15S 28.22E
95 M2 **Brakpan** S Africa 26.15S 28.22E
95 H6 **Brakpan** *salt pan* S Africa 30.32S 24.35E
95 G7 **Brakpoort** S Africa 31.21S 23.21E
95 K2 **Brakspruit** S Africa 26.40S 26.35E
95 N4 **Brakwal** S Africa 28.23S 29.27E
94 D4 **Brakwater** Namibia 22.24S 17.06E
103 N3 **Braleys** Massachusetts 41.44N 70.58W
43 H3 **Brali** Kazakhstan U.S.S.R. 48.52N 65.30E
63 U7 **Bralitz** E Germany 52.50N 14.01E
84 D4 **Brállos** Greece 38.44N 22.28E
101 M10 **Bralorne** Br Col 50.46N 122.51W
72 J9 **Bram** France 43.14N 2.07E
109 N5 **Braman** Oklahoma 36.55N 97.20W
103 D3 **Braman** Pennsylvania 41.49N 75.10W
71 K6 **Bramans** France 45.13N 6.47E
Brambach *see* **Radiumbad-Brambach**
65 F7 **Bramberg** Austria 47.17N 12.21E
56 J5 **Bramdean** Hants Eng 51.03N 1.07W
53 C5 **Bramdrupdam** Denmark 55.32N 9.29E
72 G3 **Brame** *R* France
60 O11 **Bramel** Netherlands 52.08N 6.17E
56 P3 **Bramfield** Suffolk Eng 52.19N 1.31E
56 O3 **Bramford** Suffolk Eng 52.04N 1.06E
57 L5 **Bramham** W Yorks Eng 53.53N 1.21W
57 L5 **Bramham Cross Roads** W Yorks Eng 53.50N 1.20W
29 F7 **Bramhapuri** Maharashtra India 20.36N 79.54E
56 K5 **Bramley** Surrey Eng 51.11N 0.35W
57 L6 **Bramley** S Yorks Eng 53.26N 1.15W
103 E2 **Bramley Mt** New York 42.17N 74.48W
63 H6 **Bramloge** W Germany 53.22N 8.06E
53 B6 **Bramming** Denmark 55.28N 8.42E
79 B6 **Bram,Monte** Italy 44.22N 7.14E
66 F7 **Bramois** Switzerland 46.15N 7.25E
52 K4 **Bramön** *Lt Ho* Sweden 62.15N 17.57E
56 L3 **Brampton** Cambs Eng 52.19N 0.14W
57 H3 **Brampton** Cumbria Eng 54.57N 2.43W
108 N3 **Brampton** N Dakota 46.00N 97.46W
99 L9 **Brampton** Ontario 43.42N 79.46W
56 P3 **Brampton** Suffolk Eng 52.23N 1.35E
13 J5 **Brampton I** Queensland 20.49S 149.18E
63 F8 **Bramsche** W Germany 52.28N 7.23E
63 G8 **Bramsche** W Germany 52.25N 7.59E
56 H2 **Bramshall** Staffs Eng 52.54N 1.55W
13 G1 **Bramwell** Queensland 12.07S 142.40E
104 D9 **Bramwell** W Virginia 37.20N 81.20W
76 H2 **Braña Caballo** *mt* Spain 43.00N 5.38W
81 M8 **Brancaleone** Italy 37.58N 16.05E
56 N2 **Brancaster** Norfolk Eng 52.58N 0.39E
57 K3 **Brancepeth** Durham Eng 54.44N 1.39W
106 H6 **Branch** Michigan 43.57N 86.02W
98 T7 **Branch** Newfoundland 46.53N 53.59W
103 E3 **Branch** New York 42.00N 74.30W
103 B5 **Branchdale** Pennsylvania 40.41N 76.19W
61 K4 **Branchon** Belgium 50.37N 4.58E
104 H4 **Branchport** New York 42.36N 77.11W
103 E4 **Branchville** New Jersey 41.08N 74.45W
105 G4 **Branchville** S Carolina 33.14N 80.50W
91 G10 **Branco** Angola 12.29S 20.38E
89 O10 **Branco** *isld* Cape Verde 16.40N 24.42W
118 B7 **Branco** *R* Mato Grosso do Sul Brazil
117 J8 **Branco,C** Brazil 7.08S 34.45W
120 G2 **Branco,R** Amazonas Brazil
121 B2 **Branco,R** Argentina
120 G3 **Branco,R** Mato Grosso Brazil
118 A3 **Branco,R** Mato Grosso/Rondônia Brazil
120 F3 **Branco,R** Rondônia Brazil
119 H7 **Branco,R** Roraima Brazil
64 O3 **Brand** Czechoslovakia 50.19N 12.56E
65 M4 **Brand** Nieder-Österreich Austria 48.53N 15.01E
63 T8 **Brand** Potsdam E Germany 52.02N 13.44E
65 A7 **Brand** Vorarlberg Austria 47.07N 9.45E
69 L2 **Brand** W Germany 50.45N 6.10E
50 E3 **Brandafell** *mt* Iceland 65.34N 20.50W
94 C3 **Brandberg** *mt* Namibia 21.10S 14.33E
52 J4 **Brändbo** Sweden 62.04N 16.15E
53 C5 **Brande** Denmark 55.57N 9.08E
63 L5 **Brande-Hörnerkirchen** W Germany 53.52N 9.44E
108 D4 **Brandenberg** Montana 45.51N 106.11W
63 R8 **Brandenburg** E Germany 52.25N 12.34E
107 K4 **Brandenburg** Kentucky 38.00N 86.11W
64 P2 **Brand-Erbisdorf** Karl-Marx-Stadt E Germany 50.52N 13.20E
58 F6 **Brander,Pass of** Strathclyde Scotland 56.24N 5.08W
53 C6 **Branderup** Denmark 55.08N 9.05E
72 F3 **Brandes** *reg* France 46.22N 0.42E
57 N5 **Brandesburton** Humberside Eng 53.55N 0.18W
95 K4 **Brandfort** S Africa 28.42S 26.28E
Brandhei *see* **Gråtånes**
63 R10 **Brandis** E Germany 51.21N 12.38E
66 P3 **Brandner Tal** *V* Austria
67 P11 **Brando** Corsica 42.46N 9.27E
51 J11 **Brändö** Finland 60.25N 21.05E
109 H3 **Brandon** Colorado 38.26N 102.26W
100 S9 **Brandon** Manitoba 49.50N 99.57W
107 G9 **Brandon** Mississippi 32.16N 89.59W
108 J9 **Brandon** Nebraska 40.49N 101.53W
13 H4 **Brandon** Queensland 19.30S 147.21E
56 N3 **Brandon** Suffolk Eng 52.27N 0.37E
104 M3 **Brandon** Vermont 43.47N 73.05W
106 F6 **Brandon** Wisconsin 43.44N 88.46W
59 B7 **Brandon B** Kerry Irish Rep 52.15N 10.05W
59 B7 **Brandon Hd** Kerry Irish Rep 52.16N 10.15W
59 B7 **Brandon,Mt** Kerry Irish Rep 52.14N 10.15W
104 L3 **Brandreth** New York 43.56N 74.52W
95 E9 **Brandrivier** S Africa 33.53S 21.02E
57 L4 **Brandsby** N Yorks Eng 54.08N 1.06W
53 U16 **Brandsfonn** *mt* Norway 61.27N 6.15E
53 D6 **Brandsø** *isld* Denmark 55.22N 9.43E
53 S15 **Brandsøy** *isld* Norway 61.35N 5.08E
53 Y13 **Brandstad** Norway 62.37N 8.20E
107 E5 **Brandsville** Missouri 36.40N 91.44W
108 O5 **Brandt** S Dakota 44.39N 96.39W
92 G6 **Brandt** Tanzania 8.46S 34.08E
41 B3 **Brandta,Zaliv** *gulf* Novaya Zemlya U.S.S.R.
50 E8 **Brandur** *isld* Iceland 63.23N 20.21W
52 G6 **Brandval** Norway 60.18N 12.02E
94 F8 **Brandvlei** S Africa 30.27S 20.29E
94 R13 **Brandvlei** S Africa 26.08S 27.36E
95 C9 **Brandvlei** *L* S Africa 33.43S 19.25E
104 H8 **Brandy** Virginia 38.30N 77.56W
62 H5 **Brandýs-nad-Laben** Czech 50.12N 14.30E
65 O1 **Brandýs nad Orlice** Czech 50.01N 16.18E
104 J8 **Brandywine** Maryland 38.42N 76.51W
82 K6 **Braneşti** Romania 44.27N 26.21E
103 J4 **Branford** Connecticut 41.17N 72.48W
105 E8 **Branford** Florida 29.59N 82.57W
71 G3 **Branges** France 46.38N 5.11E
62 M1 **Braniewo** Poland 54.24N 19.50E
79 P3 **Branik** Yugoslavia 45.51N 13.47E
18 J4 **Brani,Pulau** *isld* Singapore
62 M6 **Branisko** *mts* Czechoslovakia
71 C1 **Branlin** *R* France 47.45N 3.06E
51 J6 **Brännberg** Sweden 65.48N 21.10E
72 D6 **Branne** France 44.50N 0.10W
64 N8 **Brannenburg** W Germany 47.44N 12.05E
82 K8 **Brannitsa** *mts* Bulgaria
76 L3 **Brañosera** Spain 42.56N 4.18W
76 C14 **Branqueira** Portugal 37.06N 8.12W
120 D2 **Branquinho** *R* Brazil
13 F8 **Bransby** Queensland 27.40S 142.00E
111 A2 **Branscomb** California 39.40N 123.37W
123 E14 **Bransfield Str** Antarctica
109 G4 **Branson** Colorado 37.02N 103.54W
107 C5 **Branson** Missouri 36.38N 93.14W
57 N6 **Branston** Lincs Eng 53.12N 0.28W
100 D8 **Brant** Alberta 50.34N 113.27W
18 K10 **Brantas** *R* Java Indonesia
57 M6 **Brant Broughton** Lincs Eng 53.05N 0.38W
108 M2 **Brantford** N Dakota 47.36N 98.58W
99 K9 **Brantford** Ontario 43.09N 80.17W
60 M6 **Brantgum** Netherlands 53.22N 5.56E
107 K10 **Brantley** Alabama 31.35N 86.19W
72 F5 **Brantôme** France 45.22N 0.40E
12 F7 **Branxholme** Victoria 37.51S 141.49E
79 G2 **Branzi** Italy 46.01N 9.46E
75 C5 **Braojos** Spain 41.03N 3.39W
61 M7 **Bras** Belgium 49.58N 5.24E
117 A6 **Brás** Brazil 2.07S 58.08W
118 G10 **Brás** *dist* São Paulo Brazil
15 C3 **Bras** *isld* Mapia Is, Irian Jaya 0.56N 134.20E
98 M7 **Bras d'Or** C Breton I, Nova Scotia 46.15N 60.16W
98 M8 **Bras d'Or,L** C Breton I, Nova Scotia
107 D1 **Brashear** Missouri 40.09N 92.22W
120 D1 **Brasil** Brazil 4.31S 71.30W
118 E4 **Brasilândia** Brazil 15.41S 48.12W
118 F9 **Brasilandia, di** *dist* São Paulo Brazil
120 E4 **Brasileia** Brazil 10.59S 68.45W
118 F4 **Brasília** Brazil 15.45S 47.57W
118 G5 **Brasília** Brazil 16.13S 44.29W
117 B6 **Brasília Legal** Brazil 3.45S 55.42W
46 F2 **Braslav** Belorussiya U.S.S.R. 55.34N 27.06E
61 E4 **Brasmenil** Belgium 50.33N 3.33E
82 K5 **Braşov** Romania 45.39N 25.35E
26 V15 **Bras-Panon** Réunion Ind Oc 20.59S 55.41E
70 C5 **Brasparts** France 48.18N 3.58W
90 C9 **Brass** Nigeria 4.20N 6.15E
90 C9 **Brass** *R* Nigeria
72 J8 **Brassac** Tarn France 43.37N 2.29E
71 C6 **Brassac-les-Mines** France 45.25N 3.20E
61 H1 **Brasschaat** Belgium 51.17N 4.30E
13 C6 **Brassey Mt** N Terr Australia 23.00S 134.59E
14 D6 **Brassey Ra** W Australia
18 M3 **Brassey Range** Sabah Malaysia
12 G5 **Brassi** New S Wales 35.33S 144.42E
53 D4 **Brassø** *L* Denmark 56.09N 9.36E
105 D3 **Brasstown Bald** *mt* Georgia 34.52N 83.48W
104 Q1 **Brassua L** Maine
66 A5 **Brassus,le** Switzerland 46.35N 6.13E
71 D2 **Brassy** France 47.15N 3.57E
56 M5 **Brasted** Kent Eng 51.17N 0.07E
39 E2 **Brat** U.S.S.R. 67.00N 152.29E
53 X15 **Bråtådalen** *V* Norway 61.53N 7.50E
82 H4 **Bratca** Romania 46.55N 22.38E
40 M8 **Brat Chirpoyev** *vol* Kuril Is U.S.S.R. 46.28N 150.49E
82 L5 **Brates, L** Romania 45.30N 28.05E
65 Q5 **Bratislava** Czechoslovakia 48.10N 17.10E
40 E6 **Bratolyubovka** U.S.S.R. 50.46N 129.19E
82 J8 **Bratsigovo** Bulgaria 42.01N 24.20E
42 G4 **Bratsk** U.S.S.R. 56.20N 101.50E
45 C9 **Bratskoye** Ukraine U.S.S.R. 47.50N 31.33E
42 G4 **Bratskoye Vdkhr** *res* U.S.S.R.
46 G5 **Bratslav** Ukraine U.S.S.R. 48.49N 28.51E
48 U15 **Brattahlidh** *anc site* Greenland 61.00N 45.25W
53 W20 **Bratteli** Norway 59.20N 7.07E
53 V19 **Brattlandsdalen** *V* Norway 59.41N 6.46E
104 N4 **Brattleboro** Vermont 42.51N 72.33W
Brattle I *see* **Tortuga, I.**
53 U13 **Brattvåg** Norway 62.36N 6.27E
53 V19 **Bråtveit** Norway 59.36N 6.48E
64 D3 **Braubach** W Germany 50.16N 7.39E
D3 **Braubach, Ndr** W Germany 50.17N 7.38E
64 D3 **Braubach, Obr** W Germany 50.17N 7.35E
64 G2 **Brauerschwend** W Germany 50.42N 9.20E
56 M4 **Braughing** Herts Eng 51.55N 0.01E
66 S5 **Braulio** *mt* Italy 46.31N 10.23E
65 H5 **Braunau am Inn** Austria 48.16N 13.03E
69 M4 **Brauneberg** W Germany 49.54N 6.59E
64 E2 **Braunfels** W Germany 50.31N 8.24E
63 N9 **Braunlage** W Germany 51.44N 10.37E
63 P10 **Braunsbedra** E Germany 51.18N 11.53E
Braunsberg *see* **Braniewo**
95 L8 **Braunschweig** S Africa 32.47S 27.23E
63 M8 **Braunschweig** W Germany 52.15N 10.30E
56 C5 **Braunton** Devon Eng 51.07N 4.10W
66 M4 **Braunwald** Switzerland 46.57N 9.00E
71 L9 **Braus,Col de** France 43.52N 7.23E
50 D6 **Brautarholt** Iceland 64.15N 21.54W
53 U14 **Brautaset** Norway 62.10N 6.15E
87 K10 **Brava** Somalia 1.02N 44.02E
89 O11 **Brava** *isld* Cape Verde
76 C5 **Bravais** Portugal 41.48N 8.28W
104 E7 **Brave** Pennsylvania 39.44N 80.27W
69 G8 **Bravelogne-Beauvoir** France 47.58N 4.18E
52 J8 **Bråviken** *inlet* Sweden
121 J7 **Bravo** *R* Chile
120 F7 **Bravo,Cerro** *pk* Bolivia 17.45S 64.41W
121 D12 **Bravo, Cerro** *pk* Chile 26.38S 69.16W
119 B10 **Bravo,Cerro** *pk* Peru 5.32S 79.20W
115 H3 **Bravo del Norte, Río** Mexico
121 C2 **Bravo, L** Argentina
67 P12 **Bravone** *R* Corsica
121 D2 **Bravo,Sa** *mts* Argentina
76 B14 **Bravura, Barragem da** *res* Portugal 37.10N 8.45W
111 J9 **Brawley** California 32.59N 115.30W
61 G5 **Bray** Belgium 50.26N 4.06E
59 K5 **Bray** Wicklow Irish Rep 53.12N 6.06W
69 D1 **Bray-Dunes** France 51.04N 2.30E
56 W10 **Braye** Chan Is Eng Chan 49.42N 2.12W
69 E5 **Braye** France 49.26N 3.23E
70 M6 **Braye,R** France
70 O3 **Bray-et-Lû** France 49.08N 1.40E
56 D5 **Brayford** Devon Eng 51.06N 3.53W
59 B8 **Bray Hd** Kerry Irish Rep 51.53N 10.25W
59 K5 **Bray Hd** Wicklow Irish Rep 53.12N 6.05W
97 M4 **Bray I** N W Terr 69.20N 77.00W
107 C2 **Braymer** Missouri 39.33N 93.47W
69 E7 **Bray-sur-Seine** France 48.25N 3.15E
69 D4 **Bray-sur-Somme** France 49.57N 2.43E
66 Q3 **Braz** Austria 47.09N 9.55E
15 E6 **Braza** *R* Irian Jaya
77 H3 **Brazatortas** Spain 38.40N 4.18W
101 P9 **Brazeau** Alberta 52.29N 116.05W
100 B6 **Brazeau Dam** Alberta 52.58N 115.30W
101 P9 **Brazeau,Mt** Alberta 52.34N 117.22W
101 P9 **Brazeau R** Alberta
71 G2 **Brazey-en-Plaine** France 47.08N 5.13E
89 D8 **Brazier Pt** Liberia 6.06N 10.20W
107 J2 **Brazil** Indiana 39.31N 87.09W
117 H2 **Brazil** *rep* S America
96 H11 **Brazil Basin** Atlantic Oc
98 G10 **Brazil Lake** Nova Scotia 44.00N 66.00W
119 D3 **Brazo de Loba** *R* Colombia
95 N7 **Brazon Hd** S Africa 31.43S 29.25E
112 M6 **Brazoria** Texas 29.03N 95.36W
112 M6 **Brazos** *R* Texas
91 D6 **Brazzaville** Congo 4.14S 15.14E
82 E6 **Brčko** Yugoslavia 44.52N 18.49E
62 K2 **Brda** *R* Poland
62 K6 **Brdo** *mt* Czechoslovakia 49.11N 17.20E
62 H6 **Brdy** *mts* Czechoslovakia
66 N7 **Bre** Switzerland 46.02N 9.01E
119 A10 **Brea** Peru 4.42S 81.08W
75 G4 **Brea** Spain 41.31N 1.36W
13 E6 **Breadalbane** Queensland 23.50S 139.39E
58 H6 **Breadalbane** *dist* Central/Tayside Scotland
14 E7 **Breaden Bluff** *hill* W Australia 26.59S 124.36E
14 F7 **Breaden,L** W Australia
75 D7 **Brea de Tajo** Spain 40.14N 3.07W
56 T9 **Breage** Cornwall Eng 50.06N 5.20W
103 F1 **Breakabeen** New York 42.32N 74.25W
13 K1 **Breakfast Creek** *dist* Brisbane, Qnsld
95 K9 **Breakfast Vlei** S Africa 33.05S 26.57E
58 E4 **Breakish** Skye, Highland Scotland 57.14N 5.51W
11 A12 **Breaksea I** New Zealand 45.36S 166.37E
11 C13 **Breaksea Is** New Zealand
11 A12 **Breaksea Sd** New Zealand
13 L6 **Breaksea Spit** Queensland
70 G5 **Bréal-sous-Montfort** France 48.03N 1.52W
56 F4 **Bream** Glos Eng 51.46N 2.35W
11 J2 **Bream B** New Zealand
11 J2 **Bream Hd** New Zealand 35.52S 174.37E
57 J2 **Breamish, R** Northumb Eng
11 J3 **Bream Tail** *C* New Zealand 36.03S 174.37E
121 D2 **Brea Pozo** Argentina 28.11S 64.01W
52 G10 **Breared** Sweden 56.44N 13.10E
120 D11 **Breas** Chile 25.30S 70.22W
58 C2 **Breasclete** Lewis, W Isles Scotland 58.13N 6.45W
70 L2 **Bréaute** France 49.37N 0.25E
107 E11 **Breaux Bridge** Louisiana 30.17N 91.55W
18 H9 **Brebes** Java Indon 6.54S 109.00E
18 H9 **Brebes, Tanjung** *C* Java Indonesia 6.45S 109.00E
98 B5 **Brébeuf,L** Quebec
70 H4 **Brécey** France 48.44N 1.10W
70 E6 **Brech** France 47.43N 3.00W
69 C5 **Breche** *R* France
64 E3 **Brechen** W Germany 50.21N 8.12E
99 L8 **Brechin** Ontario 44.32N 79.11W
58 L5 **Brechin** Tayside Scotland 56.44N 2.40W
70 F3 **Brechou** *isld* Channel Is Eng Chan 49.26N 2.24W
61 J1 **Brecht** Belgium 51.21N 4.38E
109 D2 **Breckenridge** Colorado 39.29N 106.03W
108 O3 **Breckenridge** Minnesota 46.14N 96.35W
107 C2 **Breckenridge** Missouri 39.46N 93.49W
112 J3 **Breckenridge** Texas 32.45N 98.56W
63 F10 **Breckerfeld** W Germany 51.15N 7.30E
64 C1 **Breckerfeld** W Germany 51.15N 7.30E
56 N3 **Breckland** *reg* Norfolk and Suffolk Eng
Brecknock *co see*
Powys, Gwent, Mid Glam. *new counties*
121 K10 **Brecknock** *pen* Chile
65 P4 **Břeclav** Czechoslovakia 48.47N 16.54E
56 E4 **Brecon** Powys Wales 51.57N 3.24W
56 E4 **Brecon Beacons** *mts* Powys Wales
72 K1 **Brécy** France 47.08N 2.36E
108 Q7 **Breda** Iowa 42.10N 94.59W
60 H13 **Breda** Netherlands 51.35N 4.46E
75 Q4 **Breda** Spain 41.45N 2.34E
79 M3 **Breda di Piave** Italy 45.43N 12.20E
51 J6 **Bredåker** Sweden 65.55N 21.21E
52 J10 **Bredåkra** Sweden 56.15N 15.15E
52 G9 **Bredaryd** Sweden 57.10N 13.45E
95 D10 **Bredasdorp** S Africa 34.32S 20.02E
12 J6 **Bredbo** New S Wales 35.57S 149.10E
63 Q7 **Breddin** E Germany 52.53N 12.15E
63 K6 **Breddorf** W Germany 53.17N 9.05E
53 B6 **Brede** Denmark 55.04N 8.50E
56 N6 **Brede** E Sussex Eng 50.56N 0.36E
53 B6 **Brede Å** *R* Denmark
56 D6 **Bredebro** Denmark 55.03N 8.51E
63 J10 **Bredelar** W Germany 51.25N 8.45E
100 P8 **Bredenbury** Saskatchewan 50.58N 102.05W
61 B2 **Bredene** Belgium 51.14N 2.59E
63 R5 **Bredenfelde** E Germany 53.36N 12.57E
63 S6 **Bredereiche** E Germany 53.09N 13.15E
53 C7 **Bredevad** Denmark 54.59N 9.09E
60 P12 **Bredevoort** Netherlands 51.57N 6.37E
56 M5 **Bredhurst** Kent Eng 51.20N 0.35E
56 G3 **Bredon** Hereford & Worcs Eng 52.02N 2.07W
89 F9 **Brédou** Ivory Coast 4.58N 7.09W
52 H7 **Bredsjö** Sweden 59.52N 14.45E
63 J3 **Bredstedt** W Germany 54.38N 8.57E
53 C5 **Bredsten** Denmark 55.42N 9.23E
52 L3 **Bredträsk** Sweden 63.54N 18.35E
43 F2 **Bredy** U.S.S.R. 52.23N 60.16E
41 O2 **Bredy,Ostrov** *isld* Franz Josef Land U.S.S.R.
61 N2 **Bree** Belgium 51.08N 5.36E
95 C9 **Breede** *R* S Africa
63 S3 **Breege** E Germany 54.37N 13.22E
61 H2 **Breendonk** Belgium 51.03N 4.20E
95 C9 **Breërivier** S Africa 33.31S 19.13E
107 G3 **Breese** Illinois 38.37N 89.29W
63 Q5 **Breesen** E Germany 53.55N 12.22E
103 A2 **Breesport** New York 42.10N 76.45W
60 H8 **Breezand** Netherlands 52.54N 4.48E
60 J7 **Breezand** Netherlands
66 P6 **Bregaglia,Val** Switzerland
82 G9 **Bregalnica** *R* Yugoslavia
79 L3 **Breganze** Italy 45.42N 11.35E
64 E8 **Brege** *R* W Germany
64 E8 **Bregenbach** W Germany 48.00N 8.21E
65 A6 **Bregenz** Austria 47.31N 9.46E
65 A7 **Bregenzer Ache** *R* Austria
65 A7 **Bregenzer Wald** *mts* Austria
66 N8 **Breggia** *R* Italy/Switz
53 G5 **Bregninge** Denmark 55.42N 11.19E
82 H6 **Bregovo** Bulgaria 44.08N 22.39E
79 J2 **Breguzzo** Italy 46.01N 10.42E
70 G4 **Bréhal** France 48.54N 1.30W
70 E4 **Bréhat** *isld* France 48.50N 3.00W
98 B1 **Bréhat, Lac** Quebec
63 Q9 **Brehna** E Germany 51.34N 12.12E
63 T9 **Brehnitz** E Germany 51.41N 13.36E
53 V18 **Breiavatn** *L* Hordaland Norway 60.03N 6.52E
53 X14 **Breidalsvatn** *L* Opland Norway 62.02N 7.35E
53 U16 **Breidalsvatn** *L* Sogn og Fjordane Norway 61.16N 6.06E
64 E2 **Breidenbach** W Germany 50.53N 8.28E
64 E2 **Breidenstein** W Germany 50.55N 8.29E
50 E4 **Breidhabólsstadhur** Húnavatnssýsla, Vestur Iceland 65.28N 20.44W
50 E7 **Breidhabólsstadhur** Rangárvallasýsla Iceland 63.44N 20.08W
50 G7 **Breidhabólsstadhur** Skaftafellssýsla, Vestur Iceland 63.50N 18.01W
50 C4 **Breidhabólsstadhur** Snæfellsnessýsla Iceland 65.02N 22.25W
50 B4 **Breidhafjördhur** *B* Iceland
50 J6 **Breidhamerkurjökull** *ice cap* Iceland 64.05N 16.20W
50 J7 **Breidhamerkursandur** *sand reg* Iceland
50 C2 **Breidhaskardhshnúkur** *mt* Iceland 66.22N 22.25W
50 D5 **Breidhavatn** *L* Iceland 65.54N 21.05W
50 M4 **Breidhavík** Múlasýsla, Sudhur Iceland 65.03N 13.52W
50 M4 **Breidhavík** *inlet* Múlasýsla, Nordhur Iceland
50 B5 **Breidhavík** *inlet* Snæfellsnessýsla Iceland
50 H2 **Breidhavík** *inlet* Thingeyjarsýsla, Sudhur Iceland
50 G6 **Breidhbakur** *mt* Iceland 64.11N 18.20W
50 L5 **Breidhdalsheidhi** *heath* Iceland
50 L5 **Breidhdalsvík** Iceland 64.48N 14.00W
50 M5 **Breidhdalsvík** *inlet* Iceland
53 W16 **Breidsnes** Norway 61.02N 7.04E
53 Y20 **Breidvik** Norway 59.07N 8.05E
108 K3 **Breien** N Dakota 46.23N 100.58W
53 V19 **Breifonn** Norway 59.49N 6.47E
53 V19 **Breifonn** *glacier* Norway 59.45N 6.53E
53 V19 **Breifonn** *mt* Norway 59.45N 6.52E
66 N4 **Breil** Switzerland 46.47N 9.04E
70 L5 **Breil-sur-Mérize,le** France 48.01N 0.29E
71 M9 **Breil-sur-Roya** France 43.55N 7.31E
53 U15 **Breim** Norway 61.44N 6.25E
53 U15 **Breimsvatn** *L* Norway 61.42N 6.24E
95 K6 **Breipaal** S Africa 30.06S 26.12E
64 D7 **Breisach** W Germany 48.02N 7.36E
64 D7 **Breisgau** *reg* W Germany
53 S18 **Breistein** Norway 60.29N 5.23E
53 Y16 **Breistølen** Norway 61.01N 8.03E
53 T14 **Breisundet** *sound* Norway 62.27N 5.52E
66 G2 **Breitenbach** Switzerland 47.25N 7.33E
64 Q6 **Breitenberg** W Germany 48.43N 13.49E
64 M5 **Breitenbrunn** W Germany 49.05N 11.38E
63 Q10 **Breitenfeld** E Germany 51.25N 12.21E
65 O5 **Breitenfurth** Austria 48.08N 16.09E
64 K4 **Breitengüssbach** W Germany 49.58N 10.54E
63 P9 **Breitenhagen** E Germany 51.56N 11.56E
63 M7 **Breitenhees** W Germany 52.49N 10.29E
64 O3 **Breitenhof** E Germany 50.29N 12.44E
63 S6 **Breiter Luzinsee** *L* E Germany
66 H8 **Breithorn** Italy/Switz 45.57N 7.46E
66 H6 **Breithorn** *mt* Switzerland 46.29N 7.52E
63 Q4 **Breitling** *B* E Germany 54.09N 12.10E
64 J2 **Breitungen** W Germany 50.47N 10.19E
53 W19 **Breivatn** *L* Aust Agder Norway 59.38N 7.26E
53 S16 **Breivatn** *L* Norway 61.17N 5.21E
53 W19 **Breive** Norway 59.33N 7.18E
51 J1 **Breivikbotn** Norway 70.35N 22.17E
53 R17 **Breiviksund** Norway 60.34N 4.51E
118 E2 **Brejinho de Nazaré** Brazil 11.00S 48.33W
53 B4 **Brejning** Denmark 56.07N 8.31E
117 F6 **Brejo** Brazil 3.41S 42.50W
117 E9 **Brejo da Porta** Brazil 8.27S 45.45W
118 G2 **Brejo da Serra** Brazil 10.08S 43.19W
117 F7 **Brejo de São Félix** Brazil 5.17S 43.29W
76 B13 **Brejo Longo** Portugal 37.39N 8.48W
117 F9 **Brejo, R** Brazil
118 G3 **Brejo Velho** Brazil 12.29S 43.57W
106 K6 **Brekenridge** Michigan 43.24N 84.27W
41 D5 **Brekhovskiye Ostrova** *islds* U.S.S.R.
50 L4 **Brekka** Iceland 65.05N 14.51W
50 M4 **Brekka** Iceland 65.13N 13.48W
53 S16 **Brekke** Norway 61.01N 5.27E
52 F4 **Brekken** Norway 62.39N 11.52E
53 U17 **Brekkhus** Norway 60.44N 6.09E
63 J3 **Breklum** W Germany 54.36N 9.00E
52 E3 **Brekstad** Norway 63.42N 9.40E
53 R15 **Bremanger** Norway 61.51N 4.57E
53 R15 **Bremangerlandet** *isld* Norway
79 G3 **Brembana,Val** *V* Italy
79 G3 **Brembo** *R* Italy
105 B4 **Bremen** Georgia 33.42N 85.09W
106 H8 **Bremen** Indiana 41.27N 86.10W
104 C7 **Bremen** Ohio 39.43N 82.26W
63 J6 **Bremen** W Germany 53.05N 8.48E
13 D1 **Bremer** *I* N Terr Australia 12.04S 136.49E
14 C10 **Bremer B** W Australia
14 C10 **Bremer Bay** W Australia 34.21S 119.20E
63 J5 **Bremerhaven** W Germany 53.33N 8.35E
14 D10 **Bremer Ra** W Australia
110 C2 **Bremerton** Washington 47.34N 122.40W
63 K6 **Bremervörde** W Germany 53.29N 9.09E
66 K2 **Bremgarten** Switzerland 47.21N 8.21E
113 Q6 **Bremner** *R* Alaska
53 S19 **Bremnes** Norway 59.48N 5.11E
71 L2 **Bremoncourt** France 47.20N 7.02E
112 L4 **Bremond** Texas 31.12N 96.41W
51 B6 **Bremsteinen** *Lt Ho* Norway 65.35N 11.03E
120 B9 **Breña** *dist* Lima Peru
96 P10 **Breña Alta** La Palma Canary Is 28.39N 17.49W
96 P10 **Breña Baja** La Palma Canary Is 28.38N 17.47W
77 F5 **Breña,Embalse de la** *L* Spain 37.51N 5.02W
12 H3 **Brenda** New S Wales 29.31S 147.14E
13 H8 **Brenda** Queensland 29.00S 147.12E
53 D6 **Brenderup** Denmark 55.29N 9.59E
79 K4 **Brendola** Italy 45.29N 11.28E
56 E5 **Brendon Hills** Somerset Eng
77 E5 **Brenes** Spain 37.33N 5.53W
66 B5 **Brenet, L** Switzerland 46.41N 6.20E
66 C3 **Brenets,les** Switzerland 47.04N 6.43E
112 L5 **Brenham** Texas 30.09N 96.24W
71 E1 **Brenne** *R* Côte d'Or France 47.32N 4.27E
70 M6 **Brenne** *R* Indre-et-Loire France
72 G2 **Brenne** *reg* France
65 E7 **Brenner** Austria 47.02N 11.32E
110 M5 **Brenner** Montana 44.58N 113.16W
79 L1 **Brénnero** Italy 47.01N 11.31E
65 E7 **Brenner Pass** Austria/Italy 47.02N 11.32E
64 D8 **Brennet** W Germany 47.35N 7.55E
66 M6 **Brenno** *R* Switzerland
79 H3 **Breno** Italy 45.57N 10.18E
71 H4 **Brénod** France 46.03N 5.36E
72 H8 **Brens** France 43.53N 1.53E
64 C5 **Brenschelbach** W Germany 49.09N 7.22E
107 J9 **Brent** Alabama 32.57N 87.11W
99 M6 **Brent** Ontario 46.02N 78.29W
66 D6 **Brent** Switzerland 46.28N 6.54E
55 D3 **Brent** *bor* London Eng
54 M1 **Brent** *oil field* North Sea 61.07N 1.40E
79 L3 **Brenta** *R* Italy
79 J2 **Brenta,Gruppo di** *mts* Italy
55 D4 **Brentford** London England 51.29N 0.19W
108 M4 **Brentford** S Dakota 45.09N 98.18W
79 J3 **Brentónico** Italy 45.49N 10.57E
98 T4 **Brenton Rock** Newfoundland 49.45N 53.17W
55 D3 **Brent, R** London England
55 D3 **Brent Res** London England 51.34N 0.15W
111 C4 **Brentwood** California 37.56N 121.41W
56 M4 **Brentwood** Essex Eng 51.38N 0.18E
103 H5 **Brentwood** Long I, N Y 40.47N 73.14W
94 U13 **Brentwood Park** S Africa 26.08S 28.17E
64 J6 **Brenz** *R* W Germany
56 N5 **Brenzett** Kent Eng 51.01N 0.52E
71 J8 **Bréole,la** France 44.27N 6.17E
79 K1 **Bréonie,Alpi** *mts* Italy
95 O2 **Brereton Park** S Africa 26.57S 30.28E
79 J5 **Brescello** Italy 44.54N 10.31E
79 H3 **Brescia** Italy 45.33N 10.13E
79 H3 **Brescia** *prov* Italy
60 B3 **Breskens** Netherlands 51.24N 3.34E
Breslau *see* **Wrocław**
69 B4 **Bresle** *R* France
69 C5 **Bresles** France 49.25N 2.15E
14 C6 **Bresnahan,Mt** W Australia 23.46S 117.55E
79 F4 **Bressana Bottarone** Italy 45.05N 9.08E
79 L1 **Bressanone** Italy 46.43N 11.40E
58 Q9 **Bressay** *isld* Shetland Scotland 60.08N 1.05W
71 G4 **Bresse** *reg* France
69 M8 **Bresse,la** France 48.00N 6.52E
79 F7 **Bresso** *dist* Milan Italy
72 G8 **Bressols** France 43.58N 1.20E
72 D2 **Bressuire** France 46.50N 0.29W

46 E4 Brest Belorussiya U.S.S.R. 52.08N 23.40E
70 B5 Brest France 48.23N 4.30W
70 D5 Brest à Nantes, Canal de France
66 J2 Brestenberg Switzerland 47.19N 8.13E
Brest Litovsk see Brest U.S.S.R
70 A5 Brest,Rade de B France 48.20N 4.30W
46 E4 Brestskaya Oblast' prov Belorussiya U.S.S.R.
67 C4 Bretagne prov France
72 E8 Bretagne-d'Armagnac France 43.53N 0.09E
26 T15 Bretagne,Pte.de Réunion Ind Oc 21.12S 55.17E
70 N4 Bretagnolles France 48.57N 1.22E
120 C1 Bretana Peru 5.18S 74.17W
96 T1 Bretanha Azores 37.38N 25.47W
66 E6 Bretaye Switzerland 46.19N 7.04E
82 K4 Bretçu Romania 46.02N 26.19E
72 H6 Bretenoux France 44.55N 1.50E
70 M4 Breteuil-sur-Iton France 48.50N 0.55E
69 C4 Breteuil-sur-Noye France 49.38N 2.18E
56 H3 Bretforton Hereford & Worcs Eng 52.06N 1.51W
72 A2 Brétignolles-sur-Mer France 46.38N 1.51W
69 C6 Brétigny France 48.37N 2.19E
100 C5 Breton Alberta 53.06N 114.28W
98 N8 Breton,C C Breton I, Nova Scotia 45.57N 59.47W
116 E4 Breton,Cayo isld Cuba 21.06N 79.25W
70 M5 Bretoncelles France 48.26N 0.53E
107 G12 Breton I Louisiana 29.28N 89.11W
26 P16 Bretonne, B Kerguelen Ind Oc
72 B3 Breton,Pertuis str France
107 G12 Breton Sd Louisiana
66 C3 Bretonvillers France 47.13N 6.38E
103 F6 Breton Woods New Jersey 40.03N 74.08W
65 K7 Bretstein Austria 47.20N 14.24E
11 J2 Brett,C New Zealand 35.12S 174.22E
64 F5 Bretten W Germany 49.02N 8.42E
70 K3 Bretteville France 49.02N 0.20W
70 K3 Bretteville-l'Orgueilleuse France 49.12N 0.30W
64 J5 Brettheim W Germany 49.17N 10.06E
50 H2 Brettingsstadhir Iceland 66.07N 17.52W
75 F3 Bretún Spain 42.04N 2.23W
64 G5 Bretzfeld W Germany 49.11N 9.28E
66 G2 Bretzwil Switzerland 47.24N 7.40E
64 G4 Breuberg W Germany 49.48N 9.02E
117 D6 Breu Branco Brazil 4.00S 49.37W
69 L8 Breuches France 47.48N 6.20E
18 A3 Breueh isld Sumatra Indon
60 L13 Breugel Netherlands 51.30N 5.30E
79 C3 Breuil-Cervínia Italy 45.57N 7.38E
70 L3 Breuil-en-Auge,le France 49.13N 0.14E
71 D4 Breuil,le Allier France 46.11N 3.39E
69 F6 Breuil,le Marne France 48.59N 3.39E
72 C3 Breuil-Magné France 46.00N 0.57W
70 N4 Breuilpont France 48.58N 1.26E
60 J11 Breukelen Netherlands 52.11N 5.01E
119 F9 Breu, R Amazonas Brazil
120 C3 Breu, R Brazil/Peru
66 A1 Breurey France 47.46N 6.07E
69 K7 Breuvannes France 48.06N 5.37E
69 B6 Bréval France 48.57N 1.32E
105 E2 Brevard N Carolina 35.13N 82.46W
71 K5 Brevent,le France 45.56N 6.51E
117 D5 Breves Brazil 1.38S 50.25W
69 G7 Bréviandes France 48.17N 4.06E
52 E7 Brevik Norway 59.05N 9.42E
66 C4 Brévine,la Switzerland 46.59N 6.37E
66 C7 Brevon R France
69 G7 Brevonnes France 48.22N 4.25E
106 K3 Brevoort L Michigan 46.00N 84.55W
106 J3 Brevort Michigan 46.02N 85.02W
12 H3 Brewarrina New S Wales 29.57S 147.54E
104 R2 Brewer Maine 44.48N 68.44W
104 J3 Brewerton New York 43.15N 76.09W
89 D8 Brewerville Liberia 6.26N 10.47W
105 F10 Brewster Florida 27.45N 81.59W
109 J2 Brewster Kansas 39.21N 101.23W
103 O3 Brewster Massachusetts 41.46N 70.05W
108 L8 Brewster Nebraska 41.57N 99.52W
103 G4 Brewster New York 41.24N 73.37W
104 D6 Brewster Ohio 40.43N 81.37W
110 F1 Brewster Washington 48.05N 119.50W
48 V12 Brewster, Kap C Greenland 70.10N 22.00W
12 H5 Brewster, L New S Wales 33.30S 145.38E
11 D11 Brewster,Mt New Zealand 44.05S 169.29E
107 J10 Brewton Alabama 31.07N 87.04W
63 D10 Breyell W Germany 51.17N 6.15E
95 N2 Breyten S Africa 26.18S 29.59E
82 C5 Brežice Yugoslavia 45.55N 15.37E
88 O5 Brèzina Algeria 33.03N 1.18E
71 G6 Brezins France 45.21N 5.18E
65 J2 Březnice Czechoslovakia 49.34N 13.57E
82 H8 Breznik Bulgaria 42.44N 22.50E
62 M7 Brezno Czechoslovakia 48.49N 19.40E
65 M8 Brezno Yugoslavia 46.36N 15.18E
70 N4 Brezolles France 48.42N 1.05E
76 K3 Brezo,Sierra del mts Spain
65 P2 Březová Czechoslovakia 49.40N 16.32E
65 J2 Březové Hory Czechoslovakia 49.41N 13.59E
82 J8 Brezovo Bulgaria 42.20N 25.06E
90 K8 Bria Cent Afr Rep 6.32N 22.00E
72 G4 Briance R France
71 K7 Briançon France 44.53N 6.39E
111 M4 Brian Head mt Utah 37.42N 112.50W
79 F3 Brianza reg Italy
103 G4 Briarcliff Manor New York 41.10N 73.50W
71 B1 Briare France 47.38N 2.44E
72 H8 Briatexte France 43.44N 1.53E
81 M6 Briatico Italy 38.43N 16.02E
79 M2 Bribano Italy 46.06N 12.06E
12 J5 Bribbaree New S Wales 34.07S 147.51E
13 L7 Bribie I Queensland
112 G1 Brice Texas 34.43N 100.53W
110 B9 Briceland California 40.07N 123.55W
108 R6 Bricelyn Minnesota 43.32N 93.50W
46 F5 Brichany Moldavia U.S.S.R. 48.20N 27.01E
79 B5 Bricherasio Italy 44.49N 7.18E
59 E4 Brickeens Mayo Irish Rep 53.44N 8.53W
107 F7 Brickeys Arkansas 34.52N 90.35W
69 H7 Bricon France 48.05N 4.58E
98 M2 Briconnet,L Quebec
70 G3 Bricquebec France 49.28N 1.38W
70 G4 Bricqueville-sur-Mer France 48.55N 1.31W
57 E4 Bride Isle of Man U.K. 54.23N 4.24W
56 B3 Bridell Dyfed Wales 52.03N 4.40W
59 G7 Bride,R Waterford etc Irish Rep
71 K6 Brides-les-Bains France 45.27N 6.35E
56 C6 Bridestowe Devon Eng 50.41N 4.06W
100 U3 Bridgar Manitoba 55.36N 97.05W
110 M7 Bridge Idaho 42.09N 113.20W
110 A6 Bridge Oregon 43.02N 124.01W
105 D6 Bridgeboro Georgia 31.26N 83.58W
103 K5 Bridgehampton Long I, N Y 40.57N 72.18W
58 K4 Bridgehaugh Grampian Scotland 57.24N 3.06W
110 P9 Bridgeland Utah 40.09N 110.14W
59 H1 Bridgend Donegal Irish Rep 55.02N 7.23W
58 D7 Bridgend Islay, Strathclyde Scotland 55.48N 6.16W
56 D4 Bridgend Mid Glam Wales 51.31N 3.35W
58 K6 Bridgend Tayside Scotland 56.24N 3.26W
58 L4 Bridge of Alford Grampian Scotland 57.14N 2.44W
58 J6 Bridge of Allan Central Scotland 56.09N 5.58W
58 K5 Bridge of Cally Tayside Scotland 56.39N 3.25W
58 M4 Bridge of Don Grampian Scotland 57.11N 2.05W
58 K6 Bridge of Earn Tayside Scotland 56.24N 3.25W
58 K4 Bridge of Gairn Grampian Scotland 57.04N 3.05W
58 G5 Bridge of Orchy Strathclyde Scotland 56.31N 4.44W
58 G7 Bridge of Weir Strathclyde Scotland 55.52N 4.35W
107 L7 Bridgeport Alabama 34.58N 85.42W
101 G11 Bridgeport Br Col 49.12N 123.08W
111 E3 Bridgeport California 38.14N 119.15W
103 H4 Bridgeport Connecticut 41.12N 73.12W
109 N3 Bridgeport Kansas 38.39N 97.37W
108 G8 Bridgeport Nebraska 41.40N 103.06W
103 D7 Bridgeport New Jersey 39.48N 75.21W
104 E6 Bridgeport Ohio 40.04N 80.45W
109 M6 Bridgeport Oklahoma 35.33N 98.23W
110 H5 Bridgeport Oregon 44.30N 117.43W
103 D6 Bridgeport Pennsylvania 40.06N 75.20W
112 K2 Bridgeport Texas 33.14N 97.46W
110 F2 Bridgeport Washington 47.59N 119.38W
104 E7 Bridgeport W Virginia 39.17N 80.16W
112 K2 Bridgeport L Texas
111 E3 Bridgeport Res California 38.16N 119.14W
105 L12 Bridge Pt Bahamas 25.35N 76.42W
101 M10 Bridge R Br Col
110 R4 Bridger Montana 45.17N 108.55W
110 P4 Bridger Pk Montana 45.49N 110.56W
108 C8 Bridger Pk Wyoming 41.11N 107.12W
59 E6 Bridget,L Clare Irish Rep 52.52N 8.39W
105 K2 Bridgeton N Carolina 35.06N 77.00W
103 D8 Bridgeton New Jersey 39.26N 75.14W
103 B7 Bridgeton Pennsylvania 39.47N 76.25W
116 O6 Bridgetown Barbados 13.06N 59.37W
103 C8 Bridgetown Maryland 39.02N 75.53W
98 G9 Bridgetown Nova Scotia 44.50N 65.20W
56 G2 Bridgetown Staffs Eng 52.41N 2.01W
14 B10 Bridgetown W Australia 33.57S 116.05E
59 J7 Bridgetown Wexford Irish Rep 52.14N 6.33W
110 B9 Bridgeville California 40.29N 123.50W
104 K8 Bridgeville Delaware 38.43N 75.36W
98 K8 Bridgeville Nova Scotia 45.26N 62.36W
103 H3 Bridgewater Connecticut 41.33N 73.23W
104 R7 Bridgewater Maine 46.26N 67.50W
103 N3 Bridgewater Massachusetts 42.00N 70.59W
98 H9 Bridgewater Nova Scotia 44.23N 64.32W
108 N6 Bridgewater S Dakota 43.33N 97.30W
104 G8 Bridgewater Virginia 38.23N 78.58W
12 F7 Bridgewater,C Victoria 38.25S 141.28E
106 H8 Bridgman Michigan 41.57N 86.32W
30 G5 Bridgmanganj Uttar Prad India 27.13N 83.20E
48 T1 Bridgman, Kap C Greenland 83.10N 29.00W
56 G2 Bridgnorth Shropshire Eng 52.33N 2.25W
104 P2 Bridgton Maine 44.04N 70.42W
56 E5 Bridgwater Somerset Eng 51.08N 3.00W
56 E5 Bridgwater B Somerset Eng
57 N4 Bridlington Humberside Eng 54.05N 0.12W
57 N4 Bridlington B Humberside Eng
56 F6 Bridport Dorset Eng 50.44N 2.46W
12 H8 Bridport Tasmania 40.59S 147.24E
72 E4 Brie France 45.45N 0.14E
69 D6 Brie reg France
70 B5 Briec France 48.06N 4.00W
68 J5 Brie-Comte-Robert France 48.42N 2.37E
69 D6 Brie-Comte Robert France 48.41N 2.37E
Brieg see Brzeg
61 B3 Brielen Belgium 50.52N 2.51E
60 E12 Brielle Netherlands 51.54N 4.10E
69 H7 Brienne-le-Château France 48.24N 4.32E
66 N8 Brienno Italy 45.56N 9.08E
71 E4 Briennon France 46.09N 4.04E
69 F8 Brienon-sur-Armançon France 48.00N 3.36E
66 J4 Brienz Bern Switzerland 46.46N 8.02E
66 P5 Brienz Graubünden Switzerland 46.41N 9.36E
81 L3 Brienza Italy 40.28N 15.37E
66 J4 Brienzer Rothorn mt Switzerland 46.48N 8.02E
66 H5 Brienzer See L Switzerland
66 J4 Brienzwiler Switzerland 46.45N 8.06E
105 F4 Brier Cr Georgia
100 M8 Briercrest Saskatchewan 50.12N 105.21W
100 F4 Briereville Alberta 54.29N 111.53W
57 J5 Brierfield Lancs Eng 53.50N 2.14W
98 F9 Brier I Nova Scotia 44.15N 66.22W
56 G3 Brierley Hill W Midlands Eng 52.29N 2.07W
63 U8 Briescht E Germany 52.07N 14.09E
63 S7 Brieselang E Germany 52.35N 13.02E
69 H5 Brieulles-sur-Bar France 49.28N 4.52E
70 O4 Brieval France 48.57N 1.31E
69 K5 Briey France 49.15N 5.57E
71 B5 Briffons France 45.43N 2.38E
66 H6 Brig Switzerland 46.19N 8.00E
66 K9 Briga Italy 45.44N 8.28E
64 E7 Brigach R W Germany
80 B3 Brigantina,Pta Italy 42.34N 10.06E
103 F8 Brigantine New Jersey 39.24N 74.22W
60 B2 Brigdamme Netherlands 51.31N 3.35E
99 H10 Brigden Ontario 42.48N 82.17W
Brigels see Breil
57 N5 Brigg Humberside Eng 53.34N 0.30W
112 K5 Briggs Texas 30.54N 97.56W
109 F1 Briggsdale Colorado 40.38N 104.20W
110 N8 Brigham City Utah 41.30N 112.02W
101 G11 Brighouse Br Col 49.10N 123.09W
57 K5 Brighouse W Yorks Eng 53.42N 1.47W
56 J6 Brighstone I of Wight Eng 50.38N 1.24W
12 H6 Bright Victoria 36.42S 146.58E
111 M5 Bright Angel Point Arizona 36.14N 112.03W
56 M6 Brightling E Sussex Eng 50.58N 0.25E
56 O4 Brightlingsea Essex Eng 51.49N 1.02E
109 F2 Brighton Colorado 39.59N 104.50W
56 L6 Brighton E Sussex Eng 50.50N 0.10W
105 F10 Brighton Florida 27.13N 81.06W
107 F2 Brighton Illinois 39.02N 90.08W
106 C8 Brighton Iowa 41.10N 91.48W
106 L7 Brighton Michigan 42.32N 83.46W
99 N8 Brighton Ontario 44.03N 77.44W
12 E6 Brighton S Australia 35.03S 138.32E
116 N2 Brighton Trinidad & Tobago 10.15N 61.38W
12 D8 Brighton dist Melbourne, Vic
12 D8 Brighton Beach Melbourne, Vic
13 F6 Brighton Downs Queensland 23.20S 141.34E
12 L8 Brighton-le-Sands dist Sydney, N S W 33.57S 151.09E
94 P12 Brightwater Cape Town S Africa 34.17S 18.24E
11 H8 Brightwater New Zealand 41.22S 173.08E
56 O3 Brightwell Suffolk Eng 52.03N 1.16E
117 G9 Brigida,R.da Brazil
71 F5 Brignais France 45.40N 4.45E
72 F8 Brignemont France 43.47N 1.00E
70 B4 Brignogan-Plage France 48.40N 4.20W
71 J10 Brignoles France 43.25N 6.03E
72 F4 Brigueuil France 45.57N 0.52E
98 T6 Brigus Newfoundland 47.31N 53.13W
75 E6 Brihuega Spain 40.45N 2.52W
29 E5 Brijnagar Rajasthan India 24.45N 76.10E
89 A5 Brikama The Gambia 13.15N 16.39W
53 V15 Briksdal Norway 61.40N 6.50E
118 C7 Brilhante R Brazil
72 F3 Brillac France 46.04N 0.46E
109 F5 Brilliant New Mexico 36.57N 104.34W
106 F5 Brillion Wisconsin 44.11N 88.02W
69 J6 Brillon-en-Barrois France 48.43N 5.06E
63 J10 Brilon W Germany 51.24N 8.34E
106 E9 Brimfield Illinois 40.51N 89.54W
103 K2 Brimfield Massachusetts 42.07N 72.12W
50 B5 Brimilsvellir Iceland 64.54N 23.35W
57 L6 Brimington Derbys Eng 53.16N 1.23W
50 M4 Brimnes Múlasýsla, Nordhur Iceland 65.19N 13.47W
53 V18 Brimnes Norway 60.28N 6.54E
50 L2 Brimnes Thingeyjarsýsla, Nordhur Iceland 66.20N 14.59W
75 E2 Briñas Spain 42.36N 2.50W
18 B7 Brinchang Pen Malaysia 4.27N 101.21E
76 D12 Brinches Portugal 38.02N 7.36W
40 G1 Brindakit U.S.S.R. 60.05N 137.20E
81 Q11 Bríndisi Italy 40.37N 17.57E
81 Q11 Bríndisi prov Italy
58 S12 Bring Deeps Orkney Scotland 58.54N 3.15W
12 C4 Bring,L S Australia 30.19S 133.03E
82 C5 Brinje Yugoslavia 45.01N 15.09E
88 N7 Brinkene Algeria 28.25N 0.12W
104 C6 Brinkhaven Ohio 40.28N 82.11W
107 E6 Brinkley Arkansas 34.53N 91.12W
56 M3 Brinkley Cambs Eng 52.11N 0.23E
56 J3 Brinklow Warwicks Eng 52.25N 1.20W
121 E3 Brinkmann Argentina 30.52S 62.01W
95 G6 Brinkspan salt pan S Africa 30.20S 23.38E
63 J6 Brinkum W Germany 53.01N 8.48E
12 E5 Brinkworth S Australia 33.42S 138.24E
56 H4 Brinkworth Wilts Eng 51.34N 1.59W
71 C2 Brinon-sur-Beuvron France 47.17N 3.29E
70 P6 Brinon-sur-Sauldre France 47.34N 2.15E
108 L1 Brinsmade N Dakota 48.12N 99.20W
105 C7 Brinson Georgia 30.58N 84.43W
99 P1 Brinston Ontario 44.57N 75.22W
69 L6 Brin-sur-Seille France 48.47N 6.22E
52 H6 Brintbodarna Sweden 60.43N 14.10E
58 T11 Brinyan Orkney Scotland 59.08N 3.00W
70 J6 Briollay France 47.32N 0.32W
72 H2 Brion Indre France 46.58N 1.42E
71 C7 Brion Lozère France 44.45N 3.04E
76 B3 Brión Spain 42.51N 8.40W
66 M6 Brione Switzerland 46.18N 8.48E
75 E2 Briones Spain 42.33N 2.47W
111 C8 Briones Reservoir California
98 L6 Brion I Madeleine Is, Que 47.48N 61.30W
70 M3 Brionne France 49.11N 0.43E
72 D1 Brion-près-Thouet France 47.03N 0.11W
69 H8 Brion-sur-Ource Côte d'Or France 47.55N 4.40E
71 C6 Brioude France 45.18N 3.23E
72 D3 Brioux-sur-Boutonne France 46.08N 0.13W
70 K4 Briouze France 48.42N 0.22W
Brîqa see Bariqah
26 N16 Brisants de l'Héroïne reefs Crozet Is Ind Oc
13 L8 Brisbane Queensland 27.30S 153.00E
13 L7 Brisbane R Queensland
103 C2 Brisben New York 42.22N 75.41W
112 D8 Briscoe Texas 35.35N 100.17W
72 B9 Briscous France 43.28N 1.19W
66 K4 Brisen mt Switzerland 46.54N 8.28E
79 L6 Brisighella Italy 44.13N 11.46E
53 X18 Briskevatn L Norway 60.02N 7.36E
56 N2 Brisley Norfolk Eng 52.45N 0.53E
66 B7 Brison France 46.03N 6.27E
Bris,Ras see Berīs,Ra's cape
70 K7 Brissac France 47.22N 0.26W
70 K7 Brissac-Quincé France 47.22N 0.26W
66 L7 Brissago Switzerland 46.08N 8.43E
66 L7 Brissago, I. di Switzerland
66 L4 Bristen Switzerland 46.46N 8.42E
66 L5 Bristenstock mt Switzerland 46.44N 8.42E
80 O1 Bristivica Yugoslavia 43.34N 16.10E
56 F5 Bristol Avon Eng 51.27N 2.35W
109 H3 Bristol Colorado 38.07N 102.20W
103 J3 Bristol Connecticut 41.41N 72.57W
105 C7 Bristol Florida 30.27N 84.58W
105 E6 Bristol Georgia 31.27N 82.13W
106 J8 Bristol Indiana 41.43N 85.47W
98 E7 Bristol New Brunswick 46.28N 67.34W
104 O3 Bristol New Hampshire 43.36N 71.46W
103 E6 Bristol Pennsylvania 40.06N 74.52W
99 O7 Bristol Quebec 45.32N 76.29W
103 M3 Bristol Rhode I 41.41N 71.12W
108 N4 Bristol S Dakota 45.20N 97.44W
105 E1 Bristol Tenn/Virginia 36.35N 82.12W
104 M2 Bristol Vermont 44.09N 73.06W
103 M3 Bristol co Massachusetts
103 M3 Bristol co Rhode I
113 G8 Bristol B Alaska
56 C5 Bristol Channel England/Wales
123 A14 Bristol I S Sandwich Is Atl Oc 59.00S 26.30W
111 J7 Bristol L California 34.29N 115.40W
111 J7 Bristol Mts California
111 K3 Bristol Silver Nevada 38.06N 114.37W
56 O2 Briston Norfolk Eng 52.52N 1.05E
109 O6 Bristow Oklahoma 35.51N 96.24W
15 G8 Bristow I Papua New Guinea 9.06S 143.15E
11 B7 Bristow Pt Auckland Is Pacific Oc 50.45S 165.54E
99 C9 Britannia Bay Ontario 45.23N 75.49W
101 M11 Britannia Beach Br Col 49.34N 123.13W
123 H6 Britannia Ra Antarctica
48 U6 Britannia Sø L Greenland 77.08N 23.30W
41 N2 Britanskiy Kanal,Proliv str Franz Josef Land U.S.S.R.
123 C12 British Antarctic Terr Antarctica
97 G6 British Columbia prov Canada
97 L1 British Empire Ra N W Terr
British Guiana see Guyana
26 British Indian Ocean Terr colony Indian Ocean
113 Q2 British Mts Alaska/Yukon Terr
British North Borneo see Sabah Malaysia
11 C5 British Pk mt New Zealand 41.15S 174.44E
15 L2 British Solomon Is Pacific Oc
116 M5 British Virgin Is W Indies
91 E8 Brito Godins Angola 8.57S 16.32E
98 M7 Briton Cove C Breton I, N S 46.30N 60.26W
56 D4 Briton Ferry W Glam Wales 51.38N 3.49W
95 L1 Brits S Africa 25.39S 27.47E
95 G6 Britstown S Africa 30.36S 23.30E
60 M6 Britsum Netherlands 53.15N 5.47E
95 G6 Britsville S Africa 30.42S 23.59E
108 R6 Britt Iowa 43.05N 93.48W
99 K7 Britt Ontario 45.46N 80.35W
Brittany prov see Bretagne prov
59 K5 Brittas Dublin Irish Rep 53.14N 6.27W
59 K6 Brittas B Wicklow Irish Rep 52.53N 6.03W
59 H4 Brittas L W Meath Irish Rep 53.34N 7.17W
52 H9 Brittatorp Sweden 57.03N 14.58E
95 J3 Britten S Africa 27.44S 25.21E
58 D4 Brittle, L Skye, Highland Scotland 57.10N 6.20W
66 H2 Brittnau Switzerland 47.16N 7.57E
108 N4 Britton S Dakota 45.48N 97.43W
12 C2 Britton,Mt S Australia 26.31S 134.40E
47 E5 Britvino U.S.S.R. 61.23N 44.22E
63 T7 Britz E Germany 52.53N 13.50E
72 H5 Brive-la-Gaillarde France 45.09N 1.32E
75 D2 Briviesca Spain 42.33N 3.19W
70 G2 Brix France 49.33N 1.35W
Brixen see Bressanone
65 F7 Brixental V Austria
56 D7 Brixham Devon Eng 50.23N 3.30W
65 E7 Brixlegg Austria 47.25N 11.53E
55 F4 Brixton London Eng 51.28N 0.06W
13 G6 Brixton Queensland 23.30S 144.59E
56 K3 Brixworth Northants Eng 52.20N 0.54W
72 D4 Brizambourg France 45.49N 0.28W
50 B3 Brjánslækur Iceland 65.31N 23.10W
43 L5 Brlik Kazakhstan U.S.S.R. 43.41N 73.54E
43 L5 Brlik Kazakhstan U.S.S.R. 44.07N 73.30E
65 P3 Brno Czech 49.13N 16.40E
52 G7 Bro Sweden 59.13N 13.02E
105 D3 Broad R Georgia
105 F3 Broad R S Carolina
100 J6 Broadacres Saskatchewan 52.02N 108.59W
104 L3 Broadalbin New York 43.03N 74.14W
14 D9 Broad Arrow W Australia 30.32S 121.20E
58 D2 Broad B Lewis, W Isles Scotland
97 M7 Broadback R Quebec
99 M1 Broadback R Ontario
11 N12 Broad Bay New Zealand 45.51S 170.37E
110 A6 Broadbent Oregon 43.01N 124.09W
103 J3 Broad Brook Connecticut 41.55N 72.32W
56 E6 Broad Clyst Devon Eng 50.46N 3.26W
13 C4 Broad Cr N Terr Australia
112 N4 Broaddus Texas 31.20N 94.17W
59 E6 Broadford Clare Irish Rep 52.48N 8.38W
59 E7 Broadford Limerick Irish Rep 52.20N 8.58W
58 E4 Broadford Skye, Highland Scotland 57.14N 5.54W
12 H6 Broadford Victoria 37.16S 145.03E
56 A4 Broad Haven Dyfed Wales 51.47N 5.06W
59 C3 Broadhaven B Mayo Irish Rep 54.18N 9.55W
56 H5 Broad Hinton Wilts Eng 51.30N 1.51W
14 D5 Broadhurst Ra W Australia
108 M5 Broadland S Dakota 44.30N 98.20W
57 G2 Broad Law mt Borders Scotland 55.30N 3.22W
12 C6 Broadmeadows dist Melbourne, Vic
13 J7 Broadmere Queensland 25.30S 149.30E
113 N5 Broad Pass Alaska 63.11N 149.20W
105 G5 Broad,River S Carolina
13 J5 Broad Sound Queensland
13 K5 Broad Sound Chan Queensland
13 J6 Broadsound Ra Queensland
56 O5 Broadstairs Kent Eng 51.22N 1.27E
56 O2 Broads,The dist Norfolk Eng
108 E4 Broadus Montana 45.28N 105.22W
110 R3 Broadview Montana 46.06N 108.54W
109 G7 Broadview New Mexico 34.50N 103.12W
100 P8 Broadview Saskatchewan 50.22N 102.31W
56 G3 Broadwas Hereford & Worcs Eng 52.12N 2.21W
108 H8 Broadwater Nebraska 41.38N 102.52W
12 L3 Broadwater New S Wales 28.59S 13.16E
56 G6 Broadway Dorset Eng 50.39N 2.29W
56 H3 Broadway Hereford & Worcs Eng 52.02N 1.50W
104 G8 Broadway Virginia 38.36N 78.48W
56 F6 Broadwinsor Dorset Eng 50.49N 2.48W
11 H2 Broadwood New Zealand 35.17S 173.24E
53 D7 Broager Denmark 54.43N 9.53E
52 H10 Broby Sweden 56.15N 14.05E
66 E5 Broc Switzerland 46.37N 7.07E
72 C7 Brocas France 44.03N 0.32W
100 Q1 Brochet Manitoba 57.55N 101.40W
101 X6 Brochet, L Manitoba
98 C4 Brochet, L Quebec 49.40N 69.37W
63 G8 Brochterbeck W Germany 52.14N 7.45E
99 Q4 Brochu, L Quebec
108 P9 Brock Nebraska 40.28N 95.59W
100 J7 Brock Saskatchewan 51.26N 108.40W
63 L6 Brockel W Germany 53.06N 9.31E
63 M7 Bröckel W Germany 52.31N 10.13E
63 N9 Brocken mt E Germany 51.48N 10.37E
56 H6 Brockenhurst Hants Eng 50.49N 1.34W
100 D9 Brocket Alberta 49.34N 113.43W
108 M1 Brocket N Dakota 48.18N 98.21W
97 H2 Brock I N W Terr 78.00N 114.30W
57 N5 Brocklesby Lincs Eng 53.36N 0.17W
14 B6 Brockman,Mt W Australia 22.33S 117.24E
104 H3 Brockport New York 43.13N 77.56W
13 B2 Brock's Creek N Terr Australia 13.29S 131.26E
103 M2 Brockton Massachusetts 42.06N 71.01W
108 F1 Brockton Montana 48.10N 104.55W
99 P8 Brockville Ontario 44.35N 75.44W
108 E2 Brockway Montana 47.19N 105.45W
104 G5 Brockway Pennsylvania 41.15N 78.48W
118 K7 Brocoió,I.do Brazil 22.44S 43.08W
107 J2 Brocton Illinois 39.44N 87.56W
104 F4 Brocton New York 42.23N 79.27W
82 E5 Brod Yugoslavia 45.09N 18.00E
82 G9 Brod Yugoslavia 41.30N 21.15E
82 F7 Brodarevo Yugoslavia 43.14N 19.44E
45 W2 Brod Chuvashskiy U.S.S.R. 54.44N 50.04E
50 D3 Broddanes Iceland 65.35N 21.10W
100 L7 Broderick Saskatchewan 51.30N 106.54W
97 L3 Brodeur Pen N W Terr
106 E7 Brodhead Wisconsin 42.37N 89.23W
103 D5 Brodheadsville Pennsylvania 40.56N 75.25W
82 G6 Brodica Yugoslavia 44.29N 21.48E
104 G10 Brodnax Virginia 36.42N 78.03W
62 L2 Brodnica Poland 53.15N 19.23E
47 J7 Brodokalmak U.S.S.R. 55.35N 62.01E
46 F4 Brody Ukraine U.S.S.R. 50.05N 25.08E
61 J2 Broechem Belgium 51.10N 4.36E
95 J2 Broedersput S Africa 26.48S 25.08E
60 M6 Broek Friesland Netherlands 53.16N 6.00E
60 J10 Broek Noord-Holland Netherlands 52.26N 5.00E
60 N14 Broekhuizen Netherlands 51.29N 6.10E
60 N10 Broekland Netherlands 52.22N 6.12E
61 M3 Broekom Belgium 50.47N 5.20E
60 H9 Broek-op-Langendijk Netherlands 52.41N 4.48E
95 J6 Broekpoort R S Africa
48 V9 Broer Ruys,Kap C Greenland 73.30N 20.20W
18 B9 Broga Pen Malaysia 2.56N 101.55E
110 H5 Brogan Oregon 44.15N 117.30W
70 M3 Broglie France 49.01N 0.32E
66 L6 Broglio Switzerland 46.23N 8.40E
103 B7 Brogueville Pennsylvania 39.52N 76.29W
70 F5 Brohinière,la France 48.13N 2.08W
64 C3 Brohl-Lützing W Germany 50.28N 7.20E
71 G2 Broin France 47.04N 5.07E
63 M8 Broistedt W Germany 52.11N 10.20E
62 N3 Brok Poland 52.43N 21.50E
106 E4 Brokaw Wisconsin 45.03N 89.38W
63 K5 Brokdorf W Germany 53.52N 9.20E
109 P5 Broken Arrow Oklahoma 36.03N 95.47W
108 L8 Broken Bow Nebraska 41.26N 99.38W
109 Q7 Broken Bow Oklahoma 34.03N 94.45W
109 Q7 Broken Bow Res Oklahoma
Broken Hill see Kabwe Zambia
12 F4 Broken Hill New S Wales 31.57S 141.30E
50 C4 Brokey isld Iceland 65.05N 22.29W
39 E5 Brokhovo U.S.S.R. 59.39N 154.18E
117 B2 Brokopondo Surinam 5.05N 55.04W
117 B2 Brokopondo dist Surinam
63 L5 Brokstedt W Germany 53.59N 9.49E
66 M7 Brolla, Pass Switzerland 46.11N 8.46E
81 J7 Brolo Sicily 38.09N 14.50E
51 K12 Bromarv Finland 60.00N 23.03E
64 D8 Brombach W Germany 47.38N 7.42E
Bromberg see Bydgoszcz
63 N7 Brome W Germany 52.36N 10.57E
56 F3 Bromfield Shropshire Eng 52.23N 2.46W
56 G5 Bromham Wilts Eng 51.23N 2.03W
100 O9 Bromhead Saskatchewan 49.12N 103.42W
55 G3 Bromley Tower Hamlets, London England 51.31N 0.01W
92 E11 Bromley Zimbabwe 18.02S 31.28E
55 H5 Bromley bor London England
96 G12 Bromley Plat Atlantic Oc
52 E6 Bromma Norway 60.31N 9.13E
53 H6 Bromme Denmark 55.29N 11.32E
18 K9 Bromo mt Java Indon 7.55S 112.55E
108 S9 Brompton Iowa 40.57N 92.45W
116 H2 Brompton Jamaica, W I 18.05N 77.54W
57 M4 Brompton N Yorks Eng 54.13N 0.33W
56 G3 Bromsgrove Hereford & Worcs Eng 52.20N 2.03W
56 F3 Bromyard Hereford & Worcs Eng 52.11N 2.30W
56 D3 Bronant Dyfed Wales 52.17N 3.59W
107 B4 Bronaugh Missouri 37.42N 94.28W
75 G6 Bronchales Spain 40.30N 1.35W
52 E9 Brønderslev Denmark 57.16N 9.58E
53 A5 Brøndum Denmark 55.33N 8.30E
89 H8 Brong-Ahafo reg Ghana
79 F4 Broni Italy 45.04N 9.15E
95 M1 Bronkhorstspruit S Africa 25.50S 28.45E
95 M1 Bronkhorstspruitdam res S Africa 25.55S 28.41E
56 E3 Bronllys Powys Wales 52.01N 3.16W
48 T2 Brønlund Fd Greenland
64 L4 Bronn W Germany 49.43N 11.28E
52 H10 Brönnestad Sweden 56.05N 13.43E
47 K6 Bronnikovo U.S.S.R. 58.30N 68.29E
45 K1 Bronnitsy U.S.S.R. 55.25N 38.16E
51 C6 Brønnøysund Norway 65.38N 12.15E
64 H2 Bronnzell W Germany 50.31N 9.41E
53 B6 Brøns Denmark 55.12N 8.44E
105 E8 Bronson Florida 29.26N 82.39W
106 J8 Bronson Michigan 41.54N 85.12W
112 N4 Bronson Texas 31.23N 94.02W
99 L9 Bronte Ontario 43.23N 79.43W
81 J8 Bronte Sicily 37.47N 14.50E
112 G4 Bronte Texas 31.53N 100.20W
12 H8 Bronte Park Tasmania 42.10S 146.10E
103 M6 Bronx bor New York
103 L6 Bronxville New York 40.57N 73.49W
79 K2 Bronzolo Italy 46.24N 11.20E
98 D3 Brooch L Quebec
95 N2 Broodsnyersplaas S Africa 26.04S 29.29E
106 G9 Brook Indiana 40.52N 87.24W
103 C3 Brookdale Pennsylvania 41.59N 75.47W
104 H8 Brooke Virginia 38.23N 77.26W
59 H3 Brookeborough Fermanagh N Ireland 54.19N 7.24W
112 O4 Brookeland Texas 31.10N 94.00W
56 L3 Brook End Beds Eng 52.15N 0.26W
105 E8 Brooker Florida 29.53N 82.20W
14 B10 Brookes Inlet W Australia 34.53S 116.20E
19 H7 Brooke's Point Philippines 8.50N 117.52E
103 H4 Brookfield Connecticut 41.29N 73.24W
103 K2 Brookfield Massachusetts 42.13N 72.06W
107 C2 Brookfield Missouri 39.46N 93.04W
98 J8 Brookfield Nova Scotia 45.15N 63.18W
104 N2 Brookfield Vermont 44.03N 72.36W
106 P3 Brookfield dist Chicago, Illinois
103 J5 Brookhaven Long I, N Y 40.46N 72.49W
107 F10 Brookhaven Mississippi 31.36N 90.28W
100 N9 Brooking Saskatchewan 49.33N 104.26W
110 A7 Brookings Oregon 42.04N 124.17W
108 O5 Brookings S Dakota 44.19N 96.47W
13 H4 Brook Is.Lt.Ho Queensland 18.10S 146.20E
56 N6 Brookland Kent Eng 51.00N 0.50E
104 H5 Brookland Pennsylvania 41.51N 77.47W
100 A1 Brooklands Manitoba 49.55N 97.14W
104 C3 Brooklawn dist Philadelphia, Penn
105 F5 Brooklet Georgia 32.22N 81.40W
99 L9 Brooklin Ontario 43.58N 79.00W
104 P9 Brookline dist Boston, Mass
94 P11 Brooklyn Cape Town S Africa 33.54S 18.29E
103 L3 Brooklyn Connecticut 41.47N 71.57W
107 K2 Brooklyn Indiana 39.32N 86.23W
108 S8 Brooklyn Iowa 41.44N 92.26W
106 K7 Brooklyn Michigan 42.07N 84.18W
107 G10 Brooklyn Mississippi 31.03N 89.12W
12 L5 Brooklyn New S Wales 33.34S 151.13E
98 H9 Brooklyn Nova Scotia 44.04N 64.42W
103 C3 Brooklyn Pennsylvania 41.45N 75.49W
103 L8 Brooklyn bor New York
104 E2 Brooklyn dist Baltimore, Md
12 B7 Brooklyn dist Melbourne, Vic
11 C6 Brooklyn dist Wellington New Zealand
101 N11 Brookmere Br Col 49.48N 120.50W
104 G9 Brookneal Virginia 37.02N 78.57W
108 R4 Brook Park Minnesota 45.58N 93.02W
107 H4 Brookport Illinois 37.08N 88.40W
100 F8 Brooks Alberta 50.35N 111.54W
104 Q2 Brooks Maine 44.32N 69.09W
110 Q2 Brooks Montana 47.12N 109.26W
101 G5 Brooks Brook Yukon Terr 60.25N 133.10W
103 F2 Brooksburg New York 42.18N 74.12W
100 N5 Brooksby Saskatchewan 53.01N 104.19W
112 M6 Brookshire Texas 29.48N 95.59W
111 B8 Brooks I California 37.53N 122.20W
112 G9 Brookside Texas 29.35N 95.20W
113 K7 Brooks,L Alaska 58.30N 156.00W
113 D4 Brooks Mt Alaska 65.30N 167.09W
113 M5 Brooks,Mt Alaska 63.11N 150.41W
113 H2 Brooks Ra Alaska
106 H9 Brookston Indiana 40.36N 86.52W
108 S3 Brookston Minnesota 46.50N 92.35W
112 M2 Brookston Texas 33.38N 95.43W
56 M4 Brook Street Essex Eng 51.37N 0.17E
103 J4 Brooksvale Connecticut 41.28N 72.56W
105 E9 Brooksville Florida 28.34N 82.24W
104 S1 Brookton Maine 45.33N 67.47W
14 B9 Brookton W Australia 32.22S 116.59E
103 B2 Brooktondale New York 42.23N 76.24W
12 M6 Brookvale dist Sydney, N S W
107 M2 Brookville Indiana 39.25N 85.00W
109 N3 Brookville Kansas 38.46N 97.54W
107 H8 Brookville Mississippi 33.15N 88.37W
104 F5 Brookville Pennsylvania 41.10N 79.06W
13 H5 Brookville Queensland 20.11S 146.52E
107 J8 Brookwood Alabama 33.18N 87.19W
13 L7 Brooloo Queensland 26.30S 152.40E
103 D7 Broomall Pennsylvania 39.59N 75.22W
98 K4 Broom B Anticosti I, Que
14 D4 Broome W Australia 17.58S 122.15E
103 F2 Broome Center New York 42.27N 74.22W
14 C10 Broome Hill W Australia 33.50S 117.35E
14 F3 Broome, Mt W Australia 17.22S 125.22E
56 M4 Broomfield Essex Eng 51.47N 0.28E
58 F3 Broom,L Highland Scotland
57 K3 Broomley Northumb Eng 54.56N 1.56W
58 F3 Broom, Little L Highland Scotland
58 F3 Broom,R Highland Scotland
70 F5 Broons France 48.19N 2.15W
108 P4 Brooten Minnesota 45.30N 95.09W
14 F7 Brophy,Mt W Australia 26.45S 126.16E
14 G4 Brophy,Mt W Australia 19.17S 128.48E
119 C3 Broquelles,Pta Colombia 9.15N 76.13W
58 J2 Brora Highland Scotland 58.01N 3.51W
58 J2 Brora, L Highland Scotland 58.02N 3.57W
58 H2 Brora, R Highland Scotland
53 C6 Brørup Denmark 55.29N 9.01E
52 H11 Brösarp Sweden 55.43N 14.10E
56 G2 Broseley Shropshire Eng 52.37N 2.29W
59 G5 Brosna,R Offaly Irish Rep
59 F5 Brosna R.,Lit Tipperary etc Irish Rep
72 D5 Brossac France 45.20N 0.03W
99 T10 Brossard Quebec 45.28N 73.32W
79 B5 Brossasco Italy 44.34N 7.21E
82 H6 Broşteni Romania 44.46N 22.58E
82 K3 Broşteni Romania 47.14N 25.43E
76 C11 Brotas Portugal 38.52N 8.09W
118 G3 Brotas de Macaúbas Brazil 12.03S 42.39W
110 E6 Brothers Oregon 43.49N 120.36W
28 G7 Brothers islds Andaman Is
10 C10 Brothers Pt Macquarie I Pacific Oc 54.35S 158.57E
11 J8 Brothers, The I New Zealand 41.06S 174.27E
33 A3 Brothers,The islds Red Sea
33 K10 Brothers,The islds Socotra Ind Oc
75 K2 Broto Spain 42.36N 0.07W
64 J2 Brotterode E Germany 50.49N 10.27E
57 M3 Brotton Cleveland Eng 54.34N 0.56W
70 N5 Brou France 48.13N 1.10E
72 B4 Brouage France 45.51N 1.04W
57 J3 Brough Cumbria Eng 54.32N 2.19W
58 Q9 Brough Shetland Scotland 60.29N 1.12W
58 R9 Brough Whalsay, Shetland Scotland 60.22N 0.59W
58 S11 Brough Hd Orkney Scotland 59.09N 3.19W
58 T12 Brough Ness prom Orkney Scotland 58.44N 2.57W
59 K2 Broughshane Antrim N Ireland 54.54N 6.12W
57 G1 Broughton Borders Scotland 55.37N 3.25W
56 K3 Broughton Bucks Eng 52.04N 0.42W
57 H6 Broughton Clwyd Wales 53.10N 3.00W
57 G4 Broughton Cumbria Eng 54.17N 3.13W
107 H4 Broughton Illinois 37.56N 88.28W
109 N2 Broughton Kansas 39.18N 97.03W
57 H5 Broughton Lancs Eng 53.49N 2.44W
56 K3 Broughton Northants Eng 52.23N 0.46W
13 H5 Broughton Queensland 20.07S 146.26E
12 E5 Broughton R S Australia
12 K5 Broughton Island New S Wales 32.37S 152.20E
97 N4 Broughton Island N W Terr 67.30N 64.00W
99 T6 Broughton Sta Quebec 46.10N 71.10W
58 L6 Broughty Ferry Tayside Scotland 56.28N 2.53W
72 E8 Brouilh, le France 43.40N 0.24E
71 L9 Brouis,Col de France 43.55N 7.28E
34 C5 Broummānā Lebanon 33.53N 35.34E
62 J5 Broumov Czechoslovakia 50.36N 16.20E
40 M8 Broutona,O isld Kuril Is U.S.S.R. 46.40N 150.43E
72 L3 Broût-Vernet France 46.11N 3.16E
69 M7 Brouvelieures France 48.14N 6.44E
60 C2 Brouwershaven Netherlands 51.44N 3.55E
60 B1 Brouwershavensche Gat channel Netherlands
72 B2 Brouzils,les France 46.53N 1.20W
45 B6 Brovary Ukraine U.S.S.R. 50.30N 30.45E
66 L8 Brovello Italy 45.51N 8.32E
53 D2 Brovst Denmark 57.06N 9.32E
105 B10 Broward County Aerodrome Florida 26.06N 80.08W
108 Q3 Browerville Minnesota 46.06N 94.51W
15 J8 Brown R Papua New Guinea
116 G4 Brown Bank Atlantic Oc
106 M6 Brown City Michigan 43.13N 82.59W
Brown Cliffs see Roan Cliffs
109 L3 Brownell Kansas 38.38N 99.46W
14 E7 Browne Ra W Australia
112 E2 Brownfield Texas 33.11N 102.16W
12 B8 Brown Hill pk S Australia 34.59S 138.39E
56 H2 Brownhills W Midlands Eng 52.39N 1.55W
107 C1 Browning Missouri 40.03N 93.10W
110 M1 Browning Montana 48.33N 113.00W
100 P9 Browning Saskatchewan 49.26N 102.38W
11 F9 Browning Pass New Zealand 42.58S 171.20E
48 V11 Brown,Kap C Greenland 71.50N 22.25W
14 C9 Brown,L W Australia
108 K7 Brownlee Nebraska 42.18N 100.38W
100 M8 Brownlee Saskatchewan 50.43N 105.59W
59 K3 Brownlow Armagh N Ireland 54.28N 6.21W
12 E5 Brown,Mt S Australia 32.33S 138.02E
14 A3 Brown,Mt W Australia 32.11S 115.47E
12 C5 Brown,Pt S Australia 32.32S 133.52E
13 G3 Brown R Queensland
99 J3 Brownrigg Ontario 49.44N 81.28W
107 H3 Browns Illinois 38.23N 88.00W
11 C13 Browns New Zealand 46.10S 168.23E
112 M3 Brownsboro' Texas 32.19N 95.38W
107 K2 Brownsburg Indiana 39.50N 86.24W
99 Q7 Brownsburg Quebec 45.42N 74.25W
11 E2 Browns I New Zealand 30.50S 174.54E
103 E7 Browns Mills New Jersey 39.58N 74.35W
108 G8 Brownson Nebraska 41.12N 103.08W
12 F9 Browns R Tasmania
107 K3 Brownstown Indiana 38.52N 86.01W
116 J1 Brown's Town Jamaica, W I 18.28N 77.22W
103 B6 Brownstown Pennsylvania 40.08N 76.13W
108 O4 Browns Valley Minnesota 45.35N 96.50W
107 M2 Brownsville Indiana 39.40N 85.00W
107 K4 Brownsville Kentucky 37.10N 86.18W
110 C5 Brownsville Oregon 44.24N 122.59W
104 F6 Brownsville Pennsylvania 40.01N 79.55W
107 G6 Brownsville Tennessee 35.35N 89.15W
112 K10 Brownsville Texas 25.54N 97.30W
108 Q5 Brownton Minnesota 44.42N 94.20W
106 E7 Browntown Wisconsin 42.34N 89.49W
107 J8 Brownville Alabama 33.25N 87.45W
108 P9 Brownville Nebraska 40.23N 95.40W
104 K2 Brownville New York 44.01N 75.59W
104 Q1 Brownville Junc Maine 45.21N 69.06W
56 B6 Brown Willy mt Cornwall Eng 50.35N 4.36W
112 J4 Brownwood Texas 31.42N 98.59W
112 J4 Brownwood,L Texas
14 E2 Browse I Indian Ocean 14.04S 123.31E
58 K7 Broxburn Lothian Scotland 55.57N 3.29W
57 H6 Broxton Cheshire Eng 53.05N 2.47W
105 E6 Broxton Georgia 31.36N 82.57W
66 D4 Broye R Switzerland
66 E4 Broye R Switzerland
71 H2 Broye-lès-Pesmes-Aubigney-Montseugny France 47.19N 5.30E
69 F6 Broyes France 48.46N 3.47E
76 F9 Brozas Spain 39.37N 6.47W
79 K7 Brozzi Italy 43.48N 11.10E
79 H3 Brozzo Italy 45.44N 10.13E
65 N3 Brtnice Czechoslovakia 49.19N 15.41E
79 P4 Brtonigla Yugoslavia 45.23N 13.37E
50 K4 Brú Iceland 65.07N 15.33W
53 S15 Bru Norway 61.32N 5.11E
58 K2 Bruan Highland Scotland 58.20N 3.10W
50 E6 Brúará R Iceland
50 C5 Brúarfoss Iceland 64.44N 22.18W
50 J5 Brúarjökull ice cap Iceland 64.42N 16.10W
58 J5 Bruar Water R Tayside Scotland
Bruas see Beruas
Bruas R see Beruas R
69 D3 Bruay-en-Artois Pas de Calais France 50.29N 2.33E
69 F3 Bruay-sur-l'Escaut France 50.24N 3.33E
100 F5 Bruce Alberta 53.10N 112.00W
116 P6 Bruce Barbados 13.13N 59.34W
107 G7 Bruce Mississippi 34.00N 89.21W
108 O5 Bruce S Dakota 44.28N 96.52W
106 C4 Bruce Wisconsin 45.27N 91.18W
12 A5 Bruce dist Canberra Australia
11 D10 Bruce Bay New Zealand 43.37S 169.38E
106 E3 Bruce Crossing Michigan 46.32N 89.10W
99 J9 Brucefield Ontario 43.31N 81.32W
76 D9 Bruceira dam Portugal 39.30N 7.35W
99 G6 Bruce Mines Ontario 46.19N 83.48W
14 C6 Bruce,Mt W Australia 22.40S 117.06E
99 J7 Bruce Peninsula Ontario
14 C9 Bruce Rock W Australia 31.52S 118.09E
59 K1 Bruce's Castle Antrim N Ireland 55.17N 6.13W
107 H5 Bruceton Tennessee 36.02N 88.15W
112 K4 Bruceville Texas 31.20N 97.16W
69 N6 Bruche R France
63 K7 Bruchhausen-Vilsen W Germany 52.51N 9.01E
64 F3 Bruchköbel W Germany 50.10N 8.54E
64 F5 Bruchsal W Germany 49.07N 8.35E
65 G7 Bruck Austria 47.18N 12.49E
64 L4 Bruck Bayern W Germany 49.34N 11.00E
63 R8 Brück E Germany 52.12N 12.46E
65 P5 Bruck an der Leitha Austria 48.02N 16.47E
65 M7 Bruck an der Mur Austria 47.25N 15.17E
64 M6 Bruckberg W Germany 48.30N 12.00E
Brückenau see Bad Brückenau
64 N5 Bruck in der Oberpfalz Bayern W Germany 49.15N 12.19E
65 L8 Brückl Austria 46.45N 14.32E
81 K9 Brucoli Sicily 37.17N 15.11E
70 K3 Brucourt France 49.15N 0.06W
100 E5 Bruderheim Alberta 53.45N 112.51W
71 H9 Brue-Auriac France 43.31N 5.56E
63 P5 Brüel E Germany 53.44N 11.44E
56 F5 Brue, R Somerset Eng
72 J2 Bruère-Allichamps France 46.47N 2.25E
59 E7 Bruff Limerick Irish Rep 52.29N 8.33W
72 B1 Bruffière,la France 47.01N 1.13W
79 H3 Bruffione,Monte Italy 45.56N 10.29E
53 S15 Brufjord B Norway 61.32N 5.08E
95 J5 Brug,De S Africa 29.09S 25.49E
61 F4 Brugelette Belgium 50.36N 3.51E
Bruges Belgium see Brugge
72 D9 Bruges-Capbis-Mifaget France 43.06N 0.17W
66 J2 Brugg Switzerland 47.29N 8.13E
61 C2 Brugge Belgium 51.13N 3.14E
64 D1 Brügge W Germany 51.13N 7.04E
64 A1 Brüggen W Germany 51.15N 6.12E
79 L4 Brùgine Italy 45.18N 12.00E
79 F5 Brugneto,L.di L Italy
72 G8 Bruguières France 43.44N 1.25E
64 B2 Brühl W Germany 50.50N 6.55E
58 D7 Bruichladdich Islay, Strathclyde Scotland 55.46N 6.22W
104 F5 Bruin Pennsylvania 41.03N 79.44W
60 E13 Bruinisse Netherlands 51.40N 4.05E
111 O2 Bruin Pt mt Utah 39.39N 110.20W
28 L1 Bruint Assam India 29.07N 96.08E
95 J8 Bruintjieshoogte S Africa 32.40S 25.20E
115 F11 Bruja Pt Panama Canal Zone 8.53N 79.35W
86 L5 Brûk,Gebel el hill Egypt 30.11N 33.42E
94 E5 Brukkaros Namibia 25.40S 18.04E
94 D5 Brukkaros, Mt Namibia 25.54S 17.45E
86 L5 Brûk,Wâdi el watercourse Egypt
101 P9 Brûlé Alberta 53.17N 117.55W
108 J8 Brule Nebraska 41.06N 101.52W
106 C3 Brule Wisconsin 46.34N 91.35W
98 E2 Brûlé, L Quebec 51.05N 67.42W
99 N6 Brûlé, L Quebec 46.57N 77.13W
99 M7 Brûle Lake Sta Ontario 45.38N 78.49W
26 U14 Brûle, Le Réunion Ind Oc 20.55S 55.27E
66 O2 Brülisau Switzerland 47.17N 9.27E
70 K6 Brûlon France 47.58N 0.14W
61 J7 Brûly Belgium 49.58N 4.32E
61 H6 Brûly-de-Pesche Belgium 50.00N 4.28E
121 F3 Brum Uruguay 30.42S 57.20W
118 H4 Brumado Brazil 14.14S 41.38W
69 O6 Brumath France 48.44N 7.43E
57 M5 Brumby Humberside Eng 53.35N 0.40W
15 L9 Brumer Is Papua New Guinea 10.44S 150.14E
60 N11 Brummen Netherlands 52.05N 6.10E
52 F6 Brumunddal Norway 60.54N 11.00E
80 C3 Bruna R Italy
50 K3 Brunahvammur Iceland 65.32N 15.25W
50 H7 Brunasandur reg Iceland
66 N8 Brunate Italy 45.49N 9.07E
66 R5 Bruna, Val V Italy
50 M3 Brúnavík inlet Iceland
81 C3 Bruncu Spina mt Sardinia 40.02N 9.19E
112 H7 Brundage Texas 28.34N 99.42W
53 F5 Brundby Denmark 55.49N 10.37E
107 L10 Brundidge Alabama 31.42N 85.50W
110 K7 Bruneau Idaho 42.54N 115.49W
110 K7 Bruneau R Idaho
110 K7 Bruneau E. Fork R Idaho
110 K7 Bruneau W. Fork R Idaho
69 G4 Brunehamel France 49.46N 4.11E
18 L3 Brunei state Borneo S E Asia
18 L3 Brunei B Sabah Malaysia
Brunei Town see Bandar Seri Begawan
76 L8 Brunete Spain 40.25N 4.00W
13 D4 Brunette Cr N Terr Australia

13 D4 Brunette Downs N Terr Australia 18.33S 135.54E
98 R6 Brunette I Newfoundland 47.17N 55.55W
70 L2 Bruneval France 49.40N 0.10E
52 H3 Brunflo Sweden 63.04N 14.50E
76 B13 Brunheira Portugal 37.45N 8.45W
112 J8 Bruni Texas 27.26N 98.51W
79 L1 Brunico Italy 46.47N 11.57E
66 J4 Brünigen Switzerland 46.45N 8.09E
66 J4 Brünig Pass Switzerland 46.45N 8.07E
72 H7 Bruniquel France 44.03N 1.40E
53 Y20 Brunkeberg Norway 59.26N 8.29E
100 U9 Brunkild Manitoba 49.35N 97.38W
Brünn see Brno
65 N4 Brunn Austria 48.42N 15.32E
65 O5 Brunn Austria 48.06N 16.17E
64 N2 Brunn E Germany 50.39N 12.18E
50 J2 Brunna R Iceland
66 N2 Brunnadern Switzerland 47.21N 9.08E
53 K4 Brunnby Sweden 56.16N 12.36E
66 G7 Brunnegghorn mt Switzerland 46.08N 7.45E
66 L4 Brunnen Switzerland 46.59N 8.38E
11 F9 Brunner New Zealand 42.28S 171.12E
11 F9 Brunner, L New Zealand 42.37S 171.28E
50 K6 Brunnholl Iceland 64.18N 15.26W
66 L3 Brunni Switzerland 47.03N 8.43E
108 S3 Bruno Minnesota 46.15N 92.40W
100 M6 Bruno Saskatchewan 52.17N 105.31W
75 Q4 Bruñola Spain 41.54N 2.41E
68 G5 Brunoy France 48.42N 2.30E
63 K5 Brunsbüttelkoog W Germany 53.54N 9.08E
63 P4 Brunshaupten E Germany 54.09N 11.45E
63 L5 Brunshausen W Germany 53.38N 9.31E
60 T17 Brunssum Netherlands 50.57N 5.59E
53 V14 Brunstadhorn mt Norway 62.15N 6.40E
66 F1 Brunstatt France 47.43N 7.20E
Brunswick see Braunschweig W Germany
105 F6 Brunswick Georgia 31.09N 81.30W
104 Q3 Brunswick Maine 43.55N 69.59W
104 H7 Brunswick Maryland 39.19N 77.37W
107 C2 Brunswick Missouri 39.26N 93.08W
104 D5 Brunswick Ohio 41.14N 81.50W
12 C7 Brunswick dist Melbourne, Vic
14 E3 Brunswick B W Australia
14 B10 Brunswick Junction W Australia 33.15S 115.45E
99 G3 Brunswick L Ontario 49.00N 83.25W
121 K9 Brunswick,Pen.de Chile
62 K6 Bruntál Czechoslovakia 50.00N 17.27E
12 H9 Bruny I Tasmania
53 V18 Bruravik Norway 60.30N 6.52E
59 E7 Bruree Limerick Irish Rep 52.26N 8.36W
51 D6 Brurskanken mt Norway 65.46N 13.45E
Brusa see Bursa
79 K2 Brusago Italy 46.12N 11.19E
82 H7 Brusartsi Bulgaria 43.41N 23.01E
79 D4 Brusasco Italy 45.09N 8.04E
66 O5 Bruschg Horn mt Switzerland 46.38N 9.19E
53 U14 Brusdalsvatn L Norway 62.28N 6.26E
47 E5 Brusenets U.S.S.R. 60.16N 44.05E
109 G1 Brush Colorado 40.15N 103.36W
104 L2 Brushton New York 44.51N 74.30W
105 F1 Brushy Mts N Carolina
46 G4 Brusilov Ukraine U.S.S.R. 50.19N 29.35E
43 C2 Brusilovka Kazakhstan U.S.S.R. 50.39N 54.59E
66 R6 Brúsio Switzerland 46.16N 10.08E
115 M2 Brus Laguna Honduras 15.46N 84.32W
42 D2 Brusovo U.S.S.R. 60.36N 87.29E
121 J1 Brusque Brazil 27.07S 48.54W
72 K8 Brusque France 43.46N 2.57E
61 H3 Brussegem Belgium 50.56N 4.16E
61 S9 Brussel dist Bruxelles Belgium
Brussels Belgium see Bruxelles
99 J9 Brussels Ontario 43.44N 81.15W
95 H3 Brussels S Africa 27.08S 24.45E
106 G5 Brussels Wisconsin 44.44N 87.37W
79 C3 Brusson Italy 45.46N 7.44E
63 U6 Brüssow E Germany 53.25N 14.09E
61 L3 Brustem Belgium 50.48N 5.13E
46 C3 Brüster Ort C U.S.S.R. 54.58N 20.00E
12 J7 Bruthen Victoria 37.44S 147.49E
56 G5 Bruton Somerset Eng 51.07N 2.27W
50 V12 Bruun,Kapp C Spitsbergen 80.15N 25.15E
53 T18 Bruvik Norway 60.29N 5.40E
61 H3 Bruxelles Belgium 50.50N 4.21E
61 T9 Bruxelles National Aéroport Bruxelles Belgium 50.54N 4.29E
61 D4 Bruyelle Belgium 50.33N 3.26E
69 M7 Bruyères Vosges France 48.13N 6.43E
69 F4 Bruyères-et-Montbérault Aisne France 49.32N 3.41E
95 O5 Bruyns Hill S Africa 29.27S 30.40E
103 F3 Bruynswick New York 41.40N 74.15W
70 G5 Bruz France 48.01N 1.44W
119 E3 Bruzual Venezuela 8.03N 69.20W
79 E7 Bruzzano dist Milan Italy
81 M7 Bruzzano,C Italy 38.02N 16.09E
69 F3 Bry France 50.19N 3.41E
104 A5 Bryan Ohio 41.30N 84.34W
112 L5 Bryan Texas 30.41N 96.24W
110 Q8 Bryan Wyoming 41.35N 109.40W
123 G12 Bryan Coast Antarctica
45 K8 Bryanka Ukraine U.S.S.R. 48.32N 38.45E
42 E3 Bryanka U.S.S.R. 59.08N 93.30E
12 E5 Bryan,Mt S Australia 33.26S 138.27E
45 F3 Bryansk U.S.S.R. 53.15N 34.09E
44 H3 Bryanskaya Kosa,Mys C U.S.S.R. 44.24N 47.02E
46 H3 Bryanskaya Oblast' prov U.S.S.R.
44 H3 Bryanskoye U.S.S.R. 44.22N 47.00E
107 D7 Bryant Arkansas 34.38N 92.29W
106 K9 Bryant Indiana 40.32N 84.58W
40 D4 Bryanta R U.S.S.R.
107 D5 Bryant Cr Missouri
104 P2 Bryant Pond Maine 44.23N 70.38W
69 C3 Bryas France 50.25N 2.23E
111 M4 Bryce Canyon Nat.Park Utah 37.35N 112.13W
11 C13 Brydone New Zealand 46.15S 168.50E
61 J4 Brye Belgium 50.32N 4.33E
53 S15 Bryggja Norway 61.56N 5.25E
56 Q8 Bryher isld Is of Scilly Eng 49.57N 6.21W
56 D4 Bryn-amman Dyfed Wales 51.49N 3.52W
56 D4 Bryncethin Mid Glam Wales 51.33N 3.34W
56 C2 Bryn-crug Gwynedd Wales 52.36N 4.04W
11 M9 Bryndwr dist Christchurch New Zealand
52 B8 Bryne Norway 58.43N 5.40E
57 G6 Bryneglwys Clwyd Wales 53.01N 3.16W
57 E6 Bryngwran Gwynedd Wales 53.16N 4.29W
51 J1 Brynilen Norway 70.14N 21.10E
46 L6 Bryn'kovskaya U.S.S.R. 46.02N 38.39E
56 E4 Brynmawr Gwent Wales 51.49N 3.11W
103 D6 Bryn Mawr Pennsylvania 40.02N 75.19W
82 L2 Brynzen U.S.S.R. 48.02N 27.10E
53 D4 Bryrup Denmark 56.02N 9.32E
112 J2 Bryson Texas 33.11N 98.23W
105 D2 Bryson City N Carolina 35.26N 83.27W
99 N6 Bryson,L Quebec
68 H3 Bry-sur-Marne France 48.50N 2.32E
44 C2 Bryukhovetskaya U.S.S.R. 45.48N 39.00E
39 B3 Bryuneyade R U.S.S.R.
39 C3 Bryungyadinskiye Gory mts U.S.S.R.
41 N2 Bryusa,Ostrov isld Franz Josef Land U.S.S.R.
82 G6 Brza Palanka Yugoslavia 44.30N 22.25E
62 K5 Brzeg Poland 50.52N 17.27E
62 M6 Brzesko Poland 49.59N 20.34E
62 M4 Brzeziny Poland 51.49N 19.42E
62 L4 Brzeźnica Poland 51.03N 19.10E
62 N6 Brzozów Poland 49.41N 22.00E
Bseïra see Buseire
70 O4 Bû France 48.48N 1.30E
53 V18 Bu Norway 60.28N 6.50E
33 F8 Bū Yemen 16.18N 45.07E
91 C7 Bua Angola 7.12S 13.12E
25 L7 Bua Assam India 27.50N 93.58E
19 B5 Bua Celebes Indon 3.05S 120.15E
92 G8 Bua R Malawi
89 J9 Buabin Ghana 5.53N 1.45W
19 M6 Buad isld Philippines 11.40N 124.50E
9 A8 Buada Lagoon Nauru, Pacific Oc 0.31S 166.55E
70 J4 Buais France 48.32N 0.57W
9 D4 Buakonikai Ocean I Pacific Oc 0.52S 169.36E
15 L3 Buala Santa Isabel I Solomon Is 8.11S 159.37E
85 E6 Bū al Hidān watercourse Libya
33 E9 Bū'ān Yemen 15.11N 43.59E
89 G7 Buandougou Ivory Coast 8.18N 5.32W
19 D2 Buang isld Indonesia 3.56N 125.44E
19 B6 Buapinang Celebes Indon 4.46S 121.38E
53 U18 Buarbre glacier Norway 60.04N 6.25E
76 B8 Buarcos Portugal 40.10N 8.53W
39 D2 Buar-Yuryakh R U.S.S.R.
85 D5 Bū ash Shawk R Libya
85 C4 Bū Athla Libya 30.09N 15.39E
85 G7 Bu Athla Libya 25.40N 22.07E
85 F5 Bū Athlah Libya 29.45N 21.29E
Bua Yai see Ban Bua Yai
33 J4 Bu'ayj Saudi Arabia 24.36N 50.40E
89 B6 Buba Guinea-Bissau 11.36N 14.55W
76 D5 Bubal R Spain
91 F1 Bubanda Zaïre 4.14N 19.41E
93 C5 Bubango Uganda 0.45N 31.04E
93 A9 Bubanza Burundi 3.05S 29.22E
84 Y21 Bubaqra Malta 35.49N 14.29E
89 B6 Bubaque Guinea-Bissau 11.16N 15.51W
87 J6 Bubasa Ethiopia 9.02N 42.11E
79 D5 Búbbio Italy 44.40N 8.18E
93 D6 Bubeke I Uganda 0.20S 32.37E
66 G2 Bubendorf Switzerland 47.27N 7.45E
63 S7 Buberow E Germany 52.58N 13.11E
92 D11 Bubi dist Zimbabwe
92 D11 Bubi R Zimbabwe
93 K3 Bubisa Kenya 2.44N 38.05E
33 M9 Būbiyān, Jazīrat isld Kuwait
70 D6 Bubry France 47.58N 3.10W
39 C3 Bubr-Yuryakh R U.S.S.R.
15 L6 Bubu New Britain 5.16S 151.02E
92 G4 Bubu R Tanzania
19 K8 Bubuan isld Philippines 6.20N 121.59E
19 K9 Bubuan isld Philippines 5.23N 120.20E
92 J12 Bububu Zanzibar 6.06S 39.13E
18 A7 Bubu,Gunong mt Pen Malaysia 4.41N 100.47E
93 F5 Bubulo Uganda 0.56N 34.18E
91 F3 Buburu Zaïre 1.25N 18.03E
57 M5 Bubwith Humberside Eng 53.48N 0.55W
92 E12 Bubye R Zimbabwe
36 C4 Buca Turkey 38.22N 27.10E
76 C8 Buçaco Portugal 40.22N 8.21W
76 C8 Buçaco mt Portugal 40.22N 8.21W
36 E5 Bucak Burdur Turkey 37.28N 30.37E
37 E8 Bucak Diyarbakır Turkey 37.51N 39.03E
36 G6 Bucakkışla Turkey 36.56N 33.02E
119 D4 Bucaramanga Colombia 7.08N 73.10W
19 M7 Bucas Grande isld Philippines 9.38N 125.58E
119 B9 Bucay Ecuador 2.10S 79.10W
14 E3 Buccaneer Arch W Australia
81 J9 Buccheri Sicily 37.08N 14.51E
80 K4 Bucchianico Italy 42.18N 14.10E
80 M7 Buccino Italy 40.37N 15.23E
66 K8 Buccione Italy 45.46N 8.26E
82 K3 Bucecea Romania 47.45N 26.30E
76 A11 Bucelas Portugal 38.54N 9.07W
71 H2 Bucey-lès-Gy France 47.25N 5.50E
46 F5 Buchach Ukraine U.S.S.R. 49.09N 25.20E
12 J6 Buchan Victoria 37.30S 148.09E
58 M3 Buchan dist Grampian Scotland
105 B4 Buchanan Georgia 33.48N 85.13W
89 D9 Buchanan Liberia 5.57N 10.02W
106 H8 Buchanan Michigan 41.50N 86.24W
108 M2 Buchanan N Dakota 47.03N 98.49W
109 F7 Buchanan New Mexico 34.25N 104.47W
103 G4 Buchanan New York 41.16N 73.58W
100 P7 Buchanan Saskatchewan 51.41N 102.42W
104 F9 Buchanan Virginia 37.33N 79.43W
13 D4 Buchanan R N Terr Australia
112 J5 Buchanan Dam Texas 30.44N 98.26W
13 B4 Buchanan Hills N Terr Australia
13 H5 Buchanan,L Queensland
14 E7 Buchanan,L W Australia 25.30S 123.00E
112 J5 Buchanan Res Texas
58 N4 Buchan,Bullers of rocks Grampian Scotland 57.26N 1.49W
97 M3 Buchan G N W Terr
58 N4 Buchan Ness headland Grampian Scotland 57.28N 1.47W
98 Q5 Buchans Newfoundland 48.49N 56.53W
98 Q5 Buchans Junction Newfoundland 48.51N 56.28W
121 D5 Buchardo Argentina 34.44S 63.29W
Bucharest see Bucureşti
64 N7 Buchbach W Germany 48.18N 12.18E
66 L1 Buchberg Switzerland 47.34N 8.34E
65 A7 Buchboden Austria 47.16N 9.57E
66 F3 Buchegg Berg Switzerland
29 C2 Bucheki Pakistan 31.20N 73.42E
64 G4 Buchen Baden-Württemberg W Germany 49.32N 9.21E
63 N6 Büchen Schleswig Holstein W Germany 53.28N 10.38E
64 C4 Büchenbeuren W Germany 49.56N 7.16E
64 L1 Buchenwald site E Germany 51.03N 11.15E
92 F3 Buchenzi Tanzania 2.25S 32.20E
63 R8 Buchholz E Germany 52.09N 12.55E
63 L6 Buchholz W Germany 53.20N 9.53E
64 K8 Buching W Germany 47.38N 10.49E
64 K7 Buchloe W Germany 48.04N 10.45E
58 H6 Buchlyvie Central Scotland 56.07N 4.18W
111 D6 Buchon,Pt California 35.15N 120.54W
66 J2 Buchs Aargau Switzerland 47.24N 8.04E
66 O3 Buchs St Gallen Switzerland 47.10N 9.28E
60 T16 Buchten Netherlands 51.02N 5.48E
93 K9 Buchuma Kenya 3.38S 38.54E
121 A6 Buchupureo Chile 36.05S 72.46W
70 N2 Buchy France 49.35N 1.22E
75 F7 Buciegas Spain 40.20N 2.27W
80 E2 Búcine Italy 43.28N 11.37E
109 C6 Buck New Mexico 35.47N 107.43W
103 B7 Buck Pennsylvania 39.52N 76.14W
12 H4 Buckambool Mt New S Wales 31.55S 145.40E
107 H10 Buckatunna Mississippi 31.32N 88.33W
56 L6 Buck Barn W Sussex Eng 51.00N 0.21W
56 L3 Buckden Cambs Eng 52.18N 0.15W
57 J4 Buckden N Yorks Eng 54.12N 2.05W
63 K8 Bückeburg W Germany 52.16N 9.03E
63 K7 Bücken W Germany 52.47N 9.08E
111 M8 Buckeye Arizona 33.25N 112.34W
104 C7 Buckeye Lake Ohio 39.56N 82.30W
104 H7 Buckeystown Maryland 39.22N 77.25W
56 D7 Buckfastleigh Devon Eng 50.29N 3.46W
104 E8 Buckhannon W Virginia 38.59N 80.14W
104 E7 Buckhannon R W Virginia
58 K6 Buckhaven Fife Scotland 56.11N 3.03W
105 C4 Buckhead Georgia 33.50N 84.23W
103 D4 Buck Hill Falls Pennsylvania 41.12N 75.17W
112 K5 Buckholts Texas 30.54N 97.08W
108 F5 Buckhorn Wyoming 44.10N 104.05W
55 H2 Buckhurst Hill Essex Eng 51.38N 0.03E
105 L8 Buck I Virgin Is 17.47N 64.39W
58 L3 Buckie Grampian Scotland 57.40N 2.58W
56 K3 Buckingham Bucks Eng 52.00N 1.00W
103 D6 Buckingham Pennsylvania 40.18N 75.03W
99 P7 Buckingham Quebec 45.35N 75.25W
112 O8 Buckingham Texas 32.54N 96.44W
104 G9 Buckingham Virginia 37.33N 78.34W
56 K4 Buckingham co England
13 D1 Buckingham B N Terr Australia
13 E5 Buckingham Downs Queensland 22.04S 139.45E
55 F3 Buckingham Palace London Eng 51.30N 0.08W
100 C5 Buck L Alberta 53.00N 114.42W
13 B4 Buck,L N Terr Australia
113 G4 Buckland Alaska 65.59N 161.19W
113 G4 Buckland R Alaska
56 G5 Buckland Denham Somerset Eng 51.16N 2.22W
100 V1 Buckland L Manitoba
11 E2 Bucklands Beach New Zealand 36.52S 174.54E
13 J6 Buckland Tableland Queensland
12 D5 Buckleboo S Australia 32.52S 136.08E
14 G2 Buckle Hd W Australia 14.24S 127.51E
123 K5 Buckle I Antarctica 66.50S 163.20E
10 C10 Buckles B Macquarie I Pacific Oc
106 F9 Buckley Illinois 40.35N 88.04W
106 J5 Buckley Michigan 44.31N 85.41W
110 C2 Buckley Washington 47.10N 122.04W
13 E5 Buckley R Queensland
65 O6 Bucklige Welt reg Austria
109 L4 Bucklin Kansas 37.33N 99.39W
107 D2 Bucklin Missouri 39.47N 92.54W
103 C5 Buck Mt Pennsylvania 40.58N 75.48W
Buckner Bay see Nakagusuku-wan
108 D6 Bucknum Wyoming 43.03N 106.35W
63 U7 Buckow E Germany 52.34N 14.06E
103 C7 Buck Run Pennsylvania 39.56N 75.52W
111 C2 Bucks California 39.51N 121.10W
103 D6 Bucks co Pennsylvania
58 M4 Bucksburn Grampian Scotland 57.11N 2.10W
56 L5 Bucks Green W Sussex Eng 51.05N 0.28W
111 L7 Buckskin Mts Arizona
111 C2 Bucks Mt California 39.58N 121.10W
104 R2 Bucksport Maine 44.35N 68.47W
63 Q7 Bückwitz E Germany 52.52N 12.29E
65 Q3 Bucovice Czechoslovakia 49.09N 17.01E
91 C6 Buco Zau Angola 4.45S 12.34E
69 D3 Bucquoy France 50.09N 2.43E
98 H7 Buctouche New Brunswick 46.28N 64.46W
82 K6 Bucureşti Romania 44.25N 26.07E
19 K8 Bucutua isld Philippines 6.09N 121.50E
69 F4 Bucy-les-Pierrepont France 49.39N 3.54E
108 H3 Bucyrus N Dakota 46.04N 102.50W
104 C6 Bucyrus Ohio 40.47N 82.57W
52 C4 Bud Norway 62.54N 6.56E
112 K5 Buda Texas 30.05N 97.52W
93 F4 Budadiri Uganda 1.12N 34.20E
62 L8 Budafok Hungary 47.27N 19.01E
42 G6 Budagovo U.S.S.R. 54.37N 100.08E
Budai'a see Budayyi,Al
75 M6 Buda,I.de Spain 40.42N 0.50E
93 E4 Budaka Uganda 1.02N 33.58E
45 B4 Buda-Koshelevo Belorussiya U.S.S.R. 52.43N 30.34E
25 C1 Budalin Burma 22.24N 95.08E
92 E1 Budana Zaïre 1.40N 30.07E
62 L8 Budapest Hungary 47.30N 19.03E
30 C4 Budaun Uttar Prad India 28.02N 79.07E
30 B4 Budaun dist Uttar Prad India
33 E5 Budayyi'ah Saudi Arabia 22.56N 43.38E
33 J3 Budayyi,Al Bahrain, The Gulf 26.11N 50.28E
87 L8 Bud Bud Somalia 4.11N 46.27E
29 L2 Bud Bud W Bengal India 23.25N 87.30E
57 L6 Budby Notts Eng 53.14N 1.05W
12 G4 Budda New S Wales 31.12S 144.16E
123 F2 Budd Coast Antarctica
30 H8 Buddh Gaya Bihar India 24.42N 85.00E
87 J8 Buddi Ethiopia 5.32N 43.02E
14 B8 Budd,Mt W Australia 29.16S 115.48E
103 E7 Buddtown New Jersey 39.57N 74.42W
81 C2 Buddusò Sardinia 40.34N 9.16E
56 B6 Bude Cornwall Eng 50.50N 4.33W
107 F10 Bude Mississippi 31.29N 90.50W
60 L14 Budel Netherlands 51.17N 5.35E
60 L15 Budel-Dorplein Netherlands 51.14N 5.35E
81 C1 Budelli, I Sardinia 41.17N 9.22E
63 L4 Büdelsdorf W Germany 54.19N 9.37E
41 F1 Budennogo,Mys C U.S.S.R. 80.08N 90.40E
46 R4 Budennovka Kazakhstan U.S.S.R. 50.52N 52.49E
Budennovka Ukraine U.S.S.R. see Novoazovsk
Budennovsk see Prikumsk
44 F3 Budennovsk U.S.S.R. 44.46N 44.10E
44 D1 Budennovskaya U.S.S.R. 46.56N 41.33E
Budennovskiy see Oktyabr'skiy Rostov U.S.S.R
Budennoye see Krasnogvardeyskoye
43 K6 Budennyy Kirgiziya U.S.S.R. 42.28N 72.29E
76 B14 Budens Portugal 37.05N 8.50W
63 E9 Büderich W Germany 51.37N 6.35E
63 G9 Büderich W Germany 51.32N 7.51E
69 K4 Büderscheid Luxembourg 49.56N 5.57E
82 K6 Budeşti Romania 44.13N 26.30E
29 L6 Budge-Budge W Bengal India 22.29N 88.11E
50 B5 Budhahraun lava field Iceland
30 A3 Budhana Uttar Prad India 29.17N 77.29E
31 E8 Budhapur Pakistan 25.36N 68.23E
50 D4 Búdhardalur Iceland 65.06N 21.46W
50 L4 Budhareyrí Iceland 65.02N 14.12W
50 F6 Búdharháls ridge Iceland
50 B5 Búdhavík inlet Iceland
50 L5 Búdhir Múlasýsla, Sudhur Iceland 64.57N 14.01W
50 B5 Búdhir Snæfellsnessýsla Iceland 64.49N 23.25W
86 K6 Budhîya,Gebel ra Egypt
29 D3 Budhlada Punjab India 29.54N 75.38E
75 E6 Budia Spain 40.38N 2.46W
121 A7 Budi,L.del Chile
32 G7 Būding Iran 26.02N 57.57E
61 L3 Budingen Belgium 50.52N 5.06E
64 G3 Büdingen W Germany 50.17N 9.07E
65 O3 Budišov Czechoslovakia 49.17N 16.01E
88 H8 Budit Morocco 26.38N 10.41W
91 F2 Budjala Zaïre 2.38N 19.48E
58 N7 Budle B Northumb Eng 55.37N 1.46W
56 E6 Budleigh Salterton Devon Eng 50.38N 3.20W
31 F1 Budob Afghanistan 38.10N 70.50E
46 J1 Budogoshch U.S.S.R. 59.16N 32.30E
79 N2 Budoia Italy 46.03N 12.32E
90 C7 Budon Nigeria 8.20N 6.23E
18 N6 Budongbudong Sulawesi Indonesia 2.03S 119.14E
24 H8 Budongquan Qinghai China 35.32N 93.54E
79 L5 Budrio Italy 44.32N 11.32E
35 C6 Budrus Jordan 31.58N 34.59E
93 F4 Bududa Uganda 1.00N 34.19E
33 H5 Budū', Sabkhat al salt marsh Saudi Arabia
82 E8 Budva Yugoslavia 42.17N 18.50E
Budweis see České Budějovice
45 H7 Budy Ukraine U.S.S.R. 49.54N 36.02E
90 D9 Buea Cameroon 4.09N 9.13E
85 M7 Bûêb Egypt 24.45N 32.57E
85 E4 Bueb,B.of Libya
71 H8 Buech R France
69 A6 Buéi France 48.56N 1.25E
70 N4 Buéil France 48.56N 1.27E
35 E2 Bu'eina Israel 32.49N 35.22E
91 D6 Buela Angola 5.54S 14.40E
111 D7 Buellton California 34.38N 120.13W
75 H6 Buena Spain 40.43N 1.16W
75 F8 Buenache de Alarcón Spain 39.39N 2.10W
75 F7 Buenache de la Sierra Spain 40.08N 2.00W
121 D5 Buena Esperanza Argentina 34.45S 65.15W
119 C6 Buenaventura Colombia 3.54N 77.02W
115 F3 Buenaventura Mexico 29.50N 107.30W
119 C6 Buenaventura,B.de Colombia 3.51N 77.06W
120 F7 Buena Vista Bolivia 17.28S 63.37W
109 D3 Buena Vista Colorado 38.50N 106.08W
105 C5 Buena Vista Georgia 32.18N 84.32W
115 H7 Buenavista Jalisco Mexico 20.57N 102.30W
115 H8 Buenavista Michoacan Mexico 19.12N 102.34W
19 M7 Buenavista Mindanao Philippines 8.58N 125.27E
19 K5 Buenavista Philippines 13.16N 121.56E
96 Q14 Buenavista Tenerife Canary Is 28.22N 16.51W
104 F9 Buena Vista Virginia 37.44N 79.22W
75 P8 Buenavista dist Madrid Spain
111 E6 Buena Vista dry lake California 35.10N 119.20W
77 N2 Buenavista mt Spain 39.13N 1.59W
116 E3 Buena Vista,B.de Cuba 22.30N 79.00W
76 K3 Buenavista de Valdavia Spain 42.38N 4.37W
75 E7 Buendía Spain 40.21N 2.45W
75 E7 Buendía,Embalse de res Spain 40.22N 2.43W
53 W16 Buene Norway 61.04N 7.03E
Buenë R see Bojana R
94 N3 Buene, I Mozambique 20.28S 34.40E
121 A8 Bueno R Chile
118 E4 Buenolândia Brazil 15.47S 50.19W
111 E9 Bueno Park dist Los Angeles, Cal
118 G5 Buenópolis Brazil 17.58S 44.10W
119 E9 Buenos Aires Amazonas Colombia 3.10S 69.59W
121 F5 Buenos Aires Argentina 34.40S 58.30W
120 C3 Buenos Aires Brazil 8.30S 72.55W
119 D7 Buenos Aires Caqueta Colombia 1.33N 73.16W
115 N5 Buenos Aires Costa Rica 9.10N 83.23W
115 F10 Buenos Aires Panama 9.11N 79.37W
121 J6 Buenos Aires L Arg/Chile
121 E6 Buenos Aires prov Argentina
116 N2 Buenos Ayres Trinidad & Tobago 10.06N 61.41W
121 K5 Buen Pasto Argentina 45.08S 69.30W
121 L8 Buen Tiempo,C Argentina 51.30S 69.00W
63 H8 Buer Niedersachsen W Germany 52.14N 8.24E
118 H4 Buerarema Brazil 14.59S 39.19W
119 C7 Buesaco Colombia 1.22N 77.07W
19 N4 Buet isld Truk Is Pacific Oc 7.34N 151.53E
71 K4 Buet,Mt France 46.01N 6.53E
76 B4 Bueu Spain 42.19N 8.47W
119 C4 Buey,Alto del mt Colombia 6.05N 77.12W
109 G6 Bueyeros New Mexico 35.58N 103.41W
77 P3 Bufalí Spain 38.53N 0.31W
115 G4 Búfalo Mexico 27.17N 105.10W
15 E5 Bufareh Irian Jaya 2.15S 138.50E
100 G8 Buffalo Alberta 50.49N 110.42W
109 P4 Buffalo Kansas 37.43N 95.43W
107 L4 Buffalo Kentucky 37.29N 85.41W
108 R4 Buffalo Minnesota 45.11N 93.50W
107 C4 Buffalo Missouri 37.40N 93.08W
110 Q3 Buffalo Montana 46.49N 109.50W
108 N3 Buffalo N Dakota 46.56N 97.32W
104 G4 Buffalo New York 42.52N 78.55W
109 L5 Buffalo Oklahoma 36.51N 99.38W
105 F3 Buffalo S Carolina 34.43N 81.41W
108 G4 Buffalo S Dakota 45.25N 103.35W
112 L4 Buffalo Texas 31.27N 96.04W
104 D8 Buffalo W Virginia 38.39N 81.57W
108 D5 Buffalo Wyoming 44.21N 106.40W
100 E6 Buffalo L Alberta
101 Q6 Buffalo R Alberta/N W Terr
107 C6 Buffalo R Arkansas
108 O3 Buffalo R Minnesota
95 O4 Buffalo R S Africa
107 J6 Buffalo R Tennessee
112 F9 Buffalo R Texas
106 C5 Buffalo R Wisconsin
110 Q5 Buffalo Bill Dam Wyoming 44.30N 109.10W
110 Q5 Buffalo Bill Res Wyoming 44.30N 109.15W
108 R6 Buffalo Center Iowa 43.25N 93.58W
109 E2 Buffalo Creek Colorado 39.22N 105.16W
100 M9 Buffalo Gap Saskatchewan 49.04N 105.17W
108 G6 Buffalo Gap S Dakota 43.30N 103.20W
23 B8 Buffalo Hill Hong Kong 22.23N 114.13E
101 Q5 Buffalo L N W Terr
112 E1 Buffalo L Texas
12 H6 Buffalo,Mt Victoria 36.47S 146.03E
100 J3 Buffalo Narrows Saskatchewan 55.52N 108.28W
100 M8 Buffalo Pound Prov.Park Saskatchewan
101 Q5 Buffalo River N W Terr 60.53N 115.02W
93 J5 Buffalo Springs Kenya 0.33N 37.39E
84 R14 Buffavento Castle Cyprus 35.17N 33.24E
116 L1 Buff Bay Jamaica, W I 18.18N 76.40W
95 D10 Buffeljagsrivier S Africa 34.03S 20.33E
95 O3 Buffels R S Africa
94 D7 Buffels watercourse S Africa
94 P12 Buffelsbaai B Cape Town S Africa
95 F9 Buffelsdrif S Africa 33.44S 22.47E
71 F4 Buffières France 46.26N 4.32E
105 D3 Buford Georgia 34.09N 83.59W
108 G1 Buford N Dakota 48.00N 103.59W
108 E8 Buford Wyoming 41.08N 105.16W
82 K6 Buftea Romania 44.34N 25.58E
63 S3 Bug E Germany 54.37N 13.14E
46 E4 Bug R Poland/U.S.S.R.
62 O4 Bug R Poland/U.S.S.R.
46 E4 Bug R Ukraine U.S.S.R.
119 C6 Buga Colombia 3.53N 76.17W
93 E5 Bugaia I Uganda 0.03N 33.16E
119 C5 Bugalagrande Colombia 4.11N 76.07W
93 D6 Bugala I Uganda
12 J4 Bugaldie New S Wales 31.02S 149.08E
93 A8 Buganda Burundi 2.56S 29.13E
72 J10 Bugarach, Pic de France 42.52N 2.22E
93 B8 Bugarama Tanzania 2.51S 30.35E
42 K5 Bugarikhta U.S.S.R. 54.05N 115.00E
41 F8 Bugarikta U.S.S.R. 64.48N 90.16E
75 J8 Bugarra Spain 39.36N 0.47W
22 E3 Bugat Mongolia 47.54N 101.17E
93 E4 Bugaya Uganda 1.05N 33.13E
82 N4 Bugaz U.S.S.R. 46.03N 30.25E
87 K8 Bugda Acable Somalia 4.03N 45.10E
87 K8 Bugda Cosar Somalia 4.31N 44.50E
37 E3 Buğdaylı Turkey 40.13N 27.46E
43 C7 Bugdayli Turkmeniya U.S.S.R. 38.34N 54.34E
72 H4 Bugeat France 45.36N 1.55E
18 J9 Bugel Tanjung Java Indon 6.25S 111.02E
77 V14 Búger Balearic Is 39.46N 2.59E
93 C7 Bugere Tanzania 1.35S 31.09E
71 H5 Bugey reg France
61 G2 Buggenhout Belgium 51.01N 4.12E
60 M15 Buggenum Netherlands 51.14N 5.59E
81 A5 Buggerru Sardinia 39.24N 8.23E
Buggs Island L see Kerr L Virginia
84 Y20 Bugibba Malta 35.57N 14.25E
96 R8 Bugio isld Madeira Is 32.25N 16.29W
76 A11 Bugio Lt Ho Portugal 38.40N 9.17W
93 E5 Bugiri Uganda 0.34N 33.46E
72 C9 Bugnein France 43.21N 0.46W
82 D6 Bugojno Yugoslavia 44.03N 17.28E
93 C10 Bugomba Tanzania 4.01S 31.59E
93 D6 Bugombe Uganda 0.05S 32.46E
93 E4 Bugondo Uganda 1.37N 33.18E
93 B9 Bugongo mt Burundi 3.41S 30.21E
42 H2 Bugorkan U.S.S.R. 62.02N 108.10E
42 C4 Bugotak U.S.S.R. 55.10N 83.49E
51 O2 Bugøynes Norway 69.58N 29.40E
88 G8 Bu Graa Morocco 26.21N 12.57W
47 F2 Bugrino U.S.S.R. 68.45N 49.15E
45 C10 Bugskiy Liman lagoon Ukraine U.S.S.R.
19 H7 Bugsuk isld Philippines 8.15N 117.17E
21 B3 Bugt Nei Monggol Zizhiqu China 48.45N 121.58E
31 E6 Bugti reg Pakistan
72 F6 Bugue,le France 44.55N 0.56E
19 K2 Buguey Luzon Philippines 18.16N 121.52E
19 L5 Bugui Pt Philippines 12.36N 123.15E
42 H5 Bugul'deyka U.S.S.R. 52.32N 106.05E
46 R3 Bugul'ma U.S.S.R. 54.32N 52.46E
43 F4 Bugun' Kazakhstan U.S.S.R. 46.07N 61.14E
93 B8 Bugungu mt Burundi 2.58S 30.24E
Bugur see Luntai
24 E4 Bugur Tau mts Xinjiang Uygur Zizhiqu China
46 Q3 Buguruslan U.S.S.R. 53.36N 52.30E
43 J5 Bugyn'skoye,Vdkhr res Kazakhstan U.S.S.R.
28 J2 Buha Assam India 27.44N 93.59E
32 F5 Būhābād Iran 31.50N 55.56E
85 D4 Bū Hādi, Qr Libya 31.02N 16.40E
33 K5 Bu Hasa oil field U.A.E. 23.35N 53.20E
86 H5 Buheirat-Murrat-el-Kubra L Egypt 30.20N 32.23E
86 J5 Buheirat-Murrat-el-Sughra L Egypt 30.14N 32.32E
35 G10 Buheithan,Jeb.el mt Jordan 30.55N 35.52E
93 F7 Buhemba Tanzania 1.47S 34.07E
92 E11 Buhera Zimbabwe 19.18S 31.29E
92 E11 Buhera dist Zimbabwe
22 E8 Buh He R Qinghai China
19 L5 Buhi Luzon Philippines 13.25N 123.33E
92 E3 Buhiga Burundi 3.00S 30.09E
Buhkanum see Ban Bu Khanum
110 L7 Buhl Idaho 42.37N 114.46W
108 S2 Buhl Minnesota 47.30N 92.45W
64 E6 Bühl W Germany 48.41N 8.08E
66 O2 Bühler Switzerland 47.23N 9.26E
69 P6 Bühlertal W Germany 48.41N 8.11E
64 H5 Bühlertann W Germany 49.02N 9.55E
Buhnabad see Bohnābād
93 F5 Buholo Kenya 0.12N 34.23E
93 A9 Buhonga Burundi 3.25S 29.25E
93 B10 Buhoro Tanzania 4.30S 30.46E
92 G6 Buhoro Flats V Tanzania
34 M5 Buhriz Iraq 33.42N 44.40E
95 O2 Buhrmannskop S Africa 26.28S 30.02E
37 G8 Bühtan R Turkey
93 B4 Buhuka Uganda 1.14N 30.45E
82 K4 Buhuşi Romania 46.41N 26.45E
86 F3 Buhût Egypt 31.10N 31.19E
79 O2 Buia Italy 46.14N 13.06E
101 N7 Buick Br Col 56.57N 121.30W
89 H7 Bui Dam Ghana 8.11N 2.10W
58 E6 Buie, L Mull, Strathclyde Scotland 56.20N 5.53W
93 K10 Buiko Tanzania 4.38S 38.02E
60 H10 Buiksloot Netherlands 52.24N 4.55E
93 E5 Buikwe Uganda 0.21N 33.03E
56 F2 Buildwas Shropshire Eng 52.39N 2.33W
56 E3 Builth Wells Powys Wales 52.09N 3.24W
15 J2 Buin Bougainville I Papua New Guinea 6.52S 155.42E
121 B4 Buin Chile 33.45S 70.48W
32 D3 Bū'in Iran 35.47N 50.04E
60 Q8 Buinen Netherlands 52.56N 6.48E
66 R4 Buin,Piz mt Switz/Austria 46.52N 10.07E
45 T1 Buinsk Cheboksary U.S.S.R. 55.11N 47.04E
45 U2 Buinsk Tatar A.S.S.R. U.S.S.R. 54.58N 48.15E
89 J7 Buipe Ghana 8.51N 1.32W
117 H9 Buíque Brazil 8.35S 37.05W
64 B2 Buir W Germany 50.51N 6.35E
69 B3 Buire-le-Sec France 50.22N 1.51E
69 F4 Buironfosse France 49.58N 3.50E
71 G8 Buis-les-Baronnies France 44.16N 5.16E
71 H6 Buisse,la France 45.20N 5.37E
61 E4 Buissenal Belgium 50.40N 3.39E
72 F6 Buisson-Cussac, le Dordogne France 44.50N 0.58E
71 C7 Buisson-de-Cadouin, Le Lozère France 44.38N 3.13E
61 L6 Buissonville Belgium 50.13N 5.12E
60 N7 Buitenpost Netherlands 53.15N 6.09E
23 D9 Bui Thon Vietnam 19.43N 105.48E
98 J2 Buit, L Quebec 51.00N 63.12W
75 C6 Buitrago del Lozoya Spain 41.00N 3.38W
77 N4 Buitre mt Spain 38.10N 1.54W
94 F3 Buitsivango watercourse Botswana
61 H4 Buizingen Belgium 50.44N 4.15E
77 H5 Bujalance Spain 37.54N 4.23W
72 H4 Bujaleuf France 45.48N 1.38E
76 B2 Buján Spain 43.02N 8.37W
82 G8 Bujanovac Yugoslavia 42.27N 21.46E
75 K5 Bujaraloz Spain 41.29N 0.10W
Bujd see Bojd
82 B5 Buje Yugoslavia 45.25N 13.40E
Bujnurd see Bojnūrd
82 L5 Bujor Târg Romania 45.51N 27.57E
29 K6 Bujudih Bihar India 23.36N 86.32E
93 A9 Bujumbura Burundi 3.22S 29.19E
63 P4 Buk E Germany 54.09N 11.40E
65 P7 Bük Hungary 47.24N 16.48E
15 G8 Buk Papua New Guinea 8.30S 142.28E
42 K5 Bukachacha U.S.S.R. 53.00N 116.58E
15 J1 Buka I Papua New Guinea 5.15S 154.35E
93 D6 Bukakata Uganda 0.17S 32.03E
91 J8 Bukama Zaïre 9.13S 25.52E
24 E8 Buka Mangna Range mt ra Xizang Zizhiqu China
85 A3 Bū Kammāsh Libya 33.07N 11.43E
Bukan see Bowkān
32 E5 Būkand Iran 31.59N 52.50E
42 C5 Bukanskoye U.S.S.R. 52.45N 81.45E
43 G5 Bukantau,Gory mts Uzbekistan U.S.S.R.
15 J1 Buka Pass Papua New Guinea
93 D6 Bukasa I Uganda 0.25S 32.32E
15 J7 Bukauo Papua New Guinea 6.45S 147.17E
93 A8 Bukavu Zaïre 2.30S 28.50E
33 E3 Bukayriyah,Al Saudi Arabia 26.12N 43.36E
93 F4 Bukedea Uganda 1.21N 34.05E
61 J3 Buken Belgium 50.56N 4.37E
93 D10 Bukene Tanzania 4.15S 32.51E
93 D7 Bukerebe I Tanzania 1.27S 32.06E
93 C6 Bukeri Uganda 0.28S 31.48E
93 A9 Bukeya Burundi 3.10S 29.31E
43 G7 Bukhara Uzbekistan U.S.S.R. 39.47N 64.26E
35 B1 Bukhariya sub Jerusalem
44 D8 Bukhta Ukraine U.S.S.R. 46.05N 35.01E
41 N2 Bukhta Tikhaya Franz Josef Land U.S.S.R. 80.23N 52.58E
46 H5 Buki Ukraine U.S.S.R. 49.02N 30.29E
19 D2 Bukide isld Indonesia 3.47N 125.35E
93 E7 Bukima Tanzania 1.49S 33.26E
93 B7 Bukinda Uganda 0.10S 30.09E
18 B7 Bukit Betong Pen Malaysia 4.14N 101.55E
18 B8 Bukit Fraser Pen Malaysia 3.44N 101.44E
18 A6 Bukit Mertajam hill Pen Malaysia 5.21N 100.27E
18 H2 Bukit Panjang Singapore 1.23N 103.47E
18 C9 Bukit Serok Pen Malaysia 2.54N 102.50E
18 H3 Bukit Timah Singapore 1.20N 103.46E
18 H3 Bukit Timah dist Singapore
18 D6 Bukittinggi Sumatra Indon 0.18S 100.20E
62 M7 Bükk mts Hungary
34 C8 Bukka, Jebel el mt Jordan 30.47N 35.38E
28 C3 Bukkapatnam Andhra Prad India 14.12N 77.46E
53 T15 Bukkenibba mt Norway 61.48N 5.46E
62 K9 Bükkösd Hungary 46.07N 18.00E
46 Q2 Buklyan U.S.S.R. 55.36N 52.15E
63 Q9 Buko E Germany 51.57N 12.25E
93 C7 Bukoba Tanzania 1.19S 31.49E
91 E2 Bükoli Cent Afr Rep 3.00N 16.19E
93 D5 Bukoloto Uganda 0.44N 32.55E
93 D9 Bukombe Tanzania 3.32S 32.04E
93 C9 Bukombekombe Tanzania 3.27S 31.52E
93 C8 Bukondo Tanzania 2.39S 31.56E
93 C6 Bukoto Uganda 0.22S 31.42E
82 J2 Bukovina old prov U.S.S.R.
65 L3 Bukovsko Czechoslovakia 49.11N 14.35E
62 J1 Bukowo, Jezioro L Poland 54.20N 16.20E
45 L2 Bukrino U.S.S.R. 54.21N 39.55E
29 L4 Buksa Duar W Bengal India 26.43N 89.39E
48 S13 Buksefjorden B Greenland
Buksnes see Leknes
39 F3 Buksunda U.S.S.R. 62.31N 156.37E
42 K6 Bukuka U.S.S.R. 51.10N 116.40E
42 J7 Bukukun U.S.S.R. 49.25N 111.08E
91 J7 Bukunga Zaïre 7.44S 25.47E
90 D7 Bukuru Nigeria 9.46N 8.51E
18 F6 Buku, Tanjung C Indonesia 0.41S 104.22E
93 C5 Bukuya Uganda 0.42N 31.52E
93 E8 Bukwimba Tanzania 2.47S 33.24E
90 B5 Bukwium Nigeria 12.10N 5.30E
19 G5 Bula Moluccas Indon 3.07S 130.27E
46 P2 Bula R U.S.S.R.
91 D8 Bula Atumba Angola 8.41S 14.52E
19 H1 Bulacan Luzon Philippines 14.48N 120.55E
66 L1 Bülach Switzerland 47.32N 8.32E
87 G7 Bulad Ethiopia 7.49N 39.13E
42 F5 Bulag U.S.S.R. 52.47N 99.42E
42 J6 Bulagan U.S.S.R. 52.24N 110.18E
22 L4 Bulag Sum Nei Monggol Zizhiqu China 45.42N 117.23E
12 K4 Bulahdelal New S Wales 32.24S 152.12E
Bulair see Bolayır
42 K6 Bulak U.S.S.R. 51.04N 115.20E
19 K6 Bulalacao isld Philippines 11.47N 120.10E
92 C11 Bulalima-Mangwe dist Zimbabwe
19 H7 Bulaloc B Philippines 8.46N 117.23E
42 F5 Bulambuk U.S.S.R. 52.53N 96.27E
19 L5 Bulan Luzon Philippines 12.40N 123.53E
18 E5 Bulan isld Indonesia
19 K8 Bulan isld Philippines 6.07N 121.51E
47 N4 Bulanash U.S.S.R. 57.19N 61.59E
43 D2 Bulanavo U.S.S.R. 52.30N 55.08E
37 D5 Bulancak Turkey 40.57N 38.14E
50 G7 Buland Iceland 63.46N 18.30W
30 A4 Bulandshahr Uttar Prad India 28.30N 77.49E
30 A4 Bulandshahr dist Uttar Prad India
50 B5 Búlandshöfdhi mt Iceland 64.56N 23.27W
50 L5 Búlandstindur pk Iceland 64.43N 14.26W
37 G6 Bulanık Turkey 39.04N 42.16E
46 S4 Bulanovo U.S.S.R. 52.27N 55.12E
91 G6 Bulape Zaïre 4.39S 21.35E
85 L7 Bûlâq Egypt 25.10N 30.38E
86 Q12 Bûlâq dist Cairo Egypt
26 R7 Bulatkohupitiya Sri Lanka 7.06N 80.20E
45 L7 Bulavinovka Ukraine U.S.S.R. 49.24N 39.00E
92 D12 Bulawayo Zimbabwe 20.10S 28.43E
43 K1 Bulayevo Kazakhstan U.S.S.R. 54.55N 70.29E
53 C2 Bulbjerg mt Denmark 57.09N 9.03E
82 M4 Bulboki U.S.S.R. 46.50N 29.20E
90 M6 Bulbul,Wâdi watercourse Sudan
Buldaji see Boldaji
36 D4 Buldan Turkey 38.03N 28.50E
29 E7 Buldana Maharashtra India 20.31N 76.18E
29 E7 Buldana dist Maharashtra India
36 D4 Buldan Barajı res Turkey 38.24N 28.50E
120 B3 Buldibuyo Peru 8.07S 77.22W
113 M9 Buldir I Aleutian Is 52.20N 175.55E
29 E2 Buldur Himachal Prad India 31.47N 77.58E
43 C3 Buldurty Kazakhstan U.S.S.R. 49.56N 52.56E
31 B7 Buleda reg Pakistan
88 J7 Bu Legmaden, Oued watercourse Algeria/Morocco
87 K8 Bulei Ethiopia 5.56N 44.50E
18 L10 Buleleng Bali Indon 8.06S 115.12E
93 A7 Bulera, L Rwanda
56 H5 Bulford Wilts Eng 51.12N 1.46W
22 B3 Bulgan Mongolia 46.06N 91.25E
22 F2 Bulgan Mongolia 48.50N 103.29E
22 J2 Bulgan Mongolia 48.04N 113.30E
22 F2 Bulgan prov Mongolia
22 B3 Bulgan Gol R Mongolia
49 J8 Bulgaria rep S Europe
37 C2 Bülğarköy Turkey 40.52N 26.41E
36 D4 Bulgaz Dağ mt Turkey 38.35N 29.47E
33 D4 Bulghah Saudi Arabia 25.04N 41.34E
81 K3 Bulgheria,Monte Italy 40.04N 15.26E
69 K7 Bulgnéville France 48.12N 5.51E
13 G7 Bulgroo Queensland 25.41S 143.45E
87 L8 Bulhale Somalia 5.20N 46.23E
87 K5 Bulhar Somalia 10.24N 44.26E
19 F3 Buli Halmahera Indon 0.54N 128.16E
15 J8 Bulidobu Papua New Guinea 9.42S 147.48E
19 H7 Bulilluyan,C Philippines 8.21N 117.12E
18 H3 Bulim Singapore 1.22N 103.43E
13 K1 Bulimba dist Brisbane, Qnsld
13 L2 Bulimba Cr Brisbane, Qnsld
92 D2 Bulindi Zaïre 0.49S 29.05E
89 H7 Bulinga Ghana 9.58N 2.08W
93 C3 Bulisa Uganda 2.06N 31.25E
19 F3 Buli, Teluk B Halmahera Indonesia 0.48N 128.20E
23 D6 Buliu He R Guangxi China
53 U17 Bulken Norway 60.38N 6.16E
Bu'l Khair see Buol Kheyr
87 F7 Bulki Ethiopia 6.11N 36.31E
101 K8 Bulkley R Br Col
101 K8 Bulkley Ranges Br Col
32 E5 Būl,Kūh-e mt Iran 30.50N 52.46E
15 F8 Bulla Papua New Guinea 9.07S 141.15E
14 D9 Bullabulling W Australia 31.05S 120.52E
61 Q5 Büllange Belgium 50.24N 6.15E
44 J8 Bulla,Ostrova isld Azerbaydzhan U.S.S.R. 40.00N 49.39E
76 L10 Bullaque R Spain
112 M3 Bullard Texas 32.09N 95.20W
52 F8 Bullaresjö R Sweden
77 N4 Bullas Spain 38.02N 1.40W
13 G8 Bullawarra L Queensland 27.54S 143.31E
64 C3 Bullay W Germany 50.03N 7.09E
105 H5 Bull B S Carolina
116 L2 Bull Bay Jamaica, W I 17.56N 76.41W
66 E5 Bulle Switzerland 46.37N 7.04E
12 F4 Bullea, L New S Wales 30.11S 141.55E
113 O1 Bullen Alaska 70.10N 146.50W
101 W3 Bullen R N W Terr
116 B1 Bullen Baai B Curaçao W I
11 F8 Buller Gorge New Zealand
12 H6 Buller,Mt Victoria 37.11S 146.26E
11 G8 Buller R New Zealand
14 C9 Bullfinch W Australia 30.59S 119.06E
12 K5 Bulli New S Wales 34.15S 150.57E
105 H5 Bull I S Carolina 32.54N 79.38W
87 D4 Bulli I Sudan 12.20N 32.47E
111 H7 Bullion Mts California
13 B3 Bullita N Terr Australia 16.06S 130.29E
59 B8 Bull Lt.Ho.,The Cork Irish Rep 51.35N 10.19W
110 R3 Bull Mts Montana
13 A3 Bullo R N Terr Australia
13 G6 Bullock R Queensland
13 G4 Bullock Creek Queensland 17.43S 144.31E
13 G8 Bulloo R Queensland
13 G8 Bulloo Downs Queensland 28.30S 142.45E
13 F8 Bulloo, L Queensland
13 G8 Bulloo L Queensland
12 G4 Bulloo R New S Wales
56 C5 Bull Point Devon Eng 51.13N 4.12W
100 B9 Bull R Br Col
11 B8 Bull Rock Campbell I Pacific Oc 52.27S 169.14E
11 K7 Bulls New Zealand 40.10S 175.22E
116 J2 Bull Savannah Jamaica, W I 17.53N 77.36W
105 D1 Bulls Gap Tennessee 36.16N 83.05W
107 D5 Bull Shoals L Missouri/Ark
103 F3 Bullville New York 41.32N 74.22W
71 D5 Bully Loire France 45.56N 4.00E
69 D3 Bully Pas de Calais France 50.26N 2.44E
110 C9 Bully Choop Mt California 40.33N 122.46W
13 C2 Bulman N Terr Australia 13.32S 134.20E
13 C2 Bulman Gorge N Terr Australia 13.17S 134.10E
57 M4 Bulmer N Yorks Eng 54.06N 0.56W
101 N4 Bulmer L N-W Terr
121 A6 Bulnes Chile 36.45S 72.22W
93 D5 Bulo Uganda 0.07N 32.00E
87 K9 Bulo Burti Somalia 3.50N 45.33E
18 B8 Buloh R Pen Malaysia
18 J2 Buloh R Pen Malaysia
18 B4 Bulohsama Sumatra Indon 2.35N 97.40E
43 M7 Bulok Tadzhikistan U.S.S.R. 40.37N 70.28E
12 G6 Buloke, L Victoria
31 E3 Bulola Afghanistan 34.56N 68.02E
15 J7 Bulolo Papua New Guinea 7.13S 146.35E
14 D9 Bulong W Australia 30.44S 121.48E
93 E5 Bulopa Uganda 0.50N 33.15E
12 F5 Bulpunga New S Wales 33.44S 141.50E
29 C7 Bulsar Gujarat India 20.40N 72.55E
61 A2 Bulskamp Belgium 51.03N 2.39E
81 C3 Bultei Sardinia 40.27N 9.04E
19 E1 Bulu Indonesia 4.34N 126.45E
19 M8 Buluan Mindanao Philippines 6.40N 124.50E
19 M8 Buluan, L Mindanao Philippines
19 E1 Bulude Indonesia 4.30N 126.44E
18 M4 Bulu, Gunung mt Kalimantan Indonesia 2.51N 116.01E
93 H1 Buluk Kenya 4.13N 36.39E
89 D8 Bulukai Liberia 7.18N 10.02W
19 B6 Bulukumba Celebes Indon 5.35S 120.13E
91 G4 Bulukutu Zaïre 0.10S 21.46E
91 K6 Bulula Zaïre 5.26S 27.24E
87 G7 Bululta Ethiopia 6.12N 39.03E
91 E7 Bululundu Zaïre 6.02S 17.10E
39 C5 Bulun Khabarovsk U.S.S.R. 59.48N 143.18E
41 N5 Bulun U.S.S.R. 70.45N 127.20E
39 F2 Bulun R Magadan U.S.S.R.
93 D10 Bulunde Tanzania 4.18S 32.57E
91 F6 Bulungu Zaïre 4.36S 18.34E
91 G7 Bulungu Zaïre 6.02S 21.54E
93 D10 Bulungwa Tanzania 4.03S 32.15E
19 M5 Bulusan Luzon Philippines 12.46N 124.08E
19 C4 Bulutumpu,Gunung mt Celebes Indonesia 1.02S 122.22E
100 F6 Bulwark Alberta 52.18N 111.36W
95 E8 Bulwater S Africa 32.30S 21.49E
95 N5 Bulwer S Africa 29.48S 29.46E
13 L1 Bulwer I Brisbane, Qnsld
56 K2 Bulwick Northants Eng 52.32N 0.35W
100 N8 Bulyea Saskatchewan 50.59N 104.51W
81 B2 Bulzi Sardinia 40.52N 8.50E
15 M3 Buma Malaita I Solomon Is 8.55S 160.46E
91 F6 Bumba Zaïre 5.10S 18.41E
91 F7 Bumba Zaïre 6.58S 19.19E
91 H2 Bumba Zaïre 2.10N 22.30E
89 D7 Bumban Sierra Leone 9.10N 11.53W

95 P9 Bumbeni S Africa 27.48S 32.19E
82 H5 Bumbeşti Jiu Romania 45.10N 23.22E
94 E2 Bumbi Namibia 18.19S 19.56E
93 C7 Bumbiri Tanzania 1.37S 31.54E
93 C7 Bumbiri I Tanzania
111 M7 Bumble Bee Arizona 34.13N 112.08W
87 E5 Bumbodi Ethiopia 11.16N 35.01E
19 C3 Bumbulan Celebes Indon 0.31N 122.04E
91 G5 Bumbuli Zaïre 3.24S 20.32E
18 N3 Bum-Bum isld Sabah Malaysia
89 D7 Bumbuna Sierra Leone 9.02N 11.49W
92 J11 Bumbwini Zanzibar 5.58S 39.12E
93 F8 Bumera Tanzania 2.48S 34.11E
25 N7 Bumhkang Burma 26.55N 97.39E
23 A5 Bumhpa Bum mt Burma 26.42N 97.15E
18 H9 Bumiayu Java Indon 7.16S 108.59E
110 D3 Bumping L Washington 46.52N 121.20W
101 R1 Bumpus, Mt Victoria I, N W Terr 69.56N 113.40W
93 B3 Bu,Mt Zaïre 2.09N 30.22E
28 H2 Bumtang R Bhutan
93 A2 Bumva Zaïre 3.30N 29.21E
93 L3 Buna Kenya 2.48N 39.32E
15 K8 Buna Papua New Guinea 8.37S 148.23E
112 O5 Buna Texas 30.25N 93.59W
91 F5 Buna Zaïre 3.14S 18.59E
Bunab see Bonāb
15 H6 Bunabufi Papua New Guinea 4.36S 145.32E
Bunai see Mapei
59 C3 Bunaveela,L Mayo Irish Rep 54.02N 9.32W
33 J5 Bunayyān Saudi Arabia 23.06N 50.59E
85 G3 Bunbah Libya 32.25N 23.09E
85 G3 Bunbah,G.of Libya
59 H4 Bunbrosna W Meath Irish Rep 53.37N 7.25W
14 B10 Bunbury W Australia 33.20S 115.34E
107 D3 Bunceton Missouri 38.47N 92.49W
109 Q6 Bunch Oklahoma 35.41N 94.47W
59 J6 Bunclody Wexford Irish Rep 52.39N 6.39W
59 H1 Buncrana Donegal Irish Rep 55.08N 7.27W
13 K6 Bundaberg Queensland 24.50S 152.21E
13 F5 Bunda Bunda Queensland 20.06S 142.11E
26 T9 Bundala Sri Lanka 6.12N 81.15E
13 H8 Bundaleer Queensland 28.39S 146.31E
13 C4 Bundara crater N Terr Australia
12 K4 Bundarra New S Wales 30.11S 151.04E
63 F6 Bunde Niedersachsen W Germany 53.12N 7.16E
63 J8 Bünde Nordrhein-Westfalen W Germany 52.12N 8.35E
12 M9 Bundeena New S Wales 34.06S 151.07E
64 D5 Bundenthal W Germany 49.05N 7.50E
13 D5 Bundey R N Terr Australia
14 D7 Bundey,Mt W Australia 25.03S 122.12E
29 D5 Bundi Rajasthan India 25.28N 75.42E
29 D5 Bundi dist Rajasthan India
93 B5 Bundibugyo Uganda 0.43N 30.04E
107 C11 Bundick L Louisiana 30.45N 93.08W
107 C11 Bundicks Cr Louisiana
13 C6 Bundooma N Terr Australia 24.55S 134.19E
59 F3 Bundoran Donegal Irish Rep 54.28N 8.17W
29 J2 Bundu Bihar India 23.08N 85.19E
91 F2 Bundu tribe Zaïre
25 K6 Bun Duc Vietnam 12.55N 105.58E
32 C5 Būneh isld Iran 30.10N 49.10E
35 G6 Buneiyat, El Jordan 31.53N 35.53E
31 G3 Buner reg Pakistan
75 L3 Buñero mt Spain 42.04N 0.19E
58 D6 Bunessan Mull, Strathclyde Scotland 56.19N 6.14W
31 G6 Bunga Pakistan 29.30N 72.05E
50 K3 Bunga mt Iceland 65.48N 15.50W
90 D6 Bunga R Nigeria
14 F5 Bungabinni Well W Australia 22.12S 125.05E
12 M5 Bungan Hd New S Wales 33.41S 151.20E
12 K5 Bungaree Norah Pt New S Wales 33.19S 151.08E
56 O3 Bungay Suffolk Eng 52.28N 1.26E
25 F5 Bung Boraphet L Thailand
41 Q3 Bunge, Zemlya isld U.S.S.R.
13 J7 Bungil R Queensland
19 C5 Bunginkela isld Celebes Indon 3.04S 122.24E
19 B5 Bungku Celebes Indon 2.33S 121.59E
91 D7 Bungo Angola 7.26S 15.33E
93 F5 Bungoma Kenya 0.34N 34.34E
20 F9 Bungo-suidō channel Japan
20 E8 Bungo-Takada Japan 33.34N 131.28E
Bung Sai see Ban Bung Sai
63 N4 Bungsberg mt W Germany 54.14N 10.44E
90 C5 Bungudu Nigeria 12.18N 6.35E
17 G11 Bunguran isld Indonesia
18 H4 Bunguran Selatan islds Indonesia
76 B14 Bunheiras Portugal 37.22N 8.49W
90 F6 Buni Nigeria 11.11N 12.00E
93 B4 Bunia Zaïre 1.33N 30.13E
91 G5 Bunianga II Zaïre 3.28S 20.11E
75 C3 Buniel Spain 42.18N 3.49W
14 E9 Buningonia W Australia 31.29S 123.41E
12 G7 Buninyong Victoria 37.41S 143.58E
93 D6 Bunjako I Uganda 0.03S 32.12E
31 H3 Bunji Kashmir 35.40N 74.40E
53 K5 Bunkeflo Sweden 55.34N 12.59E
107 E4 Bunker Missouri 37.27N 91.13W
13 K6 Bunker Grp islds Gt Barrier Reef Australia
113 E4 Bunker Hill Alaska 65.10N 164.40W
112 F9 Bunker Hill Houston, Texas 29.46N 95.32W
107 G2 Bunker Hill Illinois 39.02N 89.58W
106 H9 Bunker Hill Indiana 40.40N 86.06W
109 M3 Bunker Hill Kansas 38.54N 98.43W
31 B10 Bunker I Pakistan 24.49N 66.58E
111 K5 Bunkerville Nevada 36.45N 114.08W
91 K9 Bunkeya Zaïre 10.22S 27.01E
107 D11 Bunkie Louisiana 30.57N 92.09W
90 L7 Bunkuku,Jebel mt Sudan 9.09N 23.37E
20 E2 Bunkyō dist Tōkyō Japan
59 H7 Bunmahon Waterford Irish Rep 52.08N 7.23W
Bunneh see Būneh
105 F8 Bunnell Florida 29.28N 81.16W
60 J11 Bunnik Netherlands 52.04N 5.12E
56 J2 Bunny Notts Eng 52.52N 1.07W
59 E5 Bunny,L Clare Irish Rep 53.01N 8.56W
11 K7 Bunnythorpe New Zealand 40.15S 175.38E
25 J7 Bu Noi Vietnam 11.43N 107.08E
77 P2 Buñol Spain 39.25N 0.47W
77 V14 Buñola Balearic Is 39.42N 2.42E
93 M5 Bun Plains Kenya
59 E6 Bunratty Castle Limerick Irish Rep 52.42N 8.49W
61 K3 Bunsbeek Belgium 50.51N 4.57E
60 K11 Bunschoten Netherlands 52.15N 5.23E
90 C5 Bunsuru R Nigeria
25 F2 Bun Tai Laos 21.21N 101.59E
14 B8 Buntine W Australia 29.57S 116.33E
56 L4 Buntingford Herts Eng 51.57N 0.01W
18 L6 Buntok Borneo Indon 1.45S 114.47E
18 L7 Buntui Borneo Indon 2.54S 114.10E
101 H10 Buntzen, L Br Col 49.22N 122.52W
75 H4 Buñuel Spain 41.59N 1.26W
85 C4 Bū-Nujaym Libya 30.37N 15.22E
90 D6 Bununu Nigeria 10.01N 9.35E
90 D7 Bununu Nigeria 9.54N 9.40E
18 K5 Bunut Borneo Indon 0.46N 112.32E
12 J6 Bunyan New S Wales 36.11S 149.09E
36 H4 Bünyan Turkey 38.51N 35.50E
13 K1 Bunyaville dist Brisbane, Qnsld
93 A7 Bunyonyi, L Uganda 1.17S 29.55E
18 M4 Bunyu isld Borneo Indon
93 A5 Bunyuka Zaïre 0.09N 29.25E
25 F3 Bun Yun Thailand 18.33N 100.42E
66 K2 Bünz R Switzerland
66 K2 Bünzen Switzerland 47.19N 8.19E
66 K4 Buochs Switzerland 46.58N 8.26E
19 B3 Buol Celebes Indon 1.12N 121.28E
41 L4 Buolkalakh U.S.S.R. 72.57N 119.45E
41 L5 Buolkalakh R U.S.S.R.
32 D6 Buol Kheyr Iran 28.30N 51.06E
81 L3 Buonabitacolo Italy 40.16N 15.37E
18 H3 Buona Vista Singapore 1.17N 103.47E
80 D2 Buonconvento Italy 43.08N 11.29E
25 J6 Buong Long Cambodia 13.41N 106.58E
81 L4 Buonvicino Italy 39.41N 15.53E
39 D2 Buordakh R U.S.S.R.
41 O5 Buorkhaya,Guba gulf U.S.S.R.
41 O5 Buorkhaya,Mys C U.S.S.R. 71.58N 132.45E
40 C1 Buotama R U.S.S.R. China
28 G1 Bup R Xizang Zizhiqu
15 F7 Bupul Irian Jaya 7.37S 140.52E
35 G1 Buq'ata Syria 33.12N 35.47E
33 E3 Buqay'a Saudi Arabia 26.17N 42.56E
Buqayq see Abqaiq
85 H4 Buqbuq Egypt 31.30N 25.32E
35 E2 Buqei'a Israel 32.58N 35.20E
118 J2 Buquim Brazil 11.07S 37.37W
53 A4 Bur Denmark 56.22N 8.27E
42 H3 Bur U.S.S.R. 58.48N 107.00E
50 L3 Búr reg Iceland
93 K9 Bura Kenya 3.30S 38.19E
93 L7 Bura Kenya 1.06S 39.58E
93 K9 Bura watercourse Kenya
29 K7 Burabalang R Orissa India
87 K9 Bur Acaba Somalia 2.50N 44.05E
93 M3 Burada Kenya 2.06N 40.40E
Buraida see Buraydah
33 L4 Buraimi Oman 24.16N 55.48E
33 E9 Bura,Jabal mt Yemen 14.50N 43.26E
14 B9 Burakin W Australia 30.30S 117.08E
Buraku I see Mbarukua I
39 A2 Buralakh R U.S.S.R.
90 M6 Buram Sudan 10.51N 25.09E
14 E10 Buraminya,Mt W Australia 33.13S 123.05E
43 Q3 Buran Kazakhstan U.S.S.R. 48.02N 85.12E
87 M5 Buran Somalia 10.10N 48.46E
13 K2 Buranda dist Brisbane, Qnsld
40 G4 Burandzha U.S.S.R. 54.35N 136.15E
24 D10 Burang Xizang Zizhiqu China 30.16N 81.11E
118 H5 Buranhaém Brazil 16.33S 40.04W
118 H5 Buranhaém, R Brazil
43 C2 Burannoye U.S.S.R. 51.01N 54.31E
79 M4 Burano Italy 45.29N 12.25E
80 D4 Burano,Lago di Italy
87 K6 Burao Somalia 9.31N 45.33E
87 L6 Burao prov Somalia
34 D5 Burāq Syria 33.11N 36.28E
107 G12 Buras Louisiana 29.21N 89.32W
30 H4 Burathum Nepal 28.04N 84.50E
19 M6 Burauen Philippines 10.58N 124.56E
33 E3 Buraydah Saudi Arabia 26.20N 43.59E
47 H7 Burayevo U.S.S.R. 55.52N 55.24E
33 J6 Burayhimah Saudi Arabia 21.41N 50.42E
Burayi,Al see Br'aij,El
29 D7 Buray R Maharashtra India
64 E2 Burbach W Germany 50.45N 8.05E
56 H5 Burbage Wilts Eng 51.22N 1.40W
75 H5 Burbaguena Spain 41.01N 1.20W
111 F7 Burbank California 34.10N 118.25W
43 O8 Burbash Kirgiziya U.S.S.R. 40.19N 72.23E
81 C5 Burcei Sardinia 39.21N 9.22E
108 O9 Burchard Nebraska 40.08N 96.22W
66 H6 Bürchen Switzerland 46.18N 7.49E
12 H5 Burcher New S Wales 33.32S 147.18E
108 R6 Burchinal Iowa 43.04N 93.15W
61 H2 Burcht Belgium 51.12N 4.21E
87 N6 Bur Cohleh reg Somalia
30 A7 Burda Madhya Prad India 25.50N 77.35E
87 L6 Bur Dab Ra Somalia
77 E2 Búrdalo R Spain
43 G7 Burdalyk Turkmeniya U.S.S.R. 38.29N 64.28E
13 H5 Burdekin R Queensland
13 H5 Burdekin Falls Queensland 20.35S 147.09E
101 M7 Burden,Mt Br Col 56.10N 123.09W
100 F9 Burdett Alberta 49.50N 111.33W
104 J4 Burdett New York 42.27N 76.51W
61 L4 Burdinne Belgium 50.35N 5.05E
87 K8 Burdo Somalia 4.07N 44.40E
46 N1 Burdovo U.S.S.R. 58.55N 44.00E
82 K3 Burdujeni Romania 47.39N 26.20E
36 E5 Burdur Turkey 37.44N 30.17E
36 E5 Burdur Gölü L Turkey
29 L2 Burdwan W Bengal India 23.15N 87.52E
29 L6 Burdwan dist W Bengal India
96 F14 Burdwood Bank Atlantic Oc
61 M6 Bure Belgium 50.05N 5.15E
66 E2 Bure Switzerland 47.27N 7.01E
52 N2 Bureå Sweden 64.36N 21.15E
99 P4 Bureau, L Quebec
75 D2 Bureba,La plat Spain
87 E6 Burei Ethiopia 8.19N 35.08E
40 F6 Bureinskiy,Khrebet mts U.S.S.R.
35 H4 Bureiqa Jordan 32.27N 36.01E
76 L3 Burejo R Spain
87 L8 Bur,El Somalia 4.42N 46.32E
76 E1 Burela,C Spain 43.40N 7.21W
71 F1 Bure-les-Templiers France 47.44N 4.53E
60 M6 Buren Ameland Netherlands 53.27N 5.48E
22 F3 Büren Mongolia 46.50N 104.58E
60 K12 Buren Netherlands 51.55N 5.20E
66 F3 Büren Switzerland 47.08N 7.23E
63 J9 Büren W Germany 51.33N 8.33E
42 F6 Buren-Khem U.S.S.R. 51.42N 95.03E
66 N2 Büren,Nieder Switzerland 47.28N 9.13E
66 N2 Büren,Ober Switzerland 47.27N 9.10E
71 H7 Bure,Pic de France 44.37N 5.55E
56 P2 Bure, R Norfolk Eng
30 C8 Burero Madhya Prad India 24.39N 79.06E
76 B3 Bures Spain 42.42N 8.45W
56 N4 Bures Suffolk Eng 51.59N 0.46E
40 L9 Burevestnik Kuril Is U.S.S.R. 44.56N 147.38E
40 E7 Bureya U.S.S.R. 49.49N 129.50E
40 E6 Bureya R U.S.S.R.
50 E6 Búrfell mt Árnessýsla Iceland 64.06N 20.56W
50 F6 Búrfell mt Árnessýsla Iceland 64.05N 19.50W
50 D3 Búrfell mt Strandasýsla Iceland 65.57N 21.40W
50 K3 Búrfell mt Thingeyjarsýsla, Nordhur Iceland 65.59N 15.59W
50 H2 Búrfell mt Thingeyjarsýsla, Sudhur Iceland 66.03N 17.08W
50 J3 Búrfell mt Thingeyjarsýsla, Sudhur Iceland 65.33N 16.40W
50 K3 Búrfellsheidhi heath Iceland
50 J3 Búrfellshraun lava field Iceland
99 K9 Burford Ontario 43.04N 80.28W
56 H4 Burford Oxon Eng 51.49N 1.38W
86 H3 Bûr Fu'ad Egypt 31.16N 32.19E
63 U9 Burg Cottbus E Germany 51.50N 14.10E
72 E9 Burg France 43.12N 0.20E
63 K5 Burg Schleswig Holstein W Germany 54.00N 9.16E
66 F2 Burg Switzerland 47.28N 7.26E
39 D4 Burgagy U.S.S.R. 61.35N 147.56E
39 C4 Burgakhchan U.S.S.R. 61.07N 142.40E
39 D2 Burgaly R U.S.S.R.
82 L8 Burgas Bulgaria 42.30N 27.29E
65 O7 Burgau Austria 47.09N 16.07E
76 B14 Burgau Portugal 37.04N 8.46W
64 J7 Burgau W Germany 48.25N 10.25E
39 B2 Burgavli U.S.S.R. 66.21N 137.29E
105 K3 Burgaw N Carolina 34.33N 77.56W
86 E9 Burgâya,El Egypt 28.09N 30.44E
37 F2 Burgaz Turkey 40.53N 29.04E
37 F2 Burgaz isld Turkey 40.52N 29.03E
83 K6 Burgaz Daği mts Turkey
63 P8 Burg bei Magdeburg E Germany 52.17N 11.51E
64 J5 Burgbernheim W Germany 49.27N 10.21E
110 K4 Burgdorf Idaho 45.18N 115.55W
66 G3 Burgdorf Switzerland 47.03N 7.38E
63 M8 Burgdorf W Germany 52.27N 10.01E
64 K4 Burgebrach W Germany 49.50N 10.45E
64 M2 Bürgel E Germany 50.55N 11.42E
86 E2 Burg,El Egypt 31.36N 30.59E
86 C4 Burg el'Arab Egypt 30.54N 29.32E
65 O7 Burgenland prov Austria
66 K4 Bürgenstock mt Switzerland 46.59N 8.24E
98 P6 Burgeo Newfoundland 47.37N 57.38W
65 M6 Bürger-Alpe mt Austria 47.48N 15.22E
66 O3 Burgerau Switzerland 47.09N 9.29E
95 K6 Burgersdorp S Africa 31.00S 26.20E
94 L5 Burgersfort S Africa 24.43S 30.21E
95 H6 Burgervilleweg S Africa 30.50S 24.17E
104 J9 Burgess Store Virginia 37.51N 76.21W
85 J9 Burget Tuyur dist Sudan
63 O4 Burg (Fehmarn) isld W Germany 54.27N 11.12E
57 G3 Burgh Cumbria Eng 54.56N 3.03W
60 B2 Burgh Netherlands 51.41N 3.45E
64 H2 Burghaun W Germany 50.42N 9.43E
64 O7 Burghausen W Germany 48.08N 12.50E
58 J3 Burghead Grampian Scotland 57.42N 3.30W
87 J9 Bur Gheider Idda mt Somalia 3.47N 43.45E
64 L6 Burgheim W Germany 48.43N 11.03E
56 J5 Burghfield Berks Eng 51.25N 1.03W
58 T11 Burgh Hd Orkney Scotland 59.06N 2.31W
57 O6 Burgh le Marsh Lincs Eng 53.10N 0.15E
60 C2 Burghsluis Netherlands 51.40N 3.45E
81 F8 Burgio Sicily 37.36N 13.17E
64 H3 Burgjoss W Germany 50.13N 9.30E
64 L3 Burgkunstadt W Germany 50.09N 11.16E
66 N1 Bürglen Thurgau Switz 47.33N 9.09E
66 L4 Bürglen Uri Switz 46.53N 8.40E
64 N5 Burglengenfeld W Germany 49.12N 12.03E
86 D3 Burg Migheizil Egypt 31.28N 30.24E
90 F5 Burgo Nigeria 12.40N 12.17E
77 G7 Burgo Spain 36.48N 4.56W
75 D4 Burgo de Osma,El Spain 41.35N 3.04W
76 K8 Burgohondo Spain 40.24N 4.47W
71 G5 Burgoin France 45.35N 5.17E
75 C5 Burgomillodo,Embalse de res Spain
76 J4 Burgo Ranero,El Spain 42.25N 5.13W
115 K5 Burgos Mexico 24.56N 98.48W
81 B3 Burgos Sardinia 40.23N 9.00E
75 C3 Burgos Spain 42.21N 3.41W
74 E2 Burgos prov Spain
98 T5 Burgoyne's Cove Newfoundland 48.11N 53.43W
64 K3 Burgpreppach W Germany 50.08N 10.40E
64 H3 Burgsinn W Germany 50.09N 9.39E
63 O4 Burgstaaken W Germany 54.26N 11.12E
64 O2 Burgstädt E Germany 50.55N 12.49E
64 G4 Bürgstadt W Germany 49.42N 9.17E
63 S6 Burg Stargard E Germany 53.30N 13.19E
63 F8 Burgsteinfurt W Germany 52.09N 7.21E
52 L9 Burgsvik Sweden 57.03N 18.19E
75 H2 Burguete Spain 42.59N 1.20W
75 H2 Burgui Spain 42.44N 1.00W
76 K8 Burguillo,Embalse de res Spain
77 E5 Burguillos Spain 37.36N 5.58W
77 C4 Burguillos del Cerro Spain 38.23N 6.35W
75 C8 Burguillos de Toledo Spain 39.48N 3.59W
Burgundy see Bourgogne
64 F2 Burgwald W Germany 50.59N 8.45E
63 L7 Burgwedel W Germany 52.30N 9.51E
64 K4 Burgwindheim W Germany 49.50N 10.37E
30 K8 Burhai Bihar India 24.21N 86.33E
22 D9 Burhan Budai Shan mt ra Qinghai China
36 B3 Burhaniye Balikesir Turkey 39.29N 26.59E
36 D5 Burhaniye Denizli Turkey 37.58N 28.49E
29 E7 Burhanpur Madhya Prad India 21.18N 76.08E
63 H5 Burhave W Germany 53.35N 8.21E
30 B5 Burhganga R Uttar Prad India
30 L6 Burhi R Nepal
30 J6 Burhi Gandak R Bihar India
30 F5 Burhi Rapti R Uttar Prad India
56 W10 Burhou isld Chan Is 49.43N 2.15W
91 E8 Buri Angola 9.53S 16.25E
118 E8 Buri Brazil 23.46S 48.39W
93 C2 Buri Sudan 3.48N 31.32E
29 E2 Buria Haryana India 30.09N 77.21E
19 L5 Burias isld Philippines
79 B5 Buriasco Italy 44.52N 7.24E
19 L5 Burias Pass Luzon Philippines
43 E2 Buribay Bashkir U.S.S.R. 52.00N 58.00E
115 N5 Burica,Pta C Panama 8.02N 82.52W
28 K2 Buri Dihing R Assam India
72 D4 Burie France 45.47N 0.25W
29 J4 Buri Gandak R Nepal
93 C8 Burigi, L Tanzania
98 R6 Burin Newfoundland 47.03N 55.11W
47 N5 Burino U.S.S.R. 56.02N 61.40E
98 R6 Burin Pen Newfoundland
87 G3 Buri Pen Ethiopia
25 G5 Buriram Thailand 15.01N 103.06E
87 B4 Bur Islam Sudan 13.41N 28.41E
118 E7 Buritama Brazil 21.09S 50.00W
117 F6 Buriti Brazil 3.56S 42.57W
118 E6 Buriti Alegre Brazil 18.09S 49.04W
117 F7 Buriti Bravo Brazil 5.50S 43.51W
117 E9 Buriti, Cachoeira do rapids Brazil 9.43S 46.15W
117 E7 Buriticupu, R R Brazil
117 G6 Buriti dos Lopes Brazil 3.11S 41.50W
118 B3 Buriti, R Brazil
118 G2 Buritirama Brazil 10.57S 43.39W
118 F4 Buritis Brazil 15.38S 46.29W
31 D5 Burj Pakistan 30.19N 66.40E
75 K8 Burjasot Spain 39.33N 0.26W
33 A2 Burj,El Saudi Arabia 29.28N 35.00E
35 C8 Burj el Baiyara Jordan 31.27N 34.54E
87 F8 Burji Ethiopia 5.29N 37.51E
Burj-i Chin see Borj-e Chin
87 E6 Burka Badessa Ethiopia 8.30N 34.50E
87 H7 Burka Darro Ethiopia 7.02N 41.19E
87 H7 Burkai Ethiopia 6.08N 40.45E
53 C7 Burkal Denmark 54.56N 9.05E
43 M6 Burkan R Kirgiziya U.S.S.R.
112 J1 Burkburnett Texas 34.05N 98.34W
110 K2 Burke Idaho 47.31N 115.46W
108 L6 Burke S Dakota 43.10N 99.17W
112 N4 Burke Texas 31.15N 94.48W
13 E6 Burke R Queensland
13 F5 Burke R Queensland
101 K9 Burke Chan Br Col
123 H11 Burke I Antarctica 73.00S 105.00W
15 G9 Burke I Torres Str, Qnsld 10.10S 142.30E
66 S4 Bürkelkopf mt Switz/Austria 46.59N 10.22E
11 E11 Burke Pass New Zealand 44.04S 170.40E
107 L5 Burkesville Kentucky 36.48N 85.21W
13 E4 Burketown Queensland 17.43S 139.30E
112 H4 Burkett Texas 31.59N 99.14W
104 G9 Burkeville Virginia 37.12N 78.13W
39 D3 Burkhala U.S.S.R. 62.38N 149.05E
64 O2 Burkhardtsdorf E Germany 50.42N 12.56E
39 B1 Burkhaybyt U.S.S.R. 68.00N 139.32E
108 L4 Burkmere S Dakota 45.04N 99.16W
99 L7 Burk's Falls Ontario 45.37N 79.25W
43 N1 Burla U.S.S.R. 53.20N 78.20E
42 B5 Burla R U.S.S.R.
64 G7 Burladingen W Germany 48.16N 9.06E
9 B3 Burle isld Marshall Is Pacific Oc 9.02N 167.32E
13 G5 Burleigh Queensland 20.17S 143.05E
112 K3 Burleson Texas 32.32N 97.19W
110 M7 Burley Idaho 42.32N 113.48W
57 K5 Burley W Yorks Eng 53.55N 1.45W
56 F3 Burley Gate Hereford & Worcs Eng 52.07N 2.35W
12 A6 Burley Griffin,L Canberra Australia
46 R4 Burli Kazakhstan U.S.S.R. 51.29N 52.40E
43 F1 Burli Kustanay, Kazakhstan U.S.S.R. 53.37N 61.53E
111 B4 Burlingame California 37.35N 122.25W
109 P3 Burlingame Kansas 38.45N 95.52W
109 H2 Burlington Colorado 39.17N 102.17W
103 J3 Burlington Connecticut 41.47N 72.58W
106 C9 Burlington Iowa 40.50N 91.07W
109 P3 Burlington Kansas 38.11N 95.46W
105 H1 Burlington N Carolina 36.05N 79.27W
98 R4 Burlington Newfoundland 49.46N 56.00W
103 E6 Burlington New Jersey 40.05N 74.51W
99 L9 Burlington Ontario 43.19N 79.48W
103 A3 Burlington Pennsylvania 41.47N 76.37W
104 M2 Burlington Vermont 44.28N 73.14W
110 C1 Burlington Washington 48.28N 122.20W
106 F7 Burlington Wisconsin 42.41N 88.17W
104 G7 Burlington W Virginia 39.20N 78.56W
108 B5 Burlington Wyoming 44.28N 108.29W
103 E7 Burlington co New Jersey
107 A1 Burlington Junc Missouri 40.26N 95.04W
56 F2 Burlton Shropshire Eng 52.50N 2.49W
47 H8 Burly U.S.S.R. 54.09N 56.28E
43 N4 Burlyu-Tobe Kazakhstan U.S.S.R. 46.33N 79.09E
35 G5 Burma Jordan 32.13N 35.47E
47 J5 Burmantovo U.S.S.R. 61.19N 60.28E
16 K6 Burma,Union of rep S E Asia
93 M3 Bur Mayo mt Kenya 2.55N 40.13E
61 Q9 Burmerange Luxembourg 49.28N 6.20E
110 N9 Burmester Utah 40.42N 112.28W
45 M3 Burminka U.S.S.R. 53.35N 40.15E
100 C9 Burmis Alberta 49.34N 114.17W
101 H11 Burnaby Br Col 49.16N 122.58W
101 H11 Burnaby, Mt Br Col 49.17N 122.55W
11 G9 Burnbrae New Zealand 42.04S 172.17E
101 H11 Burnby, L Br Col
57 K4 Burneston N Yorks Eng 54.15N 1.32W
112 J5 Burnet Texas 30.46N 98.14W
13 K7 Burnett R Queensland
13 K6 Burnett Hd Queensland 24.43S 152.22E
110 D9 Burney California 40.55N 121.40W
121 J9 Burney,Mte Chile 52.20S 73.28W
14 C10 Burngup W Australia 33.00S 118.39E
56 N4 Burnham Essex Eng 51.38N 0.49E
104 Q2 Burnham Maine 44.42N 69.26W
11 G10 Burnham New Zealand 43.37S 172.27E
104 H6 Burnham Pennsylvania 40.39N 77.36W
56 F5 Burnham Somerset Eng 51.15N 3.00W
56 N2 Burnham Deepdale Norfolk Eng 52.58N 0.41E
56 N2 Burnham Market Norfolk Eng 52.57N 0.44E
71 L1 Burnhaupt France 47.44N 7.10E
66 E1 Burnhaupt-le-Bas France 47.43N 7.10E
66 E1 Burnhaupt-le-Haut France 47.44N 7.09E
58 N4 Burnhaven Grampian Scotland 57.29N 1.48W
12 H8 Burnie Tasmania 41.03S 145.55E
57 N4 Burniston N Yorks Eng 54.19N 0.27W
57 J5 Burnley Lancs Eng 53.48N 2.14W
57 K3 Burnopfield Tyne and Wear Eng 54.55N 1.43W
43 K5 Burnoye Kazakhstan U.S.S.R. 42.36N 70.46E
109 D2 Burns Colorado 39.53N 106.54W
110 F6 Burns Oregon 43.36N 119.03W
108 F8 Burns Wyoming 41.12N 104.23W
57 K4 Burnsall N Yorks Eng 54.03N 1.57W
107 M5 Burnside Kentucky 36.59N 84.36W
103 F4 Burnside New York 41.28N 74.14W
104 G6 Burnside Pennsylvania 40.48N 78.47W
95 O4 Burnside S Africa 28.12S 30.08E
12 B8 Burnside dist Adelaide, S Aust 34.56S 138.39E
101 T2 Burnside R N W Terr
101 L8 Burns Lake Br Col 54.14N 125.45W
108 L3 Burnstad N Dakota 46.25N 99.39W
107 H7 Burnsville Mississippi 34.51N 88.20W
105 E2 Burnsville N Carolina 35.56N 82.18W
98 G6 Burnsville New Brunswick 47.42N 65.10W
104 E8 Burnsville W Virginia 38.50N 80.40W
Burnt Creek see Schefferville
110 P8 Burntfork Wyoming 41.00N 110.00W
116 G3 Burnt Ground Long I Bahamas 23.37N 75.17W
58 K6 Burntisland Fife Scotland 56.03N 3.15W
98 J1 Burnt Lake Quebec
95 O2 Burntop S Africa 26.49S 30.53E
110 H5 Burnt R Oregon
110 B9 Burnt Ranch California 40.51N 123.30W
99 M8 Burnt River Ontario 44.41N 78.43W
100 R3 Burntwood L Manitoba
100 R3 Burntwood R Manitoba
103 C3 Burnwood Pennsylvania 41.47N 75.32W
93 K2 Buroli Kenya 3.36N 38.33E
76 J2 Burón Spain 43.02N 5.03W
66 J3 Büron Switzerland 47.14N 8.05E
44 F5 Buron U.S.S.R. 42.47N 44.04E
79 D4 Buronzo Italy 45.29N 8.16E
72 D9 Buros France 43.21N 0.17W
63 S5 Burow E Germany 53.47N 13.17E
35 D4 Burqa Jordan 32.18N 35.12E
33 M10 Burqan oil field Kuwait
33 M10 Burqān, Al Kuwait 28.58N 47.58E
35 E4 Burqin Jordan 32.27N 35.15E
24 E2 Burqin Xinjiang Uygur Zizhiqu China 47.44N 86.55E
24 F1 Burqin He R Xinjiang Uygur Zizhiqu China
120 B10 Burquillo dist Lima Peru
100 M6 Burr Saskatchewan 52.03N 105.08W
90 D6 Burra Nigeria 11.00N 8.56E
12 E5 Burra S Australia 33.40S 138.57E
14 C9 Burracoppin W Australia 31.22S 118.30E
58 R8 Burrafirth Shetland Scotland 60.48N 0.53W
58 R8 Burra Ness pt Shetland Scotland 60.38N 0.59W
101 G11 Burrard Inlet Br Col
58 Q8 Burra Voe Shetland Scotland 60.35N 1.20W
58 Q9 Burravoe Shetland Scotland 60.23N 1.20W
58 Q9 Burravoe Yell, Shetland Scotland 60.30N 1.03W
58 T12 Burray isld Orkney Scotland 58.51N 2.54W
82 D9 Burrel Albania 41.36N 20.01E
13 C6 Burrell,Mt N Terr Australia 24.35S 134.00E
58 K5 Burrelton Tayside Scotland 56.32N 3.18W
59 D5 Burren reg Clare Irish Rep
12 J4 Burrendong Res New S Wales 32.29S 149.32E
12 J4 Burren Junction New S Wales 30.08S 148.59E
72 G10 Burret France 42.57N 1.28E
12 K6 Burrewarra Pt New S Wales 35.51S 150.12E
75 K8 Burriana Spain 39.54N 0.05W
12 J6 Burrinjuck New S Wales 35.01S 148.33E
12 J5 Burrinjuck Res New S Wales
115 J3 Burro Mexico 29.10N 101.50W
106 C6 Burr Oak Iowa 43.28N 91.51W
109 M2 Burr Oak Kansas 39.53N 98.17W
106 J8 Burr Oak Michigan 41.51N 85.19W
119 J5 Burro Burro,R Guyana
111 L7 Burro Cr Arizona
115 H3 Burro,Serranías del mts Mexico
105 K11 Burrow Cay Bahamas 26.27N 77.46W
13 F3 Burrowes, Pt Queensland 17.00S 149.58E
57 E3 Burrow Hd Dumfries & Galloway Scotland 54.41N 4.24W
109 N3 Burrton Kansas 38.02N 97.41W
13 B2 Burrundie N Terr Australia 13.32S 131.40E
120 F12 Burruyacú Argentina 26.30S 64.45W
107 G13 Burrwood Louisiana 28.57N 89.24W
56 C4 Burry Inlet Wales
56 C4 Burry Port Dyfed Wales 51.42N 4.15W
66 Q3 Bürs Austria 47.09N 9.49E
37 F3 Bursa Turkey 40.12N 29.04E
85 M6 Bûr Safâga Egypt 26.43N 33.55E
Bûr Sa'îd see Port Said
64 C1 Burscheid W Germany 51.06N 7.08E
57 H5 Burscough Bridge Lancs Eng 53.37N 2.51W
66 Q3 Bürserberg Austria 47.09N 9.47E
52 G9 Burseryd Sweden 57.14N 13.15E
63 L9 Bursfelde W Germany 51.32N 9.38E
66 B6 Bursinel Switzerland 46.27N 6.19E
57 J6 Burslem Staffs Eng 53.02N 2.12W
53 G7 Bursø Denmark 54.44N 11.30E
61 F3 Burst Belgium 50.54N 3.55E
69 P4 Bürstadt W Germany 49.38N 8.27E
100 H8 Burstall Saskatchewan 50.40N 109.56W
108 Q6 Burt Iowa 43.11N 94.12W
108 H3 Burt N Dakota 46.22N 102.09W
12 F4 Burta New S Wales 32.30S 141.05E
86 J6 Bûr Taufiq Egypt 29.57N 32.34E
66 B6 Burtigny Switzerland 46.29N 6.16E
106 K4 Burt, L Michigan
56 B4 Burton Dyfed Wales 51.43N 4.55W
57 M6 Burton Lincs Eng 53.16N 0.34W
108 L7 Burton Nebraska 42.56N 99.35W
112 L5 Burton Texas 30.12N 96.37W
57 N4 Burton Agnes Humberside Eng 54.03N 0.19W
57 H4 Burton in Kendal Cumbria Eng 54.12N 2.43W
57 H4 Burton in Lonsdale N Yorks Eng 54.09N 2.32W
105 D3 Burton L Georgia 34.50N 83.33W
57 K4 Burton Leonard N Yorks Eng 54.04N 1.30W
56 H2 Burton on Trent Staffs Eng 52.48N 1.36W
59 F2 Burtonport Donegal Irish Rep 54.59N 8.26W
52 M2 Burträsk Sweden 64.31N 20.40E
98 F7 Burtts Corner New Brunswick 46.03N 66.52W
12 F5 Burtundy New S Wales 33.45S 142.22E
86 F5 Burtus Egypt 30.09N 31.07E
Burtville see Merolia
13 C6 Burt Well N Terr Australia 23.10S 133.46E
19 E5 Buru isld Moluccas Indonesia
43 L4 Burubaytal Kazakhstan U.S.S.R. 45.07N 73.59E
Burud,Al see Barūd, Al
Burui see Jama Papua New Guinea
76 L9 Burujón Spain 39.54N 4.18W
39 D1 Burulgun U.S.S.R. 70.49N 148.45E
Burultokay see Fuhai
60 N6 Burum Netherlands 53.16N 6.14E
33 H9 Burūm S Yemen 14.24N 48.58E
86 F7 Burumbul,El Egypt 29.19N 31.14E
90 D6 Burumburum Nigeria 11.20N 8.46E
33 H9 Burūm,Ra's C S Yemen 14.20N 49.00E
87 D5 Burun reg Sudan
43 M5 Burunday Kazakhstan U.S.S.R. 43.22N 76.50E
73 G6 Burundi kingdom Central Africa
46 P3 Burunduki U.S.S.R. 54.49N 47.35E
18 E5 Burung Sumatra Indon 0.25N 103.32E
45 S9 Burunnyy U.S.S.R. 47.34N 46.45E
93 A9 Bururi Burundi 3.57S 29.35E
39 C3 Burustakh U.S.S.R. 64.21N 144.44E
90 B9 Burutu Nigeria 5.21N 5.31E
22 E4 Buruun Bayan-Ulaan Mongolia 45.32N 101.41E
56 F3 Burwarton Shropshire Eng 52.28N 2.34W
56 M6 Burwash E Sussex Eng 51.00N 0.24E
99 K6 Burwash Ontario 46.14N 80.52W
101 D5 Burwash Landing Yukon Terr 61.21N 139.01W
56 M3 Burwell Cambs Eng 52.16N 0.19E
57 O6 Burwell Lincs Eng 53.19N 0.02E
108 L8 Burwell Nebraska 41.48N 99.09W
58 T12 Burwick Orkney Scotland 58.44N 2.57W
11 M9 Burwood dist Christchurch New Zealand
12 D8 Burwood dist Melbourne, Vic
63 S10 Burxdorf E Germany 51.28N 13.17E
61 E4 Bury Belgium 50.33N 3.36E
57 J5 Bury Greater Manchester Eng 53.36N 2.17W
99 T7 Bury Quebec 45.29N 71.30W
Buryat Mongol'skaya A.S.S.R see Buryatskaya A.S.S.R
38 K3 Buryatskaya A.S.S.R U.S.S.R.
87 F5 Burye Ethiopia 10.40N 37.04E
45 E5 Buryn' Ukraine U.S.S.R. 51.13N 33.50E
44 L2 Burynshik U.S.S.R. 45.24N 51.45E
56 N3 Bury St.Edmunds Suffolk Eng 52.15N 0.43E
71 E7 Burzet France 44.44N 4.15E
31 H3 Burzil Pass Kashmir 34.50N 75.04E
81 B3 Busachi Sardinia 40.03N 8.54E
Busaiya,Al see Buşayyah,Al
79 E5 Busalla Italy 44.34N 8.56E
81 F8 Busambra, Rocca mt Sicily 37.52N 13.24E
79 H6 Busana Italy 44.22N 10.19E
19 L8 Busan B Mindanao Philippines
91 H4 Busanga Zaïre 0.53S 22.07E
91 J9 Busanga Zaïre 10.12S 25.23E
92 C9 Busanga Swamp Zambia
91 J8 Busango Zaïre 8.33S 25.30E
42 J4 Busani,Ozero L U.S.S.R. 55.23N 113.30E
33 C2 Busayţā', Al area Saudi Arabia
34 E8 Busayţā,Al plat Saudi Arabia
34 O8 Buşayyah,Al Iraq 30.05N 46.07E
100 D5 Busby Alberta 53.58N 113.54W
108 D4 Busby Montana 45.30N 106.58W
79 B5 Busca Italy 44.31N 7.28E
81 J9 Buscemi Sicily 37.06N 14.54E
63 R7 Buschow E Germany 52.35N 12.38E
63 J4 Buschsand isld W Germany
86 P4 Buşeirā Jordan 30.45N 35.36E
34 H3 Buseire Syria 35.10N 40.26E
93 E5 Busembatia Uganda 0.46N 33.37E
81 E7 Buseto-Palizzolo Sicily 38.01N 12.42E
82 G9 Buševa Planina mts Yugoslavia
86 F7 Bûsh Egypt 29.09N 31.07E
Bushairiya see Bushayrīyah
83 D3 Bushat Albania 41.58N 19.32E
34 M3 Bushayrīyah Iraq 35.15N 44.16E
32 D6 Būshehr Iran 28.59N 50.50E
32 D6 Būshehr prov Iran
101 T6 Bushell Saskatchewan 59.32N 108.50W
24 D9 Bushêngcaka Xizang Zizhiqu China 32.55N 82.14E
93 B6 Bushenyi Uganda 0.32S 30.13E
55 C2 Bushey Herts England 51.39N 0.22W
59 F6 Bushfield Tipperary Irish Rep 52.48N 8.21W
19 N4 Bush I Truk Is Pacific Oc 7.26N 151.56E
Bushire see Būshehr
103 D4 Bushkill Pennsylvania 41.36N 75.01W
103 D4 Bushkill Falls Pennsylvania 41.07N 75.01W
112 B8 Bushland Texas 35.12N 102.05W
94 E7 Bushman Land, Great reg S Africa
94 E7 Bushman Land, Little reg S Africa
95 N5 Bushman's R S Africa
59 J1 Bushmills Antrim N Ireland 55.12N 6.32W
48 S4 Bushnans Ø isld Greenland 76.00N 64.58W
105 E9 Bushnell Florida 28.41N 82.08W
106 D9 Bushnell Illinois 40.32N 90.31W
108 G8 Bushnell Nebraska 41.15N 103.53W
99 L6 Bushnell Ontario 46.49N 79.36W
59 K1 Bush R Antrim N Ireland
103 B8 Bush R Maryland
Bushruiyah see Boshruyeh
92 D12 Bushtick Zimbabwe 20.15S 28.58E
109 M3 Bushton Kansas 38.31N 98.25W
33 F2 Bushūk,Al dist Saudi Arabia
42 K5 Bushuley U.S.S.R. 52.48N 117.18E
103 K7 Bushwick New York 40.42N 73.55W
103 C3 Bushwick Pennsylvania 41.32N 75.31W
13 E5 Bushy Park Queensland 21.15S 139.45E
92 D10 Busi R Zimbabwe
93 F5 Busia Kenya 0.28N 34.07E
93 F5 Busia Uganda 0.29N 34.05E
69 E3 Busigny France 50.02N 3.29E
93 D5 Busika Uganda 0.35N 32.39E
91 G2 Businga Zaïre 3.16N 20.59E
66 L1 Büsingen W Germany 47.42N 8.41E
66 L1 Büsingen enclave W Germany
91 F4 Busira R Zaïre
93 C8 Busirayombo Tanzania 2.48S 31.47E
93 F5 Busiu Uganda 0.53N 34.12E
82 J1 Busk U.S.S.R. 49.58N 24.35E
53 Y17 Buskerud co Norway
62 M5 Busko Poland 50.28N 20.42E
64 P3 Buškovice Czechoslovakia 50.14N 13.21E
43 F1 Buskul' Kazakhstan U.S.S.R. 53.45N 61.12E
19 F2 Busobuso Moluccas Indon 2.14N 128.38E
93 E5 Busoga dist Uganda
93 E5 Busolwe Uganda 0.51N 33.57E
77 Q4 Busot Spain 38.29N 0.25W
77 K7 Busquistar Spain 36.57N 3.17W
34 D6 Busra Syria 32.30N 36.29E
Busra ash Sham see Busra
35 J2 Busra el Hariri Syria 32.50N 36.21E
87 F8 Bussa Ethiopia 5.38N 37.10E
72 D5 Bussac-Forêt France 45.13N 0.22W
69 M8 Bussang France 47.53N 6.51E
69 M8 Bussang,Col de pass France 47.53N 6.55E
40 D6 Busse U.S.S.R. 51.13N 126.57E
72 C2 Busseau,le France 46.35N 0.35W
14 B10 Busselton W Australia 33.43S 115.15E
66 G2 Busserach Switzerland 47.23N 7.33E
87 A7 Busseri Sudan 7.32N 28.00E
87 A7 Busseri watercourse Sudan
71 D4 Busset France 46.03N 3.31E
79 H5 Busseto Italy 44.59N 10.02E
108 S8 Bussey Iowa 41.11N 92.51W
72 F4 Bussière Badil France 45.40N 0.38E
72 H3 Bussière Dunoise France 46.15N 1.40E
72 G4 Bussière-Galant France 45.38N 1.02E
72 F3 Bussiere Poitevine France 46.14N 0.55E
69 K8 Bussières-lès-Belmont France 47.45N 5.32E
66 C5 Bussigny Switzerland 46.33N 6.33E
66 L1 Büsslingen W Germany 47.47N 8.41E
79 J4 Bussolengo Italy 45.28N 10.51E
79 B4 Bussoleno Italy 45.08N 7.09E
40 M8 Bussol', Proliv str Kuril Is U.S.S.R.
60 J10 Bussum Netherlands 52.17N 5.10E
66 F3 Busswil Switzerland 47.06N 7.19E
69 E7 Bussy-en-Othe France 48.01N 3.30E
71 F1 Bussy-le-Grand France 47.34N 4.32E
41 Q4 Bustakh,Ozero L U.S.S.R.
115 J4 Bustamante Mexico 26.33N 100.32W
121 L5 Bustamente,B Argentina
43 G6 Bustan Uzbekistan U.S.S.R. 40.06N 64.52E
Bustaneh,Ras see Bostāneh,Ra's-e cape
35 D2 Bustan HaGalil Israel 32.57N 35.04E
86 E9 Bustân, Wâdî El watercourse Egypt
13 K6 Bustard Hd Queensland 24.02S 151.48E
50 K3 Bustarfell Iceland 65.36N 15.07W
75 C6 Bustarviejo Spain 40.51N 3.42W
35 H2 Bustas Syria 33.00N 36.02E
75 G4 Buste,El Spain 41.52N 1.36W
82 K5 Bustenari Romania 45.09N 25.49E
115 F3 Bustillos, L Mexico
79 E3 Busto Arsizio Italy 45.37N 8.51E
76 G1 Busto,C Spain 43.34N 6.28W
19 J5 Busuanga Philippines 12.13N 119.53E
19 J5 Busuanga isld Philippines
91 G3 Busu Djanoa Zaïre 1.42N 21.23E
91 G3 Busu Gongo Zaïre 1.52N 21.44E
63 J4 Büsum W Germany 54.08N 8.52E
91 G3 Busu Melo Zaïre 1.44N 20.05E
91 F3 Busu Modanda Zaïre 1.43N 19.58E
93 D5 Busunju Uganda 0.35N 32.16E
89 J7 Busunu Ghana 9.17N 1.31W
91 G3 Bususulu Zaïre 0.48N 20.46E
93 C5 Buta Uganda 0.49N 31.34E
91 J2 Buta Zaïre 2.49N 24.50E
121 G2 Butai R Brazil
87 G6 Buta Jira Ethiopia 8.08N 38.24E
31 B6 Butak Pakistan 29.09N 63.18E
18 K9 Butak,Gunung mt Java Indon 7.58S 112.26E
93 B6 Butale Uganda 0.17S 30.24E
93 E5 Butaleja Uganda 0.54N 33.58E
29 E3 Butana Haryana India 29.11N 76.41E
87 E3 Butana,El reg Sudan
25 E9 Butang Grp islds Thailand
118 F10 Butanta dist São Paulo Brazil
121 B6 Buta Ranquil Argentina 37.01S 69.51W
93 A8 Butare Rwanda 2.35S 29.44E
Butaritari atoll see Makin atoll
19 L4 Butauanan isld Philippines 14.07N 123.17E
33 F4 Buţayn,Al area Saudi Arabia
28 B8 Butcher I Maharashtra India 18.58N 72.54E
12 E5 Bute S Australia 33.24S 138.01E
Bute co see Strathclyde reg
58 F7 Bute I Strathclyde Scotland
93 B5 Butebe Uganda 0.38N 30.13E
101 J9 Butedale Br Col 53.12N 128.45W
93 J1 Bute Giarti Ethiopia 4.34N 37.47E
35 F10 Buteina Jordan 30.52N 35.38E
101 L10 Bute Inlet Br Col
87 F8 Bute Jarti Ethiopia 4.35N 37.46E
58 F7 Bute,Kyles of channel Strathclyde Scotland
93 C4 Butemba Uganda 1.09N 31.37E
93 A5 Butembo Zaïre 0.09N 29.17E
81 H9 Butera Sicily 37.12N 14.12E
93 F5 Butere Kenya 0.14N 34.31E
58 F7 Bute,Sd.of Strathclyde Scotland
61 P5 Bütgenbach Belgium 50.26N 6.12E
95 M4 Butha Buthe Lesotho 28.46S 28.15E
95 M4 Buthabuthe dist Lesotho
21 B3 Butha Qi Nei Monggol Zizhiqu China 48.02N 122.45E
25 B2 Buthidaung Burma 20.50N 92.35E
66 F8 Buthier R Italy
93 C4 Butiaba Uganda 1.48N 31.21E
121 H3 Butiá Guaíba Brazil 30.10S 51.17W
92 F2 Butiama Tanzania 1.45S 33.54E
94 M3 Butiro Mozambique 20.40S 33.31E
93 F5 Butiru Uganda 0.50N 34.18E
93 B5 Butiti Uganda 0.38N 30.30E
63 H5 Butjadingen reg W Germany
47 J7 Butka U.S.S.R. 56.45N 63.45E
47 F4 Butkan U.S.S.R. 63.17N 49.02E
25 C3 Butle R Burma
107 H9 Butler Alabama 32.04N 88.15W
105 C5 Butler Georgia 32.33N 84.16W
106 K8 Butler Indiana 41.25N 84.54W
107 M3 Butler Kentucky 38.48N 84.23W
103 A7 Butler Maryland 39.32N 76.44W
107 B3 Butler Missouri 38.17N 94.21W
103 F4 Butler New Jersey 41.00N 74.20W
104 C6 Butler Ohio 40.35N 82.26W
109 L6 Butler Oklahoma 35.39N 99.13W
104 F6 Butler Pennsylvania 40.51N 79.55W
108 N4 Butler S Dakota 45.15N 97.42W
123 E12 Butler Island Antarctica 72.25S 60.16W
59 H3 Butlers Bridge Cavan Irish Rep 54.03N 7.22W
13 B7 Butlers Dome mt N Terr Australia 25.40S 130.08E
59 E8 Butlerstown Cork Irish Rep 51.35N 8.44W
35 J4 Butm watercourse Syria
34 K2 Butmah Iraq 36.43N 42.42E
35 G2 Butmiye Syria 32.57N 35.52E
93 D5 Butolo Uganda 0.05N 32.15E
47 M3 Buton U.S.S.R. 58.06N 58.52E
18 L6 Butong Borneo Indon 1.06S 114.50E
45 F4 Butre U.S.S.R. 52.58N 34.40E
83 D5 Butrintit, Liqen i L Albania 39.47N 20.00E
13 E5 Butru Queensland 21.30S 139.42E
66 N2 Bütschwil Switzerland 47.23N 9.05E
56 K6 Butser Hill Hants Eng 50.59N 0.59W
26 T8 Buttala Sri Lanka 6.46N 81.15E
79 K4 Buttapietra Italy 45.21N 11.00E
110 N3 Butte Montana 46.00N 112.31W
108 K2 Butte N Dakota 47.50N 100.40W
108 M7 Butte Nebraska 42.56N 98.51W
110 C7 Butte Falls Oregon 42.34N 122.35W
64 L1 Buttelstedt E Germany 51.04N 11.22E
110 D9 Butte Meadows California 40.06N 121.34W
64 G7 Buttenhausen W Germany 48.22N 9.28E
64 L4 Buttenheim W Germany 49.48N 11.02E
64 K6 Buttenwiesen W Germany 48.35N 10.44E
110 F4 Butter Cr Oregon
108 Q6 Butterfield Minnesota 43.58N 94.48W
14 D8 Butterfly W Australia 29.15S 121.30E
57 G3 Buttermere Cumbria Eng 54.33N 3.17W
57 G3 Buttermere L Cumbria Eng 54.32N 3.16W
106 D4 Butternut Wisconsin 42.02N 90.29W
103 D1 Butternut Cr New York
18 A6 Butterworth Pen Malaysia 5.24N 100.22E
95 M8 Butterworth S Africa 32.20S 28.09E
66 C4 Buttes Switzerland 46.54N 6.34E
59 E7 Buttevant Cork Irish Rep 52.14N 8.40W
14 G6 Buttfield, Mt W Australia 24.45S 128.12E
60 B2 Buttinge Netherlands 51.31N 3.37E
56 E2 Buttington Powys Wales 52.41N 3.07W
66 J3 Buttisholz Switzerland 47.07N 8.06E
64 H2 Buttlar E Germany 50.45N 9.58E
52 L9 Buttle Sweden 57.25N 18.31E
101 L11 Buttle Lake Br Col
97 K6 Button Bay Manitoba
97 N5 Button Is N W Terr
111 E6 Buttonwillow California 35.24N 119.29W
79 O2 Búttrio Italy 46.02N 13.20E
64 L1 Buttstädt E Germany 51.08N 11.25E
14 D10 Butty Harb W Australia
14 D10 Butty Hd W Australia 33.52S 121.35E
108 N3 Buttzville N Dakota 46.32N 97.38W
103 E5 Buttzville New Jersey 40.50N 75.00W
19 M7 Butuan Mindanao Philippines 8.56N 125.31E
19 M7 Butuan B Mindanao Philippines
89 J7 Butugu Ghana 8.33N 0.20W
19 D1 Butulan Mindanao Philippines 5.35N 125.30E
86 M7 Butum, Wâdî el watercourse Egypt
19 C6 Butung isld Indonesia
19 C6 Butung, Selat str Indonesia
23 C5 Butuo Sichuan China 27.46N 102.52E
45 Q1 Buturlino U.S.S.R. 55.34N 44.55E
45 M6 Buturlinovka U.S.S.R. 50.50N 40.38E
25 J6 Bu Tu Suay Vietnam 12.19N 107.33E
42 J5 Butuy U.S.S.R. 53.26N 112.20E
30 G5 Butwal Nepal 27.43N 83.27E
46 M2 Butylitsy U.S.S.R. 55.29N 41.30E
47 E5 Butyrskaya U.S.S.R. 62.20N 44.40E
64 F3 Butzbach W Germany 50.26N 8.40E
63 P5 Bützow E Germany 53.52N 11.58E
60 K12 Buurmalsen Netherlands 51.54N 5.18E
60 Q11 Buurse Netherlands 52.08N 6.50E
60 P11 Buurser beek R Netherlands
66 H1 Buus Switzerland 47.31N 7.53E
22 D3 Buutsagaan Mongolia 46.05N 98.44E
53 Y17 Buvatn L Norway 60.45N 8.05E
52 F4 Buvika Norway 62.06N 11.41E
61 G5 Buvrinnes Belgium 50.23N 4.12E
93 E5 Buvuma isld Uganda
Buwair see Buwayr, Al
34 J2 Buwaitir, Wādī watercourse Iraq

33 C4 **Buwāţah** Saudi Arabia 24.38N 39.16E
85 G7 **Buwaymah** Libya 24.15N 23.25E
33 C4 **Buwayr, Al** Saudi Arabia 25.00N 39.01E
35 H4 **Buweida, El** Jordan 32.28N 36.04E
35 H10 **Buwei'ija** *watercourse* Jordan
86 O4 **Buweirida, Wādī el** *watercourse* Jordan
93 E5 **Buwenge** Uganda 0.35N 33.11E
33 M7 **Buwī, Al** Oman 19.40N 57.21E
30 G7 **Buxar** Bihar India 25.35N 84.00E
72 E2 **Buxerolles** France 46.37N 0.22E
72 H1 **Buxeuil** France 47.07N 1.42E
72 K3 **Buxières-les-Mines** France 46.29N 2.57E
63 L6 **Buxtehude** W Germany 53.29N 9.42E
57 K6 **Buxton** Derbys Eng 53.15N 1.55W
117 A1 **Buxton** Guyana 6.45N 58.05W
105 M2 **Buxton** N Carolina 35.16N 75.32W
95 H3 **Buxton** S Africa 27.38S 24.38E
71 F3 **Buxy** France 46.43N 4.41E
46 M1 **Buy** U.S.S.R. 58.23N 41.27E
47 H7 **Buy** *R* U.S.S.R.
89 J7 **Buya** Ghana 8.20N 0.08W
93 C6 **Buyaga B** Uganda
15 E8 **Buyake** *str* Irian Jaya
22 H4 **Buyant** Mongolia 45.35N 110.50E
Buyanta Tsagān Gol *see* **Buutsagaan**
22 B3 **Buyant Gol** *R* Mongolia
22 G4 **Buyant-Ovoo** Mongolia 44.30N 107.10E
42 E5 **Buyba** U.S.S.R. 52.40N 93.28E
100 K2 **Buyck** Minnesota 48.08N 92.30W
93 E4 **Buyende** Uganda 1.11N 33.11E
Būyīn *see* **Bū'īn**
44 H5 **Buynaksk** U.S.S.R. 42.48N 47.07E
46 G4 **Buynovichi** Belorussiya U.S.S.R. 51.50N 28.30E
89 F8 **Buyo** Ivory Coast 6.21N 7.05W
76 E1 **Buyo, Mtes. del** Spain
93 A10 **Buyonga** Tanzania 4.37S 29.50E
22 L3 **Buyr Nuur** *L* Mongolia
37 F2 **Büyük** *isld* Turkey
36 F2 **Büyük** *R* Bolu Turkey
37 F5 **Büyük** *R* Rize Turkey
37 G2 **Büyükada** Turkey 40.52N 29.08E
37 C3 **Büyük Anafarta** Turkey 40.17N 26.20E
36 H5 **Büyük Çakır** Turkey 37.46N 35.27E
37 F1 **Büyükçekmece** Turkey 41.02N 28.35E
37 F1 **Büyükçekmece Gölü** *L* Turkey
37 F2 **Büyükçekmece Koya** *cove* Turkey
37 F5 **Büyük Dağı** *mt* Turkey 40.57N 41.55E
37 H2 **Büyük Derbent** Turkey 40.43N 30.08E
37 F1 **Büyükdere** Turkey 41.10N 29.02E
36 G6 **Büyük Egri Dağ** *mt* Turkey 36.45N 33.33E
36 C1 **Büyük Karıştiran** Turkey 41.18N 27.32E
37 B3 **Büyük Kemikli Burun** *C* Turkey 40.19N 26.13E
Büyükliman *see* **Vakfıkebir**
36 C5 **Büyük Menderes** *R* Turkey
36 D3 **Büyük Orhan** Turkey 39.45N 28.52E
36 J4 **Büyük Örtülü** Turkey 38.32N 36.42E
34 M4 **Büyük Yenija** Iraq 34.52N 44.33E
39 E3 **Buyunda** *R* U.S.S.R.
44 L2 **Buzachi, Poluostrov** *pen* Kazakhstan U.S.S.R.
31 H2 **Buzai Gumbad** Afghanistan 37.08N 74.02E
44 J1 **Buzan** *R* U.S.S.R.
72 G2 **Buzançais** France 46.53N 1.26E
69 H5 **Buzancy** France 49.26N 4.58E
82 K5 **Buzău** Romania 45.09N 26.49E
82 K5 **Buzăul** *R* Romania
82 K5 **Buzăului, Munţii** *mts* Romania
85 G7 **Buzaymah** Libya 24.47N 22.03E
31 B3 **Buzbai** Afghanistan 35.28N 63.22E
37 D7 **Buz Dağı** *mt* Turkey 38.04N 38.03E
46 R3 **Buzdyak** U.S.S.R. 54.38N 54.31E
20 E8 **Buzen** Japan 33.37N 131.06E
61 N8 **Buzenol** Belgium 49.38N 5.36E
61 H4 **Buzet** Belgium 50.32N 4.22E
72 E7 **Buzet-sur-Baïse** Lot-et-Garonne France 44.15N 0.18E
72 H8 **Buzet-sur-Tarn** France 43.47N 1.37E
45 K1 **Buzhaninovo** U.S.S.R. 56.21N 38.18E
94 M3 **Buzi** *R* Mozambique
82 G5 **Buziaş** Romania 45.38N 21.36E
33 N8 **Buzīyeh** Iran 30.40N 48.42E
Buznabad *see* **Boznābād**
45 R4 **Buzovlevo** U.S.S.R. 52.45N 45.40E
46 S3 **Buzov'yazy** U.S.S.R. 54.20N 55.49E
43 H2 **Buzuluk** Kazakhstan U.S.S.R. 51.53N 66.09E
46 Q3 **Buzuluk** U.S.S.R. 52.49N 52.19E
46 Q4 **Buzuluk** *R* Orenburg U.S.S.R.
46 N4 **Buzuluk** *R* Volgograd U.S.S.R.
33 J9 **Buzun** S Yemen 15.40N 50.54E
72 D9 **Buzy** Basses-Pyrénées France 43.08N 0.27W
69 K5 **Buzy** Meuse France 49.10N 5.44E
103 N3 **Buzzards B** Massachusetts
15 M9 **Bwagaoia** Louisiade Arch 10.39S 152.48E
91 F1 **Bwaka** *tribe* Zaïre
91 F6 **Bwalenge** Zaïre 5.03S 19.16E
92 D8 **Bwana Mkubwa** Zambia 13.01S 28.41E
91 F5 **Bwasa** Zaïre 3.55S 18.24E
15 L9 **Bwasiaia** D'Entrecasteaux Is Papua New Guinea 10.06S 150.58E
89 D7 **Bwedu** Sierra Leone 8.22N 10.21W
92 K12 **Bwejuu** Zanzibar 6.14S 39.32E
87 A8 **Bwendi** Zaïre 4.01N 26.42E
91 K1 **Bwendi** Zaïre 4.01N 26.42E
92 J5 **Bweni** Mafia I E Africa 7.41S 39.55E
93 C9 **Bweru** Tanzania 3.46S 31.13E
93 C4 **Bwijanga** Uganda 1.31N 31.33E
93 D8 **Bwiru** Tanzania 2.02S 32.54E
93 B6 **Bwizibwera** Uganda 0.25S 30.36E
56 E4 **Bwlch** Powys Wales 51.54N 3.15W
52 J6 **By** Sweden 60.15N 16.30E
28 B3 **Byadgi** Karnataka India 14.38N 75.31E
28 H2 **Byakar** Bhutan 27.32N 90.29E
82 K7 **Byala** Bulgaria 43.28N 25.44E
82 L8 **Byala** Bulgaria 42.53N 27.55E
82 H7 **Byala Slatina** Bulgaria 43.29N 22.55E
97 J2 **Byam Martin Chan** N W Terr
97 J2 **Byam Martin I** N W Terr 75.20N 104.30W
44 J8 **Byandovan** Azerbaydzhan U.S.S.R. 39.46N 49.23E
44 J8 **Byandovan, Mys** *C* Azerbaydzhan U.S.S.R. 39.43N 49.26E
109 N7 **Byars** Oklahoma 34.54N 97.03W
Byblos *see* **Jubail** Lebanon
62 O4 **Bychawa** Poland 51.01N 22.32E
41 H5 **Bychezhnyy** U.S.S.R. 72.05N 104.13E
45 B1 **Bychikha** Belorussiya U.S.S.R. 55.40N 29.59E
45 N3 **Bychki** U.S.S.R. 53.01N 41.57E
28 A8 **Byculla** *dist* Bombay India
62 L4 **Byczyna** Poland 51.07N 18.10E
62 K3 **Bydgoszcz** Poland 53.16N 18.00E
42 F3 **Bydumskiy Byk, Shiv** *falls* U.S.S.R. 58.20N 95.15E
Byelorussia *see* **Belorussiya S.S.R.**
100 E6 **Byemoor** Alberta 52.00N 112.17W
109 F2 **Byers** Colorado 39.43N 104.14W
112 J1 **Byers** Texas 34.04N 98.13W
99 J4 **Byers, Mt** Ontario 48.38N 81.48W
13 G3 **Byerstown** Queensland 16.00S 144.41E
104 D7 **Byesville** Ohio 39.58N 81.33W
56 J3 **Byfield** Northants Eng 52.11N 1.14W
53 S18 **Byfjorden** *inlet* Norway 60.25N 5.15E
53 T20 **Byfjorden** *inlet* Norway 59.02N 5.37E
55 B5 **Byfleet** Surrey England 51.21N 0.29W
52 M2 **Bygdeå** Sweden 64.03N 20.50E
52 M2 **Bygdeträsk** Sweden 64.25N 20.30E
53 Y16 **Bygdin** *L* Norway
52 M2 **Bygdsiljum** Sweden 64.21N 20.30E
53 D5 **Bygholm Å** *R* Denmark
52 D8 **Bygland** Norway 58.50N 7.49E
52 D8 **Byglandsfjord** Norway 58.40N 7.50E
13 F8 **Bygrave, Mt** Queensland 28.55S 142.03E
53 T16 **Bygstad** Norway 61.23N 5.40E
107 G7 **Byhalia** Mississippi 34.52N 89.40W
45 B3 **Bykhov** Belorussiya U.S.S.R. 53.30N 30.15E
53 W20 **Bykle** Norway 59.21N 7.20E
53 W20 **Bykleheiene** *moor* Norway 59.26N 7.09E
53 W20 **Bykleheiene** *mts* Norway
40 J8 **Bykov** Sakhalin U.S.S.R. 47.19N 142.32E
46 G6 **Bykovets** Moldavia U.S.S.R. 47.12N 28.29E
47 F5 **Bykovo** Arkhangel'sk U.S.S.R. 61.02N 48.09E
45 J5 **Bykovo** Kursk U.S.S.R. 51.36N 37.54E
45 R7 **Bykovo** Volgograd U.S.S.R. 49.40N 45.19E
41 N5 **Bykovskaya Protoka** *channel* U.S.S.R.
41 N5 **Bykovskiy** U.S.S.R. 72.03N 129.06E
41 N5 **Bykovskiy Poluostrov** *pen* U.S.S.R.
57 F6 **Bylchau** Clwyd Wales 53.09N 3.31W
53 C7 **Bylderup** Denmark 54.58N 9.07E
42 B2 **Bylino** U.S.S.R. 60.45N 76.45E
43 M3 **Bylkyldak** Kazakhstan U.S.S.R. 48.15N 75.05E
39 C3 **Byllar** U.S.S.R. 63.08N 143.32E
97 M3 **Bylot I** N W Terr 73.30N 79.00W
44 E4 **Bylym** U.S.S.R. 43.27N 43.02E
47 M4 **Byn'gi** U.S.S.R. 57.34N 60.19E
99 K7 **Byng Inlet** Ontario 45.45N 80.33W
13 F4 **Bynoe** *R* Queensland
13 B2 **Bynoe Harbour** N Terr Australia 12.30S 130.30E
110 N2 **Bynum** Montana 47.58N 112.20W
110 N2 **Bynum Res** Montana 47.58N 112.28W
41 E4 **Bynyuda** *R* U.S.S.R.
107 F9 **Byram** Mississippi 32.11N 90.17W
41 M5 **Byraya-Tas, Vozvyshennost'** *heights* U.S.S.R.
123 H6 **Byrd Glacier** Antarctica
99 O5 **Byrd, L** Quebec 47.02N 76.56W
123 H10 **Byrd Land** Antarctica
42 K6 **Byrka** U.S.S.R. 50.40N 118.40E
53 S17 **Byrkjeland** Norway 60.54N 5.18E
53 R17 **Byrknesøy** *isld* Norway 60.53N 4.54E
57 J2 **Byrness** Northumb Eng 55.19N 2.22W
14 B7 **Byro** W Australia 26.05S 116.05E
12 H4 **Byrock** New S Wales 30.40S 146.25E
105 D5 **Byromville** Georgia 32.11N 83.54W
111 C4 **Byron** California 37.50N 121.39W
106 E7 **Byron** Illinois 42.09N 89.17W
104 P2 **Byron** Maine 44.44N 70.37W
108 B5 **Byron** Wyoming 44.48N 108.20W
12 L3 **Byron Bay** New S Wales 28.43S 153.34E
101 T1 **Byron Bay** Victoria I, N W Terr
12 L3 **Byron, C** New S Wales 38.47S 153.11E
121 H6 **Byron I** Chile 46.45S 75.15W
14 B7 **Byro Plains** W Australia
41 F4 **Byrranga, Gory** *mts* U.S.S.R.
53 G2 **Byrum** Denmark 57.15N 11.01E
41 M8 **Byrykan** *R* U.S.S.R.
47 G6 **Byserovo** U.S.S.R. 59.04N 53.15E
52 N2 **Byske** Sweden 64.58N 21.10E
51 H6 **Byske älv** *R* Sweden
40 E5 **Byssa** U.S.S.R. 52.24N 130.28E
40 E5 **Byssa** *R* U.S.S.R.
62 M6 **Bystrá** *mt* Czechoslovakia 49.10N 19.50E
39 F6 **Bystraya** *R* Kamchatka U.S.S.R.
39 F7 **Bystraya** *R* U.S.S.R.
41 D4 **Bystraya** *R* U.S.S.R.
65 O2 **Bystré** Czechoslovakia 49.38N 16.21E
65 L2 **Bystřice** Czechoslovakia 49.44N 14.39E
65 O2 **Bystřice nad Pernšteynem** Czech 49.32N 16.16E
42 H7 **Bystrinskiy Golets, Gora** *mt* U.S.S.R. 49.45N 110.00E
46 E5 **Bystritsa** *R* Ukraine U.S.S.R.
43 M5 **Bystrovka** Kirgiziya U.S.S.R. 42.45N 75.13E
47 L6 **Bystryy** U.S.S.R. 57.49N 74.00E
42 C6 **Bystryy Istok** U.S.S.R. 52.24N 84.29E
62 K5 **Bystrzyca Kłodzka** Poland 50.19N 16.39E
41 O8 **Bysyttakh** U.S.S.R. 63.20N 132.00E
41 O6 **Bytantay** *R* U.S.S.R.
62 L6 **Bytča** Czechoslovakia 49.15N 18.30E
46 F3 **Byten'** Belorussiya U.S.S.R. 52.50N 25.28E
56 L3 **Bythorn** Cambs Eng 52.22N 0.27W
62 L5 **Bytom** Poland 50.21N 18.51E
45 F3 **Bytosh'** U.S.S.R. 53.49N 34.06E
62 K1 **Bytów** Poland 54.10N 17.29E
39 C3 **Byuchennyakh** U.S.S.R. 62.51N 143.19E
32 F1 **Byurgyutli** Turkmeniya U.S.S.R. 38.12N 55.32E
52 K9 **Byxelkrok** Sweden 57.18N 17.02E
39 D1 **Byyangnyr** U.S.S.R. 69.55N 145.18E
13 J7 **Byzantium** Queensland 27.15S 147.35E
Byzantium *anc city see* **İstanbul**
47 N4 **Byzovo** U.S.S.R. 57.33N 60.52E
44 C4 **Bzipi** Georgia U.S.S.R. 43.15N 40.24E
62 M3 **Bzura** *R* Poland
44 D4 **Bzyb** *R* U.S.S.R.
44 D4 **Bzybskiy Khrebet** *mts* Georgia U.S.S.R.
44 C4 **Bzych** U.S.S.R. 43.50N 39.45E
118 B9 **Caacupé** Paraguay 25.23S 57.05W
118 C9 **Caaguazú** Paraguay 25.25S 56.02W
118 C9 **Caaguazú** *dept* Paraguay
118 C9 **Caaguazú, Cord. de** *mts* Paraguay
119 H9 **Caapiranga** Brazil 3.18S 61.13W
118 B10 **Caapucú** Paraguay 26.14S 57.10W
118 C8 **Caarapó** Brazil 22.30S 54.51W
118 F5 **Caatinga** Brazil 17.07S 45.55W
118 C10 **Caazapá** Paraguay 26.09S 56.25W
118 C10 **Caazapá** *dept* Paraguay
91 C7 **Cabaą da Cabra, Farol de** *pt* Angola 6.29S 12.30E
118 B4 **Cabaçal, R** Brazil
117 H8 **Cabaceiras** Brazil 7.26S 36.15W
76 G7 **Cabaco, El** Spain 40.34N 6.08W
116 E3 **Cabaiguán** Cuba 22.04N 79.32W
Cabalantian *see* **Guagua**
119 H9 **Cabaliana, L** Brazil 3.28S 61.00W
72 D10 **Cabaliros** *mt* France 42.56N 0.07W
120 B6 **Caballas** Peru 14.58S 75.29W
75 P3 **Caballera. Sierra** *mts* Spain
77 Y13 **Caballeria, C** Balearic Is 40.05N 4.05E
109 C9 **Caballo** New Mexico 32.59N 107.20W
19 G2 **Caballo** *isld* Luzon Philippines 14.22N 120.37E
76 F9 **Caballo** *mt* Spain 39.59N 6.49W
77 K6 **Caballo, Cerro del** *mt* Spain 47.01N 3.27W
119 E9 **Caballococha** Peru 3.55S 70.30W
109 C9 **Caballo Res** New Mexico
115 G3 **Caballos Mesteños, Llano de los** *plain* Mexico
120 A3 **Cabana** Ancash Peru 8.24S 78.00W
120 C6 **Cabana** Ayacucho Peru 14.18S 74.02W
76 B2 **Cabana** Spain 43.13N 8.58W
72 E9 **Cabanac** France 43.17N 0.14E
120 D6 **Cabanaconde** Peru 15.37S 71.59W
76 H2 **Cabañaquinta** Spain 43.10N 5.37W
76 C2 **Cabañas** Spain 43.25N 8.11W
77 L5 **Cabañas** *mt* Spain 37.49N 2.56W
76 H9 **Cabañas del Castillo** Spain 39.33N 5.30W
75 C2 **Cabañas de Virtus** Spain 43.00N 3.52W
19 K4 **Cabanatuan** Luzon Philippines 15.30N 120.58E
75 L7 **Cabanes** Spain 40.09N 0.02E
87 J9 **Cabangifa** Somalia 3.30N 43.30E
91 E9 **Cabango** Angola 10.09S 16.33E
75 G3 **Cabanillas** Spain 42.03N 1.31W
72 H10 **Cabannes, les** France 42.46N 1.41E
98 D6 **Cabano** Quebec 47.40N 68.56W
120 E8 **Cabaraya, Cerro** *pk* Bolivia/Chile 19.10S 68.45W
19 K3 **Cabarruyan** *isld* Luzon Philippines 16.20N 120.00E
71 J10 **Cabasse** France 43.26N 6.14E
60 H12 **Cabauw** Netherlands 51.58N 4.54E
13 K7 **Cabawin** Queensland 27.18S 150.18E
13 K1 **Cabbage Tree Cr** Brisbane, Qnsld
19 G2 **Cabcaben** Luzon Philippines 14.27N 120.37E
76 D4 **Cabe** *R* Spain
76 D13 **Cabeça Gorda** Portugal 37.55N 7.47W
76 C11 **Cabeção** Portugal 38.57N 8.04W
118 F4 **Cabeceiras** Brazil 15.45S 47.00W
76 D5 **Cabeceiras de Basto** Portugal 41.31N 8.00W
76 E9 **Cabeço Alto** *mt* Portugal 39.44N 7.03W
76 D10 **Cabeço de Vide** Portugal 39.08N 7.35W
76 D9 **Cabeço Rainha** *mt* Portugal 39.52N 7.54W
121 F3 **Cabellos** Uruguay 30.40S 57.20W
72 C6 **Cabenac-et-Villagrains** France 44.35N 0.34W
60 S17 **Caberg** Netherlands 50.52N 5.40E
106 F8 **Cabery** Illinois 41.01N 88.13W
76 F9 **Cabeza Araya** *mt* Spain 39.36N 6.39W
77 F3 **Cabeza de Buey** Spain 38.44N 5.13W
77 K3 **Cabeza de Buey** *mt* Spain 38.38N 3.12W
76 G7 **Cabeza de Diego Gómez** *mt* Spain 40.55N 6.04W
76 M7 **Cabeza de Hierro** *mt* Spain
121 C9 **Cabeza del Buey** Argentina 43.50S 68.07W
76 F6 **Cabeza del Caballo** Spain 41.08N 6.34W
76 E4 **Cabeza de Manzaneda** *mt* Spain 42.15N 7.19W
120 D12 **Cabeza de Vaca, Pta** *C* Chile 26.50S 70.52W
120 A4 **Cabeza Lagarto, Pta** *C* Peru 10.06S 78.12W
77 D4 **Cabeza la Vaca** Spain 38.05N 6.24W
75 D8 **Cabezamesada** Spain 39.48N 3.06W
77 H3 **Cabezarados** Spain 38.50N 4.18W
77 H3 **Cabezarrubias del Puerto** Spain 38.37N 4.11W
120 F8 **Cabezas** Bolivia 18.45S 63.22W
115 O10 **Cabezas** Guatemala 14.11N 90.08W
105 K7 **Cabezas de San Juan** *pt* Puerto Rico 18.25N 65.38W
77 E7 **Cabezas de San Juan, Las** Spain 36.59N 4.56W
77 B5 **Cabezas Rubias** Spain 37.44N 7.05W
76 F4 **Cabezo** *mt* Spain 42.18N 6.42W
77 B5 **Cabezo Gordo** *mt* Spain 37.50N 7.09W
109 C6 **Cabezon** New Mexico 35.37N 107.07W
76 K5 **Cabezón** Spain 41.42N 4.39W
76 L2 **Cabezón de la Sal** Spain 43.19N 4.14W
76 K2 **Cabezón de Liébana** Spain 43.08N 4.35W
76 H8 **Cabezuela del Valle** Spain 40.11N 5.48W
77 F3 **Cabezza de Buey, Sierra de** *mts* Spain
75 L7 **Cabicorp, Pta** *pt* Spain 40.13N 0.16E
19 L7 **Cabilao** *isld* Philippines 9.54N 123.46E
121 E7 **Cabildo** Argentina 38.28S 61.50W
121 B4 **Cabildo** Chile 32.30S 71.05W
119 E2 **Cabimas** Venezuela 10.26N 71.27W
109 P5 **Cabin Creek** Oklahoma
91 C6 **Cabinda** Angola 5.34S 12.12E
91 C6 **Cabinda** *exclave* Angola
110 J1 **Cabinet Gorge Dam** Idaho 48.06N 116.02W
110 J1 **Cabinet Mts** Idaho/Montana
19 K9 **Cabingan** *isld* Philippines 5.40N 121.04E
91 C8 **Cabiri** Angola 8.56S 13.40E
106 C3 **Cable** Wisconsin 46.12N 91.17W
96 B13 **Cable Sta** St Helena 15.57S 5.43W
117 J9 **Cabo** Brazil 8.16S 35.00W
87 L8 **Cabobe, El** Somalia 4.12N 47.40E
121 M6 **Cabo Blanco** Argentina 47.15S 65.47W
88 F8 **Cabo Bojador** *C* Morocco 26.06N 14.33W
96 U3 **Cabo da Praia** Azores 38.43N 27.04W
77 M7 **Cabo de Gata, El** Spain 36.48N 2.14W
77 M7 **Cabo de Gata, Sierra de** *mts* Spain
92 J8 **Cabo Delgado** *dist* Mozambique
118 G8 **Cabo Frio** Brazil 22.51S 42.03W
88 G8 **Cabo Juby** *C* Morocco 27.59N 12.54W
75 F5 **Cabolafuente** Spain 41.13N 2.03W
99 O5 **Cabonga, Rés** Quebec
107 D4 **Cabool** Missouri 37.08N 92.08W
13 L7 **Caboolture** Queensland 27.05S 152.50E
119 C8 **Cabo Pantoja** Peru 0.59S 75.14W
92 F9 **Cabora Bassa Dam** Mozambique 15.34S 32.42E
121 D10 **Cabo Raso** Argentina 44.23S 65.15W
115 C2 **Caborca** Mexico 30.42N 112.10W
105 J8 **Cabo Rojo** *C* Puerto Rico
107 E7 **Cabot** Arkansas 35.00N 92.00W
99 J7 **Cabot Head** Ontario 45.15N 81.17W
98 M6 **Cabot Strait** Nfld/Nova Scotia
70 K3 **Cabourg** France 49.17N 0.07W
Cabo Verde, Ilhas do *see* **Cape Verde Islands**
76 D7 **Cabra** Portugal 40.34N 7.35W
77 H6 **Cabra** Spain 37.28N 4.28W
19 K5 **Cabra** *isld* Philippines 13.53N 120.04E
76 B5 **Cabração** Portugal 41.50N 8.39W
77 K5 **Cabra del Santo Cristo** Spain 37.42N 3.16W
75 J7 **Cabra de Mora** Spain 40.19N 0.49W
28 J7 **Cabra I** Nicobar Is 7.19N 93.50E
116 J5 **Cabral** Dominican Rep 18.16N 71.11W
Cabrales *see* **Carreña**
118 G5 **Cabral, Sierra do** *mts* Brazil
76 J2 **Cabranes** Spain 43.25N 5.25W
81 B4 **Cabras** Sardinia 39.52N 8.31E
77 H6 **Cabras** *mt* Spain 37.06N 4.10W
76 E7 **Cabras** *R* Portugal
91 A12 **Cabras, I.das** São Tomé São Tomé & Principe, Gulf of Guinea 0.24N 6.43E
77 H5 **Cabra, Sierra de** *mts* Spain
75 D5 **Cabras, Sierra de las** *mts* Guadalajara etc Spain
77 O3 **Cabras, Sierra de las** *mts* Murcia Spain
77 E7 **Cabras, Sierra de las** *mts* Spain
71 H7 **Cabre, Col de** *pass* France 44.32N 5.36E
121 F2 **Cabred** Argentina 30.00S 57.40W
76 C5 **Cabreira** *mt* Portugal 41.38N 8.03W
76 D2 **Cabreiros** Spain 43.24N 7.46W
75 F7 **Cabrejas, Altos de** *hills* Spain
75 E4 **Cabrejas del Pinar** Spain 41.48N 2.51W
75 E4 **Cabrejas, Sierra de** *mts* Spain
76 C11 **Cabrela** Portugal 38.36N 8.28W
121 D4 **Cabrera** Argentina 32.49S 63.50W
116 K5 **Cabrera** Dominican Rep 19.40N 69.54W
74 J5 **Cabrera** *isld* Balearic Is Spain
77 H4 **Cabrera** *R* Jaeń Spain
76 F4 **Cabrera** *R* León Spain
77 V15 **Cabrera, Pto** *B* Balearic Is
116 F4 **Cabreras** *R* Cuba
77 N6 **Cabrera, Sierra** *mts* Almería Spain
76 F4 **Cabrera, Sierra** *mts* León/Zamora Spain
72 H6 **Cabrerets** France 44.31N 1.39E
121 A6 **Cabrero** Chile 37.00S 72.28W
100 J8 **Cabri** Saskatchewan 50.38N 108.28W
75 G8 **Cabriel** *R* Spain
71 J9 **Cabrière, la** France 43.39N 6.23E
71 G10 **Cabriès** France 43.27N 5.22E
76 C7 **Cabril** Beira Alta Portugal 40.58N 8.06W
76 D8 **Cabril** Beira Baixa Portugal 40.05N 7.52W
76 C9 **Cabril, Barragem de** *res* Portugal 39.45N 8.10W
76 C9 **Cabril do Zezere** *dam* Portugal 39.55N 8.08W
76 G3 **Cabrillanes** Spain 42.57N 6.09W
76 G7 **Cabrillas** Spain 40.45N 6.12W
75 G6 **Cabrillas** *R* Spain
111 G9 **Cabrillo Nat. Mon** California 32.40N 117.15W
76 D6 **Cabris** Portugal 41.27N 7.48W
77 E8 **Cabrito, Pto. del** *pass* Spain 36.04N 5.32W
116 L4 **Cabrits, I** Martinique W I 14.23N 60.53W
117 G9 **Cabrobó** Brazil 8.30S 39.19W
119 F4 **Cabruta** Venezuela 7.40N 66.16W
19 K8 **Cabucan** *isld* Philippines 6.09N 120.55E
119 E2 **Cabudare** Venezuela 10.02N 69.14W
19 K3 **Cabugao** Luzon Philippines 17.47N 120.28E
19 K6 **Cabulauan** *isld* Philippines 11.22N 120.05E
115 E2 **Cabullona** Mexico 31.10N 109.32W
19 D1 **Caburah** Mindanao Philippines 5.59N 125.40E
91 D8 **Cabuta** Angola 9.48S 14.58E
19 L2 **Cabutunan Pt** Luzon Philippines 18.04N 122.12E
119 D5 **Cabuyaro** Colombia 4.21N 72.47W
76 F3 **Cacabelos** Spain 42.36N 6.44W
118 E10 **Caçador** Brazil 26.51S 50.54W
115 K9 **Cacahuatepec** Mexico 16.37N 98.10W
82 F7 **Čačak** Yugoslavia 43.54N 20.22E
117 C2 **Cacao** Fr Guiana 4.37N 52.29W
119 E9 **Cacao, I** Colombia 3.52S 70.23W
98 F3 **Cacaoui L** Quebec
118 F8 **Caçapava** Brazil 23.05S 45.40W
121 H3 **Caçapava do Sul** Brazil 30.28S 53.29W
104 G7 **Cacapon** *R* W Virginia
76 G5 **Caçarelhos** Portugal 41.33N 6.30W
119 C4 **Cácares** Colombia 7.36N 75.23W
37 F7 **Cacas** Turkey 38.25N 41.17E
25 J2 **Cac Ba, I** Vietnam 20.47N 107.00E
81 G8 **Caccamo** Sicily 37.56N 13.40E
81 A2 **Caccia, C** Sardinia 40.34N 8.09E
80 O6 **Caccia, Monte** Italy 41.02N 16.14E
66 M8 **Caccivio** Italy 45.46N 9.00E
76 D14 **Cacela** Portugal 37.09N 7.33W
121 G2 **Cacequi** Brazil 29.55S 54.50W
118 B5 **Cáceres** Brazil 16.05S 57.40W
76 G10 **Cáceres** Spain 39.29N 6.23W
74 C5 **Cáceres** *prov* Spain
118 B6 **Cáceres, L** Bolivia 18.52S 57.44W
68 E4 **Cachan** France 48.47N 2.20E
28 J3 **Cachar** *dist* Assam India
109 M7 **Cache** Oklahoma 34.38N 98.37W
107 E6 **Cache** *R* Arkansas
107 G4 **Cache** *R* Illinois
99 L6 **Cache Bay** Ontario 46.22N 79.59W
101 N10 **Cache Creek** Br Columbia 50.49N 121.20W
111 B3 **Cache Creek** California
88 O4 **Cacherou** Algeria 35.18N 0.20E
89 A5 **Cacheu** Guinea-Bissau 12.12N 16.10W
89 A5 **Cacheu** *R* Guinea-Bissau
120 E11 **Cachi** Argentina 25.05S 66.10W
120 E11 **Cachi** *R*
75 J2 **Cachilla** *mt* Spain 42.58N 0.54W
117 B9 **Cachimbo** Brazil 9.21S 54.58W
117 B9 **Cachimbo, Sa. do** *mts* Brazil
91 G8 **Cachimo** Angola 8.21S 21.24E
91 G8 **Cachimo** *R* Angola/Zaïre
120 D11 **Cachina** *R* Chile
120 D11 **Cachinal** Chile 25.56S 69.30W
120 E11 **Cachi, Nev. de** *pk* Argentina 24.48S 66.39W
91 E10 **Cachingues** Angola 13.06S 16.46E
119 D4 **Cáchira** Colombia 7.44N 73.07W
91 H10 **Cachiriavinha** Angola 12.50S 22.11E
121 B2 **Cachiyuyu** Chile 29.03S 70.58W
118 J3 **Cachoeira** Brazil 12.35S 38.59W
117 E8 **Cachoeira** *R* Brazil
118 E6 **Cachoeira Alta** Brazil 18.53S 50.54W
118 E5 **Cachoeira de Goiás** Brazil 16.40S 50.39W
117 D5 **Cachoeira do Arari** Brazil 1.00S 48.58W
121 H3 **Cachoeira do Sul** Brazil 30.03S 52.52W
118 F8 **Cachoeira Paulista** Brazil 22.39S 45.01W
118 H7 **Cachoeiro de Itapemirim** Brazil 20.51N 41.07W
76 D14 **Cachopo** Portugal 37.20N 7.49W
76 F9 **Cachorrilla** Spain 39.54N 6.40W
121 B1 **Cachos, Pta. de** Chile 27.40S 71.06W
91 E11 **Cachueca** Angola 15.17S 16.53E
120 F4 **Cachuela Esperanza** Bolivia 10.32S 65.38W
111 E7 **Cachuma, L** California 34.35N 119.57W
91 G10 **Cachungo** Angola 13.30S 21.52E
76 E16 **Cacilhas** Portugal 38.41N 9.09W
76 D16 **Cacilhas, Pta de** *C* Portugal
91 B12 **Cacimba** Angola 16.47S 11.53E
117 G9 **Cacimbas** Brazil 9.10S 41.56W
77 J6 **Cacin** Spain 37.04N 3.55W
77 J6 **Cacin** *R* Spain
82 D5 **Cačinci** Yugoslavia 45.36N 17.50E
89 B6 **Cacine** Guinea-Bissau 11.08N 14.57W
89 B6 **Cacine** *R* Guinea-Bissau
117 C3 **Caciporé** *R* Brazil
117 C3 **Caciporé, C** Brazil 3.55N 51.07W
19 J6 **Cacnipa** *isld* Philippines 10.25N 119.01E
91 F9 **Cacolo** Angola 10.09S 19.21E
91 D10 **Caconda** Angola 13.43S 15.03E
98 C6 **Cacouna** Quebec 47.55N 69.32W
111 N8 **Cactus** Arizona 33.39N 112.00W
112 H8 **Cactus** Texas 27.54N 99.25W
100 H6 **Cactus Lake** Saskatchewan 52.08N 109.50W
111 H4 **Cactus Ra** Nevada
118 D6 **Caçu** Brazil 18.38S 51.08W
91 C8 **Cacuaco** Angola 8.47S 13.21E
91 D11 **Cacula** Angola 14.33S 14.04E
91 E8 **Caculama** Angola 9.29S 16.54E
118 G4 **Caculé** Brazil 14.32S 42.09W
91 D12 **Caculuvar** *R* Angola
118 D5 **Caçununga** Brazil 16.02S 53.37W
91 D8 **Cacuso** Angola 9.26S 15.43E
75 D1 **Cadagua** Spain 43.04N 3.21W
75 D1 **Cadagua** *R* Spain
56 D2 **Cadair Idris** *mt* Gwynedd Wales 52.42N 3.54W
72 H8 **Cadalen** France 43.50N 1.58E
76 L8 **Cadalso de los Vidrios** Spain 40.18N 4.26W
75 R3 **Cadaqués** Spain 42.17N 3.16E
13 K7 **Cadarga** Queensland 26.05S 150.58E
76 A10 **Cadaval** Portugal 39.15N 9.06W
76 G1 **Cadavedo** Spain 43.32N 6.22W
56 D6 **Cadbury** Devon Eng 50.50N 3.33W
62 L6 **Čadca** Czechoslovakia 49.26N 18.45E
109 O7 **Caddo** Oklahoma 34.08N 96.16W
112 J3 **Caddo** Texas 32.43N 98.40W
107 C7 **Caddo** *R* Arkansas
112 N3 **Caddo L** Louisiana/Texas
112 L2 **Caddo Mills** Texas 33.03N 96.14W
72 E10 **Cadéac** France 42.53N 0.21E
76 E3 **Cadebo, Mtes del** Spain
56 J2 **Cadeby** Leics Eng 52.38N 1.22W
79 J5 **Cadelbosco di sopra** Italy 44.46N 10.36E
107 F12 **Cade, L.de** Louisiana 29.24N 90.52W
13 C1 **Cadell** *R* N Terr Aust
13 F5 **Cadell** *R* Queensland
79 F3 **Cadenabbia** Italy 45.59N 9.13E
66 M7 **Cadenazzo** Switzerland 46.09N 8.57E
63 K5 **Cadenberge** W Germany 53.47N 9.04E
71 G9 **Cadenet** France 43.44N 5.22E
79 G5 **Cadèo** Italy 44.58N 9.49E
115 K5 **Cadereyta** Mexico 25.38N 99.59W
105 H4 **Cades** S Carolina 33.46N 79.48W
75 O3 **Cadí** *mt* Spain 42.18N 1.35E
77 K7 **Cádiar** Spain 36.57N 3.10W
12 D3 **Cadibarrawirracanna, L** S Australia
60 T17 **Cadier** Netherlands 50.50N 5.45E
71 H10 **Cadière-d'Azur** France 43.11N 5.45E
19 L4 **Cadig Mts** Luzon Philippines
72 D6 **Cadillac** France 44.40N 0.20W
106 J5 **Cadillac** Michigan 44.15N 85.23W
99 M4 **Cadillac** Quebec 48.14N 78.25W
100 K9 **Cadillac** Saskatchewan 49.43N 107.44W
25 H3 **Ca Dinh, Nam** *R* Laos
75 O3 **Cadí, Sierra del** *mts* Spain
111 J7 **Cadiz** California 34.30N 115.30W
107 J5 **Cadiz** Kentucky 36.52N 87.50W
104 E6 **Cadiz** Ohio 40.15N 81.00W
19 L6 **Cadiz** Philippines 10.57N 123.18E
77 D7 **Cádiz** Spain 36.32N 6.18W
74 D8 **Cádiz** *prov* Spain
77 D7 **Cádiz, B.de** Spain
77 C7 **Cádiz, G.de** Spain
111 J7 **Cadiz L** California 34.15N 115.25W
19 J6 **Cadlao** *isld* Philippines 11.15N 119.22E
56 H6 **Cadnam** Hants Eng 50.56N 1.34W
100 G6 **Cadogan** Alberta 52.20N 110.28W
64 K5 **Cadolzburg** W Germany 49.27N 10.53E
101 P9 **Cadomin** Alberta 53.02N 117.20W
75 K6 **Cadoñera, La** Spain 40.56N 0.06W
66 N9 **Cadorago** Italy 45.44N 9.02E
79 M2 **Cadore** *reg* Italy
103 D3 **Cadosia** New York 41.58N 75.15W
106 C5 **Cadott** Wisconsin 44.55N 91.08W
101 P7 **Cadotte** *R* Alberta
72 F6 **Cadouin** France 44.48N 0.54E
72 G8 **Cadours** France 43.44N 1.03E
14 B9 **Cadoux** W Australia 30.47S 117.05E
75 G3 **Cadreita** Spain 42.13N 1.41W
75 J4 **Cadrete** Spain 41.34N 0.57W
79 J3 **Cadria, Monte** Italy 45.56N 10.42E
66 M7 **Cadro** Switzerland 46.03N 8.59E
60 A3 **Cadzand** Netherlands 51.22N 3.25E
118 H2 **Caém** Brazil 10.45S 40.18W
79 L4 **Ca Emo** Italy 45.05N 11.58E
70 K3 **Caen** France 49.11N 0.22W
57 M6 **Caenby Corner** Lincs Eng 53.24N 0.33W
57 G6 **Caergwrle** Clwyd Wales 53.07N 3.03W
56 F4 **Caerleon** Gwent Wales 51.37N 2.57W
57 E6 **Caernarfon** Gwynedd Wales 53.08N 4.16W
57 D6 **Caernarfon B** Wales
Caernarvon *co see* **Gwynedd** *co*
56 E4 **Caerphilly** Mid Glam Wales 51.35N 3.14W
56 E2 **Caersws** Powys Wales 52.31N 3.26W
56 F4 **Caerwent** Gwent Wales 51.37N 2.46W
57 G6 **Caerwys** Clwyd Wales 53.15N 3.18W
Caesarea *anc site see* **Qesari, Har**
Caesarea Mazaca *anc site see* **Kayseri**
Caesarea Philippi *anc site see* **Bāniyās**
105 E2 **Caesars Head** S Carolina 35.05N 82.39W
118 G6 **Caeté** Brazil 19.54S 43.37W
117 E5 **Caeté, B. do** Brazil
120 D3 **Caeté, R** Brazil
118 G3 **Caetité** Brazil 13.59S 42.32W
120 E12 **Cafayate** Argentina 26.02S 66.00W
76 D9 **Cafede** Portugal 39.55N 7.32W
118 E7 **Cafelândia** Brazil 21.47S 49.35W
119 E5 **Cafifi** Colombia 5.15N 71.04W
26 U15 **Cafres, Plaine des** Réunion Ind Oc
91 D12 **Cafu** Angola 16.30S 15.14E
117 A4 **Cafuini** *R* Brazil
118 J10 **Cagarra, I** Brazil 23.02S 43.12W
36 F6 **Çaga Tepe** *mt* Turkey 36.22N 32.39E
19 J8 **Cagayan** Philippines 6.59N 118.30E
19 K7 **Cagayan** *isld* Philippines 9.36N 121.14E
19 K7 **Cagayan** *islds* Philippines
19 K2 **Cagayan** *R* Luzon Philippines
19 M7 **Cagayan de Oro** Mindanao Philippines 8.29N 124.40E
19 J8 **Cagayan Sulu** *isld* Philippines 7.00N 118.28E
91 D8 **Cage** Angola 8.22S 14.20E
80 M7 **Caggiano** Italy 40.35N 15.28E
36 D5 **Çağırgan** Turkey 37.19N 29.00E
36 C3 **Çağış** Turkey 39.31N 28.02E
36 F3 **Çağlayik** Turkey 39.50N 31.55E
79 N7 **Cagli** Italy 43.33N 12.38E
81 C5 **Cagliari** Sardinia 39.13N 9.08E
81 B4 **Cagliari** *prov* Sardinia
81 C5 **Cagliari,G.di** Sardinia
67 P13 **Cagna, Mtgne.de** Corsica
80 N5 **Cagnano Varano** Italy 41.49N 15.47E
71 L9 **Cagnes** France 43.40N 7.09E
19 M6 **Cagosoan Pt** Philippines 10.42N 125.48E
19 L5 **Cagraray** *isld* Philippines 13.19N 123.52E
119 D7 **Caguán** *R* Colombia
105 K7 **Caguas** Puerto Rico 18.14N 66.04W
59 C8 **Caha** *mt* Kerry Irish Rep 51.46N 9.40W
107 J9 **Cahaba** *R* Alabama
70 J3 **Cahagnes** France 49.03N 0.46W
91 D12 **Cahama** Angola 16.16S 14.23E
59 C8 **Caha Mts** Kerry Irish Rep
59 G7 **Caher** Tipperary Irish Rep 52.22N 7.55W
59 F6 **Caherconlish** Limerick Irish Rep 52.36N 8.28W
59 C7 **Caherconree** *mt* Kerry Irish Rep 52.12N 9.51W
59 B4 **Caher I** Mayo Irish Rep 53.43N 10.01W
59 B8 **Cahersiveen** Kerry Irish Rep 51.57N 10.13W
103 A3 **Cahill Mt** Pennsylvania 41.37N 76.35W
59 K6 **Cahore Pt** Wexford Irish Rep 52.34N 6.11W
72 G7 **Cahors** France 44.28N 0.26E
120 B1 **Cahuapanas** Peru 5.14S 76.59W
120 B1 **Cahuapanas R** Peru
119 D8 **Cahuinari, R** Colombia
115 N5 **Cahuita, Pta** *C* Costa Rica 9.45N 82.48W
92 G10 **Caia** Mozambique 17.50S 35.21E
94 N1 **Caia** Mozambique 17.50S 35.21E
76 E11 **Caia** Portugal 38.58N 7.07W
76 E10 **Caia, Barragem do** *res* Portugal 39.00N 7.15W
118 C3 **Caiabis, Sa. dos** *mts* Brazil
37 C1 **Çaialahmet** *R* Turkey
119 G9 **Caiambe, L** Brazil
91 H9 **Caianda** Angola 11.00S 23.29E
80 K6 **Caianello** Italy 41.18N 14.03E
118 D5 **Caiapônia** Brazil 16.59S 51.48W
118 D5 **Caiapó, R** Brazil
118 D5 **Caiapó, Serra do** *mts* Brazil
80 K6 **Caiazzo** Italy 41.10N 14.22E
116 E3 **Caibarién** Cuba 22.31N 79.29W
25 J7 **Cai Be** Vietnam 10.20N 106.03E
119 F4 **Caicara** Bolívar Venezuela 7.38N 66.10W
117 J8 **Caicara** Brazil 6.30S 35.26W
119 G3 **Caicara** Monagas Venez 9.52N 63.38W
119 G9 **Caicara, R** Brazil
119 C5 **Caicedonia** Colombia 4.21N 75.50W
117 H8 **Caicó** Brazil 6.25S 37.04W
116 H4 **Caicos Bank** W I
116 H4 **Caicos Is** West Indies
116 H4 **Caicos Pass** Caicos Is/Bahamas W I
116 H4 **Caicos, West** / Caicos Is W I 21.42N 72.30W
Caidian *see* **Hanchuan**
Caidian *see* **Hanyang**
Caidian *see* **Hanyang (Caidian)**
91 G9 **Caifuche** Angola 11.22S 21.27E
72 C2 **Caillère, la** France 46.37N 0.55W
98 E1 **Cailleteau, L** Quebec 52.06N 67.30W
120 D6 **Cailloma** Peru 15.09S 71.45W
107 F12 **Caillou B** Louisiana
107 F12 **Caillou L** Louisiana 29.15N 90.45W
116 G5 **Caimanera** Cuba 19.59N 75.11W
120 F5 **Caimanes** *L* Bolivia 12.38S 65.10W
119 E6 **Caimán, L** Colombia 3.39N 69.30W
19 J4 **Caiman Pt** Luzon Philippines 15.55N 119.45E
91 D10 **Caimbamba** Angola 12.58S 14.01E
115 F11 **Caimito** *R* Panama
112 J5 **Cain City** Texas 30.13N 98.50W
91 C11 **Cainde** Angola 15.29S 13.24E
120 F8 **Caine, R** Bolivia
23 C2 **Cainnyigoin** Sichuan China 32.42N 102.08E
98 G7 **Cains R** New Brunswick
107 C1 **Cainsville** Missouri 40.27N 93.48W
25 H8 **Cai Nuoc** Vietnam 8.59N 105.58E
91 D7 **Caiongo** Angola 7.47S 15.59E
80 J5 **Caira, Monte** Italy 41.33N 13.46E
117 D6 **Cairari** Brazil 2.31S 49.05W
123 C10 **Caird Coast** Antarctica
104 G6 **Cairnbrook** Pennsylvania 40.06N 78.49W
12 G6 **Cairn Curran Dam** Victoria 37.04S 144.02E
58 G6 **Cairndow** Strathclyde Scotland 56.16N 4.55W
58 J4 **Cairn Gorm** *mt* Highland Scotland 57.07N 3.40W
58 J4 **Cairngorm Mts** Highland/Grampian Scotland
113 K6 **Cairn Mt** Alaska 61.10N 155.20W
58 L5 **Cairn o'Mounth** *mt* Grampian Scotland 56.55N 2.36W
57 C3 **Cairn Ryan** Dumfries & Galloway Scotland 54.58N 5.02W
13 H3 **Cairns** Queensland 16.51S 145.43E
57 E3 **Cairnsmore of Fleet** *mt* Dumfries & Galloway Scotland 54.59N 4.20W
57 E2 **Cairn Table** Strathclyde Scotland 55.29N 4.02W
58 J4 **Cairn Toul** *mt* Grampian Scotland 57.04N 3.44W
58 K5 **Cairnwell, The** *mt* Tayside/Grampian Scotland 56.53N 3.26W
86 F5 **Cairo** Egypt 30.03N 31.15E
105 C7 **Cairo** Georgia 30.52N 84.12W
107 G4 **Cairo** Illinois 37.01N 89.09W
107 D2 **Cairo** Missouri 39.30N 92.26W
108 M8 **Cairo** Nebraska 41.00N 98.33W
103 F2 **Cairo** New York 42.17N 74.00W
104 A6 **Cairo** Ohio 40.49N 84.04W
104 D7 **Cairo** W Virginia 39.14N 81.12W
79 D6 **Cáiro Montenotte** Italy 44.23N 8.16E
118 J3 **Cairu** Brazil 13.36S 39.00W
23 C5 **Caishentang** Guizhou China 27.15N 104.36E
23 H3 **Caishi** Anhui China 31.43N 118.30E
56 P2 **Caister** Norfolk Eng 52.39N 1.44E
57 N5 **Caistor** Lincs Eng 53.30N 0.20W
Caithness *co see* **Highland** *reg*
91 C11 **Caitou** Angola 14.28S 13.07E
91 E11 **Caiundo** Angola 15.43S 17.30E
82 K4 **Căiuţi** Romania 46.12N 26.53E
80 K7 **Caivano** Italy 40.57N 14.18E
13 G8 **Caiwarro** Queensland 28.38S 144.45E
69 D4 **Caix** France 49.49N 2.38E
Caiyuanzhen *see* **Shengsi**
120 F9 **Caiza** Bolivia 20.02S 65.40W
Caiza Tarija Bolivia *see* **Villa Ingavi**
23 H3 **Caizi Hu** *L* Anhui China
76 D7 **Caja** *R* Portugal
119 B8 **Cajabamba** Ecuador 1.45S 78.46W
120 A2 **Cajabamba** Peru 7.37S 78.03W
120 B4 **Cajacay** Peru 10.08S 77.25W
105 J8 **Caja de Muertos** *isld* Puerto Rico 17.52N 66.32W
120 A2 **Cajamarca** Peru 7.09S 78.32W
120 A2 **Cajamarca** *dept* Peru
120 A2 **Cajamarca** *R* Peru
119 C6 **Cajambre, I** Colombia 3.31N 77.21W
117 F6 **Cajapió** Brazil 3.00S 44.46W
72 H7 **Cajarc** France 44.29N 1.50E
117 E6 **Cajari** Brazil 3.22S 45.00W
120 B4 **Cajatambo** Peru 10.31S 77.01W
118 E9 **Cajati** Brazil 24.42S 48.07W
117 H8 **Cajàzeiras** Brazil 6.52S 38.31W
82 F7 **Čajetina** Yugoslavia 43.47N 19.42E
19 L5 **Cajidiocan** Philippines 12.20N 122.41E
75 M3 **Cajigar** *R* Spain
82 E7 **Čajniče** Yugoslavia 43.34N 19.05E
116 C6 **Cajones, Cayos** *islds* Caribbean Sea 16.05N 83.00W
118 J9 **Cajú** Brazil 22.53S 43.13W
120 E7 **Cajuata** Bolivia 16.44S 67.17W
117 F6 **Cajueiro, L.do** Brazil 3.30S 42.15W
117 F6 **Caju, I.do** Brazil 2.43S 42.10W
118 F7 **Cajuru** Brazil 21.15S 47.18W
117 E5 **Cajutuba** *isld* Brazil 0.35S 47.40W
22 E8 **Caka** Qinghai China 36.48N 99.15E
37 E2 **Çakaköy** Turkey 40.21N 28.08E
37 D8 **Çakal** *R* Turkey
Caka'lho *see* **Yanjing**
22 E8 **Caka Yanhu** *L* Qinghai China
37 E5 **Çakırgöl Dağı** *mt* Turkey 40.33N 39.40E
36 E6 **Çakırlar** Turkey 36.52N 30.32E
37 D3 **Çakıroba** *R* Turkey
36 H5 **Çakıt** *R* Turkey
36 F3 **Çakmak** Eskişehir Turkey 39.11N 31.51E
36 G5 **Çakmak** Konya Turkey 37.33N 34.19E
37 G6 **Çakmak Dağ** *mt* Turkey 39.46N 42.14E
37 H2 **Çakmakmlar** Turkey 40.59N 29.53E
82 C4 **Čakovec** Yugoslavia 46.24N 16.26E
Çal Hakkâri Turkey *see* **Çukurca**
36 D4 **Çal** Turkey 38.05N 29.22E
95 L7 **Cala** S Africa 31.31S 27.41E
77 D5 **Cala** Spain 37.58N 6.19W
37 G4 **Cala** Turkey 41.03N 43.20E
77 D5 **Cala** *R* Spain
77 Y14 **Cala Alcaufar** Balearic Is 39.50N 4.17E
90 D9 **Calabar** Nigeria 4.56N 8.22E
111 O10 **Calabasas** Arizona 31.29N 110.58W
77 V15 **Cala Blava** Balearic Is 39.28N 2.43E
99 O7 **Calabogie** Ontario 45.18N 76.46W
77 W14 **Cala Bona** Balearic Is 39.37N 3.22E
119 F3 **Calabozo** Venezuela 8.58N 67.28W
119 E2 **Calabozo, Ensenada de** *B* Venezuela
81 M7 **Calábria** *reg* Italy
81 L7 **Calábria, Réggio di** *prov* Italy
79 M6 **Calabrine** Italy 44.11N 12.17E
80 M7 **Calabritto** Italy 40.47N 15.15E
19 J6 **Calabugdong** *isld* Philippines 11.06N 119.41E
77 G7 **Cala Burras, Pta.de** Spain 36.31N 4.38W
75 L5 **Calaceite** Spain 41.01N 0.11E
81 E9 **Cala Cinque Denti** Pantelleria I Italy 36.50N 11.59E
120 E7 **Calacoto** Bolivia 17.16S 68.38W
67 O12 **Calacuccia** Corsica 42.20N 9.00E
77 W14 **Cala de San Vicente** *B* Balearic Is
81 D2 **Cala di Sant' Anna** Sardinia 40.43N 9.44E
81 A1 **Cala d'Oliva** Sardinia 41.05N 8.20E
81 A5 **Cala Domestica** *B* Sardinia 39.23N 8.22E
77 W15 **Cala d'Or** Balearic Is 39.23N 3.14E
77 D5 **Cala, Embalse de** *res* Spain 37.43N 6.05W
75 O4 **Calaf** Spain 41.44N 1.31E
81 B1 **Cala Falsa** *inlet* Sardinia 41.03N 8.53E
82 H7 **Calafat** Romania 43.59N 22.57E
121 J8 **Calafate** Argentina 50.19S 72.15W
75 O5 **Calafell** Spain 41.12N 1.35E
77 W15 **Cala Figuera** Balearic Is 39.20N 3.10E
77 V15 **Cala Figuera, C** Balearic Is 39.27N 2.31E
121 A7 **Calafquén, L** Chile
81 D3 **Cala Ginepro** *B* Sardinia 40.26N 9.48E
19 L6 **Calagnaan** *isld* Philippines 11.30N 123.13E
19 L4 **Calagua Is** Philippines
Calah *see* **Nimrud** *anc site*
75 G3 **Calahorra** Spain 42.19N 1.58W
91 F12 **Calai** Angola 17.47S 19.41E
69 B2 **Calais** France 50.57N 1.52E
104 S1 **Calais** Maine 45.11N 67.16W
Calais, Pas de *see* **Dover, Strait of**
120 E11 **Calalaste, Cerro** *pk* Argentina 25.47S 67.37W
120 E11 **Calalaste, Sierra** *mts* Argentina
79 M2 **Calalzo** Italy 46.28N 12.23E
120 G3 **Calama** Brazil 8.05S 62.52W
120 E10 **Calama** Chile 22.30S 68.55W
119 D2 **Calamar** Bolívar Colombia 10.16N 74.55W
119 D7 **Calamar** Vaupés Colombia 1.58N 72.30W
120 E7 **Calamarca** Bolivia 16.53S 68.07W
19 J2 **Calamba** Luzon Philippines 14.12N 121.10E
19 J5 **Calamian Grp** *islds* Philippines
77 W14 **Cala Millor** Balearic Is 39.35N 3.22E
106 D7 **Calamine** Wisconsin 42.44N 90.10W
75 H6 **Calamocha** Spain 40.54N 1.18W
81 F8 **Calamonaci** Sicily 37.32N 13.17E
77 D3 **Calamonte** Spain 38.53N 6.24W
77 G8 **Cala Moral, Pta.de** *pt* Spain 36.29N 4.41W
77 W15 **Cala Murada** Balearic Is 39.28N 3.16E
106 D8 **Calamus** Iowa 41.49N 90.43W
119 G8 **Calanaque** Brazil 0.15S 64.04W
77 C5 **Calañas** Spain 37.40N 6.53W
66 N6 **Calancasca** *R* Switzerland
66 N6 **Calanca, Val** Switzerland
75 K6 **Calanda** Spain 40.56N 0.15W
66 O4 **Calanda** *mts* Switzerland
19 K6 **Calandagan** *isld* Philippines 10.38N 120.15E
18 A3 **Calang** Sumatra Indon 4.37N 95.37E
81 C2 **Calangianus** Sardinia 40.56N 9.12E
70 D5 **Calanhel** France 48.25N 3.25W
85 F5 **Calanscio** Libya 28.15N 21.10E
85 G5 **Calanscio Sand Sea** Libya
85 F5 **Calanscio Serir** *gravel des* Libya
19 K5 **Calapan** Philippines 13.23N 121.10E
81 B6 **Cala Piombo** *inlet* Sardinia 38.53N 8.38E
110 C5 **Calapooia** *R* Oregon
77 L6 **Calar Alto** *mt* Spain 37.13N 2.31W
82 L6 **Călăraşi** Romania 44.12N 27.22E
77 W14 **Cala Ratjada** Balearic Is 39.43N 3.27E
119 C5 **Calarca** Colombia 4.31N 75.38W
77 M4 **Calar del Mundo** *mts* Spain
81 A2 **Cala Retondata** *B* Sardinia
70 D5 **Calarhel** France 48.27N 3.28W
95 L7 **Cala Road** S Africa 31.24S 27.41E
67 P13 **Cala Rossa** Corsica Mediterranean Sea 41.38N 9.20E
77 K7 **Calar, Sierra del** *mts* Spain
77 S12 **Cala Sabina** Balearic Is 38.44N 1.26E
77 W15 **Cala Santany** Balearic Is 39.20N 3.09E
66 J7 **Calasca** Italy 46.01N 8.11E
81 H8 **Calascibetta** Sicily 37.36N 14.17E
81 A5 **Calasetta** Sardinia 39.07N 8.22E
77 N4 **Calasparra** Spain 38.14N 1.41W
81 A3 **Cala Su Palosu** *B* Sardinia 40.03N 8.25E
81 E8 **Calatafimi** Sicily 37.54N 12.52E
75 E4 **Calatañazor** Spain 41.42N 2.50W
75 G5 **Calatayud** Spain 41.21N 1.39W
82 H4 **Călăţele** Romania 46.47N 23.01E
75 H4 **Calatorao** Spain 41.31N 1.20W
63 T9 **Calau** E Germany 51.45N 13.57E
19 L5 **Calauag** Luzon Philippines 13.58N 122.17E
19 J2 **Calauan** Luzon Philippines 14.08N 121.18E
81 J7 **Calavà, C** Sicily 38.11N 14.55E
77 S12 **Cala Vadella** *B* Balearic Is
81 C1 **Cala Vall'Alta** *inlet* Sardinia 41.10N 9.10E
111 C4 **Calaveras Res** California 37.28N 121.50W
77 F4 **Calaveruela** *mt* Spain 38.14N 5.29W
19 K5 **Calavite, C** Philippines 13.25N 120.20E
19 K5 **Calavite Pass** Philippines
19 J5 **Calawit** *isld* Philippines 12.18N 119.54E
19 K2 **Calayan** *isld* Philippines 19.20N 121.30E
19 M5 **Calbayog** Philippines 12.04N 124.38E
63 P9 **Calbe (Saale)** E Germany 51.54N 11.45E
19 M6 **Calbiga** Philippines 11.37N 125.01E
66 N7 **Calbiga, Monte** Italy 46.01N 9.10E
121 A8 **Calbuco** *pk* Chile 41.20S 72.38W
120 D5 **Calca** Peru 13.22S 71.54W
117 J7 **Calcanhar, Pta do** *C* Brazil 5.06S 35.30W
107 D11 **Calcasieu** *R* Louisiana
107 C12 **Calcasieu L** Louisiana
119 B8 **Calceta** Ecuador 0.51S 80.07W
120 F9 **Calcha** Bolivia 20.23S 65.25W
121 E2 **Calchaqui** Argentina 29.56S 60.14W
79 J7 **Calci** Italy 43.44N 10.31E
79 H4 **Calcinato** Italy 45.27N 10.24E
79 G3 **Calcio** Italy 45.31N 9.50E
117 D3 **Calçoene** Brazil 2.30N 50.55W
117 C3 **Calçoene** *R* Brazil
28 G4 **Calcutta** West Bengal India 22.30N 88.20E
79 K2 **Caldaro** Italy 46.25N 11.15E

80 H2 Caldarola Italy 43.08N 13.13E
79 K2 Caldaro, L. di *L* 46.23N 11.16E
76 H3 Caldas Spain 42.57N 5.52W
119 C5 Caldas *div* Colombia
76 A10 Caldas da Rainha Portugal 39.24N 9.08W
76 C6 Caldas das Taipas Portugal 41.29N 8.22W
75 Q4 Caldas de Malavella Spain 41.50N 2.48E
75 P4 Caldas de Mombuy Spain 41.38N 2.11E
76 B14 Caldas de Monchique Portugal 37.15N 8.33W
76 H2 Caldas de Oviedo Spain 43.20N 5.55W
76 B3 Caldas de Reyes Spain 42.36N 8.39W
76 C6 Caldas de Vizela Portugal 41.22N 8.18W
76 C5 Caldas do Gerês Portugal 41.44N 8.10W
118 E5 Caldas Novas Brazil 17.41S 48.39W
92 G10 Caldas Xavier Mozambique 16.01S 34.05E
57 G3 Caldbeck Cumbria Eng 54.45N 3.02W
56 K2 Caldecott Leics Eng 52.32N 0.43W
96 P1 Caldeira *mt* Azores 39.43N 31.08W
96 P4 Caldeira *vol* Azores 38.36N 28.43W
96 R2 Caldeira *vol* Azores 39.02N 27.58W
96 U3 Caldeira *vol* Terceira Canary Is 38.44N 27.19W
92 J10 Caldeira, I Mozambique 16.38S 39.42E
119 H9 Caldeirão Amazonas Brazil 3.15S 60.15W
120 F3 Caldeirão Rondônia Brazil 9.19S 64.36W
76 D14 Caldeirão, Sa.do *mts* Portugal
63 K10 Calden W Germany 51.25N 9.24E
101 G7 Calder Alaska 56.10N 133.35W
110 J2 Calder Idaho 47.16N 116.10W
100 Q7 Calder Saskatchewan 51.10N 101.45W
121 B1 Caldera Chile 27.05S 70.48W
79 K5 Calderara di Reno Italy 44.34N 11.16E
57 G4 Calder Bridge Cumbria Eng 54.27N 3.29W
58 J7 Caldercruix Strathclyde Scotland 55.53N 3.55W
57 F4 Calder Hall Cumbria 54.26N 3.31W
77 J2 Calderina *mt* Spain 39.20N 3.48W
77 J2 Calderina, Sierra de la *mts* Spain
115 P8 Calderitas Mexico 18.38N 88.19W
58 J1 Calder, L Highland Scotland 58.31N 3.36W
58 H7 Caldermill Strathclyde Scotland 55.39N 4.08W
77 F6 Calderón, L.de Spain 37.21N 5.08W
57 K5 Calder, R W Yorks Eng
13 H7 Caldervale Queensland 25.06S 146.49E
57 H3 Caldew *R* Cumbria Eng
56 F4 Caldicot Gwent Wales 51.36N 2.45W
79 K4 Caldiero Italy 45.24N 11.11E
37 H6 Çaldiran Turkey 39.10N 43.52E
79 K3 Caldonazzo Italy 45.59N 11.16E
79 K2 Caldonazzo, L. di *L* Italy
110 J6 Caldwell Idaho 43.39N 116.40W
109 N4 Caldwell Kansas 37.03N 97.37W
103 J6 Caldwell New Jersey 40.50N 74.16W
104 D7 Caldwell Ohio 39.44N 81.32W
112 L5 Caldwell Texas 30.32N 96.42W
119 B6 Caldwell I Galápagos Is 1.22S 90.22W
56 B4 Caldy I Dyfed Wales 51.38N 4.42W
95 C10 Caledon S Africa 34.14S 19.25E
59 J3 Caledon Tyrone N Ireland 54.21N 6.50W
95 K6 Caledon *R* S Africa
13 D2 Caledon B N Terr Australia
106 J7 Caledonia Michigan 42.46N 85.32W
106 C6 Caledonia Minnesota 43.37N 91.30W
104 H4 Caledonia New York 42.59N 77.52W
98 G9 Caledonia Nova Scotia 44.24N 65.02W
98 K8 Caledonia Nova Scotia 45.17N 62.20W
104 C6 Caledonia Ohio 40.38N 82.59W
99 L9 Caledonia Ontario 43.05N 79.57W
13 D2 Caledon,Mt N Terr Australia 12.55S 136.30E
75 Q4 Calella de la Costa Spain 41.37N 2.40E
13 J5 Calen Queensland 20.51S 148.53E
91 F10 Calengo Angola 13.00S 18.20E
67 O12 Calenzana Corsica 42.30N 8.51E
107 K8 Calera Alabama 33.05N 86.45W
115 G3 Calera Chihuahua Mexico 28.46N 105.56W
115 H6 Calera Zacatecas Mexico 22.58N 102.41W
77 D4 Calera de León Spain 38.06N 6.19W
96 O15 Calera, La Gomera Canary Is 28.07N 17.20W
76 K9 Calera y Chozas Spain 39.53N 4.59W
75 D4 Caleruega Spain 41.49N 3.29W
79 H5 Calestano Italy 44.36N 10.08E
96 V7 Caleta Graciosa Canary Is 29.13N 13.31W
120 D8 Caleta Buena Chile 19.55S 70.05W
121 K9 Caleta Clarencia Chile 52.57S 70.05W
121 K8 Caleta Coig *estuary* Argentina
120 D11 Caleta el Cobre Chile 24.17S 70.32W
121 K9 Caleta Josefina Chile 53.23S 69.14W
120 D9 Caleta Lobos Chile 21.04S 70.12W
121 L6 Caleta Olivia Argentina 46.21S 67.37W
120 D9 Caleta Pabellón de Pica Chile 21.00S 70.11W
81 D2 Caletta Sardinia 40.37N 9.46E
121 D5 Caleufú Argentina 35.33S 64.33W
121 B8 Caleufu *R* Argentina
111 J9 Calexico California 32.39N 115.28W
66 O4 Calfeisen Tal *V* Switzerland
37 D6 Calgal Dağ *mt* Turkey 39.06N 38.05E
37 D8 Çalgan Turkey 37.35N 38.19E
100 C7 Calgary Alberta 51.05N 114.05W
58 D5 Calgary Mull, Strathclyde Scotland 56.35N 6.16W
109 F2 Calhan Colorado 39.03N 104.17W
96 R3 Calheta Azores 38.37N 28.02W
96 O7 Calheta Madeira Is 32.42N 17.12W
105 C3 Calhoun Georgia 34.31N 84.56W
107 J4 Calhoun Kentucky 37.32N 87.15W
107 D9 Calhoun Louisiana 32.31N 92.21W
107 G8 Calhoun City Mississippi 33.50N 89.20W
105 E3 Calhoun Falls S Carolina 34.05N 82.36W
119 C6 Cali Colombia 3.24N 76.30W
37 F3 Çali Turkey 40.11N 28.54E
77 J6 Calicasas Spain 37.17N 3.37W
79 G6 Calice al Cornoviglio Italy 44.14N 9.50E
79 D6 Calice Ligure Italy 44.12N 8.18E
19 M6 Calicoan *isld* Philippines 11.00N 125.50E
107 D5 Calico Rock Arkansas 36.05N 92.09W
28 G7 Calicut Andaman Is 11.35N 92.42E
28 B5 Calicut Kerala India 11.15N 75.45E
28 B5 Calicut *dist* Kerala India
111 F6 Caliente California 35.18N 118.39W
111 K4 Caliente Nevada 37.36N 114.31W
103 E5 Califon New Jersey 40.43N 74.50W
107 D3 California Missouri 38.39N 92.35W
104 F6 California Pennsylvania 40.04N 79.54W
116 O2 California Trinidad & Tobago 10.24N 61.28W
102 B3 California *state* U.S.A.
111 F7 California Aqueduct California
115 B2 California, G.de Mexico
111 F6 California Hot Springs California 35.54N 118.40W
75 L7 Cálig Spain 40.28N 0.21E
72 E7 Calignac France 44.08N 0.25E
120 F10 Calilegua Argentina 23.45S 64.42W
82 J5 Călimaneşti Romania 45.14N 24.20E
82 J3 Călimanilor, Munţii *mts* Romania
81 R12 Calimera Italy 40.15N 18.17E
28 D5 Calimere, Pt Tamil Nadu India 10.17N 79.52E
82 J5 Călinesti Romania 45.21N 24.18E
Calingapatam *see* Kalingapatnam
121 B3 Calingasta Argentina 31.20S 69.20W
14 B9 Calingiri W Australia 31.07S 116.27E
Calīno *isld see* Kálimnos *I*
107 D8 Calion Arkansas 33.20N 92.32W
111 J8 Calipatria California 33.09N 115.30W
110 H1 Calispell Pk Washington 48.29N 117.30W
19 K6 Calis Pt Philippines 11.49N 120.15E
111 B3 Calistoga California 38.37N 122.35W
80 M7 Calitri Italy 40.54N 15.26E
95 E9 Calitzdorp S Africa 33.32S 21.41E
79 D6 Calizzano Italy 44.14N 8.07E
115 O7 Calkiní Mexico 20.21N 90.03W
112 O5 Call Texas 30.37N 93.51W
12 F3 Callabonna *R* S Australia
12 F3 Callabonna, L S Australia
87 K8 Callafo Ethiopia 5.37N 44.10E
111 H2 Callaghan, Mt Nevada 39.43N 116.57W
105 F7 Callahan Florida 30.33N 81.51W
120 D6 Callalli Peru 15.31S 71.24W
59 H6 Callan Kilkenny Irish Rep 52.33N 7.23W
58 H6 Callander Central Scotland 56.15N 4.13W
99 L6 Callander Ontario 46.14N 79.21W
19 K3 Callang Luzon Philippines 17.02N 121.37E
58 C2 Callanish Lewis, W Isles Scotland 58.12N 6.45W
12 E3 Callanna S Australia 29.39S 137.55E
60 G8 Callantsoog Netherlands 52.50N 4.41E
107 D2 Callao Missouri 39.44N 92.38W
120 B5 Callao Peru 12.05S 77.08W
111 L2 Callao Utah 39.54N 113.44W
104 J9 Callao Virginia 37.57N 76.35W
71 K9 Callas France 43.35N 6.33E
108 P3 Callaway Minnesota 46.59N 95.56W
108 L8 Callaway Nebraska 41.18N 99.55W
75 G8 Callejas *mt* Spain 39.37N 1.50W
72 D7 Callen France 44.18N 0.28W
61 E4 Callenelle Belgium 50.32N 3.32E
115 K6 Calles Mexico 23.02N 98.42W
14 E3 Calliance Reef W Australia 15.25S 123.09E
79 D4 Calliano Italy 45.01N 8.15E
79 K3 Calliano Italy 45.56N 11.06E
80 M7 Calliano Italy 40.43N 15.17E
103 D3 Callicoon New York 41.46N 75.03W
103 E3 Callicoon Center New York 41.51N 74.56W
13 K6 Callide Queensland 24.15S 150.28E
112 J7 Calliham Texas 28.30N 98.21W
100 D3 Calling L Alberta 55.18N 113.10W
100 E3 Calling R Alberta 55.07N 112.50W
56 C6 Callington Cornwall Eng 50.30N 4.18W
13 K6 Calliope Queensland 24.02S 151.11E
87 M6 Callis Somalia 8.20N 49.06E
101 H6 Callison Ranch Br Col 58.35N 131.48W
59 J3 Callon *R* Armagh N Ireland
77 Q3 Callosa de Ensarria Spain 38.40N 0.08W
77 P4 Callosa de Segura Spain 38.07N 0.53W
14 B7 Callytharra Springs W Australia 25.44S 115.15E
100 D5 Calmar Alberta 53.18N 113.46W
106 C6 Calmar Iowa 43.12N 91.53W
64 F6 Calmbach W Germany 48.46N 8.35E
71 E9 Calmette, la France 43.55N 4.15E
100 L2 Calm L Ontario 48.45N 92.00W
72 K7 Calmont Aveyron France 44.15N 2.32E
72 H9 Calmont Haute-Garonne France 43.17N 1.37E
66 B1 Calmoutier France 47.39N 6.17E
75 P3 Calm, Puig se *mt* Spain 42.08N 2.24E
56 G5 Calne Wilts Eng 51.27N 2.00W
77 O5 Calnegre, Pta.de *pt* Spain 37.31N 1.24W
115 O5 Calobre Panama 8.18N 80.49W
79 F3 Calolziocorte Italy 45.48N 9.26E
75 G7 Calomarde Spain 40.22N 1.35W
91 C8 Calomboloca Angola 9.14S 13.53E
91 G8 Calonda Angola 8.31S 20.38E
91 D11 Calonga *R* Angola
75 R4 Calonge Spain 41.52N 3.04E
72 E7 Calonges France 44.23N 0.15E
61 D4 Calonne Belgium 50.35N 3.26E
19 H1 Caloocan Luzon Philippines 14.38N 120.58E
105 F11 Caloosahatchee *R* Florida
81 N4 Calopezzati Italy 39.33N 16.46E
80 L6 Calore *R* Italy
80 M8 Calore *R* Italy
115 P7 Calotmul Mexico 21.01N 88.10W
77 R3 Calpe Spain 38.39N 0.03E
110 P7 Calpet Wyoming 42.18N 110.14W
111 D2 Calpine California 39.40N 120.26W
115 K8 Calpulálpan Mexico 19.36N 98.26W
118 B6 Cal, R.de la Bolivia
99 F3 Calstock Ontario 49.48N 84.10W
81 F8 Caltabellotta Sicily 37.35N 13.13E
81 J9 Caltagirone Sicily 37.14N 14.31E
81 J9 Caltagirone *R* Sicily
81 H9 Caltanissetta Sicily 37.29N 14.04E
81 G8 Caltanissetta *prov* Sicily
81 G8 Caltavuturo Sicily 37.49N 13.54E
57 H3 Calthwaite Cumbria Eng 54.46N 2.50W
37 D6 Çaltı *R* Turkey
36 D3 Çaltılıbük Turkey 39.57N 28.35E
75 E5 Caltojar Spain 41.24N 2.45W
59 F5 Caltra Galway Irish Rep 53.26N 8.26W
79 K3 Caltrano Italy 45.46N 11.28E
91 F8 Caluango Angola 8.20S 19.39E
91 E9 Calucinga Angola 11.18S 16.12E
71 F5 Caluire-et-Cuire France 45.48N 4.50E
91 D9 Calulo Angola 10.01S 14.56E
91 C8 Calumbo Angola 9.08S 13.24E
106 F2 Calumet Michigan 47.17N 88.28W
109 M6 Calumet Oklahoma 35.36N 98.07W
99 Q7 Calumet Quebec 45.39N 74.41W
106 R4 Calumet Park *dist* Chicago, Illinois
91 H10 Calunda Angola 12.04S 23.26E
91 F10 Calundau Angola 12.05S 19.10E
91 F12 Calunga Angola 16.30S 19.56E
23 C4 Caluo Sichuan China 29.12N 102.21E
91 D10 Caluquembe Angola 13.47S 14.40E
19 K7 Calusa *isld* Philippines 9.35N 121.02E
79 C4 Caluso Italy 45.18N 7.53E
19 K6 Caluya *isld* Philippines 11.57N 121.34E
111 O8 Calva Arizona 33.12N 110.13W
67 E3 Calvados *dept* France
15 M9 Calvados Chain, The Louisiade Arch
79 K7 Calvana, Monti della *mts* Italy
76 H7 Calvarrasa de Abajo Spain 40.57N 5.34W
76 H7 Calvarrasa de Arriba Spain 40.54N 5.35W
57 H6 Calveley Cheshire Eng 53.08N 2.38W
81 L3 Calvello Italy 40.28N 15.51E
57 K6 Calver Derbys Eng 53.16N 1.38W
107 H10 Calvert Alabama 31.09N 88.01W
103 C7 Calvert Maryland 39.43N 75.59W
112 L5 Calvert Texas 30.58N 96.40W
13 D3 Calvert *R* N Terr Aust
107 H4 Calvert City Kentucky 37.02N 88.22W
13 D3 Calvert Hills N Terr Australia 17.12S 137.20E
101 J10 Calvert I Br Col 51.30N 128.00W
103 J5 Calverton Long I, N Y 40.55N 72.46W
104 H8 Calverton Virginia 38.38N 77.41W
14 E6 Calvert Ra W Australia
76 D5 Calves de Randín Spain 41.55N 7.36W
67 O11 Calvi Corsica 42.34N 8.44E
77 U14 Calvia Balearic Is 39.33N 2.29E
80 G4 Calvi dell Umbria Italy 42.24N 12.34E
72 H7 Calvignac France 44.27N 1.46E
115 H7 Calvillo Mexico 21.53N 102.41W
80 C2 Calvi, Monte Italy 43.06N 10.37E
108 M1 Calvin N Dakota 48.51N 98.56W
109 O7 Calvin Oklahoma 34.58N 96.15W
72 J6 Calvinet France 44.44N 2.21E
94 E8 Calvinia S Africa 31.25S 19.47E
80 K6 Calvi Risorta Italy 41.13N 14.09E
79 H4 Calvisano Italy 45.21N 10.20E
71 E9 Calvisson France 43.47N 4.11E
76 H8 Calvitero *mt* Spain 40.17N 5.45W
80 N5 Calvo, Monte Italy 41.45N 15.47E
80 H4 Calvo, Mte Italy 42.24N 13.12E
81 H10 Calvo, Mte Sicily 36.59N 14.30E
63 O8 Calvörde E Germany 52.24N 11.19E
77 H3 Calvo Satelo, Embalse *res* Spain 38.33N 4.08W
64 F6 Calw-Hirsau W Germany 48.42N 8.44E
68 K2 Calye-Souilly France 48.57N 2.41E
105 J2 Calypso N Carolina 35.09N 78.07W
120 B2 Calzada Peru 6.01S 77.04W
77 J3 Calzada de Calatrava, La Spain 38.42N 3.46W
76 J9 Calzada de Oropesa Spain 39.52N 5.16W
115 G10 Calzada Larga Panama 9.11N 79.34W
76 F8 Calzadilla Spain 40.04N 6.31W
77 D4 Calzadilla de los Barros Spain 38.19N 6.19W
66 N6 Cama Switzerland 46.17N 9.11E
91 D8 Camabatela Angola 8.20S 15.26E
79 M5 Camacchio, Valli di *lagoon* Italy
96 Q7 Camacha Madeira Is 32.41N 16.52W
99 O5 Camachigama, L Quebec 47.50N 76.20W
115 H5 Camacho Mexico 24.25N 102.20W
59 K5 Camaderry *mt* Wicklow Irish Rep 53.01N 6.23W
119 F3 Camaguán Venezuela 8.09N 67.37W
116 F4 Camagüey Cuba 21.25N 77.55W
116 E4 Camagüey *prov* Cuba
116 E3 Camagüey, Arch.de Cuba
79 H7 Camaiore Italy 43.56N 10.18E
117 A8 Camaiú, R Brazil
116 E3 Camajuaní Cuba 22.27N 79.43W
Çamalan *see* Gülek
117 D5 Camaleão, I Brazil 0.10S 48.50W
91 F8 Camalengue Angola 8.10S 18.07E
76 K2 Camaleño Spain 43.09N 4.39W
75 Q3 Camallera Spain 42.06N 2.57E
115 C3 Camalli, Sierra de *ra* Mexico
118 H3 Camamu Brazil 13.57S 39.11W
120 C7 Camana Peru 16.38S 72.29W
120 C7 Camaná *R* Peru
119 H8 Camananaú, R Brazil
106 D8 Camanche Iowa 41.47N 90.16W
19 M6 Camandag *isld* Philippines 11.59N 124.27E
110 C1 Camano I Washington 48.10N 122.30W
118 C6 Camapuã Brazil 19.34S 54.04W
121 H3 Camaquã Rio Grande do Sul Brazil 30.50S 51.47W
121 H3 Camaquã, R Brazil
119 H9 Camará Brazil 3.58S 62.42W
18 G9 Camara Java Indonesia 6.01S 107.24E
88 E5 Câmara de Lôbos Madeira Is 32.40N 17.01W
96 P7 Câmara de Lobos Madeira Is 32.38N 16.59W
117 D6 Camaraipi *R* Brazil
119 F7 Camarão Brazil 1.16N 68.48W
118 B3 Camararé, R Brazil
75 M4 Camarasa Spain 41.52N 0.52E
75 M4 Camarasa, Embalse de *res* Spain 41.55N 0.52E
71 K10 Camarat, C France 43.12N 6.41E
76 E15 Camarate Portugal 38.48N 9.06W
118 J3 Camarçari Brazil 12.44S 38.16W
36 H5 Çamardı Turkey 37.49N 35.00E
76 L8 Camarena Spain 40.06N 4.08W
75 H7 Camarena de la Sierra Spain 40.09N 1.03W
72 K8 Camarès France 43.49N 2.53E
70 A5 Camaret Finistère France 48.16N 4.37W
120 F9 Camargo Bolivia 20.38S 65.15W
109 L5 Camargo Oklahoma 36.02N 99.18W
75 C1 Camargo Spain 43.24N 3.52W
115 G4 Camargo, Ciudad Mexico 27.41N 105.10W
71 F9 Camargue, Ile de la France
121 B5 Camarico Chile 35.15S 71.27W
75 J6 Camarillas Spain 40.36N 0.46W
77 N4 Camarillas, Embalse de *L* Spain 38.21N 1.38W
111 E7 Camarillo California 34.13N 119.02W
77 E8 Camarinal, Pta *pt* Spain 36.05N 5.48W
76 A2 Camariñas Spain 43.08N 9.12W
76 D15 Camarões Portugal 38.49N 9.14W
115 F11 Camarón Panama 8.53N 79.37W
115 M2 Camarón, C Honduras 15.59N 85.00W
115 F6 Camaronero, L. del Mexico
120 D8 Camarones *R* Chile
121 D10 Camarones, Bahía Argentina
77 D7 Camarón, Pta. del *pt* Spain 36.44N 6.26W
59 J7 Camaross Wexford Irish Rep 52.22N 6.42W
72 D6 Camarsac France 44.50N 0.21W
76 G5 Camarzana de Tera Spain 42.00N 6.02W
110 N5 Camas Idaho 44.02N 112.13W
77 D6 Camas Spain 37.24N 6.01W
110 C4 Camas Washington 45.35N 122.26W
110 L6 Camas Cr Idaho
110 N5 Camas Cr Idaho
81 G9 Camastra Sicily 37.16N 13.47E
110 B6 Camas Valley Oregon 43.04N 123.40W
91 D7 Camatambo Angola 6.31S 15.21E
120 F9 Camatindi Bolivia 20.57S 63.25W
91 F8 Camaxilo Angola 8.19S 18.53E
76 E4 Camba *R* Spain
76 B3 Cambados Spain 42.31N 8.49W
91 D8 Cambamba Angola 8.07S 14.45E
91 E10 Cambândua Angola 12.32S 17.20E
118 B5 Cambara Brazil 16.35S 57.50W
Cambay *see* Khambhat
Cambay, Gulf of *see* Khambhat, Gulf of
56 B6 Cambeak *prom* Cornwall Eng 50.45N 4.39W
70 H3 Cambe, la France 49.21N 1.01W
91 E9 Cambembe Angola 11.25S 17.32E
69 P3 Camberg W Germany 50.18N 8.17E
56 K5 Camberley Surrey Eng 51.21N 0.45W
70 H3 Cambernon France 49.04N 1.23W
55 F4 Camberwell London Eng 51.28N 0.05W
12 D7 Camberwell *dist* Melbourne, Vic
72 D6 Cambes France 44.45N 0.28W
77 J5 Cambil Spain 37.40N 3.33W
91 G9 Cambo Angola 10.55S 20.06E
91 E8 Cambo *R* Angola
17 F9 Cambodia *rep* S E Asia
91 E11 Cambole Angola 14.04S 16.28E
72 B9 Cambo-les-Bains France 43.22N 1.24W
91 D10 Cambonda, Sa *mts* Angola
91 D9 Cambongo *R* Angola
13 K7 Camboon Queensland 25.03S 150.37E
118 E10 Camboriú Brazil 27.01S 48.38W
56 T9 Camborne Cornwall Eng 50.12N 5.19W
91 D7 Camboso Angola 6.41S 15.54E
103 B4 Cambra Pennsylvania 41.12N 76.18W
69 E3 Cambrai France 50.10N 3.14E
72 J11 Cambras, d'Azè *mt* France 42.27N 2.09E
109 C9 Cambray New Mexico 32.12N 107.21W
76 C2 Cambre Spain 43.18N 8.21W
70 L3 Cambremer France 49.10N 0.04E
76 D6 Cambres Portugal 41.07N 7.49W
111 C6 Cambria California 35.34N 121.05W
106 E6 Cambria Wisconsin 43.32N 89.09W
56 D3 Cambrian Mts Wales
11 D11 Cambrians New Zealand 44.54S 169.48E
56 M3 Cambridge Cambs England 52.12N 0.07E
56 G4 Cambridge Glos Eng 51.44N 2.22W
110 J5 Cambridge Idaho 44.35N 116.40W
106 D8 Cambridge Illinois 41.18N 90.12W
108 R8 Cambridge Iowa 41.53N 93.30W
116 H1 Cambridge Jamaica, W I 18.18N 77.54W
109 O4 Cambridge Kansas 37.20N 96.41W
104 J8 Cambridge Maryland 38.34N 76.04W
103 M2 Cambridge Massachusetts 42.22N 71.06W
108 R4 Cambridge Minnesota 45.34N 93.11W
108 K9 Cambridge Nebraska 40.18N 100.11W
104 M3 Cambridge New York 43.02N 73.23W
11 K4 Cambridge New Zealand 37.53S 175.29E
104 D6 Cambridge Ohio 40.02N 81.36W
99 K9 Cambridge Ontario 43.22N 80.20W
104 P9 Cambridge *dist* Boston, Mass
Cambridge *isld* Chile *see* Diego de Almagro
101 V1 Cambridge Bay Victoria I, N W Terr 69.09N 105.00W
107 L2 Cambridge City Indiana 39.48N 85.11W
13 G5 Cambridge Downs Queensland 20.25S 142.52E
14 G2 Cambridge G W Australia
56 M3 Cambridge & Isle of Ely *co* England
103 M2 Cambridge Res Massachusetts 42.25N 71.16W
104 E5 Cambridge Springs Pennsylvania 41.47N 80.04W
75 N5 Cambrils Spain 41.05N 1.03E
69 D3 Cambrin France 50.30N 2.45E
69 B3 Cambron France 50.07N 1.46E
77 K4 Cambrón *mt* Spain 38.30N 3.19W
61 F4 Cambron-Casteau Belgium 50.35N 3.53E
61 F4 Cambron-Saint-Vincent Belgium 50.35N 3.55E
118 G10 Cambuci *dist* São Paulo Brazil
91 G7 Cambulo Angola 7.49S 21.15E
118 F7 Cambuquira Brazil 21.52S 45.19W
64 M1 Camburg E Germany 51.03N 11.43E
37 D4 Çam Burun *C* Turkey 41.19N 37.48E
58 L4 Cambus o' May Grampian Scotland 57.04N 2.58W
26 U14 Cambuston Réunion Ind Oc 20.56S 55.39E
119 B4 Cambutal, Cerro *pk* Panama 7.18N 80.34W
107 J10 Camden Alabama 32.00N 87.19W
107 D8 Camden Arkansas 33.32N 92.49W
103 C8 Camden Delaware 39.06N 75.34W
104 Q2 Camden Maine 44.13N 69.04W
106 K8 Camden Michigan 41.45N 84.45W
103 D7 Camden New Jersey 39.52N 75.07W
12 K5 Camden New S Wales 34.04S 150.40E
104 K3 Camden New York 43.21N 75.45W
105 G3 Camden S Carolina 34.16N 80.36W
107 H5 Camden Tennessee 36.03N 88.07W
112 N5 Camden Texas 30.55N 94.46W
55 E3 Camden *bor* London England
103 D7 Camden *co* Pennsylvania
113 P1 Camden B Alaska
121 J10 Camden, Is Chile
104 E8 Camden on Gauley W Virginia 38.23N 80.37W
14 E3 Camden Sd W Australia
107 D3 Camdenton Missouri 38.01N 92.44W
66 L7 Cámedo Switzerland 46.09N 8.37E
91 G9 Cameia, Parque Nacional da Angola
56 B6 Camelford Cornwall Eng 50.37N 4.41W
95 J3 Camelford S Africa 27.59S 24.59E
36 D5 Çameli Turkey 37.05N 29.24E
96 V14 Camello, Pta *pt* Gran Canaria Canary Is 28.10N 15.32W
58 J6 Camelon Central Scotland 56.00N 3.50W
56 B6 Camel, R Cornwall Eng
11 K3 Camels Back *mt* New Zealand 36.57S 175.36E
91 D8 Camembe Angola 8.08S 14.19E
70 L4 Camembert France 48.52N 0.10E
79 P7 Camerano Italy 43.32N 13.33E
79 O7 Camerata Picena Italy 43.35N 13.21E
71 F8 Cameret-sur-Aigues Vaucluse France 44.10N 4.53E
79 E3 Cameri Italy 45.30N 8.39E
80 H2 Camerino Italy 43.08N 13.04E
66 N8 Camerlata Italy 45.48N 9.05E
111 N6 Cameron Arizona 35.51N 111.25W
106 D9 Cameron Illinois 40.54N 90.32W
107 C12 Cameron Louisiana 29.47N 93.19W
107 B2 Cameron Missouri 39.43N 94.12W
110 O4 Cameron Montana 45.14N 111.39W
105 H2 Cameron N Carolina 35.20N 79.15W
109 G7 Cameron New Mexico 34.54N 103.22W
104 H4 Cameron New York 42.13N 77.24W
104 E7 Cameron Ohio 39.50N 80.20W
104 G5 Cameron Pennsylvania 41.28N 78.11W
112 L5 Cameron Texas 30.52N 97.00W
106 C4 Cameron Wisconsin 45.24N 91.43W
92 E6 Cameron Bay Zambia
13 G5 Cameron Downs Queensland 21.21S 144.18E
121 D10 Camerones Argentina 44.46S 65.45W
99 B3 Cameron Falls Ontario 49.08N 88.20W
18 B7 Cameron Highlands Pen Malaysia 4.30N 101.34E
101 O6 Cameron Hills Alberta
97 J2 Cameron I N W Terr
23 B9 Cameron, Mt Hong Kong 22.16N 114.10E
11 A13 Cameron Mts New Zealand
95 K8 Cameron's Glen S Africa 32.26S 26.04E
73 F5 Cameroon *fed rep* Equat Africa
Cameroun *rep see* Cameroon *rep*
90 D9 Cameroon, Mt Cameroon 4.13N 9.10E
90 D10 Cameroons B Cameroon
81 K3 Camerota Italy 40.02N 15.23E
121 F6 Camet Argentina 37.50S 57.37W
120 F2 Cametá Amazonas Brazil 6.09S 64.14W
117 D6 Cametá Pará Brazil 2.12S 49.30W
95 F9 Camfer S Africa 33.50S 22.26E
13 B3 Camfield *R* N Terr Australia
80 J4 Camicia, Monte Italy 42.27N 13.44E
81 M5 Camigliatello-Silano Italy 39.20N 16.27E
19 K2 Camiguin *isld* Philippines 18.55N 121.55E
19 M7 Camiguin *isld* Philippines
Cami, L *see* Fagnano ó Cami, L.
Camili *see* Liz
19 K4 Camiling Luzon Philippines 15.38N 120.26E
105 C6 Camilla Georgia 31.14N 84.13W
120 D8 Camiña Chile 19.18S 69.26W
76 B5 Caminha Portugal 41.52N 8.50W
111 D3 Camino California 38.43N 120.43W
76 G8 Caminomorisco Spain 40.21N 6.08W
79 H3 Camino, Pizzo *mt* Italy 45.59N 10.10E
75 H6 Caminreal Spain 40.50N 1.19W
117 E5 Camiranga Brazil 1.47S 46.15W
120 F9 Camiri Bolivia 20.08S 63.33W
79 L3 Camisano Vicentino Italy 45.32N 11.43E
120 C4 Camisea Peru 11.32S 72.43W
120 C4 Camisea *R* Peru
36 J2 Camı Tepe *mt* Turkey 40.36N 36.16E
96 Q15 Camizo, Pta *pt* Tenerife Canary Is 28.04N 16.44W
101 R4 Camlaren N W Terr 63.00N 113.12W
36 J2 Çamlıbel Turkey 40.05N 36.31E
36 J3 Çamlıbel Dağları *mts* Turkey
37 E8 Çamlidere Turkey 37.08N 39.04E
59 G4 Camlin R Longford Irish Rep
59 K3 Camlough Armagh N Ireland 54.11N 6.29W
58 M4 Cammachmore Grampian Scotland 57.03N 2.10W
104 H5 Cammal Pennsylvania 41.24N 77.28W
81 G8 Cammarata Sicily 37.38N 13.38E
81 G8 Cammarata, Mte Sicily 37.37N 13.37E
72 J9 Cammazes, les France 43.24N 2.04E
63 R8 Cammer E Germany 52.15N 12.40E
115 E4 Camoa Mexico 27.11N 109.17W
115 M3 Camoapa Nicaragua 12.25N 85.30W
117 G6 Camocim Brazil 2.55S 40.50W
66 N7 Camoghe *mt* Switzerland 46.08N 9.04E
79 F6 Camogli Italy 44.21N 9.09E
59 K6 Camolin Wexford Irish Rep 52.37N 6.25W
79 H3 Camonica, Val *V* Italy
13 G6 Camoola Queensland 23.00S 144.30E
13 E4 Camooweal Queensland 19.55S 138.06E
117 C3 Camopi Fr Guiana 3.12N 52.19W
117 C3 Camopi *R* Fr Guiana
118 H10 Camorim, L.de Brazil
77 G7 Camorro Alto *mt* Spain 36.59N 4.36W
70 E6 Camors France 47.51N 3.00W
28 H7 Camorta *isld* Nicobar Is
66 H8 Camoscio, Corno *mt* Italy 45.54N 7.53E
19 M6 Camotes Is Philippines
19 M6 Camotes Sea Philippines
115 G8 Camotlán de Miraflores Mexico 19.14N 104.12W
59 C7 Camp Kerry Irish Rep 53.13N 9.55W
80 M7 Campagna Italy 40.40N 15.06E
72 L7 Campagnac France 44.26N 3.05E
72 J10 Campagna-de-Sault France 42.48N 2.03E
80 G5 Campagna di Roma *reg* Italy
79 M4 Campagna Lúpia Italy 45.21N 12.06E
80 F4 Campagnano di Roma Italy 42.08N 12.23E
80 D3 Campagnático Italy 42.53N 11.17E
72 F6 Campagne Dordogne France 44.55N 0.58E
72 C8 Campagne Landes France 43.52N 0.36W
69 B3 Campagne-lès-Hesdin France 50.24N 1.53E
115 L2 Campamento Honduras 14.36N 86.38W
72 E9 Campan France 43.01N 0.11E
121 F5 Campana Argentina 34.10S 59.55W
81 N5 Campana Italy 39.24N 16.50E
115 H4 Campana Mexico 26.09N 103.30W
119 D7 Campana, Cerro *mt* Colombia 1.36N 73.03W
121 H7 Campana I Chile
77 F5 Campana, La Spain 37.34N 5.24W
121 C9 Campana Mahuida *reg* Argentina
118 H6 Campanário Brazil 18.13S 41.40W
118 C8 Campanario Mato Grosso do Sul Brazil 22.40S 54.57W
77 E3 Campanario Spain 38.52N 5.36W
76 G5 Campanario *mt* Spain 41.49N 6.02W
121 B5 Campanario *pk* Arg/Chile 35.56S 70.29W
80 K7 Campanella, Pta Italy 40.34N 14.20E
77 V14 Campanet Balearic Is 39.47N 2.57E
118 F7 Campanha Brazil 21.50S 45.24W
12 H9 Campania Tasmania 42.47S 147.23E
78 F7 Campania *reg* Italy
101 J9 Campania I Br Col 53.06N 129.24W
77 G7 Campanillas Spain 36.44N 4.32W
77 D8 Campano Spain 36.22N 6.09W
119 C10 Campanquiz, Cerros *mts* Peru
66 R6 Campascio *mt* Switzerland 46.24N 10.03E
13 H5 Campaspe *R* Queensland
76 L6 Campaspero Spain 41.29N 4.11W
11 D6 Camp Bay North I New Zealand
11 N10 Camp Bay South I New Zealand
111 C2 Camp Beale California 39.06N 121.23W
111 C4 Campbell California 37.24N 121.58W
107 F5 Campbell Missouri 36.30N 90.05W
108 M9 Campbell Nebraska 40.18N 98.43W
104 H4 Campbell New York 42.14N 77.11W
104 E5 Campbell Ohio 41.04N 80.34W
95 G4 Campbell S Africa 28.49S 23.44E
12 B6 Campbell *dist* Canberra Australia
13 J6 Campbell *R* Queensland
101 V1 Campbell Bay N W Terr
15 L6 Campbell, C New Britain 5.04S 150.10E
11 J8 Campbell, C New Zealand 41.44S 174.18E
101 K12 Campbell Cr Br Col
99 N8 Campbellford Ontario 44.19N 77.47W
103 F4 Campbell Hall New York 41.27N 74.16W
25 E7 Campbell I Burma
11 B8 Campbell I Pacific Oc 52.30S 169.02E
114 A5 Campbell Industrial Park Hawaiian Is 21.18N 158.06W
101 J9 Campbell Island Br Col 52.09N 128.10W
101 G1 Campbell, L N W Terr 68.12N 133.20W
101 U4 Campbell, L N W Terr 63.15N 106.25W
15 G7 Campbell, L Papua New Guinea 6.45S 142.34E
13 B5 Campbell, Mt N Terr Australia 21.48S 131.45E
101 D3 Campbell, Mt Yukon Terr 64.23N 138.43W
31 G4 Campbellpore Pakistan 33.46N 72.26E
31 F4 Campbellpore *dist* Pakistan
14 G2 Campbell Ra W Australia
101 L10 Campbell River Vancouver I, Br Col 50.01N 125.18W
99 O7 Campbell's Bay Quebec 45.43N 76.36W
107 L3 Campbellsburg Kentucky 38.31N 85.12W
106 F6 Campbellsport Wisconsin 43.36N 88.16W
107 L4 Campbellsville Kentucky 37.20N 85.21W
98 F6 Campbellton New Brunswick 48.00N 66.41W
98 S4 Campbellton Newfoundland 49.18N 54.58W
112 J7 Campbellton Texas 28.44N 98.19W
12 K5 Campbelltown New S Wales 34.04S 150.49E
103 A6 Campbelltown Pennsylvania 40.17N 76.35W
12 J8 Campbell Town Tasmania 41.55S 147.30E
12 B8 Campbelltown *dist* Adelaide, S Aust
57 B2 Campbeltown Strathclyde Scotland 55.26N 5.36W
70 G7 Campbon France 47.26N 1.59W
72 H11 Campcardos, P *mt* Spain 42.29N 1.45E
108 G4 Camp Crook S Dakota 45.32N 103.59W
77 U14 Camp. de Mar Balearic Is 39.32N 2.25E
75 P3 Campdevanol Spain 42.14N 2.11E
106 D6 Camp Douglas Wisconsin 43.56N 90.17W
76 D6 Campea Portugal 41.17N 7.52W
69 B4 Campeaux France 49.37N 1.46E
115 O8 Campeche Mexico 19.50N 90.30W
115 O8 Campeche *state* Mexico
96 B6 Campeche Bank Gulf of Mexico
115 N8 Campeche, B. de Mexico
116 F4 Campechuela Cuba 20.15N 77.17W
81 B3 Campeda *R* Sardinia
76 D14 Campeiros Portugal 37.15N 7.31W
77 Q4 Campello Spain 38.26N 0.24W
80 G3 Campello sul Clitunno Italy 42.49N 12.47E
76 C9 Campelo Portugal 39.59N 8.13W
76 A10 Campelos Portugal 39.12N 9.14W
93 K8 Camp Emusiya Kenya 2.41S 38.56E
70 F6 Campénéac France 47.58N 2.17W
82 H4 Câmpeni Romania 46.23N 23.05E
115 F10 Campéon Panama 9.15N 79.46W
105 L9 Camperdown New Providence I Bahamas 25.03N 77.17W
95 O5 Camperdown S Africa 29.45S 30.34E
12 G7 Camperdown Victoria 38.15S 143.14E
66 J8 Campertogno Italy 45.48N 8.02E
100 R6 Camperville Manitoba 52.01N 100.08W
71 C9 Campestre-et-Luc France 43.56N 3.24E
107 L9 Camp Hill Alabama 32.48N 85.40W
13 K2 Camphill *dist* Brisbane, Qnsld
79 K7 Campi Bisenzio Italy 43.49N 11.08E
81 B4 Campidano *V* Sardinia
80 K7 Campi Flegrei *dist* Italy
80 C2 Campiglia Marittima Italy 43.03N 10.37E
79 C3 Campiglia Soana Italy 45.32N 7.32E
67 P12 Campile Corsica 42.29N 9.21E
76 B13 Campilhas *R* Portugal
76 B13 Campilhas, Barragem de *res* Portugal 37.50N 8.39W
75 H7 Campillo Spain 40.19N 1.14W
75 G8 Campillo de Altobuey Spain 39.36N 1.49W
77 J5 Campillo de Arenas Spain 37.34N 3.38W
76 F7 Campillo de Azaba Spain 40.30N 6.42W
76 H9 Campillo de Deleitosa Spain 39.43N 5.34W
75 G6 Campillo de Dueñas Spain 40.53N 1.41W
76 J9 Campillo de la Jara, El Spain 39.36N 5.03W
77 E3 Campillo de Llerena Spain 38.30N 5.50W
77 G6 Campillos Spain 37.04N 4.51W
75 G8 Campillos Paravientos Spain 39.58N 1.34W
117 D7 Campina Brazil 5.46S 48.21W
117 J8 Campina Grande Brazil 7.15S 35.50W
77 F5 Campiña, La *reg* Spain
118 F8 Campinas Brazil 22.54S 47.06W
118 E6 Campina Verde Brazil 19.36S 49.25W
76 E12 Campinho Portugal 38.22N 7.29W
66 M8 Campione Italy 45.58N 8.58E
79 F3 Campione d'Italia Italy 45.57N 9.06E
75 C5 Campisábalos Spain 41.15N 3.08W
81 R12 Campi Salentina Italy 40.23N 18.01E
67 P11 Campitello Corsica 42.32N 9.18E
79 L2 Campitello Italy 46.29N 11.45E
80 J3 Campli Italy 42.43N 13.42E
19 C9 Camplong Timor Indon 10.05S 123.57E
111 F5 Camp Nelson California 36.10N 118.38W
111 H9 Campo California 32.35N 116.28W
91 A2 Campo Cameroon 2.22N 9.50E
109 H4 Campo Colorado 37.06N 102.35W
92 H10 Campo Mozambique 17.46S 39.12E
76 D12 Campo Portugal 38.20N 7.31W
66 M5 Campo Switzerland 46.33N 8.57E
119 C6 Campoalegre Colombia 2.49N 75.19W
80 L5 Campobasso Italy 41.33N 14.39E
80 K5 Campobasso *prov* Italy
81 G9 Campobello di Licata Sicily 37.16N 13.55E
81 E8 Campobello di Mazara Sicily 37.38N 12.45E
98 F9 Campobello I New Brunswick
118 F7 Campo Belo Brazil 20.52S 45.16W
121 J1 Campo Belo do Sul Brazil 27.46S 50.46W
66 R6 Campocologno Switzerland 46.15N 10.09E
66 R6 Campo, Corno di *mt* Italy/Switz 46.26N 10.07E
79 L3 Campo d'Arsego Italy 45.30N 11.55E
75 H5 Campo de Cariñena *reg* Spain
77 K2 Campo de Criptana Spain 39.25N 3.07W
77 L7 Campo de Dalías *reg* Spain
118 D2 Campo de Diauarum Brazil 11.26S 53.04W
77 E8 Campo de Gibraltar *physical reg* Spain
66 M8 Campo dei Fiori, Monte Italy 45.53N 8.46E
76 K3 Campo de la Villa *reg* Spain
121 E1 Campo del Cielo Argentina 27.50S 61.45W
67 O13 Campo del Oro *airport* Corsica 41.55N 8.47E
77 P3 Campo de Mirra Spain 38.42N 0.47W
77 L3 Campo de Montiel *physical reg* Spain
77 M7 Campo de Níjar *physical reg* Spain
75 C5 Campo de San Pedro Spain 41.25N 3.34W
79 L1 Campo di Trens Italy 46.53N 11.30E
77 J3 Campo do Calatrava *physical reg* Spain
76 C5 Campo do Gerês Portugal 41.45N 8.12W
79 F2 Campodolcino Italy 46.24N 9.21E
118 H9 Campo dos Afonsos Brazil 22.53S 43.23W
118 D10 Campo Erê Brazil 26.22S 53.08W
118 B8 Campo Esperanza Paraguay 22.17S 59.40W
81 G8 Campofelice Sicily 37.54N 13.53E
81 F8 Campofiorito Sicily 37.46N 13.15E
118 E6 Campo Florido Brazil 19.49S 48.38W
79 O2 Campofórmido Italy 46.02N 13.10E
118 H2 Campo Formoso Brazil 10.31S 40.19W
81 G8 Campofranco Sicily 37.31N 13.43E
79 J5 Campogalliano Italy 44.42N 10.50E
120 G12 Campo Gallo Argentina 26.32S 62.51W
117 A9 Campo Grande Amazonas Brazil 8.44S 59.14W
118 C7 Campo Grande Mato Grosso do Sul Brazil 20.24S 54.35W
76 E15 Campo Grande Portugal 38.45N 9.09W
118 B9 Campo Grande *airport* Paraguay 25.13S 57.35W
76 B3 Campo Lameiro Spain 42.33N 8.32W
120 G12 Campo Largo Argentina 26.45S 60.52W
118 E9 Campo Largo Brazil 25.25S 49.30W
81 K9 Campolato, C Sicily 37.18N 15.12E
79 E5 Campo Ligure Italy 44.32N 8.42E
76 H10 Campo-Lugar Spain 39.13N 5.46W
117 F7 Campo Maior Brazil 4.50S 42.12W
76 E10 Campo Maior Portugal 39.01N 7.04W
76 H2 Campomanes Spain 43.06N 5.49W
80 M5 Campomarino Italy 41.57N 15.03E
67 O13 Campomora, Pta. di Corsica 41.38N 8.48E
79 E5 Campomorone Italy 44.31N 8.54E
118 D9 Campo Mourão Brazil 24.01S 52.24W
116 N9 Campona, L Venezuela
80 B3 Campo nell'Elba Italy 42.45N 10.13E
79 M4 Camponogara Italy 45.23N 12.04E
121 H1 Campo Novo Brazil 27.41S 53.46W
75 D7 Campo Real Spain 40.20N 3.23W
81 F8 Camporeale Sicily 37.54N 13.05E
79 H6 Camporgiano Italy 44.09N 10.19E
121 E2 Campo Rico Argentina 29.45S 62.46W
76 K3 Camporredondo Spain 42.53N 4.45W
76 K3 Camporredondo, Embalse de *res* Spain
75 M4 Camporrélls Spain 41.58N 0.31E
75 H8 Camporrobles Spain 39.39N 1.24W
118 H7 Campos Brazil 21.46S 41.21W
75 J6 Campos Spain 40.43N 0.44W
118 F6 Campos Altos Brazil 19.47S 46.13W
79 L3 Camposampiero Italy 45.34N 11.56E
120 F11 Campo Santo Argentina 24.36S 65.09W
79 K5 Camposanto Italy 44.47N 11.08E
80 L6 Camposauro *mt* Italy 41.10N 14.36E
118 F3 Campos Belos Brazil 13.09S 47.03W
77 W15 Campos del Puerto Balearic Is 39.26N 3.01E
118 F8 Campos do Jordão Brazil 22.45S 45.33W
119 D8 Campo Serio Peru 1.52S 74.42W
121 H1 Campos Novos Brazil 27.26S 51.50W
102 F7 Campos, Pta *C* Mexico 19.05N 104.22W
77 V15 Campos, Pto.de Balearic Is 39.19N 2.59E
117 G8 Campos Sales Brazil 7.01S 40.21W
77 J6 Campotéjar Spain 37.29N 3.36W
66 L6 Campo Tencia *mt* Switzerland 46.26N 8.44E
80 H3 Campotosto Italy 42.34N 13.23E
80 H3 Campotosto, L.di Italy
119 F5 Campo Troco Colombia 4.54N 68.11W
79 L1 Campo Tures Italy 46.55N 11.57E
66 L6 Campo, Val di Switzerland
106 C9 Camp Point Illinois 40.03N 91.04W
111 D6 Camp Roberts California 35.47N 120.44W
75 P3 Camprodór Spain 42.19N 2.23E
75 E3 Camprovin Spain 42.21N 2.43W
112 H5 Camp San Saba Texas 31.00N 99.17W
94 P11 Camp's Bay *dist* Cape Town S Africa
58 H6 Campsie Fells *hills* Central Scotland
71 J10 Camps-la-Source France 43.24N 6.05E
107 C10 Campti Louisiana 31.56N 93.09W
104 B9 Campton Kentucky 37.44N 83.35W
104 O3 Campton New Hampshire 43.53N 71.38W
111 C2 Camptonville California 39.28N 121.01W
57 H2 Camptown Borders Scotland 55.24N 2.30W
103 B3 Camptown Pennsylvania 41.44N 75.15W
119 D8 Campuya Peru 1.46S 73.31W
119 D8 Campuya, R Peru
111 N7 Camp Verde Arizona 34.36N 111.51W
112 G6 Camp Wood Texas 29.41N 100.02W
56 L3 Cam, R Cambs Eng
25 K7 Cam Ranh Vietnam 11.54N 109.14E
100 E5 Camrose Alberta 53.01N 112.48W
101 S4 Camsell, L N W Terr
101 T6 Camsell Portage Saskatchewan 59.39N 109.12W
101 M4 Camsell Ra N W Terr
91 C11 Camucuio Angola 14.09S 13.20E
91 E10 Camué Angola 13.46S 16.58E
79 K6 Camugnano Italy 44.10N 11.06E
77 K2 Camunas Spain 39.26N 3.28W
72 H10 Camura France 42.48N 1.54E
105 J7 Camuy Puerto Rico 18.28N 66.52W
36 C2 Çan Çanakkale Turkey 40.03N 27.03E
37 E6 Çan Elâzığ Turkey 39.09N 40.12E
37 D3 Çan *R* Turkey
25 K7 Ca Na Vietnam 11.21N 108.53E
103 H2 Canaan Connecticut 42.02N 73.20W
98 G7 Canaan New Brunswick 46.15N 65.05W
104 N3 Canaan New Hampshire 43.38N 72.02W
103 H2 Canaan New York 42.25N 73.27W
116 M1 Canaan Tobago W I 11.09N 60.49W
104 O2 Canaan Vermont 45.00N 71.32W
111 N4 Canaan Pk *mt* Utah 37.37N 111.49W
98 G8 Canaan R New Brunswick
118 F5 Canabrava Brazil 17.23S 45.52W
117 C8 Cana Brava *R* Pará Brazil
118 E3 Canabrava, R Goiás Brazil
117 B8 Cana Brava, R Pará Brazil
19 H7 Canabungan *isld* Philippines 8.10N 117.11E
91 D8 Canacassala Angola 8.08S 14.07E
28 B3 Canacona Goa India 15.01N 74.04E
91 E10 Canacupa Angola 12.01S 17.22E
77 P3 Cañada Spain 38.41N 0.49W
97 Canada *dominion* N America
75 F5 Cañada *R* Spain
77 C6 Cañada, Arroyo de la *R* Spain
98 Q3 Canada Bay Newfoundland
75 J6 Cañada de Benatanduz Spain 40.35N 0.33W
121 E4 Cañada de Gómez Argentina 32.50S 61.23W
75 G8 Cañada del Hoyo Spain 39.58N 1.55W
104 P8 Canada Falls Deadwater Maine 45.54N 69.59W
121 C3 Cañada Honda Argentina 32.00S 68.35W
75 F8 Cañadajuncosa Spain 39.33N 2.15W
77 M7 Cañada, la Spain 36.50N 2.24W
77 F5 Cañada Rosal Spain 37.36N 5.13W
75 J6 Cañada Vellida Spain 40.42N 0.56W
Cañada Verde *see* Villa Huidobro
Canadel, le *see* Rayol-Canadel-sur-Mer, le
103 D4 Canadensis Pennsylvania 41.12N 75.15W
112 D8 Canadian Texas 35.54N 100.23W
109 K6 Canadian *R* New Mexico etc
121 K8 Cañadón de las Vacas Argentina 50.38S 69.15W
121 B10 Cañadon Grande, Sa *ra* Argentina
121 L6 Cañadón Seco Argentina 46.31S 67.46W
105 G4 Canadys S Carolina 33.03N 80.37W
91 G10 Canage *R* Angola
118 B9 Canaglaé, L Argentina
37 H1 Çanak *R* Turkey
37 C3 Çanakkale Turkey 40.09N 26.25E
37 C3 Çanakkale Boğazı *str* Turkey
9 B13 Canala New Caledonia 21.30S 165.58E
78 B11 Canal de la Galite *str* Tunisia
79 C5 Canale Italy 44.48N 8.00E
121 C5 Canalejas Argentina 35.14S 66.34W
76 L5 Canalejas de Peñafiel Spain 41.31N 4.07W
75 D3 Canales Spain 42.09N 3.01W
75 J8 Canales Spain 39.51N 0.47W
79 L2 Canale San Bovo Italy 46.09N 11.44E
101 Q10 Canal Flats Br Col 50.09N 115.50W
107 G5 Canalou Missouri 36.45N 89.41W
105 G11 Canal Point Florida 26.51N 80.38W
72 G8 Canals France 43.52N 1.18E
77 P3 Canáls Spain 38.58N 0.35W
104 C7 Canal Winchester Ohio 39.51N 82.48W
75 F7 Cañamares Spain 40.27N 2.14W
77 L3 Cañamares *R* Spain
120 D4 Canamari Brazil 10.15S 69.17W
76 J10 Cañamero Spain 39.23N 5.24W
104 H4 Canandaigua New York 42.53N 77.19W
104 H4 Canandaigua, L New York
115 D2 Cananea Mexico 30.59N 110.20W
118 F9 Cananéia Brazil 24.59S 47.54W
119 F6 Canapiare, Cerro *mt* Colombia 2.50N 68.23W
80 H3 Canapine, Forca *pass* Italy 42.45N 13.11E
69 C3 Canaples France 50.04N 2.15E
118 E6 Canápolis Brazil 18.45S 49.15W
119 B9 Cañar Ecuador 2.38S 78.57W
77 K7 Cañar Spain 36.56N 3.24W
119 B9 Cañar *prov* Ecuador
Cañar *R see* Naranjal, R
67 P11 Canari Corsica 42.50N 9.19E
117 G6 Canárias, I.das Brazil
Canarias, Islas *see* Canary Is
116 C4 Canarroes, Arch.de los Cuba 21.40N 82.30W
103 K8 Canarsie New York 40.38N 73.54W
96 H6 Canary Basin Atlantic Oc
96 T11 Canary Is Atlantic Oc 28.30N 14.10W
19 H2 Cañas *R* Luzon Philippines
115 O8 Canasayab Mexico 19.20N 90.36W
76 D8 Canas de Senhorim Portugal 40.29N 7.54W
115 M4 Canas Dulces Costa Rica 10.46N 85.29W

101 W4 Carey L N W Terr
14 D8 Carey, L W Australia
48 R4 Carey Øer islds Greenland 76.35N 72.00W
11 N12 Careys Bay New Zealand 45.48S 170.39E
89 D8 Careysburg Liberia 6.30N 10.32W
58 L7 Carfraemill Borders Scotland 55.47N 2.47W
26 E7 Cargados Carajos islds Ind Oc
67 O12 Cargèse Corsica 42.08N 8.36E
99 J8 Cargill Ontario 44.12N 81.14W
58 K5 Cargill Tayside Scotland 56.31N 3.25W
11 M12 Cargill, Mt New Zealand 45.49S 170.33E
13 G5 Cargoon Queensland 20.00S 144.44E
13 G5 Cargoon, L Queensland 20.10S 144.50E
70 C5 Carhaix-Plouguer France 48.16N 3.35W
56 E5 Carhampton Somerset Eng 51.11N 3.25W
Carhar see Silchar
98 E1 Carheil, L Quebec 52.40N 67.06W
120 B4 Carhuamayo Peru 10.55S 76.03W
120 B3 Carhuáz Peru 9.15S 77.39W
121 E6 Carhué Argentina 37.10S 62.45W
76 E8 Caria Portugal 40.18N 7.21W
118 H2 Cariacá R Brazil
118 H7 Cariacica Brazil 20.15S 40.23W
119 G2 Cariaco Venezuela 10.33N 63.37W
119 G2 Cariaco, G.de Venezuela
117 C6 Cariaí, R Brazil
119 B10 Cariamanga Ecuador 4.20S 79.37W
91 D9 Cariango Angola 10.34S 15.21E
81 N5 Cariati Italy 39.30N 16.56E
119 C3 Caribana, Pta Colombia 8.37N 76.54W
102 L7 Caribbean Sea C America
101 N9 Cariboo Mts Br Col
113 P4 Caribou Alaska 64.39N 145.50W
104 R7 Caribou Maine 46.52N 68.01W
98 K8 Caribou Nova Scotia 45.44N 62.40W
113 G9 Caribou R Alaska
101 K5 Caribou R N W Terr
101 K7 Caribou Hide Br Col 57.25N 127.35W
101 N10 Caribou Highway Br Col
101 R5 Caribou, Is Gt Slave L, N W Terr
98 K8 Caribou Island Nova Scotia 45.46N 62.46W
99 E5 Caribou Island Ontario 47.23N 85.48W
99 A2 Caribou, L Ontario
110 O6 Caribou Mt Idaho 43.07N 111.18W
101 Q6 Caribou Mts Alberta
101 F2 Caribou R Yukon Terr
115 F4 Carichic Mexico 27.55N 107.05W
76 D12 Caridade Portugal 38.27N 7.34W
100 Q9 Carievale Saskatchewan 49.11N 101.40W
19 M6 Carigara Philippines 11.16N 124.42E
19 M6 Carigara B Philippines
69 J4 Carignan France 49.38N 5.10E
79 C5 Carignano Italy 44.54N 7.40E
99 Q7 Carillon Quebec 45.35N 74.23W
87 M5 Carin Somalia 10.56N 49.11E
12 J4 Carinda New S Wales 30.29S 147.45E
75 H5 Cariñena Spain 41.20N 1.13W
12 L8 Caringbah New S Wales 34.03S 151.07E
118 G4 Carinhanha Brazil 14.18S 43.46W
118 F4 Carinhanha, R Brazil
81 F7 Carini Sicily 38.08N 13.11E
81 F7 Carini, G.di Sicily
58 B3 Carinish N Uist, W Isles Scotland 57.31N 7.19W
95 P1 Carino S Africa 25.31S 31.09E
76 D1 Cariño Spain 43.44N 7.51W
80 J6 Carinola Italy 41.12N 13.59E
Carinthia see Kärnten
118 J9 Carioca, Sa da mts Brazil
91 H10 Caripande Angola 12.59S 22.42E
118 F2 Cariparé Brazil 11.31S 45.04W
119 D7 Caripaya, R Colombia
119 G2 Caripe Venezuela 10.13N 63.30W
117 E5 Caripi Brazil 1.08S 47.29W
119 G2 Caripito Venezuela 10.07N 63.07W
117 G6 Cariré Brazil 3.58S 40.25W
117 A7 Cariri Brazil 4.23S 57.07W
117 G8 Caririaçu Brazil 7.05S 39.16W
117 G8 Cariris Novos, Sa. dos mts Brazil
56 J6 Carisbrooke I of Wight Eng 50.41N 1.19W
119 G3 Caris, R Venezuela
120 F3 Caritíanas Brazil 9.25S 63.06W
117 G8 Cariús Brazil 6.31S 39.28W
57 H4 Cark Lancs Eng 54.11N 2.59W
59 G2 Cark, Mt Donegal Irish Rep 54.53N 7.52W
59 J4 Carlanstown Meath Irish Rep 53.46N 6.50W
72 K6 Carlat France 44.52N 2.33E
109 N5 Carl Blackwell L Oklahoma 36.07N 97.15W
81 K9 Carlentini Sicily 37.17N 15.16E
69 E4 Carlepont France 49.31N 3.03E
77 P2 Carlet Spain 39.14N 0.31W
106 L7 Carleton Michigan 42.03N 83.11W
108 N9 Carleton Nebraska 40.18N 97.41W
98 F5 Carleton Quebec 48.08N 66.10W
98 F6 Carleton, Mt New Brunswick 47.24N 66.52W
99 O7 Carleton Place Ontario 45.08N 76.09W
98 K4 Carleton Pt Anticosti I, Que 49.45N 62.56W
95 L2 Carletonville S Africa 26.22S 27.25E
108 F5 Carlile Wyoming 44.26N 104.46W
110 J9 Carlin Nevada 40.44N 116.06W
69 M5 Carling France 49.10N 6.43E
59 K3 Carlingford Louth Irish Rep 54.02N 6.11W
12 K6 Carlingford dist Sydney, New S Wales
59 K3 Carlingford, L Irish Rep 54.05N 6.14W
99 C9 Carlington Ontario 45.23N 75.45W
107 G2 Carlinville Illinois 39.17N 89.52W
107 E7 Carlisle Arkansas 34.47N 91.42W
57 H3 Carlisle Cumbria Eng 54.54N 2.55W
107 J3 Carlisle Indiana 38.57N 87.23W
107 M3 Carlisle Kentucky 38.19N 84.02W
104 H6 Carlisle Pennsylvania 40.12N 77.12W
105 F3 CArlisle S Carolina 34.36N 81.29W
14 B2 Carlisle dist Perth, W Australia
116 O6 Carlisle B Barbados 13.05N 59.37W
95 K9 Carlisle Bridge S Africa 33.04S 26.14E
113 B10 Carlisle I Aleutian Is 52.55N 170.05W
95 K1 Carlisonia S Africa 25.59S 26.12E
72 H10 Carlit, Pic France 42.34N 1.55E
81 A5 Carloforte Sardinia 39.08N 8.17E
81 A5 Carloforte, G.di Sardinia
58 K7 Carlops Borders Scotland 55.48N 3.20W
121 D9 Carlos Ameghino, Istmo isthmus Argentina
121 H2 Carlos Barbosa Brazil 29.18S 51.32W
121 E5 Carlos Casares Argentina 35.32S 61.20W
118 H5 Carlos Chagas Brazil 17.42S 40.46W
121 J10 Carlos, I Chile 54.05S 73.20W
92 G12 Carlos, Ponta Don pt Mozambique 21.40S 35.29E
13 E6 Carlo Springs Queensland 23.23S 138.50E
121 G4 Carlos Reyles Uruguay 33.00S 56.30W
121 E5 Carlos Tejedor Argentina 35.25S 62.25W
77 G5 Carlota, La Spain 37.41N 4.56W
59 J6 Carlow Irish Rep 52.50N 6.55W
59 J6 Carlow co Irish Rep
58 C2 Carloway Lewis, W Isles Scotland 58.17N 6.47W
111 G8 Carlsbad California 33.09N 117.20W
Carlsbad Czechoslovakiasee Karlovy Vary
109 F9 Carlsbad New Mexico 32.25N 104.14W
109 F9 Carlsbad Caverns Nat.Park New Mexico
48 V11 Carlsberg Fd Greenland
26 E4 Carlsberg Ridge Indian Oc
61 L7 Carlsbourg Belgium 49.53N 5.05E
64 O3 Carlsfeld E Germany 50.26N 12.36E
106 G3 Carlshend Michigan 46.20N 87.14W
108 S3 Carlton Minnesota 46.40N 92.24W
57 L6 Carlton Notts Eng 53.22N 1.06W
57 M6 Carlton Notts Eng 53.10N 0.48W
57 K4 Carlton N Yorks Eng 54.15N 1.54W
57 L5 Carlton N Yorks Eng 53.43N 1.02W
110 B4 Carlton Oregon 45.19N 123.10W
95 H7 Carlton S Africa 31.16S 24.57E
100 L6 Carlton Saskatchewan 52.51N 106.29W
112 J4 Carlton Texas 31.54N 98.11W
14 G3 Carlton Hill W Australia 15.28S 128.37E
57 L4 Carlton Miniott N Yorks Eng 54.13N 1.24W
110 D3 Carlton Pass Washington 46.46N 121.27W
58 J7 Carluke Strathclyde Scotland 55.45N 3.51W
72 G6 Carlux France 44.53N 1.21E
107 G3 Carlyle Illinois 38.39N 89.20W
108 F3 Carlyle Montana 46.40N 104.03W
100 P9 Carlyle Saskatchewan 49.39N 102.18W
107 G3 Carlyle Lake res Illinois
101 E4 Carmacks Yukon Terr 62.04N 136.21W
79 C5 Carmagnola Italy 44.51N 7.43E
100 U9 Carman Manitoba 49.32N 97.59W
100 D8 Carmangay Alberta 50.10N 113.06W
98 S4 Carmanville Newfoundland 49.23N 54.19W
Carmarthen co see Dyfed co
56 B4 Carmarthen B Dyfed Wales
72 J7 Carmaux France 44.03N 2.09E
111 C5 Carmel California 36.34N 121.56W
104 Q2 Carmel Maine 44.46N 69.05W
103 D8 Carmel New Jersey 39.26N 75.08W
103 G4 Carmel New York 41.25N 73.40W
100 M6 Carmel Saskatchewan 52.14N 105.22W
Carmel, Cape see Karmel, Cape
57 D6 Carmel Hd Gwynedd Wales 53.24N 4.34W
115 O9 Carmelita Guatemala 17.30N 90.08W
35 D3 Carmel, Mt Israel 32.45N 35.02E
121 F5 Carmelo Uruguay 34.00S 58.20W
111 C5 Carmel Valley California 36.29N 121.47W
120 E4 Carmen Bolivia 11.40S 67.51W
121 F5 Carmen Buenos Aires Arg 34.25S 59.48W
120 D12 Carmen Chile 26.28S 70.15W
119 C3 Carmen Colombia 9.46N 75.06W
110 M4 Carmen Idaho 45.15N 113.52W
115 J5 Carmen Nuevo León Mexico 25.57N 100.24W
109 M5 Carmen Oklahoma 36.35N 98.28W
19 M7 Carmen Philippines 9.48N 124.11E
121 E4 Carmen Santa Fé Arg 33.44S 61.45W
121 G4 Carmen Uruguay 33.08S 56.02W
115 D5 Carmen I Mexico
115 F3 Carmen R Mexico
76 L9 Carmena Spain 39.57N 4.24W
120 D10 Carmen Alto Chile 23.06S 69.35W
120 B9 Carmen de la Legua-Reynosa dist Lima Peru
118 C10 Carmen del Paraná Paraguay 27.13S 56.12W
121 E8 Carmen de Patagones Argentina 40.45S 63.00W
76 H3 Cármenes Spain 42.58N 5.34W
115 O8 Carmen, I.del Mexico
121 C5 Carmensa San Luis Argentina 35.12S 67.40W
112 E7 Carmen, Sierra del mts Mexico
121 K9 Carmen Silva, Sa.de mts Chile
107 H3 Carmi Illinois 38.05N 88.11W
105 L9 Carmichael New Providence I Bahamas 25.01N 77.25W
100 J8 Carmichael Saskatchewan 50.03N 108.38W
13 J5 Carmila Queensland 21.55S 149.25E
112 L5 Carmine Texas 30.10N 96.44W
118 G7 Carmo Brazil 21.54S 42.37W
118 F7 Carmo da Cachoeira Brazil 21.24S 45.15W
118 F6 Carmo do Paranaíba Brazil 18.59S 46.20W
14 C9 Carmody, L W Australia 32.30S 119.20E
79 D6 Carmo, Monte Italy 44.10N 8.11E
19 J2 Carmona Luzon Philippines 14.18N 121.04E
77 E6 Carmona Spain 37.28N 5.38W
Carmona Angola see Uige
77 D2 Carmonita Spain 39.09N 6.21W
59 J2 Carn Londonderry N Ireland 54.54N 6.50W
59 C5 Carna Galway Irish Rep 53.20N 9.49W
57 N4 Carnaby Humberside Eng 54.04N 0.15W
70 D6 Carnac France 47.35N 3.05W
59 J3 Carnagh Armagh N Ireland 54.12N 6.43W
14 B8 Carnamah W Australia 29.41S 115.53E
12 F4 Carnanto, L S Australia 30.55S 140.45E
95 F6 Carnarvon S Africa 30.59S 22.08E
14 A6 Carnarvon W Australia 24.51S 113.45E
13 J7 Carnarvon Ra Queensland
14 D7 Carnarvon Ra W Australia
28 C6 Carnatic reg Tamil Nadu India
117 G7 Carnaúbas Brazil 5.51S 39.45W
76 A11 Carnaxide Portugal 38.43N 9.14W
58 H4 Carn Ban mt Highland Scotland 57.06N 4.18W
59 L2 Carncastle Antrim N Ireland 54.54N 5.53W
59 H1 Carndonagh Donegal Irish Rep 55.15N 7.15W
100 Q9 Carnduff Saskatchewan 49.11N 101.50W
57 F6 Carnedd Llwyelyn mt Gwynedd Wales 53.10N 3.58W
109 M6 Carnegie Oklahoma 35.06N 98.36W
104 E6 Carnegie Pennsylvania 40.24N 80.06W
14 E7 Carnegie W Australia 25.41S 123.00E
14 E7 Carnegie, L W Australia
122 S8 Carnegie Ridge Pacific Oc
70 K4 Carneille, la France 48.47N 0.27W
109 M3 Carneiro Kansas 38.45N 98.02W
121 A6 Carnero, B. del Chile
77 F8 Carnero, Pta.del pt Spain 36.05N 5.25W
105 D3 Carnesville Georgia 34.23N 83.13W
59 K6 Carnew Wicklow Irish Rep 52.43N 6.30W
106 G4 Carney Michigan 45.36N 87.34W
109 N6 Carney Oklahoma 35.50N 97.00W
123 J11 Carney isld Antarctica
57 H4 Carnforth Lancs Eng 54.08N 2.46W
58 M7 Carnham Northumberland England 55.38N 2.18W
79 O2 Carnia Italy 46.23N 13.07E
79 N2 Carnia Alpi mts Italy
76 E7 Carniçais Portugal 40.44N 7.18W
28 H6 Car Nicobar isld Nicobar Is
79 N1 Carnico, Passo di pass Italy/Austria 46.37N 12.57E
76 D15 Carnide Portugal 38.46N 9.12W
61 G5 Carnières Belgium 50.27N 4.15E
69 E3 Carnières France 50.10N 3.21E
11 B7 Carnley Harb inlet Auckland Is Pacific Oc
59 L2 Carnlough Antrim N Ireland 55.00N 6.00W
56 D2 Carno Powys Wales 52.33N 3.32W
70 C5 Carnoët France 48.22N 3.31W
71 D9 Carnon France 43.32N 3.58E
74 J8 Carnot Algeria 36.16N 1.43E
90 G9 Carnot Cent Afr Rep 4.59N 15.56E
76 A3 Carnota Spain 42.49N 9.05W
14 D3 Carnot B W Australia 17.15S 122.12E
12 D5 Carnot, C S Australia 34.55S 135.35E
89 L7 Carnotville Benin 8.47N 2.23E
71 J10 Carnoules France 43.18N 6.12E
58 L5 Carnoustie Tayside Scotland 56.30N 2.44W
59 K7 Carnsore Pt Wexford Irish Rep 52.10N 6.22W
58 J7 Carnwath Strathclyde Scotland 55.43N 3.38W
101 J2 Carnwath R N W Terr
113 N3 Caro Alaska 67.10N 148.20W
106 L6 Caro Michigan 43.29N 83.24W
119 J7 Caroaebe, R Brazil
75 J9 Caroch mt Spain 39.05N 1.04E
91 B12 Caroço, I São Tomé & Principe, Gulf of Guinea 1.32N 7.27E
121 J5 Caro, L Chile
13 K4 Carola Cay isld Gt Barrier Reef Australia 19.02S 152.20E
105 B10 Carol City Florida 25.54N 80.16W
105 F2 Caroleen N Carolina 35.15N 81.47W
117 E8 Carolina Brazil 7.20S 47.25W
105 K7 Carolina Puerto Rico 18.23N 65.57W
95 O2 Carolina S Africa 26.05S 30.07E
105 K3 Carolina Beach N Carolina 34.02N 77.56W
77 J4 Carolina, La Spain 38.16N 3.36W
100 C6 Caroline Alberta 52.07N 114.45W
11 C12 Caroline New Zealand 45.52S 168.24E
103 C9 Caroline co Maryland
122 E7 Caroline Basin, E Pacific Oc
122 E7 Caroline Basin, W Pacific Oc
10 A11 Caroline Cove Macquarie I Pacific Oc 54.45S 158.50E
122 M9 Caroline I Line Is Pacific Oc 10.00S 150.15W
17 O10 Caroline Is Pacific Oc
13 D6 Caroline, L N Terr Australia
63 G5 Carolinensiel W Germany 53.42N 7.48E
11 B12 Caroline Pk mt New Zealand 45.58S 167.15E
14 F3 Caroline Ra W Australia
70 G4 Carolles France 48.45N 1.34W
71 G8 Caromb France 44.06N 5.05E
100 M8 Caron Saskatchewan 50.28N 105.52W
79 G2 Carona Italy 46.02N 9.47E
119 B7 Carondelet Ecuador 1.05N 78.43W
10 S3 Carondelet Reef Phoenix Is Pacific Oc 5.33S 173.50W
116 O1 Caroni Trinidad & Tobago 10.36N 61.23W
116 O2 Caroni co Trinidad & Tobago
81 H7 Caronia Sicily 38.02N 14.27E
Caronie, Monti see Nebrodi, Monti
116 O1 Caroni R Trinidad & Tobago
119 H3 Caroní R Venezuela
119 H3 Caroní River Hydro-Electric Scheme Venezuela 8.15N 62.45W
116 O1 Caroni Swamp Trinidad & Tobago
66 M9 Caronno Italy 45.44N 8.49E
79 F3 Caronno Pertus Italy 45.36N 9.02E
119 E2 Carora Venezuela 10.12N 70.07W
81 P12 Carosino Italy 40.28N 17.24E
66 A7 Carouge Switzerland 46.12N 6.09E
81 Q11 Carovigno Italy 40.43N 17.40E
80 K5 Carovilli Italy 41.43N 14.18E
111 K4 Carp Nevada 37.07N 114.31W
99 O7 Carp Ontario 45.21N 76.02W
79 G5 Carpaneto Piacentino Italy 44.55N 9.48E
84 T13 Carpasia ruins Cyprus 35.37N 34.23E
49 J7 Carpathians mts Cent Europe
82 H5 Carpaţii Meridionali, Munţii mts Romania
79 H4 Carpenèdolo Italy 45.22N 10.25E
79 E5 Carpeneto Italy 44.41N 8.36E
13 G4 Carpentaria Downs Queensland 18.40S 144.18E
13 E2 Carpentaria, G. of Australia
108 F8 Carpenter Wyoming 41.04N 104.22W
110 A7 Carpenterville Oregon 42.14N 124.20W
71 G8 Carpentras France 44.03N 5.03E
79 J5 Carpi Italy 44.47N 10.53E
71 G10 Carpiagne mt France 43.15N 5.29E
81 R12 Carpignano Italy 40.12N 18.21E
79 D3 Carpignano Sesia Italy 45.32N 8.25E
117 J8 Carpina Brazil 7.50S 35.15W
80 N6 Carpinelli, Monte Italy 41.11N 15.34E
79 J6 Carpineti Italy 44.27N 10.31E
80 H5 Carpineto Romano Italy 41.36N 13.06E
82 F5 Cărpiniş Romania 45.46N 20.53E
80 N5 Carpino Italy 41.51N 15.52E
80 K5 Carpinone Italy 41.35N 14.19E
111 E7 Carpinteria California 34.25N 119.31W
108 J1 Carpio N Dakota 48.25N 101.44W
76 J6 Carpio Spain 41.13N 5.07W
76 L9 Carpio de Tajo, El Spain 39.53N 4.28W
77 H5 Carpio, El Spain 37.56N 4.30W
111 M2 Carp L Utah 39.16N 112.50W
101 M8 Carp Lake Br Col 54.48N 123.20W
106 K4 Carp Lake Michigan 45.43N 84.47W
12 F6 Carpolac Victoria 36.45S 141.20E
72 B1 Carquefou France 47.18N 1.29W
71 J10 Carqueiranne France 43.06N 6.05E
109 F1 Carr Colorado 40.54N 104.54W
105 C8 Carrabelle Florida 29.52N 84.40W
76 F3 Carracedelo Spain 42.33N 6.44W
100 O6 Carragana Saskatchewan 52.34N 103.10W
76 F5 Carragosa Portugal 41.52N 6.48W
119 D2 Carraipía Colombia 11.19N 72.21W
59 D4 Carra, L Mayo Irish Rep 53.40N 9.15W
76 C2 Carral Spain 43.14N 8.22W
12 K7 Carramar dist Sydney, N S W
59 D8 Carran mt Kerry Irish Rep 51.50N 9.22W
75 C7 Carranque Spain 40.10N 3.55W
75 D1 Carranza Spain 43.13N 3.22W
121 A5 Carranza, C Chile 35.35S 72.42W
115 M9 Carranza, Jesús Mexico 17.27N 95.01W
119 H4 Carrao, R Venezuela
76 B14 Carrapateira Portugal 37.11N 8.53W
79 H6 Carrara Italy 44.04N 10.06E
111 H5 Carrara Nevada 36.47N 116.41W
121 F9 Carrascal dist Santiago Chile
75 K6 Carrascal mt Spain 40.40N 0.06W
75 C5 Carrascal del Rio Spain 41.21N 3.54W
76 J9 Carrascalejo Spain 39.39N 5.13W
77 D2 Carrascalejo, El Spain 39.01N 6.21W
77 P3 Carrascal, Sierra del mts Spain
121 G5 Carrasco airport Uruguay 34.53S 55.50W
120 D9 Carrasco pk Chile 20.58S 70.05W
75 F6 Carrascosa Spain 40.35N 2.10W
75 E7 Carrascosa del Campo Spain 40.02N 2.45W
77 O5 Carrascoy, Sierra de mts Spain
12 H5 Carrathool New S Wales 34.25S 145.24E
77 G7 Carratraca Spain 36.51N 4.49W
59 C8 Carrauntoohil mt Kerry Irish Rep 52.00N 9.45W
76 E6 Carrazeda d'Anciães Portugal 41.14N 7.16W
117 C5 Carrazedo Brazil 1.35S 51.50W
76 E5 Carrazedo de Monte Negro Portugal 41.34N 7.25W
14 G3 Carr Boyd Ra W Australia
58 J4 Carrbridge Highland Scotland 57.17N 3.49W
123 H4 Carr.C Antarctica 66.10S 131.00E
87 J8 Carre, El Ethiopia 5.50N 42.05E
76 B10 Carregado Portugal 39.01N 8.58W
76 C8 Carregal do Sal Portugal 40.26N 8.00W
76 D13 Carreiras R Portugal
76 K2 Carreña Spain 43.20N 4.50W
121 B9 Carrenleufu R Argentina
121 B6 Carrero, Cerro pk Argentina 37.28S 69.46W
72 C9 Carresse-Cassaber France 43.29N 0.59W
Carrhae anc site see Harran Turkey
116 O8 Carriacou I Grenadines W I 12.29N 61.26W
59 E2 Carrick Donegal Irish Rep 54.39N 8.38W
57 D2 Carrick dist Strathclyde Scotland
59 K1 Carrick-a-rede I Antrim N Ireland 55.14N 6.20W
59 K3 Carrickarnon Louth Irish Rep 54.06N 6.22W
59 H7 Carrickbeg Waterford Irish Rep 52.20N 7.25W
59 L2 Carrickfergus Antrim N Ireland 54.43N 5.49W
59 J4 Carrickmacross Monaghan Irish Rep 53.58N 6.43W
59 H2 Carrickmore Tyrone N Ireland 54.36N 7.02W
59 F4 Carrick-on-Shannon Leitrim Irish Rep 53.57N 8.05W
59 H7 Carrick-on-Suir Tipperary Irish Rep 52.21N 7.25W
56 T9 Carrick Rds inlet Cornwall Eng
107 G11 Carriere Mississippi 30.35N 89.40W
99 N5 Carrière, L Quebec
68 D3 Carrières-sur-Seine France 48.55N 2.10E
107 H4 Carriers Mills Illinois 37.40N 88.40W
12 E4 Carrieton S Australia 32.28S 138.34E
59 E8 Carrigadrohid Res Cork Irish Rep
59 C6 Carrigaholt Clare Irish Rep 52.36N 9.42W
59 F8 Carrigaline Cork Irish Rep 51.49N 8.23W
59 G4 Carrigallen Leitrim Irish Rep 53.59N 7.39W
59 H2 Carrigans Donegal Irish Rep 54.57N 7.25W
59 G1 Carrigart Donegal Irish Rep 55.10N 7.48W
59 C6 Carrig I Limerick Irish Rep 52.32N 9.32W
59 F8 Carrigtohill Cork Irish Rep 51.55N 8.16W
121 F5 Carril Argentina 35.45S 59.30W
76 B3 Carril Spain 42.36N 8.46W
121 B8 Carri Lafquén, L Argentina
115 H4 Carrillo Mexico 26.54N 103.55W
121 D3 Carrilobo Argentina 31.55S 63.03W
108 L2 Carrington N Dakota 47.28N 99.08W
77 J2 Carrión de Calatrava Spain 39.01N 3.49W
77 D6 Carrión de los Céspedes Spain 37.22N 6.20W
76 K4 Carrión de los Condes Spain 42.20N 4.37W
115 F2 Carrizal Chihuahua Mexico 30.35N 106.39W
119 D1 Carrizal Colombia 12.01N 72.10W
96 V16 Carrizal Gran Canaria Canary Is 27.55N 15.22W
119 C4 Carrizal, Alto de mt Colombia 7.28N 76.28W
121 B2 Carrizal Bajo Chile 28.08S 71.15W
121 B2 Carrizal, Pta C Chile 29.10S 71.32W
76 H3 Carrizo Spain 42.35N 5.50W
111 H9 Carrizo Cr California
109 G5 Carrizo Cr New Mexico
111 P5 Carrizo Mts Arizona
115 K5 Carrizos Mexico 24.22N 99.20W
77 L3 Carrizosa Spain 38.51N 2.59W
112 H7 Carrizo Springs Texas 28.33N 99.54W
109 E8 Carrizozo New Mexico 33.39N 105.54W
77 M2 Carro mt Spain 39.10N 2.25W
76 H3 Carrocera Spain 42.47N 5.44W
79 G6 Carrodano Italy 44.15N 9.40E
108 Q7 Carroll Iowa 42.05N 94.51W
100 R9 Carroll Manitoba 49.38N 100.02W
108 N7 Carroll Nebraska 42.17N 97.12W
123 G12 Carroll Inlet Antarctica
107 H8 Carrollton Alabama 33.16N 88.06W
105 B4 Carrollton Georgia 33.34N 85.06W
107 F2 Carrollton Illinois 39.20N 90.24W
107 L3 Carrollton Kentucky 38.41N 85.09W
107 G8 Carrollton Mississippi 33.31N 89.59W
107 C2 Carrollton Missouri 39.20N 93.30W
104 A7 Carrollton Ohio 39.43N 84.16W
104 D6 Carrollton Ohio 40.34N 81.05W
112 O8 Carrollton Texas 32.55N 96.55W
104 G6 Carrolltown Pennsylvania 40.36N 78.43W
106 G7 Carrollville Wisconsin 42.53N 87.52W
100 V4 Carrol, R Manitoba
13 F4 Carron R Queensland
57 F2 Carronbridge Dumfries & Galloway Scotland 55.16N 3.48W
58 E4 Carron, L Highland Scotland
58 G3 Carron, R Highland Scotland
58 H6 Carron, Res Central Scotland 56.02N 4.05W
79 E5 Carrósio Italy 44.40N 8.50E
100 N5 Carrot R Saskatchewan
100 O5 Carrot River Saskatchewan 53.18N 103.32W
70 K4 Carrouges France 48.34N 0.08W
59 G1 Carrowkeel Donegal Irish Rep 55.08N 7.40W
59 H1 Carrowkeel Donegal Irish Rep 55.07N 7.12W
59 C3 Carrowmore, L Mayo Irish Rep 54.12N 9.47W
57 J3 Carr Shield Northumb Eng 54.50N 2.19W
79 C6 Carrù Italy 44.28N 7.52E
100 H6 Carruthers Saskatchewan 52.54N 109.15W
110 C8 Carrville California 41.04N 122.44W
57 K3 Carrville Durham Eng 54.47N 1.31W
59 L2 Carryduff Down N Ireland 54.31N 5.53W
104 L2 Carry Falls Res New York 44.20N 74.50W
71 G10 Carry-le-Rouet France 43.20N 5.10E
87 H6 Carsa Ethiopia 9.30N 41.49E
36 J1 Çarşamba Turkey 41.13N 36.43E
36 F5 Çarşamba R Turkey
37 E7 Çarsancak Turkey 38.53N 39.42E
100 D8 Carseland Alberta 50.53N 113.24W
80 H4 Carseolani, Monti Italy
57 F3 Carsethorn Dumfries & Galloway Scotland 54.55N 3.35W
55 E5 Carshalton London Eng 51.22N 0.10W
80 H4 Carsoli Italy 42.07N 13.06E
108 P8 Carson Iowa 41.14N 95.25W
108 J3 Carson N Dakota 46.26N 101.34W
110 D4 Carson Washington 45.45N 121.50W
111 E2 Carson R Nevada
106 K6 Carson City Michigan 43.11N 84.50W
111 E2 Carson City Nevada 39.10N 119.46W
111 F2 Carson L dry lake Nevada
14 F3 Carson, R W Australia
111 F2 Carson Sink dry lake Nevada 39.50N 118.30W
106 M6 Carsonville Michigan 43.26N 82.40W
71 L1 Carspach France 47.37N 7.13E
57 E2 Carsphairn Dumfries & Galloway Scotland 55.13N 4.16W
100 C7 Carstairs Alberta 51.35N 114.02W
58 J7 Carstairs Strathclyde Scotland 55.42N 3.42W
101 T6 Carswell, L Saskatchewan
121 B4 Cartagena Chile 33.32S 71.39W
119 C2 Cartagena Colombia 10.24N 75.33W
77 P5 Cartagena Spain 37.36N 0.59W
111 F5 Cartago California 36.20N 118.01W
119 C5 Cartago Colombia 4.45N 75.55W
115 N5 Cartago Costa Rica 9.50N 83.52W
77 G7 Cártama Spain 36.43N 4.38W
112 G6 Carta Valley Texas 29.48N 100.41W
120 A8 Cartavao Peru 7.54S 79.10W
76 B10 Cartaxo Portugal 39.10N 8.47W
77 B6 Cartaya Spain 37.16N 7.09W
72 C5 Cartélègue France 45.11N 0.35W
76 C4 Cartelle Spain 42.15N 8.04W
Cartensz Gunung mt see Jaya, Puntjak
110 P2 Carter Montana 47.48N 110.58W
109 L6 Carter Oklahoma 35.14N 99.31W
110 P8 Carter Wyoming 41.27N 110.25W
57 J2 Carter Bar road summit Scot/Eng 55.21N 2.27W
70 G3 Carteret France 49.22N 1.48W
103 J8 Carteret New Jersey 40.35N 74.14W
13 G2 Carter, Mt Queensland 13.00S 143.15E
105 C3 Cartersville Georgia 34.09N 84.49W
108 D3 Cartersville Montana 46.18N 106.28W
11 K8 Carterton New Zealand 41.01S 175.30E
107 G4 Carterville Illinois 37.44N 89.03W
107 D7 Carthage Arkansas 34.03N 92.33W
106 C9 Carthage Illinois 40.25N 91.09W
107 L2 Carthage Indiana 39.45N 85.33W
107 G9 Carthage Mississippi 32.42N 89.31W
107 B4 Carthage Missouri 37.10N 94.20W
105 H2 Carthage N Carolina 35.21N 79.27W
109 D8 Carthage New Mexico 33.53N 106.34W
104 K3 Carthage New York 43.59N 75.37W
108 N5 Carthage S Dakota 44.10N 97.42W
107 L5 Carthage Tennessee 36.14N 85.59W
112 N3 Carthage Texas 32.10N 94.21W
88 T3 Carthage ruins Tunisia 36.54N 10.16E
99 J6 Cartier Ontario 46.43N 81.34W
14 E1 Cartier I Timor Sea 12.31S 123.29E
99 Q9 Cartierville Airport Quebec 45.31N 73.45W
69 F3 Cartignies France 50.06N 3.51E
57 H4 Cartmel Lancs Eng 54.12N 2.57W
79 N7 Cartoceto Italy 43.46N 12.53E
82 J6 Cârtojani Romania 44.26N 25.29E
97 O7 Cartwright Labrador, Nfld 53.40N 57.00W
100 S9 Cartwright Manitoba 49.05N 99.20W
108 G2 Cartwright N Dakota 47.52N 103.57W
12 F8 Cartwright Pt Tasmania 42.56S 147.22E
119 H3 Caruachi Venezuela 8.06N 62.53W
117 J9 Caruarú Brazil 8.15S 35.55W
117 D6 Caruçambaba Brazil 2.06S 49.15W
76 F4 Carucedo Spain 42.29N 6.45W
120 D7 Carumas Peru 16.45S 70.43W
91 F7 Carumbo Zaïre 7.47S 19.58E
80 L5 Carunchio Italy 41.55N 14.32E
91 C10 Carunjamba R Angola
91 D10 Caruombolo Angola 13.52S 15.10E
119 G2 Carúpano Venezuela 10.39N 63.14W
117 E5 Carutapera Brazil 1.13S 46.00W
107 G5 Caruthersville Missouri 36.11N 89.40W
122 U12 Carvajal, B Juan Fernández, Is Pacific Oc 33.39S 78.45W
117 C6 Carvalho Brazil 2.16S 51.29W
76 B6 Carvalhos Portugal 41.04N 8.35W
104 B9 Carver Kentucky 37.36N 83.06W
103 N3 Carver Massachusetts 41.54N 70.46W
76 F6 Carviçais Portugal 41.10N 6.54W
69 D3 Carvin France 50.30N 2.58E
76 A10 Carvoeira Portugal 39.05N 9.04W
76 A11 Carvoeira Portugal 38.56N 9.24W
76 D9 Carvoeira Portugal 39.38N 7.55W
119 H8 Carvoeiro Brazil 1.30S 61.59W
76 C6 Carvoeiro Portugal 41.03N 8.28W
76 A10 Carvoeiro, C Portugal 39.21N 9.24W
76 C14 Carvoeiro,C Lt Ho Portugal 37.05N 8.27W
110 M1 Carway Alberta 49.00N 113.23W
13 H6 Carwell Queensland 24.50S 147.00E
63 S6 Carwitz E Germany 53.18N 13.26E
107 F9 Cary Mississippi 32.48N 90.56W
105 J2 Cary N Carolina 35.47N 78.48W
105 G12 Carysfort Reef Florida
79 K6 Carzolano, Monte Italy 44.04N 11.29E
119 D4 Casabe Colombia 7.04N 73.56W
77 H7 Casabermeja Spain 36.54N 4.26W
120 E10 Casabindo, Cerro de Argentina 23.00S 66.10W
121 B4 Casablanca Chile 33.20S 71.25W
88 K5 Casablanca Morocco 33.39N 7.35W
81 N5 Casabona Italy 39.15N 16.57E
118 F7 Casa Branca Brazil 21.45S 47.06W
76 B12 Casa Branca Portugal 38.18N 8.44W
76 D11 Casa Branca Portugal 38.57N 7.48W
76 D16 Casa Branca Portugal 38.44N 9.14W
76 C12 Casa Branca sta Portugal 38.30N 8.10W
80 L5 Casacalenda Italy 41.44N 14.50E
80 K4 Casacanditella Italy 42.15N 14.12E
81 J8 Casa Cantoniera Sicily 37.42N 15.00E
66 P6 Casáccia Switzerland 46.24N 9.40E
116 O2 Casa Cruz, C Trinidad & Tobago 10.04N 61.10W
115 E2 Casa de János Mexico 30.40N 108.26W
113 E4 Casadepaga Alaska 64.49N 164.20W
81 C1 Casa Garibaldi Sardinia 41.13N 9.28E
91 G9 Casage Angola 11.04S 20.39E
79 K6 Casaglia, Colla di pass Italy 44.02N 11.29E
72 K10 Casagnes France 42.44N 2.36E
111 N9 Casa Grande Arizona 32.52N 111.46W
111 N9 Casa Grande Nat.Mon Arizona 33.00N 111.31W
81 R12 Casalabate Italy 40.30N 18.08E
80 L4 Casalanguida Italy 42.03N 14.30E
75 E2 Casalarreina Spain 42.32N 2.55W
80 L4 Casalbordino Italy 42.09N 14.35E
79 C4 Casalborgone Italy 45.08N 7.56E
81 L3 Casalbuono Italy 40.13N 15.40E
79 G4 Casalbuttano Italy 45.15N 9.58E
80 K6 Casal di Principe Italy 41.01N 14.08E
80 D2 Casale Italy 43.03N 1.18E
79 K6 Casalecchio di Reno Italy 44.28N 11.17E
79 D4 Casale Monferrato Italy 45.08N 8.27E
79 G4 Casaletto Ceredano Italy 45.20N 9.37E
81 L3 Casaletto Spartano Italy 40.09N 15.36E
79 G4 Casaletto Vaprio Italy 45.25N 9.37E
79 J5 Casalgrande Italy 44.34N 10.44E
121 F6 Casalins Argentina 36.16S 58.32W
79 H5 Casalmaggiore Italy 44.58N 10.25E
79 G4 Casalmorano Italy 45.17N 9.54E
80 M5 Casalnuovo Monterotaro Italy 41.37N 15.07E
79 H4 Casaloldo Italy 45.15N 10.28E
79 G4 Casalpusterlengo Italy 45.11N 9.39E
118 A4 Casalvasco Brazil 15.20S 60.01W
80 M5 Casalvecchio di Puglia Italy 41.35N 15.07E
81 K3 Casal Velino Italy 40.11N 15.07E
79 D4 Casalvolone Italy 45.24N 8.28E
89 A5 Casamance isld Senegal 12.40N 16.45W
89 A5 Casamance reg Senegal
75 O2 Casamanya, Pic de mt Andorra 42.35N 1.34E
81 N2 Casamassima Italy 40.57N 16.55E
80 J7 Casamicciola Italy 40.44N 13.54E
67 P11 Casamozza Corsica 42.31N 9.26E
66 R5 Casana Pass Italy/Switz 46.33N 10.04E
66 R5 Casana,Piz mt Italy/Switz 46.35N 10.05E
119 D5 Casanare div Colombia
119 E4 Casanare, R Colombia
66 Q4 Casanna mt Switzerland 46.52N 9.50E
117 G9 Casa Nova Brazil 9.25S 41.04W
120 B4 Casapalca Peru 11.44S 76.14W
112 C6 Casa Piedra Texas 29.44N 104.05W
75 D6 Casar mt Spain 40.41N 3.26W
77 G7 Casarabonela Spain 36.48N 4.50W
81 R12 Casarano Italy 40.01N 18.10E
76 G9 Casar de Cáceres Spain 39.34N 6.25W
76 K8 Casar de Escalona, El Spain 40.03N 4.31W
76 G8 Casar de Palomero Spain 40.18N 6.15W
75 D4 Casarejos Spain 41.47N 3.02W
121 E2 Casares Argentina 28.58S 62.47W
115 L4 Casares Nicaragua 11.40N 86.20W
77 F8 Casares Spain 36.27N 5.16W
77 G6 Casariche Spain 37.18N 4.45W
76 L8 Casarrubios del Monte Spain 40.11N 4.02W
79 N3 Casarsa della Delizia Italy 45.58N 12.50E
75 H7 Casas Bajas Spain 40.02N 1.15W
76 J5 Casasda de Arión Spain 41.35N 5.15W
77 M2 Casas de Benítez Spain 39.22N 2.08W
76 G10 Casas de Don Antonio Spain 39.14N 6.18W
76 F8 Casas de Don Gómez Spain 40.00N 6.35W
77 F2 Casas de Don Pedro Spain 39.06N 5.19W
77 M2 Casas de Haro Spain 39.20N 2.16W
77 O2 Casas de Juan Gil Spain 39.08N 1.15W
77 N2 Casas de Juan Núñez Spain 39.07N 1.34W
77 M3 Casas de Lázaro Spain 38.46N 2.15W
76 H8 Casas del Monte Spain 40.12N 5.58W
77 M2 Casas de los Pinos Spain 39.20N 2.23W
76 G9 Casas de Millán Spain 39.49N 6.20W
76 H9 Casas de Miravete Spain 39.44N 5.45W
77 E4 Casas de Reina Spain 38.12N 5.58W
77 O2 Casas de Ves Spain 39.15N 1.20W
115 E2 Casas Grandes Mexico 30.22N 108.00W
115 F2 Casas Grandes R Mexico
77 O2 Casas Ibáñez Spain 39.17N 1.28W
77 M2 Casasimarro Spain 39.24N 2.02W
77 N5 Casas Nuevas Spain 37.56N 1.36W
Casas Viejas see Benalup de Sidonia
76 H4 Casas Viejas mt Spain 42.13N 5.55W
76 H9 Casatejada Spain 39.54N 5.40W
118 F9 Casa Verde dist São Paulo Brazil
76 K8 Casavieja Spain 40.17N 4.46W
112 O9 Casa View Texas 32.49N 96.40W
79 G3 Casazza Italy 45.44N 9.54E
121 E6 Casbas Argentina 36.48S 62.30W
121 H2 Casca Brazil 28.36S 52.00W
101 O11 Cascade Br Col 49.00N 118.06W
110 J5 Cascade Idaho 44.30N 116.04W
106 C7 Cascade Iowa 42.19N 91.01W
26 S14 Cascade Mahé I Seychelles, Ind Oc 4.39S 55.29E
110 O2 Cascade Montana 47.16N 111.41W
104 O2 Cascade New Hampshire 44.25N 71.14W
10 V10 Cascade B Norfolk I Pacific Oc 29.02S 167.59E
110 D4 Cascade Locks Oregon 45.40N 121.53W
101 N11 Cascade Mts Canada/U.S.A.
110 D1 Cascade Pass Washington 48.28N 121.04W
11 C11 Cascade Pt New Zealand 44.02S 168.21E
11 C11 Cascade R New Zealand
102 B2 Cascade Ra U.S.A.
110 J5 Cascade Res Idaho 44.35N 116.06W
12 F8 Cascades dist Hobart, Tasmania
26 N13 Cascades waterfalls Amsterdam I Indian Ocean
26 V15 Cascades, Pte.des Réunion Indian Ocean 21.10S 55.50E
110 D2 Cascade Tunnel Washington 47.44N 121.05W
110 C5 Cascadia Oregon 44.25N 122.30W
118 H9 Cascadura Brazil 22.53S 43.20W
76 A11 Cascais Portugal 38.41N 9.25W
76 B16 Cascais, B.de B Portugal
119 B10 Cascajal, R Peru
115 M4 Cascal, Paso del pk Nicaragua 11.50N 84.42W
75 G3 Cascante Spain 42.00N 1.40W
98 F5 Cascapedia R Quebec
80 G3 Cascata d Marmore Italy
77 V14 Ca's Catalá Balearic Is 39.33N 2.35E
117 H7 Cascavel Ceará Brazil 4.10S 38.15W
118 D9 Cascavel Paraná Brazil 24.59S 53.29W
80 H3 Cascia Italy 42.43N 13.01E
80 C1 Casciana Terme Italy 43.32N 10.36E
79 J7 Cascina Italy 43.41N 10.33E
104 P2 Casco Maine 44.01N 70.33W
106 G5 Casco Wisconsin 44.34N 87.36W
104 P3 Casco Bay Maine
75 H2 Caseda Spain 42.31N 1.22W
81 D5 Case della Marina Sardinia 39.12N 9.35E
79 E4 Casei Gerola Italy 45.01N 8.56E
63 U6 Casekow E Germany 53.13N 14.14E
79 E5 Casella Italy 44.32N 8.59E
79 C4 Caselle Torinese Italy 45.10N 7.39E
79 M6 Casemurate Italy 44.15N 12.13E
80 G3 Casenove Italy 42.58N 12.51E
79 L7 Casentino V Italy
81 E8 Case Parrini Sicily 37.42N 12.29E
81 B5 Case Pauceris Sardinia 39.08N 8.53E
116 L4 Case-Pilot Martinique W I 14.38N 61.08W
75 L5 Caseras Spain 41.02N 0.15E
77 K3 Caserío de Pozo de la Serna Spain 38.47N 3.14W
121 J4 Caseros Buenos Aires Arg 34.36S 58.34W
121 F4 Caseros Entre Ríos Arg 32.28S 58.30W
75 O3 Caserras Spain 42.00N 1.50E
80 K6 Caserta Italy 41.04N 14.20E
80 J6 Caserta prov Italy
77 O4 Cases del Puerto Spain 38.25N 1.14W
76 C13 Casével Portugal 37.46N 8.10W
106 L6 Caseville Michigan 43.56N 83.16W
107 J2 Casey Illinois 39.18N 88.00W
99 Q5 Casey Quebec 47.54N 74.11W
123 F2 Casey Aust Base Antarctica 66.17S 110.32E
123 A5 Casey B Antarctica
59 C5 Cashel Galway Irish Rep 53.25N 9.48W
59 G6 Cashel Tipperary Irish Rep 52.31N 7.53W
92 F11 Cashel Zimbabwe 19.31S 32.45E
59 G6 Cashel,Rock of Tipperary Irish Rep 52.32N 7.53W
59 C7 Cashen R Kerry Irish Rep
109 N6 Cashion Oklahoma 35.48N 97.42W
13 J8 Cashmere Queensland 27.46S 148.27E
110 E2 Cashmere Washington 47.31N 120.29W
11 M10 Cashmere dist Christchurch New Zealand
56 G6 Cashmoor Corner Dorset Eng 50.55N 2.03W
106 D6 Cashton Wisconsin 43.44N 90.48W
119 D6 Casibare, R Colombia
81 M7 Casignana Italy 38.06N 16.06E
119 D3 Casigua Venezuela 8.46N 72.30W
119 E2 Casigua Venezuela 11.04N 70.57W
19 L3 Casiguran Luzon Philippines 16.22N 122.07E
19 L4 Casiguran Philippines 14.44N 122.26E
19 L3 Casiguran B Luzon Philippines 16.15N 122.05E
19 K3 Casiguran Sd Luzon Philippines 16.05N 121.50E
121 E4 Casilda Argentina 33.05S 61.10W
116 E4 Casilda Cuba 21.45N 80.00W
76 F8 Casilla de Flores Spain 40.22N 6.45W
76 F9 Casillas de Coria Spain 39.57N 6.38W
96 T10 Casillas del Angel Fuerteventura Canary Is 28.29N 13.59W
82 L6 Casimcea Romania 44.45N 28.23E
118 G8 Casimiro de Abreu Brazil 22.28S 42.12W
79 H5 Casina Italy 44.31N 10.30E
12 L3 Casino New S Wales 28.50S 153.02E
75 J8 Casinos Spain 39.42N 0.43W
119 F6 Casiquiare, Can R Venezuela
115 D2 Çasita Mexico 31.00N 110.52W
65 M2 Čáslav Czechoslovakia 49.56N 15.24E
66 N8 Caslino Italy 45.50N 9.15E
120 A3 Çasma Peru 9.30S 78.18W
82 D5 Časma Yugoslavia 45.46N 16.38E
120 A3 Çasma R Peru
82 D5 Časma R Yugoslavia
111 D7 Casmalia California 34.50N 120.30W
66 N8 Casnate Italy 45.46N 9.05E
76 J2 Caso Spain 43.11N 5.20W
66 K6 Caso di Frua waterfall Italy 46.25N 8.25E
19 M6 Casogoran B Philippines 10.45N 125.45E
79 H6 Casola in Lunigiana Italy 44.12N 10.11E
79 L6 Casola Valsenio Italy 44.13N 11.37E
80 D2 Casole d'Elsa Italy 43.20N 11.02E
80 K4 Casoli Italy 42.07N 14.18E
112 N2 Cason Texas 33.02N 94.50W
79 F4 Casorate Primo Italy 45.18N 9.01E
80 K7 Casória Italy 40.54N 14.18E
79 K3 Casotto Italy 45.54N 11.21E
111 A2 Caspar California 39.25N 123.48W
75 K5 Caspe Spain 41.14N 0.03W
108 D7 Casper Wyoming 42.50N 106.20W
107 C9 Caspiana Louisiana 32.16N 93.31W
38 E5 Caspian Sea U.S.S.R./Iran
70 F2 Casquets Lt.Ho English Chan 49.43N 2.24W
107 C6 Cass Arkansas 35.40N 93.51W
11 F10 Cass New Zealand 43.03S 171.44E
104 F8 Cass W Virginia 38.23N 79.56W
108 F7 Cassa Wyoming 42.23N 104.56W
75 Q4 Cassá de la Selva Spain 41.53N 2.52E
72 F9 Cassagnabère-Tournas France 43.14N 0.48E
72 K7 Cassagnes Bégonhès France 44.10N 2.31E
66 O9 Cassago Italy 45.45N 9.18E
91 G9 Cassai Angola 10.33S 21.59E
91 G9 Cassai R Angola
Cassaigne see Sidi Ali
91 G10 Cassamba Angola 13.07S 20.20E
72 J6 Cassaniouze France 44.40N 2.22E
79 G3 Cassano d'Adda Italy 45.32N 9.31E
81 N2 Cassano delle Murge Italy 40.53N 16.46E
81 M4 Cassano Ionio Italy 39.47N 16.20E
79 E5 Cassano Spinola Italy 44.47N 8.52E
91 F8 Cassanzade Angola 9.37S 18.12E
120 G5 Cassara Brazil 13.10S 62.09W
66 M7 Cassarate Switzerland 46.01N 8.58E
106 L6 Cass City Michigan 43.37N 83.11W
69 C2 Cassel France 50.48N 2.29E
99 P7 Casselman Ontario 45.18N 75.05W
108 N3 Casselton N Dakota 46.55N 97.11W
71 J6 Casse Massion mt France 45.12N 6.22E
72 F7 Casseneuil France 44.27N 0.38E
118 F7 Cássia Brazil 20.36S 46.54W
101 H6 Cassiar Mts Br Col 60.15N 131.10W
81 K10 Cassibile Sicily 36.58N 15.12E
118 D6 Cassilândia Brazil 18.59S 51.59W
12 J4 Cassilis New S Wales 32.01S 149.59E
13 G5 Cassilis Queensland 21.13S 142.55E
79 E5 Cassine Italy 44.45N 8.31E
91 E11 Cassinga Angola 15.08S 16.04E
14 F2 Cassini I W Australia 13.59S 125.36E
121 H4 Cassino Brazil 32.14S 52.10W
80 J6 Cassino Italy 41.29N 13.50E
71 H10 Cassis France 43.13N 5.32E
108 Q2 Cass L Minnesota
108 Q2 Cass Lake Minnesota 47.22N 94.35W
91 D8 Cassoalala Angola 9.29S 14.20E
109 O3 Cassoday Kansas 38.02N 96.41W
79 E4 Cassolnovo Italy 45.22N 8.48E
91 D9 Cassongue Angola 11.53S 15.02E
106 J8 Cassopolis Michigan 41.56N 86.00W
11 M10 Cass Pk New Zealand 43.38N 172.38E
106 L6 Cass, R Michigan
11 E10 Cass R New Zealand
72 K6 Cassuejouls France 44.44N 2.48E
91 E9 Cassumbe Angola 11.13S 16.36E
107 C5 Cassville Missouri 36.42N 93.52W
103 F6 Cassville New Jersey 40.07N 74.24W
106 D7 Cassville Wisconsin 42.43N 90.57W
70 B5 Cast France 48.09N 4.09W
67 O13 Castagna, Pta. di a Corsica 41.47N 8.42E
79 K4 Castagnaro Italy 45.08N 11.25E
80 C2 Castagneto Carducci Italy 43.09N 10.36E
79 D5 Castagnole Lanze Italy 44.45N 8.09E
111 F7 Castaic California 34.30N 118.38W
77 L7 Castala Spain 36.54N 2.55W
77 P3 Castalla Spain 38.36N 0.40W
77 P4 Castalla R Spain
76 J9 Castañar de Ibor Spain 39.38N 5.25W
75 E3 Castañares de Rioja Spain 42.30N 2.55W
72 F11 Castanesa Spain 42.29N 0.40E
72 G8 Castanet-Tolosan France 43.31N 1.28E
120 G2 Castanhal Brazil 6.31S 62.18W
117 E5 Castanhal Pará Brazil 1.16S 47.55W
76 B11 Castanheira Portugal 39.00N 8.58W
76 C8 Castanheira de Pêra Portugal 40.01N 8.12W
119 G8 Castanheiro Brazil 0.16S 65.37W
76 E6 Castanheiro Portugal 41.13N 7.22W
120 G2 Castanho Brazil 7.33S 60.24W
119 H9 Castanho, L Brazil 3.45S 60.30W
121 B3 Castaño Argentina 31.01S 69.35W
77 F5 Castaño mt Spain 37.57N 5.06W
121 B3 Castaño R Argentina
79 E3 Castano Primo Italy 45.33N 8.47E
115 J4 Castaños Mexico 26.48N 101.26W
116 M1 Castara Tobago W I 11.17N 60.41W
116 M1 Castara B Tobago W I
77 K7 Castaras Spain 36.56N 3.15W
66 P6 Castasegna Switzerland 46.20N 9.31E
61 G4 Casteau Belgium 50.31N 4.01E
79 F4 Casteggio Italy 45.01N 9.07E
75 G3 Castejón Spain 42.10N 1.41W
75 L4 Castejón del Puente Spain 41.57N 0.09E
75 K4 Castejón de Monegros Spain 41.37N 0.15W
75 M2 Castejón de Sos Spain 42.30N 0.30E
75 J4 Castejón de Valdejasa Spain 41.59N 1.00W
75 H4 Castejón, Montes de Spain
79 J4 Castelbelforte Italy 45.13N 10.53E
79 L6 Castel Bolognese Italy 44.19N 11.48E
81 H8 Castelbuono Sicily 37.56N 14.05E
81 G7 Casteldaccia Sicily 38.03N 13.32E
79 J4 Castel d'Ario Italy 45.12N 10.58E
75 J6 Castel de Cabra Spain 40.49N 0.42W
79 B5 Casteldelfino Italy 44.35N 7.04E

80 J4 Castel del Monte Italy 42.22N 13.43E
80 O6 Castel del Monte Italy 41.05N 16.15E
80 E3 Castel del Piano Italy 42.53N 11.32E
79 K6 Castel del Rio Italy 44.12N 11.30E
80 F5 Castel di Guido Italy 41.54N 12.18E
81 J9 Castel di Iudica Sicily 37.30N 14.39E
81 H8 Castel di Lucio Sicily 37.53N 14.19E
80 K5 Castel di Sangro Italy 41.47N 14.07E
80 J2 Castelfidardo Italy 43.28N 13.32E
79 J7 Castelfiorentino Italy 43.36N 10.58E
75 K4 Castelflorite Spain 41.48N 0.01W
80 J6 Castelforte Italy 41.18N 13.50E
80 M7 Castelfranci Italy 40.55N 15.03E
79 L7 Castelfranco di Sopra Italy 43.37N 11.33E
79 K5 Castelfranco Emilia Italy 44.36N 11.03E
80 M6 Castelfranco in Miscano Italy 41.18N 15.05E
79 L3 Castelfranco Veneto Italy 45.40N 11.56E
80 K4 Castelfrentano Italy 42.12N 14.22E
80 G5 Castel Gandolfo Italy 41.45N 12.38E
80 E3 Castel Giorgio Italy 42.42N 11.58E
80 F4 Castel Giuliano Italy 42.03N 12.07E
79 H4 Castel Goffredo Italy 45.18N 10.27E
79 K3 Castelgomberto Italy 45.35N 11.24E
80 M7 Castelgrande Italy 40.47N 15.26E
72 E7 Casteljaloux France 44.19N 0.06E
112 J5 Castell Texas 30.43N 98.59W
64 J4 Castell W Germany 49.44N 10.22E
110 C8 Castella California 41.09N 122.20W
81 J3 Castellabate Italy 40.16N 14.57E
79 D5 Castell Alfero Italy 44.59N 8.13E
81 E7 Castellammare del Golfo Sicily 38.02N 12.53E
80 K7 Castellammare di Stabia Italy 40.47N 14.29E
81 E7 Castellammare, G.di Sicily
79 C4 Castellamonte Italy 45.23N 7.42E
81 O2 Castellana Grotte Italy 40.53N 17.10E
71 K9 Castellane France 43.50N 6.30E
81 N2 Castellaneta Italy 40.38N 16.57E
76 F10 Castellano R Spain
77 L3 Castellanos mt Spain 38.37N 2.52W
79 E3 Castellanza Italy 45.37N 8.53E
79 J5 Castellarano Italy 44.31N 10.43E
77 F8 Castellar de la Frontera Spain 36.20N 5.27W
75 G6 Castellar de la Muela Spain 40.49N 1.46W
75 N3 Castellar de la Ribera Spain 42.01N 1.25E
75 P4 Castellar del Vallés Spain 41.37N 2.05E
75 P3 Castellar de Nuch Spain 42.17N 2.01E
77 K3 Castellar de Santiago Spain 38.33N 3.17W
77 K4 Castellar de Santisteban Spain 38.16N 3.08W
75 J7 Castellar, El Spain 40.22N 0.50W
75 J4 Castellar, El reg Spain
79 G5 Castell'Arquato Italy 44.51N 9.52E
79 M2 Castellavazzo Italy 46.18N 12.19E
79 E5 Castellazzo Bórmida Italy 44.51N 8.34E
75 M5 Castelldans Spain 41.29N 0.46E
75 O5 Castelldefels Spain 41.17N 1.57E
77 K7 Castell de Ferro Spain 36.44N 3.20W
77 W14 Castell del Rey ruins Balearic Is 39.55N 3.00E
79 G4 Castelleone Italy 45.17N 9.46E
79 J3 Castelletto di Brenzone Italy 45.41N 10.45E
75 K6 Castellfort Spain 40.30N 0.11W
75 Q3 Castellfullit de la Roca Spain 42.13N 2.33E
121 F6 Castelli Buenos Aires Arg 36.07S 57.47W
80 J4 Castelli Italy 42.30N 13.43E
118 A9 Castelli, J.J Chaco Arg 25.59S 60.38W
80 D2 Castellina in Chianti Italy 43.28N 11.17E
80 C2 Castellina Marittima Italy 43.25N 10.34E
66 L8 Castello Italy 45.58N 8.40E
66 P6 Castello, Cima di mt Switzerland 46.18N 9.39E
79 D5 Castello d'Annone Italy 44.53N 8.19E
75 R3 Castelló de Ampurias Spain 42.15N 3.04E
75 M4 Castelló de Farfaña Spain 41.50N 0.43E
79 K2 Castello di Fiemme Italy 46.17N 11.27E
79 K6 Castello di Serravalle Italy 44.26N 11.02E
80 A2 Castello, Monte Italy 43.03N 9.52E
74 G4 Castellón prov Spain
75 K8 Castellón de la Plana Spain 39.59N 0.03W
77 Q3 Castellón de Rugat Spain 38.53N 0.24W
66 N6 Castello, Sasso di mt Switzerland 46.17N 9.15E
75 K6 Castellote Spain 40.48N 0.20W
79 L2 Castello Tesino Italy 46.04N 11.39E
81 Q11 Castello Villanuova Italy 40.47N 17.35E
75 N3 Castells Spain 42.18N 1.10E
75 O4 Castelltallat mts Spain
75 P4 Castelltersol Spain 41.45N 2.08E
79 J4 Castellúcchio Italy 45.09N 10.38E
81 L3 Castelluccio Italy 40.01N 15.58E
80 M6 Castelluccio de'Sauri Italy 41.18N 15.29E
80 M6 Castelluccio Valmaggiore Italy 41.20N 15.13E
81 J7 Castell'Umberto Sicily 38.05N 14.48E
75 O4 Castellvell Spain 41.38N 1.51E
80 G5 Castel Madama Italy 41.58N 12.53E
79 K5 Castel Maggiore Italy 44.34N 11.21E
79 B6 Castelmagno Italy 44.24N 7.12E
79 K4 Castelmassa Italy 45.02N 11.19E
80 L5 Castelmauro Italy 41.49N 14.43E
72 F7 Castelmoron-sur-Lot France 44.24N 0.30E
72 F8 Castelnau-Barbarens France 43.35N 0.44E
72 H9 Castelnaudary France 43.18N 1.57E
72 F7 Castelnaud-de-Gratecambe France 44.30N 0.40E
72 K8 Castelnau-de-Brassac France 43.39N 2.31E
72 C5 Castelnau-de-Médoc France 45.02N 0.48W
72 H8 Castelnau de Montmiral France 43.58N 1.49E
72 G8 Castelnau d'Estestefonds France 43.47N 1.21E
72 F9 Castelnau-Magnoac France 43.18N 0.30E
72 G7 Castelnau-Montratier France 44.17N 1.21E
72 D8 Castelnau-Rivière-Basse France 43.35N 0.01W
79 J5 Castelnovo di Sotto Italy 44.48N 10.34E
79 H6 Castelnovo ne'Monti Italy 44.26N 10.24E
80 D2 Castelnuovo Berardenga Italy 43.21N 11.29E
80 M5 Castelnuovo della Daunia Italy 41.34N 15.07E
79 H6 Castelnuovo di Garfagnana Italy 44.06N 10.24E
79 H6 Castelnuovo di Magra Italy 44.06N 10.01E
80 G4 Castelnuovo di Porto Italy 42.07N 12.30E
80 C2 Castelnuovo di Val di Cecina Italy 43.12N 10.54E
79 J4 Castelnuovo di Verona Italy 45.26N 10.46E
79 C4 Castelnuovo Don Bosco Italy 45.03N 7.58E
79 E5 Castelnuovo Scrivia Italy 44.59N 8.52E
118 H7 Castelo Brazil 20.33S 41.14W
96 P4 Castelo Branco Azores 38.32N 28.44W
76 E9 Castelo Branco Portugal 39.50N 7.30W
76 F6 Castelo Branco Portugal 41.15N 6.45W
76 E9 Castelo Branco dist Portugal
Castelo de Paiva see Sobrado de Paiva
76 E10 Castelo de Vide Portugal 39.25N 7.27W
117 G7 Castelo do Piauí Brazil 5.20S 41.33W
76 C6 Castelões Portugal 41.14N 8.13W
76 B2 Castelo, Mte Spain 43.05N 8.42W
96 S6 Castelo, Pico do mt Madeira Is 33.05N 16.21W
96 Q7 Castelo Pta do Madeira Is 32.44N 16.42W
96 V5 Castelo, Pta.do pt Azores 36.56N 25.02W
80 H2 Castelplanio Italy 43.30N 13.05E
80 H2 Castelraimondo Italy 43.12N 13.04E
80 G3 Castel Ritaldi e San Giovanni Italy 42.49N 12.41E
79 L1 Castelrotto Italy 46.34N 11.34E
72 F7 Castelsagrat France 44.11N 0.57E
80 D2 Castel San Gimignano Italy 43.24N 11.02E
80 L7 Castel San Giorgio Italy 40.47N 14.42E
79 F4 Castel San Giovanni Italy 45.04N 9.25E
81 K3 Castel San Lorenzo Italy 40.24N 15.14E
80 E1 Castel San Niccolo Italy 43.44N 11.43E
79 L6 Castel San Pietro Terme Italy 44.24N 11.36E
81 L3 Castelsaraceno Italy 40.10N 16.00E
81 B2 Castelsardo Sardinia 40.55N 8.43E
72 G7 Castelsarrasin France 44.02N 1.06E
75 K6 Castelserás Spain 40.59N 0.10W
81 G8 Casteltermini Sicily 37.33N 13.38E
80 J4 Castelvecchio Subequo Italy 42.07N 13.44E
80 L6 Castelvetere in Val Fortore Italy 41.27N 14.57E
81 E8 Castelvetrano Sicily 37.41N 12.47E
80 F3 Castel Viscardo Italy 42.50N 12.00E
75 J7 Castelvispal Spain 40.17N 0.32W
80 J6 Castel Volturno Italy 41.02N 13.57E
79 K5 Castenaso Italy 44.31N 11.28E
Castendo see Penalvo do Castelo
79 H4 Castenedolo Italy 45.28N 10.18E
60 N14 Castenraij Netherlands 51.29N 6.01E
72 E8 Castera-Verduzan France 43.48N 0.25E
95 C2 Caster, Banc du Madagascar
60 J14 Casteren Netherlands 51.23N 5.14E
104 K3 Casterland New York 43.54N 75.32W
57 H4 Casterton Cumbria Eng 54.13N 2.35W
12 F7 Casterton Victoria 37.35S 141.25E
72 C9 Castetnau France 43.20N 0.47W
72 B8 Castets Landes France 43.53N 1.08W
72 D6 Castets-en-Dorthe France 44.33N 0.08W
81 D5 Castiadas Sardinia 39.14N 9.31E
66 P4 Castiel Switzerland 46.51N 9.36E
75 H7 Castielfabib Spain 40.08N 1.19W
75 J2 Castiello de Jaca Spain 42.38N 0.33W
67 P12 Castifao Corsica 42.30N 9.06E
80 B2 Castiglioncello Italy 43.24N 10.24E
79 G6 Castiglione Chiavari Italy 44.17N 9.31E
79 G4 Castiglione d'Adda Italy 45.13N 9.42E
79 K6 Castiglione dei Pepoli Italy 44.08N 11.10E
80 F2 Castiglione del Lago Italy 43.07N 12.03E
80 C3 Castiglione della Pescáia Italy 42.46N 10.53E
79 H4 Castiglione delle Stiviere Italy 45.23N 10.29E
79 H6 Castiglione di Garfagnana Italy 44.08N 10.24E
79 F3 Castiglione d'Intelvi Italy 45.57N 9.05E
81 K8 Castiglione di Sicília Sicily 37.53N 15.08E
80 E2 Castiglione d'Orcia Italy 43.01N 11.37E
80 F3 Castiglione in Teverina Italy 42.38N 12.13E
80 K5 Castiglione Messer Marino Italy 41.52N 14.27E
79 E3 Castiglione Olona Italy 45.46N 8.52E
79 L7 Castiglion Fibocchi Italy 43.32N 11.45E
80 E2 Castiglion Fiorentino Italy 43.20N 11.55E
76 J10 Castilblanco Spain 39.17N 5.05W
77 E5 Castilblanco de los Arroyos Spain 37.41N 5.59W
75 D3 Castildelgado Spain 42.26N 3.05W
104 G4 Castile New York 42.38N 78.04W
80 J3 Castilenti Italy 42.32N 13.56E
75 H3 Castiliscar Spain 42.22N 1.16W
120 D10 Castilla Chile 23.53S 69.48W
121 B1 Castilla Chile 27.52S 70.37W
119 B10 Castilla Peru 5.16S 80.36W
76 L4 Castilla, Can.de Spain
74 E5 Castilla la Nueva reg Spain
74 D4 Castilla la Vieja reg Spain
77 D7 Castilla, Playa de beach Spain
115 L1 Castilla, Pto C Honduras 16.01N 86.01W
77 L5 Castiléjar Spain 37.43N 2.38W
119 H4 Castillejo Venezuela 6.48N 61.14W
75 G8 Castillejo de Iniesta Spain 39.31N 1.47W
75 F7 Castillejo del Romeral Spain 40.09N 2.30W
76 F7 Castillejo de Martín Viejo Spain 40.42N 6.39W
75 D4 Castillejo de Robledo Spain 41.33N 3.30W
19 K4 Castillejos Luzon Philippines 14.54N 120.15E
77 G3 Castillejo, Sierra de mts Spain
119 E2 Castilletes Colombia 11.55N 71.20W
121 H7 Castillo, Canal del str Chile
121 B4 Castillo, Cerro del pk Arg/Chile 33.59S 69.56W
76 K8 Castillo de Bayuela Spain 40.06N 4.41W
77 D5 Castillo de las Guardas, El Spain 37.41N 6.19W
77 J5 Castillo de Locubín Spain 37.32N 3.56W
105 F8 Castillo de San Marcos Nat.Mon Florida
61 H6 Castillon Belgium 50.15N 4.21E
72 G10 Castillon-en-Couserans France 42.55N 1.01E
72 D6 Castillon-la-Bataille Gironde France 44.51N 0.02W
72 F6 Castillonnès France 44.39N 0.36E
75 H2 Castillo Nuevo Spain 42.41N 1.03W
121 L5 Castillo, Pampa del plain Arg
121 H5 Castillos Uruguay 34.12S 53.52W
121 H5 Castillos, L Uruguay
75 E6 Castilmimbre Spain 40.43N 2.47W
75 G6 Castilnuevo Spain 40.49N 1.52W
104 R2 Castine Maine 44.23N 68.50W
79 D5 Cástino Italy 44.37N 8.11E
66 N7 Castione Switzerland 46.14N 9.03E
79 H3 Castione della Presolana Italy 45.54N 10.02E
79 O3 Castions di Strada Italy 45.54N 13.11E
56 N2 Castle Acre Norfolk Eng 52.42N 0.41E
59 D4 Castlebar Mayo Irish Rep 53.52N 9.17W
59 D4 Castlebar, L Mayo Irish Rep 53.50N 9.20W
58 B5 Castlebay Barra, W Isles Scotland 56.58N 7.30W
59 K4 Castlebellingham Louth Irish Rep 53.54N 6.23W
107 J10 Castleberry Alabama 31.18N 87.02W
59 J3 Castleblayney Monaghan Irish Rep 54.07N 6.44W
59 K7 Castlebridge Wexford Irish Rep 52.23N 6.27W
56 H2 Castle Bromwich W Midlands Eng 52.30N 1.45W
56 K2 Castle Bytham Lincs Eng 32.46N 0.32W
59 G3 Castle Caldwell Fermanagh N Ireland 54.29N 7.58W
57 H3 Castle Carrock Cumbria Eng 54.54N 2.42W
56 F5 Castle Cary Somerset Eng 51.06N 2.31W
59 H6 Castlecomer Kilkenny Irish Rep 52.48N 7.12W
59 E6 Castleconnell Limerick Irish Rep 52.43N 8.30W
59 B8 Castle Cove Kerry Irish Rep 51.47N 10.02W
110 J7 Castle Cr Idaho
103 C2 Castle Creek New York 42.13N 75.55W
111 N2 Castle Dale Utah 39.12N 111.00W
59 J2 Castle Dawson Londonderry N Ireland 54.47N 6.33W
59 G2 Castlederg Tyrone N Ireland 54.42N 7.35W
59 J6 Castledermot Kildare Irish Rep 52.55N 6.50W
111 K8 Castle Dome Mts Arizona
56 J2 Castle Donington Leics Eng 52.51N 1.19W
57 F3 Castle Douglas Dumfries & Galloway Scotland 54.57N 3.56W
57 L3 Castle Eden Durham Eng 54.45N 1.21W
57 F2 Castlefern Dumfries & Galloway Scotland 55.09N 3.59W
59 G2 Castlefinn Donegal Irish Rep 54.47N 7.35W
110 L7 Castleford Idaho 42.32N 114.52W
57 L5 Castleford W Yorks Eng 43.44N 1.21W
101 P11 Castlegar Br Col 49.18N 117.41W
111 O2 Castle Gate Utah 39.44N 110.52W
59 B7 Castlegregory Kerry Irish Rep 52.15N 10.01W
96 C1 Castle Harbour Bermuda
105 K3 Castle Hayne N Carolina 34.20N 77.54W
56 N4 Castle Hedingham Essex Eng 51.59N 0.37E
111 M8 Castle Hot Springs Arizona 33.59N 112.19W
116 G3 Castle Island Bahamas 22.10N 74.20W
59 D7 Castleisland Kerry Irish Rep 52.14N 9.27W
59 H5 Castlejoroan Meath Irish Rep 53.24N 7.06W
57 D3 Castle Kennedy Dumfries & Galloway Scotland 54.54N 4.57W
59 C7 Castlemaine Kerry Irish Rep 52.10N 9.42W
12 G6 Castlemaine Victoria 37.05S 144.19E
59 F8 Castlemartyn Cork Irish Rep 51.55N 8.03W
111 D6 Castle Mt California 35.57N 120.20W
105 H5 Castle Pinckney Nat.Mon S Carolina 32.46N 79.56W
110 L5 Castle Pk Idaho 44.02N 114.35W
59 F4 Castleplunket Roscommon Irish Rep 53.45N 8.20W
11 L7 Castlepoint New Zealand 40.54S 176.15E
59 H4 Castlepollard W Meath Irish Rep 53.41N 7.17W
59 F4 Castlerea Roscommon Irish Rep 53.46N 8.29W
12 J4 Castlereagh R New S Wales
13 D1 Castlereagh B N Terr Australia
56 M2 Castle Rising Norfolk Eng 52.48N 0.29E
109 F2 Castle Rock Colorado 39.23N 104.53W
28 B3 Castle Rock Karnataka India 15.25N 74.22E
59 J1 Castlerock Londonderry N Ireland 55.09N 6.47W
108 G5 Castle Rock S Dakota 44.58N 103.25W
110 O8 Castle Rock Utah 41.09N 111.11W
110 C3 Castle Rock Washington 46.16N 122.55W
96 A14 Castle Rock Pt St Helena 16.02S 5.45W
106 E6 Castle Rock Res Wisconsin
57 K3 Castleside Durham Eng 54.50N 1.52W
57 H2 Castleton Borders Scotland 55.12N 2.46W
57 K6 Castleton Derbys Eng 53.21N 1.46W
56 E4 Castleton Gwent Wales 51.33N 3.04W
116 L2 Castleton Jamaica, W I 18.11N 76.50W
57 M4 Castleton N Yorks Eng 54.27N 0.56W
111 P3 Castleton Utah 38.36N 109.19W
104 M3 Castleton Vermont 43.36N 73.11W
103 G1 Castleton on Hudson New York 42.31N 73.45W
56 G6 Castletown Dorset Eng 50.34N 2.26W
58 K1 Castletown Highland Scotland 58.35N 3.23W
57 D4 Castletown Isle of Man U.K. 54.04N 4.38W
59 H6 Castletown Leix Irish Rep 52.59N 7.30W
59 H5 Castletown W Meath Irish Rep 53.27N 7.29W
59 C8 Castletown Bere Cork Irish Rep 51.39N 9.55W
59 F7 Castletownroche Cork Irish Rep 52.10N 8.28W
59 D8 Castletownshend Cork Irish Rep 51.32N 9.11W
59 L3 Castlewellan Down Irish Rep 54.16N 5.57W
108 N5 Castlewood S Dakota 44.42N 97.01W
112 D6 Castolon Texas 29.10N 103.32W
56 N2 Caston Norfolk Eng 52.33N 0.52E
100 F6 Castor Alberta 52.14N 111.54W
56 L2 Castor Cambs Eng 52.35N 0.20W
107 C9 Castor Louisiana 32.15N 93.09W
66 H8 Castor mt Italy/Switz 45.56N 7.48E
107 D9 Castor R Louisiana
107 F4 Castor R Missouri
75 H7 Castralvo Spain 40.19N 1.05W
76 K3 Castrejón de la Peña Spain 42.48N 4.36W
76 E5 Castrelo del Valle Spain 41.59N 7.25W
76 C4 Castrelo de Miño Spain 42.18N 8.03W
76 B2 Castrelo, Embalse de res Spain 43.01N 9.00W
76 F5 Castrelos Portugal 41.50N 6.52W
70 H3 Castre, Mt France 49.17N 1.30W
72 J8 Castres France 43.36N 2.14E
72 D6 Castres-Gironde France 44.43N 0.27W
60 G9 Castricum Netherlands 52.33N 4.40E
71 D9 Castries France 43.41N 3.59E
116 O7 Castries St Lucia, W I 14.01N 60.59W
81 R13 Castrignano del Capo Italy 39.50N 18.21E
77 L5 Castril Spain 37.48N 2.46W
77 L5 Castril R Spain
76 F4 Castrillo de Cabrera Spain 42.20N 6.33W
76 L5 Castrillo de Don Juan Spain 41.47N 4.04W
76 L5 Castrillo de Duero Spain 41.34N 4.01W
75 D4 Castrillo de la Reina Spain 41.59N 3.15W
75 C4 Castrillo de la Vega Spain 41.39N 3.46W
75 B3 Castrillo de Valdavia Spain 42.27N 4.29W
Castrillon see Piedras Blancas
76 L5 Castrillo-Tejeriego Spain 41.42N 4.22W
118 E9 Castro Brazil 24.46S 50.03W
121 A9 Castro Chile 42.30S 73.46W
81 R13 Castro Italy 40.00N 18.26E
118 H3 Castro Alves Brazil 12.46S 39.33W
76 H4 Castrocalbón Spain 42.12N 6.00W
76 E4 Castro Caldelas Spain 42.23N 7.24W
79 L6 Castrocaro Italy 44.10N 11.56E
76 G4 Castrocontrigo Spain 42.11N 6.11W
76 D7 Castro Daire Portugal 40.54N 7.55W
77 M6 Castro de Filabres Spain 37.11N 2.25W
80 H5 Castro dei Volci Italy 41.30N 13.25E
77 H5 Castro del Río Spain 37.41N 4.29W
76 E2 Castro de Rey Spain 43.12N 7.24W
76 K5 Castrodeza Spain 41.38N 4.58W
76 G5 Castro, Embalse de res Spain
81 G9 Castrofilippo Sicily 37.21N 13.45E
76 L4 Castrogeriz Spain 42.17N 4.09W
76 H5 Castrogonzalo Spain 41.59N 5.36W
76 C4 Castro Laboreiro Portugal 42.02N 8.10W
76 E14 Castro Marim Portugal 37.13N 7.26W
76 K4 Castromocho Spain 42.02N 4.50W
76 J5 Castromonte Spain 41.46N 5.03W
76 J3 Castromudarra Spain 42.37N 5.04W
76 H5 Castrón R Spain
76 H5 Castronuevo Spain 41.43N 5.33W
76 J6 Castronuño Spain 41.23N 5.16W
81 M3 Castronuovo Italy 40.11N 16.10E
81 G8 Castronuovo di Sicilia Sicily 37.41N 13.36E
80 L5 Castropignano Italy 41.37N 14.34E
76 G3 Castropodame Spain 42.35N 6.28W
76 E1 Castropol Spain 43.32N 7.01W
63 F9 Castrop-Rauxel W Germany 51.33N 7.18E
76 A2 Castro, R.del Spain
81 K7 Castroreale Sicily 38.06N 15.13E
75 D1 Castro-Urdiales Spain 43.23N 3.11W
76 C13 Castro Verde Portugal 37.42N 8.05W
76 E2 Castroverde Spain 43.02N 7.20W
76 C13 Castro Verde Almodôvar Portugal 37.18N 8.07W
76 J5 Castroverde de Campos Spain 41.58N 5.19W
81 M4 Castrovillari Italy 39.48N 16.12E
111 C5 Castroville California 36.45N 121.47W
112 J6 Castroville Texas 29.22N 98.55W
120 B5 Castrovirreyna Peru 13.19S 75.16W
Castrum Harench castle see Harim
77 E3 Castuera Spain 38.44N 5.33W
92 J10 Casuarina, I Mozambique 17.09S 39.01E
14 G2 Casuarina, Mt W Australia 14.35S 127.43E
93 M9 Casuarina Pt Kenya 3.18S 40.07E
113 N6 Caswell Alaska 61.57N 150.09W
11 B11 Caswell Sd New Zealand
37 F6 Çat Turkey 39.40N 41.03E
62 L8 Čata Czechoslovakia 47.58N 18.38E
91 D10 Catabola Angola 13.07S 15.10E
120 E7 Catacajes, R Bolivia
115 M2 Catacamas Honduras 14.55N 85.54W
91 C8 Catacanha Angola 8.01S 13.14E
119 B10 Catacaos Peru 5.22S 80.40W
119 B10 Catacocha Ecuador 4.03S 79.40W
77 P2 Catadau Spain 39.17N 0.34W
116 H1 Catadupa Jamaica, W I 18.16N 77.53W
118 G7 Cataguases Brazil 21.23S 42.39W
107 D10 Catahoula L Louisiana
19 L5 Cataiñgan Philippines 12.02N 123.58E
37 G7 Çatak Turkey 38.02N 43.05E
37 G8 Çatak R Turkey
36 F1 Çatalağzi Turkey 41.30N 31.51E
36 H5 Çatalan Turkey 37.13N 35.14E
81 A4 Catalano, I Sardinia 39.53N 8.15E
118 F6 Catalão Brazil 18.12S 47.54W
37 F1 Çatalca Turkey 41.09N 28.28E
36 C3 Çatal Dağı mt Turkey 39.53N 28.19E
37 H2 Çataldere Turkey 40.40N 29.59E
98 T5 Catalina Newfoundland 48.32N 53.06W
116 K5 Catalina, I Dominican Rep 18.23N 69.00W
19 M1 Catalina Pt Guam Pacific Oc 13.32N 144.56E
121 L9 Catalina, Pta C Argentina 52.34S 68.46W
37 B2 Çatal Tepe mt Turkey 40.44N 26.11E
74 H3 Cataluna reg Spain
36 G1 Çatalzeytin Turkey 41.58N 34.11E
87 H9 Catàma Somalia 2.25N 41.49E
12 H9 Catamaran Tasmania 4.33S 146.49E
121 D2 Catamarca Argentina 28.28S 65.46W
121 C1 Catamarca prov Argentina
119 B10 Catamayo, R Ecuador
90 M8 Catambour Cent Afr Rep 6.08N 24.40E
19 L5 Catanauan Luzon Philippines 13.37N 122.20E
94 M2 Catandica Mozambique 18.05S 33.10E
19 M5 Catanduanes isld Philippines
118 E7 Catanduva Brazil 21.05S 49.00W
118 D9 Catanduvas Brazil 25.08S 53.13W
81 K8 Catania Sicily 37.31N 15.06E
81 J9 Catania prov Sicily
81 K9 Catania, Golfo di Sicily
81 J9 Catania, Piana di plain Sicily
121 B7 Catán-Lil Argentina 39.45S 70.38W
81 N6 Catanzaro Italy 38.54N 16.36E
81 M6 Catanzaro prov Italy
107 F12 Cataouatche, L Louisiana
91 D11 Catape R Angola
120 F4 Cataqueamã Brazil 11.08S 63.10W
107 K2 Cataract L Indiana 39.29N 86.50W
119 B8 Catarama Ecuador 1.36S 79.29W
112 H7 Catarina Texas 28.23N 99.38W
19 M5 Catarman Philippines 12.29N 124.35E
19 N8 Catarman Pt Mindanao Philippines 8.00N 126.23E
77 Q2 Catarroja Spain 39.24N 0.24W
103 D5 Catasauqua Pennsylvania 40.39N 75.27W
12 D5 Catastrophe, C S Australia 35.00S 135.59E
91 D10 Catata Nova Angola 13.24S 15.26E
103 B2 Catatonk New York 42.09N 76.19W
119 D3 Catatumbo, R Venezuela
105 C5 Cataula Georgia 32.37N 84.54W
120 E8 Catavi Bolivia 18.23S 66.37W
105 G3 Catawba S Carolina 34.51N 80.57W
106 D4 Catawba Wisconsin 45.33N 90.32W
105 F2 Catawba L S Carolina 35.05N 81.05W
105 F3 Catawba, R S Carolina
103 B5 Catawissa Pennsylvania 40.56N 76.27W
103 B5 Catawissa Cr Pennsylvania
92 F9 Cataxa Mozambique 15.59S 33.11E
19 M6 Catbalogan Philippines 11.46N 124.55E
57 J2 Catcleugh Res Northumb Eng 55.19N 2.25W
110 R2 Cat Creek Montana 47.05N 108.02W
69 F3 Cateau, Le France 50.07N 3.33E
91 D8 Cateco-Cangola Angola 8.28S 15.51E
120 A12 Catedral,Roca Pacific Oc 26.20S 80.06W
19 N8 Cateel Mindanao Philippines 7.48N 126.25E
19 N8 Cateel B Mindanao Philippines
91 H12 Catehu Angola 17.32S 22.24E
70 E3 Catel Channel Is 49.27N 2.35W
69 E3 Catelet, le France 50.00N 3.15E
115 M8 Catemaco Mexico 18.28N 95.10W
94 M6 Catembe Mozambique 26.00S 32.32E
121 B4 Catemu Chile 32.45S 70.52W
81 L4 Catena Costiera mts Italy
80 H4 Catena di Monte Sirente mts Italy
80 H4 Catena di Monte Velino mts Italy
81 J8 Catenanuova Sicily 37.34N 14.42E
91 G9 Catende Angola 11.16S 21.31E
117 J9 Catende Brazil 8.43S 35.36W
91 C10 Catengue Angola 12.59S 13.39E
91 D12 Catequero Angola 16.32S 14.54E
100 J5 Cater Saskatchewan 52.23N 108.04W
67 Q12 Cateraggio Corsica 42.06N 9.30E
56 L5 Caterham Surrey Eng 51.17N 0.04W
67 O11 Cateri Corsica 42.34N 8.53E
91 C8 Catete Angola 9.09S 13.40E
117 B8 Catete, R Brazil
56 P2 Catfield Norfolk Eng 52.45N 1.32E
58 Q9 Catfirth Shetland Scotland 60.16N 1.14W
55 G4 Catford London England 51.26N 00.000
109 L3 Catharine Kansas 38.57N 99.13W
108 L2 Cathay N Dakota 47.34N 99.24W
12 J6 Cathcart New S Wales 36.49S 149.25E
95 L8 Cathcart S Africa 32.18S 27.09E
112 D5 Cathedral Mt Texas 30.11N 103.40W
95 N4 Cathedral Peak S Africa 28.57S 29.12E
107 D7 Catherine, L Arkansas 34.25N 92.55W
59 H2 Catherine, L Tyrone N Ireland 54.42N 7.26W
111 M2 Catherine, Mt Utah 39.01N 112.09W
96 A11 Catherine Pt Ascension I 7.56S 14.26W
116 L2 Catherine's Pk Jamaica, W I 18.05N 76.43W
95 N5 Cathkin Pk S Africa 29.05S 29.22E
110 B3 Cathlamet Washington 46.13N 123.22W
106 L4 Cathro Michigan 45.09N 83.31W
116 G2 Cat I Bahamas
107 G11 Cat I Mississippi 30.13N 89.10W
75 L7 Catí Spain 40.28N 0.01E
80 J4 Catignano Italy 42.21N 13.57E
121 B6 Catillo Chile 36.19S 71.40W
69 F3 Catillon-sur-Sambre France 50.04N 3.39E
79 L2 Catinaccio mt Italy 46.28N 11.38E
121 C2 Catinzaco Argentina 29.40S 67.27W
89 B6 Catió Guinea-Bissau 11.13N 15.10W
81 D3 Catirina, Pta Sardinia 40.28N 9.33E
119 G5 Catisimiña Venezuela 4.07N 63.40W
117 F9 Catita Brazil 9.30S 42.56W
115 E9 Cativá Panama 9.21N 79.49W
76 D7 Cativelos Portugal 40.32N 7.41W
97 K7 Cat Lake Ontario 51.40N 91.50W
104 C8 Catlettsburg Kentucky 38.24N 82.37W
106 G9 Catlin Illinois 40.03N 87.43W
11 D13 Catlins R New Zealand
75 N5 Catllal Spain 41.10N 1.20E
104 J3 Cato New York 43.10N 76.35W
115 Q7 Catoche, C Mexico 21.38N 87.08W
104 H7 Catoctin Mt Virginia/Maryland
66 E7 Catogne mt Switzerland 46.03N 7.07E
10 M6 Cato I Coral Sea 23.14S 155.29E
76 B3 Catoira Spain 42.40N 8.43W
117 H8 Catolé do Rocha Brazil 6.16S 37.44W
57 H4 Caton Lancs Eng 54.04N 2.43W
103 A8 Catonsville Maryland 39.17N 76.44W
115 J6 Catorce Mexico 23.42N 100.54W
95 O5 Cato Ridge S Africa 29.44S 30.36E
91 E10 Catota Angola 13.57S 17.30E
76 G3 Catoute mt Spain 42.48N 6.20W
77 P4 Catral Spain 38.10N 0.47W
80 G2 Catria, Monte Italy 43.28N 12.42E
121 D6 Catrilo Argentina 36.28S 63.20W
119 H7 Catrimani Brazil 0.24N 61.45W
119 H6 Catrimani, R Brazil
103 G2 Catskill New York 42.14N 73.52W
103 F2 Catskill Cr New York
103 E2 Catskill Mts New York
103 F2 Catskill State Park New York
57 L5 Cattal N Yorks Eng 53.59N 1.19W
104 G4 Cattaraugus New York 42.20N 78.54W
69 L5 Cattenom France 49.24N 6.15E
57 K4 Catterick N Yorks Eng 54.22N 1.38W
57 K4 Catterick Bridge N Yorks Eng 54.23N 1.39W
79 N7 Cattolica Italy 43.58N 12.44E
81 F9 Cattolica Eraclea Sicily 37.27N 13.24E
120 E10 Catúa Argentina 23.55S 67.00W
95 P8 Catuane Mozambique 26.50S 32.18E
91 C10 Catumbela Angola 12.27S 13.31E
91 D10 Catumbela R Angola
118 J9 Catumbi Brazil 22.56S 43.13W
121 C3 Catuna Argentina 30.59S 66.18W
92 G8 Catur Mozambique 13.42S 35.34E
119 F9 Caturiá, I Brazil 3.30S 68.24W
72 G6 Catus France 44.34N 1.20E
81 G8 Catuso, Mte Sicily 37.43N 13.59E
119 F7 Cauaburi, R Brazil
91 E7 Cauale R Angola
119 H6 Cauamé, R Brazil
117 D7 Cauaxi, R Brazil
19 L7 Cauayan Philippines 9.58N 122.37E
119 C6 Cauca div Colombia
117 H6 Caucaia Brazil 3.44S 38.45W
119 C4 Cauca, R Colombia
119 C4 Caucasia Colombia 8.00N 75.16W
Caucasus mts see Bol'shoy Kavkaz mts
120 E10 Cauchari, Salar de salt pan Arg
100 V3 Cauchon L Manitoba
66 N6 Cauco Switzerland 46.21N 9.09E
104 P7 Caucomgomoc L Maine 46.13N 69.36W
72 F6 Caudau R France
75 H7 Caudé Spain 40.25N 1.12W
70 M2 Caudebec France 49.32N 0.44E
70 N3 Caudebec-les-Elbeuf France 49.17N 1.02E
77 P3 Caudete Spain 38.42N 0.59W
75 H8 Caudete de las Fuentes Spain 39.33N 1.18W
75 J8 Caudiel Spain 39.57N 0.35W
72 J10 Caudiès-de-Fenouillèdes France 42.49N 2.20E
72 C6 Caudos France 44.33N 0.59W
69 E3 Caudry France 50.07N 3.25E
92 E9 Cauese Mts Mozambique
99 R7 Caughnawaga Quebec 45.24N 73.44W
99 R10 Caughnawaga Ind.Res Quebec
19 N7 Cauit Pt Mindanao Philippines 9.19N 126.12E
87 M10 Cauitti Somalia 0.30S 41.10E
72 G9 Caujac France 43.18N 1.26E
101 F11 Caulfield Br Col 49.21N 123.15W
12 D8 Caulfield dist Melbourne, Vic
70 F5 Caulnes France 48.18N 2.10W
81 M7 Caulonia Italy 38.23N 16.24E
Cau Mau, Pte de see Mui Bai Bung
91 G8 Caumbue Angola 9.58S 20.20E
72 G9 Caumont Ariège France 43.02N 1.05E
72 F7 Caumont Tarn-et-Garonne France 44.01N 0.59E
70 J3 Caumont-l'Eventé France 49.05N 0.48W
71 F9 Caumont-sur-Durance Vaucluse France 43.53N 4.57E
116 E4 Caunao R Cuba
72 K9 Caunes-Minervois France 43.19N 2.30E
91 F8 Caungula Angola 8.26S 18.38E
91 G7 Caungula Angola 7.30S 20.13E
120 E6 Caupolican prov Bolivia
121 A5 Cauquenes Chile 35.58S 72.22W
119 G4 Caura, R Venezuela
70 D5 Caurel France 48.12N 3.03W
76 E3 Caurel Spain 42.38N 7.09W
76 E3 Caurel, Sierra del mts Spain
119 G8 Caurés, R Brazil
67 O13 Cauro Corsica 41.55N 8.55E
98 E5 Causapscal Quebec 48.22N 67.14W
59 C7 Causeway Kerry Irish Rep 52.25N 9.44W
72 H7 Caussade France 44.10N 1.32E
120 F4 Cautário, R Brazil
72 D10 Cauterets France 42.53N 0.06W
121 A7 Cautin prov Chile
116 F4 Cauto R Cuba
28 C4 Cauvery Falls Karnataka India 12.17N 77.08E
28 C5 Cauvery R Tamil Nadu/Karnataka India
70 L2 Cauville France 49.36N 0.08E
66 D6 Caux Switzerland 46.27N 6.57E
70 L2 Caux reg France
58 S12 Cava isld Orkney Scotland 58.53N 3.10W
75 C1 Cavada, La Spain 43.20N 3.41W
80 L7 Cava de'Tirreni Italy 40.42N 14.42E
76 B5 Cavado R Portugal
81 K9 Cavadonna, R Sicily
79 D4 Cavaglià Italy 45.24N 8.06E
88 O3 Cavaignac Algeria 36.28N 1.10E
71 G9 Cavaillon France 43.50N 5.02E
75 M6 Cava, La Spain 40.44N 0.43E
71 K10 Cavalaire France 43.11N 6.32E
71 K10 Cavalaire, B de France 43.10N 6.35E
71 K10 Cavalaire-sur-Mer France 43.12N 6.32E
118 F3 Cavalcante Brazil 13.48S 47.30W
120 F3 Cavalcante Rondônia Brazil 8.22S 63.23W
118 F3 Cavalcante, Serra do mts Brazil
76 B13 Cavaleiro Portugal 37.36N 8.43W
72 L7 Cavalerie, la France 44.01N 3.09E
79 K2 Cavalese Italy 46.18N 11.28E
108 N1 Cavalier N Dakota 48.48N 97.38W
71 J10 Cavalière France 43.10N 6.25E
79 C5 Cavallermaggiore Italy 44.43N 7.40E
11 H1 Cavalli Is New Zealand
79 N1 Cavallino, Monte Italy/Austria 46.40N 12.32E
88 Q3 Cavallo, C Algeria 36.50N 5.33E
67 O11 Cavallo, C. au C Corsica 42.31N 8.40E
67 P14 Cavallo, I Corsica 41.22N 9.15E
112 L7 Cavallo, Pass Texas 28.23N 96.24W
80 L4 Cavalluccio, Pta di Italy 42.16N 14.30E
89 E8 Cavally R Ivory Coast/Liberia
79 F4 Cava Manara Italy 45.09N 9.06E
59 H4 Cavan Cavan Irish Rep 54.00N 7.21W
95 O3 Cavan S Africa 27.47S 30.05E
59 H4 Cavan co Irish Rep
12 A7 Cavan dist Adelaide, S Aust
14 G7 Cavanagh Ra W Australia
59 F2 Cavangarden Donegal Irish Rep 54.31N 8.09W
79 K2 Cavareno Italy 46.25N 11.08E
79 F2 Cavargna Italy 46.06N 9.07E
79 M4 Cavárzere Italy 45.08N 12.05E
79 N2 Cavasso Nuovo Italy 46.13N 12.46E
79 O2 Cavazzo Carnico Italy 46.23N 13.03E
79 O2 Cavazzo, L. di Italy 46.19N 13.05E
80 G5 Cave Italy 41.49N 12.56E
11 E11 Cave New Zealand 44.16S 170.56E
107 E6 Cave City Arkansas 35.58N 91.34W
107 L4 Cave City Kentucky 37.08N 85.59W
111 N8 Cavecreek Arizona 33.51N 111.56W
79 P2 Cave del Predil Italy 46.27N 13.34E
79 J3 Cavédine Italy 46.00N 10.59E
14 D9 Cave Hill W Australia 31.40S 121.05E
107 H4 Cave in Rock Illinois 37.28N 88.11W
118 H4 Caveira, R Brazil
121 J1 Caveiras, R Brazil
96 Q4 Caveiro, Cabeço do mt Azores 38.26N 28.13W
110 B7 Cave Junction Oregon 42.10N 123.38W
99 C2 Cavell Ontario 50.14N 87.01W
100 J6 Cavell Saskatchewan 53.19N 108.40W
100 G8 Cavendish Alberta 50.50N 110.28W
56 N3 Cavendish Suffolk Eng 52.05N 0.38E
12 F7 Cavendish Victoria 37.32S 142.06E
79 M5 Ca Venier Italy 44.58N 12.20E
121 G3 Cavera R Brazil
66 L6 Cavergno Switzerland 46.21N 8.37E
25 D7 Cavern I Burma 10.20N 98.00E
118 D9 Cavernoso, Serra do mts Brazil
11 B7 Cavern Pk mt Auckland Is Pacific Oc 50.44S 166.06E
121 G3 Cavero, Serra do mts Brazil
99 C4 Cavers Ontario 48.55N 87.41W
56 K5 Caversham Berks Eng 51.29N 0.58W
11 L13 Caversham dist Dunedin New Zealand
105 B3 Cave Spring Georgia 34.05N 85.21W
59 F4 Cavetown L Roscommon Irish Rep 53.56N 8.15W
111 K3 Cave Valley Nevada 38.39N 114.50W
117 D4 Caviana, I Brazil
66 M7 Caviano Switzerland 46.07N 8.46E
72 D5 Cavignac France 45.06N 0.23W
19 K7 Cavili isld Philippines 9.16N 120.50E
91 D10 Cavimbe Angola 12.12S 14.16E
120 E5 Cavinas Bolivia 12.32S 66.45W
19 H2 Cavite Luzon Philippines 14.29N 120.54E
81 D5 Cavoli, I.dei Sardinia 39.05N 9.33E
80 G5 Cavo, Monte Italy 41.45N 12.43E
81 N3 Cavone, R Italy
91 F10 Cavongo Angola 12.46S 18.10E
79 B5 Cavour Italy 44.47N 7.22E
108 M5 Cavour S Dakota 44.24N 98.03W
79 J5 Cavriago Italy 44.42N 10.31E
82 E8 Cavtat Yugoslavia 42.35N 18.13E
Cavungo see Nana Candundo
36 F5 Çavuş Turkey 37.37N 31.57E
36 F4 Çavuşcu Gölü L Turkey
58 J3 Cawdor Highland Scotland 57.32N 3.55W
109 M2 Cawker City Kansas 39.31N 98.27W
12 F4 Cawndilla L New S Wales 32.30S 142.18E
Cawnpore see Kanpur
57 L5 Cawood N Yorks Eng 53.50N 1.07W
99 O7 Cawood Quebec 45.49N 76.13W
56 O2 Cawston Norfolk Eng 52.46N 1.10E
118 G7 Caxambu Brazil 21.59S 44.54W
119 E10 Caxias Amazonas Brazil 4.30S 71.17W
117 F7 Caxias Maranhão Brazil 4.53S 43.20W
76 C16 Caxias Portugal 38.42N 9.16W
121 H2 Caxias do Sul Brazil 29.14S 51.10W
91 E8 Caxinda Angola 9.34S 17.04E
91 H9 Caxita Angola 11.14S 22.33E
91 C8 Caxito Angola 8.34S 13.38E
117 C5 Caxiuana, B.de Brazil
56 L3 Caxton Cambs Eng 52.13N 0.06W
56 L3 Caxton Gibbet Cambs Eng 52.14N 0.07W
36 E4 Çay Turkey 38.35N 31.01E
119 B7 Cayambe Ecuador 0.02N 78.08W
119 C7 Cayambe, Vol Ecuador 0.02N 77.58W
119 B7 Cayapas, R Ecuador
Çaybaşı see Çayeli
105 F4 Cayce S Carolina 33.57N 81.10W
36 F1 Çaycuma Turkey 41.24N 32.06E
25 G8 Cay Dua, B Cambodia
37 F4 Çayeli Turkey 41.07N 40.44E
117 C2 Cayenne Fr Guiana 4.55N 52.18W
117 C2 Cayenne dept Fr Guiana
116 H5 Cayes, Les Haiti 18.15N 73.46W
69 B3 Cayeux-sur-Mer France 50.11N 1.30E
105 K7 Cayey Puerto Rico 18.08W 66.11W
Çayhan see Çayeli
Çayhan see Çakmak. Konya
36 H3 Çayıralan Turkey 39.20N 35.40E
36 F2 Çayırhan Turkey 40.06N 31.38E
37 E5 Çaykara Turkey 40.43N 40.19E
37 E8 Çaylarbaşı Turkey 37.41N 39.01E
71 C9 Caylar, le France 43.51N 3.20E
100 D8 Cayley Alberta 50.30N 113.51W
72 H7 Caylus France 44.14N 1.46E
116 E5 Cayman Brac isld Caribbean Sea 19.44N 79.48W
116 D5 Cayman, Grand isld Caribbean Sea 19.20N 81.15W
116 D5 Cayman Is W Indies
116 D5 Cayman, Lit isld Caribbean Sea 19.42N 80.00W
116 C5 Cayman Trench Caribbean Sea
25 H7 Cay Mit Vietnam 10.38N 104.59E
56 F3 Caynham Shropshire Eng 52.21N 2.39W
119 B8 Cayo Ecuador 1.23S 80.44W
71 K8 Cayolle, Col de la France 44.15N 6.45E
116 P3 Cayon St Kitts West Indies 17.21N 62.43W
76 B2 Cayon Spain 43.19N 8.36W
105 L9 Cay Point New Providence I Bahamas 24.59N 77.24W
72 K6 Cayrol, Le France 44.35N 2.46E
116 D3 Cay Sal Bank Bahamas
57 N4 Cayton N Yorks Eng 54.14N 0.23W
111 D6 Cayucos California 35.28N 120.54W
107 J2 Cayuga Indiana 39.57N 87.28W
108 N3 Cayuga N Dakota 46.05N 97.22W
99 L10 Cayuga Ontario 42.57N 79.50W
112 M4 Cayuga Texas 31.59N 95.59W
104 J4 Cayuga L New York
103 A2 Cayuta New York 42.17N 76.42W
103 A2 Cayuta Cr New York
103 A2 Cayuta L New York 42.22N 76.45W
76 K8 Cazalegas Spain 40.00N 4.42W
76 K8 Cazalegas,Embalse de res Spain
72 D7 Cazalis France 44.21N 0.23W
77 E5 Cazalla de la Sierra Spain 37.56N 5.46W
72 G6 Cazals Lot France 44.39N 1.14E
72 H7 Cazals Tarn-et-Garonne France 44.07N 1.42E
82 L6 Căzăneşti Romania 44.36N 27.03E
121 G2 Caza Pava Argentina 28.18S 56.10W
72 D8 Cazaubon France 43.56N 0.04W
72 B6 Cazaux France 44.32N 1.08W
72 B6 Cazaux et de Sanguinet, Lac de France 44.30N 1.08W
71 C8 Caze, la France 44.18N 3.21E
104 K4 Cazenovia New York 42.54N 75.51W
72 G9 Cazères France 43.13N 1.04E
72 G7 Cazes Mondenard France 44.15N 1.13E
82 C6 Cazin Yugoslavia 44.59N 15.57E
66 O5 Cazis Switzerland 46.44N 9.26E
91 F9 Cazôa Angola 10.43S 19.51E
91 H9 Cazombo Angola 11.54S 22.56E
77 L5 Cazorla Spain 37.55N 3.00W
119 F3 Cazorla Venezuela 8.02N 66.59W
77 L4 Cazorla, Sierra de mts Spain
72 G6 Cazoulès France 44.53N 1.26E
71 C10 Cazouls-les-Béziers France 43.24N 3.05E
92 F9 Cazula Mozambique 15.28S 33.40E
66 L8 Cazzago Italy 45.47N 8.44E
76 J4 Cea Spain 42.27N 5.00W
76 J3 Cea R Spain
76 G5 Ceadea Spain 41.40N 6.15W
82 K3 Ceahlau Romania 47.03N 25.58E
82 K4 Ceahlău mt Romania 46.57N 25.57E
Ceanannas Mór see Kells Meath
75 E1 Ceánuri Spain 43.06N 2.45W
Ceará see Fortaleza
117 G7 Ceará state Brazil
117 J7 Ceará Mirim Brazil 5.38S 35.25W
117 J7 Ceará Mirim, R Brazil
72 G6 Céau R France
70 J5 Ceauce France 48.29N 0.38W
71 D6 Céaux-d'Allègre France 45.12N 3.45E
72 E1 Ceaux-en-Loudun France 47.02N 0.14E
100 P5 Ceba Saskatchewan 53.07N 102.14W
115 O6 Cebaco,I Panama
115 G4 Ceballos Mexico 26.33N 104.07W
76 J3 Cebanico Spain 42.43N 5.02W
71 C5 Cebazat France 45.50N 3.05E
76 D8 Cebola Portugal 40.10N 7.47W
109 D5 Cebolla New Mexico 36.32N 106.30W
76 K9 Cebolla Spain 39.57N 4.34W
121 C2 Cebollar Argentina 29.08S 66.33W
77 B6 Cebollar mt Spain 37.22N 7.05W
121 H4 Cebollatí Uruguay 33.15S 53.46W
121 G4 Cebollatí R Uruguay
75 E4 Cebollera mt Spain 42.00N 2.40W
75 E3 Cebollera,Sierra mts Spain
109 C6 Cebollita New Mexico 35.11N 107.23W
76 L8 Cebreros Spain 40.27N 4.28W
77 E5 Cebrõn mt Spain 37.40N 5.56W
76 H4 Cebrones del Río Spain 42.15N 5.50W
19 L6 Cebu Philippines 10.17N 123.56E
19 L7 Cebu isld Philippines
80 H5 Ceccano Italy 41.34N 13.20E
62 L9 Cece Hungary 46.46N 18.39E
79 L2 Çece,Cima de mt Italy 46.16N 11.42E
65 M2 Čechtice Czechoslovakia 49.37N 15.04E
103 E7 Cecil New Jersey 39.38N 74.56W
104 A5 Cecil Ohio 41.14N 84.37W
106 F5 Cecil Wisconsin 44.49N 88.27W
103 B7 Cecil co Maryland
107 L4 Cecilia Kentucky 37.38N 85.59W
15 G7 Cecilia R Papua New Guinea
53 V15 Ceciliekruna mt Norway 61.47N 6.46E
13 K8 Cecil Plains Queensland 27.32S 151.07E
14 D7 Cecil Rhodes, Mt W Australia 25.14S 121.52E
103 C8 Cecilton Maryland 39.24N 75.52W
110 B8 Cecilville California 41.09N 123.09W
80 B2 Cecina Italy 43.18N 10.31E
80 C2 Cecina R Italy
81 N5 Cecita,Lago di Italy 39.23N 16.31E
76 F9 Ceclavín Spain 39.48N 6.47W
76 F2 Cecos Spain 43.01N 6.50W
109 M2 Cedar Kansas 39.40N 98.56W
108 M8 Cedar R Nebraska
94 E9 Cedar Berg mt S Africa 32.21S 19.10E
107 H8 Cedarbluff Mississippi 33.34N 88.53W
104 D9 Cedar Bluff Virginia 37.05N 81.45W
109 L3 Cedar Bluff Res Kansas
109 K2 Cedar Bluffs Kansas 39.58N 100.33W
108 O8 Cedar Bluffs Nebraska 41.25N 96.36W
111 M4 Cedar Breaks Nat.Mon Utah 37.37N 112.50W
103 E7 Cedar Brook New Jersey 39.42N 74.54W
106 G6 Cedarburg Wisconsin 43.17N 87.59W
108 J6 Cedar Butte S Dakota 43.36N 101.08W
107 D3 Cedar City Missouri 38.36N 92.09W
111 L4 Cedar City Utah 37.40N 113.04W
108 H3 Cedar Cr N Dakota
103 F7 Cedar Cr New Jersey
112 K5 Cedar Creek Texas 30.06N 97.30W
110 L7 Cedar Creek Res Idaho 42.14N 114.54W
112 L3 Cedar Creek Res Texas
112 O9 Cedar Crest Dallas, Texas 32.43N 96.46W
108 S7 Cedar Falls Iowa 42.34N 92.26W
116 P4 Cedar Grove Antigua W I 17.10N 61.48W
103 F5 Cedar Grove New Jersey 40.51N 74.14W
106 G6 Cedar Grove Wisconsin 43.33N 87.50W
104 D8 Cedar Grove W Virginia 38.13N 81.28W
105 L3 Cedar I N Carolina 34.58N 76.20W
104 K9 Cedar I Virginia 37.37N 75.36W
105 D8 Cedar Key Florida 29.08N 83.03W
106 G8 Cedar L Indiana 41.21N 87.21W
100 R5 Cedar L Manitoba
112 E3 Cedar L Texas 32.48N 102.16W
112 M7 Cedar Lane Texas 28.56N 95.44W
95 N2 Cedarmont S Africa 26.50S 29.00E
111 G3 Cedar Mts Nevada
104 B5 Cedar Pt Ohio 41.42N 83.20W
106 C8 Cedar,R Iowa
106 G4 Cedar R Michigan 45.25N 87.18W
106 K5 Cedar,R Michigan
106 C8 Cedar Rapids Iowa 41.59N 91.39W
108 M8 Cedar Rapids Nebraska 41.34N 98.08W

104 H5 **Cedar Run** Pennsylvania 41.31N 77.26W
106 J6 **Cedar Springs** Michigan 43.12N 85.34W
99 H10 **Cedar Springs** Ontario 42.16N 82.03W
105 B3 **Cedartown** Georgia 34.01N 85.15W
109 O4 **Cedar Vale** Kansas 37.05N 96.31W
109 E7 **Cedarvale** New Mexico 34.23N 105.43W
116 L2 **Cedar Valley** Jamaica, W I 18.00N 76.36W
110 E8 **Cedarville** California 41.33N 120.11W
106 K3 **Cedarville** Michigan 46.01N 84.20W
103 D8 **Cedarville** New Jersey 39.20N 75.12W
104 B7 **Cedarville** Ohio 39.44N 83.47W
95 N6 **Cedarville** S Africa 30.23S 29.03E
109 F4 **Cedarwood** Colorado 37.57N 104.37W
79 H2 **Cedégolo** Italy 46.04N 10.21E
76 C1 **Cedeira** Spain 43.39N 8.04W
76 K9 **Cedena** *R* Spain
76 E9 **Cedillo** Spain 39.39N 7.30W
76 E9 **Cedillo, Embalse de** *res* Portugal
76 E9 **Cedillo, Embalse de** *res* Portugal
104 H8 **Cedon** Virginia 38.05N 77.31W
100 O9 **Cedoux** Saskatchewan 49.54N 103.54W
76 E6 **Cedovim** Portugal 40.01N 7.18W
115 Q7 **Cedral** Quintana Roo **Mexico** 20.18N 86.59W
115 J6 **Cedral** San Luis Potosí **Mexico** 23.50N 100.42W
75 J7 **Cedrillas** Spain 40.26N 0.52W
81 D3 **Cedrino** *R* Sardinia
117 G8 **Cedro** Brazil 6.34S 39.03W
75 D8 **Cedrón, A** *R* Spain
96 P3 **Cedros** Azores 38.38N 28.42W
115 L2 **Cedros** Honduras 14.38N 87.06W
115 E4 **Cedros** Sonora **Mexico** 27.42N 109.19W
115 J5 **Cedros** Zacatecas **Mexico** 24.42N 101.48W
115 B3 **Cedros** *I* Mexico
116 N2 **Cedros Pt** Trinidad & Tobago 10.07N 61.49W
12 C4 **Ceduna** S Australia 32.07S 133.42E
63 U7 **Cedynia** Poland 52.52N 14.15E
76 A3 **Cee** Spain 42.57N 9.11W
81 H7 **Cefalù** Sicily 38.03N 14.03E
69 H7 **Ceffonds** France 48.28N 4.46E
76 K6 **Cega** *R* Spain
79 N3 **Céggia** Italy 45.41N 12.38E
62 M8 **Cegléd** Hungary 47.10N 19.47E
81 Q11 **Ceglie Messapico** Italy 40.39N 17.31E
77 N4 **Cehegín** Spain 38.06N 1.48W
23 D6 **Ceheng** Guizhou **China** 24.58N 105.51E
90 K6 **Cehep** Chad 11.15N 20.31E
82 H3 **Cehu Silvaniei** Romania 47.24N 23.12E
105 K7 **Ceiba** Puerto Rico 18.16N 65.40W
82 G4 **Ceica** Romania 46.53N 22.10E
76 E8 **Ceife** *R* Portugal
71 C9 **Ceilhes-et-Rocozels** France 43.48N 3.07E
76 J4 **Ceinos** Spain 42.02N 5.09W
69 L6 **Ceintrey** France 48.31N 6.10E
76 C8 **Ceira** Portugal 40.11N 8.28W
76 B9 **Çeissa** Portugal 39.40N 8.31W
65 P4 **Čejc** Czechoslovakia 48.57N 16.57E
65 M3 **Čejle Kostelec** Czechoslovakia 49.22N 15.30E
77 D5 **Cejo** *mt* Spain 37.33N 6.24W
36 H2 **Çekerek** Turkey 40.04N 35.30E
36 H2 **Çekerek** *R* Turkey
76 C7 **Cela** Portugal 40.55N 8.12W
76 H7 **Celadas** Spain 40.29N 1.09W
37 C6 **Celâlh** Turkey 39.44N 37.26E
80 J4 **Celano** Italy 42.06N 13.33E
76 D4 **Celanova** Spain 42.09N 7.58W
115 J7 **Celaya** Mexico 20.32N 100.48W
59 J5 **Celbridge** Kildare **Irish Rep** 53.20N 6.32W
72 H6 **Célé** *R* France
Celebes *see* **Sulawesi**
36 G3 **Celebi** Turkey 39.28N 33.32E
77 E8 **Celemin, Embalse de** *res* Spain
120 A2 **Celendin** Peru 6.53S 78.09W
80 L5 **Celenza sul Trigno** Italy 41.52N 14.35E
80 L5 **Celenza Val Fortore** Italy 41.33N 14.59E
66 Q5 **Celerina** Switzerland 46.31N 9.52E
112 L2 **Celeste** Texas 33.18N 96.13W
115 O7 **Celestún** Mexico 20.50N 90.22W
119 B10 **Celica** Ecuador 4.09S 79.58W
81 M5 **Celico** Italy 39.18N 16.21E
66 A6 **Celigny** Switzerland 46.22N 6.13E
37 D7 **Celıkân** Turkey 38.04N 38.18E
104 A6 **Celina** Ohio 40.34N 84.35W
107 L5 **Celina** Tennessee 36.32N 85.30W
112 L2 **Celina** Texas 33.20N 96.48W
80 E8 **Celio, Monte** *hill* Roma **Italy**
82 C4 **Celje** Yugoslavia 46.15N 15.16E
75 H7 **Cella** Spain 40.27N 1.18W
58 D2 **Cellar Hd** Lewis, W Isles **Scotland** 58.25N 6.11W
62 K8 **Celldömölk** Hungary 47.16N 17.10E
62 M7 **Celle** W Germany 52.37N 10.05E
79 B6 **Celle di Macra** Italy 44.28N 7.11E
79 F3 **Celleno** Italy 42.34N 12.08E
80 E3 **Céllere** Italy 42.30N 11.46E
72 H10 **Celles** Ariège France 42.55N 1.40E
61 D4 **Celles** Hainaut **Belgium** 50.42N 3.28E
61 L4 **Celles** Liège **Belgium** 50.39N 5.15E
61 L6 **Celles** Namur **Belgium** 50.13N 5.00E
72 F1 **Celle-St.Avant,la** France 47.02N 0.36E
72 D3 **Celles-sur-Belle** France 46.16N 0.13W
69 G7 **Celles-sur-Ource** Aube France 48.05N 4.25E
70 N6 **Cellettes** France 47.32N 1.23E
79 N2 **Cellina** *R* Italy
80 J3 **Cellino Attanasio** Italy 42.35N 13.52E
72 G2 **Celon** France 46.31N 1.30E
80 M6 **Celone** *R* Italy
76 E7 **Celorico da Beira** Portugal 40.38N 7.24W
76 C6 **Celorico de Basto** Portugal 41.23N 8.00W
37 E5 **Çeltikçi** Turkey 37.33N 30.28E
57 E6 **Cemaes** Gwynedd **Wales** 53.24N 4.27W
37 F6 **Cemal Dağı** *mt* Turkey 39.33N 40.33E
18 L5 **Cemaru, Gunung** *mt* Borneo **Indon** 1.15N 114.05E
79 K2 **Cembra** Italy 46.11N 11.14E
109 M7 **Cement** Oklahoma 34.56N 98.08W
106 K7 **Cement City** Michigan 42.03N 84.18W
103 G2 **Cementon** New York 42.08N 73.55W
103 C5 **Cementon** Pennsylvania 40.42N 75.31W
82 F7 **Čemerna Pl** *mts* Yugoslavia
82 D6 **Čemernica** *mts* Yugoslavia
82 E7 **Čemerno** Yugoslavia 43.15N 18.35E
36 H2 **Cemilbey** Turkey 40.22N 35.03E
36 D6 **Çemişgezek** Turkey 39.04N 38.56E
56 B3 **Cemmaes Hd** Dyfed **Wales** 52.07N 4.44W
56 D2 **Cemmaes Road** Powys **Wales** 52.37N 3.44W
18 N10 **Cempi, Teluk** *B* Indonesia
115 L8 **Cempoala Pyramids** *ruins* **Mexico** 19.28N 96.20W
77 N4 **Cenajo, Embalse del** *res* **Spain** 38.54N 1.50W
79 L2 **Cencenighe** Italy 46.22N 11.58E
87 F7 **Cencia** Ethiopia 6.18N 37.37E
37 E6 **Cenciğe** Turkey 39.34N 39.39E
15 B4 **Cendrawasih** *pen* Irian Jaya
15 C5 **Cendrawasih, Teluk** *B* Irian Jaya
72 F6 **Cendrieux** France 45.00N 0.50E
37 D1 **Çene** *R* Turkey
36 G4 **Çeneközü** *R* Turkey
120 A1 **Cenepa,R** Peru
37 K2 **Çengelköy** Turkey 41.03N 29.07E
37 D6 **Çengelli Dağ** *mt* Turkey 39.39N 38.13E
37 D6 **Çengerli** Turkey 39.50N 38.51E
75 M6 **Cenia** *R* Spain
75 E3 **Cenicero** Spain 42.29N 2.38W
76 L8 **Cenicientos** Spain 40.15N 4.28W
77 N2 **Cenizate** Spain 39.19N 1.40W
76 C4 **Cenlle** Spain 42.20N 8.05W
37 H6 **Cennetabat** Turkey 39.59N 44.10E
79 G5 **Ceno** *R* Italy
72 C6 **Cenon** France 44.51N 0.33W
96 S5 **Cenouras** *isld* Madeira Is 33.07N 16.18W
19 A5 **Cenrana** Celebes Indon 3.17S 118.53E
79 C5 **Centallo** Italy 44.30N 7.35E
75 P4 **Centellas** Spain 41.48N 2.14E
118 D8 **Centenario do Sul** Brazil 22.48S 51.36W
105 H3 **Centenary** S Carolina 34.03N 79.22W
92 E10 **Centenary** Zimbabwe 16.44S 31.11E
77 J4 **Centenillo** Spain 38.20N 3.45W
108 D8 **Centennial** Wyoming 41.18N 106.09W
111 L8 **Centennial Wash** *R* Arizona
108 D4 **Center** Colorado 37.45N 106.07W
107 E2 **Center** Missouri 39.30N 91.33W
107 J2 **Center** N Dakota 47.08N 101.19W
111 N4 **Center** Texas 31.49N 94.10W
103 E6 **Center Bridge** Pennsylvania 40.23N 74.58W
104 C6 **Centerburg** Ohio 40.19N 82.41W
104 S4 **Center City** Minnesota 45.25N 92.48W
104 J9 **Center Cross** Virginia 37.48N 76.48W
103 L3 **Centerdale** Rhode I 41.53N 71.30W
105 E9 **Center Hill** Florida 28.40N 82.00W
107 L5 **Center Hill Res** Tennessee
122 V7 **Center L** Palmyra I **Pacific Oc**
103 B2 **Center Lisle** New York 42.21N 76.05W
103 C4 **Center Moreland** Pennsylvania 41.25N 75.55W
103 J5 **Center Moriches** Long I, N Y 40.48N 72.47W
103 O3 **Center Ossipee** New Hampshire 43.46N 71.10W
112 H6 **Center Point** Texas 29.56N 99.04W
103 D6 **Center Square** Pennsylvania 40.10N 75.17W
103 D7 **Centerton** New Jersey 39.32N 75.10W
103 D5 **Center Valley** Pennsylvania 40.32N 75.23W
103 C2 **Center Village** New York 42.10N 75.37W
111 J9 **Centerville** Alabama 32.57N 87.08W
108 S9 **Centerville** Iowa 40.47N 92.51W
107 E12 **Centerville** Louisiana 29.44N 91.27W
104 F6 **Centerville** Pennsylvania 40.04N 79.59W
108 O6 **Centerville** S Dakota 43.07N 96.56W
107 J6 **Centerville** Tennessee 35.45N 87.29W
112 M4 **Centerville** Texas 31.17N 95.59W
110 O9 **Centerville** Utah 40.56N 111.54W
110 E4 **Centerville** Washington 45.45N 120.56W
115 H3 **Centinela,Picacho del** *pk* Mexico 29.05N 102.34W
79 K5 **Cento** Italy 44.43N 11.17E

79 G6 **Cento Croci, Passo di** *pass* Italy 44.25N 9.37E
81 K3 **Centola** Italy 40.04N 15.19E
66 L7 **Centovalli** *V* Switzerland
109 O7 **Centrahoma** Oklahoma 34.37N 96.20W
113 P4 **Central** Alaska 65.34N 144.54W
118 G2 **Central** Brazil 11.00S 42.15W
120 D10 **Central** Chile 22.06S 70.00W
109 B9 **Central** New Mexico 32.47N 108.09W
103 B4 **Central** Pennsylvania 41.18N 76.21W
105 E3 **Central** S Carolina 34.44N 82.48W
111 L4 **Central** Utah 37.26N 113.38W
118 B9 **Central** *dept* Paraguay
94 H3 **Central** *dist* Botswana
93 H6 **Central** *prov* Kenya
92 F8 **Central** *prov* Malawi
26 S7 **Central** *prov* Sri Lanka
92 D9 **Central** *prov* Zambia
89 J9 **Central** *reg* Ghana
58 H6 **Central** *reg* Scotland
73 F5 **Central African Empire** Equat Africa
102 H8 **Central America** *reg* America
11 J3 **Central Auckland** *stat area* New Zealand
31 D6 **Central Brahui Ra** Pakistan
100 L8 **Central Butte** Saskatchewan 50.50N 106.30W
109 E2 **Central City** Colorado 39.48N 105.31W
106 C7 **Central City** Iowa 42.12N 91.32W
107 J4 **Central City** Kentucky 37.17N 87.08W
108 M8 **Central City** Nebraska 41.08N 98.00W
104 G6 **Central City** Pennsylvania 40.05N 78.47W
106 C7 **Central City Res** Iowa
120 F8 **Central,Cord** *mts* Bolivia
119 C7 **Central,Cord** *mts* Colombia
116 J5 **Central,Cord** *mts* Dominican Rep
19 K3 **Central,Cord** *mts* Luzon **Philippines**
120 A1 **Central,Cord** *mts* Peru
66 L5 **Centrale,Pizzo** *mt* Switzerland 46.34N 8.37E
103 M3 **Central Falls** Rhode I 41.53N 71.24W
93 H2 **Central I** Kenya 3.29N 36.02E
107 G3 **Centralia** Illinois 38.32N 89.08W
109 O2 **Centralia** Kansas 39.43N 96.09W
107 D2 **Centralia** Missouri 39.12N 92.08W
99 J9 **Centralia** Ontario 43.17N 81.29W
110 C3 **Centralia** Washington 46.43N 122.58W
104 E8 **Centralia** W Virginia 38.35N 80.36W
103 H5 **Central Islip** Long I, N Y 40.47N 73.43W
94 G4 **Central Kalahari Game Reserve** Botswana
106 J4 **Central Lake** Michigan 45.05N 85.17W
31 B7 **Central Makran Ra** Pakistan
13 C5 **Central Mt. Stewart** N Terr Aust
110 C7 **Central Point** Oregon 42.23N 122.57W
95 M5 **Central Ra** Lesotho
15 G6 **Central Range** *mts* Papua New Guinea
104 J3 **Central Square** New York 43.18N 76.10W
110 C9 **Central Valley** California 40.42N 122.24W
103 F4 **Central Valley** New York 41.20N 74.07W
103 L3 **Central Village** Connecticut 41.44N 71.54W
107 L7 **Centre** Alabama 34.10N 85.41W
89 K7 **Centre** *dept* Benin
89 G8 **Centre** *dept* Ivory Coast
26 V12 **Centre de Flacq** Mauritius, Indian Oc 20.12S 57.43E
11 B13 **Centre Island** New Zealand 46.27S 167.54E
89 F8 **Centre-Ouest** *dept* Ivory Coast
90 E9 **Centre-Sud** *reg* Cameroon
103 B8 **Centreville** Maryland 39.03N 76.04W
103 O3 **Centreville** Massachusetts 41.38N 70.21W
106 J8 **Centreville** Michigan 41.57N 85.32W
107 E10 **Centreville** Mississippi 31.05N 91.05W
98 E7 **Centreville** New Brunswick 46.26N 67.42W
98 F9 **Centreville** Nova Scotia 44.32N 66.02W
118 K9 **Centro** Brazil 22.54S 43.07W
75 O8 **Centro** *dist* Madrid **Spain**
81 J8 **Centuripe** Sicily 37.37N 14.44E
107 J11 **Century** Florida 30.59N 87.18W
104 E7 **Century** W Virginia 39.06N 80.13W
23 D6 **Cenwanglao Shan** *mt* Guangxi **China**
23 E7 **Cenxi** Guangxi **China** 22.57N 110.57E
80 K4 **Cepagatti** Italy 42.22N 14.05E
76 G8 **Cepeda** Spain 40.28N 6.03W
76 J8 **Cepeda la Mora** Spain 40.27N 5.04W
71 H10 **Cépet,C** France 43.04N 5.57E
Cephalonia *isld see* **Kefallinía**
79 P2 **Čepovan** Yugoslavia 46.03N 13.47E
79 C7 **Ceppo,Monte** Italy 43.57N 7.45E
66 J8 **Ceppomorelli** Italy 45.58N 8.05E
80 J5 **Ceprano** Italy 41.33N 13.32E
18 J9 **Cepu** Java Indon 7.07S 111.35E
Ceram *see* **Seram** *isld*
81 J8 **Cerami** Sicily 37.48N 14.31E
81 J8 **Cerami** *R* Sicily
17 L12 **Ceram Sea** Indonesia
79 E4 **Cerano** Italy 45.25N 8.46E
70 L6 **Cérans-Foulletourte** France 47.50N 0.05E
81 K3 **Ceraso** Italy 40.11N 15.15E
81 D2 **Ceraso,C** Sardinia 40.56N 9.39E
119 F4 **Cerbatana, Sa. de la** *mt* Venezuela 6.39N 66.25W
111 K6 **Cerbat Mts** Arizona
72 L11 **Cerbère** France 42.26N 3.10E
67 P13 **Cerbicales, Is** Corsica 41.33N 9.22E
75 L6 **Cerbol** *R* Spain
80 C3 **Cerboli** *isld* Italy 42.52N 10.33E
76 B10 **Cercal** Portugal 39.14N 8.59W
76 B13 **Cercal** Portugal 37.48N 8.40W
75 D2 **Cerca,La** Spain 42.59N 3.25W
76 B13 **Cercal, Sa do** *mts* Portugal
65 L2 **Čerčany** Czechoslovakia 49.51N 14.43E
76 C2 **Cerceda** Spain 43.11N 8.28W
76 L7 **Cercedilla** Spain 40.44N 4.04W
79 C5 **Cercenasco** Italy 44.52N 7.30E
81 M4 **Cerchiara di Calábria** Italy 39.52N 16.23E
64 O5 **Cerchov** *mt* Czechoslovakia 49.23N 12.47E
79 N1 **Cercivento** Italy 46.32N 12.58E
70 O6 **Cercottes** France 47.59N 1.53E
72 D5 **Cercoux** France 45.07N 0.14W
71 D3 **Cercy-la-Tour** France 46.52N 3.38E
81 G8 **Cerda** Sicily 37.54N 13.49E
77 P2 **Cerdá** Spain 38.59N 0.35W
75 O3 **Cerdaña,La** *reg* Spain
76 C3 **Cerdedo** Spain 42.32N 8.23W
76 D8 **Cerdeira** Portugal 40.15N 7.56W
76 E7 **Cerdeira** Portugal 40.31N 7.02W
76 C1 **Cerdido** Spain 43.37N 8.00W
71 G4 **Cerdon** Ain France 46.05N 5.28E
71 A1 **Cerdon** Loiret France 47.38N 2.22E
72 K6 **Cère** *R* France
79 K4 **Cerea** Italy 45.12N 11.13E
100 G7 **Cereal** Alberta 51.25N 110.50W
121 D6 **Cereales** Argentina 36.50S 63.32W
76 J5 **Cerecinos de Campos** Spain 41.54N 5.29W
79 L4 **Ceregnano** Italy 45.03N 11.53E
76 F6 **Cerejais** Portugal 41.17N 6.55W
72 G1 **Ceré-la-Ronde** France 47.15N 1.12E
18 H9 **Cereme, Gunung** *mt* Java Indonesia 6.55S 108.25E
70 H4 **Cérences** France 48.55N 1.26W
81 N5 **Cerenzia** Italy 39.14N 16.47E
121 E2 **Ceres** Argentina 29.55S 61.55W
118 E4 **Ceres** Brazil 15.21S 49.34W
111 D4 **Ceres** California 37.36N 120.58W
58 L6 **Ceres** Fife **Scotland** 56.18N 2.59W
79 B4 **Ceres** Italy 45.19N 7.22E
104 G4 **Ceres** New York 42.01N 78.16W
95 C9 **Ceres** S Africa 33.23S 19.19E
80 H3 **Ceresa,Monte** Italy 42.48N 13.21E
79 J4 **Ceresara** Italy 45.16N 10.33E
79 C5 **Ceresole Alba** Italy 44.48N 7.49E
79 B4 **Ceresole Reale** Italy 45.26N 7.13E
71 H9 **Céreste** France 43.51N 5.35E
72 K11 **Céret** France 42.30N 2.44E
119 C3 **Cereté** Colombia 8.54N 75.51W
76 G5 **Cerezal de Aliste** Spain 41.35N 6.03W
76 G8 **Cerezo** Spain 40.14N 6.14W
75 C5 **Cerezo de Abajo** Spain 41.13N 3.35W
75 D3 **Cerezo de Riotirón** Spain 42.29N 3.08W
26 S14 **Cerf I** Mahé I Seychelles, Ind Oc 4.38S 55.30E
99 P6 **Cerf,L.du** Quebec
61 H6 **Cerfontaine** Belgium 50.10N 4.25E
26 V12 **Cerfs,Is.aux** Mauritius, Indian Oc 20.16S 57.47E
79 E4 **Cergnago** Italy 45.12N 8.46E
69 C5 **Cergy-Pontoise** France 49.03N 2.05E
65 M1 **Cerhenice** Czechoslovakia 50.05N 15.04E
79 D6 **Ceriale** Italy 44.06N 8.13E
79 C7 **Ceriana** Italy 43.53N 7.46E
80 N6 **Cerignola** Italy 41.16N 15.54E
Cerigo *isld see* **Kíthira**
72 K2 **Cérilly** France 46.37N 2.49E
81 M5 **Cerisano** Italy 39.16N 16.11E
69 F7 **Cerisiers** France 48.08N 3.30E
70 J3 **Cerisy-la Forêt** France 49.11N 0.56W
70 H3 **Cerisy-la-Salle** France 49.01N 1.17W
72 C2 **Cérizay** France 46.49N 0.40W
36 F2 **Çerkeş** Turkey 40.49N 32.52E
36 C1 **Çerkesköy** Turkey 41.17N 28.00E
82 B5 **Cerknica** Yugoslavia 45.47N 14.20E
82 G4 **Cermei** Romania 46.33N 21.51E
37 D8 **Cermelek** *R* Turkey
80 J3 **Cermignano** Italy 42.36N 13.47E
37 E7 **Çermik** Turkey 38.09N 39.27E
82 L5 **Cerna** Romania 45.06N 28.18E
82 H5 **Cerna** *R* Romania
82 J6 **Cerna** *R* Romania
76 C8 **Cernache** Portugal 40.08N 8.29W
65 P3 **Černá Hora** *mt* Czechoslovakia 49.25N 16.36E
82 L6 **Cernavodă** Romania 44.20N 28.03E
65 K4 **Černá v Pošumaví** Czechoslovakia 48.44N 14.05E
69 N8 **Cernay** France 47.49N 7.11E
69 H5 **Cernay-en-Dormois** France 49.13N 4.47E
56 G6 **Cerne Abbas** Dorset **England** 50.49N 2.29W
75 C2 **Cernégula** Spain 42.38N 3.37W
66 D3 **Cernier** Switzerland 47.04N 6.55E

82 D5 **Cernik** Yugoslavia 45.17N 17.22E
79 F3 **Çernóbbio** Italy 45.50N 9.05E
64 O4 **Černošín** Czechoslovakia 49.50N 12.53E
65 L3 **Černovice** Czechoslovakia 49.23N 14.58E
75 K6 **Cerollera** Spain 40.50N 0.04W
72 J7 **Cérou** *R* France
61 J4 **Céroux-Mousty** Belgium 50.39N 4.31E
118 F10 **Cerquiera César** *dist* São Paulo **Brazil**
76 F7 **Cerralbo** Spain 40.58N 6.35W
115 K4 **Cerralvo** Mexico 26.10N 99.40W
115 E5 **Cerralvo** *I* Mexico
37 G8 **Cerran Dağları** *mts* Turkey
76 L5 **Cerrato,Valles de** Spain
80 G2 **Cerreto d'Esi** Italy 43.18N 13.00E
80 G3 **Cerreto di Spoleta** Italy 42.49N 12.55E
79 J7 **Cerreto Guidi** Italy 43.46N 10.53E
79 H6 **Cerreto,Passo del** *pass* Italy 44.18N 10.13E
80 L6 **Cerreto Sannita** Italy 41.17N 14.34E
57 F6 **Cerrig-y Druidion** Clwyd **Wales** 53.02N 3.33W
83 D3 **Cerrik** Albania 41.01N 20.02E
120 F11 **Cerrillos** Argentina 24.55S 65.30W
109 D6 **Cerrillos** New Mexico 35.27N 106.07W
119 C6 **Cerrito** Colombia 3.45N 76.16W
115 J6 **Cerritos** Mexico 22.27N 100.19W
118 E9 **Cêrro Azul** Brazil 24.48S 49.14W
120 B5 **Cerro Azul** Peru 13.05S 76.29W
121 G4 **Cerro Chato** Uruguay 33.04S 55.08W
77 C5 **Cerro de Andévalo, El** Spain 37.45N 6.57W
77 E5 **Cerro del Hierro,El** Spain 37.58N 5.35W
120 B4 **Cerro de Pasco** Peru 10.43S 76.15W
105 J7 **Cerro de Punta** *mts* Puerto Rico
76 H8 **Cerro,El** Spain 40.20N 5.55W
107 H2 **Cerro Gordo** Illinois 39.53N 88.43W
118 C10 **Cerro Largo** Brazil 28.10S 54.43W
121 G4 **Cerro Largo** *dept* Uruguay
121 K9 **Cerro Manantiales** Chile 52.35S 69.23W
77 K7 **Cerrón** *mt* Granada **Spain** 36.50N 3.06W
77 M5 **Cerrón** *mt* Murcia **Spain** 37.51N 2.28W
119 E2 **Cerrón Cerro** *mt* Venezuela 10.21N 70.40W
120 D10 **Cerro Negro** Chile 23.55S 69.32W
115 F4 **Cerro Prieto** Mexico 26.23N 106.14W
121 C7 **Cerros Colorados, Embalse** *res* Argentina
72 D1 **Cersay** France 47.03N 0.20W
79 K7 **Certaldo** Italy 43.33N 11.03E
79 C6 **Certosa di Pesio** Italy 44.14N 7.40E
79 F4 **Certoza di Pavia** Italy 45.16N 9.09E
76 E3 **Cervantes** Spain 42.52N 7.04W
121 J8 **Cervantes,Cerro** *pk* Argentina 50.33S 73.08W
14 B9 **Cervantes I** W Australia 30.33S 115.02E
80 J6 **Cervaro** Italy 41.28N 13.54E
80 N6 **Cervaro** *R* Italy
66 K8 **Cervarolo** Italy 45.51N 8.16E
80 N6 **Cervaro, Staz. di** *sta* Italy 41.22N 15.34E
81 K3 **Cervati,Monte** Italy 40.17N 15.29E
76 K4 **Cervatos de la Cueza** Spain 42.17N 4.45W
66 J8 **Cervatto** Italy 45.53N 8.10E
79 H5 **Çervellino,Monte** Italy 44.31N 10.04E
65 M2 **Červená Řečice** Czechoslovakia 49.31N 15.11E
65 M2 **Červené Janovice** Czechoslovakia 49.51N 15.17E
65 P1 **Červené Voda** Czechoslovakia 50.03N 16.45E
75 N4 **Cervera** Spain 41.40N 1.16E
77 P4 **Cervera,C** Spain 30.01N 0.38W
75 F8 **Cervera del Llano** Spain 39.47N 2.26W
75 L7 **Cervera del Maestre** Spain 40.27N 0.16E
76 K8 **Cervera de los Montes** Spain 40.03N 4.49W
75 G3 **Cervera del Rio Alhama** Spain 42.00N 1.58W
76 L3 **Cervera de Pisuerga** Spain 42.51N 4.30W
79 C5 **Cervere** Italy 44.38N 7.47E
80 F5 **Cerveteri** Italy 41.59N 12.06E
79 M6 **Cérvia** Italy 44.16N 12.21E
80 M7 **Cervialto, Monte** Italy 40.47N 15.08E
79 O3 **Cervignano del Friuli** Italy 45.49N 13.20E
79 K1 **Cervina,Pta** *mt* Italy 46.44N 11.17E
80 L6 **Cervinara** Italy 41.02N 14.36E
Cervinia *see* **Breuil-Cervínia**
Cervin, Mt *see* **Matterhorn** *mt*
Cervino, Mt *see* **Matterhorn** *mt*
67 P12 **Cervione** Corsica 42.40N 9.28E
79 D7 **Cervo** Italy 43.56N 8.07E
76 E1 **Cervo** Spain 43.40N 7.24W
79 D3 **Cervo** *R* Italy
71 D2 **Cervon** France 47.14N 3.45E
81 M4 **Cerzeto** Italy 39.31N 16.08E
79 A5 **Cesana Torinese** Italy 44.57N 6.48E
79 E8 **Cesano Boscone** *dist* Milan **Italy**
119 D3 **Cesar** *div* Colombia
66 K8 **Cesara** Italy 45.50N 8.22E
66 B9 **Cesarches** France 45.42N 6.25E
81 J8 **Cesarò** Sicily 37.51N 14.43E
119 D2 **César,R** Colombia
79 M6 **Cesena** Italy 44.09N 12.15E
79 M6 **Cesenatico** Italy 44.12N 12.24E
79 M3 **Cesen,Monte** Italy 45.57N 12.01E
66 N7 **Cesero, Campo d** *mt* Switzerland 46.11N 9.10E
79 C6 **Césio** Italy 44.01N 7.58E
79 L2 **Cesio Maggiore** Italy 46.05N 11.58E
36 J4 **Çeşir** *R* Turkey
46 F2 **Cēsis** Latvia **U.S.S.R.** 57.18N 25.18E
65 N2 **Česká Bělá** Czechoslovakia 49.39N 15.42E
64 O5 **Česká Kubice** Czechoslovakia 49.21N 12.52E
62 H5 **Česká Lípa** Czechoslovakia 50.43N 14.35E
65 O2 **Česká Třebová** Czechoslovakia 49.54N 16.27E
65 K4 **České Budějovice** Czechoslovakia 48.58N 14.29E
65 L4 **České Velenice** Czechoslovakia 48.47N 14.58E
62 H6 **České Zemé** *rep* Czechoslovakia
65 N3 **Českomoravská** *reg* Czechoslovakia
65 P1 **Český Bohdikov** Czechoslovakia 50.02N 16.55E
65 L1 **Český Brod** Czechoslovakia 50.05N 14.52E
65 K4 **Český Krumlov** Czechoslovakia 48.48N 14.18E
64 O4 **Česky Les Šumava** *mts* Czechoslovakia
62 L6 **Český Těšín** Czechoslovakia 49.44N 18.33E
36 B4 **Çeşme** Turkey 38.19N 26.20E
37 E1 **Çeşmeli** Turkey 41.03N 27.50E
65 K3 **Češnovice** Czechoslovakia 49.02N 14.22E
76 H7 **Cespedosa** Spain 40.32N 5.35W
89 E9 **Cess** *R* Liberia
71 B10 **Cesse** *R* France
71 C10 **Cessenon** France 43.27N 3.03E
100 F7 **Cessford** Alberta 51.04N 111.34W
12 K5 **Cessnock** New S Wales 32.51S 151.21E
69 D6 **Cesson** France 48.33N 2.37E
65 J3 **Cestice** Czechoslovakia 49.11N 13.47E
75 F1 **Cestona** Spain 43.15N 2.15W
89 E9 **Cestos Pt** Liberia 5.25N 9.35W
76 C2 **Cesuras** Spain 43.10N 8.12W
82 H6 **Cetate** Romania 44.06N 23.01E
75 G5 **Cetina** Spain 41.18N 1.58W
82 D7 **Cetina** *R* Yugoslavia
82 E8 **Cetinje** Yugoslavia 42.25N 18.56E
37 D6 **Çetinkaya** Turkey 39.11N 37.36E
36 E5 **Çetmi** Turkey 37.27N 31.28E
79 H2 **Ceto** Italy 46.00N 10.21E
70 M5 **Ceton** France 48.13N 0.45E
80 E3 **Cetona** Italy 42.58N 11.54E
81 L4 **Cetraro** Italy 39.32N 15.57E
72 C10 **Cette Eygun** France 42.56N 0.35W
19 L1 **Cetti B** Guam **Pacific Oc**
65 L4 **Cetviny** Czechoslovakia 48.37N 14.33E
71 H7 **Ceuse,Pic de** France 44.30N 5.57E
77 F9 **Ceuta** *exclave* Spain 35.53N 5.19W
77 O4 **Ceuti** Spain 38.05N 1.15W
79 D6 **Ceva** Italy 44.23N 8.02E
79 J2 **Cevedale** *mt* Italy 46.26N 10.37E
71 C9 **Cevennes** *mts* France
76 L5 **Cevico de la Torre** Spain 41.51N 4.24W
76 L5 **Cevico Navero** Spain 41.52N 4.10W
71 J5 **Cevins** France 45.35N 6.28E
66 L6 **Cevio** Switzerland 46.19N 8.37E
36 F5 **Cevizli** Turkey 37.11N 31.45E
Cevizlik Trabzon Turkey *see* **Maçka**
37 G7 **Cevizlik** Turkey 38.09N 42.16E
36 H5 **Ceyhan** Turkey 37.02N 35.48E
36 H6 **Ceyhan** *R* Turkey
37 E9 **Ceylânpınar** Turkey 36.50N 40.02E
Ceylon *see* **Sri Lanka**
108 Q6 **Ceylon** Minnesota 43.33N 94.38W
100 N9 **Ceylon** Saskatchewan 49.30N 104.37W
71 H10 **Ceyreste** France 43.13N 5.37E
71 G4 **Ceyzériat** France 46.10N 5.20E
95 O9 **Ceza** S Africa 27.59S 31.23E
72 K5 **Cézallier, Monts** *mts* France
71 E8 **Cèze** *R* France
43 F8 **Chaacha** Turkmeniya **U.S.S.R.** 36.50N 60.30E
45 R3 **Chaadayevka** U.S.S.R. 53.08N 45.56E
42 E6 **Chaa-Khol'** U.S.S.R. 51.37N 92.31E
60 H13 **Chaam** Netherlands 51.30N 4.52E
88 P6 **Chaamba el Mouadhi** *tribe* Algeria
88 Q6 **Chaamba Guebala** *tribe* Algeria
92 J11 **Chaani** Zanzibar 5.57S 39.18E
Chaar,Jebel *mt see* **Sha'ar, Jebel** *mt*
87 F4 **Chaba** Ethiopia 12.20N 36.48E
72 F4 **Chabanais** France 45.52N 0.43E
121 E4 **Chabas** Argentina 33.16S 61.23W
40 F2 **Chabda** U.S.S.R. 59.50N 134.40E
71 H8 **Chabeston** France 44.28N 5.47E
71 G7 **Chabeuil** France 44.54N 5.02E
14 A6 **Chabjuwardoo B** W Australia
71 J4 **Chablais** *dist* France
115 O8 **Chablé** Mexico 17.52N 91.48W
66 E7 **Châble** Switzerland 46.05N 7.13E
69 F8 **Chablis** France 47.49N 3.48E
111 C9 **Chabot,L** California 37.44N 122.06W
88 P4 **Chabounia** Albania 35.32N 2.35E
72 F4 **Chabrac** France 45.56N 0.44E

71 D5 **Chabreloche** France 45.52N 3.42E
71 H8 **Chabre,Mtgne,de** France
71 J8 **Chabrières** France 44.00N 6.17E
72 H1 **Chabris** France 47.15N 1.38E
28 K2 **Chabua** Assam **India** 27.30N 95.09E
91 H10 **Chaca** Angola 12.24S 22.47E
120 D8 **Chaca** Chile 18.47S 70.10W
121 E5 **Chacabuco** Argentina 34.40S 60.27W
116 N1 **Chacachacare I** Trinidad & Tobago 10.41N 61.45W
115 L9 **Chacaltongo** Mexico 17.04N 97.37W
120 D10 **Chacance** Chile 22.27S 69.30W
121 A8 **Chacao,œCan de** Chile 41.50S 73.34W
120 E7 **Chacarilla** Bolivia 17.32S 68.14W
120 B9 **Chacarilla** *dist* Lima **Peru**
121 C6 **Chachahuen, Sa** *ra* Argentina
29 G5 **Chachai Falls** Madhya Prad **India** 24.44N 81.18E
120 D7 **Chachani,Nevada de** *pk* Peru 16.11S 71.31W
120 B2 **Chachapoyas** Peru 6.13S 77.54W
121 D6 **Chacharramendi** Argentina 37.20S 65.38W
25 F6 **Chachoengsao** Thailand 13.39N 101.03E
31 F6 **Chachran** Pakistan 28.50N 70.29E
31 F8 **Chachro** Pakistan 25.09N 70.18E
41 O9 **Chachygyy** U.S.S.R. 62.12N 131.42E
76 F6 **Chacim** Portugal 41.28N 6.54W
66 Q5 **Chaclavuot** Switzerland 46.39N 9.50E
118 A6 **Chaco** *dept* Paraguay
120 G11 **Chaco** *prov* Argentina
109 B5 **Chaco** *R* New Mexico
121 E1 **Chaco Austral** *reg* Argentina
118 B7 **Chaco Boreal** *plain* Paraguay
109 B5 **Chaco Canyon Nat. Mon** New Mexico
113 W9 **Chacon,C** Alaska 54.42N 132.00W
117 A8 **Chacorão,Cachoeira da** *falls* Brazil 6.20S 58.16W
120 C4 **Chacra de Piros** Peru 11.15S 72.36W
109 C6 **Chacra Mesa** *tableland* New Mexico
47 H7 **Chad** U.S.S.R. 56.30N 57.11E
73 F4 **Chad** *rep* Equat Africa
43 N7 **Chadak** Uzbekistan **U.S.S.R.** 40.58N 70.40E
42 E6 **Chadan** U.S.S.R. 51.20N 91.39E
105 J3 **Chadbourn** N Carolina 34.20N 78.51W
Chaddādi *see* **Shedadi**
56 G3 **Chaddesley Corbett** Hereford & Worcs England 52.22N 2.09W
96 A2 **Chaddock Bar** Bermuda 32.15N 64.55W
103 C7 **Chadds Ford** Pennsylvania 38.52N 75.35W
32 D4 **Chādegān** Iran 32.44N 50.39E
121 C6 **Chadileo, R** Argentina
Chadir *see* **Yeyungou**
92 F9 **Chadiza** Zambia 14.04S 32.27E
Chadka *see* **Shadhka**
90 F5 **Chad, L** Chad etc 13.20N 14.20E
42 F3 **Chadobets** U.S.S.R. 58.44N 98.54E
42 F3 **Chadobets** *R* U.S.S.R.
108 G7 **Chadron** Nebraska 42.50N 103.01W
106 E7 **Chadwick** Illinois 42.02N 89.55W
82 M4 **Chadyr Lunga** U.S.S.R. 46.03N 28.51E
25 E3 **Chae Hom** Thailand 18.40N 98.52E
21 C8 **Chaeryŏng** N Korea 38.20N 125.37E
74 F9 **Chafarinas, Islas** *islds* Spain 35.10N 2.24W
107 G4 **Chaffee** Missouri 37.10N 89.40W
104 G4 **Chaffee** New York 42.34N 78.29W
121 A10 **Chaffers,Is** Chile 44.15S 74.10W
66 B4 **Chaffois** France 46.55N 6.16E
119 D6 **Chafurray** Colombia 3.08N 73.12W
31 C6 **Chagai** Pakistan 29.20N 64.44E
31 B6 **Chagai** *dist* Pakistan
31 B6 **Chagai Hills** Pakistan
28 D3 **Chagalmurri** Andhra Prad **India** 15.00N 78.35E
46 Q4 **Chagan** *R* U.S.S.R.
42 D6 **Chagan-Uzun** U.S.S.R. 50.09N 88.15E
40 E2 **Chagda** U.S.S.R. 58.44N 130.38E
66 C1 **Chagey** France 47.37N 6.44E
56 D6 **Chagford** Devon **England** 50.41N 3.50W
92 H3 **Chagga** *tribe* Tanzania
Chaghadak *see* **Choghadāk**
32 D5 **Chaghā Khūr** Iran 31.55N 50.56E
31 C4 **Chaghaman** Afghanistan 33.10N 64.35E
Chāghir Bāzār *see* **Kagher Bazār**
43 J1 **Chaglinka** *R* Kazakhstan **U.S.S.R.**
71 F3 **Chagny** France 46.55N 4.45E
30 K3 **Chago** *mt* Nepal/Xizang Zizhiqu 27.57N 87.03E
46 K1 **Chagoda** U.S.S.R. 59.11N 35.15E
46 K1 **Chagodoshcha** *R* U.S.S.R.
27 L11 **Chagos Arch** Br Indian Oc Terr
45 U4 **Chagra** *R* U.S.S.R.
43 E4 **Chagrayskoye Plato** Kazakhstan **U.S.S.R.**
115 F10 **Chagres, R** Panama/Panama Canal Zone
104 D5 **Chagrin Falls** Ohio 41.25N 81.24W
116 O2 **Chaguanas** Trinidad & Tobago 10.31N 61.25W
116 O1 **Chaguaramas** Trinidad & Tobago 10.41N 61.38W
119 F3 **Chaguaramas** Venezuela 9.23N 66.18W
113 T9 **Chagulak I** Aleutian Is 52.35N 171.10W
43 D6 **Chagyl** Turkmeniya **U.S.S.R.** 40.46N 55.25E
43 J7 **Chagyr** Kirgiziya **U.S.S.R.** 39.45N 70.00E
24 G10 **Cha'gyüngoinba** Xizang Zizhiqu **China** 31.10N 90.42E
31 B5 **Chahah Burjak** Afghanistan 30.17N 62.06E
32 H4 **Chāhak** Iran 33.18N 58.55E
32 H4 **Chāh Akhvor** Iran 32.41N 59.40E
32 E5 **Chah'Ali** Iran 31.21N 52.51E
32 G3 **Chah'Ali Akbar** Iran 34.54N 57.07E
31 F3 **Chaharbagh** Afghanistan 34.32N 70.20E
31 D3 **Chahar Chashma** Afghanistan 35.49N 67.42E
32 H3 **Chahār Takāb** Iran 35.27N 59.55E
31 C3 **Chahartu** Afghanistan 35.48N 64.50E
Chah Asilu *see* **Chāh-e 'Asalū**
21 C3 **Chahayang** Heilongjiang **China** 48.25N 124.16E
Chahba *see* **Shahba**
32 F3 **Chāh Baba** Iran 35.55N 55.05E
32 E4 **Chāh Badam** Iran 33.56N 52.22E
Chah Bagh *see* **Chāh-e Bāgh**
32 J8 **Chāh Bahār** Iran 25.16N 60.14E
32 J8 **Chāh Bahār,Khalij-e** *B* Iran
Chah Bala Band *see* **Chāh-e Bālā Band**
32 J2 **Chahchaheh** Iran 36.35N 60.22E
32 F6 **Chāh Darāz** Iran 29.29N 54.02E
32 F5 **Chāh-e'Asalū** Iran 30.58N 54.02E
32 H4 **Chāh-e Bābā** Iran 32.49N 58.40E
32 F5 **Chāh-e Bāgh** Iran 30.17N 54.53E
32 H4 **Chāh-e Bālā Band** Iran 32.46N 58.10E
32 F6 **Chāh-e Bāzargānī** Iran 29.46N 54.42E
32 F5 **Chāh-e Dow Chāhi** Iran 31.03N 54.04E
32 F6 **Chāh-e Gaz** Iran 29.52N 55.28E
32 E4 **Chāh-e Gonbad** Iran 33.03N 53.57E
32 G3 **Chah-e Kavir** Iran 34.30N 56.50E
32 F3 **Chāh-e Khorāsān** Iran 34.32N 54.10E
32 G4 **Chāh-e Khoshāb** Iran 33.45N 57.50E
32 E4 **Chāh-e Malek** Esfahān Iran 33.25N 53.20E
32 H6 **Chāh-e Malek** Kermān Iran 28.36N 59.07E
32 F5 **Chāh-e Malek Mīrza** Iran 30.45N 54.15E
32 E4 **Chāh-e Mīrzā** Iran 33.42N 53.20E
32 F3 **Chāh-e Mūjān** Iran 34.01N 55.02E
32 E4 **Chāh-e Nūklok** Iran 33.34N 53.51E
32 F3 **Chāh-e Pansu** Iran 34.12N 55.02E
32 F6 **Chāh-e Qeysar** Iran 28.46N 55.50E
32 E3 **Chāh-e Qobād** Iran 34.10N 52.20E
32 F6 **Chāh-e Rāh** Iran 29.11N 55.18E
32 J5 **Chāh-e Raḥmān** Iran 30.30N 60.05E
31 A4 **Chah-e-Rig** Afghanistan 32.50N 61.05E
32 E3 **Chāh-e Shūr** Esfahān Iran 34.07N 52.45E
32 F4 **Chāh-e Shūr** Esfahān Iran 33.40N 55.24E
32 E5 **Chāh-e Tāqestān** Iran 31.25N 53.25E
32 H4 **Chāh-e Tūnī** Iran 32.53N 58.04E
Chah Gaz *see* **Chāh-e Gaz**
32 J6 **Chāh Gheybi,Hāmūn-e** *salt waste* Iran
Chāh Gūbād *see* **Chāh-e Qobād**
Chah Gumbaz *see* **Chāh-e Gonbad**
32 F3 **Chāh Haji Abdulla** Iran 35.36N 54.29E
Chah Haq *see* **Chāh Ḥaqq**
32 F6 **Chāh Ḥaqq** Iran 29.47N 54.16E
31 E2 **Chah-i-Ab** Afghanistan 37.30N 69.50E
Chah-i-Bazargani *see* **Chāh-e Bāzargānī**
31 B4 **Chah-i-Jahan** Afghanistan 33.08N 62.27E
Chah-i-Kisur *see* **Chāh-e Qeysar**
Chah-i-Malik *see* **Chāh-e Malek**
Chāh-i-Shūrak *see* **Qal'eh ye Shūrak**
Chah-i-Siah *see* **Chāleh Siāh**
32 A3 **Chah-i-Sirkh** Iraq 34.42N 45.37E
Chah Kavir *see* **Chāh-e Kavīr**
Chah Khurasan *see* **Chāh-e Khorāsān**
32 E5 **Chāh Kūh** Iran 31.54N 53.22E
Chah Malik *see* **Chāh-e Malek**
Chah Malik Mirza *see* **Chāh-e Malek Mīrza**
Chah Mirza *see* **Chāh-e Mīrzā**
Chah Mujun *see* **Chāh-e Mūjān**
32 F4 **Chāh Nigu** Iran 33.54N 54.09E
Chah Nukluk *see* **Chāh-e Nūklok**
21 D7 **Ch'aho** N Korea 40.11N 128.38E
Chah Pansu *see* **Chāh-e Pansu**
32 E4 **Chāh Pās** Iran 33.00N 53.22E
Chah Rahman *see* **Chāh-e-Raḥmān**
32 H5 **Chāh Ru'i** Iran 31.05N 59.40E
Chahrusehi *see* **Chāh Rūstā'ī**
32 D6 **Chāh Rūstā'ī** Iran 29.32N 50.45E
31 B6 **Chah Sandan** Pakistan 28.58N 63.28E
32 F3 **Chāh Shirin** Iran 35.22N 54.01E
Chah Shur *see* **Chāh-e Shūr**
Chah Shurgaz *see* **Shūr Gaz**
Chah Tuni *see* **Chāh-e Tūnī**
115 M9 **Chahuites** Mexico 16.20N 94.10W
32 E4 **Chāh Zangūl, Kūh-e** *mt* Iran 33.13N 52.50E
92 K7 **Chai** Mozambique 11.58S 40.10E
91 G7 **Chaiambo** Angola 7.58S 20.27E
25 F5 **Chai Badan** Thailand 15.08N 101.03E
Chaibasa *see* **Chaibassa**
29 J6 **Chaibassa** Bihar **India** 22.31N 85.50E
25 G3 **Chai Buri** Thailand 18.20N 103.38E
Chaigoubu *see* **Huai'an**

31 E8 **Chailar** Pakistan 24.58N 69.58E
72 G3 **Chaillac** France 46.26N 1.18E
70 J5 **Chailland** France 48.13N 0.52W
72 B3 **Chaillé lès Marais** France 46.25N 1.02W
72 B4 **Chaillevette** France 45.44N 1.03W
69 F7 **Chailley** France 48.05N 3.42E
71 J7 **Chaillol-le-Vieux** *mt* France 44.44N 6.12E
69 D7 **Chailly-en Bière** France 48.27N 2.37E
69 E6 **Chailly-en Brie** France 48.48N 3.08E
25 G7 **Chaine de l'Elephant** *ra* Cambodia
100 C8 **Chain Lakes Prov. Park** Alberta
30 G7 **Chainpur** Bihar **India** 25.02N 83.31E
30 E3 **Chainpur** Nepal 29.33N 81.12E
30 L5 **Chainpur** Nepal 27.18N 87.19E
69 G6 **Chaintrix-Bierges** France 48.54N 4.07E
119 D7 **Chaira,L.de** Colombia 1.15N 74.52W
61 K7 **Chairière** Belgium 49.52N 4.57E
71 D6 **Chaise-Dieu,la** France 45.19N 3.42E
25 F5 **Chai Si** *R* Thailand
Ch'ai-ta-mu P'en-ti *basin see* **Qaidam Pendi** *basin*
121 A9 **Chaitén** Chile 42.55S 72.43W
35 E1 **Chaïtîyè, Ech** Lebanon 33.12N 35.16E
30 K5 **Chaitya** Nepal 27.06N 86.53E
23 B9 **Chai Wan** Hong Kong 22.15N 114.14E
24 F4 **Chaiwopu** Xinjiang Uygur Zizhiqu **China** 43.32N 87.55E
25 E8 **Chaiya** Thailand 9.25N 99.13E
25 F5 **Chaiyaphum** Thailand 15.46N 101.55E
72 B2 **Chaize-le-Vicomte,la** France 46.40N 1.18W
121 D4 **Chaján** Argentina 33.33S 65.00W
Chajara,Ech *see* **Shajara,Esh**
121 F3 **Chajarí** Argentina 30.45S 57.55W
24 F9 **Chajing Tso** *L* Xizang Zizhiqu **China** 32.05N 87.20E
113 L6 **Chakachamna, L** Alaska 61.11N 152.40W
30 K8 **Chakai** Bihar **India** 24.34N 86.24E
31 G3 **Chakai** Pakistan 35.00N 72.57E
31 H4 **Chak Amru** Pakistan 32.23N 75.14E
30 H8 **Chakand** Bihar **India** 24.54N 84.59E
115 P8 **Chakantak** Mexico 19.10N 89.23W
92 D11 **Chakari** Zimbabwe 18.05S 29.51E
31 E6 **Chakar R** Pakistan
87 A6 **Chak Chak** Sudan 8.40N 26.50E
29 M2 **Chakdaha** W Bengal **India** 23.03N 88.32E
31 G3 **Chakdarra** Pakistan 34.40N 72.05E
92 J4 **Chake Chake** Pemba I **Indian Ocean** 5.12S 39.44E
Chakhab *see* **Shaqhab**
31 B5 **Chakhansur** Afghanistan 31.11N 62.02E
Chakhan-Tsulaotu *see* **Ch'a-han-ch'i-la-tu**
31 C3 **Chakhcharan** Afghanistan 34.28N 65.01E
30 J6 **Chakia** Bihar **India** 26.25N 85.03E
30 G7 **Chakia** Uttar Prad **India** 25.03N 83.13E
31 F2 **Chakir** Afghanistan 37.35N 70.32E
31 G5 **Chak Jhumra** Pakistan 31.33N 73.14E
30 E2 **Chakko** Xizang Zizhiqu 30.35N 81.50E
31 D7 **Chakku** Pakistan 27.48N 67.12E
24 E10 **Chaklam La** *pass* Xizang Zizhiqu **China** 31.44N 84.41E
31 H2 **Chakmaktin L** Afghanistan
24 G10 **Ch'a-k'o Shan-k'ou** *pass* Xizang Zizhiqu China 30.08N 91.18E
Chakra *see* **Shaqra**
29 J2 **Chakradharpur** Bihar **India** 22.42N 85.38E
30 A2 **Chakrata** Uttar Prad **India** 30.42N 77.52E
30 H2 **Chakri** *mt* Nepal 27.57N 86.48E
30 H2 **Chakri La** *pass* Nepal 27.58N 86.47E
29 K3 **Chakuha** Bihar **India** 22.29N 86.45E
44 D6 **Chakva** Georgia **U.S.S.R.** 41.45N 41.45E
31 G4 **Chakwal** Pakistan 32.56N 72.53E
92 G8 **Chala** Mozambique 13.39S 35.05E
120 C6 **Chala** Peru 15.51S 74.13W
92 E5 **Chala** Tanzania 7.38S 31.17E
92 E7 **Chalabesa** Zambia 11.30S 30.55E
72 J10 **Chalabre** France 42.59N 2.01E
37 H8 **Chalachor Dāgh** *mt* Iran 37.32N 44.40E
71 H3 **Chalain,L.de** France 46.40N 5.47E
72 E5 **Chalais** France 45.16N 0.03E
66 G6 **Chalais** Switzerland 46.16N 7.32E
71 G5 **Chalamont** France 46.00N 5.15E
31 H9 **Chalan Bil** *marsh* Bangladesh
31 C4 **Chalap Dalam** *mts* Afghanistan
120 C6 **Chala Pta** Peru 15.51S 74.26W
115 P10 **Chalatenango** El Salvador 14.04N 88.53W
92 J10 **Chalaua** Mozambique 16.05S 39.10E
25 E9 **Chalaung** Thailand 7.49N 98.21E
23 A1 **Chalaxung** Qinghai **China** 34.08N 97.44E
34 H6 **Chalb abū Muntar** *watercourse* Iraq
34 H6 **Chalb al Chiachi** Iraq
93 J2 **Chalbi Desert** Kenya
115 H6 **Chalchihuites** Mexico 23.30N 103.52W
115 P10 **Chalchuapa** El Salvador 14.00N 89.41W
115 K8 **Chalco** Mexico 19.18N 98.52W
42 K5 **Chaldonka** U.S.S.R. 53.50N 119.20E
56 J6 **Chale** I of Wight **England** 50.36N 1.19W
32 D4 **Chāleh Siāh** Iran 32.52N 51.25E
72 F4 **Chaleix** France 45.31N 0.57E
71 F7 **Chalençon** France 44.51N 4.35E
22 C7 **Chalengkou** Qinghai **China** 38.02N 93.54E
93 L10 **Chale Pt** Kenya 4.26S 39.32E
71 K6 **Chalets-de-Laval** France 45.02N 6.33E
69 D7 **Châlette-sur-Loing** France 48.01N 2.45E
98 G5 **Chaleurs, Baie des** Que/New Brunswick
56 K4 **Chalfont St.Giles** Bucks **England** 51.39N 0.35W
56 G4 **Chalford** Glos **England** 51.45N 2.09W
29 H6 **Chalgali** Madhya Prad **India** 23.20N 83.40E
120 C6 **Chalhuanca** Peru 14.17S 73.15W
121 K5 **Chalía, R** Argentina
121 K7 **Chalía, R** Argentina
87 E5 **Chali el Fil** Sudan 10.12N 34.03E
92 D7 **Chali, L** Zambia 11.45S 29.54E
72 K5 **Chalinargues** France 45.09N 2.54E
69 J8 **Chalindrey** France 47.48N 5.26E
23 F5 **Chaling** Hunan **China** 26.58N 113.31E
92 J5 **Chalinze** Tanzania 6.36S 38.22E
29 D7 **Chalisgaon** Maharashtra **India** 20.29N 75.10E
28 C5 **Chalisseri** Kerala **India** 10.53N 76.05E
72 K2 **Chalivoy-Milon** France 46.52N 2.42E
108 F4 **Chalk Buttes** Montana 45.36N 104.45W
Chalkedon *see* **Kadiköy**
112 K3 **Chalk Mountain** Texas 32.10N 97.54W
99 N6 **Chalk River** Ontario 46.01N 77.28W
43 N5 **Chalkudysu** Kazakhstan **U.S.S.R.** 42.54N 79.34E
11 A13 **Chalky I** New Zealand 46.04S 166.32E
11 A13 **Chalky Inlet** New Zealand
113 Q3 **Chalkyitsik** Alaska 66.38N 143.49W
121 C7 **Challacó** Argentina 38.56S 68.59W
120 D9 **Challacollo** Chile 20.58S 69.23W
70 H6 **Challain-la-Potherie** France 47.39N 1.03W
28 C3 **Challakere** Karnataka **India** 14.19N 76.40E
72 A2 **Challans** France 46.51N 1.52W
79 C3 **Challant St.Anselme** Italy 45.43N 7.44E
66 G8 **Challant,Valle di** Italy
120 E8 **Challapata** Bolivia 18.50S 66.45W
17 O9 **Challenger Deep** *trough* **Pacific Oc** 11.19N 142.15E
97 L1 **Challenger Mts** N W Terr
69 H5 **Challerange** France 49.18N 4.46E
110 L5 **Challis** Idaho 44.30N 114.15W
11 M13 **Challis** *dist* Dunedin **New Zealand**
57 D3 **Challoch** Dumfries & Galloway **Scotland** 54.58N 4.32W
71 D5 **Chalmazel** France 45.42N 3.53E
106 H9 **Chalmers** Indiana 40.39N 86.52W
107 G12 **Chalmette Nat.Hist.Park** Louisiana 29.55N 89.55W
47 D3 **Chal'mny Varre** U.S.S.R. 67.13N 37.40E
71 D3 **Chalmoux** France 46.36N 3.51E
31 H10 **Chalna** Bangladesh 22.38N 89.30E
47 C5 **Chalna** U.S.S.R. 61.51N 34.09E
70 J7 **Chalonnes** France 47.21N 0.45W
69 G6 **Châlons-sur-Marne** France 48.58N 4.22E
71 F3 **Chalon-sur-Saône** France 46.47N 4.51E
71 K1 **Châlonvillars-Mandrevillars** France 47.39N 6.47E
31 H2 **Chalt** Kashmir 36.13N 74.19E
45 L9 **Chaltyr'** U.S.S.R. 47.18N 39.30E
21 C6 **Chaluhe** Jilin **China** 43.42N 125.58E
Cha-lun *see* **Ts'o-k'o-cha**
72 F4 **Châlus** France 45.39N 0.59E
32 D2 **Chālūs** Iran 36.40N 51.25E
32 D2 **Chālūs,Rud-e** *R* Iran
Cha-lu-t'e-ch'i *see* **Jarud Qi**
120 E10 **Chalviri,Salar de** *salt pan* Bolivia
43 F6 **Chalysh** Uzbekistan **U.S.S.R.** 41.37N 60.44E
66 K3 **Cham** Switzerland 47.11N 8.28E
64 O5 **Cham** W Germany 49.13N 12.41E
64 O5 **Cham** *R* W Germany
109 E4 **Chama** Colorado 37.10N 105.23W
109 D5 **Chama** New Mexico 36.54N 106.36W
35 D1 **Chamaa** Lebanon 33.09N 35.13E
18 B6 **Chamah,Gunong** *mt* Pen Malaysia 5.13N 101.33E
121 D5 **Chamaico** Argentina 35.05S 65.05W
94 C6 **Chamais Bay** Namibia 27.56S 15.40E
94 D6 **Chamaites** Namibia 27.15S 17.52E
71 G7 **Chamaloc** France 44.48N 5.23E
31 D5 **Chaman** Pakistan 30.55N 66.27E
32 G2 **Chaman Bid** Iran 37.26N 56.38E
31 C3 **Chaman-i-Bed** Afghanistan 35.16N 64.01E
25 F6 **Chamao,Khao** *mt* Thailand 12.59N 101.42E
109 D5 **Chama,R** New Mexico
119 E3 **Chama,R** Venezuela
75 P6 **Chamartin** *dist* Madrid **Spain**
120 A2 **Chamaya** *R* Peru
29 E1 **Chamba** Himachal Prad **India** 32.33N 76.10E
92 H7 **Chamba** Tanzania 11.35S 37.00E
42 G2 **Chamba** U.S.S.R. 60.25N 102.02E
29 E1 **Chamba** *dist* Himachal Prad **India**
92 G4 **Chambalo** Tanzania 5.15S 36.00E
29 E5 **Chambal R** Madhya Prad/Rajasthan **India**
71 G6 **Chambarand,Plat de** France
116 E3 **Chambas** Cuba 22.12N 78.57W
72 H4 **Chamberet** France 45.35N 1.42E
75 P8 **Chamberí** *dist* Madrid **Spain**
71 H4 **Chambéria** France 46.27N 5.33E

100 M8 Chamberlain Saskatchewan 50.53N 105.37W
108 L6 Chamberlain S Dakota 43.49N 99.18W
104 P7 Chamberlain L Maine
14 G3 Chamberlain R W Australia
113 P2 Chamberlin,Mt Alaska 69.14N 144.59W
111 P6 Chambers Arizona 35.12N 109.25W
108 M7 Chambers Nebraska 42.11N 98.45W
13 B1 Chambers B N Terr Australia
104 H7 Chambersburg Pennsylvania 39.57N 77.40W
106 G4 Chambers,I Wisconsin 45.12N 87.21W
13 C6 Chambers Pillar pk N Terr Australia 24.52S 133.46E
71 H5 Chambéry France 45.34N 5.55E
92 E7 Chambeshi R Zambia
88 S4 Chambi, Jebel mt Tunisia 35.13N 8.38E
71 D4 Chambilly France 46.18N 4.00E
119 C10 Chambira,R Loreto Peru
119 D9 Chambira,R Loreto Peru
92 D8 Chambishi Zambia 12.39S 28.01E
69 K5 Chambley France 49.03N 5.55E
69 C5 Chambly France 49.10N 2.15E
70 L4 Chambois France 48.48N 0.06E
71 E6 Chambon-Feugerolles, le Loire France 45.24N 4.20E
72 K4 Chambon, Lac L France
72 H3 Chambon St. Croix France 46.21N 1.45E
71 E6 Chambon-sur-Lignon, le Haute-Loire France 45.04N 4.18E
72 J3 Chambon-sur-Voueize France 46.11N 2.26E
70 O6 Chambord France 47.37N 1.32E
99 S4 Chambord Quebec 48.25N 72.06W
31 C7 Chambor Kalat Pakistan 26.09N 64.45E
72 H5 Chamboulive France 45.26N 1.42E
72 F1 Chambourg-sur-Indre France 47.11N 0.58E
71 J6 Chambre,la France 45.22N 6.18E
69 L6 Chambrey France 48.47N 6.27E
15 G6 Chambri L Papua New Guinea
42 J2 Chamcha U.S.S.R. 60.48N 114.45E
43 G7 Chamchakly Turkmeniya U.S.S.R. 37.59N 63.05E
34 M3 Chamchamāl Iraq 35.32N 44.50E
25 K5 Cham,Cu Lao isld Vietnam 15.59N 108.30E
Chamdo see Qamdo
115 P5 Chame Panama 8.34N 79.51W
71 H6 Chamechaude mt France 45.18N 5.48E
32 C4 Cham-e Ḩannā Iran 32.37N 49.52E
115 G8 Chamela Mexico 19.31N 105.02W
115 P5 Chame,Pta C Panama 8.41N 79.46W
32 C4 Chameshk Iran 33.15N 48.15E
66 D2 Chamesol France 47.21N 6.50E
91 F9 Cha Messengue Angola 11.04S 18.56E
69 H8 Chamesson France 47.47N 4.33E
72 H5 Chameyrat France 45.14N 1.40E
32 D5 Cham-e Zeydun Iran 30.22N 50.09E
32 D4 Chamgordan Iran 32.28N 51.13E
121 C3 Chamical Argentina 30.22S 66.27W
34 N3 Cham i Dēwāna R Iraq
Cham-i Hena see Cham-e Ḩannā
28 H2 Chamka R Bhutan
32 D4 Cham,Kūh-e mt Iran 32.08N 50.13E
30 K4 Chamlang mt Nepal 27.47N 86.59E
30 D3 Chamlia R Nepal
92 G2 Chamliho mt Tanzania 1.55S 34.10E
44 D3 Chamlyk R U.S.S.R.
34 P5 Cham Mehr Iran 33.07N 47.33E
66 G8 Chamois Italy 45.50N 7.37E
107 E3 Chamois Missouri 38.41N 91.48W
87 F8 Chamo,L Ethiopia 5.55N 37.35E
30 C2 Chamoli Uttar Prad India 30.22N 79.19E
30 C2 Chamoli dist Uttar Prad India
71 K5 Chamonix-Mont-Blanc France 45.55N 6.52E
66 D8 Chamonix, Vallée de France
66 E7 Chamoson Switzerland 46.13N 7.14E
66 E6 Chamossaire mt Switzerland 46.20N 7.05E
71 H8 Chamouse,Mtgne,de France 44.15N 5.37E
71 J5 Chamousset France 45.34N 6.13E
71 J5 Chamoux-sur-Gelon France 45.31N 6.13E
Champ see Chānf
29 H6 Champa Madhya Prad India 22.02N 82.42E
72 J5 Champagnac Cantal France 45.22N 2.24E
72 F5 Champagnac-de-Belair France 45.24N 0.42E
71 C6 Champagnac-le-Vieux France 45.21N 3.30E
67 H4 Champagne prov France
72 H1 Champagne Berrichonne reg France
95 N5 Champagne Castle mt Lesotho 29.06S 29.20E
72 C4 Champagne Charentaise dist France
71 H5 Champagne-en-Valromey France 45.54N 5.41E
72 B3 Champagné-les-Marais France 46.23N 1.07W
72 E4 Champagne-Mouton France 45.59N 0.25E
66 C6 Champagnes France 46.23N 6.35E
72 E3 Champagné St. Hilaire France 46.19N 0.20E
71 K1 Champagney France 47.42N 6.42E
71 H3 Champagnole France 46.44N 5.55E
72 C4 Champagnolles France 45.31N 0.38W
14 E3 Champagny Is W Australia 15.25S 124.10E
106 F9 Champaign Illinois 40.07N 88.14W
28 H2 Champamati R Assam India
121 D3 Champaqui pk Argentina 31.59S 64.59W
120 B3 Champara mt Peru 8.37S 77.49W
30 H6 Champaran dist Bihar India
69 F6 Champaubert France 48.52N 3.47E
30 D3 Champawat Uttar Prad India 29.20N 80.06E
99 N4 Champcoeur Quebec 48.43N 77.40W
29 M2 Champdani W Bengal India 22.49N 88.21E
72 D3 Champdeniers-St. Denis France 46.29N 0.24W
71 E1 Champ d'Oiseau France 47.33N 4.20E
71 G2 Champdôtre France 47.11N 5.18E
69 N7 Champ-du-Feu mt France 48.24N 7.15E
66 D4 Champ du Moulin Switzerland 46.58N 6.47E
69 H6 Champeaubert,Res.de France
71 C5 Champeix France 45.35N 3.07E
72 H2 Champenoise,la France 46.56N 1.48E
115 O10 Champerico Guatemala 14.20N 91.52W
66 D7 Champéry Switzerland 46.11N 6.52E
66 E7 Champex Switzerland 46.02N 7.08E
66 C1 Champey France 47.35N 6.40E
69 L6 Champey-sur-Moselle France 48.58N 6.05E
66 Q6 Champfèr Switzerland 46.29N 9.49E
69 F6 Champfleury France 48.37N 4.00E
70 K5 Champgeneteux France 48.16N 0.22W
28 J4 Champhai Mizoram India 23.32N 93.18E
71 G6 Champier France 45.27N 5.18E
70 J6 Champigné France 47.40N 0.34W
69 E8 Champignelles France 47.47N 3.03E
69 L6 Champigneulles France 48.44N 6.10E
69 H7 Champignol-lez-Mondeville France 48.08N 4.41E
70 N6 Champigny France 47.43N 1.15E
69 E7 Champigny Yonne France 48.19N 3.08E
72 E2 Champigny le Sec France 46.43N 0.09E
68 H4 Champigny-sur-Marne France 48.49N 2.31E
72 E1 Champigny-sur-Veude France 47.04N 0.20E
72 J2 Champillet France 46.33N 2.06E
100 D8 Champion Alberta 50.17N 113.08W
61 K5 Champion Belgium 50.30N 4.54E
106 G3 Champion Michigan 46.32N 87.58W
14 A8 Champion B W Australia
104 E5 Champion Heights Ohio 41.18N 80.52W
104 M2 Champlain New York 44.59N 73.29W
99 S6 Champlain Quebec 46.27N 72.21W
104 J8 Champlain Virginia 38.01N 76.59W
104 M3 Champlain Canal New York
104 M2 Champlain,L Vermont/N Y
79 A5 Champlas du Col Italy 44.56N 6.50E
71 C2 Champlemy France 47.17N 3.22E
72 L1 Champlemy France 47.18N 3.21E
71 H1 Champlitte France 47.37N 5.31E
61 N6 Champlon Belgium 50.07N 5.30E
72 H4 Champnetery France 45.50N 1.34E
72 E4 Champniers France 45.42N 0.13E
71 J7 Champoléon France 44.44N 6.15E
66 G8 Champoluc Italy 45.49N 7.44E
71 D5 Champoly France 45.51N 3.50E
79 C3 Champorcher Italy 45.38N 7.37E
41 O2 Champ,Ostrov isld Franz Josef Land U.S.S.R.
115 O8 Champotón Mexico 19.20N 90.43W
70 N5 Champrond France 48.24N 1.05E
72 F4 Champsac France 45.42N 0.58E
72 B2 Champ St.Père,le France 46.31N 1.20W
71 J7 Champsaur mts France
70 J4 Champsecret France 48.36N 0.33W
71 H1 Champsevraine France 47.45N 5.32E
72 K5 Champs-sur-Tarentaine-Marchal France 45.24N 2.33E
71 J8 Champtercier France 44.06N 6.10E
70 J7 Champtocé France 47.25N 0.52W
70 H7 Champtoceaux France 47.21N 1.16W
71 G2 Champvans France 47.07N 5.25E
28 C5 Chamrajnagar Karnataka India 11.58N 76.54E
71 H6 Chamrousse France 45.06N 5.53E
30 F5 Chamrupur Uttar Prad India 27.19N 82.29E
Chams ed Dine Gharbi see Shams ed Din-Gharbi
66 Q5 Chamuera, V Switzerland
66 Q5 Chamues-chamuera Switzerland 46.35N 9.56E
76 C10 Chamusca Portugal 39.21N 8.29W
43 L6 Chamyndy Kirgiziya U.S.S.R. 41.30N 74.25E
45 R2 Chamzinka U.S.S.R. 54.23N 45.45E
25 F9 Chana Thailand 6.55N 100.46E
93 J7 Chana watercourse Kenya
29 E1 Chanab R Himachal Prad India
71 C8 Chanac France 44.28N 3.21E
Chanak Kale see Çanakkale
115 N9 Chanal Mexico 16.45N 92.25W
121 D3 Chañar La Rioja Argentina 30.33S 65.56W
121 C7 Chañar Neuquén Argentina 38.32S 68.27W
120 D12 Chañaral Chile 26.23S 70.40W
121 B2 Chañaral R Chile
121 B2 Chañaral, I Chile
32 H2 Chanārān Iran 36.36N 59.05E
121 B1 Chañarcillo Chile 27.47S 70.27W
121 D4 Chanares Argentina 32.10S 63.30W
119 G5 Chanaro,Cerro mt Venezuela 5.30N 63.53W
71 H5 Chanaz France 45.48N 5.47E
76 D10 Chança Portugal 39.15N 7.49W
76 E13 Chança R Portugal
120 B4 Chancay Peru 11.36S 77.14W
120 A2 Chancay R Peru
71 F1 Chanceaux France 47.31N 4.43E
108 N6 Chancellor S Dakota 43.22N 97.01W
42 H5 Chanchur U.S.S.R. 53.50N 107.00E
121 A5 Chanco Chile 35.43S 72.35W
120 B3 Chancos Peru 9.18S 77.28W
66 A7 Chancy Switzerland 46.09N 5.58E
Chanda see Chandrapur Maharashtra
30 F6 Chanda Uttar Prad India 26.06N 82.18E
70 M4 Chandai France 48.45N 0.45E
113 N3 Chandalar Alaska 67.30N 148.35W
113 P2 Chandalar R Alaska
113 N3 Chandalar L Alaska 67.32N 148.35W
30 K8 Chandan Bihar India 24.38N 86.40E
30 D4 Chandan Chauki Uttar Prad India 28.32N 80.43E
30 F5 Chandanpur Uttar Prad India 27.40N 82.39E
30 F5 Chandapar Uttar Prad India 27.24N 82.59E
29 H7 Chandarpur Madhya Prad India 21.42N 83.16E
30 G7 Chandauli Uttar Prad India 25.15N 83.17E
30 K8 Chandauri Bihar India 24.37N 86.03E
30 A4 Chandausi Aligarh, Uttar Prad India 28.06N 77.50E
30 B4 Chandausi Uttar Prad India 28.27N 78.43E
30 C7 Chandaut Uttar Prad India 25.54N 79.40E
29 K7 Chandbali Orissa India 20.46N 86.49E
107 H12 Chandeleur Is Louisiana
107 H12 Chandeleur Sound Louisiana
30 B7 Chandera Madhya Prad India 25.06N 78.59E
30 B8 Chanderi Guna, Madhya Prad India 24.43N 78.08E
30 C8 Chanderi Tikamgarh, Madhya Prad India 24.49N 79.17E
29 M2 Chandernagore W Bengal India 22.52N 88.21E
30 J7 Chandi Bihar India 25.20N 85.25E
29 E2 Chandigarh Union Terr India 30.43N 76.47E
30 A2 Chandigarh Mandir Haryana India 30.44N 76.54E
29 J2 Chandil Bihar India 22.58N 86.04E
30 D7 Chandla Madhya Prad India 25.05N 80.12E
111 N8 Chandler Arizona 33.19N 111.49W
109 O6 Chandler Oklahoma 35.43N 96.54W
98 H5 Chandler Quebec 48.21N 64.41W
112 M3 Chandler Texas 32.19N 95.29W
113 M2 Chandler R Alaska
113 L2 Chandler L Alaska 68.15N 152.40W
12 C2 Chandler,Mt S Australia 27.04S 133.17E
56 J6 Chandler's Ford Hants England 50.59N 1.23W
106 D9 Chandlerville Illinois 40.03N 90.10W
120 D3 Chandless,R Brazil
22 B3 Chandmanĭ Mongolia 47.52N 92.39E
22 D4 Chandmanĭ Mongolia 45.20N 97.59E
29 C7 Chandod Gujarat India 22.00N 73.30E
66 G6 Chandolin Switzerland 46.16N 7.36E
41 P5 Chandon R U.S.S.R.
29 D7 Chandor Maharashtra India 20.20N 74.18E
30 D7 Chandpur Atehpur, Uttar Prad India 25.56N 80.21E
30 H7 Chandpur Ballia, Uttar Prad India 25.55N 84.20E
31 H9 Chandpur Bangladesh 23.15N 90.40E
30 B3 Chandpur Bijnor, Uttar Prad India 29.08N 78.16E
29 K3 Chandra W Bengal India 22.28N 87.10E
31 J10 Chandragana Bangladesh 22.27N 92.09E
28 D4 Chandragiri Andhra Prad India 13.36N 79.20E
29 L2 Chandrakona W Bengal India 22.44N 87.31E
29 F8 Chandrapur Maharashtra India 19.58N 79.21E
29 F8 Chandrapur dist Maharashtra India
76 E4 Chandreja de Queija Spain 42.15N 7.23W
30 A6 Chandupura Madhya Prad India 26.10N 75.50E
29 E7 Chandur Amraoti, Maharashtra India 21.18N 77.49E
29 F7 Chandur Amraoti, Maharashtra India 20.48N 78.02E
30 F7 Chandwak Uttar Prad India 25.36N 83.00E
43 H7 Chandyr Uzbekistan U.S.S.R. 38.54N 65.13E
32 G1 Chandyr R Turkmeniya U.S.S.R.
32 J7 Chānf Iran 26.39N 60.31E
25 E8 Chang isld Thailand 9.40N 98.22E
41 H6 Changada R U.S.S.R.
94 M6 Changalane Mozambique 26.16S 32.13E
Chang'an see Rong'an
23 E1 Chang'an Shaanxi China 34.12N 108.57E
28 C6 Changanacheri Kerala India 9.26N 76.31E
94 M4 Changane R Mozambique
92 F10 Changara Mozambique 16.50S 33.17E
21 D7 Changbai Jilin China 41.29N 128.12E
Changbai Chaoxianzu Zizhixian see Changbai
21 D6 Changbai Shan mts Jilin China
22 C7 Changcaogou Gansu China 39.28N 94.15E
25 K3 Changcheng Guangdong China 19.23N 109.05E
23 D2 Changchi Sichuan China 29.07N 108.45E
Chang-chia-wan see Dehui
21 D9 Ch'angch'on-ni S Korea 37.50N 128.15E
Changchow Fujian see Zhangzhou
Changchow Jiangsu see Changzhou
21 C6 Changchun Jilin China 43.50N 125.20E
21 C5 Changchunling Jilin China 45.25N 125.31E
23 H3 Changdang Hu L Jiangsu China
23 F4 Changde Hunan China 29.03N 111.35E
98 S4 Change Islands Newfoundland 49.38N 54.23W
23 H2 Changfeng Anhui China 38.45N 116.22E
23 F1 Changge Henan China 34.15N 113.50E
21 B8 Changhai Liaoning China 39.15N 122.37E
21 D9 Changhowŏn S Korea 37.10N 127.37E
23 F3 Chang Hu L Hubei China 30.24N 112.23E
23 J6 Chang-hua Taiwan 24.06N 120.31E
23 H3 Changhua Zhejiang China 30.13N 119.11E
23 E9 Changhua Jiang R Guangdong China
21 D10 Changhŭng S Korea 34.40N 126.53E
18 D10 Changi Singapore 1.22N 103.58E
18 K3 Changi dist Singapore
18 K2 Changi Tanjong C Singapore 1.23N 104.00E
24 F3 Changji Xinjiang Uygur Zizhiqu China 44.00N 87.20E
23 E9 Changjiang Guangdong China 19.23N 109.05E
23 C6 Changjiang Yunnan China 24.40N 102.50E
23 H3 Chang Jiang R Anhui China
23 G4 Chang Jiang R Jiangxi China
23 E3 Chang Jiang R Sichuan China
21 D7 Changjin N Korea 40.21N 127.20E
21 D7 Changjin R N Korea
21 D7 Changjin Resr N Korea
21 D8 Changjŏn N Korea 38.41N 128.10E
30 J2 Chang La pass Xizang Zizhiqu 28.01N 86.56E
24 F10 Changla Pod La pass Xizang Zizhiqu China 30.09N 87.08E
23 H6 Changle Fujian China 25.55N 119.31E
22 L8 Changle Shandong China 36.45N 118.45E
23 J4 Changle Zhejiang China 29.27N 121.37E
22 L7 Changli Hebei China 39.44N 119.13E
21 C5 Changling Jilin China 44.16N 123.57E
18 D2 Changlun Pen Malaysia 6.25N 100.22E
31 J3 Changlung Kashmir 34.54N 77.33E
24 C8 Changlung La pass Xinjiang Uygur Zizhiqu China
31 J1 Changlung Pass Kashmir 34.37N 78.45E
22 D7 Changma Gansu China 39.54N 96.56E
31 K1 Changmar Xizang Zizhiqu China 34.24N 79.56E
30 M4 Changmu Xizang Zizhiqu 28.09N 88.00E
23 F5 Changning Hunan China 26.27N 112.23E
23 C4 Changning Sichuan China 28.40N 104.56E
23 B6 Changning Yunnan China 24.51N 99.44E
21 C8 Changnyŏn N Korea 38.35N 125.19E
22 K6 Changping Beijing China 40.14N 116.11E
Changpuzhen see Suining
22 K8 Changqing Shandong China 36.35N 116.41E
30 H2 Changri La pass Nepal 28.00N 86.47E
21 C8 Changsan-got C N Korea 38.05N 124.38E
23 F4 Changsha Hunan China 28.10N 113.00E
23 H4 Changshan Zhejiang China 28.54N 118.30E
21 B8 Changshan Qundao islds Liaoning China
22 L6 Changshanyu Hebei China 40.37N 118.03E
23 J3 Changshou Jiangsu China 31.39N 120.45E
23 D4 Changshou Sichuan China 29.50N 107.00E
23 D5 Changshun Guizhou China 25.57N 106.30E
23 H6 Changtai Fujian China 24.35N 117.47E
23 G6 Changting Fujian China 25.47N 116.17E
21 D5 Changting Heilongjiang China 44.28N 128.56E
30 J2 Changtse mt Xizang Zizhiqu 28.02N 86.55E
21 C6 Changtu Liaoning China 42.50N 123.59E
115 N5 Changuinola Panama 9.28N 82.31W
22 B7 Changweiliang Qinghai China 38.24N 92.08E
25 M7 Changwinti Assam India 27.58N 96.51E
23 D1 Changwu Gansu China 35.09N 107.42E
21 C5 Changwu Heilongjiang China 45.58N 125.31E
23 H3 Changxing Jiangsu China 31.03N 119.54E
21 B8 Changxing Dao isld Liaoning China 39.40N 121.30E
23 F3 Changyang Hubei China 30.32N 111.12E
22 L8 Changyi Shandong China 36.52N 119.20E
21 C8 Changyŏn N Korea 38.16N 125.04E
43 L6 Changyrtash Kirgiziya U.S.S.R. 40.52N 72.50E
23 G1 Changyuan Henan China 35.11N 114.38E
Changzha see Changshun
Changzhai see Changshun
22 J8 Changzhi Shanxi China 36.05N 113.12E
23 F1 Changzhi Shanxi China 36.11N 113.06E
23 F1 Changzhi Shanxi China 36.05N 113.12E
23 J3 Changzhou Jiangsu China 31.39N 120.45E
23 G3 Changzhuyuan Henan China 31.30N 115.19E
Chanh see Lang Chanh
Chan-hua see Zhanhua
121 D5 Chanilao Argentina 35.20S 64.01W
120 F11 Chañi,Nev.de pk Argentina 24.03S 65.42W
26 Q2 Chankanai Sri Lanka 9.45N 79.59E
113 H8 Chankliut I Alaska 56.10N 158.10W
23 C1 Chankou Gansu China 35.42N 104.28E
41 E5 Chankyagyarbyak, Ozero L U.S.S.R.
93 K5 Chanler's Falls Kenya 0.48N 38.03E
61 L6 Chanly Belgium 50.05N 5.10E
28 B3 Channagiri Karnataka India 14.03N 75.54E
28 C4 Channapatna Karnataka India 12.43N 77.14E
28 C4 Channaravapatna Karnataka India 12.54N 76.22E
Channarayapatna see Channaravapatna
70 L7 Channay-sur-Lathan France 47.30N 0.15E
11 K3 Channel I New Zealand 36.26S 175.22E
111 E8 Channel Is California
70 E3 Channel Is English Chan British Isles
Channel Is Nat. Mon see Anacapa Is and Santa Barbara I
98 N6 Channel Port aux Basques Newfoundland 47.34N 59.09W
14 C10 Channel Pt W Australia 34.51S 118.20E
116 F3 Channel Rock Bahamas 22.52N 76.45W
100 Q4 Channing Manitoba 54.46N 101.50W
106 F3 Channing Michigan 46.08N 88.06W
112 B8 Channing Texas 35.41N 102.21W
100 Q4 Channing airfield Saskatchewan 54.45N 101.50W
87 G6 Channo Ethiopia 9.42N 39.55E
Channun see Mian Channun
29 C5 Chanod Rajasthan India 25.32N 73.12E
71 F6 Chanos-Curzon France 45.04N 4.55E
76 C7 Chans mt Portugal 40.50N 8.12W
76 D3 Chantada Spain 42.36N 7.46W
39 K1 Chantal'skiy mt U.S.S.R. 67.48N 178.05E
39 L1 Chantal'veyergyn R U.S.S.R.
72 L3 Chantelle France 46.14N 3.08E
61 N8 Chantemelle Belgium 49.39N 5.39E
70 K6 Chantenay Sarthe France 47.55N 0.09W
25 G6 Chanthaburi Thailand 12.35N 102.08E
69 C5 Chantilly France 49.12N 2.28E
72 B2 Chantonnay France 46.41N 1.03W
71 J2 Chantrans France 47.03N 6.08E
101 Z1 Chantrey Inlet N W Terr
70 J4 Chanu France 48.43N 0.40W
28 H7 Chanumla Nicobar Is 8.18N 93.02E
109 P4 Chanute Kansas 37.41N 95.26W
31 G4 Chanuwala Pakistan 32.50N 73.09E
42 B4 Chany U.S.S.R. 55.20N 76.45E
42 B5 Chany,Ozero L U.S.S.R.
77 B5 Chanza R Spain
72 C1 Chanzeaux France 47.16N 0.38W
120 A3 Chao Peru 8.36S 78.45W
96 R8 Chão isld Madeira Is 32.34N 16.33W
23 G7 Chao'an Guangdong China 23.42N 116.36E
23 G1 Chaocheng Shandong China 36.03N 115.35E
23 H3 Chao Hu L Anhui China
120 A3 Chao,I Peru 8.46S 78.50W
92 K8 Chaonde Mozambique 13.43S 40.31E
25 F5 Chao Phraya R Thailand
21 B3 Chaor Nei Monggol Zizhiqu China 48.25N 121.25E
21 B4 Chaor He R Nei Monggol Zizhiqu China
Chaouen see Chechaouen
88 L4 Chaouen Morocco 35.10N 5.16W
69 G7 Chaource France 48.03N 4.08E
24 H9 Chaowula Shan mts Qinghai China
23 H3 Chao Xian Anhui China 31.36N 117.57E
Chaoyang see Jiayin
Chaoyang see Human
Chaoyang see Huinan
23 G7 Chaoyang Guangdong China 23.17N 116.33E
22 M6 Chaoyang Liaoning China 41.36N 120.25E
21 C2 Chaoyangcun Nei Monggol Zizhiqu China 50.02N 124.20E
22 H9 Chaoyi Shaanxi China 34.47N 110.08E
21 B2 Chaozhong Nei Monggol Zizhiqu China 50.57N 121.30E
Chaozhou see Chao'an
76 C6 Chapa Portugal 41.18N 8.04W
40 E4 Chapa U.S.S.R. 55.45N 129.19E
25 G1 Cha Pa Vietnam 22.20N 103.50E
118 C4 Chapada dos Guimarães Brazil 15.20S 55.44W
117 F8 Chapada Grande plat Brazil
117 F6 Chapadinha Brazil 3.45S 43.23W
99 Q3 Chapais Quebec 49.47N 74.54W
31 C2 Chapak Guzar Afghanistan 36.44N 64.54E
115 H7 Chapala Mexico 20.20N 103.10W
92 H9 Chapala Mozambique 15.53S 37.37E
115 H7 Chapala,L.de Mexico
40 F2 Chapanda U.S.S.R. 59.20N 132.17E
120 F7 Chapare R Bolivia
71 H6 Chapareillan France 45.29N 5.59E
30 G8 Chapari Bihar India 24.55N 83.48E
116 F4 Chaparra Cuba 21.15N 76.27W
120 C6 Cháparra Peru 15.44S 73.54W
119 C6 Chaparral Colombia 3.45N 75.30W
28 J4 Chapa Tong mt Mizoram India 22.25N 92.55E
45 Q9 Chapayeva, im Kalmyk A.S.S.R. U.S.S.R. 47.44N 44.54E
43 G8 Chapayeva, im Turkmeniya U.S.S.R. 36.46N 62.30E
39 E3 Chapayeva imeni Magadan U.S.S.R. 63.13N 152.05E
45 V5 Chapayeva, imeni Saratov U.S.S.R. 51.50N 49.09E
45 D7 Chapayevka Ukraine U.S.S.R. 49.33N 32.12E
46 Q4 Chapayevo Kazakhstan U.S.S.R. 50.12N 51.09E
45 V4 Chapayevsk U.S.S.R. 52.58N 49.44E
45 T1 Chapayevskiy U.S.S.R. 56.06N 47.15E
42 K2 Chapayev-Zheday U.S.S.R. 60.10N 117.15E
119 F6 Chapazón Venezuela 2.05N 67.07W
46 P5 Chapchachi Kazakhstan U.S.S.R. 47.50N 47.52E
71 B5 Chapdes-Beaufort France 45.54N 2.51E
71 D4 Chapeau France 46.30N 3.31E
99 N7 Chapeau Quebec 45.54N 77.05W
121 H1 Chapecó Brazil 27.14S 52.41W
118 D10 Chapecó,R Brazil
118 D10 Chapecózinho R Brazil
72 J3 Chapelaude,la France 46.26N 2.28E
57 K6 Chapel-en-le-Frith Derbys England 53.20N 1.54W
105 H2 Chapel Hill N Carolina 35.55N 79.04W
107 K6 Chapel Hill Tennessee 35.38N 86.43W
56 H4 Chapel House Oxon Eng 51.57N 1.31W
61 E4 Chapelle-á-Oie Belgium 50.36N 3.40E
72 G5 Chapelle Aubareil, la France 45.01N 1.10E
71 D3 Chapelle-au-Mans,la France 46.38N 3.58E
70 K5 Chapelle-au-Riboul,la France 48.19N 0.24W
69 L7 Chapelle-aux-Bois,la France 48.02N 6.21E
61 E4 Chapelle-á-Wattines Belgium 50.37N 3.40E
72 B1 Chapelle Basse Mer, la France 47.17N 1.19W
72 F1 Chapelle, Blanche-St. Martin, la France 47.06N 0.47E
70 G6 Chapelle-Bouexic,la France 47.56N 1.55W
70 K6 Chapelle d'Aligné, la France 47.44N 0.14W
71 A2 Chapelle-d'Angillon,la France 47.22N 2.26E
71 F4 Chapelle-de-Guinchay,la France 46.13N 4.45E
70 F7 Chapelle-des-Marais,la France 47.27N 2.14W
71 J7 Chapelle-en-Valgaudemar,la France 44.50N 6.11E
71 G7 Chapelle-en-Vercors,la France 44.58N 5.25E
69 D6 Chapelle-Gauthier,la France 48.32N 2.54E
70 H6 Chapelle-Glain,la France 47.38N 1.11W
72 B1 Chapelle-Heulin,la France 47.10N 1.20W
69 J4 Chapelle,la Ardennes France 49.44N 5.02E
66 D6 Chapelle, la France 46.18N 6.46E
70 F6 Chapelle,La Morbihan France 47.52N 2.25W
68 F3 Chapelle,La Paris France 48.53N 2.22E
69 D7 Chapelle-la-Reine, La France 48.18N 2.34E
98 L3 Chapelle,L.de la Quebec
61 H5 Chapelle-lez-Herlaimont Belgium 50.28N 4.17E
70 K4 Chapelle-Moche,la France 48.32N 0.29W
70 J5 Chapelle-Rainsouin,la France 48.06N 0.30W
70 N5 Chapelle Royale France 48.08N 1.03E
71 C2 Chapelle-St. André, la France 47.24N 3.20E
72 D2 Chapelle St. Laurent, la France 46.44N 0.28W
70 O6 Chapelle-st.Mesmin,la France 47.53N 1.50E
71 H2 Chapelle-St.Quillain,la France 47.30N 5.48E
72 A1 Chapelle-sur-Erdre, La France 47.18N 1.32W
71 L1 Chapelle-sur-Rougemont,la France 47.43N 7.01E
72 H3 Chapelle Taillefert, la France 46.06N 1.50E
58 M4 Chapel of Garioch Grampian Scotland 57.18N 2.28W
71 B2 Chapelotte,la France 47.21N 2.35E
57 O6 Chapel St.Leonards Lincs England 53.14N 0.20E
116 K2 Chapelton Jamaica, W I 18.05N 77.16W
58 H7 Chapelton Strathclyde Scotland 55.43N 4.05W
59 L3 Chapeltown Down N Ireland 54.17N 5.35W
57 L6 Chapeltown S Yorks England 53.28N 1.27W
121 F3 Chapicuy Uruguay 31.40S 57.52W
71 K5 Chapieux,les France 45.42N 6.47E
120 C5 Chapimarca Peru 13.59S 73.06W
107 F2 Chapin Illinois 39.45N 90.23W
76 L8 Chapinería Spain 40.22N 4.13W
99 G5 Chapleau Ontario 47.50N 83.24W
99 H4 Chapleau-Nemegosenda Wild River Prov. Park Ontario
99 G4 Chapleau R Ontario
103 K3 Chaplin Connecticut 41.48N 72.08W
100 L8 Chaplin Saskatchewan 50.29N 106.40W
44 C8 Chaplinka Ukraine U.S.S.R. 46.21N 33.33E
45 H8 Chaplino Ukraine U.S.S.R. 48.07N 36.15E
39 M3 Chaplino U.S.S.R. 64.25N 172.16W
45 L3 Chaplygin U.S.S.R. 53.15N 40.00E
107 K10 Chapman Alabama 31.42N 86.43W
109 N3 Chapman Kansas 38.58N 97.00W
110 R1 Chapman Montana 48.54N 108.09W
108 M8 Chapman Nebraska 41.02N 98.10W
103 C5 Chapman Pennsylvania 40.35N 75.37W
101 T1 Chapman Is N W Terr
101 O10 Chapman,Mt Br Col 51.56N 118.19W
14 F3 Chapman R W Australia
112 K8 Chapman Ranch Texas 27.35N 97.27W
94 P12 Chapmans B Cape Town S Africa
94 P12 Chapman's Pk Cape Town S Africa 34.05S 18.21E
104 C9 Chapmanville W Virginia 37.58N 82.01W
47 D3 Chapoma U.S.S.R. 66.05N 38.59E
61 M4 Chapon-Seraing Belgium 50.37N 5.16E
103 G4 Chappaqua New York 41.10N 73.45W
103 O4 Chappaquiddick I Massachusetts
40 G1 Chappayeva, Im Yakutsk U.S.S.R. 61.00N 135.20E
108 H8 Chappell Nebraska 41.06N 102.29W
112 L5 Chappell Hill Texas 30.08N 96.16W
12 J8 Chappell Is Tasmania
41 O9 Chappiyedey U.S.S.R. 61.48N 133.35E
30 H7 Chapra Bihar India 25.46N 84.44E
29 L6 Chapra W Bengal India 23.31N 88.40E
31 C3 Chapri Pass Afghanistan 34.20N 65.35E
104 J8 Chaptico Maryland 38.22N 76.47W
28 G1 Chapting Xizang Zizhiqu 29.56N 89.20E
44 H3 Chapur'yey Kosa,Os isld U.S.S.R. 44.51N 47.19E
72 B4 Chapus,le France 45.51N 1.10W
99 K4 Chaput Hughes Ontario 48.08N 80.05W
93 E10 Chaputwa Tanzania 4.29S 33.25E
35 E1 Chaqra Lebanon 33.12N 35.28E
120 F8 Chaqui Bolivia 19.34S 65.31W
32 H5 Chaqvīr,Poshteh-ye mt Iran 31.10N 58.39E
31 J4 Char Kashmir 33.15N 77.10E
88 G11 Char Mauritania 21.34N 12.57W
89 C1 Char Mauritania 21.34N 12.57W
40 A3 Chara U.S.S.R. 56.58N 118.20E
42 K3 Chara U.S.S.R. 58.48N 118.05E
42 L2 Chara R U.S.S.R.
121 F1 Charadai Argentina 27.38S 59.52W
120 F8 Charagua Bolivia 19.47S 63.14W
Charak see Band-e Chārak
29 A6 Charakra Doi Gujarat India 23.57N 69.20E
119 D4 Charalá Colombia 6.17N 73.09W
40 F1 Charan U.S.S.R. 60.20N 134.20E
120 D7 Charana Bolivia 17.35S 69.25W
119 D8 Charapita Colombia 0.39S 74.21W
121 E1 Charata Argentina 27.13S 61.14W
71 H6 Charavines France 45.26N 5.31E
115 E4 Charay Mexico 26.01N 108.50W
21 C3 Charbaqi Nei Monggol Zizhiqu China 48.35N 123.06E
71 L6 Charbonel,Pointe de France 45.17N 7.02E
66 A9 Charbon, Montagne de France 45.42N 6.11E
108 G2 Charbonneau N Dakota 47.50N 103.44W
71 F5 Charbonnières-les-Bains France 45.47N 4.44E
69 E8 Charbuy France 47.50N 3.27E
115 J6 Charcas Mexico 23.09N 101.10W
71 G8 Charce,la France 44.28N 5.28E
71 H2 Charcenne France 47.22N 5.47E
Charchan see Qiemo
Charchan Darya R see Qarqan He
77 L6 Charches Spain 37.18N 2.56W
Charchi see Qarqi
70 K5 Charchigné France 48.25N 0.25W
71 H4 Charchilla France 46.28N 5.43E
28 J1 Char Chu R Xizang Zizhiqu
112 K7 Charco Texas 28.45N 97.37W
115 N5 Charco Azul.B.de Panama
96 P10 Charco,El La Palma Canary Is 28.31N 17.51W
115 K5 Charco Escondido Mexico 25.45N 98.20W
123 F13 Charcot I Antarctica
100 G3 Chard Alberta 55.50N 110.54W
56 F6 Chard Somerset England 50.53N 2.58W
32 B2 Chārdagh Iran 36.30N 47.21E
43 H6 Chardara Kazakhstan U.S.S.R. 41.18N 67.56E
43 J6 Chardarinskoye Vdkhr res Uzbekistan/Kazakhstan U.S.S.R.
Chardavar see Chardāvol
32 B4 Chardāvol Iran 33.44N 46.42E
32 F2 Chardeh Iran 36.24N 54.19E
29 F1 Charding, La pass Xizang Zizhiqu 32.31N 79.28E
104 D5 Chardon Ohio 41.34N 81.12W
43 G7 Chardzhou Turkmeniya U.S.S.R. 39.09N 63.34E
88 P4 Charef Algeria 34.37N 2.53E
71 B5 Charensat France 45.58N 2.36E
67 E7 Charente dept France
72 C4 Charente R France
67 E7 Charente-Maritime dept France
72 K2 Charenton-du-Cher France 46.44N 2.38E
68 F4 Charenton-le-Pont France 48.49N 2.25E
70 M3 Charentonne R France
44 F7 Charentsavan Armenia U.S.S.R. 40.25N 43.37E
88 M5 Charet watercourse Morocco
71 G3 Charette France 46.55N 5.12E
71 H1 Chargey-lès-Gray France 47.31N 5.34E
30 D8 Charhanta Madhya Prad India 24.24N 80.55E
29 J1 Charhi Bihar India 23.51N 85.27E
90 G5 Chari R Cameroon/Chad
90 J7 Chari R Chad
90 H6 Chari Baguirmi div Chad
Char-i-Daraz see Chāh Darāz
31 E3 Charikar Afghanistan 35.02N 69.13E
30 K5 Charikot Nepal 27.39N 86.03E
56 N5 Charing Kent England 51.13N 0.48E
113 E2 Chariot Alaska 68.10N 165.15W
71 C2 Charité, la France 47.11N 3.01E
72 L1 Charité-sur-Loire,la France 47.11N 3.01E
108 R8 Chariton Iowa 41.00N 93.18W
107 D2 Chariton R Iowa/Missouri
117 A1 Charity Guyana 7.25N 58.38W
106 L5 Charity Is Michigan
47 G3 Charkabozh U.S.S.R. 65.43N 54.35E
47 G3 Charkayuvom U.S.S.R. 65.43N 54.33E
30 C7 Charkhari Uttar Prad India 25.24N 79.45E
29 E3 Charkhi Dadri Punjab India 28.37N 76.19E
Charkhlik see Ruoqiang
44 J6 Charkhy Azerbaydzhan U.S.S.R. 41.25N 48.53E
42 E5 Charkov U.S.S.R. 53.42N 90.30E
43 M8 Charku Tadzhikistan U.S.S.R. 39.56N 70.35E
39 B2 Charky R U.S.S.R.
39 B2 Charky-Togoy U.S.S.R. 65.51N 137.20E
56 J4 Charlbury Oxon England 51.53N 1.29W
95 N2 Charl Cilliers S Africa 26.40S 29.11E
59 J3 Charlemont Armagh N Ireland 54.27N 6.41W
61 H5 Charleroi Belgium 50.25N 4.27E
104 F6 Charleroi Pennsylvania 40.08N 79.56W
100 Q3 Charles Manitoba 55.33N 101.01W
103 M2 Charles R Massachusetts
98 P8 Charlesbourg Quebec 46.51N 71.16W
104 K9 Charles,C Virginia 37.08N 75.59W
108 S6 Charles City Iowa 43.05N 92.40W
104 H9 Charles City Virginia 37.21N 77.05W
Charles I Galápagos Is see Santa María, I
97 M5 Charles I N W Terr 62.35N 74.30W
101 S6 Charles L Alberta
15 C6 Charles Louis, Pegunungan mts Irian Jaya
11 O12 Charles,Mt New Zealand 45.52S 170.42E
14 B8 Charles,Mt W Australia 27.48S 117.27E
14 D10 Charles Pk W Australia 32.41S 121.10E
13 B1 Charles Pt N Terr Australia 12.25S 130.34E
14 A6 Charles, Pt W Australia 24.30S 113.24E
11 B12 Charles Sd New Zealand
107 B6 Charleston Arkansas 35.19N 94.02W
107 H2 Charleston Illinois 39.30N 88.11W
107 F7 Charleston Mississippi 34.00N 90.02W
107 G5 Charleston Missouri 36.54N 89.22W
11 F8 Charleston New Zealand 41.55S 171.26E
110 A6 Charleston Oregon 43.21N 124.21W
105 H5 Charleston S Carolina 32.48N 79.58W
107 M6 Charleston Tennessee 35.17N 84.45W
104 D8 Charleston W Virginia 38.23N 81.40W
111 J5 Charleston Pk mt Nevada 36.16N 115.41W
58 M4 Charlestown Grampian Scotland 57.06N 2.07W
107 L3 Charlestown Indiana 38.28N 85.40W
103 C7 Charlestown Maryland 39.35N 75.59W
59 E4 Charlestown Mayo Irish Rep 53.58N 8.47W
116 P4 Charlestown Nevis I W I 17.08N 62.37W
104 N3 Charlestown New Hampshire 43.14N 72.25W
103 L4 Charlestown Rhode I 41.24N 71.38W
95 N3 Charlestown S Africa 27.25S 29.52E
104 H7 Charles Town W Virginia 39.18N 77.54W
91 G6 Charlesville Zaïre 5.27S 21.59E
14 D7 Charles Wells Cr W Australia
100 A1 Charleswood Manitoba 49.51N 97.15W
70 N3 Charleval France 49.22N 1.23E
69 H4 Charleville France 49.46N 4.43E
13 H7 Charleville Queensland 26.25S 146.13E
106 J4 Charlevoix Michigan 45.19N 85.16W
106 J4 Charlevoix,L Michigan
113 Q4 Charley R Alaska
101 N7 Charlie Lake Br Col 56.15N 120.58W
71 E4 Charlieu France 46.10N 4.10E
121 C4 Charloni Argentina 33.44S 66.20W
106 D8 Charlotte Iowa 41.57N 90.28W
106 K7 Charlotte Michigan 42.33N 85.50W
105 G2 Charlotte N Carolina 35.03N 80.50W
112 J7 Charlotte Texas 28.52N 98.44W
105 L7 Charlotte Amalie Virgin Is 18.22N 64.56W
25 J9 Charlotte Bank S China Sea
103 E2 Charlotte Cr New York
105 E11 Charlotte Harbor Florida 26.58N 82.04W
101 L9 Charlotte L Br Col 52.11N 125.19W
52 G7 Charlottenberg Sweden 59.53N 12.17E
63 A1 Charlottenburg dist W Berlin
63 S9 Charlottenfelde E Germany 51.59N 13.19E
104 G8 Charlottesville Virginia 38.02N 78.29W
Charlotte Town see Gouyave
98 J7 Charlottetown Prince Edward I 46.14N 63.09W
103 E1 Charlotteville New York 42.33N 74.41W
116 M1 Charlotteville Tobago W I 11.19N 60.33W
55 H4 Charlton London England 51.29N 0.03E
99 K5 Charlton Ontario 47.50N 80.02W
12 G6 Charlton Victoria 36.18S 143.27E
103 L2 Charlton City Massachusetts 42.09N 71.59W
97 M7 Charlton I James B, N W Terr 52.00N 79.30W
56 G4 Charlton Kings Glos England 51.53N 2.03W
56 L5 Charlwood Surrey England 51.10N 0.15W
69 E6 Charly France 48.59N 3.17E
72 E4 Charmé France 45.57N 0.07E
71 C4 Charmeil France 46.10N 3.23E
69 L7 Charmes France 48.22N 6.17E
66 E5 Charmey Switzerland 46.38N 7.10E
69 L7 Charmois-l'Orgueilleux France 48.06N 6.17E
69 G7 Charmont-sous-Barbuise France 48.25N 4.09E
56 F6 Charmouth Dorset England 50.45N 2.55W
31 H9 Charmugria Bangladesh 23.06N 90.15E
76 B16 Charneca Portugal 38.44N 9.27W
76 E15 Charneca Portugal 38.47N 9.08W
61 O4 Charneux Belgium 50.40N 5.48E
72 F2 Charnizay France 46.55N 0.59E
14 F3 Charnley,R W Australia
56 J2 Charnwood Forest Leics England
98 A7 Charny Quebec 46.43N 71.15W
69 E8 Charny Yonne France 47.54N 3.06E
69 J5 Charny-sur-Meuse Meuse France 49.12N 5.21E
71 E3 Charollais,Mts.du France
71 E4 Charolles France 46.26N 4.17E
Charol Tso L see Lumajangdong Co
74 H8 Charon Algeria 36.03N 1.08E
72 J2 Charost France 46.59N 2.07E
88 N7 Charouïne Algeria 29.01N 0.16W
47 D5 Charozero U.S.S.R. 60.30N 38.36E
71 D7 Charpal,L.de France
98 J2 Charpeney,L Quebec 51.06N 63.50W
66 D3 Charquemont France 47.13N 6.48E
71 K2 Charquemont France 47.13N 6.48E
77 T11 Charraca,Cala de B Balearic Is
66 E7 Charrat Switzerland 46.08N 7.09E
94 N1 Charre Mozambique 17.13S 35.08E
99 P4 Charrier, L Quebec
71 D3 Charrin France 46.48N 3.36E
68 F3 Charronne Paris France 48.52N 2.24E
72 E3 Charroux France 46.09N 0.25E
69 B5 Chars France 49.09N 1.59E
31 F3 Charsadda Pakistan 34.12N 71.46E
43 H7 Charshanga Turkmeniya U.S.S.R. 37.04N 66.00E
43 O3 Charsk Kazakhstan U.S.S.R. 49.37N 81.02E
43 N7 Chartak Uzbekistan U.S.S.R. 41.05N 71.50E
92 E11 Charter dist Zimbabwe
11 N11 Charteris B New Zealand
11 N11 Charteris Bay New Zealand 43.38S 172.43E
108 P7 Charter Oak Iowa 42.05N 95.34W
13 H5 Charters Towers Queensland 20.02S 146.20E
30 F5 Charthari Uttar Prad India 27.06N 82.59E
30 A3 Charthawal Uttar Prad India 29.30N 77.37E
98 A8 Chartierville Quebec 45.19N 71.12W
70 M6 Chartre,la France 47.44N 0.35E
70 N5 Chartres France 48.27N 1.30E
71 J10 Chartreuse-de-la Verne France 43.15N 6.25E
71 K4 Chartreuse-du-Reposoir France 46.01N 6.33E
32 G5 Chārū Iran 30.05N 56.57E
46 M3 Charus U.S.S.R. 54.49N 40.46E
66 F9 Charvensod Italy 45.43N 7.19E
71 J5 Charvin,Mt France 45.49N 6.26E
71 J5 Charvonnex France 45.58N 6.10E
9 S7 Charybdis Reef Fiji 17.13S 178.00E
42 B3 Charymovo U.S.S.R. 58.30N 77.45E
43 N5 Charyn Kazakhstan U.S.S.R. 43.47N 79.24E
43 N5 Charyn R Kazakhstan U.S.S.R.
21 C8 Ch'aryon'gwan N Korea 39.50N 124.43E
42 C6 Charysh R U.S.S.R.
42 C6 Charyshskoye U.S.S.R. 51.25N 83.30E
121 F5 Chas Argentina 35.55S 58.40W
29 J1 Chas Bihar India 22.38N 86.20E
121 C1 Chaschuil Argentina 27.44S 68.14W
121 F5 Chascomas Argentina 35.34S 58.00W
101 O10 Chase Br Col 50.49N 119.41E
109 M3 Chase Kansas 38.22N 98.22W
103 B8 Chase Maryland 39.22N 76.22W
106 C6 Chaseburg Wisconsin 43.41N 91.06W
104 G10 Chase City Virginia 36.59N 78.30W
11 B13 Chase I New Zealand 47.12S 167.43E
108 L3 Chase L N Dakota 47.00N 99.35W
41 D7 Chasel'ka U.S.S.R. 65.07N 81.30E
42 B1 Chasel'ka R U.S.S.R.
99 Q2 Chase Mills New York 44.52N 75.05W
103 E1 Chaseville New York 42.33N 74.52W
47 J7 Chashi U.S.S.R. 55.56N 64.53E
43 F7 Chashkent Turkmeniya U.S.S.R. 38.00N 61.24E
31 F4 Chashma Barrage Pakistan 32.30N 71.22E
32 F3 Chashmeh Baluch Iran 35.44N 55.53E
Chashmeh Chah Shirin see Chāh Shirin
Chashmeh Girdab see Girdab
Chashmeh-i-Ab-i-Garm see Chashmeh-ye Ab-e Garm
Chashmeh-i-Mukik see Chashmeh ye Mūkīk
Chashmeh-i-Shuturun see Chashmeh ye Shotoran
32 G3 Chashmeh Nūrī Iran 35.33N 56.34E
Chashmeh Sefid see Chashmeh ye Safīd
32 E3 Chashmeh Tuleh Iran 34.31N 52.46E
Chashmeh Tulha see Chashmeh Tuleh
32 G4 Chashmeh-ye Ab-e-Garm Iran 32.50N 57.29E
32 H4 Chashmeh-ye Garm Āb Iran 32.26N 58.20E
32 G4 Chashmeh-ye Magu Iran 33.17N 56.41E
32 G4 Chashmeh-ye Mūkīk Iran 32.19N 57.30E
32 E3 Chashmeh-ye Palasi Iran 34.25N 52.45E
32 G4 Chashmeh-ye Safīd Iran 33.03N 56.32E
32 E3 Chashmeh-ye Safīd Āb Iran 34.19N 52.20E
32 F4 Chashmey-ye Shotoran Iran 33.16N 55.58E
46 G3 Chashniki Belorussiya U.S.S.R. 54.49N 29.09E
32 E3 Chāsht Khvāran Iran 35.41N 53.38E
121 C9 Chasico Argentina 42.50S 66.54W
121 E7 Chasi Co Argentina 32.28S 62.45W
108 R5 Chaska Minnesota 44.49N 93.32W
11 D13 Chaslands Mistake pt New Zealand 46.39S 169.22E
101 N10 Chasm Br Col 51.13N 121.31W
11 C11 Chasm Pass New Zealand 44.17S 168.52E
21 D7 Chasong N Korea 41.24N 126.40E
42 K5 Chasovaya U.S.S.R. 53.28N 119.58E
47 D4 Chasovenskaya U.S.S.R. 62.55N 39.42E
41 E6 Chasovnya U.S.S.R. 69.20N 88.35E
40 F3 Chasovnya-Uchurskaya U.S.S.R. 57.14N 132.14E
47 G5 Chasovo U.S.S.R. 62.00N 50.45E
45 J8 Chasov Yar Ukraine U.S.S.R. 48.35N 37.48E
25 L8 Chassad Manipur India 24.53N 94.31E
105 E9 Chassahowitzka B Florida 28.41N 82.39W
106 F2 Chassell Michigan 47.02N 88.32W
72 E4 Chasseneuil-sur-Bonnieure France 45.49N 0.28E
72 F4 Chassenon France 45.51N 0.45E
61 M8 Chassepierre Belgium 49.42N 5.16E
71 D7 Chasseradès France 44.33N 3.49E
66 E3 Chasseral mts Switzerland

66 C4 Chasseron,Le mt Switzerland 46.51N 6.33E
71 F5 Chasse-sur-Rhône France 45.35N 4.50E
71 E8 Chassezac R France
72 H2 Chassignoles France 46.33N 1.55E
71 G1 Chassigny-Aisey France 47.43N 5.23E
70 K5 Chassille France 48.01N 0.06W
72 B3 Chassiron,Phare de Lt Ho France 46.03N 1.25W
32 F4 Chastab, Kūh-e mts Iran
72 J5 Chastang, Barrage du France 45.09N 2.00E
47 K7 Chastoozerskoye U.S.S.R. 55.34N 67.55E
61 H5 Chastres Belgium 50.16N 4.28E
61 J4 Chastre-Villeroux-Blanmont Belgium 50.37N 4.38E
46 R2 Chastyye U.S.S.R. 57.20N 54.52E
120 B2 Chasuta Peru 6.32S 76.10W
32 F2 Chāt Iran 37.52N 55.27E
72 C2 Châtaigneraie,la France 46.39N 0.44W
42 J6 Chatanga U.S.S.R. 50.20N 110.45E
113 O4 Chatanika Alaska 65.06N 147.39W
113 O4 Chatanika R Alaska
68 C3 Château Yvelines France 48.54N 2.06E
116 O8 Chateaubelair St Vincent, W I 13.15N 61.05W
72 A1 Chateau Bougon airport France 47.10N 1.38W
70 H5 Châteaubourg France 48.07N 1.22W
70 H6 Châteaubriant France 47.43N 1.22W
72 G4 Château-Chervix France 45.35N 1.21E
71 D2 Château Chinon France 47.04N 3.56E
69 G8 Château d'Ancy-le-Franc France 47.47N 4.10E
79 C3 Château des Dames mt Italy 45.55N 7.34E
71 G10 Chateau d' If France 43.17N 5.20E
66 E6 Château d'Oex Switzerland 46.29N 7.08E
72 B4 Chateau d'Oléron, le France 45.52N 1.12W
70 L6 Château-du-Loir France 47.42N 0.25E
70 N5 Châteaudun France 48.04N 1.20E
69 C6 Châteaufort France 48.45N 2.05E
72 E3 Château Garnier France 46.16N 0.26E
104 L2 Chateaugay New York 44.55N 74.06W
70 H5 Châteaugiron France 48.03N 1.30W
70 J6 Château-Gontier France 47.49N 0.42W
99 Q10 Châteauguay Quebec 45.22N 73.44W
69 D7 Château-Landon France 48.09N 2.43E
70 L6 Château-la-Vallière France 47.33N 0.20E
72 F5 Château l'Evêque France 45.15N 0.42E
70 B5 Châteaulin France 48.12N 4.07W
72 J2 Châteaumeillant France 46.34N 2.11W
71 D7 Châteauneuf-de-Randon France 44.38N 3.40E
70 G4 Châteauneuf-d'Ille-et-Vilaine France 48.34N 1.56W
71 F6 Châteauneuf-d'Isère France 45.01N 4.56E
70 C5 Châteauneuf-du-Faou France 48.11N 3.50W
71 F8 Châteauneuf-du-Pape France 44.04N 4.50E
71 F8 Châteauneuf-du-Rhône France 44.28N 4.42E
70 N4 Châteauneuf-en-Thymerais France 48.35N 1.16E
72 H4 Châteauneuf-la-Forêt France 45.42N 1.36E
71 B4 Châteauneuf-les-Bains France 46.01N 2.53E
72 D4 Châteauneuf-sur-Charente France 45.36N 0.03W
72 J2 Châteauneuf-sur-Cher France 46.52N 2.18E
71 F6 Châteauneuf-sur-Isère France 45.14N 4.57E
70 P6 Châteauneuf-sur-Loire France 47.52N 2.13E
70 J6 Châteauneuf-sur-Sarthe France 47.40N 0.30W
71 C2 Châteauneuf Val-de-Bargis France 47.16N 3.12E
72 A2 Château-Olonne France 46.31N 1.44W
72 G3 Châteauponsac France 46.08N 1.17E
69 G4 Château-Porcien France 49.32N 4.15E
70 D4 Château,Pte.du France 48.52N 3.13W
71 K7 Château-Queyras France 44.45N 6.47E
71 J8 Châteauredon France 44.01N 6.13E
71 F9 Châteaurenard Bouches-du-Rhône France 43.53N 4.51E
69 D8 Châteaurenard Loiret France 47.57N 2.56E
70 M6 Château-Renault France 47.36N 0.56E
98 A7 Chateau Richer Quebec 47.00N 71.00W
71 K7 Châteauroux Hautes-Alpes France 44.37N 6.32E
72 H2 Châteauroux Indre France 46.49N 1.41E
69 M6 Château-Salins France 48.49N 6.30E
69 E5 Château-Thierry France 49.03N 3.24E
11 K6 Château Tongariro New Zealand 39.12S 175.31E
99 R5 Chateauvert,L Quebec
69 H7 Châteauvillain France 48.02N 4.56E
71 J8 Châteaux-Arnoux France 44.05N 6.00E
116 O4 Châteaux, Pte. des Guadeloupe W I 16.14N 61.11W
101 O6 Chateh Alberta 58.43N 118.47W
66 D6 Châtel France 46.17N 6.50E
72 B3 Châtelaillon-Plage France 46.05N 1.05W
71 J5 Châtelard,le France 43.40N 6.10E
70 E4 Châtelaudren France 48.32N 2.59W
71 D1 Châtel Censoir France 47.32N 3.37E
72 L3 Châtel-de-Neuvre France 46.24N 3.18E
71 D5 Châteldon France 45.59N 3.31E
61 J5 Châtelet Belgium 50.24N 4.32E
69 D7 Châtelet-en-Brie,le France 48.30N 2.48E
72 J2 Châtelet,le France 46.39N 2.17E
70 N5 Châtelets,les France 48.26N 1.10E
71 K3 Chateleu, Mt France 46.59N 6.33E
71 E1 Châtel Gérard France 47.38N 4.06E
71 C5 Châtelguyon France 45.55N 3.04E
61 J5 Châtelineau Belgium 50.25N 4.31E
71 F1 Châtellenot France 47.43N 4.49E
72 F2 Châtellerault France 46.49N 0.33E
71 D4 Châtel-Montagne France 46.07N 3.40E
66 D5 Châtel St.Denis Switzerland 46.32N 6.55E
69 L7 Châtel-sur-Moselle France 48.19N 6.23E
72 H4 Châtelus-le-Marcheix France 46.00N 1.36E
72 J3 Châtelus Malvaleix France 46.18N 2.01E
68 E4 Châtenay-Malabry France 48.46N 2.18E
69 N7 Châtenois Bas-Rhin France 48.17N 7.25E
66 D1 Châtenois Haute-Saône France 47.34N 6.51E
69 K7 Châtenois Vosges France 48.18N 5.50E
100 U8 Chatfield Manitoba 50.45N 97.35W
108 S6 Chatfield Minnesota 43.52N 92.11W
113 U8 Chatham Alaska 57.30N 135.00W
107 G2 Chatham Illinois 39.40N 89.42W
56 N5 Chatham Kent Eng 51.23N 0.32E
107 D9 Chatham Louisiana 32.19N 92.28W
103 O3 Chatham Massachusetts 41.40N 69.57W
98 G6 Chatham New Brunswick 47.02N 65.30W
103 F5 Chatham New Jersey 40.44N 74.23W
103 G2 Chatham New York 42.22N 73.36W
99 H10 Chatham Ontario 42.24N 82.11W
103 C7 Chatham Pennsylvania 39.52N 75.49W
104 F10 Chatham Virginia 36.49N 79.26W
103 G2 Chatham Center New York 42.25N 73.37W
98 G7 Chatham Head New Brunswick 46.59N 65.35W
11 K11 Chatham I Chatham Is Pacific Oc
121 J8 Chatham, I Chile 50.40S 74.30W
Chatham I Galápagos Is see San Cristóbal,I
11 K10 Chatham Is Pacific Oc
10 Q10 Chatham Rise Pacific Oc
101 H8 Chatham Sd Br Col
113 U8 Chatham Str Alaska
30 H6 Chatia Bihar India 26.33N 84.34E
61 N8 Châtillon Belgium 49.37N 5.42E
66 C7 Châtillon France 46.05N 6.35E
68 E4 Châtillon France 48.48N 2.18E
79 C3 Châtillon Italy 45.45N 7.37E
69 D8 Châtillon-Coligny France 47.50N 2.51E
71 D2 Châtillon-en-Bazois France 47.03N 3.39E
71 G7 Châtillon-en-Diois France 44.41N 5.29E
71 H4 Châtillon-en-Michaille France 46.09N 5.48E
70 H5 Châtillon-en-Vendelais France 48.12N 1.11W
71 G5 Châtillon-la-Palud France 45.58N 5.15E
71 F4 Châtillon-sur-Chalaronne France 46.07N 4.57E
72 G2 Châtillon-sur-Indre France 46.59N 1.11E
71 B1 Châtillon-sur-Loire France 47.36N 2.44E
69 F5 Châtillon-sur-Marne France 49.06N 3.46E
69 H8 Châtillon-sur-Seine France 47.52N 4.35E
43 K6 Chatkal R Kirgiziya U.S.S.R.
43 K6 Chatkal'skiy Khrebet mts U.S.S.R.
121 A9 Chato pk Arg/Chile 42.35S 72.04W
107 H10 Chatom Alabama 31.28N 88.17W
71 G6 Châtonnay France 45.30N 5.12E
84 S14 Chatos Cyprus 35.15N 33.37E
68 C3 Chatou France 48.53N 2.09E
29 J5 Chatra Bihar India 24.14N 84.57E
30 L6 Chatra Nepal 26.50N 87.09E
29 J8 Chatrapur Orissa India 19.26N 85.02E
72 H2 Châtre, la France 46.35N 1.59E
72 G3 Châtre-Langlin, la France 46.24N 1.23E
29 D4 Chatsa Rajasthan India 26.40N 75.59E
12 L6 Chatswood dist Sydney, N S W
105 C3 Chatsworth Georgia 34.49N 84.46W
106 F9 Chatsworth Illinois 40.45N 88.18W
103 E7 Chatsworth New Jersey 39.49N 74.32W
99 K8 Chatsworth Ontario 44.27N 80.54W
13 F5 Chatsworth Queensland 22.00S 140.15E
57 K6 Chatsworth Park Derbys Eng 53.14N 1.34W
105 C7 Chattahoochee Florida 30.42N 84.51W
105 B6 Chattahoochee,R Ala/Georgia
109 M7 Chattanooga Oklahoma 34.26N 98.39W
107 L6 Chattanooga Tennessee 35.02N 85.18W
110 H2 Chattaroy Washington 47.55N 117.19W
104 C9 Chattaroy W Virginia 37.43N 82.17W
30 H8 Chattarpur Bihar India 24.23N 84.11E
56 M3 Chatteris Cambs England 52.27N 0.03E
11 D12 Chatto Creek New Zealand 45.09S 169.32E
57 K1 Chatton Northumb England 55.33N 1.55W
105 B3 Chattooga,R Ala/Georgia
105 D3 Chattooga,R S Carolina
25 F5 Chatturat Thailand 15.30N 101.43E
105 D2 Chatuge L N Carolina 35.00N 83.46W
44 C10 Chatyr Dag mt Ukraine U.S.S.R. 44.44N 34.17E
43 M6 Chatyrkël',Oz L Kirgiziya U.S.S.R.
43 M6 Chatyrtash Kirgiziya U.S.S.R. 40.57N 76.25E
31 F5 Chaubara Pakistan 30.55N 71.30E
30 C3 Chaubattia Uttar Prad India 29.38N 79.25E
30 C6 Chaubia Uttar Prad India 26.52N 79.08E
103 L2 Chaubunagungamaug,L Massachusetts
72 B2 Chauché France 46.50N 1.16W
77 J6 Chauchina Spain 37.12N 3.46W
44 D10 Chauda Mys C Ukraine U.S.S.R. 45.00N 35.50E
69 K8 Chaudenay France 47.49N 5.30E
72 L6 Chaudes Aigues France 44.51N 3.00E
71 D7 Chaudeyrac France 44.40N 3.45E
61 N4 Chaudfontaine Belgium 50.35N 5.39E
98 P10 Chaudière Bassin Quebec 46.44N 71.16W
99 C8 Chaudière Falls Quebec 45.26N 75.44W
Chau Doc see Chau Phu
72 C1 Chaudron-en-Mauges France 47.17N 0.59W
69 E5 Chaudun France 49.19N 3.17E
31 F5 Chaudwan Pakistan 31.39N 70.26E
113 H6 Chauekuktuli L Alaska 60.05N 159.00W
71 E4 Chauffailles France 46.12N 4.21E
71 J7 Chauffayer France 44.45N 6.00E
25 C2 Chauk Burma 20.52N 94.50E
30 C8 Chauka Madhya Prad India 24.52N 79.31E
Chauka R see Sarda R Uttar Pradesh
30 C3 Chaukhutia Uttar Prad India 29.52N 79.20E
31 A9 Chauki Pakistan 24.55N 66.57E
30 A6 Chaukrauda Madhya Prad India 26.35N 77.57E
23 A9 Chau Kung isld Hong Kong 22.16N 114.03E
28 A1 Chaul Maharashtra India 18.35N 72.57E
69 D4 Chaulnes France 49.50N 2.49E
69 H8 Chaume,la France 47.53N 4.50E
71 G3 Chaumergy France 46.50N 5.30E
69 D6 Chaumes-en-Brie France 48.40N 2.51E
69 J7 Chaumont France 48.07N 5.08E
104 J2 Chaumont New York 44.04N 76.08W
71 J2 Chaumont mt France 47.02N 6.25E
66 D3 Chaumont mt Switzerland 47.02N 6.57E
69 B5 Chaumont-en-Vexin France 49.16N 1.53E
61 J4 Chaumont-Gistoux Belgium 50.41N 4.44E
69 G4 Chaumont-Porcien France 49.38N 4.15E
70 N7 Chaumont-sur-Loire France 47.29N 1.11E
70 O6 Chaumont-sur-Tharonne France 47.37N 1.54E
39 J1 Chaun R U.S.S.R.
72 E3 Chaunay France 46.13N 0.10E
104 C7 Chauncey Ohio 39.24N 82.07W
25 L9 Chaungwa Burma 23.00N 94.23E
25 E6 Chaungwabyin Burma 13.40N 98.24E
25 D4 Chaungzon Burma 16.22N 97.33E
39 J1 Chaunskaya U.S.S.R. 68.47N 170.41E
39 H1 Chaunskaya Guba gulf U.S.S.R.
69 E4 Chauny France 49.37N 3.14E
30 A2 Chaupal Himachal Prad India 30.56N 77.35E
30 J8 Chauparan Bihar India 24.24N 85.15E
25 H7 Chau Phu Vietnam 10.42N 105.03E
121 A9 Chauques,Is Chile 42.20S 73.15W
28 H7 Chaura isld Nicobar Is 8.28N 93.01E
29 F6 Chauragarh Madhya Prad India 22.49N 78.59E
30 G5 Chauraha Uttar Prad India 27.20N 83.36E
29 F6 Chaurai Madhya Prad India 22.02N 79.18E
30 G7 Chausa Bihar India 25.31N 83.54E
70 G4 Chausey Is France 48.52N 1.50W
26 N13 Chaussée des Otaries reef Amsterdam I Ind Oc 37.49S 77.32E
26 N15 Chaussée du Phoque reef St Paul I Ind Oc 38.42S 77.29E
61 F4 Chaussée-Notre-Dame-Louvignies Belgium 50.36N 4.00E
69 H6 Chaussee-sur-Marne,la France 48.50N 4.32E
69 C4 Chaussée-Tirancourt,la France 49.58N 2.09E
71 G3 Chaussin France 46.58N 5.25E
45 B3 Chausy Belorussiya U.S.S.R. 53.49N 30.57E
104 F4 Chautauqua New York 42.12N 79.30W
104 F4 Chautauqua,L New York
31 D5 Chauter Pakistan 30.20N 68.00E
43 K6 Chauvay Kirgiziya U.S.S.R. 40.06N 72.13E
70 G7 Chauvé France 47.12N 1.59W
70 N6 Chauvigny Loir-et-Cher France 47.58N 1.05E
72 F2 Chauvigny Vienne France 46.35N 0.39E
100 G6 Chauvin Alberta 52.42N 110.10W
66 D1 Chaux France 47.43N 6.50E
66 D3 Chaux de Fonds,La Switzerland 47.07N 6.51E
71 H3 Chaux-du-Dombief,la France 46.36N 5.55E
66 C3 Chaux du Milieu,la Switzerland 47.01N 6.43E
72 B2 Chavagnes-en-Paillers France 46.53N 1.15W
26 R2 Chavakachcheri Sri Lanka 9.38N 80.10E
117 G6 Chaval Brazil 3.05S 41.14W
75 F4 Chavaler Spain 41.51N 2.28W
71 F6 Chavanay France 45.25N 4.43E
47 D3 Chavan'ga U.S.S.R. 66.06N 37.51E
69 H6 Chavanges France 48.31N 4.33E
71 G4 Chavannes-sur-Suran France 46.16N 5.25E
118 D4 Chavantina Brazil 14.45S 52.20W
32 B4 Chavār Iran 33.43N 46.15E
117 D5 Chaves Brazil 0.10S 49.58W
76 E5 Chaves Portugal 41.44N 7.28W
120 A1 Chaves Valdivia Peru 4.29S 78.11W
104 B9 Chavies Kentucky 37.21N 83.22W
69 F5 Chavignon France 49.28N 3.31E
68 D4 Chaville France 48.48N 2.12E
119 D5 Chaviva Colombia 4.22N 72.18W
43 J6 Chavlisay Uzbekistan U.S.S.R. 41.06N 69.45E
66 C5 Chavornay Switzerland 46.43N 6.34E
92 A8 Chavuma Zambia 13.04S 22.40E
92 A8 Chavuma Falls Zambia 13.05S 22.40E
31 D6 Chawal R Pakistan
25 E8 Chawang Thailand 8.21N 99.34E
31 G5 Chaweka Pakistan 30.05N 73.25E
56 K5 Chawton Hants England 51.09N 0.59W
92 G4 Chaya Tanzania 5.35S 34.05E
42 H3 Chaya R Irkutsk U.S.S.R.
42 C3 Chaya R Tomsk U.S.S.R.
92 E7 Chaya,L Zambia 11.27S 30.31E
43 J5 Chayan Kazakhstan U.S.S.R. 42.59N 69.22E
120 F8 Chayanta,R Bolivia
40 H5 Chayatyn,Khrebet ra U.S.S.R.
41 N8 Chaydakh U.S.S.R. 64.25N 125.47E
41 O7 Chaydakh U.S.S.R. 66.04N 132.44E
43 L6 Chayek Kirgiziya U.S.S.R. 41.55N 74.28E
34 H6 Chayia Iraq 32.09N 40.58E
Chāyid at Tahir see Ka'id aṭ Ṭāhir
34 M4 Chāy Khānah Iraq 34.20N 44.34E
46 R2 Chaykovskiy U.S.S.R. 56.40N 54.10E
41 Q4 Chay-Povarnya U.S.S.R. 72.50N 140.19E
Chayul see Qayü
40 J5 Chayvo Zaliv gulf Sakhalin U.S.S.R.
72 E4 Chazelles France 45.38N 0.23E
71 E5 Chazelles-sur-Lyon France 45.38N 4.23E
70 J6 Chazé-sur-Argos France 47.37N 0.53W
47 G5 Chazhegovo U.S.S.R. 60.04N 54.16E
121 D4 Chazón Argentina 33.05S 63.15W
104 M2 Chazy New York 44.53N 73.29W
104 M2 Chazy,West New York 44.50N 73.31W
Chbeit,Jebel see Shubeit,Jebel
88 H8 Chbika watercourse Morocco
100 D7 Cheadle Alberta 51.03N 113.28W
57 J6 Cheadle Greater Manchester England 53.24N 2.13W
57 K7 Cheadle Staffs England 52.59N 1.59W
107 L8 Cheaha Mt Alabama 33.29N 85.49W
55 E5 Cheam London England 51.21N 0.13W
23 A9 Cheang Chau Ching I Hong Kong
121 J6 Cheap,Canal str Chile
104 F7 Cheat R W Virginia
107 J5 Cheatham L Tennessee 36.17N 87.15W
64 N3 Cheb Czechoslovakia 50.08N 12.28E
47 M6 Chebarkul' U.S.S.R. 55.00N 60.21E
47 M6 Chebarkul', Oz L U.S.S.R. 54.57N 60.20E
88 M5 Chebka Tioudadine hills Morocco
45 T1 Cheboksary U.S.S.R. 56.08N 47.12E
106 K4 Cheboygan Michigan 45.40N 84.28W
46 L1 Chebsara U.S.S.R. 59.14N 38.59E
91 H10 Chebula Angola 12.27S 23.49E
75 G6 Checa Spain 40.35N 1.47W
29 D5 Chechat Rajasthan India 24.46N 75.58E
39 D2 Chechelyugyun R U.S.S.R.
44 F4 Checheno Ingushskaya A.S.S.R U.S.S.R.
44 H4 Chechen'Ostrova isld U.S.S.R.
45 B4 Chechersk Belorussiya U.S.S.R. 52.54N 30.54E
39 M2 Chechin U.S.S.R. 66.46N 171.21W
21 D9 Chech'ŏn S Korea 37.05N 128.09E
42 H3 Chechuysk U.S.S.R. 58.08N 108.40E
62 M5 Chęciny Poland 50.49N 20.28E
57 K7 Checkley Staffs England 52.56N 1.57W
109 P6 Checotah Oklahoma 35.29N 95.32W
69 C8 Chécy France 47.53N 2.00E
98 L8 Chedabucto B Nova Scotia
56 F5 Cheddar Somerset England 51.17N 2.46W
71 K5 Chedde France 45.55N 6.43E
57 J6 Cheddleton Staffs England 53.04N 2.02W
26 R4 Cheddlkulam Sri Lanka 8.40N 80.18E
90 H5 Cheddra Chad 13.24N 16.03E
42 E6 Cheder U.S.S.R. 51.28N 94.45E
90 J5 Chediba Chad 12.28N 19.07E
25 B3 Cheduba Burma 18.52N 93.44E
25 B3 Cheduba I Burma
25 B3 Cheduba Str Burma
101 S7 Cheecham Alberta 56.15N 110.50W
59 J7 Cheekpoint Waterford Irish Rep 52.16N 7.00W
99 J2 Cheepash R Ontario
99 G1 Cheepay, R Ontario
13 G7 Cheepie Queensland 26.36S 145.00E
100 O1 Cheeseman L Ontario 49.28N 89.20W
109 E2 Cheesman L Colorado 39.12N 105.17W
12 B3 Cheesmans Pk S Australia 27.30S 130.22E
123 K5 Cheetham,C Antarctica 70.26S 162.40E
72 D3 Chef-Boutonne France 46.07N 0.04W
90 F2 Cheffadene Niger 19.57N 12.11E
107 G11 Chef Menteur Louisiana 30.04N 89.48W
Chefoo see Yantai
113 E6 Chefornak Alaska 60.12N 164.18W
99 R3 Chef,R.du Quebec
94 M4 Chefu Mozambique 22.13S 32.28E
91 G9 Chefumage R Angola
88 F9 Cheg Morocco 25.19N 14.49W
40 F6 Chegdomyn U.S.S.R. 51.09N 133.01E
44 E4 Chegem R U.S.S.R.
88 Q4 Chegga Algeria 34.29N 5.53E
88 L9 Chegga Mauritania 25.27N 5.45W
39 M2 Chegitun R U.S.S.R.
39 M2 Chegytun' U.S.S.R. 66.35N 171.10W
110 C3 Chehalis Washington 46.40N 122.58W
110 B3 Chehalis R Washington
32 G2 Chehār Burj Iran 36.58N 57.11E
31 E3 Chehardar Afghanistan 35.24N 68.36E
31 E3 Chehardar Pass Afghanistan 35.11N 68.42E
32 G4 Chehardeh Iran 33.41N 56.46E
34 P6 Chehariz anc site Iraq 32.13N 47.18E
23 D6 Chehe Guangxi China 24.53N 107.38E
32 B3 Chehel Chashmeh,Kūh-e mt Iran 35.50N 46.35E
32 J5 Chehel Dokhtarān, Kūh-e mt Iran 30.37N 60.38E
32 G5 Chehel Pāyeh Iran 31.55N 57.12E
Chehil Payeh see Chehel Pāyeh
Cheikh Ibrâhîm see Sheikh Ibrāhīm
Cheikh,Jebel ech mt see Sheikh,Jebel esh mt
Cheikh Meskîne see Sheikh Miskin
Cheikh Saad see Sheikh Sa'd
88 L9 Cheikria Algeria 25.27N 5.29W
44 J7 Cheil'dag Azerbaydzhan U.S.S.R. 40.17N 49.17E
72 E1 Cheillé France 47.16N 0.25E
71 K9 Cheiron,Mtgne.du France 43.49N 6.59E
21 D11 Cheju S Korea 33.31N 126.29E
21 D11 Cheju Do isld S Korea
21 D11 Cheju haehyŏp str S Korea
45 H2 Chekalin U.S.S.R. 54.06N 36.15E
46 R3 Chekan U.S.S.R. 54.50N 53.31E
42 G4 Chekanovskiy U.S.S.R. 56.07N 101.28E
41 M5 Chekanovskogo,Kryazh ridge U.S.S.R.
31 B3 Chekao Afghanistan 34.47N 63.03E
Chek Chue see Stanley Hong Kong
45 J1 Chekhov Moscow U.S.S.R. 55.07N 37.30E
40 J8 Chekhov Sakhalin U.S.S.R. 47.28N 142.00E
Chekiang prov China see Zhejiang
41 B3 Chekina,Zaliv gulf Novaya Zemlya U.S.S.R.
42 B3 Chekino U.S.S.R. 57.34N 76.30E
18 K2 Chek Jawa,Tanjong C Singapore 1.24N 103.59E
40 F6 Chekunda U.S.S.R. 50.47N 132.04E
41 N5 Chekurovka U.S.S.R. 71.04N 127.10E
47 D4 Chekuyevo U.S.S.R. 63.33N 38.58E
94 M5 Chékwé Mozambique 24.31S 32.59E
Chel see Kuru watercourse
18 E3 Chelah,Gunong mt Pen Malaysia 4.35N 102.48E
72 F9 Chélan France 43.21N 0.33E
100 O6 Chelan Saskatchewan 52.38N 103.22W
110 E2 Chelan Washington 47.50N 120.00W
110 E1 Chelan,L Washington 48.10N 120.32W
110 E1 Chelan Ra Washington
Chelas see Areeiro
91 C11 Chela,Sa.da mts Angola
40 G3 Chelasin U.S.S.R. 57.41N 137.24E
40 G3 Chelasin R U.S.S.R.
40 G2 Chelat,Khrebet mts U.S.S.R.
113 M5 Chelatna L Alaska 62.29N 151.30W
44 C1 Chelbas R U.S.S.R.
44 C2 Chelbasskaya U.S.S.R. 45.59N 39.21E
76 A11 Cheleiros Portugal 38.53N 9.19W
43 C7 Cheleken Turkmeniya U.S.S.R. 39.26N 53.11E
43 C7 Cheleken, Poluostrov pen Turkmeniya U.S.S.R.
77 B5 Cheles Spain 38.31N 7.16W
57 J6 Chelford Cheshire England 53.16N 2.17W
121 C7 Chelforó Argentina 39.04S 66.33W
88 Q3 Chelghóum el Aid Algeria 36.10N 6.08E
93 E10 Cheli watercourse Tanzania
88 R4 Chélia,Djebel mt Algeria 35.19N 6.42E
88 O3 Cheliff R Algeria
94 N4 Cheline Mozambique 22.30S 35.02E
47 H7 Chelkakovo U.S.S.R. 55.40N 55.05E
43 E3 Chelkar Aktyubinsk, Kazakhstan U.S.S.R. 47.48N 59.39E
77 P2 Chella Spain 39.03N 0.39W
69 D6 Chelles France 48.53N 2.35E
87 M6 Chellihet Somalia 8.46N 49.10E
62 O4 Chełm Poland 51.08N 23.29E
62 L2 Chełmno Poland 53.20N 18.25E
56 M4 Chelmsford Essex England 51.44N 0.28E
99 J6 Chelmsford Ontario 46.34N 81.13W
95 N3 Chelmsford Dam res S Africa 27.58S 29.40E
47 D4 Chelmuzhi U.S.S.R. 62.34N 35.40E
62 L2 Chełmża Poland 53.11N 18.34E
39 D4 Chelomdzha R U.S.S.R.
42 J3 Chelonchen R U.S.S.R.
42 D6 Chelosh U.S.S.R. 51.32N 87.50E
31 K1 Chelpanguk mt Xizang Zizhiqu China 35.40N 80.15E
108 S8 Chelsea Iowa 41.56N 92.24W
55 E4 Chelsea London England 51.29N 0.10W
103 M2 Chelsea Massachusetts 42.24N 71.02W
106 K7 Chelsea Michigan 42.19N 84.01W
103 G3 Chelsea New York 41.32N 73.57W
109 P5 Chelsea Oklahoma 36.33N 95.27W
103 D7 Chelsea Pennsylvania 39.52N 75.28W
95 J9 Chelsea S Africa 33.57S 25.25E
104 N3 Chelsea Vermont 43.58N 72.29W
104 Q9 Chelsea dist Boston, Mass
12 D8 Chelsea dist Melbourne, Victoria
55 J5 Chelsfield London England 51.22N 0.08E
55 G6 Chelsham Surrey England 51.19N 0.02W
56 G4 Cheltenham Glos England 51.54N 2.04W
12 A7 Cheltenham dist Adelaide, S Aust
23 H2 Chelue Jiangsu China 33.00N 19.33E
70 H6 Chelun France 47.51N 1.12W
23 H2 Cheluo Jiangsu China 32.43N 119.27E
75 H8 Chelva Spain 39.45N 1.00W
44 J9 Chelvand Iran 38.17N 49.03E
56 F5 Chelwood Avon England 51.22N 2.32W
47 M6 Chelyabinsk U.S.S.R. 55.12N 61.25E
38 F3 Chelyabinskaya Oblast' prov U.S.S.R.
29 K1 Chelyama W Bengal India 23.36N 86.34E
104 D8 Chelyan W Virginia 38.11N 81.31W
41 H2 Chelyuskin U.S.S.R. 77.42N 104.05E
41 H2 Chelyuskin,Mys C U.S.S.R. 77.44N 103.55E
101 M11 Chemainus Vancouver I, Br Col 48.54N 123.42W
42 D6 Chemal U.S.S.R. 51.29N 86.04E
115 Q7 Chemax Mexico 20.38N 87.55W
70 J6 Chemaze France 47.47N 0.47W
92 G10 Chemba Mozambique 17.11S 34.53E
92 D7 Chembe Zambia 11.58S 28.45E
28 B7 Chembur dist Bombay India 19.03N 72.54E
Chemchemal oil bore see Chamchamāl
42 G3 Chemdal'sk U.S.S.R. 59.35N 103.25E
93 G6 Chemelil Kenya 0.06S 35.08E
43 F8 Chemen-i-Bit Turkmeniya U.S.S.R. 35.29N 62.25E
45 C5 Chemer Ukraine U.S.S.R. 51.05N 31.13E
70 N7 Chemery France 47.21N 1.29E
69 H4 Chémery-sur-Bar France 49.35N 4.52E
72 C1 Chemillé France 47.14N 0.43W
70 M6 Chemillé-sur-Dême France 47.39N 0.39E
72 L2 Chemilly France 46.30N 3.18E
71 G3 Chemin France 46.59N 5.20E
26 U13 Chemin Grenier Mauritius, Indian Oc 20.29S 57.28E
69 H6 Cheminon France 48.44N 4.55E
70 K6 Chemiré-le-Gaudin France 47.55N 0.01W
Chemlāne,Sabkhet see Shemlān, Sabkhat
18 B7 Chemor Pen Malaysia 4.44N 101.06E
104 P8 Chemquassabamticook L Maine
42 C5 Chemskiy U.S.S.R. 54.54N 83.00E
103 A2 Chemung New York 42.01N 76.38W
103 A2 Chemung co New York
104 H4 Chemung R New York
113 O4 Chena R Alaska
31 G5 Chenab R Pakistan
72 C4 Chenac d'Uzet France 45.31N 0.50W
88 L8 Chenachane Algeria 26.04N 4.15W
88 M9 Chenachane watercourse Algeria
113 O4 Chena Hot Springs Alaska 65.03N 146.10W
103 C2 Chenango co New York
104 K4 Chenango R New York
103 C2 Chenango Bridge New York 42.10N 75.53W
103 C2 Chenango Forks New York 42.14N 75.53W
21 A3 Chen Barag Qi Nei Monggol Zizhiqu China 49.30N 119.31E
42 J4 Chencha U.S.S.R. 55.58N 111.00E
Chenchar see Shinshār
90 D8 Chenchenji Nigeria 7.31N 9.55E
Ch'en-ch'ien Tao islds see Chenqian Shan
18 B7 Chenderiang Pen Malaysia 4.14N 101.14E
18 A7 Chenderoh, Tasek L Pen Malaysia
66 C1 Chenebier France 47.39N 6.43E
66 A7 Chêne-Bourg Switzerland 46.12N 6.12E
71 H2 Chenecey-Buillon France 47.08N 5.58E
61 N4 Chênée Belgium 50.37N 5.37E
113 N6 Chenega Alaska 60.18N 148.09W
69 G6 Chêne,le France 48.33N 4.10E
72 J3 Chénerailles France 46.07N 2.10E
99 P7 Chénéville Quebec 45.53N 75.04W
109 N4 Cheney Kansas 37.39N 97.47W
110 H2 Cheney Washington 47.29N 117.35W
109 N4 Cheney Res Kansas
107 D10 Cheneyville Louisiana 31.01N 92.18W
28 D4 Chengam Tamil Nadu India 12.20N 78.46E
22 K8 Cheng'an Hebei China 36.27N 114.41E
23 D6 Chengbihe Sk res Guangxi China
23 E5 Chengbu Miaozu Zizhixian Hunan China 26.28N 110.11E
23 E1 Chengcheng Shaanxi China 35.07N 109.48E
Chengchow see Zhengzhou
22 L6 Chengde Hebei China 40.48N 118.06E
22 L6 Chengde Hebei China 40.59N 117.52E
23 G2 Chengdong Hu L Anhui China
23 C3 Chengdu Sichuan China 30.37N 104.06E
43 M5 Chengel'dy Alma-Ata, Kazakhstan U.S.S.R. 44.01N 77.30E
43 J6 Chengel'dy Kazakhstan U.S.S.R. 41.49N 68.56E
28 L1 Chengele Assam India 28.44N 96.18E
23 C6 Chenggong Yunnan China 24.55N 102.47E
23 D2 Chenggu Shaanxi China 33.09N 107.10E
23 G7 Chenghai Guangdong China 23.30N 116.42E
23 B5 Cheng Hai L Yunnan China
Ch'eng-hua see Altay
31 G4 Chengi Pakistan 32.43N 72.24E
22 L7 Chengkou Shandong China 38.07N 117.45E
23 E3 Chengkou Sichuan China 31.58N 108.51E
Cheng-lan Chi see Shenlang (Xulun Ho) Qi
23 E9 Chengmai Guangdong China 19.50N 110.01E
23 C6 Chengong Yunnan China 24.55N 102.47E
39 C2 Chën,Gora mt U.S.S.R. 65.16N 141.50E
21 D3 Chengqingqiao Heilongjiang China 49.08N 127.12E
21 B9 Chengshan Jiao headland Shandong China 37.23N 122.40E
Ch'eng-to see Chindu
Chengtu see Chengdu
23 G1 Chengwu Shandong China 35.00N 115.56E
23 D2 Cheng Xian Gansu China 33.42N 105.36E
23 G2 Chengxi Hu L Anhui China
23 J1 Chengyang Shandong China 36.15N 120.22E
23 H4 Chengyang Zhejiang China 30.01N 119.44E
21 B8 Chengzitan Liaoning China 39.28N 122.30E
Chen-hsi see Barkol
99 O6 Chénier Quebec 46.07N 76.08W
72 H3 Chéniers France 46.20N 1.50E
56 K4 Chenies Bucks England 51.41N 0.32W
113 K7 Chenik Alaska 59.13N 154.12W
98 N2 Chenil,L Quebec
69 M7 Cheniménil France 48.08N 6.35E
22 L9 Cheniu Shan isld Shandong China
23 H1 Chenjiagang Jiangsu China 34.20N 119.51E
26 U6 Chenkaladi Sri Lanka 7.47N 81.35E
115 O8 Chenkán Mexico 19.08N 90.58W
39 H1 Chenkuul',Ostrov isld U.S.S.R. 69.55N 169.14E
23 G1 Chenliu Henan China 34.39N 114.35E
Chen-nan see Nanhua
68 H4 Chennevières-sur-Marne France 48.48N 2.33E
106 F9 Chenoa Illinois 40.44N 88.43W
69 E6 Chenoise France 48.37N 3.12E
70 N7 Chenonceaux France 47.19N 1.02E
72 G1 Chenonceaux France 47.20N 1.04E
23 J3 Chenqian Shan isld Shanghai China
66 B6 Chens France 46.20N 6.17E
Chentu see Tiandeng
70 L6 Chenu France 47.37N 0.20E
23 E4 Chenxi Hunan China 28.00N 110.03E
23 F6 Chen Xiang Hunan China 25.34N 112.57E
69 F8 Cheny France 47.57N 3.32E
Chenying see Wannian
Chen-yüen see Yiwu Yunnan
25 H5 Cheom Ksan Cambodia 14.15N 104.55E
103 L3 Chepachet Rhode I 41.55N 71.40W
23 H5 Chepan Jiangxi China 27.58N 117.47E
45 H7 Chepel' Ukraine U.S.S.R. 49.20N 36.55E
120 A8 Chepen Peru 7.15S 79.23W
9 C13 Chépénéhé Loyalty Is Pacific Oc 20.43S 167.15E
121 C3 Chepes Argentina 31.19S 66.40W
115 P5 Chepigana Panama 8.12N 78.02W
115 P5 Chepo Panama 9.09N 79.03W
69 H5 Cheppe, la France 49.03N 4.31E
56 F4 Chepstow Gwent Wales 51.39N 2.41W
69 G6 Chepy France 48.54N 4.27E
32 B4 Cheqad Kabūd Iran 33.57N 46.39E
106 D3 Chequamegon B Wisconsin
67 G5 Cher dept France
70 M7 Cher R France
75 J8 Chera Spain 39.35N 0.59W
92 H6 Chera Tanzania 8.50S 36.50E
72 D4 Chérac France 45.43N 0.27W
81 P12 Cheradi,le isld Italy 40.27N 17.10E
18 D9 Cherai,Bukit hill Pen Malaysia 2.47N 103.04E
61 O6 Cherain Belgium 50.11N 5.52E
28 C6 Cheramnahadev Tamil Nadu India 8.42N 77.31E
92 F10 Chera, Mt Mozambique/Zimbabwe 16.35S 32.43E
115 J8 Cherán Mexico 19.40N 101.58W
93 G4 Cherangany Kenya 1.00N 35.15E
93 G4 Cherangany Hills Kenya
87 E6 Cherari Ethiopia 9.56N 35.55E
79 C5 Cherasco Italy 44.39N 7.52E
31 F4 Cherat Pakistan 33.50N 71.58E
61 N4 Cheratte Belgium 50.41N 5.40E
72 C9 Chéraute France 43.13N 0.51W
109 G3 Cheraw Colorado 38.07N 103.30W
107 G10 Cheraw Mississippi 31.08N 89.52W
105 H3 Cheraw S Carolina 34.41N 79.55W
42 E6 Cherbi U.S.S.R. 51.56N 94.35E
70 G2 Cherbourg France 49.38N 1.37W
88 P3 Cherchell Algeria 36.36N 2.11E
87 G4 Chercher Ethiopia 12.33N 39.50E
87 H6 Chercher reg Ethiopia
77 M6 Chercos Spain 37.15N 2.15W
61 D4 Chercq Belgium 50.35N 3.26E
45 U2 Cherdakly U.S.S.R. 54.23N 48.51E
43 P3 Cherdoyak Kazakhstan U.S.S.R. 48.49N 84.00E
47 H5 Cherdyn' U.S.S.R. 60.25N 56.22E
70 G6 Chère R France
44 F4 Cherek R U.S.S.R.
46 G1 Cherekha R U.S.S.R.
45 J5 Cheremisinovo U.S.S.R. 51.54N 37.16E
47 N4 Cheremiska U.S.S.R. 57.28N 60.54E
42 G5 Cheremkhovo U.S.S.R. 53.08N 103.01E
82 J2 Cheremosh R U.S.S.R.
47 M5 Cheremshanka U.S.S.R. 56.09N 60.15E
40 G9 Cheremshany U.S.S.R. 44.42N 135.42E
47 H5 Cheremukhovo U.S.S.R. 60.24N 59.59E
81 B2 Cheremule Sardinia 40.31N 8.43E
47 F5 Cheremushskiy U.S.S.R. 61.19N 47.27E
40 A1 Cherendey U.S.S.R. 60.10N 119.15E
42 C5 Cherepanovo U.S.S.R. 54.13N 83.28E
45 H2 Cherepet' U.S.S.R. 54.08N 36.24E
89 K6 Chereponi Ghana 10.09N 0.19E
46 L1 Cherepovets U.S.S.R. 59.09N 37.50E
47 C6 Chereptsovo U.S.S.R. 59.36N 33.15E
47 F5 Cherevkovo U.S.S.R. 61.52N 45.13E
88 T4 Chergui isld Tunisia
100 C5 Cherhill Alberta 53.50N 114.40W
56 H5 Cherhill Wilts England 51.27N 1.56W
90 E5 Chéri Niger 13.26N 11.21E
88 R4 Chéria Algeria 35.14N 7.44E
28 D2 Cherial Andhra Prad India 17.59N 79.00E
45 C3 Cherikov Belorussiya U.S.S.R. 53.35N 31.23E
79 G3 Cherio R Italy
70 N4 Cherisy France 48.44N 1.26E
56 J5 Cheriton Hants England 51.03N 1.10W
28 A5 Cheriyam isld Laccadive Is Ind Oc 10.09N 73.41E
42 H3 Cherkashina U.S.S.R. 58.40N 108.32E
Cherkasskaya Aut.Oblast' see Karachayevo-Cherkesskaya Aut Oblast'
45 J8 Cherkasskoye Ukraine U.S.S.R. 48.51N 37.25E
45 T4 Cherkasskoye U.S.S.R. 52.26N 47.11E
45 D7 Cherkassy Ukraine U.S.S.R. 49.27N 32.04E
41 O9 Chërkëkh U.S.S.R. 62.20N 133.28E
42 C3 Cherkesovo U.S.S.R. 57.50N 84.14E
45 O6 Cherkesovskiy U.S.S.R. 50.43N 42.35E
44 E3 Cherkessk U.S.S.R. 44.14N 42.05E
44 H5 Cherkey U.S.S.R. 42.57N 46.50E
82 J7 Cherkovitsa Bulgaria 43.41N 24.49E
45 L1 Cherkutino U.S.S.R. 56.10N 39.40E
28 E1 Cherla Andhra Prad India 18.05N 80.55E
47 L8 Cherlak U.S.S.R. 54.10N 74.52E
47 L8 Cherlakskiy U.S.S.R. 53.48N 74.29E
46 R3 Chermasan R U.S.S.R.
91 G10 Chermenze Angola 12.21S 20.01E
47 H6 Chermoz U.S.S.R. 58.46N 56.01E
13 K1 Chermside dist Brisbane, Qnsld
45 H3 Chern' U.S.S.R. 53.25N 36.55E
113 H9 Chernabura I Alaska 54.47N 159.35W
43 J5 Chernak Kazakhstan U.S.S.R. 43.18N 68.01E
45 K4 Chernava Lipetsk U.S.S.R. 52.30N 38.01E
45 L3 Chernava Ryazan' U.S.S.R. 53.37N 39.11E
47 H2 Chernaya Arkhangel'sk U.S.S.R. 68.34N 56.29E
41 E5 Chernaya U.S.S.R. 70.32N 89.02E
47 H2 Chernaya R Arkhangel'sk U.S.S.R.
47 J6 Chernaya R Sverdlovsk U.S.S.R.
39 F7 Chernaya,Gora mt U.S.S.R. 54.52N 158.30E
41 F3 Chernaya,Gory mts U.S.S.R.
47 G6 Chernaya Kholunitsa U.S.S.R. 58.53N 51.43E
45 B2 Chernevka Belorussiya U.S.S.R. 54.05N 30.46E
82 K9 Chernichevo Bulgaria 41.22N 25.49E
45 C5 Chernigov Ukraine U.S.S.R. 51.30N 31.18E
45 H9 Chernigovka Ukraine U.S.S.R. 47.11N 36.12E
40 F9 Chernigovka U.S.S.R. 44.20N 132.41E
44 C3 Chernigovskaya U.S.S.R. 44.40N 39.41E
45 C5 Chernigovskaya Oblast' prov Ukraine U.S.S.R.
44 C3 Chernigovskoye U.S.S.R. 44.15N 39.46E
113 F9 Cherni I Alaska 54.40N 162.21W
47 H8 Chernikovsk U.S.S.R. 54.51N 56.06E
82 K7 Cherni Lom R Bulgaria
82 H8 Cherni Vrŭkh mt Bulgaria 42.34N 23.16E
45 D7 Chernobay Ukraine U.S.S.R. 49.40N 32.22E
45 B5 Chernobyl' Ukraine U.S.S.R. 51.17N 30.15E
40 M8 Chernogo vol Kuril Is U.S.S.R. 46.32N 150.53E
42 E5 Chernogorsk U.S.S.R. 53.48N 91.16E
47 M4 Chernoistochinsk U.S.S.R. 57.48N 59.52E
40 G1 Chernolesskaya U.S.S.R. 61.30N 136.13E
44 B3 Chernomorokiy U.S.S.R. 44.51N 38.30E
44 B9 Chernomorskoye Ukraine U.S.S.R. 45.30N 32.40E
41 E8 Chernoostrovskoye U.S.S.R. 64.36N 87.45E
43 M1 Chernoretskoye Kazakhstan U.S.S.R. 52.47N 76.40E
46 F5 Chernovitskaya Oblast' prov Ukraine U.S.S.R.
42 J6 Chernovskiye Kopi U.S.S.R. 52.05N 113.18E
46 F5 Chernovtsy Ukraine U.S.S.R. 48.19N 25.52E
47 K6 Chernoye Tyumen U.S.S.R. 57.40N 69.09E
Chernoye More sea see Black Sea
47 K7 Chernoye,Oz L U.S.S.R.
39 E4 Chernoye-Ozero U.S.S.R. 61.02N 151.47E
44 H2 Chernozemel'skoye U.S.S.R. 45.27N 46.35E
45 P1 Chernukha U.S.S.R. 55.36N 43.46E
45 D6 Chernukhi Ukraine U.S.S.R. 50.18N 32.56E
45 K8 Chernukhino Ukraine U.S.S.R. 48.20N 38.34E
47 H7 Chernushka U.S.S.R. 56.30N 56.00E
47 F4 Chernut'yevo U.S.S.R. 63.46N 48.38E
46 G4 Chernyakhov Ukraine U.S.S.R. 50.30N 28.38E
46 D3 Chernyakhovsk U.S.S.R. 54.36N 21.48E
45 J6 Chernyanka U.S.S.R. 50.56N 37.48E
40 D5 Chernyayevo U.S.S.R. 52.50N 126.01E
45 G3 Chernysheno U.S.S.R. 53.52N 35.16E
47 H3 Chernysheva, Kryazh ridge U.S.S.R.
43 E4 Chernysheva,Zaliv gulf Kazakhstan U.S.S.R.
45 P4 Chernyshevo U.S.S.R. 52.56N 43.05E
42 K5 Chernyshevsk U.S.S.R. 52.38N 117.01E
Chernyshevskaya see Sovetskaya
41 K8 Chernyshevskiy U.S.S.R. 63.00N 112.30E
62 O1 Chernyshevskoye U.S.S.R. 54.39N 22.44E
45 O8 Chernyshkovskiy U.S.S.R. 48.26N 42.13E
45 S8 Cherny Yar U.S.S.R. 48.05N 46.07E
44 B3 Chernyy Aul U.S.S.R. 44.39N 38.23E
40 M8 Chernyye Brat'ya,O-va islds Kuril Is U.S.S.R.
42 D5 Chernyy Etap U.S.S.R. 54.34N 87.28E
44 G1 Chernyye Zemli reg U.S.S.R.
39 F1 Chernyy Mys U.S.S.R. 68.00N 156.40E
42 C4 Chernyy Mys U.S.S.R. 55.32N 80.03E
41 B2 Chernyy,Mys C Novaya Zemlya U.S.S.R. 75.30N 57.47E
41 A4 Chernyy,Myse C Novaya Zemlya U.S.S.R. 70.50N 53.24E
42 E2 Chernyy Ostrov U.S.S.R. 61.44N 91.14E
43 D2 Chernyy Otrog U.S.S.R. 51.55N 56.00E
107 J7 Cherokee Alabama 34.44N 87.59W
108 P7 Cherokee Iowa 42.45N 95.32W
109 Q4 Cherokee Kansas 37.22N 94.50W
109 M5 Cherokee Oklahoma 36.45N 98.22W
112 J5 Cherokee Texas 31.00N 98.44W
105 D1 Cherokee Dam Tennessee 36.10N 83.32W
105 D1 Cherokee L Tennessee
112 N3 Cherokee,L Texas 32.20N 94.44W
105 K11 Cherokee Pt Bahamas 26.27N 77.03W
105 K11 Cherokee Sound Great Abaco I Bahamas 26.28N 77.03W
69 E7 Chéroy France 48.12N 3.00E
121 B7 Cherquenco Chile 38.42S 72.00W
28 H3 Cherrapunji Meghalaya India 25.16N 91.42E
99 P4 Cherrier, Lake Quebec
Cherrife oil bore see Sherifa oil bore
70 G4 Cherrueix France 48.36N 1.40W
10 O4 Cherry isld Santa Cruz Is Pacific Oc 11.35S 169.51E
111 K2 Cherry Creek Nevada 39.54N 114.53W
104 F4 Cherry Creek New York 42.17N 79.06W
108 J5 Cherry Creek S Dakota 44.38N 101.30W
110 L9 Cherry Creek Mt Nevada 40.05N 114.53W
104 L9 Cherrydale Virginia 38.54N 77.06W
104 S2 Cherryfield Maine 44.36N 67.55W
103 H5 Cherry Grove Long I, N Y 40.40N 73.05W
103 C7 Cherry Hill Maryland 39.40N 75.51W
101 O7 Cherry Point Alberta 56.11N 119.57W
109 P4 Cherryvale Kansas 37.17N 95.33W
104 L4 Cherry Valley New York 42.49N 74.46W
105 F2 Cherryville N Carolina 35.23N 81.23W
39 G1 Cherskiy U.S.S.R. 68.45N 161.15E
42 H4 Cherskogo,Gora mt U.S.S.R. 55.10N 108.52E
42 J6 Cherskogo,Khrebet mts Chita U.S.S.R.
39 C2 Cherskogo, Khrebet ra U.S.S.R.
75 L6 Chert Spain 40.32N 0.09E
75 L6 Cherta Spain 40.54N 0.29E
47 M6 Chertala R U.S.S.R.
45 M7 Chertkovo U.S.S.R. 49.22N 40.12E
45 E1 Chertolino U.S.S.R. 56.12N 33.53E
40 G1 Chertovo-Ulovo U.S.S.R. 60.15N 136.22E
11 F10 Chertsey New Zealand 43.48S 171.57E
55 A5 Chertsey Surrey England 51.23N 0.30W
45 M1 Cherusti U.S.S.R. 55.33N 40.00E
47 F5 Cherva U.S.S.R. 62.15N 48.45E
72 G5 Cherveix-Cubas France 45.18N 1.07E
46 G3 Cherven' Belorussiya U.S.S.R. 53.40N 28.28E
82 J7 Cherven Bryag Bulgaria 43.17N 24.07E
44 G4 Chervlennaya U.S.S.R. 43.32N 45.54E
45 E8 Chervonaya Kamenka Ukraine U.S.S.R. 48.39N 33.29E
43 G4 Chervonnaya Zemlya Kazakhstan U.S.S.R. 45.14N 64.08E
46 G4 Chervonnoye,Oz L Belorussiya U.S.S.R.
46 F4 Chervonoarmeysk Ukraine U.S.S.R. 50.10N 25.20E
46 E4 Chervonograd Ukraine U.S.S.R. 50.25N 24.10E
45 F9 Chervono-Grigorovka Ukraine U.S.S.R. 47.38N 34.34E
45 L8 Chervonopartizansk Ukraine U.S.S.R. 48.05N 39.47E
45 F5 Chervonoye Ukraine U.S.S.R. 51.50N 34.02E
82 N3 Chervonoznamenka Ukraine U.S.S.R. 47.01N 30.16E
45 H7 Chervonyy Donets Ukraine U.S.S.R. 49.32N 36.34E
42 F3 Chervyanka U.S.S.R. 57.39N 99.31E
56 J4 Cherwell, R Oxon England
106 K6 Chesaning Michigan 43.12N 84.08W
104 C8 Chesapeake Ohio 38.26N 82.28W
104 J10 Chesapeake Virginia 36.45N 76.15W
104 J8 Chesapeake B Maryland etc
103 C7 Chesapeake City Maryland 39.32N 75.49W
103 C7 Chesapeake-Delaware Can Maryland/Delaware
104 K10 Chesapeake Lightship Virginia 36.58N 75.43W
66 C5 Cheseaux Switzerland 46.36N 6.37E
66 A6 Chéserex Switzerland 46.24N 6.11E
56 K4 Chesham Bucks England 51.43N 0.38W
92 D6 Cheshi, L Zambia 8.55S 29.43E
103 J3 Cheshire Connecticut 41.30N 72.25W
104 M4 Cheshire Massachusetts 42.34N 73.09W
57 H6 Cheshire co England
32 G2 Cheshmeh-ye-Khān Iran 37.17N 56.05E
43 F7 Cheshme 2-oy Turkmeniya U.S.S.R. 38.40N 61.13E
47 F3 Chëshskaya Guba gulf U.S.S.R.
56 L4 Cheshunt Herts England 51.43N 0.02W
66 E6 Chesières Switzerland 46.18N 7.03E
56 F6 Chesil Beach Dorset England 50.36N 2.32W
69 G8 Chesley France 47.59N 4.07E
99 J8 Chesley Ontario 44.18N 81.07W
43 F1 Chesma U.S.S.R. 52.40N 60.40E
68 C4 Chesnay,le France 48.50N 2.08E
105 F2 Chesnee S Carolina 35.08N 81.53W
69 H4 Chesne,le Ardennes France 49.31N 4.46E
70 M4 Chesne,le Eure France 48.53N 0.58E
42 D5 Chesnokovo U.S.S.R. 53.06N 86.06E
56 J6 Chessell I of Wight England 50.40N 1.25W
55 D5 Chessington Surrey England 51.21N 0.18W
55 B1 Chess, R Herts/Bucks England
69 F7 Chessy-les-Prés France 48.01N 3.55E
75 J8 Cheste Spain 39.30N 0.41W
107 B6 Chester Arkansas 35.40N 94.13W
110 D9 Chester California 40.20N 121.14W
57 H6 Chester Cheshire England 53.12N 2.54W
103 K4 Chester Connecticut 41.24N 72.26W
110 O5 Chester Idaho 44.00N 111.34W
107 G4 Chester Illinois 37.55N 89.50W
103 B9 Chester Maryland 38.59N 76.16W
103 J2 Chester Massachusetts 42.17N 72.59W

110 P1 **Chester** Montana 48.31N 110.58W
108 N9 **Chester** Nebraska 40.01N 97.38W
103 E5 **Chester** New Jersey 40.47N 74.42W
103 F4 **Chester** New York 41.23N 74.16W
98 H9 **Chester** Nova Scotia 44.33N 64.16W
103 D7 **Chester** Pennsylvania 39.50N 75.23W
105 F3 **Chester** S Carolina 34.43N 81.14W
112 N5 **Chester** Texas 30.57N 94.38W
104 N3 **Chester** Vermont 43.16N 72.38W
104 H9 **Chester** Virginia 37.22N 77.27W
104 E6 **Chester** W Virginia 40.36N 80.35W
103 C6 **Chester** *co* Pennsylvania
98 H9 **Chester Basin** Nova Scotia 44.35N 64.20W
116 H1 **Chester Castle** Jamaica, W I 18.20N 77.58W
103 C8 **Chester Cr** Maryland
103 K4 **Chesterfield** Connecticut 41.26N 72.13W
57 L6 **Chesterfield** Derbys England 53.15N 1.25W
110 O7 **Chesterfield** Idaho 42.53N 111.52W
107 F2 **Chesterfield** Illinois 39.15N 90.02W
103 J2 **Chesterfield** Massachusetts 42.24N 72.50W
104 N4 **Chesterfield** New Hampshire 42.53N 72.30W
105 G3 **Chesterfield** S Carolina 34.44N 80.04W
104 H9 **Chesterfield** Virginia 37.23N 77.32W
10 M5 **Chesterfield,Îles** Coral Sea
97 K5 **Chesterfield Inlet** N W Terr
104 D7 **Chesterhill** Ohio 39.27N 81.52W
12 K7 **Chester Hill** *dist* Sydney, N S W
57 K3 **Chester le Street** Durham England 54.52N 1.34W
106 G8 **Chesterton** Indiana 41.37N 87.03W
103 B8 **Chestertown** Maryland 39.13N 76.04W
104 M3 **Chestertown** New York 43.38N 73.49W
103 C8 **Chesterville** Maryland 39.16N 75.55W
99 P7 **Chesterville** Ontario 45.06N 75.16W
107 C9 **Chestnut** Louisiana 32.03N 93.00W
104 F6 **Chestnut Ridge** Pennsylvania
11 G10 **Chest Pk** *mt* New Zealand 43.06S 172.02E
104 P7 **Chesuncook** Maine 46.02N 69.27W
104 P7 **Chesuncook L** Maine
103 C8 **Cheswold** Delaware 39.13N 75.36W
42 D4 **Chet'** *R* U.S.S.R.
88 R3 **Chetaibi** Algeria 37.05N 7.23E
28 G8 **Chetamale** Andaman Is 10.45N 92.36E
106 C4 **Chetek** Wisconsin 45.20N 91.39W
98 L7 **Cheticamp** C Breton I, Nova Scotia 46.39N 61.01W
27 L7 **Chetlat** *isld* Laccadive Is Ind Oc 11.46N 72.50E
Chetnet es Salmâss,Ouâdi *see* **Shetnet es Salmas, Wādī** *watercourse*
109 P4 **Chetopa** Kansas 37.02N 95.07W
30 K8 **Chetro** Bihar India 24.28N 86.15E
43 M7 **Chetsu** Uzbekistan U.S.S.R. 41.05N 70.15E
115 P8 **Chetumal** Mexico 18.30N 88.17W
40 N6 **Chetvertyy Kuril'skiy Proliv** *str* Kuril Is U.S.S.R.
11 J7 **Chetwode Is** New Zealand
101 N8 **Chetwynd** Br Columbia 55.42N 121.36W
39 G1 **Chetyrekhstolbovoy,Ostrov** *isld* U.S.S.R. 70.38N 162.29E
40 E6 **Cheugda** U.S.S.R. 50.18N 130.26E
39 B2 **Cheulik** U.S.S.R. 66.17N 137.50E
23 B9 **Cheung Sha Wan** Hong Kong 22.20N 114.08E
71 D3 **Chevagnes** France 46.37N 3.33E
113 E6 **Chevak** Alaska 61.30N 165.35W
71 G9 **Cheval-Blanc** France 43.48N 5.04E
71 J8 **Cheval-Blanc,le** *mt* France 44.07N 6.26E
11 C2 **Chevalier,Pt** Auckland New Zealand 36.51N 174.42E
70 G7 **Chevallerais, La** Loire-Atlantique France 47.28N 1.41W
72 D5 **Chevanceaux** France 45.18N 0.14W
69 E8 **Chevannes** France 47.45N 3.30E
120 E6 **Chevejecure** Bolivia 14.52S 66.06W
66 E2 **Chevenez** Switzerland 47.24N 7.01E
104 N8 **Cheverly** *dist* Maryland
61 L6 **Chevetogne** Belgium 50.13N 5.07E
66 E6 **Cheville, Passe de** Switzerland 46.18N 7.12E
69 J6 **Chevillon** France 48.32N 5.08E
69 B7 **Chevilly** France 48.02N 1.53E
68 F4 **Chevilly-Larue** France 48.46N 2.22E
11 H9 **Cheviot** New Zealand 42.50S 173.18E
100 L6 **Cheviot** Saskatchewan 52.04N 106.21W
57 H2 **Cheviot Hills** Scot/Eng
13 G7 **Cheviot Ra** Queensland
57 J2 **Cheviot,The** *mt* Northumb England 55.29N 2.09W
70 K6 **Cheviré-le-Rouge** France 47.36N 0.10W
70 A5 **Chèvre, C. de la** France 48.12N 4.34W
107 E12 **Chevreuil, Pt** Louisiana 29.31N 91.33W
68 B5 **Chevreuse** France 48.43N 2.03E
69 C6 **Chevreuse** France 48.42N 2.03E
71 K6 **Chevril,L** France
72 A1 **Chevrolière, la** France 47.06N 1.37W
61 N5 **Chevron** Belgium 50.23N 5.44E
66 D4 **Chevroux** Switzerland 46.54N 6.55E
104 M8 **Chevy Chase** *dist* Washington D C/Md
92 F9 **Chewa** *tribe* Mozambique
92 F8 **Chewa** *tribe* Zambia/Malawi
93 H1 **Chew Bahir, L** Ethiopia
110 H1 **Chewelah** Washington 48.17N 117.44W
56 F5 **Chew Stoke** Avon England 51.22N 2.38W
66 D6 **Chexbres** Switzerland 46.30N 6.47E
72 D3 **Chey** France 46.18N 0.03W
109 L6 **Cheyenne** Oklahoma 35.37N 99.43W
112 D4 **Cheyenne** Texas 31.59N 103.05W
108 F8 **Cheyenne** Wyoming 41.08N 104.50W
108 H5 **Cheyenne** *R* S Dakota
108 K4 **Cheyenne Agency** S Dakota 45.02N 100.19W
109 M3 **Cheyenne Bottoms** Kansas 38.27N 98.42W
108 E8 **Cheyenne Pass** Wyoming 41.18N 105.32W
109 H3 **Cheyenne Wells** Colorado 38.49N 102.10W
72 K5 **Cheylade** France 45.12N 2.42E
71 E7 **Cheylard,le** France 44.54N 4.25E
14 C10 **Cheyne B** W Australia
14 E10 **Cheyney Pt** W Australia 33.54S 122.32E
66 D4 **Cheyres** Switzerland 46.49N 6.48E
28 E4 **Cheyur** Tamil Nadu India 12.23N 80.01E
28 D4 **Cheyyar R** Tamil Nadu India
101 M9 **Chezacut** Br Col 52.25N 123.58W
72 J2 **Chezal-Benoît** France 46.50N 2.06E
72 D10 **Chèze** France 42.54N 0.01W
70 E5 **Chèze,la** France 48.07N 2.39W
71 H4 **Chézery-Forens** France 46.13N 5.53E
69 E6 **Chézy-sur-Marne** France 48.59N 3.23E
29 E5 **Chhabra** Rajasthan India 24.39N 76.50E
30 A2 **Chhachhrauli** Haryana India 30.14N 77.22E
30 A3 **Chhapar** Uttar Prad India 29.34N 77.46E
29 F6 **Chhapara** Madhya Prad India 22.22N 79.35E
30 A3 **Chhaprauli** Uttar Prad India 29.12N 77.10E
30 A4 **Chhaprawat** Uttar Prad India 28.32N 77.48E
30 A7 **Chharchh** Madhya Prad India 25.24N 77.12E
30 B5 **Chharra** Uttar Prad India 27.56N 78.24E
30 A5 **Chhata** Uttar Prad India 27.43N 77.30E
31 J8 **Chhatak** Bangladesh 25.02N 91.39E
30 L6 **Chhatapur** Bihar India 26.12N 87.01E
30 C8 **Chhatarpur** Madhya Prad India 24.54N 79.35E
30 C8 **Chhatarpur** *dist* Madhya Prad India
31 E6 **Chhatr** Pakistan 28.52N 68.25E
30 C7 **Chhechh** *R* Uttar Prad India
30 C5 **Chhibramau** Uttar Prad India 27.09N 79.30E
30 E3 **Chhibro** Nepal 29.55N 81.52E
29 F6 **Chhindwara** Chindwara, Madhya Prad India 22.04N 78.58E
29 F6 **Chhindwara** Narsingpur, Madhya Prad India 23.02N 79.32E
29 F6 **Chhindwara** *dist* Madhya Prad India
30 G5 **Chhitauni** Uttar Pradesh India 27.09N 83.59E
25 H6 **Chhlong** Cambodia 12.13N 105.58E
Chhor *see* **Chor**
31 B10 **Chhota Andai** *isld* Pakistan 24.49N 67.00E
29 G7 **Chhuikhadan** Madhya Prad India 21.32N 81.02E
25 H7 **Chhuk** Cambodia 10.50N 104.28E
28 G2 **Chhukha** Bhutan 27.02N 89.36E
30 G2 **Chhule** Nepal 27.58N 86.37E
Chia-ch'a *see* **Gyaea**
Chia-chi *see* **Qionghai**
113 H9 **Chiachi I** Alaska 55.53N 159.10W
88 J6 **Chiadma** *tribe* Morocco
25 L9 **Chiahpui** Assam India 24.02N 93.11E
23 J7 **Chia-i** Taiwan 23.38N 120.27E
18 J3 **Chia Keng** Singapore 1.21N 103.52E
79 B4 **Chialamberto** Italy 45.21N 7.20E
23 J7 **Chia-li** Taiwan 23.09N 120.11E
93 N7 **Chiamboni** Somalia 1.36S 41.36E
87 M10 **Chiamboni** *C* Somalia 1.35S 41.35E
79 K3 **Chiampo** Italy 45.33N 11.17E
79 K3 **Chiampo** *R* Italy
80 E2 **Chiana,Val di** Italy
80 E2 **Chianciano Terme** Italy 43.03N 11.50E
Chiang Dao *see* **Ban Chiang Dao**
91 C11 **Chiange** Angola 15.45S 13.58E
Chiang-hsi *see* **Jiangxi** *prov*
25 F3 **Chiang Kham** Thailand 19.31N 100.20E
25 E3 **Chiang Mai** Thailand 18.48N 98.59E
Chiang Rai *see* **Muang Chiang Rai**
25 F2 **Chiang Saen** Thailand 20.17N 100.09E
Chiang-su *see* **Jiangsu** *prov*
80 C2 **Chianni** Italy 43.29N 10.38E
80 D2 **Chianti** *dist* Italy
79 K7 **Chianti,Monti del** *mts* Italy
115 N9 **Chiapa** Mexico 16.42N 92.59W
115 N9 **Chiapas** *state* Mexico
115 N9 **Chiapilla** Mexico 16.31N 92.42W
85 G8 **Chiapo, Sarir** Libya
81 J9 **Chiaramonte Gulfi** Sicily 37.02N 14.42E
81 B2 **Chiaramonti** Sardinia 40.45N 8.49E
79 O7 **Chiaravalle** Italy 43.36N 13.19E
81 M6 **Chiaravalle Centrale** Italy 38.41N 16.25E
79 F4 **Chiaravalle Milanese** Italy 45.25N 9.13E
79 G3 **Chiari** Italy 45.32N 9.55E
81 M3 **Chiaromonte** Italy 40.07N 16.13E
80 G2 **Chiascio** *R* Italy
66 N8 **Chiasso** Switzerland 45.51N 9.02E
34 N4 **Chia Surkh** *oil field* Iraq 34.37N 45.38E
44 E5 **Chiatura** Georgia U.S.S.R. 42.15N 43.17E
115 K8 **Chiautla** Mexico 18.18N 98.34W
79 F6 **Chiavari** Italy 44.19N 9.19E
67 O13 **Chiavari,Pt.de** Corsica 41.48N 8.45E
79 F2 **Chiavenna** Italy 46.19N 9.24E
Chia-yin *see* **Jiayin**
20 D3 **Chiba** Japan 35.38N 140.07E
20 O6 **Chiba** *prefect* Japan 35.58N 140.07E
94 M3 **Chibabava** Mozambique 20.17S 33.39E
39 B1 **Chibagalakh** U.S.S.R. 68.20N 139.15E
39 C2 **Chibagalakh** *R* U.S.S.R.
20 P9 **Chibana** Okinawa Japan 26.21N 127.49E
Chibchang Tso *L* *see* **Ch'ih-pu-chang Hu**
91 D11 **Chibemba** Angola 15.43S 14.07E
92 E12 **Chibi** Zimbabwe 20.18S 30.25E
92 E12 **Chibi** *dist* Zimbabwe
42 D6 **Chibit** U.S.S.R. 50.16N 87.32E
42 E5 **Chibizhek** U.S.S.R. 54.25N 93.45E
25 F5 **Chi Bon Dam** Thailand 15.50N 101.38E
92 D7 **Chibondo** Zambia 10.49S 28.40E
92 D6 **Chibote** Zambia 9.52S 29.33E
99 Q3 **Chibougamau** Quebec 49.56N 74.24W
99 P3 **Chibougamau** *R* Quebec
99 Q3 **Chibougamau L** Quebec
99 R3 **Chibougamau, Parc de** Quebec
120 C5 **Chibquiro** Peru 12.01S 74.06W
92 D8 **Chibuluma** Zambia 12.52S 28.08E
20 G5 **Chiburi-shima** *isld* Japan 36.00N 133.00E
94 M5 **Chibuto** Mozambique 24.40S 33.33E
92 D9 **Chibwe** Zambia 14.12S 28.31E
Chicacole *see* **Srikakulam**
106 G8 **Chicago** Illinois 41.50N 87.45W
113 T8 **Chicagof** Alaska 57.41N 136.09W
106 G8 **Chicago Heights** Illinois 41.31N 87.39W
106 Q1 **Chicago, R** Chicago, Illinois
106 F8 **Chicago Ship Can** Illinois
77 K2 **Chica, L** *L* Spain 39.28N 3.20W
91 E10 **Chicala** Angola 12.49S 17.03E
91 F9 **Chicala** Angola 11.55S 19.38E
121 C6 **Chical Có** Argentina 36.35S 67.50W
120 A2 **Chicama** Peru 7.53S 79.07W
120 A2 **Chicama** *R* Peru
91 C6 **Chicamba** Angola 4.58S 12.05E
119 D4 **Chicamocha** *R* Colombia
119 H4 **Chicanán, R** Venezuela
91 G8 **Chicapa** *R* Angola/Zaïre
121 D3 **Chica, Sa** *ra* Argentina
40 B4 **Chicatka** U.S.S.R. 54.04N 121.14E
98 F5 **Chic-Chocs, Parc des** Quebec
90 J3 **Chicha** Chad 16.57N 18.34E
113 T8 **Chichagof** *isld* Alaska 57.40N 136.00W
31 C7 **Chichak R** Pakistan
88 J6 **Chichaoua** Morocco 31.30N 8.47W
120 E9 **Chichas,Cord.de** *mts* Bolivia
72 D2 **Chiché** France 46.48N 0.21W
56 K3 **Chicheley** Bucks Eng 52.06N 0.41W
22 K6 **Chicheng** Hebei China 40.56N 115.50E
115 P7 **Chichén Itzá** *ruins* Mexico 20.40N 88.32W
103 F2 **Chichester** New York 42.06N 74.20W
56 K6 **Chichester** W Sussex Eng 50.50N 0.48W
14 C5 **Chichester Ra** W Australia
29 G7 **Chichgarh** Maharashtra India 20.54N 80.26E
20 N6 **Chichibu** Japan 36.00N 139.08E
20 M5 **Chichibu Tama Nat.Park** Japan
115 L3 **Chichigalpa** Nicaragua 12.35N 87.04W
21 J11 **Chichi-jima rettō** *islds* Ogasawara-Guntō Pacific Oc
31 H1 **Chichiklik Davan** *pass* Xinjiang Uygur Zizhiqu China 38.04N 75.20E
119 F2 **Chichiriviche** Venezuela 10.58N 68.17W
42 D3 **Chichka-Yul** *R* U.S.S.R.
29 F6 **Chichli** Madhya Prad India 22.48N 78.52E
31 G5 **Chichoki** Pakistan 31.37N 73.58E
29 E6 **Chichola** Madhya Prad India 22.00N 77.48E
29 E2 **Chichot** Himachal Prad India 31.32N 77.02E
Chi Chu Wan *see* **Stanley Bay**
104 H9 **Chickahominy** *R* Virginia
113 N6 **Chickaloon** Alaska 61.45N 148.30W
105 B3 **Chickamauga** Georgia 34.52N 85.18W
107 L6 **Chickamauga Dam** Tennessee 35.06N 85.12W
107 M6 **Chickamauga L** Tennessee
107 H10 **Chickasawhay** *R* Mississippi
109 N6 **Chickasha** Oklahoma 35.03N 97.57W
Chickballapur *see* **Chikballapur**
113 R4 **Chicken** Alaska 64.04N 142.00W
58 D2 **Chicken Hd** Lewis, W Isles Scotland 58.11N 6.15W
57 D4 **Chicken Rock** Isle of Man U.K. 54.02N 4.50W
123 G2 **Chick I** Antarctica 65.18S 126.01E
56 G5 **Chicklade** Wilts Eng 51.07N 2.08W
Chickmagalur *see* **Chikmagalur**
121 E5 **Chiclana** Argentina 35.44S 61.40W
77 K4 **Chiclana** Spain 38.19N 3.02W
77 K4 **Chiclana** *mt* Spain 38.19N 3.05W
77 D8 **Chiclana de la Fronterra** Spain 36.26N 6.09W
77 L4 **Chiclana,Loma de** *hills* Spain
120 A7 **Chiclayo** Peru 6.47S 79.47W
111 C2 **Chico** California 39.46N 121.50W
110 H4 **Chico** Oregon 45.45N 117.08W
112 K2 **Chico** Texas 33.19N 97.49W
19 K3 **Chico** *R* Luzon Philippines
120 F11 **Chicoana** Argentina 25.07S 65.32W
99 M4 **Chicobi,L** Quebec 48.52N 78.30W
91 D11 **Chicomba** Angola 14.10S 14.52E
94 N5 **Chicomo** Mozambique 24.33S 34.11E
115 N10 **Chicomucelo** Mexico 15.48N 92.16W
92 G8 **Chicono no** Mozambique 12.56S 35.44E
115 K7 **Chicontepec** Mexico 21.00N 98.10W
103 J2 **Chicopee** Massachusetts 42.09N 72.37W
121 K8 **Chico, R** Arg/Chile
121 B9 **Chico, R** Chubut Argentina
121 C10 **Chico, R** Chubut Argentina
121 K7 **Chico, R** Santa Cruz Argentina
121 D1 **Chico, R** Tucumán Argentina
26 U14 **Chicots,Plaine des** Réunion Ind Oc
98 A5 **Chicoutimi** Quebec 48.26N 71.06W
99 T5 **Chicoutimi** *R* Quebec
98 A5 **Chicoutimi Nord** Quebec 48.25N 71.05W
98 B5 **Chicoutimi, Parc des** Quebec
119 E6 **Chicuaco, L** Colombia 2.58N 69.08W
94 L4 **Chicualacuala** Mozambique 22.30S 31.39E
94 L4 **Chicualacula** Mozambique 22.06S 31.42E
91 D10 **Chicuma** Angola 13.26S 14.50E
28 D5 **Chidambaram** Tamil Nadu India 11.25N 79.42E
56 K5 **Chiddingfold** Surrey Eng 51.07N 0.39W
94 N5 **Chidenguele** Mozambique 24.55S 34.11E
56 F6 **Chideock** Dorset Eng 50.44N 2.50W
107 D8 **Chidester** Arkansas 33.41N 93.00W
97 N5 **Chidley, C** Labrador, Nfld 60.30N 64.30W
94 N5 **Chiducuane** Mozambique 24.35S 34.25E
91 D12 **Chiede** Angola 17.08S 15.58E
110 F1 **Chief Joseph Dam** Washington 48.04N 119.43W
105 E8 **Chiefland** Florida 29.30N 82.53W
9 J5 **Chiefs Pt** Ontario 44.39N 81.19W
Ch'ieh-la *see* **Karasay**
25 H1 **Chiem Hoa** Vietnam 22.07N 105.16E
64 O8 **Chieming** W Germany 47.53N 12.33E
64 N8 **Chiemsee** *L* W Germany
92 D6 **Chiengi** Zambia 8.40S 29.11E
Ch'ien-nan *see* **Quannan**
80 H2 **Chienti** *R* Italy
24 D3 **Chierh Davan** *pass* Xinjiang Uygur Zizhiqu China 45.38N 82.35E
79 C4 **Chieri** Italy 45.01N 7.49E
69 J5 **Chiers** *R* France
79 G2 **Chiesa** Italy 46.16N 9.50E
79 J2 **Chiese** *R* Italy
80 K4 **Chieti** Italy 42.21N 14.10E
80 K4 **Chieti** *prov* Italy
115 K8 **Chietla** Mexico 18.31N 98.32W
80 M5 **Chieuti** Italy 41.50N 15.10E
95 N4 **Chieveley** S Africa 28.50S 29.49E
61 F4 **Chièvres** Belgium 50.35N 3.49E
22 L5 **Chifeng** Nei Monggol Zizhiqu China 42.17N 118.56E
93 L7 **Chifiri** Kenya 1.18S 39.42E
12 A6 **Chifley** *dist* Canberra Australia
118 H5 **Chifre,Serra do** *mts* Brazil
91 F11 **Chifuaco** Angola 14.54S 19.47E
43 L4 **Chiganak** Kazakhstan U.S.S.R. 45.10N 73.55E
42 C3 **Chigara** U.S.S.R. 58.39N 81.45E
18 B7 **Chigar Perah** Pen Malaysia 4.25N 101.56E
20 A4 **Chigasaki** Japan 35.20N 139.24E
Chigelik *see* **Luobuzhuang**
Chigha Khur *see* **Chaghā Khūr**
31 F3 **Chigha Sarai** Afghanistan 34.52N 71.10E
113 J8 **Chiginigak** *mt* Alaska 57.10N 157.00W
45 D7 **Chigirin** Ukraine U.S.S.R. 49.04N 32.38E
45 A3 **Chigirinka** Belorussiya U.S.S.R. 53.24N 29.50E
113 L6 **Chigmit Mts** Alaska
115 K8 **Chignahuapán** Mexico 19.51N 98.02W
98 H8 **Chignecto Bay** Nova Scotia/New Bruns
113 H8 **Chignik** Alaska 56.18N 158.27W
113 H8 **Chignik B** Alaska
113 H8 **Chignik L** Alaska 56.18N 158.50W
71 J5 **Chignin** France 45.31N 6.00E
119 C4 **Chigorodó** Colombia 7.42N 76.45W
99 R3 **Chigoubiche, L** Quebec
121 B3 **Chigualoco** Chile 31.45S 71.35W
120 E9 **Chiguana** Bolivia 21.05S 67.58W
120 E9 **Chiguana, Salar de** Bolivia
121 A6 **Chiguayante** Chile 36.55S 73.00W
119 C8 **Chiguaza** Ecuador 1.59S 77.59W
94 M4 **Chigubo** Mozambique 22.50S 33.34E
24 G11 **Chigu Co** *L* Xizang Zizhiqu China 28.40N 91.45E
92 J7 **Chigugu** Tanzania 10.34S 38.59E
40 H3 **Chigul'bach** U.S.S.R. 57.37N 138.02E
55 J2 **Chigwell** Essex England 51.37N 0.05E
12 E7 **Chigwell** Tasmania 42.49S 147.17E
21 D8 **Chigyŏng** N Korea 39.50N 127.26E
35 E1 **Chihine** Lebanon 33.07N 35.15E
Chihli,Gulf of *see* **Po Hai Wan**
24 G9 **Ch'ih-pu-chang Hu** *L* Qinghai/Xizang Zizhiqu China 33.30N 90.15E
115 F3 **Chihuahua** Mexico 28.40N 106.06W
115 F3 **Chihuahua** *state* Mexico
121 B7 **Chihuido Medio** *pk* Argentina 38.01S 69.40W
43 H5 **Chiili** Kazakhstan U.S.S.R. 44.10N 66.37E
22 D6 **Chijinpu** Gansu China 40.01N 97.33E
42 C4 **Chik** U.S.S.R. 55.01N 82.29E
29 E7 **Chikalda** Maharashtra India 21.29N 77.21E
23 E8 **Chikan** Guangdong China 21.15N 110.12E
42 H5 **Chikan** U.S.S.R. 54.52N 105.40E
109 N5 **Chikaskia** *R* Oklahoma
39 J3 **Chikayevo** U.S.S.R. 64.45N 174.18E
28 C4 **Chikballapur** Karnataka India 13.29N 77.43E
41 R5 **Chikhacheva** U.S.S.R. 72.16N 146.57E
46 G2 **Chikhachevo** U.S.S.R. 57.19N 29.49E
29 E7 **Chikhli** Maharashtra India 20.21N 76.19E
Chikhu Wan *see* **Stanley B**
43 C7 **Chikishlyer** Turkmeniya U.S.S.R. 37.36N 53.57E
20 K2 **Chikiu-misaki** *C* Japan 42.19N 140.19E
Chikkai *see* **Chixi**
28 B4 **Chikmagalur** Karnataka India 13.20N 75.46E
28 B4 **Chikmagalur** *dist* Karnataka India
28 C4 **Chiknayakanhalli** Karnataka India 13.25N 76.36E
28 B2 **Chikodi** Karnataka India 16.27N 74.37E
28 B2 **Chikodi Road** Karnataka India 16.25N 74.51E
44 F4 **Chikola** U.S.S.R. 43.12N 43.54E
92 D9 **Chikonkomene** Zambia 14.48S 28.21E
42 H6 **Chikoy** U.S.S.R. 50.18N 106.55E
42 H6 **Chikoy** *R* U.S.S.R.
25 H6 **Chikreng** *R* Cambodia
20 D8 **Chikugo** Japan 33.15N 130.27E
20 D8 **Chikugo** *R* Japan
20 M5 **Chikuma** *R* Japan
92 D9 **Chikumbi** Zambia 15.11S 28.20E
113 H6 **Chikuminuk, L** Alaska 60.15N 159.00W
92 E9 **Chikunda** *tribe* Mozambique
20 N7 **Chikura** Japan 34.57N 139.58E
40 N6 **Chikurachki** *vol* Kuril Is U.S.S.R. 50.20N 155.28E
92 G10 **Chikwawa** Malawi 16.02S 34.54E
25 B2 **Chi-kyaw** Burma 20.18N 93.55E
91 D10 **Chila** Angola 12.03S 14.29E
115 L9 **Chila** Mexico 17.59N 97.51W
92 C8 **Chilabombwe** Zambia 12.20S 27.52E
115 L8 **Chilac,San Gabriel** Mexico 18.20N 97.24W
115 M3 **Chilamate** Nicaragua 12.00N 84.35W
Chilan *see* **Aqal**
92 D9 **Chilanga** Zambia 15.39S 28.19E
30 K5 **Chilankha** Nepal 27.47N 86.08E
101 L9 **Chilanko Forks** Br Col 52.10N 124.10W
115 K9 **Chilapa** Guerrero Mexico 17.38N 99.11W
115 L9 **Chilapa** Oaxaca Mexico 17.31N 97.47W
31 H3 **Chilas** Kashmir 35.24N 74.11E
31 H3 **Chilas** *dist* Kashmir
26 Q6 **Chilaw** Sri Lanka 7.34N 79.48E
120 B5 **Chilca** Peru 12.35S 76.41W
121 C2 **Chilca** San Juan Argentina 29.59S 68.21W
121 C5 **Chilca** San Luis Arg 35.04S 67.37W
120 D6 **Chilca,Cord. de** *mts* Peru
120 B5 **Chilca,Pta** Peru 12.33S 76.46W
120 D8 **Chilcaya** Chile 18.48S 69.00W
75 K8 **Chilches** Spain 39.47N 0.12W
40 B3 **Chil'chi** *R* U.S.S.R.
111 D2 **Chilcoot** California 39.49N 120.08W
101 M10 **Chilcotin** *R* Br Col
13 K3 **Chilcott I** Gt Barrier Reef Aust 16.55S 150.00E
13 K7 **Childers** Queensland 25.12S 152.13E
107 K8 **Childersburg** Alabama 33.16N 86.21W
112 G1 **Childress** Texas 34.25N 100.14W
111 M9 **Childs** Arizona 32.28N 112.50W
105 F10 **Childs** Florida 27.12N 81.21W
103 C3 **Childs** Pennsylvania 41.33N 75.32W
117 G4 **Chile** *rep* S America
122 R13 **Chile Basin** Pacific Oc
121 K6 **Chile Chico** Chile 46.34S 71.44W
121 C2 **Chilecito** La Rioja Argentina 29.10S 67.30W
92 G9 **Chileka** *airport* Malawi 15.35S 34.58E
120 A2 **Chilete** Peru 7.17S 78.48W
87 F4 **Chilga** Ethiopia 12.35N 37.05E
44 G1 **Chilgir** U.S.S.R. 46.29N 45.05E
30 H5 **Chilha** Nepal 27.37N 84.08E
56 N5 **Chilham** Kent Eng 51.15N 0.57E
30 G7 **Chilhar** Bihar India 25.26N 83.59E
107 C3 **Chilhowee** Missouri 38.35N 93.50W
104 D10 **Chilhowie** Virginia 36.49N 81.41W
82 M5 **Chilia** *R* Romania
31 G4 **Chilianwala** Pakistan 32.40N 73.39E
91 G11 **Chiliba** Angola 15.45S 20.10E
115 F10 **Chilibre** Panama 9.10N 79.34W
43 N5 **Chilik** Alma-Ata, Kazakhstan U.S.S.R. 43.36N 78.14E
46 R4 **Chilik** Kazakhstan U.S.S.R. 51.09N 54.01E
43 N5 **Chilik** *R* Kazakhstan U.S.S.R.
113 K6 **Chilikadrotna** *R* Alaska
92 E11 **Chilimanzi** Zimbabwe 19.37S 30.43E
92 E11 **Chilimanzi** *dist* Zimbabwe
42 C4 **Chilino** U.S.S.R. 55.51N 83.33E
81 B2 **Chilivani** Sardinia 40.37N 8.56E
75 E3 **Chilizarrias** *mt* Spain 42.17N 2.57W
29 J8 **Chilka Lake** Orissa India
113 U7 **Chilkat** *R* Alaska
101 M10 **Chilko** *R* Br Col
101 L10 **Chilko L** Br Col
119 B9 **Chilla,Cord.de** *mts* Ecuador
13 G3 **Chillagoe** Queensland 17.07S 144.32E
87 G7 **Chillalo** Ethiopia 7.42N 39.22E
121 A6 **Chillán** Chile 36.37S 72.10W
121 B6 **Chillán,Nevados** *mts* Chile
121 F6 **Chillar** Argentina 37.16S 59.58W
75 F7 **Chillarón de Cuenca** Spain 40.07N 2.13W
69 C7 **Chilleurs-aux-Bois** France 48.05N 2.08E
41 L8 **Chilli** *R* U.S.S.R.
106 E9 **Chillicothe** Illinois 40.56N 89.30W
107 C2 **Chillicothe** Missouri 39.47N 93.33W
104 B7 **Chillicothe** Ohio 39.20N 83.00W
112 H1 **Chillicothe** Texas 34.15N 99.32W
120 D7 **Chilliculco** Peru 17.08S 70.45W
57 K1 **Chillingham** Northumb Eng 55.31N 1.54W
12 G6 **Chillingollah** Victoria 35.17S 143.07E
31 H2 **Chillinji** Kashmir 36.47N 74.02E
103 A4 **Chillisquaque Cr** Pennsylvania
101 N11 **Chilliwack** Br Col 49.09N 121.54W
110 D1 **Chilliwack** *R* Br Col
110 D1 **Chilliwack, L** Br Columbia 49.03N 121.25W
77 G3 **Chillón** Spain 38.48N 4.52W
66 D6 **Chillon** Switzerland 46.25N 6.56E
120 B4 **Chillón** *R* Peru
71 H4 **Chilly** France 46.00N 5.58E
110 M5 **Chilly** Idaho 44.04N 113.51W
43 C6 **Chil'mamedkum, Peski** *sand des* Turkmeniya U.S.S.R.
31 H8 **Chilmari** Bangladesh 25.32N 89.42E
103 N4 **Chilmark** Massachusetts 41.20N 70.45W
29 C4 **Chilo** Rajasthan India 27.25N 73.34E
94 N3 **Chiloane, I** Mozambique 20.40S 34.56E
121 A9 **Chiloé** *prov* Chile
75 D6 **Chiloeches** Spain 40.34N 3.09W
121 A9 **Chiloé,Isla de** Chile
91 H10 **Chilombo** Angola 12.23S 22.35E
92 E8 **Chilonga** Zambia 12.01S 31.21E
110 D7 **Chiloquin** Oregon 42.35N 121.53W
115 K9 **Chilpancingo** Mexico 17.33N 99.30W
31 G2 **Chilpi** Kashmir 36.14N 73.52E
12 H6 **Chiltern** Victoria 36.11S 146.36E
56 J4 **Chiltern Hills** England
106 F5 **Chilton** Wisconsin 44.04N 88.10W
56 H5 **Chilton Foliat** Wilts Eng 51.27N 1.32W
91 G8 **Chiluage** Angola 9.30S 21.50E
92 D7 **Chilubi** Zambia 11.10S 29.55E
92 E7 **Chilubula** Zambia 10.14S 30.51E
92 G7 **Chilumba** Malawi 10.25S 34.18E
23 J6 **Chi-lung** Taiwan 25.10N 121.43E
31 J4 **Chilung Pass** Kashmir 33.54N 76.17E
92 G9 **Chilwa, L** Malawi 15.15S 35.49E
30 E5 **Chilwaria** Uttar Prad India 27.30N 81.43E
56 J6 **Chilworth** Hants Eng 50.58N 1.26W
92 G6 **Chimala** Tanzania 8.52S 34.02E
115 M9 **Chimalapa** Mexico 16.43N 94.44W
39 C2 **Chimalginskiy Khrebet** *ra* U.S.S.R.
115 O10 **Chimaltenango** Guatemala 14.40N 90.48W
115 P5 **Chimán** Panama 8.42N 78.35W
119 G2 **Chimanas,Is** Venezuela
61 H6 **Chimay** Belgium 50.03N 4.20E
109 E6 **Chimayo** New Mexico 36.00N 105.56W
121 C3 **Chimbas** Argentina 31.28S 68.33W
43 E5 **Chimbay** Uzbekistan U.S.S.R. 42.56N 59.46E
120 D12 **Chimbero** Chile 26.55S 69.56W
119 B9 **Chimbo** *R* Ecuador
119 B8 **Chimborazo** *mt* Ecuador 1.29S 78.52W
119 B8 **Chimborazo** *prov* Ecuador
120 A3 **Chimbote** Peru 9.04S 78.34W
120 A3 **Chimbote,B de** Peru 9.07S 78.36W
92 E8 **Chimbwingombe** *mt* Zambia 13.04S 31.11E
41 M8 **Chimchan** U.S.S.R. 63.38N 122.30E
39 H2 **Chimchememel'** U.S.S.R. 66.27N 166.30E
77 J6 **Chimenaes** Spain 37.07N 3.49W
47 K7 **Chimeyevo** U.S.S.R. 56.01N 65.27E
43 K6 **Chimgan** Uzbekistan U.S.S.R. 41.33N 70.00E
119 D3 **Chimichaguá** Colombia 9.19N 73.51W
41 L7 **Chimidikyan** *R* U.S.S.R.
43 N8 **Chimion** Uzbekistan U.S.S.R. 40.20N 71.30E
46 G6 **Chimishliya** Moldavia U.S.S.R. 46.30N 28.50E
43 J6 **Chimkent** Kazakhstan U.S.S.R. 42.16N 69.05E
109 E9 **Chimney Peak** New Mexico 32.42N 105.20W
26 R12 **Chimney Rocks** Seychelles, Ind Oc 4.26S 55.51E
92 F11 **Chimoio** Mozambique 19.08S 33.29E
94 M2 **Chimoio** Mozambique 19.08S 33.29E
91 E12 **Chimomo** *watercourse* Angola
77 G4 **Chimorra, Sierra de** *mts* Spain
121 C7 **Chimpay** Argentina 39.10S 66.06W
92 D6 **Chimpembe** Zambia 9.31S 29.33E
91 C6 **Chimpeze** Congo 4.29S 12.33E
31 J4 **Chimray** Kashmir 33.54N 77.58E
43 J7 **Chimtarga** *mt* Tadzhikistan U.S.S.R.
100 E9 **Chin** Alberta 49.46N 112.25W
25 B1 **Chin** *dist* Burma
21 D10 **Chin** *isld* S Korea
104 Q2 **China** Maine 44.29N 69.34W
115 K5 **China** Mexico 25.42N 99.15W
17 F5 **China** *rep* Asia
43 O7 **Chinabad** Uzbekistan U.S.S.R. 40.54N 71.58E
25 D4 **China Bakir** *R* Burma
26 T4 **China Bay** Sri Lanka 8.33N 81.11E
115 G5 **Chinacates** Mexico 25.00N 105.14W
119 D4 **Chinácota** Colombia 7.34N 72.36W
105 G2 **China Grove** N Carolina 35.36N 80.33W
115 O9 **Chinajá** Guatemala 16.05N 90.12W
111 G6 **China L** California 35.45N 117.36W
104 Q2 **China L** Maine 44.26N 69.35W
111 G6 **China Lake** California 35.40N 117.40W
115 P11 **Chinameca** El Salvador 13.30N 88.20W
China, Nat. Rep of *see* **Taiwan**
115 L3 **Chinandega** Nicaragua 12.35N 87.10W
15 G5 **Chinapelli** Papua New Guinea 3.17S 142.30E
111 F9 **China Pt** California 32.48N 118.26W
Chinaran *see* **Chanārān**
31 D4 **Chinartu** Afghanistan 32.10N 66.14E
112 K4 **China Spring** Texas 31.39N 97.20W
18 J4 **China,Tanjong** *C* Singapore 1.14N 103.50E
112 C6 **Chinati Mts** Texas
99 J7 **Chin,C** Ontario 45.05N 81.17W
119 B7 **Chinca** Ecuador 0.40N 79.35W
120 B5 **Chincha Alta** Peru 13.25S 76.07W
101 O6 **Chinchaga** *R* Alberta
120 B5 **Chincha,I de** Peru 13.39S 76.25W
34 M4 **Chinchāl** *R* Iraq
120 C5 **Chincheros** Peru 13.29S 73.44W
13 K7 **Chinchilla** Queensland 26.42S 150.35E
77 N3 **Chinchilla de Monte Aragón** Spain 38.56N 1.44W
119 C5 **Chinchina** Colombia 4.59N 75.37W
119 B10 **Chinchipe** *R* Ecuador
28 C2 **Chincholi** Karnataka India 17.29N 77.23E
75 D7 **Chinchón** Spain 40.08N 3.26W
Chin-chou *see* **Jin Xian**
Chinchow *see* **Jin Xian**
121 B4 **Chincolco** Chile 32.13S 70.53W
104 K9 **Chincoteague** Virginia 37.55N 75.23W
104 K8 **Chincoteague B** Maryland
42 D7 **Chindagatuy** Kazakhstan U.S.S.R. 49.24N 87.00E
92 H11 **Chinde** Mozambique 18.35S 36.28E
91 E10 **Chinder** Angola 12.52S 17.39E
94 N1 **Chindio** Mozambique 17.40S 35.19E
89 J7 **Chindiri** Ghana 8.09N 0.06W
71 H5 **Chindrieux** France 45.49N 5.52E
23 A2 **Chindu** Qinghai China 33.25N 96.36E
24 J9 **Chindu** Qinghai China 33.25N 96.36E
25 C1 **Chindwin** *R* Burma
20 P10 **Chinen** Okinawa Japan 26.07N 127.49E
92 G8 **Chinengue** Mozambique 13.45S 35.20E
31 H4 **Chineni** Kashmir 33.01N 75.20E
30 A6 **Chineni** Madhya Prad India 26.24N 77.33E
92 J9 **Chinga** Mozambique 15.14S 38.40E
40 J5 **Chingay** Sakhalin U.S.S.R. 52.43N 141.59E
Ch'ing-chou *see* **Yidu**
42 E6 **Chinge-Kat** U.S.S.R. 50.46N 90.30E
55 G2 **Chingford** London England 51.37N 00.000
Ch'ing-hua-chen *see* **Boai**
42 C5 **Chingis** U.S.S.R. 54.06N 81.44E
43 N3 **Chingiz-Tau, Khrebet** *mts* Kazakhstan U.S.S.R.
28 E4 **Chingleput** Tamil Nadu India 12.42N 80.01E
28 D4 **Chingleput** *dist* Tamil Nadu India
Ch'ing-ning Fujian *see* **Ning hua**
91 C11 **Chingo** Angola 14.17S 12.51E
92 C8 **Chingola** Zambia 12.31S 27.53E
92 D9 **Chingombe** Zambia 14.25S 29.56E
23 J6 **Ch'ing-shui** Taiwan 24.12N 120.33E
91 E11 **Chinguanja** Angola 14.59S 17.21E
91 E10 **Chinguar** Angola 12.33S 16.25E
89 C1 **Chinguetti** Mauritania 20.25N 12.24W
91 G7 **Chingufo** Angola 7.41S 20.30E
90 J6 **Chinguil** Chad 10.35N 19.00E
94 N3 **Chingune** Mozambique 20.38S 34.55E
21 D10 **Chinhae** S Korea 35.05N 128.47E
91 E10 **Chinhama** Angola 13.05S 16.27E
92 F9 **Chinhanda** Mozambique 15.51S 32.24E
30 E6 **Chinhat** Uttar Prad India 26.52N 81.02E
Chin-hsien *see* **Jin Xian (Dalinghe)**
21 D8 **Chinhŭng-ni** N Korea 39.26N 127.27E
113 L8 **Chiniak,C** Alaska 57.39N 152.10W
120 E6 **Chiñijo** Bolivia 15.24S 68.25W
Chining *see* **Jining**
31 G5 **Chiniot** Pakistan 31.40N 73.00E
115 E4 **Chinipas** Mexico 27.22N 108.32W
18 C8 **Chini,Tasek** *L* Pen Malaysia
113 L7 **Chinitna B** Alaska
92 G11 **Chiniziua** Mozambique 18.57S 35.08E
21 D10 **Chinju** S Korea 35.10N 128.06E
43 D6 **Chink Kaplankyr** *ridge* U.S.S.R.
90 M9 **Chinko** *R* Cent Afr Rep
111 P5 **Chinle** Arizona 36.09N 109.34W
111 P5 **Chinle Cr** Arizona
111 P5 **Chinle Val** Arizona
28 E3 **Chinna Ganjam** Andhra Prad India 15.43N 80.26E
28 C6 **Chinnamanur** Tamil Nadu India 9.50N 77.24E
21 C8 **Chinnamp'o** N Korea 38.51N 125.10E
28 D5 **Chinna Salem** Tamil Nadu India 11.40N 78.52E
56 K4 **Chinnor** Oxon Eng 51.43N 0.56W
28 D1 **Chinnur** Andhra Prad India 18.53N 79.49E
111 M6 **Chino** Arizona 35.20N 112.56W
20 M6 **Chino** Japan 35.59N 138.08E
14 C10 **Chinocup, L** W Australia 33.30S 118.22E
72 E1 **Chinon** France 47.10N 0.15E
100 G7 **Chinook** Alberta 51.28N 110.59W
110 Q1 **Chinook** Montana 48.35N 109.14W
110 D3 **Chinook Pass** Washington 46.54N 121.30W
111 M7 **Chino Valley** Arizona 34.45N 112.28W
92 F7 **Chinsali** Zambia 10.33S 32.05E
29 M2 **Chinsura** W Bengal India 22.53N 88.25E
28 E1 **Chintalnar** Madhya Prad India 18.21N 81.16E
28 D4 **Chintamani** Karnataka India 13.26N 78.05E
92 G7 **Chinteche** Malawi 11.50S 34.13E
119 C3 **Chinú** Colombia 9.07N 75.25W
92 H7 **Chinunje** Tanzania 11.20S 37.20E
61 M8 **Chiny** Belgium 49.44N 5.21E
47 M7 **Chinyavino** U.S.S.R. 55.30N 75.28E
91 D8 **Chio** Angola 9.49S 14.01E
96 Q14 **Chio** Tenerife Canary Is 28.14N 16.48W
92 F10 **Chioco** Mozambique 16.26S 32.55E
79 M4 **Chioggia** Italy 45.13N 12.17E
93 J6 **Chiokarige** Kenya 0.14S 37.57E
79 A4 **Chiomonte** Italy 45.07N 6.58E
Chios *see* **Khíos**
29 E5 **Chipa Barod** Rajasthan India 24.35N 76.42E
92 F8 **Chipata** Zambia 13.40S 32.42E
91 F11 **Chipaue** Angola 15.50S 19.01E
115 O10 **Chipaxché** Guatemala 15.33N 90.01W
31 J3 **Chip Chap R** Kashmir
121 C9 **Chipchihua,Sa de** *ra* Argentina
92 D9 **Chipembi** Zambia 14.57S 28.38E
92 C10 **Chipepo** Zambia 16.50S 27.54E
92 F9 **Chipera** Mozambique 15.22S 32.35E
92 G10 **Chiperone** *mt* Mozambique 16.30S 35.44E
91 E10 **Chipeta** Angola 12.15S 17.10E
100 T1 **Chipewyan L** Manitoba
101 R7 **Chipewyan Lake** Alberta 56.55N 113.30W
92 D7 **Chipili** Zambia 10.45S 29.04E
91 D10 **Chipindo** Angola 13.49S 15.48E
22 K8 **Chiping** Shandong China 36.40N 116.12E
92 F12 **Chipinga** Zimbabwe 20.12S 32.28E
92 F12 **Chipinga** *dist* Zimbabwe
77 D7 **Chipiona** Spain 36.44N 6.26W
91 D10 **Chipipa** Angola 12.34S 15.39E
100 B5 **Chip, L** Alberta 53.40N 115.20W
105 B7 **Chipley** Florida 30.48N 85.32W
28 A2 **Chiplun** Maharashtra India 17.32N 73.32E
98 G7 **Chipman** New Brunswick 46.11N 65.54W
99 P2 **Chipman** New York 44.47N 75.12W
99 D3 **Chipman L** Ontario 50.00N 86.15W
92 H5 **Chipogolo** Tanzania 6.52S 36.03E
92 G8 **Chipoka** Malawi 13.55S 34.33E
105 B7 **Chipola** *R* Florida
92 C9 **Chiposhya, L** Zambia 14.26S 27.45E
25 J7 **Chi Pou** Cambodia 11.00N 106.01E
99 L9 **Chippawa** Ontario 43.03N 79.04W
56 G5 **Chippenham** Wilts Eng 51.28N 2.07W
108 P4 **Chippewa** *R* Minnesota
106 C4 **Chippewa** *R* Wisconsin
106 C5 **Chippewa Falls** Wisconsin 44.56N 91.25W
106 C4 **Chippewa, L** Wisconsin 45.56N 91.10W
57 H5 **Chipping** Lancs Eng 53.54N 2.35W
56 H3 **Chipping Campden** Glos Eng 52.03N 1.46W
56 H4 **Chipping Norton** Oxon Eng 51.56N 1.32W
56 M4 **Chipping Ongar** Essex Eng 51.43N 0.15E
56 G4 **Chipping Sodbury** Avon Eng 51.33N 2.24W
66 G6 **Chippis** Switzerland 46.17N 7.33E
75 K5 **Chiprana** Spain 41.15N 0.08W
82 H7 **Chiprovtsi** Bulgaria 43.22N 22.50E
28 F1 **Chipurupalle** Vishakhapatnam, Andhra Prad India 18.17N 83.45E
28 F2 **Chipurupalle** Vishakhapatnam, Andhra Prad India 17.34N 83.10E
98 E8 **Chiputneticook Lakes** Maine/New Bruns
120 B4 **Chiquian** Peru 10.09S 77.08W
115 Q7 **Chiquilá** Mexico 21.18N 87.17W
115 P10 **Chiquimula** Guatemala 14.48N 89.32W
115 O10 **Chiquimulilla** Guatemala 14.06N 90.23W
120 D9 **Chiquinata,B.de** Chile
119 D5 **Chiquinquira** Colombia 5.37N 73.51W
121 E5 **Chiquita, Mar** *L* Buenos Aires Argentina
91 C10 **Chiquite** Angola 13.46S 13.07E
45 O8 **Chir** *R* U.S.S.R.
87 F7 **Chira** Ethiopia 8.23N 36.11E
93 L9 **Chira** Kenya 3.30S 39.35E
119 B10 **Chira** *R* Peru
71 C7 **Chirac** France 44.32N 3.16E
89 J8 **Chiradeso** Ghana 7.20N 1.40W
92 G9 **Chiradzulu** Malawi 15.41S 35.09E
31 D1 **Chirakchi** Uzbekistan U.S.S.R. 39.00N 66.30E
44 H6 **Chirakh** U.S.S.R. 41.50N 47.27E
28 B5 **Chirakkal** Kerala India 11.56N 75.22E
28 E3 **Chirala** Guntur, Andhra Prad India 15.52N 80.26E
28 E3 **Chirala** Guntur, Andhra Prad India 15.59N 80.05E
92 G10 **Chiramba** Mozambique 16.55S 34.40E
119 C5 **Chirambirá,Pta** Colombia 4.19N 77.36W
31 C3 **Chiras** Afghanistan 35.17N 65.45E
29 D3 **Chirawa** Rajasthan India 28.12N 75.42E
28 C6 **Chirayinkil** Kerala India 8.40N 76.50E
56 E2 **Chirbury** Shropshire Eng 52.35N 3.06W
43 J6 **Chirchik** Uzbekistan U.S.S.R. 41.28N 69.31E
43 J6 **Chirchik** *R* Uzbekistan U.S.S.R.
30 D2 **Chirchin** Xizang Zizhiqu 30.41N 80.14E
87 K8 **Chirchirri** Somalia 4.44N 44.40E
92 G10 **Chire** Mozambique 16.38S 35.22E
92 E12 **Chiredzi** Zimbabwe 21.00S 31.38E
92 E12 **Chiredzi** *R* Zimbabwe
112 N4 **Chireno** Texas 31.30N 94.22W
90 F1 **Chirfa** Niger 20.55N 12.22E
42 F6 **Chirgalandy** U.S.S.R. 50.34N 97.15E
30 B7 **Chirgaon** Uttar Prad India 25.34N 78.49E
119 F3 **Chirgua, R** Venezuela
30 G7 **Chiriakot** Uttar Prad India 25.53N 83.20E
119 D7 **Chiribiquete,Sa de** *mts* Colombia
111 P9 **Chiricahua Nat.Mon** Arizona 32.00N 109.20W
111 P10 **Chiricahua Pk** *mt* Arizona 31.50N 109.17W
81 J6 **Chirica,Mte** Lipari Is Italy 38.31N 14.57E
119 D3 **Chiriguana** Colombia 9.24N 73.38W
113 K9 **Chirikof, I** Alaska 55.50N 155.40W
42 E3 **Chirimba** U.S.S.R. 59.43N 92.58E
41 H6 **Chirinda** U.S.S.R. 67.44N 100.30E
31 J10 **Chiringa** Bangladesh 21.45N 92.04E
40 N7 **Chirinkotan** *vol* Kuril Is U.S.S.R. 48.59N 153.29E
40 N7 **Chirinkotan, O** *isld* Kuril Is U.S.S.R. 48.59N 153.29E
119 B10 **Chirinos** Peru 5.21S 78.58W
115 N5 **Chiriqui, G.de** Panama
115 N5 **Chiriquí Grande** Panama 8.58N 82.08W
115 N5 **Chiriquí,L.de** Panama
119 A3 **Chiriquí,Pta.** *C* Panama 9.10N 81.54W
77 M5 **Chirivel** Spain 37.35N 2.15W
57 G7 **Chirk** Clwyd Wales 52.56N 3.03W
51 Q8 **Chirka** *R* Karelia U.S.S.R.
51 Q7 **Chirka Kem** Karelia U.S.S.R. 64.22N 32.10E
29 J1 **Chirki** Bihar India 24.02N 86.09E
29 H6 **Chirmiri** Madhya Prad India 23.18N 82.26E
82 L7 **Chirnogeni** Romania 43.55N 28.14E
58 M7 **Chirnside** Borders Scot 55.48N 2.11W
92 G10 **Chiromo** Malawi 16.33S 35.10E
66 M6 **Chironico** Switzerland 46.26N 8.52E
15 K2 **Chirovanga** Choiseul I Solomon Is 6.40S 156.38E
92 E12 **Chirowandoma Falls** Zimbabwe 21.18S 31.55E
82 J8 **Chirpan** Bulgaria 42.10N 25.19E
115 N5 **Chirripó** Costa Rica 9.50N 83.25W
115 N5 **Chirripó** *pk* Costa Rica 9.31N 83.30W
Chiru *see* **Bandar-e Chīrū**
Chirua, L *see* **Chilwa, L**
92 D10 **Chirundu** Zambia 16.03S 28.50E
69 D4 **Chiry-Ourscamps** France 49.33N 2.58E
92 D9 **Chisamba** Zambia 15.00S 28.22E
92 G8 **Chisamula** *isld* Malawi 12.01S 34.39E
113 R5 **Chisana** Alaska 62.03N 142.08W
113 R5 **Chisana** *R* Alaska
113 Q6 **Chisana Glacier** Alaska 61.50N 142.40W
92 G7 **Chisanga** Malawi 10.52S 34.13E
30 K6 **Chisapani** Nepal 26.56N 86.08E
30 J5 **Chisapani Garhi** Nepal 27.35N 85.09E
115 O10 **Chisec** Guatemala 15.50N 90.18W
92 C10 **Chisekesi** Zambia 16.26S 27.28E
100 R4 **Chisel Lake** Manitoba 54.52N 100.05W
92 F6 **Chisenga** Malawi 9.59S 33.25E
92 D7 **Chishinga** *tribe* Zambia
46 S3 **Chishmy** U.S.S.R. 54.36N 55.22E
100 C4 **Chisholm** Alberta 54.55N 114.09W
104 P2 **Chisholm** Maine 44.30N 70.12W
108 S2 **Chisholm** Minnesota 47.29N 92.52W
23 H6 **Chishui** Fujian China 25.42N 118.03E
23 D4 **Chishui** Sichuan China 28.29N 105.37E
23 D5 **Chishui He** *R* Guizhou China
92 D7 **Chisi I** Zambia 11.05S 29.50E
87 N9 **Chisimaio** Somalia 0.25S 42.31E
Chişinau *see* **Kishinev**
82 G4 **Chişineu Criş** Romania 46.31N 21.31E
41 G8 **Chiskovo** U.S.S.R. 64.05N 95.30E
56 H4 **Chisledon** Wilts Eng 51.31N 1.44W
55 H5 **Chislehurst** London England 51.25N 0.05E
92 E8 **Chisomo** Zambia 13.35S 30.38E
79 B5 **Chisone** *R* Italy
91 G10 **Chisongo** Angola 13.59S 21.58E
112 D6 **Chisos Mts** Texas
112 C5 **Chispa Cr** Texas
91 G8 **Chissengue** Angola 9.13S 20.34E
94 N3 **Chissinguane** Mozambique 20.12S 34.10E
44 H2 **Chistaya Banka, Ostrov** *isld* U.S.S.R.
31 G6 **Chistian Mandi** Pakistan 29.44N 72.54E
113 P5 **Chistochina** Alaska 62.34N 144.43W
43 M1 **Chistoozernoye** U.S.S.R. 54.45N 76.35E
45 W1 **Chistopol'** U.S.S.R. 55.22N 50.33E
43 H1 **Chistopol'ye** Kazakhstan U.S.S.R. 52.37N 67.14E
43 M1 **Chistovo** U.S.S.R. 54.43N 75.31E
43 K1 **Chistyakovka** Kazakhstan U.S.S.R. 53.29N 71.16E
55 D4 **Chiswick** London Eng 51.29N 0.16W
120 E9 **Chita** Bolivia 20.06S 67.01W
119 D4 **Chita** Colombia 6.13N 72.28W
42 J6 **Chita** U.S.S.R. 52.03N 113.35E
91 C12 **Chitado** Angola 17.21S 13.58E
29 B5 **Chitalwana** Rajasthan India 24.55N 71.44E
92 E8 **Chitambo** Zambia 12.55S 30.40E
113 L4 **Chitanana** *R* Alaska
93 B6 **Chitanda** *mt* Uganda 0.58S 30.57E
20 K7 **Chita-wan** *gulf* Japan
47 F5 **Chitayevo** U.S.S.R. 60.20N 49.29E
100 K5 **Chitek** Saskatchewan 53.48N 107.46W
100 S6 **Chitek L** Manitoba
91 E10 **Chitembo** Angola 13.33S 16.47E
79 L7 **Chitignano** Italy 43.39N 11.53E
113 P6 **Chitina** Alaska 61.30N 144.31W
113 Q6 **Chitina** *R* Alaska
38 L3 **Chitinskaya Oblast'** *prov* U.S.S.R.
92 F6 **Chitipa** Malawi 9.41S 33.19E
30 B1 **Chitkul** Himachal Prad India 31.21N 78.24E
92 A8 **Chitokoloki** Zambia 13.50S 23.13E
92 F10 **Chitomba** *mt* Zimbabwe 16.54S 32.42E
91 G10 **Chitombue** Angola 12.43S 21.34E
Chitor *see* **Chittaurgarh**
20 L2 **Chitose** Japan 42.50N 141.39E
30 E7 **Chitpalgarh** Uttar Prad India 25.44N 81.52E
29 H1 **Chitpur** *dist* Calcutta, W Bengal
28 C3 **Chitradurga** Karnataka India 14.16N 76.23E
28 C3 **Chitradurga** *dist* Karnataka India
30 D7 **Chitrakut** Uttar Prad India 25.13N 80.48E
31 F3 **Chitral** Pakistan 35.52N 71.58E
31 F2 **Chitral** *reg* Pakistan
31 F3 **Chitral R** Pakistan
28 C3 **Chitravati R** Andhra Prad India
115 O6 **Chitré** Panama 7.59N 80.25W
29 B6 **Chitrod** Gujarat India 23.25N 70.42E
31 J10 **Chittagong** Bangladesh 22.20N 91.48E
31 J10 **Chittagong** *dist* Bangladesh
31 J9 **Chittagong Hill Tracts** *dist* Bangladesh
29 K1 **Chittaranjan** Bihar India 23.52N 86.40E
29 D5 **Chittaurgarh** Rajasthan India 24.54N 74.42E
29 D5 **Chittaurgarh** *dist* Rajasthan India
28 D4 **Chittoor** Andhra Prad India 13.13N 79.06E
28 D4 **Chittoor** *dist* Andhra Prad India
28 C5 **Chittur** Kerala India 10.42N 76.46E
Ch'i-tung *see* **Qidong**
Chiu-an-hua *see* **Meichengzhen**
115 P8 **Chiuchanhá** Mexico 18.10N 89.13W
120 E10 **Chiuchiu** Chile 22.18S 68.41W
30 E2 **Chiu Gompa** Xizang Zizhiqu 30.48N 81.21E
92 H8 **Chiulézi** *R* Mozambique
Chiu-ling Shan *mts see* **Jiuling Shan**
91 E10 **Chiumbe** Angola 12.29S 16.08E
91 G8 **Chiumbe** *R* Angola
91 G11 **Chiume** Angola 15.08S 21.11E
92 J8 **Chiure** Mozambique 13.24S 39.56E

79 L1 Chiusa Italy 46.38N 11.34E
79 C6 Chiusa di Pesio Italy 44.19N 7.40E
79 O2 Chiusaforte Italy 46.24N 13.19E
81 F8 Chiusa Sclafani Sicily 37.41N 13.16E
80 D2 Chiusdino Italy 43.09N 11.05E
Chiu-sha-wan see Lao sha wan
80 E2 Chiusi Italy 43.02N 11.57E
79 L7 Chiusi di Verna Italy 43.42N 11.56E
80 E2 Chiusi,Lago di Italy 43.03N 11.58E
92 F9 Chiuta Mozambique 15.29S 33.20E
92 G9 Chiuta, L Malawi 14.50S 35.50E
77 P2 Chiva Spain 39.29N 0.43W
119 F4 Chivapuri, R Venezuela
79 C4 Chivasso Italy 45.11N 7.53E
115 D4 Chívato, Pta Mexico 27.05N 111.58W
120 D6 Chivay Peru 15.28S 71.20W
120 E5 Chive Bolivia 12.22S 68.36W
115 M9 Chivela Mexico 16.42N 95.04W
121 E5 Chivilcoy Argentina 34.55S 60.00W
109 H3 Chivington Colorado 38.25N 102.33W
92 F12 Chivirira Falls Zimbabwe 21.10S 32.19E
69 F4 Chivy-les-Étouvelles France 49.32N 3.36E
92 G7 Chiwanda Tanzania 11.21S 34.55E
23 F6 Chiwei Guangdong China 24.36N 113.33E
23 F8 Chixi Guangdong China 21.59N 113.00E
115 O10 Chixoy R Mexico/Guatemala
43 O8 Chiyirchik,Pereval pass Kirgiziya U.S.S.R. 40.15N 73.34E
20 E2 Chiyoda dist Tōkyō Japan
72 D3 Chizé France 46.08N 0.20W
92 B8 Chizela Zambia 13.10S 25.02E
47 E3 Chizha U.S.S.R. 67.04N 44.20E
42 B3 Chizhapka R U.S.S.R.
43 A2 Chizhinskiye Razlivy flood area Kazakhstan U.S.S.R.
Chizhou see Guichi
45 V6 Chizhsa Vtoraya Kazakhstan U.S.S.R. 50.53N 49.39E
20 H6 Chizu Japan 35.13N 134.14E
Chkalov see Orenburg
43 K1 Chkalovo Kazakhstan U.S.S.R. 53.38N 70.28E
46 N2 Chkalovsk U.S.S.R. 56.48N 43.00E
42 E6 Chkalovskiy U.S.S.R. 52.02N 93.32E
40 F9 Chkalovskoye U.S.S.R. 44.54N 133.01E
44 E5 Chkhorotsku Georgia U.S.S.R. 42.32N 42.10E
58 H2 Chlàir, Loch a' Highland Scot 58.17N 4.06W
Ch-li-ya Shan-k'ou pass see Keriya Shankou pass
111 K6 Chloride Arizona 35.24N 114.09W
65 K4 Chlum mt Czechoslovakia 48.54N 14.04E
62 J5 Chlumec nad Cidlinou Czechoslovakia 50.10N 15.26E
65 L4 Chlum u Třeboně Czechoslovakia 48.59N 14.57E
40 H5 Chlya Ozero L U.S.S.R. 53.25N 140.06E
62 M5 Chmielnik Poland 50.37N 20.43E
Ch-mu-lang-ma Feng mt see Everest, Mt
88 J8 Chnaynat reg Morocco
21 C8 Cho isld N Korea
21 D10 Cho isld S Korea
92 F11 Choa Mozambique 18.03S 33.00E
18 F2 Choa Chu Kang Singapore 1.22N 103.41E
18 G3 Choa Chu Kang dist Singapore
76 C9 Choã de Codes Portugal 39.37N 8.04W
121 B3 Choapo, R Chile
Choārta see Chwārtā
93 K3 Choba Kenya 2.27N 38.03E
93 K3 Choba Gof mt Kenya 2.27N 38.04E
34 E2 Choban Bey Syria 36.36N 37.28E
94 H2 Chobe dist Botswana
94 G2 Chobe R Botswana/Namibia
94 H2 Chobe National Park Botswana
56 K5 Chobham Surrey Eng 51.21N 0.37W
93 D3 Chobi Lodge Uganda 2.15N 32.10E
25 H2 Cho Bo Vietnam 20.45N 105.11E
76 D6 Chocalho, Barragem res Portugal 41.07N 7.47W
120 E9 Chocaya Bolivia 20.52S 66.16W
120 B5 Chocca mt Peru 12.55S 75.20W
65 O1 Choceň Czechoslovakia 50.00N 16.15E
30 A8 Choch R Madhya Prad India
99 O5 Chochocouane R Quebec
25 H2 Cho Chu Vietnam 21.54N 105.39E
41 N8 Chochumskiy Khrebet mts U.S.S.R.
62 J4 Chocianów Poland 51.26N 15.57E
120 B5 Choclococha, L Peru 13.13S 75.04W
119 C5 Chocó div Colombia
111 K8 Chocolate Mts Arizona
111 J8 Chocolate Mts California
119 D5 Chocontá Colombia 5.08N 73.41W
103 C3 Choconut Pennsylvania 41.58N 75.59W
104 O3 Chocorua New Hampshire 43.54N 71.14W
105 K2 Chocowinity N Carolina 35.31N 77.07W
107 H9 Choctaw Alabama 32.12N 88.08W
109 N6 Choctaw Oklahoma 35.31N 97.17W
107 L10 Choctawhatchee R Ala/Florida
107 K11 Choctawhatchee B Florida
28 E2 Chodavaram Andhra Prad India 17.28N 81.50E
18 B9 Chodoi Pen Malaysia 2.50N 101.26E
23 D7 Cho Don Vietnam 22.10N 105.38E
75 K7 Chodos Spain 40.15N 0.18W
64 O3 Chodov Czechoslovakia 50.15N 12.45E
42 D6 Chodro U.S.S.R. 50.51N 88.32E
42 F6 Choduralyg U.S.S.R. 51.25N 96.27E
62 K3 Chodzież Poland 53.00N 16.55E
28 L1 Chö Dzong Xizang Zizhiqu 29.57N 96.08E
121 D7 Choele Choel Argentina 39.16S 65.38W
92 E9 Chofombo Mozambique 14.42S 31.45E
20 C3 Chōfu dist Tōkyō Japan 35.39N 139.33E
24 E4 Choga Davan mt pass Xinjiang Uygur Zizhiqu China
24 E4 Choga Davan pass Xinjiang Uygur Zizhiqu China 43.26N 85.42E
40 F4 Chogar R U.S.S.R.
32 D6 Choghadāk Iran 28.59N 51.02E
31 C2 Choghli Tepe Afghanistan 37.30N 65.49E
25 J7 Cho Giua Vietnam 10.36N 106.39E
20 C5 Chōgo Kanagawa Japan
31 H3 Chogo Lungma Glacier Kashmir
93 J6 Chogoria Kenya 0.12S 37.40E
44 F2 Chogray R U.S.S.R.
29 B5 Chohtan Rajasthan India 25.27N 71.08E
100 N5 Choiceland Saskatchewan 53.30N 104.33W
93 K3 Choichuf Kenya 2.36N 38.55E
69 J7 Choignes France 40.06N 5.10E
58 H2 Choire, L Highland Scot 58.13N 4.20W
15 K2 Choiseul I Solomon Is
121 E10 Choiseul Sound Falkland Is
71 J4 Choisy France 46.00N 6.04E
69 D5 Choisy-au-Bac France 49.27N 2.53E
68 G4 Choisy-le-Roi France 48.47N 2.26E
115 E4 Choix Mexico 26.45N 108.23W
62 H3 Chojna Poland 52.57N 14.26E
62 K2 Chojnice Poland 53.42N 17.32E
62 J4 Chojnów Poland 51.18N 15.58E
20 O2 Chōkai-san mt Japan 39.08N 140.04E
87 F5 Choke Mountains Ethiopia
44 E5 Chokhatauri Georgia U.S.S.R. 42.01N 42.15E
61 M4 Chokier Belgium 50.35N 5.25E
108 O4 Chokio Minnesota 45.35N 96.10W
43 L5 Choknar Kazakhstan U.S.S.R. 43.46N 74.29E
28 J1 Chokorgye Xizang Zizhiqu 29.23N 92.38E
43 M5 Choktal Kirgiziya U.S.S.R. 42.34N 76.38E
39 D1 Chokurdakh U.S.S.R. 70.39N 147.50E
91 G9 Chokwe tribe Angola
30 H2 Chola Col pass Nepal 27.57N 86.46E
30 H3 Chola Glacier Nepal
111 D6 Cholame California 35.44N 120.16W
111 D6 Cholame Cr California
30 H3 Chola Og Nepal 27.56N 86.48E
30 H3 Chola Pokhari L Nepal 27.55N 86.47E
23 A2 Chola Shan mts Sichuan China
Cholatse see Jobo Lhaptshan
30 H3 Cholatse pk Nepal 27.55N 86.46E
28 C6 Cholavandan Tamil Nadu India 10.00N 78.00E
56 H5 Cholderton Wilts Eng 51.11N 1.41W
92 J5 Chole Mafia I Tanzania 8.00S 39.45E
72 C1 Cholet France 47.04N 0.53W
121 B9 Cholila Argentina 42.33S 71.28W
57 J2 Chollerford Northumb Eng 55.02N 2.08W
57 J2 Chollerton Northumb Eng 55.03N 2.05W
115 Q10 Choloma Honduras 15.36N 87.57W
25 J7 Cho Lon Vietnam 10.45N 106.39E
24 C8 Cholpanglik mt pk Xinjiang Uygur Zizhiqu/Kashmir China 35.47N 79.55E
43 M6 Cholpon Kirgiziya U.S.S.R. 42.09N 75.24E
43 M5 Cholpon Ata U.S.S.R. 42.38N 77.03E
65 N2 Choltice Czechoslovakia 49.59N 15.38E
115 K8 Cholula Mexico 19.05N 98.20W
115 L3 Choluteca Honduras 13.15N 87.10W
92 C10 Choma Zambia 16.51S 27.04E
99 Q9 Chomedy Quebec 45.32N 73.45W
71 D6 Chomelix France 45.17N 3.50E
71 F7 Chomérac France 44.42N 4.39E
25 G7 Chomna Cambodia 11.44N 103.35E
Chomo see Yadong
Chomo Dzong see Qomo
25 H2 Cho Moi Vietnam 21.51N 105.36E
24 F12 Chomo Lhari pk Xizang Zizhiqu/Bhutan 27.53N 89.16E
30 L3 Chomo Lonzo mt Xizang Zizhiqu 27.56N 87.07E
Chomo Lungma mt see Everest, Mt.
29 L3 Chomo Yummo mt Sikkim India 28.02N 88.34E
25 E3 Chom Thong Thailand 18.25N 98.44E
29 D4 Chomun Rajasthan India 27.09N 75.44E
64 P3 Chomutov Czechoslovakia 50.27N 13.25E
64 Q3 Chomutovka R Czechoslovakia
42 J2 Chona R U.S.S.R.
21 D9 Ch'ŏnan S Korea 36.50N 127.09E
25 F6 Chon Buri Thailand 13.24N 100.59E
121 A9 Chonchi Chile 42.42S 73.46W
25 F4 Chon Daen Thailand 16.12N 100.55E
92 D8 Chondwe Zambia 13.16S 28.45E
119 B8 Chone Ecuador 0.44S 80.04W
119 B8 Chone, R Ecuador
23 H5 Chong'an Fujian China 27.45N 117.58E
23 J3 Chongde Zhejiang China 30.33N 120.27E
Chonggye Dzong see Qonggyai
21 C8 Chŏngiu N Korea 39.39N 125.17E
21 E7 Ch'ŏngjin N Korea 41.50N 129.55E
21 D9 Ch'ŏngju S Korea 36.39N 127.27E
25 G6 Chong Kal Cambodia 13.58N 103.35E
Chong Kara Jol see Karajül
23 A3 Chongkü Xizang Zizhiqu China 31.27N 96.36E
24 J10 Chongkü Xizang Zizhiqu China 31.27N 96.36E
22 K6 Chongli Hebei China 40.57N 115.12E
23 F5 Chongling Shui R Hunan China
21 B12 Chongming Shanghai China 31.38N 121.27E
23 J3 Chongming Dao isld Shanghai China
23 G1 Chongmou Henan China 34.44N 114.01E
21 K1 Chongno-gu dist Seoul S Korea
21 K1 Ch'ŏngnyangni dist Seoul S Korea
91 D10 Chongoroi Angola 13.32S 14.02E
23 C3 Chongqing Sichuan China 30.40N 103.35E
23 D4 Chongqing Sichuan China 29.30N 106.35E
23 G5 Chongren Jiangxi China 27.48N 115.99E
23 G6 Chongshi Jiangxi China 25.23N 115.26E
21 D9 Chŏngsŏn S Korea 37.26N 128.38E
21 E6 Chongsong N Korea 42.42N 129.46E
24 C8 Chongtash Xizang Zizhiqu China 35.30N 78.34E
94 M5 Chonguene Mozambique 25.03S 33.49E
21 D10 Chŏngŭp S Korea 35.35N 126.50E
92 D9 Chongwe R Zambia
23 D1 Chongxin Gansu China 35.15N 107.30E
23 G4 Chongyang Hubei China 29.35N 114.03E
23 H5 Chongyang Xi R Fujian China
23 G6 Chongyi Jiangxi China 25.45N 114.29E
42 E6 Chongyz-Tayga,Gora mt U.S.S.R. 51.02N 94.17E
23 D7 Chongzuo Guangxi China 22.28N 107.32E
21 D10 Chŏnju S Korea 35.50N 127.05E
28 L2 Chonkham Assam India 27.48N 96.03E
58 G6 Chon, L Central Scotland 56.13N 4.34W
121 A10 Chonos,Arch.de los Chile
43 M5 Chon-Saryoy Kirgiziya U.S.S.R. 42.38N 76.55E
120 B5 Chonta, P. De pass Peru 13.05S 75.05W
25 J7 Chon Thanh Vietnam 11.25N 106.38E
30 G1 Cho Oyu mt Xizang Zizhiqu/Nepal 28.06N 86.40E
82 G2 Chop U.S.S.R. 48.26N 22.13E
30 G8 Chopan Uttar Prad India 24.32N 83.02E
29 D7 Chopda Maharashtra India 21.15N 75.20E
57 L4 Chop Gate N Yorks Eng 54.23N 1.08W
25 J7 Cho Phuoc Hai Vietnam 10.25N 107.18E
77 N4 Chopillo R Spain
118 D9 Chopim, R Brazil
118 D9 Chopimzinho Brazil 25.49S 52.32W
30 K3 Cho Polu mt Nepal 27.56N 86.59E
103 C9 Choptank R Maryland
120 E7 Choquecamata Bolivia 16.51S 66.38W
31 E8 Chor Pakistan 23.35N 69.48E
25 H1 Cho Ra Vietnam 22.28N 105.42E
42 G4 Chora R U.S.S.R.
120 F8 Choreti Bolivia 20.00S 63.30W
30 C3 Chorgallia Uttar Prad India 29.06N 79.42E
71 J7 Chorges France 44.33N 6.16E
30 E8 Chorhat Madhya Prad India 24.26N 81.39E
87 N5 Chor Hordio gulf Somalia 10.30N 51.10E
63 T7 Chorin E Germany 52.53N 13.54E
Chorinchen see Chorin
76 L10 Chorito,Sierra del mts Spain
43 K7 Chorku Tadzhikistan U.S.S.R. 39.59N 70.36E
57 H5 Chorley Lancs Eng 53.40N 2.38W
55 B2 Chorleywood Herts Eng 51.40N 0.29W
65 P2 Chornice Czechoslovakia 49.41N 16.45E
120 E9 Chorolque,Nev pk Bolivia 20.59S 66.05W
121 B2 Choros R Chile
121 B2 Choros,Is.de los Chile
62 O2 Choroszcz Poland 53.10N 22.59E
13 G6 Chorregon Queensland 22.41S 143.30E
120 B5 Chorrillos Peru 12.10S 77.01W
120 B10 Chorrillos dist Lima Peru
117 G9 Chorrochó Brazil 8.55S 39.03W
46 F5 Chortkov Ukraine U.S.S.R. 49.01N 25.42E
43 M8 Chorukh-Dayron Tadzhikistan U.S.S.R. 40.25N 69.42E
29 B7 Chorwad Gujarat India 21.00N 79.19E
21 D8 Chŏrwŏn S Korea 38.10N 127.15E
62 M2 Chorzele Poland 53.16N 20.52E
62 L5 Chorzów Poland 50.19N 18.56E
21 C7 Chosan N Korea 40.47N 125.44E
Chōsen-kaikyō see Nishi-suidō
20 O6 Chōshi Japan 35.43N 140.51E
Choshjin Res see Changjin Res
120 B4 Chosica Peru 11.55S 76.38W
121 B6 Chos Malal Argentina 37.25S 69.17W
121 C4 Chosmes Argentina 33.23S 66.52W
21 D8 Choson-Man B N Korea
92 E9 Chossavo Mozambique 15.16S 30.24E
62 J2 Choszczno Poland 53.10N 15.24E
120 A2 Chota Peru 6.21S 78.39W
Chotan see Chohtan
29 H6 Chotanagpur reg India
119 B11 Chotano R Peru
28 G2 Chota Sinchula mt Bhutan 26.49N 89.36E
29 D6 Chota Udaipur Gujarat India 22.19N 74.03E
110 N2 Choteau Montana 47.49N 112.10W
109 P5 Choteau Oklahoma 36.12N 95.22W
65 N2 Chotěboř Czechoslovakia 49.44N 15.41E
30 M4 Choten Nyima Gompa Xizang Zizhiqu 28.06N 88.12E
64 P4 Chotěšov Czechoslovakia 49.40N 13.13E
31 F6 Choti Pakistan 29.49N 70.31E
29 B6 Chotila Gujarat India 22.23N 71.18E
88 O4 Chott ech Chergui salt L Algeria
88 S5 Chott el Fedjadj salt L Tunisia
88 N5 Chott el Gharbi salt L Algeria
88 R4 Chott el Gharsa salt L Tunisia
88 Q4 Chott el Hodna salt L Algeria
88 S5 Chott Jerid salt L Tunisia
88 R4 Chott Melrhir salt L Algeria
88 Q4 Chott Merouane salt L Algeria
65 L3 Chotýčany Lišov Czechoslovakia 49.02N 14.38E
88 L8 Chouikhia Algeria 27.50N 4.11W
69 G5 Chouilly France 49.01N 4.02E
74 K8 Choukchof mt Algeria 36.02N 4.13E
88 G11 Choum Mauritania 21.18N 12.58E
Choumarijé,Jebel see Shōmarīye, Jebel
Choura see Shawrah
Chou-shan Tao isld see Zhoushan isld
22 E6 Choushuidun Gansu China 40.17N 99.04E
65 L3 Choustník Czechoslovakia 49.20N 14.52E
76 C10 Chouto Portugal 39.16N 8.21W
69 D8 Choux,les France 47.48N 2.40E
72 E1 Chouzé-sur-Loire France 47.15N 0.08E
70 N6 Chouzy-sur-Cisse France 47.32N 1.15E
75 K8 Chóvar Spain 39.51N 0.20W
105 L1 Chowan R N Carolina
111 D4 Chowchilla California 37.07N 120.14W
14 B10 Chowerup W Australia 34.05S 116.35E
28 C5 Chowghat Kerala India 10.34N 76.01E
113 J8 Chowiet I Alaska 56.02N 156.45W
12 F5 Chowilla Dam S Australia 34.03S 140.55E
32 C2 Chowkam Iran 37.20N 49.40E
101 O9 Chown Mt Alberta 53.23N 119.26W
121 D2 Choya Argentina 28.30S 64.50W
42 D6 Choya U.S.S.R. 52.01N 86.33E
22 K2 Choybalsan Mongolia 48.02N 114.32E
71 H2 Choye France 47.24N 5.45E
76 H3 Chozas de Abajo Spain 42.30N 5.41W
Chozas de la Sierra see Soto del Real
76 E7 Chozendo Portugal 40.58N 7.29W
65 N2 Chrast Czech 49.54N 15.56E
64 Q4 Chrast Plzeň Czechoslovakia 49.48N 13.30E
89 C1 Chrerick Mauritania 21.17N 12.28W
62 K6 Chřiby mts Czechoslovakia
112 L5 Chriesman Texas 30.36N 96.46W
107 J2 Chrisman Illinois 39.48N 87.40W
95 O2 Chrissiesmeer S Africa 26.17S 30.13E
95 O2 Chrissiesmeer L S Africa 26.20S 30.13E
11 G9 Christabel, L New Zealand 42.25S 172.15E
56 H6 Christchurch Dorset Eng 50.44N 1.45W
11 G10 Christchurch New Zealand 43.33S 172.40E
116 P6 Christchurch parish Barbados
113 P3 Christian Alaska 67.30N 145.25W
113 P3 Christian R Alaska
103 C7 Christiana Delaware 39.40N 75.39W
116 J1 Christiana Jamaica, W I 18.13N 77.29W
103 C7 Christiana Pennsylvania 39.58N 76.00W
104 J7 Christiana Pennsylvania 39.57N 76.01W
95 J3 Christiana S Africa 27.55S 25.10E
97 N3 Christian, C N W Terr 70.35N 68.20W
99 K8 Christian I Ontario 44.50N 80.14W
122 U11 Christian,Pt Pitcairn I Pacific Oc 25.04S 130.08W
104 A6 Christiansburg Ohio 40.03N 84.01W
104 E9 Christiansburg Virginia 37.07N 80.26W
113 U9 Christian Sd Alaska
53 C6 Christiansfeld Denmark 55.21N 9.30E
48 T9 Christianshåb Greenland 68.50N 51.10W
53 C4 Christianshede Denmark 56.07N 9.22E
53 Q12 Christiansø isld Bornholm Denmark 55.19N 15.12E
105 L8 Christiansted Virgin Is 17.46N 64.44W
101 S4 Christie B N W Terr
25 D8 Christie Island Burma 9.37N 97.58E
121 J7 Christie, L Chile
100 V2 Christie L Manitoba
12 C4 Christie Mt S Australia 30.49S 133.26E
110 Q2 Christina Montana 47.22N 109.20W
110 G1 Christina L Br Col 49.08N 118.15W
100 G3 Christina Lake Alberta 55.37N 110.55W
11 C11 Christina, Mt New Zealand 44.48S 168.03E
100 G2 Christina River Alberta
112 J7 Christine Texas 28.47N 98.31W
103 C5 Christmans Pennsylvania 40.57N 75.38W
14 F4 Christmas Cr W Australia
14 F4 Christmas Creek W Australia 18.55S 125.56E
17 G14 Christmas I Indian Oc 10.30S 105.40E
122 U9 Christmas I Line Is Pacific Oc 2.00N 157.30W
26 K6 Christmas Rise Indian Oc
107 G4 Christopher Illinois 37.59N 89.02W
99 H2 Christopher Falls Ontario 50.02N 82.30W
14 G6 Christopher, L W Australia 24.41S 127.42E
112 G4 Christoval Texas 31.13N 100.30W
121 H3 Christovão Pereira, Pta Brazil
65 K4 Chroboly Czechoslovakia 48.57N 14.05E
109 D4 Chromo Colorado 37.02N 106.51W
65 N2 Chroustovice Czechoslovakia 49.58N 15.59E
65 N2 Chrudim Czechoslovakia 49.57N 15.47E
65 N2 Chrudimka R Czechoslovakia
84 R14 Chrysostomos Monastery Cyprus 35.15N 33.25E
62 L5 Chrzanow Poland 50.10N 19.21E
34 C5 Chtaura Lebanon 33.48N 35.50E
43 L5 Chu Kazakhstan U.S.S.R. 43.34N 73.44E
43 K5 Chu R Kazakhstan U.S.S.R.
115 O10 Chuacús,Sa.de ra Guatemala
31 G9 Chuadanga Bangladesh 23.38N 88.52E
94 M5 Chualo, L Mozambique 25.01S 32.55E
94 N3 Chuambo Mozambique 21.49S 35.18E
Ch'üan-hsien see Quanzhou
23 H4 Chuankeng Jiangxi China 28.05N 118.06E
22 H8 Chuankou Shaanxi China 36.35N 108.44E
21 B12 Chuansha Shanghai China 31.13N 121.42E
15 H7 Chuave Papua New Guinea 6.08S 145.10E
23 A4 Chubalung Sichuan China 29.48N 99.00E
43 N3 Chubartau Kazakhstan U.S.S.R. 48.11N 78.40E
111 J7 Chubbuck California 34.22N 115.20W
20 L5 Chūbu Sangaku Nat. Park Japan
121 B9 Chubut terr Argentina
121 B9 Chubut, R Argentina
Chu-chia-k'an see Longjiang
Chu Chiang estuary see Zhujiangkou estuary
45 N2 Chuchkovo U.S.S.R. 54.16N 41.29E
65 K1 Chuchle Czechoslovakia 50.02N 14.23E
41 L8 Chuchukan U.S.S.R. 63.56N 116.58E
104 J10 Chuckatuck Virginia 36.53N 76.37W
111 J8 Chuckwalla Mts California
120 A9 Chucuito dist Callao Peru
121 D4 Chucul Argentina 33.00S 64.11W
121 C3 Chucuma Argentina 31.13S 67.17W
119 C3 Chucunaque R Panama
64 P5 Chudenice Czechoslovakia 49.28N 13.11E
43 F1 Chudinovo U.S.S.R. 54.39N 62.30E
56 D6 Chudleigh Devon Eng 50.36N 3.45W
99 K6 Chudleigh Ontario 46.40N 80.24W
13 G4 Chudleigh Park Queensland 19.41S 144.06E
46 G4 Chudnov Ukraine U.S.S.R. 50.05N 28.01E
46 H1 Chudovo U.S.S.R. 59.10N 31.41E
46 G1 Chudskoye,Oz L U.S.S.R.
75 C8 Chueca Spain 39.44N 3.57W
69 D8 Chuelles France 48.00N 2.57E
45 T2 Chufarovo U.S.S.R. 54.05N 47.17E
40 B3 Chuga R U.S.S.R.
113 M7 Chugach Is Alaska
113 O6 Chugach Mts Alaska
30 H3 Chugima Nepal 27.56N 86.43E
113 C10 Chuginadak I Aleutian Is 52.50N 169.45W
20 F7 Chugoku-sanchi mts Japan
Chugoy see Xiaoguai
Chuguchak see Tacheng
113 R10 Chugul I Aleutian Is 51.58N 175.50W
42 D5 Chugunash U.S.S.R. 52.55N 87.45E
47 L7 Chugunly U.S.S.R. 56.35N 72.46E
44 C4 Chugush mt U.S.S.R. 43.49N 40.16E
45 H7 Chuguyev Ukraine U.S.S.R. 49.51N 36.44E
40 F9 Chuguyevka U.S.S.R. 44.11N 133.53E
108 F8 Chugwater Wyoming 41.46N 104.50W
108 F8 Chugwater Cr Wyoming
Chu-ho see Shangzhi
121 H4 Chuí Brazil 33.45S 53.23W
87 B7 Chui Bet Sudan 7.01N 29.18E
111 N9 Chuichu Arizona 32.44N 111.47W
43 L5 Chu-Iliyskiye Gory mts Kazakhstan U.S.S.R.
113 J6 Chuilnuk Mts Alaska
93 J6 Chuka Kenya 0.20S 37.38E
23 A4 Chuka Xizang Zizhiqu China 29.39N 98.38E
18 E3 Chukai Pen Malaysia 4.16N 103.26E
32 D6 Chukak Iran 29.50N 51.39E
41 L8 Chukar U.S.S.R. 63.41N 118.12E
40 G6 Chukchagirskoye, Ozero L U.S.S.R.
48 O2 Chukchi Sea Arctic Oc
40 G8 Chuken U.S.S.R. 47.45N 136.35E
23 J7 Chu-k'eng Taiwan 22.08N 120.43E
46 N1 Chukhloma U.S.S.R. 58.41N 42.39E
46 N1 Chukhlomskoye,Oz L U.S.S.R.
30 L4 Chukhor Xizang Zizhiqu 28.16N 87.23E
30 J3 Chukhung Nepal 27.54N 86.52E
30 J3 Chukhung mt Nepal 27.57N 86.53E
30 J3 Chukhung Glacier Nepal
Chukkai see Qujie
39 F1 Chukochiy Mys C U.S.S.R. 70.05N 159.59E
39 F1 Chukoch'ye R U.S.S.R.
39 G1 Chukoch'ye,Ozero L U.S.S.R.
39 J1 Chukotskiy Khrebet mts U.S.S.R.
39 M3 Chukotskiy,Mys C U.S.S.R. 64.16N 173.04W
39 H1 Chukotskiy Natsional'nyy Okrug dist U.S.S.R.
39 L2 Chukotskiy Poluostrov pen U.S.S.R.
Chukotsk,Sea of see Chukchi Sea
39 F1 Chukrop U.S.S.R. 68.45N 56.50E
21 D10 Chukt'ori S Korea 34.54N 128.39E
39 D1 Chukuchany U.S.S.R. 69.01N 147.33E
93 E1 Chukudum Sudan 4.12N 33.32E
92 J12 Chukwani Zanzibar 6.15S 39.13E
105 D6 Chula Georgia 31.34N 83.36W
107 C2 Chula Missouri 39.55N 93.29W
104 H9 Chula Virginia 37.24N 77.56W
42 H3 Chula R U.S.S.R.
25 K5 Chu Lai Vietnam 15.25N 108.45E
43 J5 Chulak-Kurgan Kazakhstan U.S.S.R. 43.42N 69.10E
44 B8 Chulakovka Ukraine U.S.S.R. 46.21N 32.22E
47 F4 Chulasa U.S.S.R. 64.38N 46.08E
111 G9 Chula Vista California 32.36N 117.05W
75 J8 Chulilla Spain 39.39N 0.54W
113 N5 Chulitna Alaska 62.55N 149.39W
113 N5 Chulitna R Alaska
45 O1 Chulkovo Gor'kiy U.S.S.R. 55.56N 42.46E
42 D1 Chulkovo Krasnoyarsk U.S.S.R. 62.49N 88.30E
77 L6 Chullo mt Spain 37.06N 3.00W
12 L7 Chullora dist Sydney, N S W
40 C3 Chul'man U.S.S.R. 56.54N 124.55E
56 D6 Chulmleigh Devon England 50.55N 3.52W
121 B1 Chulo Chile 27.18S 70.10W
119 B10 Chulucanas Peru 5.08S 80.10W
120 E7 Chulumani Bolivia 16.22S 67.30W
31 J3 Chulung Pass Kashmir 34.59N 77.03E
22 E2 Chuluut Gol R Mongolia
42 C4 Chulym U.S.S.R. 55.09N 80.59E
42 C3 Chulym R U.S.S.R.
42 D6 Chulyshman R U.S.S.R.
42 D6 Chulyshmanskiy Khrebet mts U.S.S.R.
42 D6 Chulyshmanskoye Ploskogor'ye tableland U.S.S.R.
47 J3 Chum U.S.S.R. 67.05N 63.15E
120 E6 Chuma Bolivia 15.29S 68.54W
42 B4 Chumakovo U.S.S.R. 55.41N 79.03E
31 K4 Chumar Kashmir 32.38N 78.36E
31 K4 Chumatang Kashmir 33.25N 78.20E
93 K1 Chumba Ethiopia 4.35N 38.17E
92 J12 Chumbe I Zanzibar 6.17S 39.11E
28 G2 Chumbi Xizang Zizhiqu 27.28N 89.00E
121 C2 Chumbicha Argentina 28.54S 66.15W
30 H2 Chumbu mt Nepal/Xizang Zizhiqu 28.02N 86.48E
24 I9 Chumda Qinghai China 33.00N 97.06E
Chumdo see Qomdo
43 Q3 Chumek Kazakhstan U.S.S.R. 48.45N 85.31E
82 K8 Chumerna mt Bulgaria 42.46N 25.59E
40 G4 Chumikan U.S.S.R. 54.40N 135.15E
75 K5 Chumilla, Llano de la plain Spain
41 A3 Chum,Mys C Novaya Zemlya U.S.S.R. 72.50N 52.35E
31 K4 Chumo L Kashmir 33.16N 78.05E
Chum Phae see Ban Chum Phae
25 E7 Chumphon Thailand 10.30N 99.11E
120 C6 Chumpi Peru 15.07S 73.45W
25 F5 Chum Saeng Thailand 15.52N 100.18E
107 J11 Chumuckla Florida 30.46N 87.15W
21 D9 Chumunjin S Korea 37.55N 127.44E
42 C5 Chumysh R U.S.S.R.
42 F3 Chuna R U.S.S.R.
121 D2 Chuñaguasi Argentina 29.56S 64.07W
23 H4 Chun'an Zhejiang China 29.35N 119.02E
30 F7 Chunar Uttar Prad India 25.08N 82.54E
117 E5 Chun,B.do Brazil
119 B9 Chunchi Ecuador 2.17S 78.55W
21 D9 Ch'unch'ŏn S Korea 37.56N 127.40E
107 H11 Chunchula Alabama 30.54N 88.12W
26 S2 Chundikkulam Sri Lanka 9.27N 80.35E
43 N5 Chundzha Kazakhstan U.S.S.R. 43.31N 79.26E
91 J11 Chunga Zambia 14.58S 25.57E
120 D8 Chungara, L Chile
21 K1 Chung-gu dist Seoul S Korea
Chung-hsing see Siyang
21 C8 Chunghwa N Korea 38.52N 125.49E
21 D9 Ch'ungju S Korea 36.59N 127.53E
23 J6 Chung-li Taiwan 24.55N 121.08E
Chung-pa see Zhongba
21 C8 Chŭngsan N Korea 39.05N 125.25E
Ch'ung-shan see Chongzuo
24 E11 Ch'ung-tui Xizang Zizhiqu 28.03N 85.59E
31 E3 Chungur,Koh-i mt Afghanistan 36.00N 68.17E
21 E6 Chunhua Jilin China 43.15N 131.01E
23 E1 Chunhua Shaanxi China 34.50N 108.37E
115 P8 Chunhubub Mexico 19.34N 88.40W
31 H5 Chunian Pakistan 30.57N 74.01E
24 E10 Chunit Tso L Xizang Zizhiqu China 30.55N 84.30E
42 F2 Chunku R U.S.S.R.
23 E4 Chunmuying Hubei China 30.02N 109.41E
26 Q2 Chunnakam Sri Lanka 9.46N 80.02E
26 R3 Chunnavil Sri Lanka 9.21N 80.10E
42 F4 Chunoyar U.S.S.R. 57.28N 97.18E
42 F4 Chunskiy U.S.S.R. 56.05N 99.45E
Chunthang see Tsunthang
46 K1 Chuny U.S.S.R. 59.20N 36.30E
92 F6 Chunya Tanzania 8.31S 33.30E
42 F2 Chunya R U.S.S.R.
21 E6 Chunyang Jilin China 43.42N 129.32E
21 D9 Ch'unyang S Korea 36.58N 128.54E
20 E2 Chūō dist Tōkyō Japan
51 R5 Chupa Karelia U.S.S.R. 66.18N 33.04E
45 F6 Chupakhovka Ukraine U.S.S.R. 50.23N 34.35E
116 O1 Chupara Pt Trinidad & Tobago 10.48N 61.22W
32 B2 Chūplū Iran 36.29N 46.59E
107 H8 Chuquatonchee Creek Mississippi
120 C6 Chuquibamba Peru 15.47S 72.44W
120 C6 Chuquibambilla Peru 14.06S 72.44W
120 E10 Chuquicamata Chile 22.20S 68.56W
121 C2 Chuquis Argentina 28.55S 66.54W
120 F9 Chuquisaca dept Bolivia
66 P4 Chur Switzerland 46.52N 9.32E
46 R2 Chur U.S.S.R. 57.08N 52.55E
45 T1 Churachiki U.S.S.R. 55.43N 47.24E
47 H6 Churaki U.S.S.R. 59.38N 55.15E
42 L2 Churan U.S.S.R. 60.45N 125.00E
41 O9 Churapcha U.S.S.R. 62.03N 132.20E
46 S2 Churayevo U.S.S.R. 55.38N 55.39E
43 M8 Churbek Kirgiziya U.S.S.R. 39.59N 67.53E
100 Q8 Churchbridge Saskatchewan 50.55N 101.58W
104 J8 Church Creek Maryland 38.30N 76.10W
103 C8 Church Hill Maryland 39.08N 75.59W
105 E1 Church Hill Tennessee 36.33N 82.33W
110 M7 Churchill Idaho 42.21N 113.54W
97 K6 Churchill Manitoba 58.45N 94.00W
56 F5 Churchill Somerset England 51.21N 2.48W
97 K6 Churchill,C Manitoba 58.45N 93.00W
97 N7 Churchill Falls Labrador, Nfld 53.38N 64.19W
97 N7 Churchill Falls waterfall Nfld/Labrador 53.30N 64.10W
104 P7 Churchill L Maine
100 J2 Churchill L Saskatchewan
123 G7 Churchill Mts Antarctica
101 L6 Churchill Pk Br Col 58.19N 125.04W
97 J6 Churchill R Manitoba
100 W2 Churchill R.,Lit Manitoba
56 E6 Churchingford Somerset England 50.56N 3.08W
56 K2 Church Langton Leics England 52.32N 0.55W
107 D11 Church Point Louisiana 30.22N 92.15W
98 F9 Church Point Nova Scotia 44.21N 66.06W
108 L1 Churchs Ferry N Dakota 48.18N 99.11W
56 F2 Church Stretton Shropshire Eng 52.32N 2.49W
103 A9 Churchton Maryland 38.48N 76.31W
59 J7 Churchtown Wexford Irish Rep 52.08N 6.55W
59 K7 Churchtown Wexford Irish Rep 52.12N 6.21W
103 B7 Churchville Maryland 39.34N 76.15W
104 H3 Churchville New York 43.06N 77.54W
104 F8 Churchville Virginia 38.14N 79.11W
108 Q7 Churdan Iowa 42.08N 94.29W
42 E6 Chureg-Tag,Gora mt U.S.S.R. 50.35N 91.05E
30 A7 Churelkhera Madhya Prad India 25.44N 77.44E
66 N3 Churfirsten mts Switzerland
29 H6 Churi Madhya Prad India 22.29N 82.40E
30 J5 Churia Ghati Hills Nepal
30 E4 Churia Ra Nepal
45 P4 Churikovo U.S.S.R. 52.07N 43.15E
120 B4 Churin Peru 10.49S 76.52W
30 G8 Churk Uttar Prad India 24.40N 83.06E
Churkang see Jaggang
29 F1 Churkang Xizang Zizhiqu 32.52N 79.50E
41 P4 Churkin,Mys C U.S.S.R. 72.31N 139.45E
93 H5 Churo Kenya 0.44N 36.27E
45 D4 Churovichi U.S.S.R. 52.08N 32.01E
120 F12 Churqui Argentina 26.25S 63.38W
77 J6 Churriana la Vega Spain 37.09N 3.38W
75 M8 Churruca, I Spain 39.50N 0.40E
56 D7 Churston Ferrers Devon England 50.23N 3.33W
29 D3 Churu Rajasthan India 28.18N 75.00E
29 D3 Churu dist Rajasthan India
Churubay Nura see Abay
106 J8 Churubusco Indiana 41.14N 85.18W
119 E2 Churuguara Venezuela 10.52N 69.35W
115 J8 Churumuco Mexico 18.36N 101.40W
94 D6 Churutabis Namibia 27.29S 17.28E
66 P4 Churwalden Switzerland 46.47N 9.33E
120 C5 Chuschi Peru 13.31S 74.20W
31 J2 Chushal Kashmir 33.37N 78.40E
31 K4 Chushal Kashmir 33.30N 80.30E
47 E5 Chushevitsy U.S.S.R. 60.30N 41.40E
43 E4 Chushkakul', Gory mts Kazakhstan U.S.S.R.
43 E4 Chushkakyl' Kazakhstan U.S.S.R. 47.09N 57.50E
24 G11 Ch'ü-shui Xizang Zizhiqu 29.23N 90.43E
Chushul Dzong see Qüxü
109 B5 Chuska Mts New Mexico/Arizona
47 H6 Chusovaya R U.S.S.R.
47 H6 Chusovoy U.S.S.R. 58.18N 57.50E
47 M4 Chusovoye U.S.S.R. 57.21N 59.12E
47 H5 Chusovskoy U.S.S.R. 61.10N 56.31E
43 K6 Chust Uzbekistan U.S.S.R. 40.59N 71.14E
30 C1 Chusu Xizang Zizhiqu 31.40N 79.05E
45 O4 Chutanovka U.S.S.R. 52.37N 42.45E
98 D4 Chute-aux-Outardes Quebec 49.07N 68.30W
98 A4 Chute-des-Passes Quebec 49.52N 71.18W
28 J2 Chutia Assam India 26.45N 93.00E
29 J6 Chutia Bihar India 23.22N 85.23E
101 H7 Chutine Br Columbia 57.40N 131.35W
45 G7 Chutovo Ukraine U.S.S.R. 49.43N 35.14E
21 E7 Chuŭronjang N Korea 41.31N 129.37E
47 H5 Chuval U.S.S.R. 60.56N 58.58E
39 H3 Chuvanskiye Gory mts U.S.S.R.
39 J2 Chuvanskoye U.S.S.R. 65.52N 173.16E
45 S1 Chuvashskaya A.S.S.R U.S.S.R.
23 H2 Chu Xian Anhui China 32.20N 118.18E
23 B6 Chuxiong Yunnan China 25.03N 101.33E
42 J3 Chuya U.S.S.R. 59.14N 112.20E
42 J3 Chuya R U.S.S.R.
42 G1 Chuyengo U.S.S.R. 62.38N 103.45E
20 N5 Chūzenji-ko L Japan
42 B3 Chuzik R U.S.S.R.
65 L1 Chvaly Czechoslovakia 50.07N 14.36E
92 K12 Chwaka Zanzibar 6.10S 39.26E
92 K12 Chwaka B Zanzibar
32 A3 Chwārtā Iraq 35.43N 45.35E
30 K6 Chyabari Nepal 26.54N 86.33E
30 L5 Chyangthapu Nepal 27.17N 87.58E
41 M8 Chybyda R U.S.S.R.
65 L3 Chýnov Czechoslovakia 49.25N 14.49E
41 M7 Chyrchi U.S.S.R. 65.21N 123.19E
64 P3 Chyše Czechoslovakia 50.06N 13.15E
40 E3 Chyul'be U.S.S.R. 57.45N 131.15E
93 J8 Chyulu Ra Kenya
75 C3 Ciadoncha Spain 42.10N 3.55W
72 F9 Ciadoux France 43.16N 0.44E
79 B4 Ciamarella,Uia de mt Italy 45.19N 7.09E
18 H9 Ciamis Java Indon 7.20S 108.21E
80 G5 Ciampino Italy 41.48N 12.36E
81 F8 Cianciana Sicily 37.32N 13.26E
18 G9 Cianjur Java Indon 6.50S 107.09E
79 H5 Ciano d'Enza Italy 44.36N 10.24E
76 H2 Ciaño de Santa Ana Spain 43.17N 5.38W
118 D8 Cianorte Brazil 23.42S 52.31W
18 G9 Cibadak Java Indon 6.54S 106.45E
18 G9 Cibatu Java Indon 7.10S 107.59E
76 G2 Cibea Spain 43.04N 6.26W
111 O7 Cibecue Arizona 34.02N 110.30W
82 H5 Cibinului, Munții mts Romania
111 K8 Cibola Arizona 33.21N 114.40W
72 A9 Ciboure France 43.23N 1.41W
18 G9 Cibuni R Java Indon
115 D2 Cibuta Mexico 31.05N 110.56W
79 F6 Çicagna Italy 44.24N 9.14E
82 B5 Čičarija mts Yugoslavia
81 L7 Ciccia,Mte Sicily 38.14N 15.32E
80 L7 Cicciano Italy 40.58N 14.33E
36 G3 Çiçekdağı Turkey 39.37N 34.24E
81 K3 Cicerale Italy 40.20N 15.08E
106 H9 Cicero Indiana 40.07N 86.01W
104 J3 Cicero New York 43.12N 76.09W
106 Q2 Cicero dist Chicago, Illinois
118 J2 Cícero Dantas Brazil 10.36S 38.22W
82 G7 Ćićevac Yugoslavia 43.44N 21.26E
23 J4 Cicheng Zhejiang China 30.01N 121.29E
95 L4 Cicilia S Africa 28.40S 27.47E
79 H4 Cicognolo Italy 45.10N 10.11E
75 F3 Cidacos R Spain
75 C1 Cidad Spain 43.02N 3.46W
76 E7 Cidadêlhe Portugal 40.55N 7.06W
118 J8 Cidade Universitária, I. da Brazil
36 G1 Cide Turkey 41.53N 33.01E
62 J5 Cidlina R Czechoslovakia
75 E4 Cidones Spain 41.49N 2.39W
18 G9 Cidua Java Indon 7.30S 107.15E
62 M3 Ciéchanow Poland 52.52N 20.38E
62 N3 Ciechanowiec Poland 52.41N 22.30E
62 L3 Ciechocinek Poland 52.53N 18.49E
116 E4 Ciego de Avila Cuba 21.51N 78.47W
75 C7 Ciempozuelos Spain 40.10N 3.37W
119 D2 Ciénaga Colombia 11.01N 74.15W
119 C3 Ciénaga de Oro Colombia 8.54N 75.39W
119 C3 Ciénaga Grande marshy lake Colombia
119 D2 Ciénaga Grande de Sta Marta marshy L Colombia
115 J5 Ciénega Mexico 25.30N 101.59W
109 E9 Cienega New Mexico 32.05N 105.06W
115 J4 Ciénega de Flores Mexico 26.00N 100.10W
115 G5 Cieneguilla Mexico 24.02N 104.02W
115 D3 Cieneguita Mexico 28.22N 111.04W
116 D3 Cienfuegos Cuba 22.10N 80.27W
72 F10 Cier-de-Luchon France 42.52N 0.36E
61 L6 Ciergnon Belgium 50.10N 5.05E
72 F10 Cierp France 42.55N 0.38E
77 O4 Cierva, Embalse de la res Spain 38.03N 1.29W
75 G7 Cierva,La Spain 40.03N 1.52W
76 B4 Cíes,Islas Spain 42.13N 8.54W
62 O5 Cieszanow Poland 50.16N 23.09E
62 L6 Cieszyn Poland 49.45N 18.35E
72 E9 Cieutat France 43.08N 0.13E
72 G4 Cieux France 45.59N 1.03E
77 O4 Cieza Spain 38.14N 1.25W
62 M6 Ciężkowice Poland 49.47N 20.58E
37 F1 Çiftalan Turkey 41.15N 28.57E
36 E3 Çifteler Turkey 39.20N 31.02E
37 F6 Çiftlik Erzurum Turkey 39.48N 40.44E
36 G4 Çiftlik Turkey 38.10N 34.29E
75 E6 Cifuentes Spain 40.47N 2.37W
76 K5 Cigales Spain 41.45N 4.42W
79 D4 Cigliano Italy 45.18N 8.01E
75 C2 Cigüenza Spain 42.56N 3.35W
36 F4 Cihanbeyli Turkey 38.40N 32.55E
37 J2 Cihangir dist İstanbul Turkey 41.02N 28.58E
18 G9 Cihara Java Indon 6.50S 106.06E
115 G8 Cihuatlán Mexico 19.12N 104.35W
77 G2 Cijara,Embalse de res Spain
18 H9 Cijulang Java Indon 7.44S 108.30E
18 G9 Cikajang Java Indon 7.20S 107.52E
18 G9 Cikampek Java Indon 6.21S 107.25E
83 D4 Çikës,Mal i mts Albania
37 F7 Cikse Turkey 38.31N 40.54E
18 H9 Cilacap Java Indon 7.44S 109.00E
26 U15 Cilaos Réunion Ind Oc 21.08S 55.28E
26 U15 Cilaos,Cirque de Réunion Ind Oc
79 E4 Cilavegna Italy 45.18N 8.45E
37 G4 Çıldır Turkey 41.08N 43.08E
37 G4 Çıldır Gölü L Turkey
36 E3 Çıldırım R Turkey
36 F3 Çile Dağı mt Turkey 39.46N 32.10E
18 H9 Ciledug Java Indon 6.56S 108.43E
81 K3 Cilento reg Italy
23 F4 Cili Hunan China 29.24N 110.59E
36 G6 Cilicia reg Turkey
36 H5 Cilician Gates pass Turkey 37.17N 34.46E
76 L3 Cillamayor Spain 42.52N 4.16W
75 G6 Cillas Spain 40.56N 1.51W
76 F8 Cilleros Spain 40.07N 6.46W
75 C4 Cilleruelo de Abajo Spain 41.53N 3.48W
75 C4 Cilleruelo de Arriba Spain 41.54N 3.39W
76 K2 Cillórigo Castro Spain 43.12N 4.36W
37 H8 Cilo Dağı mt Turkey 37.30N 44.00E
56 D3 Cilycwm Dyfed Wales 52.03N 3.50W
111 J6 Cima California 35.14N 115.30W
66 N7 Cima Italy 46.02N 9.06E
96 S6 Cima I Madeira Is 33.03N 16.17W
80 B3 Cima d.Monte Italy 42.47N 10.23E
18 G9 Cimahi Java Indon 6.54S 107.27E
66 K6 Cimalmotto Switzerland 46.17N 8.30E
18 H9 Cimanuk R Java Indon
109 C3 Cimarron Colorado 38.26N 107.34W
109 K4 Cimarron Kansas 37.49N 100.20W
109 F5 Cimarron New Mexico 36.28N 104.56W
109 M5 Cimarron R Oklahoma etc
75 G5 Cimballa Spain 41.05N 1.46W
66 G8 Cime Bianche,Colle pass Italy 45.55N 7.42E
65 K3 Čimelice Czechoslovakia 49.28N 14.04E
36 G4 Çimeliyeni Turkey 38.29N 33.52E
37 E5 Çimil R Turkey
37 E6 Çimin Turkey 39.34N 39.43E
80 F4 Cimini,Monti Italy
81 G8 Ciminna Sicily 37.53N 13.34E
80 F4 Cimino,Monte Italy 42.24N 12.13E
81 O6 Cimiti,C Italy 38.57N 17.10E
62 O2 Cimochy Poland 53.59N 22.40E
79 M2 Cimoláis Italy 46.18N 12.27E
79 J6 Cimone,Monte Italy 44.12N 10.42E
82 H4 Cîmpia Turzii Romania 46.33N 23.53E
82 K5 Cîmpina Romania 45.08N 25.44E
19 B5 Cimpu Celebes Indonesia 3.22S 120.21E
82 J5 Cîmpulung Romania 45.16N 25.03E
82 K3 Cîmpulung Moldovenesc Romania 47.32N 25.34E
82 K4 Cîmpuri Romania 46.01N 26.49E
37 E8 Çınar Turkey 37.45N 40.22E
37 F3 Çınarcık Bursa Turkey 40.03N 28.47E
37 F2 Çınarcık İstanbul Turkey 40.39N 29.08E
119 F4 Cinaruco,R Venezuela
18 F8 Cina, Tanjung C Sumatra Indon 5.57S 104.44E
75 L4 Cinca R Spain
82 D7 Činčer mt Yugoslavia 43.55N 17.05E
108 S9 Cincinnati Iowa 40.38N 92.56W
104 A7 Cincinnati Ohio 39.10N 84.30W
103 C1 Cincinnatus New York 42.33N 75.55W
116 E4 Cinco Balas,Cayos islds Cuba 21.06N 79.20W
77 K2 Cinco Casas Spain 39.10N 3.14W
121 D8 Cinco Chanares Argentina 40.43S 65.10W
121 C7 Cinco Saltos Argentina 38.45S 68.07W
75 K6 Cinctorres Spain 40.35N 0.14W
113 J8 Cinder R Alaska
56 G4 Cinderford Glos England 51.50N 2.29W
82 K5 Cîndeşti Romania 45.15N 26.42E
82 H5 Cîndrelu mt Romania 45.35N 23.48E
36 C5 Çine Turkey 37.37N 28.03E
36 C5 Çine R Turkey
61 L5 Ciney Belgium 50.17N 5.06E
76 C6 Cinfães Portugal 41.04N 8.06W
37 E3 Cinge Turkey 40.18N 27.52E
37 D8 Cingife Turkey 37.23N 37.34E
80 H2 Cingoli Italy 43.22N 13.13E
80 D3 Cinigiano Italy 42.53N 11.23E
79 F7 Cinisello Balsamo dist Milan Italy
18 N6 Cinoka, Tanjung C Celebes Indon 1.42S 119.17E
70 L7 Cinq Mars France 47.21N 0.29E
81 M7 Cinquefrondi Italy 38.25N 16.06E
28 G7 Cinque Is Andaman Is
115 N9 Cintalapa Mexico 16.42N 93.40W
72 H9 Cintegabelle France 43.19N 1.31E
79 N3 Cinto Caomaggiore Italy 45.49N 12.47E
67 O12 Cinto, Mt Corsica 42.23N 8.57E
88 E10 Cintra,Golfo di Mauritania
69 K8 Cintrey France 47.46N 5.45E
75 G3 Cintruénigo Spain 42.05N 1.50W
118 E8 Cinzas R Brazil
82 L6 Cioara Doiceşti Romania 44.49N 27.31E
80 H5 Ciociaria dist Italy
82 J6 Ciolăveşti Romania 44.17N 25.04E
76 G5 Cional Spain 41.57N 6.20W
75 F2 Ciordia Spain 42.52N 2.14W
71 H10 Çiotat,La France 43.10N 5.36E
80 O1 Čiovo,I Yugoslavia 43.30N 16.17E
18 H9 Cipatuja Java Indon 7.45S 108.02E
76 G7 Ciperez Spain 40.58N 6.17W
23 G5 Ciping Jiangxi China 26.46N 114.07E
61 F6 Ciply Belgium 50.25N 3.57E
118 J2 Cipó Brazil 11.06S 38.30W
117 B5 Cipoal Brazil 1.38S 55.25W
121 C7 Cipolletti Argentina 38.55S 68.00W
121 B5 Cipreses Hydro-Electric Sta Chile 35.48S 70.54W
70 K5 Ciral France 48.29N 0.08W
75 K7 Cirat Spain 40.04N 0.28W
75 G2 Cirauqui Spain 42.41N 1.54W
82 H6 Cîrbeşti Romania 44.56N 23.10E
119 C5 Circasia Colombia 4.37N 75.37W
80 H6 Circeo,Monte Italy 41.14N 13.03E
80 H6 Circeo,Parco Nazionale del park Italy
37 E8 Cırcıp, Bucak watercourse Turkey
36 J2 Çırçır Turkey 40.05N 36.47E
113 P4 Circle Alaska 65.50N 144.05W
108 E2 Circle Montana 47.27N 105.34W
113 P4 Circle Hot Springs Alaska 65.29N 144.40W
103 F3 Circleville New York 41.31N 74.23W
104 C7 Circleville Ohio 39.36N 82.57W
111 M3 Circleville Utah 38.10N 112.19W
15 J5 Circular Reef Bismarck Arch 3.23S 147.45E
18 H9 Cirebon Java Indon 6.46S 108.33E
81 L4 Cirella,I.di Italy 39.42N 15.49E
56 H4 Cirencester Glos England 51.44N 1.59W
69 C5 Cires-les-Mello France 49.16N 2.21E
69 M6 Cirey-sur-Vezouse France 48.35N 6.57E
115 F10 Cirí R Panama
75 G4 Ciria Spain 41.37N 1.58W
79 C4 Ciriè Italy 45.14N 7.36E
120 F3 Ciriquiri,R Brazil
75 G2 Ciriza Spain 42.48N 1.50W
81 O5 Cirò Italy 39.22N 17.04E

120 F10 **Ciro Echesortu** Argentina 22.38S 63.47W
81 O5 **Cirò Marina** Italy 39.22N 17.08E
72 G2 **Ciron** France 46.38N 1.16E
72 D7 **Ciron** *R* France
37 H3 **Çırp** *R* Turkey
75 C8 **Ciruelos** Spain 39.56N 3.38W
75 J6 **Cirugeda** Spain 40.45N 0.42W
79 G6 **Cisa,Passo d** *pass* Italy 44.28N 9.55E
106 F9 **Cisco** Illinois 40.01N 88.44W
112 J3 **Cisco** Texas 32.23N 98.59W
111 P3 **Cisco** Utah 38.59N 109.20W
95 L8 **Ciskei** *Bantu Homeland* S Africa
76 J7 **Cisla** Spain 40.58N 5.01W
82 K5 **Cislău** Romania 45.14N 26.23E
63 N4 **Cismar** W Germany 54.12N 11.00E
79 L2 **Cismon** *R* Italy
79 L3 **Cismon del Grappa** Italy 45.55N 11.44E
62 N6 **Cisna** Poland 49.12N 22.20E
82 J5 **Cisnădie** Romania 45.42N 24.09E
107 H3 **Cisne** Illinois 38.31N 88.28W
119 C4 **Cisneros** Colombia 6.32N 75.04W
76 K4 **Cisneros** Spain 42.13N 4.52W
121 E2 **Cisnes,Ls.de los** Argentina
121 A10 **Cisnes,R** Chile
79 M3 **Cison di Valmarino** Italy 45.59N 12.09E
110 D3 **Cispus** *R* Washington
110 D3 **Cispus Pass** Washington 46.28N 121.25W
72 C5 **Cissac-Médoc** France 45.14N 0.50W
70 N6 **Cisse** *R* France
64 O3 **Čistá** Czechoslovakia 50.05N 12.45E
64 Q3 **Čistá** Czechoslovakia 50.02N 13.35E
66 J6 **Cistella** *mt* Italy 46.16N 8.15E
112 K6 **Cistern** Texas 29.50N 97.15W
80 G5 **Cisterna di Latina** Italy 41.35N 12.50E
81 P11 **Cisternino** Italy 40.45N 17.26E
76 J3 **Cistierna** Spain 42.47N 5.08W
117 B4 **Citaré** *R* Brazil
18 G9 **Citarum** *R* Java Indon
89 A1 **Cité de Cansado** Mauritania 20.50N 17.03W
80 F3 **Citernella,Monte** Italy 42.41N 12.19E
71 J1 **Citers** France 47.44N 6.23E
84 S15 **Citium** *ruins* Cyprus 34.53N 33.38E
115 L8 **Citlaltepetl, Vol** Mexico 19.00N 97.18W
72 K9 **Citou** France 43.22N 2.31E
105 E8 **Citra** Florida 29.24N 82.06W
117 C2 **Citron** French Guiana **S America** 4.49N 53.55W
107 H10 **Citronelle** Alabama 31.05N 88.15W
94 E9 **Citrusdal** S Africa 32.37S 18.58E
79 L3 **Cittadella** Italy 45.39N 11.48E
80 F3 **Citta della Pieve** Italy 42.57N 12.00E
80 F2 **Citta di Castello** Italy 43.27N 12.14E
80 G4 **Cittaducale** Italy 42.24N 12.57E
81 M7 **Cittanova** Italy 38.21N 16.05E
80 H3 **Cittareale** Italy 42.37N 13.10E
80 K3 **Citta Sant'Angelo** Italy 42.31N 14.04E
66 L8 **Cittiglio** Italy 45.54N 8.40E
55 F3 **City** London England 51.31N 0.05W
14 A1 **City Beach** *dist* Perth, W Aust
103 L6 **City I** New York 40.51N 73.47W
55 F3 **City of London, County of the** *bor* London England
105 G9 **City Point** Florida 28.24N 80.47W
99 C9 **City View** Ontario 45.22N 75.43W
87 N10 **Ciuài I** Somalia 0.58S 42.10E
82 K5 **Ciucas** *mt* Romania 45.31N 25.56E
82 H4 **Ciucea** Romania 46.58N 22.50E
82 K4 **Ciucului, Munţii** *mts* Romania
115 J3 **Ciudad Acuña** Mexico 29.20N 100.58W
115 J8 **Ciudad Altamirano** Mexico 18.20N 100.40W
119 G3 **Ciudad Bolívar** Venezuela 8.06N 63.36W
119 E3 **Ciudad Bolivia** Venezuela 8.22N 70.37W
115 G4 **Ciudad Camargo** Mexico 27.41N 105.10W
115 K4 **Ciudad Camargo** Tamaulipas **Mexico** 26.19N 98.50W
115 O10 **Ciudad Cuauhtémoc** Mexico 15.38N 91.59W
115 O8 **Ciudad del Carmen** Mexico 18.38N 91.50W
115 G3 **Ciudad Delicias** Mexico 28.10N 105.30W
115 K6 **Ciudad del Maíz** Mexico 22.26N 99.36W
119 E3 **Ciudad de Nutrias** Venezuela 8.10N 69.20W
115 K7 **Ciudad de Valles** Mexico 22.00N 99.00W
77 X13 **Ciudadela** Balearic Is 40.00N 3.50E
121 J4 **Ciudadela** Buenos Aires **Argentina** 34.38S 58.33W
75 F7 **Ciudad Encantada** *hist ruins* Spain 40.13N 2.01W
119 H3 **Ciudad Guayana** Venezuela 8.22N 62.37W
115 F3 **Ciudad Guerrero** Mexico 28.33N 107.28W
115 H8 **Ciudad Guzmán** Mexico 19.40N 103.30W
115 J8 **Ciudad Hidalgo** Mexico 19.40N 100.34W
115 M9 **Ciudad Ixtepec** Mexico 16.32N 95.10W
115 F2 **Ciudad Juárez** Mexico 31.42N 106.29W
115 H5 **Ciudad Lerdo** Mexico 25.34N 103.30W
115 L6 **Ciudad Madero** Mexico 22.19N 97.50W
115 K6 **Ciudad Mante** Mexico 22.44N 98.59W
115 J7 **Ciudad Manuel Doblado** Mexico 20.44N 101.56W
115 L8 **Ciudad Mendoza** Mexico 18.49N 97.14W
115 K4 **Ciudad Mier** Mexico 26.28N 99.10W
112 H9 **Ciudad Miguel Alemán** Mexico 26.25N 99.01W
115 E4 **Ciudad Obregón** Mexico 27.28N 109.59W
119 E2 **Ciudad Ojeda** Venezuela 10.12N 71.17W
119 G4 **Ciudad Piar** Venezuela 7.25N 63.19W
77 J3 **Ciudad Real** Spain 38.59N 3.55W
74 D6 **Ciudad Real** *prov* Spain
115 K5 **Ciudad Río Bravo** Mexico 25.58N 98.04W
76 F7 **Ciudad Rodrigo** Spain 40.36N 6.33W
Ciudad Trujillo *see* **Santo Domingo** Dominican Rep
75 N7 **Ciudad Universitaria** Madrid Spain
115 K6 **Ciudad Victoria** Mexico 23.43N 99.10W
87 M10 **Ciula I** Somalia 1.00S 42.06E
82 L6 **Ciulniţa** Romania 44.26N 27.22E
82 G4 **Ciumeghiu** Romania 46.43N 21.35E
82 L5 **Ciuşlea** Romania 45.48N 27.20E
75 N4 **Ciutadilla** Spain 41.33N 1.09E
36 J1 **Civa Burun** *C* Turkey 41.23N 36.37E
66 O8 **Civate** Italy 45.50N 9.22E
79 F3 **Civenna** Italy 45.56N 9.16E
79 M2 **Civetta** *mt* Italy 46.22N 12.03E
79 K2 **Civezzano** Italy 46.06N 11.11E
66 K8 **Civiasco** Italy 45.48N 8.17E
79 O2 **Cividale del Fruili** Italy 46.06N 13.25E
29 B1 **Civil Lines** *dist* Delhi India
81 M4 **Civita** Italy 39.50N 16.19E
80 L5 **Civitacampomarano** Italy 41.47N 14.42E
80 F4 **Civita Castellana** Italy 42.17N 12.25E
80 J2 **Civitanova Alta** Italy 43.18N 13.41E
80 K5 **Civitanova del Sannio** Italy 41.39N 14.24E
80 J2 **Civitanova Marche** Italy 43.17N 13.44E
80 E4 **Civitavecchia** Italy 42.05N 11.47E
80 J3 **Civitella del Tronto** Italy 42.47N 13.40E
79 L6 **Civitella di Romagna** Italy 44.01N 11.56E
80 E2 **Civitella in Val di Chiana** Italy 43.25N 11.43E
80 E3 **Civitella,Monte** Italy 42.47N 11.41E
80 H5 **Civitella Roveto** Italy 41.54N 13.26E
79 B4 **Civrari,Monte** Italy 45.11N 7.19E
72 J2 **Civray** Cher France 46.57N 2.09E
72 E3 **Civray** Vienne **France** 46.09N 0.18E
36 D4 **Çivril** Turkey 38.18N 29.43E
81 B5 **Cixerri** *R* Sardinia
81 B5 **Cixerri** *V* Sardinia
23 J3 **Cixi** Zhejiang **China** 30.17N 121.09E
22 K8 **Ci Xian** Hebei **China** 36.20N 114.20E
65 M3 **Čižkov** Czechoslovakia 49.26N 15.07E
65 K3 **Čížová** Czechoslovakia 49.21N 14.06E
37 G8 **Cizre** Turkey 37.21N 42.11E
65 J3 **Čkyně** Czechoslovakia 49.08N 13.50E
61 G4 **Clabecq** Belgium 50.42N 4.14E
58 E7 **Clachan** Strathclyde **Scotland** 55.45N 5.34W
110 C4 **Clackamas** *R* Oregon
14 B9 **Clackline** W Australia 31.44S 116.30E
58 J6 **Clackmannan** Central **Scotland** 56.06N 3.46W
Clackmannan *co see* **Central** *reg*
56 O4 **Clacton-on-Sea** Essex **England** 51.48N 1.09E
58 F6 **Cladich** Strathclyde **Scotland** 56.21N 5.05W
59 G2 **Clady** Tyrone **N Ireland** 54.47N 7.32W
109 M3 **Claflin** Kansas 38.31N 98.34W
58 E5 **Claggan** Highland **Scotland** 56.36N 5.44W
110 J1 **Clagstone** Idaho 48.01N 116.50W
103 B9 **Claiborne** Maryland 38.51N 76.16W
58 C3 **Claidh,L** Lewis, W Isles **Scotland** 57.55N 6.37W
70 E6 **Claie,R** France
72 E2 **Clain** *R* France
98 D6 **Clair** New Brunswick 47.15N 68.38W
100 N6 **Clair** Saskatchewan 52.01N 104.01W
72 E7 **Clairac** France 44.22N 0.23E
108 N4 **Claire City** S Dakota 45.52N 97.06W
Clairefontaine *see* **Aouinet,El**
66 C1 **Clairegoutte** France 47.40N 6.37E
101 R6 **Claire,L** Alberta
112 G2 **Clairemont** Texas 33.11N 100.46W
110 C9 **Clair Engle Lake** *res* California
25 H1 **Claire, R** Vietnam
91 A4 **Clairette, Pte** Gabon 0.39S 8.50E
104 F6 **Clairton** Pennsylvania 40.17N 79.56W
69 H7 **Clairvaux** Aube **France** 48.09N 4.47E
72 J7 **Clairvaux-d'Aveyron** France 44.26N 2.24E
71 H3 **Clairvaux-les-Lacs** France 46.34N 5.45E
72 G2 **Claise** *R* France
71 H6 **Claix** France 45.07N 5.40E
110 A1 **Clallam Bay** Washington 48.16N 124.16W
68 E4 **Clamart** France 48.48N 2.16E
71 D2 **Clamecy** France 47.27N 3.31E
71 E2 **Clamercy** France 47.22N 4.26E
59 H2 **Clanabogan** Tyrone **N Ireland** 54.34N 7.22W
111 G2 **Clan Alpine Mts** Nevada
11 F11 **Clandeboye New Zealand** 44.13S 171.24E
100 G5 **Clandonald** Alberta 53.36N 110.42W
59 J5 **Clane** Kildare **Irish Rep** 53.18N 6.41W
56 J6 **Clanfield** Hants **England** 50.57N 1.00W
56 H4 **Clanfield** Oxon **England** 51.44N 1.35W
71 L9 **Clans** France 44.00N 7.09E
107 K9 **Clanton** Alabama 32.50N 86.38W
100 S8 **Clanwilliam** Manitoba 50.22N 99.50W
94 E9 **Clanwilliam** S Africa 32.10S 18.52E
94 E9 **Clanwilliam Dam** S Africa 32.12S 18.50E
58 F7 **Claonaig** Strathclyde **Scotland** 55.45N 5.23W
72 L9 **Clape,Mtgne.de la** France 43.09N 3.05E
55 F4 **Clapham** London **England** 51.27N 0.08W
109 G5 **Clapham** New Mexico 36.11N 103.24W
57 J4 **Clapham** N Yorks **England** 54.07N 2.23W
72 L8 **Clapier,le** France 43.50N 3.10E
79 B6 **Clapier,Monte** Italy 44.07N 7.25E
121 F3 **Clara** Argentina 31.50S 58.48W
105 D8 **Clara** Florida 29.49N 83.21W
59 G5 **Clara** Offaly **Irish Rep** 53.20N 7.36W
13 F4 **Clara** *R* Queensland
13 H7 **Clara** *R* Queensland
108 P5 **Clara City** Minnesota 44.58N 95.21W
25 D7 **Clara i** Burma
121 D9 **Clara,Pta** *C* Argentina 43.57S 65.15W
75 N4 **Claravalls** Spain 41.43N 1.08E
13 F4 **Claraville** Queensland 18.39S 141.41E
121 F6 **Claraz** Argentina 37.56S 59.18W
59 K3 **Clare** Down **N Ireland** 54.24N 6.21W
108 Q7 **Clare** Iowa 42.35N 94.20W
106 K6 **Clare** Michigan 43.49N 84.47W
Clare Queensland *see* **Millaroo**
12 E5 **Clare** S Australia 33.50S 138.38E
56 N3 **Clare** Suffolk **England** 52.05N 0.35E
59 D6 **Clare** *co* Irish Rep
59 E6 **Clarecastle** Clare **Irish Rep** 52.49N 8.57W
12 G5 **Clare Corner** New S Wales 33.27S 143.55E
59 G5 **Clareen** Offaly **Irish Rep** 53.04N 7.47W
59 E5 **Claregalway** Galway **Irish Rep** 53.21N 8.57W
59 B4 **Clare,I** Mayo **Irish Rep** 53.49N 10.00W
94 P11 **Claremont** Cape Town **S Africa** 33.59S 18.26E
116 K1 **Claremont** Jamaica, W I 18.23N 77.11W
104 N3 **Claremont** New Hampshire 43.23N 72.21W
108 M4 **Claremont** S Dakota 45.40N 98.00W
12 H9 **Claremont** Tasmania 42.48S 147.12E
14 A2 **Claremont** *dist* Perth, W Aust
13 G2 **Claremont Is** Gt Barrier Reef **Australia**
14 A2 **Claremont,L** Perth, W Australia 31.59S 115.46E
109 P5 **Claremore** Oklahoma 36.20N 95.37W
59 E4 **Claremorris** Mayo **Irish Rep** 53.44N 9.00W
106 C8 **Clarence** Iowa 41.53N 91.03W
107 D10 **Clarence** Louisiana 31.50N 93.00W
107 D2 **Clarence** Missouri 39.44N 92.15W
11 H9 **Clarence New Zealand** 42.09S 173.56E
12 L3 **Clarence** *R* New S Wales
96 A11 **Clarence Bay** Ascension I 7.55S 14.25W
103 G4 **Clarence Fahnestock Park** New York
57 G2 **Clarencefield** Dumfries & Galloway **Scotland** 55.00N 3.26W
121 K10 **Clarence, I** Chile 54.05S 71.55W
123 D15 **Clarence I** South Shetland Is **Antarctica** 61.10S 54.00W
11 H9 **Clarence R New Zealand**
113 V9 **Clarence Str** Alaska
Clarence Str Iran *see* **Khūran** *strait*
13 B1 **Clarence Str** N Terr **Australia**
116 G3 **Clarence Town** Long I **Bahamas** 23.06N 74.58W
107 E7 **Clarendon** Arkansas 34.41N 91.19W
99 O8 **Clarendon** Ontario 44.52N 76.43W
104 F5 **Clarendon** Pennsylvania 41.46N 79.06W
112 G1 **Clarendon** Texas 34.57N 100.54W
104 M9 **Clarendon** Virginia 38.53N 77.06W
116 J2 **Clarendon** *parish* Jamaica, W I
116 J2 **Clarendon Park** Jamaica, W I 18.00N 77.23W
95 M4 **Clarens** S Africa 28.31S 28.25E
66 D6 **Clarens** Switzerland 46.27N 6.53E
71 E9 **Clarensac** France 43.49N 4.12E
98 S5 **Clarenville** Newfoundland 48.10N 54.00W
59 E5 **Clare,R** Galway **Irish Rep**
75 G4 **Clarés de Ribota** Spain 41.32N 1.51W
100 D8 **Claresholm** Alberta 50.02N 113.33W
71 H8 **Claret** Alpes de Haute Provence **France** 44.22N 5.57E
71 D9 **Claret** Hérault **France** 43.52N 3.54E
108 F6 **Clareton** Wyoming 43.42N 104.42W
63 H9 **Clarholz** W Germany 51.55N 8.08E
75 O4 **Clariana** Spain 41.56N 1.37E
66 M4 **Claridenstock** *mt* Switzerland 46.51N 8.53E
Clarie Coast *see* **Wilkes Coast**
13 F4 **Clarina** *R* Queensland
59 E5 **Clarinbridge** Galway **Irish Rep** 53.14N 8.53W
108 P9 **Clarinda** Iowa 40.45N 95.01W
119 G3 **Clarines** Venezuela 9.56N 65.11W
104 E7 **Clarington** Ohio 39.47N 80.53W
104 F5 **Clarington** Pennsylvania 41.21N 79.08W
108 R7 **Clarion** Iowa 42.43N 93.43W
104 F5 **Clarion** Pennsylvania 41.14N 79.24W
104 F5 **Clarion** *R* Pennsylvania
116 H4 **Clarion Bank** Atlantic Oc 20.55N 74.00W
122 N6 **Clarion Fracture Zone** Pacific Oc
115 B8 **Clarión,I** Mexico
104 G5 **Clarion River, East Branch Res** Pennsylvania 41.40N 79.33W
109 O7 **Clarita** Oklahoma 34.28N 96.37W
109 D1 **Clark** Colorado 40.42N 106.54W
107 D2 **Clark** Missouri 39.17N 92.20W
108 N5 **Clark** S Dakota 44.53N 97.44W
110 Q5 **Clark** Wyoming 44.55N 109.10W
111 H8 **Clark** *L* California 33.20N 116.17W
110 N5 **Clark Canyon Res** Montana 44.59N 112.55W
111 M7 **Clarkdale** Arizona 34.49N 112.03W
101 W4 **Clarke** *R* N W Terr
13 G4 **Clarke** *R* Queensland
95 M7 **Clarkebury** S Africa 31.47S 28.18E
98 F3 **Clarke City** Quebec 50.11N 66.39W
12 J8 **Clarke I** Tasmania 40.30S 148.10E
100 K4 **Clarke L** Saskatchewan 54.25N 107.00W
13 J5 **Clarke Ra** Queensland
13 H4 **Clarke River** Queensland 19.08S 145.25E
13 F3 **Clarkes Cr** Queensland
105 D3 **Clarkesville** Georgia 34.36N 83.32W
108 P5 **Clarkfield** Minnesota 44.47N 95.49W
110 J1 **Clark Fork** Idaho 48.10N 116.10W
110 M3 **Clark Fork** *R* Montana
110 Q5 **Clark Fork** *R* Wyoming
105 E4 **Clark Hill Dam** Georgia 33.39N 82.12W
105 E4 **Clark Hill Res** S Carolina/Georgia
110 J2 **Clarkia** Idaho 47.00N 116.15W
113 K6 **Clark,L** Alaska 60.15N 154.20W
111 J6 **Clark Mt** California 35.31N 115.35W
101 L3 **Clark,Mt** N W Terr 64.23N 124.11W
109 E1 **Clark Pk** Colorado 40.36N 105.56W
99 J8 **Clark Pt** Ontario 44.04N 81.46W
107 D9 **Clarks** Louisiana 32.01N 92.08W
108 N8 **Clarks** Nebraska 41.14N 97.51W
103 F6 **Clarksburg** New Jersey 40.12N 74.27W
107 H6 **Clarksburg** Tennessee 35.53N 88.23W
104 E7 **Clarksburg** W Virginia 39.16N 80.22W
107 F7 **Clarksdale** Mississippi 34.12N 90.33W
108 R6 **Clarks Grove** Minnesota 43.45N 93.20W
98 G10 **Clark's Harbour** Nova Scotia 43.25N 65.38W
106 H9 **Clarks Hill** Indiana 40.14N 86.45W
11 E12 **Clarks Junction New Zealand** 45.43S 170.05E
108 N8 **Clarkson** Nebraska 41.44N 97.08W
99 L9 **Clarkson** Ontario 43.30N 79.38W
95 H10 **Clarkson** S Africa 34.01S 24.20E
14 E4 **Clarkson, Mt** W Australia 17.36S 123.21E
113 H7 **Clarks Point** Alaska 58.50N 158.31W
103 C4 **Clarks Summit** Pennsylvania 41.29N 75.43W
106 L7 **Clarkston** Michigan 42.44N 83.26W
110 O3 **Clarkston** Montana 46.02N 111.25W
110 H3 **Clarkston** Washington 46.26N 117.02W
116 J1 **Clark's Town** Jamaica, W I 18.25N 77.33W
103 A4 **Clarkstown** Pennsylvania 41.12N 76.43W
107 C6 **Clarksville** Arkansas 35.29N 93.29W
108 S7 **Clarksville** Iowa 42.45N 92.39W
106 J7 **Clarksville** Michigan 42.50N 85.14W
107 F2 **Clarksville** Missouri 39.23N 90.55W
11 D13 **Clarksville New Zealand** 46.09S 169.58E
107 J5 **Clarksville** Tennessee 36.31N 87.21W
112 M2 **Clarksville** Texas 33.37N 95.04W
104 G10 **Clarksville** Virginia 36.35N 78.35W
105 J3 **Clarkton** N Carolina 34.29N 78.40W
112 K8 **Clarkwood** Texas 27.46N 97.34W
110 E5 **Clarno** Oregon 44.56N 120.27W
66 N6 **Claro** Switzerland 46.16N 9.02E
121 E7 **Claromecó** Argentina 38.50S 60.05W
66 N6 **Claro, Pizzo di** *mt* Switzerland 46.18N 9.04E
118 D4 **Claro, R** Goiás Brazil
118 D6 **Claro, R** Goiás Brazil
69 E3 **Clary** France 50.04N 3.24E
103 E3 **Claryville** New York 41.55N 74.34W
58 H3 **Clashmore** Highland **Scotland** 57.52N 4.07W
59 G7 **Clashmore** Waterford **Irish Rep** 52.00N 7.49W
58 F2 **Clashnessie** Highland **Scotland** 58.13N 5.20W
110 B3 **Clatskanie** Oregon 46.06N 123.13W
58 L4 **Clatt** Grampian **Scotland** 57.19N 2.46W
112 C8 **Claude** Texas 35.06N 101.22W
13 H6 **Claude** *R* Queensland
118 G7 **Cláudio** Brazil 20.24S 44.45W
121 E7 **Claudio Molina** Argentina 38.06S 60.18W
59 H2 **Claudy** Londonderry **N Ireland** 54.54N 7.09W
63 M8 **Clauen** W Germany 52.15N 10.02E
112 E2 **Clauene** Texas 33.27N 102.24W
57 H4 **Claughton** Lancs **Eng** 54.06N 2.40W
48 T8 **Claushavn** Greenland 69.00N 51.00W
64 P2 **Clausnitz** E Germany 50.45N 13.30E
64 O2 **Claussnitz** E Germany 50.56N 12.54E
63 M9 **Clausthal-Zellerfeld** W Germany 51.48N 10.20E
79 N2 **Claut** Italy 46.17N 12.31E
79 N2 **Clauzetto** Italy 46.14N 12.54E
66 Q4 **Clavadel** Switzerland 46.47N 9.49E
71 G8 **Clavelière, Mt. de la** France 44.19N 5.30E
103 G2 **Claverack** New York 42.13N 73.43W
19 K2 **Claveria** Luzon **Philippines** 18.35N 121.04E
48 V8 **Clavering Ø** *isld* Greenland
13 H7 **Claverton** Queensland 27.24S 145.55E
100 L6 **Clavet** Saskatchewan 52.01N 106.23W
71 F6 **Claveyson** France 45.11N 4.55E
61 M5 **Clavier** Belgium 50.25N 5.22E
79 A5 **Claviere** Italy 44.56N 6.46E
56 C6 **Clawton** Devon **Eng** 50.46N 4.20W
105 F5 **Claxton** Georgia 32.10N 81.54W
111 C3 **Clay** California 38.20N 121.10W
107 J4 **Clay** Kentucky 37.28N 87.50W
112 L5 **Clay** Texas 30.24N 96.23W
104 D8 **Clay** W Virginia 38.28N 81.17W
109 N2 **Clay Center** Kansas 39.23N 97.09W
108 M9 **Clay Center** Nebraska 40.32N 98.02W
107 H3 **Clay City** Illinois 38.41N 88.22W
107 J2 **Clay City** Indiana 39.15N 87.07W
104 B9 **Clay City** Kentucky 37.52N 83.56W
57 L6 **Clay Cross** Derbys **Eng** 53.10N 1.24W
100 J9 **Claydon** Saskatchewan 49.12N 108.59W
56 O3 **Claydon** Suffolk **Eng** 52.06N 1.07E
69 D6 **Claye-Souilly** France 48.57N 2.42E
71 E4 **Clayette,la** France 46.17N 4.18E
55 D5 **Claygate** Surrey **Eng** 51.22N 0.20W
111 L5 **Clayhole Wash** *crater* Arizona
100 J1 **Clay Lake** Ontario 50.05N 93.30W
103 D7 **Claymont** Delaware 39.48N 75.58W
54 K4 **Claymore** *oil field* **North Sea** 58.25N 0.18W
101 L11 **Clayoquot** Vancouver I, Br Col 49.08N 125.58W
14 E8 **Clay Pan** W Australia 29.59S 124.45E
111 O8 **Claypool** Arizona 33.25N 110.55W
111 O7 **Clay Springs** Arizona 34.22N 110.20W
104 E6 **Claysville** Pennsylvania 40.07N 80.26W
107 L10 **Clayton** Alabama 31.53N 85.29W
103 C8 **Clayton** Delaware 39.17N 75.39W
105 D3 **Clayton** Georgia 34.52N 83.24W
110 L5 **Clayton** Idaho 44.16N 114.25W
106 D9 **Clayton** Illinois 40.02N 90.56W
107 K2 **Clayton** Indiana 39.41N 86.31W
109 K2 **Clayton** Kansas 39.44N 100.11W
105 J2 **Clayton** N Carolina 35.39N 78.28W
103 D7 **Clayton** New Jersey 39.39N 75.06W
109 G5 **Clayton** New Mexico 36.27N 103.12W
104 J2 **Clayton** New York 44.15N 76.06W
109 P7 **Clayton** Oklahoma 34.36N 95.24W
56 L6 **Clayton** W Sussex **Eng** 50.55N 0.09W
12 E3 **Clayton** *R* S Australia
104 P7 **Clayton L** Maine 46.40N 69.32W
57 J5 **Clayton le Moors** Lancs **Eng** 53.47N 2.23W
104 E9 **Claytor L** Virginia
104 K4 **Clayville** New York 42.59N 75.16W
103 L3 **Clayville** Rhode I 41.47N 71.42W
121 F4 **Clé** *R* Argentina
57 L3 **Cleadon** Durham **Eng** 54.57N 1.23W
109 O7 **Clear Boggy Cr** Oklahoma
108 P2 **Clearbrook** Minnesota 47.40N 95.27W
11 E11 **Clearburn New Zealand** 44.20S 170.00E
59 C9 **Clear, C** Cork **Irish Rep** 51.26N 9.31W
104 E8 **Clearco** W Virginia 38.06N 80.35W
111 O7 **Clear Cr** Arizona
108 D5 **Clear Cr** Wyoming
110 B8 **Clear Creek** California 41.43N 123.28W
112 G9 **Clear Creek** Texas
113 O7 **Cleare C** Alaska 59.46N 147.50W
108 Q9 **Clearfield** Iowa 40.49N 94.29W
104 G5 **Clearfield** Pennsylvania 41.02N 78.27W
110 N8 **Clearfield** Utah 41.07N 112.03W
112 G3 **Clear Fork** *R* Texas
101 O7 **Clear Hills** Alberta
59 D9 **Clear I** Cork **Irish Rep** 51.26N 9.30W
111 B2 **Clear L** California 39.05N 122.50W
108 R6 **Clear L** Iowa
107 C9 **Clear L** Louisiana 32.10N 93.37W
100 S8 **Clear L** Manitoba 50.40N 100.00W
99 N7 **Clear, L** Ontario 45.26N 77.12W
108 R6 **Clear Lake** Iowa 43.09N 93.22W
107 C10 **Clear Lake** Louisiana 31.55N 93.05W
108 R4 **Clear Lake** Minnesota 45.28N 94.00W
108 O5 **Clear Lake** S Dakota 44.44N 96.40W
111 M2 **Clear Lake** Utah 39.07N 112.45W
106 B4 **Clear Lake** Wisconsin 45.14N 92.19W
112 M6 **Clear Lake City** Texas 29.33N 95.07W
111 B3 **Clearlake Highlands** California 38.58N 122.38W
110 D8 **Clear L.Res** California 41.50N 121.10W
108 D5 **Clearmont** Wyoming 44.39N 106.26W
101 O7 **Clear Prairie** Alberta 56.35N 119.30W
14 D10 **Clear Streak Well** W Australia 32.37S 122.19E
101 N10 **Clearwater** Br Columbia 51.38N 120.02W
105 E10 **Clearwater** Florida 27.57N 82.48W
110 K3 **Clearwater** Idaho 46.02N 115.55W
109 N4 **Clearwater** Kansas 37.32N 97.31W
108 M7 **Clearwater** Nebraska 42.10N 98.11W
101 S7 **Clearwater** *R* Alberta
110 J3 **Clearwater** *R* Idaho
108 P2 **Clearwater** *R* Minnesota
23 C9 **Clear Water B** Hong Kong
Clearwater Lake *see* **Eau Claire, L à L'**
107 F4 **Clearwater Lake** *res* Missouri 37.09N 90.48W
100 Q4 **Clearwater Lake Prov. Park** Manitoba
110 K3 **Clearwater Mts** Idaho
110 K3 **Clearwater, N. Fork** *R* Idaho
100 B6 **Clearwater R** Alberta
110 K4 **Clearwater S. Fork** Idaho
57 F3 **Cleator** Cumbria **Eng** 54.31N 3.32W
57 G3 **Cleator Moor** Cumbria **England** 54.31N 3.30W
14 D7 **Cleaver, Mt** W Australia 26.40S 120.35E
112 K3 **Cleburne** Texas 32.21N 97.24W
70 K4 **Clécy** France 48.55N 0.29W
56 B4 **Cleddau, East** *R* Dyfed **Wales**
56 B4 **Cleddau, West** *R* Dyfed **Wales**
70 B4 **Cléder** France 48.40N 4.08W
56 F3 **Cleehill** Shropshire **Eng** 52.23N 2.36W
110 E2 **Cle Elum** Washington 47.12N 120.57W
110 D2 **Cle Elum L** Washington 47.19N 121.07W
57 N5 **Cleethorpes** Humberside **Eng** 53.34N 0.02W
100 H5 **Cleeves** Saskatchewan 53.28N 109.02W
69 K7 **Clefmont** France 48.06N 5.30E
70 K6 **Clefs** France 47.37N 0.04W
66 B8 **Clefs, les** France 45.52N 6.20E
112 J7 **Clegg** Texas 28.08N 98.18W
70 D5 **Cléguérec** France 48.07N 3.05W
58 J6 **Cleish Hills** Tayside **Scotland**
13 B6 **Cleland Hills** N Terr **Australia**
71 H7 **Clelles** France 44.49N 5.37E
111 N7 **Clemenceau** Arizona 34.44N 111.59W
61 O8 **Clémency** Luxembourg 49.36N 5.53E
117 C3 **Clément** Fr Guiana 3.25N 52.24W
121 J5 **Clemente, I** Chile 45.40S 74.45W
14 B6 **Clement, Mt** W Australia 22.52S 116.09E
103 D7 **Clementon** New Jersey 39.48N 75.00W
111 C3 **Clements** California 38.10N 121.05W
97 N1 **Clements Markham Inlet** N W Terr
98 G9 **Clementsport** Nova Scotia 44.39N 65.36W
98 G9 **Clementsvale** Nova Scotia 44.36N 65.35W
105 E3 **Clemson** South Carolina 34.41N 82.51W
104 D8 **Clendenin** W Virginia 38.29N 81.23W
104 D6 **Clendening Res** Ohio
56 G3 **Clent** Hereford & Worcs **Eng** 52.25N 2.06W
56 G3 **Clent Hills** Hereford & Worcs **Eng**
56 G3 **Cleobury Mortimer** Shropshire **Eng** 52.23N 2.29W
56 F3 **Cleobury North** Shropshire **Eng** 52.29N 2.34W
103 B6 **Cleona** Pennsylvania 40.20N 76.28W
71 F7 **Cléon-d'Andran** France 44.37N 4.57E
19 J6 **Cleopatra Needle** *mt* **Philippines** 10.08N 119.00E
109 M5 **Cleo Springs** Oklahoma 36.24N 98.26W
70 L7 **Cléré** France 47.25N 0.23E
70 N2 **Clères** France 49.36N 1.06E
69 G7 **Clérey** France 48.13N 4.11E
72 H5 **Clergoux** France 45.16N 1.58E
99 M4 **Cléricy** Quebec 48.22N 78.53W
69 L8 **Clerjus, le** France 47.57N 6.19E
14 C3 **Clerke Reef** Indian Oc 17.23S 119.23E
71 F4 **Clermain** France 46.22N 4.35E
72 G9 **Clermont** Ariège **France** 43.03N 1.17E
105 F9 **Clermont** Florida 28.33N 81.47W
106 C7 **Clermont** Iowa 43.00N 91.38W
61 M4 **Clermont** Liège **Belgium** 50.34N 5.24E
61 H5 **Clermont** Namur **Belgium** 50.16N 4.19E
103 G2 **Clermont** New York 42.05N 73.50W
69 C5 **Clermont** Oise **France** 49.23N 2.26E
104 G5 **Clermont** Pennsylvania 41.42N 78.30W
98 B6 **Clermont** Quebec 47.42N 70.15W
13 J6 **Clermont** Queensland 22.48S 147.40E
70 K6 **Clermont-Créans** France 47.43N 0.01W
72 F6 **Clermont-de-Beauregard** France 44.58N 0.40E
69 J5 **Clermont-en-Argonne** France 49.07N 5.05E
71 C5 **Clermont-Ferrand** France 45.47N 3.05E
71 C9 **Clermont-l'Hérault** France 43.37N 3.25E
61 O4 **Clermont-sous-Huy** Liège **Belgium** 50.40N 5.53E
66 A3 **Cléron** France 47.05N 6.05E
71 J2 **Clerval** France 47.23N 6.30E
99 L4 **Clerval** Quebec 48.47N 79.27W
61 P6 **Clervaux** Luxembourg 50.03N 6.02E
61 P7 **Clervé** *R* Luxembourg
69 B5 **Cléry-en-Vexin** France 49.08N 1.51E
70 O6 **Cléry-St. André** France 47.49N 1.45E
69 D4 **Cléry-sur-Somme** France 49.58N 2.54E
79 K2 **Cles** Italy 46.23N 11.02E
72 D2 **Clessé** France 46.42N 0.25W
58 R9 **Clett Hd** Shetland **Scotland** 60.20N 0.59W
12 D5 **Cleve** S Australia 33.37S 136.32E
56 F5 **Clevedon** Avon **Eng** 51.27N 2.51W
107 D6 **Cleveland** Arkansas 35.23N 92.42W
105 F11 **Cleveland** Florida 26.57N 81.58W
105 D3 **Cleveland** Georgia 34.43N 83.48W
110 O7 **Cleveland** Idaho 42.21N 111.44W
108 R5 **Cleveland** Minnesota 44.19N 93.50W
107 F8 **Cleveland** Mississippi 33.43N 90.46W
110 Q1 **Cleveland** Montana 48.16N 109.10W
105 G2 **Cleveland** N Carolina 35.44N 80.42W
108 L3 **Cleveland** N Dakota 46.56N 99.08W
104 K3 **Cleveland** New York 43.15N 75.50W
104 D5 **Cleveland** Ohio 41.30N 81.41W
109 O5 **Cleveland** Oklahoma 36.19N 96.31W
105 E2 **Cleveland** S Carolina 35.04N 82.31W
107 M6 **Cleveland** Tennessee 35.10N 84.51W
112 M5 **Cleveland** Texas 30.22N 95.05W
111 O2 **Cleveland** Utah 39.21N 110.53W
106 G6 **Cleveland** Wisconsin 43.56N 87.45W
57 L3 **Cleveland** *co* Eng
13 H4 **Cleveland B** Queensland
13 H4 **Cleveland, C** Queensland 19.10S 147.02E
57 L4 **Cleveland Hills** N Yorks **Eng**
118 D10 **Clevelândia** Brazil 26.24S 52.23W
117 C3 **Clevelândia do Norte** Brazil 3.47N 51.50W
113 C10 **Cleveland, Mt** Aleutian Is 52.51N 169.42W
110 M1 **Cleveland, Mt** Montana 48.55N 113.50W
12 H8 **Cleveland, Mt** Tasmania 41.23S 145.20E
57 L4 **Cleveland Tontine** N Yorks **Eng** 54.23N 1.19W
57 G5 **Cleveley** Lancs **Eng** 53.53N 3.03W
59 C4 **Clew B** Mayo **Irish Rep** 53.50N 9.50W
95 N1 **Clewer** S Africa 25.55S 29.07E
105 G11 **Clewiston** Florida 26.44N 80.56W
56 O2 **Cley** Norfolk **Eng** 52.58N 1.03E
57 H3 **Cliburn** Cumbria **Eng** 54.38N 2.38W
68 E3 **Clichy** France 48.54N 2.19E
105 D1 **Clichy, R** Tenn/Virginia
68 H3 **Clichy-sous-Bois** France 48.55N 2.32E
59 B5 **Clifden** Galway **Irish Rep** 53.29N 10.01W
11 B13 **Clifden New Zealand** 46.04S 167.43E
109 B9 **Cliff** New Mexico 32.58N 108.36W
13 E3 **Cliffdale** *R* Queensland
110 D3 **Cliffdell** Washington 46.58N 121.02W
56 M5 **Cliffe** Kent **Eng** 51.28N 0.30E
19 J6 **Cliff Hd Philippines** 10.17N 118.58E
110 O5 **Cliff Lake** Montana 44.49N 111.30W
58 R8 **Cliff, L. of** Shetland **Scotland** 60.47N 0.54W
112 K8 **Cliff Maus** *airport* Texas 27.45N 97.28W
59 F3 **Cliffony** Sligo **Irish Rep** 54.26N 8.27W
56 E3 **Clifford** Hereford & Worcs **Eng** 52.06N 3.06W
103 N3 **Clifford** Massachusetts 41.44N 70.56W
106 L6 **Clifford** Michigan 43.19N 83.11W
108 N2 **Clifford** N Dakota 47.21N 97.24W
99 K9 **Clifford** Ontario 43.58N 81.00W
95 L7 **Clifford** S Africa 31.05S 27.27E
104 F9 **Clifford** Virginia 37.38N 79.03W
106 D4 **Clifford** Wisconsin 45.34N 90.02W
110 H7 **Cliffs** Idaho 42.40N 117.00W
105 F2 **Cliffside** N Carolina 35.13N 81.46W
103 K6 **Cliffside Park** New Jersey 40.50N 73.59W
14 B10 **Cliffy Hd** W Australia 34.58S 116.24E
58 Q9 **Clift Hills** Shetland **Scotland**
111 P8 **Clifton** Arizona 33.04N 109.17W
56 F5 **Clifton** Avon **Eng** 51.29N 2.37W
57 H3 **Clifton** Cumbria **Eng** 54.39N 2.43W
57 K7 **Clifton** Derbys **Eng** 53.00N 1.45W
106 G9 **Clifton** Illinois 40.56N 87.57W
109 N2 **Clifton** Kansas 39.34N 97.17W
103 K6 **Clifton** New Jersey 40.53N 74.09W
105 K9 **Clifton** New Providence I **Bahamas** 25.01N 77.33W
11 N10 **Clifton New Zealand** 43.34S 172.44E
31 B10 **Clifton** Pakistan 24.49N 67.02E
13 K8 **Clifton** Queensland 27.55S 151.50E
112 K4 **Clifton** Texas 31.47N 97.36W
108 F6 **Clifton** Wyoming 43.38N 104.05W
94 P11 **Clifton B** Cape Town **S Africa**
104 F9 **Clifton Forge** Virginia 37.49N 79.50W
12 E2 **Clifton Hills** S Australia 27.05S 138.52E
105 K9 **Clifton Pt** New Providence I **Bahamas** 25.01N 77.33W
101 O1 **Clifton Pt** N W Terr 69.14N 118.39W
109 D2 **Climax** Colorado 39.22N 106.11W
105 C7 **Climax** Georgia 30.53N 84.26W
106 J7 **Climax** Michigan 42.14N 85.20W
108 O2 **Climax** Minnesota 47.36N 96.50W
100 J9 **Climax** Saskatchewan 49.12N 108.22W
107 M6 **Clinch** *R* Tennessee
105 E1 **Clinch** *R* Tenn/Virginia
88 O4 **Clinchant Algeria** 35.41N 0.23E
104 C9 **Clinchco** Virginia 37.09N 82.09W
104 C10 **Clinch Mts** Tenn/Virginia
104 C10 **Clinchport** Virginia 36.41N 82.45W
112 G6 **Cline** Texas 29.14N 100.06W
101 P9 **Cline Mt** Alberta 52.05N 116.48W
60 E14 **Clinge Netherlands** 51.16N 4.06E
64 K1 **Clingen** E Germany 51.14N 10.55E
105 D2 **Clingmans Dome** *mt* Tennessee 35.34N 83.29W
107 D6 **Clinton** Arkansas 35.34N 92.28W
101 N10 **Clinton** Br Columbia 51.05N 121.38W
103 J4 **Clinton** Connecticut 41.16N 72.32W
106 F9 **Clinton** Illinois 40.10N 88.59W
107 J2 **Clinton** Indiana 39.40N 87.25W
106 D8 **Clinton** Iowa 41.51N 90.12W
107 H5 **Clinton** Kentucky 36.39N 89.00W
107 E11 **Clinton** Louisiana 30.52N 91.01W
104 Q2 **Clinton** Maine 44.38N 69.31W
103 L2 **Clinton** Massachusetts 42.25N 71.41W
106 L7 **Clinton** Michigan 42.04N 83.57W
108 O4 **Clinton** Minnesota 45.25N 96.25W
107 F9 **Clinton** Mississippi 32.21N 90.20W
107 C3 **Clinton** Missouri 38.22N 93.48W
110 M3 **Clinton** Montana 46.46N 113.41W
105 J2 **Clinton** N Carolina 35.00N 78.20W
103 E5 **Clinton** New Jersey 40.38N 74.55W
104 K3 **Clinton** New York 43.04N 75.23W
11 D13 **Clinton New Zealand** 46.14S 169.23E
109 M6 **Clinton** Oklahoma 35.32N 98.59W
99 J9 **Clinton** Ontario 43.36N 81.33W
105 F3 **Clinton** S Carolina 34.27N 81.52W
107 M5 **Clinton** Tennessee 36.07N 84.08W
106 F7 **Clinton** Wisconsin 42.33N 88.51W
101 U4 **Clinton-Colden Lake** N W Terr
103 G3 **Clinton Corners** New York 41.50N 73.45W
101 C3 **Clinton Creek** Yukon Terr 64.24N 140.33W
101 C3 **Clinton Creek** Yukon Terr 64.25N 140.37W
103 F3 **Clintondale** New York 41.42N 74.03W
106 F5 **Clintonville** Wisconsin 44.37N 88.46W
111 N7 **Clints Well** Arizona 34.35N 111.19W
107 L10 **Clio** Alabama 31.41N 85.39W
108 R9 **Clio** Iowa 40.39N 93.26W
106 L6 **Clio** Michigan 43.11N 83.43W
105 H3 **Clio** S Carolina 34.34N 79.33W
72 G2 **Clion** France 46.56N 1.14E
122 O7 **Clipperton Fracture Zone** Pacific Oc
102 E8 **Clipperton I** Pacific Oc 10.20N 109.13W
58 C3 **Clisham** *mt* Harris, W Isles **Scotland** 57.58N 6.50W
72 B1 **Clisson** France 47.05N 1.16W
57 J5 **Clitheroe** Lancs **Eng** 53.53N 2.23W
80 G3 **Clitunno** *R* Italy
100 D6 **Clive** Alberta 52.30N 113.30W
11 L6 **Clive New Zealand** 39.36S 176.58E
110 M9 **Clive** Utah 40.43N 113.07W
101 O4 **Clive L** N W Terr 63.15N 118.55W
120 F7 **Cliza** Bolivia 17.34S 65.57W
100 J6 **Cloan** Saskatchewan 52.37N 108.44W
14 A6 **Cloates, Pt** W Australia 22.41S 113.40E
58 G7 **Cloch Pt** Strathclyde **Scotland** 55.57N 4.53W
95 L4 **Clocolan** S Africa 28.55S 27.34E
121 D1 **Clodomira** Argentina 27.35S 64.14W
59 K2 **Clogh** Antrim **N Ireland** 54.58N 6.18W
59 H6 **Clogh** Kilkenny **Irish Rep** 52.52N 7.10W
59 K6 **Clogh** Wexford **Irish Rep** 52.38N 6.20W
59 G2 **Cloghan** Donegal **Irish Rep** 54.50N 7.56W
59 G5 **Cloghan** Offaly **Irish Rep** 53.13N 7.53W
59 B7 **Cloghane** Kerry **Irish Rep** 52.14N 10.10W
59 G7 **Clogheen** Tipperary **Irish Rep** 52.17N 8.00W
59 H3 **Clogher** Tyrone **N Ireland** 54.25N 7.10W
59 K4 **Clogher Head** Louth **Irish Rep** 53.48N 6.15W
59 K4 **Clogherhead** Louth **Irish Rep** 53.48N 6.13W
59 K2 **Clogh Mills** Antrim **N Ireland** 55.00N 6.20W
59 F3 **Cloghore** Donegal **Irish Rep** 54.29N 8.07W
59 M3 **Cloghy** Down **N Ireland** 54.26N 5.29W
70 C6 **Clohars** France 47.48N 3.35W
58 N4 **Clola** Grampian **Scotland** 57.29N 1.59W
13 F5 **Clonagh** Queensland 20.10S 140.39E
59 E8 **Clonakilty** Cork **Irish Rep** 51.37N 8.54W
59 E8 **Clonakilty B** Cork **Irish Rep**
59 J6 **Clonamon** Wexford **Irish Rep** 52.38N 6.37W
59 H5 **Clonaslee** Leix **Irish Rep** 53.09N 7.31W
59 E4 **Clonbern** Galway **Irish Rep** 53.34N 8.39W
59 H5 **Clonbulloge** Offaly **Irish Rep** 53.15N 7.05W
59 D4 **Clonbur** Galway **Irish Rep** 53.33N 9.22W
13 F5 **Cloncurry** Queensland 20.41S 140.30E
13 F4 **Cloncurry** *R* Queensland
59 K5 **Clondalkin** Dublin **Irish Rep** 53.19N 6.24W
59 K5 **Clonee** Meath **Irish Rep** 53.25N 6.26W
59 C8 **Clonee Ls** Kerry **Irish Rep** 51.49N 9.43W
59 G7 **Cloneen** Tipperary **Irish Rep** 52.28N 7.36W
59 J6 **Clonegal** Carlow **Irish Rep** 52.42N 6.38W
59 H3 **Clones** Monaghan **Irish Rep** 54.11N 7.14W
59 F5 **Clonfert** Galway **Irish Rep** 53.14N 8.03W
59 G5 **Clonmacnoise** Offaly **Irish Rep** 53.19N 8.00W
59 H1 **Clonmany** Donegal **Irish Rep** 55.15N 7.25W
59 G7 **Clonmel** Tipperary **Irish Rep** 52.21N 7.42W
59 H4 **Clonmellon** W Meath **Irish Rep** 53.40N 7.01W
59 J6 **Clonmore** Carlow **Irish Rep** 52.50N 6.34W
59 J7 **Clonroche** Wexford **Irish Rep** 52.27N 6.43W
59 K5 **Clontarf** Dublin **Irish Rep** 53.22N 6.12W
108 P4 **Clontarf** Minnesota 45.23N 95.42W
59 H3 **Clontivrim Bridge** Fermanagh **N Ireland** 54.10N 7.15W
59 H5 **Clonygowan** Offaly **Irish Rep** 53.11N 7.16W
59 E3 **Cloonacool** Sligo **Irish Rep** 54.06N 8.47W
59 E4 **Cloonagh L** Roscommon **Irish Rep** 53.50N 8.41W
59 B8 **Cloonaghlin L** Kerry **Irish Rep** 51.52N 10.01W
59 G4 **Cloone** Leitrim **Irish Rep** 53.57N 7.47W
59 E4 **Cloonfad** Roscommon **Irish Rep** 53.41N 8.45W
59 C8 **Cloon L** Kerry **Irish Rep** 51.53N 9.56W
59 E6 **Cloonlara** Clare **Irish Rep** 52.43N 8.34W
110 A1 **Clo-oose** Vancouver I, Br Col 48.40N 124.49W
56 L3 **Clophill** Beds **Eng** 52.02N 0.25W
63 H7 **Cloppenburg** W Germany 52.52N 8.02E
108 S3 **Cloquet** Minnesota 46.43N 92.28W
118 B9 **Clorinda** Argentina 25.16S 57.45W
57 F2 **Closeburn** Dumfries & Galloway **Scotland** 55.12N 3.45W
123 A5 **Close, C** Antarctica 65.51S 52.52E
103 G5 **Closter** New Jersey 40.58N 73.58W
98 M3 **Cloudberry Pt** Quebec 50.12N 60.56W
109 E9 **Cloudcroft** New Mexico 32.58N 105.46W
108 C5 **Cloud Pk** Wyoming 44.23N 107.11W
11 J8 **Cloudy B New Zealand**
113 J5 **Cloudy Mt** Alaska 63.10N 156.08W
72 F3 **Clouère** *R* France
59 L3 **Clough** Down **N Ireland** 54.18N 5.50W
59 F6 **Cloughjordan** Tipperary **Irish Rep** 52.57N 8.02W
57 N4 **Cloughton** N Yorks **Eng** 54.20N 0.27W
99 L4 **Cloutier** Quebec 48.02N 79.12W
72 B2 **Clouzeaux, les** France 46.38N 1.30W
99 P4 **Clova** Quebec 48.07N 75.24W
58 K5 **Clova** Tayside **Scotland** 56.50N 3.06W
56 C5 **Clovelly** Devon **Eng** 51.00N 4.24W
12 M7 **Clovelly** *dist* Sydney, N S W
58 L7 **Clovenfords** Borders **Scotland** 55.37N 2.53W
105 F2 **Clover** S Carolina 35.05N 81.14W
104 G10 **Clover** Virginia 36.51N 78.46W
101 J11 **Cloverdale** Br Col 49.06N 122.44W
111 A3 **Cloverdale** California 38.46N 123.01W
107 K2 **Cloverdale** Indiana 39.30N 86.49W
109 B10 **Cloverdale** New Mexico 31.25N 108.47W
112 G8 **Cloverleaf** Texas 29.47N 95.10W
107 K4 **Cloverport** Kentucky 37.49N 86.38W
111 E5 **Clovis** California 36.47N 119.43W
109 G7 **Clovis** New Mexico 34.14N 103.13W
58 F5 **Clovulin** Highland **Scotland** 56.43N 5.17W
56 G3 **Clows Top** Hereford & Worcs **Eng** 52.21N 2.25W
70 N6 **Cloyes** France 48.00N 1.15E
59 J1 **Cloyfin** Londonderry **N Ireland** 55.09N 6.37W
59 F8 **Cloyne** Cork **Irish Rep** 51.52N 8.07W
58 F4 **Cluanie Bridge** Highland **Scotland** 57.09N 5.11W
58 F4 **Cluanie, L** Highland **Scotland** 57.08N 5.05W
72 H2 **Cluis** France 46.33N 1.44E
82 H4 **Cluj** Romania 46.47N 23.37E
71 J8 **Clumanc** France 44.03N 6.24E
56 E3 **Clun** Shropshire **Eng** 52.26N 3.02W
12 G6 **Clunes** Victoria 37.20S 143.51E
56 E3 **Clun Forest** Shropshire **Eng**
56 F3 **Clun, R** Shropshire **Eng**
100 E8 **Cluny** Alberta 50.50N 112.42W
71 F4 **Cluny** France 46.25N 4.39E
13 E6 **Cluny** Queensland 24.31S 139.32E
110 J9 **Cluro** Nevada 40.36N 116.20W
71 J5 **Clusaz, la** France 45.55N 6.25E
71 J3 **Cluse et Mijoux, la** France 46.53N 6.22E
71 H4 **Cluse, la** Ain **France** 46.10N 5.35E
71 H7 **Cluse, la** Hautes-Alpes **France** 44.38N 5.50E
71 K4 **Cluses** France 46.04N 6.35E
79 G3 **Clusone** Italy 45.53N 9.56E
99 K3 **Clute** Ontario 49.13N 81.00W
11 D12 **Clutha R New Zealand**
108 S7 **Clutier** Iowa 42.04N 92.22W
14 F6 **Clutterbuck Hills** W Australia
57 G6 **Clwyd** *co* Wales
57 G6 **Clwydian Ra** Clwyd **Wales**
57 G6 **Clwyd R** Clwyd **Wales**
105 D7 **Clyattville** Georgia 30.41N 83.20W
100 D4 **Clyde** Alberta 54.10N 113.39W
109 N2 **Clyde** Kansas 39.36N 97.25W
108 M1 **Clyde** N Dakota 48.47N 98.52W
104 J3 **Clyde** New York 43.05N 76.53W
11 D12 **Clyde New Zealand** 45.11S 169.22E
97 N3 **Clyde** N W Terr 70.30N 68.30W
104 C5 **Clyde** Ohio 41.17N 82.18W
112 H3 **Clyde** Texas 32.23N 99.30W
58 H7 **Clydebank** Strathclyde **Scotland** 55.54N 4.24W
58 J7 **Clyde, Falls of** Strathclyde **Scotland** 55.40N 3.49W
58 F7 **Clyde, Firth of Scotland**
99 O7 **Clyde Forks** Ontario 45.07N 76.41W
97 N3 **Clyde Inlet** N W Terr
110 P4 **Clyde Park** Montana 45.54N 110.36W
98 G10 **Clyde R** Nova Scotia
58 G7 **Clyde R Scotland**
57 E6 **Clyder Fawr** *mt* Gwynedd **Wales** 53.06N 4.01W
95 L2 **Clydesdale** S Africa 26.54S 27.55E
11 D13 **Clydevale New Zealand** 46.06S 169.32E
106 F6 **Clyman** Wisconsin 43.16N 88.43W
104 F6 **Clymer** Pennsylvania 40.42N 79.01W
57 E6 **Clynnog-fawr** Gwynedd **Wales** 53.01N 4.23W
56 E3 **Clyro** Powys **Wales** 52.06N 3.09W
56 E6 **Clyst Honiton** Devon **Eng** 50.44N 3.26W
56 E6 **Clyst St. Mary** Devon **Eng** 50.43N 3.26W
56 D2 **Clywedog Res** Powys **Wales**
36 C6 **Cnidus Nova** *anc site* **Turkey** 36.40N 27.22E
Cnossos *see* **Knossós**
76 E7 **Coa** *R* Portugal
59 E8 **Coachford** Cork **Irish Rep** 51.55N 8.47W
98 M3 **Coacoachou L** Quebec
115 F5 **Coacoyole** Mexico 24.37N 106.36W
59 J2 **Coagh** Tyrone **N Ireland** 54.39N 6.37W
112 F3 **Coahoma** Texas 32.18N 101.17W
115 J8 **Coahuayutla de Guerrero** Mexico 18.19N 101.42W
115 H4 **Coahuila** *state* Mexico
104 D8 **Coal** *R* W Virginia
101 K5 **Coal** *R* Yukon Terr
12 L5 **Coal and Candle Cr** New S Wales
92 H10 **Coalane** Mozambique 17.46S 37.00E
95 L2 **Coalbrook** S Africa 26.51S 27.53E
57 F1 **Coalburn** Strathclyde **Scotland** 55.36N 3.54W
106 F8 **Coal City** Illinois 41.17N 88.18W
115 H8 **Coalcomán** Mexico 18.46N 103.08W
113 Q4 **Coal Creek** Alaska 65.20N 143.25W
11 D12 **Coal Creek New Zealand** 45.30S 169.20E
100 E9 **Coaldale** Alberta 49.45N 112.38W
111 G3 **Coaldale** Nevada 38.02N 117.52W
103 C5 **Coaldale** Pennsylvania 40.49N 75.54W
11 F10 **Coalgate New Zealand** 43.29S 171.58E
109 O7 **Coalgate** Oklahoma 34.33N 96.15W
104 C8 **Coal Grove** Ohio 38.29N 82.36W
107 C6 **Coal Hill** Arkansas 35.26N 93.39W
100 E9 **Coalhurst** Alberta 49.45N 112.56W
11 A13 **Coal I New Zealand** 46.07S 166.38E
111 D5 **Coalinga** California 36.08N 120.22W
59 J2 **Coalisland** Tyrone **N Ireland** 54.33N 6.42W
109 D1 **Coalmont** Colorado 40.33N 106.27W
104 G6 **Coalport** Pennsylvania 40.43N 78.33W
101 K6 **Coal River** Br Columbia 59.38N 126.58W
104 C7 **Coalton** Ohio 39.06N 82.37W
56 J2 **Coalville** Leics **Eng** 52.44N 1.20W
95 N2 **Coalville** S Africa 26.02S 29.10E
110 O9 **Coalville** Utah 40.55N 111.25W
108 E4 **Coalwood** Montana 45.43N 105.35W
105 J7 **Coamo** Puerto Rico 18.05N 66.22W
76 F2 **Coaña** Spain 43.30N 6.45W
118 H4 **Coaraci** Brazil 14.37S 39.37W
120 F1 **Coari** Brazil 4.08S 63.07W
120 F1 **Coari, L** Brazil
120 F1 **Coari, R** Brazil
72 D9 **Coarraze** Pyrénées Atlantiques **France** 43.10N 0.12W
120 D6 **Coasa** Peru 14.06S 70.01W
93 L9 **Coast** *prov* Kenya
92 J5 **Coast** *reg* Tanzania
103 F7 **Coastal Plain** New Jersey
101 G7 **Coast Mts** Br Col/Alaska
97 N6 **Coast of Labrador** *reg* Nfld/Labrador
13 K7 **Coast Ra** Queensland
102 B2 **Coast Ra** U.S.A.
58 H7 **Coatbridge** Strathclyde **Scotland** 55.52N 4.01W
115 L8 **Coatepec** Mexico 19.29N 96.59W
115 K8 **Coatepec Harinas** Mexico 18.56N 99.41W
115 O10 **Coatepeque** Guatemala 14.42N 91.50W
103 C7 **Coatesville** Pennsylvania 39.59N 75.50W
99 T7 **Coaticook** Quebec 45.08N 71.43W
115 L9 **Coatlán** Mexico 16.25N 96.50W
109 M4 **Coats** Kansas 37.32N 98.49W
105 J2 **Coats** N Carolina 35.25N 78.32W
97 L5 **Coats I** N W Terr 62.30N 83.00W
123 C10 **Coats Land** Antarctica
107 D1 **Coatsville** Missouri 40.34N 92.38W
115 M8 **Coatzacoalcos** Mexico 18.10N 94.25W
115 L7 **Coatzintla** Mexico 20.30N 97.28W
76 D2 **Coba da Serpe, Mte** Spain 43.05N 7.54W
110 L4 **Cobalt** Idaho 45.03N 114.15W
99 L5 **Cobalt** Ontario 47.24N 79.41W
115 O10 **Cobán** Guatemala 15.28N 90.20W
37 F6 **Çobandede** Turkey 39.59N 41.59E
36 E6 **Çobanisa** Turkey 36.52N 30.01E
36 E4 **Çobanlar** Turkey 38.41N 30.45E
12 H4 **Cobar** New S Wales 31.32S 145.51E
12 J6 **Cobargo** New S Wales 36.24S 149.52E
75 J6 **Cobatillas** Spain 40.40N 0.45W
106 D7 **Cobb** Wisconsin 42.59N 90.18W
104 K9 **Cobb I** Virginia 37.20N 75.44W
12 C2 **Cobberas, Mt** Victoria 36.56S 148.13E
14 F6 **Cobb, L** W Australia 24.15S 126.18E

103 J2 **Cobble Mountain Res** Massachusetts 42.08N 72.55W
58 G6 **Cobbler, The** *mt* Strathclyde **Scotland** 56.13N 4.48W
11 G8 **Cobb, Mt New Zealand** 41.02S 172.30E
11 G8 **Cobb River** *H E Station* **New Zealand** 41.06S 172.43E
96 B2 **Cobbs Hill** Bermuda 32.17N 64.49W
77 M6 **Cobdar Spain** 37.16N 2.12W
107 G4 **Cobden** Illinois 37.32N 89.16W
99 O7 **Cobden** Ontario 45.36N 76.54W
12 G7 **Cobden** Victoria 38.21S 143.07E
98 J8 **Cobequid Bay** Nova Scotia
98 H8 **Cobequid Mountains** Nova Scotia
75 F6 **Cobeta Spain** 40.52N 2.09W
59 F8 **Cóbh** Cork **Irish Rep** 51.51N 8.17W
56 M5 **Cobham** Kent **Eng** 51.24N 0.25E
55 C6 **Cobham** Surrey **England** 51.20N 0.24W
13 B1 **Cobham B** N Terr **Australia**
12 F4 **Cobham L** New S Wales 30.09S 142.05E
120 E4 **Cobija Bolivia** 11.01S 68.45W
120 D10 **Cobija Chile** 22.32S 70.15W
104 L4 **Cobleskill** New York 42.41N 74.30W
99 M8 **Coboconk** Ontario 44.40N 78.48W
113 U8 **Cobol** Alaska 57.31N 135.51W
115 L7 **Cobos Mexico** 20.57N 97.20W
99 M9 **Cobourg** Ontario 43.58N 78.11W
13 B1 **Cobourg Pen** N Terr **Australia**
14 B6 **Cobra** W Australia 24.10S 116.29E
12 H6 **Cobram** Victoria 35.56S 145.40E
118 J9 **Cobras, I. das Brazil** 22.54S 43.10W
110 L8 **Cobre** Nevada 41.07N 114.25W
116 K2 **Cobre, R Jamaica, W I**
76 F4 **Cobreros Spain** 42.06N 6.41W
120 E10 **Cobres Argentina** 23.42S 66.15W
92 G8 **Cobue Mozambique** 12.10S 34.50E
110 B5 **Coburg** Oregon 44.09N 123.03W
64 K3 **Coburg W Germany** 50.15N 10.58E
12 C7 **Coburg** *dist* Melbourne, Vic
97 M2 **Coburg I** N W Terr 76.00N 79.30W
104 H6 **Coburn** Pennsylvania 40.52N 77.30W
119 C8 **Coca Ecuador** 0.28S 76.56W
76 K6 **Coca Spain** 41.13N 4.32W
120 D7 **Cocachacra Peru** 17.05S 71.45W
117 G6 **Cocal Brazil** 3.29S 41.34W
115 O6 **Cocal Panama** 7.46N 80.16W
118 E4 **Cocalinho Brazil** 14.25S 50.58W
Cocanada *see* **Kakinada**
120 E7 **Cocapata Bolivia** 16.55S 66.44W
79 H2 **Coca, Pizzo di** *mt* **Italy** 46.04N 10.01E
119 C8 **Coca, R Ecuador**
79 M6 **Coccolia Italy** 44.18N 12.06E
79 D4 **Cocconato Italy** 45.05N 8.02E
81 L3 **Coccovello, Monte Italy** 40.03N 15.43E
77 Q3 **Cocentaina Spain** 38.45N 0.27W
120 E7 **Cochabamba Bolivia** 17.26S 66.10W
120 E7 **Cochabamba** *dept* **Bolivia**
120 F7 **Cochabamba, Cord de** *mts* **Bolivia**
119 C7 **Cocha, L. de la Colombia** 1.05N 77.08W
121 A8 **Cochamo Chile** 41.30S 72.17W
103 D3 **Cochecton** New York 41.42N 75.03W
119 G2 **Coche, I Venezuela** 10.50N 63.59W
64 C3 **Cochem W Germany** 50.08N 7.10E
109 D3 **Cochetopa Pass** Colorado 38.10N 106.37W
28 C6 **Cochin** Kerala **India** 9.56N 76.15E
25 J7 **Cochin Chine** *reg* **Vietnam**
120 F10 **Cochinoca Argentina** 22.45S 65.53W
116 D3 **Cochinos, B. de Cuba** 22.05N 81.10W
19 G2 **Cochinos Pt** Luzon **Philippines** 14.25N 120.30E
111 P9 **Cochise** Arizona 32.06N 109.56W
111 P9 **Cochise Head** *mt* Arizona 32.04N 109.18W
103 M2 **Cochituate** Massachusetts 42.19N 71.21W
26 N16 **Cochons, Î. aux** Crozet Is **Ind Oc** 46.07S 50.10E
105 D5 **Cochran** Georgia 32.22N 83.21W
100 C7 **Cochrane** Alberta 51.15N 114.25W
121 J6 **Cochrane Chile** 47.16S 72.33W
99 J3 **Cochrane** Ontario 49.04N 81.02W
101 W6 **Cochrane** *R* Saskatchewan
Cochrane, Cerro *see* **San Lorenzo, Cerro**
121 J6 **Cochrane, L Arg/Chile**
104 E5 **Cochranton** Pennsylvania 41.32N 80.03W
103 C7 **Cochranville** Pennsylvania 39.54N 75.55W
63 O9 **Cochstedt** E **Germany** 51.53N 11.24E
14 E3 **Cockatoo I** W Australia 16.06S 123.08E
58 K4 **Cock Bridge** Grampian **Scotland** 57.10N 3.15W
12 F4 **Cockburn** S Australia 32.05S 141.00E
13 G3 **Cockburn** *R* Queensland
15 B9 **Cockburn, C** N Terr **Aust** 11.22S 132.55E
121 K10 **Cockburn, Canal** *channel* **Chile**
116 J4 **Cockburn Harb** South Caicos I **Bahamas** 21.30N 71.30W
99 G7 **Cockburn I** Ontario
99 G7 **Cockburn Island** Ontario 45.56N 83.20W
13 A7 **Cockburn, Mt** N Terr **Australia** 25.58S 129.26E
14 G3 **Cockburn Ra** W Australia
14 A3 **Cockburn Sd** W Australia
58 M7 **Cockburnspath** Borders **Scotland** 55.56N 2.21W
116 A2 **Cockburn Town** San Salvador I **Bahamas** 24.04N 74.32W
58 L7 **Cockenzie** Lothian **Scotland** 55.58N 2.58W
57 H5 **Cockerham** Lancs **Eng** 53.59N 2.50W
57 G3 **Cockermouth** Cumbria **Eng** 54.40N 3.21W
103 A8 **Cockeysville** Maryland 39.29N 76.39W
14 F9 **Cocklebiddy** W Australia 32.05S 126.10E
116 J1 **Cockpit** *mt* **Jamaica, W I** 18.16N 77.39W
116 J1 **Cockpit Country, The** *reg* **Jamaica, W I**
112 N9 **Cockrell Hill** Texas 32.44N 96.53W
95 H9 **Cockscomb** *mt* **S Africa** 33.35S 24.47E
60 H7 **Cocksdorp, De** Texel **Netherlands** 53.09N 4.53E
56 F2 **Cockshutt** Shropshire **Eng** 52.51N 2.51W
115 O5 **Coclé Panama** 8.29N 80.24W
119 B3 **Coclé del Norte Panama** 9.06N 80.35W
115 M2 **Coco** *R* **Hond/Nicaragua**
105 G9 **Cocoa** Florida 28.21N 80.46W
105 G9 **Cocoa Beach** Florida 28.19N 80.36W
26 A12 **Cocoa I** Rodriguez I **Ind Oc** 19.43S 63.18E
91 A3 **Cocobeach Gabon** 0.59N 9.34E
116 E3 **Coco, Cayo** *isld* **Cuba** 22.30N 78.30W
28 G6 **Coco Chan** Andaman Is
107 F12 **Cocodrie** Louisiana 29.16N 90.41W
115 N3 **Coco Haulover Nicaragua** 13.43N 83.30W
122 S7 **Coco, I. del Pacific Oc** 5.33N 87.00W
110 J1 **Cocolalla** Idaho 48.06N 116.37W
115 F11 **Cocolí** Panama **Canal Zone** 8.58N 79.36W
115 F3 **Cocomórachic Mexico** 28.42N 107.56W
111 M6 **Coconino Plat** Arizona
12 H5 **Cocoparra Ra** New S Wales
119 C6 **Coco, Pta** *pt* **Colombia** 2.58N 77.44W
117 D9 **Côco, R Brazil**
119 C4 **Cocorná** Colombia 6.03N 75.07W
119 K6 **Cocoro** *isld* **Philippines** 10.54N 121.12E
118 G4 **Côcos Brazil** 14.15S 44.30W
116 P2 **Cocos B** Trinidad & Tobago
Cocos, I Costa Rica *see* **Coco, I. del**
19 L1 **Cocos I** Guam **Pacific Oc** 13.14N 144.39E
17 E14 **Cocos (Keeling) Is Indian Oc**
115 E9 **Coco Solo** Panama **Canal Zone** 9.22N 79.53W
122 S8 **Cocos Ridge Pacific Oc**
118 J8 **Cocotá Brazil** 22.49S.43.11W
26 U13 **Cocotte, Mt Mauritius, Indian Oc** 20.27S 57.27E
66 L8 **Cocquio Italy** 45.52N 8.42E
119 H3 **Cocuinita, Caño** *crater* **Venezuela**
115 H7 **Cocula Mexico** 20.22N 103.50W
72 E7 **Cocumont France** 44.27N 0.03E
81 M5 **Cocuzzo, Mte Italy** 39.13N 16.08E
54 M5 **Cod** *oil field* **North Sea** 57.07N 2.25E
81 D2 **Coda Cavallo, C** Sardinia 40.51N 9.44E
82 L4 **Codăești Romania** 46.50N 27.48E
119 H9 **Codajás Brazil** 3.55S 62.00W
119 H9 **Codajás, I Brazil** 3.50S 62.12W
109 L2 **Codell** Kansas 39.12N 99.11W
81 D4 **Code, Mte** Sardinia 39.43N 9.32E
119 F2 **Codera, C Venezuela** 10.37N 66.06W
66 O7 **Codera, Val Italy**
100 L8 **Coderre** Saskatchewan 50.11N 106.31W
75 F2 **Codés** *mt* **Spain** 42.38N 2.20W
76 C3 **Codeseda Spain** 42.37N 8.25W
100 N5 **Codette** Saskatchewan 53.16N 104.01W
11 B13 **Codfish I New Zealand** 46.43S 167.40E
97 N6 **Cod I** Labrador, Nfld 57.45N 61.45E
56 L4 **Codicote** Herts **Eng** 51.52N 0.15W
79 M5 **Codigoro Italy** 44.50N 12.07E
82 J5 **Codlea Romania** 45.43N 25.27E
117 F7 **Codó Brazil** 4.28S 43.51W
79 G4 **Codogna Italy** 45.10N 9.42E
Codoñera, La *see* **Cadoñera, La**
121 J6 **Codorniz, Paso** *pass* **Arg/Chile** 47.57S 72.35W
103 A6 **Codorus Cr** Pennsylvania
75 H5 **Codos Spain** 41.17N 1.22W
76 E10 **Codosera, La Spain** 39.13N 7.10W
117 F7 **Codòzinho Brazil** 4.40S 44.14W
116 O6 **Codrington** Barbuda **W I** 17.43N 61.49W
79 N3 **Codroipo Italy** 45.58N 12.59E
81 B2 **Codrongianus** Sardinia 40.40N 8.41E
98 N6 **Codroy** Newfoundland 47.52N 59.21W
98 O5 **Codroy Pond** Newfoundland 48.04N 58.52W
82 G4 **Codrului, Munții** *mts* **Romania**
59 B8 **Cod's Hd** Cork **Irish Rep** 51.40N 10.06W
108 J7 **Cody** Nebraska 42.58N 101.16W
98 G8 **Cody** New Brunswick 45.52N 65.50W
110 Q5 **Cody** Wyoming 44.31N 109.04W
104 C10 **Coeburn** Virginia 36.57N 82.27W
95 J9 **Coega S Africa** 33.46S 25.40E
99 N8 **Coe Hill** Ontario 44.51N 77.50W
117 F7 **Coelho Neto Brazil** 4.15S 43.00W
76 F5 **Coelhoso Portugal** 41.39N 6.40W
76 D1 **Coelleira, I Spain** 43.45N 7.38W
119 D5 **Coello Colombia** 4.15N 74.52W
13 G2 **Coen** Queensland 13.50S 143.11E
13 F2 **Coen** *R* Queensland
76 C8 **Coentral Portugal** 40.04N 8.10W
95 J9 **Coerney S Africa** 33.28S 25.43E
117 A3 **Coeroeni** *R* **Surinam**
63 F9 **Coesfeld W Germany** 51.57N 7.10E
26 E6 **Coëtivy Is** Seychelles, **Ind Oc**
110 J2 **Coeur d'Alene** Idaho 47.40N 116.46W
110 J2 **Coeur d'Alene** *R* Idaho
110 J2 **Coeur d'Alene L** Idaho 47.30N 116.51W
69 E5 **Cœuvres-et-Valsery France** 49.19N 3.10E
60 P9 **Coevorden Netherlands** 52.39N 6.45E
70 K5 **Coevrons, les** *mts* **France**
72 A2 **Coëx France** 46.42N 1.46W
103 G2 **Coeymans** New York 42.28N 73.47W
103 G2 **Coeymans Hollow** New York 42.27N 73.54W
96 R11 **Cofete** Fuerteventura **Canary Is** 28.04N 14.24W
105 E6 **Coffee** Georgia 31.31N 82.20W
95 N7 **Coffee Bay S Africa** 31.59S 29.08E
110 P2 **Coffee Creek** Montana 47.21N 110.05W
101 D4 **Coffee Creek** Yukon Terr 62.50N 139.10W
107 G2 **Coffeen** Illinois 39.04N 89.22W
107 L10 **Coffee Springs** Alabama 31.09N 85.58W
107 G8 **Coffeeville** Mississippi 33.59N 89.40W
109 P4 **Coffeyville** Kansas 37.02N 95.37W
12 D5 **Coffin B** S Australia
12 D5 **Coffin Bay** S Australia 34.40S 136.22E
98 L6 **Coffin I** Madeleine Is, Que 47.35N 61.30W
12 L4 **Coff's Harbour** New S Wales 30.19S 153.05E
95 L8 **Cofimvaba S Africa** 32.01S 27.35E
115 P10 **Cofradía Honduras** 15.20N 88.09W
115 L8 **Cofre de Perote** *pk* **Mexico** 19.30N 97.10W
77 O2 **Cofrentes Spain** 39.14N 1.04W
82 M6 **Cogealac Romania** 44.36N 28.36E
76 L5 **Cogeces del Monte Spain** 41.30N 4.19W
56 N4 **Coggeshall** Essex **Eng** 51.52N 0.41E
79 D3 **Coggiola Italy** 45.41N 8.11E
106 C7 **Coggon** Iowa 42.16N 91.33W
78 C8 **Coghinas** *mt* Sardinia 40.42N 9.18E
81 B2 **Coghinas** *R* Sardinia
81 C2 **Coghinas, L. del** Sardinia
14 G4 **Coghlan, Mt** W Australia 18.01S 127.59E
79 N1 **Coglians, Monte Italy/Austria** 46.37N 12.53E
13 C7 **Coglin** *R* N Terr/S Aust
66 L6 **Coglio Switzerland** 46.17N 8.41E
72 D4 **Cognac France** 45.42N 0.19W
72 G4 **Cognac-le-Froid France** 45.50N 1.00E
72 L3 **Cognat-Lyonne France** 46.07N 3.16E
79 B3 **Cogne Italy** 45.37N 7.21E
67 O13 **Cognocoli-Montichi** Corsica 41.50N 8.55E
91 A3 **Cogo Equat Guinea** 1.06N 9.41E
118 B9 **Cogoi Argentina** 24.50S 59.08W
79 E6 **Cogoleto Italy** 44.23N 8.38E
71 K10 **Cogolin France** 43.15N 6.32E
79 K3 **Cogollo Italy** 45.47N 11.26E
75 C3 **Cogollos Spain** 42.12N 3.42W
75 C3 **Cogollos** *R* **Spain**
77 J6 **Cogollos-Vega Spain** 37.17N 3.34W
75 D6 **Cogolludo Spain** 40.56N 3.06W
77 K6 **Cogollos de Guadix Spain** 37.15N 3.09W
79 J2 **Cógolo Italy** 46.21N 10.42E
89 B6 **Cogon** *R* **Guinea**
108 N3 **Cogswell** N Dakota 46.08N 97.48W
36 G3 **Çogun Turkey** 39.21N 34.07E
94 N5 **Cõguno Mozambique** 24.23S 34.32E
108 D2 **Cohagen** Montana 47.05N 106.36W
103 D8 **Cohansey Cr** New Jersey
103 N2 **Cohasset** Massachusetts 42.15N 70.49W
120 C4 **Cohengua, R Peru**
66 B8 **Cohennoz France** 45.45N 6.29E
70 E5 **Cohiniac France** 48.27N 2.58W
104 H4 **Cohocton** New York 42.30N 77.30W
104 H4 **Cohocton** *R* New York
104 M4 **Cohoes** New York 42.45N 73.43W
12 G6 **Cohuna** Victoria 35.47S 144.15E
105 C3 **Cohutta** Georgia 34.59N 84.58W
87 N10 **Coiama I Somalia** 0.40S 42.20E
115 O6 **Coiba, I Panama**
58 F3 **Coigach** *dist* Highland **Scotland**
58 H4 **Coignafearn Lodge** Highland **Scotland** 57.13N 4.11W
69 B6 **Coignières France** 48.44N 1.55E
121 K8 **Coig R Argentina**
121 J5 **Coihaique Chile** 45.35S 72.08W
121 K5 **Coihaique Alto Chile** 45.28S 71.38W
121 A6 **Coihüe Chile** 37.32S 72.40W
121 B6 **Coihueco Chile** 36.35S 71.45W
58 D4 **Coillore** Skye, Highland **Scotland** 57.21N 6.24W
28 C5 **Coimbatore** Tamil Nadu **India** 11.00N 76.57E
28 C5 **Coimbatore** *dist* Tamil Nadu **India**
76 C8 **Coimbra Portugal** 40.12N 8.25W
76 C8 **Coimbra** *dist* **Portugal**
76 B9 **Coimbrão Portugal** 39.54N 8.53W
108 P9 **Coin** Iowa 40.40N 95.12W
77 G7 **Coín Spain** 36.40N 4.45W
69 E5 **Coincy France** 49.10N 3.26E
71 K5 **Coin, Mt France** 45.38N 6.37E
66 A7 **Cointrin Switzerland** 46.14N 6.06E
120 E8 **Coipasa, L. de Bolivia**
120 E8 **Coipasa, Salar de** *salt pan* **Bolivia**
Coire *see* **Chur Switzerland**
71 F7 **Coiron, Mts. du France**
76 C2 **Coiros Spain** 43.15N 8.10W
115 L9 **Coixtlahuaca Mexico** 17.44N 97.22W
120 D6 **Cojata Peru** 15.02S 69.25W
119 F3 **Cojedes** *state* **Venezuela**
119 F3 **Cojedes, R Venezuela**
119 B7 **Cojimíes Ecuador** 0.21N 80.01W
82 H4 **Cojocna Romania** 46.45N 23.50E
119 E2 **Cojoro Venezuela** 11.39N 71.51W
121 K6 **Cojudo Blanco, Cerro** *pk* **Argentina** 47.04S 69.18W
115 P11 **Cojutepeque El Salvador** 13.42N 88.58W
36 J5 **Çokak Turkey** 37.44N 36.18E
108 Q4 **Cokato** Minnesota 45.05N 94.10W
104 E6 **Cokeburg** Pennsylvania 40.05N 80.04W
110 P7 **Cokeville** Wyoming 42.05N 110.57W
12 F4 **Coko Ra** *mts* New S Wales
28 A8 **Colaba** *dist* Bombay **India**
28 A8 **Colaba Pt** Bombay **India** 18.54N 72.49E
11 B13 **Colac New Zealand** 46.22S 167.54E
12 G7 **Colac** Victoria 38.22S 143.38E
71 C7 **Colagne** *R* **France**
Colair L *see* **Kolleru L.**
121 B2 **Colanguil, Cerro de** *mts* **Argentina**
37 E9 **Colap** *R* **Turkey**
117 D5 **Colares Brazil** 0.55S 48.15W
76 A11 **Colares Portugal** 38.47N 9.27W
76 B15 **Colares, R. de Portugal**
118 H6 **Colatina Brazil** 19.35S 40.37W
72 F7 **Colayrac-St-Cirq France** 44.13N 0.33E
87 M9 **Colba Somalia** 0.20S 41.39E
64 F2 **Cölbe W Germany** 50.51N 8.48E
123 B4 **Colbeck Arch Antarctica** 67.23S 61.00E
123 J8 **Colbeck, C Antarctica** 77.00S 158.00W
110 H2 **Colbert** Washington 47.50N 117.20W
63 P8 **Colbitz** E **Germany** 52.20N 11.36E
63 P8 **Colbitz-Letzlinger Heide** *heath* E **Germany**
99 N8 **Colborne** Ontario 44.03N 77.53W
121 B5 **Colbún Chile** 35.42S 71.28W
109 J2 **Colby** Kansas 39.24N 101.04W
106 D5 **Colby** Wisconsin 44.54N 90.20W
120 C6 **Colca** *R* **Peru**
121 B5 **Colchagua** *prov* **Chile**
103 K3 **Colchester** Connecticut 41.35N 72.19W
56 N4 **Colchester** Essex **Eng** 51.54N 0.54E
106 D9 **Colchester** Illinois 40.25N 90.46W
103 D2 **Colchester** New York 42.10N 75.05W
95 J9 **Colchester S Africa** 33.41S 25.49E
56 G5 **Cold Ashton** Avon **Eng** 51.28N 2.22W
113 F9 **Cold B** Alaska
58 H2 **Coldbackie** Highland **Scotland** 58.29N 4.23W
103 F2 **Cold Brook** New York 42.02N 74.18W
104 G4 **Colden** New York 42.40N 78.41W
58 M7 **Coldingham** Borders **Scotland** 55.53N 2.10W
79 C7 **Col di Rodi Italy** 43.48N 7.43E
64 O1 **Colditz** E **Germany** 51.08N 12.49E
100 G4 **Cold L** Alberta
100 G4 **Cold Lake** Alberta 54.28N 110.15W
100 Q3 **Cold Lake** Manitoba 55.08N 101.06W
56 N4 **Cold Norton** Essex **Eng** 51.41N 0.39E
108 Q4 **Cold Spring** Minnesota 45.28N 94.24W
103 E9 **Cold Spring** New Jersey 38.58N 74.55W
103 G4 **Cold Spring** New York 41.25N 73.55W
103 D3 **Cold Spring** Pennsylvania 41.44N 75.19W
112 M5 **Coldspring** Texas 30.34N 95.10W
103 H5 **Cold Spring Harbor** Long I, N Y 40.53N 73.27W
58 M7 **Coldstream** Borders **Scotland** 55.39N 2.15W
95 G9 **Coldstream S Africa** 33.58S 23.42E
109 L4 **Coldwater** Kansas 37.16N 99.20W
106 J8 **Coldwater** Michigan 41.57N 85.01W
104 A6 **Coldwater** Ohio 40.28N 84.37W
99 L8 **Coldwater** Ontario 44.43N 79.39W
107 F7 **Coldwater** *R* Mississippi
112 C7 **Coldwater Cr** Texas
99 D4 **Coldwell** Ontario 48.46N 86.31W
103 H3 **Colebrook** Connecticut 41.59N 73.05W
104 O2 **Colebrook** New Hampshire 44.53N 71.30W
12 H8 **Colebrook** Tasmania 42.30S 147.21E
107 C3 **Cole Camp** Missouri 38.27N 93.13W
56 F4 **Coleford** Glos **Eng** 51.48N 2.37W
95 N5 **Coleford S Africa** 29.58S 29.28E
104 G5 **Colegrove** Pennsylvania 41.44N 78.24W
100 C9 **Coleman** Alberta 49.38N 114.28W
105 E9 **Coleman** Florida 28.45N 82.05W
106 K6 **Coleman** Michigan 43.46N 84.35W
112 H4 **Coleman** Texas 31.50N 99.27W
13 F2 **Coleman** *R* Queensland
69 B2 **Colembert France** 50.44N 1.50E
Çölemerik *see* **Hakkâri**
95 N4 **Colenso S Africa** 28.44S 29.50E
59 J1 **Coleraine** Londonderry **N Ireland** 55.08N 6.40W
108 R2 **Coleraine** Minnesota 47.19N 93.22W
99 T7 **Coleraine** Quebec 45.59N 71.22W
12 F7 **Coleraine** Victoria 37.34S 141.44E
100 G9 **Coleridge** Alberta 49.58N 110.38W
108 N7 **Coleridge** Nebraska 42.31N 97.12W
11 F10 **Coleridge, L New Zealand** 43.19S 171.30E
28 D5 **Coleroon** Tamil Nadu **India** 11.20N 79.44E
28 D5 **Coleroon R** Tamil Nadu **India**
76 D4 **Coles Spain** 42.24N 7.50W
12 J8 **Coles Bay** Tasmania 42.04S 148.20E
95 J6 **Colesberg S Africa** 30.44S 25.05E
56 G4 **Colesborne** Glos **Eng** 51.50N 2.00W
56 H3 **Coleshill** Warwicks **Eng** 52.30N 1.42W
120 D7 **Coles, Pta. de** *C* **Peru** 17.45S 71.25W
103 E4 **Colesville** New Jersey 41.16N 74.38W
111 E3 **Coleville** California 38.34N 119.30W
100 H7 **Coleville** Saskatchewan 51.42N 109.16W
111 D2 **Colfax** California 39.07N 120.56W
106 F9 **Colfax** Illinois 40.35N 88.36W
106 H9 **Colfax** Indiana 40.11N 86.40W
108 R8 **Colfax** Iowa 41.40N 93.15W
107 D10 **Colfax** Louisiana 31.32N 92.42W
109 F5 **Colfax** New Mexico 36.35N 104.46W
100 O9 **Colfax** Saskatchewan 49.56N 104.00W
110 H3 **Colfax** Washington 46.54N 117.21W
106 C5 **Colfax** Wisconsin 45.00N 91.36W
75 C5 **Colgadizos** *mt* **Spain** 41.07N 3.39W
59 F3 **Colgagh** Sligo **Irish Rep** 54.17N 8.24W
100 O9 **Colgate** Saskatchewan 49.22N 103.57W
30 L7 **Colgong** Bihar **India** 25.15N 87.15E
58 R8 **Colgrave Sd** Shetland **Scotland**
121 L5 **Colhué Huapí, L Argentina**
79 F5 **Coli Italy** 44.44N 9.25E
121 B5 **Coliauco Chile** 34.18S 71.10W
121 A6 **Colico Chile** 37.25S 73.20W
79 F2 **Colico Italy** 46.08N 9.22E
121 B7 **Colico, L Chile**
71 G4 **Coligny France** 46.23N 5.20E
95 K2 **Coligny S Africa** 26.20S 26.20E
115 K9 **Colihuala Mexico** 17.36N 98.11W
60 C2 **Colijnsplaat Netherlands** 51.36N 3.51E
115 H8 **Colima Mexico** 19.14N 103.41W
115 G8 **Colima** *state* **Mexico**
121 B4 **Colina Chile** 33.13S 70.45W
117 F8 **Colinas Brazil** 6.02S 44.15W
76 H4 **Colinas de Trasmonte Spain** 42.01N 5.49W
75 D1 **Colindres Spain** 43.24N 3.25W
98 T7 **Colinet I, Gt** Newfoundland
58 L6 **Colinsburgh** Fife **Scotland** 56.13N 2.50W
100 D4 **Colinton** Alberta 54.38N 113.16W
58 F7 **Colintraive** Strathclyde **Scotland** 55.56N 5.09W
58 C5 **Coll** *isld* Strathclyde **Scotland**
66 N7 **Colla Switzerland** 46.06N 9.03E
75 C5 **Collado Hermoso Spain** 41.03N 3.55W
75 F7 **Collados Spain** 40.16N 2.12W
75 C6 **Collado-Villalba Spain** 40.39N 4.00W
58 Q8 **Colla Firth** Shetland **Scotland** 60.32N 1.20W
58 Q8 **Collafirth** Shetland **Scotland** 60.32N 1.21W
79 H6 **Collagna Italy** 44.21N 10.16E
120 E9 **Collahuasi Chile** 21.01S 68.43W
79 K1 **Collalbo Italy** 46.33N 11.28E
79 M1 **Collalto** *mt* **Italy** 46.54N 12.08E
76 H2 **Collanzo Spain** 43.08N 5.33W
75 K2 **Collarada, Peña** *mt* **Spain** 42.43N 0.28W
12 J3 **Collarenebri** New S Wales 29.33S 148.35E
12 M6 **Collaroy** New S Wales 33.44S 151.18E
66 N7 **Colla, V Switzerland**
80 F3 **Collazzone Italy** 42.54N 12.26E
109 C2 **Collbran** Colorado 39.14N 107.57W
79 H5 **Collecchio Italy** 44.45N 10.13E
79 J2 **Collécchio** *mt* **Italy** 46.27N 10.47E
80 K5 **Colledimezzo Italy** 41.58N 14.23E
80 D2 **Colle di Val d'Elsa Italy** 43.25N 11.08E
113 O4 **College** Alaska 64.54N 147.55W
107 M2 **College Corner** Indiana 39.34N 84.49W
107 K6 **College Grove** Tennessee 35.47N 86.41W
105 C4 **College Park** Georgia 33.39N 84.28W
104 J7 **College Park** Maryland 39.00N 76.57W
110 G3 **College Place** Washington 46.03N 118.21W
112 L5 **College Station** Texas 30.38N 96.21W
79 C4 **Collegno Italy** 45.05N 7.35E
79 K1 **Colle Isarco Italy** 46.57N 11.27E
80 J5 **Collelongo Italy** 41.53N 13.36E
81 R12 **Collepasso Italy** 40.04N 18.10E
12 H3 **Collerina** New S Wales 29.22S 146.32E
79 H7 **Colle Salvetti Italy** 43.36N 10.28E
80 L6 **Colle Sannita Italy** 41.22N 14.50E
81 G8 **Collesano** Sicily 37.55N 13.57E
71 D8 **Collet-de-Dèze, le France** 44.15N 3.54E
80 L5 **Colletorto Italy** 41.39N 14.58E
103 B3 **Colley** Pennsylvania 41.32N 76.17W
112 M8 **Colleyville** Texas 32.51N 97.08W
80 K5 **Colli al Volturno Italy** 41.36N 14.07E
12 J4 **Collie** New S Wales 31.41S 148.22E
14 B10 **Collie** W Australia 33.20S 116.06E
14 B10 **Collie Cardiff** W Australia 33.27S 116.09E
112 F8 **Collier Airfield** Texas 29.52N 95.28W
14 E3 **Collier B** W Australia
14 C6 **Collier Ranges** *mts* W Australia
103 E2 **Colliersville** New York 42.29N 74.59W
107 G6 **Collierville** Tennessee 35.04N 89.40W
58 N4 **Collieston** Grampian **Scotland** 57.21N 1.56W
75 F7 **Cólliga Spain** 40.02N 2.16W
57 F2 **Collin** Dumfries & Galloway **Scotland** 55.04N 3.32W
79 J6 **Collina, Passo di** *pass* **Italy** 44.02N 10.56E
70 E5 **Collinée France** 48.18N 2.31W
70 O3 **Collines-du-Vexin, Plaine et France**
56 H5 **Collingbourne Kingston** Wilts **Eng** 51.18N 1.39W
57 M6 **Collingham** Notts **Eng** 53.09N 0.45W
57 L5 **Collingham** W Yorks **Eng** 53.55N 1.25W
103 D7 **Collingswood** New Jersey 39.55N 75.04W
104 C3 **Collingswood** *dist* Philadelphia, Penn
11 G7 **Collingwood New Zealand** 40.41S 172.41E
99 K8 **Collingwood** Ontario 44.30N 80.14W
13 F5 **Collingwood** Queensland 22.20S 142.30E
12 D7 **Collingwood** *dist* Melbourne, Vic
15 K8 **Collingwood B Papua New Guinea**
105 E5 **Collins** Georgia 32.15N 82.10W
107 G10 **Collins** Mississippi 31.38N 89.33W
107 C4 **Collins** Missouri 37.55N 93.39W
110 O2 **Collins** Montana 47.56N 111.49W
104 G4 **Collins** New York 42.32N 78.56W
100 O1 **Collins** Ontario 50.19N 89.30W
10 V10 **Collins Hd** Norfolk I **Pacific Oc** 29.04S 167.59E
99 K5 **Collins, Mt** Ontario 47.50N 80.59W
23 C9 **Collinson, C** Hong Kong 22.15N 114.15E
23 C9 **Collinson Hd** Hong Kong 22.18N 114.20E
23 B9 **Collinson, Mt** Hong Kong 22.14N 114.13E
101 X1 **Collinson Pen** Victoria I, N W Terr
107 E9 **Collinston** Louisiana 32.41N 91.52W
59 K5 **Collinstown** Dublin **Irish Rep** 53.26N 6.15W
107 L7 **Collinsville** Alabama 34.16N 85.51W
103 J3 **Collinsville** Connecticut 41.49N 72.55W
107 G3 **Collinsville** Illinois 38.40N 89.58W
109 P5 **Collinsville** Oklahoma 36.22N 95.51W
13 J5 **Collinsville** Queensland 20.31S 147.50E
107 J6 **Collinwood** Tennessee 35.10N 87.45W
79 H3 **Collio Italy** 45.48N 10.20E
72 L10 **Collioure France** 42.32N 3.05E
121 A6 **Collipulli Chile** 37.55S 72.30W
99 J1 **Collis** Ontario 51.04N 81.04W
63 S10 **Collmberg** *mt* E **Germany** 51.19N 13.02E
64 Q1 **Cölln** E **Germany** 51.10N 13.30E
88 R3 **Collo Algeria** 37.06N 6.35E
71 J10 **Collobrières France** 43.15N 6.20E
66 D6 **Collombey Switzerland** 46.17N 6.56E
59 K4 **Collon** Louth **Irish Rep** 53.47N 6.29W
121 B8 **Collon Cura** *R* **Argentina**
66 A6 **Collonge Switzerland** 46.16N 6.13E
71 H4 **Collonges France** 46.08N 5.55E
66 E7 **Collonges Switzerland** 46.11N 7.02E
66 G8 **Collon, Mt Switzerland** 45.59N 7.30E
59 F3 **Collooney** Sligo **Irish Rep** 54.11N 8.29W
120 F8 **Collpa Bolivia** 19.55S 64.45W
120 E9 **Collpa, L Bolivia**
59 C8 **Colly** *mt* Kerry **Irish Rep** 51.57N 9.58W
109 K2 **Collyer** Kansas 39.03N 100.07W
56 K2 **Colly Weston** Northants **Eng** 53.37N 0.32W
111 A9 **Colma** California 37.42N 122.29W
121 F6 **Colman Argentina** 36.26S 59.10W
69 N7 **Colmar France** 48.05N 7.21E
71 K8 **Colmars France** 44.13N 6.37E
64 J5 **Colmberg W Germany** 49.22N 10.26E
76 C8 **Colmeal Portugal** 40.08N 8.00W
121 E2 **Colmena Argentina** 28.45S 60.06W
77 H7 **Colmenar Spain** 36.54N 4.20W
76 L8 **Colmenar del Arroyo Spain** 40.25N 4.12W
75 D5 **Colmenar de la Sierra Spain** 41.04N 3.24W
75 D7 **Colmenar de Oreja Spain** 40.06N 3.25W
76 L7 **Colmenarejo Spain** 40.33N 4.01W
75 C6 **Colmenar Viejo Spain** 40.39N 3.46W
71 C2 **Colmery France** 47.20N 3.14E
112 N5 **Colmesneil** Texas 30.54N 94.27W
57 D2 **Colmonell** Strathclyde **Scotland** 55.08N 4.55W
70 J5 **Colmont** *R* **France**
109 F5 **Colmor** New Mexico 36.13N 104.41W
56 K5 **Colnbrook** Berks **Eng** 51.29N 0.32W
57 J5 **Colne** Lancs **Eng** 53.52N 2.09W
56 N4 **Colne, R** Essex **Eng**
108 R8 **Colo** Iowa 42.00N 93.18W
12 K5 **Colo** *R* New S Wales
81 M3 **Colobraro Italy** 40.12N 16.26E
79 K4 **Cologna Veneta Italy** 45.19N 11.23E
72 F8 **Cologne France** 43.44N 0.59E
108 R5 **Cologne** Minnesota 44.46N 93.44W
103 E7 **Cologne** New Jersey 39.30N 74.37W
Cologne W Germany *see* **Köln**
79 G3 **Cologno al Sério Italy** 45.35N 9.42E
79 F7 **Cologno Monzese** *dist* Milan **Italy**
87 J9 **Colole Bar Somalia** 2.00N 43.35E
106 H7 **Coloma** Michigan 42.12N 86.18W
106 E5 **Coloma** Wisconsin 44.03N 89.32W
71 L9 **Colomars France** 43.46N 7.12E
70 K3 **Colombelles France** 49.12N 0.17W
68 D2 **Colombes France** 48.55N 2.14E
69 K6 **Colombey-les-Belles France** 48.31N 5.55E
69 H7 **Colombey-les-deux-Églises France** 48.13N 4.54E
118 E7 **Colômbia Brazil** 20.11S 48.45W
119 D6 **Colombia Colombia** 3.24N 74.49W
115 K4 **Colombia Mexico** 27.42N 99.45W
117 G1 **Colombia** *rep* **S America**
96 C7 **Colombian Basin Caribbean Sea**
66 A1 **Colombier France** 47.40N 6.14E
66 D4 **Colombier** Neuchâtel **Switz** 46.58N 6.53E
66 B5 **Colombier** Vaud **Switz** 46.34N 6.29E
99 N4 **Colombière** Quebec 48.05N 77.35W
72 J7 **Colombiès France** 44.21N 2.20E
79 H3 **Colombine Monte Italy** 45.51N 10.22E
26 Q8 **Colombo Sri Lanka** 6.55N 79.52E
70 G3 **Colomby France** 49.27N 1.30W
108 L6 **Colome** S Dakota 43.15N 99.41W
77 J6 **Colomera Spain** 37.22N 3.42W
77 J6 **Colomera** *R* **Spain**
77 Y14 **Colom, I** Balearic Is 39.58N 4.16E
72 G8 **Colomiers France** 43.37N 1.20E
115 P11 **Colomoncagua Honduras** 13.54N 88.12W
121 F4 **Colón** Entre Ríos **Arg** 32.10S 58.16W
106 J8 **Colon** Michigan 41.58N 85.18W
115 E9 **Colón Panama** 9.21N 79.54W
120 D4 **Colón Peru** 11.56S 71.16W
121 E4 **Colón** Santa Fé **Arg** 33.55S 61.05W
119 D3 **Colón Venezuela** 8.02N 72.17W
12 B4 **Colona** S Australia 31.39S 132.04E
Colón, Arch. de *see* **Galápagos Is**
119 B8 **Colonche, Cord. de** *mts* **Ecuador**
Colon-Ecuador Ridge *see* **Carnegie Ridge**
30 E5 **Colonelganj** Uttar Prad **India** 27.07N 81.42E
116 G3 **Colonel Hill** Crooked I **Bahamas** 22.50N 74.21W
115 A2 **Colonet, C Mexico** 30.58N 116.20W
121 F5 **Colonia** *dept* **Uruguay**
121 D7 **Colonia Choele Choel I Argentina**
121 F5 **Colonia del Sacramento Uruguay** 34.29S 57.48W
115 F2 **Colonia Díaz Mexico** 31.14N 107.59W
121 E2 **Colonia Dora Argentina** 28.34S 62.59W
118 B10 **Colonia Elisa Argentina** 26.55S 59.31W
121 D7 **Colonia Josefa Argentina** 39.44S 65.28W
121 K6 **Colonia Las Heras Argentina** 46.30S 68.59W
121 F3 **Colonia Lavelleja Uruguay** 31.10S 57.02W
104 J8 **Colonial Beach** Virginia 38.16N 76.59W
104 H9 **Colonial Heights** Virginia 37.15N 77.25W
11 C4 **Colonial Knob** *mt* **New Zealand** 41.09S 174.48E
104 J9 **Colonial Nat. Hist. Park** Virginia
118 H4 **Colônia, R Brazil**
77 V15 **Colonia Sant Jordi** Balearic Is 39.20N 3.00E
121 F5 **Colonia Suiza Uruguay** 34.22S 57.10W
121 C5 **Colonia Urdaniz Argentina** 35.10S 66.04W
119 A3 **Colón, I. de Panama** 9.27N 82.25W
115 M2 **Colón, Montañas de** *ra* **Honduras**
81 O5 **Colonne, C. delle Italy** 39.02N 17.13E
80 J3 **Colonnella Italy** 42.52N 13.52E
81 A5 **Colonne, Pta. delle** Sardinia 39.05N 8.16E
66 N8 **Colonno Italy** 45.58N 9.10E
100 M7 **Colonsay** Saskatchewan 51.59N 105.52W
58 D6 **Colonsay** *isld* Strathclyde **Scotland** 56.05N 6.10W
109 P3 **Colony** Kansas 38.04N 95.23W
103 B7 **Colora** Maryland 39.41N 76.06W
120 E10 **Colorada, L Bolivia**
119 G3 **Coloradito Venezuela** 8.45N 63.30W
115 J7 **Colorado Mexico** 20.38N 100.15W
121 C2 **Colorado** *R* Catamarca **Argentina**
121 B5 **Colorado** *R* **Chile**
102 D3 **Colorado** *R* Colorado etc
102 G4 **Colorado** *R* Texas
102 E3 **Colorado** *state* **U.S.A.**
111 J10 **Colorado, Cerro** *mt* **Mexico** 31.30N 115.32W
112 G3 **Colorado City** Texas 32.24N 100.51W
121 E7 **Colorado, Delta del R Arg**
111 H8 **Colorado Des** California
121 D7 **Colorado Grande, L Argentina**
121 C10 **Colorado, L Argentina**
109 B2 **Colorado Nat. Mon** Colorado 39.03N 108.43W
111 M5 **Colorado Plat** Colorado etc
120 G5 **Colorado, R Brazil**
121 D7 **Colorado, R** La Pampa **Arg**
115 B1 **Colorado, R Mexico**
121 B3 **Colorado, R** San Juan **Argentina**
120 E12 **Colorados, Cerro** *pk* **Arg/Chile** 26.10S 68.22W
109 F3 **Colorado Springs** Colorado 38.50N 104.50W
79 H5 **Colorno Italy** 44.56N 10.22E
76 C13 **Colos Portugal** 37.44N 8.28W
76 C10 **Colos** *mt* **Portugal** 39.21N 8.05W
Colossae *see* **Honaz**
71 J9 **Colostre** *R* **France**
115 L10 **Colotepec Mexico** 15.52N 96.59W
115 H6 **Colotlán Mexico** 22.08N 103.15W
36 E4 **Çölovası Turkey** 38.18N 30.22E
70 E6 **Colpo France** 47.49N 2.48W
99 K8 **Colpoys B** Ontario
58 L4 **Colpy** Grampian **Scotland** 57.23N 2.36W
120 E8 **Colquechaca Bolivia** 18.40S 66.00W
120 E7 **Colquiri Bolivia** 17.22S 67.08W
105 C6 **Colquitt** Georgia 31.11N 84.43W
56 K2 **Colsterworth** Lincs **Eng** 52.48N 0.37W
108 D4 **Colstrip** Montana 45.52N 106.38W
112 D8 **Coltexo** Texas 35.28N 100.46W
56 O2 **Coltishall** Norfolk **Eng** 52.44N 1.22E
111 G7 **Colton** California 34.05N 117.20W
104 J8 **Colton** Maryland 38.14N 76.46W
104 L2 **Colton** New York 44.33N 74.56W
108 O6 **Colton** S Dakota 43.47N 96.54W
111 N2 **Colton** Utah 39.51N 111.00W
110 H3 **Colton** Washington 46.36N 117.08W
103 F6 **Colts Neck** New Jersey 40.17N 74.11W
77 O5 **Columbares** *mt* **Spain** 37.55N 1.01W
107 L10 **Columbia** Alabama 31.18N 85.08W
103 K3 **Columbia** Connecticut 41.43N 72.18W
105 E7 **Columbia** Florida 30.04N 82.42W
107 F3 **Columbia** Illinois 38.26N 90.11W
107 L4 **Columbia** Kentucky 37.05N 85.19W
107 D9 **Columbia** Louisiana 32.05N 92.04W
103 A8 **Columbia** Maryland 39.13N 76.51W
107 G10 **Columbia** Mississippi 31.14N 89.51W
107 D3 **Columbia** Missouri 38.58N 92.20W
105 L2 **Columbia** N Carolina 35.55N 76.15W
103 D5 **Columbia** New Jersey 40.56N 75.06W
104 J6 **Columbia** Pennsylvania 40.02N 76.30W
105 G4 **Columbia** S Carolina 34.00N 81.00W
108 M4 **Columbia** S Dakota 45.38N 98.19W
107 J6 **Columbia** Tennessee 35.37N 87.02W
104 G9 **Columbia** Virginia 37.45N 78.10W
103 G2 **Columbia** *co* New York
103 A4 **Columbia** *co* Pennsylvania
110 E4 **Columbia** *R* Wash/Oregon
110 F2 **Columbia Basin** Washington
97 M1 **Columbia, C** N W Terr 83.10N 70.30W
106 J8 **Columbia City** Indiana 41.09N 85.29W
104 M8 **Columbia, District of U.S.A.**
104 S2 **Columbia Falls** Maine 44.41N 67.44W
110 L1 **Columbia Falls** Montana 48.24N 114.11W
113 O6 **Columbia Glacier** Alaska
101 Q10 **Columbia Lake** Br Columbia 50.15N 115.51W
101 P9 **Columbia, Mt** Alberta/Br Col 52.09N 117.25W
97 G7 **Columbia Mts** Br Col
107 K8 **Columbiana** Alabama 33.11N 86.37W
104 E6 **Columbiana** Ohio 40.53N 80.40W
101 P10 **Columbia, R** Br Col/Washington
110 E2 **Columbia River** Washington 47.16N 120.05W
108 M4 **Columbia Road Res** S Dakota 45.45N 98.15W
115 B3 **Columbia, Sa., range Mexico**
103 G2 **Columbiaville** New York 42.19N 73.45W
109 D1 **Columbine** Colorado 40.53N 106.57W
108 D6 **Columbine** Wyoming 43.22N 106.19W
95 A8 **Columbine, C S Africa** 32.50S 17.51E
75 M8 **Columbrete Grande, I Spain** 39.53N 0.41E
75 M8 **Columbretes, Is Spain**
13 J6 **Columbria** Queensland 22.54S 149.18E
105 C5 **Columbus** Georgia 32.28N 84.59W
107 L2 **Columbus** Indiana 39.12N 85.57W
109 Q4 **Columbus** Kansas 37.09N 94.52W
107 H8 **Columbus** Mississippi 33.30N 88.27W
110 Q4 **Columbus** Montana 45.08N 109.16W
108 H1 **Columbus** N Dakota 48.55N 102.46W
108 N8 **Columbus** Nebraska 41.27N 97.21W
103 E6 **Columbus** New Jersey 40.05N 74.44W
109 C10 **Columbus** New Mexico 31.50N 107.40W
104 B7 **Columbus** Ohio 39.59N 83.03W
112 L6 **Columbus** Texas 29.42N 96.35W
106 E6 **Columbus** Wisconsin 43.20N 89.02W
116 G4 **Columbus Bank Bahamas**
104 A6 **Columbus Grove** Ohio 40.56N 84.04W
106 C8 **Columbus Junc** Iowa 41.15N 91.22W
116 A2 **Columbus Mon** San Salvador I **Bahamas** 24.04N 74.26W
116 G2 **Columbus Pt** Cat I **Bahamas** 24.09N 75.16W
116 M1 **Columbus Pt** Tobago **W I** 11.08N 60.48W
76 J2 **Colunga Spain** 43.29N 5.16W
120 D10 **Colupo, Cerro** *pk* **Chile** 22.26S 69.59W
111 B2 **Colusa** California 39.11N 122.00W
104 G6 **Colver** Pennsylvania 40.33N 78.48W
11 K3 **Colville New Zealand** 36.38S 175.32E
110 H1 **Colville** Washington 48.33N 117.55W
113 L2 **Colville** *R* Alaska
110 H1 **Colville** *R* Washington
11 K3 **Colville B New Zealand**
11 K3 **Colville, C New Zealand** 36.29S 175.21E
11 K3 **Colville Chan New Zealand**
101 L2 **Colville L** N W Terr
14 F8 **Colville, Lake** W Australia 29.35S 126.32E
101 Q1 **Colville Mts** Victoria I, N W Terr
10 Q8 **Colville Ridge Pacific Oc**
108 S6 **Colwell** Iowa 43.08N 92.35W
56 H2 **Colwich** Staffs **Eng** 52.47N 1.58W
57 F6 **Colwyn Bay** Clwyd **Wales** 53.18N 3.43W
72 G5 **Coly France** 45.05N 1.16E
56 E6 **Colyford** Devon **Eng** 50.44N 3.05W
66 L8 **Comabbio Italy** 45.47N 8.41E
24 G11 **Comai** Xizang Zizhiqu **China** 28.28N 09.133
18 H9 **Comal** *R* Java **Indon**
115 O10 **Comalapa Guatemala** 14.43N 90.51W
115 M3 **Comalapa Nicaragua** 12.15N 85.30W
115 N8 **Comalcalco Mexico** 18.16N 93.10W
121 B8 **Comallo** *R* **Argentina**
82 K6 **Comana Romania** 44.10N 26.10E
36 J2 **Comana** *anc site* **Turkey** 40.22N 36.36E
109 N7 **Comanche** Oklahoma 34.23N 97.58W
112 J4 **Comanche** Texas 31.55N 98.36W
117 C5 **Comandai, I. do Brazil**
118 B9 **Comandante Fontana Argentina** 25.19S 59.42W
121 C4 **Comandante Salas Argentina** 33.56S 68.01W
82 K4 **Comănești Romania** 46.25N 26.29E
79 J2 **Cománo Italy** 46.02N 10.58E
75 N2 **Coma Pedrosa** *mt* **Andorra** 42.35N 1.26E
120 F7 **Comarapa Bolivia** 17.53S 64.30W
77 H7 **Comares Spain** 36.51N 4.15W
115 L2 **Comayagua Honduras** 14.30N 87.39W
105 G5 **Combahee, R** S Carolina
66 E6 **Comballaz Switzerland** 46.23N 7.06E
121 B3 **Combarbalá Chile** 31.15S 71.03W
76 G3 **Combarros Spain** 42.32N 6.10W
71 H1 **Combeaufontaine France** 47.43N 5.53E
56 C5 **Combe Martin** Devon **Eng** 51.13N 4.02W
59 L2 **Comber** Down **N Ireland** 54.33N 5.45W
99 H10 **Comber** Ontario 42.14N 82.33W
99 N7 **Combermere** Ontario 45.22N 77.37W
25 B3 **Combermere B Burma**
112 K9 **Combes** Texas 26.17N 97.45W
66 F8 **Combin de Corbassière** *mt* **Switzerland** 45.59N 7.17E
66 F8 **Combin, Grand** *mt* **Switzerland** 45.57N 7.18E
61 N5 **Comblain-au-Pont Belgium** 50.28N 5.35E
61 N5 **Comblain-Fairon Belgium** 50.27N 5.33E
69 D3 **Combles France** 50.00N 2.52E
66 C8 **Combloux France** 45.54N 6.38E
87 H7 **Combolchia Ethiopia** 7.32N 41.11E
79 H2 **Cómbolo, Monte** *mt* **Italy** 46.13N 10.02E
94 M4 **Combomune Mozambique** 23.27S 32.26E
70 G5 **Combourg France** 48.25N 1.45W
12 K4 **Comboyne** New S Wales 31.35S 152.27E
66 D4 **Combremont-le-Grand Switz** 46.46N 6.48E
70 N5 **Combres France** 48.20N 1.05E
72 J5 **Combressol France** 45.28N 2.08E
70 B6 **Combrit France** 47.53N 4.09W
71 C5 **Combronde France** 45.59N 3.05E
104 B9 **Combs** Kentucky 37.14N 83.15W
68 H6 **Combs-la-Ville France** 48.40N 2.34E
12 J4 **Come-by-Chance** New S Wales 30.22E 148.31E
121 D4 **Comechingones, Sa. de** *ra* **Arg**
79 N1 **Comeglians Italy** 46.31N 12.52E
79 N1 **Comelico Superiore Italy** 46.35N 12.31E
76 D10 **Comenda Portugal** 39.24N 7.47W
118 E6 **Comendador Gomes Brazil** 19.44S 49.03W
118 F6 **Comendador Viana Brazil** 19.27S 45.52W
107 L9 **Comer** Alabama 32.02N 85.23W
105 D3 **Comer** Georgia 34.03N 83.09W
59 G7 **Comeragh Mts** Waterford **Irish Rep**
118 H5 **Comercinho Brazil** 16.22S 41.52W
105 J7 **Comerio** Puerto Rico 18.14N 66.12W
108 F1 **Comertown** Montana 48.55N 104.16W
13 J6 **Comet** Queensland 23.35S 148.32E
13 J6 **Comet** *R* Queensland
13 J6 **Comet Downs** Queensland 23.52S 148.31E
94 N3 **Cometela Mozambique** 21.51S 34.29E
14 D8 **Comet Vale** W Australia 29.57S 121.05E
112 J6 **Comfort** Texas 29.58N 98.56W
116 M2 **Comfort Castle Jamaica, W I** 18.03N 76.25W
108 Q5 **Comfrey** Minnesota 44.08N 94.54W
31 J9 **Comilla Bangladesh** 23.28N 91.10E
31 H9 **Comilla** *dist* **Bangladesh**
76 L2 **Comillas Spain** 43.23N 4.17W
61 B3 **Comines Belgium** 50.46N 3.00E
69 E2 **Comines France** 50.46N 3.00E
84 Y19 **Comino** *isld* **Mediterranean Sea**
81 D2 **Comino, C** Sardinia 40.32N 9.50E
84 X19 **Comino Chan., N Medit Sea**
84 X20 **Comino Chan., S Medit Sea**
84 X19 **Cominotto, I Medit Sea** 36.01N 14.19E
106 K5 **Comins** Michigan 44.48N 84.03W
81 J10 **Comiso** Sicily 36.57N 14.37E
115 N9 **Comitán de Domínguez Mexico** 16.18N 92.09W
81 G9 **Comitini** Sicily 37.25N 13.39E
79 M5 **Commacchio Italy** 44.42N 12.11E
70 C5 **Commana France** 48.25N 3.57W
99 L7 **Commanda** Ontario 45.57N 79.36W
71 G3 **Commenailles France** 46.47N 5.28E
72 C7 **Commensacq France** 44.13N 0.48W
72 K3 **Commentry France** 46.17N 2.43E
72 A2 **Commequiers France** 46.46N 1.51W
70 J5 **Commer France** 48.13N 0.36W
105 D3 **Commerce** Georgia 34.12N 83.29W
109 Q5 **Commerce** Oklahoma 36.56N 94.54W
112 M2 **Commerce** Texas 33.15N 95.54W
109 F2 **Commerce City** Colorado 39.50N 104.56W
69 K6 **Commercy France** 48.46N 5.36E
79 J4 **Commessággio Italy** 45.02N 10.32E
117 B2 **Commewijne** *dist* **Surinam**
72 F9 **Comminges** *reg* **France**
99 S4 **Commissaires, L. des** Quebec
96 B1 **Commissioner's Pt** Bermuda 32.20N 64.51W
97 L4 **Committee B** N W Terr
95 K9 **Committees S Africa** 33.10S 26.50E
15 L6 **Commodore B** New Britain
12 M5 **Commodore Heights** New S Wales 33.35S 151.18E
95 O3 **Commondale S Africa** 27.17S 30.54E
123 J3 **Commonwealth B Antarctica**
12 C3 **Commonwealth Hill** S Australia 29.57S 133.55E
123 G7 **Commonwealth Ra** *mts* **Antarctica**
109 E2 **Como** Colorado 39.19N 105.56W
79 F3 **Como Italy** 45.48N 9.05E
107 G7 **Como** Mississippi 34.31N 89.58W
12 L8 **Como** New S Wales 34.00S 151.04E
79 F3 **Como** *prov* **Italy**
121 L5 **Comodoro Rivadavia Argentina** 45.50S 67.30W
79 F3 **Como, L. di** *L* **Italy**
66 L7 **Comologno Switzerland** 46.13N 8.35E
92 J8 **Comomba Mozambique** 12.04S 39.16E
115 D4 **Comondú Mexico** 26.02N 111.49W
115 J7 **Comonfort Mexico** 20.48N 100.46W
28 C6 **Comorin, C** Tamil Nadu **India** 8.04N 77.35E
95 A1 **Comoro Is** *rep* **Indian Oc**
26 D6 **Comoro Ridge Indian Ocean**
71 B6 **Compains France** 45.26N 2.56E
91 B1 **Company Cameroon** 5.13N 10.06E
103 C6 **Compass** Pennsylvania 40.02N 75.56W
100 G7 **Compeer** Alberta 51.51N 110.02W
77 J7 **Cómpeta Spain** 36.50N 3.58W
69 D5 **Compiègne France** 49.25N 2.50E
69 D5 **Compiègne, Forêt de France**
72 J7 **Compolibat France** 44.23N 2.07E
76 B12 **Comporta Portugal** 38.22N 8.46W
115 G7 **Compostela Mexico** 21.12N 104.52W
19 N8 **Compostela** Mindanao **Philippines** 7.40N 126.01E
72 G4 **Compreignac France** 46.00N 1.17E
118 J10 **Comprida, I** Rio de Janeiro **Brazil** 23.03S 43.13W
118 F9 **Comprida, I** São Paulo **Brazil**
71 K9 **Comps-sur-Artuby France** 43.43N 6.31E
111 A2 **Comptche** California 39.16N 123.36W
111 F8 **Compton** California 33.55N 118.14W
106 E8 **Compton** Illinois 41.41N 89.06W
58 J6 **Comrie** Tayside **Scotland** 56.23N 4.00W
104 M3 **Comstock** New York 43.27N 73.29W
112 F6 **Comstock** Texas 29.40N 101.11W
117 C2 **Comté** *R* **Fr Guiana**
80 H3 **Comunanza Italy** 42.57N 13.25E
120 D5 **Comunidad Peru** 13.59S 69.21W
79 M4 **Cona Italy** 45.11N 12.02E
24 G12 **Cona** Xizang Zizhiqu **China** 27.59N 91.54E
24 G9 **Co Nag** *L* Xizang Zizhiqu **China** 32.00N 91.15E
89 C7 **Conakry Guinea** 9.30N 13.43W
121 C9 **Cona, L Argentina**
119 C8 **Conambo Ecuador** 1.55S 76.51W
119 C9 **Conambo, R Ecuador**
103 M3 **Conanicut I** Rhode I
121 C8 **Cona Niyeo Argentina** 41.50S 67.10W
12 H8 **Conara Junction** Tasmania 41.48S 147.30E
105 C3 **Conasauga, R** Georgia
108 H6 **Conata** S Dakota 43.45N 102.10W
121 B2 **Conay Chile** 28.56S 70.10W
67 P13 **Conca** Corsica 41.44N 9.20E
79 N7 **Conca** *R* **Italy**
80 H4 **Conca del Fucino Italy**
112 H6 **Concan** Texas 29.29N 99.44W
121 D4 **Concarán Argentina** 32.34S 65.15W
70 C6 **Concarneau France** 47.53N 3.55W
81 D2 **Concas** Sardinia 40.39N 9.34E
119 H9 **Conceição** Amazonas **Brazil** 3.05S 61.07W
119 H6 **Conceiçao Brazil** 2.10N 60.55W
117 A8 **Conceição** Mato Grosso **Brazil** 7.21S 58.08W
94 O2 **Conceição Mozambique** 18.47S 36.08E
117 H8 **Conceição** Paraíba **Brazil** 7.30S 38.28W
76 C13 **Conceição Portugal** 37.47N 8.14W
76 D14 **Conceição Portugal** 37.08N 7.36W
120 G4 **Conceição** Rondônia **Brazil** 10.19S 61.52W
118 F5 **Conceição** *R* **Brazil**
118 H6 **Conceição da Barra Brazil** 18.36S 39.46W
118 E6 **Conceição das Alagoas Brazil** 19.55S 48.22W
117 D9 **Conceição do Araguaia Brazil** 8.15S 49.15W
118 H2 **Conceição do Coité Brazil** 11.37S 39.14W
118 G6 **Conceição do Mato Dentro Brazil** 19.06S 43.22W

119 B7 **Esmeraldas, R** Ecuador
120 E5 **Esmeraldo, R** Bolivia
108 L1 **Esmond** N Dakota 48.03N 99.45W
108 N5 **Esmond** S Dakota 44.15N 97.44W
76 B7 **Esmoriz** Portugal 40.57N 8.38W
99 D2 **Esnagami** *R* Ontario
99 D2 **Esnagami L** Ontario 50.19N 86.50W
99 F4 **Esnagi L** Ontario
69 E3 **Esnes** Nord France 50.07N 3.18E
69 J5 **Esnes-en-Argonne** Meuse France 49.12N 5.13E
61 N4 **Esneux** Belgium 50.32N 5.34E
103 G3 **Esopus** New York 41.49N 73.57W
91 G2 **Esoumba, I** Zaïre 2.00N 21.15E
52 F6 **Espa** Norway 60.35N 11.17E
75 K8 **Espadán** *mt* Spain 39.54N 0.24W
76 G6 **Espadaña** Spain 41.04N 6.18W
76 G4 **Espadañedo** Spain 42.06N 6.25W
75 K8 **Espadán, Sierra de** *mts* Spain
119 E1 **Espada, Pta** Colombia 12.08N 71.08W
75 K7 **Espadilla** Spain 40.02N 0.22W
32 J7 **Espakeh** Iran 26.53N 60.12E
Espalha, R *see* **São Francisco, R** Acre Brazil
72 K6 **Espalion** France 44.32N 2.46E
77 S12 **Espalmador, I** Balearic Is 38.48N 1.26E
71 D6 **Espaly, St. Marcel** France 45.03N 3.52E
105 F8 **Espanola** Florida 29.31N 81.20W
109 D6 **Española** New Mexico 35.59N 106.05W
99 J6 **Espanola** Ontario 46.15N 81.46W
119 B6 **Española** *isld* Galápagos Is 1.27S 89.40W
77 S12 **Espardell, I** Balearic Is 38.48N 1.30E
77 D3 **Esparragalejo** Spain 38.57N 6.27W
77 E3 **Esparragosa de la Serena** Spain 38.39N 5.35W
77 F3 **Esparragosa del Caudillo** Spain 38.58N 5.15W
75 O4 **Esparraguera** Spain 41.33N 1.52E
71 H9 **Esparron** France 43.35N 5.51E
72 E9 **Esparros** France 43.02N 0.19E
115 Q10 **Esparta** Honduras 15.44N 87.12W
77 F6 **Esparteros** *mt* Spain 37.05N 5.29W
77 D6 **Espartinas** Spain 37.23N 6.07W
111 B3 **Esparto** California 38.40N 122.03W
77 S12 **Esparto, I** Balearic Is 38.57N 1.12E
115 M5 **Esparza** Costa Rica 9.59N 84.40W
75 H2 **Esparza** Spain 42.51N 1.05W
76 D1 **Espasante** Spain 43.43N 7.47W
53 E6 **Espe** Denmark 55.12N 10.25E
43 L5 **Espe** Kazakhstan U.S.S.R. 43.50N 74.10E
53 V18 **Espe** Norway 60.12N 6.36E
52 E5 **Espedalsvatn** *L* Norway 61.25N 9.35E
76 F7 **Espeja** Spain 40.34N 6.44W
77 G5 **Espejo** Spain 37.40N 4.34W
119 D7 **Espejo, L** Colombia 1.11N 72.18W
60 L9 **Espel** Netherlands 52.44N 5.39E
53 S18 **Espeland** Norway 60.23N 5.28E
72 B9 **Espelette** France 43.20N 1.26W
63 J8 **Espelkamp** W Germany 52.23N 8.36E
71 F7 **Espeluche** France 44.31N 4.49E
77 J4 **Espelúy** Spain 38.02N 3.51W
113 E3 **Espenberg, C** Alaska 66.34N 163.40W
64 N1 **Espenhain** E Germany 51.11N 12.29E
77 E7 **Espera** Spain 36.53N 5.48W
92 H8 **Esperança** Mozambique 13.30S 36.06E
14 D10 **Esperance** W Australia 33.49S 121.52E
14 D10 **Esperance B** W Australia
11 M3 **Espérance Rock, L'** Kermadec Is Pacific Oc 31.26S 178.54W
117 F6 **Esperantina** Brazil 3.53S 42.18W
117 F7 **Esperantinópolis** Brazil 4.55S 44.55W
115 E4 **Esperanza** Mexico 27.32N 109.55W
120 D3 **Esperanza** Peru 9.44S 70.49W
19 M6 **Esperanza** Philippines 11.44N 124.04E
95 O6 **Esperanza** S Africa 30.20S 30.40E
121 K8 **Esperanza** Santa Cruz Arg 51.05S 70.45W
121 E3 **Esperanza** Santa Fé Arg 31.29S 61.00W
112 B4 **Esperanza** Texas 31.08N 105.43W
123 D14 **Esperanza** *Arg Base* Graham Land Antarctica 63.24S 57.00W
121 J8 **Esperanza, I** Chile 51.05S 74.15W
96 R3 **Esperanza, Pico da** *mt* Azores 38.39N 28.05W
112 F8 **Esperanzas** Mexico 27.44N 101.22W
115 M2 **Esperanza, Sa. de la** *ra* Honduras
72 J10 **Espéraza** France 42.56N 2.13E
53 K5 **Espergærde** Denmark 55.59N 12.35E
80 J6 **Espéria** Italy 41.23N 13.41E
53 S19 **Espevær** *Lt Ho* Norway 59.36N 5.09E
53 T20 **Espevik** Norway 59.20N 5.42E
72 J10 **Espezel** France 42.49N 2.01E
76 A12 **Espichel, C. de** *Lt Ho* Portugal 38.24N 9.13W
77 F4 **Espiel** Spain 38.11N 5.01W
118 E10 **Espigão, Serra do** *mts* Brazil
76 K3 **Espigüete** *mt* Spain 42.56N 4.48W
71 E10 **Espiguette, Pte. de l'** France 43.29N 4.08E
75 L6 **Espina** *mt* Spain 40.52N 0.21E
119 D5 **Espinal** Colombia 4.08N 74.53W
76 G2 **Espina, La** Spain 43.24N 6.20W
76 K2 **Espinama** Spain 43.09N 4.47W
Espinar *see* **Yauri**
75 B6 **Espinar, El** Spain 40.43N 4.16W
71 J8 **Espinasses** France 44.28N 6.13E
115 J4 **Espinazo** Mexico 26.19N 101.08W
96 P9 **Espindola** La Palma Canary Is 28.48N 17.45W
76 B14 **Espinhaço de Cão** Portugal
76 B14 **Espinhaço de Cão, Sa de** *mts* Portugal
118 G6 **Espinhaço, Serra do** *mts* Brazil
76 C8 **Espinhal** Portugal 40.00N 8.20W
76 B6 **Espinho** Portugal 41.01N 8.38W
121 G2 **Espinilho, Serra do** *ra* Brazil
76 L2 **Espinilla** Spain 43.00N 4.14W
119 F3 **Espino** Venezuela 8.38S 66.01W
118 G4 **Espinosa** Brazil 14.58S 42.49W
75 C4 **Espinosa de Cerrato** Spain 41.58N 3.57W
75 D6 **Espinosa de Henares** Spain 40.54N 3.04W
75 C1 **Espinosa de los Monteros** Spain 43.05N 3.34W
76 L4 **Espinosa de Villagonzalo** Spain 42.28N 4.22W
76 K9 **Espinoso del Rey** Spain 39.39N 4.47W
71 B9 **Espinouse, Mts. de l'** France
37 J8 **Espir** *isld* Iran 37.30N 45.28E
72 K10 **Espira-de-l'Agly** France 42.47N 2.50E
Espírito Santo Brazil *see* **Vila Velha**
76 D13 **Espirito Santo** Portugal 37.32N 7.39W
120 G4 **Espírito Santo** Rondônia Brazil 10.05S 62.35W
118 H6 **Espírito Santo** *state* Brazil
19 K3 **Espiritu** Luzon Philippines 17.59N 120.32E
120 F7 **Espiritu Santo** Bolivia 17.05S 65.39W
115 D5 **Espíritu Santo** *I* Mexico
115 Q8 **Espíritu Santo, B. del** Mexico
121 L9 **Espíritu Santo, C** Argentina 52.40S 68.32W
19 M5 **Espiritu Santo, C** Philippines 12.35N 125.10E
9 B10 **Espíritu Santo I** New Hebrides
115 P7 **Espita** Mexico 21.00N 88.18W
76 B9 **Espite** Portugal 39.46N 8.39W
37 D5 **Espiye** Turkey 40.57N 38.43E
118 J2 **Esplanada** Brazil 11.49S 37.56W
61 D4 **Esplechin** Belgium 50.34N 3.18E
75 N5 **Espluga de Francolí** Spain 41.24N 1.07E
75 L4 **Esplús** Spain 41.47N 0.16E
98 R6 **Espoir, B. de** Newfoundland
75 Q3 **Espolla** Spain 42.23N 3.00E
51 L11 **Espoo** Finland 60.10N 24.42E
77 V14 **Esporlas** Balearic Is 39.40N 2.35E
76 C5 **Esporões** Portugal 41.31N 8.25W
76 B5 **Esposende** Portugal 41.32N 8.47W
75 N2 **Espot** Spain 42.34N 1.05E
71 J1 **Esprels** France 47.32N 6.22E
77 N5 **Espuña** *mt* Spain 37.51N 1.35W
77 N5 **Espuña, Sierra de** *mts* Spain
92 F12 **Espungabera** Mozambique 20.29S 32.48E
103 B4 **Espy** Pennsylvania 41.00N 76.25W
110 F3 **Esquatzel Coulee** *R* Washington
115 E2 **Esqueda** Mexico 30.41N 109.34W
121 B9 **Esquel** Argentina 42.55S 71.20W
69 C2 **Esquelbecq** France 50.53N 2.26E
80 E7 **Esquilino, Monte** *hill* Roma Italy
110 B1 **Esquimalt** Vancouver I, Br Col 48.26N 123.27W
121 F2 **Esquina** Argentina 30.00S 59.30W
96 T9 **Esquinza, Pta de** *pt* Fuerteventura Canary Is 28.36N 14.03W
115 P10 **Esquipulas** Guatemala 14.36N 89.22W
115 M3 **Esquipulas** Nicaragua 12.30N 85.55W
51 H3 **Esrange** *reg* Sweden
53 J4 **Esrum Sø** *L* Denmark 56.00N 12.25E
93 K1 **Ess** *mt* Ethiopia 4.30N 38.44E
47 J5 **Ess** *R* U.S.S.R.
89 J3 **Essaloua** *watercourse* Mali
88 J6 **Essaouira** Morocco 31.30N 9.48W
71 G3 **Essards-Taignevaux, les** France 46.55N 5.25E
69 B6 **Essarts-le-Roi, les** France 48.43N 1.55E
72 B2 **Essarts, les** Vendée France 46.47N 1.14W
70 L4 **Essay** France 48.33N 0.14E
91 B1 **Essé** Cameroon 4.01N 11.57E
51 K8 **Esse** Finland 63.36N 23.04E
88 O5 **Es Seggeur** *watercourse* Algeria
88 T4 **Es-Sekhira** Tunisia 34.16N 10.03E
63 L7 **Essel** W Germany 52.42N 9.39E
61 H1 **Essen** Belgium 51.28N 4.28E
63 G7 **Essen** Niedersachsen W Germany 52.43N 7.56E
63 E10 **Essen** Nordrhein-Westfalen W Germany 51.27N 6.57E
64 N6 **Essenbach** W Germany 48.37N 12.13E
12 C7 **Essendon** *dist* Melbourne, Vic
12 C7 **Essendon Airport** Melbourne, Vic 37.44S 144.55E
14 D6 **Essendon, Mt** W Australia 24.59S 120.29E
61 G3 **Essene** Belgium 50.54N 4.08E
117 A2 **Essequibo** *co* Guyana
117 A2 **Essequibo** *R* Guyana
71 G2 **Essertenne-et-Cecey** France 47.24N 5.29E
66 D5 **Essertes** Switzerland 46.34N 6.47E
66 C5 **Essertines** Switzerland 46.43N 6.38E
111 J7 **Essex** California 34.45N 115.15W
103 K4 **Essex** Connecticut 41.21N 72.23W
108 P9 **Essex** Iowa 40.50N 95.20W
103 B8 **Essex** Maryland 39.18N 76.27W
110 M1 **Essex** Montana 48.19N 113.37W
104 M2 **Essex** New York 44.18N 73.23W
99 H10 **Essex** Ontario 42.10N 82.50W
95 L7 **Essex** S Africa 31.59S 27.00E
56 M4 **Essex** *co* England
103 F5 **Essex** *co* New Jersey
104 M2 **Essex Junction** Vermont 44.30N 73.06W
119 A6 **Essex, Pta** *pt* Galápagos Is 1.00S 91.27W
92 D12 **Essexvale** Zimbabwe 20.21S 29.01E
106 L6 **Essexville** Michigan 43.39N 83.50W
69 L7 **Essey, Côte d'** *mt* France 48.25N 6.29E
69 K6 **Essey-et-Maizerais** France 48.55N 5.49E
64 M6 **Essing** W Germany 48.56N 11.49E
64 J6 **Essingen** W Germany 48.49N 10.02E
69 E6 **Essises** France 48.58N 3.26E
66 L2 **Esslingen** Switzerland 47.17N 8.43E
64 G6 **Esslingen am Neckar** W Germany 48.45N 9.19E
39 F6 **Esso** U.S.S.R. 55.58N 158.38E
69 E5 **Essômes-sur-Marne** France 49.02N 3.23E
69 C6 **Essonne** *dept* France
69 C7 **Essonne** *R* France
Essonnes *see* **Corbeil-Essonnes**
91 D5 **Essou** Congo 2.18S 15.18E
69 H7 **Essoyes** France 48.03N 4.32E
47 C5 **Essoyla** U.S.S.R. 61.47N 33.11E
60 K12 **Est** Netherlands 51.51N 5.19E
89 H7 **Est** *dept* Ivory Coast
90 F9 **Est** *reg* Cameroon
77 V14 **Establiments** Balearic Is 39.38N 2.36E
110 C4 **Estacada** Oregon 45.18N 122.20W
76 D1 **Estaca de Bares, Pta. de la** *pt* Spain 43.47N 7.41W
Estação *see* **Armação**
111 K10 **Estación Doctor** Mexico 31.57N 114.42W
111 K10 **Estación France** Mexico 31.48N 114.30W
111 K9 **Estación Mèdanos** Mexico 32.03N 114.51W
75 L3 **Estadilla** Spain 42.04N 0.16E
121 M10 **Estados, I. de los** Argentina
12 E3 **Estadunna** S Australia 28.40S 138.35E
72 K10 **Estagel** France 42.46N 2.41E
19 L3 **Estagno Pt** Luzon Philippines 17.19N 122.24E
32 F6 **Eşţahbānāt** Iran 29.05N 54.05E
61 D4 **Estaimbourg** Belgium 50.41N 3.20E
61 D4 **Estaimpuis** Belgium 50.42N 3.16E
72 K6 **Estaing** France 44.34N 2.40E
99 K6 **Estaire** Ontario 46.19N 80.48W
69 D2 **Estaires** France 50.39N 2.44E
77 U14 **Estallenchs** Balearic Is 39.39N 2.29E
75 K5 **Estanca, La** *L* Spain 41.04N 0.12W
118 J2 **Estância** Brazil 11.15S 37.28W
109 D7 **Estancia** New Mexico 34.45N 106.04W
95 N2 **Estancia** S Africa 26.20S 29.53E
121 K9 **Estancia Camerón** Chile 53.38S 69.35W
32 J5 **Estand, Kūh-e-** *mt* Iran 31.17N 60.03E
72 D8 **Estang** France 43.52N 0.06W
77 V15 **Estanyol** Balearic Is 39.22N 2.55E
115 O9 **Estapilla** Mexico 17.35N 91.24W
71 G10 **Estaque, Chaine de l'** France
71 G10 **Estaque, Rade de l'** *B* France 43.20N 5.18E
32 H6 **Estārm** Iran 28.20N 58.21E
76 B7 **Estarreja** Portugal 40.45N 8.35W
75 R3 **Estartit** Spain 42.03N 3.12E
75 R4 **Estartit** Spain 41.56N 3.09E
75 N2 **Estats, Pic d'** *mt* Spain 42.40N 1.23E
66 D4 **Estavayer le lac** Switzerland 46.52N 6.51E
95 E3 **Est, C** Madagascar 15.14S 50.28E
95 N4 **Estcourt** S Africa 29.00S 29.53E
79 L4 **Este** Italy 45.13N 11.40E
76 B6 **Este** *R* Portugal
63 L6 **Este** *R* W Germany
75 J4 **Esteban** *mt* Spain 41.56N 0.57W
120 F10 **Esteban de Urizar** Argentina 23.32S 64.05W
121 E2 **Esteban Rams** Argentina 29.54S 61.30W
77 D6 **Este, Brazo del** *R* Spain
76 A10 **Estelas** *islds* Portugal 39.25N 9.30W
115 L3 **Estelí** Nicaragua 13.04N 86.20W
103 A3 **Estella** Pennsylvania 41.31N 76.38W
76 B6 **Estella** Portugal 41.26N 8.46W
75 F2 **Estella** Spain 42.41N 2.02W
72 K10 **Estelle, Pic de l'** *mt* France 42.30N 2.33E
108 O5 **Estelline** S Dakota 44.34N 96.52W
112 G1 **Estelline** Texas 34.33N 100.26W
103 E8 **Estellville** New Jersey 39.23N 74.45W
76 G10 **Estena** *mt* Spain 39.13N 6.29W
76 K10 **Estena** *R* Spain
76 K10 **Estenilla** *R* Spain
77 G6 **Estepa** Spain 37.17N 4.52W
75 C3 **Estepar** Spain 42.16N 3.54W
77 F8 **Estepona** Spain 36.26N 5.09W
105 L7 **Este, Pta** *pt* Puerto Rico 18.09N 65.19W
113 N4 **Ester** Alaska 64.50N 148.09W
77 G3 **Esteras** *R* Spain
75 F5 **Esteras de Medina** Spain 41.06N 2.26W
108 E7 **Esterbrook** Wyoming 42.28N 105.22W
75 J6 **Estercuel** Spain 40.51N 0.39W
71 K10 **Estérel, l'** *mts* France
72 B9 **Estérençuby** France 43.07N 1.11W
100 P8 **Esterhazy** Saskatchewan 50.40N 102.02W
91 A3 **Esterias, C** Gabon 0.40N 9.20E
69 F6 **Esternay** France 48.44N 3.34E
105 F11 **Estero** Florida 26.26N 81.50W
111 C6 **Estero B** California
105 F11 **Estero B** Florida
71 K9 **Estéron** *R* France
115 K6 **Esteros** Mexico 22.32N 98.08W
118 A8 **Esteros** Paraguay 23.44S 60.59W
75 N2 **Esterri de Aneu** Spain 42.38N 1.07E
63 G6 **Esterwegen** W Germany 53.00N 7.35E
81 C4 **Esterzili** Sardinia 39.47N 9.17E
109 E1 **Estes Park** Colorado 40.24N 105.32W
76 D9 **Esteval** Portugal 39.38N 7.50W
100 P9 **Estevan** Saskatchewan 49.09N 102.59W
101 J9 **Estevan Group** Br Col 53.08N 129.40W
101 K11 **Estevan Point** Vancouver I, Br Col 49.23N 126.32W
100 G7 **Esther** Alberta 51.40N 110.18W
13 C5 **Esther Mt** N Terr Australia 21.55S 133.21E
108 Q6 **Estherville** Iowa 43.28N 94.49W
57 H4 **Esthwaite Water** *L* Lancs Eng 54.22N 2.59W
26 O16 **Est, Î. de l'** Crozet Is Ind Oc 46.27S 52.10E
105 F5 **Estill** S Carolina 32.44N 81.14W
92 F9 **Estima** Mozambique 15.43S 32.46E
61 G5 **Estinnes-au-Mont** Belgium 50.24N 4.06E
61 G5 **Estinnes-au-Val** Belgium 50.25N 4.06E
69 F7 **Estissac** France 48.16N 3.50E
117 F8 **Estiva** *R* Brazil
72 K3 **Estivareilles** France 46.24N 2.37E
75 K8 **Estivella** Spain 39.43N 0.21W
Estiyé *see* **Isriya**
100 N8 **Estlin** Saskatchewan 50.17N 104.35W
76 D14 **Estói** Portugal 37.05N 7.54W
95 K5 **Estoire** S Africa 29.05S 26.16E
117 F8 **Estolado** *R* Brazil
76 K10 **Estomiza** *R* Spain
57 L3 **Eston** Cleveland Eng 54.34N 1.07W
95 O5 **Eston** S Africa 29.53S 30.31E
100 J7 **Eston** Saskatchewan 51.09N 108.42W
Estonia *see* **Estoniya S.S.R**
46 E1 **Estoniya S.S.R** U.S.S.R.
76 A11 **Estoril** Portugal 38.42N 9.23W
76 F9 **Estorninos** Spain 39.45N 6.55W
71 J9 **Estoublon** France 43.56N 6.10E
26 O15 **Est, Pte** *C* St Paul I Ind Oc 38.44S 77.32E
76 C3 **Estrada, La** Spain 42.40N 8.30W
69 C2 **Estrée-Blanche** France 50.35N 2.20E
69 D5 **Estrées-St.Denis** France 49.26N 2.39E
121 H3 **Estreito** Brazil 31.50S 51.45W
76 D9 **Estreito** Portugal 39.57N 7.48W
118 G2 **Estreito, Serra do** *mts* Brazil
121 H2 **Estrela** Brazil 29.32S 51.58W
76 E12 **Estrela** Portugal 38.16N 7.23W
76 D8 **Estrela** *mt* Portugal 40.19N 7.36W
118 F6 **Estrêla do Indaiá** Brazil 19.32S 45.46W
118 F6 **Estrêla do Sul** Brazil 18.45S 47.43W
76 D8 **Estrêla, Serra da** *mts* Portugal
111 M9 **Estrella** Arizona 33.00N 112.25W
77 J4 **Estrella** *mt* Spain 38.25N 3.35W
111 D6 **Estrella** *R* California
15 L2 **Estrella B** Santa Isabel I Solomon Is 7.58S 159.17E
76 J9 **Estrella, La** Spain 39.42N 5.05W
115 B2 **Estrella, Pta** *pt* Mexico 30.58N 114.42W
111 M8 **Estrella, Sierra** *mts* Arizona
120 C3 **Estrema** Acre Brazil 8.09S 72.59W
120 F3 **Estrema** Amazonas Brazil 8.38S 65.40W
76 A11 **Estremadura** *hist reg* Portugal
74 A6 **Estremadura** *prov* Portugal
75 D7 **Estremera** Spain 40.11N 3.07W
76 D11 **Estremoz** Portugal 38.50N 7.35W
120 G7 **Est Rio Grande** Bolivia 17.13S 62.55W
117 D9 **Estrondo.Sa, do** *mts* Brazil
53 E3 **Estruplund** Denmark 56.33N 10.22E
91 A3 **Estuaire** *reg* Gabon
100 H8 **Estuary** Saskatchewan 50.57N 109.52W
32 C3 **Estūh** Iran 34.18N 49.18E
53 B3 **Estvad** Denmark 56.32N 8.59E
90 E8 **Esu** Cameroon 6.36N 10.04E
58 Q9 **Eswick, Moul of** *headland* Shetland Scotland 60.16N 1.06W
62 L8 **Esztergom** Hungary 47.46N 18.42E
70 E4 **Étables** France 48.37N 2.50W
72 F4 **Étagnac** France 45.54N 0.47E
48 R2 **Etah** Greenland 78.15N 72.00W
30 B5 **Etah** Uttar Prad India 27.33N 78.39E
30 B5 **Etah** *dist* Uttar Prad India
69 K5 **Étain** France 49.13N 5.38E
71 C1 **Étais-la-Sauvin** France 47.31N 3.21E
58 M7 **Etal** Northumb Eng 55.39N 2.07W
66 B3 **Étalans** France 47.09N 6.17E
71 F1 **Étalante** France 47.37N 4.46E
61 N8 **Étalle** Belgium 49.40N 5.36E
98 N3 **Étamamiou** Quebec 50.16N 59.58W
69 C7 **Étampes** France 48.26N 2.10E
12 E2 **Etamunbanie, L** S Australia
35 B7 **Etan** Israel 31.34N 34.45E
98 L6 **Étang-du-Nord** Madeleine Is, Que 47.24N 61.58W
26 T16 **Étang-Salé** Réunion Indian Oc 21.15S 55.21E
69 L5 **Étangs, les** France 49.09N 6.22E
71 E3 **Étang-sur-Arroux** France 46.52N 4.11E
69 B2 **Étaples** France 50.31N 1.39E
72 B4 **Etaules** France 45.44N 1.05W
72 C5 **Etauliers** France 45.14N 0.36W
29 F5 **Etawa** Madhya Prad India 24.08N 78.13E
29 E5 **Etawah** Rajasthan India 25.31N 76.22E
30 C6 **Etawah** Uttar Prad India 26.46N 79.01E
30 C6 **Etawah** *dist* Uttar Prad India
100 V1 **Etawney L** Manitoba
9 A2 **Etcharai** *islet* Marshall Is Pacific Oc 9.20N 167.08E
98 R10 **Etchemin, R** Quebec
115 E4 **Etchojoa** Mexico 26.56N 109.40W
66 B7 **Eteaux** France 46.04N 6.18E
70 D6 **Etel** France 47.39N 3.11W
52 L9 **Etelhem** Sweden 57.20N 18.32E
63 K7 **Etelsen** W Germany 52.59N 9.06E
19 N4 **Eten** *isld* Truk Is Pacific Oc 7.22N 151.53E
122 B4 **Etena** Swains I Pacific Oc 11.03S 171.04W
19 N4 **Eten Anchorage** Truk Is Pacific Oc 7.23N 151.54E
41 Q4 **Eterikan, Proliv** *str* U.S.S.R.
98 B5 **Eternité, L** Quebec 48.14N 70.33W
123 E13 **Eternity Ra** Antarctica
71 J2 **Eternoz** France 47.00N 6.01E
108 N6 **Ethan** S Dakota 43.32N 97.59W
61 N8 **Ethe** Belgium 49.35N 5.35E
107 E11 **Ethel** Louisiana 30.47N 91.09W
107 G8 **Ethel** Mississippi 33.07N 89.29W
107 D2 **Ethel** Missouri 39.54N 92.44W
104 D9 **Ethel** W Virginia 37.53N 81.56W
100 R7 **Ethelbert** Manitoba 51.32N 100.25W
13 A5 **Ethel Cr** N Terr Australia
13 G3 **Ethel Cr** Queensland
14 D6 **Ethel Creek** W Australia 23.05S 120.14E
88 M7 **Ethel, el** *watercourse* Algeria
14 C6 **Ethel R** W Australia
9 R7 **Ethel Reefs** Fiji 17.01S 177.10E
107 H8 **Ethelsville** Alabama 33.25N 88.12W
100 N6 **Ethelton** Saskatchewan 52.48N 104.57W
13 G4 **Etheridge** *R* Queensland
110 R6 **Ethete** Wyoming 43.03N 108.47W
73 H5 **Ethiopia** *empire* E Africa
26 R2 **Ethiopia Shoal** Sri Lanka 9.45N 80.21E
110 N1 **Ethridge** Montana 48.34N 112.10W
61 E3 **Etikhove** Belgium 50.48N 3.38E
36 B3 **Etili** Turkey 40.00N 26.53E
36 F3 **Etimesğut** Turkey 39.57N 32.40E
90 C9 **Etiti** Nigeria 5.36N 7.21E
71 H3 **Étival** Jura France 46.30N 5.47E
69 M7 **Étival-Clairefontaine** Vosges France 48.21N 6.51E
66 E6 **Etivaz, l'** Switzerland 46.26N 7.09E
58 F6 **Etive, L** Strathclyde Scotland
71 E1 **Etivey** France 47.41N 4.09E
113 J2 **Etivluk** *R* Alaska
94 D3 **Etjo Mt** Namibia 21.09S 16.30E
115 L9 **Etla** Mexico 17.13N 96.49W
110 C8 **Etna** California 41.28N 122.54W
104 Q2 **Etna** Maine 44.48N 69.09W
103 B2 **Etna** New York 42.28N 76.24W
104 F6 **Etna** Pennsylvania 40.31N 79.57W
110 M8 **Etna** Utah 41.40N 113.58W
52 E5 **Etna** *R* Norway
81 K8 **Etna, Mte** *vol* Sicily 37.45N 15.00E
53 T19 **Etne** Norway 59.40N 5.57E
52 E6 **Etnedal** Norway 60.54N 9.37E
53 T19 **Etnefjord** *inlet* Norway 59.39N 5.50E
93 L6 **Eto** Kenya 0.23S 39.18E
90 C8 **Etobe** Nigeria 7.21N 6.45E
99 B10 **Etobicoke** Ontario 43.38N 79.30W
69 F6 **Etoges** France 48.53N 3.52E
112 N4 **Etoile** Texas 31.25N 94.28W
91 K9 **Etoile** Zaïre 11.37S 27.33E
95 B8 **Étoile, Banc de l'** Madagascar
71 H10 **Etoile, Chaine de l'** *mts* France
71 F7 **Etoile-sur-Rhône** France 44.49N 4.53E
91 H3 **Etoka** Zaïre 0.12N 23.20E
113 D6 **Etolin, C** Alaska 60.25N 166.10W
113 V8 **Etolin I** Alaska 56.10N 132.30W
113 E6 **Etolin Str** Alaska
100 P6 **Etomami** Saskatchewan 52.45N 102.22W
56 K4 **Eton** Berks Eng 51.31N 0.37W
69 K5 **Eton** France 49.17N 5.41E
99 F5 **Eton** Ontario 47.33N 84.32W
13 J5 **Eton** Queensland 21.15S 148.58E
94 C2 **Etosha Game Reserve** Namibia
94 D2 **Etosha Pan** *salt L* Namibia
91 D3 **Etoumbi** Congo 0.01N 14.49E
107 M6 **Etowah** Tennessee 35.20N 84.30W
105 B3 **Etowah, R** Georgia
66 B6 **Etoy** Switzerland 46.30N 6.25E
66 C2 **Etrappe** France 47.28N 6.35E
69 F4 **Etréaupont** France 49.54N 3.55E
69 C7 **Etrechy** France 48.29N 2.10E
69 E4 **Etreillers** France 49.50N 3.10E
70 O3 **Étrépagny** France 49.19N 1.37E
70 L2 **Étretat** France 49.42N 0.12E
69 F4 **Etreux** France 49.58N 3.40E
69 D3 **Étricourt-Manancourt** France 50.03N 2.59E
71 F3 **Etrigny** France 46.35N 4.48E
69 F3 **Etrœungt** France 50.04N 3.56E
82 H8 **Etropole** Bulgaria 42.50N 24.00E
95 C7 **Etrotroka** Madagascar 22.52S 47.36E
79 B3 **Etroubles** Italy 45.49N 7.14E
72 C10 **Etsaut** France 42.54N 0.34W
28 D6 **Ettaiyapuram** Tamil Nadu India 9.09N 78.01E
12 M4 **Ettalong** New S Wales 33.31S 151.21E
61 P7 **Ettelbrück** Luxembourg 49.51N 6.06E
61 C2 **Ettelgem** Belgium 51.11N 3.02E
60 O12 **Etten** Gelderland Netherlands 51.54N 6.21E
60 G13 **Etten** Noord-Brabant Netherlands 51.34N 4.37E
64 D7 **Ettenheim** W Germany 48.16N 7.52E
64 D7 **Ettenheimmünster** W Germany 48.15N 7.54E
112 C7 **Etter** Texas 36.03N 102.00W
61 S9 **Etterbeck** *dist* Bruxelles Belgium
58 F7 **Etterick B** Strathclyde Scotland 55.51N 5.10W
110 A9 **Ettersburg** California 40.10N 124.00W
64 L1 **Ettersburg** E Germany 51.02N 11.17E
64 J2 **Etterwinden** E Germany 50.53N 10.17E
56 H3 **Ettington** Warwicks Eng 52.09N 1.36W
64 O6 **Ettling** W Germany 48.42N 12.50E
64 E6 **Ettlingen** W Germany 48.56N 8.25E
11 D12 **Ettrick** New Zealand 45.40S 169.24E
14 C5 **Ettrick** W Australia 20.37S 119.45E
106 C5 **Ettrick** Wisconsin 44.10N 91.15W
57 H1 **Ettrick Bridge End** Borders Scotland 55.30N 2.58W
57 G1 **Ettrick Forest** Borders Scotland
57 G2 **Ettrick Pen** Dumfries & Galloway/Borders Scotland 55.21N 3.16W
57 G2 **Ettrick, R** Borders Scotland
89 J2 **Ett Touil** Mali 18.58N 1.24W
28 C6 **Ettumanur** Kerala India 9.39N 76.34E
86 P2 **Et Tuneib** Jordan 31.48N 35.56E
91 K4 **Etumba** Zaïre 0.55S 26.07E
71 H2 **Etuz** France 47.21N 5.56E
56 H2 **Etwall** Derbys Eng 52.54N 1.35W
42 K6 **Etyka** U.S.S.R. 51.03N 116.50E
39 D2 **Etykan** U.S.S.R. 66.45N 145.58E
115 G7 **Etzatlán** Mexico 20.48N 104.05W
64 P1 **Etzdorf** E Germany 51.03N 13.11E
66 J1 **Etzgen** Switzerland 47.34N 8.07E
100 F9 **Etzikom** Alberta 49.30N 111.04W
100 F9 **Etzikom Coulee** *R* Alberta
66 M1 **Etzwilen** Switzerland 47.40N 8.49E
70 N1 **Eu** France 50.03N 1.25E
9 S11 **'Eua** *isld* Tonga, Pacific Oc 21.23S 174.55W
12 H5 **Euabalong** New S Wales 33.07S 146.28E
9 S10 **Eua Iki** *isld* Tonga, Pacific Oc 21.07S 174.57W
9 R12 **Euakafa** *islet* Tonga, Pacific Oc 18.45S 174.05W
107 M4 **Eubank** Kentucky 37.16N 84.40W
77 S11 **Eubarca, C** Balearic Is 39.04N 1.22E
64 H4 **Eubigheim** W Germany 49.31N 9.34E
Euboea *isld see* **Évvoia**
14 G9 **Eucla** W Australia 31.40S 128.51E
108 O2 **Euclid** Minnesota 47.59N 96.39W
104 D5 **Euclid** Ohio 41.34N 81.33W
118 H2 **Euclides da Cunha** Brazil 10.33S 39.04W
12 J6 **Eucumbene, L** New South Wales
98 G3 **Eudistes, L. des** Quebec
107 E8 **Eudora** Arkansas 33.09N 91.19W
12 E5 **Eudunda** S Australia 34.09S 139.04E
64 J3 **Euerdorf** W Germany 50.09N 10.01E
107 L10 **Eufala** Alabama 31.55N 85.10W
109 P6 **Eufaula** Oklahoma 35.16N 95.36W
109 P6 **Eufaula Res** Oklahoma
79 L4 **Euganei, Colli** *hills* Italy
110 B5 **Eugene** Oregon 44.03N 123.04W
115 B4 **Eugenia, Pta** *C* Mexico 27.50N 115.05W
118 B2 **Eugênia, R** Brazil
118 C8 **Eugênic Penzo** Brazil 22.16S 55.46W
72 D8 **Eugénie-les-Bains** France 43.42N 0.23W
118 C8 **Eugênio Penzo** Brazil 22.16S 55.47W
61 F5 **Eugies** Belgium 50.23N 3.53E
51 K8 **Eugmo** *isld* Finland 63.48N 22.50E
12 J5 **Eugowra** New S Wales 33.24S 148.25E
64 O1 **Eula** *R* E Germany
75 F2 **Eulate** Spain 42.46N 2.12W
112 N9 **Euless** Texas 32.49N 97.04W
88 Q3 **Eulma, El** Algeria 36.08N 5.40E
13 H8 **Eulo** Queensland 28.09S 145.02E
105 F6 **Eulonia** Georgia 31.32N 81.27W
76 D2 **Eume** *R* Spain
76 D2 **Eume, Embalse de** *res* Spain 43.23N 7.58W
12 J4 **Eumungerie** New S Wales 31.57S 148.39E
107 D11 **Eunice** Louisiana 30.30N 92.26W
109 G9 **Eunice** New Mexico 32.26N 103.09W
61 P4 **Eupen** Belgium 50.38N 6.02E
61 P4 **Eupen, Lac d'** *res* Belgium
27 E3 **Euphrates** *R* Iraq etc
107 G8 **Eupora** Mississippi 33.32N 89.18W
51 J10 **Eura** Finland 61.08N 22.12E
51 J10 **Eurajoki** Finland 61.13N 21.45E
67 F3 **Eure** *dept* France
70 N3 **Eure** *R* France
67 F4 **Eure-et-Loir** *dept* France
113 M4 **Eureka** Alaska 65.10N 150.20W
110 A9 **Eureka** California 40.49N 124.10W
106 E9 **Eureka** Illinois 40.44N 89.16W
109 O4 **Eureka** Kansas 37.51N 96.17W
110 K1 **Eureka** Montana 48.52N 115.04W
111 J2 **Eureka** Nevada 39.31N 115.58W
103 E3 **Eureka** New York 41.52N 74.32W
97 L1 **Eureka** N W Terr 80.00N 85.40W
95 P1 **Eureka** S Africa 25.42S 31.10E
108 L4 **Eureka** S Dakota 45.46N 99.37W
111 M2 **Eureka** Utah 39.57N 112.09W
110 G3 **Eureka** Washington 46.18N 118.37W
113 O6 **Eureka Lodge** Alaska 61.56N 147.11W
101 O7 **Eureka River** Alberta 56.23N 118.40W
97 L2 **Eureka Sd** N W Terr
107 C5 **Eureka Springs** Arkansas 36.25N 93.45W
111 G4 **Eureka Val** California
12 F4 **Eurinilla** *R* S Australia
12 F4 **Euriowie** New S Wales 31.22S 141.42E
12 H6 **Euroa** Victoria 36.46S 145.35E
13 J7 **Eurombah** Queensland 25.49S 149.35E
13 J7 **Eurombah** *R* Queensland
26 D8 **Europa** *isld* Mozambique Chan 22.20S 40.20E
76 K2 **Europa, Picos de** *mts* Spain
77 F8 **Europa Pt** Gibraltar Mediterranean Sea 36.06N 5.21W
90 D10 **Europa, Pta.de** Fernando Póo Gulf of Guinea 3.48N 8.41E
49 **Europe** *continent*
60 E12 **Europoort** Netherlands 51.59N 4.06E
60 O8 **Eursinge** Netherlands 52.47N 6.27E
64 B2 **Euskirchen** W Germany 50.40N 6.47E
112 L3 **Eustace** Texas 32.18N 96.02W
105 F9 **Eustis** Florida 28.53N 81.42W
108 K9 **Eustis** Nebraska 40.42N 100.02W
12 G5 **Euston** New S Wales 34.34S 142.49E
56 N3 **Euston** Suffolk Eng 52.22N 0.47E
107 J9 **Eutaw** Alabama 32.51N 87.53W
105 G4 **Eutawville** S Carolina 33.23N 80.23W
63 N4 **Eutin** W Germany 54.08N 10.37E
64 F7 **Eutingen** W Germany 48.29N 8.45E
101 K9 **Eutsuk, L** Br Col
63 R9 **Eutzsch** E Germany 51.50N 12.39E
69 K6 **Euville** France 48.45N 5.38E
71 E8 **Euzet** France 44.05N 4.15E
84 C7 **Éva** Greece 37.07N 21.58E
107 E10 **Eva** Louisiana 31.25N 91.47W
109 J5 **Eva** Oklahoma 36.46N 101.55W
13 C4 **Eva Downs** N Terr Australia 17.58S 134.55E
91 D12 **Evale** Angola 16.34S 15.46E
108 Q5 **Evan** Minnesota 44.20N 94.50W
12 J8 **Evandale** Tasmania 41.03S 147.12E
84 C8 **Evangelismós** Greece 36.50N 21.46E
53 U17 **Evanger** Norway 60.39N 6.05E
110 H1 **Evans** Washington 48.44N 118.00W
11 C6 **Evans B** Wellington New Zealand
96 A2 **Evans Bay** Bermuda 32.16N 64.52W
100 B5 **Evansburg** Alberta 53.35N 115.01W
97 L1 **Evans, C** N W Terr 82.40N 83.30W
104 E6 **Evans City** Pennsylvania 40.45N 80.03W
11 M11 **Evansdale** New Zealand 45.43S 170.34E
103 B4 **Evans Falls** Pennsylvania 41.28N 76.02W
12 L3 **Evans Hd** New S Wales 29.06S 153.25E
97 M7 **Evans, L** Quebec 51.00N 77.00W
101 O9 **Evans, Mt** Alberta 52.26N 118.08W
109 E2 **Evans, Mt** Colorado 39.35N 105.39W
110 M3 **Evans, Mt** Montana 46.04N 113.10W
11 N10 **Evans, Mt** New Zealand 43.39S 172.47E
97 L5 **Evans Str** N W Terr
106 G7 **Evanston** Illinois 42.02N 87.41W
110 P8 **Evanston** Wyoming 41.16N 110.58W
106 S1 **Evanston** *dist* Chicago, Illinois
113 M3 **Evansville** Alaska 66.53N 151.40W
107 G3 **Evansville** Illinois 38.04N 89.56W
107 J3 **Evansville** Indiana 38.00N 87.33W
108 P3 **Evansville** Minnesota 46.00N 95.41W
99 H7 **Evansville** Ontario 45.49N 82.35W
106 E7 **Evansville** Wisconsin 42.46N 89.18W
108 D7 **Evansville** Wyoming 42.51N 106.16W
112 J4 **Evant** Texas 31.29N 98.09W
58 H3 **Evanton** Highland Scotland 57.39N 4.21W
57 F2 **Evan Water** *R* Dumfries & Galloway Scotland
106 J6 **Evart** Michigan 43.55N 85.14W
105 D1 **Evarts** Kentucky 36.51N 83.12W
95 C7 **Evato** Madagascar 22.37S 47.40E
95 L2 **Evaton** S Africa 26.32S 27.53E
72 J3 **Évaux-les-Bains** France 46.10N 2.28E
32 E7 **Evaz** Iran 27.48N 53.58E
36 B3 **Evciler** Turkey 39.46N 26.45E
84 Q15 **Evdhimou** Cyprus 34.41N 32.46E
61 N4 **Evegnée-Tignée** Belgium 50.38N 5.43E
108 S2 **Eveleth** Minnesota 47.29N 92.46W
61 L5 **Evelette** Belgium 50.25N 5.11E
58 H3 **Evelix** Highland Scotland 57.53N 4.05W
12 C3 **Evelyn Cr** S Australia
13 C2 **Evelyn, Mt** N Terr Australia 13.31S 132.54E
51 F3 **Evenes** Norway 68.28N 16.45E
107 E5 **Evening Shade** Arkansas 36.02N 91.37W
42 E1 **Evenkiyskiy Nats. Okrug** *dist* U.S.S.R.
56 J4 **Evenlode, R** Oxon Eng
35 E1 **Even Menahem** Israel 33.05N 35.18E
35 D6 **Even Sapir** Israel 31.46N 35.08E
35 C7 **Even Shemu'el** Israel 31.34N 34.45E
39 F4 **Evensk** U.S.S.R. 61.56N 159.30E
35 C4 **Even Yehuda** Israel 32.16N 34.53E
35 D3 **Even Yizhaq** Israel 32.34N 35.05E
13 G2 **Eve Pk** Queensland 13.12S 143.35E
66 G8 **Evêque, l'** *mt* Switzerland 45.58N 7.30E
99 B4 **Everard** Ontario 48.55N 88.22W
12 J7 **Everard, C** Victoria 37.50S 149.16E
12 D4 **Everard, L** S Australia
13 C6 **Everard, Mt** N Terr Australia 23.34S 133.45E
12 B2 **Everard, Mt** S Australia 26.17S 132.00E
12 C2 **Everard Park** S Australia 27.00S 132.41E
12 B2 **Everard Ra** S Australia
61 F3 **Everbeek** Belgium 50.46N 3.49E
61 J3 **Everberg** Belgium 50.53N 4.35E
56 F5 **Evercreech** Somerset Eng 51.09N 2.30W
60 J12 **Everdingen** Netherlands 51.58N 5.10E
53 H6 **Everdrup** Denmark 55.13N 11.58E
61 H3 **Evere** Belgium 50.53N 4.25E
Everek Gümüşane Turkey *see* **Maden**
Everek Kayseri Turkey *see* **Develi**
98 S7 **Everell** Quebec 46.51N 71.11W
109 P2 **Everest** Kansas 39.41N 95.26W
30 K2 **Everest, Mt** Xizang Zizhiqu/Nepal 27.59N 86.56E
104 G6 **Everett** Pennsylvania 40.01N 78.23W
110 C2 **Everett** Washington 47.59N 122.14W
104 Q9 **Everett** *dist* Boston, Mass
103 H2 **Everett** *mt* Massachusetts 42.06N 73.26W
105 F6 **Everett City** Georgia 31.24N 81.39W
61 E2 **Evergem** Belgium 51.07N 3.43E
105 F12 **Everglades City** Florida 26.52N 81.22W
105 G12 **Everglades Nat. Park** Florida
105 G12 **Everglades, The** *swamp reg* Florida
107 K10 **Evergreen** Alabama 31.25N 86.59W
109 E2 **Evergreen** Colorado 39.38N 105.20W
105 J3 **Evergreen** N Carolina 34.24N 78.55W
106 R4 **Evergreen Park** *dist* Chicago, Illinois
57 M5 **Everingham** Humberside Eng 53.53N 0.47W
112 M10 **Everman** Texas 32.38N 97.17W
52 H11 **Everöd** Sweden 55.53N 14.05E
63 H10 **Eversberg** W Germany 51.22N 8.20E
63 K6 **Eversen** W Germany 53.03N 9.20E
56 K5 **Eversley** Hants Eng 51.21N 0.53W
117 A1 **Everton** Guyana 6.14N 57.32W
56 H3 **Evesham** Hereford & Worcs Eng 52.06N 1.56W
13 G6 **Evesham** Queensland 23.00S 143.40E
100 H6 **Evesham** Saskatchewan 52.24N 109.52W
56 H3 **Evesham, Vale of** England
71 K1 **Evette-Salbert** France 47.41N 6.48E
91 A3 **Eviando, Pta** *pt* Equat Guinea
71 K4 **Evian-les-Bains** France 46.24N 6.35E
58 S11 **Evie** Orkney Scotland 59.07N 3.06W
51 K8 **Evijärvi** Finland 63.22N 23.30E
66 E3 **Evilard** Switzerland 47.09N 7.15E
66 A3 **Evillers** France 47.00N 6.15E
91 B3 **Evinayong** Equat Guinea 1.26N 10.39E
84 C5 **Evinokhórion** Greece 38.21N 21.32E
84 C5 **Évinos** *R* Greece
66 E7 **Evionnaz** Switzerland 46.11N 7.02E
66 A7 **Evires** France 46.03N 6.15E
67 O12 **Evisa** Corsica 42.15N 8.48E
52 D8 **Evje** Norway 58.36N 7.51E
Evoghlu *see* **Evowghlī**
66 G7 **Evolène** Switzerland 46.07N 7.30E
76 B9 **Évora** Portugal 39.31N 8.59W
76 D11 **Évora** Portugal 38.34N 7.54W
76 D11 **Évora** *dist* Portugal
76 D11 **Évora Monte** Portugal 38.46N 7.41W
40 C3 **Evota** *mt* U.S.S.R. 57.32N 125.08E
32 A1 **Evowghlī** Iran 38.42N 45.10E
84 C5 **Evpálion** Greece 38.25N 21.55E
70 G5 **Evran** France 48.23N 1.59W
70 K3 **Evrecy** France 49.06N 0.30W
61 D4 **Evregnies** Belgium 50.43N 3.17E
61 K5 **Evrehailles** Belgium 50.19N 4.55E
37 C2 **Evreşe** Çanakkale Turkey 40.41N 26.54E
70 N3 **Évreux** France 49.03N 1.11E
84 C3 **Evritanía** *prov* Greece
70 K5 **Évron** France 48.09N 0.24W
35 D2 **Evron** Israel 33.00N 35.06E
83 E3 **Evropos** Greece 41.03N 22.10E
83 H4 **Évros** *R* Greece
84 D5 **Evrostíni** Greece 38.04N 22.24E
84 E8 **Evrótas** *R* Greece
69 C6 **Evry** France 48.38N 2.34E
84 Q14 **Evrykhou** Cyprus 35.01N 32.55E
35 B7 **Evtah** *watercourse* Israel
84 G4 **Évvoia** *isld* Greece
84 G4 **Évvoia** *prov* Greece
84 E3 **Evxinoúpolis** Greece 39.11N 22.44E
114 A5 **Ewa** Hawaiian Is 21.20N 158.02W
114 A5 **Ewa** *dist* Hawaiian Is
Ewab *islds see* **Kai, Kep** *Is*
114 A5 **Ewa Beach** Hawaiian Is 21.18N 158.01W
13 H4 **Ewan** Queensland 19.06S 145.50E
110 H2 **Ewan** Washington 47.06N 117.45W
13 C6 **Ewaninga** N Terr Australia 23.58S 133.59E
113 P5 **Ewan L** Alaska 62.27N 145.50W
116 K2 **Ewarton** Jamaica, W I 18.11N 77.06W
92 J1 **Ewaso Ngiri** *R* Kenya
93 G7 **Ewaso Ngiro** Kenya 1.09S 35.45E
93 H7 **Ewaso Ngiro** *R* Kenya
15 L6 **Ewasse** New Britain 5.22S 151.02E
95 G2 **Ewbank** S Africa 26.13S 23.34E
58 E3 **Ewe, L** Highland Scotland
55 E5 **Ewell** London England 51.21N 0.15W
21 A3 **Ewenkizu Zizhiqi** Nei Monggol Zizhiqu China
56 D5 **Ewenni** Mid Glam Wales 51.29N 3.35W
57 H2 **Ewes Water** *R* Dumfries & Galloway Scotland
56 L5 **Ewhurst** Surrey Eng 51.09N 0.27W
60 L12 **Ewijk** Netherlands 51.52N 5.45E
104 B8 **Ewing** Kentucky 38.22N 83.53W
107 E1 **Ewing** Missouri 40.00N 91.43W
108 M7 **Ewing** Nebraska 42.16N 98.20W
123 E13 **Ewing I** Antarctica 69.55S 61.10W
11 B7 **Ewing I** Auckland Is Pacific Oc 50.32S 166.19E
13 D6 **Ewing, Mt** N Terr Australia 22.56S 137.10E
91 D4 **Ewo** Congo 0.48S 14.47E
90 C9 **Ewu** Nigeria 5.25N 6.01E
120 F5 **Exaltación** Bolivia 13.17S 65.15W
84 E6 **Examília** Greece 37.54N 22.55E
84 E4 **Exarchos** Greece 38.35N 22.57E
56 D6 **Exbourne** Devon Eng 50.48N 3.59W
100 G7 **Excel** Alberta 51.22N 110.32W
95 F8 **Excelda** S Africa 32.17S 22.07E
95 L4 **Excelsior** S Africa 28.56S 27.04E
111 E3 **Excelsior Mt** California 38.02N 119.19W
111 F3 **Excelsior Mts** Nevada
107 B2 **Excelsior Springs** Missouri 39.20N 94.14W
103 A4 **Exchange** Pennsylvania 41.07N 76.41W
72 G5 **Excideuil** France 45.20N 1.04E
101 F6 **Excursion** Alaska 58.23N 135.23W
64 K3 **Exdorf** E Germany 50.27N 10.33E
123 J10 **Executive Committee Ra** Antarctica
106 C4 **Exeland** Wisconsin 45.42N 91.16W
56 E6 **Exe, R** Devon Eng
111 E5 **Exeter** California 36.17N 119.09W
56 D6 **Exeter** Devon Eng 50.43N 3.31W
107 C5 **Exeter** Missouri 36.41N 93.58W
108 N9 **Exeter** Nebraska 40.39N 97.29W
104 P4 **Exeter** New Hampshire 42.59N 70.56W
99 J9 **Exeter** Ontario 43.21N 81.30W
103 L3 **Exeter** Rhode I 41.35N 71.31W
101 S3 **Exeter L** N W Terr 64.46N 110.50W
56 D5 **Exford** Somerset Eng 51.08N 3.38W
72 F4 **Exideuil** France 45.54N 0.41E
79 A4 **Exilles** Italy 45.06N 6.55E
108 Q8 **Exira** Iowa 41.36N 94.51W
108 S9 **Exline** Iowa 49.39N 92.49W
60 Q8 **Exloo** Netherlands 52.52N 6.52E
70 L4 **Exmes** France 48.45N 0.10E
56 E6 **Exminster** Devon Eng 50.41N 3.29W
56 D5 **Exmoor** *moorland* Somerset/Devon Eng
104 K9 **Exmore** Virginia 37.32N 75.49W
60 K7 **Exmorra** Netherlands 53.03N 5.27E
56 E6 **Exmouth** Devon Eng 50.37N 3.25W
14 A5 **Exmouth** W Australia 21.54S 114.10E
14 A5 **Exmouth Gulf** W Australia 22.20S 114.09E
101 Q3 **Exmouth L** N W Terr 65.04N 115.59W
121 J7 **Exmouth, Pen** Chile
26 K7 **Exmouth Plateau** Indian Ocean
84 D8 **Exokhóri** Greece 36.54N 22.15E
84 D8 **Exo Nímfi** Greece 36.34N 22.28E
13 J6 **Expedition Ra** Queensland
98 R5 **Exploits R** Newfoundland
9 U2 **Exploring Is** Fiji
100 B7 **Exshaw** Alberta 51.07N 115.08W
63 K8 **Extertal** W Germany 52.05N 9.07E
56 D5 **Exton** Somerset Eng 51.05N 3.31W
74 C5 **Extremadura** *reg* Spain
76 C5 **Extremo** Portugal 41.57N 8.29W
91 F12 **Extremo Sul** Angola 16.20S 18.04E
66 G8 **Extrepieraz** Italy 45.47N 7.43E
117 G8 **Exú** Brazil 7.28S 39.45W
116 G3 **Exuma, Great** *I* Bahamas 23.40N 76.00W
116 G3 **Exuma, Little** *I* Bahamas 23.30N 75.35W
116 F2 **Exuma Sd** Bahamas
113 P6 **Eyak** Alaska 60.31N 145.35W
41 K7 **Eyakit-Tërdë** U.S.S.R. 66.22N 113.54E
35 C5 **Eyal** Israel 32.13N 34.59E
91 H5 **Eyangu** Zaïre 2.24S 23.14E
93 F9 **Eyasi, L (Soda)** Tanzania
71 H6 **Eybens** France 45.08N 5.45E
72 H5 **Eyburie** France 45.29N 1.38E
52 D8 **Eydehavn** Norway 58.31N 8.53E
56 L2 **Eye** Cambs Eng 52.36N 0.11W
56 O3 **Eye** Suffolk Eng 52.19N 1.09E
101 V4 **Eyeberry L** N W Terr 63.09N 104.40W
100 L8 **Eyebrow** Saskatchewan 50.48N 106.09W
41 N5 **Eyekit** *R* U.S.S.R.
58 J3 **Eye, L** Highland Scotland 57.47N 3.57W
58 M7 **Eyemouth** Borders Scotland 55.52N 2.06W
58 D2 **Eye Pen** Lewis, W Isles Scotland 58.13N 6.12W
60 U17 **Eygelshoven** Netherlands 50.53N 6.04E
71 G9 **Eyguières** France 43.42N 5.01E
72 J4 **Eygurande** Corrèze France 45.40N 2.26E
72 E5 **Eygurande-et-Gardedeuil** France 45.04N 0.15E
41 L7 **Eyik** U.S.S.R. 66.00N 117.30E
50 F7 **Eyjafjallajökull** *ice cap* Iceland 63.38N 19.37W
50 G4 **Eyjafjardhará** *R* Iceland
50 G2 **Eyjafjardjarsýsla** *co* Iceland
50 G2 **Eyjafjördhur** *B* Iceland
50 D3 **Eyjar** Iceland 65.50N 21.16W
40 H3 **Eykan Mys** *C* U.S.S.R. 57.00N 138.54E
72 F10 **Eylie** France 42.51N 0.58E
72 E6 **Eymet** France 44.41N 0.25E
72 H4 **Eymoutiers** France 45.44N 1.44E
61 P4 **Eynatten** Belgium 50.42N 6.05E
32 B4 **Eyn Gazān** Iran 32.33N 47.21E
58 S11 **Eynhallow Sd** Orkney Scotland
Eynihal *see* **Kale**
32 E3 **Eyn or Rashid** Iran 34.42N 52.09E
58 B4 **Eynort, L** S Uist, W Isles Scotland 57.13N 7.15W
55 K5 **Eynsford** Kent England 51.22N 0.13E
56 J4 **Eynsham** Oxon Eng 51.48N 1.22W
108 S6 **Eyota** Minnesota 44.00N 92.12W
71 F9 **Eyragues** France 43.49N 4.50E
72 C5 **Eyrans** France 45.11N 0.38W
50 D7 **Eyrarbakki** Iceland 63.52N 21.08W
50 B5 **Eyrarfjall** *mt* Iceland 65.00N 23.10W
100 H7 **Eyre** Saskatchewan 51.17N 109.50W
14 F9 **Eyre** W Australia 32.11S 126.15E
13 E6 **Eyre** *R* Queensland
59 F5 **Eyrecourt** Galway Irish Rep 53.12N 8.08W
72 H5 **Eyrein** France 45.20N 1.54E
12 D3 **Eyre, L (North)** S Australia
12 D3 **Eyre, L (South)** S Australia
12 E4 **Eyre, Mt** S Australia 31.49S 138.10E
11 C12 **Eyre Mts** New Zealand
12 D5 **Eyre Pen** S Australia
11 C12 **Eyre Pk** *mt* New Zealand 45.21S 168.27E
121 J7 **Eyre, Seno** *inlet* Chile
50 C3 **Eyri** Bardhastrandarsýsla, Austur Iceland 65.37N 22.28W
50 C2 **Eyri** Ísafjardharsýsla, Nordhur Iceland 66.01N 22.55W
100 R1 **Eyrie L** Manitoba
64 L5 **Eysölden** W Germany 49.08N 11.13E
53 N9 **Eystnes** *C* Faeroes 62.04N 6.41W
50 H6 **Eystrafjall** *mt* Iceland 64.05N 17.25W
50 E7 **Eystri Rangá** *R* Iceland
63 K7 **Eystrup** W Germany 52.47N 9.13E
Eysturoy *I see* **Østerø**
37 J2 **Eyüp** *dist* İstanbul Turkey 41.03N 28.51E
32 E3 **Eyvānaki** Iran 35.21N 52.04E
50 K4 **Eyvindará** *R* Iceland
50 L4 **Eyvindarárdalur** *V* Iceland
50 F7 **Eyvindarhólar** Iceland 63.31N 19.37W
50 G5 **Eyvindarkvísl** *R* Iceland
72 G6 **Eyzies-de-Tayac-Sireuil, les** France 44.56N 1.02E
71 F6 **Eyzin-Pinet** France 45.28N 5.00E
86 G3 **'Ezab el Basârta** Egypt 31.24N 31.46E
76 A3 **Ezaro** Spain 42.54N 9.09W
86 Q12 **Ezbekîya** *dist* Cairo Egypt
37 D5 **Ezbider** Turkey 40.05N 38.21E
75 D3 **Ezcaray** Spain 42.19N 3.00W
75 G1 **Ezcurra** Spain 43.05N 1.50W
121 F5 **Ezeiza** *airport* Argentina 34.50S 58.40W
61 K3 **Ezemaal** Belgium 50.47N 5.00E
121 C7 **Ezequiel Ramos Mexia, Embalse** *res* Argentina
82 J5 **Ezeru** *mt* Romania 45.28N 24.57E
47 G5 **Ezhva** U.S.S.R. 61.48N 50.43E
36 B3 **Ezine** Turkey 39.46N 26.20E
36 J2 **Ezinepazar** Turkey 40.32N 36.02E
60 O6 **Ezinge** Netherlands 53.18N 6.26E
95 C8 **Ezira** Madagascar 24.00S 46.59E
39 E3 **Ezop, Gora** *mt* U.S.S.R. 63.16N 151.11E
84 Q15 **Ezouza** *R* Cyprus
Ezraa *see* **Izra'**
Ezraa Station *see* **Mahattat Izra'**
32 B5 **Ezra's Tomb** *anc site* Iraq 31.18N 47.25E
88 K5 **Ez-Zhiliga** Morocco 33.18N 6.30W

122 B11 **Faaa** Tahiti Pacific Oc 17.32S 149.36W
27 L8 **Faaippolu** Maldives, Ind Oc
122 D15 **Faaite** *atoll* Tuamotu Is Pacific Oc 16.40S 145.15W
65 J8 **Faaker See** *L* Austria 46.35N 13.56E
122 C12 **Faaone** Tahiti Pacific Oc 17.39S 149.18W
122 B11 **Faaupo, Pt** *C* Society Is Pacific Oc 17.28S 149.45W
53 C4 **Fåbæk** Denmark 56.22N 9.05E
89 E7 **Fabala** Guinea 9.44N 9.00W
75 L5 **Fabara** Spain 41.10N 0.10E
72 G9 **Fabas** France 43.06N 1.06E
79 F5 **Fabbrica Curone** Italy 44.47N 9.09E
81 J7 **Fabbrica, La** Lipari Is Italy 38.25N 14.58E
79 J5 **Fabbrico** Italy 44.52N 10.48E
18 J3 **Faber** *mt* Singapore 1.17N 103.49E
52 E5 **Fåberg** Opland Norway 61.10N 10.22E
53 W15 **Fåberg** Sogn og Fjordane Norway 61.40N 7.20E
101 P4 **Faber L** N W Terr
76 F3 **Fabero** Spain 42.45N 6.38W
53 E6 **Fåborg** Fyn Denmark 55.06N 10.15E
53 B5 **Fåborg** Ribe Denmark 55.35N 8.45E
99 L5 **Fabre** Quebec 47.12N 79.23W
71 D9 **Fabrègues** France 43.33N 3.47E
72 K9 **Fabrezan** France 43.09N 2.42E
80 G2 **Fabriano** Italy 43.20N 2.54E
118 J9 **Fábrica das Chitas** Brazil 22.57S 43.14W
Fábrica de Papel *see* **Têlemaco Borba**
43 M5 **Fabrichnyy** Kazakhstan U.S.S.R. 43.08N 76.25E
81 M7 **Fabrizia** Italy 38.28N 16.18E
80 F3 **Fabro** Italy 42.52N 12.01E
82 L6 **Făcăeni** Romania 44.31N 27.55E
119 D5 **Facatativá** Colombia 4.48N 74.32W
91 G7 **Facauma** Angola 8.26S 21.20E
90 E2 **Fachi** Niger 18.06N 11.34E
11 A12 **Facile Harb** New Zealand
77 E8 **Facinas** Spain 36.09N 5.41W
13 K6 **Facing I** Queensland
19 L1 **Facpi Pt** Guam Pacific Oc 13.21N 144.38E
103 C3 **Factoryville** Pennsylvania 41.34N 75.47W
72 C6 **Facture** France 44.39N 0.58W
121 K5 **Facundo** Argentina 45.15S 70.01W
90 K3 **Fada** Chad 17.14N 21.32E
76 E10 **Fadagosa** Portugal 39.29N 7.23W
79 M2 **Fadalto** Italy 46.05N 12.21E
32 F6 **Fadāmī** Iran 28.10N 55.06E
89 K5 **Fada-N'Gourma** Upper Volta 12.05N 0.26E
39 K3 **Faddeya, Mys** *C* U.S.S.R. 62.40N 179.43E
41 J3 **Faddeya, Ostrova** *islds* U.S.S.R. 76.58N 108.00E
41 J3 **Faddeya, Zaliv** *gulf* U.S.S.R.
41 Q3 **Faddeyevskiy, Ostrov** *isld* U.S.S.R.
87 D6 **Faddoi** Sudan 8.05N 32.15E
Fadhili *oil field see* **Fādilī**
33 J5 **Faḍilah** Saudi Arabia 22.05N 50.26E
33 H3 **Fāḍilī** *oil field* Saudi Arabia 27.01N 49.10E
27 L8 **Fadippolu Atoll** Maldive Is, Indian Oc 5.13N 73.20E
59 H1 **Fad L** Donegal Irish Rep 55.14N 7.23W
33 F10 **Faḍli** *tribe* S Yemen
Fadrhāmi *see* **Tell Fajāmi**
89 D7 **Fadugu** Sierra Leone 9.35N 11.40W
79 O2 **Faédis** Italy 46.09N 13.21E
53 D6 **Fænø** *isld* Denmark 55.29N 9.43E
79 L6 **Faenza** Italy 44.17N 11.53E
48 S13 **Færingehavn** Greenland 63.45N 51.25W
54 E1 **Faeroe Bank** N Atlantic Oc
49 C4 **Færøerne** *islds* N Atlantic Oc 62.00N 7.00W
Faeroes *see* **Færøerne**
53 R16 **Færøy** *isld* Norway 61.12N 5.50E
80 D3 **Faete, Monte** Italy 42.40N 11.28E
89 K4 **Fafa** Mali 15.22N 0.48E
9 S10 **Fafa** *islet* Tonga, Pacific Oc 21.05S 175.10W
90 J8 **Fafa** *R* Cent Afr Rep
15 A4 **Fafanlap** Irian Jaya 1.57S 130.18E
87 J6 **Fafan,R** Ethiopia
76 C6 **Fafe** Portugal 41.27N 8.11W
89 K5 **Faga** *R* Upper Volta
79 O2 **Fagagna** Italy 46.07N 13.05E
122 C2 **Fagaloa B** W Samoa, Pacific Oc 13.54S 171.30W
90 E6 **Fagam** Nigeria 11.01N 10.01E
122 B1 **Fagamalo** W Samoa, Pacific Oc 13.27S 172.24W
87 C8 **Fagar** Sudan 4.15N 31.40E
93 C1 **Fagar** Sudan 4.10N 31.40E
82 J5 **Făgăraş** Romania 45.50N 24.59E
82 J5 **Făgaraşului, Munţii** *mts* Romania
122 D1 **Fagatogo** Amer Samoa Pacific Oc 14.17S 170.41W
52 H5 **Fågelsjö** Sweden 61.50N 14.35E
52 J9 **Fagerhult** Sweden 57.08N 15.40E
52 E6 **Fagernes** Norway 60.59N 9.17E
52 J7 **Fagersta** Sweden 59.59N 15.49E
82 G5 **Faget** Romania 45.50N 22.09E
82 H3 **Făgetului, Munţii** *mts* Romania
79 L6 **Faggiola, Monte** Italy 44.09N 11.31E
15 A4 **Fagita** Irian Jaya 1.47S 130.24E
80 J4 **Fagnano Alto** Italy 42.15N 13.35E
121 L10 **Fagnano O Cami, L** Arg/Chile
69 G3 **Fagnes** *hills* Belgium
61 J6 **Fagnolle** Belgium 50.07N 4.34E
90 D5 **Fagolawa** Nigeria 12.22N 8.37E
50 C7 **Fagradalsfjall** *mt* Gullbringusýsla Iceland 63.54N 22.17W
50 J5 **Fagradalsfjall** *mt* Múlasýsla, Nordhur Iceland 64.55N 16.10W
50 F3 **Fagranes** Skagafjardharsýsla Iceland 65.48N 19.42W
50 L2 **Fagranes** Thingeyjarsýsla, Nordhur Iceland 66.13N 14.54W
50 C5 **Fagraskogarfjall** *mt* Iceland 64.47N 22.10W
50 L3 **Fagridalur** Iceland 65.47N 14.26W
50 L4 **Fagridalur** *V* Iceland
89 G3 **Faguibine,L** Mali 16.45N 4.00W
50 J7 **Fagurhólsmýri** Iceland 63.53N 16.39W
87 C6 **Fagwir** Sudan 9.05N 30.48E
33 N10 **Fahaheel** Kuwait 29.02N 48.08E
32 G4 **Fahālanj** Iran 33.20N 57.10E
59 H1 **Fahan** Donegal Irish Rep 55.05N 7.28W
86 M5 **Fahdi, Wâdî el** *watercourse* Egypt
35 G2 **Fahham, El** Syria 32.58N 35.50E
88 Q6 **Fahl, El** *watercourse* Algeria
35 D4 **Fahma** Jordan 32.23N 35.11E
66 K2 **Fahr** Switzerland 47.24N 8.26E
32 F5 **Fahraj** Esfahān Iran 31.48N 54.39E
32 H6 **Fahraj** Kermān Iran 28.58N 58.51E
37 F7 **Fahran** Turkey 39.00N 40.39E
64 D8 **Fahrnau** W Germany 47.40N 7.50E
66 J2 **Fahrwangen** Switzerland 47.18N 8.15E
78 C12 **Fahs, El** Tunisia 36.20N 9.54E
33 M5 **Fahud** *oil bore* Oman 22.15N 56.31E
33 M5 **Fahūd, Jabal** *mt* Oman 22.19N 56.30E
66 D2 **Fahy** Switzerland 47.25N 6.57E
59 C3 **Fahy L** Mayo Irish Rep 54.03N 9.53W
79 K2 **Fai** Italy 46.11N 11.04E
96 Q7 **Faial** Madeira Is 32.47N 16.53W
96 O4 **Faial** *I* Azores 38.35N 28.42W
96 P4 **Faial, Can. do** Azores
96 V2 **Faial da Terra** Azores 37.29N 25.12W
Faid *see* **Fayd**
85 F3 **Fā'idīyah, Al** Libya 32.41N 21.59E
66 M6 **Faido** Switzerland 46.29N 8.48E
Faifa *see* **Fayfā**
Faifo *see* **Hoi An**
Failakai *isld see* **Faylakah**
93 K1 **Faille** Ethiopia 4.18N 38.06E
99 O4 **Faillon, L** Quebec 48.21N 76.40W
61 L4 **Faimes** Liège Belgium 50.40N 5.15E
71 E1 **Fain** France 47.37N 4.24E
9 S12 **Faioa** *atoll* Tonga, Pacific Oc 18.40S 173.50W
109 D9 **Fairacres** New Mexico 32.18N 106.52W
13 J6 **Fairbairn Res** Queensland
111 O10 **Fairbank** Arizona 31.44N 110.11W
106 B7 **Fairbank** Iowa 42.38N 92.02W
113 O4 **Fairbanks** Alaska 64.50N 147.50W
104 P2 **Fairbanks** Maine 44.44N 70.12W
112 M6 **Fairbanks** Texas 29.51N 95.34W
99 Q3 **Fairbault** Quebec 49.48N 74.29W
105 H3 **Fair Bluff** N Carolina 34.19N 79.03W
104 A7 **Fairborn** Ohio 39.48N 84.03W
105 C4 **Fairburn** Georgia 33.35N 84.36W
108 G6 **Fairburn** S Dakota 43.41N 103.12W
106 F9 **Fairbury** Illinois 40.45N 88.32W
108 N9 **Fairbury** Nebraska 40.08N 97.11W
104 F7 **Fairchance** Pennsylvania 39.48N 79.45W
106 D5 **Fairchild** Wisconsin 44.39N 90.59W
108 M1 **Fairdale** N Dakota 48.30N 98.12W
103 C3 **Fairdale** Pennsylvania 41.47N 75.59W
11 F8 **Fairdown** New Zealand 41.44S 171.43E
107 L9 **Fairfax** Alabama 32.48N 85.10W
108 Q5 **Fairfax** Minnesota 44.32N 94.43W
107 A1 **Fairfax** Missouri 40.20N 95.25W
11 C13 **Fairfax** New Zealand 46.13S 168.02E
109 O5 **Fairfax** Oklahoma 36.34N 96.43W
105 F5 **Fairfax** S Carolina 32.57N 81.15W
108 M6 **Fairfax** S Dakota 43.02N 98.52W
104 N2 **Fairfax** Vermont 44.41N 73.00W
104 H8 **Fairfax** Virginia 38.51N 77.19W
110 C2 **Fairfax** Washington 47.01N 122.01W
107 K8 **Fairfield** Alabama 33.29N 86.59W
116 O5 **Fairfield** Barbados 13.17N 59.37W
111 B3 **Fairfield** California 38.14N 122.03W
103 H4 **Fairfield** Connecticut 41.09N 73.15W
110 L6 **Fairfield** Idaho 43.21N 114.46W
107 H3 **Fairfield** Illinois 38.22N 88.23W
106 C8 **Fairfield** Iowa 41.01N 91.59W
104 Q2 **Fairfield** Maine 44.36N 69.37W
110 O2 **Fairfield** Montana 47.37N 111.59W
105 L2 **Fairfield** N Carolina 35.33N 76.14W
108 G2 **Fairfield** N Dakota 47.12N 103.14W
108 M9 **Fairfield** Nebraska 40.27N 98.06W
104 H7 **Fairfield** Pennsylvania 39.46N 77.23W
112 L4 **Fairfield** Texas 31.43N 96.10W
104 N2 **Fairfield** Vermont 44.46N 72.56W
110 H2 **Fairfield** Washington 47.23N 117.10W

103 H4 **Fairfield** *co* Connecticut
12 D6 **Fairfield** *dist* Melbourne, Vic
112 L4 **Fairfield, L** Texas
56 H4 **Fairford** Glos Eng 51.44N 1.47W
100 T7 **Fairford** Manitoba 51.36N 98.42W
95 K8 **Fairford** S Africa 32.22S 26.55E
107 C4 **Fair Grove** Missouri 37.24N 93.10W
103 N3 **Fairhaven** Massachusetts 41.39N 70.54W
106 M7 **Fair Haven** Michigan 42.42N 82.39W
104 J3 **Fair Haven** New York 43.20N 76.44W
104 M3 **Fair Haven** Vermont 43.35N 73.16W
59 K1 **Fair Hd** Antrim N Ireland 55.13N 6.09W
110 B1 **Fairholm** Washington 48.04N 123.57W
100 J5 **Fairholme** Saskatchewan 53.26N 108.32W
107 J11 **Fairhope** Alabama 30.31N 87.55W
19 H6 **Fairie Queen** *bank* S China Sea 10.40N 117.38E
58 P10 **Fair Isle** Shetland Scotland 59.32N 1.38W
109 Q5 **Fairland** Oklahoma 36.45N 94.54W
103 L2 **Fairlawn** Massachusetts 42.17N 71.44W
103 L5 **Fairlawn** New Jersey 40.57N 74.07W
103 B8 **Fairlee** Maryland 39.13N 76.11W
11 E11 **Fairlie** New Zealand 44.05S 170.50E
58 G7 **Fairlie** Strathclyde Scotland 55.46N 4.51W
11 C12 **Fairlight** New Zealand 45.27S 168.41E
13 G3 **Fairlight** Queensland 15.42S 144.09E
13 G5 **Fairlight** Queensland 20.39S 144.11E
100 Q9 **Fairlight** Saskatchewan 49.53N 101.40W
108 Q6 **Fairmont** Minnesota 43.39N 94.27W
105 H3 **Fairmont** N Carolina 34.30N 79.08W
108 N9 **Fairmont** Nebraska 40.39N 97.36W
109 N5 **Fairmont** Oklahoma 36.22N 97.43W
104 E7 **Fairmont** W Virginia 39.28N 80.08W
101 Q10 **Fairmont Hot Springs** Br Col 50.20N 115.56W
105 C3 **Fairmount** Georgia 34.26N 84.40W
106 J9 **Fairmount** Indiana 40.25N 85.39W
104 K8 **Fairmount** Maryland 38.05N 75.50W
108 O3 **Fairmount** N Dakota 46.04N 96.37W
100 H7 **Fairmount** Saskatchewan 51.24N 109.16W
97 M5 **Fair Ness** *C* N W Terr 63.25N 72.00W
57 H1 **Fairnilee** Borders Scotland 55.35N 2.52W
107 E6 **Fairoaks** Arkansas 35.12N 91.02W
111 C3 **Fair Oaks** California 38.37N 121.18W
106 G8 **Fair Oaks** Indiana 41.03N 87.14W
109 D2 **Fairplay** Colorado 39.13N 106.00W
107 C4 **Fair Play** Missouri 37.38N 93.36W
109 L2 **Fairport** Kansas 39.02N 99.03W
106 H4 **Fairport** Michigan 45.38N 86.39W
104 H3 **Fairport** New York 43.06N 77.27W
104 J9 **Fair Port** Virginia 37.52N 76.18W
104 D5 **Fairport Harbor** Ohio 41.45N 81.17W
103 D8 **Fairton** New Jersey 39.23N 75.13W
101 O7 **Fairview** Alberta 56.03N 118.28W
106 D9 **Fairview** Illinois 40.39N 90.09W
109 P2 **Fairview** Kansas 39.50N 95.44W
106 K5 **Fairview** Michigan 44.44N 84.03W
108 F2 **Fairview** Montana 47.52N 104.02W
103 K7 **Fairview** New Jersey 40.49N 74.01W
109 M5 **Fairview** Oklahoma 36.16N 98.29W
104 E4 **Fairview** Pennsylvania 42.02N 80.14W
13 G3 **Fairview** Queensland 15.29S 144.15E
108 O6 **Fairview** S Dakota 43.12N 96.30W
111 N2 **Fairview** Utah 39.38N 111.27W
104 E7 **Fairview** W Virginia 39.35N 80.14W
113 T7 **Fairweather, C** Alaska 58.49N 137.59W
113 T7 **Fairweather, Mt** Alaska/Br Col 58.50N 137.55W
58 C4 **Fairy Bridge** Skye, Highland Scotland 57.28N 6.34W
100 N5 **Fairy Glen** Saskatchewan 53.03N 104.34W
110 J7 **Fairylawn** Idaho 42.34N 116.59W
17 O10 **Fais** *I* Caroline Is Pacific Oc 9.45N 140.31E
31 G5 **Faisalabad** Pakistan 31.25N 73.09E
31 G5 **Faisalabad** *dist* Pakistan
105 J2 **Faison** N Carolina 35.06N 78.09W
69 H4 **Faissault** France 49.36N 4.32E
108 H4 **Faith** S Dakota 45.02N 102.03W
58 P8 **Faither, The** *pt* Shetland Scotland 60.33N 1.32W
86 B5 **Faiyâda, El** *hill* Egypt 30.18N 29.21E
86 E7 **Faiyûm** *div* Egypt
86 E7 **Faiyûm, El** Egypt 29.19N 30.50E
31 C2 **Faizabad** Afghanistan 36.17N 64.49E
31 F2 **Faizabad** Badakhshan Afghanistan 37.05N 70.40E
Faizabad China*see* **Jiashi**
Faizabad Iran*see* **Feyzābād**
30 F6 **Faizabad** Uttar Prad India 26.46N 82.08E
30 F6 **Faizabad** *dist* Uttar Prad India
96 T1 **Fajã de Cima** Azores 37.32N 25.39W
96 O2 **Fajã Grande** Azores 39.27N 31.16W
76 D8 **Fajão** Portugal 40.09N 7.55W
87 C7 **Fajarial,L** Sudan 6.20N 31.29E
96 O2 **Fajãsinha** Azores 39.27N 31.15W
34 N7 **Fajir** Iraq 31.55N 45.58E
34 J8 **Fajj as Salubi** *watercourse* Saudi Arabia
72 H10 **Fajolle,la** France 42.46N 1.57E
33 B2 **Fajr, Wādī** *watercourse* Saudi Arabia
122 F14 **Fakaina** *atoll* Tuamotu Is Pacific Oc 16.00S 140.05W
33 E8 **Fakām** Yemen 16.38N 43.50E
10 S3 **Fakaofo** *isld* Tokelau Is Pacific Oc 9.30S 171.15W
122 C14 **Fakarava** *atoll* Tuamotu Is Pacific Oc 16.02S 145.36W
46 R1 **Fakel** U.S.S.R. 57.38N 53.00E
56 N2 **Fakenham** Norfolk Eng 52.50N 0.51E
43 A3 **Fakeyev** Kazakhstan U.S.S.R. 48.57N 49.55E
15 B5 **Fakfak** Irian Jaya 2.55S 132.17E
87 D3 **Fakhakhir** Sudan 14.15N 32.46E
30 E5 **Fakharpur** Uttar Prad India 27.26N 81.32E
33 G9 **Fakhdh** *mt* S Yemen 14.47N 46.50E
32 F5 **Fakhrābād** Iran 31.20N 54.02E
36 H3 **Fakılı** Turkey 39.14N 34.56E
28 H2 **Fakiragram** Assam India 26.22N 90.15E
82 L8 **Fakiya** Bulgaria 42.10N 27.06E
53 J6 **Fakse** Denmark 55.16N 12.08E
53 J6 **Fakse Bugt** *B* Denmark
52 G5 **Faksefjel** *mt* Norway 61.20N 12.50E
53 J6 **Fakse Ladeplads** Denmark 55.14N 12.11E
21 C6 **Faku** Liaoning China 42.30N 123.24E
122 B4 **Fala Ane Pt** Swains I Pacific Oc 11.03S 171.06W
89 D7 **Falaba** Sierra Leone 9.54N 11.22W
19 N4 **Fala-beguets** *isld* Truk Is Pacific Oc 7.22N 151.40E
76 D1 **Faladoira, Sierra della** *mts* Spain
61 K5 **Falaën** Belgium 50.17N 4.48E
87 C6 **Falagh** Sudan 8.39N 31.04E
84 D2 **Fálaina** Greece 39.43N 22.24E
70 K4 **Falaise** France 48.54N 0.11W
101 P5 **Falaise L** N W Terr
29 L4 **Falakata** W Bengal India 26.32N 89.16E
31 C3 **Falakhar Pass** Afghanistan 35.15N 65.15E
83 F3 **Falakrón** *mts* Greece
19 N4 **Falalu** *isld* Truk Is Pacific Oc 7.39N 151.41E
25 B1 **Falam** Burma 22.58N 93.45E
89 E6 **Falama** Guinea 10.40N 8.32W
35 D5 **Falama** Jordan 32.13N 35.01E
19 N4 **Falas** *isld* Truk Is Pacific Oc 7.32N 151.45E
19 N5 **Falasit** *isld* Truk Is Pacific Oc 7.14N 151.38E
32 D4 **Falâvârjan** Iran 32.33N 51.28E
79 L2 **Falcade** Italy 46.22N 11.52E
59 F1 **Falcarragh** Donegal Irish Rep 55.08N 8.06W
75 G3 **Falces** Spain 42.24N 1.48W
82 L4 **Fălciu** Romania 46.17N 28.10E
77 S12 **Falcó, C** Balearic Is 38.50N 1.23E
76 A3 **Falcoeiro, Pta** *pt* Spain 42.31N 9.02W
109 F3 **Falcon** Colorado 38.56N 104.37W
9 S13 **Falcon** *islet* Tonga, Pacific Oc 20.20S 175.20W
119 E2 **Falcón** *state* Venezuela
81 M5 **Falconara Albanese** Italy 39.16N 16.05E
79 O7 **Falconara Marittima** Italy 43.37N 13.23E
99 K6 **Falconbridge** Ontario 46.35N 80.48W
74 G9 **Falcon, C** Algeria 35.47N 0.48W
77 V15 **Falcon, C** Balearic Is 39.07N 2.57E
112 H9 **Falcon Dam** Texas/Mexico 26.32N 99.10W
81 K7 **Falcone** Sicily 38.07N 15.06E
81 A2 **Falcone, C** Sardinia 40.57N 8.12E
81 C1 **Falcone, Pta** *pt* Sardinia 41.16N 9.14E
104 F4 **Falconer** New York 42.06N 79.12W
77 X13 **Falconera** *mt* Balearic Is 40.03N 3.57E
112 H9 **Falcon L** Texas/Mexico
100 F1 **Falcon Lake** Manitoba 49.44N 95.18W
53 E6 **Faldsled** Denmark 55.09N 10.10E
89 D5 **Faléa** Mali 12.16N 11.21W
19 M4 **Faleallej Pass** Truk Is Pacific Oc 7.27N 151.33E
122 A1 **Falealupo** W Samoa, Pacific Oc 13.25S 172.45W
122 B1 **Faleasiu** W Samoa, Pacific Oc 13.48S 171.56W
122 C2 **Falefa** W Samoa, Pacific Oc 13.53S 171.34W
53 V15 **Faleide** Norway 61.54N 6.38E
122 A1 **Falelima** W Samoa, Pacific Oc 13.30S 172.41W
46 Q1 **Falenki** U.S.S.R. 58.22N 51.31E
19 N4 **Faleosicz** *isld* Truk Is Pacific Oc 7.25N 151.39E
81 M5 **Falerna** Italy 39.00N 16.10E
52 J8 **Falerum** Sweden 58.07N 16.15E
46 G6 **Faleshty** Moldavia U.S.S.R. 47.30N 27.45E
88 S10 **Falesles** Algeria 23.43N 9.06E
19 N5 **Faleu** *isld* Truk Is Pacific Oc 7.15N 151.47E
122 B1 **Faleula** W Samoa, Pacific Oc 13.46S 171.48W
122 B2 **Falevai** W Samoa, Pacific Oc 13.53S 172.00W
112 J8 **Falfurrias** Texas 27.17N 98.10W
101 P8 **Falher** Alberta 55.45N 117.18W
33 E9 **Falībī** Yemen 15.36N 43.46E
61 J5 **Falisolle** Belgium 50.25N 4.37E
110 A9 **Falk** California 40.42N 124.07W
66 P3 **Falkais** *mt* Switz/Liechtenstein 47.04N 9.34E
87 G2 **Falkat,R** Ethiopia

63 S9 **Falkenberg** Cottbus E Germany 51.35N 13.14E
63 T7 **Falkenberg** Frankfurt E Germany 52.48N 13.58E
64 O7 **Falkenberg** Nieder-Bayern W Germany 48.26N 12.45E
64 N4 **Falkenberg** Oberpfalz, Bayern W Germany 49.51N 12.14E
52 G10 **Falkenberg** Sweden 56.55N 12.30E
99 L7 **Falkenburg** Ontario 45.06N 79.21W
63 Q6 **Falkenhagen** E Germany 53.13N 12.13E
63 S7 **Falkensee** E Germany 52.35N 13.06E
64 N3 **Falkenstein** E Germany 50.28N 12.23E
64 O5 **Falkenstein** W Germany 49.06N 12.31E
53 Y18 **Falkenutbrotet** *mt* Norway 60.16N 8.15E
53 H7 **Falkerslev** Denmark 54.50N 11.52E
53 Y16 **Falketind** *mt* Norway 61.23N 8.06E
58 J7 **Falkirk** Central Scotland 56.00N 3.48W
101 O10 **Falkland** Br Columbia 50.30N 119.35W
58 K6 **Falkland** Fife Scotland 56.15N 3.13W
121 E10 **Falkland, East I** Falkland Is
121 E10 **Falkland Islands** Atlantic Oc
121 E10 **Falkland Sd** Falkland Is
121 D9 **Falkland, West I** Falkland Is
121 C8 **Falkner** Argentina 40.30S 67.00W
107 H7 **Falkner** Mississippi 34.51N 88.56W
103 J4 **Falkner I** Connecticut 41.13N 72.39W
84 G8 **Falkonéra** *isld* Greece 36.50N 23.52E
52 G8 **Falköping** Sweden 58.10N 13.32E
107 K7 **Falkville** Alabama 34.21N 86.53W
109 O4 **Fall** *R* Kansas
61 L4 **Fallais** Belgium 50.37N 5.10E
66 L2 **Fällanden** Switzerland 47.22N 8.38E
111 G8 **Fall Brook** California 33.23N 117.15W
110 D2 **Fall City** Washington 47.34N 121.54W
106 C5 **Fall Creek** Wisconsin 44.47N 91.18W
87 G6 **Falle** Ethiopia 9.18N 38.35E
79 B3 **Fallère** *mt* Italy 45.47N 7.12E
63 N8 **Fallersleben** W Germany 52.25N 10.44E
51 H6 **Fällfors** Sweden 65.08N 20.46E
53 E5 **Falling** Denmark 55.54N 10.09E
63 L7 **Fallingbostel** W Germany 52.52N 9.41E
107 H7 **Fall Line Hills** Alabama
105 D5 **Fall Line Hills** Georgia
66 B1 **Fallon** France 47.31N 6.30E
108 E3 **Fallon** Montana 46.50N 105.08W
111 F2 **Fallon** Nevada 39.29N 118.47W
121 H7 **Fallos, Canal** *str* Chile
103 M3 **Fall River** Massachusetts 41.42N 71.08W
110 D8 **Fall River Mills** California 41.00N 121.27W
109 O4 **Fall River Res** Kansas
103 C4 **Falls** Pennsylvania 41.27N 75.50W
104 H8 **Falls Church** Virginia 38.54N 77.11W
108 P9 **Falls City** Nebraska 40.03N 95.36W
110 B5 **Falls City** Oregon 44.52N 123.28W
112 J7 **Falls City** Texas 29.00N 98.02W
104 G5 **Falls Creek** Pennsylvania 41.08N 78.48W
103 B7 **Fallston** Maryland 39.31N 76.25W
103 H3 **Falls Village** Connecticut 41.57N 73.21W
34 L5 **Fallūjah, Al** Iraq 33.21N 43.46E
61 K6 **Falmagne** Belgium 50.12N 4.54E
66 L7 **Falmenta** Italy 46.04N 8.36E
56 L6 **Falmer** E Sussex Eng 50.52N 0.05W
89 L5 **Falmey** Niger 12.32N 2.32E
61 K6 **Falmignoul** Belgium 50.12N 4.53E
116 P4 **Falmouth** Antigua W I 17.02N 61.47W
56 T9 **Falmouth** Cornwall Eng 50.08N 5.04W
116 J1 **Falmouth** Jamaica, W I 18.29N 77.39W
107 M3 **Falmouth** Kentucky 38.40N 84.20W
103 N3 **Falmouth** Massachusetts 41.33N 70.37W
106 J5 **Falmouth** Michigan 44.14N 85.05W
103 A6 **Falmouth** Pennsylvania 40.07N 76.42W
104 H8 **Falmouth** Virginia 38.20N 77.29W
56 T9 **Falmouth Bay** Cornwall Eng 50.08N 5.04W
104 P3 **Falmouth Foreside** Maine 43.44N 70.14W
53 S20 **Falnes** Norway 59.09N 5.18E
19 N4 **Falo** *isld* Truk Is Pacific Oc 7.29N 151.53E
56 B7 **Fal, R** Cornwall Eng
120 D9 **Falsa Chipana, Pta** *C* Chile 21.25S 70.05W
False B *see* **Valsbaai** *B*
14 A7 **False Ent** W Australia 26.20S 113.19E
113 F9 **False Pass** Aleutian Is 54.51N 163.30W
13 F2 **False Pera Hd** Queensland 13.05S 141.40E
106 L4 **False Presque Isle** Michigan 45.16N 83.23W
29 K7 **False Pt** Orissa India 20.22N 86.52E
75 M5 **Falset** Spain 41.08N 0.49E
117 C4 **Falsino** *R* Brazil
120 E12 **Falso Azufre, Nevado** *pk* Arg/Chile 26.47S 68.20W
116 J6 **Falso, C** Dominican Rep 17.49N 71.39W
116 C7 **Falso, C** Honduras 15.10N 83.20W
115 D6 **Falso, C** Mexico 22.50N 110.00W
121 L10 **Falso Cabo de Hornos** Chile 55.45S 68.02W
53 H7 **Falster** *isld* Denmark
52 G11 **Falsterbo** Sweden 55.23N 12.50E
57 J2 **Falstone** Northumb Eng 55.11N 2.25W
29 L6 **Falta** W Bengal India 22.18N 88.08E
79 L7 **Falterona, Monte** Italy 43.53N 11.43E
82 K3 **Fălticeni** Romania 47.27N 26.20E
52 J6 **Falun** Sweden 60.37N 15.40E
79 M1 **Falzárego, Passo di** *pass* Italy 46.32N 12.02E
84 S14 **Famagusta** Cyprus 35.07N 33.57E
84 S14 **Famagusta Bay** Cyprus
121 D1 **Famaillá** Argentina 27.05S 65.23W
121 C2 **Famatina** Argentina 28.58S 67.46W
121 C2 **Famatina, Sierra de** *mts* Argentina
91 E5 **Fambono** Zaïre 3.48S 17.19E
61 J6 **Famenne** *reg* Belgium
14 E7 **Fame Ra** W Australia
53 N10 **Famien** Faeroes 61.32N 6.52W
61 G4 **Familleureux** Belgium 50.32N 4.13E
14 F6 **Family Well** W Australia 22.35S 126.10E
77 Q3 **Famorca** Spain 38.44N 0.15W
89 E7 **Famorodougou** Guinea 8.33N 8.39W
111 E6 **Famoso** California 35.36N 119.14W
95 E3 **Fampotabe** Madagascar 15.54S 50.09E
32 D6 **Fāmūr, Daryācheh-ye** *salt marsh* Iran
91 A3 **Fan** *tribe* Gabon
59 G1 **Fanad Hd** Donegal Irish Rep 55.17N 7.38W
53 S18 **Fanahammeren** Norway 60.15N 5.23E
Fanaitis, Al *see* **Funaytis, Al**
11 K2 **Fanal I** New Zealand 35.57S 175.11E
19 N4 **Fanamar** *isld* Truk Is Pacific Oc 7.32N 151.47E
95 E2 **Fanambana** Madagascar 13.32S 49.58E
19 N5 **Fanan** *isld* Truk Is Pacific Oc 7.12N 151.59E
19 N4 **Fananan** *isld* Truk Is Pacific Oc 7.17N 151.56E
95 D5 **Fanandrana** Madagascar 18.15S 49.15E
79 J6 **Fanano** Italy 44.12N 10.47E
86 H5 **Fanâra** Egypt 30.14N 32.23E
84 C3 **Fanárion** Greece 39.25N 21.48E
84 C3 **Fanárion Magoúlas** Greece 39.27N 21.48E
23 H3 **Fanchang** Anhui China 31.06N 118.04E
107 H5 **Fancy Farm** Kentucky 36.48N 88.48W
95 C6 **Fandriana** Madagascar 20.14S 47.21E
66 N5 **Fanella Horn** *mt* Switzerland 46.33N 9.08E
59 K4 **Fane, R** Louth Irish Rep
84 V17 **Fánes** Rhodes 36.20N 28.00E
19 N4 **Faneu** *isld* Truk Is Pacific Oc 7.17N 151.54E
25 E3 **Fang** Thailand 19.56N 99.14E
87 C6 **Fangak** Sudan 9.05N 30.52E
122 E14 **Fangatau** *atoll* Tuamotu Is Pacific Oc 15.45S 140.50W
9 S10 **Fanga Uta** *lagoon* Tonga, Pacific Oc
23 E8 **Fangcheng** Guangxi China 21.47N 108.23E
23 F2 **Fangcheng** Henan China 33.18N 112.59E
23 E3 **Fangdou Shan** *mts* Sichuan China
53 E6 **Fangel** Denmark 55.18N 10.20E
57 M5 **Fangfoss** Humberside Eng 53.58N 0.50W
22 J7 **Fanglan** Shanxi China 38.32N 113.03E
23 J7 **Fang-liao** Taiwan 22.22N 120.36E
67 O12 **Fango** *R* Corsica
22 K7 **Fangshan** Beijing China 39.42N 115.58E
23 E2 **Fang Xian** Hubei China 34.45N 116.39E
21 D5 **Fangzheng** Heilongjiang China 45.50N 128.50E
22 L8 **Fangzi** Shandong China 36.44N 119.10E
15 A3 **Fani** *isld* Irian Jaya 1.03N 131.16E
33 N5 **Fanjah** Oman 23.30N 58.08E
95 C6 **Fanjakana** Madagascar 21.10S 46.51E
72 J9 **Fanjeaux** France 43.11N 2.02E
21 C6 **Fanjiatun** Jilin China 43.42N 125.05E
75 K2 **Fanlo** Spain 42.35N 0.01W
53 X15 **Fannaraken** *mt* Norway 61.31N 7.55E
112 N6 **Fannett** Texas 29.55N 94.17W
58 F3 **Fannich, L** Highland Scotland 57.37N 4.59W
107 G9 **Fannin** Mississippi 32.24N 89.58W
112 K7 **Fannin** Texas 28.42N 97.16W
122 U8 **Fanning I** *atoll* Line Is Pacific Oc 3.52N 159.22W
52 E3 **Fannrem** Norway 63.16N 9.50E
32 H7 **Fannūj** Iran 26.35N 59.40E
101 L11 **Fanny Bay** Vancouver I, Br Col 49.30N 124.50W
100 U9 **Fannystelle** Manitoba 49.44N 97.48W
79 O7 **Fano** Italy 43.51N 13.01E
53 A6 **Fanø** *isld* Denmark 55.25N 8.25E
80 J3 **Fano Adriano** Italy 42.33N 13.33E
53 A6 **Fanø Bugt** *B* Denmark
59 D5 **Fanore Bridge** Clare Irish Rep 53.07N 9.17W
22 J7 **Fanshi** Shanxi China 39.12N 113.05E
25 G1 **Fan Si Pan** *mt* Vietnam 22.19N 103.46E
33 N9 **Fanṭās, Al** Kuwait 29.10N 48.07E
86 E8 **Fant, El** Egypt 28.45N 30.52E
53 S18 **Fantoft** Norway 60.20N 5.21E
9 R12 **Fanua Unga** *islet* Tonga, Pacific Oc 18.45S 173.57W
Fanuch *see* **Fannūj**
19 N4 **Fanuela** *isld* Truk Is Pacific Oc 7.35N 151.51E
19 M4 **Fanueranu** *isld* Truk Is Pacific Oc 7.18N 151.30E
19 N4 **Fanuet** *isld* Truk Is Pacific Oc 7.33N 151.49E

19 N4 **Fanurmot** *isld* Truk Is Pacific Oc 7.19N 151.41E
23 G1 **Fan Xian** Henan China 35.59N 115.31E
87 C7 **Fanyok** Sudan 7.52N 31.49E
Fao Iraq*see* **Fâw, Al**
76 B5 **Fão** Portugal 41.31N 8.46W
Faouâr *watercourse see* **Fawwar** *watercourse*
70 D5 **Faouët,le** France 48.01N 3.29W
66 E4 **Faoug** Switzerland 46.54N 7.05E
70 B5 **Faou,le** France 48.18N 4.11W
32 D6 **Faqih Ahmadān** Iran 28.22N 51.21E
86 F8 **Faqîra, Wâdî** *watercourse* Egypt
35 E4 **Faqqu'a** Jordan 32.29N 35.24E
35 F8 **Faqu** Jordan 31.22N 35.42E
86 G4 **Fâqûs** Egypt 30.44N 31.47E
50 E6 **Far** *R* Iceland
35 F4 **Fara** Jordan 32.22N 35.39E
58 S12 **Fara** *isld* Orkney Scotland 58.51N 3.10W
43 G7 **Farab** Turkmeniya U.S.S.R. 39.14N 63.40E
89 D5 **Faraba** Mali 12.29N 10.52W
89 E6 **Faraba** Mali 11.52N 8.08W
43 G7 **Farab-Pristan'** Turkmeniya U.S.S.R. 39.12N 63.38E
13 H6 **Faraday, Mt** Queensland 24.54S 147.18E
93 A2 **Faradje** Zaïre 3.45N 29.43E
95 C7 **Farafangana** Madagascar 22.50S 47.50E
85 K6 **Farafra Oasis** Egypt
32 E5 **Farāgheh** Iran 31.04N 53.02E
87 E5 **Faragimendo,Jeb** *mt reg* Ethiopia
80 K7 **Faraglioni** Italy 40.32N 14.15E
31 B4 **Farah** Afghanistan 32.23N 62.08E
30 A5 **Farah** Uttar Prad India 27.20N 77.47E
31 B4 **Farah** *prov* Afghanistan
32 E2 **Faraḥābād** Iran 36.48N 53.07E
31 B4 **Farah Rud** *R* Afghanistan
Fara I *see* **Fera I**
80 G4 **Fara in Sabina** Italy 42.13N 12.44E
33 D7 **Fara Is** Saudi Arabia
32 A8 **Farajābād** *sub* Tehrān Iran
33 J6 **Farajah** Saudi Arabia 21.35N 50.38E
77 F7 **Faraján** Spain 36.38N 5.10W
Farajia *see* **Farajah**
87 D9 **Farajok** Sudan 3.51N 32.27E
31 E3 **Farakhulm** Afghanistan 34.31N 68.08E
30 L8 **Farakka** W Bengal India 24.50N 87.54E
29 K5 **Farakka Barrage** N Bengal India 24.43N 87.55E
84 C7 **Farakládha** Greece 37.12N 21.37E
84 F8 **Faraklón** Greece 36.32N 23.05E
89 F6 **Farako** Mali 10.45N 6.50W
17 P8 **Farallon de Medinilla** *isld* Marianas Pacific Oc 16.01N 146.04E
17 O7 **Farallon de Pajaros** *islds* Marianas Pacific Oc 20.33N 144.54E
77 D8 **Farallón Grande** *isld* Spain 36.23N 6.14W
111 A4 **Farallon Is** California 37.40N 123.00W
89 D6 **Faranah** Guinea 10.01N 10.47W
79 D3 **Fara Novara** Italy 45.33N 8.27E
33 D8 **Farasān** *oil well* Farasān Is Red Sea 16.44N 41.50E
33 D8 **Farasān Is** Red Sea
75 H3 **Farasdués** Spain 42.13N 1.05W
95 C5 **Faratsiho** Madagascar 19.24S 46.57E
17 O10 **Faraulep** *atoll* Caroline Is Pacific Oc 8.36N 144.33E
85 N8 **Farâyid,Gebel El** *mts* Egypt
87 K9 **Farbarachi** Somalia 2.29N 45.29E
107 E2 **Farber** Missouri 39.17N 91.34W
51 F6 **Fårberg** Sweden 65.39N 16.40E
82 J3 **Farcăului** *mt* Romania 47.55N 24.29E
61 J5 **Farciennes** Belgium 50.26N 4.33E
53 Y20 **Fardal** Norway 59.09N 8.03E
53 X16 **Fardalen** *V* Norway 61.21N 7.45E
81 M3 **Fardella** Italy 40.07N 16.10E
52 E7 **Farder** *Lt Ho* Norway 59.01N 10.06E
77 K6 **Fardes** *R* Spain
53 A4 **Fåre** Denmark 56.28N 8.17E
122 A15 **Fare** Society Is Pacific Oc 16.42S 151.02W
69 M5 **Farebersviller** France 49.07N 6.50E
56 J6 **Fareham** Hants Eng 50.51N 1.10W
71 G9 **Fare les Oliviers, la** France 43.32N 5.12E
69 D6 **Faremoutiers** France 48.47N 3.00E
53 H6 **Farendløse** Denmark 55.24N 11.54E
53 G5 **Fårevejle** Denmark 55.48N 11.28E
113 L5 **Farewell** Alaska 62.30N 154.00W
Farewell, C Greenland*see* **Farvel, Kap** *cape*
11 G7 **Farewell, C** New Zealand 40.30S 172.42E
11 G7 **Farewell Spit** New Zealand
119 C7 **Farfán** Ecuador 0.08N 76.37W
72 K1 **Farges-en-Septaine** France 47.05N 2.38E
105 E7 **Fargo** Georgia 30.42N 82.34W
109 L5 **Fargo** Oklahoma 36.23N 99.37W
72 E7 **Fargues-sur-Ourbise** France 44.15N 0.09E
103 E5 **Far Hills** New Jersey 40.40N 74.39W
53 K4 **Farhult** Sweden 56.13N 12.44E
53 C7 **Fårhus** Denmark 54.52N 9.20E
35 E5 **Fari'a** *R* Jordan
31 C2 **Fariab** *prov* Afghanistan
35 E5 **Fari'a el Jiftlick** Jordan 32.08N 35.30E
108 R5 **Faribault** Minnesota 44.19N 93.15W
30 A4 **Faridabad** Haryana India 28.24N 77.18E
29 D2 **Faridkot** Punjab India 30.42N 74.47E
31 H9 **Faridpur** Bangladesh 23.29N 89.31E
30 C4 **Faridpur** Uttar Prad India 28.12N 79.32E
31 H9 **Faridpur** *dist* Bangladesh
85 F4 **Fārigh** *watercourse* Libya
85 D7 **Fārigh, al** *watercourse* Libya
86 E5 **Fârigh, Wâdi el** *watercourse* Egypt
79 C5 **Fārigliano** Italy 44.31N 7.56E
52 J5 **Färila** Sweden 61.48N 15.55E
94 C4 **Farilhao Point** *C* Namibia 22.07S 14.15E
76 A10 **Farilhões** *islds* Portugal 39.28N 9.31W
89 B5 **Farim** Guinea-Bissau 12.30N 15.09W
32 H3 **Farīmān** Iran 35.46N 59.49E
12 E4 **Farina** S Australia 30.05S 138.20E
80 J4 **Farindola** Italy 42.27N 13.50E
56 H4 **Faringdon** Oxon Eng 51.40N 1.35W
52 L7 **Faringe** Sweden 59.55N 18.07E
117 E8 **Farinha, R** Brazil
79 G5 **Farini d'Olmo** Italy 44.43N 9.34E
96 V7 **Fariones, Pta** *pt* Lanzarote Canary Is 29.14N 13.24W
85 M7 **Fâris** Egypt 24.34N 32.54E
33 J6 **Fāris** Saudi Arabia 20.12N 50.58E
43 H6 **Farish** Uzbekistan U.S.S.R. 40.33N 66.51E
109 E4 **Farisita** Colorado 37.44N 105.03W
36 F6 **Fariske** Turkey 36.37N 32.37E
86 G3 **Fâriskûr** Egypt 31.20N 31.43E
76 G6 **Fariza** Spain 41.25N 6.16W
35 G2 **Farj** Syria 32.58N 35.50E
52 J10 **Färjestaden** Sweden 56.38N 16.30E
25 L9 **Farkawno** Assam India 23.08N 93.16E
31 E2 **Farkhar** Afghanistan 36.39N 69.43E
41 E7 **Farkovo** U.S.S.R. 65.46N 87.07E
92 G4 **Farkwa** Tanzania 5.25S 35.35E
100 H1 **Farlane** Ontario 50.00N 94.10W
71 J10 **Farlède, la** France 43.10N 6.03E
55 G6 **Farleigh** London Eng 51.20N 0.02W
13 J5 **Farleigh** Queensland 21.05S 149.08E
75 J4 **Farlete** Spain 41.40N 0.31W
106 C7 **Farley** Iowa 42.26N 91.01W
109 F5 **Farley** New Mexico 36.21N 104.03W
99 O6 **Farley** Quebec 46.18N 76.00W
80 D2 **Farma** *R* Italy
32 C3 **Farmahin** Iran 34.29N 49.41E
56 G5 **Farmboro** Avon Eng 51.22N 2.29W
108 N6 **Farmer** S Dakota 43.55N 97.40W
106 F9 **Farmer City** Illinois 40.15N 88.39W
112 N9 **Farmers Branch** Texas 32.53N 96.54W
107 J2 **Farmersburg** Indiana 39.15N 87.22W
106 C7 **Farmersburg** Iowa 42.57N 91.22W
112 L2 **Farmersville** Texas 33.10N 96.21W
107 D9 **Farmerville** Louisiana 32.46N 92.23W
103 H5 **Farmingdale** Long I, N Y 40.45N 73.26W
103 F6 **Farmingdale** New Jersey 40.12N 74.10W
108 H6 **Farmingdale** S Dakota 43.58N 102.52W
101 N8 **Farmington** Br Columbia 55.55N 120.30W
111 C4 **Farmington** California 37.56N 121.00W
103 J3 **Farmington** Connecticut 41.44N 72.50W
103 C9 **Farmington** Delaware 38.52N 75.35W
106 D9 **Farmington** Illinois 40.43N 90.01W
106 C9 **Farmington** Iowa 40.38N 91.43W
104 P2 **Farmington** Maine 44.41N 70.11W
108 R5 **Farmington** Minnesota 44.34N 93.07W
107 F4 **Farmington** Missouri 37.46N 90.26W
104 O3 **Farmington** New Hampshire 43.23N 71.06W
109 B5 **Farmington** New Mexico 36.43N 108.12W
110 O9 **Farmington** Utah 40.59N 111.55W
110 H2 **Farmington** Washington 47.06N 117.04W
104 E7 **Farmington** W Virginia 39.32N 80.16W
103 J3 **Farmington** *R* Connecticut
106 J9 **Farmland** Indiana 40.12N 85.06W
60 Q6 **Farmsum** Netherlands 53.19N 6.56E
105 K2 **Farmville** N Carolina 35.35N 77.35W
104 G9 **Farmville** Virginia 37.17N 78.25W
108 K9 **Farnam** Nebraska 40.45N 100.14W
56 K5 **Farnborough** Hants Eng 51.17N 0.46W
55 H5 **Farnborough** London England 51.22N 0.04E
57 H6 **Farndon** Cheshire Eng 53.06N 2.53W
54 K7 **Farne Deep** North Sea
58 N7 **Farne Is** Northumb Eng 55.38N 1.36W
107 M6 **Farner** Tennessee 35.09N 84.20W
53 V16 **Farnes** Norway 61.15N 6.32E
80 E3 **Farnese** Italy 42.33N 11.43E
56 G6 **Farnham** Dorset Eng 50.56N 2.04W
104 F4 **Farnham** New York 42.36N 79.06W
99 S7 **Farnham** Quebec 45.17N 72.59W
56 O3 **Farnham** Suffolk Eng 52.12N 1.26E
56 K5 **Farnham** Surrey Eng 51.13N 0.49W
101 P10 **Farnham, Mt** Br Columbia 50.27N 116.37W
56 K4 **Farnham Royal** Bucks Eng 51.33N 0.38W
55 K5 **Farningham** Kent England 51.23N 0.14E
66 H2 **Farnsberg** *mt* Switzerland 47.30N 7.52E
57 L6 **Farnsfield** Notts Eng 53.07N 1.03W
112 D7 **Farnsworth** Texas 36.19N 100.58W
57 J5 **Farnworth** Greater Manchester Eng 53.33N 2.24W
117 B6 **Faro** Brazil 2.10S 56.39W
76 D14 **Faro** Portugal 37.01N 7.56W

87 M5 **Faro** Somalia 11.01N 48.44E
52 L9 **Fåro** Sweden 57.55N 19.10E
101 G4 **Faro** Yukon Terr 62.15N 133.30W
101 G4 **Faro** Yukon Terr 62.11N 133.22W
76 D14 **Faro** *dist* Portugal
53 H7 **Farø** *isld* Denmark 54.58N 12.00E
90 F7 **Faro** *R* Cameroon
76 D12 **Faro do Alentejo** Portugal 38.09N 7.57W
19 M7 **Farol Pt** Philippines 9.05N 124.45E
79 B3 **Faroma** *mt* Italy 45.48N 7.26E
119 D2 **Faro,Pta** Colombia 11.06N 74.51W
81 L7 **Faro, Pta. del** Sicily 38.17N 15.39E
76 D3 **Faro,Sierra del** *mts* Spain
52 L9 **Fårösund** Sweden 57.51N 19.05E
107 E12 **Far, Pt. Au** Louisiana 29.20N 91.21W
14 A6 **Farquhar, C** W Australia 23.50S 113.35E
26 D6 **Farquhar Is** Seychelles, Ind Oc
79 M2 **Farra d'Alpago** Italy 46.07N 12.22E
79 M3 **Farra di Soligo** Italy 45.54N 12.07E
79 P3 **Farra d'Isonzo** Italy 45.55N 13.31E
Farradiya *see* **Parod**
59 C7 **Farranfore** Kerry Irish Rep 52.10N 9.33W
58 G4 **Farrar,R** Highland Scotland
13 F6 **Farrars Cr** Queensland
32 E6 **Farrāshband** Iran 28.53N 52.07E
33 E7 **Farrâsh,Jabal al** *mt* Saudi Arabia 19.36N 43.25E
104 E5 **Farrell** Pennsylvania 41.13N 80.31W
99 P7 **Farrellton** Quebec 45.44N 75.55W
12 A6 **Farrer** *dist* Canberra Australia
100 K1 **Farrington** Ontario 48.49N 92.42W
56 F5 **Farrington Gurney** Avon Eng 51.19N 2.33W
53 C6 **Farris** Denmark 55.23N 9.17E
103 L8 **Far Rockaway** New York 40.36N 73.46W
32 H4 **Farrokhī** Iran 33.50N 59.30E
76 E9 **Farroupa** Portugal 39.45N 7.25W
77 W14 **Farruch, C** Balearic Is 39.48N 3.20E
30 C5 **Farrukhabad** *dist* Uttar Prad India
Farrukhi *see* **Farrokhī**
29 E3 **Farrukhnagar** Haryana India 28.28N 76.51E
32 E6 **Fārs** *prov* Iran
32 B1 **Farsabad** Iran 39.28N 48.00E
84 D3 **Fársala** Greece 39.17N 22.23E
85 M6 **Farshût** Egypt 26.03N 32.09E
31 B4 **Farsi** Afghanistan 33.46N 63.12E
88 J8 **Farsia,El** Morocco 27.06N 9.50W
86 F4 **Farsîs** Egypt 30.40N 31.14E
33 B8 **Farsiyah B** Bahrain, The Gulf
53 C3 **Farsø** Denmark 56.47N 9.21E
87 J6 **Farso** Ethiopia 8.22N 42.57E
106 B8 **Farson** Iowa 41.06N 92.16W
110 Q7 **Farson** Wyoming 42.08N 109.26W
52 C8 **Farsund** Norway 58.05N 6.49E
33 J9 **Fartak,Jabal** *mts* S Yemen
33 K9 **Fartak,Ra's** *C* S Yemen 15.38N 52.16E
88 N5 **Fartassa Gharbia** Algeria 32.51N 1.18W
56 J3 **Farthinghoe** Northants Eng 52.03N 1.12W
118 D10 **Fartura,Serra da** *mts* Brazil
32 H2 **Fārūj** Iran 37.10N 58.15E
53 J5 **Farum** Denmark 55.49N 12.23E
32 G2 **Farūmād** Iran 36.30N 56.40E
53 B6 **Farup** Denmark 55.22N 8.45E
53 D3 **Fårup** Denmark 56.33N 9.53E
33 H4 **Farūq,Al** *hills* Saudi Arabia
Farur *see* **Forūr**
66 E5 **Farvagny** Switzerland 46.44N 7.05E
53 D4 **Fårvang** Denmark 56.16N 9.45E
48 V16 **Farvel, Kap** *C* Greenland 59.45N 43.30W
106 K6 **Farwell** Michigan 43.50N 84.51W
108 M8 **Farwell** Nebraska 41.14N 98.34W
112 D1 **Farwell** Texas 34.23N 103.03W
32 G6 **Fāryāb** Iran 28.07N 57.14E
32 E6 **Fasā** Iran 28.55N 53.39E
33 K7 **Fasad** Oman 18.28N 53.08E
81 P11 **Fasano** Italy 40.50N 17.21E
87 D4 **Fashashoya,El** Sudan 13.25N 32.34E
90 M5 **Fasher,El** Sudan 13.37N 25.22E
112 J7 **Fashing** Texas 28.48N 98.09W
35 E7 **Fashkha,Ras** *C* Jordan 31.42N 35.27E
86 E8 **Fashn,El** Egypt 28.49N 30.54E
87 C6 **Fashoda** Sudan 9.50N 32.00E
58 J5 **Faskally,L** Tayside Scotland 56.43N 3.47W
50 L5 **Fáskrúdhsfjördhur** Múlasýsla, Sudhur Iceland 64.57N 14.01W
50 M5 **Fáskrúdhsfjördhur** *B* Iceland
96 R14 **Fasnia** Tenerife Canary Is 28.14N 16.27W
89 E8 **Fassangouni** Guinea 8.01N 9.24W
103 A3 **Fassett** Pennsylvania 41.59N 76.47W
86 B6 **Fassûlet Rammâk** *area* Egypt
35 E1 **Fassûta** Israel 33.03N 35.18E
58 M7 **Fast Castle** Borders Scotland 55.56N 2.12W
32 J8 **Fāsteh,Ra's-e-** *C* Iran 25.03N 61.27E
53 B5 **Faster** Denmark 55.59N 8.36E
53 C4 **Fasterholt** Denmark 56.01N 9.07E
59 C9 **Fastnet Rock Lt.Ho** Cork Irish Rep 51.24N 9.35W
46 G4 **Fastov** Ukraine U.S.S.R. 50.08N 29.59E
89 D5 **Fatafé** Mali 13.18N 10.15W
96 V16 **Fataga** Gran Canaria Canary Is 27.52N 15.35W
15 A5 **Fatagar, Tg** *C* Irian Jaya 2.46S 132.00E
Fatahgarj *see* **Fatehgarj Sharki**
93 B3 **Fataki** Zaïre 2.01N 30.37E
89 C6 **Fatala** *R* Guinea
75 L5 **Fatarella** Spain 41.10N 0.28E
75 L5 **Fatarella, Mtes.de** Spain
29 D3 **Fatehabad** Haryana India 29.30N 75.32E
30 B5 **Fatehabad** Uttar Prad India 27.01N 78.18E
29 E5 **Fatehgarh** Madhya Prad India 24.47N 77.00E
30 C5 **Fatehgarh** Uttar Prad India 27.22N 79.38E
30 C4 **Fatehgarj Sharki** Uttar Prad India 28.06N 79.38E
31 G4 **Fatehjang** Pakistan 33.33N 72.43E
30 J8 **Fatehpur** Bihar India 24.38N 85.14E
30 D7 **Fatehpur** Fatehpur, Uttar Prad India 25.56N 80.55E
30 K6 **Fatehpur** Nepal 26.44N 86.56E
31 F5 **Fatehpur** Pakistan 31.12N 71.13E
29 D4 **Fatehpur** Rajasthan India 27.59N 75.01E
30 A2 **Fatehpur** Uttar Prad India 30.03N 77.45E
30 E5 **Fatehpur** Uttar Prad India 27.11N 87.12E
30 D7 **Fatehpur** *dist* Uttar Prad India
30 J7 **Fatehpur Shahba** Bihar India 25.32N 85.20E
24 B12 **Fatehpur Sikri** India 27.06N 77.40E
30 A5 **Fatehpur Sikri** Uttar Prad India 27.06N 77.39E
80 H6 **Fate, Monte delle** Italy 41.24N 13.18E
77 E8 **Fates, Sierra de** *mts* Spain
45 F4 **Fateyevka** U.S.S.R. 52.05N 34.54E
45 G4 **Fatezh** U.S.S.R. 52.05N 35.53E
45 G4 **Fatezh** U.S.S.R. 52.06N 35.50E
33 L4 **Fath** *oil field* The Gulf 25.28N 54.22E
Fat-Ha *see* **Fatḥah, Al**
32 F6 **Fathābād** Iran 28.36N 54.49E
34 L3 **Fatḥah, Al** Iraq 35.03N 43.34E
87 C6 **Fathai** Sudan 8.03N 31.45E
99 P3 **Father L** Quebec
Father,The *mt see* **Ulawun,Mt.**
29 E7 **Fathkhelda** Maharashtra India 20.13N 76.29E
89 A4 **Fatick** Senegal 14.19N 16.27W
37 J2 **Fatih** *dist* İstanbul Turkey 41.01N 28.52E
98 L6 **Fatima** Madeleine Is, Que 47.26N 61.54W
76 B9 **Fátima** Portugal 39.37N 8.39W
33 K8 **Fatk,Al** S Yemen 16.32N 52.44E
Fatmah *see* **Bīr Fatmah**
89 E6 **Fatoya** Guinea 11.37N 9.10W
Fatq *see* **Fatk, Al**
37 D4 **Fatsa** Turkey 41.02N 37.31E
66 M4 **Fätschbach-Falls** Switzerland 46.54N 8.59E
Fatshan *see* **Fo-shan** Kwangtung
87 D3 **Fattasha** Sudan 15.31N 32.11E
23 C9 **Fat Tau Pt** Hong Kong 22.15N 114.17E
122 V15 **Fatu Hiva** *isld* Marquesas Is Pacific Oc 10.27S 138.39W
122 V14 **Fatu Huku** *I* Marquesas Is Pacific Oc 9.26S 138.55W
9 R12 **Fatumanga** *islet* Tonga, Pacific Oc 18.52S 174.10W
9 T12 **Fatumanongi** *atoll* Tonga, Pacific Oc 19.45S 174.45W
91 E5 **Fatunda** Zaïre 4.00S 17.19E
15 C7 **Fatural** Moluccas Indon 6.39S 134.08E
30 J7 **Fatwa** Bihar India 25.30N 85.18E
15 M3 **Fauabu** Malaita I Solomon Is 8.34S 160.43E
35 G3 **Fau'ara** Jordan 32.37N 35.46E
107 B2 **Faucett** Missouri 39.35N 94.48W
71 J5 **Faucigny** *dist* France
71 J4 **Faucille, Col de la** *mt* France 46.22N 6.03E
69 L7 **Faucilles, Mts** France
69 M8 **Faucogney** France 47.51N 6.33E
87 E3 **Fau, El** Sudan 14.08N 34.19E
71 C9 **Faugères** France 43.34N 3.12E
59 H2 **Faughan,R** Londonderry N Ireland
79 J7 **Fauglia** Italy 43.34N 10.31E
66 O3 **Faulegg** *mt* Switzerland 47.01N 9.17E
66 G5 **Faulensee** Switzerland 46.41N 7.43E
66 O3 **Faulfirst** *mt* Switzerland 47.08N 9.24E
66 H5 **Faulhorn** *mt* Switzerland 46.41N 7.59E
108 L4 **Faulkton** S Dakota 45.03N 99.08W
69 M5 **Faulquemont** France 49.03N 6.36E
61 L5 **Faulx-les-Tombes** Belgium 50.26N 5.01E
15 B4 **Faumi, Gunung** *mt* Irian Jaya 1.16S 132.45E
107 J9 **Faunsdale** Alabama 32.27N 87.37W
81 J8 **Fau, Pizzo** *mt* Sicily 37.54N 14.31E
69 C2 **Fauquembergues** France 50.35N 2.06E
101 O11 **Fauquier** Br Col 49.52N 118.02W
75 K8 **Faura** Spain 39.43N 0.16W
95 B10 **Faure** S Africa 34.01S 18.45E
82 L5 **Făurei** Romania 45.05N 27.15E
14 A7 **Faure I** W Australia 25.45S 113.50E
95 J5 **Fauresmith** S Africa 29.45S 25.19E
71 H7 **Faurie la** France 44.34N 5.45E
61 G5 **Faurœulx** Belgium 50.22N 4.06E
15 J2 **Fauro I** Solomon Is 6.55S 156.05E

53 E4 Faūsing Denmark 56.27N 10.18E
51 E4 Fauske Norway 67.17N 15.25E
100 B3 Faust Alberta 55.19N 115.33W
104 L2 Faust New York 44.15N 74.31W
110 N9 Faust Utah 40.11N 112.24W
70 M2 Fauville France 49.39N 0.36E
61 N7 Fauvillers Belgium 49.52N 5.40E
72 F6 Faux France 44.47N 0.38E
95 B8 Faux Cap Madagascar 25.31S 45.31E
72 H4 Faux-la-Montagne France 45.45N 1.56E
76 E6 Favaios Portugal 41.16N 7.30W
81 G9 Favara Sicily 37.24N 13.40E
81 G9 Favarella Sicily 37.28N 13.59E
77 Q2 Favareta Spain 39.08N 0.17W
77 Y14 Favaritx,C Balearic Is 40.00N 4.16E
71 J5 Faverges France 45.45N 6.18E
72 L6 Faverolles Cantal France 44.56N 3.08E
70 O4 Faverolles Eure France 48.42N 1.36E
56 N5 Faversham Kent Eng 51.20N 0.53E
69 K7 Favières France 48.27N 5.57E
81 E8 Favignana Egadi Is Italy 37.56N 12.22E
81 E6 Favignana isld Egadi Is Italy
11 D3 Favona New Zealand 36.57S 174.48E
67 P13 Favone Corsica 41.46N 9.23E
53 C4 Favrholt Denmark 56.11N 9.10E
34 Q9 Fāw, Al Iraq 29.55N 48.26E
100 C4 Fawcett Alberta 54.34N 114.06W
100 D3 Fawcett L Alberta 55.20N 113.55W
56 J6 Fawley Hants Eng 50.49N 1.20W
97 L7 Fawn R Ontario
103 B7 Fawn Grove Pennsylvania 39.44N 76.26W
95 O5 Fawnleas S Africa 29.21S 30.44E
35 G1 Fawwar watercourse Syria
33 E3 Fawwārah,Al Saudi Arabia 26.02N 42.40E
50 B6 Faxaflói B Iceland
52 K3 Faxälven R Sweden
109 M6 Fay Oklahoma 35.51N 98.39W
Fayal isld see Faial
90 J3 Faya-Largeau Chad 17.58N 19.06E
45 F2 Fayansovyy U.S.S.R. 54.05N 34.24E
69 C8 Fay-aux-Loges France 47.57N 2.09E
72 H6 Faycelles France 44.34N 1.59E
33 E3 Fayd Saudi Arabia 27.08N 42.34E
33 F4 Faydah, Al Saudi Arabia 25.22N 44.28E
33 E7 Fayd,Al Saudi Arabia 18.01N 43.42E
33 K8 Faydamī,Al S Yemen 16.26N 52.30E
70 G7 Fay-de-Bretagne France 47.26N 1.47W
Faydemi see Faydamī
72 C1 Faye-d'Anjou France 47.18N 0.32W
100 Q3 Faye L Manitoba 55.01N 101.08W
72 E3 Faye,la France 46.01N 0.08E
72 E2 Faye-la-Vineuse France 46.57N 0.21E
71 K9 Fayence France 43.38N 6.43E
71 K5 Fayet,le France 45.54N 6.43E
107 J8 Fayette Alabama 33.42N 87.50W
106 C7 Fayette Iowa 42.50N 91.48W
106 H4 Fayette Michigan 45.43N 86.37W
107 E10 Fayette Mississippi 31.44N 91.04W
107 D2 Fayette Missouri 39.09N 92.40W
104 A5 Fayette Ohio 41.41N 84.20W
111 N2 Fayette Utah 39.14N 111.51W
107 B5 Fayetteville Arkansas 36.03N 94.10W
105 C4 Fayetteville Georgia 33.26N 84.28W
105 J2 Fayetteville N Carolina 35.03N 78.53W
107 N2 Fayetteville Ohio 39.11N 83.56W
107 K6 Fayetteville Tennessee 35.08N 86.33W
112 L6 Fayetteville Texas 29.54N 96.42W
104 D8 Fayetteville W Virginia 38.03N 81.09W
33 E8 Fayfā Saudi Arabia 17.18N 43.05E
34 L9 Fayhān, Wādī watercourse Saudi Arabia
86 H5 Fâyid Egypt 30.18N 32.16E
33 N9 Faylakah isld Kuwait 29.26N 48.20E
69 K8 Fayl-la-Forêt France 47.47N 5.36E
69 M8 Faymont France 47.57N 6.33E
61 P5 Faymonville Belgium 50.24N 6.08E
75 L5 Fayón Spain 41.15N 0.20E
34 K1 Fayshkhābūr Iraq 37.03N 42.22E
61 L7 Fays-lez-Veneurs Belgium 49.52N 5.10E
71 E7 Fay-sur-Lignon France 44.59N 4.15E
112 J9 Faysville Texas 26.26N 98.08W
61 F5 Fayt-le-Franc Belgium 50.21N 3.46E
61 G5 Fayt-lez-Manage Belgium 50.29N 4.14E
34 D9 Fazair al Ghrazi watercourse Saudi Arabia
89 K7 Fazao Togo 8.45N 0.46E
35 G1 Fazarah Syria 33.01N 35.49E
33 K8 Fazāyiḥ Bay Oman
76 A10 Faz do Arelho Portugal 39.26N 9.13W
90 E2 Fazeï Niger 18.50N 11.50E
56 H2 Fazeley Staffs Eng 52.37N 1.41W
33 E9 Fāzih,Al Yemen 14.08N 43.06E
93 N8 Fazi I Kenya 2.00S 41.12E
29 D2 Fazilka Punjab India 30.26N 74.04E
31 F6 Fazilpur Pakistan 29.18N 70.31E
33 H3 Fazran oil well Saudi Arabia 26.15N 49.10E
33 H3 Fazrān,Jabal hill Saudi Arabia 26.15N 49.15E
88 G10 Fderik Mauritania 22.40N 12.41W
59 E6 Feakle Clare Irish Rep 52.56N 8.39W
59 J4 Fea, L Monaghan Irish Rep 53.57N 6.45W
59 D7 Feale,R Kerry Irish Rep
105 K4 Fear, C N Carolina 33.51N 77.59W
58 J3 Fearn Highland Scotland 57.46N 3.58W
58 H5 Fearnan Tayside Scotland 56.35N 4.05W
72 C9 Féas France 43.10N 0.40W
111 C3 Feather R California
111 C2 Feather Falls California 39.36N 121.15W
111 C2 Feather Middle Fork R California
11 K8 Featherston New Zealand 41.07S 175.19E
95 L3 Featherstone S Africa 27.44S 27.17E
92 E11 Featherstone Zimbabwe 18.42S 30.55E
12 H6 Feathertop, Mt Victoria 36.53S 147.10E
110 K6 Featherville Idaho 43.38N 115.16W
89 F8 Febiaso Ivory Coast 7.47N 6.44W
11 A12 Febrero Pt New Zealand 45.16S 166.50E
70 L2 Fécamp France 49.45N 0.23E
69 N7 Fecht R France
56 H3 Feckenham Hereford & Worcs Eng 52.15N 1.59W
59 E6 Fedamore Limerick Irish Rep 52.33N 8.36W
121 F3 Federación Argentina 31.00S 57.55W
108 E8 Federal Wyoming 41.15N 105.05W
90 C7 Federal Capital Terr Nigeria
108 Q2 Federal Dam Minnesota 47.12N 94.11W
104 K8 Federalsburg Maryland 38.42N 75.46W
32 E6 Fedeshkūh Iran 28.49N 53.44E
53 R17 Fedje Norway 60.47N 4.43E
53 R17 Fedjefjord inlet Norway 60.45N 4.47E
108 N5 Fedora S Dakota 44.01N 97.45W
43 D1 Fedorovka Bashkir U.S.S.R. 53.13N 55.10E
46 K6 Fedorovka Kaporozh'ye, Ukraine U.S.S.R. 47.07N 35.19E
46 Q4 Fedorovka Kazakhstan U.S.S.R. 51.12N 52.00E
45 D8 Fedorovka Kirovograd, Ukraine U.S.S.R. 48.21N 32.10E
43 G1 Fedorovka Kustanay, Kazakhstan U.S.S.R. 53.38N 62.36E
45 V3 Fedorovka Kuybyshev U.S.S.R. 53.30N 49.30E
43 M1 Fedorovka Pavlodar, Kazakhstan U.S.S.R. 53.23N 76.16E
45 Q3 Fedorovka Penza U.S.S.R. 53.10N 44.15E
45 K9 Fedorovka Rostov U.S.S.R. 47.21N 38.25E
46 O4 Fedorovka Saratov U.S.S.R. 51.26N 47.29E
44 B2 Fedorovskaya U.S.S.R. 45.04N 38.29E
41 Q4 Fedorovskiy U.S.S.R. 73.52N 140.30E
44 F1 Fedoseyevka U.S.S.R. 46.54N 43.59E
44 D8 Fedotova, Kosa sand spit Ukraine U.S.S.R.
47 D5 Fedovo Arkhangel'sk U.S.S.R. 62.22N 39.21E
46 J2 Fedovo Kalinin U.S.S.R. 57.28N 34.31E
47 K4 Fedulki U.S.S.R. 65.00N 66.10E
29 C4 Fedusar Rajasthan India 26.14N 72.59E
59 C4 Feeagh, L Mayo Irish Rep 53.57N 9.35W
59 C4 Fee, L Galway Irish Rep 53.35N 9.50W
59 E7 Feenagh Limerick Irish Rep 52.24N 8.53W
59 H2 Feeny Londonderry N Ireland 54.53N 7.01W
95 P4 Feessaal S Africa 28.10S 31.08E
19 N4 Fefan isld Truk Is Pacific Oc
89 C6 Féfine R Guinea/Guinea-Bissau
69 O7 Fegersheim France 48.29N 7.41E
53 B3 Feggesund inlet Denmark 56.58N 8.55E
70 F6 Fégréac France 47.35N 2.03W
88 M7 Feguiguira Algeria 29.38N 2.35W
Fehlunj see Fahālanj
63 O4 Fehmarn isld W Germany
63 O3 Fehmarn Belt str W Germany/Denmark
63 O4 Fehmarnsund W Germany 54.24N 11.08E
63 O4 Fehmarnsund str W Germany
66 M2 Fehraltdorf Switzerland 47.23N 8.45E
63 R7 Fehrbellin E Germany 52.49N 12.46E
65 O8 Fehring Austria 46.57N 16.01E
118 H8 Feia, L Brazil 22.00S 41.21W
22 K8 Feicheng Shandong China 36.19N 116.49E
23 H3 Feidong Anhui China 31.56N 117.24E
35 E10 Feifa watercourse Jordan
53 W16 Feigumfoss waterfall Norway 61.23N 7.28E
86 M6 Feiḥi, Wâdi el watercourse Egypt
23 G1 Fei Huang He R Anhui China
120 D3 Feijó Brazil 8.07S 70.27W
23 F7 Feilai Xia Bei Jiang R Guangdong China
11 K7 Feilding New Zealand 40.12S 175.37E
71 F4 Feillens France 46.21N 4.53E
Feilnbach see Bad Feilnbach
53 V16 Feios Norway 61.08N 6.46E
92 E9 Feira Zambia 15.36S 30.27E
118 J3 Feira de Santana Brazil 12.17S 38.53W
86 L8 Feiran Egypt 28.43N 33.35E
86 M8 Feirâni, Gebel hill Egypt 28.31N 34.19E
86 K8 Feirân, Wâdi watercourse Egypt
71 J5 Feissons-sur-Isère France 45.34N 6.28E
65 J8 Feistritz Austria 46.42N 13.40E
65 N7 Feistritz R Austria
65 K8 Feistritzim Ros Austria 46.32N 14.11E
76 D14 Feiteira Portugal 37.17N 7.51W
23 H3 Feixi Anhui China 31.43N 117.13E
23 H1 Fei Xian Shandong China 35.19N 117.59E
22 K8 Feixiang Hebei China 36.32N 114.47E
82 E3 Fejer co Hungary
53 G7 Fejø isld Denmark 54.57N 11.25E
53 F4 Fejrup Århus Denmark 56.08N 10.31E
36 H5 Feke Turkey 37.52N 35.56E
62 K10 Fekete Viz R Hungary
88 S4 Fekka, el R Tunisia
40 G4 Feklistova, Ostrov isld U.S.S.R.
93 E8 Fela Tanzania 2.38S 33.03E
36 H3 Felâhiye Turkey 39.14N 35.35E
77 W15 Felanitx Balearic Is 39.28N 3.08E
65 G7 Felber-Tauern tunnel Austria
56 L5 Felbridge Surrey Eng 51.09N 0.03W
106 G3 Felch Michigan 46.00N 87.50W
63 U6 Felchow E Germany 53.03N 14.07E
64 L8 Feldafing W Germany 47.56N 11.18E
64 G2 Feldatal W Germany 50.40N 9.09E
65 N8 Feldbach Austria 46.58N 15.53E
53 F4 Feldballe Denmark 56.17N 10.37E
63 S6 Feldberg E Germany 53.21N 13.27E
64 E8 Feldberg mt W Germany 47.51N 8.02E
53 T14 Felden mt Norway 62.02N 5.56E
53 C3 Feldingbjerg Denmark 56.31N 9.08E
66 O4 Feldis Switzerland 46.48N 9.26E
65 A7 Feldkirch Austria 47.15N 9.38E
65 K8 Feldkirchen Austria 46.44N 14.06E
64 M7 Feldkirchen W Germany 48.07N 11.44E
64 M8 Feldkirchen-Westerham W Germany 47.54N 11.51E
76 J2 Felechosa Spain 43.07N 5.30W
61 K6 Felenne Belgium 50.04N 4.51E
9 R12 Feletoa Tonga, Pacific Oc 18.36S 173.59W
79 C4 Feletto Italy 45.18N 7.45E
76 F6 Felgar Portugal 41.12N 6.58W
76 C6 Felgueiras Portugal 41.22N 8.12W
76 H2 Felguera, La Spain 43.19N 5.40W
67 O11 Feliceto Corsica 42.33N 8.56E
121 F3 Feliciano R Argentina
26 R12 Felicité I Seychelles, Ind Oc 4.19S 55.52E
104 A8 Felicity Ohio 38.50N 84.06W
27 L9 Felidu Atoll Maldives, Ind Oc 3.30N 73.30E
71 D6 Félines France 45.17N 3.45E
79 H5 Felino Italy 44.42N 10.14E
77 N2 Felipa La Spain 39.03N 1.43W
115 P8 Felipe Carrillo Puerto Mexico 19.36N 88.02W
81 K3 Felitto Italy 40.22N 15.15E
77 L7 Félix Spain 36.52N 2.39W
92 E11 Felixburg Zimbabwe 19.29S 30.51E
92 E11 Felixburg Road Zimbabwe 19.31S 30.45E
101 Z1 Felix, C N W Terr 69.55N 97.59W
118 G6 Felixlândia Brazil 18.46S 44.52W
109 F8 Felix, R New Mexico
56 O4 Felixstowe Suffolk Eng 51.58N 1.20E
95 O10 Felixton S Africa 28.50S 31.53E
115 G2 Félix U. Gómez Mexico 30.38N 105.50W
79 D5 Felizzano Italy 44.54N 8.26E
50 F2 Fell Skagafjardharsýsla Iceland 66.02N 19.22W
50 D3 Fell Strandasýsla Iceland 65.34N 21.27W
64 B4 Fell W Germany 49.46N 6.47E
50 J6 Fell mt Iceland
79 O2 Fella R Italy
50 L4 Fellaheidhi heath Iceland
64 G6 Fellbach W Germany 48.48N 9.15E
72 J4 Felletin France 45.53N 2.10E
57 K3 Felling Tyne and Wear Eng 54.57N 1.33W
87 G2 Fellit Ethiopia 16.40N 38.01E
111 E6 Fellows California 35.10N 119.32W
116 L2 Fellowship Jamaica, W I 18.08N 76.27W
105 G10 Fellsmere Florida 27.47N 80.37W
79 K5 Felonica Italy 44.59N 11.21E
56 K6 Felpham W Sussex Eng 50.47N 0.39W
66 O4 Felsberg Switzerland 46.51N 9.29E
64 G1 Felsberg W Germany 51.08N 9.25E
53 D7 Felsted Denmark 54.59N 9.31E
109 H5 Felt Oklahoma 36.33N 102.48W
55 C4 Feltham London Eng 51.27N 0.25W
111 B4 Felton California 37.02N 122.05W
103 C8 Felton Delaware 39.01N 75.35W
105 B4 Felton Georgia 33.54N 85.14W
108 O2 Felton Minnesota 47.04N 96.31W
57 K2 Felton Northumb Eng 55.18N 1.42W
103 A7 Felton Pennsylvania 39.52N 76.33W
79 L2 Feltre Italy 46.01N 11.55E
61 G4 Feluy Belgium 50.33N 4.15E
80 H3 Fema, Monte Italy 42.57N 13.03E
118 F3 Femeas, R Brazil
53 G7 Femer Bælt str Denmark/W Germany
15 A5 Femin Irian Jaya 2.12S 130.17E
81 N5 Femminamorta, mte Italy 39.07N 16.40E
81 F7 Femmine, I.di Sicily 38.13N 13.14E
53 F4 Femmøller Denmark 56.15N 10.36E
53 H7 Femø isld Denmark 54.59N 11.33E
53 G7 Femø Sund str Denmark 54.59N 11.30E
52 F4 Femund L Norway
96 U1 Fenaes da Ajuda Azores 37.36N 25.20W
59 G3 Fenagh Leitrim Irish Rep 54.01N 7.50W
95 B8 Fenambosy, Pte Madagascar 25.14S 44.21E
87 G4 Fenaroa Ethiopia 13.05N 39.03E
19 L1 Fena Valley Res Guam Pacific Oc 13.23N 144.41E
109 B7 Fence Lake New Mexico 34.40N 108.41W
23 F1 Fencheng Shanxi China 35.50N 111.16E
31 J9 Fenchuganj Bangladesh 24.40N 92.00E
11 L9 Fendalton dist Christchurch New Zealand
72 H9 Fendeille France 43.15N 1.55E
77 E9 Fendek, El Morocco 35.35N 5.36W
76 C2 Fene Spain 43.28N 8.10W
99 M8 Fenelon Falls Ontario 44.32N 78.45W
15 F6 Feneng R Papua New Guinea
37 E1 Fener Turkey 41.09N 28.15E
37 J2 Fener dist Istanbul Turkey 41.02N 28.53E
37 K3 Fenerbahçe Turkey 40.58N 29.06E
37 E4 Fener Burun C Trabzon Turkey 41.08N 39.27E
37 K3 Fener Burun C Turkey 40.58N 29.05E
Fénérive see Fenoarivo Atsinanana
79 B4 Fenestrelle Italy 45.02N 7.03E
69 N6 Fénétrange France 48.51N 7.01E
66 F8 Fenetre, Col de pass Italy/Switz 45.54N 7.17E
70 J6 Feneu France 47.35N 0.35W
37 B2 Fengari Oros mts Samothráki Greece
23 G4 Fengcheng Jiangxi China 28.11N 115.47E
23 F7 Fengchuan Guangdong China 23.23N 111.30E
23 D4 Fengdu Sichuan China 29.58N 107.45E
23 D5 Fenggang Guizhou China 26.10N 107.49E
23 J4 Fenghua Zhejiang China 29.40N 121.25E
23 E5 Fenghuang Hunan China 27.54N 109.29E
23 E2 Fenghuangzui Shaanxi China 33.30N 109.20E
Fengjiaba see Wangcang
23 E3 Fengjie Sichuan China 31.06N 109.30E
23 F7 Fengkai Guangdong China 23.28N 111.30E
21 C5 Fengle Heilongjiang China 45.45N 125.24E
23 F3 Fengle Hubei China 31.29N 112.29E
23 G7 Fengliang Guangdong China 23.56N 116.13E
23 J7 Feng-lin Taiwan 23.48N 121.26E
23 E1 Fenglingdu Shaanxi China 34.41N 110.24E
22 L7 Fengnan Hebei China 39.31N 118.01E
Feng-ning see Fengning
22 K6 Fengning Hebei China 41.10N 116.41E
23 J4 Fengqiao Zhejiang China 29.47N 120.24E
23 B6 Fengqing Yunnan China 24.35N 99.55E
23 G1 Fengqiu Henan China 34.45N 114.23E
22 L7 Fengrun Hebei China 39.50N 118.10E
23 D6 Fengshan Guangxi China 24.39N 107.05E
22 L6 Fengshan Hebei China 41.08N 119.41E
21 C1 Fengshui Shan mt pk Heilongjiang China 52.25N 123.21E
23 G2 Fengtai Anhui China 32.43N 116.38E
23 H6 Fengting Fujian China 25.12N 118.45E
Fengweiba see Zhenkang
23 D7 Fengwu Guangxi China 23.24N 107.41E
23 G1 Feng Xian Jiangsu China 34.45N 116.39E
23 D2 Feng Xian Shaanxi China 33.56N 106.12E
23 J3 Fengxian Shanghai China 30.55N 121.27E
Fengxiang see Luobei
23 D1 Fengxiang Shaanxi China 34.30N 107.30E
23 G4 Fengxin Jiangxi China 28.46N 115.28E
23 H2 Fengyang Anhui China 32.49N 117.33E
23 B6 Fengyi Yunnan China 25.34N 100.12E
Fengyizhen see Maowen Qiangzu Zizhixian
Fengyizhen see Maowen
22 J6 Fengzhen Nei Monggol Zizhiqu China 40.28N 113.06E
22 J7 Fen He R Shanxi China
22 J8 Fen He R Shanxi China
23 F1 Fen He R Shanxi China
31 J9 Feni Bangladesh 23.00N 91.24E
113 H2 Feniak L Alaska 68.16N 158.20W
15 M6 Feni Is Papua New Guinea
113 Q9 Fenimore Pass Aleutian Is
72 D2 Fenioux France 46.33N 0.29W
59 C7 Fenit Kerry Irish Rep 52.17N 9.51W
110 J4 Fenn Idaho 45.58N 116.15W
111 J7 Fenner California 34.50N 115.10W
106 D7 Fennimore Wisconsin 42.59N 90.40W
106 H7 Fennville Michigan 42.36N 86.06W
31 J9 Fenny R Bangladesh/India
56 K3 Fenny Stratford Bucks Eng 52.00N 0.43W
95 C7 Fenoambony Madagascar 23.50S 47.32E
95 B7 Fenoarivo Madagascar 23.46S 44.29E
95 C5 Fenoarivo Madagascar 18.25S 46.32E
95 C6 Fenoarivo Madagascar 21.42S 46.22E
95 C6 Fenoarivo Madagascar 20.52S 46.52E
95 D4 Fenoarivo Atsinanana Madagascar 17.21S 49.25E
67 P14 Feno, Capo di Corsica 41.22N 9.10E
67 O13 Feno, C. di Corsica 41.58N 8.35E
72 G8 Fenouillet France 43.41N 1.23E
53 R17 Fensfjord inlet Norway 60.50N 4.57E
Fen-shui see Wu sheng
53 H6 Fensmark Denmark 55.17N 11.48E
56 L3 Fenstanton Cambs Eng 52.18N 0.05W
64 N5 Fensterbach W Germany 49.23N 12.02E
56 M3 Fens, The reg England
108 Q6 Fenton Iowa 43.12N 94.26W
107 D11 Fenton Louisiana 30.21N 92.56W
106 L7 Fenton Michigan 42.48N 83.42W
100 M5 Fenton Saskatchewan 53.00N 105.35W
104 J10 Fentress Virginia 36.42N 76.13W
122 L10 Fenua Ura Society Is Pacific Oc 16.30S 154.40W
58 N7 Fenwick Northumb Eng 55.38N 1.54W
99 L9 Fenwick Ontario 43.02N 79.23W
58 H7 Fenwick Strathclyde Scotland 55.40N 4.26W
104 E8 Fenwick W Virginia 38.14N 80.36W
58 H7 Fenwick Water R Strathclyde Scotland
100 O7 Fenwood Saskatchewan 51.01N 103.01W
106 D5 Fenwood Wisconsin 44.53N 90.01W
22 J8 Fenxi Shanxi China 36.36N 111.30E
Fenxiang see Luobei
22 J8 Fenyang Shanxi China 37.14N 111.43E
23 G5 Fenyi Jiangxi China 27.48N 114.39E
44 D9 Feodosiya Ukraine U.S.S.R. 45.03N 35.23E
44 D9 Feodosiyskiy Zaliv B Ukraine U.S.S.R.
44 C10 Feolent, Mys C Ukraine U.S.S.R. 44.30N 33.17E
58 D7 Feolin Jura, Strathclyde Scotland 55.51N 6.06W
69 H3 Fépin France 50.02N 4.43E
87 L6 Feradli Hills Somalia
52 F4 Feragen L Norway 62.35N 11.55E
Feragha see Farāgheh
15 L3 Fera I Solomon Is 8.07S 159.38E
59 G5 Ferbane Offaly Irish Rep 53.16N 7.49W
88 R3 Fer, C de Algeria 37.08N 7.10E
Ferdaus see Ferdow
110 J3 Ferdinand Idaho 46.08N 116.21W
107 K3 Ferdinand Indiana 38.14N 86.52W
63 T5 Ferdinandshof E Germany 53.41N 13.54E
32 H3 Ferdow Iran 34.00N 58.09E
88 G8 Ferduja Morocco 26.53N 12.14W
69 F6 Fère-Champenoise France 48.45N 4.00E
89 E7 Feredougouba R Guinea/Ivory Coast
69 F5 Fère-en-Tardenois France 49.12N 3.32E
33 H2 Fereidoon oil field The Gulf 28.40N 49.46E
70 F7 Férel France 47.29N 2.21W
69 E4 Fère, la France 49.40N 3.22E
52 F3 Feren L Norway 63.34N 11.50E
80 G3 Ferentillo Italy 42.38N 12.48E
80 H5 Ferentino Italy 41.41N 13.15E
77 M4 Férez Spain 38.21N 2.01W
87 K8 Ferfer Somalia 5.04N 45.09E
43 K6 Fergana Uzbekistan U.S.S.R. 40.23N 71.19E
43 O8 Fergana Basin U.S.S.R.
Ferganskaya Dolina see Fergana Basin
43 L6 Ferganskiy Khrebet mts Kirgiziya U.S.S.R.
Ferghana Valley see Fergana Basin
110 Q2 Fergus Montana 47.19N 109.04W
99 K9 Fergus Ontario 43.43N 80.24W
108 O3 Fergus Falls Minnesota 46.18N 96.07W
33 K8 Ferguson Field Oman 17.58N 53.30E
101 V1 Ferguson L Victoria I, N W Terr
59 E6 Fergus, R Clare Irish Rep 52.45N 9.00W
13 B2 Fergusson R N Terr Australia
15 L8 Fergusson I Papua New Guinea
77 C3 Feria Spain 38.30N 6.35W
88 S4 Fériana Tunisia 34.53N 8.30E
100 E6 Ferintosh Alberta 52.46N 112.56W
66 K8 Feriolo Italy 45.56N 8.29E
50 D5 Ferjukot Iceland 64.36N 21.40W
88 R4 Ferkane Algeria 34.33N 7.25E
89 G7 Ferkéssédougou Ivory Coast 9.30N 5.10W
53 S20 Ferkingstad Norway 59.13N 5.12E
81 J9 Ferla Sicily 37.08N 14.57E
65 K8 Ferlach Austria 46.32N 14.18E
99 B2 Ferland Ontario 50.19N 88.27W
65 G7 Ferleiten Austria 47.11N 12.49E
89 B4 Ferlo reg Senegal
89 B4 Ferlo,Vallée du Senegal
59 G3 Fermanagh co N Ireland
70 H2 Fermanville France 49.41N 1.28W
99 P6 Ferme Neuve Quebec 46.42N 75.28W
76 B7 Fermentelos Portugal 40.34N 8.32W
63 S9 Fermerswalde E Germany 51.40N 13.12E
79 N7 Fermignano Italy 43.41N 12.39E
76 C6 Fermil Portugal 41.25N 8.00W
111 D10 Fermin, Pt California 33.43N 118.18W
80 J2 Fermo Italy 43.09N 13.44E
76 G6 Fermoselle Spain 41.19N 6.24W
59 F7 Fermoy Cork Irish Rep 52.08N 8.16W
58 L5 Fern Tayside Scotland 56.45N 2.50W
77 J2 Fernancaballero Spain 39.08N 3.54W
121 D1 Fernández Argentina 27.55S 63.50W
105 F7 Fernandina Beach Florida 30.30N 81.26W
119 A5 Fernandina, I Galápagos Is 0.23S 91.32W
26 N13 Fernand,le pk Amsterdam I Ind Oc 37.50S 77.31E
117 E1 Fernando de Noronha,I Atl Oc 3.50S 32.25W
118 E7 Fernandópolis Brazil 20.18S 50.13W
Fernando Póo prov see Macias Nguema Biyogo isld prov
88 Q4 Fernane, Djebel mt Algeria 34.59N 4.19E
77 G5 Fernán Núñez Spain 37.40N 4.44W
118 G5 Fernão Dias Brazil 16.23S 44.27W
110 A9 Ferndale California 40.35N 124.16W
103 A8 Ferndale Maryland 39.11N 76.38W
103 E3 Ferndale New York 41.42N 74.44W
94 S13 Ferndale S Africa 26.06S 28.00E
110 C1 Ferndale Washington 48.51N 122.36W
106 M1 Ferndale dist Detroit, Michigan
92 K9 Ferndo Veloso, B.de Mozambique 14.29S 40.41E
56 H6 Ferndown Dorset Eng 50.48N 1.55W
58 J4 Ferness Highland Scotland 57.28N 3.45W
108 M4 Ferney S Dakota 45.18N 98.08W
71 J4 Ferney-Voltaire France 46.15N 6.06E
56 K5 Fernhurst W Sussex Eng 51.03N 0.44W
101 Q11 Fernie Br Columbia 49.30N 115.00W
65 M8 Fernitz Austria 46.59N 15.30E
59 G1 Fern, L Donegal Irish Rep 55.03N 7.43W
13 H8 Fernlee Queensland 28.12S 147.05E
111 E2 Fernley Nevada 39.36N 119.14W
65 C7 Fernpass Austria 47.22N 10.50E
110 B5 Fern Ridge Res Oregon
59 J6 Ferns Wexford Irish Rep 52.35N 6.30W
11 G10 Fernside New Zealand 43.19S 172.32E
12 F8 Ferntree Tasmania 42.56S 147.00E
64 F2 Fernwald W Germany 50.31N 8.48E
110 J2 Fernwood Idaho 47.06N 116.24W
107 F10 Fernwood Mississippi 31.10N 90.29W
28 B5 Ferokh Kerala India 11.10N 75.50E
81 M6 Feroleto Antico Italy 38.58N 16.23E
98 P2 Ferolle Pt Newfoundland 51.01N 57.06W
29 D2 Ferozeshalir Punjab India 30.54N 74.50E
66 G7 Ferpècle Switzerland 46.04N 7.33E
76 B14 Ferragudo Portugal 37.07N 8.31W
83 H4 Férrai Greece 40.53N 26.10E
72 K9 Ferrals-les-Corbières France 43.09N 2.43E
81 M3 Ferrandina Italy 40.29N 16.28E
80 M9 Ferrara Cent Afr Rep 5.24N 25.50E
79 L5 Ferrara Italy 44.50N 11.38E
79 K5 Ferrara prov Italy
79 J3 Ferrara di Monte Baldo Italy 45.40N 10.52E
123 H6 Ferrar Glacier Antarctica 77.40S 161.00E
76 C16 Ferraria Portugal 38.45N 9.17W
96 T1 Ferraria, Pta pt Azores 37.37N 25.51W
76 B12 Ferrarias Portugal 38.13N 8.38W
88 N4 Ferrat,C Algeria 35.54N 0.25W
71 L9 Ferrat,C France 43.40N 7.20E
81 D5 Ferrato,C Sardinia 39.18N 9.39E
34 C4 Ferraya Lebanon 34.01N 35.48E
76 B8 Ferreira Portugal 40.15N 8.45W
95 K5 Ferreira S Africa 29.12S 26.10E
76 E1 Ferreira Spain 43.33N 7.25W
76 D3 Ferreira R Spain
76 C12 Ferreira do Alentejo Portugal 38.04N 8.06W
76 C9 Ferreira do Zêzere Portugal 39.41N 8.17W
117 C4 Ferreira Gomes Brazil 0.52N 51.08W
95 H10 Ferreiratown S Africa 34.02S 24.55E
118 D7 Ferreiros Brazil 20.24S 52.38W
70 H5 Ferré, le France 48.30N 1.17W
120 A7 Ferreñafe Peru 6.42S 79.45W
66 J8 Ferrera Italy 45.52N 8.12E
75 M8 Ferrera, I. La Spain 39.52N 0.40E
76 G5 Ferreras de Abajo Spain 41.54N 6.05W
77 Y14 Ferrerias Balearic Is 39.59N 4.00E
75 H5 Ferreruela de Huerva Spain 41.04N 1.15W
66 E8 Ferret Switzerland 45.55N 7.07E
72 B6 Ferret, C France 44.38N 1.16W
66 E8 Ferret, Col pass Italy/Switz 45.53N 7.04E
71 L2 Ferrette France 47.30N 7.19E
79 B3 Ferret, Tête Cap pass Italy/Switz 45.54N 7.04E
66 E8 Ferret, V Switzerland
66 D8 Ferret, Valle di Italy
107 E10 Ferriday Louisiana 31.39N 91.32W
100 C6 Ferrier Alberta 52.26N 114.56W
79 F5 Ferriere Italy 44.38N 9.29E
70 K4 Ferrière-aux-Étangs,la France 48.39N 0.30W
72 D2 Ferriere,la Deux Sèvres France 46.40N 0.03W
72 B2 Ferrière,la Vendée France 46.43N 1.18W
61 N5 Ferrières Belgium 50.24N 5.37E
72 C3 Ferrières Charente-Maritime France 46.14N 0.51W
69 D7 Ferrières Loiret France 48.06N 2.48E
70 O2 Ferrières-en-Bray France 49.30N 1.46E
71 J3 Ferriere-sous-Jougne,la France 46.45N 6.23E
72 L5 Ferrières-St. Mary France 45.12N 3.04E
71 D4 Ferrières-sur-Sichon France 46.02N 3.38E
70 M4 Ferrière-sur-Risle,la France 48.58N 0.47E
53 A3 Ferring Denmark 56.32N 8.08E
53 A3 Ferring Sø L Denmark 56.33N 8.10E
106 C9 Ferris Illinois 40.29N 91.11W
112 L3 Ferris Texas 32.32N 96.41W
104 M2 Ferrisburg Vermont 44.13N 73.15W
108 C7 Ferris Mts Wyoming
53 F6 Ferritslev Denmark 55.18N 10.35E
76 E8 Ferro Portugal 40.14N 7.25W
Ferro isld Canary Issee Hierro
96 R6 Ferro isld Madeira Is 33.02N 16.25W
81 N4 Ferro R Italy
81 J9 Ferro R Sicily
81 D1 Ferro, C Sardinia 41.09N 9.32E
81 E6 Ferro, C. del Egadi Is Italy 37.57N 12.18E
76 C2 Ferrol del Caudillo, El Spain 43.29N 8.14W
120 A3 Ferrol, Pen.de Peru 9.12S 78.36W
66 R5 Ferro, Monte del Italy 46.34N 10.12E
118 C3 Ferro, R Brazil
118 G6 Ferros Brazil 19.17S 43.02W
98 N2 Ferru, L Quebec
104 E10 Ferrum Virginia 36.56N 80.03W
81 B3 Ferru, Mte Cagliari, Sardinia
81 D5 Ferru, Mte Cagliari, Sardinia 39.18N 9.37E
81 D4 Ferru, Mte Nuoro, Sardinia 39.44N 9.38E
113 N5 Ferry Alaska 64.00N 149.10W
106 H6 Ferry Michigan 43.35N 86.14W
57 L5 Ferrybridge W Yorks Eng 53.43N 1.15W
57 K3 Ferryhill Durham Eng 54.41N 1.33W
59 K3 Ferryhill Louth Irish Rep 54.07N 6.18W
98 T6 Ferryland Newfoundland 47.01N 52.53W
106 H6 Ferrysburg Michigan 43.05N 86.14W
56 C4 Ferryside Dyfed Wales 51.47N 4.22W
Ferryville Tunisiasee Menzel Bourgiba
106 C6 Ferryville Wisconsin 43.22N 91.06W
43 E1 Fershampenuaz U.S.S.R. 53.33N 59.50E
53 H5 Ferslev Denmark 55.47N 11.56E
41 J3 Fersmana, Gora mt U.S.S.R. 76.41N 105.57E
69 C7 Ferté-Alais,la France 48.29N 2.21E
70 M5 Ferté-Bernard,la France 48.11N 0.40E
69 F4 Ferté-Chevrésis, la France 49.45N 3.35E
70 M4 Ferté-Fresnel, la France 48.50N 0.30E
69 E6 Ferté-Gaucher,la France 48.47N 3.19E
72 L3 Ferté Hauterive, La France 46.24N 3.20E
70 O7 Ferté-Imbault,la France 47.23N 1.56E
69 E8 Ferté-Loupière,la France 47.54N 3.14E
70 K4 Ferté-Macé,la France 48.35N 0.22W
69 E5 Ferté-Milon,la France 49.11N 3.08E
70 O6 Ferté-St.Aubin,la France 47.43N 1.56E
70 O6 Ferté-St. Cyr,la France 47.39N 1.40E
69 E6 Ferté-sous-Jouarre,la France 48.57N 3.08E
70 M4 Ferté-Vidame,la France 48.37N 0.55E
108 O2 Fertile Minnesota 47.31N 96.19W
81 A2 Fertilia Sardinia 40.36N 8.18E
90 M7 Fertit tribe Sudan
Fertö see Neusiedler See
65 P6 Fertöd Hungary 47.36N 16.54E
65 P6 Fertörákos Hungary 47.43N 16.40E
65 P6 Fertöszentmiklos Hungary 47.35N 16.55E
80 K4 Feruccio,Pta.di Italy 42.22N 14.23E
70 L3 Fervaques France 49.02N 0.15E
60 M6 Ferwerd Netherlands 53.21N 5.49E
45 H2 Ferzikovo U.S.S.R. 54.31N 36.45E
88 L4 Fès Morocco 34.05N 5.00W
37 J8 Fesandūz Iran 37.06N 45.53E
61 K6 Feschaux Belgium 50.09N 4.55E
91 F7 Feshi Zaïre 6.08S 18.12E
58 J4 Feshiebridge Highland Scotland 57.07N 3.53W
108 L2 Fessenden N Dakota 47.39N 99.38W
69 O8 Fessenheim France 47.56N 7.33E
88 T5 Fessi watercourse Tunisia
66 O5 Fess, Piz mt Switzerland 46.44N 9.17E
53 U14 Festøy Norway 62.22N 6.20E
71 H7 Festre,Col du pass France 44.39N 5.51E
69 D2 Festubert France 50.33N 2.44E
107 F3 Festus Missouri 38.12N 90.24W
53 W16 Fet Norway 61.22N 7.15E
87 G6 Feta, El Ethiopia 9.09N 38.02E
96 P4 Feteira Azores 38.32N 28.40W
96 T1 Feteiras Azores 37.33N 25.47W
89 G8 Fetekro Ivory Coast 7.56N 4.42W
66 C6 Fèternes France 46.21N 6.34E
82 L6 Feteşti Romania 44.22N 27.51E
58 Q8 Fethaland, Pt of Shetland Scotland 60.38N 1.18W
59 G7 Fethard Tipperary Irish Rep 52.28N 7.41W
59 J7 Fethard Wexford Irish Rep 52.11N 6.50W
Fethiye Malatya Turkeysee Yazıhan
36 D6 Fethiye Turkey 36.37N 29.08E
36 D6 Fethiye Körfezi gulf Turkey
44 M5 Fetisovo Kazakhstan U.S.S.R. 42.46N 52.38E
58 R8 Fetlar isld Shetland Scotland 60.37N 0.52W
81 E8 Feto, C Sicily 37.40N 12.31E
80 B3 Fetovàia, Pta.di Italy 42.44N 10.10E
58 L5 Fettercairn Grampian Scotland 56.51N 2.35W
88 R3 Fetzara L Algeria 36.52N 7.22E
64 L5 Feucht W Germany 49.22N 11.13E
65 C7 Feuchten Austria 47.02N 10.46E
64 J5 Feuchtwangen W Germany 49.11N 10.22E
100 K7 Feudal Saskatchewan 51.52N 107.40W
66 J4 Feuerstein mt Switzerland 46.53N 8.04E
66 L1 Feuerthalen Switzerland 47.42N 8.38E
72 E7 Feugarolles France 44.13N 0.22E
58 L4 Feugh, Water of R Grampian Scotland
70 O3 Feuillie, la France 49.28N 1.31E
98 M3 Feu, L.du Quebec
69 B4 Feuquières France 49.39N 1.51E
69 B3 Feuquières-en-Vimeu France 50.04N 1.37E
71 E5 Feurs France 45.44N 4.13E
36 J5 Fevzipaşa Turkey 37.07N 36.38E
103 C4 F E Walter Reservoir Pennsylvania
61 M4 Fexhe-le-Haut-Clocher Belgium 50.40N 5.24E
61 N4 Fexhe-Slins Belgium 50.44N 5.34E
66 C5 Fey Switzerland 46.42N 6.41E
85 A8 Feyler, Ga mt Niger 22.32N 11.30E
72 G4 Feytiat France 45.48N 1.22E
32 F5 Feyzābād Kermān Iran 30.12N 55.35E
32 H3 Feyzābād Khorāsān Iran 35.00N 58.47E
71 F5 Feyzin France 45.41N 4.51E
37 G2 Feyziye Turkey 40.37N 29.30E
Fez see Fès
85 A7 Fezzan reg Libya
88 L6 Fezzou Morocco 30.53N 4.53W
57 F7 Ffestiniog Gwynedd Wales 52.58N 3.55W
56 C3 Ffostrasol Dyfed Wales 52.06N 4.23W
31 H8 Fhulchari* Bangladesh 25.10N 89.36E
72 H8 Fiac France 43.42N 1.53E
95 D6 Fiadanana Madagascar 20.25S 48.23E
121 C1 Fiambalá Argentina 27.45S 67.37W
121 C1 Fiambala R Argentina
80 H4 Fiamignano Italy 42.16N 13.08E
95 C6 Fianarantsoa Madagascar 21.27S 47.05E
90 G7 Fianga Chad 9.57N 15.09E
79 C4 Fiano Italy 45.13N 7.31E
80 H2 Fiastra, L.di Italy
82 G5 Fibiş Romania 45.57N 21.26E
76 E13 Ficalho mt Portugal 37.58N 7.17W
81 F7 Ficarazzi Sicily 38.06N 13.28E
67 O11 Ficarella R Corsica
79 K5 Ficarolo Italy 44.57N 11.26E
87 J6 Fich Ethiopia 8.10N 42.19E
87 G6 Fiche Ethiopia 9.50N 38.46E
98 R2 Fichot Is Newfoundland
64 M3 Fichtelberg W Germany 50.00N 11.52E
64 O3 Fichtelberg mt E Germany 50.26N 12.55E
64 M3 Fichtelgebirge mts W Germany
64 J5 Fichtenau W Germany 49.03N 10.16E
95 L4 Ficksburg S Africa 28.52S 27.53E
80 F3 Ficulle Italy 42.50N 12.04E
81 J9 Ficuzza R Sicily
81 F8 Ficuzza, Rocca mt Sicily 37.35N 13.08E
33 M5 Fidā Oman 23.31N 56.28E
33 K7 Fidā' Saudi Arabia 19.59N 52.26E
117 F8 Fidalgo R Brazil
34 C8 Fidan, Wādī watercourse Jordan
86 O4 Fidān, Wādī el watercourse Jordan
59 H7 Fiddown Kilkenny Irish Rep 52.20N 7.19W
79 H5 Fidenza Italy 44.52N 10.04E
66 P4 Fideris Switzerland 46.55N 9.45E
86 E7 Fidimîn Egypt 29.23N 30.46E
95 C5 Fidirana Madagascar 19.30S 46.34E
Fidishkuh see Fedeshkūh
90 A8 Fiditi Nigeria 7.41N 3.55E
53 V21 Fidjeland Norway 58.58N 6.55E
100 V1 Fidler L Manitoba
58 L6 Fidra isld Firth of Forth Scotland 56.05N 2.47W
79 L1 Fiè Italy 46.32N 11.30E
89 E6 Fié watercourse Guinea/Mali
65 G7 Fieberbrunn Austria 47.29N 12.33E
122 O4 Fieberling Tablemount Pacific Oc 32.24N 127.47W
109 C7 Field New Mexico 34.32N 107.28W
99 K6 Field Ontario 46.32N 80.03W
104 F10 Fieldale Virginia 36.42N 79.59W
13 B1 Field I N Terr Australia 12.05S 132.26E
100 K6 Fielding Saskatchewan 52.33N 107.35W
110 G7 Fields Oregon 42.17N 118.41W
110 A9 Fields Landing California 40.44N 124.14W
12 H9 Field West, Mt Tasmania 42.42S 146.28E
79 L2 Fiemme, Val di V Italy
69 B2 Fiennes France 50.49N 1.48E
83 D4 Fier Albania 40.44N 19.33E
79 L2 Fiera di Primiero Italy 46.10N 11.50E
66 G8 Fiernaz Italy 45.49N 7.36E
71 H5 Fier,R France
51 E5 Fierras mt Sweden 66.29N 15.55E
109 B9 Fierro New Mexico 32.51N 108.05W
66 G8 Fiery Italy 45.53N 7.44E
13 E4 Fiery Cr Queensland
66 J6 Fiesch Switzerland 46.25N 8.09E
66 J5 Fiescherhorn, Grosser mt Switz 46.33N 8.04E
66 L6 Fiesso Switzerland 46.30N 8.43E
112 H4 Fife Texas 31.23N 99.25W
Fife co see Fife reg
58 K6 Fife reg Scotland
58 K6 Fife, Howe of dist Fife Scotland
58 L3 Fife Keith Grampian Scotland 57.33N 2.58W
100 M9 Fife L Saskatchewan 49.13N 105.50W
100 M9 Fife Lake Saskatchewan 49.11N 105.49W
58 L6 Fife Ness prom Fife Scotland 56.17N 2.36W
87 K7 Fi-fi Somalia 7.40N 44.00E
90 M6 Fifi, El Sudan 10.04N 25.00E
12 J5 Fifield New S Wales 32.49S 147.31E
106 D4 Fifield Wisconsin 45.54N 90.26W
50 C5 Fíflholt Mýrasýsla Iceland 64.41N 22.09W
50 E7 Fíflholt Rangárvallasýsla Iceland 63.40N 20.18W
108 B5 Fifteen Mile Cr Wyoming
85 M10 Fifth Cataract Sudan 18.22N 33.45E
87 D1 Fifth Cataract rapids Sudan 18.29N 33.42E
84 C7 Figalia Greece 37.23N 21.51E
121 D8 Figalli Podesta Argentina 40.13S 64.06W
88 N4 Figalo,C Algeria 35.38N 1.14W
81 D2 Figari,C Sardinia 41.00N 9.40E
72 J6 Figeac France 44.37N 2.01E
52 K9 Figeholm Sweden 57.12N 16.35E
66 N9 Figino Italy 45.43N 9.08E
79 K7 Figline Valdarno Italy 43.37N 11.28E
75 O3 Figols Spain 42.11N 1.50E
116 P4 Fig Tree Nevis I W I 17.07N 62.35W
92 D12 Figtree Zimbabwe 20.24S 28.21E
76 D10 Figueira Portugal 39.03N 7.45W
76 C12 Figueira R Portugal
76 B8 Figueira da Foz Portugal 40.09N 8.51W
76 F7 Figueira de Castelo Rodrigo Portugal 40.54N 6.58W
76 C12 Figueira dos Cavaleiros Portugal 38.06N 8.12W
76 D7 Figueiredo da Alva Portugal 40.50N 7.59W
76 D10 Figueiró R Portugal
76 C9 Figueiró dos Vinhos Portugal 39.55N 8.16W
75 Q3 Figueras Spain 42.16N 2.57E
121 D1 Figueroa Argentina 27.40S 63.30W
121 A10 Figueroa, R Chile
75 K7 Figueroles Spain 40.07N 0.15W
76 G5 Figueruela Arriba Spain 41.52N 6.26W
88 N5 Figuig Morocco 32.10N 1.15W
90 F7 Figuil Cameroon 9.45N 13.59E
81 B3 Figulada, Mte Sardinia 40.21N 8.41E
41 Q3 Figurina, Ostrov isld U.S.S.R. 76.19N 141.37E
34 D9 Fiha al 'Inab reg Jordan
95 C5 Fihaonana Madagascar 18.34S 47.12E
9 T3 Fiji island grp Pacific Oc
10 P5 Fiji Basin, North Pacific Oc
10 P6 Fiji Basin, South Pacific Oc
60 F13 Fijnaart Netherlands 51.38N 4.29E
50 H3 Fijotsheidhi heath Iceland
90 E6 Fika Nigeria 11.19N 11.15E
84 E6 Fikhtia Greece 37.43N 22.43E
84 C2 Fiki Greece 39.31N 21.39E
53 V13 Fiksdal Norway 62.37N 6.52E
Fila see Vila
77 L6 Filabres, Sierra de los mts Spain
92 D12 Filabust Zimbabwe 20.34S 29.20E
120 E4 Filadelfia Bolivia 11.23S 68.45W
117 E8 Filadélfia Brazil 7.18S 47.30W
115 M4 Filadelfia Costa Rica 10.28N 85.33W
81 M6 Filadelfia Italy 38.47N 16.17E
118 A8 Filadelfia Paraguay 22.17S 60.03W
62 M7 Filakovo Czechoslovakia 48.17N 19.50E
56 P2 Filby Norfolk Eng 52.40N 1.40E
123 D3 Filchner,C Antarctica 66.30S 92.20E
123 E10 Filchner Ice Shelf Antarctica
66 G5 Filderich R Switzerland
64 G6 Filderstadt W Germany 48.41N 9.17E
100 R4 File L Manitoba 54.50N 100.20W
110 L7 Filer Idaho 42.36N 114.37W
80 H5 Filettino Italy 41.53N 13.20E
57 N4 Filey N Yorks Eng 54.12N 0.17W
84 Y21 Filfla isld Malta 35.48N 14.25E
84 G5 Filí Greece 38.06N 23.40E
84 D3 Filia Greece 39.15N 22.03E
84 D6 Filia Greece 37.51N 22.07E
82 H6 Filiaşi Romania 44.32N 23.31E
83 D5 Filiátes Greece 39.38N 20.16E
84 C7 Filiatrá Greece 37.09N 21.35E
81 J6 Filicudi isld Lipari Is Italy 38.35N 14.35E
80 K5 Filignano Italy 41.33N 14.04E
47 L6 Filimonovo Chelyabinsk U.S.S.R. 54.43N 60.04E
42 F4 Filimonovo U.S.S.R. 56.09N 95.32E
89 L4 Filingué Niger 14.21N 3.22E
42 G5 Filiopovskiy U.S.S.R. 53.55N 102.05E
62 O1 Filipów Poland 54.12N 22.38E
84 B1 Filippaioi Greece 40.05N 21.09E
40 G4 Filippa, Mys C U.S.S.R. 54.45N 137.40E
122 M8 Filippo Reef Line Is Pacific Oc 6.15S 150.45W
52 H7 Filipstad Sweden 59.44N 14.10E
66 P5 Filisur Switzerland 46.41N 9.42E
53 Y16 Fillefjell mt Norway 61.10N 8.05E
66 A8 Fillière R France
69 C3 Fillièvres France 50.19N 2.10E
111 F7 Fillmore California 34.25N 118.55W
108 L1 Fillmore N Dakota 48.13N 99.46W
104 G4 Fillmore New York 42.31N 78.05W
100 O9 Fillmore Saskatchewan 49.53N 103.30W
111 M3 Fillmore Utah 38.58N 112.20W
61 N5 Filot Belgium 50.26N 5.34E
80 H2 Filottrano Italy 43.26N 13.21E
64 H6 Fils R W Germany
53 C5 Filskov Denmark 55.49N 9.02E
53 A5 Filsø L Denmark 55.43N 8.14E
56 F4 Filton Avon Eng 51.31N 2.35W
87 H8 Filtu Ethiopia 5.08N 40.35E
87 H8 Filtu,Mt Ethiopia 5.20N 40.50E
36 F1 Filyos R Turkey
66 S4 Fimber Tal V Switz/Austria
123 B9 Fimbulheimen ra Antarctica
91 E5 Fimi R Zaïre
59 L2 Finaghy Antrim N Ireland 54.34N 5.58W
19 M1 Finaguayac Guam Pacific Oc 13.35N 144.52E
79 D6 Finalborgo Italy 44.11N 8.19E
81 H7 Finale Sicily 38.02N 14.10E
79 K5 Finale Emilia Italy 44.50N 11.18E
79 D6 Finale Ligure Italy 44.10N 8.21E
79 D6 Finale Pia Italy 44.11N 8.22E
77 L6 Finana Spain 37.10N 2.50W
89 E5 Fina, Res de Mali 13.25N 8.35W
104 F9 Fincastle Virginia 37.30N 79.54W
99 P7 Finch Ontario 45.09N 75.07W
87 F6 Finchaa Dam Ethiopia 9.40N 37.21E
56 M4 Finchingfield Essex Eng 51.58N 0.28E
55 E2 Finchley London England 51.36N 0.10W
53 C4 Finderup Denmark 56.25N 9.18E
58 J3 Findhorn Grampian Scotland 57.39N 3.37W
58 J3 Findhorn, R Grampian/Highland Scotland
37 F8 Fındık Turkey 37.31N 41.58E
37 G2 Fındıklı Bursa Turkey 40.30N 29.16E
37 C2 Fındıklı Çanakkale Turkey 40.27N 26.33E
37 F4 Fındıklı Çoruh Turkey 41.17N 41.07E
36 G6 Fındıkpınar Turkey 36.53N 34.22E
100 M8 Findlater Saskatchewan 50.49N 105.29W
107 H2 Findlay Illinois 39.31N 88.45W
104 B5 Findlay Ohio 41.02N 83.40W
101 P10 Findlay, Mt Br Col 50.04N 116.10W
58 L3 Findochty Grampian Scotland 57.42N 2.55W
58 M4 Findon Grampian Scotland 57.04N 2.06W
56 L6 Findon W Sussex Eng 50.52N 0.25W
12 A8 Findon dist Adelaide, S Aust
56 K3 Finedon Northants Eng 52.20N 0.39W
66 L7 Finero Italy 46.08N 8.32E
75 O3 Finestras, Sierra mts Spain
77 Q3 Finestrat Spain 38.35N 0.13W
108 N3 Fingal N Dakota 46.47N 97.48W
12 J8 Fingal Tasmania 41.37S 147.59E
58 D6 Fingal's Cave Staffa, Strathclyde Scotland 56.26N 6.21W
107 H6 Finger Tennessee 35.21N 88.39W
97 K7 Finger L Ontario 53.00N 93.00W
104 J4 Finger Lakes reg New York
59 K5 Finglas Dublin Irish Rep 53.24N 6.18W
92 E9 Fingoe Zimbabwe 15.10S 31.51E
92 E9 Fingoe mt Mozambique 15.08S 31.56E
72 G8 Finhan France 43.55N 1.13E
66 D7 Finhaut Switzerland 46.05N 6.59E
71 D8 Finiels, Pic de mt France 44.25N 3.44E
36 E6 Finike Turkey 36.18N 30.08E
36 E6 Finike Körfezi B Turkey
67 C4 Finistère dept France
76 A3 Finisterre Spain 42.54N 9.16W
76 A3 Finisterre, C Spain 42.52N 9.16W
15 H6 Finisterre Ra Papua New Guinea
113 F4 Fink Creek Alaska 65.51N 163.18W
13 C7 Finke N Terr Australia 25.30S 134.38E
13 B1 Finke B N Terr Australia
12 D2 Finke Flood Flats S Australia
13 C6 Finke Gorge N Terr Australia
12 C4 Finke,Mt S Australia 31.00S 134.20E
13 D7 Finke, R N Terr Australia
106 C2 Finland Minnesota 47.24N 91.16W
49 J4 Finland rep N Europe
49 K5 Finland, Gulf of N Europe
101 K7 Finlay R Br Col
108 S3 Finlayson Minnesota 46.10N 92.54W
108 N2 Finley N Dakota 47.31N 97.51W
12 H6 Finley New S Wales 35.40S 145.34E
109 P7 Finley Oklahoma 34.21N 95.30W
100 N2 Finmark Ontario 48.36N 89.44W
56 J4 Finmere Oxon Eng 52.00N 1.05W
53 U16 Finnabotn Norway 61.02N 6.16E
50 K2 Finnafjördhur B Iceland
58 G6 Finnart Strathclyde Scotland 56.07N 4.50W
53 X20 Finndøla R Norway 59.13N 7.55E
64 L1 Finne mts E Germany
59 H4 Finnea W Meath Irish Rep 53.47N 7.23W
100 E7 Finnegan Alberta 51.11N 112.08W
51 E4 Finneid Norway 67.16N 15.28E
63 G10 Finnentrop W Germany 51.10N 7.57E
64 D1 Finnentrop W Germany 51.10N 7.57E
61 K6 Finnevaux Belgium 50.09N 4.56E
52 M2 Finnforsfallet Sweden 64.46N 20.20E
13 H3 Finnigan, Mt Queensland 15.45S 145.15E
13 B2 Finniss R N Terr Australia 12.50S 130.40E
12 C5 Finniss, C S Australia 33.08S 134.50E
59 F2 Finn, L Donegal Irish Rep 54.51N 8.08W
51 K1 Finnmark co Norway
113 J6 Finn Mt Alaska 60.37N 157.11W

87 H9 **Finno** *mt* Somalia 3.30N 41.33E
53 T20 **Finnøy** *isld* Norway 59.10N 5.50E
59 G2 **Finn, R** Donegal Irish Rep
53 Y14 **Finnset** Norway 62.25N 8.20E
52 G6 **Finnskog** Norway 60.43N 12.23E
51 G2 **Finnsnes** Norway 69.16N 18.00E
51 J6 **Finnträsk** *L* Sweden 65.09N 21.20E
80 J4 **Fino** *R* Italy
79 F3 **Fino Mornasco** Italy 45.44N 9.03E
63 T7 **Finow** E Germany 52.50N 13.56E
63 T7 **Finowfurt** E Germany 52.49N 13.40E
63 T7 **Finow Kanal** E Germany
69 E3 **Fins** France 50.02N 3.03E
33 N5 **Fins** Oman 22.58N 59.12E
55 F3 **Finsbury** London Eng 51.32N 0.06W
15 J7 **Finschhafen** Papua New Guinea 6.35S 147.51E
53 X17 **Finse** Norway 60.36N 7.30E
66 C3 **Fins, les** France 47.05N 6.38E
52 J8 **Finspång** Sweden 58.42N 15.45E
66 J5 **Finsteraarhorn** *mt* Switzerland 46.32N 8.08E
63 T9 **Finsterwalde** E Germany 51.38N 13.43E
60 R7 **Finsterwolde** Netherlands 53.12N 7.05E
58 S11 **Finstown** Orkney Scotland 59.01N 3.07W
51 H11 **Finström** Finland 60.15N 19.55E
33 K9 **Fintās,Ra's** *C* S Yemen 15.52N 52.15E
64 E4 **Finthen** W Germany 49.59N 8.11E
59 H3 **Fintona** Co Tyrone N Ireland 54.30N 7.18W
59 F2 **Fintown** Donegal Irish Rep 54.52N 8.07W
58 H6 **Fintry Hills** Central Scotland
Finuana I *see* **Tobona I**
14 C5 **Finucane I** W Australia 20.20S 118.38E
13 F5 **Finucane Ra** Queensland
59 C7 **Finuge** Kerry Irish Rep 52.26N 9.32W
80 G3 **Fionchi, Monte** Italy 42.41N 12.37E
66 F7 **Fionnay** Switzerland 46.03N 7.18E
58 F3 **Fionn, L** Highland Scotland
80 E3 **Fiora** *R* Italy
79 J5 **Fiorano Modenese** Italy 44.32N 10.49E
11 B11 **Fiordland Nat. Park** New Zealand
79 G5 **Fiorenzuola d'Arda** Italy 44.56N 9.54E
79 N7 **Fiorenzuola di Focara** Italy 43.57N 12.49E
80 J3 **Fiori, Monte** Italy 42.46N 13.37E
79 L3 **Fior, Monte** Italy 45.55N 11.36E
92 E5 **Fip** *tribe* Tanzania
Fiq *see* **Afiq**
35 H2 **Fiqa', El** Syria 32.57N 36.10E
85 N8 **Fiqû, Wadi** *watercourse* Egypt
35 D4 **Firasin** Jordan 32.25N 35.06E
37 D8 **Firat** *R* Turkey
95 C5 **Firavahana** Madagascar 18.36S 46.50E
57 H4 **Firbank** Cumbria Eng 54.21N 2.35W
Firch, Sha'ib *watercourse see* **Firk, Sha'ib** *water course*
86 H4 **Firdân, El** Egypt 30.42N 32.23E
101 S7 **Firebag, R** Alberta
111 D5 **Firebaugh** California 36.51N 120.30W
113 M6 **Fire I** Alaska 61.09N 150.15W
103 H5 **Fire Island Lt. Ho** Long I, N Y 40.36N 73.11W
103 H5 **Fire Island National Seashore** Long I, N Y
79 K7 **Firenze** Italy 43.47N 11.15E
79 K7 **Firenze** *prov* Italy
79 K6 **Firenzuola** Italy 44.07N 11.23E
99 G4 **Fire River** Ontario 48.47N 83.36W
108 J4 **Firesteel** S Dakota 45.26N 101.18W
89 D8 **Firestone Plantation** Liberia 6.25N 10.15W
96 V15 **Firgas** Gran Canaria Canary Is 28.07N 15.33W
89 D5 **Firghia** Guinea 12.06N 10.56W
95 N2 **Firham** S Africa 26.59S 29.16E
119 G5 **Firiña** Venezuela 4.45N 64.35W
82 H3 **Firiza** Romania 47.42N 23.38E
90 G4 **Firkachi** Niger 15.40N 14.20E
85 L9 **Firket, Jebel** *mt* Sudan 20.51N 30.40E
89 K4 **Firkou** Niger 14.56N 0.59E
34 M8 **Firk, Sha'ib** *watercourse* Iraq
121 E4 **Firmat** Argentina 33.29S 61.29W
72 J6 **Firmi** France 44.33N 2.18E
71 E6 **Firminy** France 45.23N 4.18E
81 M4 **Firmo** Italy 39.43N 16.10E
100 L9 **Fir Mountain** Saskatchewan 49.23N 106.32W
46 J1 **Firovo** U.S.S.R. 57.30N 33.48E
31 F6 **Firoza** Pakistan 28.49N 70.57E
30 B5 **Firozabad** Uttar Prad India 27.09N 78.24E
29 B2 **Firozabad** *anc site* Delhi India 28.38N 77.14E
31 B3 **Firozkoh** *reg* Afghanistan
29 D2 **Firozpur** Punjab India 30.55N 74.38E
29 D2 **Firozpur** *dist* Punjab India
29 E4 **Firozpur Jhirka** Haryana India 27.45N 76.58E
40 J8 **Firsovo** Sakhalin U.S.S.R. 47.42N 142.33E
85 M7 **First Cataract** Egypt
104 O1 **First Connecticut L** New Hampshire
105 F2 **First R** N Carolina
58 Q9 **Firth** Shetland Scotland 60.26N 1.11W
101 C1 **Firth** *R* Yukon Terr
58 S11 **Firth, B of** Orkney Scotland 59.01N 3.04W
32 E6 **Firūzābād** Fārs Iran 28.51N 52.35E
Firuzabad Iran*see* **Rāsk**
32 G2 **Firūzeh** Iran 37.20N 57.19E
32 E3 **Firūzkūh** Iran 35.44N 52.50E
43 E7 **Firyuza** Turkmeniya U.S.S.R. 37.55N 58.03E
75 K3 **Fiscal** Spain 42.30N 0.07W
64 K7 **Fischach** W Germany 48.17N 10.40E
65 P5 **Fischamend Markt** Austria 48.08N 16.37E
64 C4 **Fischbach** W Germany 49.45N 7.24E
66 O1 **Fischbach** W Germany 47.40N 9.24E
65 M7 **Fischbacher Alpen** *mts* Austria
63 Q7 **Fischbeck** E Germany 52.33N 12.02E
64 E2 **Fischelbach** W Germany 50.53N 8.21E
64 L8 **Fischen** W Germany 47.56N 11.10E
65 B7 **Fischen** W Germany 47.28N 10.17E
66 M2 **Fischenthal** Switzerland 47.19N 8.56E
112 J6 **Fischer** Texas 29.58N 98.18W
63 K6 **Fischerhude** W Germany 53.07N 9.04E
94 C5 **Fischersbrunn** Namibia 24.40S 14.41E
63 S6 **Fischerwall** E Germany 53.04N 13.12E
66 M2 **Fischingen** Switzerland 47.24N 8.58E
94 D5 **Fish** *watercourse* Namibia
94 F8 **Fish** *watercourse* S Africa
56 J6 **Fishbourne** I of Wight Eng 50.44N 1.12W
111 E4 **Fish Camp** California 37.28N 119.36W
113 L1 **Fish Cr** Alaska
110 M6 **Fish Creek Res** Idaho 43.26N 113.49W
105 F10 **Fisheating Creek** Florida
107 C10 **Fisher** Louisiana 31.30N 93.29W
108 O2 **Fisher** Minnesota 47.48N 96.49W
99 N4 **Fisher** Quebec 48.29N 77.49W
12 B4 **Fisher** S Australia 30.34S 130.58E
12 A6 **Fisher** *dist* Canberra Australia
123 J4 **Fisher B** Antarctica
100 U7 **Fisher B** Manitoba
100 U7 **Fisher Branch** Manitoba 51.04N 97.38W
123 C5 **Fisher Glacier** Antarctica
95 E10 **Fisheries, The** S Africa 34.21S 21.50E
14 A9 **Fisherman I** W Australia 30.09S 115.00E
33 C10 **Fisherman's B** S Yemen
104 K9 **Fishermans I** Virginia 37.05N 75.59W
103 L4 **Fishers I** New York
97 L5 **Fisher Strait** N W Terr
113 E9 **Fisher Vol** Aleutian Is 54.45N 164.35W
94 D6 **Fish, Gr** *watercourse* Namibia
56 B4 **Fishguard** Dyfed Wales 51.59N 4.59W
56 B3 **Fishguard B** Dyfed Wales
95 B10 **Fish Hoek** S Africa 34.08S 18.25E
104 J8 **Fishing Creek** Maryland 38.21N 76.15W
100 N8 **Fishing Lakes, The** Saskatchewan 50.47N 104.00W
103 G3 **Fishkill** New York 41.32N 73.54W
103 G3 **Fishkill Cr** New York
113 M4 **Fish L** Alaska 65.09N 151.25W
101 M4 **Fish L** N W Terr 63.10N 122.35W
111 N3 **Fish L** Utah 38.34N 111.42W
58 E5 **Fishnish Pt.** Mull, Strathclyde Scotland 56.31N 5.49W
106 L6 **Fish Pt** Michigan 43.43N 83.31W
13 E4 **Fish River** N Terr Australia 17.52S 137.45E
111 A3 **Fish Rock** California 38.47N 123.34W
103 D3 **Fishs Eddy** New York 41.58N 75.10W
44 C4 **Fisht** *mt* U.S.S.R. 43.59N 39.54E
110 Q4 **Fishtail** Montana 45.28N 109.31W
110 M4 **Fishtrap** Montana 45.52N 113.15W
104 C9 **Fishtrap Res** Kentucky 37.21N 82.18W
53 T14 **Fiskå** Möre og Romsdal Norway 62.06N 5.35E
53 S20 **Fiskå** Norway 59.20N 5.18E
53 S20 **Fiskå** Rogaland Norway 59.20N 5.18E
53 U20 **Fiskå** Rogaland Norway 59.07N 6.00E
50 E7 **Fiská** *R* Iceland
83 D6 **Fiskárdho** Greece 38.29N 20.31E
53 C3 **Fiskbæk** Denmark 56.31N 9.19E
103 K2 **Fiskdale** Massachusetts 42.07N 72.07W
100 J7 **Fiske** Saskatchewan 51.29N 108.24W
123 E12 **Fiske, C** Antarctica 74.27S 60.28W
48 R13 **Fiskenæs Banke** Greenland
48 S13 **Fiskenæsset** Greenland 63.05N 50.40W
50 E5 **Fiskivötn** *lakes* Iceland
69 F5 **Fismes** France 49.18N 3.42E
89 A4 **Fissel** Senegal 14.32N 16.39W
53 U20 **Fister** Norway 59.10N 6.05E
95 C6 **Fitampito** Madagascar 20.59S 46.18E
104 O4 **Fitchburg** Massachusetts 42.35N 71.50W
103 K3 **Fitchville** Connecticut 41.34N 72.09W
75 G3 **Fitero** Spain 42.04N 1.52W
58 Q10 **Fitful Hd** Shetland Scotland 59.55N 1.23W
50 E4 **Fitjá** *R* Iceland
50 F6 **Fitjaásar** *ridge* Iceland
50 D6 **Fitjar** Iceland 64.28N 21.13W
53 S19 **Fitjar** Norway 59.55N 5.20E
122 C2 **Fito** *pk* W Samoa, Pacific Oc 13.54S 171.43W
72 K10 **Fitou** France 42.53N 2.58E
95 A7 **Fitsitika** Madagascar 23.00S 43.30E
53 C5 **Fitting** Denmark 55.38N 9.08E
56 K6 **Fittleworth** W Sussex Eng 50.58N 0.35W
90 H5 **Fittri** *L* Chad 12.43N 17.17E
120 D4 **Fitzcarrald** Peru 11.49S 72.14W
101 S6 **Fitzgerald** Alberta 59.51N 111.41W
105 D6 **Fitzgerald** Georgia 31.43N 83.16W
12 E5 **Fitzgerald B** S Australia
109 O7 **Fitzhugh** Oklahoma 34.41N 96.45W
101 K10 **Fitzhugh Sd** Br Columbia
69 C5 **Fitz-James** France 49.24N 2.27E
13 B2 **Fitzmaurice** *R* N Terr Australia
99 S5 **Fitzpatrick** Quebec 47.29N 72.46W
121 L6 **Fitz Roy** Argentina 47.00S 67.20W
12 D7 **Fitzroy** *dist* Melbourne, Vic
13 K6 **Fitzroy** *R* Queensland
121 J7 **Fitzroy, Cerro** *pk* Arg/Chile 49.16S 73.03W
14 F4 **Fitzroy Crossing** W Australia 18.13S 125.33E
99 O7 **Fitzroy Harbour** Ontario 45.29N 76.14W
13 H3 **Fitzroy I** Queensland 16.54S 146.00E
14 E4 **Fitzroy R** W Australia
99 J7 **Fitzwilliam I** Ontario 45.30N 81.47W
80 H5 **Fiuggi** Italy 41.48N 13.14E
79 J6 **Fiumalbo** Italy 44.11N 10.38E
Fiume *see* **Rijeka**
81 M5 **Fiumefreddo Bruzio** Italy 39.14N 16.04E
81 K8 **Fiumefreddo di Sicilia** Sicily 37.47N 15.13E
81 O5 **Fiumenicà, Pta** Italy 39.29N 17.02E
80 F5 **Fiumicino** Italy 41.46N 12.14E
59 J2 **Five Cross Road** Londonderry N Ireland 54.59N 6.50W
103 E9 **Five Fathom Bank Lt. Ship** U.S.A. 38.48N 74.36W
11 A12 **Five Fingers Pen** New Zealand
98 H8 **Five Islands** Nova Scotia 45.24N 64.05W
56 B6 **Five Lanes** Cornwall Eng 50.35N 4.31W
108 B6 **Fivemile Cr** Wyoming
59 H3 **Fivemiletown** Tyrone N Ireland 54.23N 7.19W
11 C12 **Five Rivers** New Zealand 45.37S 168.29E
58 F4 **Five Sisters** *mts* Highland Scotland 57.11N 5.23W
79 H6 **Fivizzano** Italy 44.14N 10.07E
92 D8 **Fiwila** Zambia 14.00S 29.34E
71 F2 **Fixin** France 47.15N 4.59E
71 D6 **Fix-St.Geneys** France 45.08N 3.40E
11 B8 **Fizeau, Mt** Campbell I Pacific Oc 52.31S 169.09E
61 M4 **Fize-Fontaine** Belgium 50.35N 5.17E
92 D4 **Fizi** Zaïre 4.18S 28.56E
44 H8 **Fizuli** Azerbaydzhan U.S.S.R. 39.35N 47.07E
53 U19 **Fjæra** Hordaland Norway 59.53N 6.25E
52 D8 **Fjære** Aust Agder Norway 58.23N 8.36E
53 V16 **Fjærland** Norway 61.24N 6.45E
50 J4 **Fjallagjía Glœdhur** *rift* Iceland
50 J2 **Fjallahöfn** *harb* Iceland
51 H4 **Fjällåsen** Sweden 67.33N 20.05E
51 D6 **Fjällfjällen** *mt* Sweden 65.10N 14.45E
50 K4 **Fjallgardhar** *mts* Iceland
52 G4 **Fjällnäs** Sweden 62.38N 12.10E
52 J3 **Fjällsjö** Sweden 63.49N 16.25E
53 A4 **Fjaltring Kirke** Denmark 56.29N 8.09E
50 D3 **Fjardharhorn** Iceland 65.34N 21.25W
50 D4 **Fjardharhorn** Iceland 65.09N 21.06W
53 T19 **Fjelberg** Norway 59.45N 5.43E
53 H7 **Fjelde** Denmark 54.45N 11.40E
53 S18 **Fjell** Norway 60.19N 5.05E
53 F3 **Fjellerup** Denmark 56.30N 10.36E
53 X18 **Fjellsjåberget** *mt* Norway 60.07N 7.40E
53 X15 **Fjellsliseter** Norway 61.37N 7.35E
53 E6 **Fjelsted** Denmark 55.26N 10.01E
53 D6 **Fjelstrup** Denmark 55.19N 9.34E
53 C2 **Fjerritslev** Denmark 57.06N 9.17E
50 J2 **Fjöll** Iceland 66.05N 16.56W
53 T20 **Fjøløy** *Lt Ho* Norway 59.06N 5.35E
53 Y20 **Fjone** Norway 59.10N 8.28E
53 W14 **Fjøra** Norway 62.18N 7.21E
50 G5 **Fjórdhungakvísl** *R* Iceland
50 H5 **Fjórdhungsalda** *mt* Iceland 64.52N 18.00W
50 G5 **Fjórdhungsvatn** *L* Iceland 64.53N 18.04W
50 L4 **Fjórdhur** Iceland 65.11N 14.02W
53 S18 **Fjøsanger** Norway 60.21N 5.20E
52 C8 **Fjotland** Norway 58.29N 7.02E
88 K5 **Fkih-beni-Salah** Morocco 32.32N 6.44W
52 E6 **Flå** Buskerud Norway 60.25N 9.26E
52 E3 **Flå** Sör-Tröndelag Norway 63.13N 10.18E
50 K6 **Fláajökull** *ice cap* Iceland 64.24N 15.45W
64 K5 **Flachslanden** W Germany 49.24N 10.32E
99 O2 **Flackville** New York 44.40N 75.21W
58 Q9 **Fladdabister** Shetland Scotland 60.04N 1.14W
48 V2 **Flade Isblink** *ice field* Greenland
53 A3 **Flade Sø** *L* Denmark 56.47N 8.17E
65 M7 **Fladnitz** Austria 47.18N 15.28E
53 B6 **Fladså** *R* Denmark
64 J2 **Fladungen** W Germany 50.32N 10.09E
50 G7 **Flaga** Iceland 63.40N 18.30W
109 G2 **Flagler** Colorado 39.17N 103.05W
105 F8 **Flagler Beach** Florida 29.29N 81.08W
72 J6 **Flagnac** France 44.36N 2.15E
111 N6 **Flagstaff** Arizona 35.12N 111.38W
95 N7 **Flagstaff** S Africa 31.05S 29.30E
11 L12 **Flagstaff** *mt* New Zealand 45.50S 170.28E
96 B13 **Flagstaff B** St Helena
96 B13 **Flagstaff Hill** St Helena 15.55S 5.42W
12 G8 **Flagstaff Hill** Tasmania 42.51S 147.24E
104 P1 **Flagstaff L** Maine
110 F7 **Flagstaff L** Oregon 42.36N 119.49W
110 K1 **Flagstone** Br Columbia 49.04N 115.10W
53 X17 **Flakavatn** *L* Norway 60.38N 7.35E
53 G6 **Flakkebjerg** Denmark 55.19N 11.24E
51 C3 **Flakstad** Norway 68.06N 13.20E
53 W17 **Flåm** Norway 60.50N 7.08E
26 V12 **Flamand, I** Mauritius, Indian Oc 20.19S 57.48E
70 G2 **Flamanville** France 49.32N 1.53W
66 F4 **Flamatt** Switzerland 46.53N 7.19E
106 D4 **Flambeau, R** Wisconsin
106 D3 **Flambeau Res** Wisconsin 45.05N 90.11W
69 E7 **Flamboin** France 48.28N 3.18E
57 N4 **Flamborough** Humberside Eng 54.07N 0.07W
57 N4 **Flamborough Hd** Humberside Eng 54.06N 0.04W
84 C2 **Flambourési** Greece 39.48N 21.45E
121 E8 **Flamenco, I** Argentina
120 D12 **Flamenco, Pta** *C* Chile 26.34S 70.43W
96 P4 **Flamengos** Azores 38.33N 28.39W
61 N6 **Flamierge** Belgium 50.02N 5.36E
63 R8 **Fläming** *reg* E Germany
105 G12 **Flamingo** Florida 25.08N 80.07W
110 Q8 **Flamingo Gorge Res** Utah/Wyoming
15 D6 **Flamingo, Teluk** *B* Irian Jaya
75 M3 **Flamisell** *R* Spain
64 D2 **Flammersfeld** W Germany 50.39N 7.32E
53 W17 **Flåmsdalen** *V* Norway 60.47N 7.07E
116 O2 **Flanagin Town** Trinidad & Tobago 10.25N 61.19W
103 J5 **Flanders** Long I, N Y 40.54N 72.37W
103 E5 **Flanders** New Jersey 40.50N 74.42W
100 L2 **Flanders** Ontario 48.45N 92.04W
69 C2 **Flandre** *prov* France
108 O5 **Flandreau** S Dakota 44.04N 96.36W
91 F4 **Flandria** Zaïre 0.23S 19.05E
110 F9 **Flanigan** Nevada 40.11N 119.54W
58 A2 **Flannan Is** W Isles Scotland 58.16N 7.35W
52 L3 **Flärke** Sweden 63.35N 19.00E
66 P3 **Fläsch** Switzerland 47.02N 9.31E
108 J3 **Flasher** N Dakota 46.28N 101.14W
52 J2 **Flåsjön** *L* Sweden 64.05N 15.40E
75 Q3 **Flassá** Spain 42.03N 2.57E
71 J10 **Flassans-sur-Issole** France 43.22N 6.14E
113 J5 **Flat** Alaska 62.28N 158.01W
112 K4 **Flat** Texas 31.19N 97.39W
101 K5 **Flat** *R* N W Terr
98 O5 **Flat Bay** Newfoundland 48.24N 58.35W
100 C4 **Flatbush** Alberta 54.40N 114.09W
103 K8 **Flatbush** New York 40.39N 73.56W
107 J8 **Flat Creek** Alabama 33.39N 87.07W
53 Z19 **Flatdal** Norway 59.34N 8.35E
53 X20 **Flateland** Norway 59.16N 7.30E
53 U16 **Flåten** Norway 61.23N 6.14E
50 C4 **Flatey** Iceland 65.22N 22.55W
50 H2 **Flatey** *isld* Iceland 66.10N 17.50W
50 H2 **Flateyjardalsheidhi** *heath* Iceland
50 B2 **Flateyri** Iceland 66.03N 23.28W
110 L2 **Flathead** *R* Montana
110 L2 **Flathead L** Montana 47.55N 114.05W
110 M1 **Flathead Middle Fork** *R* Montana
110 K1 **Flathead Mts** Montana
111 M1 **Flathead S. Fork** *R* Montana
56 E5 **Flatholm** *isld* Somerset Eng 51.23N 3.08W
26 U11 **Flat I** Mauritius, Indian Oc 19.52S 57.38E
98 O3 **Flat I** Quebec 50.44N 58.50W
13 J5 **Flat I** Queensland
100 E4 **Flat L** Alberta 54.40N 112.50W
53 X14 **Flatmark** Norway 62.26N 7.59E
11 B12 **Flat Mt** New Zealand 45.38S 167.28E
112 K6 **Flatonia** Texas 29.41N 97.08W
11 L8 **Flat Pt** New Zealand 41.12S 176.00E
106 J6 **Flat, R** Michigan
107 F4 **Flat River** Missouri 37.52N 90.31W
107 J3 **Flat Rock** Illinois 38.53N 87.40W
107 L2 **Flat Rock** Indiana 39.23N 85.50W
65 H8 **Flattach** Austria 46.57N 13.08E
13 H2 **Flattery, C** Queensland 14.58S 145.20E
110 A1 **Flattery, C** Washington 48.24N 124.43W
65 K8 **Flattnitz** Austria 46.57N 14.02E
104 D9 **Flat Top** W Virginia 37.35N 81.07W
96 C1 **Flatts Village** Bermuda 32.19N 64.44W
110 R3 **Flatwillow** Montana 46.50N 108.24W
104 E8 **Flatwoods** W Virginia 38.43N 80.39W
53 E2 **Flauenskjold** Denmark 57.15N 10.18E
65 D7 **Flaurling** Austria 47.18N 11.08E
50 K2 **Flautafell** *mt* Iceland 66.10N 15.46W
52 D7 **Flåv** *L* Norway 59.17N 8.55E
71 F7 **Flaviac** France 44.44N 4.40E
72 G4 **Flavignac** France 45.42N 1.06E
69 F4 **Flavigny-le-Grand-et-Beaurain** France 49.53N 3.41E
69 L6 **Flavigny-sur-Moselle** France 48.33N 6.12E
71 F1 **Flavigny-sur-Ozerain** France 47.32N 4.31E
72 K7 **Flavin** France 44.17N 2.35E
61 J5 **Flavion** Belgium 50.15N 4.43E
53 T14 **Flavœr** *Lt Ho* Norway 62.18N 5.36E
79 K2 **Flavón** Italy 46.18N 11.02E
69 E4 **Flavy-le-Martel** France 49.43N 3.12E
66 N2 **Flawil** Switzerland 47.25N 9.12E
61 K5 **Flawinne** Belgium 50.27N 4.49E
56 F5 **Flax Bourton** Avon Eng 51.26N 2.44W
100 H7 **Flaxcombe** Saskatchewan 51.28N 109.36W
113 P1 **Flaxsman I** Alaska 70.12N 146.00W
108 H1 **Flaxton** N Dakota 48.55N 102.24W
108 E1 **Flaxville** Montana 48.50N 105.10W
61 Q8 **Flaxweiler** Luxembourg 49.40N 6.21E
71 J9 **Flayosc** France 43.32N 6.24E
70 B4 **Flèche** *R* France
70 K6 **Flèche, La** France 47.42N 0.04W
63 O8 **Flechtingen** E Germany 52.20N 11.15E
105 K9 **Fleeming Pt** New Providence I Bahamas 24.59N 77.29W
100 F6 **Fleet** Alberta 52.10N 111.48W
56 K5 **Fleet** Hants Eng 51.16N 0.50W
58 H3 **Fleet, Loch** Highland Scotland
58 H3 **Fleet, R** Highland Scotland
103 C3 **Fleetville** Pennsylvania 41.36N 75.43W
57 E3 **Fleet, Water of** *R* Dumfries & Galloway Scotland
57 G5 **Fleetwood** Lancs Eng 53.56N 3.01W
103 C6 **Fleetwood** Pennsylvania 40.27N 75.48W
13 H5 **Fleetwood** Queensland 22.15S 145.44E
64 G5 **Flein** W Germany 49.06N 9.14E
103 E2 **Fleischmanns** New York 42.10N 74.34W
72 E6 **Fleix, le** France 44.52N 0.16E
53 S16 **Flekke** Norway 61.19N 5.21E
52 C8 **Flekkefjord** Norway 58.17N 6.40E
52 D8 **Flekkerøy** *isld* Norway 58.05N 8.03E
50 C4 **Flekkudalsá** *R* Iceland
61 M4 **Flémalle-Haute** Belgium 50.36N 5.28E
Flemhude *see* **Quarnbek**
109 H1 **Fleming** Colorado 40.40N 102.51W
100 Q8 **Fleming** Saskatchewan 50.05N 101.34W
17 O7 **Fleming Deep** *trough* Pacific Oc 24.00N 144.20E
104 B8 **Flemingsburg** Kentucky 38.26N 83.43W
103 E5 **Flemington** New Jersey 40.31N 74.52W
103 E5 **Flemington Junc** New Jersey 40.32N 74.51W
96 F4 **Flemish Cap** Atlantic Oc 46.42N 45.00W
53 E6 **Flemløse** Denmark 55.15N 10.04E
52 K7 **Flen** Sweden 59.04N 16.39E
53 K4 **Fleninge** Sweden 56.07N 12.50E
53 D7 **Flensborg Fjord** *inlet* Denmark/W Germany
63 K3 **Flensburg** W Germany 54.47N 9.27E
63 L3 **Flensburger Förde** *B* W Ger/Den
61 F5 **Flénu** Belgium 50.26N 3.53E
72 G1 **Fléré-la-Rivière** France 47.01N 1.06E
61 N4 **Fléron** Belgium 50.37N 5.41E
69 D3 **Flers** France 50.03N 2.50E
70 J4 **Flers** France 48.45N 0.34W
110 N2 **Flesher** Montana 47.00N 112.32W
99 K8 **Flesherton** Ontario 44.16N 80.32W
95 E10 **Flesh Pt** S Africa 34.18S 21.55E
19 D3 **Flesko, Tanjung** *C* Celebes Indonesia 0.27N 124.31E
53 S18 **Flesland** Norway 60.17N 5.14E
66 R4 **Fless, Piz** *mt* Switzerland 46.48N 10.02E
105 E2 **Fletcher** N Carolina 35.26N 82.31W
109 M7 **Fletcher** Oklahoma 34.50N 98.15W
101 T4 **Fletcher L** N W Terr
10 B11 **Fletcher, Mt** Macquarie I Pacific Oc 54.44S 158.51E
106 L5 **Fletcher Pond** Michigan 45.00N 83.53W
66 J7 **Fletschhorn** *mt* Switzerland 46.11N 8.00E
72 F8 **Fleurance** France 43.51N 0.40E
98 Q3 **Fleur de Lys** Newfoundland 50.09N 56.08W
98 H2 **Fleur-de-May, L** Labrador, Nfld
66 D2 **Fleurey** France 47.18N 6.46E
72 L3 **Fleuriel** France 46.17N 3.11E
66 C4 **Fleurier** Switzerland 46.55N 6.36E
61 J5 **Fleurus** Belgium 50.28N 4.33E
72 L9 **Fleury** France 43.14N 3.08E
69 B8 **Fleury-les-Aubrais** France 47.56N 1.55E
69 J5 **Fleury-sur-Aire** France 49.01N 5.09E
70 N3 **Fleury-sur-Andelle** France 49.21N 1.21E
89 B3 **Fleuve** *reg* Senegal
25 H7 **Fleuve Bassac** *R* Cambodia
25 H1 **Fleuve Rouge** *R* Vietnam
84 G6 **Fléves** *isld* Greece 37.46N 23.45E
69 K5 **Fléville-Lixières** France 49.15N 5.49E
71 D2 **Flez Cuzy** France 47.22N 3.37E
64 H3 **Flieden** W Germany 50.25N 9.35E
41 O1 **Fligeli, Mys** *C* Franz Josef Land U.S.S.R. 81.45N 59.15E
57 F3 **Flimby** Cumbria Eng 54.41N 3.31W
66 O4 **Flims** Switzerland 46.51N 9.17E
56 M5 **Flimwell** E Sussex Eng 51.03N 0.27E
13 F4 **Flinders** *R* Queensland
14 B10 **Flinders B** W Australia
15 H8 **Flinders Ent** Gt Barrier Reef Australia
13 G2 **Flinders Group** *islds* Gt Barrier Reef Australia
12 C5 **Flinders I** S Australia 33.38S 134.50E
12 J7 **Flinders I** Tasmania
12 E4 **Flinders Ra** S Australia
13 J4 **Flinders Reefs** Gt Barrier Reef Australia
69 E3 **Flines les Râches** France 50.26N 3.11E
100 Q4 **Flin Flon** Manitoba 54.47N 101.51W
69 B6 **Flins** France 48.58N 1.52E
57 G6 **Flint** Clwyd Wales 53.15N 3.07W
106 L6 **Flint** Michigan 43.03N 83.40W
Flint *co see* **Clwyd** *co*
107 K7 **Flint** *R* Ala/Tenn
33 C10 **Flint I** Aden S Yemen 12.48N 44.59E
122 M9 **Flint I** Line Is Pacific Oc 11.25S 151.48W
99 E3 **Flint L** Ontario 49.54N 85.54W
100 L9 **Flintoft** Saskatchewan 49.29N 106.20W
13 J8 **Flinton** Queensland 27.55S 149.33E
105 C4 **Flint, R** Georgia
106 L6 **Flint, R** Michigan
9 A6 **Flipper Pt** Peale I Pacific Oc 19.18N 168.35E
107 D5 **Flippin** Arkansas 36.16N 92.38W
69 K6 **Flirey** France 48.52N 5.51E
65 B7 **Flirsch** Austria 47.09N 10.25E
52 G6 **Flisa** Norway 60.36N 12.02E
52 G6 **Flisa** *R* Norway
53 X19 **Flisegga** *mt* Norway 59.50N 7.50E
52 J9 **Fliseryd** Sweden 57.06N 16.15E
41 D2 **Flissingskiy, Mys** *C* Novaya Zemlya U.S.S.R. 76.43N 69.09E
56 N2 **Flitcham** Norfolk Eng 52.49N 0.34E
75 M5 **Flix** Spain 41.14N 0.32E
69 C3 **Flixecourt** France 50.00N 2.05E
75 M5 **Flix, Embalse de** *res* Spain 41.14N 0.31E
57 N4 **Flixton** N Yorks Eng 54.12N 0.24W
69 H4 **Flize** France 49.42N 4.47E
50 B2 **Fljótavik** *B* Iceland
50 K4 **Fljótsdalsheidhi** *heath* Iceland
50 F7 **Fljótshlídh** *reg* Iceland
53 T14 **Flø** Möre og Romsdal Norway 62.25N 5.53E
53 W15 **Flo** Sogn og Fjordane Norway 61.57N 7.03E
50 E5 **Flóávatn** *L* Iceland 64.57N 20.51W
61 F4 **Flobecq** Belgium 50.44N 3.45E
57 K5 **Flockton** W Yorks Eng 53.38N 1.38W
52 G9 **Floda** Sweden 57.47N 12.20E
58 A5 **Flodday** *isld* W Isles Scotland 56.54N 7.35W
58 M7 **Flodden Field** Northumb Eng 55.38N 2.10W
58 D3 **Flodigarry** Skye, Highland Scotland 57.40N 6.15W
69 F8 **Flogny** France 47.57N 3.52E
64 P2 **Flöha** E Germany 50.52N 13.04E
64 P2 **Flöha** *R* E Germany
50 E7 **Flói** *dist* Iceland
72 C6 **Floirac** France 44.49N 0.32W
84 C6 **Flóka** Greece 37.39N 21.37E
50 D5 **Flókadalur** *V* Iceland
107 J11 **Flomaton** Alabama 31.00N 87.20W
112 G1 **Flomot** Texas 34.14N 100.59W
61 M4 **Flône** Belgium 50.33N 5.20E
64 E4 **Flonheim** W Germany 49.48N 8.03E
123 J10 **Flood Ra** Antarctica
108 S3 **Floodwood** Minnesota 46.56N 92.58W
56 J3 **Floore** Northants Eng 52.14N 1.04W
107 H3 **Flora** Illinois 38.40N 88.30W
106 H9 **Flora** Indiana 40.33N 86.32W
107 F9 **Flora** Mississippi 32.32N 90.19W
110 H4 **Flora** Oregon 45.54N 117.18W
13 B2 **Flora** *R* N Terr Australia
71 D8 **Florac** France 44.20N 3.35E
107 K10 **Florala** Alabama 31.01N 86.20W
105 E9 **Floral City** Florida 28.44N 82.18W
14 B5 **Flora, Mt** W Australia 21.50S 117.02E
41 N2 **Flora, Mys** *C* Franz Josef Land U.S.S.R. 79.57N 50.01E
13 H3 **Flora Pass** Gt Barrier Reef Australia 16.47S 146.27E
13 E4 **Floraville** Queensland 18.09S 139.52E
120 D11 **Flor de Chile** Chile 25.19S 69.47W
120 C1 **Flor de Punga** Peru 5.27S 74.05W
14 A1 **Floreat Park** *dist* Perth, W Aust
61 L5 **Florée** Belgium 50.22N 5.04E
61 K5 **Floreffe** Belgium 50.26N 4.46E
107 J7 **Florence** Alabama 34.48N 87.40W
111 N8 **Florence** Arizona 33.02N 111.22W
109 E3 **Florence** Colorado 38.23N 105.07W
110 J4 **Florence** Idaho 45.31N 116.01W
Florence Italy*see* **Firenze**
109 O3 **Florence** Kansas 38.15N 96.56W
107 M3 **Florence** Kentucky 38.59N 84.40W
103 J2 **Florence** Massachusetts 42.20N 72.40W
107 F9 **Florence** Mississippi 32.09N 90.08W
110 L3 **Florence** Montana 46.39N 114.05W
103 E6 **Florence** New Jersey 40.07N 74.48W
110 A6 **Florence** Oregon 43.59N 124.05W
105 H3 **Florence** S Carolina 34.12N 79.44W
108 N4 **Florence** S Dakota 45.04N 97.20W
112 K5 **Florence** Texas 30.50N 97.49W
112 N9 **Florence** Texas 32.42N 97.01W
106 F4 **Florence** Wisconsin 45.55N 88.14W
111 N8 **Florence Junc** Arizona 33.19N 111.20W
111 F4 **Florence L** California 37.15N 118.57W
12 E3 **Florence,L** S Australia
98 E7 **Florenceville** New Brunswick 46.26N 67.36W
119 C7 **Florencia** Colombia 1.37N 75.37W
121 F2 **Florencia** Corrientes Argentina 28.03S 59.15W
120 G11 **Florencia** Taiwan 24.04S 62.13W
121 F4 **Florencio Sánchez** Uruguay 33.55S 57.20W
61 J6 **Florennes** Belgium 50.15N 4.36E
71 C10 **Florensac** France 43.23N 3.28E
121 C9 **Florentino Ameghino, Embalse** *res* Argentina
61 M8 **Florenville** Belgium 49.42N 5.19E
115 P9 **Flores** Guatemala 16.58N 89.50W
117 H8 **Flores** Pernambuco Brazil 7.50S 37.55W
117 F8 **Flores** Piauí Brazil 7.45S 42.56W
121 F4 **Flores** *dept* Uruguay
121 K4 **Flores** *dist* Buenos Aires Arg
96 O2 **Flores** *isld* Azores 39.30N 31.13W
19 B8 **Flores** *isld* Indonesia
121 F5 **Flores** *R* Argentina
120 E3 **Florescência** Brazil 9.36S 68.34W
46 G5 **Floreshty** Moldavia U.S.S.R. 47.52N 28.12E
101 K11 **Flores I** Vancouver I, Br Col 49.20N 126.10W
117 F7 **Flores, R** Brazil
17 J13 **Flores Sea** Indonesia
117 H9 **Floresta** Brazil 8.33S 38.38W
81 J8 **Floresta** Sicily 37.59N 14.55E
112 J6 **Floresville** Texas 29.09N 98.10W
112 E3 **Florey** Texas 32.31N 102.30W
84 Z20 **Floriana** Malta 35.54N 14.31E
117 F8 **Floriano** Brazil 6.45S 43.00W
120 E3 **Floriano Peixoto** Brazil 9.07S 67.24W
121 J1 **Florianopólis** Brazil 27.35S 48.31W
121 J3 **Florida** Argentina 34.32S 58.30W
120 F8 **Florida** Bolivia 18.30S 63.30W
121 A6 **Florida** Chile 36.55S 72.45W
116 E4 **Florida** Cuba 21.32N 78.14W
109 C9 **Florida** New Mexico 32.26N 107.34W
103 F4 **Florida** New York 41.20N 74.22W
104 A5 **Florida** Ohio 41.21N 84.13W
94 S13 **Florida** S Africa 26.11S 27.55E
121 G5 **Florida** Uruguay 34.04S 56.14W
121 G4 **Florida** *dept* Uruguay
102 J4 **Florida** *state* U.S.A.
105 F12 **Florida B** Florida
105 B11 **Florida, Cape** Florida 25.38N 80.07W
105 G12 **Florida City** Florida 25.27N 80.30W
15 L3 **Florida Is** Solomon Is
105 F13 **Florida Keys** *islds* Florida
102 K6 **Florida, Straits of** U.S.A.
81 K9 **Floridia** Sicily 37.06N 15.09E
65 O5 **Floridsdorf** Austria 48.16N 16.24E
107 C10 **Florien** Louisiana 31.27N 93.29W
61 K5 **Floriffoux** Belgium 50.27N 4.46E
103 A6 **Florin** Pennsylvania 40.07N 76.32W
Florina *see* **Karolta**
83 E4 **Flórina** Greece 40.48N 21.26E
81 B2 **Florinas** Sardinia 40.39N 8.40E
106 B9 **Floris** Iowa 40.52N 92.20W
95 K9 **Florisbad** S Africa 28.46S 26.05E
109 E3 **Florissant** Colorado 38.56N 105.19W
53 S15 **Florø** Norway 61.36N 5.04E
14 B6 **Florry, Mt** W Australia 23.04S 115.55E
64 G3 **Flörsbach** W Germany 50.07N 9.26E
37 F2 **Florya** Turkey 40.59N 28.48E
50 E5 **Flosaskardh** *pass* Iceland 64.43N 20.26W
64 N4 **Floss** W Germany 49.43N 12.17E
64 N4 **Flossenbürg** W Germany 49.42N 12.20E
61 L5 **Flostoy** Belgium 50.23N 5.11E
53 W19 **Flothyl** Norway 59.45N 7.29E
58 S12 **Flotta** *isld* Orkney Scotland 58.49N 3.07W
72 B3 **Flotte, la** France 46.11N 1.20W
100 J4 **Flotten L** Saskatchewan
52 K7 **Flottsund** Sweden 59.47N 17.40E
95 L6 **Floukraal** S Africa 30.58S 27.05E
72 J9 **Floure** France 43.11N 2.29E
111 M3 **Flowell** Utah 38.59N 112.27W
98 Q2 **Flower's Cove** Newfoundland 51.18N 56.41W
109 G7 **Floyd** New Mexico 34.13N 103.36W
104 E10 **Floyd** Virginia 36.55N 80.22W
108 O7 **Floyd** *R* Iowa
112 F2 **Floydada** Texas 33.58N 101.20W
103 M8 **Floyd Bennett Field** *airfield* New York 40.36N 73.54W
111 M6 **Floyd, Mt** Arizona 35.24N 112.44W
53 U20 **Fløyrli** Norway 59.01N 6.26E
52 E6 **Fluberg** Norway 60.45N 10.16E
66 R4 **Flucht Horn** *mt* Switz/Austria 46.54N 10.14E
66 Q4 **Flüela Pass** Switz 46.46N 9.57E
66 Q4 **Flüela-Tal** *V* Switzerland
66 L4 **Flüelen** Switzerland 46.54N 8.38E
66 K4 **Flüeli** Switzerland 46.53N 8.17E
70 O6 **Fluery les Aubrais** France 47.56N 1.56E
60 L8 **Fluessen, De** *L* Netherlands 52.55N 5.31E
50 F3 **Flugumýri** Iceland 65.35N 19.20W
66 F2 **Flüh** Switzerland 47.30N 7.30E
66 M3 **Fluh Berg** *mt* Switzerland 47.04N 8.53E
66 J4 **Flühli** Switzerland 46.53N 8.01E
19 E4 **Fluk** Moluccas Indon 1.39S 127.44E
107 F11 **Fluker** Louisiana 30.50N 90.30W
70 G5 **Flume** *R* France
75 K4 **Flumen** *R* Spain
81 C4 **Flumendosa** *R* Sardinia
81 C4 **Flumendosa, L.di** Sardinia
71 K5 **Flumet** France 45.49N 6.32E
81 C4 **Flumineddu** *R* Sardinia
81 D3 **Flumineddu** *R* Sardinia
81 A5 **Fluminimaggiore** Sardinia 39.27N 8.29E
66 O3 **Flums** Switzerland 47.06N 9.21E
64 E7 **Fluorn** W Germany 48.18N 8.29E
59 K3 **Flurry Bridge** Louth Irish Rep 54.06N 6.22W
106 L6 **Flushing** Michigan 43.04N 83.51W
Flushing Netherlands*see* **Vlissingen**
103 N7 **Flushing** New York 40.46N 73.49W
104 D6 **Flushing** Ohio 40.09N 81.06W
103 L7 **Flushing B** New York
112 F3 **Fluvanna** Texas 32.54N 101.09W
75 Q3 **Fluviá** *R* Spain
53 C4 **Fly** Denmark 56.29N 9.02E
15 F7 **Fly** *R* Irian Jaya/Papua New Guinea
56 G3 **Flyford Flavell** Hereford & Worcs Eng 52.12N 2.01W
123 H12 **Flying Fish, C** Antarctica 71.53S 100.50W
26 V3 **Flying Fish Cove** Christmas I Indian Oc
13 C2 **Flying Fox Cr** N Terr Australia
53 A4 **Flynder Kirke** Denmark 56.27N 8.19E
53 B4 **Flynder Sø** *L* Denmark 56.30N 8.56E
112 L4 **Flynn** Texas 31.10N 96.07W
10 B11 **Flynn L** Macquarie I Pacific Oc 54.39S 158.52E
13 C4 **Flynn Mem** N Terr Australia 19.21S 134.15E
50 H3 **Fnjóská** *R* Iceland
9 U12 **Foa** *isld* Tonga, Pacific Oc 19.45S 174.20W
100 O7 **Foam Lake** Saskatchewan 51.38N 103.31W
27 L10 **Foa Mulaku I** Maldives, Ind Oc 0.17S 72.26E
79 D3 **Fobello** Italy 45.53N 8.10E
36 B4 **Foça** Turkey 38.40N 26.45E
82 E7 **Foča** Yugoslavia 43.30N 18.48E
37 C2 **Foca Br** *C* Turkey 40.25N 26.24E
119 A10 **Foca, I** Peru 5.15S 81.17W
61 L6 **Focant** Belgium 50.08N 5.02E
58 K3 **Fochabers** Grampian Scotland 57.37N 3.07W
90 G2 **Fochi** Chad 18.59N 15.50E
90 J2 **Fochi** Chad 19.28N 19.42E
26 Q15 **Foch, I** Kerguelen Ind Oc
90 H2 **Fochimi** Chad 18.53N 16.03E
60 O8 **Fochteloo** Netherlands 52.59N 6.20E
95 L2 **Fochville** S Africa 26.30S 27.30E
78 E4 **Foci del Po** *river mths* Italy
82 L5 **Focşani** Romania 45.41N 27.12E
53 H6 **Fodby** Denmark 55.15N 11.41E
41 B3 **Fod'kino** Novaya Zemlya U.S.S.R. 74.10N 55.02E
72 J1 **Foëcy** France 47.11N 2.09E
13 D3 **Foelsche** *R* N Terr Australia
97 O5 **Færingehavn** Greenland 63.50N 51.20W
9 R12 **Fofoa** *islet* Tonga, Pacific Oc 18.42S 174.08W
23 F7 **Fogang** Guangdong China 23.57N 113.27E
13 B2 **Fog B** N Terr Australia
103 C5 **Fogelsville** Pennsylvania 40.35N 75.40W
88 P8 **Foggaret el Arab** Algeria 27.13N 2.49E
88 P8 **Foggaret ez Zoua** Algeria 27.23N 2.53E
80 N6 **Foggia** Italy 41.28N 15.33E
80 M5 **Foggia** *prov* Italy
79 N7 **Foglia** *R* Italy
80 G6 **Fogliano, Lago di** Italy
51 H11 **Föglö** Finland 60.02N 20.25E
53 T20 **Fogn** *isld* Norway 59.08N 5.56E
98 S4 **Fogo** Newfoundland 49.43N 54.18W
89 O11 **Fogo** *I* Cape Verde
98 T4 **Fogo, C** Newfoundland 49.39N 54.00W
92 J10 **Fogo, I** Mozambique 17.15S 38.51E
98 S4 **Fogo I** Newfoundland
96 U1 **Fogo, L do** Azores 37.31N 25.29W
43 J6 **Fogolevo** Kazakhstan U.S.S.R. 42.01N 69.30E
50 G6 **Fögrufjöll** *mt* Iceland 64.10N 18.15W
53 D4 **Fogstrup** Denmark 56.04N 9.32E
Fo-hia *see* **Menghai**
65 L7 **Fohnsdorf** Austria 47.13N 14.40E
63 H3 **Föhr** *isld* W Germany
69 M4 **Föhren** W Germany 49.52N 6.46E
76 B14 **Foia** *mt* Portugal 37.18N 8.37W
80 E2 **Foiano di Chiana** Italy 43.15N 11.49E
80 L6 **Foiano in Val Fortore** Italy 41.22N 14.59E
59 B8 **Foilclogh** Kerry Irish Rep 51.54N 10.10W
58 G2 **Foinaven** *mt* Highland Scotland 58.24N 4.51W
71 G4 **Foissiat** France 46.23N 5.10E
72 H10 **Foix** France 42.57N 1.35E
67 G10 **Foix** *prov* France
75 O5 **Foix** *R* Spain
82 D7 **Fojnica** Yugoslavia 44.00N 17.51E
Fo-kang *see* **Fogang**
46 R2 **Foki** U.S.S.R. 56.42N 54.20E
45 F3 **Fokina, imeni** U.S.S.R. 53.10N 34.25E
46 J4 **Fokino** U.S.S.R. 53.28N 34.22E
84 D4 **Fokís** *prov* Greece
90 B6 **Fokku** Nigeria 11.36N 4.32E
65 O8 **Fokovci** Yugoslavia 46.45N 16.18E
52 E4 **Fokstua** Norway 62.09N 9.18E
95 B5 **Folakara** Madagascar 18.19S 45.02E
93 C2 **Fola Rapids** Sudan 3.38N 32.00E
53 X17 **Folarskarnut** *mt* Norway 60.36N 7.47E
51 D4 **Folda** *inlet* Nordland Norway
52 F2 **Folda** *inlet* Nord-Tröndelag Norway
62 M9 **Földeák** Hungary 46.19N 20.30E
53 C6 **Folding** Denmark 55.28N 9.02E
53 B6 **Foldingbro** Denmark 55.27N 9.00E
53 B6 **Fole** Denmark 55.19N 8.59E
83 G8 **Folégandros** *isld* Greece
67 Q12 **Folelli-Orezza** Corsica 42.26N 9.30E
107 J11 **Foley** Alabama 30.24N 87.41W
94 J3 **Foley** Botswana 21.34S 27.21E
105 D7 **Foley** Florida 30.04N 83.33W
108 R4 **Foley** Minnesota 45.49N 93.52W
99 H4 **Foleyet** Ontario 48.15N 82.26W
97 M4 **Foley I** N W Terr 68.30N 75.00W
91 D11 **Folgares** Angola 14.56S 15.04E
79 K3 **Folgaria** Italy 45.55N 11.11E
76 C10 **Folgas** Portugal 39.14N 8.15W
53 U18 **Folgefonn** *glacier* Norway
66 F1 **Folgensbourg** France 47.33N 7.27E
113 J5 **Folger** Alaska 63.30N 156.12W
70 B4 **Folgoët, le** France 48.33N 4.21W
76 D6 **Folgosa** Portugal 41.08N 7.41W
76 G3 **Folgoso de la Ribera** Spain 42.38N 6.19W
80 G3 **Foligno** Italy 42.57N 12.43E
53 U14 **Folkestad** Norway 62.07N 6.02E
56 O5 **Folkestone** Kent Eng 51.05N 1.11E
57 N7 **Folkingham** Lincs Eng 52.54N 0.24W
105 E7 **Folkston** Georgia 30.49N 82.02W
105 K3 **Folkstone** N Carolina 34.33N 77.30W
52 E4 **Folla** *R* Norway
52 F3 **Follafoss** Norway 63.59N 11.05E
52 E4 **Folldal** Norway 62.07N 10.03E
53 E4 **Følle** Denmark 56.18N 10.26E
53 G5 **Føllenslev** Denmark 55.44N 11.22E
53 S19 **Follerøyhamn** Norway 59.48N 5.18E
112 D7 **Follett** Texas 36.27N 100.08W
70 H4 **Folligny** France 48.49N 1.25W
79 M3 **Follina** Italy 45.58N 12.07E
52 H3 **Föllinge** Sweden 63.40N 14.40E
52 F7 **Follo** *reg* Norway
80 C3 **Follonica** Italy 42.56N 10.45E
80 C3 **Follónica, G.di** Italy
105 H5 **Folly Beach** S Carolina 32.38N 79.57W
110 G6 **Follyfarm** Oregon 43.03N 118.12W
61 O7 **Folschette** Luxembourg 49.49N 5.53E
111 C3 **Folsom** California 38.40N 121.10E
107 F11 **Folsom** Louisiana 30.39N 90.11W
109 G5 **Folsom** New Mexico 36.51N 103.56W
111 C3 **Folsom L** California
82 L5 **Folteşti** Romania 45.45N 28.00E
53 X20 **Folurvatn** *L* Norway 59.23N 7.40E
79 G4 **Fombio** Italy 45.08N 9.41E
95 A2 **Fomboni** Comoros, Indian Oc 12.18S 43.46E
116 E3 **Fomento** Cuba 22.04N 79.44W
41 J5 **Fomich** *R* U.S.S.R.
46 N6 **Fomin** U.S.S.R. 46.58N 43.31E
45 O1 **Fominki** U.S.S.R. 55.57N 42.22E
47 F3 **Fominskaya** U.S.S.R. 65.00N 48.45E
47 E6 **Fominskoye** U.S.S.R. 59.45N 42.03E
84 Y20 **Fomm ir-Rih B** Malta 35.54N 14.21E
71 J3 **Foncine-le-Bas** France 46.38N 6.02E
108 Q7 **Fonda** Iowa 42.36N 94.50W
108 K1 **Fonda** N Dakota 48.42N 100.01W
104 L4 **Fonda** New York 42.57N 74.24W
101 U6 **Fond-du-Lac** Saskatchewan 59.20N 107.09W
106 F6 **Fond du Lac** Wisconsin 43.48N 88.27W
101 V6 **Fond-du-Lac R** Saskatchewan
26 U11 **Fond du Sac** Mauritius, Indian Oc 20.02S 57.35E
105 D1 **Fonde** Kentucky 36.36N 83.53W
70 M7 **Fondettes** France 47.25N 0.37E
80 H6 **Fondi** Italy 41.22N 13.27E
80 H6 **Fondi, Lago di** Italy
79 K2 **Fondo** Italy 46.27N 11.08E
77 L7 **Fondón** Spain 36.59N 2.51W
116 L3 **Fond-St-Denis** Martinique W I 14.44N 61.08W
77 K6 **Fonelas** Spain 37.25N 3.10W
89 C6 **Fonfe** Guinea 10.34N 12.57W
76 E2 **Fonfría** Lugo Spain 43.09N 7.02W
76 G5 **Fonfría** Zamora Spain 41.37N 6.09W
91 B3 **Fong** *tribe* Cameroon/Gabon
52 F3 **Fongen** *mt* Norway 63.12N 11.36E
89 C5 **Fongolambi** Senegal 12.28N 12.00W
53 V15 **Fonn** Norway 61.36N 6.45E
50 L4 **Fönn** *mt* Iceland 65.09N 14.05W
53 S17 **Fonnebostsjøen** Norway 60.46N 5.10E
53 R17 **Fonnes** Norway 60.48N 4.59E
81 C3 **Fonni** Sardinia 40.08N 9.16E
53 S19 **Fonno** *isld* Norway 59.57N 5.17E
9 T12 **Fonoifua** *atoll* Tonga, Pacific Oc 20.16S 174.39W
72 E6 **Fonroque** France 44.43N 0.26E
76 E2 **Fonsagrada** Spain 43.08N 7.04W
119 D2 **Fonseca** Colombia 10.53N 72.51W
115 Q11 **Fonseca,G.de** El Salvador/Hond
53 D6 **Fønsskov** *pen* Denmark 55.27N 9.45E
66 B2 **Fontaine** France 47.25N 6.29E
71 L1 **Fontaine** Haut-Rhin France 47.40N 7.01E
71 H6 **Fontaine** Isère France 45.12N 5.42E
70 N6 **Fontaine** Loir-et-Cher France 47.53N 1.11E
69 D7 **Fontainebleau** France 48.24N 2.42E
94 S13 **Fontainebleau** S Africa 26.06S 27.57E
69 D7 **Fontainebleau, Forêt de** France
72 D4 **Fontaine Chalendray** France 45.57N 0.11W
71 G9 **Fontaine-de-Vaucluse** France 43.55N 5.08E
71 G1 **Fontaine Française** France 47.32N 5.22E
101 U6 **Fontaine L** Saskatchewan
26 T15 **Fontaine, La** Réunion Ind Oc 21.09S 55.20E
70 M3 **Fontaine-l'Abbé** France 49.05N 0.41E
70 N2 **Fontaine-le-Bourg** France 49.33N 1.10E
70 M2 **Fontaine-le-Dun** France 49.48N 0.51E
69 L8 **Fontaine-lès-Luxeuil** France 47.51N 6.20E
61 H5 **Fontaine-l'Evêque** Belgium 50.25N 4.19E
70 K6 **Fontaine-Milon** France 47.30N 0.15W
79 C3 **Fontainemore** Italy 45.38N 7.52E
71 F3 **Fontaines** Saône-et-Loire France 46.50N 4.46E
71 C1 **Fontaines** Yonne France 47.42N 3.15E
70 L6 **Fontaine-St. Martin,la** France 47.47N 0.03E
71 F5 **Fontaines-sur-Saône** France 45.50N 4.52E
61 G5 **Fontaine-Valmont** Belgium 50.19N 4.13E
71 M8 **Fontan** France 44.00N 7.33E
103 B6 **Fontana** Pennsylvania 40.17N 76.30W
66 L5 **Fontana** Switzerland 46.31N 8.33E
121 B10 **Fontana, L** Argentina
105 D2 **Fontana L** N Carolina
80 J5 **Fontana Liri** Italy 41.37N 13.35E
75 D6 **Fontanar** Spain 40.43N 3.10W
76 K10 **Fontanarejo** Spain 39.13N 4.30W
81 K9 **Fontana Rossa** *airport* Sicily 37.28N 15.05E
76 B15 **Fontanelas** Portugal 38.51N 9.26W
79 L6 **Fontanelice** Italy 44.16N 11.34E
79 H5 **Fontanellato** Italy 44.55N 10.10E
79 M3 **Fontanelle** Italy 45.51N 12.27E
71 E9 **Fontanes** France 43.50N 4.05E
79 D4 **Fontanetto Po** Italy 45.12N 8.12E
72 J3 **Fontanières** France 46.08N 2.29E
79 L3 **Fontaniva** Italy 45.38N 11.46E
47 N3 **Fontanka** *canal* Leningrad U.S.S.R.
77 G3 **Fontanosas** Spain 38.46N 4.32W
76 E2 **Fontao** Spain 43.05N 7.15W
101 N6 **Fontas** Br Col 58.17N 121.43W
101 N6 **Fontas** *R* Br Col
71 J6 **Fontcouvert** France 45.15N 6.18E
80 D2 **Fontebecci** Italy 43.21N 11.18E
80 D3 **Fonte Blanda** Italy 42.34N 11.10E
119 G9 **Fonte Boa** Brazil 2.33S 65.59W
76 B13 **Fonte Boa** Portugal 37.37N 8.36W
79 L3 **Fonte, Cima di** *mt* Italy 45.48N 11.30E
118 B4 **Fonte do Pau-d'Agua** Brazil 14.32S 58.33W
75 G3 **Fontellas** Spain 42.02N 1.35W
91 A1 **Fontem** Cameroon 5.32N 9.47E
68 E4 **Fontenay-aux-Roses** France 48.47N 2.18E
72 C3 **Fontenay-le-Comte** France 46.28N 0.48W
69 B5 **Fontenay-St.Père** France 49.02N 1.45E
68 G3 **Fontenay-sous-Bois** France 48.51N 2.28E
69 D6 **Fontenay-Trésigny** France 48.42N 2.53E
98 L2 **Fonteneau, L** Quebec
61 H5 **Fontenelle** Belgium 50.15N 4.23E
98 H5 **Fontenelle** Quebec 48.54N 64.33W
110 P7 **Fontenelle Fork** *R* Wyoming
110 P7 **Fontenelle Reservoir** Wyoming
61 L8 **Fontenoille** Belgium 49.43N 5.14E
66 A2 **Fontenois** France 47.29N 6.14E
71 C1 **Fontenoy** France 47.39N 3.17E
69 L8 **Fontenoy-le-Château** France 47.58N 6.13E
69 K6 **Fontenoy-sur-Moselle** France 48.43N 5.59E
72 E1 **Fontevrault l'Abbaye** France 47.11N 0.03E
119 D5 **Fontibón** Colombia 4.40N 74.06W
75 C4 **Fontioso** Spain 41.56N 3.44W
76 K7 **Fontiveros** Spain 40.55N 4.58W
56 G6 **Fontmell Magna** Dorset Eng 50.57N 2.11W
69 L5 **Fontoy** France 49.22N 6.00E
72 J10 **Font Romeu-Odeillo-Via** France 42.30N 2.03E
71 K7 **Font Sancte** *mt* France 44.36N 6.48E
59 J5 **Fontstown** Kildare Irish Rep 53.03N 6.53W
50 L2 **Fontur** *C* Iceland 66.23N 14.30W
71 F9 **Fontvieille** France 43.43N 4.42E
9 S13 **Fonuafo'ou** *isld* Tonga, Pacific Oc 20.19S 175.25W
9 R12 **Fonuafu'u** *islet* Tonga, Pacific Oc 18.47S 173.58W
9 U9 **Fonualei** *I* Tonga, Pacific Oc 18.01S 174.20W
9 R12 **Fonua'one'one** *islet* Tonga, Pacific Oc 18.47S 174.05W

62 K9 Fonyód Hungary 46.45N 17.33E
75 L3 Fonz Spain 42.01N 0.16E
79 L2 Fonzaso Italy 46.02N 11.48E
Foochow see Fuzhou
111 M2 Fool Creek Res Utah 39.27N 112.21W
66 N4 Foostock mt Switzerland 46.58N 9.15E
101 P9 Foothills Alberta 53.04N 116.47W
55 J4 Foots Cray London Eng 51.25N 0.08E
12 C7 Footscray dist Melbourne, Victoria
106 E7 Footville Wisconsin 42.40N 89.14W
61 M4 Fooz Belgium 50.41N 5.26E
23 E2 Foping Shaanxi China 33.31N 107.59E
79 D2 Foppiano Italy 46.20N 8.24E
52 K9 Föra Sweden 57.00N 16.55E
80 K4 Fora R Italy
109 O5 Foraker Oklahoma 36.54N 96.34W
113 M5 Foraker, Mt Alaska 62.59N 151.29W
58 Q10 Fora Ness prom Shetland Scotland 59.57N 1.22W
80 G4 Forano Italy 42.18N 12.36E
66 Q6 Fora, Piz mt Italy/Switz 46.22N 9.47E
32 F3 Forat Iran 35.55N 54.20E
77 P2 Forata, Embalse de res Spain 39.20N 0.52W
69 M5 Forbach France 49.11N 6.54E
64 E6 Forbach W Germany 48.40N 8.21E
108 S2 Forbes Minnesota 47.21N 92.38W
108 M4 Forbes N Dakota 45.57N 98.48W
12 J5 Forbes New S Wales 33.24S 148.03E
30 L6 Forbesganj Bihar India 26.18N 87.16E
59 G4 Forbes L Longford Irish Rep 53.47N 7.53W
101 P10 Forbes, Mt Alberta 51.53N 116.59W
95 P2 Forbes Reef Swaziland 26.10S 31.05E
90 B9 Forcados Nigeria 5.21N 5.25E
90 B9 Forcados R Nigeria
75 K6 Forcall Spain 40.39N 0.12W
71 J10 Forcalqueiret France 43.20N 6.05E
71 H9 Forcalquier France 43.56N 5.46E
76 C3 Forcarey Spain 42.35N 8.21W
72 E6 Force, la France 44.52N 0.23E
64 L4 Forchheim W Germany 49.43N 11.05E
61 H5 Forchies-la-Marche Belgium 50.27N 4.19E
64 H5 Forchtenberg W Germany 49.17N 9.35E
66 E7 Forclaz, Col de la pass Switz 46.03N 7.01E
56 C6 Ford Devon Eng 51.00N 4.16W
109 L4 Ford Kansas 37.38N 99.46W
107 M4 Ford Kentucky 37.52N 84.13W
58 M7 Ford Northumb Eng 55.38N 2.05W
58 F6 Ford Strathclyde Scotland 56.10N 5.26W
59 K6 Ford Wexford Irish Rep 52.31N 6.17W
15 A7 Fordate isld Moluccas Indon 7.03S 131.58E
13 A2 Ford, C N Terr Australia 13.26S 129.55E
111 E6 Ford City California 35.09N 119.28W
104 F6 Ford City Pennsylvania 40.44N 79.34W
53 S19 Førde Hordaland Norway 59.37N 5.30E
53 T16 Førde Sogn og Fjordane Norway 61.02N 5.49E
53 T16 Førde Sogn og Fjordane Norway 61.27N 5.51E
53 U15 Førde Sogn og Fjordane Norway 61.37N 6.28E
53 T16 Førdefjord inlet Norway 61.28N 5.35E
11 K6 Fordell New Zealand 39.57S 175.12E
63 P9 Förderstedt E Germany 51.54N 11.38E
53 S20 Førdesfjord Norway 59.25N 5.23E
53 S20 Førdesfjord inlet Norway 59.21N 5.22E
88 S9 Ford Gardel Algeria 24.51N 8.26E
56 M3 Fordham Cambs Eng 52.19N 0.24E
56 M2 Fordham Norfolk Eng 52.34N 0.23E
114 E8 Ford I Hawaiian Is 21.22N 157.58W
100 C8 Fording Alberta 50.12N 114.47W
56 H6 Fordingbridge Hants Eng 50.56N 1.47W
111 J8 Ford L California 33.40N 115.00W
107 D4 Fordland Missouri 37.08N 92.58W
62 L2 Fordon Poland 53.09N 18.08E
81 B4 Fordongianus Sardinia 39.59N 8.48E
106 G3 Ford, R Michigan
123 J9 Ford Ranges Antarctica
12 H3 Ford's Bridge New S Wales 29.46S 145.25E
59 J4 Fordstown Meath Irish Rep 53.40N 6.54W
107 K4 Fordsville Kentucky 37.38N 86.41W
112 K6 Fordtran Texas 29.04N 97.01W
108 N1 Fordville N Dakota 48.16N 97.48W
107 D8 Fordyce Arkansas 33.49N 92.23W
108 N7 Fordyce Nebraska 42.42N 97.22W
51 D5 Fore Norway 66.55N 13.40E
89 C7 Forecariah Guinea 9.28N 13.06W
56 J6 Foreland headland I of Wight Eng 50.41N 1.04W
56 D5 Foreland Pt Devon Eng 51.16N 3.47W
48 V12 Forel, Mt Greenland 67.00N 37.00W
107 B8 Foreman Arkansas 33.43N 94.24W
100 F9 Foremost Alberta 49.30N 111.34W
80 N7 Forenza Italy 40.52N 15.52E
61 E4 Forest Belgium 50.40N 3.33E
110 J3 Forest Idaho 46.08N 116.40W
107 G9 Forest Mississippi 32.22N 89.30W
104 B6 Forest Ohio 40.47N 83.31W
99 H9 Forest Ontario 43.05N 82.00W
61 R10 Forest dist Bruxelles Belgium
13 F4 Forest R Queensland
70 C6 Forést, B.de la France
100 E6 Forestburg Alberta 52.35N 112.01W
103 E3 Forestburg New York 41.35N 74.45W
112 K2 Forestburg Texas 33.33N 97.34W
108 R6 Forest City Iowa 43.16N 93.39W
105 F2 Forest City N Carolina 35.18N 81.53W
103 D3 Forest City Pennsylvania 41.39N 75.29W
104 M3 Forest Dale Vermont 43.51N 73.04W
14 B3 Forestdale dist Perth, W Aust
107 C7 Forester Arkansas 34.48N 93.50W
106 M6 Forester Michigan 43.30N 82.34W
110 B9 Forest Glen California 40.25N 123.22W
110 Q3 Forest Grove Montana 47.00N 109.05W
110 B4 Forest Grove Oregon 45.32N 123.07W
111 D2 Foresthill California 39.02N 120.49W
55 G4 Forest Hill London Eng 51.26N 0.03W
107 D10 Forest Hill Louisiana 31.02N 92.32W
103 B7 Forest Hill Maryland 39.35N 76.24W
112 M9 Forest Hill Texas 32.39N 97.16W
12 E7 Forest Hill dist Melbourne, Vic
13 G4 Forest Home Queensland 18.14S 143.00E
12 J8 Forestier, C Tasmania 42.10S 148.20E
12 J9 Forestier Pen Tasmania
103 E3 Forestine New York 41.38N 74.52W
108 S4 Forest Lake Minnesota 45.16N 92.59W
103 C3 Forest Lake Pennsylvania 41.53N 75.57W
100 D7 Forest Lawn Alberta 51.05N 114.00W
108 R4 Foreston Minnesota 45.44N 93.42W
104 D1 Forest Park dist Baltimore, Md
104 K3 Forestport New York 43.27N 75.13W
108 N1 Forest River N Dakota 48.16N 97.29W
56 M5 Forest Row E Sussex Eng 51.06N 0.02E
111 B3 Forestville California 38.29N 122.55W
103 J3 Forestville Connecticut 41.41N 72.54W
106 M6 Forestville Michigan 43.40N 82.37W
104 F4 Forestville New York 42.29N 79.11W
98 C5 Forestville Quebec 48.45N 69.04W
106 G5 Forestville Wisconsin 44.42N 87.29W
12 M6 Forestville dist Sydney, N S W
98 C5 Forestville, Parc de Quebec
53 S20 Føresvik Norway 59.14N 5.26E
61 N4 Forêt Belgium 50.35N 5.42E
61 N7 Forêt d'Anlier Belgium
61 M8 Forêt de Chiny Belgium
61 M6 Forêt de Freyr forest Belgium
61 P4 Forêt d' Eupen forest Belgium
69 G7 Forêt d'Orient, Lac de la res France
70 C6 Forêt, la France 47.55N 3.59W
69 C7 Forêt-Ste Croix, la France 48.22N 2.15E
71 D5 Forez plain France
71 D5 Forez, Mts.du France
58 L5 Forfar Tayside Scotland 56.38N 2.54W
109 K5 Forgan Oklahoma 36.55N 100.34W
100 K7 Forgan Saskatchewan 51.16N 107.50W
79 N2 Forgária nel Friuli Italy 46.14N 12.58E
69 M7 Forge, la France 48.04N 6.43E
64 K8 For9gen-See L W Germany
61 G7 Forge-Philippe Belgium 49.58N 4.15E
61 H6 Forges Belgium 50.02N 4.20E
72 H5 Forgès Corrèze France 45.09N 1.52E
70 E5 Forges, les France 48.01N 2.37W
70 O2 Forges-les-Eaux France 49.37N 1.32E
99 O4 Forget Quebec 48.20N 76.58W
100 P9 Forget Saskatchewan 49.40N 102.56W
65 C6 Forggensee L W Germany
98 H5 Forillon, Parc Nat Quebec
80 J7 Forio Italy 40.44N 13.51E
76 B5 Forjães Portugal 41.36N 8.45W
103 B8 Fork Maryland 39.28N 76.26W
107 G6 Forked Deer R Tennessee
103 F7 Forked River New Jersey 39.51N 74.12W
100 S7 Fork River Manitoba 51.30N 100.00W
110 A2 Forks Washington 47.58N 124.24W
11 E10 Forks, The New Zealand 43.15S 170.14E
103 B3 Forkston Pennsylvania 41.33N 76.07W
103 A4 Forksville Pennsylvania 41.30N 76.36W
104 G9 Fork Union Virginia 37.47N 78.16W
50 S14 Forlandsundet sound Spitsbergen
79 M6 Forlì Italy 44.13N 12.02E
79 M6 Forli prov Italy
80 K5 Forli del Sannio Italy 41.42N 14.11E
79 M6 Forlimpopoli Italy 44.12N 12.07E
81 H9 Formaggio, Mte Sicily 37.17N 14.16E
108 N3 Forman N Dakota 46.08N 97.38W
79 D2 Formazza Italy 46.23N 8.26E
66 K6 Formazza, Valle Italy
57 G5 Formby Merseyside Eng 53.34N 3.05W
12 D6 Formby B S Australia
57 G5 Formby Pt Merseyside Eng 53.34N 3.07W
80 F4 Formello Italy 42.05N 12.24E
74 H6 Formentera isld Balearic Is Spain
77 W14 Formentor, C.de Balearic Is 39.58N 3.13E
69 B4 Formerie France 49.39N 1.45E
80 J6 Formia Italy 41.16N 13.37E
80 D4 Formica di Burano Italy 42.20N 11.20E
75 J7 Formiche Alto Spain 40.20N 0.54W
75 J7 Formiche Bajo Spain 40.18N 0.54W
80 C3 Formiche di Grosseto isld Italy 42.35N 10.54E
81 K10 Formiche, Pta.delle Sicily 36.40N 15.04E
118 F7 Formiga Brazil 20.30S 45.27W
76 C9 Formigais Portugal 39.43N 8.27W
116 G5 Formigas Bank Caribbean Sea
88 D2 Formigas, Ilheus das isld Azores 37.14N 24.45W
79 J5 Formigine Italy 44.34N 10.50E
79 L5 Formignana Italy 44.51N 11.53E
70 J3 Formigny France 49.20N 0.54W
72 J10 Formiguères France 42.37N 2.06E
52 G2 Formofoss Norway 64.24N 12.24E
Formosa see Taiwan
118 B10 Formosa Argentina 26.07S 58.14W
118 F4 Formosa Brazil 15.30S 47.22W
118 B9 Formosa terr Argentina
93 M8 Formosa B Kenya
118 F2 Formosa do Rio Prêto Brazil 11.03S 45.14W
95 G9 Formosa Pk S Africa 33.52S 23.41E
118 C3 Formosa, Sa mts Brazil
Formosa Str see T'aiwan Haixia
118 E2 Formoso Brazil 11.48S 49.24W
118 F4 Formoso Brazil 14.58S 46.14W
109 M2 Formoso Kansas 39.47N 98.00W
118 G3 Formoso, R Bahia Brazil
118 E2 Formoso, R Goiás Brazil
89 B6 Formoza,I Guinea-Bissau 11.30N 16.00W
53 F4 Fornæs C Denmark 56.27N 10.58E
77 V14 Fornalutx Balearic Is 39.47N 2.44E
50 H3 Fornastadhafjall mt Iceland 65.47N 17.45W
81 A2 Fornelli Sardinia 41.00N 8.14E
77 Y13 Fornells Balearic Is 40.04N 4.07E
76 C4 Fornelos de Montes Spain 42.20N 8.26W
112 L3 Forney Texas 32.44N 96.28W
56 N3 Fornham St. Martin Suffolk Eng 52.16N 0.43E
79 N1 Forni Avoltri Italy 46.35N 12.47E
79 N2 Forni di Sopra Italy 46.26N 12.34E
79 N2 Forni di Sotto Italy 46.23N 12.39E
50 D5 Fornihvammur Iceland 64.55N 21.10W
79 L2 Forno Italy 46.21N 11.38E
79 B4 Forno Alpi Graie Italy 45.22N 7.13E
79 L2 Forno Canale Italy 46.21N 11.58E
79 M2 Forno di Zoldo Italy 46.21N 12.10E
66 K7 Forno, Pizzo mt Italy 46.15N 8.24E
76 D7 Fornos de Algodres Portugal 40.38N 7.32W
79 H5 Fornovo di Taro Italy 44.42N 10.07E
87 J4 Foroddu Ethiopia 12.57N 42.08E
75 E2 Foronda Spain 42.54N 2.44W
Føroyar see Færøerne
53 V20 Førre Norway 59.19N 6.35E
58 J3 Forres Grampian Scotland 57.37N 3.38W
53 V20 Förresheiene moor Norway 59.24N 6.45E
106 F9 Forrest Illinois 40.45N 88.25W
100 S9 Forrest Manitoba 49.58N 99.56W
12 G7 Forrest Victoria 38.33S 143.47E
14 G9 Forrest W Australia 30.49S 128.03E
12 A6 Forrest dist Canberra Australia
123 E10 Forrestal Ra Antarctica
107 F6 Forrest City Arkansas 35.01N 90.48W
113 V9 Forrester I Alaska 54.50N 133.35W
14 C2 Forrestfield dist Perth, W Aust
101 T7 Forrest L Saskatchewan
14 G8 Forrest Lakes W Australia
14 G6 Forrest, Mt W Australia 24.45S 127.46E
106 E7 Forreston Illinois 42.07N 89.36W
14 G3 Forrest, R W Australia
14 G3 Forrest River Mission W Aust 15.30S 127.47E
53 W19 Førrevatn L Norway 59.33N 7.11E
61 M6 Forrières Belgium 50.08N 5.17E
72 D3 Fors France 46.14N 0.24W
52 J6 Fors Kopparberg Sweden 60.14N 16.20E
52 K3 Fors Sweden 63.01N 16.40E
51 F3 Forsa Norway 68.17N 16.40E
52 K5 Forsa Sweden 61.45N 17.00E
50 F4 Forsæludalskvislar reg Iceland
112 F3 Forsan Texas 32.07N 101.23W
13 G4 Forsayth Queensland 18.31S 143.32E
52 K6 Forsbacka Sweden 60.37N 16.55E
52 H7 Forshaga Sweden 59.33N 13.29E
52 G8 Forshem Sweden 58.38N 13.30E
58 J2 Forsinard Highland Scotland 58.20N 3.54W
52 G10 Förslöv Sweden 56.20N 12.50E
52 L6 Forsmark Sweden 60.22N 18.10E
52 K3 Forsmo Sweden 63.15N 17.15E
51 G5 Forsnäs Sweden 66.16N 18.35E
52 D3 Forsnes Norway 63.26N 8.25E
51 K11 Forssa Finland 60.49N 23.40E
58 J1 Forss, Bridge of Highland Scotland 58.35N 3.40W
58 J1 Forss Water R Highland Scotland
62 H4 Forst E Germany 51.46N 14.39E
69 N2 Forst W Germany 50.58N 7.28E
12 K4 Forster New S Wales 32.11S 152.30E
123 A13 Forsters Passage S Sandwich Is Atlantic Oc
105 D4 Forsyth Georgia 33.02N 83.58W
107 H2 Forsyth Illinois 39.55N 88.56W
108 D3 Forsyth Montana 46.15N 106.40W
99 O4 Forsythe Quebec 48.14N 76.28W
11 J7 Forsyth I New Zealand 40.56S 174.05E
13 E3 Forsyth Is Queensland 16.46S 139.05E
13 G6 Forsyth Ra Queensland
28 B8 Fort dist Bombay India
31 G6 Fort Abbas Pakistan 29.12N 73.00E
107 E10 Fort Adams Mississippi 31.04N 91.32W
97 L7 Fort Albany Ontario 52.15N 81.35W
117 H6 Fortaleza Ceará Brazil 3.45S 38.35W
120 E5 Fortaleza Pando Bolivia 12.07S 66.51W
120 F3 Fortaleza Pando Bolivia 9.48S 65.31W
120 B4 Fortaleza R Peru
120 E2 Fortaleza de Ituxi Brazil 7.30S 66.20W
118 K9 Fortaleza de São João Brazil 22.57S 43.09W
121 H4 Fortaleza Santa Teresa Uruguay 33.57S 53.30W
115 G10 Fort Amador Panama Canal Zone 8.56N 79.32W
75 J6 Fortanete Spain 40.30N 0.33W
98 G9 Fort Anne Nat. Hist. Park Nova Scotia 44.44N 65.29W
104 G7 Fort Ashby W Virginia 39.29N 78.46W
100 C4 Fort Assiniboine Alberta 54.21N 114.46W
106 F7 Fort Atkinson Wisconsin 42.57N 88.50W
58 G4 Fort Augustus Highland Scotland 57.09N 4.41W
95 K8 Fort Beaufort S Africa 32.47S 26.38E
98 H8 Fort Beauséjour Nat. Hist. Park New Brunswick
110 R1 Fort Belknap Agency Montana 48.29N 108.47W
105 C5 Fort Benning Georgia 32.20N 84.58W
110 P2 Fort Benton Montana 47.49N 110.40W
104 J7 Fort Berlin Pennsylvania 39.56N 76.59W
110 E8 Fort Bidwell California 41.51N 120.10W
100 K3 Fort Black Saskatchewan 55.25N 107.47W
111 A2 Fort Bragg California 39.29N 123.46W
105 J2 Fort Bragg N Carolina 35.09N 78.59W
107 J3 Fort Branch Indiana 38.15N 87.33W
110 P8 Fort Bridger Wyoming 41.19N 110.23W
95 K9 Fort Brown S Africa 33.08S 26.38E
Fort Brussaux see Markounda
108 O8 Fort Calhoun Nebraska 41.26N 96.01W
104 F2 Fort Carroll Maryland 39.13N 76.31W
84 X19 Fort Chambray Gozo Mediterranean Sea 36.01N 14.18E
Fort Charlet see Djanet
97 N6 Fort Chimo Quebec 58.10N 68.15W
101 S6 Fort Chipewyan Alberta 56.45N 111.05W
108 J2 Fort Clark N Dakota 47.16N 101.18W
115 F10 Fort Clayton Panama Canal Zone 9.00N 79.35W
109 M6 Fort Cobb Oklahoma 35.08N 98.28W
109 M6 Fort Cobb Res Oklahoma 35.10N 98.30W
109 E1 Fort Collins Colorado 40.35N 105.05W
13 F5 Fort Constantine Queensland 20.30S 140.32E
99 O7 Fort Coulonge Quebec 45.50N 76.45W
104 L2 Fort Covington New York 44.59N 74.32W
Fort Dauphin see Taolañar
107 L9 Fort Davis Alabama 32.15N 85.43W
115 E9 Fort Davis Panama Canal Zone 9.16N 79.55W
112 D5 Fort Davis Texas 30.35N 103.54W
72 K11 Fort-de-Bellegarde France 42.28N 2.51E
111 P6 Fort Defiance Arizona 35.45N 109.06W
116 L4 Fort de France Martinique W I 14.36N 61.05W
116 L4 Fort-de-France, Baie de Martinique W I
Fort de Polignac see Illizi
107 K10 Fort Deposit Alabama 32.00N 86.36W
122 C12 Fort de Taravao Tahiti Pacific Oc 17.42S 149.18W
110 A8 Fort Dick California 41.54N 124.10W
103 E6 Fort Dix New Jersey 40.01N 74.38W
108 Q7 Fort Dodge Iowa 42.31N 94.10W
107 J5 Fort Donelson Nat. Mil. Park Tennessee
105 G10 Fort Drum Florida 27.31N 80.49W
98 Q2 Forteau Labrador, Nfld 51.28N 56.59W
91 G9 Forte Cameia Angola 11.40S 20.53E
118 B6 Forte Coimbra Brazil 19.55S 57.48W
79 H7 Forte d Marmi Italy 43.58N 10.10E
94 K4 Fort Edward S Africa 23.15S 29.52E
81 A2 Forte, Mte Sardinia 40.43N 8.16E
91 G7 Forte Nordeste Angola 7.21S 21.49E
99 M10 Fort Erie Ontario 42.55N 78.56W
Forte Roçadas see Roçadas
103 D8 Fortescue New Jersey 39.14N 75.10W
14 B5 Fortescue R W Australia
14 C5 Fortescue, R W Australia
104 J9 Fort Eustis Virginia 37.10N 76.36W
117 C7 Forte Veneza Brazil 5.05S 52.57W
79 L1 Fortezza Italy 46.48N 11.37E
80 B4 Fortezza, Monte della Italy 42.20N 10.18E
80 B4 Fortezza, Pta.della Italy 42.22N 10.19E
104 R7 Fort Fairfield Maine 46.45N 67.50W
105 K4 Fort Fisher N Carolina 33.57N 77.56W
Fort Flatters see Bordj Omar Dr
Fort Foureau see Koussleri
100 J2 Fort Frances Ontario 48.37N 93.23W
101 M3 Fort Franklin N W Terr 65.10N 123.30W
101 L8 Fort Fraser Br Col 54.03N 124.30W
105 F6 Fort Frederica Nat. Mon Georgia 31.14N 81.23W
105 B6 Fort Gaines Georgia 31.37N 85.04W
109 E4 Fort Garland Colorado 37.26N 105.26W
100 U9 Fort Garry Manitoba 49.50N 97.09W
104 C8 Fort Gay W Virginia 38.07N 82.35W
58 H3 Fort George Highland Scotland 57.35N 4.05W
97 M7 Fort George Quebec 53.50N 79.01W
109 P6 Fort Gibson Oklahoma 35.49N 95.14W
109 P5 Fort Gibson Res Oklahoma
101 J2 Fort Good Hope N W Terr 66.16N 128.37W
Fort Gouraud see Fderik
105 F10 Fort Green Florida 27.38N 81.57W
12 F3 Fort Grey New S Wales 29.04S 141.13E
112 H3 Fort Griffin Texas 32.55N 99.13W
115 E9 Fort Gulick Panama Canal Zone 9.19N 79.52W
58 J7 Forth Strathclyde Scotland 55.46N 3.42W
110 N6 Fort Hall Idaho 43.03N 112.26W
Fort Hall Kenyasee Murango
112 B4 Fort Hancock Texas 31.17N 105.53W
58 K6 Forth Bridge Scotland 56.00N 3.25W
Fort Hertz see Putao
58 K6 Forth, Firth of Scotland
59 J7 Forth Mt Wexford Irish Rep 52.19N 6.33W
97 L7 Fort Hope Ontario 51.30N 88.00W
103 B8 Fort Howard Maryland 39.12N 76.27W
58 H6 Forth, R Scotland
111 O10 Fort Huachuca Arizona 31.34N 110.24W
99 S6 Fortierville Quebec 46.28N 72.04W
54 L5 Forties oil field North Sea 57.44N 0.53E
98 H9 Forties Settlement Nova Scotia 44.46N 64.34W
111 K3 Fortification Ra Nevada
117 H7 Fortim Brazil 4.30S 37.46W
118 A8 Fortín Ávalos Sánchez Paraguay 23.28S 60.14W
118 B8 Fortín Boquerón Paraguay 22.50S 59.58W
121 E2 Fortín Cabeza de Chauco Arg 28.30S 61.20W
118 A8 Fortín Capitán Demattei Paraguay 22.43S 60.47W
118 B7 Fortín Carlos Antonio López Paraguay 21.20S 59.43W
118 B7 Fortín Coronel Bogado Paraguay 20.44S 59.09W
118 A8 Fortín Corrales Paraguay 22.21S 60.35W
110 L1 Fortine Montana 48.46N 114.54W
118 B8 Fortín Falcón Paraguay 23.06S 59.50W
58 H5 Fortingall Tayside Scotland 56.36N 4.04W
118 B6 Fortín Galpón Paraguay 19.54S 58.10W
118 B9 Fortín General Caballero Paraguay 24.10S 59.30W
118 B7 Fortín General Díaz Alto Paraguay Paraguay 21.05S 58.30W
118 A8 Fortín General Díaz Boquerón Paraguay 23.31S 60.34W
118 A7 Fortín General Eugenio Garay Paraguay 20.30S 61.56W
118 A7 Fortín General Mendoza Paraguay 20.05S 61.55W
118 A7 Fortín Hernandarías Paraguay 21.58S 61.33W
118 A7 Fortín Infante Rivarola Paraguay 21.43S 62.20W
118 B8 Fortín Juan de Zalazar Paraguay 23.01S 59.15W
98 E3 Fortin,L Quebec
120 G9 Fortín Lagerenza Paraguay 20.04S 61.04W
118 A9 Fortín Lavalle Argentina 25.41S 60.13W
118 A7 Fortín Leonardo Britos Paraguay 21.37S 62.15W
120 G10 Fortín Leonida Escobar Paraguay 23.23S 61.13W
118 A8 Fortín Linares Paraguay 23.13S 61.45W
118 B7 Fortín Madrejón Paraguay 20.35S 59.52W
118 B7 Fortín Madrejoncito Paraguay 20.49S 59.51W
118 A8 Fortín May Alberto Gardel Paraguay 22.43S 62.14W
120 G9 Fortín Nueva Asunción Paraguay 20.54S 61.55W
121 E2 Fortín Olmos Argentina 29.01S 60.22W
118 B6 Fortín Paredes Bolivia 19.15S 59.59W
120 G10 Fortín Pilcomayo Argentina 23.51S 60.58W
118 B8 Fortín Presidente Ayala Paraguay 23.29S 59.43W
118 A6 Fortín Ravelo Bolivia 19.20S 60.39W
118 B8 Fortín Rojas Silva Paraguay 22.37S 59.01W
118 B9 Fortín Sargento Primero Leyes Argentina 24.32S 59.16W
118 A6 Fortín Suárez Arana Bolivia 18.43S 60.13W
118 B8 Fortín Teniente Montania Paraguay 22.01S 59.52W
118 A7 Fortín Tte. Agripino Enciso Paraguay 21.15S 61.30W
118 B6 Fortín Tte. Américo Picco Paraguay 19.46S 59.47W
118 A7 Fortín Tte. Juan E. López Paraguay 21.03S 61.46W
118 B6 Fortín Tte. Primero H. Mendoza Paraguay 19.58S 59.46W
118 A9 Fortín Tte. Rojas Silva Paraguay 24.01S 60.06W
121 D7 Fortín Uno Argentina 38.50S 65.26W
95 L8 Fort Jackson S Africa 32.55S 27.42E
Fort Jameson see Chipata
105 E13 Fort Jefferson Nat. Mon Florida 24.40N 82.50W
110 C8 Fort Jones California 41.37N 122.51W
100 G4 Fort Kent Alberta 54.19N 110.38W
104 Q6 Fort Kent Maine 47.15N 68.35W
110 C7 Fort Klamath Oregon 42.42N 122.00W
107 L4 Fort Knox Kentucky 37.54N 85.59W
Fort Lallemand see Belhir
101 K11 Fort Langley Br Columbia 49.11N 122.35W
Fort Laperrine Algeriasee Tamanrasset
108 F7 Fort Laramie Wyoming 42.12N 104.30W
108 F7 Fort Laramie Nat. Mon Wyoming 42.10N 104.31W
105 G11 Fort Lauderdale Florida 26.08N 80.08W
105 G3 Fort Lawn S Carolina 34.41N 80.56W
103 K6 Fort Lee New Jersey 40.51N 73.58W
110 C2 Fort Lewis Washington 47.06N 122.36W
101 M5 Fort Liard N W Terr 60.14N 123.28W
116 J5 Fort Liberté Haiti 19.42N 71.51W
108 K3 Fort Lincoln N Dakota 46.47N 100.45W
31 F4 Fort Lockhart Pakistan 33.33N 70.58E
107 M6 Fort Loudoun Dam Tennessee 35.46N 84.15W
107 M6 Fort Loudoun L Tennessee
109 F1 Fort Lupton Colorado 40.04N 104.49W
109 G3 Fort Lyon Colorado 38.05N 103.08W
112 G5 Fort McKavett Texas 30.51N 100.07W
101 S7 Fort MacKay Alberta 57.12N 111.41W
108 C5 Fort Mackenzie Wyoming 44.48N 107.00W
100 D9 Fort Macleod Alberta 49.44N 113.24W
Fort McMahon see El Homr
Fort McMurray see McMurray
101 S7 Fort McMurray Alberta 56.40N 111.07W
101 F2 Fort McPherson N W Terr 67.29N 134.50W
106 C9 Fort Madison Iowa 40.38N 91.21W
69 B3 Fort Mahon Plage France 50.20N 1.34E
Fort Manning see Mchinji
105 F8 Fort Matanzas Nat. Mon Florida 29.43N 81.16W
105 F10 Fort Meade Florida 27.43N 81.49W
103 A8 Fort Meade Maryland 39.06N 76.45W
105 G2 Fort Mill S Carolina 35.01N 80.56W
92 G9 Fort Mlangeni Malawi 14.41S 34.40E
60 N10 Fortmond Netherlands 52.22N 6.05E
109 G1 Fort Morgan Colorado 40.14N 103.48W
Fort Motylinski see Tarahouahout
66 F7 Fort, Mt Switzerland 46.05N 7.19E
31 F6 Fort Munro Pakistan 29.51N 70.05E
105 F11 Fort Myers Florida 26.39N 81.51W
74 K8 Fort National Algeria 36.39N 4.14E
101 M6 Fort Nelson Br Columbia 58.48N 122.44W
101 M6 Fort Nelson R Br Columbia
101 L3 Fort Norman N W Terr 64.55N 125.29W
105 F10 Fort Ogden Florida 27.05N 81.56W
80 M5 Fortore R Italy
107 L7 Fort Payne Alabama 34.25N 85.42W
108 D1 Fort Peck Montana 48.01N 106.28W
108 D2 Fort Peck Res Montana
105 G10 Fort Pierce Florida 27.28N 80.20W
105 G10 Fort Pierce Inlet Florida 27.29N 80.16W
108 K5 Fort Pierre S Dakota 44.21N 100.23W
104 L4 Fort Plain New York 42.56N 74.39W
93 B5 Fort Portal Uganda 0.40N 30.17E
101 P5 Fort Providence N W Terr 61.03N 117.40W
105 G5 Fort Pulaski Nat. Mon Georgia 32.03N 80.54W
100 O8 Fort Qu'Appelle Saskatchewan 50.46N 103.48W
105 M2 Fort Raleigh Nat. Hist.Site N Carolina 35.55N 75.44W
113 F9 Fort Randall Alaska 55.10N 162.47W
108 M6 Fort Randall Dam S Dakota 43.03N 98.34W
115 E9 Fort Randolph Panama Canal Zone 9.23N 79.53W
104 A6 Fort Recovery Ohio 40.25N 84.46W
101 R5 Fort Resolution N W Terr 61.10N 113.39W
110 Q5 Fortress Mt Wyoming 44.21N 109.49W
108 K3 Fort Rice N Dakota 46.31N 100.34W
109 O2 Fort Riley Kansas 39.05N 96.47W
108 Q3 Fort Ripley Minnesota 46.11N 94.21W
92 D12 Fort Rixon Zimbabwe 20.01S 29.18E
108 G7 Fort Robinson Nebraska 42.41N 103.29W
110 D6 Fort Rock Oregon 43.21N 121.04W
58 H3 Fortrose Highland Scotland 57.34N 4.09W
11 C13 Fortrose New Zealand 46.32S 168.50E
Fort Rosebery see Mansa Zambia
111 A3 Fort Ross California 38.36N 123.21W
91 D4 Fort Rousset Congo 0.27S 15.44E
99 M1 Fort Rupert Quebec 51.30N 79.45W
28 D5 Fort St. David Tamil Nadu India 11.46N 79.46E
28 C7 Fort St. George Tamil Nadu India 13.03N 80.17E
101 L8 Fort St. James Br Columbia 54.26N 124.15W
101 N7 Fort St. John Br Columbia 56.14N 120.55W
71 L9 Fort-Ste. Marguerite France 43.31N 7.03E
31 E5 Fort Sandeman Pakistan 31.21N 69.31E
100 D5 Fort Saskatchewan Alberta 53.42N 113.12W
109 Q4 Fort Scott Kansas 37.52N 94.43W
97 L6 Fort Severn Ontario 56.00N 87.40W
110 B9 Fort Seward California 40.14N 123.40W
115 E9 Fort Sherman Panama Canal Zone 9.21N 79.57W
44 K3 Fort Shevchenko Kazakhstan U.S.S.R. 44.31N 50.15E
109 M7 Fort Sill Oklahoma 34.41N 98.25W
101 N5 Fort Simpson N W Terr 61.52N 121.15W
107 B6 Fort Smith Arkansas 35.22N 94.27W
101 S5 Fort Smith N W Terr 60.01N 111.55W
29 C7 Fort Songad Gujarat India 21.12N 73.42E
91 D3 Fort Soufflay Congo 2.00N 14.54E
108 D8 Fort Steele Wyoming 41.47N 106.58W
112 E5 Fort Stockton Texas 30.54N 102.54W
109 F7 Fort Sumner New Mexico 34.27N 104.16W
105 H5 Fort Sumter Nat. Mon S Carolina 32.44N 79.55W
109 L5 Fort Supply Oklahoma 36.35N 99.35W
109 L5 Fort Supply Res Oklahoma 36.32N 99.35W
103 K4 Fort Terry Long I, N Y 41.12N 72.11W
111 P8 Fort Thomas Arizona 33.03N 109.59W
108 L5 Fort Thompson S Dakota 44.04N 99.25W
109 P7 Fort Towson Oklahoma 34.02N 95.16W
Fort Trinquet see Bir Moghreim
53 X16 Fortun Norway 61.29N 7.42E
110 A9 Fortuna California 40.36N 124.09W
108 G1 Fortuna N Dakota 48.55N 103.47W
77 O4 Fortuna Spain 38.11N 1.07W
Fortuna Ledge see Marshall Alaska
98 R6 Fortune Newfoundland 47.05N 55.52W
98 R6 Fortune B Newfoundland
56 G6 Fortuneswell Dorset Eng 50.33N 2.27W
109 E6 Fort Union Nat. Mon New Mexico 35.55N 105.02W
53 X15 Fortunsdalen V Norway 61.33N 7.44E
40 N7 Fortuny, Proliv str Kuril Is U.S.S.R.
105 D5 Fort Valley Georgia 32.32N 83.56W
101 Q6 Fort Vermilion Alberta 58.22N 115.59W
92 E12 Fort Victoria Zimbabwe 20.10S 30.49E
107 L2 Fortville Indiana 39.56N 85.51W
107 K11 Fort Walton Beach Florida 30.27N 86.38W
110 R6 Fort Washakie Wyoming 43.02N 108.53W
106 J8 Fort Wayne Indiana 41.05N 85.08W
117 A1 Fort Wellington Guyana 6.25N 57.39W
25 L9 Fort White Burma 23.17N 93.50E
105 E8 Fort White Florida 29.55N 82.44W
100 A2 Fort Whyte Manitoba 49.49N 97.13W
29 H2 Fort William Calcutta, W Bengal 22.33N 88.20E
58 F5 Fort William Highland Scotland 56.49N 5.07W
Fort William Ontario see Thunder Bay
112 K3 Fort Worth Texas 32.45N 97.20W
108 K3 Fort Yates N Dakota 46.06N 100.39W
11 K11 Forty Fours, The islds Chatham Is Pacific Oc
113 R5 Fortymile R Alaska
113 P3 Fort Yukon Alaska 66.35N 145.20W
75 E1 Forua Spain 43.20N 2.40W
32 F7 Forūr isld Iran
61 L4 Forville Belgium 50.34N 5.00E
100 N9 Forward Saskatchewan 49.40N 104.30W
81 K8 Forza d'Agrò Sicily 37.55N 15.21E
72 F10 Fos France 42.53N 0.44E
79 H6 Fosdinovo Italy 44.08N 10.02E
47 G6 Fosforitnaya U.S.S.R. 59.33N 52.28E
71 F10 Fos, G.de France 43.23N 4.55E
23 F7 Foshan Guangdong China 23.03N 113.08E
97 L2 Fosheim Pen N W Terr
53 S20 Fosn isld Norway 59.18N 5.22E
52 E3 Fosna reg Norway
53 S14 Fosnavåg Norway 62.22N 5.39E
52 F2 Fosnes Norway 64.38N 11.17E
53 R17 Fosnøy isld Norway 60.46N 4.55E
89 J9 Foso Ghana 5.43N 1.13W
71 F10 Fos, Port de France 43.25N 4.46E
50 H7 Foss Iceland 63.51N 17.51W
53 Y19 Foss Norway 59.52N 8.28E
109 L6 Foss Oklahoma 35.29N 99.11W
89 B3 Foss Senegal 16.08N 15.49W
50 F6 Fossá R Árnessýsla Iceland
50 E3 Fossá R Húnavatnssýsla, Austur Iceland
50 F3 Fossá R Skagafjardharsýsla Iceland
50 G4 Fossá R Skagafjardharsýsla Iceland
80 K4 Fossacesia Italy 42.15N 14.30E
79 M3 Fossalta di Piave Italy 45.39N 12.30E
79 N3 Fossalta di Portogruaro Italy 45.48N 12.54E
79 C5 Fossano Italy 44.33N 7.43E
50 L5 Fossárdalur V Iceland
50 K5 Fossarvötn lakes Iceland
72 G9 Fossat, le France 43.11N 1.24E
80 G2 Fossato di Vico Italy 43.18N 12.46E
53 Z15 Fossberg Norway 61.50N 8.32E
61 O5 Fosse Liège Belgium 50.21N 5.50E
53 T17 Fosse Norway 60.35N 5.53E
72 F5 Fossemagne France 45.07N 0.59E
53 T17 Fossen Norway 60.54N 5.38E
61 J5 Fosses-la-Ville Namur Belgium 50.24N 4.42E
56 J2 Fosse Way hist route Eng
50 B3 Fossfjördhur B Iceland
50 B3 Fossheidhi heath Iceland
53 Z15 Fossheim Norway 61.50N 8.35E
50 H3 Fosshóll Iceland 65.43N 17.31W
110 E4 Fossil Oregon 45.01N 120.14W
110 P8 Fossil Wyoming 41.49N 110.45W
123 F13 Fossil Bluff U.K. Base Antarctica 71.20S 68.17W
13 G4 Fossilbrook Queensland 17.49S 144.23E
108 G6 Fossil Cycad Nat. Mon S Dakota 43.22N 103.44W
14 F4 Fossil Downs W Australia 18.12S 125.48E
95 O7 Fossil Hd S Africa 31.06S 30.11E
53 W18 Fossli Norway 60.26N 7.15E
99 L6 Fossmill Ontario 46.04N 79.07W
79 N7 Fossombrone Italy 43.42N 12.48E
109 L7 Foss Res Oklahoma
108 P2 Fosston Minnesota 47.33N 95.46W
100 O6 Fosston Saskatchewan 52.12N 103.49W
71 F10 Fos-sur-Mer France 43.26N 4.56E
50 L4 Fossvellir Iceland 65.27N 14.36W
108 N7 Foster Nebraska 42.17N 97.41W
110 C5 Foster Oregon 44.24N 122.40W
99 S7 Foster Quebec 45.18N 72.30W
103 L3 Foster Rhode I 41.52N 71.45W
12 H7 Foster Victoria 38.41S 146.11E
101 V7 Foster R Saskatchewan
48 V9 Foster Bugt B Greenland
106 G4 Foster City Michigan 45.57N 87.43W
103 E3 Fosterdale New York 41.42N 74.57W
101 V7 Foster Lakes Saskatchewan
113 U7 Foster, Mt Yukon Terr 59.50N 135.35W
100 J8 Fosterton Saskatchewan 50.30N 108.21W
107 K6 Fosterville Tennessee 35.39N 86.25W
104 B5 Fostoria Ohio 41.10N 83.25W
112 M5 Fostoria Texas 30.20N 95.12W
95 B8 Fotadrevo Madagascar 24.01S 45.00E
23 H6 Fotan Fujian China 24.09N 117.52E
57 N6 Fotherby Lincs Eng 53.25N 0.02W
14 F5 Fotheringham, Mt W Australia 20.46S 126.38E
53 T17 Fotlandsvåg Norway 60.35N 5.31E
121 B9 Foto Cahuel Argentina 42.24S 70.38W
9 T12 Fotuha'a atoll Tonga, Pacific Oc 19.50S 174.38W
89 E7 Fouala Guinea 9.05N 8.21W
70 O2 Foucarmont France 49.51N 1.34E
26 A12 Fouce, Pte.la C Rodriguez I Ind Oc 19.43S 63.20E
69 N7 Fouday France 48.26N 7.12E
70 B6 Fouesnant France 47.54N 4.00W
91 B4 Fougamou Gabon 1.16S 10.30E
70 H5 Fougères France 48.21N 1.12W
26 U14 Fougères, Plaine des Réunion Ind Oc
69 L8 Fougerolles France 47.53N 6.24E
70 J5 Fougerolles-du-Plessis France 48.28N 0.58W
61 P7 Fouhren Luxembourg 49.55N 6.12E
72 J7 Fouillade, la France 44.14N 2.01E
69 D4 Fouilloy France 49.54N 2.30E
90 J3 Fouka Chad 16.48N 18.07E
107 C8 Fouke Arkansas 33.16N 93.55W
58 O9 Foula isld Shetland Scotland 60.08N 2.05W
89 B5 Fouladou reg Senegal
69 J7 Foulain France 48.02N 5.12E
89 F6 Foulalaba Mali 10.41N 7.19W
89 C5 Foula More Guinea 12.08N 13.49W
85 N8 Foul B Egypt
61 F4 Fouleng Belgium 50.37N 3.55E
91 A4 Foulenzem Gabon 1.18S 9.05E
25 C3 Foul I Burma 18.03N 94.05E
Fou-liang see Jingdezhen
56 N4 Foulness Pt Essex Eng 51.38N 0.57E
57 G4 Foulney I Cumbria Eng 54.04N 3.09W
26 T4 Foul Pt Sri Lanka 8.31N 81.18E
11 F8 Foulwind, C New Zealand 41.45S 171.26E
89 D2 Foum Ajar Mauritania 18.36N 10.13W
90 E9 Foumban Cameroon 5.43N 10.50E
91 B1 Foumbot Cameroon 5.31N 10.28E
88 J7 Foum el Hisn Morocco 28.59N 8.55W
88 K6 Foum Zguid Morocco 30.04N 6.54W
91 B4 Founa Gabon 0.24S 11.21E
89 A4 Foundiougne Senegal 14.08N 16.30W
109 F3 Fountain Colorado 38.40N 104.44W
106 H5 Fountain Michigan 44.03N 86.12W
108 S6 Fountain Minnesota 43.46N 92.10W
105 K2 Fountain N Carolina 35.41N 77.39W
111 N2 Fountain Green Utah 39.38N 111.37W
58 L7 Fountainhall Borders Scotland 55.45N 2.55W
107 E8 Fountain Hill Arkansas 33.21N 91.50W
103 D5 Fountain Hill Pennsylvania 40.36N 75.25W
105 E3 Fountain Inn S Carolina 34.41N 82.12W
76 D14 Foupana R Portugal
72 E4 Fouquebrune France 45.32N 0.12E
13 D3 Four Archers mt N Terr Australia 15.28S 135.26E
72 B4 Fouras France 45.59N 1.06W
108 E1 Four Buttes Montana 48.50N 105.38W
72 E8 Fources France 43.59N 0.14E
71 C2 Fourchambault France 47.02N 3.05E
70 M5 Fourche, la France 48.23N 0.54E
107 B7 Fourche la Fave R Arkansas
98 M8 Fourchu C Breton I, Nova Scotia 45.43N 60.17W
111 P4 Four Corners Utah/Col/New Mex/Ariz 37.00N 109.03W
108 F5 Four Corners Wyoming 44.05N 104.08W
13 A1 Fourcroy, C N Terr Australia 11.50S 130.02E
71 J3 Fourgs, les France 46.50N 6.24E
95 M4 Fouriesburg S Africa 28.37S 28.13E
123 C3 Four Ladies Bank Antarctica
70 E7 Four, le I France 47.18N 2.40W
69 G3 Fourmies France 50.01N 4.03E
113 B10 Four Mountains, Is. of the Aleutian Is
26 V16 Fournaise, Piton de la vol Réunion Ind Oc 21.14S 55.43E
84 C3 Fournás Greece 39.04N 21.53E
26 T13 Fourneau I Mauritius, Indian Oc 20.28S 57.20E
98 P2 Fournel, L Quebec
71 C7 Fournels France 44.48N 3.07E
69 D2 Fournes-en-Weppes France 50.35N 2.54E
66 D3 Fournet France 47.10N 6.50E
11 K11 Fournier, C Chatham Is Pacific Oc 44.03S 176.18W
98 G2 Fournier, L Quebec
83 H7 Foúrnoi isld Greece
71 D5 Fournols France 45.32N 3.35E
56 H2 Four Oaks W Midlands Eng 52.35N 1.49W
90 K9 Fouroumbala Cent Afr Rep 4.33N 21.49E
116 K2 Four Paths Jamaica, W I 17.58N 77.18W
Fourqloss see Furqlus
71 F9 Fourques Gard France 43.41N 4.35E
72 K10 Fourques Pyrénées Orientales France 42.35N 2.46E
72 E7 Fourques-sur-Garonne France 44.27N 0.10E
116 O1 Four Roads Trinidad & Tobago 10.42N 61.33W
71 D3 Fours Nièvre France 46.49N 3.43E
71 K8 Fours (St. Laurent) Alpes de Haute Provence France 44.20N 6.42E
106 E3 Fourteen Mile Pt Michigan 46.59N 89.06W
95 H4 Fourteen Streams S Africa 28.05S 24.53E
85 M10 Fourth Cataract Sudan 18.44N 32.03E
95 L6 Fourth Reverse S Africa 30.48S 27.15E
19 N5 Fourup isld Truk Is Pacific Oc 7.14N 151.46E
71 L1 Foussemagne France 47.38N 7.02E
72 G9 Fousseret, le France 43.17N 1.04E
89 B4 Fouta reg Senegal
89 C6 Fouta Djallon mt reg Guinea
90 J6 Foutounga Chad 11.37N 19.23E
116 H5 Foux, Cap-à- Haiti 19.43N 73.27W
71 K8 Foux, la France 44.16N 6.35E
56 G5 Fovant Wilts Eng 51.03N 2.00W
11 B13 Foveaux Str New Zealand
53 C3 Fovlum Denmark 56.45N 9.16E
103 A7 Fowblesburg Maryland 39.33N 76.50W
56 B7 Fowey Cornwall Eng 50.20N 4.38W
56 B7 Fowey, R Cornwall Eng
105 G12 Fowey Rocks Florida 25.35N 80.05W
116 F2 Fowl Cay isld Bahamas 24.16N 76.30W
109 F3 Fowler Colorado 38.07N 104.03W
106 G9 Fowler Indiana 40.37N 87.19W
109 K4 Fowler Kansas 37.23N 100.13W
106 K6 Fowler Michigan 43.01N 84.41W
110 O1 Fowler Montana 48.20N 111.49W
11 B12 Fowler Pass New Zealand 45.20S 167.20E
12 B4 Fowler, Pt S Australia 32.02S 132.28E
12 B4 Fowlers Bay S Australia 31.59S 132.26E
12 C4 Fowlers Bay S Australia
112 J7 Fowlerton Texas 28.28N 98.49W
106 K7 Fowlerville Michigan 42.40N 85.04W
107 G6 Fowlkes Tennessee 35.58N 89.23W
56 M3 Fowlmere Cambs Eng 52.05N 0.05E
105 C7 Fowlstown Georgia 30.48N 84.34W
32 C2 Fowman Iran 37.15N 49.19E
106 G4 Fox Michigan 45.30N 87.19W
110 F5 Fox Oregon 44.39N 119.09W
97 K6 Fox R Manitoba
107 E1 Fox R Missouri
13 H5 Fox R Queensland
98 L4 Fox Bay Anticosti I, Que 49.18N 61.51W
103 M2 Foxborough Massachusetts 42.05N 71.15W
104 F5 Foxburg Pennsylvania 41.10N 79.41W
101 P8 Fox Creek Alberta 54.25N 116.57W
57 D4 Foxdale Isle of Man U.K. 54.10N 4.38W
97 L4 Foxe Basin N W Terr
97 L4 Foxe Chan N W Terr
52 F7 Foxen L Sweden 59.25N 11.55E
97 M5 Foxe Pen N W Terr
59 D4 Foxford Mayo Irish Rep 53.59N 9.07W
100 M5 Foxford Saskatchewan 53.28N 105.08W
11 E10 Fox Glacier New Zealand 43.30S 170.05E
98 R1 Fox Harbour Labrador, Nfld 52.22N 55.41W
57 N4 Foxholes N Yorks Eng 54.08N 0.28W
108 O3 Foxhome Minnesota 46.20N 96.20W
106 J4 Fox I., North Michigan 45.29N 85.47W
113 D10 Fox Is Aleutian Is
106 J4 Fox I., South Michigan 45.25N 85.50W
14 C10 Fox, L W Australia 32.51S 119.30E
101 Q6 Fox Lake Alberta 58.27N 114.34W
106 F6 Fox Lake Wisconsin 43.33N 88.54W
108 D8 Foxpark Wyoming 41.04N 106.08W
11 E10 Fox Pk mt New Zealand 43.49S 170.42E
98 L4 Fox Pt Anticosti I, Que 49.19N 61.51W
101 L7 Fox, R Br Columbia
106 F8 Fox, R Illinois
106 H3 Fox, R Michigan
106 F5 Fox, R Wisconsin
59 K5 Foxrock Dublin Irish Rep 53.16N 6.10W
56 K2 Foxton Leics Eng 52.30N 0.58W
11 K7 Foxton New Zealand 40.27S 175.18E
100 H8 Fox Valley Saskatchewan 50.29N 109.29W
100 Q8 Foxwarren Manitoba 50.30N 101.09W
107 G10 Foxworth Mississippi 31.13N 89.54W
58 H4 Foyers Highland Scotland 57.15N 4.30W
59 G4 Foygh Longford Irish Rep 53.36N 7.49W
59 H1 Foyle, L Irish Rep/N Ireland 55.05N 7.10W
59 D6 Foynes Limerick Irish Rep 52.37N 9.06W
61 K5 Foy-Notre-Dame Belgium 50.15N 4.59E
50 V12 Foynøya isld Spitsbergen 80.28N 26.00E
76 E1 Foz Spain 43.34N 7.15W
76 D9 Foz dam Portugal 39.35N 7.42W
79 L3 Foza Italy 45.54N 11.32E
120 D2 Foz de Gregório Brazil 6.51S 70.44W
120 C3 Foz do Breu Brazil 9.21S 72.46W
119 G9 Foz do Copeá Brazil 3.53S 63.16W
91 B12 Foz do Cunene Angola 17.15S 11.48E
76 B6 Foz do Douro Portugal 41.09N 8.41W
118 C9 Foz do Iguaçú Brazil 25.33S 54.31W
120 F3 Foz do Jamari Brazil 8.29S 63.29W
120 D3 Foz do Jordão Brazil 9.22S 71.58W
119 F9 Foz do Jutaí Brazil 2.46S 66.55W
119 F9 Foz do Mamoriá Brazil 2.25S 66.36W
120 E2 Foz do Pauiní Brazil 7.47S 67.07W
120 D2 Foz do Riosinho Brazil 7.15S 71.50W
120 D2 Foz do Tarauacá Brazil 6.44S 69.49W
23 G3 Foziling Sk res Anhui China 31.15N 116.20E
76 J2 Foz, La Spain 43.09N 5.15W
64 N7 Frabertsham W Germany 48.01N 12.24E
79 C6 Frabosa Soprana Italy 44.17N 7.48E
80 F4 Frabrica di Roma Italy 42.20N 12.18E
103 B5 Frackville Pennsylvania 40.46N 76.12W
56 B7 Fraddon Cornwall Eng 50.23N 4.56W
76 C2 Frades Spain 43.04N 8.16W
76 H7 Frades de la Sierra Spain 40.40N 5.47W
96 U4 Frades, Ponta dos Azores 37.01N 25.09W
121 D4 Fraga Argentina 33.32S 65.46W
75 L4 Fraga Spain 41.32N 0.21E
81 P12 Fragagnano Italy 40.26N 17.29E
76 C6 Fragil, Barragem res Portugal 41.04N 8.01W
119 C7 Fragua, Picos de la mts Colombia
76 B10 Fráguas Portugal 39.22N 8.50W
121 G4 Fraile Muerto Uruguay 32.30S 54.30W
77 J6 Frailes Spain 37.29N 3.50W
120 E8 Frailes, Cord de los mts Bolivia
61 N4 Fraipont Belgium 50.34N 5.43E
61 J5 Fraire Belgium 50.16N 4.31E
71 H2 Fraisans France 47.09N 5.45E
71 B9 Fraisse-sur-Agout France 43.37N 2.48E
61 M5 Fraiture Belgium 50.28N 5.25E
69 M7 Fraize France 48.11N 7.00E
123 C3 Fram Bank Antarctica
66 D3 Frambouhans France 47.13N 6.45E
50 H4 Frambruni lava field Iceland
61 F5 Frameries Belgium 50.25N 3.54E
103 M2 Framingham Massachusetts 42.18N 71.25W
56 O3 Framlingham Suffolk Eng 52.13N 1.21E
64 G3 Frammersbach W Germany 50.03N 9.29E
53 V17 Framnes Norway 60.47N 6.34E
53 V17 Framnes Norway 60.47N 6.34E
123 B5 Framnes Mts Antarctica
61 L7 Framont Belgium 49.55N 5.10E
62 O5 Frampol Poland 50.40N 22.40E
81 E9 Fram, Pta Pantelleria I Italy 36.49N 11.56E
53 X15 Framrusta Norway 61.55N 7.50E
118 H2 França Bahia Brazil 11.36S 40.36W
76 F5 Franca Portugal 41.54N 6.44W
118 F7 Franca São Paulo Brazil 20.33S 47.27W
26 P15 Française, B Kerguelen Ind Oc
9 A12 Français, Récif des reef New Caledonia
67 P12 Francardo Corsica 42.24N 9.11E

80 K4 Francavilla al Mare Italy 42.25N 14.16E
81 K8 Francavilla di Sicília Sicily 37.54N 15.08E
81 Q11 Francavilla Fontana Italy 40.32N 17.35E
81 M3 Francavilla in Sinni Italy 40.04N 16.12E
49 E7 France *rep* W Europe
48 V5 France, Île de *isld* Greenland 77.50N 17.30W
12 F6 Frances S Australia 36.41S 140.59E
110 B3 Frances Washington 46.32N 123.30W
101 J5 Frances *R* Yukon Terr
72 E7 Francescas France 44.04N 0.26E
13 B2 Frances Creek N Terr Australia 13.29S 131.51E
81 C1 Francesi, Pta. di li Sardinia 41.08N 9.03E
110 N1 Frances, L Montana 48.18N 112.15W
101 J5 Frances Lake Yukon Terr 61.15N 129.12W
101 J5 Frances Lake Yukon Terr
116 C4 Francés, Pta Pinos, I de Cuba 21.37N 83.10W
116 K5 Francés Viejo, C Dominican Rep 19.44N 69.55W
106 H9 Francesville Indiana 40.59N 86.54W
91 C4 Franceville Gabon 1.40S 13.31E
67 J6 Franche Comté *prov* France
66 D3 Franches Montagnes Switzerland
72 L2 Franchesse France 46.39N 3.02E
61 J6 Franchimont Belgium 50.12N 4.38E
121 G4 Francia Uruguay 32.30S 56.40W
76 G7 Francia, Peña de *mt* Spain 40.31N 6.10W
109 O7 Francis Oklahoma 34.53N 96.37W
100 O8 Francis Saskatchewan 50.08N 103.57W
116 F4 Francisco Cuba 20.51N 77.36W
119 C8 Francisco de Orellana Ecuador 0.28S 77.00W
119 D9 Francisco de Orellana Peru 3.21S 72.43W
115 H5 Francisco I. Madero Coahuila Mexico 25.48N 103.18W
115 G5 Francisco I. Madero Durango Mexico 24.28N 104.20W
121 F6 Francisco Meeks Argentina 37.01S 59.35W
118 G5 Francisco Sá Brazil 16.21S 43.30W
94 C5 Franciscus Bay Namibia
98 R1 Francis Harbour Labrador, Nfld 52.34N 55.44W
123 E13 Francis I Antarctica 67.45S 64.55W
104 O1 Francis, L New Hampshire 45.02N 71.20W
108 L6 Francis, L S Dakota
94 J3 Francistown Botswana 21.11S 27.32E
76 E6 Franco Portugal 41.26N 7.21W
76 F1 Franco, El Spain 43.33N 6.49W
81 J9 Francofonte Sicily 37.14N 14.53E
98 Q6 François Newfoundland 47.34N 56.45W
91 E7 François Joseph, Chutes *rapids* Zaïre 7.34S 17.14E
101 L8 François L Br Columbia
75 N5 Francolí *R* Spain
79 L5 Francolino Italy 44.54N 11.41E
68 D2 Franconville France 48.59N 2.15E
61 O5 Francorchamps Belgium 50.27N 5.57E
75 D5 Francos Spain 41.22N 3.22W
72 G6 Francoules France 44.32N 1.29E
110 Q6 Francs Pk Wyoming 43.58N 109.20W
70 N7 Francueil France 47.18N 1.02E
72 G1 Francueil France 47.19N 1.04E
60 L7 Franeker Netherlands 53.11N 5.33E
84 A2 Frangádhes Greece 39.50N 20.53E
84 C4 Frangísta Greece 38.57N 21.36E
71 H4 Frangy France 46.01N 5.56E
61 J5 Franière Belgium 50.27N 4.44E
100 C9 Frank Alberta 49.36N 114.24W
64 F1 Frankenau W Germany 51.05N 8.57E
64 F2 Frankenbach W Germany 50.40N 8.35E
64 P2 Frankenberg E Germany 50.55N 13.03E
64 F1 Frankenberg/Eder W Germany 51.04N 8.49E
65 H5 Frankenburg Austria 48.04N 13.30E
65 M6 Frankenfels Austria 47.59N 15.20E
64 J5 Frankenhardt W Germany 49.06N 10.01E
64 J5 Frankenhöhe *mts* W Germany
65 H6 Frankenmarkt Austria 47.59N 13.27E
106 L6 Frankenmuth Michigan 43.19N 83.44W
64 D5 Frankenstein W Germany 49.27N 8.00E
64 E4 Frankenthal (Pfalz) W Germany 49.32N 8.22E
64 M3 Frankenwald *mts* E & W Germany
116 J2 Frankfield Jamaica, W I 18.08N 77.22W
Frankford Irish Rep *see* Kilcormac
107 E2 Frankford Missouri 39.30N 91.20W
99 N8 Frankford Ontario 44.12N 77.36W
104 E9 Frankford W Virginia 37.56N 80.25W
104 C2 Frankford *dist* Philadelphia, Penn
106 H9 Frankfort Indiana 40.16N 86.31W
109 O2 Frankfort Kansas 39.43N 96.26W
107 M3 Frankfort Kentucky 38.11N 84.53W
106 H5 Frankfort Michigan 44.39N 86.13W
104 K3 Frankfort New York 43.03N 75.06W
104 B7 Frankfort Ohio 39.25N 83.11W
95 L8 Frankfort S Africa 32.44S 27.27E
95 M3 Frankfort S Africa 27.16S 28.30E
108 M5 Frankfort S Dakota 44.53N 98.19W
63 T7 Frankfurt *reg* E Germany
64 F3 Frankfurt am Main W Germany 50.06N 8.41E
62 H3 Frankfurt an der Oder E Germany 52.20N 14.32E
64 K6 Fränkische Alb *mts* W Germany
64 L4 Fränkische Schweiz *mts* W Germany
12 J7 Frankland, C Tasmania 39.53S 147.44E
14 B10 Frankland, R W Australia
103 K3 Franklin Connecticut 41.37N 72.08W
105 B4 Franklin Georgia 33.15N 85.06W
110 O7 Franklin Idaho 42.01N 111.49W
107 K2 Franklin Indiana 39.29N 86.02W
107 K5 Franklin Kentucky 36.42N 86.35W
107 E12 Franklin Louisiana 29.48N 91.31W
104 R2 Franklin Maine 44.36N 68.14W
103 M2 Franklin Massachusetts 42.05N 71.25W
110 Q3 Franklin Montana 46.24N 109.16W
105 D2 Franklin N Carolina 35.12N 83.23W
108 M9 Franklin Nebraska 40.04N 98.56W
104 O3 Franklin New Hampshire 43.26N 71.42W
103 E4 Franklin New Jersey 41.07N 74.35W
103 D2 Franklin New York 42.20N 75.09W
104 A7 Franklin Ohio 39.33N 84.17W
104 F5 Franklin Pennsylvania 41.24N 79.49W
95 N6 Franklin S Africa 30.19S 29.27E
107 K6 Franklin Tennessee 35.55N 86.52W
112 L4 Franklin Texas 31.02N 96.30W
104 J10 Franklin Virginia 36.41N 76.58W
104 F8 Franklin W Virginia 38.39N 79.21W
97 H3 Franklin *dist* N W Terr
101 K1 Franklin B N W Terr
103 A3 Franklindale Pennsylvania 41.43N 76.34W
101 R1 Franklin, district of N W Terr
110 G1 Franklin D. Roosevelt L Washington 48.05N 118.15W
103 C3 Franklin Forks Pennsylvania 41.55N 75.51W
106 E8 Franklin Grove Illinois 41.50N 89.20W
12 D5 Franklin Harb S Australia 33.42S 136.22E
123 J6 Franklin I Antarctica 76.10S 168.28E
99 K7 Franklin I Ontario 45.25N 80.20W
110 K9 Franklin L Nevada 40.25N 115.20W
101 Z2 Franklin L N W Terr 66.43N 96.20W
113 P2 Franklin Mts Alaska
11 B11 Franklin Mts New Zealand
101 K3 Franklin Mts N W Terr
101 M5 Franklin Mts N-W Terr
103 E6 Franklin Park New Jersey 40.26N 74.32W
106 P2 Franklin Park *dist* Chicago, Illinois
113 H1 Franklin, Pt Alaska 70.53N 159.00W
12 J8 Franklin Sd Tasmania
97 K3 Franklin Str N W Terr
107 F11 Franklinton Louisiana 30.52N 90.10W
105 J1 Franklinton N Carolina 36.05N 78.28W
103 F1 Franklinton New York 42.32N 74.19W
105 H2 Franklinville N Carolina 35.46N 79.44W
103 D7 Franklinville New Jersey 39.37N 75.05W
104 G4 Franklinville New York 42.20N 78.28W
110 J6 Franklin Whitney *airport* Idaho 43.33N 116.11W
11 G9 Franklyn, Mt New Zealand 42.03S 172.42E
60 L10 Frankrijk Netherlands 52.21N 5.34E
64 J3 Fränk Saale *R* W Germany
106 G7 Franksille Wisconsin 42.45N 87.56W
112 M3 Frankston Texas 32.05N 95.30W
12 H7 Frankston Victoria 38.08S 145.07E
11 C12 Frankton New Zealand 45.02S 168.44E
108 B5 Frannie Wyoming 44.59N 108.39W
71 H2 Franois France 47.13N 5.55E
72 L10 Franqui, la France 42.56N 3.02E
95 C9 Franschhoek S Africa 33.55S 19.08E
95 F5 Fransenhof S Africa 29.37S 22.25E
94 C3 Fransfontein Namibia 20.12S 15.01E
94 C3 Fransfontein Range *mts* Namibia
48 V5 Franske Øer *islds* Greenland
51 E9 Fränsta Sweden 62.30N 16.10E
56 M5 Frant E Sussex Eng 51.06N 0.16E
64 N3 Františkovy Lázně Czechoslovakia 50.07N 12.21E
38 D1 Frantsa Iosifa, Zemlya *arch* Arctic Oc
99 F4 Franz Ontario 48.28N 84.25W
63 R4 Franzburg E Germany 54.12N 12.53E
11 E10 Franz Josef Glacier New Zealand 43.28S 170.10E
Franz Josef Land *see* Zemlya Frantsa Iosifa
65 G7 Franz-Josefs Höhe Austria 47.05N 12.46E
81 A4 Frasca, C.di Sardinia 39.47N 8.27E
81 J9 Frasca, Mte Sicily 37.18N 14.33E
80 G5 Frascati Italy 41.48N 12.41E
66 E4 Fräschels Switzerland 47.00N 7.13E
81 M4 Frascineto Italy 39.50N 16.15E
66 M6 Frasco Switzerland 46.21N 8.48E
64 N8 Frasdorf W Germany 47.48N 12.18E
109 E2 Fraser Colorado 39.56N 105.50W
101 O9 Fraser *R* Br Columbia
95 E7 Fraserburg S Africa 31.55S 21.31E
58 M3 Fraserburgh Grampian Scotland 57.42N 2.00W
95 E8 Fraserburg Road S Africa 32.45S 21.59E
99 J3 Fraserdale Ontario 49.52N 81.37W
13 L7 Fraser I Queensland
14 A6 Fraser I W Australia 22.39S 113.35E
101 H11 Fraser Mills Br Col 49.14N 122.52W
14 C7 Fraser, Mt W Australia 25.33S 118.25E
14 E3 Fraser, R W Australia
14 E9 Fraser Ra W Australia
14 E9 Fraser Range W Australia 32.00S 122.47E
103 E2 Frasers New York 42.15N 74.58W
11 M5 Frasertown New Zealand 38.57S 177.26E
100 U8 Fraserwood Manitoba 50.39N 97.14W
83 D4 Frashër Albania 40.23N 20.26E
82 K6 Frasinet Romania 44.17N 26.50E
66 O1 Frasnacht Switzerland 47.32N 9.25E
71 J3 Frasne France 46.51N 6.09E
71 H2 Frasne-le-Château France 47.27N 5.53E
61 J6 Frasnes Belgium 50.05N 4.31E
61 E4 Frasnes-lez-Buissenal Belgium 50.40N 3.37E
61 H4 Frasnes-lez-Gosselies Belgium 50.32N 4.27E
75 H5 Frasno, El Spain 41.25N 1.29W
79 E4 Frassineto Po Italy 45.08N 8.32E
79 B5 Frássino Italy 44.34N 7.16E
79 J6 Frassinoro Italy 44.18N 10.34E
66 P3 Frastanz Austria 47.13N 9.38E
Frat *see* Forat
76 D9 Fratel Portugal 39.37N 7.45W
99 F5 Frater Ontario 47.21N 84.34W
65 M4 Fratres Austria 48.58N 15.22E
79 L4 Fratta Polésine Italy 45.02N 11.39E
80 F3 Fratta Todina Italy 42.52N 12.22E
66 G3 Fraubrunnen Switzerland 47.06N 7.32E
65 K6 Frauenberg Austria 47.36N 14.24E
66 M1 Frauenfeld Switzerland 47.34N 8.54E
63 T10 Frauenhain E Germany 51.23N 13.30E
66 Q4 Frauenkirch Switzerland 46.47N 9.48E
65 P6 Frauenkirchen Austria 47.50N 16.57E
64 Q2 Frauenstein E Germany 50.48N 13.33E
64 O5 Frauenstein *mt* W Germany 49.28N 12.33E
64 K2 Frauenwald E Germany 50.34N 10.52E
53 E6 Fraugde Denmark 55.21N 10.29E
121 F4 Fray Bentos Uruguay 33.10S 58.20W
121 G5 Fray Marcos Uruguay 34.13S 55.43W
72 G6 Frayssinet-le-Gélat France 44.35N 1.10E
70 N5 Frazé France 48.16N 1.07E
108 P3 Frazee Minnesota 46.42N 95.40W
108 D1 Frazer Montana 48.04N 106.02W
99 B3 Frazer L Ontario 49.15N 88.31W
76 C4 Freás de Eiras Spain 42.11N 8.02W
76 E6 Frechas Portugal 41.24N 7.10W
64 B2 Frechen W Germany 50.54N 6.48E
76 K4 Frechilla Spain 42.08N 4.50W
63 G9 Freckenhorst W Germany 51.55N 7.58E
106 F2 Freda Michigan 47.06N 88.48W
108 J3 Freda N Dakota 46.20N 101.10W
81 E8 Freddo *R* Sicily
64 E1 Fredeburg W Germany 51.12N 8.18E
63 L9 Freden W Germany 51.55N 9.55E
41 P2 Freden, Ostrov *isld* Franz Josef Land U.S.S.R. 81.30N 62.00E
53 J5 Fredensborg Denmark 55.59N 12.24E
106 K5 Frederic Michigan 44.47N 84.44W
106 B4 Frederic Wisconsin 45.42N 92.28W
104 K7 Frederica Delaware 39.01N 75.28W
53 D5 Fredericia Denmark 55.34N 9.47E
104 H7 Frederick Maryland 39.25N 77.25W
109 L7 Frederick Oklahoma 34.24N 99.03W
108 M4 Frederick S Dakota 45.50N 98.30W
13 D2 Frederick Hills N Terr Australia
99 J3 Frederick House *R* Ontario
99 K4 Frederick House L Ontario
14 B6 Frederick, R W Australia
10 L6 Frederick Reef Coral Sea 21.00S 154.26E
106 B7 Fredericksburg Iowa 42.57N 92.11W
103 B6 Fredericksburg Pennsylvania 40.27N 76.26W
104 H8 Fredericksburg Virginia 38.18N 77.30W
113 U8 Frederick Sd Alaska
48 S14 Frederickshåb Greenland 62.00N 49.47W
103 C6 Fredericksville Pennsylvania 40.27N 75.43W
103 C8 Fredericktown Maryland 39.23N 75.52W
107 F4 Fredericktown Missouri 37.33N 90.19W
104 C6 Fredericktown Ohio 40.29N 82.32W
117 A3 Frederick Willem IV Vallen *falls* Surinam 3.33N 57.32W
98 F8 Fredericton New Brunswick 45.57N 66.40W
98 F8 Fredericton Junc New Brunswick 45.40N 66.38W
106 D9 Frederiek Illinois 40.04N 90.26W
53 C4 Frederiks Denmark 56.21N 9.15E
53 J5 Frederiksberg Denmark 55.42N 12.29E
53 H6 Frederiksberg *Vestsjælland* Denmark 55.25N 11.34E
53 J5 Frederiksborg *co* Denmark
48 U16 Frederiksdal Greenland 59.59N 44.31W
53 C5 Frederikshåb Denmark 55.40N 9.12E
48 S14 Frederikshabs Banke Greenland
48 S14 Frederikshåbs Isblink *ice field* Greenland
53 F2 Frederikshavn Denmark 57.28N 10.33E
60 N8 Frederiksoord Netherlands 52.50N 6.11E
53 J5 Frederikssund Denmark 55.51N 12.05E
95 L2 Frederikstad S Africa 26.31S 27.09E
53 J5 Frederiksværk Denmark 55.58N 12.02E
75 L6 Fredes Spain 40.43N 0.10E
111 M5 Fredonia Arizona 36.57N 112.31W
119 C5 Fredonia Colombia 5.57N 75.42W
109 P4 Fredonia Kansas 37.32N 95.50W
107 H4 Fredonia Kentucky 37.11N 88.05W
108 L3 Fredonia N Dakota 46.20N 99.08W
104 F4 Fredonia New York 42.27N 79.22W
112 J5 Fredricksburg Texas 30.18N 98.54W
52 L2 Fredrika Sweden 64.03N 18.25E
Fredrikshamn *see* Hamina
52 F7 Fredrikstad Norway 59.15N 10.55E
26 B14 Fred's Hill Marion I Ind Oc 46.54S 37.50E
107 G3 Freeburg Illinois 38.25N 89.57W
107 E3 Freeburg Missouri 38.19N 91.57W
104 H6 Freeburg Pennsylvania 40.45N 77.10W
110 J4 Freedom Idaho 45.39N 116.16W
107 K2 Freedom Indiana 39.11N 86.53W
109 L5 Freedom Oklahoma 36.47N 99.06W
110 E9 Freedonyer Pk California 40.43N 120.35W
103 F6 Freehold New Jersey 40.16N 74.16W
103 F2 Freehold New York 42.22N 74.03W
106 K6 Freeland Michigan 43.34N 84.09W
103 C4 Freeland Pennsylvania 40.01N 75.53W
12 E4 Freeling Heights *mt* S Australia 30.10S 139.16E
13 C6 Freeling Mt N Terr Australia 22.34S 133.00E
111 E3 Freel Pk *mt* California 38.50N 119.56W
98 T4 Freels, Cape Newfoundland 49.13N 53.29W
108 N6 Freeman S Dakota 43.23N 97.25W
50 U14 Freemanbreen *glacier* Spitsbergen 78.20N 21.30E
106 H9 Freeman, L Indiana 40.43N 86.45W
100 B4 Freeman R Alberta
50 U14 Freemansundet *sound* Spitsbergen
107 G12 Freemason I Louisiana 29.50N 89.00W
59 E7 Freemount Cork Irish Rep 52.17N 8.53W
107 K11 Freeport Florida 30.30N 86.10W
105 J11 Freeport Grand Bahama I Bahamas 26.30N 78.47W
106 E7 Freeport Illinois 42.17N 89.38W
103 G5 Freeport Long I, N Y 40.40N 73.35W
104 P3 Freeport Maine 43.51N 70.07W
103 N8 Freeport New York
98 F9 Freeport Nova Scotia 44.17N 66.19W
104 D6 Freeport Ohio 40.13N 81.17W
104 F6 Freeport Pennsylvania 40.42N 79.43W
112 M7 Freeport Texas 28.56N 95.20W
112 J8 Freer Texas 27.53N 98.37W
106 H5 Freesoil Michigan 44.07N 86.13W
116 P4 Freetown Antigua W I 17.02N 61.42W
116 F2 Freetown Eleuthera I Bahamas 24.51N 76.18W
107 K3 Freetown Indiana 38.59N 86.09W
98 J7 Freetown Prince Edward I 46.22N 63.38W
89 C7 Freetown Sierra Leone 8.30N 13.17W
103 B1 Freeville New York 42.31N 76.21W
108 D7 Freezeout Mts Wyoming
77 C4 Fregenal de la Sierra Spain 38.10N 6.39W
77 C4 Fregenal, Sierra de *mts* Spain
80 F5 Fregene Italy 41.52N 12.12E
76 F7 Fregeneda, La Spain 41.00N 6.52W
75 M6 Freginals Spain 40.40N 0.30E
79 M2 Fregona Italy 46.00N 12.21E
118 H9 Freguesia Rio de Janeiro Brazil 22.57S 43.21W
118 J8 Freguesia Rio de Janeiro Brazil 22.48S 43.11W
117 B6 Freguesia do Andirá Brazil 2.55S 57.00W
70 F4 Fréhel France 48.40N 2.20W
89 A1 Freh, El Mauritania 20.04N 16.15W
70 F4 Fréhel, C France 48.41N 2.19W
52 D3 Frei Norway 63.03N 7.52E
64 P2 Freiberg E Germany 50.55N 13.21E
66 G6 Freiberg W Germany 48.56N 9.15E
66 N4 Freiberg *reg* Switzerland
64 Q2 Freiberger Mulde *R* E Germany
63 K5 Freiburg Niedersachsen W Germany 53.49N 9.17E
64 D7 Freiburg im Breisgau Baden-Württemberg W Germany 48.00N 7.52E
64 G1 Freienhagen W Germany 51.17N 9.04E
63 H10 Freienohl W Germany 51.22N 8.10E
64 G3 Freiensteinau W Germany 50.26N 9.24E
Freihöls *see* Fensterbach
64 M4 Freihung W Germany 49.37N 11.55E
77 L5 Freila Spain 37.32N 2.53W
65 M8 Freiland Austria 46.52N 15.08E
64 O8 Freilassing W Germany 47.50N 12.59E
64 D2 Freilingen W Germany 50.33N 7.50E
65 M6 Frein Austria 47.45N 15.29E
76 F7 Freineda Portugal 40.35N 6.53W
121 E3 Freire Argentina 31.11S 62.05W
121 A7 Freire Chile 38.54S 72.38W
121 B2 Freirina Chile 28.32S 71.10W
64 C4 Freisen W Germany 49.32N 7.15E
64 M7 Freising W Germany 48.24N 11.45E
71 K7 Freissinières France 44.45N 6.31E
65 L4 Freistadt Austria 48.31N 14.31E
Freistett *see* Rheinau
69 L5 Freistroff France 49.17N 6.29E
64 Q1 Freital E Germany 51.00N 13.40E
76 C5 Freitas Portugal 41.42N 8.13W
64 E4 Frei-Weinheim W Germany 49.59N 8.02E
76 E7 Freixedas Portugal 40.41N 7.09W
76 C9 Freixianda Portugal 39.45N 8.28W
76 E6 Freixiel Portugal 41.17N 7.15W
76 D7 Freixiosa Portugal 40.36N 7.41W
76 B5 Freixo Portugal 41.39N 8.35W
76 D11 Freixo Portugal 38.39N 7.37W
76 F6 Freixo de Espada á Cinta Portugal 41.05N 6.49W
72 J8 Frejairolles France 43.52N 2.15E
53 D2 Frejlev Denmark 57.01N 9.50E
71 K10 Fréjus France 43.26N 6.44E
71 K6 Fréjus, Col de *pass* France/Italy 45.08N 6.41E
71 K10 Fréjus, G.de France 43.25N 6.45E
53 S17 Frekhaug Norway 60.31N 5.13E
14 B9 Fremantle W Australia 32.07S 115.44E
111 O3 Fremond *R* Utah
106 K8 Fremont Indiana 41.44N 84.55W
106 J6 Fremont Michigan 43.28N 85.58W
105 K2 Fremont N Carolina 35.32N 77.59W
108 O8 Fremont Nebraska 41.26N 96.30W
104 B5 Fremont Ohio 41.21N 83.08W
103 D3 Fremont Center New York 41.51N 75.02W
110 N8 Fremont I Utah 41.10N 112.25W
110 Q7 Fremont L Wyoming 42.57N 109.49W
109 D2 Fremont Pass Colorado 39.24N 106.12W
110 Q6 Fremont Pk Wyoming 43.07N 109.36W
70 F4 Frênaye, B.de la France 48.38N 2.18W
103 L2 French *R* Massachusetts
11 B3 French Bay New Zealand
105 E2 French Broad, R N Carolina/Tenn
104 B9 Frenchburg Kentucky 37.58N 83.37W
116 H4 French Cay *isld* Caicos Is W I 21.31N 72.14W
116 H3 French Cays *islds* Bahamas
110 J4 French Creek Idaho 45.27N 116.04W
104 E5 French Creek *R* Pennsylvania
114 C2 French Frigate Shoals Hawaiian Is
110 G7 Frenchglen Oregon 42.48N 118.56W
117 H1 French Guiana *dept* S America
110 C9 French Gulch California 40.42N 122.39W
12 H7 French I Victoria 38.20S 145.20E
107 K3 French Lick Indiana 38.34N 86.38W
111 F2 Frenchman Nevada 39.17N 118.16W
104 R2 Frenchman B Maine
100 H5 Frenchman Butte Saskatchewan 53.36N 109.36W
12 H8 Frenchman Cap *mt* Tasmania 42.27S 145.54E
108 C1 Frenchman Cr Montana/Sasketchewan
111 J5 Frenchman Flat *dry lake* Nevada 36.48N 115.55W
109 J1 Frenchman Fork Colo/Nebraska
108 J9 Frenchman Fork *R* Nebraska
98 O4 Frenchman's Cove Newfoundland 49.03N 58.12W
59 F4 Frenchpark Roscommon Irish Rep 53.53N 8.24W
11 H7 French Pass *str* New Zealand
French Rocks *see* Pandavapura
12 M6 French's Forest New S Wales 33.46S 151.14E
French Somaliland *see* Djibouti
103 D5 Frenchtown New Jersey 40.32N 75.04W
69 B2 Frencq France 50.33N 1.42E
88 O4 Frenda Algeria 35.04N 1.03E
69 L7 Frenelle-la-Grande France 48.21N 6.06E
71 J6 Frêne, Pic du *mt* France 45.20N 6.12E
70 M3 Freneuse-sur-Risle France 49.14N 0.41E
71 J6 Freney d'Oisans, le France 45.03N 6.09E
66 G1 Frenkendorf Switzerland 47.30N 7.44E
64 K4 Frensdorf W Germany 49.49N 10.53E
62 L6 Frenštát Czechoslovakia 49.33N 18.10E
80 K5 Frentani, Monti dei Italy
95 N4 Frere S Africa 28.53S 29.46E
63 G8 Freren W Germany 52.29N 7.33E
14 D7 Frere Ra W Australia
66 Q2 Freschen, Hoher *mt* Austria 47.18N 9.47E
89 G9 Fresco Ivory Coast 5.03N 5.31W
117 C8 Fresco, R Brazil
116 F2 Fresh Creek Andros Bahamas 24.45N 77.48W
123 J4 Freshfield, C Antarctica 68.30S 151.05E
59 H6 Freshford Kilkenny Irish Rep 52.44N 7.23W
11 C12 Freshford New Zealand 45.46S 168.49E
110 A9 Freshwater California 40.46N 124.04W
14 A2 Freshwater B W Australia
56 H6 Freshwater Bay I of Wight Eng 50.40N 1.30E
121 A8 Fresia Chile 41.10S 73.25W
70 L5 Fresnay France 48.16N 0.02E
70 L5 Fresnaye-sur-Chédouet, la France 48.27N 0.15E
77 J3 Fresneda *R* Spain
75 F7 Fresneda de la Sierra Spain 40.23N 2.09W
75 L6 Fresneda, La Spain 40.56N 0.04E
76 F3 Fresnedo Spain 42.40N 6.35W
76 F9 Fresnedosa *R* Spain
68 E4 Fresnes France 48.45N 2.20E
71 H1 Fresne St. Mamés France 47.33N 5.52E
69 K5 Fresnes-en-Wœvre France 49.06N 5.38E
69 K8 Fresnes-sur-Apance Haute-Marne France 47.56N 5.50E
69 F3 Fresnes-sur-Escaut France 50.26N 3.30E
53 V16 Fresnikbreen *mt* Norway 61.02N 6.48E
115 H6 Fresnillo Mexico 23.10N 102.54W
111 E5 Fresno California 36.41N 119.47W
111 E4 Fresno *R* California
76 H7 Fresno Alhàndiga Spain 40.42N 5.37W
75 C5 Fresno de la Fuente Spain 41.23N 3.39W
76 H5 Fresno de la Ribera Spain 41.32N 5.34W
76 H6 Fresno de Sayago Spain 41.19N 5.58W
76 J6 Fresno el Viejo Spain 41.12N 5.09W
110 P1 Fresno Res Montana 48.40N 110.00W
70 N2 Fresnoy-Folny France 49.53N 1.27E
69 E4 Fresnoy-le-Grand France 49.56N 3.24E
66 C1 Fresse France 47.46N 6.39E
71 H3 Fresse, Mt.de France 46.47N 5.57E
69 B3 Fressenneville France 50.04N 1.35E
56 O3 Fressingfield Suffolk Eng 52.21N 1.19E
53 V16 Fresvik Norway 61.03N 6.55E
58 K1 Freswick Highland Scotland 58.35N 3.06W
70 N6 Fréteval France 47.53N 1.13E
53 W17 Fretheim Norway 60.51N 7.08E
71 H2 Fretigney-et-Velloreille France 47.29N 5.57E
70 A5 Fret,le France 48.17N 4.32W
71 G6 Frette, la France 45.23N 5.22E
77 W14 Freu, C Balearic Is 39.45N 3.27E
48 S1 Freuchen Land Greenland
58 J5 Freuchie, L Tayside Scotland 56.31N 3.51W
64 G4 Freudenberg Baden-Württemberg W Germany 49.44N 9.20E
64 D2 Freudenberg Nordrhein-Westfalen W Germany 50.54N 7.54E
64 B4 Freudenburg W Germany 49.32N 6.32E
64 E7 Freudenstadt W Germany 48.28N 8.25E
61 M7 Freux Belgium 49.58N 5.27E
69 C3 Frévent France 50.17N 2.18E
13 D5 Frew *R* N Terr Australia
12 D3 Frew *R* S Australia
13 D4 Frewena N Terr Australia 19.20S 135.10E
104 F4 Frewsburg New York 42.03N 79.11W
64 M1 Freyburg (Unstrut) E Germany 51.13N 11.46E
14 A10 Freycinet, C W Australia 34.05S 115.00E
14 A7 Freycinet Estuary *inlet* W Aust
12 J8 Freycinet Pen Tasmania
63 Q6 Freyenstein E Germany 53.18N 12.22E
69 M5 Freyming France 49.09N 6.48E
64 L5 Freystadt W Germany 49.12N 11.20E
64 Q6 Freyung W Germany 48.49N 13.34E
89 C6 Fria Guinea 10.27N 13.38W
94 B2 Fria, C Namibia 18.28S 12.01E
111 E5 Friant California 36.58N 119.44W
111 E5 Friant Dam California 36.59N 119.43W
107 F7 Friar Point Mississippi 34.22N 90.38W
26 U7 Friar's Hood Sri Lanka 7.25N 81.30E
121 D2 Frias Argentina 28.35S 65.06W
75 D2 Frías Spain 42.45N 3.18W
66 E4 Fribourg Switzerland 46.50N 7.10E
66 E5 Fribourg *canton* Switzerland
66 J1 Frick Switzerland 47.31N 8.02E
64 G8 Frickingen W Germany 47.50N 9.15E
69 D3 Fricourt France 50.00N 2.44E
110 B1 Friday Harbor Washington 48.33N 123.04W
13 F1 Friday I Queensland 10.37S 142.10E
57 M4 Fridaythorpe Humberside Eng 54.01N 0.40W
50 F4 Fridhmundarvötn *L* Iceland
64 F7 Fridingen W Germany 48.01N 8.57E
123 G8 Fridtjof Nansen, Mt Antarctica 85.20S 166.00W
15 F6 Frieda *R* Papua New Guinea
65 O7 Friedberg Austria 47.27N 16.04E
64 K7 Friedberg Bayern W Germany 48.20N 10.59E
64 F3 Friedberg Hessen W Germany 50.20N 8.45E
65 H5 Friedburg Austria 48.02N 13.15E
63 P9 Friedeburg E Germany 51.38N 11.45E
63 A2 Friedenau *dist* W Berlin W Germany
103 B5 Friedensburg Pennsylvania 40.37N 76.14W
64 H8 Friederichshafen W Germany 47.39N 9.30E
65 M4 Friedersbach Austria 48.36N 15.17E
63 T8 Friedersdorf E Germany 52.18N 13.48E
95 K3 Friedesheim S Africa 27.56S 26.43E
64 H2 Friedewald W Germany 50.53N 9.51E
63 J8 Friedewalde W Germany 52.22N 8.51E
63 T5 Friedland E Germany 53.41N 13.34E
63 L10 Friedland W Germany 51.25N 9.55E
64 K2 Friedrichroda E Germany 50.51N 10.34E
64 F3 Friedrichsdorf W Germany 50.15N 8.39E
94 C3 Friedrichsfelde Namibia 21.59S 15.59E
63 T8 Friedrichshagen E Germany 52.27N 13.39E
63 C1 Friedrichshain *dist* E Berlin
63 J4 Friedrichskoog W Germany 54.01N 8.54E
63 P5 Friedrichsruhe E Germany 53.32N 11.45E
63 K4 Friedrichstadt W Germany 54.23N 9.06E
63 T6 Friedrichswalde E Germany 53.02N 13.43E
64 K2 Friedrichswerth E Germany 51.00N 10.34E
64 G2 Frielendorf W Germany 50.58N 9.20E
109 K3 Friend Kansas 38.14N 100.56W
108 N9 Friend Nebraska 40.40N 97.18W
104 Q3 Friendship Maine 43.59N 69.21W
104 G4 Friendship New York 42.13N 78.09W
104 B8 Friendship Ohio 38.43N 83.06W
117 B2 Friendship Surinam 5.50N 56.16W
106 E6 Friendship Wisconsin 43.58N 89.48W
103 A8 Friendship *airport* Maryland 39.12N 76.39W
116 K1 Friendship *mt* Jamaica, W I 18.18N 77.10W
104 E3 Friendship Internat. Airport Maryland 39.11N 76.38W
104 F7 Friendsville Maryland 39.40N 79.25W
103 B3 Friendsville Pennsylvania 41.54N 76.02W
52 E7 Frierfjord *inlet* Norway
55 F2 Friern Barnet London Eng 51.37N 0.09W
104 E10 Fries Virginia 36.43N 81.00W
65 K8 Friesach Austria 46.57N 14.25E
63 R7 Friesack E Germany 52.45N 12.35E
60 N6 Friesche Gat *channel* Netherlands
60 M6 Friesche Wad *flats* Netherlands
64 J3 Friesenhausen W Germany 50.10N 10.30E
64 D7 Friesenheim W Germany 48.23N 7.53E
64 J8 Friesenhofen W Germany 47.45N 10.05E
60 L7 Friesland *prov* Netherlands
63 G6 Friesoythe W Germany 53.02N 7.52E
66 E1 Friessen France 47.35N 7.10E
26 R12 Frigate I Seychelles, Ind Oc 4.35S 55.56E
80 M6 Frigento Italy 41.01N 15.06E
54 M3 Frigg *oil field* North Sea 59.56N 2.00E
77 J7 Frigiliana Spain 36.48N 3.54W
79 J6 Frignano *reg* Italy
69 H6 Frignicourt France 48.42N 4.36E
89 C7 Friguiagbe Guinea 9.58N 12.57W
53 X14 Friisbua Norway 62.07N 7.50E
115 F10 Frijoles Panama Canal Zone 9.11N 79.48W
56 O4 Frinton Essex Eng 51.50N 1.14E
115 H6 Frío Mexico 23.40N 103.33W
112 J7 Frio *R* Texas
118 G8 Frio, C Brazil 22.59S 42.00W
58 L5 Friockheim Tayside Scotland 56.38N 2.40W
76 D2 Friol Spain 43.02N 7.47W
64 F6 Friolzheim W Germany 48.50N 8.50E
112 E1 Friona Texas 34.38N 102.44W
76 D9 Fripeiro *R* Portugal
80 K4 Frisa Italy 42.16N 14.22E
58 D5 Frisa, L Mull, Strathclyde Scotland 56.34N 6.05W
61 P8 Frisange Luxembourg 49.31N 6.12E
112 L2 Frisco Texas 33.09N 96.50W
107 J10 Frisco City Alabama 31.26N 87.26W
111 L3 Frisco, Mt Utah 38.33N 113.16W
112 C8 Fritch Texas 35.39N 101.36W
65 E7 Fritzens Austria 47.19N 11.35E
64 G1 Fritzlar W Germany 51.08N 9.16E
79 M2 Friuli *reg* Italy
69 B3 Friville-Escarbotin France 50.06N 1.33E
40 L9 Friza, Proliv *str* Kuril Is U.S.S.R.
52 E3 Froan Norway 64.00N 9.10E
52 D3 Froan *islds* Norway
100 P9 Frobisher Saskatchewan 49.13N 102.25W
97 N5 Frobisher B N W Terr
97 N5 Frobisher Bay N W Terr 63.45N 68.30W
101 T7 Frobisher L Saskatchewan
53 E6 Frobjerg Bavnehøj *mt* Denmark 55.22N 10.08E
50 B5 Frodha Iceland 64.53N 23.36W
50 F5 Frodha *R* Iceland
79 H2 Frodolfo *R* Italy
57 H6 Frodsham Cheshire Eng 53.18N 2.44W
71 H6 Froges France 45.16N 5.56E
100 G5 Frog L Alberta
52 E3 Frohavet *inlet* Norway
64 O1 Frohburg E Germany 51.03N 12.34E
66 L4 Frohnalpstock *mt* Switzerland 46.58N 8.39E
65 M7 Frohnleiten Austria 47.17N 15.20E
63 P8 Frohse E Germany 52.02N 11.43E
108 F1 Froid Montana 48.21N 104.30W
61 H6 Froid-Chapelle Belgium 50.09N 4.20E
61 L6 Froidfontaine Belgium 50.03N 5.00E
61 D4 Froidmont Belgium 50.35N 3.20E
118 F5 Fróis Brazil 16.30S 45.58W
69 C4 Froissy France 49.34N 2.13E
64 B2 Froitzheim W Germany 50.43N 6.35E
53 X20 Frolandsheiene *moor* Norway 59.29N 7.38E
45 P7 Frolovo U.S.S.R. 49.45N 43.40E
47 G5 Frolovskaya U.S.S.R. 61.15N 53.25E
47 K5 Froly U.S.S.R. 60.50N 69.35E
110 R4 Fromberg Montana 45.24N 108.55W
62 M1 Frombork Poland 54.21N 19.40E
116 H1 Frome Jamaica, W I 18.17N 78.09W
13 G3 Frome Queensland 15.52S 143.46E
56 G5 Frome Somerset Eng 51.14N 2.20W
12 E3 Frome *R* S Australia
12 E4 Frome Downs S Australia 31.14S 139.49E
12 E4 Frome, L S Australia
69 D2 Fromelles France 50.37N 2.52E
72 G3 Fromental France 46.10N 1.24E
70 K4 Fromentel France 48.43N 0.15W
69 F6 Fromentières France 48.54N 3.43E
70 F8 Fromentine France 46.53N 2.09W
56 G3 Fromes Hill Hereford & Worcs Eng 52.07N 2.28W
76 L4 Fromista Spain 42.16N 4.25W
63 G10 Fröndenberg W Germany 51.28N 7.46E
64 F2 Fronhausen W Germany 50.42N 8.43E
53 W16 Frønningen, indre Norway 61.07N 7.10E
53 W16 Frønningen, ytre Norway 61.06N 7.05E
72 D6 Fronsac Gironde France 44.55N 0.17W
72 F10 Fronsac Haute-Garonne France 42.57N 0.39E
33 C10 Front B S Yemen 12.47N 45.03E
91 E7 Fronteira Angola 6.36S 16.40E
76 D10 Fronteira Portugal 39.03N 7.39W
117 G8 Fronteiras Brazil 7.02S 40.32W
72 C3 Frontenay-Rohan-Rohan France 46.15N 0.33W
64 O6 Frontenhausen W Germany 48.32N 12.33E
96 P12 Frontera Hierro Canary Is 27.46N 18.01W
115 N8 Frontera Mexico 18.32N 92.39W
75 F7 Frontera, La Spain 40.24N 2.13W
115 N8 Frontera, Pta Mexico 18.37N 92.38W
115 E2 Fronteras Mexico 30.51N 109.33W
100 J9 Frontier Saskatchewan 49.12N 108.34W
110 P8 Frontier Wyoming 41.50N 110.34W
71 D10 Frontignan France 43.27N 3.45E
119 C4 Frontino Colombia 6.46N 76.10W
72 G8 Fronton France 43.51N 1.23E
105 J8 Frontón de la Brea *pt* Puerto Rico 17.37N 66.54W
109 E1 Front Ra Colorado
104 G8 Front Royal Virginia 38.56N 78.13W
61 M5 Fronville Belgium 50.18N 5.25E
53 F6 Frørup Denmark 55.15N 10.43E
63 O9 Frose E Germany 51.48N 11.23E
80 D2 Frosini Italy 43.12N 11.09E
80 H5 Frosinone Italy 41.38N 13.22E
80 H5 Frosinone *prov* Italy
53 B3 Frøslev Denmark 56.49N 8.44E
80 K5 Frosolone Italy 41.36N 14.27E
72 A1 Frossay France 47.16N 1.55W
112 L3 Frost Texas 32.03N 96.48W
52 F3 Frosta Norway 63.35N 10.46E
104 G7 Frostburg Maryland 39.39N 78.56W
57 K3 Frosterley Durham Eng 54.44N 1.57W
105 F10 Frostproof Florida 27.44N 81.33W
53 B2 Frøstrup Denmark 57.05N 8.59E
64 K2 Fröttstädt E Germany 50.56N 10.35E
69 L6 Frouard France 48.46N 6.08E
100 O9 Froude Saskatchewan 49.40N 103.15W
84 B3 Froúsa *mt* Greece 39.19N 21.22E
84 D6 Frousina Greece 37.43N 22.25E
76 C1 Frouxeira, Pta *pt* Spain 43.37N 8.11W
52 J7 Frövi Sweden 59.28N 15.24E
53 R15 Frøya *isld* Sogn og Fjordane Norway 61.48N 4.51E
52 D3 Frøya *isld* Sör-Tröndelag Norway 63.45N 8.45E
52 C3 Fröyabanken Norwegian Sea 63.50N 7.25E
61 D4 Froyennes Belgium 50.37N 3.22E
53 R15 Frøysjøen *inlet* Norway 61.45N 5.00E
53 V16 Frudalsbreen *glacier* Norway 61.52N 6.48E
69 C2 Fruges France 50.31N 2.08E
57 G2 Fruid Res Borders Scotland 55.27N 3.27W
109 B2 Fruita Colorado 39.08N 108.44W
107 H10 Fruitdale Alabama 31.20N 88.24W
108 G5 Fruitdale S Dakota 44.40N 103.42W
112 O9 Fruitdale Texas 32.43N 96.46W
121 A8 Fruitillar Chile 41.12S 73.03W
110 J5 Fruitland Idaho 44.00N 116.55W
109 B5 Fruitland New Mexico 36.43N 108.24W
110 P9 Fruitland Utah 40.14N 110.51W
11 D12 Fruitlands New Zealand 45.21S 169.21E
110 J5 Fruitvale Idaho 44.49N 116.26W
90 B9 Frukama Nigeria 5.25N 5.50E
76 L6 Frumales Spain 41.23N 4.13W
82 K3 Frumuşica Romania 47.30N 26.56E
43 K6 Frunze Kirgiziya U.S.S.R. 40.07N 71.44E
43 L5 Frunze Kirgiziya U.S.S.R. 42.53N 74.46E
44 D8 Frunze Ukraine U.S.S.R. 46.17N 34.51E
46 C7 Frunze *dist* Moscow U.S.S.R.
41 F1 Frunze, Mys *C* U.S.S.R. 80.20N 91.31E
45 F8 Frunzenskiy Ukraine U.S.S.R. 48.33N 34.56E
43 N8 Frunzenskoye Kirgiziya U.S.S.R. 40.09N 71.44E
46 G6 Frunzovka Ukraine U.S.S.R. 47.19N 29.44E
82 F5 Fruška Gora *mts* Yugoslavia
118 E7 Frutal Brazil 20.02S 48.55W
66 G5 Frutigen Switzerland 46.36N 7.39E
111 B2 Fruto California 39.36N 122.27W
45 K1 Fryanovo U.S.S.R. 56.08N 38.28E
108 G3 Fryburg N Dakota 46.54N 103.20W
82 E1 Frýdek Místek Czechoslovakia 49.42N 18.20E
62 J5 Frýdlant Severomoravský Czech 50.56N 15.05E
104 P2 Fryeburg Maine 44.02N 70.59W
52 G6 Fryksände Sweden 60.09N 13.03E
65 K4 Frymburk Czechoslovakia 48.40N 14.11E
65 O4 Fryšava Czechoslovakia 48.53N 16.21E
F.T.A.I *see* French Territory of the Afars and the Issas *see* Djibouti
66 R4 Ftan Switzerland 46.48N 10.14E
83 E5 Ftéri, mt Greece 39.10N 21.31E
84 D4 Fthiótis *prov* Greece
9 S10 Fua'amotu Tonga, Pacific Oc 21.16S 175.08W
9 R12 Fuamotu *islet* Tonga, Pacific Oc 18.47S 174.00W
23 H5 Fu'an Fujian China 27.06N 119.36E
66 C3 Fuans France 47.08N 6.35E
23 C3 Fubian Sichuan China 31.18N 102.27E
91 C6 Fubo Chimbuande Angola 5.36S 12.32E
79 J7 Fucecchio Italy 43.44N 10.48E
22 K8 Fucheng Hebei China 37.56N 116.10E
23 F1 Fucheng Shanxi China 35.40N 113.09E
Fu-chien *see* Fukien
64 E2 Fuchskauten *mt* W Germany 50.40N 8.05E
20 G7 Fuchū Japan 34.35N 133.12E
20 C2 Fuchū *dist* Tōkyō Japan
23 F6 Fuchuan Guangxi China 24.50N 111.05E
23 H4 Fuchun Jiang *R* Zhejiang China
79 J2 Fucine Italy 46.19N 10.43E
20 P1 Fudai Japan 40.00N 141.54E
87 J7 Fud, El Ethiopia 7.13N 42.50E
15 B5 Fudi, Gunung *mt* Irian Jaya 3.13S 133.49E
87 F5 Fudi,Jeb *mt* Ethiopia 10.57N 36.50E
23 J5 Fuding Fujian China 27.21N 120.10E
33 G5 Fudul *tribe* Saudi Arabia
33 H4 Fudūl, Al Saudi Arabia 25.22N 49.45E
96 U8 Fuego, Montañas del Lanzarote Canary Is
19 G2 Fuego Pt Luzon Philippines 14.08N 120.34E
77 H4 Fuencaliente Spain 38.25N 4.18W
96 P10 Fuencaliente de la Palma La Palma Canary Is 28.29N 17.50W
96 P11 Fuencaliente, Pta. de *pt* La Palma Canary Is 28.27N 17.50W
75 C7 Fuencarral Spain 40.30N 3.41W
75 H4 Fuendejalón Spain 41.45N 1.29W
75 J5 Fuendetodos Spain 41.20N 0.57W
75 H6 Fuenferrada Spain 40.52N 1.01W
77 G7 Fuengirola Spain 36.32N 4.38W
75 C7 Fuenlabrada Spain 40.16N 3.49W
77 G2 Fuenlabrada de los Montes Spain 39.08N 4.55W
77 L3 Fuenllana Spain 38.46N 2.57W
75 E3 Fuenmayor Spain 42.29N 2.34W
76 L8 Fuensalida Spain 40.04N 4.13W
77 M2 Fuensanta Spain 39.15N 2.05W
77 J5 Fuensanta de Martos Spain 37.39N 3.54W
77 M4 Fuensanta, Embalse de la *res* Spain 38.22N 2.15W
77 O3 Fuente Álamo Spain 38.42N 1.26W
77 O5 Fuente Álamo de Murcia Spain 37.44N 1.10W
77 N2 Fuentealbilla Spain 39.17N 1.34W
76 D3 Fuenteboa Spain 42.45N 7.45W
77 F5 Fuente Carreteros Spain 37.41N 5.09W
75 C4 Fuentecén Spain 41.38N 3.52W
77 D4 Fuente de Cantos Spain 38.15N 6.18W
77 E4 Fuente del Arco Spain 38.10N 5.53W
77 D3 Fuente del Maestre Spain 38.31N 6.28W
75 D8 Fuente de Pedro Naharro Spain 39.55N 3.01W
77 G6 Fuente de Piedra Spain 37.08N 4.44W
77 G6 Fuente de Piedra, L de Spain 37.06N 4.45W
76 G7 Fuente de San Esteban, La Spain 40.48N 6.15W
77 J2 Fuente el Fresno Spain 39.14N 3.46W
75 D6 Fuente el Saz del Jarama Spain 40.38N 3.30W
76 K6 Fuente el Sol Spain 41.10N 4.56W
76 H4 Fuente Encalada Spain 42.07N 6.00W
77 Q3 Fuente Encarroz Spain 38.55N 0.10W
76 F8 Fuenteguinaldo Spain 40.26N 6.41W
77 C5 Fuenteheridos Spain 37.54N 6.39W
77 P3 Fuente la Higuera Spain 38.48N 0.53W
77 F4 Fuente la Lancha Spain 38.26N 5.03W
76 J6 Fuentelapeña Spain 41.15N 5.23W
75 C4 Fuentelcésped Spain 41.35N 3.39W
75 H8 Fuentelespino de Moya Spain 39.55N 1.29W
75 F5 Fuentelmonje Spain 41.25N 2.11W
75 G5 Fuentelsaz Spain 41.04N 1.50W
76 L7 Fuentemilanos Spain 40.52N 4.14W
75 D7 Fuentenovilla Spain 40.21N 3.05W
77 F4 Fuente-Obejuna Spain 38.15N 5.25W
77 F5 Fuente Palmera Spain 37.43N 5.06W
76 L6 Fuentepelayo Spain 41.13N 4.10W
75 E4 Fuentepinilla Spain 41.33N 2.46W
75 G1 Fuenterrabía Spain 43.22N 1.48W
75 C5 Fuenterrebollo Spain 41.19N 3.57W
75 H8 Fuenterrobles Spain 39.35N 1.22W
75 F8 Fuentes Spain 39.57N 2.02W
76 J6 Fuentesauco Spain 41.14N 5.30W
77 F6 Fuentes de Andalucía Spain 37.28N 5.20W
75 G5 Fuentes de Jiloca Spain 41.14N 1.32W
77 C4 Fuentes de León Spain 38.05N 6.32W
76 K4 Fuentes de Nava Spain 42.05N 4.48W
76 F7 Fuentes de Oñoro Spain 40.35N 6.49W
76 L4 Fuentes de Valdepero Spain 42.04N 4.30W
75 L6 Fuentespalda Spain 40.48N 0.03E
77 H5 Fuente Tójar Spain 37.31N 4.09W
75 C5 Fuentidueña Spain 41.26N 3.59W
75 D7 Fuentidueña de Tajo Spain 40.07N 3.10W
119 C3 Fuerte *isld* Colombia 9.24N 76.13W
121 K9 Fuerte Bulnes Chile 53.37S 70.58W
77 J5 Fuerte del Rey Spain 37.53N 3.53W
75 F7 Fuerte-Escusa Spain 40.29N 2.11W
118 B7 Fuerte Olimpo Paraguay 21.02S 57.51W
96 S10 Fuerteventura *isld* Canary Is 28.25N 14.00W
22 G9 Fufeng Shaanxi China 34.55N 108.06E
23 D1 Fufeng Shaanxi China 34.20N 107.55E
19 K2 Fuga *isld* Philippines 18.54N 121.22E
65 E7 Fügen Austria 47.21N 11.51E
71 K8 Fugeret, le France 44.00N 6.40E
50 B7 Fuglasker *rock* Iceland 63.42N 23.00W
53 M9 Fuglebjærge Faeroes 62.10N 7.15W
53 H6 Fuglebjerg Denmark 55.18N 11.33E
53 N9 Fuglefjord Faeroes 62.14N 6.49W
53 T16 Fuglesetfjord *inlet* Norway 61.05N 5.50E
53 O9 Fuglø *isld* Faeroes 62.21N 6.15W
Fugloy *see* Fuglø
51 H1 Fugløya *isld* Norway 70.15N 20.10E
53 F7 Fuglsbølle Denmark 54.54N 10.47E
23 A5 Fugong Yunnan China 27.00N 98.52E
23 G1 Fugou Henan China 34.09N 114.21E
22 J7 Fugu Shaanxi China 39.09N 111.12E
Fuguo *see* Zhanhua
24 F2 Fuhai Xinjiang Uygur Zizhiqu China 47.04N 87.20E
24 F2 Fuhai Linchang Xinjiang Uygur Zizhiqu China 47.42N 88.48E
Fuhaimi *see* Fuḩaymī
34 K4 Fuḩaymī Iraq 34.18N 42.10E
35 G5 Fuheis Jordan 32.01N 35.46E
63 Q9 Fuhne *R* E Germany
63 L7 Fuhrberg W Germany 52.33N 9.51E
72 B1 Fuilet, le France 47.16N 1.08W
33 M4 Fujairah U.A.E. 25.10N 56.20E
20 M6 Fuji Japan 35.10N 138.37E
20 M6 Fuji *R* Japan
23 H5 Fujian *prov* China
23 D3 Fu Jiang *R* Sichuan China
22 G6 Fujiawan Nei Monggol Zizhiqu China 40.02N 106.44E
20 M7 Fujieda Japan 34.54N 138.15E
20 M6 Fuji Hakone Izu Nat. Park Japan
20 N7 Fuji Hakone Izu Nat. Park Japan
21 F4 Fujin Heilongjiang China 47.15N 131.59E
20 M6 Fujinomiye Japan 35.16N 138.33E
20 M5 Fujioka Japan 36.15N 139.00E
20 O1 Fujisaki Japan 40.38N 140.29E
20 M6 Fuji-san *vol* Japan 35.23N 138.42E
20 B4 Fujisawa Japan 35.22N 139.29E
Fujiyama *see* Fuji San *vol*
20 M6 Fuji-Yoshida Japan 35.30N 138.48E
85 J4 Fûka Egypt 31.04N 27.57E
34 P6 Fuka Iraq 32.01N 47.40E
90 C7 Fuka Nigeria 9.37N 6.57E
20 L1 Fukagawa Japan 43.44N 142.03E
24 F3 Fukang Xinjiang Uygur Zizhiqu China 44.10N 87.56E
20 N1 Fukaura Japan 40.38N 139.57E
9 S10 Fukave *islet* Tonga, Pacific Oc 21.06S 175.02W
20 C5 Fukaya Kanagawa Japan
21 B1 Fukeshan Heilongjiang China 52.39N 121.57E
Fukien *prov* China *see* Fujian
20 J6 Fukuchiyama Japan 35.19N 135.08E
20 C5 Fukuda Kanagawa Japan
20 B9 Fukue Japan 32.41N 128.52E
20 B9 Fukue-jima *isld* Japan 32.40N 128.50E
20 K5 Fukui Japan 36.04N 136.12E
20 K6 Fukui *prefect* Japan
20 D8 Fukuma Japan 33.47N 130.27E
20 K5 Fukuno Japan 36.38N 136.47E

20 P1 Fukuoka Honshu Japan 40.16N 141.20E
20 D8 Fukuoka Kyūshū Japan 33.39N 130.21E
20 D8 Fukuoka *prefect* Japan
20 N2 Fukura Yamagata Japan 39.04N 139.52E
20 L7 Fukuroi Japan 34.44N 137.53E
20 K3 Fukushima Hokkaido Japan 41.31N 140.16E
20 O4 Fukushima Honshu Japan 37.44N 140.28E
20 L6 Fukushima Nagano Japan 35.52N 137.40E
20 N4 Fukushima *prefect* Japan
20 J6 Fukusumi Japan 35.03N 135.19E
20 G7 Fukuyama Honshu Japan 34.29N 133.21E
20 D10 Fukuyama Kyūshū Japan 31.42N 130.46E
20 H7 Fukuzaki Japan 34.58N 134.43E
89 B6 Fulacunda Guinea-Bissau 11.44N 15.03W
32 E2 Fūlād Maḩalleh Iran 36.05N 53.50E
87 B5 Fula, El Sudan 11.44N 28.20E
50 F5 Fúlakvísl *R* Iceland
9 U3 Fulango *isld* Fiji 19.10S 178.39W
33 N5 Fulayj Oman 22.23N 59.25E
34 O10 Fulayj al Janūbī *watercourse* Saudi Arabia
34 N10 Fulayj ash Shimālī *watercourse* Saudi Arabia
Fulaykā *isld see* Faylakah
87 C7 Ful Bura Sudan 7.50N 31.59E
108 P6 Fulda Minnesota 43.52N 95.34W
64 H2 Fulda W Germany 50.33N 9.41E
63 L10 Fulda *R* W Germany
64 H1 Fulda *R* W Germany
64 G1 Fuldabrück W Germany 51.12N 9.28E
57 L5 Fulford N Yorks Eng 53.56N 1.04W
86 J7 Fûl, Gebel *hill* Egypt 29.21N 32.59E
55 E4 Fulham London Eng 51.29N 0.13W
Fulin *see* Hanyuan
23 H5 Fuling Fujian China 27.52N 118.37E
23 D4 Fuling Sichuan China 29.44N 107.22E
95 G9 Fullarton S Africa 33.12S 23.50E
116 N2 Fullarton Trinidad & Tobago 10.05N 61.54W
13 F5 Fullarton *R* Queensland
111 G8 Fullerton California 33.53N 117.55W
104 C8 Fullerton Kentucky 38.43N 82.59W
107 D10 Fullerton Louisiana 31.01N 92.59W
103 A8 Fullerton Maryland 39.23N 76.30W
108 M8 Fullerton Nebraska 41.20N 98.00W
66 G1 Füllinsdorf Switzerland 47.30N 7.44E
66 E7 Fully Switzerland 46.08N 7.08E
21 C5 Fulongquan Jilin China 44.24N 124.35E
62 L9 Fülöpszállás Hungary 46.50N 19.15E
65 D7 Fulpmes Austria 47.09N 11.21E
107 J10 Fulton Alabama 31.48N 87.42W
121 F6 Fulton Argentina 37.25S 58.45W
107 C8 Fulton Arkansas 33.38N 93.49W
106 D8 Fulton Illinois 41.52N 90.08W
106 H9 Fulton Indiana 40.58N 86.16W
109 Q3 Fulton Kansas 38.01N 94.43W
107 H5 Fulton Kentucky 36.31N 88.52W
107 H7 Fulton Mississippi 34.17N 88.25W
107 E3 Fulton Missouri 38.50N 91.57W
104 J3 Fulton New York 43.20N 76.26W
104 C6 Fulton Ohio 40.26N 82.50W
108 N6 Fulton S Dakota 43.45N 97.48W
104 L4 Fultonham New York 42.34N 74.26W
104 L4 Fultonville New York 42.56N 74.24W
87 C6 Ful Turuk Sudan 8.38N 31.57E
21 C4 Fulu Heilongjiang China 47.41N 124.40E
52 G5 Fuluälven *R* Sweden
52 G5 Fulufjället *mt* Sweden 61.33N 12.40E
52 G5 Fulunäs Sweden 61.19N 13.05E
61 L4 Fumal Belgium 50.35N 5.11E
94 M5 Fumane Mozambique 24.29S 34.00E
93 J1 Fuman Guba Ethiopia 4.25N 37.57E
69 H4 Fumay France 49.59N 4.42E
92 J12 Fumba Zanzibar 6.19S 39.17E
92 J5 Fumba *isld* Tanzania 6.30S 39.02E
72 F6 Fumel France 44.30N 0.58E
88 G8 Fum El Uad Morocco 27.12N 13.22W
Fumen *see* Fowman
23 C6 Fumin Yunnan China 25.11N 102.32E
79 J2 Fumo, Monte Italy 46.08N 10.33E
20 D2 Funabashi Japan 35.42N 139.59E
9 D8 Funafuti *atoll* Tuvalu, Pacific Oc 8.30S 179.12E
20 E10 Funahiki Japan 31.51N 131.23E
20 B5 Funako Kanagawa Japan
Funan *see* Fusui
Funan *see* Fushun (Funan)
23 G2 Funan Anhui China 32.41N 115.34E
87 F8 Funan Guba Ethiopia 4.22N 37.53E
20 H1 Funao Chiba Japan
52 G4 Funäsdalen Sweden 62.34N 12.35E
33 N9 Funayţis, Al Kuwait 29.14N 48.06E
88 E5 Funchal Madeira Is 32.40N 16.55W
96 P7 Funchal Madeira Is 32.38N 16.53W
92 E9 Funchal Mozambique 15.59S 30.33E
76 C13 Funcheira Portugal 37.44N 8.21W
91 C8 Funda Angola 8.51S 13.34E
119 D2 Fundación Colombia 10.31N 74.09W
76 C9 Fundada Portugal 39.43N 8.08W
118 H6 Fundão Brazil 19.58S 40.24W
76 D8 Fundão Portugal 40.08N 7.30W
53 C4 Funder Denmark 56.09N 9.29E
37 G2 Fundıçık Turkey 40.22N 29.21E
115 E4 Fundición Mexico 27.18N 109.43W
53 N9 Funding Faeroes 62.18N 6.57W
53 U20 Fundingsland Norway 59.17N 6.28E
79 L1 Fundres Italy 46.53N 11.43E
82 K6 Fundulea Romania 44.27N 26.33E
35 D5 Funduq, El Jordan 32.11N 35.08E
65 C7 Fundusfeiler *mt* Austria 47.07N 10.52E
98 F9 Fundy, Bay of Nova Scotia/New Brunswick
98 G8 Fundy Nat. Pk New Brunswick
Fünen *see* Fyn
111 H5 Funeral Pk *mt* California 36.07N 116.38W
119 C7 Funes Colombia 0.59N 77.27W
79 L1 Funes, Val di *V* Italy
86 N9 Fungur, El *B* Saudi Arabia
94 N4 Funhalouro Mozambique 23.03S 34.25E
22 L7 Funing Hebei China 39.52N 119.15E
23 H2 Funing Jiangsu China 33.49N 119.51E
23 D7 Funing Yunnan China 23.35N 105.37E
23 F2 Funiu Shan *mts* Henan China
108 L9 Funk Nebraska 40.28N 99.15W
98 T4 Funk I Newfoundland 49.46N 53.13W
108 Q2 Funkley Minnesota 47.45N 94.25W
13 J5 Funnel *R* Queensland
59 F4 Funshinagh L Roscommon Irish Rep 53.31N 8.05W
89 J6 Funsi Ghana 10.21N 1.54W
101 F6 Funter Alaska 58.17N 134.53W
90 C6 Funtua Nigeria 11.34N 7.17E
58 R8 Funzie Shetland Scotland 60.35N 0.48W
93 L10 Funzi I Kenya 4.35S 39.26E
66 M5 Fuorns Switzerland 46.38N 8.52E
22 K7 Fuping Hebei China 38.54N 114.10E
23 E1 Fuping Shaanxi China 34.48N 109.10E
85 D6 Fuqahā', Al Libya 27.51N 16.21E
23 H6 Fuqing Fujian China 25.43N 119.21E
105 J2 Fuquay Springs N Carolina 35.35N 78.50W
119 D5 Fúquené, L. de Colombia 5.31N 73.45W
53 C3 Fur Denmark 56.49N 9.02E
53 C3 Fur *isld* Denmark 56.49N 9.02E
90 L6 Fur *tribe* Sudan
76 B7 Furadouro Portugal 40.52N 8.41W
88 P10 Furana Algeria 23.48N 3.11E
92 F9 Furancungo Mozambique 14.51S 33.39E
20 M1 Furano Japan 43.23N 142.24E
21 E3 Furao Heilongjiang China 49.15N 129.39E
Furāt, Al *R see* Euphrates *R*
80 L4 Furci Italy 42.00N 14.36E
82 J7 Furculeşti Romania 43.51N 25.07E
35 C3 Fureidis Israel 32.36N 34.57E
35 G10 Fureifira Sta Jordan 30.54N 35.59E
20 M2 Furenai Japan 42.44N 142.18E
53 J5 Furesø *L* Denmark 55.48N 12.26E
64 G5 Fürfeld Baden-Württemberg W Germany 49.12N 9.04E
64 D4 Fürfeld Rheinland-Pfalz W Germany 49.47N 7.55E
61 K6 Furfooz Belgium 50.13N 4.57E
32 F6 Fūrg Iran 28.19N 55.10E
Furglus *see* Furqlus
32 G7 Fūrgun, Kūh-e *mt* Iran 27.55N 56.23E
66 K6 Furka Pass Italy/Switz 46.18N 8.27E
66 K5 Furka Pass Switzerland 46.34N 8.25E
105 F5 Furman S Carolina 32.38N 81.14W
46 M2 Furmanov U.S.S.R. 57.10N 41.09E
43 L5 Furmanovka Kazakhstan U.S.S.R. 44.15N 72.53E
43 A3 Furmanovo Kazakhstan U.S.S.R. 49.43N 49.28E
40 F9 Furmanovo U.S.S.R. 44.02N 134.40E
66 P4 Furna Switzerland 46.57N 9.42E
58 F6 Furnace Strathclyde Scotland 56.09N 5.12W
111 H5 Furnace Creek California 36.28N 116.52W
59 C4 Furnace L Mayo Irish Rep 53.55N 9.35W
96 U1 Furnas Azores 37.32N 25.19W
118 J10 Furnas Brazil 22.58S 43.17W
77 T11 Furnas *mt* Balearic Is 39.03N 1.32E
118 F7 Furnas Dam Brazil 20.40S 46.22W
96 U1 Furnas, L. das Azores 37.30N 25.20W
61 J5 Furnaux Belgium 50.18N 4.42E
12 J8 Furneaux Grp *islds* Tasmania
12 F6 Furner S Australia 37.20S 140.19E
Furnes *see* Veurne
100 H5 Furness Saskatchewan 53.08N 109.58W
57 G4 Furness *dist* Cumbria Eng
86 G5 Furn, Wâdi el *watercourse* Egypt
23 D4 Furong Jiang *R* Sichuan China
23 D4 Furong Jiang *R* Sichuan China
23 G5 Furong Shan *mt* Jiangxi China
34 E4 Furqlus Syria 34.38N 37.08E
93 K2 Furroli *mt* Ethiopia 3.42N 38.02E
63 G7 Fürstenau W Germany 52.32N 7.41E
64 F8 Fürstenberg Baden-Württemberg W Germany 47.54N 8.33E
63 S6 Fürstenberg E Germany 53.11N 13.10E
64 F1 Fürstenberg Hessen W Germany 51.10N 8.50E
63 J9 Fürstenberg Nordrhein-Westfalen W Germany 51.31N 8.45E
65 O7 Fürstenfeld Austria 47.03N 16.05E
64 L7 Fürstenfeldbruck W Germany 48.10N 11.15E
63 U8 Fürstenwalde E Germany 52.22N 14.04E
63 T6 Fürstenwerder E Germany 53.24N 13.36E
64 P6 Fürstenzell W Germany 48.31N 13.20E
81 B4 Furtei Sardinia 39.34N 8.57E
64 L5 Fürth Bayern W Germany 49.28N 11.00E
64 F4 Fürth Hessen W Germany 49.40N 8.48E
64 O5 Furth im Wald W Germany 49.19N 12.51E
64 E7 Furtwangen W Germany 48.03N 8.14E
20 K1 Furubira Japan 43.17N 140.39E
50 C2 Furufjördhur Iceland 66.16N 22.15W
50 C2 Furufjördhur *B* Iceland
20 L5 Furukawa Japan 36.16N 137.11E
20 O3 Furukawa Japan 38.34N 140.56E
33 F4 Furūthi, Al Saudi Arabia 25.41N 45.06E
97 L4 Fury and Hecla Str N W Terr
53 T18 Fusa Norway 60.12N 5.39E
53 T18 Fusafjord *inlet* Norway 60.09N 5.33E
119 D5 Fusagasugá Colombia 4.22N 74.21W
80 K7 Fusaro,Lago del Italy 40.48N 14.03E
81 M5 Fuscaldo Italy 39.25N 16.02E
65 G7 Fusch Austria 47.14N 12.49E
65 H6 Fuschl Austria 47.48N 13.18E
65 H6 Fuschlsee *L* Austria 47.49N 13.18E
63 M8 Fuse *R* W Germany
25 K3 Fushan Guangdong China 19.50N 109.55E
22 M8 Fushan Shandong China 37.29N 121.14E
23 F1 Fushan Shanxi China 36.01N 111.52E
58 K7 Fushiebridge Lothian Scotland 55.50N 3.01W
Fu-shih *see* Yan'an
20 L5 Fushiki Japan 36.49N 137.02E
20 L1 Fushiko-Uryū Japan 43.40N 141.52E
20 J7 Fushimi Japan 34.57N 135.46E
21 C7 Fushun Liaoning China 41.51N 123.53E
21 C7 Fushun Liaoning China 41.50N 123.54E
23 C4 Fushun Sichuan China 29.12N 104.52E
21 C7 Fushun (Funan) Liaoning China 41.44N 123.55E
122 C2 Fusi W Samoa, Pacific Oc 13.52S 171.36W
79 L6 Fusignano Italy 44.28N 11.58E
100 H7 Fusilier Saskatchewan 51.50N 109.44W
79 M4 Fusina Italy 45.25N 12.15E
79 P2 Fusine in Valromana Italy 46.30N 13.39E
66 L6 Fusio Switzerland 46.27N 8.40E
21 D6 Fusong Jilin China 42.15N 127.20E
40 N6 Fuss *vol* Kuril Is U.S.S.R. 50.16N 155.15E
20 A2 Fussa Tōkyō Japan
41 F3 Fussa, Mys *C* U.S.S.R. 76.10N 93.30E
Fussa, Pik *see* Fuss *vol*
65 C6 Füssen W Germany 47.35N 10.43E
69 M2 Füssenich W Germany 50.43N 6.37E
53 D4 Fussing Sø *L* Denmark 56.28N 9.53E
75 H3 Fustiñana Spain 42.02N 1.29W
23 D7 Fusui Guangxi China 22.40N 107.56E
20 L7 Futagawa Japan 34.42N 137.27E
20 E8 Futago-san *mt* Japan 33.34N 131.35E
121 B9 Futalaufquén, L Argentina
121 B9 Futaleufú Chile 43.14S 71.54W
20 C4 Futamatagawa Kanagawa Japan
20 D7 Futaoi-jima *isld* Japan 34.08N 130.46E
79 K6 Futa, Passo di *pass* Italy 44.06N 11.17E
20 O1 Futatsui Japan 40.12N 140.16E
20 N9 Futatsu-ne *rocks* Iwo Jima Pacific Oc 24.46N 141.18E
20 P9 Futemma Okinawa Japan 26.15N 127.44E
91 C6 Futila Angola 5.25S 12.14E
66 R4 Futschöl Pass Switz/Austria 46.53N 10.13E
10 R4 Futuna *isld* Îles de Horn Pacific Oc 14.25S 178.20W
9 D12 Futuna *isld* New Hebrides 19.32S 170.12E
23 H5 Futun Xi *R* Fujian China
71 H10 Fuveau France 43.27N 5.34E
86 E3 Fuwa Egypt 31.12N 30.33E
33 G10 Fuwad S Yemen 13.36N 46.42E
32 B6 Fuwaris *oil well* Saudi Arabia 28.20N 47.50E
33 J3 Fuwayrit Qatar, The Gulf 26.03N 51.20E
21 B8 Fu Xian Liaoning China 39.36N 122.00E
23 E1 Fu Xian Shaanxi China 36.02N 109.17E
23 C6 Fuxian Hu *L* Yunnan China
21 B6 Fuxin Liaoning China 42.04N 121.39E
Fuxing *see* Wangmo
21 B6 Fuxin Monggolzu Zizhixian Liaoning China 42.06N 121.46E
23 G2 Fuyang Anhui China 32.56N 115.51E
23 G7 Fuyang Guangdong China 23.43N 116.57E
22 K8 Fuyang He *R* Hebei China
23 J5 Fuying Dao *isld* Fujian China 26.32N 120.10E
23 B7 Fuyong Yunnan China 22.54N 99.50E
21 C4 Fuyu Heilongjiang China 47.46N 124.21E
21 C5 Fuyu Jilin China 45.10N 124.40E
Fu-Yüan *see* Jimsar
21 F3 Fuyuan Heilongjiang China 48.17N 134.17E
23 C6 Fuyuan Yunnan China 25.44N 104.09E
24 F2 Fuyun Xinjiang Uygur Zizhiqu China 47.15N 89.37E
62 M8 Füzesabony Hungary 47.46N 20.25E
62 N8 Füzesgyarmat Hungary 47.07N 21.10E
76 D14 Fuzeta Portugal 37.02N 7.45W
23 H5 Fuzhou Fujian China 26.09N 119.17E
23 G4 Fuzhou Jiangxi China 28.03N 116.15E
21 B8 Fuzhoucheng Liaoning China 39.45N 121.49E
56 M4 Fyfield Essex Eng 51.45N 0.16E
56 H5 Fyfield Wilts Eng 51.26N 1.47W
53 U18 Fykse Norway 60.24N 6.16E
53 U18 Fyksesund *sound* Norway
57 H5 Fylde *reg* Lancs Eng
48 R13 Fyllas Banke Greenland
53 E6 Fyn *co* Denmark
53 E6 Fyn *isld* Denmark
58 F6 Fyne, L Strathclyde Scotland
53 D7 Fynshav Denmark 54.59N 9.59E
53 F5 Fyns Hoved *C* Denmark 55.38N 10.37E
48 U3 Fynske Alper *mts* Greenland
48 U3 Fyns Sø *L* Greenland 80.30N 25.00W
53 U14 Fyrde Norway 62.04N 6.20E
53 Y20 Fyresdal Norway 59.12N 8.05E
53 Y21 Fyresdalsåna *R* Norway
53 X20 Fyresdalsheiene *moor* Norway 59.15N 7.50E
53 Y20 Fyresvatn *L* Norway
12 B6 Fyshwick *dist* Canberra Australia
58 M4 Fyvie Grampian Scotland 57.26N 2.24W
116 O2 Fyzabad Trinidad & Tobago 10.11N 61.33W
88 G8 Gaada, El *reg* Morocco
65 L7 Gaal Austria 47.18N 14.40E
87 M5 Gaan Somalia 11.13N 48.20E
60 O12 Gaanderen Netherlands 51.55N 6.21E
61 G3 Gaasbeek Belgium 50.48N 4.12E
48 T12 Gaase Fd Greenland
48 T12 Gaase Land Greenland
35 C5 Ga'ash Israel 32.14N 34.49E
Gaast *see* Rotster-Gaast
60 K7 Gaast Netherlands 53.01N 5.25E
60 L8 Gaasterland *dist* Netherlands
60 L8 Gaastmeer Netherlands 52.58N 5.33E
18 K5 Gaat *R* Sarawak Malaysia
88 P8 Gaa Taatzebar, El *reg* Algeria
88 H8 Gaat Chbabien *reg* Morocco
Ga'aton *see* Evron
87 N6 Gabàh Somalia 8.10N 50.02E
75 G8 Gabaldón Spain 39.38N 1.57W
86 E9 Gabal El Ţeir Egypt 28.14N 30.45E
Gabandi *see* Gāvbandī
47 C5 Gabanova U.S.S.R. 60.44N 32.46E
Gabar *see* Gīvar
72 E8 Gabarret France 43.59N 0.02E
98 M9 Gabarus C Breton I, Nova Scotia 45.50N 60.09W
98 M8 Gabarus B C Breton I, Nova Scotia
72 D10 Gabas France 42.53N 0.25W
72 D9 Gabas *R* France
90 D5 Gabasawa Nigeria 12.15N 9.00E
15 G8 Gabba I Torres Str, Qnsld 9.45S 142.37E
87 E6 Gabba,R Ethiopia
111 G3 Gabbs Nevada 38.53N 117.57W
111 F3 Gabbs Valley Ra Nevada
31 A8 Gabd Pakistan 25.22N 61.50E
76 C1 Gabeiras, Is Spain 43.31N 8.21W
91 D9 Gabela Angola 10.56S 14.24E
86 F8 Gabel el Nûr Egypt 28.57N 31.02E
66 G7 Gabelhorn, Ober *mt* Switz 46.03N 7.40E
65 L7 Gaberl Pass Austria 47.07N 14.55E
Gaberones *see* Gaborone
65 N8 Gabersdorf Austria 46.47N 15.37E
88 T5 Gabès Tunisia 33.52N 10.06E
88 T4 Gabès, Golfe de Tunisia
85 M9 Gabgaba Wadi *watercourse* Sudan
91 E6 Gabia Zaïre 4.37S 17.14E
77 J6 Gabia la Grande Spain 37.09N 3.40W
71 C9 Gabian France 43.31N 3.17E
79 D4 Gabiano Italy 45.09N 8.11E
111 C5 Gabilan Ra California
62 M3 Gąbin Poland 52.23N 19.41E
87 A4 Gabir Sudan 12.37N 26.42E
93 B7 Gabiro Rwanda 1.33S 30.25E
94 E4 Gabiz, Great *salt L* Namibia
11 N5 Gable End Foreland *C* New Zealand 38.32S 178.19E
101 K9 Gable Mt Br Col 53.10N 127.00W
12 J7 Gabo I Victoria 37.34S 149.25E
53 C6 Gabøl Denmark 55.16N 9.08E
91 A3 Gabon *estuary* Gabon
73 F6 Gabon *rep* Equat Africa
94 H5 Gaborone Botswana 24.45S 25.55E
121 E4 Gaboto Argentina 32.25S 60.50W
Gabredarre *see* K'ebri Dehār
41 F5 Gabrey, Vozvyshennost' *heights* U.S.S.R.
72 K7 Gabriac France 44.27N 2.48E
26 U11 Gabriel I Mauritius, Indian Oc 19.53S 57.40E
104 L2 Gabriels New York 44.26N 74.13W
120 F8 Gabriel Vera Bolivia 19.13S 65.50W
76 G8 Gabriel y Galán, Embalse *res* Spain
Gabrig *see* Gābrīk
32 H8 Gābrīk Iran 25.42N 58.27E
32 H8 Gābrīk *R* Iran
66 O2 Gäbris *mt* Switzerland 47.23N 9.26E
87 J7 Gabro Ethiopia 6.20N 43.18E
82 J8 Gabrovo Bulgaria 42.52N 25.19E
87 A9 Gabu Zaïre 3.24N 27.04E
92 D2 Gabu, Mt Zaïre 0.54S 29.34E
15 L8 Gabwina I Trobriand Is Papua New Guinea 8.23S 150.13E
79 C3 Gaby Italy 45.43N 7.53E
26 Q16 Gaby Î Kerguelen Indian Oc 49.40S 69.45E
70 L4 Gacé France 48.47N 0.18E
Gach-i-Sar *see* Gach Sār
32 D2 Gach Sār Iran 36.07N 51.21E
32 D5 Gach Sārān *oil field* Iran 30.12N 50.50E
70 F6 Gacilly, la France 47.46N 2.07W
108 L3 Gackle N Dakota 46.38N 99.10W
82 E7 Gacko Yugoslavia 43.10N 18.33E
90 C5 Gada *R* Nigeria
87 J6 Gadabursi *tribe* Ethiopia/Somalia
28 G2 Gadadhar *R* Assam/Bengal India
28 B3 Gadag Karnataka India 15.26N 75.42E
15 K9 Gadaisu Papua New Guinea 10.19S 149.45E
42 G5 Gadaley U.S.S.R. 54.24N 100.50E
90 E6 Gadam Nigeria 10.30N 11.10E
87 F2 Gadamai Sudan 17.11N 36.10E
87 E6 Gadame Ethiopia 9.00N 34.38E
18 B6 Gadang *hill* Pen Malaysia 5.30N 101.12E
29 F6 Gadarwara Madhya Prad India 22.52N 78.50E
90 E6 Gadau Nigeria 11.50N 10.05E
53 C5 Gadbjerg Denmark 55.46N 9.19E
52 H2 Gäddede Sweden 64.30N 14.15E
63 J8 Gadderbaum W Germany 52.02N 8.31E
23 B1 Gadê Qinghai China 34.07N 100.11E
63 O5 Gadebusch E Germany 53.42N 11.07E
87 B6 Gadein Sudan 8.10N 28.45E
55 B2 Gade, R Herts England
79 L1 Gadera *R* Italy
93 C2 Gaderu Sudan 3.54N 31.29E
29 B7 Gadhada Bhaunagar, Gujarat India 21.59N 71.40E
29 B6 Gadhada Kutch, Gujarat India 23.50N 70.25E
31 D8 Gadhap Pakistan 25.11N 67.10E
29 B7 Gadhia Gujarat India 21.11N 71.13E
28 B2 Gad Hinglaj Maharashtra India 16.15N 74.27E
29 A6 Gadhka Gujarat India 22.08N 69.28E
29 B7 Gadhra Gujarat India 20.53N 71.00E
35 D3 Gadish Israel 32.33N 35.14E
Gadistan *see* Gazestān
66 K5 Gadmen Switzerland 46.45N 8.21E
66 K5 Gadmen Bach *R* Switzerland
92 D11 Gado Zimbabwe 19.00S 29.51E
117 E8 Gado Bravo, Sa.do Brazil
81 C4 Gadoni Sardinia 39.55N 9.12E
77 M7 Gádor Spain 36.56N 2.29W
77 L7 Gádor, Sierra de *mts* Spain
35 F1 Gadot Israel 33.02N 35.37E
31 F8 Gadra Hyderabad Pakistan 25.40N 70.38E
31 D7 Gadra Kalat Pakistan 26.26N 66.22E
44 H8 Gadrut Azerbaydzhan U.S.S.R. 39.32N 47.00E
100 E6 Gadsby Alberta 52.20N 112.22W
107 L8 Gadsden Alabama 34.00N 86.00W
111 K9 Gadsden Arizona 32.33N 114.46W
53 J5 Gadstrup Denmark 55.34N 12.07E
28 C2 Gadwal Andhra Prad India 16.15N 77.50E
45 F6 Gadyach Ukraine U.S.S.R. 50.21N 34.00E
43 G7 Gadyn Turkmeniya U.S.S.R. 39.19N 63.25E
92 E11 Gadzema Zimbabwe 18.02S 30.16E
90 H9 Gadzi Cent Afr Rep 4.54N 16.39E
70 F5 Gaël France 48.07N 2.13W
48 V9 Gael Hamkes Bugt *B* Greenland
57 E6 Gaerwen Gwynedd Wales 53.13N 4.16W
82 J6 Găeşti Romania 44.42N 25.19E
80 J6 Gaeta Italy 41.13N 13.36E
80 H6 Gaeta, Golfo di Italy
60 G13 Gaete Netherlands 51.42N 4.42E
86 E8 Gafâdûn, El Egypt 28.49N 30.48E
76 C11 Gafanhoeira Portugal 38.45N 8.05W
Gaferiyat *see* Ilisira
17 P10 Gaferut *isld* Caroline Is Pacific Oc 9.14N 145.23E
76 D10 Gafete Portugal 39.24N 7.41W
105 F2 Gaffney S Carolina 35.03N 81.40W
88 S7 Gafgaf, El Algeria 29.31N 8.43E
19 E3 Gafi *isld* Moluccas Indon 0.10N 127.08E
65 L6 Gaflenz Austria 47.54N 14.43E
41 H3 Gafnera, Zaliv *gulf* U.S.S.R.
88 S3 Gafour Tunisia 36.19N 9.22E
86 G5 Gafra, Wâdi el *watercourse* Egypt
88 S4 Gafsa Tunisia 34.28N 8.43E
43 J6 Gafuron Tadzhikistan U.S.S.R. 40.11N 69.42E
15 A4 Gag *isld* Irian Jaya 0.25S 129.53E
85 L7 Gâga, El Egypt 24.57N 30.44E
9 B3 Gagan *islet* Marshall Is Pacific Oc 9.17N 167.33E
31 H3 Gagangir Kashmir 34.17N 75.12E
45 F1 Gagarin Smolensk U.S.S.R. 55.38N 35.00E
46 C8 Gagarin *dist* Moscow U.S.S.R.
109 B9 Gage New Mexico 32.15N 108.05W
109 L5 Gage Oklahoma 36.19N 99.46W
98 H7 Gage, C Prince Edward I 46.54N 64.15W
Gage I *see* Ghaghe I
106 E4 Gagen Wisconsin 45.52N 89.06W
90 C5 Gagere *R* Nigeria
71 G7 Gagère, Pic de la *mt* France 44.53N 5.20E
61 F4 Gages Belgium 50.37N 3.54E
98 F8 Gagetown New Brunswick 45.46N 66.09W
64 E6 Gaggenau W Germany 48.47N 8.20E
79 F4 Gaggiano Italy 45.24N 9.01E
45 R1 Gagino U.S.S.R. 55.14N 45.01E
81 J8 Gagliano Castelferrato Sicily 37.13N 14.03E
81 R13 Gagliano del Capo Italy 39.50N 18.23E
50 J3 Gagndagahnúkur *mt* Iceland 65.58N 16.04W
52 J6 Gagnef Sweden 60.35N 15.05E
50 L4 Gagnheidhi *heath* Iceland
71 E8 Gagnières France 44.18S 4.09E
89 G8 Gagnoa Ivory Coast 6.04N 5.55W
98 D2 Gagnon Quebec 51.56N 68.16W
99 P6 Gagnon, L Quebec 46.07N 75.09W
68 H3 Gagny France 48.53N 2.33E
Gago Çoutinho *see* Lumbala
92 E9 Gago Çoutinho Mozambique 14.32S 31.53E
89 H7 Gagouli Upper Volta 9.58N 3.24W
44 C4 Gagra Georgia U.S.S.R. 43.21N 40.16E
29 E5 Gagraun Rajasthan India 24.40N 76.12E
47 G5 Gagshor U.S.S.R. 60.45N 50.10E
119 D7 Gaguán, R Colombia
90 J7 Gagui Chad 9.05N 19.14E
23 C1 Gahai Gansu China 34.12N 102.16E
30 G7 Gahmar Uttar Prad India 25.30N 83.49E
65 N6 Gahns *mt* Austria 47.44N 15.54E
32 B3 Gahvāreh Iran 34.19N 46.25E
19 J9 Gaïa Sabah Malaysia 4.35N 118.45E
94 E6 Gaiab *watercourse* Namibia
90 D8 Gaiama Cameroon 6.52N 9.55E
118 B5 Gaíba, L Bolivia/Brazil
31 H8 Gaibanda Bangladesh 25.21N 89.36E
82 L4 Găiceana Romania 46.19N 27.13E
22 E8 Gaidain'goinba Qinghai China 37.16N 99.51E
84 N12 Gaidhouronísi *isld* Crete 34.53N 25.41E
112 F3 Gail Texas 32.47N 101.26W
65 G8 Gail *R* Austria
64 H6 Gaildorf W Germany 49.00N 9.46E
56 G2 Gailey Staffs Eng 52.42N 2.08W
66 M1 Gailingen W Germany 47.42N 8.45E
72 K7 Gaillac d'Aveyron France 44.22N 2.55E
72 C5 Gaillan-en-Médoc France 45.20N 0.58W
98 E1 Gaillarbois, L Quebec
115 F10 Gaillard Cut Panama Canal Zone
103 J4 Gaillard, L Connecticut 41.22N 72.47W
70 O2 Gailléfontaine France 49.40N 1.37E
Gaillimh *see* Galway
70 N3 Gaillon France 49.10N 1.19E
65 H8 Gailtaler Alpen *mts* Austria
121 D9 Gaimán Argentina 43.15S 65.30W
64 L6 Gaimersheim W Germany 48.48N 11.24E
30 E4 Gaindakanda Nepal 28.38N 81.19E
106 L7 Gaines Michigan 42.53N 83.54W
107 L5 Gainesboro Tennessee 36.20N 85.41W
107 H9 Gainesville Alabama 32.50N 88.10W
105 E8 Gainesville Florida 29.40N 82.20W
105 D3 Gainesville Georgia 34.17N 83.50W
107 D5 Gainesville Missouri 36.37N 92.28W
112 K2 Gainesville Texas 33.39N 97.08W
57 K3 Gainford Durham Eng 54.32N 1.44W
30 F5 Gainsari Uttar Prad India 27.31N 82.32E
57 M6 Gainsborough Lincs Eng 53.24N 0.48W
100 Q9 Gainsborough Saskatchewan 49.11N 101.30W
80 D2 Gaiole in Chianti Italy 43.28N 11.26E
65 J7 Gaipahöhe *mt* Austria 47.01N 13.45E
12 D4 Gairdner, L S Australia
14 C10 Gairdner, R W Australia
58 E3 Gair L Highland Scotland
58 E3 Gairloch Highland Scotland 57.43N 5.40W
58 G5 Gairlochy Highland Scotland 56.55N 4.59W
58 K4 Gairn, R Grampian Scotland
81 D4 Gairo Sardinia 39.50N 9.31E
58 T11 Gairsay *isld* Orkney Scotland 59.05N 2.58W
79 L1 Gais Italy 46.50N 11.57E
66 O2 Gais Switzerland 47.22N 9.27E
65 H6 Gaisberg *mt* Austria 47.49N 13.08E
65 L7 Gaishorn Austria 47.30N 14.33E
65 F7 Gaisstein *mt* Austria 47.21N 12.30E
104 H7 Gaithersburg Maryland 39.08N 77.13W
94 D5 Gaitsabis Namibia 24.48S 17.39E
21 B7 Gai Xian Liaoning China 40.24N 122.17E
25 F9 Gajah Hutan, Bukit *hill* Thailand 6.15N 101.04E
75 E6 Gajanejos Spain 40.50N 2.54W
29 H8 Gajapatinagaram Andhra Prad India 18.20N 83.29E
31 C7 Gajar Pakistan 27.08N 65.38E
65 P5 Gajary Czechoslovakia 48.29N 16.56E
21 E13 Gaja shima *isld* Japan 29.54N 129.37E
30 D6 Gajner Uttar Prad India 26.17N 80.04E
29 L5 Gajol W Bengal India 25.10N 88.16E
39 F6 Gakankoy U.S.S.R. 57.23N 158.30E
95 G3 Gakarosa *mt* S Africa 27.53S 23.35E
87 D2 Gakdul Sudan 17.42N 32.57E
90 D8 Gakem Nigeria 6.48N 8.56E
113 P5 Gakona Alaska 62.20N 145.19W
113 P5 Gakona Junction Alaska 62.19N 145.20W
40 G5 Gaktsynka U.S.S.R. 52.30N 137.00E
31 G2 Gakuch Kashmir 36.10N 73.50E
47 D5 Gakugsa U.S.S.R. 61.32N 36.29E
90 G8 Gala Cameroon 7.51N 14.50E
24 F11 Gala Xizang Zizhiqu China 28.04N 89.19E
43 G7 Galaassiya Uzbekistan U.S.S.R. 39.52N 64.29E
24 F11 Gala Co *L* Xizang Zizhiqu China
87 M8 Galad, El Somalia 5.25N 48.24E
87 L7 Galadi Ethiopia 6.56N 46.21E
90 C6 Galadima Kogo Nigeria 10.01N 6.55E
Galag *see* Kālak
26 R7 Galagedara Sri Lanka 7.22N 80.31E
37 B2 Gala Gölü *L* Turkey
26 S7 Galaha Sri Lanka 7.12N 80.40E
100 F6 Galahad Alberta 52.30N 111.56W
93 M3 Galahameia Kenya 2.52N 40.15E
Galaib ar Rafaifat *see* Qalīb ar Rufayfāt
45 Q5 Galakhovo U.S.S.R. 51.52N 44.26E
86 H7 Galâla el Baḥarîya, Gebel el *ra* Egypt
86 H8 Galâla el Qiblîya, Gebel el *ra* Egypt
72 E9 Galan France 43.13N 0.25E
93 L9 Galana *R* Kenya
120 E11 Galán, Cerro *pk* Argentina 26.00S 66.50W
32 F2 Galand Iran 37.01N 55.04E
18 F5 Galang *isld* Indonesia
91 D10 Galanga Angola 12.04S 15.09E
91 E10 Galangue Angola 13.42S 16.09E
91 D11 Galangue *tribe* Angola
42 E3 Galanino U.S.S.R. 57.35N 93.15E
51 K3 Galanito Norway 68.54N 22.50E
62 K7 Galanta Czechoslovakia 48.11N 17.45E
19 N2 Galap Palau Is Pacific Oc 7.38N 134.39E
76 L7 Galapagar Spain 40.35N 4.00W
75 D6 Galápagos Spain 40.41N 3.21W
117 F2 Galápagos Is Pacific Oc
75 G2 Galar Spain 42.46N 1.43W
84 A6 Galaróon Greece 37.47N 20.47E
77 C5 Galaroza Spain 37.56N 6.43W
57 H1 Galashiels Borders Scotland 55.37N 2.49W
93 H2 Galass Kenya 3.27N 36.31E
110 O1 Galata Montana 48.29N 111.20W
37 J2 Galata *dist* İstanbul Turkey 41.01N 28.57E
84 E6 Galatás Greece 37.50N 22.34E
84 F7 Galatás Greece 37.30N 23.26E
109 G3 Galatea Colorado 38.30N 103.02W
11 L5 Galatea New Zealand 38.23S 176.44E
28 J8 Galathea B Nicobar Is
82 L5 Galaţi Romania 45.27N 28.02E
81 K7 Galati Sicily 38.07N 15.30E
84 T14 Galatia Cyprus 35.25N 34.05E
107 H4 Galatia Illinois 37.50N 88.38W
109 M3 Galatia Kansas 38.38N 98.57W
36 F3 Galatia *reg* Turkey
81 R12 Galatina Italy 40.10N 18.10E
81 R12 Galatone Italy 40.09N 18.05E
Galatz *see* Galaţi
77 U14 Galatzó *mt* Balearic Is 39.38N 2.29E
71 G6 Galaure *R* France
58 L7 Gala Water *R* Borders Scotland
104 E10 Galax Virginia 36.40N 80.56W
84 D5 Galaxídhion Greece 38.22N 22.23E
89 E8 Galay Guinea 7.44N 9.04W
37 G1 Galaza Burun *C* Turkey 41.15N 29.15E
59 F7 Galbally Limerick Irish Rep 52.25N 8.18W
75 F2 Galbarra Spain 42.44N 2.14W
13 F3 Galbraith Queensland 16.23S 141.35E
87 L7 Galcaio Somalia 6.47N 47.21E
87 H7 Galchia Ethiopia 6.42N 40.40E
75 D1 Galdames Spain 43.14N 3.06W
96 U14 Galdar Gran Canaria Canary Is 28.09N 15.40W
53 Y15 Galdhøpiggen *mt* Norway 61.38N 8.19E
87 H8 Galdima Ethiopia 5.52N 41.18E
89 E5 Galé Mali 12.34N 9.33W
115 F2 Galeana Chihuahua Mexico 30.08N 107.38W
115 J5 Galeana Nuevo León Mexico 24.51N 100.08W
118 J8 Galeão Brazil 22.50S 43.14W
118 J8 Galeão, Aeroporto Brazil 22.49S 43.14W
79 L7 Galeata Italy 44.00N 11.54E
87 E4 Galegu *watercourse* Sudan/Ethiopia
32 E7 Galeh Dār Iran 27.38N 52.42E
87 N5 Gal, El Somalia 11.21N 50.23E
19 E3 Galela Halmahera Indon 1.50N 127.49E
89 D8 Galema Liberia 7.49N 10.18W
Galena *see* Geraldine W Australia
113 J4 Galena Alaska 64.43N 157.00W
106 D7 Galena Illinois 42.25N 90.26W
109 Q4 Galena Kansas 37.05N 94.39W
103 C8 Galena Maryland 39.21N 75.52W
107 C5 Galena Missouri 36.50N 93.29W
112 M6 Galena Park Texas 29.44N 95.16W
63 T5 Galenbecker See *L* E Germany
76 F4 Galende Spain 42.06N 6.40W
66 K5 Galenstock *mt* Switzerland 46.37N 8.25E
116 P2 Galeota Pt Trinidad & Tobago 10.08N 60.59W
77 L5 Galera Spain 37.45N 2.33W
77 L5 Galera *R* Spain
115 F10 Galera, Cerro *hill* Panama Canal Zone 8.56N 79.38W
75 L6 Galera, La Spain 40.41N 0.27E
116 P1 Galera Pt Trinidad & Tobago 10.49N 60.54W
119 B7 Galera, Pta *C* Ecuador 0.49N 80.03W
115 L10 Galera, Pta *C* Mexico 15.59N 97.45W
121 A8 Galera, Pta. de la *C* Chile 40.00S 73.45W
119 C2 Galera, Pta. de la *C* Colombia 10.48N 75.18W
118 B4 Galera, R Brazil
67 O12 Galeria Corsica 42.24N 8.38E
67 O12 Galeria, G.de Corsica 42.26N 8.38E
47 M2 Galernyy Ostrov *isld* Leningrad U.S.S.R.
106 D9 Galesburg Illinois 40.58N 90.22W
106 J7 Galesburg Michigan 42.17N 85.26W
103 A9 Galesville Maryland 38.50N 76.33W
106 C5 Galesville Wisconsin 44.05N 91.21W
109 F1 Galeton Colorado 40.32N 104.34W
99 K1 Galeton Ontario 51.09N 80.55W
104 H5 Galeton Pennsylvania 41.43N 77.39W
26 T14 Galets. Pte des Réunion Ind Oc 20.54S 55.17E
26 T14 Galets, R.des Réunion Ind Oc
26 S6 Galewela Sri Lanka 7.45N 80.35E
59 D7 Galey, R Kerry Irish Rep
87 L5 Galgal Somalia 10.09N 46.59E
26 R5 Galgamuwa Sri Lanka 8.01N 80.17E
87 H10 Galgasc Somalia 0.10N 41.37E
57 H5 Galgate Lancs Eng 54.00N 2.47W
39 F1 Gal'gavaam *R* U.S.S.R.
26 T9 Galge Sri Lanka 6.32N 81.18E
60 M11 Galgenberg *mt* Netherlands 52.04N 5.56E
66 M3 Galgenen Switzerland 47.12N 8.53E
26 R6 Galgiriya *mt* Sri Lanka 7.55N 80.23E
87 M6 Gal Goble Somalia 9.54N 49.50E
59 K2 Galgorm Antrim N Ireland 54.52N 6.19W
87 M7 Gal Hagar Somalia 7.21N 49.12E
118 F3 Galheirão, R Brazil
118 F3 Galheiros Brazil 13.18S 46.27W
44 D5 Gali Georgia U.S.S.R. 42.37N 41.46E
29 D6 Galiakot Rajasthan India 23.32N 74.02E
101 M11 Galiano I Br Col 48.55N 123.30W
34 M2 Galiāwa Iraq 36.24N 44.11E
71 J6 Galibier, Col.du *pass* France 45.04N 6.24E
110 B7 Galice Oregon 42.35N 123.36W
46 M1 Galich U.S.S.R. 58.20N 42.12E
82 J1 Galich U.S.S.R. 49.11N 24.44E
82 H7 Galiche Bulgaria 43.34N 22.50E
46 M1 Galichskoye, Oz *L* U.S.S.R.
74 B2 Galicia *reg* Spain
106 H8 Galien Michigan 41.48N 86.30W
103 L4 Galilee Rhode I 41.23N 71.31W
13 H5 Galilee *L* Queensland
35 D1 Galilee *reg* Israel
Galilee, Sea of *see* Tiberias, L
90 F8 Galim Cameroon 7.06N 12.25E
91 B1 Galim Cameroon 5.40N 10.16E
39 F4 Galimyy U.S.S.R. 62.15N 156.06E
116 L1 Galina Pt Jamaica, W I 18.24N 76.58W
91 C8 Galinda Angola 9.35S 13.34E
76 H7 Galinduste Spain 40.40N 5.32W
84 T13 Galinoporni Cyprus 35.30N 34.19E
104 C6 Galion Ohio 40.44N 82.46W
116 L3 Galion, B.du Martinique W I
93 D4 Galiraya Uganda 1.21N 32.49E
98 K2 Galissonnière, Lac la Quebec
76 G9 Galisteo Spain 39.58N 6.16W
Galite *see* Jezîret Jālita *I*
111 O9 Galiuro Mts Arizona
47 J7 Galkino U.S.S.R. 55.40N 62.51E
44 J2 Galkin, Ostrov *isld* U.S.S.R.
30 G4 Galkot Nepal 28.12N 83.26E
87 G7 Galla *tribe* Ethiopia
87 F4 Gallabat Sudan 12.57N 36.10E
87 L8 Gal Laghet Somalia 4.10N 47.10E
59 H1 Gallagh Road Londonderry N Ireland 55.02N 7.20W
93 M6 Galla Hills Kenya
61 E4 Gallaix Belgium 50.36N 3.35E
58 B2 Gallan Hd Lewis, W Isles Scotland 58.14N 7.01W
79 E3 Gallarate Italy 45.39N 8.47E
70 O4 Gallardon France 48.32N 1.42E
107 C2 Gallatin Missouri 39.54N 93.57W
107 K5 Gallatin Tennessee 36.22N 86.28W
112 M4 Gallatin Texas 31.55N 95.10W
110 O4 Gallatin *R* Montana
110 O4 Gallatin Gateway Montana 45.36N 111.12W
110 O4 Gallatin Pk Montana 45.23N 111.21W
110 P4 Gallatin Ra Montana/Wyo
26 R10 Galle Sri Lanka 6.01N 80.13E
75 D4 Gallega, La Spain 41.54N 3.16W
66 O6 Gallegione, Piz *mt* Switzerland 46.23N 9.30E
75 K2 Gállego *R* Spain
109 G6 Gallegos New Mexico 35.36N 103.44W
121 H6 Gallegos, C Chile 46.33S 75.40W
76 F7 Gallegos de Argañan Spain 40.38N 6.44W
76 G5 Gallegos del Rio Spain 41.44N 6.10W
76 J7 Gallegos de Sobrinos Spain 40.43N 5.08W
121 L8 Gallegos, Puerto *inlet* Argentina
121 K8 Gallegos, R Argentina
76 J4 Galleguillos de Campos Spain 42.19N 5.04W
79 J7 Galleno Italy 43.47N 10.42E
29 J7 Galleri Orissa India 20.06N 84.36E
98 O2 Gallet, L Quebec
59 E8 Galley Hd Cork Irish Rep 51.32N 8.57W
79 E4 Galliate Italy 45.29N 8.41E
79 H6 Gallicano Italy 44.03N 10.26E
80 G5 Gallicano nel Lazio Italy 41.52N 12.50E
81 L7 Gallico Italy 38.10N 15.40E
Galliéni Algeria*see* Bou Aci
26 Q16 Galliéni, Presq'île *pen* Kerguelen Ind Oc
83 F4 Gallikós *R* Greece
63 Q5 Gallin E Germany 53.32N 12.09E
81 L7 Gallina Italy 38.05N 15.41E
66 P3 Gallina Kogel *mt* Austria/Liechtenstein 47.09N 9.37E
109 D5 Gallina Pk *mt* New Mexico 36.28N 106.46W
79 D6 Gallinara *isld* Italy 44.02N 8.14E
109 E7 Gallinas New Mexico 34.09N 105.41W
109 C7 Gallinas Mts New Mexico
109 E7 Gallinas Pk New Mexico 34.16N 105.47W
119 E1 Gallinas, Pta *C* Colombia 12.27N 71.44W
120 D9 Gallinazos Chile 20.30S 69.45W
79 L3 Gallio Italy 45.54N 11.34E
81 Q12 Gallipoli Italy 40.03N 17.59E
Gallipoli Turkey*see* Gelibolu
104 C8 Gallipolis Ohio 38.49N 82.14W
75 K6 Gallipuén, Embalse de *res* Spain
104 G6 Gallitzin Pennsylvania 40.30N 78.32W
51 H4 Gällivare Sweden 67.10N 20.40E
65 L8 Gallizien Austria 46.34N 14.30E
65 K5 Gallneukirchen Austria 48.22N 14.25E
80 K6 Gallo Italy 41.28N 14.14E
52 J4 Gällö Sweden 62.57N 15.15E
75 G6 Gallo *R* Spain
81 F7 Gallo, C Sicily 38.13N 13.18E
75 H6 Gallocanta, L.de Spain 40.58N 1.30W
109 B8 Gallo Mts New Mexico
104 J3 Galloo I New York 43.54N 76.24W
54 M11 Galloper Lightship North Sea
57 D2 Galloway *dist* Scotland
11 J13 Galloway, Mt Antipodes Is Pacific Oc 49.42S 178.47E
56 M4 Gallows Corner London Eng 51.36N 0.13E
52 G9 Gallstad Sweden 57.39N 13.25E
109 B6 Gallup New Mexico 35.30N 108.45W
75 H4 Gallur Spain 41.52N 1.19W
81 C2 Gallura *reg* Sardinia
79 K7 Galluzzo Italy 43.44N 11.14E
43 J7 Gallya-Aral Uzbekistan U.S.S.R. 40.01N 67.32E
41 B3 Gallya, Mys *C* Novaya Zemlya U.S.S.R. 72.41N 56.00E
41 O2 Gallya, Ostrov *isld* Franz Josef Land U.S.S.R.
61 F3 Galmaarden Belgium 50.45N 3.58E
93 M7 Galma Galla Kenya 1.12S 40.49E
50 D3 Gálmaströnd *coast* Iceland
93 L6 Galmathi *watercourse* Kenya
66 E4 Galmiz Switzerland 46.58N 7.10E
93 M7 Galole Kenya 1.25S 40.02E
93 L7 Galole *watercourse* Kenya
35 C7 Gal'on Israel 31.38N 34.51E
12 J5 Galong New S Wales 34.37S 148.34E
99 O2 Galop I New York 44.46N 75.22W
26 S5 Gal Oya Sri Lanka 8.08N 80.50E
26 U7 Gal Oya *R* Sri Lanka
77 T11 Gal, Pta.de *pt* Balearic Is 39.07N 1.33E
Galsharain *see* Galshir
22 H3 Galshir Mongolia 46.34N 110.48E
58 D2 Galson Lewis, W Isles Scotland 58.27N 6.23W
53 C6 Galsted Denmark 55.10N 9.13E
57 E1 Galston Strathclyde Scotland 55.36N 4.24W
111 C3 Galt California 38.16N 121.20W
107 C1 Galt Missouri 40.08N 93.25W
87 K9 Gal Tardò Somalia 3.34N 45.58E
81 D3 Galtelli Sardinia 40.23N 9.38E
53 D4 Galten Denmark 56.09N 9.54E
53 E4 Galten Denmark 56.21N 10.04E
51 K1 Galten Norway 70.44N 22.40E
52 K4 Galtström Sweden 62.10N 17.30E
65 B8 Galtür Austria 46.59N 10.12E
59 F7 Galtymore *mt* Limerick Irish Rep 52.23N 8.11W
59 F7 Galty,Mts Irish Rep
91 K9 Galu Zaïre 11.20S 26.41E
32 H3 Galūgāh-e Āsīyeh Iran 34.00N 59.55E
32 F7 Galūgāh, Kūh-e *mts* Iran
92 F6 Galula Tanzania 8.38S 33.01E
19 A5 Galumpang Celebes Indon 2.27S 119.28E
106 D8 Galva Illinois 41.10N 90.03W
75 J6 Galve Spain 40.39N 0.54W
75 D5 Galve de Sorbe Spain 41.13N 3.10W
76 D10 Galveias Portugal 39.10N 8.00W
106 H9 Galveston Indiana 40.34N 86.11W
112 N6 Galveston Texas 29.17N 94.48W
112 N6 Galveston B Texas
112 N6 Galveston I Texas
121 E4 Galvez Argentina 32.03S 61.14W
76 L9 Gálvez Spain 39.42N 4.16W
30 E3 Galwa Nepal 29.39N 81.52E
59 D5 Galway Galway Irish Rep 53.16N 9.03W
59 D5 Galway *co* Irish Rep
59 D5 Galway B Galway Irish Rep
Galyāwh *see* Galiāwa
94 F3 Gam Namibia 20.13S 20.49E
15 A4 Gam *isld* Irian Jaya
19 F4 Gam *isld* Irian Jaya 1.38S 129.55E
121 E8 Gama *isld* Argentina
69 B4 Gamaches France 50.00N 1.34E
95 F3 Gamagara *V* S Africa
20 L7 Gamagōri Japan 34.49N 137.15E
31 J3 Gama Hanu Kashmir 34.39N 76.38E
107 L5 Gamaliel Kentucky 36.38N 85.48W
86 R12 Gamâlîya *dist* Cairo Egypt
86 G3 Gamâlîya, El Egypt 31.12N 31.52E
72 C8 Gamarde-les-Bains France 43.44N 0.52W
119 D3 Gamarra Colombia 8.21N 73.46W
87 H5 Gamarri,L Ethiopia 11.32N 41.40E
90 E5 Gamawa Nigeria 12.10N 10.31E
19 M5 Gamay B Philippines 12.21N 125.19E
91 E9 Gamba Angola 11.45S 17.07E
91 B5 Gamba Gabon 2.40S 10.01E
24 F11 Gamba Xizang Zizhiqu China 28.13N 88.32E
89 J6 Gambaga Ghana 10.31N 0.22W
69 B6 Gambais France 48.46N 1.40E
18 D8 Gambang Pen Malaysia 3.42N 103.05E
79 H4 Gámbara Italy 45.16N 10.18E
79 J7 Gambassi Italy 43.32N 10.57E
80 L5 Gambatesa Italy 41.30N 14.55E
91 B1 Gambé Cameroon 5.50N 11.29E
Gambeila *see* Gambēla
87 E6 Gambēla Ethiopia 8.15N 34.35E
113 B5 Gambell St Lawrence I Bering Sea 63.46N 171.45W
79 M6 Gambéttola Italy 44.07N 12.20E
29 E4 Gambhir R Rajasthan India
89 B5 Gambia R The Gambia/Senegal
89 B5 Gambia, The *rep* W Africa
89 C5 Gambie *watercourse*
105 K9 Gambier New Providence I Bahamas 25.04N 77.29W
104 C6 Gambier Ohio 40.23N 82.24W
13 B1 Gambier, C N Terr Australia 11.57S 130.55E
122 R16 Gambier Is Pacific Oc 23.10S 135.00W
12 D6 Gambier Is S Australia 35.10S 136.28E
93 M8 Gambi, L Kenya 2.10S 40.30E
57 H3 Gamblesby Cumbria Eng 54.45N 2.36W
98 S5 Gambo Newfoundland 48.48N 54.15W
118 J9 Gambôa Brazil 22.55S 43.12W
115 F10 Gamboa Panama Canal Zone 9.08N 79.42W
87 K9 Gambole, El Somalia 3.02N 45.11E
79 E4 Gambolò Italy 45.16N 8.51E
91 D4 Gamboma Congo 1.50S 15.58E
13 G3 Gamboola Queensland 16.30S 143.36E
90 G9 Gamboula Cent Afr Rep 4.05N 15.10E
19 C3 Gambuta, Gunung *mt* Celebes Indonesia 0.40N 123.20E
19 F3 Gamcaka, Tanjung *C* Halmahera Indon 1.32N 128.43E
Gamda *see* Kamtang
117 J9 Gameleira Brazil 8.32S 35.15W
60 J12 Gameren Netherlands 51.48N 5.12E
76 B5 Gamil Portugal 41.31N 8.35W
65 M6 Gaming Austria 47.56N 15.06E
95 F8 Gamka *R* S Africa
19 E3 Gamkunoro, Gunung *mt* Halmahera Indon 1.30N 127.32E
19 E3 Gamlaba Halmahera Indon 1.27N 127.59E
50 C5 Gamlaeyri *isld* Iceland 64.45N 22.28W
Gamlakarleby *see* Kokkola
52 J9 Gamleby Sweden 57.54N 16.25E

26 B14 Gamma Kop *hill* Marion I Ind Oc 46.54S 37.45E
53 B5 Gammel Blåhøj Denmark 55.52N 9.00E
53 C4 Gammel Hampen Denmark 56.01N 9.23E
53 D4 Gammel-Rye Vejle Denmark 56.05N 9.43E
53 F1 Gammel Skagen Denmark 57.44N 10.32E
51 J6 Gammelstad Sweden 65.38N 22.05E
64 G7 Gammertingen W Germany 48.15N 9.13E
103 O3 Gammon, Pt *C* Massachusetts 41.36N 70.15W
76 J7 Gamo *R* Spain
94 E7 Gamoep S Africa 29.56S 18.25E
Gamo-Gofa *prov see* Gemu-Gwefa
89 C5 Gamon Senegal 13.25N 13.00W
76 K9 Gamonal Spain 39.57N 4.58W
90 D4 Gamou Niger 14.20N 9.54E
40 E10 Gamova, Mys *C* U.S.S.R. 42.32N 131.12E
26 Q7 Gampaha Sri Lanka 7.05N 80.00E
66 G6 Gampel Switzerland 46.19N 7.45E
66 P3 Gamperdona Tal *V* Austria
26 S7 Gampola Sri Lanka 7.10N 80.34E
66 O3 Gams Switzerland 47.13N 9.27E
66 H6 Gamser Tal *V* Switzerland
65 H6 Gamsfeld *mt* Austria 47.38N 13.29E
32 J6 Gamshadzai Kūh *mts* Iran
57 M6 Gamston Notts Eng 53.17N 0.56W
87 J10 Gamsuma Somalia 0.13N 42.45E
23 A3 Gamtog Xizang Zizhiqu China 31.37N 98.42E
95 H9 Gamtoos S Africa 33.55S 24.56E
95 H9 Gamtoos *R* S Africa
93 K1 Gamud *mt* Ethiopia 4.06N 38.05E
51 N1 Gamvik Norway 71.03N 28.10E
72 D9 Gan France 43.14N 0.23W
27 L10 Gan *isld* Maldives, Ind Oc 0.42S 73.10E
23 B2 Gana Sichuan China 32.05N 101.05E
64 O6 Ganacker W Germany 48.44N 12.42E
111 P6 Ganado Arizona 35.43N 109.34W
112 L6 Ganado Texas 29.04N 96.33W
86 E4 Ganâg Egypt 31.00N 30.46E
87 H8 Ganale Dorya,R Ethiopia
39 F7 Ganal'skiye Vostryaki, Khrebet *ra* U.S.S.R.
39 F7 Ganaly U.S.S.R. 53.44N 157.37E
76 G6 Gàname Spain 41.24N 6.02W
87 H6 Ganami Ethiopia 8.59N 41.32E
87 J9 Ganane Somalia 3.49N 42.34E
87 D1 Gananita Sudan 18.22N 33.50E
99 O8 Gananoque Ontario 44.21N 76.11W
32 D6 Ganāveh Iran 29.34N 50.33E
Ganaweh *see* Ganāveh
24 F5 Gancaogou *well* Xinjiang Uygur Zizhiqu China
23 E9 Gancheng Guangdong China 18.55N 108.41E
Gand *see* Gent Belgium
Ganda *see* Mariano Machado
91 C10 Ganda *tribe* Angola
19 A5 Gandadiwata, Bukit *mt* Celebes Indonesia 2.44S 119.25E
29 G7 Gandai Madhya Prad India 21.41N 81.10E
24 G11 Gandaingoin Xizang Zizhiqu China 29.46N 91.28E
91 H7 Gandajika Zaïre 6.46S 23.58E
30 H6 Gandak *R* Bihar India
30 G5 Gandak Dam Nepal 27.31N 83.58E
Gandakun *see* Ganjgān
31 A4 Gandalak Afghanistan 33.52N 61.58E
76 B5 Gandara Portugal 41.46N 8.31W
76 C6 Gandarela Portugal 41.27N 8.02W
31 A4 Gandarra Afghanistan 33.57N 61.20E
31 H5 Ganda Singhwala Pakistan 31.02N 74.30E
31 D6 Gandava Pakistan 28.36N 67.30E
98 S5 Gander Newfoundland 48.58N 54.34W
98 S4 Gander Bay Newfoundland 49.15N 54.30W
63 J6 Ganderkesee W Germany 53.02N 8.33E
98 S5 Gander L Newfoundland
92 D10 Ganderowe Falls Zimbabwe 17.20S 29.10E
98 R5 Gander R Newfoundland
Gandersheim *see* Bad Gandersheim
75 L5 Gandesa Spain 41.03N 0.26E
29 C7 Gandevi Gujarat India 20.48N 73.05E
29 B6 Gandhi Dham Gujarat India 23.07N 70.10E
29 C6 Gandhinagar Gujarat India 23.15N 72.45E
29 D5 Gandhi Sagar Dam Rajasthan etc India 24.39N 75.41E
90 B5 Gandi Nigeria 12.55N 5.49E
90 C5 Gandi *R* Nigeria
77 Q3 Gandía Spain 38.59N 0.11W
90 G8 Gandinang Cameroon 6.50N 14.32E
79 G3 Gandino Italy 45.48N 9.54E
89 A4 Gandiol Senegal 15.50N 16.29W
92 D2 Gandjo Zaïre 1.23S 29.00E
30 C1 Gandok Xizang Zizhiqu 31.41N 79.01E
32 D5 Gandomān Iran 31.50N 51.07E
89 K6 Gando-Namoni Togo 10.25N 0.50E
96 V15 Gando, Punta de Gran Canaria Canary Is 27.55N 15.19W
91 E2 Gandou Congo 2.25N 17.25E
53 E2 Gandrup Denmark 57.03N 10.12E
118 H3 Gandu Brazil 13.44S 39.38W
91 G3 Gandu Zaïre 1.25N 20.44E
Ganduman *see* Gandomān
51 O1 Gandvik Norway 70.02N 28.42E
111 K2 Gandy Utah 39.28N 114.01W
44 F6 Gandzani Georgia U.S.S.R. 41.22N 43.46E
89 D2 Ganeb Mauritania 18.29N 10.08W
113 J5 Ganes Creek Alaska 63.06N 156.26W
26 R6 Ganewatta Sri Lanka 7.38N 80.21E
27 O5 Ganga *R* India
89 H4 Gangafani Upper Volta 14.19N 2.21W
29 K2 Gangajalghati W Bengal India 23.25N 87.07E
28 C1 Gangakher Maharashtra India 18.58N 76.35E
28 G5 Ganga, Mouths of the Bangladesh
90 F8 Ganga, Mt.de Cameroon 7.20N 14.00E
Gangan *see* Kangān
121 C9 Gangán Argentina 42.34S 68.15W
29 C3 Ganganagar Rajasthan India 29.54N 73.56E
29 C3 Ganganagar *dist* Rajasthan India
121 C9 Gangán, Pampa de *plain* Arg
29 D8 Gangapur Maharashtra India 19.45N 75.04E
29 E4 Gangapur Rajasthan India 26.30N 76.49E
90 D4 Gangara Niger 14.36N 8.29E
87 G7 Gangarro Ethiopia 7.21N 39.10E
29 L7 Ganga Sâgar W Bengal India 21.39N 88.05E
29 B5 Ganga Sara Rajasthan India 24.57N 71.23E
30 C8 Gangau *res* Madhya Prad India
28 B3 Gangavali R Karnataka India
25 C1 Gangaw Burma 22.11N 94.09E
25 M9 Gangaw *ra* Burma
28 C3 Gangawati Karnataka India 15.30N 76.36E
22 E8 Gangca Qinghai China 37.16N 100.23E
31 J3 Gangche *dist* Kashmir
24 D10 Gangdisê Shan *mt ra* Xizang Zizhiqu China
64 A2 Gangelt W Germany 51.00N 6.00E
71 D9 Ganges France 43.56N 3.43E
Ganges *R see* Ganga *R*
29 D6 Ganghar Rajasthan India 23.56N 75.42E
52 G9 Gånghester Sweden 57.43N 13.00E
81 H8 Gangi Sicily 37.48N 14.13E
81 H8 Gangi *R* Sicily
30 B5 Gangiri Uttar Prad India 27.51N 78.27E
64 O7 Gangkofen W Germany 48.25N 12.35E
24 G10 Ganglungri *mt* Xizang Zizhiqu China 31.40N 90.04E
30 D3 Gangolihat Uttar Prad India 29.39N 80.02E
30 A3 Gangon Uttar Prad India 29.48N 77.16E
30 C2 Gangotri Uttar Prad India 30.56N 79.02E
30 B2 Gangotri *mt* Uttar Prad India 30.52N 78.56E
21 C7 Gangou Jilin China 41.52N 125.43E
23 D1 Gangouyi Gansu China 35.57N 105.06E
29 L4 Gangtok Sikkim India 27.20N 88.39E
24 D10 Gangto Tang Tso *L* Xizang Zizhiqu 31.10N 82.35E
23 D1 Gangu Gansu China 34.36N 105.29E
91 J1 Gangu *R* Zaïre
91 E10 Ganguelas *tribe* Angola
91 C9 Gangula Angola 10.59S 13.57E
22 H8 Ganguyi Shaanxi China 36.47N 109.44E
91 G5 Gangwa Zaïre 3.30S 20.54E
94 F5 Gangwi Pan *salt pan* Botswana 24.34S 21.36E
35 B6 Gan HaDarom Israel 31.49N 34.42E
21 C2 Gan He *R* Nei Monggol Zizhiqu China
24 F3 Ganhezi Xinjiang Uygur Zizhiqu China 44.09N 88.13E
19 F4 Gani Halmahera Indon 0.44S 128.11E
32 G7 Gāni Iran 26.34N 57.28E
29 E6 Ganial R Madhya Prad India
42 E4 Ganina Gar' U.S.S.R. 57.07N 91.24E
30 D8 Ganj Madhya Prad India 24.24N 80.25E
29 J8 Ganjam Orissa India 19.28N 85.05E
29 J8 Ganjam *dist* Orissa India
30 B7 Ganj Dinara Madhya Prad India 25.29N 78.19E
32 D5 Ganjgān Iran 30.25N 51.49E
23 G5 Gan Jiang *R* Jiangxi China
23 C4 Ganluo Sichuan China 28.58N 102.59E
12 H5 Ganmam New S Wales 34.47S 147.01E
21 C4 Gannan Heilongjiang China 47.53N 123.29E
81 M3 Gannano.L.di Italy 40.18N 16.27E
51 J5 Gannarsbyn Sweden 66.07N 21.50E
72 L3 Gannat France 46.06N 3.11E
71 D3 Gannay-sur-Loire France 46.43N 3.37E
87 D3 Ganneb Sudan 14.50N 33.15E
66 M5 Ganneretsch, Piz *mt* Switzerland 46.37N 8.47E
11 J4 Gannet I New Zealand 37.57S 174.33E
110 L6 Gannett Idaho 43.22N 114.12W
110 Q6 Gannett Pk Wyoming 43.10N 109.38W
108 M5 Gannvalley S Dakota 44.01N 98.59W
9 B8 Ganokoro Nauru, Pacific Oc 0.31S 166.57E
29 D6 Ganora Rajasthan India 23.44N 74.16E
37 D2 Ganos Dağı *mt* Turkey
22 B8 Ganq Qinghai China 37.23N 92.23E
22 H8 Ganquan Shaanxi China 36.24N 109.20E
95 C10 Gansbaai S Africa 34.35S 19.20E
66 F2 Gänsbrunnen Switzerland 47.16N 7.28E
120 C3 Ganse Azul *oil well* Peru 8.48S 74.41W
65 P5 Gänserndorf Austria 48.21N 16.43E
35 C4 Gan Shemuel Israel 32.27N 34.57E
61 R9 Ganshoren *dist* Bruxelles Belgium
66 J1 Gansingen Switzerland 47.33N 8.08E
94 J5 Ganskuil S Africa 24.54S 26.42E
95 H3 Ganspan S Africa 27.57S 24.47E
22 F8 Gansu *prov* China
89 E8 Ganta Liberia 7.15N 8.59W
Gantang *see* Taiping
29 H7 Gantapara Orissa India 20.34N 83.42E
60 H12 Gantelwijk Netherlands 51.48N 4.56E
14 A8 Gantheaume B W Australia
12 E6 Gantheaume, C S Australia 36.00S 137.32E
14 D4 Gantheaume Pt W Australia 18.00S 122.13E
44 C4 Gantiadi Georgia U.S.S.R. 43.24N 40.08E
72 F9 Ganties France 43.04N 0.48E
57 N4 Ganton N Yorks Eng 54.11N 0.29W
66 F5 Gantrisch *mt* Switzerland 46.43N 7.27E
46 F3 Gantsevichi Belorussiya U.S.S.R. 52.49N 26.29E
18 H7 Gantung Belitung Indonesia 3.00S 108.10E
77 O5 Ganuelas Spain 37.40N 1.25W
29 K6 Ganutia W Bengal India 23.32N 87.53E
30 J8 Ganwan Bihar India 24.38N 85.56E
23 G6 Gan Xian Jiangxi China 25.53N 115.02E
Ganxiangying *see* Xide
22 G8 Ganyanchi Ningxia China 36.42N 105.05E
35 B6 Gan Yavne Israel 31.47N 34.43E
90 F7 Ganye Nigeria 8.25N 12.04E
95 H2 Ganyesa S Africa 26.35S 24.11E
95 H2 Ganyesalaagte *watercourse* S Africa
35 C4 Gan Yoshiyya Israel 32.21N 34.59E
23 H1 Ganyu Jiangsu China 34.52N 119.11E
93 L4 Ganyuri Kenya 1.43N 39.57E
46 P6 Ganyushkino Kazakhstan U.S.S.R. 46.38N 49.12E
22 L6 Ganzhao Liaoning China 41.16N 119.56E
23 G6 Ganzhou Jiangxi China 25.52N 114.51E
87 A8 Ganzi Zaïre 4.31N 26.59E
63 Q6 Ganzlin E Germany 53.23N 12.15E
86 F4 Ganzûr Egypt 30.41N 31.02E
42 H6 Ganzurino U.S.S.R. 51.35N 107.16E
89 J3 Gao Mali 16.19N 0.09W
23 G4 Gao'an Jiangxi China 28.28N 115.26E
Gaobeidian *see* Xincheng
22 K7 Gaocheng Hebei China 38.03N 114.51E
23 H3 Gaochun Jiangsu China 31.20N 118.49E
Gaocun *see* Mayang
22 J7 Gaocun Shanxi China 38.13N 112.45E
22 F7 Gaohe Guangdong China 22.44N 112.59E
23 G3 Gaohebu Anhui China 30.43N 116.23E
22 H7 Gaojiabu Shaanxi China 39.47N 112.27E
22 H8 Gaojiawan Shaanxi China 35.57N 110.01E
22 F8 Gaolan Gansu China 36.23N 103.55E
Gaoliangjian *see* Hongze
23 A5 Gaoligong Shan *mt ra* Yunnan China
23 B5 Gaoligong Shan *mt ra* Yunnan China
23 E6 Gaoling Guangxi China 24.05N 108.03E
23 E1 Gaoling Shaanxi China 34.33N 109.04E
23 D6 Gaolou Ling *mt* Guangxi China
23 H1 Gaomi Shandong China 36.23N 119.35E
23 G6 Gaopi Guangdong China 24.26N 116.35E
23 F1 Gaoping Shanxi China 35.48N 113.00E
22 M6 Gaoqiaozhen Liaoning China 40.58N 120.59E
22 L8 Gaoqing Shandong China 37.11N 117.47E
23 E5 Gaosha Hunan China 26.58N 110.40E
22 J6 Gaoshan Shanxi China 40.05N 112.59E
22 E7 Gaotai Gansu China 39.20N 99.52E
21 B6 Gaotaishan Liaoning China 42.03N 122.55E
22 K8 Gaotang Shandong China 36.55N 116.11E
89 H6 Gaoua Upper Volta 10.18N 3.12W
89 C6 Gaoual Guinea 11.44N 13.14W
90 F6 Gaouar Cameroon 10.30N 13.50E
89 H7 Gaouy Ivory Coast 9.04N 3.57W
23 C4 Gao Xian Sichuan China 28.25N 104.21E
23 G1 Gaoxianji Henan China 34.14N 114.45E
22 K7 Gaoyang Hebei China 38.44N 115.47E
23 F7 Gaoyao Guangdong China 23.03N 112.27E
22 K8 Gaoyi Hebei China 37.36N 114.35E
23 H2 Gaoyou Jiangsu China 32.48N 119.26E
23 H2 Gaoyou Hu *L* Jiangsu China
23 E8 Gaozhou Guangdong China 21.50N 110.56E
71 J7 Gap France 44.33N 6.05E
103 B7 Gap Pennsylvania 40.00N 76.01W
19 K4 Gapan Luzon Philippines 15.18N 120.58E
30 F8 Gapat *R* Madhya Prad India
11 J11 Gap Pt Chatham Is Pacific Oc 44.04S 176.38W
31 B7 Gar Pakistan 26.50N 63.31E
24 C9 Gar Xizang Zizhiqu China 32.11N 79.59E
40 D5 Gar' *R* U.S.S.R.
90 K5 Gara Chad 14.00N 21.27E
34 P10 Gara, Al *plain* Saudi Arabia
88 S10 Garaa Tin Bakeze *hill* Algeria 23.24N 9.04E
75 H8 Garaballa Spain 39.49N 1.23W
121 E2 Garabato Argentina 28.57S 60.08W
91 C3 Garabinzam Congo 1.36N 13.30E
96 Q14 Garachico Tenerife Canary Is 28.22N 16.46W
115 P5 Garachiné Panama 8.03N 78.21E
119 B3 Garachiné, Pta *pt* Panama 8.07N 78.37W
87 M7 Garad Somalia 6.56N 49.17E
87 G8 Garadasa Ethiopia 5.04N 38.10E
59 G3 Garadice L Leitrim Irish Rep 54.03N 7.43W
88 K8 Gara-Djebilet Algeria 27.00N 7.34W
88 K5 Gara, El Morocco 33.21N 7.12W
88 R4 Garaet et Tarf *L* Algeria
78 C11 Garaet Ichkeul *L* Tunisia
Garagagh, Kuh-i- *see* Galūgāh, Kūh-e *mts*
32 J6 Garagheh Iran 29.59N 60.21E
119 D5 Garagoa Colombia 5.05N 73.20W
12 J3 Garah New S Wales 29.05S 149.40E
31 G3 Garai Pakistan 35.17N 72.39E
15 J7 Garaina Papua New Guinea 7.53S 147.10E
96 O15 Garajonay *mt* Gomera Canary Is 28.07N 17.14W
82 K7 Gara Khitrino Bulgaria 43.25N 26.57E
59 F4 Gara, L Sligo Irish Rep 53.56N 8.26W
85 B6 Garama *ruins* Libya 26.38N 12.59E
93 A2 Garamba *R* Zaïre
93 A1 Garamba, Parc Nat.de la Zaïre
32 D6 Garangan *oil well* Iran 29.58N 50.59E
33 J2 Garangan *oil field* Iran 30.18N 50.35E
117 H9 Garanhuns Brazil 8.53S 36.28W
18 M10 Garantah Indonesia 9.02S 117.11E
89 C3 Garaouel Mauritania 17.29N 12.22W
118 F5 Garapuava Brazil 16.05S 46.33W
15 K8 Garara Papua New Guinea 8.35S 148.16E
30 D7 Garara *R* Uttar Prad India
85 F4 Garārah Libya 30.44N 20.59E
90 K6 Garar, Plaine de Chad
87 K8 Garas, El Somalia 4.12N 44.11E
87 L8 Garàs, El Somalia 5.10N 47.31E
19 N2 Garasuun Palau Is Pacific Oc 7.22N 134.33E
19 E1 Garat *isld* Indonesia 4.46N 127.04E
30 C7 Garautha Uttar Prad India 25.35N 79.17E
89 F9 Garawe Liberia 4.30N 7.58W
86 F6 Garawi, Wâdi *watercourse* Egypt
Garayan, Al *see* Quryān, Al
75 H2 Garayoa Spain 42.55N 1.14W
79 E4 Garbagna Novarese Italy 45.23N 8.39E
87 J9 Garba Hanre Somalia 3.20N 42.11E
87 H3 Garbanna Ethiopia 14.14N 40.45E
93 K5 Garba Tula Kenya 0.31N 38.30E
77 G2 Garbayuela Spain 39.03N 5.00W
77 F2 Garbayuela, Sierra de *mts* Spain
109 N5 Garber Oklahoma 36.26N 97.35W
110 B9 Garberville California 40.07N 123.48W
42 F5 Garbokaray U.S.S.R. 54.11N 99.56E
56 N3 Garboldisham Norfolk Eng 52.24N 0.56E
32 D4 Garbosh, Kūh-e *mt* Iran 32.36N 50.02E
63 L8 Garbsen W Germany 52.25N 9.36E
30 D2 Garbyang Uttar Prad India 30.08N 80.54E
118 E8 Garça Brazil 22.14S 49.36W
118 D4 Garças, *R* Mato Grosso Brazil
117 G9 Garças, R Pernambuco Brazil
68 D3 Garches France 48.51N 2.11E
64 M7 Garching W Germany 48.14N 11.40E
64 O7 Garching W Germany 48.08N 12.36E
109 E4 Garcia Colorado 37.02N 105.33W
75 M5 García Spain 41.08N 0.39E
77 F2 García de Sola, Embalse de *res* Spain
118 D7 Garcias Brazil 20.31S 52.14W
76 H10 Garciaz Spain 39.25N 5.38W
76 L7 Garcillán Spain 40.59N 4.16W
75 E7 Garcinarro Spain 40.13N 2.46W
67 H8 Gard *dept* France
71 E9 Gard *R* France
79 J3 Garda Italy 45.34N 10.43E
44 G6 Gardabani Georgia U.S.S.R. 41.27N 45.06E
79 J3 Garda, L.di *L* Italy
31 E3 Gardan Divāl Afghanistan 34.30N 68.15E
31 B4 Gardaneh-i-Akhri *pass* Afghanistan 33.40N 63.34E
71 G10 Gardanne France 43.27N 5.27E
108 N1 Gardar N Dakota 48.37N 97.52W
52 K10 Gårdby Sweden 56.35N 16.40E
71 J10 Garde-Freinet, la France 43.19N 6.28E
101 U4 Garde L N W Terr 62.50N 106.15W
63 O7 Gardelegen E Germany 52.33N 11.24E
106 H4 Garden Michigan 45.47N 86.32W
111 D9 Gardena California 33.53N 118.19W
110 J6 Gardena Idaho 43.58N 116.10W
108 K1 Gardena N Dakota 48.45N 100.31W
79 L1 Gardena, Val *V* Italy
107 K7 Garden City Alabama 34.01N 86.55W
105 F5 Garden City Georgia 32.07N 81.09W
109 K4 Garden City Kansas 37.57N 100.54W
107 B3 Garden City Missouri 38.35N 94.12W
108 N5 Garden City S Dakota 44.59N 97.35W
112 F4 Garden City Texas 31.51N 101.30W
110 O8 Garden City Utah 41.57N 111.24W
112 H7 Gardendale Texas 28.32N 99.14W
111 G8 Garden Grove California 33.48N 117.52W
108 R9 Garden Grove Iowa 40.49N 93.32W
106 J4 Garden I Michigan 45.48N 85.30W
12 A7 Garden I S Australia 34.49S 138.31E
14 A3 Garden I W Australia 32.13S 115.42E
14 B9 Garden I W Australia 32.15S 115.09E
107 G12 Garden Island B Louisiana 29.02N 89.09W
13 B1 Garden Point N Terr Australia 11.25S 130.27E
29 G2 Garden Reach *dist* Calcutta, W Bengal
99 F6 Garden River Ontario 46.33N 84.10W
58 M3 Gardenstown Grampian Scotland 57.40N 2.20W
100 V9 Gardenton Manitoba 49.05N 96.42W
99 O10 Gardenvale Quebec 45.25N 73.54W
110 K5 Garden Valley Idaho 44.05N 115.56W
60 L11 Garderen Netherlands 52.14N 5.43E
58 Q9 Garderhouse Shetland Scotland 60.13N 1.25W
52 F6 Gardermoen *airport* Norway 60.12N 11.11E
121 F6 Gardey Argentina 37.16S 59.21W
31 E4 Gardez Afghanistan 33.37N 69.09E
50 C6 Gardhar Iceland 64.06N 22.00W
84 B2 Gardhíki Greece 39.33N 21.16E
84 C4 Gardhíki Greece 38.50N 21.58E
50 J2 Gardhur Thingeyjarsýsla, Nordhur Iceland 66.05N 16.45W
50 K2 Gardhur Thingeyjarsýsla, Nordhur Iceland 66.12N 15.42W
50 H3 Gardhur Thingeyjarsýsla, Sudhur Iceland 65.53N 17.26W
50 H3 Gardhur Thingeyjarsýsla, Sudhur Iceland 65.53N 17.52W
30 H5 Gardi Bihar India 27.24N 84.06E
104 Q2 Gardiner Maine 44.13N 69.48W
110 P4 Gardiner Montana 45.03N 110.42W
109 F5 Gardiner New Mexico 36.53N 104.31W
103 F3 Gardiner New York 41.41N 74.10W
99 J3 Gardiner Ontario 49.19N 81.02W
110 A6 Gardiner Oregon 43.45N 124.07W
100 L7 Gardiner Dam Saskatchewan 51.17N 106.55W
13 C5 Gardiner, Mt N Terr Australia 22.10S 132.40E
14 G4 Gardiner Ra Australia
103 K4 Gardiners B Long I, N Y
12 E8 Gardiner's Cr Victoria
103 K4 Gardiners I Long I, N Y
13 B6 Gardiner's Range N Terr Australia
63 J4 Garding W Germany 54.19N 8.47E
90 J4 Gardjian Chad 15.49N 19.54E
109 E4 Gardner Colorado 37.47N 105.11W
105 F10 Gardner Florida 27.21N 81.48W
106 F8 Gardner Illinois 41.11N 88.20W
102 O4 Gardner Massachusetts 42.33N 71.59W
119 B6 Gardner, I Galápagos Is 1.23S 90.18W
10 S2 Gardner I Phoenix Is Pacific Oc 4.40S 174.30W
123 E11 Gardner Inlet Antarctica
104 S2 Gardner L Maine
13 E6 Gardner, Mt N Terr Australia 23.35S 138.00E
114 C1 Gardner Pinnacles Hawaiian Is
14 B10 Gardner, R W Australia
111 E3 Gardnerville Nevada 38.56N 119.44W
62 K1 Gardno, Jezioro *L* Poland
87 M6 Gardò Somalia 9.30N 49.06E
71 D8 Gardon-d'Ales *R* France
71 D8 Gardon-de-Mialet *R* France
71 D8 Gardon-de St.Jean *R* France
79 J3 Gardone Riviera Italy 45.37N 10.33E
79 H3 Gardone Valtrompia Italy 45.41N 10.11E
87 K6 Gardor Ethiopia 8.04N 44.34E
72 H9 Gardouch France 43.23N 1.40E
51 E6 Gardsjönäs Sweden 65.27N 16.26E
52 H8 Gårdskö Sweden 58.54N 14.20E
52 K10 Gårdslösa Sweden 56.46N 16.45E
Gardula *see* Gidole
Garduliwara *see* Garhdiwala
Gar Dzong *see* Gar
72 C7 Garein France 44.03N 0.39W
58 G6 Gare L Strathclyde Scotland
58 G6 Garelochhead Strathclyde Scotland 56.05N 4.50W
113 P10 Gareloi I Aleutian Is 51.49N 178.50W
30 F5 Garenkhuti Nepal 27.58N 82.34E
68 E3 Garenne-Colombes, la France 48.55N 2.15E
71 J10 Garéoult France 43.20N 6.03E
82 D5 Garešnica Yugoslavia 45.33N 16.56E
79 D6 Garessio Italy 44.12N 8.02E
88 Q9 Garet el Djenoun *mt* Algeria 25.11N 5.25E
117 C2 Gare Tigre Fr Guiana 4.58N 53.09W
79 H6 Garfagnana *R* Italy
107 C5 Garfield Arkansas 36.28N 93.59W
105 E5 Garfield Georgia 32.39N 82.06W
109 L3 Garfield Kansas 38.04N 99.16W
103 L6 Garfield New Jersey 40.52N 74.05W
110 N9 Garfield Utah 40.44N 112.11W
110 H2 Garfield Washington 47.01N 117.08W
110 N5 Garfield Mt Montana 44.31N 112.36W
86 L7 Garf, Wâdi el *watercourse* Egypt
84 C7 Gargaliánoi Greece 37.04N 21.38E
77 F2 Gargáliga *R* Spain
77 E2 Gargáligas Spain 39.03N 5.38W
75 J6 Gargallo Spain 40.50N 0.35W
72 H4 Gargan, Mt France 45.37N 1.39E
80 N5 Gargano, Prom.del Italy
80 O5 Gargano, Testa del *hd* Italy 41.49N 16.12E
76 H8 Garganta la Olla Spain 40.06N 5.47W
76 H8 Gargantilla Spain 40.15N 5.55W
99 E5 Gargantua, C Ontario 47.36N 85.03W
44 G9 Gargar Āzārbāījān-e Bākhtarī Iran 38.50N 45.41E
32 C5 Gargar Khuzestān Iran 30.45N 48.59E
79 K1 Gargazzone Italy 46.36N 11.12E
65 A8 Gargellen Austria 46.58N 9.55E
51 K2 Gargia Norway 69.47N 23.30E
79 J3 Gargnano Italy 45.41N 10.39E
51 G6 Gargnäs Sweden 65.19N 18.00E
75 E6 Gárgoles de Abajo Spain 40.44N 2.37W
87 H5 Gargori Ethiopia 11.47N 41.30E
87 H5 Gargori, L Ethiopia 11.45N 41.32E
89 K4 Gargouna Mali 15.58N 0.13E
57 J5 Gargrave N Yorks Eng 53.59N 2.06W
76 H8 Gargüera Spain 40.04N 5.56W
76 H9 Gargüera, Embalse de *L* Spain 39.59N 5.54W
58 H6 Gargunnock Hills Central Scotland
Gargunsa *see* Gar
46 D2 Gargždai Lithuania U.S.S.R. 55.42N 21.21E
30 E8 Garh Madhya Prad India 24.49N 81.39E
29 F6 Garha Madhya Prad India 23.10N 79.57E
29 F6 Garhakota Madhya Prad India 23.47N 79.10E
30 H7 Garhani Bihar India 25.25N 84.32E
29 D2 Garhdiwala Punjab India 31.41N 75.50E
29 F6 Garhi Madhya Prad India 23.22N 78.10E
29 D6 Garhi Rajasthan India 23.36N 74.10E
30 A4 Garhi Harsaru Haryana India 28.26N 76.55E
31 F6 Garhi Ikhtiar Khan Pakistan 28.43N 70.38E
31 D6 Garhi Khairo Pakistan 28.02N 67.58E
30 B4 Garhmuktesar Uttar Prad India 28.47N 78.06E
29 E2 Garhshankar Punjab India 31.12N 76.11E
24 E8 Garhun Tso *L* Xizang Zizhiqu China 35.00N 85.30E
30 G8 Garhwa Uttar Prad India 24.44N 83.12E
47 J6 Gari U.S.S.R. 59.28N 62.19E
87 C8 Garia Sudan 5.06N 30.23E
Garian *see* Gharyān
15 C5 Gariau Irian Jaya 3.45S 134.55E
31 E4 Garibai Pass Afghanistan 32.01N 68.20E
121 H2 Garibaldi Brazil 29.16S 51.35W
101 M11 Garibaldi Br Col 49.58N 123.09W
110 B4 Garibaldi Oregon 45.35N 123.55W
101 M11 Garibaldi Prov.Park Br Col
94 D8 Garies S Africa 30.30S 18.00E
80 J6 Garigliano *R* Italy
60 M7 Garijp Netherlands 53.10N 5.57E
19 B6 Garincing Celebes Indon 4.59S 120.18E
34 Q4 Garin, Kūh-i- *mts* Iran
75 G2 Garinoain Spain 42.35N 1.39E
93 L6 Garissa Kenya 0.27S 39.39E
93 L6 Garissa *dist* Kenya
30 C3 Garjia Uttar Prad India 29.28N 79.08E
30 H7 Garkha Bihar India 25.51N 84.51E
90 F6 Garkida Nigeria 10.27N 12.36E
90 D6 Garko Nigeria 11.45N 8.53E
90 C6 Garku Nigeria 10.31N 7.51E
109 Q4 Garland Kansas 37.45N 94.38W
100 R7 Garland Manitoba 51.38N 100.27W
105 J3 Garland N Carolina 34.47N 78.25W
108 O9 Garland Nebraska 40.58N 96.58W
104 F5 Garland Pennsylvania 41.48N 79.28W
112 O9 Garland Texas 32.50N 96.37W
110 N8 Garland Utah 41.45N 112.10W
108 B5 Garland Wyoming 44.48N 108.40W
79 E4 Garlasco Italy 45.12N 8.55E
79 F3 Garlate, L.di Italy
57 E3 Garliestown Dumfries & Galloway Scotland 54.48N 4.22W
72 D8 Garlin France 43.34N 0.15W
77 F3 Garlitos Spain 38.53N 5.03W
58 M4 Garlogie Grampian Scotland 57.08N 2.21W
107 K10 Garlrand Alabama 31.31N 86.51W
63 M6 Garlstorf W Germany 53.14N 10.05E
43 K7 Garm Tadzhikistan U.S.S.R. 39.04N 70.23E
31 C4 Garmab Afghanistan 32.12N 65.00E
34 Q3 Garmāb Gīlān Iran 35.50N 48.13E
Garmāb Iran *see* Garmeh
32 H4 Garm Āb Iran 33.55N 59.40E
Garmab Khorāsān Iran *see* Chashmeh-ye Garm Āb
32 G3 Garmab Semnān Iran 35.24N 56.50E
87 N6 Garmal Somalia 8.36N 50.19E
32 C5 Garmdasht Iran 30.40N 48.10E
32 F4 Garmeh Esfahān Iran 33.32N 54.59E
32 G2 Garmeh Khorāsān Iran 36.58N 56.14E
42 G4 Garmenka U.S.S.R. 56.58N 101.55E
Garmi *see* Germi
65 D6 Garmisch-Partenkirchen W Germany 47.30N 11.05E
32 E7 Garmosht Iran 27.57N 52.48E
58 K3 Garmouth Grampian Scotland 57.40N 3.07W
32 E3 Garmsar Iran 35.15N 52.20E
31 B5 Garmsel *reg* Afghanistan
72 A2 Garnache, la France 46.54N 1.50W
71 D3 Garnat-sur-Engièvre France 46.38N 3.39E
106 C7 Garnavillo Iowa 42.53N 91.14W
98 J2 Garneau, R Quebec
110 Q3 Garneill Montana 46.45N 109.46W
108 R6 Garner Iowa 43.06N 93.33W
105 J2 Garner N Carolina 35.43N 78.38W
100 F4 Garner Lake Prov. Park Alberta
103 F4 Garnerville New York 41.13N 74.00W
53 S18 Garnes Norway 60.26N 5.28E
106 J3 Garnet Michigan 46.11N 85.12W
110 M3 Garnet Montana 46.49N 113.20W
97 M4 Garnet B N W Terr
109 P3 Garnett Kansas 38.16N 95.15W
61 O8 Garnich Luxembourg 49.37N 5.57E
98 R6 Garnish Newfoundland 47.14N 55.22W
60 O6 Garnwerd Netherlands 53.18N 6.30E
89 G5 Garo Mali 13.12N 5.59W
87 M6 Garoe Somalia 8.17N 48.20E
28 H3 Garo Hills *dist* Assam India
77 K5 Garoiez Spain 37.52N 3.27W
29 F5 Garola Madhya Prad India 24.02N 78.26E
75 M2 Garona *R* Spain
72 E7 Garonne *R* France
121 J2 Garopaba Brazil 28.03S 48.40W
90 F7 Garoua Cameroon 9.17N 13.22E
90 G9 Garoua-Boulai Cameroon 5.54N 14.33E
15 K6 Garove I Bismarck Arch 4.40S 149.30E
50 D4 Garpsdalur Iceland 65.27N 21.50W
23 C2 Gar Qu *R* Sichuan China
86 L10 Garra *oil well* Egypt 27.59N 33.44E
58 D2 Garrabost Lewis, W Isles Scotland 58.13N 6.15W
75 O5 Garraf Spain 41.16N 1.54E
76 H3 Garrafe de Torio Spain 42.44N 5.31W
75 H2 Garralda Spain 42.57N 1.18W
12 A6 Garran *dist* Canberra Australia
55 E4 Garratt London Eng 51.26N 0.11W
30 C7 Garrauli Madhya Prad India 25.06N 79.21E
100 V3 Garraway Manitoba 55.56N 96.10W
75 F4 Garray Spain 41.49N 2.26W
63 G8 Garrel W Germany 52.58N 8.00E
60 Q6 Garrelsweer Netherlands 53.18N 6.45E
19 N2 Garreru *isld* Palau Is Pacific Oc 7.20N 134.33E
53 W14 Garretind *mt* Norway 62.21N 7.12E
108 O6 Garretson S Dakota 43.42N 96.30W
106 J8 Garrett Indiana 41.21N 85.08W
104 F7 Garrett Pennsylvania 39.53N 79.06W
108 E7 Garrett Wyoming 42.06N 105.37W
104 D5 Garrettsville Ohio 41.17N 81.07W
100 N5 Garrick Saskatchewan 53.30N 104.23W
59 D7 Garries Bridge Kerry Irish Rep 52.00N 9.20W
75 P4 Garriga, La Spain 41.41N 2.18E
71 C9 Garrigues *mts* France
71 E8 Garrigues *reg* France
59 F3 Garrison Fermanagh N Ireland 54.25N 8.05W
106 B7 Garrison Iowa 42.09N 92.08W
104 B8 Garrison Kentucky 38.37N 83.12W
108 R3 Garrison Minnesota 46.18N 93.49W
110 N3 Garrison Montana 46.30N 112.48W
108 J2 Garrison N Dakota 47.39N 101.25W
103 G4 Garrison New York 41.22N 73.57W
112 N4 Garrison Texas 31.50N 94.30W
111 K3 Garrison Utah 38.54N 114.01W
108 J2 Garrison Dam N Dakota 47.30N 101.26W
59 K4 Garristown Dublin Irish Rep 53.34N 6.23W
115 M3 Garrobo Nicaragua 13.35N 85.32W
77 D5 Garrobo, El Spain 37.37N 6.10W
75 K6 Garrocha, Sierra La *mts* Spain
59 L1 Garron Pt Antrim N Ireland 55.03N 5.58W
59 L1 Garron Tower Hotel Antrim N Ireland 55.04N 5.58W
77 D3 Garrovilla, La Spain 38.55N 6.29W
76 F9 Garrovillas Spain 39.42N 6.34W
77 N6 Garrucha Spain 37.11N 1.49W
121 G2 Garruchos Brazil 28.12S 55.35W
31 C6 Garruk Pakistan 28.25N 65.43E
101 F1 Garry I N W Terr 69.29N 135.40W
58 G4 Garry, L Highland Scotland
101 X3 Garry L N W Terr
58 H5 Garry, L Tayside Scotland 56.48N 4.15W
108 C4 Garryowen Montana 45.31N 107.28W
58 F4 Garry, R Highland Scotland
58 J5 Garry, R Tayside Scotland
65 N4 Gars Austria 48.37N 15.40E
64 N7 Gars W Germany 48.09N 12.17E
57 J4 Garsdale Cumbria Eng 54.18N 2.22W
66 P3 Garsella Kops *mt* Liechtenstein 47.11N 9.34E
93 M8 Garsen Kenya 2.16S 40.07E
90 L5 Garsila Sudan 12.25N 23.09E
95 J8 Garslands S Africa 32.11S 25.16E
53 D5 Gårslev Denmark 55.38N 9.37E
52 H11 Gärsnäs Sweden 55.33N 14.03E
100 G2 Garson L Alberta 56.22N 110.05W
63 M7 Garssen W Germany 52.39N 10.08E
57 H5 Garstang Lancs Eng 53.55N 2.47W
65 K5 Garsten Austria 48.02N 14.25E
60 P6 Garsthuizen Netherlands 53.22N 6.43E
57 H6 Garston Merseyside Eng 53.21N 2.53W
11 C12 Garston New Zealand 45.29S 168.42E
53 U20 Garsundfjord Norway 59.14N 6.00E
Gartang Cho *see* Garmosht
59 G2 Gartan L Donegal Irish Rep 54.59N 7.55W
Gartar *see* Qianning
72 F3 Gartempe *R* France
56 D4 Garth Mid Glam Wales 51.36N 3.38W
56 D3 Garth Powys Wales 52.08N 3.32W
58 Q10 Garthbanks Shetland Scotland 59.54N 1.21W
56 E2 Garthmyl Powys Wales 52.35N 3.13W
57 M5 Garthorpe Humberside Eng 53.40N 0.42W
58 H6 Gartmore Central Scotland 56.08N 4.23W
58 E7 Gartnagrenach Strathclyde Scotland 55.47N 5.31W
58 G6 Gartocharn Strathclyde Scotland 56.02N 4.32W
Gartog *see* Markam
Gartok *see* Garyarsa
63 O6 Gartow W Germany 53.02N 11.28E
63 U6 Gartz E Germany 53.13N 14.24E
94 D6 Garub Namibia 26.33S 16.00E
34 Q5 Garus, Kūh-e- *mt* Iran 33.58N 48.30E
18 G9 Garut Java Indon 7.15S 107.55E
59 J2 Garvagh Londonderry N Ireland 54.59N 6.41W
58 L7 Garvald Lothian Scotland 55.56N 2.39W
76 C13 Garvão Portugal 37.42N 8.21W
58 G3 Garve Highland Scotland 57.36N 4.41W
58 G3 Garve, L Highland Scotland 57.35N 4.40W
11 C12 Garvie Mts New Zealand
29 H5 Garwa Bihar India 24.09N 83.52E
30 B3 Garwhal *dist* Uttar Prad India
62 N4 Garwolin Poland 51.55N 21.38E
110 J2 Garwood Idaho 47.50N 116.47W
112 L6 Garwood Texas 29.25N 96.26W
109 G1 Gary Colorado 40.04N 103.36W
106 G8 Gary Indiana 41.34N 87.20W
108 O2 Gary Minnesota 47.22N 96.18W
108 O5 Gary S Dakota 44.48N 96.29W
112 N3 Gary Texas 32.01N 94.22W
104 D9 Gary W Virginia 37.23N 81.34W
24 C10 Garyarsa Xizang Zizhiqu China 31.46N 80.21E
29 G2 Garyarsa Xizang Zizhiqu China 31.46N 80.21E
42 H4 Garyn' U.S.S.R. 55.32N 107.48E
58 C2 Garynahine Lewis, W Isles Scotland 58.11N 6.43W
20 F7 Garyū-zan *mt* Japan 34.42N 132.12E
63 Q6 Garz E Germany 53.04N 12.06E
63 S4 Garz E Germany 54.19N 13.21E
121 D2 Garza Argentina 28.08S 63.30W
115 J5 Garza García Mexico 25.40N 100.25W
112 L2 Garza Little Elm Res Texas
37 F7 Garzan Turkey 38.03N 41.33E
37 F8 Garzan *R* Turkey
24 C9 Gar Zangbo *R* Xizang Zizhiqu China
23 B3 Garzê Sichuan China 31.37N 100.00E
119 C6 Garzón Colombia 2.14N 75.37W
80 J5 Gasalvieri Italy 41.37N 13.43E
43 C7 Gasan-Kuli Turkmeniya U.S.S.R. 37.31N 53.59E
53 Z14 Gåsbu Norway 62.18N 8.40E
65 B8 Gaschurn Austria 46.59N 10.03E
64 N1 Gaschwitz E Germany 51.15N 12.23E
106 J9 Gas City Indiana 40.28N 85.37W
67 E9 Gascogne *prov* France
67 D8 Gascogne, G.de France
107 E3 Gasconade *R* Missouri
98 H5 Gascons Quebec 48.14N 64.50W
108 G3 Gascoyne N Dakota 46.06N 103.10W
14 B7 Gascoyne Junction W Australia 25.02S 115.15E
14 B6 Gascoyne, Mt W Australia 24.56S 116.40E
14 A6 Gascoyne, R W Australia
75 E7 Gascueña Spain 40.18N 2.31W
75 D5 Gascueña de Bornoba Spain 41.09N 3.02W
87 F3 Gash *watercourse* Ethiopia/Sudan
90 F5 Gashagar Nigeria 13.22N 12.47E
90 E8 Gashaka Nigeria 7.20N 11.29E
31 J3 Gasherbrum *mt* Kashmir 35.46N 76.38E
32 J7 Gasht Iran 27.47N 61.59E
24 G6 Gas Hu *L* Qinghai China
90 E5 Gashua Nigeria 12.53N 11.05E
46 N6 Gashun U.S.S.R. 47.20N 42.39E
22 C6 Gashur *water hole* Xinjiang Uygur Zizhiqu China 41.20N 93.40E
24 H5 Gashur *well* Xinjiang Uygur Zizhiqu China 41.20N 93.40E
25 L7 Gasigaon Assam India 27.45N 94.24E
32 H4 Gask Iran 33.02N 59.36E
51 E4 Gaskacokka *mt* Norway 67.38N 16.10E
58 B3 Gasker *isld* W Isles Scotland 57.59N 7.17W
15 L7 Gasmata New Britain 6.18S 150.21E
15 L7 Gasmata I New Britain 6.20S 150.20E
70 O3 Gasny France 49.05N 1.36E
116 E4 Gaspar Cuba 21.44N 78.34W
116 J5 Gaspar Hernández Dominican Rep 19.41N 70.18W
105 E11 Gasparilla *isld* Florida 26.45N 82.17W
18 G7 Gaspar, Selat *str* Indonesia
98 H5 Gaspé Quebec 48.50N 64.30W
98 H5 Gaspé, B.de Quebec 48.50N 64.30W
98 H5 Gaspé, C Quebec 48.46N 64.11W
Gaspé Passage *see* Honguedo Str
98 E5 Gaspé Pen Quebec
98 G7 Gaspereau Forks New Brunswick 46.15N 65.52W
98 H9 Gaspereau L Nova Scotia 44.57N 64.35W
81 N6 Gasperina Italy 38.44N 16.31E
98 F5 Gaspésie, Parc de la Quebec
110 B8 Gasquet California 41.51N 124.00W
89 G3 Gassa Mali 16.25N 4.15W
20 O3 Gas-san *mt* Japan 38.32N 140.01E
89 B4 Gassane Senegal 14.54N 15.16W
104 E8 Gassaway W Virginia 38.41N 80.48W
60 M13 Gassel Netherlands 51.44N 5.46E
60 Q8 Gasselte Netherlands 52.58N 6.46E
60 Q8 Gasselternijeveen Netherlands 52.59N 6.51E
75 C9 Gasset, Embalse de *res* Spain 39.08N 3.58W
88 Q6 Gassi, El Algeria 31.05N 5.40E
79 C4 Gassino Italy 45.08N 7.49E
88 R6 Gassi Touil Algeria 30.35N 6.23E
88 R7 Gassi Touil *reg* Algeria
90 E7 Gassol Nigeria 8.32N 10.30E
111 J5 Gass Pk Nevada 36.23N 115.12W
53 E3 Gassum Denmark 56.34N 10.01E
65 H7 Gastein Tal *V* Austria
40 J7 Gastello Sakhalin U.S.S.R. 49.06N 142.57E
39 D4 Gastello, Imeni U.S.S.R. 61.32N 158.05E
66 G6 Gastern Tal *V* Switzerland
69 E6 Gastins France 48.38N 3.02E
110 B4 Gaston Oregon 45.25N 123.09W
105 F2 Gastonia N Carolina 35.14N 81.12W
104 G10 Gaston Res Virginia/N Car
77 F7 Gastor, El Spain 36.52N 5.19W
84 B6 Gastouni Greece 37.51N 21.15E
84 W22 Gastoúr Corfu 39.34N 19.54E
121 B9 Gastre Argentina 42.20S 69.18W
53 R16 Gåsvær *isld* Norway 61.10N 4.41E
35 C7 Gat Israel 31.38N 34.47E
Gat Libya *see* Ghāt
89 P10 Gata Cape Verde 16.12N 22.43E
76 F8 Gata Spain 40.15N 6.35W
87 A9 Gata Zaïre 3.43N 27.33E
84 R15 Gata *C* Cyprus
77 M7 Gata, C.de Spain 36.44N 2.10W
77 R3 Gata de Gorgos Spain 38.47N 0.05E
101 K6 Gataga *R* Br Col
82 G5 Gataia Romania 45.24N 21.26E
76 F8 Gata, Sierra de *mts* Spain
74 F8 Gata, Sierra del Cabo de *mts* Spain
122 S15 Gatavaké, B.de Mangaréva Pacific Oc 23.07S 134.58W
103 B7 Gatchellville Pennsylvania 39.46N 76.28W
51 P12 Gatchina U.S.S.R. 59.32N 30.09E
109 K5 Gate Oklahoma 36.51N 100.05W
104 C10 Gate City Virginia 36.38N 82.37W
57 E3 Gatehouse of Fleet Dumfries & Galloway Scotland 54.53N 4.11W
Gatere *see* Ghatere
15 K3 Gateri Solomon Is 8.06S 157.02E
110 C5 Gates Oregon 44.46N 122.25W
57 K3 Gateshead Tyne and Wear Eng 54.58N 1.35W
101 X1 Gateshead I N W Terr 70.38N 100.20W
110 O3 Gates of the Mountains *pass* Montana 46.53N 111.58W
105 L1 Gatesville N Carolina 36.24N 76.46W
112 K4 Gatesville Texas 31.26N 97.46W
109 B3 Gateway Colorado 38.41N 108.59W
110 K1 Gateway Montana 48.59N 115.10W
110 D5 Gateway Oregon 44.47N 121.05W
120 D10 Gatico Chile 22.29S 70.15W
69 C7 Gâtinais *plain* France
70 L7 Gâtine *reg* France
99 P7 Gatineau Quebec 45.29N 75.40W
99 P5 Gatineau *R* Quebec
99 P7 Gatineau, Parc de la Quebec
72 C2 Gâtine Hauteurs de *hills* France 46.38N 0.38W
95 G3 Ga-Tlhose S Africa 27.52S 23.15E
105 D2 Gatlinburg Tennessee 35.44N 83.32W
77 G4 Gato *R* Spain
35 D1 Ga'ton Israel 33.00N 35.12E
92 D11 Gatooma Zimbabwe 18.16S 29.55E
75 J8 Gátova Spain 39.46N 0.33W
32 F6 Gatrūyeh Iran 29.10N 54.40E
95 L2 Gatsrand *ridge* S Africa
20 N3 Gatsugi Japan 38.29N 139.30E
70 H2 Gatteville France 49.41N 1.18W
71 L9 Gattières France 43.45N 7.10E
79 D3 Gattinara Italy 45.37N 8.22E
13 K8 Gatton Queensland 27.33S 152.15E
30 A2 Gatu Himachal Prad India 30.33N 77.32E
115 E9 Gatún Panama Canal Zone 9.16N 79.55W
115 F9 Gatún *R* Panama
115 F10 Gatun L Panama/Panama Canal Zone
32 C4 Gatvand Iran 32.16N 48.49E
Gatwick *see* London (Gatwick) Airport
108 P1 Gatzke Minnesota 48.26N 95.49W
64 E4 Gau-Algesheim W Germany 49.58N 8.02E
87 H5 Gauani Ethiopia 10.12N 40.40E
77 F7 Gaucín Spain 36.31N 5.19W
Gaud-i-Mukh *see* Gowd-e Mokh
31 B6 Gaud-i-Zirreh *salt des* Afghanistan
98 K3 Gaudreault, L Quebec
100 U1 Gauer L Manitoba
15 K6 Gauffre, C New Britain 5.28S 148.38E
59 F2 Gaugin Mt Donegal Irish Rep 54.48N 8.02W
31 F5 Gauharwala Pakistan 31.41N 71.40E
28 H2 Gauhati Assam India 26.10N 91.45E
46 E2 Gauja *R* Latvia U.S.S.R.
53 W21 Gaukheihytta Norway 59.56N 7.19E
52 F4 Gauldalen *V* Norway
104 D8 Gauley Bridge W Virginia 38.11N 81.13W
70 M5 Gault, le France 48.06N 1.00E
98 R6 Gaultois Newfoundland 47.36N 55.55W
70 N5 Gault-St.Denis, le France 48.14N 1.28E
50 E7 Gaulverjabær Iceland 63.50N 20.54W
75 F2 Gauna Spain 42.49N 2.30W
30 E6 Gauniganj Uttar Prad India 26.12N 81.42E
64 E4 Gau-Odernheim W Germany 49.45N 8.10E
69 P4 Gau-Odernheim W Germany 49.45N 8.10E
53 W16 Gaupne Norway 61.25N 7.18E
30 J7 Gaupur Bihar India 25.46N 85.42E
29 L5 Gaur *ruins* W Bengal India 24.54N 88.16E
61 D4 Gaurain-Ramecroix Belgium 50.35N 3.29E
121 H1 Gaurama Brazil 27.37S 52.10W
30 E6 Gaura Umarni Uttar Prad India 26.07N 81.10E
43 H7 Gaurdak Turkmeniya U.S.S.R. 37.39N 66.03E
29 L2 Gaurhati W Bengal India 22.45N 87.47E
28 C4 Gauribidanūr Karnataka India 13.38N 77.26E
30 D7 Gaurihar Madhya Prad India 25.16N 80.12E
30 D4 Gauri Phanta Uttar Prad India 28.41N 80.36E
31 H9 Gaurnadi Bangladesh 22.59N 90.11E
52 E5 Gausdal, Østre Norway 61.15N 10.10E
52 E5 Gausdal, Vestre Norway 61.12N 10.09E
48 U9 Gauss Halvø *pen* Greenland
52 D7 Gausta *mt* Norway 59.51N 8.42E
64 L7 Gauting W Germany 48.03N 11.24E
50 E5 Gautlönd *land* Iceland
93 H3 Gautoro Kenya 2.36N 36.20E
53 Z14 Gautsjøen *L* Norway 62.17N 8.42E
31 C3 Gauzan Afghanistan 35.41N 64.30E
75 P5 Gavá Spain 41.18N 2.00E
43 N7 Gava Uzbekistan U.S.S.R. 41.10N 71.08E
32 E6 Gāvakān Iran 29.37N 53.10E
84 C4 Gavaloú Greece 38.32N 21.31E
77 Q3 Gavanes Spain 38.49N 0.25W
39 F5 Gavanka U.S.S.R. 57.58N 158.25E
79 H3 Gavardo Italy 45.35N 10.26E
32 H2 Gavāreshg Iran 36.35N 59.31E
72 D10 Gavarnie France 42.44N 0.01W
72 D10 Gavarnie, Cirque de France 42.42N 0.01W
75 Q4 Gavarras, Mts Spain
32 J8 Gavāter Iran 25.10N 61.31E
32 E7 Gāvbandī Iran 27.12N 53.04E
32 E7 Gāvbūs, Kūh-e *mts* Iran
84 J12 Gavdhopoúla *isld* Crete 34.56N 24.00E
84 K12 Gávdhos *isld* Crete 34.50N 24.05E
76 C4 Gávea Portugal 42.02N 8.17W
118 J10 Gávea Rio de Janeiro Brazil 23.00S 43.16W
118 J10 Gavea Rio de Janeiro Brazil 22.58S 43.14W
72 C9 Gave d'Aspe *R* France
72 D9 Gave-de-Pau *R* France
72 C9 Gave d'Oloron *R* France
72 C9 Gave d'Ossau *R* France
32 B3 Gaveh *R* Iran
118 J10 Gavelândia Brazil 23.00S 43.16W
39 H4 Gavena, Poluostrov *pen* U.S.S.R.
61 E3 Gavere Belgium 50.56N 3.40E
44 G10 Gāvgān Iran 37.48N 45.53E
79 E5 Gavi Italy 44.42N 8.48E
76 D10 Gavião Portugal 39.28N 7.56W
118 H4 Gavião, R Brazil
120 E2 Gaviãozinho Brazil 6.30S 68.45W
80 H7 Gavi, I.di Italy 40.56N 13.00E
109 C5 Gavilan New Mexico 36.22N 107.03W

32 B3 **Gavīleh** Iran 35.42N 46.21E
58 M7 **Gavinton** Borders Scotland 55.46N 2.22W
111 D7 **Gaviota** California 34.28N 120.14W
79 E3 **Gavirate** Italy 45.51N 8.42E
Gāvkan *see* **Gāvakān**
Gav Khaneh *see* **Gav Khūni**
32 E4 **Gav Khūni** Iran 32.20N 52.51E
32 G6 **Gāv Koshī** Iran 28.40N 57.15E
44 H9 **Gavlān** Iran 38.50N 47.27E
52 K6 **Gävle** Sweden 60.41N 17.10E
52 J5 **Gävleborg** *dist* Sweden
52 K6 **Gävlebukten** *B* Sweden 60.45N 17.30E
81 C3 **Gavoi** Sardinia 40.09N 9.12E
80 C3 **Gavorrano** Italy 42.56N 10.49E
70 H4 **Gavray** France 48.54N 1.20W
70 G6 **Gavre, le** France 47.32N 1.44W
87 F4 **Gavriel** Ethiopia 13.20N 37.29E
39 K4 **Gavrilla, Guba** *gulf* U.S.S.R.
40 E4 **Gavrilova** U.S.S.R. 54.36N 129.24E
45 H6 **Gavrilovka** Ukraine U.S.S.R. 50.00N 36.03E
45 O4 **Gavrilovka 2-aya** U.S.S.R. 52.53N 42.45E
46 L2 **Gavrilov Yam** U.S.S.R. 57.18N 39.49E
46 N1 **Gavrino** U.S.S.R. 58.38N 44.01E
83 G7 **Gávrion** Greece 37.54N 24.44E
84 C5 **Gavrolímni** Greece 38.23N 21.38E
37 F5 **Gâvur Dağları** *mts* Erzurum Turkey
36 J6 **Gâvur Dağları** *mts* Hatay Turkey
94 D6 **Gawachab** Namibia 27.03S 17.50E
25 N7 **Gawai** Burma 27.59N 97.30E
15 L8 **Gawa I** Papua New Guinea 9.00S 151.58E
34 M2 **Gawāra** Iraq 36.46N 44.28E
60 E14 **Gawege** Netherlands 51.25N 4.07E
65 P5 **Gaweinstal** Austria 48.30N 16.35E
87 C6 **Gaweir** *tribe* Sudan
29 E7 **Gawilgarh** Maharashtra India 21.28N 77.25E
29 E7 **Gawilgarh Hills** Maharashtra/Madhya Prad India
12 E5 **Gawler** S Australia 34.38S 138.44E
12 D5 **Gawler Ras** *mts* S Australia
52 J3 **Gåxsjö** Sweden 63.40N 15.10E
22 E5 **Gaxun Nur** *L* Nei Monggol Zizhiqu China
106 F2 **Gay** Michigan 47.13N 88.10W
30 H8 **Gaya** Bihar India 24.48N 85.00E
89 L6 **Gaya** Niger 11.52N 3.28E
90 D6 **Gaya** Nigeria 11.53N 9.01E
30 H8 **Gaya** *dist* Bihar India
18 M2 **Gaya** *isld* Sabah Malaysia 6.01N 116.02E
75 N5 **Gayá** *R* Spain
21 E6 **Gaya He** *R* Jilin China
31 G3 **Gayal Gah** Kashmir 35.35N 73.37E
18 L9 **Gayam** Indonesia 7.11S 114.20E
93 B6 **Gayaza** Uganda 0.46S 30.49E
59 H5 **Gaybrook** W Meath Irish Rep 53.28N 7.19W
56 J3 **Gaydon** Warwicks Eng 52.11N 1.27W
44 B3 **Gayduk** U.S.S.R. 44.47N 37.43E
103 N4 **Gay Head** *C* Massachusetts 41.21N 70.50W
56 K3 **Gayhurst** Bucks Eng 52.07N 0.46W
109 M2 **Gaylord** Kansas 39.41N 98.50W
106 K4 **Gaylord** Michigan 45.02N 84.41W
108 Q5 **Gaylord** Minnesota 44.33N 94.12W
110 A7 **Gaylord** Oregon 42.57N 124.07W
13 K7 **Gayndah** Queensland 25.36S 151.32E
47 G5 **Gayny** U.S.S.R. 60.17N 54.15E
18 D9 **Gayong** *hill* Pen Malaysia 2.56N 103.12E
46 G5 **Gaysin** Ukraine U.S.S.R. 48.50N 29.29E
106 D6 **Gays Mills** Wisconsin 43.20N 90.50W
56 N2 **Gayton** Norfolk Eng 52.45N 0.34E
46 L1 **Gayutino** U.S.S.R. 58.41N 38.30E
108 N7 **Gayville** S Dakota 42.54N 97.11W
46 G5 **Gayvoron** Ukraine U.S.S.R. 48.20N 29.52E
56 M2 **Gaywood** Norfolk Eng 52.46N 0.26E
Gaz Balūchestān va Sīstān *see* **Hanjīrak**
32 G7 **Gaz** Banāder va Jazāyer-e Baḩr-e Oman Iran 26.25N 57.14E
32 D4 **Gaz** Esfahān Iran 32.49N 51.39E
35 A8 **Gaza** Gaza Strip 31.30N 34.28E
94 M4 **Gaza** *dist* Mozambique
43 F6 **Gaz-Achak** Uzbekistan U.S.S.R. 41.09N 61.25E
32 H7 **Gazak** Balūchestān va Sīstān Iran 27.35N 59.55E
32 G5 **Gazak** Kermān Iran 30.42N 57.18E
43 J6 **Gazalkent** Uzbekistan U.S.S.R. 41.31N 69.45E
Gazamahu *see* **Gaz Māhū**
90 E4 **Gazamni** Niger 14.20N 10.34E
31 D6 **Gazan** Pakistan 28.27N 66.36E
90 C5 **Gazaoua** Nigeria 13.40N 7.55E
35 A8 **Gaza Strip** *terr* Egypt
32 H6 **Gāzbor** Iran 28.06N 58.50E
121 D6 **Gazcón, A** Argentina 37.31S 63.15W
31 E4 **Gazdarra Pass** Afghanistan 32.57N 68.25E
110 C8 **Gazelle** California 41.33N 122.33W
15 L5 **Gazelle Chan** New Ireland
15 L6 **Gazelle Pen** New Britain
9 B13 **Gazelle, Récif de la** *reef* Loyalty Is Pacific Oc 20.10S 165.28E
69 B6 **Gazeran** France 48.38N 1.46E
26 A16 **Gazert, C** Heard I Antarctica 53.04S 73.22E
32 F4 **Gazestān** Iran 32.29N 54.32E
43 H6 **Gazgan** Uzbekistan U.S.S.R. 40.35N 65.28E
93 L10 **Gazi** Kenya 4.25S 39.29E
91 J3 **Gazi** Zaïre 1.04N 24.30E
37 C8 **Gaziantep** Turkey 37.04N 37.21E
Gazibenli *see* **Yahyalı**
32 J4 **Gazīk** Iran 33.00N 60.15E
37 D2 **Gaziköy** Turkey 40.45N 27.21E
40 A5 **Gazimur** *R* U.S.S.R.
42 K6 **Gazimurskiy Khrebet** *mts* U.S.S.R.
42 K6 **Gazimurskiy Zavod** U.S.S.R. 51.35N 118.25E
36 F6 **Gazipaşa** Turkey 36.16N 32.18E
Gazir *see* **Gezīr**
35 E3 **Gazit** Israel 32.39N 35.27E
43 G7 **Gazli** Uzbekistan U.S.S.R. 40.10N 63.28E
32 H7 **Gaz Māhū** Iran 26.35N 58.35E
32 E2 **Gaznāsarā** Iran 36.20N 52.09E
43 N8 **Gaznau** Uzbekistan U.S.S.R. 40.11N 71.04E
79 J4 **Gazoldo degli Ippoliti** Italy 45.12N 10.34E
Gaz Sala *see* **Gaz Şāleḩ**
32 G6 **Gaz Şāleḩ** Iran 28.25N 57.45E
66 M8 **Gazzada** Italy 45.46N 8.48E
79 K4 **Gazzo Veronese** Italy 45.08N 11.05E
79 J4 **Gazzuolo** Italy 45.04N 10.35E
89 E8 **Gbanga** Liberia 7.19N 9.13W
89 C8 **Gbangbama** Sierra Leone 7.47N 12.18W
89 C8 **Gbangbatok** Sierra Leone 7.50N 12.23W
89 E7 **Gbanhala** *R* Guinea/Ivory Coast
90 B7 **Gbarijuko** Nigeria 9.37N 5.55E
89 E8 **Gbarnga** Liberia 7.02N 9.26W
Gbeibe *see* **Gubeiba**
90 B8 **Gbekebo** Nigeria 6.20N 4.56E
89 E7 **Gbéléba** Ivory Coast 9.39N 8.03W
89 C7 **Gbinti** Sierra Leone 8.59N 12.32W
90 D8 **Gboko** Nigeria 7.15N 9.09E
90 B8 **Gbongan** Nigeria 7.27N 4.21E
91 G2 **Gbwado** Zaïre 3.50N 20.53E
94 H2 **Gcoverega** Botswana 19.08S 24.18E
62 L1 **Gdańsk** Poland 54.22N 18.41E
46 G1 **Gdov** U.S.S.R. 58.48N 27.52E
74 G9 **Gdyel** Algeria 35.47N 0.26W
62 L1 **Gdynia** Poland 54.31N 18.30E
35 B7 **Ge'a** Israel 31.38N 34.36E
75 H7 **Gea de Albarracin** Spain 40.25N 1.21W
110 B3 **Gearhart** Oregon 46.01N 123.55W
110 E7 **Gearhart Mt** Oregon 42.30N 120.50W
109 M6 **Geary** Oklahoma 35.38N 98.20W
59 H5 **Geashill** Offaly Irish Rep 53.14N 7.19W
72 D8 **Geaune** France 43.39N 0.22W
89 B5 **Geba** Guinea-Bissau 12.09N 14.43W
89 B5 **Geba** *R* Guinea-Bissau/Senegal
90 E6 **Gebai** Nigeria 11.07N 11.39E
19 F4 **Gebe** *isld* Moluccas Indon
85 O10 **Gebeit** Sudan 18.58N 36.48E
85 O9 **Gebeit Mine** Sudan 21.03N 36.29E
86 C5 **Gebel Khashm el Qa'ûd** *ruins* Egypt 30.30N 29.51E
37 D5 **Gebeme** Turkey 40.38N 37.48E
64 K1 **Gebesee** E Germany 51.07N 10.57E
44 F5 **Gebi** Georgia U.S.S.R. 42.46N 43.30E
87 J6 **Gebile** Somalia 9.41N 43.40E
36 E5 **Gebiz** Turkey 37.07N 30.57E
108 B6 **Gebo** Wyoming 43.47N 108.18W
64 H8 **Gebrazhofen** W Germany 47.47N 9.57E
24 E11 **Gebuk La** *pass* Xizang Zizhiqu 29.35N 85.10E
37 G2 **Gebze** Turkey 40.48N 29.26E
87 E7 **Gechia** Ethiopia 7.27N 35.18E
87 F4 **Gedabiet** Ethiopia 13.19N 36.20E
18 D7 **Gedang, Gunung** *mt* Sumatra Indon 2.44S 101.53E
87 E3 **Gedaref** Sudan 14.01N 35.24E
108 M6 **Geddes** S Dakota 43.14N 98.40W
13 F3 **Geddes** *R* Queensland
56 K3 **Geddington** Northants Eng 52.26N 0.40W
87 K6 **Gedeis** Somalia 9.59N 45.29E
37 G2 **Gedelek** Turkey 40.27N 29.17E
35 C6 **Gedera** Israel 31.48N 34.46E
64 G3 **Gedern** W Germany 50.25N 9.12E
53 H7 **Gedesby** Denmark 54.37N 11.57E
18 G9 **Gede, Tanjung** *C* Java Indon 7.44S 107.47E
53 C4 **Gedhus** Denmark 56.17N 9.08E
93 M9 **Gedi** Kenya 3.18S 40.01E
90 M5 **Gedid Ras el Fil** Sudan 12.45N 25.45E
61 K7 **Gedinne** Belgium 49.59N 4.56E
87 C5 **Gedir,Jeb** *mt* Sudan 10.50N 31.08E
36 D3 **Gediz** Turkey 39.04N 29.25E
36 D4 **Gediz** *R* Turkey
56 L2 **Gedney Hill** Lincs Eng 52.41N 0.01W
Gedong *see* **Fangshan**
18 J5 **Gedong** Sarawak Malaysia 1.15N 110.41E
18 B9 **Gedong Lalang** Pen Malaysia 2.42N 101.59E
72 E10 **Gèdre** France 42.47N 0.02E
53 H7 **Gedser** Denmark 54.35N 11.57E
53 H7 **Gedser Odde** *C* Denmark 54.34N 11.58E
53 C3 **Gedsted** Denmark 56.42N 9.21E
94 U13 **Geduld** S Africa 26.12S 28.26E
61 K2 **Geel** Belgium 51.10N 4.59E
12 G7 **Geelong** Victoria 38.10S 144.26E
14 A8 **Geelvink Chan** W Australia
61 L4 **Geer** Belgium 50.40N 5.10E
60 H13 **Geertruidenberg** Netherlands 51.43N 4.52E
63 J5 **Geestekanal** W Germany
63 J5 **Geestenseth** W Germany 53.31N 8.51E
60 P11 **Geesteren** Gelderland Netherlands 52.08N 6.31E
60 P10 **Geesteren** Overijssel Netherlands 52.25N 6.44E
63 M6 **Geesthacht** W Germany 53.26N 10.23E
61 L3 **Geetbets** Belgium 50.53N 5.07E
12 H9 **Geeveston** Tasmania 43.11S 147.53E
85 A3 **Gefara Plain** Libya/Tunisia
64 M3 **Gefell** E Germany 50.26N 11.51E
35 C7 **Gefen** Israel 31.45N 34.53E
60 K13 **Geffen** Netherlands 51.44N 5.28E
50 J2 **Gefla** *mt* Iceland 66.26N 16.26W
64 M3 **Gefrees** W Germany 50.06N 11.45E
44 F7 **Gegamskiy Khrebet** *mts* Armenia U.S.S.R.
89 D8 **Gegbwema** Sierra Leone 7.39N 11.03W
21 B5 **Gegenmiao** Nei Monggol Zizhiqu China 46.55N 122.20E
22 L7 **Gegu** Tianjin China 39.00N 117.29E
24 C9 **Gê'gyai** Xizang Zizhiqu China 32.25N 84.05E
Geh *see* **Nīkshahr**
21 D10 **Gehaku** *isld* S Korea 34.02N 127.35E
64 G2 **Gehau** W Germany 50.47N 9.28E
72 G1 **Gehée** France 47.03N 1.30E
Gehēr, Jabal ha- *see* **Ha-Gehēr, Jabal** *mt*
63 L8 **Gehrden** W Germany 52.19N 9.37E
64 L2 **Gehren** E Germany 50.39N 11.00E
23 H3 **Ge Hu** *L* Jiangsu China
Gehua *see* **Alotau**
90 E5 **Geidam** Nigeria 12.55N 11.55E
65 E7 **Geier Spitze** *mt* Austria 47.08N 11.38E
87 D5 **Geigar** Sudan 11.58N 32.49E
103 C6 **Geigertown** Pennsylvania 40.13N 75.50W
60 N13 **Geijsteren** Netherlands 51.33N 6.03E
101 V7 **Geikie** *R* Saskatchewan
99 B2 **Geikie I** Ontario 50.01N 88.37W
13 G2 **Geikie Ra** Queensland
64 A2 **Geilenkirchen** W Germany 50.58N 6.08E
87 D2 **Geili, El** Sudan 16.01N 32.37E
53 Y17 **Geilo** Norway 60.32N 8.13E
12 F7 **Geilston Bay** Hobart, Tasmania
93 N2 **Geilu Hills** Kenya
64 E5 **Geinsheim** W Germany 49.18N 8.15E
69 P4 **Geinsheim** W Germany 49.53N 8.24E
53 W14 **Geiranger** Norway 62.06N 7.13E
53 V14 **Geirangerfjorden** *inlet* Norway 62.05N 7.00E
50 B7 **Geirfugladrangur** *rock* Iceland 63.41N 23.05W
50 E8 **Geirfuglasker** *isld* Iceland 63.19N 20.30W
50 G7 **Geirland** Iceland 63.49N 18.04W
50 G7 **Geirlandsa** *R* Iceland
50 G7 **Geirlandshraun** *mt* Iceland 63.52N 18.19W
50 D2 **Geirólfsnúpur** *C* Iceland 66.16N 21.56W
50 H6 **Geirvörtur** *mt* Iceland 64.13N 17.43W
64 H2 **Geisa** E Germany 50.43N 9.57E
60 P11 **Geiselaar** Netherlands 52.10N 6.31E
64 N6 **Geiselhöring** W Germany 48.50N 12.25E
64 J4 **Geiselwind** W Germany 49.47N 10.30E
64 M6 **Geisenfeld** W Germany 48.41N 11.40E
64 N7 **Geisenhausen** W Germany 48.28N 12.16E
64 D3 **Geisenheim** W Germany 50.01N 7.53E
64 F8 **Geisingen** W Germany 47.55N 8.40E
64 F7 **Geislingen** W Germany 48.17N 8.50E
64 H6 **Geislingen an der Steige** W Germany 48.37N 9.50E
64 J1 **Geismar** E Germany 51.41N 10.08E
69 O6 **Geispolsheim** France 48.31N 7.39E
66 K1 **Geisslingen** W Germany 47.37N 8.23E
65 M7 **Geistthal** Austria 47.11N 15.09E
93 D8 **Geita** Tanzania 2.52S 32.12E
53 R16 **Geita** *Lt Ho* Norway 61.17N 4.48E
50 D6 **Geitaberg** Iceland 64.28N 21.31W
50 L5 **Geitdalur** *V* Iceland
53 X17 **Geiterygghytta** Norway 60.43N 7.35E
64 O1 **Geithain** E Germany 51.03N 12.42E
50 L5 **Geithellur** Iceland 64.36N 14.35W
52 E7 **Geithus** Norway 59.56N 9.58E
50 E5 **Geitlandsjökull** *ice cap* Iceland 64.37N 20.34W
90 E7 **Geji** *R* Nigeria
23 C7 **Gejiu** Yunnan China 23.25N 103.05E
39 K3 **Geka, Mys** *C* U.S.S.R. 64.29N 178.14E
32 F2 **Gekcheh Dagh** *mts* Iran
87 B7 **Gel** *watercourse* Sudan
81 H9 **Gela** Sicily 37.04N 14.15E
29 K3 **Gela** *mt* Xizang Zizhiqu 29.14N 86.25E
81 H9 **Gela** *R* Sicily
81 H9 **Gela, Golfo di** Sicily
89 D8 **Gelahun** Liberia 7.55N 10.28W
93 H8 **Gelai** *mt* Tanzania 2.37S 36.06E
18 J7 **Gelam** *isld* Kalimantan Indonesia
37 G8 **Gelamemi Dağ** *mt* Turkey 37.33N 42.55E
18 E3 **Gelang, Tanjong** *C* Pen Malaysia 4.10N 103.27E
63 Q4 **Gelbensande** E Germany 54.14N 12.21E
61 K4 **Gelbressée** Belgium 50.31N 4.57E
64 J4 **Gelchsheim** W Germany 49.35N 10.02E
60 M11 **Gelderland** *prov* Netherlands
60 K12 **Geldermalsen** Netherlands 51.53N 5.17E
63 D9 **Geldern** W Germany 51.31N 6.19E
50 D4 **Geldingafell** *mt* Iceland 65.05N 21.16W
50 F6 **Geldingafell** *mt* Iceland 64.18N 19.50W
50 K5 **Geldingafen** *mt* Iceland 64.40N 15.17W
60 L14 **Geldrop** Netherlands 51.25N 5.34E
91 F2 **Gele** Zaïre 2.40N 19.16E
85 F3 **Gel Ebia** Libya 32.38N 21.26E
60 T17 **Geleen** Netherlands 50.58N 5.50E
36 F2 **Gelegra** Turkey 40.02N 31.50E
34 O5 **Geleh Jār** Iran 33.43N 46.20E
64 O2 **Gelenau** E Germany 50.43N 12.59E
36 C3 **Gelenbe** Turkey 39.12N 27.50E
36 E4 **Gelendost** Turkey 38.07N 31.00E
44 B3 **Gelendzhik** U.S.S.R. 44.34N 38.07E
99 M8 **Gelert** Ontario 44.56N 78.37W
89 L3 **Gelgiet** Mali 17.52N 3.07E
87 D5 **Gelhak** Sudan 11.02N 32.42E
87 J7 **Geli** Ethiopia 6.48N 42.59E
87 J10 **Gelib** Somalia 0.26N 42.48E
87 K10 **Gelib** Somalia 1.45N 44.55E
37 C2 **Gelibolu** Turkey 40.25N 26.41E
75 O5 **Gélida** Spain 41.26N 1.52E
36 E6 **Gelidonya Burun** *C* Turkey 36.14N 30.25E
37 F7 **Geliguzan** Turkey 38.37N 41.26E
61 M3 **Gelinden** Belgium 50.46N 5.16E
23 H6 **Geling** Fujian China 25.53N 119.04E
26 S7 **Gelioya** Sri Lanka 7.12N 80.36E
72 E7 **Gelise** *R* France
19 C8 **Geliting** Indonesia 8.39S 122.16E
12 C8 **Gellibrand, Pt** Victoria 37.53S 144.55E
61 N3 **Gellik** Belgium 50.53N 5.36E
66 B5 **Gellin** France 46.45N 6.15E
9 B3 **Gellinam** *islet* Marshall Is Pacific Oc 9.05N 167.43E
61 M3 **Gelmen** Belgium 50.47N 5.16E
66 K5 **Gelmer See** *L* Switzerland 46.37N 8.20E
32 G4 **Gelmord** Iran 33.25N 56.16E
45 C7 **Gel'myazov** Ukraine U.S.S.R. 49.45N 31.50E
64 G3 **Gelnhausen** W Germany 50.12N 9.13E
87 C8 **Gel,R** Sudan
61 K3 **Gelrode** Belgium 50.58N 4.48E
75 K5 **Gelsa** Spain 41.24N 0.28W
53 C6 **Gelså** *R* Denmark
Gelsdorf *see* **Grafschaft**
63 F10 **Gelsenkirchen** W Germany 51.30N 7.05E
53 D6 **Gelsted** Denmark 55.24N 9.58E
66 H22 **Gelterkinden** Switzerland 47.27N 7.52E
63 L3 **Gelting** W Germany 54.44N 9.54E
95 H3 **Geluk** S Africa 27.03S 24.17E
95 N4 **Geluksburg** S Africa 28.31S 29.21E
61 B3 **Geluveld** Belgium 50.50N 2.59E
61 C3 **Geluwe** Belgium 50.48N 3.05E
36 G4 **Gelveri** Turkey 38.16N 34.23E
77 D6 **Gelves** Spain 37.20N 6.01W
100 E8 **Gem** Alberta 50.58N 112.11W
109 K2 **Gem** Kansas 39.25N 100.54W
112 D8 **Gem** Texas 35.47N 100.07W
18 C9 **Gemas** Pen Malaysia 2.35N 102.35E
61 L6 **Gembes** Belgium 50.00N 5.04E
87 E6 **Gembi** Ethiopia 9.12N 35.50E
61 J4 **Gembloux** Belgium 50.34N 4.42E
15 H6 **Gembogl** Papua New Guinea 5.52S 145.06E
90 E8 **Gembu** Nigeria 6.42N 11.10E
19 E1 **Gemeh** Indonesia 4.33N 126.51E
63 E9 **Gemen** W Germany 51.51N 6.52E
91 F2 **Gemena** Zaïre 3.13N 19.48E
71 H10 **Géménos** France 43.17N 5.37E
36 J3 **Gemerek** Turkey 39.13N 36.05E
60 L13 **Gemert** Netherlands 51.33N 5.41E
14 F3 **Gemini Hills** W Australia
37 G2 **Gemlik** Turkey 40.26N 29.10E
37 F2 **Gemlik Körfezi** *gulf* Turkey
87 C8 **Gemmeiza** Sudan 5.43N 31.50E
66 H5 **Gemmenalp Horn** *mt* Switz 46.44N 7.48E
61 O4 **Gemmenich** Belgium 50.45N 6.00E
64 F5 **Gemmingen** W Germany 49.10N 8.58E
66 G6 **Gemmi Pass** Switzerland 46.24N 7.37E
18 E10 **Gemoh, Tanjong** *C* Pen Malaysia 1.46N 104.12E
79 O2 **Gemona** Italy 46.17N 13.08E
72 C4 **Gémozac** France 45.35N 0.40W
86 L10 **Gemsa** Egypt 27.39N 33.35E
95 E9 **Gemsbok** S Africa 33.06S 21.23E
94 F5 **Gemsbok Nat. Park** Botswana
95 H1 **Gemsbokvlakte** S Africa 25.55S 24.30E
87 F8 **Gemu-Gwefa** *prov* Ethiopia
64 B2 **Gemünd** W Germany 50.34N 6.30E
64 H3 **Gemünden** Bayern W Germany 50.03N 9.42E
64 C4 **Gemünden** Rheinland-Pfalz W Germany 49.54N 7.29E
64 F2 **Gemünden an der Wohra** Hessen W Germany 50.59N 8.59E
72 E4 **Genac** France 45.48N 0.01E
95 C10 **Genadendal** S Africa 34.02S 19.33E
77 F7 **Genal** *R* Spain
77 F7 **Genalguacil** Spain 36.34N 5.14W
61 H4 **Genappe** Belgium 50.37N 4.27E
52 G11 **Genarp** Sweden 55.36N 13.25E
77 L4 **Genave** Spain 38.26N 2.44W
71 E1 **Genay** France 47.32N 4.17E
80 G5 **Genazzano** Italy 41.50N 12.59E
37 F7 **Genç** Turkey 38.44N 40.35E
36 F5 **Gencek** Turkey 37.25N 31.32E
31 E6 **Gendari Mt** Pakistan 29.05N 69.45E
121 K8 **Gendarme Barreto** Argentina 50.20S 70.52W
60 J13 **Genderen** Netherlands 51.44N 5.05E
87 F4 **Gendoa,R** Ethiopia
29 E5 **Gendoli** Rajasthan India 25.32N 76.02E
71 H2 **Gendrey** France 47.12N 5.42E
60 O12 **Gendringen** Netherlands 51.53N 6.24E
109 N7 **Gene Autry** Oklahoma 34.16N 97.04W
103 C2 **Genegantslet Cr** New York
90 L5 **Geneina** Sudan 13.27N 22.30E
90 L5 **Geneina Fort** Sudan 13.30N 22.29E
71 E3 **Génelard** France 46.35N 4.15E
60 N9 **Genemuiden** Netherlands 52.38N 6.02E
95 M4 **Generaalsnek** S Africa 28.45S 28.04E
71 E9 **Générac** France 43.44N 4.21E
121 D6 **General Acha** Argentina 37.25S 64.38W
General Alvarado *see* **Miramar** Argentina
121 E6 **General Alvear** Buenos Aires Argentina 36.02S 60.00W
121 E3 **General Alvear** Entre Ríos Arg 31.58S 60.40W
121 C5 **General Alvear** Mendoza Arg 34.59S 67.40W
118 C9 **General Aquino** Paraguay 24.20S 56.47W
121 E5 **General Arenales** Argentina 34.21S 61.20W
118 C10 **General Artigas** Paraguay 26.52S 56.16W
121 F5 **General Belgrano** Argentina 35.47N 58.30W
123 D11 **General Belgrano** *Arg Base* Antarctica 77.49S 38.02W
123 E **General Bernardo O'Higgins** *Chile Base* Graham Land Antarctica 63.19S 57.54W
115 K5 **General Bravo** Mexico 25.47N 99.10W
121 H2 **General Câmara** Brazil 29.53S 51.45W
121 E1 **General Capdevila** Argentina 27.25S 61.30W
118 D4 **General Carneiro** Brazil 15.45S 52.40W
General Carrera *L see* **Buenos Aires** *L*
115 J5 **General Cepeda** Mexico 25.24N 101.30W
121 F6 **General Conesa** Buenos Aires Argentina 36.30S 57.18W
121 D8 **General Conesa** Rio Negro Argentina 40.06S 64.26W
121 H4 **General Enrique Martínez** Uruguay 33.13S 53.47W
115 J5 **General Escobedo** Mexico 25.50N 100.21W
111 F5 **General Grant Grove Section** *nat park* California
121 F6 **General Guido** Argentina 36.36S 57.45W
75 H8 **Generalisimo, Embalse del** *res* Spain 39.45N 1.09W
82 L5 **Generalisimul Suverov** Romania 45.31N 27.09E
118 B10 **General José de San Martin** Argentina 26.30N 59.20W
120 D7 **General Lagos** Chile 17.39S 69.38W
121 E6 **General Lamadrid** Argentina 37.17S 61.20W
121 G6 **General Lavalle** Argentina 36.25S 56.56W
121 D4 **General Levalle** Argentina 34.00S 63.50W
19 N7 **General Luna** Philippines 9.49N 126.09E
19 M6 **General MacArthur** Philippines 11.18N 125.31E
General Machado *see* **Canacupa**
121 F6 **General Madariaga** Argentina 37.00S 57.09W
120 F11 **General Martin Miguel de Guemes** Argentina 24.35S 65.05W
115 L8 **General Miguel Alemán** Mexico 18.11N 96.07W
121 F1 **General Paz** Argentina 27.45S 57.36W
121 B9 **General Paz, L** Arg/Chile
121 D5 **General Pico** Argentina 35.43S 63.45W
121 E1 **General Pinedo** Argentina 27.17S 61.20W
121 E5 **General Pinto** Argentina 34.45S 61.50W
121 F6 **General Pirau** Argentina 37.16S 57.46W
121 F5 **General Plaz** Argentina 35.30S 58.20W
121 C7 **General Roca** Argentina 39.00S 67.35W
120 F7 **General Saavedra** Bolivia 17.15S 63.13W
118 E7 **General Salgado** Brazil 20.37S 50.17W
117 G7 **General Sampaio** Brazil 4.01S 39.24W
117 G7 **General Sampaio, Açude** *res* Brazil
121 J3 **General San Martín** Buenos Aires Arg 34.34S 58.30W
19 M8 **General Santos** Mindanao Philippines 6.05N 125.15E
115 H5 **General Simón Bolívar** Mexico 24.42N 103.15W
115 K5 **General Terán** Mexico 25.18N 99.40W
82 L7 **General Toshevo** Bulgaria 43.42N 28.06E
112 H9 **General Treviño** Mexico 26.13N 99.30W
115 F3 **General Trías** Mexico 28.20N 106.20W
121 G2 **General Vargas** Brazil 29.42S 54.41W
121 E5 **General Viamonte** Argentina 35.01S 61.00W
115 H6 **General Vicente Guerrero** Mexico 23.45N 103.58W
121 E5 **General Villegas** Argentina 35.01S 62.59W
General Vintter, L *see* **General Paz, L**
37 D2 **Generli** Turkey 40.59N 27.08E
66 N8 **Generoso, Monte** Italy/Switz 45.56N 9.02E
110 J3 **Genesee** Idaho 46.35N 116.55W
106 L6 **Genesee** Michigan 43.07N 83.37W
104 G4 **Genesee** *R* New York
106 D8 **Geneseo** Illinois 41.27N 90.10W
109 M3 **Geneseo** Kansas 38.31N 98.10W
104 H4 **Geneseo** New York 42.46N 77.49W
72 A1 **Geneston** France 47.03N 1.31W
87 G6 **Genet** Ethiopia 9.01N 38.30E
70 H4 **Genêts** France 48.41N 1.28W
107 L10 **Geneva** Alabama 31.03N 85.51W
105 C5 **Geneva** Georgia 32.34N 84.33W
106 F8 **Geneva** Illinois 41.54N 88.20W
106 K9 **Geneva** Indiana 40.35N 84.57W
108 N9 **Geneva** Nebraska 40.30N 97.38W
104 J4 **Geneva** New York 42.53N 76.59W
104 E5 **Geneva** Ohio 41.48N 80.57W
99 J6 **Geneva** Ontario 46.48N 81.30W
95 L3 **Geneva** S Africa 27.50S 27.08E
Geneva Switzerland *see* **Genève**
112 O4 **Geneva** Texas 31.30N 93.58W
106 F7 **Geneva, L** Wisconsin 42.33N 88.30W
Geneva, Lake of Switzerland *see* **Léman, Lac**
66 A7 **Genève** Switzerland 46.13N 6.09E
75 F2 **Genevilla** Spain 42.39N 2.23W
71 H6 **Genevrey, le** France 45.02N 5.38E
Genf *see* **Genève**
80 G2 **Genga** Italy 43.26N 12.56E
92 C6 **Genge** Zaïre 8.48S 27.44E
64 E7 **Gengenbach** W Germany 48.24N 8.02E
23 B7 **Gengma** Yunnan China 23.31N 99.24E
91 H5 **Gengwa** Zaïre 3.10S 22.50E
Genhe *see* **Ergun Zuoqi**
21 B2 **Gen He** *R* Nei Monggol Zizhiqu China
87 D7 **Geni** *watercourse* Sudan
44 D8 **Genichesk** Ukraine U.S.S.R. 46.10N 34.49E
99 J3 **Genier** Ontario 49.10N 81.02W
77 H6 **Genil** *R* Spain
72 G1 **Génillé** France 47.11N 1.06E
81 C5 **Genis, Mte** Sardinia 39.25N 9.20E
71 H4 **Genissiat Dam** France 46.03N 5.48E
Genjem *see* **Genyem**
29 C6 **Genji** Rajasthan India 23.42N 73.46E
61 N3 **Genk** Belgium 50.58N 5.30E
20 C8 **Genkai-nada** *sea* Japan
39 M2 **Genkanyy, Khrebet** *mts* U.S.S.R.
71 G2 **Genlis** France 47.14N 5.13E
61 F5 **Genly** Belgium 50.23N 3.55E
24 F10 **Genmar** *R* Xizang Zizhiqu
81 C4 **Gennargentu, Monti del** Sardinia
81 C5 **Genn'Argiolas, Mte** Sardinia 39.25N 9.29E
60 M13 **Gennep** Netherlands 51.43N 5.58E
53 C6 **Genner** Denmark 55.08N 9.27E
70 K7 **Gennes** Maine-et-Loire France 47.21N 0.14W
70 J6 **Gennes** Mayenne France 47.51N 0.36W
70 H6 **Gennes-sur-Seiche** France 47.59N 1.07W
70 L6 **Genneteil** France 47.35N 0.02E
68 E2 **Gennevilliers** France 48.56N 2.17E
Gennossar *see* **Ginnosar**
109 G2 **Genoa** Colorado 39.16N 103.30W
105 E7 **Genoa** Florida 30.24N 82.53W
106 F7 **Genoa** Illinois 42.06N 88.41W
Genoa Italy *see* **Genova**
108 N8 **Genoa** Nebraska 41.28N 97.48W
111 E2 **Genoa** Nevada 39.01N 119.51W
104 B5 **Genoa** Ohio 41.32N 83.12W
112 G9 **Genoa** Texas 29.36N 95.11W
12 J6 **Genoa** Victoria 37.29S 149.35E
106 C6 **Genoa** Wisconsin 43.33N 91.12W
106 F7 **Genoa City** Wisconsin 42.30N 88.21W
121 B10 **Genoa, R** Argentina
15 B5 **Genofo, Geb** *mt* Irian Jaya 3.19S 133.43E
79 C5 **Genola** Italy 44.35N 7.39E
71 D8 **Génolhac** France 44.21N 3.57E
81 C4 **Genoni** Sardinia 39.48N 9.01E
110 O1 **Genou** Montana 48.00N 111.18W
72 H3 **Genouillac** France 46.21N 1.59E
72 E3 **Genouillé** France 46.07N 0.20E
72 H1 **Genouilly** Cher France 47.12N 1.52E
71 F3 **Genouilly** Saône-et-Loire France 46.40N 4.35E
79 E6 **Genova** Italy 44.24N 8.56E
79 E6 **Genova** *prov* Italy
79 E6 **Genova, G.di** *B* Italy
119 B5 **Genovesa, I** Galápagos Is 0.21N 89.58W
38 P1 **Genriyetty, Ostrov** *isld* U.S.S.R.
72 E6 **Gensac** France 44.48N 0.04E
61 E2 **Gent** Belgium 51.02N 3.42E
60 M12 **Gent** Netherlands 51.52N 5.59E
66 K5 **Gental** *V* Switzerland
61 F2 **Gentbrugge** Belgium 51.02N 3.46E
18 G9 **Genteng** Java Indon 7.21S 106.20E
18 K9 **Genteng** *isld* Indonesia 7.13S 113.52E
63 Q8 **Genthin** E Germany 52.25N 12.10E
66 A6 **Genthod** Switzerland 46.16N 6.10E
100 C2 **Genthon** Manitoba 49.51N 97.05W
68 E4 **Gentilly** France 48.49N 2.20E
107 J12 **Gentilly** *dist* New Orleans, Louisiana
61 J4 **Gentinnes** Belgium 50.35N 4.35E
118 G2 **Gentio do Ouro** Brazil 11.21S 42.30W
72 H4 **Gentioux-Pigerolles** France 45.47N 2.00E
53 K5 **Gentofte** Denmark 55.46N 12.32E
107 B5 **Gentry** Arkansas 36.15N 94.30W
107 B1 **Gentry** Missouri 40.20N 94.26W
18 C9 **Genuang** Pen Malaysia 2.27N 102.56E
32 G7 **Genū, Kūhhā-ye** *mt* Iran 27.25N 56.10E
61 H4 **Genval** Belgium 50.43N 4.30E
15 F5 **Genyem** Irian Jaya 2.48S 140.10E
81 M2 **Genzano di Lucania** Italy 40.51N 16.02E
80 G5 **Genzano di Roma** Italy 41.42N 12.42E
82 H5 **Geoagiu** Romania 45.56N 23.11E
14 B10 **Geographe B** W Australia
14 A6 **Geographe Chan** W Australia
48 U10 **Geographical Society Ø** *isld* Greenland
109 M2 **Geographic Center of U.S** Kansas 39.52N 98.36W
44 H7 **Geokchay** Azerbaydzhan U.S.S.R. 40.38N 47.43E
44 H7 **Geokchay** *R* Azerbaydzhan U.S.S.R.
43 E7 **Geok-Tepe** Turkmeniya U.S.S.R. 38.11N 57.59E
39 E4 **Geologicheskiy** U.S.S.R. 62.20N 152.37E
41 M2 **Georga, Zemlya** *isld* Franz Josef Land U.S.S.R.
108 O6 **George** Iowa 43.20N 96.00W
95 F9 **George** S Africa 33.57S 22.28E
113 J5 **George** *R* Alaska
97 N6 **George** *R* Quebec
12 D3 **George** *R* S Australia
26 R16 **George, C** Kerguelen Ind Oc 49.41S 70.12E
98 L8 **George, C** Nova Scotia 45.55N 61.52W
13 B6 **George Gills Ra** N Terr Australia
121 E10 **George I** Falkland Is 52.20S 59.45W
23 B10 **George I** Hong Kong 22.13N 114.06E
96 C14 **George I** St Helena 15.59S 5.38W
113 N6 **George, L** Alaska 61.15N 148.35W
113 P5 **George L** Alaska 63.46N 144.30W
59 E6 **George, L** Clare Irish Rep 52.59N 8.57W
105 F8 **George, L** Florida
12 J6 **George, L** New S Wales
104 M3 **George, L** New York
99 G6 **George, L** Ontario
12 F6 **George, L** S Australia 37.26S 140.00E
93 B6 **George, L** Uganda
14 E5 **George, L** W Australia
George Land *see* **Georga, Zemlya**
64 L5 **Georgensgmünd** W Germany 49.11N 11.01E
64 K2 **Georgenthal** E Germany 50.49N 10.40E
56 D6 **George Nympton** Devon Eng 50.59N 3.51W
14 B5 **George R** W Australia
96 D4 **Georges Bank** Atlantic Oc
11 B11 **George Sd** New Zealand
12 L8 **Georges R** New S Wales
107 E6 **Georgetown** Arkansas 35.07N 91.28W
96 A11 **Georgetown** Ascension I 7.56S 14.25W
111 D3 **Georgetown** California 38.53N 120.50W
103 H4 **Georgetown** Connecticut 41.15N 73.25W
104 K8 **Georgetown** Delaware 38.43N 75.05W
105 F8 **Georgetown** Florida 29.24N 81.39W
105 B6 **Georgetown** Georgia 31.03N 85.07W
116 D5 **Georgetown** Grand Cayman I W I 19.20N 81.23W
116 G3 **George Town** Great Exuma Bahamas 23.33N 75.47W
117 A1 **Georgetown** Guyana 6.46N 58.10W
110 O7 **Georgetown** Idaho 42.29N 111.21W
107 J2 **Georgetown** Illinois 39.58N 87.38W
107 M3 **Georgetown** Kentucky 38.13N 84.30W
103 C8 **Georgetown** Maryland 39.22N 75.52W
108 O2 **Georgetown** Minnesota 47.04N 96.48W
107 F10 **Georgetown** Mississippi 31.52N 90.10W
11 E11 **Georgetown** New Zealand 44.55N 170.50E
104 B8 **Georgetown** Ohio 38.52N 83.54W
99 L9 **Georgetown** Ontario 43.39N 79.56W
George Town Pen Malaysia *see* **Pinang**
98 K7 **Georgetown** Prince Edward I 46.12N 62.32W
13 G4 **Georgetown** Queensland 18.15S 143.30E
116 O8 **Georgetown** St Vincent, W I 13.19N 61.09W
12 E5 **Georgetown** S Australia 33.25S 138.24E
105 H4 **Georgetown** S Carolina 33.23N 79.18W
12 H8 **George Town** Tasmania 41.04S 146.48E
112 K5 **Georgetown** Texas 30.39N 97.42W
89 B5 **Georgetown** The Gambia 13.31N 14.50W
28 C7 **George Town** *dist* Madras, Tamil Nadu India
99 S7 **Georgeville** Quebec 45.08N 72.15W
123 F12 **George VI Sound** Antarctica
123 J4 **George V Land** Antarctica
104 J8 **George Washington Birth Place Nat. Mon** Virginia 38.13N 76.58W
112 J7 **George West** Texas 28.21N 98.08W
105 B6 **George, W.F., Res** Alabama/Georgia
102 K4 **Georgia** *state* U.S.A.
107 K10 **Georgiana** Alabama 31.39N 86.47W
99 J7 **Georgian B** Ontario
99 K8 **Georgian Bay Is.Nat.Park** Ontario
Georgia, S.S.R. *see* **Gruzinskaya, S.S.R.**
101 L11 **Georgia, Str. of** Br Col
13 E5 **Georgina** *R* N Terr/Qnsld
13 E4 **Georgina Cr** N Terr Australia
45 L5 **Georgiu-Dezh** U.S.S.R. 51.00N 39.30E
43 L5 **Georgiyevka** Dzhambul, Kazakhstan U.S.S.R. 43.03N 74.43E
43 J6 **Georgiyevka** Kazakhstan U.S.S.R. 42.12N 70.00E
43 O3 **Georgiyevka** Kazakhstan U.S.S.R. 48.50N 81.30E
44 E3 **Georgiyevsk** U.S.S.R. 44.10N 43.30E
44 C3 **Georgiyevskoye** U.S.S.R. 44.10N 39.06E
63 F7 **Georgsdorf** W Germany 52.34N 7.05E
63 F6 **Georgsheil** W Germany 53.29N 7.21E
63 H8 **Georgsmarienhütte** W Germany 52.13N 8.02E
65 C8 **Gepatschhaus** Austria 46.54N 10.46E
12 A7 **Gepps Cross** Adelaide, S Aust 34.51S 138.36E
70 J4 **Ger** France 48.41N 0.47W
64 N2 **Gera** E Germany 50.51N 12.11E
66 O7 **Gera** Italy 46.10N 9.23E
53 E2 **Gerå** *R* Denmark
64 K1 **Gera** *R* E Germany
64 M2 **Gera** *reg* E Germany
61 F3 **Geraardsbergen** Belgium 50.47N 3.53E
64 H5 **Gerabronn** W Germany 49.15N 9.55E
81 M7 **Gerace** Italy 38.16N 16.13E
81 H8 **Geraci Siculo** Sicily 37.52N 14.10E
107 E3 **Gerald** Missouri 38.24N 91.19W
100 Q8 **Gerald** Saskatchewan 50.40N 101.48W
118 F3 **Geral de Goiás, Serra** *mts* Brazil
110 P2 **Geraldine** Montana 47.36N 110.16W
11 F11 **Geraldine** New Zealand 44.04S 171.12E
14 A8 **Geraldine** W Australia 27.50S 114.40E
118 F4 **Geral do Paraná, Serra** *hills* Brazil
39 N1 **Geral'd, Ostrov** *isld* U.S.S.R. 71.24N 175.29W
99 D3 **Geraldton** Ontario 49.44N 86.59W
14 A8 **Geraldton** W Australia 28.49S 114.36E
121 J1 **Geral, Serra** *ra* Brazil
35 B8 **Gerar** *R* Israel
69 M7 **Gérardmer** France 48.04N 6.53E
14 E7 **Gerard, Mt** W Australia 27.15S 122.46E
65 N4 **Geras** Austria 48.48N 15.41E
35 G4 **Gerasa** *anc site* Jordan 32.17N 35.53E
32 F7 **Gerāsh** Iran 27.40N 54.10E
47 L6 **Gerasimovka** U.S.S.R. 58.34N 71.59E
87 K7 **Gerasleh** Ethiopia 6.05N 45.03E
69 G7 **Géraudot** France 48.19N 4.19E
87 D5 **Gerawid** Sudan 10.52N 33.29E
39 E4 **Gerba** U.S.S.R. 61.44N 152.12E
69 M7 **Gerbépal** France 48.08N 6.55E
110 C9 **Gerber** California 40.04N 122.10W
110 D7 **Gerber Res** Oregon 42.12N 121.05W
69 M7 **Gerbéviller** France 48.30N 6.31E
71 E7 **Gerbier-de-Jonc** *mt* France 44.50N 4.12E
63 P9 **Gerbstedt** E Germany 51.38N 11.37E
64 H4 **Gerchsheim** W Germany 49.42N 9.48E
37 F8 **Gercüş** Turkey 37.34N 41.22E
34 P3 **Gerdakāneh ye 'Olyā** Iran 35.05N 47.35E
95 K2 **Gerdau** S Africa 26.28S 26.06E
87 F7 **Gerdessa** Ethiopia 6.02N 37.29E
50 C6 **Gerdhar** Iceland 64.04N 22.39W
50 B3 **Gerdhhamrar** Iceland 65.57N 23.38W
90 K7 **Gerdil** Cent Afr Rep 9.40N 21.51E
113 L6 **Gerdine, Mt** Alaska 61.35N 152.30W
Gerede *see* **Beydili**
36 F2 **Gerede** Turkey 40.48N 32.13E
36 F2 **Gerede** *R* Turkey
77 D5 **Gerena** Spain 37.31N 6.10W
72 C3 **Gères** *R* Charente-Maritime France
76 C5 **Gerês, Sa. do** *mts* Portugal
18 D8 **Geret** *hill* Pen Malaysia 3.22N 103.04E
64 L8 **Geretsried** W Germany 47.53N 11.30E
77 L6 **Gérgal** Spain 37.07N 2.31W
44 H5 **Gergebil'** U.S.S.R. 42.29N 47.04W
37 D8 **Gerger** Turkey 37.58N 38.50E
71 F3 **Gergy** France 46.52N 4.56E
15 J7 **Gerhards, C** Papua New Guinea 6.46S 147.35E
64 K3 **Gerhardtsgereuth** E Germany 50.28N 10.46E
Geriban *see* **Hamurre, El**
119 H4 **Geri, Embalse de** *res* Venezuela
89 D8 **Gerihun** Sierra Leone 7.56N 11.35W
18 B6 **Gerik** Pen Malaysia 5.23N 101.09E
32 H4 **Gerīmenj** Iran 33.53N 58.55E
61 K6 **Gerin** Belgium 50.14N 4.49E
66 E4 **Gerine** *R* Switzerland
108 G8 **Gering** Nebraska 41.50N 103.30W
64 O1 **Geringswalde** E Germany 51.05N 12.54E
87 J5 **Geriso** Somalia 10.43N 43.30E
35 E5 **Gerizim** *anc site* Jordan 32.12N 35.16E
110 F9 **Gerlach** Nevada 40.40N 119.21W
62 M6 **Gerlachovsky** *mt* Czechoslovakia 49.09N 20.05E
64 H4 **Gerlachsheim** W Germany 49.35N 9.44E
66 G3 **Gerlafingen** Switzerland 47.10N 7.35E
53 J5 **Gerlev** Frederiksborg Denmark 55.50N 12.02E
53 G6 **Gerlev** Vestjælland Denmark 55.21N 11.21E
121 K4 **Gerli** Buenos Aires Arg 34.41S 58.22W
64 G6 **Gerlingen** W Germany 48.47N 9.03E
65 J8 **Gerlitzen** *mt* Austria 46.43N 13.53E
87 K7 **Gerlogubi** Ethiopia 6.53N 45.03E
65 F7 **Gerlos** Austria 47.14N 12.02E
65 E7 **Gerlostal** *V* Austria
76 D2 **Germade** Spain 43.21N 7.49W
98 F2 **Germain, Grand L** Quebec
121 E5 **Germania** Argentina 34.38S 62.00W
120 D4 **Germânia** Brazil 10.42S 70.07W
48 V6 **Germania Land** Greenland
Germanicea Marqasi *anc site see* **Maraş**
101 L8 **Germansen Landing** Br Col 55.47N 124.42W
107 G3 **Germantown** Illinois 38.34N 89.30W
104 H7 **Germantown** Maryland 39.11N 77.17W
103 G2 **Germantown** New York 42.08N 73.54W
104 A7 **Germantown** Ohio 39.37N 84.21W
107 G6 **Germantown** Tennessee 35.05N 89.50W
104 B1 **Germantown** *dist* Philadelphia, Penn
49 G6 **Germany, East** *rep* Cent Europe
49 F6 **Germany, West** *rep* W Europe
69 J7 **Germay** France 48.24N 5.21E
36 C5 **Germencik** Turkey 37.52N 27.37E
64 L7 **Germering** W Germany 48.07N 15.21E
64 E5 **Germersheim** W Germany 49.13N 8.23E
106 J3 **Germfask** Michigan 46.15N 85.57W
32 C1 **Germi** Iran 39.00N 48.04E
66 L8 **Germignago** Italy 45.59N 8.44E
37 D6 **Germili** Turkey 39.06N 38.47E
95 M2 **Germiston** S Africa 26.15S 28.10E
Germiter *see* **Balaban**
18 M7 **Germuru** Borneo Indon 4.00S 116.05E
63 M10 **Gernrode** Erfurt E Germany 51.24N 10.25E
63 O9 **Gernrode** Halle E Germany 51.44N 11.09E
64 E6 **Gernsbach** W Germany 48.46N 8.21E
64 F4 **Gernsheim** W Germany 49.45N 8.30E
20 L6 **Gero** Japan 35.50N 137.15E
86 O6 **Gerofit** Israel 29.56N 35.04E
79 G2 **Gerola Alta** Italy 46.04N 9.33E
64 B3 **Gerolstein** W Germany 50.13N 6.40E
64 J4 **Gerolzhofen** W Germany 49.53N 10.23E
110 G1 **Gerome** Washington 48.02N 118.18W
61 K4 **Gérompont** Belgium 50.39N 4.53E
75 Q4 **Gerona** Spain 41.59N 2.49E
74 J2 **Gerona** *prov* Spain
72 C9 **Géronce** France 43.15N 0.41W
111 O8 **Geronimo** Arizona 33.06N 110.03W
109 M7 **Geronimo** Oklahoma 34.30N 98.25W
61 M8 **Gérouville** Belgium 49.37N 5.26E
72 D10 **Ger, Pic de** *mt* France 42.56N 0.21W
61 J5 **Gerpinnes** Belgium 50.20N 4.31E
50 M4 **Gerpir** *C* Iceland 65.06N 13.32W
66 M6 **Gerra** Switzerland 46.19N 8.48E
56 U9 **Gerrans B** Cornwall Eng
56 K4 **Gerrard's Cross** Bucks Eng 51.35N 0.34W
81 C5 **Gerrei** *reg* Sardinia
75 N3 **Gerri** Spain 42.20N 1.04E
12 K5 **Gerringong** New S Wales 34.47S 150.46E
67 F9 **Gers** *dept* France
72 F8 **Gers** *R* France
66 L4 **Gersau** Switzerland 46.59N 8.32E
66 H1 **Gersbach** W Germany 47.42N 7.56E
66 K4 **Gerschnialp** Switzerland 46.48N 8.24E
64 H3 **Gersfeld** W Germany 50.27N 9.57E
53 E6 **Gerskov** Denmark 55.29N 10.28E
28 B3 **Gersoppa** Karnataka India 14.12N 74.41E
28 B3 **Gersoppa Falls** Karnataka India 14.13N 74.45E
64 F4 **Gersprenz** *R* W Germany
64 J6 **Gerstetten** W Germany 48.37N 10.02E
64 K7 **Gersthofen** W Germany 48.26N 10.53E
113 P5 **Gerstle** *R* Alaska
64 J2 **Gerstungen** E Germany 50.58N 10.05E
63 T6 **Gerswalde** E Germany 53.11N 13.45E
18 A6 **Gertak Sanggul, Tanjong** *C* Pen Malaysia 5.16N 100.11E
13 B3 **Gertrude, Mt** N Terr Australia 15.14S 131.24E
48 T1 **Gertrud Rask Land** Greenland
46 F5 **Gertsa** Ukraine U.S.S.R. 48.05N 26.13E
71 G7 **Gervanne** *R* France
60 L14 **Gerwen** Netherlands 51.29N 5.34E
Geryville *see* **Bayadh, El**
71 C5 **Gerzat** France 45.50N 3.08E
36 H1 **Gerze** Turkey 41.48N 35.13E
24 E9 **Gêrzê** Xizang Zizhiqu China 32.16N 84.12E
64 N6 **Gerzen** W Germany 48.30N 12.27E
63 E9 **Gescher** W Germany 51.57N 7.00E
65 O7 **Geschriebenstein** *mt* Austria 47.21N 16.25E
63 J9 **Geseke** W Germany 51.38N 8.31E
19 G5 **Geser** Moluccas Indon 3.52S 130.54E
75 K3 **Gesera** Spain 42.23N 0.18W
35 F3 **Gesher** Israel 32.37N 35.33E
35 D1 **Gesher HaZiv** Israel 33.03N 35.06E
36 H4 **Gesi** Turkey 38.48N 35.39E
87 K10 **Gesira** Somalia 1.58N 45.12E
15 G8 **Gesoa** Papua New Guinea 8.23S 143.36E
69 H4 **Gespunsart** France 49.49N 4.50E
41 B3 **Gessena, Mys** *C* Novaya Zemlya U.S.S.R. 72.12N 55.44E
Gessenay *see* **Saanen**
64 K7 **Gessertshausen** W Germany 48.19N 10.45E
81 A2 **Gessiera** *C* Sardinia 40.38N 8.09E
121 E3 **Gessler** Argentina 31.55S 61.08W
79 B6 **Gesso** *R* Italy
75 J8 **Gestalgar** Spain 39.36N 0.51W
72 B1 **Gesté** France 47.11N 1.08W
76 B8 **Gesteira** Portugal 40.05N 8.40W
53 C5 **Gesten** Denmark 55.32N 9.12E
66 Q1 **Gestratz** W Germany 47.39N 9.59E
81 C4 **Gesturi** Sardinia 39.44N 9.02E
80 M6 **Gesualdo** Italy 41.00N 15.05E
52 J3 **Gesunden** *L* Sweden 63.08N 15.50E
61 L5 **Gesves** Belgium 50.24N 5.04E
51 H11 **Geta** Finland 60.23N 19.50E
75 C7 **Getafe** Spain 40.18N 3.44W
32 E3 **Getcheh, Kūh-e** *mt* Iran 34.59N 52.40E
110 H8 **Getchell Mine** Nevada 41.14N 117.10W
61 L3 **Gete** *R* Belgium
87 D3 **Geteina, El** Sudan 14.50N 32.22E
63 E8 **Getelo** W Germany 52.28N 6.51E
35 B1 **Gethsemane** *biblical site* Jerusalem
98 M3 **Gethsémani** Quebec 50.14N 60.40W
93 B4 **Geti** Zaïre 1.12N 30.11E
40 C4 **Getkan** *R* U.S.S.R.
71 K4 **Gets, Col des** *pass* France 46.10N 6.40E
66 C7 **Gets, les** France 46.10N 6.40E
87 A7 **Getti** *watercourse* Sudan
66 H3 **Gettnau** Switzerland 47.09N 7.58E
63 L4 **Gettorf** W Germany 54.25N 9.58E
53 A3 **Gettrup** Denmark 56.44N 8.22E
104 H7 **Gettysburg** Pennsylvania 39.50N 77.16W
108 L5 **Gettysburg** S Dakota 45.00N 99.58W
23 D6 **Getu He** *R* Guizhou China
121 H1 **Getúlio Vargas** Brazil 27.55S 52.14W
123 J10 **Getz Ice Shelf** Antarctica
109 N4 **Geuda Springs** Kansas 37.06N 97.09W
35 B2 **Ge'ulim** *sub* Jerusalem
60 S17 **Geulle** Netherlands 50.55N 5.44E
18 B3 **Geumpang** Sumatra Indon 4.56N 96.09E
84 R14 **Geunyeli** Cyprus 35.12N 33.16E
18 B3 **Geureudong, Gunung** *mt* Sumatra Indon 4.50N 96.45E
12 J4 **Geurie** New S Wales 32.25S 148.56E
94 G1 **Geusha** Namibia 17.50S 22.50E
35 C3 **Geva' Karmel** Israel 32.39N 34.57E
32 H7 **Gevān-e Ţāleb Khānī** Iran 27.54N 59.15E
35 B7 **Gevar'am** Israel 31.36N 34.37E
37 H8 **Gevar Ovası** *plat* Turkey
37 G7 **Gevaş** Turkey 38.16N 43.05E
71 D8 **Gevaudan** *reg* France
76 B4 **Geve** Spain 42.28N 8.35W
63 F10 **Gevelsberg** W Germany 51.19N 7.20E
70 G5 **Geveze** France 48.13N 1.48W
63 S5 **Gevezin** E Germany 53.34N 13.08E
82 G9 **Gevgelija** Yugoslavia 41.09N 22.30E
35 B7 **Gevim** Israel 31.31N 34.36E
76 E10 **Gévora** *R* Spain
29 D8 **Gevrai** Maharashtra India 19.18N 75.48E
71 F2 **Gevrey-Chambertin** France 47.14N 4.59E
35 A9 **Gevulot** Israel 31.13N 34.27E
71 J4 **Gex** France 46.20N 6.03E
Gexianzhuang *see* **Qinghe**
Gey *see* **Nīkshahr**
64 O2 **Geyer** E Germany 50.37N 12.55E
64 G4 **Geyersberg** *mt* W Germany 49.54N 9.26E
44 G7 **Geygel** Azerbaydzhan U.S.S.R. 40.26N 46.19E
36 F6 **Geyik Dağ** *mt* Turkey 36.53N 32.12E
36 B3 **Geyikli** Turkey 39.49N 26.12E
87 E6 **Geyo** Ethiopia 8.01N 35.22E
95 J2 **Geysdorp** S Africa 26.31S 25.19E
110 P2 **Geyser** Montana 47.16N 110.30W
95 C2 **Geyser, Banc du** *rocks* Madagascar 12.24S 46.25E
50 E6 **Geysir** Iceland 64.19N 20.19W
36 E2 **Geyve** Turkey 40.32N 30.18E
86 L10 **Gezâir Ashrâfi** *islds* Egypt 27.47N 33.41E
86 L10 **Gezâir Gûbâl** *islds* Egypt 27.40N 33.48E
86 L10 **Gezâir Qeisûm** *islds* Egypt 27.42N 33.43E
86 L10 **Gezâir Siyûl** *islds* Egypt 27.34N 33.52E
86 L10 **Gezâir Ţawîla** *islds* Egypt 27.35N 33.46E
44 J10 **Gezāz** Iran 37.42N 48.20E
35 C6 **Gezer** Israel 31.53N 34.57E
32 F7 **Gezīr** Iran 26.44N 54.55E
86 Q12 **Gezîra, El** *dist* Cairo Egypt
87 D3 **Gezira, El** *reg* Sudan
86 Q12 **Gezîra el Rôda** *isld* Cairo Egypt
86 N7 **Gezîra Fara'ûn** *isld* Egypt 29.28N 34.52E

86 L10 Gezîra Ghânim isld Egypt 27.30N 34.00E
86 D3 Gezîra Gheroo isld Egypt 31.21N 30.06E
86 L10 Gezîra Shadwân isld Egypt 27.30N 34.00E
86 Q11 Gezîra Warrâq el Ḥadr isld Cairo Egypt
85 O8 Gezîret Halâib isld Egypt 22.19N 36.33E
86 Q11 Gezîret Muḥammad Cairo Egypt
34 O3 Gezmel Iran 35.42N 46.49E
65 M4 Gföhl Austria 48.32N 15.30E
84 X19 Ggantija, Il Gozo Medit Sea 36.03N 14.16E
33 M6 Ghāba reg Oman
87 C1 Ghaba, El Sudan 18.10N 30.42E
34 D5 Ghabāghib Syria 33.10N 36.12E
35 H1 Ghabaghib Syria 33.10N 36.14E
87 C7 Ghabat el Inderab Sudan 7.40N 30.34E
87 B6 Ghabat el Warrana Sudan 8.45N 28.45E
86 L6 Ghabîya, Wâdî el watercourse Egypt
87 C4 Ghabsha, El Sudan 12.54N 31.34E
34 D7 Ghadaf, Wādi el watercourse Jordan
31 F3 Ghadai Pakistan 34.57N 71.46E
Ghadames see Ghudāmis
34 H6 Ghadfat al Mahafur watercourse Iraq
33 B10 Ghadīr S Yemen 12.45N 44.53E
35 G2 Ghadir al Bustan Syria 32.55N 35.55E
34 G5 Ghadir al Mulūşī water hole Iraq 33.15N 39.46E
85 D6 Ghadīr ar Razzah Libya 27.20N 17.19E
35 H4 Ghadir el Abyad watercourse Jordan
34 E6 Ghadir Minqār salt marsh Syria
85 D6 Ghadīr Qāhirah Libya 26.46N 17.09E
32 E2 Ghaem Shahr Iran 36.28N 52.52E
15 L3 Ghaeta Solomon Is 9.10S 160.18E
33 M5 Ghāfāt, Al Oman 22.59N 57.04E
33 H9 Ghafīt S Yemen 14.44N 49.12E
31 G6 Ghaggar, Dry Bed of India/Pakistan
30 G8 Ghaghar Res Uttar Prad India 24.38N 83.11E
15 K2 Ghaghe I Solomon Is 7.23S 158.14E
30 G6 Ghaghra R Uttar Prad India
30 D5 Ghagra R Uttar Prad India
31 D7 Ghaibi Dero Pakistan 27.35N 67.42E
30 K7 Ghaibnath Siva Bihar India 25.15N 86.44E
86 M8 Gha'îb, Wâdî el watercourse Egypt
34 H6 Ghaida watercourse Iraq
Ghail see Ghayl, Al
35 F1 Ghajar Lebanon 33.16N 35.37E
84 X19 Ghajnsielem Gozo Medit Sea 36.01N 14.18E
84 X20 Ghajn Tuffieha B Malta
32 J5 Ghalend Iran 30.44N 61.40E
43 G3 Ghalkarteniz, Solonchak salt marsh Kazakhstan U.S.S.R.
87 B5 Ghalla,Wadi El watercourse Sudan
84 Y20 Ghallis Rocks Malta 35.58N 14.27E
86 P10 Ghāl, Wādī el watercourse Saudi Arabia
Ghamās, Al see Ghammās, Al
33 K7 Ghamghīmah, 'Abl des area Saudi Arabia
34 M7 Ghammās, Al Iraq 31.43N 44.37E
86 O4 Ghamr Jordan 30.31N 35.13E
73 D5 Ghana rep W Africa
33 L4 Ghanādah, Rās C U.A.E.
33 M7 Ghanāh Oman 18.40N 56.44E
85 B3 Ghanam, Al Libya 32.19N 12.34E
34 N8 Ghanami, Sha'īb al watercourse Iraq
87 L8 Ghan, El Somalia 4.26N 47.56E
33 L7 Ghanīm des area Saudi Arabia/Oman
29 C4 Ghanliala Rajasthan India 27.20N 72.54E
90 N5 Ghannama Sudan 12.40N 26.20E
88 T5 Ghannouche Tunisia 33.59N 10.02E
15 K3 Ghanongga I Solomon Is
30 H4 Ghanpokhara Nepal 28.18N 84.19E
29 B6 Ghantila Gujarat India 23.10N 71.19E
34 E4 Ghantūr Syria 34.24N 37.09E
29 B7 Ghantwar Gujarat India 20.56N 70.50E
33 H3 Ghanwā Saudi Arabia 27.00N 48.32E
94 F3 Ghanzi Botswana 21.42S 21.39E
94 F4 Ghanzi dist Botswana
78 C11 Ghar Tunisia 37.11N 10.10E
35 E7 Ghar watercourse Jordan
Gharabīya, Sha'īb al watercourse see Gharībīyah, Sha'īb al
33 E6 Gharāmīl, Jabal al mts Saudi Arabia
86 K9 Gharamûl, Gebel hill Egypt 28.02N 33.08E
86 O5 Gharandal Jordan 30.05N 35.12E
86 J7 Gharandal, Wâdî watercourse Egypt
86 E7 Gharaq El Sulṭâni, El Egypt 29.08N 30.41E
30 A3 Gharaunda Haryana India 29.32N 76.58E
84 X19 Gharb Gozo Medit Sea 36.04N 14.13E
86 B4 Gharbânîyât El Egypt 30.52N 29.29E
86 G6 Gharba, Wâdî watercourse Egypt
88 T4 Gharbi isld Tunisia
34 G3 Gharbi, Jebel mt Syria 35.20N 39.12E
86 E4 Gharbiya div Egypt
85 B4 Gharbīyah, al Libya 30.25N 13.22E
85 K6 Ghard Abu Muharik sand dune Egypt
86 A6 Ghard Abu Sennân watercourse Egypt
88 P5 Ghardaïa Algeria 32.20N 3.40E
Ghārdāqah, Al see Hurghada
86 B6 Ghard el Diw watercourse Egypt
86 B5 Ghard el Hallif watercourse Egypt
86 C5 Ghard el Ḥineishât watercourse Egypt
86 C5 Ghard el Ḥineishât el Wostâni watercourse Egypt
86 C6 Ghard el Kalb watercourse Egypt
86 D5 Ghard el Libeiṭa watercourse Egypt
86 C5 Ghard el Mashrûka watercourse Egypt
86 D6 Ghard el Qattânîya watercourse Egypt
86 B6 Ghard el Rammâk watercourse Egypt
86 C6 Ghard el Tafasikh watercourse Egypt
88 S3 Ghardimaou Tunisia 36.24N 8.28E
86 B7 Ghard Misa'da watercourse Egypt
86 B6 Ghard Mubârak watercourse Egypt
88 T3 Ghar-el-Melh Tunisia 37.10N 10.10E
31 C3 Ghargharib Afghanistan 34.01N 65.40E
84 Y20 Gharghur Malta 35.56N 14.28E
86 O6 Gharia, Wādī el watercourse Jordan
85 F3 Gharīb, Al Libya 32.35N 21.08E
86 J9 Ghârib, Gebel hill Egypt 28.06N 32.54E
34 N9 Gharībīyah, Sha'īb al watercourse Iraq
86 K9 Ghârib, Wâdî watercourse Egypt
31 G4 Gharibwal Pakistan 32.46N 73.14E
30 F5 Ghari Ghat Uttar Prad India 27.01N 82.30E
33 D6 Gharīth, Al Saudi Arabia 21.35N 41.50E
35 H3 Ghariyah el Garbiyah Syria 32.41N 36.14E
35 J3 Ghariyah esh Sharqiyah Syria 32.41N 36.15E
Ghariyé Charkiyé see Ghariyah esh Sharqiyah
33 H4 Ghār Mihnān Saudi Arabia 24.51N 49.32E
33 M7 Gharm, Wādī watercourse Oman
31 D8 Gharo Pakistan 24.44N 67.35E
32 C3 Gharq Abad Iran 35.06N 49.50E
34 O7 Gharraf Iraq 31.18N 46.15E
34 O7 Gharraf, Shatt al R Iraq
86 L6 Gharra, Gebel el hill Egypt 29.56N 33.42E
34 J9 Gharrah, Jāl al plat Saudi Arabia
33 H3 Ghār, Ra's al C Saudi Arabia 27.30N 49.15E
87 L9 Gharun, El Somalia 3.14N 46.35E
85 B3 Gharyān Libya 32.12N 13.02E
33 M8 Gharzaut / Arabian Sea 17.36N 56.04E
Ghasami see Qasamī
35 J3 Ghasm Syria 32.33N 36.22E
88 O5 Ghassoul Algeria 33.25N 1.14E
30 A7 Ghaswani Madhya Prad India 25.54N 77.31E
31 D4 Ghat Afghanistan 33.45N 66.45E
85 A7 Ghāt Libya 24.59N 10.11E
33 F3 Ghāṭ, Al Saudi Arabia 26.03N 45.00E
29 L2 Ghatal W Bengal India 22.40N 87.44E
30 D6 Ghatampur Uttar Prad India 26.10N 80.11E
30 A8 Ghat Bamori Madhya Prad India 24.15N 77.57E
15 L2 Ghatere Santa Isabel I Solomon Is 7.50S 159.08E
29 J7 Ghatgaon Madhya Prad India 21.21N 85.58E
33 G4 Ghatghat, Al anc site Saudi Arabia 24.30N 46.19E
30 A6 Ghatigaon Madhya Prad India 26.03N 77.56E
29 K6 Ghatsila Bihar India 22.36N 86.34E
34 E7 Ghatti Saudi Arabia 31.16N 37.31E
94 D2 Ghaub Namibia 19.30S 17.42E
30 D5 Ghausganj Hardoi, Uttar Prad India 27.04N 80.18E
30 C6 Ghausganj Kanpur, Uttar Prad India 26.10N 79.58E
31 E6 Ghauspur Pakistan 28.08N 69.10E
33 H4 Ghawar oil field Saudi Arabia 25.22N 49.23E
84 Z20 Ghaxaq Malta 35.51N 14.32E
86 D4 Ghayata, El Egypt 30.56N 30.06E
33 K8 Ghayḍah S Yemen 16.12N 52.16E
33 H9 Ghayḍah al Khaḍrā',Al S Yemen 14.14N 48.47E
33 G5 Ghayl, Al Saudi Arabia 22.35N 46.20E
33 H9 Ghayl Bā Wazīr S Yemen 14.49N 49.22E
33 H9 Ghayl Bin Yumayn S Yemen 15.35N 49.31E
33 F9 Ghaymān Yemen 15.17N 44.24E
35 H2 Ghazāle watercourse Syria
87 D1 Ghazalī Sudan 18.30N 33.02E
86 G4 Ghazâli, El Egypt 30.50N 31.49E
88 N4 Ghazaouet Algeria 35.08N 1.50W
30 A4 Ghaziabad Uttar Prad India 28.39N 77.26E
31 F5 Ghazi Ghat Pakistan 30.05N 70.55E
34 K4 Ghazīla, Wādī watercourse Iraq
30 D7 Ghazipur Fatehpur, Uttar Prad India 25.48N 80.45E
30 G7 Ghazipur Ghazipur, Uttar Prad India 25.36N 83.36E
30 G7 Ghazipur dist Uttar Prad India
86 N7 Ghazlâni, Gebel hill Egypt 29.23N 34.43E
31 D5 Ghazluna Pakistan 31.25N 67.52E
31 E4 Ghazni Afghanistan 33.33N 68.28E
31 D4 Ghazni prov Afghanistan
31 E4 Ghazni R Afghanistan
31 D4 Ghazoor Afghanistan 33.37N 66.32E
33 D3 Ghazzālah Saudi Arabia 26.47N 41.23E
32 G4 Ghebar Gumbad Iran 33.24N 57.43E
87 L8 Ghedalei Somalia 5.14N 47.54E
79 H4 Ghedi Italy 45.24N 10.16E
87 F6 Ghedo Ethiopia 9.02N 37.25E
108 S2 Gheen Minnesota 47.58N 92.48W
85 N7 Gheir, Gebel el mt Egypt 24.04N 34.12E
86 K6 Gheita, Wâdî watercourse Egypt
35 G9 Gheith watercourse Jordan
87 G3 Gheleb Ethiopia 15.49N 38.50E
87 H6 Ghelemso Ethiopia 8.50N 40.32E
87 L7 Ghelinsor Somalia 6.28N 46.39E
33 J4 Ghemeis, Rās C U.A.E. 24.22N 51.37E
87 E6 Ghemi,Jeb mt Sudan/Ethiopia 9.02N 34.10E
79 D3 Ghemme Italy 45.36N 8.25E
30 F3 Ghengkuru mt Nepal 26.59N 86.34E
107 L3 Ghent Kentucky 38.44N 85.02W
108 P5 Ghent Minnesota 44.30N 95.52W
103 G2 Ghent New York 42.19N 73.37W
82 K4 Gheorgheni Romania 46.43N 25.36E
28 B2 Gherdi Maharashtra India 17.17N 75.22E
82 K4 Gherghiului, Munţii mts Romania
93 N4 Gherille Somalia 1.41N 41.04E
82 H3 Gherla Romania 47.02N 23.55E
93 N6 Ghersei Somalia 0.33S 41.07E
87 N5 Ghesselei Somalia 11.44N 50.32E
79 E3 Ghiffa Italy 45.58N 8.37E
81 B3 Ghilarza Sardinia 40.08N 8.51E
46 N5 Ghiloaksayskaya U.S.S.R. 48.00N 43.59E
82 H3 Ghilvaci Romania 47.41N 22.40E
31 D5 Ghilzai reg Afghanistan
Ghimbi see Gembi
82 K4 Ghimeş Făget Romania 46.34N 26.03E
87 E6 Ghimitu Ethiopia 9.15N 35.03E
33 C1 Ghinah, Wādī al watercourse Saudi Arabia
34 F8 Ghīnah, Wādī al watercourse Saudi Arabia/Jordan
87 G3 Ghinda Ethiopia 15.26N 39.07E
87 H3 Ghira, mt Ethiopia 14.09N 41.01E
87 H4 Ghiriffo Ethiopia 13.14N 41.29E
30 B5 Ghiror Uttar Prad India 27.11N 78.47E
61 F4 Ghislenghien Belgium 50.39N 3.53E
67 P12 Ghisonaccia Corsica 42.01N 9.24E
67 P12 Ghisoni Corsica 42.06N 9.12E
31 D4 Ghizao Afghanistan 33.20N 66.19E
31 G2 Ghizar Kashmir 36.10N 72.48E
31 G2 Ghizar dist Kashmir
31 B10 Ghizri Pakistan 24.49N 67.03E
31 D8 Ghizri Creek Pakistan
15 L2 Ghizunabeana Is Solomon Is 7.34S 158.41E
86 M8 Ghlim, Gebel hill Egypt 28.54N 34.22E
61 F5 Ghlin Belgium 50.28N 3.54E
28 A1 Ghod Maharashtra India 19.04N 73.50E
28 B1 Ghod R Maharashtra India
30 L7 Ghoga Bihar India 25.13N 87.09E
87 L8 Ghohò Somalia 5.02N 47.20E
29 C7 Gholvad Maharashtra India 20.03N 72.48E
31 C3 Ghor prov Afghanistan
29 D6 Ghora Madhya Prad India 22.25N 74.34E
31 D8 Ghorabari Pakistan 24.12N 67.36E
31 G4 Ghora Gali Pakistan 33.52N 73.23E
31 H8 Ghoraghat Bangladesh 25.18N 89.20E
31 C4 Ghorak Afghanistan 32.03N 65.10E
29 H7 Ghorari Madhya Prad India 21.13N 82.08E
30 J6 Ghorasahan Bihar India 26.50N 85.09E
30 F8 Ghorawal Uttar Prad India 24.46N 82.46E
31 E3 Ghorband R Afghanistan
31 E3 Ghorband Pass Afghanistan 34.10N 69.29E
31 C4 Ghordang Afghanistan 32.25N 65.35E
35 E6 Ghor, El V Israel/Jordan
101 Q4 Ghost L N W Terr 63.50N 115.10W
101 P9 Ghost Mt Br Col 52.22N 117.55W
100 L1 Ghost River Ontario 50.10N 91.27W
31 E7 Ghotki Pakistan 28.00N 69.21E
Ghouna see Ghūna
32 F6 Ghowrī Iran 29.31N 54.28E
61 F4 Ghoy Belgium 50.44N 3.49E
34 E5 Ghuba, Al salt marsh Syria
34 P8 Ghubayshīyah, Al Iraq 30.42N 47.05E
86 L10 Ghubba el Gemsa B Egypt
86 L10 Ghubba el Zeit B Egypt
33 M3 Ghubbat al Ghazira inlet Oman
33 N6 Ghubbat Ḥashish B Oman
87 L5 Ghubbat Ḱalwait B Somalia
87 L5 Ghubbat Raguda B Somalia
33 K10 Ghubbat Shu'b B Socotra Ind Oc
87 N5 Ghubbet Binnah B Somalia 11.12N 51.05E
86 H6 Ghubbet el Bûs B Egypt
87 A4 Ghubeish Sudan 12.10N 27.22E
33 M7 Ghubr, Al reg Oman
34 K6 Ghudāf, Wādī al watercourse Iraq
85 A4 Ghudāmis Libya 30.10N 9.30E
Ghugas see Ghugus
30 K7 Ghugri R Bihar India
29 F8 Ghugus Maharashtra India 19.57N 79.12E
31 H2 Ghujak Bai Xinjiang Uygur Zizhiqu China 37.13N 75.18E
31 E5 Ghulam Haidar Kili Afghanistan 31.58N 68.44E
31 E8 Ghulam Mohammed Barrage Pakistan 25.28N 68.25E
30 J5 Ghumthang Nepal 27.52N 85.51E
34 H2 Ghūna Syria 36.22N 41.00E
30 L5 Ghunsa Nepal 27.40N 87.57E
86 F8 Ghurab, Gebel hill Egypt 28.58N 31.16E
33 H8 Ghuraf, Al S Yemen 16.00N 49.00E
30 B7 Ghurari R Madhya Prad India
Ghuri see Ghowrī
31 A3 Ghurian Afghanistan 34.20N 61.26E
30 L6 Ghurna Bihar India 26.27N 87.06E
33 F4 Ghurrab, Jabal mts Saudi Arabia
87 E3 Ghurr,Jeb mt Sudan 14.50N 34.19E
33 E5 Ghurūb, Jabal mts Saudi Arabia
29 G6 Ghutipari Madhya Prad India 22.52N 81.30E
33 J4 Ghuwayr, Al Qatar, The Gulf 25.54N 51.17E
34 F9 Ghuwayṭah, Nafūd al des Saudi Arabia
86 H6 Ghuweibba, Wâdî watercourse Egypt
35 G9 Ghuweir Jordan 31.08N 35.45E
33 M5 Ghuzayn Oman 23.52N 56.58E
86 J9 Ghweirib, Gebel hill Egypt 28.01N 32.52E
69 D1 Ghyvelde France 51.03N 2.32E
25 J7 Gia Dinh Vietnam 10.48N 106.43E
Giado see Jādū
44 C3 Giaginskaya U.S.S.R. 44.52N 40.04E
87 N5 Giahel watercourse Somalia
79 N2 Giais Italy 46.07N 12.36E
28 J1 Gia La pass Xizang Zizhiqu 29.49N 92.30E
Gialo see Wabat Jālū Oasis
85 F5 Gialo Libya 28.45N 21.12E
87 J10 Giamame Somalia 0.01N 42.44E
87 E7 Giamchar Ethiopia 6.44N 34.31E
Giamdo Chu R see Nyang Chu R
80 B7 Gianicolo, Monte hill Roma Italy
80 D4 Giannutri, I.di Italy 42.15N 11.06E
80 G3 Giano dell'Umbria Italy 42.50N 12.35E
95 N5 Giant's Castle mt S Africa 29.20S 29.30E
59 J1 Giant's Causeway prom Antrim N Ireland 55.14N 6.32W
26 Q4 Giant's Tank Sri Lanka
Giarabub see Jaghbūb, Al
93 N6 Giara El Somalia 0.22S 41.23E
25 H8 Gia Rai Vietnam 9.14N 105.28E
81 B4 Giara, Planu sa plat Sardinia
81 K8 Giardini Sicily 37.50N 15.17E
87 G8 Giari Bule Ethiopia 5.35N 38.30E
81 J9 Giarratana Sicily 37.03N 14.43E
81 K8 Giarre Sicily 37.44N 15.12E
71 A5 Giat France 45.48N 2.27E
81 B3 Giave Sardinia 40.28N 8.45E
79 B4 Giaveno Italy 45.03N 7.21E
79 K3 Giazza Italy 45.39N 11.08E
81 B5 Giba Sardinia 39.05N 8.38E
77 E7 Gibalbín mt Spain 36.50N 5.58W
77 H6 Gibalto mt Spain 37.04N 4.15W
116 F4 Gibara Cuba 21.09N 76.11W
77 E5 Gibarroyo mt Spain 37.54N 5.35W
87 F7 Gibbe watercourse Ethiopia
108 M9 Gibbon Nebraska 40.46N 98.49W
110 G4 Gibbon Oregon 45.43N 118.23W
110 M4 Gibbons Pass Montana 45.46N 113.58W
110 M4 Gibbonsville Idaho 45.35N 113.55W
14 F3 Gibb R W Australia
14 F3 Gibb River W Australia 16.29S 126.20E
106 F3 Gibbs City Michigan 46.13N 88.42W
96 B2 Gibb's Hill Bermuda 32.15N 64.51W
123 D15 Gibbs I S Shetland Is Antarctica 61.31S 55.26W
14 C10 Gibbs, Mt W Australia 32.55S 119.59E
103 D7 Gibbstown New Jersey 39.50N 75.18E
61 F4 Gibecq Belgium 50.38N 3.53E
86 L9 Gibeil Egypt 28.11N 33.38E
81 E8 Gibellina Sicily 37.47N 12.59E
94 D5 Gibeon Namibia 25.09S 17.43E
66 E5 Gibloux mt Switzerland 46.42N 7.03E
51 G2 Gibostad Norway 69.22N 18.01E
77 C6 Gibraleón Spain 37.23N 6.58W
77 F8 Gibraltar colony S W Europe 36.09N 5.21W
57 O6 Gibraltar Pt Lincs Eng 53.06N 0.20E
99 D10 Gibraltar Pt Ontario 43.37N 79.24W
77 E9 Gibraltar, Str. of Spain/Africa
107 C9 Gibsland Louisiana 32.34N 93.01W
110 C8 Gibson California 41.02N 122.25W
105 E4 Gibson Georgia 33.13N 82.38W
110 Q3 Gibson Montana 46.01N 109.30W
103 C3 Gibson Pennsylvania 41.47N 75.40W
104 B5 Gibsonburg Ohio 41.22N 83.20W
106 F9 Gibson City Illinois 40.28N 88.23W
14 D6 Gibson Des W Australia
103 B8 Gibson I Maryland 39.05N 76.25W
101 M11 Gibsons Br Col 49.24N 123.32W
14 D10 Gibson Soak W Australia 33.35S 121.44E
105 E10 Gibsonton Florida 27.51N 82.22W
105 H1 Gibsonville N Carolina 36.06N 79.33W
22 D4 Gichgeniyn Nuruu mts Mongolia
90 D8 Gidan Akwarra Nigeria 7.15N 8.53E
90 D7 Gidan Aondo Busu Nigeria 8.00N 8.42E
90 D7 Gidan Arichen Nigeria 8.01N 9.00E
90 E8 Gidan Nama Nigeria 7.08N 10.38E
90 D8 Gidan Sabe Nigeria 6.56N 8.55E
31 D6 Gidar Pakistan 28.16N 66.05E
47 G6 Gidayevo U.S.S.R. 59.59N 52.28E
28 D3 Giddalur Andhra Prad India 15.23N 78.56E
86 L9 Giddat el 'Illa, Gebel hill Egypt 28.26N 33.51E
86 K5 Giddi, Gebel el hill Egypt 30.10N 33.09E
112 L5 Giddings Texas 30.12N 96.59W
86 J5 Giddi, Wâdî el watercourse Egypt
52 L3 Gideå Sweden 63.29N 19.00E
52 L3 Gide älv R Sweden
55 K2 Gidea Park London Eng 51.35N 0.11E
107 G5 Gideon Missouri 36.28N 89.56W
13 F6 Gideon, Mt Queensland 22.54S 141.20E
12 F3 Gidgelpa S Australia 27.57S 140.00E
14 F8 Gidgi, L W Australia 29.15S 126.04E
30 K8 Gidhaur Bihar India 24.51N 86.11E
85 K7 Gidîda, El Egypt 25.35N 28.53E
62 L5 Gidle Poland 50.59N 19.29E
87 F8 Gidole Ethiopia 5.38N 37.28E
35 E3 Gid'ona Israel 32.33N 35.21E
35 D10 Gidron watercourse Israel
45 P1 Gidrotorf U.S.S.R. 56.28N 43.31E
64 H4 Giebelstadt W Germany 49.39N 9.57E
63 M9 Gieboldehausen W Germany 51.37N 10.12E
60 M7 Giekerk Netherlands 53.14N 5.54E
63 R5 Gielow E Germany 53.42N 12.45E
71 B1 Gien France 47.41N 2.37E
64 J6 Giengen an der Brenz W Germany 48.37N 10.15E
71 J10 Giens France 43.02N 6.06E
71 J10 Giens, G.de France 43.03N 6.05E
71 J10 Giens, Presqu'ile de pen France 43.02N 6.05E
71 F5 Gier R France
61 K1 Gierle Belgium 51.16N 4.52E
60 N12 Giesbeek Netherlands 52.00N 6.05E
95 G6 Giesenskraal S Africa 30.32S 23.18E
63 P7 Giesenslage E Germany 52.49N 11.57E
66 J5 Giessbach Switzerland 46.44N 8.02E
60 J12 Giessen Netherlands 51.47N 5.02E
64 F2 Giessen W Germany 50.35N 8.42E
60 Q7 Gieten Netherlands 53.00N 6.45E
60 Q7 Gieterveen Netherlands 53.02N 6.50E
60 N9 Giethoorn Netherlands 52.43N 6.06E
60 N9 Giethoornse Meer L Netherlands
66 A8 Giez France 45.45N 6.15E
32 G2 Gīfan Iran 37.52N 57.27E
33 A3 Gifatin islds Egypt 27.16N 33.56E
98 R7 Giffard Quebec 46.51N 71.13W
66 F6 Gifferhorn mt Switzerland 46.28N 7.22E
66 E4 Giffers Switzerland 46.47N 7.13E
105 G10 Gifford Florida 27.42N 80.25W
108 R7 Gifford Iowa 42.19N 93.05W
58 L7 Gifford Lothian Scotland 55.54N 2.45W
110 G1 Gifford Washington 48.20N 118.08W
66 C7 Giffre R France
63 N8 Gifhorn W Germany 52.28N 10.33E
20 K6 Gifu Japan 35.27N 136.46E
20 K6 Gifu prefect Japan
44 D1 Gigant U.S.S.R. 46.31N 41.20E
115 D5 Giganta, Sa.de la ra Mexico
119 C6 Gigante Colombia 2.24N 75.34W
115 E10 Gigante Panama Canal Zone 9.07N 79.50W
77 N5 Gigante mt Spain 37.44N 1.59W
79 A3 Gigante, Col du pass France/Italy 45.51N 6.57E
115 G3 Gigantes, Llanos de los plains Mexico
71 D9 Gigean France 43.30N 3.43E
58 E7 Gigha I Strathclyde Scotland 55.41N 5.45W
58 E7 Gigha, Sound of Strathclyde Scotland
15 B4 Gigi, Anggi L Irian Jaya 1.23S 133.53E
80 C4 Giglio Castello Italy 42.23N 10.54E
80 C4 Giglio, I.del Italy
80 C4 Giglio Porto Italy 42.22N 10.55E
71 D9 Gignac Herault France 43.39N 3.33E
71 H9 Gignac Vaucluse France 43.55N 5.32E
71 G10 Gignac-la Nerthe France 43.24N 5.14E
79 B3 Gignod Italy 45.47N 7.17E
Gigüela R see Záncara R
85 L6 Giheina Egypt 26.40N 31.30E
Giji, Anggi L see Gigi, Anggi L
76 H1 Gijón Spain 43.32N 5.40W
61 A3 Gijverinkhove Belgium 50.58N 2.40E
61 G3 Gijzegem Belgium 50.59N 4.04E
50 L4 Gil Múlasýsla, Nordhur Iceland 65.24N 14.39W
50 G4 Gil Skagafjardharsýsla Iceland 65.16N 18.59W
109 B9 Gila New Mexico 32.58N 108.34W
111 M8 Gila R Arizona
111 M9 Gila Bend Arizona 32.56N 112.42W
111 L8 Gila Bend Mts Arizona
109 B8 Gila Cliff Dwellings Nat.Mon New Mexico 33.14N 108.17W
111 L9 Gila Desert Arizona
111 K9 Gila Mts Arizona
34 N4 Gīlān-e Gharb Iran 34.08N 45.58E
32 A3 Gilan Garb Iran 34.09N 45.56E
99 R5 Gilardo Dam Quebec 47.12N 73.48W
35 B8 Gilat Israel 31.20N 34.38E
82 H4 Gilău Romania 46.45N 23.23E
86 H4 Gilbâna Egypt 30.56N 32.28E
111 N8 Gilbert Arizona 33.22N 111.46W
108 S2 Gilbert Minnesota 47.28N 92.26W
111 G3 Gilbert Nevada 38.13N 117.41W
104 D9 Gilbert W Virginia 37.37N 81.52W
13 F3 Gilbert R Queensland
Gilbert Is see Tuvalu
121 K10 Gilbert Is Chile 55.00S 71.15W
113 N6 Gilbert, Mt Alaska 61.10N 148.19W
101 L10 Gilbert, Mt Br Col 50.50N 124.15W
103 B5 Gilberton Pennsylvania 40.48N 76.13W
13 G4 Gilberton Queensland 19.14S 143.38E
107 H10 Gilbertown Alabama 31.53N 88.21W
110 P9 Gilbert Pk Utah 40.50N 110.17W
100 R7 Gilbert Plains Manitoba 51.09N 100.28W
13 G4 Gilbert River Queensland 18.08S 142.50E
103 D2 Gilbertsville New York 42.27N 75.20W
103 C6 Gilbertsville Pennsylvania 40.18N 75.34W
103 K2 Gilbertville Massachusetts 42.18N 72.13W
53 J4 Gilbjerghovod C Denmark 56.08N 12.18E
103 F2 Gilboa New York 42.23N 74.28W
35 E4 Gilboa', Hare hills Israel
117 E9 Gilbués Brazil 9.50S 45.22W
108 N1 Gilby N Dakota 48.07N 97.28W
32 G3 Gil Chashmeh Iran 35.25N 56.20E
40 D7 Gilchin U.S.S.R. 49.55N 127.52E
109 F1 Gilcrest Colorado 40.17N 104.46W
51 D4 Gildeskal Norway 67.04N 14.05E
110 P1 Gildford Montana 48.35N 110.19W
92 J10 Gilé Mozambique 16.10S 38.17E
104 P2 Gilead Maine 44.24N 70.59W
108 N9 Gilead Nebraska 40.05N 97.25W
34 C6 Gilead reg Jordan
44 H5 Gileb U.S.S.R. 42.06N 46.47E
Gilehdar see Galeh Dār
32 G6 Gilek, Tang-e pass Iran 28.05N 56.43E
77 G6 Gilena Spain 37.15N 4.54W
61 P4 Gileppe, Lac de la Belgium 50.35N 6.00E
112 G1 Giles Texas 34.50N 100.35W
10 F7 Giles W Australia 25.10S 128.30E
13 B3 Giles Cr N Terr Australia
14 C8 Giles, L W Australia 29.30S 119.40E
13 B5 Giles Ra N Terr Australia
85 H8 Gilf Kebir Plateau Egypt
59 K3 Gilford Down N Ireland 54.23N 6.22W
12 K3 Gilgai New S Wales 29.49S 151.09E
35 E6 Gilgal Jordan 31.59N 35.27E
12 J4 Gilgandra New S Wales 31.42S 148.40E
76 H8 Gilgarcia Spain 40.18N 5.35W
93 H6 Gilgil Kenya 0.29S 36.19E
12 J3 Gil Gil R New S Wales
31 H3 Gilgit Kashmir 35.54N 74.20E
31 G2 Gilgit dist Kashmir
31 H2 Gilgit dist Kashmir
31 G2 Gilgit R Kashmir
31 H3 Gilgit Wazarat dist Kashmir
12 H4 Gilgunnia New S Wales 32.25S 146.04E
101 J9 Gil I Br Col 53.10N 129.15W
18 L10 Gilimanuk Bali Indonesia 8.12S 114.27E
36 G6 Gilindire Turkey 36.08N 33.18E
50 E3 Giljá Iceland 65.33N 20.21W
82 F7 Giljeva Planina mts Yugoslavia
109 F1 Gill Colorado 40.28N 104.33W
97 K6 Gillam Manitoba 56.25N 94.45W
53 J4 Gilleleje Denmark 56.08N 12.19E
13 C6 Gillen R N Terr Australia
14 E7 Gillen, L W Australia 26.11S 124.34E
13 C6 Gillen, Mt N Terr Australia 23.42S 133.45E
12 D5 Gilles, L S Australia
111 M8 Gillespie Arizona 33.16N 112.58W
107 G2 Gillespie Illinois 39.08N 89.49W
11 D10 Gillespie Pt New Zealand 43.24S 169.52E
107 E7 Gillett Arkansas 34.08N 91.23W
104 J5 Gillett Pennsylvania 41.56N 76.47W
112 K6 Gillett Texas 29.08N 97.49W
106 F5 Gillett Wisconsin 44.54N 88.20W
108 E5 Gillette Wyoming 44.18N 105.30W
66 B3 Gilley France 47.03N 6.29E
107 B7 Gillham Arkansas 34.10N 94.21W
52 H4 Gillhov Sweden 62.40N 14.50E
107 C2 Gilliam Missouri 39.13N 93.00W
13 F5 Gilliat Queensland 20.40S 141.26E
13 F5 Gilliat R Queensland 20.40S 141.26E
57 K4 Gilling N Yorks Eng 54.26N 1.43W
57 L4 Gilling N Yorks Eng 54.10N 1.04W
56 G5 Gillingham Dorset Eng 51.02N 2.17W
56 N5 Gillingham Kent Eng 51.24N 0.33E
107 C11 Gillis Louisiana 30.22N 93.11W
59 B7 Gill, L Kerry Irish Rep 52.15N 10.02W
59 F3 Gill, L Sligo Irish Rep 54.15N 8.25W
113 L9 Gillon Pt Aleutian Is 52.25N 173.20E
96 C14 Gill Pt St Helena 15.59S 5.38W
58 K1 Gills Highland Scotland 58.38N 3.10W
106 G4 Gills Rock Wisconsin 45.17N 87.00W
61 H5 Gilly Belgium 50.26N 4.29E
66 B6 Gilly Switzerland 46.28N 6.18E
71 D3 Gilly-sur-Loire France 46.33N 3.47E
106 F9 Gilman Illinois 40.46N 88.01W
108 S8 Gilman Iowa 41.52N 92.45W
110 N2 Gilman Montana 47.31N 112.21W
106 D4 Gilman Wisconsin 45.12N 90.48W
107 C1 Gilman City Missouri 40.08N 93.53W
112 M3 Gilmer Texas 32.44N 94.58W
58 J6 Gilmerton Tayside Scotland 56.23N 3.50W
110 M5 Gilmore Idaho 44.28N 113.16W
13 G7 Gilmore Queensland 25.21S 144.40E
108 Q7 Gilmore City Iowa 42.43N 94.25W
99 N8 Gilmour Ontario 44.48N 77.37W
Gilolo see Halmahera I
87 E7 Gilo,R Ethiopia
82 H6 Gilortul R Romania
13 F7 Gilpeppee Queensland 26.08S 141.35E
101 N9 Gilpin Br Col 52.27N 121.04W
58 F6 Gilp, L Strathclyde Scotland 56.01N 5.26W
111 C4 Gilroy California 37.00N 121.34W
100 L8 Gilroy Saskatchewan 50.56N 106.43W
50 L5 Gilsá R Iceland
50 L4 Gilsárdalur V Iceland
50 K4 Gilsárvötn L Iceland
50 D5 Gilsbakki Iceland 64.43N 21.02W
50 D4 Gilsfjördhur B Iceland
108 M9 Giltner Nebraska 40.47N 98.09W
15 G7 Giluwe, Mt Papua New Guinea 6.06S 143.54E
56 E4 Gilwern Gwent Wales 51.51N 3.06W
40 D4 Gilyuy R U.S.S.R.
60 H13 Gilze Netherlands 51.33N 4.56E
90 M5 Gimbala, Jebel mt Sudan 12.59N 24.20E
69 P4 Gimbsheim W Germany 49.47N 8.23E
66 B5 Gimel Switzerland 46.31N 6.19E
116 O8 Gimie mt St Lucia, W I 13.54N 61.00W
81 N6 Gimigliano Italy 38.58N 16.32E
110 L6 Gimlet Idaho 43.35N 114.21W
100 V8 Gimli Manitoba 50.39N 97.00W
61 J6 Gimnée Belgium 50.08N 4.43E
52 L6 Gimo Sweden 60.11N 18.12E
47 C4 Gimoly U.S.S.R. 63.06N 31.25E
72 F8 Gimone R France
72 F8 Gimont France 43.38N 0.53E
69 J7 Gimont, Mt France 48.20N 5.04E
71 C3 Gimouille France 46.57N 3.05W
51 D3 Gimsoy Norway 68.18N 14.15E
35 C6 Gimzo Israel 31.56N 34.57E
94 N5 Ginabai Mozambique 24.28S 34.23E
85 L7 Ginâh Egypt 25.21N 30.30E
44 G7 Ginaldag mt Azerbaydzhan U.S.S.R. 40.22N 45.59E
71 H9 Ginasservis France 43.40N 5.50E
86 G5 Gindali, Wâdî el watercourse Egypt
13 J6 Gindie Queensland 23.45S 148.06E
86 E8 Gindîya, El Egypt 28.34N 30.50E
75 K6 Ginebrosa, La Spain 40.52N 0.09W
86 H5 Gineifa Egypt 30.12N 32.25E
86 G3 Gineina, El Egypt 31.06N 31.41E
86 G8 Gineinet el 'Atash hill Egypt 28.52N 31.47E
96 T8 Gines, Pta Lanzarote Canary Is 28.53N 13.52W
72 K9 Ginestas France 43.16N 2.52E
77 N2 Gineta, La Spain 39.08N 2.00W
96 T1 Ginetes Azores 37.35N 25.51W
15 M8 Ginetu I Papua New Guinea 9.30S 152.42E
50 U14 Ginevrabotnen str Spitsbergen
26 R9 Gin Ganga R Sri Lanka
28 D4 Gingee Tamil Nadu India 12.16N 79.24E
61 L3 Gingelom Belgium 50.45N 5.08E
64 H6 Gingen W Germany 48.40N 9.46E
116 H1 Ginger Hill Jamaica, W I 18.12N 77.57W
13 K6 Gin Gin Queensland 25.00S 151.58E
14 B9 Gingin W Australia 31.50S 115.50E
95 O10 Gingindlovu S Africa 29.01S 31.35E
82 H7 Gîngiova Romania 43.54N 23.50E
19 M7 Gingoog Mindanao Philippines 8.50N 125.08E
19 M7 Gingoog B Mindanao Philippines
63 S4 Gingst E Germany 54.28N 13.16E
87 H7 Ginir Ethiopia 7.06N 40.40E
35 E3 Ginnegar Israel 32.40N 35.15E
60 H13 Ginneken Netherlands 51.35N 4.47E
53 F4 Ginnerup Denmark 56.25N 10.45E
12 A5 Ginninderra, L Canberra Australia
35 F2 Ginnosar Israel 32.51N 35.31E
72 J10 Ginoles France 42.52N 2.09E
81 N2 Ginosa Italy 40.35N 16.45E
81 K6 Ginostra Lipari Is Italy 38.47N 15.12E
20 P9 Ginowan Okinawa Japan 26.14N 127.45E
69 P4 Ginsheim-Gustavsberg W Germany 49.59N 8.20E
26 R10 Gintota Sri Lanka 6.05N 80.10E
20 E2 Ginza dist Tōkyō Japan
76 D4 Ginzo de Limia Spain 42.04N 7.44W
76 D14 Giões Portugal 37.28N 7.42W
Giof see Jawf, Al
Giofra see Jufrah Oasis, Al
79 J1 Giogaia di Tessa mt Italy 46.44N 10.58E
79 K6 Giogo di Scarperia pass Italy 44.02N 11.23E
87 K9 Gioher Somalia 2.48N 45.30E
81 K3 Gioi Italy 40.17N 15.13E
80 J5 Gioia dei Marsi Italy 41.57N 13.42E
81 N2 Giòia del Colle Italy 40.47N 16.56E
81 L7 Giòia, G. di Italy
80 K6 Gioia Sannitica Italy 41.18N 14.27E
81 L7 Giòia Táuro Italy 38.26N 15.55E
81 M7 Gioiosa Iónica Italy 38.20N 16.19E
81 J7 Gioiosa Marea Sicily 38.10N 14.54E
121 K6 Gio, L Argentina
84 D4 Gióna Óros mts Greece
66 M6 Giornico Switzerland 46.24N 8.53E
Giosc see Jawsh, Al
80 N5 Giovannicchio, Monte Italy 41.50N 15.59E
80 F3 Giove Italy 42.30N 12.19E
66 M6 Giove, Madone di mt Switzerland 46.17N 8.47E
66 K6 Giove, Monte Italy 46.22N 8.23E
79 J1 Gioveretto mt Italy 46.30N 10.47E
79 K7 Giovi, Monte Italy 43.53N 11.26E
81 N1 Giovinazzo Italy 41.11N 16.40E
79 J6 Giovo, Monte Italy 44.08N 10.34E
79 K1 Giovo, Passo di pass Italy 46.52N 11.19E
66 J1 Gipf Switzerland 47.30N 8.01E
12 H7 Gippsland reg Victoria
66 F5 Gipsera Switzerland 46.41N 7.18E
117 H7 Giqui Brazil 4.46S 37.45W
29 B4 Girab Rajasthan India 26.02N 70.40E
93 K6 Giraffe Pool Kenya 0.29S 38.55E
86 N6 Girâfi, Wâdi watercourse Egypt
67 P11 Giraglia, I. de la Corsica 43.02N 9.24E
14 A6 Giralia W Australia 22.32S 114.25E
62 N6 Giraltovce Czechoslovakia 49.07N 21.30E
32 H7 Giran Iran 26.37N 59.01E
69 L7 Girancourt France 48.10N 6.19E
32 H6 Gīrān Rig mt Iran 28.08N 59.21E
29 F7 Girar Maharashtra India 20.40N 79.11E
30 B8 Girar Uttar Prad India 24.19N 78.55E
107 G2 Girard Illinois 39.26N 89.47W
109 Q4 Girard Kansas 37.30N 94.50W
104 E5 Girard Ohio 41.09N 80.42W
104 E4 Girard Pennsylvania 42.01N 80.20W
112 G2 Girard Texas 33.22N 100.41W
119 D5 Girardot Colombia 4.19N 74.47W
103 B5 Girardville Pennsylvania 40.48N 76.17W
Girash see Gerāsh
91 C11 Giraúl R Angola
91 C11 Giraúl-de-Cima Angola 15.02S 12.10E
91 C11 Giraúl, Pta.de pt Angola 15.04S 12.06E
86 M7 Girâ'. Wâdî watercourse Egypt
86 H5 Girba, Gebel el hill Egypt 30.16N 32.03E
32 G3 Girdab Iran 35.15N 56.37E
31 E3 Girdah Afghanistan 35.25N 68.14E
31 D4 Girdanai Pass Afghanistan 32.16N 67.26E
31 E5 Girdao Pakistan 31.49N 69.30E
31 C7 Girdar Dhor R Pakistan
32 J5 Girdi Iran 30.20N 61.05E
58 M4 Girdle Ness, Lt.Ho Grampian Scotland 57.08N 2.02W
113 N6 Girdwood Alaska 60.57N 149.18W
32 G7 Gireh, Kūh-e mt Iran 27.47N 57.36E
85 K10 Gir, El Sudan 19.50N 28.18E
87 C3 Gir, El watercourse Sudan
Giresor see Narlı Van Turkey
37 D5 Giresun Turkey 40.55N 38.25E
29 B7 Gir Forest Gujarat India
85 L6 Girga Egypt 26.17N 31.58E
87 B3 Girgil Sudan 14.03N 29.24E
15 H5 Girgir, C Papua New Guinea 3.50S 144.36E
90 F7 Giri Nigeria 9.21N 12.33E
91 F3 Giri R Zaïre
30 J7 Giriak Bihar India 25.03N 85.33E
29 K5 Giridih Bihar India 24.10N 86.20E
81 M6 Girifalco Italy 38.48N 16.26E
Girikamo see Silopi
12 H4 Girilambone New S Wales 31.14S 146.55E
Girimanj see Gerimenj
31 C5 Girishk Afghanistan 31.50N 64.35E
26 S6 Giritale Sri Lanka 8.00N 80.55E
26 R7 Giriulla Sri Lanka 7.19N 80.07E
29 D7 Girja R Maharashtra India
58 Q9 Girlsta Shetland Scotland 60.14N 1.14W
37 F8 Girmeli Turkey 37.15N 41.26E
29 C7 Girna R Maharashtra India
93 A2 Giro Zaïre 3.09N 29.09E
67 O12 Girolata, G.di Corsica 42.20N 8.35E
71 K1 Giromagny France 47.45N 6.49E
119 B9 Girón Ecuador 3.10S 79.09W
67 E8 Gironde dept France
72 C5 Gironde R France
72 D6 Gironde-sur-Dropt France 44.35N 0.06W
75 O3 Gironella Spain 42.02N 1.53E
69 K6 Gironville France 48.48N 5.41E
31 G4 Girot Pakistan 32.04N 72.17E
66 C8 Girotte, Lac de la France 45.45N 6.39E
72 H8 Girou R France
100 V9 Giroux Manitoba 49.38N 96.36W
44 D8 Girsovka Ukraine U.S.S.R. 46.37N 35.24E
56 L3 Girtford Bridge Beds Eng 52.08N 0.19W
56 M3 Girton Cambs Eng 52.14N 0.05E
90 B6 Giru Nigeria 11.45N 4.12E
13 H4 Giru Queensland 19.30S 147.05E
121 G2 Giruá Brazil 28.02S 54.23W
57 D2 Girvan Strathclyde Scotland 55.15N 4.51W
57 D2 Girvan, Water of R Strathclyde Scotland
100 M7 Girvin Saskatchewan 51.11N 105.57W
112 E4 Girvin Texas 31.05N 102.24W
30 E4 Girwa R Nepal
30 D7 Girwan Uttar Prad India 25.19N 80.23E
113 H4 Gisasa R Alaska
11 N5 Gisborne New Zealand 38.41S 178.02E
98 S6 Gisborne L Newfoundland
57 J5 Gisburn Lancs Eng 53.57N 2.15W
101 M8 Giscome Br Col 54.04N 122.22W
72 D7 Giscos France 44.16N 0.10W
111 N7 Gisela Arizona 34.09N 111.16W
93 A7 Gisenye Rwanda 1.41S 29.15E
66 K3 Gisikon Switzerland 47.08N 8.25E
52 G9 Gislaved Sweden 57.19N 13.30E
53 F6 Gislev Denmark 55.13N 10.37E
66 J2 Gislifluh mt Switzerland 47.26N 8.07E
53 H5 Gislinge Denmark 55.45N 11.33E
70 O3 Gisors France 49.17N 1.47E
64 K1 Gispersleben E Germany 51.02N 10.59E
43 J7 Gissar Tadzhikistan U.S.S.R. 38.30N 68.36E
43 J7 Gissarskiy Khrebet mts U.S.S.R.
80 L4 Gissi Italy 42.02N 14.33E
61 B2 Gistel Belgium 51.09N 2.58E
76 D1 Gistral, Sierra del mts Spain
66 J4 Giswil Switzerland 46.50N 8.11E
15 B4 Gita, Anggi L Irian Jaya 1.25S 133.58E
93 A8 Gitarama Rwanda 2.04S 29.45E
90 C7 Gitata Nigeria 9.08N 7.53E
Gitcha, Kūh-i- see Getcheh Kūh-e mts
93 A9 Gitega Burundi 3.24S 29.56E
61 C3 Gits Belgium 51.00N 3.06E
63 M9 Gittelde W Germany 51.48N 10.11E
35 E5 Gittit Jordan 32.06N 35.24E
93 A8 Gitwe Rwanda 2.14S 29.42E
87 J9 Giuba, Alto reg Somalia
87 J10 Giuba, Basso reg Somalia
87 M10 Giuba,Is Somalia
87 J10 Giuba,R Somalia
66 N7 Giubiasco Switzerland 46.11N 9.01E
66 L5 Giuf, Piz mt Switzerland 46.42N 8.42E
80 K7 Giugliano in Campania Italy 40.55N 14.12E
30 D1 Giugti La pass Xizang Zizhiqu 31.48N 80.35E
87 H4 Giuletti L Ethiopia
79 N3 Giulia reg Italy
80 H5 Giuliano di Roma Italy 41.33N 13.17E
80 J3 Giulianova Italy 42.45N 13.58E
82 J3 Giumalău mt Romania 47.26N 25.28E
87 J10 Giumbo Somalia 0.16S 42.35E
80 C3 Giuncarico Italy 42.55N 10.59E
82 L6 Giurgeni Romania 45.44N 27.51E
82 K7 Giurgiu Romania 43.53N 25.58E
79 F3 Giussano Italy 45.43N 9.12E
79 D6 Giusvalla Italy 44.27N 8.24E
32 G2 Gīvar Semnān Iran 36.03N 56.04E
35 D3 Giv'at 'Ada Israel 32.31N 35.00E
35 C6 Giv'at Brenner Israel 31.52N 34.48E
35 B1 Givat Hamivtar dist Jerusalem
35 E3 Giv'at Hamore hill Israel 32.37N 35.22E
35 B1 Giv'at Hanania dist Jerusalem
35 A1 Giv'at Havradim dist Jerusalem
35 B10 Giv'at Ḥayil hill Israel 30.59N 34.40E
35 C4 Giv'at Ḥayyim Israel 32.24N 34.56E
35 B7 Giv'ati Israel 31.43N 34.41E
35 B10 Giv'at 'Ivḥa hill Israel 30.56N 34.33E
35 C5 Giv'at Koaḥ Israel 32.02N 34.56E
35 A2 Giv'at Mordechai dist Jerusalem
35 D3 Giv'at Nili Israel 32.34N 35.02E
35 D3 Giv'at 'Oz Israel 32.34N 35.12E
35 B10 Giv'at Rut hill Israel 30.53N 34.32E
35 A1 Giv'at Shaul sub Jerusalem
35 D6 Giv'at Ye'arim Israel 31.47N 35.05E
35 C7 Giv'at Yesha'yahu Israel 31.40N 34.57E
35 C5 Giv'atyim Israel 32.04N 34.48E
35 F2 Giv'at Yo'ay Syria 32.48N 35.41E
35 D9 Giv'at Zafit hill Israel 31.03N 35.11E
53 C5 Give Denmark 55.51N 9.15E
69 D3 Givenchy-en-Gohelle France 50.23N 2.46E
69 H3 Givet France 50.08N 4.49E
35 B8 Giv'olim Israel 31.23N 34.35E
71 F5 Givors France 45.35N 4.47E
61 G5 Givry Belgium 50.23N 4.02E
71 F3 Givry France 46.47N 4.45E
19 N5 Givry isld Truk Is Pacific Oc 7.08N 151.52E
69 H6 Givry-en-Argonne France 48.57N 4.54E
53 C5 Givskud Denmark 55.49N 9.22E
86 F6 Gîza div Egypt
86 Q12 Gîza, El Cairo Egypt
86 E5 Gizai Egypt 30.28N 30.51E
86 F6 Giza Pyramids Egypt 29.59N 31.07E
80 O1 Gizdavac Yugoslavia 43.39N 16.28E
44 F4 Gizel' U.S.S.R. 43.02N 44.36E
44 F5 Gizel'don R U.S.S.R.
70 L7 Gizeux France 47.24N 0.13E
43 G6 Gizhduvan Uzbekistan U.S.S.R. 40.07N 64.15E
39 G4 Gizhiga U.S.S.R. 62.00N 160.34E
39 G4 Gizhiga R U.S.S.R.
39 F4 Gizhiginskaya Guba gulf U.S.S.R.
15 K3 Gizo Solomon Is 8.04S 156.45E
15 K3 Gizo I Solomon Is 8.04S 156.45E
Gizvan see Jazvān
69 F4 Gizy France 49.36N 3.47E
62 N1 Gizycko Poland 54.03N 21.48E
81 M6 Gizzeria Italy 38.59N 16.13E
50 G6 Gjáfjöll mt Iceland 64.22N 18.28W
50 J3 Gjástykki rift reg Iceland
53 T15 Gjegnet mt Norway 61.48N 5.50E
53 S16 Gjelsvik Norway 61.28N 5.22E
53 U15 Gjemmestad Norway 61.45N 6.10E
53 Z16 Gjende L Norway 61.29N 8.37E
53 Y16 Gjendebu Norway 61.27N 8.28E
52 D5 Gjendesheim Norway 61.30N 8.51E
53 T15 Gjengedal Norway 61.40N 5.56E
53 T19 Gjerde Hordaland Norway 59.40N 5.57E
53 U18 Gjerde Hordaland Norway 60.08N 6.20E
53 W15 Gjerde Sogn og Fjordane Norway 61.38N 7.15E
53 V15 Gjerdeaksla mt Norway 61.44N 6.55E
53 E3 Gjerlev Denmark 56.35N 10.08E
53 W13 Gjermundnes Norway 62.37N 7.10E
53 T18 Gjermundshamn Norway 60.03N 5.56E
53 D4 Gjern Denmark 56.14N 9.45E
53 C5 Gjerndrup Denmark 55.31N 9.02E
53 F4 Gjerrild Denmark 56.30N 10.51E
53 F4 Gjerrild Klint cliff Denmark 56.33N 10.52E
52 D8 Gjerstad Aust Agder Norway 58.54N 9.00E
53 T18 Gjerstad Hordaland Norway 60.30N 5.32E
52 G2 Gjersvik Norway 64.53N 13.25E
52 E4 Gjevil-Vatn L Norway 62.43N 9.25E
83 D4 Gjirokastër Albania 40.05N 20.10E
101 Z1 Gjoa Haven King William I, N W Terr 68.39N 96.08W
50 D3 Gjögur Iceland 66.00N 21.18W
50 G2 Gjögur C Iceland 66.10N 18.15W
53 D2 Gjøl Denmark 57.04N 9.44E
53 C3 Gjørup Denmark 56.39N 9.22E
53 U13 Gjøsund Norway 62.32N 6.09E
53 N9 Gjov Faeroes 62.20N 6.56W
52 D8 Gjovdal Norway 58.55N 8.19E
52 F6 Gjøvik Norway 60.47N 10.41E
83 C4 Gjuhëzës, Kep i C Albania 40.26N 19.16E
53 Y13 Gjuratind mt Norway 62.33N 8.03E
53 Y19 Gjuvikfjell mt Norway 59.59N 8.04E
53 X18 Gjuvsjå L Norway 60.04N 7.50E
61 H4 Glabais Belgium 50.38N 4.27E
61 K3 Glabbeek Zuurbemde Belgium 50.52N 4.57E
98 N7 Glace Bay C Breton I, Nova Scotia 46.11N 59.58W
70 G2 Glacerie, la France 49.36N 1.34W
101 P10 Glacier Br Col 51.16N 117.31W
110 D1 Glacier Washington 48.53N 121.57W
113 T7 Glacier B Alaska
113 T7 Glacier Bay Nat.Mon Alaska
Glacier Creek P.O see Sixtymile
113 O6 Glacier I Alaska 60.53N 147.10W
113 R4 Glacier Mt Alaska 64.46N 141.50W
101 P10 Glacier Nat.Park Br Col
110 M1 Glacier Nat.Park Montana
110 D1 Glacier Pk Washington 48.07N 121.06W
66 D8 Glaciers, Aiguille des mt France/Italy 45.48N 6.48E
97 M2 Glacier Str N W Terr
63 E9 Gladbeck W Germany 51.34N 6.59E
108 S7 Gladbrook Iowa 42.11N 92.42W
109 L2 Glade Kansas 39.41N 99.19W
11 B11 Glade House New Zealand 44.56S 167.58E
64 F2 Gladenbach W Germany 50.46N 8.35E
109 B3 Glade Park Colorado 38.59N 108.45W
104 D10 Glade Spring Virginia 36.48N 81.47W
12 L7 Gladesville dist Sydney, N S W
112 N3 Gladewater Texas 32.33N 94.57W
39 H7 Gladkovskaya mt Komandorskiye O-va U.S.S.R. 54.52N 166.20E
100 N9 Gladmar Saskatchewan 49.12N 104.31W
100 T8 Gladstone Manitoba 50.14N 98.56W
106 G4 Gladstone Michigan 45.52N 87.02W
108 H3 Gladstone N Dakota 46.53N 102.32W
109 G5 Gladstone New Mexico 36.19N 103.59W
11 K8 Gladstone New Zealand 41.06S 175.39E
13 K6 Gladstone Queensland 23.52S 151.16E
12 E5 Gladstone S Australia 33.17S 138.22E
12 J8 Gladstone Tasmania 40.57S 148.01E
106 K6 Gladwin Michigan 43.59N 84.28W
104 F8 Glady W Virginia 38.47N 79.44W
104 F9 Gladys Virginia 37.10N 79.07W
101 G6 Gladys L Br Col 59.50N 132.52W
53 G6 Glænø isld Denmark 55.11N 11.27E
50 G3 Glæsibær Iceland 65.45N 18.08W
52 G7 Glafsfjörden L Sweden
50 C3 Gláma mt Iceland 65.46N 22.59W
52 F4 Glåma R Norway
111 J8 Glamis California 33.00N 115.06W
100 K7 Glamis Saskatchewan 51.23N 107.53W
58 K5 Glamis Tayside Scotland 56.37N 3.01W
82 D6 Glamoc Yugoslavia 44.03N 16.51E
Glamorgan co see Glamorgan W., Mid, & South three new counties
53 E6 Glamsbjerg Denmark 55.17N 10.07E
19 M9 Glan Mindanao Philippines 5.49N 125.11E
52 J8 Glan L Sweden 58.37N 16.00E
65 K8 Glan R Austria
64 D4 Glan R W Germany
59 D7 Glanaruddery Mts Kerry Irish Rep

66 B6 Gland Switzerland 46.26N 6.16E
71 H7 Glandage France 44.41N 5.35E
71 G7 Glandasse mt France 44.45N 5.28E
72 G5 Glandon France 45.28N 1.14E
71 J6 Glandon, Col du pass France 45.14N 6.11E
65 K8 Glandorf Austria 46.45N 14.23E
63 G8 Glandorf W Germany 52.06N 8.00E
66 E4 Glâne R Switzerland
63 G8 Glane R W Germany
65 K8 Glanegg Austria 46.44N 14.13E
66 D4 Glâne, Pt Switzerland 46.50N 6.55E
60 R11 Glanerbrug Netherlands 52.13N 6.59E
61 D4 Glanerie, La Belgium 50.32N 3.18E
63 H7 Glane-Visbek W Germany 52.50N 8.19E
59 F8 Glanmire Cork Irish Rep 51.55N 8.25W
59 C8 Glanmore L Kerry Irish Rep 51.44N 9.46W
64 C5 Glan Münchweiler W Germany 49.28N 7.27E
93 G5 Glanville Kenya 0.58N 35.05E
59 F7 Glanworth Cork Irish Rep 52.11N 8.21W
66 Q5 Glaris Switzerland 46.44N 9.46E
66 M4 Glarner Alpen mts Switzerland
66 M3 Glärnisch mt Switzerland 47.00N 9.00E
66 N3 Glarus Switzerland 47.03N 9.04E
66 N3 Glarus canton Switzerland
109 N2 Glasco Kansas 39.22N 97.51W
103 G2 Glasco New York 42.03N 73.52W
66 F2 Glaser Berg mt France 47.27N 7.17E
106 E9 Glasford Illinois 40.35N 89.49W
103 L3 Glasgo Connecticut 41.33N 71.53W
116 G1 Glasgow Jamaica, W I 18.21N 78.13W
107 L5 Glasgow Kentucky 36.59N 85.56W
107 D2 Glasgow Missouri 39.14N 92.48W
108 D1 Glasgow Montana 48.12N 106.37W
58 H7 Glasgow Strathclyde Scotland 55.53N 4.15W
104 F9 Glasgow Virginia 37.38N 79.29W
64 Q2 Glashütte Dresden E Germany 50.52N 13.47E
63 U5 Glashütte Neubrandenburg E Germany 53.34N 14.15E
65 M8 Glashütten Austria 46.50N 15.03E
59 J3 Glaslough Monaghan Irish Rep 54.19N 6.54W
100 J5 Glaslyn Saskatchewan 53.23N 108.22W
58 K5 Glas Maol mt Tayside Scotland 56.52N 3.22W
100 M9 Glasnevin Saskatchewan 49.33N 105.08W
59 G5 Glassan W Meath Irish Rep 53.28N 7.52W
103 D7 Glassboro New Jersey 39.42N 75.07W
59 L3 Glassdrummond Down N Ireland 54.08N 5.54W
57 E3 Glasserton Dumfries & Galloway Scotland 54.43N 4.28W
58 G3 Glass, L Highland Scotland 57.43N 4.30W
111 F4 Glass Mt California 37.45N 118.42W
112 D5 Glass Mts Texas
57 H5 Glasson Lancs England 54.00N 2.51W
113 U8 Glass Pen Alaska
58 G4 Glass, R Highland Scotland
103 J3 Glastonbury Connecticut 41.43N 72.36W
56 F5 Glastonbury Somerset Eng 51.09N 2.43W
58 G2 Glasven mt Highland Scotland 58.11N 4.58W
66 L2 Glatt R Switzerland
66 N2 Glatt R Switzerland
66 K1 Glattfelden Switzerland 47.33N 8.30E
56 L3 Glatton Cambs Eng 52.28N 0.19W
Glatz see Kłodzko
64 O2 Glauchau E Germany 50.48N 12.32E
50 F3 Glaumbær Iceland 65.35N 19.30W
82 K7 Glavinitsa Bulgaria 43.55N 26.48E
84 E2 Glavkí Greece 39.37N 22.35E
45 V5 Glavnyy Kazakhstan U.S.S.R. 51.05N 49.45E
44 H4 Glavnyy Kut U.S.S.R. 43.32N 47.26E
112 D7 Glazier Texas 36.02N 100.16W
45 M3 Glazok U.S.S.R. 53.06N 40.42E
46 R1 Glazov U.S.S.R. 58.09N 52.42E
41 B2 Glazova, Guba gulf Novaya Zemlya U.S.S.R.
45 H4 Glazunovka U.S.S.R. 52.30N 36.20E
45 O7 Glazunovskaya U.S.S.R. 49.49N 42.50E
62 K2 Głda R Poland
58 G3 Gleann Mor V Highland Scotland
107 H5 Gleason Tennessee 36.13N 88.36W
106 E4 Gleason Wisconsin 45.18N 89.30W
104 H5 Gleasonton Pennsylvania 41.22N 77.43W
57 G4 Gleaston Cumbria Eng 54.08N 3.09W
66 J5 Gleckstein Switzerland 46.36N 8.07E
111 P10 Gleeson Arizona 31.43N 109.50W
88 G9 Gleib Chileh Morocco 24.09N 13.30W
64 K3 Gleichberg mt E Germany 50.23N 10.37E
100 D8 Gleichen Alberta 50.52N 113.02W
64 M1 Gleina E Germany 51.15N 11.44E
65 M7 Glein-alpe mts Austria
65 N7 Gleisdorf Austria 47.07N 15.43E
Gleiwitz see Gliwice
61 O5 Gleize, La Belgium 50.25N 5.51E
53 B5 Glejbjerg Denmark 55.34N 8.50E
108 G7 Glen Nebraska 42.37N 103.36W
104 O2 Glen New Hampshire 44.06N 71.10W
95 K4 Glen S Africa 28.58S 26.21E
110 A6 Glenada Oregon 43.58N 124.04W
59 F3 Glenade L Leitrim Irish Rep 54.22N 8.16W
58 F4 Glen Affric V Highland Scotland
11 K4 Glen Afton New Zealand 37.37S 175.02E
99 P7 Glen Almond Quebec 45.42N 75.30W
58 H6 Glen Almond V Tayside Scotland
105 F2 Glen Alpine N Carolina 35.45N 81.47W
59 C3 Glenamoy R Mayo Irish Rep
70 C6 Glénans, Iles de France 47.43N 3.57W
57 C2 Glen App V Strathclyde Scotland 55.01N 5.02W
11 C12 Glenaray New Zealand 45.37S 168.58E
58 F6 Glen Aray V Strathclyde Scotland
59 K1 Glenariff, R Antrim N Ireland
59 L2 Glenarm Antrim N Ireland 54.58N 5.57W
59 L2 Glenarm, R Antrim N Ireland
59 K6 Glenart Castle Wicklow Irish Rep 52.50N 6.11W
58 H6 Glen Artney V Tayside Scotland
103 B2 Glen Aubrey New York 42.15N 76.01W
95 K7 Glen Avon S Africa 31.41S 26.12E
100 O8 Glenavon Saskatchewan 50.11N 103.05W
58 J4 Glen Avon V Grampian Scotland
59 K2 Glenavy Antrim N Ireland 54.36N 6.13W
11 F11 Glenavy New Zealand 44.56S 171.06E
59 E2 Glen B Donegal Irish Rep 54.43N 8.48W
100 K9 Glenbain Saskatchewan 49.51N 107.01W
57 B1 Glenbarr Strathclyde Scotland 55.34N 5.40W
12 K4 Glenbawn Res New S Wales 32.04S 150.55E
59 C8 Glenbeg L Cork Irish Rep 51.43N 9.52W
59 C7 Glenbeigh Kerry Irish Rep 52.03N 9.56W
100 S9 Glenboro Manitoba 49.35N 99.20W
103 G4 Glenbrook Connecticut 41.04N 73.31W
108 J1 Glenburn N Dakota 48.32N 101.14W
103 A8 Glen Burnie Maryland 39.10N 76.37W
98 P4 Glenburnie Newfoundland 49.27N 57.54W
12 F7 Glenburnie S Australia 37.49S 140.56E
100 K5 Glenbush Saskatchewan 53.16N 108.00W
94 P12 Glencairn Cape Town S Africa 34.10S 18.26E
58 F4 Glen Cannich V Highland Scotland
111 N5 Glen Canyon gorge Arizona/Utah 36.55N 111.32W
57 F2 Glencaple Dumfries & Galloway Scotland 55.00N 3.35W
59 C7 Glencar Kerry Irish Rep 52.01N 9.52W
59 F3 Glencar L Sligo etc Irish Rep 54.20N 8.23W
58 F3 Glencarron Highland Scotland 57.30N 5.15W
58 F4 Glen Carron V Highland Scotland
58 K6 Glencarse Tayside Scotland 56.23N 3.19W
58 G2 Glen Cassley V Highland Scotland
103 C2 Glen Castle New York 42.10N 75.56W
72 E3 Glençay France 46.23N 0.24E
58 K5 Glen Clova V Tayside Scotland
58 K5 Glen Clunie V Grampian Scotland
107 L8 Glencoe Alabama 33.55N 85.57W
108 Q5 Glencoe Minnesota 44.45N 94.10W
109 E8 Glencoe New Mexico 33.24N 105.27W
99 J10 Glencoe Ontario 42.45N 81.44W
95 O4 Glencoe S Africa 28.10S 30.10E
12 F7 Glencoe S Australia 37.41S 140.05E
58 F5 Glen Coe V Highland Scotland
59 E2 Glencolumbkille Donegal Irish Rep 54.42N 8.44W
95 J9 Glenconnor S Africa 33.24S 25.09E
103 M6 Glen Cove Long I, N Y 40.53N 73.36W
108 K4 Glencross S Dakota 45.26N 100.54W
111 M8 Glendale Arizona 33.34N 112.10W
111 F7 Glendale California 34.09N 118.20W
107 K11 Glendale Florida 30.52N 86.10W
109 N3 Glendale Kansas 38.55N 97.54W
111 K5 Glendale Nevada 36.40N 114.36W
104 A7 Glendale Ohio 39.16N 84.28W
110 B7 Glendale Oregon 42.44N 123.25W
95 P5 Glendale S Africa 29.20S 31.06E
104 E7 Glendale W Virginia 39.56N 80.44W
92 E10 Glendale Zimbabwe 17.22S 31.05E
101 L10 Glendale Cove Br Col 50.39N 125.40W
59 K5 Glendalough, Vale of Wicklow Irish Rep
58 F6 Glendaruel V Strathclyde Scotland
12 K5 Glen Davis New S Wales 33.07S 150.22E
109 E1 Glendevey Colorado 40.47N 105.56W
58 J6 Glendevon Tayside Scotland 56.13N 3.38W
58 J6 Glen Devon V Tayside Scotland
108 F2 Glendive Montana 47.08N 104.42W
108 E7 Glendo Wyoming 42.30N 105.02W
100 F4 Glendon Alberta 54.16N 111.05W
107 F8 Glendora Mississippi 33.51N 90.20W
11 D2 Glendowie New Zealand 36.52S 174.53E
59 K1 Glendun, R Antrim N Ireland
13 H4 Gleneagle Queensland 18.13S 145.18E
58 J6 Gleneagles Tayside Scotland 56.17N 3.45W
58 J6 Glen Eagles V Tayside Scotland
59 K6 Glenealy Wicklow Irish Rep 52.58N 6.08W
11 B2 Glen Eden bor Auckland New Zealand
109 M2 Glen Elder Kansas 39.31N 98.18W
109 M2 Glen Elder Res Kansas
58 E4 Glenelg Highland Scotland 57.13N 5.37W
12 E5 Glenelg S Australia 34.59S 138.31E
12 F6 Glenelg R Victoria
14 E3 Glenelg, R W Australia
100 S8 Glenella Manitoba 50.34N 99.11W
58 L5 Glen Esk V Tayside Scotland
58 F5 Glen Etive V Strathclyde Scotland
100 P9 Glen Ewen Saskatchewan 49.14N 102.02W
11 M12 Glenfalloch gardens New Zealand 45.53S 170.37E
58 G6 Glen Falloch V Central Scotland
58 K6 Glenfarg Tayside Scotland 56.17N 3.25W
58 J4 Glen Feshie V Highland Scotland
108 M2 Glenfield N Dakota 47.28N 98.36W
104 K3 Glenfield New York 43.42N 75.24W
11 C1 Glenfield New Zealand 36.46S 174.43E
58 F5 Glenfinnan Highland Scotland 56.53N 5.27W
112 L6 Glen Flora Texas 29.22N 96.12W
14 B6 Glen Florrie W Australia 23.01S 116.03E
103 F2 Glenford New York 42.00N 74.08W
59 H1 Glengad Hd Donegal Irish Rep 55.20N 7.11W
58 K4 Glen Gairn V Grampian Scotland
103 E5 Glen Gardner New Jersey 40.42N 74.56W
59 C8 Glengariff Cork Irish Rep 51.45N 9.33W
58 F4 Glen Garry V Highland Scotland
58 H5 Glen Garry V Tayside Scotland
14 C7 Glengarry Ra W Australia
116 K2 Glengoffe Jamaica, W I 18.09N 76.54W
59 L2 Glengormly Antrim N Ireland 54.41N 5.58W
13 E6 Glengyle Queensland 24.45S 139.20E
103 G3 Glenham New York 41.31N 73.56W
11 C13 Glenham New Zealand 46.26S 168.53E
108 K4 Glenham S Dakota 45.30N 100.16W
95 H8 Glen Harry S Africa 32.07S 24.43E
13 C6 Glen Helen N Terr Aust 23.15S 132.35E
13 C6 Glen Helen Gorge N Terr Australia 23.34S 132.37E
11 G8 Glenhope New Zealand 41.39S 172.40E
72 H3 Glénic France 46.13N 1.56E
59 D5 Glenicmurrin L Clare Irish Rep 53.18N 9.30W
12 K3 Glen Innes New S Wales 29.42S 151.45E
12 D8 Glen Iris dist Melbourne, Vic
58 K5 Glenisla Tayside Scotland 56.44N 3.17W
57 E2 Glenkens V Dumfries & Galloway Scot
100 K8 Glen Kerr Saskatchewan 50.36N 107.03W
59 G1 Glen L Donegal Irish Rep 55.06N 7.50W
106 H5 Glen L Michigan 44.53N 86.01W
59 G4 Glen L W Meath Irish Rep 53.39N 7.35W
58 K4 Glen Livet V Grampian Scotland
58 H5 Glen Lochay V Central Scotland
58 F4 Glen Loyne V Highland Scotland
57 D3 Glenluce Dumfries & Galloway Scotland 54.53N 4.49W
12 G4 Glen Lyon New S Wales 31.41S 142.06E
103 B4 Glen Lyon Pennsylvania 41.11N 76.02W
58 H5 Glen Lyon V Tayside Scotland
11 K4 Glen Massey New Zealand 37.42S 175.05E
103 D7 Glen Mills Pennsylvania 39.55N 75.30W
107 D11 Glenmora Louisiana 31.00N 92.35W
59 H7 Glenmore Kilkenny Irish Rep 52.21N 7.02W
13 J7 Glenmorgan Queensland 27.19S 149.40E
58 G4 Glen Moriston V Highland Scotland
58 K5 Glen Muick V Grampian Scotland
111 B2 Glenn California 39.32N 122.00W
113 P5 Glennallen Alaska 62.08N 145.38W
59 E4 Glennamaddy Galway Irish Rep 53.37N 8.33W
66 N5 Glenner R Switzerland
106 L5 Glennie Michigan 44.34N 83.43W
12 H7 Glennie I Victoria 39.06S 146.14E
111 P10 Glenn, Mt Arizona 31.56N 110.00W
111 F6 Glennville California 35.43N 118.42W
105 F6 Glennville Georgia 31.55N 81.57W
59 C5 Glenoalough,L Galway Irish Rep 53.28N 9.44W
59 L2 Glenoe Antrim N Ireland 54.48N 5.50W
58 H6 Glen Ogle V Central Scotland
11 D13 Glenomaru New Zealand 46.25S 169.44E
79 H2 Gleno, Monte Italy 46.03N 10.06E
101 H7 Glenora Br Col 57.50N 131.24W
13 G4 Glenora Queensland 19.00S 142.58E
11 C11 Glenorchy New Zealand 44.52S 168.26E
12 F8 Glenorchy dist Hobart, Tasmania 42.50S 147.18E
58 G6 Glen Orchy V Strathclyde Scotland
11 D13 Glenore New Zealand 46.07S 169.53E
13 F4 Glenore Queensland 17.47S 141.06E
13 E6 Glenormiston Queensland 22.58S 138.49E
58 G4 Glen Orrin V Highland Scotland
12 B8 Glen Osmond dist Adelaide, S Aust
58 K5 Glen Prosen V Tayside Scotland
12 L4 Glenreagh New S Wales 30.02S 153.00E
57 H3 Glenridding Cumbria Eng 54.33N 2.58W
109 G6 Glenrio New Mexico 35.11N 103.03W
99 Q7 Glen Robertson Ontario 45.22N 74.30W
103 J5 Glen Rock Pennsylvania 39.47N 76.13W
108 E7 Glenrock Wyoming 42.52N 105.52W
112 K3 Glen Rose Texas 32.14N 97.45W
58 K6 Glenrothes Fife Scotland 56.12N 3.10W
13 E5 Glenroy Queensland 20.24S 139.45E
94 U14 Glenroy S Africa 26.24S 28.18E
14 F3 Glenroy W Australia 17.23S 126.01E
12 C6 Glenroy dist Melbourne, Vic
58 G5 Glen Roy V Highland Scotland
104 M3 Glens Falls New York 43.17N 73.41W
110 K7 Glens Ferry Idaho 42.57N 115.19W
59 J2 Glenshane Pass Londonderry N Ireland 54.52N 6.51W
58 K5 Glen Shee V Tayside Scotland
59 K1 Glenshesk, R Antrim N Ireland
58 F4 Glen Shiel V Highland Scotland
58 F6 Glen Shira V Strathclyde Scotland
11 C5 Glenside New Zealand 41.12S 174.47E
95 O5 Glenside S Africa 29.23S 30.47E
100 L7 Glenside Saskatchewan 51.27N 106.50W
58 G5 Glen Spean V Highland Scotland
103 E4 Glen Spey New York 41.29N 74.48W
53 D3 Glenstrup Sø L Denmark 56.36N 9.53E
103 C4 Glen Summit Pennsylvania 41.08N 75.50W
108 D1 Glentana Montana 48.52N 106.15W
58 L5 Glen Tanar V Grampian Scotland
58 G4 Glen Tarff V Highland Scotland
95 K8 Glenthorn S Africa 32.29S 26.15E
59 F2 Glenties Donegal Irish Rep 54.47N 8.17W
58 J5 Glen Tilt V Tayside Scotland
58 H5 Glen Tromie V Highland Scotland
57 D2 Glentrool Dumfries & Galloway Scotland 55.05N 4.35W
58 H5 Glen Truim V Highland Scotland
11 F10 Glentunnel New Zealand 43.29S 171.56E
100 L9 Glentworth Saskatchewan 49.25N 106.40W
108 J3 Glen Ullin N Dakota 46.50N 101.50W
58 G4 Glen Urquhart V Highland Scotland
13 H6 Glenusk Queensland 24.14S 145.35E
99 K5 Glenvale Ontario 47.52N 80.09W
106 G7 Glenview Illinois 42.05N 87.49W
108 R6 Glenville Minnesota 43.35N 93.14W
108 M9 Glenville Nebraska 40.30N 98.14W
103 A7 Glenville Pennsylvania 39.45N 76.48W
104 E8 Glenville W Virginia 38.57N 80.51W
105 D2 Glenville L N Carolina 35.10N 83.09W
12 E8 Glen Waverley dist Melbourne, Vic
103 E3 Glen Wild New York 41.38N 74.35W
107 K10 Glenwood Alabama 31.40N 86.11W
107 C7 Glenwood Arkansas 34.20N 93.35W
105 E5 Glenwood Georgia 32.11N 82.43W
114 C8 Glenwood Hawaiian Is 19.29N 155.09W
107 L2 Glenwood Indiana 39.37N 85.18W
108 P8 Glenwood Iowa 41.04N 95.46W
108 P4 Glenwood Minnesota 45.39N 95.22W
107 D1 Glenwood Missouri 40.31N 92.36W
105 F2 Glenwood N Carolina 35.38N 82.00W
98 S5 Glenwood Newfoundland 49.00N 54.53W
103 E4 Glenwood New Jersey 41.15N 74.30W
109 B8 Glenwood New Mexico 33.19N 108.53W
110 B4 Glenwood Oregon 45.39N 123.16W
103 C3 Glenwood Pennsylvania 41.39N 75.44W
111 N3 Glenwood Utah 38.45N 111.59W
110 D3 Glenwood Washington 46.01N 121.17W
106 B4 Glenwood Wisconsin 45.03N 92.09W
104 C8 Glenwood W Virginia 38.34N 82.13W
109 C2 Glenwood Springs Colorado 39.33N 107.21W
100 D9 Glenwoodville Alberta 49.24N 113.28W
50 G3 Glerá R Iceland
50 D4 Glerárskógar Iceland 65.12N 21.43W
50 G3 Glerárthorp Iceland 65.42N 18.05W
66 D2 Glère France 47.21N 7.00E
53 F4 Glesborg Denmark 56.29N 10.44E
63 N4 Gleschendorf W Germany 54.02N 10.40E
66 K5 Gletsch Switzerland 46.33N 8.22E
50 M3 Glettinganes C Iceland 65.31N 13.36W
121 F5 Glew Argentina 34.55S 58.25W
100 H7 Glidden Saskatchewan 51.14N 109.09W
106 D3 Glidden Wisconsin 46.09N 90.36W
110 B6 Glide Oregon 43.19N 123.05W
63 S8 Glienick E Germany 52.15N 13.22E
63 S7 Glienicke E Germany 52.37N 13.19E
63 U8 Glienicke E Germany 52.12N 14.05E
84 G6 Glifádha Greece 37.52N 23.45E
61 K4 Glimes Belgium 50.41N 4.50E
59 D6 Glin Limerick Irish Rep 52.34N 9.17W
82 C5 Glina Yugoslavia 45.20N 16.06E
82 C5 Glina R Yugoslavia
63 M5 Glinde W Germany 53.33N 10.12E
39 H7 Glinka Komandorskiye O-va U.S.S.R. 54.41N 168.02E
45 D2 Glinka Smolensk U.S.S.R. 54.38N 32.54E
59 E4 Glinn L Roscommon Irish Rep 53.50N 8.33W
62 M3 Glinojeck Poland 52.49N 20.19E
84 C2 Glínos Greece 39.31N 21.52E
45 D8 Glinsk Kirovograd, Ukraine U.S.S.R. 48.57N 32.54E
45 E6 Glinsk Sumy, Ukraine U.S.S.R. 50.39N 33.20E
47 N4 Glinskoye U.S.S.R. 57.30N 61.24E
82 J1 Glinyany U.S.S.R. 49.50N 24.31E
66 D6 Glion Switzerland 46.27N 6.56E
66 H6 Glis Switzerland 46.19N 7.59E
52 H4 Glissjöberg Sweden 62.07N 14.05E
53 Z15 Glittertind mt Norway 61.40N 8.32E
62 L5 Gliwice Poland 50.20N 18.40E
50 F6 Gljúfurleitafoss waterfall Iceland 64.19N 19.15W
83 D4 Gllavë Albania 40.31N 19.59E
111 O8 Globe Arizona 33.23N 110.48W
45 E7 Globino Ukraine U.S.S.R. 49.23N 33.16E
Glogau see Głogów
65 N6 Gloggnitz Austria 47.41N 15.57E
62 J4 Głogów Poland 51.40N 16.06E
62 K5 Głogówek Poland 50.21N 17.50E
63 Q8 Gloine E Germany 52.11N 12.14E
58 F4 Glomach, Falls Highland Scotland 57.16N 5.19W
70 D5 Glomel France 48.13N 3.24W
51 D5 Glomfjord Norway 66.49N 14.00E
52 F7 Glomma R Norway
51 H6 Glommersträsk Sweden 65.17N 19.40E
52 K10 Glömminge Sweden 56.43N 16.30E
64 M8 Glonn W Germany 47.49N 11.52E
61 N4 Glons Belgium 50.45N 5.33E
Gloppen see Vereid Gloppen
Gloppen see Vereide
53 U15 Gloppenfjord inlet Norway 61.49N 6.05E
50 G3 Gloppufjall mt Iceland 65.46N 18.44W
50 G4 Gloppufjall mt Iceland 65.30N 18.34W
59 H4 Glore, L W Meath Irish Rep 53.42N 7.15W
79 J1 Glorenza Italy 46.40N 10.33E
117 H9 Glória Bahia Brazil 9.12S 38.20W
118 J9 Glória Rio de Janeiro Brazil 22.56S 43.11W
119 E7 Gloria, Salto falls Colombia 1.59N 71.58W
109 E6 Glorieta New Mexico 35.35N 105.46W
95 C1 Glorieuses, Is Madagascar 11.34S 47.19E
113 A6 Glory of Russia C St Matthew I Bering Sea 60.35N 172.55W
70 L3 Glos France 49.07N 0.18E
95 G4 Glosam S Africa 28.06S 23.03E
70 M4 Glos-la-Ferrière France 48.51N 0.36E
84 G3 Glóssa Greece 39.11N 23.37E
57 K6 Glossop Derbys Eng 53.27N 1.57W
123 G9 Glossopteris, Mt Antarctica 84.45S 114.00W
70 M3 Glos-sur-Risle France 49.17N 0.41E
107 E10 Gloster Mississippi 31.12N 91.01W
53 J5 Glostrup Denmark 55.41N 12.25E
45 S3 Glotovka U.S.S.R. 53.58N 46.43E
47 F4 Glotovo U.S.S.R. 63.25N 49.28E
56 G4 Gloucester Glos Eng 51.53N 2.14W
104 P4 Gloucester Massachusetts 42.37N 70.41W
12 K4 Gloucester New S Wales 31.59S 151.58E
104 J9 Gloucester Virginia 37.26N 76.33W
56 G4 Gloucester co England
103 D7 Gloucester co New Jersey
103 D7 Gloucester City New Jersey 39.53N 75.08W
13 J4 Gloucester I Queensland 20.00S 148.27E
66 E2 Glovelier Switzerland 47.20N 7.12E
98 P5 Glover I Newfoundland
115 Q9 Glover Reef Belize
104 L3 Gloversville New York 43.03N 74.19W
98 S5 Glovertown Newfoundland 48.40N 54.03W
63 Q7 Glöwen E Germany 52.55N 12.06E
62 M4 Głowno Poland 51.59N 19.41E
62 K5 Głubczyce Poland 50.20N 17.21E
62 K5 Głubczyce Poland 50.13N 17.50E
46 K3 Glubki U.S.S.R. 53.04N 36.54E
47 H6 Glubokaya U.S.S.R. 58.47N 59.51E
39 J4 Glubokaya, Bukhta gulf U.S.S.R.
45 M8 Glubokiy Rostov U.S.S.R. 48.31N 40.20E
45 O9 Glubokiy Rostov U.S.S.R. 47.01N 42.47E
47 K4 Glubokiy Poluy R U.S.S.R.
46 G2 Glubokoye Belorussiya U.S.S.R. 55.07N 27.42E
43 O2 Glubokoye Kazakhstan U.S.S.R. 50.08N 82.16E
42 C5 Glubokoye U.S.S.R. 53.00N 80.45E
43 O1 Glubokoye U.S.S.R. 53.00N 80.49E
41 F6 Glubokoye, Ozero L U.S.S.R.
63 L3 Glücksburg W Germany 54.51N 9.34E
95 P3 Gluckstadt S Africa 27.57S 31.02E
63 K5 Glückstadt W Germany 53.47N 9.26E
53 D5 Glud Denmark 55.49N 10.00E
53 C4 Gludsted Denmark 56.02N 9.19E
53 N10 Gluggarnir Faeroes 61.33N 6.54W
53 W19 Gluggvardegga mt Norway 59.49N 7.28E
71 F7 Gluiras France 44.50N 4.32E
45 E5 Glukhov Ukraine U.S.S.R. 51.40N 33.54E
45 P1 Glukhovo U.S.S.R. 55.05N 43.30E
53 K5 Glumslöv Sweden 55.57N 12.49E
53 H6 Glumsø Denmark 55.22N 11.42E
46 G3 Glusha Belorussiya U.S.S.R. 53.03N 28.55E
45 F5 Glushkovo U.S.S.R. 51.22N 34.39E
46 G3 Glussk Belorussiya U.S.S.R. 52.51N 28.40E
47 K8 Glyadyanskoye U.S.S.R. 54.51N 65.05E
82 K2 Glyboka U.S.S.R. 48.04N 25.56E
59 K4 Glyde, R Louth Irish Rep
57 G7 Glyn-Ceiriog Clwyd Wales 52.56N 3.11W
56 D4 Glyncorrwg W Glam Wales 51.41N 3.38W
14 E6 Glynde Hill W Australia 23.37S 123.12E
103 A8 Glyndon Maryland 39.29N 76.48W
108 O3 Glyndon Minnesota 46.51N 96.35W
53 B3 Glyngøre Denmark 56.46N 8.53E
59 L2 Glynn Antrim N Ireland 54.50N 5.49W
56 D4 Glynneath W Glam Wales 51.46N 3.38W
56 D4 Glyntawe Powys Wales 51.51N 3.40W
45 S6 Gmelinka U.S.S.R. 50.24N 46.54E
65 J8 Gmünd Kärnten Austria 46.55N 13.33E
65 L4 Gmünd Nieder-Österreich Austria 48.47N 14.59E
64 M8 Gmund W Germany 47.45N 11.45E
65 J6 Gmunden Austria 47.56N 13.48E
63 P9 Gnadau E Germany 51.58N 11.46E
104 D6 Gnadenhutten Ohio 40.22N 81.25W
66 N1 Gnaden-See L W Germany 47.43N 9.03E
52 K4 Gnarp Sweden 62.03N 17.20E
63 K6 Gnarrenburg W Germany 53.23N 9.01E
65 N8 Gnas Austria 46.53N 15.50E
89 H2 Gnefideh Mali 18.46N 2.22W
84 Y20 Gnejna B Malta 35.56N 14.21E
53 G4 Gniben C Denmark 56.01N 11.18E
62 L2 Gniew Poland 53.50N 18.48E
62 K3 Gniezno Poland 52.32N 17.32E
65 H6 Gnigl Austria 47.49N 13.06E
Gniloye More see Sivash lagoon
63 M4 Gnissau W Germany 54.01N 10.29E
82 G8 Gnjilane Yugoslavia 42.26N 21.26E
63 R5 Gnoien E Germany 53.58N 12.42E
91 A4 Gnonié, Pte pt Gabon 0.07S 9.15E
56 G2 Gnosall Staffs Eng 52.47N 2.15W
66 N7 Gnosca Switzerland 46.15N 9.02E
64 K5 Gnotzheim W Germany 49.04N 10.44E
14 C10 Gnowangerup W Australia 33.57S 117.58E
14 B9 Gnuka W Australia 31.08S 117.24E
63 L4 Gnutz W Germany 54.08N 9.50E
91 B4 Gnyoungou Gabon 1.29S 11.10E
28 A3 Goa Goa India 15.31N 73.56E
28 B3 Goa, Damān & Diu terr India
12 K6 Goalen Hd New S Wales 36.36S 150.03E
28 H2 Goalpara Assam India 26.10N 90.38E
28 H2 Goalpara dist Assam India
31 H9 Goalundo Ghat Bangladesh 23.44N 89.49E
90 M8 Goangoa R Cent Afr Rep
87 F4 Goang,R Ethiopia
15 H7 Goaribari I Papua New Guinea 7.50S 144.17E
94 B2 Goas Namibia 19.28S 13.02E
115 L3 Goascorán Honduras 13.36N 87.44W
89 H8 Goaso Ghana 6.49N 2.27W
58 F7 Goat Fell mt Arran, Strathclyde Scotland 55.38N 5.12W
57 M4 Goathland N Yorks Eng 54.23N 0.44W
110 M1 Goat Mt Montana 48.11N 113.00W
87 G7 Goba Ethiopia 7.01N 39.59E
94 M6 Goba Mozambique 26.12S 32.11E
33 K10 Goba Socotra Ind Oc 12.35N 53.46E
94 E4 Gobabis Namibia 22.30S 18.58E
29 L6 Gobardanga W Bengal India 22.52N 88.46E
30 H5 Gobardhana Bihar India 27.20N 84.19E
94 E6 Gobas Namibia 26.42S 18.02E
59 L2 Gobbins Cliff Path,The Antrim N Ireland 54.46N 5.40W
93 L1 Gobbo Ethiopia 4.31N 39.46E
15 K8 Gobe Papua New Guinea 9.05S 148.06E
36 C2 Göbel Turkey 40.01N 28.10E
65 J5 Göbels Berg mt Austria 48.06N 13.32E
77 K6 Gobernador Spain 37.29N 3.19W
121 E3 Gobernador Crespo Argentina 30.23S 60.20W
Gobernador Gordillo see Chamical
121 K7 Gobernador Gregores Argentina 48.45S 70.05W
121 K8 Gobernador Mayer Argentina 51.17S 70.17W
121 G2 Gobernador Virasoro Argentina 28.05S 56.04W
93 M1 Gobetto Ethiopia 4.25N 40.36E
22 F4 Gobi des Mongolia etc
30 H6 Gobindganj Bihar India 26.29N 84.39E
29 K1 Gobindpur Dhanbad, Bihar India 23.51N 86.32E
30 J8 Gobindpur Gaya, Bihar India 24.48N 85.42E
29 J6 Gobindpur Ranchi, Bihar India 23.03N 85.03E
20 J8 Gobō Japan 33.52N 135.09E
56 E2 Gobowen Shropshire Eng 52.54N 3.02W
28 G1 Gobshi Xizang Zizhiqu 28.50N 89.45E
87 M9 Gòbuin Somalia 0.19S 42.35E
46 H2 Gobza R U.S.S.R.
81 B3 Goceano, Catena del mts Sardinia
63 D9 Goch W Germany 51.40N 6.10E
94 E5 Gochas Namibia 24.55S 18.55E
61 K6 Gochenée Belgium 50.11N 4.45E
87 E6 Gocho Ethiopia 8.34N 35.55E
64 F5 Gochshelm W Germany 49.06N 8.45E
25 J7 Go Cong Vietnam 10.22N 106.41E
31 G9 Godagari Bangladesh 24.30N 88.24E
26 S9 Godakewala Sri Lanka 6.29N 80.41E
75 L6 Godall Spain 40.40N 0.28E
56 K5 Godalming Surrey Eng 51.11N 0.37W
31 A6 Godar-i-Shah ruins Afghanistan 29.56N 61.24E
61 H5 Godarville Belgium 50.30N 4.17E
27 N6 Godavari R India
28 F2 Godavari, C Andhra Prad India 16.41N 82.25E
28 E2 Godavari, East dist Andhra Prad India
28 F2 Godavari, Mouths of the Andhra Prad India
29 D8 Godavari R Maharashtra India
28 E2 Godavari, West dist Andhra Prad India
98 E4 Godbout Quebec 49.20N 67.38W
98 E4 Godbout, R Quebec
30 L8 Godda Bihar India 24.50N 87.13E
101 F7 Goddard Alaska 56.50N 135.20W
109 N4 Goddard Kansas 37.40N 97.35W
111 F4 Goddard, Mt California 37.07N 118.43W
14 E9 Goddards Cr W Australia
64 F4 Goddelau-Wolfskehlen W Germany 49.50N 8.30E
87 J8 God Dere Ethiopia 5.07N 43.58E
117 B2 Goddo Surinam 4.01N 55.33W
53 S19 Goddo isld Norway 59.50N 5.07E
85 C6 Goddua Libya 26.28N 14.17E
76 C11 Godeal mt Portugal 38.49N 8.16W
82 H7 Godech Bulgaria 43.01N 23.00E
79 M3 Godega di San Urbano Italy 45.56N 12.24E
52 J8 Godegård Sweden 58.45N 15.05E
92 H5 Godegode Tanzania 6.30S 35.40E
63 K9 Godelheim W Germany 51.44N 9.21E
77 P2 Godelleta Spain 39.26N 0.41W
36 E6 Gödene Turkey 36.33N 30.21E
99 J9 Goderich Ontario 43.43N 81.43W
70 L2 Goderville France 49.38N 0.22E
36 G5 Gödet Turkey 37.02N 33.29E
69 D2 Godewaersvelde France 50.47N 2.38E
107 F3 Godfrey Illinois 38.59N 90.11W
99 O8 Godfrey Ontario 44.32N 76.41W
50 H3 Godhafoss waterfall Iceland 65.42N 17.31W
48 S8 Godhavn Greenland 69.18N 53.40W
50 F4 Godhdalir Iceland 65.19N 19.04W
29 C6 Godhra Gujarat India 22.49N 73.40E
29 A6 Godia Cr Gujarat India
79 F5 Godiasco Italy 44.54N 9.03E
87 L8 Godinlave Somalia 5.52N 46.31E
61 K5 Godinne Belgium 50.22N 4.52E
112 K3 Godley Texas 32.27N 97.34W
11 E10 Godley Glacier New Zealand 43.28S 170.30E
11 O10 Godley Hd New Zealand 43.35S 172.48E
11 E10 Godley R New Zealand
56 L3 Godmanchester Cambs Eng 52.19N 0.11W
15 D6 Godman, Geb mt Irian Jaya 4.13S 136.58E
56 G6 Godmanstone Dorset Eng 50.46N 2.29W
19 D4 Godo, Bukit mt Moluccas Indon 1.49S 124.45E
87 G3 Godofelassi Ethiopia 14.55N 38.52E
77 B4 Godolid R Spain
62 L8 Gödöllő Hungary 47.36N 19.20E
53 U13 Godøv Norway 62.30N 6.03E
53 T14 Godøy isld Norway 62.28N 5.59E
121 C4 Godoy Cruz Argentina 32.56S 68.52W
53 T18 Godøysund Norway 60.04N 5.35E
56 T9 Godrevy I Cornwall Eng 50.14N 5.24W
56 H6 Godshill Hants Eng 50.56N 1.44W
56 J6 Godshill I of Wight Eng 50.38N 1.14W
97 K7 God's Lake Manitoba 54.45N 94.00W
56 L5 Godstone Surrey Eng 51.15N 0.04W
48 S12 Godthåb Greenland 64.15N 51.35W
95 O1 Godwanerivier S Africa 25.37S 30.38E
29 C5 Godwar reg Rajasthan India
105 J2 Godwin N Carolina 35.13N 78.41W
Godwin Austen mt see K2, Mt
61 O4 Goé Belgium 50.36N 5.57E
15 F8 Goe Papua New Guinea 8.10S 141.33E
Goede Hoop, Tg C see Gude Hoop, Tg. C.
95 K6 Goedemoed S Africa 30.34S 26.25E
60 C1 Goedereede Netherlands 51.50N 3.59E
95 L2 Goedgedag S Africa 26.08S 27.14E
Goedgegun see Nhlangano
61 F3 Goeferdinge Belgium 50.46N 3.50E
61 F5 Goegnies-Chaussée Belgium 50.21N 3.57E
Goeie Hoop, Kaap de see Good Hope, C of
99 O3 Goeland Quebec 49.32N 76.16W
98 A4 Goéland, L Quebec
99 O3 Goëland, L. au Quebec
60 C1 Goeree isld Netherlands
60 C2 Goes Netherlands 51.30N 3.54E
50 J3 Gœsafjoll mt Iceland 65.47N 16.54W
50 J2 Gœsavatn L Iceland 66.10N 16.12W
61 O7 Goesdorf Luxembourg 49.55N 5.58E
61 L5 Goesnes Belgium 50.27N 5.13E
109 P2 Goff Kansas 39.39N 95.39W
93 N3 Goff Somalia 2.40N 41.02E
87 K8 Goffado Somalia 5.20N 45.30E
111 J7 Goffs California 34.56N 115.04W
104 O3 Goffstown New Hampshire 43.02N 71.34W
66 P3 Göfis Austria 47.14N 9.38E
44 E2 Gofitskoye U.S.S.R. 45.05N 43.04E
41 P2 Gofmana, Ostrov isld Franz Josef Land U.S.S.R.
99 J5 Gogama Ontario 47.42N 81.44W
30 D3 Gogan Nepal 29.12N 80.25E
29 D7 Gogaon Madhya Prad India 21.54N 75.46E
34 N3 Gögasür R Iraq
20 F6 Gō-gawa R Japan
106 E3 Gogebic Michigan 46.20N 89.29W
106 E3 Gogebic, L Michigan
106 D3 Gogebic Ra Michigan
23 A4 Gogên Xizang Zizhiqu China 29.10N 97.20E
87 G6 Gogetti Ethiopia 8.18N 38.30E
64 K7 Göggingen W Germany 48.20N 10.53E
29 C7 Gogha Gujarat India 21.40N 72.20E
56 D3 Goginan Dyfed Wales 52.25N 3.55W
56 M3 Gog Magog Hills Cambs Eng
69 M6 Gogney France 48.37N 6.51E
69 F3 Gognies-Chausée France 50.20N 3.58E
14 F4 Gogo W Australia 18.17S 125.35E
92 G5 Gogo tribe Tanzania
15 H6 Gogol R Papua New Guinea
29 B7 Gogola Gujarat India 20.43N 71.08E
40 D5 Gogolevka U.S.S.R. 52.46N 127.40E
45 E7 Gogolevo Ukraine U.S.S.R. 49.58N 33.45E
43 L2 Gogolevskiy Kazakhstan U.S.S.R. 52.08N 72.35E
62 L5 Gogolin Poland 50.30N 18.00E
Gogra R see Ghaghra R
30 K7 Gogri Bihar India 25.27N 86.36E
87 B6 Gogrial Sudan 8.30N 28.08E
Gog Tepe see Göktepe
89 E4 Gogui Mali 15.45N 9.23W
29 C5 Gogunda Rajasthan India 24.29N 73.38E
30 H8 Goh Bihar India 24.59N 84.38E
87 E5 Goha Ethiopia 10.23N 34.31E
30 B6 Gohad Madhya Prad India 26.25N 78.26E
29 E3 Gohana Haryana India 29.06N 76.43E
30 C7 Gohand Uttar Prad India 25.42N 79.33E
29 E6 Goharganj Madhya Prad India 23.02N 77.42E
62 D3 Gohfeld W Germany 52.12N 8.45E
63 Q9 Gohrau E Germany 51.50N 12.30E
63 N6 Göhrde W Germany 53.08N 10.54E
63 T4 Göhren E Germany 54.21N 13.46E
66 O1 Göhren-Berg mt W Germany 47.44N 9.24E
20 H4 Goi Chiba Japan 35.32N 140.10E
117 J8 Goiana Brazil 7.30S 35.00W
118 E6 Goiandira Brazil 18.06S 48.07W
118 E4 Goianésia Brazil 15.21S 49.02W
118 E5 Goiânia Brazil 16.43S 49.18W
117 J8 Goianinha Brazil 6.14S 35.14W
118 E4 Goiás Brazil 15.57S 50.07W
118 E3 Goiás state Brazil
118 E6 Goiatuba Brazil 18.01S 49.18W
19 N2 Goikul Palau Is Pacific Oc 7.23N 134.36E
90 F7 Goila Nigeria 9.57N 12.41E
58 G6 Goil, L Strathclyde Scotland 56.07N 4.54W
92 C5 Goi Mani Zaïre 7.44S 26.34E
90 N9 Goindji Cent Afr Rep 5.31N 27.12E
23 A3 Goinsargoin Xizang Zizhiqu China 31.56N 98.04E
24 J10 Goinxab Qinghai China 31.59N 96.38E
118 D9 Goio-Erê Brazil 24.11S 53.01W
76 D2 Goiriz Spain 43.19N 7.36W
60 J13 Goirle Netherlands 51.31N 5.04E
76 C8 Gois Portugal 40.10N 8.06W
65 J6 Goisern Austria 47.38N 13.38E
79 J4 Goito Italy 45.16N 10.40E
75 G1 Goizueta Spain 43.10N 1.52W
87 F4 Goja Ethiopia 12.08N 37.01E
87 F7 Gojab,R Ethiopia
Gojam prov see Gwejam
20 J7 Gojō Japan 34.21N 135.42E
20 O2 Gojōnome Japan 39.57N 140.06E
31 G5 Gojra Pakistan 31.10N 72.43E
37 D8 Gök R Adıyaman Turkey
36 D2 Gök R Bursa Turkey
37 E8 Gök R Diyarbakır Turkey
36 D3 Gök R Kütahya Turkey
37 G1 Gök R Turkey
28 B2 Gokak Karnataka India 16.13N 74.54E
28 B3 Gokarn Karnataka India 14.34N 74.21E
36 D5 Gökbel mt Turkey 37.45N 28.55E
36 F5 Gök Çay R Turkey
37 B3 Gökçe Gökçeada Turkey 40.12N 25.54E
37 B3 Gökçeada isld Turkey
36 H1 Gökçeağaç Turkey 41.39N 34.32E
36 D3 Gökçedağ Turkey 39.33N 28.55E
36 C4 Gokçen Turkey 38.06N 27.55E
36 F3 Gök Dağ mt Turkey 39.02N 32.21E
37 E7 Gökdere Elâzığ Turkey 38.44N 40.06E
36 J2 Gökdere Tokat Turkey 40.26N 36.44E
36 F6 Gökdore R Turkey
63 K4 Gokels W Germany 54.07N 9.29E
28 H1 Gokhar La pass Xizang Zizhiqu 29.31N 91.22E
36 G1 Gökirmak R Turkey
43 D6 Goklenkuy, Solonchak salt marsh Turkmeniya U.S.S.R.
37 F6 Gökoğlan Turkey 39.32N 41.20E
20 G1 Gokōmutsumi Chiba Japan
89 K7 Gokoron Ghana 8.26N 0.38E
Gökova see Ula
31 B8 Gokprosh Hills Pakistan
37 G6 Göksu Turkey 39.34N 42.02E
37 G6 Göksu R Erzurum Turkey
36 H5 Göksu R Seyhan Turkey
37 G3 Gök Su R Turkey
36 J4 Göksun Turkey 38.03N 36.30E
36 J4 Göksun R Turkey
36 G6 Göksu Nehir R Turkey
37 F4 Göktas Turkey 41.15N 41.33E
25 D1 Gokteik Burma 22.20N 96.54E
34 N3 Gök Tepe Iraq 35.16N 45.11E
36 D5 Göktepe Turkey 37.23N 28.32E
36 E3 Gök Tepe mt Afyon Turkey 39.10N 30.42E
36 C5 Gök Tepe mt Muğla Turkey 37.22N 28.23E
36 D6 Gök Tepe mt Muğla Turkey 36.53N 29.16E
87 J5 Gokti Ethiopia 10.07N 42.51E
30 A5 Gokul Uttar Prad India 27.27N 77.44E
92 D11 Gokwe Zimbabwe 18.07S 28.58E
30 H2 Gokyo Nepal 27.57N 86.42E
52 D6 Gol Norway 60.43N 8.55E
29 J2 Gola Bihar India 23.32N 85.44E
30 G6 Gola Bazar Uttar Prad India 26.21N 83.20E
76 D3 Golada Spain 42.45N 8.00W
28 J2 Golaghat Assam India 26.30N 93.59E
30 D4 Gola Gokarannath Uttar Prad India 28.04N 80.28E
59 F1 Gola I Donegal Irish Rep 55.05N 8.21W
28 G2 Golakganj Assam India 26.09N 89.55E
35 F2 Golan reg Syria
62 K3 Gołańcz Poland 52.57N 17.18E
Golan Heights see Golan Reg
32 G7 Goläshkerd Iran 27.59N 57.14E
87 J6 Golaski Ethiopia 8.51N 42.43E
37 G2 Gölavağı R Turkey
45 D10 Golaya Pristan' Ukraine U.S.S.R. 46.30N 32.32E
93 M8 Golbanti Kenya 2.27S 40.12E
36 F3 Gölbaşı Turkey 39.48N 32.48E
65 F8 Gölbnerjoch mt Austria 46.49N 12.30E
87 H8 Golbo Ethiopia 4.40N 40.38E
41 D5 Gol'chikha U.S.S.R. 71.45N 83.30E
28 D2 Golconda Andhra Prad India 17.24N 78.23E
107 H4 Golconda Illinois 37.20N 88.29W
110 H9 Golconda Nevada 40.58N 117.28W
Gölcük Çanakkale Turkey see Etili
37 G2 Gölcük Kocaeli Turkey 40.44N 29.50E
Gölcük Niğde Turkey see Misli
37 E8 Gölcük Urfa Turkey 37.28N 39.06E
65 M2 Golčův Jeníkov Czechoslovakia 49.49N 15.29E
104 H5 Gold Pennsylvania 41.52N 77.52W
66 O2 Goldach Switzerland 47.28N 9.28E
37 D6 Gol Dağı mt Turkey 39.02N 38.23E
62 N1 Gołdap Poland 54.19N 22.19E
66 L3 Goldau Switzerland 47.03N 8.33E
110 A7 Gold Beach Oregon 42.25N 124.27W
63 P7 Goldbeck E Germany 52.44N 11.51E
63 Q5 Goldberg E Germany 53.36N 12.06E
66 R3 Gold Berg mt Austria 47.11N 10.02E
98 L8 Goldboro Nova Scotia 45.10N 61.38W
110 M5 Goldburg Idaho 44.25N 113.38W
110 O1 Gold Butte Montana 48.53N 111.25W
89 J9 Gold Coast Ghana
13 L8 Gold Coast Queensland Australia 27.59S 153.22E
113 N5 Gold Creek Alaska 62.45N 149.44W
63 K3 Goldelund W Germany 54.40N 9.07E
111 L8 Golden Arizona 33.55N 113.18W
101 P10 Golden Br Col 51.19N 116.58W
109 E2 Golden Colorado 39.45N 105.15W
110 K4 Golden Idaho 45.49N 115.40W
106 C9 Golden Illinois 40.05N 91.01W
59 G7 Golden Tipperary Irish Rep 52.30N 7.58W
112 G9 Golden Acres Texas 29.39N 95.09W
11 G7 Golden B New Zealand
103 G4 Goldenbridge New York 41.17N 73.40W
107 B4 Golden City Missouri 37.24N 94.08W
110 E4 Goldendale Washington 45.50N 120.50W
63 N10 Goldene Aue reg E Germany
111 B4 Golden Gate channel California
111 J4 Golden Gate Ra Nevada
116 M2 Golden Grove Jamaica, W I 17.56N 76.17W
23 B8 Golden Hill Hong Kong 22.23N 114.08E
Golden Horn, The see Haliç
99 N7 Golden Lake Ontario 45.35N 77.16W
107 F12 Golden Meadow Louisiana 29.24N 90.18W
107 H5 Golden Pond Kentucky 36.48N 88.04W
100 H8 Golden Prairie Saskatchewan 50.13N 109.37W
14 D9 Golden Ridge W Australia 30.51S 121.42E
116 P3 Golden Rock airport St Kitts West Indies 17.18N 62.41W
63 H7 Goldenstedt W Germany 52.47N 8.25E
31 J3 Golden Throne mt Kashmir 35.37N 76.40E
59 F6 Golden Vale Limerick Irish Rep
95 J8 Golden Valley S Africa 32.49S 25.47E
92 D11 Golden Valley Zimbabwe 18.11S 29.50E
98 K8 Goldenville Nova Scotia 45.07N 62.00W
87 J7 Golder Ethiopia 7.09N 43.41E
55 E3 Golders Green London England 51.35N 0.13W
108 R7 Goldfield Iowa 42.43N 93.56W
111 G4 Goldfield Nevada 37.42N 117.15W
112 J7 Goldfinch Texas 28.53N 98.53W
110 M9 Gold Hill Utah 40.10N 113.50W
66 G4 Goldiwil Switzerland 46.47N 7.42E
33 B10 Gold Mohur B S Yemen
111 G4 Gold Point Nevada 37.22N 117.22W
101 K11 Gold River Br Col 49.46N 126.03W
100 K1 Gold Rock Ontario 49.28N 92.40W
100 Q1 Goldsand L Manitoba 57.00N 101.00W
103 C8 Goldsboro Maryland 39.02N 75.47W
105 K2 Goldsboro N Carolina 35.23N 78.00W
103 A6 Goldsboro Pennsylvania 40.09N 76.45W
Goldshöfe see Hofen
112 E3 Goldsmith Texas 31.59N 102.36W
111 H6 Goldstone L California 35.21N 116.55W
14 C5 Goldsworthy W Australia 20.20S 119.31E
14 C5 Goldsworthy, Mt W Australia 20.20S 119.33E
112 J4 Goldthwaite Texas 31.28N 98.35W
37 G5 Göle Turkey 40.47N 42.36E
88 P6 Golea, El Algeria 30.35N 2.51E
37 E3 Gölecik R Turkey
113 Q2 Goleen R Alaska
76 C10 Golegã Portugal 39.24N 8.29W
82 K8 Golema Kamchiva R Bulgaria
82 J8 Golemo Konare Bulgaria 42.16N 24.32E
62 H2 Goleniów Poland 53.34N 14.50E
39 G5 Golenishcheva, Mys C U.S.S.R. 59.14N 164.31E
31 B4 Golestān Afghanistan 32.37N 63.39E
32 F5 Golestānak Iran 30.38N 54.14E
111 E7 Goleta California 34.26N 119.50W
42 H5 Golets Davydov, Gora mt U.S.S.R. 52.35N 107.30E
42 J4 Golets-Inyaptuk, Gora mt U.S.S.R. 56.25N 110.05E
42 K3 Golets-Longdor, Gora mt U.S.S.R. 58.25N 116.50E
40 F3 Golets Oblachnyy mt U.S.S.R. 57.32N 132.41E
42 J3 Golets-Purpula, Gora mt U.S.S.R. 59.29N 114.50E
40 A3 Golets-Skalistyy mt Irkutsk U.S.S.R. 56.25N 119.21E
40 E4 Golets Skalistyy mt Yakutsk U.S.S.R. 55.53N 130.30E
71 L9 Golfe-Juan France 43.33N 7.03E
115 N5 Golfito Costa Rica 8.42N 83.10W
115 B2 Golfo de Santa Clara town Mexico 31.48N 114.40W
96 P11 Golfo, El Hierro Canary Is
87 H10 Gòlgia Somalia 0.41N 41.45E
12 F5 Gol Gol New S Wales 34.10S 142.17E
87 M7 Golgol Somalia 6.32N 48.32E
120 F11 Golgota Argentina 24.36S 65.47W
36 D5 Gölhisar Turkey 37.11N 29.30E
112 K7 Goliad Texas 28.40N 97.26W
93 M3 Golija, El Kenya 2.52N 40.57E
82 F7 Golija Planina mts Yugoslavia
90 M3 Goli, Jebel mt Sudan 16.05N 24.40E
21 B5 Golin Baixing Nei Monggol Zizhiqu China 44.53N 121.50E
72 K6 Golinhac France 44.37N 2.34E
45 Q3 Golitsyno U.S.S.R. 53.40N 44.05E
29 K1 Goljor Bara Bihar India 23.56N 87.06E
37 D5 Gölköy Turkey 40.42N 37.37E
11 D6 Gollans, R New Zealand
Gollel see Lavumisa
65 O5 Göllersdorf Austria 48.30N 16.07E
Göllet see Kölmürlü
69 P4 Göllheim W Germany 49.36N 8.03E
63 T6 Gollin E Germany 53.03N 13.37E
65 H6 Golling Austria 47.37N 13.11E
65 J7 Golling, Hoch mt Austria 47.16N 13.45E
66 C5 Gollion Switzerland 46.35N 6.31E
63 T9 Gollmitz E Germany 51.43N 13.53E
32 A2 Golmānkhāneh Iran 37.36N 45.10E
36 C4 Gölmarmara Turkey 38.42N 27.52E
63 S8 Golmberg mt E Germany 52.01N 13.21E
64 M2 Golmsdorf E Germany 50.58N 11.40E
24 H7 Golmud Qinghai China 36.22N 94.55E
19 K5 Golo isld Philippines 13.37N 120.23E
67 P11 Golo R Corsica
47 G2 Golodnaya Guba, Ozero L U.S.S.R.
43 J6 Golodnaya Step' U.S.S.R.
87 H6 Gololcha Ethiopia 8.12N 40.03E
92 G9 Golomoti Malawi 14.19S 34.40E
121 E2 Golondrina Argentina 28.31S 60.02W
46 H5 Golovanevsk Ukraine U.S.S.R. 48.25N 30.30E
45 M2 Golovanovo U.S.S.R. 54.56N 40.29E
45 B3 Golovenchitsy Belorussiya U.S.S.R. 53.43N 30.49E
113 F4 Golovin Alaska 64.32N 163.00W

113 F4 Golovin B Alaska
45 Q3 Golovinshchino U.S.S.R. 53.20N 44.00E
42 G5 Golovinskaya U.S.S.R. 53.28N 102.45E
40 K10 Golovnina caldera Kuril Is U.S.S.R. 43.53N 145.32E
40 M7 Golovnina Proliv str Kuril Is U.S.S.R.
40 K10 Golovnino Kuril Is U.S.S.R. 43.46N 145.26E
42 H4 Golovskoye U.S.S.R. 55.29N 105.35E
32 D4 Golpāyegan Iran 33.23N 50.18E
36 E2 Gölpazarı Turkey 40.16N 30.18E
76 H6 Golpejas Spain 41.00N 5.55W
31 G4 Golra Pakistan 33.40N 73.00E
65 P6 Gols Austria 47.54N 16.55E
32 J7 Golshahr Iran 27.20N 60.58E
113 G5 Golsovia Alaska 63.33N 161.10W
58 J3 Golspie Highland Scotland 57.58N 3.58W
63 T9 Golssen E Germany 51.58N 13.36E
53 D2 Gølstrup Denmark 57.25N 9.50E
32 C3 Gol Tappeh Iran 35.17N 48.14E
109 M5 Goltry Oklahoma 36.33N 98.09W
45 R3 Gol'tsovka U.S.S.R. 53.37N 45.09E
42 F3 Gol'tyavino U.S.S.R. 58.26N 98.29E
62 L2 Gołub Poland 53.07N 19.00E
40 G8 Golubitsa U.S.S.R. 46.05N 135.28E
82 C4 Golubovec Yugoslavia 46.11N 16.03E
43 L1 Golubovka Kazakhstan U.S.S.R. 53.08N 74.00E
87 H6 Golufa Ethiopia 8.20N 41.36E
42 G5 Golumet' U.S.S.R. 53.05N 102.22E
91 D8 Golungo Alto Angola 9.10S 14.45E
108 G3 Golva N Dakota 46.45N 103.59W
58 J1 Golval Highland Scotland 58.32N 3.53W
32 J4 Gol Vardeh Iran 33.02N 60.25E
Gölveren see Çiftlik Erzurum Turkey
Gölviran see Beyviran
82 J9 Golyam Perelik Bulgaria 41.36N 24.33E
46 N3 Golyayevka U.S.S.R. 52.36N 43.30E
39 E7 Golygino U.S.S.R. 51.50N 156.44E
62 M3 Gołymin Poland 52.49N 20.48E
45 C2 Golynki U.S.S.R. 54.51N 31.29E
47 K7 Golyshmanovo U.S.S.R. 56.26N 68.22E
63 R8 Golzow E Germany 52.17N 12.37E
93 A7 Goma Zaïre 1.40S 29.14E
24 F10 Gomang Co L Xizang Zizhiqu China 31.10N 89.10E
Gomang Tso L see Gomang Co
22 E9 Gomangxung Qinghai China 35.48N 101.09E
75 F4 Gómara Spain 41.37N 2.13W
Gomara reg Morocco see Rhomara
92 J7 Gomba Mozambique 11.19S 38.19E
87 B9 Gombari Zaïre 2.45N 29.03E
91 D8 Gombe Angola 8.03S 14.11E
90 E6 Gombe Nigeria 10.17N 11.14E
93 D5 Gombe Uganda 0.30N 32.28E
91 E4 Gombe Zaïre 0.45S 17.36E
93 C10 Gombe R Tanzania
91 F3 Gombe tribe Zaïre
91 D10 Gombealamba Angola 13.20S 15.07E
92 J4 Gombelo Tanzania 5.00S 38.58E
91 D6 Gombe Matadi Zaïre 4.59S 14.42E
92 C5 Gombe Mts Zaïre
90 F6 Gombi Nigeria 10.06N 12.44E
79 H7 Gombo Italy 43.43N 10.17E
18 H9 Gombong Java Indon 7.36S 109.29E
44 G6 Gombori Georgia U.S.S.R. 41.52N 45.14E
26 B12 Gombrani I Rodriguez I Ind Oc 19.46S 63.25E
Gömeç see Armutova
76 H6 Gomecello Spain 41.03N 5.32W
45 B4 Gomel' Belorussiya U.S.S.R. 52.25N 31.00E
45 B4 Gomel'skaya Oblast' prov Belorussiya U.S.S.R.
Gömel Su R see Gömil R
Gomen see Nangoku
96 O14 Gomera isld Canary Is 28.08N 17.14W
76 C13 Gomes Aires Portugal 37.31N 8.11W
76 C4 Gomesende Spain 42.10N 8.06W
58 D6 Gometra isld Strathclyde Scotland 56.29N 6.18W
115 F3 Gomez Farias Mexico 29.20N 107.42W
115 G2 Gómez, Félix U Mexico 30.38N 105.50W
115 H5 Gómez Palacio Mexico 25.39N 103.30W
119 B9 Gómez Rendón Ecuador 2.25S 80.22W
34 L2 Gömil R Iraq
32 F2 Gomishan Iran 37.04N 54.05E
70 F5 Gommené France 48.10N 2.28W
63 P8 Gommern E Germany 52.05N 11.50E
24 E9 Gomo Xizang Zizhiqu China 34.00N 85.16E
24 E8 Gomo Co L Xizang Zizhiqu China 34.03N 85.30E
15 C7 Gomo Gomo Moluccas Indon 6.39S 134.43E
29 K1 Gomoh Bihar India 23.50N 86.15E
93 K2 Gomo, mt Ethiopia 3.40N 38.33E
Gomo Selung see Gomo
Gomo Tshakha L see Gomo Co
66 J6 Goms dist Switzerland
19 E4 Gomumu isld Moluccas Indonesia 1.50S 127.35E
61 N4 Gomze-Andoumont Belgium 50.33N 5.40E
Gona see Garara
30 B8 Gona Uttar Prad India 24.24N 78.33E
Gonabad see Jūymand
32 H2 Gonābād Iran 36.30N 59.18E
32 D4 Gonahrān Iran 32.59N 50.41E
116 H5 Gonaïves Haiti 19.29N 72.42W
40 E3 Gonam U.S.S.R. 57.15N 131.15E
40 E3 Gonam R U.S.S.R.
116 H5 Gonâve, Île de la Haiti
30 J7 Gonawan Bihar India 25.22N 85.37E
32 F2 Gonbad-e Kāvūs Iran 37.15N 55.11E
62 N7 Gönc Hungary 48.29N 21.14E
71 H6 Goncelin France 45.16N 6.00E
30 E5 Gonda Uttar Prad India 27.08N 81.58E
30 E5 Gonda dist Uttar Prad India
29 B7 Gondal Gujarat India 21.59N 70.52E
Gondar see Gonder
119 D8 Gondar Colombia 1.35S 72.07W
36 G5 Göndelen Turkey 37.42N 34.15E
37 D5 Göndelic Tepe mt Turkey 40.33N 38.10E
64 F5 Gondelsheim W Germany 49.04N 8.39E
87 F4 Gonder Ethiopia 12.39N 37.29E
29 G7 Gondia Maharashtra India 21.23N 80.14E
66 H3 Gondiswil Switzerland 47.09N 7.53E
66 J7 Gondo Switzerland 46.13N 8.08E
94 M2 Gondola Mozambique 19.10S 33.40E
87 K6 Gondolibah Ethiopia 8.17N 45.08E
76 B6 Gondomar Portugal 41.10N 8.35W
76 B4 Gondomar Spain 42.07N 8.45W
69 N3 Gondorf W Germany 50.18N 7.27E
76 C5 Gondŏriz Portugal 41.53N 8.25W
89 H5 Gondoro Upper Volta 13.29N 2.40W
69 K5 Gondrecourt-Aix Meurthe-et-Moselle France 49.15N 5.46E
69 K6 Gondrecourt-le-Château Meuse France 48.31N 5.31E
61 F4 Gondregnies Belgium 50.37N 3.55E
72 E8 Gondrin France 43.53N 0.14E
35 F1 Gonen Israel 33.07N 35.38E
37 D3 Gönen Turkey 40.06N 27.39E
35 A2 Gonen dist Jerusalem
37 D3 Gönen R Turkey
69 C6 Gonesse France 48.59N 2.27E
71 J10 Gonfaron France 43.20N 6.17E
58 Q9 Gonfirth Shetland Scotland 60.20N 1.20W
70 L2 Gonfreville l'Orcher France 49.31N 0.14E
91 F11 Gonga Angola 15.47S 19.17E
26 S9 Gongala mt Sri Lanka 6.23N 80.38E
23 F3 Gong'an Hubei China 30.00N 112.10E
24 H11 Gongbo'gyamda Xizang Zizhiqu China 30.03N 93.10E
23 E6 Gongcheng Guangxi China 24.55N 110.39E
24 G11 Gonggar Xizang Zizhiqu China 29.17N 90.46E
23 B4 Gongga Shan mt pk Sichuan China 29.34N 101.53E
22 E8 Gonghe Qinghai China 36.20N 100.46E
23 B6 Gonglang Yunnan China 24.50N 100.20E
89 E9 Gonglee Liberia 5.48N 9.24W
24 D4 Gongliu Xinjiang Uygur Zizhiqu China 43.30N 82.10E
Gonglüe see Donggu
91 E6 Gongo Zaïre 4.31S 17.45E
118 H4 Gongogi, R Brazil
90 E6 Gongola R Nigeria
12 H4 Gongolgon New S Wales 30.22S 146.56E
93 M9 Gongoni Kenya 3.04S 40.07E
91 H5 Gongo Piete Zaïre 3.24S 23.13E
91 A4 Gongoué Gabon 0.31S 9.13E
23 F5 Gongpingxu Hunan China 26.13N 112.47E
22 D6 Gongpoquan Gansu China 41.50N 97.00E
23 A5 Gongshan Drungzu Nuzu Zizhixian Yunnan China 27.34N 98.36E
23 F4 Gongtian Hunan China 29.08N 113.28E
23 C6 Gongwan Shan mt ra Yunnan China
23 F1 Gong Xian Henan China 34.45N 112.57E
23 C4 Gong Xian Sichuan China 28.22N 104.50E
22 L6 Gongyingzi Liaoning China 41.21N 119.49E
Gongzhuling see Huaide
121 G4 Goñi Uruguay 33.30S 56.24W
62 O2 Goniadz Poland 53.30N 22.44E
93 K10 Gonja Tanzania 4.15S 38.02E
23 A3 Gonjo Xizang Zizhiqu China 30.37N 98.26E
23 A3 Gonjo Xizang Zizhiqu China 30.45N 98.17E
81 A5 Gonnesa Sardinia 39.17N 8.27E
81 A5 Gonnesa, G. di Sardinia
64 G7 Gönningen W Germany 48.27N 9.08E
Gonnord see Valanjou
84 D2 Gónnos Greece 39.52N 22.29E
81 B5 Gonnosfanadiga Sardinia 39.30N 8.39E
81 B4 Gonnosnò Sardinia 39.47N 8.53E
94 F2 Gono Namibia 19.01S 20.50E
20 P1 Gonohe Japan 40.30N 141.20E
30 D8 Gonour Madhya Prad India 24.27N 80.15E
20 C8 Gōnoura Japan 33.47N 129.40E
61 H6 Gonrieux Belgium 50.02N 4.25E
71 J2 Gonsans France 47.14N 6.17E
72 E7 Gontaud-de-Nogaret France 44.28N 0.18E
66 O2 Gonten Switzerland 47.20N 9.21E
61 F3 Gontrode Belgium 50.59N 3.48E
95 M8 Gonubie Mouth S Africa 32.56S 28.01E
37 F6 Gönük Turkey 39.08N 40.53E
37 F6 Gönük R Turkey
121 C8 Gonumillo Argentina 40.54S 67.26W
108 P2 Gonvick Minnesota 47.42N 95.31W
87 E6 Gonza Ethiopia 9.38N 34.28E
79 J5 Gonzaga Italy 44.58N 10.49E
111 C5 Gonzales California 36.30N 121.28W
107 F11 Gonzales Louisiana 30.15N 90.56W
115 K6 Gonzáles Mexico 22.50N 98.25W
112 K6 Gonzales Texas 29.31N 97.29W
121 E7 Gonzales Cháves Argentina 38.02S 60.05W
121 J10 Gonzalez, Canal str Chile
120 A12 González I Pacific Oc 26.27S 80.04W
96 T10 Gonzalo, Pta pt Fuerteventura Canary Is 28.25N 13.51W
119 B3 Gonzalo Vasquez Panama 8.26N 78.30W
119 B10 Gonzanama Ecuador 4.13S 79.28W
64 C4 Gonzerath W Germany 49.51N 7.08E
40 C5 Gonzha U.S.S.R. 53.37N 125.19E
93 K3 Goochi Kenya 2.24N 38.57E
104 H9 Goochland Virginia 37.42N 77.54W
15 K8 Goodenough B Papua New Guinea
123 H2 Goodenough, C Antarctica 66.15S 126.35E
15 L8 Goodenough I D'Entrecasteaux Is Papua New Guinea
26 N13 Goodenough, Pte C Amsterdam I Ind Oc 37.49S 77.31E
99 M8 Gooderham Ontario 44.54N 78.24W
100 O7 Goodeve Saskatchewan 51.03N 103.11W
106 J5 Good Harbor B Michigan
106 J4 Good Hart Michigan 45.33N 85.05W
95 E7 Good Hope S Africa 31.51S 21.54E
113 E4 Goodhope R Alaska
113 F3 Goodhope B Alaska
95 B10 Good Hope, C.of S Africa 34.20S 18.25E
101 L10 Good Hope, Mt Br Col 51.08N 124.10W
94 E7 Goodhouse S Africa 28.53S 18.15E
108 S5 Goodhue Minnesota 44.26N 92.39W
110 L7 Gooding Idaho 42.56N 114.44W
105 F12 Goodland Florida 25.55N 81.42W
109 J2 Goodland Kansas 39.20N 101.43W
100 R9 Goodlands Manitoba 49.05N 100.35W
26 U11 Goodlands Mauritius, Indian Oc 20.02S 57.39E
112 H1 Goodlett Texas 34.22N 99.56W
107 K5 Goodlettsville Tennessee 36.19N 86.43W
106 F4 Goodman Wisconsin 45.39N 88.21W
55 J3 Goodmayes London Eng 51.34N 0.07E
113 G7 Goodnews R Alaska
113 G7 Goodnews B Alaska
113 G7 Goodnews Bay Alaska 59.06N 161.38W
112 C8 Goodnight Texas 35.02N 101.12W
12 H3 Goodooga New S Wales 29.08S 147.30E
13 B2 Goodparla N Terr Australia 13.29S 132.15E
113 P4 Goodpaster R Alaska
109 F3 Good Pasture Colorado 38.05N 104.56W
109 F1 Goodrich Colorado 40.22N 104.04W
56 F4 Goodrich Hereford & Worcs Eng 51.53N 2.37W
110 J5 Goodrich Idaho 44.40N 116.35W
108 K2 Goodrich N Dakota 47.29N 100.09W
112 N5 Goodrich Texas 30.34N 94.57W
106 D4 Goodrich Wisconsin 45.10N 90.04W
13 B1 Goodrich Bank N Terr Australia 10.44S 130.16E
108 P1 Goodridge Minnesota 48.10N 95.57W
101 P10 Goodsir, Mt Br Col 51.10N 116.29W
100 H4 Goodsoil Saskatchewan 54.24N 109.12W
100 P7 Good Spirit L Saskatchewan
100 P7 Good Spirit Lake Prov. Park Saskatchewan
111 J6 Goodsprings Nevada 35.50N 115.26W
107 K8 Good Water Alabama 33.02N 86.02W
100 O9 Goodwater Saskatchewan 49.22N 103.40W
109 J5 Goodwell Oklahoma 36.35N 101.38W
56 B3 Goodwick Dyfed Wales 52.00N 5.00W
111 M7 Goodwin Arizona 34.24N 112.21W
99 L4 Goodwin Ontario 48.54N 79.42W
108 O5 Goodwin S Dakota 44.53N 96.55W
56 P5 Goodwin Sands Kent Eng
94 Q11 Goodwood Cape Town S Africa 33.54S 18.32E
11 E12 Goodwood New Zealand 45.34S 170.42E
12 A8 Goodwood dist Adelaide, S Aust
61 G3 Gooik Belgium 50.47N 4.07E
60 J10 Gooimeer L Netherlands
57 M5 Goole Humberside Eng 53.42N 0.52W
12 H5 Goolgowi New S Wales 34.01S 145.45E
12 J4 Goolma New S Wales 32.21S 149.20E
12 J5 Gooloogong New S Wales 33.37S 148.43E
12 E6 Goolwa S Australia 35.31S 138.45E
13 C1 Goomadeer R N Terr Australia
14 B9 Goomalling W Australia 31.19S 116.49E
12 H3 Goombalie New S Wales 29.59S 145.24E
13 K7 Goombungee Queensland 27.21S 151.50E
13 K7 Goomeri Queensland 26.10S 152.00E
29 J8 Goomsur Orissa India 19.50N 84.40E
94 M2 Goonda Mozambique 19.51S 34.00E
13 K8 Goondiwindi Queensland 28.30S 150.17E
14 D9 Goongarrie W Australia 30.04S 121.07E
14 D8 Goongarrie, L W Australia 30.00S 121.10E
13 J5 Goonyella Queensland 21.50S 148.00E
60 P11 Goor Netherlands 52.14N 6.35E
101 P8 Goose R Alberta
97 N7 Goose Bay Labrador, Nfld 53.15N 60.20W
108 B5 Gooseberry Cr Wyoming
100 G6 Gooseberry L. Prov. Park Alberta 52.07N 110.48W
98 R2 Goose Cove Newfoundland 51.18N 55.37W
110 M7 Goose Cr Idaho
110 M8 Goose Cr. Mts Utah
110 M7 Goose Cr. Res Idaho 42.10N 113.56W
108 D7 Goose Egg Wyoming 42.46N 106.30W
121 E10 Goose Green Falkland Is 51.52S 59.00W
113 F9 Goose I Alaska 54.41N 162.11W
110 E8 Goose L Cal/Oregon
100 Q4 Goose L Manitoba 54.23N 101.20W
100 K7 Goose L Saskatchewan 51.45N 107.25W
100 P5 Goose L Saskatchewan 53.36N 103.30W
28 C3 Gooty Andhra Prad India 15.08N 77.36E
29 K8 Gop Orissa India 19.59N 86.00E
31 H9 Gopalganj Bangladesh 23.00N 89.48E
31 H6 Gopalganj Bihar India 26.28N 84.26E
31 H9 Gopalpur Bangladesh 24.14N 89.03E
29 J8 Gopalpur Orissa India 19.20N 85.00E
30 D5 Gopamau Uttar Prad India 27.31N 80.18E
18 B7 Gopeng Pen Malaysia 4.28N 101.10E
65 M4 Gopfritz Austria 48.44N 15.25E
28 C5 Gopichettipalayam Tamil Nadu India 11.28N 77.27E
30 F7 Gopiganj Uttar Prad India 25.17N 82.27E
62 L3 Gopło, Jezioro L Poland 52.35N 18.17E
66 H6 Goppenstein Switzerland 46.23N 7.46E
66 P1 Goppertsweiler W Germany 47.39N 9.44E
64 H6 Göppingen W Germany 48.43N 9.39E
77 L6 Gor Spain 37.23N 2.58W
87 J6 Gora Ethiopia 9.07N 42.29E
30 A7 Gora Madhya Prad India 25.16N 77.43E
62 K4 Góra Poland 51.40N 16.32E
92 D3 Gora Rwanda 2.10S 29.15E
23 B3 Gora Sichuan China 31.38N 101.28E
51 R4 Gora Chesnachorr mt U.S.S.R. 67.46N 33.27E
87 E6 Goracho,Jeb mt Ethiopia 8.26N 35.18E
93 H7 Goradai Kenya 1.11S 36.04E
44 H8 Goradiz Azerbaydzhan U.S.S.R. 39.27N 47.19E
77 K6 Gorafe Spain 37.29N 3.01W
87 G6 Gora Gorfu mts Ethiopia
44 G4 Goragorskiy U.S.S.R. 43.30N 45.07E
111 K10 Gora, I Mexico 31.42N 114.39W
62 N4 Góra Kalwaria Poland 51.59N 21.11E
30 G6 Gorakhpur Uttar Prad India 26.45N 83.23E
30 G6 Gorakhpur dist Uttar Prad India
87 N5 Gor Ali Ra Somalia
87 G4 Gor Amba Ethiopia 12.23N 38.43E
87 K8 Goran, El Ethiopia 5.01N 44.18E
84 D8 Goránoi Greece 36.55N 22.25E
82 E7 Goransko Yugoslavia 43.07N 18.51E
44 D4 Gora Psish mt U.S.S.R. 43.26N 41.15E
51 O5 Gora Rakhmoayvi mt Karelia 66.51N 29.10E
34 N4 Gōrashala Iraq 34.44N 45.29E
44 D4 Gora Urup mt U.S.S.R. 43.38N 41.00E
82 E7 Goražde Yugoslavia 43.41N 18.59E
45 J3 Gorbachevo U.S.S.R. 53.35N 37.10E
45 P1 Gorbatov U.S.S.R. 56.08N 43.05E
45 P1 Gorbatovka U.S.S.R. 56.16N 43.45E
45 O7 Gorbatovskiy U.S.S.R. 49.21N 42.03E
121 A7 Gorbea Chile 39.08S 72.45W
40 G2 Gorbi R U.S.S.R.
40 A5 Gorbitsa U.S.S.R. 53.06N 119.09E
41 E6 Gorbiyachin R U.S.S.R.
45 B3 Gorbovichi Belorussiya U.S.S.R. 53.48N 30.41E
41 B2 Gorbovy, Ostrova isld Novaya Zemlya U.S.S.R.
47 M3 Gorbunovo U.S.S.R. 57.52N 59.58E
105 K11 Gorda Cay isld Bahamas 26.06N 77.32W
117 G8 Gorda, Pta C Brazil 2.53S 40.50W
110 A9 Gorda, Pta C California 40.15N 124.21W
120 D8 Gorda, Pta C Chile 19.19S 70.18W
96 Q4 Gorda, Serra plat Azores
77 H3 Gorda, Sierra mt Ciudad Real Spain 38.50N 4.15W
77 H6 Gorda, Sierra mt Granada Spain 37.03N 4.12W
71 G9 Gordes France 43.55N 5.12E
36 C4 Gördes Turkey 38.55N 28.17E
66 L7 Gordevio Switzerland 46.14N 8.45E
45 C4 Gordeyevka U.S.S.R. 52.55N 31.59E
53 B6 Gørding Ribe Denmark 55.29N 8.48E
53 A4 Gørding Ringkøbing Denmark 56.21N 8.19E
36 F3 Gordium anc site Turkey 39.36N 32.00E
107 J8 Gordo Alabama 33.20N 87.55W
66 M7 Gördola Switzerland 46.12N 8.52E
113 R2 Gordon Alaska 69.39N 141.18W
109 F4 Gordon Colorado 37.40N 104.51W
105 D5 Gordon Georgia 32.52N 83.21W
108 H7 Gordon Nebraska 42.48N 103.12W
103 B5 Gordon Pennsylvania 40.45N 76.20W
112 J3 Gordon Texas 32.33N 98.23W
106 C3 Gordon Wisconsin 46.14N 91.47W
12 L6 Gordon dist Sydney, N S W
12 H9 Gordon R Tasmania
79 F2 Gordona Italy 46.18N 9.22E
13 B1 Gordon B N Terr Australia
76 J4 Gordoncillo Spain 42.09N 5.24W
108 J7 Gordon Cr Nebraska
13 B3 Gordon Cr N Terr Australia
14 G4 Gordon Downs W Australia 18.43S 128.33E
121 K10 Gordon I Chile 55.00S 69.43W
100 G2 Gordon L Alberta
101 R4 Gordon L N W Terr
101 F4 Gordon Landing Yukon Terr 63.35N 135.20W
14 B10 Gordon, R W Australia
95 B10 Gordons Bay S Africa 34.10S 18.52E
58 K3 Gordonstoun Grampian Scotland 57.42N 3.23W
107 L5 Gordonsville Tennessee 36.08N 85.57W
104 G8 Gordonsville Virginia 38.08N 78.12W
13 H3 Gordonvale Queensland 17.05S 145.45E
66 N7 Gorduno Switzerland 46.13N 9.02E
90 H8 Gore Chad 7.57N 16.31E
87 E6 Gore Ethiopia 8.10N 35.29E
11 C13 Gore New Zealand 46.06S 168.58E
109 P6 Gore Oklahoma 35.32N 95.06W
11 H9 Gore Bay New Zealand 42.53S 173.18E
99 H7 Gore Bay Ontario 45.54N 82.28W
58 K7 Gorebridge Lothian Scotland 55.51N 3.02W
Goreda see Gariau
36 J5 Göredin Turkey 37.45N 36.49E
112 H2 Goree Texas 33.28N 99.33W
37 D4 Görele Turkey 41.03N 38.59E
45 J2 Gorelki U.S.S.R. 54.15N 37.38E
39 F1 Gorelova U.S.S.R. 68.15N 158.39E
45 N4 Goreloye U.S.S.R. 52.55N 41.30E
39 F7 Gorelyy Khrebet, Sopka vol Kamchatka U.S.S.R. 52.34N 158.02E
104 O2 Gore Mt Vermont 44.54N 71.48W
35 D1 Goren Israel 33.03N 35.14E
36 C3 Görenez Dağı mt Turkey 39.00N 28.00E
45 D3 Gorenovo U.S.S.R. 53.52N 32.51E
113 M7 Gore Pt Alaska 59.15N 151.00W
13 E4 Gore Pt Queensland 17.37S 139.57E
35 D9 Gorer watercourse Israel
109 D2 Gore Ra Colorado
59 J6 Goresbridge Kilkenny Irish Rep 52.37N 7.00W
107 H4 Goreville Illinois 37.32N 89.00W
70 F3 Gorey Channel Is 49.12N 2.02W
59 K6 Gorey Wexford Irish Rep 52.40N 6.18W
32 H6 Gorg Iran 29.30N 59.40E
93 N3 Gorgala Somalia 2.18N 41.03E
32 F2 Gorgān Iran 36.50N 54.29E
32 E2 Gorgān B Iran
32 F2 Gorgān, Rūd-e R Iran
14 C5 Gorge Ra W Australia
13 H4 Gorge Ra., The Queensland
79 N3 Gorgo al Monticano Italy 45.47N 12.33E
89 C3 Gorgol R Mauritania
89 C3 Gorgol blanc R Mauritania
89 C3 Gorgol noir watercourse Mauritania
84 A3 Gorgómilos Greece 39.19N 20.56E
119 B6 Gorgona, I Colombia 3.00N 78.19W
80 A2 Gorgona, I.di Italy 43.25N 9.54E
79 F3 Gorgonzola Italy 45.32N 9.23E
87 F4 Gorgora Ethiopia 12.15N 37.17E
90 E5 Gorgoram Nigeria 12.40N 10.45E
110 O9 Gorgorza Utah 40.45N 111.34W
77 R3 Gorgos R Spain
109 L3 Gorham Kansas 38.54N 99.01W
104 P3 Gorham Maine 43.41N 70.28W
104 O2 Gorham New Hampshire 44.23N 71.11W
104 H4 Gorham New York 42.48N 77.08W
29 J1 Gorhar Bihar India 24.07N 85.43E
87 G6 Gori Ethiopia 8.41N 38.01E
44 F6 Gori Georgia U.S.S.R. 41.59N 44.05E
65 P9 Gorican Yugoslavia 46.23N 16.42E
83 D4 Goricë Albania 40.54N 20.57E
30 D2 Goriganga R Uttar Prad India
107 D1 Gorin Missouri 40.22N 92.02W
60 H12 Gorinchem Netherlands 51.50N 4.59E
56 J4 Goring Oxon Eng 51.32N 1.09W
52 J5 Göringen Sweden 61.14N 15.20E
44 G8 Goris Armenia U.S.S.R. 39.31N 46.22E
Gor-i Shala see Gōrashala
46 K2 Goritsy U.S.S.R. 57.10N 36.41E
63 Q9 Göritz Halle E Germany 51.59N 12.29E
63 T6 Göritz Neubrandenburg E Germany 53.25N 13.55E
84 E7 Goritzá Greece 37.02N 22.33E
40 F9 Goriyy U.S.S.R. 44.55N 133.52E
79 P3 Gorizia Italy 45.57N 13.37E
79 P3 Gorizia prov Italy
82 H5 Gorj div Romania
82 C5 Gorjanci mts Yugoslavia
47 F4 Gorka U.S.S.R. 62.46N 46.14E
44 F3 Gor'kaya Balka ravine U.S.S.R.
30 H4 Gorkha Nepal 28.01N 84.37E
45 B2 Gorki Belorussiya U.S.S.R. 54.17N 30.59E
46 O1 Gorki Gor'kiy U.S.S.R. 57.36N 45.04E
47 K3 Gorki Tyumen U.S.S.R. 65.05N 65.20E
82 N1 Gorki Tikich R U.S.S.R.
45 Q1 Gor'kiy U.S.S.R. 56.20N 44.00E
45 S7 Gor'kosolenoye, Oz L U.S.S.R.
46 N2 Gor'kovskaya Oblast' prov U.S.S.R.
47 L7 Gor'kovskoye U.S.S.R. 55.22N 74.20E
46 N2 Gor'kovskoye Vdkhr res U.S.S.R.
42 C5 Gor'koye, Ozero L Altay U.S.S.R.
42 C6 Gor'koye, Ozero L Altay U.S.S.R.
47 M8 Gor'koye, Ozero L Omsk U.S.S.R.
79 F7 Gorla dist Milan Italy
63 O6 Gorleben W Germany 53.03N 11.21E
56 P2 Gorleston Norfolk Eng 52.36N 1.43E
53 G5 Gørlev Denmark 55.33N 11.14E
62 N6 Gorlice Poland 49.40N 21.09E
47 E4 Gorlichevskaya U.S.S.R. 62.33N 42.59E
62 H4 Görlitz E Germany 51.09N 15.00E
53 J5 Gørløse Denmark 55.54N 12.13E
63 O6 Gorlosen E Germany 53.12N 11.27E
45 K8 Gorlovka Ukraine U.S.S.R. 48.17N 38.05E
45 L3 Gorlovo U.S.S.R. 53.50N 39.02E
111 F7 Gorman California 34.48N 118.50W
108 K5 Gorman S Dakota 44.55N 100.04W
112 J3 Gorman Texas 32.13N 98.41W
104 F7 Gormania Maryland 39.18N 79.23W
59 K4 Gormanston Meath Irish Rep 53.38N 6.14W
12 H8 Gormanston Tasmania 42.06S 145.37E
30 B6 Gormi Madhya Prad India 26.36N 78.30E
29 H7 Gorna Orissa India 20.20N 83.00E
81 J9 Gornalunga R Sicily
82 K7 Gorna Oryakhovitsa Bulgaria 43.07N 25.40E
45 Q7 Gornaya Proleyka U.S.S.R. 49.24N 44.58E
47 K6 Gornaya Subbota U.S.S.R. 59.50N 69.57E
66 H8 Gorner Glacier Switzerland
66 H8 Gornergrat Switzerland 49.59N 7.47E
80 O2 Gornje Selo Yugoslavia 43.22N 16.21E
82 F6 Gornji Milanovac Yugoslavia 44.01N 20.29E
82 D7 Gornji Vakuf Yugoslavia 43.57N 17.34E
79 G3 Gorno Italy 45.52N 9.50E
42 D6 Gorno-Altaysk U.S.S.R. 51.59N 85.56E
42 D6 Gorno-Altayskaya Aut. Oblast aut prov U.S.S.R.
43 L7 Gorno-Badakhshanskaya Aut. Oblast' aut prov Tadzhikistan U.S.S.R.
42 J3 Gorno-Chuyskiy U.S.S.R. 57.38N 111.40E
47 K5 Gorno-Filinskoye U.S.S.R. 60.06N 69.58E
47 K6 Gorno Slinkina U.S.S.R. 58.50N 68.48E
40 G2 Gornostakhskiy, Khrebet ra U.S.S.R.
47 F2 Gornostal'ya Guba gulf U.S.S.R.
45 E9 Gornostayevka Ukraine U.S.S.R. 47.00N 33.45E
46 H4 Gornostaypol Ukraine U.S.S.R. 51.04N 30.11E
45 Q7 Gorno-Vodyanoye U.S.S.R. 49.15N 44.56E
43 Q3 Gornoye Kazakhstan U.S.S.R. 48.02N 85.00E
44 D4 Gornoye U.S.S.R. 43.32N 21.34E
40 J8 Gornozavodsk Sakhalin U.S.S.R. 46.35N 141.47E
42 C6 Gornyak Altay U.S.S.R. 50.59N 81.30E
45 L3 Gornyak Ryazan' U.S.S.R. 53.36N 39.29E
45 M8 Gornyatskiy U.S.S.R. 48.17N 40.55E
47 J3 Gornyatskiy U.S.S.R. 67.30N 64.03E
40 F9 Gornye Klyuchi U.S.S.R. 45.15N 133.30E
44 E4 Gornyy Kabardino-Balkar A.S.S.R. U.S.S.R. 43.22N 42.50E
40 G6 Gornyy Khabarovsk U.S.S.R. 50.48N 136.14N
45 U5 Gornyy Saratov U.S.S.R. 51.46N 48.34E
51 P2 Gornyy U.S.S.R. 69.20N 30.40E
45 R7 Gornyy Balykley U.S.S.R. 49.34N 45.04E
47 K3 Gornyy Kazymsk U.S.S.R. 66.33N 68.30E
42 G5 Gornyy Kuy U.S.S.R. 54.39N 103.05E
42 K6 Gornyy Zerentuy U.S.S.R. 51.13N 119.32E
90 J7 Goro Chad 8.33N 18.08E
79 M5 Goro Italy 44.52N 12.18E
46 F5 Gorodenka Ukraine U.S.S.R. 48.40N 25.30E
46 N2 Gorodets U.S.S.R. 56.34N 43.29E
47 E2 Gorodetski, B., Mys C U.S.S.R. 67.41N 41.00E
45 A3 Gorodishche Belorussiya U.S.S.R. 53.45N 29.45E
46 F3 Gorodishche Belorussiya U.S.S.R. 53.18N 26.00E
46 G3 Gorodishche Belorussiya U.S.S.R. 53.40N 29.45E
45 C7 Gorodishche Cherkassy, Ukraine U.S.S.R. 49.19N 31.27E
45 L7 Gorodishche Lugansk, Ukraine U.S.S.R. 49.05N 39.40E
45 R3 Gorodishche Penza U.S.S.R. 53.16N 45.44E
46 J3 Gorodishche Smolensk U.S.S.R. 54.47N 34.19E
45 T2 Gorodishche Tatar A.S.S.R. U.S.S.R. 54.33N 47.30E
45 Q8 Gorodishche Volgograd U.S.S.R. 48.48N 44.30E
46 F4 Gorodnitsa Ukraine U.S.S.R. 50.50N 27.19E
45 C5 Gorodnya Ukraine U.S.S.R. 51.54N 31.37E
46 H2 Gorodnya U.S.S.R. 57.20N 31.25E
45 A1 Gorodok Belorussiya U.S.S.R. 55.28N 29.29E
46 E5 Gorodok Ukraine U.S.S.R. 49.48N 23.39E
46 M6 Gorodovikovsk U.S.S.R. 46.06N 41.57E
15 H7 Goroka Papua New Guinea 6.02S 145.22E
12 F6 Goroke Victoria 35.43S 141.30E
46 E4 Gorokhov Ukraine U.S.S.R. 50.30N 24.46E
45 O1 Gorokhovets U.S.S.R. 56.11N 42.42E
40 J5 Goromay Sakhalin U.S.S.R. 52.31N 143.05E
89 J4 Gorom-Gorom Upper Volta 14.27N 0.14W
15 A6 Gorong Moluccas Indon 4.06S 131.20E
15 A6 Gorong, Kepulauan arch Moluccas Indon
94 N3 Gorongose R Mozambique
94 N2 Gorongoza Mt Mozambique 18.30S 34.03E
19 C3 Gorontalo Celebes Indon 0.33N 123.05E
90 B5 Goronyo Nigeria 13.26N 5.40E
41 E7 Goroshikha U.S.S.R. 66.27N 87.33E
62 M1 Górowo Iławeckie Poland 54.18N 20.31E
65 N8 Gor. Radgona Yugoslavia 46.41N 15.59E
Gorrahei see Gorshe
60 N7 Gorredijk-Kortezwaag Netherlands 53.00N 6.04E
79 F5 Gorreto Italy 44.37N 9.17E
99 J9 Gorrie Ontario 43.53N 81.06W
79 D5 Gorrino Italy 44.33N 8.13E
70 J5 Gorron France 48.25N 0.49W
63 S9 Görsdorf E Germany 51.54N 13.30E
56 C4 Gorseinon Wales 51.41N 4.02W
61 L3 Gorsem Belgium 50.50N 5.10E
87 K7 Gorshe Ethiopia 6.34N 44.25E
45 K5 Gorshechnoye U.S.S.R. 51.31N 38.02E
45 K8 Gorskoye Ukraine U.S.S.R. 48.45N 38.31E
43 N7 Gorskoye Uzbekistan U.S.S.R. 40.29N 70.46E
60 N11 Gorssel Netherlands 52.13N 6.12E
59 E5 Gort Galway Irish Rep 53.04N 8.50W
77 D10 Gortazar-Tzenin Morocco 35.24N 6.01W
59 E5 Gorteen Galway Irish Rep 53.22N 8.35W
59 E4 Gorteen Sligo Irish Rep 54.00N 8.31W
60 M10 Gortel Netherlands 52.18N 5.53E
59 H2 Gortin Tyrone N Ireland 54.43N 7.14W
84 L11 Gortis ruins Crete 35.04N 24.56E
93 K5 Goruffa Kenya 0.21N 38.51E
29 K6 Gorumahisani Orissa India 22.21N 86.22E
59 C5 Gorumna I Galway Irish Rep 53.15N 9.40W
93 D6 Goru Pt Uganda 0.05S 32.07E
118 G4 Gorutuba, R Brazil
45 B4 Gorval' Belorussiya U.S.S.R. 52.34N 30.10E
64 E8 Görwihl W Germany 47.39N 8.05E
42 D4 Goryachegorsk U.S.S.R. 55.26N 88.54E
44 G4 Goryacheistochnenskaya U.S.S.R. 43.24N 45.46E
46 Q4 Goryachenskiy Kazakhstan U.S.S.R. 50.06N 51.15E
44 E3 Goryachevodskaya U.S.S.R. 44.02N 43.06E
42 H5 Goryachinsk U.S.S.R. 53.00N 108.20E
44 C3 Goryachiy Klyuch Krasnodar U.S.S.R. 44.36N 39.08E
39 E4 Goryachiy Klyuch Magadan U.S.S.R. 61.07N 152.30E
40 M8 Goryashchaya Sopka vol Kuril Is U.S.S.R. 46.50N 151.45E
46 F4 Goryn' R Belorussiya/Ukraine U.S.S.R.
62 M5 Góry Świętokrzyskie mts Poland
45 U3 Goryushka U.S.S.R. 53.35N 48.22E
31 B4 Gorzanak Afghanistan 32.54N 63.24E
80 H3 Gorzano, Monte Italy 42.37N 13.24E
69 L5 Gorzé France 49.03N 6.00E
79 D5 Gorzegno Italy 44.31N 8.08E
63 Q8 Görzke E Germany 52.11N 12.23E
62 L4 Gorzów Poland 51.01N 18.21E
62 J3 Gorzów Wielkopolski Poland 52.42N 15.12E
87 K6 Gos Ethiopia 8.18N 44.31E
30 F6 Gosainganj Faizabad, Uttar Prad India 26.34N 82.23E
30 E6 Gosainganj Lucknow, Uttar Prad India 26.46N 81.06E
30 J4 Gosainkund Nepal 28.06N 85.25E
Gosainthan see Xixabangma Feng
79 L2 Gosaldo Italy 46.13N 11.58E
65 J6 Gosau Austria 47.35N 13.32E
65 J6 Gosausee L Austria 47.32N 13.31E
87 L6 Gosawein Somalia 9.03N 46.50E
57 N7 Gosberton Lincs Eng 52.52N 0.09W
66 L5 Göschenen Switzerland 46.40N 8.36E
66 L5 Göschenental V Switzerland
66 K5 Göscheneralpsee L Switz 46.38N 8.30E
15 L9 Goschen Str Papua New Guinea
64 M2 Göschwitz E Germany 50.52N 11.35E
20 N4 Gosen Japan 37.45N 139.11E
56 N4 Gosfield Essex Eng 51.56N 0.35E
12 K5 Gosford New S Wales 33.25S 151.18E
57 G4 Gosforth Cumbria Eng 54.26N 3.27W
31 C7 Goshanak Pakistan 26.17N 64.56E
111 E5 Goshen California 36.20N 119.26W
103 H3 Goshen Connecticut 41.50N 73.13W
106 J8 Goshen Indiana 41.34N 85.49W
103 J2 Goshen Massachusetts 42.26N 72.48W
103 E8 Goshen New Jersey 39.08N 74.51W
103 F4 Goshen New York 41.24N 74.20W
110 B6 Goshen Oregon 44.00N 123.00W
95 L8 Goshen S Africa 32.15S 27.08E
111 N2 Goshen Utah 39.57N 111.54W
104 F9 Goshen Virginia 37.58N 79.32W
84 S15 Goshi Cyprus 34.58N 33.30E
20 O1 Goshogawara Japan 40.48N 140.27E
116 N4 Gosier Guadeloupe W I 16.12N 61.30W
63 M9 Goslar W Germany 51.55N 10.25E
70 H5 Gosné France 48.14N 1.28W
14 C2 Gosnells dist Perth, W Aust
82 C6 Gospić Yugoslavia 44.33N 15.22E
56 J6 Gosport Hants Eng 50.48N 1.08W
107 K2 Gosport Indiana 39.20N 86.40W
107 G10 Goss Mississippi 31.21N 89.54W
63 Q9 Gossa E Germany 51.42N 12.27E
89 A4 Gossas Senegal 14.28N 16.00W
66 O2 Gossau St Gallen Switzerland 47.25N 9.16E
66 M2 Gossau Zürich Switzerland 47.18N 8.46E
65 L7 Gosseck Austria 47.26N 14.54E
61 H5 Gosse'lies Belgium 50.28N 4.26E
14 B10 Gosselin, C W Australia 34.25S 115.24E
52 C4 Gossen isld Norway 62.50N 6.45E
13 C4 Gosse R N Terr Australia
89 J4 Gossi L Mali 15.48N 1.20W
90 M7 Gossinga Sudan 8.36N 25.59E
65 J6 Gossl Austria 47.38N 13.54E
65 H8 Gössnitz Austria 46.56N 13.05E
64 N2 Gössnitz E Germany 50.53N 12.26E
90 K7 Gosso Cent Afr Rep 9.30N 21.03E
45 H6 Gostishchevo U.S.S.R. 50.47N 36.40E
82 F9 Gostivar Yugoslavia 41.47N 20.55E
65 L6 Göstling Austria 47.49N 14.56E
65 L6 Göstlinger Alpen mts Austria
45 B6 Gostomel' Ukraine U.S.S.R. 50.41N 30.15E
62 K4 Gostyn Poland 51.52N 17.00E
62 L3 Gostynin Poland 52.25N 19.27E
52 G8 Göta, älv R Sweden
52 J8 Göta kanal Sweden
20 F2 Gotanno dist Tōkyō Japan
29 B4 Gotaru Rajasthan India 27.18N 70.02E
53 N9 Gøte Faeroes 62.13N 6.44W
93 B3 Gote Zaïre 2.13N 30.47E
109 M6 Gotebo Oklahoma 35.04N 98.53W
52 F9 Göteborg Sweden 57.45N 12.00E
52 F8 Göteborg och Bohus dist Sweden
87 L8 Got, El Somalia 4.35N 46.04E
61 M3 Gotem Belgium 50.48N 5.19E
20 M6 Gotemba Japan 35.20N 138.58E
64 K2 Gotha E Germany 50.57N 10.43E
106 D6 Gotham Wisconsin 43.13N 90.18W
52 L9 Gothem Sweden 57.35N 18.47E
108 K9 Gothenburg Nebraska 40.57N 100.10W
Gothenburg Sweden see Göteborg
89 K5 Gotheye Niger 13.52N 1.34E
31 B9 Goth Goli Mār dist Karachi Pakistan
Goth Ibrāhīm Haidari see Korangi
31 B9 Goth Sher Shāh dist Karachi Pakistan
31 B9 Goth Warayo Gado Pakistan 24.54N 67.04E
29 F6 Gotitoria Madhya Prad India 22.42N 78.50E
52 L9 Gotland dist Sweden
52 L9 Gotland isld Sweden
52 J7 Götlunda Sweden 59.20N 15.40E
19 F3 Gotowasi Halmahera Indon 0.37N 128.24E
82 H9 Gotse Delchev Bulgaria 41.33N 23.45E
52 L8 Gotska Sandön isld Sweden 58.25N 19.25E
20 F6 Gōtsu Japan 35.02N 132.13E
61 D3 Gottem Belgium 50.58N 3.27E
95 L3 Gottenburg S Africa 27.08S 27.54E
79 G6 Gottero, Monte Italy 44.21N 9.41E
63 J3 Gotteskoog-see L W Germany
64 O6 Gotteszell W Germany 48.57N 12.59E
61 G5 Gottignies Belgium 50.29N 4.04E
64 F2 Göttingen Hessen W Germany 50.52N 8.47E
63 L9 Göttingen Niedersachsen W Germany 51.32N 9.57E
64 F8 Gottmadingen W Germany 47.43N 8.47E
66 M1 Gottmadingen W Germany 47.44N 8.47E
52 L3 Gottne Sweden 63.27N 18.25E
79 H4 Gottolengo Italy 45.17N 10.16E
20 B8 Gottō-rettō islds Japan
63 L3 Gottorf W Germany 54.31N 9.33E
101 M10 Gott Pk Br Col 50.18N 122.16W
53 C2 Gøttrup Denmark 57.03N 9.13E
103 A5 Gottshalls Pennsylvania 40.45N 76.39W
62 K6 Gottwaldov Czechoslovakia 49.14N 17.40E
65 A7 Götzis Austria 47.21N 9.40E
69 E7 Gouaix France 48.29N 3.18E
89 K6 Gouande Benin 10.49N 0.59E
70 D5 Gouarec France 48.13N 3.11W
21 B7 Goubangzi Liaoning China 41.22N 121.46E
90 N9 Goubére Cent Afr Rep 5.50N 26.48E
87 J5 Goubeto Djibouti 11.26N 43.04E
90 H1 Goubon Chad 20.46N 17.09E
60 G11 Gouda Netherlands 52.01N 4.43E
95 C9 Gouda S Africa 33.19S 19.03E
71 E8 Goudargues France 44.13N 4.28E
69 F4 Goudelancourt-les-Pierrepont France 49.40N 3.52E
121 C5 Goudge Argentina 34.43S 68.10W
56 M5 Goudhurst Kent Eng 51.07N 0.28E
95 C9 Goudini S Africa 33.40S 19.15E
89 C4 Goudiri Senegal 14.12N 12.41W
90 E5 Goudoumaria Niger 13.40N 11.10E
121 D5 Goudra Argentina 34.45S 63.18W
99 F4 Goudreau Ontario 48.16N 84.32W
60 H12 Goudriaan Netherlands 51.54N 4.54E
94 R14 Goudryk S Africa 26.19S 27.35E
60 F12 Goudswaard Netherlands 51.47N 4.16E
89 F7 Gouekan Ivory Coast 8.05N 7.48W
70 G4 Gouesnière, la France 48.36N 1.54W
70 B5 Gouesnou France 48.27N 4.28W
70 E5 Gouet R France
89 F7 Gouétougou Ivory Coast 8.15N 6.54W
72 F3 Gouex France 46.23N 0.42E
70 C5 Gouézec France 48.10N 3.59W
71 H6 Gouffre Berger France 45.13N 5.37E
72 H6 Gouffre-de-Padirac France 44.51N 1.44E
59 D8 Gouganebarra,L Cork Irish Rep 51.50N 9.20W
105 E4 Gough Georgia 33.06N 82.13W
96 J13 Gough Island S Atlantic Oc 40.20S 10.00W
100 E6 Gough L Alberta 52.00N 112.25W
61 J5 Gougnies Belgium 50.22N 4.35E
89 M4 Gougoufena Niger 14.11N 4.50E
71 J1 Gouhenans France 47.36N 6.28E
99 Q4 Gouin, Rés Quebec
21 B3 Goukou Nei Monggol Zizhiqu China 48.37N 122.05E
58 L3 Goukstone Grampian Scotland 57.35N 2.51W
99 F6 Goulais River Ontario 46.44N 84.24W
12 H7 Goulbourn R Victoria
12 J5 Goulburn New S Wales 34.47S 149.43E
12 K4 Goulburn R New S Wales
12 H6 Goulburn R Victoria
13 C1 Goulburn Is N Terr Australia
107 E8 Gould Arkansas 33.59N 91.32W
109 D1 Gould Colorado 40.32N 106.02W
109 L7 Gould Oklahoma 34.42N 99.47W
99 T7 Gould Quebec 45.35N 71.24W
106 J3 Gould City Michigan 46.05N 85.41W
123 G8 Gould Coast Antarctica
14 B7 Gould, Mt W Australia 25.46S 117.24E
105 G12 Goulds Florida 25.33N 80.24W
103 D4 Gouldsboro Pennsylvania 41.15N 75.27W
90 G5 Goulfey Cameroon 12.25N 14.50E
88 H7 Goulimime Morocco 28.56N 10.04W
89 M4 Goulmi Niger 14.00N 5.48E
88 L6 Goulmima Morocco 31.42N 5.00W
90 D4 Goulouiski Niger 15.01N 9.05E
84 C5 Goumaíoi Greece 38.26N 21.58E
89 E5 Goumbanko Mali 12.58N 9.29W
89 F4 Goumbou Mali 15.02N 7.25W
83 E4 Gouménissa Greece 40.56N 22.27E
90 J1 Goumeur Chad 20.34N 18.35E
66 C5 Goumoëns la Ville Switzerland 46.40N 6.37E
71 K2 Goumois France 47.15N 6.56E
89 H4 Goundaka Mali 14.28N 3.58W
89 H3 Goundam Mali 16.27N 3.39W
90 H10 Goundi Cent Afr Rep 3.37N 17.01E
90 H7 Goundi Chad 9.22N 17.21E
89 F5 Gouni Mali 12.56N 7.25W
90 G7 Gounou-Gaya Chad 9.37N 15.30E
89 G3 Gounsao Mali 16.39N 4.08W
84 D6 Goúra Greece 37.56N 22.20E
90 H3 Gouradi Chad 16.26N 17.10E
88 N7 Gourara reg Algeria
88 O3 Gouraya Algeria 36.35N 1.55E
70 F5 Gouray, le France 48.20N 2.29W
116 M4 Gourbeyre Guadeloupe W I 15.59N 61.41W
89 H5 Gourcy Upper Volta 13.13N 2.20W
89 H5 Gourcy Upper Volta 13.16N 2.18W
72 F9 Gourdan-Polignan France 43.04N 0.35E
61 H5 Gourdinne Belgium 50.17N 4.27E
72 G6 Gourdon France 44.45N 1.22E
15 H6 Gourdon, C Papua New Guinea 4.25S 145.20E
90 E5 Gouré Niger 13.59N 10.15E
89 C4 Gourel Kea Senegal 14.08N 13.40W
69 G6 Gourgançon France 48.41N 4.01E
72 D2 Gourgé France 46.43N 0.10W
90 H2 Gouri Chad 18.50N 16.49E
70 C5 Gourin France 48.08N 3.37W
90 J2 Gouring Chad 18.44N 19.10E
31 H8 Gouripur Bangladesh 24.47N 90.35E
95 E9 Gourits R S Africa
99 F4 Gourlay L Ontario 48.54N 84.55W
89 K6 Gourma reg Niger/Upper Volta
89 J3 Gourma-Rharous Mali 16.58N 1.50W
70 O3 Gournay-en-Bray France 49.29N 1.44E
84 N11 Gourniá ruins Crete 35.06N 25.47E
90 J2 Gouro Chad 19.36N 19.36E
58 G7 Gourock Strathclyde Scotland 55.58N 4.49W
12 J6 Gourock Ra New S Wales
89 F8 Gouros tribe Ivory Coast
89 H6 Gourounsi reg Ghana/Upper Volta
88 L5 Gourrama Morocco 32.20N 4.01W
89 G1 Gours Oulad Ahmed reg Mali
84 B5 Gouryiá Greece 38.28N 21.16E
68 G1 Goussainville France 49.01N 2.27E
72 C8 Gousse France 43.47N 0.53W
90 D5 Goutchi Niger 13.32N 9.31E
71 B5 Goutelle, la France 45.51N 2.45E
72 E5 Goût Rossignol France 45.24N 0.24E
84 M11 Goúvais Crete 35.19N 25.19E
76 D8 Gouveia Portugal 40.29N 7.35W
76 E7 Gouveia Portugal 40.40N 7.10W
104 K2 Gouverneur New York 44.21N 75.29W
100 K9 Gouverneur Saskatchewan 49.46N 107.34W
84 F3 Goúves Greece 39.00N 23.15E
84 W22 Gouviá Corfu 39.39N 19.50E
70 P3 Gouvieux France 49.11N 2.26E
70 G3 Gouville France 49.06N 1.35W
60 J10 Gouwzee shallow sea Netherlands
71 J3 Goux-les-Usiers France 46.58N 6.15E
116 P5 Gouyave Grenada, W I 12.10N 61.44W
61 H5 Gouy-lez-Piéton Belgium 50.29N 4.20E
69 E3 Gouzeaucourt France 50.03N 3.07E
72 J3 Gouzon France 46.11N 2.14E
100 N7 Govan Saskatchewan 51.19N 105.00W
34 M1 Govanda Plat Iraq/Turkey
30 A5 Govardhan Uttar Prad India 27.30N 77.27E
109 K3 Gove Kansas 38.58N 100.30W
13 D1 Gove N Terr Australia 11.56S 136.51E
70 G5 Goven France 48.01N 1.50W
39 H5 Govena, Mys C U.S.S.R. 59.50N 166.01E
100 H9 Govenlock Saskatchewan 49.14N 109.51W
13 D1 Gove Pen N Terr Australia
82 J2 Goverla mt U.S.S.R. 48.09N 24.30E
118 J8 Governador, I. do Brazil
118 H6 Governador Valadares Brazil 18.51S 41.57W
110 D4 Government Camp Oregon 45.19N 121.46W
19 N8 Governor Generoso Mindanao Philippines 6.38N 126.07E
98 K8 Governor L Nova Scotia
11 M10 Governors Bay New Zealand 43.37S 172.39E
103 L7 Governors I New York 40.42N 74.01W
22 C4 Govĭaltay prov Mongolia
58 B3 Govick Harris, W Isles Scotland 57.58N 7.04W
29 H5 Govind Ballash Pant Sagar L Bihar India
30 E8 Govindgarh Madhya Prad India 24.22N 81.18E
30 A5 Govindgarh Rajasthan India 27.31N 77.00E
29 E2 Govind Sagar L Himachal Prad India
22 G3 Govĭ-Ugtaal Mongolia 46.04N 107.25E
79 D5 Govone Italy 44.48N 8.07E
41 N5 Govorovo U.S.S.R. 70.14N 126.00E
29 J2 Gowai R Bihar/W Bengal India
31 E5 Gowal Pakistan 30.44N 68.52E
11 G8 Gowanbridge New Zealand 41.43S 172.34E
104 G4 Gowanda New York 42.28N 78.57W
13 G6 Gowan Ra Queensland
11 G8 Gowan Valley New Zealand 41.46S 172.35E
31 C6 Gowārān Afghanistan 29.44N 65.43E
32 F5 Gowd-e Aḩmad Iran 30.05N 55.54E
32 G4 Gowd-e-Hasht Tekkeh Iran 32.34N 56.11E
32 F6 Gowd-e Mokh Iran 28.09N 54.06E
107 B2 Gower Missouri 39.37N 94.34W
56 C4 Gower pen W Glam Wales
10 E11 Gower I Lord Howe I Pacific Oc 31.36S 159.05E
10 E11 Gower, Mt Lord Howe I Pacific Oc 31.36S 159.05E
99 K5 Gowganda Ontario 47.41N 80.46W
32 G6 Gowk Iran 29.51N 57.44E
31 E4 Gowmal Kalay Afghanistan 32.29N 68.55E
59 G4 Gowna, L Longford Irish Rep 53.50N 7.34W
59 H6 Gowran Kilkenny Irish Rep 52.38N 7.04W
108 Q7 Gowrie Iowa 42.18N 94.18W
58 K6 Gowrie, Carse of dist Tayside Scotland
44 H9 Gowyjeh Soltān Iran 38.32N 46.41E
92 C5 Goy Zaïre 6.19S 27.51E
121 F2 Goya Argentina 29.10S 59.15W
116 N4 Goyave Guadeloupe W I 16.09N 61.35W
13 C7 Goyder R N Terr Australia
13 D2 Goyder R N Terr Australia
12 F2 Goyder, L S Australia
98 M3 Goyelle, L Quebec
121 E6 Goyena Argentina 37.44S 62.36W
120 B4 Goyllarisquizga Peru 10.31S 76.24W
36 E2 Göynük Turkey 40.24N 30.45E
36 E2 Göynük R Turkey

20 P2 Goyō-zan mt Honshu Japan 39.12N 141.44E
53 Z19 Goysen mt Norway 59.32N 8.31E
53 Y18 Gøystvatn L Norway 60.00N 8.18E
90 K5 Goz Beïda Chad 12.10N 21.20E
61 H5 Gozée Belgium 50.20N 4.21E
86 L3 Gôz el Dab'a hill Egypt 31.03N 33.51E
24 D8 Gozha Co L Xizang Zizhiqu China
43 G6 Gozhdye Uzbekistan U.S.S.R. 40.23N 63.20E
36 H6 Gözne Turkey 37.00N 34.32E
Gozón see Luanco
87 E2 Goz Regeb Sudan 16.03N 35.33E
79 D3 Gozzano Italy 45.45N 8.26E
95 H8 Graaff-Reinet S Africa 32.15S 24.32E
94 E9 Graafwater S Africa 32.08S 18.32E
60 E14 Graauw Netherlands 51.20N 4.07E
64 E5 Graben-Neudorf W Germany 49.10N 8.30E
64 J3 Grabfeld reg W Germany
89 F9 Grabo Ivory Coast 4.57N 7.30W
84 J10 Graboúsa isld Crete 35.37N 23.34E
95 C10 Grabouw S Africa 34.09S 19.01E
43 L1 Grabovo Kazakhstan U.S.S.R. 53.08N 74.50E
45 R3 Grabovo U.S.S.R. 53.25N 45.01E
63 P8 Grabow Magdeburg E Germany 52.15N 11.57E
62 L4 Grabów Poland 51.30N 18.05E
63 P6 Grabow Schwerin E Germany 53.17N 11.34E
63 O6 Grabow W Germany 53.01N 11.07E
66 O3 Grabs Switzerland 47.11N 9.27E
82 C6 Gračac Yugoslavia 44.20N 15.52E
82 E6 Gračanica Yugoslavia 44.43N 18.18E
72 H1 Graçay France 47.09N 1.51E
110 O7 Grace Idaho 42.35N 111.45W
108 M2 Grace City N Dakota 47.32N 98.48W
99 O6 Gracefield Quebec 46.05N 76.05W
61 M4 Grâce-Hollogne Belgium 50.38N 5.28E
98 G1 Grace L Labrador, Nfld
14 C10 Grace, L W Australia
Grace McKinley mt see McKinley Pk
109 M6 Gracemont Oklahoma 35.13N 98.16W
11 D6 Grace, Mt New Zealand 41.20S 174.56E
105 B7 Graceville Florida 30.58N 85.31W
108 O4 Graceville Minnesota 45.34N 96.26W
13 K2 Graceville dist Brisbane, Qnsld
107 J5 Gracey Kentucky 36.52N 87.40W
66 H7 Grächen Switzerland 46.12N 7.50E
45 L4 Grachevka Lipetsk U.S.S.R. 52.05N 40.00E
46 R3 Grachevka Orenburg U.S.S.R. 52.54N 52.56E
45 V5 Grachev Kust U.S.S.R. 51.59N 49.47E
45 O6 Grachi U.S.S.R. 50.54N 42.17E
115 P10 Gracías Honduras 14.36N 88.30W
115 N2 Gracias á Dios, C Nicaragua 15.00N 83.10W
96 R1 Graciosa isld Azores 39.03N 28.03W
96 V7 Graciosa isld Canary Is 29.15N 13.31W
65 O8 Grad Yugoslavia 46.48N 16.07E
82 E6 Gradačac Yugoslavia 44.52N 18.26E
117 C8 Gradaús Brazil 7.43S 51.10W
117 D8 Gradaús, Sa. dos mts Brazil
51 E5 Graddis Norway 66.45N 15.46E
76 J3 Gradefes Spain 42.37N 5.14W
65 K8 Grades Austria 46.59N 14.17E
82 G9 Gradeška Planina mts Yugoslavia
82 K8 Gradets Bulgaria 42.10N 26.05E
82 K8 Gradets Bulgaria 42.46N 26.30E
72 C6 Gradignan France 44.47N 0.36W
76 A11 Gradil Portugal 38.59N 9.17W
79 O3 Gradisca d'Isonzo Italy 45.53N 13.30E
82 H5 Grădistea Muncelului Romania 45.37N 23.11E
63 S9 Graditz E Germany 51.33N 13.04E
45 E7 Gradizhsk Ukraine U.S.S.R. 49.14N 33.07E
79 O3 Grado Italy 45.40N 13.23E
76 G2 Grado Spain 43.23N 6.04W
75 L3 Grado, El Spain 42.09N 0.13E
80 E3 Gradoli Italy 42.38N 11.51E
45 O4 Gradskiy Umet U.S.S.R. 52.31N 42.59E
82 G9 Gradsko Yugoslavia 41.33N 21.59E
13 J8 Gradule Queensland 28.32S 149.10E
107 E7 Grady Arkansas 34.02N 91.41W
109 G7 Grady New Mexico 34.50N 103.19W
53 A6 Grådyb headland Denmark 55.28N 8.19E
14 B9 Grady, L W Australia 30.21S 117.28E
103 D7 Gradyville Pennsylvania 39.57N 75.28W
111 D2 Graeagle California 39.45N 120.37W
48 S13 Grædefjorden Greenland 63.17N 51.07W
53 D5 Grædstrup Denmark 55.54N 9.32E
58 S12 Graemsay isld Orkney Scotland 58.56N 3.17W
53 H7 Grænge Denmark 54.47N 11.47E
50 D4 Grænumýrartunga Iceland 65.05N 21.04W
53 J4 Græsted Denmark 56.04N 12.18E
108 Q6 Graettinger Iowa 43.14N 94.45W
Grafarkirkja see Gröf
64 L7 Gräfelfing W Germany 48.06N 11.27E
64 P6 Grafenau W Germany 48.51N 13.25E
64 L4 Gräfenberg W Germany 49.38N 11.15E
63 Q9 Gräfenhainichen E Germany 51.45N 12.28E
66 K1 Grafenhausen W Germany 47.46N 8.16E
64 K2 Gräfenroda E Germany 50.45N 10.48E
65 M5 Grafenschlag Austria 48.30N 15.11E
65 K8 Grefenstein Austria 46.37N 14.28E
64 L2 Gräfenthal E Germany 50.31N 11.18E
64 K1 Gräfentonna E Germany 51.06N 10.45E
64 M4 Grafenwöhr W Germany 49.43N 11.55E
65 N5 Grafenwörth Austria 48.25N 15.47E
80 F3 Graffignano Italy 42.34N 12.13E
56 L3 Grafham Water L Cambs Eng 52.18N 0.20W
60 M9 Grafhorst Netherlands 52.35N 5.56E
Gräfinau see Angstedt-Gräfinau
64 M7 Grafing W Germany 48.02N 11.58E
64 O6 Grafling W Germany 48.54N 12.59E
66 P6 Graf, Monte Italy 46.18N 9.31E
112 J3 Graford Texas 32.56N 98.16W
64 C2 Grafschaft W Germany 50.35N 7.03E
60 H9 Graft Netherlands 52.33N 4.49E
107 F3 Grafton Illinois 38.59N 90.26W
108 R6 Grafton Iowa 43.20N 93.04W
103 L2 Grafton Massachusetts 42.13N 71.40W
108 N1 Grafton N Dakota 48.28N 97.25W
12 L3 Grafton New S Wales 29.40S 152.56E
104 M4 Grafton New York 42.47N 73.26W
104 C5 Grafton Ohio 41.16N 82.04W
106 G6 Grafton Wisconsin 43.20N 87.58W
104 E7 Grafton W Virginia 39.21N 80.03W
13 H3 Grafton, C Queensland 16.51S 146.00E
121 J10 Grafton, Is Chile
111 K3 Grafton, Mt Nevada 38.42N 114.46W
13 H3 Grafton Pass Gt Barrier Reef Australia 16.35S 146.15E
80 L7 Gragnano Italy 40.42N 14.31E
118 K9 Gragoatá Brazil 22.56S 43.08W
103 E4 Graham New York 41.26N 74.36W
100 M1 Graham Ontario 49.16N 90.33W
112 J2 Graham Texas 33.07N 98.36W
101 M7 Graham R Br Col
Graham Bell I see Greem Bell, Ostrov
101 G9 Graham I Br Col
97 K2 Graham I N W Terr 77.20N 90.30W
100 C2 Graham L Alberta
104 R2 Graham L Maine
123 E14 Graham Land pen Antarctica
111 P9 Graham, Mt Arizona 32.41N 109.53W
95 K9 Grahamstown S Africa 33.18S 26.32E
103 E3 Grahamsville New York 41.51N 74.32W
89 D3 Grahane, El Mauritania 16.30N 11.49W
82 E8 Grahovo Yugoslavia 42.40N 18.41E
88 T4 Graïba Tunisia 34.33N 10.12E
61 L7 Graide Belgium 49.57N 5.04E
79 A3 Graie, Alpi mts Italy/France
59 J6 Graigue Leix Irish Rep 52.56N 6.57W
56 N5 Grain Kent Eng 51.28N 0.43E
89 D9 Grain Coast Liberia
66 H9 Graine Italy 45.44N 7.46E
109 K2 Grainfield Kansas 39.07N 100.29W
56 N5 Grain, I of Kent Eng 51.28N 0.42E
108 J9 Grainton Nebraska 40.50N 101.15W
72 K6 Graissac France 44.46N 2.46E
71 C9 Graissessac France 43.41N 3.05E
18 L10 Grajagan Java Indon 8.35S 114.14E
76 J4 Grajal de Campos Spain 42.19N 5.01W
120 C3 Grajaú Acre Brazil 8.34S 72.49W
117 E7 Grajaú Brazil 5.50S 46.04W
118 J9 Grajaú Rio de Janeiro Brazil 22.56S 43.17W
117 E7 Grajaú, R Brazil
75 C5 Grajera Spain 41.22N 3.37W
62 N2 Grajewo Poland 53.40N 22.29E
46 Q2 Grakhovo U.S.S.R. 56.01N 51.50E
76 C7 Gralheira,Serra mts Portugal
53 C6 Gram Denmark 55.18N 9.03E
82 H7 Gramada Bulgaria 43.49N 22.39E
120 A4 Gramadal, Pta Peru 10.27S 78.03W
119 D4 Gramalote Colombia 7.54N 72.45W
117 B2 Gramankondre Surinam 4.25N 55.49W
72 H6 Gramat France 44.46N 1.42E
72 H6 Gramat, Causse de plat France
82 L8 Gramatikovo Bulgaria 42.03N 27.38E
65 P5 Gramatneusiedl Austria 48.02N 16.30E
63 U6 Grambow E Germany 53.25N 14.22E
121 D1 Gramilla Argentina 27.16S 64.35W
63 H7 Gramke W Germany 52.31N 8.06E
61 D3 Grammene Belgium 50.58N 3.29E
81 J9 Grammichele Sicily 37.13N 14.39E
66 D6 Grammont mt Switzerland 46.23N 6.49E
83 D4 Grámmos mt Greece/Albania 40.23N 20.45E
84 E8 Grámmousa Greece 36.55N 22.39E
63 R4 Grammow E Germany 54.04N 12.38E
42 D5 Gramoteino U.S.S.R. 54.34N 86.24E
14 C9 Gramphorne, Mt W Australia 31.44S 118.45E
12 F6 Grampian mts Victoria
58 K4 Grampian reg Scotland
58 G5 Grampian Mts Scotland
56 B7 Grampound Cornwall Eng 50.18N 4.54W
60 P9 Gramsbergen Netherlands 52.36N 6.40E
83 D4 Gramsh Albania 40.52N 20.12E
84 J10 Grámvoúsa isld Crete 35.39N 23.34E
63 U6 Gramzow E Germany 53.13N 14.00E
117 B2 Gran R Surinam
79 B6 Grana R Italy
100 B5 Granada Alberta 53.38N 115.20W
109 H3 Granada Colorado 38.03N 102.20W
115 M4 Granada Nicaragua 11.58N 85.59W
77 J6 Granada Spain 37.10N 3.35W
74 E7 Granada prov Spain
77 D5 Granada de Riotinto, La Spain 37.46N 6.30W
77 J5 Granada, R. de Spain
75 M5 Granadella Spain 41.21N 0.39E
76 G8 Granadilla Spain 40.16N 6.06W
96 R15 Granadilla de Abona Tenerife Canary Is 28.08N 16.34W
77 B5 Granado, El Spain 37.31N 7.25W
77 B5 Granado, Sierra del mts Spain
121 K7 Gran Altiplanície Central reg Argentina
53 W18 Grananut mt Norway 60.14N 7.15E
59 H4 Granard Longford Irish Rep 53.47N 7.30W
79 K5 Granarolo dell'Emilia Italy 44.33N 11.26E
65 G7 Granat Spitze mt Austria 47.08N 12.35E
77 J3 Granátula Spain 38.48N 3.45W
121 K7 Gran Baja San Julián reg Argentina
121 L6 Gran Bajo plain Argentina
121 C7 Gran Bajo Salitroso salt L Argentina
112 K3 Granbury Texas 32.27N 97.47W
109 N9 Granbury, Lake Texas
109 E1 Granby Colorado 40.05N 105.56W
103 J3 Granby Connecticut 41.57N 72.47W
103 J2 Granby Massachusetts 42.15N 72.31W
107 B5 Granby Missouri 36.53N 94.18W
99 S7 Granby Quebec 45.23N 72.44W
109 E1 Granby L Colorado 40.10N 105.52W
96 U15 Gran Canaria isld Canary Is 28.00N 15.35W
71 G1 Grancey-le-Château France 47.41N 5.02E
120 G10 Gran Chaco reg Arg/Paraguay
116 O2 Gran Couva Trinidad & Tobago 10.24N 61.23W
69 J7 Grand France 48.22N 5.28E
107 E11 Grand R Louisiana
107 B1 Grand R Missouri
108 J4 Grand R S Dakota
119 D6 Granda Colombia 3.33N 73.44W
76 C13 Grandaços Portugal 37.40N 8.10W
76 F2 Grandas de Salime Spain 43.13N 6.53W
66 N8 Grandate Italy 45.47N 9.04E
70 H6 Grand-Auverne France 47.35N 1.19W
99 B3 Grand B Ontario
105 J11 Grand Bahama I Bahamas
98 R6 Grand Bank Newfoundland 47.06N 55.48W
96 F4 Grand Banks of Newfoundland Atlantic Oc
Grand Bassa see Buchanan Liberia
89 H9 Grand Bassam Ivory Coast 5.14N 3.45W
26 U15 Grand Bassin Réunion Indian Oc 21.10S 55.32E
91 A2 Grand Batanga Cameroon 2.50N 9.55E
107 G12 Grand Bay Louisiana 29.20N 89.20W
98 F8 Grand Bay New Brunswick 45.19N 66.14W
100 V8 Grand Beach Manitoba 50.34N 96.38W
100 V8 Grand Beach Prov.Park Manitoba
26 U15 Grand Benard mt Réunion Ind Oc 21.07S 55.26E
99 J9 Grand Bend Ontario 43.21N 82.45W
71 K8 Grand Bérard mt France 44.28N 6.39E
106 L7 Grand Blanc Michigan 42.55N 83.36W
71 J5 Grand Bornand, le France 45.57N 6.25E
116 N4 Grand Bourg Marie Galante, Guadeloupe W I 15.53N 61.19W
72 H3 Grand Bourg, le France 46.10N 1.38E
98 O6 Grand Bruit Newfoundland 47.40N 58.16W
26 V16 Grand Brûlé mt slope Réunion Ind Oc
116 J4 Grand Caicos isld Caicos Is W I 21.49N 71.45W
70 H3 Grandcamp-Maisy France 49.23N 1.01W
59 J5 Grand Canal Dublin etc Irish Rep
107 C9 Grand Cane Louisiana 32.06N 93.50W
111 M5 Grand Canyon Arizona 36.02N 112.09W
111 M5 Grand Canyon gorge Arizona
111 M5 Grand Canyon Nat.Mon Arizona 36.20N 112.55W
111 M5 Grand Canyon Nat.Park Arizona
105 J10 Grand Cays islds Bahamas 27.14N 78.20W
100 G4 Grand Centre Alberta 54.25N 110.13W
89 E9 Grand Cess Liberia 4.36N 8.12W
70 E6 Grand Champ France 47.46N 2.50W
70 G7 Grand-champ France 47.22N 1.37W
107 D12 Grand Chenier Louisiana 29.44N 92.59W
71 H5 Grand Colombier mt France 45.55N 5.44E
110 F2 Grand Coulee Washington 47.58N 119.00W
110 F2 Grand Coulee canyon Washington
110 G2 Grand Coulee Dam Washington 47.59N 118.58W
66 D4 Grandcour Switzerland 46.53N 6.57E
70 N3 Grand Couronne France 49.21N 1.01E
70 O2 Grandcourt France 49.54N 1.31E
71 K8 Grand Coyer mt France 44.06N 6.41E
71 F5 Grand Croix, la France 45.31N 4.35E
116 N3 Grand Cul de Sac Marin B Guadeloupe W I
119 E2 Grand de Oro airport Venezuela 10.44N 72.39W
76 D10 Grande R Portugal
77 G7 Grande R Spain
77 J4 Grande R Spain
77 P2 Grande R Spain
116 O3 Grande Anse Guadeloupe W I 16.17N 61.04W
98 G6 Grande-Anse New Brunswick 47.49N 65.12W
121 L8 Grande B Argentina
26 U11 Grande Baie Mauritius, Indian Oc 20.01S 57.35E
79 L5 Grande Bonificazione Ferrarese reg Italy
70 F7 Grande Brière reg France
101 O9 Grande Cache Alberta 53.53N 119.07W
98 G5 Grande-Cascapédia Quebec 48.15N 65.54W
71 K6 Grande Casse mt France 45.25N 6.50E
116 E4 Grande, Cayo isld Cuba 20.56N 79.09W
116 L9 Grande, Cayo isld Lesser Antilles 11.49N 66.38W
71 H6 Grande Chartreuse mts France
66 C3 Grande Combe, la France 47.02N 6.34E
71 E8 Grande Combe, la France 44.13N 4.02E
95 A1 Grande Comore isld Comoros, Indian Oc
121 H2 Grande, Coxilha mts Brazil
121 G4 Grande, Cuchilla mts Uruguay
120 F10 Grande de Jujuy, R Argentina
121 G4 Grande del Durazno, Cuchilla mts Uruguay
116 G4 Grande de Moa, Cayo isld Cuba 20.44N 74.56W
120 E10 Grande de San Juan R Arg/Bolivia
120 F10 Grande de Tarija R Arg/Bolivia
66 E6 Grande Eau R Switzerland
61 K3 Grande Gette R Belgium
98 H5 Grande Grève Quebec 48.46N 64.14W
61 L4 Grande Hallet Belgium 50.41N 5.02E
70 C4 Grande, I France 48.48N 3.35W
81 Q12 Grande, I Italy 40.15N 17.53E
117 C6 Grande, I Pará Brazil
118 G8 Grande, I Rio de Janeiro Brazil 23.15S 44.25W
81 E8 Grande, I Sicily 37.53N 12.28E
121 G4 Grande Inferior, Cuchilla mts Uruguay
121 L6 Grande, L Argentina
117 D10 Grande, L Brazil
117 B6 Grande, L Pará Brazil
77 K2 Grande, L Spain 39.27N 3.20W
77 K2 Grande, L Spain 39.30N 3.14W
79 M6 Grande, Monte Italy 44.01N 12.01E
81 E9 Grande, Mte Pantelleria I Italy 36.48N 12.00E
81 E8 Grande, Mte Sicily 37.53N 12.46E
120 G8 Grande ó Guapay, R Bolivia
26 B12 Grande Passe Rodriguez I Ind Oc 19.46S 63.27E
101 O8 Grande Prairie Alberta 55.10N 118.52W
120 D11 Grande, Pta C Chile 25.05S 70.46W
121 L9 Grande, R Argentina/Chile
118 G2 Grande, R Bahia Brazil
Grande, R Guinea-Bissausee Corubal, R
121 B6 Grande, R Mendoza Arg
118 E6 Grande, R Minas Gerais Brazil
115 M3 Grande, R Nicaragua
120 B6 Grande, R Peru
118 H9 Grande, R Rio de Janeiro Brazil
71 H10 Grande Rade B France 43.05N 5.57E
90 F2 Grand Erg de Bilma sand dune reg Niger
88 N7 Grand Erg Occidental sand dune reg Algeria
88 Q7 Grand Erg Oriental sand dune reg Algeria
98 H5 Grande Rivière Quebec 48.24N 64.30W
116 P1 Grande Rivière Trinidad & Tobago 10.50N 61.03W
97 M6 Grande Rivière de la Baleine Quebec
116 H5 Grande Rivière du-Nord Haiti 19.36N 72.10W
26 T13 Grande Rivière Noire B Mauritius, Indian Oc
26 V12 Grande Rivière S.E Mauritius, Indian Oc 20.17S 57.46E
79 B3 Grande Rochère mt Italy 45.49N 7.04E
110 B4 Grande Ronde Oregon 45.06N 123.37W
110 H4 Grande Ronde R Oregon
121 D3 Grande Sa mts Argentina
120 G3 Grande, Sa mts Rondônia Brazil
119 H6 Grande, Sa mt Roraima Brazil 2.35N 60.45W
120 D9 Grande, Salar salt pan Chile
71 K5 Grande Sassière mt France 45.30N 7.00E
98 C5 Grandes Bergeronnes Quebec 48.16N 69.35W
70 M2 Grandes Dalles, les France 49.49N 0.31E
66 E8 Grandes Jorasses mts France/Italy
72 B8 Grandes Landes reg France
99 S6 Grandes Piles Quebec 46.41N 72.42W
71 J6 Grandes Rousses mts France
120 F10 Grandes, Salinas salt pans Arg
70 N2 Grandes Ventes, les France 49.46N 1.15E
98 L7 Grand Etang C Breton I, Nova Scotia 46.32N 61.02W
116 P5 Grand Etang L Grenada, W I 12.06N 61.42W
26 U15 Grand Etang L Réunion Ind Oc 21.05S 55.39E
116 N3 Grande Terre I Guadeloupe W I
66 K7 Grande, V Italy
98 G4 Grande Vallèe Quebec 49.14N 65.08W
116 N3 Grande Vigie, Pte. de la Guadeloupe W I 16.31N 61.28W
93 K6 Grand Falls Kenya 0.17S 38.01E
98 E6 Grand Falls New Brunswick 47.02N 67.46W
98 R5 Grand Falls Newfoundland 48.57N 55.40W
112 E4 Grandfalls Texas 31.21N 102.52W
111 N6 Grand Falls waterfall Arizona 35.29N 111.15W
98 E8 Grand Falls L Maine
105 F1 Grandfather Mt N Carolina 36.06N 81.50W
109 M7 Grandfield Oklahoma 34.14N 98.43W
71 L6 Grand Fond Albaron mt France 45.21N 7.05E
101 O11 Grand Forks Br Col 49.02N 118.30W
108 N2 Grand Forks N Dakota 47.57N 97.05W
69 C2 Grand Fort Philippe France 51.00N 2.06E
70 G6 Grand Fougeray, le France 47.44N 1.43W
71 K7 Grand Glaiza, Pic du mt France/Italy 44.50N 6.53E
Grandglise see Stambruges-Grandglise
66 E8 Grand Golliaz mt Switz/Italy 45.52N 7.07E
103 E2 Grand Gorge New York 42.22N 74.32W
116 J5 Grand Gosier Haiti 18.13N 71.55W
61 O5 Grand-Halleux Belgium 50.20N 5.55E
61 M5 Grandhan Belgium 50.20N 5.25E
84 Z20 Grand Harbour Malta
98 F9 Grand Harbour New Brunswick 44.41N 66.46W
106 H6 Grand Haven Michigan 43.04N 86.13W
99 M9 Grand I New York 43.02N 79.00W
105 F8 Grandin Florida 29.43N 81.56W
107 F5 Grandin Missouri 36.50N 90.50W
108 O2 Grandin N Dakota 47.14N 97.00W
101 O3 Grandin, L N W Terr
42 F5 Grandioznyy, Pik pk U.S.S.R. 53.54N 96.09E
107 G11 Grand Island Louisiana 30.09N 89.21W
106 H3 Grand Island Michigan 46.32N 86.40W
108 M9 Grand Island Nebraska 40.56N 98.21W
107 G12 Grand Isle Louisiana 29.12N 90.00W
104 Q6 Grand Isle Maine 47.18N 68.10W
104 M2 Grand Isle Vermont 44.44N 73.18W
109 B2 Grand Junction Colorado 39.04N 108.33W
108 Q7 Grand Junction Iowa 42.01N 94.14W
106 H7 Grand Junction Michigan 42.24N 86.04W
107 G6 Grand Junction Tennessee 35.03N 89.10W
107 E11 Grand L Louisiana
98 E7 Grand L New Brunswick/Maine
89 G9 Grand Lahau Ivory Coast 5.09N 5.01W
109 E1 Grand Lake Colorado 40.15N 105.50W
107 C11 Grand Lake Louisiana 30.01N 93.16W
107 D12 Grand Lake Louisiana 29.52N 92.45W
107 G12 Grand Lake Louisiana 29.41N 89.49W
104 S1 Grand Lake Maine
106 L4 Grand Lake Michigan 45.18N 83.30W
98 F8 Grand Lake New Brunswick
98 P4 Grand Lake Newfoundland
104 A6 Grand Lake Ohio
109 Q5 Grand Lake O' The Cherokees Oklahoma
104 Q7 Grand Lakes L Maine 46.13N 68.50W
106 K7 Grand Ledge Michigan 42.45N 85.44W
61 K4 Grand-Leez Belgium 50.35N 4.46E
71 G6 Grand-Lemps, le France 45.24N 5.25E
72 A1 Grand Lieu, Lac de France 47.06N 1.40W
53 H5 Grandløse Denmark 55.41N 11.45E
104 Q7 Grand L Seboeis Maine 46.16N 68.38W
70 L6 Grand-Lucé, le France 47.52N 0.28E
98 F9 Grand Manan isld New Brunswick
104 S2 Grand Manan Chan Maine
106 J3 Grand Marais Michigan 46.39N 86.00W
106 D2 Grand Marais Minnesota 47.45N 90.20W
61 N5 Grandmenil Belgium 50.17N 5.40E
99 S6 Grand-Mère Quebec 46.36N 72.41W
109 C2 Grand Mesa Colorado 39.03N 107.55W
98 E2 Grandmesnil, L Quebec
61 E4 Grandmetz Belgium 50.37N 3.38E
101 P10 Grand Mt Br Col 51.02N 117.22W
71 K5 Grand Mt France 45.37N 6.32E
66 E7 Grand Muveran mt Switzerland 46.14N 7.08E
98 R2 Grandois Newfoundland 51.07N 55.46W
66 N7 Grandola Italy 46.03N 9.13E
76 B12 Grândola Portugal 38.10N 8.34W
76 B12 Grândola, Sa.de mts Portugal
65 O2 Grándorf Czechoslovakia 49.43N 16.28E
107 C2 Grand Pass Missouri 39.11N 93.26W
9 A12 Grand Passage str New Caledonia
66 A7 Grand Piton mt France 46.06N 6.07E
89 K8 Grand Popo Benin 6.19N 1.57E
106 E2 Grand Portage Minnesota 47.57N 89.41W
112 N9 Grand Prairie Texas 32.45N 97.00W
69 H5 Grandpré France 49.21N 4.52E
72 F2 Grand Pressigny, le France 46.56N 0.48E
70 N3 Grand Quevilly France 49.26N 1.03E
106 J6 Grand, R Michigan
104 D5 Grand R Ohio
100 S5 Grand Rapids Manitoba 53.12N 99.19W
106 J7 Grand Rapids Michigan 42.57N 86.40W
108 R2 Grand Rapids Minnesota 47.13N 93.31W
9 C14 Grand Récif du Sud reef New Caledonia
61 G5 Grand-Reng Belgium 50.20N 4.05E
61 G6 Grandrieu Belgium 50.12N 4.10E
71 D7 Grandrieu France 44.47N 3.38E
71 D5 Grandrif France 45.31N 3.48E
71 E4 Grandris France 46.03N 4.28E
98 M8 Grand River C Breton I, Nova Scotia 45.38N 60.41W
108 R9 Grand River Iowa 40.49N 93.58W
116 L3 Grand' Rivière Martinique W I 14.52N 61.11W
61 K4 Grand-Rosière-Hottomont Belgium 50.38N 4.52E
116 P5 Grand Roy Grenada, W I 12.08N 61.44W
26 U12 Grand R, S.E Mauritius, Indian Oc
66 E8 Grand St.Bernard pass Switz/Italy 45.53N 7.11E
112 M3 Grand Saline Texas 32.41N 95.43W
117 B2 Grand Santi Fr Guiana 4.19N 54.24W
71 G6 Grand-Serre, le France 45.16N 5.06E
66 D8 Grands Mulets mt France 45.53N 6.52E
66 C4 Grandson Switzerland 46.49N 6.39E
107 G12 Grand Terre Is Louisiana
110 P6 Grand Teton mt Wyoming 43.45N 110.50W
110 P6 Grand Teton Nat. Park Wyoming
107 G4 Grand Tower Illinois 37.37N 89.30W
58 J5 Grandtully Castle Tayside Scotland 56.38N 3.49W
55 B3 Grand Union Canal London/Herts/Bucks England
72 J6 Grand-Vabre France 44.38N 2.21E
66 F2 Grandval Switzerland 47.16N 7.26E
72 L6 Grandval, Barrage de France 44.58N 3.07E
109 B2 Grand Valley Colorado 39.27N 108.03W
99 K9 Grand Valley Ontario 43.54N 80.20W
71 H2 Grandvelle-et-le-Perrenot France 47.31N 6.00E
71 H7 Grand Veymont mt France 44.53N 5.30E
110 J7 Grand View Idaho 43.00N 116.06W
100 R7 Grandview Manitoba 51.11N 100.41W
112 K3 Grandview Texas 32.16N 97.12W
110 F3 Grandview Washington 46.16N 119.54W
66 E5 Grandvillard Switzerland 46.32N 7.06E
71 K1 Grandvillars France 47.33N 6.58E
106 J7 Grandville Michigan 42.54N 85.48W
69 H4 Grandville, la France 49.47N 4.48E
69 M7 Grandvillers France 48.15N 6.40E
69 B4 Grandvilliers France 49.40N 1.56E
61 M7 Grandvoir Belgium 49.52N 5.22E
111 L5 Grand Wash crater Arizona
111 L6 Grand Wash Cliffs mts Arizona
71 F7 Grâne France 44.43N 4.56E
51 C6 Grane Norway 65.35N 13.25E
52 L2 Graned Sweden 64.30N 18.20E
75 K4 Grañén Spain 41.56N 0.22W
75 P4 Granera, Sierra mts Spain
79 B5 Granero, Monte Italy 44.43N 7.04E
121 D1 Graneros Argentina 27.35S 65.29W
121 B5 Graneros Chile 34.05S 70.45W
121 L7 Gran Escorial reg Argentina
99 N5 Granet, L Quebec
59 E6 Graney, L Clare Irish Rep 52.59N 8.40W
52 H6 Grangärde Sweden 60.15N 15.00E
57 G3 Grange Cumbria Eng 54.33N 3.09W
57 H4 Grange Lancs Eng 54.12N 2.55W
104 F2 Grange Maryland 39.15N 76.30W
59 E3 Grange Sligo Irish Rep 54.24N 8.31W
59 K4 Grangebellew Louth Irish Rep 53.49N 6.20W
55 J2 Grange Hill Essex Eng 51.36N 0.05E
116 H1 Grange Hill Jamaica, W I 18.19N 78.11W
58 J6 Grangemouth Central Scotland 56.01N 3.44W
71 E6 Grangent, Barrage de France 45.28N 4.15E
71 K4 Grange, Pte. de France 46.16N 6.47E
107 E1 Granger Missouri 40.28N 91.59W
112 K5 Granger Texas 30.44N 97.28W
110 E3 Granger Washington 46.21N 120.10W
110 Q8 Granger Wyoming 41.37N 109.58W
66 F6 Granges Valais Switz 46.16N 7.28E
66 D4 Granges Vaud Switz 46.46N 6.53E
52 J6 Grängesberg Sweden 60.06N 15.00E
66 B4 Granges St. Marie France 46.48N 6.17E
69 M7 Granges-sur-Vologne France 48.09N 6.47E
110 J4 Grangeville Idaho 45.56N 116.07W
118 B9 Gran Guardia Argentina 25.50S 58.54W
53 X21 Granheim Norway 58.59N 7.35E
66 J2 Gränichen Switzerland 47.22N 8.07E
52 K3 Graninge Sweden 63.03N 17.00E
101 K8 Granisle Br Columbia 54.55N 126.14W
109 L7 Granite Oklahoma 34.58N 99.24W
110 G5 Granite Oregon 44.49N 118.25W
94 K4 Granite S Africa 23.08S 29.41E
108 E8 Granite Wyoming 41.06N 105.09W
101 L10 Granite Bay Br Col 50.14N 125.17W
107 M12 Granite City Illinois 38.43N 90.04W
98 P5 Granite Dam Newfoundland
108 P5 Granite Falls Minnesota 44.49N 95.31W
105 F2 Granite Falls N Carolina 35.48N 81.26W
110 D1 Granite Falls Washington 48.05N 121.58W
113 N7 Granite I Alaska 59.40N 149.46W
106 G3 Granite I Michigan 46.44N 87.24W
110 H9 Granite Mt Nevada 40.19N 117.49W
111 J7 Granite Mts California 34.46N 115.43W
111 J8 Granite Mts ra California 33.58N 115.07W
111 H6 Granite Pass California 35.25N 116.34W
110 Q4 Granite Pk Montana 45.10N 109.50W
110 H8 Granite Pk Nevada 41.41N 117.36W
110 M9 Granite Pk Utah 40.07N 113.16W
110 R7 Granite Pk Wyoming 42.32N 108.54W
106 G3 Granite Pt Michigan 46.38N 87.27W
110 F9 Granite Ra Nevada
113 Q6 Granite Range Alaska
13 B5 Granites, The N Terr Australia 20.38S 130.22E
13 B5 Granites, The pk N Terr Australia 20.37S 130.20E
105 F4 Graniteville S Carolina 33.34N 81.48W
103 H8 Graniteville Staten I, N Y 40.38N 74.10W
45 J9 Granitnoye Ukraine U.S.S.R. 47.28N 37.51E
117 G8 Granito Brazil 7.44S 39.35W
43 L5 Granitogorsk Kazakhstan U.S.S.R. 42.38N 73.24E
81 E8 Granitola Sicily 37.34N 12.34E
81 E8 Granitola, C Sicily 37.33N 12.41E
11 F8 Granity New Zealand 41.38S 171.54E
63 T4 Granitz E Germany 54.23N 13.37E
117 G6 Granja Brazil 3.07S 40.51W
76 B6 Granja Portugal 41.03N 8.39W
76 E6 Granja Portugal 41.01N 7.24W
76 E12 Granja Portugal 38.18N 7.15W
75 L5 Granja de Escarpe Spain 41.25N 0.21E
76 H5 Granja de Moreruela Spain 41.48N 5.44W
77 E4 Granja de Torrehermosa Spain 38.19N 5.35W
76 C15 Granja do Marquês airport Portugal 38.50N 9.20W
116 J5 Granja, Pta. de la Dominican Rep 19.56N 71.38W
77 F4 Granjuela, La Spain 38.22N 5.21W
51 L11 Grankulla Finland 60.12N 24.45E
52 K9 Grankullavik Sweden 57.20N 17.06E
100 F9 Granlea Alberta 49.41N 111.12W
52 H3 Granlunda Sweden 63.33N 14.15E
79 O2 Gran Monte Italy 46.17N 13.22E
115 F3 Gran Morelos Mexico 28.15N 106.30W
52 H8 Gränna Sweden 58.02N 14.30E
107 B7 Grannis Arkansas 34.17N 94.21W
108 J1 Grano N Dakota 48.38N 101.36W
75 P4 Granollers Spain 41.37N 2.18E
52 L2 Granön Sweden 64.17N 18.40E
120 C4 Gran Pajonal hill ridge Peru
120 E9 Gran Pampa Salada salt L Bolivia
79 B3 Gran Paradiso mts Italy 45.33N 7.17E
79 L1 Gran Pilastro mt Switz/Italy 46.58N 11.45E
109 D7 Gran Quivira Nat.Mon New Mexico 34.16N 106.06W
66 E8 Gran San Bernardo, Valle del Italy
80 J4 Gran Sasso d'Italia mts Italy
63 S6 Gransee E Germany 53.00N 13.10E
59 L2 Gransha Antrim N Ireland 54.48N 5.43W
105 G10 Grant Florida 27.55N 80.34W
108 Q8 Grant Iowa 41.06N 94.58W
106 J6 Grant Michigan 43.20N 85.49W
110 M4 Grant Montana 45.00N 113.04W
108 J9 Grant Nebraska 40.50N 101.42W
109 P8 Grant Oklahoma 33.56N 95.32W
99 D2 Grant Ontario 50.06N 86.18W
96 T11 Gran Tarajal Fuerteventura Canary Is 28.12N 14.02W
107 B1 Grant City Missouri 40.29N 94.25W
113 L4 Grant Creek Alaska 65.11N 152.59W
14 D7 Grant Duff Ra W Australia
57 M7 Grantham Lincs Eng 52.55N 0.39W
13 C1 Grant I N Terr Australia 11.11S 132.55E
101 P3 Grant L N W Terr
113 D4 Grantley Harbor Alaska
111 F3 Grant, Mt Nevada 38.34N 118.48W
111 G2 Grant, Mt Nevada 39.42N 117.48W
14 E8 Grant, Mt W Australia 28.10S 123.27E
58 K7 Granton Lothian Scotland 55.59N 3.14W
103 D2 Granton New York 42.07N 75.16W
99 J9 Granton Ontario 43.13N 81.20W
106 D5 Granton Wisconsin 44.35N 90.28W
79 C3 Gran Tournalin mt Italy 45.52N 7.41E
58 J4 Grantown-on-Spey Grampian Scotland 57.20N 3.38W
111 J3 Grant Ra Nevada
14 E4 Grant Ra W Australia
52 L2 Granträsk Sweden 64.20N 18.20E
113 M6 Grants Alaska 61.13N 150.58W
109 C6 Grants New Mexico 35.10N 107.51W
106 B4 Grantsburg Wisconsin 45.47N 92.40W
110 L3 Grantsdale Montana 46.12N 114.10W
58 M7 Grantshouse Borders Scotland 55.53N 2.19W
110 B7 Grants Pass Oregon 42.26N 123.20W
14 D4 Grant Spring W Australia 19.44S 121.31E
110 N9 Grantsville Utah 40.36N 112.29W
104 D8 Grantsville W Virginia 38.55N 81.07W
105 C4 Grantville Georgia 33.14N 84.51W
103 A6 Grantville Pennsylvania 40.23N 76.39W
100 D9 Granum Alberta 49.54N 113.29W
70 G4 Granville France 48.50N 1.35W
106 E8 Granville Illinois 41.15N 89.16W
108 P6 Granville Iowa 43.00N 95.51W
103 J2 Granville Massachusetts 42.04N 72.52W
108 K1 Granville N Dakota 48.18N 100.51W
104 M3 Granville New York 43.24N 73.16W
104 C6 Granville Ohio 40.03N 82.31W
104 H6 Granville Pennsylvania 40.33N 77.38W
12 K7 Granville dist Sydney, N S W
98 G9 Granville Ferry Nova Scotia 44.45N 65.33W
100 R2 Granville L Manitoba
103 A3 Granville Summit Pennsylvania 41.44N 76.43W
53 V17 Granvin Norway 60.33N 6.44E
79 J2 Gran Zebrù mt Italy 46.28N 10.34E
63 P5 Granzin E Germany 53.31N 11.56E
75 K10 Grao, El Spain 39.00N 0.10W
77 Q3 Grao, El Spain 38.59N 0.10W
118 G5 Grão Mogol Brazil 16.32S 42.50W
112 M4 Grapeland Texas 31.30N 95.31W
111 F7 Grapevine California 34.56N 118.56W
112 N8 Grapevine Texas 32.54N 97.06W
112 N8 Grapevine Dam Texas 32.56N 97.03W
111 G5 Grapevine Mts California/Nevada
112 K3 Grapevine Res Texas 33.00N 97.05W
61 M7 Grapfontaine Belgium 49.49N 5.24E
79 L3 Grappa, Monte Italy 45.52N 11.49E
116 G5 Grappler Bank Caribbean Sea
52 J6 Gräsberg Sweden 60.15N 15.15E
63 M8 Grasdorf W Germany 52.07N 10.10E
53 U17 Gråsida mts Norway 60.35N 6.20E
53 U18 Gråsida mt Norway 60.12N 6.16E
94 L5 Graskop S Africa 24.58S 30.49E
101 S3 Gras, L. de N W Terr
66 C4 Gras, les France 46.59N 6.32E
57 G4 Grasmere Cumbria Eng 54.28N 3.02W
95 L2 Grasmere S Africa 26.26S 27.52E
52 L6 Gräsö Sweden 60.22N 18.30E
103 B9 Grasonville Maryland 38.58N 76.12W
53 T14 Grasøyane isld Norway 62.26N 5.46E
95 H5 Graspan S Africa 29.19S 24.27E
95 H6 Graspan salt pan S Africa 30.40S 24.30E
94 C6 Grasplatz Namibia 26.43S 15.18E
104 K2 Grass R New York
81 M2 Grassano Italy 40.38N 16.17E
108 B6 Grass Creek Wyoming 43.56N 108.39W
71 K9 Grasse France 43.40N 6.56E
99 M3 Grasset, L Quebec
57 K4 Grassington N Yorks Eng 54.04N 1.59W
110 C8 Grass L California 41.38N 122.13W
112 F2 Grassland Texas 33.08N 101.36W
11 J8 Grassmere, L New Zealand 41.44S 174.11E
14 D10 Grass Patch W Australia 33.14S 121.40E
100 T3 Grass R Manitoba
99 Q2 Grass R New York
110 R2 Grassrange Montana 47.02N 108.49W
95 J7 Grassridge Dam res S Africa 31.45S 25.27E
99 S2 Grass River Lock New York 44.59N 74.48W
100 Q4 Grass River Prov. Park Manitoba
111 C2 Grass Valley California 39.13N 121.04W
110 E4 Grass Valley Oregon 45.22N 120.47W
12 G7 Grassy King I, Tasmania 40.04S 144.09E
108 G2 Grassy Butte N Dakota 47.26N 103.18W
116 F3 Grassy Cr Andros Bahamas 23.53N 77.49W
100 G7 Grassy Island L Alberta 51.50N 110.20W
104 E8 Grassy Knob mt W Virginia 38.04N 80.31W
100 F9 Grassy Lake Alberta 49.50N 111.42W
94 Q12 Grassy Park Cape Town S Africa 34.02S 18.31E
53 D7 Gråsten Denmark 54.55N 9.37E
52 G8 Grästorp Sweden 58.19N 12.45E
51 D5 Gråtånes Norway 66.54N 14.44E
51 F3 Gratangen Norway 68.40N 17.40E
72 G9 Gratens France 43.19N 1.06E
98 T5 Grate's Cove Newfoundland 48.09N 52.56W
60 M15 Grathem Netherlands 51.12N 5.51E
106 D7 Gratiot Wisconsin 42.34N 90.02W
104 A7 Gratis Ohio 39.38N 84.32W
51 H6 Gråträsk Sweden 65.30N 19.50E
71 K10 Gratteloup, Col de pass France 43.23N 6.37E
81 G8 Gratteri Sicily 37.58N 13.58E
65 M7 Gratwein Austria 47.08N 15.20E
61 G4 Graty Belgium 50.38N 4.00E
103 A5 Gratz Pennsylvania 40.37N 76.43W
87 H6 Graua Ethiopia 9.07N 41.51E
53 D4 Grauballe Denmark 56.13N 9.38E
66 N5 Graubünden canton Switzerland
71 E9 Grau-du-Roi, le France 43.32N 4.08E
66 O4 Graue Hörner mts Switzerland
72 H8 Graulhet France 43.45N 1.58E
75 L3 Graus Spain 42.11N 0.20E
61 J5 Graux Belgium 50.20N 4.43E
75 F3 Grávalos Spain 42.06N 2.01W
117 J9 Gravata Brazil 8.10S 35.32W
117 G8 Gravata R Brazil
121 J2 Gravataí Brazil 29.56S 51.00W
53 Y15 Gravdalen V Norway 61.01N 8.08E
60 L12 Grave Netherlands 51.45N 5.45E
79 F2 Gravedona Italy 46.09N 9.18E
71 J6 Grave, la France 45.03N 6.18E
100 L9 Gravelbourg Saskatchewan 49.53N 106.33W
101 V4 Gravel Hill L N W Terr
69 C2 Gravelines France 50.59N 2.08E
70 H5 Gravelle, la France 48.05N 1.00W
79 D3 Gravellona Toce Italy 45.56N 8.26E
69 L5 Gravelotte France 49.07N 6.03E
99 L8 Gravenhurst Ontario 44.55N 79.22W
64 E3 Grävenwiesbach W Germany 50.23N 8.28E
110 L3 Grave Pk Idaho 46.26N 114.45W
72 B4 Grave, Pte de France 45.35N 1.04W
56 M5 Gravesend Kent Eng 51.27N 0.24E
12 K3 Gravesend New S Wales 29.35S 150.20E
103 N2 Graves Lt. Ho., The Massachusetts 42.22N 70.53W
71 F9 Graveson France 43.51N 4.47E
107 B5 Gravette Arkansas 36.25N 94.29W
53 W17 Gravhalst pass Norway 60.43N 7.05E
84 D4 Graviá Greece 38.40N 22.26E
70 N3 Gravigny France 49.03N 1.11E
70 L2 Graville France 49.31N 0.10E
81 M2 Gravina R Italy
81 M2 Gravina di Puglia Italy 40.48N 16.25E
113 W9 Gravina I Alaska 55.20N 131.45W
58 D2 Gravir Lewis, W Isles Scotland 58.03N 6.26W
108 Q9 Gravity Iowa 40.45N 94.44W
53 D3 Gravlev Denmark 56.51N 9.50E
116 H5 Gravois, Pte.-à- Haiti 18.02N 73.56W
67 O12 Gravone R Corsica
57 H4 Gravrigg Cumbria Eng 54.22N 2.39W
52 F2 Gravvik Norway 64.58N 11.45E
106 J5 Grawn Michigan 44.41N 85.41W
71 H2 Gray France 47.27N 5.35E
105 D4 Gray Georgia 33.01N 83.33W
108 Q8 Gray Iowa 41.49N 94.59W
104 P3 Gray Maine 43.52N 70.20W
109 K5 Gray Oklahoma 36.33N 100.50W
100 N8 Gray Saskatchewan 50.12N 104.31W
72 B5 Grayan et l'Hôpital France 45.27N 1.07W
101 T5 Gray L N W Terr
110 A3 Grayland Washington 46.48N 124.05W
113 G5 Grayling Alaska 62.55N 160.04W
106 K5 Grayling Michigan 44.40N 84.43W
101 L6 Grayling R Br Col
101 C2 Grayling Fork
113 R3 Grayling Fork, R Alaska
13 C4 Grayling, Mt N Terr Australia 18.14S 133.50E
56 M5 Grays Essex Eng 51.29N 0.20E
110 A3 Grays Harb Washington
110 O6 Grays L Idaho 43.04N 111.25W
106 F7 Grays L Illinois 42.21N 88.02W
110 O6 Grays L.Outlet R Idaho
104 C8 Grayson Kentucky 38.21N 82.59W
107 D9 Grayson Louisiana 32.03N 92.05W
100 P8 Grayson Saskatchewan 50.45N 102.41W
99 A2 Grayson L Ontario 50.53N 89.25W
109 E2 Grays Pk Colorado 39.37N 105.47W
106 J4 Grays Reef Lt.Ho Michigan 45.45N 85.10W
110 B3 Grays River Washington 46.22N 123.36W
107 K11 Grayton Beach Florida 30.20N 86.10W
107 H3 Grayville Illinois 38.15N 88.00W
45 G6 Grayvoron U.S.S.R. 50.29N 35.40E
65 M7 Graz Austria 47.05N 15.22E
71 E6 Grazac France 45.11N 4.10E
77 F7 Grazalema Spain 36.46N 5.23W
77 F7 Grazalema, Sierra de mts Spain
61 L3 Grazen Belgium 50.52N 5.07E
82 G8 Grdelica Yugoslavia 42.55N 22.03E
89 E8 Gre Liberia 6.45N 8.44W
82 K6 Greaca, Lacul L Romania 44.05N 26.25E
72 H6 Gréalou France 44.32N 1.52E
57 L6 Greasbrough S Yorks Eng 53.28N 1.21W
101 M4 Greasy L N W Terr 62.55N 122.17W
57 H3 Great Asby Cumbria Eng 54.31N 2.30W
9 S3 Great Astrolabe Reef Fiji 18.45S 178.30E
Great Aughrabies Falls see Groot Aughrabies Falls
10 F8 Great Australian Bight Australia
56 M4 Great Baddow Essex Eng 51.43N 0.29E
116 E2 Great Bahama Bank Bahamas
56 M4 Great Bardfield Essex Eng 51.57N 0.26E
13 G1 Great Barrier Reef Australia
103 H2 Great Barrington Massachusetts 42.12N 73.22W
110 J9 Great Basin Nevada
26 U9 Great Basses isld Sri Lanka 6.11N 81.29E
104 P3 Great Bay New Hampshire
103 F7 Great Bay New Jersey
101 L3 Great Bear R N W Terr
101 N2 Great Bear L N W Terr
109 M3 Great Bend Kansas 38.22N 98.47W
108 O3 Great Bend N Dakota 46.09N 96.49W
103 C3 Great Bend Pennsylvania 41.58N 75.45W
56 O3 Great Blakenham Suffolk Eng 52.06N 1.05E
59 A7 Great Blasket I Kerry Irish Rep 52.05N 10.32W
98 F3 Great Boule I Quebec 50.09N 66.18W
98 R2 Great Brehat Newfoundland 51.26N 55.31W
Great Britain see United Kingdom of Great Britain and N Ireland
57 H6 Great Budworth Cheshire Eng 53.18N 2.31W
98 Q5 Great Burnt L Newfoundland
104 G7 Great Cacapon W Virginia 39.37N 78.20W
105 L7 Great Camanoe, I Virgin Is 18.30N 64.35W
56 K2 Great Casterton Leics Eng 52.41N 0.32W
56 N5 Great Chart Kent Eng 51.09N 0.50E
56 M3 Great Chesterford Cambs Eng 52.04N 0.11E
56 O4 Great Clacton Essex Eng 51.49N 1.09E
28 G6 Great Coco I Andaman Is
57 K7 Great Cubley Derbys Eng 52.57N 1.44W
56 K2 Great Dalby Leics Eng 52.44N 0.54W
100 K6 Great Deer Saskatchewan 52.36N 107.05W
109 C1 Great Divide Colorado 40.47N 107.51W
10 K5 Great Dividing Ra Qnsld/N S W
57 N4 Great Driffield Humberside Eng 54.01N 0.26W
99 H7 Great Duck I Ontario 45.40N 82.58W
56 M4 Great Dunmow Essex Eng 51.53N 0.22E
56 M4 Great Easton Essex Eng 51.54N 0.20E
103 E8 Great Egg Harbor R New Jersey
103 E8 Great Egg Harbor Inlet New Jersey
56 N2 Great Ellingham Norfolk Eng 52.32N 0.57E
123 C9 Greater Antarctica Antarctica
116 D4 Greater Antilles islds West Indies
Greater Khingan Range see Da Hinggan Ling
22 M3 Greater Khingan Range mt ra Nei Monggol Zizhiqu China
57 J6 Greater Manchester co Eng
11 H1 Great Exhibition B New Zealand
119 H5 Great Fall Guyana 5.42N 61.07W
110 O2 Great Falls Montana 47.30N 111.16W
105 G3 Great Falls S Carolina 34.34N 80.56W
107 L6 Great Falls Dam Tennessee 35.48N 83.39W
107 L6 Great Falls L Tennessee
56 N3 Great Finborough Suffolk Eng 52.10N 0.56E
95 K9 Great Fish R S Africa
54 M6 Great Fisher Bank North Sea
95 L9 Great Fish Pt S Africa 33.31S 27.07E
11 K7 Greatford New Zealand 40.06S 175.25E
57 G4 Great Gable mt Cumbria Eng 54.29N 3.13W
56 J2 Great Glen Leics Eng 52.35N 1.02W
58 G4 Great Glen, The V Highland Scotland
116 K2 Great Goat I Jamaica, W I 17.52N 77.03W
57 M7 Great Gonerby Lincs Eng 52.56N 0.40W
105 K11 Great Guana Cay isld Bahamas 26.41N 77.07W
116 F2 Great Guana Cay isld Bahamas 24.04N 76.20W
57 L3 Greatham Cleveland Eng 54.39N 1.14W
56 K5 Greatham Hants Eng 51.04N 0.54W
98 Q3 Great Harbour Deep Newfoundland 50.22N 56.32W
57 J5 Great Harwood Lancs Eng 53.48N 2.24W
11 A12 Great I New Zealand 46.00S 166.33E
11 G1 Great I Three Kings Is New Zealand 34.09S 172.08E
105 H11 Great Isaac I Bahamas 26.02N 79.05W
95 E8 Great Karroo reg S Africa
95 L8 Great Kei R S Africa
95 L8 Great Kei Drift S Africa 32.16S 27.40E
13 K6 Great Keppel isld Queensland 23.10S 150.58E
105 K3 Great L N Carolina 34.52N 77.04W
12 H8 Great L Tasmania
57 N5 Great Limber Lincs Eng 53.34N 0.19W
56 G3 Great Malvern Hereford & Worcs Eng 52.07N 2.19W
56 N2 Great Massingham Norfolk Eng 52.46N 0.40E

11 K3 **Great Mercury I** New Zealand 36.38S 175.48E
56 K4 **Great Missenden** Bucks Eng 51.43N 0.43W
57 J3 **Great Musgrave** Cumbria Eng 54.31N 2.21W
103 N7 **Great Neck** New York 40.48N 73.44W
28 J7 **Great Nicobar** *isld* Nicobar Is
15 G8 **Great North East Chan** Qnsld/Papua New Guinea
85 L7 **Great Oasis, The** Egypt
56 L4 **Great Offley** Herts Eng 51.56N 0.21W
57 F6 **Great Ormes Hd** Gwynedd Wales 53.21N 3.53W
56 M2 **Great Ouse, R** Norfolk England
95 G4 **Great Pan, The** *salt pan* S Africa 28.18S 23.35E
15 G7 **Great Papuan Plat** Papua New Guinea
116 J2 **Great Pedro Bluff** *C* Jamaica, W I 17.51N 77.45W
57 H5 **Great Plumpton** Lancs Eng 53.48N 2.56W
104 R2 **Great Pond** Maine 44.56N 68.16W
56 K2 **Great Ponton** Lincs Eng 52.52N 0.38W
103 O4 **Great Pt** Massachusetts 41.23N 70.03W
98 G10 **Great Pubnico L** Nova Scotia
103 N3 **Great Quittacas Pond** *L* Massachusetts
116 H1 **Great R** Jamaica, W I
92 G5 **Great Ruaha** *R* Tanzania
105 J11 **Great Sale Cay** *isld* Bahamas
110 N8 **Great Salt L** Utah 41.10N 112.40W
110 M8 **Great Salt L.Des** Utah
109 M5 **Great Salt Plains Res** Oklahoma
103 L4 **Great Salt Pond** Rhode I
109 E4 **Great Sand Dunes, Nat.Mon** Colorado
14 D5 **Great Sandy Desert** W Australia
13 L7 **Great Sandy I** Queensland
96 A2 **Great Sd** Bermuda
9 R1 **Great Sea Reef** Fiji
113 Q9 **Great Sitkin I** Aleutian Is 52.05N 176.10W
101 Q5 **Great Slave L** N W Terr
57 L4 **Great Smeaton** N Yorks Eng 54.26N 1.29W
105 D2 **Great Smoky Mts** N Carolina
105 D2 **Great Smoky Mts.Nat.Park** Tenn/N Car
101 L7 **Great Snow Mt** Br Col 57.26N 124.00W
54 D13 **Great Sole Bank** Atlantic Oc
103 H5 **Great South Bay** Long I, N Y
103 J5 **Great South Beach** Long I, N Y
66 L4 **Great Spannort** *mt* Switzerland 46.47N 8.32E
105 K12 **Great Stirrup Cay** Bahamas 25.50N 77.55W
56 N6 **Greatstone-on-Sea** Kent Eng 50.58N 0.58E
96 B14 **Great Stone Tor** *mt* St Helena 15.59S 5.39W
59 K5 **Great Sugar Loaf** *mt* Wicklow Irish Rep 53.09N 6.09W
94 E4 **Great Ums** Namibia 23.09S 18.58E
95 P8 **Great Usutu** *R* S Africa/Moz
105 C2 **Great Val** Tennessee
10 F7 **Great Victoria Des** S Australia/W Australia
98 J8 **Great Village** Nova Scotia 45.25N 63.36W
56 N4 **Great Wakering** Essex Eng 51.34N 0.48E
56 M4 **Great Waltham** Essex Eng 51.48N 0.26E
104 S2 **Great Wass I** Maine 44.28N 67.35W
56 K3 **Great Weldon** Northants Eng 52.29N 0.38W
12 H8 **Great Western Tiers** *mts* Tasmania
25 D7 **Great West Torres Is** Burma
57 K4 **Great Whernside** *mt* N Yorks Eng 54.10N 1.59W
66 L4 **Great Windgälle** *mt* Switz 46.48N 8.44E
95 C9 **Great Winterhoek** *mt* S Africa 33.07S 19.10E
56 G3 **Great Witley** Hereford & Worcs Eng 52.18N 2.21W
56 P2 **Great Yarmouth** Norfolk Eng 52.37N 1.44E
52 F8 **Grebbestad** Sweden 58.42N 11.15E
64 G2 **Grebenau** W Germany 50.45N 9.29E
64 G3 **Grebenhain** W Germany 50.29N 9.21E
45 D6 **Grebenka** Ukraine U.S.S.R. 50.07N 32.25E
42 E3 **Grebenskiy Byk, Shiv** *falls* U.S.S.R. 58.10N 94.55E
63 K10 **Grebenstein** W Germany 51.27N 9.24E
65 K7 **Grebenzen** *mt* Austria 47.02N 14.20E
88 S11 **Greboun, Mt** Niger 20.00N 8.38E
79 F7 **Greco** *dist* Milan Italy
84 T15 **Greco, C** Cyprus 34.57N 34.05E
80 J5 **Greco, Monte** Italy 41.48N 14.00E
64 L5 **Greding** W Germany 49.02N 11.23E
76 J8 **Gredos, Sierra de** *mts* Spain
53 B6 **Gredstedbro** Denmark 55.24N 8.45E
121 K9 **Greec** Chile 52.30S 69.27W
49 J9 **Greece** *rep* S Europe
109 F1 **Greeley** Colorado 40.26N 104.43W
108 M8 **Greeley** Nebraska 41.34N 98.31W
103 E4 **Greeley** Pennsylvania 41.25N 75.00W
97 L1 **Greely Fd** N W Terr
41 P2 **Greem Bell, Ostrov** Franz Josef Land U.S.S.R.
109 N2 **Green** Kansas 39.26N 97.01W
107 J4 **Green** *R* Kentucky
110 Q9 **Green** *R* Utah/Colorado/Wyoming
105 G11 **Greenacres City** Florida 26.37N 80.09W
104 K9 **Greenbackville** Virginia 37.59N 75.26W
11 C3 **Green Bay** New Zealand 36.56S 174.41E
106 F5 **Green Bay** Wisconsin 44.32N 88.00W
106 G5 **Green Bay** Wisconsin
103 A8 **Greenbelt** Maryland 39.00N 76.53W
12 L4 **Green Bluff** New S Wales
103 A5 **Greenbrier** Pennsylvania 40.43N 76.38W
104 E8 **Greenbrier** *R* W Virginia
103 N2 **Greenbush** Massachusetts 42.11N 70.44W
106 L5 **Greenbush** Michigan 44.35N 83.20W
108 O1 **Greenbush** Minnesota 48.42N 96.10W
14 B10 **Greenbushes** W Australia 33.50S 116.00E
12 K6 **Green C** New S Wales 37.17S 150.03E
59 J1 **Greencastle** Donegal Irish Rep 55.12N 6.59W
59 K3 **Greencastle** Down N Ireland 54.02N 6.06W
107 K2 **Greencastle** Indiana 39.39N 86.51W
104 H7 **Greencastle** Pennsylvania 39.47N 77.44W
116 F2 **Green Cay** *isld* Bahamas 24.03N 77.12W
107 D1 **Green City** Missouri 40.15N 92.58W
100 B4 **Green Court** Alberta 54.00N 115.10W
105 F8 **Green Cove Springs** Florida 29.00N 81.42W
99 E8 **Green Cr** Ontario
103 E8 **Green Creek** New Jersey 39.03N 74.54W
103 G2 **Greendale** New York 42.12N 73.51W
108 S7 **Greene** Iowa 42.56N 92.46W
108 J1 **Greene** N Dakota 48.38N 101.37W
103 C2 **Greene** New York 42.20N 75.45W
103 L3 **Greene** Rhode I 41.42N 72.45W
63 L9 **Greene** W Germany 51.52N 9.57E
103 F2 **Greene** *co* New York
14 G6 **Greene, Mt** W Australia 23.12S 128.19E
105 E1 **Greeneville** Tennessee 36.10N 82.50W
111 C5 **Greenfield** California 36.20N 121.15W
111 E6 **Greenfield** California 35.15N 119.00W
57 G6 **Greenfield** Clwyd Wales 53.18N 3.13W
107 F2 **Greenfield** Illinois 39.21N 90.21W
107 L2 **Greenfield** Indiana 39.48N 85.46W
108 Q8 **Greenfield** Iowa 41.18N 94.27W
104 N4 **Greenfield** Massachusetts 42.36N 72.37W
107 C4 **Greenfield** Missouri 37.23N 93.50W
104 B7 **Greenfield** Ohio 39.21N 83.24W
109 M6 **Greenfield** Oklahoma 35.44N 98.24W
107 H5 **Greenfield** Tennessee 36.10N 88.48W
103 H4 **Greenfield Hill** Connecticut 41.11N 73.17W
103 E3 **Greenfield Park** New York 41.44N 74.31W
55 C3 **Greenford** London Eng 51.32N 0.21W
107 C5 **Green Forest** Arkansas 36.20N 93.25W
59 H4 **Greengates** Cavan Irish Rep 53.52N 7.26W
103 N2 **Green Harbor** Massachusetts 42.05N 70.40W
14 A9 **Green Hd** W Australia 30.03S 114.59E
57 H3 **Greenhead** Northumb Eng 54.59N 2.31W
116 O1 **Green Hill** Trinidad & Tobago 10.44N 61.34W
13 B1 **Greenhill I** N Terr Australia 11.40S 132.05E
11 C13 **Greenhills** New Zealand 46.34S 168.19E
14 B9 **Greenhills** W Australia 31.58S 117.01E
11 C1 **Greenhithe** New Zealand 36.46S 174.40E
111 F6 **Greenhorn Mts** California
57 K4 **Greenhow** N Yorks Eng 54.04N 1.49W
113 O6 **Green I** Alaska 60.15N 147.25W
23 B9 **Green I** Hong Kong 22.17N 114.06E
98 Q2 **Green I** Newfoundland 51.24N 56.33W
11 C13 **Green I** New Zealand 46.47S 168.36E
13 H3 **Green I** Queensland 16.43S 146.00E
14 B9 **Green I** W Australia 30.44S 115.08E
99 Q4 **Greening** Quebec 48.07N 75.00W
116 G1 **Green Island** Jamaica, W I 18.23N 78.17W
11 E12 **Green Island** New Zealand 45.54S 170.25E
19 J6 **Green Island B** Philippines
15 J1 **Green Islands** Papua New Guinea
11 A13 **Green Islets** New Zealand
101 N10 **Green L** Br Col 51.26N 121.12W
106 F6 **Green L** Wisconsin 43.49N 89.00W
106 F6 **Green L** Wisconsin
100 K4 **Green Lake** Saskatchewan 54.18N 107.49W
112 L7 **Green Lake** Texas 28.32N 96.49W
116 P6 **Greenland** Barbados 13.16N 59.35W
97 P1 **Greenland** *isld* N America
48 **Greenland** *terr* Arctic
48 G11 **Greenland Basin** Arctic Oc
48 C10 **Greenland-Iceland Rise** N Atlantic Oc
11 D12 **Greenland Res** New Zealand 45.26S 169.39E
95 L3 **Greenlands** S Africa 27.08S 27.41E
48 G10 **Greenland Sea** Arctic Oc
103 D6 **Green Lane** Pennsylvania 40.20N 75.28W
58 M7 **Greenlaw** Borders Scotland 55.43N 2.28W
109 O2 **Greenleaf** Kansas 39.43N 96.58W
58 J6 **Greenloaning** Tayside Scotland 56.14N 3.54W
57 F2 **Green Lowther** *mt* Strathclyde Scotland 55.23N 3.45W
98 P2 **Greenly I** Quebec 51.23N 57.12W
12 C5 **Greenly I** S Australia 34.39S 134.50E
11 L6 **Greenmeadows** New Zealand 39.32S 176.52E
109 D2 **Green Mountain Res** Colorado
96 B12 **Green Mt** Ascension I
104 M3 **Green Mts** Vermont
108 C7 **Green Mts** Wyoming
58 G7 **Greenock** Strathclyde Scotland 55.57N 4.45W
57 G4 **Greenodd** Cumbria Eng 54.14N 3.04W
59 K3 **Greenore** Louth Irish Rep 54.02N 6.08W
59 K7 **Greenore Pt** Wexford Irish Rep 52.15N 6.18W
113 R2 **Greenough Mt** Alaska 69.10N 141.40W
14 B8 **Greenough, R** W Australia
94 P11 **Green Point** *dist* Cape Town S Africa
105 G5 **Green Pond** South Carolina 32.43N 80.33W
103 K4 **Greenport** Long I, N Y 41.06N 72.22W
10 A12 **Green Pt** Macquarie I Pacific Oc 54.46S 158.48E
105 E2 **Green, R** N Carolina
98 D6 **Green, R** New Brunswick
111 O3 **Green R** Utah 39.00N 110.10W
103 H2 **Green River** New York 42.16N 73.28W
15 F5 **Green River** Papua New Guinea 3.54S 141.08E
110 Q8 **Green River** Wyoming 41.33N 109.27W
107 L4 **Green River Res** Kentucky
112 G9 **Greens Bayou** Houston, Texas 29.45N 95.12W
107 J9 **Greensboro** Alabama 32.42N 87.38W
105 C7 **Greensboro** Florida 30.34N 84.45W
105 D4 **Greensboro** Georgia 33.33N 83.10W
103 C9 **Greensboro** Maryland 38.58N 75.49W
105 H1 **Greensboro** N Carolina 36.03N 79.50W
104 N2 **Greensboro** Vermont 44.36N 72.16W
107 L2 **Greensburg** Indiana 39.20N 85.29W
109 L4 **Greensburg** Kansas 37.36N 99.17W
107 L4 **Greensburg** Kentucky 37.14N 85.30W
107 F11 **Greensburg** Louisiana 30.50N 90.41W
104 F6 **Greensburg** Pennsylvania 40.17N 79.34W
13 K2 **Greenslopes** *dist* Brisbane, Qnsld
98 T4 **Greenspond** Newfoundland 49.04N 53.36W
104 G7 **Green Spring** W Virginia 39.32N 78.37W
104 B5 **Green Springs** Ohio 41.15N 83.03W
58 E3 **Greenstone Pt** Highland Scotland 57.55N 5.37W
105 J3 **Green Swamp** N Carolina
12 J5 **Greenthorpe** New S Wales 33.59S 148.22E
107 D1 **Greentop** Missouri 40.20N 92.34W
106 J9 **Greentown** Indiana 40.28N 85.57W
103 D4 **Greentown** Pennsylvania 41.19N 75.19W
105 K11 **Green Turtle Cay** *isld* Bahamas 26.51N 77.22W
107 H2 **Greenup** Illinois 39.15N 88.10W
103 N7 **Greenvale** New York
13 H4 **Greenvale** Queensland 18.55S 145.05E
14 G3 **Greenvale** W Australia 17.05S 127.50E
110 C8 **Greenview** California 41.33N 122.55W
107 K10 **Greenville** Alabama 31.50N 86.40W
110 E9 **Greenville** California 40.09N 120.57W
105 D7 **Greenville** Florida 30.29N 83.39W
107 G3 **Greenville** Illinois 38.54N 89.24W
107 J4 **Greenville** Kentucky 37.11N 87.11W
89 E9 **Greenville** Liberia 5.01N 9.03W
104 Q1 **Greenville** Maine 45.28N 69.36W
106 J6 **Greenville** Michigan 43.11N 85.13W
107 E8 **Greenville** Mississippi 33.23N 91.03W
107 F4 **Greenville** Missouri 37.06N 90.26W
105 K2 **Greenville** N Carolina 35.36N 77.23W
104 O4 **Greenville** New Hampshire 42.46N 71.49W
103 F2 **Greenville** New York 42.25N 74.02W
104 A6 **Greenville** Ohio 40.06N 84.37W
104 E5 **Greenville** Pennsylvania 41.24N 80.24W
105 E3 **Greenville** S Carolina 34.52N 82.25W
112 L2 **Greenville** Texas 33.09N 96.07W
104 F8 **Greenville** Virginia 38.01N 79.12W
100 M2 **Greenwater L** Ontario 48.35N 90.28W
100 O6 **Greenwater Lake Prov. Park** Saskatchewan 52.35N 103.30W
100 S9 **Greenway** Manitoba 49.23N 99.08W
108 L4 **Greenway** S Dakota 45.56N 99.42W
103 G4 **Greenwich** Connecticut 41.02N 73.37W
109 N4 **Greenwich** Kansas 37.47N 97.14W
55 G4 **Greenwich** London Eng 51.29N 00.000
103 D8 **Greenwich** New Jersey 39.23N 75.21W
104 M3 **Greenwich** New York 43.07N 73.30W
104 C5 **Greenwich** Ohio 41.02N 82.32W
111 N3 **Greenwich** Utah 38.26N 111.55W
55 H4 **Greenwich** *bor* London England
123 E15 **Greenwich I** S Shetland Is Antarctica 62.33S 59.58W
107 B6 **Greenwood** Arkansas 35.13N 94.17W
110 G1 **Greenwood** Br Col 49.08N 118.41W
111 D3 **Greenwood** California 38.51N 120.55W
103 C9 **Greenwood** Delaware 38.48N 75.36W
107 K2 **Greenwood** Indiana 39.36N 86.07W
107 M5 **Greenwood** Kentucky 36.52N 84.30W
107 C9 **Greenwood** Louisiana 32.26N 93.59W
107 F8 **Greenwood** Mississippi 33.31N 90.10W
108 O9 **Greenwood** Nebraska 40.58N 96.26W
13 C5 **Greenwood** N Terr 20.15S 134.13E
105 E3 **Greenwood** S Carolina 34.11N 82.10W
108 M7 **Greenwood** S Dakota 42.55N 98.12W
106 D5 **Greenwood** Wisconsin 44.47N 90.36W
105 F3 **Greenwood L** S Carolina 34.16N 82.00W
103 F4 **Greenwood Lake** New York 41.13N 74.17W
107 H8 **Greenwood Springs** Mississippi 33.53N 88.20W
110 J3 **Greer** Idaho 46.24N 116.10W
105 E3 **Greer** S Carolina 34.55N 82.14W
107 D6 **Greers Ferry Res** Arkansas
59 J6 **Greese, R** Kildare Irish Rep
107 C7 **Greeson,L** Arkansas
63 F5 **Greetsiel** W Germany 53.31N 7.06E
70 M5 **Greez** France 48.08N 0.46E
90 K9 **Gréfodé** Cent Afr Rep 5.48N 21.29E
63 D10 **Grefrath** W Germany 51.20N 6.20E
100 S9 **Gregg** Manitoba 49.58N 99.20W
112 N3 **Greggton** Texas 32.30N 94.49W
100 F2 **Gregoire L** Alberta 56.27N 111.10W
120 D2 **Gregório, R** Brazil
108 L6 **Gregory** S Dakota 43.14N 99.25W
13 E4 **Gregory** *R* Queensland
13 E4 **Gregory Downs** Queensland 18.36S 139.09E
12 E3 **Gregory, L** S Australia
14 C7 **Gregory, L** W Australia 25.35S 119.40E
14 G5 **Gregory L** W Australia
13 G4 **Gregory Ra** Queensland
14 D5 **Gregory Ra** W Australia
105 L12 **Gregory Town** Bahamas 25.23N 76.33W
58 A4 **Greian Head** Barra, W Isles Scotland 57.02N 7.32W
50 A3 **Greidhavík** Bardhastrandarsýsla, Vestur Iceland 65.33N 24.20W
65 H8 **Greifenburg** Austria 46.46N 13.12E
66 L2 **Greifensee** Switzerland 47.22N 8.41E
66 L2 **Greifensee** *L* Switzerland 47.18N 8.42E
65 O5 **Greifenstein** Austria 48.22N 16.15E
63 T6 **Greiffenberg** E Germany 53.06N 13.57E
63 S4 **Greifswald** E Germany 54.06N 13.24E
63 T4 **Greifswalder Bodden** *B* E Germany
63 T4 **Greifswalder Oie** *isld* E Germany 54.15N 13.55E
122 V9 **Greig Pt** Fanning I Pacific Oc 3.50N 159.21W
65 K7 **Greimberg** *mt* Austria 47.15N 14.10E
65 L5 **Grein** Austria 48.14N 14.50E
66 M5 **Greina Pass** Switzerland 46.37N 8.58E
92 D4 **Greinerville** Zaïre 5.58S 29.06E
65 L4 **Greiner Wald** *woods* Austria
56 F5 **Greinton** Somerset Eng 51.08N 2.50W
64 L5 **Greisselbach** W Germany 49.12N 11.29E
64 N2 **Greiz** E Germany 50.40N 12.11E
53 D5 **Grejs Dal** *V* Denmark 55.43N 9.31E
84 C6 **Gréka** Greece 37.33N 21.42E
66 G2 **Grellingen** Switzerland 47.27N 7.35E
61 G2 **Grembergen** Belgium 51.03N 4.06E
47 D2 **Gremikha** U.S.S.R. 68.03N 39.38E
63 N4 **Gremsmühlen** W Germany 54.10N 10.33E
45 E4 **Gremyach** Ukraine U.S.S.R. 52.21N 33.16E
42 H5 **Gremyachinsk** Buryat U.S.S.R. 52.48N 108.00E
47 H6 **Gremyachinsk** Perm U.S.S.R. 58.37N 57.58E
45 R4 **Gremyachka** U.S.S.R. 52.06N 45.45E
45 L5 **Gremyach'ye** U.S.S.R. 51.30N 39.01E
53 F4 **Grenå** Denmark 56.25N 10.53E
110 C8 **Grenada** California 41.39N 122.33W
107 G8 **Grenada** Mississippi 33.47N 89.49W
116 P5 **Grenada** *I* Windward Is W I
107 G8 **Grenada L** Mississippi
72 G8 **Grenade** France 43.47N 1.18E
72 D8 **Grenade-sur-l'Adour** France 43.47N 0.25W
116 O8 **Grenadines, The** *islds* Windward Is W I
66 F3 **Grenchen** Switzerland 47.13N 7.24E
53 C5 **Grene** Denmark 55.44N 9.04E
68 E3 **Grenelle** Paris France 48.51N 2.18E
53 F1 **Grenen** *headland* Denmark 57.45N 10.40E
12 J5 **Grenfell** New S Wales 33.54S 148.11E
100 P8 **Grenfell** Saskatchewan 50.24N 102.56W
66 J6 **Grengiols** Switzerland 46.23N 8.06E
50 G3 **Grenivík** Iceland 65.57N 18.09W
50 H3 **Grenjadharstadhur** Iceland 65.47N 17.14W
103 D7 **Grenloch** New Jersey 39.47N 75.03W
57 E3 **Grennoch, L** Dumfries & Galloway Scotland 55.00N 4.17W
71 H6 **Grenoble** France 45.11N 5.43E
109 O4 **Grenola** Kansas 37.22N 96.27W
108 G1 **Grenora** N Dakota 48.38N 103.55W
57 L6 **Grenoside** S Yorks Eng 53.27N 1.30W
66 F1 **Grentzingen** France 47.35N 7.18E
116 P5 **Grenville** Grenada, W I 12.07N 61.37W
109 G5 **Grenville** New Mexico 36.36N 103.37W
108 N4 **Grenville** S Dakota 45.27N 97.22W
13 G1 **Grenville C** Queensland 12.00S 143.13E
101 J9 **Grenville Chan** Br Col
101 L10 **Grenville, Mt** Br Col 50.59N 124.31W
64 D8 **Grenzach-Wyhlen** W Germany 47.33N 7.40E
64 A1 **Grenzlandring** W Germany
71 H9 **Gréoux-les-Bains** France 43.45N 5.53E
66 K3 **Greppen** Switzerland 47.04N 8.26E
63 Q9 **Greppin** W Germany 51.38N 12.18E
63 Q4 **Gresenhorst** E Germany 54.09N 12.25E
31 C7 **Greshag** Pakistan 27.44N 65.09E
31 D7 **Greshak** Pakistan 27.38N 66.04E
110 C4 **Gresham** Oregon 45.30N 122.25W
72 H7 **Grésigne, Forêt de** France
18 K9 **Gresik** Java Indon 7.12S 112.38E
18 E7 **Gresik** Sumatra Indon 2.17S 103.51E
58 D2 **Gress** Lewis, W Isles Scotland 58.18N 6.18W
51 C7 **Gressamoen Nat.Park** Norway
71 H7 **Gresse** *R* France
71 H7 **Gresse-en-Vercors** France 44.53N 5.35E
79 C3 **Gressoney la Trinité** Italy 45.50N 7.49E
79 C3 **Gressoney St.Jean** Italy 45.47N 7.50E
66 H8 **Gressoney, Valle di** Italy
12 G7 **Gressy** Victoria 38.03S 143.43E
65 M6 **Gresten** Austria 47.59N 15.02E
71 H5 **Grésy-sur-Aix** France 45.43N 5.56E
71 J5 **Grésy-sur-Isère** France 45.35N 6.15E
12 K5 **Greta** New S Wales 32.40S 151.21E
107 J13 **Gretna** Louisiana 29.55N 90.02W
100 U9 **Gretna** Manitoba 49.01N 97.34W
104 F10 **Gretna** Virginia 36.57N 79.23W
57 G2 **Gretna Green** Dumfries & Galloway Scotland 55.00N 3.04W
69 D6 **Gretz-Armainvilliers** France 48.44N 2.45E
64 K1 **Greussen** E Germany 51.14N 10.58E
69 K7 **Greux** France 48.27N 5.40E
53 J5 **Greve** Denmark 55.35N 12.15E
79 K7 **Greve** Italy 43.35N 11.19E
72 B4 **Grève, la** France 45.47N 1.08W
60 E13 **Grevelingen** *estuary* Netherlands
63 G8 **Greven** W Germany 52.07N 7.38E
84 B1 **Grevená** Greece 40.05N 21.26E
84 B2 **Grevena** *prefect* Greece
60 T16 **Grevenbicht** Netherlands 41.02N 5.46E
69 M1 **Grevenbroich** W Germany 51.06N 6.36E
63 L5 **Grevenkop** W Germany 53.51N 9.33E
61 Q8 **Grevenmacher** Luxembourg 49.41N 6.27E
63 O5 **Grevesmühlen** E Germany 53.53N 11.11E
53 J5 **Greve Strand** Denmark 55.34N 12.17E
53 K4 **Grevie** Sweden 56.23N 12.50E
11 H7 **Greville Harb** *inlet* New Zealand
53 H5 **Grevinge** Denmark 55.48N 11.34E
121 L10 **Grévy, I** Chile 55.35S 67.40W
57 K4 **Grewelthorpe** N Yorks Eng 54.11N 1.39W
59 L2 **Grey Abbey** Down N Ireland 54.32N 5.33W
108 B5 **Greybull** Wyoming 44.30N 108.02W
108 B5 **Greybull** *R* Wyoming
13 D2 **Grey, C** N Terr Australia 13.00S 136.35E
110 Q4 **Greycliff** Montana 45.46N 109.46W
44 G1 **Greydernoye** U.S.S.R. 46.52N 45.05E
108 Q4 **Grey Eagle** Minnesota 45.49N 94.45W
101 F4 **Grey Hunter Pk** Yukon Terr 63.40N 135.40W
98 R3 **Grey Is** Newfoundland
98 R3 **Grey Is. Harbour** Newfoundland 50.43N 55.36W
95 M2 **Greylingstad** S Africa 26.45S 28.45E
11 C2 **Grey Lynn** *dist* Auckland New Zealand
11 F9 **Greymouth** New Zealand 42.28S 171.12E
101 F11 **Grey, Pt** Br Col 49.16N 123.16W
12 G7 **Grey, Pt** Victoria 38.36S 144.02E
Grey R *see* **Little R** Newfoundland
11 F9 **Grey R** New Zealand
13 G8 **Grey Ra** Queensland/N S W
98 Q5 **Grey Res** Newfoundland
110 P6 **Greys** *R* Wyoming
14 A7 **Grey's Plains** W Australia
57 H3 **Greystoke** Cumbria Eng 54.40N 2.52W
109 B1 **Greystone** Colorado 40.36N 108.41W
95 H9 **Greystone** S Africa 33.10S 24.54E
92 D12 **Greystone** Zimbabwe 20.06S 29.30E
59 K5 **Greystones** Wicklow Irish Rep 53.09N 6.04W
11 K8 **Greytown** New Zealand 41.04S 175.29E
Greytown Nicaragua*see* **San Juan del Norte**
95 C10 **Greytown** S Africa 34.03S 19.35E
95 O5 **Greytown** S Africa 29.04S 30.35E
61 J4 **Grez-Doiceau** Belgium 50.44N 4.42E
70 J6 **Grez-en-Bouère** France 47.52N 0.31W
79 K3 **Grezzana** Italy 45.32N 11.01E
79 P2 **Grgar** Yugoslavia 46.00N 13.40E
59 H1 **Grianan of Aileach** Donegal Irish Rep 55.01N 7.25W
66 S4 **Griankopf** *mt* Italy 46.47N 10.27E
66 N8 **Griante** Italy 45.59N 9.15E
83 D4 **Griba** *mts* Albania
45 N5 **Gribanovskiy** U.S.S.R. 51.28N 41.59E
56 B7 **Gribbin Hd** Cornwall Eng 50.19N 4.40W
26 H11 **Gribb Seamount** Southern Oc 62.00S 88.30E
90 J8 **Gribingui** *R* Cent Afr Rep
89 E8 **Gribo** Liberia 6.22N 8.28W
45 K2 **Gribovka** U.S.S.R. 54.20N 38.30E
47 C3 **Gridino** U.S.S.R. 66.00N 34.39E
111 C2 **Gridley** California 39.24N 121.42W
106 F9 **Gridley** Illinois 40.44N 88.54W
109 P3 **Gridley** Kansas 38.05N 95.54W
66 L7 **Gridone** *mt* Switzerland 46.08N 8.39E
75 G7 **Griegos** Spain 40.26N 1.43W
60 K6 **Griend** *isld* Netherlands
60 M14 **Griendtsveen** Netherlands 51.27N 5.52E
79 K1 **Gries** Italy 46.30N 11.20E
65 D7 **Gries am Brenner** Austria 47.03N 11.30E
Griesbach *see* **Untergriesbach**
64 P7 **Griesbach im Rottel** Bayern W Germany 48.27N 13.12E
65 C7 **Griesen** W Germany 47.30N 10.58E
64 F4 **Griesheim** W Germany 49.51N 8.33E
65 D7 **Gries im Sellrain** Austria 47.12N 11.09E
65 J5 **Grieskirchen** Austria 48.14N 13.51E
66 K6 **Gries Pass** Switz/Italy 46.28N 8.23E
Griessen *see* **Klettgau**
65 G7 **Griessen Pass** Austria 47.28N 12.40E
60 N11 **Grietelo** Netherlands 51.12N 6.07E
63 D9 **Grieth** W Germany 51.47N 6.19E
65 L8 **Griffen** Austria 46.43N 144.44E
105 C4 **Griffin** Georgia 33.15N 84.17W
100 O9 **Griffin** Saskatchewan 49.39N 103.29W
105 F9 **Griffin, L** Florida 28.54N 81.52W
113 Q1 **Griffin Pt** Alaska 70.05N 142.50W
12 H5 **Griffith** New S Wales 34.18S 146.04E
12 A6 **Griffith** *dist* Canberra Australia
97 K3 **Griffith I** N W Terr 74.40N 95.30W
107 E6 **Griffithville** Arkansas 35.10N 91.39W
105 K2 **Grifton** N Carolina 35.23N 77.26W
103 E6 **Griggstown** New Jersey 40.27N 74.36W
107 F2 **Griggsville** Illinois 39.42N 90.42W
81 B4 **Grighini, Mte** Sardinia 39.57N 8.49E
79 F3 **Grigna** *mt* Italy 45.58N 9.23E
71 F8 **Grignan** France 44.25N 4.55E
79 D3 **Grignasco** Italy 45.41N 8.20E
79 L2 **Grigno** Italy 46.01N 11.38E
72 D7 **Grignols** France 44.23N 0.02W
71 F5 **Grigny** France 45.37N 4.47E
46 G6 **Grigoriopol'** Moldavia U.S.S.R. 47.08N 29.18E
44 D2 **Grigoripolisskaya** U.S.S.R. 45.17N 41.04E
45 D5 **Grigorovka** Ukraine U.S.S.R. 51.03N 32.51E
44 A8 **Grigor'yevka** Ukraine U.S.S.R. 30.39N 46.38E
45 C10 **Grigor'yevka** Ukraine U.S.S.R. 46.52N 31.04E
45 H8 **Grigor'yevka** Ukraine U.S.S.R. 48.15N 36.45E
60 O6 **Grijpskerk** Netherlands 53.15N 6.18E
Grik *see* **Gerik**
90 J9 **Griko** Cent Afr Rep 5.42N 19.26E
Grikwastad *see* **Griquatown**
41 O2 **Grili, Ostrov** *isld* Franz Josef Land U.S.S.R.
71 F8 **Grillon** France 44.23N 4.56E
66 A6 **Grilly** France 46.20N 6.08E
82 K1 **Grimailov** U.S.S.R. 49.21N 26.00E
81 M5 **Grimaldi** Italy 39.08N 16.14E
90 K9 **Grimari** Cent Afr Rep 5.43N 20.06E
71 K10 **Grimaud** France 43.16N 6.32E
72 E2 **Grimaudière, la** France 46.49N 0.02E
61 H3 **Grimbergen** Belgium 50.56N 4.22E
12 G8 **Grim, C** Tasmania 40.45S 144.45E
66 G7 **Grimentz** Switzerland 46.12N 7.35E
111 C2 **Grimes** California 39.04N 121.55W
110 K5 **Grimes Pass** Idaho 44.02N 115.51W
58 B3 **Griminish Pt** N Uist, W Isles Scotland 57.40N 7.29W
64 O1 **Grimma** E Germany 51.14N 12.43E
63 S4 **Grimmen** E Germany 54.07N 13.04E
Grimmenthal *see* **Obermassfeld-Grimmenthal**
66 F5 **Grimmialp** Switzerland 46.35N 7.30E
58 T12 **Grim Ness** *prom* Orkney Scotland 58.49N 2.52W
63 T7 **Grimnitzsee** *L* E Germany
53 V18 **Grimo** Norway 60.22N 6.38E
57 O6 **Grimoldby** Lincs Eng 53.22N 0.05E
50 D5 **Grimsá** *R* Iceland
57 N5 **Grimsby** Humberside Eng 53.35N 0.05W
99 L9 **Grimsby** Ontario 43.12N 79.35W
66 K5 **Grimsel-pass** Switzerland 46.34N 8.22E
66 K5 **Grimsel See** *L* Switzerland 46.34N 8.18E
58 T12 **Grimsetter** *aer* Orkney Scotland 58.57N 2.52W
50 H1 **Grímsey** *isld* Iceland 66.33N 18.00W
50 D3 **Grimsey** *isld* Strandasýsla Iceland 65.42N 21.21W
101 P7 **Grimshaw** Alberta 56.11N 117.37W
50 E6 **Grímsnes** *reg* Iceland
50 J3 **Grímsstadhir** Iceland 65.39N 16.09W
52 D8 **Grimstad** Norway 58.20N 8.35E
53 B5 **Grimstrup** Denmark 55.32N 8.39E
50 E4 **Grímstunga** Iceland 65.19N 20.10W
50 E4 **Grímstunguheidhi** *heath* Iceland
50 H6 **Grímsvötn** *mt* Iceland 64.26N 17.20W
103 C5 **Grimville** Pennsylvania 40.35N 75.48W
53 Z16 **Grindaheim** Norway 61.08N 8.33E
53 Y16 **Grindane** *mt* Norway 61.06N 8.30E
50 C7 **Grindavík** Iceland 63.50N 22.27W
53 V16 **Grinde** Norway 61.11N 6.45E
53 T20 **Grindefjord** *inlet* Norway 59.27N 5.31E
66 J5 **Grindelwald** Switzerland 46.38N 8.03E
53 C3 **Grinderslev** Denmark 56.42N 9.05E
53 U19 **Grindheim** Norway 59.40N 6.02E
53 B5 **Grindsted** Denmark 55.46N 8.56E
104 Q8 **Grindstone** Maine 45.46N 68.35W
98 L6 **Grindstone I** Madeleine Is, Que 47.20N 61.55W
98 L6 **Grindstone Island** Madeleine Is, Que 47.25N 61.54W
100 U7 **Grindstone Prov. Park** Manitoba
100 V7 **Grindstone Pt** *C* Manitoba 51.22N 96.37W
45 E4 **Grinevo** Bryansk U.S.S.R. 52.35N 33.05E
46 H3 **Grinevo** Smolensk U.S.S.R. 54.36N 32.07E
57 M6 **Gringley on the Hill** Notts Eng 53.25N 0.53W
108 S8 **Grinnell** Iowa 41.45N 92.42W
109 K2 **Grinnell** Kansas 39.08N 100.38W
97 K2 **Grinnell Pen** N W Terr
75 C7 **Griñón** Spain 40.13N 3.51W
82 B4 **Grintaveo** *mt* Yugoslavia 46.20N 14.32E
57 K4 **Grinton** N Yorks Eng 54.23N 1.55W
75 H5 **Grio** *R* Spain
58 B2 **Griomaval** *mt* Lewis, W Isles Scotland 58.05N 7.04W
52 D3 **Grip** *Lt Ho* Norway 63.14N 7.40E
72 E10 **Gripp** France 42.56N 0.13E
63 O6 **Grippel** W Germany 53.04N 11.19E
95 M6 **Griqualand East** *reg* S Africa
95 G4 **Griquatown** S Africa 28.51S 23.15E
66 O5 **Grisch, Piz** *mt* Switzerland 46.33N 9.29E
97 L2 **Grise Fiord** N W Terr 76.10N 83.15W
75 H4 **Grisén** Spain 41.44N 1.10W
50 C5 **Grísthóll** Iceland 64.59N 22.46W
79 L4 **Grisignano di Zocco** Italy 45.28N 11.42E
69 B2 **Gris-Nez, C** France 50.52N 1.35E
81 L4 **Grisolia** Italy 39.43N 15.51E
72 G8 **Grisolles** France 43.50N 1.18E
Grisons *canton see* **Graubünden**
52 L6 **Grisslehamn** Sweden 60.04N 18.50E
108 P8 **Griswold** Iowa 41.12N 95.09W
82 L1 **Gritsev** U.S.S.R. 49.59N 27.12E
47 G5 **Griva** U.S.S.R. 60.35N 50.58E
47 L5 **Grivenka** U.S.S.R. 55.38N 59.37E
44 B2 **Grivenskaya** U.S.S.R. 45.39N 38.11E
69 C4 **Grivesnes** France 49.41N 2.29E
45 Q5 **Grivki** U.S.S.R. 51.56N 44.05E
79 B3 **Grivola, mt** Italy 45.36N 7.16E
84 D2 **Grízanon** Greece 39.38N 22.03E
57 G4 **Grizebeck** Cumbria Eng 54.15N 3.10W
63 P9 **Grizeline** E Germany 51.56N 11.47E
88 M9 **Grizim** Algeria 25.20N 2.55W
101 N3 **Grizzly Bear Mt** N W Terr 65.24N 120.49W
50 J3 **Grjót** *stony reg* Iceland
50 K4 **Grjót** *stony reg* Iceland
50 F5 **Grjótá** *R* Iceland
50 K5 **Grjótá** *R* Múlasýsla, Nordhur Iceland
50 G7 **Grjotá** *R* Skaftafellssýsla, Vestur Iceland
50 H4 **Grjotá** *R* Thingeyjarsýsla, Sudhur Iceland
50 K4 **Grjótárvatn** *L* Iceland 65.28N 15.00W
50 J2 **Grjótnes** Iceland 66.28N 16.31W
82 C6 **Grmeč Planina** *mts* Yugoslavia
98 R3 **Groais I** Newfoundland
63 S10 **Gröba** E Germany 51.20N 13.17E
61 K2 **Grobbendonk** Belgium 51.12N 4.45E
63 Q10 **Gröbers** E Germany 51.26N 12.08E
46 D2 **Grobina** Latvia U.S.S.R. 56.31N 21.15E
94 K5 **Groblersdal** S Africa 25.15S 29.25E
65 J7 **Gröbming** Austria 47.28N 13.55E
56 J2 **Groby** Leics Eng 52.40N 1.12W
63 P9 **Gröbzig** E Germany 51.42N 11.52E
53 V15 **Grodås** Norway 61.58N 6.32E
63 J3 **Gröde-Appeland** *isld* W Germany
66 F5 **Grodei** Switzerland 46.31N 7.25E
62 O2 **Gródek** Poland 53.08N 23.39E
Grodekovo *see* **Pogranichnyy**
65 H6 **Grödig** Austria 47.45N 13.03E
62 K5 **Grodków** Poland 50.41N 17.21E
63 S10 **Grödlitz** E Germany 51.25N 13.26E
46 E3 **Grodnenskaya Oblast'** *prov* Belorussiya U.S.S.R.
46 E3 **Grodno** Belorussiya U.S.S.R. 53.40N 23.50E
62 J3 **Grodzisk** Poland 52.14N 16.21E
62 M3 **Grodzisk Mazowiecki** Poland 52.09N 20.38E
46 G3 **Grodzyanka** Belorussiya U.S.S.R. 53.30N 28.41E
60 A3 **Groede** Netherlands 51.23N 3.30E
95 G6 **Groen** *R* S Africa
50 H6 **Grœnajall** *mt* Iceland 64.12N 17.22W
50 H6 **Grœnalón** *L* Iceland 64.10N 17.25W
50 F6 **Grœnavatn** *L* Árnessýsla Iceland 64.24N 19.36W
50 G6 **Grœnavatn** *L* Iceland 64.08N 18.41W
50 H3 **Grœnavatn** *L* Iceland 65.33N 17.01W
95 L3 **Groenebloem** S Africa 27.18S 27.03E
60 C3 **Groenendijk** Zeeland Netherlands 51.22N 4.00E
Groenendijk Zuid Holland Netherlands*see* **Hazerswoude-Rijndijk**
95 J9 **Groenheuwels** S Africa 33.15S 25.59E
50 G6 **Grœnifjallgardhur** *ridge* Iceland
60 P11 **Groenlo** Netherlands 52.02N 6.36E
95 O3 **Groenvlei** S Africa 27.28S 30.14E
95 F4 **Groenwater** *R* S Africa
112 L4 **Groesbeck** Texas 31.31N 96.35W
60 M12 **Groesbeek** Netherlands 51.47N 5.56E
60 N12 **Groessen** Netherlands 51.56N 6.01E
60 G9 **Groet** Netherlands 52.44N 4.40E
50 G7 **Gröf** Iceland 63.43N 18.32W
18 L10 **Grogak** Bali Indon 8.12S 114.45E
18 F3 **Grogol Hilir** Jakarta Indonesia 6.13S 106.47E
18 F3 **Grogol, Kali** *R* Indonesia
63 K8 **Grohnde** W Germany 52.01N 9.25E
80 O2 **Grohote** Yugoslavia 43.23N 16.17E
69 F3 **Groise, la** France 50.04N 3.40E
64 N1 **Groitzsch** E Germany 51.09N 12.17E
70 D6 **Groix** France 47.39N 3.27W
70 D6 **Groix, I de** France 47.38N 3.26W
62 M4 **Grójec** Poland 51.54N 20.51E
45 B5 **Grokhov** Belorussiya U.S.S.R. 51.53N 30.29E
66 E4 **Grolley** Switzerland 46.50N 7.05E
60 P8 **Grolloo** Netherlands 52.56N 6.40E
88 T3 **Grombalia** Tunisia 36.38N 10.29E
63 N4 **Grömitz** W Germany 54.09N 10.59E
79 G3 **Gromo** Italy 45.58N 9.55E
45 P8 **Gromoslavka** U.S.S.R. 48.14N 43.39E
72 K1 **Gron** France 47.07N 2.44E
53 C7 **Grønå** *R* Denmark
53 W18 **Grøna** *R* Norway
53 U19 **Grønaheinuten** *mt* Norway 59.44N 6.18E
50 B2 **Grönahlídh** *coast* Iceland
63 L8 **Gronau** Niedersachsen W Germany 52.05N 9.46E
63 F8 **Gronau in Westfalen** Nordrhein-Westfalen W Germany 52.13N 7.02E
53 B4 **Grønbjerg** Denmark 56.10N 8.33E
53 U15 **Grøndalsvatn** *L* Norway 61.58N 6.17E
64 J8 **Grönenbach** W Germany 47.53N 10.13E
53 Y16 **Grønevatn** *L* Norway 61.12N 8.04E
52 G2 **Grong** Norway 64.27N 12.19E
53 C4 **Grønhøj** Denmark 56.23N 9.13E
53 U16 **Grøning** Norway 61.26N 6.27E
63 O9 **Gröningen** E Germany 51.57N 11.13E
60 P7 **Groningen** Netherlands 53.13N 6.35E
117 B2 **Groningen** Surinam 5.45N 55.31W
60 O6 **Groningen** *prov* Netherlands
60 O6 **Groninger Wad** *flats* Netherlands
50 O10 **Grønkapp** *C* Jan Mayen I 70.58N 8.40W
79 K2 **Gronlait** *mt* Italy 46.06N 11.22E
100 N5 **Gronlid** Saskatchewan 53.06N 104.28W
48 T15 **Grønnedal** Greenland 61.25N 48.00W
53 X18 **Grønnut** *mt* Norway 60.24N 7.55E
66 N7 **Grono** Switzerland 46.15N 9.09E
51 C5 **Grønøy** Norway 66.48N 13.30E
53 T18 **Grønsdal** Norway 60.26N 5.50E
52 L7 **Grönskär** *Lt Ho* Sweden 59.26N 19.03E
52 J9 **Grönskåra** Sweden 57.05N 15.45E
53 J7 **Grønsund** *sound* Denmark 54.50N 12.12E
60 S17 **Gronsveld** Netherlands 50.48N 5.44E
53 X14 **Grønvatn** *L* Norway 62.07N 7.38E
112 C8 **Groom** Texas 35.12N 101.03W
56 M5 **Groombridge** E Sussex Eng 51.07N 0.12E
59 L2 **Groomsport** Down N Ireland 54.41N 5.37W
95 D9 **Groot** *R* S Africa
95 H9 **Groot** *R* S Africa
60 H12 **Groot-Ammers** Netherlands 51.55N 4.50E
94 F7 **Groot Aughrabies Falls** S Africa 28.34S 20.19E
94 D4 **Groot Barmen** Namibia 22.08S 16.43E
95 B8 **Groot-Berg** *R* S Africa
61 H3 **Groot-Bijgaarden** Belgium 50.52N 4.16E
95 F10 **Groot-Brakrivier** S Africa 34.03S 22.13E
95 G5 **Grootdoring** S Africa 29.58S 23.02E
94 F7 **Groot Drink** S Africa 28.33S 21.42E
13 D2 **Groote Eylandt** *isld* N Terr Australia
60 O7 **Grootegast** Netherlands 53.13N 6.16E
94 D5 **Grootfontein** Namibia 25.02S 16.48E
95 J4 **Groot-Gannapan** *salt pan* S Africa 28.04S 25.35E
95 N4 **Groothoek** S Africa 28.01S 29.25E
94 F3 **Groot Laagte** *watercourse* Botswana
94 L4 **Groot Letaba** *R* S Africa
61 M3 **Groot-Loon** Belgium 50.47N 5.22E
95 K1 **Groot-Marico** S Africa 25.37S 26.26E
95 K1 **Grootpan** S Africa 25.59S 26.34E
95 G9 **Grootrivierhoogte** *mts* S Africa 33.10S 24.15E
60 H9 **Grootschermer** Netherlands 52.35N 4.50E
61 N3 **Groot-Spouwen** Belgium 50.50N 5.33E
95 O3 **Grootspruit** S Africa 27.25S 30.40E
95 F9 **Groot-Swartberge** *mts* S Africa
95 G7 **Groot-Tafelberg** *mt* S Africa 31.07S 23.56E
95 J8 **Groot-Vis** *R* S Africa
95 M2 **Grootvlei** S Africa 26.48S 28.31E
94 F7 **Groot Vloer** *salt L* S Africa
95 K8 **Groot-Winterberg** *mt* S Africa 32.21S 26.25E
95 H9 **Groot-Winterhoekberge** *mts* S Africa
79 E4 **Gropello Cairoli** Italy 45.11N 9.00E
61 F4 **Grosage** Belgium 50.33N 3.46E
77 P5 **Grosa, I** Spain 37.44N 0.41W
69 N5 **Grosbliederstroff** France 49.09N 7.01E
71 F2 **Grosbois-en-Montagne** France 47.20N 4.35E
72 A2 **Grosbreuil** France 46.33N 1.37W
61 O7 **Grosbus** Luxembourg 49.50N 5.58E
79 H2 **Grósio** Italy 46.18N 10.17E
116 O7 **Gros Islet** St Lucia, W I 14.06N 60.59W
52 H9 **Grosjö** Sweden 57.25N 13.42E
68 F2 **Groslav** France 48.59N 2.21E
56 F4 **Grosmont** Gwent Wales 51.55N 2.52W
116 H5 **Gros Morne** Haiti 19.45N 72.46W
116 L3 **Gros Morne** Martinique W I 14.42N 61.01W
98 G4 **Gros Morne** Quebec 49.16N 65.33W
98 P4 **Gros Morne** *pk* Newfoundland 49.36N 57.47W
26 U15 **Gros Morne, Le** *mt* Réunion Ind Oc 21.07S 55.28E
98 P4 **Gros Morne Nat. Park** Newfoundland
71 F3 **Grosne** *R* France
70 F3 **Grosnez Pt** Channel Is 49.15N 2.15W
98 P3 **Gros Pate** *pk* Newfoundland 50.12N 57.22W
105 F7 **Gross** Florida 30.22N 81.42W
65 F7 **Gross Ache** *R* Austria
64 M4 **Gross Albershof** W Germany 49.32N 11.45E
64 H1 **Grossalmerode** W Germany 51.16N 9.47E
65 L6 **Gross Alp Koge** *mt* Austria 47.50N 14.34E
63 O9 **Gross Alsleben** E Germany 51.59N 11.15E
63 P8 **Gross Ammensleben** E Germany 52.14N 11.32E
91 C11 **Grossa, Pta** Angola 14.11S 12.20E
117 D4 **Grossa, Pta** Brazil 1.15N 49.53W
64 P5 **Gross Arber** *mt* W Germany 49.07N 13.09E
65 H7 **Gross Arl** Austria 47.14N 13.12E
64 F3 **Grossauheim** W Germany 50.05N 8.57E
63 S8 **Grossbeeren** E Germany 52.21N 13.18E
63 T8 **Grossbesten** E Germany 52.15N 13.39E
63 M10 **Grossbodungen** E Germany 51.29N 10.30E
65 K7 **Gross Bosenstein** *mt* Austria 47.26N 14.25E
64 O1 **Gross Bothen** E Germany 51.12N 12.45E
64 G6 **Grossbottwar** W Germany 49.00N 9.19E
64 L2 **Gross-Breitenbach** E Germany 50.35N 11.01E
65 L6 **Gross Buchstein** *mt* Austria 47.37N 14.37E
Grossburgwedel *see* **Burgwedel**
66 H3 **Grossdietwil** Switzerland 47.10N 7.53E
63 T7 **Gross-Dölln** E Germany 52.59N 13.32E
63 J8 **Grosse Aue** *R* W Germany
64 M2 **Gross Ebersdorf** E Germany 50.47N 11.58E
98 L6 **Grosse I** Madeleine Is, Que 47.39N 61.32W
64 K1 **Grossen Behringen** E Germany 51.02N 10.32E
63 O4 **Grossenbrode** W Germany 54.23N 11.07E
64 F2 **Grossenbuseck** W Germany 50.35N 8.48E
64 K1 **Grossenehrich** E Germany 51.15N 10.50E
63 O7 **Gross Engersen** E Germany 52.38N 11.21E
63 T10 **Grossenhain** E Germany 51.18N 13.33E
63 H7 **Grossenkneten** W Germany 52.57N 8.16E
69 Q2 **Grossenlinden** W Germany 50.32N 8.39E
64 N2 **Grossenstein** E Germany 50.53N 12.12E
53 C7 **Grossenwiehe** W Germany 54.42N 9.15E
65 P5 **Gross Enzersdorf** Austria 48.12N 16.33E
116 N4 **Grosse Pointe** Marie Galante, Guadeloupe W I 16.00N 61.17W
106 P1 **Grosse Pointe Farms** *dist* Detroit, Michigan
106 O2 **Grosse Pointe Park** *dist* Detroit, Michigan
106 P1 **Grosse Pointe Woods** *dist* Detroit, Michigan
66 M3 **Grosser Aubrig** *mt* Switzerland 47.06N 8.53E
63 S3 **Grosser Jasmunder Bodden** *B* E Germany
66 L3 **Grosser Mythen** *mt* Switzerland 47.02N 8.42E
63 T10 **Grosse Röder** *R* E Germany
63 M4 **Grosser Plöner See** *L* W Germany
63 S6 **Grosser Stechlinsee** *L* E Germany 53.09N 13.02E
66 Q3 **Grosser Walser Tal** *V* Austria
80 D3 **Grosseto** Italy 42.46N 11.07E
80 C3 **Grosseto** *prov* Italy
40 H8 **Grossevichi** U.S.S.R. 47.59N 139.26E
64 D5 **Gross Eyberg** *mt* W Germany 49.07N 7.44E
64 E3 **Gross Feldberg** *mt* W Germany 50.13N 8.28E
63 T6 **Gross Fredenwalde** E Germany 53.08N 13.48E
64 F4 **Gross-Gerau** W Germany 49.55N 8.29E
65 L4 **Gross Gerungs** Austria 48.35N 14.58E
63 M8 **Gross Gleidingen** W Germany 52.13N 10.25E
65 G7 **Gross Glockner** *mt* Austria 47.05N 12.44E
65 G7 **Gross Glockner Pass** Austria 47.06N 12.51E
63 P6 **Gross-Godems** E Germany 53.22N 11.47E
64 N1 **Gross Görschen** E Germany 51.13N 12.11E
63 N5 **Gross Gronau** W Germany 53.48N 10.44E
63 M5 **Gross Hansdorf** W Germany 53.40N 10.17E
65 N7 **Gross Hartmannsdorf** Austria 47.09N 15.55E
64 P2 **Gross Hartmannsdorf** E Germany 50.48N 13.20E
63 F5 **Grossheide** W Germany 53.36N 7.18E
64 M1 **Gross Heringen** E Germany 51.06N 11.39E
63 F7 **Gross Hesepe** W Germany 52.38N 7.13E
66 G4 **Gross Höchstetten** Switzerland 46.55N 7.38E
63 R4 **Gross-Hohrdorf** E Germany 54.24N 12.56E
65 L6 **Grosshollenstein** Austria 47.48N 14.47E
63 M8 **Gross Ilsede** W Germany 52.17N 10.13E
63 M7 **Gross-Kain** W Germany 52.42N 10.28E
65 M4 **Gross Kamp** *R* Austria
64 E4 **Gross Karlbach** W Germany 49.33N 8.13E
63 O4 **Gross Klütz-höved** *C* E Germany 54.02N 11.12E
64 L2 **Gross Kochberg** E Germany 50.46N 11.20E
64 N1 **Gross Korbetha** E Germany 51.16N 12.03E
63 T8 **Gross Köris** E Germany 52.10N 13.40E
63 R8 **Gross Kreutz** E Germany 52.24N 12.46E
64 N6 **Gross Laaber** *R* W Germany
64 J4 **Gross-Langheim** W Germany 49.45N 10.15E
63 U8 **Gross Leuthen** E Germany 52.02N 14.03E
64 H2 **Grosslüder** W Germany 50.35N 9.32E
63 S8 **Gross-Machnow** E Germany 52.17N 13.29E
64 M6 **Grossmehring** W Germany 48.45N 11.32E
65 J4 **Gross Mühl** *R* Austria
81 E7 **Grosso, C** Egadi Is Italy 38.02N 12.22E
63 M7 **Gross-Oesingen** W Germany 52.38N 10.28E
64 G4 **Grossostheim** W Germany 49.55N 9.06E
79 H2 **Grossotto** Italy 46.17N 10.15E
72 K2 **Grossouvre** France 46.53N 2.56E
65 L4 **Gross Pertholz** Austria 48.38N 14.50E
65 O7 **Grosspetersdorf** Austria 47.15N 16.19E
65 K6 **Gross Priel** *mt* Austria 47.44N 14.05E
64 P6 **Gross Rachel** *mt* W Germany 48.58N 13.27E
65 L6 **Grossraming** Austria 47.54N 14.33E
63 U9 **Gross Räschen** E Germany 51.35N 14.01E
65 L6 **Gross Reifling** Austria 47.40N 14.43E
63 K4 **Gross-Rheide** W Germany 54.27N 9.26E
63 M9 **Gross Rhüden** W Germany 51.56N 10.08E
63 U10 **Gross Röhrsdorf** E Germany 51.09N 14.02E
64 B5 **Grossrosseln** W Germany 49.12N 6.52E
64 L1 **Gross Rudestedt** E Germany 51.06N 11.06E
65 M8 **Gross St Florian** Austria 46.50N 15.20E
65 L8 **Gross Saualpe** Austria 46.52N 14.40E
63 T7 **Gross Schönebeck** E Germany 52.55N 13.32E
63 P7 **Gross Schwechten** E Germany 52.42N 11.47E
65 P5 **Gross Schweinbarth** Austria 48.25N 16.38E
63 T8 **Gross Selchower See** *L* E Germany
65 M4 **Gross Sieghards** Austria 48.48N 15.25E
63 N8 **Gross-Sisbeck** W Germany 52.22N 10.57E
Gross Spelk Kogel *see* **Koralpe**
66 G6 **Grossstrubel** *mt* Switzerland 46.25N 7.34E
64 H6 **Gross Süssen** W Germany 48.41N 9.45E
66 J4 **Grossteil** Switzerland 46.50N 8.08E
64 F4 **Gross-Umstadt** W Germany 49.52N 8.56E
64 P2 **Gross Waltersdorf** E Germany 50.47N 13.16E
66 J3 **Grosswangen** Switzerland 47.08N 8.03E
63 P6 **Gross-Warnow** Schwerin E Germany 53.14N 11.37E
65 N5 **Gross Weikersdorf** Austria 48.29N 15.59E
63 Q6 **Gross Welle** E Germany 53.02N 12.06E
63 L4 **Gross-Wittensee** W Germany 54.24N 9.46E
63 Q7 **Gross Wudicke** E Germany 52.36N 12.15E
63 R5 **Gross Wüstenfelde** E Germany 53.54N 12.34E
63 Q8 **Gross Wusterwitz** E Germany 52.22N 12.23E
63 T7 **Gross Ziethen** E Germany 52.57N 13.55E
64 F4 **Gross-Zimmern** W Germany 49.52N 8.50E
69 M6 **Grostenquin** France 48.58N 6.44E
70 M3 **Gros Theil, le** France 49.13N 0.49E
82 B5 **Grosuplje** Yugoslavia 45.57N 14.40E
112 H4 **Grosvenor** Texas 31.53N 99.10W
103 L3 **Grosvenor Dale** Connecticut 41.59N 71.54W

13 J5 Grosvenor Downs Queensland 22.02S 148.04E
113 K7 Grosvenor, L Alaska 58.40N 155.20W
110 P6 Gros Ventre Ra Wyoming
53 T17 Grøsvik Norway 60.41N 5.41E
60 L8 Grote Brekken L Netherlands 52.52N 5.41E
61 N2 Grote-Brogel Belgium 51.09N 5.30E
63 J9 Grotenberg mt W Germany 51.54N 8.50E
61 F3 Grotenberge Belgium 50.52N 3.50E
61 K2 Grote Nete R Belgium
53 X14 Grotli Norway 62.01N 7.40E
103 K4 Groton Connecticut 41.22N 72.05W
104 O4 Groton Massachusetts 42.36N 71.35W
104 J4 Groton New York 42.36N 76.23W
108 M4 Groton S Dakota 45.28N 98.07W
104 N2 Groton Vermont 44.13N 72.13W
51 D4 Grøtøy Norway 67.51N 14.45E
80 K7 Grotta Azzurra cave Italy 40.34N 14.13E
80 H6 Grotta delle Capre Italy 41.13N 13.05E
79 P3 Grotta Gigante cave Italy 45.43N 13.46E
81 P11 Grottaglie Italy 40.32N 17.26E
80 M6 Grottaminarda Italy 41.04N 15.04E
80 J3 Grottammare Italy 42.59N 13.52E
53 Y14 Grøttavatn L Norway 62.29N 8.00E
80 J2 Grottazzolina Italy 43.07N 13.36E
81 G9 Grotte Sicily 37.24N 13.42E
71 C8 Grotte-de-Dargilan France 44.12N 3.22E
72 G5 Grotte-de-Lascaux France 45.03N 1.10E
71 D9 Grotte-des-Demoiselles France 43.54N 3.45E
80 E3 Grotte di Castro Italy 42.40N 11.52E
81 M7 Grotteria Italy 38.22N 16.16E
72 D9 Grottes-de-Betharram France 43.06N 0.11W
71 F8 Grottes-de-St.Marcel France 44.20N 4.33E
104 G8 Grottoes Virginia 38.16N 78.50W
81 M2 Gróttole Italy 40.36N 16.23E
64 F5 Grotzingen W Germany 49.01N 8.30E
88 K5 Grou R Morocco
100 A3 Grouard Alberta 55.30N 116.02W
101 P3 Grouard L N-W Terr
70 G4 Grouin, Pte.du France 48.43N 1.50W
89 H8 Groumania Ivory Coast 7.55N 3.56W
99 H4 Groundhog R Ontario
110 M6 Grouse Idaho 43.41N 113.36W
110 M8 Grouse Creek Utah 41.44N 113.54W
101 G10 Grouse Mt Br Col 49.24N 123.05W
94 L7 Groutville S Africa 29.25S 31.14E
60 M7 Grouw Netherlands 53.06N 5.50E
88 N5 Grouz, Jbel mts Morocco
52 D8 Grovane Norway 58.17N 8.00E
53 X13 Grøvdal Norway 62.35N 7.56E
109 Q5 Grove Oklahoma 36.34N 94.46W
76 B4 Grove Spain 42.30N 8.52W
53 U16 Grovebre glacier Norway 61.29N 6.30E
104 B7 Grove City Ohio 39.53N 83.06W
104 E5 Grove City Pennsylvania 41.10N 80.05W
101 O8 Grovedale Alberta 55.02N 118.50W
107 J10 Grove Hill Alabama 31.42N 87.48W
13 B2 Grove Hill N Terr Australia 13.29S 131.33E
53 C4 Grove Kirke Denmark 56.19N 9.03E
111 D4 Groveland California 37.50N 120.14W
52 G4 Grövelsjön Sweden 64.05N 12.20E
123 D5 Grove Mts Antarctica
76 B4 Grove, Pen.del Spain
109 F1 Grover Colorado 40.52N 104.14W
110 P7 Grover Wyoming 42.47N 110.56W
111 D6 Grover City California 35.06N 120.35W
112 O6 Groves Texas 29.55N 93.53W
104 O2 Groveton New Hampshire 44.35N 71.32W
112 M4 Groveton Texas 31.04N 95.08W
105 E4 Grovetown Georgia 33.27N 82.12W
11 H8 Grovetown New Zealand 41.30S 173.59E
110 P5 Grovont Wyoming 43.39N 110.41W
111 L9 Growler Arizona 32.49N 113.47W
111 L9 Growler Mts Arizona
82 L7 Grozd'ovo Bulgaria 43.01N 27.33E
79 P4 Grožnjan Yugoslavia 45.22N 13.43E
43 K5 Groznoye Kirgiziya U.S.S.R. 42.33N 71.10E
44 G4 Groznyy U.S.S.R. 43.21N 45.42E
53 W21 Grubbåfjell mt Norway 59.57N 7.00E
60 N14 Grubbenvorst Netherlands 51.25N 6.10E
63 O4 Grube W Germany 54.14N 11.03E
63 U9 Grube Ilse E Germany 51.34N 14.01E
66 S3 Grübele Kopf mt Switz/Austria 47.01N 10.24E
63 L9 Grubenhagen W Germany 51.46N 9.50E
66 F5 Grubenwald Switzerland 46.35N 7.23E
82 D5 Grubišno Polje Yugoslavia 45.41N 17.11E
64 P6 Grubweg W Germany 48.35N 13.30E
70 M2 Gruchet-le-Valasse France 49.33N 0.30E
82 E8 Gruda Yugoslavia 42.31N 18.22E
82 L8 Grudovo Bulgaria 42.21N 27.10E
62 M2 Grudusk Poland 53.03N 20.40E
62 L2 Grudziadz Poland 53.29N 18.45E
72 B3 Grues France 46.24N 1.18W
120 D9 Gruesa, Pta C Chile 20.26S 70.12W
98 B6 Grues, I aux Quebec
69 L7 Gruey-lès-Surance France 48.02N 6.12E
58 F3 Gruinard Highland Scotland 57.52N 5.26W
58 F3 Gruinard B Highland Scotland
58 F3 Gruinard, Little Highland Scotland 57.50N 5.27W
58 D7 Gruinart, L Islay, Strathclyde Scotland 55.52N 6.20W
72 L9 Gruissan France 43.07N 3.06E
Gruissan, Étang de see Ayrolle, Étang de l'
61 N2 Gruitrode Belgium 51.05N 5.36E
112 J9 Grulla Texas 26.16N 98.41W
50 T14 Grumantbyen Land Spitsbergen 78.10N 15.15E
64 D4 Grumbach W Germany 49.39N 7.33E
81 L3 Grumento Nova Italy 40.17N 15.53E
92 G3 Grumeti R Tanzania
93 F8 Grummetti watercourse Tanzania
81 N1 Grumo Appula Italy 41.02N 16.43E
52 G7 Grums Sweden 59.20N 13.05E
45 F6 Grun Ukraine U.S.S.R. 50.15N 34.37E
64 O2 Grüna E Germany 50.48N 12.47E
65 J6 Grünau Austria 47.51N 13.58E
63 T8 Grunau E Germany 52.25N 13.36E
94 E6 Grunau Namibia 27.47S 18.23E
65 N6 Grunbach Austria 47.49N 15.59E
64 G6 Grunbach W Germany 48.49N 9.25E
Grünberg Poland see Zielona Góra
64 F2 Grünberg W Germany 50.35N 8.58E
50 D5 Grund Borgarfjardharsýsla Iceland 64.35N 21.35W
50 G3 Grund Eyjafjardharsýsla Iceland 65.32N 18.06W
50 B5 Grundarfjördhur Iceland 64.55N 23.16W
50 B5 Grundarfjördhur B Iceland
64 G3 Gründau W Germany 50.13N 9.07E
Gründelhardt see Frankenhardt
48 R11 Grundene bank Greenland
56 O3 Grundisburgh Suffolk Eng 52.07N 1.15E
65 J6 Grundl-see L Austria 47.37N 13.52E
52 L3 Grundsunda Sweden 63.21N 19.20E
52 K3 Grundtjärn Sweden 63.32N 17.25E
108 S7 Grundy Center Iowa 42.22N 92.43W
99 K7 Grundy Lake Prov.Park Ontario
61 M6 Grune Belgium 50.09N 5.23E
53 X19 Grungebru Norway 59.42N 7.50E
53 X19 Grungedal Norway 59.44N 7.43E
53 X19 Grungevatn L Norway 59.44N 7.45E
115 J5 Gruñidora Mexico 24.12N 101.57W
63 Q8 Grüningen E Germany 52.17N 12.28E
66 M2 Grüningen Switzerland 47.17N 8.47E
50 C2 Grunnavik inlet Iceland
64 H4 Grünsfeld W Germany 49.36N 9.46E
64 E4 Grünstadt W Germany 49.34N 8.10E
65 B6 Grüntensee L W Germany 47.39N 10.29E
64 M7 Grünwald W Germany 48.02N 11.35E
61 M6 Grupont Belgium 50.06N 5.17E
95 G4 Gruqualand West reg S Africa
71 D3 Grury France 46.41N 3.55E
66 P4 Grüsch Switzerland 46.59N 9.38E
58 Q9 Gruting Shetland Scotland 60.14N 1.30W
58 Q10 Grutness Shetland Scotland 59.52N 1.17W
66 H5 Grütschalp Switzerland 46.37N 7.53E
112 C7 Gruver Texas 36.14N 101.25W
66 E5 Gruyère, L.de Switzerland
66 E5 Gruyères Switzerland 46.35N 7.05E
46 E2 Gruzdžiai Lithuania U.S.S.R. 56.02N 23.11E
38 D4 Gruzinskaya S.S.R U.S.S.R.
42 H4 Gruznovka U.S.S.R. 55.10N 105.20E
41 J5 Gryada-Khara-Tas heights U.S.S.R.
41 P3 Gryada Shmidta mts Novosibirskiye O-va U.S.S.R.
45 L4 Gryazi U.S.S.R. 52.30N 39.56E
45 L2 Gryaznoye Ryazan' U.S.S.R. 54.02N 39.08E
45 Q7 Gryaznoye Volgograd U.S.S.R. 49.41N 44.39E
45 U2 Gryaznukha U.S.S.R. 54.15N 48.15E
39 D3 Gryaznyy U.S.S.R. 63.15N 146.43E
46 M1 Gryazovets U.S.S.R. 58.52N 40.12E
62 M6 Grybów Poland 49.38N 20.54E
52 J6 Grycksbo Sweden 60.41N 15.30E
58 G7 Gryfe Water R Strathclyde Scotland
62 J2 Gryfice Poland 53.55N 15.11E
62 H2 Gryfino Poland 53.15N 14.30E
108 P1 Grygla Minnesota 48.19N 95.38W
66 E6 Gryon Switzerland 46.17N 7.04E
53 U13 Grytefjorden inlet Norway 62.32N 6.25E
53 T20 Grytenuten mt Norway 59.25N 5.59E
53 W14 Grytevatn L Norway 62.27N 7.06E
52 H7 Grythyttan Sweden 59.53N 14.32E
51 E3 Grytøya isld Norway 68.55N 16.30E
53 S16 Grytøyra Norway 61.17N 5.01E
53 X13 Grytten Norway 62.33N 7.42E
121 G8 Grytviken S Georgia 54.17S 36.30W
62 J2 Grzmiąca Poland 53.50N 16.29E
65 D7 Gschnitz Austria 47.03N 11.21E
64 H6 Gschwend W Germany 48.56N 9.45E
66 H5 Gspaltenhorn Switzerland 46.31N 7.50E
66 F6 Gstaad Switzerland 46.28N 7.17E
64 N8 Gstadt W Germany 47.53N 12.26E
66 F6 Gsteig Switzerland 46.23N 7.17E
58 G7 Gt Cumbrae I Strathclyde Scotland 55.46N 4.55W
29 J6 Gua Bihar India 22.16N 85.24E
92 G10 Gua Mozambique 17.12S 35.10E
92 F5 Gua Tanzania 7.50S 32.28E
Guabiruparaná,R see Eiru, R
115 N5 Guabito Panama 9.30N 82.36W
119 D6 Guacamayas Colombia 2.16N 74.57W
116 F4 Guacanayabo, G.de Cuba
119 F2 Guacara Venezuela 10.15N 67.53W
119 E5 Guacharía, R Colombia
111 M9 Gu Achi Arizona 32.19N 112.03W
120 F11 Guachipas Argentina 25.31S 65.31W
120 F11 Guachipas, R Argentina
115 N4 Guácimo Costa Rica 10.10N 83.40W
118 C8 Guaçu Brazil 22.07S 54.31W
118 H7 Guaçuí Brazil 20.44S 41.40W
77 K5 Guadahortuna Spain 37.33N 3.24W
77 E6 Guadaira R Spain
77 E6 Guadairilla R Spain
77 C3 Guadajira R Spain
77 E5 Guadajoz Spain 37.35N 5.40W
77 G5 Guadajoz R Spain
115 H7 Guadalajara Mexico 20.40N 103.20W
75 D6 Guadalajara Spain 40.37N 3.10W
74 F4 Guadalajara prov Spain
75 G7 Guadalaviar Spain 40.23N 1.44W
75 H7 Guadalaviar R Spain
77 G4 Guadalbarbo R Spain
77 J5 Guadalbullón R Spain
77 E7 Guadalcacin, Embalse de res Spain 36.40N 5.45W
77 E4 Guadalcanal Spain 38.06N 5.49W
15 L3 Guadalcanal I Solomon Is
77 G5 Guadalcazar Spain 37.46N 4.56W
77 E3 Guadalefra R Spain
77 K4 Guadalén R Spain
77 K4 Guadalen, Embalse de res Spain 38.14N 3.25W
77 L5 Guadalentin R Spain
77 N5 Guadalentín R Spain
121 C5 Guadales Argentina 34.30S 67.55W
77 D7 Guadalete R Spain
77 J7 Guadalfeo R Spain
77 G7 Guadalhorce R Spain
77 G7 Guadalhorce, Embalse de res Spain
77 K4 Guadalimar R Spain
77 H7 Guadalmedina R Spain
74 D6 Guadalmellato R Spain
77 G4 Guadalmellato, Embalse del res Spain 38.04N 4.41W
77 L3 Guadalmena R Spain
77 L4 Guadalmena, Embalse de res Spain
77 G3 Guadalmez R Spain
75 K5 Guadalope Spain
77 F5 Guadalquivir R Spain
121 C5 Guadal, Sa.de ra Argentina
77 G7 Guadalteba R Spain
77 G7 Guadalteba, Embalse de res Spain 36.55N 4.50W
96 R2 Guadalupe Azores 39.04N 28.01W
115 A1 Guadalupe Baja California Mexico 32.04N 116.35W
117 F8 Guadalupe Brazil 6.42S 43.45W
111 D7 Guadalupe California 34.57N 120.33W
115 H6 Guadalupe Mexico 22.47N 102.30W
115 J5 Guadalupe Nuevo León Mexico 25.43N 100.15W
120 A8 Guadalupe Peru 7.17S 79.28W
115 L8 Guadalupe Puebla Mexico 19.12N 97.28W
76 J10 Guadalupe Spain 39.27N 5.19W
102 C5 Guadalupe I Mexico
111 H9 Guadalupe R Mexico
112 J6 Guadalupe R Texas
115 F2 Guadalupe Bravos Mexico 31.25N 106.08W
76 J10 Guadalupejo R Spain
112 C4 Guadalupe Mountains Nat. Pk Texas 31.55N 104.52W
109 E9 Guadalupe Mts New Mexico
76 J10 Guadalupe, Sierra de mts Spain
115 G5 Guadalupe Victoria Mexico 24.30N 104.08W
115 F4 Guadalupe y Calvo Mexico 26.04N 106.58W
75 E7 Guadamajud R Spain
77 E3 Guadamez R Spain
76 L9 Guadamur Spain 39.49N 4.09W
76 L7 Guadarrama Spain 40.40N 4.06W
119 F3 Guadarrama Venezuela 8.30N 68.03W
76 L8 Guadarrama R Spain
76 L7 Guadarrama, Pto.de pass Spain 40.41N 4.09W
75 C6 Guadarrama, Sierra de mts Spain
77 F3 Guadarramilla R Spain
76 J10 Guadarranque Spain
77 F8 Guadarranque, Embalse del res Spain 36.20N 5.29W
77 Q2 Guadasuar Spain 39.11N 0.28W
75 G8 Guadazaón R Spain
116 N4 Guadeloupe I Lesser Antilles W I
116 N6 Guadeloupe Passage Lesser Antilles W I
115 G5 Guadelupe Aguilera Mexico 24.28N 104.41W
77 D6 Guadiamar R Spain
74 C6 Guadiana R Portugal/Spain
77 L3 Guadiana Alto R Spain
116 B3 Guadiana, B.de Cuba
77 K2 Guadiana, Can.del Spain
77 K5 Guadiana Menor R Spain
77 F8 Guadiaro R Spain
77 G4 Guadiato R Spain
75 E7 Guadiela R Spain
76 J8 Guadiervas R Spain
76 G10 Guadiloba R Spain
77 K6 Guadix Spain 37.19N 3.08W
76 F5 Guadramil Portugal 41.54N 6.34W
121 A9 Guafo, G. de Chile
121 A9 Guafo, I Chile 43.40S 74.45W
81 Q12 Guagnano Italy 40.24N 17.57E
67 O12 Guagno-les-Bains Corsica 42.09N 8.58E
19 G1 Guagua Luzon Philippines 14.57N 120.38E
116 P1 Guaico Trinidad & Tobago 10.35N 61.09W
118 G5 Guaicuí Brazil 17.10S 44.49W
118 C7 Guaicuras Brazil 20.07S 56.44W
119 B7 Guaillabamba, R Ecuador
115 L2 Guaimaca Honduras 14.34N 86.49W
116 F4 Guáimaro Cuba 21.02N 77.24W
119 G5 Guaina Venezuela 5.09N 63.37W
119 F6 Guaina, R Venez/Colombia
119 E6 Guainía div Colombia
119 G5 Guaiquinima, Cerro mt Venez 5.47N 63.42W
118 C9 Guaíra Brazil 24.05S 54.15W
118 C9 Guaíra dept Paraguay
Guaíra Falls see Salto das Sete Quedas
121 A9 Guaitecas Is Chile
116 F4 Guajaba, Cayo isld Cuba 21.53N 77.32W
96 Q14 Guajara mt Tenerife Canary Is 28.14N 16.36W
117 D5 Guajará Açu Brazil 1.37S 48.07W
120 F4 Guajará Mirim Brazil 10.50S 65.21W
117 C6 Guajara, R Brazil
120 G1 Guajaratuba Brazil 5.05S 62.45W
75 B8 Guajaraz, Embalse de res Spain
77 J7 Guajar Faraguit Spain 36.51N 3.35W
120 E2 Guajarraã Brazil 7.44S 66.54W
115 H3 Guaje, Llano de plain Mexico
115 L2 Guajiniquil Honduras 14.22N 86.08W
119 D2 Guajira div Colombia
119 E1 Guajira, Pen. de Colombia
115 N5 Gualaca Panama 8.33N 82.19W
119 B9 Gualaceo Ecuador 2.56S 78.48W
120 D10 Gualaguala, Pta Chile 22.45S 70.18W
89 E7 Gualako Guinea 9.45N 9.52W
111 A3 Gualala California 38.45N 123.31W
115 P10 Gualán Guatemala 15.06N 89.22W
119 B9 Gualaquiza Ecuador 3.32S 78.38W
77 F5 Gualbacarejo R Spain
77 K7 Gualchos Spain 36.45N 3.24W
80 G2 Gualdo Tadino Italy 43.13N 12.47E
72 C4 Gua, le Charente-Maritime France 45.44N 0.57W
71 H6 Guâ, le Isère France 45.00N 5.37E
121 F4 Gualeguay Argentina 33.10S 59.14W
121 F4 Gualeguay R Argentina
121 F4 Gualeguaychu Argentina 33.03S 59.31W
121 D8 Gualicho, Salina salt pan Arg
76 J9 Gualija R Spain
121 B9 Gualjaina Argentina 42.43S 70.30W
120 D8 Guallatiri vol Chile 18.25S 69.08W
121 A5 Gualleco Chile 35.10S 72.03W
79 J5 Gualtieri Italy 44.54N 10.37E
19 L1 Guam isld Pacific Oc
117 E5 Guamá Brazil 1.35S 47.29W
119 F2 Guama Venezuela 10.18N 68.49W
119 D3 Guamal Colombia 9.10N 74.15W
119 B10 Guamani, Cord de mts Peru
117 E5 Guamá, R Brazil
121 A10 Guamblin, I Chile 44.50S 75.10W
121 E6 Guamini Argentina 37.01S 62.28W
119 D5 Guamo Colombia 4.02N 74.57W
116 F4 Guamo Cuba 20.39N 76.58W
119 B8 Guamote Ecuador 1.58S 78.46W
119 G5 Guampí, Sa.de mts Venezuela
115 E5 Guamúchil Mexico 25.28N 108.10W
119 C7 Guamués R Colombia
18 B7 Gua Musang Pen Malaysia 4.52N 101.59E
22 K7 Gu'an Hebei China 39.26N 116.19E
116 C3 Guanabacoa Cuba 23.08N 82.18W
120 D4 Guanabara Brazil 10.46S 70.08W
118 J8 Guanabara, B.de Brazil
115 M4 Guanacaste, Cord. de ra Costa Rica
115 F5 Guanacevi Mexico 25.56N 105.57W
116 B4 Guanahacabibes, Pen. de Cuba
105 L7 Guana I Virgin Is 18.30N 64.37W
115 M1 Guanaja Honduras 16.29N 85.52W
116 C3 Guanajay Cuba 22.56N 82.42W
115 J7 Guanajuato Mexico 21.00N 101.16W
115 J7 Guanajuato state Mexico
118 G4 Guanambi Brazil 14.14S 42.44W
119 F6 Guaname R Venezuela
120 A3 Guañape, I.de Peru 8.32S 78.59W
116 O1 Guanapo Trinidad & Tobago 10.35N 61.16W
30 H2 Guanara Glacier Nepal
119 E3 Guanare Venezuela 9.04N 69.45W
119 E3 Guanare Viejo, R Venezuela
119 E3 Guanarito Venezuela 8.43N 69.12W
119 E3 Guanarito, R Venezuela
96 U14 Guanarteme, Pta. de Gran Canaria Canary Is 28.11N 15.38W
119 F5 Guanay, Sierra mts Venezuela
22 J7 Guancen Shan mt ra Shanxi China
23 E8 Guanchang Guangdong China 20.38N 110.18E
121 C2 Guandacol Argentina 29.32S 68.37W
22 L5 Guandegong Nei Monggol Zizhiqu China 42.54N 118.03E
21 D6 Guandi Jilin China 43.34N 128.31E
23 E3 Guandiankou Hubei China 34.18N 111.01E
116 B3 Guane Cuba 22.13N 84.07W
23 H4 Guanfeng Jiangxi China 28.20N 118.11E
23 D3 Guang'an Sichuan China 30.25N 106.41E
23 G5 Guangchang Jiangxi China 26.48N 116.06E
23 H3 Guangde Anhui China 30.55N 119.23E
23 F7 Guangdong prov China
23 H4 Guangfeng Jiangxi China 28.20N 118.11E
23 C3 Guangfu Sichuan China 30.45N 104.55E
23 C3 Guanghan Sichuan China 30.59N 104.18E
23 C1 Guanghe Gansu China 35.30N 103.25E
23 F2 Guanghua Hubei China 32.24N 111.40E
23 F1 Guanghua Shanxi China 36.03N 111.12E
23 G4 Guangji Hubei China 29.51N 115.38E
22 K7 Guangling Shanxi China 39.45N 114.10E
21 B8 Guanglu Dao isld Liaoning China
23 B5 Guangmao Shan mt Yunnan China
23 H3 Guangming Ding mt pk Anhui China 30.05N 118.04E
23 D6 Guangnan Yunnan China 24.05N 105.04E
23 F7 Guangning Guangdong China 23.37N 112.26E
22 K8 Guangping Hebei China 36.29N 114.54E
22 L8 Guangrao Shandong China 37.04N 118.22E
23 G2 Guangshan Henan China 32.03N 115.00E
23 G3 Guangshui Hubei China 31.37N 114.00E
23 D7 Guangxi prov China
23 H3 Guangyang Anhui China 30.24N 117.59E
23 F6 Guangyang Guangxi China 25.32N 110.54E
23 D2 Guangyuan Sichuan China 32.25N 105.56E
23 H5 Guangze Fujian China 27.33N 117.24E
23 F7 Guangzhou Guangdong China 23.08N 113.20E
22 K8 Guangzong Hebei China 37.05N 115.10E
118 G6 Guanhães Brazil 18.46S 42.58W
118 G6 Guanhães R Brazil
105 J8 Guánica Puerto Rico 17.59N 66.55W
115 O6 Guánico Panama 7.20N 80.21W
119 H3 Guanipa, R Venezuela
23 F5 Guanjiazui Hunan China 26.56N 111.50E
Guankou see Ningshan
23 D6 Guanling Guizhou China 26.00N 105.40E
23 E3 Guanmian Shan mts Sichuan China
23 H1 Guannan Jiangsu China 34.09N 119.25E
119 B8 Guano Ecuador 1.38S 78.40W
119 H2 Guanoca Venezuela 10.09N 62.51W
110 F7 Guano L Oregon 42.10N 119.31W
21 D4 Guansongzhen Heilongjiang China 46.12N 128.55E
Guansuo see Guanling
119 G2 Guanta Venezuela 10.15N 64.38W
116 G4 Guantánamo Cuba 20.09N 75.14W
116 G5 Guantánamo, B.de Cuba 19.59N 75.10W
22 K8 Guantao Hebei China 36.40N 115.22E
22 K6 Guanting Sk L Hebei China 40.22N 115.20E
22 K6 Guanting Sk res Hebei China
22 K8 Guan Xian Shandong China 36.29N 115.21E
23 C3 Guan Xian Sichuan China 31.01N 103.40E
23 D2 Guanyinsi Shaanxi China 33.23N 106.26E
23 C3 Guanyinyan Sichuan China 30.30N 102.09E
119 C4 Guapà Colombia 7.34N 76.38W
118 F7 Guapé Brazil 20.45S 45.52W
119 C6 Guapí Colombia 2.36N 77.54W
115 N4 Guápiles Costa Rica 10.15N 83.46W
121 A9 Guapi Quilán isld Chile
116 N2 Guapo B Trinidad & Tobago
121 H2 Guaporé Rio Grande do Sul Brazil 28.55S 51.55W
Guaporé fed terr see Rondônia
121 H2 Guaporé R Rio Grande do Sul Brazil
120 F5 Guaporé, R Bolivia/Brazil
120 E7 Guaqui Bolivia 16.38S 68.50W
118 F3 Guará R Brazil
117 J8 Guarabira Brazil 6.46S 35.25W
119 B8 Guaranda Ecuador 1.36S 79.30W
118 H7 Guarapari Brazil 20.39S 40.31W
118 D9 Guarapuava Brazil 25.22S 51.28W
118 E9 Guaraqueçaba Brazil 25.18S 48.23W
118 E7 Guararapes Brazil 21.17S 50.38W
117 J9 Guararapes airport Brazil 8.14S 34.55W
115 O6 Guararé Panama 7.50N 80.18W
75 K3 Guara, Sierra de mts Spain
89 E7 Guarasso Guinea 8.01N 8.13W
118 F8 Guaratinguetá Brazil 22.49S 45.09W
118 E9 Guaratuba Brazil 25.53S 48.38W
118 E9 Guaratuba, B Brazil 25.52S 48.40W
120 E5 Guarayos Bolivia 13.20S 68.50W
120 G6 Guarayos, R Bolivia
96 P11 Guarazoca Hierro Canary Is 27.48N 17.58W
80 H5 Guarcino Italy 41.48N 13.20E
76 E7 Guarda Portugal 40.32N 7.17W
66 R4 Guarda Switzerland 46.47N 10.09E
76 E7 Guarda dist Portugal
87 N5 Guardafui, C Somalia 11.50N 51.16E
77 L5 Guardal R Spain
77 E3 Guarda, La Spain 38.48N 5.43W
77 P4 Guardamar de Segura Spain 38.05N 0.39W
118 F5 Guarda Mor Brazil 17.43S 47.06W
119 F3 Guardatinajas Venezuela 9.04N 67.23W
81 N6 Guardavalle Italy 38.31N 16.30E
58 L6 Guard Bridge Fife Scotland 56.22N 2.54W
80 F3 Guardea Italy 42.37N 12.18E
77 J5 Guardia de Jaén, La Spain 37.44N 3.41W
121 E2 Guardia Escolta Argentina 28.59S 62.05W
80 K4 Guardiagrele Italy 42.12N 14.14E
75 D8 Guardia, La Spain 39.47N 3.29W
76 B5 Guardia, La Spain 41.54N 8.53W
121 L7 Guardián, C Argentina 48.22S 66.22W
81 M5 Guardia Piemontese Italy 39.28N 16.00E
80 L6 Guardia Sanframondi Italy 41.15N 14.36E
75 O3 Guardiola Spain 42.13N 1.53E
75 O4 Guardiola Spain 41.40N 1.46E
80 C2 Guardistallo Italy 43.19N 10.37E
76 K3 Guardo Spain 42.47N 4.50W
76 D8 Guardunha, Sa. da mts Portugal
77 D3 Guareña Spain 38.51N 6.06W
76 J6 Guareña R Spain
75 K3 Guarga R Spain
15 J8 Guari Papua New Guinea 8.06S 146.53E
119 G9 Guariba, R Amazonas Brazil
117 C7 Guaribas, Cachoeira rapids Brazil 4.25S 52.40W
120 G3 Guaribe Mato Grosso Brazil
120 G3 Guaribe R Brazil
119 F3 Guárico state Venezuela
116 G4 Guarico, Pta C Cuba 20.40N 74.46W
119 F3 Guárico, R Venezuela
119 G3 Guario Venezuela 9.25N 64.31W
115 P10 Guarita Honduras 14.10N 88.46W
121 H1 Guarita R Brazil
118 A3 Guaritire, R Brazil
77 G7 Guaro Spain 36.40N 4.50W
77 K4 Guarrizás R Spain
77 J4 Guarrizas, Embalse del res Spain 38.15N 3.35W
119 E5 Guarrojo, R Colombia
77 J4 Guarromán Spain 38.11N 3.41W
75 M3 Guart R Spain
118 F9 Guarujá Brazil 24.00S 46.22W
118 G9 Guarulhos dist São Paulo Brazil
119 F6 Guasacavi, Cerro mt Colombia 2.54N 68.15W
119 F6 Guasacavi, R Colombia
15 M8 Guasapa Papua New Guinea 9.12S 152.58E
119 D2 Guasare, R Venezuela
115 E5 Guasave Mexico 25.33N 108.30W
119 E4 Guasdualito Venezuela 7.15N 70.40W
81 C4 Guasila Sardinia 39.34N 9.03E
115 K7 Guasima Mexico 20.55N 97.52W
119 H4 Guasipati Venezuela 7.28N 61.58W
118 C9 Guassú, R Brazil
79 J5 Guastalla Italy 44.56N 10.39E
29 L7 Guasuba R W Bengal India
120 D9 Guatacondo Chile 20.56S 69.06W
115 O10 Guatemala Guatemala 14.38N 90.22W
102 H7 Guatemala rep Central America
119 D5 Guateque Colombia 5.02N 73.25W
121 E4 Guatimozin Argentina 33.29S 62.24W
119 F2 Guatire Venezuela 10.30N 66.33W
96 V7 Guatiza Lanzarote Canary Is 29.05N 13.29W
75 K3 Guatizalema R Spain
121 D6 Guatraché Argentina 37.40S 63.12W
121 D9 Guatrochi Argentina 42.16S 65.07W
116 P2 Guatuaro Pt Trinidad & Tobago 10.20N 60.58W
15 L9 Guaugurina Papua New Guinea 10.36S 150.28E
15 L9 Guaugurina B Papua New Guinea
15 G7 Guavi R Papua New Guinea
119 E6 Guaviare, R Colombia
121 G2 Guaviravi Argentina 29.20S 56.50W
118 F7 Guaxupé Brazil 21.17S 46.44W
98 S8 Guay Quebec 46.48N 71.11W
58 J5 Guay Tayside Scotland 56.38N 3.39W
119 C4 Guayabal Antioquia Colombia 6.34N 76.53W
119 E5 Guayabal Boyaca Colombia 4.46N 71.25W
116 F4 Guayabal Cuba 20.42N 77.36W
119 D6 Guayabero, R Meta/Vaupes Colombia
119 F5 Guayabero, R Vichada Colombia
121 B3 Guayacán Chile 30.00S 71.26W
121 C3 Guayaguas, Sa.de ra Argentina
116 P2 Guayaguayare Trinidad & Tobago 10.09N 61.02W
96 F8 Guayana Basin Atlantic Oc
119 F5 Guayapo, R Venezuela
119 B9 Guayaquil Ecuador 2.13S 79.54W
119 A9 Guayaquil, G.de Ecuador
120 F4 Guayaramerin Bolivia 10.51S 65.23W
119 B9 Guayas prov Ecuador
119 C7 Guayas, R Colombia
120 F10 Guayatayoc, L.de Argentina
118 B10 Guaycuru R Argentina
121 H6 Guayeco, Arch Chile
115 D4 Guaymas Mexico 27.59N 110.54W
121 F3 Guayquiraro R Argentina
23 H1 Guayun Jiangsu China 34.27N 119.20E
115 O10 Guazacapán Guatemala 14.03N 90.26W
23 H2 Guazhou Jiangsu China 32.12N 119.28E
94 D2 Gub Namibia 19.37S 16.12E
87 G8 Guba Ethiopia 4.52N 39.18E
91 K9 Guba Zaïre 10.38S 26.27E
87 M5 Gubado Somalia 10.19N 48.05E
47 H1 Guba Dolgaya U.S.S.R. 70.17N 58.40E
23 C4 Gubai Sichuan China 28.58N 104.18E
47 H6 Gubakha U.S.S.R. 58.55N 57.30E
87 J5 Guban reg Somalia
19 M5 Gubat Luzon Philippines 12.55N 124.08E
87 E5 Gubba Ethiopia 11.17N 35.20E
93 K2 Gubbadummi Ethiopia 3.53N 38.31E
28 C4 Gubbi Karnataka India 13.20N 76.56E
80 G2 Gubbio Italy 43.21N 12.35E
44 H5 Gubden U.S.S.R. 42.34N 47.34E
47 H5 Gubdor U.S.S.R. 60.12N 56.40E
34 J2 Gubeiba Syria 36.12N 41.10E
22 L6 Gubeikou Beijing China 40.45N 117.11E
87 A9 Gubeli Zaïre 3.32N 27.01E
Guben see Wilhelm-Pieck-Stadt
47 M5 Gubernskoye U.S.S.R. 55.28N 60.35E
77 B5 Gubica R Spain
62 H4 Gubin Poland 51.59N 14.43E
45 G8 Gubinikha Ukraine U.S.S.R. 48.48N 35.15E
90 F5 Gubio Nigeria 12.32N 12.44E
45 J5 Gubkin U.S.S.R. 51.17N 37.32E
86 E6 Gubr, Gebel hill Egypt 29.59N 30.31E
93 F6 Gucha R Kenya
94 D2 Guchab Namibia 19.40S 17.47E
72 E10 Guchen France 42.52N 0.20E
22 K8 Gucheng Hebei China 37.09N 115.50E
23 F2 Gucheng Hubei China 32.20N 111.30E
23 C2 Gucheng Sichuan China 32.25N 104.55E
Guchi see Qūshchi
22 F4 Guchin-Us Mongolia 45.27N 102.24E
28 C6 Gudalur Madura, Madras India 9.41N 77.17E
28 C5 Gudalur Nilgiris, Tamil Nadu India 11.30N 76.30E
75 J7 Gúdar Spain 40.26N 0.44W
29 H8 Gudari Orissa India 19.24N 83.50E
75 J7 Gúdar, Sierra de mts Spain
44 D4 Gudauta Georgia U.S.S.R. 43.08N 40.10E
53 F6 Gudbjerg Denmark 55.09N 10.40E
52 D4 Gudbrandsdalen V Norway
53 T16 Guddal Norway 61.14N 5.32E
28 D4 Guddiyatam Tamil Nadu India 13.00N 78.51E
31 E6 Guddu Barrage Pakistan 28.23N 69.47E
15 B4 Gude Hoop, Tanjung de C Irian Jaya 0.19S 132.24E
53 D4 Gudenå R Denmark
64 G1 Gudensberg W Germany 51.10N 9.21E
44 G4 Gudermes U.S.S.R. 43.22N 46.06E
53 D7 Guderup Denmark 55.00N 9.52E
29 D4 Gudha Rajasthan India 26.58N 75.10E
Gud Hasht Takkeh see Gowd-e-Hasht Tekkeh
53 P12 Gudhjem Bornholm Denmark 53.13N 14.59E
76 E4 Gudiña, La Spain 42.04N 7.08W
28 E2 Gudivada Andhra Prad India 16.28N 81.03E
84 Z20 Gudja Malta 35.51N 14.31E
53 F6 Gudme Denmark 55.09N 10.43E
69 J7 Gudmont France 48.21N 5.08E
23 A6 Gudong Yunnan China 25.21N 98.29E
31 C7 Gudri R Pakistan
87 F6 Gudr,R Ethiopia
87 K6 Gudubi Somalia 8.48N 45.00E
23 F1 Gudui Shanxi China 35.14N 111.46E
36 F2 Güdül Turkey 40.12N 32.14E
53 G6 Gudum Denmark 55.26N 11.24E
53 A3 Gudumbro Denmark 56.31N 8.28E
53 E3 Gudumholm Denmark 56.58N 10.07E
53 A3 Gudum Kirke Denmark 56.31N 8.28E
28 D3 Gudur Kurnool, Andhra Prad India 15.45N 78.30E
28 D3 Gudur Nellore, Andhra Prad India 14.10N 79.51E
53 V17 Gudvangen Norway 60.52N 6.50E
40 F6 Gudzhal R U.S.S.R.
89 G4 Guébou Mali 15.04N 4.35W
69 N8 Guebwiller France 47.55N 7.13E
75 D1 Guecho Spain 43.21N 3.01W
70 M5 Gué-de-la-Chaîne France 48.22N 0.31E
70 O4 Gue-de-Longroi, le France 48.30N 1.43E
119 G9 Guedes, L. do Brazil 2.22S 65.38W
72 C3 Gué-de-Velluire, le France 46.23N 0.55W
90 M9 Guedimba Cent Afr Rep 5.34N 25.21E
88 M4 Guefaït Morocco 34.14N 2.23W
70 E6 Guegon France 47.56N 2.34W
99 N4 Guéguen, L Quebec
70 E6 Guéhenno France 47.54N 2.38W
76 A3 Gueixol, Pta. de pt Spain 42.44N 9.05W
119 D6 Güejar, R Colombia
77 K6 Güéjar Sierra Spain 37.10N 3.26W
89 D7 Guékédou Guinea 8.35N 10.11W
88 Q4 Guelalia Algeria 35.15N 4.44E
90 G6 Guélengdeng Chad 10.55N 15.31E
88 R3 Guelma Algeria 36.29N 7.25E
108 M3 Guelph N Dakota 46.02N 98.14W
99 K9 Guelph Ontario 43.34N 80.16W
88 P10 Gueltâs d 'In Ziza Algeria 23.33N 2.34E
88 G9 Guelta Zemmur Morocco 24.10N 12.20W
88 P4 Guelt es Stel Algeria 35.10N 3.02E
89 J1 Guem Mali 20.46N 1.13W
89 J2 Guem Mali 18.12N 0.13W
88 R5 Guemar Algeria 33.34N 6.49E
69 N7 Guémar France 48.12N 7.25E
70 G6 Guémene-Penfao France 47.38N 1.50W
70 D5 Guéméné-sur-Scorff France 48.04N 3.13W
Guéna see Bilala
89 D3 Guendel Mauritania 17.41N 11.25W
89 G3 Guendouch Mali 16.13N 5.01W
89 L6 Guéné Benin 11.44N 3.16E
75 D1 Güeñes Spain 43.11N 3.05W
99 P6 Guénette Quebec 46.33N 75.16W
121 K5 Guenguel, R Argentina
70 G6 Guenroue France 47.32N 1.57W
89 A4 Gueoul Senegal 15.30N 16.20W
70 F6 Guer France 47.54N 2.06W
89 A1 Güera Morocco 20.49N 17.06W
90 H6 Guera div Chad
90 J6 Guera, Mt.du Chad 11.59N 18.14E
70 F7 Guérande France 47.20N 2.25W
119 G3 Güera, R Venezuela
88 Q5 Guerara Algeria 32.53N 4.22E
70 H6 Guerche-de-Bretagne, la France 47.57N 1.13W
72 K2 Guerche-sur-l'Aubois, la France 46.57N 2.56E
88 M4 Guercif Morocco 34.15N 3.21W
90 J7 Guére Chad 9.14N 18.10E
90 J1 Guere watercourse Chad
90 L4 Guéréda Chad 14.30N 22.05E
85 F8 Guerende Libya 23.25N 21.21E
72 H3 Guéret France 46.10N 1.52E
72 L1 Guérigny France 47.05N 3.11E
99 L5 Guérin Quebec 47.40N 79.19W
70 F8 Guérinière, la France 46.58N 2.14W
92 H10 Guerissa Mozambique 17.19S 35.58E
70 D5 Guerlédan, L.de France
70 D5 Guern France 48.02N 3.05W
88 P11 Guernene Algeria 21.43N 2.34E
75 E1 Guernica y Luno Spain 43.19N 2.40W
100 M7 Guernsey Saskatchewan 51.52N 105.12W
108 F7 Guernsey Wyoming 42.17N 104.45W
70 E3 Guernsey I Channel Is 49.27N 2.35W
108 F7 Guernsey Res Wyoming 42.20N 104.47W
70 M4 Gueroulde, la France 48.49N 0.53E
92 G8 Guerra Mozambique 13.05S 35.12E
112 J9 Guerra Texas 26.54N 98.54W
88 R3 Guerrah, El Algeria 36.09N 6.35E
76 C9 Guerreira Portugal 39.32N 8.23W
76 E14 Guerreiros do Rio Portugal 37.22N 7.28W
115 J3 Guerrero Nuevo León Mexico 28.21N 100.22W
115 K4 Guerrero Tamaulipas Mexico 26.49N 99.20W
77 C2 Guerrero R Spain
115 J9 Guerrero state Mexico
115 F3 Guerrero, Ciudad Mexico 28.33N 107.28W
115 B3 Guerrero Negro Mexico 28.00N 114.10W
72 E10 Guerreys, Pic de mt France 42.44N 0.22E
119 E3 Guerrilandia Venezuela 8.56N 69.45W
70 O2 Guerville France 49.57N 1.32E
88 N7 Guerzim Algeria 29.39N 1.40W
75 H2 Güesa Spain 42.48N 1.05W
90 F1 Guesebida Niger 22.00N 13.54E
123 J9 Guest Peninsula Antarctica 76.30S 148.00W
89 E5 Guetalo Mali 13.57N 9.24W
75 F1 Guetaria Spain 43.18N 2.11W
72 A9 Guéthary France 43.25N 1.36W
88 M10 Guettara, El Mali 22.08N 2.59W
88 S4 Guettar, El Tunisia 34.20N 8.55E
71 E3 Gueugnon France 46.36N 4.03E
107 D11 Gueydan Louisiana 30.01N 92.30W
89 F9 Guéyo Ivory Coast 5.25N 6.04W
90 J1 Guezendi Chad 21.34N 18.14E
87 B3 Gufala Sudan 14.20N 29.00E
66 N3 Gufelstock mt Switzerland 47.02N 9.09E
66 N5 Güferhorn mt Switzerland 46.32N 9.04E
65 E6 Guffert-Spitze mt Austria 47.33N 11.48E
50 C3 Gufudalur Iceland 65.35N 22.24W
50 D6 Gufunes Iceland 64.09N 21.50W
40 G5 Guga U.S.S.R. 52.45N 137.31E
30 F5 Gugauli Uttar Prad India 27.39N 82.18E
87 J10 Gugeleje Somalia 1.14N 43.11E
31 G5 Gugera Pakistan 30.55N 73.21E
32 E3 Gūgerd, Kūh-e mts Iran
66 F4 Guggisberg Switzerland 46.47N 7.21E
56 R8 Gugh isld Is of Scilly Eng 49.54N 6.19W
87 F7 Gughe mt Ethiopia 6.16N 37.25E
32 G6 Gügher Iran 29.28N 56.27E
28 C2 Gugi Karnataka India 16.43N 76.42E
Gugird, Kuh-i see Gūgerd, Kūh-e mts
121 E3 Guglieri Argentina 30.45S 62.40W
64 F5 Güglingen W Germany 49.04N 9.00E
80 L5 Guglionesi Italy 41.54N 14.55E
82 H5 Gugu mt Romania 45.17N 22.40E
17 P8 Guguan isld Marianas Pacific Oc 17.20N 145.51E
87 G6 Gugu Mts Ethiopia
30 B6 Guhisar Madhya Prad India 26.15N 78.32E
32 H7 Gūh Kūh mt Iran 26.06N 58.23E
63 R6 Gühlen-Glienecke E Germany 53.04N 12.46E
118 C4 Guia Brazil 15.21S 56.15W
76 B9 Guia Portugal 39.57N 8.47W
76 C14 Guia Portugal 37.07N 8.17W
96 U15 Guía de Gran Canaria Gran Canaria Canary Is 28.08N 15.38W
96 Q14 Guia de Isora Tenerife Canary Is 28.13N 16.47W
76 F4 Guiana mt Spain 42.26N 6.35W
89 L5 Guiaoue Niger 13.01N 3.57E
89 F7 Guiborosso Ivory Coast 8.53N 7.01W
71 E3 Guiche, la France 46.33N 4.27E
70 G6 Guichen France 47.58N 1.47W
12 E6 Guichen B S Australia 37.10S 139.45E
23 H3 Guichi Anhui China 30.42N 117.25E
115 M9 Guichicovi Mexico 16.59N 95.09W
121 F4 Guichón Uruguay 32.20S 57.13W
70 C4 Guiclan France 48.34N 3.58W
89 N5 Guidam-Roumji Niger 13.38N 6.38E
22 E8 Guide Qinghai China 36.02N 101.34E
90 G7 Guidein Chad 9.05N 15.18E
70 D6 Guidel France 47.47N 3.28W
90 F7 Guider Cameroon 9.55N 13.59E
108 M9 Guide Rock Nebraska 40.03N 98.20W
79 J3 Guidicarie, Val V Italy
90 D5 Guidimouni Niger 13.40N 9.31E
23 D5 Guiding Guizhou China 26.36N 107.10E
79 J4 Guidizzolo Italy 45.20N 10.34E
23 F5 Guidong Hunan China 26.07N 113.56E
89 B3 Guier, L.de Senegal
71 H5 Guiers R France
Guigan see Gorgān
79 J6 Guiglia Italy 44.26N 10.57E
89 F8 Guiglo Ivory Coast 6.40N 7.28W
70 G6 Guignen France 47.55N 1.51W
69 D6 Guignes France 48.38N 2.49E
61 D4 Guignies Belgium 50.33N 3.22E
61 M3 Guigoven Belgium 50.50N 5.24E
119 F2 Güigüe Venezuela 10.05N 67.48W
99 L5 Guigues Quebec 47.29N 79.26W
Guihua see Mingxi
94 M5 Guija Mozambique 24.31S 33.02E
23 F7 Gui Jiang R Guangdong China
23 E6 Gui Jiang R Guangxi China
23 J4 Guiji Shan mts Zhejiang China
77 G4 Guijo Spain 38.30N 4.48W
76 G8 Guijo de Coria Spain 40.06N 6.28W
76 G8 Guijo de Galisteo Spain 40.05N 6.25W
76 G8 Guijo de Granadilla Spain 40.12N 6.10W
76 H8 Guijo de Santa Bárbara Spain 40.10N 5.39W
76 H7 Guijuelo Spain 40.34N 5.40W
56 L3 Guilden Morden Cambs Eng 52.04N 0.09W
56 K5 Guildford Surrey Eng 51.14N 0.35W
14 B9 Guildford W Australia 31.55S 115.55E
104 O2 Guildhall Vermont 44.34N 71.36W
58 K6 Guildtown Tayside Scotland 56.28N 3.25W
89 C6 Guiledji Guinea 11.43N 13.27W
21 B4 Guiler Gol R Nei Monggol Zizhiqu China
103 J4 Guilford Connecticut 41.16N 72.41W
104 Q1 Guilford Maine 45.11N 69.24W
103 C2 Guilford New York 42.25N 75.32W
104 E1 Guilford dist Baltimore, Md
105 H1 Guilford College N Carolina 36.03N 79.56W
105 H1 Guilford Ct.Ho.Nat.Mil.Park N Carolina 36.08N 79.51W
91 C6 Guilherme Capelo Angola 5.11S 12.10E
76 C5 Guilhofrei, Barragem de res Portugal 41.35N 8.07W
23 E6 Guilin Guangxi China 25.21N 110.11E
70 F6 Guillac France 47.56N 2.28W
76 B4 Guillarey Spain 42.04N 8.37W
91 E7 Guillaume, Chutes rapids Zaïre 7.42S 17.20E
71 K8 Guillaumes France 46.05N 6.51E
77 D5 Guillena Spain 37.32N 6.03W
75 P4 Guillerías reg Spain
71 K7 Guillestre France 44.39N 6.40E
70 F5 Guilliers France 48.03N 2.24W
66 B2 Guillon France 47.19N 6.24E
71 E1 Guillon France 47.31N 4.05E
71 J2 Guillon-les-Bains France 47.19N 6.23E
72 C6 Guillos France 44.33N 0.30W
91 D7 Guilo Pombe Angola 7.07S 15.45E
70 B6 Guilvinec, le France 47.48N 4.17W
96 R14 Güimar Tenerife Canary Is 28.19N 16.25W
117 F6 Guimarães Brazil 2.07S 44.42W
76 C6 Guimarães Portugal 41.26N 8.19W
19 L6 Guimaras isld Philippines
19 L6 Guimaras Str Philippines
76 D2 Guimaray Spain 43.00N 7.47W
96 R14 Güimar, Pta. de Tenerife Canary Is 28.19N 16.22W
70 B5 Guimiliau France 48.29N 4.00W
107 J8 Guin Alabama 33.59N 87.56W
115 M3 Güina Nicaragua 14.00N 85.14W
22 E9 Guinan Qinghai China 35.47N 100.46E
23 B1 Guinan Qinghai China 35.47N 100.46E
19 L6 Guinauayan isld Philippines 11.49N 123.55E
116 E3 Guinchos Cay isld Cuba 22.46N 78.08W
111 B3 Guinda California 38.48N 122.12W
75 Q7 Guindalera, La dist Madrid Spain
19 M7 Guindulman Philippines 9.45N 124.30E
28 C8 Guindy dist Madras, Tamil Nadu India
89 C6 Guinea rep W Africa
96 K8 Guinea Basin Atlantic Oc
89 B5 Guinea-Bissau rep W Africa
50 N10 Guineabukta B Jan Mayen I 70.53N 9.05W
92 D11 Guinea Fowl Zimbabwe 19.31S 29.55E
73 E5 Guinea, G.of W Africa
98 C3 Guinecourt, L Quebec
116 C3 Güines Cuba 22.50N 82.02W
69 B2 Guînes France 50.51N 1.52E
89 F7 Guinetéguela Ivory Coast 8.22N 7.22W
70 D4 Guingamp France 48.34N 3.09W
90 G6 Guingler Cameroon 10.48N 14.41E
89 B4 Guinguinéo Senegal 14.20N 15.57W
90 L8 Guinod Cent Afr Rep 6.50N 23.04E
19 L6 Guintacan isld Philippines 11.18N 123.54E
19 L4 Guintinua isld Philippines 14.25N 122.58E
107 E6 Guion Arkansas 35.56N 91.58W
115 M5 Guiones, Pta C Costa Rica 9.56N 85.40W
70 B5 Guipavas France 48.27N 4.25W
23 E7 Guiping Guangxi China 23.20N 110.04E
89 F9 Guipolo Liberia 5.02N 7.38W
74 F1 Guipúzcoa prov Spain
89 H2 Guir Mali 18.52N 2.52W
88 M6 Guir R Morocco
88 M6 Guir watercourse Algeria
116 C3 Güira de Melena Cuba 22.47N 82.33W
118 D5 Guiratinga Brazil 16.19S 53.43W
89 F4 Guirel Mali 15.31N 7.03W
119 H2 Güiria Venezuela 10.37N 62.21W
88 H7 Guir, Jbel mts Morocco
61 O8 Guirsch Belgium 49.43N 5.51E
117 C2 Guisanbourg Fr Guiana 4.27N 51.54W
71 J7 Guisane R France
57 L3 Guisborough Cleveland Eng 54.32N 1.04W
69 E4 Guiscard France 49.40N 3.04E
70 C5 Guiscriff France 48.04N 3.39W
69 F4 Guise France 49.54N 3.39E
57 K5 Guiseley W Yorks Eng 53.53N 1.42W
75 N4 Guisona Spain 41.47N 1.18E
72 D5 Guîsres France 45.03N 0.12W
70 B4 Guisseny France 48.38N 4.24W
88 K5 Guisser Morocco 32.39N 7.48W
56 N2 Guist Norfolk Eng 52.47N 0.58E
90 L9 Guita Koulouba Cent Afr Rep 5.58N 23.21E
59 D7 Guitane L Kerry Irish Rep 52.00N 9.25W
115 L7 Guitérrez Zamora Mexico 20.30N 97.06W
76 D2 Guitiriz Spain 43.10N 7.52W
89 G9 Guitri Ivory Coast 5.31N 5.14W
19 M6 Guiuan Philippines 11.02N 125.44E
69 E4 Guivry France 49.40N 3.07E
23 H4 Guixi Jiangxi China 28.16N 117.09E
23 E7 Gui Xian Guangxi China 23.06N 109.36E
23 D5 Guiyang Guizhou China 26.35N 106.40E
23 F6 Guiyang Hunan China 25.51N 112.31E
23 D5 Guizhou prov China
32 G5 Gūjahr Iran 31.34N 56.35E
72 B6 Gujan-Mestras France 44.39N 1.04W
29 B6 Gujarat state India
31 G4 Gujar Khan Pakistan 33.19N 73.23E
90 E6 Gujiba Nigeria 11.30N 11.55E
90 F6 Gujiba Nigeria 11.34N 12.03E
31 H4 Gujranwala Pakistan 32.06N 74.11E
31 G4 Gujranwala dist Pakistan
31 H4 Gujrat Pakistan 32.35N 74.06E
31 G4 Gujrat dist Pakistan
23 E3 Gujunba Sichuan China 31.46N 108.01E
Gujur see Gūjahr
Guk see Gowk
44 F6 Gukasyan Armenia U.S.S.R. 41.01N 43.50E
41 N2 Gukera, Ostrov isld Franz Josef Land U.S.S.R.
111 N9 Gu Komelik Arizona 32.31N 111.56W
45 L8 Gukovo U.S.S.R. 48.05N 39.59E
32 A2 Gūk Tappeh Iran 36.49N 45.49E

29 E2 Gula Haryana India 30.02N 76.21E
31 J4 Gulabgarh Kashmir 33.17N 76.12E
53 S17 Gulafjord inlet Norway 60.57N 5.04E
22 F8 Gulang Gansu China 37.32N 103.00E
23 A5 Gulang Yunnan China 26.05N 48.38E
90 E6 Gulani Nigeria 10.46N 11.46E
30 A4 Gulaothi Uttar Prad India 28.36N 77.47E
12 J4 Gulargambone New S Wales 31.21S 148.32E
31 E3 Gulbahar Afghanistan 35.13N 69.19E
31 A9 Gulbāi Pakistan 24.53N 66.58E
Gulbān Laiya see Qulbān Layyah
28 C2 Gulbarga Karnataka India 17.22N 76.47E
28 C2 Gulbarga dist Karnataka India
46 F2 Gulbene Latvia U.S.S.R. 57.10N 26.42E
31 H5 Gulberg Pakistan 31.32N 74.23E
31 C4 Gulbina Afghanistan 32.46N 65.26E
43 L6 Gul'cha Kirgiziya U.S.S.R. 40.21N 73.26E

36 H6 Gülcihan Turkey 36.29N 35.55E
53 A5 Guldager Denmark 55.32N 8.25E
53 E5 Guldbjerg Denmark 55.32N 10.09E
53 H7 Guldborg Denmark 54.53N 11.45E
53 H7 Guldborg Sund sound Denmark
64 D4 Guldental W Germany 49.53N 7.52E
52 H7 Guldsmeds-hyttan L Sweden 59.40N 15.10E
36 H5 Gülek Turkey 37.12N 34.48E
37 E7 Guleman Turkey 38.25N 39.54E
53 S17 Gulen Norway 60.58N 5.04E
53 S15 Gulen, Midt inlet Norway 61.44N 5.10E
53 S15 Gulen, Nord inlet Norway 61.47N 5.12E
45 D4 Gulevka U.S.S.R. 52.38N 32.15E
105 H2 Gulf N Carolina 35.30N 79.20W
107 J11 Gulf Beach Florida 30.18N 87.28W
13 G4 Gulf Highway rd Queensland
Gulf of Chihli see Bohai Wan
Gulf of Chihli see Bo Hai

Gulf of Liaotung see Liaodong Wan
107 G12 Gulf Outlet Louisiana
105 E10 Gulfport Florida 27.44N 82.44W
107 G11 Gulfport Mississippi 30.21N 89.08W
103 C2 Gulf Summit New York 42.02N 75.32W
30 C8 Gulganj Madhya Prad India 24.42N 79.22E
51 O1 Gulgofjorden Norway 70.40N 28.40E
12 J4 Gulgong New S Wales 32.20S 149.49E
87 D4 Guli Sudan 13.31N 32.32E
21 B1 Gulian Heilongjiang China 52.55N 122.20E
87 D5 Guli,Jeb mt Sudan 11.50N 33.38E
23 D4 Gulin Sichuan China 28.07N 105.50E
75 G2 Gulina Spain 42.55N 1.47W
92 K11 Gulioni Zanzibar 5.59S 39.23E
31 D5 Gulistan Afghanistan 30.30N 66.30E
43 J6 Gulistan Uzbekistan U.S.S.R. 40.31N 68.47E
Gulistanak see Golestānak
19 N2 Gulitel mt Palau Is Pacific Oc 7.36N 134.38E
63 P6 Gülitz E Germany 53.13N 11.57E
21 B3 Guliya Shan mt pk Nei Monggol Zizhiqu China 49.47N 122.28E
Gulja see Yining

31 E5 Gul Kach Pakistan 31.57N 69.33E
113 P5 Gulkana Alaska 62.15N 145.30W
113 P5 Gulkana R Alaska
44 D2 Gul'kevichi U.S.S.R. 45.21N 40.43E
32 D6 Gulkhari oil well Iran 29.30N 50.46E
33 J2 Gulkhari oil field Iran 29.38N 50.47E
59 D8 Gullaba Hill Kerry Irish Rep 51.52N 9.27W
52 J10 Gullabo Sweden 56.26N 15.50E
58 L6 Gullane Lothian Scotland 56.02N 2.50W
100 O1 Gull Bay Ontario 49.50N 89.05W
53 U17 Gullbrå Norway 60.50N 6.15E
50 C7 Gullbringusýsla co Iceland
61 C3 Gullegem Belgium 50.51N 3.12E
53 D4 Gullev Denmark 56.21N 9.42E
53 T18 Gullfjell mt Norway 60.23N 5.35E
50 E6 Gullfoss waterfall Iceland 64.20N 20.08W
Gullhúsá see Sandeyri
106 J4 Gull I Michigan 45.42N 85.50W
106 H3 Gulliver Michigan 46.01N 86.00W
100 D6 Gull L Alberta 52.30N 114.00W
108 Q3 Gull L Minnesota
100 J8 Gull Lake Saskatchewan 50.05N 108.30W
51 G6 Gullön Sweden 65.40N 18.15E
11 N13 Gull Rocks islds New Zealand 45.55S 170.39E
52 H8 Gullspång Sweden 58.58N 14.05E
51 J5 Gullträsk Sweden 66.10N 21.15E
36 G2 Güllüce Turkey 40.47N 33.24E
36 C5 Güllük Turkey 37.14N 27.36E
90 B5 Gulma Nigeria 12.40N 4.23E
31 H3 Gulmarg Kashmir 34.04N 74.25E
66 N3 Gulmen mt Switzerland 47.03N 9.13E
30 G4 Gulmikot Nepal 28.01N 83.18E
36 G6 Gülnar Turkey 36.18N 33.24E
21 C5 Gulong Heilongjiang China 45.50N 124.08E
Gulpaigan see Golpāyegan
31 C3 Gul Pass Afghanistan 34.49N 65.20E
60 T17 Gulpen Netherlands 50.49N 5.54E
63 Q7 Gülper See L E Germany
36 B3 Gülpınar Turkey 39.31N 26.08E
31 A3 Gulran Afghanistan 35.06N 61.41E
Gülşehir see Arapsun
52 K3 Gulsele Sweden 63.48N 17.10E
43 L4 Gul'shad Kazakhstan U.S.S.R. 46.37N 74.22E
18 G3 Gul, Tanjong C Singapore 1.18N 103.40E
63 S5 Gültz E Germany 53.45N 13.12E
90 C7 Gulu Nigeria 8.42N 6.38E
93 D3 Gulu Uganda 2.46N 32.21E
13 J7 Guluguba Queensland 26.16S 150.03E
13 D1 Guluwuru I N Terr Australia 11.30S 136.20E
58 F5 Gulvain mt Highland Scotland 56.57N 5.16W
92 H5 Gulwe Tanzania 6.29S 36.29E
40 B4 Gulya U.S.S.R. 54.45N 121.04E
44 C1 Gulyay Borisovka U.S.S.R. 46.36N 40.15E
47 H2 Gulyayevskiye Koshki, Ostrova islds U.S.S.R.
45 H9 Gulyaypole Ukraine U.S.S.R. 47.39N 36.16E
63 S4 Gülzow E Germany 54.02N 13.07E
30 F3 Gum Nepal 29.33N 82.09E

Guma see Pishan
31 E4 Gumal R Pakistan
31 F4 Gumal Pass Pakistan 32.02N 70.10E
87 F5 Gumar Ethiopia 10.29N 36.50E
32 D3 Gümargan Iran 35.38N 50.40E
13 G7 Gumbardo Queensland 26.05S 144.51E
31 E5 Gumbaz Pakistan 30.02N 69.00E
87 C6 Gumbie Sudan 8.34N 30.38E
87 C8 Gumbiri,Jeb mt Sudan 4.20N 30.56E
92 G7 Gumbiro Tanzania 10.19S 35.40E
52 N2 Gumboda Sweden 64.13N 21.00E
13 B5 Gum Cr N Terr Australia
90 D5 Gumel Nigeria 12.38N 9.21E
Gümgüm see Varto
29 J1 Gumia Bihar India 23.48N 85.50E
75 C4 Gumiel de Hizán Spain 41.46N 3.42W
75 C4 Gumiel del Mercado Spain 41.45N 3.48W
30 H4 Gumila Nepal 27.45N 86.43E
15 H7 Gumire Papua New Guinea 6.11S 144.55E
31 D4 Gum Kol Afghanistan 33.05N 67.09E
29 J6 Gumla Bihar India 23.03N 84.36E
12 G5 Gum Lake New S Wales 32.42S 143.12E
20 M5 Gumma prefect Japan
66 E4 Gümmenen Switzerland 46.57N 7.15E
64 D1 Gummersbach W Germany 51.02N 7.34E
66 E6 Gummfluh mt Switzerland 46.27N 7.12E
90 B5 Gummi Nigeria 12.09N 5.10E
18 B3 Gumpang R Sumatra Indon
65 O5 Gumpoldskirchen Austria 48.03N 16.17E
Gumshan see Gomīshan
30 F7 Gumti R Uttar Prad India
63 Q7 Gumtow E Germany 52.58N 12.17E
95 L4 Gumtree S Africa 28.51S 27.43E
23 C7 Gumu Yunnan China 23.17N 104.18E
87 D7 Gumuru Sudan 6.42N 32.54E
37 E5 Gümüşane Turkey 40.26N 39.26E
36 H2 Gümüşhacıköy Turkey 40.52N 35.14E
36 E2 Gümüşova Turkey 40.52N 30.53E
87 G6 Guna Ethiopia 8.18N 39.52E
30 A8 Guna Madhya Prad India 24.39N 77.18E
29 E5 Guna dist Madhya Prad India
87 G5 Guna mt Ethiopia 11.40N 38.20E
Gunabad see Gonābād
14 E6 Gunanya Spring W Australia 23.14S 122.39E
Gunbad-i-Qabus see Gonbad-e Kāvūs
12 H5 Gunbar New S Wales 34.04S 145.25E
24 H11 Güncang Xizang Zizhiqu China 29.45N 94.14E
105 H12 Gun Cay isld Bahamas 25.36N 79.19W
42 J5 Gunda U.S.S.R. 52.48N 111.45E
91 F7 Gunda Zaïre 6.17S 19.25E
12 J6 Gundagai New S Wales 35.07S 148.05E
Gundalpet see Gundlupet
29 G7 Gundardehi Madhya Prad Ind 20.56N 81.21E
91 C6 Gunda Sundi Zaïre 4.47S 12.54E
36 J3 Gündelen R Turkey
64 J6 Gundelfingen W Germany 48.33N 10.23E
64 G5 Gundelsheim W Germany 49.18N 9.10E
28 C4 Gunderi Karnataka India 13.59N 76.09E
53 C3 Gundersted Denmark 56.55N 9.29E
65 G5 Gundertshausen Austria 48.05N 12.59E
53 E3 Gunderup Denmark 56.57N 10.02E
64 E4 Gundheim W Germany 49.40N 8.15E
18 J9 Gundih Java Indon 7.12S 110.51E
91 G2 Gundji Zaïre 2.03N 21.31E
28 D3 Gundlakamma R Andhra Prad India
28 C5 Gundlupet Karnataka India 11.49N 76.40E
37 F2 Gündoğdu Bursa Turkey 40.21N 29.02E
36 C2 Gündoğdu Çanakkale Turkey 40.17N 27.08E
37 F4 Gündoğdu Rize Turkey 41.03N 40.38E
36 F6 Gündoğmuş Turkey 36.50N 32.07E
53 H7 Gundsley Denmark 54.54N 11.57E

Güney Antalya Turkey see Kızılağaç
36 D4 Güney Denizli Turkey 38.24N 28.50E
37 E5 Güneyce Turkey 40.52N 40.29E
37 F5 Güneysu Turkey 40.56N 40.40E
100 M2 Gunflint L Minnesota 48.06N 90.40W
39 B3 Gungkhada R U.S.S.R.
25 N7 Gunglilap Burma 27.17N 98.15E
91 D9 Gungo Angola 11.44S 14.10E
91 D9 Gungo Angola 10.58S 15.30E
91 F6 Gungu Zaïre 5.43S 19.20E
91 D10 Gungue Angola 13.44S 15.25E
31 H3 Gunial Kashmir 34.43N 75.49E
44 H5 Gunib U.S.S.R. 42.23N 46.57E
100 V5 Gunisao L Manitoba
100 U5 Gunisao R Manitoba
Gunjial see Quaidabad
53 U20 Gunlanut mt Norway 59.18N 6.14E
111 L4 Gunlock Utah 37.17N 113.47W
56 D5 Gunn Devon Eng 51.06N 3.56W
58 C5 Gunna isld Strathclyde Scotland 56.34N 6.44W
86 M8 Gunna, Gebel ra Egypt
101 T6 Gunnar Saskatchewan 59.25N 108.50W
22 F4 Günnariyn Mongolia 45.39N 102.01E
51 F6 Gunnarn Sweden 65.01N 17.40E
50 K2 Gunnarstadhir Iceland 66.10N 15.23W
30 B4 Gunnaur Uttar Prad India 28.14N 78.25E
13 H4 Gunnawarra Queensland 17.55S 145.11E
97 R4 Gunnbjørn mt Greenland 68.54N 29.48W
52 K9 Gunnebo Sweden 57.44N 16.33E
12 K4 Gunnedah New S Wales 30.59S 150.15E
57 J4 Gunnerside N Yorks Eng 54.23N 2.04W
26 U11 Gunners Quoin isld Mauritius, Indian Oc 19.57S 57.37E
123 A7 Gunnerus Bank Antarctica
12 J5 Gunning New S Wales 34.48S 149.16E
56 C6 Gunnislake Cornwall Eng 50.31N 4.12W
109 D3 Gunnison Colorado 38.33N 106.55W
111 N2 Gunnison Utah 39.09N 111.50W
109 B3 Gunnison R Colorado
110 N8 Gunnison I Utah 41.21N 112.53W
50 K2 Gunnólfsvikurfjall mt Iceland 66.09N 15.04W
13 B1 Gunn Pt N Terr Australia 12.10S 131.00E
53 V16 Gunnvorbreen mt Norway 61.17N 6.50E
100 J7 Gunnworth Saskatchewan 51.20N 108.10W
18 J4 Gunong Ayer Sarawak Malaysia 2.09N 111.24E
13 E4 Gunpowder R Queensland
103 B8 Gunpowder R Maryland
22 G7 Gun Qarag Nei Monggol Zizhiqu China 39.49N 107.40E
30 H7 Gunri Bihar India 25.39N 84.38E
29 E8 Gun Sangari Maharashtra India 19.30N 76.02E
65 O6 Günselsdorf Austria 47.57N 16.17E
65 J5 Gunskirchen Austria 48.08N 12.58E
43 K7 Gunt R Tadzhikistan U.S.S.R.
28 C3 Guntakal Andhra Prad India 15.11N 77.24E
66 G5 Gunten Switzerland 46.43N 7.43E
110 B6 Gunter Oregon 43.49N 123.30W
112 L2 Gunter Texas 33.29N 96.46W
63 N9 Güntersberge E Germany 51.39N 10.58E
64 E4 Guntersblum W Germany 49.48N 8.21E
65 O4 Guntersdorf Austria 48.39N 16.03E
107 K7 Guntersville Alabama 34.20N 86.18W
107 K7 Guntersville Dam Alabama 34.23N 86.24W
107 K7 Guntersville L Alabama
76 D3 Guntín Spain 42.53N 7.41W
100 U8 Gunton Manitoba 50.18N 97.18W
56 O2 Gunton Norfolk Eng 52.52N 1.19E
107 H7 Guntown Mississippi 34.26N 88.40W
65 O5 Guntramsdorf Austria 48.03N 16.19E
18 B10 Guntung Sumatra Indon 1.36N 101.35E
28 E2 Guntur Andhra Prad India 16.20N 80.27E
28 D2 Guntur dist Andhra Prad India
Gunugu see Kanūgar
19 E7 Gunungapi isld Moluccas Indon 6.37S 126.38E
18 B5 Gunungsitoli Indonesia 1.16N 97.34E
18 F8 Gunungsugih Sumatra Indon 5.00S 105.16E
18 C5 Gunungtua Sumatra Indon 1.24N 99.36E
29 H8 Gunupur Orissa India 19.04N 83.52E
14 B9 Gunyidi W Australia 30.09S 116.04E
36 F3 Günyüzü Turkey 39.22N 31.49E
64 J7 Günz R W Germany
64 J7 Günzburg W Germany 48.27N 10.18E
64 K5 Gunzenhausen W Germany 49.07N 10.46E
63 N9 Günzerode E Germany 51.32N 10.41E
23 G2 Guo He R Anhui China
23 D7 Guohua Guangxi China 23.24N 107.22E
22 K6 Guojiatun Hebei China 41.40N 116.56E
23 D1 Guojiazhen Gansu China 35.00N 105.32E
Guoluezhen see Lingbao
23 G2 Guoyang Anhui China 33.30N 116.12E
22 J7 Guoyangzhen Shanxi China 38.52N 112.45E
90 C7 Gupa Nigeria 8.29N 6.40E
23 H1 Gupei Jiangsu China 34.05N 118.01E
31 G2 Gupis Kashmir 36.12N 73.30E
90 F6 Gur Nigeria 10.49N 12.16E
87 C5 Gur watercourse Sudan
87 G3 Gura Ethiopia 15.02N 39.01E
90 D6 Gura mt Nigeria 10.19N 8.58E
87 E2 Gura watercourse Sudan
85 N10 Gurad, Jebel mt Sudan 18.53N 35.05E
86 M3 Gura, El reg Egypt
87 F6 Guraghe reg Ethiopia
31 H3 Gurais Kashmir 34.37N 74.53E
42 G5 Guran U.S.S.R. 54.45N 100.45E
93 L2 Gurar Kenya 3.23N 39.32E
90 C7 Gurara R Nigeria
93 M4 Gurati Kenya 1.09N 40.46E
30 E6 Gurbakhshganj Uttar Prad India 26.18N 81.10E
Gurban Bulagin see Gurvanbulag
22 J5 Gurban Obo Nei Monggol Zizhiqu China 43.07N 112.30E
Gurban Sayhan mts see Gurvan Sayhan Uul
24 F3 Gurbantünggüt Shamo basin Xinjiang Uygur Zizhiqu China
87 A8 Gurba, R Zaïre
66 G4 Gürbe R Switzerland
87 G8 Gurbi,Mt Ethiopia 4.32N 39.05E
29 D1 Gurdaspur Punjab India 32.04N 75.28E
29 D2 Gurdaspur dist Punjab India
32 J8 Gürdim Iran 25.13N 60.10E
107 C8 Gurdon Arkansas 33.55N 93.10W
44 G6 Gurdzhaani Georgia U.S.S.R. 41.45N 45.49E
87 H7 Gure Ethiopia 7.26N 40.37E
36 D4 Güre Turkey 38.40N 29.11E
87 K7 Gureharago Ethiopia 6.22N 45.38E
9 A3 Gurer islet Marshall Is Pacific Oc 9.04N 167.17E
Gurg see Gorg
30 A4 Gurgaon Haryana India 28.27N 77.01E
30 A4 Gurgaon dist Haryana India
90 M5 Gurgei, Jebel mt Sudan 13.52N 24.20E
82 J4 Gurghiului, Munţii mts Romania
117 F9 Gurgueia, R Brazil
87 H7 Gurgura Ethiopia 7.46N 41.25E
30 E8 Gurh Madhya Prad India 24.30N 81.30E
29 B5 Gurha Rajasthan India 25.11N 71.49E
90 F6 Guri Nigeria 11.19N 12.45E
87 J8 Guriale Somalia 4.12N 42.40E
75 D1 Guriezo Spain 43.21N 3.19W
15 H7 Gurimatu Papua New Guinea 6.42S 144.45E
90 F7 Gurin Nigeria 9.05N 12.54E
24 G10 Guring La pass Xizang Zizhiqu China 30.17N 90.13E
118 E6 Gurinhatã Brazil 19.16S 49.45W
117 E5 Guripi, R Brazil
82 F10 Gur-i-Topit mt Albania 40.49N 20.28E
117 G6 Guriu Brazil 2.52S 40.32W
65 K8 Gurk Austria 46.53N 14.18E
65 J8 Gurk R Austria
32 H6 Gur Khar Iran 28.30N 59.35E
65 L8 Gurk, R Austria
65 K8 Gurktal Austria
65 J8 Gurktaler Alpen mts Austria
59 E6 Gur, L Limerick Irish Rep 52.32N 8.32W
43 F6 Gurlen Uzbekistan U.S.S.R. 41.51N 60.23E
37 D6 Gürlevik Dağı mt Turkey 39.34N 37.32E
107 K7 Gurley Alabama 34.41N 86.25W
108 H8 Gurley Nebraska 41.20N 102.59W
28 C2 Gurmatkal Karnataka India 16.55N 77.25E
Gurmeh Khane see Golmānkhānen
56 S9 Gurnard's Head Cornwall Eng 50.11N 5.36W
103 N2 Gurnet Pt C Massachusetts 42.00N 70.35W
66 F4 Gurnigelbad Switzerland 46.46N 7.27E
92 F10 Guro Mozambique 17.28S 33.18E
92 F10 Guro Mozambique 17.45S 34.42E
94 M1 Guro Mozambique 17.26S 33.16E
45 E8 Gurovka Ukraine U.S.S.R. 48.05N 33.05E
37 G7 Gürpinar Turkey 38.18N 43.26E
37 H7 Gürpınar Turkey 38.08N 43.32E
87 H8 Gurra tribe Ethiopia
28 D4 Gurramkonda Andhra Prad India 13.48N 79.35E
75 J3 Gurrea de Gállego Spain 42.01N 0.45W
66 L7 Gurro Italy 46.06N 8.35E
30 C7 Gursarai Uttar Prad India 23.37N 79.12E
53 T14 Gursken Norway 62.14N 5.39E
53 T14 Gurskøy isld Norway 62.16N 5.42E
40 H6 Gurskoye Khabarovsk U.S.S.R. 50.21N 138.06E
37 G3 Gürsü Turkey 40.13N 29.13E
66 F4 Gurten mt Switzerland 46.56N 7.27E
66 P3 Gurtis Spitze mt Austria 47.12N 9.38E
66 L5 Gurtnellen Switzerland 46.44N 8.38E
94 F2 Guru Namibia 19.42S 20.40E
29 L3 Guru Xizang Zizhiqu China 28.04N 89.19E
30 H8 Gurua Bihar India 24.41N 84.47E
92 H9 Gurué Mozambique 15.30S 36.58E
36 G1 Güruh Dağ mt Turkey
82 K3 Guru Humorului Romania 47.31N 25.57E
94 D4 Gurumana Namibia 23.02S 16.49E

43 N7 Gurumsaray Uzbekistan U.S.S.R. 40.49N 70.58E
37 C7 Gürün Turkey 38.44N 37.15E
93 F1 Gurungu Kenya 4.26N 34.32E
117 C5 Gurupá Brazil 1.25S 51.36W
117 C5 Gurupa, I.Grande de Brazil
118 E2 Gurupi Brazil 11.44S 49.01W
117 E5 Gurupi, C Brazil 0.56S 46.08W
117 D7 Gurupi, Sa. do mts Brazil
86 M4 Gurûr, Wâdi el watercourse Egypt
29 C5 Guru Sikhar mt Rajasthan India 24.43N 72.53E
28 D2 Guruzala Andhraprad India 16.33N 79.36E
22 D3 Gurvanbulag Mongolia 47.16N 98.35E
22 F3 Gurvanbulag Mongolia 47.38N 103.35E
22 K2 Gurvandzagal Mongolia 49.39N 115.00E
22 G4 Gurvansayhan Mongolia 45.22N 106.54E
22 F5 Gurvan Sayhan Uul mts Mongolia
90 E5 Gurvi Nigeria 12.45N 10.29E
43 B4 Gur'yev Kazakhstan U.S.S.R. 47.08N 51.59E
45 T3 Gur'yevka U.S.S.R. 53.37N 47.09E
42 D5 Gur'yevsk U.S.S.R. 54.20N 86.00E
31 C4 Gurz Afghanistan 32.46N 64.32E
69 L2 Gürzenich W Germany 50.47N 6.27E
44 C10 Gurzuf Ukraine U.S.S.R. 44.33N 34.15E
93 H2 Gus Kenya 3.02N 36.52E
46 M2 Gus' R U.S.S.R.
Gusair see Quşayr oil well
31 F3 Gusalik Afghanistan 35.01N 70.52E
81 C3 Gusana, L.di Sardinia 40.08N 9.12E
90 C5 Gusau Nigeria 12.12N 6.40E
66 O3 Guscha mt Switzerland 47.03N 9.19E
63 P8 Güsen E Germany 52.21N 11.59E
46 D3 Gusev U.S.S.R. 54.32N 22.12E
45 E1 Gusevo U.S.S.R. 56.06N 33.21E
21 C8 Gushan Liaoning China 39.50N 123.03E
45 J5 Gushchino U.S.S.R. 51.20N 37.15E
110 Q9 Gusher Utah 40.19N 109.50W
35 E1 Gush Halav anc site Israel 33.01N 35.27E
23 G2 Gushi Henan China 32.07N 115.53E
89 J7 Gushiago Ghana 9.56N 0.13W
20 P10 Gushikami Okinawa Japan 26.05N 127.45E
20 P9 Gushikawa Okinawa Japan 26.21N 127.50E
Gushk Pain see Kushk-e Pā'īn
Gusht see Gasht
15 B5 Gusi Irian Jaya 3.00S 133.53E
18 M2 Gusi Sabah Malaysia 6.06N 117.12E
41 J4 Gusikha Krasnoyarsk U.S.S.R. 73.39N 107.30E
46 P3 Gusikha Tatar A.S.S.R. U.S.S.R. 54.50N 49.30E
41 J4 Gusikha R U.S.S.R.
41 R5 Gusinaya, Guba gulf U.S.S.R.
41 A4 Gusinaya Zemlya, P-ov pen Novaya Zemlya U.S.S.R.
82 F8 Gusinje Yugoslavia 42.35N 19.50E
39 C4 Gusinka R U.S.S.R.
45 C2 Gusino U.S.S.R. 54.42N 30.20E
42 H6 Gusinoozersk U.S.S.R. 51.20N 106.35E
42 H6 Gusinoye Ozero U.S.S.R. 51.10N 106.15E
42 H6 Gusinoye, Ozero L U.S.S.R.
29 L2 Guskhara W Bengal India 23.28N 87.45E
45 M1 Gus'-Khrustal'nyy U.S.S.R. 55.38N 40.44E
83 D4 Gusmar Albania 40.13N 19.53E
39 G1 Gusmp, Ostrov isld U.S.S.R.
23 D4 Gusong Sichuan China 28.25N 105.09E
81 B4 Guspini Sardinia 39.33N 8.38E
79 H3 Gussago Italy 45.36N 10.09E
65 O7 Güssing Austria 47.03N 16.19E
79 H4 Gussola Italy 45.01N 10.21E
65 M6 Gusswerk Austria 47.45N 15.19E
52 H6 Gust Adolf Sweden 60.05N 13.55E
50 U13 Gustav Adolf Land Spitsbergen
48 V13 Gustav Holm, Kap C Greenland 66.30N 34.30W
116 N6 Gustavia St Barthélemy Lesser Antilles 17.55N 62.50W
Gustavo A.Madero see Villa de Guadalupe
115 C2 Gustavo Sotelo Mexico 31.33N 113.45W
113 U7 Gustavus Alaska 58.25N 135.50W
50 U12 Gustav V Land Spitsbergen
63 P9 Güsten E Germany 51.49N 11.38E
64 E2 Gusternhain W Germany 50.40N 8.11E
111 C4 Gustine California 37.14N 121.00W
112 J4 Gustine Texas 31.50N 98.25W
63 S4 Gustow E Germany 54.18N 13.14E
63 Q5 Güstrow E Germany 53.48N 12.11E
52 K8 Gusum Sweden 58.15N 16.30E
82 K1 Gusyatin U.S.S.R. 49.04N 26.11E
45 N1 Gus'-Zheleznyy U.S.S.R. 55.04N 41.10E
93 E8 Guta Tanzania 2.03S 33.45E
64 D7 Gutach W Germany 48.07N 7.59E
64 E7 Gutach W Germany 48.14N 8.13E
42 F5 Gutarskiy Khrebet mts U.S.S.R.
65 L5 Gutau Austria 48.25N 14.38E
42 H7 Gutay U.S.S.R. 49.59N 108.15E
58 Q8 Gutcher Shetland Scotland 60.40N 1.00W
87 L8 Gut, El Somalia 5.35N 47.39E
64 E7 Gütenbach W Germany 48.03N 8.10E
65 M5 Gutenbrunn Austria 48.22N 15.08E
64 M3 Gutenfürst E Germany 50.25N 11.58E
65 N6 Gutenstein Austria 47.53N 15.53E
63 P9 Güterglück E Germany 51.59N 11.59E
63 H9 Gütersloh W Germany 51.54N 8.22E
14 B8 Gutha W Australia 29.04S 115.58E
107 J5 Guthrie Kentucky 36.40N 87.10W
108 Q2 Guthrie Minnesota 47.18N 94.47W
108 K1 Guthrie N Dakota 48.00N 100.23W
109 N6 Guthrie Oklahoma 35.53N 97.26W
112 G2 Guthrie Texas 33.38N 100.21W
108 Q8 Guthrie Center Iowa 41.40N 94.30W
100 R3 Guthrie L Manitoba
103 C6 Guthriesville Pennsylvania 40.02N 75.46W
23 H5 Gutian Fujian China 26.36N 118.50E
120 F8 Gutiérrez Bolivia 19.25S 63.30W
Guting see Yutai
63 S8 Gut-Neuhof E Germany 52.05N 13.25E
30 E7 Gutni Uttar Prad India 25.42N 81.24E
44 H6 Guton mt U.S.S.R. 41.53N 46.46E
63 Q5 Gutow E Germany 53.46N 12.08E
61 M3 Gutschoven Belgium 50.46N 5.19E
66 K5 Guttannen Switzerland 46.38N 8.18E
65 L8 Guttaring Austria 46.54N 14.31E
106 C7 Guttenberg Iowa 42.48N 91.06W
103 J7 Guttenberg New Jersey 40.48N 74.02W
66 O1 Güttingen Switzerland 47.36N 9.18E
92 E11 Gutu Zimbabwe 19.41S 31.09E
92 E11 Gutu dist Zimbabwe
Gutwand see Gatvand
45 G6 Guty Ukraine U.S.S.R. 50.07N 35.21E
63 S5 Gützkow E Germany 53.57N 13.25E
36 F2 Güvem Turkey 40.34N 32.40E
36 J6 Güvenç Turkey 36.43N 36.30E
35 C7 Guvrin watercourse Israel
Guwair see Guwer
86 L4 Guwârîr, El reg Egypt
34 L2 Guwer Iraq 36.02N 43.30E
64 G1 Guxhagen W Germany 51.12N 9.29E
22 J8 Gu Xian Shanxi China 36.17N 111.55E
105 K8 Guyama Puerto Rico 18.00N 66.07W
37 G8 Güyan Turkey 37.29N 42.43E
117 A2 Guyana rep S America
104 C8 Guyandotte R W Virginia
22 H6 Guyang Nei Monggol Zizhiqu China 41.07N 110.10E
99 M4 Guyenne Quebec 48.48N 78.29W
67 E8 Guyenne prov France
12 F8 Guy Fawkes R Tasmania
56 M2 Guyhirn Cambs Eng 52.37N 0.05E
Guyi see Sanjiang
109 J5 Guymon Oklahoma 36.42N 101.30W
32 E6 Güyom Iran 29.53N 52.18E
113 R6 Guyot Glacier Alaska 60.10N 141.50W
12 K4 Guyra New S Wales 30.14S 151.40E
98 L8 Guysborough Nova Scotia 45.23N 61.30W
105 F5 Guyton Georgia 32.20N 81.23W
22 K6 Guyuan Hebei China 41.33N 115.40E
23 D1 Guyuan Ningxia China 35.56N 106.50E
43 H7 Guzar Uzbekistan U.S.S.R. 38.37N 66.15E
31 C3 Guzar Bash Afghanistan 34.12N 65.52E
31 C3 Guzar-i-Pam Afghanistan 34.05N 64.36E
37 G6 Güzel R Turkey
37 G7 Güzel R Turkey
36 F6 Güzelsu Turkey 36.53N 31.51E
23 E4 Guzhang Hunan China 28.39N 109.58E
23 H2 Guzhen Anhui China 33.20N 117.19E
Guzhou see Rongjiang
115 F2 Guzmán Mexico 31.14N 107.24W
115 H8 Guzmán, Ciudad Mexico 19.40N 103.29W
115 F2 Guzmán, L.de Mexico
20 C4 Guzo Kanagawa Japan
44 E4 Gvandra mt U.S.S.R. 43.13N 42.08E
Gvan-i-Tālāb Khāni see Gevān-e Tāleb Khāni
82 K1 Gvardeiskoe U.S.S.R. 49.20N 26.40E
39 D4 Gvardeyets U.S.S.R. 62.00N 147.14E
44 C9 Gvardeyskoye Ukraine U.S.S.R. 45.08N 34.01E
52 E7 Gvarv Norway 59.23N 9.11E
Gvatar see Gavāter
50 H4 Gvendarhnjukur mt Iceland 65.08N 17.47W
82 J2 Gvozdets U.S.S.R. 48.37N 25.17E
25 C4 Gwa Burma 17.36N 94.34E
12 J4 Gwabegar New S Wales 30.34S 149.00E
65 G8 Gwabl Austria 46.53N 12.40E
90 C7 Gwada Nigeria 9.46N 6.49E
90 B5 Gwadabawa Nigeria 13.28N 5.15E
31 B8 Gwadar Pakistan 25.09N 62.21E
15 L8 Gwadarab I Trobriand Is Papua New Guinea 8.20S 150.11E
31 B8 Gwadar West B Pakistan
92 C11 Gwai Zimbabwe 19.15S 27.42E
92 C11 Gwai R Zimbabwe
57 E6 Gwalchmai Gwynedd Wales 53.15N 4.25W
29 F2 Gwaldam Uttar Prad India 30.02N 79.34E
14 D8 Gwalia W Australia 28.56S 121.20E
29 D5 Gwalior Chitorgarh, Madhya Prad India 24.54N 74.55E

30 B6 Gwalior Gwalior, Madhya Prad India 26.12N 78.09E
30 A6 Gwalior dist Madhya Prad India
13 J7 Gwambegwine Queensland 25.12S 149.36E
Gwamongga mt see Lina, Gunung mt
92 D12 Gwanda Zimbabwe 19.15S 27.42E
92 D12 Gwanda dist Zimbabwe
90 B5 Gwandu Nigeria 12.30N 4.41E
91 J1 Gwane Zaïre 4.42N 25.54E
91 J1 Gwane R Zaïre
90 E6 Gwani Nigeria 10.25N 11.38E
90 E6 Gwara Nigeria 10.03N 11.56E
90 D6 Gwaram Nigeria 11.15N 9.52E
87 G5 Gwarradit Ethiopia 11.21N 38.20E
90 C6 Gwarzo Nigeria 11.55N 7.55E
31 C6 Gwash Pakistan 28.29N 65.33E
90 B6 Gwashi Nigeria 11.51N 5.45E
31 A8 Gwatar Bay Iran/Pakistan
66 G5 Gwatt Switzerland 46.44N 7.37E
56 B3 Gwbert-on-Sea Dyfed Wales 52.08N 4.41W
92 E10 Gwebi Zimbabwe 17.40S 30.40E
25 C2 Gwebin Burma 20.56N 94.41E
59 F2 Gweebarra B Donegal Irish Rep 54.53N 8.30W
59 F1 Gweedore Donegal Irish Rep 55.03N 8.14W
56 T9 Gweek Cornwall Eng 50.05N 5.13W
87 F5 Gwejam prov Ethiopia
92 D11 Gwelo Zimbabwe 19.25S 29.50E
92 D11 Gwelo dist Zimbabwe
92 D11 Gwelo R Zimbabwe
92 C10 Gwembe Zambia 16.30S 27.42E
110 E4 Gwendolen Oregon 45.22N 120.07W
56 F4 Gwent co Wales
56 F4 Gwent reg Gwent Wales
93 E4 Gweri Uganda 1.43N 33.44E
92 D3 Gweshe Zaïre 2.40S 28.36E
94 H3 Gweta Botswana 20.13S 25.15E
106 G3 Gwinn Michigan 46.16N 87.26W
108 N3 Gwinner N Dakota 46.15N 97.38W
90 E7 Gwona Nigeria 9.40N 10.55E
87 C8 Gworolorongo Sudan 4.52N 31.01E
90 F6 Gwoza Nigeria 11.07N 13.43E
56 C4 Gwyddelwern Dyfed Wales 52.00N 4.15W
12 K4 Gwydir R New S Wales
57 E7 Gwynedd co Wales
100 D6 Gwynne Alberta 52.58N 113.12W
71 H2 Gy France 47.24N 5.48E
30 H1 Gyachung Glacier Xizang Zizhiqu
30 H1 Gyachung Kang mt Xizang Zizhiqu/Nepal 28.06N 86.45E
24 G11 Gyaea Xizang Zizhiqu China 29.13N 92.43E
23 C1 Gyagartang Gansu China 34.53N 102.31E
Gya'gya see Saga

Gyaisi see Jiulong
28 K1 Gyakateng Xizang Zizhiqu 29.28N 94.49E
24 E11 Gyala Shankou pass Xizang Zizhiqu China 28.42N 84.34E

Gyamda Dzong see Gongbo'gyamda
Gyamo Ngo Chu R see Salween R
Gyamo Ngo Chu R see Nu Jiang
44 G7 Gyamysh mt Azerbaydzhan U.S.S.R. 40.16N 46.21E
24 E10 Gyangrang Xizang Zizhiqu China 30.47N 85.09E
Gyangtse see Gyangzê
24 F11 Gyangzê Xizang Zizhiqu China 28.53N 89.35E
30 F7 Gyanpur Uttar Prad India 25.20N 82.28E
29 F6 Gyaraspur Madhya Prad India 23.44N 78.10E
23 A1 Gyaring Qinghai China 35.06N 97.39E
24 F10 Gyaring Co L Xizang Zizhiqu China 31.05N 88.00E
23 A1 Gyaring Hu L Qinghai China
28 K1 Gyarishing Assam India 28.59N 95.44E
Gyatsa Dzong see Gyaea
32 F1 Gyaur watercourse Turkmeniya U.S.S.R.
43 E7 Gyaurs Turkmeniya U.S.S.R. 37.48N 58.44E
23 B4 Gyawa Sichuan China 29.46N 100.24E
41 C5 Gyda U.S.S.R. 70.57N 78.32E
Gydan, Khrebet see Kolymskiy, Khrebet
41 C5 Gydanskaya Guba gulf U.S.S.R.
41 C5 Gydanskiy, Poluostrov pen U.S.S.R.
41 B4 Gydanskiy Proliv str U.S.S.R.
24 H11 Gyêmdong Xizang Zizhiqu China 29.00N 93.25E
69 G7 Gyé-sur-Seine France 48.02N 4.26E
24 C10 Gye Tsaka L Xizang Zizhiqu China
53 U18 Gygrastolen mt Norway 60.03N 6.10E
Gyigang see Zayü
Gyigang see Zayü (Gyigang)
24 G10 Gyimda Xizang Zizhiqu China 30.06N 92.54E
24 E11 Gyirong Xizang Zizhiqu China 28.27N 85.13E
24 E11 Gyirong Xizang Zizhiqu China 28.57N 85.12E
23 A3 Gyitang Xizang Zizhiqu China 30.45N 97.26E
24 H9 Gyiza Qinghai China 33.06N 96.13E
97 P5 Gyldenløves Fd Greenland
53 H5 Gyldenløves Høj hill Denmark 55.33N 11.52E
59 F8 Gyleen Cork Irish Rep 51.48N 8.11W
51 K5 Gyljen Sweden 66.22N 22.45E
53 E5 Gylling Denmark 55.53N 10.11E
53 E5 Gylling Næs C Denmark 55.52N 10.13E
13 L7 Gympie Queensland 26.10S 152.35E
40 E3 Gynym R U.S.S.R.
40 E3 Gynymskaya U.S.S.R. 57.44N 130.44E
25 C3 Gyobingauk Burma 18.14N 95.39E
20 N5 Gyōda Japan 36.10N 139.27E
62 M9 Gyoma Hungary 46.56N 20.50E
62 M8 Gyöngyös Hungary 47.46N 20.00E
62 M8 Gyöngyös R Hungary
65 P7 Gyöngyös R Hungary/Austria
62 L9 Gyönk Hungary 46.34N 18.26E
82 D3 Győr Hungary 47.41N 17.40E
82 D3 Győr-Sopron co Hungary
65 P8 Györvár Hungary 46.58N 16.52E
109 D2 Gypsum Colorado 39.38N 106.56W
109 N3 Gypsum Kansas 38.44N 97.26W
14 F7 Gypsum L W Australia 27.10S 127.29E
101 Q5 Gypsum Pt Gt Slave L, N W Terr 61.52N 114.36W
100 T7 Gypsumville Manitoba 51.47N 98.38W
53 Y17 Gyrinosvatn L Norway 60.50N 8.14E
53 H6 Gyrstinge Denmark 55.29N 11.42E
53 H5 Gyrstinge Sø L Denmark 55.30N 11.43E
52 K6 Gysinge Sweden 60.17N 16.55E
82 G8 Gyueshovo Bulgaria 42.13N 22.28E
62 N9 Gyula Hungary 46.39N 21.17E
44 H8 Gyulably Azerbaydzhan U.S.S.R. 39.52N 46.55E
44 J6 Gyul'gerychay R U.S.S.R.
30 D1 Gyun-go Xizang Zizhiqu China 31.12N 80.03E
44 K7 Gyurgyan Azerbaydzhan U.S.S.R. 40.23N 50.16E
46 J2 Gzhat' R U.S.S.R.
42 B4 Gzhatsk Novosibirsk U.S.S.R. 55.36N 78.13E
84 Y20 Gzira Malta 35.54N 14.30E

28 G2 Ha Bhutan 27.17N 89.22E
50 H6 Háabunga mt Iceland 64.21N 17.25W
61 J3 Haacht Belgium 50.58N 4.38E
50 D3 Háafell mt Strandasýsla Iceland 65.55N 21.30W
50 H3 Háafell mt Thingeyjarsýsla, Sudhur Iceland 65.39N 17.44W
9 T12 Ha'afeva atoll Tonga, Pacific Oc 19.55S 174.44W
60 J12 Haaften Netherlands 51.49N 5.14E
65 L5 Haag Neider Österreich Austria 48.07N 14.34E
64 N7 Haag Ober-Bayern W Germany 48.09N 12.12E
65 J5 Haag Ober-Österreich Austria 48.11N 13.38E
64 M4 Haag Oberpfalz, Bayern W Germany 49.40N 11.46E
66 O3 Haag Switzerland 47.13N 9.30E
50 S13 Haakon V11 Land reg Spitsbergen
50 O9 Haakon V11 topp ra Jan Mayen I 71.05N 8.12W
60 Q11 Haaksbergen Netherlands 52.09N 6.45E
9 S12 Ha'alaufuli Tonga, Pacific Oc 18.36S 173.56W
61 G3 Haaltert Belgium 50.54N 4.00E
60 B2 Haamstede Netherlands 51.42N 3.45E
69 N1 Haan W Germany 51.11N 7.01E
22 C2 Haanhöhiy Uul mts Mongolia
9 U12 Ha'ano isld Tonga, Pacific Oc 19.40S 174.16W
9 U12 Ha'apai Group islds Tonga, Pacific Oc
51 L8 Haapajärvi Finland 63.45N 25.20E
51 L9 Haapamäki Finland 62.15N 24.25E
51 N11 Haapasaari I Finland 60.21N 27.28E
51 L7 Haapavesi Finland 64.09N 25.25E
122 A11 Haapiti Society Is Pacific Oc 17.33S 149.52W
46 E1 Haapsalu Estonia U.S.S.R. 58.58N 23.32E
64 M7 Haar W Germany 48.05N 11.44E
35 E10 Ha'arava watercourse Israel
64 D5 Haardt mts W Germany
60 J13 Haaren Netherlands 51.36N 5.13E
63 J9 Haaren W Germany 51.34N 8.44E
60 O10 Haarle Netherlands 52.22N 6.22E

60 G10 Haarlem Netherlands 52.23N 4.38E
95 G9 Haarlem S Africa 33.45S 23.20E
60 G10 Haarlemmer Meer area Netherlands
60 J13 Haarsteeg Netherlands 51.43N 5.12E
63 G9 Haarstrang reg W Germany
94 F7 Haartbees watercourse S Africa
60 H11 Haarzuilens Netherlands 52.07N 5.00E
60 T17 Haasdal Netherlands 50.54N 5.49E
61 G2 Haasdonk Belgium 51.11N 4.15E
61 J3 Haasrode Belgium 50.50N 4.44E
11 D10 Haast New Zealand 43.53S 169.04E
13 B6 Haast Bluff N Terr Australia 23.20S 131.56E
11 D11 Haast Pass New Zealand 44.07S 169.22E
11 D10 Haast R New Zealand
11 C11 Haast Ra New Zealand
60 H12 Haastrecht Netherlands 52.00N 4.46E
9 S11 Ha'atua Tonga, Pacific Oc 21.25S 174.58W
Haba see Lihābah, Al
64 L8 Habach W Germany 47.44N 11.17E
50 E7 Hábær Iceland 63.45N 20.36W
24 E1 Habahe Xinjiang Uygur Zizhiqu China 47.52N 86.09E
35 G4 Habaka Jordan 32.28N 35.51E
33 E2 Habakah, Al Saudi Arabia 29.51N 42.21E
77 E3 Haba, La Spain 38.55N 5.49W
116 C3 Habana Cuba 23.07N 82.25W
116 C3 Habana prov Cuba
89 G2 Haba Oukdour Mali 19.58N 5.30W
88 L12 Haba Oukdour reg Mali
Habap see Girmeli
26 S5 Habarane Sri Lanka 8.02N 80.45E
50 G7 Hábarmur mt Iceland 63.57N 18.54W
33 J5 Habarōn Saudi Arabia 22.50N 51.40E
33 K8 Habarūt Oman 17.19N 52.45E
72 C8 Habas France 43.34N 0.55W
88 F8 Habas Morocco 26.27N 14.08W
35 F8 Habashina, Jebel el mts Jordan
93 L4 Habaswein Kenya 1.02N 39.30E
Habauna, Wadi see Habawnāh, Wādī watercourse
101 O6 Habay Alberta 58.48N 118.40W
61 N8 Habay-la-Neuve Belgium 49.43N 5.39E
61 N8 Habay-la-Vieille Belgium 49.43N 5.38E
33 G9 Habbān S Yemen 14.21N 47.04E
34 L5 Habbānīyah Iraq 33.22N 43.35E
34 L5 Habbānīyah, Hawr al L Iraq
31 D8 Hab Chauki Pakistan 25.05N 66.55E
88 O6 Habeilat watercourse Algeria
61 O8 Habergy Belgium 49.37N 5.45E
34 Q4 Habībābād Iran 34.19N 48.12E
74 G9 Habibas Lt Ho Algeria 35.45N 1.08W
30 H6 Habibnagar Bihar India 26.11N 84.19E
85 L6 Habib, Wadi watercourse Egypt
64 G1 Habichts-wald wood W Germany 51.18N 9.22E
31 J9 Habiganj Bangladesh 24.24N 91.25E
22 K5 Habirag Nei Monggol Zizhiqu China 42.18N 115.42E
35 G7 Habis watercourse Jordan
33 K8 Habka Oman 17.28N 53.41E
66 H5 Habkern Switzerland 46.44N 7.52E
Habkob see Dharmjaygarh
35 C5 Habla Jordan 32.10N 34.59E
52 L9 Hablingbo Sweden 57.12N 18.16E
52 H9 Habo Sweden 57.55N 14.05E
40 L10 Habomai shoto islds Kuril Is Pacific Ocean
35 C3 Ha Bonim Israel 32.38N 34.56E
21 J5 Haboro Japan 44.23N 141.43E
58 D2 Habost Lewis, W Isles Scotland 58.29N 6.15W
31 D8 Hab R Pakistan
87 J6 Habr Awal tribe Somalia/Ethiopia
87 J6 Habr Gerhajis tribe Somalia/Ethiopia
87 K6 Habr Toljaalo tribe Somalia
65 M2 Habry Czechoslovakia 49.45N 15.29E
87 K7 Habr Yunis tribe Somalia/Ethiopia
66 J2 Habsburg Switzerland 47.28N 8.11E
33 K5 Habshān oil field U.A.E. 23.49N 53.38E
71 L1 Habsheim France 47.44N 7.25E
33 H8 Habshīyah, Jabal mts S Yemen
20 N7 Habuminato Japan 34.42N 139.26E
61 N4 Haccourt Belgium 50.44N 5.40E
37 D1 Hace R Turkey
119 C8 Hacha Colombia 0.02S 75.30W
121 B7 Hachado, Paso de pass Arg/Chile 38.41S 70.59W
88 P7 Hachchana, El Algeria 29.32N 3.44E
77 E9 Hachef R Morocco
63 G10 Hachen W Germany 51.23N 7.59E
64 D2 Hachenburg W Germany 50.40N 7.50E
88 H10 Hachia, El reg Mauritania
20 N8 Hachijō-jima isld Japan
Hachiman see Ōmi-Hachiman
20 K6 Hachiman Japan 35.48N 136.58E
20 O1 Hachimori Japan 40.20N 140.02E
20 K1 Hachinai-dake mt Japan 43.05N 140.36E
20 P1 Hachinohe Japan 40.30N 141.30E
20 N6 Hachiōji Japan 35.40N 139.20E
109 B10 Hachita New Mexico 31.55N 108.20W
61 O6 Hachiville Luxembourg 50.07N 5.55E
61 N8 Hachy Belgium 49.42N 5.41E
36 G2 Hacıbayram Turkey 40.38N 34.22E
36 H4 Hacıbektaş Turkey 38.56N 34.34E
37 G5 Hacıhalil Dağı mt Turkey 40.25N 43.09E
37 C2 Hacıköy Edirne Turkey 40.59N 26.33E
37 G5 Hacıköy Kars Turkey 40.21N 43.09E
Hacıköy Yozgat Turkey see Çekerek
110 D8 Hackamore California 41.34N 121.10W
52 H4 Hackås Sweden 62.56N 14.30E
111 L6 Hackberry Arizona 35.22N 113.44W
107 C12 Hackberry Louisiana 29.59N 93.20W
109 K3 Hackberry Cr Kansas
103 J6 Hackensack New Jersey 40.53N 74.03W
103 F4 Hackensack R New Jersey/New York
59 J6 Hacketstown Carlow Irish Rep 52.52N 6.33W
107 B6 Hackett Arkansas 35.10N 94.25W
12 B6 Hackett dist Canberra Australia
103 E5 Hackettstown New Jersey 40.52N 74.50W
107 J7 Hackleburg Alabama 34.15N 87.51W
12 E4 Hack, Mt S Australia 30.44S 138.45E
57 M4 Hackness N Yorks Eng 54.17N 0.31W
55 G3 Hackney London England 51.33N 0.03W
55 G3 Hackney bor London Eng
37 G7 Haçlı Gölü L Turkey 39.00N 42.15E
91 D9 Haco Angola 10.15S 15.44E
25 J2 Ha Coi Vietnam 21.25N 107.45E
19 N5 Hacq isld Truk Is Pacific Oc 7.01N 151.56E
61 E4 Hacquegnies Belgium 50.39N 3.36E
37 F7 Haçreş Dağları mts Turkey
88 O4 Hactne Algeria 35.34N 0.03E
33 H5 Hadabat al Budū gravel plain Saudi Arabia
28 B3 Hadagalli Karnataka India 15.04N 75.54E
85 N10 Hadaiamet, Jebel mt Sudan 18.38N 35.35E
85 N9 Hadai-Aweb, Jeb mt Sudan 21.51N 35.23E
87 H7 Hada Kumbi Ethiopia 6.03N 41.40E
87 F2 Hadaliya Sudan 16.10N 36.10E
64 E3 Hadamar W Germany 50.27N 8.04E
31 D5 Hada Mts Afghanistan
33 F2 Hadaqah, Al Saudi Arabia 28.28N 44.23E
108 N7 Hadar Nebraska 42.08N 97.29W
33 D7 Hadārah isld Saudi Arabia 18.26N 41.11E
33 B5 Hadarba,Ras C Sudan 22.05N 36.53E
35 C5 Hadar Ramatayim Israel 32.09N 34.54E
33 G9 Hadā, Wādī watercourse S Yemen
33 E5 Hadbah, Al plain Saudi Arabia
33 L8 Hadbarah Oman 17.40N 55.14E
Hadb Hamar see Hudb Humar plat
33 C6 Haddā' Saudi Arabia 21.26N 39.35E
86 E3 Haddâdi,El Egypt 31.20N 30.47E
33 J3 Hadd,Al Bahrain, The Gulf 26.15N 50.42E
33 N5 Hadd, Al Oman 22.31N 59.45E
103 J4 Haddam Connecticut 41.28N 72.30W
109 N2 Haddam Kansas 39.52N 97.18W
33 F6 Haddār, Al Saudi Arabia 21.59N 45.53E
35 E1 Haddâsse Lebanon 33.10N 35.23E
56 M3 Haddenham Cambs Eng 52.21N 0.09E
58 L7 Haddington Lothian Scotland 55.58N 2.47W
123 E14 Haddington, Mt Antarctica 64.20S 57.30W
56 P2 Haddiscoe Norfolk Eng 52.31N 1.35E
105 D4 Haddock Georgia 33.02N 83.28W
13 F7 Haddon Corner Qnsld/S Aust 26.00S 141.00E
12 F2 Haddon Downs S Australia 26.19S 140.45E
103 D7 Haddonfield New Jersey 39.53N 75.01W
26 Q12 Haddon Pt Seychelles, Ind Oc 4.28S 55.13E
27 L9 Haddunmahti Atoll Maldives, Ind Oc 1.55N 73.25E
87 L5 Haded reg Somalia
87 L6 Haded Plain Somalia
90 E5 Hadejia Nigeria 12.30N 10.03E
90 D5 Hadejia R Nigeria
52 E6 Hadeland reg Norway
63 J5 Hadelner Kanal W Germany
63 K4 Hademarschen W Germany 54.08N 9.26E
13 K7 Haden Queensland 27.15S 151.52E
87 F2 Hadendowa tribe Sudan
35 C4 Hadera Israel 32.26N 34.55E
35 C4 Hadera R Israel
65 N5 Hadersdorf Austria 48.28N 15.42E
53 D6 Haderslev Denmark 55.15N 9.30E
Haderslev co see Sønderjylland
53 B4 Haderup Denmark 56.23N 9.00E
29 E8 Hadgaon Maharashtra India 19.30N 77.42E
33 D5 Hadhah Saudi Arabia 22.34N 40.38E
Hadhal see Hatgal
85 C5 Hadh, al watercourse Libya
85 D7 Hadh, Al watercourse Libya
33 E2 Hadhālil, Al reg Saudi Arabia
33 J6 Hādhat al Hārrah sand area Saudi Arabia
33 H6 Hadh Banī Zaynān sand area Saudi Arabia
33 J6 Hadh Fāris sand area Saudi Arabia
33 J6 Hadh Mazayriq sand area Saudi Arabia
Hadhr see Hadr, Al
33 G9 Hadhramaut, Wādī watercourse S Yemen
33 J7 Hadh Shakwah sand area Saudi Arabia
33 K10 Hadiboh Socotra Ind Oc 12.36N 53.59E
33 K10 Hadibū Socotra Ind Oc 12.36N 53.59E
35 C6 Hadid Israel 31.58N 34.55E

33 J6 Hadidah, Al met craters Saudi Arabia 21.32N 50.30E
86 D5 Hadîd, Gebel hill Egypt 30.19N 30.06E
87 E2 Hadiga Sudan 17.52N 34.41E
34 D8 Hādi, Jebel el mts Jordan
24 E7 Hadilik Xinjiang Uygur Zizhiqu China 37.51N 86.10E
36 F6 Hadım Turkey 36.58N 32.27E
Hadimköy see Boyalık
86 K5 Hadîra, Wâdî el watercourse Egypt
35 F8 Haditha Jordan 31.18N 35.33E
34 E7 Hadīthah, Al Saudi Arabia 31.26N 37.10E
88 R3 Hadjar, El Algeria 36.44N 7.44E
90 K6 Hadjera Chad 10.10N 21.06E
88 Q5 Hadjira, El Algeria 32.40N 5.28E
88 P3 Hadjout Algeria 36.33N 2.20E
56 N4 Hadleigh Essex Eng 51.34N 0.36E
56 N3 Hadleigh Suffolk Eng 52.02N 0.57E
103 J2 Hadley Massachusetts 42.21N 72.35W
97 J3 Hadley B N W Terr
56 M5 Hadlow Kent Eng 51.14N 0.20E
11 F11 Hadlow New Zealand 44.22S 171.11E
98 R9 Hadlow Crique B Quebec 46.46N 71.12W
63 O9 Hadmersleben E Germany 52.00N 11.20E
56 F2 Hadnall Shropshire Eng 52.47N 2.42W
87 J7 Hado Ethiopia 7.21N 43.46E
69 L7 Hadol France 48.06N 6.27E
21 D10 Hadong S Korea 35.00N 127.30E
25 H2 Hadong Vietnam 20.58N 105.46E
34 E8 Hadraj, Wādī watercourse Saudi Arabia/Jordan
34 K3 Hadr, Al Iraq 35.34N 42.42E
33 G9 Hadramawt reg S Yemen
34 L3 Hadrānīyah Iraq 35.36N 43.14E
51 D3 Hadsel Norway 68.33N 15.00E
51 D3 Hødseløya isld Norway 68.32N 14.50E
53 E4 Hadsten Denmark 56.19N 10.03E
53 E3 Hadsund Denmark 56.43N 10.08E
93 H2 Hadu Hills Kenya
85 J5 Hadûn, Gebel mt Egypt 29.06N 26.19E
113 N3 Hadweenzic R Alaska
121 G3 Haedo,Cuchilla de mts Uruguay
53 Y20 Hægefjell mt Norway 59.16N 8.25E
21 C8 Haeju N Korea 38.04N 125.40E
21 C9 Haeju-man B N Korea/S Korea
50 C2 Hælavík Iceland 66.27N 22.35W
60 M15 Haelen Netherlands 51.14N 5.57E
50 D5 Hælsheidhi heath Iceland
114 E3 Haena Hawaiian Is 22.13N 159.33W
21 D10 Haenam S Korea 34.35N 126.35E
114 E3 Haena Pt Hawaiian Is 22.13N 159.33W
94 K5 Haenertsburg S Africa 24.00S 29.50E
50 A3 Hænuvík Iceland 65.37N 24.11W
89 B3 Haéré-Lao Senegal 16.24N 14.21W
Ha-erh-pin see Harbin
85 K10 Hafair, El Sudan 18.50N 29.47E
Hafar Saudi Arabiasee Hafar al Bāţin
35 F1 Hafar Syria 33.06N 35.41E
33 D2 Hafar, Al Saudi Arabia 28.40N 41.19E
33 G4 Hafar al 'Atk Saudi Arabia 25.58N 46.34E
33 F2 Hafar al Bāţin Saudi Arabia 28.29N 46.00E
Hafar 'Atj see Hafar al 'Atk
65 D7 Hafelekar-Spitze mt Austria 47.19N 11.25E
35 C6 Hafez Hayyim Israel 31.47N 34.47E
33 M4 Haffah, Ra's C Oman 25.45N 56.19E
Haffe see Babenna
63 N4 Haffkrug-Scharbeutz W Germany 54.03N 10.43E
48 T4 Haffners Bjerg mt Greenland 76.30N 63.00W
100 K6 Hafford Saskatchewan 52.45N 107.21W
78 C13 Haffouz Tunisia 35.38N 9.39E
89 C5 Hafia Guinea 12.09N 13.19W
37 C6 Hafik Turkey 39.53N 37.24E
85 L10 Hafir Sudan 19.32N 30.17E
35 H9 Hafira watercourse Jordan
33 C3 Hafirat al 'Aydā Saudi Arabia 26.28N 39.08E
33 L5 Hafit Oman 23.57N 55.52E
33 L4 Hafit, Jabal hills Oman/U.A.E.
31 G4 Hafizabad Pakistan 32.03N 73.42E
53 U19 Håfjell mt Norway 59.43N 6.01E
28 J3 Hāflong Assam India 25.07N 92.51E
50 D6 Hafnarfjall mt Iceland 64.30N 21.50W
50 D6 Hafnarfjördhur Iceland 64.04N 21.58W
50 M5 Hafnarnes C Iceland 64.53N 13.45W
65 H7 Hafner mt Austria 47.05N 13.25E
65 N5 Hafnerbach Austria 48.14N 15.33E
50 C7 Hafnir Iceland 63.56N 22.41W
50 E2 Hafnir Iceland 66.04N 20.22W
50 K3 Hafralón L Iceland 65.51N 15.35W
50 K2 Hafralónsá R Iceland
50 D4 Hafratindur pk Iceland 65.19N 21.57W
50 D6 Hafravatn L Iceland 64.08N 21.40W
53 T21 Hafsfjord inlet Norway 58.58N 5.33E
53 W16 Hafslo Norway 61.19N 7.10E
53 W16 Hafslovatn L Norway 61.18N 7.10E
Haftavan see Haftvān
32 C5 Haft Gel Iran 31.28N 49.35E
Haft Kel oil field see Haft Gel
31 B3 Haftqala R Afghanistan
32 E7 Haftvān Iran 27.46N 53.18E
Hafun see Dante Somali Rep
87 N5 Hafun, B.di Somalia
50 G7 Hafursey mt Iceland 63.31N 18.49W
50 E5 Hafursfell mt Iceland 64.42N 20.32W
50 C5 Hafursfjördhur B Iceland
50 H4 Hafursstadhaheidhi heath Iceland
21 B3 Hag Nei Monggol Zizhiqu China 49.10N 121.07E
66 H1 Häg W Germany 47.44N 7.55E
87 D4 Hag 'Abdullah Sudan 13.59N 33.35E
93 M5 Hagadera Kenya 0.02N 40.17E
95 M8 Haga-Haga S Africa 32.45S 28.15E
Hagalil reg see Galilee
105 F5 Hagan Georgia 32.09N 81.47W
50 F2 Haganesvík Iceland 66.05N 19.10W
50 K3 Hágangaheidhi heath Iceland
50 G5 Háganganyrdhri mt Iceland 64.35N 18.15W
50 G5 Háganga sydhri mt Iceland 64.32N 18.15W
87 E3 Hagar el Abiad Sudan 14.30N 35.53E
28 C3 Hagari R Karnataka India
93 M4 Hagarta Kenya 1.37N 40.33E
Hagaruhi see Hauraha
52 K6 Hagaström Sweden 60.41N 17.05E
50 B4 Hagavadhall inlet Iceland
50 E6 Hagavatn L Iceland 64.29N 20.20W
63 F5 Hage W Germany 53.36N 7.16E
69 L7 Hagécourt France 48.14N 6.09E
63 R8 Hagelsberg mt E Germany 52.09N 12.32E
113 G7 Hagemeister I Alaska 58.40N 161.00W
113 G7 Hagemeister Str Alaska
63 J6 Hagen Niedersachsen W Germany 53.22N 8.39E
63 F10 Hagen Nordrhein-Westfalen W Germany 51.22N 7.27E
100 M6 Hagen Saskatchewan 52.56N 105.31W
63 K8 Hagenburg W Germany 52.26N 9.19E
48 U2 Hagen Fjord Greenland
65 H6 Hagen Gebirge mts Austria
15 H6 Hagen, Mt Papua New Guinea 5.45S 144.05E
63 O6 Hagenow E Germany 53.27N 11.12E
66 F1 Hagenthal France 47.32N 7.29E
85 F7 Hager el Bahri Libya 25.44N 21.05E
110 L7 Hagerman Idaho 42.50N 114.55W
103 J5 Hagerman Long I, N Y 40.46N 72.57W
109 F8 Hagerman New Mexico 33.06N 104.20W
52 J8 Hägerstad Sweden 58.05N 15.55E
107 L2 Hagerstown Indiana 39.56N 85.09W
104 H7 Hagerstown Maryland 39.39N 77.44W
99 K10 Hagersville Ontario 42.58N 80.04W
60 J12 Hagestein Netherlands 51.59N 5.07E
72 C8 Hagetaubin France 43.31N 0.36W
72 C8 Hagetmau France 43.39N 0.35W
52 H6 Hagfors Sweden 60.03N 13.45E
87 K7 Haggarih Ethiopia 7.05N 45.50E
52 H3 Häggenås Sweden 63.24N 14.55E
93 M6 Haggerso Kenya 0.46S 40.12E
58 N7 Haggerston Northumberland Eng 55.41N 1.56W
66 J2 Hägglingen Switzerland 47.23N 8.15E
52 H3 Häggsjön Sweden 63.53N 14.15E
86 J5 Hâgg, Wâdî el watercourse Egypt
50 B4 Hagi Bardhastrandarsýsla, Vestur Iceland 65.30N 23.25W
20 E7 Hagi Japan 34.25N 131.22E
50 E7 Hagi Rangárvallasýsla Iceland 63.59N 20.26W
25 H1 Ha Giang Vietnam 22.50N 104.58E
82 K4 Hăgimas mt Romania 46.41N 25.49E
86 G4 Hâgir, El Egypt 30.41N 31.49E
20 L6 Hagiwara Japan 35.52N 137.12E
56 G3 Hagley Hereford & Worcs Eng 52.26N 2.08W
11 M9 Hagley Pk Christchurch New Zealand
66 O1 Hagnau W Germany 47.40N 9.19E
87 K6 Hagoga Ethiopia 8.06N 45.20E
Ha Golan reg see Golan reg
69 L5 Hagondange France 49.16N 6.11E
50 J3 Hagong mt Iceland 65.45N 16.40W
50 G6 Hágonguhraun lava field Iceland
50 H6 Hagöngur mt Iceland 64.11N 17.45W
19 G1 Hagonoy Luzon Philippines 14.51N 120.44E
105 G3 Hagood S Carolina 34.04N 80.34W
35 C5 Hagor Israel 32.08N 34.57E
35 F1 Ha Gosherim Israel 33.13N 35.37E
84 Y21 Hagras-Sewda C Malta 35.50N 14.25E
59 D6 Hags Hd Clare Irish Rep 52.57N 9.28W
108 L3 Hague N Dakota 46.03N 100.00W
104 M3 Hague New York 43.45N 73.31W
100 L6 Hague Saskatchewan 52.33N 106.24W
70 G2 Hague, C. de la France 49.44N 1.56W
69 O6 Haguenau France 48.49N 7.47E
109 E1 Hagues Pk Colorado 40.30N 105.38W
Hague, The see 's Gravenhage
86 H6 Hagûl, Wâdî watercourse Egypt
24 D9 Hagung Tso L Xizang Zizhiqu China 32.50N 81.42E
88 G8 Hagunia Morocco 27.30N 12.27W
88 J6 Haha tribe Morocco
98 O3 Ha Ha B Quebec
98 N3 Ha Ha Bay Quebec 50.57N 59.00W
21 J11 Haha-jima-rettō isld Ogasawara-Guntō Pacific Oc
98 B5 Ha Ha, L Quebec 48.02N 70.50W
87 K6 Hahe Somalia 9.16N 44.59E
53 W20 Håhellerhytta Norway 59.02N 7.10E
105 D7 Hahira Georgia 30.59N 83.23W
64 M4 Hahnbach W Germany 49.32N 11.50E
69 O2 Hahn-bei-Wallmerod W Germany 50.31N 7.54E
65 F7 Hahnen-Kamm mt Austria 47.26N 12.22E
63 M9 Hahnenklee-Bockswiese W Germany 51.53N 10.18E
62 K9 Hahót Hungary 46.40N 16.57E
35 C3 HaHoterim Israel 32.45N 34.57E
86 O5 Hai Jordan 30.21N 35.29E
25 E9 Hai isld Thailand 7.25N 99.00E
23 E8 Hai'an Guangdong China 20.15N 110.10E
23 J2 Hai'an Jiangsu China 32.31N 120.31E
94 E7 Haib watercourse Namibia
Haibak see Samangan
21 D4 Haibei Heilongjiang China 47.42N 126.52E
23 H6 Haicheng Fujian China 24.24N 117.53E
21 B7 Haicheng Liaoning China 40.53N 122.45E
30 E6 Haidargarh Uttar Prad India 26.36N 81.21E
65 J5 Haiding Austria 48.13N 13.59E
64 Q6 Haidmühle W Germany 48.50N 13.48E
88 S4 Haïdra Tunisia 35.32N 8.25E
64 O5 Haidstein mt W Germany 49.13N 12.49E
25 J2 Hai Duong Vietnam 20.56N 106.21E
86 F6 Hai, El Egypt 29.39N 31.18E
88 M4 Hai, El R Morocco
35 C2 Haifa Israel 32.49N 34.59E
35 D2 Haifa, B. of Israel
23 G7 Haifeng Guangdong China 22.56N 115.19E
50 F6 Háifoss waterfall Iceland 64.13N 19.41W
14 F9 Haig W Australia 30.58S 126.06E
86 G6 Hai, Gebel el Egypt 29.42N 31.36E
64 E2 Haiger W Germany 50.44N 8.13E
64 F7 Haigerloch W Germany 48.22N 8.50E
101 P7 Haig L Alberta 56.54N 116.03W
101 P7 Haig Lake Alberta 56.54N 116.06W
108 J10 Haigler Nebraska 40.00N 101.55W
22 L7 Hai He R Tianjin China
20 A2 Haijima Tōkyō Japan
23 E8 Haikang Guangdong China 20.54N 110.05E
20 C8 Haiki Japan 33.09N 129.48E
87 G5 Haik,L Ethiopia 11.20N 39.43E
23 E8 Haikou Guangdong China 20.05N 110.25E
114 E6 Haiku Hawaiian Is 20.55N 156.20W
33 D3 Hā'il Saudi Arabia 27.31N 41.45E
28 J3 Hailakandi Assam India 24.40N 92.34E
21 A3 Hailar Nei Monggol Zizhiqu China 49.15N 119.41E
22 L2 Hailar He R Heilongjiang China
21 B3 Hailar He R Nei Monggol Zizhiqu China
110 L6 Hailey Idaho 43.31N 114.19W
99 L5 Haileybury Ontario 47.27N 79.39W
109 P7 Haileyville Oklahoma 34.54N 95.36W
21 E5 Hailin Heilongjiang China 44.37N 129.24E
23 F8 Hailing Dao isld Guangdong China 21.35N 111.47E
61 L5 Haillot Belgium 50.26N 5.09E
21 C6 Hailong Jilin China 42.26N 125.42E
21 C6 Hailong Jilin China 42.39N 125.48E
56 M6 Hailsham E Sussex Eng 50.52N 0.16E
21 D4 Hailun Heilongjiang China 47.29N 126.58E
Hai-lung see Hailong
51 L6 Hailuoto Finland 65.01N 24.45E
51 L6 Hailuoto isld Finland 65.10N 24.45E
Hailut see Urad Zhongu Liaheqi
33 D3 Hā'il, Wādī watercourse Saudi Arabia
34 G4 Hail, Wādī watercourse Syria
63 M8 Haimar W Germany 52.18N 10.04E
23 J3 Haimen Jiangsu China 31.58N 121.11E
23 J4 Haimen Zhejiang China 28.40N 121.27E
65 C7 Haiming Austria 47.16N 10.53E
116 J5 Haina Dominican Rep 18.27N 70.02W
87 F1 Haina,Jeb mt Sudan 18.02N 37.45E
23 E9 Hainan Dao isld Guangdong China
23 F8 Hainan Dao isld Guangdong China
25 D2 Hai-nang Burma 21.01N 97.58E
61 G4 Hainaut prov Belgium
69 E3 Hainaut reg France
65 P5 Hainburg Austria 48.09N 16.57E
113 U7 Haines Alaska 59.11N 135.23W
110 H5 Haines Oregon 44.55N 117.55W
61 G5 Haine-St.Paul Belgium 50.27N 4.12E
61 G5 Haine-St.Pierre Belgium 50.27N 4.13E
103 D5 Hainesburg New Jersey 40.57N 75.03W
105 F9 Haines City Florida 28.06N 81.39W
103 F2 Haines Falls New York 42.13N 74.06W
101 E5 Haines Highway Yukon Terr
101 E5 Haines Junction Yukon Terr 60.45N 137.21W
103 E4 Hainesville New Jersey 41.15N 74.48W
65 N5 Hainfeld Austria 48.03N 15.47E
64 J1 Hainich reg E Germany
64 P2 Hainichen E Germany 50.58N 13.08E
61 F5 Hainin Belgium 50.26N 3.46E
23 J3 Haining Zhejiang China 30.31N 120.35E
63 N10 Hainleite reg E Germany
64 Q2 Hainsberg E Germany 50.59N 13.38E
25 J2 Haiphong Vietnam 20.50N 106.41E
21 F4 Haiqing Heilongjiang China 47.52N 134.35E
22 E8 Hairag Qinghai China 37.15N 100.23E
33 G4 Ha'ir,Al Saudi Arabia 24.22N 46.50E
22 F6 Hairhan Namag Nei Monggol Zizhiqu China 41.25N 102.02E
69 J6 Haironville France 48.41N 5.05E
100 F5 Hairy Hill Alberta 53.46N 111.58W
21 B6 Haisgai Nei Monggol Zizhiqu China 43.05N 122.32E
116 H5 Haiti rep West Indies
23 E9 Haitou Guangdong China 19.34N 109.03E
21 C5 Haituo Jilin China 45.17N 124.00E
62 M8 Haivan Hungary 47.40N 19.41E
111 N9 Haivana Nakya Arizona 32.01N 111.39W
15 G7 Haivare Papua New Guinea 7.16S 143.19E
111 G5 Haiwee Res California 36.11N 117.57W
22 L7 Haixing Hebei China 38.09N 117.29E
22 E8 Haixin Shan mt Qinghai China
85 O10 Haiya Sudan 18.17N 36.21E
87 F1 Haiya Junction Sudan 18.20N 36.21E
25 M2 Haiyan Guangdong China 21.50N 112.33E
22 E8 Haiyan Qinghai China 36.55N 100.54E
23 J3 Haiyan Zhejiang China 30.33N 120.57E
35 H4 Haiyan el Mushrif Jordan 32.16N 36.09E
35 H5 Haiyan er Ruweibid Jordan 32.15N 36.07E
22 M8 Haiyang Shandong China 36.45N 121.15E
21 C8 Haiyang Dao isld Liaoning China
Haiyou see Samen
22 F8 Haiyuan Gansu China 36.36N 104.40E
23 D7 Haiyuan Guangxi China 22.10N 107.35E
22 G8 Haiyuan Ningxia China 36.34N 105.52E
23 B6 Haizidi Yunnan China 24.35N 101.46E
33 C5 Hajar Saudi Arabia 22.07N 39.33E
Hajarain see Hajarayn, Al
33 N5 Hājar, Al Oman 23.24N 58.32E
Hajar al Gharbi, Al mts see Hajar, Western
Hajar ash Sharquī, al mts see Hajar, Eastern
33 H9 Hajarayn, Al S Yemen 15.28N 48.20E
33 N5 Hajar, Eastern mts Oman
33 C3 Hajar, Jabal mts Saudi Arabia
33 M5 Hajar, Western mts Oman
82 G3 Hajdú-Bihar co Hungary
62 N8 Hajdúböszörmény Hungary 47.40N 21.29E
62 N8 Hajdúdorog Hungary 47.48N 21.29E
62 N8 Hajdúhadház Hungary 47.40N 21.40E
62 N8 Hajdúnanás Hungary 47.50N 21.26E
62 N8 Hajdúszoboszló Hungary 47.27N 21.21E
88 L5 Hajeb, El Morocco 33.43N 5.13W
88 S4 Hajeb el Aïoun Tunisia 35.24N 9.33E
33 K10 Hajhir mt Socotra Indian Oc 12.36N 54.02E
84 C7 Haji Greece 37.01N 21.50E
31 D6 Haji Pakistan 29.16N 67.51E
31 C4 Haji Alam Afghanistan 32.20N 65.33E
34 M1 Hājī Beg R Iraq
34 M2 Hajī Ebrāhīm, Kūhe mt Iran/Iraq 36.32N 44.59E
31 E3 Hajigak Pass Afghanistan 34.38N 68.08E
20 M3 Hajiki-saki C Japan 38.20N 138.32E
30 J7 Hajipur Bihar India 25.41N 85.13E
33 E9 Hājir Yemen 14.41N 43.34E
33 H4 Hajir tribe Saudi Arabia
Hajir, Jabal see Ha-Geher, Jabal mt
34 K5 Hājiyah, Wādī watercourse Iraq
33 B2 Hajj Saudi Arabia 29.01N 36.13E
32 D3 Hājjābād-e Māsileh Iran 34.50N 51.09E
33 E9 Hajjah Yemen 15.45N 43.34E
32 F6 Hājjiābād Banāder va Jazāyer-e Bahr-e Oman Iran 28.19N 55.54E
32 G7 Hājjiābād Banāder va Jazāyer-e Bahr-e Oman Iran 27.10N 56.55E
32 F4 Hājjiābād Esfahān Iran 32.03N 54.12E
32 F6 Hājjiābād Fārs Iran 28.22N 54.26E
32 F2 Hājjiābād Māzandarān Iran 36.40N 54.20E
32 F4 Hājjiābād-e Zarrīn Iran 33.09N 54.54E
44 H10 Hājjī Aqā Iran 37.52N 46.45E
34 N6 Hājjī Muhsin Iraq 32.36N 45.29E
33 M7 Hajmah Oman 19.55N 56.15E
Hajmi see 'Ajami
34 G7 Hajm, Khabarī al marshes Saudi Arabia
62 O3 Hajnówka Poland 52.45N 23.32E
28 H2 Hajo Assam India 26.16N 91.35E
21 D10 Hajo isld S Korea
33 D6 Hajrah Saudi Arabia 20.13N 41.02E
33 G8 Hajr, Al S Yemen 16.11N 47.45E
Hajr, Jabal see Ha-Geher, Jabal mt
33 H9 Hajr, Wādī R S Yemen
22 D5 Haju Nei Monggol Zizhiqu China 42.09N 98.35E
25 B1 Haka Burma 22.42N 93.41E
87 P4 Hakabi Socotra S Yemen 12.23N 54.02E
114 C7 Hakalau Hawaiian Is 19.53N 155.15W
35 G3 Hakama Jordan 32.35N 35.53E
122 U14 Hakamui Marquesas Is Pacific Oc 9.22S 140.01W
91 J8 Hakansson, Mts Zaïre
52 G8 Håkantorp Sweden 58.18N 12.55E
11 A13 Hakapoua, L New Zealand
Hakarmel, Har ridge see Carmel, Mt
20 N4 Hakase-yama mt Japan 37.22N 139.43E
11 E11 Hakataramea New Zealand 44.43S 170.28E
11 E11 Hakataramea R New Zealand
20 G7 Hakata-shima isld Japan
9 R9 Hakau Mama'o reef Tonga, Pacific Oc 20.59S 175.13W
121 B8 Hakelhuincul, Altiplanicie de plat Argentina
26 S8 Hakgala mt Sri Lanka 6.55N 80.48E
37 G7 Hakif Turkey 38.07N 42.34E
34 C8 Hakippa, Har mt Israel 30.22N 35.02E
37 E6 Hakis Turkey 39.18N 39.52E
37 H8 Hakkâri Turkey 37.36N 43.45E
51 J5 Hakkas Sweden 66.53N 21.36E
20 O1 Hakkōda-san mt Japan 40.39N 140.51E
Hak Kok Tau see Collinson, C.
26 S10 Hakmana Sri Lanka 6.05N 80.40E
20 K3 Hakodate Japan 41.46N 140.44E
20 K3 Hakodate-wan B Japan
20 A2 Hakonegasaki Tōkyō Japan
94 D4 Hakos Mts Namibia
94 F6 Hakskeenpan salt L S Africa
20 K5 Hakui Japan 36.55N 136.46E
20 K5 Haku-san vol Japan 36.10N 136.46E
20 K5 Hakusan Nat.Pk Japan
31 E8 Hala Pakistan 25.47N 68.28E
33 F5 Halabān Saudi Arabia 23.30N 44.19E
34 N3 Halabja Iraq 35.11N 45.59E
115 O7 Halachó Mexico 20.29N 90.02W
21 C5 Halahai Jilin China 44.43N 124.59E
87 G3 Halai Ethiopia 15.00N 39.20E
85 O8 Halaib Egypt 22.12N 36.35E
86 L4 Halâl, Gebel hill Egypt 30.38N 33.59E
114 D4 Halalii L Hawaiian Is
53 T18 Hålandsdal Norway 60.14N 5.51E
53 U20 Hålandsosen Norway 59.21N 6.15E
61 N8 Halanzy Belgium 49.33N 5.45E
35 G1 Halas Syria 33.14N 35.56E
62 N8 Halastó L Hungary 47.39N 21.05E
34 D9 Halat 'Ammar Saudi Arabia 29.11N 36.09E
93 L3 Halati Kenya 2.32N 39.38E
89 L7 Halatia Benin 9.04N 2.30E
82 K3 Hălăuceşti Romania 47.06N 26.50E
114 B6 Halawa Hawaiian Is 20.13N 155.47W
114 D5 Halawa Hawaiian Is 21.09N 157.15W
35 F4 Halawa Jordan 32.23N 35.39E
114 D5 Halawa Bay Hawaiian Is
114 D5 Halawa, C Hawaiian Is 21.10N 156.43W
114 E8 Halawa Heights Hawaiian Is 21.23N 157.55W
87 E4 Halawa,Jeb mt Sudan/Ethiopia 12.36N 35.40E
34 D4 Halba Lebanon 34.33N 36.04E
63 T8 Halbe E Germany 52.07N 13.42E
65 N8 Halbenrein Austria 46.44N 15.58E
63 O9 Halberstadt E Germany 51.54N 11.04E
56 E6 Halberton Devon Eng 50.55N 3.25W
100 O9 Halbrite Saskatchewan 49.30N 103.34W
65 P6 Halbturn Austria 47.52N 16.59E
11 K7 Halcombe New Zealand 40.07S 175.31E
56 E5 Halcon Corner Somerset Eng 51.01N 3.05W
19 K5 Halcon, Mt Philippines 13.16N 120.59E
103 F2 Halcott Center New York 42.12N 74.30W
103 E2 Halcottsville New York 42.14N 74.37W
95 M6 Halcyon Drift S Africa 30.56S 28.28E
101 P10 Halcyon Hot Springs Br Col 50.30N 117.56W
53 E3 Hald Århus Denmark 56.33N 10.08E
50 F6 Hald Iceland 64.11N 19.25W
53 C3 Hald Viborg Denmark 56.36N 9.12E
53 H6 Haldagerlille Denmark 55.20N 11.32E
101 N2 Haldane R N W Terr
11 D13 Haldane B New Zealand
52 F7 Halden Norway 59.08N 11.13E
65 C7 Halden See L Austria 47.30N 10.35E
63 O8 Haldensleben E Germany 52.18N 11.25E
66 P4 Haldenstein Switzerland 46.53N 9.33E
53 M9 Haldersvig Faeroes 62.16N 7.06W
29 L6 Haldia W Bengal India 22.02N 88.02E
29 L4 Haldibari W Bengal India 26.19N 88.53E
29 K6 Haldi R W Bengal India
53 C4 Hald Sø L Denmark 56.23N 9.23E
53 E4 Haldum Denmark 56.17N 10.03E
30 C3 Haldwani Uttar Prad India 29.13N 79.31E
121 E6 Hale Argentina 36.04N 60.52W
109 H2 Hale Colorado 39.37N 102.09W
57 J6 Hale Greater Manchester Eng 53.22N 2.20W
106 L5 Hale Michigan 44.23N 83.49W
107 C2 Hale Missouri 39.36N 93.20W
13 D6 Hale R N Terr Australia
114 E6 Haleakala Crater Hawaiian Is 20.43N 156.10W
114 E6 Haleakala Nat. Park Hawaiian Is
114 E6 Haleakala Nat. Pk Hawaiian Is
Haleb see Aleppo
87 J4 Haleb I Ethiopia 12.55N 43.00E
112 F1 Hale Center Texas 34.04N 101.52W
103 F5 Haledon New Jersey 40.56N 74.11W
103 D2 Hale Eddy New York 42.01N 75.24W
50 D5 Háleiksvatn L Iceland 64.49N 21.51W
114 A4 Haleiwa Hawaiian Is 21.36N 158.07W
31 B5 Haleli Afghanistan 31.17N 62.26E
14 B7 Hale, Mt W Australia 26.04S 117.13E
61 L3 Halen Belgium 50.57N 5.07E
114 C5 Halena Hawaiian Is 21.05N 157.14W
30 A5 Halena Rajasthan India 27.07N 77.10E
87 F3 Halenga tribe Sudan
114 C7 Halepiula Hawaiian Is 19.55N 155.24W
107 L6 Hales Bar Dam Tennessee 35.03N 85.30W
95 J8 Halesowen S Africa 32.15S 25.40E
56 G3 Halesowen W Midlands Eng 52.26N 2.05W
56 M5 Hale Street Kent Eng 51.14N 0.24E
56 O3 Halesworth Suffolk Eng 52.21N 1.30E
104 E2 Halethorpe Maryland 39.14N 76.40W
107 J7 Haleyville Alabama 34.12N 87.38W
85 K9 Halfa dist Sudan
89 H9 Half Assini Ghana 5.03N 2.53W
34 P7 Halfāyah, Al Iraq 31.48N 47.28E
50 B3 Hálfdánarfell mt Iceland 65.38N 23.39W
37 D8 Halfeti Turkey 37.12N 37.53E
64 N8 Halfing W Germany 47.57N 12.18E
33 N6 Halfīn,Wādī watercourse Oman
Hal Flood Ra see Flood Ra
111 A10 Half Moon B California
11 C13 Half Moon B Stewart I New Zealand
12 D8 Half Moon B Victoria
109 K2 Halford Kansas 39.22N 100.53W
56 H3 Halford Warwicks Eng 52.07N 1.36W
104 H7 Halfway Maryland 39.36N 77.47W
110 H5 Halfway Oregon 44.53N 117.07W
112 F1 Halfway Texas 34.12N 101.57W
101 M7 Halfway R Br Col
95 M2 Halfway House S Africa 26.00S 28.08E
26 B14 Halfway Kop hill Marion I Ind Oc 46.54S 37.48E
113 K6 Halfway Mt Alaska 60.47N 155.29W
55 J4 Halfway Street London Eng 51.26N 0.06E
60 H10 Halfweg Netherlands 52.22N 4.45E
22 L3 Halhīn Gol R China/Mongolia
53 S18 Halhjem Norway 60.09N 5.28E
35 D7 Halhul Jordan 31.34N 35.07E
37 E2 Hali isld Turkey 40.28N 28.05E
33 D7 Hali oasis Saudi Arabia 18.38N 41.22E
30 F8 Halia Uttar Prad India 24.50N 82.19E
30 E6 Haliapur Uttar Prad India 26.31N 81.47E
35 B7 Halib watercourse Gaza Strip
Haliban see Halabān
99 M7 Haliburton Ontario 45.03N 78.30W
99 M7 Haliburton Highlands reg Ontario
37 J2 Haliç inlet İstanbul Turkey
Halicarnassus anc site see Bodrum
26 T8 Hali-ela Sri Lanka 6.57N 81.02E
103 N3 Halifax Massachusetts 42.00N 70.52W
105 K1 Halifax N Carolina 36.19N 77.37W
98 J9 Halifax Nova Scotia 44.38N 63.35W
104 J6 Halifax Pennsylvania 40.28N 76.56W
13 H4 Halifax Queensland 18.33S 146.16E
57 K5 Halifax W Yorks Eng 53.44N 1.52W
13 H4 Halifax B Queensland
13 H4 Halifax, Mt Queensland 19.08S 146.20E
51 K11 Halikko Finland 60.24N 23.05E
37 F3 Halilbey isld Turkey 40.11N 28.35E
37 F6 Halilçavus Turkey 39.16N 41.40E
32 D6 Halileh, Ra's-e C Iran 28.49N 50.54E
87 A7 Halima Sudan 7.32N 27.50E
34 D4 Halimet el Qabu mt Syria 34.12N 36.37E
36 F6 Halimiye Turkey 36.44N 32.42E
18 G3 Halim Perdanakusuma airport Jakarta Indonesia 6.16S 106.54E
18 G9 Halimun, Gunung mt Java Indon 6.42S 106.26E
87 M6 Halin Somalia 9.02N 48.36E
29 M2 Halisahar W Bengal India 22.26N 88.27E
33 D7 Hali,Wādī watercourse Saudi Arabia
33 H8 Haliyā S Yemen 17.02N 49.45E
28 B3 Haliyal Karnataka India 15.21N 74.51E
33 H3 Haliyatah, Jabal al mt Saudi Arabia 26.45N 48.09E
51 K4 Halju mt Sweden 67.58N 22.40E
53 D6 Halk Denmark 55.12N 9.39E
36 F2 Halkavun Turkey 40.12N 32.39E
113 M1 Halkett, C Alaska 70.50N 152.18W
100 E6 Halkirk Alberta 52.18N 112.08W
58 K1 Halkirk Highland Scotland 58.30N 3.30W
51 L2 Halkkavarre mt Norway 69.58N 25.24E
65 K6 Hall Austria 47.38N 14.28E
103 A9 Hall Maryland 38.54N 76.44W
110 M3 Hall Montana 46.35N 113.12W
52 K3 Hälla Sweden 63.56N 17.20E
61 J2 Hallaar Belgium 51.05N 4.44E
103 A6 Hallam Pennsylvania 40.00N 76.36W
66 K1 Hallan Switzerland 47.43N 8.28E
56 M6 Halland E Sussex Eng 50.56N 0.08E
52 G3 Håland Sweden 63.19N 13.20E
52 G10 Halland dist Sweden
105 G12 Hallandale Florida 25.58N 80.09W
52 G10 Hallandsås hills Sweden
53 K4 Hallands Väderö isld Sweden 56.28N 12.35E
33 M8 Hallānīyah / Arabian Sea 17.30N 56.00E
21 D11 Halla San mt S Korea 33.25N 126.30E
95 J3 Hallatt's Hope S Africa 27.02S 25.23E
12 D5 Hall B S Australia
97 N1 Hall Basin Greenland
97 L4 Hall Beach N W Terr 68.48N 76.10W
100 S8 Hallboro Manitoba 50.09N 99.26W
48 U11 Hall Bredning inlet Greenland
61 J2 Halle Antwerp Belgium 51.14N 4.39E
61 G4 Halle Brabant Belgium 50.44N 4.14E
63 P10 Halle E Germany 51.28N 11.58E
60 O12 Halle Netherlands 51.59N 6.26E
63 H8 Halle W Germany 52.04N 8.22E
63 O9 Halle reg E Germany
52 J10 Hälleberga Sweden 56.51N 15.40E
61 L3 Halle-Booienhoven Belgium 50.48N 5.07E
99 G3 Hallebourg Ontario 49.39N 83.29W
53 G5 Halleby Å R Denmark
110 K9 Halleck Nevada 40.59N 115.28W
52 H7 Hällefors Sweden 59.46N 14.30E
65 H6 Hallein Austria 47.41N 13.06E
52 H3 Hallen Sweden 63.10N 14.05E
52 J3 Hallen Sweden 63.44N 15.30E
64 F1 Hallenberg W Germany 51.06N 8.38E
69 B4 Hallencourt France 50.00N 1.52E
53 F4 Hallendrup Denmark 56.21N 10.43E
63 P10 Halle-Neustadt E Germany 51.29N 11.54E
64 M6 Hallertau dist W Germany
52 J4 Hällesjö Sweden 62.55N 16.15E
112 L6 Hallettsville Texas 29.27N 96.57W
61 M6 Halleux Belgium 50.10N 5.30E
107 E8 Halley Arkansas 33.31N 91.20W
123 D11 Halley U.K. Base Antarctica 75.31S 26.36W
113 A6 Hall I Bering Sea 60.39N 173.00W
Hall I Franz Josef Land see Gallya, Ostrov
108 H2 Halliday N Dakota 47.22N 102.21W
101 T5 Halliday L N W Terr 61.22N 108.55W
109 E1 Halligan Res Colorado 40.53N 105.22W
63 J3 Halligen, Die islds W Germany
52 D6 Hallingdal V Norway
52 E6 Hallingdalselv R Norway
53 X17 Hallingskarvet mts Norway
53 W17 Hallingskeid Norway 60.40N 7.15E
50 E5 Hallmundarhraun lava field Iceland
52 K6 Hållnäs Uppsala Sweden 60.32N 17.50E
52 M2 Hällnäs Västerbotten Sweden 64.18N 19.40E
108 O1 Hallock Minnesota 48.48N 96.56W
100 K8 Hallonquist Saskatchewan 50.07N 107.21W
50 L4 Hallormsstadhaskogur wood Iceland
50 L4 Hallormsstadhur Iceland 65.05N 14.42W
57 M6 Halloughton Notts Eng 53.04N 0.59W
97 N5 Hall Pen N W Terr
14 E3 Hall Pt W Australia 15.40S 124.22E
107 G6 Halls Tennessee 35.51N 89.24W
56 D7 Hallsands Devon Eng 50.14N 3.40W
112 G8 Halls Bayou R Texas
52 H7 Hallsberg Sweden 59.05N 15.07E
14 G4 Halls Creek W Australia 18.17S 127.38E
15 J8 Hall Sd Papua New Guinea 8.50S 146.30E
64 K4 Hallstadt W Germany 49.55N 10.54E
52 J7 Hallstahammar Sweden 59.26N 16.17E
65 J6 Hallstatt Austria 47.34N 13.39E
65 J6 Hallstätter-See L Austria
52 L6 Hallstavik Sweden 60.06N 18.42E
103 C3 Hallstead Pennsylvania 41.57N 75.45W
107 C9 Hall Summit Louisiana 32.10N 93.19W
107 D2 Hallsville Missouri 39.05N 92.12W
112 N3 Hallsville Texas 32.30N 94.34W
26 D8 Hall Tablemount Indian Oc 21.52S 39.03E
26 C8 Hall Table Mt Mozambique Chan
65 D7 Halltal Austria 47.20N 11.30E
57 G4 Hallthwaites Cumbria Eng 54.16N 3.16W
104 G5 Hallton Pennsylvania 41.26N 78.56W
35 H8 Hallufa watercourse Jordan
69 E2 Halluin France 50.47N 3.08E
60 M6 Hallum Netherlands 53.18N 5.47E
53 E2 Hallund Denmark 57.15N 10.07E
53 C5 Hallundbæk Denmark 55.52N 9.03E
66 J2 Hallwiler See L Switzerland 47.18N 8.13E
61 L6 Halma Belgium 50.05N 5.08E
108 O1 Halma Minnesota 48.40N 96.34W
61 L3 Halmaal Belgium 50.48N 5.10E
82 H4 Hălmagiu Romania 46.16N 22.37E
19 F3 Halmahera isld Moluccas Indon
19 F4 Halmahera Sea Moluccas Indon
82 H3 Halmeu Romania 47.59N 23.02E
52 G10 Halmstad Sweden 56.41N 12.55E
53 X18 Halnefjord L Norway 60.23N 7.45E
53 X18 Halnekollen mt Norway 60.26N 7.41E
30 A1 Halog Himachal Prad India 31.10N 77.11E
87 H3 Haloll Ethiopia 14.22N 41.02E
94 D6 Haloog Namibia 27.22S 17.55E
78 C12 Halq el Oued Tunisia 36.52N 10.18E
53 E3 Hals Denmark 57.00N 10.19E
50 H3 Háls Iceland 65.44N 17.50W
64 P6 Hals W Germany 48.36N 13.29E
52 D3 Halsa Norway 63.05N 8.20E
50 K6 Hálsaós str Iceland
64 F2 Halsdorf W Germany 50.55N 8.57E
108 K8 Halsey Nebraska 41.55N 100.16W
110 B5 Halsey Oregon 44.23N 123.07W
19 J6 Halsey Harb Philippines 11.47N 119.59E
103 B2 Halsey Valley New York 42.08N 76.27W
53 H5 Halsnæs pen Denmark 55.59N 11.59E
53 T20 Halsne Norway 59.12N 5.58E
53 T19 Halsnøy isld Hordaland Norway 59.45N 5.47E
53 T19 Halsnøy Kloster Norway 59.48N 5.40E
51 C6 Halsøy Norway 65.51N 13.10E
53 G6 Halsskov Denmark 55.21N 11.08E
53 G6 Halsskov Odde C Denmark 55.21N 11.07E
108 O2 Halstad Minnesota 47.20N 96.50W
56 N4 Halstead Essex Eng 51.57N 0.38E
109 N3 Halstead Kansas 38.01N 97.32W
55 J6 Halstead Kent Eng 51.20N 0.08E
60 F13 Halsteren Netherlands 51.32N 4.16E
69 L5 Halstroff France 49.23N 6.29E
51 L8 Halsua Finland 63.28N 24.10E
11 L10 Halswell New Zealand 43.35S 172.35E
11 C6 Halswell, Pt Wellington New Zealand 41.17S 174.49E
11 L10 Halswell R New Zealand
37 F8 Haltan watercourse Turkey
22 D7 Haltang He R Gansu China
22 C7 Haltang He R Qinghai China
52 F4 Haltdalen Norway 62.56N 11.10E
52 E2 Halten isld Norway 64.11N 9.25E
52 D2 Haltenbanken bank Norwegian Sea 64.45N 9.00E
63 F9 Haltern W Germany 51.45N 7.10E
51 J2 Haltia mt Finland 69.17N 21.21E
66 G1 Haltingen W Germany 47.37N 7.37E
61 L5 Haltinne Belgium 50.27N 5.04E
112 M9 Haltom City Texas 32.46N 97.17W
57 J4 Halton Gill N Yorks Eng 54.12N 2.11W
115 O8 Haltunchén Mexico 19.30N 90.43W
57 J3 Haltwhistle Northumb Eng 54.58N 2.27W
Haluan see Halvān
33 K4 Halūl isld The Gulf 25.40N 52.25E
35 C10 Haluqim, Har hills Israel
35 A9 Haluza, Holot sand dunes Israel
29 B6 Halvad Gujarat India 23.02N 71.18E
32 G4 Halvān Iran 33.57N 56.13E
64 C1 Halver W Germany 51.12N 7.28E
53 V20 Halvfarheia moor Norway 59.01N 6.47E
50 U15 Halvmåneøya isld Spitsbergen 77.15N 23.15E
48 S4 Halvø reg Greenland
100 L8 Halvorgate Saskatchewan 50.38N 106.42W
53 D2 Halvrimmen Denmark 57.07N 9.36E
34 G10 Halwān hill Saudi Arabia 28.24N 39.15E
33 C3 Halwān, Jabal mts Saudi Arabia
56 D7 Halwell Devon Eng 50.22N 3.43W
13 K7 Haly, Mt Queensland 26.14S 151.30E
Halys R see Kızıl Irmak
90 G6 Ham Chad 10.01N 15.35E
69 E4 Ham France 49.45N 3.05E
35 G3 Ham Jordan 32.31N 35.48E
55 D4 Ham London Eng 51.26N 0.19W
58 O9 Ham Shetland Scotland 60.08N 2.04W
20 F7 Hama Japan 34.01N 132.48E
34 D3 Hamā Syria 35.09N 36.44E
20 F7 Hamada Japan 34.56N 132.04E
88 J8 Hamada reg Morocco
88 M7 Hamada de la Daoura plat Algeria
88 Q7 Hamada de Tinrhert plat Algeria
88 K7 Hamada du Dra plat Algeria
88 M10 Hamada el Haricha plat Mali
37 H6 Hama Dağ mt Turkey 39.45N 43.56E
85 J5 Hamâda, Gebel mt Egypt 28.35N 27.15E
34 F6 Hamad, Al des Jordan/Saudi Arabia
85 B8 Hamada Mangueni plat Niger
32 C3 Hamadān Iran 34.46N 48.35E
32 C3 Hamadān prov Iran
88 Q6 Hamada, Région de Algeria
88 L10 Hamada Safia plat Mali
88 L9 Hamada Safra tribe Algeria
88 L7 Hamada Tounassine plat Algeria
88 P7 Hamadet el Atchane reg Algeria
35 F3 Hamadya Israel 32.32N 35.31E
20 P9 Hamahika-jima isld Okinawa Japan
Hamaidan see Khawr Hamīdān
35 C10 Hamakhtesh, Hagadol canyon Israel
35 D10 Hamakhtesh Haqatan canyon Israel
20 L7 Hamakita Japan 34.46N 137.44E
114 B7 Hamakua dist Hawaiian Is
36 J6 Hamam Turkey 36.21N 36.35E
Hamam Yozgat Turkeysee Sarıkaya
35 H4 Hamama Jordan 32.19N 36.02E
20 L1 Hamamasu Japan 43.38N 141.22E
20 L7 Hamamatsu Japan 34.42N 137.42E
20 L7 Hamana ko L Japan
77 E4 Hamapega mt Spain 38.04N 5.46W
35 C4 HaMa'pil Israel 32.22N 34.59E
50 B3 Hamar Iceland 65.30N 23.20W
108 M2 Hamar N Dakota 47.50N 98.35W
52 F6 Hamar Norway 60.57N 10.55E
33 G5 Hamar, Al Saudi Arabia 22.23N 46.11E
50 H6 Hamarinn mt Iceland 64.28N 17.50W
35 E9 Hamarmar watercourse Israel
35 D9 Hamarmar, Har hills Israel
33 M7 Hamar Nafūr isld Oman 27.09N 57.52E
51 E3 Hamarøy Norway 68.05N 15.40E
87 J7 Hamarro Hadad Ethiopia 7.30N 42.11E
50 L5 Hamarsfjördhur B Iceland
34 G2 Hamar, Wādī watercourse Syria
33 G5 Hamar,Wādī al watercourse Saudi Arabia
86 M5 Hamar, Wâdi el watercourse Egypt
20 H6 Hamasaka Japan 35.40N 134.28E
85 N7 Hamâta, Gebel mt Egypt 24.11N 35.01E
35 F3 Hamat Gader anc site Jordan 32.41N 35.40E
21 J5 Hama-Tombetsu Japan 45.08N 142.24E
86 K4 Hamâyir, Gebel hill Egypt 30.39N 33.12E
69 N5 Hambach France 49.04N 7.03E
26 T9 Hambantota Sri Lanka 6.07N 81.07E
108 L2 Hamberg N Dakota 47.48N 99.31W
50 T15 Hambergbukta glacier Spitsbergen 77.05N 17.30E
63 J6 Hambergen W Germany 53.19N 8.49E
50 R11 Hambergfjellet Spitsbergen 74.21N 19.09E
101 O9 Hamber Prov.Park Br Col
56 J6 Hambledon Hants Eng 50.56N 1.04W
57 L5 Hambleton N Yorks Eng 53.46N 1.11W
57 L4 Hambleton Hills N Yorks Eng
105 L8 Ham Bluff pt Virgin Is 17.46N 64.56W
110 D8 Hambone California 41.20N 121.41W
48 R11 Hamborgerland isld Greenland 65.28N 53.00W
Hamborn see Duisburg
56 F6 Hambridge Somerset Eng 50.59N 2.53W
56 F4 Hambrook Avon Eng 51.31N 2.31W
63 L7 Hambühren W Germany 52.37N 9.59E
107 E8 Hamburg Arkansas 33.13N 91.50W
110 B8 Hamburg California 41.47N 123.05W
103 K4 Hamburg Connecticut 41.23N 72.20W
108 P9 Hamburg Iowa 40.36N 95.40W
103 E4 Hamburg New Jersey 41.09N 74.35W
104 G4 Hamburg New York 42.44N 78.50W
103 C5 Hamburg Pennsylvania 40.33N 75.59W
95 L9 Hamburg S Africa 33.18S 27.28E
63 M5 Hamburg W Germany 53.33N 10.00E
70 H4 Hambye France 48.56N 1.17W
21 D9 Hamch'ang S Korea 36.50N 127.40E
33 E7 Hamdah Saudi Arabia 19.05N 43.39E
89 B5 Hamdallaha Senegal 13.08N 14.49W
33 D7 Hamdānah Saudi Arabia 19.58N 40.35E
34 D3 Hamdānīya Syria 35.27N 36.51E
103 J4 Hamden Connecticut 41.23N 72.55W
103 D2 Hamden New York 42.43N 75.01W
104 C7 Hamden Ohio 39.10N 82.32W
Hamdh, Wadi see Hamd, Wādī al watercourse
36 C3 Hamdibey Turkey 39.50N 27.15E
Hamdun see Gölcük
33 B4 Hamd,Wādī al watercourse Saudi Arabia
51 K10 Hämeenkyrö Finland 61.39N 23.10E
51 L10 Hämeenlinna Finland 61.00N 24.25E
51 K10 Häme, lääni Finland
88 K10 Hameidmat Mauritania 22.49N 6.39W
23 B10 Ha Mei Wan B Hong Kong
14 A10 Hamelin B W Australia 34.10S 115.00E
14 B10 Hamelin, C W Australia 34.15S 115.01E
14 A7 Hamelin Pool W Australia 26.25S 114.13E
14 A7 Hamelin Pool inlet W Australia
63 K8 Hameln W Germany 52.07N 9.22E
110 N6 Hamer Idaho 43.57N 112.12W
63 O8 Hamersleben E Germany 52.04N 11.06E
14 C5 Hamersley W Australia 22.20S 117.58E
14 B5 Hamersley Ra W Australia
63 P7 Hamerten E Germany 52.36N 11.59E
58 O9 Hametoun Shetland Scotland 60.07N 2.05W
21 D8 Hamhŭng N Korea 39.54N 127.35E
33 H9 Hāmī S Yemen 14.51N 49.56E
24 H4 Hami Xinjiang Uygur Zizhiqu China 42.37N 93.32E
32 C5 Hamīd Iran 31.10N 48.29E
86 E6 Hâmid, Gebel hill Egypt 29.50N 30.36E
Hamidieh see Hamidīya
Hamidiya Israelsee Hamadya
34 C4 Hamidīya Syria 34.43N 35.57E
36 E3 Hamidiye Turkey 39.35N 30.54E
37 E3 Hamidiye Turkey 40.07N 28.12E
30 H7 Hamidnagar Bihar India 25.04N 84.39E
33 N5 Hāmil, Al Oman 22.14N 58.15E
107 J7 Hamilton Alabama 34.09N 88.00W
113 F5 Hamilton Alaska 62.55N 164.00W
96 B2 Hamilton Bermuda 32.18N 64.48W
109 C1 Hamilton Colorado 40.23N 107.36W
105 C5 Hamilton Georgia 32.44N 84.54W
106 C9 Hamilton Illinois 40.23N 91.22W
106 K8 Hamilton Indiana 41.32N 84.56W
109 O4 Hamilton Kansas 37.59N 96.09W
106 H7 Hamilton Michigan 42.41N 86.01W
107 B2 Hamilton Missouri 39.44N 94.01W
110 L3 Hamilton Montana 46.15N 114.10W
108 N1 Hamilton N Dakota 48.49N 97.28W
104 K4 Hamilton New York 42.50N 75.33W
11 K4 Hamilton New Zealand 37.46S 175.18E
104 A7 Hamilton Ohio 39.23N 84.33W
99 L9 Hamilton Ontario 43.15N 79.50W
110 F5 Hamilton Oregon 44.45N 119.19W
13 F6 Hamilton Queensland 22.47S 140.34E
58 H7 Hamilton Strathclyde Scotland 55.47N 4.03W
12 H9 Hamilton Tasmania 42.32S 146.46E
112 J4 Hamilton Texas 31.42N 98.08W
12 F7 Hamilton Victoria 37.45S 142.04E
110 D1 Hamilton Washington 48.32N 122.00W
104 E1 Hamilton dist Baltimore, Md
13 F6 Hamilton R Queensland
12 C2 Hamilton R S Australia
111 B2 Hamilton City California 39.45N 122.01W
108 B6 Hamilton Dome Wyoming 43.47N 108.30W
13 C6 Hamilton Downs N Terr Australia 23.30S 132.20E
97 O7 Hamilton Inlet Labrador, Nfld
107 C7 Hamilton, L Arkansas
111 C4 Hamilton, Mt California 37.20N 121.37W
10 B11 Hamilton, Mt Macquarie I Pacific Oc 54.42S 158.51E
111 J2 Hamilton, Mt Nevada 39.13N 115.33W
Hamilton, R Labrador, Nfld see Churchill R
59 J3 Hamiltons Bawn Armagh N Ireland 54.20N 6.33W
85 G4 Hamin watercourse Libya
51 N11 Hamina Finland 60.33N 27.15E
100 R8 Hamiota Manitoba 50.11N 100.38W
61 M7 Hamipré Belgium 49.50N 5.27E
35 J2 Hamir Syria 32.57N 36.18E
Hamir Yemensee Khamir
29 E2 Hamirpur Himachal Prad India 31.38N 76.36E
30 D7 Hamirpur Uttar Prad India 25.57N 80.08E
30 C7 Hamirpur dist Uttar Prad India
34 J7 Hāmir, Wādī watercourse Arabia/Iraq
Hamitabat see Isparta
53 U17 Hamlagrøvatn L Norway 60.32N 6.07E
104 A5 Hamler Ohio 41.14N 84.02W
106 H8 Hamlet Indiana 41.23N 86.36W
105 H3 Hamlet N Carolina 34.54N 79.44W
108 J9 Hamlet Nebraska 40.25N 101.14W
14 B6 Hamlet, Mt W Australia 23.13S 115.24E
12 E5 Hamley Bridge S Australia 34.21S 138.40E
104 H3 Hamlin New York 43.17N 77.56W
103 D4 Hamlin Pennsylvania 41.24N 75.25W
112 G3 Hamlin Texas 32.54N 100.07W
104 C8 Hamlin W Virginia 38.16N 82.07W
106 H5 Hamlin L Michigan 44.03N 86.28W
25 J8 Ham Luong, Gua river mth Vietnam
61 P8 Hamm Luxembourg 49.37N 6.10E
63 G9 Hamm W Germany 51.40N 7.49E
69 O2 Hamm W Germany 50.46N 7.42E
88 S5 Hamma Tunisia 33.59N 8.05E
88 M6 Hammada du Guir reg Algeria/Morocco
85 A5 Hammādah al Hamrā plat Libya
85 A7 Hammādat Marzūq stony des Libya
35 F3 Hamma, El Israel 32.41N 35.40E
88 S5 Hamma, El Tunisia 33.50N 9.45E
35 H7 Hammam watercourse Jordan
34 M7 Hammâm, Al Iraq 31.08N 44.04E
88 N4 Hammam bou Hadjar Algeria 35.22N 0.58W
86 B4 Hammam, El Egypt 30.51N 29.23E
88 L5 Hammam, El Morocco 33.12N 5.30W
88 T3 Hammamet Tunisia 36.25N 10.40E
88 T3 Hammamet, Golfe de B Tunisia
88 H10 Hammami plat Mauritania
78 C12 Hammam Lif Tunisia 36.46N 10.24E
88 Q4 Hamman es Salahine Algeria 34.53N 5.36E
86 J7 Hammân Far'ûn, Gebel Egypt 29.12N 32.59E
94 K5 Hammanskraal S Africa 25.28S 28.16E
34 O8 Hammār, Al Iraq 30.58N 46.51E
34 O8 Hammār, Hawr Al L Iraq
51 H11 Hammarland Finland 60.13N 19.45E
52 G6 Hammarsbyn Sweden 60.59N 13.15E
51 M3 Hammastunturi mt Finland 68.34N 27.00E
86 L4 Hamma, Wâdi el watercourse Egypt
61 H3 Hamme Brabant Belgium 50.55N 4.17E
61 G2 Hamme Oost Vlaanderen Belgium 51.06N 4.08E
63 J6 Hamme R W Germany
53 D4 Hammel Denmark 56.15N 9.53E
64 H3 Hammelburg W Germany 50.07N 9.53E
53 F4 Hammelev Århus Denmark 56.27N 10.54E
53 C6 Hammelev Sønderjylland Denmark 55.15N 9.24E
63 S6 Hammelspring E Germany 53.04N 13.26E
61 J3 Hamme-Mille Belgium 50.47N 4.43E

52 J3 **Hammerdal** Sweden 63.35N 15.20E
53 P12 **Hammeren** Bornholm Denmark 55.18N 14.47E
51 K1 **Hammerfest** Norway 70.40N 23.44E
53 D4 **Hammershøj** Denmark 56.30N 9.46E
53 P12 **Hammershus** *ruin* Bornholm Denmark 55.17N 14.46E
55 E4 **Hammersmith** London England 51.30N 0.14W
64 C3 **Hammerstein** W Germany 50.28N 7.22E
53 C4 **Hammerum** Denmark 56.08N 9.04E
110 K7 **Hammett** Idaho 42.56N 115.26W
63 E9 **Hamminkeln** W Germany 51.43N 6.36E
109 L6 **Hammon** Oklahoma 35.38N 99.24W
107 H2 **Hammond** Illinois 39.48N 88.37W
106 G8 **Hammond** Indiana 41.37N 87.30W
107 F11 **Hammond** Louisiana 30.31N 90.28W
108 F4 **Hammond** Montana 45.14N 104.53W
104 K2 **Hammond** New York 44.27N 75.43W
110 B3 **Hammond** Oregon 46.11N 123.58W
12 E5 **Hammond** S Australia 32.33S 138.20E
106 B5 **Hammond** Wisconsin 44.59N 92.27W
106 K4 **Hammond B** Michigan
13 F1 **Hammond I** Queensland 10.34S 142.10E
104 H4 **Hammondsport** New York 42.24N 77.15W
98 G8 **Hammondvale** New Brunswick 45.33N 65.34W
12 K8 **Hammondville** *dist* Sydney, N S W
95 L4 **Hammonia** S Africa 28.45S 27.48E
111 C2 **Hammonton** California 39.12N 121.24W
103 E7 **Hammonton** New Jersey 39.38N 74.49W
88 N8 **Hammoudia** Algeria 26.33N 0.07W
87 F8 **Hammur Koke** Ethiopia 5.12N 36.42E
58 Q9 **Hamnavoe** Shetland Scotland 60.25N 1.05W
58 Q9 **Hamnavoe** Shetland Scotland 60.06N 1.20W
58 Q8 **Hamnavoe** Yell, Shetland Scotland 60.30N 1.05W
58 P8 **Hamna Voe** *B* Shetland Scotland 60.30N 1.34W
58 Q9 **Hamna Voe** *B* Yell, Shetland Scotland 60.30N 1.06W
51 L1 **Hamnbukt** Norway 70.06N 25.04E
51 H2 **Hamneidet** Norway 69.55N 20.56E
51 P1 **Hamningberg** Norway 70.32N 30.35E
25 H7 **Ham Ninh** Vietnam 10.11N 104.01E
99 T7 **Ham Nord** Quebec 45.53N 71.37W
37 D6 **Hamo** Turkey 39.31N 38.14E
90 F3 **Hamodji** Niger 16.39N 13.39E
61 N5 **Hamoir** Belgium 50.26N 5.32E
61 L5 **Hamois** Belgium 50.21N 5.09E
51 H4 **Hamojåkk** Sweden 67.20N 20.10E
37 D8 **Hamon** Turkey 37.15N 37.33E
61 N1 **Hamont** Belgium 51.15N 5.33E
37 F6 **Hamorit Dağ** *mt* Turkey 39.12N 41.53E
103 C7 **Hamorton** Pennsylvania 39.52N 75.42W
87 G2 **Hamoyet,Jeb** *mt* Sudan 17.37N 38.01E
103 K2 **Hampden** Massachusetts 42.04N 72.25W
108 M1 **Hampden** N Dakota 48.35N 98.40W
98 Q4 **Hampden** Newfoundland 49.32N 56.51W
11 E12 **Hampden** New Zealand 45.20S 170.50E
103 J2 **Hampden** *co* Massachusetts
104 R2 **Hampden Highlands** Maine 44.44N 68.54W
28 C3 **Hampi** Karnataka India 15.20N 76.25E
69 M6 **Hampont** France 48.51N 6.35E
56 J5 **Hampshire** *co* England
103 J2 **Hampshire** *co* Massachusetts
55 E3 **Hampstead** London Eng 51.33N 0.11W
104 J7 **Hampstead** Maryland 39.38N 76.52W
105 K3 **Hampstead** N Carolina 34.23N 77.43W
98 F8 **Hampstead** New Brunswick 45.38N 66.08W
61 M5 **Hampteau** Belgium 50.16N 5.28E
107 D8 **Hampton** Arkansas 33.33N 92.28W
103 K3 **Hampton** Connecticut 41.47N 72.03W
105 E8 **Hampton** Florida 29.52N 82.08W
105 C4 **Hampton** Georgia 33.23N 84.18W
108 R7 **Hampton** Iowa 42.46N 93.12W
55 C5 **Hampton** London England 51.25N 0.22W
108 N9 **Hampton** Nebraska 40.52N 97.55W
98 G8 **Hampton** New Brunswick 45.30N 65.50W
104 P4 **Hampton** New Hampshire 42.56N 70.51W
103 E5 **Hampton** New Jersey 40.42N 74.57W
110 E6 **Hampton** Oregon 43.41N 120.15W
105 F5 **Hampton** S Carolina 32.52N 81.06W
104 J9 **Hampton** Virginia 37.02N 76.23W
110 P8 **Hampton** Wyoming 41.31N 110.19W
103 J5 **Hampton Bays** Long I, N Y 40.53N 72.32W
55 D5 **Hampton Court** London Eng 51.24N 0.19W
14 B5 **Hampton Harb** W Australia
14 F9 **Hampton Tableland** W Australia
55 D5 **Hampton Wick** London Eng 51.25N 0.19W
35 E5 **Hamra** Jordan 32.12N 35.26E
33 M5 **Hamrā** Oman 23.00N 57.09E
52 J5 **Hamra** Sweden 61.40N 15.00E
33 E9 **Ḩamrā'** Yemen 15.03N 42.56E
85 H8 **Hamra** *watercourse* Egypt
33 M5 **Hamra, Al** Oman 23.07N 57.17E
33 C5 **Ḩamrā', Al** Saudi Arabia 23.58N 38.53E
86 M8 **Ḩamra, Gebel** *hill* Egypt 28.35N 34.30E
86 N6 **Ḩamra, Gebel el** *hill* Egypt 29.40N 34.47E
86 F7 **Ḩamrâi, Gebel** *hill* Egypt 29.25N 31.26E
35 F8 **Ḩamra, Jebel el** *hill* Jordan 31.28N 35.38E
33 H4 **Hamrā Jūdah** *plat* Saudi Arabia
90 M3 **Hamra Koila, Jebel** *mt* Sudan 16.10N 25.10E
52 K6 **Hamrånge** Sweden 60.59N 17.05E
Hamrâte *see* **Hamrat, El**
34 D4 **Hamrat, El** Syria 34.28N 36.54E
87 A3 **Hamrat esh Sheikh** Sudan 14.38N 27.56E
53 S17 **Hamre** Norway 60.33N 5.20E
34 M4 **Hamrīn, Jabal** *mts* Iraq
33 L4 **Hamriyyah** U.A.E. 25.30N 55.33E
84 Y20 **Hamrun** Malta 35.53N 14.30E
88 K7 **Hamsailik, Jbel** *mt* Morocco 29.50N 7.03W
110 P7 **Hams Fork** *R* Wyoming
56 N5 **Ham Street** Kent Eng 51.05N 0.52E
61 H5 **Ham-sur-Heure** Belgium 50.19N 4.23E
61 J5 **Ham-sur-Sambre** Belgium 50.27N 4.40E
25 J7 **Ham Tan** Vietnam 10.39N 107.47E
29 E1 **Hamta Pass** Himachal Prad India 32.15N 77.27E
106 L7 **Hamtramck** Michigan 42.26N 83.02W
106 N1 **Hamtramck** *dist* Detroit, Michigan
15 C5 **Hamuku** Irian Jaya 3.23S 135.09E
86 F3 **Hâmûl, El** Egypt 31.19N 31.09E
33 H9 **Hamūm** *tribe* S Yemen
50 L3 **Hámundarstadhir** Iceland 65.51N 14.47W
31 A5 **Hāmun-e Şāberi** *salt marsh* Afghanistan
31 C6 **Hamun-i-Lora** *salt L* Pakistan
31 B6 **Hamun-i-Mashkel** *flood area* Iran/Pakistan
32 J7 **Hamunt Kūh** *mt* Iran 27.03N 61.15E
37 G6 **Hamur** Turkey 39.36N 43.00E
87 M7 **Hamurre, El** Somalia 7.12N 48.57E
86 G5 **Ḩamza, Gebel el** *hill* Egypt 30.15N 31.38E
44 F9 **Ḩamzīān Pass** Iran 38.45N 44.54E
89 H6 **Han** Ghana 10.46N 2.22W
52 H4 **Hån** Sweden 62.19N 14.05E
114 E6 **Hana** Hawaiian Is 20.45N 156.00W
116 D3 **Hanábana** *R* Cuba
116 D3 **Hanabanilla** Cuba 22.07N 80.05W
53 X14 **Hånådalstind** *mt* Norway 62.20N 7.48E
Ḩanādir Escarpment *see* **Tirāq, J. al**
114 E6 **Hana, dist** Hawaiian Is
15 J1 **Hanahan** Papua New Guinea 5.10S 154.43E
114 C7 **Hanaipoe** Hawaiian Is 19.56N 155.28W
37 G4 **Hanak** Turkey 41.14N 42.51E
20 E10 **Hanaki** Japan 31.48N 131.09E
33 D4 **Ḩanākīyah,Al** Saudi Arabia 24.53N 40.30E
Hanakpınar *see* **Çınar**
33 B4 **Ḩanalc** Saudi Arabia 25.32N 37.00E
114 E3 **Hanalei** Hawaiian Is 22.12N 159.30W
114 E3 **Hanalei** *dist* Hawaiian Is
114 F3 **Hanalei B** Hawaiian Is
20 P2 **Hanamaki** Japan 39.25N 141.04E
114 E6 **Hanamanioa, C** Hawaiian Is 20.34N 156.26W
114 F4 **Hanamaulu** Hawaiian Is 22.00N 159.22W
28 D1 **Hanamkonda** Andhra Prad India 18.04N 79.34E
94 D5 **Hanam Plateau** Namibia
93 G10 **Hanang** *mt* Tanzania 4.27S 35.24E
114 E4 **Hanapepe** Hawaiian Is 21.56N 159.37W
114 E4 **Hanapepe** *R* Hawaiian Is
114 E4 **Hanapepe B** Hawaiian Is
20 N9 **Hanare-iwa** *rocks* Iwo Jima Pacific Oc 24.49N 141.21E
87 A4 **Hanatir** Sudan 13.22N 27.52E
64 F3 **Hanau** W Germany 50.08N 8.56E
114 B5 **Hanauma Bay** Hawaiian Is
122 V15 **Hanavavé** Marquesas Is Pacific Oc 10.27S 138.39W
20 O1 **Hanawa** Japan 40.11N 140.48E
33 F3 **Ḩanbalī, Al** *area* Saudi Arabia
22 G5 **Hanbogd** Mongolia 43.06N 107.35E
99 L5 **Hanbury** Ontario 47.36N 79.40W
107 K7 **Hanceville** Alabama 34.03N 86.48W
101 M10 **Hanceville** Br Col 51.55N 123.02W
22 L7 **Hancheng** Hebei China 39.15N 117.44E
23 E1 **Hancheng** Shaanxi China 35.28N 110.55E
23 E2 **Hancheng** Shaanxi China 32.48N 108.38E
21 C8 **Hanch'ŏn** N Korea 39.14N 125.25E
23 F3 **Hanchuan** Hubei China 30.38N 113.49E
104 R2 **Hancock** Maine 44.32N 68.16W
104 G7 **Hancock** Maryland 39.42N 78.13W
106 F2 **Hancock** Michigan 47.08N 88.34W
108 P4 **Hancock** Minnesota 45.28N 95.50W
103 D3 **Hancock** New York 41.58N 75.17W
106 E5 **Hancock** Wisconsin 44.09N 89.31W
105 F10 **Hancock, L** Florida 27.59N 82.50W
103 D7 **Hancocks Bridge** New Jersey 39.30N 75.27W
20 K7 **Handa** Japan 34.52N 136.57E
87 N5 **Handa** Somalia 10.40N 51.07E
58 F2 **Handa** *isld* Highland Scotland 58.23N 5.11W
22 K8 **Handan** Hebei China 36.37N 114.25E
22 K8 **Handan** Hebei China 36.35N 114.31E
53 B4 **Handbjerg** Denmark 56.28N 8.44E
56 L5 **Handcross** W Sussex Eng 51.03N 0.13W
66 K5 **Handegg** Switzerland 46.37N 8.18E
66 K5 **Handegg Fall** Switzerland 46.37N 8.18E
60 L13 **Handel** Netherlands 51.35N 5.44E
100 J6 **Handel** Saskatchewan 52.04N 108.41W
52 L7 **Handen** Sweden 59.12N 18.09E
92 J4 **Handeni** Tanzania 5.25S 38.04E
53 D3 **Handest** Denmark 56.34N 9.50E
30 F7 **Handia** Uttar Prad India 25.22N 82.12E
65 N6 **Handles Berg** *mt* Austria 47.50N 15.45E
56 G6 **Handley** Dorset Eng 50.58N 2.00W
112 K3 **Handley** Texas 32.44N 97.13W
62 L7 **Handlová** Czechoslovakia 48.45N 18.45E
10 C10 **Handspike Pt** Macquarie I Pacific Oc 54.28S 158.55E
100 P9 **Handsworth** Saskatchewan 49.53N 102.56W
57 L6 **Handsworth** S Yorks Eng 53.23N 1.23W
61 B2 **Handzame** Belgium 51.02N 3.00E
20 A2 **Hane** Tōkyō Japan
20 E3 **Haneda Airport** Japan 35.33N 139.46E
61 M4 **Haneffe** Belgium 50.38N 5.19E
Hanegev *reg see* **Negev** *region*
34 B8 **Haneqarot** *watercourse* Israel
63 K4 **Hanerau** W Germany 54.07N 9.27E
101 K11 **Haney** Br Col 49.13N 122.36W
111 E5 **Hanford** California 36.19N 119.39W
110 F3 **Hanford** Washington 46.35N 119.23W
Hanga *see* **Hanh**
28 B3 **Hangal** Karnataka India 14.49N 75.14E
25 D5 **Hangan** Burma 15.10N 97.53E
21 D9 **Hangang** *R* S Korea
122 T16 **Hanga Piko** Easter I Pacific Oc 27.09S 109.27W
122 U16 **Hanga Roa** Easter I Pacific Oc 27.09S 109.26W
11 M5 **Hangaroa** New Zealand 38.42S 177.38E
11 K5 **Hangatiki** New Zealand 38.15S 175.12E
22 E3 **Hangay** Mongolia 47.56N 99.30E
42 F7 **Hangayn Nuruu** *mts* Mongolia
Hangchow *see* **Hangzhou**
63 T8 **Hangelsberg** E Germany 52.24N 13.56E
52 H9 **Hånger** Sweden 57.06N 13.58E
22 G6 **Hanggin Houqi** Nei Monggol Zizhiqu China 40.52N 107.04E
22 H7 **Hanggin Qi** Nei Monggol Zizhiqu China 39.51N 108.42E
23 C9 **Hang Hau** Hong Kong 22.18N 114.16E
87 M5 **Hanghei** Somalia 10.11N 49.04E
104 C8 **Hanging Rock** Ohio 38.34N 82.45W
95 B10 **Hangklip, Kaap** *C* S Africa 34.23S 18.50E
110 H2 **Hangman Cr** Washington
21 D8 **Hangnyang** N Korea 39.05N 127.50E
51 K12 **Hangö** Finland 59.50N 23.00E
66 O4 **Hangsackgrat** *mt* Switzerland 46.58N 9.19E
24 C4 **Hangtengri Feng** *mt pk* Xinjiang Uygur Zizhiqu China 42.13N 80.16E
22 L7 **Hangu** Hebei China 39.15N 117.44E
31 F4 **Hangu** Pakistan 33.32N 71.04E
23 F6 **Hanguang** Guangdong China 24.15N 113.08E
26 S7 **Hanguranketa** Sri Lanka 7.10N 80.47E
23 J3 **Hangzhou** Zhejiang China 30.18N 120.07E
23 J3 **Hangzhou Wan** *B* Zhejiang China
22 E1 **Hanh** Mongolia 51.29N 100.46E
91 D10 **Hanha** *R* Angola
91 C10 **Hanha** *tribe* Angola
53 C2 **Hanherreder** *reg* Denmark
22 F5 **Hanhongor** Mongolia 43.51N 104.22E
37 E7 **Hani** Turkey 38.26N 40.23E
33 H3 **Ḩanīdh** Saudi Arabia 26.35N 48.40E
63 M8 **Hänigsen** W Germany 52.29N 10.05E
35 E1 **Hanine** *R* Lebanon
86 O4 **Haniqra** *watercourse* Israel
35 D1 **Haniqra, Rosh** *C* Israel 33.05N 35.06E
33 E10 **Ḩanīsh al 'Kabīr,Al** *isld* Yemen 13.45N 42.45E
87 J4 **Hanish Is** Red Sea
35 D1 **Hanita** Israel 33.05N 35.10E
34 N9 **Ḩanīyah, Al** *ridge* Iraq
18 K7 **Hanjalipan** Borneo Indon 2.17S 112.48E
23 C1 **Hanjiaji** Gansu China 35.30N 102.58E
Hanjiang *see* **Yangzhou**
23 H6 **Hanjiang** Fujian China 25.33N 119.08E
23 G7 **Han Jiang** *R* Guangdong China
22 G8 **Hanjiaoshui** Ningxia China 37.05N 105.37E
32 J7 **Hanjirak** Iran 27.56N 61.59E
34 P5 **Hanjis, Kūh-e-** *mts* Iran
60 H13 **Hank** Netherlands 51.44N 4.54E
51 M9 **Hankasalmi** Finland 62.21N 26.30E
60 O10 **Hankate** Netherlands 52.26N 6.26E
88 J10 **Hank, El** *reg* Mauritania
37 E7 **Hankendi** Turkey 38.36N 39.04E
63 N7 **Hankensbüttel** W Germany 52.44N 10.35E
95 H9 **Hankey** S Africa 33.50S 24.53E
103 D3 **Hankins** New York 41.48N 75.10W
108 O3 **Hankinson** N Dakota 46.04N 96.55W
Hanko *see* **Hangö**
23 G3 **Hankou** Hubei China 30.45N 114.30E
111 O3 **Hanksville** Utah 38.21N 110.44W
31 K4 **Hanle** Kashmir 32.46N 79.01E
100 L7 **Hanley** Saskatchewan 51.38N 106.25W
57 J6 **Hanley** Staffs Eng 53.01N 2.10W
56 G3 **Hanley Castle** Hereford & Worcs Eng 52.05N 2.14W
108 P5 **Hanley Falls** Minnesota 44.40N 95.35W
36 J3 **Hanlı** Turkey 39.28N 36.40E
57 H7 **Hanmer** Clwyd Wales 52.57N 2.49W
99 K6 **Hanmer** Ontario 46.40N 80.57W
11 G9 **Hanmer R** New Zealand
11 G9 **Hanmer Springs** New Zealand 42.31S 172.52E
13 G3 **Hann** *R* Queensland
100 F7 **Hanna** Alberta 51.38N 111.56W
110 P9 **Hanna** Utah 40.27N 110.50W
108 D8 **Hanna** Wyoming 41.52N 106.32W
108 M2 **Hannaford** N Dakota 47.19N 98.11W
108 M1 **Hannah** N Dakota 48.59N 98.40W
99 L1 **Hannah B** Ontario
59 K2 **Hannastown** Antrim N Ireland 54.35N 6.02W
50 O10 **Hannberget** Jan Mayen I 70.57N 8.36W
61 L4 **Hannêche** Belgium 50.35N 5.03E
107 E2 **Hannibal** Missouri 39.41N 91.20W
106 D4 **Hannibal** Wisconsin 45.16N 90.48W
53 B4 **Hanning** Denmark 56.01N 8.31E
14 F3 **Hann, Mt** W Australia 15.55S 125.57E
69 K5 **Hannonville-sous-les-Côtes** France 49.03N 5.40E
108 J2 **Hannover** N Dakota 47.09N 101.26W
63 L8 **Hannover** W Germany 52.23N 9.44E
14 F3 **Hann, R** W Australia
13 C6 **Hann Ra** N Terr Australia
61 L4 **Hannut** Belgium 50.40N 5.05E
36 G4 **Hanobası** Turkey 38.35N 33.48E
52 J11 **Hanöbukten** *B* Sweden
25 H2 **Hanoi** Vietnam 21.01N 105.52E
53 X16 **Hånosa** *mt* Norway 61.06N 7.40E
Hânoûté, El *see* **Hānūt, El**
103 K3 **Hanover** Connecticut 41.39N 72.04W
109 O2 **Hanover** Kansas 39.54N 96.53W
103 N2 **Hanover** Massachusetts 42.07N 70.49W
108 R4 **Hanover** Minnesota 45.09N 93.40W
110 Q2 **Hanover** Montana 47.07N 109.34W
104 N3 **Hanover** New Hampshire 43.42N 72.17W
99 J8 **Hanover** Ontario 44.10N 81.03W
104 J7 **Hanover** Pennsylvania 39.47N 76.59W
95 H7 **Hanover** S Africa 31.05S 24.27E
116 G1 **Hanover** *parish* Jamaica, W I
121 J8 **Hanover, I** Chile
95 H6 **Hanover Road** S Africa 30.57S 24.32E
105 L9 **Hanover Sd** New Providence I Bahamas 25.06N 77.17W
15 J1 **Hanpan, C** Papua New Guinea 5.02S 154.35E
82 E6 **Han Pijesak** Yugoslavia 44.04N 18.59E
61 K4 **Hanret** Belgium 50.35N 4.57E
62 K8 **Hanság** *reg* Hungary/Austria
101 N8 **Hansard** Br Col 54.06N 121.55W
61 E2 **Hansbeke** Belgium 51.05N 3.32E
108 L1 **Hansboro** N Dakota 48.59N 99.22W
53 W18 **Hansbu** Norway 60.05N 7.26E
30 L8 **Hansdiha** Bihar India 24.36N 87.05E
99 F3 **Hansen** Ontario 49.17N 84.03W
123 B5 **Hansen mts** Antarctica
23 H3 **Hanshan** Hubei China 31.40N 117.48E
23 F4 **Hanshou** Hunan China 28.53N 111.50E
23 F3 **Han Shui** *R* Hubei China
23 E2 **Han Shui** *R* Shaanxi China
29 E3 **Hansi** Haryana India 29.06N 76.01E
52 H5 **Hansjö** Sweden 61.10N 14.40E
105 L7 **Hans Lollick Is** Virgin Is 18.26N 64.56W
15 M6 **Hans Meyer Ra** New Ireland
103 N2 **Hanson** Massachusetts 42.05N 70.51W
13 C5 **Hanson** *R* N Terr Australia
11 K11 **Hanson B** Chatham Is Pacific Oc
100 P4 **Hanson L** Saskatchewan
12 D4 **Hanson, L** S Australia 31.02S 136.13E
53 D5 **Hansted** Vejle Denmark 55.53N 9.52E
53 B2 **Hanstholm** *harb* Denmark 57.08N 8.36E
29 K7 **Hansua** Orissa India 20.39N 86.52E
22 L4 **Han Sum** Nei Monggol Zizhiqu China 44.36N 119.59E
61 L6 **Han-sur-Lesse** Belgium 50.07N 5.11E
69 L6 **Han-sur-Nied** France 49.00N 6.26E
60 C3 **Hansweert** Netherlands 51.27N 4.00E
87 M5 **Hantara,Jeb** *mt* Somalia 11.20N 49.40E
22 F2 **Hantay** Mongolia 49.39N 102.50E
61 G5 **Hantes-Wihéries** Belgium 50.18N 4.10E
30 K7 **Hanti** Bihar India 25.55N 86.15E
Hanting *see* **Wei Xian**
98 H8 **Hantsport** Nova Scotia 45.04N 64.12W
18 A7 **Hantu, Tanjong** *C* Pen Malaysia 4.18N 100.33E
69 N7 **Hantz, Col du** *pass* France 48.24N 7.05E
22 L4 **Han Ul** Nei Monggol Zizhiqu China 45.10N 119.49E
29 D3 **Hanumangarh** Rajasthan India 29.33N 74.21E
30 K6 **Hanumannagar** Nepal 26.30N 86.53E
33 L8 **Hanun** Oman 17.25N 54.11E
34 E3 **Hānūt, El** Syria 35.49N 37.18E
22 E2 **Hanuy Gol** *R* Mongolia
70 B5 **Hanvec** France 48.20N 4.10W
23 C3 **Hanwang** Sichuan China 31.17N 104.30E
55 C3 **Hanwell** London Eng 51.30N 0.21W
26 R8 **Hanwella** Sri Lanka 6.55N 80.06E
55 C4 **Hanworth** London Eng 51.26N 0.23W
22 D7 **Hanxia** Gansu China 39.50N 97.05E
117 B3 **Hany** *R* Fr Guiana
23 G3 **Hanyang** Hubei China 30.37N 114.02E
23 E2 **Hanyin** Shaanxi China 32.56N 108.40E
23 C4 **Hanyuan** Sichuan China 29.20N 102.45E
20 A4 **Hanzaike** Kanagawa Japan
23 D2 **Hanzhong** Shaanxi China 33.09N 107.03E
23 H1 **Hanzhuang** Shandong China 34.39N 117.26E
61 J5 **Hanzinelle** Belgium 50.18N 4.33E
61 J5 **Hanzinne** Belgium 50.18N 4.32E
122 E15 **Hao** *atoll* Tuamotu Is Pacific Oc 18.04S 141.00W
89 H4 **Haogoundou,L** Mali 15.45N 3.15W
21 E4 **Haolianghe** Heilongjiang China 46.42N 129.35E
35 F3 **HaOn** Israel 32.44N 35.38E
90 K3 **Haouach** *watercourse* Chad
88 Q6 **Haoud el Hamra** Algeria 31.59N 5.42E
88 Q6 **Haouds, Région d'** Algeria
89 C3 **Haoussinia, El** Mauritania 17.46N 12.19W
77 F9 **Haouz, Jebel** *mts* Morocco
51 L6 **Haparanda** Sweden 65.50N 24.10E
60 J14 **Hapert** Netherlands 51.22N 5.15E
19 F2 **Hapo** Moluccas Indon 2.33N 128.24E
28 J2 **Hāpoli** Assam India 27.36N 93.42E
56 P2 **Happisburgh** Norfolk Eng 52.50N 1.32E
112 F1 **Happy** Texas 34.44N 101.52W
110 B8 **Happy Camp** California 41.48N 123.24W
13 E5 **Happy Cr** N Terr Australia
28 H3 **Happy Valley** Meghalaya India 25.33N 91.55E
60 M13 **Haps** Netherlands 51.42N 5.52E
21 D7 **Hapsu** N Korea 41.12N 128.48E
11 H9 **Hapuku** New Zealand 42.19S 173.44E
30 A4 **Hapur** Uttar Prad India 28.43N 77.47E
26 S8 **Haputale** Sri Lanka 6.46N 80.58E
114 B8 **Ha Puu a Pele** *pk* Hawaiian Is 19.03N 155.52W
35 A1 **Ha-Qirya** *sub* Jerusalem
34 B9 **Ḩaql** Saudi Arabia 29.14N 34.56E
33 J5 **Ḩaqshah** Saudi Arabia 22.48N 50.11E
33 E8 **Ḩaqū, Al** Saudi Arabia 17.32N 42.41E
33 E7 **Ḩaqw** Saudi Arabia 18.06N 42.15E
15 B6 **Har** Moluccas Indon 5.21S 133.10E
22 G2 **Hara** Mongolia 49.00N 106.00E
22 G2 **Haraa Gol** *R* Mongolia
87 J4 **Hara Alol** Djibouti 12.01N 42.16E
87 H7 **Hara Bonel** Ethiopia 6.19N 41.02E
Hara Buhain Gol *R see* **Haruuhin Gol**
87 H7 **Hara Buri** Ethiopia 6.31N 41.20E
93 N3 **Hara Cadera** Somalia 2.10N 41.03E
33 E8 **Ḩarad** Yemen 16.27N 43.04E
33 H4 **Ḩarad** *well* Saudi Arabia 24.22N 49.08E
33 H4 **Ḩaradh** Saudi Arabia 24.12N 49.07E
34 C9 **Harad, Jebel el** *mt* Jordan 29.39N 35.48E
51 J5 **Harads** Sweden 66.06N 21.00E
86 P6 **Harad, Wādī** *watercourse* Jordan
87 H7 **Hara Fanna** Ethiopia 6.03N 41.10E
107 H12 **Harahan** *dist* New Orleans, Louisiana
87 H8 **Hara Harba** Ethiopia 5.50N 41.30E
122 D15 **Haraiki** *atoll* Tuamotu Is Pacific Oc 17.28S 143.30W
Haraim *see* **Haraym**
30 L6 **Haraincha** Nepal 26.37N 87.22E
30 F6 **Haraiya** Uttar Prad India 26.48N 82.28E
33 E8 **Ḩaraja** Saudi Arabia 17.57N 43.22E
93 M6 **Ḩara Jilo** Kenya 0.38S 40.56E
35 J3 **Harak, El** Syria 32.45N 36.18E
53 T19 **Haraldseidvågen** Norway 59.32N 5.35E
53 S20 **Haraldshaugen** Norway 59.26N 5.15E
20 O4 **Haramachi** Japan 37.38N 140.59E
20 B4 **Hara-Machida** Tōkyō Japan
53 U13 **Haramsøy** *isld* Norway 62.39N 6.12E
31 H3 **Haramukh** *mt* Kashmir 34.25N 74.53E
Hara Nariin Uula *see* **Lang Shan**
77 K6 **Harana, Sierra** *mts* Spain
53 Y18 **Hårånatten** Norway 60.22N 8.09E
25 K8 **Harangajao** Assam India 25.09N 92.54E
Hara Nor *L see* **Har Hu** *lake*
31 G5 **Harappa Road** Pakistan 30.35N 72.56E
Harar *see* **Hārer**
Harar *prov see* **Hārergē**
87 L8 **Harardera** Somalia 4.40N 47.50E
86 N4 **Har Ardon** *hill* Israel 30.39N 34.57E
86 N5 **Har 'Arif** *hill* Israel 30.25N 34.44E
86 N4 **Har Arikha** *hill* Israel 30.39N 34.47E
85 F5 **Harash** Libya 28.30N 20.55E
67 P13 **Harata, Col de** *pass* Corsica 41.42N 9.12E
87 G2 **Harat I** Ethiopia 16.05N 39.26E
87 F6 **Haratu** Ethiopia 9.23N 37.06E
37 H7 **Haravil Dağ** *mt* Turkey 38.14N 44.24E
33 K7 **Haraym** Saudi Arabia 19.40N 52.46E
22 H4 **Har-Ayrag** Mongolia 45.42N 109.14E
87 C3 **Haraza, Jeb** *mt* Sudan 15.01N 30.25E
90 J5 **Haraz-Djombo** Chad 13.50N 19.31E
90 K7 **Harazé** Chad 9.58N 20.47E
33 C4 **Harb** *tribe* Saudi Arabia
53 X15 **Harbardsbreen** *glacier* Norway 61.42N 7.41E
64 J8 **Harbatshofen** W Germany 47.36N 10.01E
89 D8 **Harbel** Liberia 6.19N 10.20W
21 D5 **Harbin** Heilongjiang China 45.45N 126.41E
37 J2 **Harbiye** *dist* İstanbul Turkey 41.03N 28.59E
33 A3 **Harb, Jabal** *mt* Saudi Arabia 27.58N 35.41E
52 K6 **Harbo** Sweden 60.06N 17.15E
31 D6 **Harboi Hills** Pakistan
53 J7 **Hårbølle** Denmark 54.54N 12.12E
69 D4 **Harbonnières** France 49.51N 2.40E
53 A3 **Harboør** Denmark 56.38N 8.12E
53 A3 **Harboør Tange** *pen* Denmark 56.43N 8.12E
110 A7 **Harbor** Oregon 42.04N 124.14W
106 M6 **Harbor Beach** Michigan 43.51N 82.40W
12 M6 **Harbord** New S Wales 33.47S 151.18E
106 K4 **Harbor Springs** Michigan 45.25N 84.59W
57 J2 **Harbottle** Northumb Eng 55.20N 2.07W
98 R6 **Harbour Breton** Newfoundland 47.29N 55.50W
98 S6 **Harbour Buffett** Newfoundland 47.33N 54.06W
105 K12 **Harbour Cay, Great** *isld* Bahamas 25.45N 77.52W
105 K12 **Harbour Cay, Little** *isld* Bahamas 25.33N 77.42W
11 N12 **Harbour Cone** *hill* New Zealand 45.52S 170.38E
98 T6 **Harbour Grace** Newfoundland 47.42N 53.17W
105 L12 **Harbour I** Bahamas 25.31N 76.36W
98 S6 **Harbour Mille** Newfoundland 47.37N 54.55W
121 E10 **Harbours, B of** Falkland Is
98 H8 **Harbourville** Nova Scotia 45.08N 64.51W
63 L6 **Harburg** Hamburg W Germany 53.28N 9.57E
64 K6 **Harburg** W Germany 48.47N 10.41E
53 E6 **Hårby** Denmark 55.13N 10.07E
29 G6 **Harchoka** Madhya Prad India 23.48N 81.48E
98 G7 **Harcourt** New Brunswick 46.29N 65.18W
111 L8 **Harcuvar Mts** Arizona
66 P2 **Hard** Austria 47.29N 9.42E
29 E6 **Harda** Madhya Prad India 22.22N 77.08E
33 H8 **Ḩardah, Wādī** *watercourse* S Yemen
53 U18 **Hardanger** *dist* Norway
53 T19 **Hardangerfjorden** *inlet* Norway
52 C6 **Hardanger-Jukulen** *glacier* Norway
53 W18 **Hardangervidda** *plat* Norway
94 D5 **Hardap Dam** Namibia 24.28S 17.48E
107 F9 **Hardee** Mississippi 32.34N 90.52W
105 F5 **Hardeeville** S Carolina 32.18N 81.05W
60 M7 **Hardegarijp** Netherlands 53.13N 5.57E
65 N4 **Hardegg** Austria 48.52N 15.53E
63 L9 **Hardegsen** W Germany 51.38N 9.49E
69 B2 **Hardelot-Plage** France 50.38N 1.35E
Harden *see* **Murrumburrah**
60 P9 **Hardenberg** Netherlands 52.34N 6.38E
18 L3 **Harden, Bukit** *mt* Borneo Indonesia 4.08N 115.48E
66 H5 **Harder** *mt* Switzerland 46.43N 7.52E
60 L10 **Harderwijk** Netherlands 52.21N 5.37E
109 J5 **Hardesty** Oklahoma 36.37N 101.13W
60 M10 **Harde, t'** Netherlands 52.25N 5.53E
14 B6 **Hardey, R** W Australia
64 G4 **Hardheim** W Germany 49.36N 9.28E
Hardi *see* **Narkatiaganj**
107 F2 **Hardin** Illinois 39.10N 90.38W
107 C2 **Hardin** Missouri 39.16N 93.50W
108 C4 **Hardin** Montana 45.44N 107.35W
108 Q3 **Harding** Minnesota 46.08N 94.02W
95 N6 **Harding** S Africa 30.35S 29.53E
101 P1 **Harding** *R* N W Terr
31 H9 **Hardinge Bridge** Bangladesh 24.02N 89.01E
113 M6 **Harding Icefield** Alaska
105 B5 **Harding L** Georgia
100 T2 **Harding L** Manitoba
14 B5 **Harding R** W Australia
107 K4 **Hardinsburg** Kentucky 37.46N 86.29W
60 H12 **Hardinxveld-Giessendam** Netherlands 51.50N 4.51E
100 F6 **Hardisty** Alberta 52.42N 111.19W
101 P3 **Hardisty L** N W Terr
69 C4 **Hardivillers** France 49.37N 2.14E
110 F4 **Hardman** Oregon 45.10N 119.40W
14 E4 **Hardman, Mt** W Australia 18.18S 124.37E
35 D8 **Hardof** *watercourse* Israel/Jordan
30 D5 **Hardoi** Uttar Prad India 27.23N 80.06E
30 C5 **Hardoi** *div* Uttar Prad India
57 J4 **Hardraw** N Yorks Eng 54.19N 2.12W
99 D3 **Hardrock Mines** Ontario 49.41N 86.59W
30 B5 **Harduaganj** Uttar Prad India 27.56N 78.09E
30 B3 **Hardwar** Uttar Prad India 29.58N 78.09E
56 K4 **Hardwick** Bucks Eng 51.52N 0.50W
103 K2 **Hardwick** Massachusetts 42.21N 72.12W
108 O6 **Hardwick** Minnesota 43.48N 96.10W
104 N2 **Hardwick** Vermont 44.30N 72.23W
56 G4 **Hardwicke** Glos Eng 51.49N 2.18W
12 D5 **Hardwicke B** S Australia
88 O4 **Hardy** Algeria 35.30N 1.47E
107 E5 **Hardy** Arkansas 36.19N 91.29W
110 O2 **Hardy** Montana 47.11N 111.49W
100 N9 **Hardy** Saskatchewan 49.31N 104.49W
11 M4 **Hardy, Mt** New Zealand 37.49S 177.48E
121 L10 **Hardy, Pen** Chile
106 J6 **Hardy Res** Michigan
98 R2 **Hare B** Newfoundland
98 S5 **Hare Bay** Newfoundland 48.50N 54.01W
55 B2 **Harefield** London Eng 51.36N 0.28W
53 U14 **Hareid** Norway 62.22N 6.02E
86 M4 **Hareidin, Wâdi** *watercourse* Egypt
53 T14 **Hareidlandet** *isld* Norway 62.55N 5.55E
35 C6 **Har'el** Israel 31.49N 34.57E
61 D3 **Harelbeke** Belgium 50.51N 3.19E
61 M3 **Haren** Belgium 50.47N 5.24E
61 S9 **Haren** Bruxelles Belgium
60 P7 **Haren** Groningen Netherlands 53.10N 6.36E
60 L12 **Haren** Noord-Brabant Netherlands 51.48N 5.36E
63 F7 **Haren** W Germany 52.48N 7.15E
60 P7 **Harendermolen** Netherlands 53.08N 6.38E
48 S7 **Hareøen** *isld* Greenland 70.25N 54.50W
87 J6 **Hārer** Ethiopia 9.20N 42.10E
87 J7 **Hārergē** *prov* Ethiopia
88 O8 **Haret** *watercourse* Algeria
57 K5 **Harewood** W Yorks Eng 53.54N 1.30W
56 F4 **Harewood End** Hereford & Worcs Eng 51.57N 2.41W
Hareyek *see* **Hureiyik, El**
Harfa *see* **Hurfah**
Harfaz *see* **Barınç**
70 L2 **Harfleur** France 49.31N 0.12E
103 B2 **Harford** New York 42.25N 76.15W
103 C3 **Harford** Pennsylvania 41.46N 75.42W
103 B7 **Harford** *co* Maryland
103 B2 **Harford Mills** New York 42.24N 76.13W
52 L6 **Harg** Sweden 60.13N 18.25E
90 K9 **Harga** Cent Afr Rep 5.16N 21.50E
30 D5 **Hargam** Uttar Prad India 27.45N 80.44E
22 L2 **Hargant** Nei Monggol Zizhiqu China 49.10N 118.29E
69 M5 **Hargarten-aux-Mines** France 49.13N 6.36E
87 K6 **Hargeisa** Somalia 9.31N 44.02E
87 J5 **Hargeisa** *prov* Somalia
82 J4 **Harghita** *div* Romania
82 K4 **Harghitei, Munţii** *mts* Romania
69 E4 **Hargicourt** France 49.58N 3.10E
112 J9 **Hargill** Texas 26.27N 98.01W
61 M6 **Hargimont** Belgium 50.11N 5.18E
69 H3 **Hargnies** France 50.01N 4.48E
100 Q9 **Hargrave** Manitoba 49.55N 101.05W
100 S4 **Hargrave L** Manitoba
15 L6 **Hargy, L** New Britain 5.22S 151.09E
37 F6 **Harhal Dağ** *mt* Turkey 39.34N 41.08E
86 N4 **Har Haluqim** *hill* Israel 30.55N 34.50E
86 N4 **Har Ḩamran** *hill* Israel 30.41N 34.34E
86 N5 **Har Ḩarif** *hill* Israel 30.29N 34.33E
22 G7 **Harhatan** Nei Monggol Zizhiqu China 38.29N 107.13E
86 N4 **Har Hemet** *hill* Israel 30.36N 34.42E
22 D7 **Har Hu** *L* Qinghai China
37 G8 **Harhur** Turkey 37.51N 42.21E
20 M4 **Hari** Japan 37.03N 138.20E
18 E6 **Hari** *R* Sumatra Indon
96 V7 **Haria** Lanzarote Canary Is 29.09N 13.30W
Hariana *state see* **Haryana**
89 L3 **Hariat** Mali 16.11N 2.30E
33 F9 **Harib** Yemen 15.01N 45.30E
89 H3 **Haribonga,L** Mali 16.10N 2.20W
Harid, Wadi *see* **Kharid, Wādī al** *watercourse*
86 J10 **Ḩariet Marrîma** *hill* Egypt 27.43N 32.40E
34 B8 **Harif, Har** *mt* Egypt/Israel 30.30N 34.33E
28 B3 **Harihar** Karnataka India 14.33N 75.44E
30 H8 **Harihargan** Bihar India 24.33N 84.17E
11 E10 **Harihari** New Zealand 43.11S 170.32E
28 B4 **Hariharpur** Karnataka India 13.31N 75.14E
29 B6 **Harij** Gujarat India 23.45N 71.56E
29 D2 **Harike Barrage** Punjab India 31.09N 75.00E
34 D2 **Harim** Syria 36.13N 36.30E
35 G3 **Harima** Jordan 32.37N 35.52E
20 H7 **Harima-nada** *sea* Japan
33 M4 **Harīm, Jabal al** *mt* Oman
55 F3 **Haringey** *bor* London Eng
31 H10 **Haringhat R** Bangladesh
60 E12 **Haringvliet** *estuary* Netherlands
60 L7 **Harinxma, V, Kanaal** *canal* Netherlands
28 C6 **Haripad** Kerala India 9.17N 76.26E
30 M7 **Haripur** Bangladesh 25.50N 88.08E
31 G4 **Haripur** Pakistan 34.00N 73.01E
29 D5 **Haripur** Rajasthan India 26.00N 74.04E
87 C5 **Hariqa,El** Sudan 11.49N 31.41E
33 G5 **Ḩariq,Al** Saudi Arabia 23.34N 46.35E
34 M2 **Ḩarir** Iraq 36.34N 44.22E
35 H2 **Harir** *watercourse* Syria
32 J3 **Hari Rūd** *R* Afghanistan
35 D5 **Haris** Jordan 32.07N 35.09E
35 E1 **Hârîs** Lebanon 33.10N 35.23E
94 D4 **Haris** Namibia 22.48S 16.52E
107 F6 **Harisburg** Arkansas 35.33N 90.44W
34 P8 **Hārithah, Al** Iraq 30.43N 47.44E
33 E7 **Ḩarjab,Wādī** *watercourse* Saudi Arabia
52 H5 **Härjån** *R* Sweden
51 J10 **Harjavalta** Finland 61.19N 22.10E
86 N5 **Har Karkom** *mt* Israel 30.16N 34.43E
105 L3 **Harkers I** N Carolina 34.42N 76.34W
86 O3 **Har Kidod** Israel 31.15N 35.12E
103 B7 **Harkins** Maryland 39.43N 76.27W
30 J6 **Harlakhi** Bihar India 26.38N 85.59E
108 P8 **Harlan** Iowa 41.39N 95.20W
109 M2 **Harlan** Kansas 39.37N 98.46W
104 B10 **Harlan** Kentucky 36.50N 83.19W
108 L9 **Harlan County Res** Nebraska
65 N5 **Harland** Austria 48.10N 15.39E
61 O7 **Harlange** Luxembourg 49.55N 5.47E
63 G5 **Harle** W Germany 53.43N 7.49E
56 C2 **Harlech** Gwynedd Wales 52.52N 4.07W
105 E4 **Harlem** Georgia 33.26N 82.20W
110 R1 **Harlem** Montana 48.33N 108.47W
103 K7 **Harlem** New York 40.49N 73.57W
103 G2 **Harlemville** New York 42.17N 73.35W
63 G5 **Harlesiel** W Germany 53.38N 7.45E
56 O3 **Harleston** Norfolk Eng 52.24N 1.18E
53 E4 **Harlev** Denmark 56.08N 10.00E
53 J6 **Hårlev** Roskilde Denmark 55.22N 12.14E
103 D6 **Harleysville** Pennsylvania 40.17N 75.24W
105 G4 **Harleyville** S Carolina 33.14N 80.26W
60 K7 **Harlingen** Netherlands 53.10N 5.25E
112 K9 **Harlingen** Texas 26.12N 97.43W
63 G5 **Harlinger Land** *reg* W Germany
63 M9 **Harlingerode** W Germany 51.54N 10.25E
55 B4 **Harlington** London Eng 51.29N 0.25W
52 H11 **Harlösa** Sweden 55.44N 13.30E
56 M4 **Harlow** Essex Eng 51.47N 0.08E
108 L1 **Harlow** N Dakota 48.11N 99.30W
110 Q3 **Harlowton** Montana 46.26N 109.50W
86 N5 **Har Loz** *hill* Israel 30.28N 34.35E
64 P2 **Harlsbrucke** E Germany 50.57N 13.21E
32 E6 **Harm** Iran 28.13N 53.43E
28 G1 **Harm** Xizang Zizhiqu 29.05N 88.36E
33 H4 **Harmaliyah** *oil field* Saudi Arabia 24.34N 49.38E
104 F8 **Harman** W Virginia 38.55N 79.32W
12 B6 **Harman** *dist* Canberra Australia
36 D3 **Harmancık** Turkey 39.42N 29.10E
52 K5 **Harmånger** Sweden 61.55N 17.20E
103 A8 **Harmans** Maryland 39.10N 76.41W
60 H11 **Harmelen** Netherlands 52.06N 4.58E
56 F2 **Harmerhill** Shropshire Eng 52.48N 2.45W
103 D8 **Harmersville** New Jersey 39.30N 75.25W
61 G5 **Harmignies** Belgium 50.24N 4.01E
87 H2 **Harmil Is** Ethiopia 16.30N 40.10E
109 L5 **Harmon** Oklahoma 36.09N 99.34W
55 B4 **Harmondsworth** London Eng 51.29N 0.28W
100 A2 **Harmon R** Alberta
104 Q2 **Harmony** Maine 44.58N 69.34W
106 B6 **Harmony** Minnesota 43.33N 92.00W
103 D5 **Harmony** New Jersey 40.44N 75.09W
103 L3 **Harmony** Rhode I 41.54N 71.36W
28 C4 **Harnahalli** Karnataka India 13.15N 76.13E
28 A2 **Harnai** Maharashtra India 17.45N 73.07E
31 E5 **Harnai** Pakistan 30.05N 68.00E
31 F4 **Harnauli** Pakistan 32.16N 71.33E
53 E6 **Harndrup** Denmark 55.28N 10.02E
110 G6 **Harney** Oregon 43.38N 118.47W
110 E6 **Harney Basin** Oregon
105 F9 **Harney, L** Florida 28.45N 81.02W
110 F6 **Harney L.(dry)** Oregon 43.15N 119.10W
108 G6 **Harney Pk** S Dakota 43.50N 103.33W
61 N8 **Harnoncourt** Belgium 49.32N 5.30E
52 K4 **Härnösand** Sweden 62.37N 17.55E
22 K2 **Har Nuden** Nei Monggol Zizhiqu China 48.55N 116.51E
21 B5 **Har Nur** Nei Monggol Zizhiqu China 45.37N 120.05E
22 C2 **Har Nuur** *L* Dzavhan Mongolia
22 C2 **Har Nuur** *L* Hovd Mongolia
75 E2 **Haro** Spain 42.34N 2.52W
35 C10 **Haro'A** *watercourse* Israel
35 E3 **Harod** *R* Israel
55 K2 **Harold Hill** London Eng 51.36N 0.14E
58 R8 **Haroldswick** Shetland Scotland 60.47N 0.50W
69 L7 **Haroué** France 48.28N 6.10E
52 C4 **Harøya** *isld* Norway 62.55N 6.29E
28 B3 **Harpanahalli** Karnataka India 14.48N 75.56E
Harpelunde Station *see* **Sandby**
56 L4 **Harpenden** Herts Eng 51.49N 0.22W
109 M4 **Harper** Kansas 37.16N 98.02W
89 F9 **Harper** Liberia 4.25N 7.43W
110 H6 **Harper** Oregon 43.53N 117.37W
112 H5 **Harper** Texas 30.18N 99.18W
113 M4 **Harper Bend** Alaska 65.00N 151.45W
101 Q6 **Harper Cr** Alberta
111 G6 **Harper L** California 35.02N 117.15W
113 Q4 **Harper Mt** Alaska 64.14N 143.55W
101 C3 **Harper, Mt** Yukon Terr 64.48N 140.04W
11 F9 **Harper Pass** New Zealand 42.43S 171.52E
104 H7 **Harpers Ferry** W Virginia 39.19N 77.46W
103 E2 **Harpersfield** New York 42.26N 74.42W
13 C5 **Harper Springs** N Terr Australia 22.10S 134.05E
107 J5 **Harpeth** *R* Tennessee
56 N2 **Harpley** Norfolk Eng 52.49N 0.39E
52 G10 **Harplinge** Sweden 56.45N 12.45E
58 D4 **Harport L** Skye, Highland Scotland 57.18N 6.22W
63 J7 **Harpstedt** W Germany 52.55N 8.35E
110 K4 **Harpster** Idaho 45.59N 115.58W
100 M9 **Harptree** Saskatchewan 49.19N 105.26W
103 C2 **Harpursville** New York 42.11N 75.37W
37 E7 **Harput** Turkey 38.44N 39.15E
86 M4 **Har Qeren** *hill* Israel 31.00N 34.29E
86 O5 **Har Qetura** *hill* Israel 30.03N 35.03E
22 L6 **Harqin Qi** Nei Monggol Zizhiqu China 42.00N 118.36E
22 L6 **Harqin Zuoyi Monggolzu Zizhixian** Liaoning China 41.06N 119.46E
111 L8 **Harquahala Mts** Arizona
89 C4 **Harr** Mauritania 15.21N 12.28W
74 K8 **Harrach** *R* Algeria
88 P3 **Harrach, El** Algeria 36.45N 3.07E
85 K5 **Harra, El** Egypt 28.22N 29.02E
35 H1 **Hārra, El** Syria 33.03N 36.00E
85 O3 **Harra, El** *reg* Jordan
109 N6 **Harrah** Oklahoma 35.30N 97.11W
33 C1 **Harrah, Al** *reg* Saudi Arabia
29 F6 **Harrai** Madhya Prad India 22.38N 79.19E
86 N4 **Har Ramon** *hill* Israel 30.30N 34.38E
52 G2 **Harran** Norway 64.34N 12.29E
35 J2 **Harran** Syria 32.53N 36.22E
31 F6 **Harrand** Pakistan 29.31N 70.10E
64 K3 **Harras** E Germany 50.24N 10.52E
33 D8 **Ḩarrāt ad Dahīn** *lava flow* Saudi Arabia
33 E6 **Ḩarrāt al Buqūm** *lava flow* Saudi Arabia
33 B3 **Ḩarrat ar Rahāh** *lava flow* Saudi Arabia
33 E8 **Ḩarrāt as Sarat** *lava flow* Saudi Arabia/Yemen
33 D7 **Ḩarrāt Habhab ash Shaykh** *lava flow* Saudi Arabia
33 D6 **Ḩarrāt Ḩadan** *lava flow* Saudi Arabia
33 D3 **Ḩarrāt Ḩutaym** *lava flow* Saudi Arabia
33 C4 **Ḩarrat Khaybar** *lava flow* Saudi Arabia
33 D5 **Ḩarrāt Kishb** *lava flow* Saudi Arabia
33 D4 **Ḩarrāt Kuramā** *lava flow* Saudi Arabia
33 B4 **Ḩarrat Lunayyir** *lava flow* Saudi Arabia
33 E6 **Ḩarrāt Nawāşīf** *lava flow* Saudi Arabia
33 D5 **Ḩarrat Rahaţ** *lava flow* Saudi Arabia
58 S11 **Harray, L of** Orkney Scotland 59.03N 3.15W
61 N5 **Harre** Belgium 50.22N 5.40E
53 B3 **Harre** Denmark 56.43N 8.55E
30 F5 **Harrebarre** Nepal 27.50N 82.59E
107 D8 **Harrell** Arkansas 33.30N 92.22W
60 P12 **Harreveld** Netherlands 51.58N 6.31E
69 K7 **Harréville-les-Chanteurs** France 48.16N 5.38E
99 L2 **Harricanaw R** Ontario/Quebec
53 E4 **Harridslev** Denmark 56.30N 10.08E
87 J9 **Harriento** Somalia 2.32N 42.20E
56 N5 **Harrietsham** Kent Eng 51.15N 0.41E
106 J5 **Harrietta** Michigan 44.19N 85.42W
30 J5 **Harriharpur Garhi** Nepal 27.19N 85.30E
103 F4 **Harriman** New York 41.18N 74.09W
107 M6 **Harriman** Tennessee 35.57N 84.32W
103 C9 **Harrington** Delaware 38.55N 75.35W
104 S2 **Harrington** Maine 44.37N 67.48W
110 G2 **Harrington** Washington 47.28N 118.15W
98 N3 **Harrington Harbour** Quebec 50.31N 59.30W
96 C1 **Harrington Sd** Bermuda
100 P2 **Harriott L** Saskatchewan
110 B9 **Harris** California 40.05N 123.40W
107 C1 **Harris** Missouri 40.18N 93.22W
100 K7 **Harris** Saskatchewan 51.46N 107.34W
58 C3 **Harris** *div* W Isles Scotland
107 H4 **Harrisburg** Illinois 37.40N 88.10W
108 G8 **Harrisburg** Nebraska 41.33N 103.46W
104 B7 **Harrisburg** Ohio 39.50N 83.11W
110 B5 **Harrisburg** Oregon 44.16N 123.10W
103 A6 **Harrisburg** Pennsylvania 40.18N 76.49W
95 K3 **Harrisburg** S Africa 27.08S 26.25E
108 O6 **Harrisburg** S Dakota 43.27N 96.40W
58 C3 **Harris, Forest of** Harris, W Isles Scotland
100 H2 **Harris Hill** Ontario 48.55N 94.34W
105 F9 **Harris, L** Florida 28.47N 81.49W
12 D4 **Harris, L** S Australia
53 C7 **Harrislee** W Germany 54.49N 9.25E
95 N4 **Harrismith** S Africa 28.16S 29.08E
14 C10 **Harrismith** W Australia 32.55S 117.50E
13 A6 **Harris, Mt** N Terr Australia 24.50S 129.23E
11 C11 **Harris Mts** New Zealand
107 C5 **Harrison** Arkansas 36.13N 93.07W
105 E5 **Harrison** Georgia 32.50N 82.45W
110 J2 **Harrison** Idaho 47.27N 116.46W
106 K5 **Harrison** Michigan 44.02N 84.46W
110 O4 **Harrison** Montana 45.43N 111.48W
108 G7 **Harrison** Nebraska 42.42N 103.53W
103 H7 **Harrison** New Jersey 40.45N 74.09W
103 G5 **Harrison** New York 40.58N 73.42W
108 M6 **Harrison** S Dakota 43.28N 98.30W
113 M1 **Harrison B** Alaska
107 E10 **Harrisonburg** Louisiana 31.48N 91.50W
104 G8 **Harrisonburg** Virginia 38.27N 78.54W
97 O7 **Harrison, C** Labrador, Nfld 54.55N 58.00W
101 N11 **Harrison L** Br Col
26 S14 **Harrison, Mt** Mahé I Seychelles, Ind Oc 4.42S 55.27E
107 B3 **Harrisonville** Missouri 38.40N 94.21W
103 D7 **Harrisonville** New Jersey 39.42N 75.17W
Harris Ridge *see* **Lomonosov Ridge**
58 B3 **Harris, Sd of** W Isles Scotland
99 K9 **Harriston** Ontario 43.54N 80.52W
106 L5 **Harrisville** Michigan 44.41N 83.19W
104 K2 **Harrisville** New York 44.09N 75.20W
103 L3 **Harrisville** Rhode I 41.58N 71.41W
104 D7 **Harrisville** W Virginia 39.13N 81.04W
107 K2 **Harrodsburg** Indiana 39.01N 86.32W
107 M4 **Harrodsburg** Kentucky 37.45N 84.51W
57 K5 **Harrogate** N Yorks Eng 54.00N 1.33W
108 L5 **Harrold** S Dakota 44.31N 99.42W
112 H1 **Harrold** Texas 34.05N 99.02W
55 C2 **Harrow** London England 51.35N 0.20W
99 H10 **Harrow** Ontario 42.02N 82.55W
103 D6 **Harrow** Pennsylvania 40.29N 75.10W
100 Q8 **Harrowby** Manitoba 50.45N 101.28W
55 C3 **Harrow on the Hill** London Eng 51.34N 0.21W
52 J2 **Harrsjön** Sweden 64.23N 15.20E
108 K9 **Harry Strunk L** Nebraska
86 N4 **Har Sa'ad** *hill* Israel 30.43N 34.50E
86 N5 **Har Saggi** *hill* Israel 30.21N 34.38E
63 K6 **Harsefeld** W Germany 53.27N 9.29E
63 H9 **Harsewinkel** W Germany 51.58N 8.14E
33 E8 **Harshaf** Saudi Arabia 17.40N 43.57E
87 L5 **Harshau** Somalia 11.08N 47.21E
30 A7 **Harsi** *res* Madhya Prad India
61 M6 **Harsin** Belgium 50.11N 5.21E
32 B3 **Harsin** Iran 34.15N 47.38E
37 D5 **Harşit** Turkey 40.46N 38.55E
37 E5 **Harsit** *R* Turkey
60 M11 **Harskamp** Netherlands 52.08N 5.45E
53 E6 **Hårslev** Denmark 55.30N 10.06E
53 K5 **Härslöv** Sweden 55.57N 12.54E
51 H5 **Harsprånget** Sweden 66.51N 19.50E
51 F3 **Harstad** Norway 68.48N 16.30E
56 M3 **Harston** Cambs Eng 52.08N 0.04E
29 E6 **Harsud** Madhya Prad India 22.02N 76.42E
63 L8 **Harsum** W Germany 52.13N 9.58E
52 E2 **Harsvik** Norway 64.03N 10.00E
53 B4 **Harsyssel** *reg* Denmark
57 L3 **Hart** Cleveland Eng 54.43N 1.17W
106 H6 **Hart** Michigan 43.43N 86.22W
100 M9 **Hart** Saskatchewan 49.11N 105.42W
112 E1 **Hart** Texas 34.23N 102.07W
37 E5 **Hart** Turkey 40.24N 40.10E
101 E3 **Hart** *R* Yukon Terr
35 G3 **Harta** Jordan 32.41N 35.51E
88 N8 **Harta, El** Algeria 26.37N 1.48W
21 B6 **Hartao** Liaoning China 42.30N 122.06E
95 K2 **Hartbeesfontein** S Africa 26.45S 26.25E
95 L1 **Hartbeespoort** S Africa 25.44S 27.52E
95 L1 **Hartbeespoortdam** *res* S Africa 25.46S 27.50E
65 N7 **Hartberg** Austria 47.18N 15.58E
57 K2 **Hartburn** Northumb Eng 55.10N 1.52W
53 W18 **Hårteigen** *mt* Norway 60.11N 7.05E
100 C8 **Hartell** Alberta 50.40N 114.12W
95 F10 **Hartenbos** S Africa 34.08S 22.05E
69 E5 **Hartennes-et-Taux** France 49.17N 3.21E
64 E2 **Hartenrod** W Germany 50.45N 8.27E
64 O2 **Hartenstein** E Germany 50.40N 12.40E
64 J5 **Hartershofen** W Germany 49.25N 10.15E
57 G2 **Hart Fell** *mt* Dumfries & Galloway/Borders Scotland 55.25N 3.25W
56 M5 **Hartfield** E Sussex Eng 51.06N 0.06E
107 L10 **Hartford** Alabama 31.05N 85.43W
107 B6 **Hartford** Arkansas 35.01N 94.24W
103 J3 **Hartford** Connecticut 41.45N 72.42W
109 P3 **Hartford** Kansas 38.19N 95.58W
107 K4 **Hartford** Kentucky 37.26N 86.57W
106 H7 **Hartford** Michigan 42.13N 86.10W
104 C6 **Hartford** Ohio 40.15N 82.42W
105 D2 **Hartford** Tennessee 35.47N 83.15W
106 F6 **Hartford** Wisconsin 43.18N 88.23W
103 J3 **Hartford** *co* Connecticut
106 J9 **Hartford City** Indiana 40.28N 85.21W
64 O1 **Hartha** E Germany 51.06N 13.00E
Hartha Iraq *see* **Hārithah, Al**
64 O2 **Harthau** E Germany 50.46N 12.56E
101 M8 **Hart Highway** Br Col
58 J7 **Harthill** Strathclyde Scotland 55.52N 3.45W
103 L6 **Hart I** New York 40.52N 73.46W
57 K6 **Hartington** Derbys Eng 53.09N 1.48W

108 N7 Hartington Nebraska 42.36N 97.16W
98 D2 Hart-Jaune R Quebec
64 P7 Hartkirchen W Germany 48.24N 13.24E
52 H2 Hartkjølen mt Norway 64.19N 14.00E
110 F7 Hart L Oregon 42.25N 119.51W
12 D4 Hart, L S Australia 31.09S 136.20E
56 C6 Hartland Devon Eng 50.59N 4.29W
104 Q2 Hartland Maine 44.53N 69.28W
98 E7 Hartland New Brunswick 46.18N 67.31W
95 P3 Hartland S Africa 27.27S 31.04E
56 B5 Hartland Pt Devon Eng 51.02N 4.31W
56 B6 Hartland Quay Devon Eng 50.59N 4.31W
56 G3 Hartlebury Hereford & Worcs Eng 52.20N 2.14W
57 L3 Hartlepool Cleveland Eng 54.41N 1.13W
108 P6 Hartley Iowa 43.10N 95.28W
112 B8 Hartley Texas 35.54N 102.24W
92 E11 Hartley Zimbabwe 18.10S 30.14E
92 D11 Hartley dist Zimbabwe
101 J9 Hartley Bay Br Col 53.27N 129.18W
56 K5 Hartley Wintney Hants Eng 51.19N 0.55W
110 F2 Hartline Washington 47.41N 119.08W
103 C8 Hartly Delaware 39.09N 75.14W
64 P5 Hartmanice Czechoslovakia 49.11N 13.28E
64 O2 Hartmannsdorf E Germany 50.53N 12.48E
64 G3 Hartmannshain W Germany 50.27N 9.17E
100 Q6 Hart Mt Manitoba 52.30N 101.24W
110 F7 Hart Mt Oregon 42.29N 119.45W
14 F3 Hart, Mt W Australia 16.57S 125.00E
100 R9 Hartney Manitoba 49.29N 100.31W
51 M10 Hartola Finland 61.35N 26.04E
95 J2 Harts R S Africa
94 D3 Hartseer Namibia 20.13S 16.20E
109 E2 Hartsel Colorado 39.02N 105.48W
107 K7 Hartselle Alabama 34.26N 86.58W
64 J6 Härtsfeld mts W Germany
109 P7 Hartshorne Oklahoma 34.53N 95.34W
12 C5 Harts I S Australia 32.39S 133.08E
13 C6 Harts Range N Terr Australia 22.57S 134.55E
105 G3 Hartsville S Carolina 34.23N 80.05W
107 K5 Hartsville Tennessee 36.23N 86.11W
95 H3 Hartswater S Africa 27.46S 24.49E
35 C6 Hartuv Israel 31.45N 35.00E
107 D4 Hartville Missouri 37.14N 92.30W
108 F7 Hartville Wyoming 42.18N 104.43W
105 E3 Hartwell Georgia 34.22N 82.57W
105 D3 Hartwell Res Georgia/S Car 34.30N 83.00W
103 E3 Hartwood New York 41.32N 74.41W
99 H3 Harty Ontario 49.29N 82.43W
33 E8 Ḥarūb Saudi Arabia 17.28N 42.55E
19 F5 Haruku isld Moluccas Indon 3.34S 128.28E
Harunabad see Shahabad
36 J5 Haruniye Turkey 37.18N 36.27E
34 C8 Hārūn, Jebel mt Jordan 30.18N 35.24E
28 D4 Harur Tamil Nadu India 12.01N 78.29E
93 M7 Haruru Kenya 1.20S 40.13E
21 B3 Har Us Nei Monggol Zizhiqu China 48.10N 122.30E
22 B2 Har Us Nuur L Hovd Mongolia
22 B2 Har Us Nuur L Uvs Mongolia
33 K8 Harūt S Yemen 16.03N 52.13E
85 D6 Harūt al Aswad, Al reg Libya
31 A4 Harut R Afghanistan
31 A5 Harut Rud Afghanistan 31.47N 61.16E
22 F3 Haruuhin Gol R Mongolia
35 C6 Ḥaruvit Israel 31.45N 34.51E
Ḥaruz see Harūz-e Bala
32 G5 Harūz-e Bala Iran 30.48N 57.05E
32 F6 Harvand Iran 28.25N 55.44E
111 H7 Harvard California 34.58N 116.40W
110 J3 Harvard Idaho 46.56N 116.44W
106 F7 Harvard Illinois 42.25N 88.37W
108 M9 Harvard Nebraska 40.39N 98.06W
103 D2 Harvard New York 42.02N 75.07W
113 O6 Harvard Glacier Alaska 61.20N 147.40W
109 D3 Harvard Mt Colorado 38.55N 106.21W
61 F5 Harveng Belgium 50.24N 3.59E
14 F7 Harvest, Mt W Australia 25.54S 126.33E
106 G8 Harvey Illinois 41.38N 87.40W
108 S8 Harvey Iowa 41.18N 92.55W
108 L2 Harvey N Dakota 47.47N 99.57W
14 B10 Harvey W Australia 33.06S 115.50E
107 J13 Harvey dist New Orleans, Louisiana
110 D9 Harvey Mt California 40.45N 121.04W
103 B4 Harveys L Pennsylvania
98 F8 Harvey Station New Brunswick 45.44N 67.00W
109 P3 Harveyville Kansas 38.47N 95.57W
103 B4 Harveyville Pennsylvania 41.14N 76.15W
107 F5 Harviell Missouri 36.40N 90.29W
56 J4 Harwell Oxon Eng 51.37N 1.18W
56 O4 Harwich Essex Eng 51.57N 1.17E
103 O3 Harwich Massachusetts 41.40N 70.03W
103 O3 Harwich Port Massachusetts 41.38N 70.03W
103 H3 Harwinton Connecticut 41.47N 73.04W
11 N12 Harwood New Zealand 45.48S 170.41E
112 K6 Harwood Texas 29.40N 97.32W
64 E4 Harxheim W Germany 49.38N 8.08E
29 D3 Haryana state India
63 M9 Harz mts Germany
61 N5 Harzé Belgium 50.27N 5.40E
63 O9 Harzgerode E Germany 51.39N 11.09E
34 C8 Hāsā Jordan 30.47N 35.56E
35 F10 Hasa R Jordan
33 H4 Hasā, Al tribe Saudi Arabia
22 C3 Hasagt Mongolia 46.24N 95.21E
87 D3 Hasaheisa Sudan 14.44N 33.20E
Hasakah, Al see Haseke, El
24 B7 Hasalbag Xinjiang Uygur Zizhiqu China 37.46N 76.47E
32 B2 Hasan Iran 36.02N 46.18E
32 E4 Ḥasanābād Esfahān Iran 32.08N 52.44E
34 O4 Ḥasanābād Kermānshāh Iran 34.37N 46.44E
37 F3 Hasanağa R Turkey
86 L5 Ḥasana, Gebel el hill Egypt 30.26N 33.47E
Ḥasan al Lacha see Ḥasan al Lajī
34 L5 Ḥasan al Lajī Iraq 33.28N 43.58E
86 L5 Ḥasana, Wâdî watercourse Egypt
37 D7 Hasançelebi Turkey 38.58N 37.54E
36 G4 Hasan Dağı mt Turkey 38.07N 34.10E
30 D6 Hasanganj Uttar Prad India 26.46N 80.38E
33 B4 Ḥasānī, Al isld Saudi Arabia 25.00N 37.08E
33 E5 Ḥasan,Jabal mts Saudi Arabia
37 F8 Ḥasankeyf Turkey 37.44N 41.23E
44 K10 Hasan Kīādeh Iran 37.26N 49.56E
32 G7 Ḥasan Langī Iran 27.24N 56.51E
28 D1 Ḥasanparti Andhra Prad India 18.08N 79.33E
30 A5 Hasanpur Haryana India 27.58N 77.30E
30 B4 Hasanpur Uttar Prad India 28.43N 78.17E
30 K7 Hasanpur Road Bihar India 25.43N 86.12E
34 O2 Ḥasan Salaran Iran 36.03N 46.17E
28 C5 Ḥasanur Tamil Nadu India 11.40N 77.06E
32 H8 Hasār Iran 25.47N 58.11E
35 E7 Hasasa watercourse Jordan
35 G10 Hasa Sta Jordan 30.49N 35.58E
34 E8 Hasa, Wādī watercourse Jordan
34 C8 Hāsā, Wādī el R Jordan
34 J2 Hasawīya Fawqāni Syria 36.49N 41.28E
34 C5 Hâsbaiya Lebanon 33.24N 35.41E
36 H3 Hasbek Turkey 39.33N 35.32E
63 G8 Hasbergen W Germany 52.14N 7.57E
64 B5 Hasborn-Dautweiler W Germany 49.29N 6.58E
103 J6 Hasbrouck Heights New Jersey
34 L7 Ḥasb, Sha'ib watercourse Iraq
56 K5 Ḥascombe Surrey Eng 51.09N 0.35W
58 R8 Hascosay isld Shetland Scotland 60.36N 1.00W
29 H6 Hasdo R Madhya Prad India
63 G8 Hase R W Germany
34 H2 Haseke, El Syria 36.32N 40.44E
64 K2 Hasel R E Germany
63 L5 Haseldorf W Germany 53.38N 9.36E
63 G7 Haselünne W Germany 52.41N 7.30E
63 U8 Hasenfelde E Germany 52.25N 14.12E
121 F3 Hasenkamp Argentina 31.31S 59.46W
22 F3 Hashaat Mongolia 47.29N 103.09E
90 M5 Hashab Sudan 13.20N 25.29E
87 D3 Hashaba Sudan 14.19N 32.15E
32 K7 Hashak Iran 27.25N 62.15E
Hasharon see Sharon, Plain of
86 N8 Hasha, Wādī el watercourse Saudi Arabia
20 A4 Hashiba Kanagawa Japan
87 J2 Hashid tribe Yemen
34 M6 Ḥashimīyah, Al Iraq 32.22N 44.42E
20 J7 Hashimoto Japan 34.19N 135.33E
20 A3 Hashimoto dist Kanagawa Japan
Hashır see Pervari
Hashniz see Heshnīz
32 D3 Hashtjerd Iran 35.58N 50.40E
32 C2 Hashtpar Iran 37.59N 48.57E
32 B2 Hashtrūd Iran 37.29N 47.05E
33 F6 Ḥasī, Al Saudi Arabia 20.09N 45.30E
33 K8 Ḥasī 'Awfayr S Yemen 17.02N 52.14E
85 A6 Ḥasi Haghe Libya 26.18N 10.32E
33 L8 Ḥāsik Oman 17.25N 55.15E
33 L8 Ḥāsikīyah isld Arabian Sea 17.28N 55.37E
19 F4 Ḥasil isld Moluccas Indon 1.08S 128.23E
31 G6 Hasilpur Pakistan 29.42N 72.40E
Hasineh see Band-e Hasīneh
87 E4 Hasira, El Sudan 13.20N 34.22E
85 A6 Hasi Tin Ihédan Libya 27.14N 9.58E
52 J3 Håsjö Sweden 63.02N 16.20E
107 D7 Haskell Arkansas 34.30N 92.38W
109 P6 Haskell Oklahoma 35.50N 95.40W
112 H2 Haskell Texas 33.10N 99.45W
60 M8 Haskerhorne Netherlands 52.57N 5.50E
37 G5 Hasköy Turkey 40.59N 42.54E
37 J2 Hasköy dist İstanbul Turkey 41.02N 28.54E
87 K6 Haskul Ethiopia 8.42N 44.47E
65 K4 Haslach Austria 48.35N 14.03E
64 E7 Haslach W Germany 48.16N 8.06E
66 G3 Hasle Bern Switzerland 47.01N 7.40E
53 P12 Hasle Bornholm Denmark 55.12N 14.43E
66 J4 Hasle Luzern Switzerland 46.58N 8.04E
56 K5 Haslemere Surrey Eng 51.06N 0.43W
66 O2 Haslen Appenzell Switzerland 47.23N 9.22E
66 N4 Haslen Switzerland 46.59N 9.04E
112 M8 Haslet Texas 32.57N 97.21W
53 H6 Haslev Denmark 55.20N 11.59E
57 J5 Haslingden Lancs Eng 53.43N 2.18W
66 J5 Haslital V Switzerland
53 E4 Haslund Denmark 56.25N 10.02E
53 E5 Hasmark Denmark 55.33N 10.28E
69 E3 Hasnon France 50.25N 3.23E
35 D3 HaSolelim Israel 32.45N 35.14E
34 O2 Hāşol, Kūh-e- mt Iran 36.02N 46.39E
72 B9 Hasparren France 43.23N 1.18W
69 E3 Haspres France 50.16N 3.25E
37 G8 Hasrās Turkey 37.58N 42.18E
36 J6 Hassa Turkey 36.48N 36.30E
93 L8 Hassa Bodala Kenya 2.21S 39.50E
32 A3 Hassan Iraq 35.26N 44.24E
28 C4 Hassan Karnataka India 13.01N 76.03E
28 C4 Hassan dist Karnataka India
31 G4 Hassan Abdal Pakistan 33.49N 72.48E
87 C2 Hassanawi watercourse Sudan
87 D3 Hassaniya tribe Sudan
Hassaouîye Faouqâni see Hasawīya Fawqāni
111 M8 Hassayampa R Arizona
64 K3 Hassberge mts W Germany
51 F9 Hassel Sweden 62.15N 16.45E
69 N5 Hassel W Germany 49.16N 7.10E
52 K4 Hassela Sweden 62.06N 16.45E
10 C10 Hasselborough B Macquarie I Pacific Oc
63 N9 Hasselfelde E Germany 51.42N 10.52E
97 K2 Hassel Sd N W Terr
61 M3 Hasselt Belgium 50.56N 5.20E
60 N9 Hasselt Netherlands 52.36N 6.05E
53 F4 Hassensør C Denmark 56.09N 10.44E
63 N9 Hasserode E Germany 51.50N 10.46E
Hassetché see Haseke, El
64 K3 Hassfurt W Germany 50.02N 10.32E
88 N8 Hassi Ambrosini Algeria 27.50N 1.45W
88 M7 Hassi Azrar Algeria 30.00N 3.35W
88 O7 Hassi Barouda Algeria 28.35N 1.50E
88 P6 Hassi Bedjiaf Algeria 30.51N 2.43E
88 L7 Hassi Beida Algeria 29.30N 5.32W
88 R7 Hassi Bel Guebbour Algeria 28.46N 6.21E
88 R6 Hassi bel Hairane Algeria 31.15N 6.10E
88 R6 Hassi bel Kiouta Algeria 31.31N 6.01E
88 H7 Hassi Ben Khcheiba Morocco 28.04N 11.22W
74 F10 Hassi Berkane Morocco 34.51N 2.55W
88 R6 Hassi Bottine Algeria 31.17N 6.42E
88 K7 Hassi bou Agba Algeria 29.22N 6.17W
88 K7 Hassi Bou Akba Algeria 28.53N 7.37W
88 N6 Hassi bou Amama Algeria 31.13N 1.49W
88 Q7 Hassi Bou Krechba Algeria 29.45N 5.45E
88 N6 Hassi bou Krelala Algeria 30.15N 0.27W
88 L7 Hassi Bou Laadam Algeria 29.43N 4.05W
88 S9 Hassi Bourahla Algeria 24.40N 8.25E
88 R6 Hassi Bou Safia Algeria 31.36N 6.46E
88 P6 Hassi Bou Tali Algeria 30.38N 2.01E
88 O6 Hassi Bou Zid Algeria 31.49N 1.50E
88 L7 Hassi Chaamba Algeria 29.25N 4.25W
88 P7 Hassi Chebaba Algeria 29.25N 3.00E
88 O6 Hassi Cheïkr Algeria 31.20N 1.24E
88 P6 Hassi Djaafar Algeria 31.27N 3.03E
88 P6 Hassi Djafou Algeria 30.56N 3.31E
88 N6 Hassi Djedid Algeria 30.28N 0.03W
Hassié see Hisya
88 M7 Hassi el Aamri Algeria 29.02N 2.22W
88 N7 Hassi el Amri Algeria 29.40N 0.18W
88 Q7 Hassi el Biod Algeria 28.30N 5.58E
82 J8 Hassi el Fokra salt L Mauritania
88 P6 Hassi el Hadadra Algeria 31.38N 3.33E
88 Q6 Hassi el Hadjar Algeria 31.24N 4.55E
Hassi el Homcur see Fort MacMahon
88 P8 Hassi el Krenig Algeria 26.33N 3.05E
88 K7 Hassi el Mounir Algeria 29.07N 7.07W
88 P6 Hassi Erg Sedra Algeria 30.03N 2.03E
88 P8 Hassi Ersoum el Lil Algeria 27.35N 3.28E
88 N6 Hassi Fokra Algeria 30.10N 1.24W
88 O6 Hassi Gour Raoua Algeria 30.59N 1.10E
88 P8 Hassi Habadra Algeria 26.30N 3.47E
88 S7 Hassi Imoulaye Algeria 29.59N 9.12E
88 O7 Hassi Imzirene Algeria 29.15N 1.15E
88 N7 Hassi Inifeg Algeria 28.15N 1.30W
88 P7 Hassi Inifel Algeria 29.50N 3.38E
88 Q8 Hassi In Kelemet Algeria 26.55N 5.50E
88 P7 Hassi Insokki Algeria 28.28N 3.31E
88 O6 Hassi Irziz Algeria 30.06N 1.40E
88 S8 Hassi Issendjell Algeria 26.53N 8.45E
88 O6 Hassi Izi Algeria 31.35N 1.45E
88 P7 Hassi Krezrez Algeria 28.55N 2.02E
88 N6 Hassi Malah Algeria 30.34N 1.55W
88 N6 Hassi Mamoura Algeria 31.45N 0.24W
88 M7 Hassi Mana Algeria 28.48N 2.37W
88 P6 Hassi Marraket Algeria 30.13N 3.00E
88 N7 Hassi Massine Algeria 28.59N 1.27W
88 M7 Hassi Mdakane Algeria 28.25N 2.15W
88 P6 Hassi Mebrouka Algeria 30.14N 2.23E
88 P6 Hassi Mechgarden Algeria 30.11N 3.03E
88 L7 Hassi Menngoub Algeria 29.47N 5.19W
88 N6 Hassi Merhimine Algeria 31.04N 1.25W
88 Q6 Hassi-Messaoud Algeria 31.52N 5.57E
88 P6 Hassi Mestour Algeria 31.33N 2.03E
88 N6 Hassi Mezou Algeria 31.28N 1.21W
88 N6 Hassi Morra Algeria 31.28N 1.53W
88 R7 Hassi Mouilah Maatallah Algeria 28.52N 6.01E
88 P7 Hassi Mouilokh Algeria 29.05N 2.05E
88 O6 Hassi Mouïna Algeria 30.48N 0.24E
88 O7 Hassi Mouley Guenndouz Algeria 29.50N 1.19E
88 O8 Hassi Moya Achem Algeria 27.07N 0.50E
88 Q7 Hassi Msegguem Algeria 28.17N 4.39E
53 A3 Hassing Denmark 56.50N 8.29E
88 S8 Hassi Ouan Sidi mt Algeria 27.58N 9.43E
88 O6 Hassi Ouchen Algeria 30.18N 0.37E
88 L6 Hassi Oudika Algeria 30.03N 4.10W
88 P5 Hassi-R'Mel Algeria 33.10N 3.12E
33 E8 Hassis oil bore Farasān Is Red Sea 16.41N 42.05E
88 R7 Hassi Tabankort Algeria 28.41N 7.02E
88 S8 Hassi Tadjenout Algeria 26.30N 8.50E
88 O7 Hassi Targui Algeria 29.33N 1.25E
88 R6 Hassi Tartrat Algeria 30.03N 6.26E
88 O8 Hassi Teraga Algeria 27.19N 1.54E
88 S7 Hassi Timellouline Algeria 29.12N 8.29E
88 S7 Hassi Tin Fouchaye Algeria 29.28N 8.54E
88 S9 Hassi Tin Kéouéne Algeria 25.40N 9.33E
88 M7 Hassi Tinouradj Algeria 29.10N 2.38W
88 Q8 Hassi Tioukeline Algeria 26.28N 4.43E
88 R6 Hassi Tournize Algeria 31.48N 7.02E
88 M6 Hassi Zerzour Algeria 30.40N 3.56W
88 L6 Hassi Zhuilma Morocco 30.10N 5.09W
88 P6 Hassi Zirara Algeria 31.18N 3.18E
88 O6 Hassi Zirara Rharbia Algeria 31.13N 1.25E
34 E3 Hass, Jebel el mts Syria
64 L3 Hasslach W Germany 50.17N 11.19E
64 K1 Hassleben Erfurt E Germany 51.06N 11.00E
63 T6 Hassleben Neubrandenburg E Germany 53.13N 13.42E
52 H10 Hässleholm Sweden 56.09N 13.45E
52 H8 Hasslerör Sweden 58.45N 13.57E
64 E5 Hassloch W Germany 49.22N 8.15E
58 K2 Haster Highland Scotland 58.26N 3.10W
52 H8 Hästholmen Sweden 58.16N 14.40E
61 K6 Hastière-Lavaux Belgium 50.13N 4.49E
61 K6 Hastière-par-delà Belgium 50.13N 4.50E
116 O6 Hastings Barbados 13.05N 59.36W
56 N6 Hastings E Sussex Eng 50.51N 0.36E
105 F8 Hastings Florida 29.42N 81.31W
108 P8 Hastings Iowa 41.00N 95.30W
106 J7 Hastings Michigan 42.38N 85.17W
108 S5 Hastings Minnesota 44.40N 92.52W
108 M9 Hastings Nebraska 40.37N 98.22W
11 L6 Hastings New Zealand 39.39S 176.52E
109 M7 Hastings Oklahoma 34.14N 98.06W
99 N8 Hastings Ontario 44.19N 77.57W
104 G6 Hastings Pennsylvania 40.41N 78.42W
12 H9 Hastings Tasmania 43.23S 146.50E
12 L4 Hastings R New S Wales
15 L9 Hastings I Louisiade Arch 10.17S 151.50E
103 G5 Hastings-on-Hudson New York 40.58N 73.54W
12 K4 Hastings Ra New S Wales
53 E6 Håstrup Denmark 55.10N 10.12E
52 H10 Hästveda Sweden 56.16N 13.55E
109 H3 Hasty Colorado 38.08N 102.58W
51 J1 Hasvik Norway 70.29N 22.09E
30 D7 Haswa Uttar Prad India 25.52N 80.52E
33 K9 Ḥaşwayn S Yemen 15.35N 52.08E
109 G3 Haswell Colorado 38.27N 103.09W
57 L3 Haswell Durham England 54.47N 1.23W
Hasyah see Hisya
30 G6 Hata Uttar Prad India 26.45N 83.45E
85 M9 Hatab, Wadi El Sudan
11 C6 Hataitai dist Wellington New Zealand
22 H5 Hatanbulag Mongolia 43.08N 109.05E
93 M6 Hatatesa Kenya 0.45S 40.55E
Hatay see Antakya
104 K6 Hatboro Pennsylvania 40.11N 75.08W
109 C9 Hatch New Mexico 32.39N 107.10W
111 M4 Hatch Utah 37.39N 112.26W
112 H4 Hatchel Texas 31.52N 99.57W
13 D5 Hatches Cr N Terr Australia 21.00S 135.19E
101 W6 Hatchet L Saskatchewan 58.36N 103.40W
107 G6 Hatchie R Tennessee
103 N3 Hatchville Massachusetts 41.38N 70.34W
110 D9 Hat Creek California 40.48N 121.31W
108 F7 Hat Creek Wyoming 42.58N 104.22W
82 H5 Haţeg Romania 45.35N 22.57E
23 K6 Hateruma isld Japan 24.03N 123.44E
30 G5 Hatewa Ghat Uttar Prad India 27.18N 83.32E
107 B7 Hatfield Arkansas 34.30N 94.22W
56 L4 Hatfield Herts Eng 51.46N 0.13W
103 J2 Hatfield Massachusetts 42.23N 72.36W
108 O6 Hatfield Minnesota 43.57N 96.11W
12 G5 Hatfield New S Wales 33.53S 143.47E
103 D6 Hatfield Pennsylvania 40.17N 75.18W
100 M7 Hatfield Saskatchewan 51.26N 105.00W
57 M5 Hatfield S Yorks Eng 53.36N 0.59W
56 M4 Hatfield Heath Essex Eng 51.50N 0.13E
56 N4 Hatfield Peverel Essex Eng 51.47N 0.35E
22 E1 Hatgal Mongolia 50.27N 100.12E
29 H6 Hath Madhya Prad India 22.16N 83.10E
108 D3 Hathaway Montana 46.16N 106.10W
56 C6 Hatherleigh Devon Eng 50.49N 4.04W
12 F6 Hatherleigh S Australia 37.30S 140.14E
56 J2 Hathern Leics Eng 52.48N 1.14W
57 K6 Hathersage Derbys Eng 53.19N 1.38W
30 B5 Hathras Uttar Prad India 27.36N 78.02E
30 H6 Hathwa Bihar India 26.21N 84.19E
101 X1 Hat I N W Terr 68.20N 100.19W
31 J10 Hatia Bangladesh 22.26N 90.13E
30 L5 Hatia Nepal 27.44N 87.21E
31 J10 Hatia R Bangladesh
31 J10 Hatia I Bangladesh 22.40N 91.00E
33 C6 Ḥātibah, Ra's C Saudi Arabia 21.55N 38.57E
25 H7 Ha Tien Vietnam 10.24N 104.30E
33 F3 Ḥatīfah, Al area Saudi Arabia
105 J7 Ḥatillo Puerto Rico 18.29N 66.50W
35 G3 Hatim Jordan 32.38N 35.46E
29 E3 Hatin Haryana India 28.02N 77.17E
25 H3 Ha Tinh Vietnam 18.21N 105.55E
36 F5 Hatip Turkey 37.44N 32.25E
35 D10 Hatira watercourse Israel
35 C10 Ḥatira, Hare hills Israel
30 A1 Hat Kot Haryana India 31.04N 76.57E
53 T18 Hatlestrand Norway 60.03N 5.55E
88 S4 Hatob, el R Tunisia
116 B1 Hato, Bocht van B Curaçao W I
119 E4 Hato Corozal Colombia 6.08N 71.45W
20 E1 Hatogaya Japan 35.50N 139.45E
116 K5 Hato Mayor Dominican Rep 18.49N 69.16W
Hatra anc site see Ḥadr, Al
61 M6 Hatrival Belgium 50.01N 5.21E
94 D4 Hatsamas Namibia 22.50S 17.35E
Hat Sao see Ban Hat Sao
20 F7 Hatsukaichi Japan 34.22N 132.20E
29 G7 Hatta Balaghat, Madhya Prad India 21.42N 80.21E
29 F5 Hatta Panna, Madhya Prad Ind 24.09N 79.40E
12 F5 Hattah Victoria 34.52S 142.23E
18 N3 Hattan mt Sabah Malaysia 5.14N 118.38E
60 N10 Hattem Netherlands 52.29N 6.04E
69 O6 Hatten France 48.54N 7.59E
105 M2 Hatteras N Carolina 35.14N 75.41W
105 M2 Hatteras, C N Carolina 35.14N 75.31W
105 M2 Hatteras Inlet N Carolina 35.12N 75.44W
64 E3 Hattersheim W Germany 50.04N 8.23E
53 O9 Hattervig Faeroes 62.20N 6.14W
51 D6 Hattfjelldal Norway 65.35N 14.00E
107 G10 Hattiesburg Mississippi 31.20N 89.19W
69 M6 Hattigny France 48.38N 6.58E
30 A4 Hattin Haryana India 28.02N 77.13E
53 D5 Hatting Denmark 55.51N 9.46E
63 F10 Hattingen W Germany 51.24N 7.10E
95 O4 Hattingspruit S Africa 28.05S 30.08E
29 H8 Hatti R Orissa India
69 C5 Hatton France 49.29N 2.19E
58 N4 Hatton Grampian Scotland 57.25N 1.55W
108 N2 Hatton N Dakota 47.38N 97.28W
100 H8 Hatton Saskatchewan 50.02N 109.50W
26 S8 Hatton Sri Lanka 6.54N 80.35E
56 H3 Hatton Warwicks Eng 52.18N 1.38W
110 G3 Hatton Washington 46.46N 118.49W
25 D6 Hattras Pass Burma
69 N7 Hattstatt France 48.01N 7.19E
51 L10 Hattula Finland 61.06N 24.20E
Hattusas anc site see Boğazkale
19 D8 Hatudo Indonesia 9.08S 125.35E
116 F4 Hatuey Cuba 21.11N 77.33W
11 L7 Hatuma New Zealand 40.03S 176.32E
36 F5 Hatunsaray Turkey 37.35N 32.22E
19 F5 Hatunuru Moluccas Indon 2.50S 128.40E
122 U13 Hatutu I Marquesas Is Pacific Oc 7.56S 140.38W
65 O8 Hatzendorf Austria 46.59N 16.01E
64 C3 Hatzenport W Germany 50.14N 7.26E
64 F2 Hatzfeld W Germany 50.59N 8.32E
15 H6 Hatzfeldthaven Papua New Guinea 4.26S 145.11E
66 N4 Hätzingen Switzerland 46.58N 9.02E
60 N13 Hau W Germany 51.44N 6.09E
25 K6 Hau Bon Vietnam 13.22N 108.25E
69 E2 Haubourdin France 50.37N 3.00E
87 K6 Haud tribe Ethiopia
66 G7 Haudères Switzerland 46.05N 7.31E
53 Y13 Hauduken mt Norway 62.32N 8.06E
66 H2 Hauenstein Switzerland 47.23N 7.52E
35 G4 Haufa Jordan 32.29N 35.50E
35 F3 Haufa R Jordan
50 F4 Haugakvísi R Iceland
53 X17 Haugastøl Norway 60.30N 7.50E
53 C4 Hauge Denmark 56.15N 9.22E
52 C8 Hauge Norway 58.20N 6.17E
53 W16 Hauge Sogn og Fjordane Norway 61.05N 7.30E
53 V14 Haugen Möre og Romsdal Norway 62.07N 6.45E
53 V14 Haugen Norway 62.07N 6.45E
53 V14 Haugen Sogn og Fjordane Norway 62.00N 6.40E
106 C4 Haugen Wisconsin 45.35N 91.45W
53 S20 Haugesund Norway 59.25N 5.16E
53 Y20 Haugfoss waterfall Norway 59.14N 8.05E
107 C9 Haughton Louisiana 32.31N 93.30W
53 T17 Haugsdal Norway 60.51N 5.31E
65 O4 Haugsdorf Austria 48.43N 16.05E
53 T19 Haugsfjell mt Norway 59.38N 5.44E
53 S14 Haugshavn Norway 62.10N 5.25E
50 K3 Haugsöræfi reg Iceland
50 K3 Haugsvatn L Iceland 65.45N 15.45W
51 L10 Hauho Finland 61.12N 24.32E
15 M3 Hauhui Malaita I Solomon Is 9.18S 161.06E
11 K5 Hauhungaroa Ra New Zealand
66 G1 Hauingen W Germany 47.39N 7.42E
50 D4 Haukadalsvatn L Iceland 65.03N 21.38W
50 E6 Haukadalur Árnessýsla Iceland 64.20N 20.17W
50 B3 Haukadalur Ísafjardharsýsla, Vestur Iceland 65.53N 23.36W
53 U16 Haukedal Norway 61.25N 6.23E
53 U16 Haukedalsvatn L Norway 61.24N 6.20E
53 S18 Haukeland Norway 60.21N 5.27E
53 X19 Haukeligrend Norway 59.45N 7.33E
53 W19 Haukeliseter Norway 59.49N 7.14E
51 L6 Haukipudas Finland 65.12N 25.20E
51 N9 Haukivesi L Finland 62.10N 28.30E
51 N9 Haukivuori Finland 62.02N 27.15E
50 K3 Hauksstadhaheidhi heath Iceland
50 K3 Haukstadhir Iceland 65.40N 15.10W
61 G5 Haulchin Belgium 50.23N 4.05E
60 O7 Haule Netherlands 53.02N 6.20E
34 J2 Haul, El Syria 36.24N 41.09E
60 O7 Haulerwijk Netherlands 53.03N 6.20E
11 L6 Haumoana New Zealand 39.37S 176.59E
121 E1 Haumonia Argentina 27.30S 60.10W
11 H9 Haumuri Bluff C New Zealand 42.33S 173.32E
64 H2 Haune R W Germany
64 H2 Hauneck W Germany 50.50N 9.44E
64 H2 Haunetal Hessen W Germany 50.46N 9.42E
64 K7 Haunstetten W Germany 48.17N 10.55E
11 F9 Haupiri, L New Zealand 42.34S 171.41E
64 O5 Hauptenberg mt W Germany 49.01N 12.35E
95 K2 Hauptsrus S Africa 26.33S 26.17E
66 O2 Hauptwil Switzerland 47.28N 9.16E
Haur see Ḥūr
Haura see Ḥawrā, Al
15 M4 Hauraha San Cristobal I Solomon Is 10.47S 161.55E
11 K3 Hauraki G New Zealand
Haurān, Wādī watercourse see Ḥawrān, Wādī
11 B12 Hauroko, L New Zealand
122 A11 Hauru, Pt Society Is Pacific Oc 17.29S 149.55W
65 J7 Haus Austria 47.25N 13.46E
53 S18 Haus Norway 60.27N 5.30E
64 E7 Hausach W Germany 48.17N 8.11E
63 J8 Hausberge W Germany 52.14N 8.55E
66 H1 Hausen W Germany 47.41N 7.51E
110 O3 Hauser Lake Dam Montana 46.46N 111.54W
64 E8 Häusern W Germany 47.45N 8.10E
64 M8 Hausham W Germany 47.44N 11.51E
65 O5 Hausleiten Austria 48.24N 16.07E
65 H5 Hausruck mts Austria
Haussez, Is. d' see Mercury Is
66 N4 Hausstock mt Switzerland 46.53N 9.04E
51 O5 Hautajärvi Finland 66.29N 29.04E
88 K6 Haut Atlas mts Morocco
69 B3 Haut Banc, Pte.du France 50.24N 1.34E
69 J8 Haut-du-Sec mt France 47.48N 5.11E
69 M8 Haut-du-Them, le France 47.51N 6.44E
66 F7 Haute Switzerland 46.12N 7.18E
69 K8 Haute-Amance France 47.51N 5.34E
67 P12 Haute-Corse dept Corsica
71 G4 Hautecourt-Romanèche France 46.09N 5.25E
72 G5 Hautefort France 45.16N 1.08E
67 F9 Haute-Garonne dept France
66 A5 Haute Joux mts France
90 L8 Haute Kotto dist Cent Afr Rep
67 H7 Haute-Loire dept France
71 K5 Hauteluce France 45.45N 6.36E
67 J4 Haute-Marne dept France
99 R4 Haute-Mauricie, Parc de Quebec
71 C4 Hauterive France 46.05N 3.26E
98 D4 Hauterive Quebec 49.11N 68.16W
71 G6 Hauterives France 45.15N 5.01E
67 K8 Hautes-Alpes dept France
90 G9 Haute Sangha div Cent Afr Rep
67 K5 Haute-Saône dept France
67 K7 Haute-Savoie dept France
61 P4 Hautes Fagnes moor Belgium
67 E9 Hautes-Pyrénées dept France
69 H4 Hautes Riviéres France 49.53N 4.51E
61 O7 Haute Sûre, Lac de la res Luxembourg
67 F7 Haute-Vienne dept France
71 H5 Hauteville-Lompnès France 45.58N 5.36E
70 G4 Hauteville-sur-Mer France 48.58N 1.33W
Haute Volta rep see Upper Volta
61 L6 Haut-Fays Belgium 50.00N 5.01E
66 A5 Haut Foncine, le France 46.40N 6.05E
66 D7 Hautforts mt France 46.10N 6.46E
104 R2 Haut, I.au Maine
61 H4 Haut-Ittre Belgium 50.39N 4.18E
61 K5 Haut-le-Wastia Belgium 50.18N 4.50E
90 M8 Haut-M'Bomou dist Cent Afr Rep
69 F3 Hautmont France 50.15N 3.55E
Haut, Mt see Cornillet, Mt
91 C4 Haut-Ogooué reg Gabon
61 F5 Hautrage Belgium 50.28N 3.46E
67 K5 Haut-Rhin dept France
68 D3 Hauts-de-Seine dept France
88 N5 Hauts Plateaux Algeria
69 F5 Hautvillers France 49.05N 3.57E
Haut-Zaïre see Zaïre Supérieure
114 B4 Hauula Hawaiian Is 21.36N 157.55W
11 J8 Hauwai New Zealand 41.46S 174.11E
86 C4 Hauwârîya El Egypt 30.57N 29.41E
72 C9 Haux France 43.04N 0.49W
Hauz see Ḥowz
32 J5 Hauzdār Iran 30.32N 61.15E
64 Q6 Hauzenberg W Germany 48.40N 13.39E
Hauz-i-Dumbitu see Ḥowz-e Dūmatu
87 G4 Hauzien Ethiopia 13.58N 39.25E
Hauz-i-Giaur see Ḥowz-e Gīvar
Hauz-i-Khan see Ḥowz-i-Khan
Hauz-i-Kulut see Ḥowz-e Kalūt
Hauz-i-Mian-i-Tak see Ḥowz-i-Mian-i-Tak
Hauz-i-Panj see Ḥowz-e Panj
31 C5 Hauz Qala Afghanistan 31.03N 64.50E
37 E6 Havaçor Turkey 39.21N 39.06E
107 C6 Havana Arkansas 35.07N 93.33W
Havana Cubasee Habana
105 C7 Havana Florida 30.38N 84.25W
106 D9 Havana Illinois 40.17N 90.04W
109 P4 Havana Kansas 37.05N 95.57W
108 N4 Havana N Dakota 45.58N 97.38W
69 L5 Havange France 49.23N 6.00E
26 U8 Havannavela Sri Lanka 6.40N 81.31E
56 K6 Havant Hants Eng 50.51N 0.59W
111 K7 Havasu L Cal/Arizona
61 F5 Havay Belgium 50.22N 3.59E
53 C3 Havbro Denmark 56.48N 9.27E
53 J5 Havdrup Denmark 55.33N 12.08E
63 Q7 Havel R E Germany
61 M5 Havelange Belgium 50.23N 5.15E
63 Q7 Havelberg E Germany 52.50N 12.05E
31 G5 Haveli Pakistan 31.10N 72.13E
31 G3 Havelian Pakistan 34.05N 73.14E
63 Q7 Havelland reg E Germany
63 R7 Havelland Grosser Hauptkanal E Germany
105 L3 Havelock N Carolina 34.54N 76.57W
108 H3 Havelock N Dakota 46.29N 102.47W
98 G8 Havelock New Brunswick 45.59N 65.20W
11 H8 Havelock New Zealand 41.17S 173.48E
99 N8 Havelock Ontario 44.26N 77.53W
95 P1 Havelock Swaziland 25.58S 31.08E
13 C2 Havelock Falls N Terr Australia 12.42S 133.49E
28 G7 Havelock I Andaman Is
11 L6 Havelock North New Zealand 39.40S 176.53E
63 S7 Havel See L W Berlin W Germany
60 N8 Havelte Netherlands 52.46N 6.15E
60 N8 Havelterberg Netherlands 52.46N 6.13E
109 N4 Haven Kansas 37.54N 97.47W
103 E3 Haven New York 41.33N 74.32W
60 A3 Haven Cadzand Netherlands 51.22N 3.24E
109 O2 Havensville Kansas 39.31N 96.05W
95 M8 Haven, The S Africa 32.12S 28.57E
56 B4 Haverfordwest Dyfed Wales 51.49N 4.58W
104 O4 Haverhill Massachusetts 42.47N 71.07W
104 N2 Haverhill New Hampshire 44.01N 72.06W
56 M3 Haverhill Suffolk Eng 52.05N 0.26E
28 B3 Haveri Karnataka India 14.46N 75.26E
55 K3 Havering bor London Eng
55 K2 Havering atte Bower London Eng 51.37N 0.11E
95 M2 Haverklip S Africa 26.15S 28.54E
52 L6 Häverö Stockholm Sweden 60.03N 18.42E
52 J4 Häverö Västernorrland Sweden 62.25N 15.05E
53 C2 Haverslev Denmark 57.03N 9.24E
53 D3 Haverslev Denmark 56.48N 9.42E
103 G4 Haverstraw New York 41.12N 73.58W
109 L4 Haviland Kansas 37.37N 99.06W
104 A5 Haviland Ohio 41.01N 84.36W
99 F6 Haviland Bay Ontario 46.55N 84.26W
61 D4 Havinnes Belgium 50.37N 3.28E
82 K2 Havîrna Romania 48.04N 26.43E
62 L6 Havířov Czechoslovakia 49.46N 18.20E
65 N2 Havlíčhkova Borová Czechoslovakia 49.38N 15.46E
65 N2 Havlíčkův Brod Czechoslovakia 49.38N 15.34E
53 D6 Havnbjerg Denmark 55.03N 9.18E
53 E3 Havndal Denmark 56.40N 10.13E
53 B6 Havneby Denmark 55.06N 8.34E
53 G5 Havnsø Denmark 55.46N 11.21E
53 B4 Havnstrup Denmark 56.07N 8.47E
51 L1 Havøysund Norway 70.59N 24.35E
64 Q3 Havraň Czechoslovakia 50.27N 13.37E
36 C3 Havran Turkey 39.33N 27.05E
61 G5 Havré Belgium 50.28N 4.03E
120 D2 Havre Brazil 7.50S 71.20W
110 Q1 Havre Montana 48.34N 109.40W
98 L6 Havre Aubert Madeleine Is, Que 47.15N 61.51W
53 G6 Havrebjerg Denmark 55.28N 11.20E
98 L8 Havre Boucher Nova Scotia 45.41N 61.32W
103 B7 Havre de Grace Maryland 39.33N 76.06W
11 M2 Havre Rock Kermadec Is Pacific Oc 31.17S 178.56W
98 J3 Havre St.Pierre Quebec 50.16N 63.36W
10 Q8 Havre Trough Pacific Oc
36 B1 Havsa Turkey 41.32N 26.49E
52 J2 Havsnäs Sweden 64.04N 15.50E
36 H2 Havza Turkey 40.57N 35.40E
Hawa see Hsia-wa
87 D2 Hawad,El watercourse Sudan
114 B7 Hawaii isld Hawaiian Is
114 Hawaii state U.S.A.
102 U13 Hawaiian Is Pacific Oc
122 J5 Hawaiian Ridge Pacific Oc
114 B7 Hawaii County Hawaiian Is
114 C8 Hawaii Volcanoes Nat. Park Hawaiian Is
33 M9 Ḥawallī Kuwait 29.20N 48.00E
35 G3 Ḥawar Jordan 32.36N 35.45E
35 G3 Hawara Jordan 32.32N 35.54E
57 G6 Hawarden Clwyd Wales 53.11N 3.02W
108 O6 Hawarden Iowa 43.00N 96.30W
11 G9 Hawarden New Zealand 42.55S 172.40E
100 L7 Hawarden Saskatchewan 51.26N 106.37W
86 J9 Hawashîya, Wâdi watercourse Egypt
87 E4 Hawata, El Sudan 13.25N 34.42E
87 C3 Hawawir tribe Sudan
33 H6 Ḥawāyā, Al des area Saudi Arabia
85 C5 Ḥawd al Milh marsh Libya
12 E6 Hawdon, L S Australia 37.09S 139.54E
11 D11 Hawea Flat New Zealand 44.40S 169.20E
11 D11 Hawea, L New Zealand
114 D5 Hawea Pt Hawaiian Is 21.01N 156.40W
11 J6 Hawera New Zealand 39.35S 174.19E
111 G7 Hawes California 34.57N 117.21W
57 J4 Hawes N Yorks Eng 54.18N 2.12W
11 B12 Hawes Hd New Zealand 45.02S 167.02E
107 K4 Hawesville Kentucky 37.53N 86.47W
57 H3 Hawes Water L Cumbria Eng 54.31N 2.49W
114 B6 Hawi Hawaiian Is 29.13N 155.48W
57 H2 Hawick Borders Scotland 55.25N 2.47W
Hawisia see Bîr Hawisia
87 L8 Hawiya tribe Somalia
33 D6 Hawiyah, Al Saudi Arabia 21.26N 40.29E
34 P7 Ḥawizah, Hawr al marsh Iraq
Ḥawizeh, Haur al see Ḥawizah, Hawr al marsh
33 C2 Hawjā',Al Saudi Arabia 28.59N 38.37E
105 F13 Hawk Channel Florida
11 D11 Hawkdun Ra New Zealand
11 M6 Hawke B New Zealand
12 L4 Hawke, C New S Wales 32.12S 152.33E
56 N3 Hawkedon Suffolk Eng 52.09N 0.37E
12 E4 Hawker S Australia 31.43S 138.25E
12 F3 Hawker Gate New S Wales 29.46S 141.00E
11 L6 Hawke's Bay stat area New Zealand
99 Q7 Hawkesbury Ontario 45.36N 74.38W
13 F1 Hawkesbury I Queensland
13 C1 Hawkesbury Pt N Terr Australia 11.53S 134.05E
12 M5 Hawkesbury R New S Wales
123 F9 Hawkes, Mt Antarctica 84.30S 54.00W
56 N5 Hawkhurst Kent Eng 51.02N 0.30E
113 U7 Hawk Inlet Alaska 58.06N 134.44W
111 L4 Hawkins Pk mt Utah 37.29N 113.56W
105 D5 Hawkinsville Georgia 32.16N 83.29W
99 F4 Hawk Junction Ontario 48.04N 84.34W
100 H1 Hawk Lake Ontario 49.49N 94.00W
107 E3 Hawk Point Missouri 38.58N 91.10W
106 L4 Hawks Michigan 45.18N 83.53W
116 F2 Hawksbill Cay isld Bahamas 24.31N 76.45W
57 G4 Hawkshead Cumbria Eng 54.23N 3.00W
116 G2 Hawks nest Pt Cat I Bahamas 24.10N 75.33W
108 F8 Hawk Springs Wyoming 41.48N 104.15W
13 K7 Hawkwood Queensland 25.46S 150.48E
Hawler see Arbil
109 G4 Hawley Colorado 37.59N 103.44W
108 O3 Hawley Minnesota 46.51N 96.20W
103 D4 Hawley Pennsylvania 41.28N 75.11W
112 H3 Hawley Texas 32.37N 99.50W
103 C2 Hawleyton New York 42.01N 75.56W
25 E2 Hawng Luk Burma 20.33N 99.59E
109 Q8 Haworth Oklahoma 33.52N 94.40W
57 K5 Haworth W Yorks Eng 53.50N 1.57W
105 H2 Haw R N Carolina
33 H9 Hawra S Yemen 15.40N 48.15E
33 G10 Ḥawrā,Al S Yemen 13.52N 47.35E
34 J5 Ḥawrān, Wādī watercourse Iraq
34 C10 Ḥawşal plat Saudi Arabia
33 F5 Ḥawshah, Jibāl al mts Saudi Arabia
95 C10 Hawston S Africa 34.24S 19.08E
33 G9 Ḥawṭah, Al S Yemen 14.25N 47.25E
33 G5 Ḥawṭah, Al oasis Saudi Arabia
105 E8 Hawthorn Florida 29.33N 82.05W
12 D7 Hawthorn dist Melbourne, Vic
111 F3 Hawthorne Nevada 38.31N 118.37W
103 F5 Hawthorne New Jersey 40.57N 74.09W
99 E8 Hawthorne Ontario 45.23N 75.39W
106 C3 Hawthorne Wisconsin 46.31N 91.51W
111 D9 Hawthorne dist Los Angeles, California
11 D6 Hawtrey hill New Zealand 41.17S 174.55E
35 D5 Hawwara Jordan 32.09N 35.15E
35 G7 Hawwara Jordan 31.41N 35.51E
33 E5 Ḥawzah,Jabal mts Saudi Arabia
21 C5 Ḥaxat Jilin China 44.45N 124.30E
22 J4 Haxat Hudag Nei Monggol Zizhiqu China 44.50N 112.45E
108 D2 Haxby Montana 47.47N 106.25W
57 M6 Haxey Humberside Eng 53.29N 0.50W
109 H1 Haxtun Colorado 40.38N 102.37W
12 G5 Hay New S Wales 34.31S 144.31E
56 E3 Hay Powys Wales 52.04N 3.07W
110 H3 Hay Washington 46.41N 117.55W
101 N6 Hay R Alberta/Br Col
19 F5 Haya Moluccas Indon 3.27S 129.31E
92 E2 Haya tribe Tanzania
20 P2 Hayachine-san mt Japan 39.33N 141.30E
20 L2 Hayakita Japan 42.45N 141.50E
69 L5 Hayange France 49.20N 6.04E
87 L8 Hayarab Hills Somalia
20 B4 Hayashi Kanagawa Japan
20 B1 Hayashi Saitama Japan
20 E8 Hayasui-seto channel Japan
36 J2 Hayati Turkey 40.41N 36.46E
109 D1 Haybro Colorado 40.20N 106.58W
57 N4 Hayburn Wyke N Yorks Eng 54.21N 0.27W
13 A2 Hay, C N Terr Australia 14.00S 129.32E
113 G4 Haycock Alaska 65.11N 161.19W
33 E4 Ḥayd, Al Saudi Arabia 24.56N 43.39E
32 A2 Ḥaydarābād Iran 37.09N 45.27E
37 F2 Haydariye Turkey 40.31N 29.07E
37 K3 Haydarpaşa Turkey 41.00N 29.04E
111 O8 Hayden Arizona 33.01N 110.48W
109 C1 Hayden Colorado 40.31N 107.17W
110 J2 Hayden L Idaho 47.45N 116.45W
103 J2 Haydenville Massachusetts 42.23N 72.42W
13 F4 Haydon Queensland 17.55S 141.27E
57 J3 Haydon Bridge Northumb Eng 54.58N 2.14W
70 G3 Haye-du-Puits, la France 49.17N 1.33W
70 N3 Haye, la France 49.28N 1.23E
70 H4 Haye-Pesnel, la France 48.47N 1.23W
55 H5 Hayes Bromley, London Eng 51.23N 0.01E
55 B3 Hayes Hillingdon, London Eng 51.31N 0.25W
107 D11 Hayes Louisiana 30.05N 92.58W
108 J5 Hayes S Dakota 44.23N 101.01W
97 K6 Hayes R Manitoba
48 R3 Hayes reg Greenland
70 M4 Haye-St.Sylvestre, la France 48.54N 0.36E
108 J9 Hayes Center Nebraska 40.30N 101.02W
113 L6 Hayes Glaciers Alaska
25 D7 Hayes I Burma
113 O5 Hayes, Mt Alaska 63.39N 146.45W
100 V4 Hayes R Manitoba
105 D2 Hayesville N Carolina 35.03N 83.49W
23 C9 Ha Yeung Hong Kong 22.18N 114.17E
57 K6 Hayfield Derbys Eng 53.23N 1.57W
108 S6 Hayfield Minnesota 43.54N 92.50W
111 J8 Hayfield Res California 33.42N 115.36W
110 B9 Hayfork California 40.34N 123.13W
57 J4 Haygarth Cumbria Eng 54.22N 2.27W
64 G7 Hayingen W Germany 48.17N 9.30E
86 F6 Hayîra, Wâdî watercourse Egypt
37 D2 Hayırsız isld Turkey 40.39N 27.30E
33 F8 Hayjān Yemen 16.46N 44.10E
101 O6 Hay L Alberta 58.50N 118.41W
33 M4 Hayl Oman 24.12N 56.10E
100 D5 Hay Lakes Alberta 53.12N 113.02W
56 T9 Hayle Cornwall Eng 50.10N 5.25W
68 F4 Haÿ-les-Roses, l' France 48.47N 2.21E
56 K6 Hayling, I Hants Eng 50.48N 0.59W
105 E7 Haylow Georgia 30.49N 82.56W
36 F3 Haymana Turkey 39.26N 32.30E
13 J5 Hayman I Queensland 20.04S 148.52E
104 H8 Haymarket Virginia 38.48N 77.40W
122 L11 Haymet Rocks Pacific Oc 27.11S 160.00W
13 C6 Hay, Mt N Terr Australia 23.29S 133.01E
108 H4 Haynes N Dakota 45.59N 102.28W
103 C2 Haynes New York 42.28N 75.34W
107 C9 Haynesville Louisiana 32.57N 93.09W
104 R8 Haynesville Maine 45.51N 67.58W
107 K9 Hayneville Alabama 32.11N 86.35W
33 H9 Haynin S Yemen 15.48N 48.13E
35 D3 HaYogev Israel 32.37N 35.12E
70 N2 Hayons, les France 49.41N 1.23E
13 J5 Hay Point Queensland 21.18S 149.12E
13 D6 Hay R N Terr Australia
106 C4 Hay, R Wisconsin
37 D1 Hayrabolu Turkey 41.14N 27.04E
37 D1 Hayrabolu R Turkey
101 Q5 Hay River N W Terr 60.51N 115.42W
100 F8 Hays Alberta 50.06N 111.49W
109 L3 Hays Kansas 38.53N 99.20W
110 R2 Hays Montana 48.00N 108.40W
33 E10 Ḥays Yemen 13.57N 43.30E
108 H7 Hay Springs Nebraska 42.41N 102.42W
48 V7 Haystack pt Greenland 75.40N 19.25W
110 K8 Haystack Mt Nevada 41.40N 115.38W
111 L2 Haystack Pk mt Utah 39.50N 113.55W
100 G6 Hayter Alberta 52.24N 110.08W
107 G5 Hayti Missouri 36.14N 89.47W
108 N5 Hayti S Dakota 44.40N 97.22W
57 M5 Hayton Humberside Eng 53.54N 0.47W
56 D6 Haytor Vale Devon Eng 50.35N 3.44W
28 L1 Hayuliang Assam India 28.06N 96.30E
111 B4 Hayward California 37.40N 122.07W
108 R6 Hayward Minnesota 43.40N 93.14W
109 N5 Hayward Oklahoma 36.15N 97.32W
106 C3 Hayward Wisconsin 46.02N 91.26W
13 B2 Hayward, Mt N Terr Australia 13.40S 130.37E
56 L5 Haywards Heath W Sussex Eng 51.00N 0.06W
100 T9 Haywood Manitoba 49.40N 98.12W
33 N6 Ḥayy Oman 20.45N 58.15E
34 O6 Ḥayy, Al Iraq 32.11N 46.03E
34 K10 Ḥayyānīyah Saudi Arabia 28.42N 42.16E
33 B8 Ḥayyan, Ra's C Bahrain, The Gulf 26.03N 50.39E
Hazak see İdil
37 E7 Hazar Turkey 38.26N 39.32E
43 K8 Hazara Afghanistan 36.59N 70.10E
31 G3 Hazara dist Pakistan
31 C4 Hazarajat reg Afghanistan
32 G6 Hazārān, Kūh-e mt Iran 29.32N 57.22E
104 B9 Hazard Kentucky 37.14N 83.11W
103 J3 Hazardville Connecticut 41.59N 72.32W
37 E7 Hazar Gölü L Turkey 38.16N
29 J6 Hazaribagh Bihar India 24.00N 85.23E
29 J5 Hazaribagh dist Bihar India
29 H6 Hazaribagh Ra Bihar/Madhya Prad India
32 H2 Hazār Masjed, Kūh-e mts Iran
Hazar Masjid, Kuh-i- see Hazār Masjed, Kūh-e- mts
34 F8 Ḥazawzā salt marsh Saudi Arabia
69 D2 Hazebrouck France 50.43N 2.32E
107 H5 Hazel Kentucky 36.31N 88.20W
108 O1 Hazel Minnesota 48.01N 96.06W
108 N5 Hazel S Dakota 44.47N 97.22W
105 E6 Hazelhurst Georgia 31.53N 82.34W
107 F10 Hazelhurst Mississippi 31.52N 90.25W
106 M1 Hazel Park dist Detroit, Michigan
100 E1 Hazelridge Manitoba 49.57N 96.44W
101 K8 Hazelton Br Col 55.15N 127.38W
109 M4 Hazelton Kansas 37.06N 98.24W
108 K3 Hazelton N Dakota 46.30N 100.15W
107 E7 Hazen Arkansas 34.45N 91.35W
108 J2 Hazen N Dakota 47.19N 101.38W
111 E2 Hazen Nevada 39.34N 119.01W
113 E6 Hazen B Alaska
97 N1 Hazen, L N W Terr 81.50N 70.00W
100 K9 Hazenmore Saskatchewan 49.42N 107.11W
97 H2 Hazen Str N W Terr
35 B9 Ḥazerim Israel 31.14N 34.43E
60 G11 Hazerswoude Netherlands 52.06N 4.35E
60 G11 Hazerswoude-Rijndijk Zuid Holland Netherlands 52.08N 4.35E
35 D10 Ḥazeva Israel 30.49N 35.15E
35 D10 Ḥazeva anc site Israel 30.48N 35.15E
105 E2 Hazewood N Carolina 35.28N 83.00W
31 D2 Hazhdanahr reg Afghanistan
86 M7 Hazim, El reg Egypt
103 C5 Hazleton Pennsylvania 40.58N 75.59W
14 G5 Hazlett, L W Australia
64 N3 Hazlov Czechoslovakia 50.10N 12.17E
33 M5 Ḥazm Oman 23.32N 57.20E
33 B2 Ḥazm, Al Saudi Arabia 28.42N 36.17E
34 H8 Ḥazm al Badarīyāt plat Saudi Arabia
Ḥazo see Kozluk
35 F2 Ḥazor Israel 32.59N 35.33E
35 B6 Ḥazor Ashdod Israel 31.46N 34.44E
35 D3 HaZorea Israel 32.39N 35.06E
35 E3 HaZore'im Israel 32.45N 35.30E
30 J7 Hazrat Jandaha Bihar India 25.44N 85.31E
31 D2 Hazrat Sultan Afghanistan 36.29N 67.54E
31 G4 Hazro Pakistan 33.55N 72.33E
37 F7 Hazro Turkey 38.15N 40.44E
94 E6 Hazuur Namibia 26.40S 19.52E
35 F2 Hazzan Syria 32.56N 35.45E
56 N2 Heacham Norfolk Eng 52.55N 0.30E

56 N5 Headcorn Kent Eng 51.11N 0.37E
59 D5 Headford Galway Irish Rep 53.28N 9.06W
98 E9 Head Harbour I Maine 44.31N 67.32W
13 E5 Headingly Queensland 21.19S 138.17E
107 L10 Headland Alabama 31.21N 85.21W
92 F11 Headlands Zimbabwe 18.14S 32.03E
11 C11 Headlong Pk *mt* New Zealand 44.33S 168.39E
12 B4 Head of Bight *B* S Australia
110 K3 Headquarters Idaho 46.38N 115.48W
26 V3 Headridge Hill Christmas I Indian Oc 10.26S 105.44E
110 A7 Heads, The Oregon 42.45N 124.30W
106 E4 Heafford Junc Wisconsin 45.32N 89.43W
57 L5 Healaugh W Yorks Eng 53.55N 1.14W
111 B3 Healdsburg California 38.36N 122.53W
109 N7 Healdton Oklahoma 34.14N 97.31W
95 K8 Healdtown S Africa 32.44S 26.43E
12 H7 Healesville Victoria 37.40S 145.31E
113 N5 Healy Alaska 63.50N 149.01W
109 K3 Healy Kansas 38.35N 100.38W
113 P5 Healy L Alaska 63.59N 144.40W
113 P4 Healy, R Alaska
100 Q3 Heaman Manitoba 55.55N 101.19W
57 L6 Heanor Derbys Eng 53.01N 1.22W
92 D12 Heany Junction Zimbabwe 20.06S 28.54E
11 G7 Heaphy R New Zealand
26 G10 Heard I Antarctica 53.07S 73.20E
100 M8 Hearne Saskatchewan 50.05N 105.10W
112 L5 Hearne Texas 30.54N 96.36W
101 Q1 Hearne, C N W Terr 68.13N 114.33W
101 R4 Hearne L N W Terr
111 A2 Hearst California 39.31N 123.12W
99 G3 Hearst Ontario 49.42N 83.40W
123 E13 Hearst I Antarctica 69.30S 62.20W
108 H3 Heart *R* N Dakota
100 F4 Heart L Alberta
110 P5 Heart L Wyoming 44.16N 110.30W
100 A3 Heart R Alberta
98 T6 Heart's Content Newfoundland 47.52N 53.21W
98 T6 Heart's Delight Newfoundland 47.47N 53.29W
57 L6 Heath Derbys Eng 53.12N 1.19W
12 K9 Heathcote New S Wales 34.06S 151.01E
12 G6 Heathcote Victoria 36.54S 144.42E
11 M10 Heathcote R Christchurch New Zealand
11 N10 Heathcote Valley New Zealand 43.35S 172.42E
98 O5 Heatherton Newfoundland 48.19N 58.43W
94 P12 Heathfield Cape Town S Africa 34.02S 18.28E
98 L4 Heath Pt Anticosti I, Que 49.05N 61.44W
120 E5 Heath, R Peru/Bolivia
55 B4 Heathrow (London) Airport London Eng 51.28N 0.27W
105 G3 Heath Springs S Carolina 34.35N 80.42W
98 F6 Heath Steel Mines New Brunswick 47.19N 66.07W
104 J9 Heathsville Virginia 37.55N 76.29W
95 J1 Heathview S Africa 25.57S 25.24E
95 O10 Heatonville S Africa 28.40S 31.48E
109 Q7 Heavener Oklahoma 34.54N 94.35W
112 J8 Hebbronville Texas 27.19N 98.41W
57 K5 Hebden Bridge W Yorks Eng 53.45N 2.00W
23 C8 Hebe Haven Hong Kong
22 K7 Hebei *prov* China
13 J8 Hebel Queensland 28.55S 147.49E
111 O7 Heber Arizona 34.28N 110.36W
110 O9 Heber Utah 40.31N 111.25W
63 L6 Heber W Germany 53.06N 9.52E
107 D6 Heber Springs Arkansas 35.30N 92.01W
26 N13 Hébert, Cratère Amsterdam I Ind Oc 37.51S 77.32E
99 P3 Hébert, L Quebec
99 T4 Hébertville Station Quebec 48.25N 71.44W
110 O5 Hebgen L Montana 44.45N 111.15W
23 G1 Hebi Henan China 35.57N 114.08E
110 B4 Hebo Oregon 45.15N 123.51W
49 C5 Hebrides *islds* Scotland
58 C4 Hebrides, Sea of the Scotland
109 D1 Hebron Colorado 40.36N 106.25W
103 K3 Hebron Connecticut 41.39N 72.22W
106 F7 Hebron Illinois 42.27N 88.29W
106 G8 Hebron Indiana 41.18N 87.14W
35 D7 Hebron Jordan 31.32N 35.06E
97 N6 Hebron Labrador, Nfld 58.05N 62.30W
108 H3 Hebron N Dakota 46.55N 102.02W
108 N9 Hebron Nebraska 40.10N 97.35W
98 F10 Hebron Nova Scotia 43.57N 66.03W
104 C7 Hebron Ohio 39.58N 82.31W
103 M3 Hebronville Massachusetts 41.54N 71.18W
52 K7 Heby Sweden 59.56N 16.53E
101 H9 Hecate Str Br Col
115 O7 Hecelchakán Mexico 20.10N 90.09W
110 A5 Heceta Hd Oregon 44.10N 124.08W
113 V9 Heceta I Alaska 55.46N 133.40W
72 E9 Hèches France 43.01N 0.22E
23 E6 Hechi Guangxi China 24.39N 108.02E
64 F7 Hechingen W Germany 48.21N 8.58E
75 J2 Hecho Spain 42.45N 0.45W
61 M2 Hechtel Belgium 51.07N 5.22E
63 K5 Hechthausen W Germany 53.38N 9.15E
23 D3 Hechuan Sichuan China 30.02N 106.15E
63 T7 Heckelberg E Germany 52.44N 13.51E
56 K5 Heckfield Hants Eng 51.21N 0.58W
57 N7 Heckington Lincs Eng 52.59N 0.18W
63 P9 Hecklingen E Germany 51.52N 11.32E
57 K5 Heckmondwike W Yorks England 53.43N 1.45W
103 H5 Heckscher State Park Long I, N Y
100 V7 Hecla Manitoba 51.09N 96.40W
108 M4 Hecla S Dakota 45.53N 98.09W
58 B4 Hecla *mt* S Uist, W Isles Scotland 57.17N 7.16W
97 H2 Hecla & Griper B N W Terr
100 V7 Hecla I Manitoba
100 V7 Hecla Prov. Park Manitoba
98 F9 Hectanooga Nova Scotia 44.04N 66.02W
111 H7 Hector California 34.47N 116.28W
108 Q5 Hector Minnesota 44.46N 94.43W
11 F8 Hector New Zealand 41.35S 171.55E
11 K7 Hector *mt* New Zealand 40.57S 175.18E
101 P10 Hector, Mt Alberta 51.35N 116.18W
94 L5 Hectorspruit S Africa 25.27S 31.41E
116 M2 Hector's River Jamaica, W I 18.00N 76.17W
52 J7 Hed Sweden 59.42N 15.46E
35 C9 Hed *watercourse* Israel
20 M7 Heda Japan 34.58N 138.46E
52 E6 Hedal Norway 60.37N 9.41E
26 U8 Heda Oya *R* Sri Lanka
93 J10 Hedaru Tanzania 4.30S 37.51E
69 D3 Hédauville France 50.03N 2.35E
51 G6 Hedberg Sweden 65.26N 18.50E
52 E7 Heddal Norway 59.36N 9.09E
64 F4 Heddesheim W Germany 49.31N 8.38E
57 K3 Heddon on the Wall Tyne and Wear Eng 55.00N 1.46W
Hede *see* Sheyang
70 G5 Hédé France 48.17N 1.48W
52 H4 Hede Sweden 62.27N 13.30E
53 J5 Hedehusene Denmark 55.39N 12.12E
60 K13 Hedel Netherlands 51.45N 5.15E
52 J6 Hedemora Sweden 60.13N 16.00E
63 L10 Hedemünden W Germany 51.23N 9.46E
53 E6 Heden Denmark 55.15N 10.23E
51 K5 Hedenäset Sweden 66.12N 23.40E
53 D5 Hedensted Denmark 55.47N 9.43E
63 O9 Hedersleben E Germany 51.52N 11.15E
52 K6 Hedesunda Sweden 60.25N 17.00E
51 F11 Hedesundafjärdarna *L* Sweden 60.20N 17.00E
52 K6 Hedesundafjord *inlet* Sweden
52 H4 Hedeviken Sweden 62.25N 13.45E
11 C13 Hedgehope New Zealand 46.12S 168.32E
110 Q3 Hedgesville Montana 46.28N 109.30W
104 G7 Hedgesville W Virginia 39.33N 78.01W
50 G2 Hédhinsfjördhur *B* Iceland
23 C7 Hedi He *R* Yunnan China
115 J5 Hedionda Grande Mexico 25.09N 100.51W
23 E8 Hedi Sk *res* Guangdong China
33 C10 Hedjuff, Ra's *C* S Yemen 12.48N 45.00E
101 N11 Hedley Br Columbia 49.21N 120.02W
112 G1 Hedley Texas 34.53N 100.40W
53 W18 Hedlo Norway 60.18N 7.10E
52 F5 Hedmark *co* Norway
52 F6 Hedmark *reg* Norway
20 Q8 Hedo-misaki *C* Okinawa Japan 26.55N 128.15E
57 N5 Hedon Humberside Eng 53.44N 0.12W
20 Q8 Hedo-zaki Okinawa Japan 26.54N 128.15E
106 B8 Hedrick Iowa 41.10N 92.19W
53 A4 Hee Denmark 56.09N 8.18E
63 F7 Heede W Germany 53.00N 7.18E
60 L8 Heeg Netherlands 52.58N 5.36E
60 L8 Heegermeer *L* Netherlands
63 T7 Heegermühle E Germany 52.50N 13.45E
63 F8 Heek W Germany 52.07N 7.04E
60 T16 Heel Netherlands 51.11N 5.54E
9 B6 Heel Pt Wake I Pacific Oc 19.19N 166.37E
60 G9 Heemskerk Netherlands 52.31N 4.40E
60 G10 Heemstede Netherlands 52.21N 4.37E
60 F13 Heen, De Netherlands 51.37N 4.16E
63 J8 Heepen W Germany 52.03N 8.36E
61 K6 Heer Belgium 50.10N 4.50E
60 S17 Heer Netherlands 50.50N 5.44E
66 P2 Heerbrugg Switzerland 47.25N 9.37E
60 N10 Heerde Netherlands 52.23N 6.02E
60 M8 Heerenveen Netherlands 52.57N 5.55E
60 K12 Heerewaarden Netherlands 51.49N 5.23E
60 H9 Heerhugowaard Netherlands 52.40N 4.50E
50 T15 Heer Land Spitsbergen
60 T17 Heerlen Netherlands 50.53N 5.59E
60 T17 Heerlerheide Netherlands 50.55N 5.57E
61 M3 Heers Belgium 50.45N 5.18E
61 N3 Hees Belgium 50.51N 5.37E
60 J13 Heesbeen Netherlands 51.43N 5.07E
60 L13 Heesch Netherlands 51.44N 5.32E
61 D3 Heestert Belgium 50.47N 3.25E
60 K13 Heeswijk Netherlands 51.39N 5.29E
60 L14 Heeze Netherlands 51.23N 5.35E
23 H3 Hefei Anhui China 31.55N 117.18E
23 E4 Hefeng Hubei China 29.55N 109.52E
61 H2 Heffen Belgium 51.03N 4.25E
61 P7 Heffingen Luxembourg 49.46N 6.14E
101 N10 Heffley Br Col 50.46N 120.17W
107 L8 Heflin Alabama 33.38N 85.36W
21 E4 Hegang Heilongjiang China 47.36N 130.30E
64 F8 Hegau *dist* W Germany
53 W21 Hegestøl Norway 58.57N 7.29E
53 X16 Hegg Norway 61.04N 7.55E
28 C4 Heggadadevankote Karnataka India 12.05N 76.18E
53 T16 Heggheim Norway 61.14N 5.40E
50 D4 Heggstadhanes *C* Iceland 65.27N 21.14W
15 G7 Hegigio *R* Papua New Guinea
103 B5 Hegins Pennsylvania 40.40N 76.29W
66 N1 Hegne W Germany 47.43N 9.06E
50 F3 Hegranes *pen* Iceland 65.43N 19.30W
20 K4 Hegura-jima *isld* Japan 37.52N 136.56E
35 D10 HeHalaq, Har *escarp* Israel
92 G6 Hehe *tribe* Tanzania
25 D2 Heho Burma 20.48N 96.50E
87 C5 Heiban Sudan 11.11N 30.35E
22 J7 Heicha Shan *mt* Shanxi China 38.15N 111.14E
52 E5 Heidal Norway 61.45N 9.20E
35 F8 Heidan *R* Jordan
94 D4 Heide Namibia 23.31S 17.22E
63 K4 Heide W Germany 54.12N 9.06E
64 L5 Heideck W Germany 49.08N 11.09E
107 N4 Heidelberg Kentucky 37.32N 83.50W
107 H10 Heidelberg Mississippi 31.53N 89.00W
95 D10 Heidelberg S Africa 34.05S 20.57E
95 M2 Heidelberg S Africa 26.31S 28.21E
64 F5 Heidelberg W Germany 49.25N 8.42E
12 D7 Heidelberg *dist* Melbourne, Vic
64 F5 Heidelsheim W Germany 49.06N 8.38E
66 P2 Heiden Switzerland 47.27N 9.32E
64 M4 Heide Naab *R* W Germany
64 J6 Heidenheim Baden-Württemberg W Germany 48.41N 10.10E
64 K5 Heidenheim Bayern W Germany 49.01N 10.46E
65 M4 Heidenreichstein Austria 48.53N 15.08E
64 D3 Heidenrod W Germany 50.08N 7.58E
69 O3 Heidenrod W Germany 50.10N 7.57E
61 O7 Heidersheid Luxembourg 49.53N 5.59E
94 Q11 Heideveld Cape Town S Africa 33.58S 18.33E
50 K2 Heidharhöfn Iceland 66.17N 15.02W
50 D6 Heidharhorn *mt* Iceland 64.29N 21.45W
66 P5 Heid See *L* Switzerland 46.45N 9.33E
60 J12 Hei-en-Boeicop Netherlands 51.57N 5.05E
20 P2 Hei-gawa *R* Japan
57 K3 Heighington Durham Eng 54.36N 1.37W
106 K5 Heights, The Michigan 44.21N 84.47W
20 F8 Heigun-tō *isld* Japan
Heihe *see* Aihui
22 E7 Hei He *R* Gansu China
114 D8 Heiheiahula *mt* Hawaiian Is 19.25N 154.59W
Hei-Ho *R see* Salween
60 M13 Heijen Netherlands 51.41N 5.59E
60 M14 Heijthuizen Netherlands 51.15N 5.54E
60 J13 Heikant Noord-Brabant Netherlands 51.36N 5.05E
60 C3 Heikant Zeeland Netherlands 51.15N 4.00E
Heike *see* St.Willebrord
53 E8 Heikendorf W Germany 54.22N 10.12E
61 G4 Heikruis Belgium 50.44N 4.07E
95 M3 Heilbron S Africa 27.17S 27.58E
64 G5 Heilbronn W Germany 49.08N 9.14E
58 K1 Heilen, L Highland Scotland 58.35N 3.17W
64 G8 Heiligenberg W Germany 47.51N 9.19E
65 G7 Heiligenblut Austria 47.03N 12.51E
63 P4 Heiligendamm E Germany 54.09N 11.51E
63 N4 Heiligenhafen W Germany 54.22N 11.00E
63 E10 Heiligenhaus W Germany 51.20N 6.49E
65 O7 Heiligenkreuz Austria 47.00N 16.16E
63 M10 Heiligenstadt E Germany 51.23N 10.09E
64 L4 Heiligenstadt W Germany 49.52N 11.11E
60 R7 Heiligerlee Netherlands 53.09N 7.00E
23 H1 Heilin Jiangsu China 35.02N 118.53E
23 A9 Hei Ling Chau *isld* Hong Kong
60 A3 Heille Netherlands 51.16N 3.23E
Heilong Jiang *see* Amur R
21 C4 Heilongjiang *prov* China
21 F4 Heilong Jiang *R* Heilongjiang China
60 G9 Heiloo Netherlands 52.36N 4.43E
48 T2 Heilprin Land Greenland
64 K5 Heilsbronn W Germany 49.21N 10.50E
69 H6 Heiltz-le-Maurupt France 48.48N 4.49E
Heilungkiang *prov* China*see* Heilongjiang
Heil, Wadi el *see* Hail, Wādī *water course*
50 E8 Heimaey *isld* Iceland 63.25N 20.17W
22 E8 Heimahe Qinghai China 36.40N 100.00E
64 A2 Heimbach W Germany 50.38N 6.29E
66 G4 Heimberg Switzerland 46.48N 7.37E
64 G4 Heimbuchenthal W Germany 49.52N 9.17E
63 N9 Heimburg E Germany 51.50N 10.56E
108 L2 Heimdal N Dakota 47.49N 99.38W
54 M3 Heimdal *oil field* North Sea 59.38N 2.06E
123 C10 Heime frontfjella *ra* Antarctica
66 Q1 Heimenkirch W Germany 47.37N 9.55E
69 M2 Heimersheim W Germany 50.43N 6.55E
66 G3 Heimiswil Switzerland 47.03N 7.40E
53 T15 Heimseta Norway 61.41N 5.50E
64 F6 Heimsheim W Germany 48.48N 8.52E
66 Q4 Heim Spitze *mt* Austria 46.58N 9.57E
50 K6 Heinabergsjökull *ice cap* Iceland 64.18N 15.50W
15 H4 Heina Is Bismarck Arch 1.09S 144.24E
51 O9 Heinävesi Finland 62.26N 28.40E
61 H2 Heindonk Belgium 51.04N 4.24E
64 H1 Heinebach W Germany 51.03N 9.42E
113 N4 Heine Creek Alaska 65.35N 148.30W
60 F12 Heinenoord Netherlands 51.50N 4.29E
61 P6 Heinerscheid Luxembourg 50.06N 6.05E
64 L3 Heinersdorf E Germany 50.22N 11.16E
60 C3 Heinkenszand Netherlands 51.28N 3.49E
60 N10 Heino Netherlands 52.26N 6.14E
51 M10 Heinola Finland 61.13N 26.05E
63 P8 Heinrichsburg E Germany 52.17N 11.45E
64 A1 Heinsberg W Germany 51.04N 6.06E
100 G5 Heinsburg Alberta 53.47N 110.30W
61 O8 Heinsch Belgium 49.42N 5.45E
63 S9 Heinsdorf E Germany 51.56N 13.20E
25 D5 Heinz B Burma
25 D5 Heinze Is Burma
88 N8 Heïrane, Djebel *mt* Algeria 27.55N 0.46W
25 L8 Heirnkut Burma 25.15N 94.47E
87 L5 Heis Somalia 10.52N 46.50E
21 B7 Heishan Liaoning China 41.41N 122.04E
22 K5 Heishanton Nei Monggol Zizhiqu China 43.22N 116.57E
21 A2 Heishantou Nei Monggol Zizhiqu China 50.10N 119.29E
23 C2 Heishui Sichuan China 31.57N 103.19E
23 E4 Heishui Sichuan China 29.02N 108.48E
22 H8 Heishuisi Shaanxi China 36.03N 108.55E
100 E6 Heisler Alberta 52.40N 112.13W
103 E8 Heislerville New Jersey 39.13N 75.00W
61 J2 Heist-op-den-Berg Belgium 51.05N 4.44E
35 G2 Heit Syria 32.45N 35.54E
35 G2 Heital Syria 32.48N 35.46E
86 K5 Heiţân, Gebel *hill* Egypt 30.02N 33.08E
66 F4 Heitenried Switzerland 46.50N 7.18E
66 K2 Heitersberg *mt* Switzerland 47.23N 8.22E
66 K2 Heitersberg Tunnel Switzerland
64 D8 Heitersheim W Germany 47.53N 7.41E
65 C7 Heiterwand *mt* Austria 47.18N 10.44E
65 C7 Heiterwang Austria 47.28N 10.45E
57 J1 Heiton Borders Scotland 55.34N 2.27W
21 C5 Heiyupao Jilin China 45.51N 123.12E
85 K5 Heiz, El Egypt 28.02N 28.36E
Hejāz *prov see* Hijāz
22 H7 Hejialiang Shaanxi China 38.26N 109.55E
22 K7 Hejian Hebei China 38.27N 116.02E
23 E8 Hejiang Guangdong China 21.55N 110.33E
23 D4 Hejiang Sichuan China 28.46N 105.47E
23 F6 He Jiang *R* Guangxi China
23 F6 Hejie Guangxi China 24.23N 111.30E
23 E1 Hejin Shanxi China 35.32N 110.41E
24 E4 Hejing Xinjiang Uygur Zizhiqu China 42.15N 86.22E
53 D6 Hejls Denmark 55.23N 9.36E
53 D6 Hejlsminde Denmark 55.22N 9.37E
53 B5 Hejnsvig Denmark 55.42N 9.00E
53 D6 Hejsager Denmark 55.13N 9.37E
61 G3 Hekelgem Belgium 50.54N 4.06E
11 M6 Hekerangi Pt New Zealand
114 D6 Hekili Pt Hawaiian Is 20.47N 156.37W
37 D7 Hekımhan Turkey 38.50N 37.56E
50 F7 Hekla *mt* Iceland 64.00N 19.41W
Hekou *see* Yanshan
22 F8 Hekou Gansu China 36.10N 103.24E
23 F7 Hekou Guangdong China 23.11N 112.52E
22 J6 Hekou Nei Monggol Zizhiqu China 40.15N 111.13E
23 C7 Hekou Yunnan China 22.30N 103.54E
95 L1 Hekpoort S Africa 25.55S 27.38E
61 M3 Heks Belgium 50.46N 5.22E
62 L1 Hel Poland 54.36N 18.48E
44 J10 Helābād Iran 37.57N 48.24E
52 G4 Helagsfjället *mt* Sweden 62.58N 12.25E
28 J2 Helam Assam India 27.50N 93.20E
22 G7 Helan Ningxia China 38.36N 106.23E
22 G7 Helan Shan *mt ra* Ningxia China
64 K1 Helbe *R* E Germany
53 E3 Helberskov Denmark 56.44N 10.18E
63 P9 Helbra E Germany 51.34N 11.30E
61 M2 Helchteren Belgium 51.03N 5.23E
64 K3 Heldburg E Germany 50.17N 10.47E
60 N14 Helden Netherlands 51.20N 6.00E
64 F3 Heldenbergen W Germany 50.14N 8.51E
116 P3 Helden's Pt St Kitts W I 17.25N 62.51W
61 F3 Heldergem Belgium 50.53N 3.57E
64 L1 Heldrungen E Germany 51.18N 11.13E
77 F3 Helechal Spain 38.40N 5.23W
76 K10 Helechosa Spain 39.19N 4.54W
28 J2 Helem Assam India 26.52N 93.30E
105 D3 Helen Georgia 34.43N 83.44W
107 K8 Helena Alabama 33.18N 86.52W
107 F7 Helena Arkansas 34.30N 90.35W
110 B9 Helena California 40.48N 123.09W
105 E5 Helena Georgia 32.02N 82.58W
117 A1 Helena Guyana 6.40N 57.55W
110 N3 Helena Montana 46.35N 112.00W
99 S2 Helena New York 44.56N 74.43W
109 M5 Helena Oklahoma 36.34N 98.16W
60 M14 Helenaveen Netherlands 51.23N 5.55E
111 G7 Helendale California 34.45N 117.19W
100 J5 Hélène L Saskatchewan 53.33N 108.12W
123 D3 Helen Glacier Antarctica 66.38S 94.40E
14 E6 Helen Hill W Australia 22.49S 123.38E
15 A2 Helen I Caroline Is Pacific Oc 2.56N 131.45E
99 B3 Helen L Ontario 49.05N 88.16W
111 H4 Helen, Mt Nevada 37.30N 116.45W
13 F5 Helen, Mt Queensland 21.35S 141.08E
17 M11 Helen Reef Caroline Is Pacific Oc 2.43N 131.46E
58 G6 Helensburgh Strathclyde Scotland 56.01N 4.44W
25 N3 Helen Shoal S China Sea
13 C4 Helen Springs N Terr Australia 18.24S 133.55E
11 J3 Helensville New Zealand 36.40S 174.28E
Helets *oil well see* Helez
35 B7 Helez *oil well* Israel 31.36N 34.39E
88 Q6 Hel Fedj Algeria 31.57N 5.56E
65 K4 Helfenberg Austria 48.33N 14.09E
56 T9 Helford R Cornwall Eng
63 P9 Helfta E Germany 51.30N 11.35E
50 C4 Helgafell Iceland 65.02N 22.44W
50 E8 Helgafell *mt* Iceland 63.26N 20.15W
50 E4 Helgavatn Iceland 65.27N 20.20W
50 F6 Helgavatn *L* Iceland 64.22N 19.30W
51 C6 Helgeland *reg* Norway
52 E7 Helgen Norway 59.15N 9.22E
53 F4 Helgenæs *C* Denmark 56.08N 10.31E
53 U15 Helgheim Norway 61.33N 6.25E
62 D1 Helgoland *isld* W Germany 54.09N 7.52E
63 H4 Helgoländer Bucht *B* W Germany
51 G1 Helgøy Norway 70.08N 19.25E
52 K3 Helgum Sweden 63.12N 16.55E
21 E4 Heli Heilongjiang China 47.15N 130.16E
53 Z16 Helin *L* Norway 61.03N 8.37E
86 R11 Heliopolis Cairo Egypt
22 E7 Heli Shan *mts* Gansu China
50 K3 Heljardalsfjö'll *mt* Iceland 65.52N 15.45W
50 G3 Heljarfjall *mt* Iceland 65.49N 18.51W
61 D4 Helkijn Belgium 50.44N 3.23E
52 F3 Hell Norway 63.25N 10.54E
50 E7 Hella Iceland 63.50N 20.25W
53 V16 Hella Norway 61.12N 6.37E
50 G2 Hella *C* Iceland 66.12N 18.51W
53 V19 Hellandsbygd Norway 59.41N 6.31E
63 O7 Hellberg *mt* E Germany 52.35N 11.18E
26 U15 Hell-Bourg Réunion Ind Oc 21.03S 55.32E
53 X20 Helle Aust Agder Norway 59.03N 7.35E
53 K4 Hellebæk Denmark 56.04N 12.34E
61 F4 Hellebecq Belgium 50.40N 3.53E
32 D6 Helleh *R* Iran
51 F4 Hellemobotn Norway 67.50N 16.34E
60 O10 Hellendoorn Netherlands 52.23N 6.27E
64 A3 Hellenthal W Germany 50.29N 6.26E
53 K5 Hellerup Denmark 55.44N 12.36E
37 B3 Helles *C* Turkey 40.02N 26.12E
53 J6 Hellested Denmark 55.20N 12.16E
53 S16 Hellestrand Sogn og Fjordane Norway 61.20N 5.07E
53 V14 Hellesylt Norway 62.05N 6.52E
53 E2 Hellevad Nordjylland Denmark 57.13N 10.11E
53 C6 Hellevad Sønderjylland Denmark 55.05N 9.13E
53 W19 Hellevassbu Norway 59.59N 7.14E
53 S16 Hellevik Norway 61.18N 5.10E
60 E12 Hellevoetsluis Netherlands 51.49N 4.08E
57 J4 Hellifield N Yorks Eng 54.01N 2.12W
51 H2 Helligskogen Norway 69.14N 20.40E
51 D4 Helligvær *isld* Norway 67.25N 13.55E
77 N3 Hellín Spain 38.31N 1.43W
58 Q9 Helli Ness *prom* Shetland Scotland 60.02N 1.10W
50 G7 Hellisa *R* Iceland
58 B4 Hellisay *isld* W Isles Scotland 57.01N 7.21W
50 E8 Hellisey *isld* Iceland 63.22N 20.21W
50 D6 Hellisheidhi *heath* Árnessýsla Iceland
50 L3 Hellisheidhi *heath* Múlasýsla, Nordhur Iceland
53 R17 Hellisøy *isld* Norway 60.46N 4.45E
50 B5 Hellissandur Snæfellsnessýsla Iceland 64.55N 23.54W
65 K5 Hellmonsödt Austria 48.27N 14.19E
50 B5 Hellnanes *C* Iceland 64.44N 23.38W
50 B5 Hellnar Iceland 64.45N 23.39W
30 L5 Hellok Nepal 27.31N 87.48E
60 J12 Hellouw Netherlands 51.50N 5.10E
Hell's Canyon *see* Snake River Canyon
116 K2 Hellshire Hills Jamaica, W I
50 F5 Helluhraun *lava field* Iceland
53 E2 Hellum Denmark 57.16N 10.11E
60 Q7 Hellum Netherlands 53.14N 6.51E
95 D2 Hell-Ville Madagascar 13.24S 48.17E
63 F9 Hellweg *reg* W Germany
63 K6 Hellwege W Germany 53.04N 9.13E
111 D5 Helm California 36.31N 120.09W
31 B5 Helmand *prov* Afghanistan
31 B5 Helmand R Afghanistan
63 K9 Helmarshausen W Germany 51.37N 9.26E
64 M3 Helmbrechts W Germany 50.14N 11.43E
63 N10 Helme *R* E Germany
64 J2 Helmershausen E Germany 50.33N 10.17E
60 L14 Helmond Netherlands 51.28N 5.40E
63 J4 Helmsand *isld* W Germany
58 J2 Helmsdale Highland Scotland 58.07N 3.40W
58 J2 Helmsdale, R Highland Scotland
53 U15 Helmseter Norway 61.50N 6.07E
57 L4 Helmsley N Yorks Eng 54.14N 1.04W
64 F5 Helmstadt W Germany 49.19N 8.59E
63 O8 Helmstedt W Germany 52.14N 11.01E
110 N3 Helmville Montana 46.52N 112.56W
53 E6 Helnæs Denmark 55.08N 10.02E
53 E6 Helnæs Bugt *B* Denmark 55.09N 10.04E
51 M1 Helnes, Lt.Ho Norway 71.04N 26.10E
21 C5 Helong Jilin China 44.06N 125.12E
21 D6 Helong Jilin China 42.38N 128.58E
112 J6 Helotes Texas 29.34N 98.43W
111 O2 Helper Utah 39.40N 110.51W
95 O4 Helpmekaar S Africa 28.27S 30.26E
63 T6 Helpter Berge *mt* E Germany 53.29N 13.37E
64 H1 Helsa-Wickenrode W Germany 51.16N 9.41E
57 H6 Helsby Cheshire Eng 53.16N 2.46W
66 J6 Helsenhorn *mt* Italy/Switz 46.18N 8.10E
52 G10 Helsingborg Sweden 56.05N 12.45E
53 J4 Helsinge Denmark 56.02N 12.12E
Helsingfors *see* Helsinki
53 K4 Helsingør Denmark 56.03N 12.38E
51 L11 Helsinki Finland 60.08N 25.00E
53 V14 Helstad Norway 62.15N 6.55E
56 T9 Helston Cornwall Eng 50.05N 5.16W
63 L7 Helstorf W Germany 52.35N 9.36E
53 O9 Heltnin *C* Faeroes 62.14N 7.40W
107 K3 Heltonville Indiana 38.56N 86.22W
121 E3 Helvecia Argentina 31.09S 60.09W
118 H5 Helvécia Brazil 17.48S 39.39W
57 G3 Helvellyn *mt* Cumbria Eng 54.32N 3.02W
95 K5 Helvetia S Africa 29.52S 26.34E
59 G7 Helvick Hd Waterford Irish Rep 52.03N 7.32W
60 J13 Helvoirt Netherlands 51.38N 5.14E
86 F6 Helwân Egypt 29.51N 31.20E
60 J9 Hem Netherlands 52.40N 5.11E
53 D4 Hem Vejle Denmark 56.02N 9.48E
53 B3 Hem Viborg Denmark 56.36N 8.58E
87 M6 Heman Basin Somalia
35 E9 Hemar *watercourse* Israel
100 F7 Hemaruka Alberta 51.48N 111.10W
64 M5 Hemau W Germany 49.03N 11.48E
26 S7 Hembarawa Sri Lanka 7.30N 80.59E
66 N2 Hemberg Switzerland 47.18N 9.11E
63 E9 Hemden W Germany 51.52N 6.36E
35 C5 Hemed Israel 32.01N 34.50E
56 L4 Hemel Hempstead Herts Eng 51.46N 0.28W
60 K8 Hemelum Netherlands 52.53N 5.28E
61 F3 Hemelveerdegem Belgium 50.48N 3.52E
15 M9 Hemenahei I Louisiade Arch 11.12S 153.05E
63 G10 Hemer W Germany 51.24N 7.46E
111 H8 Hemet California 33.45N 116.58W
64 H8 Hemigkofen W Germany 47.36N 9.41E
61 H2 Hemiksem Belgium 51.09N 4.20E
69 M6 Héming France 48.42N 6.58E
108 G7 Hemingford Nebraska 42.20N 103.04W
100 Q4 Heming Lake Manitoba 54.53N 101.10W
105 H4 Hemingway S Carolina 33.44N 79.27W
103 H4 Hemlock Res Connecticut 41.18N 73.17W
13 L1 Hemmant *dist* Brisbane, Qnsld
63 J4 Hemme W Germany 54.17N 8.58E
53 F4 Hemmed Denmark 56.30N 10.45E
63 G7 Hemmelte W Germany 52.46N 7.58E
63 L8 Hemmendorf W Germany 52.05N 9.36E
Hemmerwurth *see* Hemme
53 A5 Hemmet Denmark 55.51N 8.23E
63 L8 Hemmingen W Germany 52.18N 9.45E
99 R7 Hemmingford Quebec 45.03N 73.36W
63 K5 Hemmoor W Germany 53.42N 9.08E
52 F7 Hemnes Norway 59.43N 11.26E
51 D5 Hemnesberget Norway 66.14N 13.40E
112 O4 Hemphill Texas 31.21N 93.50W
56 O2 Hempnall Norfolk Eng 52.30N 1.19E
103 N8 Hempstead New York
112 L5 Hempstead Texas 30.06N 96.06W
103 M6 Hempstead Harb New York
61 J6 Hemptinne Belgium 50.14N 4.34E
61 K4 Hemptinne Belgium 50.36N 4.59E
91 H7 Hemptinne Zaïre 6.19S 22.31E
30 D5 Hempur Uttar Prad India 27.38N 80.34E
56 P2 Hemsby Norfolk Eng 52.42N 1.41E
52 L9 Hemse Sweden 57.14N 18.25E
53 Z17 Hemsedal Norway 60.52N 8.34E
53 Y17 Hemsedalsfjellene *plat* Norway
52 D6 Hemsil *R* Norway
37 F4 Hemşin Turkey 41.02N 40.53E
52 H10 Hemsjö Sweden 56.18N 14.45E
63 L6 Hemslingen W Germany 53.05N 9.37E
52 L4 Hemsö Sweden 62.42N 18.10E
57 L5 Hemsworth W Yorks Eng 53.38N 1.21W
87 J7 Hen Ethiopia 7.48N 43.45E
23 F1 Henan *prov* China
70 F4 Hénanbihen France 48.34N 2.23W
23 B1 Henan Monggolzu Zizhixian Qinghai China 34.40N 101.35E
70 F4 Hénansal France 48.32N 2.27W
75 F5 Henar *R* Spain
75 H8 Henarejos Spain 39.51N 1.29W
75 E5 Henares *R* Spain
20 N1 Henashi-zaki *C* Japan 40.36N 139.52E
66 N2 Henau Switzerland 47.28N 9.08E
13 C6 Henbury N Terr Australia 24.33S 133.14E
75 E6 Henche Spain 40.42N 2.43W
11 J2 Hen & Chicken Is New Zealand
88 S4 Henchir Souatir Tunisia 34.38N 8.24E
93 F9 Hendawashi Tanzania 3.57S 34.17E
72 A9 Hendaye France 43.22N 1.46W
69 D3 Hendecourt-lès-Cagnicourt France 50.12N 2.58E
36 E2 Hendek Turkey 40.47N 30.45E
121 E6 Henderson Argentina 36.18S 61.43W
103 C8 Henderson Maryland 39.04N 75.46W
105 J1 Henderson N Carolina 36.20N 78.26W
111 K5 Henderson Nevada 36.01N 115.00W
104 J3 Henderson New York 43.50N 76.08W
107 H6 Henderson Tennessee 35.27N 88.40W
112 N3 Henderson Texas 32.11N 94.48W
104 C8 Henderson W Virginia 38.50N 82.08W
11 B2 Henderson *bor* Auckland New Zealand
11 B2 Henderson Cr *inlet* New Zealand
122 O11 Henderson I Pacific Oc 24.20S 128.20W
122 P5 Henderson Seamount Pacific Oc
105 E2 Hendersonville N Carolina 35.19N 82.28W
32 C5 Hendījān Iran 30.17N 49.43E
32 C5 Hendijan *oil well* The Gulf 30.02N 49.55E
55 E2 Hendon London Eng 51.35N 0.14W
13 K8 Hendon Queensland 28.09S 151.54E
100 O6 Hendon Saskatchewan 52.08N 103.50W
55 E2 Hendon Aerodrome London Eng 51.36N 0.15W
32 E7 Hendorābī Iran
82 J4 Hendorf Romania 46.04N 24.50E
13 K1 Hendra *dist* Brisbane, Qnsld
56 E4 Hendreforgan Mid Glam Wales 51.36N 3.28W
108 O5 Hendricks Minnesota 44.30N 96.22W
104 F7 Hendricks W Virginia 39.04N 79.39W
94 H2 Hendrick's Pan Botswana 19.07S 25.52E
60 G12 Hendrik-Ido-Ambacht Netherlands 51.51N 4.38E
117 B2 Hendrik Top, pk Surinam 4.11N 56.15W
95 J6 Hendrik Verwoerd Dam *res* S Africa 30.40S 25.45E
95 N2 Hendrina S Africa 26.10S 29.43E
56 C4 Hendy Dyfed Wales 51.43N 4.04W
56 B4 Hendy-gwyn Dyfed Wales 51.50N 4.37W
110 O8 Henefer Utah 41.01N 111.30W
56 L6 Henfield W Sussex Eng 50.56N 0.17W
15 H7 Henganofi Papua New Guinea 6.14S 145.32E
Hengchow *see* Heng-yang
23 J7 Heng-ch'un Taiwan 22.03N 120.45E
23 C2 Hengdan Gansu China 32.49N 104.53E
21 E5 Hengdaohezi Heilongjiang China 44.46N 129.03E
21 D6 Hengdaozi Jilin China 43.20N 127.20E
23 F5 Hengdong Hunan China 27.05N 112.53E
23 A4 Hengduan Shan *mt ra* Xizang Zizhiqu China
60 O11 Hengelo Gelderland Netherlands 52.03N 6.18E
60 Q10 Hengelo Overijssel Netherlands 52.16N 6.46E
64 P6 Hengersberg W Germany 48.47N 13.05E
60 P11 Hengevelde Netherlands 52.12N 6.38E
23 H4 Hengfeng Jiangxi China 28.21N 117.33E
50 L4 Hengifoss *waterfall* Iceland 65.05N 14.54W
50 L4 Hengifossarvatn Iceland 65.10N 14.57W
50 D6 Hengill *mt* Iceland 64.05N 21.19W
23 C4 Heng Jiang *R* Sichuan China
23 F4 Henglongqiao Hunan China 28.23N 112.27E
23 F5 Hengnan Hunan China 26.52N 112.32E
23 F5 Hengshan Hunan China 27.18N 112.45E
22 H8 Hengshan Shaanxi China 37.54N 108.55E
23 F5 Heng Shan *mt pk* Hunan China 27.18N 112.40E
22 J7 Heng Shan *mts* Shanxi China
22 K8 Hengshui Hebei China 37.45N 115.44E
60 C3 Hengstdijk Netherlands 51.20N 4.00E
64 J5 Hengstfeld W Germany 49.13N 10.06E
23 E7 Heng Xian Guangxi China 22.38N 109.22E
23 F5 Hengyang Hunan China 26.59N 112.22E
23 F5 Hengyang Hunan China 26.58N 112.31E
28 J8 Henhoaha Nicobar Is 6.48N 93.49E
Henin *see* Haynin
69 D3 Hénin-Liétard France 50.25N 2.58E
11 E12 Henley New Zealand 45.59S 170.11E
98 R2 Henley Harbour Labrador, Nfld 52.00N 55.50W
56 H3 Henley-in-Arden Warwicks Eng 52.17N 1.46W
56 K4 Henley-on-Thames Oxon Eng 51.32N 0.56W
111 B2 Henleyville California 39.59N 122.18W
103 D9 Henlopen, C Delaware 38.48N 75.05W
56 L3 Henlow Beds Eng 52.02N 0.18W
112 J5 Henly Texas 30.13N 98.14W
12 A8 Henly and Grange *dist* Adelaide, S Aust
20 P9 Henna Okinawa Japan 26.18N 127.54E
52 J4 Hennan Sweden 62.01N 15.55E
65 H6 Henndorf Austria 47.54N 13.12E
53 A5 Henne Denmark 55.44N 8.14E
64 J2 Henneberg E Germany 50.30N 10.23E
70 D6 Hennebont France 47.48N 3.16W
64 C2 Hennef (Sieg) W Germany 50.47N 7.17E
64 K5 Hennenbach W Germany 49.17N 10.35E
95 L3 Hennenman S Africa 27.58S 27.01E
106 E8 Hennepin Illinois 41.14N 89.21W
70 L3 Hennequeville France 49.23N 0.06E
109 N5 Hennessey Oklahoma 36.06N 97.54W
69 L7 Hennezel France 48.03N 6.07E
63 S8 Hennickendorf E Germany 52.10N 13.06E
66 D5 Henniez Switzerland 46.45N 6.53E
63 S7 Hennigsdorf E Germany 52.38N 13.13E
106 G9 Henning Illinois 40.20N 87.43W
108 P3 Henning Minnesota 46.18N 95.27W
95 K7 Henning S Africa 31.16S 26.07E
107 G6 Henning Tennessee 35.40N 89.32W
51 D3 Henningsvær Norway 68.08N 14.14E
53 S15 Hennøystranda Norway 61.49N 5.14E
63 K4 Hennstedt W Germany 54.17N 9.10E
61 G4 Hennuyères Belgium 50.38N 4.10E
69 C5 Hénonville France 49.12N 2.03E
32 F7 Henqām *isld* Iran 26.40N 55.55E
100 M5 Henribourg Saskatchewan 53.27N 105.40W
61 O4 Henri-Chapelle Belgium 50.41N 5.56E
72 K1 Henrichemont France 47.19N 2.30E
112 J2 Henrietta Texas 33.49N 98.13W
Henrietta I *see* Genriyetty, Ostrov
97 L6 Henrietta Maria C Hudson B, N W Terr 55.05N 82.30W
111 N4 Henrieville Utah 37.34N 111.59W
101 L7 Henri Mt Br Columbia 56.31N 124.48W
61 G4 Henripont Belgium 50.36N 4.11E
Henrique de Carvalho *see* Suarimo
110 O7 Henry Idaho 42.54N 111.30W
106 E8 Henry Illinois 41.07N 89.23W
104 K10 Henry, C Virginia 36.56N 76.00W
109 O6 Henryetta Oklahoma 35.27N 96.00W
123 E15 Henryk Arctowski *Pol. Base* Antarctica 62.09S 58.28W
97 N4 Henry Kater Pen N W Terr
105 A4 Henry L Alabama 33.50N 86.05W
28 G7 Henry Lawrence I Andaman Is
110 K1 Henry, Mt Montana 48.50N 115.30W
111 O3 Henry Mts Utah
14 B6 Henry, R W Australia
110 O5 Henrys Fork *R* Idaho
110 O5 Henrys L Idaho 44.39N 111.24W
107 L3 Henryville Indiana 38.33N 85.47W
103 D4 Henryville Pennsylvania 41.06N 75.14W
99 J9 Hensall Ontario 43.26N 81.31W
59 C5 Hens Castle Galway Irish Rep 53.27N 9.31W
107 H4 Henshaw Kentucky 37.35N 88.03W
111 H8 Henshaw, L California 33.15N 116.44W
61 E5 Hensies Belgium 50.26N 3.41E
112 N9 Hensley Airfield Texas 32.44N 96.58W
15 M3 Henslow, C Guadalcanal I Solomon Is 9.58S 160.38E
14 G3 Hensman, Mt W Australia 15.57S 128.55E
103 F2 Hensonville New York 42.15N 74.13W
63 L5 Henstedt-Ulzburg W Germany 53.48N 9.58E
56 G6 Henstridge Somerset Eng 50.59N 2.24W
22 H2 Hentiy Mongolia 48.05N 109.50E
22 H2 Hentiy *prov* Mongolia
22 H2 Hentiyn Nuruu *mts* Mongolia
28 J7 Hentoin Nicobar Is 8.00N 93.31E
12 H6 Henty New S Wales 35.30S 147.03E
25 C4 Henzada Burma 17.36N 95.26E
20 P9 Henza-jima *I* Okinawa Japan 26.21N 127.57E
100 L6 Hepburn Saskatchewan 52.34N 106.43W
101 S2 Hepburn I N W Terr 67.52N 111.00W
23 G3 Hepeng Anhui China 31.12N 116.47E
105 E4 Hephzibah Georgia 33.19N 82.06W
Heping *see* Yanhe
23 G6 Heping Guangdong China 24.27N 114.52E
Hepo *see* Jiexi
61 L2 Heppen Belgium 51.07N 5.14E
61 P5 Heppenbach Belgium 50.22N 6.13E
64 B2 Heppendorf W Germany 50.55N 6.38E
64 F4 Heppenheim an der Bergstrasse W Germany 49.38N 8.39E
61 H5 Heppignies Belgium 50.28N 4.30E
110 F4 Heppner Oregon 45.21N 119.32W
35 F2 Heptapegon *anc site* Israel 32.52N 35.31E
23 E8 Hepu Guangxi China 21.37N 109.11E
99 J8 Hepworth Ontario 44.37N 81.09W
23 B5 Heqing Yunnan China 26.34N 100.12E
22 J7 Hequ Shanxi China 39.20N 111.22E
Heraclea *anc site see* Ereğli Zonguldak
50 L3 Héradhsflói *B* Iceland
50 L3 Héradhssandur *sand reg* Iceland
52 F6 Heradsbygd Norway 60.58N 11.38E
Hérak *see* Harak, El
37 G8 Herakol Dağ *mt* Turkey 37.47N 42.35E
13 J3 Herald Cays *islds* Gt Barrier Reef Australia 17.00S 149.06E
103 A8 Herald Harbor Maryland 39.03N 76.34W
11 B1 Herald I New Zealand 36.47S 174.39E
Herald I U.S.S.R.*see* Geral'd, Ostrov
11 N1 Herald Islets Kermadec Is Pacific Oc
65 M2 Herálec Czechoslovakia 49.32N 15.28E
53 U18 Herand Norway 60.20N 6.24E
31 B3 Herat Afghanistan 34.20N 62.10E
31 A3 Herat *prov* Afghanistan
Herat-i-Khurreh *see* Tājābād
Herauabad *see* Herowābād
67 H9 Hérault *dept* France
71 D9 Hérault *R* France
71 G6 Herbasse *R* France
70 F7 Herbaudiere, Pte.de l' France 47.02N 2.18W
70 N6 Herbault France 47.37N 1.09E
63 F10 Herbede W Germany 51.25N 7.15E
63 G9 Herbern W Germany 51.44N 7.39E
11 E12 Herbert New Zealand 45.15S 170.49E
100 K8 Herbert Saskatchewan 50.26N 107.12W
13 E5 Herbert *R* N Terr Australia
13 H4 Herbert *R* Queensland
28 G7 Herbertabad Andaman Is 11.42N 92.34E
13 E6 Herbert Downs Queensland 23.00S 139.12E
15 F7 Herbert Hoover, L Papua New Guinea 7.14S 141.04E
113 B10 Herbert I Aleutian Is 52.49N 170.10W
64 G7 Herbertingen W Germany 48.04N 9.27E
13 B4 Herbert, Mt N Terr Australia 18.10S 130.20E
15 H6 Herbert, Mt Papua New Guinea 5.40S 144.59E
14 F3 Herbert, Mt W Australia 17.15S 125.12E
13 H3 Herberton Queensland 17.20S 145.55E
30 A2 Herbertpur Uttar Prad India 30.26N 77.43E
95 E10 Herbertsdale S Africa 34.01S 21.45E
59 F6 Herbertstown Limerick Irish Rep 52.32N 8.28W
11 L7 Herbertville New Zealand 40.29S 176.32E
98 A5 Hérbertville Quebec 48.23N 71.42W
75 K6 Herbés Spain 40.44N 0.01W
61 L7 Herbeumont Belgium 49.47N 5.14E
72 B2 Herbiers, les France 46.52N 1.00W
70 F7 Herbignac France 47.28N 2.19W
69 G6 Herbisse France 48.38N 4.07E
69 N5 Herbitzheim France 49.01N 7.05E
100 S4 Herb Lake Manitoba 54.47N 99.45W
68 C2 Herblay France 49.00N 2.09E
64 D7 Herbolzheim W Germany 48.15N 7.47E
53 B4 Herborg Denmark 56.04N 8.36E
64 E2 Herborn W Germany 50.41N 8.19E
64 J6 Herbrechtingen W Germany 48.36N 10.12E
66 H7 Herbriggen Switzerland 46.08N 7.48E
64 G2 Herbstein W Germany 50.33N 9.21E
62 L5 Herby Poland 50.45N 18.50E
82 E8 Herceg Novi Yugoslavia 42.26N 18.35E
61 F4 Herchies Belgium 50.32N 3.51E
97 K6 Herchmer Manitoba 57.30N 94.00W
64 H4 Herchsheim W Germany 49.37N 9.57E
Herculânea *see* Coxim
76 C2 Hercules *mt* Spain 43.23N 8.24W
109 O5 Herd Oklahoma 36.52N 96.13W
63 F10 Herdecke W Germany 51.24N 7.26E
61 N3 Herderen Belgium 50.48N 5.35E
61 G3 Herdersem Belgium 50.58N 4.04E
50 J4 Herdhubreidh *mt* Iceland 65.10N 16.22W
50 J4 Herdhubreidharfjöll *mts* Iceland
50 J4 Herdhubreidhartögl *mt* Iceland 65.05N 16.25W
53 R17 Herdla Norway 60.34N 4.56E
53 S17 Herdlafjord *inlet* Norway 60.32N 5.05E
69 O2 Herdorf W Germany 50.47N 7.58E
115 M4 Heredia Costa Rica 10.00N 84.08W
109 F1 Hereford Colorado 40.58N 104.18W
56 F3 Hereford Hereford & Worcs Eng 52.04N 2.43W
103 A7 Hereford Maryland 39.35N 76.40W
103 C6 Hereford Pennsylvania 40.26N 75.34W
112 E1 Hereford Texas 34.49N 102.25W
Hereford *co see* Hereford & Worcester *co*
103 E8 Hereford Inlet New Jersey
56 F3 Hereford & Worcester *co* Eng
52 D8 Herefoss Norway 58.32N 8.23E
122 D16 Héréhérétué *atoll* Tuamotu Is Pacific Oc 19.58S 144.58W
37 G2 Hereke Turkey 40.49N 29.38E
11 H2 Herekino New Zealand 35.16S 173.14E
11 H2 Herekino Harb *inlet* New Zealand
89 D7 Heremakono Guinea 9.55N 11.06W
66 F7 Hérémence, V. d' Switzerland
77 K2 Herencia Spain 39.22N 3.21W
66 F7 Hérens, Val d' Switzerland
61 J3 Herent Belgium 50.54N 4.40E
61 K2 Herentals Belgium 51.11N 4.50E
61 K2 Herenthout Belgium 51.09N 4.45E
71 C9 Hérépian France 43.35N 3.08E
11 D10 Heretaniwha Pt New Zealand 43.35S 169.35E
61 G4 Herfelingen Belgium 50.45N 4.06E
53 J6 Herfølge Denmark 55.25N 12.09E
63 J8 Herford W Germany 52.07N 8.40E
64 H8 Hergatz W Germany 47.39N 9.49E
61 P4 Hergenrath Belgium 50.42N 6.02E
66 Q1 Hergensweiler W Germany 47.37N 9.47E
50 C4 Hergilsey *isld* Iceland 65.26N 22.59W
66 H3 Hergiswil Luzern Switzerland 47.05N 7.58E
66 K4 Hergiswil Unterwalden Switzerland 46.59N 8.18E
76 H10 Herguijuela Spain 39.23N 5.45W
Herheri *see* Çaylarbaşı
70 G7 Heric France 47.26N 1.39W
71 K1 Héricourt France 47.35N 6.45E
71 K2 Hérimoncourt France 47.26N 6.52E
63 N10 Heringen E Germany 51.27N 10.54E
Heringsdorf *see* Seebad Heringsdorf
63 O4 Heringsdorf W Germany 54.18N 11.01E
109 O3 Herington Kansas 38.40N 96.56W
61 D4 Hérinnes Belgium 50.42N 3.22E
58 L7 Heriot Borders Scotland 55.47N 2.56W
11 D12 Heriot New Zealand 45.51S 169.20E
101 L10 Heriot Bay Br Col 50.06N 125.12W
32 B1 Heris Iran 38.15N 47.08E
66 O2 Herisau Switzerland 47.23N 9.17E
72 K2 Hérisson France 46.31N 2.42E
19 N4 Herit *isld* Truk Is Pacific Oc 7.25N 151.56E
123 F10 Heritage Ra Antarctica
53 X13 Herjevatn *L* Norway 62.38N 7.36E
61 L3 Herk-de-Stad Belgium 50.56N 5.10E
60 U16 Herkenbosch Netherlands 51.09N 6.04E
104 L3 Herkimer New York 43.02N 74.59W
60 E13 Herkingen Netherlands 51.42N 4.05E
123 J11 Herlacher, C Antarctica 74.00S 114.00W
64 N2 Herlasgrün E Germany 50.33N 12.13E
Herlen Gol *see* Kerulen
22 K2 Herlen He *R* Nei Monggol Zizhiqu China
64 J1 Herleshausen W Germany 51.01N 10.11E
53 J5 Herlev Denmark 55.44N 12.28E
53 H6 Herlufmagle Denmark 55.19N 11.47E
48 V15 Herluf Trolle, Kap *C* Greenland 61.05N 42.30W
97 R1 Herluf Trolles Land Greenland
72 B8 Herm France 43.48N 1.08W
70 F3 Herm *isld* Channel Is 49.28N 2.27W
65 H8 Hermagor Austria 46.38N 13.23E
61 M4 Hermalle-sous-Huy Belgium 50.33N 5.22E
106 F3 Herman Michigan 46.40N 88.21W
108 O4 Herman Minnesota 45.50N 96.10W
108 O8 Herman Nebraska 41.41N 96.15W
19 J4 Hermana Mayor *isld* Luzon Philippines 15.49N 119.48E
115 J4 Hermanas Mexico 27.18N 101.14W
109 C10 Hermanas New Mexico 31.51N 107.58W
66 B6 Hermance Switzerland 46.18N 6.16E
58 R8 Herma Ness *prom* Shetland Scotland 60.50N 0.54W
107 E3 Hermann Missouri 38.43N 91.26W
63 M7 Hermannsberg W Germany 52.49N 10.06E
13 C6 Hermannsburg N Terr Australia 23.58S 132.37E
64 P4 Heřmanova Hut' Czechoslovakia 49.43N 13.05E
53 V16 Hermansverk Norway 61.11N 6.52E
106 G4 Hermansville Michigan 45.43N 87.36W
95 C10 Hermanus S Africa 34.25S 19.14E
65 N2 Heřmanuv Městec Czechoslovakia 49.57N 15.40E
107 F10 Hermanville Mississippi 31.59N 90.51W
61 N4 Hermée Belgium 50.42N 5.37E
34 D4 Hermel, El Lebanon 34.25N 36.23E
72 C2 Hermenault, l' France 46.31N 0.55W
71 B5 Herment France 45.45N 2.34E
69 C5 Hermes France 49.22N 2.15E
95 N7 Hermes, C S Africa 31.39S 29.32E
64 B4 Hermeskeil W Germany 49.39N 6.57E

61 K6 Hermeton-sur-Meuse Belgium 50.12N 4.49E
76 K2 Hermida, La Spain 43.15N 4.37W
12 H4 Hermidale New S Wales 31.33S 146.44E
69 E3 Hermies France 50.07N 3.01E
96 O14 Hermigüa Gomera Canary Is 28.11N 17.11W
76 F5 Hermisende Spain 41.58N 6.53W
110 F4 Hermiston Oregon 45.50N 119.18W
107 D8 Hermitage Arkansas 33.27N 92.10W
98 R6 Hermitage Newfoundland 47.35N 55.55W
11 E10 Hermitage New Zealand 43.47S 170.06E
98 Q6 Hermitage B Newfoundland
70 E5 Hermitage, l' France 48.20N 2.50W
14 B5 Hermite I W Australia 20.30S 115.31E
121 L10 Hermite, Is Chile
70 M6 Hermites, les France 47.40N 0.47E
13 B2 Hermit Hill N Terr Australia 13.45S 130.25E
15 H4 Hermit Is Bismarck Arch
111 M5 Hermits Rest Arizona 36.03N 112.18W
112 G3 Hermleigh Texas 32.37N 100.46W
95 B9 Hermon S Africa 33.26S 18.58E
Hermōn, Mt *see* Sheikh, Jebel esh
69 F5 Hermonville France 49.20N 3.55E
109 C4 Hermosa Colorado 37.22N 107.50W
19 G1 Hermosa Luzon Philippines 14.50N 120.31E
108 G6 Hermosa S Dakota 43.50N 103.11W
111 D9 Hermosa Beach California 33.51N 118.25W
119 E5 Hermosa, Caño de la *crater* Colombia
115 D3 Hermosillo Mexico 29.15N 110.59W
Hermsdorf *see* Ottendorf-Okrilla
64 M2 Hermsdorf Gera E Germany 50.53N 11.51E
118 C9 Hernandarias Paraguay 25.20S 54.40W
121 E4 Hernandez Argentina 32.22S 60.00W
109 D5 Hernandez New Mexico 36.05N 106.06W
105 E9 Hernando Florida 28.54N 82.23W
107 G7 Hernando Mississippi 34.50N 90.00W
75 G1 Hernani Spain 43.16N 1.59W
108 Q8 Herndon Iowa 41.51N 94.21W
109 K2 Herndon Kansas 39.55N 100.47W
107 J5 Herndon Kentucky 36.44N 87.37W
104 J6 Herndon Pennsylvania 40.43N 76.50W
104 H8 Herndon Virginia 38.58N 77.25W
104 D9 Herndon W Virginia 37.30N 81.21W
61 G4 Herne Belgium 50.43N 4.02E
56 O5 Herne Kent Eng 51.21N 1.08E
63 F9 Herne W Germany 51.32N 7.12E
56 O5 Herne Bay Kent Eng 51.23N 1.08E
60 L12 Hernen Netherlands 51.50N 5.41E
53 B4 Herning Denmark 56.08N 8.59E
75 F1 Hernio, Mte Spain 43.11N 2.08W
Heroiva *see* Herat
95 F9 Herold S Africa 33.51S 22.27E
64 L4 Heroldsberg W Germany 49.32N 11.10E
61 L4 Héron Belgium 50.33N 5.05E
110 K1 Heron Montana 48.04N 115.57W
99 D4 Heron Bay Ontario 48.41N 86.20W
37 G6 Heronek *R* Turkey
13 K6 Heron I Gt Barrier Reef Australia 23.25S 151.55E
11 F10 Heron, L New Zealand 43.29S 171.11E
108 P6 Heron Lake Minnesota 43.48N 95.20W
99 S10 Hérons, I.aux Quebec 45.26N 73.35W
32 C2 Herowābād Iran 37.36N 48.36E
53 T14 Heroy Norway 62.18N 5.45E
53 T19 Herøysundet Norway 59.55N 5.48E
82 B5 Herpelje Kozina Yugoslavia 45.35N 13.58E
60 L12 Herpen Netherlands 51.46N 5.38E
60 J13 Herpt Netherlands 51.44N 5.10E
61 E4 Herquegies Belgium 50.38N 3.35E
76 K7 Herradón, El Spain 40.33N 4.34W
118 B10 Herradura Argentina 26.28S 58.19W
115 J6 Herradura Mexico 23.01N 101.45W
75 D2 Herramelluri Spain 42.30N 3.01W
72 D7 Herré France 44.01N 0.01W
108 K4 Herreid S Dakota 45.50N 100.03W
Herrenalb *see* Bad Herrenalb
64 F6 Herrenberg W Germany 48.36N 8.52E
64 E6 Herrenwies W Germany 48.38N 8.17E
121 D2 Herrera Argentina 28.27S 63.06W
77 G6 Herrera Spain 37.22N 4.50W
75 H5 Herrera *mt* Spain 41.10N 1.06W
76 E9 Herrera de Alcántara Spain 39.39N 7.25W
76 J10 Herrera del Duque Spain 39.10N 5.03W
75 H5 Herrera de los Navarros Spain 41.12N 1.04W
76 L3 Herrera de Pisuerga Spain 42.35N 4.20W
77 M3 Herrera, La Spain 38.58N 2.08W
77 G6 Herrera, L.de Spain 37.06N 4.35W
115 G5 Herreras Mexico 25.10N 105.30W
75 G6 Herrería Guadalajara Spain 40.53N 1.58W
76 E3 Herrería Lugo Spain 42.40N 7.18W
77 L2 Herrería *mt* Spain 39.01N 2.44W
77 B5 Herrerías Spain 37.37N 7.18W
77 J7 Herrero *mt* Spain 36.57N 3.41W
115 Q8 Herrero, Pta Mexico 19.20N 87.23W
75 E4 Herreros Spain 41.49N 2.43W
76 J7 Herreros de Suso Spain 40.48N 5.02W
76 F10 Herreruela Spain 39.28N 6.55W
53 F6 Herrested Denmark 55.17N 10.37E
56 J5 Herriard Hants Eng 51.13N 1.03W
108 L6 Herrick S Dakota 43.07N 99.11W
12 J8 Herrick Tasmania 41.04S 147.53E
103 C3 Herrick Center Pennsylvania 41.45N 75.30W
103 B3 Herrickville Pennsylvania 41.48N 76.16W
64 J5 Herrieden W Germany 49.15N 10.30E
107 G4 Herrin Illinois 37.48N 89.01W
98 S4 Herring Neck Newfoundland 49.37N 54.35W
107 M4 Herrington L Kentucky
100 Q2 Herriot Manitoba 56.24N 101.17W
66 H1 Herrischried W Germany 47.40N 8.00E
53 H7 Herritslev Denmark 54.42N 11.40E
64 H7 Herrlingen W Germany 48.26N 9.55E
69 O6 Herrlisheim France 48.44N 7.55E
52 G8 Herrljunga Sweden 58.05N 13.02E
64 E4 Herrnsheim W Germany 49.40N 8.20E
64 L8 Herrsching W Germany 48.00N 11.11E
64 C4 Herrstein W Germany 49.47N 7.20E
77 N2 Herrumblar, El Spain 39.24N 1.37W
72 K1 Herry France 47.13N 2.56E
72 H8 Hers *R* France
64 L4 Hersbruck W Germany 49.31N 11.26E
64 D1 Herscheid W Germany 51.11N 7.42E
95 L6 Herschel S Africa 30.37S 27.10E
100 J7 Herschel Saskatchewan 51.38N 108.21W
101 D1 Herschel Yukon Terr 69.34N 139.00W
121 L10 Herschel, I Chile 55.53S 67.20W
101 D1 Herschel I Yukon Terr
106 F8 Herscher Illinois 41.03N 88.05W
64 J3 Herschfeld W Germany 50.20N 10.16E
61 C4 Herseaux Belgium 50.43N 3.14E
61 K2 Herselt Belgium 51.03N 4.53E
106 J6 Hersey Michigan 43.52N 85.28W
55 C5 Hersham Surrey Eng 51.22N 0.23W
103 A6 Hershey Pennsylvania 40.16N 76.39W
121 E3 Hersilia Argentina 30.00S 61.48W
53 D5 Herslev Denmark 55.35N 9.36E
53 D3 Hersom Denmark 56.33N 9.34E
61 N4 Herstal Belgium 50.40N 5.38E
61 M4 Herstappe Belgium 50.43N 5.26E
56 M6 Herstmonceux E Sussex Eng 50.53N 0.20E
53 R16 Hersvik Norway 61.10N 4.53E
61 D4 Hertain Belgium 50.37N 3.17E
87 H6 Hertale,L Ethiopia 9.55N 40.23E
60 T16 Herten Netherlands 51.11N 5.59E
63 F9 Herten W Germany 51.36N 7.08E
66 K3 Hertenstein Switzerland 47.02N 8.25E
56 L4 Hertford Herts Eng 51.48N 0.05W
105 L1 Hertford N Carolina 36.11N 76.30W
56 L4 Hertford *co* England
61 P4 Hertogenwald *forest* Belgium
61 D2 Hertsberge Belgium 51.07N 3.16E
48 U6 Hertugen of Orleans Land Greenland
95 J4 Hertzogville S Africa 28.07S 25.30E
35 C5 Herut Israel 32.14N 34.55E
76 H8 Hervás Spain 40.16N 5.52W
61 O4 Herve Belgium 50.38N 5.48E
61 N4 Herve *plat* Belgium
13 L7 Hervey B Queensland
122 L10 Hervey Is Cook Is Pacific Oc 19.21S 158.58W
99 S6 Hervey Junction Quebec 46.52N 72.29W
13 H4 Hervey Ra Queensland
53 T20 Hervik Norway 59.19N 5.36E
60 N12 Herwen Netherlands 51.53N 6.07E
64 E5 Herxheim W Germany 49.08N 8.12E
63 S9 Herzberg Cottbus E Germany 51.42N 13.14E
63 M9 Herzberg am Harz W Germany 51.40N 10.20E
63 R7 Herzberg (Mark) Potsdam E Germany 52.54N 12.58E
61 F3 Herzele Belgium 50.53N 3.55E
63 T8 Herzfelde E Germany 52.30N 13.52E
63 G7 Herzlake W Germany 52.42N 7.37E
35 C5 Herzliyya Israel 32.10N 34.50E
64 K4 Herzogenaurach W Germany 49.34N 10.54E
66 G3 Herzogenbuchsee Switzerland 47.12N 7.43E
65 N5 Herzogenburg Austria 48.18N 15.43E
64 A2 Herzogenrath W Germany 50.51N 6.06E
63 Q6 Herzsprung E Germany 53.05N 12.29E
32 D6 Heşār Banāder va Jazāyer-e Khalīj-e Fārs Iran 29.52N 50.18E
32 C3 Heşār Tehrān Iran 35.50N 49.01E
61 K4 Hesbaye *plat* Belgium
69 B2 Hesdigneul-lès-Boulogne France 50.40N 1.40E
69 C3 Hesdin France 50.22N 2.03E
63 G6 Hesel W Germany 53.19N 7.36E
32 E7 Heshnīz Iran 27.04N 53.31E
23 E1 Heshui Gansu China 35.49N 108.02E
23 F7 Heshui Guangdong China 22.16N 111.43E
22 J8 Heshun Shaanxi China 37.22N 113.35E
66 G1 Hésingue France 47.35N 7.31E
52 C8 Heskestad Norway 58.28N 6.22E
108 L2 Hesper N Dakota 47.59N 99.36W
61 P8 Hesperange Luxembourg 49.34N 6.10E
111 G7 Hesperia California 34.25N 117.19W
106 H6 Hesperia Michigan 43.33N 86.03W
109 B4 Hesperus Colorado 37.16N 108.03W
109 B4 Hesperus Pk Colorado 37.26N 108.03W
101 G4 Hess *R* Yukon Terr
53 U14 Hessa *isld* Norway 62.28N 6.07E
113 N4 Hess Cr Alaska
106 K3 Hessel Michigan 46.01N 84.25W
53 F6 Hesselager Denmark 55.10N 10.44E
64 K5 Hesselberg *mt* W Germany 49.05N 10.34E
53 H4 Hesselø *isld* Denmark 56.11N 11.45E
63 N8 Hessen E Germany 52.01N 10.47E
62 D5 Hessen *land* W Germany
64 F1 Hessenstein W Germany 51.06N 8.50E
64 H5 Hessenthal W Germany 49.06N 9.50E
64 H1 Hessisch Lichtenau W Germany 51.12N 9.44E
63 K8 Hessisch Oldendorf W Germany 52.11N 9.15E
57 N5 Hessle Humberside Eng 53.44N 0.26W
101 G4 Hess Mts Yukon Terr
12 D4 Hesso S Australia 32.08S 137.58E
109 N3 Hesston Kansas 38.07N 97.26W
53 T16 Hestad Norway 61.20N 5.57E
53 Y15 Hestbrepiggane *mt* Norway 61.45N 8.05E
53 Y15 Hestedalshødga *mt* Norway 61.48N 8.03E
53 J7 Hestehoved *C* Denmark 54.50N 12.11E
53 U15 Hestenesøyri Norway 61.50N 6.01E
50 C2 Hesteyrarfjördhur *B* Iceland
50 C2 Hesteyri Iceland 66.20N 22.52W
50 E6 Hestfjall *mt* Árnessýsla Iceland 64.00N 20.40W
50 G3 Hestfjall *mt* Eyjafjardharsýsla Iceland 65.56N 18.42W
50 C3 Hestfjördhur *B* Iceland
51 C5 Hestmona *isld* Norway 66.33N 12.50E
53 N10 Hestø Faeroes 61.58N 6.53W
53 N10 Hestø *isld* Faeroes 61.58N 6.53W
55 C4 Heston London Eng 51.29N 0.23W
61 G5 Hestre, La Belgium 50.28N 4.14E
69 G3 Hestrud France 50.12N 4.09E
Hestur *see* Hestø
50 E6 Hestvatn *L* Iceland 64.01N 20.42W
57 G6 Heswall Merseyside Eng 53.20N 3.06W
30 J5 Hetauda Nepal 27.26N 85.02E
111 E4 Hetch Hetchy Res California 37.56N 119.45W
60 O10 Heten Netherlands 52.20N 6.17E
60 M12 Heteren Netherlands 51.58N 5.46E
56 O2 Hethersett Norfolk Eng 52.36N 1.11E
23 G7 Hetian Guangdong China 23.23N 115.38E
103 B4 Hetlerville Pennsylvania 41.01N 76.16W
25 K2 Hetou Guangdong China 21.04N 109.50E
69 L5 Hettange-Grande France 49.25N 6.09E
Hettenhausen *see* Ebersburg
60 N12 Hettenheuvel *mt* Netherlands 51.55N 6.14E
64 E4 Hettenleidelheim W Germany 49.32N 8.05E
108 H3 Hettinger N Dakota 46.00N 102.39W
26 R6 Hettipola Sri Lanka 7.36N 80.05E
66 L1 Hettlingen Switzerland 47.33N 8.42E
57 L3 Hetton le Hole Tyne and Wear Eng 54.50N 1.27W
63 P9 Hettstedt E Germany 51.39N 11.31E
60 C3 Het Veer Netherlands 51.18N 3.56E
64 F4 Hetzbach W Germany 49.35N 8.59E
64 B4 Hetzerath W Germany 49.53N 6.49E
61 D1 Het Zoute Belgium 51.21N 3.19E
64 H6 Heubach W Germany 48.47N 9.56E
64 F7 Heuberg *reg* W Germany
69 C3 Heuchin France 50.29N 2.16E
63 N9 Heudeber E Germany 51.54N 10.51E
69 K6 Heudicourt-sous-les-Côtes France 48.56N 5.43E
60 S17 Heugem Netherlands 50.50N 5.42E
13 B6 Heughlin, Mt N Terr Australia 23.17S 132.11E
Heuglin, Kapp *see* Pechuel Løsche, Kapp
61 C3 Heule Belgium 50.50N 3.15E
64 C2 Heumar W Germany 50.55N 7.07E
88 O3 Heumis, les Algeria 36.23N 1.15E
95 H5 Heuningneskloof S Africa 29.12S 24.33E
95 L3 Heuningspruit S Africa 27.27S 27.25E
95 G2 Heuningvleisoutpan *salt pan* S Africa 26.18S 23.09E
70 N3 Heuqueville France 49.17N 1.21E
61 M5 Heure Belgium 50.18N 5.18E
61 H5 Heure *R* Belgium
15 M4 Heuri Solomon Is 10.16S 160.29E
60 P12 Heurne, De Netherlands 51.54N 6.35E
61 M2 Heusden Limburg Belgium 51.02N 5.17E
60 J13 Heusden Netherlands 51.44N 5.09E
61 F2 Heusden Oost Vlaanderen Belgium 51.02N 3.48E
64 J3 Heustreu W Germany 50.21N 10.17E
66 G5 Heustrich Switzerland 46.39N 7.41E
61 O4 Heusy Belgium 50.35N 5.52E
104 K2 Heuvelton New York 44.37N 75.24W
70 L2 Hève, C.de la France 49.30N 0.04E
61 J3 Hever Belgium 50.59N 4.33E
56 M5 Hever Kent Eng 51.11N 0.06E
35 E8 Hever *watercourse* Israel/Jordan
61 J3 Heverlee Belgium 50.52N 4.42E
57 H4 Heversham Cumbria Eng 54.15N 2.47W
62 M8 Heves Hungary 47.36N 20.17E
82 F3 Heves *co* Hungary
Hevik *see* Shirābād
61 J4 Hévillers Belgium 50.37N 4.37E
65 O4 Hevlin Czechoslovakia 48.45N 16.23E
53 E4 Hevring Å *R* Denmark
35 C8 Hevron *watercourse* Israel
100 O9 Heward Saskatchewan 49.44N 103.10W
54 M9 Hewett *oil field* North Sea 53.02N 1.51E
103 F4 Hewitt New Jersey 41.08N 74.19W
103 L6 Hewlett Pt New York 40.50N 73.45W
65 B7 Hexen Kopf *mt* Austria 47.02N 10.28E
57 J3 Hexham Northumb Eng 54.58N 2.06W
23 H6 Hexi Fujian China 24.57N 117.14E
23 C5 Hexi Sichuan China 27.46N 102.08E
23 C6 Hexi Yunnan China 24.08N 102.39E
23 H3 He Xian Anhui China 31.42N 118.21E
23 F6 He Xian Guangxi China 24.49N 111.23E
22 L5 Hexigten Qi Nei Monggol Zizhiqu China 43.20N 117.22E
95 C9 Hexrivier S Africa 33.30S 19.35E
95 C9 Hexrivierberge *mts* S Africa
112 H5 Hext Texas 30.53N 99.34W
23 E1 Heyang Shaanxi China 35.14N 110.02E
23 H1 Heyang Shandong China 35.26N 118.30E
37 F2 Heybeli Turkey 40.53N 29.06E
37 F2 Heybeli *isld* Turkey
110 M7 Heyburn Idaho 42.33N 113.46W
109 O6 Heyburn Res Oklahoma
61 N5 Heyd Belgium 50.22N 5.34E
50 L5 Heydalir Iceland 64.49N 14.10W
32 E4 Heydarābād Esfahān Iran 32.15N 52.22E
32 F5 Heydarābād Kermān Iran 30.37N 55.35E
32 H6 Heydarābād Kermān Iran 29.14N 59.50E
32 J5 Heydarābād Khorāsān Iran 31.02N 60.03E
71 G5 Heyrieux France 45.37N 5.03E
61 S9 Heysel Bruxelles Belgium
57 H4 Heysham Lancs Eng 54.02N 2.54W
94 J5 Heystekrand Transvaal S Africa 25.17S 27.14E
56 G5 Heytesbury Wilts Eng 51.11N 2.07W
23 G7 Heyuan Guangdong China 23.41N 114.45E
50 C5 Heyvatn *L* Iceland 64.33N 22.09W
11 N11 Heyward Pt New Zealand 45.45S 170.41E
57 J5 Heywood Greater Manchester Eng 53.36N 2.13W
12 F7 Heywood Victoria 38.08S 141.40E
37 F7 Hezan Turkey 38.20N 40.36E
37 C7 Hezanlı Dağ *mt* Turkey 38.37N 37.16E
23 G1 Heze Shandong China 35.16N 115.27E
23 C1 Hezheng Gansu China 35.29N 103.36E
37 G8 Hezil *R* Turkey
35 D8 Hezron, Har *hills* Israel
23 C1 Hezuo Gansu China 35.00N 102.58E
53 W15 Høebru Norway 61.30N 7.00E
85 F5 H Husayn Libya 29.55N 21.19E
105 G12 Hialeah Florida 25.49N 80.17W
105 D3 Hiawassee Georgia 34.58N 83.44W
109 P2 Hiawatha Kansas 39.51N 95.34W
111 N2 Hiawatha Utah 39.29N 111.00W
85 L5 Hîba, El Egypt 28.46N 30.58E
33 K7 Hibāk, Al *des area* Saudi Arabia
57 M5 Hibaldstow Humberside Eng 53.31N 0.32W
33 E8 Hibata *reg* Saudi Arabia
99 Q5 Hibbard Quebec 47.52N 74.04W
95 O6 Hibberdene S Africa 30.35S 30.35E
108 S2 Hibbing Minnesota 47.25N 92.55W
12 H9 Hibbs, Pt Tasmania 42.39S 145.16E
103 F5 Hibernia New Jersey 40.57N 74.30W
14 E1 Hibernia Reef Timor Sea 12.00S 123.25E
20 D7 Hibiki-nada *B* Japan
22 E1 Hibing Gol *R* Mongolia
19 M6 Hibuson *isld* Philippines 10.26N 125.29E
32 J7 Hīchān Iran 26.20N 60.07E
Hîché, El *see* Hishe, El
93 K2 Hichunne, El Ethiopia 3.45N 38.34E
114 E8 Hickam A.F. Base *airport* Hawaiian Is
111 M9 Hickiwan Arizona 32.22N 112.28W
57 L5 Hickleton S Yorks Eng 53.33N 1.15W
107 G5 Hickman Kentucky 36.33N 89.11W
108 O9 Hickman Nebraska 40.36N 96.39W
109 C7 Hickman New Mexico 34.33N 107.57W
120 F10 Hickmann Argentina 23.11S 63.30W
98 T5 Hickman's Harbour Nfld 48.08N 53.40W
109 J4 Hickok Kansas 37.34N 101.14W
103 B7 Hickory Maryland 39.34N 76.20W
107 G9 Hickory Mississippi 32.19N 89.01W
105 F2 Hickory N Carolina 35.44N 81.23W
105 F2 Hickory, L N Carolina
103 C4 Hickory Run State Park Pennsylvania
107 G6 Hickory Valley Tennessee 35.09N 89.06W
112 M8 Hicks Texas 32.54N 97.24W
11 N4 Hick's Bay New Zealand 37.36S 178.21E
115 P9 Hicks Cays *islds* Belize 17.40N 88.10W
101 Y5 Hicks L N W Terr
99 K9 Hickson Ontario 43.14N 80.49W
103 G5 Hicksville Long I, N Y 40.47N 73.32W
104 A5 Hicksville Ohio 41.18N 84.45W
112 J4 Hico Texas 31.54N 98.02W
82 H3 Hida Romania 47.01N 23.19E
20 M2 Hidaka Japan 42.53N 142.28E
20 J8 Hidaka *R* Japan
20 M2 Hidaka *sub-prefect* Hokkaido Japan
20 M2 Hidaka-sammyaku *mts* Japan
115 K4 Hidalgo Coahuila Mexico 27.49N 99.50W
115 K5 Hidalgo Tamaulipas Mexico 24.16N 99.28W
115 K7 Hidalgo *state* Mexico
115 J8 Hidalgo, Ciudad Mexico 19.40N 100.34W
115 G4 Hidalgo del Parral Mexico 26.58N 105.40W
115 E4 Hidalgo, M., Presa *res* Mexico
96 S13 Hidalgo, Pta. del *pt* Tenerife Canary Is 28.34N 16.19W
115 M9 Hidalgotitlán Mexico 17.46N 94.39W
115 L9 Hidalgo Yalalag Mexico 17.14N 96.10W
30 L6 Hidalwa Nepal 26.43N 87.06E
Hidd *see* Hadd, Al
63 J8 Hiddenhausen W Germany 52.10N 8.37E
63 S3 Hiddensee *isld* E Germany
13 H4 Hidden Valley Queensland 19.06S 145.56E
63 J9 Hiddesen W Germany 51.55N 8.50E
90 K4 Hid el Hassan Chad 15.19N 20.30E
85 M9 Hidiglib, Wadi *watercourse* Sudan
118 E5 Hidrolândia Brazil 16.59S 49.11W
118 E4 Hidrolina Brazil 14.45S 49.23W
65 L6 Hieflau Austria 47.37N 14.45E
75 D5 Hiendelaencina Spain 41.05N 3.00W
9 B13 Hienghène New Caledonia 20.40S 164.54E
75 J8 Hierbas *mt* Spain 39.31N 0.53W
60 L10 Hierden Netherlands 52.22N 5.40E
70 C5 Hière *R* France
69 C3 Hiermont France 50.11N 2.04E
96 P12 Hierro *isld* Canary Is 27.45N 18.00W
75 C6 Hierro *mt* Spain 40.48N 3.55W
75 G2 Higa *mt* Spain 42.41N 1.31W
20 P8 Higashieue Okinawa Japan 26.44N 127.47E
20 M6 Higashigawa Japan 35.15N 138.06E
20 O9 Higashi-iwa *rocks* Iwo Jima Pacific Oc 24.47N 141.22E
20 H7 Higashi-Katakimi Japan 34.45N 134.10E
20 B2 Higashi-Kurume Tōkyō Japan
20 N5 Higashi-Matsuyama Japan 36.02N 139.25E
20 B2 Higashi-Murayama Tōkyō Japan
20 D2 Higashi-Ōizumi Tōkyō Japan
20 P9 Higashi-Onna Okinawa Japan 26.23N 127.48E
20 C8 Higashi-suidō *str* Japan
20 B3 Higashi-Teragata Tōkyō Japan
20 B2 Higashi-Yamato Tōkyō Japan
86 K5 Higâyib, Wâdi el *watercourse* Egypt
107 D2 Higbee Missouri 39.17N 92.30W
103 J3 Higganum Connecticut 41.30N 72.34W
112 D7 Higgins Texas 36.17N 100.03W
12 A5 Higgins *dist* Canberra Australia
106 K5 Higgins L Michigan
107 C2 Higginsville Missouri 39.03N 93.43W
14 D9 Higginsville W Australia 31.46S 121.43E
95 G5 Higg's Hope S Africa 29.20S 23.15E
56 K3 Higham Ferrers Northants Eng 52.18N 0.36W
55 G2 Higham Hill London Eng 51.36N 0.02W
56 C6 Highampton Devon Eng 50.49N 4.09W
109 G4 Highbee Colorado 37.47N 103.25W
57 J4 High Bentham N Yorks Eng 54.08N 2.30W
26 B13 High Bluff Prince Edward I Ind Oc 46.40S 37.54E
56 F5 Highbridge Somerset Eng 51.13N 2.59W
56 J5 Highclere Hants Eng 51.22N 1.22W
11 M13 Highcliff New Zealand 45.53S 170.35E
106 F5 High Cliff Wisconsin 44.09N 88.17W
110 E6 High Des Oregon
56 F2 High Ercall Shropshire Eng 52.46N 2.36W
103 F3 High Falls New York 41.50N 74.08W
106 F4 High Falls Res Wisconsin 45.18N 88.12W
95 O6 Highflats S Africa 30.15S 30.12E
116 K1 Highgate Jamaica, W I 18.16N 76.53W
55 F3 Highgate London Eng 51.34N 0.09W
14 B1 Highgate *dist* Perth, W Aust
57 M4 High Hawsker N Yorks Eng 54.27N 0.34W
57 H3 High Hesket Cumbria Eng 54.48N 2.48W
100 W3 High Hill L Manitoba
25 E7 High I Burma 11.02N 98.17E
23 C8 High I Hong Kong
106 J4 High I Michigan 45.43N 85.40W
11 B9 High I Snares Is Pacific Oc 48.00S 166.35E
112 N6 High Island Texas 29.32N 94.24W
23 C9 High Junk Pk Hong Kong 22.17N 114.16E
103 D3 High Lake Pennsylvania 41.48N 75.19W
111 G7 Highland California 34.08N 117.11W
107 G3 Highland Illinois 38.45N 89.40W
109 P2 Highland Kansas 39.51N 95.16W
103 G3 Highland New York 41.43N 73.58W
106 D6 Highland Wisconsin 43.02N 90.21W
58 F3 Highland *reg* Scotland
103 G4 Highland Falls New York 41.22N 73.58W
112 F8 Highland Heights Houston, Texas 29.52N 95.26W
103 H3 Highland L Connecticut 41.55N 73.06W
107 G3 Highland L *res* Illinois
103 F4 Highland Mills New York 41.21N 74.07W
106 G7 Highland Park Illinois 42.10N 87.48W
106 L7 Highland Park Michigan 42.26N 83.05W
99 C9 Highland Park Ontario 45.23N 75.46W
106 M1 Highland Park *dist* Detroit, Michigan
111 E3 Highland Pk *mt* California 38.33N 119.45W
111 K4 Highland Pk *mt* Nevada 37.55N 114.36W
105 F12 Highland Pt Florida 26.31N 81.14W
105 D2 Highlands N Carolina 35.03N 83.14W
103 G6 Highlands New Jersey 40.24N 73.59W
95 K9 Highlands S Africa 33.20S 26.18E
112 M6 Highlands Texas 29.48N 95.04W
104 H9 Highland Springs Virginia 37.33N 77.19W
104 F2 Highlandtown *dist* Baltimore, Md
101 P6 High Level Alberta 58.31N 117.08W
29 K7 High Level Canal Orissa India
108 L5 Highmore S Dakota 44.31N 99.26W
13 K5 High Peak I Queensland 21.58S 150.38E
96 A14 High Pk St Helena 15.59S 5.44W
105 H2 High Point N Carolina 35.58N 80.00W
100 K8 High Point Saskatchewan 50.59N 107.58W
103 E4 High Point State Park New Jersey
101 P8 High Prairie Alberta 55.27N 116.28W
100 D8 High River Alberta 50.35N 113.50W
105 J11 High Rock Bahamas 26.36N 78.20W
100 R3 Highrock Manitoba 55.50N 100.22W
105 G2 High Rock N Carolina 35.36N 80.13W
103 D3 High Rock *mt* Pennsylvania 41.55N 75.25W
100 R3 Highrock L Manitoba
105 G2 High Rock L N Carolina
101 V7 Highrock L Saskatchewan 57.15N 105.30W
12 H9 High Rocky Pt Tasmania 42.17S 145.24E
14 F8 High Sand Hill W Australia 28.13S 126.40E
14 F8 High Sand Ridge W Australia 27.59S 126.40E
105 E8 High Springs Florida 29.49N 82.36W
103 E6 Hightstown New Jersey 40.16N 74.33W
106 G7 Highwood Illinois 42.13N 87.50W
110 P2 Highwood Montana 47.35N 110.47W
56 H4 Highworth Wilts Eng 51.38N 1.43W
56 K4 High Wycombe Bucks Eng 51.38N 0.46W
93 M7 Higlet Kenya 1.04S 40.20E
87 G8 Higo Ethiopia 4.22N 38.23E
115 E5 Higuera da Zaragoza Mexico 25.58N 109.20W
77 D5 Higuera de Aracena Spain 37.50N 6.27W
77 J5 Higuera de Arjona Spain 37.58N 3.59W
77 H5 Higuera de Calatrava Spain 37.49N 4.09W
77 E3 Higuera de la Serena Spain 38.39N 5.45W
77 E4 Higuera de Llerena Spain 38.23N 5.59W
77 C4 Higuera de Real Spain 38.09N 6.41W
77 C4 Higuera de Vargas Spain 38.27N 6.57W
77 H6 Higueral, El Spain 37.20N 4.15W
77 L7 Higuera, Punta de la *mt* Spain 36.52N 2.48W
75 G1 Higuer, C Spain 43.24N 1.48W
105 H7 Higuero, Pta *pt* Puerto Rico 18.23N 67.18W
119 F2 Higuerote Venezuela 10.30N 66.07W
77 O3 Higueruela Spain 38.58N 1.28W
75 J8 Higueruelas Spain 39.47N 0.53W
116 K5 Higüey Dominican Rep 18.40N 68.43W
11 K6 Hihitahi New Zealand 39.33S 175.42E
86 G4 Hihya Egypt 30.41N 31.35E
46 D1 Hiiumaa *isld* Estonia U.S.S.R.
Hijanah *see* Hijāne, El
Hijanah, Buhayrat al *L see* Hijâne, Bahret el *L*
34 D5 Hijâne, Bahret el *L* Syria
34 D5 Hijâne, El Syria 33.22N 36.33E
34 G5 Hijān, Wādī *watercourse* Syria
75 K5 Hijar Spain 41.10N 0.27W
34 M8 Hijārah, Şahrā *des* Iraq
77 L6 Hijate, El Spain 37.23N 2.35W
18 E7 Hijau, Gunung *mt* Sumatra Indonesia 2.58S 102.30E
33 B3 Hijâz *prov* Saudi Arabia
33 E8 Hijaz *reg* Saudi Arabia
20 E8 Hiji Japan 33.22N 131.32E
29 K7 Hijili *reg* W Bengal India
Hijjané, Bahret *L see* Hijâne, Bahret al *L*
Hijjané, El *see* Hijâne, El
60 O8 Hijken Netherlands 52.53N 6.30E
60 O8 Hijkersmilde Netherlands 52.56N 6.25E
60 L7 Hijlaard Netherlands 53.10N 5.43E
19 M8 Hijo Mindanao Philippines 7.21N 125.51E
60 M6 Hijum Netherlands 53.17N 5.46E
20 E8 Hikari Japan 33.59N 131.56E
20 N6 Hikawa Japan 35.49N 139.08E
20 H7 Hiketa Japan 34.13N 134.23E
20 J8 Hiki Japan 33.36N 135.29E
20 J8 Hikigawa Japan 33.35N 135.22E
20 J8 Hiki-gawa *R* Japan
26 R9 Hikkaduwa Sri Lanka 6.08N 80.06E
111 J4 Hiko Nevada 37.36N 115.15W
20 K6 Hikone Japan 35.17N 136.13E
20 D8 Hiko-san *mt* Japan 33.29N 130.58E
11 K4 Hikuai New Zealand 37.04S 175.48E
122 E15 Hikuéru *atoll* Tuamotu Is Pacific Oc 17.32S 142.32W
11 J2 Hikurangi New Zealand 35.37S 174.18E
11 N4 Hikurangi *mt* New Zealand 37.56S 178.04E
122 A10 Hikurangi *pk* Rarotonga Pacific Oc 21.12S 159.45W
11 K4 Hikutaia New Zealand 37.17S 175.40E
19 E7 Hila Indon 7.36S 127.25E
30 G3 Hilajug Nepal 27.51N 86.40E
87 J7 Hilala Ethiopia 6.05N 43.50E
87 D3 Hilaliya Sudan 14.58N 33.15E
108 C6 Hiland Wyoming 43.08N 107.20W
120 D9 Hilaricos Chile 21.30S 69.30W
56 N2 Hilborough Norfolk Eng 52.34N 0.41E
64 E1 Hilchenbach W Germany 51.00N 8.07E
100 G8 Hilda Alberta 50.30N 110.02W
53 V18 Hildal Norway 60.00N 6.35E
94 H5 Hildavale Botswana 25.19S 25.38E
64 K3 Hildburghausen E Germany 50.25N 10.45E
110 D7 Hildebrand Oregon 42.19N 121.28W
63 E10 Hilden W Germany 51.12N 6.56E
64 B1 Hilden W Germany 51.10N 6.56E
64 J2 Hilders W Germany 50.34N 10.00E
57 J7 Hilderstone Staffs Eng 52.55N 2.05W
57 N4 Hilderthorpe Humberside Eng 54.04N 0.11W
63 L8 Hildesheim W Germany 52.09N 9.58E
53 U13 Hildre Norway 62.36N 6.20E
108 L9 Hildreth Nebraska 40.20N 99.01W
114 B8 Hilea Hawaiian Is 19.08N 155.32W
33 N6 Hilf, Ra's *C* Oman 20.39N 58.56E
122 K8 Hilgard Deep Pacific Oc 2.40S 167.20W
56 M2 Hilgay Norfolk Eng 52.33N 0.23E
110 Q2 Hilger Montana 47.16N 109.22W
31 H8 Hili Bangladesh 25.16N 89.04E
18 B5 Hiliotaluwa Indonesia 0.37N 97.52E
18 B5 Hilisimaetano Indonesia 0.36N 97.42E
110 O1 Hill Montana 48.47N 111.09W
104 O3 Hill New Hampshire 43.33N 71.44W
Hilla *see* Hillah, Al
116 P6 Hillaby, Mt Barbados 13.12N 59.35W
85 M7 Hilla, El Egypt 25.16N 32.35E
87 A4 Hilla, El Sudan 13.24N 27.02E
34 M6 Hillah, Al Iraq 32.28N 44.29E
33 G5 Hillah, Al Saudi Arabia 23.29N 46.54E
108 J5 Hilland S Dakota 44.16N 101.51W
95 D9 Hillandale S Africa 33.05S 20.35E
52 G9 Hillared Sweden 57.37N 13.10E
123 H6 Hillary Coast Antarctica
115 P9 Hill Bank Belize 17.37N 88.40W
103 F4 Hillburn New York 41.08N 74.08W
110 K6 Hill City Idaho 43.19N 115.02W
109 L2 Hill City Kansas 39.23N 99.51W
108 R3 Hill City Minnesota 46.59N 93.44W
108 G6 Hill City S Dakota 43.57N 103.36W
111 P2 Hill Cr Utah
100 C9 Hillcrest Alberta 49.35N 114.22W
11 C1 Hillcrest New Zealand 36.46S 174.43E
95 O5 Hillcrest S Africa 29.47S 30.47E
61 F3 Hillegem Belgium 50.53N 3.51E
60 F12 Hillegersberg Netherlands 51.58N 4.30E
60 G10 Hillegom Netherlands 52.18N 4.35E
63 J8 Hillegossen W Germany 52.00N 8.37E
Hilleh *R see* Helleh *R*
53 J5 Hillerød Denmark 55.56N 12.19E
53 E6 Hillerslev Fyn Denmark 55.13N 10.22E
53 B2 Hillerslev Viborg Denmark 57.01N 8.45E
64 B3 Hillesheim W Germany 50.17N 6.40E
51 G2 Hillesøy Norway 69.36N 18.00E
53 T21 Hillevåg Norway 58.57N 5.45E
12 K4 Hillgrove New S Wales 30.35S 151.57E
11 E12 Hillgrove New Zealand 45.22S 170.50E
13 H4 Hill Grove Queensland 19.37S 145.50E
108 N4 Hillhead S Dakota 45.50N 97.24W
100 E5 Hilliard Alberta 53.40N 112.30W
105 F7 Hilliard Florida 30.40N 81.58W
55 B3 Hillingdon *bor* London Eng
56 N2 Hillington Norfolk Eng 52.49N 0.33E
70 E4 Hillion France 48.32N 2.40W
101 T5 Hill Island L N W Terr
106 L4 Hillman Michigan 45.04N 83.53W
108 R3 Hillman Minnesota 46.01N 93.53W
14 B9 Hillman, L W Australia 30.10S 117.00E
100 H5 Hillmond Saskatchewan 53.26N 109.41W
14 B9 Hill.R W Australia
109 G1 Hillrose Colorado 40.19N 103.32W
106 C8 Hills Iowa 41.33N 91.33W
108 O6 Hills Minnesota 43.32N 96.21W
105 D4 Hillsboro Georgia 33.10N 83.40W
107 G2 Hillsboro Illinois 39.10N 89.28W
106 C9 Hillsboro Iowa 40.50N 91.43W
109 N3 Hillsboro Kansas 38.22N 97.14W
107 F3 Hillsboro Missouri 38.13N 90.33W
105 H1 Hillsboro N Carolina 36.04N 79.06W
108 N2 Hillsboro N Dakota 47.25N 97.07W
104 O3 Hillsboro New Hampshire 43.07N 71.54W
109 C9 Hillsboro New Mexico 32.55N 107.35W
104 B7 Hillsboro Ohio 39.12N 83.37W
110 C4 Hillsboro Oregon 45.32N 122.59W
112 K3 Hillsboro Texas 32.01N 97.08W
106 D6 Hillsboro Wisconsin 43.38N 90.22W
104 E8 Hillsboro W Virginia 38.08N 80.15W
105 G11 Hillsboro Can Florida
111 B10 Hillsborough California 37.33N 122.21W
116 O8 Hillsborough Carriacou I W I 12.28N 61.28W
59 K3 Hillsborough Down Irish Rep 54.28N 6.05W
98 H8 Hillsborough New Brunswick 45.56N 64.40W
11 C2 Hillsborough *dist* Auckland New Zealand
98 J7 Hillsborough B Prince Edward I
13 J5 Hillsborough, C Queensland 20.55S 149.04E
99 K9 Hillsburgh Ontario 43.46N 80.10W
64 D3 Hillscheid W Germany 50.24N 7.42E
106 K8 Hillsdale Michigan 41.56N 84.37W
103 G2 Hillsdale New York 42.11N 73.31W
99 L8 Hillsdale Ontario 44.35N 79.46W
108 F8 Hillsdale Wyoming 41.15N 104.30W
103 A4 Hillsgrove Pennsylvania 41.27N 76.42W
111 M7 Hillside Arizona 34.26N 112.55W
109 E3 Hillside Colorado 38.15N 105.37W
58 M4 Hillside Grampian Scotland 57.04N 2.08W
103 H8 Hillside New Jersey 40.42N 74.14W
14 C5 Hillside W Australia 21.47S 119.20E
56 G4 Hillsley Glos Eng 51.37N 2.20W
99 E3 Hillsport Ontario 49.27N 85.34W
12 H5 Hillston New S Wales 33.30S 145.33E
59 F4 Hill Street Roscommon Irish Rep 53.53N 8.05W
12 D5 Hills View S Australia 33.04S 136.31E
108 L4 Hillsview S Dakota 45.50N 99.32W
103 K2 Hillsville Massachusetts 42.17N 72.01W
104 E10 Hillsville Virginia 36.46N 80.44W
58 Q9 Hillswick Shetland Scotland 60.28N 1.30W
105 F5 Hilltonia Georgia 32.53N 81.41W
95 N5 Hilltop S Africa 29.40S 29.45E
57 L5 Hill Top W Yorks Eng 53.39N 1.30W
59 K3 Hilltown Down N Ireland 54.12N 6.09W
107 F2 Hillview Illinois 39.25N 90.32W
111 D4 Hilmar California 37.25N 120.51W
86 R11 Hilmîya Cairo Egypt
114 C7 Hilo Hawaiian Is 19.42N 155.04W
114 C7 Hilo B Hawaiian Is
105 G10 Hilolo Florida 22.27N 80.47W
64 L5 Hilpoltstein W Germany 49.11N 11.13E
57 G4 Hilpsford Pt Cumbria Eng 54.03N 3.10W
30 J7 Hilsa Bihar India 25.19N 85.17E
64 F5 Hilsbach W Germany 49.11N 8.53E
69 O7 Hilsenheim France 48.19N 7.36E
66 G5 Hilterfingen Switzerland 46.44N 7.41E
104 H3 Hilton New York 43.16N 77.46W
99 G6 Hilton Beach Ontario 46.16N 83.56W
105 G5 Hilton Head I S Carolina 32.12N 80.45W
123 E12 Hilton Inlet Antarctica
95 O5 Hilton Road S Africa 29.35S 30.19E
64 L4 Hiltpoltstein W Germany 49.40N 11.20E
63 G9 Hiltrup W Germany 51.54N 7.38E
110 C8 Hilts California 41.59N 122.39W
51 N10 Hiltula Finland 61.57N 28.30E
37 D8 Hilvan Turkey 37.35N 38.58E
60 J14 Hilvarenbeek Netherlands 51.29N 5.08E
60 J11 Hilversum Netherlands 52.14N 5.10E
33 G5 Hilwah, Al Saudi Arabia 23.27N 46.50E
33 F7 Himá Saudi Arabia 18.15N 44.27E
29 E2 Himachal Pradesh *state* India
33 D4 Himá Dariyah,Jabal *mts* Saudi Arabia
27 M3 Himalaya *mts* India etc
29 J3 Himalchuli *mt* Nepal 28.25N 84.39E
51 K7 Himanka Finland 64.04N 23.40E
33 H3 Himārah, Al Saudi Arabia 26.34N 49.02E
83 D4 Himarë Albania 40.08N 19.43E
11 K7 Himatangi New Zealand 40.23S 175.20E
29 C6 Himatnagar Gujarat India 23.38N 73.02E
65 O5 Himberg Austria 48.05N 16.27E
63 N6 Himbergen W Germany 53.06N 10.45E
Himeida,Al *see* Humaydah, Al
20 H7 Himeji Japan 34.50N 134.40E
20 P2 Himekami dake *pk* Japan 39.50N 141.16E
108 B5 Himes Wyoming 44.42N 108.10W
20 M3 Hime-saki *C* Japan 38.04N 138.36E
20 E8 Hime-shima *isld* Japan
95 N5 Himeville S Africa 29.45S 29.31E
20 K5 Himi Japan 36.54N 136.59E
65 K8 Himmelberg Austria 46.45N 14.03E
53 D4 Himmelberg *mt* Denmark 56.06N 9.42E
63 K5 Himmelpforten W Germany 53.37N 9.18E
53 D3 Himmerland *reg* Denmark
36 H4 Himmetdede Turkey 38.56N 35.08E
63 K9 Himmighausen W Germany 51.48N 9.02E
93 J9 Himo Tanzania 3.24S 37.32E
19 L6 Himogaan Philippines 10.57N 123.24E
90 F6 Hina Cameroon 10.18N 13.49E
20 D9 Hinagu Japan 32.27N 130.34E
18 B5 Hinako *isld* Indonesia 0.52N 97.15E
11 K8 Hinakura New Zealand 41.19S 175.40E
19 N7 Hinatuan Mindanao Philippines 8.20N 126.18E
19 N7 Hinatuan B Mindanao Philippines
19 M7 Hinatuan Pass Philippines
116 H5 Hinche Haiti 19.10N 72.01W
87 F8 Hinchenni *mt* Ethiopia 4.35N 37.00E
113 O6 Hinchinbrook Entrance *str* Alaska
113 O6 Hinchinbrook I Alaska 60.20N 146.30W
13 H4 Hinchinbrook I Queensland
100 P6 Hinchliffe Saskatchewan 52.04N 102.40W
56 J2 Hinckley Leics Eng 52.33N 1.21W
108 S3 Hinckley Minnesota 46.01N 92.57W
111 M2 Hinckley Utah 39.20N 112.40W
104 K3 Hinckley Res New York 43.20N 75.05W
30 A3 Hindan *R* Uttar Prad India
Hindarabi *isld see* Hendorābī I
30 A6 Hindaun Rajasthan India 26.44N 77.02E
87 F5 Hinde Ethiopia 10.06N 36.20E
65 B6 Hindelang W Germany 47.31N 10.23E
66 G3 Hindelbank Switzerland 47.03N 7.33E
60 K8 Hindeloopen Netherlands 52.57N 5.24E
Hindenburg *see* Lindenhagen
63 J3 Hindenburg-damm W Germany
51 K6 Hindersön *isld* Sweden 65.34N 22.35E
57 M3 Hinderwell N Yorks Eng 54.32N 0.46W
112 J7 Hindes Texas 28.44N 98.44W
56 K5 Hindhead Surrey Eng 51.07N 0.44W
93 M8 Hindi Kenya 2.11S 40.48E
Hindian *see* Hendījān
33 B7 Hindi Gider *Lt Ho* Sudan 19.22N 37.55E
50 E3 Hindisvík *inlet* Iceland
34 M6 Hindīyah,Al Iraq 32.32N 44.14E
34 M6 Hindīyah Barrage Iraq 32.43N 44.18E
57 H5 Hindley Greater Manchester Eng 53.32N 2.35W
12 A8 Hindmarsh *dist* Adelaide, S Aust
12 F6 Hindmarsh, L Victoria
29 J7 Hindol Orissa India 20.40N 85.16E
29 D5 Hindoli Rajasthan India 25.34N 75.38E
11 E12 Hindon New Zealand 45.45S 170.20E
56 G5 Hindon Wilts Eng 51.06N 2.08W
29 F6 Hindoria Madhya Prad India 23.52N 79.38E
28 C3 Hindri R Andhra Prad India
11 F10 Hinds New Zealand 44.02S 171.33E
98 Q4 Hinds Hill *pk* Newfoundland 49.00N 56.58W
53 F5 Hindsholm *pen* Denmark 55.30N 10.40E
98 P5 Hinds L Newfoundland 48.58N 57.00W
31 D5 Hindubagh Pakistan 30.51N 67.50E
27 K2 Hindu Kush *mts* Afghanistan
28 C4 Hindupur Andhra Prad India 13.49N 77.29E
100 G5 Hindville Alberta 53.11N 110.40W
86 P7 Hind, Wādī el *watercourse* Saudi Arabia
110 F6 Hines Oregon 43.33N 119.03W
104 M2 Hinesburg Vermont 44.19N 73.07W
101 O7 Hines Creek Alberta 56.13N 118.39W
105 F6 Hinesville Georgia 31.53N 81.36W
29 F7 Hinganghat Maharashtra India 20.32N 78.52E
53 D4 Hinge Denmark 56.16N 9.32E
61 H2 Hingene Belgium 51.07N 4.16E
61 L4 Hingeon Belgium 50.32N 5.00E
103 N2 Hingham Massachusetts 42.15N 70.53W
110 P1 Hingham Montana 48.34N 110.28W
56 N2 Hingham Norfolk Eng 52.34N 0.58E
Hingho *see* Xinghe
Hinghwa Wan *B see* Xinghua Wan
Hingi *see* Xingyi
Hingkwo *see* Xingguo
31 C8 Hinglaj Pakistan 25.30N 65.32E
70 F5 Hinglé, le France 48.23N 2.05W
Hing-ning *see* Xingning
29 E8 Hingoli Maharashtra India 19.45N 77.12E
31 D7 Hingol R Pakistan
Hing-ping *see* Xingping
Hing-shan *see* Xingshan
26 S5 Hingurakgoda Sri Lanka 8.02N 80.57E
Hin Heup *see* Ban Hin Heup
26 R9 Hiniduma Sri Lanka 6.19N 80.20E
76 H5 Hiniesta,La Spain 41.33N 5.49W
37 F6 Hiniş Turkey 39.22N 41.44E
37 F6 Hiniş *R* Turkey
111 G7 Hinkley California 34.57N 117.14W
14 G7 Hinkley, Mt W Australia 26.10S 128.58E
56 E5 Hinkley Pt Somerset Eng 51.12N 3.09W
50 T13 Hinlopenstretet *str* Spitsbergen
90 E6 Hinna Nigeria 10.20N 11.35E
53 T21 Hinna Norway 58.55N 5.45E
33 H3 Hinnāh, Al Saudi Arabia 26.56N 48.46E
51 J11 Hinnerjoki Finland 61.00N 22.00E
53 E4 Hinnerup Denmark 56.16N 10.05E
35 B1 Hinnom,Val of Jerusalem
51 E3 Hinnøya *isld* Norway 68.35N 15.50E
20 B2 Hino Tōkyō Japan 35.41N 139.25E
20 K5 Hino *R* Japan
19 L7 Hinobaan Philippines 9.34N 122.30E
75 E4 Hinodejo *mt* Spain 41.42N 2.41W
76 G9 Hinojal Spain 39.42N 6.22W
77 C4 Hinojales Spain 38.00N 6.35W
77 L5 Hinojares Spain 37.43N 3.00W
121 E6 Hinojo Argentina 36.55S 60.10W
77 L5 Hinojora *mt* Spain 37.32N 2.31W
77 D6 Hinojos Spain 37.17N 6.23W
75 G5 Hinojosa Spain 41.02N 1.56W
76 F7 Hinojosa de Duero Spain 40.59N 6.47W
77 F4 Hinojosa del Duque Spain 38.30N 5.09W
77 D4 Hinojosa del Valle Spain 38.29N 6.10W
76 K8 Hinojosa de San Vicente Spain 40.06N 4.44W
75 F8 Hinojosa, La Spain 39.44N 2.25W
77 H3 Hinojosas Spain 38.37N 4.08W
20 E9 Hinokage Japan 32.40N 131.24E
20 F6 Hinomi-saki *C* Japan 35.28N 132.36E
106 G8 Hinsdale Illinois 41.48N 87.55W
103 H2 Hinsdale Massachusetts 42.26N 73.08W
108 C1 Hinsdale Montana 48.25N 107.05W
104 N4 Hinsdale New Hampshire 42.48N 72.29W
104 G4 Hinsdale New York 42.11N 78.20W
56 G2 Hinstock Shropshire Eng 52.51N 2.28W
65 F7 Hinterbichl Austria 47.01N 12.20E
64 E3 Hintermeilingen W Germany 50.30N 8.08E
66 N5 Hinterrhein Switzerland 46.32N 9.13E
65 D7 Hinter Riss Austria 47.29N 11.29E
66 O3 Hinterruck *mt* Switzerland 47.09N 9.19E
64 O8 Hinter See W Germany 47.36N 12.50E
65 H6 Hinter See *L* Austria 47.46N 13.15E
66 N4 Hinter Steinibach Switzerland 46.54N 9.08E
65 K6 Hinterstoder Austria 47.42N 14.09E
65 E7 Hinter Tux Austria 47.07N 11.40E
64 D5 Hinter Weidenthal W Germany 49.12N 7.46E
64 E8 Hinterzarten W Germany 47.54N 8.07E
56 O3 Hintlesham Suffolk Eng 52.03N 1.03E
101 P9 Hinton Alberta 53.24N 117.35W
56 H6 Hinton Dorset Eng 50.46N 1.43W
109 M6 Hinton Oklahoma 35.29N 98.23W
104 E9 Hinton W Virginia 37.42N 80.54W
20 O5 Hi-numa *L* Japan
34 F7 Hinw, Al *hill* Saudi Arabia 31.17N 38.17E
66 M2 Hinwil Switzerland 47.18N 8.51E
72 C8 Hinx France 43.42N 0.55W
36 H6 Hınzır Burun *C* Turkey 36.20N 35.45E
36 J4 Hınzır Dağı *mt* Turkey 38.56N 36.12E
120 D7 Hipocapac, Nev. de *pk* Peru 16.33S 70.33W
115 J5 Hipólito Mexico 25.42N 101.23W
121 C4 Hipólito Irogoyen Argentina 32.51S 66.23W
60 H8 Hippolytushoef Netherlands 52.54N 4.57E
Hippos *anc site see* Susitha
94 C2 Hirabis Namibia 19.36S 15.06E
37 H7 Hirabit Dağ *mt* Turkey 38.21N 44.03E
20 C8 Hirado Japan 33.22N 129.31E
20 C8 Hirado-jima *isld* Japan
88 Q10 Hirafok Algeria 23.40N 5.46E
29 H7 Hirakud Dam Orissa India 21.32N 83.55E
29 H7 Hirakud Res Orissa India
104 P3 Hiram Maine 43.52N 70.49W
93 L7 Hiraman *watercourse* Kenya
87 K8 Hiran Somalia 4.48N 45.12E
87 K8 Hiran *prov* Somalia
20 N1 Hiranai Japan 40.57N 140.58E
30 C8 Hirapur Madhya Prad India 24.21N 79.12E
21 H8 Hirasawa Japan 39.14N 139.57E
20 C8 Hira-shima *isld* Japan 33.00N 129.14E
20 F6 Hirata Japan 35.25N 132.45E
20 N6 Hiratsuka Japan 35.20N 139.19E
20 B3 Hirayama Tōkyō Japan
Hirbiya *see* Karmiyya
28 B3 Hirekerur Karnataka India 14.29N 75.26E
36 G3 Hirfanlı Barajı *dam* Turkey 39.18N 33.31E
Hirgis Nur *L see* Hyargas Nuur
28 C4 Hiriyur Karnataka India 13.56N 76.35E
Hiriz *see* Heris
82 K3 Hîrlău Romania 47.26N 26.54E
87 H6 Hirna Ethiopia 9.12N 41.05E
20 N2 Hiroo Japan 42.17N 143.17E
20 O1 Hirosaki Japan 40.34N 140.28E
20 G6 Hirose Japan 35.22N 133.09E
20 F7 Hiroshima Japan 34.23N 132.27E
20 F7 Hiroshima *prefect* Japan
20 P3 Hirota-wan *B* Japan
33 J5 Hirrah, Al Saudi Arabia 22.36N 51.14E
64 F6 Hirsau W Germany 48.44N 8.44E
64 L4 Hirschaid W Germany 49.50N 10.59E
64 M4 Hirschau W Germany 49.32N 11.56E
64 M3 Hirschberg E Germany 50.24N 11.50E
Hirschberg Poland *see* Jelenia Góra
65 L7 Hirschegg Austria 47.02N 14.58E
64 O6 Hirschenstein *mt* W Germany 48.58N 12.53E
64 F5 Hirschhorn W Germany 49.28N 8.54E
53 F2 Hirsholmene *Lt Ho* Denmark 57.29N 10.38E
71 L1 Hirsingue France 47.35N 7.15E
69 G4 Hirson France 49.56N 4.05E
82 L6 Hîrşova Romania 44.41N 27.56E
58 A1 Hirta *isld* W Isles Scotland 57.49N 8.34W
53 D1 Hirtshals Denmark 57.36N 9.58E
66 E1 Hirtzbach France 47.36N 7.14E
61 O8 Hirtzenberg *mt* Belgium 49.40N 5.47E
51 M10 Hirvensalmi Finland 61.40N 26.51E
51 L7 Hirvineva Finland 64.44N 25.10E
56 D4 Hirwain Mid Glam Wales 51.45N 3.30W

20 B9 **Hisaka-shima** *I* Japan 32.50N 128.50E
Hisār *see* **Ḥeşār**
29 D3 **Hisar** Haryana **India** 29.10N 75.45E
32 C2 **Hisar** Iran 36.02N 48.49E
29 D3 **Hisar** *dist* Haryana **India**
Hisarköy *see* **Domaniç**
36 F1 **Hisarönü** Turkey 41.33N 32.01E
53 R17 **Hisarøy** *isld* Norway 60.59N 4.59E
35 G6 **Hisban** Jordan 31.48N 35.48E
35 F6 **Hisban** *R* Jordan
Hisb,Sh'ib *watercourse see* **Ḥasb, Sha'ib**
34 G2 **Hishe, El** Syria 36.24N 39.02E
52 G10 **Hishult** Sweden 56.25N 13.20E
33 F8 **Hishwah, Al** *area* Yemen
15 J8 **Hisiu** Papua New Guinea 9.02S 146.48E
108 J6 **Hisle** S Dakota 43.24N 101.45W
33 B2 **Hismā** *reg* Saudi Arabia
34 C10 **Hismā, Al** *plain* Saudi Arabia
33 F10 **Hiṣn, Al** S Yemen 13.17N 45.18E
Hisn al Abr *see* **Huṣn Al 'Abr**
33 H8 **Hiṣn al Fuḍūl** S Yemen 16.21N 48.16E
33 G10 **Hiṣn Bal'īd** S Yemen 13.34N 46.58E
116 H4 **Hispaniola** *isld* West Indies
31 H2 **Hispar Glacier** Kashmir
Hissar Iran*see* **Hisar**
56 M3 **Histon** Cambs **Eng** 52.15N 0.06E
30 J8 **Hisua** Bihar **India** 24.51N 85.26E
33 B9 **Ḥiswah, Al** S Yemen 12.50N 44.57E
86 P6 **Ḥiswa, Wādī el** *watercourse* Jordan
34 D4 **Hisya** Syria 34.25N 36.45E
34 K5 **Hīt** Iraq 33.38N 42.50E
20 D8 **Hita** Japan 33.19N 130.55E
75 D6 **Hita** Spain 40.49N 3.03W
20 O5 **Hitachi** Japan 36.35N 140.40E
32 J7 **Hītak** Iran 26.17N 60.22E
20 C7 **Hitakatsu** Japan 34.41N 129.27E
50 C5 **Hítará** *R* Iceland
50 C5 **Hítarnes** *C* Iceland 64.40N 22.25W
50 D5 **Hítarvatn** *L* Iceland 64.52N 21.58W
56 N3 **Hitcham** Suffolk **Eng** 52.07N 0.54E
109 M6 **Hitchcock** Oklahoma 35.58N 98.22W
100 O9 **Hitchcock** Saskatchewan 49.12N 103.03W
108 M5 **Hitchcock** S Dakota 44.39N 98.25W
112 M6 **Hitchcock** Texas 29.21N 95.02W
56 L4 **Hitchin** Herts **Eng** 51.57N 0.17W
109 P6 **Hitchita** Oklahoma 35.33N 95.44W
86 O9 **Hiteibi, Wādī el** *watercourse* Saudi Arabia
103 K4 **Hither Hills State Park** Long I, N Y
122 D15 **Hiti** *I* Tuamotu Is **Pacific Oc** 16.30S 144.10W
122 C12 **Hitiaa** Tahiti **Pacific Oc** 17.35S 149.17W
75 E8 **Hito, El** Spain 39.51N 2.43W
75 E8 **Hito, L.de El** Spain 39.52N 2.42W
20 D9 **Hitoyoshi** Japan 32.12N 130.48E
52 D3 **Hitra** Norway 63.37N 8.46E
52 D3 **Hitra** *isld* Norway
63 L6 **Hittfeld** W Germany 53.23N 9.58E
65 A7 **Hittisau** Austria 47.28N 9.58E
63 O6 **Hitzacker** W Germany 53.09N 11.04E
66 K3 **Hitzkirch** Switzerland 47.14N 8.16E
20 N5 **Hiuchi-dake** *pk* Japan 36.58N 139.19E
20 G7 **Hiuchi-nada** *sea* Japan
95 P9 **Hiuhluwe** S Africa 28.02S 32.17E
122 V14 **Hiva Oa** *isld* Marquesas Is **Pacific Oc** 9.45S 139.00W
61 N6 **Hives** Belgium 50.09N 5.35E
Hivris *see* **Simek**
85 M6 **Hiw** Egypt 26.01N 32.18E
9 B9 **Hiw** *isld* New Hebrides 13.07S 166.34E
29 E7 **Hiwarkhed** Maharashtra **India** 21.10N 76.58E
20 H8 **Hiwasa** Japan 33.42N 134.32E
107 M6 **Hiwassee** *R* Tennessee
105 C2 **Hiwassee Dam** N Carolina 35.08N 84.02W
105 C2 **Hiwassee L** N Carolina 35.08N 84.13W
86 P10 **Hiweit,El** Saudi Arabia 27.42N 35.38E
13 L5 **Hixson Cay** *isld* Gt Barrier Reef **Australia** 22.20S 152.36E
20 J2 **Hiyama** *sub-prefect* Hokkaido **Japan**
34 C8 **Hiyon** *watercourse* **Israel**
20 D3 **Hiyoshi** *dist* Tōkyō **Japan**
86 N5 **Hiyyon** *watercourse* **Israel**
37 G7 **Hizan** Turkey 38.10N 42.26E
21 J8 **Hizume** Japan 39.33N 141.12E
50 C3 **Hjallar** Iceland 65.35N 22.09W
53 E2 **Hjallerup** Denmark 57.10N 10.10E
50 D7 **Hjalli** Iceland 63.57N 21.18W
52 J7 **Hjälmaren** *L* Sweden
101 T5 **Hjalmar L** N W Terr
50 E3 **Hjaltabakki** Iceland 65.38N 20.19W
50 F3 **Hjaltadalur** *V* Iceland
50 L3 **Hjaltastadhur** Iceland 65.31N 14.11W
50 G3 **Hjalteyri** Iceland 65.51N 18.10W
53 C3 **Hjarbæk** Denmark 56.32N 9.20E
53 C3 **Hjarbæk Fjord** *inlet* Denmark 56.33N 9.20E
53 B2 **Hjardemål** Denmark 57.04N 8.49E
50 C5 **Hjardharfell** Iceland 64.53N 22.45W
50 D4 **Hjardharholt** Dalasýsla **Iceland** 65.07N 21.42W
50 D5 **Hjardharholt** Mýrasýsla **Iceland** 64.43N 21.31W
53 E5 **Hjarnø** *isld* Denmark 55.49N 10.05E
52 D7 **Hjartdal** Norway 59.37N 8.41E
51 D6 **Hjartfjell** *mt* Norway 65.52N 14.25E
53 C6 **Hjarup** Denmark 55.27N 9.21E
53 W15 **Hjelle** Norway 61.55N 7.08E
53 J7 **Hjelm** Denmark 54.54N 12.15E
53 F4 **Hjelm** *isld* Denmark 56.08N 10.48E
53 J7 **Hjelm Bugt** *B* Denmark 54.56N 12.22E
53 R17 **Hjelme** Norway 60.39N 4.49E
53 U20 **Hjelmelandsvågen** Norway 59.13N 6.11E
53 S15 **Hjelmevatn** *L* Norway 61.48N 5.25E
51 L1 **Hjelmsøya** *isld* Norway 71.05N 24.40E
53 R17 **Hjeltefjord** *inlet* Norway 60.33N 4.56E
53 G5 **Hjembæk** Denmark 55.42N 11.25E
52 E4 **Hjerkinn** Norway 62.14N 9.29E
53 B4 **Hjerm** Denmark 56.27N 8.39E
53 C6 **Hjerndrup** Denmark 55.19N 9.25E
53 B6 **Hjerpsted** Denmark 55.02N 8.40E
53 A5 **Hjerting** Denmark 55.32N 8.22E
53 C6 **Hjerting** Haderslev **Denmark** 55.23N 9.03E
52 H8 **Hjo** Sweden 58.17N 14.07E
53 C4 **Hjøllund** Denmark 56.04N 9.23E
53 W18 **Hjølmo** Norway 60.22N 7.10E
53 C6 **Hjordkær** Denmark 55.03N 9.19E
50 G8 **Hjörleifshöfdhi** *mt* Iceland 63.25N 18.45W
53 D2 **Hjørring** Denmark 57.28N 9.59E
Hjørring *co see* **Nordjylland**
50 C5 **Hjörsey** *isld* Iceland 64.32N 22.21W
53 E7 **Hjortø** Denmark 54.58N 10.30E
53 E7 **Hjortø** *isld* Denmark 54.58N 10.30E
53 E4 **Hjortshøj** Denmark 56.15N 10.17E
53 D5 **Hjortsvang** Denmark 55.54N 9.31E
53 U14 **Hjørundfjord** Norway 62.12N 6.26E
53 U14 **Hjørundfjorden** *inlet* Norway 62.20N 6.25E
53 U14 **Hjørungavåg** Norway 62.22N 6.05E
51 H7 **Hjuken** Sweden 64.19N 19.35E
52 E7 **Hjuksebø** Norway 59.32N 9.20E
25 N7 **Hkakabo Razi** *mt* Burma 28.17N 97.46E
25 E2 **Hkok** *R* Burma
25 N7 **Hkring Bum** *mt* Burma 27.04N 97.22E
95 O9 **Hlabisa** S Africa 28.10S 31.53E
25 C4 **Hlaing** *R* Burma
24 F11 **Hlako Kangri** *mt pk* Xizang Zizhiqu **China** 28.48N 87.40E
94 L6 **Hlatikulu** Swaziland 26.58S 31.28E
25 D4 **Hlegu** Burma 17.05N 96.16E
33 J9 **Hleime** S Yemen 15.31N 50.55E
50 D6 **Hlidhar** *mt* Iceland 64.17N 21.20W
50 F7 **Hlídharendi** Iceland 63.44N 19.55W
50 J3 **Hlídharfjall** *mt* Iceland 65.42N 16.53W
50 L3 **Hlídharfjöll** *mts* Iceland
50 D7 **Hlídharvatn** *L* Árnessýsla **Iceland** 63.52N 21.45W
50 C5 **Hlidharvatn** *L* Snæfellsnessýsla **Iceland** 64.54N 22.10W
64 P3 **Hlinec** *R* Czechoslovakia
65 N2 **Hlinsko** Czechoslovakia 49.46N 15.54E
50 C2 **Hljódhabunga** *mt* Iceland 66.11N 22.15W
95 O3 **Hlobane** S Africa 27.42S 31.00E
50 E6 **Hlödhufell** *mt* Iceland 64.25N 20.31W
62 K7 **Hlohovec** Czechoslovakia 48.27N 17.50E
65 K3 **Hluboká nad Vltava** Czech 49.04N 14.27E
95 O9 **Hluhluwe** *R* S Africa
25 N9 **Hlung-Tan** Burma 23.13N 98.26E
95 O8 **Hluti** Swaziland 27.12S 31.35E
25 L9 **Hnahlan** Assam **India** 23.44N 93.24E
50 E3 **Hnausar** Iceland 65.30N 20.21W
50 K4 **Hnefilsdalsa** *R* Iceland
50 G5 **Hnífá** *R* Iceland
50 B2 **Hnífsdalur** Iceland 66.07N 23.06W
50 A3 **Hnjótur** Iceland 65.34N 24.07W
50 G4 **Hnjúkskvísl** *R* Iceland
53 A5 **Ho** Denmark 55.34N 8.15E
89 K8 **Ho** Ghana 6.38N 0.38E
25 H2 **Hoa Binh** Vietnam 20.49N 105.20E
25 K7 **Hoa Da** Vietnam 11.13N 108.34E
100 C6 **Hoadley** Alberta 52.51N 114.22W
94 E4 **Hoaganas** Namibia 23.55S 18.04E
108 K8 **Hoagland** Nebraska 41.31N 100.32W
25 K5 **Hoai Nhon** Vietnam 14.24N 109.00E
25 H1 **Hoang Su Phi** Vietnam 22.47N 104.40E
94 B2 **Hoanib** *watercourse* Namibia
20 E8 **Hoashi** Japan 33.20N 131.11E
110 P6 **Hoback** *R* Wyoming
110 P6 **Hoback Pk** Wyoming 43.05N 110.33W
106 G8 **Hobart** Indiana 41.32N 87.14W
103 E2 **Hobart** New York 42.22N 74.40W
109 L6 **Hobart** Oklahoma 35.03N 99.04W
12 H9 **Hobart** Tasmania 42.54S 147.18E
13 H6 **Hobartville** Queensland 23.20S 146.32E
100 D6 **Hobbema** Alberta 52.50N 113.27W
109 G9 **Hobbs** New Mexico 32.42N 103.08W
123 J10 **Hobbs Coast** Antarctica
107 K7 **Hobbs Island** Alabama 34.31N 86.30W
Hobdo *see* **Hovd**
105 G10 **Hobe Sound** Florida 27.03N 80.09W
88 N6 **Hobeur, El** *reg* Algeria
105 K1 **Hobgood** N Carolina 36.02N 77.24W
95 L5 **Hobhouse** S Africa 29.31S 27.08E
57 H2 **Hobkirk** Borders **Scotland** 55.24N 2.40W
119 C6 **Hobo** Colombia 2.34N 75.28W
93 J1 **Hobok** Ethiopia 4.22N 37.15E
61 H2 **Hoboken** Belgium 51.11N 4.21E
105 E6 **Hoboken** Georgia 31.11N 82.09W
103 L7 **Hoboken** New Jersey 40.45N 74.03W
24 E2 **Hoboksar** Xinjiang Uygur Zizhiqu **China** 46.47N 85.50E
22 H6 **Hobq Shamo** *des* Nei Monggol Zizhiqu China
61 O8 **Hobscheid** Luxembourg 49.42N 5.55E
Höbsögöl Dalay *L see* **Hövsgöl Nuur**
110 Q3 **Hobson** Montana 47.00N 109.51W
11 D2 **Hobson B** Auckland **New Zealand**
11 K3 **Hobson, Mt** New Zealand 36.12S 175.27E
12 C8 **Hobsons B** Victoria
11 B1 **Hobsonville** New Zealand 36.48S 174.39E
105 L2 **Hobucken** N Carolina 35.16N 76.33W
53 A5 **Ho Bugt** *B* Denmark 55.34N 8.16E
52 L10 **Hoburgen** *Lt Ho* Sweden 56.55N 18.05E
Hobyo *see* **Obbia**
37 C2 **Hoçaâli** Turkey 40.41N 26.21E
115 P7 **Hocabá** Mexico 20.49N 89.29W
36 D4 **Hocalar** Turkey 38.38N 29.53E
88 M4 **Hoceima, Al** Morocco 35.14N 3.56W
65 H7 **Hochalm Spitze** *mt* Austria 47.02N 13.20E
66 O2 **Hochalp** *mt* Switzerland 47.17N 9.16E
65 M7 **Hochalpe** *mt* Austria 47.21N 15.13E
66 N5 **Hochberg Horn** *mt* Switzerland 46.31N 9.07E
66 K3 **Hochdorf** Switzerland 47.10N 8.16E
66 Q5 **Hoch Ducan** *mt* Switzerland 46.42N 9.52E
65 N8 **Hocheck** *mt* Austria 46.59N 15.42E
69 O6 **Hochfelden** France 48.46N 7.34E
65 G7 **Hochfilzen** Austria 47.28N 12.37E
65 C8 **Hoch Finstermünz** Austria 46.57N 10.30E
66 L3 **Hochfluh** *mt* Switzerland 47.01N 8.35E
65 F8 **Hochgrabe** *mt* Austria 46.52N 12.26E
64 K2 **Hochheim** E Germany 50.57N 10.59E
112 K6 **Hochheim** Texas 29.19N 97.19W
64 E3 **Hochheim** W Germany 50.01N 8.23E
25 J7 **Ho Chi Minh** Vietnam 10.46N 106.43E
Ho Chi Minh City *see* **Saigon**
65 L6 **Hochkar** *mt* Austria 47.43N 14.55E
65 H7 **Hochkönig** *mt* Austria 47.27N 13.04E
65 H8 **Hochkreuz** *mt* Austria 46.49N 13.05E
65 M7 **Hochlantsch** *mt* Austria 47.23N 15.26E
69 L1 **Hochneukirch** W Germany 51.06N 6.27E
65 K8 **Hochobir** *mt* Austria 46.31N 14.29E
Hochow *see* **Ho-ch'uan**
65 C6 **Hochplatte** *mt* W Germany 47.33N 10.53E
65 L7 **Hochreichart** *mt* Austria 47.22N 14.41E
65 N6 **Hochschneeberg** *mts* Austria
65 M6 **Hochschwab** *mt* Austria 47.37N 15.08E
65 M6 **Hochschwab** *mts* Austria
64 D5 **Hochspeyer** W Germany 49.26N 7.54E
Höchst *see* **Frankfurt am Main**
64 F4 **Hochst** W Germany 49.47N 8.59E
65 M6 **Hochstadl** *mt* Austria 47.43N 15.05E
64 K4 **Höchstadt** Oberfranken, Bayern W Germany 49.42N 10.50E
64 K6 **Höchstädt** Schwaben, Bayern **W Germany** 48.35N 10.35E
66 F1 **Hochstatt** France 47.42N 7.16E
65 K7 **Hochstein** *mt* Austria 47.26N 14.12E
64 D2 **Höchstenbach** W Germany 50.38N 7.45E
64 G8 **Höchster** *mt* W Germany 47.50N 9.25E
69 O4 **Hochstetten-Dhaun** W Germany 49.48N 7.31E
48 V7 **Hochstetter Forland** *prom* Greenland
11 F9 **Hochstetter,L** New Zealand 42.27S 171.38E
65 K9 **Hochstuhl** *mt* Yugoslavia/Austria 46.25N 14.10E
65 G7 **Hochtor** *mt* Salzburg **Austria** 47.07N 12.59E
65 L6 **Hochtor** *mt* Steiermark **Austria** 47.34N 14.38E
23 B8 **Ho Chung** Hong Kong 22.22N 114.14E
65 B7 **Hochvoget** *mt* Austria 47.23N 10.26E
66 G2 **Hochwald** Switzerland 47.27N 7.38E
66 P4 **Hochwang** *mt* Switzerland 46.52N 9.36E
65 N6 **Hochwechsel** *mt* Austria 47.33N 15.55E
65 O6 **Hochwolkersdorf** Austria 47.40N 16.18E
64 F5 **Hockenheim** W Germany 49.19N 8.34E
56 O2 **Hockering** Norfolk **Eng** 52.41N 1.03E
104 C7 **Hocking** *R* Ohio
104 D7 **Hockingport** Ohio 39.12N 81.47W
112 M5 **Hockley** Texas 30.02N 95.53W
56 H3 **Hockley Heath** W Midlands **Eng** 52.21N 1.46W
56 K4 **Hockliffe** Beds **Eng** 51.56N 0.36W
115 P7 **Hoctúm** Mexico 20.48N 89.14W
29 E4 **Hodal** Haryana **India** 27.52N 77.22E
Hodar *see* **Hüvār**
87 K7 **Hodayu Wein** Ethiopia 7.42N 45.08E
53 B5 **Hodde** Denmark 55.42N 8.39E
57 J5 **Hodder, R** Lancs **Eng**
56 L4 **Hoddesdon** Herts **Eng** 51.46N 0.01W
95 N6 **Hode** S Africa 30.50S 29.09E
Hodeida *see* **Hudaydah, Al**
85 N8 **Hodein, Wadī** *watercourse* **Egypt**
107 D9 **Hodge** Louisiana 32.18N 92.42W
107 L4 **Hodgenville** Kentucky 37.34N 85.45W
108 F3 **Hodges** Montana 46.58N 104.25W
105 E3 **Hodges** S Carolina 34.16N 82.15W
98 R4 **Hodges Hill** *pk* Newfoundland 49.04N 55.52W
111 G8 **Hodges,L** California 33.04N 117.05W
100 L8 **Hodgeville** Saskatchewan 50.07N 106.58W
100 U7 **Hodgson** Manitoba 51.13N 97.35W
13 C3 **Hodgson Downs** N Terr **Aust** 15.15S 134.07E
89 E3 **Hodh** *reg* Mauritania
61 M6 **Hodister** Belgium 50.12N 5.30E
35 B7 **Hodiyya** Israel 31.40N 34.37E
62 M9 **Hódmezővásárhely** Hungary 46.26N 20.21E
88 Q4 **Hodna, Mts. du** Algeria
53 T20 **Hodne** Norway 59.05N 5.46E
56 F2 **Hodnet** Shropshire **Eng** 52.51N 2.35W
20 D4 **Hodogaya** Japan 35.26N 139.36E
65 O4 **Hodonice** Czechoslovakia 48.51N 16.11E
62 K7 **Hodonín** Czechoslovakia 48.52N 17.10E
82 C4 **Hodos** Yugoslavia 46.49N 16.20E
53 B4 **Hodsager** Denmark 56.19N 8.52E
11 N12 **Hodson Hill** New Zealand 45.47S 170.40E
95 N5 **Hodson's Peak** *mt* S Africa 29.38S 29.17E
37 D3 **Hodul Dağ** *mt* Turkey
36 H4 **Hodul Daği** *mt* Turkey
61 N5 **Hody** Belgium 50.29N 5.30E
113 N3 **Hodzana** *R* Alaska
114 B6 **Hoea** Hawaiian Is 20.15N 155.52W
53 F4 **Hoed** Denmark 56.19N 10.49E
60 C3 **Hoedekenskerke** Netherlands 51.25N 3.55E
70 E7 **Hoëdic** *isld* France 47.21N 2.53W
61 K3 **Hoegaarden** Belgium 50.47N 4.53E
109 F4 **Hoehne** Colorado 37.17N 104.24W
61 H3 **Hoeilaart** Belgium 50.46N 4.28E
60 C3 **Hoek** Netherlands 51.18N 3.47E
95 B8 **Hoek,De** S Africa 32.57S 18.45E
61 D1 **Hoeke** Belgium 51.17N 3.20E
94 P12 **Hoek van Bobbejaan** *C* Cape Town S Africa 34.18S 18.24E
60 E12 **Hoek-van-Holland** Netherlands 51.59N 4.07E
61 K3 **Hoeleden** Belgium 50.52N 4.59E
53 Y13 **Hoemsbu** Norway 62.33N 8.07E
60 M11 **Hoenderloo** Netherlands 52.07N 5.53E
64 A2 **Hoengen** W Germany 50.52N 6.13E
21 D9 **Hoengsŏng** S Korea 37.29N 127.59E
60 T17 **Hoensbroek** Netherlands 50.55N 5.55E
77 F9 **Ho era** *R* Morocco
21 E6 **Hoeryong** N Korea 42.29N 129.45E
61 M3 **Hoeselt** Belgium 50.51N 5.30E
60 K11 **Hoevelaken** Netherlands 52.10N 5.27E
60 G13 **Hoeven** Netherlands 51.35N 4.35E
61 H1 **Hoevenen** Belgium 51.18N 4.24E
100 M6 **Hoey** Saskatchewan 52.52N 105.49W
65 H6 **Hof** Austria 47.49N 13.13E
50 E3 **Hof** Húnavatnssýsla, Austur **Iceland** 65.55N 20.20W
50 L3 **Hof** Múlasýsla, Nordhur **Iceland** 65.39N 14.58W
50 J7 **Hof** Skaftafellssýsla, Austur **Iceland** 63.54N 16.44W
50 F3 **Hof** Skagafjardharsýsla **Iceland** 65.54N 19.24W
50 F4 **Hof** Skagafjardharsýsla **Iceland** 65.17N 19.01W
64 M3 **Hof** W Germany 50.19N 11.56E
64 H2 **Hofbieber** W Germany 50.35N 9.51E
50 G8 **Hofdhabrekka** Iceland 63.26N 18.54W
50 G7 **Höfdhabrekkujökull** *ice cap* Iceland 63.35N 18.53W
50 G3 **Höfdhahverfi** Iceland 65.57N 18.05W
50 E3 **Höfdhakaupstadhur** Iceland 65.50N 20.19W
50 F3 **Höfdhavatn** *L* Iceland 65.57N 19.28W
50 F3 **Höfdhi** Iceland 65.58N 19.23W
64 F6 **Höfen** W Germany 48.49N 8.35E
64 J6 **Hofen** W Germany 48.54N 10.10E
Ho-feng *see* **Hoxtolgay**
50 K6 **Hoffell** Iceland 64.23N 15.19W
50 L5 **Hoffell** *mt* Iceland 64.59N 14.05W
50 K6 **Hoffelsjökull** *ice cap* Iceland 64.28N 15.35W
108 P4 **Hoffman** Minnesota 45.49N 95.49W
105 H2 **Hoffman** N Carolina 35.02N 79.34W
103 J8 **Hoffman I** New York 40.35N 74.04W
63 K10 **Hofgeismar** W Germany 51.29N 9.22E
64 E3 **Hofheim** Hessen **W Germany** 50.05N 8.27E
64 K3 **Hofheim in Unterfranken** Bayern W Germany 50.08N 10.32E
65 J5 **Hofkirchen** Austria 48.29N 13.49E
64 P6 **Hofkirchen** W Germany 48.41N 13.08E
92 E9 **Hofmeyer** Zambia 14.40S 30.52E
95 J7 **Hofmeyr** S Africa 31.40S 25.48E
50 C2 **Höfn** Ísafjardharsýsla, Nordhur **Iceland** 66.26N 22.29W
50 B3 **Höfn** Ísafjardharsýsla, Vestur **Iceland** 65.55N 23.49W
50 M3 **Höfn** Múlasýsla, Nordhur **Iceland** 65.32N 13.45W
50 D6 **Höfn** Mýrasýsla **Iceland** 64.28N 21.58W
50 K6 **Höfn** Skaftafellssýsla, Austur **Iceland** 64.16N 15.10W
85 E5 **Hofra** Libya 29.17N 18.09E
90 M7 **Hofrat en Nahas** Sudan 9.49N 24.16E
50 K3 **Hofsá** *R* Múlasýsla, Nordhur **Iceland**
50 G4 **Hofsá** *R* Skagafjardharsýsla **Iceland**
50 K3 **Hofsárdalur** *V* Iceland
50 G5 **Hofsjökull** *ice cap* Iceland 64.50N 18.50W
50 F3 **Hofsós** Iceland 65.54N 19.25W
61 H3 **Hofstade** Brabant **Belgium** 50.59N 4.30E
61 G3 **Hofstade** Oost Vlaanderen **Belgium** 50.57N 4.02E
50 F3 **Hofstadhir** Iceland 65.42N 19.24W
50 D6 **Hofsvík** *inlet* Iceland
50 L4 **Hofteigur** Iceland 65.22N 14.53W
20 E7 **Höfu** Japan 34.02N 131.34E
Hofūf *see* **Hufūf,Al**
86 F6 **Hôf, Wâdî** *watercourse* **Egypt**
53 K4 **Höganäs** Sweden 56.13N 12.34E
12 H7 **Hogan Grp** *islds* Tasmania 39.14S 146.59E
53 X16 **Høganosa** *mt* Norway 61.08N 7.34E
111 D3 **Hogan Res** California 38.09N 120.48W
99 T2 **Hogansburg** New York 44.59N 74.41W
105 C4 **Hogansville** Georgia 33.10N 84.55W
13 H7 **Hoganthulla** *R* Queensland
99 B3 **Hogarth** Ontario 49.12N 98.17W
13 D5 **Hogarth, Mt** N Terr **Australia** 21.52S 137.00E
113 K3 **Hogatza** Alaska 66.15N 155.53W
113 K3 **Hogatza** *R* Alaska
110 N5 **Hogback Mt** Montana 44.55N 112.07W
52 G7 **Högboda** Sweden 59.35N 13.05E
52 K9 **Högby** Sweden 57.10N 17.00E
53 Y21 **Høgefoss** *waterfall* **Norway** 58.58N 8.30E
53 W18 **Høgehæ** *mt* Norway 60.18N 7.26E
94 E7 **Hogeis** Namibia 28.20S 19.13E
110 R1 **Hogeland** Montana 48.51N 108.39W
52 J7 **Högfors** Sweden 59.58N 15.03E
88 P11 **Hoggar** *reg* **Algeria**
88 Q10 **Hoggar** *reg* **Algeria**
53 X14 **Høggjøymen** *mt* Norway 62.05N 7.55E
100 V1 **Hogg L** Manitoba
82 J5 **Hoghiz** Romania 45.59N 25.19E
57 H5 **Hoghton** Lancs **Eng** 53.44N 2.35W
106 J4 **Hog I** Michigan 45.48N 85.22W
105 L9 **Hog I** New Providence I **Bahamas**
104 K9 **Hog I** Virginia 37.25N 75.43W
53 B4 **Høgild** Denmark 56.03N 9.00E
35 C4 **Hogla** Israel 32.23N 34.56E
61 M5 **Hogne** Belgium 50.15N 5.17E
50 E6 **Högnhöfdhi** *mt* Iceland 64.22N 20.30W
22 J2 **Högnö** Mongolia 48.35N 113.49E
61 M4 **Hognoul** Belgium 50.41N 5.27E
92 H4 **Hogoro** Tanzania 5.56S 36.27E
99 D9 **Hogs Back** Ontario 45.22N 75.42W
56 K5 **Hog's Back** *ridge* Surrey **Eng**
52 J9 **Högsby** Sweden 57.10N 16.03E
53 T21 **Høgsfjorden** *inlet* Norway 58.57N 6.00E
52 K4 **Högsjö** Sweden 62.47N 17.55E
53 W14 **Høgstolen** *mt* Norway 62.23N 7.30E
116 H4 **Hogsty Reef** Atlantic Oc 21.41N 73.48W
53 T17 **Hogsvær** Norway 60.54N 5.32E
53 X14 **Høgtunga** *mt* Norway 62.15N 7.46E
51 D5 **Høgtuvbre** *mt* Norway 66.27N 13.40E
110 A2 **Hoh** *R* Washington
95 N6 **Hoha** S Africa 30.08S 29.36E
63 R10 **Hohburg** E Germany 51.25N 12.48E
64 C3 **Hohe Acht** *mt* W Germany 50.22N 7.00E
66 M3 **Hohe Etzel** *mt* Switzerland 47.10N 8.46E
65 C7 **Hohe Geige** *mt* Austria 47.01N 10.55E
64 K6 **Hohen-Altheim** W Germany 48.45N 10.35E
65 P4 **Hohenau** Austria 48.37N 16.55E
65 N6 **Hohenberg** Austria 47.54N 15.38E
64 M3 **Hohenberg** W Germany 50.12N 11.39E
64 N3 **Hohenberg** W Germany 50.06N 12.14E
63 U10 **Hohenbocka** E Germany 51.26N 14.00E
63 S9 **Hohenbucke** E Germany 51.46N 13.28E
64 M5 **Hohenburg** W Germany 49.17N 11.49E
64 K1 **Hohenebra** E Germany 51.18N 10.50E
63 M8 **Hoheneggelsen** W Germany 52.12N 10.10E
64 H1 **Hoheneiche** W Germany 51.08N 9.58E
65 A7 **Hohenems** Austria 47.23N 9.43E
64 M5 **Hohenfels** W Germany 49.12N 11.51E
63 Q7 **Hohengöhren** E Germany 52.38N 12.03E
Hohenheim *see* **Ostfildern**
64 M7 **Hohenkammer** W Germany 48.25N 11.32E
63 C5 **Hohenkirchen** W Germany 53.40N 7.55E
63 Q10 **Hohenleina** E Germany 51.28N 12.28E
64 N2 **Hohenleuben** E Germany 50.43N 12.03E
63 G10 **Hohenlimburg** W Germany 51.22N 7.34E
64 M7 **Hohenlinden** W Germany 48.09N 11.59E
63 L5 **Hohenlockstedt** W Germany 53.57N 9.37E
63 S5 **Hohenmocker** E Germany 53.49N 13.12E
64 N1 **Hohenmölsen** E Germany 51.10N 12.05E
63 Q7 **Hohennauen** E Germany 52.41N 12.21E
63 S7 **Höhen-Neuendorf** W Germany 52.41N 13.16E
65 K6 **Hohe Nock** *mt* Austria 47.48N 14.20E
64 H2 **Hohenroda** W Germany 50.50N 9.50E
65 C6 **Hohenschwangau** W Germany 47.34N 10.46E
63 Q8 **Hohenseeden** E Germany 52.19N 12.01E
63 S9 **Hohenseefeld** E Germany 51.53N 13.18E
64 F2 **Hohensolms** W Germany 50.39N 8.30E
64 M4 **Hohenstadt** W Germany 49.30N 11.30E
64 H6 **Hohenstaufen** W Germany 48.45N 9.43E
64 G7 **Hohenstein** W Germany 48.20N 9.18E
64 O2 **Hohenstein-Ernstthal** E Germany 50.48N 12.43E
66 J4 **Hohenstollen** *mt* Switzerland 46.47N 8.15E
65 K7 **Hohentauern** Austria 47.26N 14.30E
66 K1 **Hohentengen** W Germany 47.34N 8.26E
107 J6 **Hohenwald** Tennessee 35.33N 87.31W
64 L6 **Hohenwart** W Germany 48.32N 11.25E
65 K7 **Hohenwart** *mt* Austria 47.20N 14.14E
64 M2 **Hohenwarte Talsperre** *res* E Germany 50.35N 11.32E
66 Q1 **Hohenweiler** Austria 47.36N 9.47E
63 K9 **Hohenwepel** W Germany 51.32N 9.07E
63 L4 **Hohenwestedt** W Germany 54.06N 9.39E
63 N6 **Hohenzethen** W Germany 53.03N 10.49E
63 S6 **Hohen Zieritz** E Germany 53.27N 13.07E
64 F7 **Hohenzollern** W Germany 48.20N 8.59E
64 O5 **Hoher Bogen** *mts* W Germany
64 J3 **Hohe Rhön** *mts* W Germany
65 B7 **Hoher Ifen** *mt* Austria 47.22N 10.07E
66 O2 **Hoher Kasten** *mt* Switzerland 47.17N 9.26E
66 L3 **Hohe Rone** *mt* Switzerland 47.09N 8.41E
65 F7 **Hohe Salve** *mt* Austria 47.29N 12.13E
65 B7 **Hohes Licht** *mt* Austria 47.17N 10.17E
64 J5 **Hohe Steig** *mt* W Germany 49.25N 10.23E
65 F7 **Hohe Tauern** *mts* Austria
66 G2 **Hohe Winde** *mt* Switzerland 47.21N 7.35E
66 H4 **Hohgant** *mt* Switzerland 46.48N 7.50E
66 H6 **Hohgleifen** *mt* Switzerland 46.23N 7.48E
22 J6 **Hohhot** Nei Monggol Zizhiqu **China** 40.49N 111.37E
69 N2 **Hohkeppel** W Germany 50.59N 7.19E
64 E6 **Hohloh** *mt* W Germany 48.42N 8.27E
63 L4 **Hohn** W Germany 54.18N 9.30E
69 O2 **Höhn** W Germany 50.37N 7.59E
63 M7 **Hohne** W Germany 52.35N 10.23E
69 N7 **Hohneck** *mt* France 48.02N 7.01E
63 N6 **Hohnstorf** W Germany 53.22N 10.33E
89 K8 **Hohoe** Ghana 7.08N 0.32E
103 F4 **Hohokus** New Jersey 41.00N 74.07W
113 J6 **Hoholitna** *R* Alaska
64 D3 **Höhr-Grenzhausen** W Germany 50.26N 7.40E
24 H8 **Hoh Sai Hu** *L* Qinghai **China**
63 N4 **Hohwacht** W Germany 54.19N 10.40E
63 N4 **Hohwachter Bucht** *B* W Germany
69 N7 **Hohwald, le** France 48.24N 7.20E
24 G8 **Hoh Xil Hu** *L* Qinghai **China**
24 F8 **Hoh Xil Shan** *mt ra* Qinghai/Xizang Zizhiqu China
22 D8 **Hoh Yanchi** *L* Qinghai **China**
22 D8 **Hoh Yanchi** *L* Qinghai **China**
25 K5 **Hoi An** Vietnam 15.54N 108.19E
Hoifung *see* **Haifeng**
Hoihow *see* **Haikou**
93 C4 **Hoima** Uganda 1.25N 31.22E
109 M3 **Hoisington** Kansas 38.32N 98.47W
Hoitow *see* **Haikou**
22 D8 **Hoit Taria** Qinghai **China** 37.25N 96.42E
25 H2 **Hoi Xuan** Vietnam 20.22N 105.09E
53 K4 **Höja** Sweden 56.14N 12.58E
28 J2 **Hojai** Assam **India** 26.00N 92.54E
53 E6 **Højby** Fyn **Denmark** 55.20N 10.27E
53 H5 **Højby** Vestjælland **Denmark** 55.55N 11.37E
53 D5 **Højen** Denmark 55.41N 9.31E
Højen Nordjylland *see* **Gammel Skagen**
53 B7 **Højer** Denmark 54.58N 8.38E
53 J6 **Højerup** Denmark 55.18N 12.27E
20 F8 **Hōjō** Japan 33.58N 132.47E
20 H7 **Hōjō** Japan 34.56N 134.50E
53 B6 **Højrup** Denmark 55.14N 8.59E
53 C3 **Højslev** Denmark 56.35N 9.13E
25 E2 **Hok** *R* Burma
106 C6 **Hokah** Minnesota 43.46N 91.22W
Hokang *see* **Hegang**
87 G6 **Hokecho** Ethiopia 8.02N 39.59E
52 L6 **Hökhuvud** Sweden 60.14N 18.14E
11 H2 **Hokianga Harb** *inlet* **New Zealand**
20 N5 **Hōki-gawa** *R* Japan
11 E9 **Hokitika** New Zealand 42.42S 170.59E
11 E9 **Hokitika R** New Zealand
20 M1 **Hokkaido** *I* Japan
20 M1 **Hokkaido** *prefect* Japan
52 E7 **Hokksund** Norway 59.45N 9.55E
32 G2 **Hokmābād** Iran 36.37N 57.34E
20 O5 **Hokota** Japan 36.10N 140.30E
Hok Tsui *see* **D'Aguilar,C**
20 K6 **Hokunku Tunnel** Japan 35.45N 136.10E
20 K6 **Hokunō** Japan 35.55N 136.47E
53 Y17 **Hol** Norway 60.36N 8.21E
50 G4 **Hóla** Iceland 65.20N 18.12W
50 J2 **Hólaheidhi** *heath* Iceland
28 C3 **Holalkere** Karnataka **India** 14.03N 76.11E
Höland *see* **Løken**
120 F6 **Holanda** Bolivia 14.07S 64.49W
9 R12 **Holanga** Tonga, Pacific Oc 18.35S 173.58W
19 N4 **Holap** *isld* Truk Is **Pacific Oc** 7.39N 151.54E
50 G4 **Hólar** Iceland 65.20N 18.12W
50 F3 **Hólar** Skagafjardharsýsla **Iceland** 65.44N 19.07W
50 H3 **Hólar** Thingeyjarsýsla, Sudhur **Iceland** 65.42N 17.09W
50 G3 **Holárfjall** *mt* Iceland 65.45N 18.35W
53 X15 **Holåtindan** *mt* Norway 61.45N 7.53E
53 E3 **Holbæk** Denmark 56.33N 10.19E
53 H5 **Holbæk** Denmark 55.43N 11.44E
Holbæk *co see* **Vestjælland**
53 H5 **Holbæk Fjord** *inlet* Denmark 55.44N 11.44E
95 O2 **Holbank** S Africa 26.35S 30.15E
56 M2 **Holbeach** Lincs **Eng** 52.49N 0.01E
56 M2 **Holbeach Marsh** Lincs **Eng**
101 K10 **Holberg** Vancouver I, Br Col 50.39N 128.00W
53 C7 **Holbøl** Denmark 54.53N 9.27E
55 F3 **Holborn** London **Eng** 51.31N 0.07W
13 J4 **Holborne I** Queensland 19.42S 148.21E
115 Q7 **Holbox** Mexico 21.34N 87.16W
111 O7 **Holbrook** Arizona 34.54N 110.11W
110 N7 **Holbrook** Idaho 42.10N 112.40W
103 N2 **Holbrook** Massachusetts 42.10N 71.00W
108 L9 **Holbrook** Nebraska 40.19N 100.00W
12 H6 **Holbrook** New S Wales 35.46S 147.20E
53 Y13 **Holbua** Norway 62.31N 8.27E
57 J5 **Holcombe** Greater Manchester **Eng** 53.39N 2.20W
106 C4 **Holcombe** Wisconsin 45.14N 91.05W
100 E5 **Holden** Alberta 53.13N 112.11W
103 L2 **Holden** Massachusetts 42.21N 71.52W
107 B3 **Holden** Missouri 38.44N 94.00W
111 M2 **Holden** Utah 39.06N 112.18W
104 C9 **Holden** W Virginia 37.50N 82.04W
109 O6 **Holdenville** Oklahoma 35.05N 96.25W
12 A6 **Holder** *dist* Canberra **Australia**
57 N5 **Holderness** *pen* Humberside **Eng**
100 M8 **Holdfast** Saskatchewan 50.58N 105.28W
12 A8 **Holdfast B** S Australia
121 L5 **Holdich** Argentina 45.58S 68.15W
108 Q4 **Holdingford** Minnesota 45.42N 94.28W
63 H7 **Holdorf** W Germany 52.36N 8.08E
108 L9 **Holdrege** Nebraska 40.28N 99.28W
48 V9 **Hold with Hope** *pen* Greenland
53 G7 **Holeby** Denmark 54.43N 11.29E
122 V7 **Holei I** Palmyra I **Pacific Oc** 5.52N 162.04W
95 N8 **Hole in the Wall** S Africa 32.02S 29.06E
Hôl,El *see* **Haul,El**
52 F7 **Hølen** Norway 59.33N 10.45E
28 C4 **Hole Narsipur** Karnataka **India** 12.46N 76.14E
62 K6 **Holešov** Czechoslovakia 49.20N 17.35E
116 O6 **Holetown** Barbados 13.11N 59.38W
95 L3 **Holfontein** S Africa 27.53S 27.05E
94 U13 **Holfontein** Transvaal **S Africa** 26.08S 28.29E
104 A5 **Holgate** Ohio 41.15N 84.08W
76 G9 **Holguera** Spain 39.53N 6.21W
116 F4 **Holguín** Cuba 20.54N 76.15W
22 F6 **Hol Hudag** Nei Monggol Zizhiqu **China** 40.35N 103.02E
62 K7 **Holič** Czechoslovakia 48.50N 17.10E
65 N1 **Holice** Czechoslovakia 50.05N 15.59E
113 H5 **Holikachuk** Alaska 62.52N 159.39W
87 N5 **Holim** *reg* Somalia
113 J6 **Holitna** *R* Alaska
52 G6 **Höljes** Sweden 60.54N 12.35E
60 K11 **Holk** Netherlands 52.14N 5.27E
33 C10 **Holkat B** S Yemen 12.47N 45.04E
56 N2 **Holkham** Norfolk **Eng** 52.58N 0.48E
50 K2 **Hölkná** *R* Iceland
50 B2 **Hóll** Ísafjardharsýsla, Nordhur **Iceland** 66.09N 23.13W
50 J2 **Hóll** Thingeyjarsýsla, Nordhur **Iceland** 66.03N 16.36W
50 K2 **Hóll** Thingeyjarsýsla, Nordhur **Iceland** 66.25N 15.55W
65 O4 **Hollabrunn** Austria 48.34N 16.05E
61 D4 **Hollain** Belgium 50.32N 3.26E
94 C5 **Hollam's Bird Is** Namibia 24.38S 14.33E
100 T9 **Holland** Manitoba 49.36N 98.52W
103 K2 **Holland** Massachusetts 42.04N 72.09W
106 H7 **Holland** Michigan 42.46N 86.06W
108 O5 **Holland** Minnesota 44.05N 96.12W
104 G4 **Holland** New York 42.39N 78.32W
110 B7 **Holland** Oregon 42.08N 123.34W
112 K5 **Holland** Texas 30.53N 97.26W
56 L2 **Holland** *div* Lincs **Eng**
107 F8 **Hollandale** Mississippi 33.10N 90.53W
116 M2 **Holland B** Jamaica, W I
99 K8 **Holland Centre** Ontario 44.24N 80.48W
Hollandia *see* **Jayapura**
14 C9 **Holland,Mt** W Australia 32.12S 119.47E
13 K2 **Holland Park** *dist* Brisbane, Qnsld
60 P9 **Hollandscheveld** Netherlands 52.42N 6.32E
60 G11 **Hollandsch Ijssel** *R* Netherlands
60 F13 **Hollands diep** *channel* Netherlands
12 E2 **Hollands Hill** S Australia 26.52S 137.52E
61 N7 **Hollange** Belgium 49.54N 5.41E
63 M8 **Holle** W Germany 52.05N 10.09E
61 B3 **Hollebeke** Belgium 50.48N 2.56E
63 N5 **Hollenbek** W Germany 53.36N 10.51E
65 J6 **Höllen-Gebirge** *mts* Austria
63 L6 **Hollenstedt** W Germany 53.22N 9.43E
• 65 N6 **Hollen-tal** *V* Austria
65 F7 **Hollersbach** Austria 47.17N 12.25E
104 G3 **Holley** New York 43.17N 78.04W
64 L4 **Hollfeld** W Germany 49.46N 11.18E
123 G10 **Hollick Kenyon Plat** Antarctica
112 J2 **Holliday** Texas 33.48N 98.43W
104 G6 **Hollidaysburg** Pennsylvania 40.26N 78.24W
56 N5 **Hollingbourne** Kent **Eng** 51.17N 0.39E
63 K4 **Hollingstedt** W Germany 54.27N 9.20E
103 L7 **Hollis** New York 40.43N 73.47W
109 L7 **Hollis** Oklahoma 34.42N 99.56W
111 C5 **Hollister** California 36.49N 121.25W
110 L7 **Hollister** Idaho 42.22N 114.35W
107 C5 **Hollister** Missouri 36.39N 93.12W
109 M7 **Hollister** Oklahoma 34.21N 98.53W
103 M2 **Holliston** Massachusetts 42.13N 71.25W
15 L6 **Hollman,C** New Britain 4.59S 150.06E
Hollogne-aux-Pierres *see* **Grâce-Hollogne**
61 L4 **Hollogne-sur-Geer** Belgium 50.40N 5.13E
55 F3 **Holloway** London **Eng** 51.34N 0.08W
107 D10 **Holloway** Louisiana 31.22N 92.16W
103 G2 **Hollowville** New York 42.13N 73.41W
60 L6 **Hollum** Netherlands 53.27N 5.38E
53 K6 **Höllviken** *B* Sweden 55.25N 12.55E
109 H3 **Holly** Colorado 38.04N 102.09W
106 L7 **Holly** Michigan 42.46N 83.35W
107 F9 **Holly Bluff** Mississippi 32.50N 90.42W
101 G11 **Hollyburn** Br Col 49.20N 123.10W
11 C11 **Hollyford R** New Zealand
107 E7 **Holly Grove** Arkansas 34.36N 91.13W
105 F8 **Holly Hill** Florida 29.04N 81.03W
105 G4 **Holly Hill** S Carolina 33.19N 80.26W
59 D4 **Hollymount** Mayo **Irish Rep** 53.40N 9.07W
105 K3 **Holly Ridge** N Carolina 34.30N 77.33W
107 G7 **Holly Springs** Mississippi 34.47N 89.25W
105 G11 **Hollywood** Florida 26.01N 80.09W
104 J8 **Hollywood** Maryland 38.21N 76.36W
59 J5 **Hollywood** Wicklow **Irish Rep** 53.06N 6.35W
111 D8 **Hollywood** *dist* Los Angeles, California
53 D6 **Holm** Denmark 55.03N 9.43E
51 C6 **Holm** Norway 65.12N 12.10E
52 K4 **Holm** Sweden 62.40N 16.40E
Holma *see* **Valstad**
109 E5 **Holman** New Mexico 36.02N 105.22W
Holmand *see* **Homand**
101 P1 **Holman Island** Victoria I, N W Terr 70.42N 117.41W
50 L4 **Holmar** Múlasýsla, Sudhur **Iceland** 65.03N 14.04W
50 E7 **Hólmar** Rangárvallasýsla **Iceland** 63.35N 20.09W
50 E4 **Holmavatn** *L* Húnavatnssýsla, Austur Iceland 65.14N 20.19W
50 E5 **Holmavatn** *L* Húnavatnssýsla, Vestur Iceland 64.59N 20.29W
50 E5 **Hólmavatn** *L* Mýrasýsla **Iceland** 64.48N 20.55W
53 W19 **Holmavatn** *L* Rogaland **Norway** 59.41N 7.09E
50 D3 **Hólmavík** Iceland 65.43N 21.39W
103 F6 **Holmdel** Monmouth, New Jersey 40.21N 74.12W*see* **Macclesfield Bank**
95 N2 **Holmdene** S Africa 26.51S 29.05E
56 L3 **Holme** Cambs **Eng** 52.28N 0.16W
57 H4 **Holme** Cumbria **Eng** 54.13N 2.44W
53 E4 **Holme** Denmark 56.07N 10.12E
57 M5 **Holme** Humberside **Eng** 53.49N 0.46W
57 J5 **Holme** Lancs **Eng** 53.46N 2.09W
53 T15 **Holme** Norway 61.45N 5.57E
53 B5 **Holme Å** *R* Denmark
123 B4 **Holme B** Antarctica
53 S16 **Holmedal** Norway 61.22N 5.10E
53 T18 **Holmefjord** Norway 60.17N 5.42E
106 C6 **Holmen** Wisconsin 43.58N 91.18W
53 R17 **Holmengra** *Lt Ho* Norway 60.51N 4.39E
103 G3 **Holmes** New York 41.32N 73.38W
105 K12 **Holmes Cay** *isld* Bahamas 25.38N 77.44W
57 J6 **Holmes Chapel** Cheshire **Eng** 53.12N 2.22W
57 K6 **Holmesfield** Derbys **Eng** 53.18N 1.30W
100 V1 **Holmes L** Manitoba
110 P5 **Holmes, Mt** Wyoming 44.50N 110.52W
13 J3 **Holmes Reef** Gt Barrier Reef **Australia** 16.30S 147.47E
52 E7 **Holmestr** Norway 59.29N 10.20E
53 V20 **Holmevatn** *L* Aust Agder **Norway** 59.29N 6.59E
53 W18 **Holmevatn** *L* Hordaland **Norway** 60.02N 7.05E
100 S9 **Holmfield** Manitoba 49.10N 99.30W
57 K5 **Holmfirth** W Yorks **Eng** 53.35N 1.46W
51 G6 **Holmfors** Sweden 65.16N 18.10E
119 J5 **Holmia** Guyana 4.58N 59.35W
48 V3 **Holm Land** Greenland
52 M3 **Holmögadd** Sweden 63.37N 20.45E
52 M3 **Holmön** Sweden 63.47N 20.55E
53 U15 **Holmøyane** Norway 61.56N 6.25E
57 O5 **Holmpton** Humberside **Eng** 53.42N 0.04E
97 O3 **Holms** *isld* Greenland 74.10N 57.00W
50 G7 **Hólmsá** *R* Iceland
52 E7 **Holmsbu** Norway 59.34N 10.26E
95 J6 **Holmsgrove** S Africa 30.34S 25.59E
52 K3 **Holmsjö** Sweden 63.40N 17.30E
52 J4 **Holmsjön** *L* Sweden 62.26N 15.20E
53 A4 **Holmsland Klit** *dunes* **Denmark**
53 E6 **Holmstrup** Fyn **Denmark** 55.21N 10.17E
53 G5 **Holmstrup** Vestjælland **Denmark** 55.38N 11.24E
52 M3 **Holmsund** Sweden 63.41N 20.20E
52 L9 **Holmudden** *Lt Ho* Sweden 57.57N 19.20E
107 C11 **Holmwood** Louisiana 30.06N 93.08W
56 G6 **Holnest** Dorset **Eng** 50.53N 2.30W
64 M5 **Holnstein** W Germany 49.07N 11.32E
52 K7 **Hölö** Sweden 59.02N 19.36E
92 D5 **Holoholo** *tribe* Tanzania
105 F9 **Holopaw** Florida 28.08N 81.04W
35 C5 **Holot** Israel 32.01N 34.46E
14 F2 **Holothuria Banks** W Australia 13.35S 126.00E
52 F4 **Holøydal** Norway 62.13N 11.25E
13 F2 **Holroyd** *R* Queensland
50 E7 **Hólsa** *R* Iceland
53 U16 **Holsavatn** *L* Norway 61.25N 6.05E
61 K3 **Holsbeek** Belgium 50.55N 4.46E
53 U16 **Holsen** Norway 61.25N 6.10E
53 S17 **Holsenøy** *isld* Norway 60.34N 5.07E
50 B5 **Hólsfjall** *mt* Iceland 64.53N 23.01W
95 M3 **Holspruit** *R* S Africa
50 J3 **Hólssandur** *sand reg* Iceland
50 J3 **Hólssel** Iceland 65.42N 16.11W
53 B4 **Holstebro** Denmark 56.22N 8.38E
53 B5 **Holsted** Denmark 55.31N 8.55E
53 B6 **Holsted Stationsby** Denmark 55.29N 8.55E
108 P7 **Holstein** Iowa 42.29N 95.35W
108 M9 **Holstein** Nebraska 40.28N 98.38W
99 K8 **Holstein** Ontario 44.04N 80.45W
66 H2 **Hölstein** Switzerland 47.26N 7.46E
53 G6 **Holsteinborg** Denmark 55.14N 11.28E
63 N4 **Holsteinische Schweiz** W Germany 54.12N 10.35E
48 R10 **Holsteinsborg** Greenland 66.55N 53.30W
105 D1 **Holston R** Tenn/Virginia
56 C6 **Holsworthy** Devon **Eng** 50.49N 4.21W
107 J8 **Holt** Alabama 33.14N 87.30W
57 H6 **Holt** Clwyd **Wales** 53.05N 2.54W
50 D4 **Holt** Dalasýsla **Iceland** 65.24N 21.54W
107 K11 **Holt** Florida 30.42N 86.47W
50 B2 **Holt** Ísafjardharsýsla, Vestur **Iceland** 66.00N 23.25W
106 K7 **Holt** Michigan 42.38N 85.31W
108 O1 **Holt** Minnesota 48.20N 96.11W
56 O2 **Holt** Norfolk **Eng** 52.55N 1.05E
50 F7 **Holt** Rangárvallasýsla **Iceland** 63.33N 19.49W
50 G7 **Holt** Skaftafellssýsla, Vestur **Iceland** 63.46N 18.13W
12 A5 **Holt** *dist* Canberra **Australia**
50 E7 **Holt** *dist* **Iceland**
50 E3 **Holtastadhir** Iceland 65.35N 20.04W
108 L7 **Holt Cr** Nebraska
53 J5 **Holte** Denmark 55.50N 12.29E
63 O9 **Holtemme** *R* E Germany
60 O10 **Holten** Netherlands 52.16N 6.25E
110 O3 **Holter L.Dam** Montana 47.00N 112.00W
56 G3 **Holt Heath** Hereford & Worcs **Eng** 52.16N 2.16W
63 O5 **Holthusen** E Germany 53.33N 11.21E
107 L2 **Holton** Indiana 39.05N 85.25W
109 P2 **Holton** Kansas 39.27N 95.44W
106 H6 **Holton** Michigan 43.26N 86.03W
22 L4 **Holt Sum** Nei Monggol Zizhiqu **China** 44.18N 117.39E
60 T16 **Holtum** Netherlands 51.03N 5.49E
53 C4 **Holtum Å** *R* Denmark
111 J9 **Holtville** California 32.47N 115.22W
103 B7 **Holtwood** Pennsylvania 39.50N 76.19W
99 K4 **Holtyre** Ontario 48.29N 80.16W
114 B7 **Holualoa** Hawaiian Is 19.37N 155.57W
52 D8 **Holum** Norway 58.06N 7.32E
23 J6 **Ho-lung** Taiwan 24.37N 120.46E
53 Y19 **Holvik** Norway 59.50N 8.19E
60 M6 **Holwerd** Netherlands 53.22N 5.54E
60 Q6 **Holwierde** Netherlands 53.22N 6.53E
56 K5 **Holybourne** Hants **Eng** 51.10N 0.57W
113 H5 **Holy Cross** Alaska 62.10N 159.53W
56 G3 **Holy Cross** Hereford & Worcs **Eng** 52.24N 2.06W
95 N7 **Holy Cross** S Africa 31.09S 29.40E
59 G6 **Holycross** Tipperary **Irish Rep** 52.38N 7.52W
109 D2 **Holy Cross, Mt.of the** Colorado 39.27N 106.26W
57 D6 **Holyhead** Gwynedd **Wales** 53.19N 4.38W
57 D6 **Holyhead Bay** Gwynedd **Wales**
57 D6 **Holyhead Mt** Gwynedd **Wales** 53.19N 4.40W
59 F6 **Holy I** Clare **Irish Rep** 52.55N 8.27W
57 D6 **Holy I** Gwynedd **Wales** 53.16N 4.39W
58 N7 **Holy I** Northumb **Eng** 55.41N 1.48W
57 C1 **Holy I** Strathclyde **Scotland** 55.32N 5.05W
100 G4 **Holyoke** Alberta 54.06N 110.35W
109 H1 **Holyoke** Colorado 40.34N 102.20W
103 J2 **Holyoke** Massachusetts 42.12N 72.37W
109 M3 **Holyrood** Kansas 38.35N 98.25W
98 T6 **Holyrood** Newfoundland 47.24N 53.10W
60 J10 **Holysloot** Netherlands 52.25N 5.01E
64 P4 **Holýšov** Czechoslovakia 49.36N 13.06E
57 G6 **Holywell** Clwyd **Wales** 53.17N 3.13W
56 F6 **Holywell** Dorset **Eng** 50.50N 2.35W
59 L2 **Holywood** Down **N Ireland** 54.38N 5.50W
64 D3 **Holzappel** W Germany 50.20N 7.55E
63 S9 **Holzdorf** E Germany 51.48N 13.07E
63 P5 **Holzendorf** E Germany 53.41N 11.37E
63 H8 **Holzhausen** W Germany 52.13N 8.02E
64 D3 **Holzhausen an der Haide** W Germany 50.13N 7.55E
64 K6 **Holzheim** W Germany 48.36N 10.57E
64 M8 **Holzkirchen** W Germany 47.52N 11.42E
63 K9 **Holzminden** W Germany 51.49N 9.26E
63 G9 **Holzwickede** W Germany 51.31N 7.38E
53 H6 **Høm** Denmark 55.25N 114.48E
32 C4 **Homā** Iran 33.08N 49.48E
36 D4 **Homa** Turkey 38.15N 29.59E
93 F6 **Homa Bay** Kenya 0.31S 34.30E
26 Q8 **Homagama** Sri Lanka 6.51N 80.00E
25 L8 **Homalin** Burma 24.50N 94.59E
32 H4 **Homand** Iran 32.28N 59.35E
32 D4 **Homâyunshahr** Iran 32.42N 51.28E
61 H2 **Hombeek** Belgium 51.01N 4.27E
64 G1 **Homberg** Hessen **W Germany** 51.03N 9.25E
64 G2 **Homberg** Hessen **W Germany** 50.44N 9.00E
63 E10 **Homberg** Nordrhein-Westfalen **W Germany** 51.27N 6.41E
66 J2 **Hom Berg** *mt* Switzerland 47.17N 8.11E
69 E4 **Homblières** France 49.51N 3.23E
89 J4 **Hombori** Mali 15.16N 1.40W
89 J4 **Hombori,Mts du** Mali
61 O4 **Hombourg** Belgium 50.43N 5.55E
69 M5 **Hombourg-Haut** France 49.08N 6.46E
75 G6 **Hombrados** Spain 40.48N 1.41W
120 E11 **Hombre Muerto, Salar del** *salt pan* Argentina
87 F3 **Hombul** *watercourse* Ethiopia
Homburg *see* **Nümbrecht**
64 H4 **Homburg** Bayern **W Germany** 49.47N 9.37E
64 C5 **Homburg** Rheinland-Pfalz **W Germany** 49.20N 7.20E
97 N4 **Home B** N W Terr
9 D5 **Home B** Ocean I **Pacific Oc**
110 J6 **Homedale** Idaho 43.37N 116.55W
13 H4 **Home Hill** Queensland 19.38S 147.25E
26 V2 **Home I** Cocos Is **Ind Oc** 12.07S 96.53E
105 E7 **Homeland** Georgia 30.52N 82.03W
76 C5 **Homem** *R* Portugal
11 J2 **Home Pt** New Zealand 35.20S 174.23E
113 M7 **Homer** Alaska 59.40N 151.37W
106 G9 **Homer** Illinois 40.03N 87.58W
107 C9 **Homer** Louisiana 32.48N 93.02W
106 K7 **Homer** Michigan 42.08N 84.49W
104 F6 **Homer City** Pennsylvania 40.33N 79.11W
56 O3 **Homersfield** Suffolk **Eng** 52.25N 1.22E
11 B11 **Homer Tunnel** *road tunnel* **New Zealand** 44.47S 167.58E
105 E6 **Homerville** Georgia 31.02N 82.44W
105 G12 **Homestead** Florida 25.29N 80.29W
106 C8 **Homestead** Iowa 41.44N 91.51W
108 F1 **Homestead** Montana 48.26N 104.32W
109 M5 **Homestead** Oklahoma 36.10N 98.24W
110 J4 **Homestead** Oregon 45.02N 116.52W
13 H5 **Homestead** Queensland 20.20S 145.37E
108 O9 **Homestead Nat.Mon** Nebraska 40.18N 96.49W
107 K8 **Homewood** Alabama 33.28N 86.50W
11 L8 **Homewood** New Zealand 41.11S 176.00E
28 G7 **Homfray's Str** Andaman Is
36 G2 **Homi** *R* Turkey
109 O5 **Hominy** Oklahoma 36.26N 96.24W
109 O5 **Hominy** *R* Oklahoma
53 T17 **Hømmelfoss** *waterfall* **Norway** 60.53N 5.38E
51 C6 **Hommelstø** Norway 65.32N 12.20E
52 F3 **Hommelvik** Norway 63.24N 10.48E
72 F10 **Homme,Pic de l'** *mt* France 42.48N 0.56E
53 T21 **Hommersåk** Norway 58.56N 5.52E
60 L8 **Hommerts** Netherlands 52.59N 5.39E
70 L7 **Hommes** France 47.26N 0.18E
28 C2 **Homnabad** Karnataka **India** 17.44N 77.11E
107 E10 **Homochitto** *R* Mississippi
94 N4 **Homoine** Mozambique 23.52S 35.09E
65 K4 **Homole** Czechoslovakia 48.57N 14.26E
82 G6 **Homoljske Planina** *mts* Yugoslavia

19 M6 **Homonhon** *isld* Philippines 10.45N 125.41E
82 J4 **Homorod** Romania 46.03N 25.15E
105 E9 **Homosassa** Florida 28.47N 82.37W
105 E9 **Homosassa Is** Florida
61 N7 **Hompré** Belgium 49.57N 5.41E
87 C3 **Homra, El** Sudan 14.15N 31.30E
86 K10 **Homra el Girigab** *hill* Egypt 27.46N 33.19E
Homs Libya*see* **Khums,Al**
34 D4 **Homs** Syria 34.44N 36.43E
34 D4 **Homs,Bahret** *L* Syria
86 K7 **Homur, Wâdî el** *watercourse* Egypt
88 R10 **Honag** Algeria 23.28N 7.52E
88 S10 **Honag** *watercourse* Algeria
Honan *see* **Luoyang**
Honan *prov* China*see* **Henan**
114 B8 **Honaunau** Hawaiian Is 19.25N 155.55W
28 C4 **Honavalli** Karnataka India 13.20N 76.22E
28 B3 **Honavar** Karnataka India 14.19N 74.27E
36 D5 **Honaz** Turkey 37.46N 29.15E
36 D5 **Honaz Dağı** *mt* Turkey 37.42N 29.18E
25 J8 **Hon Ba** *isld* Vietnam
25 H7 **Hon Chong** Vietnam 10.25N 104.30E
25 H8 **Hon Chuoi** *isld* Vietnam 9.00N 104.31E
25 K7 **Hon,Cu Lao** *isld* Vietnam 11.15N 108.49E
111 C2 **Honcut** California 39.20N 121.31W
119 D5 **Honda** Colombia 5.15N 74.50W
29 J7 **Honda** Orissa India 21.22N 85.39E
119 E1 **Honda,B** Colombia 12.21N 71.47W
19 J7 **Honda B** Philippines
29 J7 **Hondapa** Orissa India 20.59N 84.44E
95 H6 **Hondeblaf** *R* S Africa
94 D8 **Hondeklip Baai** S Africa 30.20S 17.18E
61 O8 **Hondelange** Belgium 49.38N 5.50E
95 D9 **Hondewater** S Africa 33.39S 20.45E
100 C3 **Hondo** Alberta 55.04N 114.02W
20 D9 **Hondo** Japan 32.28N 130.12E
109 E8 **Hondo** New Mexico 33.22N 105.17W
112 H6 **Hondo** Texas 29.21N 99.09W
115 P8 **Hondo** *R* Mexico/Belize
77 P4 **Hondón de las Nieves** Spain 38.19N 0.51W
111 E9 **Hondo, R** California
109 F8 **Hondo,R** New Mexico
69 D2 **Hondschoote** France 50.59N 2.35E
60 P7 **Hondsrug** *reg* Netherlands
102 J8 **Honduras** *rep* Cent America
115 L1 **Honduras,C.de** Honduras 16.01N 86.01W
102 J7 **Honduras G.of** Cent America
115 Q9 **Honduras, G. of** Central America
100 Q2 **Hone** Manitoba 56.14N 101.20W
105 E3 **Honea Path** S Carolina 34.26N 82.24W
64 H2 **Hönebach** W Germany 50.56N 9.56E
52 E6 **Hønefoss** Norway 60.08N 10.16E
66 H4 **Honegg** *mt* Switzerland 46.48N 7.49E
103 D3 **Honesdale** Pennsylvania 41.34N 75.15W
115 K7 **Honey** Mexico 20.16N 98.11W
103 C6 **Honey Brook** Pennsylvania 40.06N 75.55W
110 A9 **Honeydew** California 40.15N 124.08W
94 S13 **Honeydew** S Africa 26.05S 27.56E
108 N1 **Honeyford** N Dakota 48.03N 97.28W
112 M2 **Honey Grove** Texas 33.36N 95.54W
112 N5 **Honey Island** Texas 30.24N 94.26W
110 E9 **Honey L** California 40.15N 120.20W
11 B8 **Honey,Mt** Campbell I Pacific Oc 52.34S 169.10E
99 K8 **Honeywood** Ontario 44.14N 80.08W
70 L3 **Honfleur** France 49.25N 0.14E
53 G5 **Høng** Denmark 55.31N 11.18E
25 H1 **Hong** *R* Vietnam
25 J2 **Hon Gai** Vietnam 20.57N 107.06E
23 G3 **Hong'an** Hubei China 31.20N 114.42E
22 F8 **Hongchengzi** Gansu China 36.22N 103.16E
21 D9 **Hongch'ŏn** S Korea 37.44N 127.53E
22 G8 **Hongde** Gansu China 36.43N 107.11E
66 K2 **Höngg** Switzerland 47.24N 8.30E
23 G7 **Honghai Wan** *B* Guangdong China
23 C7 **Honghe** Yunnan China 23.25N 102.25E
23 G2 **Hong He** *R* Henan China
23 F4 **Honghu** Hubei China 29.51N 113.27E
23 F4 **Hong Hu** *L* Hubei China
Hongjialou *see* **Licheng**
23 E5 **Hongjiang** Hunan China 27.08N 109.51E
23 G7 **Hong Kong** *colony* S E Asia
23 H6 **Honglai** Fujian China 25.04N 118.30E
22 C6 **Hongliuhe** Gansu China 41.31N 94.45E
22 C6 **Hongliuyan** Gansu China 41.04N 95.32E
22 F7 **Hongliuyuan** Gansu China 38.49N 103.18E
25 H7 **Hong Ngu** Vietnam 10.50N 105.21E
Hongning *see* **Wulian**
20 E2 **Hongō** *dist* Tōkyō Japan
Hongor Ömnögovĭ *see* **Hanhongor**
22 J4 **Hongor** Sühbaatar Mongolia 45.45N 112.56E
21 D5 **Hongqi** Jilin China 44.25N 126.31E
Hongqiao *see* **Qidong**
24 H4 **Hongqicun** Xinjiang Uygur Zizhiqu China 42.30N 94.00E
24 G4 **Hongqikan** Xinjiang Uygur Zizhiqu China 43.08N 91.44E
23 E9 **Hongqizhen** Guangdong China 18.47N 109.29E
66 E6 **Hongrin** *R* Switzerland
25 F3 **Hongsa** Laos 19.42N 101.23E
23 F2 **Hongshiyan** Henan China 33.13N 113.40E
23 E7 **Hongshui He** *R* Guangxi China
23 D6 **Hongshui He** *R* Guizhou China
21 D9 **Hongsŏng** S Korea 36.37N 126.38E
22 J7 **Hongtao Shan** *mt* Shanxi China 39.40N 112.42E
22 J8 **Hongtong** Shanxi China 36.15N 111.41E
20 J8 **Hongū** Japan 33.49N 135.47E
98 H4 **Honguedo Pass** Que/New Brunswick
30 K3 **Hongu Glacier** Nepal
30 K4 **Hongu Khola** *R* Nepal
30 J4 **Hongu South Peak** *mt* Nepal 27.49N 86.56N
Hongwansi *see* **Sunan Yugurzu Zizhixian**
21 D7 **Hongwŏn** N Korea 40.00N 127.56E
23 C4 **Hongxi** Sichuan China 28.36N 103.02E
23 C4 **Hongya** Sichuan China 29.55N 103.26E
21 C3 **Hongyan** Nei Monggol Zizhiqu China 49.30N 125.04E
23 C2 **Hongyuan** Sichuan China 32.42N 102.42E
23 H2 **Hongze** Jiangsu China 33.10N 118.53E
23 H2 **Hongze Hu** *L* Jiangsu China
15 L3 **Honiara** Guadalcanal I Solomon Is 9.28S 159.57E
15 G7 **Honinabi** Papua New Guinea 6.08S 142.14E
56 O2 **Honingham** Norfolk Eng 52.40N 1.07E
56 N3 **Honington** Suffolk Eng 52.20N 0.48E
57 G3 **Honister Hause** *ridge* Cumbria England 54.31N 3.18W
56 E6 **Honiton** Devon Eng 50.48N 3.13W
20 N5 **Honjō** Japan 36.16N 139.09E
20 O2 **Honjō** Japan 39.22N 140.02E
51 J10 **Honkajoki** Finland 62.00N 22.15E
20 B3 **Hon-Machida** Tōkyō Japan
25 H3 **Hon Matt** *isld* Vietnam 18.52N 105.58E
25 H3 **Hon Me** *isld* Vietnam 19.23N 105.53E
28 B3 **Honnali** Karnataka India 14.15N 75.35E
61 L6 **Honnay** Belgium 50.05N 5.03E
25 J3 **Hon Ne, I** Vietnam 19.57N 106.01E
51 M1 **Honningsvåg** Norway 70.58N 25.59E
114 C7 **Honohina** Hawaiian Is 19.54N 155.10W
114 C6 **Honokaa** Hawaiian Is 20.04N 155.27W
114 D5 **Honokahua** Hawaiian Is 21.00N 156.40W
11 M4 **Honokawa** *mt* New Zealand 37.50S 177.59E
114 B7 **Honokohau** Hawaiian Is 19.41N 155.58W
114 D5 **Honokohau** Hawaiian Is 21.01N 156.37W
114 D6 **Honokowai** Hawaiian Is 20.56N 156.41W
114 B5 **Honolulu** Hawaiian Is 21.19N 157.50W
114 B5 **Honolulu** *dist* Hawaiian Is
114 B4 **Honolulu County** *div* Hawaiian Is
114 E9 **Honolulu Ht** Hawaiian Is
114 D7 **Honolulu Landing** Hawaiian Is 19.33N 154.55W
114 E6 **Honomaee** Hawaiian Is 20.47N 156.03W
114 E6 **Honomanu Bay** Hawaiian Is
114 C7 **Honomu** Hawaiian Is 19.51N 155.06W
118 H8 **Honorio Gurgel** Brazil 22.51S 43.21W
114 A5 **Honouliuli** Hawaiian Is 21.22N 158.03W
25 G8 **Hon Panjang** *isld* Gulf of Thailand 9.18N 103.28E
75 F8 **Honrubia** Spain 39.36N 2.17W
75 C4 **Honrubia de la Cuesta** Spain 41.31N 3.41W
60 E11 **Honselersdijk** Netherlands 52.00N 4.14E
61 K3 **Honsem** Belgium 50.48N 4.50E
20 H6 **Honshu** *isld* Japan
53 H5 **Hønsinge** Denmark 55.52N 11.34E
53 Z15 **Honsjo** *L* Norway 61.54N 8.32E
76 L6 **Hontalbilla** Spain 41.20N 4.08W
75 E8 **Hontanaya** Spain 39.42N 2.51W
72 D8 **Hontanx** France 43.49N 0.15W
75 F8 **Hontecillos** Spain 39.41N 2.11W
60 B3 **Honte,De** *channel* Netherlands
75 D7 **Hontoba** Spain 40.27N 3.03W
75 D4 **Hontoria del Pinar** Spain 41.50N 3.10W
25 K5 **Hon Trau** *isld* Vietnam
25 H8 **Hon Trung Lon** *isld* Vietnam 8.38N 106.11E
25 H8 **Hon Trung Nho** *isld* Vietnam 8.36N 106.08E
114 B8 **Honuapo** Hawaiian Is 19.06N 155.33W
114 B8 **Honuapo B** Hawaiian Is
28 B2 **Honwad** Karnataka India 16.49N 75.30E
94 H5 **Honye** Botswana 24.58S 24.49E
56 N5 **Hoo** Kent Eng 51.26N 0.34E
101 T2 **Hood** *R* N W Terr
113 U8 **Hood Bay** Alaska 57.25N 134.27W
Hood I *see* **Española, I.**
110 D4 **Hood, Mt** Oregon 45.24N 121.41W
14 C10 **Hood Pt** W Australia 34.19S 119.30E
13 G8 **Hood Ra** Queensland
103 A6 **Hood Res** Pennsylvania
110 D4 **Hood River** Oregon 45.44N 121.31W
110 B2 **Hoodsport** Washington 47.24N 123.10W
64 G1 **Hoof** W Germany 51.17N 9.21E
60 G10 **Hoofddorp** Netherlands 52.18N 4.41E
60 B3 **Hoofdplaat** Netherlands 51.22N 3.40E
60 G10 **Hoofd vaart** *canal* Netherlands
60 T17 **Hoogcruts** Netherlands 50.47N 5.50E
63 J3 **Hooge** *isld* W Germany
60 K14 **Hoogeloon** Netherlands 51.23N 5.16E
60 J14 **Hooge Mierde** Netherlands 51.23N 5.08E
60 F14 **Hoogerheide** Netherlands 51.25N 4.19E
60 O9 **Hoogeveen** Netherlands 52.43N 6.29E
60 O9 **Hoogeveensche Vaart** *canal* Netherlands
60 Q7 **Hoogezand** Netherlands 53.10N 6.45E
60 G13 **Hooge Zwaluwe** Netherlands 51.41N 4.45E
60 P8 **Hooghalen** Netherlands 52.55N 6.32E
29 K6 **Hooghly** *dist* W Bengal India
29 K7 **Hooghly R** W Bengal India
60 J9 **Hoogkarspel** Netherlands 52.42N 5.10E
60 O7 **Hoogkerk** Netherlands 53.13N 6.30E
61 C3 **Hooglede** Belgium 50.58N 3.05E
60 G11 **Hoogmade** Netherlands 52.10N 4.35E
60 M11 **Hoog-Soeren** Netherlands 52.13N 5.52E
61 A3 **Hoogstade** Belgium 50.58N 2.42E
61 K1 **Hoogstraten** Belgium 51.24N 4.46E
95 M3 **Hoogte** S Africa 27.28S 28.04E
60 F12 **Hoogvliet** Netherlands 51.52N 4.22E
60 H9 **Hoogwoud** Netherlands 52.44N 4.56E
65 J7 **Hoohwildstelle** *mt* Austria 47.20N 13.50E
56 K5 **Hook** Hants Eng 51.17N 0.58W
55 D5 **Hook** London England 51.22N 0.18W
11 F11 **Hook** New Zealand 44.42S 171.09E
114 B8 **Hookena** Hawaiian Is 19.23N 155.54W
109 J5 **Hooker** Oklahoma 36.51N 101.13W
123 K5 **Hooker, C** Antarctica 63.16S 162.00W
26 B15 **Hooker,C** Marion I Ind Oc 46.59S 37.50E
13 B4 **Hooker Creek** N Terr Australia 18.17S 130.38E
Hooker I *see* **Gukera, Ostrov**
59 J7 **Hook Hd** Wexford Irish Rep 52.07N 6.55W
13 J5 **Hook I** Queensland
13 L7 **Hook Pt** Queensland 25.47S 153.02E
13 J4 **Hook Reef** Gt Barrier Reef Australia 19.50S 149.15E
112 N2 **Hooks** Texas 33.29N 94.19W
104 O3 **Hooksett** New Hampshire 43.05N 71.25W
63 H5 **Hooksiel** W Germany 53.38N 8.02E
114 C5 **Hoolehua** Hawaiian Is 21.11N 157.06W
11 M10 **Hoon Hay** *dist* Christchurch New Zealand
60 N10 **Hoonhorst** Netherlands 52.29N 6.14E
110 B8 **Hoopa** California 41.05N 123.42W
109 E4 **Hooper** Colorado 37.44N 105.54W
108 O8 **Hooper** Nebraska 41.38N 96.32W
110 N8 **Hooper** Utah 41.10N 112.08W
110 G3 **Hooper** Washington 46.45N 118.09W
113 D6 **Hooper B** Alaska
113 D6 **Hooper Bay** Alaska 61.29W 166.10W
114 B8 **Hooper Camp** Hawaiian Is 19.19N 155.47W
104 J8 **Hooper I** Maryland 38.16N 76.11W
11 G1 **Hooper Pt** New Zealand 34.24S 172.53E
11 N12 **Hoopers Inlet** New Zealand
106 G9 **Hoopeston** Illinois 40.28N 87.41W
98 Q3 **Hooping Harbour** Newfoundland 50.38N 56.11W
108 N1 **Hoople** N Dakota 48.34N 97.38W
95 J3 **Hoopstad** S Africa 27.50S 25.54E
114 B8 **Hoopuloa** Hawaiian Is 19.12N 155.55W
95 D10 **Hoop Vlei,De** *L* S Africa 34.27S 20.22E
52 H11 **Höör** Sweden 55.55N 13.33E
60 K6 **Hoorn** Netherlands 53.24N 5.21E
60 J9 **Hoorn** Noord-Holland Netherlands 52.38N 5.03E
122 J10 **Hoorn,Is de** Pacific Oc
60 J9 **Hoornse Hop** *B* Netherlands
60 N7 **Hoornsterzwaag** Netherlands 53.00N 6.11E
104 M4 **Hoosick Falls** New York 42.54N 73.22W
100 H7 **Hoosier** Saskatchewan 51.36N 109.50W
108 G4 **Hoover** S Dakota 45.06N 103.17W
111 K5 **Hoover Dam** Nevada/Arizona 36.01N 114.45W
106 M9 **Hoover Res** Ohio 40.05N 82.52W
104 G6 **Hooversville** Pennsylvania 40.08N 78.54W
53 S18 **Hop** Norway 60.20N 5.21E
50 E3 **Hóp** *L* Iceland 65.32N 20.30W
37 F4 **Hopa** Turkey 41.26N 41.22E
103 E5 **Hopatcong** New Jersey 40.57N 74.40W
103 E5 **Hopatcong, L** New Jersey
103 C3 **Hop Bottom** Pennsylvania 41.42N 75.46W
56 J4 **Hopcroft's Holt** Oxon Eng 51.55N 1.19W
113 N6 **Hope** Alaska 60.55N 149.45W
111 L8 **Hope** Arizona 33.44N 113.42W
107 C8 **Hope** Arkansas 33.40N 93.36W
101 N11 **Hope** Br Col 49.21N 121.28W
107 L2 **Hope** Indiana 39.18N 85.47W
109 N3 **Hope** Kansas 38.42N 97.05W
103 C8 **Hope** Maryland 39.03N 75.59W
108 N2 **Hope** N Dakota 47.20N 97.44W
103 E5 **Hope** New Jersey 40.54N 74.58W
109 F9 **Hope** New Mexico 32.48N 104.44W
53 T15 **Hope** Norway 61.44N 5.53E
103 L3 **Hope** Rhode I 41.44N 71.34W
116 L2 **Hope Bay** Jamaica, W I 18.12N 76.34W
56 F2 **Hope Bowdler** Shropshire Eng 52.32N 2.47W
97 N6 **Hopedale** Labrador, Nfld 55.30N 60.10W
103 L2 **Hopedale** Massachusetts 42.08N 71.33W
95 B9 **Hopefield** S Africa 33.05S 18.20E
Hopeh *prov* China*see* **Hebei**
58 G2 **Hope,L** Highland Scotland 58.27N 4.38W
12 E3 **Hope,L** S Australia
14 D10 **Hope,L** W Australia
115 P8 **Hopelchén** Mexico 19.46N 89.50W
12 E3 **Hopeless, Mt** S Australia 29.41S 139.41E
58 K3 **Hopeman** Grampian Scotland 57.42N 3.26W
105 J3 **Hope Mills** N Carolina 34.57N 78.57W
12 H5 **Hope,Mt** New S Wales 32.50S 145.52E
48 J12 **Hopen** *isld* Arctic Oc
11 G9 **Hope Pass** New Zealand 42.38S 172.05E
113 D2 **Hope Pt** Alaska 68.20N 166.49W
101 P1 **Hope Pt** N W Terr 69.00N 116.20W
11 G9 **Hope R** New Zealand
56 E7 **Hopes Nose** *headland* Devon Eng 50.28N 3.28W
12 F6 **Hopetoun** Victoria 35.43S 142.20E
14 D10 **Hopetoun** W Australia 33.52S 120.08E
105 L11 **Hope Town** Elbow Cay Bahamas 26.37N 76.57W
95 H5 **Hopetown** S Africa 29.37S 24.05E
56 F3 **Hope-under-Dinmore** Hereford & Worcs Eng 52.11N 2.42W
103 L3 **Hope Valley** Rhode I 41.31N 71.42W
103 E6 **Hopewell** New Jersey 40.24N 74.45W
98 K8 **Hopewell** Nova Scotia 45.29N 62.41W
104 G6 **Hopewell** Pennsylvania 40.07N 78.17W
104 H9 **Hopewell** Virginia 37.17N 77.19W
97 M6 **Hopewell Is** Hudson B, N W Terr
103 G3 **Hopewell Junc** New York 41.35N 73.47W
65 C6 **Hopfensee** *L* W Germany 47.37N 10.44E
65 F8 **Hopfgarten** Öst Tirol Austria 46.56N 12.30E
65 F7 **Hopfgarten** Tirol Austria 47.28N 12.09E
111 O6 **Hopi Buttes** *mts* Arizona
25 M8 **Hopin** Burma 24.58N 96.34E
71 J2 **Hôpital-du-Grosbois.l** France 47.10N 6.12E
71 J3 **Hôpitaux-Neufs, les** France 46.47N 6.22E
106 J7 **Hopkins** Michigan 42.37N 85.47W
107 B1 **Hopkins** Missouri 40.33N 94.50W
12 G6 **Hopkins** *R* Victoria
14 G6 **Hopkins,L** W Australia
11 D10 **Hopkins,Mt** New Zealand 43.48S 169.59E
107 J5 **Hopkinsville** Kentucky 36.50N 87.30W
103 L2 **Hopkinton** Massachusetts 42.14N 71.31W
103 L4 **Hopkinton** Rhode I 41.27N 71.46W
111 A3 **Hopland** California 38.58N 123.08W
Hopoi *see* **Bukauo**
25 D2 **Hopong** Burma 20.50N 97.15E
63 T7 **Hoppegarten** E Germany 52.31N 13.41E
101 P1 **Hoppner** *R* N W Terr
69 N4 **Hoppstädten-Weiersbach** W Germany 49.37N 7.11E
51 N1 **Hopseidet** Norway 70.48N 27.44E
63 G8 **Hopsten** W Germany 52.23N 7.37E
56 P2 **Hopton** Norfolk Eng 52.33N 1.43E
53 C6 **Hoptrup** Denmark 55.11N 9.29E
Ho-p'u *see* **Hepu**
104 F7 **Hopwood** Pennsylvania 39.52N 79.42W
13 G5 **Hopwood,Mt** Queensland 21.50S 144.25E
91 C11 **Hoque** Angola 14.40S 13.55E
110 B3 **Hoquiam** Washington 46.59N 123.55W
86 E10 **Hôr** Egypt 27.52N 30.44E
23 B1 **Hor** Qinghai China 35.11N 101.00E
65 N3 **Hora** *mt* Czechoslovakia 49.10N 15.42E
87 G7 **Hora Abyate,L** Ethiopia
26 T7 **Horabora Wewa** *L* Sri Lanka
109 J3 **Horace** Kansas 38.27N 101.50W
75 M8 **Horadada, I. la** Spain 39.51N 0.40E
87 J6 **Hora Kalifo** Ethiopia 8.52N 43.07E
26 R8 **Horana** Sri Lanka 6.42N 80.04E
37 G5 **Horasan** Turkey 40.03N 42.10E
64 P2 **Hora Svatého šebestiána** Czech 50.31N 13.17E
64 P2 **Hora Svaté Kateřing** Czech 50.36N 13.27E
107 B8 **Horatio** Arkansas 33.56N 94.25W
65 J3 **Horaždovice** Czechoslovakia 49.19N 13.42E
64 F7 **Horb am Neckar** W Germany 48.27N 8.41E
53 J7 **Horbelev** Denmark 54.49N 12.04E
64 O7 **Horbering** W Germany 48.21N 12.34E
66 Q1 **Hörbranz** Austria 47.33N 9.46E
100 B6 **Horburg** Alberta 52.27N 115.11W
53 D3 **Hørby** Nordjylland Denmark 56.40N 9.46E
53 E2 **Hørby** Nordjylland Denmark 57.19N 10.24E
52 H11 **Hörby** Sweden 55.50N 13.50E
75 E7 **Horcajada de la Torre** Spain 40.02N 2.35W
76 J8 **Horcajada La** Spain 40.25N 5.28W
76 K10 **Horcajo de los Montes** Spain 39.20N 4.39W
75 D8 **Horcajo de Santiago** Spain 39.50N 3.01W
77 H3 **Horcajo,El** Spain 38.31N 4.25W
77 M3 **Horcajo, El** Spain 38.44N 2.28W
76 J7 **Horcajo Medianero** Spain 40.38N 5.25W
115 G3 **Horcasitas** Mexico 28.20N 105.50W
75 D6 **Horche** Spain 40.34N 3.04W
64 E4 **Horchheim** W Germany 49.36N 8.20E
77 G3 **Horcón** *mt* Spain 38.37N 4.56W
115 N5 **Horconcitos** Panama 8.20N 82.10W
120 F11 **Horcones R** Argentina
53 R17 **Hordabø** Norway 60.42N 4.55E
53 T18 **Hordaland** *co* Norway
15 F5 **Horden** *R* Papua New Guinea
87 N5 **Hordio** Somalia 10.36N 51.08E
35 D7 **Hordos, Har** *mt* Jordan 31.40N 35.15E
112 H4 **Hords Creek Res** Texas
53 A3 **Hørdum** Denmark 56.51N 8.30E
56 C3 **Horeb** Dyfed Wales 52.03N 4.21W
92 E6 **Hore B** Zambia
65 M2 **Hořepník** Czechoslovakia 49.31N 15.07E
35 C5 **Horeshim** Israel 32.08N 34.58E
82 H5 **Horezu** Romania 45.06N 24.00E
50 G3 **Horgá** *R* Iceland
50 G3 **Hörgardalur** *V* Iceland
66 L2 **Horgen** Switzerland 47.16N 8.36E
23 B1 **Horgorgoinba** Qinghai China 34.15N 99.01E
82 F4 **Horgos** Yugoslavia 46.09N 19.59E
50 H7 **Horgsland** Iceland 63.52N 17.58W
66 K1 **Horheim** W Germany 47.39N 8.21E
22 G5 **Hörh Uul** *mts* Mongolia
62 J5 **Hořice** Czechoslovakia 50.23N 15.39E
65 K4 **Hořice na Šumavě** Czechoslovakia 48.46N 14.12E
106 F6 **Horicon** Wisconsin 43.27N 88.39W
20 B1 **Horigane** Saitama Japan
22 J6 **Horinger** Nei Monggol Zizhiqu China 40.20N 111.50E
20 B1 **Horinouchi** Saitama Japan
61 M4 **Horion-Hozémont** Belgium 50.38N 5.23E
100 M9 **Horizon** Saskatchewan 49.32N 105.17W
122 K11 **Horizon Depth** Pacific Oc 23.15S 174.46W
120 E3 **Horizonte** Brazil 9.44S 68.25W
62 H4 **Horka** E Germany 51.19N 14.55E
52 H6 **Hörken** Sweden 60.03N 14.55E
37 E5 **Horlar Dağı** *mt* Turkey 40.17N 39.41E
56 L5 **Horley** Surrey Eng 51.11N 0.11W
123 G8 **Horlick Mts** Antarctica
32 J6 **Hormak** Iran 30.00N 60.50E
53 E2 **Hørmested** Denmark 57.28N 10.16E
77 P5 **Hormigas, I** Spain 37.39N 0.38W
75 E3 **Hormilla** Spain 42.27N 2.47W
32 F7 **Hormoz** Iran 27.31N 54.56E
32 G7 **Hormoz** *isld* Iran 27.05N 56.30E
32 F7 **Hormoz,Küh-e** *mt* Iran 27.25N 55.08E
32 F7 **Hormūd-e Bāgh** Iran 27.29N 54.19E
Hormuz *see* **Hormoz**
33 M3 **Hormuz,Strait of** The Gulf etc
65 N4 **Horn** Austria 48.40N 15.40E
60 M15 **Horn** Netherlands 51.12N 5.56E
52 J9 **Horn** Sweden 57.54N 15.50E
66 O2 **Horn** Switzerland 47.29N 9.28E
66 M1 **Horn** W Germany 47.42N 8.59E
15 B4 **Horna** Irian Jaya 1.37S 133.48E
77 D3 **Hornachos** Spain 38.34N 6.04W
77 D3 **Hornachos,Sierra de** *mts* Spain
77 F5 **Hornachuelos** Spain 37.50N 5.14W
62 M7 **Hornad** *R* Czechoslovakia
101 M1 **Hornaday** *R* N W Terr
50 K6 **Hornafjardharós** *str* Iceland
50 K6 **Hornafjördhur** *B* Iceland
50 B3 **Hornatœr** *ridge* Iceland
51 F5 **Hornavan** *L* Sweden 66.15N 17.40E
64 C5 **Hornbach** W Germany 49.11N 7.23E
63 J9 **Horn-Bad Meinog** W Germany 51.52N 8.56E
53 J4 **Hornbæk** Frederiksborg Denmark 56.06N 12.29E
53 D4 **Hornbæk** Viborg Denmark 56.28N 10.00E
107 C10 **Hornbeck** Louisiana 31.19N 93.24W
64 E7 **Hornberg** W Germany 48.13N 8.14E
52 G8 **Hornborgasjön** *L* Sweden 58.20N 13.35E
110 C8 **Hornbrook** California 41.56N 122.34W
50 L5 **Hornbrynja** *mt* Iceland 64.51N 14.57W
63 N8 **Hornburg** W Germany 52.02N 10.38E
57 H4 **Hornby** Lancs Eng 54.07N 2.38W
11 C3 **Horn,C** Auckland New Zealand 36.56S 174.44E
Horn,C Chile*see* **Hornos,C.de**
50 C2 **Horn, C** Iceland 66.28N 22.27W
57 N6 **Horncastle** Lincs Eng 53.13N 0.07W
55 K3 **Hornchurch** London Eng 51.34N 0.13E
52 J6 **Horndal** Sweden 60.17N 16.25E
53 V17 **Horndalsnut** *mt* Norway 60.38N 6.42E
56 J6 **Horndean** Hants Eng 50.55N 1.00W
56 M4 **Horndon** Essex Eng 51.32N 0.25E
63 N6 **Horndorf** W Germany 53.13N 10.34E
53 E6 **Horne** Denmark 55.07N 10.11E
53 D1 **Horne** Nordjylland Denmark 57.34N 9.59E
53 B5 **Horne** Ribe Denmark 55.44N 8.32E
63 L5 **Horneburg** W Germany 53.31N 9.35E
52 M3 **Hörnefors** Sweden 63.36N 19.55E
53 E6 **Horneland** *pen* Denmark 55.06N 10.10E
53 S15 **Hornelen** *mt* Norway 61.51N 5.13E
104 H4 **Hornell** New York 42.19N 77.39W
99 F3 **Hornepayne** Ontario 49.14N 84.48W
Hörnerkirchen *see* **Brande-Hörnerkirchen**
103 E6 **Hornerstown** New Jersey 40.07N 74.31W
107 F5 **Hornersville** Missouri 36.03N 90.08W
52 D8 **Hornesund** Norway 58.37N 7.55E
53 G2 **Hornfiskrøn** *isld* Denmark 57.13N 11.01E
63 O8 **Hornhausen** E Germany 52.03N 11.10E
59 G1 **Horn Hd** Donegal Irish Rep 55.13N 7.59W
60 O6 **Hornhuizen** Netherlands 53.23N 6.22E
107 H11 **Horn I** Mississippi 30.13N 88.40W
13 F1 **Horn I** Queensland
62 L6 **Horní Benešov** Czechoslovakia 49.59N 17.37E
64 O3 **Horní Blatná** Czechoslovakia 50.23N 12.47E
65 M3 **Horní Cerekev** Czechoslovakia 49.19N 15.20E
65 K4 **Horni Dvořiště** Czechoslovakia 48.37N 14.25E
65 O1 **Horní Jelení** Czechoslovakia 50.04N 16.05E
10 R4 **Horn, Iles De** *island grp* Pacific Oc
115 E4 **Hornillos** Mexico 26.30N 108.30W
53 V15 **Hornindal** Norway 61.59N 6.32E
53 U15 **Hornindalsvatn** *L* Norway
53 E4 **Hørning** Denmark 56.05N 10.02E
65 K4 **Horni Planá** Czechoslovakia 48.47N 14.03E
64 E6 **Hornisgrinde** *mt* W Germany 48.36N 8.14E
64 O3 **Horní Slavkov** Czechoslovakia 50.08N 12.49E
65 J4 **Horní Vitavice** Czechoslovakia 48.58N 13.46E
65 K3 **Horni Záhoří** Czechoslovakia 49.20N 14.13E
94 D4 **Hornkranz** Namibia 23.22S 16.25E
66 M2 **Hörnli** *mt* Switzerland 47.23N 8.56E
113 H6 **Horn Mts** Alaska
101 N4 **Horn Mts** N W Terr
52 D8 **Hornnes** Norway 58.34N 7.45E
15 J5 **Horno Is** Admiralty Is
121 A8 **Hornopiren, V** *mt* Chile 41.50S 72.30W
115 H5 **Hornos** Mexico 25.22N 102.56W
77 L4 **Hornos** Spain 38.13N 2.43W
121 L10 **Hornos, C.de** Chile 56.00S 67.15W
121 L10 **Hornos,I** Chile 55.59S 67.15W
69 B4 **Hornoy-le Bourg** France 49.51N 1.54E
101 O4 **Horn R** N W Terr
12 K5 **Hornsby** New S Wales 33.11S 151.06E
107 H6 **Hornsby** Tennessee 35.13N 88.50W
56 C6 **Horns Cross** Devon Eng 50.59N 4.18W
57 N5 **Hornsea** Humberside Eng 53.55N 0.10W
55 F3 **Hornsey** London Eng 51.35N 0.08W
52 M3 **Hörnsjö** Sweden 63.48N 19.30E
53 E4 **Hornslet** Denmark 56.19N 10.20E
35 E2 **Horns of Hittin** *anc site* Israel 32.48N 35.28E
64 K1 **Hornsömmern** E Germany 51.12N 10.50E
11 J11 **Horns, The** *mt* Chatham Is Pacific Oc 44.07S 176.37W
63 P5 **Hornstorf** E Germany 53.56N 11.32E
53 D5 **Hornstrup** Denmark 55.45N 9.34E
50 T16 **Hornsund** *sound* Spitsbergen
50 L6 **Hornsvik** *inlet* Iceland
61 F5 **Hornu** Belgium 50.27N 3.50E
53 C3 **Hornum** Nordjylland Denmark 56.51N 9.27E
53 D5 **Hornum** Vejle Denmark 55.45N 9.50E
63 H3 **Hörnum** W Germany 54.46N 8.18E
63 H3 **Hörnum** *prom* W Germany
66 J1 **Hornussen** Switzerland 47.30N 8.04E
50 C2 **Hornvík** *inlet* Iceland
20 M2 **Horoizumi** Japan 42.01N 143.07E
89 H3 **Horo,L** Mali 16.15N 3.45W
21 J5 **Horonobe** Japan 45.03N 141.51E
11 K6 **Horopito** New Zealand 39.21S 175.23E
11 F10 **Hororata** New Zealand 43.33S 171.59E
37 E5 **Horos Dağları** *mts* Turkey
20 M2 **Horoshiri-dake** *mt* Japan 42.43N 142.40E
22 H7 **Horo Sum** Nei Monggol Zizhiqu China 39.21N 109.29E
65 J2 **Hořovice** Czechoslovakia 49.55N 13.50E
11 K7 **Horowhenua Plain** New Zealand
26 S4 **Horowupotana** Sri Lanka 8.32N 80.50E
61 M3 **Horpmaal** Belgium 50.46N 5.20E
70 K5 **Horps,le** France 48.23N 0.28W
21 B5 **Horqin** Jilin China 45.10N 121.38E
21 B4 **Horqin Youyi Qianqi** Nei Monggol Zizhiqu China 46.02N 122.00E
21 B6 **Horqin Zuoyi Houqi** Nei Monggol Zizhiqu China 43.00N 122.14E
21 C5 **Horqin Zuoyi Zhongqi** Nei Monggol Zizhiqu China 44.08N 123.19E
118 B8 **Horqueta** Paraguay 23.20S 57.03W
118 A9 **Horqueta, L** Argentina 25.00S 61.00W
93 L6 **Horrade** Kenya 0.59S 39.22E
75 C4 **Horra,La** Spain 41.44N 3.52W
53 H7 **Horreby** Denmark 54.49N 12.00E
52 G9 **Horred** Sweden 57.22N 12.25E
11 G10 **Horrelville** New Zealand 43.21S 172.22E
64 B2 **Horrem** W Germany 50.55N 6.43E
24 G10 **Horru** Xizang Zizhiqu China 30.30N 91.32E
61 G4 **Horrues** Belgium 50.37N 4.03E
26 V2 **Horsburgh I** Cocos Is Ind Oc 12.05S 96.50E
64 J1 **Hörschel** E Germany 51.00N 10.15E
65 K5 **Horsching** *airport* Austria 8.14N 14.12E
107 K4 **Horse Branch** Kentucky 37.27N 86.41W
56 M6 **Horsebridge** E Sussex Eng 50.52N 0.15E
107 L4 **Horse Cave** Kentucky 37.10N 85.56W
109 G3 **Horse Cr** Colorado
107 C4 **Horse Cr** Missouri
13 D6 **Horse Cr** N Terr Australia
108 F8 **Horse Cr** Wyoming
108 E8 **Horse Creek** Wyoming 41.25N 105.11W
101 N9 **Horsefly** Br Col 52.20N 121.25W
108 L2 **Horsehead L** N Dakota
104 J4 **Horseheads** New York 42.11N 76.51W
98 R3 **Horse Is** Newfoundland
98 R3 **Horse Islands** Newfoundland 50.12N 55.43W
110 E9 **Horse L** California 40.40N 120.30W
64 J2 **Hörsel** *R* E Germany
64 J2 **Hörsel Berge** *mt* E Germany 50.58N 10.28E
59 E5 **Horseleap** Galway Irish Rep 53.28N 8.40W
56 K5 **Horsell** Surrey Eng 51.20N 0.35W
103 M3 **Horseneck Beach** Massachusetts 41.30N 71.02W
53 E2 **Horsens** Nordjylland Denmark 57.07N 10.07E
53 D5 **Horsens** Vejle Denmark 55.53N 9.53E
53 E5 **Horsens Fjord** *inlet* Denmark 55.50N 10.06E
100 F2 **Horse R** Alberta
96 A14 **Horse Ridge** *mt* St Helena 16.00S 5.45W
105 D8 **Horseshoe** Florida 29.27N 83.17W
14 C7 **Horse Shoe** W Australia 25.27S 118.32E
96 B2 **Horseshoe B** Bermuda 32.15N 64.50W
101 F10 **Horseshoe B** Br Col
101 F10 **Horseshoe Bay** Br Col 49.22N 123.17W
110 J6 **Horse Shoe Bend** Idaho 43.55N 116.11W
13 C7 **Horseshoe Bend** N Terr Australia 25.13S 134.14E
116 P3 **Horse Shoe Pt** St Kitts W I 17.12N 62.39W
111 N7 **Horseshoe Res** Arizona 34.04N 111.42W
95 G7 **Horseshoe,The** *mt* S Africa 31.40S 23.16E
109 B8 **Horse Springs** New Mexico 33.55N 108.12W
56 P2 **Horsey** Norfolk Eng 52.46N 1.39E
57 K5 **Horsforth** W Yorks Eng 53.51N 1.39W
86 N4 **Horsha** *watercourse* Israel
56 O2 **Horsham** Norfolk Eng 52.41N 1.16E
103 D6 **Horsham** Pennsylvania 40.11N 75.08W
100 H8 **Horsham** Saskatchewan 50.25N 109.57W
12 F6 **Horsham** Victoria 36.45S 142.15E
56 L5 **Horsham** W Sussex Eng 51.04N 0.21W
53 J5 **Hørsholm** Denmark 55.53N 12.30E
53 G7 **Horslunde** Denmark 54.54N 11.13E
64 O4 **Horšovsky Týn** Czechoslovakia 49.32N 12.55E
60 L12 **Horssen** Netherlands 51.52N 5.37E
63 S4 **Horst** E Germany 54.08N 13.13E
60 N14 **Horst** Limburg Netherlands 51.27N 6.04E
63 L5 **Horst** Schleswig Holstein W Germany 53.48N 9.37E
53 T15 **Horstadvatnet** *L* Norway 61.33N 5.40E
56 O2 **Horstead** Norfolk Eng 52.44N 1.21E
63 G8 **Hörstel** W Germany 52.18N 7.35E
63 D10 **Hörstgen** W Germany 51.30N 6.28E
63 F8 **Horstmar** W Germany 52.05N 7.19E
62 L7 **Hor Štubňa** Czechoslovakia 48.50N 18.50E
Horsunlu *see* **Kuyucak** Aydın Turkey
88 B1 **Horta** Azores 38.32N 28.40W
96 P4 **Horta** Azores 38.32N 28.38W
75 L6 **Horta de San Juan** Spain 40.57N 0.19E
52 E7 **Horten** Norway 59.25N 10.30E
105 F6 **Hortense** Georgia 31.20N 81.58W
75 E5 **Hortezuela** Spain 41.29N 2.50W
75 D3 **Hortigüela** Spain 42.04N 3.25W
51 J6 **Hortlax** Sweden 65.18N 21.24E
56 H6 **Horton** Dorset Eng 50.52N 1.58W
109 P2 **Horton** Kansas 39.39N 95.32W
103 D3 **Horton** New York 41.58N 75.00W
56 F6 **Horton** Somerset Eng 50.56N 2.57W
101 K1 **Horton** *R* N W Terr
57 J4 **Horton in Ribblesdale** N Yorks Eng 54.09N 2.17W
55 K5 **Horton Kirby** Kent Eng 51.24N 0.15E
103 D3 **Hortonville** New York 41.46N 75.01W
36 G6 **Hortu** Turkey 36.23N 33.14E
Horudha *see* **Huraydah, Al**
87 L6 **Horufadi** Somalia 8.35N 46.22E
53 C5 **Hørup** Denmark 55.46N 9.29E
63 K3 **Hörup** W Germany 54.44N 9.08E
53 D7 **Hørup Halvø** *pen* Denmark 54.53N 9.58E
53 G5 **Hørve** Denmark 55.46N 11.28E
52 H10 **Hörvik** Sweden 56.02N 14.45E
35 B9 **Horvot Haljza** *ruins* Israel 31.06N 34.39E
35 B9 **Horvot Rehovot** *anc site* Israel 31.02N 34.34E
35 D9 **Horvot 'Uza** *ruins* Israel 31.12N 35.10E
66 K3 **Horw** Switzerland 47.02N 8.18E
57 H5 **Horwich** Greater Manchester Eng 53.37N 2.33W
99 H4 **Horwood L** Ontario
62 H5 **Hory Lužické** *mts* Czech/E Ger 50.53N 14.40E
64 P5 **Hory Matky Boží** Czechoslovakia 49.16N 13.27E
62 J5 **Hory Orlické** *mts* Czechoslovakia
36 D5 **Horzom** *R* Turkey
87 F7 **Hosa'ina** Ethiopia 7.30N 37.47E
53 S17 **Hosanger** Norway 60.35N 5.29E
37 H7 **Hoşap** Turkey 38.21N 43.47E
64 G3 **Hösbach** W Germany 50.00N 9.12E
61 P7 **Hoscheid** Luxembourg 49.57N 6.05E
28 C4 **Hosdurga** Karnataka India 13.49N 76.14E
18 K4 **Hose Mts** Sarawak Malaysia
35 E1 **Hosen** Israel 33.00N 35.17E
63 U10 **Hosena** E Germany 51.27N 14.02E
85 F8 **Hosenofu** Libya 23.41N 21.04E
34 Q4 **Hoseynābād** Hamadān Iran 34.05N 48.29E
32 G6 **Hoseynābād** Kermān Iran 29.55N 56.20E
32 B3 **Hoseynābād** Kordestān Iran 35.30N 47.09E
34 P2 **Hoseynābād** Kordestān Iran 36.16N 47.46E
32 C4 **Hoseynābād** Lorestān Iran 32.43N 48.20E
32 D3 **Hoseynābād-e Shebānī** Iran 34.15N 51.09E
32 C5 **Hoseynīyeh** Iran 30.56N 48.09E
34 Q6 **Hoseynīyeh ye Khodā Dād** Iran 32.42N 48.17E
105 C7 **Hosford** Florida 30.23N 84.49W
31 B7 **Hoshab** Pakistan 26.02N 63.55E
29 E6 **Hoshangabad** Madhya Prad India 22.44N 77.45E
29 E6 **Hoshangabad** *reg* Madhya Prad India
87 D3 **Hosh,El** Sudan 14.07N 33.27E
29 D2 **Hoshiarpur** Punjab India 31.30N 75.59E
29 D2 **Hoshiarpur** *dist* Punjab India
86 D4 **Hôsh 'Isa** Egypt 30.55N 30.17E
24 F6 **Hoshu Kuduk** *well* Xinjiang Uygur Zizhiqu China 38.47N 87.32E
32 G6 **Hoshūn** Iran 29.16N 56.20E
61 P6 **Hosingen** Luxembourg 50.01N 6.05E
Hoskâr *see* **Sancak**
108 N7 **Hoskins** Nebraska 42.07N 97.19W
15 L6 **Hoskins** New Britain 5.30S 150.27E
28 C4 **Hoskote** Karnataka India 13.06N 77.47E
50 E3 **Höskuldsstadhir** Húnavatnssýsla, Austur Iceland 65.44N 20.15W
50 L5 **Höskuldsstadhir** Múlasýsla, Sudhur Iceland 64.52N 14.27W
53 W20 **Hoslemo** Norway 59.26N 7.25E
108 L4 **Hosmer** S Dakota 45.33N 99.28W
37 E6 **Hösnek** Turkey 39.17N 40.29E
20 E9 **Hososhima** Japan 32.25N 131.38E
109 C6 **Hospah** New Mexico 35.43N 107.46W
66 L5 **Hospenthal** Switzerland 46.37N 8.34E
28 C3 **Hospet** Karnataka India 15.16N 76.20E
72 F10 **Hospice-de-France** France 42.43N 0.39E
71 K5 **Hospice-Petit-St.Bernard** France 45.40N 6.53E
59 F7 **Hospital** Limerick Irish Rep 52.29N 8.25W
121 G3 **Hospital,Cuchilla del** *mts* Uruguay
76 H4 **Hospital de Órbigo** Spain 42.27N 5.53W
75 P5 **Hospitalet** Barcelona Spain 41.21N 2.06E
75 M6 **Hospitalet** Tarragona Spain 41.00N 0.55E
72 H10 **Hospitalet-près-l'Andorre, l'** France 42.35N 1.47E
66 J7 **Hospiz** Switzerland 46.15N 8.02E
51 O6 **Hossa** Finland 65.29N 29.36E
72 B8 **Hossegor** France 43.39N 1.25W
Hosseina *see* **Hosa'ina**
119 J3 **Hossororo** Guyana 8.05N 59.50W
109 B6 **Hosta Butte** *mt* New Mexico 35.34N 108.11W
75 Q4 **Hostalrich** Spain 41.45N 2.38E
121 K10 **Hoste, I** Chile
53 S17 **Hosteland** Norway 60.50N 5.15E
72 C6 **Hostens** France 44.30N 0.38W
65 O4 **Hostěradice** Czechoslovakia 48.58N 16.16E
65 N3 **Hostím** Czechoslovakia 49.02N 15.53E
65 K1 **Hostivice** Czechoslovakia 50.06N 14.16E
65 K2 **Hostomice** Czechoslovakia 49.50N 14.03E
64 O4 **Hostouň** Czechoslovakia 49.34N 12.47E
53 A5 **Hostrup** Ribe Denmark 55.34N 8.22E
53 B7 **Hostrup** Sønderjylland Denmark 54.58N 8.58E
53 C7 **Hostrup Sø** *L* Denmark 54.58N 9.27E
28 C4 **Hosur** Tamil Nadu India 12.45N 77.51E
58 Q9 **Hoswick** Shetland Scotland 60.00N 1.15W
25 E3 **Hot** Thailand 18.07N 98.34E
52 H3 **Hotagen** Sweden 63.59N 14.15E
95 D10 **Hotagterklip** S Africa 34.47S 20.02E
20 L5 **Hotaka** Japan 36.22N 137.52E
36 G5 **Hotamış** Turkey 37.38N 33.20E
24 C7 **Hotan** Xinjiang Uygur Zizhiqu China 37.07N 79.57E
24 C7 **Hotan** Xinjiang Uygur Zizhiqu China 37.07N 79.57E
24 C6 **Hotan He** *R* Xinjiang Uygur Zizhiqu China
95 G3 **Hotazel** S Africa 27.17S 23.01E
101 P7 **Hotchkiss** Alberta 57.00N 117.40W
109 C3 **Hotchkiss** Colorado 38.47N 107.42W
111 H3 **Hot Creek Ra** Nevada
19 G5 **Hote** Moluccas Indonesia 0.03S 130.18E
77 W14 **Hotel Formentor** *ruin* Balearic Is 39.55N 3.08E
63 O8 **Hötensleben** E Germany 52.08N 11.03E
28 C2 **Hotgi** Maharashtra India 17.37N 76.03E
13 B1 **Hotham,C** N Terr Australia 12.03S 131.17E
113 F3 **Hotham Inlet** Alaska
12 H6 **Hotham, Mt** Victoria 36.58S 147.11E
14 B10 **Hotham,R** W Australia
52 J2 **Hoting** Sweden 64.08N 16.15E
95 B6 **Hoto** Madagascar 21.59S 45.21E
22 H7 **Hotong Qagan Nur** *L* Nei Monggol Zizhiqu China
22 F3 **Hotont** Mongolia 47.21N 102.30E
107 C7 **Hot Springs** Arkansas 34.30N 93.02W
110 L2 **Hot Springs** Montana 47.37N 114.40W
105 E2 **Hot Springs** N Carolina 35.54N 82.52W
108 G6 **Hot Springs** S Dakota 43.26N 103.29W
112 D6 **Hot Springs** Texas 29.13N 103.01W
104 F9 **Hot Springs** Virginia 37.59N 79.51W
107 C7 **Hot Springs Nat Park** Arkansas 34.30N 93.02W
109 D1 **Hot Sulphur Springs** Colorado 40.04N 106.06W
101 O3 **Hottah L** N W Terr
116 G5 **Hotte,Massif de la** *mts* Haiti
94 C6 **Hottentot Bay** Namibia 26.08S 14.59E
94 C6 **Hottentot Point** *C* Namibia 26.10S 14.59E
95 C9 **Hottentotskloof** S Africa 33.15S 19.37E
61 M5 **Hotton** Belgium 50.16N 5.27E
50 L4 **Höttur** *mt* Iceland 65.07N 14.28W
122 V16 **Hotuiti** Easter I Pacific Oc 27.07S 109.17W
112 B4 **Hot Wells** Texas 31.00N 105.02W
66 J1 **Hotzenwald** *mts* W Germany
63 L6 **Hötzingen** W Germany 53.01N 9.58E
53 E2 **Hou** Nordjylland Denmark 57.04N 10.23E
9 B13 **Houaïlu** New Caledonia 21.18S 165.33E
Houaïz *see* **Huweid**
70 E7 **Houat** *isld* France 47.24N 2.58W
58 R8 **Houbie** Shetland Scotland 60.36N 0.51W
71 K5 **Houches,les** France 45.53N 6.49E
69 D3 **Houdain** France 50.27N 2.32E
69 B6 **Houdan** France 48.48N 1.36E
69 J6 **Houdelaincourt** France 48.33N 5.28E
61 N8 **Houdemont** Belgium 49.43N 5.35E
61 G5 **Houdeng-Aimeries** Belgium 50.29N 4.09E
61 G5 **Houdeng-Gœgnies** Belgium 50.29N 4.10E
61 K7 **Houdremont** Belgium 49.57N 4.57E
69 K7 **Houécourt** France 48.17N 5.55E
72 E7 **Houeillès** France 44.12N 0.03E
72 E9 **Houeydets** France 43.10N 0.22E
61 O6 **Houffalize** Belgium 50.08N 5.48E
72 D8 **Houga,le** France 43.47N 0.11W
109 J5 **Hough** Oklahoma 36.53N 101.37W
106 F2 **Houghton** Michigan 47.06N 88.34W
104 G4 **Houghton** New York 42.27N 78.10W
108 M4 **Houghton** S Dakota 45.44N 98.11W
13 H4 **Houghton** *R* Queensland
106 K5 **Houghton L** Michigan
57 L3 **Houghton le Spring** Tyne and Wear Eng 54.51N 1.28W
11 H1 **Houhora** New Zealand 34.48S 173.06E
25 G2 **Houie Moc,Pou** *mt* Laos 21.33N 102.07E
68 D2 **Houilles** France 48.56N 2.11E
11 D13 **Houipapa** New Zealand 46.30S 169.34E
53 D4 **Houlbjerg** Denmark 56.21N 9.53E
35 F1 **Hoûlé** Lebanon 33.13N 35.31E
70 K3 **Houlgate** France 49.18N 0.04W
107 G7 **Houlka** Mississippi 34.03N 89.02W
70 N2 **Houlme,le** France 49.30N 1.02E
104 R7 **Houlton** Maine 46.09N 67.50W
107 F12 **Houma** Louisiana 29.35N 90.44W
23 F1 **Houma** Shanxi China 35.36N 111.15E
9 R10 **Houma** Tonga, Pacific Oc 21.10S 175.18W
9 S11 **Houma** Tonga, Pacific Oc 21.19S 174.55W
9 R12 **Houma Fakalele** *pt* Tonga, Pacific Oc 18.34S 174.00W
9 S10 **Houma Toloa** *pt* Tonga, Pacific Oc 21.16S 175.08W
25 N1 **Houmen** Guangdong China 22.48N 115.07E
88 T5 **Houmet Essouq** Tunisia 33.55N 10.52E
89 H6 **Houndé** Upper Volta 11.34N 3.31W
55 C4 **Hounslow** London England 51.28N 0.21W
61 L6 **Hour** Belgium 50.10N 5.02E
58 E4 **Hourn,L** Highland Scotland
72 B5 **Hourtin** *L* France 45.12N 1.04W
72 B5 **Hourtin, Lac d'** France
103 H2 **Housatonic** Massachusetts 42.15N 73.22W
103 H3 **Housatonic** *R* Conn/Mass
109 G7 **House** New Mexico 34.39N 103.56W
98 L6 **House Harbour** Madeleine Is, Que 47.26N 61.50W
100 E3 **House R** Alberta
111 L2 **House Ra** Utah
Houssainiyet *see* **Husayniyat**
Houssaïnîyet ech Cheikh Aali *see* **Huseiniyat esh Sheikh 'Ali**
26 T15 **Houssaye, Cap la** Réunion Ind Oc 21.00S 55.14E
101 K8 **Houston** Br Col 54.24N 126.39W
103 C9 **Houston** Delaware 38.55N 75.30W
106 C6 **Houston** Minnesota 43.45N 91.35W
107 G8 **Houston** Mississippi 33.54N 89.01W
107 E4 **Houston** Missouri 37.19N 91.59W
112 M6 **Houston** Texas 29.45N 95.25W
112 M4 **Houston County L** Texas
112 F8 **Houston Heights** Houston, Texas 29.48N 95.24W
107 C3 **Houstonia** Missouri 38.53N 93.22W
112 G9 **Houston Internat. Airport** Texas 29.39N 95.16W
112 M5 **Houston,L** Texas
107 C11 **Houston R** Louisiana
60 L14 **Hout** Netherlands 51.28N 5.38E
94 K4 **Hout** *R* S Africa
61 E4 **Houtaing** Belgium 50.38N 3.41E
61 H4 **Houtain-le-Val** Belgium 50.35N 4.25E
61 N4 **Houtain-St.-Siméon** Belgium 50.44N 5.37E
33 H2 **Hout, Al** *oil field* The Gulf 28.50N 49.06E
61 C2 **Houtave** Belgium 51.14N 3.07E
95 B10 **Houtbaai** S Africa 34.03S 18.21E
95 B10 **Houtbaai** *B* S Africa
61 A2 **Houtem** Belgium 51.01N 2.37E
60 J11 **Houten** Netherlands 52.02N 5.10E
61 M2 **Houthalen** Belgium 51.02N 5.22E
61 B3 **Houthem** Belgium 50.47N 2.58E
60 N14 **Houthuizen** Netherlands 51.27N 6.10E
61 B3 **Houthulst** Belgium 50.58N 2.57E
60 N7 **Houtigehage** Netherlands 53.09N 6.10E
95 L2 **Houtkop** S Africa 26.36S 27.52E
95 H6 **Houtkraal** S Africa 30.23S 24.05E
14 A8 **Houtman Abrolhos** *arch* W Australia
61 K2 **Houtvenne** Belgium 51.03N 4.49E
104 G6 **Houtzdale** Pennsylvania 40.50N 78.21W
61 K3 **Houwaart** Belgium 50.56N 4.51E
95 G6 **Houwaterdam** *res* S Africa 30.21S 23.20E
61 K5 **Houx** Belgium 50.18N 4.54E
24 F4 **Houxia** Xinjiang Uygur Zizhiqu China 43.09N 87.01E
61 L6 **Houyèt** Belgium 50.11N 5.01E
53 E5 **Hov** Århus Denmark 55.55N 10.16E
53 K4 **Hov** Sweden 56.27N 12.45E
52 H8 **Hova** Sweden 58.53N 14.13E
53 X21 **Hovatn** *L* Norway 58.58N 7.47E
53 B5 **Hovborg** Denmark 55.37N 8.57E
22 B2 **Hovd** Hovd Mongolia 48.00N 91.43E
22 F4 **Hovd** Övörhangay Mongolia 44.40N 102.11E
22 B3 **Hovd** *prov* Mongolia
53 W19 **Hovdehytta** Norway 59.33N 7.20E
53 R15 **Hovden** Norway 61.41N 4.51E
53 R15 **Hovden** *isld* Norway 61.41N 4.51E
22 B2 **Hovd Gol** *R* Mongolia
53 M9 **Høvdin** *mt* Faeroes 62.18N 7.13W
52 J4 **Hovdsjö** Sweden 62.53N 15.35E
61 H2 **Hove** Belgium 51.09N 4.29E
56 L6 **Hove** E Sussex Eng 50.49N 0.11W
53 N10 **Hove** Faeroes 61.31N 6.45W
Hove Ringkøbing Denmark*see* **Klinkby**
53 G5 **Høve** Vestjælland Denmark 55.51N 11.30E
53 D5 **Hovedgård** Denmark 55.57N 9.58E
63 J9 **Hövelhof** W Germany 51.49N 8.39E
53 B5 **Hoven** Denmark 55.52N 8.46E
108 L4 **Hoven** S Dakota 45.13N 99.44W
111 P4 **Hovenweep Nat.Mon** Utah 37.17N 109.10W
53 A4 **Hover** Denmark 56.09N 8.25E
53 A4 **Hover Å** *R* Denmark
61 G4 **Hoves** Belgium 50.40N 4.02E
53 Y17 **Hovet** Norway 60.38N 8.09E
32 C5 **Hoveyzeh** Iran 31.25N 48.06E
48 V4 **Hovgaards** *isld* Greenland 80.00N 19.00W
57 M4 **Hovingham** N Yorks Eng 54.10N 0.59W
106 E2 **Hovland** Minnesota 47.50N 89.58W
53 S16 **Hovlandsdalsvatn** *L* Norway 61.14N 5.27E
22 H5 **Hövsgöl** Mongolia 43.36N 109.40E
22 E1 **Hövsgöl** *prov* Mongolia
22 E1 **Hövsgöl Nuur** *L* Mongolia
53 C6 **Hovslund** Denmark 55.09N 9.22E
90 M3 **Howa** *watercourse* Chad/Sudan
87 H3 **Howakil I** Ethiopia 15.10N 40.16E
109 O4 **Howard** Kansas 37.27N 96.16W
104 C6 **Howard** Ohio 40.25N 82.20W
104 H5 **Howard** Pennsylvania 41.01N 77.40W
13 L7 **Howard** Queensland 25.20S 152.32E
95 H4 **Howard** S Africa 28.08S 24.01E
108 N5 **Howard** S Dakota 44.02N 97.31W
106 J6 **Howard City** Michigan 43.23N 85.30W
112 F5 **Howard Cr** Texas
13 D1 **Howard I** N Terr Australia
101 U4 **Howard L** N W Terr 62.13N 106.00W
108 Q4 **Howard Lake** Minnesota 45.05N 94.02W
113 J2 **Howard Pass** Alaska 68.12N 157.00W
61 D4 **Howardries** Belgium 50.31N 3.22E
106 G6 **Howards Grove** Wisconsin 43.51N 87.50W
57 M5 **Howden** Humberside Eng 53.45N 0.52W
110 N6 **Howe** Idaho 43.47N 113.00W
106 J8 **Howe** Indiana 41.44N 85.24W
109 Q7 **Howe** Oklahoma 34.57N 94.37W
112 L2 **Howe** Texas 33.31N 96.36W
12 J6 **Howe,C** New S Wales 37.20S 149.59E

26 Q14 Howe Î Kerguelen Indian Ocean 48.50S 69.26E
85 N9 Howeit,Jebel mt Sudan 20.08N 34.19E
106 L7 Howell Michigan 42.36N 83.55W
12 K4 Howell New S Wales 30.00S 151.00E
110 N8 Howell Utah 41.48N 112.27W
108 N8 Howells Nebraska 41.43N 97.00W
103 F4 Howells New York 41.29N 74.27W
12 C2 Howe,Mt S Australia 26.15S 133.25E
58 L5 Howe of the Mearns dist Grampian Scotland
10 U10 Howe,Pt Norfolk I Pacific Oc 29.01S 167.55E
108 H5 Howes S Dakota 44.35N 102.02W
101 M11 Howe Sd Br Col
11 E2 Howick New Zealand 36.54S 174.56E
99 R7 Howick Quebec 45.11N 73.51W
95 O5 Howick S Africa 29.30S 30.15E
13 H2 Howick Group islds Gt Barrier Reef Australia
12 E3 Howitt, L S Australia
12 H6 Howitt,Mt Victoria 37.15S 146.40E
104 R1 Howland Maine 45.15N 68.40W
9 P8 Howland I Pacific Oc 0.48N 176.38W
122 A3 Howland I Phoenix Is Pacific Oc 0.48N 176.38W
98 P4 Howley Newfoundland 49.10N 57.07W
58 B4 Howmore S Uist, W Isles Scotland 57.18N 7.23W
29 M3 Howrah W Bengal India 22.35N 88.20E
29 K6 Howrah dist W Bengal India
101 P10 Howser Br Col 50.19N 116.57W
59 K5 Howth Dublin Irish Rep 53.23N 6.04W
32 H4 Howz Iran 32.38N 58.01E
32 F4 Ḥowz-e Dūmatu Iran 33.12N 54.10E
32 F4 Ḥowz-e Gīvar Iran 32.28N 54.16E
32 F4 Ḥowz-e Kalūt Iran 32.48N 54.21E
32 F4 Ḥowz-e Panj Esfahān Iran 33.49N 54.25E
32 G5 Ḥowz-e Panj Kermān Iran 31.05N 56.57E
32 F4 Ḥowz-i Haft Farsakh Iran 32.49N 55.25E
32 G4 Ḥowz-i Khan Iran 32.12N 57.29E
32 F4 Ḥowz-i-Mian-i-Tak Iran 32.24N 54.48E
58 S12 Hoxa,Sd.of Orkney Scotland
107 F5 Hoxie Arkansas 36.01N 91.00W
109 K2 Hoxie Kansas 39.21N 100.27W
56 O3 Hoxne Suffolk Eng 52.21N 1.12E
63 K9 Höxter W Germany 51.47N 9.22E
24 E2 Hoxtolgay Xinjiang Uygur Zizhiqu China 46.34N 86.00E
24 E4 Hoxud Xinjiang Uygur Zizhiqu China 42.11N 86.48E
58 S12 Hoy isld Orkney Scotland
63 K7 Hoya W Germany 52.48N 9.08E
20 C2 Hōya dist Tōkyō Japan
77 N3 Hoya-Gonzalo Spain 38.58N 1.34W
53 U16 Høyanger Norway 61.13N 6.05E
50 N10 Hoybergodden Jan Mayen I 70.51N 9.05W
53 Y19 Høydalsmo Norway 59.30N 8.15E
53 Y15 Høydalsvatn L Norway 61.41N 8.02E
62 H4 Hoyerswerda E Germany 51.28N 14.17E
57 G6 Hoylake Merseyside Eng 53.23N 3.11W
52 G2 Høylandet Norway 64.38N 12.20E
53 T19 Høylandsbygdi Norway 59.47N 5.48E
99 J4 Hoyle Ontario 48.35N 81.03W
107 G3 Hoyleton Illinois 38.26N 89.15W
63 O9 Hoym E Germany 51.48N 11.18E
75 C6 Hoyo de Manzanares Spain 40.37N 3.54W
76 L8 Hoyo de Pinares,El Spain 40.30N 4.26W
77 J4 Hoyo,El Spain 38.24N 3.55W
58 S12 Hoy,Old Man of rock Orkney Scotland 58.53N 3.26W
76 F8 Hoyos Spain 40.10N 6.43W
36 E4 Hoyran Turkey 38.20N 30.59E
36 E4 Hoyran Gölü L Turkey
37 D3 Hoyrat Gol L Turkey 40.18N 27.28E
58 S12 Hoy Sd Orkney Scotland
109 P2 Hoyt Kansas 39.15N 95.43W
98 F8 Hoyt New Brunswick 45.34N 66.32W
51 O9 Höytiäinen L Finland 62.50N 29.40E
Hoyto Tamirin Gol R see Tamirïn Gol
110 O9 Hoyt Pk Utah 40.43N 111.11W
37 E6 Hozat Turkey 39.09N 39.13E
77 F8 Hozgarganta R Spain
75 G6 Hoz Seca,la R Spain
25 D2 Hpa Lai Burma 21.10N 97.09E
64 P4 Hrachaluská Nádrž L Czechoslovakia
62 J5 Hradec Králové Czech 50.13N 15.50E
65 O4 Hrádek Czechoslovakia 48.47N 16.17E
65 M3 Hradisko mt Czechoslovakia 49.09N 15.21E
64 P3 Hradiště mt Czechoslovakia 50.12N 13.08E
50 L4 Hrafnabjörg Iceland 65.29N 14.35W
50 D6 Hrafnagja R Iceland
50 C7 Hrafnagja rift Iceland
50 B3 Hrafnseyri Iceland 65.46N 23.24W
50 C2 Hrafnsfjördhur B Iceland
50 F7 Hrafntinnuhraun lava field Iceland
62 K6 Hranice Severomoravský Czech 49.34N 17.45E
Hranice Západočeský Czech see Rossbach
50 B3 Hraun Ísafjardharsýsla, Vestur Iceland 65.54N 23.42W
50 E2 Hraun Skagafjardharsýsla Iceland 66.07N 20.07W
50 K5 Hraun reg Iceland
50 L4 Hraundalur V Iceland
50 L5 Hraungardhur lava field Iceland
50 E7 Hraungerdhi Iceland 63.57N 20.50W
50 K1 Hraunhafnartangi pt Iceland 66.32N 15.59W
50 G6 Hraunvatn L Iceland 64.12N 18.39W
65 K2 Hřebeny mts Czechoslovakia
50 D5 Hredhavatn L Iceland 64.45N 21.34W
50 D5 Hredhavatnsskogur wood Iceland
50 E6 Hreppar reg Iceland
50 E6 Hrepphólar Iceland 64.04N 20.20W
50 G5 Hreysiskvísl R Iceland
65 K2 Hřímáždice Czechoslovakia 49.41N 14.18E
62 M7 Hriňová Czechoslovakia 48.35N 19.30E
50 G3 Hrísey Iceland 65.59N 18.20W
50 G2 Hrísey isld Iceland 66.00N 18.21W
50 L3 Hróaldstadhir Iceland 65.49N 14.55W
65 N2 Hrochuv Tynec Czechoslovakia 49.58N 15.54E
50 K6 Hrollaugseyjar islds Iceland 64.03N 15.59W
50 C2 Hrolleifsborg mt Iceland 66.09N 22.13W
50 L5 Hrómundarey isld Iceland 64.36N 14.21W
62 L7 Hron R Czechoslovakia
64 O3 Hroznětín Czechoslovakia 50.19N 12.52E
62 O5 Hrubieszów Poland 50.49N 23.53E
50 E6 Hruni Iceland 64.09N 20.16W
65 O2 Hrušová Czechoslovakia 49.55N 16.12E
65 O4 Hrušovany nad Jevišovka Czechoslovakia 48.51N 16.25E
50 F5 Hrutafell mt Iceland 64.44N 19.43W
50 K3 Hrutafjöll mt Múlasýsla, Nordhur Iceland 65.39N 15.33W
50 J3 Hrútafjoll mt Thingeyjarsýsla, Nordhur Iceland 65.50N 16.44W
50 D4 Hrútafjördhur B Iceland
82 C6 Hrvatska rep Yugoslavia
25 D2 Hsa Mong Hkam Burma 20.40N 96.59E
25 D3 Hsataw Burma 19.35N 97.34E
25 N9 Hsenwi Burma 23.16N 97.59E
Hsiang-ch'üan Ho R Xinjiang Uygur Zizhiqu see Xiangquan He
Hsiang-hsien see Xiangzhou
23 J8 Hsiao-lan Hsü isld Taiwan 21.53N 121.35E
25 D2 Hsihkip Burma 20.22N 96.41E
25 D2 Hsi-Hseng Burma 20.07N 97.17E
Hsi-Hsia-Pang-ma Feng mt pk see Xixabangma Feng
23 H7 Hsi-hsü-p'ing Hsü isld Taiwan 23.11N 119.25E
Hsi-hu see Usu
Hsi-Kuei-t'u-ch'i see Xuguit Qi
23 J7 Hsi-lo Taiwan 23.46N 120.25E
Hsin-an-chen see Xinyi
23 J6 Hsin-ch'eng Taiwan 24.07N 121.35E
23 J6 Hsin-chu Taiwan 24.48N 120.59E
23 J7 Hsing-ch'ang Taiwan 23.06N 121.22E
Hsing-k'ai Hu L see Ozero Khanka
Hsin-i see Xinyi
23 J6 Hsin-tien Taiwan 24.58N 121.31E
23 J7 Hsin-ying Taiwan 28.18N 120.18E
25 D1 Hsipaw Burma 22.32N 97.12E
23 J6 Hsüeh Shan mts Taiwan
25 D1 Hsumhsai Burma 22.18N 96.35E
Hsün-K'o see Xunke
23 H6 Hua 'An Fujian China 25.00N 117.30E
94 B3 Huab watercourse Namibia
120 B6 Huacachina Peru 14.07S 75.45W
120 B3 Huacaibamba Peru 9.03S 76.49W
120 F5 Huacaraje Bolivia 13.33S 63.48W
120 F9 Huacaya Bolivia 20.45S 63.42W
120 E8 Huachacalla Bolivia 18.47S 68.15W
119 G6 Huachamacari, Cerro mt Venez 3.44N 65.59W
120 F6 Huachi Bolivia 14.15S 63.33W
22 G8 Huachi Gansu China 36.28N 107.58E
120 F6 Huachi, L Bolivia 14.15S 63.33W
115 E2 Huachinera Mexico 30.12N 108.58W
121 A6 Huachipato Chile 36.45S 73.09W
120 B4 Huacho Peru 11.05S 77.36W
120 B4 Huachón Peru 10.40S 75.55W
120 B5 Huachos Peru 13.13S 76.30W
21 E4 Huachuan Heilongjiang China 47.08N 130.50E
120 B3 Huacrachuco Peru 8.37S 77.04W
120 D7 Huacullani Peru 16.39S 69.20W
22 J6 Huade Nei Monggol Zizhiqu China 41.58N 113.59E
21 D6 Huadian Jilin China 43.01N 126.45E
23 J4 Huading Shan mt Zhejiang China 29.18N 121.06E
120 B4 Huagaruancha(Huagaruncho) mt Peru 10.32S 75.57W
22 D6 Huahai Gansu China 40.18N 97.44E
22 C7 Huahaizi Qinghai China 38.48N 94.25E
Hua Hin see Ban Hua Hin
122 A15 Huahine isld Society Is Pacific Oc 16.45S 151.00W
Hua-hsien see Huazhou
22 K6 Huai'an Hebei China 40.48N 114.24E
23 H2 Huai 'an Jiangsu China 33.30N 119.09E
23 G1 Huaibei Anhui China 34.00N 116.48E
23 G2 Huaibin Henan China 32.32N 115.27E
21 C6 Huaide Jilin China 43.30N 124.48E
21 C6 Huaidezhen Jilin China 43.48N 124.45E
Huaidian see Shenqiu
23 H2 Huai He R Anhui China
23 G2 Huai He R Henan China
23 E5 Huaihua Hunan China 27.27N 109.50E
23 F6 Huaiji Guangdong China 24.03N 112.06E
22 K6 Huailai Hebei China 40.24N 115.31E
120 A2 Huailillas mt Peru 7.55S 78.03W
25 G4 Huai Luang R Thailand
Huai-ming see Anqing
23 H2 Huainan Anhui China 32.41N 117.06E
23 G3 Huaining Anhui China 30.23N 116.44E
22 J7 Huairen Shanxi China 39.52N 113.03E
22 K6 Huairou Beijing China 40.16N 116.38E
25 H5 Huai Samran R Thailand
120 B5 Huaitará Peru 13.36S 75.21W
23 G2 Huaiyang Henan China 33.44N 114.55E
25 G4 Huai Yang Res Thailand
23 H2 Huaiyin Jiangsu China 33.40N 119.07E
23 H2 Huaiyuan Anhui China 32.57N 117.12E
23 E6 Huaiyuan Guangxi China 24.40N 108.27E
115 L9 Huajuápan de León Mexico 17.50N 97.48W
115 K5 Hualahuises Mexico 24.56N 99.42W
111 L6 Hualapai Mts Arizona
120 E12 Hualfín Argentina 27.15S 66.53W
23 J7 Hua-lien Taiwan 23.58N 121.35E
23 G4 Hualin Jiangxi China 28.36N 115.05E
120 C5 Hualla Peru 13.44S 73.56W
120 B1 Huallaga, R Peru
120 B3 Huallanca Peru 8.47S 77.53W
22 F8 Hualong Huizu Zizhixian Gansu China 36.08N 102.24E
21 E4 Huama Heilongjiang China 47.05N 131.45E
120 A8 Huamachuco Peru 7.50S 78.01W
120 B5 Huamani Peru 13.51S 75.31W
120 B5 Huamanrazo Peru 12.54S 75.04W
115 L8 Huamantla Mexico 19.21N 97.58W
91 D10 Huambo Angola 12.47S 15.44E
91 D10 Huambo dist Angola
119 B11 Huambos Cajamarca Peru 6.31S 79.59W
120 A7 Huambos Libertad Peru 6.30S 78.59W
115 M2 Huampusirpi Honduras 15.14N 84.37W
21 E4 Huanan Heilongjiang China 46.12N 130.30E
120 E6 Huanay Bolivia 15.24S 67.54W
120 B4 Huancabamba Pasco Peru 10.30S 75.29W
119 B10 Huancabamba Piura Peru 5.17S 79.28W
119 B10 Huancabamba, R Peru
121 B9 Huancache, Sa ra Argentina
120 D6 Huancané Peru 15.10S 69.44W
120 B5 Huancano Peru 13.36S 75.37W
120 C5 Huancapi Peru 13.40S 74.05W
120 C5 Huancarama Peru 13.38S 73.07W
120 C5 Huanca Sancos Peru 13.50S 74.16W
120 B5 Huancavelica Peru 12.45S 75.03W
120 B5 Huancavelica dept Peru
120 B5 Huancayo Peru 12.05S 75.12W
120 E9 Huanchaca Bolivia 20.18S 66.40W
118 A4 Huanchaca mts Bolivia 14.37S 60.59W
118 A4 Huanchaca, Sa. de mts Brazil/Bolivia
120 A8 Huanchaco Peru 8.03S 79.06W
Huang'an see Hong'an
Huang-an see Hong'an
23 J2 Huangang Jiangsu China 32.30N 121.06E
Huangcaoba see Xingyi
23 G2 Huangchuan Henan China 32.15N 115.10E
23 G3 Huanggang Hubei China 30.27N 114.53E
22 L5 Huanggangliang mt pk Nei Monggol Zizhiqu China 43.32N 117.30E
23 H5 Huanggang Shan mt Fujian China
Huang Hai see Yellow Sea
23 J1 Huang Hai sea China
22 F8 Huang He R Gansu China
23 G1 Huang He R Henan China
23 G2 Huang He R Henan China
22 G7 Huang He R Nei Monggol Zizhiqu China
22 H6 Huang He R Nei Monggol Zizhiqu China
23 A1 Huang He R Qinghai China
23 B1 Huang He R Qinghai China
22 H8 Huang He R Shanxi/Shaanxi China
Huangheyan see Madoi
Huang Ho R see Huang He
22 L7 Huanghua Hebei China 38.26N 117.23E
23 G1 Huangkou Anhui China 34.22N 116.46E
23 G4 Huanglaomen Jiangxi China 29.27N 115.57E
23 E1 Huangling Shaanxi China 35.40N 109.12E
23 E9 Huangliu Guangdong China 18.31N 108.40E
23 E1 Huanglong Shaanxi China 35.40N 109.12E
Huanglongsi see Kaifeng
Huang-lung see Huanglong
23 G3 Huangmei Hubei China 30.06N 115.55E
23 E6 Huangmian Guangxi China 24.45N 109.39E
21 D6 Huangnihe Jilin China 43.31N 128.00E
23 G3 Huangpi Hubei China 30.58N 114.23E
23 D5 Huangpin Guizhou China 26.54N 107.51E
23 E8 Huangpo Guangdong China 21.29N 110.46E
23 F7 Huangpu Guangdong China 23.08N 113.31E
23 G4 Huangshagang Jiangxi China 28.52N 114.45E
23 H3 Huang Shan mts Anhui China
22 M8 Huangshanguan Shandong China 37.32N 120.15E
23 G3 Huangshi Hubei China 30.13N 115.05E
22 F8 Huang Shui R Gansu China
21 D6 Huangsongdian Jilin China 43.36N 127.32E
22 H8 Huangtu Gaoyuan plat Shaanxi China
22 L6 Huangtuliangzi Hebei China 41.14N 118.40E
22 M8 Huang Xian Shandong China 37.40N 120.30E
23 J4 Huangyan Zhejiang China 28.39N 121.19E
Huangyan Dao see Scarborough Reef
23 F5 Huangyangsi Hunan China 26.39N 111.40E
22 E8 Huangyuan Qinghai China 36.40N 101.27E
Huangzhai see Yangqu
Huangzhou see Huanggang
23 E9 Huangzhu Guangdong China 19.30N 110.25E
21 B12 Huaniao Shan isld Zhejiang China
23 C6 Huaning Yunnan China 24.12N 102.54E
22 C6 Huaniushan Gansu China 41.15N 95.30E
23 E6 Huanjian Guangxi China 24.49N 108.12E
23 E6 Huanjiang Guangxi China 24.49N 108.12E
22 G8 Huan Jiang R Gansu China
115 M2 Huanquibila Honduras 14.59N 85.00W
21 C7 Huanren Liaoning China 41.14N 125.22E
Huanshan see Yuhuan
120 C5 Huanta Peru 12.54S 74.13W
22 L8 Huantai Shandong China 36.57N 118.08E
120 B5 Huantán Peru 12.25S 75.44W
120 B3 Huánuco Peru 9.55S 76.11W
120 B4 Huánuco dept Peru
120 C6 Huanuhuanu Peru 15.35S 73.55W
120 E8 Huanuni Bolivia 18.15S 66.48W
22 G8 Huan Xian Gansu China 36.40N 107.20E
120 C6 Huanzo, de, Cord mts Peru
23 B5 Huaping Yunnan China 26.46N 101.25E
23 J6 Hua-p'ing Hsü isld Taiwan
120 E8 Huar Bolivia 19.00S 66.46W
120 D9 Huara Chile 20.00S 69.45W
120 B4 Huaral Peru 11.31S 77.10W
120 B3 Huaráz Peru 9.33S 77.31W
120 B3 Huari Peru 9.22S 77.14W
120 B4 Huariaca Peru 10.13S 76.06W
120 E7 Huarina Bolivia 16.14S 68.37W
119 B10 Huarmaca Peru 5.36S 79.35W
120 A3 Huarmey Peru 10.03S 78.08W
120 B5 Huarochiri Peru 12.08S 76.16W
120 C5 Huarocondo Peru 13.23S 72.15W
120 B4 Huaron Peru 11.03S 76.24W
23 F4 Huarong Hunan China 29.32N 112.33E
75 G2 Huarte Spain 42.50N 1.35W
75 G2 Huarte Araquil Spain 42.55N 1.59W
119 C9 Huasaga, R Peru
120 B3 Huascaran, Nev.de pk Peru 9.08S 77.36W
121 B2 Huasco Chile 28.30S 71.15W
121 B2 Huasco R Chile
120 E9 Huasco, Salar del salt pan Chile
23 F5 Huashi Hunan China 27.28N 112.40E
23 B1 Huashixia Qinghai China 35.13N 99.12E
22 D7 Huashugou Gansu China 39.18N 97.58E
115 M2 Huaspuc Honduras 14.38N 84.26W
115 E4 Huatabampo Mexico 26.49N 109.40W
23 D1 Huating Gansu China 35.08N 107.10E
21 B6 Hua Tugal Nei Monggol Zizhiqu China 43.51N 122.07E
120 E5 Huatunas, Lagunas Bolivia
115 L8 Huatusco Mexico 19.12N 96.58W
115 K7 Huauchinango Mexico 20.11N 98.04W
115 N3 Huaunta Nicaragua 13.30N 83.32W
120 B4 Huaura R Peru
120 B4 Huauru, I de Peru 11.30S 77.52W
115 L8 Huautla Mexico 18.10N 96.51W
23 D5 Huaxi Guizhou China 26.25N 106.40E
23 F7 Hua Xian Guangdong China 23.32N 113.22E
23 E1 Hua Xian Shaanxi China 34.33N 109.47E
23 G1 Huaxiancheng Henan China 35.33N 114.34E
120 B2 Huayabamba R Peru
115 K7 Huayacocotla Mexico 20.34N 98.27W
23 D2 Huayangzhen Shaanxi China 33.28N 107.33E
120 B4 Huayhuash,Cord mts Peru
23 E1 Huayin Shaanxi China 34.36N 110.09E
23 D3 Huaying Shan mt ra Sichuan China
120 B3 Huaylas Peru 8.52S 77.53W
120 B4 Huayllay Peru 11.03S 76.21W
120 C5 Huayopata Peru 13.00S 72.35W
23 G3 Huayuan Hubei China 31.17N 114.01E
23 E4 Huayuan Hunan China 28.36N 109.26E
120 B5 Huayucachi Peru 12.08S 75.13W
120 B6 Huayuri. Pampa de plain Peru
22 E7 Huazhaizi Gansu China 38.37N 100.24E
23 E8 Huazhou Guangdong China 21.35N 110.38E
21 C7 Huazi Liaoning China 41.25N 123.30E
Hubain see Qaryat Ḥubayn al Gharbīyah
108 R7 Hubbard Iowa 42.19N 93.18W
100 O7 Hubbard Saskatchewan 51.06N 103.20W
112 L4 Hubbard Texas 31.51N 96.49W
112 H3 Hubbard Creek Res Texas
106 L5 Hubbard L Michigan
106 L5 Hubbard Lake Michigan 44.53N 83.34W
101 D5 Hubbard, Mt Yukon/Alaska 60.16N 139.06W
98 H9 Hubbards Nova Scotia 44.38N 64.04W
108 N9 Hubbell Nebraska 40.01N 97.39W
23 F3 Hubei prov China
65 G8 Huben Öst Tirol Austria 46.56N 12.34E
65 C7 Huben Tirol Austria 47.03N 10.59E
87 M5 Hubera Somalia 10.37N 48.25E
99 Q7 Huberdeau Quebec 45.58N 74.40W
63 T7 Hubertusstock E Germany 52.55N 13.40E
28 B3 Hubli Karnataka India 15.20N 75.14E
35 G3 Hubras Jordan 32.40N 35.50E
86 J5 Hubr Umm Khisheib reg Egypt
121 D6 Hucal Argentina 37.45S 64.00W
61 L4 Huccorgne Belgium 50.34N 5.10E
63 J6 Huchting Bremen W Germany 53.03N 8.43E
64 A1 Hückelhoven-Ratheim W Germany 51.03N 6.13E
64 C1 Hückeswagen W Germany 51.09N 7.20E
13 D6 Huckitta N Terr Australia 22.30S 135.29E
57 L6 Hucknall Torkard Notts Eng 53.02N 1.11W
69 B2 Hucqueliers France 50.34N 1.55E
Hudaybu see Ḥadībū
33 E9 Ḥudaydah, Al Yemen 14.50N 42.58E
33 C3 Ḥudb Ḥumar plat Saudi Arabia
57 K5 Huddersfield W Yorks Eng 53.39N 1.47W
52 K7 Huddinge Sweden 59.15N 17.57E
63 H6 Hude W Germany 53.08N 8.26E
35 F9 Hudeira watercourse Jordan
63 L7 Hudemühlen W Germany 52.45N 9.36E
87 E2 Hudi Sudan 17.43N 34.18E
52 K5 Hudiksvall Sweden 61.45N 17.10E
70 H4 Hudimesnil France 48.52N 1.30W
109 F1 Hudson Colorado 40.04N 104.37W
105 E9 Hudson Florida 28.23N 82.42W
106 F9 Hudson Illinois 40.36N 88.59W
106 J8 Hudson Indiana 41.32N 85.03W
108 S7 Hudson Iowa 42.26N 92.26W
109 M3 Hudson Kansas 38.07N 98.40W
103 L2 Hudson Massachusetts 42.24N 71.34W
106 K8 Hudson Michigan 41.51N 84.22W
104 O4 Hudson New Hampshire 42.44N 71.26W
104 D5 Hudson Ohio 41.14N 81.27W
100 K1 Hudson Ontario 50.06N 92.09W
108 O6 Hudson S Dakota 43.08N 96.30W
106 B5 Hudson Wisconsin 44.59N 92.43W
108 B7 Hudson Wyoming 42.54N 108.35W
103 F5 Hudson co New Jersey
104 M5 Hudson R New York
97 L6 Hudson Bay Canada
100 P6 Hudson Bay Saskatchewan 52.51N 102.23W
103 G7 Hudson Canyon Atlantic Oc
121 J6 Hudson, Cerro pk Chile 46.07S 72.58W
104 M3 Hudson Falls New York 43.16N 73.36W
103 F4 Hudson Highlands hills New York
109 P5 Hudson Lake Oklahoma 36.20N 95.10W
48 U9 Hudson Land Greenland
123 H11 Hudson Mts Antarctica
101 N7 Hudson's Hope Br Col 56.03N 121.59W
97 M5 Hudson Str Canada
106 J7 Hudsonville Michigan 42.52N 85.53W
87 L6 Hudun Somalia 9.06N 47.22E
100 W5 Hudwin L Manitoba
25 J4 Hue Vietnam 16.28N 107.35E
76 F6 Huebra R Spain
121 A8 Huechucuicui, Pta C Chile 41.50S 74.00W
121 B7 Huechulafquén, L Argentina
82 H4 Huedin Romania 46.52N 23.02E
114 B7 Huehue Hawaiian Is 19.44N 155.59W
115 N10 Huehuetán Mexico 15.01N 92.25W
115 O10 Huehuetenango Guatemala 15.19N 91.26W
115 G5 Huehueto, Cerro pk Mexico 24.05N 105.45W
115 K8 Huejotzingo Mexico 19.10N 98.23W
115 H6 Huejuqilla Mexico 22.40N 103.52W
115 K7 Huejutla Mexico 21.10N 98.25W
77 K6 Huélago Spain 37.25N 3.15W
75 G7 Huélamo Spain 40.16N 1.49W
70 C5 Huelgoat France 48.22N 3.45W
77 K5 Huelma Spain 37.39N 3.28W
114 E6 Huelo Pt Hawaiian Is 20.54N 156.12W
77 C6 Huelva Spain 37.15N 6.56W
74 C7 Huelva prov Spain
77 D5 Huelva, R.de Spain
75 E7 Huelves Spain 40.02N 2.54W
121 J5 Huemules R Chile
77 L6 Huéneja Spain 37.11N 2.56W
25 H4 Huen-Hine Laos 16.11N 105.02E
121 B3 Huentelauquén Chile 31.38S 71.33W
115 D3 Huépac Mexico 29.53N 110.14W
119 E2 Hueque R Venezuela
121 A9 Huequi, Pen Chile
121 A9 Huequi, V Chile 42.27S 72.40W
77 M7 Huércal de Almería Spain 36.53N 2.26W
77 N6 Huércal Overa Spain 37.23N 1.56W
109 F3 Huerfano R Colorado
75 C2 Huérmeces Spain 42.31N 3.47W
75 G7 Huerta del Marquesado Spain 40.09N 1.42W
75 D4 Huerta del Rey Spain 41.50N 3.20W
75 C8 Huerta de Valdecarábonos Spain 39.51N 3.37W
75 F6 Huertahernando Spain 40.49N 2.17W
121 C3 Huerta, Sa.de la ra Argentina
77 Q4 Huertas, C.de las Spain 38.22N 0.24W
115 J5 Huertecillas Mexico 24.08N 101.10W
75 F3 Huérteles Spain 42.01N 2.19W
75 K4 Huerto Spain 41.56N 0.11W
75 H5 Huerva R Spain
77 K5 Huesa Spain 37.46N 3.04W
75 K3 Huesca Spain 42.08N 0.25W
74 G2 Huesca prov Spain
77 L5 Huéscar Spain 37.49N 2.32W
77 E5 Huesna R Spain
122 V12 Hueso Ballena, Pta C Juan Fernández, Is Pacific Oc 33.39S 78.16W
112 B5 Hueso, Sierra del mts Mexico
115 J8 Huétamo Mexico 18.36N 100.54W
75 E7 Huete Spain 40.09N 2.42W
77 J6 Huetor Santillan Spain 37.13N 3.30W
77 H6 Huétor Tájar Spain 37.12N 4.03W
77 J6 Huetor Vega Spain 37.09N 3.34W
115 K8 Huexotla ruins Mexico 19.30N 98.50W
33 H3 Ḥufayrah, Al Saudi Arabia 26.05N 49.11E
33 F4 Ḥufayyirah, Al Saudi Arabia 24.28N 44.42E
108 K3 Huff N Dakota 46.39N 100.40W
64 G5 Hüffenhardt W Germany 49.17N 9.05E
108 M4 Huffton S Dakota 45.36N 98.05W
64 E8 Hüfingen W Germany 47.56N 8.30E
33 C2 Ḥufrah, Al area Saudi Arabia
34 F10 Ḥufrah, Al plat Saudi Arabia
53 S18 Huftarøy isld Norway 60.03N 5.17E
33 H4 Hufūf, Al Saudi Arabia 25.20N 49.34E
66 F5 Hugeligrat mt Switzerland 46.32N 7.16E
57 M5 Huggate Humberside Eng 53.59N 0.38W
113 K4 Huggins I Alaska 65.50N 154.30W
108 K9 Hugh Butler L Nebraska 40.23N 100.43W
100 F6 Hughenden Alberta 52.31N 111.00W
13 G5 Hughenden Queensland 20.50S 144.10E
113 K3 Hughes Alaska 66.02N 154.20W
107 F7 Hughes Arkansas 34.58N 90.30W
12 A4 Hughes S Australia 30.40S 129.32E
12 A6 Hughes dist Canberra Australia
100 R2 Hughes R Manitoba
112 N3 Hughes Springs Texas 32.59N 94.38W
107 C3 Hughesville Missouri 38.49N 93.19W
103 A4 Hughesville Pennsylvania 41.15N 76.43W
13 C6 Hugh R N Terr Australia
103 G3 Hughsonville New York 41.34N 73.56W
100 K7 Hughton Saskatchewan 51.14N 107.55W
56 R8 Hugh Town Is of Scilly Eng 49.55N 6.19W
53 T19 Huglo I Norway 59.50N 5.36E
109 G2 Hugo Colorado 39.07N 103.27W
108 R4 Hugo Minnesota 45.08N 93.00W
109 P7 Hugo Oklahoma 34.01N 95.31W
110 B7 Hugo Oregon 42.35N 123.25W
109 P7 Hugo Res Oklahoma
109 J4 Hugoton Kansas 37.11N 101.22W
64 D7 Hugsweier W Germany 48.22N 7.50E
23 F1 Huguan Shanxi China 36.02N 113.38E
103 E4 Huguenot New York 41.25N 74.37W
103 K9 Huguenot Park Staten I, N Y 40.32N 74.11W
Huhehot see Hohhot
66 J5 Hühnerstock mt Switzerland 46.36N 8.13E
119 G5 Huhucunya Venezuela 4.44N 65.25W
15 J9 Huia Papua New Guinea 10.07S 147.48E
23 H6 Hui 'An Fujian China 25.03N 118.46E
22 G8 Hui'anbu Ningxia China 37.25N 106.45E
22 G8 Huianbu Ningxia China 37.25N 106.45E
11 L5 Huiarau Ra New Zealand
60 O5 Huibertgat channel Netherlands
23 G6 Huichang Jiangxi China 25.31N 115.40E
115 K7 Huichapán Mexico 20.24N 99.40W
Huicheng see She Xian
115 H6 Huicholes, Sa.de los ra Mexico
21 D7 Huichŏn N Korea 40.06N 126.20E
23 C1 Huichuan Gansu China 35.00N 104.03E
23 G7 Huidong Guangdong China 22.58N 114.43E
23 C5 Huidong Sichuan China 26.38N 102.37E
21 D5 Huifaheng Heilongjiang China 47.48N 128.35E
22 L2 Huihe Nei Monggol Zizhiqu China 48.12N 119.20E
22 L2 Hui He R Nei Monggol Zizhiqu China
60 F14 Huijbergen Netherlands 51.26N 4.23E
23 G1 Huiji He R Henan China
91 C11 Huila Angola 15.04S 13.33E
91 D11 Huila dist Angola
119 C6 Huila div Colombia
23 G7 Huilai Guangdong China 23.04N 116.17E
119 C6 Huila, Nev. de vol Colombia 3.00N 75.59W
23 C5 Huili Sichuan China 26.41N 102.15E
121 D2 Huillapima Argentina 28.45S 65.58W
115 N9 Huimanguillo Mexico 17.50N 93.22W
22 L8 Huimin Shandong China 37.36N 117.30E
120 E7 Huiñaimarca, L. de Peru/Bolivia
21 D6 Huinan Jilin China 42.50N 126.01E
121 D5 Huinca Renancó Argentina 34.51S 64.22W
23 D1 Huining Gansu China 35.39N 105.05E
119 C8 Huiririma Ecuador 0.46S 75.38W
60 G8 Huisduinen Netherlands 52.57N 4.43E
61 E3 Huise Belgium 50.54N 3.35E
23 D5 Huishui Guizhou China 26.10N 106.39E
72 E1 Huismes France 47.13N 0.16E
70 M5 Huîsne R France
70 N6 Huisseau-sur-Cosson France 47.36N 1.28E
60 L12 Huisseling Netherlands 51.47N 5.38E
60 M12 Huissen Netherlands 51.57N 5.57E
61 F4 Huissignies Belgium 50.34N 3.45E
24 G8 Huiten Nur L Qinghai China
23 G1 Huiting Henan China 34.10N 116.13E
23 E5 Huitong Hunan China 26.51N 109.40E
51 K10 Huittinen Finland 61.11N 22.40E
115 K8 Huitzuco Mexico 18.20N 99.20W
23 D2 Hui Xian Gansu China 33.47N 106.07E
23 F1 Hui Xian Henan China 35.26N 113.50E
115 N10 Huixtla Mexico 15.09N 92.30W
23 G7 Huiyang Guangdong China 23.04N 114.21E
23 C5 Huize Yunnan China 26.24N 103.08E
60 K10 Huizen Netherlands 52.17N 5.15E
23 G7 Huizhou Guangdong China 23.08N 114.28E
61 H4 Huizingen Belgium 50.45N 4.17E
60 M7 Huizum Netherlands 53.12N 5.47E
33 C2 Hūj, Al area Saudi Arabia
33 E10 Ḥujarīyah, Al area Yemen
22 F3 Hujirt Mongolia 46.52N 102.42E
33 D4 Hujr Saudi Arabia 25.52N 40.40E
11 L5 Huka Falls waterfall New Zealand 38.39S 176.07E
11 K7 Hukanui New Zealand 40.32S 175.42E
11 F9 Hukarere New Zealand 42.14S 171.42E
25 M7 Hukawng Valley Burma
11 J2 Hukerenui New Zealand 35.33S 174.12E
Hukmabad see Hokmābād
23 G4 Hukou Jiangxi China 29.42N 116.21E
94 F5 Hukuntsi Botswana 24.02S 21.48E
87 G7 Hula Ethiopia 6.33N 38.30E
109 O5 Hulah Oklahoma 36.56N 96.03W
109 O5 Hulah Res Oklahoma
Hulaiba see Ḥulaybah
Hulaifa see Ḥulayfah
Hūl, Al see Haul, El
21 D4 Hulan Heilongjiang China 45.59N 126.37E
26 R9 Hulandawa Sri Lanka 6.12N 80.28E
26 T8 Hulandawa Sri Lanka 6.52N 81.20E
21 C4 Hulan Ergi Heilongjiang China 47.14N 123.36E
21 D4 Hulan He R Heilongjiang China
35 F1 Hulata Israel 33.03N 35.37E
34 P8 Ḥulaybah Iraq 30.04N 47.16E
33 D4 Ḥulayfah Saudi Arabia 25.59N 40.45E
22 G4 Huld Mongolia 45.05N 105.31E
35 C6 Hulda Israel 31.50N 34.53E
61 J3 Huldenberg Belgium 50.47N 4.35E
108 F5 Hulett Wyoming 44.40N 104.33W
121 H3 Hulha Negra Brazil 31.20S 53.45W
28 K2 Huliagaon Assam India 27.35N 94.30E
Huliao see Dabu
Hulihale see Pawa
32 B4 Hulilan Iran 33.48N 47.09E
21 F5 Hulin Heilongjiang China 45.44N 132.59E
21 C5 Hulin He R Jilin China
21 B5 Hulin He R Nei Monggol Zizhiqu China
57 N5 Hull Humberside Eng 53.45N 0.20W
107 E2 Hull Illinois 39.42N 91.11W
108 O6 Hull Iowa 43.11N 96.08W
103 N2 Hull Massachusetts 42.19N 70.54W
108 K3 Hull N Dakota 46.02N 100.08W
99 P7 Hull Quebec 45.26N 75.45W
112 N5 Hull Texas 30.09N 94.39W
13 A6 Hull Cr N Terr Australia
87 F7 Hulle Ethiopia 7.35N 37.10E
53 C7 Hüllerup W Germany 54.43N 9.20E
123 J9 Hull Glacier Antarctica 75.25S 136.50W
10 S2 Hull I Phoenix Is Pacific Oc 4.35S 172.20W
57 N5 Hull, R Humberside Eng
61 H4 Hulpe, La Belgium 50.43N 4.30E
63 E10 Hüls W Germany 51.23N 6.30E
60 T17 Hulsberg Netherlands 50.54N 5.52E
60 L10 Hulshorst Netherlands 52.22N 5.44E
61 K2 Hulshout Belgium 51.05N 4.48E
53 E1 Hulsig Denmark 57.40N 10.28E
61 K6 Hulsonniaux Belgium 50.12N 4.57E
60 E14 Hulst Zeeland Netherlands 51.17N 4.03E
61 D3 Hulste Belgium 50.53N 3.18E
60 H13 Hulten Netherlands 51.34N 4.58E
52 J9 Hultsfred Sweden 57.30N 15.50E
21 B7 Huludao Liaoning China 40.47N 121.00E
23 D1 Hulu He R Gansu China
23 E1 Hulu He R Shaanxi China
Hu-lun see Hailar
Hulun see Hailar
22 L2 Hulun Nur L Heilongjiang China
22 K2 Hulun Nur L Nei Monggol Zizhiqu China
22 L2 Hulun Nur L Nei Monggol Zizhiqu China
Hulūn Usanī see Hujirt
21 D2 Huma Heilongjiang China 51.42N 126.39E
77 G7 Huma mt Spain 36.56N 4.44W
21 C1 Huma He R Heilongjiang China
120 F10 Humahuaca Argentina 23.13S 65.20W
61 M6 Humain Belgium 50.12N 5.15E
120 E4 Humaita Bolivia 10.53S 66.32W
120 F2 Humaitá Brazil 7.33S 63.01W
118 B10 Humaitá Paraguay 27.02S 58.31W
120 C3 Humaitá, R Brazil
21 D6 Human Jilin China 42.50N 126.01E
75 D6 Humanes Spain 40.50N 3.09W
95 H10 Humansdorp S Africa 34.01S 24.45E
107 C4 Humansville Missouri 37.48N 93.38W
85 N10 Humar, El watercourse Sudan
50 K6 Humarkló mt Iceland 64.24N 15.50W
120 B5 Humay Peru 13.44S 75.53W
34 B9 Ḥumaydah, Al Saudi Arabia 29.12N 34.55E
85 G5 Ḥumaymāt, al Libya 28.20N 22.01E
33 F4 Ḥumayyān, Jabal mt Saudi Arabia 24.33N 44.43E
33 G3 Humayyir, Jabal al mt Saudi Arabia 27.12N 47.53E
69 G6 Humbauville France 48.40N 4.25E
91 D12 Humbe Angola 16.41S 14.55E
69 H6 Humbécourt France 48.35N 4.55E
61 H3 Humbeek Belgium 50.58N 4.23E
99 C10 Humber B Ontario
98 P5 Humbermouth Newfoundland 48.58N 57.56W
57 N5 Humber, R Humberside Eng
99 B10 Humber R Ontario
57 M5 Humberside co Eng
120 D9 Humberstone Chile 20.14S 69.48W
117 F6 Humberto de Campos Brazil 2.34S 43.30W
106 D5 Humbird Wisconsin 44.32N 90.54W
53 F7 Humble Denmark 54.50N 10.43E
112 M6 Humble Texas 30.00N 95.18W
109 G9 Humble City New Mexico 32.47N 103.12W
111 M7 Humboldt Arizona 34.30N 112.15W
107 H2 Humboldt Illinois 39.34N 88.20W
108 Q7 Humboldt Iowa 42.43N 94.12W
109 P4 Humboldt Kansas 37.50N 95.26W
108 P9 Humboldt Nebraska 40.10N 95.59W
110 G9 Humboldt Nevada 40.36N 118.15W
100 M6 Humboldt Saskatchewan 52.13N 105.09W
107 H6 Humboldt Tennessee 35.50N 88.58W
110 G9 Humboldt R Nevada
111 G2 Humboldt salt marsh Nevada 39.50N 117.55W
110 A9 Humboldt B California
97 N2 Humboldt Gletscher glacier Greenland 79.40N 64.00W
111 F2 Humboldt L Nevada 40.00N 118.38W
110 H8 Humboldt, Lit R Nevada
9 B14 Humboldt, Mt New Caledonia 21.55S 166.29E
11 G9 Humboldt, Mt New Zealand 42.10S 172.38E
11 C11 Humboldt Mts New Zealand
110 K8 Humboldt N. Fork R Nevada
110 G9 Humboldt Ra Nevada
Humboldt Range see Danghe Nan Shan
22 D9 Humboldt Range Qinghai/Gansu China
15 F5 Humboldt, Teluk B Irian Jaya
Humbug B see Washow B
107 B3 Hume Missouri 38.06N 94.34W
104 G8 Hume Virginia 38.50N 78.00W
101 J3 Hume R N W Terr
13 H7 Humeburn Queensland 27.20S 145.10E
115 E10 Humedad I Panama
32 H8 Hūmedān Iran 25.27N 59.42E
87 B4 Humeir Gabir Sudan 13.08N 28.52E
62 N7 Humenné Czechoslovakia 48.57N 21.55E
87 F3 Humera Ethiopia 14.15N 36.35E
12 H6 Hume Res New S Wales/Victoria
69 J8 Humes-Jorquenay France 47.54N 5.18E
108 R9 Humeston Iowa 40.51N 93.29W
77 G6 Humilladero Spain 37.06N 4.43W
30 E3 Humla Karnali R Nepal
53 K5 Humlebæk Denmark 55.58N 12.34E
53 B3 Humlum Denmark 56.33N 8.34E
35 G5 Hummar, El Jordan 32.01N 35.49E
63 K9 Humme W Germany 51.32N 9.23E
52 F4 Hummelfjell mt Norway 62.27N 11.17E
60 N11 Hummelo Netherlands 52.00N 6.14E
103 A6 Hummelstown Pennsylvania 40.15N 76.44W
63 G7 Hümmling hills W Germany
11 E12 Hummock mt New Zealand 45.33S 170.22E
119 E3 Humocaro Bajo Venezuela 9.41N 70.00W
121 A5 Humos, C Chile 35.22S 72.35W
91 C11 Humpata Angola 15.01S 13.21E
107 E7 Humphrey Arkansas 34.25N 91.43W
110 N5 Humphrey Idaho 44.29N 112.14W
108 N8 Humphrey Nebraska 41.42N 97.30W
110 D2 Humphrey Washington 47.15N 121.43W
101 B1 Humphrey Pt Alaska 69.57N 142.30W
12 F8 Humphrey R Tasmania
111 E5 Humphreys California 36.57N 119.27W
107 C1 Humphreys Missouri 40.08N 93.20W
111 F4 Humphreys, Mt California 37.16N 118.40W
111 N6 Humphreys Pk mt Arizona 35.21N 111.41W
103 G2 Humphreysville New York 42.12N 73.46W
13 C7 Humphries, Mt N Terr Australia 25.30S 134.10E
65 M7 Humpolec Czechoslovakia 49.32N 15.22E
51 K11 Humppila Finland 60.56N 23.30E
110 B2 Humptulips Washington 47.14N 123.57W
13 B2 Humpty Doo N Terr Australia 12.37S 131.14E
33 L5 Ḥumrah, Al des area U.A.E.
86 F7 Ḥumret Shaibûn, Gebel hill Egypt 29.06N 31.15E
Ḥums see Homs Syria
35 G8 Ḥumud Jordan 31.18N 35.48E
114 C7 Humuula Hawaiian Is 19.41N 155.27W
85 C5 Hūn Libya 29.06N 15.57E
58 K1 Huna Highland Scotland 58.39N 3.07W
50 E3 Húnafjördhur B Iceland
50 D3 Húnaflói B Iceland
50 E4 Húnavatnssýsla, Austur Iceland
50 E4 Húnavatnssýsla, Vestur co Iceland
86 M9 Huna Wâdi watercourse Egypt
33 E10 Hunayshiyah Yemen 13.06N 43.36E
33 H4 Ḥunayy, Al Saudi Arabia 24.58N 48.47E
21 E6 Hunchun Jilin China 42.55N 130.28E
11 H9 Hundalee New Zealand 42.35S 173.27E
50 F5 Hundavötn lakes Iceland
53 B3 Hundborg Denmark 56.56N 8.31E
48 S8 Hunde Ejland isld Greenland 68.50N 53.10W
53 U14 Hundeidvik Möre og Romsdal Norway 62.22N 6.26E
53 B6 Hunderup Denmark 55.26N 8.43E
53 H5 Hundested Denmark 55.58N 11.53E
31 G5 Hundewali Pakistan 31.55N 72.42E
56 E3 Hundred House Powys Wales 52.11N 3.18W
101 N10 Hundred Mile House Br Col 51.39N 121.20W
53 U19 Hundseid Rogaland Norway 59.33N 6.00E
51 J6 Hundsjö Sweden 65.57N 21.50E
53 E5 Hundslund Denmark 55.55N 10.03E
65 G7 Hundstein mt Austria 47.22N 12.54E
53 T20 Hundvåg Norway 59.00N 5.45E
53 S18 Hundvåko Norway 60.08N 5.05E
53 T15 Hundvik Norway 61.53N 5.55E
53 S17 Hundvin Norway 60.40N 5.13E
66 O2 Hundwil Switzerland 47.22N 9.20E
53 D2 Hune Denmark 57.15N 9.40E
82 H5 Hunedoara Romania 45.45N 22.54E
82 H5 Hunedoara div Romania
Huneshiya see Ḥunayshīyah
64 H2 Hünfeld W Germany 50.41N 9.45E
64 E3 Hünfelden W Germany 50.19N 8.04E
69 P3 Hünfelden W Germany 50.19N 8.09E
9 R12 Hunga isld Tonga, Pacific Oc 18.40S 174.07W
9 S13 Hunga Ha'apai isld Tonga, Pacific Oc 20.33S 175.25W
49 H7 Hungary rep Cent Europe
9 S13 Hunga Tonga isld Tonga, Pacific Oc 20.32S 175.25W
Hung-chi-la-fu Ta-pan see Khunjerab Pass
52 J4 Hunge Sweden 62.46N 15.10E
64 F3 Hungen W Germany 50.28N 8.55E
56 H5 Hungerford Berks Eng 51.26N 1.30W
13 G8 Hungerford Queensland 29.00S 144.26E
112 L6 Hungerford Texas 29.24N 96.05W
21 E9 Hŭnghae S Korea 36.05N 129.22E
23 B9 Hung Hom Hong Kong 22.18N 114.11E
22 H8 Hung-liu Ho R Nei Monggol Zizhiqu China
21 D8 Hŭngnam N Korea 39.49N 127.40E
Hungry see Lime Village
96 B2 Hungry Bay Bermuda 32.17N 64.46W
59 C8 Hungry Hill mt Cork Irish Rep 51.42N 9.47W
110 L1 Hungry Horse Dam Montana 48.20N 114.00W
110 M1 Hungry Horse Res Montana 48.10N 113.45W
23 J7 Hung-t'ou Hsü isld Taiwan 22.04N 121.32E
91 E10 Hungulo Angola 13.17S 16.07E
28 C2 Hungund Karnataka India 16.04N 76.09E
22 C2 Hüngüy Gol R Mongolia
25 J2 Hung Yen Vietnam 20.38N 106.05E
21 B7 Hun He R Liaoning China
22 J6 Hun He R Nei Monggol Zizhiqu China
71 M1 Huningue France 47.36N 7.35E
89 J9 Huni Valley Ghana 5.33N 1.56W
21 D7 Hunjiang Jilin China 41.54N 126.23E
21 C7 Hun Jiang R Liaoning China
57 N4 Hunmanby N Yorks Eng 54.11N 0.19W
107 E2 Hunnewell Missouri 39.40N 91.51W
60 M15 Hunsel Netherlands 51.12N 5.50E
60 Q7 Hunsevaart Kanaal canal Netherlands
64 A2 Hünshoven W Germany 50.57N 6.09E
94 D6 Huns Mts Namibia
56 N2 Hunstanton, New Norfolk Eng 52.57N 0.30E
64 C4 Hunstrück mts W Germany
53 B2 Hunstrup Denmark 57.03N 8.49E
28 C4 Hunsur Karnataka India 12.20N 76.19E
22 L4 Hunt Nei Monggol Zizhiqu China 44.16N 120.00E
112 H5 Hunt Texas 30.04N 99.23W
99 J3 Hunta Ontario 49.06N 81.16W
63 H6 Hunte R W Germany
63 H8 Hunteburg W Germany 52.27N 8.16E
107 E6 Hunter Arkansas 35.02N 91.09W
109 M2 Hunter Kansas 39.15N 98.25W
108 N2 Hunter N Dakota 47.15N 97.15W
103 F2 Hunter New York 42.13N 74.15W
11 F11 Hunter New Zealand 44.38S 171.02E
109 N5 Hunter Oklahoma 36.34N 97.40W
103 A5 Hunter Pennsylvania 40.46N 76.44W
112 J6 Hunter Texas 29.48N 98.04W
10 P6 Hunter isld Pacific Oc 22.31S 172.06E
12 K4 Hunter R New S Wales
10 V11 Hunter, C Norfolk I Pacific Oc 29.05S 167.58E
103 D5 Hunterdon co New Jersey
30 H8 Hunterganj Bihar India 24.27N 84.49E
101 J10 Hunter I Br Col 51.58N 128.02W
12 G8 Hunter I Tasmania 40.30S 144.47E
10 P6 Hunter I.Ridge Pacific Oc
12 G8 Hunter Is Tasmania
113 M5 Hunter, Mt Alaska 62.58N 151.09W
103 F2 Hunter Mt New York 42.11N 74.15W
11 B12 Hunter Mts New Zealand
11 D11 Hunter R New Zealand
12 J5 Hunter Ra New S Wales
98 J7 Hunter River Prince Edward I 46.21N 63.22W
110 G1 Hunters Washington 48.09N 118.12W
25 B3 Hunter's B Burma
13 F6 Hunter's Gorge Queensland 23.40S 141.10E
12 L7 Hunter's Hill dist Sydney, N S W
11 E11 Hunter's Hills, The New Zealand
111 B9 Hunters Pt San Francisco, Cal
92 D11 Hunter's Road Zimbabwe 19.09S 29.49E
105 G2 Huntersville N Carolina 35.24N 80.52W
103 A4 Huntersville Pennsylvania 41.19N 76.45W
104 E8 Huntersville W Virginia 38.12N 80.02W
13 J7 Hunterton Queensland 26.11S 148.30E
106 J8 Huntertown Indiana 41.14N 85.11W
11 K6 Hunterville New Zealand 39.55S 175.36E
107 K3 Huntingburg Indiana 38.16N 86.59W
56 L3 Huntingdon Cambs Eng 52.20N 0.12W
104 G6 Huntingdon Pennsylvania 40.31N 78.02W
99 Q7 Huntingdon Quebec 45.05N 74.11W
107 H6 Huntingdon Tennessee 36.00N 88.27W
Huntingdon & Peterborough co see Cambridgeshire
98 J3 Hunting I Quebec 50.15N 63.10W
105 G5 Hunting I S Carolina 32.25N 80.35W
106 J9 Huntington Indiana 40.54N 85.30W
103 H5 Huntington Long I, N Y 40.53N 73.25W
103 J2 Huntington Massachusetts 42.15N 72.53W
110 H5 Huntington Oregon 44.20N 117.15W
112 N4 Huntington Texas 31.16N 94.34W
111 O2 Huntington Utah 39.19N 110.58W
104 C8 Huntington W Virginia 38.24N 82.26W
103 H5 Huntington Bay Long I, N Y
111 F8 Huntington Beach California 33.40N 118.00W
103 B4 Huntington Cr Pennsylvania
111 E4 Huntington L California 37.14N 119.12W
103 B4 Huntington Mills Pennsylvania 41.12N 76.15W

111 D9 Huntington Park dist Los Angeles, California
56 G4 Huntley Glos Eng 51.53N 2.25W
110 R4 Huntley Montana 45.54N 108.19W
108 L9 Huntley Nebraska 40.13N 99.19W
108 F8 Huntley Wyoming 41.58N 104.09W
63 H7 Huntlosen W Germany 52.59N 8.17E
58 L4 Huntly Grampian Scotland 57.27N 2.47W
11 K4 Huntly New Zealand 37.35S 175.10E
101 J5 Hunt, Mt Yukon Terr 61.32N 129.15W
12 D3 Hunt Pen S Australia
56 B4 Huntsman's Leap prom Dyfed Wales 51.37N 4.57W
108 C5 Hunts Mt Wyoming 44.44N 107.42W
98 H10 Hunts Point Nova Scotia 43.57N 64.46W
107 K7 Huntsville Alabama 34.44N 86.35W
107 C5 Huntsville Arkansas 36.04N 93.46W
107 D2 Huntsville Missouri 39.27N 92.31W
99 L7 Huntsville Ontario 45.20N 79.14W
112 M5 Huntsville Texas 30.43N 95.34W
110 O8 Huntsville Utah 41.15N 111.45W
115 P7 Hunucmá Mexico 21.00N 89.51W
37 F5 Hunut Turkey 40.41N 41.09E
63 E9 Hünxe W Germany 51.38N 6.46E
92 E10 Hunyani R Zimbabwe
92 E10 Hunyani Dam Zimbabwe 17.56S 31.00E
92 E10 Hunyani Ra Zimbabwe
22 J7 Hunyuan Shanxi China 39.40N 113.49E
31 H2 Hunza Kashmir 36.23N 74.43E
31 H2 Hunza reg Kashmir
31 H2 Hunza R Kashmir
24 C3 Huocheng Xinjiang Uygur Zizhiqu China 44.15N 80.49E
21 C4 Huodifangzi Heilongjiang China 47.01N 124.43E
23 F1 Huojia Henan China 35.14N 113.38E
21 C3 Huolongmen Heilongjiang China 49.49N 125.48E
22 K7 Huolu Hebei China 38.06N 114.18E
9 A12 Huon isld New Caledonia 18.03S 162.58E
12 H9 Huon R Tasmania
15 J7 Huon G Papua New Guinea
25 H3 Huong Khe Vietnam 18.14N 105.44E
25 J7 Huong My Vietnam 10.01N 106.26E
25 H3 Huong Son Vietnam 18.31N 105.30E
25 J4 Huong Thuy Vietnam 16.22N 107.43E
15 J7 Huon Penin Papua New Guinea
12 H9 Huonville Tasmania 43.01S 147.01E
23 G2 Huoqiu Anhui China 32.25N 116.12E
21 D3 Huormojin Heilongjiang China 49.32N 127.45E
23 G3 Huoshan Anhui China 31.24N 116.25E
23 J7 Huo-shao Tao isld Taiwan 22.38N 121.30E
22 J8 Huo Xian Shanxi China 36.37N 111.44E
Hupeh prov China see Hubei
21 D8 Hŭpkok N Korea 39.02N 127.45E
36 J6 Hupnik R Turkey
61 K4 Huppaye Belgium 50.42N 4.53E
60 Q11 Huppel Netherlands 52.00N 6.46E
69 B3 Huppy France 50.02N 1.46E
64 J1 Hüpstedt E Germany 51.20N 10.27E
28 K1 Hupu Assam India 28.46N 95.50E
33 M6 Huqf, Al reg Oman
35 E2 Huqoq Israel 32.52N 35.29E
32 G5 Hūr Iran 30.51N 57.05E
85 O9 Hura Sudan 21.15N 36.50E
29 K2 Hura W Bengal India 23.18N 86.40E
Huraimilāl see Huraymilā
Hurama see Hongyuan
32 B1 Hūrand Iran 38.54N 47.22E
122 C11 Hurareoa Tahiti Pacific Oc 17.30S 149.23W
33 H9 Huraydah, Al S Yemen 15.35N 48.09E
33 G4 Huraymilā Saudi Arabia 25.09N 46.08E
33 G5 Huraysān area Saudi Arabia
33 F4 Hurayyiq, Al Saudi Arabia 25.27N 45.26E
62 L8 Hurbanovo Czechoslovakia 47.53N 18.10E
52 F6 Hurdalssjøen L Norway 60.20N 11.05E
99 J7 Hurd, C Ontario 45.14N 81.44W
107 D1 Hurdland Missouri 40.07N 92.18W
10 A12 Hurd Pt Macquarie I Pacific Oc 54.47S 158.52E
108 L2 Hurdsfield N Dakota 47.28N 99.56W
72 E6 Hure France 44.33N 0.01E
86 F4 Hûrein Egypt 30.39N 31.08E
35 J2 Hureiyik, El Syria 32.45N 36.18E
87 M8 Hur,El Somalia 5.00N 48.12E
21 B6 Hure Qi Jilin China 42.46N 121.49E
22 F6 Huretin Sum Nei Monggol Zizhiqu China 40.17N 103.04E
35 G1 Hurfah Syria 33.16N 35.54E
35 E1 Hurfeish Israel 33.01N 35.21E
85 M6 Hurghada Egypt 27.17N 33.47E
Hürhe Ula mts see Hörh Uul
72 J3 Huriel France 46.22N 2.27E
93 J2 Huri Hills Kenya
99 B4 Hurkett Ontario 48.52N 88.29W
59 E6 Hurlers Cross Clare Irish Rep 52.43N 8.51W
56 D5 Hurlestone Pt Somerset Eng 51.15N 3.42W
56 K4 Hurley Berks Eng 51.33N 0.49W
107 H11 Hurley Mississippi 30.39N 88.30W
109 B9 Hurley New Mexico 32.41N 108.07W
103 F3 Hurley New York 41.56N 74.03W
108 N6 Hurley S Dakota 43.18N 97.04W
106 D3 Hurley Wisconsin 46.25N 90.15W
103 E3 Hurleyville New York 41.44N 74.40W
57 E1 Hurlford Strathclyde Scotland 55.36N 4.28W
104 K8 Hurlock Maryland 38.37N 75.52W
14 C10 Hurlstone, L W Australia 32.35S 119.28E
31 C6 Hurmagai Pakistan 28.18N 64.28E
22 F5 Hürmen Mongolia 43.19N 104.01E
56 H6 Hurn airport Dorset Eng 50.48N 1.51W
111 D5 Huron California 36.14N 120.05W
109 P2 Huron Kansas 39.37N 95.23W
104 C5 Huron Ohio 41.23N 82.33W
108 M5 Huron S Dakota 44.22N 98.12W
106 F3 Huron B Michigan
106 M5 Huron City Michigan 44.02N 82.50W
77 E7 Hurones, Embalse de res Spain 36.40N 5.32W
99 L8 Huronia reg Ontario
106 M5 Huron, L U.S.A./Canada
106 G3 Huron Mts Michigan
111 L4 Hurricane Utah 37.10N 113.16W
104 C8 Hurricane W Virginia 38.26N 82.02W
105 E6 Hurricane Cr Georgia
116 E3 Hurricane Flats Bahamas 23.40N 78.30W
107 J6 Hurricane Mills Tennessee 35.58N 87.47W
53 X16 Hurrungane mts Norway
56 J5 Hursley Hants Eng 51.02N 1.24W
112 M9 Hurst Texas 32.47N 97.11W
56 J5 Hurstbourne Priors Hants Eng 51.13N 1.23W
56 J5 Hurstbourne Tarrant Hants Eng 51.17N 1.27W
56 L6 Hurstpierpoint W Sussex Eng 50.56N 0.11W
12 L8 Hurstville dist Sydney, N S W
121 B3 Hurtado Chile 30.15S 70.44W
121 B3 Hurtado R Chile
69 L2 Hürtgenwald W Germany 50.12N 6.22E
64 B2 Hürth W Germany 50.52N 6.49E
69 M2 Hürth W Germany 50.52N 6.51E
107 L9 Hurtsboro Alabama 32.13N 85.26W
11 G9 Hurunui R New Zealand
53 A3 Hurup Viborg Denmark 56.46N 8.26E
53 D7 Hürup W Germany 54.45N 9.32E
57 K4 Hurworth Durham Eng 54.29N 1.31W
50 E5 Húsafell Iceland 64.41N 20.55W
30 B5 Husain Uttar Prad India 27.37N 78.16E
Husainabad Iran see Hoseynābād
30 J7 Husainabad Monghyr, Bihar Ind 25.06N 85.52E
30 H8 Husainabad Palamau, Bihar Ind 24.33N 84.01E
31 E5 Husain Nika Pakistan 31.53N 69.14E
35 D7 Husan Jordan 31.43N 35.08E
50 L4 Húsavatn L Iceland 65.15N 14.54W
50 M4 Húsavík Nordhur Múlasýsla Iceland 65.24N 13.38W
50 D3 Húsavík Strandasýsla Iceland 65.39N 21.37W
50 H2 Húsavík Thingeyjarsýsla, Sudhur Iceland 66.03N 17.17W
50 K2 Húsavík inlet Iceland
33 M4 Husayfin, Al Oman 24.38N 56.32E
33 F8 Husayn tribe Yemen
34 M5 Huşayn al Ghafūs Iraq 33.13N 44.33E
35 F1 Husayniyat Syria 33.05N 35.40E
56 J3 Husbands Bosworth Leics Eng 52.27N 1.03W
53 D6 Husby Fyn Denmark 55.22N 9.51E
53 A4 Husby Ringkøbing Denmark 56.17N 8.12E
63 L3 Husby W Germany 54.46N 9.34E
35 G4 Huseiniya, El Jordan 32.15N 35.47E
35 F2 Huseiniyat esh Sheikh 'Ali Syria 32.54N 35.39E
30 H6 Husepur Bihar India 26.28N 84.10E
53 N10 Husevig Faeroes 61.49N 6.41W
Huseyinabat see Alaca
37 F3 Hüseyinalani Turkey 40.08N 29.02E
Huseyınlı see Kızılırmak
95 J3 Husfeldt S Africa 27.10S 25.47E
Hushan see Cixi
21 E5 Hushan Heilongjiang China 45.33N 130.30E
Hushen see Hoshūn
82 L4 Huşi Romania 46.40N 28.05E
76 K4 Husillos Spain 42.05N 4.31W
65 J3 Husinec Czechoslovakia 49.04N 13.59E
58 B3 Husinish Harris, W Isles Scotland 57.59N 7.06W
52 H9 Huskvarna Sweden 57.47N 14.15E
Husky Lakes see Eskimo Lakes
113 J4 Huslia Alaska 65.40N 156.30W
113 J4 Huslia R Alaska
35 G4 Husn Jordan 32.29N 35.53E
33 G8 Huşn Āl 'Abr S Yemen 16.09N 47.16E
Husn el Akrād see Qal'at al Husn
53 T19 Husnes Norway 59.52N 5.46E
33 G10 Huşn Shabib S Yemen 13.54N 46.42E
110 L2 Huson Montana 47.01N 114.20W
65 P3 Husovice Czechoslovakia 49.13N 16.38E
53 R16 Husøy Norway 61.01N 4.43E
100 E7 Hussar Alberta 51.03N 112.37W
69 N8 Husseren-Wesserling France 47.53N 7.00E
52 C4 Hustadvika Norway
65 P4 Hustopeče Czechoslovakia 48.56N 16.44E
53 U19 Hustvietsata mt Norway 59.35N 6.12E
53 B6 Husum Denmark 55.05N 8.41E
53 N9 Husum Faeroes 62.16N 6.41W
53 X16 Husum Norway 61.03N 7.48E
63 K4 Husum W Germany 54.29N 9.04E
53 S15 Husvågøy isld Norway 61.55N 5.03E
121 G8 Husvik S Georgia 54.12S 36.43W
22 F2 Hutag Mongolia 49.26N 102.42E
22 D4 Hutag Nuur L Mongolia
32 G5 Hūtak Iran 30.36N 56.59E
18 A8 Hutan Melintang Pen Malaysia 3.52N 100.56E
18 C5 Hutanopan Sumatra Indon 0.40N 99.46E
29 J6 Hutar Bihar India 23.45N 84.26E
112 O9 Hutchins Texas 32.40N 96.43W
109 N3 Hutchinson Kansas 38.03N 97.56W
108 Q5 Hutchinson Minnesota 44.54N 94.22W
95 G7 Hutchinson S Africa 31.30S 23.11E
Hutchinson, C see Est, Pte
105 G10 Hutchinsons I Florida
111 N7 Hutch Mt Arizona 34.50N 111.24W
33 E8 Huth Yemen 16.21N 43.54E
25 E4 Huthi Burma 16.10N 98.48E
35 F2 Hutiye Syria 32.50N 35.42E
15 J1 Hutjen Buka I Papua New Guinea 5.25S 154.38E
21 D2 Hutongzhen Heilongjiang China 51.35N 126.42E
21 F5 Hutou Heilongjiang China 45.57N 133.43E
107 J2 Hutsonville Illinois 39.05N 87.40W
65 H7 Hüttau Austria 47.27N 13.18E
70 L5 Hutte, la France 48.18N 0.05E
64 L4 Hüttenbach W Germany 49.37N 11.18E
65 L8 Hüttenberg Austria 46.57N 14.33E
64 G3 Hüttengesäss W Germany 50.13N 9.03E
69 P2 Hüttental W Germany 50.54N 8.02E
61 Q4 Hüttgen W Germany 50.40N 6.25E
64 Q6 Hutthurm W Germany 48.41N 13.29E
107 D8 Huttig Arkansas 33.01N 92.10W
112 K5 Hutto Texas 30.34N 97.34W
56 F5 Hutton Avon Eng 51.20N 2.56W
54 L1 Hutton oil field North Sea 61.05N 1.26E
57 M4 Hutton le Hole N Yorks Eng 54.17N 0.55W
13 J7 Hutton, Mt Queensland 25.53S 148.10E
14 E6 Hutton Ra W Australia
57 L4 Hutton Rudby N Yorks Eng 54.27N 1.17W
104 E8 Huttonsville W Virginia 38.43N 80.00W
11 E4 Hutt R New Zealand
14 A8 Hutt, R W Australia
65 H7 Hüttschlag Austria 47.11N 13.14E
66 H3 Huttwil Switzerland 47.07N 7.51E
66 M1 Hüttwilen Switzerland 47.37N 8.53E
24 E3 Hutubi Xinjiang Uygur Zizhiqu China 44.11N 86.54E
24 E4 Hutubi He R Xinjiang Uygur Zizhiqu China
22 J7 Hutuo He R Hebei China
22 G7 Hut Yanchi Nei Monggol Zizhiqu China
27 L9 Huvadu Atoll Maldives, Ind Oc 0.30N 73.16E
32 J7 Hūvār Iran 26.10N 61.27E
Hüvek see Bozova Urfa Turkey
90 K8 Huvet Cent Afr Rep 6.40N 21.21E
32 H7 Hūviān, Kūh-e mts Iran
Huwaila see Huwaylah, Al
Huwaimi, Sha'ib watercourse see Juraymī, Sha'īb
33 M6 Huwaisah, Al oil field Oman 21.58N 56.02E
33 J4 Huwār Is Bahrain, The Gulf
86 O5 Huwar, Wādī watercourse Jordan
33 J4 Huwaylah, Al Qatar, The Gulf 25.56N 51.29E
33 G9 Huwaymi, Al S Yemen 14.06N 47.42E
33 F8 Huwaymil des area Saudi Arabia
33 B2 Huwaytat tribe Saudi Arabia
33 D4 Huwayyit, Al Saudi Arabia 25.34N 40.21E
34 D3 Huweid Syria 35.32N 36.22E
33 F5 Huwwah, Al Saudi Arabia 23.04N 45.49E
Huwwara see Hawwara
23 E1 Hu Xian Shaanxi China 34.06N 108.36E
100 D7 Huxley Alberta 51.56N 113.11W
108 R8 Huxley Iowa 41.53N 93.38W
113 R6 Huxley, Mt Alaska 60.20N 141.10W
11 D11 Huxley, Mt New Zealand 44.06S 169.42E
14 F4 Huxley, Mt W Australia 18.30S 126.26E
58 Q9 Huxter Shetland Scotland 60.14N 1.17W
61 L4 Huy Belgium 50.32N 5.14E
57 H6 Huyton Merseyside Eng 53.25N 2.52W
36 F5 Hüyük Turkey 38.00N 31.34E
37 F7 Huyut Turkey 38.30N 41.48E
35 C8 Huzeil Israel 31.25N 34.45E
21 C1 Huzhong Heilongjiang China 52.05N 123.40E
Huzhou see Wuxing
22 E8 Huzhu Qinghai China 36.50N 101.59E
28 D2 Huzurnagar Andhra Prad India 17.02N 79.58E
50 M5 Hvalbakur isld Iceland 64.36N 13.13W
52 F7 Hvaler isld Norway 59.07N 10.55E
50 C6 Hvaleyri Iceland 64.04N 22.00W
50 D6 Hvalfjördhur B Iceland
50 A3 Hvallátur Iceland 65.31N 24.25W
50 C4 Hvallátur isld Iceland 65.26N 22.46W
50 L6 Hvalnes Iceland 64.25N 14.35W
50 F3 Hvalnes C Iceland 66.00N 19.57W
53 C3 Hvalpsund Denmark 56.43N 9.12E
53 C3 Hvalp Sund sound Denmark 56.43N 9.12E
48 V6 Hvalrosodden B Greenland 77.00N 20.00W
50 H7 Hvalsiki str Iceland 63.45N 17.34W
50 B3 Hvalsker Iceland 65.32N 23.55W
50 C7 Hvalsnes Iceland 63.59N 22.45W
48 R3 Hvalsund sound Greenland
50 D6 Hvalvatn L Iceland 64.23N 21.10W
50 G2 Hvalvatnsfjördhur B Iceland
53 D3 Hvam Denmark 56.40N 9.31E
50 F3 Hvammsfell mt Iceland 65.39N 19.10W
50 C4 Hvammsfjördhur B Iceland
50 K3 Hvammsheidhi heath Iceland
50 E4 Hvammstangi Iceland 65.24N 20.57W
50 D4 Hvammur Dalasýsla Iceland 65.13N 21.50W
50 D5 Hvammur Mýrasýsla Iceland 64.50N 21.20W
50 G7 Hvammur Skaftafellssýsla, Vestur Iceland 63.45N 18.29W
50 F3 Hvammur Skagafjardharsýsla Iceland 65.52N 19.50W
50 K2 Hvammur Thingeyjarsýsla, Nordhur Iceland 66.08N 15.23W
50 L4 Hvanná Iceland 65.22N 14.48W
50 J6 Hvannadalshnúkur mt Iceland 64.02N 16.35W
50 D5 Hvanneyri Iceland 64.34N 21.45W
50 J3 Hvannfell mt Iceland 65.33N 16.47W
50 J3 Hvannstadhafjallgardhur mt Iceland 65.55N 16.02W
82 C7 Hvar Yugoslavia 43.11N 16.28E
82 D7 Hvar isld Yugoslavia
50 D6 Hveragerdhi Iceland 64.00N 21.10W
50 F5 Hveravellir Iceland 64.52N 19.35W
50 H3 Hveravellir Thingeyjarsýsla, Sudhur Iceland 65.53N 17.10W
50 G6 Hverfisfljot R Iceland
50 J3 Hverfjall mt Iceland 65.37N 16.52W
53 B3 Hvidbjerg Viborg Denmark 56.40N 8.32E
53 B3 Hvidbjerg Viborg Denmark 56.45N 8.39E
53 B3 Hvidbjerg Viborg Denmark 56.34N 8.57E
53 N9 Hvidenæs Faeroes 62.03N 6.46W
53 A4 Hvide Sande Denmark 56.00N 8.08E
53 B6 Hviding Denmark 55.16N 8.42E
53 E4 Hvilsager Denmark 56.23N 10.22E
53 D3 Hvilsom Denmark 56.39N 9.38E
53 E4 Hvilsted Denmark 56.01N 10.04E
50 E6 Hvítá R Árnessýsla Iceland
50 D5 Hvítá R Mýrasýsla Iceland
50 H6 Hvítá R Skaftafellssýsla, Vestur Iceland
50 C3 Hvítanes Iceland 66.00N 22.48W
50 F5 Hvitárvatn L Iceland 64.35N 19.50W
52 F7 Hvitsten Norway 59.35N 10.42E
52 E7 Hvittingfoss Norway 59.28N 10.01E
50 D4 Hvoll Iceland 65.23N 21.52W
50 E7 Hvolsvöllur Iceland 63.45N 20.14W
50 D3 Hvulsa C Iceland 65.39N 21.21W
Hwaan see Hua'an
Hwang Ho R see Huang Ho R
Hwangpaitientze see Laoling
Hwangpei see Huangling
Hweian see Huian
Hweitseh see Huize
Hwokia see Huojia
20 P10 Hyakuna Okinawa Japan 26.05N 127.48E
110 P4 Hyalite Pk Montana 45.25N 110.59W
110 B9 Hyampom California 40.39N 123.29W
103 O3 Hyannis Massachusetts 41.39N 70.16W
108 J8 Hyannis Nebraska 42.00N 101.45W
103 O3 Hyannis Port Massachusetts 41.38N 70.18W
22 C2 Hyargas Nuur L Mongolia
100 P7 Hyas Saskatchewan 51.52N 102.08W
114 E6 Hyashi Hawaiian Is 20.49N 156.29W
110 C7 Hyatt Res Oregon 42.12N 122.27W
103 A9 Hyattsville Maryland 38.57N 76.56W
108 C5 Hyattville Wyoming 44.15N 107.36W
107 J10 Hybart Alabama 31.50N 87.22W
99 N7 Hybla Ontario 45.11N 77.53W
52 J9 Hycklinge Sweden 57.55N 15.55E
113 V9 Hydaburg Alaska 55.15N 132.50W
53 Z17 Hydalseter Norway 60.59N 8.33E
57 J6 Hyde Greater Manchester Eng 53.27N 2.04W
11 E12 Hyde New Zealand 45.20S 170.16E
48 U1 Hyde Fjord, Frederick E Greenland
104 B9 Hyden Kentucky 37.08N 83.23W
14 C9 Hyden W Australia 32.30S 118.51E
103 G3 Hyde Park New York 41.47N 73.56W
12 A8 Hyde Park dist Adelaide, S Aust
113 W9 Hyder Alaska 55.55N 130.05W
111 L8 Hyder Arizona 33.01N 113.21W
28 D2 Hyderabad Andhra Prad India 17.22N 78.26E
31 E8 Hyderabad Pakistan 25.23N 68.24E
31 E8 Hyderabad div Pakistan
31 E8 Hyderabad dist Pakistan
Hydra isld see Idhra
109 M6 Hydro Oklahoma 35.34N 98.36W
112 J5 Hye Texas 30.15N 98.36W
70 H4 Hyenville France 48.59N 1.28W
71 J10 Hyères France 43.07N 6.08E
71 J10 Hyères, Iles d' France 43.01N 6.25E
71 J10 Hyères, Rade d' B France 43.03N 6.15E
66 B2 Hyèvre France 47.22N 6.25E
109 E1 Hygiene Colorado 40.12N 105.12W
101 J5 Hyland R Yukon Terr
13 A2 Hyland B N Terr Australia
101 J7 Hyland Post Br Col 57.40N 128.10W
53 V19 Hylen Norway 59.33N 6.35E
53 X20 Hylestad Norway 59.06N 7.33E
53 D5 Hylke Denmark 55.59N 9.57E
53 G7 Hyllekrog isld Denmark 54.36N 11.30E
53 S16 Hyllestad Norway 61.10N 5.18E
53 F4 Hyllested Denmark 56.17N 10.47E
53 H6 Hyllinge Denmark 55.13N 11.36E
53 H6 Hyllinge Denmark 55.16N 11.37E
53 K4 Hyllinge Sweden 56.06N 12.54E
100 E4 Hylo Alberta 54.40N 112.11W
53 U19 Hylsfjorden inlet Norway 59.32N 6.20E
110 K9 Hylton Res Nevada 40.40N 115.47W
112 F3 Hyman Texas 32.09N 101.08W
107 J2 Hymera Indiana 39.11N 87.19W
69 L7 Hymont France 48.16N 6.09E
12 F6 Hynam S Australia 36.57S 140.50E
12 K4 Hyndland, Mt New S Wales 30.09S 152.25E
104 G7 Hyndman Pennsylvania 39.50N 78.43W
110 L6 Hyndman Pk Idaho 43.46N 114.10W
104 H5 Hyner Pennsylvania 41.19N 77.37W
20 H6 Hyōgo prefect Japan
61 F5 Hyon Belgium 50.27N 3.58E
21 D8 Hyŏn-ni N Korea 38.30N 127.50E
20 H6 Hyōno-sen mt Japan 35.22N 134.50E
21 D10 Hyŏpch'ŏn S Korea 35.33N 128.12E
90 L9 Hyrra Banda Cent Afr Rep 5.58N 22.01E
110 O8 Hyrum Utah 41.39N 111.50W
51 N7 Hyrynsalmi Finland 64.41N 28.30E
108 C3 Hysham Montana 46.18N 107.13W
101 O8 Hythe Alberta 55.18N 119.33W
56 J6 Hythe Hants Eng 50.51N 1.24W
56 O5 Hythe Kent Eng 51.05N 1.05E
12 H9 Hythe Tasmania 43.20S 147.00E
20 E9 Hyūga Japan 32.25N 131.38E
51 L11 Hyvinkää Finland 60.37N 24.50E
25 K6 Ia Ayum R Vietnam
82 J3 Iacobeni Romania 47.24N 25.20E
120 D4 Iaco, R Brazil
118 H3 Iaçu Brazil 12.49S 40.10W
104 D9 Iaeger W Virginia 37.29N 81.50W
87 K9 Iaghegh Somalia 3.15N 44.00E
87 K9 Iaglei Somalia 2.26N 45.25E
95 C7 Iakora Madagascar 23.04S 46.40E
15 H7 Ialibu Papua New Guinea 6.18S 144.00E
15 H7 Ialibu, Mt Papua New Guinea 6.16S 144.02E
82 L6 Ialomita div Romania
82 K6 Ialomiţa R Romania
25 J2 Iam Vietnam 21.22N 106.31E
15 G8 Iamara Papua New Guinea 8.27S 142.58E
105 C7 Iamonia, L Florida 30.39N 84.12W
95 B7 Ianakafy Madagascar 23.20S 45.28E
82 L5 Ianca Romania 45.06N 27.29E
11 E10 Ianthe, L New Zealand 43.04S 170.38E
92 J9 Iapala Mozambique 15.01S 38.02E
117 G7 Iapi Brazil 5.37S 40.27W
82 H4 Iara Romania 46.31N 23.35E
119 H7 Iarauarune, Sa hills Brazil
59 D5 Iar Connaught reg Galway Irish Rep
15 H7 Iaro R Papua New Guinea
82 L3 Iaşi Romania 47.09N 27.38E
83 G3 Iasmos Greece 41.07N 25.12E
118 F4 Iassiara Brazil 14.09S 46.37W
112 F3 Iatan Texas 32.20N 101.06W
107 D10 Iatt, L Louisiana 31.33N 92.40W
Iaxartes R see Syr-Dar'ya
47 G5 Ib U.S.S.R. 61.15N 50.13E
19 J4 Iba Luzon Philippines 15.20N 119.59E
66 L3 Ibach Switzerland 47.01N 8.39E
90 A8 Ibadan Nigeria 7.23N 3.56E
86 F10 'Ibâda, Wâdî watercourse
119 C5 Ibagué Colombia 4.25N 75.20W
76 H10 Ibahernando Spain 39.20N 5.55W
118 E8 Ibaiti Brazil 23.49S 50.15W
87 A9 Ibambi Zaïre 2.26N 27.38E
93 B6 Ibanda Uganda 0.08S 30.30E
72 B9 Ibañeta, Pto. de pass Spain 43.01N 1.20W
121 J6 Ibáñez R Chile
91 E3 Ibangui Congo 0.31N 16.14E
110 M9 Ibapah Utah 40.04N 113.59W
82 F7 Ibar R Yugoslavia
20 G7 Ibara Japan 34.35N 133.25E
20 O5 Ibaraki prefect Japan
121 G3 Ibare Brazil 30.50S 54.15W
119 B7 Ibarra Ecuador 0.23N 78.05W
118 B9 Ibarreta Argentina 25.13S 59.50W
33 F9 Ibb Yemen 14.03N 44.10E
87 B8 Ibba Sudan 4.49N 29.02E
87 B7 Ibba watercourse Sudan
63 G8 Ibbenbüren W Germany 52.17N 7.44E
35 G4 Ibbin Jordan 32.22N 35.48E
35 G3 Ibdar Jordan 32.40N 35.47E
75 G5 Ibdes Spain 41.13N 1.51W
75 C3 Ibeas de Juarros Spain 42.20N 3.32W
90 B8 Ibekwe Nigeria 6.36N 5.44E
91 H2 Ibembo Zaïre 2.36N 23.40E
91 F2 Ibenga Congo 2.15N 18.05E
91 E2 Ibenga R Congo
121 F2 Iberá, Esteros del marshes Arg
121 F2 Iberá, L Argentina
120 C1 Iberia Loreto Peru 5.50S 74.05W
120 D4 Iberia Madre de Dios Peru 11.22S 69.35W
107 D3 Iberia Missouri 38.05N 92.18W
90 D2 Iberkom Niger 18.58N 8.32E
99 R7 Iberville Quebec 45.18N 73.15W
51 F3 Ibestad Norway 68.47N 17.10E
90 B6 Ibeto Nigeria 10.31N 5.06E
90 D7 Ibi Nigeria 8.11N 9.44E
77 P3 Ibi Spain 38.38N 0.35W
118 F6 Ibiá Brazil 19.30S 46.31W
118 G5 Ibiaí Brazil 16.48S 44.53W
117 G7 Ibiapaba Brazil 5.01S 40.56W
117 G7 Ibiapaba, Sa, da Brazil
76 F3 Ibias R Spain
118 G4 Ibiassucê Brazil 14.16S 42.18W
92 H5 Ibibo Tanzania 6.03S 37.09E
85 N8 Ibib, Wadi watercourse Sudan
118 H4 Ibicaraí Brazil 14.52S 39.37W
121 G3 Ibicí da Cruz R Brazil
117 G7 Ibicuã Brazil 5.56S 39.30W
121 G2 Ibicuí Brazil 29.25S 56.40W
121 G2 Ibicuí, R Brazil
20 K6 Ibigawa Japan 35.32N 136.31E
35 D2 I'billin Israel 32.49N 35.12E
35 G4 'Ibillin Jordan 32.21N 35.49E
90 C8 Ibillo Nigeria 7.25N 6.07E
117 H9 Ibimirim Brazil 8.30S 37.40W
92 D1 Ibina R Zaïre
118 D8 Ibiporã Brazil 23.16S 51.01W
118 H3 Ibiquera Brazil 12.43S 40.50W
118 G2 Ibiraba Brazil 10.50S 42.59W
118 H6 Ibiraçu Brazil 19.51S 40.22W
118 E10 Ibirama Brazil 27.10S 49.35W
118 H5 Ibiranhém Brazil 17.53S 40.06W
121 G3 Ibirapuita R Brazil
92 F4 Ibiri Tanzania 4.55S 32.33E
121 G2 Ibirocaí Brazil 29.45S 56.25W
118 G3 Ibitiara Brazil 12.44S 42.15W
118 E7 Ibitinga Brazil 21.43S 48.47W
118 G2 Ibitunane Brazil 11.36S 42.45W
77 S12 Ibiza isld Balearic Is 38.54N 1.26E
88 L5 Iblane, Jbel bon mts Morocco
81 J9 Iblei, Monti Sicily
86 F4 Ibnahs Egypt 30.34N 31.06E
33 F3 Ibn Buşayyiş Saudi Arabia 27.53N 45.19E
33 D7 Ibn Hādī Saudi Arabia 18.08N 41.53E
35 F8 Ibn Hammad watercourse Jordan
34 M6 Ibn Najm, Hawr L Iraq
92 K8 Ibo Mozambique 12.21S 40.40E
93 D8 Ibondo Tanzania 2.38S 32.40E
91 K4 Ibonga Zaïre 0.37S 26.53E
15 B5 Ibonma Irian Jaya 3.29S 133.30E
76 J9 Ibor R Spain
90 A8 Iboro Nigeria 7.05N 3.10E
72 D9 Ibos France 43.15N 0.02W
118 G3 Ibotirama Brazil 12.13S 43.12W
93 D10 Iboziya Tanzania 4.02S 32.33E
33 N5 Ibrā' Oman 22.43N 58.32E
36 F5 Ibradı Turkey 37.06N 31.34E
37 K2 Ibrahım Ağa R Turkey
86 G4 Ibrâhîmîya, El Egypt 30.44N 31.34E
36 G5 Ibrala Turkey 37.09N 33.31E
34 K2 Ibrat aş Şaghīra Iraq 36.24N 42.19E
90 M6 Ibra, Wâdi watercourse Sudan
45 S1 Ibresi U.S.S.R. 55.19N 47.00E
33 M5 Ibrī Oman 23.15N 56.16E
37 C2 İbrice Turkey 40.36N 26.32E
37 C2 İbrice Burun C Turkey 40.35N 26.32E
37 G1 İbriktepe Turkey 41.01N 26.30E
77 K4 Ibros Spain 38.02N 3.29W
42 E4 Ibryul' U.S.S.R. 56.15N 91.45E
86 F3 Ibshân Egypt 31.10N 31.10E
53 Q12 Ibsker Bornholm Denmark 55.06N 15.05E
56 H6 Ibsley Hants Eng 50.53N 1.47W
56 J2 Ibstock Leics Eng 52.42N 1.23W
35 H2 Ibta Syria 32.47N 36.10E
19 E3 Ibu Halmahera Indonesia 1.30N 127.33E
20 Q8 Ibu Okinawa Japan 26.47N 128.16E
19 E3 Ibu mt Halmahera Indonesia 1.29N 127.40E
19 K1 Ibuhos isld Philippines 20.21N 121.50E
93 D4 Ibuje Uganda 1.54N 32.23E
20 K2 Iburi sub-prefect Japan
20 D10 Ibusuki Japan 31.15N 130.40E
93 A8 Ibuye Burundi 2.49S 29.46E
119 F9 Içá Brazil
120 B6 Ica Peru 14.02S 75.48W
120 B6 Ica prov Peru
120 B6 Ica R Peru
119 H5 Icabaru Venezuela 4.22N 61.45W
119 H5 Icabaru, R Venezuela
116 N2 Icacos Pt Trinidad & Tobago 10.04N 61.55W
19 J6 Icadambanauan isld Philippines 10.47N 119.35E
121 G2 Icamaqua R Brazil
119 F7 Içana Brazil 0.23N 67.22W
119 E7 Içana, R Brazil
121 D2 Icaño Argentina 28.53S 65.20W
117 G6 Icaraí Ceará Brazil 3.05S 39.42W
118 K9 Icarai Rio de Janeiro Brazil 22.55S 43.07W
118 K9 Icarai, Enseada de B Brazil
117 F6 Icatu Brazil 2.45S 44.02W
111 K5 Iceberg Canyon gorge Nevada/Arizona
110 G3 Ice Harbor Dam Washington 46.16N 118.51W
Içel see Mersin
49 A4 Iceland rep N Atlantic Oc
96 J2 Iceland-Færoe Rise Atlantic Oc
88 N5 Ich Algeria 32.31N 1.01W
39 F6 Icha U.S.S.R. 55.35N 156.00E
39 F6 Icha R Kamchatka U.S.S.R.
42 C4 Icha R Novosibirsk U.S.S.R.
88 K7 Ichaf Algeria 28.08N 7.04W
29 J5 Ichak Bihar India 24.08N 85.26E
28 B2 Ichalkaranji Maharashtra India 16.40N 74.33E
30 F6 Ichara R Uttar Prad India
30 D7 Ichauli Uttar Prad India 25.32N 80.10E
29 J8 Ichchapuram Orissa India 19.10N 84.43E
64 J7 Ichenhausen W Germany 48.21N 10.20E
42 H3 Ichera U.S.S.R. 58.35N 109.45E
90 C8 Icheu Nigeria 7.42N 6.43E
20 G7 Ichi Japan 34.33N 133.05E
20 E9 Ichifusa-yama mt Japan 32.19N 131.04E
Ichig see Chegga Mauritania
39 G3 Ichigemskiy Khrebet ra U.S.S.R.
20 O6 Ichihara Japan 35.32N 140.04E
20 G2 Ichikawa Chiba Japan 35.45N 139.55E
120 F7 Ichilo, R Bolivia
20 K6 Ichinomiya Japan 35.18N 136.48E
20 O6 Ichinomiya Japan 35.22N 140.22E
20 P3 Ichinoseki Japan 38.56N 141.08E
39 F6 Ichinskaya Sopka vol U.S.S.R. 55.43N 157.45E
Ichinskiy vol see Ichinskaya Sopka vol
45 D6 Ichnya Ukraine U.S.S.R. 50.52N 32.24E
120 F6 Ichoa, R Bolivia
89 J1 Ichourad Mali 20.30N 1.18W
88 J7 Icht Morocco 29.01N 8.53W
77 F10 Ichtal Morocco 35.15N 5.18W
61 C2 Ichtegem Belgium 51.06N 3.01E
64 K2 Ichtershausen E Germany 50.52N 10.58E
39 J1 Ichun' U.S.S.R. 69.01N 171.03E
120 D7 Ichuña Peru 16.08S 70.40W
30 A7 Ichwaro Madhya Prad India 25.42N 77.32E
55 B3 Ickenham London England 51.34N 0.26W
56 N3 Icklingham Suffolk Eng 52.20N 0.36E
56 M3 Icknield Way hist route Eng
37 E7 Içme Turkey 38.37N 39.33E
117 H8 Icó Brazil 6.22S 38.51W
91 E7 Icoca Angola 6.12S 16.20E
96 Q14 Icod de los Vinos Tenerife Canary Is 28.22N 16.43W
118 H7 Iconha Brazil 20.45S 40.51W
Iconium anc site see Konya
117 D5 Icoraci Brazil 1.16S 48.28W
113 R7 Icy B Alaska
113 F1 Icy C Alaska 70.20N 162.00W
113 T7 Icy Pt Alaska 58.25N 137.05W
113 U7 Icy Str Alaska
Id see Narman
107 C9 Ida Louisiana 33.00N 93.55W
106 L8 Ida Michigan 41.55N 83.30W
95 L7 Ida S Africa 31.25S 27.32E
109 Q8 Idabel Oklahoma 33.54N 94.50W
108 P7 Ida Grove Iowa 42.20N 95.29W
90 C8 Idah Nigeria 7.05N 6.45E
102 C1 Idaho state U.S.A.
110 K6 Idaho City Idaho 43.50N 115.50W
110 N6 Idaho Falls Idaho 43.30N 112.01W
109 E2 Idaho Springs Colorado 39.44N 105.31W
109 H2 Idalia Colorado 39.43N 102.17W
95 O2 Idalia S Africa 26.53S 30.38E
Idalion see Dhali
109 J8 Idalou Texas 33.40N 101.40W
13 E6 Idamea, L Queensland 22.54S 138.45E
11 E11 Ida, Mt New Zealand 44.57S 170.07E
13 C5 Ida, Mt N Terr Australia 22.25S 134.34E
14 D8 Ida, Mt W Australia 29.14S 120.23E
110 C5 Idanha Oregon 44.42N 122.04W
76 E9 Idanha-a-Nova Portugal 39.55N 7.15W
76 E9 Idanha, Barragem de res Portugal
90 B8 Idanre Nigeria 7.05N 5.03E
29 C6 Idar Gujarat India 23.47N 73.03E
64 C4 Idar-Oberstein W Germany 49.43N 7.19E
42 F4 Idarskoye Belogor'ye mts U.S.S.R.
64 C4 Idarwald mts W Germany
11 D12 Ida Valley New Zealand 45.02S 169.51E
90 A8 Idawgaw Nigeria 6.50N 2.58E
90 E4 Idaye Niger 14.54N 11.33E
52 F7 Idd Norway 59.05N 11.25E
87 A3 Idd Abu Sufyan Sudan 15.30N 27.52E
33 K5 'Idd, Al U.A.E. 23.05N 53.32E
87 M7 Iddan Somalia 6.05N 48.55E
35 E10 'Iddan watercourse Israel
87 B3 Idd el Asoda Sudan 14.28N 29.27E
90 M6 Idd el Chanam Sudan 11.30N 24.19E
90 L6 Idd el Ghanam Sudan 11.45N 23.44E
87 B3 Idd el Merikh Sudan 14.57N 29.40E
33 K4 Idd el Sharqi oil field The Gulf 25.25N 52.20E
61 G3 Iddergem Belgium 50.52N 4.03E
100 F8 Iddesleigh Alberta 50.44N 111.20W
87 J8 Iddidole Ethiopia 5.51N 43.36E
60 P7 Ide Netherlands 53.07N 6.35E
105 C5 Ideal Georgia 32.24N 84.14W
61 F3 Idegem Belgium 50.48N 3.55E
85 B7 Idehan Marzūq sand dune reg Libya
85 A6 Idehan Ubari sand dune reg Libya
88 J7 Idehr Morocco 29.37N 9.37W
47 C4 Idel' U.S.S.R. 64.08N 34.21E
88 Q10 Idelès Algeria 23.50N 5.55E
89 K4 Idélimen Mali 15.51N 1.27E
91 B5 Idemba Gabon 2.32S 11.36E
91 A1 Idénao Cameroon 4.16N 8.56E
22 D2 Ider Mongolia 48.15N 97.24E
Iderīn Horshō see Ider
22 E2 Ideriyn Gol R Mongolia
53 H7 Idestrup Denmark 54.45N 11.58E
92 H6 Idete Tanzania 8.40S 36.20E
86 E3 Idfîna Egypt 31.18N 30.31E
85 M7 Idfu Egypt 24.55N 32.52E
35 G10 'Idham Jebel el mt Jordan 32.52N 35.46E
84 L11 Idhi Óros mts Crete
84 F7 Idhra Greece 37.20N 23.28E
84 G7 Idhra isld Greece
84 F7 Idhros, Stenón str Greece
18 B3 Idi Sumatra Indon 5.02N 97.37E
93 A6 Idi Amin Dada (L. Edward) L Uganda/Zaïre
79 K6 Idice R Italy
86 K10 Idîd el Gadân, Gebel hill Egypt 27.35N 33.03E
89 N3 Idikel Niger 17.32N 7.39E
90 C2 Idikel Niger 19.45N 7.41E
37 F8 Idil Turkey 37.21N 41.54E
33 H9 'Idim, Wādī watercourse S Yemen
91 F6 Idiofa Zaïre 5.00S 19.38E
113 H5 Iditarod Alaska 62.30N 158.11W
113 H5 Iditarod R Alaska
Idjen mts see Ijen mts
93 A8 Idjwi, I Zaïre
52 J6 Idkerberget Sweden 60.22N 15.15E
86 D3 Idku Egypt 31.18N 30.18E
57 M6 Idle, R Notts Eng
34 D3 Idlib Syria 35.57N 36.38E
86 E9 Idmu Egypt 28.09N 30.40E
35 C7 Idna Jordan 31.33N 34.58E
87 G7 Ido Ethiopia 7.30N 39.30E
90 E8 Ido Nigeria 7.15N 10.21E
75 H2 Idocin Spain 42.41N 1.28W
92 G5 Idodi Tanzania 7.49S 35.10E
87 L7 Idole Somalia 6.08N 46.58E
13 C6 Idracowra N Terr Australia 24.58S 133.48E
52 G5 Idre Sweden 61.52N 12.45E
111 D5 Idria California 36.26N 120.39W
82 B4 Idrija Yugoslavia 46.00N 14.00E
42 E5 Idrinskoye U.S.S.R. 54.21N 92.10E
85 B3 Idris Libya 32.42N 13.14E
88 L4 Idriss 1 res Morocco 34.07N 4.40W
46 G2 Idritsa U.S.S.R. 56.20N 28.50E
79 H3 Idro Italy 45.44N 10.29E
79 J3 Idro, L.di L Italy
72 D9 Idron-Lée-Ousse-Sendets France 43.17N 0.15W
53 T21 Idse isld Norway 58.59N 5.56E
53 T20 Idsefjord inlet Norway 59.01N 5.58E
60 L8 Idskenhuizen Netherlands 52.55N 5.43E
72 J2 Ids St. Roch France 46.43N 2.14E
53 L3 Idstedt W Germany 54.35N 9.31E
64 E3 Idstein W Germany 50.13N 8.16E
53 B4 Idum Denmark 56.20N 8.30E
95 M8 Idutywa S Africa 32.06S 28.20E
33 E3 'Idwah, Al Saudi Arabia 27.19N 42.16E
86 L6 'Idwet el Malh Egypt 29.35N 33.34E
40 E3 Idyum R U.S.S.R.
44 G7 Idzhevan Armenia U.S.S.R. 40.54N 45.06E
20 P8 Ie-jima isld Okinawa Japan 26.44N 127.48E
80 L5 Ielsi Italy 41.31N 14.48E
93 J1 Ienia Ethiopia 4.10N 37.31E
118 D8 Iepê Brazil 22.38S 51.06W
61 B3 Ieper Belgium 50.51N 2.53E
84 N11 Ierápetra Crete 35.00N 25.45E
I-erh-k'o-shih-t'ang see Irkeshtam
Ierhkoszetang see Irkeshtam
87 C8 Ieri Sudan 5.50N 30.09E
81 D4 Ierzu Sardinia 39.48N 9.32E
20 H7 Ie-shima isld Japan 34.40N 134.30E
87 K8 Iesomma Somalia 4.05N 45.40E
20 P8 Ie-suidō str Okinawa Japan
87 J8 Iet Somalia 4.36N 43.03E
Ieta see Hutjena
77 R3 Ifach, Peñón de pt Spain 38.38N 0.05E
95 O6 Ifafa Beach S Africa 30.28S 30.39E
87 F4 Ifag Ethiopia 12.04N 37.46E
92 H6 Ifakara Tanzania 8.10S 36.38E
33 A2 Ifal,Wadi al watercourse Saudi Arabia
95 C6 Ifanadiana Madagascar 21.19S 47.39E
95 C8 Ifarantsa Madagascar 24.55S 46.51E
90 B8 Ife Nigeria 7.33N 4.34E
89 J2 Ifei Mali 19.39N 0.10W
90 J5 Ifénat Chad 13.45N 18.35E
90 D2 Iférouane Niger 19.05N 8.24E
66 F6 Iffigen Switzerland 46.24N 7.27E
13 F4 Iffley Queensland 18.50S 141.10E
92 G6 Ifinga Tanzania 9.30S 35.30E
90 B8 Ifon Nigeria 6.58N 5.45E
95 C8 Ifotaka Madagascar 24.49S 46.09E
12 B4 Ifould L S Australia 30.55S 132.05E
88 L5 Ifrane Morocco 33.31N 5.10W
35 F9 Ifranj Jordan 31.10N 35.41E
91 G4 Ifumo Zaïre 1.49S 20.51E
33 J4 'Ifzi'iyyah, Al / U.A.E. 24.20N 51.40E
74 E10 Igá R Morocco
90 C6 Igabi Nigeria 10.45N 7.48E
92 F6 Igali Tanzania 9.04S 33.23E
48 U15 Igaliko Greenland 60.58N 45.28W
92 E4 Igalukilo Tanzania 5.59S 30.40E
92 F4 Igalula Tanzania 5.17S 33.05E
92 F4 Igalula Tanzania 5.36S 32.38E
92 F6 Igamba Tanzania 9.30S 33.28E
18 J4 Igan Sarawak Malaysia 2.51N 111.43E
18 J4 Igan R Sarawak Malaysia
90 A8 Igana Nigeria 7.57N 3.19E
92 H5 Igandu Tanzania 6.21S 36.09E
39 E4 Igandzha U.S.S.R. 60.44N 150.19E
93 E5 Iganga Uganda 0.37N 33.29E
90 A8 Igangan Nigeria 7.45N 3.14E
117 J8 Igaraçu Brazil 7.50S 34.52W
119 D8 Igara Paraná, R Colombia
118 F7 Igarapava Brazil 20.02S 47.46W
117 E5 Igarape Açú Brazil 1.07S 47.36W
117 F7 Igarapé Grande Brazil 4.40S 44.58W
117 D5 Igarapé Miri Brazil 1.58S 48.56W
118 G2 Igarité Brazil 11.36S 43.24W
41 E6 Igarka U.S.S.R. 67.31N 86.33E
118 C9 Igatimí Paraguay 24.04S 55.40W
29 C8 Igatpuri Maharashtra India 19.41N 73.38E
90 B7 Igbaja Nigeria 8.20N 4.54E
90 B7 Igbetti Nigeria 8.44N 4.08E
90 A7 Igboho Nigeria 8.53N 3.50E
19 L6 Igbon isld Philippines 11.13N 123.11E
90 A8 Igbo Ora Nigeria 7.29N 3.19E
88 J6 Igdet, Jbel mt Morocco 31.00N 8.25W
32 B1 Igdir Iran 39.20N 47.34E
36 H2 Iğdır Tokat Turkey 40.17N 35.37E
37 D5 Iğdir Dağı mt Turkey 40.19N 37.56E
48 S7 Igdlorssuit Greenland 71.15N 53.30W
70 M5 Igé France 48.19N 0.31E
90 B6 Igede Nigeria 10.05N 5.50E
64 B4 Igel W Germany 49.45N 6.35E
39 M2 Igel'veyem R U.S.S.R.
93 E7 Igenge Pt Tanzania 1.29S 33.39E
52 K5 Iggesund Sweden 61.38N 17.15E
88 S10 Igharghar watercourse Algeria
88 K6 Ighil M'Goun, Jbel mt Morocco 31.28N 6.28W
37 F7 Igik Turkey 38.16N 41.46E
48 S9 Iginiarfik Greenland 68.10N 53.15W
93 L3 Igiria hill Kenya 2.40N 39.24E
42 G4 Igirma U.S.S.R. 56.57N 103.40E
66 P4 Igis Switzerland 46.57N 9.35E
113 R10 Igitkin I Aleutian Is 51.59N 175.55W
113 K7 Igiugig Alaska 59.19N 155.58W
24 B6 Igizyar Xinjiang Uygur Zizhiqu China 38.38N 76.18E
85 N7 'Igla, Gebel mt Egypt 25.06N 34.35E
30 A5 Iglas Uttar Prad India 27.43N 77.56E
121 B3 Iglesia Argentina 30.20S 69.23W
81 B5 Iglesias Sardinia 39.19N 8.32E
75 C3 Iglesias Spain 42.19N 3.59W
81 B4 Iglesiente reg Sardinia
75 K7 Iglesuela del Cid, La Spain 40.29N 0.19W
76 K8 Iglesuela, La Spain 40.14N 4.45W
88 M6 Igli Algeria 30.28N 2.19W
47 H8 Iglino U.S.S.R. 54.52N 56.30E
108 G6 Igloo S Dakota 43.13N 103.51W
97 L4 Iglooik N W Terr 69.10N 83.59W
65 D7 Igls Austria 47.14N 11.26E
88 K7 Igma Algeria 29.05N 6.24W
86 M7 'Igma, Gebel el plat Egypt
100 L1 Ignace Ontario 49.26N 91.40W
109 C4 Ignacio Colorado 37.06N 107.38W
115 H5 Ignacio Allende Mexico 24.30N 103.59W
115 F3 Ignacio Zaragoza Mexico 29.35N 107.40W
115 K6 Ignacio Zaragoza Mexico 23.11N 98.47W
46 F2 Ignalina Lithuania U.S.S.R. 55.21N 26.10E
40 B5 Ignashino U.S.S.R. 53.30N 122.22E
41 J3 Ignatiya, Mys C U.S.S.R. 76.43N 108.15E
45 C9 Ignatovka Ukraine U.S.S.R. 47.05N 31.10E
45 T3 Ignatovka U.S.S.R. 53.56N 47.40E
36 C1 Iğne C Turkey 41.51N 28.06E
36 C1 Iğneada Turkey 41.50N 28.01E
28 G8 Ignoitijala Andaman Is 10.35N 92.24E
68 D5 Igny France 48.44N 2.14E
69 F5 Igny-Comblizy France 49.00N 3.43E
110 C9 Igo California 40.31N 122.34W
92 F5 Igoma Tanzania 7.50S 33.22E
93 E10 Igombe watercourse Tanzania
45 E1 Igorevskaya U.S.S.R. 55.26N 33.19E
71 E2 Igornay France 47.03N 4.23E
83 D5 Igoumenitsa Greece 39.32N 20.13E
90 B7 Igporin Nigeria 8.39N 4.49E
46 R1 Igra U.S.S.R. 57.31N 53.09E
76 D11 Igrejinha Portugal 38.42N 7.54W
42 G3 Igren'kina, Shiv falls U.S.S.R. 58.50N 101.00E
47 J4 Igrim U.S.S.R. 63.12N 64.30E
48 V12 Igterajivit Greenland 70.29N 22.20W
118 E9 Iguaçu, R Paraná Brazil
118 H4 Iguaí Brazil 14.50S 40.09W
119 D7 Iguaje, Mesa de Colombia
115 K8 Iguala Mexico 18.21N 99.31W
75 O4 Igualada Spain 41.35N 1.37E
77 F7 Igualeja Spain 36.38N 5.07W
115 K9 Igualtepec Mexico 17.46N 98.18W
118 F9 Iguape Brazil 24.37S 47.30W
118 G6 Iguarapé Brazil 20.08S 44.15W
117 F7 Iguará, R Brazil
118 F7 Iguatama Brazil 20.12S 45.40W
118 C8 Iguatemi Brazil 23.35S 54.30W
118 C8 Iguatemi, R Brazil
117 G8 Iguatu Brazil 6.22S 39.20W
118 C9 Iguazú, Cataratas del falls Arg/Brazil 25.35S 54.22W
91 A4 Iguéla Gabon 1.57S 9.22E
91 A4 Iguéla, Lag Gabon
76 G3 Igüeña Spain 42.44N 6.16W
71 E4 Iguerande France 46.12N 4.05E
96 S13 Igueste Tenerife Canary Is 28.30N 16.09W
93 F10 Iguguno Tanzania 4.32S 34.37E
88 K6 Iguiguil, Jbel mt Morocco 30.13N 7.53W
118 G2 Iguira Brazil 10.39S 42.39W
92 G5 Igula Tanzania 7.16S 34.40E
90 C8 Igumale Nigeria 6.47N 7.55E
92 F5 Igumira Tanzania 6.50S 33.21E
93 E10 Igunga Tanzania 4.17S 33.54E
93 E9 Igurubi Tanzania 3.59S 33.43E
92 D11 Igusi Zimbabwe 19.40S 28.06E
113 K8 Igvak, C Alaska 57.27N 156.00W
93 D9 Ihapula Tanzania 3.51S 32.16E
22 E4 Ih Bogd Uul mts Mongolia
92 G6 Iheme Tanzania 8.01S 35.28E
88 S9 Iherir Algeria 25.25N 8.22E
21 C12 Iheya shima isld Japan 27.05N 12.00E
22 H4 Ihhet Mongolia 45.58N 110.02E
88 Q11 Ihirène watercourse Algeria
22 H4 Ihjargalan Mongolia 45.30N 108.45E
86 E7 Ihnâsya El Madîna Egypt 29.06N 30.56E
72 B9 Iholdy France 43.17N 1.11W
95 C7 Ihorombe Madagascar 23.00S 47.31E
95 C7 Ihosy Madagascar 22.23S 46.09E
95 A6 Ihotry Madagascar 21.59S 43.36E
25 G6 Ihr Cambodia 13.53N 103.50E
63 F6 Ihrhove W Germany 53.10N 7.27E
64 D7 Ihringen W Germany 48.03N 7.39E
36 E3 Ihsaniye Afyon Turkey 39.02N 30.23E
37 G2 Ihsaniye Kocaeli Turkey 40.42N 29.51E
33 B10 Ihsan, Jabal mt S Yemen 12.46N 44.53E
22 E3 Ihtamir Mongolia 47.29N 100.55E
37 D6 Ihtik Turkey 39.37N 38.47E
82 H8 Ihtiman Bulgaria 42.27N 23.48E
15 H7 Ihu Papua New Guinea 7.52S 145.22E
11 C3 Ihumatao hill New Zealand 36.59S 174.45E
93 C4 Ihungu Uganda 1.39N 31.42E
22 D2 Ih-Uul Mongolia 48.30N 98.52E
51 L6 Ii Finland 65.20N 25.25E
20 L6 Iida Japan 35.32N 137.48E
20 N4 Iide-san mt Japan 37.49N 139.44E
47 C5 Ii'inskiy U.S.S.R. 61.01N 32.40E
51 N2 Iijärvi L Finland 69.27N 27.50E
51 N6 Iijoki R Finland
51 N8 Iisalmi Finland 63.32N 27.15E
51 N9 Iisvesi Finland 62.42N 27.03E
20 G5 Iitomi Chiba Japan
20 M5 Iiyama Japan 36.52N 138.22E

20 O4 Iizaka Japan 37.48N 140.21E
20 D8 Iizuka Japan 33.38N 130.40E
93 M7 Ijara Kenya 1.35S 40.31E
90 B8 Ijebu Igbo Nigeria 6.56N 4.01E
90 A8 Ijebu Ode Nigeria 6.47N 3.58E
18 L10 Ijen mts Java Indon
90 B8 Ijero Nigeria 7.51N 5.11E
60 L7 IJlst Netherlands 53.01N 5.38E
60 J10 IJmeer Pampus L Netherlands
60 G10 IJmuiden Netherlands 52.28N 4.38E
60 N10 IJssel R Netherlands
60 J8 IJsselmeer sea Netherlands
60 J8 IJsselmeer Afsluitdijk dyke Netherlands
60 G12 IJsselmonde Netherlands 51.54N 4.33E
60 F12 IJsselmonde isld Netherlands
60 M9 IJsselmuiden Netherlands 52.34N 5.55E
60 M14 IJsselsteijn Netherlands 51.29N 5.54E
60 J11 IJsselstein Netherlands 52.01N 5.02E
9 B8 Ijub Nauru, Pacific Oc 0.30S 166.57E
121 G2 Ijuí Brazil 28.23S 54.00W
121 G2 Ijuí, R Brazil
60 B3 IJzendijke Netherlands 51.19N 3.37E
61 B3 Ijzer R Belgium
Ijzim see Kerem Maharal
46 R3 Ik R U.S.S.R.
42 H3 Ika U.S.S.R. 59.20N 106.15E
51 K10 Ikaalinen Finland 61.46N 23.05E
20 M5 Ikaho Japan 36.30N 138.52E
95 C6 Ikalamavony Madagascar 21.10S 46.35E
91 G5 Ikali Zaïre 2.02S 21.04E
11 F9 Ikamatua New Zealand 42.17S 171.43E
48 S9 Ikamiut Greenland 68.50N 52.00W
24 F6 Ikanbujmal Xinjiang Uygur Zizhiqu China 39.45N 88.20E
91 G5 Ikanda Zaïre 3.07S 21.36E
90 D9 Ikang Nigeria 4.49N 8.30E
93 K7 Ikanga Kenya 1.42S 38.04E
91 F5 Ikari Zaïre 2.28S 19.59E
83 H7 Ikaria isld Greece
90 D9 Ikasa Cameroon 4.58N 8.50E
53 C4 Ikast Denmark 56.09N 9.10E
113 F9 Ikatan Aleutian Is 54.45N 163.20W
48 U14 Ikáteq Greenland 65.35N 38.05W
48 V13 Ikáteq airport Greenland 66.00N 36.45W
39 G3 Ikato U.S.S.R. 63.19N 160.28E
42 J5 Ikatskiy Khrebet mts U.S.S.R.
91 F3 Ikau Zaïre 1.13N 19.45E
30 E5 Ikauna Uttar Prad India 27.32N 81.58E
11 L5 Ikawhenua Ra New Zealand
20 N2 Ikeda Hokkaido Japan 42.56N 143.26E
20 J7 Ikeda Honshu Japan 34.52N 135.23E
20 G7 Ikeda Shikoku Japan 34.02N 133.48E
20 G8 Ikegawa Japan 33.38N 133.10E
90 A8 Ikeja Nigeria 6.37N 3.25E
20 P9 Ike-jima isld Okinawa Japan
91 H4 Ikela Zaïre 1.06S 23.06E
91 E3 Ikelemba Congo 1.12N 16.38E
91 F3 Ikelemba R Zaïre
91 F4 Ikengo Zaïre 0.10S 18.10E
48 V16 Ikeq inlet Greenland 59.50N 43.00W
90 B8 Ikeram Nigeria 7.39N 5.51E
48 V16 Ikerasagssuaq fjord Greenland
48 T7 Ikerasak Greenland 70.28N 51.30W
90 B8 Ikerre Nigeria 7.30N 5.19E
48 U14 Ikerssuaq fjord Greenland
65 P7 Ikervár Hungary 47.13N 16.58E
42 G5 Ikey U.S.S.R. 54.10N 100.05E
20 C8 Iki isld Japan 33.50N 129.40E
21 E11 Iki isld Japan
44 F2 Iki Burul U.S.S.R. 45.49N 44.41E
93 C7 Ikimba, L Tanzania
44 G6 Ikindzhi Shikhly Azerbaydzhan U.S.S.R. 41.17N 45.07E
90 B8 Ikirun Nigeria 7.54N 4.40E
20 C8 Iki-suidō str Japan
21 E11 Ikitsuki-shima I Japan 33.29N 129.28E
36 F3 Ikizce Turkey 39.36N 32.40E
37 F5 Ikizdere Turkey 40.47N 40.34E
92 G2 Ikizu Tanzania 1.55S 34.02E
53 T16 Ikjefjord Norway 61.03N 5.40E
86 K8 'Ikma, Gebel hill Egypt 28.38N 33.18E
90 B8 Ikole Nigeria 7.46N 5.37E
113 K8 Ikolik, C Alaska 57.19N 154.50W
90 D9 Ikom Nigeria 6.00N 8.41E
93 F8 Ikoma Tanzania 2.04S 34.37E
92 F6 Ikomba Tanzania 9.09S 32.20E
92 G6 Ikombe Tanzania 9.31S 34.05E
41 E5 Ikon U.S.S.R. 70.24N 89.45E
95 C6 Ikongo Madagascar 21.52S 47.27E
44 D3 Ikon Khal' U.S.S.R. 44.19N 41.57E
93 K7 Ikoo Kenya 1.10S 38.10E
95 C4 Ikopa R Madagascar
46 L4 Ikorets R U.S.S.R.
90 A8 Ikorodu Nigeria 6.36N 3.32E
90 C9 Ikot Ekpene Nigeria 5.10N 7.43E
87 D8 Ikoto Sudan 4.07N 33.08E
91 B4 Ikoy R Gabon
47 L7 Ik, Oz L U.S.S.R. 56.05N 70.30E
92 C3 Ikozi Zaïre 2.35S 27.40E
113 K1 Ikpikpuk R Alaska
86 F4 Ikrâsh Egypt 30.46N 31.30E
44 H1 Ikryanoye U.S.S.R. 46.06N 47.44E
42 C4 Iksa R U.S.S.R.
35 E3 Iksāl Israel 32.41N 35.19E
45 J1 Iksha U.S.S.R. 56.09N 37.30E
93 E5 Ikulwe Uganda 0.27N 33.29E
92 G4 Ikungi Tanzania 5.03S 34.46E
92 F4 Ikungu Tanzania 5.23S 33.42E
93 E7 Ikungu Tanzania 1.34S 33.43E
20 H6 Ikuno Japan 35.12N 134.46E
93 C8 Ikusa I Tanzania 2.08S 31.48E
20 L1 Ikushumbetsu Japan 43.17N 141.59E
93 D9 Ikusule Tanzania 3.57S 32.53E
20 C3 Ikuta Kanagawa Japan 35.37N 139.33E
93 K8 Ikutha Kenya 2.05S 38.10E
65 P6 Ikva R Hungary
86 F4 Ikwa Egypt 30.42N 31.28E
86 G4 Ikyâd Egypt 30.44N 31.53E
13 B3 Ikymbon R N Terr Australia
89 M7 Ila Nigeria 8.00N 4.54E
91 G5 Ila Zaïre 2.53S 21.07E
92 C9 Ila tribe Zambia
87 L5 Ilad Somalia 10.02N 47.50E
88 O11 Ilaferh Algeria 21.40N 1.58E
88 O11 Ilaferh watercourse Algeria
19 K3 Ilagan Luzon Philippines 17.07N 121.53E
15 L9 Ilai I Louisiade Arch 10.54S 151.37E
28 D6 Ilaiyankudi Tamil Nadu India 9.39N 78.40E
95 C6 Ilaka Madagascar 20.20S 47.10E
95 D5 Ilaka Madagascar 19.30S 48.50E
113 P10 Ilak I Aleutian Is 51.30N 178.20W
32 B4 Ilam Iran 33.37N 46.27E
30 L6 Ilam Nepal 26.55N 87.55E
32 B4 Ilām sub-prov Iran
35 D3 Ilaniyya Israel 32.45N 35.24E
42 F4 Ilanskiy U.S.S.R. 56.13N 96.09E
66 N4 Ilanz Switzerland 46.47N 9.13E
90 A8 Ilaro Nigeria 6.50N 3.05E
89 M3 Ilatan Niger 16.30N 4.45E
120 D7 Ilave Peru 16.07S 69.40W
62 M2 Iława Poland 53.35N 19.33E
42 L1 Ilbenge U.S.S.R. 62.58N 124.55E
93 H8 Ilbisil Kenya 2.06S 36.47E
93 H8 Ilbisil Kenya 2.06S 36.47E
53 E2 Ilbro Denmark 57.26N 10.03E
12 D2 Ilbunga S Australia 26.25S 135.00E
56 F5 Ilchester Somerset Eng 51.01N 2.41W
121 K10 Ildefonso Is Chile 55.50S 69.15W
99 J9 Ilderton Ontario 43.04N 81.24W
100 K3 Ile-à-la-Crosse L Saskatchewan
82 H3 Ileanda Romania 47.20N 23.39E
9 A13 Ile Art New Caledonia 19.55S 163.45E
99 P9 Ile Bizard, et I Quebec 45.29N 73.50W
91 G6 Ilebo Zaïre 4.20S 20.35E
67 G3 Ile de France prov France
69 C5 Ile de France reg France
72 A2 Ile D'Olonne France 46.34N 1.47W
46 R4 Ilek U.S.S.R. 51.32N 53.20E
46 R4 Ilek R U.S.S.R.
92 G6 Ilembula Tanzania 8.55S 34.35E
92 E2 Ilemera Tanzania 1.52S 31.39E
93 D8 Ilemera Tanzania 2.25S 32.57E
59 D8 Ilen, R Cork Irish Rep
99 O10 Ile Perrot et I Quebec 45.23N 73.53W
9 A12 Ile Pott New Caledonia 19.35S 163.35E
93 H1 Ileret Kenya 4.18N 36.14E
88 P11 Ilerh Algeria 20.57N 3.21E
88 P11 Ilerh watercourse Algeria
68 E2 Ile St.Denis, L' France 48.56N 2.20E
90 A7 Ilesha Nigeria 8.55N 3.25E
90 B8 Ilesha Nigeria 7.39N 4.38E
46 P2 Ilet' R U.S.S.R.
70 B6 Ile-Tudy France 47.51N 4.10W
63 N9 Ilfeld E Germany 51.35N 10.48E
66 H4 Ilfis R Switzerland
55 J3 Ilford London England 51.33N 0.06E
100 W2 Ilford Manitoba 56.04N 95.40W
82 K6 Ilfov div Romania
56 C5 Ilfracombe Devon Eng 51.13N 4.08W
13 G6 Ilfracombe Queensland 23.30S 144.30E
42 G5 Ilga R U.S.S.R.
36 G2 Ilgaz Turkey 40.55N 33.37E
36 G1 Ilgaz Dağları mts Turkey
36 F4 Ilgin Turkey 38.16N 31.57E
84 Z20 Il Gżira Malta 35.52N 14.35E
92 K9 Ilha dist Mozambique
118 F8 Ilhabela Brazil 23.47S 45.20W
119 G8 Ilha Grande Brazil 0.28S 65.03W
118 G8 Ilha Grande, B. de Brazil
96 R4 Ilha, Pta.da Azores 38.25N 28.03W
118 D7 Ilha Salteira Dam Brazil 20.20S 51.16W
Ilhas do Cabo Verde see Cape Verde Is
Ilhas dos Açôres see Azores Is
76 B7 Ilhavo Portugal 40.36N 8.40W
118 H4 Ilhéus Brazil 14.50S 39.06W
96 O2 Ilhéus, Pta dos pt Azores 39.23N 31.16W
Ili see Kapchagay
43 N5 Ili R Kazakhstan U.S.S.R.
82 H5 Ilia Romania 45.57N 22.40E
84 B6 Ilia prov Greece
113 K7 Iliamna Alaska 59.44N 154.55W
113 L6 Iliamna vol Alaska 60.05N 153.09W
113 K7 Iliamna L Alaska 59.30N 155.30W
19 C8 Ili Boleng vol Indonesia 8.16S 123.17E
37 D6 Ilic Turkey 39.27N 38.34E
37 H6 Ilica Agri Turkey 39.29N 43.42E
36 C3 Ilica Balikesir Turkey 39.52N 27.46E
37 F6 Ilıca Erzurum Turkey 39.58N 41.09E
43 J6 Il'ich Kazakhstan U.S.S.R. 40.50N 68.29E
44 F8 Il'ichevsk Nakhichevan' U.S.S.R. 39.22N 45.05E
44 A8 Il'ichevsk Ukraine U.S.S.R. 46.19N 30.42E
19 M4 Ilick Harb. Truk Is Pacific Oc 7.20N 151.34E
109 G1 Iliff Colorado 40.45N 103.04W
19 M7 Iligan Mindanao Philippines 8.12N 124.13E
19 L7 Iligan B Mindanao Philippines
19 L2 Iligan Pt Luzon Philippines 18.18N 122.21E
84 F5 Ilíki L Greece 38.24N 23.15E
47 M4 Ilim Sverdlovsk U.S.S.R. 57.22N 58.58E
47 M4 Ilim Sverdlovsk U.S.S.R. 57.31N 59.02E
42 G3 Ilim R U.S.S.R.
39 E1 Ilimniir U.S.S.R. 69.03N 152.10E
15 J8 Ilimo Papua New Guinea 8.58S 148.00E
42 H1 Ilimpeya R U.S.S.R.
42 G4 Ilimsk Irkutsk U.S.S.R. 56.45N 103.50E
42 G4 Ilimskiy, Khrebet mts U.S.S.R.
19 K5 Ilin isld Philippines 12.15N 121.05E
28 C3 Ilindri R Andhra Prad India
119 B8 Iliniza, Cerra mt Ecuador 0.40S 78.45W
42 H6 Il'inka Buryat U.S.S.R. 52.10N 107.15E
43 D3 Il'inka Kazakhstan U.S.S.R. 49.57N 56.26E
42 D4 Il'inka Krasnoyarsk U.S.S.R. 55.20N 90.00E
45 N8 Il'inka Rostov U.S.S.R. 48.33N 41.07E
47 N4 Il'inka Sverdlovsk U.S.S.R. 57.52N 60.55E
42 C3 Il'inka Tomsk U.S.S.R. 57.40N 80.58E
42 F6 Il'inka Tuvinsk U.S.S.R. 51.12N 95.30E
45 C1 Il'ino U.S.S.R. 55.57N 31.40E
44 D2 Il'inskaya U.S.S.R. 45.44N 40.44E
42 J6 Il'inskiy Chita U.S.S.R. 52.10N 114.10E
40 J8 Il'inskiy Sakhalin U.S.S.R. 48.00N 142.12E
47 F5 Il'insko Podomskoye U.S.S.R. 61.09N 47.50E
42 C6 Il'inskoye Altay U.S.S.R. 51.25N 85.05E
46 N1 Il'inskoye Kostroma U.S.S.R. 58.47N 44.30E
47 H6 Il'inskoye Perm U.S.S.R. 58.34N 55.42E
46 N2 Il'insko Zaborskoye U.S.S.R. 57.12N 44.28E
19 K5 Ilin Str Philippines
46 G5 Il'intsy Ukraine U.S.S.R. 49.08N 29.11E
84 G3 Iliodhrómia isld Greece
84 F7 Iliókastron Greece 37.27N 23.16E
84 A2 Iliokhóri Greece 39.58N 20.55E
19 E8 Iliômar Indonesia 9.43S 126.49E
104 K3 Ilion New York 43.01N 75.04W
114 C5 Ilio Pt Hawaiian Is 21.13N 157.16W
42 G4 Ilir U.S.S.R. 55.12N 100.45E
39 F1 Ilirgytkin, Ozero L U.S.S.R. 70.32N 159.00E
39 H1 Ilirney U.S.S.R. 67.20N 167.50E
82 B5 Ilirska Bistrica Yugoslavia 45.34N 14.14E
36 G5 Ilisira Turkey 37.12N 33.03E
31 H2 Ilisu Davan pass Kashmir/Xinjiang Uygur Zizhiqu 37.00N 75.36E
Ilium anc site see Troy
113 G5 Ilivit Mts Alaska
Iliysk see Kapchagay
42 H6 Il'ka U.S.S.R. 51.45N 108.35E
28 C3 Ilkal Karnataka India 15.59N 76.11E
57 L7 Ilkeston Derbys Eng 52.59N 1.18W
44 G10 Ilkhechi Iran 37.56N 45.58E
45 N1 Il'kino U.S.S.R. 55.12N 41.37E
57 K5 Ilkley W Yorks Eng 53.55N 1.50W
84 Y20 Il-Kullana C Malta 35.51N 14.24E
65 A7 Ill R Austria
71 L1 Ill R France 47.42N 7.17E
87 H3 Illadaban Ethiopia 14.21N 40.40E
50 F5 Illahraun lava field Iceland
120 E6 Illampu, Nev.de pk Bolivia 15.51S 68.30E
75 E7 Illana Spain 40.11N 2.54W
19 L8 Illana B Mindanao Philippines
76 F2 Illano Spain 43.20N 6.51W
121 B3 Illapel Chile 31.40S 71.13W
121 B3 Illapel, R Chile
35 D4 'Illar Jordan 32.22N 35.06E
45 G8 Illarionovo Ukraine U.S.S.R. 48.22N 35.17E
76 H2 Illas Spain 43.30N 5.59W
79 K4 Illasi Italy 45.29N 11.11E
72 D6 Illats France 44.36N 0.25W
93 J4 Illaut Kenya 1.54N 37.15E
12 C2 Illbillee, Mt S Australia 27.03S 132.30E
67 D4 Ille-et-Vilaine dept France
89 M4 Illéla Niger 14.32N 5.19E
64 J7 Iller R W Germany
64 J7 Illertissen W Germany 48.13N 10.07E
119 A10 Illesca, Cerro mt Peru 5.59S 81.06W
75 C7 Illescas Spain 40.08N 3.51W
121 G4 Illescas Uruguay 33.34S 55.20W
72 K10 Ille-sur-la-Tet France 42.40N 2.37E
66 F1 Illfurth France 47.41N 7.16E
66 L4 Illgau Switzerland 46.59N 8.44E
70 N5 Illiers-Combray France 48.18N 1.15E
66 D7 Illiez, V. d' Switzerland
70 F5 Illifaut France 48.07N 2.20W
87 K7 Illig Ethiopia 7.16N 45.32E
12 B2 Illillinna, Mt S Australia 27.10S 131.46E
120 E7 Illimani, Nev.de pk Bolivia 16.37S 67.48W
64 F6 Illingen W Germany 48.57N 8.55E
110 B7 Illinois R Oregon
102 H2 Illinois state U.S.A.
106 D8 Illinois & Mississippi Can Illinois
106 E9 Illinois, R Illinois
94 T13 Illiondale Witwatersrand S Africa 26.08S 28.11E
107 G2 Illiopolis Illinois 39.50N 89.13W
88 S8 Illizi Algeria 26.32N 8.33E
69 O6 Illkirch-Graffenstaden France 48.32N 7.44E
64 G8 Illmensee W Germany 47.53N 9.25E
65 P6 Illmitz Austria 47.46N 16.48E
107 G4 Illmo Missouri 37.13N 89.31W
89 L6 Illo Nigeria 11.32N 3.33E
13 D6 Illogwa R N Terr Australia
70 O2 Illois France 49.45N 1.40E
77 J6 Illora Spain 37.17N 3.53W
95 O6 Illovo S Africa 30.06S 30.50E
95 O6 Illovo Beach S Africa 30.07S 30.51E
64 M5 Illschwang W Germany 49.27N 11.42E
53 X14 Illstiegga mt Norway 62.15N 7.36E
75 G4 Illueca Spain 41.32N 1.38W
50 E3 Illugastadhir Húnavatnssýsla, Vestur Iceland 65.36N 20.53W
50 H3 Illugastadhir Thingeyjarsýsla, Sudhur Iceland 65.37N 17.46W
50 G6 Illugaver Iceland 64.25N 18.38W
53 E6 Illumø isld Denmark 55.08N 10.07E
53 X15 Illvatn L Norway 61.43N 7.47E
50 G2 Illvidhrahnjukur mt Iceland 66.08N 18.59W
64 L1 Ilm R E Germany
64 M6 Ilm R W Germany
51 K9 Ilmajoki Finland 62.43N 22.32E
33 F7 'Ilmān, Jabal al mts Saudi Arabia
64 K2 Ilmenau E Germany 50.41N 10.55E
63 M6 Ilmenau R W Germany
46 H1 Il'men', Ozero L U.S.S.R.
84 Y21 Il-Minkba C Malta 35.49N 14.29E
56 F6 Ilminster Somerset Eng 50.56N 2.55W
39 J3 Il'muv'ye U.S.S.R. 64.58N 173.59E
113 H8 Ilnik Alaska 56.35N 159.40W
120 D7 Ilo Peru 17.42S 71.20W
19 J6 Iloc isld Philippines 11.18N 119.40E
19 L6 Iloilo Philippines 10.41N 122.33E
19 L6 Iloilo Str Philippines
92 G5 Ilolo Tanzania 7.15S 35.20E
51 P9 Ilomantsi Finland 62.40N 30.55E
28 J2 Ilong Assam India 27.31N 93.51E
93 F10 Ilongero Tanzania 4.40S 34.50E
15 F5 Ilop Papua New Guinea 2.50S 141.13E
90 B7 Ilorin Nigeria 8.32N 4.34E
26 R12 Ilot, L' isld Seychelles, Ind Oc 4.36S 55.54E
45 R6 Ilovatka U.S.S.R. 50.30N 45.54E
45 K9 Ilovaysk Ukraine U.S.S.R. 47.55N 38.14E
45 Q7 Ilovlya U.S.S.R. 49.19N 44.01E
45 Q7 Ilovlya R U.S.S.R.
39 J4 Il'pi U.S.S.R. 61.31N 172.59E
39 J4 Il'pi R U.S.S.R.
39 G5 Il'pinskiy Poluostrov pen U.S.S.R.
39 G5 Il'pyrskiy U.S.S.R. 59.58N 164.12E
84 X19 Il-Qala Ta'San Blas B Gozo Mediterranean Sea 36.04N 14.19E
63 N8 Ilse R Germany
63 N9 Ilsenburg E Germany 51.53N 10.41E
64 G5 Ilsfeld W Germany 49.03N 9.16E
64 H5 Ilshofen W Germany 49.10N 9.55E
21 E7 Ilsin-dong N Korea 40.34N 129.05E
56 D6 Ilsington Devon Eng 50.35N 3.42W
44 B3 Il'skiy U.S.S.R. 44.52N 38.35E
53 C4 Ilskov Denmark 56.15N 9.06E
53 T19 Ilsvåg Norway 59.31N 5.49E
66 O3 Iltios Switzerland 47.11N 9.19E
120 B2 Iluambo R Peru
87 E7 Ilubabor prov Ethiopia
48 V15 Iluileq isld Greenland 60.50N 42.45W
93 E9 Ilula Tanzania 3.16S 33.20E
92 E4 Ilunde Tanzania 5.50S 30.54E
92 E4 Ilunde Tanzania 5.06S 30.34E
92 F5 Ilunde Tanzania 6.45S 32.27E
28 D5 Iluppur Tamil Nadu India 10.32N 78.37E
35 E3 'Ilūt Israel 32.43N 35.15E
47 K3 Ilval U.S.S.R. 66.33N 66.15E
82 J3 Ilva Mică Romania 47.17N 24.40E
110 A3 Ilwaco Washington 46.18N 124.03W
19 E7 Ilwaki Indon 7.55S 126.26E
86 D8 'Ilw el Ahmar el Qibli, El hill Egypt 28.57N 30.01E
86 E7 'Ilw el Bireig hill Egypt 29.00N 30.44E
41 J5 Il'ya R U.S.S.R.
42 B2 Il'yak U.S.S.R. 60.13N 77.57E
42 B3 Il'yak R U.S.S.R.
43 E6 Il'yaly Turkmeniya U.S.S.R. 41.52N 59.35E
37 G3 Ilyasbey Turkey 40.14N 29.52E
37 D2 Ilyas Daği mt Marmara I Turkey 40.37N 27.36E
47 H5 Ilych R U.S.S.R.
65 N7 Ilz Austria 47.07N 15.57E
65 N7 Ilz R Austria
64 P6 Ilz R W Germany
62 N4 Iłża Poland 51.11N 21.13E
62 N4 Iłżanka R Poland
42 K4 Ima U.S.S.R. 55.15N 115.58E
20 F7 Imabari Japan 34.04N 132.59E
20 O1 Imabetsu Japan 41.12N 140.30E
117 A5 Imabú R Brazil
20 N5 Imaichi Japan 36.43N 139.41E
20 K6 Imajō Japan 35.48N 136.10E
20 C4 Imajuku Kanagawa Japan
115 F5 Imala Mexico 24.52N 107.12W
92 J9 Imala Mozambique 14.39S 39.34E
34 M7 Imām al Ḩamzah Iraq 31.43N 44.58E
43 F8 Imambaba Turkmeniya U.S.S.R. 36.45N 62.25E
86 R12 Imâm,El Cairo Egypt
34 M5 Imām Ḩamid Iraq 33.30N 44.50E
Imam Ḩamza see Imām al Ḩamzah
Imam Quli see Emām Qolī
47 C2 Imandra U.S.S.R. 67.53N 33.30E
47 C2 Imandra, Oz L U.S.S.R.
90 C8 Imani Nigeria 7.20N 7.43E
95 B8 Imanombo Madagascar 24.25S 45.50E
121 G1 Imán, Sa. del ra Argentina
43 J1 Imantau, Oz L Kazakhstan U.S.S.R.
20 C8 Imari Japan 33.18N 129.51E
86 E10 'Imarîya, El Egypt 27.38N 30.52E
121 J2 Imaruí Brazil 28.23S 48.49W
87 F1 Imasa Sudan 18.00N 36.12E
74 D10 Imasinen Morocco 34.57N 4.31W
120 D6 Imata Peru 15.51S 71.08W
119 H3 Imataca, Serranía de mts Venezuela
20 H4 Imatomi Chiba Japan
93 D1 Imatong,Jeb mts Sudan
51 O10 Imatra Finland 61.14N 28.50E
86 B4 'Imâyid El Egypt 30.46W 29.12E
120 A1 Imaza, R R Peru
20 K6 Imazu Japan 35.25N 136.01E
86 Q12 Imbâba Cairo Egypt
87 F6 Imbabo Ethiopia 9.38N 37.38E
119 B7 Imbabura prov Ecuador
119 H5 Imbaimadai Guyana 5.44N 60.17W
116 J5 Imbert Dominican Rep 19.48N 70.50W
121 J2 Imbituba Brazil 28.15S 48.44W
118 E9 Imbituva Brazil 25.09S 50.37W
110 H4 Imbler Oregon 45.28N 117.59W
107 E5 Imboden Arkansas 36.10N 91.11W
91 F4 Imbonga Zaïre 0.43S 19.44E
15 F5 Imbrinis Papua New Guinea 2.58S 141.30E
118 H4 Imbuíra Brazil 14.09S 40.14W
41 G8 Imbukan R U.S.S.R.
89 K3 Imenas Mali 16.20N 0.40E
Imera Meridionale see Salso R
95 D4 Imerimandroso Madagascar 17.23S 48.38E
119 G7 Imerí Sa mts Venezuela
91 F2 Imese Zaïre 2.06N 18.09E
105 F7 Imeson airport Florida 30.27N 81.42W
88 F9 Imetlan reg Morocco
88 R11 Imezla watercourse Niger
88 K5 Im Fout Morocco 32.48N 7.58W
34 M10 Imghatti,Wādī watercourse Saudi Arabia
47 L6 Imgyt R U.S.S.R.
47 L6 Imgytskoye Boloto marsh U.S.S.R.
87 J7 Imi Ethiopia 6.28N 42.10E
120 E11 Imilac, Salar de salt pan Chile
88 L5 Imilchil Morocco 32.08N 5.40W
88 F10 Imilili Mauritania 23.18N 15.54W
53 Y18 Imingdalen V Norway 60.13N 8.30E
53 Z18 Imingen Norway 60.15N 8.36E
88 K6 Imini,wadi Morocco
88 J6 Imi n 'Tanout Morocco 31.10N 8.50W
88 S8 Imirhou watercourse Algeria
88 F9 Imiric-Li Labiad reg Morocco
88 F9 Imiric-Li Lahmar reg Morocco
44 J8 Imishli Azerbaydzhan U.S.S.R. 39.50N 48.03E
29 F1 Imis P Kashmir/Xizang Zizhiqu 32.19N 79.05E
88 J7 Imitek Morocco 29.40N 8.15W
84 G6 Imittós mt Greece 37.57N 23.49E
30 J3 Imja Glacier Nepal
30 J3 Imja Khola R Nepal
21 D8 Imjin R N Korea
87 D8 Imkororo Sudan 5.10N 32.30E
86 L9 Imlaha, Wâdi watercourse Egypt
39 H3 Imlan R U.S.S.R.
110 G9 Imlay Nevada 40.40N 118.07W
108 H6 Imlay S Dakota 43.42N 102.21W
106 L6 Imlay City Michigan 43.02N 83.04W
12 B4 Immarna S Australia 30.29S 132.13E
90 M4 Immaseri Sudan 15.40N 25.31E
35 D5 Immatin Jordan 32.11N 35.09E
64 F8 Immendingen W Germany 47.57N 8.44E
66 J1 Immeneich W Germany 47.42N 8.08E
63 K10 Immenhausen W Germany 51.26N 9.28E
66 K3 Immensee Switzerland 47.06N 8.27E
66 O1 Immenstaad W Germany 47.40N 9.22E
65 B6 Immenstadt W Germany 47.34N 10.14E
88 Q9 Im Meskane Algeria 24.05N 4.05E
95 J5 Immigrant S Africa 29.07S 25.36E
57 N5 Immingham Dock Humberside Eng 53.36N 0.11W
105 F11 Immokalee Florida 26.25N 81.26W
42 J3 Immyal U.S.S.R. 59.34N 111.10E
110 J4 Imnaha Idaho 45.34N 116.40W
110 J4 Imnaha R Oregon
42 B2 Imn-Lor, Ozero U.S.S.R. 61.50N 75.30E
90 C9 Imo R Nigeria
108 P9 Imogene Iowa 40.55N 95.25W
20 B2 Imokubo Tōkyō Japan
79 L6 Imola Italy 44.22N 11.43E
75 E5 Imón Spain 41.10N 2.45W
15 F5 Imonda Papua New Guinea 3.21S 141.10E
95 B8 Imongy Madagascar 25.17S 45.43E
82 D7 Imotski Yugoslavia 43.27N 17.12E
88 J6 Imouzzer Morocco 30.40N 9.30W
61 F3 Impe Belgium 50.57N 3.57E
91 D5 Impé Congo 2.45S 15.16E
95 N5 Impendle S Africa 29.36S 29.52E
39 H3 Impenveem R U.S.S.R.
120 E1 Imperatriz Amazonas Brazil 5.20S 67.13W
117 E7 Imperatriz Maranhão Brazil 5.32S 47.28W
79 C7 Imperia prov Italy
111 J9 Imperial California 32.51N 115.33W
108 J9 Imperial Nebraska 40.32N 101.40W
120 B5 Imperial Peru 13.04S 76.21W
100 M7 Imperial Saskatchewan 51.21N 105.28W
112 E4 Imperial Texas 31.16N 102.43W
111 K9 Imperial Dam Cal/Arizona 32.52N 114.28W
75 H4 Imperial de Aragón, Can Spain
111 J9 Imperial Valley California
79 D7 Imperia Porto Maurízio Italy 43.52N 8.01E
14 C4 Imperieuse Reef W Australia 17.40S 118.53E
98 J9 Imperoyal Nova Scotia 44.38N 63.30W
64 E5 Impflingen W Germany 49.09N 8.07E
91 E3 Impfondo Congo 1.36N 18.00E
28 J3 Imphal Manipur India 24.47N 93.55E
25 L8 Imphal R Manipur India
71 C3 Imphy France 46.56N 3.15E
47 C5 Impilakhti U.S.S.R. 61.38N 31.05E
79 K7 Impruneta Italy 43.42N 11.15E
91 C10 Impulo Angola 13.51S 13.39E
35 F8 Imra Jordan 31.21N 35.41E
37 K2 Imrahor dist Istanbul Turkey 41.01N 29.01E
37 F2 Imralı Turkey 40.34N 28.33E
37 F2 Imralı isld Turkey
33 F10 'Imrān S Yemen 12.45N 44.44E
86 F10 'Imrâni, Wâdi el watercourse Egypt
37 D6 Imranlı Turkey 39.53N 38.54E
Imroz see Gökçe
37 B3 Imroz C Gökçeada Turkey 40.06N 25.50E
Imroz isld see Gökçeada
Imrun see Pütürge
53 U20 Imsland Norway 59.28N 6.00E
65 C7 Imst Austria 47.14N 10.45E
34 D6 Imtān Syria 32.26N 36.50E
41 N7 Imtonzha U.S.S.R. 66.03N 129.30E
115 D2 Imuris Mexico 30.48N 110.52W
19 J6 Imuruan B Philippines
113 D4 Imuruk Basin Alaska
113 F4 Imuruk L Alaska 65.35N 163.14W
19 H2 Imus Luzon Philippines 14.27N 120.56E
95 L8 Imvani S Africa 32.02S 27.03E
35 C6 Imwas Jordan 31.50N 34.59E
21 D10 In S Korea 35.58N 126.52E
40 F7 In R U.S.S.R.
89 L7 Ina Benin 9.57N 2.47E
20 L6 Ina Japan 35.52N 137.58E
62 J2 Ina R Poland
89 J1 In Abeg Mali 20.05N 1.00W
34 D9 'Ināb,El mt Jordan 29.57N 36.57E
89 L2 I-n-Abelene Mali 18.59N 2.25E
34 D8 'Ināb, Wādī al watercourse Jordan
96 A16 Inaccessible I Tristan da Cunha 37.19S 12.44W
123 C15 Inaccessible Is Antarctica 60.45S 53.00W
112 G3 Inadale Texas 32.32N 100.42W
88 S10 In Afaleleh Algeria 23.38N 9.14E
92 H9 Inaga Mozambique 15.14S 37.29E
19 J7 Inagauan Philippines 9.32N 118.38E
20 N4 Ina-gawa R Japan
59 D6 Inagh Clare Irish Rep 52.50N 9.15W
59 C4 Inagh,L Galway Irish Rep 53.31N 9.45W
20 C3 Inagi Tōkyō Japan
116 H4 Inagua, Great I Bahamas
116 H4 Inagua, I., Little Bahamas 21.31N 73.00W
89 E3 In Ahmar Mauritania 17.24N 9.00W
120 B2 Inahuaya Peru 7.09S 75.18W
117 H9 Inajá Brazil 8.54S 37.47W
117 D9 Inaja R Brazil
117 D9 Inaja,Sa.do mts Brazil
89 L2 I-n-Akantarer watercourse Mali/Algeria
89 J2 In Akhmed Mali 19.49N 0.56W
15 L3 Inakona Guadalcanal I Solomon Is 9.54S 160.28E
89 H3 In Alay Mali 17.42N 2.30W
89 N2 I-n-Allarène Gérigéri Niger 18.14N 6.13E
20 N8 Inamba-jima I Japan 33.37N 139.18E
120 D5 Inambari Peru 12.42S 69.42W
120 D5 Inambari, R Peru
88 S7 In Amenas Algeria 28.05N 9.23E
88 Q10 In Amguel Algeria 23.41N 5.09E
20 J8 Inami Japan 33.48N 135.13E
89 G3 In Amzag Mali 16.50N 4.51W
I-nan see Yinan
18 M2 Inanam Sabah Malaysia 6.02N 116.08E
11 F8 Inangahua Junction New Zealand 41.53S 171.58E
113 C10 Inanudak B Aleutian Is
15 B5 Inanwatan Irian Jaya 2.09S 132.14E
39 D3 Inanya R U.S.S.R.
15 J8 Inaorena Papua New Guinea 8.24S 146.44E
88 L4 Inaouene R Morocco
120 D4 Iñapari Peru 10.58S 69.36W
19 L1 Inarajan Guam Pacific Oc 13.17N 144.45E
51 N3 Inari Finland 68.54N 27.05E
51 N3 Inari L Finland
89 M3 I-n-Aridal Niger 17.49N 4.23E
41 J8 Inarigda U.S.S.R. 63.15N 107.40E
51 N3 Inarijärvi L Finland
18 A6 Inas,Gunong mt Pen Malaysia 5.15N 100.56E
20 N7 Inatori Japan 34.46N 139.02E
15 J8 Inauaia Papua New Guinea 8.40S 146.32E
120 E3 Inauini,R Brazil
15 J8 Inawabui Papua New Guinea 8.40S 146.37E
20 O4 Inawashiro Japan 37.35N 140.04E
20 O4 Inawashiro-ko L Japan
88 R9 In Azaoua Algeria 25.42N 6.54E
90 C1 In Azaoua Nigeria 20.46N 7.32E
88 S11 In Azaoua watercourse Niger
89 L2 I-n-Azaraf Mali 19.29N 2.36E
35 G4 'Inba Jordan 32.29N 35.46E
89 K3 I-n-Begouene Mali 16.58N 0.19E
88 O8 In Belbel Algeria 27.54N 1.09E
89 J2 In Beriem Mali 19.23N 0.23W
77 V14 Inca Balearic Is 39.43N 2.54E
120 D12 Inca de Oro Chile 26.43S 70.00W
121 C1 Incahuasi,Nevado pk Arg/Chile 27.03S 68.20W
120 E11 Incahuasi, Salina de salt pan Argentina
121 B2 Inca, Paso del pass Arg/Chile 28.42S 69.45W
57 H6 Ince Cheshire Eng 53.17N 2.50W
36 H1 Ince C Turkey 42.05N 34.55E
36 H4 Incesu Turkey 38.39N 35.12E
59 C7 Inch Kerry Irish Rep 52.09N 9.58W
59 K6 Inch Wexford Irish Rep 52.44N 6.13W
Incha see Incheh
58 G3 Inchbae Lodge Highland Scotland 57.40N 4.41W
58 L5 Inchbare Tayside Scotland 56.47N 2.39W
58 M6 Inchcape Lt. Ho Scotland 56.26N 2.24W
58 K6 Inchcolm isld Fife Scotland 56.02N 3.18W
32 G2 Incheh Iran 37.37N 56.30E
110 G1 Inchelium Washington 48.19N 118.12W
64 L6 Inchenhofen W Germany 48.30N 11.07E
70 O1 Incheville France 50.01N 1.30E
59 G1 Inch I Donegal Irish Rep 55.04N 7.30W
59 E6 Inchicronan L Clare Irish Rep 52.55N 8.54W
59 D8 Inchigeelagh Cork Irish Rep 51.50N 9.08W
59 C8 Inchiquin L Kerry Irish Rep 51.48N 9.41W
59 D6 Inchiquin,L L Clare Irish Rep 52.56N 9.10W
89 B2 Inchiri reg Mauritania
58 K6 Inchkeith isld Scotland 56.02N 3.09W
58 F7 Inch Marnock isld Strathclyde Scotland 55.48N 5.09W
58 G2 Inchnadamph Highland Scotland 58.08N 4.58W
21 D9 Inch'ŏn S Korea 37.30N 126.38E
94 M2 Inchope Mozambique 19.15S 33.59E
39 M2 Inchoun U.S.S.R. 66.16N 170.17W
58 K6 Inchture Tayside Scotland 56.27N 3.11W
69 E3 Inchy France 50.07N 3.30E
Incili see Karasu Turkey
75 C2 Incinillas Spain 42.53N 3.35W
76 E3 Incio Spain 42.39N 7.21W
34 C2 Incirli Turkey 36.40N 35.20E
37 E8 Incir Tepesi pk Turkey 37.42N 39.49E
79 K7 Incisa in Valdarno Italy 43.40N 11.27E
79 D5 Incisa Scapaccino Italy 44.48N 8.23E
94 M5 Incomati R Mozambique
61 K4 Incourt Belgium 50.42N 4.48E
67 P13 Incudine,l' Corsica 41.51N 9.12E
58 D7 Indaal, L Islay, Strathclyde Scotland
89 H1 In Dagouber Mali 22.12N 2.32W
118 F6 Indaiá R Brazil
118 D6 Indaiá Grande R Brazil
52 K4 Indal Sweden 62.34N 17.10E
52 K4 Indalsälven R Sweden
30 G7 Indara Uttar Prad India 26.00N 83.38E
30 B7 Indargarh Madhya Prad India 25.55N 78.34E
29 E5 Indargarh Rajasthan India 25.40N 76.14E
29 L2 Indas W Bengal India 23.07N 87.40E
25 D2 Indaw Burma 21.30N 96.52E
25 M9 Indaw Burma 24.14N 96.07E
28 K4 Indaw Burma 23.40N 94.50E
25 M8 Indawgyi L Burma
115 G5 Indé Mexico 25.53N 105.10W
93 C3 Inde Uganda 2.51N 31.17E
54 M9 Indefatigable oil field North Sea 53.21N 2.30E
Indefatigable I see Santa Cruz, I
66 M7 Indémini Switzerland 46.06N 8.50E
66 G6 Inden Switzerland 46.21N 7.38E
64 A2 Inden W Germany 50.52N 6.21E
111 F5 Independence California 36.48N 118.14W
106 C7 Independence Iowa 42.28N 91.55W
109 P4 Independence Kansas 37.13N 95.43W
107 F11 Independence Louisiana 30.38N 90.30W
107 B2 Independence Missouri 39.04N 94.27W
110 B5 Independence Oregon 44.50N 123.12W
104 D10 Independence Virginia 36.38N 81.11W
106 C5 Independence Wisconsin 44.21N 91.27W
48 T2 Independence Fjord Greenland
110 J9 Independence Mts Nevada
120 E7 Independencia Bolivia 17.08S 66.52W
117 G7 Independência Brazil 5.25S 40.18W
120 B6 Independencia,B.de Peru
Inder see Jalaid Qi
87 E7 Inderacha Ethiopia 7.38N 35.17E
18 E6 Inderagiri R Sumatra Indon
18 D7 Inderapura Sumatra Indon 2.02S 100.56E
18 D7 Inderapura, Tandjung C Sumatra Indonesia 2.08S 100.48E
46 Q5 Inderborskiy Kazakhstan U.S.S.R. 48.32N 51.44E
30 C6 Indergarh Uttar Prad India 26.56N 79.40E
22 J3 Indermeg Mongolia 47.40N 111.05E
Inderöy see Strømmen
46 Q5 Inder, Oz L Kazakhstan U.S.S.R.
22 F6 Indertin Hudag Nei Monggol Zizhiqu China 40.21N 102.53E
66 D2 Indevillers France 47.19N 6.58E
110 D2 Index Washington 47.49N 121.32W
28 C2 Indi Karnataka India 17.13N 76.01E
16 H6 India rep S Asia
109 M7 Indiahoma Oklahoma 34.37N 98.46W
106 H3 Indian L Michigan
106 H3 Indian R Michigan
104 K2 Indian R New York
101 D4 Indian R Yukon Terr
13 D6 Indiana N Terr Australia 23.02S 135.36E
104 F6 Indiana Pennsylvania 40.39N 79.11W
102 J3 Indiana state U.S.A.
26 H11 Indian Antarctic Basin Southern Oc
26 J10 Indian Antarctic Ridge Southern Oc
107 K2 Indianapolis Indiana 39.45N 86.10W
101 H10 Indian Arm inlet Br Col
98 T4 Indian Bay Newfoundland 49.02N 53.52W
98 M7 Indian Brook C Breton I, Nova Scotia 46.22N 60.30W
101 P6 Indian Cabins Alberta 59.50N 117.40W
31 F7 Indian Desert India/Pakistan
103 G1 Indian Fields New York 42.30N 73.56W
97 O7 Indian Harbour Labrador, Nfld 54.25N 57.20W
98 J9 Indian Harbour Nova Scotia 44.30N 63.55W
13 L7 Indian Hd Queensland 25.00S 153.15E
104 H8 Indian Head Maryland 38.37N 77.11W
100 O8 Indian Head Saskatchewan 50.32N 103.41W
104 L3 Indian L New York
104 B6 Indian L Ohio 40.30N 83.54W
104 L3 Indian Lake New York 43.46N 74.16W
100 U1 Indian L., Northern Manitoba
100 T1 Indian L., Southern Manitoba
103 E7 Indian Mills New Jersey 39.47N 74.45W
110 P7 Indian Mt Wyoming 42.17N 110.39W
26 Indian Ocean
108 R8 Indianola Iowa 41.22N 93.32W
107 F8 Indianola Mississippi 33.25N 90.40W
108 K9 Indianola Nebraska 40.16N 100.24W
109 P6 Indianola Oklahoma 35.11N 95.46W
118 F6 Indianópolis Brazil 19.00S 47.57W
118 F10 Indianópolis dist São Paulo Brazil
103 D3 Indian Orchard Pennsylvania 41.33N 75.14W
110 Q5 Indian Pk Wyoming 44.47N 109.52W
111 L3 Indian Pk mt Utah 38.18N 113.53W
56 B7 Indian Queens Cornwall Eng 50.24N 4.55W
105 G9 Indian R Florida
105 G10 Indian River Florida
106 K4 Indian River Michigan 45.25N 84.36W
105 G9 Indian River City Florida 28.33N 80.50W
103 A7 Indian Rock Res Pennsylvania 39.55N 76.47W
111 J5 Indian Springs Nevada 36.33N 115.40W
105 G10 Indiantown Florida 27.02N 80.31W
110 J5 Indian Valley Idaho 44.34N 116.26W
111 O6 Indian Wells Arizona 35.26N 110.05W
118 J2 Indiaroba Brazil 11.31S 37.29W
98 A2 Indicateur L Quebec
91 B6 Indienne, Pte pt Congo 4.40S 11.48E
47 F2 Indiga U.S.S.R. 67.40N 49.00E
39 D1 Indigirka R U.S.S.R.
39 D1 Indigirskaya Nizmennost' lowland U.S.S.R.
39 C3 Indigirskiy U.S.S.R. 64.37N 144.20E
47 F2 Indigskaya Guba gulf U.S.S.R.
82 F5 Indija Yugoslavia 45.03N 20.06E
25 L9 Indin Burma 23.05N 94.06E
101 Q3 Indin L N W Terr
111 H8 Indio California 33.44N 116.14E
119 G7 Indios, Cachoeira dos rapids Brazil 0.55N 63.54W
10 N4 Indispensable Reefs Pacific Oc
15 L3 Indispensable Str Solomon Is
92 E11 Indiva Zimbabwe 19.23S 30.01E
88 P11 In Djezzal Algeria 20.16N 2.10E
16 L7 Indo-China reg S E Asia
16 L9 Indonesia rep S E Asia
13 K2 Indooroopilly dist Brisbane, Qnsld
29 D6 Indore Madhya Prad India 22.42N 75.54E
29 D6 Indore dist Madhya Prad India
18 H9 Indramayu Java Indon 6.22S 108.20E
18 H9 Indramayu, Tanjung C Java Indon 6.16S 108.19E
27 N6 Indravati R India
72 A1 Indre France 47.13N 1.39W
67 F6 Indre dept France
72 G1 Indre R France
67 F5 Indre-et-Loire dept France
30 A3 Indri Haryana India 29.51N 77.02E
105 G10 Indrio Florida 27.32N 80.22W
72 G1 Indrois R France
12 C2 Indulkana R S Australia
91 E11 Indungo Angola 14.50S 16.19E
79 E3 Induno Olona Italy 45.51N 8.50E
Indur see Nizamabad
62 O2 Indura Belorussiya U.S.S.R. 53.27N 23.53E
28 D2 Indurti Andhra Prad India 17.01N 78.55E
100 D8 Indus Alberta 50.57N 113.50W
27 L3 Indus R Pakistan/India
24 C9 Indus R Xizang Zizhiqu
31 G3 Indus Kohistan reg Kashmir/Pakistan
31 D8 Indus, Mouths of the Pakistan
31 E8 Indus R Pakistan
39 F7 Industrial'nyy Kamchatka U.S.S.R. 52.59N 158.45E
64 L5 Industriehafen airport W Germany 49.27N 11.05E
106 D9 Industry Illinois 40.20N 90.37W
112 L6 Industry Texas 30.00N 96.31W
95 L7 Indwe S Africa 31.28S 27.20E
95 L7 Indwe R S Africa
88 R11 In Ebeggi Algeria 21.43N 6.32E
36 G1 Inebolu Turkey 41.57N 33.45E
85 A7 In-Ebrun Algeria 24.25N 11.00E
36 C1 Inece Turkey 41.40N 27.05E
89 H1 I-n-Echaïe Mali 20.07N 2.09W
37 D2 Inecik Turkey 40.57N 27.17E
89 M3 I-n-Eddoui Niger 17.11N 5.26E
89 M2 I-n-Edek Niger 18.12N 4.28E
89 J2 In Edeman Mali 19.52N 0.39W
88 R7 Inedï Algeria 29.03N 7.59E
37 G3 Inegöl Turkey 40.06N 29.31E
36 H2 Inegöl Dağı mt Turkey 40.54N 35.04E
87 E2 Ineibis Sudan 17.58N 34.00E
88 Q9 In Ekker Algeria 24.03N 5.06E
89 K2 I-n-Emsel Mali 19.30N 0.40E
19 B8 Inerie vol Indonesia 8.52S 120.56E
82 G4 Ineu Romania 46.26N 21.51E
72 J2 Ineuil France 46.47N 2.16E
Inevi see Cihanbeyli
15 G7 Inewi Papua New Guinea 7.09S 143.50E
112 L7 Inez Texas 28.56N 96.47W
88 J6 Inezgane Morocco 30.22N 9.38E
85 A8 In-Ezzane Algeria 23.34N 11.10E
88 O11 In Ezzek Mali 20.40N 0.20E
95 D10 Infanta,C S Africa 34.27S 20.51E
119 D4 Infantas Colombia 6.52N 73.52W
77 K3 Infantes Spain 38.45N 3.01W
120 G3 Infernao, Cachoeira rapids Brazil 8.22S 60.46W
120 D12 Infielès,Pta C Chile 26.25S 70.46W
115 H8 Infiernillo,L Mexico
76 J2 Infiesto Spain 43.21N 5.21W
81 K4 Infreschi, Pta. degli Italy 40.00N 15.26E
117 J8 Ingá Brazil 7.15S 35.34W
51 L11 Inga Finland 60.04N 24.03E
91 C6 Inga Zaïre 5.34S 13.39E
25 C4 Ingabu Burma 17.47N 95.15E
89 N3 Ingal Niger 16.51N 7.01E
13 C5 Ingallanna R N Terr Australia
107 L2 Ingalls Indiana 39.57N 85.48W
109 K4 Ingalls Kansas 37.51N 100.27W
106 G4 Ingalls Michigan 45.23N 87.36W
101 V5 Ingalls L N W Terr
111 D2 Ingalls, Mt California 40.00N 120.37W
47 L7 Ingaly U.S.S.R. 55.50N 74.18E
91 G4 Inganda Zaïre 0.05S 20.59E
56 M4 Ingatestone Essex Eng 51.41N 0.22E
90 D5 Ingawa Nigeria 12.45N 8.01E
57 K5 Ingbirchworth S Yorks Eng 53.34N 1.39W
53 W16 Ingeborgfjell mt Norway 61.18N 7.30E
64 H5 Ingelfingen W Germany 49.18N 9.40E
64 E4 Ingelheim W Germany 49.58N 8.04E
61 D3 Ingelmunster Belgium 50.55N 3.16E
60 K12 Ingen Netherlands 51.58N 5.29E
66 L3 Ingenbohl Switzerland 47.01N 8.38E
91 F4 Ingende Zaïre 0.15S 18.58E
121 C5 Ingeniero Balloffet Argentina 34.55S 67.48W
120 G10 Ingeniero Guillermo Nueva Juárez Argentina 23.55S 61.50W
121 B8 Ingeniero Jacobacci Argentina 41.25S 69.37W
121 D5 Ingeniero Luiggi Argentina 35.25S 64.44W
101 L7 Ingenika R Br Col
96 V15 Ingenio Gran Canaria Canary Is 27.56N 15.26W
120 B6 Ingenio, R Peru
113 E7 Ingeramiut Alaska 59.58N 165.40W
69 N7 Ingersheim France 48.06N 7.18E
109 M5 Ingersoll Oklahoma 36.47N 98.25W
99 K9 Ingersoll Ontario 43.03N 80.53W
87 D5 Ingessana Hills Sudan
19 F3 Inggelang isld Moluccas Indon 0.36N 128.38E
22 F6 Inggen Nei Monggol Zizhiqu China 41.27N 104.46E
13 H4 Ingham Queensland 18.35S 146.12E
56 N3 Ingham Suffolk Eng 52.18N 0.43E
43 H7 Ingichka Uzbekistan U.S.S.R. 39.46N 65.59E
40 F2 Ingili U.S.S.R. 58.29N 134.55E
40 G2 Ingili R U.S.S.R.
26 R8 Ingiriya Sri Lanka 6.45N 80.10E
50 B5 Ingjaldshóll Iceland 64.54N 23.52W
57 J4 Ingleborough mt N Yorks Eng 54.10N 2.23W
57 L4 Ingleby Greenhow N Yorks Eng 54.27N 1.06W
13 F6 Ingledoon Queensland 24.00S 140.32E
48 S3 Inglefield Bredning inlet Greenland
97 N2 Inglefield Land Greenland
103 C8 Ingleside Maryland 39.05N 75.53W
99 R2 Ingleside Ontario 45.00N 75.00W
112 K8 Ingleside Texas 27.53N 97.14W
57 K3 Ingleton Durham Eng 54.35N 1.44W
57 J4 Ingleton N Yorks Eng 54.10N 2.27W
111 F8 Inglewood California 33.58N 118.22W
11 J6 Inglewood New Zealand 39.07S 174.13E
13 K8 Inglewood Queensland 28.25S 151.02E
12 G6 Inglewood Victoria 36.35S 143.56E
100 Q8 Inglis Manitoba 50.57N 101.15W
13 D1 Inglis I N Terr Australia
113 G4 Inglutalik R Alaska
42 J6 Ingoda R U.S.S.R.
92 H10 Ingode Mozambique 17.34S 36.42E
95 N3 Ingogo S Africa 27.35S 29.55E
57 O6 Ingoldmells Lincs Eng 53.12N 0.21E
100 G1 Ingolf Ontario 49.47N 95.06W
48 V3 Ingolf Fd Greenland
50 D7 Ingolfsfjall Iceland 63.59N 21.04W
50 J7 Ingólfshöfdhi prom Iceland 63.49N 16.39W
91 E6 Ingololo Zaïre 5.49S 16.53E
64 L6 Ingolstadt W Germany 48.46N 11.27E
108 C3 Ingomar Montana 46.35N 107.21W
12 C3 Ingomer S Australia 29.38S 134.48E
98 M7 Ingonish C Breton I, Nova Scotia 46.42N 60.22W
61 D3 Ingooigem Belgium 50.49N 3.27E
110 C9 Ingot California 40.44N 122.05W
89 H3 In Gouzma Mali 17.37N 2.09W
51 L1 Ingøya isld Norway 71.04N 24.00E
42 A1 Ing-Puta-Yaun-Pugol U.S.S.R. 62.32N 74.30E
112 H5 Ingram Texas 30.05N 99.16W
106 D4 Ingram Wisconsin 45.32N 90.50W
98 H9 Ingramport Nova Scotia 44.40N 64.00W
72 F2 Ingrandes Indre France 46.36N 0.58E
70 J7 Ingrandes Maine-et-Loire France 47.25N 0.55W
72 F2 Ingrandes Vienne France 46.53N 0.34E
101 P3 Ingray L N W Terr
120 F9 Ingre Bolivia 20.32S 63.53W
70 O6 Ingré France 47.56N 1.49E
55 K3 Ingrebourne R London England
123 C4 Ingrid Christensen Coast Antarctica
53 D2 Ingstrup Denmark 57.20N 9.44E
88 Q12 In Guezzam Algeria 19.37N 5.52E
70 D6 Inguiniel France 47.59N 3.17W
45 D9 Ingul R Ukraine U.S.S.R.
45 E9 Ingulets Ukraine U.S.S.R. 47.43N 33.16E
45 D10 Ingulets R Ukraine U.S.S.R.
42 J5 Ingur U.S.S.R. 53.37N 113.46E
44 E5 Inguri R Georgia U.S.S.R.
42 A2 Inguyagun R U.S.S.R.
95 O8 Ingwavuma S Africa 27.08S 32.00E
69 N6 Ingwiller France 48.52N 7.29E
56 O2 Ingworth Norfolk Eng 52.50N 1.15E
94 M6 Inhaca Mozambique 26.01S 32.58E
91 H10 Inhacalenga Angola 12.58S 23.35E

94 M6 **Inhaca Pen** Mozambique
94 M3 **Inhafenga** Mozambique 20.35S 33.53E
94 N4 **Inhambane** Mozambique 23.51S 35.29E
94 N4 **Inhambane** *dist* Mozambique
118 J2 **Inhambupe** Brazil 11.52S 38.22W
118 J3 **Inhambupe,R** Brazil
94 N2 **Inhaminga** Mozambique 18.24S 35.00E
121 G1 **Inhancora** *R* Brazil
118 C7 **Inhanduí Guaçu, R** Brazil
118 C7 **Inhanduízinho,R** Brazil
92 G10 **Inhangoma** Mozambique 17.30S 35.15E
118 G6 **Inhapim** Brazil 19.35S 42.06W
94 N5 **Inharrime** Mozambique 24.29S 35.01E
92 G10 **Inharuca** Mozambique 17.32S 35.04E
94 N3 **Inhassôro** Mozambique 21.32S 35.13E
118 J9 **Inhaúma** Brazil 22.53S 43.18W
118 G3 **Inhaúmas** Brazil 13.03S 44.39W
30 E6 **Inhauna** Uttar Prad India 26.31N 81.28E
36 E2 **Inhisar** Turkey 40.03N 30.22E
118 H4 **Inhobim** Brazil 15.17S 40.59W
91 C6 **Inhuca** Angola 4.48S 12.23E
118 E5 **Inhumas** Brazil 16.23S 49.31W
113 L3 **Iniakuk** *R* Alaska
19 B8 **Inielika** *vol* Indonesia 8.39S 120.57E
77 N2 **Iniesta** Spain 39.27N 1.45W
117 C3 **Inini** Fr Guiana 3.40N 54.00W
117 C3 **Inini** *R* Fr Guiana
88 P11 **In Inirech** Algeria 20.22N 2.36E
51 J11 **Iniö** Finland 60.24N 21.25E
88 N12 **In Irech** Mali 19.34N 0.32W
119 F6 **Inírida,R** Colombia
59 B4 **Inishark** *isld* Galway Irish Rep 53.37N 10.16W
59 F1 **Inishbofin** *isld* Donegal Irish Rep 55.10N 8.10W
59 B4 **Inishbofin** *isld* Galway Irish Rep 53.38N 10.12W
59 D3 **Inishcrone** Sligo Irish Rep 54.13N 9.05W
59 C5 **Inisheer** *isld* Galway Irish Rep 53.03N 9.31W
59 B3 **Inishglora** *isld* Mayo Irish Rep 54.13N 10.07W
59 B3 **Inishkea** *isld* Mayo Irish Rep 54.08N 10.11W
59 C5 **Inishmaan** *isld* Galway Irish Rep 53.05N 9.35W
59 C5 **Inishmore** *isld* Galway Irish Rep 53.07N 9.45W
59 E3 **Inishmurray** *isld* Sligo Irish Rep 54.26N 8.40W
59 H1 **Inishowen** *dist* Donegal Irish Rep 55.13N 7.30W
59 J1 **Inishowen Hd** Donegal Irish Rep 55.09N 6.56W
59 A7 **Inishtooskert** *isld* Kerry Irish Rep 52.08N 10.35W
59 H1 **Inishtrahull** *isld* Donegal Irish Rep 55.27N 7.14W
59 H1 **Inishtrahull Sd** Donegal Irish Rep 55.25N 7.20W
59 B4 **Inishturk** *isld* Mayo Irish Rep 53.43N 10.05W
59 B7 **Inishvickillane** *isld* Kerry Irish Rep 52.03N 10.36W
59 H7 **Inistioge** Kilkenny Irish Rep 52.29N 7.04W
34 M4 **Injānah** Iraq 34.29N 44.38E
22 L4 **Injgan Sum** Nei Monggol Zizhiqu China 44.49N 118.41E
13 J7 **Injune** Queensland 25.53S 148.30E
39 E7 **Inkanyush, Mys** *C* U.S.S.R. 51.16N 157.28E
56 H3 **Inkberrow** Hereford & Worcs Eng 52.13N 1.59W
88 O11 **In Kerett** Mali 20.53N 1.06E
98 H6 **Inkerman** New Brunswick 47.40N 64.51W
13 F3 **Inkerman** Queensland 16.20S 141.21E
51 M11 **Inkeroinen** Finland 60.42N 26.55E
42 C3 **Inkino** U.S.S.R. 58.30N 82.04E
91 D6 **Inkisi** *R* Zaïre
91 D6 **Inkisi Kisantu** Zaïre 5.08S 15.09E
101 G6 **Inklin** Br Col 58.54N 133.08W
101 G6 **Inklin** *R* Br Col
110 N7 **Inkom** Idaho 42.48N 112.15W
91 H6 **Inkongo** Zaïre 4.55S 23.15E
Inkoo *see* **Inga**
89 K2 **I-n-Koufi** Mali 19.11N 1.25E
90 D3 **In Koufouane** Niger 17.10N 8.43E
46 N1 **Inkovo** U.S.S.R. 57.38N 43.20E
95 J4 **Inkpan** *salt pan* S Africa 28.18S 25.51E
108 N1 **Inkster** N Dakota 48.10N 97.39W
42 G6 **Inkur** U.S.S.R. 50.20N 103.20E
43 F7 **Inkylap** Turkmeniya U.S.S.R. 37.51N 61.41E
113 H3 **Inland L** Alaska 66.30N 159.50W
95 L3 **Inlandsee** *L* S Africa 27.04S 27.30E
25 D2 **Inle, L** Burma 20.30N 96.55E
36 F4 **Inler** *R* Turkey
108 M7 **Inman** Nebraska 42.23N 98.31W
104 L2 **Inman** New York 44.35N 74.06W
105 E2 **Inman** S Carolina 35.03N 82.08W
101 O1 **Inman** *R* N W Terr
85 A8 **In-Maradjelah** *dist* Algeria
66 Q5 **Inn** *R* Switzerland
64 P7 **Inn** *R* W Germany/Austria
12 F3 **Innamincka** S Australia 27.47S 140.41E
53 T19 **Innbjoa** Norway 59.40N 5.40E
58 G7 **Innellan** Strathclyde Scotland 55.54N 4.57W
58 K7 **Innerleithen** Borders Scotland 55.38N 3.05W
65 J8 **Inner Leoben** Austria 46.56N 13.43E
57 D3 **Innermessan** Dumfries & Galloway Scotland 54.55N 4.59W
Inner Mongolia *aut reg* China*see* **Nei Monggol Zizhiqu**
58 E4 **Inner Sound** Highland Scotland
63 M8 **Innerste** *R* W Germany
66 J5 **Innertkirchen** Switzerland 46.43N 8.14E
65 F8 **Innervillgraten** Austria 46.49N 12.22E
58 M7 **Innerwick** Lothian Scotland 55.58N 2.24W
53 X14 **Innfjorden** Norway 62.29N 7.35E
52 F3 **Innherad** *reg* Norway
Innien *see* **Aukrug**
64 L7 **Inning** W Germany 48.04N 11.10E
59 E8 **Inniscarra Res** Cork Irish Rep
100 D6 **Innisfail** Alberta 52.01N 113.59W
13 H3 **Innisfail** Queensland 17.30S 146.00E
100 F5 **Innisfree** Alberta 53.24N 111.30W
40 E7 **Innokent'yevka** Amur U.S.S.R. 49.20N 129.37E
40 G7 **Innokent'yevka** Khabarovsk U.S.S.R. 49.41N 136.54E
41 D5 **Innokent'yevskaya** U.S.S.R. 71.37N 83.08E
40 H7 **Innokent'yevskiy** U.S.S.R. 48.37N 140.09E
113 H5 **Innoko** *R* Alaska
20 G7 **Inno-shima** *isld* Japan
50 D6 **Innrihólmur** Iceland 64.19N 21.57W
65 D7 **Innsbruch** Austria 47.17N 11.25E
51 G3 **Innset** Norway 68.41N 18.50E
52 E4 **Innset** Norway 62.44N 10.05E
53 V15 **Innvik** Norway 61.51N 6.38E
39 M2 **Innymney,Gora** *mt* U.S.S.R. 66.04N 173.19W
59 B8 **Inny,R** Kerry Irish Rep
59 G4 **Inny,R** W Meath etc Irish Rep
20 G8 **Ino** Japan 33.33N 133.23E
19 C3 **Inobonto** Celebes Indonesia 0.52N 123.58E
118 D6 **Inocência** Brazil 19.52S 51.58W
120 A12 **Inocentes, Cerro de los** *pk* Juan Fernández, Is Pacific Oc 33.46S 80.45W
109 P5 **Inola** Oklahoma 36.09N 95.31W
15 K8 **Inonda** Papua New Guinea 8.49S 148.22E
91 F4 **Inongo** Zaïre 1.55S 18.20E
119 D8 **Inonias** Peru 1.06S 74.02W
36 E3 **İnönü** Turkey 39.49N 30.07E
13 G4 **Inorunie** Queensland 18.12S 142.40E
41 D2 **Inostrantseva, Zaliv** *B* Novaya Zemlya U.S.S.R.
119 E1 **Inosu** Colombia 12.18N 71.43W
97 M6 **Inoucdjouac** Quebec 58.25N 78.15W
88 Q11 **In Oudad** Algeria 20.17N 4.38E
88 P11 **In Ouzzal** Algeria 20.41N 2.34E
62 L3 **Inowrocław** Poland 52.49N 18.12E
120 E7 **Inquisivi** Bolivia 16.55S 67.10W
88 P10 **In Rabir** Algeria 23.48N 3.53E
88 Q12 **In Rahir** Algeria 19.54N 4.20E
88 P9 **In Rellal** Algeria 25.42N 2.03E
88 O8 **In Rhar** Algeria 27.08N 1.54E
66 E3 **Ins** Switzerland 47.01N 7.07E
88 R9 **In Sakane** Algeria 24.06N 6.50E
88 P8 **In Salah** Algeria 27.12N 2.29E
45 Q3 **Insar** U.S.S.R. 53.53N 44.20E
45 R2 **Insar** *R* U.S.S.R.
58 L4 **Insch** Grampian Scotland 57.21N 2.36W
60 J7 **Inschot** *channel* Netherlands
14 A7 **Inscription,C** W Australia 25.29S 113.00E
12 M8 **Inscription Pt** New S Wales 34.00S 151.14E
25 D4 **Insein** Burma 16.54N 96.08E
64 J2 **Inselsberg** *mt* E Germany 50.51N 10.28E
58 J4 **Insh** Highland Scotland 57.06N 3.57W
90 D7 **Inshar** Nigeria 8.45N 9.42E
86 F5 **Inshâs El Raml** Egypt 30.23N 31.28E
58 J4 **Insh,L** Highland Scotland 57.07N 3.56W
100 O7 **Insinger** Saskatchewan 51.31N 103.07W
92 D11 **Insiza** Zimbabwe 19.44S 29.12E
92 D12 **Insiza** *dist* Zimbabwe
92 D11 **Insiza** *R* Zimbabwe
57 H5 **Inskip** Lancs Eng 53.51N 2.50W
62 J2 **Insko** Poland 53.27N 15.32E
69 M6 **Insming** France 48.57N 6.52E
88 P7 **In Sokki** *watercourse* Algeria
53 T17 **Instefjord** Norway 60.58N 5.30E
Insterburg *see* **Chernyakhovsk**
53 W18 **Instestølen** Norway 60.27N 7.25E
77 L7 **Instinción** Spain 37.00N 2.39W
56 C5 **Instow** Devon Eng 51.03N 4.10W
100 J9 **Instow** Saskatchewan 49.45N 108.15W
89 J9 **Insu** Ghana 5.43N 1.53W
82 L6 **Insurăţei** Romania 44.55N 27.40E
47 J3 **Inta** U.S.S.R. 66.04N 60.01E
89 K2 **I-n-Tabedog** Mali 19.48N 1.11E
89 N2 **In Tadreft** Niger 19.05N 6.38E
88 P9 **In Tafineg** Algeria 24.24N 3.17E
108 F2 **Intake** Montana 47.19N 104.32W
89 L3 **In Talak** Mali 16.22N 3.20E
89 K3 **In Tasit** Mali 17.30N 0.11E
89 K3 **In Tebezas** Mali 17.49N 1.53E
121 D5 **Intendente Alvear** Argentina 35.12S 63.32W
36 B2 **İntepe** Turkey 40.01N 26.19E
108 J6 **Interior** S Dakota 43.42N 101.59W
105 F8 **Interlachen** Florida 29.35N 81.55W
66 H5 **Interlaken** Switzerland 46.42N 7.52E
12 H8 **Interlaken** Tasmania 42.08S 147.08E
108 R1 **International Falls** Minnesota 48.38N 93.26W
100 R10 **International Peace Garden** Canada/U.S.A. 49.00N 100.05W
101 O9 **Intersection Mt** Alberta/Br Col 53.49N 119.59W
28 G6 **Interview I** Andaman Is
88 P11 **In Tideini** Algeria 20.27N 3.25E
121 E2 **Intiyaco** Argentina 28.43S 60.04W
42 B2 **Intletovy** U.S.S.R. 61.36N 75.09E
82 K5 **Intorsura Buzăuli** Romania 45.40N 26.02E
Intra *see* **Verbania**
107 D12 **Intracoastal Waterway** Louisiana etc
66 L8 **Intragna** Italy 45.59N 8.35E
66 L7 **Intragna** Switzerland 46.11N 8.42E
79 F3 **Intróbio** Italy 45.58N 9.27E
80 J4 **Introdacqua** Italy 42.00N 13.55E
63 G8 **Intrup** W Germany 52.11N 7.53E
47 E3 **Intsy** U.S.S.R. 65.56N 40.45E
18 L6 **Intu** Borneo Indon 0.15S 115.23E
92 C11 **Intundhla** Zimbabwe 18.55S 27.14E
92 J9 **Intute** Mozambique 14.08S 39.55E
119 D9 **Intutu** Peru 3.33S 74.53W
43 O4 **Intymak** Kazakhstan U.S.S.R. 46.28N 80.45E
20 O6 **Inubō-saki** *C* Japan 35.41N 140.52E
97 O3 **Inugsulik Bugt** *B* Greenland
20 E8 **Inukai** Japan 33.04N 131.38E
101 R2 **Inulik L** N W Terr
20 A2 **Inume** Tōkyō Japan
121 K9 **Inútil,B** Chile
101 G1 **Inuvik** N W Terr 68.16N 133.40W
120 C4 **Inuya** Peru 10.38S 73.38W
120 C4 **Inuya,R** Peru
47 H6 **In'va** *R* U.S.S.R.
59 F2 **Inver** Donegal Irish Rep 54.39N 8.17W
58 N3 **Inverallochy** Grampian Scotland 57.40N 1.55W
58 F6 **Inveraray** Strathclyde Scotland 56.13N 5.05W
58 G6 **Inverarnan** Central Scotland 56.20N 4.44W
58 G6 **Inverbeg** Strathclyde Scotland 56.08N 4.40W
58 M5 **Inverbervie** Grampian Scotland 56.51N 2.17W
11 C13 **Invercargill** New Zealand 46.26S 168.21E
95 C9 **Inverdoorn** S Africa 33.07S 19.49E
12 K3 **Inverell** New S Wales 29.46S 151.10E
58 J5 **Inverey** Grampian Scotland 56.59N 3.32W
58 H4 **Inverfarigaig** Highland Scotland 57.17N 4.28W
58 H3 **Invergordon** Highland Scotland 57.42N 4.10W
58 K6 **Invergowrie** Tayside Scotland 56.28N 3.04W
58 K5 **Inverharity** Tayside Scotland 56.46N 3.20W
58 E4 **Inverie** Highland Scotland 57.03N 5.41W
66 N9 **Inverigo** Italy 45.45N 9.15E
58 F4 **Inverinate** Highland Scotland 57.14N 5.28W
58 L5 **Inverkeilor** Tayside Scotland 56.38N 2.33W
58 K6 **Inverkeithing** Fife Scotland 56.02N 3.25W
58 G7 **Inverkip** Strathclyde Scotland 55.55N 4.52W
58 F2 **Inverkirkaig** Highland Scotland 58.08N 5.16W
58 F3 **Inverlael** Highland Scotland 57.49N 5.04W
13 F4 **Inverleigh** Queensland 18.00S 140.34E
100 O7 **Invermay** Saskatchewan 51.47N 103.09W
101 P10 **Invermere** Br Col 50.30N 116.00W
58 G4 **Invermoriston** Highland Scotland 57.13N 4.38W
98 L7 **Inverness** C Breton I, Nova Scotia 46.14N 61.19W
105 E9 **Inverness** Florida 28.51N 82.21W
58 H4 **Inverness** Highland Scotland 57.27N 4.15W
110 P1 **Inverness** Montana 48.33N 110.40W
99 T6 **Inverness** Quebec 46.15N 71.34W
Inverness *co see* **Highland** *reg*
58 H3 **Inverness,Firth of** Highland Scotland
58 F5 **Inversanda** Highland Scotland 56.41N 5.22W
58 H3 **Invershin** Highland Scotland 57.55N 4.25W
58 G6 **Inversnaid** Central Scotland 56.14N 4.42W
58 M4 **Inverurie** Grampian Scotland 57.17N 2.23W
13 A4 **Inverway** N Terr Australia 17.49S 129.40E
25 D6 **Investigator Chan** Burma
12 C5 **Investigator Group** *islds* S Aust
17 H10 **Investigator Shoal** S China Sea
12 D6 **Investigator Str** S Australia
28 G7 **Invisible Bank** Andaman Is
66 K8 **Invorio** Italy 45.46N 8.29E
110 D9 **Inwood** California 40.34N 121.56W
108 O6 **Inwood** Iowa 43.19N 96.28W
99 J10 **Inwood** Ontario 42.48N 81.59W
95 M7 **Inxu** *R* S Africa
42 D6 **Inya** Gorno-Altay U.S.S.R. 50.24N 86.47E
39 C5 **Inya** Khabarovsk U.S.S.R. 59.23N 144.46E
39 C5 **Inya** *R* Khabarovsk U.S.S.R.
42 C4 **Inya** *R* Novosibirsk U.S.S.R.
39 C2 **Inyali** *R* U.S.S.R.
92 F11 **Inyanga** Zimbabwe 18.13S 32.46E
92 F11 **Inyanga** *dist* Zimbabwe
92 F11 **Inyanga Nat.Park** Zimbabwe
92 F11 **Inyangani** *mt* Zimbabwe 18.18S 32.54E
108 F5 **Inyan Kara Cr** Wyoming
92 C11 **Inyantue** Zimbabwe 18.33S 26.39E
95 P3 **Inyati** S Africa 27.49S 31.04E
92 D11 **Inyati** Zimbabwe 19.39S 28.54E
92 F11 **Inyazura** Zimbabwe 18.39S 32.16E
111 G6 **Inyokern** California 35.39N 117.48W
111 F4 **Inyo Mts** California
92 F5 **Inyonga** Tanzania 6.43S 32.02E
25 M9 **Inywa** Burma 23.57N 96.18E
45 S3 **Inza** U.S.S.R. 53.51N 46.21E
45 R3 **Inza** *R* U.S.S.R.
88 N8 **Inzegmir** Algeria 27.06N 0.05W
89 K3 **I-n-Zekouane** Mali 16.39N 0.36E
64 O8 **Inzell** W Germany 47.45N 12.46E
47 H8 **Inzer** U.S.S.R. 54.12N 57.31E
47 H8 **Inzer** *R* U.S.S.R.
45 O4 **Inzhavino** U.S.S.R. 52.20N 42.30E
91 E6 **Inzia** *R* Zaïre
70 D6 **Inzinzac-Lochrist** France 47.51N 3.16W
Io *vol see* **Ebeko** *Vol*
84 A2 **Ioánnina** Greece 39.40N 20.51E
84 A2 **Ioánnina** *prov* Greece
84 A2 **Ioanninon** *L* Greece
101 H11 **Ioco** Br Col 49.18N 122.53W
83 H9 **Ioinianísia** *isld* Greece 35.48N 26.25E
Iō Jima *see* **Iō Tō**
21 J12 **Iōjima** *isld* Kazan-Rettō Pacific Oc 24.47N 141.19E
21 E12 **Iō-jima** *isld* Osumi-Guntō Japan 30.50N 130.20E
47 D2 **Iokanga** U.S.S.R. 68.00N 39.46E
47 D2 **Iokanga** *R* U.S.S.R.
15 J8 **Iokea** Papua New Guinea 8.22S 146.15E
109 C3 **Iola** Colorado 38.27N 107.05W
109 P4 **Iola** Kansas 37.57N 95.56W
103 A4 **Iola** Pennsylvania 41.09N 76.31W
112 L5 **Iola** Texas 30.46N 96.05W
79 L5 **Iolanda di Savoia** Italy 44.53N 11.59E
42 D6 **Iolgo,Khrebet** *mts* U.S.S.R.
43 F8 **Iolotan'** Turkmeniya U.S.S.R. 37.17N 62.19E
15 J8 **Ioma** Papua New Guinea 8.20S 147.51E
91 C12 **Iona** Angola 16.54S 12.34E
98 M8 **Iona** C Breton I, Nova Scotia 45.55N 60.49W
110 O6 **Iona** Idaho 43.33N 111.56W
108 P6 **Iona** Minnesota 43.56N 95.46W
103 B6 **Iona** Pennsylvania 40.19N 76.21W
108 L6 **Iona** S Dakota 43.31N 99.24W
58 D6 **Iona** *isld* Strathclyde Scotland 56.19N 6.25W
82 L6 **Ion Corvin** Romania 44.07N 27.50E
111 G3 **Ione** Nevada 38.57N 117.35W
110 F4 **Ione** Oregon 45.30N 119.49W
110 H1 **Ione** Washington 48.45N 117.25W
82 J6 **Ioneşti** Romania 44.52N 24.12E
91 H2 **Iongerloo St Norbert** Zaïre 2.35N 23.41E
91 E8 **Iongo** Angola 9.11S 17.45E
108 S6 **Ionia** Iowa 43.01N 92.27W
106 J7 **Ionia** Michigan 42.58N 85.06W
107 C3 **Ionia** Missouri 38.31N 93.20W
Ionian Islands *see* **Iónioi Nísoi.**
83 B6 **Ionian Sea** S Europe
83 D5 **Iónioi Nísoi** *islds* Greece
39 M2 **Ioniveyem** *R* U.S.S.R.
84 C2 **Ion Míkani** *R* Greece
87 J10 **Ionti** Somalia 0.05S 42.33E
81 L6 **Ioppolo** Italy 38.35N 15.54E
81 G9 **Ioppolo Giancaxio** Sicily 37.24N 13.34E
44 G6 **Iora** *R* U.S.S.R.
43 K7 **Iordan** Tadzhikistan U.S.S.R. 40.00N 71.46E
15 H7 **Iori** Papua New Guinea 7.32S 145.28E
44 G6 **Iori** *R* Georgia U.S.S.R.
83 G8 **Ios** Greece 36.44N 25.16E
83 G8 **Ios** *isld* Greece 36.44N 25.16E
47 G4 **Iosser** U.S.S.R. 62.54N 52.00E
20 N9 **Iō Tō** *isld* Japan
89 A2 **Iouik,C** Mauritania 19.45N 16.16W
107 C11 **Iowa** Louisiana 30.12N 93.01W
102 H2 **Iowa** *state* U.S.A.
106 C8 **Iowa City** Iowa 41.39N 91.31W
108 R7 **Iowa Falls** Iowa 42.28N 93.16W
112 J2 **Iowa Park** Texas 33.57N 98.41W
106 B8 **Iowa,R** Iowa
106 C6 **Iowa,R.,Upper** Iowa
115 P10 **Ipala** Guatemala 14.38N 89.38W
93 D10 **Ipala** Tanzania 4.29S 32.52E
26 R5 **Ipalogama** Sri Lanka 8.05N 80.30E
118 E5 **Ipameri** Brazil 17.44S 48.09W
118 H6 **Ipanema** Minas Gerais Brazil 19.52S 41.38W
118 J10 **Ipanema** Rio de Janeiro Brazil 22.59S 43.12W
117 H9 **Ipanema** *R* Brazil
117 H7 **Ipanguacu** Brazil 5.30S 36.52W
120 C3 **Iparía** Peru 9.17S 74.29W
121 J2 **Ipateva, L** Brazil
84 D4 **Ipáti** Greece 38.52N 22.14E
118 G6 **Ipatinga** Brazil 19.32S 42.30W
44 E2 **Ipatovo** U.S.S.R. 45.44N 42.56E
106 D9 **Ipava** Illinois 40.22N 90.19W
I-pei *see* **Minglun**
62 L7 **Ipel'** *R* Hungary/Czech
113 E2 **Ipewik** *R* Alaska
64 J4 **Iphofen** W Germany 49.42N 10.17E
119 C7 **Ipiales** Colombia 0.52N 77.38W
118 H4 **Ipiaú** Brazil 14.07S 39.43W
118 H3 **Ipirá** Brazil 12.15S 39.46W
119 E9 **Ipiranga** Amazonas Brazil 3.02N 69.36W
119 G9 **Ipiranga** Amazonas Brazil 3.13S 66.00W
120 G1 **Ipiranga** Amazonas Brazil 4.15S 61.37W
118 E9 **Ipiranga** Paraná Brazil 24.59S 50.41W
118 G10 **Ipiranga** *dist* São Paulo Brazil
83 D5 **Ipiros** *div* Greece
120 C2 **Ipixuna** Amazonas Brazil 7.34S 72.37W
117 F7 **Ipixuna** Maranhão Brazil 4.25S 44.40W
120 C2 **Ipixuna,R** Amazonas Brazil
120 F2 **Ipixuna,R** Amazonas Brazil
120 G2 **Ipixuna,R** Amazonas Brazil
117 C7 **Ipixuna,R** Pará Brazil
19 J1 **Ipo** Luzon Philippines 14.53N 121.07E
19 J1 **Ipo Dam** Luzon Philippines 14.53N 121.08E
18 B7 **Ipoh** Pen Malaysia 4.36N 101.02E
117 J9 **Ipojuca** *R* Brazil
92 F4 **Ipole** Tanzania 5.48S 32.49E
19 H7 **Ipolote B** Philippines
118 D5 **Iporá** Brazil 16.25S 51.07W
118 E9 **Iporanga** Brazil 24.34S 48.38W
46 G4 **Ippa** *R* Belorussiya U.S.S.R.
99 J9 **Ipperwash Prov.Park** Ontario 43.12N 81.57W
64 J4 **Ippesheim** W Germany 49.36N 10.15E
90 K8 **Ippy** Cent Afr Rep 6.05N 21.07E
37 C2 **Ipsala** Turkey 40.56N 26.23E
64 J4 **Ipsheim** W Germany 49.32N 10.30E
37 D5 **Ipsile** Turkey 40.13N 37.34E
84 E7 **Ipsilí** *isld* Greece 37.26N 22.58E
84 D6 **Ipsoús** Greece 37.33N 22.05E
57 K6 **Ipstones** Staffs Eng 53.03N 1.58W
116 H1 **Ipswich** Jamaica, W I 18.12N 77.50W
104 P4 **Ipswich** Massachusetts 42.41N 70.51W
13 L8 **Ipswich** Queensland 27.38S 152.40E
108 L4 **Ipswich** S Dakota 45.30N 99.01W
56 O3 **Ipswich** Suffolk Eng 52.04N 1.10E
117 G7 **Ipu** Brazil 4.23S 40.44W
117 G7 **Ipueiras** Ceará Brazil 4.31S 40.45W
118 E2 **Ipueiras** Goiás Brazil 11.13S 48.27W
18 D7 **Ipuh** Sumatra Indon 2.58S 101.28E
121 A10 **Ipún** *isld* Chile 44.35S 74.50W
118 G2 **Ipupiara** Brazil 11.51S 42.38W
92 D7 **Ipusukilo** Zambia 10.22S 30.00E
45 C4 **Iput'** *R* U.S.S.R.
22 C7 **Iqe** Qinghai China 38.04N 94.24E
22 C7 **Iqe He** *R* Qinghai China
Iqlid *see* **Eqlid**
118 B3 **Iquê,R** Brazil
120 D9 **Iquique** Chile 20.15S 70.08W
Iquiri,R *see* **Ituxi,R**
119 D9 **Iquitos** Peru 3.51S 73.13W
35 F6 **'Ira** Jordan 31.59N 35.40E
89 H5 **Ira** Mali 13.12N 3.32W
112 F5 **Iraan** Texas 30.42N 101.56W
75 H2 **Irabia, Embalse de** *res* Spain 43.00N 1.10W
89 L3 **Iracher Zegueren** *watercourse* Mali
117 C2 **Iracoubo** Fr Guiana 5.28N 53.15W
32 J7 **Irafshān** Iran 26.43N 61.58E
32 J7 **Irafshān** *reg* Iran
66 M6 **Iragna** Switzerland 46.19N 8.58E
20 L7 **Irago-misaki** *C* Japan 34.35N 137.01E
35 D8 **'Ira, Hare** *hills* Israel
118 D10 **Iraí** Brazil 27.15S 53.17W
32 F4 **Irāj** Iran 33.24N 54.50E
118 H8 **Irajá** Brazil 22.50S 43.20W
118 H8 **Irajá** *R* Brazil
26 U7 **Irakkamam** Sri Lanka 7.15N 81.45E
83 G8 **Iráklia** *isld* Greece 36.50N 25.28E
84 M11 **Iráklion** Crete 35.20N 25.08E
84 L11 **Iráklion** *prov* Crete
121 E5 **Irala** Argentina 34.45S 60.43W
118 C9 **Irala** Paraguay 25.55S 54.35W
118 H3 **Iramaia** Brazil 13.17S 41.01W
93 E7 **Iramba** Tanzania 2.00S 33.26E
92 G4 **Iramba** *tribe* Tanzania
16 F5 **Iran** *kingdom* S W Asia
26 Q3 **Iranaitivu** *isld* Sri Lanka 9.17N 79.58E
26 R3 **Iranamadu** Sri Lanka 9.21N 80.24E
26 R3 **Iranamadu Tank** Sri Lanka
118 D10 **Irani** *R* Brazil
18 K5 **Iran Penunungan** *mts* Kalimantan/Sarawak
16 F5 **Iran,Plat of** Iran
34 O2 **Irānshāh** Iran 36.08N 46.44E
32 J7 **Irānshahr** Iran 27.15N 60.41E
Irānshahr Kermān Iran*see* **Fahraj**
88 Q8 **Iraouene,Djebel** *mts* Algeria
92 G4 **Iraow** *tribe* Tanzania
119 H2 **Irapa** Venezuela 10.37N 62.35W
115 J7 **Irapuato** Mexico 20.40N 101.30W
'Irāq *see* **Arāk**
Iraq Iran*see* **Irāj**
35 F9 **Iraq** Jordan 31.05N 35.38E
27 E3 **Iraq** *rep* S W Asia
34 D9 **Iraq,Al** *hill* Saudi Arabia 29.24N 36.52E
35 G6 **'Iraq el Amir** Jordan 31.55N 35.45E
118 J3 **Irará** Brazil 12.05S 38.42W
88 Q8 **Irarrarem** *reg* Algeria
104 N2 **Irasburg** Vermont 44.47N 72.19W
117 C5 **Iratapuru** *R* Brazil
118 E9 **Irati** Brazil 25.25S 50.38W
75 H2 **Irati** *R* Spain
15 B4 **Irau, Mt** Irian Jaya 0.38S 132.56E
85 A6 **Irāwan** *watercourse* Libya
47 H4 **Irayel'** U.S.S.R. 64.23N 55.25E
90 C3 **Irayène** Niger 16.28N 7.51E
115 N5 **Irazú, Vol** *pk* Costa Rica 9.59N 83.52W
42 F3 **Irba** U.S.S.R. 58.09N 99.01E
42 F4 **Irbeyskoye** U.S.S.R. 55.40N 95.30E
35 G3 **Irbid** Jordan 32.33N 35.51E
47 J6 **Irbit** U.S.S.R. 57.44N 63.02E
47 J6 **Irbit** *R* U.S.S.R.
57 N5 **Irby** Humberside Eng 53.32N 0.12W
57 O6 **Irby** Lincs Eng 53.09N 0.12E
66 L1 **Irchel** *hill* Switzerland 47.33N 8.36E
61 F4 **Irchonwelz** Belgium 50.37N 3.46E
65 K6 **Irdning** Austria 47.32N 14.07E
45 C7 **Irdyn'** Ukraine U.S.S.R. 49.21N 31.45E
91 E4 **Irebu** Zaïre 0.40S 17.46E
57 G3 **Ireby** Cumbria Eng 54.44N 3.11W
118 H2 **Irecê** Brazil 11.22S 41.51W
87 M5 **Iredame** Somalia 10.30N 49.21E
112 K4 **Iredell** Texas 31.58N 97.50W
75 F3 **Iregua** *R* Spain
41 K9 **Irelakh** *R* U.S.S.R.
112 K4 **Ireland** Texas 31.34N 97.58W
96 B1 **Ireland I** Bermuda
49 C6 **Ireland, Republic of** W Europe
59 K5 **Ireland's Eye** *isld* Dublin Irish Rep 53.25N 6.04W
57 G4 **Ireleth** Cumbria Eng 54.11N 3.12W
42 J2 **Irelyakh** *R* U.S.S.R.
91 J4 **Irema** Zaïre 0.23S 24.14E
47 H7 **Iren** *R* U.S.S.R.
121 E7 **Irene** Argentina 38.31S 60.45W
95 M1 **Irene** S Africa 25.53S 28.13E
108 N6 **Irene** S Dakota 43.06N 97.10W
119 J5 **Ireng,R** Brazil/Guyana
37 E6 **Iresi** Turkey 39.08N 39.53E
39 E4 **Iret'** U.S.S.R. 60.03N 154.20E
108 O7 **Ireton** Iowa 42.58N 96.20W
39 E4 **Iretskiy Liman** *lagoon* U.S.S.R.
44 F3 **Irgakly** U.S.S.R. 44.21N 44.45E
35 A2 **Ir Ganim** *dist* Jerusalem
42 J6 **Irgen', Ozero** *L* U.S.S.R. 52.05N 112.30E
43 F3 **Irgiz** Kazakhstan U.S.S.R. 48.36N 61.14E
43 F3 **Irgiz** *R* Kazakhstan U.S.S.R.
81 D3 **Irgoli di Galtelli** Sardinia 40.24N 9.38E
88 O11 **Irharen** Algeria 21.35N 1.00E
88 Q9 **Irharhar** *watercourse* Algeria
88 R5 **Irharhar** *watercourse* Algeria
88 R11 **Irharrhar** *watercourse* Algeria
89 N3 **Irhazer Wan Agadès** *watercourse* Niger
88 J6 **Irherm** Morocco 30.04N 8.26W
84 F7 **Iria** Greece 37.29N 23.00E
15 C5 **Irian Jaya** *prov* Indonesia
Irian,West *see* **Irian Jaya**
90 L4 **Iriba** Chad 15.10N 22.11E
39 B1 **Irichan** *R* U.S.S.R.
117 A4 **Iricoumé, Sa** *mts* Brazil
32 B1 **Iri Dagh** *mt* Iran 38.29N 46.11E
19 L5 **Iriga** Luzon Philippines 13.26N 123.24E
76 C3 **Irijo** Spain 42.32N 8.06W
76 C2 **Irijoa** Spain 43.17N 8.04W
43 E2 **Iriklinskiy** U.S.S.R. 51.38N 58.37E
92 G5 **Iringa** Tanzania 7.49S 35.39E
92 G6 **Iringa** *reg* Tanzania
37 E7 **Iringil** Turkey 38.27N 39.03E
37 G7 **Irini Dağ** *mt* Turkey 38.43N 43.11E
28 C5 **Irinjalakuda** Kerala India 10.22N 76.14E
23 K6 **Iriomoteshima** *isld* Japan
115 M2 **Iriona** Honduras 15.55N 85.10W
117 C9 **Iriri Novo** *R* Brazil
117 C6 **Iriri,R** Brazil
Irish Rep *see* **Ireland, Rep of**
54 G9 **Irish Sea** Gt Britain/Ireland
12 G8 **Irishtown** Tasmania 40.57S 144.43E
72 B9 **Irissarry** France 43.15N 1.13W
95 C7 **Iritsoka** Madagascar 23.05S 46.05E
117 E5 **Irituia** Brazil 1.45S 47.26W
33 H3 **Irj** Saudi Arabia 26.20N 48.56E
35 F4 **Irjan** Jordan 32.24N 35.44E
86 G8 **Irkâs, Wâdi** *watercourse* Egypt
43 L7 **Irkeshtam** Kirgiziya U.S.S.R. 39.40N 73.58E
42 F3 **Irkineyeva** *R* U.S.S.R.
42 F3 **Irkineyevo** U.S.S.R. 58.31N 96.57E
45 D7 **Irkleyev** Ukraine U.S.S.R. 49.32N 32.19E
42 G6 **Irkut** *R* U.S.S.R.
42 G6 **Irkutsk** U.S.S.R. 52.18N 104.15E
38 K3 **Irkutskaya Oblast'** *prov* U.S.S.R.
57 J6 **Irlam** Greater Manchester Eng 53.28N 2.25W
100 F6 **Irma** Alberta 52.56N 111.11W
106 E4 **Irma** Wisconsin 45.21N 89.40W
36 G3 **Irmak** Turkey 39.59N 33.24E
64 E2 **Irmgarteichen** W Germany 50.52N 8.10E
81 J10 **Irminio** *R* Sicily
105 F3 **Irmo** S Carolina 34.03N 81.11W
60 M7 **Irnsum** Netherlands 53.05N 5.47E
70 G5 **Irodouer** France 48.15N 1.57W
70 A5 **Iroise** *gulf* France
90 J6 **Iro,L** Chad 10.05N 19.24E
12 D5 **Iron Baron** S Australia 32.58S 137.09E
15 L3 **Iron Bottom Sd** Solomon Is
99 G6 **Iron Bridge** Ontario 46.16N 83.13W
56 G2 **Ironbridge** Shropshire Eng 52.38N 2.30W
110 C9 **Iron Canyon Res** California
107 J6 **Iron City** Tennessee 35.02N 87.33W
113 E4 **Iron Cr** Alaska 64.57N 164.40W
107 F4 **Irondale** Missouri 37.50N 90.40W
104 E6 **Irondale** Ohio 40.34N 80.44W
99 M8 **Irondale** Ontario 44.53N 78.30W
Iron Gate *gorge see* **Portile de Fier**
12 D5 **Iron Knob** S Australia 32.44S 137.08E
59 H4 **Iron,L** W Meath Irish Rep 53.37N 7.28W
92 E11 **Iron Mine Hill** Zimbabwe 19.19S 30.25E
106 F4 **Iron Mountain** Michigan 45.51N 88.03W
110 A7 **Iron Mt** Oregon 42.42N 124.07W
111 L4 **Iron Mt** Utah 37.39N 113.24W
59 G3 **Iron Mts** Leitrim, etc Irish Rep
108 L5 **Iron Nation** S Dakota 44.07N 99.45W
13 G2 **Iron Range** Queensland 12.39S 143.13E
106 F6 **Iron Ridge** Wisconsin 43.24N 88.33W
106 F3 **Iron River** Michigan 46.05N 88.38W
106 C3 **Iron River** Wisconsin 46.34N 91.04W
106 J5 **Irons** Michigan 44.08N 85.55W
110 H5 **Ironside** Oregon 44.20N 117.58W
99 C8 **Ironside** Quebec 45.30N 75.44W
111 L4 **Iron Springs** Utah 37.45N 113.13W
106 J4 **Ironton** Michigan 45.14N 85.12W
107 F4 **Ironton** Missouri 37.37N 90.40W
106 D3 **Ironwood** Michigan 46.25N 90.07W
99 P8 **Iroquois** Ontario 44.51N 75.19W
108 N5 **Iroquois** S Dakota 44.24N 97.51W
99 P2 **Iroquois Dam** Ontario 44.50N 75.19W
99 K4 **Iroquois Falls** Ontario 48.47N 80.41W
106 G9 **Iroquois,R** Illinois
19 M5 **Irosin** Luzon Philippines 12.41N 124.01E
20 M7 **Irō-zaki** *C* Japan 34.36N 138.48E
45 B6 **Irpen'** Ukraine U.S.S.R. 50.31N 30.29E
46 G4 **Irpen'** *R* Ukraine U.S.S.R.
80 L7 **Irpinia** *reg* Italy
33 G6 **'Irq Abū Faqār** *sand ridge* Saudi Arabia
33 G10 **'Irqah** S Yemen 13.39N 47.20E
85 F5 **'Irq, al** Libya 29.05N 21.30E
33 G3 **'Irq al Harūrī** *sand ridge* Saudi Arabia
33 E3 **'Irq al Mazhūr** *dune area* Saudi Arabia
33 H6 **'Irq al Qasbā'** Saudi Arabia 21.04N 48.30E
'Irq as Subai *see* **'Irq Subay** *Sand Dunes*
33 G4 **'Irq ath Thāmām** *sand ridge* Saudi Arabia
33 G4 **'Irq Banbān** *sand dunes* Saudi Arabia
33 G3 **'Irq Jahām** *sand ridge* Saudi Arabia
33 E5 **'Irq Subay** *sand dunes* Saudi Arabia
Irqu *see* **'Irqah**
12 D3 **Irrapatana** S Australia 29.05S 136.32E
25 C4 **Irrawaddy** *div* Burma
25 C2 **Irrawaddy** *R* Burma
25 C5 **Irrawaddy,Mouths of the** Burma
64 A4 **Irrel** W Germany 49.51N 6.29E
61 P6 **Irrhausen** W Germany 50.05N 6.12E
100 D7 **Irricana** Alberta 51.19N 113.33W
89 G3 **Irrigi** *reg* Mali/Mauritania
Irrsee *see* **Zellersee**
43 D6 **Irsarybaba,Gory** *mts* Turkmeniya U.S.S.R.
64 K8 **Irsee** W Germany 47.55N 10.35E
42 E4 **Irsha** U.S.S.R. 55.54N 94.49E
31 H2 **Irshad Pass** Kashmir/Afghan 36.53N 74.10E
82 H2 **Irshava** U.S.S.R. 48.20N 23.02E
81 M2 **Irsina** Italy 40.44N 16.15E
47 F5 **Irta** U.S.S.R. 62.05N 48.52E
75 L7 **Irta,Sierra de** *mts* Spain
57 H2 **Irthing,R** Northumb/Cumbria Eng
56 K3 **Irthlingborough** Northants Eng 52.20N 0.37W
47 M5 **Irtyash,Oz** *L* U.S.S.R. 55.50N 60.45E
38 G3 **Irtysh** *R* U.S.S.R.
43 L1 **Irtyshsk** Omsk U.S.S.R. 53.55N 74.56E
43 M1 **Irtyshskoye** Kazakhstan U.S.S.R. 53.22N 75.30E
77 L5 **Iruela,La** Spain 37.56N 2.59W
75 E6 **Irueste** Spain 40.36N 2.54W
93 E7 **Irugwa I** Tanzania 1.44S 33.23E
20 A1 **Iruma** Saitama Japan
93 A4 **Irumu** Zaïre 1.32N 29.49E
75 F1 **Irumugarrieta** *mt* Spain 43.00N 2.02W
75 G1 **Irún** Spain 43.20N 1.48W
120 E7 **Irupana** Bolivia 16.29S 67.28W
75 F1 **Irura** Spain 43.10N 2.03W
75 G1 **Irurita** Spain 43.07N 1.33W
75 H2 **Irurozqui** Spain 42.46N 1.15W
75 G2 **Irurzun** Spain 42.55N 1.50W
120 F10 **Iruya** Argentina 22.40S 65.16W
47 F4 **Irva** *R* U.S.S.R.
100 G9 **Irvine** Alberta 49.58N 110.18W
111 G8 **Irvine** California 33.41N 117.50W
104 B9 **Irvine** Kentucky 37.42N 83.59W
57 D1 **Irvine** Strathclyde Scotland 55.37N 4.40W
13 H3 **Irvinebank** Queensland 17.24S 145.12E
57 D1 **Irvine Bay** Strathclyde Scotland 55.37N 4.45W
57 D1 **Irvine, R** Strathclyde Scotland
59 G3 **Irvinestown** Fermanagh N Ireland 54.29N 7.38W
112 O9 **Irving** Texas 32.47N 96.57W
14 F7 **Irving, Mt** W Australia 27.04S 126.59E
107 K4 **Irvington** Kentucky 37.51N 86.18W
103 J7 **Irvington** New Jersey 40.43N 74.14W
103 G4 **Irvington** New York 41.03N 73.52W
104 J9 **Irvington** Virginia 37.40N 76.26W
Irwad *see* **Arwad**
110 O6 **Irwin** Idaho 43.25N 11.17W
108 P8 **Irwin** Iowa 41.48N 95.12W
108 H7 **Irwin** Nebraska 42.52N 102.00W
14 B8 **Irwin** W Australia 29.16S 115.03E
14 B11 **Irwin, Pt** W Australia 35.03S 116.20E
14 B8 **Irwin, R** W Australia
105 D5 **Irwinton** Georgia 32.47N 83.10W
47 H6 **Is** U.S.S.R. 58.47N 59.40E
Is *anc site* Iraq*see* **Hit**
I-sa *see* **Honghe**
33 B8 **Isa** Bahrain, The Gulf 26.10N 50.03E
35 F10 **Isa** Jordan 30.50N 35.38E
90 C5 **Isa** Nigeria 13.11N 6.24E
13 J6 **Isaac** *R* Queensland
101 N9 **Isaac L** Br Col
59 K4 **Isaac's Bower** Dublin Irish Rep 53.37N 6.11W
98 L8 **Isaacs Harbour** Nova Scotia 45.10N 61.40W
75 J2 **Isaba** Spain 42.52N 0.55W
109 M4 **Isabel** Kansas 37.29N 98.34W
108 J4 **Isabel** S Dakota 45.23N 101.26W
19 L6 **Isabela** Philippines 10.12N 122.58E
105 J7 **Isabela** Puerto Rico 18.30N 67.02W
116 J5 **Isabela,C** Dominican Rep 19.58N 71.02W
119 A5 **Isabela,I** Galápagos Is
119 A5 **Isabel,B** Galápagos Is
121 K9 **Isabel, I** Chile 52.50S 70.40W
115 M3 **Isabelia, Cord** *ra* Nicaragua
111 F6 **Isabella** California 35.38N 118.28W
100 R8 **Isabella** Manitoba 50.18N 100.50W
106 C2 **Isabella** Minnesota 47.36N 91.21W
14 F5 **Isabella, L** W Australia 20.35S 126.45E
111 F6 **Isabella Res** California 35.40N 118.25W
106 G2 **Isabelle Pt** Michigan 47.21N 87.56W
105 K7 **Isabel Segunda** Puerto Rico 18.08N 65.30W
75 M3 **Isábena** *R* Spain
41 E3 **Isachenko,Ostrov** *isld* U.S.S.R.
97 J2 **Isachsen** N W Terr 78.50N 103.30W
97 J2 **Isachsen,C** N W Terr 79.20N 106.00W
50 B2 **Ísafjardhardjúp** *inlet* Iceland
50 C3 **Ísafjardharsýsla, Nordhur** *co* Iceland
50 B3 **Ísafjardharsýsla, Vestur** *co* Iceland
50 B2 **Ísafjördhur** Iceland 66.05N 23.08W
50 C3 **Ísafjördhur** *B* Iceland
30 A8 **Isagarh** Madhya Prad India 24.50N 77.53E
95 C7 **Isahara** Madagascar 23.42S 47.21E
20 D9 **Isahaya** Japan 32.51N 130.02E
31 C7 **Isai Kalat** Pakistan 26.58N 64.04E
92 F3 **Isaka** Tanzania 3.52S 33.00E
91 F5 **Isaka** Zaïre 2.33S 18.54E
91 G4 **Isaka** Zaïre 0.33S 20.10E
91 G4 **Isaka** Zaïre 1.49S 20.50E
31 F4 **Isa Khel** Pakistan 32.39N 71.20E
43 B1 **Isakly** U.S.S.R. 54.08N 51.07E
95 B7 **Isakoa** Madagascar 23.23S 45.51E
47 E4 **Isakogorka** U.S.S.R. 64.23N 40.31E
47 C5 **Isakovo** U.S.S.R. 60.05N 33.25E
35 F9 **Isal** *watercourse* Jordan
81 C3 **Isalle** *R* Sardinia
82 H6 **Işalniţa** Romania 44.25N 23.46E
95 B7 **Isalo, Massif ruiniforme de l'** *mts* Madagascar
30 C5 **Isan** *R* Uttar Prad India
30 C8 **Isanagar** Madhya Prad India 24.51N 79.22E
30 E5 **Isanagar** Uttar Prad India 27.54N 81.13E
119 E7 **Isana,R** Colombia
91 G5 **Isandja** Zaïre 2.59S 21.59E
94 T13 **Isando** S Africa 26.08S 28.13E
91 H4 **Isanga** Equateur Zaïre 1.30S 22.24E
92 G5 **Isanga** Tanzania 7.24S 34.16E
93 D9 **Isanga** *watercourse* Tanzania
91 J3 **Isangi** Zaïre 0.48N 24.10E
91 C6 **Isangila Falls** Zaïre 5.17S 13.36E
90 B7 **Isanlu Makatu** Nigeria 8.20N 5.50E
64 N6 **Isar** *R* W Germany
35 G3 **Is'ara** Jordan 32.37N 35.45E
33 E9 **'Isá, Ra's** *C* Yemen 15.14N 42.39E
79 L1 **Isarco** *R* Italy
84 D7 **Isari** Greece 37.22N 22.00E
20 K2 **Isari-dake** *mt* Hokkaido Japan 42.52N 140.38E
76 L2 **Isar,Sierra de** *mts* Spain
65 D6 **Isartal** *V* W Germany
18 E7 **Isauisau,Bukit** *mt* Sumatra Indon 3.58S 103.42E
30 E6 **Isauli** Uttar Prad India 26.25N 81.51E
92 D3 **Isavi** Rwanda 2.34S 29.49E
35 D6 **Isawiya** Israel 31.48N 35.15E
33 C1 **'Īsāwīyah, 'Al** Saudi Arabia 30.39N 38.03E
41 G5 **Isayevskiy** U.S.S.R. 71.52N 99.59E
89 L3 **Isazagene** Mali 16.32N 3.40E
47 E3 **Isba Bol'shaya Bab'ya** U.S.S.R. 66.26N 40.28E
43 O7 **Isbaskent** Uzbekistan U.S.S.R. 41.04N 72.21E
107 J7 **Isbell** Alabama 34.27N 87.45W
69 C2 **Isbergues** France 50.37N 2.27E
58 Q8 **Isbister** Shetland Scotland 60.36N 1.19W
76 K6 **Iscar** Spain 41.21N 4.33W
120 F9 **Iscayachi** Bolivia 21.32S 65.04W
69 K7 **Isches** France 48.01N 5.50E
65 B7 **Ischgl** Austria 47.02N 10.18E
80 J7 **Ischia** Italy 40.44N 13.57E
80 J7 **Ischia,I.d'** Italy
80 N5 **Ischitella** Italy 41.54N 15.54E
65 J6 **Ischl** *R* Austria
87 J9 **Iscia Baidoa** Somalia 3.08N 43.34E
119 C6 **Iscuandé,R** Colombia
53 S17 **Isdalstø** Norway 60.33N 5.15E
14 F3 **Isdell,R** W Australia
70 P6 **Isdes** France 47.41N 2.15E
20 K7 **Ise** Japan 34.29N 136.41E
114 C8 **Iseai Camp** Hawaiian Is 19.15N 155.28W
93 F7 **Isebania** Tanzania 1.16S 34.27E
53 H5 **Isefjord** *B* Denmark
86 G5 **'Iseili, Wâdi** *watercourse* Egypt
92 G5 **Iseke** Tanzania 6.20S 35.01E
65 D7 **Isel Berg** *mt* Austria 47.15N 11.22E
123 K7 **Iselin Bank** Ross Sea Antarctica
26 K14 **Iselin Seamount** Southern Oc 70.45S 178.15E
66 J7 **Iselle** Italy 46.13N 8.13E
65 G8 **Iselsberg Pass** Austria 46.52N 12.52E
65 G8 **Isel-tal** *V* Austria
66 H5 **Iseltwald** Switzerland 46.43N 7.58E
64 N7 **Isen** W Germany 48.12N 12.05E
69 J7 **Is-en-Bassigny** France 48.02N 5.25E
46 R2 **Isenbayevo** U.S.S.R. 56.09N 53.28E
64 D3 **Isenburg** W Germany 50.29N 7.35E
63 N8 **Isenbüttel** W Germany 52.26N 10.37E
63 N7 **Isenhagen** W Germany 52.43N 10.37E
66 L4 **Isenthal** Switzerland 46.55N 8.34E
53 C4 **Isenvad** Denmark 56.06N 9.14E
79 H3 **Iseo** Italy 45.39N 10.03E
79 H3 **Iseo,L.di** *L* Italy
66 E7 **Isérables** Switzerland 46.10N 7.15E
93 D10 **Iseramagazi** Tanzania 4.39S 32.10E
71 L6 **Iseran,Col de l'** *pass* France 45.25N 7.02E
67 J7 **Isère** *dept* France
71 G6 **Isère** *R* France
117 C2 **Isère,Pte** *C* Fr Guiana 5.45N 53.53W
63 G10 **Iserlohn** W Germany 51.23N 7.42E
80 K5 **Isernia** Italy 41.35N 14.14E
80 K5 **Isernia** *prov* Italy
20 K7 **Ise shima Nat.Park** Japan
47 K7 **Iset'** *R* U.S.S.R.
47 K7 **Isetskoye** U.S.S.R. 56.30N 65.20E
20 K7 **Ise-wan** *B* Japan
90 A8 **Iseyin** Nigeria 7.59N 3.40E
20 N5 **Isezaki** Japan 36.19N 139.11E
Isfahan *see* **Esfahān**
43 J7 **Isfana** Kirgiziya U.S.S.R. 39.51N 69.31E
Isfandak *see* **Esfandak**
Isfandaqeh *see* **Gāv Koshī**
Isfandun *see* **Esfandāran**
43 M8 **Isfara** Tadzhikistan U.S.S.R. 40.10N 70.42E
43 M8 **Isfara** *R* Kirgiziya U.S.S.R.
Isfehdeh *see* **Esfideh**
35 D3 **'Isfiya** Israel 32.43N 35.04E
53 X13 **Isfjord** *inlet* Norway 62.33N 7.42E
53 X13 **Isfjorden** Norway 62.34N 7.49E
50 S14 **Isfjorden** *inlet* Spitsbergen
50 S14 **Isfjord Radio** Spitsbergen 78.02N 13.40E
90 F6 **Isge** Nigeria 10.59N 13.17E
56 K3 **Isham** Northants Eng 52.21N 0.43W
93 A6 **Ishango** Zaïre 0.08S 29.36E
34 M6 **Ishāq** Iraq 32.15N 44.48E
44 G4 **Ishcherskaya** U.S.S.R. 43.45N 45.06E
91 H5 **Ishenga Oshwe** Zaïre 3.57S 22.33E
47 H5 **Isherim,Gora** *mt* U.S.S.R. 61.07N 59.08E
119 J6 **Isherton** Guyana 2.19N 59.23W
45 U2 **Isheyevka** U.S.S.R. 54.24N 48.15E
86 L10 **'Ish, Gebel** *hill* Egypt 27.30N 33.32E
34 O5 **'Ishiāb** Iran 33.48N 46.45E
90 C9 **Ishiago** Nigeria 5.56N 7.31E
92 E7 **Ishiba Ngandu** Zambia 11.14S 31.44E
20 P2 **Ishidoriya** Japan 39.31N 141.08E
23 K6 **Ishigakishima** *isld* Japan
20 L1 **Ishikari** Japan 43.15N 141.21E
20 L1 **Ishikari** *sub-prefect* Hokkaido Japan
20 M1 **Ishikari-dake** *mt* Hokkaido Japan 43.32N 143.00E
20 L1 **Ishikari-gawa** *R* Japan
20 K1 **Ishikari-wan** *B* Japan
20 O4 **Ishikawa** Japan 37.08N 140.29E
20 P9 **Ishikawa** Okinawa Japan 26.25N 127.47E
20 K5 **Ishikawa** *prefect* Japan
44 G8 **Ishikhly** *mt* Azerbaydzhan U.S.S.R. 39.36N 46.12E
47 K7 **Ishim** U.S.S.R. 56.10N 69.30E
43 J1 **Ishim** *R* Kazakhstan U.S.S.R.
46 S3 **Ishimbay** U.S.S.R. 53.30N 55.59E
43 J1 **Ishimskaya Step'** U.S.S.R.
43 H2 **Ishimskoye** Kazakhstan U.S.S.R. 51.23N 67.07E
20 P3 **Ishinomaki** Japan 38.25N 141.18E
20 P3 **Ishinomaki-wan** *B* Japan
20 O5 **Ishioka** Japan 36.11N 140.16E
20 J3 **Ishizaki** Japan 41.41N 140.02E
20 G8 **Ishizuchi-san** *mt* Japan 33.48N 133.11E
31 E2 **Ishkamish** Kataghan Afghanistan 36.25N 69.11E
31 F2 **Ishkashim** Badakhshan Afghanistan 36.43N 71.34E
43 K8 **Ishkashim** Tadzhikistan U.S.S.R. 36.45N 71.36E
31 G2 **Ishkuman** Kashmir 36.35N 73.50E
83 D3 **Ishm** *R* Albania
86 F7 **Ishmant** Egypt 29.12N 31.11E
91 F5 **Isho** Zaïre 2.44S 18.15E
50 H4 **Ishólsvatn** Iceland 65.20N 17.24W
106 G3 **Ishpeming** Michigan 46.30N 87.38W
Ishqābād *see* **Eshāqābād**
Ishqanan *see* **Eshkanān**
Ishtahard *see* **Eshtehārd**
31 F2 **Ishtragh** Afghanistan 36.37N 71.46E
31 H9 **Ishurdi** Bangladesh 24.10N 89.04E
120 F7 **Isiboro,R** Bolivia
61 F4 **Isières** Belgium 50.40N 3.50E
41 O2 **Isiglera, Ostrov** *isld* Franz Josef Land U.S.S.R.
70 H4 **Isigny-le-Buat** France 48.37N 1.10W
70 H3 **Isigny sur Mer** Calvados France 49.18N 1.06W
36 F2 **Işık Dağ** *mt* Turkey 40.39N 32.46E
36 D4 **Işıklı** Turkey 38.20N 29.50E
75 N2 **Isil** Spain 42.41N 1.05E
81 C4 **Isili** Sardinia 39.45N 9.07E
47 L8 **Isil'kul'** U.S.S.R. 54.55N 71.15E
93 C9 **Isilobi** *mt* Tanzania 3.29S 31.31E
19 C3 **Isimu** Celebes Indon 0.40N 122.53E
42 J5 **Isinga** U.S.S.R. 52.58N 112.00E
42 J5 **Isinginskoye,Oz** *L* U.S.S.R. 52.58N 111.58E
119 B8 **Isinlivi** Ecuador 0.41S 78.52W
93 J5 **Isiolo** Kenya 0.20N 37.36E
93 K5 **Isiolo** *dist* Kenya
95 O5 **Isipingo** S Africa 29.58S 30.57E
95 O5 **Isipingo Beach** S Africa 30.00S 30.57E
87 A9 **Isiro** Zaïre 2.50N 27.40E
13 G6 **Isisford** Queensland 24.17S 144.30E
92 G5 **Isisi** Tanzania 7.12S 35.43E
50 V13 **Isispynten** *pt* Spitsbergen 79.45N 27.00E
40 C1 **Isit'** U.S.S.R. 60.51N 125.12E
47 K7 **Iska** *R* U.S.S.R.
31 D2 **Iskabad Canal** Afghanistan
39 L2 **Iskamen',Khrebet** *mts* U.S.S.R.
31 F2 **Iskan** Afghanistan 36.35N 70.54E
Iskandarîya,El *see* **Alexandria** Egypt
34 M6 **Iskandarīyah,Al** Iraq 32.53N 44.22E
43 J6 **Iskander** Uzbekistan U.S.S.R. 41.34N 69.14E
Iskanderina *R see* **Alexander** *R*
36 C6 **İskandil Burun** *C* Turkey 36.42N 27.20E
36 C5 **İskele** Turkey 37.04N 28.20E
36 J6 **İskenderun** Turkey 36.37N 36.08E
36 H6 **İskenderun Körfezi** *gulf* Turkey
Iski *see* **Loubayed**
36 G2 **İskilip** Turkey 40.45N 34.28E
43 L6 **Iski-Naukat** Kirgiziya U.S.S.R. 40.16N 72.35E
43 C4 **Iskine** Kazakhstan U.S.S.R. 47.18N 52.40E
43 C4 **Iskininskiy** Kazakhstan U.S.S.R. 47.13N 52.52E
42 C5 **Iskitim** U.S.S.R. 54.42N 83.18E
43 N7 **Iskovat** Uzbekistan U.S.S.R. 41.19N 71.41E
42 D1 **Iskup** U.S.S.R. 63.06N 88.10E
82 H8 **Iskŭr** *R* Bulgaria
82 H8 **Iskŭr Dam** Bulgaria
101 J7 **Iskut** Br Col 57.56N 129.59W

101 H7 Iskut R Br Col
100 O3 Iskwatam L Saskatchewan
77 B6 Isla Cristina Spain 37.12N 7.19W
88 F10 Isla Herne Mauritania 23.50N 15.48W
36 J5 İslâhiye Turkey 37.02N 36.37E
Islamabad Kashmir see Anantnag
31 G4 Islamabad Pakistan 33.40N 73.08E
31 G6 Islam Barrage Pakistan 29.50N 72.31E
31 F7 Islamgarh Pakistan 27.56N 70.50E
31 F8 Islamkot Pakistan 24.40N 70.12E
30 B4 Islamnagar Uttar Prad India 28.19N 78.42E
105 G13 Islamorada Florida 24.56N 80.37W
30 J7 Islampur Patna, Bihar India 25.09N 85.13E
30 M6 Islampur Purnea, Bihar India 26.17N 88.11E
31 A3 Islam Qala Afghanistan 34.39N 61.03E
107 J4 Island Kentucky 37.27N 87.10W
101 N5 Island R N W Terr
19 J7 Island B Philippines
55 C5 Island Barn Res Surrey England
11 C6 Island Bay dist Wellington New Zealand
103 F7 Island Beach New Jersey
110 H4 Island City Oregon 45.22N 118.00W
59 D4 Islandeady L Mayo Irish Rep 53.50N 9.22W
104 Q7 Island Falls Maine 46.01N 68.16W
99 J3 Island Falls Ontario 49.36N 81.21W
100 P3 Island Falls Saskatchewan 55.31N 102.21W
13 K5 Island Hd Queensland 22.20S 150.40E
103 F7 Island Heights New Jersey 39.57N 74.09W
97 K7 Island L Manitoba 54.00N 94.50W
98 Q5 Island L Newfoundland
99 K7 Island L Ontario 45.48N 80.05W
12 D4 Island L S Australia
110 B9 Island Mountain California 40.01N 123.30W
110 O5 Island Park Idaho 44.26N 111.21W
110 O5 Island Park Res Idaho 44.25N 111.30W
30 J3 "Island Peak" mt Nepal 27.56N 86.56E
104 O2 Island Pond Vermont 44.50N 71.53W
14 B9 Island Pt W Australia 30.21S 115.01E
98 O4 Islands,B.of Newfoundland
11 J2 Islands,B.of New Zealand
58 K5 Isla,R Tayside Scotland
120 E11 Isla,Salar de la salt pan Chile
86 L9 Isla, Wâdî watercourse Egypt
100 G5 Islay Alberta 53.24N 110.32W
58 D7 Islay isld Strathclyde Scotland
120 C7 Islay,Pta C Peru 17.02S 72.06W
58 D7 Islay, Sound of Strathclyde Scotland
72 G4 Isle France 45.49N 1.14E
108 R3 Isle Minnesota 46.08N 93.26W
72 E5 Isle R France
69 C5 Isle-Adam,l' France 49.07N 2.14E
69 G6 Isle Aubigny France 48.31N 4.18E
98 O6 Isle aux Morts Newfoundland 47.35N 59.00W
104 R2 Isleboro Maine 44.18N 68.55W
71 G5 Isle d'Abeau, l' France 45.37N 5.13E
72 E8 Isle-de Noé, l' France 43.35N 0.25E
72 E4 Isle d'Espagnac,l' France 45.39N 0.13E
72 F9 Isle-en-Dodon,l' France 43.24N 0.50E
56 M3 Isleham Cambs Eng 52.21N 0.25E
72 G8 Isle Jourdain, l' Gers France 43.37N 1.05E
72 F3 Isle-Jourdain,l' Vienne France 46.14N 0.41E
66 B5 Isle,l' Switzerland 46.38N 6.25E
98 A5 Isle Maligne Quebec 48.35N 71.39W
55 G4 Isle of Dogs dist London Eng 51.30N 0.01W
105 F6 Isle of Hope Georgia 31.59N 81.59W
57 E4 Isle of Man Irish Sea
57 E3 Isle of Whithorn Dumfries & Galloway Scotland 54.42N 4.22W
56 J6 Isle of Wight co England
58 E4 Isle Ornsay Skye, Highland Scotland 57.08N 5.49W
106 F1 Isle Royale Michigan
106 F1 Isle Royale National Park Michigan
56 R8 Isles of Scilly England
69 G5 Isles-sur-Suippes France 49.21N 4.13E
71 G9 Isle-sur-la-Sorgue,l' France 43.55N 5.03E
71 K2 Isle-sur-le-Doubs,l' France 47.27N 6.34E
71 E1 Isle-sur-Serein,l' France 47.36N 4.00E
109 D7 Isleta New Mexico 34.55N 106.43W
96 V14 Isleta,La pen Gran Canaria Canary Is
77 N7 Isleta,Pta.de la pt Spain 36.54N 1.59W
111 C3 Isleton California 38.09N 121.36W
55 C4 Isleworth London Eng 51.28N 0.20W
45 T1 Isley-Pokrovskoye U.S.S.R. 56.02N 47.02E
66 M1 Islikon Switzerland 47.33N 8.51E
55 F3 Islington London England 51.33N 0.06W
11 L9 Islington New Zealand 43.32S 172.30E
103 H5 Islip Long I, N Y 40.44N 73.12W
56 J4 Islip Oxon Eng 51.50N 1.14W
116 N2 Islote Pt Trinidad & Tobago 10.04N 61.47W
120 E8 Isluga vol Chile 19.10S 68.48W
121 F4 Ismael Cortinas Uruguay 33.57S 57.05W
86 H4 Ismâ'ilîya Egypt 30.36N 32.15E
44 J7 Ismailly Azerbaydzhan U.S.S.R. 40.46N 48.10E
87 F5 Ismala Georgis Ethiopia 11.38N 36.58E
64 M7 Ismaning W Germany 48.13N 11.41E
108 F3 Ismay Montana 46.30N 104.48W
36 E3 İsmetpaşa Eskişehir Turkey 39.24N 30.54E
37 D7 İsmetpaşa Malatya Turkey 38.19N 38.19E
85 M7 Isna Egypt 25.16N 32.30E
76 D9 Isna Portugal 39.51N 7.51W
81 H8 Isnello Sicily 37.57N 14.01E
61 J4 Isnes Belgium 50.31N 4.44E
64 J8 Isny W Germany 47.42N 10.02E
95 B7 Isoanala Madagascar 23.50S 45.45E
20 B4 Isobe Kanagawa Japan
20 D5 Isogo dist Yokohama Japan
21 H9 Isohara Japan 36.49N 140.44E
51 J9 Isojoki Finland 62.07N 22.00E
92 F6 Isoka Tanzania 9.25S 33.31E
92 F7 Isoka Zambia 10.09S 32.39E
87 D8 Isoke Sudan 4.19N 33.00E
51 J8 Isokyrö Finland 63.01N 22.20E
71 L8 Isola France 44.12N 7.03E
107 F8 Isola Mississippi 33.15N 90.36W
79 C7 Isolabona Italy 43.53N 7.39E
79 D5 Isola d'Asti Italy 44.50N 8.12E
79 E5 Isola del Cantone Italy 44.39N 8.58E
80 J3 Isola del Gran Sasso d'Italia Italy 42.30N 13.40E
79 K4 Isola della Scala Italy 45.17N 11.00E
80 J5 Isola del Liri Italy 41.40N 13.35E
81 O6 Isola di Capo Rizzuto Italy 38.57N 17.06E
80 F4 Isola Farnese Italy 42.02N 12.23E
79 K4 Isola Rizza Italy 45.17N 11.12E
79 K3 Isola Vicentino Italy 45.38N 11.27E
70 C6 Isole R France
107 L5 Isoline Tennessee 36.05N 85.04W
66 M7 Isone Switzerland 46.08N 9.00E
51 M4 Iso-Poikela Finland 67.55N 26.50E
96 P12 Isora Hierro Canary Is 27.44N 17.56W
79 H4 Isorella Italy 45.19N 10.19E
66 K7 Isorno R Italy
51 N6 Iso-Syöte mt Finland 65.38N 27.40E
20 K2 Isoya Japan 42.54N 140.22E
71 D8 Ispagnac France 44.22N 3.32E
Ispakeh see Espakeh
36 E5 Isparta Turkey 37.46N 30.32E
36 E5 Isparta R Turkey
37 F1 Ispartakule Turkey 41.04N 28.43E
37 D7 İspendere Turkey 38.24N 38.29E
82 K7 Isperikh Bulgaria 43.43N 26.50E
81 J10 Ispica Sicily 36.47N 14.55E
31 B7 Ispikan Pakistan 26.14N 62.14E
37 F5 İspir Turkey 40.29N 41.02E
37 H8 İspiriz Dağları mts Turkey
31 D6 Isplinji Pakistan 29.36N 67.04E
72 B9 Ispoure France 43.10N 1.13W
79 E3 Ispra Italy 45.49N 8.36E
44 D3 Ispravnaya U.S.S.R. 44.14N 41.47E
121 J5 Isquiliac, I Chile 45.20S 74.35W
34 B6 Israel rep S W Asia
14 E10 Israelite B W Australia
34 E3 Isrīya ruins Syria 35.24N 37.47E
45 Q3 Issa U.S.S.R. 53.52N 44.50E
46 G2 Issa R U.S.S.R.
88 R10 Issakarassene, Guelta reg Algeria
88 R10 Issalane Algeria 22.38N 7.55E
71 K10 Issambres,Pte.des France 43.21N 6.43E
119 J5 Issano Guyana 5.51N 59.24W
71 E7 Issarlès Ardèche France 44.50N 4.03E
70 H6 Issé France 47.38N 1.27W
53 F5 Issehoved C Denmark 56.00N 10.34E
14 A8 Isseka W Australia 28.30S 114.35E
63 D9 Isselburg W Germany 51.48N 6.28E
63 H9 Isselhorst W Germany 51.57N 8.25E
119 H4 Isseneru Guyana 6.30N 60.21W
89 F8 Issia Ivory Coast 6.33N 6.33W
72 F6 Issigeac France 44.44N 0.38E
79 C3 Issime Italy 45.42N 7.52N
34 N7 Issin anc site Iraq 31.56N 45.14E
77 N4 Isso Spain 38.30N 1.45W
71 C5 Issoire France 45.33N 3.15E
71 J10 Issole R France
72 H2 Issoudun France 46.57N 1.59E
63 D9 Issum W Germany 51.32N 6.25E
71 G1 Is-sur-Tille France 47.32N 5.07E
43 M5 Issyk Kazakhstan U.S.S.R. 42.23N 77.25E
43 L5 Issykata Kirgiziya U.S.S.R. 42.35N 74.59E
43 M6 Issyk-Kul',Oz L Kirgiziya U.S.S.R.
43 N6 Issyk-Kul'skaya Obl Kirgiziya U.S.S.R.
68 E4 Issy-les-Moulineaux France 48.49N 2.17E
71 D3 Issy-l'Évêque France 46.43N 3.58E
33 C4 Iştabl 'Antar Saudi Arabia 25.06N 38.56E
31 E3 Istalif Afghanistan 34.51N 69.06E
77 G7 Istán Spain 36.35N 4.56W
37 F1 İstanbul Turkey 41.02N 28.57E
86 F5 Iştanha Egypt 30.28N 31.06E
Istard see Estārm
Istehbanat see Eşţahbānāt
66 G1 Istein W Germany 47.40N 7.33E
39 D1 Isteney Terde U.S.S.R. 70.01N 147.23E
53 X14 Isterdalen V Norway 62.29N 7.40E
32 C4 Istgāh-e Eznā Iran 33.27N 49.30E
44 G9 Istgāh-e Halākū Iran 38.42N 45.37E
32 E2 Istgāh-e Zīrab Iran 36.10N 52.59E
121 F3 Isthilart Argentina 31.12S 57.55W
Isthmía see Kirás Vrísi
99 J7 Isthmus B Ontario
80 D3 Istia Italy 42.47N 11.12E
84 F4 Istiaía Greece 38.57N 23.09E
37 F8 Istilil Turkey 37.14N 41.03E
Istin,Kuh-i- see Estand,Kūh-e- mt
44 G8 Istisu Azerbaydzhan U.S.S.R. 39.56N 46.00E
119 C5 Istmina Colombia 5.11N 76.39W
96 S11 Istmo de la Pared Fuerteventura Canary Is
105 F10 Istokpoga,L Florida 27.24N 81.15W
45 H1 Istra U.S.S.R. 55.55N 36.52E
82 B5 Istra pen Yugoslavia
79 M3 Istrana Italy 45.41N 12.06E
36 C1 Istranca Dağları mts Turkey
71 F9 Istres France 43.30N 4.59E
84 U17 Istrios Rhodes 36.06N 27.50E
31 H2 Istyk R Tadzhikistan U.S.S.R.
75 G4 Isuela R Zaragoza Spain
75 K3 Isuela,R Huesca Spain
75 H3 Isuerre Spain 42.29N 1.03W
15 H6 Isumrud Str Papua New Guinea
Isurugi see Oyabe
53 U16 Isvatn L Norway 61.27N 6.20E
53 V19 Isvatn L Norway 59.58N 6.50E
30 K4 Iswa Glacier Nepal
30 K4 Iswa La pass Nepal 27.48N 87.04E
31 H10 Iswaripur Bangladesh 22.20N 89.07E
95 O2 Iswepe S Africa 26.50S 30.32E
43 D2 Isyangulovo Bashkir U.S.S.R. 52.14N 56.34E
39 G4 Is Yen U.S.S.R. 61.39N 162.38E
90 F6 Isza Nigeria 11.28N 13.42E
118 B9 Itá Paraguay 25.29S 57.21W
33 J9 'Itāb S Yemen 15.19N 51.25E
117 J8 Itabaiana Paraíba Brazil 7.18S 35.17W
118 J2 Itabaiana Sergipe Brazil 10.42S 37.37W
118 J2 Itabaianinha Brazil 11.16S 37.48W
118 H7 Itabapoana Brazil 21.17S 40.59W
118 H7 Itabapoana,R Brazil
20 E2 Itabashi dist Tōkyō Japan
91 K5 Itabatshi Zaïre 3.38S 27.02E
118 E8 Itaberá Brazil 23.49S 49.09W
118 H3 Itaberaba Brazil 12.34S 40.21W
118 E5 Itaberaí Brazil 16.03S 49.43W
118 G6 Itabira Brazil 19.39S 43.14W
118 G7 Itabirito Brazil 20.21S 43.45W
120 G1 Itaboca Brazil 4.52S 62.52W
117 D7 Itaboca,Cachoeira rapids Brazil 4.33S 49.31W
33 J9 'Itāb,Ra's C S Yemen 15.15N 51.28E
117 A2 Itabru Falls Guyana 4.53N 58.15W
118 H4 Itabuna Brazil 14.48S 39.18W
117 D7 Itacaiuna, R Brazil
117 E9 Itacajá Brazil 8.18S 47.45W
118 G4 Itacarambi Brazil 15.08S 44.04W
118 J4 Itacaré Brazil 14.17S 38.59W
117 D8 Itacayunas,Sa mts Brazil
117 A6 Itacoatiara Brazil 3.06S 58.22W
119 E10 Itacuai,R Brazil
118 C9 Itacurubí del Rosario Paraguay 24.30S 56.52W
118 H3 Itaetê Brazil 13.00S 41.00W
92 F4 Itaga Tanzania 4.55S 32.45E
118 H6 Itaguaçu Brazil 19.52S 40.53W
118 D8 Itaguajé Brazil 22.35S 52.08W
118 F4 Itaguari,R Brazil
117 E7 Itaguatins Brazil 5.46S 47.31W
118 E8 Itaí Brazil 23.23S 49.05W
118 H3 Itaíba Brazil 12.25S 40.23W
118 C9 Itaimbey, R Paraguay
117 G8 Itaim,R Brazil
118 E10 Itaiópolis Brazil 26.28S 49.58W
118 C9 Itaipu Dam Brazil/Paraguay 25.22S 54.34W
117 B7 Itaituba Brazil 4.15S 55.56W
118 E10 Itajaí Brazil 26.50S 48.39W
121 J1 Itajaí Açú,R Brazil
118 F8 Itajubá Brazil 22.24S 45.25W
118 G2 Itajubaquara Brazil 11.22S 42.40W
118 H4 Itajuipe Brazil 14.39S 39.24W
92 F6 Itaka Tanzania 8.51S 32.50E
42 K5 Itaka U.S.S.R. 53.55N 118.50E
31 J9 Itakhola Bangladesh 24.09N 91.22E
20 O6 Itako Japan 35.57N 140.31E
31 J3 Italia Pass Kashmir 35.27N 77.18E
77 D6 Itálica ruins Spain 37.27N 6.04W
121 D5 Italó Argentina 34.46S 63.49W
112 L3 Italy Texas 32.11N 96.53W
49 G8 Italy rep S Europe
117 J8 Itamaracá,I.de Brazil 7.45S 34.45W
118 G5 Itamarandiba Brazil 17.52S 42.53W
117 E6 Itamataré Brazil 2.15S 46.18W
118 H6 Itambacuri Brazil 18.03S 41.41W
118 H6 Itambacuri R Brazil
118 H4 Itambé Brazil 15.14S 40.37W
118 G6 Itambé,Pico de mt Brazil 18.23S 43.21W
20 J7 Itami Japan 34.48N 135.24E
84 C3 Itamos mt Greece 39.12N 21.48E
95 A8 Itampolo Madagascar 24.40S 43.58E
28 J2 Itanagar Arunachal Pradesh India 27.02N 93.38E
95 B6 Itandrano Madagascar 21.48S 45.18E
87 E6 Itang Ethiopia 8.10N 34.16E
118 F9 Itanhaém Brazil 24.09S 46.47W
118 G8 Itanhandu Brazil 22.13S 44.55W
118 H10 Itanhanga Brazil 22.59S 43.18W
120 F1 Itanhauã,R Brazil
118 H5 Itanhém Brazil 17.06S 40.21W
118 H5 Itanhém,R Brazil
118 H5 Itaobím Brazil 16.34S 41.27W
118 E4 Itapaci Brazil 14.59S 49.32W
117 G6 Itapagé Brazil 3.45S 39.36W
118 E6 Itapajipe Brazil 19.54S 49.18W
120 F2 Itaparaná,R Brazil
118 J3 Itaparica, I Brazil 13.00S 38.38W
118 H4 Itapebi Brazil 15.55S 39.35W
121 F3 Itapebi Uruguay 31.17S 57.44W
118 F7 Itapecerica Brazil 20.28S 45.09W
118 H7 Itapemirim Brazil 21.01S 40.48W
118 H7 Itaperuna Brazil 21.14S 41.51W
118 H4 Itapetinga Brazil 15.17S 40.16W
118 E8 Itapetininga Brazil 23.36S 48.07W
118 E8 Itapeva Brazil 23.59S 48.59W
121 G2 Itapevi Brazil 29.49S 55.07W
118 H2 Itapicuru Brazil 10.28S 41.52W
117 F6 Itapicuru Mirim Brazil 3.27S 44.22W
118 H2 Itapicuru Mirim R Brazil
118 J2 Itapicuru,R Bahia Brazil
117 E8 Itapicuru, R Maranhão Brazil
117 E8 Itapicuru, Serra da mts Brazil
120 G1 Itapinima Brazil 5.23S 60.40W
117 G6 Itapipoca Brazil 3.29S 39.35W
117 A4 Itapi,R Brazil
118 F8 Itapira Brazil 22.24S 46.46W
117 A6 Itapiranga Amazonas Brazil 2.44S 58.04W
121 H1 Itapiranga Santa Catarina Brazil 27.11S 53.45W
121 F2 Itapitocai Brazil 29.50S 57.09W
117 H7 Itapiúna Brazil 4.32S 38.58W
118 E10 Itapocu,R Brazil
118 E7 Itápolis Brazil 21.32S 48.46W
117 H8 Itaporanga Paraíba Brazil 7.15S 38.00W
118 E8 Itaporanga São Paulo Brazil 23.43S 49.28W
121 H3 Itapuã Brazil 30.26S 51.02W
118 C10 Itapuá dept Paraguay
118 E4 Itapuranga Brazil 15.44S 49.55W
118 E9 Itararé Brazil 24.06S 49.23W
118 E8 Itararé R Brazil
29 E6 Itarsi Madhya Prad India 22.39N 77.48E
118 D6 Itarumã Brazil 18.46S 51.23W
112 K3 Itasca Texas 32.10N 97.09W
108 P2 Itasca, L Minnesota
108 P2 Itasca State Park Minnesota
103 C2 Itaska New York 42.17N 75.55W
95 C5 Itasy,L Madagascar 19.02S 46.47E
117 C6 Itatá,R Brazil
121 A6 Itata,R Chile
Itatiaia pk see Agulhas Negras Pk
118 F8 Itatiba Brazil 22.59S 46.51W
121 F2 Itati,L Argentina
118 E8 Itatinga Brazil 23.06S 48.36W
42 D4 Itatka U.S.S.R. 56.49N 85.35E
42 D4 Itatskiy U.S.S.R. 56.06N 89.07E
120 F1 Itatuba Brazil 5.46S 63.21W
117 C5 Itatupa Brazil 0.34S 51.15W
118 E5 Itauçu Brazil 16.13S 49.38W
117 F8 Itaueira,R Brazil
119 G9 Itaúna Amazonas Brazil 2.59S 65.57W
118 G7 Itaúna Minas Gerais Brazil 20.04S 44.30W
118 H6 Itaúnas Brazil 18.22S 39.45W
30 D5 Itaunia Uttar Prad India 27.05N 80.53E
120 C1 Itaya,R Peru
19 K1 Itbayat isld Philippines 20.47N 121.52E
56 J6 Itchen Hants Eng 50.54N 1.22W
101 R3 Itchen L N W Terr 65.35N 112.50W
56 J6 Itchen,R Hants Eng
56 J5 Itchen Stoke Hants Eng 51.06N 1.13W
90 F1 Itchouma Niger 20.14N 13.32E
120 D7 Ite Peru 17.55S 70.57W
84 D5 Itéa Greece 38.26N 22.25E
61 J2 Itegem Belgium 51.07N 4.44E
43 K2 Itemgen,Oz L Kazakhstan U.S.S.R. 52.20N 71.05E
92 G5 Itende Tanzania 6.49S 34.28E
119 D4 Ité,R Colombia
76 L4 Itero de la Vega Spain 42.16N 4.15W
Ithaca Greece see Itháki
106 K6 Ithaca Michigan 43.18N 84.36W
103 A2 Ithaca New York 42.26N 76.30W
84 A5 Itháki isld Greece
84 A5 Ithákis,Porthmós str Greece
63 L8 Ith Hils hills W Germany
34 D10 Ithil,Wādī al watercourse Saudi Arabia
84 C7 Ithómi mt Greece 37.11N 21.55E
56 E3 Ithon,R Powys Wales
34 E7 Ithrah Saudi Arabia 31.26N 37.37E
34 D8 Ithrīyat,Jebel mts Jordan
30 F5 Itiathok Uttar Prad India 27.18N 82.02E
84 C1 Itiés Greece 40.04N 21.37E
92 G4 Itigi Tanzania 5.41S 34.30E
30 B5 Itimadpur Uttar Prad India 27.14N 78.12E
93 D9 Itimbia Tanzania 3.21S 32.13E
118 H5 Itinga Brazil 16.36S 41.52W
118 C5 Itiquira Brazil 17.14S 54.13W
118 C5 Itiquira, R Brazil
118 H3 Itiruçu Brazil 13.31S 40.06W
118 H2 Itiúba Brazil 10.44S 39.52W
118 H2 Itiúba,Serra de mts Brazil
48 R10 Itivdleq Greenland 66.35N 53.25W
120 G10 Itiyura,R Argentina
29 J5 Itkhari Bihar India 24.19N 85.11E
113 M2 Itkillik R Alaska
47 M5 Itkul' U.S.S.R. 56.11N 60.34E
47 M5 Itkul,Oz L U.S.S.R. 56.08N 60.32E
86 H10 Itla el Bâsha hill Egypt 27.31N 32.20E
86 E10 Itlîdim Egypt 27.53N 30.47E
86 F4 Itmîda Egypt 30.46N 31.21E
43 C3 Itmurinkol' Oz L Kazakhstan U.S.S.R. 49.28N 52.30E
20 N7 Itō Japan 34.58N 139.04E
93 E10 Itobo Tanzania 4.09S 33.02E
92 K9 Itoculo Mozambique 14.43S 40.20E
20 L4 Itoigawa Japan 37.02N 137.52E
91 G4 Itoko Zaïre 1.00S 21.48E
20 O10 Itoman Okinawa Japan 26.05N 127.40E
95 B7 Itombona Madagascar 23.51S 44.05E
70 N4 Iton R France
120 F5 Itonamas,R Bolivia
95 B5 Itondy Madagascar 19.01S 45.20E
95 C5 Itongafeno mt Madagascar 19.57S 46.50E
77 J7 Itrabo Spain 36.48N 3.38W
80 J6 Itri Italy 41.18N 13.33E
86 E7 Itsa Egypt 29.14N 30.47E
107 F8 Itta Bena Mississippi 33.30N 90.20W
88 Q4 Ittel watercourse Algeria
66 O1 Ittendorf W Germany 47.42N 9.20E
61 H3 Itterbeek Belgium 50.50N 4.15E
60 T16 Ittervoort Netherlands 51.10N 5.50E
81 C2 Ittia,Pta mt Sardinia 40.43N 9.25E
Ittiḥād,Al see Madīnat ash Sha'b
81 B2 Ittireddu Sardinia 40.33N 8.55E
81 B2 Ittiri Sardinia 40.36N 8.34E
61 H4 Ittre Belgium 50.39N 4.16E
39 M3 Ittygran,Ostrov isld U.S.S.R. 64.38N 172.35W
118 F8 Itu Brazil 23.17S 47.18W
118 H3 Ituaçu Brazil 13.48S 41.14W
119 C4 Ituango Colombia 7.07N 75.46W
118 H3 Ituberá Brazil 13.45S 39.10W
120 D2 Itucumã R Brazil
120 D1 Itui,R Brazil
118 E6 Ituiutaba Brazil 19.00S 49.25W
92 C3 Itula Zaïre 3.30S 27.50E
113 J6 Itulilik Alaska 61.20N 157.07W
92 G5 Itumba tribe Tanzania
118 E6 Itumbiara Brazil 18.25S 49.15W
100 O7 Ituna Saskatchewan 51.09N 103.24W
92 F6 Itungi Tanzania 9.36S 33.56E
117 A2 Ituni Guyana 5.28N 58.15W
117 D7 Itupiranga Brazil 5.10S 49.20W
118 E10 Ituporanga Brazil 27.25S 49.35W
121 G2 Itú,R Brazil
118 E6 Iturama Brazil 19.44S 50.10W
120 F10 Iturbe Argentina 23.00S 65.20W
118 C10 Iturbe Paraguay 26.01S 56.30W
115 P8 Iturbide Campeche Mexico 19.36N 89.35W
115 K5 Iturbide Nuevo León Mexico 24.45N 99.53W
93 A4 Ituri R Zaïre
93 A5 Ituri Forest Zaïre
40 L9 Iturup Ostrov isld Kuril Is U.S.S.R.
118 G7 Itutinga Brazil 21.18S 44.56W
118 F7 Ituverava Brazil 20.22S 47.48W
120 F3 Ituxi, R Brazil
121 G1 Ituzaingó Argentina 27.34S 56.44W
30 F5 Itwa Uttar Prad India 27.20N 82.42E
93 E9 Itwangi Tanzania 3.50S 33.06E
72 B9 Itxassou France 43.20N 1.24W
86 E4 Ityâi el Bârûd Egypt 30.54N 30.40E
64 K3 Itz R W Germany
94 E6 Itzawisis Namibia 26.18S 18.09E
63 L5 Itzehoe W Germany 53.56N 9.32E
88 L5 Itzer Morocco 32.54N 5.03W
63 K5 Itzwärden W Germany 53.49N 9.06E
119 E7 Iuaretê Brazil 0.35N 69.13W
81 J8 Iudica,Mte Sicily 37.31N 14.37E
79 O2 Iudrio R Italy
107 H3 Iuka Illinois 38.37N 88.49W
109 M4 Iuka Kansas 37.45N 98.44W
107 H7 Iuka Mississippi 34.49N 88.11W
39 L1 Iul'tin U.S.S.R. 67.43N 178.56W
92 J9 Iulúti Mozambique 15.50S 39.00E
118 H7 Iúna Brazil 20.21S 41.32W
53 X17 Iungsdalshytta Norway 60.48N 7.55E
119 E7 Iutica Brazil 1.06N 69.28W
105 E3 Iva S Carolina 34.19N 82.41W
95 C7 Ivahona Madagascar 23.26S 46.10E
118 D8 Ivaí, R Brazil
95 C7 Ivakoany,Massif de l' mts Madagascar
51 N3 Ivalo Finland 68.40N 27.40E
51 N3 Ivalojoki R Finland
65 P7 Ivan Hungary 47.26N 16.57E
65 O3 Ivančice Czechoslovakia 49.06N 16.23E
82 E7 Ivančići Yugoslavia 44.00N 18.33E
45 D8 Ivangorod Ukraine U.S.S.R. 48.54N 32.14E
82 F8 Ivangrad Yugoslavia 42.51N 19.50E
40 L9 Ivan Groznyy vol Kuril Is U.S.S.R. 45.01N 147.52E
108 O5 Ivanhoe Minnesota 44.28N 96.12W
12 G5 Ivanhoe New S Wales 32.56S 144.22E
104 E10 Ivanhoe Virginia 36.50N 80.57W
14 G3 Ivanhoe W Australia 15.37S 128.40E
99 H4 Ivanhoe R Ontario
99 H4 Ivanhoe L Ontario 48.07N 82.33W
82 C5 Ivanić Grad Yugoslavia 45.41N 16.25E
45 M1 Ivanishchi U.S.S.R. 55.46N 40.26E
45 D6 Ivanitsa Ukraine U.S.S.R. 50.48N 32.40E
65 N8 Ivanjci Yugoslavia 46.36N 15.59E
82 F7 Ivanjica Yugoslavia 43.35N 20.12E
46 G4 Ivankov Ukraine U.S.S.R. 50.59N 29.50E
46 N1 Ivankovo Kostroma U.S.S.R. 57.59N 43.01E
45 J2 Ivan'kovo Tula U.S.S.R. 54.44N 37.58E
40 F7 Ivankovtsy U.S.S.R. 49.07N 134.30E
46 E5 Ivano-Frankovsk Ukraine U.S.S.R. 48.40N 24.40E
82 L1 Ivanopol U.S.S.R. 49.50N 28.10E
65 Q3 Ivanovice na Hane Czechoslovakia 49.18N 17.05E
40 D6 Ivanovka Amur U.S.S.R. 50.24N 128.00E
44 D8 Ivanovka Kherson, Ukraine U.S.S.R. 46.43N 34.35E
45 K8 Ivanovka Lugansk, Ukraine U.S.S.R. 48.15N 38.58E
43 M1 Ivanovka Omsk U.S.S.R. 55.09N 75.16E
43 C1 Ivanovka Orenburg U.S.S.R. 52.52N 53.47E
43 P3 Ivanovka Semipalatinsk, Kazakhstan U.S.S.R. 48.34N 82.16E
46 F4 Ivanovo Belorussiya U.S.S.R. 52.10N 25.31E
46 M2 Ivanovo U.S.S.R. 57.00N 41.00E
46 M2 Ivanovskaya Oblast' prov U.S.S.R.
43 P2 Ivanovskiy Khrebet mts Kazakhstan U.S.S.R.
45 F5 Ivanovskoye Kursk U.S.S.R. 51.37N 34.58E
45 H3 Ivanovskoye Orël U.S.S.R. 53.05N 36.16E
111 J6 Ivanpah California 35.20N 115.20W
45 J1 Ivanteyevka Moscow U.S.S.R. 55.58N 37.55E
45 V4 Ivanteyevka Saratov U.S.S.R. 52.16N 49.05E
40 L9 Ivao,Gory mt Kuril Is U.S.S.R. 45.45N 149.44E
39 G5 Ivashka U.S.S.R. 58.35N 162.16E
95 C6 Ivato Madagascar 20.38S 47.11E
95 C5 Ivato airport Madagascar 18.49S 47.30E
82 K9 Ivaylovgrad Bulgaria 41.32N 26.08E
47 J5 Ivdel' U.S.S.R. 60.45N 60.30E
57 H3 Ivegill Cumbria Eng 54.47N 2.54W
63 R5 Ivenack E Germany 53.43N 12.59E
46 F3 Ivenets Belorussiya U.S.S.R. 53.50N 26.40E
55 A3 Iver Bucks Eng 51.31N 0.30W
56 K4 Iver Heath Bucks Eng 51.33N 0.33W
107 H2 Ivesdale Illinois 39.57N 88.26W
56 G2 Ivetsey Bank Staffs Eng 52.42N 2.15W
47 K6 Iveylevo U.S.S.R. 57.36N 67.10E
88 O3 Ivi,C Algeria 36.08N 0.12E
50 E5 Ivídægra reg Iceland
48 T15 Ivigtut Greenland 61.15N 48.15W
91 C3 Ivindo R Gabon
56 K4 Ivinghoe Bucks Eng 51.51N 0.39W
118 D8 Ivinheima Brazil 22.10S 53.30W
118 D8 Ivinheima,R Brazil
113 N2 Ivishak R Alaska
117 D8 Iviti Brazil 7.48S 48.08W
Iviza isld see Ibiza
45 H5 Ivnya U.S.S.R. 51.05N 36.10E
120 F9 Ivo Bolivia 20.29S 63.20W
95 C7 Ivohibe Madagascar 22.28S 46.53E
42 H6 Ivolginsk U.S.S.R. 51.48N 107.18E
104 J10 Ivor Virginia 36.54N 76.57W
89 F9 Ivory Coast Ivory Coast
89 F7 Ivory Coast rep W Africa
103 K4 Ivoryton Connecticut 41.21N 72.26W
52 H10 Ivösjön L Sweden 56.10N 14.30E
45 F3 Ivot U.S.S.R. 53.40N 34.13E
71 A2 Ivoy-le-Pré France 47.21N 2.28E
61 M4 Ivoz-Ramet Belgium 50.36N 5.29E
79 C4 Ivrea Italy 45.28N 7.52E
36 C3 İvrindi Turkey 39.33N 27.27E
71 F2 Ivry-en-Montagne France 47.02N 4.38E
70 N4 Ivry-la-Bataille France 48.53N 1.28E
68 F4 Ivry-sur-Seine France 48.49N 2.24E
48 V12 Ivssorigseq Greenland 70.28N 22.35W
97 M5 Ivugivik Quebec 62.20N 78.00W
92 F6 Ivuna Tanzania 8.21S 32.31E
91 J6 Ivungu Zaïre 4.28S 25.10E
56 D7 Ivybridge Devon Eng 50.23N 3.56W
56 N5 Ivychurch Kent Eng 51.01N 0.55E
104 D8 Ivydale W Virginia 38.32N 81.03W
20 O3 Iwadeyama Japan 38.38N 140.52E
15 L8 Iwa I Marshall Bennett Is Papua New Guinea 8.45S 151.42E
20 O2 Iwai-gawa R Japan
20 P2 Iwaizumi Japan 39.51N 141.50E
20 O1 Iwaki-gawa R Japan
20 O1 Iwaki-san mt Japan 40.38N 140.18E
20 F7 Iwakuni Japan 34.10N 132.09E
20 L1 Iwamizawa Japan 43.12N 141.47E
18 L4 Iwan R Borneo Indon
20 K1 Iwanai Japan 43.01N 140.32E
20 O3 Iwanuma Japan 38.06N 140.51E
20 A1 Iwasawa Saitama Japan
20 O5 Iwase Japan 36.21N 140.02E
20 M5 Iwasuge-yama mt Japan 36.44N 138.34E
20 L7 Iwata Japan 34.42N 137.51E
20 P2 Iwate Japan 39.59N 141.14E
20 P2 Iwate prefect Japan
20 O2 Iwate-san mt Japan 39.53N 140.59E
20 H7 Iwaya Japan 34.35N 135.00E
86 H5 'Iweibid, Gebel Egypt 30.08N 32.13E
86 H5 'Iweibid,Gebel hill Egypt 30.06N 32.07E
90 B8 Iwo Nigeria 7.38N 4.11E
Iwō Jima isld see Iō Tō
Iwō Tō isld see Iō Tō
69 E3 Iwuy France 50.14N 3.20E
115 K9 Ixcamilpa de Guerrero Mexico 18.00N 98.42W
61 S10 Ixelles dist Bruxelles Belgium
115 K7 Ixhuatlán Mexico 20.42N 98.00W
120 E5 Ixiamas Bolivia 13.45S 68.10W
115 K7 Ixmiquilpán Mexico 20.30N 99.15W
95 O6 Ixopo S Africa 30.10S 30.05E
115 K8 Ixtaccihuatl vol Mexico 19.11N 98.38W
115 N9 Ixtacomitán Mexico 17.26N 93.05W
115 J9 Ixtapa,Pta C Mexico 17.40N 101.40W
115 M9 Ixtepec,Ciudad Mexico 16.32N 95.10W
115 H8 Ixtlahuacán Mexico 19.00N 103.40W
115 G7 Ixtlán Nayarit Mexico 21.02N 104.21W
115 L9 Ixtlán Oaxaca Mexico 17.22N 96.29W
56 N3 Ixworth Suffolk Eng 52.18N 0.50E
42 G5 Iya R U.S.S.R.
19 B8 Iya vol Indonesia 8.53S 121.40E
87 B4 Iyal Bakhit Sudan 13.20N 28.39E
33 N6 Iyal Wahibah tribe Oman
18 L9 Iyang isld Indonesia 7.00S 114.10E
37 E5 Iyidere Turkey 40.59N 40.24E
20 F8 Iyo Japan 33.43N 132.42E
20 G8 Iyomishima Japan 33.58N 133.30E
20 F8 Iyo-nada sea Japan
35 F1 Iyyon R Israel
82 J3 Iza R Romania
115 P10 Izabal Guatemala 15.22N 89.09W
115 P10 Izabal, L. de Guatemala
115 P11 Izalco El Salvador 13.43N 89.40W
75 H2 Izalzu Spain 42.55N 1.03W
115 P7 Izamal Mexico 20.56N 89.01W
96 R14 Izaña, Observatorio de Tenerife Canary Is 28.19N 16.30W
115 N10 Izapa ruins Mexico 14.54N 92.11W
75 E1 Izaro I.de Spain 43.25N 2.41W
75 E2 Izarra Spain 42.57N 2.55W
113 F6 Izaviknek R Alaska
44 H5 Izberbash U.S.S.R. 42.31N 47.52E
62 O5 Izbica Poland 50.55N 23.10E
45 E1 Izdeshkovo U.S.S.R. 55.09N 33.27E
76 F5 Izeda Portugal 41.33N 6.43W
61 C3 Izegem Belgium 50.55N 3.13E
32 C5 Izeh Iran 31.48N 49.49E
61 M8 Izel Belgium 49.42N 5.22E
21 C13 Izena shima isld Japan 26.56N 127.59E
61 A3 Izenberge Belgium 51.00N 2.40E
71 H4 Izernore France 46.13N 5.33E
71 G6 Izeron France 45.09N 5.23E
31 G3 Izgal Pakistan 35.25N 73.16E
46 R2 Izhevsk U.S.S.R. 56.49N 53.11E
45 M2 Izhevskoye U.S.S.R. 54.34N 40.53E
47 G3 Izhma U.S.S.R. 65.03N 53.48E
47 G4 Izhma R U.S.S.R.
42 D4 Izhmorskiy U.S.S.R. 56.14N 86.38E
88 G8 Izic reg Morocco
61 N5 Izier Belgium 50.23N 5.35E
71 F6 Izieux France 45.29N 4.30E
113 D10 Izigan,C Aleutian Is 53.16N 167.40W
95 O6 Izingolweni S Africa 30.47S 30.08E
33 M5 Izkī Oman 22.57N 57.46E
46 G6 Izmail Ukraine U.S.S.R. 45.20N 28.48E
45 J4 Izmalkovo U.S.S.R. 52.42N 38.00E
39 D5 Izmaylova,Mys C U.S.S.R. 59.18N 147.38E
45 T3 Izmaylovo U.S.S.R. 53.44N 47.15E
36 C4 İzmir Turkey 38.25N 27.10E
83 J6 İzmir Boz mts Turkey
36 B4 İzmir Körfezi gulf Turkey
37 H2 İzmit Turkey 40.47N 29.55E
37 G2 İzmit Körfezi gulf Turkey
77 H6 Iznájar Spain 37.15N 4.19W
77 H6 Iznájar, Embalse de res Spain 37.15N 4.15W
77 J6 Iznalloz Spain 37.24N 3.30W
77 K4 Iznatoraf Spain 38.10N 3.02W
37 G2 İznik Turkey 40.27N 29.43E
37 G2 İznik Gölü L Turkey
45 G1 Iznoski U.S.S.R. 55.00N 35.19E
45 G5 Iznoskovo U.S.S.R. 51.35N 35.07E
71 K7 Izoard,Col d' pass France 44.49N 6.44E
44 D2 Izobil'nyy U.S.S.R. 45.25N 41.44E
79 P3 Izola Yugoslavia 45.32N 13.39E
37 D7 İzolu Turkey 38.28N 38.40E
95 O6 Izotsha S Africa 30.47S 30.25E
120 G8 Izozog Bolivia 19.28S 62.55W
120 G8 Izozogog Bajo Bolivia 18.45S 62.18W
35 J2 Izra' Syria 32.52N 36.15E
35 G3 'Izrit Jordan 32.39N 35.51E
62 L9 Izsak Hungary 46.49N 19.22E
115 D10 Iztacalco dist Mexico City Mexico
115 O11 Iztapa Guatemala 13.58N 90.42W
115 D10 Iztapalapa dist Mexico City Mexico
82 J9 Iztochni Rodopi mts Bulgaria
115 K8 Izúcar de Matamoros Mexico 18.38N 98.30W
20 M7 Izu-hantō pen Japan
20 C7 Izuhara Japan 34.12N 129.18E
20 G1 Izumi Chiba Japan
20 D9 Izumi Japan 32.02N 130.20E
20 J7 Izumi-Ōtsu Japan 34.29N 135.22E
20 J7 Izumi-Sano Japan 34.23N 135.18E
20 M4 Izumozaki Japan 37.31N 138.40E
47 N4 Izumrud U.S.S.R. 57.08N 61.25E
20 N7 Izu-shotō islds Japan
41 D3 Izvestiy Tsentral'nogo Ispolnitel'nogo Komiteta, Ostrova islds U.S.S.R.
40 E7 Izvestkovyy U.S.S.R. 48.58N 131.35E
82 K4 Izvorul Oltului Romania 46.34N 25.47E
46 F4 Izyaslav Ukraine U.S.S.R. 50.10N 26.46E
43 E4 Izyndy Kazakhstan U.S.S.R. 45.48N 59.29E
45 J7 Izyum Ukraine U.S.S.R. 49.12N 37.19E

33 L4 Jaairah al Ḥamra', Al U.A.E. 25.40N 55.46E
51 M10 Jaala Finland 61.04N 26.30E
33 N5 Ja'alān reg Oman
33 F10 Ja'ar S Yemen 13.12N 45.19E
51 L5 Jaatila Finland 66.17N 25.20E
15 J2 Jaba Bougainville I Papua New Guinea 6.19S 155.13E
35 D4 Jaba Jordan 32.19N 35.14E
35 D7 Jab'a Jordan 41.40N 35.04E
35 E6 Jaba Jordan 31.52N 35.15E
32 G3 Jaba R Iran
75 F7 Jábaga Spain 40.05N 2.16W
33 D9 Jabal at Tair Lt Ho Red Sea 15.35N 41.52E
75 E7 Jabalera Spain 40.17N 2.46W
35 A7 Jabaliya Gaza Strip 31.32N 34.29E
77 K3 Jabalón R Spain
75 H7 Jabaloyas Spain 40.15N 1.24W
29 F6 Jabalpur Madhya Prad India 23.10N 79.59E
29 F6 Jabalpur dist Madhya Prad India
77 J4 Jabalquinto Spain 38.01N 3.43W
33 D3 Jabal Shammar dist Saudi Arabia
31 E3 Jabal-us-Siraj Afghanistan 35.07N 69.14E
118 G10 Jabaquara dist São Paulo Brazil
77 C2 Jabarriega mt Spain 39.08N 6.48W
33 D7 Jabbārah isld Saudi Arabia 19.29N 40.04E
61 C2 Jabbeke Belgium 51.11N 3.06E
34 E2 Jabbul Syria 36.06N 37.32E
34 E3 Jabbūl, Sabkhat al salt marsh Syria
60 T17 Jabeek Netherlands 50.58N 5.56E
63 R5 Jabel E Germany 53.33N 12.33E
22 L2 Jabhlangt Nei Monggol Zizhiqu China 48.54N 117.55E
18 C9 Jabi Pen Malaysia 2.34N 102.47E
35 H3 Jabir Jordan 32.31N 36.12E
33 N5 Jabir tribe Oman
35 H3 Jabir Sta Jordan 32.30N 36.12E
Jabisah see Jebisa oil bore
Jablah see Jeble
83 D3 Jablanica mts Albania
82 G8 Jablanica R Yugoslavia
62 J5 Jablonec nad Nisou Czechoslovakia 50.44N 15.10E
62 K7 Jablonica Czechoslovakia 48.37N 17.26E
65 P1 Jablonné nad Orlicí Czech 50.02N 16.37E
62 H5 Jablonné v Podještědí Czech 50.47N 14.45E
62 L2 Jabłonowo Poland 53.22N 19.09E
62 L6 Jablunkov Czechoslovakia 49.35N 18.45E
90 B5 Jabo Nigeria 12.28N 4.59E
117 J9 Jaboatão Brazil 8.05S 35.00W
118 E7 Jaboticabal Brazil 21.15S 48.17W
Jabrin oasis see Yabrīn oasis
77 C5 Jabugo Spain 37.55N 6.44W
80 M2 Jabuka isld Yugoslavia 43.06N 15.28E
18 F6 Jabung, Tanjung C Sumatra Indon 1.02S 104.22E
120 F1 Jaburu Amazonas Brazil 5.35S 64.05W
117 A7 Jabuti Brazil 4.07S 58.35W
9 C2 Jabwot I atoll Marshall Is Pacific Oc 7.45N 169.00E
75 J2 Jaca Spain 42.34N 0.33W
118 B6 Jacadigo,L Brazil 19.14S 57.43W
121 A10 Jacaf, Canal str Chile
115 K7 Jacala Mexico 21.01N 99.12W
115 O10 Jacaltenango Guatemala 15.39N 91.46W
121 G2 Jacaqua Brazil 29.40S 55.15W
118 G4 Jacaraci Brazil 14.52S 42.23W
118 D3 Jacaré Mato Grosso Brazil 12.02S 53.25W
120 F4 Jacaré Rondônia Brazil 10.10S 64.14W
117 A7 Jacareacanga Brazil 5.59S 57.32W
118 F8 Jacareí Brazil 23.17S 45.57W
118 H9 Jacarepaguá Brazil 22.56S 43.22W
120 F2 Jacaré,R Amazonas Brazil
118 H2 Jacaré, R Bahia Brazil
117 A9 Jacaretinga Brazil 8.30S 59.17W
118 E8 Jacarézinho Brazil 23.08S 49.58W
Jacem see Jāsim
64 L8 Jachenau W Germany 47.36N 11.26E
64 O3 Jáchymov Czechoslovakia 50.22N 12.55E
118 H5 Jacinto Brazil 16.07S 40.15W
112 G9 Jacinto City Texas 29.46N 95.15W
121 J2 Jacinto Machado Brazil 29.01S 49.49W
120 F3 Jaciparaná Brazil 9.16S 64.24W
120 F3 Jaciparanã, R Brazil
64 A1 Jackerath W Germany 51.02N 6.27E
99 D4 Jackfish Ontario 48.47N 86.56W
100 J5 Jackfish L Saskatchewan 53.05N 108.20W
101 R6 Jackfish River Alberta 59.03N 112.50W
100 U7 Jackhead Harbour Manitoba 51.52N 97.16W
97 N6 Jack Lane B Labrador, Nfld
104 P1 Jackman Maine 45.37N 70.16W
110 E1 Jack Mt Washington 48.47N 120.58W
99 C3 Jackpine Ontario 49.39N 87.50W
13 G3 Jack R Queensland
107 M5 Jacksboro Tennessee 36.19N 84.11W
112 J2 Jacksboro Texas 33.13N 98.11W
104 H6 Jacks Mt Pennsylvania
107 J10 Jackson Alabama 31.30N 87.55W
111 D3 Jackson California 38.19N 120.49W
105 D4 Jackson Georgia 33.17N 84.00W
104 B9 Jackson Kentucky 37.32N 83.24W
107 E11 Jackson Louisiana 30.50N 91.14W
106 K7 Jackson Michigan 42.15N 84.24W
108 P6 Jackson Minnesota 43.38N 95.00W
107 F9 Jackson Mississippi 32.20N 90.11W
107 G4 Jackson Missouri 37.23N 89.40W
110 M4 Jackson Montana 45.25N 113.24W
105 K1 Jackson N Carolina 36.24N 77.25W
104 C7 Jackson Ohio 39.03N 82.40W
103 C3 Jackson Pennsylvania 41.50N 75.37W
13 J7 Jackson Queensland 26.40S 149.37E
105 F4 Jackson S Carolina 33.19N 81.50W
107 H6 Jackson Tennessee 35.37N 88.50W
110 P6 Jackson Wyoming 43.28N 110.45W
104 F8 Jackson R Virginia
11 C10 Jackson B New Zealand
101 L10 Jackson Bay Br Col 50.31N 125.45W
11 C11 Jackson Bay New Zealand 44.00S 168.38E
11 J7 Jackson, C New Zealand 41.00S 174.20E
104 A6 Jackson Center Ohio 40.26N 84.02W
109 B4 Jackson Gulch Res Colorado
11 C10 Jackson Head New Zealand 43.58S 168.38E
103 K7 Jackson Heights New York 40.45N 73.53W
Jackson I see Dzheksona, Ostrov
105 C7 Jackson, L Florida 30.33N 84.17W
105 D4 Jackson L Georgia 33.22N 83.53W
110 P6 Jackson L Wyoming 43.55N 110.40W
14 C9 Jackson, Mt W Australia 30.17S 119.16E
110 G8 Jackson Mts Nevada
106 G5 Jacksonport Wisconsin 44.59N 87.11W
107 G9 Jackson Prairie Mississippi
109 F1 Jackson Res Colorado 40.24N 104.05W
11 F9 Jacksons New Zealand 42.47S 171.32E
98 Q4 Jackson's Arm Newfoundland 49.51N 56.49W
94 S14 Jacksons Drift S Africa 26.19S 27.59E
107 L8 Jacksonville Alabama 33.48N 85.47W
107 D7 Jacksonville Arkansas 34.52N 92.08W
105 F7 Jacksonville Florida 30.20N 81.40W
107 F2 Jacksonville Illinois 39.44N 90.14W
103 A7 Jacksonville Maryland 39.31N 76.33W
107 D2 Jacksonville Missouri 39.35N 92.28W
105 K3 Jacksonville N Carolina 34.45N 77.26W
103 A2 Jacksonville New York 42.30N 76.37W
112 M4 Jacksonville Texas 31.59N 95.19W
105 F7 Jacksonville Beach Florida 30.18N 81.24W
89 E9 Jacktown Liberia 5.03N 8.56W
51 F5 Jäckvik Sweden 66.23N 17.00E
113 R4 Jack Wade Alaska 64.04N 141.35W
116 H5 Jacmel Haiti 18.18N 72.32W
115 G4 Jaco Mexico 27.52N 104.00W
19 E8 Jaco isld Indonesia 8.28S 127.21E
Jacob see N 'Kayi
31 E6 Jacobabad Pakistan 28.16N 68.30E
31 E6 Jacobabad dist Pakistan
118 H2 Jacobina Brazil 11.13S 40.30W
111 M5 Jacob Lake Arizona 36.43N 112.14W
100 N1 Jacobs Ontario 50.16N 89.45W
95 H5 Jacobsdal Orange Free State S Africa 29.08S 24.46E
Jacobsdal Transvaal S Africa see Lucerne
103 E6 Jacobstown New Jersey 40.05N 74.36W
35 E5 Jacob's Well anc site Jordan 32.13N 35.17E
103 A7 Jacobus Pennsylvania 39.53N 76.43W
115 H8 Jacona Mexico 19.58N 102.19W
11 B8 Jacquemart I Campbell I Pacific Oc 52.36S 169.08E
99 R7 Jacques Cartier Quebec 45.31N 73.31W
99 T5 Jacques Cartier R Quebec
99 T5 Jacques Cartier, L Quebec 47.35N 71.15W
98 G4 Jacques Cartier, Mt Quebec 49.00N 65.55W
98 H3 Jacques-Cartier Pass Quebec
98 F6 Jacquet River New Brunswick 47.56N 66.01W
89 G9 Jacqueville Ivory Coast 5.12N 4.25W
15 L6 Jacquinot B New Britain
117 J8 Jacú R Brazil
118 F7 Jacuí Minas Gerais Brazil 21.01S 46.45W
121 H2 Jacuí Rio Grande do Sul Brazil 29.58S 53.10W
121 H2 Jacuí R Brazil
118 J3 Jacuípe Brazil 12.29S 38.35W
118 H2 Jacuípe, R Brazil
119 F8 Jacumã, R Brazil
111 H9 Jacumba California 32.36N 116.12W
117 D7 Jacunda Brazil 4.33S 49.25W
117 D6 Jacundá, R Brazil
118 F9 Jacupiranga Brazil 24.38S 47.58W
118 E4 Jaçura Brazil 15.53S 50.51W
119 F2 Jacura Venezuela 11.06N 68.54W
118 H2 Jacuricí R Brazil
35 G8 Jad'a Jordan 31.23N 35.45W
90 F7 Jada Nigeria 8.47N 12.08E
33 M9 Jadādīyah Kuwait 29.14N 47.52E
Jadaidat 'Arar see Judayyidat Ar'ar
89 L2 Jadal reg Mali/Niger
82 E6 Jadar R Yugoslavia
28 D2 Jadcherla Andhra Prad India 16.46N 78.05E
35 J2 Jaddal Syria 32.58N 36.22E
Jaddangi see Juddangi
31 B8 Jaddi, Ras C Pakistan 25.11N 63.31E
63 H6 Jade W Germany 53.22N 8.14E
63 H5 Jade estuary W Germany
63 H6 Jade R W Germany
63 H6 Jadebusen B W Germany
25 M8 Jade Mines Burma
33 D7 Jadhdhānah Saudi Arabia 19.52N 41.45E
33 K8 Jādib S Yemen 16.38N 54.00E
34 K4 Jadīd Iraq 34.15N 42.20E
88 J5 Jadida, El Morocco 33.19N 8.35W
62 N3 Jadów Poland 52.30N 21.40E
75 E6 Jadraque Spain 40.55N 2.55W
80 N1 Jadrtovac Yugoslavia 43.41N 15.58E
85 A4 Jādū Libya 31.58N 12.01E
53 H5 Jægerspris Denmark 55.52N 11.59E
26 Q7 Ja-ela Sri Lanka 7.05N 79.53E
14 C8 Jaellan, Mt W Australia 29.45S 117.40E
19 K4 Jaen Luzon Philippines 15.22N 120.53E
120 A1 Jaen Peru 5.45S 78.51W
77 J5 Jaén Spain 37.46N 3.48W
74 E7 Jaén prov Spain
52 B8 Jæren reg Norway
52 G2 Jævsjo L Norway/Sweden 64.05N 13.00E
32 D3 Ja'farābād Iran 34.50N 50.40E
32 H2 Ja'farābād Khorāsān Iran 37.13N 58.18E
32 C3 Ja'farābād Tehrān Iran 35.46N 49.18E
32 G4 Ja'fārn Iran 33.39N 56.18E
95 B8 Jafaro Madagascar 24.54S 45.31E
Ja'faru see Ja'fārn
89 F1 Jafene reg Mauritania
Jaffa see Tel Aviv-Yafo
12 E6 Jaffa, C S Australia 36.58S 139.39E
26 Q2 Jaffna Sri Lanka 9.40N 80.01E
26 R2 Jaffna Lagoon Sri Lanka
Jafi see Yafi
34 D8 Jafr, El Jordan 30.16N 36.11E
34 D8 Jafr, El salt marsh Jordan
33 J4 Jāfūrah, Al des reg Saudi Arabia
30 A2 Jagadhri Haryana India 30.11N 77.18E
92 K9 Jagaia Mozambique 15.00S 40.10E
28 C3 Jagalur Karnataka India 14.35N 76.15E
30 C6 Jagamanpur Uttar Prad India 26.24N 79.13E
31 H8 Jagannathganj Ghat Bangladesh 24.46N 89.51E
30 C5 Jagat Uttar Prad India 27.58N 79.13E
30 E6 Jagatpur Uttar Prad India 26.03N 81.16E
31 E3 Jagdalak Afghanistan 34.25N 69.45E
29 H8 Jagdalpur Madhya Prad India 19.04N 82.05E
21 C2 Jagdaqi Nei Monggol Zizhiqu China 50.29N 124.13E
30 H7 Jagdispur Bihar India 25.29N 84.25E

30 E6 Jagdispur Uttar Prad India 26.27N 81.37E
65 M4 Jagenbach Austria 48.39N 15.03E
95 O4 Jagersdrif, De S Africa 28.01S 30.25E
95 J5 Jagersfontein S Africa 29.46S 25.25E
64 N3 Jägersgrün E Germany 50.27N 12.28E
24 C9 Jaggang Xizang Zizhiqu China 32.52N 79.45E
28 E2 Jaggayyapeta Andhra Prad India 16.56N 80.08E
Jaghatai see Joghatāy
85 H5 Jaghbūb, al Libya 29.42N 24.38E
32 G7 Jaghīn Iran 27.13N 57.25E
34 J2 Jaghjagha R Syria
Jagial see Jagtial
Jagin see Jaghīn
32 H8 Jagīn R Iran
90 D7 Jagindi Nigeria 9.21N 8.15E
32 H8 Jagīn, Ra's C Iran 25.33N 58.11E
30 A6 Jagnair Uttar Prad India 26.52N 77.36E
113 Q2 Jago R Alaska
29 D2 Jagraon Punjab India 30.48N 75.36E
Jagsamka see Luding
Jagsamka see Luding
64 J5 Jagst R W Germany
64 J5 Jagstzell W Germany 49.01N 10.07E
28 D1 Jagtial Andhra Prad India 18.48N 78.55E
90 H10 Jagua Cent Afr Rep 3.55N 16.41E
118 H3 Jaguaquara Brazil 13.31S 39.56W
121 H4 Jaguarão Brazil 32.30S 53.25W
121 H4 Jaguarão, R Brazil
118 H2 Jaguarari Brazil 10.18S 40.12W
117 H7 Jaguaretama Brazil 5.38S 38.48W
121 G2 Jaguari Brazil 29.29S 54.40W
121 G2 Jaguari R Brazil
118 E9 Jaguariaíva Brazil 24.15S 49.44W
117 H7 Jaguaribe Brazil 5.54S 38.36W
117 G8 Jaguaribe, R Brazil
118 J3 Jaguaripe Brazil 13.07S 38.49W
117 H7 Jaguaruana Brazil 4.50S 37.50W
121 J2 Jaguaruna Brazil 28.40S 49.04W
121 C2 Jagüe Argentina 28.38S 68.25W
121 C2 Jagüe, R Argentina
116 D3 Jaguey Grande Cuba 22.31N 81.07W
33 E9 Jāh, Al Yemen 14.21N 43.04E
Jahama see Jahmah
30 C4 Jahanabad Bareilly, Uttar Prad India 28.38N 79.43E
30 H7 Jahanabad Bihar India 25.13N 84.59E
30 D6 Jahanabad Kanpur India 26.06N 80.21E
32 C2 Jahan Dagh mt Iran 36.26N 48.30E
30 B4 Jahangirabad Uttar Prad India 28.24N 78.06E
Jahangirnagar see Dacca
30 A4 Jahangirpur Uttar Prad India 28.12N 77.42E
Jahara, Al see Jahrah, Al
29 D5 Jahazpur Rajasthan India 25.38N 75.20E
13 B1 Jahleel Pt N Terr Australia 11.10S 131.17E
34 N9 Jahmah wells Iraq 29.45N 45.30E
30 C1 Jahnavi R Uttar Prad India
82 E7 Jahorina mt Yugoslavia 43.41N 18.36E
35 F9 Jahra Jordan 31.02N 35.39E
33 M9 Jahrah, Al Kuwait 29.22N 47.40E
32 E6 Jahrom Iran 28.29N 53.32E
90 D5 Jahun Nigeria 12.07N 9.35E
117 B3 Jai R Surinam
89 D7 Jaiama Sierra Leone 8.33N 11.00W
117 G8 Jaicós Brazil 7.17S 41.05W
28 A2 Jaigarh Maharashtra India 17.18N 73.13E
29 E2 Jaijon Doaba Punjab India 31.22N 76.08E
19 E3 Jailolo Halmahera Indon 1.05N 127.29E
Jailolo Gilolo isld see Halmahera
19 F3 Jailolo, Selat str Moluccas Indon
89 D3 Jaimamé Mauritania 16.38N 10.31E
120 D8 Jaiña Chile 19.33S 69.15W
30 J8 Jainagar Bihar India 24.23N 85.39E
22 F9 Jainca Qinghai China 35.48N 102.25E
31 J8 Jaintiapur Bangladesh 25.06N 92.08E
28 K2 Jaipur Assam India 27.14N 95.24E
28 F1 Jaipur Orissa India 18.51N 82.41E
29 D4 Jaipur Rajasthan India 26.53N 75.50E
29 J2 Jaipur W Bengal India 23.25N 86.10E
29 D4 Jaipur dist Rajasthan India
31 H8 Jaipurhat Bangladesh 25.04N 89.06E
Jairoud see Jerūd
30 E6 Jais Uttar Prad India 26.16N 81.32E
35 F10 Ja'is watercourse Jordan
29 B4 Jaisalmer Rajasthan India 26.52N 70.55E
29 B4 Jaisalmer dist Rajasthan India
30 A5 Jait Uttar Prad India 27.36N 77.36E
29 F7 Jaitgarh hill Maharashtra India 20.58N 78.40E
30 H8 Jaitiya Bihar India 24.55N 84.38E
30 C8 Jaitpur Madhya Prad India 24.19N 79.50E
30 C7 Jaitpur Uttar Prad India 25.15N 79.34E
35 D5 Jaiyus Jordan 32.12N 35.02E
30 F4 Jajarkot Nepal 28.40N 82.12E
32 G2 Jajarm Iran 36.58N 56.26E
30 A6 Jajau Uttar Prad India 26.56N 77.56E
82 D6 Jajce Yugoslavia 44.20N 17.16E
32 D3 Jaji R Iran
90 E5 Jajibiriri Nigeria 13.00N 11.50E
29 K7 Jajpur Orissa India 20.50N 86.25E
Jaju see Dayu
65 P7 Ják Hungary 47.09N 16.34E
94 D2 Jakalsberg Namibia 19.23S 17.28E
94 C4 Jakalswater Namibia 22.36S 15.19E
18 G9 Jakarta Java Indon 6.08S 106.45E
18 F2 Jakarta, Teluk B Indonesia
101 G5 Jakes Corner Yukon Terr 60.20N 133.58W
29 D3 Jakhal Haryana India 29.46N 75.51E
29 A6 Jakhau Gujarat India 23.15N 68.48E
30 B8 Jakhaura Uttar Prad India 24.54N 78.20E
30 B8 Jakhlaun Uttar Prad India 24.34N 78.18E
31 D5 Jakin mt Afghanistan 31.47N 66.03E
91 B1 Jakiri Cameroon 6.06N 10.55E
32 J7 Jakkī Kowr Iran 26.09N 61.34E
66 O2 Jakobsbad Switzerland 47.19N 9.21E
51 P2 Jakobselv R Norway/U.S.S.R.
48 T8 Jakobshavn Greenland 69.10N 51.05W
51 K8 Jakobstad Finland 63.41N 22.40E
90 B9 Jakpa Nigeria 5.51N 5.06E
82 G9 Jakupica mts Yugoslavia
92 F7 Jakwa Gorge Malawi 11.01S 33.50E
109 G9 Jal New Mexico 32.05N 103.12W
32 G7 Jalābī Iran 27.24N 56.40E
115 L8 Jalacingo Mexico 19.48N 97.19W
35 G5 Jal'ad Jordan 32.08N 35.46E
33 F7 Jaladah, Al des area Saudi Arabia
21 B4 Jalaid Qi Nei Monggol Zizhiqu China 46.44N 122.54E
22 L2 Jalai Nur Nei Monggol Zizhiqu China 49.26N 117.44E
33 F4 Jalājil Saudi Arabia 25.39N 45.29E
31 F3 Jalalabad Afghanistan 34.26N 70.25E
30 C5 Jalalabad Farukhabad, Uttar Prad India 27.06N 79.47E
29 D2 Jalalabad Punjab India 30.36N 74.17E
30 C5 Jalalabad Shahjahanpur, Uttar Prad India 27.43N 79.39E
30 A3 Jalalabad Uttar Prad India 29.37N 77.25E
30 L7 Jalalgarh Bihar India 25.59N 87.31E
30 B5 Jalali Uttar Prad India 27.51N 78.15E
33 L9 Jāl al Liyah Kuwait
30 F6 Jalalpur Faizabad, Uttar Prad India 26.19N 82.44E
29 C7 Jalalpur Gujarat India 20.58N 72.59E
30 C7 Jalalpur Hamirpur, Uttar Prad India 25.52N 79.48E
Jalalpur Pakistansee Jalalpur Pirwala
31 H4 Jalalpur Pakistan 32.39N 74.11E
30 E7 Jalalpur Dhai Uttar Prad India 26.00N 81.09E
31 F6 Jalalpur Pirwala Pakistan 29.30N 71.20E
35 E3 Jalama Jordan 32.31N 35.19E
34 G7 Jālamīd, Al Saudi Arabia 31.21N 39.57E
Ja'lān see Ja'alān reg
77 O2 Jalance Spain 39.12N 1.05W
115 P10 Jalapa Guatemala 14.39N 89.59W
115 N9 Jalapa Mexico 17.45N 92.48W
115 L3 Jalapa Nicaragua 13.56N 86.11W
115 L8 Jalapa Enríquez Mexico 19.32N 96.56W
28 D4 Jalarpet Tamil Nadu India 12.35N 78.33E
51 K9 Jalasjärvi Finland 62.30N 22.50E
31 C4 Jalauddin Afghanistan 32.20N 64.26E
30 C6 Jalaun Uttar Prad India 26.09N 79.20E
30 C6 Jalaun dist Uttar Prad India
33 M9 Jāl az Zawr Kuwait
13 C2 Jalboi R N Terr Australia
35 E4 Jalbun Jordan 32.27N 35.25E
31 D5 Jaldak Afghanistan 31.58N 66.44E
31 H8 Jaldakha R Bangladesh etc
87 J6 Jaldessa Ethiopia 9.42N 42.10E
93 K3 Jaldessa Kenya 2.10N 38.11E
28 C2 Jaldrug Karnataka India 16.17N 76.29E
30 J6 Jale Bihar India 26.23N 85.44E
118 E7 Jales Brazil 20.10S 50.38W
30 B5 Jalesar Uttar Prad India 27.29N 78.18E
30 J6 Jaleswar Nepal 26.40N 85.47E
29 K7 Jaleswar Orissa India 21.48N 87.14E
29 E7 Jalgaon Akola, Maharashtra India 21.03N 76.35E
29 D7 Jalgaon Maharashtra India 21.01N 75.39E
29 D7 Jalgaon dist Maharashtra India
61 O4 Jalhay Belgium 50.33N 5.58E
34 O8 Jalībah Iraq 30.36N 46.33E
Jalib Bakār see Qalīb Bāqūr
71 D4 Jaligny France 46.22N 3.35E
32 H3 Jalīlābād Iran 34.54N 59.43E
90 E7 Jalingo Nigeria 8.55N 11.25E
115 G7 Jalisco state Mexico
35 C5 Jaljūlya Israel 32.09N 34.57E
31 G3 Jalkot Pakistan 35.14N 73.24E
Jallabi see Jalābī
72 C1 Jallais France 47.12N 0.52W
Jallakan see Kūshkak
76 A3 Jallas R Spain
Jallieu see Bourgoin-Jallieu
66 B8 Jallouvre, Pic de mt France 46.00N 6.28E
29 D8 Jalna Maharashtra India 19.50N 75.58E
75 F3 Jalón Spain 42.13N 2.29W
77 Q3 Jalón Spain 38.45N 0.01W
75 H4 Jalón R Spain
69 G5 Jâlons France 49.01N 4.11E
Jalo Oasis see Waḥat Jālū
29 C5 Jalor Rajasthan India 25.21N 72.43E
29 C5 Jalor dist Rajasthan India
115 H7 Jalostotitlán Mexico 21.11N 102.29W
115 H7 Jalpa Guanajuato Mexico 20.52N 102.00W
115 H7 Jalpa Zacatecas Mexico 21.40N 103.00W
29 L4 Jalpaiguri W Bengal India 26.30N 88.50E
29 L4 Jalpaiguri dist W Bengal India
115 K7 Jalpan Mexico 21.13N 99.28W
29 L4 Jalpes W Bengal India 26.30N 88.59E
32 K7 Jālq Iran 27.37N 62.46E
35 E4 Jalqamus Jordan 32.25N 35.22E
31 E3 Jalrez Afghanistan 34.29N 68.36E
28 B4 Jalsur Karnataka India 12.35N 75.20E
35 E5 Jalud Jordan 32.04N 35.19E
Jālūd R see Harod R
9 C3 Jaluit atoll Marshall Is Pacific Oc 6.00N 169.35E
35 G7 Jalul Jordan 31.44N 35.51E
34 N4 Jalūlā' Iraq 34.16N 45.10E
32 E7 Jam Iran 27.49N 52.22E
32 J3 Jām R Iran
32 J3 Jām reg Iran
119 B8 Jama Ecuador 0.11S 80.12W
15 G5 Jama Papua New Guinea 3.58S 143.01E
90 D6 Jamaari Nigeria 11.42N 9.54E
61 J6 Jamagne Belgium 50.13N 4.32E
116 G4 Jamaica Cuba 20.16N 75.10W
103 N7 Jamaica New York 40.42N 73.48W
104 N3 Jamaica Vermont 43.06N 72.47W
116 M2 Jamaica / West Indies
103 K8 Jamaica B New York
103 L8 Jamaica Bay Wildlife Refuge New York
116 G5 Jamaica Chan Greater Antilles
104 P9 Jamaica Pond Boston, Mass 42.18N 71.04W
31 D7 Jama Jamot Pakistan 26.00N 66.55E
32 B2 Jamalabad Āzārbāījān-e Khāvarī Iran 37.14N 47.43E
32 C4 Jamālābād Tehrān Iran 33.55N 49.31E
120 A1 Jamalca Peru 5.55S 78.18W
33 J4 Jamalīyah, Al Qatar, The Gulf 25.42N 51.09E
31 H8 Jamalpur Bangladesh 24.54N 89.57E
30 K7 Jamalpur Bihar India 25.19N 86.30E
119 E9 Jamanari, R Brazil
66 D6 Jaman, Col de pass Switzerland 46.28N 6.58E
116 A1 Jamanota mt Aruba W I 12.29N 69.57W
117 B7 Jamanxim, R Brazil
119 B8 Jama Pta Ecuador 0.10S 80.22W
120 F3 Jamari Brazil 8.45S 63.25W
120 F3 Jamari, R Brazil
120 E10 Jama, Salinade salt pan Argentina
24 D3 Jamati Xinjiang Uygur Zizhiqu China 45.44N 83.35E
91 E10 Jamba Angola 12.46S 16.17E
91 E11 Jamba Angola 14.40S 16.02E
98 F4 Jamban, Pte Quebec 49.56N 66.59W
66 C7 Jambaz, Col de pass France 46.15N 6.31E
Jambe see Abaso
119 B9 Jambeli, Can.de Ecuador
12 K5 Jamberoo New S Wales 34.40S 150.44E
61 K5 Jambes Belgium 50.27N 4.52E
Jambi see Telanaipura
18 E6 Jambi prov Sumatra Indonesia
13 K6 Jambin Queensland 24.14S 150.21E
29 C4 Jambo Rajasthan India 27.14N 72.30E
18 B3 Jamboaye R Sumatra Indon
18 B3 Jambuair, Tanjung C Sumatra Indon 5.15N 97.30E
34 M3 Jambur Iraq 35.07N 44.33E
89 A5 Jambur The Gambia 13.16N 16.41W
29 C6 Jambusar Gujarat India 22.00N 72.50E
30 K8 Jamdaha Bihar India 24.45N 86.54E
Jamdena / see Yamdena
28 D1 Jamekunte Andhra Prad India 18.17N 79.30E
107 C5 James R Missouri
108 N6 James R N Dakota/S Dakota
101 S2 James R N W Terr
104 G9 James R Virginia
31 E8 Jamesabad Pakistan 25.16N 69.18E
97 L7 James B Canada
103 F6 Jamesburg New Jersey 40.22N 74.27W
105 K2 James City N Carolina 35.05N 77.02W
104 G5 James City Pennsylvania 41.37N 78.41W
121 A10 James I Chile 45.00S 74.10W
James I Galápagos Is see San Salvador, I.
105 G5 James I S Carolina 32.40N 80.09W
50 S13 James I Land Spitsbergen
105 F2 James, L N Carolina 35.45N 81.55W
107 C1 Jameson Missouri 40.00N 93.59W
101 S1 Jameson Is N W Terr
48 U11 Jameson Land Greenland
95 M2 Jameson Park S Africa 26.28S 28.25E
95 O4 Jameson's Drift S Africa 28.47S 30.55E
103 J5 Jamesport Long I, N Y 40.57N 72.34W
107 C2 Jamesport Missouri 39.58N 93.47W
105 L12 James Pt Bahamas 25.21N 76.23W
14 A4 James Pt W Australia 32.14S 115.45E
13 D5 James R N Terr Australia
104 J9 James R Virginia
13 C6 James Ra N Terr Australia
123 E14 James Ross I Antarctica
101 Z1 James Ross Str N W Terr
107 K2 Jamestown Indiana 39.55N 86.37W
109 N2 Jamestown Kansas 39.37N 97.53W
59 H5 Jamestown Leix Irish Rep 53.07N 7.06W
106 J7 Jamestown Michigan 42.50N 85.50W
108 M3 Jamestown N Dakota 46.54N 98.42W
104 F4 Jamestown New York 42.05N 79.15W
104 B7 Jamestown Ohio 39.39N 83.45W
Jamestown Ontario see Wawa Ontario
104 E5 Jamestown Pennsylvania 41.30N 80.25W
103 M3 Jamestown Rhode I 41.30N 71.23W
95 K7 Jamestown S Africa 31.07S 26.48E
96 B13 Jamestown St Helena 15.56S 5.44W
12 E5 Jamestown S Australia 33.12S 138.38E
105 H4 Jamestown S Carolina 33.17N 79.43W
58 G7 Jamestown Strathclyde Scotland 56.00N 4.34W
107 M5 Jamestown Tennessee 36.24N 84.58W
104 J9 Jamestown Nat.Hist.Site Virginia
108 M2 Jamestown Res N Dakota
105 L2 Jamesville N Carolina 35.49N 76.56W
104 J4 Jamesville New York 42.58N 76.05W
69 J5 Jametz France 49.26N 5.23E
110 H5 Jamieson Oregon 44.11N 117.26W
51 K10 Jämijärvi Finland 61.50N 22.40E
32 C3 Jamilābād Iran 34.24N 48.30E
115 L9 Jamiltepec Mexico 16.18N 97.51W
61 J6 Jamiolle Belgium 50.13N 4.30E
61 H5 Jamiouix Belgium 50.22N 4.25E
108 L7 Jamison Nebraska 42.59N 99.18W
28 B2 Jamkhandi Karnataka India 16.31N 75.21E
28 B1 Jamkhed Maharashtra India 18.44N 75.24E
31 H4 Jamki Pakistan 32.20N 74.24E
35 G2 Jamlah, El Syria 32.48N 35.51E
33 M5 Jammah Oman 23.35N 57.38E
28 D3 Jammalamadugu Andhra Prad India 14.51N 78.21E
Jammāma see Ruḥama
87 G5 Jamma,R Ethiopia
53 C2 Jammerbugten B Denmark
95 K5 Jammerdrif S Africa 29.42S 26.58E
53 G5 Jammerland Bugt B Denmark 55.35N 11.03E
31 H4 Jammu Kashmir 32.43N 74.54E
31 H4 Jammu dist Kashmir
31 H3 Jammu and Kashmir state S Asia
29 B6 Jamnagar Gujarat India 22.28N 70.06E
29 A6 Jamnagar dist Gujarat India
32 J3 Jamnatabad Iran 35.38N 61.08E
29 D7 Jamner Maharashtra India 20.47N 75.52E
30 B8 Jamni R Uttar Prad etc India
62 J1 Jamno, Jezioro L Poland 54.15N 16.10E
61 M8 Jamoigne Belgium 49.42N 5.25E
18 G9 Jampang Kulon Java Indon 7.18S 106.33E
31 F6 Jampur Pakistan 29.38N 70.40E
31 F3 Jamrud Pakistan 34.01N 71.28E
51 L10 Jämsä Finland 61.51N 25.10E
31 E7 Jam Sahib Pakistan 26.20N 68.39E
51 L10 Jämsänkoski Finland 61.54N 25.10E
29 J2 Jamshedpur Bihar India 22.47N 86.12E
32 A7 Jamshīdābād sub Tehrān Iran
66 R4 Jam Tal V Austria
30 F7 Jamtali Uttar Prad India 25.50N 82.08E
29 K1 Jamtara Bihar India 23.58N 86.49E
52 G3 Jämtland dist Sweden
52 J3 Jämtl Sikås Sweden 63.38N 15.15E
Jamtup, Tg C see Yamtua, Tg. C
30 K8 Jamui Bihar India 24.57N 86.14E
18 M4 Jamuk, Gunung mt Borneo Indon 2.39N 116.35E
111 H9 Jamul California 32.41N 116.51W
28 J2 Jamuna R Assam India
31 H8 Jamuna R Bangladesh
119 C6 Jamundí Colombia 3.16N 76.31W
Jamur, Danau L see Yamur, Danau L
76 G4 Jamuz R Spain
33 H3 Janā isld Saudi Arabia 27.22N 49.56E
33 M7 Janabah tribe Oman
34 D7 Janab, Wādī el watercourse Jordan
Janah see Jonāh
93 D6 Jana I Uganda 0.14S 32.35E
29 G6 Janakpur Madhya Prad India 23.40N 81.50E
30 J6 Janakpur Nepal 26.44N 85.56E
75 L6 Jana, La Spain 40.31N 0.14E
119 H9 Janauacá, L Brazil 3.25S 60.17W
118 G4 Janaúba Brazil 15.47S 43.16W
117 D4 Janaucú, I Brazil
31 B3 Janawar Afghanistan 34.26N 63.28E
31 G4 Jand Pakistan 33.30N 72.06E
118 E5 Jandaia Brazil 17.04S 50.10W
118 J2 Jandaíra Brazil 11.36S 37.48W
14 B3 Jandakot dist Perth, W Aust
14 B3 Jandakot, L W Australia 32.09S 115.56E
77 E8 Janda, Laguna de la Spain
32 F3 Jandaq Iran 34.04N 54.26E
95 D9 Jan de Boers S Africa 33.16S 20.09E
53 A5 Janderup Denmark 55.38N 8.23E
96 S11 Jandía pen Fuerteventura Canary Is
31 H5 Jandiala Pakistan 31.51N 74.38E
96 R12 Jandía, Pta. de Fuerteventura Canary Is 28.03N 14.32W
120 D1 Jandiatuba, R Brazil
31 F4 Jandola Pakistan 32.20N 70.10E
13 K7 Jandowae Queensland 26.46S 151.03E
61 K4 Jandrain-Jandrenoulle Belgium 50.40N 4.59E
77 J4 Jándula R Spain
77 J4 Jándula, Embalse del res Spain 38.15N 3.55E
77 K5 Jandulillo R Spain
64 P5 Jandvice n. Úhlavou Czechoslovakia 49.21N 13.14E
76 D8 Janeiro de Cima Portugal 40.04N 7.48W
118 F2 Janeiro, R Brazil
104 E7 Jane Lew W Virginia 39.07N 80.26W
11 C12 Jane Pk mt New Zealand 45.20S 168.21E
110 E9 Janesville California 40.19N 120.31W
108 S7 Janesville Iowa 42.38N 92.28W
108 R5 Janesville Minnesota 44.06N 93.41W
106 E7 Janesville Wisconsin 42.42N 89.02W
58 K2 Janetstown Highland Scotland 58.16N 3.23W
88 H8 Janga Morocco 26.02N 11.54W
118 D10 Jangada Brazil 26.23S 51.15W
15 J1 Jangaini isld Papua New Guinea 4.45S 155.17E
32 H3 Jangal Iran 34.40N 59.11E
94 N5 Jangamo Mozambique 24.06S 35.21E
28 D2 Jangaon Andhra Prad India 17.44N 79.10E
18 M7 Jangeru Borneo Indon 2.19S 116.31E
30 B1 Jangi Himachal Prad India 31.37N 78.26E
29 L5 Jangipur W Bengal India 24.28N 88.08E
18 L6 Jangkang Kalimantan Indonesia 1.07S 114.09E
118 C7 Jango Brazil 20.24S 55.28W
24 H9 Jangsib Qinghai China 33.50N 94.52E
18 F6 Jang, Tanjung C Indonesia 0.17S 105.00E
32 B1 Jānī Beyglū Iran 38.39N 47.11E
63 S8 Jänickendorf E Germany 52.03N 13.13E
31 F4 Jani Khel Pakistan 32.47N 70.34E
34 H3 Janīn Syria 35.22N 40.08E
18 D9 Janing hill Pen Malaysia 2.30N 103.25E
31 C5 Jani Qala Afghanistan 30.42N 64.02E
82 G8 Janjevo Yugoslavia 42.33N 21.15E
95 B6 Janjina Madagascar 20.30S 45.50E
28 A1 Janjira Maharashtra India 18.16N 72.59E
93 L5 Janju Kenya 0.43N 39.06E
95 H3 Jan Kemp S Africa 27.55S 24.51E
100 P4 Jan L Saskatchewan
18 M4 Janlonong Borneo Indon 2.17N 116.58E
49 C2 Jan Mayen isld Arctic Oc 71.00N 9.00W
34 O6 Jannah Iraq 32.38N 46.50E
12 L8 Jannali New S Wales 34.01S 151.05E
32 D3 Jannatābād Iran 34.30N 51.09E
Jannine see Janīn
115 E2 Janos Mexico 30.50N 108.10W
62 L9 Jánoshalma Hungary 46.20N 19.20E
62 K8 Jánosháza Hungary 47.06N 17.11E
63 S5 Janow E Germany 53.47N 13.25E
62 K3 Janowiec Poland 52.45N 17.29E
62 N5 Janów Lubelski Poland 50.42N 22.24E
62 O3 Janów Podlaski Poland 52.11N 23.11E
30 A3 Jansath Uttar Prad India 29.20N 77.50E
108 N9 Jansen Nebraska 40.10N 97.04W
100 N7 Jansen Saskatchewan 51.46N 104.40W
95 H8 Jansenville S Africa 32.56S 24.40E
95 M2 Jan Smuts airport S Africa 26.09S 28.15E
117 D5 Janua Cœli Brazil 1.55S 49.24W
118 G4 Januária Brazil 15.28S 44.23W
96 T8 Janubio, Laguna de Lanzarote Canary Is 28.56N 13.50W
70 O5 Janville France 48.12N 1.52E
28 C1 Janwada Karnataka India 18.01N 77.32E
31 B8 Janzar mt Pakistan 25.54N 63.42E
70 H6 Janzé France 47.58N 1.29W
31 B7 Jaodar Pakistan 27.23N 62.56E
Jao-p'ing see Sanrao
75 L3 Jaoquin Costa, Embalse de res Spain 42.09N 0.19E
29 D6 Jaora Madhya Prad India 23.40N 75.10E
Jaora Mandsaur, Madhya Prad see Malhargarh
17 M5 Japan empire E Asia
Japan Alps Nat.Park see Chūbu Sangaku Nat. Park
21 E8 Japan, Sea of E Asia
122 F4 Japan Trench Pacific Oc
118 J2 Japaratuba Brazil 10.35S 36.59W
117 D5 Japariteua Brazil 1.43S 48.22W
Japen / see Yapen /
Japen, Selat see Sorenarwa, Selat
120 C2 Japiim Brazil 7.37S 72.55W
29 D4 Japog Rajasthan India 26.52N 75.08E
115 L2 Japón Honduras 15.36N 86.20W
51 N9 Jäppilä Finland 62.24N 27.30E
119 G9 Japurá, R Brazil
28 K3 Japyo Mt Nagaland India 25.32N 94.07E
115 P6 Jaqué Panama 7.31N 78.08W
120 C6 Jaqui Peru 15.30S 74.26W
93 L6 Jara Kenya 0.44S 39.49E
75 G5 Jaraba Spain 41.11N 1.54W
116 J5 Jarabacoa Dominican Rep 19.09N 70.39W
35 F2 Jarabah Syria 32.57N 35.39E
77 Q2 Jaraco Spain 39.02N 0.12W
33 D7 Jarad Saudi Arabia 19.00N 41.25E
87 K3 Jarada, Al Yemen 15.47N 45.07E
77 O2 Jarafuel Spain 39.09N 1.05W
118 E4 Jaráguá Brazil 15.45S 49.18W
118 E10 Jaraguá do Sul Brazil 26.29S 49.07W
118 C7 Jaraguari Brazil 20.06S 54.24W
118 E10 Jaraguá, Serra mts Brazil
76 H9 Jaraicejo Spain 39.40N 5.49W
76 H8 Jaraiz de la Vera Spain 40.04N 5.45W
93 M6 Jara Jila Kenya 0.21S 40.59E
29 F1 Jara La pass Xizang Zizhiqu 32.45N 79.35E
76 J9 Jara, La reg Spain
28 K1 Jaram Assam India 28.02N 94.10E
75 C6 Jarama R Spain
121 L6 Jaramillo Argentina 47.10S 67.10W
76 H8 Jarandilla Spain 40.08N 5.39W
35 G4 Jarash Jordan 32.17N 35.54E
35 G4 Jarash R Jordan
77 N5 Jara, Sierra de la mts Spain
117 C6 Jarauçu, R Brazil
34 F8 Jarawī, Al Saudi Arabia 30.10N 38.44E
75 F4 Jaray Spain 41.41N 2.07W
110 K8 Jarbidge Nevada 41.53N 115.26W
52 K6 Järbo Sweden 60.43N 16.40E
110 K7 Jarbridge R Idaho
85 F3 Jardas Libya 32.19N 20.57E
14 B10 Jardee W Australia 34.18S 116.04E
117 G8 Jardim Ceará Brazil 7.31S 39.15W
118 C7 Jardim Mato Grosso do Sul Brazil 21.29S 56.02W
118 F10 Jardim America dist São Paulo Brazil
96 O7 Jardim do Mar Madeira Is 32.44N 17.12W
117 H8 Jardim do Serido Brazil 6.31S 36.45W
118 F10 Jardim Paulista dist São Paulo Brazil
77 M3 Jardín R Spain
85 F4 Jardinah Libya 31.48N 20.12E
13 F1 Jardine R Queensland
98 E6 Jardine Brook New Brunswick 47.23N 67.36W
116 E4 Jardines de la Reina islds Cuba
118 E6 Jardinésia Brazil 19.18S 48.42W
23 B9 Jardines Lookout mt Hong Kong 22.16N 114.11E
118 F7 Jardinópolis Brazil 20.59S 47.48W
72 A3 Jard-sur-Mer France 46.26N 1.34W
52 J9 Järeda Sweden 57.24N 15.35E
52 F6 Jaren Norway 60.24N 10.35E
65 N8 Jarenina Yugoslavia 46.37N 15.42E
30 A6 Jareru Madhya Prad India 26.03N 77.41E
76 E4 Jares R Spain
33 C4 Jarf, Al ridge Saudi Arabia
22 E2 Jargalant Arhangay Mongolia 48.45N 100.45E
22 K3 Jargalant Dornod Mongolia 46.58N 115.20E
Jargalant Hovd Mongoliasee Hovd
70 P6 Jargeau France 47.51N 2.01E
Jarh Jarh R see Jaghjagha R
31 H8 Jaria Jhanjail Bangladesh 25.00N 90.40E
120 G1 Jari, L Brazil 5.00S 62.21W
117 C4 Jari, R Brazil
90 C6 Jarji Nigeria 10.49N 7.35E
50 H3 Jarlsstadhir Iceland 65.33N 17.29W
85 B6 Jarmah Libya 26.31N 13.06E
63 S5 Jarmen E Germany 53.56N 13.21E
69 M7 Jarménil France 48.07N 6.35E
34 M3 Jarmo anc site Iraq 35.34N 44.55E
30 L8 Jarmundi Bihar India 24.25N 87.03E
52 K7 Järna Sweden 59.05N 17.35E
72 D4 Jarnac France 45.41N 0.10W
72 J3 Jarnages France 46.11N 2.05E
52 J8 Järnlunden L Sweden 58.13N 15.40E
69 K5 Jarny France 49.09N 5.54E
19 L6 Jaro Philippines 10.44N 122.30E
62 K4 Jarocin Poland 51.59N 17.30E
29 C6 Jarod Gujarat India 22.25N 73.21E
62 J5 Jaroměř Czechoslovakia 50.22N 15.55E
65 N3 Jaroměřice nad Rokytnou Czech 49.06N 15.53E
15 B5 Jarona Irian Jaya 3.43S 133.23E
116 F4 Jaronu Cuba 21.49N 77.58W
65 O4 Jaroslavice Czechoslovakia 48.46N 16.14E
62 O5 Jarosław Poland 50.00N 22.40E
109 E4 Jaroso Colorado 37.01N 105.37W
65 M3 Jarošov Czechoslovakia 49.13N 15.05E
52 G3 Järpen Sweden 63.20N 13.30E
75 G4 Jarque Spain 41.33N 1.40W
35 F8 Jarra watercourse Jordan
32 C5 Jarrāhī R Iran
34 J2 Jarrāh, Wādī R Syria
115 J7 Jarral de Berrio Mexico 21.42N 101.01W
104 H10 Jarratt Virginia 36.48N 77.29W
51 G5 Jarre mt Sweden 66.36N 18.40E
112 K5 Jarrell Texas 30.50N 97.37W
25 G3 Jarres, Plaine des Laos
103 B7 Jarrettsville Maryland 39.36N 76.29W
72 B3 Jarrie, la France 46.08N 1.01W
121 E8 Jarrillas Argentina 40.24S 62.45W
100 F6 Jarrow Alberta 52.56N 111.23W
57 L3 Jarrow Tyne and Wear Eng 54.59N 1.29W
71 B2 Jars France 47.24N 2.40E
87 F8 Jarso Ethiopia 5.17N 37.31E
87 H8 Jarso Ethiopia 4.15N 41.25E
22 G7 Jartai Nei Monggol Zizhiqu China 39.44N 105.47E
22 G7 Jartai Yanchi L Nei Monggol Zizhiqu China
120 G4 Jarú Brazil 10.24S 62.45W
33 K8 Jarūb S Yemen 16.21N 52.24E
21 B5 Jarud Qi Nei Monggol Zizhiqu China 44.36N 121.00E
120 G4 Jarú, R Brazil
46 F1 Järva-Jaani Estonia U.S.S.R. 59.03N 25.59E
51 L11 Järvenpää Finland 60.29N 25.06E
100 D4 Jarvie Alberta 54.30N 113.58W
69 L6 Jarville-la-Malgrange France 48.40N 6.14E
99 K10 Jarvis Ontario 42.52N 80.08W
122 B3 Jarvis I Line Is Pacific Oc 0.23S 160.02W
52 J5 Järvsö Sweden 61.43N 16.25E
30 F5 Jarwa Uttar Prad India 27.38N 82.32E
70 K6 Jarzé France 47.34N 0.14W
82 F5 Jaša Tomić Yugoslavia 45.26N 20.50E
29 B6 Jasdan Gujarat India 22.04N 71.19E
63 T7 Jasdorf E Germany 52.30N 13.48E
32 E5 Jashnī Iran 30.07N 53.36E
29 J6 Jashpurnagar Madhya Prad India 22.52N 84.14E
30 K8 Jasidih Bihar India 24.32N 86.39E
63 U5 Jasienica Poland 53.38N 14.35E
89 K8 Jasikan Ghana 7.28N 0.33E
35 H2 Jāsim Syria 32.59N 36.04E
34 M5 Jāsimiyah Iraq 33.46N 44.44E
18 C9 Jasin Pen Malaysia 2.18N 102.24E
32 G8 Jāsk Iran 25.40N 57.46E
32 G8 Jāsk-e Kohneh Iran 25.45N 57.48E
62 N6 Jasło Poland 49.45N 21.28E
100 O7 Jasmin Saskatchewan 51.12N 103.32W
63 T3 Jasmund pen E Germany
30 D8 Jaso Madhya Prad India 24.29N 80.30E
29 C5 Jasol Rajasthan India 25.49N 72.18E
121 D9 Jason Is Falkland Is 51.05S 61.00W
123 E14 Jason Pen Antarctica
107 J2 Jasonville Indiana 39.09N 87.13W
107 J8 Jasper Alabama 33.48N 87.18W
101 O9 Jasper Alberta 52.55N 118.05W
107 C6 Jasper Arkansas 36.00N 93.11W
105 E7 Jasper Florida 30.31N 82.58W
105 C3 Jasper Georgia 34.28N 84.27W
107 K3 Jasper Indiana 38.22N 86.58W
106 K8 Jasper Michigan 41.49N 84.01W
108 O6 Jasper Minnesota 43.47N 96.22W
107 B4 Jasper Missouri 37.20N 94.20W
104 H4 Jasper New York 42.06N 77.31W
99 P8 Jasper Ontario 44.49N 75.55W
107 L6 Jasper Tennessee 35.04N 85.36W
112 N5 Jasper Texas 30.57N 94.00W
101 O9 Jasper Nat.Park Alberta
100 D5 Jasper Place Alberta 53.33N 113.30W
30 D7 Jaspura Uttar Prad India 25.48N 80.22E
33 B8 Jasrah, Al Bahrain, The Gulf 26.09N 50.27E
30 B5 Jasrana Uttar Prad India 27.15N 78.38E
29 C4 Jasrasar Rajasthan India 27.43N 73.52E
31 H4 Jasrota Kashmir 32.29N 75.27E
34 N6 Jaṣṣān Iraq 32.57N 45.52E
71 F5 Jassans-Riottier France 46.00N 4.45E
71 G4 Jasseron France 46.13N 5.20E
Jassy see Iaşi
62 L1 Jastarnia Poland 54.41N 18.40E
82 G7 Jastrebac mts Yugoslavia
82 C5 Jastrebarsko Yugoslavia 45.41N 15.39E
65 O9 Jastrebci Yugoslavia 46.27N 16.15E
62 K2 Jastrowie Poland 53.25N 16.50E
30 B6 Jaswantnagar Uttar Prad India 26.54N 78.54E
29 C5 Jaswantpura Rajasthan India 24.50N 72.32E
62 M8 Jászapáti Hungary 47.30N 20.10E
62 M8 Jászárokszállás Hungary 47.39N 19.58E
62 M8 Jászberény Hungary 47.30N 19.56E
62 M8 Jászfenyszaru Hungary 47.32N 19.42E
62 M8 Jászladány Hungary 47.21N 20.10E
118 D5 Jataí Brazil 17.58S 51.45W
75 E1 Jata,Mte Spain 43.23N 2.50W
117 A5 Jatapu,R Brazil
77 J7 Játar Spain 36.56N 3.54W
30 C7 Jatara Madhya Prad India 25.00N 79.03E
29 B7 Jatarabad Gujarat India 20.51N 71.27E
32 B2 Ja'tarābād Kordestān Iran 36.01N 47.05E
28 B2 Jath Maharashtra India 17.01N 75.20E
30 E7 Jathwara Uttar Prad India 25.49N 81.47E
31 E8 Jati Pakistan 24.20N 68.18E
18 H9 Jatibarang Java Indonesia 6.26S 108.18E
116 E4 Jatibonico Cuba 21.56N 79.11W
75 K5 Jatiel Spain 41.13N 0.23W
18 G3 Jatinegara Jakarta Indonesia 6.12S 106.51E
77 P3 Játiva Spain 39.00N 0.32W
18 H9 Jatiwangi Java Indonesia 6.45S 108.12E
117 C7 Jatobá Pará Brazil 4.48S 52.45W
117 D7 Jatobá Pará Brazil 4.35S 49.33W
31 F6 Jatoi Pakistan 29.29N 70.58E
35 D2 Jatt Israel 32.58N 35.13E
35 D4 Jatt Israel 32.24N 35.02E
120 G2 Jatuarana Brazil 7.53S 60.41W
63 T5 Jatzke E Germany 53.37N 13.34E
63 T5 Jatznick E Germany 53.35N 13.57E
91 C11 Jau Angola 15.14S 13.31E
118 E8 Jaú Brazil 22.11S 48.35W
119 G5 Jáua,Meseta del Cerro plat Venezuela
119 H8 Jauaperi Brazil
117 C5 Jauari,Sa mts Brazil
14 D4 Jaubert,C W Australia 18.56S 121.39E
61 K4 Jauche Belgium 50.41N 4.57E
116 G4 Jauco Cuba 20.08N 74.20W
72 J10 Jau,Col de pass France 42.42N 2.15E
70 D4 Jaudy R France
65 M5 Jauerling mt Austria 48.21N 15.22E
Jauf,Al see Jawf,Al
Jauf,Wadi see Jawf, Wādī al watercourse
72 C6 Jauge France 44.43N 0.42W
31 G4 Jauharabad Pakistan 32.16N 72.17E
120 B4 Jauja Peru 11.50S 75.15W
71 E7 Jaujac France 44.38N 4.15E
30 A3 Jaula Uttar Prad India 29.16N 77.24E
72 E4 Jauldes France 45.47N 0.19E
75 J5 Jaulin Spain 41.27N 1.00W
72 E2 Jaulnay France 46.56N 0.26E
115 K6 Jaumave Mexico 23.28N 99.22W
66 F5 Jaun Switzerland 46.37N 7.17E
117 A8 Jauna, R Brazil
72 E2 Jaunay Clan France 46.43N 0.22E
46 F2 Jaunjelgava Latvia U.S.S.R. 56.34N 25.02E
66 F5 Jaun Pass Switzerland 46.36N 7.21E
46 F2 Jaunpiebalga Latvia U.S.S.R. 57.25N 26.00E
30 F7 Jaunpur Uttar Prad India 25.44N 82.41E
30 F7 Jaunpur dist Uttar Prad India
75 G2 Jaunsaras Spain 43.00N 1.49W
65 L8 Jauntal V Austria
119 H9 Jaú,R Brazil
71 B9 Jaur R France
32 J6 Jauri Iran 28.03N 60.30E
75 H2 Jaurrieta Spain 42.54N 1.08W
118 C6 Jauru Brazil 18.29S 54.18W
118 D6 Jauru,R Mato Grosso Brazil
118 B4 Jauru,R Mato Grosso do Sul Brazil
71 K8 Jausiers France 44.25N 6.44E
69 D5 Jaux France 49.23N 2.46E
35 F9 Jauza Jordan 31.09N 35.38E
Java / see Jawa /
28 D4 Javadi Hills Tamil Nadu India
Javaés,R see Formoso,R Goiás
118 E2 Javaés,Serra dos mts Brazil
75 H7 Javalambre mt Spain 40.05N 1.02W
75 H7 Javalambre, Sierra de mts Spain
75 H7 Javalón mt Spain 40.13N 1.25W
31 C3 Javand Afghanistan 35.04N 64.09E
77 H6 Javarero mt Spain 37.22N 4.03W
26 K6 Java Ridge Indian Oc
120 C1 Javari,R Brazil
17 G12 Java Sea Indonesia
77 R3 Jávea Spain 38.48N 0.10E
Javeh Khan see Kūpān
63 P7 Jävenitz E Germany 52.32N 11.31E
72 F4 Javerdot France 45.57N 0.59E
72 F4 Javerlhac-et-La-Chappelle-St.Robert France 45.34N 0.34E
Javhlant see Uliastay
71 J8 Javie,la France 44.10N 6.21E
75 H2 Javier Spain 42.35N 1.13W
121 J6 Javier isld Chile 47.10S 74.20W
61 K6 Javingue Belgium 50.06N 4.55E
82 E6 Javor mts Yugoslavia
62 L7 Javoria mt Czechoslovakia 48.27N 19.15E
65 M3 Javořice mt Czechoslovakia 49.14N 15.20E
65 K9 Javornik Yugoslavia 46.26N 14.03E
62 L6 Javorniky mts Czechoslovakia
51 J6 Jävre Sweden 65.10N 21.34E
70 K5 Javron-les-Chapelles France 48.25N 0.20W
35 G6 Jawa Jordan 31.51N 35.56E
90 E5 Jawa Nigeria 12.50N 11.08E
18 G9 Jawa isld Indonesia
18 G9 Jawa Barat prov Java Indon
29 D5 Jawad Madhya Prad India 24.35N 74.57E
29 C5 Jawai, R Rajasthan India
29 E2 Jawala Mukhi Himachal Prad India 31.51N 76.22E
34 L3 Jāwan Iraq 35.58N 43.02E
29 E7 Jawar Madhya Prad India 21.57N 76.30E
33 M7 Jawārah,Al Oman 18.56N 57.20E
18 H9 Jawa Tengah prov Java Indon
18 K9 Jawa Timur prov Java Indon
33 J5 Jawb,Al depression Saudi Arabia
85 G7 Jawf, Al Libya 24.09N 23.19E
33 C2 Jawf, Al Saudi Arabia 29.47N 39.52E
33 E7 Jawf,Al Saudi Arabia 18.13N 43.10E
34 Q10 Jawf,Al Saudi Arabia 28.07N 48.03E
33 F9 Jawf, Wādī al watercourse Yemen
29 C8 Jawhar Maharashtra India 19.56N 73.19E
18 H6 Jawi Borneo Indon 0.47S 109.15E
33 G9 Jawl ash Shaykh S Yemen 14.12N 47.40E
62 J4 Jawor Poland 51.01N 16.11E
62 L5 Jaworzno Poland 50.13N 19.11E
85 A3 Jawsh,Al Libya 32.03N 11.42E
33 B8 Jaww Bahrain, The Gulf 25.59N 50.37E
109 Q5 Jay Oklahoma 36.25N 94.49W
115 L9 Jayacatlán Mexico 17.28N 96.51W
119 B11 Jayanca Peru 6.27S 79.52W
15 D6 Jaya, Puntjak mt Irian Jaya 4.05S 137.09E
15 F5 Jayapura Irian Jaya 2.37S 140.39E
15 E6 Jayawijaya, Pegunungan mts Irian Jaya
33 C2 Jayb,Al Saudi Arabia 29.38N 39.25E
108 F7 Jay Em Wyoming 42.28N 104.21W
77 J7 Jayena Spain 36.57N 3.49W
32 C5 Jāyezān Iran 30.53N 49.52E
30 K6 Jaynagar Bihar India 26.36N 86.08E
29 L6 Jaynagar W Bengal India 22.10N 88.21E
Jayrūd see Jerūd
112 G2 Jayton Texas 33.16N 100.35W
105 J7 Jayuya Puerto Rico 18.13N 66.34W
72 E3 Jazeneuil France 46.27N 0.03E
34 H3 Jazirah,Al reg Syria/Iraq
33 E9 Jaz'ir az Zubayr isld Yemen 15.00N 42.10E
32 D6 Jazireh-ye Shīf Iran 29.05N 50.58E
115 J5 Jazminal Mexico 24.55N 101.25W
32 H7 Jaz Mūrīān, Hāmūn-e salt marsh Iran
32 C2 Jazvān Iran 37.09N 48.29E
35 G5 Jazzaza,El Jordan 32.14N 35.49E
66 H8 Jazzi,Cima di mt Italy/Switz 45.58N 7.53E
Jdeiyé see Judeiye
111 J6 Jean Nevada 35.46N 115.20W
112 J2 Jean Texas 33.18N 98.38W
107 E12 Jeanerette Louisiana 29.55N 91.41W
Jeanette I see Zhannetty, Ostrov
98 E1 Jean L Quebec 52.26N 67.33W
101 N5 Jean Marie River N W Terr 61.32N 120.40W
26 R16 Jeanne d'Arc,Presqu'île pen Kerguelen Indian Oc
104 F6 Jeannette Pennsylvania 40.20N 79.38W
116 H5 Jean Rabel Haiti 19.48N 73.05W
57 L4 Jeater Houses N Yorks Eng 54.20N 1.20W
35 G1 Jeba Syria 33.10N 35.55E
35 J1 Jebāb Syria 33.06N 36.16E
88 L4 Jebala mts Morocco
32 H6 Jebāl Bārez,Kūh-e mts Iran
90 B7 Jebba Nigeria 9.11N 4.49E
85 E5 Jebel Libya 28.40N 19.58E
87 D3 Jebel Aulia vill Sudan 15.19N 32.31E
87 D4 Jebel Biyut Sudan 13.20N 32.56E
87 D4 Jebel Dud Sudan 13.23N 33.10E
87 D4 Jebelein,El Sudan 12.38N 32.51E
87 D4 Jebel Moya Sudan 13.30N 33.22E
87 D2 Jebel Qerri vill Sudan 16.16N 32.50E
87 H3 Jebel Tair I Red Sea 15.35N 41.50E
120 B1 Jeberos Peru 5.18S 76.15W
77 G10 Jebha Morocco 35.13N 4.40W
35 D1 Jébîne, Ej Lebanon 33.07N 35.14E
88 T4 Jebiniana Tunisia 35.00N 10.53E
34 H2 Jebisa oil bore Syria 36.08N 40.50E
53 B3 Jebjerg Denmark 56.40N 9.00E
34 C3 Jeble Syria 35.22N 35.56E
31 C7 Jebri Pakistan 27.16N 65.47E
69 N7 Jebsheim France 48.08N 7.30E
18 F6 Jebus Indonesia 1.44S 105.28E
31 G4 Jech Doab interfluve Pakistan
92 G8 Jeci mt Mozambique 12.50S 35.09E
57 H2 Jedburgh Borders Scotland 55.29N 2.34W
100 P7 Jedburgh Saskatchewan 51.15N 103.00W
Jedda see Jiddah
106 M6 Jeddo Michigan 43.09N 82.36W
78 C12 Jedeida Tunisia 36.55N 9.56E
88 S3 Jedeida Tunisia 36.53N 9.57E
Jedeidé see Judeidat el Wādī
65 O2 Jedlová Czechoslovakia 49.41N 16.18E
62 M5 Jędrzejów Poland 50.39N 20.18E
62 N2 Jedwabne Poland 53.15N 22.17E
57 H2 Jed Water R Borders Scotland
101 H9 Jedway Moresby I, Br Col 52.18N 131.13W
51 M4 Jeesiö Finland 67.33N 26.05E
63 O7 Jeetze E Germany 52.45N 11.26E
63 O6 Jeetze R W Germany
Jef Fam islds see Yef Fam, Kepulauan Is
108 P5 Jeffers Minnesota 44.03N 95.11W
109 E2 Jefferson Colorado 39.23N 105.47W
105 D3 Jefferson Georgia 34.06N 83.35W
108 Q7 Jefferson Iowa 42.01N 94.22W
104 H7 Jefferson Maryland 39.23N 77.34W
103 E2 Jefferson New York 42.28N 74.37W
104 E5 Jefferson Ohio 41.44N 80.46W
109 N5 Jefferson Oklahoma 36.44N 97.46W
110 B5 Jefferson Oregon 44.44N 123.01W
108 O7 Jefferson S Dakota 42.36N 96.34W
112 N3 Jefferson Texas 32.45N 94.21W
106 F6 Jefferson Wisconsin 43.01N 88.48W
107 D3 Jefferson City Missouri 38.33N 92.10W
110 N3 Jefferson City Montana 46.24N 112.01W
105 D1 Jefferson City Tennessee 36.07N 83.30W
110 O4 Jefferson Island Montana 45.51N 111.56W
111 H3 Jefferson, Mt Nevada 38.47N 116.58W
110 D5 Jefferson,Mt Oregon 44.41N 121.46W
107 L3 Jeffersontown Kentucky 38.12N 85.35W
105 D5 Jeffersonville Georgia 32.41N 83.21W
107 L3 Jeffersonville Indiana 38.16N 85.45W
103 E3 Jeffersonville New York 41.48N 74.56W
104 B7 Jeffersonville Ohio 39.39N 83.33W
104 N2 Jeffersonville Vermont 44.39N 72.51W
108 C7 Jeffrey City Wyoming 42.30N 107.52W
95 H10 Jeffreys Bay S Africa 34.05S 24.55E
10 B11 Jeffryes,Mt Macquarie I Pacific Oc 54.44S 158.52E
90 K1 Jef-Jef El Kebir plat Chad
Jef Lio see Yeflio
90 B5 Jega Nigeria 12.16N 4.21E
66 G3 Jegenstorf Switzerland 47.03N 7.31E
37 K8 Jeghir Iran 37.36N 46.46E
53 B3 Jegind Ø isld Denmark 56.38N 8.42E
72 E8 Jégun France 43.46N 0.28E
Jehan Dagh see Jahan Dagh Mt
61 M4 Jehay-Bodegnée Belgium 50.35N 5.20E
31 A5 Jehile Pūzak salt waste Afghanistan
61 L7 Jehonville Belgium 49.54N 5.12E
34 C8 Jeib,Wadi el watercourse Israel/Jordan
121 J6 Jeinemeni,Cerro pk Chile 46.57S 72.15W
53 B7 Jejsing Denmark 54.57N 8.58E
118 C9 Jejui Guazú,R Paraguay
46 F2 Jēkabpils Latvia U.S.S.R. 56.28N 25.58E
Je-ka-la Shan-k'ou pass see Rakha La
87 D6 Jekaw Ethiopia 8.23N 33.50E
87 E7 Jeki Ethiopia 7.11N 35.18E
105 F6 Jekyll I Georgia 31.03N 81.25W
18 C7 Jelai R Pen Malaysia
87 G6 Jeldu Ethiopia 9.09N 38.10E
62 J5 Jelenia Góra Poland 50.55N 15.45E
29 L4 Jelep La pass Sikkim/Xizang Zizhiqu 27.20N 88.58E
46 E2 Jelgava Latvia U.S.S.R. 56.39N 23.40E
107 M5 Jellico Tennessee 36.35N 84.08W
99 C3 Jellicoe Ontario 49.43N 87.31W
11 J3 Jellicoe Chan New Zealand
53 C5 Jelling Denmark 55.46N 9.26E
90 E6 Jellum Nigeria 11.30N 10.51E
110 C9 Jelly California 40.21N 122.12W
62 L5 Jełowa Poland 50.50N 18.00E
32 B4 Jelow Gīr Iran 33.02N 47.54E
52 E7 Jeløy / Norway 59.40N 10.50E
53 C6 Jels Denmark 55.22N 9.13E
53 U20 Jelsa Norway 59.20N 6.02E
62 M7 Jelšava Czechoslovakia 48.37N 20.15E
60 M7 Jelsum Netherlands 53.14N 5.46E
90 D7 Jemaa Nigeria 9.29N 8.24E
88 J5 Jemâa-Shaim Morocco 32.24N 8.52W
18 F4 Jemaja isld Indonesia
18 D9 Jemaluang Pen Malaysia 2.15N 103.50E
61 F5 Jemappes Belgium 50.27N 3.53E
18 K10 Jember Java Indon 8.07S 113.45E
92 K12 Jembiana Zanzibar 6.20S 39.33E
63 N8 Jembke W Germany 52.29N 10.47E
18 M2 Jembongan isld Sabah Malaysia
88 T4 Jem, El Tunisia 35.15N 10.35E
61 M6 Jemelle Belgium 50.10N 5.16E
18 C9 Jementah Pen Malaysia 2.24N 102.39E
61 M4 Jemeppe Liège Belgium 50.37N 5.30E
61 J5 Jemeppe Namur Belgium 50.28N 4.40E
109 D6 Jemez R New Mexico
109 D6 Jemez Springs New Mexico 35.45N 106.43W
63 F6 Jemgum W Germany 53.16N 7.22E
24 E2 Jeminay Xinjiang Uygur Zizhiqu China 47.30N 85.40E
24 E2 Jeminay Xinjiang Uygur Zizhiqu China 47.30N 86.03E
78 D13 Jemmal Tunisia 35.38N 10.44E
88 T4 Jemmal Tunisia 35.38N 10.50E
88 S5 Jemna Tunisia 33.34N 9.00E
65 N3 Jemnice Czechoslovakia 49.02N 15.35E
9 C1 Jemo atoll Marshall Is Pacific Oc 10.10N 169.30E
18 M6 Jempang, Danau L Borneo Indonesia
18 C8 Jempol R Pen Malaysia
98 F8 Jemseg New Brunswick 45.51N 66.08W
90 E7 Jen Nigeria 9.25N 11.29E
64 M2 Jena E Germany 50.56N 11.35E
107 D10 Jena Louisiana 31.40N 92.05W
66 P4 Jenaz Switzerland 46.56N 9.43E
65 E7 Jenbach Austria 47.24N 11.47E
18 A8 Jendarata Pen Malaysia 3.55N 100.58E
Jende see Yende
88 S3 Jendouba Tunisia 36.30N 8.45E
89 D8 Jene Liberia 7.19N 10.45W
61 M4 Jeneffe Liège Belgium 50.39N 5.21E
61 L5 Jeneffe Namur Belgium 50.22N 5.15E
88 T6 Jeneïn Tunisia 31.44N 10.05E
90 D6 Jengre Nigeria 10.20N 8.49E
35 E4 Jenin Jordan 32.28N 35.18E
120 G1 Jenipapo Amazonas Brazil 5.36S 60.54W
104 D9 Jenkinjones W Virginia 37.18N 81.27W
104 C9 Jenkins Kentucky 37.11N 82.39W
108 Q3 Jenkins Minnesota 46.38N 94.20W
103 E7 Jenkins New Jersey 39.42N 74.32W

19 M9 **Jose Abad Santos** Mindanao Philippines 5.56N 125.40E
120 E5 **José A.de Palacios** Bolivia 13.48S 66.15W
121 G4 **José Batlle-y-Ordoñez** Uruguay 33.28S 55.08W
117 C9 **José Bispo,R** Brazil
118 A3 **José Bonifácio** Brazil 12.11S 60.14W
115 L8 **José Cardel** Mexico 19.21N 96.23W
117 F7 **José de Freitas** Brazil 4.45S 42.36W
121 B10 **José de San Martin** Argentina 44.04S 70.29W
121 F4 **José Enrique Rodo** Uruguay 33.43S 57.33W
121 E3 **Josefina** Argentina 31.30S 61.59W
118 C5 **Joselândia** Brazil 16.33S 56.08W
119 F6 **José María** Colombia 2.16N 68.07W
53 U20 **Jøsenfjord** *inlet* Norway 59.16N 6.15E
121 G3 **José Otávio** Brazil 31.15S 54.08W
19 L4 **Jose Pañganiban** Luzon Philippines 14.18N 122.40E
121 G4 **José Pedro Varela** Uruguay 33.30S 54.28W
110 J4 **Joseph** Idaho 45.49N 116.29W
110 H4 **Joseph** Oregon 45.22N 117.14W
110 H4 **Joseph** *R* Oregon
14 G2 **Joseph Bonaparte G** Australia
111 O7 **Joseph City** Arizona 34.58N 110.21W
54 M6 **Josephine** *oil field* North Sea 56.27N 2.27E
98 G1 **Joseph, L** Labrador, Nfld
99 K6 **Joseph,L** Ontario
98 K4 **Joseph Pt** Anticosti I, Que 49.26N 62.08W
15 H6 **Josephstaal** Papua New Guinea 4.42S 144.55E
11 C12 **Josephville** New Zealand 45.48S 168.25E
30 C2 **Joshimath** Uttar Prad India 30.33N 79.35E
20 M5 **Joshin-etsu Kogen Nat. Park** Japan
29 K7 **Joshipur** W Bengal India 21.59N 86.04E
112 K3 **Joshua** Texas 32.28N 97.25W
111 H7 **Joshua Tree** California 34.09N 116.20W
111 H7 **Joshua Tree Nat. Mon** *nat park* California
70 O6 **Josnes** France 47.48N 1.31E
64 H3 **Jossatal** W Germany 50.14N 9.37E
70 E6 **Josselin** France 47.58N 2.32W
69 D6 **Jossigny** France 48.50N 2.46E
52 E3 **Jøssund** Norway 63.52N 9.50E
52 F2 **Jøssund** Norway 64.23N 10.50E
53 W15 **Jostedal** Norway 61.35N 7.18E
53 W16 **Jostedalen** *V* Norway 61.25N 7.14E
53 V16 **Jostedalsbreen** *glacier* Norway
53 V16 **Jostefonn** *glacier* Norway 61.25N 6.35E
105 L7 **Jost Van Dyke I** Virgin Is 18.29N 64.47W
62 M7 **Jósvafő** Hungary 48.30N 20.33E
51 K2 **Jotkajavrre** Norway 69.45N 23.56E
53 Y15 **Jotunheimen** *mts* Norway
76 E6 **Jou** Portugal 41.28N 7.25W
Jouaïf,Ej *see* **Juwaïf,El**
35 E1 **Jouaiya** Lebanon 33.14N 35.20E
Jouaïze *see* **Juwayzah**
69 E6 **Jouarre** France 48.55N 3.08E
69 B6 **Jouars** France 48.47N 1.55E
95 G9 **Joubertina** S Africa 33.50S 23.50E
70 K4 **Joué-du-Bois** France 48.35N 0.15W
70 M7 **Joué-lès-Tours** France 47.22N 0.41E
70 H7 **Joué-sur-Erdre** France 47.29N 1.25W
72 K1 **Jouet-sur-l'Aubois** France 47.03N 2.59E
71 J3 **Jougne** France 46.46N 6.23E
72 F3 **Jouhet** France 46.30N 0.50E
Joukhadâr,El *see* **Jukhadar,Al**
51 N6 **Joukokylä** Finland 65.02N 28.00E
105 J12 **Joulters Cays** *isld* Bahamas
34 C5 **Jounié** Lebanon 33.58N 35.38E
112 J7 **Jourdanton** Texas 28.55N 98.34W
60 M8 **Joure** Netherlands 52.58N 5.48E
72 F3 **Journet** France 46.27N 0.59E
72 F6 **Journiac** France 44.58N 0.53E
Jourrein *see* **Jurein**
100 B3 **Joussard** Alberta 55.22N 115.50W
Joûssié *see* **Jūsiya**
99 M3 **Joutel** Quebec 49.32N 78.20W
51 M10 **Joutsa** Finland 61.46N 26.09E
51 N5 **Joutsijärvi** Finland 66.41N 28.00E
Jouveney I *see* **Iwa**
66 B5 **Joux, Lac de** Switzerland
71 D1 **Joux-la-Ville** France 47.38N 3.52E
66 B5 **Joux, Vallée de** Switzerland
70 O4 **Jouy** France 48.30N 1.33E
69 L5 **Jouy-aux-Arches** France 49.03N 6.05E
68 D4 **Jouy-en-Josas** France 48.46N 2.11E
69 E6 **Jouy-le-Châtel** France 48.39N 3.09E
70 O6 **Jouy-le-Potier** France 47.45N 1.48E
69 F5 **Jouy-lès-Reims** France 49.13N 3.55E
76 D1 **Jove** Spain 43.41N 7.31W
116 D3 **Jovellanos** Cuba 22.49N 81.11W
Joverega *see* **Gcoverega**
121 D5 **Jovita** Argentina 34.32S 63.56W
28 J3 **Jowai** Assam India 25.26N 92.14E
32 D2 **Jowr Deh** Iran 36.45N 50.20E
44 K10 **Jowrshar** Iran 37.22N 49.51E
32 D4 **Jowsheqān-e Qālī** Iran 33.34N 51.12E
32 C3 **Jowzān** Iran 34.15N 48.59E
31 G4 **Joya Mair** Pakistan 33.05N 72.51E
59 C4 **Joyces Country** *dist* Galway Irish Rep
71 E8 **Joyeuse** France 44.29N 4.15E
101 G4 **Joy, Mt.** Yukon Terr 63.43N 132.56W
92 K12 **Jozani** Tanzania 6.16S 39.26E
20 K1 **Jōzankei** Japan 42.58N 141.08E
71 C5 **Joze** France 45.52N 3.18E
62 N4 **Józefów** Poland 51.03N 21.50E
Jozini Dam *see* **Strijdom Dam, J.G.**
31 C2 **Jozjan** *prov* Afghanistan
Jrâba *see* **Jarabah**
Ju *see* **Yu**
87 C6 **Juai Bor** Sudan 9.21N 30.42E
113 U7 **Jualin** Alaska 58.50N 135.00W
119 F9 **Juami,R** Brazil
115 H5 **Juan Aldama** Mexico 24.20N 103.23W
121 F3 **Juan B.Arruabarrena** Argentina 30.20S 58.23W
23 G1 **Juancheng** Shandong China 35.32N 115.30E
121 F6 **Juancho** Argentina 37.09S 57.05W
13 J7 **Juandah** *R* Queensland
116 K2 **Juan de Bolas** *mt* Jamaica, W I 18.04N 77.09W
110 A1 **Juan de Fuca,Str of** Canada/U.S.A.
121 D7 **Juan de Garay** Argentina 38.53S 64.34W
95 A4 **Juan de Nova** *isld* Madagascar 17.02S 43.42E
115 G10 **Juan Díaz** Panama 9.03N 79.26W
121 E6 **Juan E.Barra** Argentina 37.51S 60.25W
120 A12 **Juan Fernández,Is** Pacific Oc
96 V16 **Juan Grande** Gran Canaria Canary Is 27.49N 15.23W
119 G2 **Juangriego** Venezuela 11.06N 63.59W
92 J6 **Juani I** Tanzania 8.00S 39.48E
121 F3 **Juan Jorge** Argentina 32.00S 58.20W
120 B2 **Juanjuí** Peru 7.10S 76.44W
51 N8 **Juankoski** Finland 63.05N 28.25E
121 F5 **Juan Lacaze** Uruguay 34.26S 57.25W
71 L9 **Juan-les Pins** France 43.39N 7.06E
115 E2 **Juan Mata Ortíz** Mexico 30.08N 108.02W
121 B2 **Juan Soldado,C.de** Chile 29.45S 71.25W
121 H6 **Juan Stuven** *isld* Chile 48.00S 75.00W
88 F9 **Juan Torno,Pta.de** *pt* Morocco 25.18N 14.52W
121 F6 **Juárez** Argentina 37.40S 59.48W
115 N9 **Juárez** Chiapas Mexico 17.40N 93.10W
115 J4 **Juaréz** Coahuila Mexico 27.39N 100.43W
115 F2 **Juárez, Ciudad** Mexico 31.42N 106.29W
111 J9 **Juárez, Sa** *ra* Mexico
115 A1 **Juárez,Sa.de** *ra* Mexico
89 E9 **Juarzon** Liberia 5.15N 8.45W
89 J8 **Juaso** Ghana 6.41N 1.07W
33 E7 **Ju'ayfirah,Al** Saudi Arabia 18.59N 43.41E
117 G9 **Juàzeiro** Brazil 9.25S 40.30W
117 G8 **Juàzeiro do Norte** Brazil 7.10S 39.18W
87 C8 **Juba** Sudan 4.50N 31.35E
Juba *R see* **Giuba** *R*
29 H6 **Juba** *ruins* Madhya Prad India 23.42N 83.29E
34 C4 **Jubail** Lebanon 34.08N 35.38E
Jubail Saudi Arabia*see* **Jubayl,Al**
Juba, Lower *reg see* **Giuba, Basso**
Juba, Upper *reg see* **Giuba, Alto**
33 H3 **Jubayl,Al** Saudi Arabia 26.59N 49.40E
33 G4 **Jubayl, Al** *area* Saudi Arabia
35 G5 **Jubba** Jordan 32.11N 35.53E
33 D2 **Jubbah** Saudi Arabia 28.03N 40.56E
30 A1 **Jubbal** Himachal Prad India 31.05N 77.40E
33 E3 **Jubb, Al** Saudi Arabia 27.12N 42.19E
35 G1 **Jubbata el Khasab** Syria 33.13N 35.50E
35 F1 **Jubbata ez Zayt** Syria 33.16N 35.44E
60 N8 **Jubbega-Schurega** Netherlands 52.58N 6.07E
Jubbulpore *see* **Jabalpur**
35 G5 **Jubeiha,El** Jordan 32.02N 35.52E
63 K3 **Jübek** W Germany 54.33N 9.24E
75 F3 **Jubera** Spain 42.19N 2.17W
33 F9 **Jubil** Yemen 14.55N 44.46E
98 R5 **Jubilee Lake** Newfoundland
14 F8 **Jubilee Lake** W Australia
111 H6 **Jubilee Pass** California 35.55N 116.35W
23 B8 **Jubilee Res** Hong Kong 22.24N 114.08E
121 F3 **Jubileo** Argentina 31.45S 58.40W
30 K5 **Jubing** Nepal 27.36N 86.41E
70 K5 **Jublains** France 48.15N 0.29W
119 B9 **Jubones,R** Ecuador
77 F7 **Jubrique** Spain 36.35N 5.13W
77 O2 **Júcar** *R* Spain
116 E4 **Júcaro** Cuba 21.37N 78.51W
117 G8 **Jucás** Brazil 6.29S 39.33W
115 L9 **Juchatengo** Mexico 16.21N 97.08W
64 A1 **Jüchen** W Germany 51.06N 6.30E
115 H7 **Juchipila** Mexico 21.25N 103.05W
115 M9 **Juchitán** Mexico 16.27N 95.05W
115 G7 **Juchitlán** Mexico 20.04N 104.06W
115 P11 **Jucuapa** El Salvador 13.30N 88.23W
118 H5 **Jucururu** Brazil 16.57S 39.57W
118 H5 **Jucururu,R** Brazil
108 M3 **Jud** N Dakota 46.32N 98.53W
106 E7 **Juda** Wisconsin 42.35N 89.31W
35 B7 **Judaea** *reg* Israel/Jordan
33 H4 **Jūdah** Saudi Arabia 25.52N 48.53E
35 F7 **Judaiyida** Jordan 31.32N 35.39E
35 G9 **Judaiyida** Jordan 31.15N 35.49E
Judaydat *see* **Judeidat el Wādī**
34 J7 **Judayyidat Ar'ar** Saudi Arabia 31.24N 41.24E
28 F2 **Juddangi** Andhra Prad India 17.30N 82.12E
98 S6 **Jude I** Newfoundland 47.15N 54.48W
35 D2 **Judeida** Israel 32.55N 35.09E
35 E4 **Judeida** Jordan 32.20N 35.18E
34 D5 **Judeidat el Wādī** Syria 33.34N 36.11E
35 F4 **Judeita** Jordan 32.25N 35.42E
35 H1 **Judeiye** Syria 33.04N 36.06E
65 O5 **Judenau** Austria 48.18N 16.00E
64 L3 **Judenbach** E Germany 50.23N 11.13E
65 L7 **Judenburg** Austria 47.10N 14.40E
75 F5 **Judes** *mt* Spain 41.07N 2.08W
11 E4 **Judgeford** New Zealand 41.07S 174.56E
23 B5 **Judian** Yunnan China 27.18N 99.40E
77 G3 **Judio** *mt* Spain 38.35N 4.32W
98 L8 **Judique** C Breton I, Nova Scotia 45.55N 61.30W
110 Q2 **Judith** *R* Montana
110 P2 **Judith Basin** Montana
110 Q3 **Judith Gap** Montana 46.40N 109.46W
103 M4 **Judith, Pt** Rhode I 41.22N 71.29W
108 J3 **Judson** N Dakota 46.50N 101.15W
107 E6 **Judsonia** Arkansas 35.17N 91.39W
Juegang *see* **Rudong**
77 K3 **Juego de Bolos** *mt* Spain 38.53N 3.05W
53 E5 **Juelsminde** Denmark 55.43N 10.02E
118 H5 **Juerana** Brazil 17.39S 39.35W
75 F6 **Juez** *mt* Spain 40.35N 2.02W
66 P6 **Juf** Switzerland 46.27N 9.35E
119 H8 **Jufari,R** Brazil
33 D3 **Jufayfah,Al** Saudi Arabia 27.07N 41.12E
33 G4 **Jufayr, Al** Saudi Arabia 24.02N 46.18E
35 F4 **Juffein** Jordan 32.29N 35.39E
85 C5 **Jufrah Oasis, al** Libya
14 E9 **Jugalinna** W Australia 30.13S 124.16E
70 F5 **Jugon-les-Lacs** France 48.25N 2.19W
Jugoslavia *see* **Yugoslavia**
33 J4 **Juh** Qatar, The Gulf 24.53N 51.04E
33 E8 **Juhā** Saudi Arabia 16.44N 42.50E
34 N9 **Juhaym** Iraq 29.37N 45.24E
33 B4 **Juhaynah** *tribe* Saudi Arabia
22 M6 **Juhua Dao** *isld* Liaoning China
115 M3 **Juigalpa** Nicaragua 12.04N 85.23W
70 H6 **Juigné-des-Moutiers** France 47.41N 1.10W
72 G5 **Juillac** France 45.19N 1.19E
72 E9 **Juillan** France 43.12N 0.02E
69 D5 **Juilly** France 49.01N 2.43E
Juimand *see* **Jūymand**
118 B2 **Juinamirim,R** Brazil
118 B3 **Juina,R** Brazil
69 C6 **Juine** *R* France
63 F5 **Juist** W Germany 53.41N 7.01E
63 E5 **Juist** *isld* W Germany
118 G7 **Juiz de Fora** Brazil 21.47S 43.23W
22 L5 **Jujinchang** Nei Monggol Zizhiqu China 42.43N 117.39E
18 D6 **Jujuhan** *R* Sumatra Indon
71 G4 **Jujurieux** France 46.03N 5.25E
120 E10 **Jujuy** *prov* Argentina
35 G2 **Jukhadar, Al** Syria 32.55N 35.51E
51 H4 **Jukkasjärvi** Sweden 67.53N 20.35E
52 D5 **Juklegga** *mt* Norway 61.03N 8.13E
53 U15 **Juklestad** Norway 61.32N 6.15E
23 F5 **Jukoupu** Hunan China 27.24N 111.15E
51 E6 **Juktån** *R* Sweden
120 E9 **Julaca** Bolivia 20.56S 67.32W
Julaida,Al *see* **Julaydah,Al**
34 N9 **Julaydah,Al** Arabia/Iraq 29.02N 45.38E
33 H3 **Julayqah,Al** Saudi Arabia 27.45N 48.30E
93 L2 **Juldessa** *mt* Ethiopia 3.55N 39.26E
61 O4 **Julémont** Belgium 50.42N 5.46E
109 H1 **Julesburg** Colorado 40.59N 102.16W
Julfa *see* **Jolfā**
120 D7 **Juli** Peru 16.15S 69.30W
119 F8 **Julia** Brazil 1.36S 68.00W
13 F5 **Julia** *R* Queensland
66 P5 **Julia** *R* Switzerland
120 D6 **Juliaca** Peru 15.29S 70.09W
13 F5 **Julia Creek** Queensland 20.40S 141.40E
110 J3 **Juliaetta** Idaho 46.35N 116.43W
111 H8 **Julian** California 33.04N 116.37W
60 G8 **Julianadorp** Netherlands 52.54N 4.45E
60 T16 **Juliana Kanaal** *canal* Netherlands
117 B3 **Juliana Top** *mt* Surinam 3.41N 56.32W
48 U15 **Julianehåb** Greenland 60.40N 46.00W
59 K4 **Julianstown** Meath Irish Rep 53.40N 6.16W
64 A2 **Jülich** W Germany 50.55N 6.21E
66 Q6 **Julier Pass** Switzerland 46.28N 9.43E
66 P6 **Julier, Piz** *mt* Switzerland 46.30N 9.45E
82 B4 **Julijske Alpe** *mts* Yugoslavia
115 G3 **Julimes** Mexico 28.25N 105.26W
121 H2 **Júlio de Castilhos** Brazil 29.13S 53.40W
35 D2 **Jūlis** Israel 32.56N 35.11E
52 J7 **Julita** Sweden 59.07N 16.04E
113 N4 **Julius** Alaska 64.30N 149.00W
70 G4 **Jullouville** France 48.47N 1.34W
29 D2 **Jullundur** Punjab India 31.18N 75.40E
29 D2 **Jullundur** *dist* Punjab India
69 G8 **Jully** France 47.47N 4.16E
53 D4 **Julsø** *L* Denmark 56.07N 9.40E
22 K8 **Julu** Hebei China 37.13N 115.00E
18 B3 **Julu Rayeu** Sumatra Indon 4.59N 97.32E
76 F9 **Jumadiel** *R* Spain
33 E7 **Jumah,Al** Saudi Arabia 18.22N 42.33E
Jumaima,Al *see* **Jumaymah,Al**
35 G8 **Jumaiyil** *anc site* Jordan 31.29N 35.54E
23 A2 **Jumanggoin** Sichuan China 32.32N 98.29E
120 F1 **Juma,R** Amazonas Brazil
34 H5 **Jumat Qa'ara** *depression* Iraq
34 L9 **Jumaymah,Al** Arabia/Iraq 29.36N 43.37E
92 H7 **Jumbe Salim's** Tanzania 10.38S 36.31E
101 P10 **Jumbo Mt** Br Col 50.19N 116.41W
71 C6 **Jumeaux** France 45.26N 3.20E
70 K7 **Jumelles** France 47.26N 0.06W
72 C1 **Jumellière,la** France 47.16N 0.44W
61 H5 **Jumet** Belgium 50.27N 4.26E
35 G3 **Jumha** Jordan 32.33N 35.46E
70 M3 **Jumièges** France 49.26N 0.50E
72 G5 **Jumilhac-le-Grand** France 45.29N 1.04E
77 O4 **Jumilla** Spain 38.28N 1.19W
30 F3 **Jumla** Nepal 29.17N 82.10E
Jumna *R see* **Yamuna**
34 C8 **Jum Suwwāna** *mt* Jordan 30.26N 35.30E
33 C6 **Jumūm,Al** Saudi Arabia 21.38N 39.43E
29 B7 **Junagadh** Gujarat India 21.32N 70.32E
29 B7 **Junagadh** *dist* Gujarat India
29 H8 **Junagarh** Orissa India 19.50N 83.00E
34 Q9 **Jūn al Kuwayt** *B* Kuwait
23 H1 **Junan** Shandong China 35.12N 118.49E
33 E6 **Junaynah,Al** Saudi Arabia 20.19N 42.50E
32 H4 **Junbuk** Iran 32.52N 58.36E
22 L4 **Jun Bulen** Nei Monggol Zizhiqu China 45.40N 118.00E
76 F8 **Juncajo** *mt* Spain 40.06N 6.51W
121 B4 **Juncal** *pk* Arg/Chile 33.05S 70.04W
121 D8 **Juncal,L** Argentina
105 K7 **Juncos** Puerto Rico 18.15N 65.56W
75 M5 **Juncosa** Spain 41.23N 0.46E
75 N5 **Juncosa** Spain 41.19N 1.27E
112 H5 **Junction** Texas 30.31N 99.48W
111 M3 **Junction** Utah 38.15N 112.14W
13 C1 **Junction B** N Terr Australia
107 D8 **Junction City** Arkansas 33.01N 92.43W
105 C5 **Junction City** Georgia 32.36N 84.28W
109 O2 **Junction City** Kansas 39.02N 96.51W
107 M4 **Junction City** Kentucky 37.33N 84.49W
110 B5 **Junction City** Oregon 44.14N 123.12W
106 E5 **Junction City** Wisconsin 44.35N 89.45W
13 G6 **Jundah** Queensland 24.48S 143.00E
118 F8 **Jundiaí** Brazil 23.10S 46.54W
22 K6 **Jundu Shan** *mts* Beijing China
113 U7 **Juneau** Alaska 58.20N 134.20W
106 F6 **Juneau** Wisconsin 43.23N 88.42W
75 M4 **Juneda** Spain 41.33N 0.49E
12 J5 **Junee** New S Wales 34.51S 147.40E
105 F10 **June in Winter,L** Florida 27.18N 81.25W
111 E4 **June Lake** California 37.46N 119.04W
115 J8 **Jungapeo** Mexico 19.30N 100.30W
22 H7 **Jungar Qi** Nei Monggol Zizhiqu China 39.43N 111.00E
66 H5 **Jungfrau** *mt* Switzerland 46.33N 7.58E
66 H5 **Jungfraujoch** Switzerland 46.33N 7.59E
24 F3 **Junggar Pendi** *basin* Xinjiang Uygur Zizhiqu China
61 Q8 **Junglinster** Luxembourg 49.43N 6.15E
110 G9 **Jungo** Nevada 40.56N 118.24W
31 D8 **Jungshahi** Pakistan 24.51N 67.46E
108 M9 **Juniata** Nebraska 40.38N 98.30W
104 H6 **Juniata** *R* Pennsylvania
72 G6 **Junies,les** France 44.33N 1.14E
121 E5 **Junín** Buenos Aires Arg 34.34S 60.55W
121 C4 **Junín** Mendoza Arg 33.10S 68.30W
120 B4 **Junín** Peru 11.11S 76.00W
120 B4 **Junín** *dept* Peru
121 B7 **Junín de los Andes** Argentina 39.57S 71.05W
120 B4 **Junín, L. de** Peru 11.02S 76.07W
104 F8 **Junior** W Virginia 38.58N 79.57W
104 R1 **Junior L** Maine
98 E7 **Juniper** New Brunswick 46.32N 67.13W
111 L6 **Juniper Mts** Arizona
111 C5 **Junipero Serra Pk** California 36.09N 121.26W
20 N1 **Jūnisho** Japan 40.13N 140.36E
69 G5 **Juniville** France 49.24N 4.21E
Jūniye *see* **Jounié**
113 O2 **Junjik** *R* Alaska
23 C9 **Junk B** Hong Kong
64 B3 **Jünkerath** W Germany 50.20N 6.36E
51 E5 **Junkerdal** Norway 66.49N 15.35E
23 C9 **Junk I** Hong Kong 22.16N 114.15E
23 C4 **Junlian** Sichuan China 28.15N 104.22E
29 C8 **Junnar** Maharashtra India 19.15N 73.58E
112 F5 **Juno** Texas 30.11N 101.09W
100 K5 **Junor** Saskatchewan 53.34N 107.53W
51 J4 **Junosuando** Sweden 67.25N 22.29E
76 D4 **Junqera de Espadañedo** Spain 42.19N 7.36W
76 D4 **Junquera de Ambia** Spain 42.12N 7.44W
75 Q3 **Junquera,La** Spain 42.25N 2.52E
52 K3 **Junsele** Sweden 63.40N 16.55E
23 G4 **Junshan Hu** *L* Jiangxi China
76 A10 **Junto,Mte** Portugal 39.11N 9.03W
22 H7 **Juntuliang** Nei Monggol Zizhiqu China 39.40N 109.04E
110 G6 **Juntura** Oregon 43.46N 118.05W
51 O6 **Juntusranta** Finland 65.12N 29.30E
23 F2 **Jun Xian** Hubei China 32.44N 111.10E
Junyah *see* **Jounié**
51 O9 **Juojärvi** *L* Finland 62.40N 28.40E
51 K5 **Juoksengi** Sweden 66.32N 23.50E
118 G2 **Jupaguá** Brazil 11.52S 44.21W
32 G5 **Jūpār** Iran 30.06N 57.09E
118 H6 **Juparanã, L** Brazil 19.16S 40.12W
118 D7 **Jupiá** Brazil 20.48S 51.32W
118 D7 **Jupiá Dam** Brazil 20.51S 51.40W
70 L6 **Jupilles** France 47.47N 0.25E
61 N4 **Jupille-sur-Meuse** Belgium 50.38N 5.38E
105 G11 **Jupiter** Florida 26.57N 80.08W
94 T13 **Jupiter** S Africa 26.13S 28.05E
98 J4 **Jupiter,R** Anticosti I, Que
61 N4 **Juprelle** Belgium 50.42N 5.32E
118 F9 **Juquiá** Brazil 24.18S 47.36W
118 F9 **Juquiá,R** Brazil
115 L9 **Juquíla, Sta. Catarina** Mexico 16.15N 97.20W
87 B6 **Jur** *R* Sudan
67 J6 **Jura** *dept* France
58 E6 **Jura** *isld* Strathclyde Scotland
67 J6 **Jura** *mts* France/Switz
118 H3 **Jurací** Brazil 13.12S 40.53W
119 C4 **Juradó** Colombia 7.07N 77.45W
62 L5 **Jura Krakowska** *mts* Poland
118 G5 **Juramento** Brazil 16.50S 43.36W
Juramento *R* Argentina*see* **Pasaje**
66 D3 **Jura, Mts** France/Switz
72 D9 **Jurançon** France 43.17N 0.23W
58 E7 **Jura,Sd.of** Strathclyde Scotland
34 L9 **Juraybah,Al** Saudi Arabia
33 G3 **Juraybiat** *oil field* Saudi Arabia 27.30N 47.43E
33 H3 **Jurayd, Al** *isld* Saudi Arabia 27.08N 49.59E
33 F4 **Jurayfah,Al** Saudi Arabia 25.29N 45.12E
34 M8 **Juraymī, Sha'īb** *watercourse* Iraq
33 E6 **Jurayr,Al** Saudi Arabia 20.12N 43.58E
46 E2 **Jurbarkas** Lithuania U.S.S.R. 55.04N 22.42E
61 F4 **Jurbise** Belgium 50.32N 3.55E
57 D4 **Jurby** Isle of Man U.K. 54.21N 4.31W
33 E4 **Jurdhāwiyah,Al** Saudi Arabia 25.16N 42.45E
Jurdi *see* **Jowr Deh**
35 J2 **Jurein** Syria 32.56N 36.24E
35 G6 **Jureina** Jordan 31.46N 35.48E
117 G9 **Juremal** Brazil 9.40S 40.21W
35 H5 **Jurf** *watercourse* Jordan
34 C8 **Jurf ed Darāwish** Jordan 30.42N 35.52E
14 E4 **Jurgurra,R** W Australia
21 B5 **Jurh** Nei Monggol Zizhiqu China 44.41N 120.31E
24 G9 **Jurhen Ul Shan** *mts* Qinghai China
30 J5 **Juribela** Nepal 27.08N 85.24E
14 B9 **Jurien B** W Australia
72 D4 **Jurignac** France 45.31N 0.01W
82 M6 **Jurilovca** Romania 44.46N 28.52E
89 D8 **Juring** Sierra Leone 7.00N 11.32W
117 B6 **Juriti Velho** Brazil 2.26S 56.17W
31 F2 **Jurm** Afghanistan 36.50N 70.52E
46 E2 **Jūrmala** Latvia U.S.S.R. 56.59N 23.35E
35 G2 **Jurmeia** Syria 32.55N 35.47E
35 G2 **Jurniye** Syria 32.54N 35.50E
76 E11 **Juromenha** Portugal 38.45N 7.14W
23 H3 **Jurong** Jiangsu China 31.56N 119.20E
18 H3 **Jurong** *dist* Singapore
18 H3 **Jurong** *R* Singapore
65 N9 **Juršinci** Yugoslavia 46.28N 15.58E
119 F9 **Juruá** Brazil 3.30S 66.05W
120 C3 **Juruá Mirim** *R* Brazil
119 F9 **Juruá, R** Brazil
33 A7 **Jurudiyah** Saudi Arabia 26.33N 49.58E
118 B3 **Juruena** Brazil 12.50S 58.58W
117 A9 **Juruena,R** Brazil
118 K9 **Jurujuba,Pta.de** Brazil 22.56S 43.08W
118 D2 **Juruna,R** Brazil
120 D3 **Jurupari,R** Brazil
117 B6 **Juruti** Brazil 2.10S 56.00W
51 J9 **Jurva** Finland 62.40N 22.00E
20 O1 **Jūsan-ko** Japan 41.00N 140.20E
119 G3 **Jusepín** Venezuela 9.47N 63.33W
61 N7 **Juseret** Belgium 49.53N 5.33E
Jushqan Esfahān Iran*see* **Jowsheqān-e Qālī**
32 G2 **Jūshqān** Khorāsān Iran 37.00N 57.25E
34 D4 **Jūsiya** Syria 34.26N 36.35E
72 J6 **Jussac** France 44.59N 2.25E
69 K8 **Jussey** France 47.49N 5.55E
66 B7 **Jussy** Switzerland 46.15N 6.17E
72 K1 **Jussy-le-Chaudrier** France 47.08N 2.55E
100 S8 **Justice** Manitoba 50.00N 99.46W
112 F2 **Justiceburg** Texas 33.03N 101.14W
112 K2 **Justin** Texas 33.06N 97.20W
121 D4 **Justo Daract** Argentina 33.52S 65.12W
117 G9 **Jutaí** Brazil 8.36S 40.15W
119 F10 **Jutaí** Brazil 5.11S 68.54W
117 D6 **Jutai, I. Grande de** Brazil
119 F9 **Jutaí, R** Brazil
117 C5 **Jutai,Sa.do** *mts* Brazil
120 D2 **Jutaizinho, R** Brazil
63 S9 **Jüterbog** E Germany 51.59N 13.05E
118 C8 **Juti** Brazil 22.44S 54.37W
115 P10 **Jutiapa** Guatemala 14.17N 89.50W
115 L2 **Jutiapa** Honduras 15.48N 86.30W
115 L2 **Juticalpa** Honduras 14.45N 86.12W
51 F5 **Jutis** Sweden 66.16N 17.15E
Jutland *see* **Jylland**
60 J11 **Jutphaas** Netherlands 52.02N 5.06E
60 L8 **Jutrijp** Netherlands 53.00N 5.40E
52 F5 **Jutulhogget** *pass* Norway 61.59N 10.55E
51 O8 **Juuka** Finland 63.13N 29.20E
51 N10 **Juva** Finland 61.54N 27.49E
115 J7 **Juventino Rosas** Mexico 20.40N 101.00W
70 H5 **Juvigné** France 48.14N 1.01W
70 H4 **Juvigny-le-Tertre** France 48.41N 1.01W
70 J4 **Juvigny-sous-Andaine** France 48.33N 0.30W
69 C6 **Juvisy** France 48.41N 2.22E
68 F5 **Juvisy-sur-Orge** France 48.42N 2.23E
53 B6 **Juvre** Denmark 55.11N 8.33E
34 E5 **Juwaïf,El** *escarp* Syria
Juwain *see* **Lāsh-e Joveyn**
Juwara *see* **Jawārah,Al**
33 J5 **Juwayfah,Al** Saudi Arabia 22.22N 50.04E
Juwayf,Aj *see* **Juwaïf,El**
35 G1 **Juwayzah** Syria 33.02N 35.50E
35 F9 **Juweir** Jordan 31.01N 35.42E
35 G6 **Juweiyida,El** Jordan 31.53N 35.57E
18 J9 **Juwono** Java Indon 6.41S 111.08E
23 H1 **Ju Xian** Shandong China 35.36N 118.50E
23 G1 **Juye** Shandong China 35.26N 116.04E
32 H3 **Jūymand** Iran 34.19N 58.40E
32 F6 **Jūyom** Iran 28.03N 54.02E
69 H7 **Juzennecourt** France 48.11N 4.48E
72 F10 **Juzet** France 42.59N 0.45E
30 B3 **Jwalapur** Uttar Prad India 29.56N 78.06E
53 G5 **Jyderup** Denmark 55.40N 11.25E
53 B4 **Jylland** *pen* Denmark
53 J5 **Jyllinge** Denmark 55.46N 12.08E
53 E2 **Jyske ås** *hills* Denmark 57.15N 10.15E
53 H5 **Jystrup** Denmark 55.31N 11.53E
51 M9 **Jyväskylä** Finland 62.16N 25.50E
91 J2 **Ka** Zaïre 3.29N 24.51E
90 B6 **Ka** *R* Nigeria
15 G7 **Ka** *R* Papua New Guinea
114 B4 **Kaaawa** Hawaiian Is 21.33N 157.47W
93 F2 **Kaabong** Uganda 3.30N 34.08E
94 F7 **Kaaing Velt** *plat* S Africa
43 E8 **Kaakhka** Turkmeniya U.S.S.R. 37.22N 59.40E
114 A4 **Kaala** *mt* Hawaiian Is 21.30N 155.12W
9 B13 **Kaala-Gomen** New Caledonia 20.44S 164.29E
51 H4 **Kaalasjärvi** *L* Sweden 67.49N 19.50E
95 M2 **Kaalfontein** S Africa 26.03S 28.15E
95 M4 **Kaallaagte** S Africa 28.08S 28.01E
95 K5 **Kaalspruit** S Africa 29.16S 26.09E
114 B9 **Kaalualu** Hawaiian Is 18.58N 155.37W
51 N2 **Kaamanen** Finland 69.05N 27.16E
87 C6 **Kaan** Sudan 9.00N 30.43E
114 D6 **Kaanapali** Hawaiian Is 20.56N 156.42W
95 O1 **Kaap** *R* S Africa
114 E6 **Kaapahu Bay** Hawaiian Is
94 L5 **Kaapmuiden** S Africa 25.33S 31.20E
95 G4 **Kaap Plato** *plat* S Africa
95 O1 **Kaapsehoop** S Africa 25.37S 30.46E
Kaapstad *see* **Cape Town**
63 O6 **Kaarssen** E Germany 53.13N 11.03E
69 M1 **Kaarst** W Germany 51.15N 6.37E
89 E5 **Kaarta** *reg* Mali
60 J13 **Kaatsheuvel** Netherlands 51.39N 5.02E
51 N9 **Kaavi** Finland 62.58N 28.30E
30 H7 **Kab** Bihar India 25.23N 84.47E
Kaba *see* **Habahe**
62 N8 **Kaba** Hungary 47.21N 21.14E
87 B3 **Kababish** *tribe* Sudan
39 G1 **Kabachkova** U.S.S.R. 69.15N 161.34E
37 D5 **Kabadüz** Turkey 40.50N 37.55E
19 B6 **Kabaena** *isld* Indonesia
93 B5 **Kabagole** Uganda 0.12N 30.55E
18 E7 **Kaba,Gunung** *mt* Sumatra Indon 3.32S 102.41E
37 D8 **Kabahaydar** Turkey 37.15N 38.56E
24 E1 **Kaba He** *R* Xinjiang Uygur Zizhiqu China
92 A9 **Kaba Hill** Zambia 14.49S 23.40E
34 P8 **Kabaish,Al** Iraq 30.58N 47.02E
89 E6 **Kaba Kangaba** Mali 11.59N 8.22W
37 E1 **Kabakça** Turkey 41.14N 28.22E
43 G7 **Kabakly** Turkmeniya U.S.S.R. 39.46N 62.31E
40 B3 **Kabaktan** U.S.S.R. 56.41N 122.23E
89 D7 **Kabala** Sierra Leone 9.40N 11.36W
93 A7 **Kabale** Uganda 1.15S 29.58E
117 A2 **Kabalebo** *R* Surinam
93 C3 **Kabalega (Murchison) Falls** Uganda 2.17N 31.41E
19 B4 **Kabali** Celebes Indonesia 1.38S 122.00E
36 H1 **Kabalı** Turkey 41.52N 35.03E
91 K7 **Kabalo** Zaïre 6.02S 26.55E
80 F1 **Kabal,Rtic** *pt* Yugoslavia 43.14N 16.32E
15 M6 **Kabaman** New Ireland 4.22S 152.48E
91 H6 **Kabamba** Zaïre 5.40S 23.50E
91 K7 **Kabamba, L** Zaïre 7.55S 27.00E
92 C4 **Kabambare** Zaïre 4.40S 27.41E
47 K8 **Kaban'** Kazakhstan U.S.S.R. 54.44N 66.30E
91 K7 **Kabango** Zaïre 6.24S 26.05E
92 D6 **Kabango** Zaïre 8.41S 28.10E
18 C4 **Kabanjahe** Sumatra Indon 3.02N 98.26E
46 Q3 **Kabanovka** U.S.S.R. 53.39N 51.10E
42 H6 **Kabansk** U.S.S.R. 52.03N 106.45E
45 K7 **Kaban'ya** Ukraine U.S.S.R. 49.13N 38.15E
40 H8 **Kaban'ya** U.S.S.R. 46.50N 138.22E
89 H3 **Kabara** Mali 16.42N 2.54W
89 G4 **Kabara,L** Mali 15.50N 4.35W
46 L7 **Kabardinka** U.S.S.R. 44.38N 37.58E
44 E4 **Kabardino-Balkarskaya A.S.S.R** U.S.S.R.
Kabardinskaya A.S.S.R *see* **Kabardino-Balkarskaya A.S.S.R**
92 D3 **Kabare** Zaïre 2.28S 28.47E
93 G5 **Kabarnet** Kenya 0.30N 35.45E
19 L8 **Kabasalan** Mindanao Philippines 7.48N 122.48E
93 D5 **Kabasanda** Uganda 0.17N 32.15E
92 D2 **Kabasha** Zaïre 0.42S 29.11E
20 C9 **Kaba-shima** *isld* Japan 32.47N 129.00E
25 D3 **Kabaung** *R* Burma
Kabauw *see* **Cabauw**
85 A4 **Kābāw** Libya 31.51N 11.17E
90 C8 **Kabba** Nigeria 7.50N 6.07E
28 C5 **Kabbani** *R* Kerala/Karnataka India
33 M10 **Kabd** *hills* Kuwait
51 H5 **Kåbdalis** Sweden 66.11N 19.58E
34 G4 **Kabd es Sārem** *hills* Syria
Kabd Ouarqa *see* **Kabd Warqa**
34 G4 **Kabd Warqa** *hills* Syria
20 F7 **Kabe** Japan 34.31N 132.29E
85 M10 **Kab,El** Sudan 19.17N 32.44E
91 K8 **Kabele, L** Zaïre 8.48S 26.08E
51 D3 **Kabelvåg** Norway 68.13N 14.30E
99 E4 **Kabenung** *L* Ontario 48.15N 85.02W
93 E4 **Kaberamaido** Uganda 1.46N 33.09E
19 B3 **Kabetan** *isld* Celebes Indon 1.04N 120.39E
108 R1 **Kabetogama** Minnesota 48.26N 93.01W
108 R1 **Kabetogama L** Minnesota
90 F5 **Kabi** Niger 13.21N 12.28E
Kabia *isld* Celebes Indonesia*see* **Selayar**
19 C7 **Kabia** *isld* Indonesia 6.55S 122.13E
90 G7 **Kabia** *R* Chad
Kabiarat *see* **Wowanda**
34 D9 **Kabid,Al** Jordan 29.47N 36.29E
15 L5 **Kabien** New Ireland 2.45S 150.45E
91 K5 **Kabilu** Zaïre 2.22S 27.21E
99 F3 **Kabinakagami** *R* Ontario
99 F4 **Kabinakagami L** Ontario
91 J7 **Kabinda** Zaïre 6.10S 24.29E
37 F7 **Kabindin Tepesı** *hill* Turkey 38.57N 41.43E
18 M3 **Kabinu** Borneo Indon 4.01N 116.06E
19 D8 **Kabir** Indonesia 8.17S 124.15E
Kabīr *R see* **Kebīr** *R*
Kābirī *see* **Kabri**
32 B4 **Kabīr Kūh** *mts* Iran
33 B9 **Kabīr,Wādī al** *watercourse* S Yemen
31 F5 **Kabirwala** Pakistan 30.24N 71.51E
43 J8 **Kabla** Tadzhikistan U.S.S.R. 37.29N 68.07E
90 J8 **Kabo** Cent Afr Rep 7.48N 18.35E
90 D6 **Kabo** Nigeria 11.50N 8.09E
92 D5 **Kaboko** Zaïre 7.13S 28.21E
92 B8 **Kabompo** Zambia 13.36S 24.10E
92 A9 **Kabompo** *R* Zambia
18 J5 **Kabong** Sarawak Malaysia 1.50N 111.07E
91 J7 **Kabongo** Zaïre 7.20S 25.34E
92 C5 **Kabonzo** Zaïre 6.41S 27.49E
25 D6 **Kabosa I** Burma
89 K7 **Kabou** Togo 9.30N 0.52E
93 C6 **Kaboyo** Uganda 0.22S 31.35E
30 C7 **Kabrai** Uttar Prad India 25.24N 80.00E
35 D1 **Kabri** Israel 33.01N 35.09E
86 H5 **Kabrit** Egypt 30.15N 32.30E
33 E4 **Kabshah,Jabal** *mts* Saudi Arabia
Kabsh, Ra's al *see* **Jibsh, Ra's al**
91 J8 **Kabubu** Zaïre 9.42S 24.40E
32 J4 **Kabūdeh** Iran 33.22N 60.48E
32 H2 **Kabūd Gonbad** Iran 37.02N 59.46E
32 C3 **Kabūd Rāhang** Iran 35.12N 48.44E
19 K3 **Kabugao** Luzon Philippines 17.59N 121.12E
31 E3 **Kabul** Afghanistan 34.30N 69.10E
35 D2 **Kābūl** Israel 32.52N 35.13E
31 E3 **Kabul** *prov* Afghanistan
93 C6 **Kabula** Uganda 0.20S 31.11E
93 C5 **Kabulasoke** Uganda 0.10N 31.50E
15 J5 **Kabuli** Admiralty Is 2.09S 146.42E
31 E3 **Kabul R** Afghanistan
91 K6 **Kabumbu** Zaïre 4.07S 26.17E
91 K7 **Kabumbulu** Zaïre 7.40S 26.48E
92 D8 **Kabunda** Zaïre 12.27S 29.21E
92 D7 **Kabunda** Zambia 11.09S 28.50E
91 K9 **Kabundi** Zaïre 10.06S 27.14E
19 E2 **Kaburuang** *isld* Indonesia
87 D2 **Kabushiya** Sudan 16.54N 33.41E
Kabutarang *see* **Kabūd Rāhang**
32 G5 **Kabūtar Khān** Iran 30.19N 56.19E
18 B6 **Kabut,Bukit** *hill* Pen Malaysia 5.28N 101.32E
18 E8 **Kabuwe** Indonesia 5.30S 102.14E
91 H7 **Kabwanga** Zaïre 7.02S 22.36E
92 D9 **Kabwe** Zambia 14.29S 28.25E
91 J7 **Kabwe Katanda** Zaïre 7.58S 24.27E
91 K8 **Kabwe, L** Zaïre 9.10S 26.02E
93 C4 **Kabwoya** Uganda 1.14N 31.07E
15 J7 **Kabwum** Papua New Guinea 6.04S 147.09E
88 Q3 **Kabylie,Gde & Petite** *mts* Algeria
47 L7 **Kabyrdak** U.S.S.R. 56.08N 72.22E
43 G2 **Kabyrga** *R* Kazakhstan U.S.S.R.
82 G8 **Kačanik** Yugoslavia 42.14N 21.15E
44 C10 **Kacha** Ukraine U.S.S.R. 44.46N 33.32E
44 C10 **Kacha** *R* Ukraine U.S.S.R.
31 C7 **Kacha Daman** Pakistan 27.14N 64.45E
93 G3 **Kachagalau** *mt* Kenya 2.16N 35.06E
31 A6 **Kacha Kuh** *ra* Iran/Pakistan
45 Q7 **Kachalinskaya** U.S.S.R. 49.07N 44.02E
92 E9 **Kachalola** Zambia 14.45S 30.37E
31 C8 **Kachari,Ras** *C* Pakistan 25.11N 65.50E
26 P3 **Kachchativu** *isld* Sri Lanka 9.23N 79.33E
90 J6 **Kaché** Chad 10.08N 19.46E
92 F8 **Kachebera** Zambia 13.50S 32.50E
113 M7 **Kachemak B** Alaska
110 D2 **Kachess,L** Washington 47.20N 121.15W
31 D5 **Kachh** Pakistan 30.25N 67.21E
31 D6 **Kachhi** *reg* Pakistan
29 D5 **Kachhola** Rajasthan India 25.26N 75.12E
90 C7 **Kachia** Nigeria 9.50N 7.55E
94 H2 **Kachikau** Botswana 18.08S 24.26E
25 M8 **Kachin** *state* Burma
93 C6 **Kachira, L** Uganda 0.35S 31.07E
43 M1 **Kachiry** Kazakhstan U.S.S.R. 53.07N 76.08E
87 F6 **Kachisi** Ethiopia 9.31N 37.50E
47 H6 **Kachkanar** U.S.S.R. 58.43N 59.28E
45 E9 **Kachkarovka** Ukraine U.S.S.R. 47.05N 33.45E
30 A8 **Kachnar** Madhya Prad India 24.26N 77.38E
31 G2 **Kach Pass** Pakistan 36.54N 72.35E
44 G6 **Kachreti** Georgia U.S.S.R. 41.38N 45.40E
61 C3 **Kachtem** Belgium 50.56N 3.12E
31 H10 **Kachua** Bangladesh 22.39N 89.54E
42 H5 **Kachug** U.S.S.R. 53.58N 105.55E
42 E5 **Kachul'ka** U.S.S.R. 53.40N 92.54E
93 D4 **Kachung** Uganda 1.55N 32.58E
37 F5 **Kaçkar Dağı** *mt* Turkey 40.50N 41.09E
37 F5 **Kaçkar Tepeleri** *hills* Turkey
65 M2 **Kácov** Czechoslovakia 49.48N 15.02E
90 J2 **Kada** Chad 19.20N 19.39E
20 J7 **Kada** Japan 34.15N 135.04E
25 D4 **Kadaingti** Burma 17.35N 97.31E
28 C6 **Kadaiyanallur** Tamil Nadu India 9.04N 77.25E
30 H8 **Kadalgori** Bihar India 24.21N 84.57E
42 J4 **Kadali** U.S.S.R. 55.30N 114.10E
93 F4 **Kadam Mt** Uganda 1.45N 34.43E
64 P3 **Kadan** Czechoslovakia 50.24N 13.16E
29 C6 **Kadana** Gujarat India 23.22N 73.52E
31 D5 **Kadanai R** Pakistan
25 E6 **Kadan Kyun** *isld* Burma
18 L8 **Kadapongan** *isld* Indonesia 4.44S 115.42E
30 J6 **Kadarbana** Nepal 26.45N 85.20E
62 K9 **Kadarkút** Hungary 46.13N 17.39E
19 C6 **Kadatuang** *isld* Indonesia 5.34S 122.31E
26 Q8 **Kadawata** Sri Lanka 7.01N 79.57E
42 K6 **Kadaya** U.S.S.R. 50.55N 119.18E
87 H5 **Kaddabasa,L** Ethiopia 10.17N 40.32E
26 T5 **Kaddaiparichchan** Sri Lanka 8.28N 81.17E
28 D1 **Kaddam** *L* Andhra Prad India 19.12N 78.41E
29 F8 **Kaddam** *res* Andhra Prad India 19.12N 78.40E
89 J8 **Kade** Ghana 6.08N 0.51W
90 G9 **Kadeï** *R* Cameroon/Cent Afr Rep
64 E8 **Kadelburg** W Germany 47.37N 8.18E
20 P9 **Kadena** Okinawa Japan 26.20N 127.45E
21 C13 **Kadena** Okinawa Japan 29.00N 128.00E
14 F7 **Kadgo L** W Australia 26.40S 126.40E
84 G4 **Kadhenoi** Greece 38.35N 23.46E
34 M5 **Kādhimain** Iraq 33.22N 44.20E
29 C6 **Kadi** Gujarat India 23.20N 72.22E
28 C6 **Kadiapattanam** Tamil Nadu India 8.07N 77.21E
Kadiene *see* **Ban Kadiene**
82 H9 **Kadijica** *mt* Bulgaria 41.49N 22.59E
37 C1 **Kadıköy** Edirne Turkey 41.05N 26.40E
37 E1 **Kadıköy** İstanbul Turkey 41.08N 28.22E
37 F2 **Kadıköy** İstanbul Turkey 40.59N 29.02E
37 G3 **Kadimi** Turkey 40.07N 29.24E
12 E5 **Kadina** S Australia 33.58S 137.14E
36 F4 **Kadınhanı** Turkey 38.15N 32.14E
89 G6 **Kadiolo** Mali 10.35N 7.41W
30 F6 **Kadipur** Uttar Prad India 26.11N 82.22E
29 D8 **Kadirabad** Maharashtra India 19.52N 75.59E
36 C6 **Kadırga Burun** *C* Turkey 36.43N 28.18E
28 D3 **Kadiri** Andhra Prad India 14.08N 78.07E
36 J5 **Kadirli** Turkey 37.22N 36.05E
31 G5 **Kadirpur** Pakistan 31.36N 72.17E
36 H3 **Kadısehri** Turkey 40.00N 35.49E
90 N9 **Kadjéma** Cent Afr Rep 5.10N 26.10E
32 H3 **Kadkan** Iran 35.33N 58.49E
27 L7 **Kadmat** *isld* Laccadive Is Ind Oc 11.08N 72.46E
Kadmus *castle see* **Qadmūs,El**
47 E6 **Kadnikov** U.S.S.R. 59.33N 40.16E
46 L3 **Kadnoye** U.S.S.R. 53.15N 37.50E
25 D4 **Kado** Burma 16.34N 97.40E
20 O1 **Kado** Japan 40.03N 140.05E
108 J6 **Kadoka** S Dakota 43.50N 101.30W
45 O2 **Kadom** U.S.S.R. 54.32N 42.30E
25 C5 **Kadonkani** Burma 15.50N 95.11E
45 Q2 **Kadoshkino** U.S.S.R. 54.02N 44.22E
15 H5 **Kadovar I** Papua New Guinea 3.37S 144.37E
82 G9 **Kadrifakovo** Yugoslavia 41.51N 22.02E
25 M9 **Kadu** Burma 24.44N 96.16E
26 S7 **Kadugannawa** Sri Lanka 7.15N 80.32E
87 B5 **Kadugli** Sudan 11.00N 29.44E
90 C6 **Kaduna** Nigeria 10.28N 7.25E
90 C7 **Kaduna** *R* Nigeria
93 E4 **Kadunguru** Uganda 1.31N 33.13E
28 C4 **Kadur** Karnataka India 13.34N 76.01E
25 M6 **Kadusam** *mt* India/Xizang Zizhiqu 28.27N 96.37E
26 Q8 **Kaduwela** Sri Lanka 6.55N 80.01E
46 K1 **Kaduy** U.S.S.R. 59.12N 37.02E
30 A8 **Kadwaha** Madhya Prad India 24.57N 77.55E
29 D8 **Kadwa R** Maharashtra India
89 K7 **Kadyamba** Togo 9.55N 0.39E
42 F6 **Kadyr-Egi-Tayga,Khrebet,mts** U.S.S.R.
46 N1 **Kadyy** U.S.S.R. 57.48N 43.10E
44 G8 **Kadzharan** Armenia U.S.S.R. 39.10N 46.07E
47 H4 **Kadzherom** U.S.S.R. 64.42N 55.59E
42 C3 **Kadzhi** U.S.S.R. 59.55N 82.40E
43 M6 **Kadzhi-Say** Kirgiziya U.S.S.R. 42.09N 77.10E
89 C3 **Kaédi** Mauritania 16.12N 13.32W
98 R5 **Kaegudeck L** Newfoundland
90 G6 **Kaélé** Cameroon 10.05N 14.28E
114 E6 **Kaeleku** Hawaiian Is 20.47N 156.03W
114 A4 **Kaena Pt** Hawaiian Is 21.35N 158.18W
114 D6 **Kaena,Pt** Hawaiian Is 20.54N 157.04W
114 D4 **Kaeo** Hawaiian Is 21.53N 160.08W
11 H2 **Kaeo** New Zealand 35.05S 173.48E
Ka-erh *see* **Gar**
Ka-erh-k'un-sha *see* **Gar**
53 D6 **Kærum** Denmark 55.16N 9.57E
21 D9 **Kaesŏng** N Korea 37.59N 126.30E
34 E7 **Kāf** Saudi Arabia 31.25N 37.29E
91 H8 **Kafakumba** Zaïre 9.42S 23.41E
44 G8 **Kafan** Armenia U.S.S.R. 39.11N 46.22E
90 D7 **Kafanchan** Nigeria 9.38N 8.20E
30 E4 **Kafara** Uttar Prad India 28.04N 81.02E
32 H3 **Kāfar Qal'eh** Iran 35.53N 59.21E
Kafer Aqqeb *see* **Kafr'Aqib**
Kafer Chams *see* **Kafr Shams**
35 F1 **Kafer Kela** Lebanon 33.17N 35.33E
48 T1 **Kaffeklubben Ø** *isld* Greenland
95 K5 **Kaffer** *R* S Africa
95 K5 **Kafferrivier** S Africa 29.26S 26.05E
95 K2 **Kafferskraaldam** *res* S Africa 26.48S 26.37E
95 N2 **Kafferspruit** S Africa 26.37S 29.50E
95 N4 **Kafferstad** S Africa 28.02S 29.00E
89 B4 **Kaffrine** Senegal 14.08N 15.34W
90 B5 **Kafi** Nigeria 13.40N 5.46E
31 F3 **Kafiristan** *reg* Pakistan
43 J8 **Kafirnigan** *R* Tadzhikistan U.S.S.R.
Kafir Qal'eh *see* **Kāfar Qal'eh**
51 K2 **Kåfjord** Norway 69.56N 22.55E
51 H2 **Kåfjord** *inlet* Norway 69.35N 20.35E
15 A5 **Kafnikalep** Misoöl I, Irian Jaya 2.01S 130.09E
35 E1 **Kafra** Lebanon 33.10N 35.21E
90 F2 **Kafra** Niger 19.02N 12.18E
35 D5 **Kafr'Ain** Jordan 32.03N 35.07E
35 D6 **Kafr'Aqab** Jordan 31.53N 35.14E
35 F2 **Kafr 'Aqib** Syria 32.52N 35.39E
35 C5 **Kafr Bārā** Israel 32.08N 34.58E
34 D3 **Kafr Behūm** Syria 35.05N 36.42E
35 D4 **Kafr Dan** Jordan 32.28N 35.15E
35 D5 **Kafr ed Dik** Jordan 32.04N 35.05E
Kafr'Ein *see* **Kafr'Ain**
35 F6 **Kafrein** Jordan 31.51N 35.39E
35 F6 **Kafrein** *R* Jordan
86 G3 **Kafr el Battîkh** Egypt 31.25N 31.44E
86 D3 **Kafr el Dauwâr** Egypt 31.08N 30.08E
86 F3 **Kafr el Garâyda** Egypt 31.14N 31.16E
86 F3 **Kafr el Gharbi,El** Egypt 31.14N 31.03E
35 G2 **Kafr el Ma** Syria 32.49N 35.49E
86 F3 **Kafr el Sharqi,El** Egypt 31.16N 31.10E
86 E3 **Kafr el Sheik** Egypt 31.07N 30.56E
86 E3 **Kafr el Sheikh** *div* Egypt
86 F4 **Kafr el Tamîmi** Egypt 30.36N 31.22E
86 E4 **Kafr el Zaiyât** Egypt 30.50N 30.49E
35 F2 **Kafr Harīb** Syria 32.45N 35.39E
35 E3 **Kafr Kama** Israel 32.43N 35.26E
35 E3 **Kafr Kanna** Israel 32.44N 35.20E
86 F4 **Kafr Kila el Bâb** Egypt 30.41N 31.08E
35 E6 **Kafr Malik** Jordan 31.59N 35.18E
35 E2 **Kafr Mandā** Israel 32.49N 35.16E
35 F1 **Kafr Naffakh** Syria 33.04N 35.44E
35 H1 **Kafr Nasij** Syria 33.09N 36.02E
35 D6 **Kafr Ni'ma** Jordan 31.55N 35.06E
Kafroûn Bachoûr *see* **Kafrun**
35 D5 **Kafr Qaddum** Jordan 32.13N 35.08E
35 D3 **Kafr Qari'** Israel 32.31N 35.04E
35 C5 **Kafr Qasim** Israel 32.07N 34.58E
35 D4 **Kafr Qud** Jordan 32.27N 35.14E
86 E4 **Kafr Rabi'** Egypt 30.42N 30.50E
35 D4 **Kafr Ra'i** Jordan 32.22N 35.09E
86 G3 **Kafr Sa'd** Egypt 31.20N 31.38E
86 G4 **Kafr Şaqr** Egypt 30.48N 31.36E
35 H1 **Kafr Shams** Syria 33.07N 36.07E
86 F5 **Kafr Shibîn** Egypt 30.18N 31.18E
86 F4 **Kafr Shukr** Egypt 30.33N 31.16E
86 D3 **Kafr Silîm** Egypt 31.09N 30.07E
35 E2 **Kafr Sumei'** Israel 32.58N 35.18E
35 D5 **Kafr Sur** Jordan 32.15N 35.04E
35 D5 **Kafr Thulth** Jordan 32.09N 35.03E
34 D4 **Kafrun** Syria 34.52N 36.14E
Kafrūn Bachur *see* **Kafrun**
35 D2 **Kafr Yasīf** Israel 32.57N 35.10E
32 C4 **Kafshgarān** Iran 33.52N 48.38E
87 F4 **Kafta** Ethiopia 13.53N 37.11E
93 C4 **Kafu** *R* Uganda
92 D7 **Kafubu** *R* Zaïre
92 D9 **Kafue** Zambia 15.44S 28.10E
92 C8 **Kafue** *R* Zambia
92 C9 **Kafue Dam** *res* Zambia
92 D9 **Kafue Gorge** Zambia 15.55S 28.45E
92 C9 **Kafue Nat.Park** Zambia
92 F7 **Kafukule** Malawi 11.27S 33.38E
92 D8 **Kafulafuta** Zambia 13.12S 28.20E
92 D6 **Kafulwe** Zambia 9.01S 29.03E
93 B7 **Kafunzo** Uganda 1.02S 30.25E
93 B9 **Kafura** Tanzania 3.48S 30.40E
43 E1 **Kaga** Bashkir U.S.S.R. 53.31N 57.45E
20 K5 **Kaga** Japan 36.20N 136.15E
84 B5 **Kagádhi** Greece 38.02N 21.27E
113 Q10 **Kagalaska I** Aleutian Is 51.49N 176.20W
44 C1 **Kagalnitskaya** U.S.S.R. 46.53N 40.10E
26 S5 **Kagama** Sri Lanka 8.05N 80.33E
20 G6 **Kagami** Japan 35.08N 133.58E
113 C10 **Kagamil I** Aleutian Is 53.00N 169.40W
31 G3 **Kagan** Pakistan 34.47N 73.36E
43 G7 **Kagan** Uzbekistan U.S.S.R. 39.45N 64.32E
23 B1 **Kagang** Qinghai China 35.27N 100.11E
Kaganovich *see* **Tovarkovskiy**
43 G8 **Kaganovicha, im** Turkmeniya U.S.S.R. 36.04N 62.44E
89 J6 **Kagao** Upper Volta 11.57N 1.57W
90 C6 **Kagara** Nigeria 10.13N 6.12E
30 A5 **Kagaraul** Uttar Prad India 27.02N 77.50E
90 C7 **Kagarko** Nigeria 9.28N 7.36E
45 B7 **Kagarlyk** Ukraine U.S.S.R. 49.50N 30.50E
113 G7 **Kagati L** Alaska 59.54N 160.08W
20 G7 **Kagawa** *prefect* Japan
99 H7 **Kagawong** Ontario 45.54N 82.15W
85 L10 **Kagbar Cataract** Sudan 19.56N 30.34E
24 H8 **Kagchinar La** *pass* Qinghai China 34.41N 93.18E
52 N2 **Kåge** Sweden 64.50N 21.00E
87 C8 **Kagelu** Sudan 4.05N 30.36E
93 B7 **Kagera** *R* Tanzania/Rwanda/Uganda
93 B7 **Kagera,Parc Nat.de la** Rwanda
53 J5 **Kagerup** Denmark 56.00N 12.17E
34 H2 **Kagher Bazār** Syria 36.54N 40.53E
30 G7 **Kaghzipur** Uttar Prad India 25.45N 83.38E
99 C2 **Kagianagami L** Ontario
99 D3 **Kagiano L** Ontario 49.17N 86.25W
66 K4 **Kägiswil** Switzerland 46.56N 8.16E
37 F1 **Kâğıthane** Turkey 41.05N 28.58E
37 J1 **Kâğıthane** Turkey 41.05N 28.56E
37 J1 **Kâğıthane** *R* Turkey
37 G5 **Kağızman** Turkey 40.08N 43.07E
101 J1 **Kaglik L** N W Terr 69.27N 129.55W
87 C3 **Kagmar** Sudan 30.25N 15.24E

93 C6 Kagologolo Uganda 0.08S 31.36E
90 H7 Kagopai Chad 8.16N 16.23E
90 D7 Kagoro Nigeria 9.36N 8.25E
20 D10 Kagoshima Japan 31.37N 130.32E
20 D10 Kagoshima *prefect* Japan
20 D10 Kagoshima-wan *gulf* Japan
15 G7 Kagua Papua New Guinea 6.28S 143.56E
46 G6 Kagul Moldavia U.S.S.R. 45.58N 28.10E
82 L5 Kagul,Ozero *L* U.S.S.R. 45.22N 28.25E
93 E4 Kagulu Uganda 1.16N 33.18E
92 H5 Kaguru *tribe* Tanzania
113 L8 Kaguyak Alaska 56.50N 153.50W
42 F6 Kagzhirba U.S.S.R. 51.42N 96.26E
Kahab *see* Qahab
114 D4 Kahaino Hawaiian Is 21.48N 160.14W
32 G2 Kāhak Khorāsān Iran 36.24N 56.45E
32 C2 Kahak Tehrān Iran 36.09N 49.45E
32 D3 Kahak Tehrān Iran 34.25N 50.54E
114 D6 Kahakuloa Hawaiian Is 21.00N 156.33W
114 F3 Kahala Pt Hawaiian Is 22.09N 159.18W
88 M7 Kahal de Tabelbala *sand dune* Algeria
86 H6 Kahalîya,Gebel *hill* Egypt 29.56N 32.10E
86 H5 Kahalîya, Wâdî *watercourse*
88 M8 Kahal Morrat *reg* Algeria
114 B5 Kahaluu Hawaiian Is 21.27N 157.50W
93 D9 Kahama Tanzania 3.48S 32.36E
31 E6 Kahan Pakistan 29.20N 68.58E
114 B4 Kahana Hawaiian Is 21.33N 157.50W
114 D6 Kahana Hawaiian Is 20.59N 156.41W
114 D6 Kahana Pt Hawaiian Is 20.58N 156.41W
28 L1 Kahao Assam India 28.17N 97.02E
11 M5 Kaharoa *mt* New Zealand 38.20S 177.12E
26 R8 Kahatapitiya Sri Lanka 6.47N 80.03E
19 E3 Kahatola *isld* Halmahera Indon 1.39N 127.29E
93 H7 Kahawa Kenya 1.11S 36.55E
26 R9 Kahawa Sri Lanka 6.11N 80.04E
26 S9 Kahawatta Sri Lanka 6.35N 80.34E
18 K6 Kahayan *R* Kalimantan Indonesia
92 H3 Kahe Tanzania 3.14S 37.22E
93 J9 Kahe Tanzania 3.30S 37.27E
93 J9 Kahe Tanzania 3.29S 37.26E
91 F7 Kahemba Zaïre 7.20S 19.00E
92 H6 Kahengwa Tanzania 8.09S 37.59E
114 A5 Kahe Pt Hawaiian Is 21.20N 158.11W
11 B12 Kaherekoau Mts New Zealand
33 H3 Kahfah,Al Saudi Arabia 27.22N 48.23E
31 F3 Kahi Afghanistan 34.08N 70.41E
92 D5 Kahia Zaïre 6.22S 28.21E
35 J3 Kahil Syria 32.37N 36.16E
88 P4 Kahil,Djebel Bou *mts* Algeria
114 B9 Kahilipali Pt Hawaiian Is 18.58N 155.36W
113 M5 Kahiltna Glacier Alaska 62.35N 151.20W
Kahiri *see* Kūhīrī
64 G3 Kahl *R* W Germany
64 M2 Kahla E Germany 50.48N 11.35E
34 P7 Kahla Iraq 31.39N 47.18E
65 O5 Kahlenberg *mt* Austria 48.17N 16.20E
64 F1 Kahler Asten *mt* W Germany 51.12N 8.30E
110 G3 Kahlotus Washington 46.39N 118.34W
32 G7 Kahn'Alī Iran 27.32N 57.55E
Kahni *see* Kohneh
Kahn-i-'Ali *see* Kahn 'Alī
89 E8 Kahnplé Liberia 7.16N 8.30W
101 N6 Kahntah Br Col 58.19N 120.52W
Kahnu *see* Kahnūj
32 G7 Kahnūj Iran 27.56N 57.46E
107 E1 Kahoka Missouri 40.24N 91.44W
20 K5 Kahoku-gata *L* Japan
114 D6 Kahoolawe *isld* Hawaiian Is 20.30N 156.40W
32 J7 Kahrād Iran 26.01N 61.15E
36 J5 Kahramanmaraş Turkey 37.34N 36.54E
31 F6 Kahror Pakistan 29.38N 71.59E
37 D8 Kâhta Turkey 37.48N 38.35E
37 D8 Kâhta *R* Turkey
32 G3 Kahugish Iran 35.00N 57.34E
11 K11 Kahuitara Pt Chatham Is Pacific Oc 44.16S 176.09W
114 B4 Kahuku Hawaiian Is 21.40N 157.56W
114 B4 Kahuku Pt Hawaiian Is 21.42N 158.00W
114 E6 Kahului Hawaiian Is 20.56N 156.29W
114 E6 Kahului B Hawaiian Is
93 B5 Kahunge Uganda 0.21N 30.27E
32 H6 Kahurak Iran 29.25N 59.38E
11 G7 Kahurangi Pt New Zealand 40.47S 172.11E
31 G4 Kahuta Pakistan 33.38N 73.27E
Kahutara Pt *see* Table Cape New Zealand
93 C1 Kaia *R* Sudan
87 C9 Kaia *watercourse* Sudan
90 A7 Kaiama Nigeria 7.35N 3.58E
90 B7 Kaiama Nigeria 9.37N 4.03E
15 J7 Kaiapit Papua New Guinea 6.12S 146.09E
11 G10 Kaiapoi New Zealand 43.24S 172.40E
100 O1 Kaiashk *R* Ontario
111 M5 Kaibab Plat Arizona
20 J6 Kaibara Japan 35.09N 135.02E
15 B6 Kai Besar *isld* Moluccas Indon
111 N5 Kaibito Plat Arizona
89 J6 Kaibo Upper Volta 11.42N 0.55W
19 F5 Kaibobo Moluccas Indon 3.12S 128.10E
15 M3 Kaichi, Mt Guadalcanal I Solomon Is 9.51S 160.30E
34 O7 Ka'id aṭ Ṭāhir Iraq 31.09N 46.29E
Kaidik *R see* Kaidu (Karaxahar) He
Kaidu *see* Qeydü
24 E4 Kaidu (Karaxahar) He *R* Xinjiang Uygur Zizhiqu China
94 C2 Kaientes Namibia 19.33S 14.20E
122 S15 Kaiepe,Pte Mangaréva Pacific Oc 23.07S 134.58W
119 J5 Kaieteur Falls Guyana 5.09N 59.29W
23 G1 Kaifeng Henan China 34.47N 114.20E
15 H6 Kaigulan Papua New Guinea 6.00S 145.53E
114 B8 Kaiholena *mt* Hawaiian Is 19.10N 155.35W
23 H4 Kaihua Zhejiang China 29.08N 118.21E
11 J6 Kai-Iwi New Zealand 39.50S 174.57E
28 C1 Kaij Maharashtra India 18.42N 76.05E
23 D3 Kaijiang Sichuan China 31.07N 107.55E
15 B6 Kai Kecil *I* Moluccas Indon
15 B6 Kai,Kep *islds* Moluccas Indonesia
Kai Ketjil *I see* Kai Kecil
11 H2 Kaikohe New Zealand 35.25S 173.49E
11 L13 Kaikorai Hill Dunedin New Zealand 45.53S 170.26E
23 D5 Kaikou Guizhou China 26.03N 107.21E
11 H9 Kaikoura New Zealand 42.24S 173.41E
11 H9 Kaikoura Pen New Zealand
11 H9 Kaikoura Ra New Zealand
21 C1 Kaikukang Heilongjiang China 53.07N 124.48E
30 C7 Kail *R* Madhya Prad India
89 D7 Kailahun Sierra Leone 8.21N 10.35W
30 D4 Kailali Nepal 28.35N 80.47E
30 A2 Kailana Uttar Prad India 30.40N 77.52E
30 A6 Kailaras Madhya Prad India 26.19N 77.37E
Kailas *mt see* Kangrinboqê Feng *mt peak*
28 H3 Kailāshahar Tripura India 24.33N 92.00E
64 G4 Kailbach W Germany 49.32N 9.06E
15 L8 Kaileuna I Trobriand Is Papua New Guinea 8.30S 150.55E
23 D5 Kaili Guizhou China 26.34N 107.58E
30 C7 Kailla Uttar Prad India 25.57N 79.00E
91 K5 Kailo Zaïre 2.41S 26.04E
93 G4 Kailongol *mt* Kenya 1.53N 35.48E
21 B6 Kailu Nei Monggol Zizhiqu China 43.35N 121.12E
114 B5 Kailua Hawaiian Is 21.24N 157.45W
114 B7 Kailua Hawaiian Is 19.43N 155.59W
114 E6 Kailua Hawaiian Is 20.53N 156.14W
114 A7 Kailua B Hawaiian Is
15 F7 Kaim *R* Papua New Guinea
11 K4 Kaimai Range *mt ra* New Zealand
83 E4 Kaïmakchalán *mt* Greece 40.55N 21.48E
15 B5 Kaimana Irian Jaya 3.39S 133.44E
11 K6 Kaimanawa Mts New Zealand
24 H9 Kaimar Qinghai China 33.10N 95.40E
11 F9 Kaimata New Zealand 42.33S 171.24E
15 B6 Kaimeer *isld* Moluccas Indon 5.10S 132.03E
93 G3 Kaimeruk Hills Kenya
30 C5 Kaimganj Uttar Prad India 27.33N 79.19E
15 F7 Kaim, L Papua New Guinea
20 D10 Kaimon-dake *pk* Japan 31.11N 130.32E
114 D8 Kaimu Hawaiian Is 19.22N 154.58W
30 E8 Kaimur *reg* Madhya Prad India
29 G5 Kaimur Ra Madhya Prad India 24.14N 80.50E
61 D4 Kain Belgium 50.38N 3.23E
51 K13 Käina Estonia 58.50N 22.49E
65 M7 Kainach Austria 47.08N 15.05E
65 M7 Kainach *R* Austria
114 B7 Kainaliu Hawaiian Is 19.32N 155.55W
20 J7 Kainan Japan 34.09N 135.12E
15 H7 Kainantu Papua New Guinea 6.16S 145.50E
83 G3 Kainchal *mt* Greece 41.31N 24.19E
43 L5 Kainda Kirgiziya U.S.S.R. 42.48N 73.39E
65 N7 Kaindorf Austria 47.14N 15.55E
91 C6 Kai Ndunga Zaïre 5.43S 12.44E
25 C2 Kaing Burma 21.26N 95.00E
11 L5 Kaingaroa Forest New Zealand 38.24S 176.36E
11 K10 Kaingaroa Harb Chatham Is Pacific Oc
11 L5 Kaingaroa Plat New Zealand
65 J6 Kainisch Austria 47.35N 13.51E
90 B7 Kainji Nigeria 9.49N 4.37E
89 M7 Kainji Dam Nigeria 9.49N 4.38E
89 M6 Kainji Res Nigeria
84 E4 Kainoúryion Greece 38.48N 22.43E
42 B4 Kainsk-Barabinskiy U.S.S.R. 55.26N 78.16E
29 J7 Kaintragarh Orissa India 20.44N 84.36E
51 K4 Kainulaisjärvi Sweden 67.00N 22.32E
19 C6 Kaioba Celebes Indonesia 5.20S 122.38E
114 D6 Kaiolohia Bay Hawaiian Is
11 J3 Kaipara Flats New Zealand 36.26S 174.35E
11 J3 Kaipara Harb *inlet* New Zealand
11 J3 Kaipara R New Zealand
111 N4 Kaiparowits Plat Utah
23 F7 Kaiping Guangdong China 22.20N 112.42E
22 L7 Kaiping Hebei China 39.40N 118.12E
Kair *R see* Kalar *R*
29 C6 Kaira Gujarat India 22.55N 72.50E
29 C6 Kaira *dist* Gujarat India
51 N4 Kairala Finland 67.12N 27.20E
30 A3 Kairana Uttar Prad India 29.24N 77.12E
19 F5 Kairatu Moluccas Indonesia 3.19S 128.18E
15 G5 Kairiru I Papua New Guinea 3.22S 143.33E
15 B4 Kaironi Irian Jaya 0.45S 133.38E
88 T4 Kairouan Tunisia 35.42N 10.01E
15 J8 Kairuku Papua New Guinea 8.50S 146.30E
15 B4 Kais *R* Irian Jaya
30 E5 Kaisarganj Uttar Prad India 27.15N 81.33E
66 F5 Kaiseregg Switzerland 46.39N 7.19E
65 F6 Kaiser Gebirge *mts* Austria
111 E4 Kaiser Pk *mt* California 37.16N 119.13W
64 C3 Kaisersesch W Germany 50.14N 7.09E
64 D5 Kaiserslautern W Germany 49.27N 7.47E
66 K1 Kaiserstuhl Switzerland 47.34N 8.25E
64 D7 Kaiserstuhl *mt* W Germany 48.05N 7.42E
63 E10 Kaiserswerth W Germany 51.18N 6.43E
46 E3 Kaisiadorys Lithuania U.S.S.R. 54.51N 24.29E
93 B4 Kaiso Uganda 1.31N 30.58E
66 J1 Kaisten Switzerland 47.32N 8.02E
93 J4 Kaisut Desert Kenya
20 F7 Kaita Japan 34.23N 132.31E
90 C5 Kaita Nigeria 13.09N 7.44E
11 H2 Kaitaia New Zealand 35.08S 173.18E
11 D13 Kaitangata New Zealand 46.18S 169.52E
15 B7 Kai Tanimbar *isld* Moluccas Indon 6.01S 132.28E
19 A5 Kai, Tanjung *C* Celebes Indon 2.51S 118.47E
11 M5 Kaitawa New Zealand 38.49S 177.08E
11 H8 Kaiteriteri New Zealand 41.03S 173.00E
29 E3 Kaithal Haryana India 29.47N 76.29E
92 G3 Kaiti Tanzania 3.45S 35.50E
11 K8 Kaitoke New Zealand 41.04S 175.10E
Kaitong *see* Tongyu
18 G7 Kait, Tanjung *C* Sumatra Indon 3.15S 106.05E
Kaitu *see* Keytū
119 J4 Kaituma *R* Guyana
51 G4 Kaitumälven *R* Sweden
51 G4 Kaitumjaure *L* Sweden 67.46N 18.30E
29 B1 Kaitwara Delhi India 28.40N 77.15E
51 H3 Kaivare *mt* Sweden 68.23N 19.56E
11 J3 Kaiwaka New Zealand 36.09S 174.28E
19 E8 Kaiwatu Indon 8.06S 127.49E
11 C5 Kaiwharawhara *dist* Wellington New Zealand
114 B5 Kaiwi Chan Hawaiian Is
23 E3 Kai Xian Sichuan China 31.14N 108.28E
23 D5 Kaiyang Guizhou China 27.03N 106.57E
21 C6 Kaiyuan Liaoning China 42.39N 124.04E
23 C7 Kaiyuan Yunnan China 23.42N 103.09E
113 H5 Kaiyuh Mts Alaska
20 J7 Kaizuka Japan 34.25N 135.20E
93 L7 Kaja Kenya 1.43S 39.01E
51 N7 Kajaani Finland 64.12N 27.45E
13 F5 Kajabbi Queensland 20.03S 140.02E
31 C4 Kajaki Afghanistan 32.16N 65.05E
18 L4 Kajan *R* Kalimantan Indonesia
19 B6 Kajang Celebes Indon 5.22S 120.20E
18 B9 Kajang Pen Malaysia 2.59N 101.46E
18 E9 Kajang,Gunong *mt* Pen Malaysia 2.46N 104.10E
90 K5 Kaja, Wadi *watercourse* Sudan
32 J7 Kajdar Iran 26.35N 61.17E
93 H7 Kajiado Kenya 1.50S 36.48E
93 H7 Kajiado *dist* Kenya
87 G8 Kajibo,Mt Ethiopia 4.11N 38.58E
91 F7 Kajiji Zaïre 7.39S 18.33E
20 M6 Kajikazawa Japan 35.35N 138.28E
20 D10 Kajiki Japan 31.45N 130.39E
87 A6 Kajok Sudan 8.20N 28.00E
87 C9 Kajo Kaji Sudan 3.56N 31.40E
31 C4 Kajrān Afghanistan 33.12N 65.28E
32 B2 Kaju Iran 37.19N 46.39E
31 E4 Kajuri Kach Pakistan 32.03N 69.54E
90 C6 Kajuru Nigeria 10.15N 7.43E
111 M9 Kaka Arizona 32.31N 112.18W
87 D5 Kaka Sudan 10.41N 32.13E
87 G7 Kaka *mt* Ethiopia 7.23N 39.05E
90 F9 Kaka *tribe* Cameroon
18 N4 Kakaban *isld* Indonesia 2.06N 118.33E
100 N2 Kakabeka Falls Ontario 48.24N 89.40W
87 G6 Kaka Dam Ethiopia 8.24N 39.06E
93 C5 Kakade *mt* Uganda 0.56N 31.43E
100 J1 Kakagi L Ontario 49.15N 93.50W
11 K5 Kakahi New Zealand 38.56S 175.23E
19 M8 Kakal *R* Mindanao Philippines
19 A4 Kakali Celebes Indonesia 1.58S 119.21E
94 F7 Kakamas S Africa 28.45S 20.33E
93 F5 Kakamega Kenya 0.17N 34.47E
28 H6 Kakana Nicobar Is 9.08N 92.48E
91 K9 Kakanda Zaïre 10.42S 26.24E
11 E12 Kakanui New Zealand 45.12S 170.54E
11 E12 Kakanui Mts New Zealand
31 D7 Kakar Pakistan 26.56N 67.40E
11 J6 Kakaramea New Zealand 39.43S 174.27E
30 B8 Kakarwao Madhya Prad India 24.27N 78.58E
91 E3 Kakassengue Congo 1.33N 17.00E
89 D8 Kakata Liberia 6.35N 10.19W
11 K6 Kakatahi New Zealand 39.41S 175.21E
37 E6 Kakbil Turkey 29.17N 39.16E
31 C2 Kakdamburid Afghanistan 36.32N 65.48E
29 L7 Kakdwip W Bengal India 21.57N 88.10E
113 U8 Kake Alaska 57.00N 134.00W
20 F7 Kake Japan 34.37N 132.18E
20 M7 Kakegawa Japan 34.47N 138.02E
92 D4 Kakelwe Zaïre 4.50S 29.00E
91 G6 Kakenge Zaïre 4.54S 21.55E
21 D12 Kakeroma jima *isld* Japan
93 F9 Kakesyo Tanzania 3.15S 34.59E
30 A7 Kaketa *res* Madhya Prad India
42 G5 Kakha U.S.S.R. 53.28N 103.58E
Ka-Khem *R see* Malyy Yenisey *R*
44 H6 Kakhi U.S.S.R. 41.30N 47.00E
44 H5 Kakhib U.S.S.R. 42.26N 46.40E
32 H3 Kākhk Iran 34.12N 58.38E
113 K7 Kakhonak Bay Alaska 59.25N 154.55W
113 K7 Kakhonak L Alaska 59.30N 154.15W
45 E10 Kakhovka Ukraine U.S.S.R. 46.50N 33.30E
45 E10 Kakhovskoye Vdkhr *res* Ukraine U.S.S.R.
39 F5 Kakhtana U.S.S.R. 58.49N 159.43E
39 G5 Kakhtana *R* U.S.S.R.
32 D6 Kākī Iran 28.19N 51.34E
92 D8 Kakielo Zaïre 12.21S 29.35E
28 F2 Kakinada Andhra Prad India 16.59N 82.20E
91 E6 Kakinga Zaïre 4.39S 16.55E
93 E5 Kakira Uganda 0.36N 33.13E
101 P5 Kakisa N W Terr 61.00N 117.40W
101 P5 Kakisa L N W Terr 60.55N 117.40W
93 B7 Kakitumba Rwanda 1.04S 30.26E
20 M4 Kakizaki Japan 37.16N 138.22E
20 H7 Kakogawa Japan 34.49N 134.52E
93 D4 Kakoge Uganda 1.03N 32.30E
93 A5 Kakola Zaïre 0.47N 29.40E
93 M8 Kakole Kenya 2.46S 40.01E
93 B9 Kakonko Tanzania 3.17S 30.56E
84 Q15 Kakopetria Cyprus 34.59N 32.55E
30 C5 Kakora Uttar Prad India 27.53N 79.02E
30 D6 Kakori Uttar Prad India 26.51N 80.48E
93 F4 Kakoro Uganda 1.10N 34.04E
72 C9 Kakouetta, Gorges de France
84 D6 Kakoúri Greece 37.40N 22.22E
84 C7 Kakóvatos Greece 37.27N 21.39E
43 H1 Kak,Oz *L* Kazakhstan U.S.S.R. 53.37N 66.14E
89 H7 Kakpin Ivory Coast 8.40N 3.41W
30 C5 Kakrala Uttar Prad India 27.54N 79.12E
29 L2 Kaksa W Bengal India 23.26N 87.29E
113 Q1 Kaktovik Alaska 70.08N 143.50W
20 O4 Kakuda Japan 37.59N 140.48E
31 G3 Kakul Pakistan 34.13N 73.19E
92 C4 Kakulu Zaïre 5.18S 27.55E
93 F2 Kakuma Kenya 3.43N 34.53E
20 O2 Kakumagawa Japan 39.24N 140.29E
92 E8 Kakumbi Zambia 13.08S 31.49E
93 C5 Kakumiro Uganda 0.47N 31.23E
32 D5 Kakun Iran 30.39N 51.46E
20 O2 Kakunodate Japan 39.37N 140.35E
18 K4 Kakus *R* Sarawak Malaysia
94 D2 Kakuse Namibia 18.41S 17.37E
93 C6 Kakuto Uganda 0.53S 31.30E
101 O8 Kakwa *R* Alberta/Br Col
30 C6 Kakwan Uttar Prad India 26.44N 79.57E
91 H9 Kakwata Zaïre 10.45S 23.33E
93 L7 Kakya Kenya 1.34S 39.03E
62 M8 Kál Hungary 47.44N 20.15E
31 F5 Kala Pakistan 30.22N 70.46E
87 C9 Kala Sudan 3.59N 31.16E
92 E5 Kala Tanzania 7.30S 31.34E
92 E6 Kala Tanzania 8.07S 30.59E
91 F2 Kala Zaïre 3.23N 18.40E
92 D5 Kala Zaïre 7.11S 29.39E
88 S4 Kalaa el Khasba Tunisia 35.40N 8.34E
78 D13 Kalaa Kebira Tunisia 35.53N 10.32E
30 A2 Kala Amb Himachal Prad India 30.30N 77.12E
88 S4 Kalaat-es-Nam Tunisia 35.48N 8.18E
Kalaat Markab *see* Qal'at el Marqab
31 F4 Kalabagh Pakistan 33.00N 71.35E
19 D8 Kalabahi Indonesia 8.14S 124.32E
84 C2 Kalabáka Greece 39.42N 21.38E
18 M3 Kalabakan Sabah Malaysia 4.22N 117.29E
37 C3 Kalabakli *R* Turkey
89 E4 Kalabana Mali 14.10N 8.34W
93 G3 Kalabata *watercourse* Kenya
28 D2 Kalabgur Andhra Prad India 17.39N 78.02E
12 F4 Kalabity S Australia 32.05S 140.16E
92 A9 Kalabo Zambia 15.00S 22.37E
45 N6 Kalach U.S.S.R. 50.26N 41.02E
31 D3 Kalacha Afghanistan 35.30N 67.40E
93 J2 Kalacha Kenya 3.09N 37.30E
47 L7 Kalachinsk U.S.S.R. 55.02N 74.40E
45 O8 Kalach-Kurtlak U.S.S.R. 49.00N 42.28E
45 P8 Kalach-na-Donu U.S.S.R. 48.43N 43.32E
45 M6 Kalachskaya Vozvyshennost' *uplands* U.S.S.R.
25 B2 Kaladan Burma 21.09N 92.58E
25 B2 Kaladan *R* Burma
99 N8 Kaladar Ontario 44.39N 77.07W
28 B2 Kaladgi Karnataka India 16.12N 75.35E
19 B5 Kaladu *R* Celebes Indon
114 C5 Kalae Hawaiian Is 21.09N 157.01W
114 B9 Ka Lae *C* Hawaiian Is 18.58N 155.24W
19 B5 Kalaena *R* Celebes Indon
114 B6 Ka Lae o Malae *pt* Hawaiian Is 20.06N 155.54W
84 V17 Kaláfou Rhodes 36.07N 28.04E
25 D1 Kalagwe Burma 22.33N 96.34E
29 H8 Kalahandi *dist* Orissa India
94 F4 Kalahari Desert *reg* Botswana
94 F6 Kalahari Game Reserve S Africa
94 F5 Kalahari Gemsbok Nat.Park S Africa
28 D4 Kalahasti Andhra Prad India 13.48N 79.42E
114 E4 Kalaheo Hawaiian Is 21.55N 159.31E
31 B5 Kala Hisam Afghanistan 31.50N 63.10E
114 E6 Kalahu Pt Hawaiian Is 20.48N 156.03W
43 K7 Kalai-Khumb Tadzhikistan U.S.S.R. 38.30N 70.46E
43 G8 Kalai-Mor Turkmeniya U.S.S.R. 35.40N 62.32E
30 J5 Kalaiya Nepal 27.03N 85.01E
51 K7 Kalajoki Finland 64.15N 24.00E
51 L8 Kalajoki *R* Finland
32 H8 Kālak Iran 25.29N 59.22E
34 L2 Kalak Iraq 36.17N 43.38E
42 K4 Kalakan U.S.S.R. 55.10N 116.45E
42 K4 Kalakan *R* U.S.S.R.
30 E7 Kalakankar Uttar Prad India 25.48N 81.21E
18 B4 Kalakepen Sumatra Indon 2.45N 97.49E
93 E4 Kalaki Uganda 1.48N 33.20E
93 G2 Kalakol *watercourse* Kenya
K'a-la-k'un-lun Shan-k'ou *see* Karakoram Pass
31 D3 Kalalak Afghanistan 35.41N 66.44E
33 A5 Kalalat,Gebel *mts* Egypt
114 E3 Kalalau Lookout Hawaiian Is 22.09N 159.38W
93 L5 Kalalut Kenya 0.49N 39.35E
44 D2 Kalaly *R* U.S.S.R.
29 F7 Kalam Maharashtra India 20.28N 78.20E
31 G3 Kalam Pakistan 35.26N 72.39E
31 G3 Kalam *dist* Pakistan
110 C3 Kalama Washington 46.01N 122.50W
19 D2 Kalama *isld* Indon 3.15N 125.28E
110 C3 Kalama *R* Washington
84 D7 Kalámai Greece 37.02N 22.07E
84 C7 Kalamará Greece 37.07N 21.57E
Kalamáta *see* Kalámai
106 J7 Kalamazoo Michigan 42.17N 85.36W
106 J7 Kalamazoo,R Michigan
18 L8 Kalambau *isld* Indon 4.55S 115.36E
92 D3 Kalambi Zaïre 3.00S 28.30E
92 E6 Kalambo Falls Tanzania 8.35S 31.13E
37 H8 Kalamerik Dağ *mt* Turkey 37.49N 43.34E
84 A3 Kalamiés Greece 39.10N 20.56E
37 K3 Kalamış Limanı *B* Turkey
44 C9 Kalamitskiy Zaliv *B* Ukraine U.S.S.R.
29 E8 Kalamnuri Maharashtra India 19.42N 77.21E
84 A4 Kálamos Greece 38.37N 20.55E
84 G5 Kálamos Greece 38.17N 23.51E
84 A4 Kálamos *isld* Greece
18 M4 Kalampising Borneo Indon 3.45N 116.45E
14 B9 Kalamunda W Australia 31.57S 116.03E
12 E3 Kalamurra,L S Australia
28 J3 Kala Naga Manipur India 24.45N 93.20E
29 D1 Kalanaur Gurdaspur, Punjab India 32.01N 75.13E
29 E3 Kalanaur Rohtak, Punjab India 28.55N 76.25E
44 C8 Kalanchak Ukraine U.S.S.R. 46.14N 33.18E
31 B6 Kalandi Pakistan 28.31N 63.14E
53 S18 Kalandseidet Norway 60.15N 5.28E
95 D3 Kalandy Madagascar 15.42S 48.43E
18 J3 Kalang *dist* Singapore
18 J3 Kalang *R* Singapore
93 K6 Kalanga Corner Kenya 0.47S 38.21E
93 D6 Kalangala Uganda 0.19S 32.18E
42 K6 Kalanguy U.S.S.R. 51.03N 116.30E
84 C5 Kalanístra Greece 38.03N 21.51E
14 B9 Kalannie W Australia 30.22S 117.05E
Kalanta *see* Kalāntarī
32 F4 Kalāntarī Iran 32.11N 54.05E
51 J11 Kalanti Finland 60.49N 21.35E
29 D3 Kalanwali Haryana India 29.51N 75.00E
Kalanzau *see* Kalān Ziād
32 H7 Kalān Ziād Iran 27.25N 59.32E
19 B7 Kalao *isld* Indonesia 7.20S 120.57E
114 B7 Kalaoa Hawaiian Is 19.43N 155.59W
19 M8 Kalaong Mindanao Philippines 6.06N 124.17E
19 B7 Kalaotoa *isld* Indonesia 7.23S 121.49E
26 Q5 Kala Oya *R* Sri Lanka
Kala Pa *see* Pa Qal'eh
114 D8 Kalapana Hawaiian Is 19.21N 154.59W
30 J2 Kala Pattar *mt* Nepal 27.59N 86.49E
21 B2 Kalaqi Nei Monggol Zizhiqu China 50.41N 122.10E
34 N4 Kalār Iraq 34.38N 45.18E
42 K4 Kalar *R* U.S.S.R.
32 J8 Kalar *watercourse* Iran
46 G6 Kalarash Moldavia U.S.S.R. 47.18N 28.16E
40 A3 Kalar, Khrebet *mts* U.S.S.R.
52 J4 Kälarne Sweden 62.59N 16.05E
26 T4 Kal Aru *R* Sri Lanka
18 L5 Kalasin Borneo Indon 0.15N 114.16E
Kalat Iran*see* Kabūd Gonbad
31 D6 Kalat Kalat Pakistan 29.01N 66.38E
31 C8 Kalat Makran Pakistan 25.22N 64.02E
31 D7 Kalat *dist* Pakistan
31 A4 Kalata Afghanistan 32.33N 61.36E
87 G5 Kalata Ethiopia 10.23N 38.41E
32 F2 Kalateh Iran 36.35N 55.40E
32 G3 Kalāteh-ye Khūr Iran 34.07N 57.54E
32 G2 Kalāteh-ye Mazīnan Iran 36.19N 56.56E
32 F2 Kalāteh-ye Mollā Iran 36.19N 54.55E
85 N8 Kalât,Gebel *mt* Egypt 23.08N 34.40E
32 H3 Kalat,Kūh-e *mt* Iran 34.18N 58.22E
9 S11 Kalau *islet* Tonga, Pacific Oc 21.30S 175.00E
114 D5 Kalaupapa Hawaiian Is 21.12N 156.59W
44 E2 Kalaus *R* U.S.S.R.
28 D2 Kalava Kol Andhra Prad India 16.16N 78.19E
84 U17 Kalavárdha Rhodes 36.20N 27.57E
84 R15 Kalavaso *mine* Cyprus 34.47N 33.16E
84 R15 Kalavasos Cyprus 34.46N 33.18E
84 D5 Kalávrita Greece 38.02N 22.06E
25 D2 Kalaw Burma 20.37N 96.35E
26 R9 Kalawana Sri Lanka 6.32N 80.25E
114 D5 Kalawao Hawaiian Is 21.12N 156.56W
19 A4 Kalawaranaputi Celebes Indonesia 1.09S 119.56E
26 S5 Kalawewa Sri Lanka 8.02N 80.32E
36 H3 Kalaycık *R* Turkey
42 J3 Kalayka U.S.S.R. 58.28N 111.50E
33 M4 Kalba U.A.E. 25.05N 56.20E
64 H3 Kalbach W Germany 50.24N 9.41E
53 N9 Kalbak Faeroes 62.04N 6.49W
33 N6 Kalbān,Al Oman 20.19N 58.40E
14 A8 Kalbarri W Australia 27.42S 114.10E
95 B9 Kalbaskraal S Africa 33.35S 18.39E
63 O7 Kalbe E Germany 52.40N 11.24E
43 P3 Kalbinskiy Khrebet *mts* Kazakhstan U.S.S.R.
33 H9 Kalb, Ra's al *C* S Yemen 14.04N 48.42E
82 B5 Kalce Yugoslavia 45.55N 14.13E
45 T3 Kalda U.S.S.R. 53.47N 47.30E
50 D7 Kaldadharnes Iceland 63.56N 21.10W
53 V17 Kaldafjell *mt* Norway 60.48N 6.48E
50 H3 Kaldakinn *dist* Iceland
50 F7 Kaldakofsjökull *ice cap* Iceland 63.53N 19.09W
50 G6 Kaldakvísl *R* Iceland
50 C2 Kaldalón *inlet* Iceland
50 C5 Kaldárós *B* Iceland
53 W19 Kaldavatn *L* Norway 59.48N 7.00E
50 D3 Kaldbaksvík *inlet* Iceland
50 B3 Kaldbakur *mt* Ísafjardharsýsla, Vestur Iceland 65.49N 23.39W
50 G7 Kaldbakur *mt* Skaftafellssýsla, Vestur Iceland 63.55N 18.05W
50 F3 Kaldbakur *mt* Skagafjardharsýsla Iceland 65.36N 19.39W
50 G2 Kaldbakur *mt* Thingeyjarsýsla, Sudhur Iceland 66.01N 18.09W
53 W14 Kaldhusseter Norway 62.10N 7.27E
36 H5 Kaldı Dağ *mt* Turkey 37.42N 35.09E
50 E5 Kaldidalur *V* Iceland
50 D3 Kaldrananes Iceland 65.47N 21.21W
50 E2 Kaldrani Iceland 66.05N 20.20W
43 C3 Kaldygayty *R* Kazakhstan U.S.S.R.
36 D6 Kale Antalya Turkey 36.15N 29.59E
Kale Bingöl Turkey*see* Karlıova
36 D5 Kale Denizli Turkey 37.27N 28.50E
37 E5 Kale Gümüşane Turkey 40.23N 39.39E
28 B2 Kale Maharashtra India 17.12N 74.14E
37 D7 Kale Malatya Turkey 38.27N 38.46E
37 C8 Kale Maraş Turkey 37.47N 37.10E
36 F6 Kaleardı Burun *C* Turkey 36.31N 32.00E
36 G2 Kalecik Turkey 40.06N 33.22E
36 F6 Kalediran Turkey 36.06N 32.34E
19 C6 Kaledupa *isld* Indonesia 5.35S 123.45E
12 A5 Kaleen *dist* Canberra Australia
101 Z2 Kaleet *R* N W Terr
25 D5 Kalegauk I Burma
46 R2 Kalegino U.S.S.R. 56.05N 54.31E
93 A8 Kalehe Zaïre 2.05S 28.52E
32 C2 Kaleh Sarai Iran 37.42N 49.04E
25 C3 Kaleindaung *R* Burma
92 D4 Kalembelembe Zaïre 4.36S 28.45E
37 F2 Kalem Burun *C* Turkey 40.39N 29.00E
93 E8 Kalemera Tanzania 2.17S 33.45E
92 D4 Kalémié Zaïre 5.57S 29.10E
36 C3 Kalemoğlu Turkey 39.04N 28.11E
25 L9 Kalemyo Burma 23.12N 94.10E
60 M8 Kalenberg Netherlands 52.47N 5.56E
63 K7 Kalenberg *reg* W Germany
92 B7 Kalene Hill Zambia 11.10S 24.12E
92 G5 Kalenga Tanzania 7.50S 35.34E
91 J7 Kalenge Zaïre 7.07S 25.30E
43 M6 Kalenina, im Kirgiziya U.S.S.R. 41.28N 76.19E
84 A3 Kalénji Greece 39.29N 20.59E
46 Q5 Kalenyy Kazakhstan U.S.S.R. 49.31N 51.40E
84 C4 Kalesménon Greece 38.56N 21.43E
62 L5 Kalety Poland 50.35N 18.50E
106 H5 Kaleva Michigan 44.23N 86.01W
47 C3 Kalevala Karelia U.S.S.R. 65.13N 31.12E
25 L9 Kalewa Burma 23.15N 94.19E
32 B1 Kaleybar Iran 38.45N 47.08E
50 H7 Kálfafell Iceland 63.57N 17.40W
50 J2 Kálfafell *mt* Iceland 66.13N 16.10W
50 J6 Kálfafellsfjöll *mt* Iceland 64.15N 16.02W
50 K6 Kálfafellsstadhur Iceland 64.11N 15.53W
87 O4 Kal Farun *I* S Yemen 12.27N 52.08E
33 J10 Kal Farun *islds* Socotra Indian Ocean 12.28N 52.14E
50 C2 Kálfatindur *pk* Iceland 66.27N 22.24W
50 C6 Kálfatjörn Iceland 64.01N 22.18W
50 H3 Kalfborgarvatn *L* Iceland 65.31N 17.20W
50 E7 Kálfholt Iceland 63.54N 20.39W
50 E2 Kálfshamarsvik Iceland 66.01N 20.26W
50 E6 Kálfstindar *mt* Iceland 64.15N 20.52W
42 K6 Kalga U.S.S.R. 50.59N 118.58E
47 D4 Kalgachikha U.S.S.R. 63.16N 36.40E
Kalgan *see* Zhangjiakou
14 C10 Kalgan,R W Australia
112 F2 Kalgary Texas 33.24N 101.09W
28 B3 Kalghatgi Karnataka India 15.11N 75.00E
113 M6 Kalgin I Alaska 60.30N 151.56W
90 B5 Kalgo Nigeria 12.20N 4.14E
14 D9 Kalgoorlie W Australia 30.49S 121.29E
32 H5 Kāl Gūsheh Iran 31.00N 58.10E
53 Y18 Kalhovd Norway 60.04N 8.23E
83 E4 Kalí Greece 40.49N 22.12E
30 D3 Kali *R* India/Nepal
36 E4 Kalı *R* Turkey
30 A3 Kali *R* Uttar Prad India
30 M8 Kaliachak W Bengal India 24.52N 88.01E
30 L6 Kaliaganj Bihar India 26.20N 87.37E
83 E6 Kaliakoúdha *mt* Greece 38.49N 21.45E
18 F8 Kalianda Sumatra Indon 5.43S 105.34E
18 K9 Kalianget Indonesia 7.04S 113.56E
15 J5 Kali Bay Admiralty Is 2.07S 146.31E
43 K1 Kalibek,Oz *L* Kazakhstan U.S.S.R.
19 L6 Kalibo Philippines 11.42N 122.20E
104 A6 Kalida Ohio 40.59N 84.13W
28 C6 Kalidaikurichchi Tamil Nadu India 8.41N 77.29E
89 E5 Kalifabougou Mali 12.55N 8.11W
31 E2 Kalifgan Afghanistan 36.48N 69.47E
30 H5 Kali Gandak *R* Nepal
31 H9 Kaliganj Bangladesh 23.58N 90.30E
28 D3 Kaligiri Andhra Prad India 14.51N 79.40E
114 F3 Kalihiwai Hawaiian Is 22.12N 159.25W
32 D6 Kalij-e-Fārs *prov* Iran
45 L4 Kalikino U.S.S.R. 52.55N 39.50E
114 F3 Kaliko *mt* Hawaiian Is 22.09N 159.29W
30 E3 Kalikot Nepal 29.05N 81.41E
91 K5 Kalima Zaïre 2.38S 26.34E
18 J7 Kalimantan *terr* Indonesia
18 J5 Kalimantan Barat *prov* Borneo Indonesia
18 L7 Kalimantan Selatan *prov* Borneo Indonesia
18 K6 Kalimantan Tengah *prov* Borneo Indonesia
18 L4 Kalimantan Timur *prov* Borneo Indonesia
31 D3 Kalim Bulag Afghanistan 35.29N 67.08E
84 H4 Kalimeriánoi Greece 38.37N 24.05E
83 H8 Kálimnos Greece 36.57N 26.59E
83 H7 Kálimnos *isld* Greece
29 L4 Kalimpong W Bengal India 27.02N 88.34E
93 G1 Kalin Kenya 4.22N 35.33E
36 J3 Kalın Turkey 39.41N 36.47E
28 B3 Kalinadi *R* Karnataka India
32 F3 Kal-i-Namak Iran 34.55N 55.06E
29 J8 Kalingapatnam Andhra Prad India 18.21N 84.11E
19 C6 Kalingsusuh,Teluk *B* Indonesia
15 F5 Kalingum Papua New Guinea 3.31S 141.54E
43 E6 Kalinin Turkmeniya U.S.S.R. 42.08N 59.41E
46 K2 Kalinin U.S.S.R. 56.49N 35.57E
46 E7 Kalinin *dist* Moscow U.S.S.R.
43 J7 Kalininabad Leninabad, Tadzhikistan U.S.S.R. 39.46N 69.09E
43 J7 Kalininabad Tadzhikistan U.S.S.R. 37.54N 68.58E
43 L7 Kalinina, im Tadzhikistan U.S.S.R. 37.45N 74.24E
46 N1 Kalinina, imeni U.S.S.R. 57.59N 45.07E
45 J1 Kaliningrad U.S.S.R. 55.56N 37.55E
46 D3 Kaliningrad U.S.S.R. 54.40N 20.30E
44 F6 Kalinino Armenia U.S.S.R. 41.07N 44.16E
44 J1 Kalinino Astrakhan' U.S.S.R. 46.20N 48.56E
45 S1 Kalinino Cheboksary U.S.S.R. 55.38N 46.50E
42 K6 Kalinino Chita U.S.S.R. 51.58N 116.45E
44 C2 Kalinino Krasnodar U.S.S.R. 45.08N 39.01E
46 S2 Kalinino Perm U.S.S.R. 57.18N 56.18E
44 F1 Kalinino U.S.S.R. 46.23N 43.52E
45 Q5 Kalininsk U.S.S.R. 51.32N 44.29E
44 B2 Kalininskaya U.S.S.R. 45.31N 38.41E
46 J2 Kalininskaya Oblast' *prov* U.S.S.R.
45 E9 Kalininskoye Ukraine U.S.S.R. 47.06N 33.00E
30 D8 Kalinjar Madhya Prad India 25.00N 80.29E
29 D6 Kalinjara Rajasthan India 23.20N 74.22E
29 F1 Kalinka La *pass* Xizang Zizhiqu 32.45N 79.56E
46 G4 Kalinkovichi Belorussiya U.S.S.R. 52.10N 29.13E
47 H6 Kalino U.S.S.R. 58.15N 57.42E
82 E7 Kalinovik Yugoslavia 43.31N 18.29E
43 D3 Kalinovka Kazakhstan U.S.S.R. 50.00N 55.24E
46 G5 Kalinovka Ukraine U.S.S.R. 49.29N 28.30E
47 M4 Kalinovo U.S.S.R. 57.14N 60.04E
44 G4 Kalinovskaya U.S.S.R. 43.36N 45.33E
44 H4 Kalinovskiy U.S.S.R. 43.58N 46.35E
28 B4 Kaliot Kerala India 12.23N 75.07E
15 M6 Kalip New Britain 5.14S 152.01E
Kalipar *see* Kaleybar
82 L6 Kalipetrovo Bulgaria 44.06N 27.14E
93 E5 Kaliro Uganda 0.54N 33.30E
18 K10 Kalisat Java Indon 8.02S 113.50E
29 E5 Kali Sindh R Rajasthan India
93 C6 Kalisizo Uganda 0.33S 31.39E
110 L1 Kalispell Montana 48.12N 114.19W
62 J2 Kalisz Koszalin Poland 53.18N 15.55E
62 L4 Kalisz Poznań Poland 51.46N 18.02E
45 M8 Kalitva *R* Rostov U.S.S.R.
46 L4 Kalitva *R* Voronezh U.S.S.R.
92 E4 Kaliua Tanzania 5.05S 31.50E
84 D3 Kalivákia Greece 39.27N 22.05E
84 B4 Kalívia Aitolía Greece 38.37N 21.18E
84 D6 Kalívia Korinthía Greece 37.55N 22.17E
84 G6 Kalívia Thorikoú Greece 37.50N 23.55E
52 O1 Kalix Sweden 65.51N 23.14E
51 H4 Kalix älv *R* Sweden
51 H4 Kalixfors Sweden 67.45N 20.10E
29 E2 Kalka Himachal Prad India 30.50N 76.55E
13 G2 Kalkah Queensland 14.50S 143.21E
93 L5 Kalkalcha Bokatelolie Plains Kenya
28 J3 Kalkalighat Assam India 24.31N 92.16E
36 D6 Kalkan Turkey 36.16N 29.25E
63 D9 Kalkar W Germany 51.44N 6.17E
106 J5 Kalkaska Michigan 44.44N 85.11W
94 P12 Kalkbaai Cape Town S Africa 34.07S 18.27E
94 P12 Kalkbaaiberg *mt* Cape Town S Africa 34.05S 18.27E
61 F2 Kalken Belgium 51.02N 3.55E
94 D3 Kalkfeld Namibia 20.53S 16.11E
94 F4 Kalkfontein Botswana 22.08S 20.53E
95 J5 Kalkfonteindam *res* S Africa 29.31S 25.15E
Kalkha *watercourse see* Kelekh *watercourse*
63 O5 Kalkhorst E Germany 53.58N 11.04E
36 C3 Kalkım Turkey 39.46N 27.12E
53 Z13 Kalkjin *mt* Norway 62.37N 8.34E
94 E5 Kalk Plateau Namibia
94 D5 Kalkrand Namibia 24.03S 17.33E
26 U6 Kalkudah Sri Lanka 7.55N 81.33E
117 A2 Kalkuni Guyana 5.30N 57.58W
95 K4 Kalkvlakte S Africa 28.03S 26.57E
64 B2 Kall W Germany 50.33N 6.33E
28 D5 Kallakkurichchi Tamil Nadu India 11.44N 78.56E
12 D2 Kallakoopah *R* S Australia
28 C1 Kallam Maharashtra India 18.36N 76.03E
46 F1 Kallaste Estonia U.S.S.R. 58.40N 27.12E
51 N9 Kallavesi *L* Finland 62.40N 27.45E
63 O7 Kallehne E Germany 52.48N 11.23E
63 H10 Kallenhardt W Germany 51.27N 8.25E
63 J8 Kalletal W Germany 52.08N 8.58E
Kallia *see* Qalya
84 E6 Kalliánoi Greece 37.53N 22.30E
64 P2 Kallich Czechoslovakia 50.34N 13.20E
84 V17 Kallidhiés Rhodes Greece 36.20N 28.11E
84 E4 Kallídhromon Óri *mts* Greece
84 C3 Kallifóni Greece 39.16N 21.57E
29 J8 Kallikota Orissa India 19.38N 85.08E
84 D2 Kallipévki Greece 39.58N 22.28E
35 F7 Kallirhoe Hot Springs Jordan 31.36N 35.34E
30 C4 Kallis *R* Uttar Prad India
84 D5 Kallithéa Fokís Greece 38.23N 22.08E
84 C8 Kallithéa Messinía Greece 36.52N 21.47E
84 D2 Kallithéa Olímbou Greece 39.58N 22.11E
83 D3 Kallmet Albania 41.51N 19.41E
64 M5 Kallmünz W Germany 49.09N 11.59E
66 E3 Kallnach Switzerland 47.02N 7.15E
61 H1 Kallo Belgium 51.15N 4.17E
83 H5 Kalloní Greece 39.16N 26.16E
83 H5 Kallonís Kolpos *G* Greece
52 G3 Kallsjön *L* Sweden 63.35N 13.00E
53 X18 Kallungsjå *L* Norway 60.06N 7.55E
51 O5 Kallunki Finland 66.38N 28.57E
28 C2 Kallur Karnataka India 16.12N 77.08E
53 N9 Kallur *C* Faeroes 62.23N 6.49W
24 D7 Kalmakkuduk Xinjiang Uygur Zizhiqu China 37.02N 82.50E
Kalmak Qaleh *see* Kalmūkh Qal'eh
42 C5 Kalmanka U.S.S.R. 52.55N 83.32E
50 E5 Kalmanstunga Iceland 64.44N 20.49W
52 J10 Kalmar Sweden 56.39N 16.20E
52 J9 Kalmar *dist* Sweden
52 J10 Kalmarsund *channel* Sweden
29 F7 Kalmeshwar Maharashtra India 21.15N 79.01E
64 E5 Kalmit *mt* W Germany 49.19N 8.05E
46 L6 Kalmius *R* Ukraine U.S.S.R.
61 H1 Kalmthout Belgium 51.23N 4.29E
32 G2 Kalmūkh Qal'eh Iran 37.57N 56.17E
26 U7 Kalmunai Sri Lanka 7.25N 81.49E
46 M4 Kalmyk U.S.S.R. 51.15N 41.59E
Kalmyk A.S.S.R *see* Kalmytskaya A.S.S.R
46 Q5 Kalmykovo Kazakhstan U.S.S.R. 49.02N 51.55E
46 N6 Kalmytskaya A.S.S.R U.S.S.R.
29 M2 Kalna W Bengal India 23.13N 88.23E
29 H6 Kalnai Madhya Prad India 22.45N 83.30E
45 B8 Kal'nibolota Ukraine U.S.S.R. 48.47N 30.58E
44 C1 Kalnibolotskaya U.S.S.R. 46.01N 40.29E
31 J9 Kalni R Bangladesh
62 L9 Kalocsa Hungary 46.31N 19.00E
82 J8 Kalofer Bulgaria 42.36N 25.00E
84 S14 Kalogrea Cyprus 35.20N 33.36E
114 C6 Kalohi Chan Hawaiian Is
84 L12 Kaloí Liménes Crete 34.55N 24.48E
84 Q14 Kalokhorin Cyprus 35.06N 32.53E
84 R15 Kalokhorio Cyprus 34.50N 33.03E
90 M5 Kalokitting Sudan 12.44N 24.19E
91 J7 Kaloko Zaïre 6.47S 25.47E
29 C6 Kalol Mehsana, Gujarat India 23.15N 72.32E
29 C6 Kalol Panch Mahals, Gujarat India 22.38N 73.32E
92 D7 Kalola Zaïre 10.00S 28.03E
91 K5 Kalole Zaïre 3.40S 27.22E
93 L9 Kaloleni Kenya 3.49S 39.38E
114 D7 Kaloli Pt Hawaiian Is 19.37N 154.57W
91 K8 Kalombo Zaïre 8.20S 26.24E
92 C10 Kalomo Zambia 17.02S 26.29E
106 C8 Kalona Iowa 41.28N 91.42W
91 E6 Kalonda Zaïre 4.56S 17.35E
91 J7 Kalonda Zaïre 6.40S 25.08E
91 J7 Kalondwe Zaïre 6.35S 24.15E
101 K9 Kalone Pk Br Col 52.41N 126.41W
84 C7 Kalonerón Greece 37.19N 21.43E
19 L4 Kalongkooan *isld* Philippines 14.55N 122.08E
83 F3 Kalón Kástron Greece 41.00N 23.20E
93 G4 Kalosia Kenya 1.39N 35.45E
19 L4 Kalotkot *isld* Philippines 14.55N 122.17E
84 C5 Kaloúsi Greece 38.02N 21.48E
53 E4 Kalø Vig *inlet* Denmark 56.12N 10.25E
32 B1 Kalow *R* Iran
82 J8 Kaloyanovo Bulgaria 42.20N 24.43E
84 C7 Kaloyerési Greece 37.11N 21.50E
30 B1 Kalpa Himachal Prad India 31.33N 78.16E
27 L7 Kalpeni I Laccadive Is Indian Ocean 10.05N 73.15E
30 C6 Kalpi Uttar Prad India 26.07N 79.44E
24 C5 Kalpin Xinjiang Uygur Zizhiqu China 40.33N 79.00E
26 Q5 Kalpitiya Sri Lanka 8.13N 79.45E
65 G7 Kals Austria 47.01N 12.39E
32 B3 Kal Safīd Iran 34.47N 47.21E
53 E5 Kalsenakke *C* Denmark 55.51N 10.12E
87 L5 Kalsheikh Somalia 10.03N 47.10E
32 G2 Kāl-Shūr,Rūd-e *R* Iran
30 A2 Kalsi Uttar Prad India 30.32N 77.50E
113 G6 Kalskag Alaska 61.29N 160.29W
53 N9 Kalsø *isld* Faeroes 62.18N 6.47W
Kalsoy *see* Kalsø
113 H4 Kaltag Alaska 64.19N 158.50W
42 D5 Kaltan U.S.S.R. 53.30N 87.17E
66 K3 Kaltbad Switzerland 47.03N 8.28E
66 N3 Kaltbrunn Switzerland 47.13N 9.02E
65 B7 Kalte Berg *mt* Austria 47.06N 10.08E
64 M4 Kaltenbrunn W Germany 49.38N 11.57E
63 L5 Kaltenkirchen W Germany 53.51N 9.58E
65 O5 Kaltenleutgeben Austria 48.08N 16.13E
66 F5 Kalte Sense *R* Switzerland
29 C3 Kalu Rajasthan India 28.23N 73.56E
45 H2 Kaluga U.S.S.R. 54.31N 36.16E
26 R8 Kalu Ganga *R* Sri Lanka
45 O4 Kalugino U.S.S.R. 52.25N 42.17E
93 C5 Kaluguza Uganda 0.47N 31.08E
18 M8 Kalukalukuang *isld* Indonesia 5.14S 117.41E
91 J8 Kalule Nord Zaïre 9.43S 25.53E
92 D8 Kalulushi Zambia 12.50S 28.03E
90 D7 Kalum Nigeria 8.39N 9.32E
14 F2 Kalumburu W Australia 14.14S 126.38E
91 J3 Kalumete *R* Zaïre
18 B8 Kalumpang Pen Malaysia 3.41N 101.31E
53 G5 Kalundborg Denmark 55.42N 11.06E
53 F5 Kalundborg Fjord *inlet* Denmark 55.40N 11.00E
92 D7 Kalundu Zambia 10.20S 29.33E
92 F6 Kalungu *R* Zambia
92 D6 Kalungwishi *R* Zambia
18 M2 Kalupis Falls Sabah Malaysia 6.04N 116.29E
29 C8 Kalu R Maharashtra India
31 F4 Kalur Kot Pakistan 32.08N 71.20E
46 E5 Kalush Ukraine U.S.S.R. 49.02N 24.20E
62 N3 Kałuszyn Poland 52.13N 21.49E
93 C9 Kalutagi *mt* Tanzania 3.13S 31.42E
26 Q9 Kalutara Sri Lanka 6.35N 79.59E
18 L4 Kalutong,Bukit *mt* Sarawak Malaysia 3.11N 114.36E
19 B5 Kaluwaja Celebes Indon 3.51S 120.20E
46 J3 Kaluzhskaya Oblast' *prov* U.S.S.R.
53 R15 Kalvåg Norway 61.47N 4.53E
53 Z16 Kalvåhøgda *mt* Norway 61.24N 8.37E
29 D7 Kalvan Maharashtra India 20.30N 74.06E
44 H9 Kalvanaq Iran 38.06N 46.58E
46 E3 Kalvarija Lithuania U.S.S.R. 54.20N 23.10E
53 U14 Kalvatn Norway 62.02N 6.25E
53 J7 Kalvehave Denmark 55.00N 12.08E
51 K8 Kälviä Finland 63.53N 23.30E
51 N10 Kalvitsa Finland 61.56N 27.20E
51 L10 Kalvola Finland 61.07N 24.07E
53 B6 Kalvslund Denmark 55.22N 8.50E
28 D2 Kalwakurti Andhra Prad India 16.39N 78.27E
65 L7 Kalwang Austria 47.26N 14.46E
30 D4 Kalwapur Nepal 28.47N 80.30E
30 F6 Kalwari Uttar Prad India 26.38N 82.41E
47 H5 Kal'ya U.S.S.R. 60.19N 59.58E
28 A1 Kalyan Maharashtra India 19.17N 73.11E
30 E5 Kalyan *R* Uttar Prad India
28 C3 Kalyandrug Andhra Prad India 14.33N 77.05E
28 C2 Kalyani Karnataka India 17.53N 76.57E
29 H8 Kalyansingapuram Orissa India 19.34N 83.21E
46 L2 Kalyazin U.S.S.R. 57.15N 37.59E
25 C3 Kama Burma 19.01N 95.04E
42 B4 Kama Novosibirsk U.S.S.R. 55.53N 77.41E
47 J5 Kama Sverdlovsk U.S.S.R. 60.09N 62.08E
46 R2 Kama U.S.S.R. 56.20N 54.08E
91 K5 Kama Zaïre 3.33S 27.09E
46 R2 Kama *R* U.S.S.R.
30 L2 Kama Chu *R* Xizang Zizhiqu China
93 C7 Kamachumu Tanzania 1.35S 31.36E
90 F1 Kamada Niger 21.30N 13.16E
20 E9 Kamae Japan 32.46N 131.57E
20 E9 Kamaeura Kyūshū Japan 32.48N 131.56E
94 D5 Kamagams Namibia 24.59S 17.18E
20 G2 Kamagaya Chiba Japan 35.46N 140.01E
114 D6 Kamaiki Pt Hawaiian Is 20.45N 156.50W
20 P2 Kamaishi Japan 39.18N 141.52E
20 N9 Kama-iwa *rock* Iwo Jima Pacific Oc 24.47N 141.17E
122 S16 Kamaka *isld* Gambier Is Pacific Oc 23.15S 134.56W
39 G6 Kamaki U.S.S.R. 56.20N 161.31E
114 D6 Kamakou *pk* Hawaiian Is 21.06N 156.52W
20 B4 Kamakura Japan 35.19N 139.33E
119 J5 Kamakusa Guyana 5.54N 59.55W
18 K9 Kamal Indonesia 7.08S 112.46E
92 E4 Kamalampa Tanzania 5.32S 30.30E
28 D3 Kamalapuram Andhra Prad India 14.38N 78.40E
30 C5 Kamalganj Uttar Prad India 27.15N 79.37E
31 G5 Kamalia Pakistan 30.14N 72.40E
114 D4 Kamalino Hawaiian Is 21.51N 160.14W
114 D5 Kamalo Hawaiian Is 21.30N 156.53W
89 C7 Kamalu Sierra Leone 9.25N 12.14W
25 D4 Kamamaung Burma 17.22N 97.39E
30 A5 Kaman Rajasthan India 27.39N 77.16E
36 G3 Kaman Turkey 39.22N 33.43E
91 J6 Kamana Zaïre 5.59S 24.58E
93 A6 Kamande Zaïre 0.35S 29.16E
42 G3 Kamanga *R* U.S.S.R.
93 A5 Kamango Zaïre 0.38N 29.54E
117 B3 Kamani *R* Surinam
94 C2 Kamanjab Namibia 19.35S 14.51E
93 A8 Kamanyola Zaïre 2.45S 28.58E
114 E6 Kamaole Hawaiian Is 20.44N 156.27W
91 F6 Kamapumpa Zaïre 5.54S 19.05E
84 D5 Kamárais Greece 38.17N 22.00E
33 E9 Kamarān Red Sea 15.21N 41.40E
119 H5 Kamarang, R Guyana
33 E9 Kamarān I Red Sea
31 D3 Kamard *reg* Afghanistan
28 D1 Kamareddi Andhra Prad India 18.19N 78.20E
29 M2 Kamarhati W Bengal India 22.45N 88.21E
84 E5 Kamári Greece 38.05N 22.34E
84 F4 Kamária Greece 38.55N 23.10E

117 A1 **Kamaria Falls** Guyana 6.28N 58.48W
37 E6 **Kamarık** Turkey 39.36N 39.19E
84 H6 **Kamárizos** Greece 37.43N 24.00E
31 B7 **Kamarod** Pakistan 27.32N 63.41E
89 D7 **Kamaron** Sierra Leone 9.26N 10.55W
Kamaruddin Karez *see* **Qamruddin Karez**
110 O9 **Kamas** Utah 40.40N 111.16W
43 H7 **Kamashi** Uzbekistan U.S.S.R. 38.49N 66.28E
30 D7 **Kamasin** Uttar Prad India 25.31N 80.54E
20 E3 **Kamata** *dist* Tōkyō Japan
91 K8 **Kamatanda** Zaïre 8.30S 27.42E
92 C11 **Kamativi** Zimbabwe 18.19S 27.07E
94 J2 **Kamativi** Zimbabwe 18.20S 27.06E
100 P2 **Kamatsi L** Saskatchewan
91 F7 **Kamayala** Zaïre 7.23S 19.09E
Kamba *see* **Gamba**
89 L6 **Kamba** Nigeria 11.50N 3.40E
91 H5 **Kamba** Zaïre 4.00S 22.22E
91 G6 **Kambadianga** Zaïre 5.33S 20.26E
Kamba Dzong *see* **Gamba**
89 C7 **Kambaia** Sierra Leone 9.53N 12.23W
25 N8 **Kambaiti** Burma 25.25N 98.06E
90 H8 **Kambakota** Cent Afr Rep 7.11N 17.45E
89 C6 **Kambala** Guinea 11.57N 13.25W
28 H1 **Kamba La** *pass* Xizang Zizhiqu 29.12N 90.34E
14 D9 **Kambalda** W Australia 31.12S 121.40E
39 E8 **Kambal'naya Sopka** *vol* U.S.S.R. 51.15N 156.49E
47 F2 **Kambal'nitskiye Koshki Ostrova** *islds* U.S.S.R.
28 C6 **Kambam** Tamil Nadu India 9.44N 77.19E
50 M5 **Kambanes** *C* Iceland 64.49N 13.51W
28 K1 **Kambang** Assam India 28.12N 94.40E
18 D6 **Kambang** Sumatra Indon 1.40S 100.42E
18 H9 **Kambangan** *isld* Java Indon
28 H1 **Kamba Partsi** Xizang Zizhiqu 29.18N 90.35E
Kambar Pakistan*see* **Qambar**
50 G6 **Kambar** *ridge* Iceland
9 U3 **Kambara** *isld* Fiji 18.57S 178.58W
46 R2 **Kambarka** U.S.S.R. 56.18N 54.13E
89 D5 **Kambaya** Mali 12.17N 10.06W
15 F5 **Kamberatoro** Papua New Guinea 3.39S 141.02E
84 A3 **Kambí** Greece 39.13N 20.54E
89 C7 **Kambia** Sierra Leone 9.09N 12.53W
26 V2 **Kambing I** Cocos Is Ind Oc 12.12S 96.51E
21 E7 **Kambo Ho** *mt* N Korea 41.45N 129.20E
89 K7 **Kambole** Togo 8.43N 1.39E
92 E6 **Kambole** Zambia 8.51S 30.49E
19 D1 **Kamboling** *isld* Indonesia 4.40N 125.25E
84 J11 **Kámbos** Crete 35.22N 23.34E
84 Q14 **Kambos** Cyprus 35.02N 32.45E
84 D8 **Kámbos** Greece 36.56N 22.12E
37 F7 **Kambos Dağı** *mt* Turkey 38.18N 41.56E
91 K9 **Kambove** Zaïre 10.50S 26.39E
19 B5 **Kambuno,Bukit** *mt* Celebes Indon 2.20S 120.05E
39 F6 **Kamchatka** *pen* U.S.S.R.
39 G6 **Kamchatka** *R* U.S.S.R.
Kamchatskaya Gora *vol see* **Klyuchevskaya Sopka** *vol*
38 Q3 **Kamchatskaya Oblast'** *prov* U.S.S.R.
39 G6 **Kamchatskiy Mys** *C* U.S.S.R. 56.03N 163.04E
39 G6 **Kamchatskiy Poluostrov** *pen* U.S.S.R.
39 G7 **Kamchatskiy Proliv** *str* U.S.S.R.
39 G6 **Kamchatskiy Zaliv** *B* U.S.S.R.
82 L7 **Kamchiya** *R* Bulgaria
47 E5 **Kamchuga** U.S.S.R. 60.01N 43.09E
95 H8 **Kamdeboo** *R* S Africa
95 G3 **Kamden** S Africa 27.22S 23.54E
31 F3 **Kamdesh** Afghanistan 35.25N 71.26E
20 F2 **Kameari** *dist* Tōkyō Japan
20 N4 **Kameda** Japan 37.54N 139.08E
21 H8 **Kameda** Japan 39.29N 140.06E
95 J2 **Kameel** S Africa 26.35S 25.03E
20 B1 **Kamegane** Saitama Japan
20 F2 **Kameido** *dist* Tōkyō Japan
K'a-mei-t'e Shan *see* **Kamet** *mt*
110 G4 **Kamela** Oregon 45.26N 118.23W
45 V5 **Kamelik** *R* U.S.S.R.
93 A8 **Kamembe** Rwanda 2.26S 28.57E
93 A8 **Kamembe** *airport* Rwanda 2.28S 28.54E
46 G2 **Kamen'** Belorussiya U.S.S.R. 55.01N 28.50E
45 E5 **Kamen'** Ukraine U.S.S.R. 51.24N 33.36E
41 G5 **Kamen'** U.S.S.R. 70.42N 95.07E
63 G9 **Kamen** W Germany 51.36N 7.39E
40 N7 **Kamen'Avos'** *isld* Kuril Is U.S.S.R. 49.45N 154.10E
91 J7 **Kamende** Zaïre 6.26S 24.35E
62 O3 **Kamenets** Belorussiya U.S.S.R. 52.23N 23.46E
46 J2 **Kamenets** U.S.S.R. 55.29N 33.40E
46 F5 **Kamenets-Podolskaya Oblast'** *prov* Ukraine U.S.S.R.
46 F5 **Kamenets Podolskiy** Ukraine U.S.S.R. 48.40N 26.36E
28 J2 **Kameng Frontier Division** Assam India
83 D4 **Kamenicë** Albania 40.32N 20.44E
65 N3 **Kamenice** Czechoslovakia 49.22N 15.47E
65 M3 **Kamenice nad Lípou** Czechoslovakia 49.18N 15.05E
44 J8 **Kamen'Ignatiya** *isld* Azerbaydzhan U.S.S.R. 39.35N 49.30E
47 E3 **Kamenka** Arkhangel'sk U.S.S.R. 65.55N 44.02E
45 D7 **Kamenka** Cherkassy, Ukraine U.S.S.R. 49.03N 32.06E
45 G2 **Kamenka** Kaluga U.S.S.R. 54.09N 35.54E
46 Q4 **Kamenka** Kazakhstan U.S.S.R. 51.10N 50.20E
42 F3 **Kamenka** Krasnoyarsk U.S.S.R. 58.34N 95.53E
46 L4 **Kamenka** Lipetsk U.S.S.R. 52.01N 38.46E
82 M2 **Kamenka** Moldavia U.S.S.R. 48.02N 28.40E
45 Q3 **Kamenka** Penza U.S.S.R. 53.10N 44.05E
40 G9 **Kamenka** Primor'ye U.S.S.R. 44.30N 136.05E
40 J7 **Kamenka** Sakhalin U.S.S.R. 49.16N 142.10E
45 R6 **Kamenka** Saratov U.S.S.R. 50.42N 45.25E
45 L7 **Kamenka** Ukraine U.S.S.R. 49.37N 39.22E
43 B2 **Kamenka** Ural'sk, Kazakhstan U.S.S.R. 51.09N 50.17E
45 L6 **Kamenka** Voronezh U.S.S.R. 50.43N 39.25E
42 F3 **Kamenka** *R* U.S.S.R.
46 E4 **Kamenka Bug'skaya** Ukraine U.S.S.R. 50.07N 24.30E
45 F9 **Kamenka-Dneprovskaya** Ukraine U.S.S.R. 47.29N 34.25E
39 G1 **Kamenka,Ostrov** *isld* U.S.S.R.
46 E4 **Kamen Kashirsky** Ukraine U.S.S.R. 51.32N 24.59E
42 C5 **Kamen'-na-Obi** U.S.S.R. 53.46N 81.18E
47 B5 **Kamennogorsk** U.S.S.R. 61.00N 29.00E
44 C3 **Kamennomostskiy** U.S.S.R. 44.18N 40.13E
47 C4 **Kamennoye, Oz** *L* U.S.S.R.
65 L2 **Kamenný Privoz** Czechoslovakia 49.53N 14.30E
39 G3 **Kamennyy,Khrebet** *ra* U.S.S.R.
41 S3 **Kamennyy,Mys** *C* U.S.S.R. 75.09N 151.09E
45 R8 **Kamennyy Yar** U.S.S.R. 48.27N 45.33E
82 L8 **Kameno** Bulgaria 42.33N 27.17E
45 M9 **Kamenolomni** U.S.S.R. 47.40N 40.14E
91 G9 **Kamenongue** Angola 11.22S 20.12E
40 E9 **Kamen'Rybolov** U.S.S.R. 44.46N 132.01E
42 H6 **Kamensk** U.S.S.R. 51.59N 106.40E
46 M5 **Kamenskiy** Rostov U.S.S.R. 49.20N 41.15E
45 R6 **Kamenskiy** Saratov U.S.S.R. 50.55N 45.30E
44 D9 **Kamenskoye** Crimea, Ukraine U.S.S.R. 45.16N 35.32E
47 K7 **Kamenskoye** Tyumen U.S.S.R. 57.18N 65.03E
39 H3 **Kamenskoye** U.S.S.R. 62.31N 166.15E
45 G9 **Kamenskoye** Zaporozh'ye, Ukraine U.S.S.R. 47.33N 35.23E
45 M8 **Kamensk-Shakhtinskiy** U.S.S.R. 48.20N 40.16E
47 N5 **Kamensk-Ural'skiy** U.S.S.R. 56.29N 61.49E
47 K8 **Kamenyy-Brod** Kazakhstan U.S.S.R. 53.05N 67.40E
45 V4 **Kamenyy Brod** U.S.S.R. 52.55N 49.59E
62 H4 **Kamenz** E Germany 51.17N 14.08E
20 J6 **Kameoka** Japan 35.02N 135.35E
60 H11 **Kamerik** Netherlands 52.07N 4.54E
58 F7 **Kames** Strathclyde Scotland 55.54N 5.15W
39 G4 **Kameshki** U.S.S.R. 62.20N 160.28E
45 M1 **Kameshkovo** U.S.S.R. 56.21N 41.00E
Kameshli *see* **Qamishliye,El**
30 C2 **Kamet** *mt* Uttar Prad India 30.55N 79.36E
20 K7 **Kameyama** Japan 34.52N 136.28E
110 J3 **Kamiah** Idaho 46.14N 116.01W
20 D2 **Kami-Akatsuka** *dist* Tōkyō Japan
20 E1 **Kami-Bamba** Saitama Japan
20 B4 **Kami-Echi** Kanagawa Japan
62 K2 **Kamien** Poland 53.32N 17.30E
62 J5 **Kamienna Góra** Poland 50.48N 16.00E
62 H2 **Kamień Pomorski** Poland 53.58N 14.49E
62 L4 **Kamieńsk** Poland 51.12N 19.29E
94 E8 **Kamiesberg** S Africa 30.14S 18.04E
94 D8 **Kamieskroon** S Africa 30.09S 17.56E
94 E8 **Kamies Saktor Berg** *mt* S Africa 30.22S 18.07E
20 M1 **Kami-Furano** Japan 43.29N 142.30E
20 B4 **Kamigo** Kanagawa Japan
20 A1 **Kami-Hirose** Saitama Japan
20 D4 **Kami-Hoshikawa** *dist* Yokohama Japan
20 M1 **Kamikawa** Japan 43.45N 142.44E
20 M1 **Kamikawa** *sub-prefect* Hokkaido Japan
20 D3 **Kami-Kitazawa** *dist* Tōkyō Japan
20 C2 **Kami-Kiyoto** Tōkyō Japan
20 C10 **Kami-Koshiki-jima** *isld* Japan
20 A3 **Kami-Kuzawa** Kanagawa Japan
13 F4 **Kamileroi** Queensland 19.20S 140.02E
101 X4 **Kamilukuak L** N W Terr
20 B3 **Kami-Mizo** Kanagawa Japan
91 J8 **Kamina** Zaïre 8.46S 25.00E
97 K5 **Kaminak L** N W Terr 62.00N 95.00W
100 N2 **Kaministikwia** Ontario 48.33N 89.37W
20 C7 **Kamino-shima** *isld* Japan
20 O3 **Kaminoyama** Japan 38.10N 140.16E
97 K5 **Kaminuriak L** N W Terr 62.50N 96.00W
20 L5 **Kamioka** Japan 36.21N 137.18E
93 F2 **Kamion** Uganda 3.43N 34.15E
91 F6 **Kamisha** *R* Zaïre
113 L7 **Kamishak B** Alaska
20 N1 **Kami-Shihoro** Japan 43.13N 143.16E
20 D9 **Kami-shima** *isld* Japan
36 H5 **Kamışlı** Turkey 37.34N 34.55E
20 C1 **Kami-Tomi** Saitama Japan
20 C4 **Kami-Tsuruma** Tōkyō Japan
92 D3 **Kamituga** Zaïre 3.01S 28.10E
20 C4 **Kami-Wada** Kanagawa Japan
20 O9 **Kamiyama-shima** *isld* Okinawa Japan 26.14N 127.35E
20 B3 **Kami-Yugi** Tōkyō Japan
43 K5 **Kamkaly** Kazakhstan U.S.S.R. 44.07N 70.02E
28 J1 **Kamla** *R* Assam India
30 K7 **Kamla** *R* Bihar India
30 D5 **Kamlapur** Uttar Prad India 27.24N 80.48E
87 D3 **Kamlin, El** Sudan 15.03N 33.11E
101 N10 **Kamloops** Br Columbia 50.39N 120.24W
101 N10 **Kamloops L** Br Col
95 F9 **Kammanassieberge** *mts* S Africa
65 J6 **Kammer Schörfling** Austria 47.57N 13.37E
Kammersee *see* **Attersee**
63 U5 **Kamminke** E Germany 53.53N 14.14E
20 E8 **Kammon-kaikyō** *str* Japan
20 D8 **Kammon Tunnels** Japan 33.58N 130.57E
65 J7 **Kammspitz** *mt* Austria 47.29N 13.51E
35 H1 **Kammunah** Syria 33.15N 36.14E
20 J6 **Kammuri-shima** *isld* Japan 35.42N 135.24E
20 F7 **Kammuri-yama** *mt* Japan 34.29N 132.03E
82 B4 **Kamnik** Yugoslavia 46.14N 14.35E
42 J4 **Kamniokan** U.S.S.R. 56.20N 111.58E
44 G7 **Kamo** Armenia U.S.S.R. 40.21N 45.07E
87 G8 **Kamo** Ethiopia 4.32N 38.26E
11 J2 **Kamo** New Zealand 35.40S 174.19E
20 N4 **Kamo** Niigata Japan 37.40N 139.05E
42 F2 **Kamo** *R* U.S.S.R.
117 A4 **Kamoa Mts** Guyana
85 O10 **Kamob Sanha** Sudan 19.12N 36.53E
20 K1 **Kamoenai** Japan 43.13N 140.23E
21 H10 **Kamogawa** Japan 35.06N 140.09E
114 D6 **Kamohio B** Hawaiian Is
20 H7 **Kamojima** Japan 34.02N 134.14E
31 H5 **Kamoke** Pakistan 31.58N 74.15E
23 B4 **Kam'ong** Sichuan China 28.10N 101.13E
20 H7 **Kamoshima** Japan 34.00N 134.36E
98 C6 **Kamouraska** Quebec 47.34N 69.51W
65 N4 **Kamp** *R* Austria
18 F6 **Kampa** Indonesia 1.46S 105.26E
93 D5 **Kampala** Uganda 0.19N 32.35E
15 K6 **Kampalap** Bismarck Arch 5.36N 148.04E
92 B8 **Kampanda** Zambia 12.01S 24.04E
18 B7 **Kampar** Pen Malaysia 4.17N 101.08E
18 D5 **Kampar** *R* Sumatra Indonesia
64 D3 **Kamp-Bornhofen** W Germany 50.13N 7.37E
92 C6 **Kampemba** Zaïre 9.00S 27.36E
60 M9 **Kampen** Netherlands 52.33N 5.55E
63 H3 **Kampen** W Germany 54.58N 8.22E
91 K5 **Kampene** Zaïre 3.35S 26.40E
60 M9 **Kampereiland** Netherlands
60 B2 **Kamperland** Netherlands 51.35N 3.43E
60 M9 **Kampernieuwstad** Netherlands 52.31N 5.53E
25 E4 **Kamphaeng Phet** Thailand 16.28N 99.31E
92 D6 **Kampinda** Zambia 8.48S 29.44E
93 G6 **Kampi ya Moto** Kenya 0.09S 35.55E
28 C3 **Kampli** Karnataka India 15.24N 76.34E
63 E10 **Kamp-Lintfort** W Germany 51.30N 6.33E
92 D7 **Kampolombo, L** Zambia 11.48S 28.49E
91 H7 **Kamponde** Zaïre 6.42S 22.57E
18 D8 **Kampong Baharu** Pen Malaysia 3.23N 103.24E
18 D8 **Kampong Benta** Pen Malaysia 3.32N 103.24E
18 C8 **Kampong Chenor** Pen Malaysia 3.28N 102.35E
18 B9 **Kampong Dingkil** Pen Malaysia 2.54N 101.42E
18 B7 **Kampong Jalong** Pen Malaysia 4.52N 101.10E
18 C7 **Kampong Kachong** Pen Malaysia 4.18N 102.24E
18 C8 **Kampong Kelola** Pen Malaysia 3.50N 102.26E
18 C7 **Kampong Kenyam** Pen Malaysia 4.30N 102.28E
18 B7 **Kampong Kepayang** Pen Malaysia 4.32N 101.08E
18 D8 **Kampong Kuala Aur** Pen Malaysia 3.02N 103.01E
18 B8 **Kampong Kuala Dong** Pen Malaysia 3.56N 101.54E
18 D8 **Kampong Lamir** Pen Malaysia 3.36N 103.19E
18 B7 **Kampong Lasah** Pen Malaysia 4.58N 101.13E
18 B7 **Kampong Lintang** Pen Malaysia 4.56N 101.06E
18 C8 **Kampong Lubok Paku** Pen Malaysia 3.30N 102.46E
18 C8 **Kampong Mengkarak** Pen Malaysia 3.18N 102.28E
18 C10 **Kampong Minyak Beku** Pen Malaysia 1.46N 102.54E
18 C7 **Kampong Pakoh** Pen Malaysia 4.45N 102.16E
18 C7 **Kampong Pengau** Pen Malaysia 4.26N 102.28E
18 C7 **Kampong Renggong** Pen Malaysia 4.30N 102.35E
18 A8 **Kampong Sekendi** Pen Malaysia 3.40N 100.57E
25 H5 **Kampong Sralao** Cambodia 14.05N 105.45E
18 B8 **Kampong Sungei Chin** Pen Malaysia 3.59N 101.47E
18 D8 **Kampong Tandjung Batu** Pen Malaysia 3.12N 103.25E
18 B6 **Kampong Tawai** Pen Malaysia 5.22N 101.03E
25 H7 **Kampot** Cambodia 10.37N 104.11E
29 F7 **Kamptee** Maharashtra India 21.12N 79.16E
89 H6 **Kampti** Upper Volta 10.07N 3.22W
15 E6 **Kampung** *R* Irian Jaya
18 K7 **Kampungtengah** Borneo Indon 3.15S 113.20E
108 R7 **Kamrar** Iowa 42.23N 93.43W
15 B5 **Kamrau, Teluk** *B* Irian Jaya
30 H7 **Kamriaon** Bihar India 25.33N 84.23E
28 H2 **Kamrup** *dist* Assam India
100 Q7 **Kamsack** Saskatchewan 51.34N 101.51W
32 J7 **Kamsaptar** Iran 27.31N 60.52E
Kamsar *see* **Qamsar**
89 B6 **Kamsar** Guinea 10.33N 14.34W
53 V20 **Kamsdalen** *V* Norway 59.08N 6.50E
35 G5 **Kamsha, El** Jordan 32.08N 35.54E
30 D3 **Kamsin** Nepal 29.56N 80.36E
47 G5 **Kamskiy** U.S.S.R. 60.05N 53.22E
45 V1 **Kamskoye Ust'ye** U.S.S.R. 55.12N 49.15E
47 H6 **Kamskoye Vdkhr** *res* U.S.S.R.
23 B2 **Kamtang** Sichuan China 32.22N 100.59E
30 J6 **Kamtaul** Bihar India 26.20N 85.50E
29 G7 **Kamtha** Maharashtra India 21.30N 80.23E
100 P2 **Kamuchawie L** Saskatchewan
93 L6 **Kamudi** Kenya 0.41S 39.49E
28 D6 **Kamudi** Tamil Nadu India 9.25N 78.23E
20 M2 **Kamui-dake** *mt* Japan 42.24N 142.56E
93 E5 **Kamuli** Uganda 0.57N 33.08E
15 B5 **Kamundan** *R* Irian Jaya
29 G5 **Kamur Ra** Madhya Prad/Uttar Prad India
20 K3 **Kamuso** Japan 41.51N 140.39E
Kamutti *see* **Kamudi**
84 C2 **Kamvoúnia Ori** *mts* Greece
93 B5 **Kamwenge** Uganda 0.12N 30.27E
32 B3 **Kāmyārān** Iran 34.45N 46.58E
65 K2 **Kamýcká nádrž** *res* Czechoslovakia
65 K3 **Kamýk** *mt* Czechoslovakia 49.14N 14.18E
42 F4 **Kamyshet** U.S.S.R. 55.11N 98.45E
45 G9 **Kamyshevakha** Zaporozh'ye, Ukraine U.S.S.R. 47.42N 35.32E
44 B1 **Kamyshevatskaya** U.S.S.R. 46.25N 37.57E
44 F1 **Kamyshevaya** *R* U.S.S.R.
47 N5 **Kamyshevo** U.S.S.R. 56.32N 61.22E
44 G4 **Kamysheye** U.S.S.R. 43.52N 45.45E
45 R6 **Kamyshin** U.S.S.R. 50.05N 45.24E
46 Q3 **Kamyshla** U.S.S.R. 54.08N 52.10E
47 J7 **Kamyshlov** U.S.S.R. 56.55N 62.41E
43 F2 **Kamyshnyy** Kazakhstan U.S.S.R. 51.57N 61.45E
45 U6 **Kamyshok** U.S.S.R. 50.16N 48.22E
45 H9 **Kamysh-Zarya** Ukraine U.S.S.R. 47.19N 36.42E
43 F4 **Kamyslybas** Kazakhstan U.S.S.R. 46.09N 61.55E
43 F4 **Kamyslybas, Ozero** *L* Kazakhstan U.S.S.R.
42 G6 **Kamyzhi** U.S.S.R. 52.35N 102.38E
44 J1 **Kamyzyak** U.S.S.R. 46.05N 48.06E
44 J1 **Kamyzyak** *R* U.S.S.R.
33 M3 **Kamzar** Oman 26.21N 56.23E
25 C1 **Kan** Burma 22.25N 94.07E
42 E4 **Kan** *R* U.S.S.R.
42 H1 **Kana** U.S.S.R. 62.55N 108.45E
87 C9 **Kana** Zaïre 3.15N 30.10E
93 B2 **Kana** Zaïre 3.13N 30.12E
93 B3 **Kana** Zaïre 2.01N 30.18E
97 M7 **Kanaaupscow** Quebec 54.00N 76.40W
97 M7 **Kanaaupscow** *R* Quebec
111 M4 **Kanab** Utah 37.03N 112.32W
111 M5 **Kanab Cr** Arizona
18 K4 **Kana, Bukit** *mt* Sarawak Malaysia 2.44N 112.47E
93 C6 **Kanabulemu** Uganda 0.56S 31.42E
45 T3 **Kanadey** U.S.S.R. 53.09N 47.30E
113 Q10 **Kanaga I** Aleutian Is 51.45N 117.20W
20 D4 **Kanagawa** *dist* Yokohama Japan
20 N6 **Kanagawa** *prefect* Japan
20 O1 **Kanagi** Japan 40.53N 140.26E
114 B7 **Kanahaha** Hawaiian Is 19.35N 155.18W
119 H4 **Kanaima Falls** Guyana 6.53N 60.21W
114 E6 **Kanaio** Hawaiian Is 20.37N 156.22W
31 D6 **Kanak** Pakistan 29.58N 66.45E
36 H3 **Kanak** *R* Turkey
113 H7 **Kanakanak** Alaska 59.00N 158.35W
28 C4 **Kanakapura** Karnataka India 12.34N 77.24E
26 R3 **Kanakarayankulam** Sri Lanka 9.02N 80.31E
35 H1 **Kanakir** Syria 33.16N 36.06E
19 D2 **Kanakitang** *isld* Indonesia 3.12N 125.31E
82 B4 **Kanal** Yugoslavia 46.08N 13.43E
84 C3 **Kanália** Kardhítsa Greece 39.24N 21.48E
84 E3 **Kanália** Magnisía Greece 39.30N 22.53E
28 J8 **Kanalla** Nicobar Is 6.52N 93.43E
90 D7 **Kanam** Nigeria 9.29N 10.00E
19 B5 **Kanan** Celebes Indonesia 2.48S 120.10E
34 M5 **Kan'an** Iraq 33.41N 44.49E
100 B8 **Kananaskis L** Alberta 50.38N 115.03W
90 C5 **Kanan Bakachi** Niger 13.51N 7.50E
41 H8 **Kananda** U.S.S.R. 63.51N 103.46E
91 H6 **Kananga** Zaïre 5.53S 22.26E
43 D1 **Kananikol'skoye** Bashkir U.S.S.R. 52.15N 57.30E
21 C9 **Kananyŏng-ni** N Korea 37.55N 125.36E
114 D6 **Kanapou B** Hawaiian Is
15 L8 **Kanapu I** Trobriand Is Papua New Guinea 8.22S 150.07E
29 E6 **Kanar** Madhya Prad India 23.39N 76.13E
92 C11 **Kana, R** Zimbabwe
29 K8 **Kanarak** Orissa India 19.53N 86.10E
42 E4 **Kanaray** U.S.S.R. 56.58N 94.40E
111 L4 **Kanarraville** Utah 37.33N 113.11W
45 T1 **Kanash** U.S.S.R. 55.30N 47.27E
42 C3 **Kanaskino** U.S.S.R. 59.15N 80.59E
24 F1 **Kanas Köl** *L* Xinjiang Uygur Zizhiqu China 48.45N 87.02E
113 K8 **Kanatak** Alaska 57.35N 156.01W
9 U6 **Kanathea** *isld* Fiji 17.15S 179.10W
Kanauj *see* **Kannauj**
47 G5 **Kanava** U.S.S.R. 61.08N 55.00E
108 R7 **Kanawha** Iowa 42.56N 93.48W
112 M2 **Kanawha** Texas 33.53N 95.16W
104 C8 **Kanawha** *R* W Virginia
104 D7 **Kanawha, Little** *R* W Virginia
20 M7 **Kanaya** Shizuoka Japan 34.49N 138.08E
21 G10 **Kanayama** Japan 35.42N 137.11E
43 O3 **Kanayka** Kazakhstan U.S.S.R. 49.38N 81.55E
39 J1 **Kanayyen** U.S.S.R. 69.50N 174.35E
20 K5 **Kanazawa** Japan 36.35N 136.38E
20 B4 **Kanazawa** *dist* Japan 35.21N 139.38E
92 E2 **Kanazi** Tanzania 1.30S 31.42E
20 K5 **Kanazu** Japan 36.13N 136.15E
25 M9 **Kanbalu** Burma 23.10N 95.31E
39 K2 **Kanchalan** U.S.S.R. 65.14N 176.35E
39 K2 **Kanchalan** *R* U.S.S.R.
25 E5 **Kanchanaburi** Thailand 14.02N 99.32E
Kanchenjunga *see* **Kangchenjunga** *mt*
92 C10 **Kanchindu** Zambia 17.07S 27.29E
28 D4 **Kanchipuram** Tamil Nadu India 12.50N 79.44E
29 M2 **Kanchrapara** W Bengal India 22.27N 88.27E
31 D5 **Kand** *mt* Pakistan 30.48N 67.33E
20 D8 **Kanda** Japan 33.48N 130.58E
31 D6 **Kanda** Pakistan 23.33N 67.52E
30 A2 **Kandaghat** Himachal Prad India 30.57N 77.08E
31 C5 **Kandahar** Afghanistan 31.36N 65.47E
28 C1 **Kandahar** Maharashtra India 18.54N 77.14E
100 N7 **Kandahar** Saskatchewan 51.45N 104.19W
31 C5 **Kandahar** *prov* Afghanistan
91 H7 **Kanda Kanda** Zaïre 6.56S 23.33E
47 C3 **Kandalaksha** U.S.S.R. 67.09N 32.31E
47 C3 **Kandalakshskaya Guba** *B* U.S.S.R.
91 F7 **Kandale** Zaïre 6.01S 19.25E
26 Q7 **Kandana** Sri Lanka 7.03N 79.55E
18 C9 **Kandang** Pen Malaysia 2.08N 102.20E
18 B4 **Kandang** Sumatra Indon 3.02N 97.20E
18 L7 **Kandangan** Borneo Indon 2.50S 115.15E
84 J11 **Kándanos** Crete 35.19N 23.44E
15 A8 **Kandar** Moluccas Indon 8.14S 131.00E
42 D4 **Kandat** U.S.S.R. 57.12N 89.00E
30 E6 **Kandaura** Uttar Prad India 26.20N 81.10E
42 C4 **Kandaurovo** U.S.S.R. 55.41N 83.15E
43 K7 **Kandav** Tadzhikistan U.S.S.R. 39.10N 71.44E
46 E2 **Kandava** Latvia U.S.S.R. 57.00N 22.42E
9 S3 **Kandavu** *I* Fiji
9 S3 **Kandavu Passage** Fiji
89 K7 **Kandé** Togo 9.58N 1.02E
92 D5 **Kandefwe** Zaïre 7.26S 29.44E
91 E3 **Kandeko** *R* Congo
64 E5 **Kandel** W Germany 49.05N 8.12E
15 G6 **Kandep** Papua New Guinea 5.54S 143.34E
66 G5 **Kander** *R* Switzerland
66 G5 **Kanderbrück** Switzerland 46.35N 7.40E
66 G5 **Kandergrund** Switzerland 46.33N 7.40E
64 D8 **Kandern** W Germany 47.42N 7.40E
66 G6 **Kandersteg** Switzerland 46.30N 7.41E
53 E1 **Kandestederne** Denmark 57.40N 10.24E
84 A4 **Kandhíla** Akarnanía Greece 38.42N 20.56E
84 D6 **Kandhíla** Arkadhía Greece 37.46N 22.22E
84 F4 **Kandhílion Óros** *mts* Greece
31 E6 **Kandhkot** Pakistan 28.15N 69.18E
30 A3 **Kandhla** Uttar Prad India 29.19N 77.17E
Kandhot *see* **Kandhkot**
31 F3 **Kandhura** Pakistan 34.35N 71.20E
28 D2 **Kandi** Andhra Prad India 17.35N 78.05E
89 L6 **Kandi** Benin 11.05N 2.59E
31 D6 **Kandi** Pakistan 28.12N 66.59E
29 L1 **Kandi** W Bengal Ind 23.57N 88.04E
89 B6 **Kandiafara** Guinea 11.17N 14.45W
31 E7 **Kandiaro** Pakistan 27.02N 68.16E
113 R4 **Kandik** *R* Alaska
37 K1 **Kandilli** Turkey 41.05N 29.08E
36 E1 **Kandıra** Turkey 41.05N 30.08E
19 B3 **Kandi, Tanjung** *C* Celebes Indonesia 1.19N 121.30E
90 J9 **Kandjia** *R* Cent Afr Rep
29 B6 **Kandla** Gujarat India 23.03N 70.11E
93 B3 **Kandoi** Zaïre 2.28N 30.18E
12 J5 **Kandos** New S Wales 32.53S 149.59E
29 J2 **Kandra** Bihar India 22.51N 86.08E
30 H5 **Kandrang Garhi** Nepal 27.43N 84.47E
95 C4 **Kandrany** Madagascar 16.01S 46.20E
95 C4 **Kandreho** Madagascar 17.27S 46.06E
29 H6 **Kandri** Madhya Prad India 23.32N 83.53E
15 K7 **Kandrian** New Britain 6.14S 149.32E
43 C1 **Kandry** U.S.S.R. 54.34N 54.13E
15 G6 **Kanduanum** Papua New Guinea 4.18S 143.49E
28 D3 **Kandukur** Andhra Prad India 15.15N 79.47E
26 S7 **Kandy** Sri Lanka 7.17N 80.40E
39 E4 **Kandychan** U.S.S.R. 60.38N 150.30E
107 F2 **Kane** Illinois 39.12N 90.21W
104 G5 **Kane** Pennsylvania 41.40N 78.48W
108 B5 **Kane** Wyoming 44.50N 108.11W
97 M2 **Kane Basin** Greenland
20 B4 **Kaneda** Kanagawa Japan
61 D2 **Kanegem** Belgium 51.01N 3.24E
32 E7 **Kaneh** *R* Iran
113 G7 **Kanektok** *R* Alaska
89 C4 **Kanel** Senegal 15.30N 13.18W
90 G4 **Kanem** *div* Chad
90 G4 **Kanem** *reg* Chad
91 J9 **Kanema** Zaïre 10.32S 24.25E
114 B5 **Kaneohe** Hawaiian Is 21.25N 157.48W
114 B5 **Kaneohe Bay** Hawaiian Is
29 D5 **Kanera** Rajasthan India 24.42N 74.56E
31 D6 **Kaneti** Pakistan 29.38N 66.30E
45 C7 **Kanev** Ukraine U.S.S.R. 49.46N 31.28E
47 D3 **Kanevka** U.S.S.R. 67.08N 39.50E
44 B1 **Kanevskaya** U.S.S.R. 46.05N 38.57E
20 O3 **Kaneyama** Japan 38.52N 140.18E
82 B5 **Kanfanar** Yugoslavia 45.06N 13.50E
94 G4 **Kang** Botswana 23.41S 22.50E
93 K8 **Kanga** Kenya 2.46S 38.14E
92 H5 **Kanga** Tanzania 6.02S 37.47E
37 C6 **Kangal** Turkey 39.15N 37.23E
41 N9 **Kangalassy** U.S.S.R. 62.25N 129.58E
48 R11 **Kangâmiut** Greenland 65.55N 53.00W
32 G8 **Kangān** Banāder va Jazāyer-e Baḩr-e Oman Iran 25.50N 57.27E
32 E7 **Kangan** Banāder va Jazāyer-e Khalīj-e Fārs Iran 27.51N 52.07E
31 H10 **Kanga R** Bangladesh
18 D2 **Kangar** Pen Malaysia 6.28N 100.10E
89 E6 **Kangare** Mali 11.36N 8.04W
24 A6 **Kangar He** *R* Xinjiang Uygur Zizhiqu China
18 D9 **Kangar Lenggor** Pen Malaysia 2.14N 103.43E
12 D6 **Kangaroo I** S Australia
13 E4 **Kangaroo Pt** Queensland 17.34S 139.46E
119 J5 **Kangaruma** Guyana 5.17N 59.10W
51 L7 **Kangas** Finland 64.10N 24.40E
51 N9 **Kangaslampi** Finland 62.16N 28.20E
51 M9 **Kangasniemi** Finland 62.01N 26.35E
48 S9 **Kangâtsiaq** Greenland 68.15N 53.30W
32 B3 **Kangāvar** Iran 34.29N 47.55E
28 C5 **Kangayam** Tamil Nadu India 11.01N 77.35E
82 M4 **Kangaz** U.S.S.R. 46.06N 28.06E
22 K6 **Kangbao** Hebei China 41.50N 114.50E
Kang-ch'a *see* **Gangca**
29 L4 **Kangchenjunga** *mt* Nepal/India 27.44N 88.11E
30 H2 **Kang Cho** *mt* Nepal 27.59N 86.43E
23 B3 **Kangding** Sichuan China 30.05N 102.04E
30 L2 **Kangdoshung Glacier** Xizang Zizhiqu
91 J8 **Kange** Zaïre 8.09S 25.52E
18 L9 **Kangean** *isld* Indonesia
18 L9 **Kangean, Pulau Pulau** *islds* Indonesia
97 N4 **Kangeeak Pt** N W Terr 68.00N 65.00W
91 K5 **Kangela** Zaïre 2.51S 26.49E
87 D7 **Kangen,R** Sudan
48 S12 **Kangeq** Greenland 64.15N 52.12W
48 S9 **Kangeq** *isld* Greenland 67.45N 53.45W
97 Q4 **Kangerdlugssuaq** *inlet* Greenland
Kangerdlugssuatsiaq *see* **Lindenow Fjord**
93 H4 **Kangetet** Kenya 1.58N 36.06E
21 D7 **Kanggye** N Korea 40.58N 126.38E
K'ang-hsien *see* **Kang Xian**
21 D9 **Kanghwa** S Korea 37.46N 126.28E
42 K6 **Kangil** U.S.S.R. 52.18N 116.25E
22 J7 **Kangjiahui** Shanxi China 38.18N 112.12E
22 J7 **Kangjiahui** Shanxi China 38.25N 112.12E
24 J11 *pass* Xizang Zizhiqu/India 29.27N 96.02E
21 D4 **Kangjinjing** Heilongjiang China 46.15N 126.50E
25 L8 **Kanglatongbi** Manipur India 25.00N 93.55E
23 C1 **Kangle** Gansu China 35.14N 103.40E
24 E10 **Kangmar** Xizang Zizhiqu China 30.45N 85.43E
24 F11 **Kangmar** Xizang Zizhiqu China 28.32N 89.41E
21 D9 **Kangnŭng** S Korea 37.48N 127.52E
91 B3 **Kango** Gabon 0.15N 10.11E
Kangogrotte *caves see* **Cango Caves**
20 N9 **Kangoku-iwa** *rocks* Iwo Jima Pacific Oc 24.48N 141.17E
93 F3 **Kangole** Uganda 2.26N 34.28E
93 J7 **Kangondi** Kenya 1.02S 37.41E
51 K4 **Kangos** Sweden 67.30N 22.40E
91 K5 **Kangosi** Zaïre 3.23S 26.44E
41 E8 **Kangotovo** U.S.S.R. 63.28N 87.25E
91 H8 **Kangoya** Zaïre 9.57S 22.47E
28 K3 **Kangpat** Manipur India 24.44N 94.30E
21 C6 **Kangping** Liaoning China 42.45N 123.20E
25 L8 **Kangpokpi** Manipur India 25.08N 93.59E
29 E1 **Kangra** Himachal Prad India 32.04N 76.16E
29 E1 **Kangra** *dist* Himachal Prad India
24 D10 **Kangrinboqê Feng** *mt pk* Xizang Zizhiqu China 31.05N 81.21E
24 E9 **Kangro** Xizang Zizhiqu China 33.00N 85.41E
23 J7 **Kang-shan** Taiwan 22.45N 120.18E
30 K2 **Kangshung Glacier** Xizang Zizhiqu
30 H4 **Kangtega** Nepal 27.48N 86.49E
19 K9 **Kang Tipayan Dakula** *isld* Philippines 5.30N 120.14E
28 J2 **Kangto** *mt* India/Xizang Zizhiqu 27.54N 92.32E
24 G12 **Kangto** *mt pk* Xizang Zizhiqu China 27.56N 92.35E
24 E9 **Kangtog** Xizang Zizhiqu China 32.40N 84.28E
21 E6 **Kangui** N Korea 42.19N 130.40E
29 H2 **Kangu La** *pass* Nepal/Xizang Zizhiqu 30.03N 82.12E
23 D2 **Kang Xian** Gansu China 33.27N 105.30E
24 C7 **Kangxiwar** Xinjiang Uygur Zizhiqu China 36.15N 78.35E
25 C4 **Kangyidaung** Burma 16.54N 94.54E
29 F7 **Kanhan** *R* Madhya Prad etc India
29 E8 **Kanhargaon** Maharashtra India 19.56N 77.11E
30 L7 **Kanharia** Bihar India 25.47N 87.42E
29 H5 **Kanhar R** Madhya Prad etc India
Kan-hsien *see* **Ganzhou**
25 C1 **Kani** Burma 22.24N 94.55E
28 K1 **Kani** Xizang Zizhiqu 29.28N 95.25E
91 J7 **Kaniama** Zaïre 7.32S 24.11E
92 C5 **Kaniambe** Zaïre 7.27S 26.59E
43 K6 **Kanibadam** Tadzhikistan U.S.S.R. 40.20N 70.18E
19 N4 **Kanibu, Eli** *isld* Truk Is Pacific Oc 7.26N 152.01E
37 K8 **Kānī Darreh** Iran 37.19N 46.45E
11 F9 **Kaniere** New Zealand 42.44S 171.00E
11 F9 **Kaniere, L** New Zealand 42.49S 171.09E
15 H4 **Kaniet Is** Bismarck Arch
28 D3 **Kanigiri** Andhra Prad India 15.25N 79.30E
31 E4 **Kaniguram** Pakistan 32.31N 69.49E
34 N3 **Kānī Harme** Iraq 35.46N 45.58E
34 L1 **Kānī Māsī** Iraq 37.13N 43.25E
34 N4 **Kānī Māsī** Iraq 34.12N 45.22E
93 K6 **Kaningo** Kenya 0.48S 38.32E
47 E2 **Kanin Kamen'** *ridge* U.S.S.R.
47 E2 **Kanin Nos** U.S.S.R. 68.35N 43.29E
47 E2 **Kanin Nos, Mys** *C* U.S.S.R. 68.38N 43.20E
47 E2 **Kanin, Poluostrov** *pen* U.S.S.R.
47 E3 **Kaninskiy Bereg** *coast* U.S.S.R.
34 M1 **Kānī Rash** Iraq 37.00N 44.27E
34 O5 **Kānī Sakht** Iraq 33.17N 46.06E
31 B4 **Kanisk** Afghanistan 32.30N 62.20E
20 O1 **Kanita** Japan 41.02N 140.38E
91 K5 **Kaniuki** Zaïre 2.49N 27.11E
12 F6 **Kaniva** Victoria 36.33S 141.17E
29 F6 **Kaniwara** Madhya Prad India 22.10N 79.46E
29 D5 **Kanjarda** Madhya Prad India 24.39N 75.18E
30 B8 **Kanjia** Madhya Prad India 24.24N 78.12E
82 F4 **Kanjiža** Yugoslavia 46.03N 20.04E
51 J10 **Kankaanpää** Finland 61.47N 22.25E
30 L6 **Kankai** *R* Bihar India
106 G8 **Kankakee** Illinois 41.08N 87.52W
106 F8 **Kankakee, R** Illinois
91 C4 **Kankan** Gabon 0.05S 12.12E
89 E6 **Kankan** Guinea 10.22N 9.11W
Kankanhalli *see* **Kanakapura**
29 G7 **Kanker** Madhya Prad India 20.17N 81.30E
26 R2 **Kankesanturai** Sri Lanka 9.48N 80.03E
31 G2 **Kankhun Pass** W Pak/Afghan 36.54N 73.04E
51 L4 **Kankonen** Finland 67.33N 24.50E
89 D4 **Kankossa** Mauritania 15.54N 11.31W
29 C5 **Kankroli** Rajasthan India 25.03N 73.58E
40 C3 **Kankunskiy** U.S.S.R. 57.36N 126.00E
37 D8 **Kanlıavşar** Turkey 37.15N 38.16E
24 G11 **Kan-lon Shan** *mt pk* Xizang Zizhiqu China 29.58N 90.02E
25 E7 **Kanmaw Kyun** *isld* Burma
42 E5 **Kanmegirskiy Khrebet** *mts* U.S.S.R.
52 H10 **Kånna** Sweden 56.45N 13.55E
29 D7 **Kannad** Maharashtra India 20.18N 75.12E
105 G2 **Kannapolis** N Carolina 35.30N 80.36W
30 C5 **Kannauj** Uttar Prad India 27.02N 79.56E
20 P9 **Kanna-zaki** *C* Okinawa Japan 26.15N 127.55E
61 N3 **Kanne** Belgium 50.49N 5.40E
28 C6 **Kanniyakumari** Tamil Nadu India 8.04N 77.35E
28 C6 **Kanniyakumari** *dist* Tamil Nadu India
29 E6 **Kannod** Madhya Prad India 22.40N 76.47E
51 L9 **Kannonkoski** Finland 62.58N 25.15E
21 F11 **Kannoura** Japan 33.35N 134.18E
51 K8 **Kannus** Finland 63.55N 23.55E
20 E7 **Kano** Japan 34.14N 131.50E
90 D6 **Kano** Nigeria 12.00N 8.31E
19 D5 **Kano** *isld* Moluccas Indon 2.03S 124.23E
90 D5 **Kano** *state* Nigeria
109 K2 **Kanona** Kansas 39.50N 100.26W
92 E8 **Kanona** Zambia 13.03S 30.37E
43 N2 **Kanonerka** Kazakhstan U.S.S.R. 50.44N 79.40E
93 C5 **Kanoni** Uganda 0.12N 31.55E
20 G7 **Kanonji** Japan 34.08N 133.38E
94 Q11 **Kanonkop** *hill* Cape Town S Africa 33.49S 18.36E
116 B2 **Kanon, Pt** Curaçao W I 12.08N 68.45W
109 M3 **Kanopolis** Kansas 38.40N 98.10W
109 N3 **Kanopolis Res** Kansas
109 H2 **Kanorado** Kansas 39.19N 102.03W
111 M3 **Kanosh** Utah 38.48N 112.31W
90 F4 **Kanouri** *reg* Nigeria
18 K4 **Kanowit** Sarawak Malaysia 2.03N 112.15E
20 D10 **Kanoya** Japan 31.22N 130.50E
51 R4 **Kan Ozero** *L* U.S.S.R. 67.02N 34.09E
29 J7 **Kanpur** Orissa India 20.25N 85.15E
31 E6 **Kanpur** Pakistan 28.10N 68.09E
30 D6 **Kanpur** Uttar Prad India 26.27N 80.14E
30 C6 **Kanpur** *dist* Uttar Prad India
31 D7 **Kanrach** *reg* Pakistan
92 C8 **Kansanshi Mine** Zambia 12.05S 26.25E
88 L4 **Kansara, El** Morocco 34.03N 5.58W
107 J2 **Kansas** Illinois 39.33N 87.58W
109 Q5 **Kansas** Oklahoma 36.14N 94.48W
109 P2 **Kansas** *R* Kansas
102 G3 **Kansas** *state* U.S.A.
109 Q2 **Kansas City** Kansas 39.05N 94.37W
107 B2 **Kansas City** Missouri 39.02N 94.33W
43 J6 **Kansay** Tadzhikistan U.S.S.R. 40.31N 69.41E
91 K9 **Kansenia** Zaïre 10.18S 26.04E
23 G6 **Kanshi** Fujian China 24.55N 116.54E
42 F4 **Kansk** U.S.S.R. 56.11N 95.48E
42 F5 **Kanskoye Belogor'ye** *mts* U.S.S.R.
30 G7 **Kanso** Uttar Prad India 25.55N 83.48E
21 D8 **Kansŏng** S Korea 38.20N 128.28E
92 C5 **Kansonge** Zaïre 7.57S 27.23E
24 A6 **Kansu** Xinjiang Uygur Zizhiqu China 39.40N 74.45E
Kansu *prov* China*see* **Gansu**
43 L5 **Kant** Kirgiziya U.S.S.R. 42.53N 74.52E
87 E7 **Kanta** Ethiopia 6.02N 35.15E
30 J6 **Kantai** Bihar India 26.12N 85.18E
51 N9 **Kantala** Finland 62.09N 27.15E
26 T5 **Kantalai** Sri Lanka 8.22N 81.00E
31 G8 **Kantanagar** Bangladesh 25.47N 88.45E
Kantang *see* **Ban Kantang**
84 S14 **Kantara Castle** Cyprus 35.23N 33.55E
88 Q4 **Kantara, El** Algeria 35.13N 5.40E
25 H5 **Kantaralak** Thailand 14.40N 104.38E
89 K5 **Kantchari** Upper Volta 12.37N 1.37E
90 D5 **Kantche** Niger 13.33N 8.26E
45 L7 **Kantemirovka** U.S.S.R. 49.40N 39.52E
60 P6 **Kantens** Netherlands 53.22N 6.39E
30 B3 **Kanth** Uttar Prad India 29.04N 78.38E
30 D6 **Kantha** Uttar Prad India 26.34N 80.45E
87 E7 **Kantiere** Ethiopia 6.28N 34.57E
29 J7 **Kantilo** Orissa India 20.20N 85.16E
113 M5 **Kantishna** Alaska 63.31N 151.07W
113 M4 **Kantishna** *R* Alaska
29 D3 **Kantli** *R* Rajasthan India
20 M6 **Kanto sanchi** *mts* Japan
89 C5 **Kantoutou** Guinea 12.19N 13.28W
25 D3 **Kantulong** Burma
59 E7 **Kanturk** Cork Irish Rep 52.10N 8.55W
32 F4 **Kanūgar** Iran 33.18N 54.37E
119 J6 **Kanuku Mts** Guyana
20 N5 **Kanuma** Japan 36.34N 139.44E
93 A6 **Kanungu** Uganda 0.54S 29.46E
28 E3 **Kanuparti** Andhra Prad India 15.38N 80.10E
94 E6 **Kanus** Namibia 27.54S 18.40E
113 M3 **Kanuti** *R* Alaska
15 G7 **Kanuwe** *R* Papua New Guinea
93 F5 **Kanyaboli L** Kenya 0.03N 34.10E
93 F6 **Kanyada** Kenya 0.41S 34.25E
93 F6 **Kanyamkago** Kenya 0.57S 34.31E
93 B10 **Kanyato** Tanzania 4.26S 30.17E
94 H5 **Kanye** Botswana 24.59S 25.19E
25 C3 **Kanyinngu** Burma 18.02N 19.15E
25 D3 **Kanyutkwin** Burma 18.19N 96.30E
20 J4 **Kanzaki** Chiba Japan
65 J8 **Kanzel** Austria 46.41N 14.54E
91 J9 **Kanzenze** Zaïre 10.29S 25.13E
93 A8 **Kanzi** Rwanda 2.40S 29.47E
9 T12 **Kao** *isld* Tonga, Pacific Oc 19.40S 175.01W
90 B6 **Kaoge** Nigeria 11.10N 4.05E
31 B3 **Kaoghan** Afghanistan 34.12N 63.01E
23 J7 **Kao-hsiung** Taiwan 22.36N 120.17E
94 B2 **Kaoko Otavi** Namibia 18.17S 13.43E
94 B1 **Kaoko Veld** *plat* Namibia
89 A4 **Kaolack** Senegal 14.09N 16.08W
82 L7 **Kaolinova** Bulgaria 43.40N 27.04E
92 B9 **Kaoma** Zambia 14.50S 24.48E
92 B8 **Kaonde** *tribe* Zambia
90 J2 **Kaortchi** Chad 18.20N 18.47E
21 C5 **Kaoshan** Jilin China 44.48N 125.37E
31 E3 **Kaoshan Pass** Afghanistan 35.16N 69.02E
89 M5 **Kaouara** Niger 13.59N 4.19E
91 D5 **Kaounga** Congo 3.33S 15.11E
9 R12 **Kapa** *isld* Tonga, Pacific Oc 18.44S 174.02W
114 F3 **Kapaa** Hawaiian Is 22.04N 159.20W
114 B6 **Kapaau** Hawaiian Is 20.14N 155.48W
92 G9 **Kapachira Falls** *waterfall* Malawi 15.49S 34.45E
29 C6 **Kapadvanj** Gujarat India 23.03N 73.09E
114 F4 **Kapaia** Hawaiian Is 21.59N 159.22W
37 F2 **Kapakali Burun** *C* Turkey 40.28N 28.59E
15 J8 **Kapakapa** Papua New Guinea 9.45S 147.29E
37 H3 **Kapaklı** Bilecik Turkey 40.05N 29.53E
37 F2 **Kapaklı** Bursa Turkey 40.28N 28.58E
43 N4 **Kapal** Kazakhstan U.S.S.R. 45.08N 79.01E
19 F8 **Kapala** *isld* Indon 8.10S 128.46E
18 A6 **Kapala Batas** Pen Malaysia 5.30N 100.24E
114 B7 **Kapalaoa** Hawaiian Is 19.54N 155.53W
36 F3 **Kapalı** *R* Turkey
91 H6 **Kapambwe** Zaïre 5.31S 22.52E
19 D8 **Kapan** Timor Indon 9.44S 124.15E
84 G5 **Kapandrítion** Greece 38.13N 23.52E
91 E6 **Kapanga** Zaïre 5.08S 17.03E
91 H8 **Kapanga** Zaïre 8.22S 22.37E
114 C8 **Kapaoo Pt** Hawaiian Is 19.11N 155.24W
18 B8 **Kapar** Pen Malaysia 3.07N 101.20E
92 C3 **Kaparangao** Zaïre 3.53S 26.35E
15 D6 **Kapare** *R* Irian Jaya
84 F5 **Kaparéli** Greece 38.13N 23.12E
32 C5 **Kaparhā** Iran 30.05N 49.40E
63 S3 **Kap Arkona** *C* E Germany 54.41N 13.26E
29 D5 **Kapasan** Rajasthan India 24.52N 74.22E
92 E6 **Kapatu** Zambia 9.41S 30.40E
15 J7 **Kapau** *R* Papua New Guinea
48 V6 **Kap Bismarck** Greenland 76.45N 18.30W
43 M5 **Kapchagay** Kazakhstan U.S.S.R. 43.51N 77.14E
43 N5 **Kapchagayskoye Vdkhr** *res* Kazakhstan U.S.S.R.
93 F4 **Kapchorwa** Uganda 1.25N 34.28E
Kap Dan *see* **Kulusuk**
93 H4 **Kapedo** Kenya 1.10N 36.04E
60 G9 **Kapel** Netherlands 52.35N 4.42E
60 C3 **Kapelle** Netherlands 51.29N 3.58E
61 H1 **Kapellen** Antwerp Belgium 51.19N 4.25E
61 K3 **Kapellen** Brabant Belgium 50.53N 4.57E
63 D9 **Kapellen** W Germany 51.34N 6.22E
61 H2 **Kapelle-op-den-Bos** Belgium 51.01N 4.21E
52 L7 **Kapellskär** Sweden 59.43N 19.00E
93 G4 **Kapenguria** Kenya 1.14N 35.08E
93 E2 **Kapeta** *watercourse* Uganda
65 M7 **Kapfenberg** Austria 47.27N 15.18E
91 F6 **Kapia** Zaïre 4.19S 19.48E
37 E2 **Kapı Dağı** *mt* Turkey 40.28N 27.50E
37 E2 **Kapıdağı Yarımadası** *pen* Turkey
36 D6 **Kapikargin** Turkey 36.41N 28.50E
87 B9 **Kapili** *R* Zaïre
84 Q15 **Kapilio** Cyprus 34.47N 32.57E
28 J2 **Kapili R** Assam India
31 H9 **Kapilmuni** Bangladesh 22.41N 89.20E
122 F7 **Kapingamarangi Rise** Pacific Oc
19 C4 **Kapinyu, Tanjung** *C* Celebes Indon 0.47S 122.10E
31 E5 **Kapip** Pakistan 31.21N 69.39E
93 E4 **Kapiri** Uganda 1.38N 33.48E
92 D8 **Kapiri Mposhi** Zambia 13.59S 28.40E
31 E3 **Kapisa** *prov* Afghanistan
48 S12 **Kapisigdlit** Greenland 64.25N 50.15W
97 L7 **Kapiskau** Ontario 52.50N 82.01W
18 K5 **Kapit** Sarawak Malaysia 2.00N 112.54E
45 B8 **Kapitanovka** Ukraine U.S.S.R. 48.55N 31.43E
39 B4 **Kapitanskaya Zaseka** U.S.S.R. 60.55N 139.37E
117 B3 **Kapiting** Brazil 2.20N 55.14W
90 K4 **Kapka, Massif du** *mt reg* Chad
107 D11 **Kaplan** Louisiana 30.00N 92.19W
84 C8 **Kapláni** Greece 36.49N 21.51E
46 O7 **Kaplan Yurt** U.S.S.R. 43.38N 46.50E
65 K4 **Kaplice** Czechoslovakia 48.45N 14.29E
92 E9 **Kapoche** Zambia 15.22S 30.21E
25 E8 **Kapoe** Thailand 9.35N 98.36E
87 D8 **Kapoeta** Sudan 4.50N 33.35E
15 J8 **Kapogere** Papua New Guinea 9.47S 147.44E
114 D8 **Kapoho** Hawaiian Is 19.30N 154.50W
114 D8 **Kapoho Pt** Hawaiian Is 19.29N 154.50W
91 H9 **Kapombo** Zaïre 10.40S 23.30E
92 D5 **Kapona** Zaïre 7.11S 29.09E
11 J6 **Kaponga** New Zealand 39.24S 174.08E
92 D5 **Kapongolo** Zaïre 7.51S 28.12E
19 A6 **Kapoposang** *isld* Indonesia 4.42S 118.59E
62 L9 **Kapos** *R* Hungary
62 K9 **Kaposvár** Hungary 46.21N 17.49E
Kapotjol *see* **Kafnikalep**
31 B8 **Kappar** Pakistan 25.18N 62.42E
53 G7 **Kappel** Denmark 54.47N 11.03E
66 N2 **Kappel** St Gallen Switzerland 47.17N 9.07E
64 C3 **Kappel** W Germany 50.01N 7.21E
66 L3 **Kappel** Zürich Switzerland 47.14N 8.31E
63 L3 **Kappeln** W Germany 54.39N 9.56E
64 E6 **Kappelrodeck** W Germany 48.36N 8.08E
52 L9 **Kappelshamn** Sweden 57.52N 18.50E
51 J2 **Kapperusvaarat** *mt* Finland 69.09N 21.10E
65 B7 **Kappl** Austria 47.05N 10.24E
50 S14 **Kapp Linne** Spitsbergen 78.02N 13.40E
29 E5 **Kapran** Rajasthan India 25.26N 76.15E
80 N1 **Kaprije** Yugoslavia 43.42N 15.43E
80 N1 **Kaprije** *I* Yugoslavia 43.42N 15.43E
61 E2 **Kaprijke** Belgium 51.13N 3.37E
65 G7 **Kaprun** Austria 47.17N 12.46E
93 G5 **Kapsabet** Kenya 0.12N 35.05E
84 H5 **Kápsala** Greece 38.08N 24.15E
30 G3 **Kapsale** *mt* Nepal 27.51N 86.41E
31 B7 **Kap Salt Swamp** Pakistan
21 D7 **Kapsan** N Korea 41.05N 128.17E
23 A9 **Kap Shui Mun** *sea* Hong Kong
28 C1 **Kapsi** Maharashtra India 18.58N 77.25E
84 D6 **Kápsia** Greece 37.37N 22.20E
93 G5 **Kapsowar** Kenya 0.59N 35.32E
46 E3 **Kapsukas** Lithuania U.S.S.R. 54.31N 23.20E
92 E9 **Kapsuku** *hill* Zimbabwe 15.40S 30.18E
37 E2 **Kapsul Burun** *C* Turkey 40.29N 28.03E
93 G5 **Kaptagat** Kenya 0.24N 35.27E
31 J10 **Kaptai Dam** Bangladesh 22.29N 92.15E
37 F5 **Kaptanpaşa** Turkey 40.56N 40.46E
90 L3 **Kapterko** Chad 16.50N 23.10E
93 F4 **Kaptokoi** Uganda 1.28N 34.26E
42 K7 **Kaptsegaytuy** U.S.S.R. 49.58N 118.45E
18 H6 **Kapuas** *R* Kalimantan Indonesia
18 L6 **Kapuas** *R* Kalimantan Indonesia
18 K5 **Kapuas Hulu, Pengunungan** *mts* Kalimantan/Sarawak
92 D6 **Kapulo** Zaïre 8.19S 29.12E
12 E5 **Kapunda** S Australia 34.19S 138.55E
11 J6 **Kapuni** New Zealand 39.25S 174.09E
29 C4 **Kapūria** Rajasthan India 26.52N 73.08E
29 D2 **Kapurthala** Punjab India 31.20N 75.26E
29 D2 **Kapurthala** *dist* Punjab India
99 H3 **Kapuskasing** Ontario 49.25N 82.26W
99 H4 **Kapuskasing** *R* Ontario
45 R8 **Kapustin Yar** U.S.S.R. 48.33N 45.42E
92 D6 **Kaputa** Zambia 8.28S 29.41E
12 K4 **Kaputar** *mt* New S Wales 30.20S 150.10E
93 G3 **Kaputir** Kenya 2.05N 35.29E
62 K8 **Kapuvár** Hungary 47.36N 17.01E
92 D6 **Kapwasa** Zaïre 9.56S 28.10E
44 G8 **Kapydzhik** *mt* U.S.S.R. 39.11N 46.00E
42 J5 **Kapylyushi, Oz** *L* U.S.S.R. 54.50N 112.15E
21 D9 **Kapy'ŏng** S Korea 37.53N 127.30E
24 B7 **Kaqung** *see* **Xaqung**
87 F8 **Kara** Ethiopia 5.55N 37.08E
30 E7 **Kara** Uttar Prad India 25.42N 81.22E
89 K7 **Kara** *R* Benin/Togo
37 E6 **Kara** *R* Erzurum Turkey
37 D8 **Kara** *R* Gaziantep Turkey
37 F7 **Kara** *R* Muş etc Turkey
47 J2 **Kara** *R* U.S.S.R.
37 H7 **Kara** *R* Van Turkey

44 M6 **Karaada Ostrov** *isld* Turkmeniya U.S.S.R. 41.31N 52.33E
37 E3 **Karaağaç** Turkey 40.11N 28.16E
37 G6 **Karaağil** Turkey 39.09N 42.08E
36 F3 **Karaali** Turkey 39.40N 32.56E
94 E5 **Karaam** Namibia 24.59S 18.37E
36 J2 **Karaaptal** Turkey 40.57N 36.10E
24 A6 **Kara Art Pass** Xinjiang Uygur Zizhiqu China
43 L7 **Karaart, Pereval** *pass* China/U.S.S.R. 39.00N 73.51E
43 N3 **Karaaul** Kazakhstan U.S.S.R. 48.58N 79.15E
36 J3 **Karababa Dağı** *mt* Turkey 39.30N 36.04E
87 D1 **Karaba, El** Sudan 18.32N 33.41E
37 F3 **Karabalçık** Turkey 40.19N 29.06E
43 L5 **Kara-Balty** Kirgiziya U.S.S.R. 42.49N 73.24E
43 M7 **Karabalyk** Uzbekistan U.S.S.R. 40.52N 69.53E
45 K1 **Karabanovo** U.S.S.R. 56.17N 38.44E
43 L3 **Karabas** Kazakhstan U.S.S.R. 49.38N 73.01E
43 M4 **Karabas** Kazakhstan U.S.S.R. 46.32N 76.12E
47 M5 **Karabash** U.S.S.R. 55.28N 60.15E
43 C3 **Karabau** Kazakhstan U.S.S.R. 48.28N 52.56E
43 M7 **Karabau** Uzbekistan U.S.S.R. 41.02N 70.04E
37 E7 **Karabegân** Turkey 38.34N 40.10E
43 G7 **Karabekaul** Turkmeniya U.S.S.R. 38.31N 64.09E
37 D2 **Karabiga** Turkey 40.24N 27.18E
37 D2 **Karabiga Liman** *B* Turkey
43 G8 **Karabil', Vozvyshennost'** *heights* Turkmeniya U.S.S.R.
37 F6 **Karabıyık** Turkey 39.57N 40.50E
37 E6 **Karaboğa Dağ** *mt* Turkey 39.05N 40.15E
43 C6 **Kara-Bogaz-Gol** Turkmeniya U.S.S.R. 41.04N 52.58E
43 C6 **Kara-Bogaz-Gol, Proliv** *str* Turkmeniya U.S.S.R.
43 C6 **Kara-Bogaz Gol, Zaliv** *B* Turkmeniya U.S.S.R.
15 A4 **Karabra** *R* Irian Jaya
44 H5 **Karabudakhkent** U.S.S.R. 42.43N 47.33E
36 F1 **Karabük** Turkey 41.12N 32.36E
42 F3 **Karabula** U.S.S.R. 58.10N 97.27E
43 P3 **Karabulak** Kazakhstan U.S.S.R. 47.34N 84.40E
43 N3 **Karabulak** Semipalatinsk U.S.S.R. 48.16N 77.41E
43 N5 **Karabulak** Taldy-Kurgan, Kazakhstan U.S.S.R. 44.53N 78.29E
44 F4 **Karabulak** U.S.S.R. 44.50N 43.17E
Kara Bura *see* **Xinyuan**
Kara Buran Köl *L see* **Taitema Hu**
24 F6 **Kara Buran Köl** *L* Xinjiang Uygur Zizhiqu China
36 B4 **Karaburun** Turkey 38.38N 26.30E
37 D2 **Kara Burun** *C* Çanakkale Turkey 40.28N 27.17E
36 B4 **Kara Burun** *C* İzmir Turkey 38.40N 26.25E
36 C6 **Kara Burun** *C* Muğla Turkey 36.32N 27.59E
37 C2 **Kara Burun** *mt* Turkey 40.25N 26.27E
83 C4 **Karaburun** *pen* Albania
43 F3 **Karabutak** Kazakhstan U.S.S.R. 49.55N 60.05E
Karaca *see* **Siran**
37 F2 **Karaca Ali** Turkey 40.29N 29.04E
37 E3 **Karacabey** Turkey 40.14N 28.22E
37 E8 **Karacadağ** Turkey 37.43N 39.38E
36 G5 **Karaca Dağ** *mt* Konya Turkey
36 J3 **Karaca Dağ** *mt* Sivas Turkey
36 F3 **Karaca Dağ** *mt* Turkey 39.12N 32.51E
37 D1 **Karacakılavuz** Turkey 41.08N 27.21E
36 C1 **Karacaköy** Turkey 41.24N 28.22E
37 E8 **Karacalı Dağları** *mts* Turkey
37 F3 **Karaçaoba** Turkey 40.13N 28.43E
36 C1 **Karacaoğlan** Turkey 41.32N 27.06E
36 D5 **Karacasu** Turkey 37.43N 28.37E
37 D6 **Karacaviran** Turkey 39.45N 38.09E
Karacaviran Urfa Turkey*see* **Sekerli**
36 J3 **Karaçayır** Turkey 39.57N 36.57E
44 J8 **Karachala** Azerbaydzhan U.S.S.R. 39.48N 48.59E
Karachay-Cherkess Aut. Oblast' *see* **Karachayevo-Cherkesskaya Aut. Oblast'**
44 D4 **Karachayevo-Cherkesskaya Aut. Oblast'** U.S.S.R.
44 D4 **Karachayevsk** U.S.S.R. 43.44N 41.57E
45 F3 **Karachev** U.S.S.R. 53.06N 35.00E
31 D8 **Karachi** Pakistan 24.51N 67.02E
31 D8 **Karachi** *div* Pakistan
31 D8 **Karachi** *dist* Pakistan
37 F6 **Karaçoban** Turkey 39.18N 41.59E
37 E7 **Karaçor** Turkey 38.42N 39.36E
Karacurun *see* **Hilvan**
28 B2 **Karad** Maharashtra India 17.19N 74.15E
44 K7 **Karadag** Azerbaydzhan U.S.S.R. 40.16N 49.35E
37 C3 **Karadağ** Turkey 40.05N 26.57E
37 E2 **Kara Dağ** *mt* Bursa Turkey 40.23N 28.16E
36 H2 **Kara Dağ** *mt* Çorum/Amasya Turkey
37 E6 **Kara Dağ** *mt* Erzincan Turkey 39.56N 39.11E
37 H8 **Kara Dağ** *mt* Hakkâri Turkey 37.42N 43.42E
36 G5 **Kara Dağ** *mt* Konya Turkey 37.25N 33.09E
37 C3 **Kara Dağı** *mt* Çanakkale Turkey
36 F1 **Kara Dağı** *mt* Turkey
37 H8 **Kara Dağları** *mts* Hakkâri Turkey
44 H6 **Karadagly** Azerbaydzhan U.S.S.R. 41.11N 47.02E
43 H6 **Kara-Dar'ya** Uzbekistan U.S.S.R. 40.01N 66.30E
43 O8 **Karadar'ya** *R* Uzbekistan/Kirgiziya U.S.S.R.
Kara Deniz *see* **Black Sea**
37 F2 **Karadeniz Boğazı** *str* Turkey
37 E5 **Karadere** Turkey 40.57N 40.23E
37 E3 **Kara Dere** *R* Bursa etc Turkey
37 G2 **Kara Dere** *R* Kocaeli etc Turkey
26 U6 **Karadiyanaru** Sri Lanka 7.42N 81.32E
24 D6 **Kara Dong** *ruins* Xinjiang Uygur Zizhiqu China 38.36N 81.37E
44 J8 **Karadonlu** Azerbaydzhan U.S.S.R. 39.47N 48.04E
46 J6 **Karadzha** Ukraine U.S.S.R. 45.23N 32.30E
43 E5 **Karadzhar** Uzbekistan U.S.S.R. 43.31N 58.43E
43 O7 **Karadzhigach** Kirgiziya U.S.S.R. 41.10N 72.23E
43 O8 **Karadzhigach** Kirgiziya U.S.S.R. 40.08N 72.05E
42 J5 **Karaftit** U.S.S.R. 54.12N 111.58E
Karafuto *isld see* **Sakhalin**
89 J7 **Karaga** Ghana 9.57N 0.22W
39 G5 **Karaga** U.S.S.R. 59.10N 162.45E
47 L6 **Karagach** U.S.S.R. 57.55N 72.30E
26 S6 **Karagahatenna** Sri Lanka 7.33N 80.42E
40 B5 **Karagan** Chita U.S.S.R. 53.30N 120.40E
44 K3 **Karagan** Kazakhstan U.S.S.R. 44.36N 50.34E
42 F5 **Karagan** Krasnoyarsk U.S.S.R. 54.51N 95.20E
43 L3 **Karaganda** Kazakhstan U.S.S.R. 49.53N 73.07E
37 C1 **Karagarlik** *R* Turkey
43 B2 **Karagay** Kazakhstan U.S.S.R. 50.45N 50.43E
47 H6 **Karagay** U.S.S.R. 58.22N 55.02E
43 M3 **Karagayly** Kazakhstan U.S.S.R. 49.20N 75.41E
Karageban *see* **Hamo**
43 C7 **Karagel'** Turkmeniya U.S.S.R. 39.23N 53.14E
32 F1 **Karagëz** Turkmeniya U.S.S.R. 38.59N 55.26E
24 D4 **Karaghai Tash Dawan** *pass* Xinjiang Uygur Zizhiqu China 42.55N 83.00E
31 C3 **Karaghaitu** Afghanistan 35.35N 65.48E
39 G5 **Karaginskiy, Ostrov** *isld* U.S.S.R.
39 G5 **Karaginskiy Zaliv** *B* U.S.S.R.
44 L4 **Karagiye Vpadina** *mud flat* Kazakhstan U.S.S.R.
92 D4 **Karago** Tanzania 5.20S 29.46E
36 D6 **Kara Göl** *L* Turkey
30 L7 **Karagola** Bihar India 25.26N 87.24E
37 F6 **Karagöl Dağı** *mt* Turkey 39.40N 41.15E
91 C3 **Karagoua** *R* Congo etc
89 G5 **Karagouana** Mali 12.32N 5.39W
90 F6 **Karaguaro** Nigeria 11.56N 12.39E
37 J2 **Karagümrük** *dist* İstanbul Turkey 41.01N 28.52E
43 P2 **Karaguzhikha** Kazakhstan U.S.S.R. 50.46N 83.20E
30 A7 **Karahal** Madhya Prad India 25.29N 77.03E
36 H1 **Karahalil** Turkey 41.08N 35.47E
36 D4 **Karahallı** Turkey 38.20N 29.32E
Karahan *see* **Dağbaşı** Urfa Turkey
37 G6 **Karahasan** Turkey 39.02N 42.31E
36 H3 **Karahasanlı** Turkey 39.18N 34.44E
36 C5 **Karahayıt** Turkey 37.48N 28.00E
30 A7 **Karai** *R* Rajasthan etc India
47 H7 **Karaidel'** U.S.S.R. 55.50N 56.50E
28 D5 **Karaikkudi** Tamil Nadu India 10.04N 78.46E
37 C2 **Karaincirli** Turkey 40.38N 26.18E
Kara Irtysh *R see* **Ertix He**
36 H5 **Karaisalı** Turkey 37.16N 35.02E
26 Q5 **Karaitivu** Sri Lanka 8.13N 79.49E
26 Q4 **Karaitivu** *isld* North Western Sri Lanka 8.30N 79.47E
26 Q2 **Karaitivu** *isld* Sri Lanka 9.46N 79.53E
32 D3 **Karaj** Iran 35.48N 50.58E
32 D3 **Karaj** *R* Iran
32 D3 **Karaj Dam** Iran 35.57N 51.10E
28 B3 **Karajgi** Karnataka India 14.55N 75.31E
24 B5 **Karajül** Xinjiang Uygur Zizhiqu China 40.15N 76.48E
35 F9 **Karak** Jordan 31.11N 35.42E
18 B8 **Karak** Pen Malaysia 3.24N 101.59E
29 F1 **Karak** Xizang Zizhiqu 32.18N 78.41E
35 F9 **Karak** *watercourse* Jordan
11 D6 **Karaka B** Wellington New Zealand
83 H6 **Karaka Burun** *C* Turkey 38.06N 26.36E
43 D7 **Kara-Kala** Turkmeniya U.S.S.R. 38.29N 56.18E
43 E5 **Karakala** Uzbekistan U.S.S.R. 43.38N 59.30E
Karakalh *see* **Ozalp**
43 D5 **Kara-Kalpakskaya A.S.S.R** Uzbekistan U.S.S.R.
43 N7 **Kara-Kalpakskaya Step'** Uzbekistan U.S.S.R.
89 L5 **Kara Kara** Niger 12.47N 3.38E
Kara Kash *see* **Moyu**
43 G6 **Karakatinskaya, Vpadina** *depression* Uzbekistan U.S.S.R.
Karakax *see* **Moyu**
37 E2 **Karakaya Burun** *C* Turkey 40.26N 27.45E
29 F6 **Karakbel** Madhya Prad India 22.57N 79.22E
37 E8 **Karakeçi** Turkey 37.25N 39.26E
36 G3 **Karakeçili** Turkey 39.36N 33.22E
35 J3 **Karak, El** Syria 32.41N 36.21E
19 E1 **Karakelong** *isld* Indonesia 4.21N 126.40E
43 G4 **Karaketken** Kazakhstan U.S.S.R. 45.14N 64.31E
42 D6 **Kara-Khol'** U.S.S.R. 51.17N 89.39E
24 D7 **Karaki** Xinjiang Uygur Zizhiqu China 37.01N 81.14E
37 G5 **Karakılise** Turkey 40.03N 42.27E
14 B9 **Karakin Ls** W Australia 31.06S 115.29E
Kara Kizil *see* **Yushugou**
37 F3 **Karakoca** Turkey 40.16N 28.34E
37 E7 **Karakoçan** Turkey 38.57N 40.02E
43 J4 **Karakoin, Ozero** *L* Kazakhstan U.S.S.R.
34 K1 **Karakök Dagh** *mt* Syria
43 M6 **Karakolka** Kirgiziya U.S.S.R. 41.31N 77.23E
43 G2 **Karakomarskoye Vdkhr** *res* Kazakhstan U.S.S.R.
43 M8 **Karakon** Tadzhikistan U.S.S.R. 40.32N 70.18E
Karaköprü *see* **Karaçoban**
31 J3 **Karakoram Pass** Kashmir 35.33N 77.51E
Karakoram Pass Kashmir/China*see* **Karakoram Shankou**
31 H2 **Karakoram Ra** Kashmir
89 D4 **Karakoro** *watercourse* Mauritania
22 F3 **Karakorum** *anc site* Mongolia 47.10N 102.50E
24 B8 **Karakorum Shankou** *pass* Xinjiang Uygur Zizhiqu China 35.33N 77.51E
37 F6 **Karaköy** Turkey 39.05N 41.45E
44 H5 **Karakoysu** *R* U.S.S.R.
42 K6 **Karaksar** U.S.S.R. 51.18N 116.00E
43 N2 **Karakuduk** Kazakhstan U.S.S.R. 51.16N 79.13E
43 K1 **Kara-Kuga** Kazakhstan U.S.S.R. 54.53N 70.53E
43 G7 **Karakul'** Bukhara, Uzbekistan U.S.S.R. 39.30N 63.52E
43 L6 **Kara-kul'** Kirgiziya U.S.S.R. 41.37N 72.40E
43 L7 **Karakul'** Tadzhikistan U.S.S.R. 39.06N 73.38E
37 E6 **Karakulak** Turkey 39.59N 40.01E
43 L6 **Kara-Kul'dzha** Kirgiziya U.S.S.R. 40.38N 73.31E
46 R2 **Karakulino** U.S.S.R. 56.05N 53.41E
43 L7 **Kara-Kul', Ozero** *L* Tadzhikistan U.S.S.R.
47 J8 **Karakul'skoye** U.S.S.R. 54.07N 62.25E
43 O3 **Karakul'tas** Kazakhstan U.S.S.R. 48.41N 80.51E
43 N4 **Karakum** Kazakhstan U.S.S.R. 46.48N 79.30E
43 C4 **Karakum, Peski** *sand des* Kazakhstan U.S.S.R.
43 G7 **Karakumskiy Kanal** Turkmeniya U.S.S.R.
43 E7 **Karakumy, Peski** *sand des* Turkmeniya U.S.S.R.
43 G8 **Karakumy, Yugo-Vostochnoye** *des* Turkmeniya U.S.S.R.
46 P8 **Karakureishi** U.S.S.R. 42.10N 47.40E
37 G5 **Karakurt** Turkey 40.11N 42.34E
94 E2 **Karakuwisa** Namibia 18.56S 19.40E
24 C7 **Karakux He** *R* Xinjiang Uygur Zizhiqu China
41 D8 **Karal'ka** *R* U.S.S.R.
42 K4 **Karalon** U.S.S.R. 57.03N 115.50E
14 C7 **Karalundi** W Australia 26.07S 118.41E
42 H4 **Karam** U.S.S.R. 55.12N 107.38E
35 F6 **Karama** Jordan 31.58N 35.34E
93 J5 **Karama** Kenya 0.15N 37.51E
19 A5 **Karama** *R* Celebes Indon
36 H3 **Karamağara** Turkey 39.42N 35.32E
Karamai *see* **Karamay**
36 G5 **Karaman** Turkey 37.11N 33.13E
36 D5 **Karamanlı** Turkey 37.22N 29.47E
44 J7 **Karamar'yan** Azerbaydzhan U.S.S.R. 40.35N 48.03E
24 E3 **Karamay** Xinjiang Uygur Zizhiqu China 45.48N 84.30E
43 M7 **Karamazor** Tadzhikistan U.S.S.R. 40.54N 69.52E
31 G2 **Karambar Pass** Pakistan 36.52N 73.44E
18 M7 **Karambu** Borneo Indon 3.52S 116.05E
11 G8 **Karamea** New Zealand 41.15S 172.07E
11 F8 **Karamea Bight** New Zealand
11 G8 **Karamea R** New Zealand
43 G7 **Karamet Niyaz** Turkmeniya U.S.S.R. 37.37N 64.32E
18 L8 **Karamian** *isld* Indonesia 5.05S 114.35E
36 E4 **Karamık Gölü** *L* Turkey
24 E7 **Karamiran He** *R* Xinjiang Uygur Zizhiqu China
24 F7 **Karamiran Shankou** Xinjiang Uygur Zizhiqu China 36.18N 87.09E
24 F7 **Karamiran Shankou** *pass* Xinjiang/Xizang China 36.16N 87.02E
39 E4 **Karamken** U.S.S.R. 60.10N 150.51E
84 C8 **Karammanóli** Greece 37.00N 21.45E
30 G7 **Karamnasa** *R* Bihar/Uttar Prad India
93 E2 **Karamoja** *dist* Uganda
Kara Muran Darya *R see* **Karamiran He**
Kara Muran Dawan *pass see* **Karamiran Shankou**
37 G2 **Karamürsel** Turkey 40.42N 29.37E
36 H5 **Karamusalı** Turkey 37.34N 35.47E
42 G3 **Karamysheva** U.S.S.R. 57.33N 100.55E
33 H3 **Karān** *isld* The Gulf 27.43N 49.50E
119 J6 **Karanambo** Guyana 3.46N 59.18W
32 B3 **Karand** Iran 34.16N 46.15E
36 H5 **Karanfil Dağı** *mt* Turkey
Karang *mt see* **Chamah, Gunong**
18 F7 **Karangagung** Sumatra Indon 2.17S 104.25E
93 H9 **Karangai** Tanzania 3.29S 36.53E
89 G5 **Karangana** Mali 12.15N 5.04W
30 K8 **Karangarh** Bihar India 24.37N 86.29E
11 D10 **Karangarua R** New Zealand
18 L10 **Karangasem** Bali Indonesia 8.24S 115.40E
18 H9 **Karangboto, Tanjung** *C* Java Indon 7.45S 109.25E
19 A7 **Karang Bril** *isld* Indonesia 6.05S 118.58E
18 G9 **Karang, Gunung** *mt* Java Indon 6.17S 106.02E
19 A4 **Karang, Tanjung** *C* Celebes Indon 0.37S 119.45E
32 C5 **Karanj** *oil well* Iran 30.37N 49.58E
29 E7 **Karanja** Maharashtra India 20.28N 77.32E
28 A1 **Karanja I** Maharashtra India 18.52N 72.45E
28 C2 **Karanja R** Karnataka India
29 G6 **Karanjia** Madhya Prad India 22.22N 80.50E
29 J7 **Karanjia** Orissa India 21.52N 85.59E
89 H6 **Karankasso** Upper Volta 10.51N 3.53W
36 H3 **Karanlık** *R* Turkey
24 H5 **Kara Nor** *L* Gansu China
29 C3 **Karanpur** Rajasthan India 29.47N 73.30E
30 F6 **Karanpur** Uttar Prad India 26.56N 82.31E
29 J6 **Karanpura** Bihar India 23.49N 85.12E
31 F3 **Karan R** Afghanistan
47 L5 **Karantraye** U.S.S.R. 55.36N 59.11E
84 S14 **Karaolas** Cyprus 35.08N 33.55E
36 C5 **Karaova** Turkey 37.07N 27.40E
43 H4 **Karaozek** Kazakhstan U.S.S.R. 45.02N 65.16E
31 D3 **Kara Pass** Afghanistan 35.26N 67.48E
91 J3 **Karapata** Zaïre 0.49N 25.10E
82 L7 **Karapelit** Bulgaria 43.40N 27.35E
37 C2 **Karapınar** Edirne Turkey 40.47N 26.39E
36 G5 **Karapınar** Konya Turkey 37.44N 33.34E
36 F1 **Karapınar** Zonguldak Turkey 41.28N 32.11E
11 K4 **Karapiro** New Zealand 37.54S 175.32E
11 K4 **Karapiro, L** New Zealand
93 G4 **Karapokot** *tribe* Kenya
30 E7 **Karari** Uttar Prad India 25.27N 81.25E
30 B7 **Kararkhera** Madhya Prad India 25.18N 78.13E
15 B5 **Karas** *isld* Irian Jaya 3.25S 132.40E
Kara Sai *see* **Karasay**
36 F2 **Karaşar** Turkey 40.20N 32.01E
43 N6 **Karasay** Kirgiziya U.S.S.R. 41.34N 77.59E
24 D7 **Karasay** Xinjiang Uygur Zizhiqu China 36.48N 83.49E
94 E6 **Karas Berg, Gt** *mts* Namibia
94 E6 **Karas Berg, Little** *mts* Namibia
94 E7 **Karasburg** Namibia 28.00S 18.43E
38 G1 **Kara Sea** U.S.S.R.
44 M7 **Karasengir, Mys** *C* Turkmeniya U.S.S.R. 40.43N 52.51E
29 E7 **Karasgaon** Maharashtra India 21.21N 77.40E
Kara Shahr *see* **Yanqi**
43 M2 **Karashoky** Kazakhstan U.S.S.R. 51.01N 75.02E
36 G3 **Karasinir Dağı** *mt* Turkey
41 E7 **Karasino** U.S.S.R. 66.53N 86.52E
51 M2 **Karasjok** Norway 69.27N 25.30E
51 L2 **Karasjokka** *R* Norway
43 M2 **Karasor** Kazakhstan U.S.S.R. 50.56N 75.45E
43 M3 **Karasor, Oz** *L* Karaganda, Kazakhstan U.S.S.R.
43 J1 **Karasor, Oz** *L* Kokchetav, Kazakhstan U.S.S.R. 54.20N 69.15E
43 M2 **Karasor, Oz** *L* Pavlodar, Kazakhstan U.S.S.R. 52.00N 75.45E
Karasu *see* **Hizan**
44 J7 **Karasu** Azerbaydzhan U.S.S.R. 40.10N 48.42E
43 P3 **Karasu** Kazakhstan U.S.S.R. 47.49N 83.24E
43 L6 **Kara Su** Kirgiziya U.S.S.R. 40.45N 73.00E
43 L1 **Karasu** Kokchetav, Kazakhstan U.S.S.R. 52.49N 73.46E
43 F2 **Karasu** Kustanay, Kazakhstan U.S.S.R. 51.22N 62.15E
43 H1 **Karasu** Kustanay, Kazakhstan U.S.S.R. 52.44N 65.29E
36 E1 **Karasu** Turkey 41.07N 30.37E
46 O8 **Kara Su** *R* Azerbaydzhan U.S.S.R.
36 J6 **Karasu** *R* Hatay Turkey
37 E1 **Karasu** *R* İstanbul Turkey
43 L1 **Karasu** *R* Kazakhstan U.S.S.R.
43 O7 **Karasu** *R* Kirgiziya U.S.S.R.
42 E6 **Kara-Sug** U.S.S.R. 51.21N 92.10E
43 N1 **Karasuk** U.S.S.R. 53.45N 78.01E
42 C5 **Karasuk** *R* U.S.S.R.
20 O5 **Karasuyama** Japan 36.39N 140.08E
47 K6 **Karas'ye, Oz** *L* U.S.S.R. 58.20N 67.50E
32 J3 **Karat** Iran 34.30N 60.34E
115 N3 **Karatá** Nicaragua 13.56N 83.30W
43 M4 **Karatal** *R* Kazakhstan U.S.S.R.
43 Q3 **Karatan** Kazakhstan U.S.S.R. 47.38N 85.10E
36 H6 **Karataş** Turkey 36.32N 35.22E
36 H6 **Karataş Burun** *C* Turkey 36.31N 35.18E
24 D8 **Kara Tash Davan** *pass* Xinjiang Uygur Zizhiqu China 35.49N 82.31E
43 K5 **Kara Tau** Kazakhstan U.S.S.R. 43.09N 70.28E
44 L3 **Karatau,Khrebet** *mts* Gur'yev, Kazakhstan U.S.S.R.
Karatchok *see* **Karakök Dagh** *mt*
36 J5 **Karatepe** *anc site* Turkey 37.22N 36.16E
25 E7 **Karathuri** Burma 10.58N 98.45E
93 J6 **Karatina** Kenya 0.29S 37.08E
Karativo I *see* **Karaitivu**
51 G5 **Karatjaure** *L* Sweden 66.44N 18.40E
43 C3 **Karatobe** Kazakhstan U.S.S.R. 49.44N 53.30E
43 F4 **Karatobe, Mys** *C* Kazakhstan U.S.S.R. 46.07N 60.00E
43 E3 **Karatogay** Kazakhstan U.S.S.R. 48.38N 59.41E
42 C7 **Karatogoy** Kazakhstan U.S.S.R. 48.25N 84.20E
43 C4 **Karaton** Kazakhstan U.S.S.R. 46.26N 53.32E
37 C7 **Karatoruk** Turkey 38.54N 37.20E
84 C6 **Karátoula** Greece 37.44N 21.32E
31 H8 **Karatoya** *R* Bangladesh
20 C8 **Karatsu** Japan 33.28N 129.58E
19 E1 **Karatung** *isld* Indonesia 4.44N 127.05E
24 F2 **Karatünggü** Xinjiang Uygur Zizhiqu China 46.50N 89.45E
43 H2 **Karaturgay** *R* Kazakhstan U.S.S.R.
42 E5 **Karatuzskoye** U.S.S.R. 53.35N 92.54E
43 D5 **Karatyuley, Sor** *mud flat* Kazakhstan U.S.S.R.
43 E4 **Karatyup, Poluostrov** *pen* Kazakhstan U.S.S.R.
Karau *see* **Parapap**
119 J6 **Karaudanawa** Guyana 2.27N 59.26W
Karaul *see* **Qongkol**
41 D5 **Karaul** Krasnoyarsk U.S.S.R. 70.08N 83.13E
47 J6 **Karaul** Sverdlovsk U.S.S.R. 59.04N 60.08E
43 G7 **Karaulbazar** Uzbekistan U.S.S.R. 39.31N 64.53E
30 A6 **Karauli** Rajasthan India 26.30N 77.00E
43 D3 **Karaulkel'dy** Kazakhstan U.S.S.R. 48.39N 55.53E
43 M6 **Karaultëbë** Kirgiziya U.S.S.R. 40.35N 75.55E
30 A3 **Karaunda** Uttar Prad India 29.22N 77.24E
30 G6 **Karaundi** Uttar Prad India 26.28N 83.55E
20 D10 **Karauni Nat. Park** Japan 31.57N 130.50E
43 O7 **Karaunkyur** *R* Kirgiziya U.S.S.R.
37 G5 **Karaurğan** Turkey 40.14N 42.14E
43 F5 **Karauzyak** Uzbekistan U.S.S.R. 43.00N 60.02E
84 C3 **Karáva** *mt* Greece 39.18N 21.34E
43 K6 **Karavan** Kirgiziya U.S.S.R. 41.29N 71.16E
43 O8 **Karavan** Kirgiziya U.S.S.R. 40.19N 72.11E
45 G7 **Karavan** Ukraine U.S.S.R. 49.35N 35.47E
84 R14 **Karavas** Cyprus 35.20N 33.12E
83 C4 **Karavastas, Kënet'e** *L* Albania
45 L1 **Karavayevo** U.S.S.R. 56.08N 39.30E
84 G8 **Karávi** *isld* Greece 36.45N 23.35E
84 Q14 **Karavostasi** Cyprus 35.08N 32.49E
43 M8 **Karavshin** *R* Kirgiziya U.S.S.R.
93 M8 **Karawa** Kenya 2.38S 40.11E
91 G2 **Karawa** Zaïre 3.14N 20.17E
18 G8 **Karawang Tanjung** *C* Java Indonesia 5.56S 107.00E
65 J8 **Karawanken** *mts* Austria
15 G6 **Karawari** *R* Papua New Guinea
15 C6 **Karaweira** / Moluccas Indonesia 5.59S 134.52E
36 J2 **Karayaka** Turkey 40.50N 36.42E
37 G6 **Karayazı** Turkey 39.41N 42.09E
Kara Yulghun *see* **Karayulgun**
24 C5 **Karayulgun** Xinjiang Uygur Zizhiqu China 41.24N 80.50E
Karayün *see* **Mamuga**
43 K4 **Karazhal** Kazakhstan U.S.S.R. 48.00N 70.55E
43 L4 **Karazhingil** Kazakhstan U.S.S.R. 46.50N 73.28E
34 M6 **Karbalā'** Iraq 32.37N 44.03E
64 F3 **Karben** W Germany 50.13N 8.52E
30 D6 **Karbigwan** Uttar Prad India 26.13N 80.28E
30 L8 **Karbindha** Bihar India 24.26N 87.19E
52 J5 **Kårböle** Sweden 61.59N 15.20E
94 P12 **Karbonkelberg** *mt* Cape Town S Africa 34.02S 18.19E
63 Q6 **Karbow-Vietlübbe** E Germany 53.25N 12.07E
Karbush, Kuh-i *see* **Garbosh, Kūh-e** *mt*
53 B3 **Karby** Denmark 56.46N 8.34E
63 L3 **Karby** W Germany 54.37N 9.58E
62 M8 **Karcag** Hungary 47.19N 20.53E
30 E7 **Karchana** Uttar Prad India 25.17N 81.55E
24 G10 **Karchen La** *pass* Xizang Zizhiqu China 31.12N 91.50E
39 H2 **Karchyk, Poluostrov** *pen* U.S.S.R.
53 W17 **Kårdal** Norway 60.45N 7.06E
30 E2 **Kardam** Xizang Zizhiqu 30.26N 81.04E
65 L3 **Kardašova Řečice** Czechoslovakia 49.12N 14.50E
84 B6 **Kardhamás** Greece 37.45N 21.20E
83 H6 **Kardhámila** Greece 38.33N 26.04E
36 B4 **Kardhámila** Khíos Greece 38.34N 26.05E
84 D8 **Kardhamíli** Greece 36.53N 22.14E
84 C3 **Kardhítsa** Greece 39.22N 21.55E
84 C3 **Kardhítsa** *prov* Greece
84 C3 **Kardhitsomagoúla** Greece 39.24N 21.55E
51 K5 **Kardis** Sweden 66.58N 23.45E
46 E1 **Kärdla** Estonia U.S.S.R. 59.00N 22.42E
45 D2 **Kardymovo** U.S.S.R. 54.54N 32.25E
44 F4 **Kardzhiy** U.S.S.R. 43.16N 44.21E
90 H7 **Karé** Chad 8.09N 17.50E
95 K4 **Karee** S Africa 28.52S 26.22E
95 F6 **Kareeberge** *mts* S Africa
95 H9 **Kareedouw** S Africa 33.58S 24.17E
95 G5 **Kareekloof** S Africa 29.49S 23.24E
95 D9 **Kareevlakte** S Africa 33.35S 20.37E
30 K7 **Kareha** *R* Bihar India
50 Q11 **Kåre, Kapp** *C* Spitsbergen 74.23N 18.58E
44 F5 **Kareli** Georgia U.S.S.R. 42.01N 43.52E
46 M3 **Kareli** U.S.S.R. 53.30N 41.50E
Karelia, A.S.S.R *see* **Karel'skaya A.S.S.R**
38 C2 **Karel'skaya A.S.S.R** U.S.S.R.
47 C4 **Karel'skaya Masel'ga** U.S.S.R. 63.10N 33.51E
92 E5 **Karema** Tanzania 6.50S 30.25E
28 G6 **Karen** Andaman Is 12.50N 92.52E
25 D3 **Karen** *state* Burma
Karend *see* **Karand**
42 K5 **Karenga** *R* U.S.S.R.
47 H5 **Karepino** U.S.S.R. 61.05N 57.08E
30 B7 **Karera** Madhya Prad India 25.27N 78.09E
51 K3 **Karesuando** Sweden 68.27N 22.30E
88 J10 **Karet** Mauritania 23.45N 8.05W
88 J10 **Karet** *reg* Mauritania
39 G1 **Karetovo** U.S.S.R. 68.48N 161.10E
32 J7 **Kārevāndar** Iran 27.50N 60.45E
11 L4 **Karewa I** New Zealand 37.30S 176.09E
31 A4 **Karez Dasht** Afghanistan 33.17N 61.30E
31 C5 **Karez-i-Ata** Afghanistan 31.30N 65.10E
Karfa *see* **Qarfah**
43 D2 **Kargala** U.S.S.R. 51.59N 55.14E
44 G4 **Kargalinskaya** U.S.S.R. 43.43N 46.30E
43 L3 **Kargaly** Kazakhstan U.S.S.R. 48.18N 74.18E
39 K2 **Karganay** U.S.S.R. 65.20N 175.07E
24 D10 **Kargan La** *pass* Xizang Zizhiqu 30.15N 82.24E
32 C2 **Karganrūd** Iran 37.48N 49.01E
37 F5 **Kargapazarı Dağı** *mt* Turkey 40.11N 41.33E
47 J7 **Kargapol'ye** U.S.S.R. 56.00N 64.21E
36 G3 **Kargasekmez Dağ** *mt* Turkey 39.12N 34.01E
42 C3 **Kargasok** U.S.S.R. 59.07N 80.58E
42 C4 **Kargat** U.S.S.R. 55.11N 80.16E
42 C4 **Kargat** *R* U.S.S.R.
89 K6 **Kargatenga** Upper Volta 11.13N 0.02E
Karghalik *see* **Yecheng**
93 J3 **Kargi** Kenya 2.30N 37.35E
36 H1 **Kargı** Turkey 41.09N 34.32E
40 H6 **Kargi** U.S.S.R. 51.13N 138.52E
31 J4 **Kargia** Kashmir 33.00N 77.17E
31 J3 **Kargil** Kashmir 34.31N 76.13E
Kargilik *see* **Yecheng**
45 N7 **Karginskaya** U.S.S.R. 49.22N 41.40E
Kargiz, Kuh-i- *see* **Karkas, Kūh-e** *mts*
41 G5 **Kargo** U.S.S.R. 71.06N 98.20E
47 D5 **Kargopol'** U.S.S.R. 61.32N 38.59E
63 R5 **Kargow** E Germany 53.31N 12.47E
62 J3 **Kargowa** Poland 52.04N 15.53E
95 N6 **Karg's Post** S Africa 30.30S 29.29E
30 B6 **Karhal** Uttar Prad India 27.00N 78.56E
29 K5 **Karharbari** Bihar India 24.10N 86.18E
101 G8 **Karheen** Alaska 55.45N 133.20W
51 M11 **Karhula** Finland 60.29N 26.58E
84 D2 **Kariá** Greece 39.59N 22.23E
84 D5 **Kariá** Greece 38.01N 22.25E
84 E6 **Kariá** Greece 37.38N 22.32E
84 D7 **Kariaí** Greece 37.18N 22.30E
95 C7 **Karianga** Madagascar 22.25S 47.22E
92 D10 **Kariba** Zimbabwe 16.32S 28.50E
92 D10 **Kariba** *dist* Zimbabwe
92 D10 **Kariba Dam** Zimbabwe/Zambia 16.31S 28.50E
92 D10 **Kariba, Lake** Zimbabwe/Zambia
20 J2 **Kariba-yama** *mt* Japan 42.36N 139.56E
94 C3 **Karibib** Namibia 21.59S 15.51E
95 J9 **Kariega** S Africa 33.26S 25.15E
95 K9 **Kariega** S Africa 33.40S 26.41E
95 G8 **Kariega** *R* S Africa
84 D3 **Kariés** Greece 39.05N 22.25E
33 H8 **Karif Salāsil** S Yemen 16.34N 48.52E
51 M2 **Karigasniemi** Finland 69.22N 25.47E
30 K8 **Karihari** Bihar India 24.27N 86.02E
51 J9 **Karijoki** Finland 62.17N 21.40E
20 H3 **Karikachi Pass** Japan 43.10N 142.45E
20 M1 **Karikachi-tōge** *pass* Hokkaido Japan 43.08N 142.47E
28 D5 **Karikal** Tamil Nadu India 10.58N 79.50E
11 H1 **Karikari, C** New Zealand 33.47S 173.27E
90 E7 **Karim** Nigeria 9.20N 11.14E
87 C1 **Karima** Sudan 18.32N 31.48E
Karimabad *see* **Hunza**
32 F4 **Karīmābād** Esfahān Iran 32.07N 54.14E
32 G5 **Karīmābād** Kermān Iran 30.31N 56.50E
18 H6 **Karimata** *isld* Indonesia
18 H6 **Karimata, Pulau Pulau** *islds* Indonesia
18 H7 **Karimata, Selat** *str* Indonesia
28 J3 **Karimganj** Assam India 24.52N 92.20E
32 D3 **Karim Khaneh** Iran 35.02N 51.50E
28 D1 **Karimnagar** Andhra Prad India 18.27N 79.06E
28 D1 **Karimnagar** *dist* Andhra Prad India
15 H7 **Karimui** Papua New Guinea 6.19S 144.48E
18 E5 **Karimun** *isld* Indonesia
18 J8 **Karimunjawa** *isld* Indonesia 5.52S 110.27E
18 J8 **Karimunjawa, Pulau Pulau** *islds* Indonesia
87 K5 **Karin** Somalia 10.50N 45.47E
36 C5 **Karıncalı Dağı** *mt* Turkey
36 D4 **Karınca Tepesi** *mt* Turkey 38.28N 28.43E
84 C8 **Kariofóra** Greece 37.00N 21.55E
11 K6 **Karioi** New Zealand 39.28S 175.32E
11 J4 **Karioi** *mt* New Zealand 37.52S 174.50E
51 K11 **Karis** Finland 60.05N 23.45E
53 J6 **Karise** Denmark 55.19N 12.13E
93 A7 **Karisimbi, Mt** Rwanda/Zaïre 1.32S 29.27E
84 H5 **Káristos** Greece 38.01N 24.25E
32 G4 **Karit** Iran 33.23N 57.10E
93 F4 **Karita** Uganda 1.34N 34.52E
84 D7 **Karítaina** Greece 37.29N 22.02E
11 E12 **Karitane** New Zealand 45.39S 170.40E
15 G7 **Karius Ra** Papua New Guinea
20 K7 **Kariya** Japan 35.00N 137.00E
92 C10 **Kariyangwe** Zimbabwe 18.00S 27.38E
31 B3 **Kariz** Afghanistan 34.02N 62.15E
32 J3 **Kārīz** Iran 34.50N 60.49E
31 A4 **Karizak** Afghanistan 32.21N 61.30E
Karjaa *see* **Karis**
28 B1 **Karjat** Ahmadnagar, Maharashtra India 18.34N 75.04E
28 A1 **Karjat** Konkan, Maharashtra India 18.54N 73.23E
87 F2 **Karkabat** Ethiopia 16.20N 37.25E
29 K6 **Karkai** *R* Bihar/Orissa India
28 B4 **Karkal** Karnataka India 13.13N 74.55E
37 G4 **Karkal Dağı** *mt* Turkey 41.26N 42.02E
28 B2 **Karkamb** Maharashtra India 17.51N 75.21E
Karkamıs *see* **Barak** Turkey
15 H6 **Karkar** Papua New Guinea 4.32S 145.58E
43 M3 **Karkaralinsk** Kazakhstan U.S.S.R. 49.21N 75.27E
44 H8 **Karkarchay** *R* Azerbaydzhan U.S.S.R.
15 J6 **Karkar I** Papua New Guinea 4.40S 146.00E
34 P4 **Karkasār** Iran 34.35N 47.29E
32 D4 **Karkas, Kūh-e** *mts* Iran
31 D7 **Karkh** Pakistan 27.42N 67.10E
29 G7 **Karkhara R** Madhya Prad India
32 C5 **Karkheh** *R* Iran
32 H8 **Kārkin Dar** *mt* Iran 25.50N 58.50E
44 B9 **Karkinitskiy Zaliv** *gulf* Ukraine U.S.S.R.
51 L11 **Karkkila** Finland 60.32N 24.10E
51 L11 **Kärkölä** Finland 60.56N 25.15E
86 N5 **Karkom** *watercourse* Israel
32 D4 **Kar-Konān** Iran 32.27N 50.09E
33 B4 **Karkūmā, Ra's** *C* Saudi Arabia 25.47N 36.37E
35 C4 **Karkur** Israel 32.29N 34.59E
41 O2 **Karla-Aleksandra, Ostrov** *isld* Franz Josef Land U.S.S.R.
31 F4 **Karlachi** Pakistan 33.47N 70.02E
45 G5 **Karla Libknekhta** U.S.S.R. 51.38N 35.30E
31 G2 **Karla Marksa** U.S.S.R. 37.12N 72.35E
43 K8 **Karla Marksa, Pik** *mt* Tadzhikistan U.S.S.R. 37.12N 72.25E
53 F4 **Karlby** Denmark 56.29N 10.53E
51 O1 **Karlebotn** Norway 70.07N 28.35E
53 J7 **Karleby** Denmark 54.47N 12.02E
50 M4 **Karlfell** *mt* Iceland 65.25N 13.57W
29 H6 **Karlidi** Madhya Prad India 23.57N 83.20E
37 G2 **Karlık Dağı** *mt* Turkey
37 C2 **Karlıköy** Turkey 40.46N 25.32E
24 H4 **Karlik Shan** *mt* Xinjiang Uygur Zizhiqu China
Karlik Tagh *ra see* **Karlik Shan**
36 J5 **Karlık Tepesi** *mt* Turkey 37.26N 36.33E
62 J1 **Karlino** Poland 54.02N 15.52E
37 F6 **Karlıova** Turkey 39.17N 41.02E
64 O2 **Karl-Marx-Stadt** E Germany 50.50N 12.55E
64 O2 **Karl-Marx-Stadt** *reg* E Germany
Karlnock *see* **Königstuhl**
82 C6 **Karlobag** Yugoslavia 44.32N 15.05E
82 C5 **Karlovac** Yugoslavia 45.30N 15.34E
45 G7 **Karlovka** Ukraine U.S.S.R. 49.28N 35.09E
82 J8 **Karlovo** Bulgaria 42.38N 24.49E
64 O3 **Karlovy Vary** Czechoslovakia 50.13N 12.52E
52 L3 **Karlsbäck** Sweden 63.51N 18.50E
64 E6 **Karlsbad** W Germany 48.55N 8.30E
52 H8 **Karlsborg** Sweden 58.32N 14.32E
41 D1 **Karlsena, Mys** *C* Novaya Zemlya U.S.S.R. 77.01N 67.30E
64 L7 **Karlsfeld** W Germany 48.12N 11.29E
63 K9 **Karlshafen** W Germany 51.38N 9.26E
52 H10 **Karlshamn** Sweden 56.10N 14.50E
52 H7 **Karlskoga** Sweden 59.19N 14.33E
52 J10 **Karlskrona** Sweden 56.10N 15.35E
53 J5 **Karlslune Strand** Denmark 55.34N 12.14E
51 H1 **Karlsøy** Norway 70.02N 19.50E
108 K1 **Karlsruhe** N Dakota 48.07N 100.38W
64 E5 **Karlsruhe** W Germany 49.00N 8.24E
108 O1 **Karlstad** Minnesota 48.35N 96.31W
52 G7 **Karlstad** Sweden 59.24N 13.32E
64 H4 **Karlstadt** W Germany 49.58N 9.47E
65 M4 **Karlstein** Austria 48.53N 15.25E
65 K2 **Karlštejn** Czechoslovakia 49.57N 14.12E
113 K8 **Karluk** Alaska 57.33N 154.32W
42 H5 **Karluk** U.S.S.R. 53.30N 105.58E
113 K8 **Karluk L** Alaska 57.20N 154.05W
50 V12 **Karl XII Øyane** Spitsbergen 80.32N 25.00E
43 H7 **Karlyuk** Turkmeniya U.S.S.R. 37.34N 66.16E
43 J7 **Karlyuk** Uzbekistan U.S.S.R. 38.10N 67.43E
89 K5 **Karma** Niger 13.38N 1.52E
30 L2 **Karma Changri** *mt* Xizang Zizhiqu 28.03N 87.06E
33 K10 **Karma, Ghubbat** *B* Socotra Ind Oc
28 B1 **Karmala** Maharashtra India 18.25N 75.15E
46 Q5 **Karmanovka** Kazakhstan U.S.S.R. 49.20N 50.20E
45 F1 **Karmanovo** U.S.S.R. 55.49N 34.51E
43 D1 **Karmaskaly** Bashkir U.S.S.R. 54.22N 56.08E
29 K1 **Karmatam** Bihar India 24.05N 86.44E
35 C2 **Karmel, C** Israel 32.50N 34.57E
35 E2 **Karmi'el** Israel 32.55N 35.18E
35 B7 **Karmiyya** Israel 31.37N 34.33E
24 D9 **Karmo Tso** *L* Xizang Zizhiqu China 32.03N 82.03E
53 S20 **Karmøy** *isld* Norway 59.15N 5.15E
31 G6 **Karmpur** Pakistan 29.55N 72.22E
53 S20 **Karmsund** *sound* Norway 59.15N 5.21E
31 C1 **Karnab** Uzbekistan U.S.S.R. 39.46N 65.31E
43 H7 **Karnabchul', Step'** Uzbekistan U.S.S.R.
112 N3 **Karnack** Texas 32.40N 94.12W
31 J10 **Karnafuli R** Bangladesh
31 J9 **Karnafuli Res** Bangladesh
107 H4 **Karnak** Illinois 37.18N 88.59W
85 M7 **Karnak, El** Egypt 25.44N 32.39E
30 A3 **Karnal** Haryana India 29.41N 76.58E
29 E3 **Karnal** *dist* Haryana India
31 E4 **Karnala Pass** Afghanistan 33.54N 68.09E
30 E3 **Karnali** *R* Nepal
30 C2 **Karnaprayag** Uttar Prad India 30.15N 79.13E
28 B3 **Karnataka** *state* India
112 K7 **Karnes City** Texas 28.54N 97.55W
65 G8 **Karnische Alpen** *mts* Austria/Italy
82 K8 **Karnobat** Bulgaria 42.39N 26.59E
90 L4 **Karnoï** Sudan 15.00N 23.17E
52 F8 **Kärnsjön** *L* Sweden 58.35N 11.38E
65 H8 **Kärnten** *prov* Austria
31 C7 **Karodi** Pakistan 27.58N 65.52E
92 D10 **Karoi** Zimbabwe 16.46S 29.45E
9 T5 **Karoko** Vanua Levu Fiji 16.30S 179.56E
25 D5 **Karokpi** Burma 15.52N 97.45E
28 H1 **Karo La** *pass* Xizang Zizhiqu 28.53N 90.09E
29 A2 **Karol Bagh** *dist* Delhi India
12 E4 **Karolta** S Australia 32.23S 139.58E
19 B7 **Karompa** *isld* Indonesia 7.18S 121.46E
30 B8 **Karonda** Madhya Prad India 24.20N 78.16E
28 K3 **Karong** Manipur India 25.18N 94.05E
92 F6 **Karonga** Malawi 9.54S 33.55E
24 E10 **Karong Tso** *L* Xizang Zizhiqu China 31.00N 84.50E
14 D9 **Karonie** W Australia 30.59S 122.39E
92 D3 **Karonje Mt** Rwanda 2.10S 29.20E
12 E6 **Karoonda** S Australia 35.09S 139.54E
31 F5 **Karor** Pakistan 31.15N 70.59E
87 G2 **Karora** Sudan 17.45N 38.20E
11 C6 **Karori** *dist* Wellington New Zealand
11 B6 **Karori R** New Zealand
11 B6 **Karori Rock** *isld* New Zealand 41.21S 174.39E
83 H8 **Káros** *isld* Greece 36.54N 25.40E
19 A4 **Karossa** Celebes Indon 1.46S 119.21E
19 A8 **Karossa, Tanjung** *C* Indonesia 9.35S 118.57E
89 K4 **Karou** Mali 15.09N 0.45E
90 K5 **Karoub** Chad 12.34N 21.33E
89 F4 **Karounga** Mali 15.19N 7.35W
84 W22 **Karousádhes** Corfu 39.47N 19.45E
63 Q8 **Karow** Magdeburg E Germany 52.22N 12.17E
63 Q5 **Karow** Schwerin E Germany 53.33N 12.17E
43 L4 **Karoy** Kazakhstan U.S.S.R. 45.50N 74.46E
46 F5 **Karpach** Moldavia U.S.S.R. 48.00N 27.10E
84 T14 **Karpas Pen** Cyprus
83 J9 **Kárpathos** *isld* Greece
84 C4 **Karpenísion** Greece 38.55N 21.47E
84 C2 **Karperón** Greece 39.57N 21.38E
87 C8 **Karpeto** Sudan 4.10N 31.41E
93 C1 **Karpeto** Sudan 4.07N 31.41E
66 N4 **Kärpf** *mt* Switzerland 45.56N 9.05E
64 P7 **Karpfham** W Germany 48.25N 13.14E
30 H7 **Karpi** Bihar India 25.10N 84.43E
46 G6 **Karpineny** Moldavia U.S.S.R. 46.46N 28.18E
47 H6 **Karpinsk** U.S.S.R. 59.48N 59.59E
47 E4 **Karpogory** U.S.S.R. 64.01N 44.30E
84 D3 **Karpokhóri** Greece 39.20N 22.00E
30 K2 **Karpo La** *pass* Xizang Zizhiqu 28.02N 87.02E
39 J1 **Karpung, Gora** *mt* U.S.S.R. 68.44N 172.39E
47 J6 **Karpuninskiy** U.S.S.R. 58.42N 61.49E
47 M4 **Karpushikha** U.S.S.R. 57.32N 59.58E
36 C5 **Karpuzlu** Aydın Turkey 37.33N 27.48E
37 C2 **Karpuzlu** Edirne Turkey 40.51N 26.18E
14 B9 **Karragullen** W Australia 32.05S 116.03E
14 A1 **Karrakatta** *dist* Perth, W Aust
97 O3 **Karrats Fd** Greenland
53 H6 **Karrebæk** Denmark 55.12N 11.40E
53 H6 **Karrebæksminde** Denmark 55.11N 11.39E
53 H6 **Karrebæksminde Bugt** *B* Denmark 55.10N 11.38E
94 F8 **Karree Berge** *mts* S Africa
14 B10 **Karridale** W Australia 34.12S 115.04E
31 B3 **Karrukh** Afghanistan 34.30N 62.36E
43 F7 **Karrychirla** Turkmeniya U.S.S.R. 37.37N 60.07E
37 G5 **Kars** Turkey 40.35N 43.05E
37 G5 **Kars** *R* Turkey
87 G8 **Karsa Dek** Ethiopia 5.13N 39.52E
30 A6 **Karsado** Rajasthan India 26.50N 77.04E
93 K3 **Karsa Gudas** Kenya 2.06N 38.02E
43 H3 **Karsakpay** Kazakhstan U.S.S.R. 47.47N 66.43E
Karsakuwigamak L *see* **Rutten L**
51 M8 **Kärsämäki** Finland 63.58N 25.50E
31 C4 **Karsang** Afghanistan 32.07N 64.21E
36 H5 **Karsantı** Turkey 37.33N 35.22E
46 G2 **Kārsava** Latvia U.S.S.R. 56.45N 27.40E
34 N7 **Kār, Shatt al** *watercourse* Iraq
43 C6 **Karshi** Turkmeniya U.S.S.R. 40.45N 52.54E
43 H7 **Karshi** Uzbekistan U.S.S.R. 38.53N 65.45E
43 G7 **Karshinskaya Step'** Uzbekistan U.S.S.R.
47 H1 **Karskiye Vorota, Proliv** *str* U.S.S.R.
41 C3 **Karskoye More** *sea* U.S.S.R.
30 A1 **Karsog** Himachal Prad India 31.23N 77.12E
63 P6 **Karstädt** E Germany 53.09N 11.45E
53 T20 **Kårstø** Norway 59.17N 5.33E
53 B5 **Karstoft** Denmark 55.57N 8.58E
51 L9 **Karstula** Finland 62.53N 24.50E
45 S2 **Karsun** U.S.S.R. 54.11N 46.58E
52 J5 **Karsvall** Sweden 61.50N 15.10E
28 J1 **Karta** Xizang Zizhiqu 28.04N 92.27E
34 C4 **Kartaba** Lebanon 34.07N 35.50E
30 K1 **Karta Changri** *mt* Xizang Zizhiqu 28.07N 87.00E
37 G2 **Kartal** Turkey 40.54N 29.12E
30 D7 **Kartal** Uttar Prad India 25.02N 80.20E
82 J9 **Kartál** *mt* Bulgaria 41.13N 25.19E
37 E8 **Kartalcircibi** *watercourse* Turkey
37 D7 **Kartal Tepesi** *mt* Turkey 38.14N 37.45E
43 F1 **Kartaly** U.S.S.R. 53.06N 60.37E
29 D2 **Kartarpur** Punjab India 31.28N 75.33E
87 H4 **Kartati** Ethiopia 12.05N 41.34E
47 G4 **Kartayël'** U.S.S.R. 64.30N 53.19E
36 G1 **Kart Dağ** *mt* Turkey 41.46N 33.19E
84 C7 **Karteróli** Greece 37.05N 21.59E
104 G5 **Karthaus** Pennsylvania 41.08N 78.07W
64 B4 **Karthaus** W Germany 49.43N 6.37E
65 G8 **Kartitsch** Austria 46.44N 12.31E
31 J3 **Kartse** Kashmir 34.18N 76.04E
51 N9 **Karttula** Finland 62.54N 27.05E
40 F9 **Kartun** U.S.S.R. 45.55N 134.55E
119 J4 **Kartuni** Guyana 6.38N 59.54W
62 L1 **Kartuzy** Poland 54.21N 18.11E
30 B6 **Karu** *R* Madhya Prad India
94 C4 **Karub** Namibia 22.10S 15.10E
92 D9 **Karubwe** Zambia 15.09S 28.23E
37 D8 **Karuç** *R* Turkey
15 B5 **Karufa** Irian Jaya 3.50S 133.25E
20 M5 **Karuizawa** Japan 36.22N 138.37E
14 F9 **Karulbie** W Australia 31.49S 126.30E
93 D3 **Karuma Falls** Uganda 2.15N 32.15E
21 J7 **Karumai** Japan 40.16N 141.30E
13 F3 **Karumba** Queensland 17.25S 140.50E
29 A6 **Karumbhar I** Gujarat India 22.27N 69.40E
93 D8 **Karumo** Tanzania 2.31S 32.49E
93 D9 **Karumwa** Tanzania 3.12S 32.38E
32 C5 **Kārūn** *R* Iran
28 C6 **Karunagapalli** Kerala India 9.03N 76.33E
51 K5 **Karungi** Sweden 66.03N 23.55E
93 F6 **Karungu** Kenya 0.49S 34.10E
19 A8 **Karuni** Indonesia 9.25S 119.15E
14 G3 **Karunjie** W Australia 16.12S 127.12E
Karunki *see* **Kukkola**
32 D5 **Kārūn, Kūh-e** *mt* Iran 31.29N 50.16E
90 A7 **Karunzi** Nigeria 9.54N 3.40E
53 C4 **Karup** Denmark 56.19N 9.10E
53 B4 **Karup Å** *R* Denmark
28 D5 **Karur** Tamil Nadu India 10.58N 78.03E
26 Q5 **Karuwalagaswewa** Sri Lanka 8.03N 79.59E
93 B9 **Karuzi** Burundi 3.04S 30.09E
109 G3 **Karval** Colorado 38.44N 103.33W
84 D8 **Karvelá** Greece 36.44N 22.28E
28 D4 **Karvetnagar** Andhra Prad India 13.27N 79.25E
51 K9 **Karvia** Finland 62.08N 22.35E
51 G2 **Kårvik** Norway 69.53N 19.00E
62 L6 **Karviná** Czechoslovakia 49.50N 18.30E
Karwanda *see* **Kārevāndar**
31 B4 **Karwangah** Afghanistan 33.42N 62.21E
28 B3 **Karwar** Karnataka India 14.50N 74.09E
65 D7 **Karwendel Gebirge** *mts* Austria
30 D7 **Karwi** Uttar Prad India 25.13N 80.54E
Karyagino *see* **Fizuli**
47 K5 **Karym** U.S.S.R. 60.03N 66.40E
39 F7 **Karymskaya Sopka** *vol* U.S.S.R. 54.05N 159.22E
42 J6 **Karymskoye** Chita U.S.S.R. 51.40N 114.20E
42 G5 **Karymskoye** Irkutsk U.S.S.R. 54.08N 101.50E
43 C6 **Karynzharyk, Peski** *sand des* Kazakhstan U.S.S.R.
33 B8 **Karzakkān** Bahrain, The Gulf 26.07N 50.30E
31 K4 **Karzok** Kashmir 32.59N 78.16E
53 D2 **Kås** Denmark 57.12N 9.42E
90 M5 **Kas** Sudan 12.30N 24.18E
36 D6 **Kaş** Turkey 36.12N 29.38E
42 D3 **Kas** *R* U.S.S.R.
29 C8 **Kasa** Maharashtra India 19.56N 73.02E
92 E4 **Kasaba** Tanzania 5.17S 30.25E
Kasaba Turkey*see* **Turgutlu**
92 E6 **Kasaba Bay** Zambia 8.32S 30.42E
92 G8 **Kasache** Malawi 13.25S 34.16E
20 F2 **Kasai** *dist* Tōkyō Japan
91 G8 **Kasai** *R* Angola/Zaïre
91 G6 **Kasai Occidental** *prov* Zaïre
92 A3 **Kasai Oriental** *prov* Zaïre
91 H9 **Kasaji** Zaïre 10.22S 23.29E
20 O5 **Kasama** Japan 36.24N 140.16E
92 E7 **Kasama** Zambia 10.10S 31.11E
93 C5 **Kasambia** Uganda 0.16N 31.21E
91 K5 **Kasambule** Zaïre 3.20S 26.10E
87 E3 **Kasamor,Jeb** *mt* Sudan 14.38N 35.24E
93 D8 **Kasamwa** Tanzania 2.51S 32.28E
93 B9 **Kasana** Tanzania 3.38S 30.27E
92 E3 **Kasanda** Tanzania 3.30S 30.51E
93 C5 **Kasanda** Uganda 0.32N 31.49E
21 D7 **Kasandonggu** N Korea 41.20N 126.50E
94 H1 **Kasane** Botswana 17.50S 25.05E
92 E6 **Kasanga** Tanzania 8.27S 31.10E
92 A6 **Kasangeshi** *R* Zaïre
87 D8 **Kasangor** *mt* Sudan 5.50N 33.59E
91 D6 **Kasangulu** Zaïre 4.33S 15.12E
92 E8 **Kasanka Nat. Park** Zambia
43 K6 **Kasansay** Uzbekistan U.S.S.R. 41.14N 71.31E
20 G7 **Kasaoka** Japan 34.31N 133.30E
28 B4 **Kasaragod** Kerala India 12.30N 74.59E
33 C7 **Kasar, Ras** *C* Sudan 18.02N 38.33E
40 L9 **Kasatka** Kuril Is U.S.S.R. 44.58N 147.46E
40 E7 **Kasatkino** U.S.S.R. 48.59N 130.05E
30 A2 **Kasauli** Himachal Prad India 30.54N 76.57E
31 J9 **Kasba** Bangladesh 23.42N 91.08E

30 L7 Kasba Bihar India 25.51N 87.32E
101 W5 Kasba, L N W Terr
88 K5 Kasba Tadla Morocco 32.34N 6.18W
65 K6 Kasberg mt Austria 47.48N 14.01E
43 H7 Kas'bi Uzbekistan U.S.S.R. 38.58N 65.23E
53 B3 Kås Bredning B Denmark 56.40N 8.42E
88 N5 Kasdir, El Algeria 33.44N 1.20W
52 H11 Kåseberga Sweden 55.23N 14.05E
20 D10 Kaseda Japan 31.25N 130.17E
113 F2 Kasegaluk L Alaska
32 B3 Kaseh Garan Iran 34.07N 46.02E
65 J3 Kasejovice Czechoslovakia 49.29N 13.45E
92 B8 Kasempa Zambia 13.28S 25.48E
64 L3 Kasendorf W Germany 50.02N 11.22E
91 J7 Kasenga Zaïre 6.20S 25.42E
92 D7 Kasenga Zaïre 10.22S 28.45E
92 C7 Kasengo Zaïre 11.22S 27.56E
93 B4 Kasenye Zaïre 1.23N 30.25E
93 B5 Kasese Uganda 0.10N 30.06E
91 K4 Kasese Zaïre 1.34S 27.14E
30 B5 Kasganj Uttar Prad India 27.48N 78.38E
Kash R see Kax He
93 M6 Kasha Kenya 0.49S 40.58E
100 M2 Kashabowie Ontario 48.40N 90.26W
32 J2 Kashaf R Iran
32 D4 Kāshān Iran 33.59N 51.35E
32 D4 Kāshān reg Iran
87 E5 Kashangaro,Jeb Sudan/Ethiopia 10.56N 34.35E
45 N7 Kashary U.S.S.R. 49.03N 41.00E
113 D10 Kashega Aleutian Is 53.31N 167.08W
113 J6 Kashegelok Alaska 60.50N 157.52W
Kashgar see Kashi
Kashgar R see Kaxgar He
43 O8 Kashgarkishlak Kirgiziya U.S.S.R. 40.39N 72.50E
Kashgar Yangi Shahr see Shule
24 B6 Kashi Xinjiang Uygur Zizhiqu China 39.29N 76.02E
20 J7 Kashihara Japan 34.28N 135.46E
20 D8 Kashima Japan 33.09N 130.08E
20 O4 Kashima Japan 37.42N 140.58E
21 H10 Kashima Japan 35.58N 140.42E
91 K9 Kashimbo Zaïre 11.11S 26.22E
46 L2 Kashin U.S.S.R. 57.22N 37.39E
45 U2 Kashinka U.S.S.R. 54.36N 48.09E
47 M5 Kashino U.S.S.R. 56.44N 60.52E
20 C5 Kashio Kanaga Japan
29 H8 Kashipur Orissa India 19.22N 83.11E
30 B3 Kashipur Uttar Prad India 29.13N 78.58E
29 K2 Kashipur W Bengal India 23.26N 86.41E
45 K2 Kashira U.S.S.R. 54.52N 38.13E
100 N1 Kashishibog L Ontario
Kashit see Keshīt
92 D8 Kashitu Zambia 13.45S 28.40E
20 B4 Kashiwagaya Kanagawa Japan
20 M4 Kashiwazaki Japan 37.22N 138.33E
47 M4 Kashka U.S.S.R. 57.38N 58.54E
43 H7 Kashkadar'inskaya Oblast' prov Uzbekistan U.S.S.R.
43 H7 Kashkadar'ya R Uzbekistan U.S.S.R.
32 B4 Kashkān R Iran
47 C5 Kashkany U.S.S.R. 61.20N 33.39E
47 D3 Kashkarantsy U.S.S.R. 66.25N 35.45E
43 M6 Kashkasu Kirgiziya U.S.S.R. 41.41N 76.15E
43 L4 Kashken Teniz Kazakhstan U.S.S.R. 45.46N 73.20E
86 L5 Kashkûl, El reg Egypt
41 D7 Kash-Ky R U.S.S.R.
45 N3 Kashma R U.S.S.R.
32 H3 Kāshmar Iran 35.13N 58.25E
Kashmir see Jammu and Kashmir
31 H3 Kashmir North dist Kashmir
31 H3 Kashmir South dist Kashmir
31 H3 Kashmir, Vale of Kashmir
31 E6 Kashmor Pakistan 28.24N 69.42E
31 F3 Kashmund ra Afghanistan
93 A8 Kashofu Zaïre 2.14S 29.02E
45 U3 Kashpirovka U.S.S.R. 53.02N 48.26E
47 M6 Kashtak U.S.S.R. 55.18N 61.22E
24 E8 K'a-shun Tso L Xizang Zizhiqu China 34.35N 86.00E
91 K7 Kashyukulu Zaïre 7.01S 26.01E
30 G6 Kasia Uttar Prad India 26.45N 83.55E
91 K7 Kasiba Zaïre 7.07S 27.00E
91 H8 Kasidishi R Zaïre
31 F3 Kasigar Afghanistan 34.47N 70.06E
Kasigluk see Akolmiut
37 D1 Kaşıkçı Turkey 41.02N 27.14E
92 D5 Kasiki Zaïre 7.39S 29.55E
34 K2 Kasik Kopit Iraq 36.25N 42.49E
91 H8 Kasileshi R Zaïre
113 M6 Kasilof Alaska 60.21N 151.17W
93 D10 Kasimani watercourse Tanzania
90 D8 Kasimbila Nigeria 6.56N 9.46E
45 N2 Kasimov U.S.S.R. 54.55N 41.25E
37 J2 Kasımpaşa dist İstanbul Turkey 41.02N 28.54E
93 A5 Kasindi Zaïre 0.03N 29.43E
91 K7 Kasinge Zaïre 6.19S 27.00E
37 F8 Kasır Turkey 37.11N 40.48E
19 E4 Kasiruta isld Moluccas Indon
19 G6 Kasiui isld Moluccas Indon 4.30S 131.39E
92 F8 Kasiya Malawi 13.46S 33.23F
43 F4 Kaskakulan Kazakhstan U.S.S.R. 45.38N 60.59E
89 B3 Kaskas Senegal 16.21N 14.06W
107 G3 Kaskaskia R Illinois
43 M5 Kaskelen Kazakhstan U.S.S.R. 43.10N 76.35E
51 G6 Kasker Sweden 65.51N 18.00E
Kaskinen see Kaskö
51 J9 Kaskö Finland 62.23N 21.10E
25 G7 Kas Kong Cambodia 11.29N 103.10E
25 G7 Kas Kong isld Cambodia 11.20N 103.00E
47 M5 Kasli U.S.S.R. 55.54N 60.45E
101 P11 Kaslo Br Columbia 49.54N 116.57W
29 K6 Kasmar Bihar India 23.36N 86.00E
101 X6 Kasmere L Manitoba
45 F1 Kasnya U.S.S.R. 55.23N 34.18E
92 B7 Kasonda Zaïre 10.13S 24.24E
91 K6 Kasongo Zaïre 4.32S 26.33E
92 B6 Kasongo Zaïre 9.24S 24.13E
91 E7 Kasongo-Lunda Zaïre 6.30S 16.51E
83 H9 Kásos isld Greece
83 H9 Kásos Str Greece
64 Q5 Kašperské Hory Czechoslovakia 49.09N 13.34E
44 F6 Kaspi Georgia U.S.S.R. 41.56N 44.25E
44 H5 Kaspiysk U.S.S.R. 42.54N 47.36E
44 H2 Kaspiyskiy U.S.S.R. 45.24N 47.21E
Kaspiyskoye More see Caspian Sea
45 C2 Kasplya U.S.S.R. 54.59N 31.44E
45 C1 Kasplya R U.S.S.R.
25 H6 Kas Preas Cambodia 13.15N 105.58E
25 G7 Kas Prins isld Cambodia 10.23N 102.58E
86 Q12 Kasr el Nîl dist Cairo Egypt
25 G7 Kas Rong isld Cambodia 10.44N 103.14E
25 G7 Kas Rong Sam Lem isld Cambodia 10.36N 103.20E
87 F3 Kassala Sudan 15.24N 36.25E
87 E2 Kassala prov Sudan
87 F3 Kassala,Jeb mt Sudan 15.21N 36.28E
43 H7 Kassan Uzbekistan U.S.S.R. 39.03N 65.35E
84 F1 Kassándra pen Greece
113 R9 Kassatochi, I Aleutian Is 52.10N 175.30W
64 H1 Kassel W Germany 51.18N 9.30E
88 S4 Kasserine Tunisia 35.13N 8.43E
117 A4 Kassikaityu R Guyana
90 J7 Kassinda Chad 8.44N 18.12E
85 L10 Kassinger Sudan 18.47N 31.51E
84 W22 Kassiópi Corfu 39.48N 19.55E
25 G7 Kas Smach isld Cambodia 10.56N 103.04E
108 S5 Kasson Minnesota 44.02N 92.45W
89 H6 Kassou Upper Volta 11.35N 2.04W
15 E7 Kassuë Irian Jaya 6.59S 139.15E
30 D5 Kasta Uttar Prad India 27.50N 80.31E
31 A8 Kastag Pakistan 25.54N 61.48E
36 G1 Kastamonu Turkey 41.22N 33.47E
84 B2 Kastana Tríkkala Greece 39.43N 21.23E
83 H3 Kastanéai Greece 41.39N 26.30E
84 D6 Kastaniá Korinthía Greece 37.52N 22.23E
53 E3 Kastbjerg Denmark 56.39N 10.10E
64 E3 Kastel W Germany 50.01N 8.18E
64 C3 Kastellaun W Germany 50.04N 7.26E
84 J11 Kastélli Crete 35.29N 23.38E
84 D4 Kastélli Greece 38.42N 22.25E
84 M11 Kastéllion Crete 35.12N 25.20E
Kastellórizon isld see Megísti
80 O1 Kaštel Lukšić Yugoslavia 43.34N 16.22E
80 O1 Kaštel Stari Yugoslavia 43.34N 16.20E
61 E3 Kaster Belgium 50.48N 3.30E
64 B1 Kaster W Germany 51.00N 6.33E
61 K2 Kasterlee Belgium 51.14N 4.58E
64 M5 Kastl W Germany 49.22N 11.41E
52 J10 Kastlösa Sweden 56.26N 16.25E
52 J10 Kastlösa isld Øland Sweden 56.26N 16.25E
63 N5 Kastorf W Germany 53.44N 10.33E
84 D7 Kastóri Greece 37.10N 22.17E
83 E4 Kastoria Greece 40.33N 21.15E
83 E4 Kastorias,L Greece
45 K5 Kastornoye U.S.S.R. 51.49N 38.09E
84 A4 Kastós isld Greece 38.35N 20.55E
84 B4 Kastráki Akarnanía Greece 38.45N 21.21E
84 C2 Kastráki Tríkkala Greece 39.43N 21.37E
84 B4 Kastrakíou, Tekhnití Limni res Greece
40 M8 Kastrikum, Mys C Kuril Is U.S.S.R. 46.13N 150.34E
84 C5 Kastrítsi Greece 38.16N 21.50E
37 B3 Kastro Gökçeada Turkey 40.14N 25.53E
83 G5 Kástron Greece 39.53N 25.04E
83 D5 Kastrosikiá Greece 39.06N 20.36E
53 K5 Kastrup København Denmark 55.39N 12.40E
53 H6 Kastrup Storstrøm Denmark 55.03N 11.55E
20 F6 Kasubuchi Japan 35.02N 132.33E
20 K6 Kasugai Japan 35.15N 136.57E
95 K9 Kasuka S Africa 33.39S 26.45E
91 J4 Kasuku Zaïre 1.50S 25.49E
93 B10 Kasulu Tanzania 4.33S 30.06E
92 C8 Kasumbalesa Zaïre 12.10S 27.48E
20 H6 Kasumi Japan 35.40N 134.37E
20 O5 Kasumiga-ura L Japan
44 H7 Kasum Ismailov Azerbaydzhan U.S.S.R. 40.35N 46.46E
44 J6 Kasumkent U.S.S.R. 41.43N 48.11E
29 E2 Kasumpti Himachal Prad India 30.57N 77.06E
18 K7 Kasungan Borneo Indonesia 2.01S 113.21E
92 F8 Kasungu Malawi 13.04S 33.29E
92 F8 Kasungu (Mission) Malawi 13.11S 33.29E
92 G9 Kasupi Malawi 15.10S 35.20E
31 H5 Kasur Pakistan 31.07N 74.30E
32 J6 Kasūr, Godār-e- pass Iran 29.44N 60.52E
42 G3 Kata U.S.S.R. 58.45N 102.45E
92 B10 Kataba Zambia 16.02S 25.03E
20 P9 Katabaru Okinawa Japan 26.30N 127.59E
19 C6 Katabu Indonesia 4.57S 122.33E
90 C7 Kataeregi Nigeria 9.20N 6.13E
90 E5 Katagum Nigeria 12.18N 10.21E
104 Q8 Katahdin Mt Maine 45.55N 68.57W
91 H8 Kataie Zaïre 9.29S 22.51E
Katakami see Bizen
31 K3 Kataklik Kashmir 34.59N 78.02E
91 J5 Katako Kombe Zaïre 3.27S 24.21E
84 B6 Katákolon Greece 37.38N 21.19E
113 P2 Katakturuk R Alaska
20 A3 Katakura Tōkyō Japan
90 C7 Katakwa Nigeria 8.12N 7.20E
93 E4 Katakwi Uganda 1.55N 33.58E
93 A7 Katale Zaïre 1.14S 29.20E
113 P6 Katalla Alaska 60.11N 144.35W
29 C6 Katana Gujarat India 22.16N 72.50E
Katana Syriasee Qatana
92 D3 Katana Zaïre 2.11S 28.50E
91 H7 Katanda Zaïre 6.23S 23.55E
93 A6 Katanda Zaïre 0.51S 29.21E
91 H6 Katanga Zaïre 5.01S 22.08E
91 J7 Katanga Zaïre 6.31S 25.49E
91 J8 Katanga prov Zaïre
29 F7 Katangi Madhya Prad India 21.46N 79.50E
40 J6 Katangli Sakhalin U.S.S.R. 51.42N 143.14E
92 D8 Katanino Zambia 13.38S 28.43E
91 K6 Katanki Zaïre 5.15S 26.22E
14 C10 Katanning W Australia 33.43S 117.32E
91 K5 Katanti Zaïre 2.19S 27.08E
91 H8 Katapakishi Zaïre 8.15S 22.47E
32 D2 Kata Pusht Iran 36.32N 50.10E
92 D3 Katara Burundi 3.00S 29.38E
26 T9 Kataragama Sri Lanka 6.26N 81.20E
30 E4 Katarnian Ghat Uttar Prad India 28.19N 81.09E
84 A6 Katastári Greece 37.50N 20.45E
20 J6 Katata Japan 35.08N 135.52E
47 H8 Katav Ivanovsk U.S.S.R. 54.45N 58.11E
84 D4 Katavíthra mt Greece 38.45N 22.19E
31 E4 Katawaz Afghanistan 32.40N 68.20E
31 E4 Katawaz-Urgun prov Afghanistan
47 J7 Kataysk U.S.S.R. 56.20N 62.30E
95 K8 Katberg S Africa 32.33S 26.41E
94 U13 Katboschfontein S Africa 26.06S 28.29E
90 C7 Katcha Nigeria 8.42N 6.14E
87 B5 Katcha Sudan 10.49N 29.41E
28 H7 Katchall isld Nicobar Is
89 C3 Katchi, Oued watercourse Mauritania
92 E5 Kate Tanzania 7.51S 31.13E
91 K6 Katea Zaïre 5.39S 26.09E
93 D6 Katebo Uganda 0.01S 32.07E
113 H4 Kateel R Alaska
93 E7 Kateguru Tanzania 1.53S 33.25E
94 T14 Kate Hamel S Africa 26.18S 28.14E
91 H9 Katende Zaïre 11.04S 22.20E
92 D4 Katenga Zaïre 5.01S 28.49E
91 J6 Katenta Zaïre 5.30S 25.50E
91 J8 Katentania Zaïre 9.46S 25.24E
91 J9 Katentania Zaïre 10.17S 25.51E
100 O8 Katepwa Saskatchewan 50.43N 103.37W
100 O8 Katepwa Prov. Park Saskatchewan
93 C5 Katera Uganda 0.45N 31.59E
83 F4 Kateríni Greece 40.15N 22.30E
45 B8 Katerinopol' Ukraine U.S.S.R. 48.55N 30.58E
59 K3 Katesbridge Down N Ireland 54.18N 6.08W
56 L2 Kate's Cabin Cambs Eng 52.33N 0.20W
93 G10 Katesh Tanzania 4.32S 35.24E
101 G7 Kates Needle mt Br Col/Alaska 57.02N 132.05W
92 F9 Katete Zambia 14.02S 32.10E
29 H6 Katghora Madhya Prad India 22.33N 82.34E
29 H7 Katgi Madhya Prad India 21.42N 82.33E
25 M9 Katha Burma 24.11N 96.20E
30 H7 Kathar Bihar India 25.36N 84.13E
86 L8 Katherîna, Gebel hill Egypt 28.30N 33.57E
13 B2 Katherine N Terr Australia 14.29S 132.20E
13 G6 Katherine R Queensland
11 K3 Katherine B New Zealand
13 C2 Katherine R N Terr Australia
30 C3 Kathgodam Uttar Prad India 29.15N 79.32E
29 D7 Kathi Maharashtra India 21.48N 74.02E
29 B6 Kathiawar pen Gujarat India
86 J4 Kathîb el Henu hill Egypt 30.38N 32.51E
86 H4 Kathîb el Kheil reg Egypt
86 J5 Kathîb el Makhâzin reg Egypt
86 L4 Kathîb el Sabakh reg Egypt
33 E9 Kathīb, Ra's al C Yemen 14.54N 42.51E
84 P15 Kathikas Cyprus 34.55N 32.25E
26 T5 Kathiraveli Sri Lanka 8.13N 81.23E
33 H8 Kathīri tribal state S Yemen
93 J5 Kathita R Kenya
29 D6 Kathiwara Madhya Prad India 22.29N 74.12E
105 E9 Kathleen Florida 28.07N 82.03W
13 B2 Kathleen Falls N Terr Australia 14.42S 131.37E
14 D7 Kathleen Valley W Australia 27.30S 120.33E
30 J5 Kathmandu Nepal 27.42N 85.19E
30 D5 Kathna R Uttar Prad India
35 F9 Kathrabba Jordan 31.08N 35.37E
100 D7 Kathryn Alberta 51.16N 113.37W
108 N3 Kathryn N Dakota 46.41N 97.59W
31 H4 Kathua Kashmir 32.23N 75.34E
31 H4 Kathua dist Kashmir
93 L7 Kathua watercourse Kenya
89 E5 Kati Mali 12.41N 8.04W
30 D8 Katia R Madhya Prad India
89 G7 Katiali Ivory Coast 9.49N 5.49W
18 K5 Katibas R Sarawak Malaysia
18 C7 Katiët Indonesia 2.22S 99.50E
93 G3 Katigithigiria Hills Kenya
30 L7 Katihar Bihar India 25.33N 87.34E
11 K4 Katikati New Zealand 37.32S 175.58E
11 L4 Katikati Ent New Zealand 37.28S 176.01E
122 V15 Katiki pk Easter I Pacific Oc 27.06S 109.16W
Katima Mulilo see Ngweze
92 B10 Katima Rapids Zambia 17.28S 24.11E
100 S6 Katimik L Manitoba
45 L3 Katino U.S.S.R. 53.55N 39.12E
89 G7 Katiola Ivory Coast 8.11N 5.04W
Katiraveli see Kathiraveli
87 D8 Katire Sudan 4.05N 32.46E
37 F2 Katırlı Turkey 40.37N 28.58E
122 D14 Katiu atoll Tuamotu Is Pacific Oc 16.24S 144.20W
51 L3 Kätkätunturi mt Finland 68.20N 25.10E
94 F8 Katkop S Africa 30.11S 20.05E
95 M6 Katkop S Africa 30.52S 28.31E
94 E8 Katkop Hills S Africa
87 B5 Katla Sudan 11.50N 29.23E
50 G7 Katla mt Iceland 63.36N 18.59W
82 M5 Katlabukh, Ozero L U.S.S.R. 45.25N 29.00E
63 M9 Katlenburg W Germany 51.42N 10.05E
31 D3 Katlish Afghanistan 34.39N 66.24E
113 K8 Katmai B Alaska
113 K7 Katmai, Mt Alaska 58.20N 154.59W
113 K7 Katmai Nat. Mon Alaska
Katmandu see Kathmandu
30 C4 Katna R Uttar Prad India
29 G6 Katni Madhya Prad India 23.47N 80.29E
84 D6 Kato Agali Greece 37.47N 22.16E
84 C5 Káto Akhaïa Greece 38.08N 21.33E
84 F5 Káto Alepochóri Greece 38.05N 23.12E
84 C5 Káto Alissós Greece 38.08N 21.35E
84 R14 Kato Dhikomo Cyprus 35.15N 33.20E
84 C7 Káto Figalía Greece 37.26N 21.46E
92 A7 Katoka Zaïre 10.40S 22.43E
84 E3 Káto Kerasiá Greece 39.28N 22.55E
84 B5 Katokhí Greece 38.24N 21.15E
84 D6 Káto Klitoría Greece 37.53N 22.07E
84 C7 Káto Kopanáki Greece 37.17N 21.48E
30 B1 Katol Himachal Prad India 31.12N 78.05E
29 F7 Katol Maharashtra India 21.19N 78.38E
84 B6 Káto Loukávitsa Greece 37.52N 21.29E
84 C5 Káto Makrinoú Greece 38.28N 21.38E
84 C7 Káto Mélpia Greece 37.20N 21.55E
92 C5 Katompi Zaïre 6.08S 26.21E
103 G4 Katonah New York 41.17N 73.40W
92 E9 Katondwe Zambia 15.15S 30.19E
83 F3 Káto Nevrokópion Greece 41.21N 23.51E
93 B5 Katonga R Uganda
18 J3 Katong, Tanjong C Singapore 1.18N 103.54E
43 Q3 Katon-Karagay Kazakhstan U.S.S.R. 49.15N 85.33E
84 D2 Kato Olimbos mt Greece 39.55N 22.23E
12 K5 Katoomba New S Wales 33.42S 150.23E
84 D3 Káto Orfana Greece 39.25N 22.12E
91 J5 Katopa Zaïre 2.53S 25.02E
84 Q14 Kato Pyrgos Cyprus 35.11N 32.41E
84 B5 Káto Rétsina Greece 38.25N 21.25E
29 C6 Katosan Gujarat India 23.30N 72.18E
84 D7 Káto Sélitsa Greece 37.00N 22.10E
84 H6 Káto Soúnion Greece 37.39N 24.01E
83 F4 Káto Stavrós Greece 40.39N 23.43E
84 B4 Katoúna Greece 38.47N 21.07E
84 G4 Katoúnia Greece 38.43N 23.44E
65 J3 Katovice Czechoslovakia 49.17N 13.49E
84 C6 Káto Vlasía Greece 38.00N 21.55E
62 L5 Katowice Poland 50.15N 18.59E
29 C7 Katpur Gujarat India 21.29N 72.46E
30 J6 Katra Bihar India 26.13N 85.39E
30 F5 Katra Gonda, Uttar Prad India 27.31N 82.03E
30 E8 Katra Madhya Prad India 24.54N 81.40E
30 C4 Katra Shahjahanpur, Uttar Prad India 28.01N 79.39E
36 E5 Katrancık Dağ mt Turkey 37.28N 30.19E
29 J1 Katras Bihar India 23.49N 86.19E
47 K3 Katravozh U.S.S.R. 66.22N 66.02E
52 J5 Katrineberg Sweden 61.03N 16.20E
52 J8 Katrineholm Sweden 58.59N 16.15E
58 G6 Katrine, L Central Scotland 56.16N 4.30W
60 C2 Kats Netherlands 51.34N 3.53E
84 H5 Katsaróni Greece 38.03N 24.23E
84 D7 Katsaroú Greece 37.13N 22.02E
65 J7 Katschberghöhe pass Austria 47.04N 13.38E
60 C2 Katscheveer Netherlands 51.33N 3.52E
95 C3 Katsepy Madagascar 15.43S 46.13E
91 K7 Katshi Zaïre 6.03S 26.10E
84 A2 Katsiká Greece 39.37N 20.53E
90 C5 Katsina Nigeria 13.00N 7.32E
90 D8 Katsina R Nigeria
90 D8 Katsina Ala Nigeria 7.10N 9.30E
20 D4 Katsuda Kanagawa Japan
20 C8 Katsumoto Japan 33.54N 129.40E
20 J6 Katsuno Japan 35.18N 136.01E
20 F2 Katsushika dist Tōkyō Japan
20 O5 Katsuta Japan 36.24N 140.32E
20 O6 Katsuura Chiba Japan 35.10N 140.20E
20 K5 Katsuyama Fukui Japan 36.00N 136.30E
20 N6 Katsuyama Honshu Japan 35.06N 139.50E
20 G6 Katsuyama Okayama Japan 35.07N 133.40E
43 H7 Kattakurgan Uzbekistan U.S.S.R. 39.54N 66.13E
14 F5 Kattamudda Well W Australia 21.17S 126.36E
33 K10 Kattānahan, Ra's pen Socotra Ind Oc 12.03N 53.36E
52 G10 Kattarp Sweden 56.07N 12.50E
31 D4 Kattasang Hills Afghanistan
84 U18 Kattaviá Rhodes 35.57N 27.46E
99 K3 Kattawagami L Ontario 49.50N 80.05W
52 F10 Kattegat, chan Den/Sweden
60 C2 Kattendijke Netherlands 51.31N 3.57E
64 J2 Kattennordheim E Germany 50.35N 10.08E
63 G8 Kattenvenne W Germany 52.07N 7.53E
52 L9 Katthammarsvik Sweden 57.27N 18.54E
52 L2 Kattisavan Sweden 64.45N 18.10E
53 D5 Kattrup Denmark 55.58N 9.55E
28 D5 Kattuputtur Tamil Nadu India 11.00N 78.13E
26 Q9 Katukurunda Sri Lanka 6.32N 79.58E
93 J7 Katulani Kenya 1.32S 37.37E
93 G2 Katulenyang Hills Kenya
93 D3 Katulikire Uganda 2.02N 32.10E
87 B3 Katul, Jeb mt Sudan 14.12N 29.25E
93 M3 Katulu Kenya 2.30N 40.40E
91 J7 Katumba Zaïre 7.43S 25.19E
29 E4 Katumbar Rajasthan India 27.18N 77.02E
92 F7 Katumbi Malawi 10.47S 33.36E
42 D6 Katun' R U.S.S.R.
26 Q7 Katunayake Sri Lanka 7.10N 79.53E
92 F5 Katunda Tanzania 7.20S 32.45E
93 M8 Katungu Kenya 2.56S 40.05E
93 B6 Katunguru Uganda 0.08S 30.05E
42 D6 Katunskiy Khrebet mts U.S.S.R.
18 N10 Katupa Indonesia 8.10S 118.08E
26 R6 Katupota Sri Lanka 7.31N 80.12E
31 E6 Katuri Pakistan 29.51N 68.39E
30 K8 Katuria Bihar India 24.46N 86.44E
29 L2 Katwa W Bengal India 23.40N 88.10E
93 A5 Katwa Zaïre 0.06N 29.21E
93 A6 Katwe Uganda 0.08S 29.53E
60 F11 Katwijk aan den Rijn Netherlands 52.12N 4.25E
60 F11 Katwijk-aan-Zee Netherlands 59.12N 4.24E
42 B3 Katyl'ga U.S.S.R. 59.07N 76.40E
41 G5 Katyryk U.S.S.R. 71.17N 99.31E
47 N4 Katyshka U.S.S.R. 57.39N 61.43E
62 K4 Katy Wrocłowskie Poland 51.01N 16.45E
64 G5 Katzenbuckel mt W Germany 49.29N 9.03E
64 D3 Katzenelnbogen W Germany 50.16N 7.59E
64 L2 Katzhütte E Germany 50.33N 11.04E
19 E3 Kau Halmahera Indon 1.11N 127.54E
Kau Somaliasee Bender Ziada
114 B8 Kau dist Hawaiian Is
94 F2 Kaua watercourse Botswana
114 F3 Kauai isld Hawaiian Is
114 F4 Kauai Chan Hawaiian Is
114 D4 Kauai County div Hawaiian Is
30 J8 Kaua Kol Bihar India 24.51N 85.54E
11 C13 Kauana New Zealand 46.01S 168.21E
64 D3 Kaub W Germany 50.05N 7.48E
94 H2 Kaucaca Pan Botswana 19.48S 25.45E
114 C8 Kau Des Hawaiian Is 19.18N 155.20W
29 F6 Kaudiya Madhya Prad India 22.53N 78.53E
122 D14 Kauehi atoll Tuamotu Is Pacific Oc 15.49S 145.10W
114 D8 Kaueleau Hawaiian Is 19.26N 154.55W
64 K8 Kaufbeuren W Germany 47.53N 10.37E
64 K7 Kaufering W Germany 48.05N 10.53E
112 L3 Kaufman Texas 32.35N 96.18W
64 H1 Kaufungen W Germany 51.17N 9.39E
90 D5 Kaugama Nigeria 12.31N 9.48E
15 H7 Kaugel R Papua New Guinea
51 J9 Kauhajoki Finland 62.26N 22.10E
51 K8 Kauhava Finland 63.06N 23.00E
114 B6 Kauhola Pt Hawaiian Is 20.14N 155.46W
114 F6 Kauiki Hd Hawaiian Is 20.45N 155.58W
114 E6 Kauiki Ho Hawaiian Is 20.45N 156.00W
Kaukaban see Kawkabān
Kaukab el Hawa see Belvoir anc site
11 J3 Kaukapakapa New Zealand 36.37S 174.30E
15 J2 Kaukauai Bougainville I Solomon Is 6.50S 155.40E
106 F5 Kaukauna Wisconsin 44.20N 88.16W
25 M9 Kaukkwe R Burma
25 M9 Kaukkwe Hills Burma
122 C14 Kaukura atoll Tuamotu Is Pacific Oc 15.47S 146.40W
94 E4 Kaukurus Namibia 22.47S 18.37E
114 D2 Kaula I Hawaiian Is 21.40N 160.33W
122 V7 Kaula I Palmyra I Pacific Oc 5.52N 162.05W
114 D3 Kaulakahi Chan Hawaiian Is
28 C1 Kaulas Andhra Prad India 18.19N 77.38E
61 N2 Kaulille Belgium 51.11N 5.31E
51 K5 Kauliranta Finland 66.26N 23.40E
92 D9 Kaulishishi mt Zambia 15.20S 28.44E
114 B8 Kauluoa Pt Hawaiian Is 19.18N 155.49W
114 E4 Kaumakani Hawaiian Is 21.56N 159.38W
114 D6 Kaumalapau Hawaiian Is 20.46N 156.58W
114 D6 Kaumalapau Harb Hawaiian Is 20.47N 156.58W
114 C7 Kaumana Hawaiian Is 19.41N 155.09W
91 J8 Kaumba Zaïre 8.26S 24.40E
65 N5 Kaumberg Austria 48.02N 15.53E
11 K4 Kaunai Ra New Zealand
114 C5 Kaunakakai Hawaiian Is 21.08N 157.02W
114 E4 Kaunalewa Hawaiian Is 22.00N 159.44W
114 B8 Kauna Pt Hawaiian Is 19.02N 155.53W
46 E3 Kaunas Lithuania U.S.S.R. 54.52N 23.55E
44 M5 Kaundy Vpadina mud flat Kazakhstan U.S.S.R.
65 C7 Kauner Tal V Austria
31 H8 Kaunia Bangladesh 25.45N 89.30E
Kauniainen see Grankulla
51 K4 Kaunisvaara Sweden 67.22N 23.22E
15 H5 Kaup Papua New Guinea 3.50S 144.01E
53 W16 Kaupanger Norway 61.11N 7.14E
50 H3 Kaupangur Iceland 65.39N 17.59W
114 E6 Kaupo Hawaiian Is 20.37N 156.08W
11 J6 Kaupokonui R New Zealand
Kaura Iransee Khūrāb
90 B5 Kaura Nigeria 13.30N 4.16E
90 C5 Kaura Namoda Nigeria 12.39N 6.38E
29 H7 Kauria Madhya Prad India 21.15N 82.34E
30 E4 Kauriala R Nepal
30 E4 Kauriala Ghat Uttar Prad India 28.22N 81.01E
93 J4 Kauro Kenya 1.02N 37.40E
90 D6 Kauro Nigeria 10.35N 8.11E
24 G5 Kauruk Bulak well Xinjiang Uygur Zizhiqu China 41.05N 90.29E
23 C8 Kau Sai Hong Kong 22.21N 114.19E
Kau Sai Chau isld see Keui I Hong Kong
82 M4 Kaushany U.S.S.R. 46.36N 29.28E
53 S18 Kausland Norway 60.13N 5.05E
51 K8 Kaustinen Finland 63.33N 23.40E
15 L5 Kaut New Ireland 2.47S 150.52E
19 E3 Kau, Teluk B Halmahera Indonesia
61 P7 Kautenbach Luxembourg 49.57N 6.01E
51 K2 Kautokeino Norway 69.00N 23.06E
51 J10 Kauttua Finland 61.07N 22.12E
65 M4 Kautzen Austria 48.57N 15.15E
93 G2 Kauwalathe watercourse Kenya
23 B8 Kau Wa San Tsuen Hong Kong 22.20N 114.07E
25 E7 Kau-ye Kyun isld Burma
23 A9 Kau Yi Chau isld Hong Kong 22.17N 114.04E
39 D5 Kava R U.S.S.R.
39 H4 Kavacha U.S.S.R. 60.17N 169.55E
36 D3 Kavacık Turkey 39.42N 28.31E
82 G9 Kavadarci Yugoslavia 41.26N 22.01E
83 D3 Kavajë Albania 41.11N 19.33E
37 C2 Kavak Çanakkale Turkey 40.37N 26.52E
36 J1 Kavak Samsun Turkey 41.04N 36.03E
37 C6 Kavak Sivas Turkey 39.18N 37.29E
37 G3 Kavaklı Turkey 40.06N 29.46E
36 C5 Kavaklıdere Turkey 37.28N 28.22E
37 F2 Kavaklı Liman B Turkey
37 C2 Kavak suyu R Turkey
37 G8 Kaval Turkey 37.30N 43.29E
92 D4 Kavala isld Zaïre 5.39S 29.22E
44 C1 Kavalerka R U.S.S.R.
40 G9 Kavalerovo U.S.S.R. 44.19N 135.08E
113 P10 Kavalga I Aleutian Is 51.35N 178.50W
28 E3 Kavali Andhra Prad India 14.57N 80.03E
40 G2 Kaval'kan U.S.S.R. 58.10N 136.40E
84 A2 Kavallári Greece 39.44N 20.55E
119 H5 Kavanayen Venezuela 5.36N 61.44W
32 E6 Kavār Iran 29.15N 52.41E
27 L7 Kavaratti isld Laccadive Is Ind Oc 10.32N 72.43E
82 L7 Kavarna Bulgaria 43.26N 28.22E
84 B6 Kavásila Greece 37.52N 21.16E
91 H8 Kavava Zaïre 8.52S 22.19E
63 Q4 Kavelstorf E Germany 54.01N 12.13E
45 N2 Kaverino U.S.S.R. 54.10N 41.50E
28 D4 Kaveripatnam Tamil Nadu India 12.25N 78.12E
29 C6 Kavi Gujarat India 22.11N 72.41E
15 L5 Kavieng New Ireland 2.34S 150.48E
113 O2 Kavik R Alaska
94 H2 Kavimba Botswana 18.02S 24.38E
32 D3 Kavir Iran 35.10N 51.59E
32 G3 Kavīr Kūshk Iran 34.58N 57.12E
92 D3 Kavivira Zaïre 3.21S 29.08E
44 A2 Kavkaz U.S.S.R. 45.20N 36.39E
44 D2 Kavkazskaya U.S.S.R. 45.26N 40.42E
42 E5 Kavkazskoye U.S.S.R. 53.59N 92.00E
52 G11 Kävlinge Sweden 55.47N 13.05E
53 K5 Kävlingeån R Sweden
84 W23 Kávos Corfu 39.24N 20.06E
84 N11 Kavoúsi Crete 35.07N 25.51E
92 E5 Kavu R Tanzania
Kavul see Kābūl Israel
117 C2 Kaw Fr Guiana 4.31N 52.00W
25 D4 Kawa Burma 17.04N 96.30E
90 F5 Kawa Nigeria 12.57N 12.33E
85 L10 Kawa ruin Sudan 19.08N 30.31E
20 A1 Kawadera Saitama Japan
87 D4 Kawa, El Sudan 13.43N 32.30E
99 M7 Kawagama L Ontario 45.17N 78.45W
20 A1 Kawagoe Japan 35.55N 139.30E
20 C2 Kawaguchi Japan 35.47N 139.42E
20 M6 Kawaguchi Japan 35.34N 138.44E
20 M3 Kawaharada Japan 38.01N 138.18E
87 A3 Kawahla tribe Sudan
20 P2 Kawai Japan 39.36N 141.42E
15 L8 Kawa I Trobriand Is Papua New Guinea 8.32S 150.15E
114 B6 Kawaihae Hawaiian Is 20.02N 155.50W
114 B6 Kawaihae B Hawaiian Is
114 F3 Kawaihau dist Hawaiian Is
114 D4 Kawaihoa Pt Hawaiian Is 21.46N 160.12W
114 E3 Kawaikini, Mt Hawaiian Is 22.03N 159.30W
114 A4 Kawailoa Hawaiian Is 21.37N 158.05W
114 A4 Kawailoa Beach Hawaiian Is 21.35N 158.05W
114 F4 Kawai Pt Hawaiian Is 21.56N 159.20W
87 B7 Kawajena Sudan 7.30N 28.20E
20 M6 Kawakami Japan 35.58N 138.31E
11 J2 Kawakawa New Zealand 35.23S 174.06E
11 K3 Kawa Kawa Bay New Zealand 36.56S 175.08E
20 E9 Kawakita Japan 32.15N 131.33E
19 D1 Kawalusu isld Indonesia 4.13N 125.21E
92 D6 Kawama Zaïre 9.28S 28.30E
92 D7 Kawama Zambia 10.10S 28.49E
20 O4 Kawamata Japan 37.39N 140.35E
92 D6 Kawambwa Zambia 9.45S 29.10E
20 N7 Kawana Japan 34.53N 139.05E
19 D3 Kawangkoan Celebes Indon 1.12N 124.43E
20 G7 Kawanoe Japan 34.01N 133.32E
11 C12 Kawarau R New Zealand
29 G6 Kawardha Madhya Prad India 22.01N 81.05E
99 M8 Kawartha L Ontario
20 C3 Kawasaki Japan 35.32N 139.41E
20 D7 Kawashiri-misaki C Honshu Japan 34.25N 130.56E
20 O1 Kawauchi Japan 41.10N 141.00E
11 J3 Kawau I New Zealand 36.25S 174.53E
20 C4 Kawawa Kanagawa Japan
109 O5 Kaw City Oklahoma 36.45N 96.53W
25 D5 Kawdut Burma 15.31N 97.49E
15 A4 Kawe isld Irian Jaya 0.04S 130.08E
111 E5 Kaweah R California
11 L6 Kaweka mt New Zealand 39.16S 176.23E
11 L6 Kaweka Ra New Zealand
114 A4 Kawela Bay Hawaiian Is
114 B6 Kawela Camp Hawaiian Is 20.07N 155.30W
100 L2 Kawene Ontario 48.46N 91.10W
11 L5 Kawerau New Zealand 38.03S 176.43E
11 J5 Kawhia New Zealand 38.03S 174.50E
11 J5 Kawhia Harb inlet New Zealand
111 H4 Kawich Ra Nevada
92 E6 Kawimbe Zambia 8.50S 31.31E
100 S6 Kawinaw L Manitoba
19 D1 Kawio isld Indonesia 4.40N 125.26E
19 D1 Kawio,Kep islds Indonesia
25 E4 Kawkareik Burma 16.33N 98.18E
25 M9 Kawlin Burma 23.48N 95.41E
25 D3 Kawludo Burma 18.30N 97.19E
25 E6 Kawmapyin Burma 12.27N 99.04E
25 N9 Kawngmeum Burma 23.04N 99.02E
109 O5 Kaw Reservoir Oklahoma
33 M5 Kawr, Jabal mt Oman 23.12N 57.00E
25 E7 Kawthaung Burma 10.01N 98.32E
25 D3 Kawthoolei State Burma
24 B6 Kaxgar (Kashgar) He R Xinjiang Uygur Zizhiqu China
24 D4 Kax He R Xinjiang Uygur Zizhiqu China
23 E3 Ka Xian Sichuan China 31.14N 108.28E
47 G5 Kay U.S.S.R. 60.00N 52.59E
64 O7 Kay W Germany 48.02N 12.46E
18 M4 Kaya Borneo Indon 2.55N 117.33E
89 J5 Kaya Upper Volta 13.04N 1.09W
18 E8 Kayaäpu Indonesia 5.30S 102.17E
Kayacık see Hotamış
36 J3 Kayadibi Turkey 39.29N 36.43E
Kayadibi Yozgat Turkeysee Salmanlı
25 D3 Kayah State Burma
93 L9 Kaya Kauma Kenya 3.38S 39.44E
44 H5 Kayakent U.S.S.R. 42.23N 47.53E
113 P7 Kayak I Alaska 59.55N 144.30W
37 H2 Kayalar Turkey 40.52N 29.52E
37 G2 Kayalı Dağ mt Turkey 40.55N 29.39E
28 D6 Kayalpatnam Tamil Nadu India 8.34N 78.07E
92 E6 Kayambi Zambia 9.29S 31.59E
25 D4 Kayan Burma 16.54N 96.35E
19 C8 Kayan Indonesia 8.20S 123.59E
18 K6 Kayan R Kalimantan Indonesia
19 N1 Kayangel Is Palau Is Pacific Oc
19 N1 Kayangel Pass Palau Is Pacific Oc
28 C6 Kayankulam Kerala India 9.10N 76.31E
93 A8 Kayanza Burundi 2.54S 29.34E
37 F8 Kayapinar Turkey 37.34N 41.07E
29 F8 Kayar Maharashtra India 19.54N 78.59E
89 A4 Kayar Senegal 14.53N 17.09W
36 G3 Kayas Turkey 39.56N 33.01E
44 G3 Kayasula U.S.S.R. 44.20N 45.01E
29 E6 Kayatha Madhya Prad India 23.11N 76.07E
108 D6 Kaycee Wyoming 43.40N 106.36W
44 M3 Kaydak,Sor mud flat Kazakhstan U.S.S.R.
95 M2 Kaydale S Africa 26.29S 28.24E
99 D2 Kayedon L Ontario
19 E5 Kayeli Moluccas Indon 3.25S 127.07E
91 H9 Kayenda Zaïre 10.48S 23.06E
111 O5 Kayenta Arizona 36.44N 110.17W
93 D9 Kayenzi Tanzania 3.16S 32.37E
93 E8 Kayenzi Tanzania 2.24S 33.05E
93 B9 Kayero Burundi 3.50S 30.03E
89 D4 Kayes Mali 14.26N 11.28W
91 J8 Kayeye Zaïre 8.37S 25.54E
92 C6 Kayeye Zaïre 8.21S 28.00E
104 D8 Kayford W Virginia 38.01N 81.29W
43 G2 Kaygy Kazakhstan U.S.S.R. 50.58N 64.45E
89 D7 Kayima Sierra Leone 8.54N 11.14W
36 C4 Kayışlar Turkey 38.51N 27.41E
61 P9 Kayl Luxembourg 49.29N 6.03E
36 C4 Kaymakçı Turkey 38.08N 28.07E
43 M1 Kaymanachikha Kazakhstan U.S.S.R. 53.35N 75.09E
37 H2 Kaymas Turkey 40.57N 30.07E
36 E3 Kaymaz Turkey 39.32N 31.12E
42 G4 Kaymonova U.S.S.R. 56.18N 103.10E
42 G4 Kaymonovo U.S.S.R. 56.50N 105.00E
42 B3 Kaymysovy U.S.S.R. 59.52N 75.52E
64 N2 Kayna E Germany 51.00N 12.15E
37 B3 Kayna Burun C Gökçeada Turkey 40.14N 25.57E
Kaynak see Karacadağ
43 M3 Kaynar Kazakhstan U.S.S.R. 49.15N 77.25E
36 J4 Kaynar Turkey 38.55N 36.29E
82 M4 Kaynary U.S.S.R. 46.40N 29.03E
39 K3 Kaynupil'gyn Laguna lagoon U.S.S.R.
20 Q9 Kayō Okinawa Japan 26.33N 128.07E
19 E3 Kayoa isld Moluccas Indon 0.05N 127.25E
91 K8 Kayombo Zaïre 9.31S 26.10E
91 K9 Kayombo Zaïre 10.15S 26.31E
93 B7 Kayonza Rwanda 1.53S 30.31E
36 J5 Kaypak Turkey 37.08N 36.28E
39 K3 Kaypil'gakuy,Oz L U.S.S.R.
101 D1 Kay Pt Yukon Terr 69.16N 138.21W
43 J6 Kayrakkum Tadzhikistan U.S.S.R. 40.13N 69.53E
43 M8 Kayrakkumskoye Vdkhr res Tadzhikistan U.S.S.R.
37 C2 Kaysatı R Turkey
45 S7 Kaysatskoye U.S.S.R. 49.44N 46.50E
117 B3 Käyser Gebergte mts Surinam
36 H4 Kayseri Turkey 38.42N 35.28E
69 N7 Kaysersberg France 48.09N 7.16E
110 O8 Kaysville Utah 41.03N 111.56W
26 Q2 Kayts Sri Lanka 9.42N 79.52E
19 B7 Kayuadi isld Indonesia 6.49S 120.50E
18 F7 Kayuagung Sumatra Indon 3.18S 104.53E
93 A10 Kayugoro Burundi 4.15S 29.47E
15 C6 Kayumerah, Teluk B Irian Jaya
39 F5 Kayuyu U.S.S.R. 57.52N 158.09E
100 M9 Kayville Saskatchewan 49.43N 105.08W
41 E6 Kayyerkan U.S.S.R. 69.25N 87.45E
90 G5 Kaza Nigeria 12.01N 14.10E
87 F4 Kaza watercourse Ethiopia
99 O7 Kazabazua Quebec 45.56N 76.01W
42 H4 Kazachinskoye Irkutsk U.S.S.R. 56.14N 107.35E
42 E3 Kazachinskoye Krasnoyarsk U.S.S.R. 57.41N 93.15E
45 P5 Kazachka U.S.S.R. 51.29N 43.59E
45 H6 Kazach'ya Lopan' Ukraine U.S.S.R. 50.20N 36.13E
41 H5 Kazach'ye Krasnoyarsk U.S.S.R. 72.03N 102.46E
41 P5 Kazach'ye Yakutsk U.S.S.R. 70.46N 136.15E
43 E5 Kazakdar'ya Uzbekistan U.S.S.R. 43.24N 59.45E
40 J6 Kazakevichi Sakhalin U.S.S.R. 50.24N 142.14E
44 G6 Kazakh Azerbaydzhan U.S.S.R. 41.05N 45.19E
38 F4 Kazakhskaya S.S.R U.S.S.R.
43 J2 Kazakhskiy Melkosopochnik mt reg Kazakhstan U.S.S.R.
44 L5 Kazakhskiy Zaliv B Kazakhstan U.S.S.R.
Kazakh S.S.R see Kazakhskaya S.S.R
46 R4 Kazakhstan Kazakhstan U.S.S.R. 51.11N 52.52E
45 K4 Kazaki U.S.S.R. 52.37N 38.15E
41 B4 Kazakova R Novaya Zemlya U.S.S.R.
43 F4 Kazalinsk Kazakhstan U.S.S.R. 45.45N 62.01E
42 C3 Kazal'tsevo U.S.S.R. 59.21N 80.37E
45 V1 Kazan' U.S.S.R. 55.45N 49.10E
97 K5 Kazan R N W Terr
36 F6 Kazancı Turkey 36.30N 32.53E
43 D7 Kazandzhik Turkmeniya U.S.S.R. 39.15N 55.31E
47 K8 Kazanka Kazakhstan U.S.S.R. 53.22N 67.21E
45 D9 Kazanka Ukraine U.S.S.R. 47.50N 32.50E
46 P2 Kazanka R U.S.S.R.
43 E5 Kazanketken Uzbekistan U.S.S.R. 43.01N 59.13E
100 J3 Kazan L Saskatchewan
82 J8 Kazanlŭk Bulgaria 42.37N 25.23E
45 K3 Kazanovka U.S.S.R. 53.45N 38.42E
42 K6 Kazanovo U.S.S.R. 51.52N 115.52E
21 J12 Kazan-rettō islds Japan
43 O3 Kazanshunkur Kazakhstan U.S.S.R. 49.34N 81.16E
45 N7 Kazanskaya U.S.S.R. 49.47N 41.10E
47 M6 Kazanskiy U.S.S.R. 54.59N 60.48E
45 M3 Kazanskoye Tambov U.S.S.R. 53.25N 40.40E
47 K7 Kazanskoye Tyumen U.S.S.R. 55.40N 69.15E
44 D9 Kazantip,Mys C Ukraine U.S.S.R. 45.29N 35.53E
44 D9 Kazantipskiy Zaliv B Ukraine U.S.S.R.
41 D6 Kazantsevo U.S.S.R. 69.53N 83.48E
43 L6 Kazarman Kirgiziya U.S.S.R. 41.23N 74.01E
42 F5 Kazas R U.S.S.R.
46 G5 Kazatin Ukraine U.S.S.R. 49.41N 28.49E
47 M7 Kazatkul' U.S.S.R. 55.02N 76.01E
43 E3 Kazatskiy Kazakhstan U.S.S.R. 49.23N 58.30E
45 E5 Kazatskoye Ukraine U.S.S.R. 51.17N 33.32E
90 D5 Kazaure Nigeria 12.42N 8.28E
85 A3 Kāzāzīyah, B. al Libya 32.21N 11.58E
44 F5 Kazbegi Georgia U.S.S.R. 42.41N 44.40E
44 F5 Kazbek mt Georgia U.S.S.R. 42.42N 44.30E
36 B3 Kaz Dağı mt Turkey 39.41N 26.52E
92 F8 Kazembe Zambia 12.10S 32.33E
32 D6 Kāzerūn Iran 29.35N 51.40E
43 K1 Kazgorodok Kokchetav, Kazakhstan U.S.S.R. 52.55N 70.40E
44 E2 Kazgulak U.S.S.R. 45.30N 43.16E
47 G5 Kazhim U.S.S.R. 60.18N 51.34E
31 B7 Kazhmak R Pakistan
Kazi Ahmad see Qazi Ahmad
43 K8 Kazidi Tadzhikistan U.S.S.R. 37.03N 71.30E
92 G4 Kazikazi Tanzania 5.36S 34.14E
44 J7 Kazi Magomed Azerbaydzhan U.S.S.R. 40.03N 48.56E
62 N4 Kazimierz Poland 51.20N 21.56E
Kāẓimīyah, Al see Kādhimain
34 M7 Kazim Matrah Iraq 31.38N 44.43E
92 H6 Kazimoto Tanzania 9.04S 36.49E
82 F2 Kazincbarcika Hungary 48.15N 20.40E
45 L4 Kazinka Lipetsk U.S.S.R. 52.33N 39.48E
45 L3 Kazinka U.S.S.R. 53.54N 39.21E
28 D2 Kazipet Andhra Prad India 17.58N 79.29E
35 E5 Kāziya er Ratrūt Jordan 32.09N 35.29E
46 E3 Kazlų Rūda Lithuania U.S.S.R. 54.35N 23.10E
44 H4 Kaz'maaul U.S.S.R. 43.26N 46.46E
32 J7 Kazmīr Iran 26.29N 60.01E
64 4 Kaznějov Czechoslovakia 49.53N 13.23E
93 B6 Kazo Uganda 0.03S 30.48E
44 F6 Kazreti Georgia U.S.S.R. 41.26N 44.12E
45 U7 Kaztalovka Kazakhstan U.S.S.R. 49.45N 48.42E
92 B11 Kazuma Pan Nat.Park Zimbabwe
91 H7 Kazumba Zaïre 6.30S 22.02E
92 B10 Kazungula Zambia 17.45S 25.20E
Kazvin see Qazvīn
93 D4 Kazwama Uganda 1.20N 32.39E
32 G1 Kazy Turkmeniya U.S.S.R. 39.15N 57.30E
47 K4 Kazym R U.S.S.R.
47 K4 Kazymskaya U.S.S.R. 63.40N 67.15E
47 K4 Kazymskiy Mys U.S.S.R. 64.44N 65.40E
42 E5 Kazyr R U.S.S.R.
62 K3 Kcynia Poland 53.00N 17.29E
64 P5 Kdyně Czechoslovakia 49.24N 13.03E
84 H6 Kéa Greece 37.38N 24.20E
84 H6 Kéa isld Greece
114 C7 Keaau Hawaiian Is 19.36N 155.02W
59 F3 Keadew Roscommon Irish Rep 54.03N 8.08W
59 J3 Keady Armagh N Ireland 54.15N 6.42W
84 H6 Kéae,Stenón str Greece
114 E9 Keahi Pt Hawaiian Is 21.19N 157.59W
114 A7 Keahole Pt Hawaiian Is 19.44N 156.03W
114 E6 Keahu Hawaiian Is 20.51N 156.22W
114 D6 Kealaikahiki Channel Hawaiian Is
114 B7 Kealakekua Hawaiian Is 19.31N 155.56W
114 B8 Kealakekua B Hawaiian Is
114 B7 Kealapuali Hawaiian Is 19.37N 155.46W
114 B8 Kealia Hawaiian Is 19.24N 155.53W
114 F3 Kealia Hawaiian Is 22.05N 159.20W
114 E6 Kealia Pond Hawaiian Is 20.48N 156.28W
58 D6 Keal,L.na Strathclyde Scotland 56.28N 6.05W
111 O6 Keams Canyon Arizona 35.49N 110.13W
114 B7 Keamuku Hawaiian Is 19.49N 155.43W
90 D7 Keana Nigeria 8.09N 8.52E
114 E6 Keanae Hawaiian Is 20.50N 156.09W
114 E6 Keanae Valley Hawaiian Is
114 C7 Keanakolu Hawaiian Is 19.54N 155.21W
114 C8 Keana Pt Hawaiian Is 19.16N 155.08W
103 F6 Keansburg New Jersey 40.27N 74.08W
114 C8 Keaoi Hawaiian Is 19.15N 155.17W
59 M3 Kearney Down N Ireland 54.24N 5.28W
108 L9 Kearney Nebraska 40.42N 99.04W
99 L7 Kearney Ontario 45.33N 79.13W
103 H7 Kearny New Jersey 40.46N 74.09W
111 F5 Kearsarge Pass California 36.47N 118.20W
95 P5 Kearsney S Africa 29.18S 31.15E
107 C9 Keatchie Louisiana 32.11N 93.56W
95 O4 Keate's Drift S Africa 28.50S 30.30E
110 H5 Keating Oregon 44.51N 117.33W
104 H5 Keating Pennsylvania 41.15N 77.56W
100 K6 Keatley Saskatchewan 52.47N 107.30W
105 D8 Keatons Beach Florida 29.51N 83.36W
114 B7 Keauhou Hawaiian Is 19.34N 155.58W
114 C7 Keaukaha Hawaiian Is 19.43N 155.03W
114 E6 Keawakapu Hawaiian Is 20.42N 156.26W
114 D4 Keawanui B Hawaiian Is
37 D7 Keban Turkey 38.48N 38.45E
37 D7 Keban Baraji dam Turkey 38.48N 38.45E
18 K5 Kebanbatu Borneo Indon 0.59N 112.16E
28 K1 Kebang Assam India 28.09N 95.01E
88 S4 Kebar, Jebel el mt Tunisia 34.53N 9.25E
18 H7 Kebatu isld Indonesia 3.47S 108.08E
18 F3 Kebayoran Jakarta Indonesia 6.15S 106.48E
90 B5 Kebbi Nigeria 12.05N 4.49E
90 F7 Kebbi R Cameroon/Chad
90 B6 Kebbi R Nigeria
31 C2 Kebcha Qala Afghanistan 36.17N 65.26E
89 A4 Kébèmer Senegal 15.24N 16.25W
42 D6 Kebezen' U.S.S.R. 51.56N 87.10E
89 F7 Kébi Ivory Coast 9.18N 6.37W
88 S5 Kebili Tunisia 33.42N 8.58E
34 C3 Kebīr R Syria
88 R3 Kebir,el R Algeria
87 H3 Kebir I Ethiopia 15.40N 40.12E
87 N5 Kebir,Jeb.El mt Somalia 11.34N 50.18E
36 F2 Kebirmir R Turkey
90 M5 Kebkabiya Sudan 13.39N 24.05E
51 G4 Kebnekaise Sweden 67.53N 18.40E
51 G4 Kebnekaise mt Sweden 67.55N 18.35E
25 J2 Ke Boa,I de Vietnam 21.10N 107.28E
58 D2 Kebock Hd Lewis, W Isles Scotland 58.02N 6.22W
87 K7 K'ebri Dehār Ethiopia 6.45N 44.17E
18 H9 Kebumen Java Indonesia 7.40S 109.41E
37 J1 Kece R Turkey
31 B7 Kech reg Pakistan
87 F8 Kecha Ethiopia 5.09N 36.43E
20 C7 Kechi Japan 34.18N 129.22E
101 K6 Kechika R Br Col
31 E6 Kechi Kalat Pakistan 29.15N 69.19E
36 E5 Keçiborlu Turkey 37.57N 30.18E
37 F2 Keçikaya Burun C Turkey 40.34N 28.48E
62 M9 Kecskemét Hungary 46.56N 19.43E
44 D6 Keda Georgia U.S.S.R. 41.35N 41.54E
44 G7 Kedabek Azerbaydzhan U.S.S.R. 40.34N 45.46E
18 A6 Kedah state Pen Malaysia
46 E2 Kėdainiai Lithuania U.S.S.R. 55.17N 23.58E
30 C2 Kedarnath Uttar Prad India 30.44N 79.03E

30 C2 **Kedarnath** mt Uttar Prad India 30.47N 79.02E
110 E9 **Keddie** California 40.00N 120.57W
Kedesh Naphtali anc site see Tel Qedesh
98 E6 **Kedgwick** New Brunswick 47.38N 67.21W
98 E6 **Kedgwick R** New Brunswick
84 D3 **Kédhron** Greece 39.13N 22.03E
84 L11 **Kédhros Óros** mt Crete 35.11N 24.37E
88 H9 **Kediat Arheniat** hills Mauritania
88 G10 **Kediat Idjil** mt Mauritania 22.42N 12.30W
87 C8 **Kediba** Sudan 5.31N 30.45E
60 J12 **Kedichem** Netherlands 51.52N 5.03E
18 K9 **Kediri** Java Indon 7.45S 112.01E
100 M8 **Kedleston** Saskatchewan 50.50N 105.06W
39 F2 **Kedon** R U.S.S.R.
21 D3 **Kedong** Heilongjiang China 48.07N 126.22E
93 D1 **Kedong.Jeb** mt Sudan 4.03N 32.39E
89 C5 **Kédougou** Senegal 12.35N 12.09W
107 D7 **Kedron** Arkansas 34.03N 92.08W
13 K1 **Kedron** dist Brisbane, Qnsld
13 K1 **Kedron Brook** Brisbane, Qnsld
47 M3 **Kedrovka** U.S.S.R. 58.10N 59.21E
47 M4 **Kedrovoye** U.S.S.R. 57.11N 60.30E
47 K5 **Kedrovyy** U.S.S.R. 61.30N 68.15E
18 H9 **Kedungwuni** Java Indon 7.01S 109.35E
47 G4 **Kedva** U.S.S.R. 64.14N 53.28E
47 G4 **Kedva** R U.S.S.R.
39 C3 **Kedyumya** R U.S.S.R.
101 N10 **Keefers** Br Col 50.03N 121.32W
114 E9 **Keehi Lagoon** Hawaiian Is
59 B4 **Keel** Mayo Irish Rep 53.58N 10.05W
57 N5 **Keelby** Lincs Eng 53.35N 0.15W
101 K3 **Keele** R N W Terr
101 H4 **Keele Pk** Yukon Terr 63.25N 130.17W
111 G5 **Keeler** California 36.30N 117.53W
100 M8 **Keeler** Saskatchewan 50.41N 105.50W
100 J4 **Keeley L** Saskatchewan
Keeling Is see Cocos Is
59 G1 **Keel L** Donegal Irish Rep 55.03N 7.45W
98 T5 **Keels** Newfoundland 48.37N 53.25W
59 G5 **Keelty** Roscommon Irish Rep 53.24N 7.59W
101 T8 **Keely L** Saskatchewan
59 G4 **Keenagh** Longford Irish Rep 53.37N 7.48W
19 J8 **Keenapusan** isld Philippines 7.12N 118.25E
111 F6 **Keene** California 35.13N 118.32W
104 N4 **Keene** New Hampshire 42.55N 72.17W
104 M2 **Keene** New York 44.15N 73.49W
107 L7 **Keener** Alabama 34.07N 85.59W
109 F1 **Keenesburg** Colorado 40.06N 104.32W
58 L5 **Keen,Mt** Tayside/Grampian Scotland 56.58N 2.59W
59 F6 **Keeper Hill** mt Tipperary Irish Rep 52.45N 8.16W
12 K4 **Keepit Res** New S Wales 30.52S 150.30E
13 A3 **Keep R** N Terr Australia
61 J2 **Keerbergen** Belgium 51.00N 4.38E
95 C9 **Keeromsberg** mt S Africa 33.33S 19.35E
95 K4 **Keeromsberg** mt S Africa 28.43S 26.30E
13 F2 **Keer-weer,C** Queensland 13.58S 141.31E
104 M2 **Keeseville** New York 44.31N 73.30W
60 C2 **Keeten** channel Netherlands
94 E6 **Keetmanshoop** Namibia 26.36S 18.08E
108 R2 **Keewatin** Minnesota 47.22N 93.02W
100 H1 **Keewatin** Ontario 49.47N 94.30W
97 K5 **Keewatin** dist N W Terr
87 F7 **Kefa** prov Ethiopia
83 D5 **Kefali,Kep** C Albania 39.55N 19.52E
84 A5 **Kefallinía** isld Greece
37 B3 **Kefalo Burun** C Gökçeada Turkey 40.08N 26.00E
36 C6 **Kefaloka** Turkey 36.58N 27.19E
84 D2 **Kefalóvriso** Greece 39.53N 22.04E
19 D8 **Kefamenanu** Timor Indonesia 9.31S 124.29E
35 C7 **Kefar Ahim** Israel 31.45N 34.45E
35 B6 **Kefar Aviv** Israel 31.49N 34.43E
35 B8 **Kefar Azza** Israel 31.29N 34.32E
35 D3 **Kefar Barukh** Israel 32.39N 35.11E
35 C6 **Kefar Bilu** Israel 31.53N 34.49E
35 F1 **Kefar Blum** Israel 33.10N 35.36E
35 C6 **Kefar Danyyel** Israel 31.56N 34.56E
35 C6 **Kefar 'Eqron** Israel 31.52N 34.49E
35 D7 **Kefar 'Ezyon** Jordan 31.39N 35.07E
35 C2 **Kefar Gallim** Israel 32.46N 34.58E
35 E3 **Kefar Gid'on** Israel 32.38N 35.17E
35 F1 **Kefar Gil'adi** Israel 33.15N 35.34E
35 D3 **Kefar Glickson** Israel 32.31N 35.00E
35 E3 **Kefar HaHoresh** Israel 32.42N 35.17E
35 C4 **Kefar Haiyim** Israel 32.21N 34.54E
35 D2 **Kefar HaMaccabi** Israel 32.47N 35.07E
35 B7 **Kefar HaNagid** Israel 31.44N 34.38E
35 C6 **Kefar HaNagid** Israel 31.54N 34.45E
35 F2 **Kefar HaNasi** Israel 32.58N 35.36E
35 C4 **Kefar HaRo'e** Israel 32.24N 34.55E
35 D3 **Kefar Hasidim** Israel 32.45N 35.06E
35 C5 **Kefar Hess** Israel 32.15N 34.56E
35 F2 **Kefar Hittim** Israel 32.48N 35.30E
35 E3 **Kefar Kisch** Israel 32.40N 35.27E
35 C5 **Kefar Mallal** Israel 32.10N 34.54E
35 D2 **Kefar Masaryk** Israel 32.53N 35.06E
35 C7 **Kefar Menahem** Israel 31.44N 34.50E
35 C4 **Kefar Monash** Israel 32.21N 34.55E
Kefar Nahum see Capernaum anc site
Kefar Ono see Qiryat Ono
Kefar Qesem see Katr Qasim
35 D1 **Kefar Rosh HaNiqra** Israel 33.05N 35.07E
35 F4 **Kefar Ruppin** Israel 32.27N 35.33E
35 A2 **Kefar Salma** sub Jerusalem
35 C5 **Kefar Sava** Israel 32.11N 34.54E
35 E2 **Kefar Shammay** Israel 32.58N 35.27E
35 A1 **Kefar Shaul** sub Jerusalem
35 C6 **Kefar Shemu'el** Israel 31.53N 34.56E
35 F1 **Kefar Szold** Israel 33.12N 35.39E
35 E3 **Kefar Tavor** Israel 32.41N 32.25E
35 C6 **Kefar Truman** Israel 31.58N 34.56E
35 C6 **Kefar Uriyya** Israel 31.47N 34.57E
35 C4 **Kefar Vitkin** Israel 32.23N 34.52E
35 B7 **Kefar Warburg** Israel 31.43N 34.44E
35 C4 **Kefar Yav'etz** Israel 32.16N 34.58E
35 E3 **Kefar Yehezqel** Israel 32.34N 35.22E
35 C4 **Kefar Yona** Israel 32.19N 34.55E
35 C7 **Kefar Zekharya** Israel 31.43N 34.57E
35 E2 **Kefar Zetim** Israel 32.49N 35.28E
78 B12 **Kef, El** Tunisia 36.10N 8.40E
Keferdiz Gaziantep Turkeysee Sakcagözü
37 E7 **Keferdiz** Malatya Turkey 38.20N 39.03E
65 L5 **Kefermarkt** Austria 48.27N 14.33E
90 C7 **Keffi** Nigeria 8.51N 7.47E
90 D5 **Keffin Hausa** Nigeria 12.13N 9.59E
36 E1 **Kefken** Turkey 41.12N 30.15E
36 E1 **Kefken Adası** isld Turkey 41.14N 30.15E
50 A3 **Keflavík** Bardhastrandarsýsla, Vestur Iceland 65.30N 24.11W
50 C6 **Keflavík** Gullbringusýsla Iceland 64.01N 22.35W
88 O4 **Kef Sidi Ali** mt Algeria 34.15N 1.35E
39 G3 **Kegali** R U.S.S.R.
26 R7 **Kegalla** Sri Lanka 7.14N 80.21E
98 L3 **Kégashka** Quebec 50.12N 61.20W
98 L3 **Kégashka L** Quebec
41 M7 **Kegechakh** U.S.S.R. 65.09N 121.09E
43 N5 **Kegen'** Kazakhstan U.S.S.R. 43.01N 79.13E
43 M5 **Kegety** Kirgiziya U.S.S.R. 42.38N 75.14E
43 E5 **Kegeyli** Uzbekistan U.S.S.R. 42.56N 59.36E
45 G7 **Kegichevka** Ukraine U.S.S.R. 49.19N 35.46E
53 D7 **Kegnæs** Denmark 54.53N 9.54E
101 P7 **Keg River** Alberta 57.48N 117.51W
90 J1 **Kegueur Terbi** mt Chad 21.24N 18.40E
45 Q10 **Kegul'ta** Kalmyk A.S.S.R. U.S.S.R. 46.56N 44.24E
46 N6 **Kegul'ta** U.S.S.R. 46.58N 44.15E
46 E2 **Kegums** Latvia U.S.S.R. 56.42N 24.50E
56 J2 **Kegworth** Leics Eng 52.50N 1.16W
29 H3 **Kehami** Nepal 29.01N 83.50E
Kéheil see Kahil
85 M10 **Keheili** Sudan 19.25N 32.50E
85 M10 **Keheili** watercourse Sudan
32 E4 **Kehi** Iran 32.36N 52.22E
64 D6 **Kehl** W Germany 48.35N 7.50E
61 P8 **Kehlen** Luxembourg 49.40N 6.02E
46 F1 **Kehra** Estonia U.S.S.R. 59.19N 25.21E
64 C3 **Kehrig** W Germany 50.16N 7.14E
66 K3 **Kehrsiten** Switzerland 47.01N 8.23E
25 D2 **Kehsi Mansam** Burma 21.56N 97.51E
90 G6 **Keia** Cameroon 10.26N 14.45E
61 B2 **Keiem** Belgium 51.05N 2.53E
57 K5 **Keighley** W Yorks Eng 53.52N 1.54W
60 O11 **Keijenborg** Netherlands 52.02N 6.17E
114 B7 **Keikiwaha Pt** Hawaiian Is 19.31N 155.58W
46 E1 **Keila** Estonia U.S.S.R. 59.18N 24.29E
15 L1 **Keila I** Solomon Is 5.27S 159.24E
87 B5 **Keilak,L** Sudan 10.49N 29.20E
87 E5 **Keili** Sudan 10.51N 34.20E
58 E7 **Keills** Strathclyde Scotland 55.58N 5.42W
12 B6 **Keilor** dist Melbourne, Vic
94 F7 **Keimoes** S Africa 28.41S 20.59E
95 M8 **Kei Mouth** S Africa 32.41S 28.23E
53 S15 **Keipen** mt Norway 61.45N 5.26E
Keiran, Bandar al see Khayrān Ra's al C
95 L8 **Kei Road** S Africa 32.42S 27.33E
91 K5 **Keisha** Zaïre 2.38S 27.17E
95 L9 **Keiskamma** R S Africa
95 L8 **Keiskammahoek** S Africa 32.41S 27.09E
95 L9 **Keiskamma Pt** S Africa 33.18S 27.29E
58 K1 **Keiss** Highland Scotland 58.32N 3.08W
89 M4 **Keita** Niger 14.45N 5.40E
90 B4 **Keïta** Niger 14.47N 5.45E
51 M8 **Keitele** Finland 63.10N 26.24E
51 M8 **Keitele** L Finland
58 L3 **Keith** Grampian Scotland 57.32N 2.57W
12 F6 **Keith** S Australia 36.06S 140.22E
101 M3 **Keith Arm** Great Bear L, N W Terr
13 B1 **Keith,C** N Terr Australia 11.36S 131.30E
101 N9 **Keithley Creek** Br Col 52.45N 121.25W
106 D8 **Keithsburg** Illinois 41.06N 90.55W
107 C9 **Keithville** Louisiana 32.21N 93.50W
94 F2 **Keitsa** Namibia 19.52S 20.25E
53 A7 **Keitum** W Germany 54.53N 8.21E
9 S8 **Keiyasi** Viti Levu Fiji 17.55S 177.45E
110 C4 **Keizer** Oregon 44.58N 123.01W
98 G9 **Kejimkujik Nat. Park** Nova Scotia
48 U9 **Kejser Franz Josephs Fjord** Greenland
114 E4 **Kekaha** Hawaiian Is 21.58N 159.43W
11 J9 **Kekerengu** New Zealand 42.01S 174.02E
62 M8 **Kékes** mt Hungary 47.52N 20.01E
15 G7 **Keketa** Papua New Guinea 6.48S 143.38E
44 G2 **Keke Usun,Oz** L U.S.S.R.
19 F4 **Kekik** isld Moluccas Indonesia 1.30S 128.37E
26 S5 **Kekirawa** Sri Lanka 8.02N 80.36E
43 L6 **Kekiyrim** Kirgiziya U.S.S.R. 41.24N 73.54E
19 N2 **Keklau** Palau Is Pacific Oc 7.36N 134.39E
114 D6 **Kekoa Pt** Hawaiian Is 20.56N 156.42W
36 D6 **Kekov** isld Turkey 36.11N 29.53E
29 D5 **Kekri** Rajasthan India 25.57N 75.13E
39 F6 **Kekuk** U.S.S.R. 56.45N 157.52E
39 H4 **Kekurnaya Gora** mt U.S.S.R. 60.25N 166.40E
47 C2 **Kekurskiy,Mys** C U.S.S.R. 69.58N 32.00E
41 M6 **Kel'** U.S.S.R. 69.21N 124.50E
88 K5 **Kelaa,El** Morocco 32.02N 7.23W
91 H8 **Kelagne Bushimaie** R Zaïre
27 L8 **Kelai** isld Maldives, Ind Oc 6.47N 73.01E
18 M5 **Kelai** R Borneo Indon
87 E8 **Kelam** Ethiopia 4.49N 35.58E
22 J7 **Kelan** Shanxi China 38.45N 111.30E
18 B9 **Kelanang** Pen Malaysia 2.47N 101.26E
18 B9 **Kelang** Pen Malaysia 3.00N 101.27E
19 E5 **Kelang** isld Moluccas Indon 3.10S 127.43E
18 B9 **Kelang, Pulau** isld Pen Malaysia
26 R8 **Kelani G** R Sri Lanka
26 Q8 **Kelaniya** Sri Lanka 6.59N 79.55E
18 E3 **Kelantan** R Pen Malaysia
18 B7 **Kelantan** state Pen Malaysia
19 A6 **Kelara** R Celebes Indon
32 D2 **Kelārdasht** Iran 36.29N 51.21E
44 G7 **Kel'badzhar** Azerbaydzhan U.S.S.R. 40.06N 46.03E
90 L6 **Kelbaria** Chad 11.30N 22.27E
64 B3 **Kelberg** W Germany 50.17N 6.56E
63 O10 **Kelbra** E Germany 51.27N 11.03E
65 F7 **Kelchsau** Austria 47.24N 12.08E
57 J4 **Keld** N Yorks Eng 54.24N 2.10W
47 E4 **Kel'da** R U.S.S.R.
53 J7 **Keldby** Denmark 54.59N 11.51E
50 K5 **Kelduá** R Iceland
50 E7 **Keldur** Iceland 63.50N 20.05W
93 E4 **Kele** Uganda 1.40N 33.10E
41 O8 **Kele** R U.S.S.R.
90 J4 **Kélèb** watercourse Chad
9 T13 **Kelefesia** atoll Tonga, Pacific Oc 20.30S 174.45W
41 Q5 **Kelegan** U.S.S.R. 70.15N 141.32E
46 J6 **Kelegei** Ukraine U.S.S.R. 46.25N 32.35E
90 E5 **Kélekam** Niger 13.40N 11.50E
35 C8 **Kelekh** watercourse Israel
36 D3 **Keles** Turkey 39.55N 29.11E
43 J6 **Keles** Uzbekistan U.S.S.R. 41.21N 69.10E
84 B6 **Keleví** Greece 37.51N 21.18E
37 E1 **Kelevı** R Turkey
100 J7 **Kelfield** Saskatchewan 51.57N 107.34W
105 K1 **Kelford** N Carolina 36.12N 77.15W
30 B8 **Kelgawan** Uttar Prad India 24.50N 78.45E
57 M6 **Kelham** Notts Eng 53.06N 0.51W
64 M6 **Kelheim** W Germany 48.55N 11.54E
78 D12 **Kelibia** Tunisia 36.50N 11.05E
43 H7 **Kelif** Turkmeniya U.S.S.R. 37.23N 66.17E
84 G1 **Kélifos** isld Greece 40.04N 23.43E
43 G7 **Kelifskiy Uzboy** salt marsh Turkmeniya U.S.S.R.
39 H1 **Kelil'vun Gora** mt U.S.S.R. 68.49N 167.00E
109 F1 **Kelim** Colorado 40.24N 104.57W
87 E6 **Kelim** Ethiopia 9.10N 34.31E
93 F4 **Kelim** R Uganda
19 B8 **Keli Mutu** vol Indonesia 8.42S 121.54E
41 M5 **Kelimyar** R U.S.S.R.
64 E3 **Kelkheim** W Germany 50.07N 8.27E
69 P3 **Kelkheim** W Germany 50.08N 8.27E
37 E5 **Kelkit** Turkey 40.07N 39.28E
37 D5 **Kelkit** R Turkey
87 E6 **Kella Dafino** Ethiopia 9.01N 35.22E
84 R15 **Kellaki** Cyprus 34.48N 33.10E
64 Q6 **Kellberg** W Germany 48.36N 13.33E
91 D4 **Kellé** Congo 0.05S 14.33E
90 E4 **Kellé** Niger 14.18N 10.07E
89 A4 **Kellé** Senegal 15.13N 16.30W
Kelleck see Kalak
112 M8 **Keller** Texas 32.54N 97.16W
104 K9 **Keller** Virginia 37.35N 75.47W
110 G1 **Keller** Washington 48.03N 118.40W
14 C9 **Kellerberrin** W Australia 31.40S 117.41E
101 N4 **Keller L** N W Terr
100 L2 **Keller L** Saskatchewan 56.03N 106.50W
43 J1 **Kellerovka** Kazakhstan U.S.S.R. 53.51N 69.15E
63 N4 **Kellersee** L W Germany
108 Q9 **Kellerton** Iowa 40.43N 94.03W
97 G3 **Kellet,C** N W Terr 72.00N 125.30W
23 B9 **Kellet I** Hong Kong 22.17N 114.10E
104 F5 **Kellettville** Pennsylvania 41.34N 79.17W
104 C5 **Kelleys I** Ohio 41.37N 82.42W
84 S15 **Kellia** Cyprus 34.58N 33.37E
108 Q2 **Kelliher** Minnesota 47.58N 94.28W
100 O7 **Kelliher** Saskatchewan 51.15N 103.41W
63 L5 **Kellinghusen** W Germany 53.57N 9.43E
64 J7 **Kellmünz** W Germany 48.07N 10.09E
42 D1 **Kellog** U.S.S.R. 62.32N 86.19E
42 D2 **Kellog** R U.S.S.R.
110 J2 **Kellogg** Idaho 47.33N 116.06W
108 S8 **Kellogg** Iowa 41.42N 92.54W
51 O5 **Kelloselkä** Finland 66.56N 28.54E
59 K2 **Kells** Antrim N Ireland 54.48N 6.14W
59 H6 **Kells** Kilkenny Irish Rep 52.32N 7.16W
59 J4 **Kells** Meath Irish Rep 53.44N 6.53W
107 J5 **Kelly** Kentucky 36.55N 87.29W
107 D10 **Kelly** Louisiana 31.58N 92.10W
Kelly Queensland see Inorunie
110 P6 **Kelly** Wyoming 43.38N 110.38W
113 F2 **Kelly** R Alaska
13 E6 **Kelly** R Queensland
56 C6 **Kelly Bray** Cornwall Eng 50.31N 4.18W
13 B7 **Kelly Hills** N Terr Australia
91 E12 **Kelly, L** Angola 16.04S 17.10E
101 K3 **Kelly L** N W Terr
59 F5 **Kellys Grove** Galway Irish Rep 53.18N 8.15W
95 K5 **Kelly's View** S Africa 29.09S 26.06E
56 K3 **Kelmarsh** Northants Eng 52.24N 0.55W
46 E2 **Kelme** Lithuania U.S.S.R. 55.38N 22.50E
82 K2 **Kelmentsy** U.S.S.R. 48.27N 26.55E
14 C3 **Kelmscott** dist Perth, W Aust
90 G7 **Kélo** Chad 9.21N 15.50E
29 F7 **Kelod** Maharashtra India 21.30N 78.58E
84 Q15 **Kelokedhara** Cyprus 34.48N 32.39E
18 M5 **Kelolokan** Borneo Indon 1.05N 117.57E
15 L1 **Keloma I** Solomon Is 5.25S 159.21E
51 J3 **Kelottijärvi** L Sweden 68.32N 22.00E
101 O11 **Kelowna** Br Col 49.50N 119.29W
Kelpin see Kalpin
57 H6 **Kelsall** Cheshire Eng 53.13N 2.43W
64 F3 **Kelsberbach** W Germany 50.03N 8.31E
Kelsefid see Kal Safid
100 V2 **Kelsey** Manitoba 56.04N 96.30W
103 D2 **Kelsey** New York 42.02N 75.21W
101 L10 **Kelsey Bay** Vancouver I, Br Col 50.22N 125.59W
100 Q5 **Kelsey Lake** Manitoba 53.42N 101.25W
111 B3 **Kelseyville** California 38.58N 122.50W
57 J1 **Kelso** Borders Scotland 55.36N 2.25W
111 J6 **Kelso** California 35.01N 115.39W
108 N2 **Kelso** N Dakota 47.21N 97.02W
11 D12 **Kelso** New Zealand 45.56S 169.16E
95 O6 **Kelso** S Africa 30.22S 30.43E
100 Q9 **Kelso** Saskatchewan 49.59N 101.59W
110 C3 **Kelso** Washington 46.08N 122.54W
57 L6 **Kelstedge** Derbys Eng 53.11N 1.29W
69 Q3 **Kelsterbach** W Germany 50.03N 8.36E
11 B2 **Kelston** Auckland New Zealand
53 H5 **Kelstrup** Denmark 55.50N 11.35E
53 D6 **Kelstrupstrand** Denmark 55.12N 9.36E
43 J5 **Kel'temashat** Kazakhstan U.S.S.R. 42.32N 70.00E
36 F1 **Kel Tepe** mt Turkey 41.04N 32.28E
41 N7 **Kel'terskiy Khrebet** mts U.S.S.R.
77 F10 **Kelti,Jebel** mt Morocco 35.21N 5.17W
110 M8 **Kelton** Utah 41.45N 113.09W
88 M4 **Keltoum** mt Morocco 34.23N 2.08W
58 K6 **Kelty** Fife Scotland 56.08N 3.24W
112 N4 **Keltys** Texas 31.23N 94.49W
18 D10 **Keluang** Pen Malaysia 2.01N 103.18E
18 K9 **Kelud,Gunung** mt Java Indon 7.56S 112.16E
56 N4 **Kelvedon** Essex Eng 51.51N 0.42E
111 O8 **Kelvin** Arizona 33.07N 110.59W
100 O6 **Kelvington** Saskatchewan 52.10N 103.30W
99 B3 **Kelvin I** Ontario 49.54N 88.38W
29 C5 **Kelwara** Rajasthan India 25.02N 73.36E
30 B8 **Kelwara** Uttar Prad India 24.44N 78.15E
100 S8 **Kelwood** Manitoba 50.38N 99.28W
47 C4 **Kem'** U.S.S.R. 64.58N 34.39E
47 C3 **Kem'** R Karelia U.S.S.R.
42 E3 **Kem'** R Krasnoyarsk U.S.S.R.
19 D3 **Kema** Celebes Indon 1.23N 125.05E
47 D5 **Kema** R U.S.S.R.
18 L3 **Kemabong** Sabah Malaysia 4.56N 115.55E
89 G5 **Ke Macina** Mali 13.59N 5.21W
37 E6 **Kemah** Turkey 39.35N 39.02E
30 A7 **Kemai** Madhya Prad India 25.46N 77.24E
37 D6 **Kemaliye** Turkey 39.16N 38.29E
36 C4 **Kemalpaşa** İzmir Turkey 38.26N 27.27E
35 F4 **Kemalpaşa** Turkey 41.30N 41.30E
15 L1 **Kemalu I** Solomon Is 5.30S 159.28E
101 K9 **Kemano** Br Col 53.39N 127.58W
18 E3 **Kemasik** Pen Malaysia 4.24N 103.26E
65 J5 **Kematen** Austria 48.10N 13.52E
18 C8 **Kemayan** Pen Malaysia 3.07N 102.22E
18 F2 **Kemayoran Airport** Jakarta Indonesia 6.09S 106.51E
91 H1 **Kemba** Cent Afr Rep 4.05N 22.22E
19 C4 **Kembani** Indonesia 1.35S 122.54E
90 K9 **Kembe** Cent Afr Rep 4.29N 21.53E
91 B4 **Kembéle** Gabon 1.43S 11.24E
63 R9 **Kemberg** E Germany 51.47N 12.39E
103 C7 **Kemblesville** Pennsylvania 39.44N 75.50W
87 G5 **Kembolcha** Ethiopia 11.00N 39.42E
91 C3 **Kemboma** Gabon 0.45N 13.31E
71 M1 **Kembs** France 47.41N 7.31E
15 L6 **Kembul** New Britain 5.59S 150.37E
42 E4 **Kemchug** R U.S.S.R.
36 E6 **Kemer** Antalya Turkey 36.39N 30.33E
37 D2 **Kemer** Çanakkale Turkey 40.25N 27.04E
36 D6 **Kemer** Muğla Turkey 36.39N 29.22E
37 D3 **Kemer** R Turkey
36 D5 **Kemer Barajı** dam Turkey 37.34N 28.32E
37 F1 **Kemerburgaz** Turkey 41.10N 28.55E
37 E5 **Kemer Dağı** mt Turkey 40.31N 40.14E
42 D4 **Kemerovo** U.S.S.R. 55.25N 86.05E
38 H3 **Kemerovskaya Oblast'** prov U.S.S.R.
51 L6 **Kemi** Finland 65.46N 24.34E
51 N5 **Kemijärvi** Finland 66.42N 27.30E
51 N5 **Kemijärvi** L Finland 66.35N 27.20E
51 M5 **Kemijoki** R Finland
Kemiö see Kimito
40 H3 **Kemkara** U.S.S.R. 57.10N 139.06E
45 R2 **Kemlya** U.S.S.R. 54.43N 45.15E
61 B3 **Kemmel** Belgium 50.47N 2.50E
61 B3 **Kemmelberg** mt Belgium 50.47N 2.48E
110 P8 **Kemmerer** Wyoming 41.47N 110.33W
Kemmuna isld see Comino
Kemmunett see Cominotto
64 M4 **Kemnath** W Germany 49.52N 11.55E
58 M4 **Kemnay** Grampian Scotland 57.14N 2.27W
100 R9 **Kemnay** Manitoba 49.50N 100.09W
63 T4 **Kemnitz** E Germany 54.05N 13.34E
90 J8 **Kémo** R Cent Afr Rep
90 J8 **Kemo Gribingui** dist Cent Afr Rep
47 D5 **Kemozero,Ozero** L U.S.S.R.
95 O2 **Kemp** S Africa 26.55S 30.46E
112 L3 **Kemp** Texas 32.27N 96.14W
18 D10 **Kempas** Pen Malaysia 1.34N 103.40E
47 J4 **Kempazh** R U.S.S.R.
121 J10 **Kempe,I** Chile 54.20S 72.30W
51 L7 **Kempele** Finland 64.56N 25.26E
63 D10 **Kempen** W Germany 51.22N 6.25E
42 K2 **Kempendyayi** U.S.S.R. 62.02N 118.42E
42 K2 **Kempendyayi** R U.S.S.R.
64 C3 **Kempenich** W Germany 50.25N 7.06E
61 M2 **Kempenland** reg Belgium
60 J14 **Kempenland** reg Netherlands
64 C4 **Kempfeld** W Germany 49.47N 7.15E
91 F5 **Kempimpi** Zaïre 3.01S 18.16E
61 L2 **Kempisch Kanaal** canal Belgium
112 H2 **Kemp, L** Texas
123 B5 **Kemp Land** Antarctica
112 K4 **Kempner** Texas 31.04N 98.00W
123 E12 **Kemp Pen** Antarctica 73.20S 60.10W
116 F2 **Kemp's Bay** Andros Bahamas 24.03N 77.34W
12 L4 **Kempsey** New S Wales 31.05S 152.50E
56 K3 **Kempston** Beds Eng 52.07N 0.30W
64 D4 **Kempten** Rheinland-Pfalz W Germany 49.58N 7.57E
66 M2 **Kempten** Switzerland 47.20N 8.49E
64 J8 **Kempten (Allgäu)** Bayern W Germany 47.44N 10.19E
99 Q5 **Kempt, L** Quebec
106 F9 **Kempton** Illinois 40.57N 88.14W
108 N2 **Kempton** N Dakota 47.49N 97.38W
12 H8 **Kempton** Tasmania 42.28S 147.10E
95 M2 **Kempton Park** S Africa 26.07S 28.14E
99 P7 **Kemptville** Ontario 45.01N 75.39W
18 J8 **Kemujan** isld Indonesia 5.47S 110.29E
61 G2 **Kemzeke** Belgium 51.12N 4.05E
30 D7 **Ken** R Madhya Prad/Uttar Prad India
35 F2 **Kena'an, Har** hill Israel 32.59N 35.30E
99 L5 **Kenabeek** Ontario 47.39N 80.00W
88 M6 **Kenadsa** Algeria 31.30N 2.30W
113 M6 **Kenai** Alaska 60.35N 151.19W
113 N6 **Kenai L** Alaska 60.25N 149.30W
113 M7 **Kenai Mts** Alaska
113 N6 **Kenai Pen** Alaska
18 E6 **Kenaliasam** Sumatra Indon 1.37S 103.38E
18 F8 **Kenam Tanjung** C Sumatra Indon 4.40S 105.55E
87 D8 **Kenamuke Swamp** Sudan
93 K8 **Kenani** Kenya 2.52S 38.19E
105 G10 **Kenansville** Florida 27.53N 80.59W
32 E6 **Kenāreh** Iran 29.54N 52.52E
31 A3 **Kenar-e-Kapeh** Afghanistan 34.11N 60.40E
100 L7 **Kenaston** Saskatchewan 51.30N 106.15W
18 L4 **Kenawang,Bukit** mt Sarawak Malaysia 2.55N 114.39E
85 J4 **Kenâyis, Gulf of** Egypt
104 G10 **Kenbridge** Virginia 36.56N 78.10W
39 B4 **Kencha** U.S.S.R. 60.45N 139.57E
47 M5 **Kenchurka** U.S.S.R. 56.16N 59.47E
29 H6 **Kenda** Madhya Prad India 22.31N 82.10E
57 H4 **Kendal** Cumbria Eng 54.20N 2.45W
116 J2 **Kendal** Jamaica, W I 18.05N 77.29W
18 J9 **Kendal** Java Indon 6.56N 110.14E
12 L4 **Kendal** New S Wales 31.28S 152.40E
95 M2 **Kendal** S Africa 26.05S 28.57E
100 O8 **Kendal** Saskatchewan 50.15N 103.35W
105 G12 **Kendall** Florida 25.39N 80.20W
109 J4 **Kendall** Kansas 37.56N 101.33W
104 G3 **Kendall** New York 43.20N 78.03W
101 P2 **Kendall** R N W Terr
13 F2 **Kendall** R Queensland
97 L5 **Kendall,C** N W Terr 63.35N 87.00W
11 G8 **Kendall,Mt** New Zealand 41.23S 172.22E
106 J8 **Kendallville** Indiana 41.27N 85.15W
18 G9 **Kendang,Gunung** mt Java Indon 7.18S 107.40E
19 C5 **Kendari** Celebes Indon 3.57S 122.36E
18 J7 **Kendawangan** Borneo Indon 2.32S 110.13E
18 J7 **Kendawangan** R Borneo Indon
14 C10 **Kendenup** W Australia 34.28S 117.35E
29 K1 **Kendghata** Bihar India 24.04N 87.10E
90 J6 **Kendigué** Chad 10.00N 18.36E
84 C7 **Kendoikón** Greece 37.17N 21.58E
29 K7 **Kendrapara** Orissa India 20.30N 89.29E
95 H8 **Kendrew** S Africa 32.31S 24.30E
110 J3 **Kendrick** Idaho 46.37N 116.40W
111 N6 **Kendrick Pk** mt Arizona 35.25N 111.50W
93 F6 **Kendu Bay** Kenya 0.22S 34.40E
43 L5 **Kendyktas** mts Kazakhstan U.S.S.R.
43 Q3 **Kendyrlik** Kazakhstan U.S.S.R. 47.30N 85.14E
43 C6 **Kendyrli Kayasanskoye,Plato** Kazakhstan U.S.S.R.
43 F5 **Kendyrli,Ostrov** isld Uzbekistan U.S.S.R. 44.22N 60.48E
43 C5 **Kendyrlisor,Solonchak** salt marsh Kazakhstan U.S.S.R.
44 M5 **Kendyrli Zaliv** B Kazakhstan U.S.S.R.
44 F2 **Kendzhe Kulau** U.S.S.R. 45.28N 43.49E
12 J4 **Kenebri** New S Wales 30.40S 149.00E
112 K7 **Kenedy** Texas 28.50N 97.52W
109 O7 **Kenefick** Oklahoma 34.10N 96.22W
95 M6 **Kenega** R S Africa
95 M6 **Kenega Drift** S Africa 30.29S 28.37E
108 K4 **Kenel** S Dakota 45.54N 100.30W
26 T7 **Kenelula** Sri Lanka 7.22N 81.13E
89 D8 **Kenema** Sierra Leone 7.55N 11.12W
18 J5 **Kenepai, Gunung** mt Borneo Indon 0.42N 111.44E
11 H8 **Kenepuru Sd** New Zealand
108 M9 **Kenesaw** Nebraska 40.39N 98.40W
42 C4 **Kenga** U.S.S.R. 57.26N 81.00E
42 C4 **Kenga** R U.S.S.R.
91 E6 **Kenge** Zaïre 4.56S 17.04E
92 J4 **Kengeja** Pemba I 5.24S 39.42E
92 B7 **Kengere** Zaïre 11.09S 25.29E
43 E5 **Kenges** Uzbekistan U.S.S.R. 43.36N 59.35E
25 E2 **Keng Hkam** Burma 21.03N 98.25E
51 K4 **Kengis** Sweden 67.10N 23.30E
25 H4 **Keng Kabao** Laos 16.48N 104.45E
25 H4 **Keng Kok** Laos 16.26N 105.13E
25 F2 **Keng Lap** Burma 20.55N 100.40E
25 E2 **Keng Lon** Burma 21.18N 98.05E
25 O9 **Keng Ma** Yunnan China 23.30N 99.10E
25 E2 **Keng Tawng** Burma 20.44N 98.18E
25 E2 **Keng Tung** Burma 21.16N 99.39E
94 F7 **Kenhardt** S Africa 29.19S 21.08E
113 L6 **Kenibuna L** Alaska 61.10N 153.00W
89 D5 **Kéniéba** Mali 12.54N 11.17W
94 P11 **Kenilworth** Cape Town S Africa 34.00S 18.28E
56 H3 **Kenilworth** Warwicks Eng 52.21N 1.34W
43 H6 **Kenimekh** Uzbekistan U.S.S.R. 40.16N 65.09E
18 M3 **Keningau** Sabah Malaysia 5.21N 116.11E
87 C7 **Kenisa** Sudan 6.50N 31.10E
88 K4 **Kenitra** Morocco 34.20N 6.34W
39 K4 **Keniut** U.S.S.R. 62.27N 179.14E
41 N8 **Kenkeme** R U.S.S.R.
90 H7 **Kenkignan** Chad 9.40N 17.49E
Kenkiyak see Shubarshi
57 E2 **Ken,L** Dumfries & Galloway Scotland 55.02N 4.07W
55 F6 **Kenley** London Eng 51.19N 0.06W
22 L8 **Kenli** Shandong China 37.44N 118.36E
105 J2 **Kenly** N Carolina 35.36N 78.08W
59 C8 **Kenmare** Kerry Irish Rep 51.53N 9.35W
108 H1 **Kenmare** N Dakota 48.40N 102.05W
59 C8 **Kenmare R** Kerry Irish Rep
58 E3 **Kenmore** Highland Scotland 57.33N 5.45W
58 H5 **Kenmore** Tayside Scotland 56.35N 4.00W
13 K2 **Kenmore** dist Brisbane, Qnsld
56 F5 **Kenn** Avon Eng 51.26N 2.50W
109 G8 **Kenna** New Mexico 33.51N 103.48W
104 D8 **Kenna** W Virginia 38.42N 81.42W
104 P1 **Kennebago Lake** Maine 45.06N 70.41W
108 L6 **Kennebec** S Dakota 43.53N 99.51W
104 Q2 **Kennebec** R Maine
104 P3 **Kennebunk** Maine 43.24N 70.33W
104 P3 **Kennebunkport** Maine 43.22N 70.28W
112 M9 **Kennedale** Texas 32.40N 97.13W
108 O1 **Kennedy** Minnesota 48.44N 96.54W
108 K7 **Kennedy** Nebraska 42.32N 100.51W
104 F4 **Kennedy** New York 42.10N 79.07W
100 P8 **Kennedy** Saskatchewan 50.01N 102.21W
92 C11 **Kennedy** Zimbabwe 18.50S 27.08E
Kennedy, C see Canaveral, C
97 N1 **Kennedy Chan** N W Terr/Greenland
13 G4 **Kennedy Highway** rd Queensland
103 N8 **Kennedy Internat.Airport** New York 40.39N 73.47W
98 O2 **Kennedy L** Quebec
100 P5 **Kennedy L** Saskatchewan 53.35N 102.55W
101 D5 **Kennedy,Mt** Yukon Terr 60.19N 139.00W
25 L9 **Kennedy Peak** mt Burma 23.35N 94.04E
13 G3 **Kennedy R** Queensland
14 B6 **Kennedy Ra** W Australia
13 G3 **Kennedy R.,N** Queensland
11 K3 **Kennedy's B** New Zealand
103 C8 **Kennedyville** Maryland 39.18N 76.00W
66 Q2 **Kennelbach** Austria 47.29N 9.46E
107 H12 **Kenner** Louisiana 30.00N 90.12W
56 D6 **Kennerleigh** Devon Eng 50.51N 3.41W
105 C4 **Kennesaw Mt.Nat.Battlefield Park** Georgia 33.56N 84.38W
56 H5 **Kennet** R Wilts etc Eng
98 J8 **Kennetcook** Nova Scotia 45.10N 63.43W
14 B6 **Kenneth Ra** W Australia
107 F5 **Kennett** Missouri 36.15N 90.04W
103 C7 **Kennett Square** Pennsylvania 39.51N 75.43W
110 F3 **Kennewick** Washington 46.13N 119.08W
106 E9 **Kenney** Illinois 40.06N 89.05W
112 L5 **Kenney** Texas 30.03N 96.20W
101 L9 **Kenney Dam** Br Col 53.38N 124.59W
113 Q6 **Kennicott** Alaska 61.29N 142.52W
56 N3 **Kenninghall** Norfolk Eng 52.26N 1.00E
10 M6 **Kenn Reef** Coral Sea 21.15S 155.45E
39 B4 **Kennya** U.S.S.R. 61.50N 138.20E
110 D7 **Keno** Oregon 42.08N 121.56W
98 A5 **Kénogami** Quebec 48.26N 71.14W
99 T4 **Kénogami** Quebec 48.26N 71.16W
99 E2 **Kenogami** R Ontario
99 T4 **Kénogami, L** res Quebec
99 K4 **Kenogami Lake** Ontario 48.07N 80.10W
99 J4 **Kenogamissi L** Ontario
101 F4 **Keno Hill** Yukon Terr 63.58N 135.22W
100 H1 **Kenora** Ontario 49.47N 94.26W
106 G7 **Kenosha** Wisconsin 42.34N 87.50W
104 C8 **Kenova** W Virginia 38.23N 82.34W
103 E3 **Kenoza Lake** New York 41.44N 74.52W
51 P7 **Kenozero** Karelia U.S.S.R. 64.56N 30.20E
47 D5 **Kenozero,Ozero** L U.S.S.R.
94 Q11 **Kenridge** Cape Town S Africa 33.51S 18.38E
108 M2 **Kensal** N Dakota 47.29N 98.44W
58 D4 **Kensaleyre** Skye, Highland Scotland 57.29N 6.19W
116 H5 **Kenscoff** Haiti 18.29N 72.18W
43 J4 **Kense** Kazakhstan U.S.S.R. 46.48N 68.17E
107 E6 **Kensett** Arkansas 35.12N 91.40W
108 R6 **Kensett** Iowa 43.22N 93.11W
103 G4 **Kensico Res** New York
103 J3 **Kensington** Connecticut 41.37N 72.47W
109 L2 **Kensington** Kansas 39.46N 99.02W
55 E3 **Kensington** London Eng 51.31N 0.12W
98 J7 **Kensington** Prince Edward I 46.26N 63.39W
55 E3 **Kensington & Chelsea** bor London Eng
103 H3 **Kent** Connecticut 41.43N 73.28W
108 Q9 **Kent** Iowa 40.58N 94.26W
108 O3 **Kent** Minnesota 46.27N 96.41W
104 D5 **Kent** Ohio 41.10N 81.20W
110 E4 **Kent** Oregon 45.14N 120.41W
112 C4 **Kent** Texas 31.04N 104.14W
110 C2 **Kent** Washington 47.24N 122.15W
103 C8 **Kent** co Delaware
56 M5 **Kent** co England
103 C8 **Kent** co Maryland
103 L3 **Kent** co Rhode I
95 M8 **Kentani** S Africa 32.30S 28.20E
43 J5 **Kentau** Kazakhstan U.S.S.R. 43.28N 68.36E
99 H10 **Kent Bridge** Ontario 42.31N 82.06W
106 J6 **Kent City** Michigan 43.13N 85.46W
103 G4 **Kent Cliffs** New York 41.27N 73.45W
103 L3 **Kent Dam** Rhode I 41.45N 71.35W
56 N3 **Kentford** Suffolk Eng 52.16N 0.30E
12 H7 **Kent Group** islds Tasmania
25 F4 **Ken Thao** Thailand 17.40N 101.19E
121 J5 **Kent,I** Chile 45.15S 74.30W
103 B9 **Kent I** Maryland
19 D6 **Kentiolo** isld Indonesia 5.44S 124.31E
98 G7 **Kent Junction** New Brunswick 46.35N 65.22W
106 G9 **Kentland** Indiana 40.46N 87.26W
57 H4 **Kentmere** Cumbria Eng 54.26N 2.50W
103 C8 **Kenton** Delaware 39.14N 75.40W
100 R9 **Kenton** Manitoba 49.58N 100.40W
106 F3 **Kenton** Michigan 46.30N 88.54W
104 B6 **Kenton** Ohio 40.38N 83.38W
109 H5 **Kenton** Oklahoma 36.55N 102.59W
107 H5 **Kenton** Tennessee 36.11N 89.00W
51 P7 **Kentozero** L Karelia U.S.S.R. 64.50N 31.09E
101 U1 **Kent Pen** N W Terr
103 B9 **Kent Pt** Maryland 38.50N 76.22W
59 J4 **Kentstown** Meath Irish Rep 53.38N 6.32W
90 E8 **Kentu** Nigeria 6.56N 10.31E
102 J3 **Kentucky** state U.S.A.
107 H5 **Kentucky Dam** Kentucky 37.00N 88.16W
107 H5 **Kentucky Lake** Kentucky/Tenn.
107 M3 **Kentucky R** Kentucky
98 H8 **Kentville** Nova Scotia 45.04N 64.30W
107 F11 **Kentwood** Louisiana 30.58N 90.31W
43 N4 **Kentyubek,Poluostrov** pen Kazakhstan U.S.S.R. 46.38N 78.54E
90 A7 **Kenu** Nigeria 9.06N 3.12E
100 Q7 **Kenville** Manitoba 52.00N 101.20W
57 E2 **Ken,Water of** R Dumfries & Galloway Scotland
14 C2 **Kenwick** dist Perth, W Aust
73 H5 **Kenya** rep E Africa
93 J6 **Kenya,Mt** Kenya 0.10S 37.19E
108 S5 **Kenyon** Minnesota 44.18N 92.59W
100 E9 **Kenyon** airport Alberta 49.37N 112.46W
123 E13 **Kenyon Pen** Antarctica 68.30S 63.30W
103 K3 **Kenyonville** Connecticut 41.56N 72.05W
41 J4 **Ken-Yuryakh** U.S.S.R. 72.41N 106.48E
20 N6 **Ken-zaki** C Japan 35.09N 139.40E
24 C9 **Kenze Tso** L Xizang Zizhiqu China 33.58N 80.57E
43 K3 **Kenzharyk** Kazakhstan U.S.S.R. 49.54N 70.45E
64 D7 **Kenzingen** W Germany 48.12N 7.46E
46 M3 **Kenzino** U.S.S.R. 53.41N 40.28E
90 G9 **Kenzou** Cent Afr Rep 4.09N 15.09E
114 B8 **Keokea** Hawaiian Is 19.24N 155.53W
114 E6 **Keokea** Hawaiian Is 20.42N 156.22W
114 E6 **Keokea** mt Hawaiian Is 20.40N 156.19W
106 C9 **Keokuk** Iowa 40.23N 91.25W
30 C7 **Keolari** R Uttar Prad India
114 B5 **Keolu Hills** Hawaiian Is
114 D6 **Keomuku** Hawaiian Is 20.50N 156.49W
114 E6 **Keoneoio** Hawaiian Is 20.36N 156.25W
25 H3 **Keo Neua,Col de** pass Laos/Vietnam 18.22N 105.10E
29 J7 **Keonjhar** Orissa India 21.38N 85.40E
29 J7 **Keonjhargarh** dist Orissa India
30 F6 **Keoripur** Uttar Prad India 26.02N 82.21E
Keos isld see Kéa
106 C9 **Keosauqua** Iowa 40.44N 91.58W
109 F1 **Keota** Colorado 40.42N 104.06W
106 C8 **Keota** Iowa 41.21N 91.57W
109 Q6 **Keota** Oklahoma 35.15N 94.55W
25 H7 **Kep** Cambodia 10.31N 104.18E
Kepa mt see Mittagskogel
18 E7 **Kepahiang** Sumatra Indon 3.40S 102.36E
43 E6 **Kepekli** Turkmeniya U.S.S.R. 41.58N 59.20E
39 H1 **Keperveyem** U.S.S.R. 67.53N 165.52E
37 C3 **Kepez** Turkey 40.07N 26.24E
15 E7 **Kepi** Irian Jaya 6.34S 139.22E
47 E3 **Kepina** U.S.S.R. 65.21N 41.50E
26 S7 **Kepitigalla** Sri Lanka 7.25N 80.33E
11 B12 **Kepler Mts** New Zealand
62 K4 **Kępno** Poland 51.18N 17.59E
18 B8 **Kepong** Pen Malaysia 3.12N 101.38E
13 K6 **Keppel B** Queensland
18 J4 **Keppel Harb** Singapore
121 E9 **Keppel I** Falkland Is 51.20S 60.00W
40 G2 **Keppyul'skaya** U.S.S.R. 58.03N 135.16E
36 C3 **Kepsut** Turkey 39.41N 28.09E
89 K8 **Képté Béna** Togo 7.26N 0.40E
42 L1 **Keptin** U.S.S.R. 62.34N 124.22E
114 C5 **Kepuhi** Hawaiian Is 21.11N 157.15W
29 J6 **Kera** Bihar India 22.44N 83.58E
32 G6 **Kerāh** Iran 29.01N 57.37E
28 B5 **Kerala** state India
15 H6 **Keram** R Papua New Guinea
21 C13 **Kerama Retto** islds Japan
84 E2 **Keramídhi** Greece 39.35N 22.55E
18 F6 **Kerandin** Indonesia 0.12S 104.44E
12 G6 **Kerang** Victoria 35.42S 143.59E
18 A7 **Kerang, Tanjong** C Pen Malaysia 4.46N 100.34E
90 F6 **Keraoua** Cameroon 11.10N 13.55E
84 G6 **Keratéa** Greece 37.48N 23.58E
14 C5 **Keraudren,C** W Australia 19.56S 119.53E
51 L11 **Kerava** Finland 60.25N 25.10E
15 L6 **Keravat** New Britain 4.20S 152.00E
84 D4 **Kerax** mt Greece 38.44N 22.07E
18 E7 **Kerbau, Tanjung** C Sumatra Indon 4.00S 102.19E
40 G5 **Kerbi** R U.S.S.R.
Kerbrat see Téven-Kerbrat
110 B7 **Kerby** Oregon 42.15N 123.40W
84 X19 **Kercem** Gozo Medit Sea 36.02N 14.14E
44 E9 **Kerch'** Ukraine U.S.S.R. 45.22N 36.27E
47 J6 **Kerchel'** U.S.S.R. 59.19N 64.49E
47 G5 **Kerchem'ya** U.S.S.R. 61.29N 53.59E
44 D9 **Kerchenskiy Poluostrov** pen Ukraine U.S.S.R.
44 A2 **Kerchenskiy Proliv** str U.S.S.R.
47 H6 **Kerchevskiy** U.S.S.R. 59.58N 56.11E
89 K3 **Kerchouel** Mali 17.12N 0.15E
83 F4 **Kerdhíllion** mt Greece 40.46N 23.35E
88 J7 **Kerdous** Morocco 29.34N 9.11W
88 K8 **Kereb Cheheïba** reg Algeria
92 J5 **Kerege** Tanzania 6.35S 39.02E
41 N8 **Kerekhtyakh** U.S.S.R. 63.15N 129.35E
42 M2 **Kerekyan** U.S.S.R. 61.40N 125.40E
15 H7 **Kerema** Papua New Guinea 7.59S 145.46E
35 E1 **Kerem Ben Zimra** Israel 33.02N 35.28E
101 O11 **Keremeos** Br Col 49.12N 119.50W
35 C3 **Kerem Maharal** Israel 32.38N 34.59E
36 G1 **Kerempe Burun** C Turkey 42.02N 33.21E
35 A9 **Kerem Shalom** Israel 31.14N 34.17E
87 G3 **Keren** Ethiopia 15.46N 38.30E
112 L3 **Kerens** Texas 32.07N 96.15W
11 K4 **Kerepehi** New Zealand 37.17S 175.39E
47 C3 **Keret'** U.S.S.R. 66.15N 33.45E
47 C3 **Keret',Ozero** L U.S.S.R.
47 D3 **Kerets,Mys** C U.S.S.R. 65.20N 39.45E
15 G7 **Kerewa,Mt** Papua New Guinea 6.00S 143.15E
89 A5 **Kerewan** The Gambia 13.29N 16.10W
47 F4 **Kerga** U.S.S.R. 62.41N 45.59E
32 G1 **Kergeli** Turkmeniya U.S.S.R. 38.12N 56.52E
70 D5 **Kergrist-Moëlou** France 48.18N 3.19W
26 F9 **Kerguelen Basin** Indian Ocean
26 F10 **Kerguelen Is** Indian Ocean 49.30S 69.30E
26 G10 **Kerguelen Ridge** Southern Oc
103 F3 **Kerhonkson** New York 41.46N 74.18W
84 A6 **Kerí** Greece 37.40N 20.49E
18 A6 **Kerian** R Pen Malaysia
93 G6 **Kericho** Kenya 0.22S 35.19E
26 S3 **Keridamadu** Sri Lanka 9.12N 80.41E
70 D5 **Kerien** France 48.23N 3.13W
18 K5 **Kerihun,mt** Borneo Indon 1.02N 113.55E
11 H2 **Kerikeri** New Zealand 35.12S 173.59E
51 O10 **Kerimäki** Finland 61.56N 29.18E
92 K7 **Kerimbas, Ilhas** Mozambique
18 D7 **Kerinci, Danau** L Sumatra Indon
18 D6 **Kerinci, Gunung** mt Sumatra Indon 1.43S 101.15E
93 H3 **Kerio** watercourse Kenya
41 O6 **Keriske** U.S.S.R. 69.55N 132.15E
Keriya see Yutian
24 D7 **Keriya He** R Xinjiang Uygur Zizhiqu China
24 D8 **Keriya Shankou** pass Xizang Zizhiqu China 35.14N 81.32E
62 K9 **Kerka** R Yugoslavia/Hungary
60 J10 **Kerkbuurt** Marken I Netherlands 52.28N 5.06E
60 K12 **Kerkdriel** Netherlands 51.47N 5.21E
63 D10 **Kerken** W Germany 51.27N 6.25E
88 T4 **Kerkenna,Iles** Tunisia
61 E3 **Kerkhove** Belgium 50.48N 3.30E
108 P4 **Kerkhoven** Minnesota 45.11N 95.20W
47 G4 **Kerki** Komi U.S.S.R. 63.41N 54.05E
43 H7 **Kerki** Turkmeniya U.S.S.R. 37.53N 65.10E
43 H7 **Kerkichi** Turkmeniya U.S.S.R. 37.55N 65.11E
82 H9 **Kerkinítis, L** Greece
84 W22 **Kérkira** Corfu 39.38N 19.55E
83 D5 **Kérkira** isld Greece
84 W22 **Kérkiras,Vórion Stenón** str Corfu/Albania
61 K3 **Kerkom** Belgium 50.52N 4.52E
61 L3 **Kerkom-Bij-St.-Truiden** Belgium 50.47N 5.11E
90 L4 **Kerkour Nourene** mt reg Chad
60 U17 **Kerkrade** Netherlands 50.52N 6.04E
61 F3 **Kerksken** Belgium 50.53N 4.00E
60 C2 **Kerkwerve** Netherlands 51.41N 3.54E
60 J12 **Kerkwijk** Netherlands 51.47N 5.13E
18 B8 **Kerling** Pen Malaysia 3.36N 101.34E
50 G3 **Kerling** mt Iceland 65.33N 18.14W
50 G6 **Kerlingar** mt Iceland 64.24N 18.00W
50 F5 **Kerlingará** R Iceland
50 F5 **Kerlingarfjöll** mt Iceland 64.38N 19.15W
50 C3 **Kerlingarfjördhur** B Iceland
50 J2 **Kerlingar-hraun** lava Iceland
58 M5 **Kerloch** mt Grampian Scotland 56.59N 2.30W
70 B4 **Kerlouan** France 48.39N 4.22W
85 L10 **Kerma** Sudan 19.33N 30.21E
9 O11 **Kermadec Is** S Pacific Oc 30.00S 178.30W
122 J11 **Kermadec Ridge** Pacific Oc
122 J11 **Kermadec Trench** Pacific Oc
111 D5 **Kerman** California 36.42N 120.04W
32 G5 **Kermān** Iran 30.18N 57.05E
32 G6 **Kermān** prov Iran
32 H6 **Kermān Des** Iran
32 B3 **Kermānshāh** prov Iran
32 B3 **Kermānshāhān** Iran 34.19N 47.04E
32 F5 **Kermānshāhān** Iran 31.28N 54.54E
36 C6 **Kerme Körfezi** B Turkey
82 K8 **Kermen** Bulgaria 42.30N 26.16E
Kermine see Navoi
45 O3 **Kermis'** U.S.S.R. 53.51N 42.05E
112 D4 **Kermit** Texas 31.49N 103.07W
104 C9 **Kermit** W Virginia 37.51N 82.24W
61 L3 **Kermt** Belgium 50.57N 5.15E
111 F5 **Kern** R California
70 D5 **Kernascléden** France 48.03N 3.20W
56 F4 **Kerne Bridge** Hereford & Worcs Eng 51.53N 2.36W
105 G1 **Kernersville** N Carolina 36.07N 80.04W
65 N6 **Kernhof** Austria 47.49N 15.34E
61 M3 **Kerniel** Belgium 50.49N 5.22E
13 B7 **Kernot Ra** N Terr Australia
66 K4 **Kerns** Switzerland 46.54N 8.17E
111 F6 **Kernville** California 35.48N 118.27W
18 B6 **Keroh** Pen Malaysia 5.44N 101.00E
47 G5 **Keros** U.S.S.R. 60.45N 52.52E
89 E7 **Kérouané** Guinea 9.16N 9.00W
15 H6 **Kerowagi** Papua New Guinea 5.56S 144.53E
12 G4 **Kerpa** New S Wales 32.14S 143.59E
64 B2 **Kerpen** W Germany 50.52N 6.42E
82 L4 **Kerpineny** Moldavia U.S.S.R. 46.46N 28.18E
123 H6 **Kerr,C** Antarctica 79.55S 160.20E
87 F8 **Kerre** Ethiopia 5.20N 36.11E
90 N9 **Kerre** R Cent Afr Rep
58 E6 **Kerrera** isld Strathclyde Scotland 56.24N 5.33W
112 B7 **Kerrick** Texas 36.30N 102.16W
87 C9 **Kerripi** Sudan 3.55N 31.52E
105 F8 **Kerr,L** Florida 29.20N 81.49W
104 G10 **Kerr L** Virginia
116 A2 **Kerr Mt** San Salvador I Bahamas 24.03N 74.27W
100 H7 **Kerrobert** Saskatchewan 51.56N 109.09W
11 H1 **Kerr Pt** New Zealand 34.24S 173.02E
104 F9 **Kerrs Creek** Virginia 37.52N 79.31W
107 G6 **Kerrville** Tennessee 35.22N 89.51W
112 H5 **Kerrville** Texas 30.03N 99.09W
56 E3 **Kerry** Powys Wales 52.30N 3.16W
59 C7 **Kerry** co Irish Rep
59 C7 **Kerry Hd** Kerry Irish Rep 52.25N 9.57W
56 E3 **Kerry Hill** Powys Wales 52.28N 3.19W
93 H1 **Kersa Bis** Kenya 4.06N 36.46E
25 J2 **Kersaint,I.du** Vietnam 21.41N 107.41E
61 K3 **Kersbeek-Miskom** Belgium 50.53N 5.00E
65 H7 **Kerschbach** Austria 47.13N 13.20E
109 F1 **Kersey** Colorado 40.23N 104.33W
56 N3 **Kersey** Suffolk Eng 52.03N 0.55E
105 G3 **Kershaw** S Carolina 34.33N 80.36W
74 E9 **Kert** R Morocco
18 H6 **Kertamulia** Borneo Indon 0.22S 109.10E
18 E3 **Kerteh** Pen Malaysia 4.28N 103.24E
53 F6 **Kerteminde** Denmark 55.27N 10.40E
84 C6 **Kérteza** Greece 37.58N 21.59E
13 E7 **Kertie Hill** N Terr Australia 25.58S 137.50E
37 G6 **Kertis** Turkey 39.04N 43.28E
18 K9 **Kertosono** Java Indon 7.36S 112.07E
93 J6 **Keruguya** Kenya 0.31S 37.18E
Kerulen R see Herlen He
22 K2 **Kerulen** R China/Mongolia
18 J5 **Kerumuk** Borneo Indon 0.58N 110.21E
28 B2 **Kerur** Karnataka India 16.01N 75.36E
63 D9 **Kervenheim** W Germany 51.38N 6.17E
70 D6 **Kervignac** France 47.45N 3.14W
88 N7 **Kerzaz** Algeria 29.27N 1.27W
66 E4 **Kerzers** Switzerland 46.59N 7.12E
45 Q1 **Kerzhenets** U.S.S.R. 56.28N 44.25E
46 N2 **Kerzhenets** R U.S.S.R.
31 H9 **Kesabpur** Bangladesh 22.54N 89.15E
99 K2 **Kesagami** R Ontario
99 K2 **Kesagami L** Ontario
51 O10 **Kesälahti** Finland 61.54N 29.50E
35 D6 **Kesalon** Israel 31.46N 35.02E
37 C2 **Kesan** Turkey 40.52N 26.37E
37 D5 **Keşap** Turkey 40.55N 38.31E
30 H6 **Kesariya** Bihar India 26.21N 84.52E
66 Q5 **Kesch,Piz** mt Switzerland 46.38N 9.53E
91 F5 **Kese** Zaïre 3.23S 18.08E
20 P3 **Kesennuma** Japan 38.54N 141.34E
59 G2 **Kesh** Fermanagh N Ireland 54.31N 7.43W
21 C3 **Keshan** Heilongjiang China 48.03N 125.55E
106 F5 **Keshena** Wisconsin 44.54N 88.37W
32 H6 **Keshīt** Iran 29.40N 58.15E
29 B7 **Keshod** Gujarat India 21.20N 70.20E
29 E5 **Keshorai Patan** Rajasthan India 25.21N 76.01E
29 L3 **Keshpur** W Bengal India 22.34N 87.29E
32 C4 **Keshvar** Iran 33.08N 48.40E
Keshwar see Keshvar
28 C3 **Kesigi** Andhra Prad India 15.51N 77.14E
37 G6 **Kesik** Turkey 39.22N 42.32E
36 J5 **Keşiş** R Turkey
37 E6 **Keşiş Dağları** mts Turkey
37 H7 **Keşiş Gölü** L Turkey 38.28N 43.35E
36 G3 **Keskin** Turkey 39.41N 33.36E
51 L9 **Keski-Suomi** dist Finland
47 C5 **Keskozero** U.S.S.R. 61.15N 33.06E
29 F7 **Keslabori** Maharashtra India 20.24N 79.20E
46 K1 **Kesova Gora** U.S.S.R. 57.34N 37.15E
89 H1 **Kesret el Gani** watercourse Mali
61 J2 **Kessel** Belgium 51.08N 4.38E
60 N14 **Kessel** Netherlands 51.18N 6.03E
60 N14 **Kesseleijk** Netherlands 51.17N 6.01E
65 G7 **Kesselfall** fall Austria 47.13N 12.43E
61 J3 **Kessel-Lo** Belgium 50.53N 4.45E
61 O2 **Kessenich** Belgium 51.09N 5.50E
56 P3 **Kessingland** Suffolk Eng 52.25N 1.42E
66 O1 **Kesswil** Switzerland 47.36N 9.19E
Kestel see Gürsü
36 E5 **Kestel Gölü** L Turkey
95 M4 **Kestell** S Africa 28.19S 28.43E
47 C3 **Kesten'ga** U.S.S.R. 65.52N 31.45E
36 D6 **Kestep** Turkey 36.30N 29.18E
61 G3 **Kester** Belgium 50.46N 4.07E

60 L12 Kesteren Netherlands 51.56N 5.35E
64 D3 Kestert W Germany 50.10N 7.40E
57 M6 Kesteven *div* Lincs Eng
51 M7 Kestilä Finland 64.23N 26.12E
55 H5 Keston London England 51.22N 0.02E
57 G3 Keswick Cumbria Eng 54.37N 3.08W
98 F8 Keswick Ridge New Brunswick 45.58N 66.52W
62 K9 Keszthely Hungary 46.47N 17.16E
42 C3 Ket' *R* U.S.S.R.
89 K9 Keta Ghana 5.55N 1.01E
50 E2 Keta Iceland 66.03N 20.02W
87 G6 Ketama Ethiopia 9.31N 38.45E
18 K2 Ketam,Pulau *isld* Singapore
39 C4 Ketanda U.S.S.R. 60.44N 141.20E
39 C5 Ketanda *R* U.S.S.R.
89 K7 Ketao Togo 9.39N 1.16E
41 F6 Keta,Ozero *L* U.S.S.R.
18 H6 Ketapang Borneo Indon 1.50S 109.59E
18 K9 Ketapang Indonesia 6.56S 113.14E
18 D7 Ketaun Sumatra Indon 3.19S 101.49E
113 W9 Ketchikan Alaska 55.25N 131.40W
110 L6 Ketchum Idaho 43.41N 114.23W
109 P5 Ketchum Oklahoma 36.33N 95.03W
112 F4 Ketchum Mt Texas 31.20N 101.04W
89 J8 Kete Ghana 7.50N 0.03W
60 L9 Ketelmeer *L* Netherlands
39 F6 Ketepana,Gora *mt* U.S.S.R. 57.03N 158.20E
41 L8 Keterdyakh U.S.S.R. 64.15N 119.56E
29 B1 Keth Wara Delhi India 28.41N 77.15E
31 D8 Keti Bandar Pakistan 24.06N 67.30E
113 H2 Ketik *R* Alaska
50 J4 Ketildyngja *mt* Iceland 65.26N 16.36W
50 L3 Ketilsstadhir Múlasýsla, Nordhur Iceland 65.41N 14.24W
50 L4 Ketilstadhir Múlasýsla, Sudhur Iceland 65.13N 14.30W
50 E5 Ketilvatn *L* Iceland 64.57N 20.39W
40 E3 Ket-Kap,Khrebet *mts* U.S.S.R.
43 N5 Ketmen'Khrebet *mts* U.S.S.R./China
89 L8 Ketou Benin 7.25N 2.45E
47 K7 Ketovo U.S.S.R. 55.24N 65.18E
40 M8 Ketoy,Ostrov *isld* Kuril Is U.S.S.R. 47.21N 152.29E
62 N1 Kętrzyn Poland 54.05N 21.24E
61 P4 Kettenis Belgium 50.39N 6.03E
56 K3 Kettering Northants Eng 52.24N 0.44W
53 D7 Ketting Denmark 54.58N 9.54E
95 E9 Ketting S Africa 33.05S 21.25E
53 H7 Kettinge Denmark 54.42N 11.45E
108 S3 Kettle *R* Minnesota
110 G1 Kettle *R* Washington
58 K6 Kettlebridge Fife Scotland 56.15N 3.08W
104 H5 Kettle Cr *R* Pennsylvania
110 G1 Kettle Falls Washington 48.38N 118.03W
99 D8 Kettle Island Quebec
111 D5 Kettleman City California 36.00N 120.00W
110 G1 Kettle River Ra Washington
57 J4 Kettlewell N Yorks Eng 54.09N 2.02W
56 K2 Ketton Leics Eng 52.38N 0.33W
63 E10 Kettwig W Germany 51.22N 6.55E
93 H8 Ketumbaine *mt* Tanzania 2.53S 36.13E
18 J5 Ketungau *R* Borneo Indon
63 R8 Ketzin E Germany 52.29N 12.52E
18 A3 Keudeteunom Sumatra Indon 4.28N 95.42E
23 C8 Keui I Hong Kong
104 H4 Keuka L New York
42 G3 Keul' U.S.S.R. 58.25N 102.45E
64 K1 Keula E Germany 51.20N 10.33E
47 L6 Keum *R* U.S.S.R.
95 G10 Keurboomsrivier S Africa 34.01S 23.24E
89 F3 Keurig Mauritania 16.59N 7.09W
51 L9 Keurusselkä *L* Finland
51 L9 Keuruu Finland 62.16N 24.38E
47 K5 Keushki U.S.S.R. 61.45N 67.28E
65 K8 Keutschacher.See *L* Austria 46.36N 14.10E
45 P3 Kevdo-Vershina U.S.S.R. 53.07N 43.26E
63 D9 Kevelaer W Germany 51.33N 6.15E
107 H4 Kevil Kentucky 37.04N 88.56W
110 O1 Kevin Montana 48.44N 111.58W
55 D4 Kew London Eng 51.29N 0.18W
116 H4 Kew N Caicos I W I 21.55N 72.04W
12 D7 Kew *dist* Melbourne, Victoria
99 M4 Kewagama Quebec 48.15N 78.25W
106 E8 Kewanee Illinois 41.14N 89.56W
107 H9 Kewanee Mississippi 32.25N 88.27W
106 H8 Kewanna Indiana 41.01N 86.24W
30 G5 Keware Nepal 27.57N 83.47E
106 G5 Kewaunee Wisconsin 44.27N 87.31W
106 F3 Keweenaw B Michigan
106 F3 Keweenaw Bay Michigan 46.52N 88.30W
106 F2 Keweenaw Pen Michigan
106 G2 Keweenaw Pt Michigan 47.23N 87.42W
119 H5 Keweigek Guyana 5.59N 60.40W
108 K6 Keyapaha S Dakota 43.06N 100.08W
108 K6 Keya Paha *R* S Dakota
43 M6 Këyaygyr Kirgiziya U.S.S.R. 40.42N 75.37E
100 S8 Keyes Manitoba 50.14N 99.08W
109 H5 Keyes Oklahoma 36.48N 102.13W
107 G3 Keyesport Illinois 38.46N 89.12W
99 K7 Key Harbour Ontario 45.53N 80.44W
108 F5 Keyhole Res Wyoming
24 D4 Keyi Xinjiang Uygur Zizhiqu China 42.15N 82.48E
99 K7 Key Junction Ontario 45.59N 80.42W
59 F3 Key,L Roscommon Irish Rep 54.00N 8.15W
105 G12 Key Largo Florida 25.07N 80.28W
13 A2 Keyling Inlet N Terr Australia
104 H7 Keymar Maryland 39.36N 77.15W
32 E2 Keymir Turkmeniya U.S.S.R. 37.48N 53.58E
56 F5 Keynsham Avon Eng 51.26N 2.30W
103 F6 Keyport New Jersey 40.27N 74.12W
110 C2 Keyport Washington 47.40N 122.36W
104 G7 Keyser W Virginia 39.25N 78.59W
105 E4 Keysille Georgia 33.14N 82.12W
106 B8 Keystone Iowa 42.00N 92.10W
108 J8 Keystone Nebraska 41.15N 101.36W
109 O5 Keystone Oklahoma 36.08N 96.18W
108 G6 Keystone S Dakota 43.55N 103.28W
104 D9 Keystone W Virginia 37.25N 81.27W
105 E8 Keystone Heights Florida 29.46N 82.02W
111 N10 Keystone Pk *mt* Arizona 31.53N 111.14W
109 O5 Keystone Res Oklahoma
100 M8 Keystown Saskatchewan 50.29N 105.08W
37 D8 Keysun Turkey 37.34N 37.51E
104 G9 Keysville Virginia 37.02N 78.30W
32 C3 Keytū Iran 35.18N 48.07E
105 F13 Key West Florida 24.34N 81.48W
46 R1 Kez U.S.S.R. 57.52N 53.40E
93 B8 Keza Tanzania 2.45S 30.40E
104 P3 Kezar Falls Maine 43.49N 70.56W
104 P2 Kezar L Maine
88 Q6 Kezdir *watercourse* Algeria
42 G3 Kezhma Krasnoyarsk U.S.S.R. 58.58N 101.08E
92 D12 Kezi Zimbabwe 20.58S 28.32E
35 D1 Keziv *R* Israel
62 M6 Kežmarok Czechoslovakia 49.09N 20.25E
94 F5 Kgalagadi *dist* Botswana
94 G4 Kgaotwe Pan Botswana 22.40S 23.16E
94 J5 Kgatleng *dist* Botswana
94 F5 Kghoti Botswana 24.58S 21.59E
95 G2 Kgokgolelaagte *watercourse* S Africa
113 F6 Kgun L Alaska 61.30N 163.41W
35 J1 Khabab Syria 33.00N 36.16E
42 J2 Khabalakh U.S.S.R. 60.05N 112.28E
90 M5 Khabaqa Sudan 12.42N 25.29E
32 F5 Khabar Iran 30.33N 54.40E
24 D2 Khabar Asu *pass* Kazakhstan/Xinjiang Uygur Zizhiqu 47.15N 83.04E
86 K4 Khabari,Gebel el *hill* Egypt 30.36N 33.10E
47 G3 Khabarikha U.S.S.R. 65.45N 52.15E
47 J2 Khabarovo U.S.S.R. 69.36N 60.25E
40 G7 Khabarovsk U.S.S.R. 48.32N 135.08E
38 O2 Khabarovskiy Kray *terr* U.S.S.R.
42 B5 Khabary U.S.S.R. 53.36N 79.30E
43 J2 Khabay *R* Kazakhstan U.S.S.R.
33 N5 Khabbah,Ra's al *C* Oman 22.12N 59.50E
34 K10 Khabb Saḩḩah *sand dunes* Saudi Arabia
33 F8 Khabb,Wādī *watercourse* Yemen
44 D3 Khabez U.S.S.R. 44.04N 41.48E
86 G5 Khabîra Umm Gidam *hill* Egypt 30.24N 32.00E
Khabis *see* Shahdāb
31 B3 Khabody Pass Afghanistan 34.40N 63.10E
Khâboûr *R see* Khābūr *R*
32 G6 Khabr Iran 28.50N 56.17E
33 D5 Khabrā al'Arn *mud flat* Saudi Arabia
Khabra al Boliya *see* Khabrat al Bawlīyah
33 G9 Khabr,Al S Yemen 14.07N 47.02E
34 O8 Khabraţ al Bawliyah *water hole* Iraq 30.12N 46.50E
85 O3 Khabrat es Seigal *salt marsh* Syria
34 E9 Khabrat Ummm ar Raqabah *mud flat* Jordan
Khabr Bala *see* Khabr
34 K1 Khābūr *R* Iraq
34 H3 Khābūr *R* Syria
33 M5 Khābūrah,Al Oman 23.59N 57.10E
Khachagia Kuh *see* Qachāghem Kūh *mt*
47 D4 Khachela U.S.S.R. 63.22N 39.02E
39 C1 Khachimiyer *R* U.S.S.R.
44 H7 Khachinchay *R* Azerbaydzhan U.S.S.R.
44 J6 Khachmas Azerbaydzhan U.S.S.R. 41.27N 48.50E
29 D6 Khachrod Madhya Prad India 23.25N 75.20E
41 N9 Khachykat U.S.S.R. 61.15N 129.00E
42 K6 Khadabulak U.S.S.R. 50.40N 116.18E
Khadain *see* Khādeyn
86 N5 Khadâkhid, Wâdi Egypt
Khadalik *see* Hadilik
33 K8 Khadam Oman 17.46N 53.35E
33 F8 Khaḑārah Saudi Arabia 17.50N 44.01E
33 F9 Khaḑārah Yemen 15.02N 44.15E
33 N5 Khaḑar, Jabal *mt* Oman 22.31N 59.13E
34 K9 Khadd, Wādī al *watercourse* Saudi Arabia
30 E7 Khaderi *R* Uttar Prad India
32 C5 Khādeyn Iran 31.06N 49.20E
35 D7 Khadr Jordan 31.42N 35.09E
33 E2 Khaḑrā', Al Saudi Arabia 28.22N 43.11E
31 E7 Khadro Pakistan 26.11N 68.50E
47 K3 Khadyta U.S.S.R. 67.00N 69.30E
47 K3 Khadytayakha *R* U.S.S.R.
44 C3 Khadyzhensk U.S.S.R. 44.24N 39.33E
Khaf *see* Khvāf
33 G3 Khafaq,Al Saudi Arabia 26.35N 47.32E
33 H2 Khafji *oil field* The Gulf 28.32N 48.59E
33 D5 Khafqān,Al *mud flat* Saudi Arabia
33 N10 Khafqi, Ra's al *C* Saudi Arabia 28.22N 48.34E
32 E6 Khafr Iran 28.45N 53.15E
33 G4 Khafs Banbān Saudi Arabia 25.31N 46.29E
33 G5 Khafs Daghrah Saudi Arabia 23.45N 47.08E
34 K7 Khaft, Sha'īb al *watercourse* Iraq
30 E7 Khaga Uttar Prad India 25.47N 81.05E
30 K7 Khagaria Bihar India 25.31N 86.27E
30 J7 Khagaul Bihar India 25.34N 85.02E
31 J9 Khagrachbari Bangladesh 23.08N 92.00E
39 B2 Khagyr U.S.S.R. 67.19N 136.15E
31 B5 Khahak Afghanistan 31.46N 62.39E
Khai *see* Ban Khai
94 B2 Khaias Namibia 19.47S 13.36E
Khaibar *see* Khaybar
30 A5 Khair Uttar Prad India 27.57N 77.50E
30 K8 Khaira Bihar India 24.53N 86.13E
Khairabad *see* Kheyrābād
31 B5 Khairabad Afghanistan 30.34N 63.37E
31 C2 Khairabad Afghanistan 36.21N 64.55E
30 D5 Khairabad Uttar Prad India 27.32N 80.45E
29 G7 Khairagarh Madhya Prad India 21.28N 81.00E
30 A6 Khairagarh Uttar Prad India 26.57N 77.49E
Khairan,Ras al *see* Khayrān,Ra's al *cape*
31 F6 Khairgarh Pakistan 28.10N 70.52E
30 D4 Khairigarh Uttar Prad India 28.20N 80.50E
31 B3 Khair Khana Afghanistan 34.55N 63.35E
84 E5 Khairónia Greece 38.30N 22.50E
94 C2 Khairos Namibia 19.48S 15.03E
31 G6 Khairpur Bahawalpur Pakistan 29.35N 72.19E
31 E7 Khairpur Khairpur Pakistan 27.30N 68.50E
31 E7 Khairpur *div* Pakistan
31 F6 Khairpur Sadat Pakistan 29.20N 70.50E
44 E5 Khaishi Georgia U.S.S.R. 42.56N 42.13E
32 D5 Khāīz,Kūh-e *mt* Iran 30.26N 50.56E
31 C2 Khaja du Koh *mt* Afghanistan 36.50N 65.34E
44 H10 Khājehghūr Iran 37.24N 47.00E
29 F5 Khajrāho *anc site* Madhya Prad India 24.50N 79.55E
30 D6 Khajuha Uttar Prad India 26.03N 80.31E
30 F6 Khajurhat Uttar Prad India 26.32N 82.08E
30 K8 Khajuri Bihar India 24.33N 86.06E
29 K7 Khajuri W Bengal India 21.57N 88.00E
42 D5 Khakasskaya Avt. Obl *prov* U.S.S.R.
31 D3 Khakdao Afghanistan 34.59N 67.11E
31 E3 Khāk-e Jabbar 34.24N 69.29E
32 E4 Khakh Iran 33.56N 52.08E
44 G5 Khakhalgi *mt* U.S.S.R. 42.50N 45.09E
40 G3 Khakhar' U.S.S.R. 57.40N 135.30E
42 G4 Khakharey U.S.S.R. 55.17N 101.22E
94 G5 Khakhea Botswana 24.51S 23.20E
41 M7 Khakhsyn U.S.S.R. 65.52N 123.21E
45 T8 Khaki,sor *salt L* Kazakhstan U.S.S.R.
34 Q4 Khākrīz Iran 34.46N 48.06E
31 C5 Khakriz *reg* Afghanistan
Khakurinokhabl' *see* Shovgenovskiy
43 G7 Khalach Turkmeniya U.S.S.R. 38.04N 64.54E
34 Q7 Khalaf Iran 31.35N 48.34E
32 C5 Khalafābād Iran 30.54N 49.25E
32 C3 Khalajestan *reg* Iran
24 F10 Khalamba La *pass* Xizang Zizhiqu China 30.01N 89.54E
84 C5 Khalandrítsa Greece 38.06N 21.47E
Khalasa *see* Horvot Halẓa
84 F6 Khalasméni Greece 37.45N 23.27E
44 F5 Khalatsa *mt* Georgia U.S.S.R. 42.33N 43.56E
31 J3 Khalatse Kashmir 34.24N 76.49E
44 H7 Khaldan Azerbaydzhan U.S.S.R. 40.42N 47.13E
30 E2 Khaleb Xizang Zizhiqu 30.54N 81.14E
42 B1 Khalesavoy U.S.S.R. 63.23N 78.20E
33 D4 Khalf,Al Saudi Arabia 25.02N 40.29E
41 K5 Khalgannakh U.S.S.R. 71.52N 114.07E
84 G5 Khália Greece 38.29N 23.33E
33 A7 Khalī,Al *isld* Saudi Arabia 26.27N 50.12E
32 D4 Khalidabad Iran 33.42N 51.59E
Khali,El *see* Hebron Jordan
86 R12 Khalifa,El *dist* Cairo Egypt
31 D5 Khalifat *mt* Pakistan 30.21N 67.45E
86 D3 Khalîg Abu Qîr *B* Egypt
86 B4 Khalîg el 'Arab *B* Egypt
86 J3 Khalîg el Tîna *B* Egypt
86 O9 Khalīj 'Aynūna *inlet* Saudi Arabia
32 D6 Khalīj-e Fārs *sub prov* Iran
32 F7 Khalīj-e Fārs va Daryā-ye 'Omān *sub-prov* Iran
Khalīj-e-Gavāter *see* Gwatar B
78 D12 Khalīj et Hammāmet *gulf* Tunisia
85 E4 Khalīj Surt *G* Libya
85 E4 Khalīj Surt *G* Libya
78 D12 Khalīj Tunis *gulf* Tunisia
84 B2 Khalíki Greece 39.41N 21.12E
32 H3 Khalilabad Iran 35.10N 58.18E
30 G6 Khalilabad Uttar Prad India 26.47N 83.04E
Khalil,El *see* Hebron Jordan
32 E7 Khalīlī Iran 27.38N 53.20E
43 E2 Khalilovo U.S.S.R. 51.27N 58.01E
84 A5 Khaliotáta Greece 38.13N 20.37E
34 M5 Khālis,Al Iraq 33.51N 44.32E
43 E5 Khalkabad Uzbekistan U.S.S.R. 42.40N 59.44E
Khalkhal *see* Herowābād
84 E2 Khálki Greece 39.34N 22.33E
83 J8 Khálki *isld* Greece
83 F4 Khalkidhiki *pen* Greece
84 G5 Khalkis Greece 38.28N 23.36E
35 E5 Khallat el Fūla Jordan 32.10N 35.28E
47 J2 Khal'mer-Yu U.S.S.R. 67.58N 64.48E
44 J7 Khaltan Azerbaydzhan U.S.S.R. 40.58N 48.40E
30 H5 Khalte Nepal 27.50N 84.19E
46 P1 Khalturin U.S.S.R. 58.38N 48.50E
45 G7 Khalturino Ukraine U.S.S.R. 49.30N 35.16E
33 N6 Khalūf Oman 20.31N 58.04E
84 C7 Khalvátsou Greece 37.08N 21.48E
41 N7 Khalygras U.S.S.R. 67.04N 129.50E
39 B4 Khalyya *R* U.S.S.R.
42 J2 Khamaky U.S.S.R. 60.15N 111.48E
31 F3 Khama Pass Afghanistan 35.40N 71.00E
42 G6 Khamar-Daban,Khrebet *mts* U.S.S.R.
33 F6 Khamāsīn Al Saudi Arabia 20.29N 44.49E
29 A6 Khambhaliya Gujarat India 22.13N 69.42E
29 C6 Khambhat Gujarat India 22.19N 72.39E
29 C6 Khambhat *dist* Gujarat India
29 C7 Khambhat (or Cambay) Gujarat India
47 L3 Khambi Yakha U.S.S.R. 65.57N 72.35E
29 E7 Khamgaon Maharashtra India 20.42N 76.40E
92 D12 Khami Zimbabwe 20.20S 28.30E
92 D11 Khami *R* Zimbabwe
31 C2 Kham-i-Ab *reg* Afghanistan
83 H9 Khamilí *isld* Greece 35.51N 26.14E
33 E8 Khamir Yemen 16.06N 43.57E
34 E10 Khamīsah Saudi Arabia 28.02N 37.15E
Khamis Mushait *see* Khamis Mushayţ
33 E7 Khamis Mushayţ Saudi Arabia 18.19N 42.45E
25 H3 Kham Keut Laos 18.17N 104.45E
33 G3 Khamma Saudi Arabia 27.03N 46.44E
28 E2 Khammam Andhra Prad India 17.16N 80.13E
28 E2 Khammam *dist* Andhra Prad India
40 G1 Khamna *R* U.S.S.R.
41 M8 Khampa U.S.S.R. 63.52N 123.10E
42 J1 Khampa Yakutsk U.S.S.R. 62.58N 115.10E
42 K1 Khampa Yakutsk U.S.S.R. 62.58N 116.32E
25 J5 Khampho *R* Laos
42 J2 Khamrà U.S.S.R. 60.18N 114.10E
42 F5 Khamsara *R* U.S.S.R.
34 L7 Khamsāt,Sha'īb abū *watercourse* Iraq
32 B2 Khamseh *reg* Iran
28 L2 Khamtis *tribe* India/Burma
Khamyak *see* Khanīyak
43 N8 Khamzaabad Kirgiziya U.S.S.R. 40.00N 71.50E
43 K6 Khamza Khakimzade Uzbekistan U.S.S.R. 40.29N 71.31E
94 C4 Khan *watercourse* Namibia
29 K6 Khana W Bengal India 23.12N 87.50E
31 E2 Khanabad Takhar Afghanistan 36.42N 69.08E
43 N7 Khanabad Uzbekistan U.S.S.R. 40.53N 70.47E
85 F4 Khanādiqīyah, M. al Libya 30.36N 29.59E
Khan Agha *see* Khānaqāh
31 E2 Khanaka Afghanistan 36.33N 69.16E
31 C2 Khanakha Afghanistan 36.06N 65.25E
34 K5 Khān al Baghdādī Iraq 33.52N 42.33E
34 M6 Khān al Ḩammād Iraq 32.20N 44.18E
34 M6 Khan al Maḩāwīl Iraq 32.39N 44.28E
34 M5 Khān al Mashāhidah Iraq 33.40N 44.15E
34 M6 Khān al Muşalla Iraq 32.09N 44.20E
28 B2 Khanapur Maharashtra India 17.19N 74.45E
32 A2 Khānaqāh Iran 37.35N 45.47E
34 N4 Khānaqīn Iraq 34.22N 45.22E
35 H4 Khanasira Jordan 32.23N 36.03E
34 J2 Khana Sor Iraq 36.28N 41.36E
32 A1 Khanasur Pass Iran/Iraq 38.14N 44.27E
34 M5 Khān Azād Iraq 33.08N 44.21E
34 E4 Khanāzīr, Jebel el *mts* Syria
32 F2 Khān Bāgh Iran 36.11N 55.22E
Khan Bani Sa'ad *see* Banī Sa'd
31 G3 Khanbari Pass Kashmir 35.52N 73.56E
44 F6 Khanchali,Oz *L* Georgia U.S.S.R.
30 G5 Khanchikot Nepal 27.56N 83.10E
12 J6 Khancoban New S Wales 36.09S 148.06E
42 H5 Khanda U.S.S.R. 54.58N 107.15E
41 P9 Khanda *R* U.S.S.R.
Khandab *see* Khondāb
42 E6 Khandagayty U.S.S.R. 50.45N 92.02E
28 A1 Khandala Kolaba, Maharashtra India 18.45N 73.25E
28 B1 Khandala Satara, Maharashtra India 18.01N 74.04E
11 C5 Khandallah *dist* Wellington New Zealand
85 L10 Khandaq,El Sudan 18.34N 30.34E
30 C5 Khandar Uttar Prad India 27.47N 79.36E
30 B5 Khandauh Uttar Prad India 27.19N 78.02E
29 D4 Khandela Rajasthan India 27.33N 75.32E
29 J7 Khandgiri Hill Orissa India 20.20N 85.50E
29 J7 Khandpara Orissa India 20.15N 85.11E
31 E4 Khand Pass Pak/Afghan 32.13N 69.20E
29 D6 Khandu Rajasthan India 23.28N 74.32E
31 G2 Khandūd Afghanistan 36.57N 72.19E
29 E7 Khandwa Madhya Prad India 21.49N 76.23E
41 P8 Khandyga U.S.S.R. 62.42N 135.35E
Khâne Cheïkhoûn *see* Khān Shiekhūn
Khâne Erennbé *see* Khan Ureinibah
32 E5 Khāneh Khowreh Iran 30.53N 53.04E
Khāneh Sūr,Gardaneh-ye *see* Khanasur Pass
35 H7 Khan ez Zabib *anc site* Jordan 31.31N 36.06E
35 H8 Khan ez Zabib Sta Jordan 31.28N 36.06E
Khanfar *see* Ja'ar
39 F7 Khangar,Gora *mt* U.S.S.R. 54.46N 157.19E
31 F6 Khangarh Pakistan 29.57N 71.14E
43 N8 Khangiz Uzbekistan U.S.S.R. 40.19N 71.32E
47 J4 Khanglasy U.S.S.R. 62.45N 61.32E
47 J5 Khangokurt U.S.S.R. 62.00N 64.23E
30 F5 Khangra Nepal 27.46N 82.17E
25 K6 Khanh Hoa Vietnam 12.15N 109.04E
25 H8 Khanh Hung Vietnam 9.36N 105.59E
40 B3 Khani U.S.S.R. 57.05N 120.57E
40 B3 Khani *R* U.S.S.R.
84 K10 Khaniá Crete 35.31N 24.01E
84 J11 Khaniá *prov* Crete
30 B7 Khaniadhana Madhya Prad India 25.02N 78.08E
44 G10 Khānīān Iran 37.30N 45.56E
45 H2 Khanino U.S.S.R. 54.13N 36.53E
84 J10 Khaníon,Kólpos *gulf* Crete
32 E6 Khanīyak Iran 29.05N 52.05E
34 M6 Khān Jadwal Iraq 32.03N 44.48E
86 F5 Khânka,El Egypt 30.12N 31.21E
40 F9 Khanka,Ozero *L* U.S.S.R./China
30 A7 Khankar Madhya Prad India 25.34N 77.43E
31 G4 Khanki Pakistan 32.22N 73.55E
43 F6 Khanki Uzbekistan U.S.S.R. 41.29N 60.45E
31 G4 Khanki Weir Pakistan 32.22N 73.53E
44 G7 Khanlar Azerbaydzhan U.S.S.R. 40.34N 46.18E
44 H8 Khanlyk Azerbaydzhan U.S.S.R. 39.16N 46.43E
34 L6 Khān Mujiddah Iraq 32.22N 43.50E
29 E2 Khanna Punjab India 30.42N 76.16E
30 D7 Khanna Uttar Prad India 25.34N 80.04E
41 O7 Khannakh *R* U.S.S.R.
25 G3 Khan,Nam *R* Laos
31 C5 Khannan Afghanistan 30.39N 65.56E
41 L7 Khannya *R* U.S.S.R.
47 J3 Khanovey U.S.S.R. 67.19N 63.48E
41 C6 Khanovey-Sede U.S.S.R. 68.14N 77.10E
31 F6 Khanpur Pakistan 23.38N 70.40E
34 M7 Khān Ruḩābah Iraq 31.44N 44.19E
31 F5 Khansar Pakistan 31.40N 71.15E
34 D3 Khān Sheikhūn Syria 35.27N 36.38E
44 C3 Khanskaya U.S.S.R. 44.41N 39.59E
44 B1 Khanskoye Ozero *L* U.S.S.R.
86 L9 Khanşûr,Gebel *hill* Egypt 28.03N 33.59E
43 L5 Khantau Kazakhstan U.S.S.R. 44.14N 73.47E
41 E6 Khantayka U.S.S.R. 68.15N 86.35E
41 E6 Khantayka *R* U.S.S.R.
41 F6 Khantayskoye,Ozero *L* U.S.S.R.
41 E6 Khantayskoye Vodokhranilishche *res* U.S.S.R.
43 O6 Khan Tengri,Pik Kirgiziya/Kazakhstan U.S.S.R. 42.13N 80.14E
47 K5 Khanty-Mansiysk U.S.S.R. 61.01N 69.00E
42 C2 Khanty Mansiyskiy Nats. Okr U.S.S.R.
25 E4 Khanu Thailand 16.05N 99.45E
34 L3 Khanuqah *oil well* Iraq 35.20N 43.14E
35 G1 Khan Ureinibah Syria 33.11N 35.53E
39 C5 Khanyangda U.S.S.R. 58.03N 140.31E
35 A8 Khan Yunis Gaza Strip 31.21N 34.18E
45 K8 Khanzhenkovo Ukraine U.S.S.R. 48.05N 38.05E
35 F4 Khanzira Jordan 32.28N 35.42E
35 F9 Khanzira Jordan 31.03N 35.36E
25 E8 Khao Chum Thong Thailand 8.08N 99.53E
25 H5 Khao Phra Vihar *ruin* Cambodia 14.25N 104.44E
25 E5 Khao Yai *mt* Thailand 15.23N 99.22E
Khao Yoi *see* Bag Khao Yoi
29 F7 Khapa Maharashtra India 21.28N 79.02E
31 J3 Khapalu Kashmir 35.12N 76.21E
42 J7 Khapcheranga U.S.S.R. 49.46N 112.20E
46 F6 Khapilovka *R* U.S.S.R.
40 C2 Khappyrastakh U.S.S.R. 59.24N 124.41E
28 A7 Khar *dist* Bombay India 19.05N 72.51E
32 C3 Khar *R* Iran
40 D3 Khara *R* U.S.S.R.
41 O8 Khara-Aldan U.S.S.R. 63.22N 133.00E
42 J2 Khara Astakh U.S.S.R. 60.30N 113.08E
33 F8 Kharāb,Al Yemen 16.24N 44.39E
45 T9 Kharabali U.S.S.R. 47.26N 47.15E
30 A1 Kharag Himachal Prad India 31.31N 77.24E
30 K8 Kharagdiha Bihar India 24.25N 86.12E
29 B6 Kharaghoda Gujarat India 23.11N 71.46E
30 K7 Kharagpur Bihar India 25.07N 86.33E
29 K6 Kharagpur W Bengal India 22.23N 87.22E
42 J6 Kharagun U.S.S.R. 51.35N 111.10E
30 A7 Kharai Madhya Prad India 25.07N 77.44E
32 D4 Kharājī Iran 32.06N 50.50E
34 O1 Kharāju Iran 37.13N 46.31E
84 M11 Khárakas Crete 35.00N 25.08E
42 G6 Khara-Khuzhar U.S.S.R. 50.50N 103.50E
32 G2 Kharakī Iran 37.45N 56.45E
28 A1 Kharakvasla L Maharashtra India 18.30N 73.45E
42 F6 Kharal U.S.S.R. 51.59N 96.41E
41 M7 Kharalakh U.S.S.R. 66.15N 124.05E
42 B1 Kharampur U.S.S.R. 64.16N 78.01E
42 B1 Kharampur *R* U.S.S.R.
31 C6 Kharan Pakistan 28.32N 65.26E
31 B7 Kharan *dist* Pakistan
32 G6 Khārān *R* Iran
32 F4 Kharānaq Iran 32.18N 54.42E
Kharan Kalat *see* Kharan
42 K6 Kharanor U.S.S.R. 50.08N 116.40E
Kharaqi *see* Kharakī
30 F8 Kharar Uttar Prad India 24.21N 82.57E
29 L2 Kharar W Bengal India 22.40N 87.45E
Kharari Rajasthan India*see* Abu Road
30 B7 Kharari Uttar Prad India 25.32N 78.31E
35 D7 Kharas Jordan 31.37N 35.02E
47 K1 Kharasavey *R* U.S.S.R.
39 E1 Khara-Tala U.S.S.R. 69.11N 154.19E
39 B2 Khara-Tas U.S.S.R. 65.44N 135.16E
41 K4 Khara-Tumus, Poluostrov *pen* U.S.S.R.
41 N5 Kharaulakh' U.S.S.R. 70.30N 129.44E
41 N5 Kharaulakh' *R* U.S.S.R.
41 N5 Kharaulakhskiy Khrebet *mts* U.S.S.R.
42 H6 Kharauz U.S.S.R. 52.20N 106.20E
44 J10 Kharāyem Iran 35.57N 48.13E
86 J10 Kharâza, Gebel el *hill* Egypt 27.56N 32.50E
41 M8 Kharbala U.S.S.R. 64.03N 120.21E
35 D6 Kharbata Jordan 31.57N 35.04E
42 H5 Kharbatovo U.S.S.R. 53.46N 106.01E
31 E4 Kharbin Pass Afghanistan 33.10N 68.34E
39 G6 Kharchino U.S.S.R. 56.35N 160.50E
28 B1 Kharda Maharashtra India 18.38N 75.32E
28 C8 Khardi Maharashtra India 19.35N 73.27E
31 J3 Khardung La *pass* Kashmir 34.18N 77.38E
31 A3 Kharez Ilias Afghanistan 35.28N 61.20E
33 G5 Kharfah,Al Saudi Arabia 22.11N 46.43E
32 B5 Kharfiyah Iraq 30.57N 47.05E
32 D6 Khārg *isld* Iran 29.14N 50.20E
32 D6 Khārg *oil field* The Gulf 29.13N 50.17E
85 L7 Khârga,El Egypt 25.27N 30.32E
42 J5 Kharga,Ozero *L* U.S.S.R. 52.55N 111.55E
30 C8 Khargapur Madhya Prad India 24.50N 79.09E
29 D7 Khargon Madhya Prad India 21.49N 75.39E
Khargpur *see* Kharagpur
40 F5 Khargu *R* U.S.S.R.
30 E5 Khargupur Uttar Prad India 27.22N 81.59E
43 L7 Khargush,Pereval *pass* Tadzhikistan U.S.S.R. 37.32N 73.02E
39 D1 Khargystyr U.S.S.R. 69.19N 147.10E
30 A5 Khari *R* Uttar Prad India
31 G4 Kharian Pakistan 32.52N 73.52E
29 H7 Khariar Orissa India 20.19N 82.50E
33 F9 Khārid,Wādī al *watercourse* Yemen
30 L7 Kharik Bihar India 25.23N 87.01E
42 G5 Kharik U.S.S.R. 54.15N 101.40E
86 L5 Kharîm,Gebel *hill* Egypt 30.16N 33.58E
40 N7 Kharimkotan *vol* Kuril Is U.S.S.R. 49.07N 154.31E
40 N7 Kharimkotan, O *isld* Kuril Is U.S.S.R. 49.07N 154.31E
29 D5 Khari R Ajmer, Rajasthan India
29 C5 Khari, R Jalor, Rajasthan India
33 J5 Kharit Saudi Arabia 23.32N 51.08E
41 E4 Kharitona Lapteva,Bereg *coast* U.S.S.R.
33 A4 Kharit,Wâdi *watercourse* Egypt
35 G3 Kharja Jordan 32.40N 35.53E
33 G5 Kharj, Al *oasis* Saudi Arabia
33 J7 Kharkhair Saudi Arabia 18.54N 51.05E
29 E3 Kharkhauda Haryana India 28.55N 76.56E
30 A4 Kharkhauda Uttar Prad India 28.50N 77.44E
45 H6 Khar'kov Ukraine U.S.S.R. 50.00N 36.15E
45 H6 Khar'kovskaya Oblast' *prov* Ukraine U.S.S.R.
32 E5 Khār Kūh *mt* Iran 31.38N 53.46E
41 N2 Kharli, Ostrov *isld* Franz Josef Land U.S.S.R. 81.16N 54.15E
47 D2 Kharlovka U.S.S.R. 68.48N 37.20E
47 C5 Kharlu U.S.S.R. 61.45N 30.55E
47 M6 Kharlushi U.S.S.R. 55.14N 60.58E
33 H4 Kharmā',Jabal *plat* Saudi Arabia
82 K9 Kharmanli Bulgaria 41.55N 25.55E
31 J4 Kharna Kashmir 33.36N 77.31E
84 C8 Kharokopión Greece 36.48N 21.55E
29 G7 Kharora Madhya Prad India 21.28N 81.58E
31 E4 Kharoti *reg* Afghanistan
47 E6 Kharovsk U.S.S.R. 59.56N 40.09E
41 G6 Kharpicha,Ozero *L* U.S.S.R.
86 L3 Kharrûba,El Egypt 31.11N 33.57E
34 L7 Kharr, Wādī al *watercourse* Iraq
33 H3 Kharsānīyah *oil well* Saudi Arabia 27.10N 49.20E
34 P3 Kharsareh, Kūh *mt* Iran 35.02N 47.48E
29 J2 Kharsawan Bihar India 22.46N 85.49E
47 L1 Kharse,Mys *C* U.S.S.R. 70.05N 73.25E
Khār,Shatt al *R see* Kār,Shatt al *R*
41 Q5 Kharstan U.S.S.R. 72.10N 140.15E
30 L4 Kharta Xizang Zizhiqu 28.04N 87.19E
30 K1 Khartachangri Glacier Xizang Zizhiqu
30 L1 Kharta Chu *R* Nepal
30 K2 Kharta Glacier Xizang Zizhiqu
31 J3 Khartaksho Kashmir 34.55N 76.14E
30 K1 Khartaphu *mt* Xizang Zizhiqu 28.04N 86.59E
87 D3 Khartoum Sudan 15.33N 32.32E
87 D3 Khartoum *prov* Sudan
87 D3 Khartoum North Sudan 15.39N 32.34E
45 K8 Khartsyzsk Ukraine U.S.S.R. 48.02N 38.10E
47 H3 Kharutayuvam U.S.S.R. 66.51N 59.31E
32 G4 Kharv-e Bālā Iran 33.37N 57.02E
47 K3 Kharvuta U.S.S.R. 67.15N 69.44E
31 E4 Kharwar *reg* Afghanistan
41 K6 Kharyyalakh U.S.S.R. 68.26N 112.16E
31 E3 Kharzar Pass Afghanistan 35.04N 68.21E
Khasab *see* Qasab
33 M3 Khaşab, Al Oman 26.14N 56.15E
33 M3 Khaşab, Khōr *gulf* Oman
41 N5 Khasalakh U.S.S.R. 70.34N 126.15E
40 E10 Khasan U.S.S.R. 42.28N 130.48E
32 G1 Khasardag,Gora *mt* Turkmeniya U.S.S.R. 38.28N 56.25E
44 E4 Khasaut U.S.S.R. 43.43N 42.34E
44 H4 Khasavyurt U.S.S.R. 43.16N 46.36E
41 D5 Khaseynto,Ozero *L* U.S.S.R.
33 L7 Khasfah,Al Oman 19.40N 54.19E
31 B5 Khash Afghanistan 31.29N 62.49E
32 J6 Khāsh Iran 28.14N 61.15E
86 F6 Khashab,Gebel el *hill* Egypt 29.56N 31.00E
86 M10 Khashabi,Gebel *hill* Egypt 27.50N 34.11E
31 B5 Khash Des Afghanistan
47 K3 Khashgort U.S.S.R. 65.25N 65.40E
22 C6 Khashi Bulak *well* Xinjiang Uygur Zizhiqu China 41.40N 93.37E
24 H5 Khashi Bulak *well* Xinjiang Uygur Zizhiqu China 41.40N 93.37E
33 G5 Khashm al Khufaysah *mt* Saudi Arabia 22.57N 47.00E
33 E3 Khashm ar Ra'an *mt* Saudi Arabia 26.53N 43.19E
33 J4 Khashm Bijrān *hill* Saudi Arabia 24.06N 50.59E
86 B4 Khashm el 'Eish Egypt
87 E3 Khashm el Girba Sudan 14.59N 35.59E
86 E5 Khashm el Kalb *hill* Egypt 30.13N 30.51E
86 O5 Khashm Imsheitī *mt* Jordan 30.02N 35.21E
33 G5 Khashm Māwān *mt* Saudi Arabia 22.49N 46.04E
33 F6 Khashm Mishlaḩ Saudi Arabia 21.08N 45.27E
33 F6 Khashm Mutarjim Saudi Arabia 20.38N 45.17E
33 B3 Khashm Şana' Saudi Arabia 27.36N 37.34E
86 J10 Khashm Umm 'Omeiyid *hill* Egypt 27.40N 32.36E
31 B5 Khash R Afghanistan
31 B5 Khash Rud *R* Afghanistan
44 F6 Khashuri Georgia U.S.S.R. 41.58N 43.35E
84 B2 Khasiá Ori *mts* Greece
33 E5 Khāşirah,Al Saudi Arabia 23.30N 43.45E
82 K9 Khaskovo Bulgaria 41.57N 25.32E
86 G9 Khasm el Raqaba *hill* Egypt 28.15N 31.46E
32 C5 Khasravī Iran 31.05N 48.50E
39 C2 Khastakh U.S.S.R. 66.43N 141.28E
39 E4 Khasyn-Ugol' U.S.S.R. 60.08N 150.49E
30 F8 Khatai Madhya Prad India 24.32N 82.34E
30 K6 Khataia Bihar India 26.19N 86.45E
33 L5 Khatam, Al *des area* U.A.E.
33 C3 Khatam,Jabal al *mts* Saudi Arabia
41 H5 Khatanga U.S.S.R. 71.59N 102.31E
41 H5 Khatanga *R* U.S.S.R.
41 J4 Khatangskiy Zaliv *gulf* U.S.S.R.
39 F3 Khataren U.S.S.R. 62.34N 155.38E
30 A3 Khatauli Uttar Prad India 29.16N 77.42E
47 H3 Khatayakha U.S.S.R. 66.25N 57.15E
30 C4 Khatima Uttar Prad India 28.56N 79.58E
31 F2 Khatinza Pass Afghan/Pakistan 36.26N 71.37E
33 M4 Khatmat al Malāha Oman 24.58N 56.22E
Khâtoûniye *see* Khātūniya
31 K4 Khatpa Thanbo Kashmir 33.32N 78.10E
33 M4 Khaţţ, Al U.A.E. 25.36N 56.03E
45 J1 Khatun' U.S.S.R. 55.01N 37.52E
32 F5 Khātūnābād Iran 30.02N 55.24E
34 J2 Khātūniya Syria 36.27N 41.15E
41 N9 Khatylyma U.S.S.R. 61.35N 129.58E
40 C3 Khatymy *R* U.S.S.R.
39 K4 Khatyn' U.S.S.R. 62.00N 175.05E
39 D3 Khatyngnakh Magadan U.S.S.R. 62.43N 150.00E
39 D4 Khatyngnakh Magadan U.S.S.R. 62.02N 148.06E
40 F1 Khatyngnakh Yakutsk U.S.S.R. 60.37N 133.44E
39 C1 Khatyngnakh *R* Yakutsk U.S.S.R.
41 L8 Khatyng-Sysy U.S.S.R. 63.39N 118.55E
39 E1 Khatyrabyt U.S.S.R. 69.09N 151.39E
43 H6 Khatyrchi Uzbekistan U.S.S.R. 40.02N 65.58E
39 K4 Khatyrka U.S.S.R. 62.05N 175.18E
39 J3 Khatyrka *R* U.S.S.R.
40 B2 Khatystakh U.S.S.R. 58.37N 121.33E
40 C2 Khatystyr Yakutsk U.S.S.R. 59.00N 125.15E
41 N7 Khatystyr Yakutsk U.S.S.R. 65.20N 126.45E
84 B3 Khatzí *mt* Greece 39.25N 21.20E
43 H7 Khaudag Uzbekistan U.S.S.R. 37.36N 67.22E
32 C5 Khāvar Iran 31.36N 48.41E
84 B6 Khávari Greece 37.51N 21.23E
29 A6 Khavda Gujarat India 23.50N 69.49E
31 E3 Khawak Pass Afghanistan 35.40N 69.51E
29 D6 Khawasa Madhya Prad India 23.05N 74.42E
33 E10 Khawkhah, Al Yemen 13.53N 43.13E
33 K10 Khawlaf,Ra's *C* Socotra Ind Oc 12.40N 54.07E
33 N9 Khawr 'Abd Allāh *B* Kuwait
33 J4 Khawr,Al Qatar, The Gulf 25.40N 51.33E
Khawr ash Shamm *crater see* Elphinstone Inlet
33 N9 Khawr aş Şabīyah *channel* Kuwait
33 A10 Khawr Bi'r Aḩmad *B* S Yemen
33 B10 Khawr Ghadīr *B* S Yemen
33 K6 Khawr Ḩamīdān *salty well* Saudi Arabia 20.44N 53.50E
33 C9 Khawr Maksar *crater* S Yemen
33 N10 Khawr Mufattaḩ Saudi Arabia 28.10N 48.22E
33 K7 Khawr Şhiban *salty well* Saudi Arabia 19.40N 52.11E
33 F10 Khawr 'Umayrah *B* S Yemen
34 G7 Khawr-Umm-Wu'āl *salt lake* Saudi Arabia
25 D5 Khawsa Burma 15.01N 97.49E
33 D7 Khawsh Saudi Arabia 19.00N 41.55E
33 E9 Khawtamah, Al *isld* Yemen 15.42N 42.16E
33 C4 Khaybar Saudi Arabia 25.48N 39.12E
33 E7 Khaybar Saudi Arabia 18.53N 42.52E
43 K7 Khaydarken Kirgiziya U.S.S.R. 39.58N 71.20E
39 H4 Khaylino U.S.S.R. 61.01N 166.50E
39 G5 Khaylyulya U.S.S.R. 58.04N 161.59E
47 H2 Khaypudyrskaya Guba *gulf* U.S.S.R.
33 N5 Khayrān Ra's al *C* Oman 23.34N 58.45E
39 F6 Khayryuzova, Mys *C* U.S.S.R. 57.08N 156.30E
42 G5 Khayryuzovka Irkutsk U.S.S.R. 53.46N 103.30E
39 C5 Khayryuzovka Khabarovsk U.S.S.R. 59.22N 144.52E
39 F6 Khayryuzovo U.S.S.R. 56.53N 157.00E
33 B10 Khaysā S Yemen 12.45N 44.55E
40 D1 Khaysardakh U.S.S.R. 60.37N 128.14E
41 O5 Khayyr U.S.S.R. 70.49N 133.30E
39 A1 Khayysardakh U.S.S.R. 67.56N 134.41E
43 F6 Khazar-Asp Uzbekistan U.S.S.R. 41.19N 61.05E
34 L4 Khāzimīyah Iraq 34.47N 43.38E
34 L2 Khāzir *R* Iraq
44 J6 Khazry Azerbaydzhan U.S.S.R. 41.30N 48.14E
Khbaïra el Khachâm *see* Khbaira el Khasham
34 J3 Khbaira el Khasham *salt swamp* Syria
25 H3 Khe Bo Vietnam 19.10N 104.39E
28 A1 Khed Poona, Maharashtra India 18.54N 73.56E
28 A2 Khed Ratnagiri, Maharashtra India 17.44N 73.25E
29 C5 Khed Brahma Gujarat India 24.03N 73.03E
32 H3 Khedri Iran 34.03N 58.45E
86 M7 Kheiyâla,Gebel *hill* Egypt 29.20N 34.14E
30 A4 Khekra Uttar Prad India 28.51N 77.17E
31 C4 Khel Afghanistan 32.24N 65.53E
28 K2 Khela Assam India 27.00N 95.25E
30 D3 Khela Uttar Prad India 29.57N 80.35E
41 E4 Khelaliturku,Ozero *L* U.S.S.R. 72.50N 89.00E
39 D4 Khel-Deli, Ozero *L* U.S.S.R. 61.41N 145.49E
25 H2 Khe Long Vietnam 21.25N 104.50E
47 C5 Khelyulya U.S.S.R. 61.43N 30.42E
42 E6 Khemchik *R* U.S.S.R.
42 E6 Khemchiksiy, Khrebet *mts* U.S.S.R.
77 E10 Khemis Beni Arous Morocco 35.19N 5.38W
88 P3 Khemis Miliana Algeria 36.15N 2.18E
88 K5 Khemisset Morocco 33.50N 6.03W
77 E9 Khems Anjra Morocco 35.40N 5.31W
89 H1 Khenachich,El *reg* Mali
88 R4 Khenchela Algeria 35.22N 7.09E
88 H10 Khénifissa Mauritania 23.32N 10.50W
88 L5 Khenifra Morocco 33.00N 5.40W
25 B1 Khenkhar Burma 22.02N 92.52E
87 H6 Khera Ethiopia 9.08N 40.31E
Kheraji *see* Kharājī
29 C6 Kheralu Gujarat India 23.57N 72.38E
32 E6 Kherāmeh Iran 29.30N 53.21E
30 D5 Kheri Uttar Prad India 27.54N 80.48E
30 D4 Kheri *dist* Uttar Prad India
29 D2 Khern Karan Punjab India 31.12N 74.36E
40 H5 Kherpuchi U.S.S.R. 53.00N 138.50E
88 Q3 Kherrata Algeria 36.30N 5.18E
32 C4 Khersan *R* Iran
45 D10 Kherson Ukraine U.S.S.R. 46.39N 32.38E
44 C10 Khersonesskiy,Mys *C* Ukraine U.S.S.R. 44.35N 33.22E
84 K10 Khersónisos Akrotíri *pen* Crete
84 F6 Khersónisos Methánon *pen* Greece
45 D10 Khersonskaya Oblast' *prov* Ukraine U.S.S.R.
44 E6 Khertvisi Georgia U.S.S.R. 41.29N 43.15E
29 C6 Kherwara Rajasthan India 23.58N 73.38E
25 J4 Khe Sanh Vietnam 16.37N 106.50E
31 E3 Khesh Afghanistan 34.41N 68.13E
32 D6 Khesht Iran 29.32N 51.19E
41 G5 Kheta Krasnoyarsk U.S.S.R. 71.33N 99.40E
39 E4 Kheta Magadan U.S.S.R. 61.05N 151.53E
41 H5 Kheta *R* U.S.S.R.
39 G1 Khetachan *R* U.S.S.R.
88 M5 Khetit Ahmed *watercourse* Morocco
47 C3 Khetolambina U.S.S.R. 66.20N 33.21E
29 D4 Khetri Rajasthan India 28.00N 75.49E
Kheurbet Chakroûb *see* Ruqays
31 G4 Khewra Pakistan 32.41N 73.04E
47 L3 Kheygiyakha *R* U.S.S.R.
32 F6 Kheyrābād Kermān Iran 29.25N 55.18E
34 Q7 Kheyrābād Khuzestān Iran 31.49N 48.23E
34 Q2 Kheyr al Malid,Kūh-e- *mt* Iran 36.54N 48.35E
41 O2 Kheysa,Ostrov *isld* Franz Josef Land U.S.S.R.
32 E7 Khīārū Iran 27.24N 52.47E
25 F5 Khiaw,Khao *mt* Thailand 14.23N 101.21E
47 C2 Khibiny *mt* U.S.S.R. 67.48N 33.48E
29 J7 Khichina Orissa India 21.54N 85.54E
33 F6 Khidā,Jabal *mts* Saudi Arabia
34 N7 Khidr,Al Iraq 31.13N 45.34E
51 O10 Khiitola Karelia U.S.S.R. 61.14N 29.40E
29 E5 Khilchipur Madhya Prad India 24.03N 76.32E
84 E6 Khiliomódhion Greece 37.48N 22.51E
39 E1 Khil'mi,Gora *mt* U.S.S.R. 69.51N 151.06E
42 J6 Khilok U.S.S.R. 51.25N 110.28E
42 H6 Khilok *R* U.S.S.R.
84 C6 Khimadhión Greece 37.45N 21.30E
45 J1 Khimki U.S.S.R. 55.53N 37.26E
44 G5 Khimoy U.S.S.R. 42.38N 45.52E
42 D6 Khindiktig Khol', Oz *L* U.S.S.R.
40 E7 Khingansk U.S.S.R. 49.10N 131.10E
42 F5 Khinguy U.S.S.R. 54.49N 99.25E
39 D4 Khinike *R* U.S.S.R.
31 E3 Khinjan Afghanistan 35.36N 68.55E
31 F8 Khinsar Pakistan 25.22N 70.29E
29 B4 Khinyan Rajasthan India 27.19N 70.50E
83 D6 Khionáta Greece 38.06N 20.44E
83 H6 Khíos Greece 38.23N 26.07E
83 H6 Khíos *isld* Greece
31 E8 Khipro Pakistan 25.50N 69.24E
35 B2 Khirbat Umm Tūbā Jordan 31.44N 35.14E
35 E5 Khirbet Abu Falah Jordan 32.01N 35.18E
35 H2 Khirbet Bajjah Syria 32.56N 36.00E
35 E5 Khirbet Beit Hasan Jordan 32.14N 35.24E
35 C7 Khirbet Beyt 'Awwa Jordan 31.31N 34.57E
35 D8 Khirbet Deir Razih Jordan 31.28N 35.02E
35 G4 Khirbet ed Dahma *ruins* Jordan 32.27N 35.55E
35 J2 Khirbet el Buweir Syria 32.56N 36.18E
35 G4 Khirbet el Kufeirat *ruins* Jordan 32.28N 35.55E
35 E6 Khirbet el Mafjir *airfield* Jordan 31.52N 35.28E
35 F4 Khirbet el Wahadina Jordan 32.20N 35.38E
35 G4 Khirbet esh Shamahid *ruins* Jordan 32.19N 35.53E
35 F3 Khirbet esh Shuna Jordan 32.36N 35.36E
35 H5 Khirbet es Samra *ruins* Jordan 32.10N 36.10E
35 H3 Khirbet et Ghazale Syria 32.44N 36.12E
35 C9 Khirbet Gharra *anc site* Israel 31.14N 34.58E
35 G4 Khirbet Harqala *ruins* Jordan 32.24N 35.49E
35 F4 Khirbet Listib *ruins* Jordan 32.23N 35.43E
35 F4 Khirbet Mar Ilyas *ruins* Jordan 32.22N 35.43E
35 C9 Khirbet Mashash *anc site* Israel 31.13N 34.58E
35 H1 Khirbet Qarinah Syria 33.10N 36.04E
35 F3 Khirbet Sheikh Husein Jordan 32.37N 35.37E
35 E9 Khirbet Sheikh 'Isa *ruins* Jordan 31.02N 35.28E
35 D8 Khirbet Susia Jordan 31.25N 35.07E
35 F10 Khirbet Tannur *anc site* Jordan 30.58N 35.42E
35 F3 Khirbet 'Uyun Syria 32.47N 35.40E
86 E4 Khirbita Egypt 30.45N 30.39E
31 F4 Khirgi Pakistan 32.15N 70.15E
30 J6 Khirhar Bihar India 26.31N 85.58E
30 E7 Khiri Uttar Prad India 25.02N 81.49E
29 E6 Khirkiya Madhya Prad India 22.12N 76.58E
84 R15 Khirokitia Cyprus 34.47N 33.21E
29 L2 Khirpai W Bengal India 22.42N 87.36E
Khirr,Wadi al Iraq*see* Kharr, Wādī al *watercourse*
33 E1 Khirr, Wādī al *watercourse* Saudi Arabia
33 J4 Khīşah,Al Saudi Arabia 24.42N 50.45E
82 J8 Khisar Bulgaria 42.30N 24.44E
Khisfin *see* Ramat Magshimim
45 D2 Khislavichi U.S.S.R. 54.12N 32.10E
Khist *see* Khesht
31 J1 Khitai Pass Kashmir 35.49N 79.28E
46 M4 Khitrovo U.S.S.R. 52.28N 41.49E
44 H6 Khiv U.S.S.R. 41.47N 47.57E
43 F6 Khiva Uzbekistan U.S.S.R. 41.25N 60.49E
32 B1 Khīyāv Iran 38.24N 47.49E
33 H3 Khizamī Saudi Arabia 26.30N 48.39E
44 D1 Khlebodarnyy U.S.S.R. 46.41N 40.55E
34 J3 Khleisia *oil well* Iraq 35.20N 41.27E
84 G5 Khlembotsárion Greece 38.17N 23.30E
45 L4 Khlevnoye U.S.S.R. 52.10N 39.05E
83 F6 Khlomón *mt* Greece 38.37N 23.00E
84 E3 Khlomón *mt* Magnisía Greece 39.05N 22.57E
84 E4 Khlomón Óros *mts* Greece
25 E5 Khlong,Mae *R* Thailand
Khlong Makham *see* Ban Khlong Makham
88 K9 Khlouia Mauritania 25.52N 6.37W
Khlung *see* Ban Khlung
Khmeizir,Jebel el *mts see* Khanāzīr, Jebel el *mts*
46 J4 Khmelev Ukraine U.S.S.R. 50.58N 33.22E
45 C8 Khmelevoye Ukraine U.S.S.R. 48.33N 31.25E
46 G5 Khmel'nik Ukraine U.S.S.R. 49.36N 27.59E
46 F5 Khmel'nitskiy Ukraine U.S.S.R. 49.25N 26.59E
17 F9 Khmer Republic S E Asia
39 D5 Khmitevskogo Poluostrov *pen* U.S.S.R.
25 H8 Khoai,Hon *isld* Vietnam 8.26N 104.48E
Khoashen *vol see* Ichinskaya Sopka *vol*
Khobar *see* Khubar,Al
Khobdo *see* Hovd Hovd Mongolia
44 D5 Khobi Georgia U.S.S.R. 42.19N 41.52E
39 C2 Khobol'chan U.S.S.R. 67.13N 140.15E
45 M3 Khobotovo U.S.S.R. 53.03N 40.24E
41 L8 Khochot U.S.S.R. 64.11N 119.41E
42 L1 Khochot U.S.S.R. 63.00N 122.05E
32 G4 Khodā Āfarīd Iran 32.51N 56.19E
32 B1 Khodā Āfarīn Iran 39.09N 46.54E
42 F5 Khodarus U.S.S.R. 52.39N 99.23E
46 E5 Khodorov Ukraine U.S.S.R. 49.20N 24.19E
39 E7 Khodutka,Sopka *vol* Kamchatka U.S.S.R. 52.04N 157.44E
45 V1 Khodyashevo-Tatarskoye U.S.S.R. 55.50N 49.49E
43 N7 Khodzha Uzbekistan U.S.S.R. 40.45N 70.58E
43 N7 Khodzhaabad Uzbekistan U.S.S.R. 40.53N 71.10E
43 G7 Khodzha Davlet Uzbekistan U.S.S.R. 39.20N 63.46E
43 D7 Khodzhakala Turkmeniya U.S.S.R. 38.45N 56.24E
44 D5 Khodzhali *mt* Georgia U.S.S.R. 42.59N 41.53E
43 G7 Khodzhambass Turkmeniya U.S.S.R. 38.09N 65.00E
43 H7 Khodzha Mubarek Uzbekistan U.S.S.R. 39.16N 65.11E
32 G1 Khodzhaolen Turkmeniya U.S.S.R. 38.46N 57.15E
43 E6 Khodzheyli Uzbekistan U.S.S.R. 42.25N 59.25E

43 O8 **Khodzhiabad** Uzbekistan **U.S.S.R.** 40.41N 72.34E
40 J6 **Khöe** Sakhalin **U.S.S.R.** 51.20N 142.07E
42 H5 **Khogot** **U.S.S.R.** 53.15N 105.54E
30 B3 **Khoh** *R* Uttar Prad **India**
Khoi *see* **Khvoy**
31 D5 **Khojak Pass** **Pakistan** 30.54N 66.29E
30 E2 **Khojarnath** Xizang Zizhiqu 30.08N 81.20E
30 K6 **Khokhaha** Bihar **India** 26.10N 86.32E
45 K5 **Khokhol** **U.S.S.R.** 51.34N 38.48E
94 F5 **Khokhowe Pan** **Botswana** 24.48S 21.25E
31 F8 **Khokhropar** **Pakistan** 25.44N 70.13E
39 E1 **Khokhur** **U.S.S.R.** 68.28N 151.02E
41 D6 **Khokiley** **U.S.S.R.** 70.00N 82.01E
Khok Kloi *see* **Ban Khok Kloi**
29 E1 **Khoksar** Punjab **India** 32.27N 77.15E
29 E7 **Kholapur** Maharashtra **India** 21.00N 77.52E
42 K6 **Kholbon** **U.S.S.R.** 51.56N 116.18E
31 D2 **Kholm** **Afghanistan** 36.42N 67.41E
46 H2 **Kholm** **U.S.S.R.** 57.10N 31.11E
45 B4 **Kholmech'** Belorussiya **U.S.S.R.** 52.07N 30.38E
45 E1 **Kholmino** **U.S.S.R.** 56.01N 33.58E
47 E4 **Kholmogorskaya** **U.S.S.R.** 63.51N 40.46E
47 E4 **Kholmogory** **U.S.S.R.** 64.12N 41.42E
40 J8 **Kholmsk** Sakhalin **U.S.S.R.** 47.02N 142.03E
45 D5 **Kholmy** Ukraine **U.S.S.R.** 51.52N 32.37E
45 E1 **Kholm-Zhirkovskiy** **U.S.S.R.** 55.30N 33.30E
46 G3 **Kholopenichi** Belorussiya **U.S.S.R.** 54.30N 28.58E
42 J5 **Kholoy** *R* **U.S.S.R.**
29 D6 **Kholvi** Rajasthan **India** 23.58N 75.50E
42 E6 **Khol-Yezhu** **U.S.S.R.** 50.45N 94.24E
42 C6 **Kholzun, Khrebet** *mts* **U.S.S.R.**
32 C2 **Khomān** **Iran** 37.24N 49.40E
94 D4 **Khomas Highland** *mts* **Namibia**
84 C8 **Khomaterón** **Greece** 36.50N 21.53E
89 A4 **Khombole** **Senegal** 14.43N 16.42W
Khombu Glacier *see* **Khumbu Glacier**
84 C4 **Khómeri** **Greece** 38.36N 21.51E
32 D4 **Khomeyn** **Iran** 33.38N 50.03E
44 F5 **Khomi** Georgia **U.S.S.R.** 42.21N 44.05E
42 H2 **Khomokashevo** **U.S.S.R.** 60.15N 106.05E
41 M8 **Khomusta** **U.S.S.R.** 63.28N 120.30E
41 L8 **Khomustakh** **U.S.S.R.** 63.06N 117.38E
45 F5 **Khomutovka** **U.S.S.R.** 51.56N 34.31E
42 G6 **Khomutovo** **U.S.S.R.** 52.32N 104.24E
45 J4 **Khomutovo** **U.S.S.R.** 52.53N 37.25E
31 D4 **Khonak Pass** **Afghanistan** 33.57N 66.35E
32 C3 **Khondāb** **Iran** 34.24N 49.14E
42 F5 **Khonda-Dzhuglymskiy,Khrebet** *mts* **U.S.S.R.**
30 E7 **Khondar** Uttar Prad **India** 25.08N 81.59E
92 G7 **Khondowe** **Malawi** 10.36S 34.10E
25 G5 **Khone Kriel** **Cambodia** 14.17N 103.39E
25 H5 **Khong** **Laos** 14.08N 105.50E
40 E1 **Khongkhoyuku** **U.S.S.R.** 61.15N 131.30E
39 E3 **Khongo** **U.S.S.R.** 63.44N 150.16E
39 C3 **Khongor** *R* **U.S.S.R.**
25 H5 **Khong Sedone** **Laos** 15.35N 105.47E
32 E7 **Khonj** **Iran** 27.54N 53.28E
92 G10 **Khonjeni** **Malawi** 16.05S 35.19E
32 E7 **Khonj,Kūh-e** *mts* **Iran**
Khon Kaen *see* **Muang Khon Kaen**
42 H6 **Khonkholoy** **U.S.S.R.** 51.08N 108.10E
28 K2 **Khonsa** Assam **India** 26.59N 95.38E
39 A1 **Khonu** Yakutsk **U.S.S.R.** 68.14N 134.48E
39 C2 **Khonu** Yakutsk **U.S.S.R.** 66.29N 143.12E
39 E2 **Khonulakh** **U.S.S.R.** 66.19N 151.27E
45 O7 **Khopër** *R* **U.S.S.R.**
42 K3 **Khoppuruo** **U.S.S.R.** 59.15N 119.20E
Khor Qatar, The Gulf*see* **Khawr,Al**
40 G8 **Khor** **U.S.S.R.** 47.59N 135.01E
40 G7 **Khor** *R* **U.S.S.R.**
84 C6 **Khóra** Arkadhía **Greece** 37.41N 21.50E
84 C7 **Khóra** Messinía **Greece** 37.03N 21.42E
31 E7 **Khora** **Pakistan** 27.25N 68.36E
84 K10 **Khorafákia** Crete 35.34N 24.05E
Khoraiba *see* **Khuraybah**
33 N9 **Khor-al-Amaya** *oil terminal* **Iraq** 29.47N 48.41E
87 J4 **Khor-Anghar** **Djibouti** 12.21N 43.22E
32 G3 **Khorāsān** *prov* **Iran**
84 K11 **Khóra Sfakíon** Crete 35.12N 24.08E
Khōr as Sabiya *channel see* **Khawr Aş Şabīyah** *chan*
88 K7 **Khorb el Ethel** **Algeria** 28.30N 6.17W
42 K1 **Khordogoy** **U.S.S.R.** 62.38N 115.40E
47 K2 **Khordype,Gora** *mt* **U.S.S.R.** 67.50N 66.00E
87 M5 **Khoreh,Las** **Somalia** 11.10N 48.16E
86 M5 **Khoreiza,Wâdi** *watercourse* **Egypt**
84 D7 **Khorémi** **Greece** 37.23N 22.05E
43 F6 **Khoremskaya Oblast'** *prov* Uzbekistan **U.S.S.R.**
47 H3 **Khoreyver** **U.S.S.R.** 67.26N 58.00E
33 M4 **Khōr Fakkān** **U.A.E.** 25.20N 56.20E
87 N5 **Khor Filuch** *B* **Somalia** 11.51N 50.34E
41 K4 **Khorgo** **U.S.S.R.** 73.30N 113.30E
Khorgos *see* **Korgas**
89 B4 **Khorhol** **Senegal** 15.26N 15.01W
42 H6 **Khorinsk** **U.S.S.R.** 52.14N 109.52E
42 L2 **Khorintsy** **U.S.S.R.** 60.42N 121.25E
94 C3 **Khorixas** **Namibia** 20.23S 14.55E
43 G4 **Khorkhut** Kazakhstan **U.S.S.R.** 45.39N 63.56E
45 K1 **Khorlovo** **U.S.S.R.** 55.20N 38.50E
33 C10 **Khormaksar** **S Yemen** 12.48N 45.02E
33 C10 **Khormaksar Airport** **S Yemen** 12.50N 45.02E
24 F3 **Khormali** *well* Xinjiang Uygur Zizhiqu **China** 45.16N 88.40E
32 D6 **Khormūj,Kūh-e** *mt* **Iran** 28.43N 51.32E
43 K8 **Khorog** Tadzhikistan **U.S.S.R.** 37.32N 71.32E
45 E7 **Khorol** Ukraine **U.S.S.R.** 49.49N 33.17E
40 F9 **Khorol** **U.S.S.R.** 44.25N 132.02E
45 E7 **Khorol** *R* Ukraine **U.S.S.R.**
40 E1 **Khoronkhu** **U.S.S.R.** 60.37N 130.14E
41 M7 **Khoronku** *R* **U.S.S.R.**
41 M7 **Khoronnokh** **U.S.S.R.** 66.21N 121.00E
43 N1 **Khorosheye** **U.S.S.R.** 53.39N 78.30E
44 H8 **Khoroslū Dāgh** *mt* **Iran**
47 L3 **Khorovaya** **U.S.S.R.** 66.12N 71.57E
32 G3 **Khorramābād** Khorāsān **Iran** 35.06N 57.57E
32 C4 **Khorramābād** Lorestān **Iran** 33.29N 48.21E
32 D2 **Khorramābād** Māzandarān **Iran** 36.45N 50.58E
32 C2 **Khorram Darreh** **Iran** 36.10N 49.14E
32 C5 **Khorramshahr** **Iran** 30.25N 48.09E
34 H4 **Khorr,Wādī el** *watercourse* **Syria**
34 L2 **Khorsabad** *anc site* **Iraq** 36.28N 43.13E
Khōr Shiban *see* **Khawr Şhiban** *salty well*
42 G5 **Khor-Tagna** **U.S.S.R.** 53.26N 101.32E
45 E6 **Khoruzhevka** Ukraine **U.S.S.R.** 50.55N 33.50E
45 D4 **Khorzhovka** **U.S.S.R.** 52.46N 32.20E
41 O6 **Khos-Alas** **U.S.S.R.** 67.39N 130.16E
47 H3 **Khoseda Khard** **U.S.S.R.** 67.04N 59.25E
47 H2 **Khosedayu** *R* **U.S.S.R.**
32 H4 **Khosf** **Iran** 32.45N 58.50E
45 T9 **Khosheutovo** **U.S.S.R.** 47.04N 47.50E
86 J7 **Khoshira,Gebel** *hill* **Egypt** 29.29N 32.55E
39 E2 **Khosko** *R* **U.S.S.R.**
32 C5 **Khosrowabad** Khuzestān **Iran** 30.10N 48.24E
32 B3 **Khosrowābād** Kordestān **Iran** 35.30N 47.39E
32 E5 **Khosrow Shīrīn** **Iran** 30.53N 52.02E
32 A3 **Khosrowvī** **Iran** 34.20N 45.35E
Khost *see* **Matun**
31 D5 **Khost** **Pakistan** 30.15N 67.35E
31 E4 **Khost** *reg* **Afghanistan**
44 C4 **Khosta** **U.S.S.R.** 43.31N 39.55E
84 E5 **Khóstia** **Greece** 38.15N 22.55E
32 F6 **Khosūyeh** **Iran** 28.31N 54.25E
29 E3 **Khot** Haryana **India** 29.22N 76.10E
Khotan *see* **Hotan**
Khotan Darya *R see* **Hotan He**
30 K5 **Khotang** **Nepal** 27.03N 86.51E
45 F5 **Khoten'** Ukraine **U.S.S.R.** 51.05N 34.47E
31 G2 **Khotgaz Pass** **Afghanistan** 36.37N 72.08E
45 D3 **Khotimsk** Belorussiya **U.S.S.R.** 53.24N 32.36E
46 F5 **Khotin** Ukraine **U.S.S.R.** 48.30N 26.31E
45 K1 **Khotkovo** **U.S.S.R.** 56.15N 38.00E
45 G6 **Khotmyzhsk** **U.S.S.R.** 50.38N 35.52E
41 O6 **Khotogor** **U.S.S.R.** 68.45N 133.00E
113 J4 **Khotol** *mt* **Alaska** 64.10N 157.50W
45 C7 **Khotski** Ukraine **U.S.S.R.** 49.55N 31.38E
45 G3 **Khotynets** **U.S.S.R.** 53.07N 35.25E
84 B2 **Khouliarádhes** **Greece** 39.33N 21.01E
84 Q15 **Khoulou** **Cyprus** 34.52N 32.35E
84 C4 **Khoúni** **Greece** 38.50N 21.33E
88 K5 **Khouribga** **Morocco** 32.54N 6.57W
43 K7 **Khovaling** Tadzhikistan **U.S.S.R.** 38.25N 70.01E
42 E6 **Khovu-Aksy** **U.S.S.R.** 51.11N 93.45E
28 H3 **Khowai** Tripura **India** 24.04N 91.36E
32 E5 **Khowrjān** **Iran** 30.25N 53.15E
32 F4 **Khowrnag,Kūh-e** *mt* **Iran** 32.10N 54.48E
45 B5 **Khoyniki** Belorussiya **U.S.S.R.** 51.54N 30.00E
44 E6 **Khozapini,Oz** *L* Georgia **U.S.S.R.**
44 F6 **Khrami** *R* Georgia **U.S.S.R.**
25 G4 **Khram,Mae Nam Song** *R* **Thailand**
84 D7 **Khránoi** **Greece** 37.19N 22.02E
45 M1 **Khrapovitskaya Dacha** **U.S.S.R.** 55.55N 40.55E
42 G4 **Khrebtovaya** **U.S.S.R.** 56.42N 104.16E
86 J9 **Khreim, Wâdî el** *watercourse* **Egypt**
45 C4 **Khrenovka** **U.S.S.R.** 52.05N 31.54E
45 M5 **Khrenovoye** **U.S.S.R.** 51.08N 40.16E
25 B2 **Khreum** **Burma** 21.25N 93.40E
28 H3 **Khri R** Assam **India**
83 G4 **Khrisoúpolis** **Greece** 40.59N 24.42E
84 B5 **Khrisovéryi** **Greece** 38.30N 21.21E
84 D6 **Khrisovitsi** **Greece** 37.32N 22.12E
83 G8 **Khristianá** *isld* **Greece** 36.14N 25.13E
82 M2 **Khristinovka** **U.S.S.R.** 48.50N 29.59E
42 G5 **Khristoforova** **U.S.S.R.** 54.00N 104.38E
45 E9 **Khristoforovka** Ukraine **U.S.S.R.** 47.59N 33.04E
47 F5 **Khristoforovo** **U.S.S.R.** 60.55N 47.10E
82 J9 **Khrojna** **Bulgaria** 41.50N 24.40E
41 Q5 **Khroma** *R* **U.S.S.R.**
41 R5 **Khromskaya Guba** *gulf* **U.S.S.R.**
43 E2 **Khrom-Tau** Kazakhstan **U.S.S.R.** 50.15N 58.22E
24 A6 **Khr Sarykolskiy** *mt ra* Xinjiang Uygur Zizhiqu **China**
28 J2 **Khru** *R* Assam **India**
45 M2 **Khrushchevo** **U.S.S.R.** 54.10N 40.00E
45 K2 **Khruslovka** **U.S.S.R.** 54.24N 38.15E
40 G9 **Khrustal'nyy** **U.S.S.R.** 44.26N 135.10E
84 P15 **Khrysokhou** **Cyprus** 35.00N 32.26E
84 P14 **Khrysokhou B** **Cyprus**
83 H7 **Khtapodhiá** *isld* **Greece** 37.24N 25.34E
Khuan Mao *see* **Ban Khuan Mao**
31 G4 **Khuar** **Pakistan** 33.18N 72.30E
33 J3 **Khubar,Al** **Saudi Arabia** 26.18N 50.06E
34 K5 **Khubbāz,Wādī** *watercourse* **Iraq**
33 H3 **Khubrah,Al** **Saudi Arabia** 27.01N 48.25E
34 G5 **Khubub,Khabari al** *salt marshes* **Iraq**
44 H6 **Khuchni** **U.S.S.R.** 41.58N 47.57E
Khuda Afarid *see* **Khodā Āfarīd**
Khuda Afarin *see* **Khodā Āfarīn**
30 J7 **Khudaganj** Bihar **India** 25.06N 85.14E
30 C5 **Khudaganj** Uttar Prad **India** 27.12N 79.40E
42 J6 **Khudan** *R* **U.S.S.R.**
86 M7 **Khudara, Gebel** *hill* **Egypt** 29.15N 34.15E
44 J6 **Khudat** Azerbaydzhan **U.S.S.R.** 41.37N 48.42E
43 C7 **Khudayberdy** Turkmeniya **U.S.S.R.** 39.59N 54.44E
33 E2 **Khudd,Wādī al** *watercourse* **Saudi Arabia**
31 H5 **Khudian** **Pakistan** 30.59N 74.19E
41 D7 **Khudoseya** *R* **U.S.S.R.**
42 F5 **Khudoyelan'** **U.S.S.R.** 54.41N 99.40E
33 H8 **Khudrah,Wādī** *watercourse* **S Yemen**
Khudran *see* **Khvodrān**
34 C5 **Khudr,Jūn el** *B* **Lebanon**
94 H4 **Khudumelapye** **Botswana** 23.52S 24.43E
42 H6 **Khudunskiy Khrebet** *mts* **U.S.S.R.**
39 C3 **Khudzh** *R* **U.S.S.R.**
39 D3 **Khudzhakh** **U.S.S.R.** 63.39N 146.27E
33 F4 **Khuff** **Saudi Arabia** 25.00N 44.45E
33 F4 **Khuff,Al** *escarp* **Saudi Arabia**
41 G7 **Khugdyungda,Khrebet** *mts* **U.S.S.R.**
31 D5 **Khugiani** **Afghanistan** 31.33N 66.15E
Khuglana *see* **Pirzada**
94 F6 **Khuis** **Botswana** 26.40S 21.49E
25 H5 **Khu Khan** **Thailand** 14.37N 104.12E
33 C5 **Khulays** **Saudi Arabia** 22.09N 39.20E
29 D7 **Khuldabad** Maharashtra **India** 20.01N 75.16E
47 J3 **Khulga** *R* **U.S.S.R.**
46 O6 **Khulkhuta** **U.S.S.R.** 46.20N 46.24E
44 G1 **Khulkuta** **U.S.S.R.** 46.20N 46.24E
33 J7 **Khullat Umm al Ghīrān** *des area* **Saudi Arabia**
31 D3 **Khulm** *R* **Afghanistan**
31 H9 **Khulna** **Bangladesh** 22.49N 89.34E
31 H10 **Khulna** *dist* **Bangladesh**
44 E6 **Khulo** Georgia **U.S.S.R.** 41.39N 42.15E
Khumain *see* **Khomeyn**
30 H3 **Khumbila** *mt* **Nepal** 27.52N 86.43E
30 G3 **Khumbu** *reg* **Nepal**
30 J2 **Khumbu Glacier** **Nepal**
30 J2 **Khumbutse** *mt* **Nepal/Xizang Zizhiqu** 28.01N 86.52E
30 H3 **Khumde** **Nepal** 27.49N 86.43E
30 H3 **Khumjung** **Nepal** 27.50N 86.44E
40 G6 **Khummi** **U.S.S.R.** 50.20N 137.05E
40 G6 **Khummi,Oz** *L* **U.S.S.R.**
33 C6 **Khumrah** **Saudi Arabia** 21.23N 39.08E
85 C3 **Khums** *reg* **Libya**
85 C3 **Khums,Al** **Libya** 32.39N 14.15E
25 G6 **Khum Svay Chek** **Cambodia** 13.47N 102.58E
24 F10 **Khumu** *R* Xizang Zizhiqu **China**
30 F6 **Khundaur** Uttar Prad **India** 26.02N 82.02E
87 C3 **Khuneiqa** *watercourse* **Sudan**
35 H6 **Khuneizir** **Jordan** 32.18N 36.03E
35 E10 **Khuneizira** *watercourse* **Jordan**
33 C2 **Khunfah,Al** *des area* **Saudi Arabia**
40 G7 **Khungari** *R* **U.S.S.R.**
32 H4 **Khūnīk Bālā** **Iran** 33.34N 59.06E
Khunj *see* **Khonj**
Khunjerab Pass *see* **Kunjirap Daban**
Khunj,Kuh-i- *see* **Khonj,Kūh-e-** *mts*
33 H5 **Khunn, Al** **Saudi Arabia** 23.34N 49.15E
Khu Noi *see* **Ban Khu Noi**
Khunsar *see* **Khvānsār**
32 D4 **Khunsār** **Iran** 33.10N 50.19E
29 J6 **Khunti** Bihar **India** 23.02N 85.19E
95 J2 **Khunwana** **S Africa** 26.22S 25.20E
Khun Yuam *see* **Ban Khun Yuam**
44 H5 **Khunzakh** **U.S.S.R.** 42.34N 46.43E
Khur *see* **Khvor**
32 H3 **Khūr** **Iran** 35.40N 58.01E
32 H4 **Khur** Khorāsān **Iran** 32.57N 58.27E
32 E6 **Khūrāb** **Iran** 28.37N 52.10E
32 G3 **Khūr,Ab** **Iran** 34.20N 57.01E
29 F5 **Khurai** Madhya Prad **India** 24.04N 78.18E
Khurais *oil well see* **Khurays**
35 H7 **Khuraiyim** *watercourse* **Jordan**
35 J8 **Khuraiyim, Jebel el** *mts* **Jordan**
32 F7 **Khūran** *str* **Iran**
32 H7 **Khūrān, Kūh-e** *mt* **Iran** 26.45N 58.15E
30 C8 **Khurar** *R* Madhya Prad **India** 24.28N
30 F5 **Khurasa** Uttar Prad **India** 27.06N 82.02E
46 P8 **Khuray** **U.S.S.R.** 41.50N 48.30E
33 H9 **Khuraybah** **S Yemen** 15.01N 48.20E
33 H4 **Khurays** *oil well* **Saudi Arabia** 25.06N 48.04E
34 J10 **Khurayzah,Al** **Saudi Arabia** 28.29N 41.51E
39 E5 **Khurchan** **U.S.S.R.** 59.50N 153.27E
29 J7 **Khurda** Orissa **India** 20.10N 85.42E
31 C4 **Khurd,Koh-i-** *mt* **Afghanistan** 33.24N 65.55E
Khurd Narvan *see* **Khvord Nārvān**
32 F3 **Khūr-e Gaz** **Iran** 34.11N 55.08E
86 O9 **Khureiba, Al** **Saudi Arabia** 28.03N 35.10E
35 G3 **Khureiba,El** **Jordan** 32.39N 35.52E
35 G6 **Khureibat es Suq** **Jordan** 31.52N 35.55E
90 N5 **Khureit** **Sudan** 13.59N 26.03E
39 D4 **Khuren** *R* **U.S.S.R.**
Khurgu *see* **Khvorgū**
Khur-i-Gaz *see* **Khūr-e Gaz**
41 E8 **Khuringda** *R* **U.S.S.R.**
Khurīyā Murīyā, Jaā'ir *see* **Kuria Muria Is**
30 A4 **Khurja** Uttar Prad **India** 28.15N 77.51E
30 G7 **Khurmabad** Bihar **India** 25.01N 83.51E
86 N9 **Khurma, El** *B* **Saudi Arabia**
33 E6 **Khurmah,Al** **Saudi Arabia** 21.55N 42.02E
Khurmala *oil field see* **Kirkuk**
31 B4 **Khurmalik** **Afghanistan** 32.18N 62.26E
Khurmuj *see* **Khvormūj**
30 F4 **Khurpa** **Nepal** 28.49N 82.01E
Khurramābād *see* **Khorramābād**
Khurramdarreh *see* **Khorram Darreh**
Khurramshahr *see* **Khorramshahr**
33 H3 **Khursānīyāh** *oil field* **Saudi Arabia** 27.14N 49.13E
Khurunaq *see* **Kharānaq**
Khurunaq, Kuh-i *see* **Khowrnag, Kūh-e** *mt*
43 J7 **Khurvatan** Uzbekistan **U.S.S.R.** 38.46N 67.47E
Khuryā Muryā,Jazā'ir *see* **Kuria Muria Is**
32 F3 **Khurz** **Iran** 35.44N 54.45E
Khusainabad *see* **Hoseynābād**
Khush Ab *see* **Khvosh āb**
31 G4 **Khushab** **Pakistan** 32.16N 72.18E
31 F4 **Khushalgarh** **Pakistan** 33.30N 71.57E
31 B3 **Khush Asia** **Afghanistan** 35.00N 62.22E
32 C2 **Khūshāvar** **Iran** 37.57N 48.58E
42 J6 **Khushenga** **U.S.S.R.** 51.28N 110.58E
32 H5 **Khushk Rud** **Iran** 31.25N 58.15E
34 D9 **Khush Shah,Wādī el** *watercourse* **Jordan**
32 F2 **Khush Yailaq** *mt* **Iran** 36.50N 55.35E
31 B4 **Khuspas** **Afghanistan** 32.00N 62.31E
30 J7 **Khusropur** Bihar **India** 25.29N 85.23E
46 E5 **Khust** Ukraine **U.S.S.R.** 48.11N 23.19E
Khustuābād *see* **Khosrowābād**
Khusu *see* **Khosūyeh**
47 L3 **Khus' Yakha** **U.S.S.R.** 66.30N 73.40E
29 G7 **Khutagaon** Maharashtra **India** 20.11N 80.15E
30 K6 **Khutauna** Bihar **India** 26.30N 86.24E
30 K7 **Khutia** Bihar **India** 25.31N 86.33E
44 E1 **Khutorskoy** **U.S.S.R.** 46.52N 43.01E
94 H4 **Khutse** **Botswana** 23.22S 24.28E
40 H7 **Khutu** *R* **U.S.S.R.**
41 E4 **Khutudabiga** *R* **U.S.S.R.**
40 H7 **Khutu Datta** **U.S.S.R.** 49.25N 139.59E
33 J3 **Khuwayr,Al** **Qatar, The Gulf** 26.05N 51.09E
87 B4 **Khuwei** **Sudan** 13.02N 29.13E
31 D7 **Khuzdar** **Pakistan** 27.49N 66.39E
32 C5 **Khuzestān** *prov* **Iran**
42 H5 **Khuzhir** Irkutsk **U.S.S.R.** 53.12N 107.25E
32 J3 **Khvāf** **Iran** 34.32N 60.05E
32 J3 **Khvāf** *reg* **Iran**
32 B1 **Khvājeh** **Iran** 38.13N 46.39E
32 J5 **Khvājeh Dow Chāhī** **Iran** 31.55N 60.35E
45 U4 **Khvalynsk** **U.S.S.R.** 52.30N 48.04E
44 E5 **Khvanchkara** Georgia **U.S.S.R.** 42.33N 43.00E
32 F6 **Khvānsār** **Iran** 29.57N 54.08E
45 G3 **Khvastovichi** **U.S.S.R.** 53.28N 35.05E
45 S4 **Khvatovka** **U.S.S.R.** 52.22N 46.32E
32 F5 **Khvodrān** **Iran** 31.23N 55.48E
44 H9 **Khvojehlī** **Iran** 38.33N 47.39E
32 F4 **Khvor** **Iran** 33.47N 55.03E
32 G3 **Khvord Nārvān** **Iran** 34.03N 56.57E
32 G7 **Khvorgū** **Iran** 27.34N 56.29E
32 D6 **Khvormūj** **Iran** 28.39N 51.23E
45 M4 **Khvorostyanka** Lipetsk **U.S.S.R.** 52.20N 40.15E
45 U4 **Khvorostyanka** **U.S.S.R.** 52.32N 48.58E
32 D6 **Khvosh āb** **Iran** 29.13N 51.08E
32 B2 **Khvosh Maqām** **Iran** 36.10N 47.23E
32 A1 **Khvoy** **Iran** 38.32N 45.02E
46 J1 **Khvoynaya** **U.S.S.R.** 58.58N 34.30E
25 E5 **Khwae Noi** *R* **Thailand**
31 F2 **Khwahan** **Afghanistan** 37.52N 70.15E
31 B5 **Khwaja Ali** **Afghanistan** 30.17N 63.05E
31 D5 **Khwaja Amran** **Pakistan** 30.37N 66.30E
31 B3 **Khwajachist** **Afghanistan** 34.21N 63.45E
Khwaja Do Chatun *see* **Khvājeh Dow Chāhī**
31 E2 **Khwaja-i-Ghar** **Afghanistan** 37.08N 69.24E
31 F4 **Khwaja Kuram** *mt* **Afghanistan** 33.42N 70.05E
31 F2 **Khwaja Muhammad Ra** **Afghanistan**
Khwash *see* **Khāsh**
31 F4 **Khyber** *dist* **Pakistan**
31 F3 **Khyber Pass** **Pak/Afghan** 34.06N 71.05E
44 J6 **Khynalyk** Azerbaydzhan **U.S.S.R.** 41.12N 48.08E
82 H1 **Khyrov** **U.S.S.R.** 49.32N 22.50E
15 K2 **Kia** Santa Isabel I **Solomon Is** 7.32S 158.26E
9 S4 **Kia** *islet* **Fiji** 16.14S 179.07E
91 J8 **Kiabukwa** **Zaïre** 8.46S 24.49E
30 K8 **Kiajori** Bihar **India** 34.32N 86.27E
Kialing Kiang *R see* **Jialing Jiang**
91 K7 **Kialo** **Zaïre** 6.18S 26.53E
85 C3 **Kiām** *watercourse* **Libya**
12 K5 **Kiama** **New S Wales** 34.41S 150.49E
91 E7 **Kiama** **Zaïre** 7.19S 17.49E
31 D8 **Kiamari** **Pakistan** 24.50N 67.00E
19 M8 **Kiamba** Mindanao **Philippines** 6.02N 124.33E
93 J6 **Kiambere** *mt* **Kenya** 0.41S 37.49E
92 D5 **Kiambi** **Zaïre** 7.20S 28.01E
91 F6 **Kiambo** **Zaïre** 5.42S 19.05E
93 H7 **Kiambu** **Kenya** 1.10S 36.51E
109 P7 **Kiamichi** *R* **Oklahoma**
109 P7 **Kiamichi Mts** **Oklahoma**
99 P6 **Kiamika** **Quebec** 46.25N 75.23W
99 P6 **Kiamika, L** **Quebec** 46.40N 75.08W
Kiamusze *see* **Jiamusi**
Kian *see* **Ji'an**
113 G3 **Kiana** **Alaska** 66.59N 160.35W
91 F6 **Kianfu** **Zaïre** 4.29S 18.02E
24 D10 **Kiang** *mt* Xizang Zizhiqu 31.38N 83.43E
13 K6 **Kianga** **Queensland** 24.39S 150.11E
Kiangan *see* **Jiang'an**
95 C4 **Kiangara** **Madagascar** 17.58S 47.02E
Kiangcheng *see* **Jiangcheng**
Kiangchow *see* **Jiangzhou**
Kiangkow *see* **Jiangkou**
93 J6 **Kiangombe** *mt* **Kenya** 0.33S 37.28E
Kiangshan *see* **Jiangshan**
Kiangsi *prov* **China***see* **Jiangxi**
Kiangsu *prov* **China***see* **Jiangsu**
Kiangti *see* **Jiangdi**
Kiangyi *see* **Jiangyi**
51 O6 **Kiantajärvi** *L* **Finland**
Kiaocheng *see* **Jiaocheng**
Kiaochow Wan *B see* **Jiazhou Wan**
Kiaoho *see* **Jiaohe**
Kiaokia *see* **Qiaojia**
91 K8 **Kiapulka** **Zaïre** 9.00S 27.21E
15 F7 **Kia R** **Irian Jaya**
32 E2 **Kīāsēh** **Iran** 36.20N 53.35E
100 U2 **Kiask L** **Manitoba**
84 E5 **Kiáton** **Greece** 38.01N 22.45E
85 N9 **Kiau, Wadi** *watercourse* **Sudan**
Kiawang *see* **Jiawang**
Kiayu *see* **Jiayu**
Kiayukwan *see* **Jiayuguan**
53 B4 **Kibæk** **Denmark** 56.03N 8.52E
91 K7 **Kibala, L** **Zaïre** 7.56S 26.57E
93 C5 **Kibale** **Uganda** 0.50N 31.06E
93 A2 **Kibali** *R* **Zaïre**
91 K6 **Kibamba** **Zaïre** 4.56S 26.36E
91 E5 **Kibambili** **Zaïre** 3.10S 17.16E
93 D5 **Kibanga Port** **Uganda** 0.13N 32.51E
91 C5 **Kibangou** **Congo** 3.30S 12.15E
91 K6 **Kibangula** **Zaïre** 4.52S 27.03E
29 F1 **Kibar** Himachal Prad **India** 32.20N 78.01E
93 E8 **Kibara** **Tanzania** 2.08S 33.29E
92 J6 **Kibata** **Tanzania** 8.24S 39.00E
92 H4 **Kibati** **Tanzania** 5.54S 37.25E
92 G6 **Kibau** **Tanzania** 8.37S 35.11E
19 M8 **Kibawe** Mindanao **Philippines** 7.28N 124.58E
92 H4 **Kibaya** **Tanzania** 5.20S 36.35E
93 A8 **Kibeho** **Rwanda** 2.38S 29.33E
91 E7 **Kibenga** **Zaïre** 7.56S 17.30E
91 D6 **Kibentele** **Zaïre** 5.35S 14.43E
92 H5 **Kiberege** **Tanzania** 7.57S 36.54E
51 P1 **Kiberg** **Norway** 70.17N 30.56E
93 B10 **Kiberie** **Tanzania** 4.39S 30.35E
89 J8 **Kibi** **Ghana** 6.11N 0.31W
92 D5 **Kibi** **Zaïre** 6.12S 29.10E
93 G6 **Kibigori** **Kenya** 0.04S 35.04E
93 A8 **Kibingo** **Rwanda** 2.45S 29.41E
93 B6 **Kibingo** **Uganda** 0.34S 30.24E .
93 J8 **Kibini** **Kenya** 2.14S 37.17E
93 C4 **Kibiro** **Uganda** 1.41N 31.18E
87 E8 **Kibish,R** **Ethiopia/Sudan**
92 J5 **Kibiti** **Tanzania** 7.40S 39.00E
93 J9 **Kibo** *vol* **Tanzania** 3.05S 37.20E
93 C5 **Kiboga** **Uganda** 0.56N 31.48E
93 J8 **Kiboko** **Kenya** 2.12S 37.43E
91 K8 **Kibola** **Zaïre** 9.42S 27.09E
91 J5 **Kibombo** **Zaïre** 3.58S 25.54E
91 J5 **Kibombo Rive** **Zaïre** 3.53S 26.00E
93 B9 **Kibondo** **Tanzania** 3.34S 30.41E
93 J9 **Kibongoto** **Tanzania** 3.11S 37.06E
93 F6 **Kibos** **Kenya** 0.04S 34.50E
87 G8 **Kibre Mengist** **Ethiopia** 5.54N 38.59E
36 F2 **Kıbrıscık** **Turkey** 40.24N 31.52E
34 B10 **Kibrit,Jabal al** *mt* **Saudi Arabia** 28.17N 34.43E
93 B8 **Kibungu** **Rwanda** 2.09S 30.33E
91 C6 **Kibunzi** **Zaïre** 5.05S 13.52E
93 A9 **Kibuye** **Burundi** 3.39S 29.58E
93 A8 **Kibuye** **Rwanda** 2.03S 29.19E
92 C7 **Kibuye** **Zaïre** 11.25S 27.50E
92 D5 **Kibwesa** **Tanzania** 6.31S 29.58E
93 J8 **Kibwezi** **Kenya** 2.25S 37.57E
56 K2 **Kibworth** Leics **Eng** 52.33N 0.59W
82 F9 **Kičevo** **Yugoslavia** 41.30N 20.59E
91 L10 **Kichaka** **Kenya** 4.19S 39.21E
93 B7 **Kicherere** *mt* **Tanzania** 1.09S 30.43E
42 G5 **Kichey** **U.S.S.R.** 54.18N 104.40E
30 C4 **Kichha** Uttar Prad **India** 28.54N 79.30E
30 C4 **Kichha** *R* Uttar Prad **India**
30 F6 **Kichhaunchha** Uttar Prad **India** 26.25N 82.46E
39 G5 **Kichiga** **U.S.S.R.** 59.54N 163.30E
20 C2 **Kichijōji** *dist* Tōkyō **Japan**
47 F5 **Kichmenga** *R* **U.S.S.R.**
47 F6 **Kichmengskiy Gorodok** **U.S.S.R.** 59.58N 45.44E
Kichow *see* **Qizhou**
46 Q3 **Kichuy** **U.S.S.R.** 54.51N 51.58E
46 Q2 **Kichuy** *R* **U.S.S.R.**
93 B6 **Kichwamba** **Uganda** 0.14S 30.06E
106 D6 **Kickapoo** *R* **Wisconsin**
101 P10 **Kicking Horse Pass** **Br Col** 51.28N 116.23W
92 G5 **Kidachi** **Tanzania** 6.43S 35.34E
89 K2 **Kidal** **Mali** 18.27N 1.25E
33 L5 **Kidan,Al** *des area* **Saudi Arabia**
19 C4 **Kidandal** **Indonesia** 1.34S 123.14E
92 H5 **Kidatu** **Tanzania** 7.41S 37.01E
55 H4 **Kidbrooke** London **Eng** 51.28N 0.02E
108 N4 **Kidder** **S Dakota** 45.53N 97.42W
56 G3 **Kidderminster** Hereford & Worcs **Eng** 52.23N 2.14W
29 G2 **Kidderpore** *dist* Calcutta, W Bengal
95 L9 **Kidd's Beach** **S Africa** 33.09S 27.41E
93 E1 **Kidepo** *watercourse* **Sudan**
93 E2 **Kidepo Nat.Park** **Uganda**
93 D4 **Kidera** **Uganda** 1.22N 32.59E
92 H5 **Kidete** **Tanzania** 6.40S 36.44E
92 H5 **Kidete** **Tanzania** 6.22S 37.19E
50 E7 **Kidhjaberg** **Iceland** 64.00N 20.46W
59 C3 **Kid I** Mayo **Irish Rep** 54.20N 9.52W
91 J6 **Kidimba** **Zaïre** 5.06S 25.28E
90 M5 **Kidingir** **Sudan** 12.48N 24.35E
89 C4 **Kidira** **Senegal** 14.35N 12.12W
56 J4 **Kidlington** Oxon **Eng** 51.50N 1.17W
31 K4 **Kidmang** **Kashmir** 33.20N 80.12E
11 M6 **Kidnappers,C** **New Zealand** 39.39S 177.17E
35 D8 **Kidod,Har** *hill* **Israel**
92 H5 **Kidodi** **Tanzania** 7.36S 37.04E
93 E4 **Kidongole** **Uganda** 1.16N 33.58E
35 B1 **Kidron,Val of** **Jerusalem**
13 G4 **Kidston** **Queensland** 18.50S 144.10E
92 J5 **Kidugallo** **Tanzania** 6.49S 38.12E
18 K4 **Kidurong, Tanjong** *C* Sarawak **Malaysia** 3.17N 113.02E
86 M9 **Kîd, Wâdî** *watercourse* **Egypt**
33 D7 **Kidwat al A'waj** **Saudi Arabia** 18.44N 41.22E
56 C4 **Kidwelly** Dyfed **Wales** 51.45N 4.18W
33 J8 **Kidyūt** **S Yemen** 16.50N 51.26E
33 J8 **Kidyūt,Wādī** *watercourse* **S Yemen**
108 K2 **Kief** **N Dakota** 47.52N 100.30W
64 N8 **Kiefersfelden** **W Germany** 47.36N 12.12E
Kiehsiu *see* **Jiexiu**
95 B9 **Kiekoesvlei** **S Africa** 33.16S 18.22E
63 M4 **Kiel** **W Germany** 54.20N 10.08E
106 F6 **Kiel** **Wisconsin** 43.55N 88.03W
62 M5 **Kielce** **Poland** 50.51N 20.39E
57 J2 **Kielder Res** Northumb **England** 55.12N 2.30W
57 J2 **Kielder Resr** Northumberland **England**
61 G1 **Kieldrecht** **Belgium** 51.17N 4.11E
63 M3 **Kieler Bucht** *B* **W Germany**
63 M4 **Kieler Förde** *B* **W Germany**
12 D5 **Kielpa** **S Australia** 33.34S 136.11E
60 Q7 **Kiel-Windeweer** **Netherlands** 53.07N 6.47E
51 J7 **Kiemensnäs** **Sweden** 64.42N 21.09E
Kienan *see* **Qian'an**
23 D8 **Kien An** **Vietnam** 20.45N 106.40E
65 M6 **Kienberg** **Austria** 47.58N 15.07E
25 H8 **Kien Binh** **Vietnam** 9.36N 105.59E
91 K9 **Kienge** **Zaïre** 10.33S 27.33E
Kienhsien *see* **Ch'ien-hsien**
25 H8 **Kien Hung** **Vietnam** 9.45N 105.22E
Kienko *see* **Jiange**
Kienli *see* **Jianli**
Kiennan *see* **Quannan**
Kienshih *see* **Jianshi**
Kiensi *see* **Qianxi**
66 G5 **Kiental** **Switzerland** 46.36N 7.43E
66 G5 **Kiental** *V* **Switzerland**
Kienyang *see* **Qianyang**
64 N1 **Kieritzsch** **E Germany** 51.10N 12.23E
64 D1 **Kierspe** **W Germany** 51.09N 7.36E
66 G4 **Kiesen** **Switzerland** 46.50N 7.35E
15 J2 **Kieta** Bougainville I **Papua New Guinea** 6.15S 155.37E
Kiev *see* **Kiyev**
12 H6 **Kiewa** *R* **Victoria**
95 G8 **Kiewietskuil** **S Africa** 32.34S 23.32E
89 D3 **Kiffa** **Mauritania** 16.38N 11.28W
71 L2 **Kiffis** **France** 47.27N 7.20E
84 G5 **Kifisiá** **Greece** 38.04N 23.49E
84 E4 **Kifisokhóri** **Greece** 38.36N 22.43E
84 E4 **Kifissós** *R* **Greece**
34 M6 **Kifl, Al** **Iraq** 32.13N 44.24E
35 D5 **Kifl Harith** **Jordan** 32.07N 35.09E
34 M4 **Kifrī** **Iraq** 34.44N 44.58E
86 J10 **Kifri,Gebel** *hill* **Egypt** 27.49N 32.50E
93 E7 **Kifuli** **Tanzania** 1.48S 33.03E
92 B5 **Kifuse** **Zaïre** 6.02S 24.36E
93 E10 **Kigahumo** **Tanzania** 4.01S 33.08E
93 B7 **Kigali** **Rwanda** 1.56S 30.04E
113 K2 **Kigalik** *R* **Alaska**
93 J6 **Kiganjo** **Kenya** 0.22S 37.01E
93 A8 **Kigeme** **Rwanda** 2.30S 29.34E
93 A6 **Kigezi** *dist* **Uganda**
37 E6 **Kiği** **Turkey** 39.19N 40.20E
87 E6 **Kigille** **Sudan** 8.44N 34.01E
41 Q4 **Kigilyakh** **U.S.S.R.** 73.20N 140.00E
41 P4 **Kigilyakh, Poluostrov** *pen* **U.S.S.R.**
113 D4 **Kigluaik Mts** **Alaska**
89 G6 **Kignan** **Mali** 11.47N 5.59E
92 D4 **Kigoma** **Tanzania** 4.52S 29.36E
93 B10 **Kigoma** *reg* **Tanzania**
92 E3 **Kigosi** *R* **Tanzania**
93 F10 **Kigota** **Tanzania** 4.34S 34.50E
113 D6 **Kigoumiut** **Alaska** 60.12N 167.01W
92 J11 **Kigunda** **Zanzibar** 5.47S 39.18E
92 F4 **Kigwa** **Tanzania** 5.10S 33.13E
92 G5 **Kigwe** **Tanzania** 6.05S 35.26E
Kığzı *see* **Havasor**
13 F7 **Kihee** **Queensland** 27.22S 142.30E
114 E6 **Kihei** Hawaiian Is 20.47N 156.27W
11 K5 **Kihikihi** **New Zealand** 38.02S 175.22E
51 K4 **Kihlanki** **Finland** 67.35N 23.35E
51 K9 **Kihniö** **Finland** 62.11N 23.10E
114 B7 **Kiholo** Hawaiian Is 19.51N 155.45W
114 B7 **Kiholo B** Hawaiian Is
30 D7 **Kihunian** Uttar Prad **India** 25.01N 80.57E
93 K10 **Kihurio** **Tanzania** 4.30S 38.04E
43 L4 **Kiik** Kazakhstan **U.S.S.R.** 47.30N 72.55E
51 K11 **Kiikala** **Finland** 60.28N 23.36E
51 K10 **Kiikka** **Finland** 61.20N 22.45E
51 K10 **Kiikoinen** **Finland** 61.27N 22.35E
114 B8 **Kiilae B** Hawaiian Is
114 D4 **Kii Landing** Hawaiian Is 21.59N 160.04W
51 N3 **Kiilopää** *mt* **Finland** 68.21N 27.35E
51 M6 **Kiiminki** **Finland** 65.08N 25.45E
20 K7 **Kii-Nagashima** **Japan** 34.11N 136.19E
20 D10 **Kiire** **Japan** 31.20N 130.30E
20 J8 **Kii-sanchi** *mts* **Japan**
20 H8 **Kii-suidō** *channel* **Japan**
93 H6 **Kijabe** **Kenya** 0.56S 36.34E
113 K6 **Kijik** **Alaska** 60.19N 154.19W
93 L9 **Kijipwa** **Kenya** 3.49S 39.48E
93 C2 **Kijo** *R* **Sudan**
20 Q8 **Kijoka** Okinawa **Japan** 26.42N 128.08E
93 C4 **Kijunjubwa** **Uganda** 1.28N 31.48E
50 B3 **Kikafell** *mt* **Iceland** 65.31N 23.15W
93 B7 **Kikagati** **Uganda** 1.02S 30.40E
85 N10 **Kikaiet,Jebel** *mt* **Sudan** 19.13N 34.39E
21 D12 **Kikai-shima** *isld* **Japan**
92 C4 **Kikalaye** **Zaïre** 4.52S 27.51E
92 J5 **Kikale** **Tanzania** 7.51S 39.13E
93 D5 **Kikamulo** **Uganda** 0.49N 32.23E
94 G4 **Kikao** **Botswana** 23.00S 24.00E
101 R2 **Kikerk L** N W Terr 67.19N 113.18W
39 F7 **Kikhchik** Kamchatka **U.S.S.R.** 53.57N 156.14E
39 G7 **Kikhpinych Sopka** *vol* Kamchatka **U.S.S.R.** 54.29N 160.15E
89 F9 **Kiki** *R* **Liberia**
41 D8 **Kikiakki** **U.S.S.R.** 63.47N 82.44E
113 L2 **Kikiakrorak** *R* **Alaska**
82 F5 **Kikinda** **Yugoslavia** 45.50N 20.30E
31 B8 **Kikki** **Pakistan** 25.42N 62.36E
83 G7 **Kikládhes** *islds* **Greece**
85 B3 **Kiklah** **Libya** 32.05N 12.49E
46 O2 **Kiknur** **U.S.S.R.** 57.12N 47.01E
114 D6 **Kikoa Pt** Hawaiian Is 20.48N 156.48E
91 J8 **Kikole** **Zaïre** 9.26S 25.55E
92 G5 **Kikombo** **Tanzania** 6.15S 36.00E
91 F6 **Kikombo** **Zaïre** 5.37S 18.50E
20 K3 **Kikonai** **Japan** 41.42N 140.27E
91 K8 **Kikondja** **Zaïre** 8.12S 26.27E
91 E6 **Kikongo** **Zaïre** 4.16S 17.17E
91 C6 **Kikonzi** **Zaïre** 5.02S 13.04E
15 H7 **Kikori** **Papua New Guinea** 7.25S 144.13E
93 C4 **Kikube** **Uganda** 1.20N 31.15E
93 D4 **Kikube** **Uganda** 1.51N 32.04E
20 D9 **Kikuchi** **Japan** 33.00N 130.49E
93 J9 **Kikuletwa** *R* **Tanzania**
45 P6 **Kikvidze** **U.S.S.R.** 50.44N 43.05E
95 J7 **Kikvorsberg** *mts* **S Africa**
92 J6 **Kikwetu** **Tanzania** 9.51S 39.45E
99 M6 **Kikwissi,L** **Quebec** 46.57N 78.33W
91 F6 **Kikwit** **Zaïre** 5.02S 18.51E
52 G7 **Kil** **Sweden** 59.30N 13.20E
110 L1 **Kila** **Montana** 48.08N 114.29W
52 K8 **Kila** **Sweden** 58.45N 16.32E
Kila Abdullah *see* **Qila Abdullah**
Kılaban Hâkkari **Turkey***see* **Güyan**
Kılaban Hâkkari **Turkey***see* **Uludere**
31 H4 **Kila Didar Singh** **Pakistan** 32.06N 74.03E
52 K5 **Kilafors** **Sweden** 61.14N 16.35E
93 K8 **Kilaguni Lodge** **Kenya** 2.54S 38.03E
15 J8 **Kila Kila** **Papua New Guinea** 9.31S 147.10E
28 D6 **Kilakkarai** Tamil Nadu **India** 9.14N 78.47E
50 J2 **Kilakot** **Iceland** 66.05N 16.49W
32 E3 **Kilan** **Iran** 35.34N 52.10E
84 Q15 **Kilani** **Cyprus** 34.50N 32.52E
29 E1 **Kilar** Himachal Prad **India** 33.04N 76.26E
Kila Saifulla *see* **Qila Saifullah**
31 H4 **Kila Sobha Singh** **Pakistan** 32.10N 74.50E
114 F3 **Kilauea** Hawaiian Is 22.13N 159.26W
114 C8 **Kilauea Crater** Hawaiian Is 19.24N 155.16W
114 C8 **Kilaueaiki Crater** Hawaiian Is 19.24N 155.15W
114 F3 **Kilauea Pt** Hawaiian Is 22.14N 159.25W
65 M5 **Kilb** **Austria** 48.07N 15.25E
59 C6 **Kilbaha** Clare **Irish Rep** 52.35N 9.52W
36 G5 **Kılbasan** **Turkey** 37.20N 33.11E
59 J4 **Kilberry** Meath **Irish Rep** 53.42N 6.41W
58 G7 **Kilbirnie** Strathclyde **Scotland** 55.46N 4.41W
11 C6 **Kilbirnie** *dist* Wellington **New Zealand**
51 C5 **Kilboghamn** **Norway** 66.28N 13.13E
57 C1 **Kilbrannan Sd** Strathclyde **Scotland**
59 H6 **Kilbricken** Leix **Irish Rep** 52.58N 7.27W
59 K5 **Kilbride** Meath **Irish Rep** 53.27N 6.24W
58 B4 **Kilbride** S Uist, W Isles **Scotland** 57.07N 7.22W
59 K5 **Kilbride** Wicklow **Irish Rep** 53.12N 6.27W
59 E8 **Kilbrittain** Cork **Irish Rep** 51.40N 8.41W
113 G6 **Kilbuck Mts** **Alaska**
98 E7 **Kilburn** New Brunswick 46.38N 67.45W
57 L4 **Kilburn** N Yorks **Eng** 54.12N 1.13W
12 A7 **Kilburn** *dist* Adelaide, S Aust
59 E2 **Kilcar** Donegal **Irish Rep** 54.38N 8.35W
58 F7 **Kilchattan** Strathclyde **Scotland** 55.45N 5.02W
58 D5 **Kilchoan** Highland **Scotland** 56.43N 6.06W
59 E5 **Kilchreest** Galway **Irish Rep** 53.11N 8.39W
21 E7 **Kilchu** **N Korea** 40.55N 129.21E
59 L3 **Kilclief** Down **N Ireland** 54.20N 5.33W
59 J5 **Kilcock** Kildare **N Ireland** 53.24N 6.40W
59 E5 **Kilcolgan** Galway **Irish Rep** 53.13N 8.52W
59 E7 **Kilcolman Castle** Cork **Irish Rep** 52.15N 8.37W
59 F5 **Kilconnell** Galway **Irish Rep** 53.20N 8.25W
58 L6 **Kilconquhar** Fife **Scotland** 56.13N 2.50W
59 K5 **Kilcoole** Wicklow **Irish Rep** 53.07N 6.04W
59 G5 **Kilcormac** Offaly **Irish Rep** 53.10N 7.43W
13 K7 **Kilcoy** **Queensland** 26.58S 152.30E
58 G7 **Kilcreggan** Strathclyde **Scotland** 55.59N 4.50W
59 J5 **Kilcullen** Kildare **Irish Rep** 53.08N 6.45W
101 K9 **Kildala Arm** **Br Col**
57 L4 **Kildale** N Yorks **Eng** 54.28N 1.04W
59 J4 **Kildalkey** Meath **Irish Rep** 53.34N 6.54W
59 J5 **Kildare** Kildare **Irish Rep** 53.10N 6.55W
112 N3 **Kildare** **Texas** 32.55N 94.17W
59 J5 **Kildare** *co* **Irish Rep**
98 J7 **Kildare,C** Prince Edward I 46.55N 63.59W
53 J5 **Kildebrønde** **Denmark** 55.37N 12.17E
60 N12 **Kilder** **Netherlands** 51.56N 6.14E
59 E6 **Kildimo** Limerick **Irish Rep** 52.37N 8.50W
47 C2 **Kil'din, Ostrov** *isld* **U.S.S.R.** 69.22N 34.15E
58 J2 **Kildonan** Highland **Scotland** 58.10N 3.51W
100 B1 **Kildonan** **Manitoba** 49.57N 97.07W
101 L11 **Kildonan** Vancouver I, **Br Col** 49.01N 125.00W
92 E10 **Kildonan** **Zimbabwe** 17.15S 30.44E
59 J5 **Kildoon** Kildare **Irish Rep** 53.06N 6.55W
59 F7 **Kildorrery** Cork **Irish Rep** 52.15N 8.25W
59 H2 **Kildrum** Donegal **Irish Rep** 54.58N 7.25W
58 L4 **Kildrummy Castle** Grampian **Scotland** 57.14N 2.55W
108 S8 **Kilduff** **Iowa** 41.38N 92.54W
91 K8 **Kileba** **Zaïre** 8.45S 27.24E
90 M6 **Kileikli Mogo** **Sudan** 11.25N 25.31E
101 L2 **Kilekale L** N W Terr
93 B5 **Kilembe** **Uganda** 0.14N 30.01E
91 F6 **Kilembe** **Zaïre** 5.47S 19.54E
53 B3 **Kilen** *L* **Denmark** 56.30N 8.34E
92 H5 **Kilengwe** **Tanzania** 7.30S 37.31E
59 D6 **Kilfenora** Clare **Irish Rep** 52.59N 9.13W
58 F7 **Kilfinan** Strathclyde **Scotland** 55.58N 5.19W
59 F7 **Kilfinnane** Limerick **Irish Rep** 52.22N 8.28W
59 F7 **Kilfrush Cross Roads** Limerick **Irish Rep** 52.27N 8.25W
39 E4 **Kil'gana** *R* **U.S.S.R.**
59 D8 **Kilgarvan** Kerry **Irish Rep** 51.54N 9.26W
59 F4 **Kilglass L** Roscommon **Irish Rep** 53.50N 8.01W
110 O5 **Kilgore** **Idaho** 44.25N 111.53W
108 K7 **Kilgore** **Nebraska** 42.58N 100.58W
112 N3 **Kilgore** **Texas** 32.23N 94.54E
93 F6 **Kilgoris** **Kenya** 1.00S 34.54E
59 E6 **Kilgory L** Clare **Irish Rep** 52.51N 8.41W
13 D3 **Kilgour** *R* N Terr **Australia**
57 N4 **Kilham** Humberside **Eng** 54.04N 0.23W
85 M7 **Kilh,El** **Egypt** 25.06N 32.48E
31 K2 **Kilian Davan** *pass* Xinjiang Uygur Zizhiqu **China** 36.45N 78.05E
93 K9 **Kilibasi** **Kenya** 3.59S 38.57E
89 L7 **Kilibo** **Benin** 8.32N 2.38E
Kiliçkaya *see* **Ersis**
36 G3 **Kılıçözü** *R* **Turkey**
37 C3 **Kilidülbahir** **Turkey** 40.09N 26.23E
Kilien Shan *mts see* **Zoulang Nanshan**
93 L9 **Kilifi** **Kenya** 3.37S 39.50E
93 L9 **Kilifi** *dist* **Kenya**
93 L9 **Kilifi Creek** **Kenya**
9 C3 **Kili I** *atoll* Marshall Is **Pacific Oc** 5.40N 169.03E
31 H2 **Kilik Pass** Xinjiang Uygur Zizhiqu/Kashmir **China** 37.02N 74.46E
93 F8 **Kilimafedha** **Tanzania** 2.17S 34.56E
93 J9 **Kilimanjaro** *mt* **Tanzania**
93 J10 **Kilimanjaro** *reg* **Tanzania**
93 M8 **Kilima Simba** **Kenya** 2.44S 40.10E
92 G4 **Kilimatinde** **Tanzania** 5.52S 34.55E
15 J1 **Kilinailau Is** **Papua New Guinea**
37 G2 **Kılınç** **Turkey** 40.38N 29.24E
92 J6 **Kilindi** **Tanzania** 8.02S 39.10E
93 L10 **Kilindini Harbour** **Kenya** 4.04S 39.33E
92 J5 **Kilindoni** Mafia I **E Africa** 7.56S 39.40E
46 E1 **Kilingi-Nõmme** Estonia **U.S.S.R.** 58.08N 24.58E
Kilingi Nymme *see* **Kilingi-Nõmme**
26 R3 **Kilinochchi** **Sri Lanka** 9.23N 80.24E
37 C9 **Kilis** **Turkey** 36.43N 37.07E
113 L8 **Kiliuda B** **Alaska**
46 G6 **Kiliya** Ukraine **U.S.S.R.** 45.30N 29.16E
59 C6 **Kilkee** Clare **Irish Rep** 52.41N 9.38W
59 K3 **Kilkeel** Down **N Ireland** 54.04N 6.00W
59 E4 **Kilkelly** Mayo **Irish Rep** 53.53N 8.51W
59 H6 **Kilkenny** Kilkenny **Irish Rep** 52.39N 7.15W
59 H6 **Kilkenny** *co* **Irish Rep**
57 B2 **Kilkenzie** Strathclyde **Scotland** 55.28N 5.40W
56 C6 **Kilkhampton** Cornwall **Eng** 50.53N 4.29W
83 F4 **Kilkís** **Greece** 40.59N 22.52E
59 E6 **Kilkishen** Clare **Irish Rep** 52.48N 8.45W
13 K7 **Kilkivan** **Queensland** 26.03S 152.09E
59 J5 **Kill** Kildare **Irish Rep** 53.15N 6.35W
59 H7 **Kill** Waterford **Irish Rep** 52.10N 7.20W
59 D6 **Killadysert** Clare **Irish Rep** 52.40N 9.07W
59 K1 **Killagan** Antrim **N Ireland** 55.01N 6.22W
59 D3 **Killala** Mayo **Irish Rep** 54.13N 9.13W
59 D3 **Killala B** **Irish Rep** 54.16N 9.08W
99 D3 **Killala L** **Ontario** 49.05N 86.33W
59 F6 **Killaloe** Clare **Irish Rep** 52.48N 8.27W
99 N7 **Killaloe** **Ontario** 45.33N 77.26W
100 P8 **Killaly** **Saskatchewan** 50.46N 102.51W
100 F6 **Killam** **Alberta** 52.48N 111.53W
59 H5 **Killane** Offaly **Irish Rep** 53.20N 7.04W
59 J6 **Killane** Wexford **Irish Rep** 52.31N 6.45W
12 L6 **Killara** *dist* Sydney, New S Wales
94 Q11 **Killarney** Cape Town **S Africa** 33.50S 18.31E
59 C7 **Killarney** Kerry **Irish Rep** 52.03N 9.30W
100 S9 **Killarney** **Manitoba** 49.12N 99.40W
13 B3 **Killarney** N Terr **Australia** 16.05S 131.52E
99 J7 **Killarney** **Ontario** 45.58N 81.31W
13 K8 **Killarney** **Queensland** 28.18S 152.15E
105 L9 **Killarney,L** New Providence I **Bahamas**
99 J6 **Killarney Prov.Park** **Ontario**
59 C4 **Killary Harb** Mayo **Irish Rep** 53.38N 9.55W
59 G3 **Killashandra** Cavan **Irish Rep** 54.01N 7.32W
59 G4 **Killashee** Longford **Irish Rep** 53.41N 7.53W
59 E7 **Killawillin** Cork **Irish Rep** 52.08N 8.31W
103 B2 **Killawog** **New York** 42.24N 76.01W
59 H5 **Killbeggan** W Meath **Irish Rep** 53.22N 7.30W
108 H2 **Killdeer** **N Dakota** 47.22N 102.44W
100 L9 **Killdeer** **Saskatchewan** 49.06N 106.22W
59 H2 **Killea** Londonderry **N Ireland** 54.58N 7.24W
59 G8 **Killeagh** Cork **Irish Rep** 51.57N 8.00W
58 E7 **Killean** Strathclyde **Scotland** 55.39N 5.40W
59 C5 **Killeany** Galway **Irish Rep** 53.06N 9.40W
58 H6 **Killearn** Central **Scotland** 56.03N 4.22W
59 K3 **Killeen** Armagh **N Ireland** 54.07N 6.21W
112 K4 **Killeen** **Texas** 31.08N 97.44W
59 H5 **Killeigh** Offaly **Irish Rep** 53.13N 7.27W
37 E3 **Killek** **Turkey** 40.14N 27.49E
87 H5 **Killelu** **Ethiopia** 10.35N 41.40E
87 H5 **Killelu** *watercourse* **Ethiopia**
59 K6 **Killena** Wexford **Irish Rep** 52.35N 6.16W
59 G6 **Killenaule** Tipperary **Irish Rep** 52.34N 7.40W
36 C3 **Kıller** *R* **Turkey**
58 J5 **Killiecrankie,Pass of** Tayside **Scotland** 56.43N 3.40W
37 D6 **Kıllık** **Turkey** 39.23N 37.42E
113 K2 **Killik** *R* **Alaska**
113 K2 **Killik Bend** **Alaska** 68.59N 154.10W
59 F5 **Killimor** Galway **Irish Rep** 53.10N 8.17W
58 K2 **Killimster** Highland **Scotland** 58.30N 3.11W
58 H6 **Killin** Central **Scotland** 56.28N 4.20W
59 K5 **Killiney** Dublin **Irish Rep** 53.15N 6.07W
52 F4 **Killingdal** **Norway** 62.47N 11.26E
57 K4 **Killinghall** N Yorks **Eng** 54.01N 1.34W
103 L3 **Killingly** **Connecticut** 41.51N 71.53W
103 J4 **Killingworth** **Connecticut** 41.22N 72.34W
57 K2 **Killingworth** Tyne and Wear **Eng** 55.02N 1.32W
84 B6 **Killíni** **Greece** 37.55N 21.08E
84 D6 **Killíni Óros** *mts* **Greece**
58 H4 **Killin,L** Highland **Scotland** 57.09N 4.26W
58 E7 **Killisport,L** Strathclyde **Scotland** 55.54N 5.39W
59 C7 **Killorglin** Kerry **Irish Rep** 52.06N 9.47W
59 L3 **Killough** Down **N Ireland** 54.16N 5.39W
103 H8 **Kill Van Kull** *R* **New York/New Jersey**
59 F2 **Killybegs** Donegal **Irish Rep** 54.38N 8.27W
59 J3 **Killylea** Armagh **N Ireland** 54.21N 6.47W
59 L3 **Killyleagh** Down **N Ireland** 54.24N 5.39W
59 G5 **Killyon** Offaly **Irish Rep** 53.06N 7.43W
59 E5 **Kilmacdoagh Church** Galway **Irish Rep** 53.04N 8.55W
58 G7 **Kilmacolm** Strathclyde **Scotland** 55.54N 4.38W
59 G1 **Kilmacrenan** Donegal **Irish Rep** 55.02N 7.47W
59 H7 **Kilmacthomas** Waterford **Irish Rep** 52.12N 7.25W
59 H7 **Kilmaganny** Kilkenny **Irish Rep** 52.27N 7.20W
59 D4 **Kilmaine** Mayo **Irish Rep** 53.35N 9.07W
59 E7 **Kilmallock** Limerick **Irish Rep** 52.25N 8.35W
58 D3 **Kilmaluag** Skye, Highland **Scotland** 57.41N 6.19W
58 L6 **Kilmany** Fife **Scotland** 56.23N 2.59W
57 E1 **Kilmarnock** Strathclyde **Scotland** 55.37N 4.30W
104 J9 **Kilmarnock** **Virginia** 37.43N 76.24W
58 F6 **Kilmartin** Strathclyde **Scotland** 56.08N 5.29W
58 G7 **Kilmaurs** Strathclyde **Scotland** 55.39N 4.32W
59 J5 **Kilmeage** Kildare **Irish Rep** 53.20N 6.50W
59 E7 **Kilmeedy** Limerick **Irish Rep** 52.25N 9.00W
58 F6 **Kilmelford** Strathclyde **Scotland** 56.16N 5.29W
46 Q2 **Kil'mez** **U.S.S.R.** 57.00N 51.02E
46 Q2 **Kil'mez** *R* **U.S.S.R.**
107 G8 **Kilmichael** **Mississippi** 33.26N 89.33W
58 F6 **Kilmichael** Strathclyde **Scotland** 56.05N 5.28W
59 K6 **Kilmichael Pt** Wexford **Irish Rep** 52.44N 6.08W
59 D6 **Kilmihil** Clare **Irish Rep** 52.44N 9.19W
58 G4 **Kilmorack** Highland **Scotland** 57.28N 4.31W
12 G6 **Kilmore** **Victoria** 37.18S 144.58E
59 J7 **Kilmore Quay** Wexford **Irish Rep** 52.11N 6.35W
58 E7 **Kilmory** Strathclyde **Scotland** 55.55N 5.41W
58 G7 **Kilmun** Strathclyde **Scotland** 55.59N 4.56W
59 D6 **Kilmurry** Clare **Irish Rep** 52.48N 9.27W
59 E6 **Kilmurry** Clare **Irish Rep** 52.47N 8.47W
59 H4 **Kilnaleck** Cavan **Irish Rep** 53.52N 7.19W

58 E6 Kilninver Strathclyde Scotland 56.20N 5.31W
57 O5 Kilnsea Humberside Eng 53.38N 0.07E
93 B4 Kilo Zaïre 1.49N 30.10E
92 F5 Kiloli Tanzania 6.51S 33.29E
92 H6 Kilombero R Tanzania
91 J5 Kilometre 28 Zaïre 3.11S 25.49E
93 B4 Kilomines Zaïre 1.48N 30.14E
87 B9 Kilo Moto Zaïre 3.21N 28.44E
92 G6 Kilondo Tanzania 9.47S 34.22E
92 G6 Kilosa Tanzania 9.10S 35.50E
92 H5 Kilosa Tanzania 6.49S 37.00E
51 H2 Kilpisjärvi Finland 69.03N 20.50E
51 H2 Kilpisjärvi L Sweden/Finland 69.00N 20.45E
51 L7 Kilpua Finland 64.22N 25.00E
59 J2 Kilrea Londonderry N Ireland 54.57N 6.34W
58 L6 Kilrenny Fife Scotland 56.15N 2.41W
59 C5 Kilronan Galway Irish Rep 53.07N 9.40W
59 D6 Kilrush Clare Irish Rep 52.39N 9.29W
56 J3 Kilsby Northants Eng 52.20N 1.09W
59 G7 Kilsheelan Tipperary Irish Rep 52.22N 7.35W
58 H7 Kilsyth Strathclyde Scotland 55.59N 4.04W
27 L7 Kiltan I Laccadive Is Indian Ocean 11.30N 73.00E
59 J6 Kiltealy Wexford Irish Rep 52.34N 6.45W
59 J5 Kilteel Kildare Irish Rep 53.14N 6.31W
59 J6 Kiltegan Wicklow Irish Rep 52.55N 6.36W
59 E4 Kiltimagh Mayo Irish Rep 53.52N 9.00W
59 F5 Kiltoom Roscommon Irish Rep 53.28N 8.01W
59 F5 Kiltormer Galway Irish Rep 53.14N 8.16W
59 E4 Kiltullagh L Galway Irish Rep 53.35N 8.35W
59 F3 Kiltyclogher Leitrim Irish Rep 54.22N 8.02W
114 F3 Kiluea B Hawaiian Is
Kilun see Kilan
32 D6 Kilūr Karīm Iran 29.51N 50.45E
32 D6 Kilur Karim oil well Iran 29.40N 50.39E
Kilvan see Aşağıhanik
51 J5 Kilvo Sweden 66.50N 21.04E
92 D6 Kilwa Zaïre 9.15S 28.21E
92 D6 Kilwa I Zambia 9.14S 28.30E
92 J6 Kilwa Kisiwani Tanzania 9.00S 39.30E
92 J6 Kilwa Kivinje Tanzania 8.45S 39.21E
92 J6 Kilwa Masoko Tanzania 8.55S 39.31E
58 G7 Kilwinning Strathclyde Scotland 55.40N 4.42W
59 F7 Kilworth Cork Irish Rep 52.10N 8.15W
59 F7 Kilworth Mts Cork Irish Rep
37 C3 Kilya Turkey 40.13N 26.22E
44 J7 Kilyazi Azerbaydzhan U.S.S.R. 40.52N 49.21E
37 F1 Kilyos Turkey 41.14N 29.02E
109 G4 Kim Colorado 37.15N 103.21W
43 M8 Kim Tadzhikistan U.S.S.R. 40.12N 70.15E
29 C7 Kim R Gujarat India
18 K2 Kim R Pen Malaysia
90 E9 Kim watercourse Cameroon
93 J7 Kima Kenya 1.58S 37.16E
91 K4 Kima Zaïre 1.26S 26.42E
15 E7 Kimaän Irian Jaya 7.54S 138.51E
93 F9 Kimali Tanzania 3.25S 34.29E
110 M7 Kimama Idaho 42.51N 113.48W
92 H5 Kimamba Tanzania 6.44S 37.10E
92 J6 Kimambi Tanzania 9.20S 38.25E
93 J8 Kimana Kenya 2.44S 37.31E
18 L3 Kimanis, Telok B Sabah Malaysia
12 D5 Kimba S Australia 33.08S 136.23E
108 G8 Kimball Nebraska 41.16N 103.40W
108 M6 Kimball S Dakota 43.44N 98.57W
104 D9 Kimball W Virginia 37.27N 81.33W
113 P5 Kimball,Mt Alaska 63.18N 144.40W
108 P8 Kimballton Iowa 41.38N 95.03W
91 F6 Kimbanda Zaïre 5.17S 19.14E
91 E6 Kimbao Zaïre 5.29S 17.39E
15 L6 Kimbe New Britain 5.36S 150.10E
15 L6 Kimbe B New Britain
101 Q11 Kimberley Br Col 49.40N 115.58W
56 O2 Kimberley Norfolk Eng 52.36N 1.03E
99 K8 Kimberley Ontario 44.24N 80.33E
95 H4 Kimberley S Africa 28.45S 24.46E
13 H3 Kimberley,C Queensland 16.15S 145.30E
14 E3 Kimberley Downs W Australia 17.20S 124.21E
10 F5 Kimberley Plat W Australia
14 F3 Kimberley Plateau W Australia
14 C7 Kimberley Ra W Australia
110 L7 Kimberly Idaho 42.32N 114.23W
111 J2 Kimberly Nevada 39.16N 115.02W
110 F5 Kimberly Oregon 44.47N 119.39W
106 F5 Kimberly Wisconsin 44.15N 88.19W
92 J5 Kimbiji Tanzania 7.00S 39.30E
103 D4 Kimbles Pennsylvania 41.28N 75.07W
56 L3 Kimbolton Cambs Eng 52.18N 0.24W
11 K7 Kimbolton New Zealand 40.02S 175.47E
91 F7 Kimbongo Zaïre 6.08S 18.01E
91 D5 Kimboto Congo 3.12S 14.08E
92 F5 Kimbu tribe Tanzania
42 G5 Kimel'tey U.S.S.R. 54.09N 101.58E
92 J11 Kimembe Zanzibar 5.52S 39.19E
21 D10 Kimhae S Korea 35.10N 128.57E
90 E8 Kimi Cameroon 6.06N 11.29E
84 H4 Kími Greece 38.38N 24.06E
Kimida see Kumdah
93 F5 Kimilili Kenya 0.47N 34.42E
51 K11 Kimito Finland 60.10N 22.45E
100 A3 Kimiwan L Alberta 55.45N 116.50W
40 E7 Kimkan U.S.S.R. 48.55N 131.26E
107 F3 Kimmswick Missouri 38.21N 90.23W
84 H8 Kímolos Greece 36.47N 24.35E
84 H8 Kímolos isld Greece
91 C6 Kimongo Congo 4.27S 12.53E
45 K3 Kimovsk U.S.S.R. 53.58N 38.35E
91 D6 Kimpako Zaïre 5.00S 15.14E
91 D6 Kimpangu Zaïre 5.52S 15.03E
91 D6 Kimpanzou Congo 4.34S 15.00E
89 G5 Kimparana Mali 12.52N 4.59W
91 D6 Kimpese Zaïre 5.29S 14.24E
91 D6 Kimpoko Zaïre 4.12S 15.33E
20 M3 Kimpoku-san mt Japan 38.09N 138.21E
46 K2 Kimry U.S.S.R. 56.51N 37.20E
25 K5 Kim Son Vietnam 14.16N 108.56E
52 J8 Kimstad Sweden 58.33N 15.58E
60 K7 Kimswerd Netherlands 53.08N 5.26E
91 D6 Kimuenza Zaïre 4.30S 15.13E
92 D5 Kimvanga Zaïre 7.32S 28.41E
91 D6 Kimvula Zaïre 5.54S 15.59E
47 E3 Kimzha U.S.S.R. 65.31N 44.40E
25 C1 Kin Burma 22.47N 94.39E
20 C7 Kin Japan 34.33N 129.27E
20 P9 Kin Okinawa Japan 26.27N 127.56E
20 P9 Kina Okinawa Japan 26.23N 127.44E
18 M2 Kinabalu, Gunong mt Sabah Malaysia 6.03N 116.32E
18 M3 Kinabatangan R Sabah Malaysia
58 L6 Kinaldy Burn Fife Scotland
59 H4 Kinale,L Longford Irish Rep 53.46N 7.25W
37 F2 Kinali isld Turkey 40.55N 29.03E
93 L10 Kinango Kenya 4.07S 39.18E
93 L9 Kinangoni Kenya 3.54S 39.14E
93 H6 Kinangop,Mt Kenya 0.37S 36.42E
93 H6 Kinangop Plat Kenya
105 F3 Kinards South Carolina 34.23N 81.48W
Kinareh see Kenāreh
83 H8 Kínaros isld Greece 36.59N 26.15E
28 E2 Kinarsani R Andhra Prad India
18 L3 Kinarut Sabah Malaysia 5.52N 116.00E
101 O10 Kinbasket Br Col 51.59N 118.02W
89 F7 Kinbirila Ivory Coast 9.46N 7.38W
58 J2 Kinbrace Highland Scotland 58.15N 3.56W
100 F8 Kinbrook Island Prov.Park Alberta
45 C10 Kinburnskaya Kosa sand spit Ukraine U.S.S.R.
109 P3 Kincaid Kansas 38.07N 95.07W
100 K9 Kincaid Saskatchewan 49.41N 107.01W
58 H3 Kincardine Highland Scotland 57.51N 4.21W
99 J8 Kincardine Ontario 44.11N 81.38W
Kincardine co see Grampian reg
58 L4 Kincardine O'Neil Grampian Scotland 57.05N 2.40W
58 J6 Kincardine on Forth Fife Scotland 56.04N 3.44W
25 N8 Kinchang Burma 26.34N 98.01E
101 J8 Kincolith Br Col 55.00N 129.57W
58 J4 Kincraig Highland Scotland 57.08N 3.56W
91 G6 Kinda Zaïre 4.48S 21.50E
91 J8 Kinda Zaïre 9.20S 25.06E
42 C3 Kindal U.S.S.R. 59.11N 80.32E
91 D5 Kindamba Congo 3.48S 14.32E
91 G7 Kindambi Zaïre 6.10S 20.21E
25 L9 Kindat Burma 23.42N 94.29E
65 M6 Kindberg Austria 47.31N 15.27E
106 M6 Kinde Michigan 43.58N 82.59W
64 L1 Kindelbrück E Germany 51.16N 11.05E
91 J8 Kindele Zaïre 8.39S 24.10E
107 D11 Kinder Louisiana 30.30N 92.51W
64 C3 Kinderbeuern W Germany 50.01N 7.01E
60 G12 Kinderdijk Netherlands 51.53N 4.38E
103 G2 Kinderhook Cr New York
100 H7 Kindersley Saskatchewan 51.27N 109.08W
89 C6 Kindia Guinea 10.03N 12.49W
42 J4 Kindikan U.S.S.R. 56.01N 115.15E
64 M6 Kinding W Germany 49.00N 11.25E
87 C5 Kindirma,Jeb mt Sudan 10.50N 30.19E
96 C1 Kindley naval air station Bermuda 32.22N 64.42W
91 E5 Kindongo Zaïre 3.53S 17.30E
108 N3 Kindred N Dakota 46.39N 97.00W
91 J5 Kindu Zaïre 3.00S 25.56E
113 G7 Kinegnak Alaska 58.50N 161.40W
46 Q3 Kinel' U.S.S.R. 53.17N 50.42E
46 Q3 Kinel' Cherkassy U.S.S.R. 53.30N 51.30E
46 M2 Kineshma U.S.S.R. 57.28N 42.08E
93 E7 Kinesi Tanzania 1.28S 33.54E
56 H3 Kineton Warwicks Eng 52.10N 1.30W
15 M6 King New Ireland 4.28S 152.49E
13 B2 King R N Terr Australia
13 C1 King R N Terr Australia
13 E6 King R Queensland
13 G2 King R Queensland
12 H8 King R Tasmania
91 F6 Kingandu Zaïre 5.31S 18.23E
91 C6 Kinganga Zaïre 5.19S 13.50E
13 K7 Kingaroy Queensland 26.32S 151.50E
121 A10 King, Canal str Chile
97 J2 King Christian I N W Terr 77.40N 102.00W
111 C5 King City California 36.13N 121.09W
107 B1 King City Missouri 40.02N 94.31W
101 K10 Kingcome Inlet Br Col 50.58N 126.15W
113 F9 King Cove Alaska 55.02N 162.19W
121 G8 King Edward Point S Georgia 54.15S 36.34W
14 F3 King Edward R W Australia
123 J8 King Edward VII Land Antarctica
Kingerban see Kingirbān
104 P2 Kingfield Maine 44.57N 70.11W
109 N6 Kingfisher Oklahoma 35.53N 97.56W
121 D9 King George B Falkland Is
123 E15 King George I South Shetland Is Antarctica
97 M6 King George Is Hudson B, N W Terr
122 C14 King George Is Tuamotu Is Pacific Oc
101 Q10 King George, Mt Br Col 50.36N 115.26W
101 D5 King George, Mt Yukon Terr 60.29N 139.42W
14 C11 King George Sd W Australia
55 G2 King George's Res London Eng
119 H5 King George VI Falls Guyana 5.46N 61.08W
55 A4 King George VI Res Surrey Eng
121 G8 King Haakon B S Georgia
110 K6 King Hill Idaho 43.00N 115.14W
14 E6 King Hill W Australia 22.35S 123.51E
58 K6 Kinghorn Fife Scotland 56.04N 3.11W
99 C3 Kinghorn Ontario 49.45N 87.20W
21 D4 Kinghua Heilongjiang China 47.03N 126.10E
35 H4 King Hussein Airport Jordan 32.22N 36.14E
113 C4 King I Alaska 65.00N 168.00W
123 H11 King I Antarctica
101 K9 King I Br Col
King I Burma see Kadan Kyun
12 G7 King I Tasmania
34 M4 Kingirbān Iraq 34.41N 44.55E
46 G1 Kingisepp U.S.S.R. 59.22N 28.40E
46 E1 Kingissepp Estonia U.S.S.R. 58.12N 22.30E
12 J6 King, L Victoria
58 K6 Kinglassie Fife Scotland 56.11N 3.15W
110 G8 King Lear mt Nevada 41.14N 118.34W
123 D3 King Leopold & Queen Astrid Coast Antarctica
14 E3 King Leopold Ra W Australia
100 E5 Kingman Alberta 53.15N 112.41W
111 K6 Kingman Arizona 35.12N 114.02W
109 M4 Kingman Kansas 37.39N 98.07W
104 R1 Kingman Maine 45.34N 68.14W
122 L7 Kingman Reef Line Is Pacific Oc 6.27N 162.24W
13 H7 King, Mt Queensland 25.10S 147.30E
112 E4 King Mt Texas 31.19N 102.18W
14 C5 King, Mt W Australia 22.20S 118.07E
91 K5 Kingombe Zaïre 2.37S 26.39E
91 K5 Kingombe Zaïre 3.51S 26.32E
91 K7 Kingombe Zaïre 7.26S 26.12E
12 D4 Kingoonya S Australia 30.55S 135.18E
91 C6 Kingoye Zaïre 4.29S 13.47E
10 E11 King Pt Lord Howe I Pacific Oc 31.36S 159.05E
14 G3 King, R W Australia
31 E5 Kingri Pakistan 30.24N 69.49E
103 G5 Kings co New York 40.37N 74.00W
107 C5 Kings R Arkansas
111 D5 Kings R California
110 G8 Kings R Nevada
113 J7 King Salmon Alaska 58.40N 156.40W
113 J7 King Salmon R Alaska
58 L6 Kingsbarns Fife Scotland 56.18N 2.39W
56 D7 Kingsbridge Devon Eng 50.17N 3.46W
56 H2 King's Bromley Staffs Eng 52.45N 1.48W
111 E5 Kingsburg California 36.30N 119.34W
112 K6 Kingsbury Texas 29.39N 97.51W
56 H2 Kingsbury Warwicks Eng 52.35N 1.40W
55 D3 Kingsbury Green London Eng 51.35N 0.16W
109 D1 Kings Canyon Colorado 40.56N 106.14W
111 F4 Kings Canyon Nat.Park California
56 J5 Kingsclere Hants Eng 51.20N 1.14W
12 L3 Kingscliff-Fingal New S Wales 28.15S 153.32E
95 N6 Kingscote S Africa 30.01S 29.22E
12 E6 Kingscote S Australia 35.40S 137.39E
59 J4 Kingscourt Cavan Irish Rep 53.55N 6.48W
98 T5 King's Cove Newfoundland 48.35N 53.21W
56 M5 Kingsdown Kent Eng 51.21N 0.17E
11 J4 Kingseat New Zealand 37.08S 174.48E
56 L5 Kingsfold W Sussex Eng 51.07N 0.20W
12 M7 Kingsford dist Sydney, N S W
56 O5 Kingsgate Kent Eng 51.24N 1.26E
12 L8 Kingsgrove dist Sydney, N S W
94 S13 Kings Kloof S Africa 26.03S 27.47E
107 D8 Kingsland Arkansas 33.52N 92.18W
105 F7 Kingsland Georgia 30.49N 81.43W
56 L4 King's Langley Herts Eng 51.43N 0.28W
57 H6 Kingsley Cheshire Eng 53.16N 2.41W
56 K5 Kingsley Hants Eng 51.08N 0.54W
108 P7 Kingsley Iowa 42.26N 95.58W
106 J5 Kingsley Michigan 44.36N 85.32W
103 C3 Kingsley Pennsylvania 41.45N 75.45W
95 O3 Kingsley S Africa 27.55S 30.32E
108 J8 Kingsley Dam Nebraska 41.15N 101.40W
56 M2 King's Lynn Norfolk Eng 52.45N 0.24E
9 C6 Kingsmill Group islds Kiribati, Pac Oc
56 V11 King's Mills Channel Is 49.28N 2.36W
105 F2 Kings Mt N Carolina 35.14N 81.21W
105 F2 Kings Mt.Nat.Mil.Pk S Carolina 35.08N 81.25W
56 H3 King's Norton W Midlands Eng 52.24N 1.56W
113 J6 King Solomon R Alaska
103 H5 Kings Park Long I, N Y 40.53N 73.15W
110 P9 Kings Pks Utah 40.46N 110.23W
103 M7 Kings Point New York 40.48N 73.45W
98 H8 Kingsport Nova Scotia 45.10N 64.22W
105 E1 Kingsport Tennessee 36.33N 82.34W
59 G6 Kings, R Tipperary Irish Rep
14 E3 Kings Sd W Australia
56 J5 Kings Somborne Hants Eng 51.05N 1.29W
56 D6 Kingsteignton Devon Eng 50.33N 3.35W
107 C5 Kingston Arkansas 36.01N 93.32W
56 G6 Kingston Dorset Eng 50.37N 2.05W
58 K3 Kingston Grampian Scotland 57.40N 3.08W
116 L2 Kingston Jamaica, W I 17.58N 76.48W
103 N2 Kingston Massachusetts 42.00N 70.44W
107 B2 Kingston Missouri 39.37N 94.03W
104 O4 Kingston New Hampshire 42.55N 71.02W
103 F3 Kingston New York 41.55N 74.00W
11 C12 Kingston New Zealand 45.21S 168.44E
10 V10 Kingston Norfolk I Pacific Oc 29.04S 167.57E
104 C7 Kingston Ohio 39.29N 82.43W
109 O8 Kingston Oklahoma 34.00N 96.45W
99 O8 Kingston Ontario 44.14N 76.30W
103 C4 Kingston Pennsylvania 41.15N 75.52W
103 L4 Kingston Rhode I 41.29N 71.31W
12 E6 Kingston S Australia 36.50S 139.50E
12 H9 Kingston Tasmania 42.57S 147.18E
110 C2 Kingston Washington 47.48N 122.30W
104 D9 Kingston W Virginia 37.58N 81.19W
12 A6 Kingston dist Canberra Australia
56 J4 Kingston Bagpuize Oxon Eng 51.42N 1.25W
12 F9 Kingston Beach Tasmania
111 J6 Kingston Pk mt California 35.43N 115.55W
Kingston-upon-Hull see Hull Humberside
55 D4 Kingston upon Thames London England 51.25N 0.18W
57 H3 Kingstown Cumbria Eng 54.56N 2.56W
Kingstown Irish Rep see Dún Laoghaire
116 O8 Kingstown St Vincent, W I 13.12N 61.14W
105 H4 Kingstree S Carolina 33.40N 79.50W
104 E5 Kingsville Ohio 41.53N 80.41W
99 H10 Kingsville Ontario 42.02N 82.44W
112 K8 Kingsville Texas 27.32N 97.53W
56 D7 Kingswear Devon Eng 50.21N 3.34W
95 J3 Kingswood S Africa 27.29S 25.46E
12 B8 Kingswood dist Adelaide, S Aust
Kingtai see Jingtai
56 E3 Kington Hereford & Worcs Eng 52.12N 3.01W
91 E6 Kinguji Zaïre 5.20S 17.58E
91 E7 Kingunda Zaïre 6.36S 16.58E
91 E6 Kingungu Zaïre 4.34S 16.02E
58 H4 Kingussie Highland Scotland 57.05N 4.04W
101 Y1 King William I N W Terr
95 L8 King William's Town S Africa 32.53S 27.24E
104 F7 Kingwood W Virginia 39.27N 79.43W
Kingyun see Qingyun
29 G7 Kinhi Madhya Prad India 21.39N 80.31E
Kinhsien see Jinxian
92 D7 Kiniama Zaïre 11.29S 28.25E
91 C6 Kiniati Zaïre 5.19S 12.58E
84 C8 Kinigós Greece 36.55N 21.45E
36 C3 Kınık Turkey 39.05N 27.25E
37 E1 Kınık R Turkey
Kinim see Karkar
100 M6 Kinistino Saskatchewan 52.58N 105.01W
30 H7 Kinjar Bihar India 25.14N 84.50E
91 D6 Kinkala Congo 4.18S 14.49E
20 P3 Kinka-san Japan 38.16N 141.34E
91 C6 Kinkenge Zaïre 4.56S 13.39E
39 G5 Kinkil' U.S.S.R. 59.20N 160.22E
95 B4 Kinkony, L Madagascar 16.09S 45.50E
98 J7 Kinkora Prince Edward I 46.19N 63.36W
91 D6 Kinkosi Zaïre 5.37S 15.46E
11 K5 Kinleith New Zealand 38.15S 175.56E
100 K6 Kinley Saskatchewan 52.05N 107.25W
11 C11 Kinloch New Zealand 44.51S 168.20E
58 F2 Kinlochbervie Highland Scotland 58.27N 5.02W
58 D4 Kinloch Castle Rum, Highland Scotland 57.01N 6.17W
58 F3 Kinlochewe Highland Scotland 57.36N 5.18W
58 F4 Kinloch Hourn Highland Scotland 57.06N 5.24W
58 G5 Kinlochleven Highland Scotland 56.43N 4.58W
58 E5 Kinlochmoidart Highland Scotland 56.48N 5.45W
58 H5 Kinloch Rannoch Tayside Scotland 56.42N 4.11W
58 J3 Kinloss Grampian Scotland 57.38N 3.33W
59 F3 Kinlough Leitrim Irish Rep 54.27N 8.17W
25 C3 Kinmaw Burma 18.32N 94.19E
20 P9 Kin-misaki C Okinawa Japan 26.25N 127.57E
99 M8 Kinmount Ontario 44.46N 78.40W
107 H3 Kinmundy Illinois 38.45N 88.51W
53 S15 Kinn Norway 61.36N 5.02E
53 R15 Kinn isld Norway 61.34N 4.46E
52 G9 Kinna Sweden 57.32N 12.42E
101 P11 Kinnaird Br Col 49.13N 117.41W
58 M3 Kinnaird's Hd Grampian Scotland 57.42N 2.00W
52 G9 Kinnared Sweden 57.02N 13.05E
50 H3 Kinnarfjöll mts Iceland
50 C3 Kinnarstadhir Iceland 65.33N 22.09W
30 B2 Kinnaur dist Himachal Prad India
108 B6 Kinnear Wyoming 43.10N 108.40W
59 H5 Kinnegad W Meath Irish Rep 53.27N 7.05W
57 F2 Kinnel Water R Dumfries & Galloway Scotland
35 F3 Kinneret Israel 32.43N 35.34E
35 A8 Kinneret-Negev-Conduit Israel
Kinneret, Yam L see Tiberias, L
59 G5 Kinnitty Offaly Irish Rep 53.06N 7.43W
26 T4 Kinniyai Sri Lanka 8.30N 81.11E
51 L8 Kinnula Finland 63.24N 25.00E
20 J7 Kino R Japan
20 K6 Kinomoto Japan 35.33N 136.12E
93 B6 Kinoni Uganda 0.39S 30.31E
93 C6 Kinoni Uganda 0.06S 31.05E
100 P1 Kinoosao Saskatchewan 57.06N 102.02W
20 H6 Kinosaki Japan 35.39N 134.47E
61 N2 Kinrooi Belgium 51.09N 5.45E
95 N2 Kinross S Africa 26.25S 29.05E
58 K6 Kinross Tayside Scotland 56.13N 3.27W
Kinross co see Tayside reg
59 E8 Kinsale Cork Irish Rep 51.42N 8.32W
104 J8 Kinsale Virginia 38.02N 76.38W
59 F8 Kinsale Harb Cork Irish Rep 51.40N 8.30W
59 E8 Kinsale, Old Hd. of C Cork Irish Rep 51.36N 8.32W
53 V18 Kinsarvik Norway 60.22N 6.44E
64 K8 Kinsau W Germany 47.53N 10.55E
91 D6 Kinsele Zaïre 5.04S 15.30E
100 F5 Kinsella Alberta 53.02N 111.34W
108 E3 Kinsey Montana 46.34N 105.40W
91 D6 Kinshasa Zaïre 4.18S 15.18E
91 D6 Kinsi Zaïre 4.47S 15.47E
Kinsiang see Jinxiang
109 L4 Kinsley Kansas 37.55N 99.26W
104 E5 Kinsman Ohio 41.27N 80.36W
53 V18 Kinso R Norway
56 H6 Kinson Dorset Eng 50.46N 1.54W
105 K2 Kinston N Carolina 35.15N 77.34W
109 P6 Kinta Oklahoma 35.07N 95.14W
18 B7 Kinta R Pen Malaysia
18 L10 Kintamali Bali Indonesia 8.14S 115.20E
89 J7 Kintampo Ghana 8.06N 1.40W
18 L7 Kintap Borneo Indon 3.54S 115.14E
92 G4 Kintinku Tanzania 5.56S 35.14E
110 L1 Kintla Pk Montana 48.57N 114.11W
103 D5 Kintnersville Pennsylvania 40.33N 75.11W
91 K8 Kintobongo-bungi Zaïre 8.56S 26.25E
19 C4 Kintom Celebes Indon 1.05S 122.40E
58 M4 Kintore Grampian Scotland 57.14N 2.21W
12 B2 Kintore, Mt S Australia 26.35S 130.25E
13 A6 Kintore Ra N Terr Australia
91 F6 Kintshua Zaïre 4.27S 19.38E
47 L5 Kintus U.S.S.R. 60.10N 71.25E
58 E7 Kintyre dist Strathclyde Scotland
57 B2 Kintyre pen Strathclyde Scotland
25 C1 Kinu Burma 22.47N 95.36E
20 N5 Kinu-gawa R Japan
100 B3 Kinuso Alberta 55.22N 115.20W
101 Q8 Kinuso Alberta 55.17N 115.30W
59 E5 Kinvarra Galway Irish Rep 53.08N 8.56W
20 P9 Kin-wan B Okinawa Japan
29 F8 Kinwat Maharashtra India 19.38N 78.16E
93 H5 Kinyang Kenya 0.56N 36.00E
93 F10 Kinyangiri Tanzania 4.27S 34.35E
92 J11 Kinyasin Zanzibar 5.59S 39.18E
87 D9 Kinyeti mt Sudan 3.56N 32.52E
91 F6 Kinzambi Zaïre 5.00S 18.47E
91 C6 Kinzao Zaïre 5.29S 13.20E
87 F5 Kinzela Ethiopia 11.54N 37.03E
103 B6 Kinzers Pennsylvania 40.00N 76.04W
43 D3 Kinzhaly Kazakhstan U.S.S.R. 48.54N 56.16E
91 F5 Kinzia Zaïre 3.36S 18.26E
64 D7 Kinzig R Baden-Württemberg W Germany
64 G3 Kinzig R Hessen W Germany
66 L4 Kinzig Pass Switzerland 46.54N 8.44E
110 E5 Kinzua Oregon 44.59N 120.04W
104 G5 Kinzua Pennsylvania 41.53N 78.58W
19 E8 Kio Indon 8.06S 127.11E
9 T5 Kioa isld Fiji 16.39S 179.55E
93 F10 Kiomboi Tanzania 4.15S 34.20E
110 F3 Kiona Washington 46.15N 119.29W
84 A5 Kióni Greece 38.27N 20.41E
91 C6 Kionzo Zaïre 5.43S 13.24E
99 M6 Kiosk Ontario 46.06N 78.53W
89 L6 Kioure Benin 10.39N 3.49E
109 F2 Kiowa Colorado 39.18N 104.27W
109 M4 Kiowa Kansas 37.02N 98.28W
109 P7 Kiowa Oklahoma 34.44N 95.56W
109 F2 Kiowa Cr Colorado
100 Q3 Kipahigan L Man/Sask
114 E6 Kipahulu Hawaiian Is 20.39N 156.04W
114 E6 Kipahulu Valley Hawaiian Is
91 K6 Kipaka Zaïre 4.10S 26.31E
92 G5 Kipampwa Tanzania 7.06S 34.02E
91 E6 Kipandi Zaïre 5.15S 16.50E
91 K8 Kipanga Zaïre 9.25S 27.25E
84 E8 Kiparíssi Lakonía Greece 36.58N 22.59E
84 E2 Kiparíssia Lárisa Greece 39.31N 22.33E
84 C7 Kiparissía Messinía Greece 37.15N 21.40E
84 B6 Kiparissiakós Kólpos gulf Greece
99 M6 Kipawa Quebec 46.47N 79.00W
99 M6 Kipawa, L Quebec
99 M5 Kipawa, Parc de Quebec
43 F6 Kipchak Uzbekistan U.S.S.R. 42.12N 60.05E
24 B5 Kipchak Pass Kirgiziya/Xinjiang Uygur Zizhiqu 40.18N 76.04E
92 F5 Kipembawe Tanzania 7.40S 33.25E
92 G6 Kipengere Ra Tanzania
92 J6 Kiperere Chini Tanzania 9.58S 38.40E
64 L6 Kipfenberg W Germany 48.57N 11.25E
92 E5 Kipili Tanzania 7.30S 30.39E
92 D8 Kipilingu Zaïre 13.14S 29.03E
93 M8 Kipini Kenya 2.31S 40.31E
93 H6 Kipipiri mt Kenya 0.25S 36.33E
93 G5 Kipkabus Kenya 0.18N 35.31E
93 F5 Kipkarren River Kenya 0.37N 34.58E
100 P8 Kipling Saskatchewan 50.08N 102.40W
113 E7 Kipnuk Alaska 59.55N 164.08W
84 A2 Kípos Greece 39.52N 20.48E
37 B2 Kipos, Ákra C Samothráki Greece 40.24N 25.42E
84 B2 Kipouryió Greece 39.57N 21.22E
100 E9 Kipp Alberta 49.48N 112.57W
57 L5 Kippax W Yorks Eng 53.46N 1.22W
66 H6 Kippel Switzerland 46.24N 7.46E
58 H6 Kippen Central Scotland 56.08N 4.11W
64 D7 Kippenheim W Germany 48.19N 7.50E
98 O5 Kippens Newfoundland 48.33N 58.40W
57 F3 Kippford Dumfries & Galloway Scotland 54.52N 3.49W
59 K5 Kippure mt Dublin Irish Rep 53.11N 6.20W
42 C5 Kiprino Altay U.S.S.R. 53.33N 82.07E
47 N4 Kiprino Sverdlovsk U.S.S.R. 57.57N 60.45E
84 E3 Kipséli Greece 39.30N 22.38E
93 J5 Kipsing R Kenya
104 K9 Kiptopeke Virginia 37.09N 75.59W
91 K9 Kipushi Zaïre 11.46S 27.15E
91 J7 Kipushia Zaïre 6.10S 25.10E
92 D8 Kipushia Zaïre 12.57S 29.30E
84 F6 Kirá isld Greece 37.42N 23.15E
37 F1 Kiraçköy Turkey 41.03N 28.39E
20 H8 Kiragawa Japan 33.20N 134.06E
30 F7 Kirakat Uttar Prad India 25.39N 82.55E
15 M4 Kirakira San Cristobal I Solomon Is 10.30S 161.55E
37 H8 Kiran Turkey 37.47N 44.00E
33 J4 Kir'ānah, Al Qatar, The Gulf 25.02N 51.03E
92 E5 Kirando Tanzania 7.27S 30.38E
89 D4 Kirané Mali 15.21N 10.19W
37 E3 Kıranlar Turkey 40.17N 28.20E
95 C5 Kiranomena Madagascar 18.17S 46.02E
93 J8 Kirasha mt Kenya 2.07S 37.14E
84 E6 Kirás Vrísi Greece 37.55N 23.00E
37 H7 Kirato Turkey 38.21N 44.23E
30 B3 Kiratpur Uttar Prad India 29.30N 78.12E
36 C4 Kiraz Turkey 38.14N 28.12E
36 B2 Kirazlı Turkey 40.02N 26.44E
Kırbaşı see Gelegra
Kirberg see Hünfelden
41 H6 Kirbey U.S.S.R. 69.11N 104.28E
41 K6 Kirbey U.S.S.R. 68.25N 110.08E
58 S12 Kirbister Orkney Scotland 58.56N 3.05W
107 C7 Kirby Arkansas 34.15N 93.40W
99 F6 Kirby Ontario 46.43N 84.17W
108 B6 Kirby Wyoming 43.49N 108.10W
57 K4 Kirby Hill N Yorks Eng 54.27N 1.47W
57 L4 Kirby Hill N Yorks Eng 54.07N 1.25W
112 O5 Kirbyville Texas 30.40N 93.56W
36 B1 Kırcasalih Turkey 41.22N 26.45E
65 N8 Kirchbach Austria 46.56N 15.38E
65 N5 Kirchberg Austria 48.27N 15.54E
64 H5 Kirchberg Baden-Württemberg W Germany 49.12N 9.59E
66 G3 Kirchberg Bern Switzerland 47.06N 7.36E
64 O2 Kirchberg E Germany 50.37N 12.31E
64 C4 Kirchberg Rheinland Pfalz W Germany 49.57N 7.24E
66 N2 Kirchberg St Gallen Switz 47.25N 9.04E
65 M5 Kirchberg am der Pielach Austria 48.02N 15.27E
65 N6 Kirchberg-am-Wechsel Austria 47.38N 15.59E
65 M4 Kirchberg-an-Walde Austria 48.45N 15.05E
65 F6 Kirchbichl Austria 47.32N 12.06E
66 J3 Kirchbuhl Switzerland 47.08N 8.12E
64 P6 Kirchdorf Bayern W Germany 48.55N 13.17E
63 O5 Kirchdorf E Germany 53.59N 11.26E
63 J7 Kirchdorf Niedersachsen W Germany 52.36N 8.49E
66 G4 Kirchdorf Switzerland 46.48N 7.33E
65 K6 Kirchdorf an der Krems Austria 47.55N 14.08E
69 O2 Kirchen W Germany 50.49N 7.53E
64 M4 Kirchenlaibach W Germany 49.52N 11.46E
64 M3 Kirchenlamitz W Germany 50.09N 11.58E
64 N7 Kirchensur W Germany 48.01N 12.22E
64 G6 Kirchentellinsfurt W Germany 48.32N 9.10E
64 M4 Kirchenthumbach W Germany 49.44N 11.45E
63 Q5 Kirch Grubenhagen E Germany 53.40N 12.30E
64 K1 Kirchheilingen E Germany 51.11N 10.44E
65 H5 Kirchheim Austria 48.13N 13.22E
64 G5 Kirchheim Baden-Württemberg W Germany 49.03N 9.10E
64 G6 Kirchheim Baden-Württemberg W Germany 48.39N 9.28E
64 J7 Kirchheim Bayern W Germany 48.10N 10.29E
69 P4 Kirchheim-Bolanden W Germany 49.40N 8.01E
63 E9 Kirchhellen W Germany 51.36N 6.55E
64 E1 Kirchhundem W Germany 51.05N 8.06E
63 O6 Kirch Jesar E Germany 53.27N 11.16E
63 H6 Kirchkimmen W Germany 53.04N 8.26E
64 K3 Kirchlauter W Germany 50.02N 10.44E
63 J8 Kirchlengern W Germany 52.12N 8.38E
63 K7 Kirchlinteln W Germany 52.56N 9.19E
64 F2 Kirchnain W Germany 50.49N 8.56E
64 O6 Kirchroth W Germany 48.57N 12.33E
65 O6 Kirchschlag Nieder-Österreich Austria 47.31N 16.18E
65 K5 Kirchschlag Ober-Österreich Austria 48.26N 14.18E
63 J7 Kirchweyhe W Germany 52.58N 8.48E
63 J6 Kirchwistedt W Germany 53.24N 8.55E
64 D8 Kirchzarten W Germany 47.58N 7.57E
43 J6 Kirda Uzbekistan U.S.S.R. 41.04N 68.59E
86 F5 Kirdâsa Egypt 30.02N 31.06E
90 J2 Kirdimi Chad 18.11N 18.31E
36 C3 Kireç Turkey 39.34N 28.23E
36 F5 Kireli Turkey 37.56N 31.32E
42 H4 Kirenga R U.S.S.R.
36 D5 Kirenis R Turkey
42 H3 Kirensk U.S.S.R. 57.45N 108.02E
43 J3 Kirey R Kazakhstan U.S.S.R.
45 J3 Kireyevsk U.S.S.R. 53.57N 37.56E
43 J2 Kirey, Ozero L Kazakhstan U.S.S.R. 50.08N 68.45E
Kirgalı see Pirinçlik
43 N8 Kirgili Uzbekistan U.S.S.R. 40.28N 71.44E
47 M4 Kirgishany U.S.S.R. 56.52N 59.10E
Kirgizia see Kirgiziya, S.S.R
43 L6 Kirgiziya S.S.R U.S.S.R.
43 C1 Kirgiz-Miyaki U.S.S.R. 53.39N 54.49E
43 K5 Kirgizskiy Khrebet mts Kirgiziya/Kazakhstan U.S.S.R.
16 F4 Kirgiz Step' Kazakhstan U.S.S.R.
39 F6 Kirgonik R U.S.S.R.
89 H5 Kiri Mali 13.59N 2.56W
91 F4 Kiri Zaïre 1.29S 19.00E
90 H3 Kiri reg Chad
84 E5 Kiriáki Greece 38.21N 22.47E
122 H8 Kiribati rep Pacific Ocean
26 S8 Kirigalpotta mt Sri Lanka 6.48N 80.45E
37 F5 Kırık Turkey 40.21N 40.56E
36 J6 Kırıkhan Turkey 36.30N 36.20E
36 G3 Kırıkkale Turkey 39.51N 33.32E
11 J2 Kirikopuni New Zealand 35.50S 174.03E
45 G6 Kirikovka Ukraine U.S.S.R. 50.22N 35.07E
47 D6 Kirillov U.S.S.R. 59.53N 38.21E
44 D8 Kirillovka Ukraine U.S.S.R. 46.23N 35.23E
45 O3 Kirillovo Penza U.S.S.R. 53.46N 42.41E
40 J8 Kirillovo Sakhalin U.S.S.R. 46.29N 142.19E
51 O11 Kirillovskoye U.S.S.R. 60.28N 29.20E
87 E6 Kirin Ethiopia 9.55N 34.20E
Kirin prov China see Jilin
93 A8 Kirinda Rwanda 2.12S 29.37E
26 T9 Kirinda Sri Lanka 6.13N 81.20E
26 T9 Kirindi Oya R Sri Lanka
11 J2 Kiripa New Zealand 35.35S 174.30E
25 E8 Kirirath, Mae R Thailand
31 F5 Kiri Shamozai Pakistan 31.25N 70.33E
46 H1 Kirishi U.S.S.R. 59.30N 32.02E
20 D10 Kirishima-yama mt Japan 31.57N 130.50E
87 L6 Kirit Somalia 8.59N 46.08E
15 F8 Kiriwa Papua New Guinea 8.26S 141.31E
Kiriwina Is see Trobriand Is
41 N9 Kiriyestyakh U.S.S.R. 62.20N 127.35E
109 H2 Kirk Colorado 39.37N 102.36W
58 K1 Kirk Highland Scotland 58.30N 3.14W
108 G8 Kirk Nebraska 41.25N 103.24W
110 D7 Kirk Oregon 42.44N 121.49W
36 H5 Kirk R Turkey
36 E3 Kırka Turkey 39.16N 30.31E
37 J2 Kırkağac İstanbul Turkey 41.03N 28.54E
36 C3 Kırkağaç Manisa Turkey 39.06N 27.40E
57 G3 Kirkbampton Cumbria Eng 54.54N 3.04W
57 F3 Kirkbean Dumfries & Galloway Scotland 54.55N 3.36W
57 G3 Kirkbride Cumbria Eng 54.54N 3.12W
32 B2 Kirk Bulāg D mt Iran 36.43N 47.19E
57 K5 Kirkburton W Yorks Eng 53.37N 1.42W
57 H6 Kirkby Merseyside Eng 53.29N 2.54W
57 H4 Kirkby Lonsdale Cumbria Eng 54.13N 2.36W
57 M4 Kirkbymoorside N Yorks Eng 54.16N 0.55W
57 J4 Kirkby Stephen Cumbria Eng 54.28N 2.20W
57 H3 Kirkby Thore Cumbria Eng 54.38N 2.33W
100 D8 Kirkcaldy Alberta 50.22N 113.10W
58 K6 Kirkcaldy Fife Scotland 56.07N 3.10W
57 C3 Kirkcolm Dumfries & Galloway Scotland 54.58N 5.05W
57 E2 Kirkconnel Dumfries & Galloway Scotland 55.23N 4.01W
57 D3 Kirkcowan Dumfries & Galloway Scotland 54.55N 4.36W
59 L3 Kirkcubbin Down N Ireland 54.30N 5.32W
57 E3 Kirkcudbright Dumfries & Galloway Scotland 54.50N 4.03W
Kirkcudbright co see Dumfries & Galloway reg
57 E3 Kirkcudbright B Dumfries & Galloway Scotland
57 L5 Kirk Deighton N Yorks Eng 53.57N 1.24W
53 N10 Kirkebø Faeroes 61.58N 6.47W
53 F6 Kirkeby Fyn Denmark 55.08N 10.33E
53 B6 Kirkeby Sønderjylland Denmark 55.07N 8.33E
28 A1 Kirkee Maharashtra India 18.36N 73.57E
53 H5 Kirke Eskildstrup Denmark 55.35N 11.42E
53 G5 Kirke Helsinge Denmark 55.31N 11.13E
53 H5 Kirke-Hvalsø Denmark 55.36N 11.52E
53 H5 Kirke Hyllinge Denmark 55.43N 11.55E
100 Q8 Kirkella Manitoba 50.02N 101.22W
64 C5 Kirkel-Neuhausel W Germany 49.17N 7.15E
69 N5 Kirkel-Neuhausel W Germany 49.17N 7.15E
52 G6 Kirkenær Norway 60.27N 12.04E
51 P2 Kirkenes Norway 69.41N 30.02E
53 H5 Kirke Såby Denmark 55.38N 11.53E
Kirkesdal see Björkas
53 G6 Kirke Stillinge Denmark 55.27N 11.15E
51 G3 Kirkestind mt Norway 68.47N 19.10E
58 J7 Kirkfieldbank Strathclyde Scotland 55.41N 3.50W
57 H5 Kirkham Lancs Eng 53.47N 2.53W
37 D5 Kirkharman Turkey 40.33N 38.32E
58 B3 Kirkibost I N Uist, W Isles Scotland 57.34N 7.25W
57 E3 Kirkinner Dumfries & Galloway Scotland 54.50N 4.27W
58 H7 Kirkintilloch Strathclyde Scotland 55.57N 4.10W
50 G7 Kirkjubæjarklaustur Iceland 63.47N 18.02W
50 L3 Kirkjubær Iceland 65.32N 14.25W
50 B2 Kirkjubol Ísafjardharsýsla, Vestur Iceland 66.01N 23.34W
50 M5 Kirkjuból Múlasýsla, Sudhur Iceland 64.51N 13.55W
53 N10 Kirkjubønes C Faeroes 61.57N 6.44W
50 G7 Kirkjufell mt Iceland 63.59N 18.55W
50 E8 Kirkjufell vol Iceland 63.27N 20.16W
50 E4 Kirkjuhvammur Iceland 65.25N 20.56W
37 C1 Kirk Kavak R Turkey
Kirkkonummi see Kyrkslätt
111 M7 Kirkland Arizona 34.26N 112.43W
106 F7 Kirkland Illinois 42.05N 88.51W
99 P10 Kirkland Quebec 45.27N 73.49W
112 G1 Kirkland Texas 34.23N 100.05W
110 C2 Kirkland Washington 47.41N 122.12W
101 G12 Kirkland I Br Col 49.07N 123.06W
99 K4 Kirkland Lake Ontario 48.10N 80.02W
36 H2 Kırklar Dağ mt Turkey 40.26N 35.10E
37 F5 Kırklar Dağları mts Turkey
36 C1 Kırklareli Turkey 41.45N 27.12E
106 H9 Kirklin Indiana 40.12N 86.22W
57 M6 Kirklington Notts Eng 53.07N 0.59W
57 K4 Kirklington N Yorks Eng 54.13N 1.31W
58 K7 Kirkliston Lothian Scotland 55.58N 3.25W
11 E11 Kirkliston Ra New Zealand
108 P8 Kirkman Iowa 41.43N 95.16W
57 D4 Kirkmichael Isle of Man U.K. 54.17N 4.35W
57 D2 Kirkmichael Strathclyde Scotland 55.21N 4.37W
58 J5 Kirkmichael Tayside Scotland 56.44N 3.31W
57 J1 Kirknewton Northumb Eng 55.34N 2.09W
58 J7 Kirk of Shotts Strathclyde Scotland 55.51N 3.50W
84 Y20 Kirkop Malta 35.51N 14.29E
57 H3 Kirkoswald Cumbria Eng 54.46N 2.41W
57 D2 Kirkoswald Strathclyde Scotland 55.20N 4.47W
57 G2 Kirkpatrick Dumfries & Galloway Scotland 55.01N 3.08W
100 F7 Kirkpatrick, L Alberta
123 G7 Kirkpatrick,Mt Antarctica 84.25S 165.30E
57 H4 Kirkstone Pass Cumbria Eng 54.29N 2.56W
107 D1 Kirksville Missouri 40.12N 92.35W
58 M4 Kirktown of Auchterless Grampian Scotland 57.28N 2.29W
34 M3 Kirkūk Iraq 35.28N 44.26E
58 T12 Kirkwall Orkney Scotland 58.59N 2.58W
111 B2 Kirkwood California 39.52N 122.10W
103 C7 Kirkwood Delaware 39.35N 75.42W
103 C2 Kirkwood New York 42.03N 75.47W
103 B7 Kirkwood Pennsylvania 39.52N 76.05W
95 J9 Kirkwood S Africa 33.24S 25.26E
108 J5 Kirley S Dakota 44.30N 101.16W
Kirmasti see Mustafa Kemalpaşa
36 D3 Kirmasti R Turkey
36 F2 Kirmir R Turkey
36 H5 Kırmıt Turkey 37.17N 35.35E
58 G7 Kirn Strathclyde Scotland 55.58N 4.55W
64 C4 Kirn W Germany 49.47N 7.28E
36 G6 Kırobası Turkey 36.44N 33.53E
92 J5 Kirongwe Mafia I E Africa 7.50S 39.50E
45 F2 Kirov Kaluga U.S.S.R. 54.05N 34.20E
46 P1 Kirov U.S.S.R. 58.38N 49.38E
42 K6 Kirova U.S.S.R. 51.00N 114.50E
44 G7 Kirovabad Azerbaydzhan U.S.S.R. 40.39N 46.20E
43 J8 Kirovabad Tadzhikistan U.S.S.R. 37.19N 69.05E
43 M4 Kirova, im Kazakhstan U.S.S.R. 46.24N 77.15E
43 J7 Kirova, im Tadzhikistan U.S.S.R. 37.48N 68.53E
44 F7 Kirovakan Armenia U.S.S.R. 40.49N 44.30E
41 F2 Kirova,Ostrov isld U.S.S.R. 77.40N 92.10E
44 J8 Kirova,Zaliv B Azerbaydzhan U.S.S.R.
47 M4 Kirovgrad U.S.S.R. 57.28N 60.00E
45 G9 Kirovo Ukraine U.S.S.R. 47.38N 35.43E
47 J7 Kirovo U.S.S.R. 55.35N 63.42E
43 N7 Kirovo Uzbekistan U.S.S.R. 40.27N 70.37E
46 Q1 Kirovo-Chepetsk U.S.S.R. 58.40N 50.02E
45 D8 Kirovograd Ukraine U.S.S.R. 48.31N 32.15E
45 D8 Kirovogradskaya Oblast' prov Ukraine U.S.S.R.
44 J9 Kirovsk Azerbaydzhan U.S.S.R. 38.47N 48.43E
43 F7 Kirovsk Turkmeniya U.S.S.R. 37.44N 60.19E
47 C2 Kirovsk U.S.S.R. 67.37N 33.39E
46 P1 Kirovskaya Oblast' prov U.S.S.R.
40 C4 Kirovskiy Amur U.S.S.R. 54.19N 124.25E
44 J2 Kirovskiy Astrakhan' U.S.S.R. 45.51N 48.09E
39 F7 Kirovskiy Kamchatka U.S.S.R. 54.25N 155.37E
43 N5 Kirovskiy Kazakhstan U.S.S.R. 44.54N 78.13E
40 F9 Kirovskiy Primor'ye U.S.S.R. 45.07N 133.30E
45 K8 Kirovskoye Donetsk, Ukraine U.S.S.R. 48.12N 38.20E
43 K5 Kirovskoye Kirgiziya U.S.S.R. 42.37N 71.33E
40 J6 Kirovskoye Sakhalin U.S.S.R. 50.40N 142.50E
44 D9 Kirovskoye Simferopol', Ukraine U.S.S.R. 45.13N 35.12E
43 D7 Kirpili Turkmeniya U.S.S.R. 39.37N 57.14E
44 B2 Kirpil'skiy Liman lagoon U.S.S.R.
90 C7 Kirri Nigeria 8.12N 6.12E
100 G7 Kirriemuir Alberta 51.56N 110.20W
58 K5 Kirriemuir Tayside Scotland 56.41N 3.01W
47 G6 Kirs U.S.S.R. 59.21N 52.10E
45 O4 Kirsanov U.S.S.R. 52.40N 42.45E
43 B2 Kirsanoy U.S.S.R. 51.29N 52.30E
36 G3 Kırşehir Turkey 39.09N 34.08E
89 L5 Kirtachi Niger 12.49N 2.29E
37 C3 Kirte Turkey 40.07N 26.14E
31 D8 Kirthar Ra Pakistan
29 A2 Kirtinagar dist Delhi India
57 G2 Kirtle Bridge Dumfries & Galloway Scotland 55.02N 3.12W
108 F7 Kirtley Wyoming 42.50N 104.06W
57 M6 Kirton Humberside Eng 53.29N 0.35W
57 N7 Kirton Lincs Eng 52.56N 0.04W
64 G2 Kirtorf W Germany 50.46N 9.06E
93 B6 Kiruhura Uganda 0.13S 30.52E
93 L10 Kirui I Tanzania 4.43S 39.13E
51 H4 Kiruna Sweden 67.53N 20.15E
91 J4 Kirundu Zaïre 0.50S 25.37E
92 G4 Kirurumo Tanzania 5.50S 34.10E
11 G10 Kirwee New Zealand 43.31S 172.13E
109 L2 Kirwin Kansas 39.41N 99.06W
109 L2 Kirwin Res Kansas
93 L9 Kirwitu Kenya 3.46S 39.50E
45 S1 Kirya U.S.S.R. 55.05N 46.52E
93 D4 Kiryandongo Uganda 1.53N 32.05E
42 G3 Kir'yanovskaya Kontora U.S.S.R. 58.20N 104.10E
20 N5 Kiryū Japan 36.26N 139.18E
42 C5 Kirza U.S.S.R. 54.14N 81.43E
45 K1 Kirzhach U.S.S.R. 56.09N 38.54E
45 R2 Kirzhemany U.S.S.R. 54.38N 45.50E
52 J9 Kisa Sweden 57.58N 15.38E
50 F6 Kisá R Iceland
92 D6 Kisabi Zaïre 8.04S 29.10E
93 F10 Kisaga Tanzania 4.24S 34.22E
92 H5 Kisahi Tanzania 7.28S 37.41E
20 N2 Kisakata Japan 39.13N 139.54E
91 E5 Kisakenda Zaïre 3.25S 17.48E
93 C4 Kisala Uganda 1.02N 31.10E
91 K8 Kisale, L Zaïre 8.25S 26.30E
91 F7 Kisambo Zaïre 6.29S 18.13E
84 J10 Kisámou,Kólpos gulf Crete
28 D2 Kisampet Andhra Prad India 16.57N 78.17E
93 C8 Kisanda mt Tanzania 2.56S 31.15E
91 F7 Kisandji Zaïre 6.18S 19.16E
91 J9 Kisanfu Zaïre 10.40S 25.55E
91 K7 Kisanga Zaïre 7.49S 26.22E
91 J3 Kisangani Zaïre 0.33N 25.14E
92 J5 Kisangire Tanzania 7.25S 38.43E
93 J9 Kisangiro Tanzania 3.37S 37.33E
19 E8 Kisar isld Indon 8.05S 127.12E
113 G6 Kisaralik R Alaska
18 C4 Kisaran Sumatra Indon 3.00N 99.36E
92 J5 Kisarawe Tanzania 6.58S 39.02E
20 D4 Kisarazu Japan 35.23N 139.57E
46 P3 Kisat' U.S.S.R. 53.26N 47.45E
92 J12 Kisauni Zanzibar 6.13S 39.14E
62 K8 Kisbér Hungary 47.30N 18.00E
100 P9 Kisbey Saskatchewan 49.40N 102.43W
41 R5 Kiseleva U.S.S.R. 71.29N 148.15E
45 Q9 Kiselevka Rostov U.S.S.R. 47.20N 44.08E
42 D3 Kiselevka Tomsk U.S.S.R. 57.59N 88.00E
45 C8 Kiselevka Ukraine U.S.S.R. 48.54N 31.14E
42 D5 Kiselevsk U.S.S.R. 54.01N 86.41E
91 H9 Kisenge Zaïre 10.42S 23.19E
91 J6 Kisengwe Zaïre 5.59S 25.50E
93 E8 Kisesse Tanzania 2.33S 33.07E
34 M6 Kish anc site Iraq 32.33N 44.39E
37 F5 Kısha Turkey 40.28N 41.26E
93 C7 Kishanda Tanzania 1.41S 31.34E
30 L6 Kishanganj Purnea, Bihar India 26.06N 87.57E
30 K7 Kishanganj Saharsa, Bihar India 25.41N 86.57E
Kishangarh see Kishengarh
29 D4 Kishangarh Rajasthan India 26.33N 74.52E
29 E4 Kishangarh Rajasthan India 27.52N 76.41E
30 E7 Kishanpur Uttar Prad India 25.39N 81.02E
30 A3 Kishanpur Bara Uttar Prad India 29.11N 77.18E
31 H3 Kishen Ganga R Kashmir
30 C8 Kishengarh Madhya Prad India 24.22N 79.45E
45 F8 Kishenki Ukraine U.S.S.R. 48.52N 34.08E
90 A7 Kishi Nigeria 9.06N 3.56E
92 D5 Kishiale Zaïre 7.59S 28.15E
43 K1 Kishikaroy,Oz L Kazakhstan U.S.S.R. 54.05N 71.20E
46 G6 Kishinev Moldavia U.S.S.R. 47.00N 28.50E
20 J7 Kishiwada Japan 34.28N 135.22E
31 B3 Kishlak-i-Khwaja Afghanistan 35.08N 63.15E

30 C5 Kishni Uttar Prad India 27.02N 79.15E
31 H9 Kishorganj Bangladesh 24.26N 90.46E
58 E4 Kishorn Ross & Crom Scotland 57.23N 5.36W
58 E4 Kishorn, L Highland Scotland
31 H4 Kishtwar Kashmir 33.20N 75.49E
Kishui see Jishui
93 F6 Kisian Kenya 0.04S 34.41E
93 K9 Kisigau mt Kenya 3.49S 38.40E
92 G5 Kisigo R Tanzania
93 F6 Kisii Kenya 0.40S 34.47E
92 J5 Kisiju Tanzania 7.25S 39.20E
37 K2 Kısıklı Turkey 41.01N 29.07E
92 G5 Kisilwa Tanzania 7.15S 35.30E
93 L3 Kisiniro Kenya 2.22N 39.42E
37 G4 Kısır Dağı mt Turkey 41.01N 43.04E
93 J10 Kisiwani Tanzania 4.05S 37.55E
93 A7 Kisizi Uganda 1.00S 29.58E
113 N9 Kiska I Aleutian Is 52.00N 177.30E
113 N9 Kiska Vol Aleutian Is 52.06N 177.33E
100 T4 Kiskittogisu L Manitoba
100 T4 Kiskitto L Manitoba
62 K9 Kiskomárom Hungary 46.33N 17.10E
62 M8 Kisköre res Hungary
62 L9 Kiskőrös Hungary 46.39N 19.20E
62 M9 Kiskundorozsma Hungary 46.17N 20.03E
62 M9 Kiskunfélegyháza Hungary 46.42N 19.52E
62 L9 Kiskunhalas Hungary 46.26N 19.29E
62 M9 Kiskunmajsa Hungary 46.30N 19.46E
29 B4 Kisliangarh Rajasthan India 27.52N 70.34E
45 J7 Kislovka Ukraine U.S.S.R. 49.37N 37.55E
45 R7 Kislovo U.S.S.R. 49.55N 45.24E
44 E4 Kislovodsk U.S.S.R. 43.56N 42.44E
47 N5 Kislovskoye U.S.S.R. 56.32N 61.32E
44 C1 Kislyakovskaya U.S.S.R. 46.37N 39.41E
Kismayu see Chisimaio
20 B3 Kiso Tōkyō Japan
20 K6 Kiso-gawa R Japan
93 B5 Kisomoro Uganda 0.34N 30.12E
93 A7 Kisoro Uganda 1.17S 29.42E
20 L6 Kiso-sammyaku mts Japan
93 A9 Kisosi Burundi 3.33S 29.39E
62 L8 Kispest Hungary 47.28N 19.08E
101 J8 Kispiox R Br Col
35 E2 Kisrâ Israel 32.57N 35.18E
88 M4 Kiss R Morocco
91 D5 Kissenguelé Congo 3.18S 14.12E
Kisseraing I Burma see Kanmaw Kyun
53 H5 Kisserup Denmark 55.48N 11.43E
89 D7 Kissidougou Guinea 9.15N 10.08W
105 F9 Kissimmee Florida 28.20N 81.24W
105 F10 Kissimmee,L Florida 27.55N 81.15W
105 F10 Kissimmee,R Florida
100 Q3 Kississing L Manitoba 55.15N 101.30W
64 H8 Kisslegg W Germany 47.47N 9.53E
84 F3 Kissós Greece 39.24N 23.08E
Kissoué see Kiswe
35 A8 Kissufim Israel 31.23N 34.24E
85 H9 Kissu,Jebel mt Sudan 21.37N 25.10E
51 H3 Kistefjeld Norway 68.37N 19.35E
53 W20 Kistefjell mt Norway 59.03N 7.29E
62 M9 Kistelek Hungary 46.27N 19.58E
45 P4 Kistendey U.S.S.R. 52.07N 43.40E
66 N4 Kisten Pass Switzerland 46.49N 9.02E
66 Q4 Kisten Stein mt Switzerland 46.53N 9.47E
62 M7 Kisterenye Hungary 48.01N 19.50E
Kistna, R see Krishna, R
51 L1 Kistrand Norway 70.27N 25.11E
50 D7 Kistufell mt Gullbringusýsla Iceland 63.57N 21.49W
50 H5 Kistufell mt Iceland 64.47N 17.13W
50 K3 Kistufell mt Múlasýsla, Nordhur Iceland 65.46N 15.17W
50 L5 Kistufell mt Múlasýsla, Sudhur Iceland 64.52N 14.33W
62 M8 Kisújszállás Hungary 47.14N 20.45E
93 F6 Kisumu Kenya 0.08S 34.47E
93 B10 Kisuzi Tanzania 4.13S 30.07E
62 N7 Kisvárda Hungary 48.13N 22.03E
Kiswah see Kiswe
34 D5 Kiswe Syria 33.21N 36.16E
92 J6 Kiswere Tanzania 9.25S 39.31E
87 D8 Kit watercourse Sudan
89 E5 Kita Mali 13.04N 9.29W
20 E2 Kita dist Tōkyō Japan
43 H7 Kitab Uzbekistan U.S.S.R. 39.08N 66.51E
91 K7 Kitabu Zaïre 6.31S 26.40E
20 B1 Kitada Saitama Japan
20 H8 Kitagawa Japan 33.47N 134.09E
20 O5 Kita-Ibaraki Japan 36.46N 140.45E
46 D7 Kitai-Gorod dist Moscow U.S.S.R.
21 J12 Kita-lō-jima isld Kazan-Rettō Pacific Oc 25.27N 141.16E
46 G6 Kitai,Oz L Ukraine U.S.S.R.
51 H5 Kitajaur Sweden 66.11N 20.00E
20 P2 Kitakami Japan 39.18N 141.05E
20 P2 Kitakami-gawa R Japan
20 N4 Kitakata Japan 37.38N 139.52E
20 D8 Kita-Kyūshū Japan 33.52N 130.49E
93 D5 Kitala Uganda 0.07N 32.33E
93 F9 Kitalala Tanzania 3.59S 34.04E
93 G4 Kitale Kenya 1.01N 35.01E
20 D2 Kitamachi dist Tōkyō Japan
91 J6 Kitambwe Zaïre 4.02S 25.31E
21 J6 Kitami Japan 43.51N 143.54E
93 B6 Kitampungu mt Uganda 0.24S 30.03E
20 C4 Kitamura Kanagawa Japan
91 K7 Kitanda Zaïre 6.37S 26.28E
92 J7 Kitangari Tanzania 10.39S 39.20E
93 F10 Kitangiri, L Tanzania
20 B1 Kitano Saitama Japan
20 N9 Kitano-hana C Iwo Jima Pacific Oc 24.49N 141.20E
20 O5 Kita-ura lagoon Japan
15 L8 Kitava I Trobriand Is Papua New Guinea 8.40S 151.20E
20 J8 Kitayama R Japan
20 J8 Kitayama-gawa R Japan
20 A1 Kita-Yaogi Saitama Japan
109 H3 Kit Carson Colorado 38.45N 102.47W
99 K9 Kitchener Ontario 43.27N 80.30W
14 E9 Kitchener W Australia 31.01S 124.20E
Kitchioh see Jieshi
105 E5 Kite Georgia 32.41N 82.33W
51 P9 Kitee Finland 62.06N 30.09E
92 H6 Kiteketa Tanzania 9.09S 36.41E
39 G3 Kitepskaya U.S.S.R. 62.48N 160.44E
92 G5 Kitete Tanzania 7.00S 34.31E
93 D2 Kitgum Uganda 3.17N 32.54E
93 E2 Kitgum Matidi Uganda 3.16N 33.04E
84 F5 Kithairón Óros mts Greece
83 F8 Kíthíra Greece 36.10N 22.59E
83 F8 Kíthíra isld Greece
84 H7 Kíthnos Greece 37.25N 24.25E
84 H7 Kíthnos isld Greece
30 A4 Kithor Uttar Prad India 28.51N 77.55E
84 S15 Kiti Cyprus 34.50N 33.35E
84 S15 Kiti,C Cyprus 34.48N 33.37E
99 H3 Kitigan Ontario 49.23N 82.16W
35 G4 Kitim Jordan 32.26N 35.54E
101 J8 Kitimat Br Col 54.05N 128.38W
101 J9 Kitimat Mill Br Col 54.00N 128.41W
51 M4 Kitinen R Finland
87 D2 Kitiyab Sudan 17.13N 33.42E
82 G8 Kitka mt Yugoslavia 42.40N 21.41E
41 H3 Kit,Mys C U.S.S.R. 76.59N 101.00E
93 C4 Kitoba Uganda 1.31N 31.23E
40 M8 Kitoboynyy Kuril Is U.S.S.R. 46.49N 151.45E
91 F6 Kitombe Zaïre 5.22S 18.59E
93 A9 Kitongo Burundi 3.12S 29.52E
92 J6 Kitopi Tanzania 8.10S 38.49E
42 G5 Kitoy U.S.S.R. 52.36N 103.55E
42 G6 Kitoyskiye Gol'tsy mts U.S.S.R.
83 F4 Kítros Greece 40.22N 22.34E
51 R3 Kitsa R U.S.S.R.
100 G5 Kitscoty Alberta 53.22N 110.22W
56 N5 Kits Coty House Kent Eng 51.20N 0.30E
46 F5 Kitsman' Ukraine U.S.S.R. 48.30N 25.50E
20 E8 Kitsuki Japan 33.24N 131.36E
20 O5 Kitsuregawa Japan 36.42N 140.00E
84 D8 Kítta Greece 36.31N 22.24E
35 G4 Kitta,El Jordan 32.17N 35.50E
12 E3 Kittakittaooloo, L S Australia
104 F6 Kittanning Pennsylvania 40.49N 79.31W
103 E4 Kittatinny Mts ra New Jersey
63 R5 Kittendorf E Germany 53.37N 12.54E
104 P3 Kittery Maine 43.05N 70.45W
114 A1 Kittery I Hawaiian Is 28.00N 176.15W
104 P3 Kittery Point Maine 43.06N 70.42W
51 L4 Kittilä Finland 67.40N 24.50E
65 Q5 Kittsee Austria 48.06N 17.03E
28 B3 Kittur Karnataka India 15.38N 74.53E
105 M1 Kitty Hawk N Carolina 36.04N 75.43W
92 C5 Kitu Zaïre 7.36S 27.41E
93 M8 Kitua,Ras pt Kenya 2.50S 40.12E
93 K7 Kitui Kenya 1.22S 38.01E
93 K7 Kitui dist Kenya
15 J7 Kitumala Pt Papua New Guinea 6.20S 147.50E
Kitumbaine mt see Ketumbaine Mt
92 F5 Kitunda Tanzania 6.48S 33.17E
101 K8 Kitwanga Br Col 55.06N 128.00W
93 B6 Kitwe Uganda 0.08S 30.30E
92 D8 Kitwe-Nkana Zambia 12.50S 28.11E
Kityang see Jieyang
93 E5 Kityerera Uganda 0.19N 33.30E
65 F7 Kitzbühel Austria 47.27N 12.23E
65 F7 Kitzbühler Alpen mts Austria
65 F7 Kitzbühler Hohe mt Austria 47.28N 12.27E
64 J4 Kitzingen W Germany 49.45N 10.11E
93 J7 Kiu Kenya 1.54S 37.10E
Kiujaoping see Sanrao
51 J10 Kiukainen Finland 61.13N 22.05E
113 L7 Kiukpalik I Alaska 58.39N 153.35W
30 K7 Kiul Bihar India 25.10N 86.06E
30 K8 Kiul R Bihar India
25 E3 Kiu Lom Dam Thailand 18.31N 99.39E
Kiulung see Jiulong
91 K6 Kiumbi Zaïre 5.31S 26.34E
93 N7 Kiunga Kenya 1.44S 41.31E
15 F7 Kiunga Papua New Guinea 6.10S 141.15E
51 M8 Kiuruvesi Finland 63.38N 26.40E
Kiutai see Jiutai
39 M3 Kivak U.S.S.R. 64.17N 172.59W
113 E3 Kivalina Alaska 67.45N 164.40W
84 E6 Kivéri Greece 37.31N 22.44E
84 Q15 Kividhes Cyprus 34.45N 32.52E
113 E3 Kividlo Alaska 66.30N 164.55W
51 L8 Kivijärvi Finland 63.09N 25.05E
52 H11 Kivik Sweden 55.40N 14.15E
51 M12 Kiviõli Estonia 59.23N 26.58E
83 E4 Kivotós Greece 40.13N 21.26E
93 A6 Kivu prov Zaïre
93 A7 Kivu, L Rwanda/Zaïre
40 G5 Kivun,Khrebet mts U.S.S.R.
15 G8 Kiwai I Papua New Guinea 8.35S 143.25E
113 G3 Kiwalik Alaska 66.00N 162.00W
11 G8 Kiwi New Zealand 41.32S 172.46E
92 G7 Kiwindi Tanzania 11.33S 35.00E
42 D4 Kiya R U.S.S.R.
43 J3 Kiyakty,Ozero L Kazakhstan U.S.S.R. 50.00N 69.15E
32 A1 Kiyāmaki Dagh mt Iran 38.42N 45.52E
20 O10 Kiyan Okinawa Japan 26.05N 127.39E
20 O10 Kiyan-zaki C Okinawa Japan 26.03N 127.40E
20 O10 Kiyan-zaki C Okinawa Japan 26.04N 127.39E
33 D7 Kiyāt Saudi Arabia 18.43N 41.21E
39 E1 Kiyeng-Kyuyel' U.S.S.R. 68.41N 153.45E
41 J4 Kiyeng-Kyuyel', Ozero L U.S.S.R. 73.00N 109.40E
45 B6 Kiyev Ukraine U.S.S.R. 50.25N 30.30E
46 C7 Kiyev dist Moscow U.S.S.R.
43 K2 Kiyevka Kazakhstan U.S.S.R. 50.15N 71.33E
40 F10 Kiyevka U.S.S.R. 42.50N 133.43E
44 E1 Kiyevka U.S.S.R. 46.06N 42.57E
45 B6 Kiyevskaya Oblast' prov Ukraine U.S.S.R.
45 B5 Kiyevskoy Vodokhranilishche res Ukraine U.S.S.R.
36 E3 Kıyır R Turkey
100 J7 Kiyiu L Saskatchewan 51.37N 108.53W
43 J2 Kiyma Kazakhstan U.S.S.R. 51.37N 67.31E
20 C1 Kiyose Tōkyō Japan
93 E5 Kiyunga Uganda 0.44N 33.20E
91 J7 Kizamba Zaïre 7.16S 24.03E
47 H6 Kizel U.S.S.R. 59.01N 57.42E
47 E5 Kizema U.S.S.R. 61.12N 44.52E
42 H6 Kizha U.S.S.R. 51.30N 108.55E
90 B7 Kizhi Nigeria 9.45N 5.13E
42 H6 Kizhinga Alaska U.S.S.R. 51.54N 109.55E
93 C4 Kizi R Uganda
93 C6 Kiziba Uganda 0.27S 31.41E
93 D5 Kiziba Uganda 0.50N 32.38E
93 B7 Kiziguru Rwanda 1.45S 30.24E
37 F2 Kızıl Adalar islds Turkey
36 F6 Kızılağaç Antalya Turkey 36.39N 31.52E
37 F7 Kızılağaç Muş Turkey 38.44N 41.20E
36 G6 Kızılalan Turkey 36.48N 33.04E
Kizil Bulak see Qizil Bulak
36 G6 Kızıl Burun C Turkey 36.03N 33.05E
36 D5 Kızılcabölük Turkey 37.36N 29.03E
36 D5 Kızılcadağ Turkey 37.01N 29.53E
36 D6 Kızılca Dağ mt Turkey 36.55N 29.52E
36 F2 Kızılcahamam Turkey 40.28N 32.37E
37 H5 Kızılçakçak Turkey 40.44N 43.38E
36 G6 Kızılcalı Turkey 36.18N 33.04E
36 H5 Kızıl Dağ mt Niğde Turkey 37.40N 34.52E
37 D6 Kızıl Dağ mt Sivas Turkey 39.55N 38.22E
36 J6 Kızıl Dağı mt Hatay Turkey 36.21N 36.01E
Kızıldikme see Akpınar
36 D5 Kızılhisar Turkey 37.35N 29.18E
37 D8 Kızılin Turkey 37.27N 38.08E
36 G2 Kızılırmak Turkey 40.20N 33.59E
36 G2 Kızıl Irmak R Turkey
36 E5 Kızılkaya Burdur Turkey 37.18N 30.28E
Kızılkaya Konya see Başkışla
Kizil Khoto see Kyzyl
36 H3 Kızılkoca Turkey 39.32N 34.45E
36 C4 Kızıllar Turkey 38.46N 28.07E
37 E1 Kızılpınar Turkey 41.15N 27.56E
43 E1 Kizil'skoye U.S.S.R. 52.44N 58.49E
37 G8 Kızılsu Turkey 37.26N 42.09E
44 A2 Kiziltashskiy Liman lagoon U.S.S.R.
37 F8 Kızıltepe Turkey 37.12N 40.36E
36 F1 Kızıl Tepe mt Turkey 41.02N 31.32E
37 F2 Kızıltoprak Turkey 40.59N 29.03E
36 F5 Kızılviran Turkey 37.52N 32.08E
44 H4 Kizil'yurt U.S.S.R. 43.13N 46.54E
92 J6 Kizimbani Tanzania 9.04S 39.20E
39 G6 Kizimen,Sopka vol Kamchatka U.S.S.R. 55.08N 160.19E
90 J3 Kizimi Chad 16.37N 18.10E
92 K12 Kizimkazi Zanzibar 6.28S 39.28E
42 E5 Kizir R U.S.S.R.
37 C2 Kızkapan Turkey 40.45N 26.29E
37 C3 Kizlar Daği mts Turkey
44 H4 Kizlyar U.S.S.R. 43.51N 46.43E
44 H3 Kizlyarskiy Zaliv B U.S.S.R.
51 Q6 Kizreka Karelia U.S.S.R. 65.33N 31.53E
91 C6 Kizu Zaïre 4.55S 13.01E
20 D3 Kizuki dist Kanagawa Japan
92 E5 Kizumbi Tanzania 7.46S 30.46E
43 D7 Kizyl-Arvat Turkmeniya U.S.S.R. 39.00N 56.23E
43 C7 Kizyl-Atrek Turkmeniya U.S.S.R. 37.37N 54.49E
43 H7 Kizyl-Ayak Turkmeniya U.S.S.R. 37.40N 65.17E
24 C8 Kizyl Jilga Xinjiang Uygur Zizhiqu China 35.18N 78.48E
43 C7 Kizyl-Su Turkmeniya U.S.S.R. 39.49N 53.01E
51 J2 Kjækan Norway 69.46N 22.04E
50 D6 Kjalarnes C Iceland 64.14N 21.55W
50 F5 Kjalfell mt Iceland 64.46N 19.32W
50 F5 Kjalhraun lava field Iceland
50 C3 Kjálkafjördhur B Iceland
50 F6 Kjalkaversfoss Iceland 64.22N 19.06W
50 C2 Kjaransvík Iceland 66.25N 22.44W
50 E5 Kjarra R Iceland
50 G3 Kjáströnd Iceland 65.55N 18.09W
53 C4 Kjellerup Denmark 56.18N 9.27E
53 V14 Kjellstadli Norway 62.02N 6.45E
53 T16 Kjelstadnakken mt Norway 61.21N 5.55E
51 M1 Kjelvik Norway 70.59N 26.00E
53 W15 Kjenndalskruna mt Norway 61.44N 7.05E
51 D4 Kjerringøy Norway 67.33N 14.50E
52 D8 Kjevik airport Norway 58.13N 8.05E
53 S14 Kjøde Norway 62.01N 5.28E
53 Z14 Kjølen mts Norway 62.03N 8.39E
50 K4 Kjölfell mt Iceland 65.23N 15.58W
51 N1 Kjøllefjord Norway 70.55N 27.21E
53 T15 Kjølsdal Norway 61.55N 5.40E
50 D6 Kjölur mt Iceland 64.19N 21.18W
50 F5 Kjölur reg Iceland
50 D4 Kjörseyri Iceland 65.14N 21.09W
53 V15 Kjos Norway 61.57N 6.30E
50 D6 Kjósarsýsla co Iceland
53 V15 Kjøsnesfjord inlet Norway 61.32N 6.30E
95 F9 Klaarstroom S Africa 33.20S 22.33E
60 F12 Klaaswaal Netherlands 51.45N 4.26E
19 D3 Klabat, Gunung mt Celebes Indon 1.28N 125.04E
82 E6 Kladanj Yugoslavia 44.14N 18.42E
80 O1 Kladnjice Yugoslavia 43.42N 16.18E
65 K1 Kladno Czechoslovakia 50.10N 14.07E
82 H6 Kladovo Yugoslavia 44.36N 22.33E
63 S8 Kladow W Berlin 52.28N 13.08E
64 O4 Kladruby Czechoslovakia 49.43N 12.59E
65 M1 Kladruby nad Labem Czech 50.04N 15.29E
18 M3 Klagan Sabah Malaysia 5.58N 117.28E
65 K8 Klagenfurt Austria 46.38N 14.20E
111 P6 Klagetoh Arizona 35.31N 109.33W
46 D2 Klaipéda Lithuania U.S.S.R. 55.43N 21.07E
18 K9 Klakah Java Indon 7.55S 113.12E
53 V15 Klakegg Norway 61.36N 6.31E
50 E5 Klakkur mt Iceland 64.34N 20.28W
53 D5 Klakring Denmark 55.43N 9.58E
53 N9 Klaksvig Faeroes 62.13N 6.34W
110 A8 Klamath California 41.32N 124.03W
110 B8 Klamath R California
110 D7 Klamath Falls Oregon 42.14N 121.47W
110 B8 Klamath Mts California
110 C8 Klamath River California 41.53N 122.44W
50 D4 Klambrafell mt Iceland 65.03N 21.15W
15 A4 Klamono Irian Jaya 1.08S 131.28E
82 C4 Klanjec Yugoslavia 46.03N 15.45E
63 J3 Klanxbüll W Germany 54.53N 8.41E
101 J7 Klappan R Br Columbia
52 G6 Klarabro Sweden 60.46N 12.50E
52 G7 Klarälven R Sweden
60 N11 Klarenbeek Netherlands 52.10N 6.04E
53 E2 Klarup Denmark 57.01N 10.05E
64 P3 Klášterec Czechoslovakia 50.24N 13.10E
18 J9 Klaten Java Indon 7.40S 110.32E
64 P5 Klatovy Czechoslovakia 49.24N 13.17E
65 K6 Klaus Austria 47.50N 14.10E
66 P2 Klaus Vorarlberg Austria 47.19N 9.39E
63 S4 Klausdorf E Germany 54.25N 13.01E
65 O5 Klausen-Leopoldsdorf Austria 48.06N 16.02E
66 M4 Klausen Pass Switzerland 46.52N 8.52E
50 E6 Klausturhólar Iceland 64.05N 20.48W
113 V9 Klawak Alaska 55.35N 133.04W
94 E8 Klawer S Africa 31.45S 18.36E
Klawock see Klawak
89 D8 Klay Liberia 6.48N 10.51W
84 A2 Klaziádhes Greece 39.38N 20.58E
60 Q9 Klazienaveen Netherlands 52.43N 7.00E
89 F5 Klé Mali 12.01N 6.28W
Klea see Abu Tuleih Battlefield
112 O9 Kleberg dist Dallas, Texas
62 K3 Kłecko Poland 52.38N 17.22E
62 L3 Kleczew Poland 52.22N 18.09E
98 J3 Kleczkowski L Quebec
Kleef see Kleve
101 L10 Kleena Kleene Br Col 51.58N 124.59W
108 C5 Kleenburn Wyoming 44.54N 107.02W
63 S5 Kleeth E Germany 53.37N 13.05E
50 B3 Kleifaheidhi heath Iceland
50 D4 Kleifar Dalasýsla Iceland 65.27N 21.40W
50 D3 Kleifar Strandasýsla Iceland 65.43N 21.34W
50 D7 Kleifarvatn L Iceland 63.55N 22.00W
110 R3 Klein Montana 46.24N 108.33W
94 F7 Kleinbegin S Africa 28.50S 21.36E
63 P6 Klein Berge E Germany 53.14N 11.52E
95 F10 Klein-Brakrivier S Africa 34.05S 22.08E
63 K8 Klein Bremen W Germany 52.15N 9.02E
116 K9 Klein Curaçao isld Lesser Antilles 12.00N 68.40W
61 M2 Kleine-Brogel Belgium 51.10N 5.27E
63 S9 Kleine Elster R E Germany
94 R13 Klein Elandsvlei S Africa 26.09S 27.39E
66 J3 Klein Emme R Switzerland
63 J9 Kleinenberg W Germany 51.34N 8.59E
61 K2 Kleine Nete R Belgium
Kleinengstingen see Engstingen
63 T4 Kleiner Jasmunder Bodden L E Germany
Kleine Sluis see Anna Paulowna
103 B6 Kleinfeltersville Pennsylvania 40.18N 76.15W
65 K8 Klein Glödnitz Austria 46.52N 14.08E
95 J2 Klein-Harts R S Africa
94 E6 Kleinkaras Namibia 27.36S 18.05E
63 R8 Klein Kreutz E Germany 52.27N 12.38E
64 N6 Klein Laaber R W Germany
66 J1 Klein Laufenburg W Germany 47.34N 8.03E
94 L4 Klein Letaba R S Africa
64 F2 Klein Linden W Germany 50.33N 8.40E
66 F2 Kleinlützel Switzerland 47.26N 7.25E
63 S8 Klein-Machnow E Germany 52.26N 13.13E
95 C10 Kleinmond S Africa 34.20S 19.01E
65 K5 Klein Munchen Austria 48.16N 14.18E
64 Q6 Klein Philippsreut W Germany 48.53N 13.41E
95 H9 Kleinpoort S Africa 33.20S 24.53E
65 L6 Klein Reifling Austria 47.50N 14.38E
95 D8 Klein Roggeveldberge mts S Africa
65 L8 Klein St.Paul Austria 46.51N 14.03E
94 D7 Kleinsee S Africa 29.43S 17.03E
65 B7 Klein-Spitze mt Austria 47.14N 10.04E
95 C9 Kleinstraat S Africa 33.24S 19.57E
95 E9 Klein-Swartberg mt S Africa 33.25S 21.21E
63 N5 Klein Thurow E Germany 53.43N 10.59E
95 H2 Klein-Tswaing S Africa 26.53S 24.10E
95 L4 Klein-Vet R S Africa
95 J8 Klein-Vis R S Africa
63 Q8 Klein Wusterwitz E Germany 52.28N 12.15E
65 N6 Klein Zell Austria 47.59N 15.44E
53 X20 Kleivegrend Norway 59.15N 7.55E
53 D3 Klejtrup Denmark 56.36N 9.39E
82 D6 Klekovača mt Yugoslavia 44.25N 16.32E
53 P12 Klemensker Bornholm Denmark 55.11N 14.49E
80 O2 Klement isld Yugoslavia 43.10N 16.23E
108 R6 Klemme Iowa 43.01N 93.33W
61 C2 Klemskerke Belgium 51.14N 3.02E
101 J9 Klemtu Br Col 52.35N 128.32W
82 F6 Klenak Yugoslavia 44.47N 19.42E
64 O5 Klenčí Pod Čerchovem Czech 49.26N 12.45E
53 Y14 Klenegga mt Norway 62.24N 8.14E
63 N7 Klenze W Germany 52.56N 10.57E
45 M6 Klepovo U.S.S.R. 50.44N 40.27E
95 G7 Klerk,De S Africa 31.15S 23.30E
61 B2 Klerken Belgium 51.00N 2.54E
95 K2 Klerksdorp S Africa 26.52S 26.39E
95 L2 Klerkskraal S Africa 26.15S 27.10E
113 G3 Klery Creek Alaska 67.10N 160.23W
62 O3 Kleszczele Poland 52.35N 23.19E
65 K4 Klet mt Czechoslovakia 48.53N 14.18E
45 E3 Kletnya U.S.S.R. 53.23N 33.14E
45 P7 Kletskaya U.S.S.R. 49.18N 43.05E
46 N5 Kletskiy U.S.S.R. 49.18N 43.05E
45 P7 Kletsko-Pochtovskiy U.S.S.R. 49.34N 43.03E
64 E8 Klettgau W Germany 47.37N 8.24E
64 E8 Klettgau reg W Ger/Switz
63 T9 Klettwitz E Germany 51.32N 13.54E
53 T16 Klevald Norway 61.10N 5.50E
46 F4 Klevan' Ukraine U.S.S.R. 50.44N 25.50E
63 D9 Kleve W Germany 51.47N 6.11E
45 V4 Klevenka U.S.S.R. 52.06N 49.30E
18 B6 Klian Intan Pen Malaysia 5.36N 101.02E
42 K6 Klichka U.S.S.R. 50.28N 118.01E
110 D4 Klickitat Washington 45.50N 121.07W
110 D3 Klickitat R Washington
84 T13 Klidhes Is Cyprus 35.42N 34.37E
63 Q7 Klietz E Germany 53.41N 12.05E
60 Q8 Klijndijk Netherlands 52.49N 6.51E
53 C2 Klim Denmark 57.06N 9.11E
42 F3 Klimino U.S.S.R. 58.40N 98.44E
60 T17 Klimmen Netherlands 50.53N 5.53E
62 N5 Klimontów Poland 50.40N 21.29E
45 C3 Klimovichi Belorussiya U.S.S.R. 53.36N 31.58E
46 Q1 Klimovka U.S.S.R. 58.52N 51.09E
45 D4 Klimovo U.S.S.R. 52.24N 32.13E
45 J1 Klimovsk U.S.S.R. 55.21N 37.31E
51 D6 Klimpfjäll Sweden 65.05N 14.50E
45 H1 Klin U.S.S.R. 56.20N 36.45E
101 L10 Klinaklini R Br Col
105 F4 Kline S Carolina 33.07N 81.20W
19 M9 Kling Mindanao Philippines 5.58N 124.38E
64 Q2 Klingenberg E Germany 50.55N 13.32E
64 G4 Klingenberg am Main W Germany 49.47N 9.12E
64 E5 Klingenmünster W Germany 49.08N 8.02E
64 N3 Klingenthal E Germany 50.21N 12.28E
103 A5 Klingerstown Pennsylvania 40.40N 76.42W
18 J5 Klingkang Ra Kalimantan/Sarawak
66 J1 Klingnau Switzerland 47.34N 8.15E
63 R6 Klink E Germany 53.30N 12.38E
53 A3 Klinkby Ringkøbing Denmark 56.33N 8.14E
64 O3 Klínovec mt Czechoslovakia 50.23N 12.57E
Klintebjerg see Gerskov
52 L9 Klintehamn Sweden 57.24N 18.14E
53 E5 Klinte Kirke Denmark 55.35N 10.16E
45 V5 Klintsovka U.S.S.R. 51.42N 49.12E
45 D4 Klintsy U.S.S.R. 52.45N 32.15E
83 H5 Klió Greece 39.20N 26.22E
95 O4 Klip R Natal S Africa
95 M3 Klip R Orange Free State S Africa
95 N3 Klip R S Africa
95 F8 Klipbank S Africa 32.27S 22.26E
95 C10 Klipdale S Africa 34.18S 19.57E
94 E6 Klipdam Namibia 27.05S 19.52E
95 H4 Klipdam S Africa 28.20S 24.38E
95 L2 Klipdrifdam res S Africa 26.36S 27.19E
95 J8 Klipfontein Cape Province S Africa 32.36S 25.45E
95 N1 Klipfontein Transvaal S Africa 25.55S 29.14E
95 F8 Klipkrans S Africa 32.46S 22.55E
53 C7 Kliplev Denmark 54.57N 9.25E
52 G10 Klippan Sweden 56.08N 13.10E
53 J6 Klippinge Denmark 55.22N 12.20E
95 H9 Klipplaat S Africa 33.02S 24.20E
94 T14 Kliprivier S Africa 26.26S 28.05E
94 S14 Klipriviersberg mt S Africa 26.17S 27.58E
94 E8 Kliprug Berg mt S Africa 31.40S 19.25E
94 S14 Kliptown S Africa 26.16S 27.53E
84 R15 Klirou Cyprus 34.59N 33.10E
82 J8 Klisura Bulgaria 42.40N 24.28E
53 B2 Klitmøller Denmark 57.03N 8.32E
63 J3 Klixbüll W Germany 54.48N 8.54E
82 D6 Ključ Yugoslavia 44.32N 16.48E
65 P4 Klobouky Czechoslovakia 48.59N 16.53E
62 L5 Kłobuck Poland 50.54N 18.54E
99 M6 Klock Ontario 46.15N 78.30W
63 U6 Klockow E Germany 53.25N 14.02E
62 L3 Kłodawa Poland 52.16N 18.51E
62 K5 Kłodzko Poland 50.28N 16.40E
60 C3 Kloetinge Netherlands 51.30N 3.55E
52 F6 Kløfta Norway 60.04N 11.06E
111 H7 Klondike California 34.40N 116.00W
101 D3 Klondike R Yukon Terr
66 M3 Klön Tal V Switzerland
66 M3 Klöntaler See L Switzerland 47.02N 9.00E
95 O5 Kloof S Africa 29.48S 30.50E
60 O6 Kloosterburen Netherlands 53.23N 6.24E
60 P9 Kloosterdijk Netherlands 52.30N 6.35E
60 P10 Kloosterhaar Netherlands 52.30N 6.40E
60 P8 Kloosterveen Netherlands 53.00N 6.31E
60 D3 Kloosterzande Netherlands 51.22N 4.01E
65 L8 Klopeiner See L Austria 46.37N 14.35E
83 D3 Klos Albania 41.28N 20.10E
53 A4 Kloster Denmark 56.08N 8.11E
63 S7 Klosterfelde E Germany 52.48N 13.30E
53 A4 Klosterhede Plantage wood Denmark 56.28N 8.27E
Klosterlausnitz see Bad Klosterlausnitz
65 B7 Klösterle Austria 47.08N 10.04E
63 Q6 Kloster Malchow E Germany 53.28N 12.26E
63 P9 Kloster Mansfeld E Germany 51.35N 11.30E
65 O5 Klosterneuburg Austria 48.19N 16.20E
64 F7 Klosterreichenbach Baden-Württemberg W Germany 48.06N 8.50E
69 P6 Klosterreichenbach W Germany 48.32N 8.24E
66 Q4 Klosters Switzerland 46.54N 9.54E
65 A7 Kloster tal V Austria
53 S18 Kloster Ulven Norway 60.11N 5.27E
63 S8 Kloster Zinna E Germany 52.02N 13.07E
52 J7 Kloten Sweden 59.54N 15.19E
66 L2 Kloten Switzerland 47.27N 8.35E
64 C3 Klotten W Germany 50.10N 7.12E
63 O7 Klötze E Germany 52.38N 11.11E
99 E3 Klotz Lake Prov. Park Ontario
64 Q1 Klotzsche E Germany 51.07N 13.46E
89 K8 Klouto Togo 6.58N 0.39E
53 C5 Klovborg Denmark 55.55N 9.30E
52 H4 Klövsjö Sweden 62.31N 14.51E
101 D5 Kluane Yukon Terr 60.59N 138.22W
101 D5 Kluane R Yukon Terr
101 D5 Kluane L Yukon Terr
101 D5 Kluane National Park Yukon Terr
Kluang see Keluang
18 E7 Kluang Sumatra Indon 2.36S 103.47E
18 J7 Kluang, Tanjung C Borneo Indon 3.03N 110.42E
62 L5 Kluczbork Poland 50.59N 18.10E
66 O1 Kluftern W Germany 47.42N 9.24E
61 E3 Kluisbergen Belgium 50.46N 3.32E
61 E2 Kluizen Belgium 51.09N 3.44E
Klukhori see Karachayevsk
44 D4 Klukhorskiy Pereval pass U.S.S.R. 43.15N 41.54E
113 U7 Klukwan Alaska 59.25N 135.55W
18 M7 Klumpeng, Teluk B Borneo Indon
60 G13 Klundert Netherlands 51.39N 4.31E
18 L10 Klungkung Bali Indonesia 8.32S 115.25E
69 N1 Klüppelberg W Germany 51.07N 7.30E
113 P6 Klutina L Alaska 61.40N 145.59W
52 M2 Klutmark Sweden 64.43N 20.40E
63 O5 Klütz E Germany 53.58N 11.10E
19 C8 Kluwang Indonesia 8.30S 123.22E
45 A1 Klyastitsy U.S.S.R. 55.48N 29.25E
46 Q3 Klyavlino U.S.S.R. 54.18N 52.00E
45 N1 Klyaz'ma R U.S.S.R.
50 M4 Klyppsstadhir Iceland 65.23N 13.55W
47 E3 Klyuchevaya U.S.S.R. 65.14N 41.18E
47 N4 Klyuchevsk U.S.S.R. 57.09N 60.57E
39 G6 Klyuchevskaya Sopka vol Kamchatka U.S.S.R. 56.03N 160.38E
42 K5 Klyuchevskiy U.S.S.R. 53.31N 119.30E
Klyuchevskoy vol see Klyuchevskaya Sopka Vol
42 J6 Klyuchi Aginskiy Buryat U.S.S.R. 50.55N 113.30E
43 N2 Klyuchi Altay U.S.S.R. 52.18N 79.07E
40 D7 Klyuchi Amur U.S.S.R. 49.45N 128.00E
47 M6 Klyuchi Chelyabinsk U.S.S.R. 54.40N 61.16E
39 G6 Klyuchi Kamchatka U.S.S.R. 56.19N 160.49E
46 S2 Klyuchi Perm U.S.S.R. 57.00N 57.30E
45 S5 Klyuchi Saratov U.S.S.R. 51.59N 46.34E
47 J6 Klyuchi Sverdlovsk U.S.S.R. 57.50N 62.55E
15 L3 Kmagha Santa Isabel I Solomon Is 8.20S 159.44E
31 J3 K2, Mt Kashmir/Xinjiang Uygur Zizhiqu 35.53N 76.32E
52 C8 Knaben Norway 58.40N 7.05E
65 J7 Knallstein,Gross mt Austria 47.19N 13.58E
28 B3 Knanapur Karnataka India 15.41N 74.38E
95 K6 Knapdaar S Africa 30.43S 26.09E
58 E7 Knapdale dist Strathclyde Scotland
106 B5 Knapp Wisconsin 44.58N 92.02W
50 J7 Knappavellir Iceland 63.55N 16.36W
60 K10 Knardijk dyke Netherlands
57 L4 Knaresborough N Yorks Eng 54.00N 1.27W
57 J3 Knarsdale Northumb Eng 54.53N 2.30W
64 M2 Knau E Germany 50.38N 11.42E
53 E4 Knebel Denmark 56.13N 10.30E
63 H5 Knechtsand sandbank W Germany
100 K3 Knee L Saskatchewan
57 M6 Kneesall Notts Eng 53.11N 0.57W
88 T4 Kneïs isld Tunisia 34.23N 10.18E
63 N7 Knesebeck W Germany 52.41N 10.43E
61 D2 Knessalare Belgium 51.08N 3.25E
64 K4 Knetsgau W Germany 50.00N 10.35E
82 J7 Knezha Bulgaria 43.30N 24.06E
112 G4 Knickerbocker Texas 31.14N 100.38W
84 C1 Knídhi Greece 40.06N 21.36E
Kniet see Ban Kniet
108 H2 Knife R N Dakota
113 K7 Knife Pk Alaska 58.22N 155.03W
106 C3 Knife River Minnesota 46.57N 91.48W
110 P8 Knight Wyoming 41.13N 110.51W
113 O6 Knight I Alaska 60.20N 147.50W
101 K10 Knight Inlet Br Columbia
56 E3 Knighton Powys Wales 52.21N 3.03W
107 L2 Knightstown Indiana 39.48N 85.30W
59 B8 Knights Town Kerry Irish Rep 51.55N 10.17W
107 J2 Knightsville Indiana 39.32N 87.05W
103 J2 Knightville Res Massachusetts 42.18N 72.52W
44 E2 Knigino U.S.S.R. 45.37N 42.52E
84 E4 Knimídhos, Dhíavlos str Greece
84 E4 Knimís mt Greece 38.45N 22.48E
82 C6 Knin Yugoslavia 44.02N 16.11E
65 P2 Knínice Czechoslovakia 49.33N 16.42E
63 H5 Kniphausen W Germany 53.33N 8.04E
112 H6 Knippa Texas 29.17N 99.38W
65 L7 Knittelfeld Austria 47.14N 14.50E
52 K7 Knivsta Sweden 59.43N 17.49E
64 Q6 Knížecí Pláně Czechoslovakia 48.58N 13.38E
65 K4 Kniž Stolec mt Czechoslovakia 48.52N 14.02E
82 G7 Knjaževac Yugoslavia 43.35N 22.12E
14 A8 Knobby Hd W Australia 29.41S 114.55E
107 F5 Knobel Arkansas 36.19N 90.38W
Knob Lake see Schefferville
14 G2 Knob Pk W Australia 14.55S 128.34E
59 D6 Knock Clare Irish Rep 52.38N 9.20W
59 D7 Knockacummer mt Cork Irish Rep 52.15N 9.05W
59 E7 Knockaderry Limerick Irish Rep 52.28N 8.58W
59 F7 Knockainy Limerick Irish Rep 52.29N 8.28W
59 D5 Knocka L Galway Irish Rep 53.18N 9.15W
59 G1 Knockalla Hills Donegal Irish Rep
59 G7 Knockanaffrin mt Waterford Irish Rep 52.17N 7.35W
58 K4 Knockandhu Grampian Scotland 57.18N 3.19W
59 D7 Knockanefune mt Kerry Irish Rep 52.14N 9.17W
59 E6 Knockannis mt Clare Irish Rep 52.58N 9.15W
59 D8 Knockboy mt Cork Irish Rep 51.48N 9.27W
59 C8 Knockbrack mt Kerry Irish Rep 51.56N 9.29W
59 F4 Knockcroghery Roscommon Irish Rep 53.35N 8.06W
59 D7 Knockfeha mt Kerry Irish Rep 52.13N 9.19W
57 J3 Knock Fell mt Cumbria Eng 54.41N 2.24W
59 K1 Knocklayd mt Antrim N Ireland 55.09N 6.15W
59 G7 Knockmealdown Mts Irish Rep
59 B8 Knocknadober mt Kerry Irish Rep 51.59N 10.11W
59 C8 Knocknagullion mt Kerry Irish Rep 51.52N 9.48W
59 F7 Knocknaskagh mt Cork Irish Rep 52.06N 8.26W
59 J6 Knockroe mt Carlow Irish Rep 52.35N 6.48W
59 H7 Knocktopher Kilkenny Irish Rep 52.29N 7.13W
95 G9 Knoetze S Africa 33.14S 23.48E
61 D1 Knokke-Heist Belgium 51.21N 3.19E
60 H9 Knollendam Netherlands 52.31N 4.47E
110 M9 Knolls Utah 40.44N 113.18W
66 K3 Knonau Switzerland 47.13N 8.28E
50 B5 Knorr Iceland 64.50N 23.30W
53 E2 Knøsen mt Denmark 57.12N 10.18E
83 G9 Knossos ruins Crete 35.18N 25.10E
84 M11 Knossós ruins Crete 35.18N 25.10E
112 F3 Knott Texas 32.25N 101.40W
57 H5 Knott End Lancs Eng 53.56N 3.00W
57 L5 Knottingley W Yorks Eng 53.43N 1.14W
56 C5 Knowle Devon Eng 51.08N 4.10W
56 H3 Knowle W Midlands Eng 52.23N 1.43W
109 K5 Knowles Oklahoma 36.52N 100.13W
99 S7 Knowlton Quebec 45.13N 72.31W
106 E5 Knowlton Wisconsin 44.45N 89.41W
106 H8 Knox Indiana 41.17N 86.37W
108 L1 Knox N Dakota 48.23N 99.40W
104 F5 Knox Pennsylvania 41.15N 79.33W
Knox Basin see Eastern Indian-Antarctic Basin
101 G8 Knox,C Graham I, Br Col 54.09N 133.05W
107 D1 Knox City Missouri 40.09N 92.00W
112 H2 Knox City Texas 33.25N 99.48W
123 E2 Knox Coast Antarctica
111 B3 Knoxville California 38.48N 122.23W
106 D9 Knoxville Illinois 40.55N 90.17W
108 R8 Knoxville Iowa 41.19N 93.05W
107 E10 Knoxville Mississippi 31.22N 91.08W
104 H5 Knoxville Pennsylvania 41.58N 77.26W
105 D1 Knoxville Tennessee 36.00N 83.57W
58 E4 Knoydart dist Highland Scotland
26 S7 Knuckles mt Sri Lanka 7.25N 80.33E
31 D7 Knude Hills Pakistan
97 R4 Knud Rasmussens Land Greenland
53 F6 Knudshoved C Denmark 55.18N 10.52E
53 H6 Knudshoved headland Denmark 55.06N 11.39E
53 H6 Knudshoved pen Denmark
53 N10 Knúkur mt Faeroes 61.47N 6.51W
64 G2 Knüllwald W Germany 50.59N 9.26E
57 J6 Knutsford Cheshire Eng 53.18N 2.23W
53 Z16 Knutsholstind mt Norway 61.26N 8.34E
53 U20 Knutsvik Norway 59.18N 6.08E
66 J3 Knutwil Switzerland 47.12N 8.04E
45 R1 Knyaginino U.S.S.R. 55.48N 45.02E
47 E6 Knyazhevo U.S.S.R. 59.40N 43.51E
45 G1 Knyazh'y Gory U.S.S.R. 56.05N 35.16E
95 G10 Knysna S Africa 34.03S 23.03E
62 O2 Knyszyn Poland 53.20N 22.52E
114 D7 Koae Hawaiian Is 19.32N 154.51W
90 H4 Koal Chad 14.26N 16.26E
114 E6 Koali Hawaiian Is 20.41N 156.02W
87 C5 Koalib,Jeb mt Sudan 11.36N 30.21E
89 J5 Koalla Upper Volta 13.30N 0.07W
114 B8 Koa Mill Hawaiian Is 19.13N 155.50W
20 E9 Koarai Japan 32.19N 131.24E
51 M2 Koarvikodds mt Finland 69.05N 26.20E
30 H7 Koath Bihar India 25.20N 84.16E
18 A6 Kob Pen Malaysia 5.25N 100.39E
18 G7 Koba Indonesia 2.30S 106.26E
20 D10 Koba Japan 31.57N 130.42E
15 C7 Koba Moluccas Indon 6.30S 134.35E
44 F5 Koban' U.S.S.R. 42.56N 44.32E
53 J6 Kobanke mt Denmark 55.14N 12.02E
82 B4 Kobarid Yugoslavia 46.16N 13.35E
20 D9 Kobayashi Japan 32.00N 130.58E
90 L4 Kobbai Sudan 14.04N 23.58E
61 G3 Kobbegem Belgium 50.54N 4.15E
48 T15 Kobberminebugt B Greenland 61.00N 48.00W
53 C3 Kobberup Denmark 56.31N 9.06E
Kobbo see K'obo
Kobdo see Hovd Hovd Mongolia
19 E3 Kobe Halmahera Indonesia 0.28N 127.54E
20 J7 Kōbe Japan 34.40N 135.12E
53 G7 Købelev Denmark 54.54N 11.07E
66 P2 Kobelwald Switzerland 47.19N 9.33E
45 F7 Kobelyaki Ukraine U.S.S.R. 49.09N 34.14E
94 E8 Kobe Mts S Africa 31.45S 19.00E
53 K5 København Denmark 55.43N 12.34E
53 J5 København co Denmark
89 E4 Kobenni Mauritania 15.58N 9.24W
65 H5 Kobernausser Wald reg Austria
64 C3 Kobern-Gondorf W Germany 50.19N 7.28E
65 O6 Kobersdorf Austria 47.37N 16.23E
19 F5 Kobi Moluccas Indonesia 2.59S 129.54E
23 K6 Kōbi sho isld Japan 25.58N 123.40E
66 P2 Koblach Austria 47.20N 9.37E
66 J1 Koblenz Switzerland 47.37N 8.14E
64 D3 Koblenz W Germany 50.21N 7.36E
44 A8 Koblevo Ukraine U.S.S.R. 46.40N 31.14E
28 K2 Kobo Assam India 27.48N 95.20E
87 G4 K'obo Ethiopia 12.06N 39.42E
91 E6 Kobo Zaïre 5.00S 17.16E
93 B2 Koboko Uganda 3.24N 30.58E
40 F5 Koboldo U.S.S.R. 53.00N 132.44E
46 K1 Kobozha U.S.S.R. 58.45N 35.00E
46 K1 Kobozha R U.S.S.R.
47 G6 Kobra R U.S.S.R.
46 E4 Kobrin Belorussiya U.S.S.R. 52.16N 24.22E
15 C7 Kobroör isld Moluccas Indonesia
20 M6 Kobuchizawa Japan 35.54N 138.19E
113 J3 Kobuk Alaska 66.55N 157.00W
113 H3 Kobuk R Alaska
44 D6 Kobuleti Georgia U.S.S.R. 41.49N 41.46E
41 N8 Kobyai U.S.S.R. 63.30N 127.14E
45 O4 Kobyaki U.S.S.R. 52.44N 42.34E
62 K4 Kobylin Poland 51.42N 17.14E
45 C6 Kobyzhcha Ukraine U.S.S.R. 50.50N 31.31E
37 D3 Koca R Balikesir Turkey
37 C3 Koca R Çanakkale Turkey
36 G1 Koca R Kastamonu Turkey
36 G5 Koca R Konya Turkey
36 D6 Koca R Muğla Turkey
36 E1 Kocaali Turkey 41.03N 30.54E
65 K2 Kocaba R Czechoslovakia
36 C2 Kocabaş R Turkey
37 D2 Koca Burun C Turkey 40.52N 27.28E
37 D3 Kocaçay R Turkey
36 J4 Koca Dağı mt Turkey 38.47N 36.15E
Kocaeli see İzmit
36 B3 Kocakatran Dağı mt Turkey
37 D8 Koçalı Turkey 37.55N 38.14E
Koçan see Göksu
82 G9 Kočani Yugoslavia 41.55N 22.25E
36 F1 Kocanoz Turkey 41.25N 32.30E
37 G6 Kocapınar Turkey 39.05N 43.10E
36 C5 Koçarlı Turkey 37.45N 27.42E
36 E4 Koca Tepe mt Turkey 38.40N 30.25E
23 B1 Kocê Gansu China 34.35N 102.05E
82 F6 Koceljevo Yugoslavia 44.28N 19.50E
82 B5 Kočevje Yugoslavia 45.39N 14.51E
30 H8 Koch Bihar India 24.56N 84.46E
44 L3 Kochak Zaliv gulf Kazakhstan U.S.S.R.
25 D8 Ko Chan isld Burma
21 D10 Kochang S Korea 35.27N 126.40E
21 D10 Kŏch'ang S Korea 35.39N 127.59E
25 G6 Ko Chang isld Thailand
26 Q7 Kochchikade Sri Lanka 7.15N 79.51E
41 H8 Kochechum R U.S.S.R.
40 A2 Kochegarovo U.S.S.R. 59.57N 119.01E
64 L8 Kochel am See W Germany 47.39N 11.20E
64 L8 Kochelsee L W Germany 47.39N 11.20E
42 C4 Kochenevo U.S.S.R. 55.03N 82.14E
42 G4 Kochenga Irkutsk U.S.S.R. 55.55N 104.00E
47 E5 Kochen'ga Vologda U.S.S.R. 60.10N 43.24E
64 H5 Kocher R W Germany
42 G4 Kocherga U.S.S.R. 55.15N 103.45E
45 Q5 Kochetovka Saratov U.S.S.R. 51.45N 44.45E
45 M4 Kochetovka Tambov U.S.S.R. 52.59N 40.30E
47 G6 Kochevo U.S.S.R. 59.39N 54.10E
42 L5 Kocheya U.S.S.R. 52.32N 120.42E
20 F7 Kōchi Honshu Japan 34.30N 132.51E
97 M4 Koch I N W Terr 69.40N 78.00W
20 G8 Kōchi Shikoku Japan 33.33N 133.32E
20 G8 Kōchi prefect Japan
41 G5 Kochikha U.S.S.R. 70.36N 95.35E
20 P10 Kochinda Okinawa Japan 26.05N 127.43E
Kochisar see Kızıltepe
47 J8 Kochkar' U.S.S.R. 54.30N 60.43E
42 C5 Kochki U.S.S.R. 54.16N 80.29E
47 C4 Kochkoma U.S.S.R. 64.03N 34.14E
43 O7 Kochkor-Ata Kirgiziya U.S.S.R. 41.03N 72.13E
43 M6 Kochkorka Kirgiziya U.S.S.R. 42.13N 75.14E
45 R2 Kochkurovo U.S.S.R. 54.03N 45.24E
47 J3 Kochmes U.S.S.R. 66.12N 60.48E
110 O4 Koch Mt Montana 45.02N 111.26W
48 S1 Koch's Fd.,J.P Greenland
44 H3 Kochubey U.S.S.R. 44.25N 46.33E
45 F7 Kochubeyevka Ukraine U.S.S.R. 49.44N 34.59E
44 D3 Kochubeyevskoye U.S.S.R. 44.41N 41.50E
41 F8 Kochumdek U.S.S.R. 64.28N 92.48E
42 D5 Kochura U.S.S.R. 52.45N 87.58E
44 G3 Kochuvey U.S.S.R. 44.57N 45.10E
62 K4 Kocie Góry mts Poland
62 N4 Kock Poland 51.39N 22.28E
37 C8 Köçke Turkey 37.14N 37.14E
60 H11 Kockengen Netherlands 52.09N 4.57E
94 R13 Kocksoord S Africa 26.13S 27.39E
63 O7 Köckte E Germany 52.33N 11.08E
62 L9 Kocsola Hungary 46.30N 18.10E
28 B3 Kod Karnataka India 14.33N 75.27E
47 H4 Kodachdikost U.S.S.R. 63.09N 55.50E
28 C5 Kodaikanal Tamil Nadu India 10.15N 77.31E
20 B2 Kodaira Tōkyō Japan 35.43N 139.30E
29 J8 Kodala Orissa India 19.36N 84.55E
Kodar see Huzurnagar
30 J5 Kodari Nepal 27.58N 85.56E
42 K4 Kodar,Khrebet mts U.S.S.R.
30 J8 Kodarma Bihar India 24.28N 85.36E
26 U6 Koddaimunnai Sri Lanka 7.45N 81.42E
26 T4 Koddiyar B Sri Lanka
62 O4 Kodeń Poland 51.54N 23.35E
45 L6 Kodentsovo U.S.S.R. 50.37N 39.29E
18 N10 Kodi Indonesia 9.36S 119.01E
91 H5 Kodi Zaïre 3.50S 22.10E
113 L8 Kodiak Alaska 57.49N 152.30W
113 L8 Kodiak I Alaska 57.20N 153.40W
26 R2 Kodikamam Sri Lanka 9.40N 80.13E
47 E5 Kodima U.S.S.R. 62.24N 43.57E
29 B7 Kodinar Gujarat India 20.44N 70.46E
47 D4 Kodino U.S.S.R. 63.43N 39.56E
26 Q1 Kodiyakharai Tamil Nadu India 10.17N 79.49E
89 K5 Kodjari Upper Volta 12.01N 1.53E
Kodna see Kudnah
87 D6 Kodok Sudan 9.51N 32.07E
20 O1 Kodomari Japan 41.09N 140.20E
20 O1 Kodomari-misaki C Japan 41.08N 140.15E
44 D5 Kodori R Georgia U.S.S.R.
44 D5 Kodori,Mys C Georgia U.S.S.R. 42.49N 41.10E
44 D5 Kodorskiy Khrebet mts Georgia U.S.S.R.
28 C3 Kodumuru Andhra Prad India 15.43N 77.46E
46 G5 Kodyma Ukraine U.S.S.R. 48.06N 29.04E
46 H5 Kodyma R Ukraine U.S.S.R.
60 G9 Koedijk Netherlands 52.40N 4.45E
94 F9 Koedoes Berge mts S Africa
94 P11 Koeëlbaai B Cape Town S Africa
95 F5 Koegas S Africa 29.18S 22.20E
94 F7 Koegrabie S Africa 29.02S 21.43E
60 G8 Koegras dist Netherlands
60 O9 Kœkange Netherlands 52.42N 6.20E
61 B2 Koekelare Belgium 51.06N 2.59E
61 R9 Koekelberg dist Bruxelles Belgium
95 K2 Koekemoer S Africa 26.50S 26.48E
94 E8 Koekenaap S Africa 31.30S 18.20E
114 D6 Koele Hawaiian Is 20.50N 156.55W
29 H5 Koel R Bihar India
30 H7 Koelwar Bihar India 25.36N 84.47E
24 F8 Ko-erh-lu-kai Shan-k'ou pass Xizang Zizhiqu China 35.36N 87.10E
Koeri see Kuri
61 O8 Koerich Luxembourg 49.40N 5.57E
61 M2 Koersel Belgium 51.04N 5.16E
94 E5 Koes Namibia 25.59S 19.08E
60 C4 Koewacht Netherlands 51.14N 3.58E
111 L8 Kofa Mts Arizona
36 C1 Kofçaz Turkey 41.58N 27.12E
64 N6 Köfering W Germany 48.56N 12.12E
95 J5 Koffiefontein S Africa 29.25S 25.01E
50 F4 Kofi Iceland 65.12N 19.05W
15 A4 Kofiau isld Irian Jaya
65 M7 Köflach Austria 47.04N 15.04E
89 J8 Koforidua Ghana 6.01N 0.12W
20 M6 Kōfu Japan 35.42N 138.34E
20 N5 Koga Japan 36.12N 139.42E
13 K7 Kogan Queensland 27.02S 150.42E
20 C2 Koganei dist Tōkyō Japan 35.43N 139.28E
12 L8 Kogarah dist Sydney, N S W
53 J6 Køge Denmark 55.28N 12.12E
53 J6 Køge Bugt B Denmark
47 H4 Kogel' R U.S.S.R.

97 D6 Kogguing Alaska 59.03N 157.11W
46 G6 Kogil'nik R Moldavia/Ukraine U.S.S.R.
87 E6 Kogo Dalla Ethiopia 8.42N 34.29E
113 H6 Kogrukluk R Alaska
50 M3 Kögur C Iceland 65.37N 13.54W
20 D7 Kogushi Japan 34.10N 130.55E
Kohala see Kapaau
114 B6 Kohala Mts Hawaiian Is
31 C8 Kohaluien Pakistan 25.30N 64.26E
31 D7 Kohan Pakistan 26.30N 66.28E
30 G5 Kohar Gari Uttar Prad India 27.04N 83.52E
31 F4 Kohat Pakistan 33.37N 71.30E
31 F4 Kohat dist Pakistan
65 O7 Koh-Fidisch Austria 47.11N 16.20E
31 C3 Koh-i-Hisar mts Afghanistan
46 E1 Kohila Estonia U.S.S.R. 59.09N 24.48E
28 K3 Kohima Nagaland India 25.40N 94.08E
28 K3 Kohima dist Nagaland India
11 D2 Kohimarama Auckland New Zealand
28 C2 Kohir Andhra Prad India 17.36N 77.38E
31 E3 Kohistan reg Afghanistan
25 H6 Koh Ker Cambodia 13.47N 104.01E
123 H11 Kohler Ra Antarctica
64 A2 Kohlscheid W Germany 50.50N 6.05E
69 L2 Kohlscheid W Germany 50.50N 6.06E
31 E6 Kohlu Pakistan 29.56N 69.20E
Kohna 'Umar see Kohneh 'Omar
32 F7 Kohneh Iran 26.37N 55.29E
32 F3 Kohneh 'Omar Iran 34.40N 54.40E
20 D4 Kōhoku dist Yokohama Japan
65 L4 Kohout mt Czechoslovakia 48.46N 14.37E
30 A2 Kohra Himachal Prad India 30.53N 76.49E
64 O1 Kohren Sahlis E Germany 51.00N 12.37E
31 A3 Kohsan Afghanistan 34.40N 61.11E
25 G7 Koh Tang isld Cambodia 10.20N 103.08E
46 F1 Kohtla-Järve Estonia U.S.S.R. 59.28N 27.20E
36 D6 Kohu Dağı mt Turkey
11 H2 Kohukohu New Zealand 35.22S 173.34E
21 D10 Kohŭng S Korea 34.38N 127.16E
11 J6 Kohuratahi New Zealand 39.04S 174.49E
93 D3 Koich Uganda 2.35N 32.14E
20 M4 Koide Japan 37.15N 138.56E
101 C5 Koidern Yukon Terr 61.58N 140.29W
28 H7 Koihoa Nicobar Is 8.10N 93.27E
Koil see Aligarh Aligarh, Uttar Prad
30 F5 Koilabas Nepal 27.40N 82.32E
84 F7 Koilás Argolís Greece 37.25N 23.06E
84 D2 Koilás Lárisa Greece 39.35N 22.18E
30 H8 Koilawan Bihar India 25.00N 84.31E
15 H5 Koil I Papua New Guinea 3.20S 144.15E
28 C2 Koilkonda Andhra Prad India 16.46N 77.46E
28 D3 Koilkuntla Andhra Prad India 15.15N 78.16E
28 H7 Koimekeah Nicobar Is 7.55N 93.17E
Koin isld see Qūyūn
47 G4 Koin R U.S.S.R.
90 L3 Koïnaména Chad 17.00N 23.14E
21 D7 Koin-dong N Korea 40.29N 126.28E
34 M2 Koi Sanjaq Iraq 36.05N 44.38E
51 P8 Koitere L Finland 63.00N 30.45E
51 L5 Koivu Finland 66.12N 25.10E
93 G6 Koiwa Kenya 0.35S 35.21E
Koja see Kaju
32 J8 Kojā, Kowr-e R Iran
20 B7 Kŏje-Do isld S Korea
89 H7 Kojei Ghana 8.12N 2.29W
65 N3 Kojetice Czechoslovakia 49.09N 15.49E
62 K6 Kojetín Czechoslovakia 49.22N 17.20E
20 G7 Kojima Japan 34.25N 133.45E
20 J3 Ko-jima isld Japan 41.22N 139.45E
20 N8 Ko-jima isld Japan 33.06N 139.44E
20 D9 Kōjiro Japan 32.54N 130.15E
21 D8 Kojŏ N Korea 38.54N 127.55E
14 B10 Kojonup W Australia 33.50S 117.05E
32 D2 Kojūr Iran 36.23N 51.41E
25 E2 Kok R Thailand
104 Q1 Kokadjo Maine 45.40N 69.28W
26 T7 Kokagala mt Sri Lanka 7.25N 81.12E
Ko Kah see Ban Ko Kah
43 G3 Kokalaat Kazakhstan U.S.S.R. 49.50N 64.00E
43 K6 Kokand Uzbekistan U.S.S.R. 40.33N 70.55E
101 P11 Kokanee Glacier Prov.Park Br Col
43 K6 Kokankishlak Uzbekistan U.S.S.R. 40.55N 72.29E
43 F4 Kokaral Kazakhstan U.S.S.R. 46.14N 60.44E
43 F4 Kokaral,Ostrov isld Kazakhstan U.S.S.R.
15 B5 Kokas Irian Jaya 2.45S 132.26E
62 M7 Kokava Czechoslovakia 48.34N 19.50E
20 J7 Kokawa Japan 34.16N 135.24E
43 J8 Kokayty Tadzhikistan U.S.S.R. 37.33N 68.35E
31 E2 Kokcha R Afghanistan
43 J1 Kokchetav Kazakhstan U.S.S.R. 53.18N 69.25E
51 K10 Kokemäenjoki R Finland
51 J10 Kokemäki Finland 61.15N 22.20E
36 H3 Kökenes Dağ mt Turkey 39.44N 35.00E
94 E7 Kokerboom Namibia 28.11S 19.25E
45 A2 Kokhanovo Belorussiya U.S.S.R. 54.29N 29.29E
35 B7 Kokhav Israel 31.37N 34.40E
Kokhav Havarden anc site see Belvoir anc.site
89 B4 Koki Senegal 15.30N 15.59W
28 B4 Kokkanisseri Kerala India 12.08N 75.13E
26 R3 Kokkavil Sri Lanka 9.15N 80.25E
26 S3 Kokkilai Sri Lanka 8.59N 80.57E
84 D8 Kókkina Louriá Greece 36.49N 22.26E
84 F4 Kokkinomiliá Greece 38.54N 23.16E
51 K8 Kokkola Finland 63.50N 23.10E
84 D1 Kokkoniplós Greece 40.06N 22.16E
24 F2 Kok Kudak well Xinjiang Uygur Zizhiqu China 46.03N 87.34E
90 B8 Koko Nigeria 6.02N 5.29E
15 J8 Kokoda Papua New Guinea 8.52S 147.44E
114 B5 Koko Head Hawaiian Is 21.15N 157.33W
113 F2 Kokolik R Alaska
114 E6 Kokomo Hawaiian Is 20.52N 156.17W
106 H9 Kokomo Indiana 40.30N 86.09W
15 D6 Kokonau Irian Jaya 4.42S 136.25E
20 E8 Kokone Japan 33.16N 131.08E
94 G5 Kokong Botswana 24.27S 23.03E
11 E12 Kokonga New Zealand 45.13S 170.15E
Koko Nor see Ching Hai Hu
15 M6 Kokopo New Britain 4.18S 152.17E
84 C6 Kokorá Greece 37.34N 21.56E
41 H4 Kokora,Ozero L U.S.S.R.
45 F4 Kokorevka U.S.S.R. 52.35N 34.16E
89 L7 Kokoro Benin 8.24N 2.41E
18 A4 Kokos isld Indonesia 3.00N 95.26E
Kokoshili Ra see Hoh Xil Shan
42 D6 Kokpash U.S.S.R. 51.21N 87.46E
43 O3 Kokpekty Kazakhstan U.S.S.R. 48.47N 82.28E
89 G5 Kokri Mali 13.57N 5.32W
113 K4 Kokrines Alaska 64.58N 154.40W
113 K4 Kokrines Hills Alaska
21 D8 Koksan N Korea 38.45N 126.40E
43 J5 Koksaray Kazakhstan U.S.S.R. 42.34N 68.06E
37 G6 Kökse Dağ mt Turkey 39.55N 42.37E
47 L8 Koksengirsor,Oz L Kazakhstan U.S.S.R. 53.02N 71.50E
43 M6 Kokshaal-Tau,Khrebet mts U.S.S.R/Xinjiang Uygur Zizhiqu
47 E5 Kokshen'ga R U.S.S.R.
61 A2 Koksijde Belgium 51.07N 2.38E
50 O9 Koksneset B Jan Mayen I 71.09N 8.10W
97 N6 Koksoak R Quebec
21 D10 Koksŏng S Korea 35.17N 127.18E
45 M8 Koksovyy U.S.S.R. 48.11N 40.39E
95 N6 Kokstad S Africa 30.32S 29.25E
43 N4 Koksu Kazakhstan U.S.S.R. 45.00N 77.40E
43 J6 Koksu Tashkent, Kazakhstan U.S.S.R. 41.31N 68.01E
43 N5 Koktal Kazakhstan U.S.S.R. 44.09N 79.50E
43 K4 Koktas Kazakhstan U.S.S.R. 47.30N 70.57E
43 K6 Kok-Tash Kirgiziya U.S.S.R. 41.08N 72.48E
24 E4 Kök Teke Dawan pass Xinjiang Uygur Zizhiqu China 42.40N 84.04E
Kok-togoy see Fuyun
Koktokay see Fuyun
43 O4 Koktuma Kazakhstan U.S.S.R. 45.33N 81.44E
43 D3 Koktyubek Kazakhstan U.S.S.R. 48.06N 56.47E
20 D10 Kokubu Japan 31.45N 130.45E
20 B2 Kokubunji dist Tōkyō Japan
41 Q5 Kokuora U.S.S.R. 71.33N 144.50E
20 D8 Kokura Japan 33.54N 130.52E
19 B6 Koku, Tanjung C Indonesia 5.30S 121.58E
26 Q2 Kokuvil Sri Lanka 9.42N 80.02E
42 K6 Kokuy U.S.S.R. 52.15N 117.35E
113 H7 Kokwok R Alaska
43 L6 Kok-Yangak Kirgiziya U.S.S.R. 41.04N 73.12E
Kök Yar see Kokyar
24 B7 Kokyar Xinjiang Uygur Zizhiqu China 37.24N 77.15E
37 G6 Kol R Turkey
39 F7 Kol' R U.S.S.R.
92 J5 Kola Tanzania 7.00S 39.00E
47 C2 Kola U.S.S.R. 68.53N 33.01E
15 C6 Kola isld Moluccas Indon
47 C2 Kola R U.S.S.R.
28 F1 Kolab R Orissa India
28 A1 Kolaba dist Maharashtra India
29 J7 Kolabira Orissa India 21.49N 84.14E
31 D7 Kolachi R Pakistan
44 F7 Kolageran Armenia U.S.S.R. 40.55N 44.36E
31 H3 Kolahoi mt Kashmir 34.12N 75.21E
89 D7 Kolahun Liberia 8.24N 10.02W
31 G3 Kolai Pakistan 35.05N 73.08E
19 B6 Kolaka Celebes Indon 4.04S 121.38E
19 L7 Kolambugan Mindanao Philippines 8.08N 123.58E
13 K6 Kolan R Queensland
25 E9 Ko Lanta isld Thailand 7.30N 99.00E
Kola Peninsula see Kol'skiy Poluostrov pen
30 A2 Kolar Himachal Prad India 30.30N 77.24E
28 D4 Kolar Karnataka India 13.10N 78.10E
28 C4 Kolar dist Karnataka India
30 A7 Kolaras Madhya Prad India 25.14N 77.36E
28 D4 Kolar Gold Fields Karnataka India 12.54N 78.16E
51 K4 Kolari Finland 67.22N 23.50E
30 A6 Kolari Rajasthan India 26.53N 77.49E
82 K7 Kolarovgrad Bulgaria 43.16N 26.55E
44 E8 Kolarovka Ukraine U.S.S.R. 46.52N 36.20E
62 K8 Kolárovo Czechoslovakia 47.55N 17.58E
53 U14 Kolås Norway 62.14N 6.18E
52 G3 Kolåsen Sweden 63.45N 13.00E
82 F8 Kolašin Yugoslavia 42.50N 19.31E
53 U14 Kolåstind mt Norway 62.16N 6.20E
29 C4 Kolayat Rajasthan India 27.56N 73.02E
40 C4 Kolbachi U.S.S.R. 54.24N 123.03E
52 J7 Kolbäck Sweden 59.33N 16.15E
19 D9 Kolbano Timor Indon 10.02S 124.31E
50 F3 Kolbeinsdalur V Iceland
50 C5 Kolbeinsstadhir Iceland 64.48N 22.16W
Kolberg see Kołobrzeg
64 N8 Kolbermoor W Germany 47.50N 12.04E
93 N7 Kolbio Kenya 1.09S 41.14E
65 H8 Kolbnitz Austria 46.53N 13.19E
52 E4 Kolbotn Norway 62.15N 10.24E
52 F6 Kolbu Norway 60.38N 10.41E
62 N5 Kolbuszowa Poland 50.15N 21.46E
53 F5 Kolby Denmark 55.48N 10.34E
53 F5 Kolby Kås Denmark 55.48N 10.33E
45 L1 Kol'chugino U.S.S.R. 56.17N 39.23E
89 B5 Kolda Senegal 12.56N 14.55W
53 B3 Koldby Denmark 56.49N 8.32E
95 K9 Kol,De S Africa 33.38S 26.19E
53 C6 Kolding Denmark 55.29N 9.30E
53 D6 Kolding Fjord inlet Denmark 55.29N 9.31E
50 H5 Koldukvislarjökull ice cap Iceland 64.34N 17.50W
45 W4 Koldyban' U.S.S.R. 52.44N 50.01E
91 F4 Kole Zaïre 1.41S 18.21E
91 H5 Kole Zaïre 3.30S 22.28E
91 J2 Kole Zaïre 2.08N 25.25E
88 P3 Koléa Algeria 36.42N 2.46E
114 E6 Kolekole pk Hawaiian Is 20.42N 156.16W
89 D6 Kolen Guinea 11.00N 11.42W
40 J5 Kolendo Sakhalin U.S.S.R. 53.54N 142.59E
46 G6 Kolesnoye Ukraine U.S.S.R. 46.05N 29.55E
64 Q3 Kolešovice Czechoslovakia 50.09N 13.37E
39 E1 Kolesovo U.S.S.R. 70.54N 151.44E
39 E1 Kolesovskiye Ostrova islds U.S.S.R.
42 D4 Koleul U.S.S.R. 56.33N 87.20E
15 E7 Kolff,Tandjung C Irian Jaya 7.23S 138.28E
50 M5 Kolfreyjustadhur Iceland 64.56N 13.49W
46 F1 Kolga Laht B Estonia U.S.S.R.
50 B5 Kolgrafafjördhur B Iceland
45 R5 Kolgrivovka U.S.S.R. 51.45N 45.20E
47 F2 Kolguyev, Ostrov isld U.S.S.R.
29 J6 Kolhan reg Bihar India
28 B2 Kolhapur Maharashtra India 16.40N 74.20E
28 B2 Kolhapur dist Maharashtra India
60 H8 Kolhorn Netherlands 52.47N 4.53E
30 G5 Kolhui Uttar Prad India 27.19N 83.19E
51 O8 Koli Finland 63.07N 29.50E
93 D3 Koli R Uganda
82 L5 Kolibash U.S.S.R. 45.43N 28.11E
25 E9 Ko Libong isld Thailand 7.16N 99.20E
113 J7 Koliganek Alaska 59.49N 157.25W
42 B2 Kolik'yegan U.S.S.R. 61.47N 79.08E
42 B2 Kolik'yegan R U.S.S.R.
84 V17 Kolimbia Rhodes 36.15N 28.10E
65 M1 Kolín Czechoslovakia 50.02N 15.11E
110 Q2 Kolin Montana 47.06N 109.45W
53 F4 Kolind Denmark 56.22N 10.37E
53 F4 Kolindsund depression Denmark 56.52N 10.45E
64 P5 Kolinec Czechoslovakia 49.18N 13.27E
84 B6 Koliri Greece 37.41N 21.29E
93 F4 Koliri Uganda 1.19N 34.11E
87 G7 Kolito Ethiopia 7.18N 38.10E
53 C4 Kølkær Denmark 56.04N 9.05E
46 E1 Kolkas rags C Latvia U.S.S.R. 57.43N 22.38E
43 J7 Kolkhozabad Tadzhikistan U.S.S.R. 37.40N 68.43E
46 F4 Kolki Ukraine U.S.S.R. 51.09N 25.40E
63 T7 Kol. Kienitz E Germany 52.51N 13.32E
50 F3 Kolkuós Iceland 65.50N 19.21W
50 F4 Kolkuskull Iceland 65.11N 19.43W
50 C3 Kollabudhir Iceland 65.37N 22.03W
50 D3 Kollafjardharnes Iceland 65.38N 21.22W
50 C3 Kollafjördhur B Bardhastrandarsýsla, Austur Iceland
50 D6 Kollafjördhur B Kjósarsýsla Iceland
28 C5 Kollangod Kerala India 10.36N 76.43E
50 K2 Kollavík inlet Iceland
53 W14 Kollbeinvatn L Norway 62.02N 7.21E
64 L1 Kölleda E Germany 51.12N 11.15E
53 N9 Kollefjord Faeroes 62.08N 6.54W
28 C4 Kollegal Karnataka India 12.08N 77.06E
28 E2 Kolleru L Andhra Prad India
66 J2 Kölliken Switzerland 47.20N 8.01E
84 D7 Kollínai Greece 37.17N 22.21E
50 J4 Kollóttadyngja mt Iceland 65.13N 16.35W
50 A3 Kollsvík Iceland 65.37N 24.17W
60 N6 Kollum Netherlands 53.17N 6.09E
60 N6 Kollumerpomp Netherlands 53.18N 6.12W
50 L3 Kollumúli headland Iceland 65.48N 14.18W
53 C4 Kollund Ringkøbing Denmark 56.06N 9.02E
53 C7 Kollund Sønderjylland Denmark 54.51N 9.28E
94 C6 Kolmanskop Namibia 26.40S 15.12W
42 E3 Kolmogorovo U.S.S.R. 59.15N 91.17E
61 M3 Kolmont Belgium 50.48N 5.25E
65 G7 Kolm Saigurn Austria 47.04N 12.59E
37 G5 Kölmürlü Turkey 40.43N 42.17E
64 B2 Köln W Germany 50.56N 6.57E
62 N2 Kolno Poland 53.26N 21.58E
114 C5 Kolo Hawaiian Is 21.06N 157.11W
62 L3 Koło Poland 52.12N 18.37E
93 G10 Kolo Tanzania 4.45S 35.49E
91 D6 Kolo Zaïre 5.30S 14.42E
91 K7 Kolo Zaïre 7.26S 26.46E
114 F4 Koloa Hawaiian Is 21.54N 159.28W
114 E4 Koloa dist Hawaiian Is
9 S12 Koloa isld Tonga, Pacific Oc 18.38S 173.56W
45 R8 Kolobovka U.S.S.R. 48.40N 45.30E
62 J1 Kołobrzeg Poland 54.10N 15.35E
63 S9 Kolochau E Germany 51.44N 13.19E
45 D2 Kolodnya U.S.S.R. 54.49N 32.10E
87 C5 Kologi Sudan 10.51N 30.59E
89 F6 Kologo Mali 11.12N 7.29W
46 N1 Kologriv U.S.S.R. 58.49N 44.19E
89 E5 Kolokani Mali 13.35N 8.01W
84 N11 Kolokithiá Crete 35.16N 25.45E
40 M8 Kolokol vol Kuril Is U.S.S.R. 46.03N 150.04E
47 G2 Kolokolkova Guba gulf U.S.S.R.
19 B4 Kololio Indonesia 0.10S 121.40E
87 H7 Kololo Ethiopia 7.29N 41.58E
45 G7 Kolomak Ukraine U.S.S.R. 49.49N 35.19E
15 K2 Kolombangara I Solomon Is 8.00S 157.10E
42 C3 Kolominskiye U.S.S.R. 57.50N 83.15E
45 K1 Kolomna U.S.S.R. 55.05N 38.45E
46 E5 Kolomyya Ukraine U.S.S.R. 48.31N 25.00E
89 F6 Kolondiéba Mali 10.52N 6.50W
13 K6 Kolonga Queensland 24.48S 151.45E
9 S10 Kolonga Tonga, Pacific Oc 21.07S 175.05W
19 E1 Kolongana Indonesia 4.02N 126.39E
84 P15 Koloni Cyprus 34.45N 32.28E
89 G5 Koloni Mali 12.48N 5.17W
89 G5 Kolonkan Mali 13.01N 4.17W
94 G6 Kolonkwanen Botswana 26.38S 22.00E
26 S9 Kolonne Sri Lanka 6.24N 80.41E
19 B5 Kolono Celebes Indonesia 2.40S 122.00E
19 C6 Kolono Celebes Indonesia 4.17S 122.43E
19 B4 Kolonodale Celebes Indonesia 1.59S 121.20E
19 F3 Kolorai isld Moluccas Indonesia 1.40N 128.03E
25 K9 Kolosib Assam India 24.14N 92.41E
47 L7 Kolosovka U.S.S.R. 56.30N 73.35E
84 Q15 Kolossi ruins Cyprus 34.40N 32.56E
93 K6 Kolotea Kenya 0.31S 38.46E
9 R10 Kolovai Tonga, Pacific Oc 21.05S 175.20W
64 P5 Koloveč Czechoslovakia 49.30N 13.07E
46 Q4 Kolovertnyy Kazakhstan U.S.S.R. 50.31N 51.08E
93 G4 Kolowa Kenya 1.11N 35.44E
39 E1 Koloyka U.S.S.R. 69.12N 153.29E
47 C2 Kolozero,Oz L U.S.S.R.
Kolozsvar see Cluj
46 K1 Kolp' R U.S.S.R.
39 F7 Kolpakova R U.S.S.R.
42 C3 Kolpashevo U.S.S.R. 58.21N 82.59E
51 P12 Kolpino U.S.S.R. 59.44N 30.39E
63 R5 Kölpin-see L E Germany
45 J4 Kolpny U.S.S.R. 52.15N 37.02E
31 D6 Kolpur Pakistan 29.55N 67.08E
63 Q10 Kölsa E Germany 51.29N 12.15E
52 H4 Kolsätt Sweden 62.02N 14.45E
47 C2 Kol'skiy, Poluostrov pen U.S.S.R.
47 C2 Kol'skiy Zaliv B U.S.S.R.
95 H5 Kolskop mt S Africa 29.15S 24.26E
53 F6 Kølstrup Denmark 55.26N 10.36E
53 N10 Kolter Faeroes 61.59N 6.58W
53 N10 Kolter isld Faeroes 61.59N 6.58W
45 Q4 Koltovskaya U.S.S.R. 52.46N 44.16E
47 M4 Kol'tsovo U.S.S.R. 56.44N 60.48E
46 Q3 Koltubanovskiy U.S.S.R. 53.00N 52.00E
Koltur see Kolter
30 K6 Koluahi Bihar India 26.28N 86.04E
82 F6 Kolubara R Yugoslavia
121 L6 Koluel Kayké Argentina 46.40S 68.18W
Kölük see Kâhta
36 F4 Kolukısa Turkey 38.32N 32.17E
27 L9 Kolumadulu Atoll Maldives, Ind Oc 2.25N 73.10E
29 G8 Kolur Madhya Prad India 19.55N 81.11E
45 M8 Kolushkino U.S.S.R. 48.38N 40.54E
62 M4 Koluszki Poland 51.44N 19.50E
43 J2 Koluton Kazakhstan U.S.S.R. 51.45N 69.45E
47 H3 Kolva R Komi U.S.S.R.
47 H5 Kolva R Perm U.S.S.R.
28 A1 Kolvan Maharashtra India 18.36N 73.35E
52 F2 Kolvereid Norway 64.53N 11.35E
51 L1 Kolvik Norway 70.16N 25.01E
47 C3 Kolvitsa U.S.S.R. 67.02N 33.12E
51 R4 Kolvitskoye,Ozero L U.S.S.R. 67.05N 33.25E
31 C7 Kolwa reg Pakistan
91 J9 Kolwezi Zaïre 10.45S 25.25E
28 A2 Kolya R Maharashtra India
45 L3 Kolybel'skoye U.S.S.R. 53.07N 39.55E
45 K1 Kolyberovo U.S.S.R. 55.16N 38.45E
39 F1 Kolyma R U.S.S.R.
39 F1 Kolymskaya U.S.S.R. 68.50N 158.35E
39 H2 Kolymskaya mt U.S.S.R. 66.26N 166.18E
39 E1 Kolymskaya Nizmennost' lowland U.S.S.R.
39 F4 Kolymskiy,Khrebet ra U.S.S.R.
39 D1 Kolymskiy Perevoz U.S.S.R. 68.26N 146.15E
45 Q4 Kolyshley U.S.S.R. 52.42N 44.32E
45 H1 Kolyubakino U.S.S.R. 55.39N 36.31E
39 K2 Kolyuchaya,Gora mt U.S.S.R. 66.39N 175.16E
39 M2 Kolyuchin,Ostrov isld U.S.S.R. 67.28N 174.25W
39 M2 Kolyuchinskaya Guba gulf U.S.S.R.
42 C6 Kolyvan' Altay U.S.S.R. 51.16N 82.31E
42 C4 Kolyvan' Novosibirsk U.S.S.R. 55.19N 82.45E
82 H7 Kom mt Bulgaria 43.09N 23.02E
91 B2 Kom R Cameroon etc
25 E5 Koma Burma 15.37N 98.13E
87 F6 Koma Ethiopia 8.29N 36.50E
42 E4 Koma U.S.S.R. 55.05N 91.24E
90 F5 Komadougou Yobe R Niger/Nigeria
90 E5 Komadugu Gana R Nigeria
20 C3 Komae dist Tōkyō Japan
20 L6 Komagane Japan 35.44N 137.54E
20 K2 Komaga-take mt Japan 42.05N 140.41E
20 N4 Komaga-take pk Japan 37.04N 139.20E
51 K1 Komagfjord Norway 70.15N 23.20E
94 D7 Komaggas Mts S Africa
31 D3 Komaghai Afghanistan 34.28N 66.29E
51 P1 Komagvær Norway 70.15N 30.34E
93 A4 Komanda Zaïre 1.25N 29.43E
39 H6 Komandorskiye Ostrova islds U.S.S.R.
45 H9 Komar Ukraine U.S.S.R. 47.59N 36.47E
45 F4 Komarichi U.S.S.R. 52.24N 34.50E
42 C6 Komarikha Altay U.S.S.R. 51.58N 82.45E
47 H6 Komarikha Perm U.S.S.R. 58.10N 57.18E
45 B5 Komarin Belorussiya U.S.S.R. 51.25N 30.25E
62 L8 Komárno Czechoslovakia 47.46N 18.05E
100 U8 Komarno Manitoba 50.30N 97.18W
39 F1 Komarok U.S.S.R. 68.18N 157.40E
62 L8 Komárom Hungary 47.43N 18.06E
82 E3 Komárom co Hungary
45 D5 Komarovka Ukraine U.S.S.R. 51.14N 32.08E
47 B5 Komarovo U.S.S.R. 60.11N 29.48E
42 B2 Komarovy U.S.S.R. 60.24N 75.53E
91 D2 Komaso Cent Afr Rep 3.43N 15.58E
95 O1 Komati R S Africa
94 L5 Komati Poort S Africa 25.25S 31.55E
111 M8 Komatke Arizona 33.17N 112.09W
87 E7 Komaton Ethiopia 7.44N 34.23E
84 T14 Koma tou Yialou Cyprus 35.25N 34.10E
20 K5 Komatsu Ishikawa Japan 36.25N 136.27E
20 O3 Komatsu Yamagata Japan 38.01N 140.01E
20 H8 Komatsushima Japan 34.00N 134.36E
20 D3 Komazawa Olympic Park Tōkyō Japan
91 J2 Komba Zaïre 2.52N 24.03E
19 C7 Komba isld Indonesia 7.48S 123.38E
92 E4 Kombe Tanzania 5.05S 31.34E
91 J6 Kombe Zaïre 4.17S 24.59E
89 D7 Kombile Sierra Leone 9.46N 11.09W
89 J5 Kombissiguiri Upper Volta 12.01N 1.27W
90 G8 Kombo Cameroon 6.25N 14.43E
90 E6 Kombo Nigeria 10.05N 11.51E
Kombolchia see Kembolcha
84 B3 Kombóti Greece 39.06N 21.05E
87 J6 Kombulcha Ethiopia 9.26N 42.06E
28 K1 Komdi mt Assam India 28.42N 95.12E
53 E3 Komdrup Denmark 56.54N 10.06E
19 N2 Komebail L Palau Is Pacific Oc
93 D8 Kome I Tanzania
93 D6 Kome I Uganda 0.05S 32.48E
85 M7 Kôm el Ahmar Egypt 25.03N 32.43E
41 O8 Komelek U.S.S.R. 64.59N 133.00E
86 F3 Kôm el Tawil,El Egypt 31.13N 31.05E
35 B1 Komemiyut dist Jerusalem
79 P3 Komen Yugoslavia 45.49N 13.45E
84 B3 Koméno Greece 39.03N 21.02E
89 F4 Komentibougou Mali 14.24N 6.18W
94 G5 Kome Pan Botswana 24.20S 22.45E
18 F7 Komering R Sumatra Indon
91 K8 Komeshia Zaïre 8.00S 27.04E
15 C6 Komfane Moluccas Indonesia 5.40S 134.48E
95 L8 Komga S Africa 32.35S 27.55E
86 E4 Kôm Hamâda Egypt 30.46N 30.41E
38 E2 Komi A.S.S.R U.S.S.R.
84 T14 Komi Kebir Cyprus 35.24N 34.00E
84 A4 Komilio Greece 38.43N 20.36E
90 C8 Kominio Nigeria 7.15N 6.28E
43 E5 Komintern Uzbekistan U.S.S.R. 43.16N 58.38E
45 B10 Kominternovskoye Ukraine U.S.S.R. 46.50N 30.57E
89 K6 Komin Yanga Upper Volta 11.46N 0.06E
86 D3 Kôm Ishu Egypt 31.06N 30.01E
45 O9 Komissarovskiy U.S.S.R. 47.30N 42.58E
80 O2 Komiža Yugoslavia 43.03N 16.11E
62 L7 Komjatice Czechoslovakia 48.10N 18.10E
82 E4 Komló Hungary 46.11N 18.15E
95 J9 Kommadagga S Africa 33.10S 25.55E
95 K3 Kommandodrif S Africa 27.29S 26.15E
95 F9 Kommandokraal S Africa 33.08S 22.52E
95 M4 Kommandonek S Africa 28.48S 28.01E
60 M12 Kommerdijk Netherlands 51.51N 5.54E
60 O6 Kommerzijl Netherlands 53.17N 6.20E
95 B10 Kommetjie S Africa 34.09S 18.20E
95 L5 Kommissiepoort S Africa 29.20S 27.17E
43 F7 Kommuna Turkmeniya U.S.S.R. 37.32N 60.30E
42 J6 Kommunal'naya U.S.S.R. 52.02N 115.10E
42 D5 Kommunar U.S.S.R. 54.23N 89.22E
41 E6 Kommunarka U.S.S.R. 69.37N 86.58E
45 K8 Kommunarsk Ukraine U.S.S.R. 48.30N 38.47E
39 K3 Kommunist U.S.S.R. 63.16N 179.06E
43 K7 Kommunizma,Pik mt Tadzhikistan U.S.S.R. 38.59N 72.01E
84 E4 Kómnina Greece 38.45N 22.41E
15 G7 Komo Papua New Guinea 6.15S 143.02E
91 B3 Komo R Gabon
19 A8 Komodo isld Indonesia
89 H7 Komoe, Parc National de la Ivory Coast
89 H9 Komoé, R Ivory Coast
85 M7 Kom Ombo Egypt 24.26N 32.57E
91 C5 Komono Congo 3.15S 13.14E
15 E7 Komoran isld Irian Jaya
20 M5 Komoro Japan 36.20N 138.26E
83 G3 Komotiní Greece 41.06N 25.25E
89 G4 Komou Mali 15.50N 4.09W
82 F8 Komovi mt Yugoslavia 42.51N 19.38E
45 D8 Kompaneyevka Ukraine U.S.S.R. 48.15N 32.30E
95 H9 Kompanjiesdrif S Africa 33.53S 24.05E
95 H7 Kompasberg mt S Africa 31.45S 24.32E
15 G6 Kompiam Papua New Guinea 5.23S 143.56E
25 H7 Kompong Cham Cambodia 11.59N 105.26E
25 H6 Kompong Chhnang Cambodia 12.16N 104.39E
25 H6 Kompong Kleang Cambodia 13.07N 104.08E
25 G7 Kompong Som Cambodia 11.03N 103.41E
25 G7 Kompong Som Cambodia 10.38N 103.28E
25 G7 Kompong Som,B.de Cambodia
25 H7 Kompong Speu Cambodia 11.25N 104.32E
25 H6 Kompong Thma Cambodia 12.25N 105.08E
25 H6 Kompong Thom Cambodia 12.42N 104.52E
25 H6 Kompong Trabek Cambodia 13.07N 105.17E
25 H7 Kompong Trabek Cambodia 11.09N 105.29E
25 H7 Kompong Trach Cambodia 10.35N 104.27E
25 H7 Kompong Trach Cambodia 11.25N 105.48E
25 H7 Kompong Tralach Cambodia 11.55N 104.46E
19 D3 Kompot Celebes Indon 0.25N 124.09E
46 G6 Komrat Moldavia U.S.S.R. 46.18N 28.40E
40 J6 Komrvo Sakhalin U.S.S.R. 51.07N 143.33E
42 D2 Komsa U.S.S.R. 61.54N 89.18E
95 D8 Komsberg S Africa 32.41S 20.46E
95 D8 Komsbergeskarp mts S Africa
44 L2 Komsomolets, Zaliv B U.S.S.R.
43 J7 Komsomolabad Tadzhikistan U.S.S.R. 39.52N 69.58E
43 F1 Komsomolets Kazakhstan U.S.S.R. 53.47N 62.01E
41 F1 Komsomolets,Ostrov isld U.S.S.R.
43 C4 Komsomolets,Zaliv gulf Kazakhstan U.S.S.R.
46 M2 Komsomol'sk Ivanovo U.S.S.R. 57.00N 40.20E
42 D4 Komsomol'sk Kemerovo U.S.S.R. 55.42N 88.13E
43 G7 Komsomol'sk Turkmeniya U.S.S.R. 39.01N 63.34E
45 E7 Komsomol'sk Ukraine U.S.S.R. 49.01N 33.38E
42 D4 Komsomol'sk U.S.S.R. 57.24N 86.00E
44 G2 Komsomol'skiy Kalmyk A.S.S.R. U.S.S.R. 45.23N 46.00E
43 C4 Komsomol'skiy Kazakhstan U.S.S.R. 47.16N 53.44E
47 J2 Komsomol'skiy Komi U.S.S.R. 67.32N 63.58E
39 J1 Komsomol'skiy Magadan U.S.S.R. 69.11N 172.42E
45 R2 Komsomol'skiy Mordovian A.S.S.R. U.S.S.R. 54.20N 45.49E
47 J5 Komsomol'skiy Tyumen U.S.S.R. 61.21N 63.18E
40 G6 Komsomol'sk-na-Amure U.S.S.R. 50.32N 136.59E
43 E5 Komsomol'sk-na-Ustyurte Uzbekistan U.S.S.R. 44.01N 58.15E
42 J3 Komsomol'sko-Melodezhnyy U.S.S.R. 57.46N 112.39E
42 J5 Komsomol'skoye Buryat U.S.S.R. 52.30N 111.02E
45 T1 Komsomol'skoye Cheboksary U.S.S.R. 55.16N 47.32E
45 K9 Komsomol'skoye Donetsk, Ukraine U.S.S.R. 47.40N 38.05E
45 H7 Komsomol'skoye Khar'kov U.S.S.R. 49.36N 36.32E
45 T6 Komsomol'skoye Saratov U.S.S.R. 50.46N 47.05E
41 J3 Komsomol'skoy Pravdy,Ostrova,Is U.S.S.R.
95 L4 Komspruit S Africa 28.01S 27.43E
90 N9 Komu R Cent Afr Rep
39 D2 Komunyuakhe R U.S.S.R.
37 B3 Kömür Burun C Gökçeada Turkey 40.10N 25.41E
111 M10 Kom Vo Arizona 31.57N 112.21W
41 O7 Komyatinova U.S.S.R. 66.00N 130.05E
45 E6 Komyshnya Ukraine U.S.S.R. 50.10N 33.42E
29 H5 Kon Uttar Prad India 24.22N 83.22E
28 F1 Konada Andhra Prad India 18.02N 83.41E
44 J6 Konakhkend Azerbaydzhan U.S.S.R. 41.04N 48.36E
84 D8 Konákia Greece 36.45N 22.28E
46 K2 Konakovo U.S.S.R. 56.40N 36.50E
36 C3 Konakpınar Balikesir Turkey 39.24N 27.49E
Konakpınar Sivas see Karatoruk
20 D5 Kōnan dist Yokohama Japan
91 C4 Konanadembe Gabon 1.24S 12.26E
31 F3 Konar prov Afghanistan
29 J1 Konar Res Bihar India
32 D6 Konār Takhteh Iran 29.24N 51.18E
109 O7 Konawa Oklahoma 34.58N 96.47W
82 D5 Končanica Yugoslavia 45.40N 17.10E
Konche Darya R see Konqi He
42 J5 Konda R Buryat U.S.S.R.
47 J6 Konda R Tyumen U.S.S.R.
29 G8 Kondagaon Madhya Prad India 19.35N 81.42E
28 F1 Kondakamberu Orissa India 18.07N 82.15E
39 F1 Kondakova U.S.S.R. 68.04N 157.28E
39 E1 Kondakovo U.S.S.R. 69.38N 152.00E
42 E3 Kondakovskiy U.S.S.R. 57.59N 94.14E
39 D1 Kondakovskiye Gory mts U.S.S.R.
28 C1 Kondalwadi Maharashtra India 18.50N 77.44E
28 E2 Kondapalle Andhra Prad India 16.38N 80.36E
28 E2 Kondavid Andhra Prad India 16.17N 80.16E
89 D7 Kondembaia Sierra Leone 9.27N 11.38W
84 R14 Kondemenos Cyprus 35.16N 33.07E
99 O6 Kondiaronk,L Quebec
14 C10 Kondinin W Australia 32.33S 118.13E
47 K5 Kondinskiy Sor L U.S.S.R.
47 K6 Kondinskoye U.S.S.R. 59.38N 67.25E
92 G4 Kondoa Tanzania 4.54S 35.46E
45 R4 Kondol' U.S.S.R. 52.49N 45.02E
91 K3 Kondolole Zaïre 1.22N 26.02E
40 G6 Kondon U.S.S.R. 51.16N 136.31E
47 C5 Kondopoga U.S.S.R. 62.12N 34.17E
32 H3 Kondor Iran 35.13N 58.08E
62 M9 Kondoros Hungary 46.45N 20.49E
84 E6 Kondóstavlos Greece 37.49N 22.45E
84 C6 Kondovázaina Greece 37.48N 21.54E
42 H2 Kondrat'yeva U.S.S.R. 61.55N 109.25E
42 F4 Kondrat'yevo U.S.S.R. 57.22N 98.15E
45 P2 Kondrovka U.S.S.R. 54.38N 43.18E
45 G2 Kondrovo U.S.S.R. 54.50N 35.51E
90 F6 Konduga Nigeria 11.40N 13.30E
45 W3 Kondurcha R U.S.S.R.
93 H10 Kondusi Tanzania 4.40S 36.08E
14 B9 Kondut W Australia 30.44S 117.06E
42 E3 Konduyak U.S.S.R. 59.14N 94.08E
9 B13 Kone New Caledonia 21.04S 164.50E
89 C7 Konebomby I Guinea 9.58N 13.45W
30 H3 Koner Nepal 27.52N 86.45E
39 L2 Konergino U.S.S.R. 65.56N 178.45W
47 H4 Konetsbor U.S.S.R. 64.55N 57.46E
47 D5 Konevo Arkhangel'sk U.S.S.R. 62.09N 39.22E
47 N4 Konevo Sverdlovsk U.S.S.R. 57.29N 60.41E
44 J1 Konevskiy Oseredok,O isld Kazakhstan U.S.S.R.
53 H6 Køng Denmark 55.05N 11.40E
89 G7 Kong Ivory Coast 9.10N 4.33W
15 J2 Konga Bougainville I Papua New Guinea 6.40S 155.32E
11 F8 Kongahue Pt New Zealand 41.28S 171.59E
113 Q2 Kongakut R Alaska
21 D12 Kongan Amami Guntō Japan 27.58N 129.00E
19 M3 Kongauru isld Palau Is Pacific Oc 7.04N 134.17E
48 T13 Kong Christian IX Land Greenland
48 T10 Kong Christian X Land Greenland
53 B6 Kongeå R Denmark
53 K5 Kongens Lyngby Denmark 55.47N 12.32E
53 D3 Kongens Tisted Denmark 56.45N 9.37E
97 P5 Kong Frederik den VI Kyst coast Greenland
48 U4 Kong Frederik V111 Land Greenland
51 M9 Konginkangas Finland 62.48N 25.40E
39 F3 Konginskiye Gory mts U.S.S.R.
21 D9 Kongju S Korea 36.28N 127.03E
Kongka Dzong see Gonggar
50 V13 Kong Karls Land islds Spitsbergen
18 M5 Kong Kat hill Borneo Indon 0.59N 116.40E
18 M5 Kongkemul mt Borneo Indon 1.55N 116.04E
19 B5 Kongkong R Celebes Indon
23 A5 Konglu Burma 27.14N 97.59E
94 G1 Kongola Namibia 17.45S 23.20E
91 K6 Kongolo Zaïre 5.20S 27.00E
87 C7 Kongor Sudan 7.09N 31.21E
48 U10 Kong Oscars Fjord Greenland
89 J5 Kongoussi Upper Volta 13.19N 1.31W
24 D10 Kongque He R Xizang Zizhiqu China
51 F3 Kongsbakktind mt Norway 68.20N 17.20E
52 E7 Kongsberg Norway 59.42N 9.39E
39 E1 Kongsey U.S.S.R. 67.53N 151.12E
51 O1 Kongsfjord Norway 70.42N 29.15E
50 S14 Kongsfjorden inlet Spitsbergen
53 B6 Kongsmark Denmark 55.08N 8.33E
52 G2 Kongsmoen Norway 64.53N 12.26E
50 V14 Kongsøya isld Spitsbergen 78.55N 29.00E
51 O1 Kongsøyfjord inlet Norway 70.43N 29.30E
53 J6 Kongsted Denmark 55.15N 12.03E
52 G6 Kongsvinger Norway 60.13N 11.59E
15 F7 Kongun, L Papua New Guinea
24 B6 Kongur Shan mt pk Xinjiang Uygur Zizhiqu China 38.35N 75.20E
92 H5 Kongwa Tanzania 6.13S 36.28E
119 J5 Kong Waruk R Guyana
48 U8 Kong Wilhelms Land Greenland
91 K9 Koni Zaïre 10.41S 27.14E
89 D4 Koniakar Mali 14.35N 10.51E
84 D2 Koniatsi Greece 39.50N 22.06E
65 P2 Konice Czechoslovakia 49.35N 16.55E
62 M5 Koniecpol Poland 50.46N 19.40E
64 H4 Königheim W Germany 49.37N 9.35E
64 F6 Königsbach W Germany 48.58N 8.37E
Königsberg U.S.S.R.see Kaliningrad
64 D4 Königsberg mt W Germany 49.35N 7.33E
64 K3 Königsberg in Bayern W Germany 50.05N 10.35E
64 J6 Königsbronn W Germany 48.44N 10.07E
63 T10 Königsbrück E Germany 51.16N 13.54E
64 K7 Königsbrunn W Germany 48.14N 10.53E
64 M8 Königsdorf W Germany 47.49N 11.30E
64 L2 Königsee E Germany 50.40N 11.05E
64 E7 Königsfeld Baden-Württemberg W Germany 48.09N 8.26E
64 L4 Königsfeld Bayern W Germany 49.57N 11.06E
Königshofen see Lauda-Königshofen
64 K3 Königshofen im Grabfeld W Germany 50.18N 10.30E
63 N8 Königslutter W Germany 52.15N 10.49E
64 P8 Königssee W Germany 47.35N 13.00E
64 P8 Königssee L W Germany 47.33N 12.59E
63 T3 Königsstuhl mt E Germany 54.34N 13.41E
64 F5 Königsstuhl mt W Germany 49.23N 8.43E
64 M4 Königstein Bayern W Germany 49.36N 11.39E
64 E3 Königstein Hessen W Germany 50.11N 8.28E
65 O5 Königstetten Austria 48.19N 16.08E
65 J8 Königstuhl mt Austria 46.57N 13.47E
65 L5 Königswiesen Austria 48.25N 14.52E
64 C2 Königswinter W Germany 50.41N 7.11E
63 T8 Königs Wusterhausen E Germany 52.18N 13.37E
62 L3 Konin Poland 52.12N 18.12E
40 G5 Konin R U.S.S.R.
60 O10 Koningsbelt mt Netherlands 52.20N 6.25E
61 J2 Koningshooikt Belgium 51.06N 4.37E
11 K7 Konini New Zealand 40.28S 175.45E
61 M3 Koninksem Belgium 50.46N 5.26E
39 E5 Koni Poluostrov pen U.S.S.R.
83 D5 Konispol Albania 39.42N 20.10E
84 H4 Konístrais Greece 38.35N 24.04E
84 A1 Kónitsa Greece 40.03N 20.45E
113 R9 Koniuji I Aleutian Is 52.15N 175.10W
21 D12 Koniya Japan 28.08N 129.19E
66 F4 Koniz Switzerland 46.56N 7.25E
87 C4 Kon,Jeb mt Sudan 13.11N 31.36E
82 D7 Konjic Yugoslavia 43.40N 17.59E
82 E6 Konjuh mt Yugoslavia 44.18N 18.32E
44 D7 Konka R Ukraine U.S.S.R.
51 J3 Könkämä älv R Sweden/Finland
28 A1 Konkan reg Maharashtra India
94 D6 Konkib watercourse Namibia
94 D6 Konkiep Namibia 26.45S 17.15E
89 H5 Konkisitenga Upper Volta 12.32N 2.18W
91 K9 Konko Zaïre 10.15S 27.27E
89 K6 Konkobiri Benin 11.16N 1.50E
92 C8 Konkola Zambia 12.12S 27.48E
89 C6 Konkoure R Guinea
42 J3 Konkudera U.S.S.R. 57.35N 112.32E
94 F4 Konkwe Pan salt pan Botswana 23.11S 21.08E
90 B6 Konkwesso Nigeria 10.50N 4.04E
89 G4 Konna Mali 14.59N 4.02W
63 P9 Könnern E Germany 51.41N 11.46E
64 N3 Konnersreuth W Germany 50.01N 12.15E
51 M9 Konnevesi Finland 62.35N 26.20E
51 M9 Konnevesi L Finland 62.32N 26.37E
51 O3 Konnostunturi mt Finland/U.S.S.R. 68.45N 28.45E
28 C8 Konnur Tamil Nadu India 13.06N 80.13E
15 M6 Konogaiang,Mt New Ireland 4.07S 152.43E
15 M5 Konogogo New Ireland 3.34S 152.07E
66 G4 Konolfingen Switzerland 46.54N 7.38E
103 K4 Konomoc, L Connecticut 41.25N 72.12W
92 E5 Konongo tribe Tanzania
15 L5 Konos New Ireland 3.09S 151.47E
47 E5 Konosha U.S.S.R. 60.58N 40.08E
41 E7 Konoshchel'ye U.S.S.R. 66.17N 87.17E
20 N5 Kōnosu Japan 36.02N 139.32E
45 E5 Konotop Ukraine U.S.S.R. 51.15N 33.14E
47 K8 Konovalovka Kazakhstan U.S.S.R. 53.40N 67.12E
45 D6 Konovka Ukraine U.S.S.R. 50.11N 32.05E
29 H6 Konpara Madhya Prad India 22.23N 83.55E
25 K5 Kon Plong Vietnam 14.36N 108.23E
24 F5 Konqi He R Xinjiang Uygur Zizhiqu China
19 N1 Konrei Palau Is Pacific Oc 7.44N 134.38E
65 L1 Konřim Czechoslovakia 50.01N 14.59E
89 G5 Konseguela Mali 12.18N 5.47W
62 M4 Końskie Poland 51.12N 20.23E
95 D9 Konstabel S Africa 33.16S 20.17E
84 C7 Konstandínoi Greece 37.16N 21.55E
41 D2 Konstantina,Mys C Novaya Zemlya U.S.S.R. 76.33N 68.57E
39 G1 Konstantinova U.S.S.R. 68.10N 161.03E
40 D7 Konstantinovka Amur U.S.S.R. 49.36N 128.00E
45 J8 Konstantinovka Donetsk, Ukraine U.S.S.R. 48.33N 37.45E
45 G7 Konstantinovka Khar'kov, Ukraine U.S.S.R. 49.57N 35.08E
45 C9 Konstantinovka Nikolayev, Ukraine U.S.S.R. 47.51N 31.07E
45 N9 Konstantinovsk Rostov U.S.S.R. 47.37N 41.08E
45 J1 Konstantinovskiy Moscow U.S.S.R. 55.24N 37.44E
64 G8 Konstanz W Germany 47.40N 9.10E
32 J7 Kont Iran 27.00N 61.57E
90 B6 Kontagora Nigeria 10.24N 5.22E
90 F8 Kontcha Cameroon 7.59N 12.15E
25 D2 Kontha Burma 21.48N 96.47E
61 H2 Kontich Belgium 51.08N 4.27E
51 N7 Kontiomäki Finland 64.21N 28.10E
84 C7 Kontovoúnia mts Greece
113 L6 Kontrashibuna L Alaska 60.12N 154.00W
25 J5 Kontum Vietnam 14.23N 108.00E
25 J6 Kontum,Plat.du Vietnam
36 G2 Konur Turkey 40.10N 33.42E
39 K1 Konus mt U.S.S.R. 67.37N 177.52E
40 E3 Konus,Gora mt U.S.S.R. 57.30N 131.45E
47 E3 Konushinskaya Korga,Mys C U.S.S.R. 67.08N 43.50E
36 F5 Konya Turkey 37.51N 32.30E
37 E2 Konya Liman B Turkey
36 F4 Konya Ovası plat Turkey
90 D9 Konye Cameroon 4.54N 9.30E
45 G5 Konyshevka U.S.S.R. 51.52N 35.17E
43 C3 Konystanu Kazakhstan U.S.S.R. 48.52N 53.14E
43 K1 Konyukhovo Kazakhstan U.S.S.R. 55.08N 70.44E
64 B4 Konz W Germany 49.42N 6.35E
93 J7 Konza Kenya 1.45S 37.07E
39 F1 Konzaboy U.S.S.R. 68.38N 157.58E
64 O5 Konzell W Germany 49.05N 12.44E
47 H6 Konzhakovskiy Kamen',Gora mt U.S.S.R. 59.40N 59.05E
60 H10 Koog aan den Zaan Netherlands 52.28N 4.49E
60 H7 Koog,De Texel Netherlands 53.06N 4.46E
61 D4 Kooigem Belgium 50.44N 3.20E
113 B5 Kookooligit Mts St Lawrence I Bering Sea
14 D8 Kookynie W Australia 29.25S 121.29E
13 F5 Koolamarra Queensland 20.11S 140.08E
14 E3 Koolan I W Australia 16.08S 123.16E
Koolanooka see Bowgada
13 F3 Koolatah Queensland 15.52S 142.29E
13 D2 Koolatong R N Terr Australia
114 B4 Koolauloa dist Hawaiian Is
114 B5 Koolaupoko dist Hawaiian Is
114 B5 Koolau Ra Hawaiian Is
13 G3 Koolburra Queensland 15.17S 144.00E
14 B6 Kooline W Australia 22.58S 116.15E
13 E6 Koolivoo,L Queensland
61 D2 Koolkerke Belgium 51.14N 3.15E
12 E3 Koolkootinnie L S Australia
61 C2 Koolskamp Belgium 51.00N 3.13E
12 E5 Koolunga S Australia 33.37S 138.21E
14 C9 Koolyanobbing W Australia 30.48S 119.29E
14 B10 Koombana B W Australia
12 A4 Koonalda S Australia 31.18S 129.48E
95 K8 Koonap S Africa 32.59S 26.39E
95 K8 Koonap R S Africa
12 G6 Koondrook Victoria 35.39S 144.11E
12 C4 Koonibba S Australia 32.02S 133.30E
39 E5 Koopgorodok U.S.S.R. 59.37N 154.10E
95 H4 Koopmansfontein S Africa 28.15S 24.03E
15 B4 Koör Irian Jaya 0.23S 132.22E
93 H7 Koora Kenya 1.50S 36.23E
12 J5 Koorawatha New S Wales 34.03S 148.34E
13 G3 Koorboora Queensland 17.21S 144.48E
14 B9 Koorda W Australia 30.50S 117.51E
14 B5 Koordarrie W Australia 22.13S 115.03E
20 O4 Koori Japan 37.51N 140.30E
63 S4 Koos isld E Germany 54.11N 13.25E
95 J3 Koosfontein S Africa 27.22S 25.26E
111 N3 Koosharem Utah 38.31N 111.54W
110 J3 Kooskia Idaho 46.09N 116.00W
100 U7 Koostatak Manitoba 51.26N 97.26W
110 K1 Kootenai R Montana
101 P11 Kootenay L Br Col
110 J1 Kootenay Landing Br Col 49.16N 116.41W
101 P10 Kootenay Nat.Park Br Col
101 P11 Kootenay R Br Col/Idaho/Montana
94 F8 Kootjieskolk S Africa 31.15S 20.21E
60 N7 Kootstertille Netherlands 53.13N 6.05E
60 M11 Kootwijk Netherlands 52.11N 5.46E
60 L11 Kootwijkerbroek Netherlands 52.10N 5.40E
89 E7 Koussa Guinea 9.36N 8.25W
113 B5 Koozata Lagoon St Lawrence I Bering Sea 63.20N 170.30W
43 M5 Kopa Kazakhstan U.S.S.R. 43.31N 75.45E
30 G6 Kopaganj Uttar Prad India 26.01N 83.34E
82 L2 Kopai Gorod U.S.S.R. 48.49N 27.50E
84 F5 Kopais dry lake Greece
91 K6 Kopakopa Zaïre 4.08S 27.25E
50 A3 Kópanes C Iceland 65.48N 24.05W
84 A3 Kopáni Greece 39.28N 20.50E
45 D10 Kopani Kherson, Ukraine U.S.S.R. 46.48N 32.15E
44 D7 Kopani Zaporozh'ye, Ukraine U.S.S.R. 47.27N 35.44E
45 S9 Kopanovka U.S.S.R. 47.28N 46.47E
82 F7 Kopaonik mts Yugoslavia
29 D8 Kopargaon Maharashtra India 19.55N 74.32E
29 K7 Kopari Orissa India 21.16N 86.28E
50 J2 Kópasker Iceland 66.18N 16.25W
50 D6 Kópavogur Iceland 64.06N 21.53W
11 B13 Kopeka B Stewart I New Zealand
36 G4 Köpek Gölü L Turkey
36 F1 Köpekkayası Burun C Turkey 41.54N 32.58E
63 T8 Kopenick E Germany 52.27N 13.36E
82 B5 Koper Yugoslavia 45.31N 13.44E
53 S20 Kopervik Norway 59.17N 5.20E
43 D7 Kopet-Dag,Khrebet mts U.S.S.R.
47 M6 Kopeysk U.S.S.R. 55.08N 61.39E
66 M3 Köpfler mt Switzerland 47.07N 8.58E
84 R15 Kophinou Cyprus 34.49N 33.25E
37 J9 Kopī L Iran 36.58N 45.52E
15 G6 Kopiago, L Papua New Guinea 5.24S 142.30E
52 J7 Köping Sweden 59.31N 16.01E
83 C2 Koplikisipërm Albania 42.14N 19.29E
47 M3 Kopna,Gora mt U.S.S.R. 58.18N 59.08E
18 K2 Kopok,Tanjong C Pen Malaysia 1.26N 104.00E
42 C6 Kopolevskiy Belok,Gora mt U.S.S.R. 51.07N 83.46E
19 C8 Kopondei, Tanjung C Indonesia 8.03S 122.52E
46 N3 Kopovka U.S.S.R. 53.32N 43.02E
28 B4 Koppa Karnataka India 13.31N 75.20E
28 C3 Koppal Karnataka India 15.21N 76.09E
52 F5 Koppang Norway 61.34N 11.04E
52 H7 Kopparberg Sweden 59.55N 14.59E
52 G5 Kopparberg dist Sweden
104 E6 Koppel Pennsylvania 40.48N 80.22W
53 M9 Koppenni mt Faeroes 62.14N 7.13W
52 F3 Kopperå Norway 63.24N 11.50E
112 K3 Kopperl Texas 32.04N 97.32W

40 H7 Koppi U.S.S.R. 48.31N 140.08E
40 H7 Koppi R U.S.S.R.
95 L3 Koppies S Africa 27.15S 27.35E
95 L3 Koppiesdam res S Africa 27.15S 27.41E
66 G3 Koppigen Switzerland 47.08N 7.37E
52 G7 Koppom Sweden 59.42N 12.08E
84 B3 Kópraina Greece 39.02N 21.04E
82 D4 Koprivnica Yugoslavia 46.09N 16.50E
82 J8 Koprivshtitsa Bulgaria 42.37N 24.19E
36 E5 Köprü R Turkey
37 E5 Koprübaşı Turkey 40.50N 40.05E
37 G3 Köprühisar Turkey 40.17N 29.46E
36 F6 Köprülü Turkey 36.43N 32.12E
36 D3 Köprüören Turkey 39.29N 29.44E
95 L7 Kopshorn mt S Africa 31.08S 27.35E
84 C3 Kópsi mt Greece 39.05N 21.44E
61 P8 Kopstal Luxembourg 49.40N 6.05E
47 J6 Koptelovo U.S.S.R. 57.45N 61.50E
46 G4 Koptsevichi Belorussiya U.S.S.R. 52.12N 28.14E
51 J13 Köpu Estonia 58.55N 22.12E
11 K4 Kopu New Zealand 37.11S 175.35E
11 K7 Kopuaranga New Zealand 40.50S 175.40E
46 F5 Kopychintsy Ukraine U.S.S.R. 49.10N 25.58E
42 D5 Kop'yevo U.S.S.R. 55.00N 89.46E
42 C3 Kopylovka U.S.S.R. 58.41N 82.24E
45 B2 Kopys Belorussiya U.S.S.R. 54.20N 30.17E
32 E5 Kor R Iran
30 L7 Kora Bihar India 25.37N 87.25E
30 D6 Kora Uttar Prad India 29.06N 80.22E
37 G5 Kora R Kars Turkey
37 E5 Kora R Trabzon Turkey
83 D3 Korab mts Albania
47 E3 Korabelnyy, Mys C U.S.S.R. 66.59N 41.17E
45 M3 Korablino U.S.S.R. 53.54N 40.00E
29 G7 Koracha Madhya Prad India 20.22N 80.41E
25 E8 Ko Ra I Thailand 9.12N 98.20E
31 C7 Korak Pakistan 26.51N 65.48E
19 N2 Korak isld Palau Is Pacific Oc 7.22N 134.36E
36 B4 Koraka Burun C Turkey 38.06N 26.36E
24 E11 Kora La pass Xizang Zizhiqu China 29.01N 86.35E
26 Q8 Koralawella Sri Lanka 6.45N 79.54E
65 L8 Koralpe mt Austria 46.48N 14.59E
24 E7 Koramlik Xinjiang Uygur Zizhiqu China 37.28N 85.40E
82 C5 Korana R Yugoslavia
90 J2 Koranga Chad 19.18N 18.10E
28 C2 Korangal Andhra Prad India 17.07N 77.35E
31 C10 Korangi Pakistan 24.48N 67.08E
95 F3 Korannaberg mts S Africa
94 F7 Koranna Land reg S Africa
15 M6 Korapun New Britain 5.27S 152.04E
28 F1 Koraput Orissa India 18.48N 82.41E
29 H8 Koraput dist Orissa India
Korat see Nakhon Ratchasima
28 D1 Koratla Andhra Prad India 18.51N 78.41E
35 F2 Korazim anc site Israel 32.54N 35.33E
29 H6 Korba Madhya Prad India 22.22N 82.46E
88 T3 Korba Tunisia 36.37N 10.54E
64 F1 Korbach W Germany 51.16N 8.53E
90 H6 Korbal Chad 10.00N 17.42E
61 J3 Korbeek-Dijle Belgium 50.51N 4.39E
61 K3 Korbeek-Lo Belgium 50.52N 4.46E
110 B9 Korbel California 40.54N 123.58W
18 B7 Korbu, Gunong mt Pen Malaysia 4.43N 101.17E
83 D4 Korcë Albania 40.38N 20.44E
42 C5 Korchino U.S.S.R. 53.01N 81.40E
37 D8 Korcik Daïg mts Turkey 37.25N 38.48E
82 D8 Korčula Yugoslavia 42.57N 17.08E
82 D8 Korčula isld Yugoslavia 42.56N 17.05E
42 F2 Korda U.S.S.R. 61.29N 98.10E
64 B4 Kordel W Germany 49.50N 6.38E
32 B3 Kordestān prov Iran
44 H10 Kord Kandī Iran 37.57N 46.55E
32 C3 Kord Khvord Iran 34.32N 49.05E
32 F2 Kord Kūy Iran 36.49N 54.05E
87 B4 Kordofan prov Sudan
42 E5 Kordovo U.S.S.R. 54.10N 93.14E
32 J7 Kords reg Iran
32 E6 Kord Sheykh Iran 28.32N 52.46E
21 C8 Korea B China/Korea
9 K6 Korea, North people's rep Asia
9 K6 Korea, South rep Asia
21 D10 Korea Str Japan/Korea
87 G5 Koreb Ethiopia 11.20N 38.56E
87 F2 Koreb mt Ethiopia 16.48N 37.03E
28 B2 Koregaon Maharashtra India 17.44N 74.16E
93 K5 Koreh Wells Kenya 0.01N 38.44E
45 H2 Korekozevo U.S.S.R. 54.21N 36.12E
50 L3 Kórekstadhir Iceland 65.33N 14.09W
47 C3 Korelaksha U.S.S.R. 65.31N 32.30E
20 C3 Koremasa Tōkyō Japan
45 F5 Korenevo U.S.S.R. 51.23N 34.55E
44 E9 Korenkovo Ukraine U.S.S.R. 45.07N 36.23E
41 J4 Korennoye U.S.S.R. 73.32N 107.20E
44 C2 Korenovsk U.S.S.R. 45.29N 39.28E
91 H3 Koret Zaïre 0.36N 23.23E
46 F4 Korets Ukraine U.S.S.R. 50.39N 27.10E
39 H4 Korf U.S.S.R. 60.18N 165.52E
39 H4 Korfa, Zaliv gulf U.S.S.R.
84 A3 Korfovoúni Greece 39.15N 20.59E
40 G7 Korfovskiy U.S.S.R. 48.20N 135.08E
37 E2 Korga Burun C Turkey 40.58N 27.53E
24 C3 Korgas Xinjiang Uygur Zizhiqu China 44.20N 80.45E
51 D5 Korgen Norway 66.04N 13.50E
89 G7 Korhogo Ivory Coast 9.22N 5.31W
20 D10 Kōri Japan 31.22N 130.28E
119 J4 Koriabo Guyana 7.37N 59.37W
29 A6 Kori Creek Gujarat India
15 C4 Korido Biak I, Irian Jaya 0.46S 135.34E
89 H4 Korienza Mali 15.22N 3.52W
84 C7 Korifásion Greece 37.00N 21.41E
90 C6 Koriga Nigeria 10.47N 6.54E
15 D4 Korim Biak I, Irian Jaya Indonesia 0.55S 136.08E
88 N5 Korima, El watercourse Algeria
32 J6 Korīn Iran 28.52N 60.25E
95 B9 Koringberg S Africa 33.01S 18.40E
95 D8 Koringplaas S Africa 32.49S 20.58E
83 F4 Korinós Greece 40.19N 22.35E
53 E6 Korinth Denmark 55.09N 10.21E
84 D6 Korinthía prov Greece
84 D5 Korinthiakós,Kólpos gulf Greece
84 E6 Kórinthos Greece 37.56N 22.55E
84 H6 Korisía Greece 37.40N 24.19E
82 F8 Koritnik mt Yugoslavia 42.05N 20.33E
Koritsa see Korcë
20 O4 Kōriyama Japan 37.23N 140.22E
45 F5 Korizh U.S.S.R. 51.23N 34.14E
32 G2 Korkī Iran 37.11N 56.32E
31 C7 Korkian Pakistan 27.21N 64.21E
47 M6 Korkino Chelyabinsk U.S.S.R. 54.55N 61.25E
42 H5 Korkino Irkutsk U.S.S.R. 54.22N 105.20E
39 E3 Korkodon U.S.S.R. 64.45N 154.02E
39 F3 Korkodon R U.S.S.R.
36 E5 Korkuteli Turkey 37.07N 30.11E
24 E5 Korla Xinjiang Uygur Zizhiqu China 41.48N 86.10E
42 C2 Korliki U.S.S.R. 61.33N 82.28E
45 B3 Korma Belorussiya U.S.S.R. 53.08N 30.47E
99 H5 Kormak Ontario 47.39N 82.59W
84 R14 Kormakiti Cyprus 35.20N 33.01E
84 Q14 Kormakiti C Cyprus 35.24N 32.55E
65 P7 Körmend Hungary 47.01N 16.36E
47 L7 Kormilovka U.S.S.R. 55.01N 74.09E
34 M3 Kor Mor oil well Iraq 35.04N 44.46E
44 F1 Kormovka U.S.S.R. 46.16N 43.32E
15 H6 Korn Papua New Guinea 5.52S 144.20E
82 C7 Kornat isld Yugoslavia 43.50N 15.20E
64 L5 Kornburg W Germany 49.21N 11.07E
64 A2 Kornelimünster W Germany 50.44N 6.11E
64 K1 Körner E Germany 51.14N 10.35E
46 G6 Korneshty Moldavia U.S.S.R. 47.21N 28.00E
95 L6 Kornetspruit R Lesotho
65 O5 Korneuburg Austria 48.22N 16.20E
43 L2 Korneyevka Karaganda, Kazakhstan U.S.S.R. 50.13N 74.15E
43 J1 Korneyevka Kazakhstan U.S.S.R. 54.01N 68.30E
45 U5 Korneyevka U.S.S.R. 51.42N 48.42E
42 C5 Kornilovo Altay U.S.S.R. 53.31N 81.11E
42 D4 Kornilovo Krasnoyarsk U.S.S.R. 55.37N 89.42E
39 E5 Kornino U.S.S.R. 59.13N 152.20E
84 R15 Kornos Cyprus 34.53N 33.25E
45 V1 Kornoukhovo U.S.S.R. 55.32N 49.52E
52 F8 Kornsjø Norway 58.55N 11.40E
53 C3 Kornum Denmark 56.58N 9.20E
60 K7 Kornwerderzand Netherlands
64 G6 Kornwestheim W Germany 48.52N 9.12E
87 F5 Koro Ethiopia 10.05N 37.57E
89 F7 Koro Ivory Coast 8.36N 7.28W
89 H4 Koro Mali 14.01N 2.57W
94 F2 Koro Namibia 18.04S 20.25E
9 S6 Koro isld Fiji 17.20S 179.25E
19 B4 Koro R Celebes Indon
15 G6 Koroba Papua New Guinea 5.46S 142.48E
43 M3 Korobovskiy Kazakhstan U.S.S.R. 49.35N 75.07E
45 J6 Korocha U.S.S.R. 50.50N 37.13E
36 F2 Köroğlu Tepesi mt Turkey 40.30N 31.53E
87 J8 Korogo Ethiopia 4.59N 43.10E
15 G6 Korogo Papua New Guinea 4.08S 143.11E
92 J4 Korogwe Tanzania 5.10S 38.30E
12 F7 Koroit Victoria 38.17S 142.26E
89 G7 Korokara Ivory Coast 9.53N 5.30W
11 D5 Korokoro New Zealand 41.12S 174.52E
11 D5 Korokoro R New Zealand
42 C4 Korolevka U.S.S.R. 56.02N 83.02E
45 C1 Korolevshchina U.S.S.R. 55.48N 31.45E
9 S8 Korolevu Viti Levu Fiji 17.53S 177.54E
9 S8 Korolevu Viti Levu Fiji 18.15S 177.43E
93 J3 Koroli Desert Kenya
90 J6 Korom watercourse Chad
9 S8 Koromba mt Viti Levu Fiji 17.54S 177.35E
Koromo see Toyota
105 F8 Korona Florida 29.22N 81.12W
93 K3 Korondere locality Kenya 2.58N 38.30E
93 L3 Korondil mt Kenya 2.59N 39.22E
92 G5 Korongo Tanzania 6.29S 34.50E
12 G6 Korong Vale Victoria 36.22S 143.45E
84 C8 Koróni Greece 36.48N 21.57E
84 S14 Koronia Cyprus 35.22N 33.54E
84 E5 Korónia Greece 38.21N 22.58E
83 F4 Korónia, L Greece
62 K2 Koronowo Poland 53.19N 17.55E
45 D5 Korop Ukraine U.S.S.R. 51.34N 32.58E
89 B5 Korope Senegal 13.12N 14.29W
82 J2 Koropets U.S.S.R. 48.55N 25.10E
84 G6 Koropí Greece 37.54N 23.52E
19 N2 Koror Palau Is Pacific Oc 7.21N 134.31E
19 N2 Koror isld Palau Is Pacific Oc
12 B7 Kororoit Cr Victoria
62 M9 Körös R Hungary
15 G6 Korosameri R Papua New Guinea
9 T6 Koro Sea Fiji
90 J1 Korossom watercourse Chad
46 G4 Korosten' Ukraine U.S.S.R. 51.00N 28.30E
47 J2 Korotaikha R U.S.S.R.
9 S5 Korotasere Vanua Levu Fiji 16.35S 179.35E
93 E4 Koroto Uganda 1.58N 33.12E
90 J3 Koro Toro Chad 16.10N 18.30E
45 L6 Korotoyak U.S.S.R. 50.58N 39.12E
45 B4 Korovatichi Belorussiya U.S.S.R. 52.14N 30.04E
84 T14 Korovia Cyprus 35.29N 34.17E
113 R9 Korovin B Aleutian Is
113 G9 Korovin I Alaska 55.26N 160.20W
45 H5 Korovino Kursk U.S.S.R. 51.24N 36.44E
43 C1 Korovino Orenburg U.S.S.R. 53.51N 53.06E
45 E6 Korovintsy Ukraine U.S.S.R. 50.50N 33.45E
113 R9 Korovin Vol Aleutian Is 52.20N 174.10W
45 D2 Korovniki U.S.S.R. 54.55N 32.46E
93 J2 Korowe Kenya 3.06N 37.24E
9 S7 Koroyanitu Viti Levu Fiji 17.40S 177.35E
64 A4 Körperich W Germany 49.55N 6.15E
51 M9 Korpilahti Finland 62.02N 25.34E
51 K5 Korpilombolo Sweden 66.51N 23.00E
51 J11 Korpo Finland 60.10N 21.35E
Korppoo see Korpo
30 K6 Korrapatti Bihar India 26.07N 87.00E
53 X14 Kors Norway 62.26N 7.52E
40 J8 Korsakov Sakhalin U.S.S.R. 46.36N 142.50E
45 J3 Korsakovo U.S.S.R. 53.16N 37.23E
52 J9 Korsberga Sweden 57.17N 15.10E
63 D10 Korschenbroich W Germany 51.21N 6.30E
64 B1 Korschenbroich W Germany 51.12N 6.31E
53 H5 Korshage C Denmark 55.59N 11.48E
82 J2 Korshev U.S.S.R. 48.39N 25.02E
53 E3 Korsholm isld Denmark 56.58N 10.21E
42 J3 Korshunovo U.S.S.R. 58.40N 110.10E
51 J9 Korsnäs Finland 62.47N 21.10E
52 J6 Korsnas Sweden 60.37N 15.50E
51 E3 Korsnes Norway 68.15N 16.04E
53 G6 Korsør Denmark 55.19N 11.09E
53 R16 Korssund Norway 61.15N 5.00E
37 F6 Körsu Turkey 39.35N 41.45E
45 C7 Korsun'-Shevchenkovskiy Ukraine U.S.S.R. 49.26N 31.15E
61 C2 Kortemark Belgium 51.02N 3.03E
61 L3 Kortenaken Belgium 50.54N 5.03E
61 J3 Kortenberg Belgium 50.53N 4.33E
60 J11 Kortenhoef Netherlands 52.13N 5.05E
51 K8 Kortesjärvi Finland 63.19N 23.10E
61 M3 Kortessem Belgium 50.52N 5.23E
52 H7 Kortfors Sweden 59.24N 14.42E
60 C2 Kortgene Netherlands 51.34N 3.48E
87 C1 Korti Sudan 18.06N 31.33E
61 L4 Kortijs Belgium 50.42N 5.09E
24 F1 Korti Linchang Xinjiang Uygur Zizhiqu China 48.13N 87.34E
89 C7 Kortimaw I Sierra Leone 8.58N 13.18W
47 G5 Kortkeros U.S.S.R. 61.49N 51.32E
103 E2 Kortright New York 42.25N 74.47W
61 D3 Kortrijk Belgium 50.50N 3.17E
61 K3 Kortrijk-Dutsel Belgium 50.56N 4.48E
46 M1 Kortsovo U.S.S.R. 58.51N 42.10E
42 E5 Kortuz U.S.S.R. 54.27N 91.38E
37 F3 Koru Bursa Turkey 40.17N 28.56E
93 G6 Koru Kenya 0.10S 35.17E
37 K2 Koru dist İstanbul Turkey 41.02N 29.04E
36 C3 Korucu Turkey 39.27N 27.22E
37 C2 Koru Dağ mt Turkey 40.46N 26.55E
32 H6 Korūk Iran 28.53N 58.29E
12 H7 Korumburra Victoria 38.26S 145.49E
91 C10 Koruteva,Sa mts Angola
51 O3 Korvatunturi mt Finland 68.03N 29.25E
Korvua see Metsäkylä
41 H7 Korvunchana R U.S.S.R.
29 F5 Korwai Madhya Prad India 24.08N 78.01E
51 O4 Korya Karelia U.S.S.R. 67.10N 29.35E
39 H4 Koryakskaya U.S.S.R. 60.38N 169.35E
39 F7 Koryakskaya Sopka vol Kamchatka U.S.S.R. 53.19N 158.41E
39 H4 Koryakskiy Khrebet mts U.S.S.R.
39 H4 Koryakskiy Nats. Okrug dist U.S.S.R.
47 F5 Koryazhma U.S.S.R. 61.18N 47.08E
21 D10 Koryŏng S Korea 35.46N 128.15E
45 D5 Koryukovka Ukraine U.S.S.R. 51.45N 32.15E
45 S2 Korznevka U.S.S.R. 54.11N 46.22E
62 K1 Korzybie Poland 54.18N 16.50E
83 J8 Kos Greece 36.53N 27.19E
83 J8 Kos isld Greece
42 H5 Kosa Buryat U.S.S.R. 54.45N 108.50E
47 G6 Kosa Perm U.S.S.R. 59.58N 54.59E
47 G6 Kosa R U.S.S.R.
43 G2 Kosagal Kazakhstan U.S.S.R. 52.00N 63.00E
43 L4 Kosagash,Mys C Kazakhstan U.S.S.R. 45.58N 73.44E
20 O1 Kosaka Japan 40.21N 140.42E
30 E7 Kosam Uttar Prad India 25.20N 81.24E
25 E8 Ko Samui Thailand 9.26N 99.58E
43 H3 Kosay Kazakhstan U.S.S.R. 48.32N 66.35E
45 J2 Kosaya Gora U.S.S.R. 54.08N 37.33E
42 F3 Kosaya,Shiv falls U.S.S.R. 58.25N 97.47E
43 G6 Kosboget Uzbekistan U.S.S.R. 42.07N 64.41E
43 C4 Koschagyl Kazakhstan U.S.S.R. 46.52N 53.48E
64 M6 Kösching W Germany 48.49N 11.32E
62 K3 Kościan Poland 52.05N 16.38E
62 K1 Kościerzyna Poland 54.08N 17.58E
107 G8 Kosciusko Mississippi 33.02N 89.36W
9 D9 Kosciusko Bank Tuvalu, Pac Oc 10.15S 179.30E
113 V8 Kosciusko I Alaska 56.00N 133.40W
12 J6 Kosciusko,Mt New S Wales 36.28S 148.17E
36 G2 Kös Dağı mt Turkey
37 E5 Köşe Turkey 40.13N 39.39E
36 G6 Köseçobanlı Turkey 37.30N 33.09E
37 D5 Köse Dağı mt Turkey 40.04N 37.57E
63 S10 Koselitz E Germany 51.23N 13.26E
63 U4 Koserow E Germany 54.03N 14.00E
42 C2 Koses R U.S.S.R.
65 M2 Košetice Czechoslovakia 49.33N 15.07E
26 R8 Kosgama Sri Lanka 6.56N 80.09E
28 C2 Kosgi Andhra Prad India 17.01N 77.43E
26 Q9 Kosgoda Sri Lanka 6.32N 80.02E
44 F7 Kosh Armenia U.S.S.R. 40.18N 44.09E
85 L9 Kosha Sudan 20.49N 30.35E
42 D7 Kosh-Agach U.S.S.R. 50.00N 88.44E
47 J6 Koshay U.S.S.R. 59.05N 61.52E
44 C3 Koshekhabl' U.S.S.R. 44.55N 40.28E
40 J7 Koshevoy Sakhalin U.S.S.R. 49.33N 142.50E
31 J1 K'o-Shih-erh-Ts'un Kashmir 35.18N 78.53E
20 K2 Koshikawa Japan 43.53N 144.47E
20 C10 Koshikijima-rettō islds Japan
20 C10 Koshiki-kaikyō str Japan
91 F6 Koshimbanda Zaïre 5.10S 19.51E
31 B3 Koshk Afghanistan 34.57N 62.15E
32 J3 Koshkak Iran 34.55N 60.45E
43 C4 Koshkar Kazakhstan U.S.S.R. 47.28N 53.24E
45 W2 Koshki U.S.S.R. 54.13N 50.29E
47 K2 Koshki isld U.S.S.R.
107 E5 Koshkonong Missouri 36.35N 91.39W
43 F6 Kosh-Kupyr Uzbekistan U.S.S.R. 41.35N 60.18E
43 C6 Koshoba Turkmeniya U.S.S.R. 40.21N 54.31E
20 M5 Koshoku Japan 36.33N 138.09E
43 L6 Koshtëbë Kirgiziya U.S.S.R. 41.06N 74.16E
30 A5 Kosi Uttar Prad India 27.47N 77.25E
30 K7 Kosi R Bihar India
30 C3 Kosi R Uttar Prad India
95 P8 Kosi B S Africa 26.55S 32.54E
62 N7 Košice Czechoslovakia 48.44N 21.15E
30 L6 Kosi Dam Nepal 26.36N 87.03E
30 L6 Kosi Dhar R Bihar India
42 C5 Kosikha U.S.S.R. 53.20N 84.40E
95 P8 Kosi L S Africa 26.59S 32.50E
43 E2 Kos-Istek Kazakhstan U.S.S.R. 50.45N 57.48E
36 C5 Köşk Turkey 37.50N 28.04E
82 E5 Koška Yugoslavia 45.33N 18.16E
98 R6 Koskaecodde L Newfoundland
36 G3 Köşker Turkey 39.27N 34.03E
51 K11 Koski Finland 60.40N 23.10E
84 H5 Kóskinon Greece 38.22N 24.10E
51 J5 Koskivaara Sweden 66.39N 21.00E
43 H3 Koskol' Kazakhstan U.S.S.R. 49.32N 67.08E
43 M5 Koskuduk Kazakhstan U.S.S.R. 44.06N 77.23E
51 H4 Koskullskulle Sweden 67.12N 20.45E
47 F4 Koslan U.S.S.R. 63.29N 48.59E
26 T8 Koslanda Sri Lanka 6.45N 81.00E
Köslin see Koszalin
Koslov see Michurinsk
47 F3 Kosma R U.S.S.R.
82 J2 Kosmach U.S.S.R. 48.18N 24.49E
84 E7 Kosmás Greece 37.05N 22.44E
84 A2 Kosmirá Greece 39.35N 20.48E
43 J5 Kosmoldyk Kazakhstan U.S.S.R. 43.52N 68.35E
95 L1 Kosmos S Africa 25.45S 27.51E
110 C3 Kosmos Washington 46.30N 122.13W
21 D8 Kosŏng N Korea 38.36N 128.21E
21 D7 Kosong-ni N Korea 40.48N 128.30E
45 H4 Kosorzha U.S.S.R. 52.07N 36.46E
82 J2 Kosov U.S.S.R. 48.19N 25.03E
82 G8 Kosovo Yugoslavia 42.37N 21.05E
82 F8 Kosovo i Metohija reg Yugoslavia
82 F8 Kosovska Mitrovica Yugoslavia 42.54N 20.52E
47 M5 Kosoy Brod U.S.S.R. 56.30N 60.20E
Kosrab see Kosrap
24 B7 Kosrap Xinjiang Uygur Zizhiqu China 37.28N 76.24E
87 F7 Kossa Ethiopia 7.53N 36.49E
63 S10 Kossdorf E Germany 51.29N 13.13E
112 L4 Kosse Texas 31.18N 96.38W
63 P9 Kösseln E Germany 51.38N 11.59E
65 F6 Kössen Austria 47.41N 12.25E
90 G6 Kosséoua Cameroon 10.43N 14.21E
64 O1 Kössern E Germany 51.11N 12.47E
64 P7 Kösslarn W Germany 48.21N 13.09E
19 N1 Kossol Pass Palau Is Pacific Oc
19 N1 Kossol Reef Palau Is Pacific Oc
89 G8 Kossou dam Ivory Coast 6.59N 5.32W
46 F3 Kossovo Belorussiya U.S.S.R. 52.40N 25.18E
62 N3 Kossów Poland 52.35N 22.08E
82 D5 Kostajnica Yugoslavia 45.13N 16.34E
Kosta-Khetagurovo see Nazran'
82 C5 Kostanjevica Yugoslavia 45.51N 15.27E
63 T9 Kostebrau E Germany 51.31N 13.50E
65 L2 Kostelec nad Černými Lesy Czechoslovakia 50.00N 14.52E
62 J5 Kostelec nad Orlicí Czechoslovakia 50.08N 16.15E
53 J7 Koster Denmark 54.59N 12.13E
95 K1 Koster S Africa 25.52S 26.54E
45 L1 Kosterevo U.S.S.R. 55.54N 39.39E
87 D4 Kosti Sudan 13.11N 32.38E
41 A4 Kostin Nos,Mys C Novaya Zemlya U.S.S.R. 70.55N 53.07E
42 F4 Kostino Irkutsk U.S.S.R. 55.39N 99.30E
41 E7 Kostino Krasnoyarsk U.S.S.R. 65.14N 88.02E
45 N8 Kostino Bystryantskiy U.S.S.R. 48.25N 41.41E
41 A4 Kostin Shar,Proliv str Novaya Zemlya U.S.S.R.
47 C4 Kostomuksa U.S.S.R. 64.39N 30.45E
46 F4 Kostopol' Ukraine U.S.S.R. 50.51N 26.22E
46 M1 Kostroma U.S.S.R. 57.46N 40.59E
46 M1 Kostroma R U.S.S.R.
46 M1 Kostromskaya Oblast' prov U.S.S.R.
62 K3 Kostrzyn Poland 52.24N 17.11E
62 H3 Kostrzyn Zielona Góra Poland 52.35N 14.40E
45 D3 Kostyukovichi Belorussiya U.S.S.R. 53.20N 32.01E
45 B4 Kostyukovka Belorussiya U.S.S.R. 52.32N 30.57E
40 D6 Kostyukovka U.S.S.R. 51.20N 127.45E
21 D10 Kosu-dong S Korea 35.39N 128.44E
20 L5 Kosugi Japan 36.44N 137.06E
25 E9 Ko Sukon isld Thailand 7.06N 99.32E
47 H6 Kos'va R U.S.S.R.
47 H3 Kos'yu U.S.S.R. 65.36N 59.00E
47 H3 Kos'yu R U.S.S.R.
47 H3 Kos'yuvom U.S.S.R. 66.19N 59.45E
62 J1 Koszalin Poland 54.10N 16.10E
65 P7 Köszeg Hungary 16.32N 16.32E
28 E3 Kota Andhra Prad India 14.04N 80.03E
18 C9 Kota Pen Malaysia 2.33N 102.10E
29 D5 Kota Rajasthan India 25.11N 75.58E
30 G8 Kota Uttar Prad India 24.27N 83.08E
29 E5 Kota dist Rajasthan India
18 F8 Kotaagung Sumatra Indon 5.30S 104.39E
30 C3 Kota Bagh Uttar Prad India 29.23N 79.17E
18 J6 Kotabaharu Borneo Indon 0.51S 111.32E
18 E2 Kota Baharu Pen Malaysia 6.07N 102.15E
18 M6 Kotabangun Borneo Indonesia 0.15S 116.36E
29 D5 Kota Barrage Rajasthan India 25.06N 75.51E
18 M7 Kotabaru Borneo Indon 3.15S 116.15E
Kotabaru Irian Jaya see Jayapura
18 D6 Kota Baru Sumatra Indon 1.02S 101.43E
18 M2 Kota Belud Sabah Malaysia 6.22N 116.19E
18 F8 Kotabumi Sumatra Indon 4.52S 104.59E
19 D3 Kotabunan Celebes Indon 0.50N 124.39E
29 D5 Kota Dam Rajasthan India 25.01N 75.43E
31 F5 Kot Addu Pakistan 30.28N 70.58E
28 C5 Kotagiri Tamil Nadu India 11.21N 76.44E
Kotah see Kota
21 D11 Ko-Takara jima isld Japan 29.14N 129.20E
18 M3 Kota Kinabalu Sabah Malaysia 5.59N 116.04E
51 O4 Kotala Finland 67.01N 29.00E
29 K2 Kotalpur W Bengal India 23.00N 87.35E
19 D3 Kotamobagu Celebes Indon 0.46N 124.21E
20 F4 Kotanishi Japan 41.03N 140.24E
31 E4 Kotanni Pass Afghanistan 33.03N 69.05E
28 F1 Kotapad Orissa India 19.06N 82.26E
18 D5 Kotapinang Baru Sumatra Indon 1.55N 100.07E
29 D5 Kotari R Rajasthan India
18 D5 Kotatengah Sumatra Indon 1.01N 100.30E
18 D10 Kota Tinggi Pen Malaysia 1.45N 103.53E
18 J7 Kotawaringin Borneo Indon 2.30S 111.29E
31 H9 Kotchandpur Bangladesh 23.25N 89.02E
101 N6 Kotcho R Br Col
101 N6 Kotcho L Br Col 59.05N 121.10W
31 E7 Kot Diji Pakistan 27.16N 68.44E
30 B3 Kotdwara Uttar Prad India 29.44N 78.33E
37 G5 Kötek Turkey 40.12N 43.01E
41 M7 Kotekh U.S.S.R. 66.35N 123.00E
82 K8 Kotel Bulgaria 42.52N 26.26E
46 P1 Kotel'nich U.S.S.R. 58.10N 48.20E
45 P9 Kotel'nikovo U.S.S.R. 47.39N 43.08E
41 P3 Kotel'nyy U.S.S.R. 75.59N 138.00E
41 P3 Kotel'nyy,Ostrov isld U.S.S.R.
45 F6 Kotel'va Ukraine U.S.S.R. 50.04N 34.46E
11 M6 Kotemaori New Zealand 39.02S 177.03E
39 D1 Kotenko U.S.S.R. 70.30N 147.28E
50 G7 Kotey Iceland 63.33N 18.10W
31 G3 Kotgala Pakistan 35.21N 73.19E
29 H8 Kotgar Orissa India 19.53N 83.46E
30 A1 Kotgarh Himachal Prad India 31.18N 77.29E
63 P9 Köthen (Anhalt) E Germany 51.46N 11.59E
30 H8 Kothi Bihar India 24.24N 84.33E
30 D8 Kothi Madhya Prad India 24.45N 80.46E
30 J7 Kothia Bihar India 25.51N 85.37E
30 F6 Kothili Uttar Prad India 27.00N 82.41E
93 F2 Kotido Uganda 3.02N 34.07E
37 H7 Kotıkı Turkey 38.54N 44.14E
40 F8 Kotikovo Khabarovsk U.S.S.R. 47.25N 134.31E
40 K7 Kotikovo Sakhalin U.S.S.R. 49.05N 144.19E
31 E7 Kot Imamgarh Pakistan 26.30N 69.18E
28 F2 Kotipalle Andhra Prad India 16.44N 82.03E
93 F3 Kotipe R Uganda
51 M11 Kotka Finland 60.26N 26.55E
29 D2 Kot Kapura Punjab India 30.35N 74.50E
29 E3 Kot Kasim Rajasthan India 28.01N 76.47E
30 A1 Kotkhai Himachal Prad India 31.06N 77.31E
47 G3 Kotkino Arkhangel'sk U.S.S.R. 67.03N 51.07E
47 M6 Kotkino Tomsk U.S.S.R. 58.15N 75.52E
30 A1 Kotla Himachal Prad India 31.43N 77.16E
85 E5 Kotla Libya 28.36N 18.59E
47 F5 Kotlas U.S.S.R. 61.15N 46.35E
31 G4 Kotli Kashmir 33.13N 73.51E
113 F5 Kotlik Alaska 63.00N 163.40W
51 O11 Kotlin, Ostrov isld U.S.S.R. 60.00N 29.40E
50 G8 Kötlutangi pt Iceland 63.24N 18.40W
51 O12 Kotly U.S.S.R. 59.36N 28.45E
40 H7 Koto U.S.S.R. 50.00N 139.50E
20 F2 Kōtō dist Tōkyō Japan
20 G7 Kotohira Japan 34.10N 133.48E
20 K1 Kotoni Japan 43.06N 141.16E
90 C7 Koton Karifi Nigeria 8.05N 6.45E
90 B6 Kotonkoro Nigeria 11.03N 5.53E
82 E8 Kotor Yugoslavia 42.27N 18.46E
65 P9 Kotoriba Yugoslavia 46.20N 16.50E
82 D6 Kotor Varoš Yugoslavia 44.38N 17.22E
21 D7 Kot'osu N Korea 40.12N 127.12E
45 F7 Kotovka Ukraine U.S.S.R. 49.07N 34.57E
45 Q6 Kotovo U.S.S.R. 50.19N 44.49E
46 G6 Kotovsk Moldavia U.S.S.R. 46.50N 28.31E
46 G5 Kotovsk Ukraine U.S.S.R. 47.42N 29.30E
45 N4 Kotovsk U.S.S.R. 52.36N 41.30E
29 E4 Kot Putli Rajasthan India 27.41N 76.11E
31 D6 Kotra Pakistan 28.33N 67.24E
29 C5 Kotra Rajasthan India 24.22N 73.15E
30 C7 Kotra Uttar Prad India 25.49N 79.18E
29 B7 Kotra Pitha Gujarat India 20.57N 71.18E
31 E8 Kotri Pakistan 25.22N 68.18E
31 D8 Kotri Allahrakhio Shah Pakistan 24.28N 67.55E
29 G8 Kotri R Madhya Prad India
84 D8 Kótronas Greece 36.38N 22.29E
43 E3 Kotr-Tas Kazakhstan U.S.S.R. 48.19N 58.57E
31 D9 Kot Sarae Pakistan 23.58N 67.52E
65 H8 Kötschach Austria 46.41N 13.01E
84 D3 Kotseri Greece 39.27N 22.10E
50 D7 Kotströnd Iceland 63.58N 21.08W
28 E2 Kottagudem Andhra Prad India 17.32N 80.39E
26 P1 Kottaippattanam Tamil Nadu India 9.57N 79.11E
28 C6 Kottarakara Kerala India 8.59N 76.45E
28 B5 Kottayam Kerala India 11.49N 75.32E
28 C6 Kottayam Kottayam, Kerala India 9.34N 76.31E
28 C6 Kottayam dist Kerala India
26 Q8 Kotte Sri Lanka 6.54N 79.55E
60 Q12 Kotten Netherlands 51.56N 6.47E
69 N3 Kottenheim W Germany 50.21N 7.15E
90 K9 Kotto R Cent Afr Rep
52 J3 Köttsjön Sweden 63.20N 16.00E
28 C3 Kotturu Karnataka India 14.50N 76.12E
9 T12 Kotu atoll Tonga, Pacific Oc 19.55S 174.50W
9 T12 Kotu Grp islds Tonga, Pacific Oc
37 G7 Kotum Turkey 38.26N 42.16E
37 H7 Kotūr R Turkey
43 C7 Koturdepe U.S.S.R. 39.25N 53.41E
41 H5 Kotuy R U.S.S.R.
41 G7 Kotuykan R Krasnoyarsk U.S.S.R.
30 H6 Kotwa Bihar India 26.31N 84.52E
30 E7 Kotwa Madhya Prad India 25.02N 81.19E
29 H6 Kotwar Pk Madhya Prad India 23.10N 83.59E
44 J1 Kotyaeka U.S.S.R. 46.30N 48.50E
45 U10 Kotyayevka Kazakhstan U.S.S.R. 46.34N 48.46E
82 M3 Kotyuzhany U.S.S.R. 47.50N 28.38E
64 Q1 Kötzchenbroda E Germany 51.07N 13.38E
113 F3 Kotzebue Alaska 66.51N 162.40W
113 E3 Kotzebue Sd Alaska
64 O5 Kötzting W Germany 49.11N 12.52E
Kouaïyé,El see Kuweiyah,El
89 K6 Kouandé Benin 10.15N 1.35E
90 J9 Kouango Cent Afr Rep 4.59N 19.59E
91 B5 Kouango, Pte pt Gabon 3.23S 10.37E
90 J4 Kouba Modounga Chad 15.41N 18.16E
90 J4 Kouba Olanga Chad 15.49N 18.20E
Koubayat see Qoubayat
98 H7 Kouchibouguac Nat. Park New Brunswick
60 G11 Koudekerk Netherlands 52.08N 4.35E
60 B3 Koudekerke Netherlands 51.29N 3.33E
89 H5 Koudougou Upper Volta 12.15N 2.23W
60 K8 Koudum Netherlands 52.55N 5.27E
94 E9 Koue Bokkeveld reg S Africa
90 F4 Koufey Niger 14.47N 13.20E
84 O12 Koufonísi isld Crete 34.56N 26.08E
83 H8 Koufonísia isld Greece 36.57N 25.35E
90 K7 Kouga Chad 9.59N 21.02E
95 H9 Kouga R S Africa
95 G9 Kougaberge mts S Africa
91 A3 Kougouleu Gabon 0.20N 9.58E
91 B6 Kouilou div Congo
91 B6 Kouilou R Congo
90 K9 Kouimba Rapids Cent Afr Rep 4.35N 20.26E
84 A6 Koúkesi Greece 37.49N 20.46E
90 H8 Kouki Cent Afr Rep 7.09N 17.13E
84 Q15 Kouklia Cyprus 34.42N 32.34E
84 S14 Kouklia Cyprus 35.06N 33.46E
90 K8 Koukourou R Cent Afr Rep
114 D4 Koula R Hawaiian Is
91 C4 Koulamoutou Gabon 1.12S 12.29E
89 A5 Koular Senegal 13.42N 16.12W
90 F4 Koulda Chad 14.20N 13.55E
25 H6 Koulen Cambodia 13.49N 104.43E
84 E8 Kouléndia Greece 36.37N 22.59E
89 F5 Koulikoro Mali 12.55N 7.31W
84 D5 Kouloúra Akhaïa Greece 38.14N 22.05E
9 B13 Koumac New Caledonia 20.32S 164.20E
13 J5 Koumala Queensland 21.35S 149.15E
91 B3 Koumameyong Gabon 0.11N 11.51E
89 C5 Koumba R Guinea
89 C6 Koumbia Guinea 11.48N 13.29W
89 H6 Koumbia Upper Volta 11.18N 3.38W
89 J6 Koumbili Upper Volta 11.21N 1.27W
90 J8 Koumi R Cent Afr Rep
89 K6 Koumongou Togo 10.12N 0.32E
89 B4 Koumpentoum Senegal 14.00N 14.32W
90 H7 Koumra Chad 8.56N 17.32E
91 E4 Kounda Congo 1.32S 16.40E
91 B6 Kounda,Pte pt Congo 4.11S 11.24E
89 C5 Koundara Guinea 12.28N 13.15W
89 H3 Koundi Mali 16.27N 3.27W
89 D5 Koundian Mali 13.10N 10.35W
89 G6 Koundougou Upper Volta 11.43N 4.40W
89 B5 Koungheul Senegal 14.00N 14.48W
89 B4 Koung Koung Senegal 14.35N 14.47W
90 M9 Koungou,Mt Cent Afr Rep 5.44N 25.20E
91 B5 Koungou, Mts Gabon
35 E1 Kounine Lebanon 33.09N 35.26E
89 F7 Kounioumassa Ivory Coast 8.28N 6.59W
90 H7 Kouno Chad 9.52N 17.39E
83 H8 Kounoupói isld Greece 36.32N 26.29E
43 L4 Kounradskiy Kazakhstan U.S.S.R. 46.58N 74.59E
89 B5 Kounthiao Senegal 13.35N 14.25W
112 N5 Kountze Texas 30.22N 94.20W
95 E9 Koup S Africa 33.08S 21.16E
89 J5 Koupéla Upper Volta 12.07N 0.21W
84 E8 Koupía Greece 36.52N 22.54E
Kouqian see Yongji
89 H3 Koura Mali 16.27N 3.08W
89 C6 Kouraia Guinea 10.19N 12.14W
42 C5 Kourak U.S.S.R. 54.48N 84.39E
89 E6 Kourémalé Mali 11.59N 8.42W
89 H5 Kouri Upper Volta 12.46N 3.28W
20 P8 Kouri-jima isld Okinawa Japan 26.43N 128.02E
84 Q15 Kouris R Cyprus
89 N4 Kournaka Niger 14.08N 7.01E
84 K11 Kournás Crete 35.20N 24.18E
117 C2 Kourou Fr Guiana 5.08N 52.37W
117 C2 Kourou R Fr Guiana
89 D5 Kourouba Mali 13.22N 10.57W
85 B8 Kourou Koubiké Niger 22.39N 13.11E
89 E6 Kouroussa Guinea 10.40N 9.50W
90 K2 Kourtidi Chad 18.31N 20.35E
95 E8 Kousberg mt S Africa 32.56S 21.10E
90 H6 Koussa Chad 11.56N 17.45E
89 E3 Koussa Mauritania 16.58N 8.15W
89 C4 Koussan Senegal 14.10N 12.22W
89 B5 Koussanar Senegal 13.52N 14.05W
90 G5 Kousséri Chad 12.05N 14.56E
84 H7 Koutalá Greece 37.08N 24.27E
89 G5 Koutiala Mali 12.20N 5.23W
95 F9 Koutjie S Africa 33.42S 22.35E
9 C14 Koutoumo isld New Caledonia 22.42S 167.32E
84 C6 Koutsokhéra Greece 37.47N 21.32E
84 D2 Koutsókheron Greece 39.36N 22.14E
84 E6 Koutsopódhi Greece 37.41N 22.43E
89 K8 Kouvé Togo 6.36N 1.24E
51 M11 Kouvola Finland 60.54N 26.45E
91 E4 Kouyou R Congo
42 G3 Kova U.S.S.R. 58.18N 100.25E
42 G3 Kova R U.S.S.R.
82 F5 Kovačica Yugoslavia 45.06N 20.37E
82 E7 Kovač Planina mts Yugoslavia
45 A2 Kovali Belorussiya U.S.S.R. 54.50N 29.55E
Kovans see Kale Gümüşane Turkey
36 E5 Kovara Gölü L Turkey
47 C3 Kovda U.S.S.R. 66.40N 32.43E
51 P4 Kovdor U.S.S.R. 67.33N 30.30E
47 C3 Kovdozero Oz L U.S.S.R.
46 E4 Kovel' Ukraine U.S.S.R. 51.12N 24.48E
47 K5 Kovenskaya R U.S.S.R.
46 N2 Kovernino U.S.S.R. 57.08N 43.41E
51 P9 Kovero Finland 62.33N 30.35E
26 Q2 Kovilan Pt Sri Lanka 9.50N 79.51E
28 C6 Kovilpatti Tamil Nadu India 9.12N 77.55E
82 F6 Kovin Yugoslavia 44.44N 20.59E
Kovno see Kaunas
45 B5 Kovpyta Ukraine U.S.S.R. 51.22N 30.51E
39 F6 Kovran U.S.S.R. 57.13N 156.55E
47 F3 Kovriga,Gora mt U.S.S.R. 67.04N 46.56E
39 G3 Kovrizhka U.S.S.R. 62.32N 163.00E
45 N1 Kovrov U.S.S.R. 56.23N 41.21E
45 P2 Kovylkino U.S.S.R. 54.02N 43.56E
46 L1 Kovzha R U.S.S.R.
47 D5 Kovzhskoye,Oz L U.S.S.R.
93 L8 Kowa Gulecha Kenya 2.40S 39.41E
11 F10 Kowai Bush New Zealand 43.18S 171.57E
62 L3 Kowal Poland 52.32N 19.05E
62 L2 Kowalewo Poland 53.09N 18.50E
94 D4 Kowas Namibia 22.55S 17.59E
91 J4 Kowe Zaïre 1.35S 25.54E
94 E5 Kowes Namibia 25.08N 18.59E
11 F9 Kowhitirangi New Zealand 42.52S 171.00E
99 C2 Kowkash Ontario 50.15N 87.14W
32 E5 Kowlī Kosh,Gardaneh-ye pass Iran 30.49N 53.09E
23 G7 Kowloon Hong Kong 22.20N 114.15E
23 B9 Kowloon Bay Hong Kong
23 B9 Kowloon City Hong Kong 22.19N 114.10E
23 B9 Kowloon Pt Hong Kong 22.17N 114.09E
21 D8 Kowŏn N Korea 39.25N 127.15E
44 H9 Kowtār Pass Iran 38.37N 47.03E
31 E3 Kowt-e 'Ashrow Afghanistan 34.27N 68.48E
24 C6 Koxlax Xinjiang Uygur Zizhiqu China 38.00N 80.30E
24 C7 Koxtag Xinjiang Uygur Zizhiqu China 37.20N 77.55E
Kōya see Koi Sanjaq
20 E3 Koyama dist Tōkyō Japan
20 E7 Kōyama-misaki C Japan 34.40N 131.34E
43 M3 Koyandy Kazakhstan U.S.S.R. 49.50N 75.38E
20 J7 Kōyasan Japan 34.13N 135.34E
20 A1 Koyata Saitama Japan
43 H1 Koybagar,Ozero L Kazakhstan U.S.S.R.
36 D6 Köyceğiz Turkey 36.57N 28.40E
36 D6 Köyceğiz Gölü L Turkey
37 C7 Köyceviran Turkey 38.25N 37.15E
47 E3 Koyda U.S.S.R. 66.20N 42.30E
47 C2 Koydor U.S.S.R. 67.32N 30.19E
47 J8 Koyelga U.S.S.R. 54.41N 60.54E
47 M6 Koyelga R U.S.S.R.
39 K2 Koyginveem R U.S.S.R.
47 G5 Koygorodok U.S.S.R. 60.29N 51.01E
37 K2 Köyici dist İstanbul Turkey 41.03N 29.01E
43 D6 Koymatdag, Gory mts Turkmeniya U.S.S.R.
28 A2 Koyna Res Maharashtra India
47 F4 Koynas U.S.S.R. 64.45N 47.31E
20 O2 Koyoshi-gawa R Japan
47 H5 Koyp,Gora mt U.S.S.R. 62.05N 59.09E
45 L9 Koysug U.S.S.R. 47.07N 39.44E
43 H6 Koytash Uzbekistan U.S.S.R. 40.14N 67.16E
113 G4 Koyuk Alaska 64.55N 161.20W
113 G4 Koyuk R Alaska
113 J4 Koyukuk Alaska 64.53N 157.50W
113 J4 Koyukuk isld Alaska
113 J4 Koyukuk R Alaska
37 D5 Koyulhisar Turkey 40.17N 37.51E
37 D2 Koyun isld Turkey 40.30N 27.35E
47 M3 Koyva R U.S.S.R.
51 P7 Koyvozero Karelia U.S.S.R. 64.49N 30.59E
21 G11 Koza Japan 33.34N 135.54E
20 P9 Koza Okinawa Japan 26.20N 127.45E
20 J8 Koza R Japan
Kozağacı see Günyüzü
36 C3 Kozak Turkey 39.15N 27.05E
20 C7 Kō-zaki C Japan 34.06N 129.12E
36 H3 Kozaklı Turkey 39.12N 34.48E
20 G7 Kōzan Japan 34.36N 133.02E
36 H5 Kozan Turkey 37.27N 35.47E
36 H3 Kozan R Turkey
83 E4 Kozáni Greece 40.18N 21.48E
82 D5 Kozara Planina mts Yugoslavia
62 L7 Kozárovce Czechoslovakia 48.20N 18.30E
45 C6 Kozelets Ukraine U.S.S.R. 50.54N 31.09E
45 E7 Kozel'shchina Ukraine U.S.S.R. 49.12N 33.52E
45 G2 Kozel'sk U.S.S.R. 54.02N 35.48E
61 L3 Kozen Belgium 50.52N 5.14E
43 F4 Kozhabaky Kazakhstan U.S.S.R. 45.40N 61.50E
43 J2 Kozhakol',Ozero L Kazakhstan U.S.S.R.
42 B1 Kozherel'-Tu,Oz L U.S.S.R. 64.02N 81.00E
41 K4 Kozhevnikovo Krasnoyarsk U.S.S.R. 73.32N 110.12E
42 B5 Kozhevnikovo Novosibirsk U.S.S.R. 55.00N 78.15E
42 C4 Kozhevnikovo U.S.S.R. 56.19N 84.00E
Kozhikode see Calicut India
47 H3 Kozhim U.S.S.R. 65.45N 59.30E
47 H3 Kozhim R U.S.S.R.
47 H4 Kozhim-Iz,Gora mt U.S.S.R. 63.10N 58.52E
47 H3 Kozhimvom U.S.S.R. 65.50N 59.20E
47 D4 Kozhozero,Ozero L U.S.S.R.
47 D4 Kozhposelok U.S.S.R. 63.10N 38.10E
42 B4 Kozhurla U.S.S.R. 55.20N 79.00E
47 H3 Kozhva U.S.S.R. 65.09N 57.00E
47 H3 Kozhva R U.S.S.R.
62 N4 Kozienice Poland 51.35N 21.31E
82 G8 Kozjak mt Yugoslavia 42.18N 21.55E
82 G9 Kozjak mt Yugoslavia 41.04N 21.56E
64 Q3 Kožlany Czechoslovakia 50.00N 13.33E
62 L5 Koźle Poland 50.20N 18.06E
39 G7 Kozlova,Mys C U.S.S.R. 54.32N 161.45E
82 J7 Kozlovets Bulgaria 43.30N 25.20E
45 U1 Kozlovka Cheboksary U.S.S.R. 55.50N 48.15E
45 R2 Kozlovka Mordovian A.S.S.R. U.S.S.R. 54.43N 45.52E
45 M6 Kozlovka Voronezh U.S.S.R. 50.54N 40.30E
45 N5 Kozlovka Voronezh U.S.S.R. 51.41N 41.16E
36 F1 Kozlu Turkey 41.23N 31.44E
37 F7 Kozluk Turkey 38.11N 41.27E
62 K4 Koźmin Poland 51.50N 17.29E
45 S1 Kozmodem'yansk U.S.S.R. 56.21N 46.35E
82 J1 Kozovo U.S.S.R. 49.25N 25.09E
62 J4 Kozuchów Poland 51.45N 15.36E
42 E4 Kozul'ka U.S.S.R. 56.11N 91.23E
20 N7 Kōzu-shima isld Japan 34.12N 139.12E
39 F6 Kozyrevsk U.S.S.R. 56.02N 159.51E
87 A7 Kpaile Sudan 7.07N 27.54E
89 K8 Kpandu Ghana 7.00N 0.25E
89 K7 Kpessi Togo 8.04N 1.20E
89 K8 Kpetoe Ghana 6.33N 0.48E
89 K8 Kra Togo 7.11N 1.10E
25 E7 Kra R Burma/Thailand
95 K6 Kraai R S Africa
95 B9 Kraaifontein S Africa 33.50S 18.43E
61 H3 Kraainem Belgium 50.52N 4.28E
95 J2 Kraaipan S Africa 26.17S 25.19E
63 O6 Kraak E Germany 53.28N 11.25E
95 H5 Kraankuil S Africa 29.53S 24.11E
39 M2 Kraasnaya Yaranga U.S.S.R. 65.40N 177.55W
60 E14 Krabbendijke Netherlands 51.25N 4.07E
25 E8 Krabi Thailand 8.04N 98.52E
25 E7 Kra Buri Thailand 10.25N 98.48E
88 P4 Krachem,El Algeria 35.34N 2.54E
66 N1 Kradolf Switzerland 47.32N 9.13E
53 X18 Kraekkjahytta Norway 60.28N 7.43E
50 J3 Krafla mt Iceland 65.43N 16.44W
64 M2 Kraftsdorf E Germany 50.52N 11.56E
18 J9 Kragan Java Indonesia 6.40S 111.33E
53 C4 Kragelund Denmark 56.12N 9.25E
53 G7 Kragenæs Denmark 54.55N 11.22E
52 E8 Kragero Norway 58.54N 9.25E
60 M9 Kraggenburg Netherlands 52.40N 5.55E
82 F6 Kragujevac Yugoslavia 44.01N 20.55E
64 G4 Krahenberg W Germany 49.35N 9.02E
64 K2 Krahnberg mt E Germany 50.58N 10.39E
Krai see Ban Krai
64 N7 Kraiburg am Inn W Germany 48.10N 12.26E
64 F5 Kraich R W Germany
64 F5 Kraichgau dist W Germany
64 F5 Kraichtal W Germany 49.08N 8.46E
65 K8 Kraig Austria 46.49N 14.23E
45 H2 Krainka U.S.S.R. 54.07N 36.20E
25 E7 Kra Isthmus of Thailand
Krakatau isld see Rakata
34 D4 Krak des Chevaliers anc site Syria 34.47N 36.18E
95 G9 Krakeelrivier S Africa 33.49S 23.43E
53 S14 Kråkenes Norway 62.02N 5.00E
53 S16 Krakhella Norway 61.09N 5.01E
25 H6 Krakor Cambodia 12.31N 104.12E
82 H1 Krakovets U.S.S.R. 49.59N 23.10E
63 Q5 Krakow E Germany 53.39N 12.17E
62 M5 Kraków Poland 50.03N 19.55E
63 Q5 Krakower See L E Germany
50 F5 Krákur mt Iceland 64.58N 19.52W
25 G6 Kralanh Cambodia 13.35N 103.26E
62 N7 Král Chlmec Czechoslovakia 48.27N 22.00E
116 K8 Kralendijk Bonaire W I 12.09N 68.18W
62 K5 Králíky Czechoslovakia 50.06N 16.45E
82 F7 Kraljevo Yugoslavia 43.44N 20.41E
62 L6 Kral'ovany Czechoslovakia 49.10N 19.05E
64 P4 Kralovice Czechoslovakia 49.59N 13.30E
65 P3 Královo Pole Czechoslovakia 49.14N 16.37E
62 H5 Kralupy Czechoslovakia 50.15N 14.20E
64 P3 Kralupy Czechoslovakia 50.26N 13.20E
18 G3 Kramatjati Jakarta Indonesia 6.16S 106.52E
45 J8 Kramatorsk Ukraine U.S.S.R. 48.43N 37.33E
108 K1 Kramer N Dakota 48.43N 100.42W
108 O9 Kramer Nebraska 40.35N 96.50W
52 K4 Kramfors Sweden 62.55N 17.50E
88 O3 Kramis,C Algeria 36.22N 0.41E
25 F6 Kram,Ko isld Thailand 12.41N 100.48E
60 E13 Krammer estuary Netherlands
51 P1 Krampenes Norway 70.07N 30.14E
53 Y19 Krâmvik Norway 59.48N 8.05E
63 D9 Kranenburg W Germany 51.47N 6.03E
52 J3 Krångede Sweden 63.09N 16.05E
Krang, Tanjong see Kerang, Tanjong
84 B2 Kraniá Greece 39.53N 21.18E
84 C2 Kraniá Dheskatis Greece 39.57N 21.58E
64 L2 Kranichfeld E Germany 50.51N 11.12E
84 F7 Kranídhion Greece 37.23N 23.09E
82 B4 Kranj Yugoslavia 46.15N 14.20E
18 H2 Kranji Singapore 1.26N 103.45E
18 H2 Kranji dist Singapore
18 H2 Kranji res Singapore
79 P2 Kranjskagora Yugoslavia 46.29N 13.48E
84 D2 Kranón Greece 39.31N 22.20E
94 J5 Kransberg mt S Africa 24.22S 27.36E
95 M4 Kransfontein S Africa 28.08S 28.35E
95 O4 Kranskop S Africa 28.58S 30.52E
95 N3 Kranskop mt S Africa 27.44S 29.43E
95 G5 Kranspan salt pan S Africa 29.31S 23.25E
80 N1 Krapanj Yugoslavia 43.41N 15.56E
82 C4 Krapina Yugoslavia 46.10N 15.52E
82 C4 Krapina R Yugoslavia
45 D2 Krapivenskiy U.S.S.R. 54.06N 32.43E
42 D4 Krapivinskiy U.S.S.R. 55.01N 86.47E
45 J3 Krapivna U.S.S.R. 53.55N 37.09E
62 K5 Krapkowice Poland 50.29N 17.56E
53 K4 Krapperup Sweden 56.17N 12.33E
65 K8 Krappfeld reg Austria
47 F5 Krasavino U.S.S.R. 60.58N 46.25E
45 P5 Krasavka Saratov U.S.S.R. 51.10N 43.20E
41 B3 Krasheninnikova,Mys C Novaya Zemlya U.S.S.R. 74.08N 58.25E
39 G5 Krasheninnikova,Mys C U.S.S.R. 58.27N 163.21E
65 P2 Krasíkov Czechoslovakia 49.52N 16.42E
46 F5 Krasilov Ukraine U.S.S.R. 49.39N 26.59E
45 C5 Krasilovka Ukraine U.S.S.R. 51.11N 31.14E
39 M1 Krasina,Zaliv B Vrangelya, Ostrov U.S.S.R.
41 A4 Krasino Novaya Zemlya U.S.S.R. 70.45N 54.30E
41 G3 Krasin,Ostrov isld U.S.S.R. 76.40N 95.00E
45 O4 Krasivka U.S.S.R. 52.15N 42.30E
46 L3 Krasiv Mecha R U.S.S.R.
40 E10 Kraskino U.S.S.R. 42.42N 130.48E
46 F2 Krāslava Latvia U.S.S.R. 55.50N 27.12E
64 O3 Kraslíce Czechoslovakia 50.21N 12.31E
65 K2 Krásna Hora Czechoslovakia 49.37N 14.17E
45 C3 Krasnaya Gora U.S.S.R. 53.00N 31.36E
45 N1 Krasnaya Gorbatka U.S.S.R. 55.47N 41.46E
45 P1 Krasnaya Gorka Gor'kiy U.S.S.R. 56.13N 43.06E
45 C2 Krasnaya Gorka Smolensk U.S.S.R. 54.41N 31.02E
39 B2 Krasnaya-Gorka Yakutsk U.S.S.R. 66.21N 137.15E
43 L3 Krasnaya Polyana Kazakhstan U.S.S.R. 49.17N 73.03E
44 C4 Krasnaya Polyana Krasnodar U.S.S.R. 43.42N 40.13E
45 J1 Krasnaya Polyana Moscow U.S.S.R. 56.02N 37.26E
44 D1 Krasnaya Polyana Rostov U.S.S.R. 46.06N 41.30E

45 J9 Krasnaya Polyana Ukraine U.S.S.R. 47.34N 37.05E
46 C7 Krasnaya Presnya *dist* Moscow U.S.S.R.
39 E4 Krasnaya Rechka U.S.S.R. 61.46N 152.12E
44 J6 Krasnaya Sloboda Azerbaydzhan U.S.S.R. 41.24N 48.33E
46 F3 Krasnaya Sloboda Belorussiya U.S.S.R. 52.51N 27.09E
45 S3 Krasnaya Sosna U.S.S.R. 53.51N 46.49E
41 O8 Krasnaya Tanda U.S.S.R. 62.40N 132.00E
39 J4 Krasnaya Yaranga Kamchatka U.S.S.R. 61.53N 174.05E
39 K3 Krasnaya Yaranga Magadan U.S.S.R. 63.37N 176.35E
45 G6 Krasnaya Yaruga U.S.S.R. 50.50N 35.41E
45 J4 Krasnaya Zarya U.S.S.R. 52.47N 37.43E
45 P4 Krasnaya Znamya U.S.S.R. 52.04N 43.31E
42 E6 Krasnaya Zvezda Krasnoyarsk U.S.S.R. 51.55N 92.50E
40 C2 Krasnaya Zvezda Yakutsk U.S.S.R. 58.10N 124.50E
40 E1 Krasnaya Zvezda Yakutsk U.S.S.R. 60.31N 131.27E
39 J3 Krasneno U.S.S.R. 64.37N 174.20E
62 N5 Krasnik Poland 50.56N 22.14E
64 O3 Krásno Czechoslovakia 50.06N 12.48E
43 J1 Krasnoarmeyesk Kazakhstan U.S.S.R. 53.52N 69.51E
45 K1 Krasnoarmeysk Moscow U.S.S.R. 56.11N 38.12E
45 R5 Krasnoarmeysk Saratov U.S.S.R. 51.01N 45.50E
45 J8 Krasnoarmeysk Ukraine U.S.S.R. 48.17N 37.14E
45 Q8 Krasnoarmeysk Volgograd U.S.S.R. 48.31N 44.34E
44 B2 Krasnoarmeyskaya U.S.S.R. 45.22N 38.13E
43 F1 Krasnoarmeyskiy Kazakhstan U.S.S.R. 52.47N 61.30E
39 J1 Krasnoarmeyskiy Magadan U.S.S.R. 69.30N 172.02E
45 O9 Krasnoarmeyskiy Rostov U.S.S.R. 47.01N 42.12E
45 T1 Krasnoarmeyskoye Cheboksary U.S.S.R. 55.45N 47.10E
Krasnoarmeyskoye Checheno-Ingushskaya *see* Urus-Martan
47 F5 Krasnoborsk U.S.S.R. 61.34N 46.05E
62 O5 Krasnobród Poland 50.32N 23.11E
42 D5 Krasnobrodskiy U.S.S.R. 54.14N 86.30E
44 B2 Krasnodar U.S.S.R. 45.02N 39.00E
46 L6 Krasnodarskiy Kray *terr* U.S.S.R.
45 L8 Krasnodon Ukraine U.S.S.R. 48.17N 39.44E
82 J1 Krasnoe U.S.S.R. 49.55N 24.36E
46 H1 Krasnofarfornyy U.S.S.R. 59.15N 31.53E
43 M5 Krasnogorka Kazakhstan U.S.S.R. 43.16N 75.09E
46 G2 Krasnogorodskoye U.S.S.R. 56.50N 28.20E
40 J7 Krasnogorsk Sakhalin U.S.S.R. 48.22N 142.09E
47 J8 Krasnogorskiy Chelyabinsk U.S.S.R. 54.37N 61.09E
45 U1 Krasnogorskiy U.S.S.R. 56.09N 48.20E
43 Q2 Krasnogorskoye Altay U.S.S.R. 52.18N 86.14E
46 R1 Krasnogorskoye Udmurt A.S.S.R. U.S.S.R. 57.42N 52.31E
42 D6 Krasnogorskoye U.S.S.R. 52.18N C86.10E
45 G7 Krasnograd Ukraine U.S.S.R. 49.22N 35.28E
43 H7 Krasnogvardeysk Uzbekistan U.S.S.R. 39.45N 67.16E
47 J7 Krasnogvardeyskiy U.S.S.R. 57.23N 62.18E
45 K6 Krasnogvardeyskoye Belgorod U.S.S.R. 50.39N 38.22E
44 D2 Krasnogvardeyskoye Stavropol' U.S.S.R. 45.51N 41.31E
44 C9 Krasnogvardeyskoye Ukraine U.S.S.R. 45.31N 34.16E
44 C2 Krasnogvardeyskoye U.S.S.R. 45.09N 39.37E
47 H6 Krasnokamsk U.S.S.R. 58.05N 55.49E
47 H7 Krasnokholmskiy Bashkir U.S.S.R. 56.00N 55.02E
45 G6 Krasnokutsk Ukraine U.S.S.R. 50.03N 35.13E
43 M1 Krasnokutskoye Kazakhstan U.S.S.R. 53.04N 75.59E
45 L5 Krasnolesniyy U.S.S.R. 51.53N 39.35E
62 N1 Krasnoles'ye U.S.S.R. 54.24N 22.21E
43 L5 Krasnooktyabr'skiy Kirgiziya U.S.S.R. 42.47N 74.15E
45 Q8 Krasnooktyabr'skiy Volgograd U.S.S.R. 48.53N 44.46E
47 B5 Krasnoostrovskiy U.S.S.R. 60.16N 28.33E
45 H7 Krasnopavlovka Ukraine U.S.S.R. 49.08N 36.20E
44 C9 Krasnoperekopsk Ukraine U.S.S.R. 45.56N 33.47E
45 C3 Krasnopol'ye Belorussiya U.S.S.R. 53.20N 31.24E
45 F8 Krasnopol'ye Dnepropetrovsk, Ukraine U.S.S.R. 48.25N 34.56E
45 G6 Krasnopol'ye Sumy, Ukraine U.S.S.R. 50.46N 35.16E
45 K5 Krasnopolye Voronezh U.S.S.R. 51.11N 38.49E
40 G9 Krasnorechenskiy U.S.S.R. 44.40N 135.18E
45 B10 Krasnoselka Ukraine U.S.S.R. 46.37N 30.45E
41 D7 Krasnosel'kup U.S.S.R. 65.45N 82.31E
44 G7 Krasnosel'sk Armenia U.S.S.R. 40.35N 45.20E
45 D8 Krasnosel'ye Ukraine U.S.S.R. 48.55N 32.28E
42 C6 Krasnoshchëkovo U.S.S.R. 51.41N 82.44E
45 P2 Krasnoslobodsk Mordovian A.S.S.R. U.S.S.R. 54.25N 43.45E
45 Q8 Krasnoslobodsk Volgograd U.S.S.R. 48.42N 44.35E
42 E5 Krasnoturansk U.S.S.R. 54.15N 91.30E
47 J6 Krasnotur'insk U.S.S.R. 59.46N 60.10E
47 H7 Krasnoufimsk U.S.S.R. 56.40N 57.49E
47 M3 Krasnoural'sk U.S.S.R. 58.25N 60.00E
43 D1 Krasnousol'skiy Bashkir U.S.S.R. 53.54N 56.30E
47 H5 Krasnovishersk U.S.S.R. 60.26N 57.02E
43 C6 Krasnovodsk Turkmeniya U.S.S.R. 40.01N 53.00E
44 M7 Krasnovodsk U.S.S.R. 40.00N 53.00E
43 C6 Krasnovodskiy Poluostrov *pen* Turkmeniya U.S.S.R.
43 C7 Krasnovodskiy Zaliv *B* Turkmeniya U.S.S.R.
32 E1 Krasnovodsk,Mys *C* Turkmeniya U.S.S.R. 39.40N 53.01E
43 C6 Krasnovodskoye Plato Turkmeniya U.S.S.R.
47 L7 Krasnoyarka Omsk U.S.S.R. 55.20N 73.10E
47 J6 Krasnoyarka Sverdlovsk U.S.S.R. 59.27N 60.30E
41 F2 Krasnoy Armii, Proliv *str* U.S.S.R.
40 D6 Krasnoyarovo U.S.S.R. 51.26N 128.25E
42 E4 Krasnoyarsk U.S.S.R. 56.05N 92.46E
43 E2 Krasnoyarskiy U.S.S.R. 51.59N 59.53E
38 H2 Krasnoyarskiy Kray *terr* U.S.S.R.
42 E5 Krasnoyarskoye Vdkhr *res* U.S.S.R.
45 K6 Krasnoye Belgorod U.S.S.R. 50.55N 38.42E
45 E3 Krasnoye Bryansk U.S.S.R. 53.03N 33.54E
Krasnoye Kalmyk A.S.S.R. U.S.S.R. *see* Ulan Erge
42 D5 Krasnoye Kemerovo U.S.S.R. 54.40N 85.26E
45 K4 Krasnoye Lipetsk U.S.S.R. 52.54N 38.47E
44 B8 Krasnoye Ukraine U.S.S.R. 46.08N 32.47E
47 E6 Krasnoye Vologda U.S.S.R. 59.43N 42.12E
45 N5 Krasnoye Voronezh U.S.S.R. 51.10N 41.30E
45 M1 Krasnoye Ekho U.S.S.R. 55.47N 40.44E
46 M1 Krasnoye-na-Volge Kostroma U.S.S.R. 57.32N 41.10E
39 J3 Krasnoye,Ozero *L* U.S.S.R.
43 F8 Krasnoye Znamya Turkmeniya U.S.S.R. 36.51N 62.28E
47 G5 Krasnozatonskiy U.S.S.R. 61.41N 51.03E
46 L2 Krasnozavodsk U.S.S.R. 56.30N 38.10E
42 B5 Krasnozerskoye U.S.S.R. 53.59N 79.15E
46 K5 Krasnoznamensk Ukraine U.S.S.R. 48.17N 37.14E
43 D1 Krasnoznamenskiy Bashkir U.S.S.R. 53.41N 55.59E
43 J2 Krasnoznamenskiy Kazakhstan U.S.S.R. 51.03N 69.27E
45 S1 Krasnye Chetai U.S.S.R. 55.41N 46.09E
82 M3 Krasnye Okny U.S.S.R. 47.30N 29.29E
62 O5 Krasnystaw Poland 51.00N 23.10E
45 C2 Krasnyy Smolensk U.S.S.R. 54.35N 31.28E
45 A4 Krasnyy Bereg Belorussiya U.S.S.R. 52.55N 29.45E
45 N1 Krasnyy Bogatyr' U.S.S.R. 56.01N 41.08E
45 T3 Krasnyy Bor Saratov U.S.S.R. 54.00N 47.14E
46 R2 Krasnyy Bor Tatar A.S.S.R. U.S.S.R. 55.52N 53.10E
42 H6 Krasnyy Chikoy U.S.S.R. 50.25N 108.45E
44 L3 Krasnyy Dolginets Kazakhstan U.S.S.R. 44.57N 51.07E
46 O2 Krasnyye Baki U.S.S.R. 57.02N 45.15E
44 H1 Krasnyye-Barrikady U.S.S.R. 46.12N 47.52E
46 L1 Krasnyye Tkachi U.S.S.R. 57.30N 39.42E
Krasnyy Kamyshanik *see* Komsomol'skiy
46 K1 Krasnyy Kholm Kalinin U.S.S.R. 58.05N 37.00E
46 R4 Krasnyy Kholm Orenburg U.S.S.R. 51.38N 54.11E
44 H1 Krasnyy Khudyk U.S.S.R. 46.19N 46.55E
47 H7 Krasnyy-Klyuch U.S.S.R. 55.25N 56.44E
45 K8 Krasnyy Kut Ukraine U.S.S.R. 48.14N 38.46E
45 T6 Krasnyy Kut U.S.S.R. 50.58N 47.00E
45 J7 Krasnyy Liman Ukraine U.S.S.R. 49.00N 37.50E
45 L5 Krasnyy Liman U.S.S.R. 51.32N 39.51E
45 L8 Krasnyy Luch Ukraine U.S.S.R. 48.10N 39.00E
45 N10 Krasnyy Manych U.S.S.R. 46.59N 41.10E
45 N1 Krasnyy Mayak U.S.S.R. 56.04N 41.22E
43 E3 Krasnyy Oktyabr' Aktyubinsk, Kazakhstan U.S.S.R. 49.53N 58.59E
43 M4 Krasnyy Oktyabr' Karaganda, Kazakhstan U.S.S.R. 46.47N 75.57E
47 J7 Krasnyy Oktyabr' Kurgan U.S.S.R. 55.39N 64.48E
45 R5 Krasnyy Oktyabr' Saratov U.S.S.R. 51.36N 45.40E
45 K1 Krasnyy Oktyabr' Vladimir U.S.S.R. 56.11N 38.54E
45 R7 Krasnyy Oktyabr' Volgograd U.S.S.R. 49.08N 45.39E
39 K3 Krasnyy Olenevod U.S.S.R. 62.45N 175.31E
46 L1 Krasnyy Pereval U.S.S.R. 57.42N 39.42E
45 E4 Krasnyy Rog U.S.S.R. 52.55N 33.45E
45 M9 Krasnyy Sulin U.S.S.R. 47.54N 40.05E
45 R5 Krasnyy Tekstil'shchik U.S.S.R. 51.22N 45.49E
45 L1 Krasnyy Tkach U.S.S.R. 55.25N 39.06E
45 N1 Krasnyy Voskhod U.S.S.R. 55.59N 41.40E
45 U10 Krasnyy Yar Astrakhan' U.S.S.R. 46.30N 48.20E
42 J5 Krasnyy Yar Chita U.S.S.R. 53.56N 114.45E
43 J1 Krasnyy Yar Kokchetav, Kazakhstan U.S.S.R. 53.22N 69.16E
45 W3 Krasnyy Yar Kuybyshev U.S.S.R. 53.28N 50.20E
47 L7 Krasnyy-Yar Omsk U.S.S.R. 55.15N 72.59E
45 S5 Krasnyy Yar Saratov U.S.S.R. 51.39N 46.26E
47 J6 Krasnyy Yar Sverdlovsk U.S.S.R. 59.22N 60.09E
42 C4 Krasnyy Yar Tomsk U.S.S.R. 57.11N 84.35E
44 J1 Krasnyy Yar U.S.S.R. 46.30N 48.25E
45 Q6 Krasnyy Yar Volgograd U.S.S.R. 50.44N 44.45E
25 J6 Kratie Cambodia 12.30N 106.03E
15 H7 Kratke Ra Papua New Guinea
82 G8 Kratovo Yugoslavia 42.03N 22.10E
84 B2 Krátsovon *mt* Greece 39.48N 21.25E
66 G5 Krattigen Switzerland 46.39N 7.44E
15 F5 Krau Irian Jaya 3.22S 140.04E
65 L7 Kraubath Austria 47.19N 14.57E
64 G7 Krauchenwies W Germany 48.01N 9.15E
64 H5 Krautheim W Germany 49.24N 9.39E
63 K5 Krautsand W Germany 53.46N 9.23E
18 G9 Krawang Java Indon 6.15S 107.15E
39 G1 Kray Lesov U.S.S.R. 69.10N 161.20E
39 G4 Krayniy,Ostrov *isld* U.S.S.R. 61.29N 163.00E
44 H4 Kraynovka U.S.S.R. 43.58N 47.22E
109 P7 Krebs Oklahoma 34.57N 95.44W
94 D8 Kreefte B S Africa 30.52S 17.35E
63 E10 Krefeld W Germany 51.20N 6.32E
53 J5 Kregme Denmark 55.57N 12.04E
64 F4 Krehberg *mt* W Germany 49.42N 8.45E
90 L7 Kreich *tribe* Cent Afr Rep
88 O4 Kreider,Le Algeria 34.09N 0.07E
63 L9 Kreiensen W Germany 51.52N 9.58E
Kreime, El *see* Mreyer, El
64 Q2 Kreischa E Germany 50.57N 13.47E
Kreis Reef *see* Circular Reef
113 D5 Krekatok I Alaska 62.01N 166.00W
53 X16 Krekjavatn,indre *L* Norway 61.15N 7.56E
53 X16 Krekjavatn,ytre *L* Norway 61.13N 7.58E
88 N6 Kreloua Sidi Brahim Algeria 30.31N 0.19W
65 M2 Křelovice Czechoslovakia 49.32N 15.10E
84 E8 Kremastí Greece 36.58N 22.52E
84 B4 Kremastón, Tekhnití Limni *res* Greece
82 H7 Kremena Bulgaria 43.10N 23.44E
45 E7 Kremenchug Ukraine U.S.S.R. 49.03N 33.25E
45 D7 Kremenchugskoye Vdkhr *res* Ukraine U.S.S.R.
46 F4 Kremenets Ukraine U.S.S.R. 50.05N 25.48E
45 J9 Kremenevka Ukraine U.S.S.R. 47.20N 37.30E
45 P2 Kremenki U.S.S.R. 55.00N 43.24E
47 M6 Kremenkul' U.S.S.R. 55.11N 61.10E
45 K7 Kremennaya Ukraine U.S.S.R. 49.03N 38.15E
46 N5 Kremenskaya U.S.S.R. 49.29N 43.30E
45 G1 Kremenskoye U.S.S.R. 55.06N 35.57E
65 M3 Křemešník *mt* Czechoslovakia 49.24N 15.20E
83 F2 Kremikovtsi Bulgaria 42.47N 23.30E
110 P1 Kremlin Montana 48.34N 110.06W
68 F4 Kremlin-Bicêtre France 48.49N 2.22E
63 S7 Kremmen E Germany 52.46N 13.02E
109 D1 Kremmling Colorado 40.03N 106.24W
63 L5 Krempe W Germany 53.50N 9.30E
65 N5 Krems Austria 48.25N 15.36E
65 M5 Krems *R* Nieder-Österreich Austria
65 K5 Krems *R* Ober-Österreich Austria
65 J8 Kremsbrücke Austria 46.58N 13.38E
65 K5 Kremsmünster Austria 48.05N 14.08E
65 K4 Křemže Czechoslovakia 48.54N 14.20E
40 N7 Krenitsyna,Pik *vol* Kuril Is U.S.S.R. 49.22N 154.43E
40 N7 Krenitsyna,Proliv *str* Kuril Is U.S.S.R.
113 D9 Krenitzin Is Aleutian Is
65 P2 Křenov Czechoslovakia 49.41N 16.37E
63 Q10 Krensitz E Germany 51.29N 12.28E
65 H8 Krenzeck-Gruppe *mts* Austria
39 J3 Krepost' U.S.S.R. 64.43N 170.45E
50 J4 Kreppa *R* Iceland
50 J5 Krepputunga *delta* Iceland
82 E7 Kreševo Yugoslavia 43.52N 18.02E
103 D5 Kresgeville Pennsylvania 40.55N 75.30W
42 B4 Kreshchenka U.S.S.R. 55.51N 80.00E
112 F1 Kress Texas 34.22N 101.46W
64 H8 Kressbronn W Germany 47.33N 9.40E
66 P1 Kressbronn W Germany 47.36N 9.35E
39 L2 Kresta,Zaliv *gulf* U.S.S.R.
46 H2 Kresti U.S.S.R. 55.48N 31.22E
47 M8 Krestiki U.S.S.R. 54.38N 75.29E
41 O8 Krest-Khal'dzhayy U.S.S.R. 62.55N 134.20E
46 J3 Krestovaya Smolensk U.S.S.R. 53.40N 32.49E
42 J3 Krestovaya Yakutsk U.S.S.R. 59.48N 113.15E
41 B3 Krestovaya, Guba Novaya Zemlya U.S.S.R. 74.08N 55.35E
47 G3 Krestovka U.S.S.R. 66.24N 52.31E
45 U2 Krestovo-Gorodishche U.S.S.R. 54.11N 48.35E
47 M1 Krestovskiy, Ostrov *isld* Leningrad U.S.S.R.
39 G1 Krestovskiy,Ostrov *isld* U.S.S.R. 70.50N 160.33E
39 E7 Krestovyy,Mys *C* Kamchatka U.S.S.R. 51.45N 158.10E
41 J3 Krestovyy,Mys *C* Krasnoyarsk U.S.S.R. 76.46N 109.40E
44 F5 Krestovyy Pereval *pass* Georgia U.S.S.R. 42.32N 44.32E
46 J1 Kresttsy U.S.S.R. 58.09N 32.48E
39 G6 Kresty Kamchatka U.S.S.R. 56.20N 160.20E
41 E5 Kresty Krasnoyarsk U.S.S.R. 70.50N 89.58E
41 H5 Kresty Krasnoyarsk U.S.S.R. 71.57N 102.19E
45 J1 Kresty Moscow U.S.S.R. 55.15N 37.07E
41 P5 Kresty U.S.S.R. 70.54N 136.15E
42 K2 Krestyakh U.S.S.R. 62.14N 116.12E
41 D4 Krest'yanka U.S.S.R. 72.55N 80.48E
46 D2 Kretinga Lithuania U.S.S.R. 55.52N 21.12E
88 M7 Krettamia Algeria 28.42N 3.32W
64 M8 Kreuth W Germany 47.39N 11.45E
66 Q4 Kreuz *mt* Switzerland 46.58N 9.47E
64 A2 Kreuzau W Germany 50.45N 6.30E
63 B2 Kreuzberg *dist* W Berlin W Germany
65 H8 Kreuzeck *mt* Austria 46.52N 13.07E
65 D7 Kreuzeck *mt* W Germany 47.28N 11.04E
66 N2 Kreuzegg *mt* Switzerland 47.18N 9.01E
65 J8 Kreuzen Kärnten Austria 46.40N 13.34E
65 L5 Kreuzen Ober-Österreich Austria 48.17N 14.48E
65 E7 Kreuzjoch *mt* Austria 47.16N 11.59E
66 N1 Kreuzlingen Switzerland 47.38N 9.12E
64 E2 Kreuztal W Germany 50.57N 8.00E
Krian *R see* Kerian *R*
78 C12 Krib,El Tunisia 36.19N 9.10E
91 A2 Kribi Cameroon 2.56N 9.56E
45 C3 Krichev Belorussiya U.S.S.R. 53.40N 31.44E
28 C4 Krichnaraja Sagara *res* Karnataka India
65 N6 Krieglach Austria 47.33N 15.34E
95 N2 Kriel S Africa 26.16S 29.14E
66 K3 Kriens Switzerland 47.03N 8.17E
66 P2 Kriesseren Switzerland 47.23N 9.36E
84 H5 Kriezá Greece 38.24N 24.08E
84 A2 Krífovon Greece 39.30N 20.55E
90 C9 Krigam Nigeria 5.12N 6.35E
39 M2 Kriguygun,Mys *C* U.S.S.R. 65.27N 171.12W
53 A3 Krik Denmark 56.47N 8.18E
53 A3 Krik Vig *inlet* Denmark 56.45N 8.16E
40 J9 Kril'on,Mys *C* Sakhalin U.S.S.R. 45.51N 142.04E
60 P9 Krim,De Netherlands 52.39N 6.39E
65 F7 Krimml Austria 47.14N 12.11E
65 F7 Krimmler Fälle *falls* Austria 47.13N 12.11E
65 F7 Krimmler Tal *V* Austria
60 G12 Krimpen aan den Lek Netherlands 51.54N 4.38E
66 N2 Krinau Switzerland 47.18N 9.03E
90 L7 Krindja Cent Afr Rep 8.21N 22.46E
52 E5 Kringen Norway 61.45N 9.35E
45 F8 Krinichki Ukraine U.S.S.R. 48.20N 34.29E
45 K8 Krinichnaya Ukraine U.S.S.R. 48.08N 38.04E
60 G12 Krinpen aan den Ijssel Netherlands 51.55N 4.35E
84 C5 Krionéri Greece 38.20N 21.35E
103 F3 Kripplebush New York 41.52N 74.14W
84 E7 Krísafa Greece 37.06N 22.32E
30 J6 Krishanagarh Bihar India 26.12N 85.01E
28 C2 Krishna Andhra Prad India 16.25N 77.19E
28 E2 Krishna *dist* Andhra Prad India
Krishnagar *see* Krishnanagar
28 D4 Krishnagiri Tamil Nadu India 12.33N 78.11E
28 H3 Krishnai R Assam India
28 E3 Krishna, Mouths of the Andhra Prad India
29 L6 Krishnanagar W Bengal India 23.22N 88.32E
28 D2 Krishna, R Andhra Prad India
28 C4 Krishnaraja Dam Karnataka India 12.25N 76.33E
28 C4 Krishnarajpet Karnataka India 12.40N 76.25E
84 D5 Krissaíos Kólpos *gulf* Greece
52 J9 Kristdala Sweden 57.24N 16.12E
88 N4 Kristel Algeria 35.50N 0.30W
52 J10 Kristianopel Sweden 56.15N 16.05E
52 D8 Kristiansand Norway 58.08N 8.01E
52 H10 Kristianstad Sweden 56.02N 14.10E
52 G10 Kristianstad *dist* Sweden
52 D3 Kristiansund Norway 63.06N 7.58E
51 J9 Kristiinan kaupunki Finland 62.16N 21.18E
52 H7 Kristinehamn Sweden 59.17N 14.09E
Kristinestad *see* Kristiinankaupunki
46 G5 Kristinovka Ukraine U.S.S.R. 48.50N 29.58E
53 E4 Kristrup Denmark 56.27N 10.05E
50 C7 Krísuvik Iceland 63.54N 22.05W
Krithia *see* Kirte
83 G9 Kríti *isld* Greece
42 D4 Kritovo U.S.S.R. 56.14N 90.00E
84 N11 Kritsá Crete 35.10N 25.38E
45 L2 Kriusha U.S.S.R. 54.57N 39.58E
82 G8 Kriva *R* Yugoslavia
82 E6 Krivaja *R* Bosnia Yugoslavia
82 F5 Krivaja *R* Vojvodina Yugoslavia
45 L1 Krivandino U.S.S.R. 55.33N 39.38E
65 J1 Křivoklát Czechoslovakia 50.03N 13.53E
42 B2 Krivolutskoye U.S.S.R. 60.14N 78.50E
45 M8 Krivorozh'ye U.S.S.R. 48.51N 40.45E
42 C4 Krivosheino U.S.S.R. 57.20N 83.55E
45 S6 Krivoyar U.S.S.R. 50.52N 46.30E
42 C4 Krivoyash U.S.S.R. 55.31N 84.14E
82 N3 Krivoye Ozero U.S.S.R. 47.58N 30.21E
45 E9 Krivoy Rog Ukraine U.S.S.R. 47.55N 33.24E
45 P3 Krivozer'ye U.S.S.R. 53.39N 43.54E
46 O1 Krivyachka U.S.S.R. 58.38N 45.19E
82 G8 Kriya Palanka Yugoslavia 42.11N 22.19E
88 S4 Kriz Tunisia 34.01N 8.15E
65 O3 Křižanov Czechoslovakia 49.24N 16.06E
82 D4 Križevci Yugoslavia 46.02N 16.33E
65 N2 Křižova Czechoslovakia 49.41N 15.51E
82 B5 Krk Yugoslavia 45.02N 14.34E
82 B5 Krk *isld* Yugoslavia 45.05N 14.34E
82 C7 Krka *R* Dalmatia Yugoslavia
82 C5 Krka *R* Slovenija Yugoslavia
62 J5 Krkonoše *mts* Czechoslovakia 50.45N 15.45E
79 P2 Krn *mt* Yugoslavia 46.16N 13.40E
62 K5 Krnov Czechoslovakia 50.05N 17.40E
62 K4 Krobia Poland 51.48N 17.00E
52 E6 Krøderen Norway 60.08N 9.48E
52 E6 Krøderen *L* Norway
117 B2 Kroetoe *pk* Surinam 4.25N 56.35W
53 B5 Krogager Denmark 55.43N 8.52E
64 P1 Krögis E Germany 51.07N 13.23E
53 E5 Krogsbølle Denmark 55.35N 10.23E
Kroh *see* Keroh
64 O6 Kröhstorf W Germany 48.37N 12.58E
50 H4 Krókdalur *V* Iceland
84 E8 Krokeaí Greece 36.53N 22.32E
52 J8 Krokek Sweden 58.40N 16.25E
51 D6 Kroken Nordland Norway 65.23N 14.15E
53 W16 Kroken Sogn og Fjordane Norway 61.20N 7.25E
84 E3 Krókion Greece 39.12N 22.45E
94 J5 Krokodil *R* S Africa
52 H3 Krokom Sweden 63.20N 14.30E
18 J5 Krokong Sarawak Malaysia 1.17N 110.02E
62 L1 Krokowa Poland 54.47N 18.09E
50 D4 Króksfjardharnes Iceland 65.27N 21.56W
50 C4 Króksfjördhur *B* Iceland
52 K2 Kroksjö Sweden 64.30N 17.55E
45 E5 Krolevets Ukraine U.S.S.R. 51.34N 33.24E
95 H10 Krom *R* S Africa
64 D2 Krombach W Germany 50.59N 7.58E
61 A3 Krombeke Belgium 50.55N 2.41E
95 N1 Kromdraai S Africa 25.48S 29.05E
62 K6 Kroměříž Czechoslovakia 49.19N 17.27E
95 N2 Kromklip S Africa 26.06S 29.12E
60 H9 Krommenie Netherlands 52.30N 4.46E
60 K11 Kromme Rijn *R* Netherlands
95 G7 Kromrivier S Africa 31.59S 23.02E
45 G4 Kromy U.S.S.R. 52.40N 35.46E
64 L3 Kronach W Germany 50.14N 11.20E
100 N8 Kronau Saskatchewan 50.20N 104.21W
64 E3 Kronberg W Germany 50.11N 8.31E
66 O2 Kronberg *mt* Switzerland 47.17N 9.21E
64 P3 Krondorf Czechoslovakia 50.20N 13.07E
64 C1 Kronenberg Nordrhein-Westfalen W Germany 51.12N 7.10E
64 A3 Kronenberg W Germany 50.20N 6.30E
25 J5 Krong Poko *R* Vietnam
28 K1 Kronli Assam India 28.25N 95.50E
52 H10 Kronoberg *dist* Sweden
51 K8 Kronoby Finland 63.44N 23.04E
39 G7 Kronoki U.S.S.R. 54.48N 161.12E
39 G7 Kronotskaya Sopka *vol* Kamchatka U.S.S.R. 54.54N 160.32E
39 G7 Kronotskiy,Mys *C* U.S.S.R. 54.45N 162.10E
39 G7 Kronotskiy Poluostrov *pen* U.S.S.R.
39 G7 Kronotskiy Zaliv *B* U.S.S.R.
39 G7 Kronotskoye Oz *L* U.S.S.R.
48 U4 Kronprins Christian Land Greenland
48 S8 Kronprinsen Ejland *isld* Greenland 69.00N 53.30W
50 O9 Kronprinsesse Märthas Bre *glacier* Jan Mayen I 71.07N 8.01W
123 B10 Kronprinsess Märtha Kyst *coast* Antarctica
97 Q4 Kronprins Frederiks Bjerge *mts* Greenland
123 A6 Kronprins Olav Kyst *coast* Antarctica
51 O12 Kronshtadt U.S.S.R. 60.00N 29.40E
25 E5 Kronwa Burma 15.24N 98.24E
64 N7 Kronwinkl W Germany 48.29N 12.03E
95 K8 Kroomie S Africa 32.46S 26.27E
95 L1 Kroondal S Africa 25.45S 27.20E
95 L3 Kroonstad S Africa 27.40S 27.15E
47 H7 Kropachevo U.S.S.R. 55.04N 57.58E
63 P4 Kröpelin E Germany 54.04N 11.49E
42 K3 Kropotkin Irkutsk U.S.S.R. 58.32N 115.25E
44 D2 Kropotkin Krasnodar U.S.S.R. 45.25N 40.35E
42 J3 Kropotkina,Khrebet *mts* U.S.S.R.
63 L4 Kropp W Germany 54.24N 9.31E
63 O9 Kroppenstedt E Germany 51.57N 11.19E
63 R9 Kropstädt E Germany 51.58N 12.44E
63 T4 Kröslin E Germany 54.08N 13.45E
62 L3 Krośniewice Poland 52.14N 19.10E
62 N6 Krosno Rzeszów Poland 49.40N 21.46E
62 J3 Krosno Zielona Góra Poland 52.03N 15.04E
50 B3 Kross Bardhastrandarsýsla, Vestur Iceland 65.31N 23.21W
50 E7 Kross Rangárvallasýsla Iceland 63.36N 20.18W
53 M9 Krossafelli *mt* Faeroes 62.08N 7.14W
50 M4 Krossanes Iceland 65.01N 13.40W
50 L6 Krossanes *C* Iceland 64.27N 14.30W
50 K2 Krossavík Iceland 66.19N 15.41W
53 Y15 Krossbu Norway 61.35N 8.01E
64 M2 Krossen E Germany 50.58N 11.59E
50 B3 Krosseyri Iceland 65.41N 23.21W
53 S18 Krossfjord *inlet* Norway 60.10N 5.15E
50 D2 Krossnesfjall *mt* Iceland 66.04N 21.32W
53 Y19 Krosso Norway 59.53N 8.27E
62 K4 Krotoszyn Poland 51.41N 17.27E
46 Q3 Krotovka U.S.S.R. 53.18N 51.02E
65 D6 Krotten Klein *mt* W Germany 47.32N 11.12E
107 E11 Krotz Springs Louisiana 30.31N 91.48W
88 R3 Kroub,El Algeria 36.15N 6.40E
89 B3 Kroufa Mauritania 17.23N 15.44W
88 S3 Kroumirie *mts* Tunisia
65 O2 Krouna Czechoslovakia 49.47N 16.02E
83 F3 Kroúsia,mt Greece 41.06N 23.06E
84 L11 Kroussón Crete 35.14N 24.59E
18 H9 Kroya Java Indon 7.37S 109.13E
83 D2 Krrab *mt* Albania 42.16N 19.58E
83 D3 Krrab *mts* Albania
82 C5 Krško Yugoslavia 45.58N 15.30E
45 Q4 Krucha U.S.S.R. 52.20N 44.45E
64 C3 Kruft-Mendig W Germany 50.24N 7.21E
99 L5 Krugerdorf Ontario 47.57N 79.54W
94 L4 Kruger Nat.Park S Africa
95 J5 Krugers S Africa 29.56S 25.49E
95 L2 Krugersdorp S Africa 26.06S 27.46E
94 R13 Krugersdorp West S Africa 26.06S 27.45E
95 H7 Krugerspoortdam *res* S Africa 31.18S 24.33E
94 L5 Krugerspost S Africa 25.00S 30.32E
47 L6 Kruglaya,Gora *mt* U.S.S.R. 54.42N 59.30E
40 G7 Kruglikovo U.S.S.R. 48.11N 135.07E
47 L5 Kruglitsa,Gora *mt* U.S.S.R. 55.18N 59.45E
113 L9 Krugloi Pt Aleutian Is 52.30N 173.45E
44 E3 Kruglolesskoye U.S.S.R. 44.42N 42.47E
45 A2 Krugloye Belorussiya U.S.S.R. 54.15N 29.50E
46 L6 Krugloye U.S.S.R. 47.01N 39.15E
18 E8 Krui Sumatra Indon 5.13S 103.56E
61 H2 Kruibeke Belgium 51.10N 4.19E
95 E8 Kruidfontein S Africa 32.51S 21.57E
60 E14 Kruiningen Netherlands 61.27N 4.03E
60 B3 Kruisdijk Netherlands 51.22N 3.32E
95 H9 Kruisfontein S Africa 34.00S 24.44E
61 E3 Kruishoutem Belgium 50.54N 3.32E
60 F13 Kruisland Netherlands 51.34N 4.24E
95 G9 Kruisvallei S Africa 33.52S 23.09E
83 D3 Krujë Albania 41.31N 19.35E
15 F5 Kru Kru Papua New Guinea 2.45S 141.27E
18 F3 Krukut, Kali *R* Indonesia
112 K2 Krum Texas 33.16N 97.16W
Krumasje *see* Yakaturo
65 M4 Krumau Austria 48.36N 15.28E
65 O6 Krumbach Austria 47.32N 16.12E
64 J7 Krumbach (Schwaben) W Germany 48.14N 10.22E
83 D2 Krumë Albania 42.12N 20.24E
66 N3 Krummenau Switzerland 47.15N 9.11E
64 D1 Krummenerl W Germany 51.05N 7.47E
63 F6 Krummhörn W Germany 53.26N 7.05E
63 T4 Krummin E Germany 54.03N 13.51E
82 K9 Krumovgrad Bulgaria 41.29N 25.38E
65 K8 Krumpendorf Austria 46.34N 14.13E
65 P1 Krumperky Czechoslovakia 50.05N 16.52E
65 D6 Krün W Germany 47.31N 11.18E
Krungkao *see* Ayutthaya
25 F6 Krung Thep Thailand 13.44N 100.30E
46 E3 Kruonis Lithuania U.S.S.R. 54.47N 24.18E
64 Q3 Krupá Czechoslovakia 50.11N 13.44E
82 E6 Krupanj Yugoslavia 44.21N 19.21E
45 F5 Krupets U.S.S.R. 51.38N 34.20E
62 L7 Krupina Czechoslovakia 48.22N 19.00E
46 G3 Krupki Belorussiya U.S.S.R. 54.19N 29.05E
113 E3 Krusenstern,C Alaska 67.10N 163.50W
101 R1 Krusenstern,C N W Terr 68.26N 113.57W
82 G7 Kruševac Yugoslavia 43.34N 21.20E
80 O1 Kruševo Yugoslavia 43.35N 16.13E
Krušné Hory *mts see* Erzgebirge *mts*
82 G9 Krušovo Yugoslavia 41.20N 21.17E
46 F2 Krustpils Latvia U.S.S.R. 56.29N 26.00E
47 G4 Krutaya U.S.S.R. 62.59N 54.45E
69 M8 Krüth France 47.56N 6.59E
42 C5 Krutikha Altay U.S.S.R. 53.59N 81.13E
47 N4 Krutikha Sverdlovsk U.S.S.R. 57.13N 61.08E
47 L7 Krutinka U.S.S.R. 56.01N 71.30E
39 F7 Krutogorova *R* U.S.S.R.
39 F7 Krutogorovo U.S.S.R. 54.59N 155.51E
42 C4 Krutologovo U.S.S.R. 55.16N 82.14E
43 G1 Krutoyarskiy U.S.S.R. 54.11N 63.07E
45 J4 Krutoye U.S.S.R. 52.25N 37.30E
40 N7 Kruzenshterna,Proliv *str* Kuril Is U.S.S.R.
113 U8 Kruzof I Alaska 57.10N 135.40W
100 K6 Krydor Saskatchewan 52.48N 107.05W
52 J6 Krylbo Sweden 60.07N 16.15E
44 C1 Krylovskaya U.S.S.R. 46.06N 39.19E
44 C1 Krylovskaya U.S.S.R. 46.18N 39.59E
62 P5 Krylów Poland 50.40N 24.01E
44 E9 Krym Ukraine U.S.S.R. 45.23N 36.36E
44 C10 Krym *pen* Ukraine U.S.S.R.
44 B3 Krymsk U.S.S.R. 44.56N 38.00E
46 J6 Krymskaya Oblast' *prov* Ukraine U.S.S.R.
44 C10 Krymskiye Gory *mts* Ukraine U.S.S.R.
62 M6 Krynica Poland 49.25N 20.56E
45 B1 Krynki Belorussiya U.S.S.R. 55.02N 30.28E
62 O2 Krynki Poland 53.18N 23.45E
Kryolitbrud *see* Ivigtut
64 P3 Kryry Czechoslovakia 50.10N 13.25E
45 B5 Kryuki Belorussiya U.S.S.R. 51.30N 30.16E
45 J1 Kryukovo U.S.S.R. 55.58N 37.10E
82 M3 Kryulyany U.S.S.R. 47.13N 29.09E
42 F5 Kryzhina,Khrebet *mt* U.S.S.R.
82 M2 Kryzhopol U.S.S.R. 48.20N 28.52E
62 L5 Krzepice Poland 50.58N 18.41E
62 N5 Krzeszów Poland 50.24N 22.20E
62 M5 Krzeszowice Poland 50.09N 19.42E
62 K4 Krzywin Poland 51.59N 16.49E
62 J3 Krzyż Poland 52.53N 16.01E
88 N7 Ksabi Algeria 29.07N 1.01W
88 L5 Ksabi Morocco 32.50N 4.26W
89 G1 Ksaib Ounane,El Mauritania 21.18N 5.34W
88 P4 Ksar Chellala Algeria 35.12N 2.20E
88 M6 Ksarel Aïd Algeria 30.55N 2.46W
89 C2 Ksar el Barka Mauritania 18.25N 12.20W
89 P4 Ksar El Boukhari Algeria 35.55N 2.47E
88 P5 Ksar el Hirane Algeria 33.48N 3.13E
88 L4 Ksar-el-Kebir Morocco 35.04N 5.56W
77 E9 Ksar Sghir Morocco 35.50N 5.34W
89 C1 Ksar Torchane Mauritania 20.42N 13.02W
88 N7 Kseïbat,El Algeria 28.04N 0.29W
88 M7 Kseïb,El Algeria 29.30N 2.12W
88 O5 Ksel,Djebel *mt* Algeria 33.44N 1.05E
21 A1 Ksen'evka U.S.S.R. 53.30N 118.42E
47 H5 Ksenofontova U.S.S.R. 61.02N 56.11E
42 K5 Ksen'yevka U.S.S.R. 53.32N 118.50E
88 Q3 Kseur,El Algeria 36.42N 4.50E
45 J5 Kshenskiy U.S.S.R. 51.53N 37.43E
62 K3 Książ Poland 52.05N 17.12E
88 T4 Ksour Essaf Tunisia 35.24N 11.00E
88 N5 Ksour, Monts des Algeria
88 T5 Ksour,Mts.des Tunisia
45 Q1 Kstovo U.S.S.R. 56.09N 44.12E
Ksudach *vol see* Shtyubelya,Sopka *vol*
Kteïbe *see* Kuteibe,El
84 E6 Kténas Óros *mt* Greece 37.34N 22.32E
Ktima *see* Paphos
84 F5 Ktipás *mt* Greece 38.24N 23.25E
18 C2 Kuah Pen Malaysia 6.20N 99.51E
23 C6 Kuaize He *R* Yunnan China
122 T16 Kuaku *isld* Gambier Is Pacific Oc 23.12S 134.51W
18 F4 Kuala Anambas Indonesia 2.59N 105.48E
18 C4 Kuala Sumatra Indon 3.35N 98.20E
18 L3 Kuala Belait Brunei 4.38N 114.12E
18 E3 Kuala Dungun Pen Malaysia 4.45N 103.24E
18 A7 Kuala Kangsar Pen Malaysia 4.50N 100.55E
18 L7 Kualakapuas Borneo Indon 3.00S 114.22E
18 C9 Kuala Kelawang Pen Malaysia 2.56N 102.03E
18 E3 Kuala Kerai Pen Malaysia 5.32N 102.12E
18 K5 Kualakeriau Borneo Indon 0.51N 113.21E
18 A6 Kuala Ketil Pen Malaysia 5.36N 100.38E
18 C8 Kuala Krau Pen Malaysia 3.42N 102.22E
18 B8 Kuala Kubu Baharu Pen Malaysia 3.35N 101.37E
18 A7 Kuala Kurau Pen Malaysia 5.00N 100.24E
18 K6 Kualakurun Borneo Indon 1.10S 113.54E
18 B3 Kualalangsa Sumatra Indon 4.31N 97.59E
18 C8 Kuala Lipis Pen Malaysia 4.11N 102.00E
18 B8 Kuala Lumpur Pen Malaysia 3.08N 101.42E
18 K6 Kualamanjual Borneo Indon 1.23S 112.01E
18 A6 Kuala Muda Pen Malaysia 5.35N 100.21E
18 D2 Kuala Nerang Pen Malaysia 6.14N 100.33E
18 K7 Kualapembuang Borneo Indon 3.28S 112.35E
18 L3 Kuala Penyu Sabah Malaysia 5.35N 115.35E
18 J7 Kualapesaguan Borneo Indon 2.02S 110.07E
18 C9 Kuala Pilah Pen Malaysia 2.44N 102.15E
114 C5 Kualapuu Hawaiian Is 21.09N 157.02W
18 D9 Kuala Rompin Pen Malaysia 2.45N 103.29E
18 B8 Kuala Selangor Pen Malaysia 3.24N 101.12E
18 C3 Kualasimpang Sumatra Indon 4.12N 98.03E
18 E3 Kuala Terengganu Pen Malaysia 5.20N 103.07E
18 E6 Kualatungkal Sumatra Indon 0.50S 103.28E
47 B3 Kualoyarvi U.S.S.R. 66.58N 29.10E
18 M3 Kuamut Sabah Malaysia 5.08N 117.30E
18 M3 Kuamut *R* Sabah Malaysia
15 M9 Kuanak I Louisiade Arch 11.10S 152.54E
22 L6 Kuancheng Hebei China 40.36N 118.30E
19 C3 Kuandang Celebes Indon 0.53N 122.58E
19 C3 Kuandang,Teluk *B* Celebes Indonesia
21 C7 Kuandian Liaoning China 40.45N 124.46E
18 B8 Kuang Pen Malaysia 3.16N 101.33E
Kuang-chou *see* Guangzhou
Kuang-hsi *see* Guangxi *province*
Kuang-tung *see* Guangdong *province*
Kuan-nan *see* Qinglan
18 D8 Kuantan Pen Malaysia 3.50N 103.19E
Kuan-yün *see* Guayun
11 K3 Kuaotunu New Zealand 35.46S 175.45E
30 L6 Kuari Bihar India 26.24N 87.26E
94 D5 Kub Namibia 24.17S 17.32E
44 J6 Kuba Azerbaydzhan U.S.S.R. 41.23N 48.33E
44 E4 Kuba U.S.S.R. 43.51N 43.27E
41 N4 Kuba-Aryta,Ostrov U.S.S.R.
34 E3 Kubaibât Syria 35.13N 37.09E
34 J2 Kubaibate Syria 36.38N 41.01E
Kubaisa *see* Kubaysah
39 C3 Kubalakh U.S.S.R. 63.03N 144.31E
41 M7 Kubalakh,Oz *L* U.S.S.R. 67.04N 124.13E
46 L6 Kuban' *R* U.S.S.R.
90 L6 Kubar Sudan 11.34N 23.05E
33 M5 Kubārah Oman 24.05N 56.54E
94 C4 Kubas Namibia 22.16S 15.39E
44 H8 Kubatly Azerbaydzhan U.S.S.R. 39.19N 46.35E
34 K5 Kubaysah Iraq 33.37N 42.37E
33 N10 Kubbar *isld* Kuwait 29.04N 48.28E
52 L3 Kubbe Sweden 63.32N 18.05E
90 L6 Kubbum Sudan 11.50N 23.42E
47 E5 Kubena *R* U.S.S.R.
47 D6 Kubenskoye,Oz *L* U.S.S.R.
45 O9 Kuberle U.S.S.R. 47.01N 42.10E
15 G7 Kubibu, L Papua New Guinea 6.21S 143.18E
45 H1 Kubinka U.S.S.R. 55.34N 36.43E
15 G6 Kubkain Papua New Guinea 4.20S 142.22E
46 G2 Kublichi Belorussiya U.S.S.R. 55.10N 28.24E
66 Q4 Küblis Switzerland 46.55N 9.47E
46 O2 Kubnya *R* U.S.S.R.
20 G8 Kubokawa Japan 33.13N 133.09E
94 D7 Kuboos S Africa 28.32S 17.00E
15 H7 Kubor, Mt Papua New Guinea 6.10S 144.43E
15 H7 Kubor Ra Papua New Guinea
82 K7 Kubrat Bulgaria 43.49N 26.31E
86 J5 Kûbri, El Egypt 30.02N 32.32E
18 L10 Kubu Bali Indon 8.15S 115.30E
18 A6 Kubu Gajah Pen Malaysia 5.08N 100.40E
42 J6 Kubukhay U.S.S.R. 50.29N 114.55E
18 L5 Kubumesaäi Borneo Indon 1.26N 115.05E
15 J8 Kubuna Papua New Guinea 8.48S 146.42E
43 H1 Kubyshevskiy U.S.S.R. 53.17N 66.16E
82 G6 Kučevo Yugoslavia 44.30N 21.40E
Kucha *see* Kuqa
29 J2 Kuchai Bihar India 22.50N 85.45E
29 D4 Kuchaman Rajasthan India 27.10N 74.54E
29 D4 Kuchaman Road Rajasthan India 27.01N 74.58E
93 G4 Kuchelebai Kenya 1.30N 35.02E
61 P4 Küchelscheid Belgium 50.31N 6.12E
64 H6 Kuchen W Germany 48.38N 9.48E
65 B7 Kuchen-Spitze *mt* Austria 47.03N 10.14E
18 J5 Kuching Sarawak Malaysia 1.32N 110.20E
21 E12 Kuchino erabu shima *isld* Japan
21 E13 Kuchino shima *isld* Japan
20 D9 Kuchinotsu Japan 32.38N 130.10E
45 C5 Kuchinovka Ukraine U.S.S.R. 51.43N 31.58E
20 F6 Kuchitagi Japan 35.10N 132.42E
65 H6 Kuchl Austria 47.38N 13.10E
42 B5 Kuchukskoye, Oz *L* U.S.S.R.
82 M3 Kuchurgan *R* U.S.S.R.
63 N5 Kücknitz W Germany 53.54N 10.49E
Kuçove *see* Qyteti Stalin
37 C3 Küçük Anafarta Turkey 40.19N 26.20E
36 B4 Küçük Bahçe Turkey 38.34N 26.25E
37 F1 Küçükçekmece Turkey 41.01N 28.47E
37 F2 Küçükçekmece Gölü *L* Turkey
37 F2 Küçükçekmece Koya *crater* Turkey
36 G3 Küçük Gölü *L* Turkey
37 B3 Küçük Kemikli Burun *C* Turkey 40.18N 26.14E
37 H1 Küçükköy Turkey 41.05N 28.47E
36 B3 Küçük Kuyu Turkey 39.32N 26.34E
36 B3 Küçük Menderes *R* Çanakkale Turkey
36 C4 Küçük Menderes *R* İzmir Turkey
29 B6 Kuda Gujarat India 23.08N 71.30E
42 G6 Kuda U.S.S.R. 52.28N 104.25E
26 R9 Kuda *R* Sri Lanka
42 G5 Kuda *R* U.S.S.R.
28 B2 Kudachi Karnataka India 16.39N 74.54E
20 P10 Kudaka-shima *isld* Okinawa Japan 26.07N 127.54E
28 A2 Kudal Maharashtra India 16.01N 73.44E
20 E7 Kudamatsu Japan 34.02N 131.51E
90 C6 Kudan Nigeria 11.20N 7.41E
18 J6 Kudangan Borneo Indon 1.36S 111.01E
26 T9 Kuda Oya Sri Lanka 6.31N 81.07E
18 E5 Kudap Sumatra Indon 1.15N 102.28E
43 L7 Kudara Tadzhikistan U.S.S.R. 38.25N 72.39E
42 H6 Kudara U.S.S.R. 52.15N 106.40E
42 H6 Kudara-Somon U.S.S.R. 50.10N 107.28E
116 A1 Kudarebe *pt* Aruba W I 12.40N 70.03W
18 M2 Kudat Sabah Malaysia 6.54N 116.47E
25 C1 Kudaw Burma 22.34N 95.04E
33 D7 Kudaya Saudi Arabia 19.22N 41.47E
60 H11 Kudelstaart Netherlands 52.15N 4.45E
47 H8 Kudeyevskiy U.S.S.R. 54.55N 56.46E
50 G7 Kúdhatljót *R* Iceland
113 F9 Kudiakof *islds* Alaska
44 J6 Kudial *R* Azerbaydzhan U.S.S.R.
46 E3 Kudirkos Naumiestis Lithuania U.S.S.R. 54.45N 22.58E
28 C3 Kudligi Karnataka India 14.55N 76.22E
35 G1 Kudnah Syria 33.01N 35.53E
113 G8 Kudobin *islds* Alaska
20 E9 Kudogawa Japan 32.30N 131.38E
28 B4 Kudremukh *mt* Karnataka India 13.09N 75.12E
42 C4 Kudryashevo U.S.S.R. 57.15N 80.39E
40 L9 Kudryavyy *vol* Kuril Is U.S.S.R. 45.23N 148.48E
14 F5 Kuduarra Well W Australia 20.45S 126.10E
43 J8 Kuduk Afghanistan 37.30N 69.54E
40 B2 Kudu-Kyuyel' U.S.S.R. 59.25N 121.06E
18 J9 Kudus Java Indon 6.46S 110.48E
86 E10 Kudyet el Islâm Egypt 27.32N 30.44E
47 G6 Kudymkar U.S.S.R. 59.01N 54.40E
Kuei-chou *see* Guizhou *prov*
Kuei-chu *see* Huaxi
23 J6 Kuei-shan Tao *isld* Taiwan
Kuei-sui *see* Hohhot
24 E3 K'uei-t'un Ho *R see* Kuytun He China
39 G3 Kuel *R* U.S.S.R.
90 M5 Ku,El *watercourse* Sudan
51 P2 Kuets'yarvi, Ozero *L* U.S.S.R. 69.25N 30.10E
Kueyang *see* Guiyang
34 M6 Kūfah, Al Iraq 32.02N 44.25E
15 A5 Kufar Moluccas Indon 3.34S 130.47E
35 G7 Kufeirat Abu Khinan Jordan 31.44N 35.48E
35 G5 Kufeir,El Jordan 32.13N 35.56E
35 G6 Kufeir el Wakhyan Jordan 31.45N 35.46E
85 E5 Kuff Libya 28.26N 18.54E
36 D4 Kûfi *R* Turkey
33 H6 Kuflah,Al Saudi Arabia 21.03N 49.02E
85 G7 Kufra, Al *oasis* Libya
35 F4 Kufr Abil Jordan 32.25N 35.40E
35 F4 Kufr Alma Jordan 32.29N 35.42E
35 G3 Kufr 'An Jordan 32.33N 35.45E
35 F3 Kufr Asad Jordan 32.35N 35.43E
35 F4 Kufr 'Awan Jordan 32.25N 35.41E
Küfre *see* Sirvan
35 F4 Kufrinja Jordan 32.18N 35.42E
35 F4 Kufrinja *R* Jordan
35 G3 Kufr Jayiz Jordan 32.37N 35.49E
35 G4 Kufr Khal Jordan 32.22N 35.53E
35 G3 Kufr Kifiya Jordan 32.30N 35.46E
35 F4 Kufr Rakib Jordan 32.27N 35.41E
35 G3 Kufr Saum Jordan 32.41N 35.48E
35 G3 Kufr Yuba Jordan 32.33N 35.48E
65 F6 Kufstein Austria 47.36N 12.11E
86 G5 Kufûr el 'Âyid Egypt 30.28N 31.35E
86 G4 Kufûr Nigm Egypt 30.45N 31.35E
20 F7 Kuga Japan 34.06N 132.04E
44 J1 Kugach *R* U.S.S.R.
101 H1 Kugaluk *R* N W Terr
43 N5 Kugaly Kazakhstan U.S.S.R. 44.30N 78.41E
37 F5 Kugans *R* Turkey
24 A5 Kugart Pass Kirgiziya/Xinjiang Uygur Zizhiqu 40.20N 74.52E
43 L6 Kugart Pass *pass* China/U.S.S.R. 40.20N 74.52E
43 K7 Kugas Afghanistan 38.27N 70.42E
45 T1 Kugesi U.S.S.R. 56.00N 47.15E
44 C1 Kugey U.S.S.R. 46.53N 39.21E
47 J4 Kugi U.S.S.R. 63.26N 62.36E
43 H7 Kugitangtau, Khrebet *mts* Turkmeniya U.S.S.R.
101 G1 Kugmallit B N W Terr
87 J7 Kugno Ethiopia 6.18N 42.30E
90 C6 Kugo Nigeria 10.05N 7.10E
44 C1 Kugo-Yeya *R* U.S.S.R.
23 B3 Kugqa Sichuan China 30.47N 101.12E
22 D9 Kugri Qinghai China 35.50N 98.28E
113 F4 Kugruk *R* Alaska
44 E2 Kugul'ta U.S.S.R. 45.23N 42.24E
Kuhaifiya *see* Kuhayfiyah, Al
Kuhak *see* Kahak
32 K7 Kūhak Iran 27.10N 63.15E
24 D10 Kuhanbokano *mt pk* Xizang Zizhiqu China 31.57N 83.15E
33 E3 Kuhayfīyah, Al Saudi Arabia 27.11N 43.00E
64 L7 Kühbach W Germany 48.29N 11.11E
Kuh Banan *see* Kūhbonān
63 Q6 Kuhbier E Germany 53.09N 12.06E
32 G5 Kūhbonān Iran 31.23N 56.16E
37 H7 Kuh Dağı *mt* Turkey
32 B4 Kūhdasht Iran 33.31N 47.39E
Kuh-e Dasht *see* Kūhdasht
Kūh-e Leylā *see* Lālī *oil field*
32 G7 Kūhestak Iran 26.50N 57.04E
32 D5 Kuhgiluyeh Iran 30.49N 50.36E
32 D6 Kuh-i-Mand *oil well* Iran 28.09N 51.26E
32 C2 Kūhīn Iran 36.18N 49.37E
32 J7 Kūhīrī Iran 26.55N 61.04E
Kuhistak *see* Kūhestak
32 J8 Kūh Lab, Ra's *C* Iran 25.17N 60.28E
63 T4 Kühlenhagen E Germany 54.03N 13.38E
51 L10 Kuhmalahti Finland 61.31N 24.35E
51 O7 Kuhmo Finland 64.04N 29.30E
97 S3 Kuhn Ø *isld* Greenland 74.50N 20.00W
65 L8 Kühnsdorf Austria 46.37N 14.38E
32 E4 Kūhpayeh Iran 32.42N 52.25E
32 G5 Kūhpāyeh *mt* Iran 30.34N 57.08E
32 G8 Kūh, Ra's-al- *C* Iran 25.47N 57.18E
63 Q5 Kuhs E Germany 53.53N 12.15E
32 J7 Kūh Sar Iran 26.25N 60.34E
63 J6 Kuhstedt W Germany 53.24N 8.58E
Ku-hua *see* Shoucheng
32 E7 Kuhvār Iran 27.06N 53.58E
Kuhwar *see* Kuhvār
15 J7 Kui Papua New Guinea 7.30S 147.16E
94 D6 Küibis Namibia 26.42S 16.51E
32 E2 Kuidzhuk Turkmeniya U.S.S.R. 37.40N 53.45E
94 G6 Kuiepan *salt pan* S Africa 27.33S 22.00E
29 K2 Kuilapal W Bengal India 22.50N 86.39E
21 C3 Kuile He *R* Nei Monggol Zizhiqu China
95 N3 Kuilen, De S Africa 27.05S 29.10E
95 K1 Kuilfontein S Africa 25.45S 26.22E
95 B9 Kuilsrivier S Africa 33.55S 18.40E
60 M8 Kuinre Netherlands 52.47N 5.50E
94 D5 Kuis Namibia 24.16S 17.35E
94 C4 Kuiseb *watercourse* Namibia

23 G7 **Kuitan** Guangdong China 23.05N 116.00E
113 U8 **Kuiu I** Alaska 56.40N 134.00W
51 L6 **Kuivajoki** *R* Finland
51 L6 **Kuivaniemi** Finland 65.35N 25.10E
33 G3 **Kū'Jabal al** *mt* Saudi Arabia 27.36N 47.04E
29 K7 **Kujang** Orissa India 20.12N 86.38E
21 D8 **Kujang-dong** N Korea 39.52N 126.00E
20 P1 **Kuji** Japan 40.10N 141.47E
20 O5 **Kuji-gawa** *R* Japan 36.29N 140.37E
20 P1 **Kuji-wan** *B* Japan
29 J1 **Kuju** Bihar India 23.44N 85.31E
93 E3 **Kuju** Uganda 2.05N 33.36E
Kujur *see* **Kojūr**
20 E8 **Kujū-san** *mt* Japan 33.07N 131.14E
Kuk *see* **Muang Kuk**
113 G1 **Kuk** *R* Alaska
42 J6 **Kuka** U.S.S.R. 51.45N 112.58E
114 C6 **Kukaiau** Hawaiian Is 20.03N 155.20W
113 K7 **Kukak** Alaska 58.19N 154.11W
113 K7 **Kukaklek L** Alaska 59.14N 155.20W
113 G6 **Kukaklik L** Alaska 61.35N 160.20W
31 J2 **Kukalang** *pass* Xinjiang Uygur Zizhiqu China 36.38N 76.40E
32 D5 **Kukālar, Kūh-e** *mts* Iran 31.45N 50.56E
94 G5 **Kukami** Botswana 24.08S 22.19E
40 F7 **Kukan** U.S.S.R. 49.10N 133.25E
99 H4 **Kukatush** Ontario 48.09N 82.15W
90 F5 **Kukawa** Nigeria 12.55N 13.31E
94 G3 **Kuke** Botswana 21.07S 22.16E
14 C10 **Kukerin** W Australia 33.11S 118.03E
83 D2 **Kukës** Albania 42.05N 20.24E
39 C5 **Kukhtuy** U.S.S.R. 59.38N 143.10E
39 C4 **Kukhtuy** *R* U.S.S.R.
21 E12 **Kukinaga** Japan 30.24N 131.00E
15 J8 **Kukipi** Papua New Guinea 8.11S 146.09E
51 L5 **Kukkola** Finland 66.01N 24.05E
46 Q2 **Kukmor** U.S.S.R. 56.09N 50.50E
46 L1 **Kukoboy** U.S.S.R. 58.41N 39.52E
113 F2 **Kukpowruk** *R* Alaska
113 E2 **Kukpuk** *R* Alaska
29 D6 **Kukshi** Madhya Prad India 22.10N 74.48E
24 H5 **Kukucher** *water hole* Xinjiang Uygur Zizhiqu China 41.10N 93.48E
24 H5 **Kukucher** *water hole* Xinjiang Uygur Zizhiqu China 41.10N 93.48E
114 B6 **Kukuihaele** Hawaiian Is 20.08N 155.35W
114 F4 **Kukuiula** Hawaiian Is 21.53N 159.28W
100 L1 **Kukukus L** Ontario 49.45N 91.58W
26 R8 **Kukulugala** *mt* Sri Lanka 6.40N 80.16E
89 C7 **Kukuna** Sierra Leone 9.23N 12.40W
28 E2 **Kukunuru** Andhra Prad India 17.34N 81.11E
18 D10 **Kukup** Pen Malaysia 1.19N 103.28E
18 D10 **Kukup** *isld* Pen Malaysia
9 A6 **Kuku Pt** Wake I Pacific Oc 19.18N 166.34E
87 D5 **Kukur** Sudan 11.30N 33.52E
37 F4 **Kükürt Tepe** *mt* Turkey 41.08N 41.26E
18 L7 **Kukusan, Gunung** *mt* Borneo Indon 3.17S 115.57E
40 D4 **Kukushka** U.S.S.R. 54.40N 126.01E
46 S1 **Kukushtan** U.S.S.R. 57.35N 56.50E
41 J6 **Kukusunda** *R* U.S.S.R.
42 H4 **Kukuyskiy Mys** U.S.S.R. 57.00N 106.20E
32 F7 **Kūl** *R* Iran
82 H7 **Kula** Bulgaria 43.53N 22.30E
36 D4 **Kula** Turkey 38.33N 28.38E
82 F5 **Kula** Yugoslavia 45.37N 19.32E
18 C5 **Kulabu, Gunung** *mt* Sumatra Indon 0.30N 99.47E
31 F5 **Kulachi** Pakistan 31.58N 70.30E
45 D4 **Kulagi** U.S.S.R. 52.54N 32.25E
46 Q5 **Kulagino** Kazakhstan U.S.S.R. 48.22N 51.35E
29 J5 **Kulaha Hill** Bihar India 24.23N 84.56E
18 D10 **Kulai** Pen Malaysia 1.41N 103.33E
24 G11 **Kula Kangri** *mt pk* Xizang Zizhiqu China 28.15N 90.34E
33 D6 **Kulākh** Saudi Arabia 21.16N 40.55E
Kulakkaya *see* **Yavuzkemal**
42 E3 **Kulakovo** U.S.S.R. 58.05N 93.50E
43 D4 **Kulakshi** Kazakhstan U.S.S.R. 47.09N 55.22E
93 H3 **Kulal, Mt** Kenya 2.44N 36.56E
44 K3 **Kulaly Ostrov** *isld* Kazakhstan U.S.S.R.
43 M6 **Kulanak** Kirgiziya U.S.S.R. 41.22N 75.18E
43 E4 **Kulandy, P-ov** *pen* Kazakhstan U.S.S.R.
31 B8 **Kulaneh** *reg* Pakistan
114 C7 **Kulani Prison** Hawaiian Is 19.32N 155.18W
43 E4 **Kulanoy** Kazakhstan U.S.S.R. 46.06N 59.32E
43 K3 **Kulanutpes** *R* Kazakhstan U.S.S.R.
31 C6 **Kulao R** Pakistan
41 O5 **Kular** U.S.S.R. 70.35N 134.34E
41 O6 **Kular, Kryazh** *ridge* U.S.S.R.
114 E6 **Kula Sanitarium** Hawaiian Is
28 D6 **Kulasekharapatnam** Tamil Nadu India 8.23N 78.05E
19 K8 **Kulassein** *isld* Philippines 6.24N 120.40E
82 H9 **Kulata** Bulgaria 41.23N 23.21E
18 M5 **Kulat, Gunung** *mt* Borneo Indon 1.21N 117.17E
31 J9 **Kulaura** Bangladesh 24.32N 92.02E
85 L9 **Kulb** Sudan 21.02N 30.42E
45 F5 **Kul'bak** U.S.S.R. 51.15N 34.45E
41 J4 **Kul'cha, Mys** *C* U.S.S.R. 73.31N 109.13E
40 H5 **Kul'chi** U.S.S.R. 53.33N 139.32E
46 D2 **Kuldīga** Latvia U.S.S.R. 56.58N 21.58E
41 K3 **Kul'dima, Bukhta** *gulf* U.S.S.R.
Kuldja *see* **Yining**
101 K8 **Kuldo** Br Columbia 55.56N 127.53W
43 G6 **Kul'dzhuktau, Gory** *mts* Uzbekistan U.S.S.R.
94 F4 **Kule** Botswana 23.05S 20.05E
37 E1 **Kule** *R* Turkey
45 O1 **Kulebaki** U.S.S.R. 55.25N 42.31E
45 G8 **Kulebovka** Ukraine U.S.S.R. 48.37N 35.10E
37 E3 **Külefli** Turkey 40.16N 27.55E
82 C6 **Kulen Vakuf** Yugoslavia 44.35N 16.02E
53 S19 **Kuleseid** Norway 59.44N 5.15E
45 L9 **Kuleshovka** U.S.S.R. 47.05N 39.35E
86 G7 **Kûlet el Qrein** *hill* Egypt 29.27N 31.56E
43 F1 **Kulevchi** U.S.S.R. 53.14N 61.24E
31 H4 **Kulgam** Kashmir 33.40N 75.03E
41 O6 **Kulgasokh** *R* U.S.S.R.
13 C7 **Kulgera** N Terr Australia 25.50S 133.02E
19 C9 **Kuli** Indonesia 10.51S 123.05E
19 N4 **Kuli** *isld* Truk Is Pacific Oc 7.26N 151.39E
53 K4 **Kulia Gunnarstorp** Sweden 56.06N 12.50E
47 G6 **Kuligi** U.S.S.R. 58.15N 53.42E
113 H7 **Kulik, L** Alaska 59.49N 158.50W
113 K7 **Kulik, L** Alaska 59.00N 154.50W
82 J1 **Kulikov** U.S.S.R. 49.59N 24.05E
45 C5 **Kulikovka** Ukraine U.S.S.R. 51.20N 31.40E
45 K3 **Kulikovo Pole** U.S.S.R. 53.25N 38.43E
45 O6 **Kulikovskiy** U.S.S.R. 50.51N 42.32E
18 A6 **Kulim** Pen Malaysia 5.20N 100.35E
14 C10 **Kulin** W Australia 32.42S 118.08E
42 G2 **Kulinda** U.S.S.R. 60.12N 103.30E
42 H2 **Kulinda** U.S.S.R. 61.43N 107.59E
26 R7 **Kuliyapitiya** Sri Lanka 7.27N 80.03E
14 B9 **Kulja** W Australia 30.28S 117.17E
43 N8 **Kul'kent** Tadzhikistan U.S.S.R. 40.09N 70.42E
31 D1 **Kulkishlak** Uzbekistan U.S.S.R. 39.27N 67.04E
43 G5 **Kulkuduk** Uzbekistan U.S.S.R. 42.31N 63.16E
12 G4 **Kulkyne** *R* New S Wales
53 K4 **Kulla Gunnarstorp** Sweden 56.07N 12.40E
53 J4 **Kullen** *pen* Sweden 56.18N 12.28E
64 J1 **Küllstedt** E Germany 51.16N 10.16E
66 J2 **Kulm** Aargau Switzerland 47.18N 8.08E
108 M3 **Kulm** N Dakota 46.19N 98.56W
66 K3 **Kulm** Schwyz Switzerland 47.03N 8.29E
64 M4 **Kulmain** W Germany 49.53N 11.55E
89 H7 **Kulmasa** Ghana 9.47N 2.25W
64 L3 **Kulmbach** W Germany 50.06N 11.28E
47 E4 **Kuloy** U.S.S.R. 64.57N 43.32E
47 E3 **Kuloy** *R* Arkhangel'sk U.S.S.R.
47 E5 **Kuloy** *R* Vologda U.S.S.R.
37 F7 **Kulp** Turkey 38.32N 41.01E
30 C7 **Kulpahar** Uttar Prad India 25.20N 79.38E
12 E5 **Kulpara** S Australia 34.07S 137.59E
89 H6 **Kulpawn** *R* Ghana
103 B5 **Kulpmont** Pennsylvania 40.47N 76.27W
103 D6 **Kulpsville** Pennsylvania 40.15N 75.21W
43 C4 **Kul'sary** Kazakhstan U.S.S.R. 46.59N 54.02E
64 H4 **Külsheim** W Germany 49.40N 9.33E
42 H6 **Kul'skiy** U.S.S.R. 52.12N 109.35E
51 M3 **Kultala** Finland 68.31N 26.44E
43 B4 **Kultay** Kazakhstan U.S.S.R. 45.20N 51.19E
44 L2 **Kultay** U.S.S.R. 45.20N 51.25E
29 K1 **Kulti** W Bengal India 23.45N 86.50E
52 J2 **Kultsjöluspen** Sweden 64.57N 15.30E
51 D6 **Kultsjön** *L* Sweden 65.00N 15.00E
42 G6 **Kultuk** U.S.S.R. 51.46N 103.45E
39 H4 **Kultushino** U.S.S.R. 60.27N 166.28E
63 R10 **Kültzschau** E Germany 51.28N 12.41E
29 E2 **Kulu** Himachal Pradesh India 31.59N 77.06E
36 G3 **Kulu** Turkey 39.06N 33.02E
39 D4 **Kulu** U.S.S.R. 61.52N 147.29E
15 K6 **Kulu** *R* New Britain
39 D4 **Kulu** *R* U.S.S.R.
43 P3 **Kuludzhun** Kazakhstan U.S.S.R. 49.05N 83.05E
87 H3 **Kululli** Ethiopia 14.26N 40.20E
92 F5 **Kululu** Tanzania 6.31S 33.04E
15 M8 **Kulumadau** Woodlark I Papua New Guinea 9.05S 152.43E
Kuluncak *see* **Ayvalı**
K'u-lun-ch'i *see* **Hure Qi**
43 N1 **Kulunda** U.S.S.R. 52.34N 78.58E
42 C5 **Kulunda** *R* U.S.S.R.
43 M1 **Kulundinskaya Step'** U.S.S.R.
42 B5 **Kulundinskoye, Oz** *L* U.S.S.R.
122 R15 **Kulu-puhi-puhi, Pte** *C* Mangaréva Pacific Oc 23.07S 135.02W
48 U14 **Kulusuk** *C* Greenland 65.32N 37.15W
42 K6 **Kulusutay** U.S.S.R. 50.14N 115.48E
28 D5 **Kulutalai** Tamil Nadu India 10.57N 78.25E
47 M6 **Kuluyevo** U.S.S.R. 55.14N 60.36E
32 F5 **Kūlvand** Iran 31.22N 54.36E
12 G6 **Kulwin** Victoria 35.02S 142.40E
43 J7 **Kulyab** Tadzhikistan U.S.S.R. 37.55N 69.47E
45 O5 **Kulyabovka** U.S.S.R. 51.47N 42.25E
42 B2 **Kul'-Yegan** *R* U.S.S.R.
42 C2 **Kulynigol** *R* U.S.S.R.
36 C4 **Kum** *R* Turkey
35 G1 **Kum** *watercourse* Syria
20 F8 **Kuma** Japan 33.41N 132.53E
90 E8 **Kuma** Nigeria 6.56N 11.21E
20 D9 **Kuma** *R* Japan
44 F3 **Kuma** *R* Stavropol' etc U.S.S.R.
47 K6 **Kuma** *R* Tyumen U.S.S.R.
15 G8 **Kumaderi Reef** Torres Str, Qnsld
20 A2 **Kumagawa** Tōkyō Japan
20 N5 **Kumagaya** Japan 36.09N 139.22E
18 J7 **Kumai** Borneo Indonesia 2.45S 111.44E
15 G7 **Kumaio** Papua New Guinea 7.18S 143.40E
20 J2 **Kumaishi** Japan 42.10N 139.58E
Kumait, Al *see* **Kumayt, Al**
18 J7 **Kumai, Teluk** *B* Borneo Indon
43 F2 **Kumak** U.S.S.R. 51.09N 60.08E
43 E2 **Kumak** *R* U.S.S.R.
117 A3 **Kumaka** Guyana 3.52N 58.25W
42 K5 **Kumakanda** U.S.S.R. 52.50N 116.55E
41 N5 **Kumakh-Surt** U.S.S.R. 71.30N 127.08E
42 J6 **Kumakhta** U.S.S.R. 51.25N 113.50E
40 E2 **Kumaky** *R* U.S.S.R.
92 D12 **Kumalo** *airport* Zimbabwe 20.03S 28.51E
15 E4 **Kumamba, Kepulauan** *islds* Irian Jaya
20 D9 **Kumamoto** Japan 32.50N 130.42E
20 D9 **Kumamoto** *prefect* Japan
44 J8 **Kumani** *isld* Azerbaydzhan U.S.S.R. 39.30N 49.30E
82 F7 **Kumanica** Yugoslavia 43.28N 20.16E
20 K8 **Kumano** Japan 33.54N 136.08E
20 K8 **Kumano-gawa** *R* Japan
82 G8 **Kumanovo** Yugoslavia 42.07N 21.40E
11 F9 **Kumara** New Zealand 42.37S 171.11E
40 D6 **Kumara** U.S.S.R. 51.34N 126.45E
11 F9 **Kumara Junction** New Zealand 42.35S 171.07E
30 L7 **Kumari** Bihar India 25.40N 87.43E
Kum Arik *R see* **Aksu He**
31 H9 **Kumarkhali** Bangladesh 23.54N 89.16E
14 D10 **Kumarl** W Australia 32.48S 121.33E
89 J8 **Kumasi** Ghana 6.45N 1.35W
30 B2 **Kumaun** *div* Uttar Prad India
15 B5 **Kumawa, Pegunungan** *ra* Irian Jaya
34 O6 **Kumayt, Al** Iraq 32.03N 46.53E
90 D9 **Kumba** Cameroon 4.39N 9.26E
Kumbak, Mt *see* **Amungwiwa, Mt**
28 D5 **Kumbakonam** Tamil Nadu India 10.59N 79.24E
24 G11 **Kumba La** *pass* Xizang Zizhiqu China 29.40N 92.21E
13 K7 **Kumbarilla** Queensland 27.20S 150.52E
90 B6 **Kumbashi** Nigeria 10.56N 5.44E
15 F8 **Kumbe** Irian Jaya 8.21S 140.12E
15 F7 **Kumbe** *R* Irian Jaya
43 M6 **Kum Bel** Kirgiziya U.S.S.R. 41.40N 75.40E
36 E3 **Kümbet** Turkey 39.11N 30.35E
29 C5 **Kumbhalgarh** Rajasthan India 25.08N 73.37E
28 A2 **Kumbharli Ghat** *mt* Maharashtra India
30 E4 **Kumbher** Nepal 28.16N 81.24E
87 H6 **Kumbi** Ethiopia 8.10N 41.38E
92 E4 **Kumbi** *tribe* Tanzania
28 B4 **Kumbla** Kerala India 12.37N 74.57E
90 E8 **Kumbo** Cameroon 6.10N 10.41E
26 T8 **Kumbukkan Oya** *R* Sri Lanka
93 K6 **Kumbulanawa** *mt* Kenya 0.17S 38.48E
9 T5 **Kumbulau Pt** Vanua Levu Fiji 16.28S 179.56E
21 D8 **Kŭmch'ŏn** N Korea 38.11N 126.25E
21 D9 **Kŭmch'ŏn** S Korea 36.07N 128.08E
43 C7 **Kum-Dag** Turkmeniya U.S.S.R. 39.14N 54.33E
33 F6 **Kumdah** Saudi Arabia 20.22N 45.08E
36 D1 **Kumdere** Turkey 41.14N 29.13E
32 E3 **Kumel** Iran 34.51N 52.10E
46 P1 **Kumeny** U.S.S.R. 58.02N 49.50E
43 D1 **Kumertau** Bashkir U.S.S.R. 52.48N 55.46E
28 H2 **Kumgiri** Assam India 26.38N 92.08E
30 A1 **Kumharsain** Himachal Prad India 31.20N 77.22E
30 A5 **Kumher** Rajasthan India 27.19N 77.23E
21 D8 **Kŭmhwa** S Korea 38.12N 127.28E
93 E4 **Kumi** Uganda 1.29N 33.56E
20 H6 **Kumihama** Japan 35.38N 134.52E
47 K6 **Kuminskiy** U.S.S.R. 58.48N 65.59E
36 B3 **Kumkale** Turkey 40.00N 26.13E
37 J2 **Kumkapı** *dist* İstanbul Turkey 41.00N 28.54E
25 M7 **Kumki** Assam India 27.10N 113.55E
24 G5 **Kumkuduk** Xinjiang Uygur Zizhiqu China 40.15N 91.55E
43 J7 **Kumkurgan** U.S.S.R. 37.50N 67.36E
52 H7 **Kumla** Ørebro Sweden 59.08N 15.09E
52 K7 **Kumla** Västmanland Sweden 59.51N 16.40E
44 G4 **Kumli** U.S.S.R. 43.59N 46.01E
51 H11 **Kumlinge** Finland 60.15N 20.45E
113 J8 **Kumliun, C** Alaska 56.31N 157.50W
36 E6 **Kumluca** Turkey 36.23N 30.17E
37 E1 **Kumluca** *R* Turkey
51 H3 **Kummavuopio** Sweden 68.55N 20.50E
63 R5 **Kummerow** Neubrandenburg E Germany 53.47N 12.51E
63 R4 **Kummerow** Rostock E Germany 54.18N 12.53E
63 R5 **Kummerower See** *L* E Germany
64 M5 **Kümmersbruck** W Germany 49.25N 11.55E
63 S8 **Kummersdorf** E Germany 52.09N 13.21E
21 D11 **Kŭmnyŏng** S Korea 33.32N 126.44E
21 D10 **Kŭmo** *isld* S Korea
43 H4 **Kumola** *R* Kazakhstan U.S.S.R.
42 F3 **Kumonda** U.S.S.R. 59.58N 97.00E
25 N8 **Kumon Range** Burma
42 J4 **Kumora** U.S.S.R. 55.52N 111.15E
25 G4 **Kumphawapi** Thailand 17.10N 102.52E
89 C7 **Kumrabai-Mamila** Sierra Leone 8.34N 12.05W
29 J7 **Kumritar** *mt* Orissa India 21.43N 85.12E
39 G6 **Kumroch, Khrebet** *ra* U.S.S.R.
37 C5 **Kumru** Turkey 40.53N 37.16E
94 E7 **Kums** Namibia 28.07S 19.40E
21 D8 **Kumsŏng** N Korea 38.29N 127.45E
28 B3 **Kumta** Karnataka India 14.25N 74.25E
61 K3 **Kumtich** Belgium 50.49N 4.53E
44 H4 **Kumtorkala** U.S.S.R. 43.01N 47.13E
91 J2 **Kumu** Zaïre 3.03N 25.13E
44 H5 **Kumukh** U.S.S.R. 42.10N 47.06E
Kumul *see* **Hami**
26 U9 **Kumuna** Sri Lanka 6.31N 81.42E
29 H7 **Kumund** Orissa India 20.31N 82.43E
Kumush *see* **Kümüx**
15 K8 **Kumusi Pt** Papua New Guinea 8.25S 148.16E
24 F4 **Kümüx** Xinjiang Uygur Zizhiqu China 42.10N 88.08E
62 O1 **Kumuzovo** U.S.S.R. 54.47N 22.50E
45 O7 **Kumylzhenskaya** U.S.S.R. 49.52N 42.35E
25 D3 **Kun** *R* Burma
113 J2 **Kuna** *R* Alaska
34 M2 **Kunagurg** Iraq 36.08N 44.03E
14 E6 **Kunanaggi Well** W Australia 23.27S 122.34E
31 F3 **Kunar** Afghanistan 34.37N 70.52E
31 F3 **Kunar R** Afghanistan
Kunār Takhteh *see* **Konār Takhteh**
24 E4 **Künas** Xinjiang Uygur Zizhiqu China 43.14N 84.40E
24 D4 **Künas Chang** Xinjiang Uygur Zizhiqu China 43.38N 82.30E
47 M5 **Kunashak** U.S.S.R. 55.42N 61.30E
40 K9 **Kunashir** *isld* Kuril Is U.S.S.R.
40 K9 **Kunashirskiy Proliv** *str* U.S.S.R./Japan
13 K6 **Kunawarara** Queensland 22.55S 150.08E
30 C7 **Kunch** Uttar Prad India 25.59N 79.08E
25 M9 **Kunchaung** Burma 23.48N 96.35E
30 H4 **Kunchha** Nepal 28.10N 84.22E
24 D9 **Kunchuk Tso** *L* Xizang Zizhiqu China 33.45N 82.42E
65 P2 **Kunčina** Czechoslovakia 49.48N 16.38E
46 F1 **Kunda** Estonia U.S.S.R. 59.30N 26.30E
30 E7 **Kunda** Uttar Prad India 25.43N 81.31E
28 C5 **Kunda Hills** Kerala/Tamil Nadu India
30 E6 **Kundanganj** Uttar Prad India 26.23N 81.09E
Kundar *see* **Kondor**
30 C5 **Kundaria** Uttar Prad India 27.50N 79.28E
31 E5 **Kundar R** Pakistan
42 D4 **Kundat** U.S.S.R. 55.10N 88.00E
92 C7 **Kundelungu Mts** Zaïre
60 M8 **Kunder of Tjonger Kanaal** *canal* Netherlands
28 B3 **Kundgol** Karnataka India 15.15N 75.19E
93 M7 **Kundi** Kenya 1.09S 40.43E
29 D5 **Kundia** Rajasthan India 25.02N 74.11E
31 F4 **Kundian** Pakistan 32.26N 71.30E
15 H6 **Kundiawa** Papua New Guinea 6.00S 144.57E
90 M6 **Kundi, L** Sudan 10.30N 25.15E
14 D10 **Kundip** W Australia 33.44S 120.11E
65 E7 **Kundl** Austria 47.28N 12.00E
29 B7 **Kundla** Gujarat India 21.20N 71.22E
47 M6 **Kundravy** U.S.S.R. 54.49N 60.10E
91 F4 **Kundu** *tribe* Zaïre
18 E5 **Kundur** *isld* Indonesia
31 E2 **Kunduz** Afghanistan 36.47N 68.51E
31 E2 **Kunduz** *prov* Afghanistan
36 H1 **Kunduz Dağı** *mt* Turkey 41.09N 35.03E
31 E2 **Kunduz R** Afghanistan
94 B1 **Kunene** *R* Namibia
Künes *see* **Xinyuan**
24 D4 **Künes He** *R* Xinjiang Uygur Zizhiqu China
89 H7 **Kunfasi** Ghana 9.32N 2.29W
Kung *see* **Band-e Kong**
91 F6 **Kunga** Zaïre 4.40S 18.33E
52 F9 **Kungälv** Sweden 57.54N 12.00E
41 J4 **Kungasalakh, Oz** *L* U.S.S.R.
Kunges *R see* **Künes He**
43 M5 **Kungey Alatau, Khrebet** *mts* Kirgiziya/Kazakhstan U.S.S.R.
24 D10 **Kunggyü Co** *L* Xizang Zizhiqu China 30.30N 82.05E
101 H9 **Kunghit I** Queen Charlotte Is, Br Col 52.02N 131.02W
Kung-ho *see* **Gonghe**
Kung-ka *see* **Gonggar**
48 V13 **Kûngmiut** Greenland 65.50N 37.05W
43 E6 **Kungrad** Uzbekistan U.S.S.R. 42.20N 59.53E
52 G9 **Kungsbacka** Sweden 57.30N 12.05E
52 J7 **Kungsör** Sweden 59.25N 16.21E
Kungtsing *see* **Tzekung**
91 F2 **Kungu** Zaïre 2.50N 19.19E
46 S2 **Kungur** U.S.S.R. 57.25N 57.10E
Kungur *mt see* **Kongur Shan**
13 J5 **Kungurri** Queensland 21.04S 148.45E
42 F6 **Kungur Tuk** U.S.S.R. 50.36N 97.32E
92 F6 **Kungutas** Tanzania 8.30S 33.15E
92 D4 **Kungwe B** Tanzania
92 D5 **Kungwe, C** Tanzania 6.01S 29.44E
25 D4 **Kungyangon** Burma 16.27N 96.00E
62 M8 **Kunhegyes** Hungary 47.22N 20.36E
25 E2 **Kunhing** Thailand 21.20N 98.26E
29 F7 **Kuni** *R* Maharashtra India
28 C4 **Kunigai** Karnataka India 13.01N 76.59E
64 C2 **Künigswinter** W Germany 50.40N 7.13E
20 E9 **Kunimi-dake** *pk* Kūshū Japan 32.32N 131.02E
18 H9 **Kuningan** Java Indon 7.02S 108.30E
21 E11 **Kunisaki** Kyūshū Japan 33.35N 131.43E
20 B2 **Kunitachi** Tōkyō Japan
29 J7 **Kunjabar** Orissa India 20.26N 84.53E
31 H4 **Kunjah** Pakistan 32.32N 74.03E
24 B7 **Kunjirap Daban** *pass* Xinjiang Uygur Zizhiqu China 36.46N 75.16E
29 B7 **Kunkavav** Gujarat India 21.38N 71.05E
66 O4 **Kunkels Pass** Switzerland 46.52N 9.25E
103 D5 **Kunkletown** Pennsylvania 40.51N 75.26W
18 C5 **Kunkun** Sumatra Indon 0.45N 99.02E
25 N9 **Kunlong** Burma 23.21N 98.39E
23 E7 **Kunlun Guan** *pass* Guangxi China 23.07N 108.40E
24 E7 **Kunlun Shan** *mt pk* Xinjiang Uygur Zizhiqu China
24 H8 **Kunlun Shankou** *pass* Qinghai China 35.40N 94.03E
30 J6 **Kunma** Bihar India 26.40N 85.38E
62 M8 **Kunmadaras** Hungary 47.29N 20.44E
40 F4 **Kun Man'ye** *R* U.S.S.R.
23 C6 **Kunming** Yunnan China 25.04N 102.41E
20 K2 **Kunnui** Japan 42.29N 140.19E
53 N9 **Kunø** Faeroes 62.18N 6.39W
53 N9 **Kunø** *isld* Faeroes 62.18N 6.39W
Kunobis *see* **Rietfontein S W Africa**
47 K4 **Kunovat** *R* U.S.S.R.
Kunoy *see* **Kunø**
60 T17 **Kunrade** Netherlands 50.53N 5.56E
Kunsa *see* **Gar**
21 D10 **Kunsan** S Korea 35.57N 126.42E
23 J3 **Kunshan** Jiangsu China 31.21N 120.57E
62 M9 **Kunszentmárton** Hungary 46.50N 20.19E
62 L9 **Kunszentmiklós** Hungary 47.00N 19.07E
86 N6 **Kuntilla, El** Egypt 30.00N 34.41E
40 N7 **Kuntomintar** *vol* Kuril Is U.S.S.R. 48.46N 154.01E
91 H5 **Kuntshankoie** Zaïre 3.22S 23.34E
39 D5 **Kuntuk** U.S.S.R. 59.49N 148.14E
30 A7 **Kunu** *R* Madhya Prad India
15 J1 **Kunua** Bougainville I Papua New Guinea 5.49S 154.48E
41 L8 **Kunu-Berete** U.S.S.R. 63.19N 119.51E
14 C9 **Kununoppin** W Australia 31.09S 117.53E
14 G3 **Kununurra** W Australia 15.42S 128.50E
21 C8 **Kunu-ri** N Korea 39.45N 125.56E
101 Y4 **Kunwak** *R* N W Terr
30 B6 **Kunwari** *R* Madhya Prad India
90 D5 **Kunya** Nigeria 12.16N 8.32E
47 H6 **Kuny'a** Perm U.S.S.R. 58.47N 56.48E
46 H2 **Kunya** Pskov U.S.S.R. 56.18N 30.59E
46 H2 **Kunya** *R* U.S.S.R.
Kunyang *see* **Jinning**
43 E6 **Kunya-Urgench** Turkmeniya U.S.S.R. 42.18N 59.10E
94 G3 **Kunyere** *R* Botswana
21 B9 **Kunyu Shan** *mts* Shandong China
65 M3 **Künžák** Czechoslovakia 49.08N 15.12E
64 H5 **Künzelsau** W Germany 49.17N 9.41E
91 E5 **Kunzulu** Zaïre 3.28S 16.12E
65 J4 **Kunžvart** Czechoslovakia 48.55N 13.44E
23 J4 **Kuocang Shan** *mts* Zhejiang China
41 P5 **Kuogastakh** U.S.S.R. 71.18N 135.02E
42 K2 **Kuokunu** U.S.S.R. 62.04N 116.25E
40 F1 **Kuoluma** *R* U.S.S.R.
41 K5 **Kuonamka, Bol'shaya** *R* U.S.S.R.
41 M7 **Kuonara** U.S.S.R. 66.49N 121.59E
19 N5 **Kuop Atoll** Truk Is Pacific Oc
51 N9 **Kuopio** Finland 62.54N 27.40E
51 M8 **Kuopio** *dist* Finland
51 N2 **Kuorboaivi** *mt* Finland 69.40N 27.40E
51 L10 **Kuorevesi** Finland 61.56N 24.40E
51 K9 **Kuortane** Finland 62.48N 23.30E
51 M10 **Kuortti** Finland 61.26N 26.25E
Kuo-te *see* **Pingguo**
51 H5 **Kuouka** Sweden 66.35N 20.35E
Kuoutatjärro *mt see* **Pädnatjärro**
41 M5 **Kuoyka** U.S.S.R. 70.30N 121.20E
41 M5 **Kubyka** *R* U.S.S.R.
82 C5 **Kupa** *R* Yugoslavia
114 C8 **Kupaahu** Hawaiian Is 19.20N 155.01W
32 E5 **Kūpān** Iran 30.17N 53.30E
19 C9 **Kupang** Timor Indon 10.13S 123.38E
19 C9 **Kupang, Teluk** *B* Timor Indon
113 N2 **Kuparuk** *R* Alaska
45 O5 **Kupava** U.S.S.R. 51.06N 42.56E
53 U15 **Kupefjellet** *mts* Norway 61.35N 6.07E
Küpeler *see* **Ertugrul**
64 M3 **Kupferberg** W Germany 50.09N 11.36E
64 H5 **Kupferzell** W Germany 49.14N 9.42E
15 K9 **Kupiano** Papua New Guinea 10.06S 148.12E
43 M1 **Kupino** U.S.S.R. 54.20N 77.21E
46 E2 **Kupiškis** Lithuania U.S.S.R. 55.50N 24.58E
37 H3 **Küplü** Bilecik Turkey 40.06N 30.00E
37 C1 **Küplü** Edirne Turkey 41.07N 26.24E
28 D4 **Kuppam** Andhra Prad India 12.45N 78.20E
64 E6 **Kuppenheim** W Germany 48.50N 8.16E
29 H8 **Kuppiti** Andhra Prad India 18.13N 83.58E
113 V8 **Kupreanof I** Alaska 56.50N 133.30W
113 H9 **Kupreanof Pt** Alaska 55.36N 159.40W
113 L7 **Kupreanof Str** Alaska
64 L3 **Küps** W Germany 50.11N 11.17E
82 C5 **Kupu** *R* Yugoslavia
40 E4 **Kupuri** *R* U.S.S.R.
45 J7 **Kupyansk** Ukraine U.S.S.R. 49.41N 37.37E
45 J7 **Kupyansk-Uzlovoy** Ukraine U.S.S.R. 49.37N 37.40E
24 D5 **Kuqa** Xinjiang Uygur Zizhiqu China 41.43N 82.58E
24 D5 **Kuqa Chang** Xinjiang Uygur Zizhiqu China 41.10N 83.42E
15 B6 **Kur** *isld* Moluccas Indonesia 5.21S 132.00E
Kur *R* Iran*see* **Kor** *R*
40 F7 **Kur** *R* U.S.S.R.
90 D6 **Kura** Nigeria 11.46N 8.25E
44 J7 **Kura** *R* Azerbaydzhan etc U.S.S.R.
44 F3 **Kura** *R* Stavropol' U.S.S.R.
33 C4 **Kurá, A1** *plat* Saudi Arabia
14 B6 **Kurabuka, R** W Australia
37 G4 **Kuraç** Turkey 41.03N 42.02E
93 M3 **Kura, El** Kenya 2.11N 40.59E
43 L5 **Kuragaty** Kazakhstan U.S.S.R. 43.06N 73.01E
42 E5 **Kuragino** U.S.S.R. 53.54N 92.40E
20 F7 **Kurahashi-jima** *isld* Japan
44 H6 **Kurakh** U.S.S.R. 41.37N 47.46E
46 P8 **Kurakh** *R* U.S.S.R.
45 J8 **Kurakhovka** Ukraine U.S.S.R. 48.03N 37.25E
45 J9 **Kurakhovo** Ukraine U.S.S.R. 47.56N 37.06E
45 S2 **Kurakino** Mordovian A.S.S.R. U.S.S.R. 54.57N 46.09E
45 Q4 **Kurakino** Penza U.S.S.R. 52.35N 44.03E
87 K7 **Kurali** Ethiopia 7.47N 44.27E
43 J6 **Kuraminskiy, Khrebet** *mts* U.S.S.R.
20 C8 **Kuramoto** Japan 33.03N 129.55E
41 O6 **Kuranakh-Yuryakh** *R* U.S.S.R.
13 H3 **Kuranda** Queensland 16.30S 145.30E
Kurandab *see* **Kūrān Dap**
32 H7 **Kūrān Dap** Iran 26.04N 59.37E
20 G5 **Kuranotani** Japan 36.10N 133.01E
30 F8 **Kuraon** Uttar Prad India 25.00N 82.04E
31 D8 **Kura Pass** Pakistan 25.58N 66.59E
43 D2 **Kurashasayskiy** Kazakhstan U.S.S.R. 50.19N 56.28E
20 G7 **Kurashiki** Japan 34.36N 133.43E
14 G4 **Kura Soak** W Australia 19.45S 127.00E
18 A7 **Kurau** *R* Pen Malaysia
40 E5 **Kuravinskoye** U.S.S.R. 52.27N 130.20E
42 F4 **Kuray** U.S.S.R. 56.41N 95.32E
32 C7 **Kurayn** *isld* The Gulf 27.39N 49.50E
20 G6 **Kurayoshi** Japan 35.27N 133.52E
42 D6 **Kurayskiy Khrebet** *mts* U.S.S.R.
42 H6 **Kurba** *R* U.S.S.R.
37 K3 **Kurbaglı** *R* Turkey
42 E4 **Kurbatovo** U.S.S.R. 55.35N 91.12E
21 D3 **Kurbin He** *R* Heilongjiang China
42 H5 **Kurbulik** U.S.S.R. 53.48N 108.59E
44 B2 **Kurchanskiy Liman** *lagoon* U.S.S.R.
45 G5 **Kurchatov** U.S.S.R. 51.38N 35.37E
43 P3 **Kurchum** Kazakhstan U.S.S.R. 48.35N 83.39E
43 P3 **Kurchum** *R* Kazakhstan U.S.S.R.
24 D4 **Kurdai Davan** *mt pass* Xinjiang Uygur Zizhiqu China
China 42.55N 82.25E
43 M5 **Kurday** Kazakhstan U.S.S.R. 43.22N 75.04E
32 E6 **Kūr Deh** Iran 28.04N 52.31E
32 F7 **Kūrdeh-e Lar** Iran 27.48N 54.24E
86 G3 **Kurdi, El** Egypt 31.11N 31.45E
37 E7 **Kurdistan** *reg* Turkey/Iraq/Iran
Kurd Kui *see* **Kord Küy**
87 H3 **Kurdumiyat,Jezt** *islds* Ethiopia 14.09N 41.40E
28 B1 **Kurduvadi** Maharashtra India 18.06N 75.31E
82 J9 **Kurdzhali** Bulgaria 41.38N 25.21E
82 J9 **Kŭrdzhali Dam** Bulgaria
44 D4 **Kurdzhinovo** U.S.S.R. 43.59N 40.58E
20 F7 **Kure** Honshu Japan 34.14N 132.32E
20 D10 **Kure** Japan 31.21N 130.32E
36 G1 **Küre** Turkey 41.48N 33.44E
30 F6 **Kurebhar** Uttar Prad India 26.24N 82.07E
37 D7 **Kürecik** Turkey 38.24N 37.55E
114 A1 **Kure I** Hawaiian Is 28.35N 178.10W
35 F4 **Kureiyima** Jordan 32.16N 35.36E
Kuressaare *see* **Kingissepp**
41 E7 **Kureyka** U.S.S.R. 66.29N 87.10E
41 E7 **Kureyka** *R* U.S.S.R.
42 J3 **Kureyskaya** U.S.S.R. 58.58N 111.25E
37 E1 **Kurfallı** Turkey 41.13N 28.19E
43 K2 **Kurgal'dzhino** Kazakhstan U.S.S.R. 50.35N 70.03E
47 K7 **Kurgan** U.S.S.R. 55.30N 65.20E
43 M7 **Kurgan** Uzbekistan U.S.S.R. 40.49N 69.58E
44 D3 **Kurganinsk** U.S.S.R. 44.54N 40.34E
47 M4 **Kurganovo** U.S.S.R. 56.38N 60.26E
38 F3 **Kurganskaya Oblast'** *prov* U.S.S.R.
43 J7 **Kurgan-Tyube** Tadzhikistan U.S.S.R. 37.52N 68.47E
43 H3 **Kurgasyn** Kazakhstan U.S.S.R. 49.15N 66.40E
47 C3 **Kurgiyevo** U.S.S.R. 65.13N 32.50E
51 N12 **Kurgolovo** U.S.S.R. 59.47N 28.08E
44 M6 **Kurguzul'skaya, Bukhta** *gulf* Turkmeniya U.S.S.R.
29 F7 **Kurhad** Maharashtra India 20.10N 78.13E
31 F2 **Kuri** Afghanistan 36.34N 70.06E
29 B4 **Kuri** Rajasthan India 26.37N 70.42E
15 C5 **Kuri** *R* Irian Jaya
90 F6 **Kuria** Nigeria 10.25N 12.12E
92 G7 **Kuria** *tribe* Tanzania
9 B5 **Kuria Is** Kiribati, Pac Oc
33 L8 **Kuria Muria B** Oman
33 L8 **Kuria Muria Is** Arabian Sea
78 D13 **Kuriate, Is** Tunisia
13 F5 **Kuridala** Queensland 21.15S 140.30E
85 L10 **Kuri, El** Sudan 18.17N 31.43E
31 H8 **Kurigram** Bangladesh 25.49N 89.39E
45 O1 **Kurikha** U.S.S.R. 55.01N 42.51E
51 J9 **Kurikka** Finland 62.36N 22.25E
20 O3 **Kurikoma-yama** *mt* Japan 38.58N 140.49E
Kuril Is *see* **Kurilskiye Ostrova**
45 U6 **Kurilovka** U.S.S.R. 50.44N 48.01E
46 M1 **Kurilovo** U.S.S.R. 58.40N 41.20E
122 G3 **Kuril Ridge** Pacific Oc
40 L9 **Kuril'sk** Kuril Is U.S.S.R. 45.10N 147.51E
40 L9 **Kurilskiye Ostrova** *islds* U.S.S.R.
39 E7 **Kuril'skoye Oz** *L* U.S.S.R.
122 G3 **Kuril Trench** Pacific Oc
65 P3 **Kuřim** Czechoslovakia 49.18N 16.32E
61 M3 **Kuringen** Belgium 50.57N 5.18E
12 L5 **Ku-Ring-Gai Chase** Sydney, N S W
94 E1 **Kuring Kuru** Namibia 17.38S 18.39E
44 J8 **Kurinskaya Kosa** *sand spit* Azerbaydzhan U.S.S.R.
11 L6 **Kuripapango** New Zealand 39.22S 176.21E
Kurit *see* **Karit**
20 L1 **Kuriyama** Japan 43.03N 141.46E
87 M5 **Kurkar Hills** Somalia
Kürkçü *see* **Sarıkavak**
45 K3 **Kurkino** U.S.S.R. 53.25N 38.43E
93 J3 **Kurkum** Kenya 2.38N 37.30E
42 D6 **Kurkure-Bazhi, Gora** *mt* U.S.S.R. 51.05N 88.25E
85 M8 **Kurkur Oasis** Egypt
28 B7 **Kurla** *dist* Bombay India 19.05N 72.53E
46 M4 **Kurlak** U.S.S.R. 51.22N 40.30E
42 C4 **Kurlek** U.S.S.R. 56.12N 84.48E
42 K6 **Kurleya** U.S.S.R. 52.12N 119.10E
45 M1 **Kurlovskiy** U.S.S.R. 55.26N 40.40E
43 B1 **Kurmanayevka** U.S.S.R. 52.33N 52.01E
87 E5 **Kurmuk** Sudan 10.36N 34.16E
45 S1 **Kurmysh** U.S.S.R. 55.48N 46.01E
64 F5 **Kürnbach** W Germany 49.05N 8.51E
12 M8 **Kurnell** New S Wales 34.01S 151.13E
12 M8 **Kurnell Pen** New S Wales
28 D3 **Kurnool** Andhra Prad India 15.51N 78.01E
28 C3 **Kurnool** *dist* Andhra Prad India
Kurnub *anc site see* **Mamshit**
20 O5 **Kurobane** Japan 36.47N 140.09E
20 L5 **Kurobe** Japan 36.55N 137.24E
20 L5 **Kurobe-gawa** *R* Japan
21 G10 **Kuroi** Japan 35.10N 135.09E
20 O1 **Kuroishi** Japan 40.37N 140.34E
20 O5 **Kuroiso** Japan 36.58N 140.02E
20 D8 **Kuroki** Japan 33.12N 130.40E
100 O7 **Kuroki** Saskatchewan 51.52N 103.30W
20 K2 **Kuromatsunai** Japan 42.39N 140.17E
31 D1 **Kuropatkino** Uzbekistan U.S.S.R. 39.57N 67.28E
85 L9 **Kuror, Jebel** *mt* Sudan 20.27N 31.30E
64 Q2 **Kurort Kipsdorf** E Germany 50.49N 13.41E
20 G6 **Kurosaka** Japan 35.14N 133.22E
21 E12 **Kuro shima** *isld* Japan 30.52N 130.00E
20 A1 **Kurosu** Saitama Japan
40 D4 **Kurovskiy** U.S.S.R. 54.26N 126.55E
45 K1 **Kurovskoye** U.S.S.R. 55.33N 38.52E
11 E11 **Kurow** New Zealand 44.44S 170.27E
62 N4 **Kurów** Poland 51.25N 22.10E
44 F4 **Kurp** U.S.S.R. 43.40N 44.28E
31 C7 **Kurragi** Pakistan 26.19N 65.37E
93 L1 **Kurraia, El** Ethiopia 4.05N 39.36E
30 C5 **Kurra Jarawan** Uttar Prad India 27.01N 79.06E
31 F4 **Kurram** Pakistan 33.51N 70.11E
31 F4 **Kurram** *reg* Pakistan
31 F4 **Kurramgarhi Dam** Pakistan 33.03N 70.36E
31 F4 **Kurram R** Pakistan
87 F8 **Kurri** Ethiopia 5.48N 36.24E
12 K5 **Kurri Kurri** New S Wales 32.49S 151.30E
44 E3 **Kursavka** U.S.S.R. 44.29N 42.32E
30 L7 **Kursela** Bihar India 25.27N 87.15E
29 L4 **Kurseong** W Bengal India 26.54N 88.21E
33 E5 **Kursh, Jabal** *mts* Saudi Arabia
30 E5 **Kursi** Uttar Prad India 27.03N 81.02E
35 F3 **Kursi, El** Jordan 32.41N 35.42E
45 H5 **Kursk** U.S.S.R. 51.45N 36.14E
44 F3 **Kurskaya** U.S.S.R. 44.01N 44.30E
46 K4 **Kurskaya Oblast'** *prov* U.S.S.R.
30 K6 **Kurson** Bihar India 26.08N 86.17E
33 K6 **Kursū', Al** *des area* Saudi Arabia
82 G7 **Kuršumlija** Yugoslavia 43.09N 20.17E
37 E2 **Kurşunlu** Bursa Turkey 40.25N 28.18E
36 G2 **Kurşunlu** Çankırı Turkey 40.49N 33.17E
37 D7 **Kurşunlu** Malatya Turkey 38.40N 37.50E
43 E6 **Kurt** Turkmeniya U.S.S.R. 42.00N 59.45E
44 F5 **Kurta** Georgia U.S.S.R. 42.16N 43.57E
37 F8 **Kurtalan** Turkey 37.58N 41.36E
47 J8 **Kurtamysh** U.S.S.R. 54.55N 64.22E
37 C1 **Kurtbey** Turkey 41.09N 26.34E
64 C1 **Kürten** W Germany 51.03N 7.15E
36 G1 **Kurtgirmez** *mt* Turkey 41.37N 33.11E
30 H7 **Kurtha** Bihar India 25.08N 84.49E
36 F4 **Kurthasanlı** Turkey 38.21N 32.11E
114 C7 **Kurtistown** Hawaiian Is 19.35N 155.04W
37 G4 **Kurtkale** Turkey 41.16N 43.09E
Kurtköy *see* **Altıntaş** Kütahya
37 G2 **Kurtköy** Turkey 40.56N 29.18E
37 G2 **Kurt Köy Dere** *R* Turkey
36 D6 **Kurtoğlu Burun** *C* Turkey 36.33N 28.50E
37 J2 **Kurtuluş** *dist* İstanbul Turkey 41.02N 28.56E
37 E5 **Kürtün** Turkey 40.40N 39.06E
42 E6 **Kurtushibinskiy, Khrebet** *mts* U.S.S.R.
43 M5 **Kurty** *R* Kazakhstan U.S.S.R.
51 K10 **Kuru** Finland 61.54N 23.45E
90 D7 **Kuru** Nigeria 9.40N 8.50E
28 H2 **Kuru** *R* Bhutan
37 D7 **Kuru** *R* Malatya Turkey
36 J2 **Kuru** *R* Tokat Turkey
87 A6 **Kuru** *watercourse* Sudan
89 D7 **Kurubonla** Sierra Leone 9.13N 10.55W
36 F1 **Kurucaşile** Turkey 41.50N 32.42E
37 D6 **Kuruçay** Turkey 39.39N 38.31E
37 F3 **Kuruçeşme** Turkey 40.08N 28.50E
37 C2 **Kurucıköy** Turkey 40.55N 26.30E
29 G7 **Kurud** Madhya Prad India 20.52N 81.42E
15 D4 **Kurudu** *isld* Irian Jaya 1.50S 137.00E
87 C1 **Kuru, El** *ruins* Sudan 18.23N 31.42E
31 E2 **Kuruk** Afghanistan 37.10N 69.26E
Kuruk Iran*see* **Korūk**
Kuruk Darya *R see* **Konqi He**
24 G4 **Kuruk Gol** *R* Xinjiang Uygur Zizhiqu China
29 E3 **Kurukshetra** Haryana India 29.59N 76.49E
24 F5 **Kuruktag** *mts* Xinjiang Uygur Zizhiqu China
Kuruk Tagh *mts see* **Kuruktag**
Kurum *see* **Dangsia**
95 G3 **Kuruman** S Africa 27.28S 23.27E
95 F2 **Kuruman** *watercourse* S Africa
95 G3 **Kuruman-Heuwels** *mts* S Africa
20 D8 **Kurume** Japan 33.20N 130.29E
42 J5 **Kurumkan** U.S.S.R. 54.20N 110.15E
87 E8 **Kurun** *watercourse* Sudan
13 C5 **Kurundi** N Terr Australia 20.30S 134.40E
13 C5 **Kurundi** *R* N Terr Australia
28 B2 **Kurundvad** Maharashtra India 16.42N 74.37E
26 R7 **Kurunegala** Sri Lanka 7.28N 80.23E
42 K2 **Kurung** U.S.S.R. 60.58N 115.28E
87 C5 **Kurun,Jeb** *mt* Sudan 11.30N 31.23E
40 G2 **Kurun Uryakh** U.S.S.R. 58.40N 137.10E
42 K6 **Kurunzulay** U.S.S.R. 50.58N 117.10E
113 K2 **Kurupa** *lakes* Alaska
113 K2 **Kurupa** *R* Alaska
29 H8 **Kurupam** Andhra Prad India 18.56N 83.37E
39 M3 **Kurupkan** U.S.S.R. 64.39N 174.05W
117 A2 **Kurupukari** Guyana 4.43N 58.40W
20 O6 **Kururi** Japan 35.16N 140.06E
43 M8 **Kurusay** Kirgiziya U.S.S.R. 40.02N 69.35E
85 L9 **Kurush, Jebel** *mts* Sudan
92 J5 **Kuruti** Tanzania 7.14S 39.23E
26 R8 **Kuruwita** Sri Lanka 6.46N 80.22E
20 L5 **Kuruyon Dam** Japan 36.36N 137.40E
42 C6 **Kur'ya** Altay U.S.S.R. 51.38N 82.15E
47 H5 **Kur'ya** Komi U.S.S.R. 61.42N 57.11E
46 Q1 **Kur'ya** Udmurt A.S.S.R. U.S.S.R. 57.42N 52.00E
41 E5 **Kur'ya** U.S.S.R. 70.25N 88.55E
45 D6 **Kuryn'ka** Ukraine U.S.S.R. 50.12N 32.45E
25 H7 **Kus** Cambodia 10.55N 104.40E
47 L5 **Kusa** U.S.S.R. 55.21N 59.28E
47 L5 **Kusa** *R* U.S.S.R.
90 C5 **Kusada** Nigeria 12.31N 7.59E
36 C5 **Kuşadası** Turkey 37.50N 27.16E
21 E12 **Kusagaki jima** *isld* Japan 30.54N 129.30E
39 A2 **Kusagan-Olokh** U.S.S.R. 66.24N 132.48E
20 H7 **Kusagi** Japan 34.56N 134.06E
18 L7 **Kusan, Pegunungan** *mts* Borneo Indon
44 J6 **Kusary** Azerbaydzhan U.S.S.R. 41.27N 48.27E
20 J6 **Kusatsu** Japan 35.02N 136.00E
20 M5 **Kusatsu** Japan 36.38N 138.35E
101 E5 **Kusawa** *R* Yukon Terr
101 E5 **Kusawa L** Yukon Terr
20 G6 **Kuse** Japan 35.06N 133.42E
35 G2 **Kuseibe** Syria 32.58N 35.58E
64 C4 **Kusel** W Germany 49.32N 7.25E
30 F8 **Kusera** Uttar Prad India 24.42N 82.30E
63 O7 **Kusey** E Germany 52.36N 11.06E
52 M2 **Kusfors** Sweden 64.58N 20.00E
37 E3 **Kuş Gölü** *L* Turkey
32 J7 **Kūsh** Iran 26.07N 60.10E
Kusha Chāpān *R see* **Qusha Chāwpān**
29 D6 **Kushalgarh** Rajasthan India 23.13N 74.29E
46 K2 **Kushalino** U.S.S.R. 57.03N 36.02E
43 N7 **Kushan** Uzbekistan U.S.S.R. 41.08N 71.47E
32 G3 **Kūshank** Iran 35.20N 57.36E
44 C1 **Kushchevskaya** U.S.S.R. 46.34N 39.39E
20 P9 **Kushi** Okinawa Japan 26.31N 128.01E
20 K7 **Kushida** *R* Japan
20 D10 **Kushikino** Japan 31.45N 130.16E
20 E10 **Kushima** Japan 31.28N 131.14E
20 J8 **Kushimoto** Japan 33.28N 135.47E
Kushing *see* **Kūshank**
21 K6 **Kushiro** Japan 42.58N 144.24E
20 F6 **Kushi-taki** Japan 35.17N 132.33E
31 B3 **Kushk** Afghanistan 34.55N 62.20E
31 B3 **Kushka** Afghanistan 35.14N 62.15E
43 F8 **Kushka** Turkmeniya U.S.S.R. 35.18N 62.22E
39 G4 **Kushka** U.S.S.R. 61.58N 160.19E
31 B3 **Kushka** *R* Afghan/U.S.S.R.
32 C4 **Kūshkak** Iran 32.08N 48.52E
32 G6 **Kushk-e Pā'īn** Iran 28.44N 56.46E
32 B4 **Kūshkī** Iran 33.25N 47.07E
47 E4 **Kushkushara** U.S.S.R. 64.56N 40.32E
30 E8 **Kushmahar** Madhya Prad India 24.18N 81.43E
43 G2 **Kushmurun** Kazakhstan U.S.S.R. 52.30N 64.37E
43 G1 **Kushmurun, Oz** *L* Kazakhstan U.S.S.R.
46 S2 **Kushnarenkovo** U.S.S.R. 55.08N 55.20E
82 H2 **Kushnitsa** Ukraine U.S.S.R. 48.29N 23.08E
43 H6 **Kushrabat** Uzbekistan U.S.S.R. 40.16N 66.30E
28 C3 **Kushtagi** Karnataka India 15.44N 76.10E
113 P6 **Kushtaka L** Alaska 60.23N 144.08W
31 H9 **Kushtia** Bangladesh 23.54N 89.07E
31 H9 **Kushtia** *dist* Bangladesh
32 H6 **Kushtih** Iran 29.41N 59.46E
46 Q4 **Kushum** Kazakhstan U.S.S.R. 50.49N 51.11E
43 B2 **Kushum** *R* Kazakhstan U.S.S.R.
47 M3 **Kushva** U.S.S.R. 58.20N 59.48E
21 D3 **Kusite** Heilongjiang China 48.47N 128.46E
113 G6 **Kuskokwim** *R* Alaska
113 E7 **Kuskokwim B** Alaska
113 H6 **Kuskokwim Mts** Alaska
113 F6 **Kuskovak** Alaska 60.10N 162.18W
Kuşluyan *see* **Gölköy**
30 G4 **Kusma** Nepal 28.14N 83.40E
66 L2 **Küsnacht** Switzerland 47.19N 8.34E
21 C8 **Kusŏng** N Korea 39.57N 125.20E
41 B4 **Kusova Zemlya, O** *isld* Novaya Zemlya U.S.S.R.
44 E4 **Kusparty** U.S.S.R. 43.07N 43.27E
87 G8 **Kussa** Ethiopia 4.09N 38.58E
66 K1 **Küssaberg** W Germany 47.35N 8.19E
21 K6 **Kussharo-ko** *L* Hokkaido Japan
66 K3 **Küssnacht** Switzerland 47.05N 8.26E
51 L4 **Küstala** Finland 67.53N 25.20E
43 G1 **Kustanay** Kazakhstan U.S.S.R. 53.15N 63.40E
51 F5 **Kustarakaise** *mt* Sweden 66.45N 16.50E
45 O2 **Kustarevka** U.S.S.R. 54.16N 42.14E
113 M6 **Kustatan** Alaska 60.45N 151.50W
51 J11 **Kustavi** Finland 60.34N 21.20E
Küstrin *see* **Kostrzyn** Zielona Góra
44 H6 **Kusur** U.S.S.R. 41.47N 46.57E
34 F7 **Kusūr,Al** *plat* Saudi Arabia
39 K1 **Kus'veem** *R* U.S.S.R.
32 C5 **Kut** Iran 31.28N 48.21E
90 C7 **Kuta** Nigeria 9.50N 6.40E
93 G9 **Kuta** Tanzania 3.58S 35.37E
42 H4 **Kuta** *R* U.S.S.R.
32 C5 **Kūt Abdollāh** Iran 31.15N 48.41E
18 B4 **Kutabuloh** Sumatra Indon 3.27N 97.05E
18 B4 **Kutacane** Sumatra Indon 3.35N 97.44E
36 D3 **Kütahya** Turkey 39.25N 29.56E
18 M6 **Kutai** *R* Borneo Indon
44 C3 **Kutais** U.S.S.R. 44.31N 39.18E
44 E5 **Kutaisi** Georgia U.S.S.R. 42.15N 42.44E
34 N6 **Kūt, Al** Iraq 32.30N 45.51E
Kut al Hai *see* **Hayy, Al**
Kūt al Imāra *see* **Kūt, Al**
86 E4 **Kutâma el Ghâba** Egypt 30.55N 30.53E
44 H3 **Kutan** U.S.S.R. 44.41N 46.34E
40 E2 **Kutana** Yakutsk U.S.S.R. 59.04N 131.45E
18 B4 **Kutanibong** Sumatra Indon 3.52N 96.24E
43 J4 **Kutansor, Oz** *L* Kazakhstan U.S.S.R.
41 F6 **Kutaramakan, Oz** *L* U.S.S.R.
11 M5 **Kutarere** New Zealand 38.03S 177.10E
42 F6 **Ku Tayga, Khrebet** *mts* U.S.S.R.
34 N6 **Kūt Barrage** Iraq 32.30N 45.48E
109 G3 **Kutch** Colorado 38.55N 103.54W
29 A6 **Kutch** *reg* India
20 K2 **Kutchan** Japan 42.54N 140.43E
29 A6 **Kutch, G. of** Gujarat India
29 A5 **Kutch, Great Rann of** *flood area* India/Pakistan
29 B6 **Kutch, Little Rann of** *flood area* Gujarat India
32 C4 **Kūt-e Gāpū** *anc site* Iran 32.20N 48.07E
35 H3 **Kuteibe, El** Syria 32.45N 36.12E
90 G6 **Kutelaha** Nigeria 11.50N 14.23E
45 K9 **Kuteynikovo** Ukraine U.S.S.R. 47.48N 38.17E
45 O9 **Kuteynikovskaya** U.S.S.R. 47.15N 42.08E
30 K6 **Kuthanwa** Nepal 26.49N 86.14E
29 F5 **Kuthara** Madhya Prad India 24.10N 79.16E
30 C6 **Kuthaund** Uttar Prad India 26.21N 79.24E
42 H3 **Kutima** U.S.S.R. 57.12N 108.15E
82 D5 **Kutina** Yugoslavia 45.29N 16.48E
Kutiyadi *see* **Kuttyadi**
25 N9 **Kutkai** Burma 23.31N 97.57E
44 H7 **Kutkashen** Azerbaydzhan U.S.S.R. 40.59N 47.50E
25 G4 **Kut Khao** Thailand 16.07N 102.23E
25 G7 **Kut, Ko** *isld* Thailand 11.40N 102.33E
45 W1 **Kutlu Bukash** U.S.S.R. 55.39N 50.35E
65 M2 **Kutná Hora** Czechoslovakia 49.57N 15.15E
30 C8 **Kutni** *R* Madhya Prad India
62 L3 **Kutno** Poland 52.13N 19.20E
18 H9 **Kutoarjo** Java Indon 7.45S 109.55E
47 L3 **Kutop'yegan** U.S.S.R. 66.18N 70.30E
28 E1 **Kutru** Madhya Prad India 19.03N 80.52E
51 K3 **Kuttainen** Sweden 68.24N 22.50E
28 C6 **Kuttalam** Tamil Nadu India 8.55N 77.17E
107 H4 **Kuttawa** Kentucky 37.04N 88.05W
66 J2 **Küttigen** Switzerland 47.25N 8.03E
28 B5 **Kuttyadi** Kerala India 11.38N 75.43E
93 J6 **Kutu** Kenya 0.32S 37.21E
91 F5 **Kutu** Zaïre 2.42S 18.10E
92 H5 **Kutu** *tribe* Tanzania
31 J10 **Kutubdia Chan** Bangladesh
31 J10 **Kutubdia I** Bangladesh
15 G7 **Kutubu, L** Papua New Guinea
36 F2 **Kütüklü Dağı** *mt* Turkey
42 G5 **Kutulik** U.S.S.R. 53.24N 102.50E
90 M4 **Kutum** Sudan 14.10N 24.40E
42 E5 **Kuturchinskoye Belogor'ye** *mts* U.S.S.R.
91 H5 **Kutu Songo** Zaïre 3.25S 22.33E
65 Q4 **Kúty** Czechoslovakia 48.39N 17.01E
82 J2 **Kuty** U.S.S.R. 48.16N 25.11E
64 J3 **Kützberg** W Germany 50.04N 10.07E
103 C5 **Kutztown** Pennsylvania 40.32N 75.46W
101 R1 **Kuuk** *R* Victoria I, N W Terr
43 C6 **Kuuli-Mayak** Turkmeniya U.S.S.R. 40.17N 52.46E
21 D7 **Kuup-Tong** N Korea 40.50N 126.01E
61 D3 **Kuurne** Belgium 50.51N 3.18E
51 L4 **Kuusajoki** Finland 67.38N 25.15E
51 O6 **Kuusamo** Finland 65.57N 29.15E
51 M11 **Kuusankoski** Finland 60.55N 26.42E
47 G6 **Kuva** U.S.S.R. 59.05N 54.03E
43 O8 **Kuva** Uzbekistan U.S.S.R. 40.34N 72.05E
45 S2 **Kuvakino** U.S.S.R. 54.59N 46.24E
43 D2 **Kuvandyk** U.S.S.R. 51.29N 57.25E
43 N8 **Kuvasay** Uzbekistan U.S.S.R. 40.20N 71.59E
47 L6 **Kuvashi** U.S.S.R. 55.06N 59.21E
45 T3 **Kuvat'** U.S.S.R. 53.27N 47.41E
39 K1 **Kuvet** *R* U.S.S.R.
50 D3 **Kúvikur** Iceland 65.57N 21.26W

46 J2 Kuvshinovo U.S.S.R. 57.03N 34.12E
85 M9 Ku,Wadi el watercourse Sudan
20 H6 Kuwahara Japan 35.26N 134.11E
33 M9 Kuwait Kuwait 29.20N 48.00E
33 M9 Kuwait sheikhdom The Gulf
20 K6 Kuwana Japan 35.04N 136.40E
30 F6 Kuwana R Uttar Prad India
85 M9 Kuwa, Wadi watercourse Sudan
Kuwayr see Guwer
Kuwayt, Al see Kuwait
33 M9 Kuwayt, Jūn al gulf Kuwait
35 G3 Kuweiyah, El Syria 32.44N 35.48E
47 E3 Kuya U.S.S.R. 65.06N 40.09E
82 N3 Kuyalnik R U.S.S.R.
44 A8 Kuyal'nitskiy Liman lagoon Ukraine U.S.S.R.
43 N7 Kuyaly-Kurgancha Uzbekistan U.S.S.R. 40.39N 70.56E
39 H3 Kuybiveem R U.S.S.R.
39 J3 Kuyboveem R U.S.S.R.
44 F7 Kuybyshev Armenia U.S.S.R. 40.46N 44.59E
Kuybyshev Novosibirsk see Kainsk-Barabinskiy
45 V2 Kuybyshev Tatar A.S.S.R. U.S.S.R. 54.57N 49.03E
46 Q3 Kuybyshev U.S.S.R. 53.10N 50.10E
46 F6 Kuybyshev dist Moscow U.S.S.R.
43 F8 Kuybysheva, im Turkmeniya U.S.S.R. 37.26N 62.09E
45 C9 Kuybyshevka Ukraine U.S.S.R. 47.38N 31.43E
Kuybyshevka-Vostochnaya see Belogorsk Amur
44 C10 Kuybyshevo Crimea, Ukraine U.S.S.R. 44.36N 33.52E
44 L3 Kuybyshevo Kazakhstan U.S.S.R. 44.12N 51.42E
40 L9 Kuybyshevo Kuril Is U.S.S.R. 45.04N 147.44E
45 K9 Kuybyshevo Rostov U.S.S.R. 47.49N 38.59E
43 N8 Kuybyshevo Uzbekistan U.S.S.R. 40.23N 71.17E
45 H9 Kuybyshevo Zaporozh'ye, Ukraine U.S.S.R. 47.20N 36.41E
46 P3 Kuybyshevskaya Oblast' prov U.S.S.R.
43 J7 Kuybyshevskiy Tadzhikistan U.S.S.R. 37.55N 68.54E
47 K8 Kuybyshevskiy U.S.S.R. 53.19N 66.55E
45 U3 Kuybyshevskoye Vdkhr res U.S.S.R.
39 C3 Kuydusun R U.S.S.R.
46 S2 Kuyeda U.S.S.R. 56.28N 55.30E

32 B1 Kūyeh Iran 38.48N 47.50E
22 H7 Kuye He R Shaanxi China
43 L4 Kuygan Kazakhstan U.S.S.R. 45.24N 74.08E
42 H6 Kuytun Buryat U.S.S.R. 51.33N 107.45E
42 G5 Kuytun Irkutsk U.S.S.R. 54.22N 101.35E
24 E3 Kuytun Xinjiang Uygur Zizhiqu China 44.30N 85.00E
42 D7 Kuytun, Gora U.S.S.R./China/Mongolia 79.15N 87.50E
24 E3 Kuytun He L Xinjiang Uygur Zizhiqu China
37 D8 Kuyucak Adıyaman Turkey 37.52N 38.21E
36 C5 Kuyucak Aydın Turkey 37.53N 28.29E
43 G2 Kuyukkol', Ozero L Kazakhstan U.S.S.R. 50.59N 64.29E
43 N7 Kuyukmazar Uzbekistan U.S.S.R. 41.05N 71.30E
39 H4 Kuyul R U.S.S.R.
42 F2 Kuyumba U.S.S.R. 61.02N 97.03E
42 D6 Kuyus U.S.S.R. 50.58N 86.18E
117 A3 Kuyuwini R Guyana
87 E7 Kuza Ethiopia 7.05N 35.28E
42 D4 Kuzbass basin U.S.S.R.
42 D5 Kuzedeyevo U.S.S.R. 53.21N 87.14E
45 F2 Kuzemki U.S.S.R. 54.25N 34.16E
45 K7 Kuzemovka Ukraine U.S.S.R. 49.30N 38.00E
36 G1 Kuzey Anadolu Dağları ra Turkey
37 K2 Kuzgunçuk İstanbul Turkey 41.02N 29.05E
42 E6 Kuzhe-Baza U.S.S.R. 51.50N 90.40E
28 C6 Kuzhittura Tamil Nadu India 8.18N 77.15E
45 Q1 Kuzhutki U.S.S.R. 55.55N 44.02E
47 M4 Kuzino U.S.S.R. 57.03N 59.28E
113 E4 Kuzitrin R Alaska
42 E2 Kuz'movka U.S.S.R. 62.21N 92.13E
45 V2 Kuznechikha U.S.S.R. 54.44N 49.37E
45 S3 Kuznetsk U.S.S.R. 53.08N 46.35E
42 D4 Kuznetskiy Alatau mts U.S.S.R.
47 M5 Kuznetskoye U.S.S.R. 55.30N 60.39E
40 D5 Kuznetsovo Amur U.S.S.R. 52.34N 126.08E
40 H8 Kuznetsovo Primor'ye U.S.S.R. 46.12N 138.01E
47 J6 Kuznetsovo Sverdlovsk U.S.S.R. 59.15N 63.21E
47 D3 Kuzomen U.S.S.R. 66.15N 36.51E
45 T3 Kuzovatovo U.S.S.R. 53.34N 47.40E
47 C3 Kuzreka U.S.S.R. 66.35N 34.48E
36 G6 Kuzucubelen Turkey 36.49N 34.25E
20 N5 Kuzuu Japan 36.25N 139.37E
36 G1 Kuzyaka Turkey 41.13N 33.44E
39 F5 Kvachina, Bukhta gulf U.S.S.R.
51 E3 Kvæfjord Norway 68.47N 16.10E
51 J2 Kvænangen Norway 69.55N 21.40E
51 H1 Kvænangen inlet Norway
51 J2 Kvænangsbotn Norway 69.43N 22.00E
53 H6 Kværkeby Denmark 55.28N 11.53E
53 F6 Kværndrup Denmark 55.11N 10.32E
53 D7 Kværs Denmark 54.56N 9.31E
53 V21 Kvæven Norway 58.57N 6.55E
44 F5 Kvaisi Georgia U.S.S.R. 42.31N 43.41E
53 N10 Kvalbø Faeroes 61.37N 6.57W
53 N10 Kvalbø Fjord inlet Faeroes 61.37N 6.55W
51 K1 Kvaløya isld Norway 70.35N 23.50E
51 G1 Kvaløy, N isld Norway 70.10N 19.10E
51 G2 Kvaløy, S isld Norway 69.40N 18.30E
51 K1 Kvalsund Norway 70.30N 24.00E
50 T15 Kvalvågen inlet Spitsbergen 77.28N 18.00E
53 M9 Kvalvig Faeroes 62.11N 7.02W
52 E5 Kvam Norway 61.40N 9.46E
53 T16 Kvamshesten mt Norway 61.25N 5.38E
53 T18 Kvamskogen Norway 60.23N 5.56E
53 U16 Kvamsøy Norway 61.07N 6.25E
53 S14 Kvamsøy isld Norway 62.13N 5.24E
48 S14 Kvanefjord inlet Greenland
53 H5 Kvanløse Denmark 55.39N 11.41E
53 V18 Kvanndal Norway 60.28N 6.36E
53 V19 Kvanndalen V Norway 59.42N 6.59E
53 U14 Kvanndalsvatn L Norway 62.07N 6.21E
53 O9 Kvannesund Faeroes 62.18N 6.29W
53 T16 Kvanngrøfjell mt Norway 61.13N 5.45E
44 G6 Kvareli Georgia U.S.S.R. 41.27N 45.47E
43 E2 Kvarkeno U.S.S.R. 52.07N 59.45E
52 H10 Kvarnamåla Sweden 56.35N 14.55E
52 G2 Kvarnbergsvattnet L Sweden
82 B6 Kvarner G Yugoslavia
82 B6 Kvarnerić Yugoslavia
52 K8 Kvarsebo Sweden 53.38N 16.40E
53 T15 Kvasshornet mt Norway 61.52N 5.40E
44 F5 Kvemo Artani Georgia U.S.S.R. 42.14N 44.59E
44 D4 Kvemo Azhara Georgia U.S.S.R. 43.07N 41.46E
53 X18 Kvenna R Norway
50 D4 Kvennabrekka Iceland 65.02N 21.40W
53 W18 Kvennsjøen L Norway 60.04N 7.12E
50 J5 Kverká R Múlasýsla, Nordhur Iceland
50 K3 Kverká R Thingeyjarsýsla, Nordhur Iceland
50 J5 Kverkárnes reg Iceland
50 H5 Kverkfjallahryggur ridge Iceland
50 J5 Kverkfjallarani reg Iceland
50 J5 Kverkfjöll Iceland 64.39N 16.42W
52 D4 Kvernes Norway 63.00N 7.46E
53 W20 Kvervenuten mt Norway 59.26N 7.20E
51 H2 Kvesmenes Norway 69.17N 20.00E
51 J8 Kevlax Finland 63.10N 21.50E
50 G2 Kvíabekkur Iceland 66.01N 18.45W
50 B5 Kvíabryggja Iceland 64.57N 23.20W
50 J7 Kviarjökull ice cap Iceland 63.58N 16.34W
113 J7 Kvichak Alaska 58.59N 156.55W
113 J7 Kvichak B Alaska
113 J7 Kvichak R Alaska
50 C3 Kvígindisfjördhur B Iceland
51 D6 Kvigtind mt Norway 65.13N 13.50E
51 F5 Kvikkjock Sweden 66.58N 17.45E
52 E4 Kvikne Norway 62.36N 10.19E
64 Q5 Kvilda Czechoslovakia 49.01N 13.35E
53 V19 Kvilldal Norway 59.31N 6.39E
52 C8 Kvina R Norway
52 C8 Kvinesdal Norway 58.18N 7.00E
53 T19 Kvinnherad Norway 60.00N 6.00E
50 J7 Kvisker Iceland 63.59N 16.27W
52 H7 Kvistbro Sweden 59.09N 14.48E
53 K5 Kvistofta Sweden 55.59N 12.50E
52 D3 Kvisvik Norway 63.05N 8.02E
53 U17 Kvitanosa mt Norway 60.46N 6.15E
53 V14 Kviteggja mt Norway 62.05N 6.44E
53 W15 Kvitekoll mt Norway 61.32N 7.03E
53 Y20 Kviteseid Norway 59.25N 8.28E
53 T18 Kvitingen Norway 60.28N 5.54E
51 O1 Kvitnes Norway 70.48N 28.45E
42 F4 Kvitok U.S.S.R. 56.05N 98.30E
50 W12 Kvitøya isld Spitsbergen
53 S20 Kvitsøy Norway 59.04N 5.26E
53 M9 Kvivig Faeroes 62.07N 7.04W
53 A5 Kvong Denmark 55.46N 8.27E
53 D4 Kvorning Denmark 56.29N 9.43E
90 D9 Kwa Nigeria 4.34N 8.00E
91 E5 Kwa R Zaïre
61 L2 Kwaadmechelen Belgium 51.06N 5.09E
101 L7 Kwadacha Wilderness Prov. Park Br Col
93 L9 Kwa Dadu Kenya 3.14S 39.42E
60 C3 Kwadendamme Netherlands 51.26N 3.53E
60 H9 Kwadijk Netherlands 52.32N 4.58E
Kwai R see Khwae Noi R
15 L8 Kwaiawata I Papua New Guinea 8.55S 151.53E
90 D9 Kwa Ibo R Nigeria
23 B8 Kwai Chung Hong Kong 22.22N 114.07E
93 N8 Kwaihu I Kenya 2.00S 41.18E
Kwaik Juna see Jāsk-e Kohneh

9 C2 Kwajalein atoll Marshall Is Pacific Oc 9.15N 167.30E
9 A3 Kwajalein Lagoon Marshall Is Pacific Oc
117 B2 Kwakoegron Surinam 5.14N 55.20W
93 G9 Kwa Kuchinja Tanzania 3.40S 35.57E
117 A2 Kwakwani Guyana 5.16N 58.04W
93 L10 Kwale Kenya 4.10S 39.27E
90 C9 Kwale Nigeria 5.49N 6.24E
93 K10 Kwale, dist Kenya
92 J12 Kwale I Zanzibar 6.24S 39.18E
89 J8 Kwamang Ghana 7.00N 1.15W
95 O10 Kwa Mbonambi S Africa 28.36S 32.05E
92 H5 Kwa Mhinda Tanzania 7.36S 37.59E
95 P9 Kwa Mnyaise S Africa 27.41S 32.25E
91 E5 Kwamouth Zaïre 3.11S 16.16E
92 G4 Kwa Mtoro Tanzania 5.14S 35.23E
21 K2 Kwanak-ku dist Seoul S Korea
93 B3 Kwandruma Zaïre 2.02N 30.52E
91 J6 Kwanga Zaïre 4.10S 25.28E
30 G4 Kwangde mt Nepal 27.48N 86.39E
21 D10 Kwangju S Korea 35.07N 126.52E
91 E5 Kwango R Zaïre
Kwangsi prov Chinasee Guangxi
Kwangtung prov Chinasee Guangdong
21 D10 Kwangyang S Korea 35.01N 127.32E
93 D4 Kwania, L Uganda
21 D7 Kwansŏ-ri N Korea 40.21N 128.42E
91 E12 Kwanyama tribe Angola
90 B7 Kwara state Nigeria
90 B7 Kwara state Nigeria
Kwaremont see Kluisbergen
99 J1 Kwataboahegan R Ontario
90 C5 Kwatarkwashi Nigeria 12.10N 6.50E
28 G8 Kwate tu Kwage Andaman Is 10.38N 92.33E
15 C5 Kwatisore Irian Jaya 3.18S 134.50E
91 G2 Kwawa Zaïre 2.49N 21.10E
90 E6 Kwaya Nigeria 10.31N 11.52E
95 O4 Kwazulu Bantu Homeland Natal S Africa
Kweichow prov Chinasee Guizhou

Kweiping see Guilin
Kweiyang see Guiyang
95 M8 Kwelega S Africa 32.54S 28.05E
94 H5 Kweneng dist Botswana
91 F6 Kwenge Zaïre 4.58S 18.40E
91 F7 Kwenge R Zaïre
113 G6 Kwethluk Alaska 60.46N 161.34W
113 G6 Kwethluk R Alaska
90 C6 Kwiambana Nigeria 11.05N 6.35E
62 L2 Kwidzyn Poland 53.44N 18.53E
113 D7 Kwigamiut Alaska 59.45N 166.10W
113 F7 Kwigillingok Alaska 59.50N 163.10W
113 E5 Kwiguk Alaska 62.45N 164.32W
15 J8 Kwikila Papua New Guinea 9.51S 147.43E
113 E5 Kwikpak Alaska 63.05N 164.30W
91 E5 Kwilu R Zaïre
93 E9 Kwimba tribe Tanzania
14 A4 Kwinana W Australia 32.15S 115.46E
113 G7 Kwinhagak Alaska 59.45N 161.59W
15 F7 Kwinia, L Papua New Guinea 7.32S 141.44E
92 H4 Kwinji Tanzania 5.28S 37.45E
62 J4 Kwisa R Poland
117 A3 Kwitaro R Guyana
119 J6 Kwitaro R Guyana
14 C10 Kwobrup W Australia 33.36S 117.55E
15 B4 Kwoka mt Irian Jaya 0.40S 132.24E
87 E8 Kwollu Ethiopia 5.59N 35.29E
90 C6 Kwongoma Nigeria 10.31N 6.26E
23 B9 Kwun Tong Hong Kong 22.18N 114.13E
52 E2 Kya isld Norway 64.28N 10.10E
90 J7 Kyabé Chad 9.28N 18.54E
13 G7 Kyabra Queensland 26.17S 143.08E
13 G7 Kyabra R Queensland
12 H6 Kyabram Victoria 36.21S 145.05E
25 C2 Kyadet Burma 21.50N 94.55E
25 D4 Kyaikkami Burma 16.04N 97.34E
25 C4 Kyaiklat Burma 16.25N 95.42E
25 D4 Kyaikto Burma 17.16N 97.01E
25 E4 Kya-in-Seikkyi Burma 16.02N 98.08E
93 C7 Kyaka Tanzania 1.16S 31.25E
42 H6 Kyakhta U.S.S.R. 50.22N 106.30E
12 G5 Kyalite New S Wales 34.57S 143.31E
31 J2 Kyam Kashmir 34.18N 79.00E
93 D6 Kyamuswa Uganda 0.25S 32.32E
93 B7 Kyamutaga Tanzania 1.30S 30.55E
12 D5 Kyancutta S Australia 33.08S 135.31E
47 D4 Kyanda U.S.S.R. 64.15N 38.02E
25 C3 Kyangin Burma 18.20N 95.15E
25 D3 Kyangin Burma 19.31N 96.16E
87 A7 Kyango Sudan 7.59N 27.43E
30 H4 Kyangshar Khola R Nepal
47 C4 Kyargozero U.S.S.R. 63.20N 34.18E
Kyaring Tso L see Gyaring Co
25 D3 Kyaukhnyat Burma 18.17N 97.30E
25 C3 Kyaukkyi Burma 18.12N 94.28E
25 D3 Kyaukkyi Burma 18.19N 96.45E
25 D1 Kyaukme Burma 22.30N 97.02E
25 C1 Kyaukmyaung Burma 22.36N 95.55E
25 C2 Kyaukpadaung Burma 20.50N 95.08E
25 B3 Kyaukpyu Burma 19.27N 93.33E
25 D2 Kyaukse Burma 21.33N 96.06E
25 B2 Kyauktaw Burma 20.48N 93.00E
25 C2 Kyaukyit Burma 21.44N 95.17E
25 C4 Kyaunggon Burma 17.04N 95.12E
46 E3 Kybartai Lithuania U.S.S.R. 54.28N 22.48E
66 M2 Kyburg Switzerland 47.28N 8.45E
12 F6 Kybybolite S Australia 36.54S 140.58E
39 D2 Kycham-Kyuyel' U.S.S.R. 65.34N 146.48E
47 E3 Kychema U.S.S.R. 65.32N 42.42E
52 H2 Kycklingvattnet Sweden 64.36N 14.10E
25 D3 Kyebogyi Burma 19.23N 97.16E
11 E12 Kyeburn New Zealand 45.08S 170.16E
93 C5 Kyegegwa Uganda 0.30N 31.05E
25 E4 Kyeikdon Burma 16.00N 98.24E
25 E4 Kyeikywa Burma 16.08N 98.22E
25 C4 Kyeintali Burma 18.00N 94.29E
29 E1 Kyelang Himachal Prad India 32.33N 77.03E
93 E5 Kyemeire Uganda 0.27N 33.43E
93 B5 Kyenjojo Uganda 0.38N 30.40E
93 E4 Kyere Uganda 1.30N 33.35E
30 K4 Kyetrak Xizang Zizhiqu 28.15N 86.35E
30 G1 Kyetrak Glacier Xizang Zizhiqu
63 O10 Kyffhäuser mt E Germany 51.25N 11.06E
14 E7 Kyffin-Thomas Hill W Australia 26.50S 123.15E
53 F5 Kyholm isld Denmark 55.57N 10.41E

25 D3 Kyidaunggan Burma 19.54N 96.13E
Kyimdong see Gyêmdong
25 B2 Kyindwe Burma 21.00N 93.51E
Kyirong see Gyirong
29 K3 Kyishong Xizang Zizhiqu 28.34N 87.19E
62 K6 Kyjov Czechoslovakia 49.00N 17.10E
84 Q15 Kykkou Monastery Cyprus 34.58N 32.45E
100 J8 Kyle Saskatchewan 50.50N 108.02W
108 H6 Kyle S Dakota 43.25N 102.10W
112 K6 Kyle Texas 30.00N 97.54W
108 D8 Kyle Wyoming 41.46N 106.15W
57 D1 Kyle dist Strathclyde Scotland
58 E4 Kyleakin Skye, Highland Scotland 57.16N 5.44W
92 E12 Kyle Dam Zimbabwe 20.15S 30.58E
59 C4 Kylemore Castle Galway Irish Rep 53.33N 9.58W
58 E4 Kyle of Lochalsh Highland Scotland 57.17N 5.43W
58 F2 Kylesku Highland Scotland 58.15N 5.01W
58 F2 Kylestrome Highland Scotland 58.16N 5.01W
64 B3 Kyll R W Germany
42 K2 Kyllakh U.S.S.R. 60.15N 119.48E
39 D1 Kyllakh R U.S.S.R.
41 N5 Kyllakh, Zaliv gulf U.S.S.R.
64 B3 Kyllburg W Germany 50.02N 6.36E
41 N8 Kylygyr U.S.S.R. 63.30N 129.45E
51 M11 Kymi dist Finland
51 M11 Kymijoki R Finland
39 L2 Kymyneyveem R U.S.S.R.
47 H6 Kyn U.S.S.R. 57.55N 58.40E
56 T10 Kynance Cove Cornwall Eng 49.57N 5.15W
12 G6 Kyneton Victoria 37.17S 144.31E
64 O3 Kynšperk nad Ohři Czechoslovakia 50.07N 12.34E
13 F5 Kynuna Queensland 21.35S 141.52E
42 E5 Kynzy-Made, Gora mt U.S.S.R. 52.55N 94.28E
20 P9 Kyoda Okinawa Japan 26.32N 127.57E
93 E4 Kyoga, L Uganda
20 J6 Kyōga-misaki C Japan 35.48N 135.12E
12 L3 Kyogle New S Wales 28.36S 152.59E
87 A6 Kyom watercourse Sudan
20 D9 Kyōmachi Japan 32.03N 130.46E
21 C8 Kyomip'o N Korea 38.55N 125.50E
25 E4 Kyondo Burma 16.35N 98.03E
25 D2 Kyong Burma 21.00N 96.30E
13 H5 Kyong Queensland 21.59S 145.50E
21 E10 Kyŏngju S Korea 35.52N 129.15E
20 B6 Kyŏngsan S Korea 35.46N 128.45E
21 E7 Kyŏngsŏng N Korea 41.38N 129.39E
Kyŏngsŏng S Koreasee Sŏul
93 C6 Kyotera Uganda 0.38S 31.34E
20 J6 Kyōto Japan 35.02N 135.45E
20 J6 Kyōto prefect Japan
43 J2 Kypshak, Ozero L Kazakhstan U.S.S.R. 50.08N 68.28E
42 J7 Kyra U.S.S.R. 49.38N 111.58E
51 J8 Kyranjoki R Finland
39 E1 Kyrbana U.S.S.R. 68.35N 153.59E
40 D1 Kyrbykan U.S.S.R. 60.05N 127.15E
39 E4 Kyrchan R U.S.S.R.
41 M6 Kyrdanyy U.S.S.R. 69.45N 124.57E
42 G6 Kyren U.S.S.R. 51.43N 102.05E
84 R14 Kyrenia Cyprus 35.20N 33.20E
84 R14 Kyrenia Mts Cyprus
41 M8 Kyrgyday U.S.S.R. 64.41N 124.25E
63 Q7 Kyritz E Germany 52.57N 12.23E
53 T16 Kyrkjebø Norway 61.10N 5.55E
53 X17 Kyrkjedørsnut mt Norway 60.38N 7.41E
53 U14 Kyrkjefjell mt Norway 62.02N 6.17E
53 V15 Kyrkjenibba mt Norway 61.57N 6.48E

52 E3 Kyrksæterøra Norway 63.17N 9.06E
51 L11 Kyrkslätt Finland 60.06N 24.20E
51 K10 Kyrösjärvi L Finland
53 U19 Kyrping Norway 59.45N 6.08E
47 H4 Kyrta U.S.S.R. 64.02N 57.40E
39 B2 Kyrt-Uyalakh U.S.S.R. 67.21N 135.21E
47 J6 Kyrtym'ya U.S.S.R. 59.02N 63.40E
47 H6 Kyr'ya U.S.S.R. 59.21N 58.58E
41 L8 Kyrynniky U.S.S.R. 63.34N 116.46E
47 M7 Kyshtovka U.S.S.R. 56.35N 76.34E
47 M5 Kyshtym U.S.S.R. 55.43N 60.32E
65 O1 Kyšperk Czechoslovakia 50.03N 16.30E
47 F4 Kyssa U.S.S.R. 64.40N 47.59E
41 M7 Kystatam U.S.S.R. 67.19N 123.25E
41 D9 Kys'yegan R U.S.S.R.
43 B3 Kysykkamys Kazakhstan U.S.S.R. 49.14N 50.17E
39 B3 Kysyl-Suluo U.S.S.R. 63.32N 138.15E
41 N8 Kysyl-Syr U.S.S.R. 62.34N 129.50E
41 K8 Kysyl-Yllyk U.S.S.R. 63.14N 113.46E
39 B1 Kysyl-Yuryakh U.S.S.R. 67.56N 139.15E
41 O6 Kytalyktakh U.S.S.R. 68.54N 134.08E
84 S14 Kythrea Cyprus 35.14N 33.30E
47 H6 Kytlym U.S.S.R. 59.31N 59.09E
42 D5 Kytmanovo U.S.S.R. 53.28N 85.30E
41 N8 Kytyl U.S.S.R. 63.23N 129.30E
40 C1 Kytyl-Zhura U.S.S.R. 60.58N 125.37E
41 K6 Kyuekh-Bulung U.S.S.R. 68.26N 113.36E
41 Q5 Kyuel'-Yuryakh R U.S.S.R.
41 K6 Kyuenelekyan R U.S.S.R.
39 C1 Kyuerelyakh U.S.S.R. 67.45N 140.45E
93 K8 Kyulu Kenya 2.56S 38.24E
30 D1 Kyunglung Xizang Zizhiqu 31.02N 80.34E
25 E5 Kyungyaung Burma 15.30N 98.14E
25 M9 Kyunhla Burma 23.22N 95.20E
101 K10 Kyuquot Vancouver I, Br Col 50.02N 127.22W
44 H7 Kyurd Azerbaydzhan U.S.S.R. 40.47N 47.08E
44 J7 Kyurdamir Azerbaydzhan U.S.S.R. 40.21N 48.09E
39 B2 Kyurelkan U.S.S.R. 67.27N 138.36E
43 D7 Kyurendag, Khrebet mts Turkmeniya U.S.S.R.
43 D4 Kyushe Kazakhstan U.S.S.R. 45.15N 56.25E
20 D9 Kyūshū isld Japan
122 D7 Kyushu-Palau Ridge Pacific Oc
20 E9 Kyūshū-sanchi mts Japan
82 H8 Kyustendil Bulgaria 42.16N 22.40E
41 N5 Kyusyur U.S.S.R. 70.44N 127.30E
39 C3 Kyuyent R U.S.S.R.
39 C3 Kyuyente U.S.S.R. 63.30N 142.05E
30 C1 Kyuyur La pass Xizang Zizhiqu 31.45N 79.42E
44 G8 Kyvrak Nakhichevan' U.S.S.R. 39.23N 45.08E
12 H6 Kywong New S Wales 35.01S 146.45E
51 L8 Kyyjärvi Finland 63.02N 24.34E
44 M3 Kyzan Kazakhstan U.S.S.R. 44.57N 52.40E
42 D6 Kyzas U.S.S.R. 52.22N 89.18E
42 D5 Kyzlasov U.S.S.R. 53.10N 89.59E
44 L5 Kyzyk Kazakhstan U.S.S.R. 42.54N 51.53E
42 E6 Kyzyl U.S.S.R. 51.45N 94.28E
43 N4 Kyzylagash Kazakhstan U.S.S.R. 45.20N 78.45E
31 G1 Kyzylart Pass Tadzhikistan U.S.S.R. 39.25N 73.21E
43 J3 Kyzyldyykan Kazakhstan U.S.S.R. 48.45N 68.17E
43 O7 Kyzyl-Dzhar Kirgiziya U.S.S.R. 41.16N 72.00E
47 L8 Kyzylkak, Oz L Kazakhstan U.S.S.R. 53.25N 73.50E
43 O3 Kyzylkesek Kazakhstan U.S.S.R. 47.56N 82.02E
42 D6 Kyzyl Khaye U.S.S.R. 50.05N 89.57E
42 F6 Kyzyl-Khem R U.S.S.R.
43 N4 Kyzylkiya Kazakhstan U.S.S.R. 47.24N 79.44E
43 K6 Kyzyl-Kiya Kirgiziya U.S.S.R. 40.15N 72.06E
43 C3 Kyzylkoga Kazakhstan U.S.S.R. 48.28N 53.05E
43 F3 Kyzylkol', Oz L Kazakhstan U.S.S.R. 48.52N 61.58E
43 J3 Kyzyl-Kommuna Kazakhstan U.S.S.R. 48.41N 67.31E
38 F4 Kyzylkum reg U.S.S.R.
43 G5 Kyzylkum, Peski sand des Kazakhstan/Uzbekistan U.S.S.R.
42 E6 Kyzyl-Mazhalyk U.S.S.R. 51.11N 90.35E
43 L7 Kyzylrabot Tadzhikistan U.S.S.R. 37.31N 74.49E
43 K7 Kyzylsu R Kirgiziya U.S.S.R.
43 L2 Kyzyltas Kazakhstan U.S.S.R. 50.43N 74.07E
47 M5 Kyzyltash, Oz L U.S.S.R. 55.44N 60.45E
43 K4 Kyzyltau Kazakhstan U.S.S.R. 47.59N 72.19E
43 K4 Kyzyltau Kazakhstan U.S.S.R. 47.50N 72.20E
43 M4 Kyzyltu Kazakhstan U.S.S.R. 47.43N 75.41E
43 H3 Kyzyluy Kazakhstan U.S.S.R. 47.45N 65.30E
43 G3 Kyzylzhar Kazakhstan U.S.S.R. 49.07N 62.32E
43 N5 Kyzylzhide Kazakhstan U.S.S.R. 43.46N 78.14E
43 J3 Kzyl-Dzhar Kazakhstan U.S.S.R. 48.15N 69.36E
43 H5 Kzyl-Orda Kazakhstan U.S.S.R. 44.52N 65.28E
43 H5 Kzyl Ordinskoye Vdkhr res Kazakhstan U.S.S.R.
43 K1 Kzyltu Kazakhstan U.S.S.R. 53.39N 72.22E

65 O4 Laa an der Thaya Austria 48.44N 16.23E
64 M5 Laaber W Germany 49.04N 11.54E
64 C3 Laacher See L W Germany 50.24N 7.18E
63 Q5 Laage E Germany 53.56N 12.21E
60 N12 Laag-Keppel Netherlands 51.59N 6.14E
60 N11 Laag-Soeren Netherlands 52.05N 6.05E
121 F10 La Aguada dist Santiago Chile
60 T16 Laak Netherlands 51.07N 5.49E
65 J6 Laakirchen Austria 47.59N 13.49E
Laaland see Lolland
121 D5 La Amarga Argentina 34.17S 64.15W
15 C5 Laamora,Danau L Irian Jaya 3.39S 134.18E
96 T10 La Ampuyenta Fuerteventura Canary Is 28.26N 13.39W
88 J8 Laanach Morocco 26.50N 9.33W
51 N3 Laanila Finland 68.24N 27.25E
96 T10 La Antigua Fuerteventura Canary Is 28.24N 14.02W
61 L3 Laar Belgium 50.47N 5.02E
88 F9 Laarch reg Morocco
61 F2 Laarne Belgium 51.02N 3.51E
64 E2 Laasphe W Germany 50.55N 8.25E
119 G2 La Asunción Venezuela 11.06N 63.53W
114 C5 Laau Pt Hawaiian Is 21.06N 157.19W
119 G4 La Aurora Venezuela 7.37N 65.08W
66 O4 Laax Switzerland 46.48N 9.16E
66 N4 Laaxer Tal V Switzerland
88 H8 Laayeram reg Morocco
89 M4 Laba Niger 14.40N 5.59E
89 H6 Laba Upper Volta 11.50N 2.39W
91 F6 Laba Zaïre 4.40S 19.50E
44 C2 Laba R U.S.S.R.
115 H3 La Babia Mexico 28.39N 102.00W
76 C3 Labacolla Spain 42.54N 8.25W
107 F3 Labadie Missouri 38.31N 90.51W
54 E12 Labadie Bank Atlantic Oc
107 F12 Labadieville Louisiana 29.50N 91.00W
75 O3 La Baelle, Embalse de res Spain
87 K5 Laba Geri Somalia 10.25N 44.37E
120 G6 La Bahia, Lag Bolivia 14.25S 61.06W
76 K7 Labajos Spain 40.50N 4.32W
19 C8 Labala Indonesia 8.31S 123.29E
71 G4 Labalme France 46.05N 5.30E
35 F10 La'ban Jordan 30.54N 35.42E
35 F10 La'ban watercourse Jordan
121 D1 La Banda Argentina 27.44S 64.14W
89 N4 Labandam Niger 14.52N 6.10E
18 K4 Labang Sarawak Malaysia 3.17N 113.30E
19 C8 Labao Indonesia 8.12S 122.49E
115 H7 La Barca Mexico 20.20N 102.33W
72 C5 Labarde France 45.02N 0.38W
110 P7 La Barge Wyoming 42.16N 110.11W
110 P7 La Barge Cr Wyoming
119 C7 La Barquilla Ecuador 0.16N 77.24W
115 N3 La Barra de Río Grande Nicaragua 12.55N 83.32W
72 F9 Labarthe-Rivière France 43.05N 0.38E
59 D6 Labasheeda Clare Irish Rep 52.35N 9.25W
72 C9 Labastide Cézeracq France 43.22N 0.32W
72 B9 Labastide Clairence France 43.26N 1.15W
72 H9 Labastide d'Anjou France 43.20N 1.52E
72 D8 Labastide d'Armagnac France 43.58N 0.11W
72 H6 Labastide Murat France 44.39N 1.33E
72 K9 Labastide Rouairoux France 43.28N 2.39E
72 E8 Labatut-Rivière France 43.32N 0.03E
25 B2 Labawa Burma 20.37N 92.40E
47 G3 Labazhskoye U.S.S.R. 67.21N 52.03E
41 G5 Labaz, Ozero L U.S.S.R.
89 B1 Labba Mauritania 20.39N 14.20W
34 J9 Labbah,Al plat Saudi Arabia
51 F5 Labbas Sweden 66.25N 17.30E
89 K4 Labbezenga Mali 15.02N 0.48E
35 D1 Labbouna Lebanon 33.05N 35.09E
85 C3 Labdah ruins Libya 32.59N 14.15E
51 O3 Labdsh'yaur,Ozero L U.S.S.R. 68.57N 29.44E
89 C6 Labé Guinea 11.17N 12.11W
62 J5 Labe R Czechoslovakia

72 J9 Labécède-Lauragais France 43.22N 2.00E
71 E7 Labégude France 44.38N 4.23E
72 F8 Labéjan France 43.32N 0.30E
105 F11 La Belle Florida 26.47N 81.27W
107 E1 La Belle Missouri 40.06N 91.56W
99 Q6 Labelle Quebec 46.17N 74.45W
99 P6 Labelle, Parc de Quebec
19 C5 Labengke isld Celebes Indon 3.28S 122.24E
72 B8 Labenne France 43.36N 1.25W
101 F5 Laberge, L Yukon Terr
71 G3 Labergement-lès-Seurre France 47.00N 5.06E
121 E7 Laberinto, Pta C Argentina 39.27S 62.04W
64 N6 Laberweinting W Germany 48.48N 12.21E
18 L3 Labi Brunei 4.26N 114.24E
18 N3 Labian,Tanjong C Sabah Malaysia 5.10N 119.15E
101 L5 La Biche R Yukon Terr
82 B5 Labin Yugoslavia 45.05N 14.07E
44 D3 Labinsk U.S.S.R. 44.39N 40.44E
18 D9 Labis Pen Malaysia 2.22N 103.01E
71 E8 Lablachère France 44.28N 4.13E
121 G10 La Blanca dist Santiago Chile
19 L4 Labo Luzon Philippines 14.09N 122.52E
19 C4 Labobo isld Indonesia 1.45S 123.20E
111 J10 La Bomba Mexico 31.53N 115.02W
108 E7 Labonte Cr Wyoming
77 K6 Laborcillas Spain 37.27N 3.17W
62 N6 Laborec R Czechoslovakia
47 K2 Laborovaya U.S.S.R. 67.38N 67.30E
19 C5 Labota Celebes Indon 2.52S 122.13E
14 C7 Labouchere, Mt W Australia 25.10S 118.18E
34 D4 Laboué,El Lebanon 34.13N 36.20E
72 C7 Labouheyre France 44.13N 0.55W
121 D5 Laboulaye Argentina 34.05S 63.20W
72 J8 Laboutarie France 43.47N 2.06E
61 F5 La-Bouverie Belgium 50.24N 3.53E
76 D2 Labrada R Spain
Labrador see Labrador, Coast of
98 K1 Labrador dist Newfoundland
97 N7 Labrador City Nfld/Labrador 52.56N 66.52W
48 R13 Labrador Sea Greenland
Labrang see Xiahe

119 D5 Labranzagrande Colombia 5.34N 72.34W
76 L2 Labra,Peña mt Spain 43.03N 4.25W
121 D4 La Brava, L Argentina
120 F2 Lábrea Brazil 7.20S 64.46W
116 N2 La Brea Trinidad & Tobago 10.14N 61.37W
La Brea, Cerros de see Amotape ó de la Brea, Cerros
115 E5 La Brecha Mexico 25.22N 108.28W
72 C6 Labrède France 44.42N 0.31W
98 C4 Labrieville Quebec 49.20N 69.37W
98 C4 Labrieville, Parc de Quebec
72 C7 Labrit France 44.06N 0.32W
100 E1 La Broquerie Manitoba 49.32N 96.30W
72 K6 Labrousse France 44.51N 2.32E
69 C3 Labroye France 50.17N 2.00E
72 J8 Labruguière France 43.32N 2.15E
76 B5 Labrujo Portugal 41.51N 8.33W
18 F9 Labuan Java Indonesia 6.25S 105.49E
18 L3 Labuan isld Sabah Malaysia
Labudalin see Ergun Youqi
19 E4 Labuha Moluccas Indon 0.35S 127.28E
19 A8 Labuhanbajo Indonesia 8.33S 119.55E
18 D4 Labuhanbatu Sumatra Indonesia 2.16N 100.14E
18 D4 Labuhanbilik Sumatra Indon 2.30N 100.10E
18 B4 Labuhanhaji Sumatra Indon 3.31N 97.00E
18 C4 Labuhanruku Sumatra Indon 3.10N 99.32E
18 F8 Labuhanwaiharu Sumatra Indon 5.45S 104.29E
61 G5 Labuissière Belgium 50.19N 4.12E
18 M3 Labuk R Sabah Malaysia
18 M2 Labuk, Telok B Sabah Malaysia
93 G1 Labur mt Kenya 4.27N 35.48E
71 B1 La Bussière France 47.45N 2.44E
25 C4 Labutta Burma 16.08N 94.45E
39 E2 Labuya U.S.S.R. 67.29N 154.03E
39 C3 Labynkyr, Ozero L U.S.S.R. 62.30N 143.32E
28 G7 Labyrinth Is Andaman Is
101 U5 Labyrinth L N W Terr 60.48N 106.20W
12 D4 Labyrinth, L S Australia 30.43S 135.07E
47 K3 Labytnangi U.S.S.R. 66.43N 66.28E
Lac see Nyanza-Lac Burundi
83 D3 Laç Albania 41.38N 19.40E
90 G5 Lac Chad
99 S5 Lac à Beauce Quebec 47.19N 72.46W
121 E3 La Cabral Argentina 30.08S 61.10W
115 G5 La Cadena Mexico 25.53N 104.10W
100 J8 Lacadena Saskatchewan 50.58N 108.22W
120 E8 Lacajahuira R Bolivia
77 K6 Lacalahorra Spain 37.11N 3.03W
61 P4 La Calamine Belgium 50.43N 6.01E
120 F11 La Caldera Argentina 24.34S 65.24W
121 D3 La Calera Argentina 31.24S 64.25W
121 B4 La Calera Chile 32.47S 71.16W
96 U7 La Caleta Lanzarote Canary Is 29.08N 13.38W
98 J3 Lac Allard Quebec 50.34N 63.27W
120 D11 Lacalle Chile 24.26S 69.48W
72 K6 Lacalm France 44.46N 2.52E
107 D10 Lacamp Louisiana 31.10N 92.57W
115 P5 La Campana Panama 8.45N 79.52W
120 B11 La Campiña dist Lima Peru
La Campine see Kempenland
121 D1 La Cañada Argentina 27.45S 63.43W
72 B6 Lacanau France 44.59N 1.05W
72 B6 Lacanau, Lac de France 44.58N 1.07W
72 B5 Lacanau Océan France 45.00N 1.12W
71 F2 Lacanche France 47.05N 4.34E
119 G3 La Canoa Venezuela 8.39N 63.53W
115 O9 Lacantum R Mexico
72 K6 Lacapelle Barres France 44.57N 2.43E
72 H6 Lacapelle Marival France 44.44N 1.54E
72 J6 Lacapelle-Viescamp France 44.55N 2.15E
77 D2 Lácara R Spain
121 B8 Lacar L Argentina
121 D4 La Carlota Argentina 33.30S 63.15W
19 L6 La Carlota Philippines 10.21N 122.55E
72 B9 Lacarre France 43.12N 1.09W
72 K8 Lacaune France 43.42N 2.41E
72 K8 Lacaune, Mts. de France
98 E5 Lac au Saumon Quebec 48.25N 67.20W
99 S5 Lac aux Brochets Quebec 47.14N 72.41W
99 S6 Lac aux Sables Quebec 46.52N 72.24W
72 H6 Lacave France 44.50N 1.33E
99 M6 La Cave Ontario 46.23N 78.44W
72 K8 Lacaze France 43.44N 2.30E
98 D6 Lac Baker New Brunswick 47.20N 68.40W
87 H10 Lac Bissigh watercourse Somalia
99 S4 Lac-Bouchette Quebec 48.16N 72.11W
Laccadive-Chagos Ridge see Maldive Ridge
27 L7 Laccadive Is Indian Oc
26 G4 Laccadive Trough Indian Oc
99 S5 Lac Chat Quebec 47.10N 72.39W
79 F4 Lacchiarella Italy 45.20N 9.08E
87 H10 Lac Dera watercourse Somalia
100 H4 Lac des Iles Saskatchewan
98 B8 Lac-Drolet Quebec 45.43N 70.52W
106 E4 Lac du Flambeau Wisconsin 45.58N 89.54W
57 N5 Laceby Humberside Eng 53.33N 0.10W
80 M6 Lacedonia Italy 41.03N 15.26E
99 S5 Lac Édouard Quebec 47.40N 72.16W
115 L2 La Ceiba Honduras 15.45N 86.45W
119 E3 La Ceiba Venezuela 9.31N 71.04W
119 C4 La Ceja Colombia 6.02N 75.30W
72 H4 Lacelle France 45.38N 1.49E
75 L6 La Cenia Spain 40.39N 0.16E
12 E6 Lacepede B S Australia
14 D3 Lacepede Is W Australia 16.52S 122.09E
94 N2 Lacerdónia Mozambique 18.01S 35.30E
79 J1 Láces Italy 46.37N 10.52E
98 B7 Lac Etchemin Quebec 46.24N 70.31W
103 B3 Laceyville Pennsylvania 41.38N 76.09W
98 B7 Lac Frontière Quebec 46.40N 70.01W
99 P6 Lac Gatineau Quebec 46.34N 75.44W
47 D5 Lacha, Ozero L U.S.S.R.
69 B5 Lachapelle-aux-Pots France 49.28N 1.55E
77 J6 Láchar Spain 37.12N 3.50W
29 L4 Lachen Sikkim India 27.46N 88.36E
66 M3 Lachen Switzerland 47.12N 8.51E
64 E5 Lachen W Germany 49.20N 8.12E
71 K9 Lachens mt France 43.45N 6.40E
121 C5 La Chilca Mendoza Argentina 34.16S 67.50W
121 D2 La Chilca Santiago del Estero Argentina 28.47S 63.51W
44 H8 Lachin Azerbaydzhan U.S.S.R. 39.38N 46.33E
106 L4 Lachine Michigan 45.04N 83.44W
99 R10 Lachine Quebec 45.27N 73.41W
99 R10 Lachine Canal Montreal, Quebec
99 R10 Lachine, Rapides de Quebec
24 H10 Lachin La pass Xizang Zizhiqu China 31.26N 95.31E
45 J5 Lachinovo U.S.S.R. 51.47N 37.55E
120 B5 La Chira, Pta Peru 12.14S 77.04W
35 C7 Lachish reg Israel
12 H5 Lachlan R New S Wales
29 E4 Lachmangarh Alwar, Rajasthan India 27.20N 76.51E
29 D4 Lachmangarh Sikar Rajasthan India 27.48N 75.06E
119 D8 La Chorrera Colombia 1.00S 73.10W
115 F11 La Chorrera Panama 8.51N 79.46W
63 M7 Lachte R W Germany
98 E5 Lac Humqui Quebec 48.22N 67.33W
29 L4 Lachung Sikkim India 27.42N 88.48E
99 Q7 Lachute Quebec 45.39N 74.21W
36 H2 Laçin Turkey 40.45N 34.57E
121 G10 La Cisterna dist Santiago Chile
115 G6 La Ciudad Durango Mexico 23.43N 105.42W
59 G2 Lack Fermanagh N Ireland 54.33N 7.35W

59 E5 Lackagh Galway Irish Rep 53.22N 8.53W
103 F3 Lackawack New York 41.48N 74.25W
104 G4 Lackawanna New York 42.49N 78.49W
103 C3 Lackawanna co Pennsylvania
103 D3 Lackawanna R Pennsylvania
103 D4 Lackawaxen Pennsylvania 41.29N 75.00W
103 D3 Lackawaxen R Pennsylvania
59 J5 Lacken Res Wicklow Irish Rep 53.10N 6.30W
56 N3 Lackford Suffolk Eng 52.18N 0.37E
19 D8 Lacla R Indonesia
100 F4 Lac la Biche Alberta 54.46N 111.59W
101 N10 Lac La Hache Br Columbia 51.50N 121.29W
101 P4 Lac La Marte N W Terr 63.15N 117.22E
100 M3 Lac La Ronge Prov.Park Saskatchewan
110 J1 Laclede Idaho 48.10N 116.44W
107 C2 Laclede Missouri 39.47N 93.10W
121 D1 La Cocha Argentina 27.47S 65.36W
56 G5 Lacock Wilts Eng 51.25N 2.08W
75 B1 La Cohilla, Embalse de res Spain
121 E6 La Colina Argentina 37.24S 61.33W
99 R7 Lacolle Quebec 45.04N 73.22W
115 D3 La Colorada Mexico 28.49N 110.32W
115 H6 La Colorada Mexico 23.48N 102.22W
100 D6 Lacombe Alberta 52.30N 113.42W
107 G11 Lacombe Louisiana 30.19N 89.57W
106 E8 Lacon Illinois 41.02N 89.24W
108 R8 Lacona Iowa 41.10N 93.22W
104 J3 Lacona New York 43.39N 76.04W
99 Q6 La Conception Quebec 46.09N 74.44W
115 N9 La Concordia Mexico 16.08N 92.38W
81 C4 Laconi Sardinia 39.51N 9.03E
104 O3 Laconia New Hampshire 43.32N 71.29W
110 C1 La Conner Washington 48.22N 122.29W
121 C1 La Constancia Argentina 27.46S 66.26W
105 E9 Lacoochee Florida 28.29N 82.19W
121 C6 La Copelina Argentina 37.14S 67.38W
121 E6 La Copeta Argentina 36.46S 61.58W
118 B9 La Cordillera dept Paraguay
99 N4 Lacorne Quebec 48.22N 78.00W
72 G10 Lacourt France 42.56N 1.09E
66 C3 Lac ou Villers France 47.03N 6.40E
116 J2 Lacovia Jamaica, W I 18.09N 77.46W
72 C9 Lacq France 43.25N 0.37W
108 O4 Lac Qui Parle L Minnesota
108 O5 Lac Qui Parle R Minnesota
108 J6 Lacreek L S Dakota
99 Q6 Lac Rémi Quebec 46.01N 74.47W
106 C6 La Crescent Minnesota 43.50N 91.19W
99 S5 La Croche Quebec 47.44N 72.44W
72 K6 Lacroix Barrez France 44.47N 2.36E
108 S1 La Croix, L Minnesota/Ontario
69 D5 Lacroix-St. Ouen France 49.20N 2.47E
106 H8 La Crosse Indiana 41.18N 86.53W
109 L3 La Crosse Kansas 38.32N 99.19W
110 H3 La Crosse Washington 46.50N 117.53W
106 C6 La Crosse Wisconsin 43.48N 91.15W
14 G2 Lacrosse I W Australia 14.44S 128.15E
121 G2 La Cruz Argentina 29.10S 56.40W
115 G4 La Cruz Chihuahua Mexico 27.50N 105.11W
119 C7 La Cruz Colombia 1.33N 76.58W
115 M4 La Cruz Costa Rica 11.05N 85.39W
115 M3 La Cruz Nicaragua 13.04N 84.12W
115 F6 La Cruz Sinaloa Mexico 23.53N 106.53W
115 K5 La Cruz Tamaulipas Mexico 24.08N 99.14W
121 G4 La Cruz Uruguay 33.54S 56.11W
99 P6 Lac Saguay Quebec 46.30N 75.08W
99 P7 Lac Ste. Marie Quebec 45.56N 75.57W
99 G3 Lac Ste. Thérèse Ontario 49.48N 83.39W
115 H3 La Cuesta Mexico 28.45N 102.26W
121 B6 La Cueva Chile 37.28S 71.21W
109 E6 La Cueva New Mexico 35.55N 105.16W
61 M8 Lacuisine Belgium 49.43N 5.20E
100 N6 Lac Vert Saskatchewan 52.32N 104.32W
109 Q3 La Cygne Kansas 38.21N 94.46W
85 N4 Lad Israel 31.59N 34.53E
45 R2 Lada U.S.S.R. 54.36N 45.24E
118 H5 Ladainha Brazil 17.39S 41.45W
31 J3 Ladakh reg Kashmir
31 J3 Ladakh Ra Kashmir
45 D6 Ladan' Ukraine U.S.S.R. 50.31N 32.35E
25 E9 Ladang isld Thailand
18 B7 Ladang Jagor Pen Malaysia 4.42N 101.34E
30 K6 Ladania Bihar India 26.37N 86.20E
18 F9 Lada, Teluk B Java Indon
56 J3 Ladbroke Warwicks Eng 52.14N 1.23W
11 L10 Ladbrooks New Zealand 43.37S 172.32E
106 E8 Ladd Illinois 41.23N 89.14W
109 J3 Ladder Cr Kansas
107 E2 Laddonia Missouri 39.13N 91.38W
17 H10 Ladd Reef S China Sea 8.44N 111.20E
103 B3 Laddsburg Pennsylvania 41.34N 76.24W
107 E8 Ladelle Arkansas 33.30N 91.49W
63 K3 Ladelund W Germany 54.50N 9.02E
115 O10 La Democracia Guatemala 14.12N 90.56W
64 F5 Ladenburg W Germany 49.28N 8.36E
65 O4 Ladendorf Austria 48.33N 16.28E
61 F4 Ladeuze Belgium 50.34N 3.47E
84 D7 Ladhá Greece 37.05N 22.13E
58 E4 Ladhar Bheinn mt Highland Scotland 57.04N 5.35W
30 B7 Ladhaura Madhya Prad India 25.04N 78.51E
Lādhiqīya, El see Latakia
30 C3 Ladhiya R Uttar Prad India
84 D6 Ládhon R Greece
72 G4 Ladignac-le-Long France 45.35N 1.07E
26 R12 La Digue I Seychelles, Ind Oc 4.20S 55.51E
36 H2 Lâdik Samsun Turkey 40.54N 35.54E
36 J2 Lâdik Tokat Turkey 40.34N 36.46E
Lâdikars see Vilâdikars
53 D4 Lading Denmark 56.13N 9.59E
72 J6 Ladinhac France 44.45N 2.29E
Ladis see Lādīz
95 E9 Ladismith S Africa 33.30S 21.15E
32 J6 Lādīz Iran 28.57N 61.20E
103 E3 Ladleton New York 41.57N 74.33W
101 H12 Ladner Br Columbia 49.06N 123.05W
108 G4 Ladner S Dakota 45.50N 103.45W
82 G6 Ladne Vode Yugoslavia 44.16N 21.31E
29 D4 Ladnun Rajasthan India 27.36N 74.26E
87 C8 Lado mt Sudan 5.10N 31.32E
76 E9 Ladoeiro Portugal 39.51N 7.16W
107 K2 Ladoga Indiana 39.56N 86.49W
Ladoga, L see Ladozhskoye Ozero L
69 D7 Ladon France 48.01N 2.32E
112 M2 Ladonia Texas 33.26N 95.57W
119 D5 La Dorado Colombia 5.28N 74.41W
44 C2 Ladozhskaya U.S.S.R. 45.20N 39.55E
47 C5 Ladozhskoye Ozero U.S.S.R. 60.13N 31.01E
47 C5 Ladozhskoye Ozero L U.S.S.R.
66 S4 Lad, Piz mt Austria/Switz/Italy 46.51N 10.28E
66 S5 Lad, Piz mt Switzerland 46.35N 10.25E
121 J9 Ladrillero pk Chile 52.58S 72.35W
121 H7 Ladrillero, Canal str Chile
119 A4 Ladrones, Is Panama 7.51N 82.27W
109 C7 Ladrones Pk New Mexico 34.27N 107.07W
28 J2 Ladu mt Assam India 27.55N 93.44E
113 R5 Ladue R Alaska
115 E3 La Dura Mexico 28.22N 109.33W
46 D3 Ladushkin U.S.S.R. 54.30N 20.05E
47 C5 Ladva Vetka Karelia U.S.S.R. 61.16N 34.23E
30 A3 Ladwa Haryana India 30.00N 77.02E
93 D2 Ladwong mt Uganda 3.06N 32.20E
97 L2 Lady Ann Str N W Terr
58 K6 Ladybank Fife Scotland 56.17N 3.08W
12 J8 Lady Barron Flinders I, Tas 40.12S 148.14E
57 K6 Ladybower Res Derbys Eng 53.23N 1.42W
95 L5 Ladybrand S Africa 29.12S 27.27E
14 F5 Lady Edith L W Australia 20.39S 126.46E
13 L6 Lady Elliot I Gt Barrier Reef Australia 24.07S 152.42E
99 K5 Lady Evelyn L Ontario
101 R1 Lady Franklin Pt Victoria I, N W Terr 68.30N 113.10W
95 L7 Lady Frere S Africa 31.42S 27.14E
41 E7 Ladyga U.S.S.R. 65.44N 85.45E
41 D5 Ladygiy Yar U.S.S.R. 70.53N 83.33E
95 L6 Lady Grey S Africa 30.43S 27.13E
96 B11 Lady Hill Ascension I 7.57S 14.23W
57 D1 Lady I Strathclyde Scotland 55.31N 4.44W
123 J6 Lady Newnes Ice Shelf Antarctica
101 P1 Lady Richardson, B Victoria I, N W Terr
59 K7 Lady's Island L Wexford Irish Rep 52.12N 6.23W
95 N4 Ladysmith S Africa 28.34S 29.47E
101 M11 Ladysmith Vancouver I, Br Col 48.57N 123.50W
106 C4 Ladysmith Wisconsin 45.27N 91.07W
43 J2 Ladyzhenka Kazakhstan U.S.S.R. 51.00N 68.42E
82 N2 Ladyzhinka U.S.S.R. 48.32N 30.15E
15 J7 Lae Papua New Guinea 6.45S 147.00E
25 F3 Lae Thailand 19.26N 100.59E
9 B2 Lae atoll Marshall Is Pacific Oc 8.57N 166.12E
19 C6 Laëa Indonesia 4.40S 123.14E
53 C5 Læborg Denmark 55.32N 9.07E
51 M2 Lævajoki Norway 69.55N 26.25E
18 A4 Laehobang Indonesia 2.34N 95.55E
50 E4 Lækjamót Iceland 65.25N 20.37W
50 L2 Læknistadhir Iceland 66.22N 14.55W
114 B7 Lae Mano pt Hawaiian Is 19.50N 155.58W
25 G6 Laem Ngop Thailand 12.10N 102.27E
25 F9 Laem Pho C Thailand
119 F3 La Encrucijada Venezuela 9.16N 67.02W
114 E6 Lae o Apole pt Hawaiian Is 20.37N 156.11W
114 D5 Lae o Kahiu Hawaiian Is 21.13N 157.02W
114 D6 Lae o Kaka pt Hawaiian Is 20.30N 156.32W
114 B8 Lae o Kamoi pt Hawaiian Is 19.05N 155.55W
114 D6 Lae o Kealaikahiki Hawaiian Is 20.31N 156.43W
114 B8 Lae o Kimo pt Hawaiian Is 19.03N 155.34W

114 D6 **Lae o Kuikui** *pt* Hawaiian Is 20.36N 156.34W
114 B8 **Lae o Puuo** *pt* Hawaiian Is 19.07N 155.31W
63 H8 **Laer** Niedersachsen W Germany 52.07N 8.05E
63 F8 **Laer** Nordrhein-Westfalen W Germany 52.03N 7.21E
53 X16 **Lærdal** *V* Norway 61.04N 7.39E
53 W16 **Lærdalsøyri** Norway 61.06N 7.28E
81 B2 **Laerru** Sardinia 40.49N 8.50E
95 G8 **Laer Sneeuberg** *mts* S Africa
121 D2 **La Esmeralda** Argentina 28.43S 64.37W
118 A8 **La Esmeralda** Paraguay/Bolivia 22.13S 62.44W
119 G6 **La Esmeralda** Venezuela 3.11N 65.33W
53 G2 **Læsø** *isld* Denmark
53 F2 **Læso Rende** *channel* Denmark
121 K6 **La Española** Argentina 47.27S 69.30W
120 F6 **La Esperanza** Beni Bolivia 14.24S 65.32W
115 P10 **La Esperanza** Honduras 14.19N 88.09W
120 F11 **La Esperanza** Jujuy Arg 24.09S 64.52W
121 C6 **La Esperanza** La Pampa Arg 36.43S 66.45W
116 C3 **La Esperanza** Pinar del Rio Cuba 22.44N 83.44W
120 G6 **La Esperanza** Santa Cruz Bolivia 14.36S 62.14W
120 F10 **La Estrella** Argentina 23.47S 64.02W
120 F7 **La Estrella** Bolivia 16.27S 63.39W
96 V15 **La Estrella** Gran Canaria Canary Is 28.02N 15.22W
90 G6 **Laf** Cameroon 10.16N 14.11E
90 B6 **Lafagu** Nigeria 11.09N 4.15E
121 D3 **La Falda** Argentina 31.01S 64.30W
106 D6 **La Farge** Wisconsin 43.33N 90.38W
106 S5 **La Fargeville** New York 44.15N 76.00W
87 K6 **Lafa Rug** Somalia 10.00N 44.42E
107 L9 **Lafayette** Alabama 32.55N 85.26W
111 C8 **Lafayette** California 37.53N 122.08W
109 E2 **Lafayette** Colorado 39.59N 105.06W
105 B3 **Lafayette** Georgia 34.42N 85.18W
106 H9 **Lafayette** Indiana 40.25N 86.54W
107 D11 **Lafayette** Louisiana 30.12N 92.01W
108 Q5 **Lafayette** Minnesota 44.26N 94.24W
103 E4 **Lafayette** New Jersey 41.06N 74.41W
103 M3 **Lafayette** Rhode I 41.35N 71.29W
107 K5 **Lafayette** Tennessee 36.31N 86.02W
104 O2 **Lafayette, Mt** New Hampshire 44.10N 71.38W
26 V12 **Lafayette, Pte** Mauritius, Indian Oc 20.07S 57.45E
111 C8 **Lafayette Res** California 37.52N 122.08W
116 B3 **La Fé** Cuba 22.02N 84.15W
112 K9 **La Feria** Texas 26.10N 97.49W
99 M4 **Laferté** Quebec 48.37N 78.48W
69 K8 **Laferté-sur-Amance** France 47.50N 5.42E
69 H7 **Laferté-sur-Aube** France 48.06N 4.47E
33 J4 **Laffān, Ra's** *C* Qatar, The Gulf 25.56N 51.32E
71 H6 **Laffrey** France 45.02N 5.47E
90 D7 **Lafia** Nigeria 8.30N 8.34E
90 B7 **Lafiagi** Nigeria 8.50N 5.23E
72 E9 **Lafitole** France 43.27N 0.05E
Lafiya *see* **Līfīyah, Al**
99 N3 **Laflamme** *R* Quebec
100 L9 **Lafleche** Saskatchewan 49.44N 106.32W
65 O7 **Lafnitz** Austria 47.27N 16.01E
65 O7 **Lafnitz** *R* Austria
9 B13 **La Foa** New Caledonia 21.40S 165.52E
107 M5 **La Follette** Tennessee 36.23N 84.09W
87 D8 **Lafon** Sudan 5.05N 32.29E
99 M5 **Laforce** Quebec 47.32N 78.45W
99 J5 **Laforest** Ontario 47.02N 81.13W
117 B2 **La Forestière** Fr Guiana 5.15N 54.17W
72 G7 **Lafrançaise** France 44.08N 1.14E
105 E3 **La France** S Carolina 34.34N 82.46W
119 D3 **La Fria** Venezuela 8.19N 72.19W
69 N6 **Lafrimbole** France 48.36N 7.01E
32 F7 **Laft** Iran 26.55N 55.46E
28 J7 **Laful** Nicobar Is 7.10N 93.50E
93 K2 **Laga Afgudud** *watercourse* Kenya
50 D6 **Lágafell** Iceland 64.10N 21.41W
50 E6 **Lagafell** *mt* Iceland 64.21N 20.58W
87 H7 **Laga Hida** Ethiopia 7.51N 41.02E
15 H6 **Lagaip** *R* Papua New Guinea
78 B11 **La Galite** *isld* Tunisia
121 E2 **La Gallareta** Argentina 29.43S 60.20W
115 G5 **La Gallega** Mexico 25.48N 105.04W
86 K4 **Lagama, Gebel el** *hill* Egypt 30.47N 33.27E
80 H3 **Laga, Monti della** Italy
52 H10 **Lagan** *R* Sweden
84 A6 **Laganá, Ormos** *B* Greece
69 M6 **Lagarde** Moselle France 48.41N 6.42E
72 H5 **Lagarde Enval** Corrèze France 45.10N 1.48E
72 G9 **Lagardelle-sur-Lèze** France 43.24N 1.23E
76 E5 **Lagarelhos** Portugal 41.40N 7.28W
76 D8 **Lagares** Portugal 40.24N 7.52W
50 L4 **Lagarfljót** *R* Iceland
50 L3 **Lagarfoss** *waterfall* Iceland 65.31N 14.22W
30 D8 **Lagargawan** Madhya Prad India 24.26N 80.48E
79 J3 **Lagarina, Val** Italy
109 D4 **La Garita Mts** Colorado
53 X18 **Lågaros** Norway 60.10N 7.48E
76 J9 **Lagartera** Spain 39.54N 5.12W
115 E10 **Lagarterito** Panama 9.09N 79.55W
118 J2 **Lagarto** Brazil 10.55S 37.40W
30 D5 **Lagcha** Uttar Prad India 27.49N 80.49E
118 H2 **Lage** Brazil 10.10S 40.58W
76 A2 **Lage** Spain 43.13N 9.00W
63 J8 **Lage** W Germany 52.00N 8.47E
60 J14 **Lage Meirde** Netherlands 51.24N 5.09E
52 E5 **Lågen** *L* Norway 61.25N 10.25E
52 E7 **Lågen** *R* Norway
53 Y18 **Lågen** *R* Norway
Lagens *see* **Lajes**
60 L13 **Lagepeel** Netherlands 51.43N 5.44E
63 L5 **Lägerdorf** W Germany 53.53N 9.35E
96 U8 **La Geria** Lanzarote Canary Is 28.57N 13.44W
76 A2 **Lage, Ría de** *estuary* Spain
66 K2 **Lägern** *mt* Switzerland 47.29N 8.22E
41 A3 **Lagernyy** Novaya Zemlya U.S.S.R. 73.19N 54.15E
45 H7 **Lagery** Ukraine U.S.S.R. 49.26N 36.32E
60 J11 **Lage Vuursche** Netherlands 52.10N 5.13E
60 G13 **Lage-Zwaluwe** Netherlands 51.42N 4.42E
57 C2 **Lagg** Arran, Strathclyde Scotland 55.27N 5.14W
58 E7 **Lagg** Jura, Strathclyde Scotland 55.57N 5.50W
58 H4 **Laggan** Highland Scotland 57.02N 4.18W
58 D7 **Laggan B** Islay, Strathclyde Scotland
58 G5 **Laggan, L** Highland Scotland
93 M4 **Lagh Bisigh** *watercourse* Kenya
93 L4 **Lagh Bogal** *watercourse* Kenya
50 L4 **Lágheidhi** *heath* Iceland
31 F3 **Laghman** *prov* Afghanistan
88 P5 **Laghouat** Algeria 33.49N 2.55E
59 E5 **Laghtgeorge** Galway Irish Rep 53.21N 8.55W
59 F2 **Laghy** Donegal Irish Rep 54.37N 8.05W
44 J7 **Lagich** Azerbaydzhan U.S.S.R. 40.49N 48.23E
83 C3 **Lagit,Kep i** *C* Albania 41.09N 19.25E
24 E9 **Lagkor Co** *L* Xizang Zizhiqu China 32.04N 84.10E
Laglag *see* **Laqlaq**
79 O1 **Laglésie San Leopoldo** Italy 46.31N 13.22E
66 N8 **Laglio** Italy 45.53N 9.09E
119 D3 **La Gloria** Colombia 8.37N 73.51W
25 J7 **Lagna** *R* Vietnam
71 G5 **Lagnieu** France 45.54N 5.20E
69 D6 **Lagny** France 48.53N 2.43E
81 M5 **Lago** Italy 39.10N 16.09E
89 D7 **Lago** Sierra Leone 8.07N 11.13W
29 K3 **Lago** Xizang Zizhiqu 29.06N 87.19E
96 T2 **Lagôa** Azores 37.30N 25.35W
76 C14 **Lagoa** Portugal 37.07N 8.27W
76 F6 **Lagõa** Portugal 41.27N 6.46W
76 F6 **Lagoaca** Portugal 41.11N 6.44W
119 C7 **Lago Agrio** *oil well* Ecuador 0.50N 76.54W
118 G6 **Lagoa Santa** Brazil 19.39S 43.44W
121 H2 **Lagoa Vermelha** Brazil 28.26S 51.36W
121 K7 **Lago Cardiel** Argentina 48.58S 71.23W
117 E7 **Lago da Pedra** Brazil 4.21S 45.08W
Lagodei, El *see* **Gardò**
44 G6 **Lagodekhi** Georgia U.S.S.R. 41.50N 46.16E
91 H9 **Lago Dilolo** Angola 11.27S 22.03E
118 E4 **Lagolândia** Brazil 15.38S 48.59W
115 O10 **La Gomera** Guatemala 14.05N 91.03W
81 L3 **Lagonegro** Italy 40.07N 15.46E
19 L5 **Lagonoy G** Luzon Philippines
13 E3 **Lagoon Cr** Queensland
121 K6 **Lago Posadas** Argentina 47.31S 71.45W
72 C9 **Lagor** France 43.24N 0.39W
121 A8 **Lago Ranco** Chile 40.20S 72.29W
71 E8 **Lagorce** France 44.22N 4.25E
116 A1 **Lago Refinery** Aruba W I 12.26N 69.54W
90 A8 **Lagos** Nigeria 6.27N 3.28E
76 B14 **Lagos** Portugal 37.05N 8.40W
89 L8 **Lagos** *reg* Nigeria
92 D4 **Lagosa** Tanzania 5.59S 29.58E
79 M5 **Lagosanto** Italy 44.45N 12.08E
115 J7 **Lagos de Moreno** Mexico 21.21N 101.55W
79 H2 **Lago Spalma, Cimo** *mt* Italy 46.23N 10.12E
77 M4 **Lagos, Sierra de** *mts* Spain
91 C8 **Lagostas, Farol das** *pt* Angola 8.46S 13.16E
88 T3 **La Goulette** Tunisia 36.52N 10.18E
120 G3 **Lago Verde** Brazil 8.27S 62.35W
121 K7 **Lago Viedma** Argentina 49.45S 72.00W
84 D6 **Lagovoúni** Greece 37.57N 22.03E
87 B5 **Lagowa, El** Sudan 11.23N 29.10E
50 T12 **Lågøya** *isld* Spitsbergen 80.20N 18.30E
110 G4 **La Grande** Oregon 45.21N 118.05W
97 M7 **La Grande-Rivière** Quebec
105 B4 **La Grange** Georgia 33.02N 85.02W
106 J8 **Lagrange** Indiana 41.38N 85.24W
107 L3 **La Grange** Kentucky 38.24N 85.23W
107 E1 **La Grange** Missouri 40.01N 91.31W
105 K2 **La Grange** N Carolina 35.18N 77.47W
104 C5 **Lagrange** Ohio 41.13N 82.08W
112 L6 **La Grange** Texas 29.55N 96.54W
14 D4 **Lagrange** W Australia 18.46S 121.49E
108 F8 **La Grange** Wyoming 41.39N 104.10W
14 D4 **Lagrange B** W Australia
103 G3 **Lagrangeville** New York 41.39N 73.45W
75 B6 **La Granja** Spain 40.52N 4.02W
119 H5 **La Gran Sabana** *reg* Venezuela
72 K9 **Lagrasse** France 43.05N 2.37E
26 U12 **Lagrave, Mt** Mauritius, Indian Oc 20.20S 57.36E
66 P6 **Lagrev, Piz** *mt* Switzerland 46.28N 9.43E
70 G6 **La Grigonnais** France 47.33N 1.39W
119 E3 **La Grita** Venezuela 8.09N 71.58W
51 H12 **Lågskär** *Lt Ho* Finland 59.50N 19.42E
119 F2 **La Guaira** Venezuela 10.38N 66.55W
120 E9 **Laguam** Bolivia 20.55S 68.15W
96 Q14 **La Guancha** Tenerife Canary Is 28.22N 16.38W
121 D2 **La Guardia** Argentina 29.33S 65.28W
121 B1 **La Guardia** Chile 27.43S 69.32W
75 E2 **Laguardia** Spain 42.33N 2.35W
103 K7 **La Guardia Airport** New York 40.47N 73.53W
75 L3 **Laguarres** Spain 42.13N 0.28E
75 K3 **Laguarta** Spain 42.25N 0.08W
72 H7 **Laguepie** France 44.09N 1.58E
72 K6 **Laguiole** France 44.41N 2.50E
121 J2 **Laguna** Brazil 28.29S 48.45W
109 C6 **Laguna** New Mexico 35.03N 107.24W
112 G6 **Laguna** Texas 29.25N 100.02W
13 L7 **Laguna B** Queensland
111 G8 **Laguna Beach** California 33.32N 117.45W
111 O5 **Laguna Cr** Arizona
111 K9 **Laguna Dam** Cal/Arizona 32.49N 114.30W
76 K5 **Laguna de Duero** Spain 41.35N 4.44W
76 H4 **Laguna de Negrillos** Spain 42.14N 5.40W
115 N3 **Laguna de Perlas** Nicaragua 12.19N 83.40W
121 K7 **Laguna Grande** Argentina 49.30S 70.08W
117 C5 **Laguna, I. da** Brazil
111 H9 **Laguna Mts** California
121 E3 **Laguna Paiva** Argentina 31.21S 60.40W
120 D9 **Lagunas** Chile 20.59S 69.37W
120 B1 **Lagunas** Peru 5.15S 75.24W
111 J9 **Laguna Salada** *dry lake* Mexico 32.20N 115.40W
77 L3 **Lagunas de Ruidera** *L* Spain 38.57N 2.52W
75 F6 **Lagunaseca** Spain 40.32N 2.02W
120 G11 **Laguna Yema** Argentina 24.15S 61.15W
19 J1 **Lagundi** Luzon Philippines 14.31N 121.14E
76 H8 **Lagunilla** Spain 40.20N 5.58W
120 F8 **Lagunillas** Bolivia 19.38S 63.39W
119 E2 **Lagunillas** Venezuela 10.07N 71.16W
120 D6 **Lagunillas,L** Peru 15.45S 70.45W
21 C7 **Lagushao** Liaoning China 40.30N 124.55E
21 C3 **Laha** Heilongjiang China 48.15N 124.34E
18 N3 **Lahad Datu** Sabah Malaysia 5.01N 118.20E
23 C7 **Lahadi** Yunnan China 23.03N 103.50E
114 D6 **Lahaina** *dist* Hawaiian Is 20.23N 156.40W
18 L5 **Laham** Borneo Indon 0.20N 115.26E
61 E4 **Lahamaide** Belgium 50.42N 3.44E
30 B6 **Lahar** Madhya Prad India 26.12N 78.56E
32 C2 **Lahargin** Iran 37.06N 48.19E
72 B7 **Laharie** France 44.03N 1.01W
106 D9 **La Harpe** Illinois 40.35N 90.57W
30 D5 **Laharpur** Uttar Prad India 27.42N 80.52E
18 B7 **Lahat** Pen Malaysia 4.32N 101.02E
18 E7 **Lahat** Sumatra Indon 3.46S 103.32E
86 J6 **Lahata, Wādî** *watercourse* Egypt
35 C8 **Lahav** Israel 31.23N 34.52E
98 H9 **La Have** Nova Scotia 44.18N 64.23W
98 H9 **La Have Is** Nova Scotia
30 C7 **Lahchuraghat** Uttar Prad India 25.21N 79.16E
63 K7 **Lahde** W Germany 52.22N 9.00E
25 M8 **Lahe** Burma 26.20N 95.28E
33 F10 **Lahej** S Yemen 13.01N 44.54E
93 L2 **Lah, El** Ethiopia 3.48N 39.14E
121 C5 **La Herradura** Argentina 35.31S 66.35W
18 B5 **Lahewa** Indonesia 1.23N 97.08E
69 J6 **Laheycourt** France 48.54N 5.02E
121 B2 **La Higuera** Chile 29.33S 71.15W
115 D4 **La Higuera** Mexico 26.20N 111.44W
32 D2 **Lāhījān** Iran 37.12N 50.00E
114 A5 **Lahilahi Pt** Hawaiian Is 21.28N 158.14W
59 D6 **Lahinch** Clare Irish Rep 52.56N 9.20W
29 G8 **Lahir** Maharashtra India 19.25N 80.48E
64 K3 **Lahm** W Germany 50.06N 10.53E
64 F2 **Lahn** W Germany 50.33N 8.40E
64 F2 **Lahn** *R* W Germany
69 O3 **Lahnstein** W Germany 50.18N 7.37E
64 F2 **Lahntal** W Germany 50.51N 8.43E
121 C6 **La Holanda** Argentina 36.51S 67.10W
52 G10 **Laholm** Sweden 56.30N 13.05E
53 K3 **Laholmsbukten** *B* Sweden 56.33N 12.50E
Lahong *see* **Baleno**
111 E2 **Lahontan** *R* Nevada 39.25N 119.10W
31 H5 **Lahore** Pakistan 31.34N 74.22E
31 H5 **Lahore** *div* Pakistan
31 H5 **Lahore** *dist* Pakistan
119 H4 **La Horqueta** Venezuela 7.55N 60.20W
64 D7 **Lahr** W Germany 48.21N 7.52E
31 E6 **Lahri** Pakistan 29.12N 68.15E
88 H8 **Lahsaiat** Morocco 27.01N 10.19W
La-hsiung Ts'o *L see* **Laxong Co**
63 M8 **Lahstedt** W Germany 52.13N 10.14E
51 M10 **Lahti** Finland 61.00N 25.40E
119 B10 **La Huaca** Peru 4.59S 80.58W
115 G8 **La Huerta** Mexico 19.29N 104.40W
26 U8 **Lahugala** Sri Lanka 6.53N 81.42E
28 G1 **Lahukrar Dzong** Xizang Zizhiqu 29.45N 89.11E
30 A1 **Lahul and Spiti** *dist* Himachal Prad India
29 E1 **Lahul and Spiti** *reg* Himachal Prad India
35 G8 **Lahun** *anc site* Jordan 31.28N 35.51E
86 E7 **Lāhûn, El** Egypt 29.13N 30.59E
19 L5 **Lahuy** *isld* Luzon Philippines 13.58N 123.50E
30 H7 **Lai** Bihar India 25.31N 84.48E
90 H7 **Lai** Chad 9.22N 16.14E
Lai Switzerland*see* **Lenzerheide**
89 J5 **Lai** Upper Volta 12.32N 1.50W
15 G6 **Laiagam** Papua New Guinea 5.31S 143.29E
23 H2 **Lai'an** Anhui China 32.24N 118.26E
80 C2 **Laiatico** Italy 43.28N 10.43E
Laibach *see* **Ljubljana**
30 J5 **Lai Bakya** *R* Nepal
23 E7 **Laibin** Guangxi China 23.43N 108.14E
66 Q1 **Laiblach** *R* Austria/W Germany
29 K7 **Laichanpur** Orissa India 21.12N 86.42E
25 G1 **Lai Chau** Vietnam 22.04N 103.10E
23 B9 **Lai Chi Kok** Hong Kong 22.19N 114.08E
64 H7 **Laichingen** W Germany 48.30N 9.41E
Lai-chou *see* **Ye Xian**
32 G6 **Laidāru** Iran 29.48N 56.13E
58 E3 **Laide** Highland Scotland 57.52N 5.33W
13 K8 **Laidley** Queensland 27.35S 152.18E
58 G5 **Laidon, L** Tayside Scotland 56.38N 4.39W
114 B4 **Laie** Hawaiian Is 21.39N 157.56W
114 B4 **Laie Pt** Hawaiian Is 21.39N 157.55W
23 E4 **Laifeng** Hubei China 29.33N 109.19E
69 H4 **Laifour** France 49.55N 4.42E
70 H5 **Laignelet** France 48.22N 1.09W
69 G8 **Laignes** France 47.51N 4.22E
115 P10 **La Iguala** Honduras 14.37N 88.26W
79 D7 **Laigueglia** Italy 43.59N 8.09E
51 J9 **Laihia** Finland 62.58N 22.00E
25 D2 **Lai-hka** Burma 21.21N 97.42E
25 D2 **Lai Hsak** Burma 21.02N 97.12E
19 A6 **Laikang, Teluk** *B* Celebes Indonesia 5.37S 119.31E
93 H5 **Laikipia** *dist* Kenya
93 H5 **Laikipia Escarpment** Kenya
Lailan *see* **Laylān**
70 O6 **Lailly-en-Val** France 47.46N 1.41E
28 K2 **Laimakuri** Assam India 27.42N 95.01E
66 P1 **Laimnau** W Germany 47.38N 9.38E
69 J6 **Laimont** France 48.51N 5.02E
83 H3 **Lainá** Greece 41.03N 26.19E
65 G8 **Lainach** Austria 46.52N 12.56E
65 L6 **Lainbach** Austria 47.39N 14.47E
11 B3 **Laingholm** New Zealand 36.58S 174.38E
95 D9 **Laingsburg** S Africa 33.12S 20.51E
51 G6 **Lainijaur** Sweden 65.16N 18.50E
51 J4 **Lainio** Sweden 67.47N 22.20E
51 J3 **Lainio älv** *R* Sweden
81 L4 **Laino Borgo** Italy 39.57N 15.59E
71 C1 **Lainsecq** France 47.32N 3.17E
65 L4 **Lainsitz** *R* Austria
79 L1 **Laión** Italy 46.37N 11.35E
29 B2 **Laipatnagar** Delhi India 28.35N 77.15E
58 K5 **Lair** Tayside Scotland 56.45N 3.25W
109 H1 **Laird** Colorado 40.06N 102.06W
100 L6 **Laird** Saskatchewan 52.44N 106.36W
103 A4 **Lairdsville** Pennsylvania 41.14N 76.37W
98 Q8 **Lairet, R** Quebec
58 H2 **Lairg** Highland Scotland 58.01N 4.25W
90 H6 **Lairi** Chad 10.50N 17.09E
19 B3 **Lais** Celebes Indonesia 0.47N 120.31E
19 M8 **Lais** Mindanao Philippines 6.16N 125.40E
18 E7 **Lais** Sumatra Indon 3.30S 102.02E
116 D3 **La Isabela** Cuba 22.56N 80.03W
93 J4 **Laisamis** Kenya 1.36N 37.48E
45 V1 **Laishevo** U.S.S.R. 55.25N 49.31E
22 K7 **Laishui** Hebei China 39.23N 115.42E
119 C4 **La Isla** Colombia 6.50N 76.59W
96 U7 **La Isleta** *I* Lanzarote Canary Is 29.07N 13.40W
70 K4 **Laison** *R* France
80 F5 **Laispoli** Italy 41.57N 12.05E
72 K7 **Laissac** France 44.23N 2.49E
66 A2 **Laissey** France 47.18N 6.15E
51 F5 **Laisvall** Sweden 66.08N 17.10E
70 C6 **Laita** *R* France
51 G4 **Laitaure** *L* Sweden 67.07N 18.20E
93 G4 **Laiteruk Hill** Kenya 1.44N 35.49E
51 J11 **Laitila** Finland 60.52N 21.40E
93 H10 **Laiverero** Tanzania 4.22S 36.43E
79 K2 **Laives** Italy 46.26N 11.21E
22 L8 **Laiwu** Shandong China 36.14N 117.40E
19 E4 **Laiwui** Moluccas Indonesia 1.20S 127.39E
22 M8 **Laixi** Shandong China 36.50N 120.40E
22 M8 **Laiyang** Shandong China 36.58N 120.40E
22 K7 **Laiyuan** Hebei China 39.19N 114.44E
70 K3 **Laize** *R* France
22 L8 **Laizhou Wan** *B* Shandong China
119 D3 **La Jagua** Colombia 9.33N 73.18W
121 B6 **Laja, L. de** Chile
121 C7 **La Japonesa** Argentina 38.42S 66.28W
121 A6 **Laja, R** Chile
109 E4 **La Jara** Colorado 37.17N 105.58W
109 D4 **La Jara Reservoir** Colorado
96 T9 **Lajares** Fuerteventura Canary Is 28.40N 13.56W
121 H2 **Lajeado** Brazil 29.28S 52.00W
118 F9 **Laje dos Santos** *isld* Brazil 24.19S 46.13W
76 F8 **Lajeosa** Portugal 40.20N 6.49W
96 U3 **Lajes** Azores 38.45N 27.07W
118 E3 **Lajes** Goiás Brazil 13.58S 48.07W
117 H7 **Lajes** Rio Grande do Norte Brazil 5.40S 36.15W
121 J1 **Lajes** Santa Catarina Brazil 27.48S 50.20W
96 O2 **Lajes das Flores** Azores 39.23N 31.12W
96 Q4 **Lajes do Pico** Azores 38.25N 28.15W
112 D6 **Lajitas** Texas 29.19N 103.47W
35 G9 **Lajjun** *anc site* Jordan 31.14N 35.52E
82 F6 **Lajkovac** Yugoslavia 44.22N 20.13E
111 G9 **La Jolla** California 32.50N 117.16W
100 N8 **Lajord** Saskatchewan 50.20N 104.13W
62 M8 **Lajosmizse** Hungary 47.02N 19.31E
66 E2 **Lajoux** Switzerland 47.17N 7.08E
115 F4 **La Joya** Mexico 27.27N 106.15W
109 D7 **La Joya** New Mexico 34.21N 106.51W
120 D7 **La Joya** Peru 16.43S 71.53W
25 M7 **Laju** Assam India 26.59N 95.36E
120 G6 **La Junta** Bolivia 15.23S 61.33W
109 G4 **La Junta** Colorado 37.59N 103.34W
115 F3 **La Junta** Mexico 28.30N 107.20W
34 Q3 **Lak** Iran 35.03N 48.21E
90 H8 **Laka** *tribe* Cent Afr Rep
90 G7 **Laka** *tribe* Chad
53 W18 **Lakadalsberga** *mt* Norway 60.08N 7.28E
19 B8 **Lakahembi** Indonesia 9.42S 120.31E
89 E4 **Lakaminé** Mali 14.35N 9.44W
30 E4 **Lakarpata** Nepal 28.44N 81.30E
52 K3 **Lakasjö** Sweden 63.55N 17.45E
84 R14 **Lakatamia** Cyprus 35.07N 33.19E
33 D7 **Lakathah** Saudi Arabia 19.09N 41.57E
95 D5 **Lakato** Madagascar 19.10S 48.26E
51 J5 **Lakaträsk** Sweden 66.17N 21.10E
93 M4 **Lak Bor** *watercourse* Kenya
93 M5 **Lak Dera** *watercourse* Kenya
93 M5 **Lak Dima** *watercourse* Kenya
110 O5 **Lake** Idaho 44.40N 111.23W
106 J6 **Lake** Michigan 43.51N 85.01W
107 G9 **Lake** Mississippi 32.20N 89.20W
103 F4 **Lake** New York 41.17N 74.17W
110 E6 **Lake** Oregon 43.15N 120.40W
105 F9 **Lake Alfred** Florida 28.04N 81.46W
100 N9 **Lake Alma** Saskatchewan 49.10N 104.18W
108 M6 **Lake Andes** S Dakota 43.09N 98.31W
103 D4 **Lake Ariel** Pennsylvania 41.27N 75.23W
107 D11 **Lake Arthur** Louisiana 30.05N 92.41W
109 F8 **Lake Arthur** New Mexico 33.01N 104.23W
108 O5 **Lake Benton** Minnesota 44.14N 96.18W
14 C10 **Lake Biddy** W Australia 33.01S 118.51E
108 O1 **Lake Bronson** Minnesota 48.44N 96.39W
14 C9 **Lake Brown** W Australia 30.57S 118.19E
105 E7 **Lake Butler** Florida 30.01N 82.21W
14 C10 **Lake Camm** W Australia 32.59S 119.35E
103 C3 **Lake Carey** Pennsylvania 41.35N 75.56W
12 H5 **Lake Cargelligo** New S Wales 33.19S 146.23E
107 C11 **Lake Charles** Louisiana 30.13N 93.13W
107 F6 **Lake City** Arkansas 35.50N 90.28W
110 E8 **Lake City** California 41.39N 120.14W
109 C3 **Lake City** Colorado 38.02N 107.19W
105 E7 **Lake City** Florida 30.12N 82.39W
108 Q7 **Lake City** Iowa 42.16N 94.43W
106 J5 **Lake City** Michigan 44.22N 85.12W
108 S5 **Lake City** Minnesota 44.27N 92.18W
104 E4 **Lake City** Pennsylvania 42.02N 80.22W
105 H4 **Lake City** S Carolina 33.52N 79.46W
108 N4 **Lake City** S Dakota 45.45N 97.26W
107 M5 **Lake City** Tennessee 36.12N 84.10W
11 F10 **Lake Coleridge** *H E Station* New Zealand 43.22S 171.33E
103 D3 **Lake Como** Pennsylvania 41.51N 75.21W
107 F7 **Lake Cormorant** Mississippi 34.54N 90.12W
110 J8 **Lake Cr** Nevada
108 Q5 **Lake Crystal** Minnesota 44.06N 94.13W
106 E6 **Lake Delton** Wisconsin 43.35N 89.49W
45 K9 **Lakedemonovka** U.S.S.R. 47.10N 38.35E
57 G4 **Lake District** England
100 F5 **Lake Eliza** Alberta 53.50N 111.11W
12 D2 **Lake Eyre Basin** S Australia
Lake Fd *see* **Tugtiliq** *fjord*
108 P6 **Lakefield** Minnesota 43.40N 95.11W
99 M8 **Lakefield** Ontario 44.25N 78.16W
13 G2 **Lakefield** Queensland 14.52S 144.10E
106 G7 **Lake Forest** Illinois 42.15N 87.50W
106 F7 **Lake Geneva** Wisconsin 42.35N 88.26W
109 E3 **Lake George** Colorado 38.58N 105.23W
104 M3 **Lake George** New York 43.25N 73.45W
14 C10 **Lake Grace** W Australia 33.06S 118.23E
97 N5 **Lake Harbour** N W Terr 62.50N 69.50W
108 E8 **Lake Hattie Res** Wyoming
111 K7 **Lake Havasu City** Arizona 34.28N 114.20W
112 O9 **Lake Highlands** *dist* Dallas, Texas
103 F2 **Lake Hill** New York 42.04N 74.12W
111 F7 **Lake Hughes** California 34.40N 118.27W
103 F6 **Lakehurst** New Jersey 40.01N 74.19W
112 M6 **Lake Jackson** Texas 29.03N 95.28W
15 J7 **Lakekama R** Papua New Guinea
103 G3 **Lake Katrine** New York 41.59N 73.59W
14 C10 **Lake King** W Australia 33.05S 119.41E
105 F9 **Lakeland** Florida 28.02N 81.59W
105 D6 **Lakeland** Georgia 31.03N 83.05W
100 N6 **Lake Lenore** Saskatchewan 52.25N 104.59W
106 F2 **Lake Linden** Michigan 47.12N 88.26W
101 P10 **Lake Louise** Alberta 51.26N 116.10W
93 G9 **Lake Manyara Nat. Park** Tanzania
9 U2 **Lakemba** *isld* Fiji 18.10S 178.49W
9 U2 **Lakemba Passage** Fiji
111 K6 **Lake Mead Nat. Rec. Area** Arizona
108 R6 **Lake Mills** Iowa 43.26N 93.30W
104 E5 **Lake Milton** Ohio 41.06N 80.58W
113 L5 **Lake Minchumina** Alaska 63.55N 152.25W
104 Q1 **Lake Moxie** Maine 45.22N 69.55W
15 F7 **Lake Murray** Papua New Guinea 6.35S 141.28E
93 H6 **Lake Nakuru Nat. Park** Kenya
13 E5 **Lake Nash** N Terr Australia 20.58S 137.52E
64 P5 **Laken Berg** *mt* W Ger/Czech 49.07N 13.19E
56 N3 **Lakenheath** Suffolk Eng 52.25N 0.31E
95 J2 **Lakensvlei** S Africa 26.52S 26.00E
106 J7 **Lake Odessa** Michigan 42.47N 85.09W
100 H1 **Lake of the Woods Prov. Park** Ontario
106 L7 **Lake Orion** Michigan 42.47N 83.13W
110 C4 **Lake Oswego** Oregon 45.25N 122.42W
109 Q5 **Lake O' The Cherokees** Oklahoma
110 P5 **Lake Outlet** Wyoming 44.35N 110.24W
11 D10 **Lake Paringa** New Zealand 43.43S 169.25E
105 G11 **Lake Park** Florida 26.48N 80.06W
105 D7 **Lake Park** Georgia 30.41N 83.12W
108 P6 **Lake Park** Iowa 43.28N 95.20W
108 O3 **Lake Park** Minnesota 46.53N 96.06W
105 F10 **Lake Placid** Florida 27.18N 81.22W
104 L2 **Lake Placid** New York 44.18N 74.01W
111 B2 **Lakeport** California 39.04N 122.56W
105 F11 **Lakeport** Florida 26.58N 81.09W
106 M6 **Lakeport** Michigan 43.07N 82.30W
108 N5 **Lake Preston** S Dakota 44.24N 97.22W
107 E9 **Lake Providence** Louisiana 32.48N 91.10W
11 E11 **Lake Pukaki** New Zealand 44.12S 170.11E
110 F9 **Lake Ra** Nevada
97 L7 **Lake River** Ontario 54.30N 82.30W
98 G9 **Lake Rossignol Res** Nova Scotia
108 H2 **Lake Sakakawea** N Dakota
12 J7 **Lakes Entrance** Victoria 37.52S 148.01E
111 E4 **Lakeshore** California 37.15N 119.14W
111 P7 **Lakeside** Arizona 34.10N 109.59W
111 H9 **Lakeside** California 32.51N 116.55W
94 P12 **Lakeside** Cape Town S Africa 34.05S 18.28E
108 H7 **Lakeside** Nebraska 42.04N 102.26W
110 N8 **Lakeside** Utah 41.13N 112.54W
12 F3 **Lake Stewart** New S Wales 29.22S 140.12E
99 F5 **Lake Superior Prov. Park** Ontario
11 E11 **Lake Tekapo** *H E Station* New Zealand 44.02S 170.29E
110 O8 **Laketown** Utah 41.50N 111.19W
99 M7 **Lake Traverse** Ontario 45.57N 78.06W
109 C9 **Lake Valley** New Mexico 32.43N 107.34W
100 L8 **Lake Valley** Saskatchewan 50.39N 106.00W
112 J5 **Lake Victor** Texas 30.56N 98.13W
108 P7 **Lake View** Iowa 42.18N 95.02W
106 J6 **Lakeview** Michigan 43.26N 85.18W
110 O5 **Lakeview** Montana 44.36N 111.48W
110 E7 **Lakeview** Oregon 42.13N 120.21W
105 H3 **Lake View** S Carolina 34.20N 79.12W
112 G1 **Lakeview** Texas 34.41N 100.43W
112 N9 **Lakeview** Texas 32.43N 96.58W
107 E8 **Lake Village** Arkansas 33.20N 91.19W
103 H3 **Lakeville** Connecticut 41.58N 73.26W
106 H8 **Lakeville** Indiana 41.32N 86.17W
103 N3 **Lakeville** Massachusetts 41.51N 70.57W
108 R5 **Lakeville** Minnesota 44.38N 93.17W
103 F4 **Lakeville** New York 41.12N 74.15W
104 H4 **Lakeville** New York 42.50N 77.42W
103 D4 **Lakeville** Pennsylvania 41.26N 75.16W
14 D7 **Lake Violet** W Australia 26.30S 120.25E
110 M7 **Lake Walcott Res** Idaho 42.40N 113.25W
105 F10 **Lake Wales** Florida 27.55N 81.36W
108 L2 **Lake Williams** N Dakota 47.09N 99.39W
111 E9 **Lakewood** California 33.49N 118.08W
103 F6 **Lakewood** New Jersey 40.06N 74.12W
109 F9 **Lakewood** New Mexico 32.39N 104.39W
104 F4 **Lakewood** New York 42.06N 79.21W
104 D5 **Lakewood** Ohio 41.29N 81.50W
103 D3 **Lakewood** Pennsylvania 41.51N 75.24W
103 M3 **Lakewood** Rhode I 41.46N 71.24W
105 G11 **Lake Worth** Florida 26.36N 80.04W
105 G11 **Lake Worth Inlet** Florida
112 L9 **Lake Worth Village** Texas 32.47N 97.26W
39 F1 **Lakeyeva** U.S.S.R. 68.40N 159.20E
29 C3 **Lakh** Rajasthan India 29.32N 73.20E
29 B4 **Lakha** Rajasthan India 26.09N 70.54E
30 J6 **Lakhandai** *R* Bihar India
84 U18 **Lakhaniá** Rhodes Greece 35.58N 27.52E
30 H6 **Lakhaura** Bihar India 26.46N 84.58E
74 H8 **Lakhdar** Algeria 36.12N 0.28E
74 K8 **Lakhdaria** Algeria 36.34N 3.36E
47 C5 **Lakhdenpokh'ya** U.S.S.R. 61.34N 30.12E
30 D5 **Lakhimpur** Uttar Prad India 27.57N 80.47E
28 K2 **Lakhimpur** *dist* Assam India
35 C7 **Lakhish** Israel 31.34N 34.51E
35 B6 **Lakhish** *watercourse* Israel
30 C6 **Lakhna** Uttar Prad India 26.39N 79.09E
29 F6 **Lakhnadon** Madhya Prad India 22.34N 79.38E
30 A3 **Lakhnauti** Uttar Prad India 29.48N 77.12E
29 A6 **Lakhpat** Gujarat India 23.49N 68.54E
28 B6 **Lakhtar** Gujarat India 22.53N 70.53E
28 K2 **Lakhuti** Nagaland India 26.16N 94.19E
50 G6 **Laki** *vol* Iceland 64.04N 18.11W
109 J4 **Lakin** Kansas 37.57N 101.16W
47 D7 **Lakinsk** U.S.S.R. 56.01N 39.58E
45 L1 **Lakinskiy** U.S.S.R. 56.01N 39.59E
84 C5 **Lákka** Greece 38.14N 21.59E
31 F4 **Lakki** Pakistan 32.35N 70.58E
37 B2 **Lákkona** Samothráki Greece 40.23N 25.34E
84 B5 **Lakkópetra** Greece 38.10N 21.28E
93 L5 **Lak Lebole** *watercourse* Kenya
28 B3 **Lakmeshwar** Karnataka India 15.10N 75.32E
53 B6 **Lakolk** Denmark 55.09N 8.30E
84 D8 **Lakonía** *prov* Greece
84 E8 **Lakonikós Kólpos** *gulf* Greece
19 F8 **Lakor** *isld* Indonesia 8.18S 128.09E
Lakor Tso *L see* **Lagkor Co**
108 Q6 **Lakota** Iowa 43.23N 94.05W
89 G9 **Lakota** Ivory Coast 5.50N 5.40W
108 M1 **Lakota** N Dakota 48.02N 98.20W
25 H3 **Lak Sao** Laos 18.12N 104.59E
26 R8 **Laksapana Falls** Sri Lanka 6.54N 80.30E
51 M1 **Laksefjord** *inlet* Norway
51 L1 **Lakselv** Norway 70.03N 24.55E
53 S18 **Laksevåg** Norway 60.23N 5.18E
51 C6 **Laksfors** Norway 65.38N 13.16E
28 A5 **Lakshadweep** *islds* India
31 J9 **Laksham** Bangladesh 23.15N 91.08E
28 D1 **Lakshettipet** Andhra Prad India 18.57N 79.06E
29 L6 **Lakshmikantapur** W Bengal Ind 22.05N 88.19E
31 D4 **Lakshuk Pass** Afghanistan 33.54N 67.10E
28 H7 **Laksi** Nicobar Is 8.13N 93.05E
15 L5 **Lakuramau** New Ireland 2.55S 151.17E
84 C6 **Lála** Greece 37.42N 21.43E
19 L8 **Lala** Mindanao Philippines 7.59N 123.45E
91 H6 **Lala** Zaïre 4.10S 23.30E
92 E8 **Lala** *tribe* Zambia
28 J3 **Lalaghat** Assam India 24.34N 92.35E
93 E9 **Lalago** Tanzania 3.27S 33.57E
121 D4 **La Laguna** Argentina 32.49S 63.15W
115 F11 **La Laguna** Panama 8.52N 79.48W
96 S13 **La Laguna** Tenerife Canary Is 28.29N 16.19W
121 A6 **La Laja** Chile 37.15S 72.45W
31 C5 **Lalak Pass** Afghanistan 31.40N 65.20E
9 R13 **Lalalolomei Bank** Tonga, Pacific Oc 18.56S 174.03W
28 C6 **Lalam** Kerala India 9.42N 76.46E
31 H4 **Lala Musa** Pakistan 32.41N 74.01E
36 B1 **Lâlapaşa** Turkey 41.52N 26.44E
91 B3 **Lalara** Gabon 0.30N 11.27E
93 H4 **Lalaro** Kenya 1.02N 36.33E
93 H3 **Lalarok** Kenya 2.15N 36.45E
92 J9 **Lalaua** Mozambique 14.22S 38.20E
30 D7 **Lalauli** Uttar Prad India 25.49N 80.33E
30 K8 **Lalbairo** Bihar India 24.53N 86.32E
29 G7 **Lalbara** Madhya Prad India 21.58N 80.08E
72 H7 **Lalbenque** France 44.20N 1.32E
30 J6 **Lalbhitti** Nepal 26.58N 85.56E
30 B3 **Lal Dhang** Uttar Prad India 29.50N 78.19E
55 B5 **Laleham** Surrey Eng 51.25N 0.29W
32 G6 **Lāleh Zār** Iran 29.33N 56.49E
32 G6 **Lāleh Zār, Kūh-e** *mt* Iran 29.28N 56.49E
63 Q5 **Lalendorf** E Germany 53.46N 12.23E
19 A4 **Lalereh, Tandjung** *C* Celebes Indon 1.59S 119.14E
56 D4 **Laleston** Mid Glam Wales 51.31N 3.38W
71 E7 **Lalevade-d'Ardèche** France 44.39N 4.20E
30 J7 **Lalganj** Bihar India 25.52N 85.10E
30 F7 **Lalganj** Mirzapur, Uttar Prad India 25.01N 82.21E
30 D6 **Lalganj** Rae Bareli, Uttar Prad India 26.10N 80.58E
30 E7 **Lalgopalganj** Uttar Prad India 25.39N 81.37E
28 D5 **Lalgudi** Tamil Nadu India 10.52N 78.52E
32 C4 **Lālī** *oil field* Iran 32.21N 49.06E
87 G4 **Lalibela** Ethiopia 12.01N 39.05E
119 B9 **La Libertad** Ecuador 2.17S 80.54W
115 P11 **La Libertad** El Salvador 13.28N 89.20W
115 O9 **La Libertad** Guatemala 16.49N 90.08W
115 M3 **La Libertad** Nicaragua 12.12N 85.10W
120 A3 **La Libertad** *dept* Peru
121 B4 **La Ligua** Chile 32.30S 71.16W
93 L8 **Lali Hills** Kenya
115 Q10 **La Lima** Honduras 15.20N 87.55W
19 C5 **Lalimbuë** Celebes Indonesia 3.51S 122.25E
21 D5 **Lalin** Heilongjiang China 45.13N 126.56E
76 C3 **Lalín** Spain 42.40N 8.06W
72 F6 **Lalinde** France 44.50N 0.45E
19 B9 **Lalindi** Indonesia 10.15S 120.14E
19 B5 **Lalindu** *R* Celebes Indonesia
21 D5 **Lalin He** *R* Heilongjiang China
21 D5 **Lalin He** *R* Jilin China
30 B8 **Lalitpur** Uttar Prad India 24.42N 78.24E
30 C3 **Lalkua** Uttar Prad India 29.04N 79.31E
88 Q3 **Lalla Kredidja** *mt* Algeria 36.25N 4.10E
71 H7 **Lalley** France 44.45N 5.41E
19 K2 **Lal-Lo** Luzon Philippines 18.12N 121.42E
31 H8 **Lalmanir Hat** Bangladesh 25.51N 89.34E
19 B6 **Laloa** Celebes Indonesia 4.51S 121.52E
101 T7 **La Loche** Saskatchewan 56.31N 109.27W
100 H2 **La Loche West** Saskatchewan 56.29N 109.39W
120 F9 **La Loma** Bolivia 20.50S 64.44W
12 D6 **Lalor** *dist* Melbourne, Vic
84 E6 **Lálouka** Greece 37.38N 22.46E
71 F6 **Lalouvesc** France 45.08N 4.32E
31 G9 **Lalpur** Bangladesh 24.12N 89.00E
30 D7 **Lalpura** Uttar Prad India 25.51N 80.03E
47 F5 **Lal'sk** U.S.S.R. 60.45N 47.34E
29 E4 **Lalsot** Rajasthan India 26.31N 76.22E
19 E4 **Laluin** *isld* Moluccas Indon 0.04S 127.24E
31 B9 **Lālūkhet** Pakistan 24.54N 67.03E
72 B8 **Laluque** France 43.51N 1.00W
115 H6 **La Luz** Mexico 23.00N 102.23W
115 M3 **La Luz** Nicaragua 13.42N 84.35W
87 C8 **Lalyo** Sudan 4.20N 31.03E
83 C3 **Lalzës, Gji i** *B* Albania
64 P5 **Lam** W Germany 49.12N 13.04E
31 J10 **Lama** Bangladesh 21.46N 92.12E
67 P11 **Lama** Corsica 42.34N 9.10E
76 B5 **Lama** Portugal 41.34N 8.32W
76 C4 **Lama** Spain 42.24N 8.26W
46 K2 **Lama** *R* U.S.S.R.
119 D6 **La Macarena** Colombia 2.03N 73.57W
93 B2 **Lamada** Sudan 3.45N 30.54E
80 K4 **Lama dei Peligni** Italy 42.03N 14.11E
109 D5 **La Madera** New Mexico 36.22N 106.04W
23 A5 **Lamadi** Yunnan China 27.26N 98.50E
22 L6 **Lamadong** Liaoning China 40.44N 119.40E
121 D1 **La Madrid** Argentina 27.37S 65.16W
115 J4 **Lamadrid** Mexico 27.05N 101.49W
18 M3 **Lamag** Sabah Malaysia 5.29N 117.50E
72 F7 **Lamagistère** France 44.08N 0.49E
72 J3 **Lamaids** France 46.18N 2.24E
61 D4 **Lamain** Belgium 50.36N 3.18E
25 D5 **Lamaing** Burma 15.31N 97.45E
89 K7 **Lama-Kara** Togo 9.36N 1.18E
19 C8 **Lamakera** Indonesia 8.26S 123.12E
24 D10 **Lama La** *pass* Xizang Zizhiqu 31.29N 81.42E
98 B6 **La Malbaie** Quebec 47.39N 70.11W
115 K8 **La Malinche** *pk* Mexico 19.14N 98.01W
98 R7 **Lamaline** Newfoundland 46.52N 55.48W
71 C9 **Lamalou-les-Bains** France 43.36N 3.05E
79 J6 **Lama Mocogno** Italy 44.18N 10.43E
115 H5 **La Mancha** Mexico 24.50N 102.51W
115 L2 **Lamaní** Honduras 14.14N 87.36W
71 G9 **Lamanon** France 43.42N 5.05E
115 M4 **La Mansión** Costa Rica 10.06N 85.21W
120 E5 **La Manza** Bolivia 13.29S 66.38W
41 F6 **Lama, Ozero** *L* U.S.S.R.
9 C11 **Lamap** New Hebrides 16.26S 167.47E
107 C6 **Lamar** Arkansas 35.26N 93.25W
109 H3 **Lamar** Colorado 38.04N 102.37W
107 G7 **Lamar** Mississippi 34.55N 89.20W
107 B4 **Lamar** Missouri 37.30N 94.18W
108 J9 **Lamar** Nebraska 40.35N 101.59W
109 O6 **Lamar** Oklahoma 35.05N 96.06W
105 G3 **Lamar** S Carolina 34.11N 80.03W
110 P5 **Lamar** *R* Wyoming
69 K7 **Lamarche** France 48.04N 5.47E
71 G2 **Lamarche-sur-Saône** France 47.16N 5.23E
32 E7 **Lamard** Iran 27.22N 53.20E
71 F1 **Lamargelle** France 47.33N 4.51E
84 G4 **Lámari** Greece 38.39N 23.54E
15 H7 **Lamari** *R* Papua New Guinea
121 C5 **La Maroma** Argentina 35.15S 66.20W
76 C10 **Lamarosa** Portugal 39.04N 8.27W
121 D7 **Lamarque** Argentina 39.25S 65.43W
72 C5 **Lamarque** France 45.06N 0.42W
98 B6 **Lamartine** Quebec 47.04N 70.21W
74 J8 **Lamartine, Barrage de** Algeria 36.05N 1.35E
121 E6 **La Martinetas** Argentina 37.14S 61.08W
120 B2 **Lamas** Peru 6.28S 76.31W
36 G6 **Lamas** Turkey 36.33N 34.17E
36 G6 **Lamas** *R* Turkey
76 D6 **Lamas de Olo** Portugal 41.22N 7.48W
87 J8 **Lama Shillindi** Ethiopia 4.50N 42.06E
115 L2 **La Masica** Honduras 15.38N 87.08W
71 F7 **Lamastre** France 44.59N 4.35E
96 T10 **La Matilla** Fuerteventura Canary Is 28.33N 13.58W
81 M6 **Lamato R** Italy
99 R5 **La Mauricie Parc Nat.** Quebec
116 G4 **La Maya** Cuba 20.11N 75.40W
50 E5 **Lambá** *R* Iceland
92 C8 **Lamba** *tribe* Zambia
65 J5 **Lambach** Austria 48.06N 13.52E
50 B3 **Lambadalsfjall** *mt* Iceland 65.54N 23.08W
50 M5 **Lambafell** *mt* Iceland 64.59N 13.58W
50 H3 **Lambafjöll** *mt* Iceland 65.54N 17.05W
50 E6 **Lambahraun** *lava field* Iceland
84 C7 **Lámbaina** Greece 37.08N 21.58E
70 E5 **Lamballe** France 48.28N 2.31W
91 B4 **Lambarené** Gabon 0.41S 10.13E
118 F7 **Lambari** Brazil 21.59S 45.21W
9 S5 **Lambasa** Vanua Levu Fiji 16.25S 179.24E
19 B6 **Lambasina** *isld* Celebes Indon 4.05S 121.23E
50 K5 **Lambatungujökull** *ice cap* Iceland 64.32N 15.25W
50 L5 **Lambatungur** *mt* Iceland 64.41N 14.47W
53 N9 **Lamba Vig** *inlet* Faeroes 62.08N 6.38W
120 A7 **Lambayeque** Peru 6.36S 79.45W
120 A7 **Lambayeque** *dept* Peru
59 K4 **Lambay I** Dublin Irish Rep 53.29N 6.01W
56 M5 **Lamberhurst** Kent Eng 51.07N 0.24E
105 F6 **Lambert** Georgia 31.45N 81.39W
107 F7 **Lambert** Mississippi 34.13N 90.18W
108 F2 **Lambert** Montana 47.42N 104.39W
15 L6 **Lambert, C** New Britain 4.13S 151.30E
11 J7 **Lambert, C** New Zealand 40.58S 174.15E
14 B5 **Lambert, C** W Australia 20.40S 117.11E
123 C5 **Lambert Glacier** Antarctica
48 U4 **Lambert Land** Greenland
108 P5 **Lamberton** Minnesota 44.13N 95.20W
94 E9 **Lamberts Bay** S Africa 32.04S 18.20E
103 E6 **Lambertville** New Jersey 40.22N 74.57W
71 G9 **Lambesc** France 43.39N 5.15E
55 F4 **Lambeth** London England 51.30N 0.07W
99 J10 **Lambeth** Ontario 42.54N 81.20W
55 F4 **Lambeth** *bor* London Eng
26 B16 **Lambeth, C** Heard I Antarctica 53.11S 73.38E
84 B6 **Lambéti** Greece 37.42N 21.27E
58 T11 **Lamb Hd** Orkney Scotland 59.05N 2.31W
30 F6 **Lambhur** Uttar Prad India 26.08N 82.14E
29 D2 **Lambi** Punjab India 30.03N 74.35E
84 C6 **Lámbia** Greece 30.50N 21.47E
89 J7 **Lambo** Ghana 8.35N 1.57W
95 B7 **Lambomakondro** Madagascar 22.41S 44.41E
15 M6 **Lambon** New Ireland 4.48S 152.50E
56 H4 **Lambourn** Berks Eng 51.31N 1.31W
64 E5 **Lambrecht** W Germany 49.22N 8.05E
79 F4 **Lambro** *R* Italy
104 E10 **Lambsburg** Virginia 36.35N 80.47W
64 E4 **Lambsheim** W Germany 49.31N 8.17E
99 T7 **Lambton** Quebec 45.50N 71.06W
101 M1 **Lambton, C** N W Terr 71.05N 123.06W
11 C5 **Lambton Harb** *B* Wellington New Zealand
99 C10 **Lambton Mills** Ontario 43.40N 79.31W
15 L5 **Lambu** New Ireland 3.14S 151.46E
61 J5 **Lambusart** Belgium 50.27N 4.33E
25 G5 **Lam Chi** *R* Thailand
25 H5 **Lam Chi** *R* Thailand
15 A7 **Lamdessar Timur** Moluccas Indonesia 7.15S 131.57E
25 H5 **Lam Dom Noi** *R* Thailand
90 G7 **Lamé** Chad 9.14N 14.33E
90 D6 **Lame** Nigeria 10.27N 9.12E
108 D4 **Lame Deer** Montana 45.36N 106.38W
76 D6 **Lamego** Portugal 41.05N 7.49W
121 C2 **La Mejicana** Argentina 29.00S 67.45W
120 C5 **La Mejorada** Peru 12.32S 74.59W
76 C6 **Lamelas** Portugal 41.17N 8.29W
119 D6 **La Mensura, Cerro** *mt* Colombia 2.40N 74.37W
116 M3 **Lamentin** Guadeloupe W I 16.16N 61.38W
9 C11 **Lamenu** New Hebrides 16.37S 168.09E
98 H6 **Lamèque** New Brunswick 47.50N 64.40W
98 H6 **Laméque, Ile** New Brunswick
121 D2 **La Merced** Argentina 28.10S 65.38W
120 B4 **La Merced** Peru 11.03S 75.16W
12 F5 **Lameroo** S Australia 35.20S 140.33E
111 H9 **La Mesa** California 32.45N 117.00W
119 D5 **La Mesa** Colombia 4.37N 74.30W
109 D9 **La Mesa** New Mexico 32.06N 106.44W
115 O5 **La Mesa** Panama 8.09N 81.10W
112 F3 **Lamesa** Texas 32.43N 101.57W
Lametta *see* **Danu**
70 G5 **La Meziére** France 48.12N 1.45W
58 Q9 **Lamgarth Hd** Shetland Scotland 60.13N 1.10W
84 D4 **Lamía** Greece 38.55N 22.26E
19 N8 **Lamigan Pt** Mindanao Philippines 6.47N 126.22E
120 B9 **La Milla** *dist* Lima Peru
61 M4 **Lamine** Belgium 50.41N 5.20E
57 F1 **Lamington** Strathclyde Scotland 55.34N 3.37W
15 K8 **Lamington, Mt** Papua New Guinea 8.55S 148.10E
115 D3 **La Misa** Mexico 28.23N 110.30W
19 L8 **Lamitan** Philippines 6.39N 122.09E
112 J4 **Lamkin** Texas 31.49N 98.18W
19 G4 **Lamlam** Irian Jaya 0.05S 130.44E
19 L1 **Lamlam** *mt* Guam Pacific Oc 13.20N 144.40E
57 C1 **Lamlash** Arran Scotland 55.32N 5.08W
24 F10 **Lamlung La** *pass* Xizang Zizhiqu China 30.57N 88.00E
87 K8 **Lamma Bar** Ethiopia 5.25N 44.57E
87 K9 **Lamma Gad** Somalia 3.10N 44.58E
23 B10 **Lamma I** Hong Kong
53 H5 **Lammefjord** *reg* Denmark 55.45N 11.34E
95 N1 **Lammerkop** S Africa 25.37S 29.25E
58 L7 **Lammer Law** *hill* Lothian Scotland 55.51N 2.46W
11 D12 **Lammerlaw Ra** New Zealand
13 G5 **Lammermoor** Queensland 21.15S 144.37E
58 L7 **Lammermuir Hills** Lothian/Borders Scotland
64 A2 **Lammersdorf** W Germany 50.38N 6.17E
18 A3 **Lammeulo** Sumatra Indonesia 5.15N 95.56E
52 H9 **Lammhult** Sweden 57.09N 14.35E
51 L10 **Lammi** Finland 61.04N 25.07E
29 K3 **Lamna La** *pass* Xizang Zizhiqu 28.19N 86.46E
70 M5 **Lamnay** France 48.07N 0.42E
30 K5 **Lamobagar** Nepal 27.54N 86.12E
30 L5 **Lamobagar Gola** Nepal 27.39N 87.21E
93 D3 **Lamogi** Uganda 2.49N 32.13E
19 N4 **Lamoil** *isld* Truk Is Pacific Oc 7.39N 151.41E
110 K9 **Lamoile** Nevada 40.44N 115.28W
106 E8 **La Moille** Illinois 41.32N 89.17W
104 N2 **Lamoille** *R* Vermont
106 D9 **La Moine, R** Illinois
79 L2 **Lamon** Italy 46.03N 11.45E
110 G2 **Lamona** Washington 47.21N 118.29W
19 K4 **Lamon B** Luzon Philippines
79 L6 **Lamone** *R* Italy
18 K9 **Lamongan** Java Indon 7.05S 112.26E
72 F7 **Lamongjoie** France 44.05N 0.32E
108 R9 **Lamoni** Iowa 40.38N 93.56W
100 E5 **Lamont** Alberta 53.44N 112.41W
111 F6 **Lamont** California 35.15N 118.56W
105 D7 **Lamont** Florida 30.22N 83.49W
110 O6 **Lamont** Idaho 43.58N 111.11W
106 C7 **Lamont** Iowa 42.36N 91.37W
109 N5 **Lamont** Oklahoma 36.43N 97.35W
108 C7 **Lamont** Wyoming 42.12N 107.28W
71 C6 **Lamontgie** France 45.29N 3.19E
72 E6 **Lamonzie St. Martin** France 44.50N 0.24E
74 G10 **Lamoricière** Algeria 34.54N 1.03W
115 G3 **La Morita** Mexico 28.33N 104.28W
61 M8 **Lamorteau** Belgium 49.32N 5.29E
72 B6 **Lamothe** Gironde France 44.38N 1.01W
71 C6 **Lamothe** Haute-Loire France 45.20N 3.25E
72 G6 **Lamothe-Cassel** France 44.37N 1.30E
72 E6 **Lamothe Londerron** France 44.34N 0.04E
17 P10 **Lamotrek** *atoll* Caroline Is Pacific Oc 7.28N 146.23E
99 M4 **La Motte** Quebec 48.19N 78.08W
70 P6 **Lamotte-Beuvron** France 47.37N 2.01E
108 M3 **La Moure** N Dakota 46.23N 98.19W
120 D6 **Lampa** Peru 15.22S 70.22W
Lampang *see* **Muang Lampang**
25 G4 **Lam Pao** *res* Thailand
112 J4 **Lampasas** Texas 31.04N 98.12W
112 K5 **Lampasas** *R* Texas
70 A5 **Lampaul-Plouarzel** France 48.27N 4.45W
115 J4 **Lampazos** Mexico 27.00N 100.30W
81 E10 **Lampedusa** Lampedusa, I di Italy 35.31N 12.37E
81 E10 **Lampedusa, I. di** Pelagie, Is Italy
61 B2 **Lampernisse** Belgium 51.02N 2.46E
64 E4 **Lampertheim** W Germany 49.36N 8.28E
63 T10 **Lampertswalde** E Germany 51.19N 13.41E
56 C3 **Lampeter** Dyfed Wales 52.07N 4.05W
103 B6 **Lampeter** Pennsylvania 40.00N 76.15W
56 B4 **Lamphey** Dyfed Wales 51.40N 4.51W
Lamphun *see* **Muang Lamphun**
81 E10 **Lampione, I. di** Pelagie, Is Italy 35.34N 12.20E
25 G5 **Lam Plai Mat** *R* Thailand
100 P9 **Lampman** Saskatchewan 49.23N 102.48W

79 J7 Lamporecchio Italy 43.49N 10.54E
56 K3 Lamport Northants Eng 52.22N 0.53W
47 E3 Lampozhnya U.S.S.R. 65.45N 44.23E
65 G6 Lamprechtshausen Austria 47.59N 12.58E
51 O6 Lämpsä Finland 65.50N 30.00E
89 A3 Lampsar Senegal 16.09N 16.18W
18 L6 Lampung Borneo Indon 1.51S 115.03E
18 F8 Lampung *prov* Sumatra Indon
18 F8 Lampung, Teluk *B* Sumatra Indon
25 H5 Lam Si Bai *R* Thailand
45 K4 Lamskoye U.S.S.R. 52.56N 38.04E
63 M9 Lamspringe W Germany 51.58N 10.02E
63 K5 Lamstedt W Germany 53.38N 9.05E
60 E14 Lamswaarde Netherlands 51.21N 4.03E
29 G6 Lamta Madhya Prad India 22.06N 80.10E
23 C9 Lam Tong I Hong Kong
25 C3 Lamu Burma 19.15N 94.10E
93 M8 Lamu Kenya 2.17S 40.54E
93 M8 Lamu *dist* Kenya
119 C11 Lamud Peru 6.09S 77.55W
93 M8 Lamu I Kenya 2.18S 40.53E
115 G3 La Mula Mexico 29.21N 104.32W
71 F4 Lamure-sur-Azergues France 46.04N 4.30E
93 H7 Lamwia *mt* Kenya 1.25S 36.38E
109 E6 Lamy New Mexico 35.28N 105.55W
41 O6 Lamy-Kyuyel, Oz *L* U.S.S.R. 69.13N 134.15E
25 F6 Lan *isld* Thailand 12.55N 100.46E
79 K1 Lana Italy 46.37N 11.09E
13 G5 Lana Queensland 22.01S 143.10E
91 B3 Lana *R* Equat Guinea
114 D6 Lanai *I* Hawaiian Is 20.50N 156.55W
114 D6 Lanai City Hawaiian Is 20.50N 156.56W
114 D6 Lanaihale *pk* Hawaiian Is 20.48N 156.54W
75 K4 Lanaja Spain 41.46N 0.20W
61 N3 Lanaken Belgium 50.53N 5.39E
31 J1 Lanak La *pass* Kashmir/Xizang Zizhiqu China 34.27N 79.32E
19 M8 Lanao, L Mindanao Philippines
71 E7 Lanarce France 44.43N 4.00E
105 C8 Lanark Florida 29.54N 84.36W
106 E7 Lanark Illinois 42.06N 89.51W
99 O7 Lanark Ontario 45.02N 76.23W
58 J7 Lanark Strathclyde Scotland 55.41N 3.48W
Lanark *co see* Strathclyde *reg*
18 M3 Lanas Sabah Malaysia 5.19N 116.38E
72 L6 Lanau, Barrage de France 44.53N 3.00E
61 N3 Lanaye Belgium 50.47N 5.42E
25 E7 Lanbi Kyun *isld* Burma
19 L7 Lanboyan Pt Mindanao Philippines 8.17N 122.57E
23 B7 Lancang Yunnan China 22.40N 99.58E
23 A3 Lancang Jiang *R* Xizang Zizhiqu China
23 B5 Lancang Jiang *R* Yunnan China
23 B7 Lancang Jiang *R* Yunnan China
76 E3 Láncara Spain 42.52N 7.20W
57 H5 Lancashire *co* England
111 F7 Lancaster California 34.42N 118.09W
107 M4 Lancaster Kentucky 37.35N 84.34W
57 H4 Lancaster Lancs Eng 54.03N 2.48W
108 O1 Lancaster Minnesota 48.51N 96.45W
107 D1 Lancaster Missouri 40.32N 92.31W
98 F8 Lancaster New Brunswick 45.16N 66.06W
104 O2 Lancaster New Hampshire 44.29N 71.34W
104 G4 Lancaster New York 42.53N 78.50W
104 C7 Lancaster Ohio 39.43N 82.37W
99 Q7 Lancaster Ontario 45.08N 74.31W
103 B6 Lancaster Pennsylvania 40.03N 76.18W
105 G3 Lancaster S Carolina 34.43N 80.47W
112 O10 Lancaster Texas 32.35N 96.46W
104 J9 Lancaster Virginia 37.48N 76.30W
106 D7 Lancaster Wisconsin 42.52N 90.43W
103 A6 Lancaster *co* Pennsylvania
122 M11 Lancaster, Récif *reef* Tubuai Is Pacific Oc 27.00S 146.30W
97 L3 Lancaster Sound N W Terr
108 F6 Lance Cr Wyoming
108 F6 Lance Creek Wyoming 43.02N 104.38W
14 B9 Lancelin W Australia 31.01S 115.19E
14 B9 Lancelin I W Australia 31.33S 115.19E
14 E7 Lancelot, Mt W Australia 26.14N 123.17E
71 G8 Lance, Mt. de la France 44.27N 5.06E
100 J8 Lancer Saskatchewan 50.48N 108.52W
18 C8 Lanchang Pen Malaysia 3.30N 102.10E
30 C1 Lanchen *R* Xizang Zizhiqu
69 B3 Lanchères France 50.09N 1.33E
57 K3 Lanchester Durham Eng 54.50N 1.44W
82 J2 Lanchin U.S.S.R. 48.34N 24.45E
44 E5 Lanchkhuti Georgia U.S.S.R. 42.06N 42.01E
Lanchow *see* Lanzhou
80 K4 Lanciano Italy 42.13N 14.23E
75 E2 Lanciego Spain 42.34N 2.31W
70 F4 Lancieux France 48.36N 2.09W
107 M5 Lancing Tennessee 36.09N 84.39W
121 A7 Lanco Chile 39.25S 72.47W
71 G9 Lançon-Provence France 43.35N 5.08E
62 N5 Łańcut Poland 50.06N 22.12E
66 A7 Lancy Switzerland 46.12N 6.08E
50 E7 Land *dist* Iceland
52 E6 Land *reg* Norway
108 K1 Landa N Dakota 48.55N 100.56W
18 H5 Landak *R* Borneo Indon
50 J7 Landáll *R* Iceland
64 O6 Landau Bayern W Germany 48.40N 12.43E
63 K10 Landau Hessen W Germany 51.21N 9.05E
64 E5 Landau in der Pfalz W Germany 49.12N 8.07E
50 G7 Landbrot *dist* Iceland
50 H7 Landbrotsvotn *rivers* Iceland
70 H5 Landéan France 48.25N 1.09W
65 C7 Landeck Austria 47.09N 10.35E
76 E5 Landedo Portugal 41.55N 7.01W
61 E2 Landegem Belgium 51.03N 3.35E
51 D4 Landegode *isld* Norway 67.25N 14.20E
70 C5 Landeleau France 48.13N 3.44W
61 H5 Landelies Belgium 50.23N 4.21E
70 H4 Landelles-et-Coupigny France 48.53N 1.01W
61 L3 Landen Belgium 50.45N 5.05E
103 C7 Landenberg Pennsylvania 39.47N 75.46W
61 L4 Landenne Belgium 50.31N 5.04E
110 R7 Lander Wyoming 42.49N 108.44W
70 B5 Landerneau France 48.27N 4.16W
66 E3 Landeron Switzerland 47.03N 7.05E
13 B5 Lander R N Terr Australia
52 G9 Landeryd Sweden 57.05N 13.15E
72 C3 Landes Charente-Maritime France 46.00N 0.36W
70 N6 Landes Loir-et-Cher France 47.40N 1.09E
104 F8 Landes W Virginia 38.55N 79.13W
67 E8 Landes *dept* France
63 K7 Landesbergen W Germany 52.34N 9.07E
53 F7 Landet Fyn Denmark 55.00N 10.36E
53 G7 Landet Storstrøm Denmark 54.46N 11.17E
121 E4 Landeta Argentina 32.00S 62.02W
75 H8 Landete Spain 39.54N 1.22W
70 D6 Landévant France 47.46N 3.07W
70 B5 Landevennec France 48.18N 4.17W
72 A2 Landevieille France 46.39N 1.48W
28 G6 Landfall I Andaman Is 13.40N 93.00E
121 J9 Landfall, I Chile 53.18S 74.12W
56 H6 Landford Wilts Eng 50.58N 1.37W
123 J9 Land Glacier Antarctica 75.45S 141.00W
63 S5 Landgraben *R* E Germany
63 J5 Land Hadeln *reg* W Germany
31 D8 Landhi Pakistan 24.51N 67.16E
31 B5 Landi Barechi Afghanistan 30.14N 62.50E
31 F3 Landi Kotal Pakistan 34.07N 71.15E
31 B5 Landi Muhammad Amin Khan Afghanistan 30.31N 63.48E
100 U3 Landing L Manitoba 55.20N 97.30W
72 D6 Landiras France 44.33N 0.26W
105 G2 Landis N Carolina 35.33N 80.35W
100 J6 Landis Saskatchewan 52.13N 108.27W
103 E7 Landisville New Jersey 39.31N 74.55W
103 B6 Landisville Pennsylvania 40.06N 76.25W
70 B5 Landivisiau France 48.30N 4.06W
70 H5 Landivy France 48.29N 1.02W
63 K5 Land Kehdingen *reg* W Germany
65 F6 Landl Austria 47.37N 12.03E
66 L3 Ländli Switzerland 47.07N 8.38E
50 F6 Landmannahellir Iceland 64.03N 19.11W
105 F3 Lando S Carolina 34.45N 81.01W
106 E3 Land O Lakes Wisconsin 46.09N 89.12W
51 D8 Landön Sweden 63.31N 14.38E
14 B7 Landor W Australia 25.06S 116.50E
71 D7 Landos France 44.51N 3.50E
52 H3 Landösjön *L* Sweden 63.35N 14.10E
30 B2 Landour Uttar Prad India 30.27N 78.06E
66 P4 Landquart Switzerland 46.58N 9.34E
66 P4 Landquart *R* Switzerland
69 F3 Landrecies France 50.08N 3.42E
69 K5 Landres Meurthe-et-Moselle France 49.19N 5.49E
69 J5 Landres-et-St.-George Ardennes France 49.23N 5.01E
66 B3 Landresse France 47.15N 6.29E
79 F4 Landriano Italy 45.19N 9.16E
99 N4 Landrienne Quebec 48.34N 77.58W
14 F4 Landrigan Cliffs W Australia
79 M1 Landro Italy 46.38N 12.14E
76 D1 Landrove, R Spain
105 E2 Landrum S Carolina 35.10N 82.11W
71 K5 Landry France 45.34N 6.45E
63 Q9 Landsberg E Germany 51.32N 12.11E
Landsberg Poland *see* Gorzów Wielkopolski
64 K7 Landsberg am Lech W Germany 48.03N 10.54E
13 L7 Landsborough Queensland 26.50S 152.50E
13 G5 Landsborough *R* Queensland
11 D10 Landsborough, R New Zealand
97 G2 Lands End *C* N W Terr 76.10N 123.00W
56 S9 Land's End *pt* Cornwall Eng 50.03N 5.44W
71 L1 Landser France 47.41N 7.23E
64 N6 Landshut W Germany 48.31N 12.10E
61 F3 Landskouter Belgium 50.58N 3.48E
53 K5 Landskrona Sweden 55.49N 12.50E
97 K1 Lands Lokk Pt N W Terr 81.40N 91.00W
60 H10 Landsmeer Netherlands 52.26N 4.55E
64 D5 Landstuhl W Germany 49.25N 7.35E
53 S17 Landsvik Norway 60.36N 5.03E
70 C5 Landudal France 48.04N 3.59W
70 B6 Landudec France 48.00N 4.21W
110 R2 Landusky Montana 47.55N 108.37W
63 L10 Landwehrhagen W Germany 51.21N 9.35E
63 J5 Land Wursten *reg* W Germany
64 N3 Landwüst E Germany 50.16N 12.20E
53 U16 Låne Norway 61.11N 6.13E
105 H4 Lane S Carolina 33.31N 79.54W
108 M5 Lane S Dakota 44.05N 98.25W
112 L6 Lane City Texas 29.12N 96.02W
12 L7 Lane Cove *dist* Sydney, New S Wales
12 L6 Lane Cove R New S Wales
56 K4 Lane End Bucks Eng 51.38N 0.52W
61 H5 Laneffe Belgium 50.17N 4.30E
121 F6 La Negra Argentina 37.50S 59.20W
120 D10 La Negra Chile 23.46S 70.18W
65 E7 Lanersbach Austria 47.09N 11.44E
103 H1 Lanesboro Massachusetts 42.31N 73.14W
106 C6 Lanesboro Minnesota 43.44N 91.57W
103 C3 Lanesboro Pennsylvania 41.57N 75.35W
59 G4 Lanesborough Roscommon Irish Rep 53.40N 8.00W
75 D1 Lanestosa Spain 43.13N 3.26W
103 F2 Lanesville New York 42.07N 74.18W
107 L9 Lanett Alabama 32.52N 85.12W
69 D5 Laneuville-Roy France 49.29N 2.35E
69 J5 Laneuville-sur-Meuse France 49.29N 5.10E
70 E5 Lanfains France 48.21N 2.55W
Lan-feng *see* Langao
Lanfeng *see* Langao
100 G7 Lanfine Alberta 51.22N 110.40W
100 N9 Lang Saskatchewan 49.55N 104.22W
53 F6 Langå Fyn Denmark 55.11N 10.43E
53 D4 Langå Viborg Denmark 56.23N 9.55E
50 D5 Langá *R* Iceland
24 D10 La'nga Co *L* Xizang Zizhiqu China
75 D4 Langa de Duero Spain 41.36N 3.24W
83 F4 Langadhás Greece 40.45N 23.04E
84 D6 Langádhia Greece 37.40N 22.01E
50 D7 Langahlidh *slope* Iceland
28 J3 Langai R Assam India
Langak Tso *L see* La'nga Co
90 C5 Langalanga Nigeria 12.01N 6.53E
91 D5 Langa Langa Zaïre 3.50S 15.59E
50 K2 Langanes *pen* Iceland
23 E2 Langao Shaanxi China 32.20N 108.59E
31 G2 Langar Badakhshan Afghanistan 37.01N 73.52E
31 A4 Langar Farah Afghanistan 32.15N 61.43E
31 C4 Langar Helmand Afghanistan 32.38N 65.15E
32 J3 Langar Iran 35.24N 60.26E
Langar Pakistan *see* Jand
31 E3 Langar Parwan Afghanistan 35.01N 68.51E
19 C6 Langara Indonesia 4.03S 123.01E
121 L6 Lángara, B Argentina
101 G8 Langara I Queen Charlotte Is, Br Col 54.12N 133.00W
50 C5 Langárfoss Iceland 64.35N 22.00W
32 D2 Langarūd Iran 37.10N 50.09E
65 N4 Langau Austria 48.51N 15.43E
58 D2 Langavat, L Lewis, W Isles Scotland 58.25N 6.14W
50 D5 Langavatn *L* Mýrasýsla Iceland 64.47N 21.45W
53 V18 Langavatn *L* Norway 60.04N 6.46E
50 H3 Langavatn *L* Thingeyjarsýsla, Sudhur Iceland 65.48N 17.07W
100 P8 Langbank Saskatchewan 50.04N 102.19W
101 L11 Lang Bay Br Columbia 49.48N 124.28W
60 K11 Langbroek Netherlands 52.02N 5.21E
23 D8 Lang Chanh Vietnam 20.08N 105.12E
29 G1 Lang Chu *R* Xizang Zizhiqu
53 X14 Langdal Norway 62.21N 7.35E
107 L9 Langdale Alabama 32.50N 85.11W
100 D8 Langdon Alberta 50.58N 113.38W
109 M4 Langdon Kansas 37.52N 98.20W
108 M1 Langdon N Dakota 48.46N 98.21W
10 C10 Langdon Pt Macquarie I Pacific Oc 54.32S 158.53E
66 K2 Langdorf Switzerland 47.16N 8.21E
61 K3 Langdorp Belgium 50.59N 4.52E
71 C6 Langeac France 45.05N 3.30E
72 E1 Langeais France 47.21N 0.26E
87 F2 Langeb *watercourse* Sudan
95 B9 Langebaan S Africa 33.06S 18.03E
95 B8 Langebaanweg S Africa 32.58S 18.09E
94 E8 Lange Berg *mts* S Africa
95 C9 Langeberg *mts* S Africa
95 F4 Langeberg *mts* S Africa
53 U16 Langedalen *mts* Norway 61.15N 6.20E
53 U15 Langedalsvatn *L* Norway 61.44N 6.10E
65 M4 Langegg Austria 48.50N 15.03E
53 X21 Langeid Norway 59.00N 7.32E
53 X19 Langeidvatn *L* Norway 59.42N 7.35E
53 F7 Langeland *isld* Denmark
53 F7 Langelands Bælt *str* Denmark
60 M8 Langelille Netherlands 52.51N 5.51E
51 L10 Längelmäki Finland 61.42N 24.40E
51 L10 Längelmävesi *L* Finland 61.33N 24.20E
60 O7 Langelo Netherlands 53.06N 6.27E
63 M9 Langelsheim W Germany 51.57N 10.19E
61 B3 Langemark Belgium 50.55N 2.55E
66 Q1 Langen Austria 47.31N 9.51E
64 F4 Langen Hessen W Germany 49.59N 8.41E
63 J5 Langen Niedersachsen W Germany 53.37N 8.36E
64 H8 Langenargen W Germany 47.35N 9.33E
66 P1 Langenargen W Germany 47.36N 9.33E
64 P2 Langenau E Germany 50.51N 13.18E
64 J7 Langenau W Germany 48.29N 10.08E
64 N2 Langenberg Gera E Germany 50.55N 12.04E
63 F10 Langenberg W Germany 51.22N 7.07E
66 H2 Langenbruck Switzerland 47.21N 7.46E
64 M4 Langenbruck W Germany 49.39N 11.49E
69 Q5 Langenbrücken W Germany 49.12N 8.38E
64 H5 Langenburg W Germany 49.16N 9.51E
51 E2 Langenes Norway 69.01N 15.15E
63 J3 Langeness *isld* W Germany
65 C7 Langenfeld Austria 47.05N 10.58E
69 M1 Langenfeld W Germany 51.06N 6.57E
63 L8 Langenhagen W Germany 52.26N 9.45E
63 J3 Langenhorn W Germany 54.41N 8.53E
64 O6 Langenisarhofen W Germany 48.44N 12.59E
65 N5 Langenlois Austria 48.29N 15.42E
64 D4 Langenlonsheim W Germany 49.55N 7.55E
63 S9 Langennaundorf E Germany 51.36N 13.21E
64 G3 Langenselbold W Germany 50.10N 9.03E
64 J4 Langensteinach W Germany 49.30N 10.13E
64 F6 Langensteinbach W Germany 48.55N 8.30E
66 H3 Langenthal Switzerland 47.13N 7.48E
53 S18 Langenuen *inlet* Norway 60.00N 5.21E
65 N6 Langenwang Austria 47.34N 15.38E
64 K5 Langenzenn W Germany 49.30N 10.50E
65 O5 Langenzersdorf Austria 48.20N 16.22E
63 F5 Langeoog W Germany 53.45N 7.29E
60 G11 Langeraar Netherlands 52.12N 4.43E
60 H12 Langerak Netherlands 51.56N 4.54E
53 E2 Langerak *inlet* Denmark 57.05N 10.07E
64 A2 Langerwehe W Germany 50.48N 6.22E
53 Y19 Langesjå *L* Telemark Norway 59.57N 8.17E
53 X18 Langesjøen *L* Buskerud Norway 60.15N 7.46E
53 F6 Langeskov Denmark 55.22N 10.36E
53 H6 Langesø *L* Denmark 55.29N 11.48E
52 E7 Langesund Norway 59.02N 9.45E
52 E8 Langesundsfjord *inlet* Norway
66 H3 Langeten *R* Switzerland
53 U14 Langevåg Norway 62.26N 6.15E
53 U15 Langevatn *L* Norway 61.37N 6.12E
53 W15 Langevatn *L* Norway 61.58N 7.22E
26 U16 Langevin, Pte de Réunion Indian Ocean 21.23S 55.39E
64 K2 Langewiesen E Germany 50.40N 10.59E
70 N5 Langey France 48.03N 1.11E
60 N8 Langezwaag Netherlands 52.59N 6.00E
Langfang *see* Anci
51 J1 Langfjord Norway 70.04N 22.18E
51 N1 Langfjord *inlet* Finnmark Norway
52 D4 Langfjord *inlet* Möre og Romsdal Norway
103 B8 Langford Maryland 39.11N 76.09W
108 N4 Langford S Dakota 45.35N 97.50W
63 H7 Langförden W Germany 52.47N 8.16E
121 J9 Langford, Seno *B* Chile
18 D5 Langgam Sumatra Indonesia 0.14N 101.47E
18 C5 Langgapayung Sumatra Indon 1.44N 99.59E
24 H11 Langgar Xizang Zizhiqu China 29.50N 93.46E
69 Q3 Lang-Göns W Germany 50.30N 8.39E
56 K2 Langham Leics Eng 52.42N 0.45W
100 L6 Langham Saskatchewan 52.22N 106.55W
79 D5 Langhe *dist* Italy
31 B4 Langhera Afghanistan 32.02N 63.42E
79 H5 Langhirano Italy 44.36N 10.16E
25 D2 Langhko Burma 20.20N 98.00E
57 G2 Langholm Dumfries & Galloway Scotland 55.09N 3.00W
50 G7 Langholt Iceland 63.35N 18.09W
103 E6 Langhorne Pennsylvania 40.11N 74.56W
30 L4 Langhphu *mt* Xizang Zizhiqu 28.01N 87.54E
50 G5 Langihryggur *mt* Iceland 64.58N 18.35W
50 G6 Langisjór *L* Iceland 64.10N 18.20W
50 E5 Langjökull *ice cap* Iceland 64.43N 20.03W
18 C2 Langkawi *isld* Pen Malaysia
19 D6 Langkesi, Pulau Pulau *islds* Indonesia
25 E8 Lang Kha Toek, Khao *mt* Thailand 9.33N 98.45E
25 H1 Lang Khuong Vietnam 22.18N 104.30E
94 F7 Langklip S Africa 28.15S 20.17E
18 M2 Langkon Sabah Malaysia 6.34N 116.45E
99 P4 Langlade Quebec 48.14N 75.59W
98 Q7 Langlade, I Atlantic Oc 46.55N 56.20W
101 K11 Langley Br Col 49.07N 122.39W
105 F4 Langley S Carolina 33.32N 81.51W
110 C1 Langley Washington 48.02N 122.25W
101 K11 Langley *co* Br Col
53 A5 Langli *isld* Denmark 55.32N 8.20E
13 H7 Langlo *R* Queensland
13 H7 Langlo Crossing Queensland 26.10S 145.42E
13 H7 Langlo Downs Queensland 25.28S 145.46E
110 A7 Langlois Oregon 42.56N 124.29W
99 N4 Langlois Village Quebec 48.55N 77.10W
63 H5 Lang-lütjen-sand *sandbank* W Germany
30 G3 Langmoche Nepal 27.52N 86.38E
30 F3 Langmoche Col *pass* Nepal 27.54N 86.34N
30 G3 Langmoche Kola *R* Nepal
Langmusi *see* Dagcanglhamo
Langmusze *see* Joerhkai
66 H4 Langnau Bern Switzerland 46.57N 7.47E
66 L2 Langnau Zürich Switzerland 47.17N 8.32E
57 D4 Langness Pt Isle of Man U.K. 54.03N 4.37W
53 J7 Langø *isld* Denmark 54.58N 12.38E
53 F5 Langø *pen* Denmark 55.35N 10.37E
71 D7 Langogne France 44.43N 3.51E
28 G1 Langoi Xizang Zizhiqu 28.24N 89.07E
72 D6 Langoiran France 44.42N 0.21W
72 D6 Langon Gironde France 44.33N 0.14W
70 G6 Langon Ille-et-Vilaine France 47.44N 1.50W
72 C3 Langon, le France 46.26N 0.58W
53 F5 Langør Denmark 55.55N 10.39E
76 C2 Langosteira, Pta Spain 43.22N 8.29W
51 D3 Langøy *isld* Norway 68.45N 15.00E
30 D1 Langpoche *R* Xizang Zizhiqu
56 F5 Langport Somerset Eng 51.02N 2.50W
Langqên Kanbab *R see* Xiangquan He
64 N6 Langquaid W Germany 48.50N 12.05E
69 J8 Langres France 47.53N 5.20E
71 F2 Langres, Plat. de France
66 O1 Langrickenbach Switzerland 47.36N 9.16E
24 C7 Langru Xinjiang Uygur Zizhiqu China 36.50N 79.44E
70 K3 Langrune France 49.19N 0.22W
100 T8 Langruth Manitoba 50.23N 98.40W
40 J5 Langry Sakhalin U.S.S.R. 53.03N 142.01E
18 B3 Langsa Sumatra Indon 4.28N 97.59E
18 B3 Langsa, Teluk *B* Sumatra Indon
65 L4 Langschlag Austria 48.36N 14.54E
65 K8 Lang See *L* Austria 46.47N 14.26E
52 K3 Långsele Sweden 63.11N 17.05E
57 K5 Langsett S Yorks Eng 53.30N 1.40W
22 G6 Langshan Nei Monggol Zizhiqu China 41.05N 107.30E
22 G6 Lang Shan *mt ra* Nei Monggol Zizhiqu China
22 H6 Lang Shan *mt ra* Nei Monggol Zizhiqu China
25 M7 Langshing Burma 26.49N 95.50E
52 J6 Långshyttan Sweden 60.26N 16.02E
53 D5 Langskov Denmark 55.49N 9.33E
25 J2 Lang Son Vietnam 21.50N 106.45E
28 H1 Lang-ta Xizang Zizhiqu 29.54N 91.09E
30 J4 Langtang Nepal 28.14N 85.36E
57 K4 Langthwaite N Yorks Eng 54.25N 1.59W
28 J3 Langting Assam India 25.28N 93.10E
57 N4 Langtoft Humberside Eng 54.05N 0.28W
57 N6 Langton Lincs Eng 53.13N 0.09W
51 H6 Långträsk Sweden 65.23N 20.20E
112 F6 Langtry Texas 29.49N 101.36W
66 Q6 Languard, Piz *mt* Switzerland 46.29N 9.57E
67 G9 Languedoc *prov* France
70 E4 Langueux France 48.30N 2.44W
Languiaru *R see* Iquê, R
70 D6 Languidic France 47.50N 3.09W
75 D5 Languilla Spain 41.26N 3.26W
107 F6 L'Anguille *R* Arkansas
121 B9 Lañguineo Argentina 43.16S 69.53W
120 D6 Langui y Layo *L* Peru 14.31S 71.15W
64 J1 Langula E Germany 51.09N 10.26E
50 E6 Langvatn *L* Iceland 64.30N 20.31W
53 Y15 Langvatn *L* Norway 61.31N 8.20E
50 F7 Langviuhraun *lava field* Iceland
95 C9 Langvlei S Africa 33.45S 19.45E
63 H5 Langwarden W Germany 53.37N 8.19E
57 H3 Langwathby Cumbria Eng 54.42N 2.39W
63 K7 Langwedel W Germany 52.58N 9.12E
60 L8 Langweer Netherlands 52.59N 5.43E
66 P4 Langwies Switzerland 46.50N 9.44E
57 N6 Langworth Lincs Eng 53.17N 0.25W
23 H3 Langxi Anhui China 31.07N 119.06E
23 D3 Langzhong Sichuan China 31.39N 105.56E
76 B5 Lanhezes Portugal 41.44N 8.41W
70 B5 Lanhouarneau France 48.35N 4.14W
99 L5 Laniel Quebec 47.03N 79.16W
100 M7 Lanigan Saskatchewan 51.50N 105.01W
114 B5 Lanikai Hawaiian Is 21.23N 157.43W
70 A5 Lanildut France 48.29N 4.45W
121 B7 Lanin, Parque Nacional Arg/Chile
121 B7 Lanín, V Arg/Chile 39.35S 71.33W
85 N7 L'ân Is Egypt 24.22N 35.21E
56 B7 Lanivet Cornwall Eng 50.27N 4.45W
18 J5 Lanjak, Bukit *mt* Sarawak Malaysia 1.25N 112.00E
77 K7 Lanjarón Spain 36.55N 3.29W
29 G7 Lanji Madhya Prad India 21.30N 80.36E
63 E10 Lank W Germany 51.18N 6.39E
63 T7 Lanke E Germany 52.46N 13.35E
108 N1 Lankin N Dakota 48.21N 97.54W
61 N2 Lanklaar Belgium 51.01N 5.44E
39 E5 Lankovaya *R* U.S.S.R.
120 D5 Lanlacuni Bajo Peru 13.28S 70.22W
90 A8 Lanlate Nigeria 7.41N 3.34E
87 M6 Lanle Somalia 8.50N 48.07E
70 E4 Lanloup France 48.43N 2.58W
70 C4 Lanmeur France 48.38N 3.44W
51 J3 Lannavaara Sweden 68.04N 22.00E
45 G7 Lannaya Ukraine U.S.S.R. 49.20N 35.19E
72 E9 Lannemezan France 43.08N 0.22E
72 E9 Lannemezan *plat* France
72 E8 Lannepax France 43.48N 0.13E
70 A4 Lannilis France 48.35N 4.32W
70 D4 Lannion France 48.44N 3.27W
99 Q6 L'Annonciation Quebec 46.24N 74.52W
69 E2 Lannoy France 50.40N 3.13E
72 K5 Lanobre France 45.26N 2.31E
103 F7 Lanoka Harbor New Jersey 39.52N 74.10W
99 R7 Lanoraie Quebec 45.57N 73.15W
120 G6 La Noria Bolivia 15.05S 61.14W
115 F6 La Noria Mexico 23.32N 106.20W
72 G5 Lanouaille France 45.24N 1.09E
82 K1 Lanovtsy U.S.S.R. 49.51N 26.03E
23 B5 Lanping Yunnan China 26.25N 99.25E
61 F4 Lanquesaint Belgium 50.39N 3.48E
51 J5 Lansån Sweden 66.29N 22.30E
71 E9 Lansargues France 43.39N 4.02E
103 D6 Lansdale Pennsylvania 40.14N 75.17W
94 Q11 Lansdowne Cape Town S Africa 33.59S 18.31E
103 A8 Lansdowne Maryland 39.15N 76.39W
99 O8 Lansdowne Ontario 44.24N 76.02W
103 D7 Lansdowne Pennsylvania 39.57N 75.16W
30 B3 Lansdowne Uttar Prad India 29.50N 78.42E
104 A2 Lansdowne *dist* Philadelphia, Penn
12 K7 Lansdowne *dist* Sydney, N S W
97 L7 Lansdowne House Ontario 52.05N 88.00W
106 F3 L'Anse Michigan 46.45N 88.27W
98 H5 L'Anse-aux-Griffons Quebec 48.56N 64.20W
63 R5 Lansen E Germany 53.36N 12.45E
71 H6 Lans-en-Vercors France 45.07N 5.35E
108 J1 Lansford N Dakota 48.39N 101.22W
103 C5 Lansford Pennsylvania 40.49N 75.54W
23 F6 Lanshan Hunan China 25.14N 112.01E
106 C6 Lansing Iowa 43.21N 91.13W
109 Q2 Lansing Kansas 39.15N 94.55W
106 K7 Lansing Michigan 42.44N 85.34W
105 F1 Lansing N Carolina 36.30N 81.32W
51 J5 Lansjärv Sweden 66.39N 22.10E
65 P2 Lanškroun Czechoslovakia 49.55N 16.38E
71 K6 Lanslebourg France 45.17N 6.53E
71 H6 Lans, Mtgnes. de France
72 H8 Lanta France 43.33N 1.38E
76 L4 Lantadilla Spain 42.20N 4.17W
105 B9 Lantana Florida 26.34N 80.06W
23 F7 Lan Tao *isld* Hong Kong 22.15N 114.00E
77 K6 Lanteira Spain 37.11N 3.08W
77 F6 Lantejuela La Spain 37.21N 5.13W
69 L8 Lanterne *R* France
72 H5 Lanteuil France 45.08N 1.39E
70 O7 Lanthenay France 47.24N 1.44E
Lantian *see* Linyuan
23 E1 Lantian Shaanxi China 34.06N 109.19E
18 D6 Lantic, Bukit *hill* Sumatra Indonesia 0.41S 100.28E
72 B6 Lanton France 44.43N 1.03W
71 L9 Lantosque France 43.58N 7.18E
108 J4 Lantry S Dakota 45.01N 101.26W
66 P5 Lantsch Switzerland 46.42N 9.33E
71 D3 Lanty France 46.48N 3.50E
84 C6 Lantzói Greece 37.42N 21.34E
71 C8 Lanuéjols France 44.08N 3.23E
72 J7 Lanuéjouls France 44.26N 2.09E
85 E4 Lanuf, Ras Libya 30.26N 18.36E
121 K5 Lanus *dist* Buenos Aires Arg
81 D4 Lanusei Sardinia 39.53N 9.33E
80 G5 Lanuvio Italy 41.40N 12.42E
19 N7 Lanuza Mindanao Philippines 9.12N 126.04E
19 N7 Lanuza B Mindanao Philippines
70 E6 Lanvaux, Landes de *reg* France
70 B5 Lanvéoc France 48.17N 4.28W
70 E4 Lanvollon France 48.38N 2.59W
21 D4 Lanxi Heilongjiang China 46.18N 126.15E
23 G3 Lanxi Hubei China 30.20N 115.10E
23 H4 Lanxi Zhejiang China 29.12N 119.27E
22 J7 Lan Xian Shanxi China 38.16N 111.30E
65 J1 Lány Czechoslovakia 50.08N 13.58E
87 C8 Lanya Sudan 5.17N 30.33E
65 K3 Lany, mt Czechoslovakia 49.10N 14.06E
Lan Yü *isld* Taiwan *see* Hung-t'ou Hsü island
63 P6 Lanz E Germany 53.05N 11.36E
75 G2 Lanz Spain 43.00N 1.37W
76 C2 Lanza Spain 43.04N 8.12W
96 U7 Lanzarote *isld* Canary Is 29.00N 13.38W
23 C1 Lanzhou Gansu China 36.01N 103.45E
21 C5 Lanzijing Jilin China 44.50N 123.30E
66 N8 Lanzo Italy 45.59N 9.02E
79 B4 Lanzo Torinese Italy 45.16N 7.28E
81 L4 Lao *R* Italy
19 K2 Laoag Luzon Philippines 18.14N 120.36E
19 M5 Laoang Philippines 12.35N 125.02E
19 M5 Laoang I Philippines 12.35N 125.00E
23 C6 Laochang Yunnan China 25.13N 104.40E
30 D1 Laoche La *pass* Xizang Zizhiqu 31.48N 80.06E
36 D5 Laodicea *anc site* Turkey 37.46N 29.02E
24 D2 Laofenkou Xinjiang Uygur Zizhiqu China 46.08N 83.30E
22 L6 Laoguo Hebei China 40.58N 118.56E
22 L5 Laoha He *R* Nei Monggol Zizhiqu China
Laohekou *see* Guanghua
Lao-ho-k'ou *see* Guanghua
59 H6 Laois *co* Irish Rep
21 B1 Laojingou Heilongjiang China 53.14N 122.17E
Laojunmiao *see* Yumen
Laojunmiao *see* Yumen (Laojunmiao)
21 C3 Laolai Heilongjiang China 48.42N 124.59E
21 D7 Laoling Jilin China 41.26N 126.19E
96 T9 La Oliva Fuerteventura Canary Is 28.36N 13.53W
Laolong *see* Longchuan
25 E3 Lao, Mae *R* Thailand
69 F4 Laon France 49.34N 3.37E
106 F4 Laona Wisconsin 45.35N 88.40W
70 N4 Laons France 48.42N 1.11E
120 B4 La Oroya Peru 11.36S 75.54W
17 G8 Laos *state* S E Asia
24 E3 Laoshawan Xinjiang Uygur Zizhiqu China 44.34N 85.50E
22 M7 Laotie Shan *mt* Liaoning China 38.46N 121.19E
77 F10 Laou *R* Morocco
Laouié *see* Lawiye
88 Q11 Laouni Algeria 20.28N 5.43E
114 D6 Lao Valley Hawaiian Is
Laowohi *pass see* Khardung La
19 B5 Laowu Celebes Indonesia 2.38S 120.40E
21 E5 Laoye Ling *mts* Heilongjiang China
21 D5 Laoye Ling *mts* Jilin China
118 E9 Lapa Brazil 25.46S 49.44W
118 J9 Lapa Brazil 22.57S 43.11W
84 B5 Lápa Greece 38.06N 21.25E
118 F9 Lapa *dist* São Paulo Brazil
19 K9 Lapac *isld* Philippines 5.34N 120.47E
121 F1 Lapachito Argentina 27.12S 59.25W
14 D9 Lapage, L W Australia
90 C7 Lapai Nigeria 9.05N 6.32E
77 C4 Lapa, La Spain 38.27N 6.31W
71 D4 Lapalisse France 46.15N 3.44E
121 D8 La Palma Argentina 41.44S 65.16W
119 D5 La Palma Colombia 5.23N 74.24W
115 P10 La Palma El Salvador 14.20N 89.10W
115 P9 La Palma Guatemala 17.30N 89.25W
115 P5 La Palma Panama 8.22N 78.08W
119 B4 La Palma Panama 7.44N 80.16W
96 P9 La Palma *isld* Canary Is 28.40N 17.50W
72 K10 Lapalme France 42.59N 3.00E
72 L10 Lapalme, Étang de *L* France 42.58N 3.01E
121 G5 La Paloma Uruguay 34.37S 54.08W
119 D3 La Paloma Venezuela 8.50N 72.34W
71 F8 Lapalud France 44.18N 4.41E
120 D5 La Pampa Peru 13.36S 69.36W
121 C6 La Pampa *prov* Argentina
111 D6 La Panza California 35.22N 120.13W
111 D6 La Panza Ra California
119 G4 La Paragua Venezuela 6.53N 63.22W
19 J9 Laparan I Philippines 5.53N 120.00E
115 G6 La Parilla Mexico 23.43N 104.08W
30 H3 Laparma Nepal 27.53N 86.44E
76 E7 Lapa, Sa. da Portugal
Lapasset *see* Lakhdar
121 K La Paternal *dist* Buenos Aires Argentina
84 S14 Lapathos Cyprus 35.16N 33.50E
99 T7 La Patrie Quebec 45.24N 71.15W
120 E7 La Paz Bolivia 16.30S 68.10W
121 F3 La Paz Entre Ríos Argentina 30.45S 59.36W
115 L2 La Paz Honduras 14.20N 87.40W
106 H8 Lapaz Indiana 41.28N 86.19W
121 C4 La Paz Mendoza Arg 33.30S 67.36W
115 D5 La Paz Mexico 24.10N 110.17W
115 L3 La Paz Nicaragua 12.20N 86.41W
119 D2 La Paz Venezuela 10.44N 72.02W
120 E6 La Paz *dept* Bolivia
120 E7 La Paz, R. de Bolivia
30 A8 Lapchaura Madhya Prad India 24.56N 77.10E
30 K4 Lapche Xizang Zizhiqu 28.08N 86.13E
24 E10 Lapchung Tso *L* Xizang Zizhiqu China 30.01N 85.25E
119 E8 La Pedrera Colombia 1.16S 69.43W
106 L6 Lapeer Michigan 43.03N 83.19W
106 J9 Lapel Indiana 40.04N 85.50W
121 E3 La Pelada Argentina 30.53S 60.53W
115 O5 La Peña Panama 8.09N 81.02W
121 K6 La Peninsular Argentina 47.51S 70.35W
115 G3 La Perla Mexico 28.18N 104.34W
120 A10 La Perla *dist* Callao Peru
100 U3 La Perouse Manitoba 55.14N 98.00W
122 V15 La Pérouse, B Easter I Pacific Oc 27.05S 109.19W
114 C2 La Pérouse Pinnacle Hawaiian Is
115 L6 La Pesca Mexico 23.46N 97.47W
72 D7 Lapeyrade France 44.04N 0.02W
71 B4 Lapeyrouse France 46.14N 2.52E
77 K6 Lapeza Spain 37.17N 3.16W
56 D6 Lapford Devon Eng 50.52N 3.47W
115 H7 La Piedad Mexico 20.20N 102.01W
119 G4 La Piña, R Venezuela
110 D6 La Pine Oregon 43.40N 121.30W
19 M5 Lapinig Samar Philippines 12.20N 125.18E
19 M6 Lapinin *isld* Philippines 10.07N 124.35E
51 N8 Lapinlahti Finland 63.21N 27.25E
47 M5 Lapino U.S.S.R. 56.18N 61.18E
119 B3 La Pintada Panama 8.37N 80.26W
84 R14 Lapithos Cyprus 35.20N 33.11E
107 F11 Laplace Louisiana 30.04N 90.30W
25 F4 Lap Lae Thailand 17.38N 100.01E
61 D4 Laplaigne Belgium 50.31N 3.27E
26 U15 La Plaine-des-Palmistes Réunion Indian Oc 21.08S 55.38E
47 C2 Laplandiya U.S.S.R. 68.16N 33.20E
108 K4 La Plant S Dakota 45.09N 100.40W
121 F5 La Plata Argentina 34.52S 57.55W
119 C6 La Plata Colombia 2.33N 75.55W
104 J8 La Plata Maryland 38.32N 76.59W
107 D1 La Plata Missouri 40.01N 92.30W
119 A8 La Plata *isld* Ecuador 1.18S 81.05W
121 D4 La Playosa Argentina 32.05S 63.03W
72 J5 Lapleau France 45.18N 2.10E
72 F7 Laplume France 44.07N 0.33E
103 C3 La Plume Pennsylvania 41.33N 75.46W
98 B6 La Pocatière Quebec 47.21N 70.04W
98 O6 La Poile Bay Newfoundland
106 D3 La Pointe Wisconsin 46.47N 90.47W
120 E11 La Poma Argentina 24.40S 66.15W
47 E4 Lapominka U.S.S.R. 64.40N 40.38E
111 D2 La Porte California 39.41N 120.58W
106 H8 La Porte Indiana 41.35N 86.44W
108 Q2 Laporte Minnesota 47.13N 94.45W
103 B4 Laporte Pennsylvania 41.25N 76.29W
100 H7 Laporte Saskatchewan 51.12N 109.30W
106 B7 La Porte City Iowa 42.19N 92.10W
19 A6 Laposo, Bukit *mt* Celebes Indon 4.30S 119.49E
93 E2 Laposs Sudan 3.55N 33.26E
26 T14 La Possession Réunion Indian Ocean 20.55S 55.20E
69 N7 Lapoutroie France 48.09N 7.10E
82 G6 Lapovo Yugoslavia 44.10N 21.02E
115 C5 La Poza Mexico 25.50N 112.00W
51 K8 Lappajärvi *L* Finland 63.08N 23.41E
13 G3 Lappa Junction Queensland 17.19S 144.55E
51 K8 Lapparjärvi Finland 63.13N 23.40E
51 N10 Lappeenranta Finland 61.04N 28.15E
51 J9 Lappfjärd Finland 62.14N 21.30E
51 J10 Lappi Turku Finland 61.07N 21.50E
51 L4 Lappi *dist* Finland
51 H3 Lappland Sweden/Finland
38 B2 Lappland *reg* Sweden/Finland/U.S.S.R.
51 K2 Lappojavrre *L* Norway 69.15N 23.47E
51 K5 Lappträsk Sweden 66.01N 23.30E
99 R7 Laprairie Quebec 45.24N 73.30W
99 S10 Laprairie Basin Quebec
108 E7 La Prele Cr Wyoming
40 C4 Lapri U.S.S.R. 55.44N 124.50E
30 F7 Lapri *R* Uttar Prad India
121 E6 Laprida Argentina 37.34S 60.45W
71 D5 Laprugne France 46.00N 3.44E
112 H7 La Pryor Texas 28.57N 99.53W
61 D1 Lapscheure Belgium 51.16N 3.21E
37 C2 Lâpseki Turkey 40.22N 26.42E
48 O9 Laptev Sea Arctic Oc
41 M3 Laptevykh More *sea* U.S.S.R.
51 K9 Lapua Finland 62.57N 23.00E
51 K8 Lapuanjoki *R* Finland
121 D2 La Puerta Catamarca Argentina 28.10S 65.46W
121 D3 La Puerta Córdoba Argentina 30.53S 63.15W
119 E3 La Puerta Venezuela 9.08N 70.46W
19 L6 Lapu-Lapu Philippines 10.18N 123.58E
121 D2 La Punta Argentina 28.23S 64.47W
120 A10 La Punta *dist* Callao Peru
119 A9 La Puntilla *pt* Ecuador 2.13S 81.00W
115 C4 La Purisima Mexico 26.10N 112.05W
110 A2 La Push Washington 47.55N 124.38W
82 H3 Lăpusului, Munţii *mts* Romania
Lapväärtti *see* Lappfjärd
62 O3 Łapy Poland 53.00N 22.50E
25 M8 Lapyep Ga Burma 26.13N 95.48E
85 K9 Laqiya Arbain Sudan 20.01N 28.01E
85 K10 Laqiya 'Umran *mt* Sudan 19.55N 28.18E
34 L4 Laqlaq Iraq 34.57N 43.33E
71 B5 Laqueuille France 45.39N 2.44E
120 F10 La Quiaca Argentina 22.08S 65.35W
103 A3 Laquin Pennsylvania 41.37N 76.39W
66 J7 Laquinhorn *mt* Switzerland 46.09N 8.00E
32 F7 Lār Iran 27.42N 54.19E
30 G6 Lar Uttar Prad India 26.11N 83.57E
119 E2 Lara *state* Venezuela
89 J7 Larabanga Ghana 9.16N 1.56W
76 B2 Laracha Spain 43.15N 8.35W
77 D10 Larache Morocco 35.12N 6.10W
59 K6 Laragh Wicklow Irish Rep 53.00N 6.18W
71 H8 Laragne-Montéglin France 44.19N 5.49E
71 F5 Larajasse France 45.37N 4.30E
32 G7 Lārak *isld* Iran 26.53N 56.21E
108 E8 Laramie Wyoming 41.20N 105.38W
108 E7 Laramie *R* Wyoming
108 E7 Laramie Pk Wyoming 42.18N 105.26W
108 D7 Laramie Ra Wyoming
Laranda *anc site see* Karaman
117 A7 Laranjal Brazil 4.16S 57.30W
118 F8 Laranjal Paulista Brazil 23.01S 47.50W
118 J9 Laranjeiras Brazil 22.56S 43.12W
118 D9 Laranjeiras do Sul Brazil 25.23S 52.23W
118 E8 Laranjinha, R Brazil
19 C8 Larantuka Indonesia 8.20S 123.00E
75 E6 Laranueva Spain 40.57N 2.33W
77 V15 La Rapita Balearic Is 39.22N 2.57E
15 A7 Larat Moluccas Indon 7.09S 131.45E
19 G6 Larat Moluccas Indonesia 4.46S 131.44E
15 A7 Larat *isld* Moluccas Indon 7.09S 131.45E
119 D3 La Raya, Ciénaga de *marshy L* Colombia 8.23N 74.31W
74 K8 L'Arba Algeria 36.33N 3.12E
88 P3 Larba Algeria 36.34N 3.05E
40 C4 Larba U.S.S.R. 55.19N 123.28E
77 E10 Larbat Ayacha Morocco 35.24N 5.55W
58 J6 Larbert Central Scotland 56.02N 3.51W
52 L9 Lärbro Sweden 57.47N 18.50E
72 B9 Larceveau-Arros-Cibits France 43.13N 1.06W
70 J5 Larchamp France 48.20N 1.00W
71 K8 Larche Alpes de Haute Provence France 44.27N 6.51E
72 G5 Larche Corrèze France 45.07N 1.24E
79 A6 Larche, Col de *pass* Italy/France 44.26N 6.55E
103 N6 Larchmont New York 40.57N 73.47W
53 Y20 Lårdal Telemark Norway 59.25N 8.10E
Lardal Vestfold Norway *see* Svarstad
92 J10 Larde Mozambique 16.27S 39.41E
80 C2 Larderello Italy 43.23N 10.53E
99 L4 Larder Lake Ontario 48.06N 79.44W
75 F3 Lardero Spain 42.26N 2.27W
84 V17 Lárdhos Rhodes 36.05N 28.01E
71 K10 Lardier, C France 43.10N 6.38E
79 F4 Lardirago Italy 45.14N 9.14E
98 M8 L'Ardoise C Breton I, Nova Scotia 45.37N 60.46W
76 E9 Lardosa Portugal 39.59N 7.27W
69 C6 Lardy France 48.31N 2.15E
93 J5 Lare Kenya 0.20N 37.56E
107 C1 Laredo Missouri 40.02N 93.28W
75 D1 Laredo Spain 43.24N 3.24W
112 H8 Laredo Texas 27.32N 99.22W
121 G9 La Reina *dist* Santiago Chile
99 L4 La Reine Quebec 48.52N 79.30W
60 O11 Laren Gelderland Netherlands 52.12N 6.22E
60 J10 Laren Noord-Holland Netherlands 52.15N 5.14E
118 J2 Larenjeiras Brazil 10.49S 37.11W
32 F3 Lārestān Iran 35.45N 54.05E
66 Q4 Laret Switzerland 46.51N 9.52E
82 K2 Larga U.S.S.R. 48.22N 26.50E
98 J3 Large I Quebec 50.14N 63.53W
58 L6 Largo Fife Scotland 56.13N 2.56W
105 E10 Largo Florida 27.54N 82.47W
103 A9 Largo Maryland 38.54N 76.50W
94 U14 Largo S Africa 26.16S 28.30E
109 C5 Largo *R* New Mexico
58 L6 Largo Bay Fife Scotland
116 D4 Largo, Cayo *isld* Cuba 21.37N 81.26W
118 H9 Largo do Tangue Brazil 22.56S 43.23W
105 G12 Largo, Key *isld* Florida
58 L6 Largo Ward Fife Scotland 56.15N 2.52W
12 A7 Largs S Australia 34.50S 138.29E
58 G7 Largs Strathclyde Scotland 55.48N 4.52W
12 A7 Largs Bay S Australia
32 B1 Lārī Iran 38.32N 47.52E
79 J7 Lari Italy 43.34N 10.35E
19 A4 Lariang Celebes Indon 1.27S 119.19E
19 A4 Lariang *R* Celebes Indon
66 A2 Larians France 47.25N 6.15E
93 H8 Lariboro Tanzania 2.59S 36.43E
121 F5 La Rica Argentina 35.00S 59.53W
32 B1 Lārījan Iran 39.16N 47.16E
31 B7 Larikand Pakistan 27.52N 63.48E
84 F4 Lárimna Greece 38.34N 23.17E
108 N2 Larimore N Dakota 47.54N 97.38W
32 E3 Lārīn Iran 35.59N 52.19E
80 L5 Larino Italy 41.48N 14.54E
42 B2 Larino U.S.S.R. 60.36N 77.37E
121 C2 La Rioja Argentina 29.26S 66.50W
121 C2 La Rioja *prov* Argentina
Lario, L. di *see* Como, L. di
84 D2 Lárisa Greece 39.38N 22.25E
84 D2 Lárisa *prov* Greece
32 F7 Laristan *reg* Iran
72 D5 Larit *R* France
100 T9 La Rivière Manitoba 49.15N 98.41W
Larjan *see* Lārījan
30 A1 Larji Himachal Prad India 31.43N 77.13E
108 J3 Lark N Dakota 46.28N 101.24W
31 E7 Larkana Pakistan 27.32N 68.18E
31 D7 Larkana *dist* Pakistan
58 J7 Larkhall Strathclyde Scotland 55.45N 3.59W
98 O4 Lark Harbour Newfoundland 49.06N 58.22W
107 K7 Larkinsville Alabama 34.41N 86.08W
31 B4 Lar Koh *mt* Afghanistan 32.25N 62.36E
13 H3 Lark Pass Gt Barrier Reef Australia 15.05S 145.45E
56 M3 Lark, R Suffolk etc Eng
109 F2 Larkspur Colorado 39.13N 104.54W
56 N3 Larling Norfolk Eng 52.28N 0.55E
42 A3 Larlomkiny U.S.S.R. 59.17N 74.32E
70 D6 Larmar-Plage France 47.42N 3.21W
84 S15 Larnaca Cyprus 34.54N 33.39E
84 S15 Larnaca Bay Cyprus
59 L2 Larne Antrim N Ireland 54.51N 5.49W
109 L3 Larned Kansas 38.12N 99.05W
59 L2 Larne L Antrim N Ireland 54.50N 5.48W
90 F7 Laro Cameroon 8.19N 12.21E
72 B3 La Rochelle France 46.10N 1.10W
71 E3 Larochemillay France 46.53N 4.00E
69 E8 Laroche-St. Cydroine France 47.58N 3.28E
61 P7 Larochette Luxembourg 49.47N 6.13E
76 E4 Laroco Spain 42.21N 7.10W
66 O5 La Rofna *R* Switzerland
77 K6 Laroles Spain 37.01N 3.01W
116 K5 La Romana Dominican Rep 18.27N 68.57W
96 R13 La Romantica Tenerife Canary Is 28.24N 16.34W
19 B5 Larompong Celebes Indon 3.31S 120.21E
19 B5 Larona Celebes Indon 2.48S 121.25E
100 M3 La Ronge Saskatchewan 55.07N 105.18W
100 M3 La Ronge, L Saskatchewan
41 P2 La-Rons'yer, Os *isld* Franz Josef Land U.S.S.R.
93 C2 Laropi Uganda 3.34N 31.51E
72 J6 Laroquebrou France 44.58N 2.11E
72 H10 Laroque d'Olmes France 42.58N 1.52E
72 F7 Laroque-Timbaut France 44.17N 0.46E
115 J5 La Rosa Mexico 25.37N 101.24W
107 F12 Larose Louisiana 29.33N 90.23W
115 J3 La Rosita Mexico 28.21N 101.38W
76 D5 Larouco *mt* Portugal 41.53N 7.44W
76 D5 Larouco, Sa do Portugal
75 G2 Larraga Spain 42.33N 1.50W
75 G2 Larrainzar Spain 42.58N 1.41W
75 F2 Larraona Spain 42.47N 2.15W
75 G2 Larrasoaña Spain 42.54N 1.32W
72 C9 Larrau France 43.01N 0.56W
72 G8 Larrazet France 43.56N 1.05E
14 C5 Larrey Pt W Australia 19.59S 119.06E
13 C3 Larrimah N Terr Australia 15.31S 133.10E
75 F2 Larríon Spain 42.42N 2.04W
121 D5 Larroude Argentina 35.01S 63.32W
98 L8 Larry's River Nova Scotia 45.13N 61.23W
34 N7 Larsa *anc site* Iraq 31.14N 45.51E
123 C4 Lars Christensen Coast Antarctica
60 L10 Larsen Netherlands 52.26N 5.32E
113 L8 Larsen Bay Alaska 57.30N 154.00W
121 G8 Larsen Harbour S Georgia
123 E13 Larsen Ice Shelf Antarctica
108 D1 Larslan Montana 48.36N 106.16W
51 K8 Larsmo Finland 63.45N 22.45E
53 T14 Larsnes Norway 62.12N 5.35E
100 N1 Larson Ontario 49.06N 90.19W
121 E3 La Rubia Argentina 30.09S 61.46W
112 M3 Larue Texas 32.07N 95.41W
72 D10 Laruns France 42.59N 0.25W
25 L8 Laruri Nagaland India 25.44N 94.29E
52 E7 Larvik Norway 59.04N 10.02E
42 C2 Lar'yak U.S.S.R. 61.10N 80.20E
72 L7 Larzac *reg* France
79 J1 Lasa Italy 46.38N 10.42E
121 F1 La Sabana Argentina 27.53S 59.59W
119 F6 La Sabana Colombia 2.24N 68.29W
87 L6 Las Adeh Somalia 10.00N 46.37E
19 F5 Lasahata Moluccas Indon 2.50S 128.27E
111 P3 La Sal Utah 38.18N 109.15W
109 F1 La Salle Colorado 40.21N 104.43W
71 D8 Lasalle France 44.03N 3.51E
106 E8 La Salle Illinois 41.20N 89.06W
100 U9 La Salle Manitoba 49.41N 97.15W
99 G10 La Salle Ontario 42.15N 83.05W

99 R10 La Salle Quebec 45.26N 73.40W
77 K7 Las Alpujarras dist Spain
18 L5 Lasan Borneo Indonesia 1.10N 115.10E
15 J7 Lasanga I Papua New Guinea 7.25S 147.16E
109 G3 Las Animas Colorado 38.03N 103.14W
115 C3 Las Animas, Pta Mexico 28.50N 113.18W
87 L6 Las Anod Somalia 8.26N 47.19E
96 U7 La Santa Lanzarote Canary Is 29.05N 13.40W
75 D1 Las Arenas Spain 43.19N 3.00W
96 S14 Las Arenitas Tenerife Canary Is 28.13N 16.21W
121 F6 Las Armas Argentina 37.01S 57.51W
99 L4 La Sarre Quebec 48.49N 79.12W
75 F1 Lasarte Spain 43.15N 2.01W
116 L9 Las Aves, Islas Lesser Antilles 11.59N 67.30W
121 E2 Las Avispas Argentina 29.55S 61.15W
115 L8 Las Bajadas airport Mexico 19.10N 96.12W
115 M3 Las Banderas Nicaragua 12.20N 85.58W
75 H3 Las Bárdenas reg Spain
76 G8 Las Batuecas V Spain
65 L5 Lasberg Austria 48.28N 14.34E
76 K7 Las Berlanas Spain 40.48N 4.45W
119 G4 Las Bonitas Venezuela 7.50N 65.40W
76 F2 Las Brañas reg Spain
118 A10 Las Breñas Argentina 27.00S 61.05W
53 D4 Låsby Denmark 56.09N 9.50E
121 B5 Las Cabras Chile 34.14S 71.30W
77 M4 Las Cabras mt Spain 38.04N 2.23W
116 J5 Lascahobas Haiti 18.51N 71.56W
76 L2 Las Caldas de Besaya Spain 43.18N 4.05W
96 S13 Las Caletillas Tenerife Canary Is 28.14N 16.20W
96 R14 Las Cañadas Tenerife Canary Is
121 D2 Las Cañas Argentina 28.10S 65.16W
115 M4 Las Cañas Costa Rica 10.26N 85.08W
96 V14 Las Canteras Gran Canaria Canary Is 28.09N 15.26W
77 L2 Las Canteras mt Spain 39.06N 2.58W
81 G8 Lascari Sicily 38.00N 13.57E
115 F10 Las Cascadas Panama Canal Zone 9.05N 79.41W
77 K6 Las Catitas mt Spain 37.11N 3.18W
120 F12 Las Cejas Argentina 26.51S 64.45W
121 C9 Las Chapas Argentina 43.38S 66.40W
98 R4 La Scie Newfoundland 49.58N 55.36W
75 H4 Las Cinco Villas reg Spain
121 B7 Las Colorados Neuquén Arg 39.32S 70.35W
121 F5 Las Conchas Argentina 34.28S 58.34W
118 B5 Las Conchas Bolivia 17.25S 59.34W
77 J4 Las Correderas Spain 38.23N 3.30W
115 D5 Las Cruces Baja Cal Mexico 24.15N 110.10W
115 F3 Las Cruces Chihuahua Mexico 29.28N 107.22W
109 D9 Las Cruces New Mexico 32.18N 106.47W
76 C3 Las Cruces Spain 42.47N 8.10W
119 D3 Las Cruces Venezuela 8.46N 72.30W
75 G6 Las Cuerlas Spain 40.57N 1.34W
75 K6 Las Cuevas de Cañart Spain 40.46N 0.26W
119 C7 Las Cuevas de los Guacharos caves Colombia 1.41N 76.00W
65 L3 Lásenice Czechoslovakia 49.05N 14.59E
121 B2 La Serena Chile 29.54S 71.18W
75 O2 Las Escaldes Andorra 42.31N 1.32E
115 J4 Las Esperancas Mexico 27.47N 101.21W
77 M5 Las Estancias, Sierra de mts Spain
121 F6 Las Flores Buenos Aires Arg 36.03S 59.08W
120 F11 Las Flores Salta Arg 24.23S 63.50W
75 L5 Las Garrigas plain Spain
Lasgird see Låsjerd
121 C10 Las Golondrinas Argentina 44.45S 67.05W
75 C9 Las Guadalerzas reg Spain
32 J7 Lāshār R Iran
87 J5 Lasharad Ethiopia 10.37N 42.28E
100 H5 Lashburn Saskatchewan 53.08N 109.36W
31 A5 Lāsh-e Joveyn Afghanistan 31.43N 61.37E
121 C4 Las Heras Argentina 32.48S 68.50W
76 K9 Las Herencias Spain 39.52N 4.55W
25 D1 Lashio Burma 22.58N 97.48E
30 B6 Lashkar Madhya Prad India 26.12N 78.08E
31 C5 Lashkar Gah Afghanistan 31.30N 64.20E
Lashkar Satma see Akfaz
45 N2 Lashma U.S.S.R. 54.55N 41.10E
120 D5 Las Hormigas Peru 12.46S 69.51W
121 K7 Las Horquetas Argentina 48.08S 71.15W
76 G8 Las Hurdes V Spain
18 B4 Lasia isld Indonesia
18 B4 Lasikin Indonesia 2.22N 96.20E
121 J9 La Silveta pk Chile 52.23S 72.11W
62 L2 Łasin Poland 53.30N 19.02E
45 N1 Lasino U.S.S.R. 55.03N 41.45E
115 M3 La Sirena Nicaragua 12.59N 84.35W
84 N11 Lasíthi prov Crete
32 E3 Läsjerd Iran 35.24N 53.06E
121 B5 Las Juntas Argentina 35.14S 69.29W
115 M4 Las Juntas Costa Rica 10.18N 85.00W
62 L4 Łask Poland 51.37N 19.10E
32 D3 Laskarak Iran 35.54N 51.34E
82 C4 Laško Yugoslavia 46.10N 15.16E
62 L2 Laskowice Poland 53.30N 18.25E
77 J2 Las Labores Spain 39.17N 3.31W
121 B7 Las Lajas Argentina 38.30S 70.28W
115 O5 Las Lajas Panama 8.15N 81.51W
119 G4 Las Lajitas Venezuela 6.57N 65.40W
115 K6 Las Lavaderos Mexico 23.31N 98.04W
75 P3 Las Llosas Spain 42.09N 2.07E
119 B10 Las Lomas Peru 4.40S 80.15W
118 A9 Las Lomitas Argentina 24.41S 60.35W
77 C6 Las Marismas marshland Spain
121 L6 Las Martinetas Argentina 47.23S 67.40W
119 F3 Las Mercedes Venezuela 9.08N 66.27W
115 L3 Las Mercedes airport Nicaragua 12.10N 86.16W
77 L2 Las Mesas Spain 39.24N 2.45W
76 F2 Las Mestas Spain 43.08N 6.31W
115 G3 Las Mesteñas Mexico 28.15N 104.34W
115 O6 Las Minas Panama 7.49N 80.41W
119 G2 Las Minas Venezuela 10.04N 64.38W
76 L10 Las Navas R Spain
76 L7 Las Navas del Marquès Spain 40.35N 4.20W
61 H4 Lasne-Chapelle-St.-Lambert Belgium 50.42N 4.29E
77 M7 Las Negras Spain 36.53N 2.01W
96 P10 Las Nieves La Palma Canary Is 28.42N 17.44W
115 G4 Las Nieves Mexico 26.26N 105.21W
66 O8 Lasnigo Italy 45.53N 9.16E
77 N6 Las Norias Spain 37.28N 1.51W
119 G2 La Sola isld Venezuela 11.22N 63.37W
19 C5 Lasolo Celebes Indonesia 3.28S 122.06E
19 B5 Lasolo R Celebes Indonesia
19 C5 Lasolo, Teluk B Celebes Indon
76 H3 Las Omañas Spain 42.40N 5.52W
65 F8 Lasorling, mt Austria 46.59N 12.20E
121 F1 Las Palmas Argentina 27.08S 58.45W
115 O5 Las Palmas Panama 8.09N 81.28W
111 H9 Las Palmas R Mexico
96 V15 Las Palmas de Gran Canaria Canary Is 28.08N 15.27W
109 C8 Las Palomas New Mexico 33.03N 107.19W
77 L2 Las Pedroñeras Spain 39.27N 2.41W
118 B5 Las Petas Bolivia 16.22S 59.10W
118 B5 Las Petas, R Bolivia
121 G5 Las Piedras Uruguay 34.42S 56.14W
119 E2 Las Piedras Venezuela 11.44N 70.12W
121 F5 Las Pipinas Argentina 35.30S 57.15W
75 Q3 Las Planas Spain 42.03N 2.32E
119 C4 Las Playos airport Colombia 6.15N 75.33W
121 C9 Las Plumas Argentina 43.43S 67.16W
76 E4 Las Portas, Embalse de res Spain 42.08N 7.20W
31 G2 Laspur Pakistan 36.03N 72.30E
115 P10 Las Quebradas Guatemala 15.21N 88.42W
101 L11 Lasqueti I Br Columbia 49.28N 124.20W
77 N5 Las Reales mt Spain 37.37N 1.32W
121 E4 Las Rosas Argentina 32.27S 61.30W
76 L3 Las Rozas Spain 42.58N 4.02W
75 C7 Las Rozas de Madrid Spain 40.30N 3.53W
87 L6 Lassada Somalia 8.35N 46.55E
63 N5 Lassahn E Germany 53.36N 10.58E
75 A2 Las Salas Spain 42.56N 5.06W
76 D5 Las Salas, Embalse de res Spain 41.55N 7.55W
63 T5 Lassan E Germany 53.57N 13.52E
118 G5 Lassance Brazil 17.50S 44.37W
70 K5 Lassay-les-Châteaux France 48.26N 0.29W
51 J5 Lassbyn Sweden 66.03N 21.50E
65 P5 Lassee Austria 48.14N 16.49E
110 D9 Lassen Pk California 40.30N 121.30W
110 D9 Lassen Volcanic Nat. Park Cal
72 D9 Lasseube France 43.13N 0.29W
69 D4 Lassigny France 49.36N 2.51E
65 L6 Lassing Austria 47.46N 14.54E
91 C4 Lassio R Gabon
123 E12 Lassiter Coast Antarctica
65 K7 Lassnitzdorf Austria 47.05N 14.12E
65 N7 Lassnitzhöhe Austria 47.06N 15.37E
99 R7 L'Assomption Quebec 45.48N 73.27W
70 J4 Lassy France 48.54N 0.40W
115 K6 Las Tablas Mexico 22.17N 99.52W
115 O6 Las Tablas Panama 7.49N 80.16W
120 E11 Lastarria vol Arg/Chile 25.10S 68.31W
109 G2 Last Chance Colorado 39.45N 103.36W
79 K3 Lastebasse Italy 45.55N 11.17E
79 L2 Lastè delle Sute mt Italy 46.14N 11.32E
84 B6 Lastéika Greece 37.42N 21.25E
121 D1 Las Termas Argentina 27.30S 64.50W
57 M4 Lastingham N Yorks Eng 54.18N 0.52W
100 N7 Last Mountain ra Saskatchewan
100 M7 Last Mountain L Saskatchewan
75 H5 Las Torcas, Embalse de res Spain 41.17N 1.05W
77 O4 Las Torres de Cotillas Spain 38.01N 1.14W
121 F2 Las Toscas Argentina 28.22S 59.20W
72 J9 Lastours France 43.20N 2.22E
91 C4 Lastoursville Gabon 0.50S 12.43E
82 D8 Lastovo isld Yugoslavia
121 E6 Lastra Argentina 37.28S 61.18W
79 K7 Lastra a Signa Italy 43.46N 11.07E
76 L6 Lastras de Cuéllar Spain 41.17N 4.06W
76 J1 Lastres, C. de Spain 43.32N 5.18W
115 F7 Las Tres Marías islds Mexico
115 C4 Las Tres Vírgenes, Vol Mexico 27.27N 112.37W
119 G4 Las Trincheras Venezuela 6.57N 64.55W
63 G7 Lastrup W Germany 52.48N 7.51E
82 D6 Lašva Yugoslavia 44.08N 17.56E
115 G3 Las Varas Chihuahua Mexico 28.09N 105.20W
119 F4 Las Varas Colombia 6.09N 68.13W
115 G7 Las Varas Nayarit Mexico 21.12N 105.10W
121 E3 Las Varillas Argentina 31.54S 62.45W
111 J5 Las Vegas Nevada 36.10N 115.10W
109 E6 Las Vegas New Mexico 35.36N 105.15W
76 H7 Las Veguillas Spain 40.43N 5.50W
76 L9 Las Ventas con Peña Aguilera Spain 39.37N 4.14W
76 J8 Las Ventas de San Julian Spain 40.00N 5.18W
115 E3 Las Veras Chihuahua Mexico 29.31N 107.58W
77 M5 Las Vertientes Spain 37.36N 2.24W
116 D3 Las Villas prov Cuba
76 J10 Las Villuercas reg Spain
29 E4 Laswari Rajasthan India 27.32N 76.50E
87 M6 Las Warwar Somalia 9.01N 48.59E
120 D7 Las Yaras Peru 17.52S 70.35W
44 D4 Lata Georgia U.S.S.R. 43.04N 41.31E
119 B8 Latacunga Ecuador 0.58S 78.36W
123 F13 Latady I Antarctica
119 D8 La Tagua Colombia 0.05S 74.39W
34 C3 Latakia Syria 35.31N 35.47E
19 E4 Latalata isld Moluccas Indon 0.15S 127.03E
51 J3 Latäseno R Finland
99 L5 Latchford Ontario 47.20N 79.47W
15 A7 Latdalam Moluccas Indon 7.59S 131.09E
9 T10 Late isld Tonga, Pacific Oc 18.49S 174.40W
53 V19 Låtefoss waterfall Norway 59.57N 6.36E
79 L2 Latemar mt Italy 46.23N 11.35E
79 L7 Laterina Italy 43.31N 11.42E
81 N2 Laterza Italy 40.37N 16.48E
112 M4 Latexo Texas 31.23N 95.31W
107 G2 Latham Illinois 39.59N 89.10W
14 B8 Latham W Australia 29.46S 116.25E
12 A5 Latham dist Canberra Australia
70 L7 Lathan R France
63 F7 Lathen W Germany 52.52N 7.19E
58 K2 Latheron Highland Scotland 58.17N 3.22W
29 B7 Lathi Gujarat India 21.45N 71.28E
29 B4 Lathi Rajasthan India 26.59N 71.37E
31 J4 Latho Kashmir 33.42N 77.43E
107 B2 Lathrop Missouri 39.32N 94.19W
111 H5 Lathrop Wells Nevada 36.38N 116.23W
72 F3 Lathus France 46.20N 0.58E
61 K4 Lathuy Belgium 50.43N 4.49E
81 Q11 Latiano Italy 40.33N 17.44E
32 F7 Lātīdān Iran 27.07N 55.47E
52 K2 Latikberg Sweden 64.39N 17.05E
33 H8 Lāṭikhiyah,Al S Yemen 17.20N 49.00E
72 E2 Latillé France 46.37N 0.05E
80 G6 Latina Italy 41.28N 12.53E
119 B10 La Tina Peru 4.33S 79.59W
80 H6 Latina dist Italy
75 N8 Latina dist Madrid Spain
121 E1 La Tinajas Argentina 27.30S 62.50W
80 G5 Latina Scalo Italy 41.32N 12.57E
109 E5 Latir Pk New Mexico 36.47N 105.28W
79 N3 Latisana Italy 45.46N 13.00E
45 K5 Latnaya U.S.S.R. 51.43N 38.55E
81 N2 Lato R Italy
119 B7 La Tola Ecuador 1.09N 79.02W
121 D4 La Toma Argentina 33.02S 65.38W
82 H2 Latoritsa R U.S.S.R.
75 N2 La Torrasa, Embalse de res Spain
119 G2 La Tortuga, I Venezuela 11.00N 65.22W
113 O6 Latouche Alaska 60.01N 147.59W
14 D4 Latouche Treville, C W Australia 18.28S 121.54E
90 G1 Latouma Niger 22.10N 14.50E
61 N8 Latour Belgium 49.33N 5.35E
71 B5 Latour-d'Auvergne France 45.32N 2.42E
72 H11 Latour-de-Carol France 42.28N 1.51E
72 K10 Latour-de-France France 42.46N 2.39E
89 H7 Latouro Ivory Coast 9.35N 3.03W
72 G9 Latrape France 43.15N 1.17E
50 B2 Látrar Iceland 66.24N 23.01W
50 C2 Latravík inlet Ísafjardharsýsla, Nordhur Iceland
50 B5 Látravik inlet Snæfellsnessýsla Iceland
75 K3 Latre Spain 42.25N 0.29W
69 H8 Latrecey France 47.59N 4.52E
118 F2 La Três Rios res Brazil
99 P3 La Trève, L Quebec
19 K3 La Trinidad Luzon Philippines 16.28N 120.37E
115 L3 La Trinidad Nicaragua 12.57N 86.15W
119 E4 La Trinidad Venezuela 7.15N 69.06W
119 E4 La Trinidad de Orichuna Venezuela 7.10N 69.45W
115 N9 La Trinitaria Mexico 16.10N 92.01W
116 L3 La Trinité Martinique W I 14.44N 60.58W
104 F6 Latrobe Pennsylvania 40.18N 79.14W
12 H8 Latrobe Tasmania 41.13S 146.23E
77 M2 Latronadero mt Spain 39.04N 2.24W
81 M3 Latronico Italy 40.05N 16.01E
72 J6 Latronquière France 44.48N 2.04E
121 C2 La Troya, R Argentina
35 C6 Latrun Jordan 31.50N 34.59E
65 H8 Latschur mt Austria 46.45N 13.25E
105 H3 Latta S Carolina 34.21N 79.28W
Lattaquie see Latakia
81 M5 Lattarico Italy 39.28N 16.08E
80 K7 Lattari, Monti Italy
60 Q10 Lattrop Netherlands 52.26N 6.59E
104 A5 Latty Ohio 41.05N 84.35W
19 D8 Latuna Indonesia 8.25S 124.06E
99 S5 La Tuque Quebec 47.26N 72.47W
50 G2 Látur Iceland 66.07N 18.17W
28 C1 Latur Maharashtra India 18.24N 76.34E
Latvia see Latviya S.S.R.
46 D2 Latviya S.S.R U.S.S.R.
La-tzu see Lhazê
15 L6 Lau New Britain 5.51S 151.20E
90 E7 Lau Nigeria 9.11N 11.19E
87 C7 Lau Sudan 6.45N 30.25E
29 J6 Laua R Madhya Prad India
64 G2 Laubach Hessen W Germany 50.33N 9.00E
64 D3 Laubach Rheinland-Pfalz W Ger 50.03N 7.31E
94 F2 Lauban Namibia 18.20S 20.33E
10 R6 Lau Basin Pacific Oc
70 H6 Laubrières France 47.57N 1.04W
64 E3 Laubuseschbach W Germany 50.23N 8.20E
120 E8 Lauca R Bolivia
64 M1 Laucha E Germany 51.14N 11.40E
63 T10 Lauchhammer E Germany 51.30N 13.48E
64 J6 Lauchheim W Germany 48.53N 10.16E
101 T1 Lauchlan R Victoria I, N W Terr
64 H4 Lauda-Königshofen W Germany 49.34N 9.43E
52 C8 Laudal Norway 58.15N 7.30E
53 V14 Laudalstinder mt Norway 62.03N 6.36E
64 H5 Laudenbach W Germany 49.25N 9.57E
58 L7 Lauder Borders Scotland 55.43N 2.45W
100 R9 Lauder Manitoba 49.24N 100.40W
107 H9 Lauderdale Mississippi 32.32N 88.30W
58 L7 Lauderdale dist Borders Scotland
105 B10 Lauderdale-by-the-Sea Florida 26.10N 80.07W
71 F8 Laudun France 44.06N 4.39E
63 K8 Lauenau W Germany 52.17N 9.22E
63 L6 Lauenbruck W Germany 53.12N 9.32E
63 N6 Lauenburg an der Elbe W Germany 53.23N 10.33E
66 F6 Lauenen Switzerland 46.27N 7.20E
63 K9 Lauenförde W Germany 51.39N 9.22E
63 L8 Lauenstein W Germany 52.04N 9.33E
64 J3 Lauer R W Germany
66 L3 Lauerz Switzerland 47.02N 8.36E
66 L3 Lauerzer See L Switzerland 47.03N 8.36E
64 L4 Lauf W Germany 49.30N 11.16E
64 G3 Laufach W Germany 50.01N 9.22E
50 F7 Laufafell mt Iceland 63.54N 19.18W
50 G3 Laufás Iceland 65.54N 18.02W
66 H2 Laufelfingen Switzerland 47.24N 7.52E
66 G2 Laufen Switzerland 47.26N 7.31E
64 O8 Laufen W Germany 47.56N 12.56E
66 J1 Laufenburg Switzerland 47.34N 8.04E
65 J6 Lauffen Austria 47.41N 13.38E
64 G5 Lauffen am Neckar W Germany 49.05N 9.11E
50 G5 Laugafell mt Iceland 65.00N 18.21W
50 E6 Laugarvatn L Iceland 64.13N 20.43W
50 E6 Laugarvatnsfjall mt Iceland 64.16N 20.45W
56 C4 Laugharne Dyfed Wales 51.47N 4.28W
106 H3 Laughing Fish Pt Michigan 46.32N 86.59W
15 M8 Laughlan Is Papua New Guinea 9.12S 153.32E
13 C6 Laughlen Mt N Terr Australia 23.20S 134.20E
109 F5 Laughlin Pk New Mexico 36.37N 104.12W
56 M6 Laughton E Sussex Eng 50.54N 0.09E
72 F7 Laugnac France 44.18N 0.37E
10 R5 Lau Group islds Fiji
64 J6 Lauingen (Donau) W Germany 48.33N 10.26E
77 L7 Laujar de Andarax Spain 37.00N 2.53W
51 M9 Laukaa Finland 62.27N 25.58E
30 K6 Laukaha Bihar India 26.33N 86.28E
30 K6 Laukahi Bihar India 26.28N 86.33E
122 C1 Laulii W Samoa, Pacific Oc 13.50S 171.42W
40 G9 Laulyu U.S.S.R. 45.47N 135.18E
114 C7 Laumaia Hawaiian Is 19.45N 155.22W
71 E1 Laumes, les France 47.33N 4.28E
25 E7 Laun Thailand 10.10N 98.45E
72 G8 Launac France 43.45N 1.11E
72 G8 Launaguet France 43.41N 1.27E
99 M4 Launay Quebec 48.39N 78.30W
70 B5 Launay, P France 48.13N 4.06W
56 C6 Launceston Cornwall Eng 50.38N 4.21W
12 H8 Launceston Tasmania 41.25S 147.07E
76 B6 Laundos Portugal 41.26N 8.44W
59 C7 Laune, R Kerry Irish Rep
25 N8 Launggyaung Burma 25.57N 98.09E
25 E6 Launglon Burma 14.00N 98.08E
25 D6 Launglon Bok Is Burma
120 G6 La Unión Bolivia 15.18S 61.10W
121 A8 La Unión Chile 40.15S 73.02W
119 C7 La Unión Colombia 1.35N 77.09W
115 Q11 La Unión El Salvador 13.20N 87.50W
115 L2 La Unión Honduras 15.02N 86.40W
120 B3 La Unión Huánuco Peru 9.47S 76.45W
115 J8 La Unión Mexico 18.00N 101.48W
109 D10 La Union New Mexico 31.57N 106.41W
119 B10 La Unión Piura Peru 5.27S 80.45W
119 F3 La Unión Venezuela 8.15N 67.46W
114 D6 Launiupoko Hawaiian Is 20.51N 156.30W
69 H4 Launois-sur-Vence France 49.39N 4.32E
65 K8 Launsdorf Austria 46.47N 14.28E
114 C7 Laupahoehoe Hawaiian Is 20.00N 155.15W
53 W14 Lauparen mt Norway 62.27N 6.06E
66 E4 Laupen Switzerland 46.57N 7.15E
66 G4 Lauperswil Switzerland 46.58N 7.45E
64 H7 Laupheim W Germany 48.13N 9.55E
19 K4 Laur Luzon Philippines 15.36N 121.15E
87 C7 Lau,R Sudan
13 G3 Laura Queensland 15.30S 144.30E
100 K7 Laura Saskatchewan 51.51N 107.18W
12 E5 Laura S Australia 33.08S 138.19E
72 H8 Lauragais reg France
72 J9 Lauraguel France 43.05N 2.10E
119 F4 La Urbana Venezuela 7.06N 66.55W
53 D4 Laurbjerg Denmark 56.22N 9.56E
81 M7 Laureana di Borrello Italy 38.29N 16.05E
104 K8 Laurel Delaware 38.32N 75.34W
107 L2 Laurel Indiana 39.31N 85.11W
103 A8 Laurel Maryland 39.06N 76.51W
107 G10 Laurel Mississippi 31.41N 89.09W
110 R4 Laurel Montana 45.40N 108.46W
108 N7 Laurel Nebraska 42.14N 97.05W
99 K9 Laurel Ontario 43.57N 80.14W
103 C6 Laureldale Pennsylvania 40.23N 75.55W
118 B10 Laureles Paraguay 27.14S 57.25W
107 K11 Laurel Hill Florida 30.58N 86.29W
104 F7 Laurel Hill Pennsylvania
103 F6 Laurelton New Jersey 40.04N 74.08W
104 C7 Laurelville Ohio 39.29N 82.56W
72 K9 Laure-Minervois France 43.16N 2.31E
58 M5 Laurencekirk Grampian Scotland 56.50N 2.29W
59 F5 Laurencetown Galway Irish Rep 53.14N 8.10W
71 C9 Laurens France 43.30N 3.12E
108 Q7 Laurens Iowa 42.51N 94.51W
103 D1 Laurens New York 42.32N 75.06W
105 E3 Laurens S Carolina 34.29N 82.01W
69 L2 Laurensberg W Germany 50.48N 6.03E
26 A16 Laurens Pen Heard I Antarctica
48 K5 Laurentian Basin Arctic Oc
99 R7 Laurentides Quebec 45.51N 73.45W
99 T5 Laurentides, Parc Prov. des Quebec
81 L3 Laurenzana Italy 40.28N 15.58E
30 C7 Lauri Madhya Prad India 25.09N 80.00E
81 L3 Lauria Italy 40.03N 15.50E
120 B4 Lauricocha, L Peru 10.19S 76.39W
Lau Ridge see South Fiji Ridge
14 E7 Laurie, Mt W Australia 26.23S 123.50E
100 Q2 Laurie R Manitoba
100 S8 Laurier Manitoba 50.55N 99.35W
72 G3 Laurière France 46.04N 1.29E
100 R2 Laurie River Manitoba 56.13N 101.00W
99 T6 Laurierville Quebec 46.17N 71.40W
57 E3 Laurieston Dumfries & Galloway Scotland 54.57N 4.03W
12 L4 Laurieton New S Wales 31.40S 152.48E
51 L6 Laurila Finland 65.50N 24.30E
110 N4 Laurin Montana 45.22N 112.07W
105 H3 Laurinburg N Carolina 34.46N 79.29W
81 K3 Laurino Italy 40.20N 15.20E
71 G9 Lauris France 43.45N 5.18E
11 F10 Lauriston New Zealand 43.44S 171.48E
81 K3 Laurito Italy 40.09N 15.24E
51 N10 Lauritsala Finland 61.05N 28.20E
106 F2 Laurium Michigan 47.16N 88.27W
30 H6 Lauriya Nandangarh Bihar India 27.00N 84.24E
80 L7 Lauro Italy 40.52N 14.37E
78 F11 Lauro, M Sicily 37.06N 14.50E
121 J2 Lauro Muller Brazil 28.25S 49.21W
66 C5 Lausanne Switzerland 46.32N 6.39E
64 L3 Lauscha E Germany 50.28N 11.10E
62 H4 Lausitz, Nieder reg E Germany
62 H4 Lausitz, Ober reg E Germany
71 E7 Laussonne France 44.58N 4.02E
72 F6 Laussou France 44.35N 0.48E
18 H6 Laut isld Borneo Indon
18 M7 Laut isld Borneo Indon
71 J6 Lautaret, Col du pass France 45.02N 6.24E
121 A7 Lautaro Chile 38.30S 72.30W
121 J7 Lautaro, Cerro pk Chile 49.00S 73.25W
19 E8 Lautem Indonesia 8.24S 126.56E
69 N8 Lautenbach France 47.57N 7.10E
63 M9 Lautenthal W Germany 51.52N 10.17E
64 O2 Lauter E Germany 50.33N 12.47E
64 D5 Lauter R W Germany
66 P2 Lauterach Austria 47.29N 9.44E
64 M5 Lauterach R W Germany
64 E7 Lauterbach Baden-Württemberg W Ger 48.14N 8.20E
64 G2 Lauterbach Hessen W Ger 50.38N 9.24E
64 O1 Lauterbach Leipzig E Germany 51.10N 12.38E
63 T4 Lauterbach Rügen E Germany 54.21N 13.30E
69 P6 Lauterbourg France 48.58N 8.10E
66 H5 Lauterbrunnen Switzerland 46.36N 7.54E
64 D4 Lauterecken W Germany 49.39N 7.36E
64 M5 Lauterhofen W Germany 49.22N 11.36E
64 G2 Lautertal W Germany 50.35N 9.15E
64 K3 Lautertal (Kr. Coburg) W Germany 50.17N 10.59E
9 U5 Lauthala isld Fiji 16.46S 179.42W
51 L6 Lautiosaari Finland 65.49N 23.27E
64 F7 Lautlingen W Germany 48.13N 8.58E
9 R7 Lautoka Viti Levu Fiji 17.36S 177.28E
72 J8 Lautrec France 43.42N 2.08E
18 L7 Laut, Selat str Borneo Indon
53 Y17 Lauvdalenseter Norway 60.45N 8.20E
53 Z15 Lauvhø mt Norway 61.45N 8.31E
53 T14 Lauvstad Norway 62.10N 5.56E
61 M4 Lauw Belgium 50.44N 5.25E
69 N8 Lauw France 47.46N 7.02E
94 E4 Lauwater Namibia 23.12S 18.00E
61 C3 Lauwe Belgium 50.48N 3.12E
60 O5 Lauwers channel Netherlands 53.32N 6.24E
60 N6 Lauwerszee B Netherlands
60 O6 Lauwerzijl Netherlands 53.18N 6.17E
72 G7 Lauzerte France 44.16N 1.08E
72 H6 Lauzès France 44.34N 1.34E
71 J8 Lauzet-Ubaye France 44.25N 6.26E
98 A7 Lauzon Quebec 46.49N 71.10W
72 E6 Lauzun France 44.38N 0.28E
110 D8 Lava Beds Nat. Mon California 41.45N 121.30W
112 L6 Lavaca R Texas
112 L7 Lavaca B Texas
61 N6 Lavacherie Belgium 50.03N 5.31E
76 B4 Lavadores Spain 42.14N 8.41W
79 F6 Lavagna Italy 44.18N 9.21E
79 F6 Lavagna R Italy
110 N7 Lava Hot Springs Idaho 42.37N 112.00W
70 J5 Laval France 48.04N 0.45W
99 R9 Laval Quebec 45.34N 73.40W
99 R9 Laval des Rapides Quebec 45.33N 73.43W
71 E6 Lavalette, Barrage de France 45.09N 4.10E
121 C4 Lavalle Argentina 32.44S 68.38W
106 D6 La Valle Wisconsin 43.34N 90.08W
121 G5 Lavalleja dept Uruguay
103 F7 Lavallette New Jersey 39.58N 74.04W
98 C5 Laval, R Quebec
65 L8 Lavamünd Austria 46.39N 14.57E
35 B10 Lavan watercourse Israel
71 J10 Lavandou, le France 43.13N 6.21E
79 L6 Lavane, Monte mt Italy 44.00N 11.37E
51 F3 Lavangen Norway 68.47N 17.50E
15 L4 Lavanggu Solomon Is 11.42S 160.15E
99 O7 Lavant Ontario 45.03N 76.44W
65 L8 Lavant R Austria
65 L8 Lavant-tal V Austria
121 A6 Lavapié, Pta C Chile 37.10S 73.37W
75 O9 Lavapiés dist Madrid Spain
Lavar see Lāvar Kabkān
28 C2 Lavara Maharashtra India 18.00N 76.23E
72 E7 Lavardac France 44.11N 0.18E
72 F8 Lavardens France 43.46N 0.31E
70 M6 Lavardin France 47.44N 0.54E
70 M5 Lavaré France 48.03N 0.40E
32 D6 Lāvar Kabkān Iran 28.14N 51.16E
32 F5 Lāvar Meydān salt flat Iran
79 K3 Lavarone Italy 45.56N 11.15E
71 B1 Lavau France 47.36N 2.58E
72 J3 Lavaufranche France 46.19N 2.14E
72 H8 Lavaur France 43.41N 1.48E
72 E2 Lavausseau France 46.33N 0.05E
61 L6 Lavaux-Ste.-Anne Belgium 50.07N 5.05E
72 J3 Lavaveix-les-Mines France 46.04N 2.05E
111 C5 Laveaga Pk mt California 36.53N 121.11W
116 J5 La Vega Dominican Rep 19.15N 70.33W
115 H7 La Vega Mexico 20.35N 103.52W
119 E2 La Vela Venezuela 11.30N 69.33W
72 H10 Lavelanet France 42.56N 1.50E
80 N6 Lavello Italy 41.03N 15.48E
53 D4 Laven Denmark 56.07N 9.44E
53 W18 Låven mts Norway 60.03N 7.19E
66 M8 Lavena Italy 45.58N 8.53E
56 K3 Lavendon Bucks Eng 52.11N 0.40W
56 N3 Lavenham Suffolk Eng 52.06N 0.47E
79 E3 Laveno Italy 45.55N 8.37E
79 H3 Lavenone Italy 45.44N 10.26E
115 L2 La Venta Honduras 14.19N 87.12W
115 M8 La Venta ruins Mexico 18.07N 94.03W
69 D2 Laventie France 50.37N 2.46E
119 F4 La Venturosa Colombia 6.07N 68.49W
15 J1 L'Averdy, C Bougainville I Papua New Guinea 5.34S 155.00E
111 L4 La Verkin Utah 37.12N 113.15W
109 L5 Laverne Oklahoma 36.43N 99.55W
112 J6 La Vernia Texas 29.22N 98.08W
56 E5 Lavernock Pt S Glam Wales 51.24N 3.11W
95 M2 Laversburg S Africa 26.25S 28.30E
14 D8 Laverton W Australia 28.49S 122.25E
109 E4 La Veta Colorado 37.30N 105.01W
109 E4 La Veta Pass Colorado 37.33N 105.14W
66 E7 Lavey Switzerland 46.14N 7.01E
19 M5 Lavezares Philippines 12.32N 124.20E
79 L5 Lavezzola Italy 44.34N 11.52E
35 E2 Lavi Israel 32.47N 35.26E
51 K10 Lavia Finland 61.36N 22.35E
80 M7 Laviano Italy 40.47N 15.18E
115 H4 La Víbora Mexico 27.10N 103.00W
119 F2 La Victoria Venezuela 10.16N 67.21W
120 B9 La Victoria dist Lima Peru
99 M7 Lavieille, L Ontario 45.50N 78.15W
74 J8 Lavigerie Algeria 36.13N 2.24E
53 S16 Lavik Norway 61.06N 5.30E
56 V11 La Villiaze airport Channel Is 49.27N 2.36W
66 R4 Lavin Switzerland 46.47N 10.07E
120 F11 La Viña Argentina 25.30S 65.33W
110 R3 Lavina Montana 46.19N 108.57W
120 A8 La Viña Peru 6.56S 79.23W
79 B3 Lavina mt Italy 45.33N 7.27E
71 K2 Laviron France 47.15N 6.32E
79 K2 Lavis Italy 46.08N 11.07E
72 F8 Lavit France 43.58N 0.56E
119 G3 La Viuda Venezuela 8.45N 63.53W
120 B4 La Viuda pass Peru 11.20S 76.28W
66 L6 Lavizzara, Val Switzerland
39 H1 Lavka Integralsoyuza U.S.S.R. 68.47N 169.56E
84 F3 Lávkos Greece 39.10N 23.15E
61 L4 Lavoir Belgium 50.33N 5.07E
122 F8 Lavongai isld Bismarck Arch
105 D3 Lavonia Georgia 34.26N 83.09W
112 L2 Lavon Res Texas
66 M6 Lavorgo Switzerland 46.27N 8.51E
76 B8 Lavos Portugal 40.06N 8.50W
71 C6 Lavoûte-Chilhac France 45.10N 3.24E
71 D6 Lavoute-sur-Loire France 45.07N 3.55E
100 F5 Lavoy Alberta 53.28N 111.52W
76 E16 Lavradio Portugal 38.39N 9.04W
118 G7 Lavras Brazil 21.15S 44.59W
117 H8 Lavras da Mangabeira Brazil 6.41S 38.55W
121 H3 Lavras do Sul Brazil 30.48S 53.55W
76 C11 Lavre Portugal 38.46N 8.22W
76 C11 Lavre R Portugal
76 B11 Lavre sta Portugal 38.47N 8.31W
39 M2 Lavrentiya U.S.S.R. 65.37N 171.02W
84 H6 Lávrion Greece 37.43N 24.03E
45 H4 Lavrovo Orël U.S.S.R. 52.50N 36.01E
46 M4 Lavrovo Tambov U.S.S.R. 52.20N 40.58E
41 J7 Lavruska, Vozvyshennost' heights U.S.S.R.
52 K2 Lavsjö Sweden 64.13N 16.40E
95 O8 Lavumisa Swaziland 27.18S 31.55E
92 E8 Lavusi mt Zambia 12.25S 30.50E
25 M8 Lawa Burma 25.35N 96.46E
31 F4 Lawa Pakistan 32.43N 71.59E
29 D4 Lawa Rajasthan India 26.20N 75.38E
117 B3 Lawa R Surinam
30 F4 Lawamjula Nepal 28.17N 82.16E
93 D4 Lawampanga Uganda 1.33N 32.31E
29 H7 Lawan Madhya Prad India 21.40N 82.27E
18 M10 Lawang isld Indonesia 8.17S 116.40E
Lawarai Pass see Lowarai Pass
112 L7 La Ward Texas 28.52N 96.29W
18 L3 Lawas Sarawak Malaysia 4.50N 115.25E
19 B5 Lawatu Celebes Indonesia 2.54S 120.20E
33 F10 Lawdar S Yemen 13.53N 45.53E
19 C6 Lawele Indonesia 5.15S 123.00E
110 G6 Lawen Oregon 43.27N 118.47W
58 H5 Lawers Tayside Scotland 56.32N 4.10W
101 R2 Lawford Is N W Terr
100 V4 Lawford L Manitoba
13 K6 Lawgi Queensland 24.45S 150.49E
15 M9 Lawik Reef Louisiade Arch
18 B6 Lawin Pen Malaysia 5.18N 101.03E
19 F4 Lawin isld Moluccas Indon 1.30S 128.43E
18 K5 Lawit, Gunong mt Kalimantan/Sarawak 1.26N 112.58E
18 E3 Lawit, Gunong mt Pen Malaysia 5.28N 102.36E
35 F2 Lawiye Syria 32.51N 35.40E
25 D2 Lawksawk Burma 21.13N 96.50E
106 B6 Lawler Iowa 43.04N 92.10W
108 R3 Lawler Minnesota 46.30N 93.07W
94 S14 Lawley S Africa 26.22S 27.50E
14 F2 Lawley, R W Australia
98 R7 Lawn Newfoundland 46.56N 55.32W
103 A6 Lawn Pennsylvania 40.13N 76.32W
112 H3 Lawn Texas 32.07N 99.47W
105 F2 Lawndale N Carolina 35.24N 81.36W
13 E4 Lawn Hill Queensland 18.32S 138.32E
13 E4 Lawn Hill Cr Queensland
19 C6 Lawowa Indonesia 4.24S 122.59E
123 C5 Law Plat Antarctica
33 E2 Lawqah Saudi Arabia 29.50N 42.46E
89 H6 Lawra Ghana 10.40N 2.49W
107 K2 Lawrence Indiana 39.50N 86.01W
109 P3 Lawrence Kansas 38.58N 95.15W
104 O4 Lawrence Massachusetts 42.41N 71.12W
108 M9 Lawrence Nebraska 40.17N 98.15W
11 D12 Lawrence New Zealand 45.56S 169.43E
107 M2 Lawrenceburg Indiana 39.06N 84.51W
107 M3 Lawrenceburg Kentucky 38.02N 84.53W
107 J6 Lawrenceburg Tennessee 35.16N 87.20W
31 G4 Lawrencepore Pakistan 33.50N 72.32E
98 E8 Lawrence Station New Brunswick 45.26N 67.12W
59 K3 Lawrencetown Down N Ireland 54.23N 6.17W
98 G9 Lawrencetown Nova Scotia 44.54N 65.10W
98 J9 Lawrencetown Nova Scotia 44.38N 63.21W
105 D4 Lawrenceville Georgia 33.58N 83.59W
107 J3 Lawrenceville Illinois 38.44N 87.42W
103 E6 Lawrenceville New Jersey 40.17N 74.42W
104 H5 Lawrenceville Pennsylvania 41.59N 77.07W
104 H10 Lawrenceville Virginia 36.45N 77.50W
14 D7 Lawrence Wells, Mt W Australia 26.52S 120.10E
111 F4 Laws California 37.24N 118.21W
107 B2 Lawson Missouri 39.26N 94.12W
100 L8 Lawson Saskatchewan 50.53N 106.37W
15 J7 Lawson, Mt Papua New Guinea 7.43S 146.35E
103 C3 Lawsville Center Pennsylvania 41.56N 75.49W
105 E7 Lawtey Florida 30.03N 82.03W
57 J6 Lawton Cheshire Eng 53.06N 2.17W
106 J7 Lawton Michigan 42.10N 85.51W
108 M1 Lawton N Dakota 48.20N 98.21W
109 M7 Lawton Oklahoma 34.36N 98.25W
103 B3 Lawton Pennsylvania 41.46N 76.06W
18 J9 Lawu, Gunung mt Java Indon 7.40S 111.13E
11 M13 Lawyers Hd New Zealand 45.55S 170.32E
34 C10 Lawz, Jabal al mt Saudi Arabia 28.39N 35.18E
66 J6 Lax Switzerland 46.24N 8.08E
52 H7 Laxå Sweden 59.00N 14.37E
50 E6 Laxa R Árnessýsla Iceland
50 D6 Laxá R Borgarfjardharsýsla Iceland
50 D4 Laxá R Dalasýsla Iceland
50 D6 Laxá R Kjósarsýsla Iceland
50 K6 Laxá R Skaftafellssýsla, Austur Iceland
50 H3 Laxá R Thingeyjarsýsla, Sudhur Iceland
50 H3 Laxamýri Iceland 65.59N 17.20W
50 D3 Laxárdalsheidhi heath Iceland
50 E3 Laxárdalur V Húnavatnssýsla, Austur Iceland
50 L4 Laxárdalur V Múlasýsla, Nordhur Iceland
50 H3 Laxárdalur V Thingeyjarsýsla, Sudhur Iceland
50 E3 Laxárvatn L Iceland 65.35N 20.10W
58 C2 Laxay Lewis, W Isles Scotland 58.06N 6.31W
58 D2 Laxdale Lewis, W Isles Scotland 58.13N 6.23W
65 O5 Laxenburg Austria 48.04N 16.22E
57 E4 Laxey Isle of Man U.K. 54.14N 4.24W
56 O3 Laxfield Suffolk Eng 52.18N 1.22E
58 F2 Laxford Bridge Highland Scotland 58.22N 5.01W
84 R14 Laxla Cyprus 35.06N 33.22E
58 Q9 Laxo Shetland Scotland 60.21N 1.11W
24 E8 Laxong Co L Xizang Zizhiqu China 34.20N 85.00E
69 L6 Laxou France 48.41N 6.08E
52 H3 Laxsjö Sweden 63.49N 14.50E
109 C1 Lay Colorado 40.32N 107.54W
72 B2 Lay R France 46.34N 1.10W
47 M3 Laya U.S.S.R. 58.04N 59.56E
47 H3 Laya R U.S.S.R.
75 H3 Layana Spain 42.18N 1.15W
18 D10 Layang Layang Pen Malaysia 1.45N 103.30E
120 D8 La Yarada Peru 18.14S 70.32W
31 B9 Layāri R Pakistan
18 M8 Layar, Tanjung C Borneo Indon 4.04S 116.06E
59 K1 Layde Ch Antrim N Ireland 55.07N 6.03W
47 F2 Laydennyy,Mys C U.S.S.R. 68.25N 46.00E
69 C7 Laye R France
19 F7 Layeni Indonesia 6.59S 129.08E
12 G7 Layers Hill Victoria 38.41S 143.27E
84 D9 Láyia Greece 36.29N 22.29E
84 E8 Láyion Greece 36.50N 22.35E
87 M3 Layjūn S Yemen 15.33N 49.10E
107 K9 Lay L Alabama
44 E5 Layla mt Georgia U.S.S.R. 42.55N 42.35E
33 G5 Laylá oasis Saudi Arabia 22.16N 46.45E
34 M3 Laylān Iraq 35.17N 44.32E
47 K6 Layma R U.S.S.R.
75 F5 Layna Spain 41.05N 2.19W
72 C1 Layon R France
76 L9 Layos Spain 39.47N 4.04W
88 G8 La'Youn Morocco 27.10N 13.11W
72 F7 Layrac France 44.08N 0.40E
43 G2 Layrent'Yevka Kazakhstan U.S.S.R. 52.28N 63.30E
69 K6 Lay-St.Remy France 48.41N 5.47E
114 B1 Laysan I Hawaiian Is 25.46N 171.44W
103 K4 Laysville Connecticut 41.20N 72.17W
47 K6 Laytamak U.S.S.R. 58.29N 67.28E
103 E4 Layton New Jersey 41.12N 74.49W
59 K4 Laytown Meath Irish Rep 53.41N 6.14W
25 N8 Laza Burma 26.31N 97.42E
76 E4 Laza Spain 42.04N 7.28W
75 F3 Lazagurria Spain 42.30N 2.14W
84 D3 Lazár Boúga Greece 39.20N 22.27E
112 H1 Lazare Texas 34.17N 99.59W
26 S14 Lazare,Pt Mahé I Ind Oc 4.45S 55.28E
76 D16 Lazareto Portugal 38.40N 9.13W
40 J5 Lazarev U.S.S.R. 52.12N 141.27E
82 F6 Lazarevac Yugoslavia 44.23N 20.19E
43 E5 Lazareva, Oz isld Aral'skoye More U.S.S.R.
51 Q8 Lazarevo Karelia U.S.S.R. 63.34N 32.57E
45 J3 Lazarevo Tula U.S.S.R. 53.54N 37.31E
44 C4 Lazarevskoye U.S.S.R. 43.55N 39.23E
115 B2 Lázaro Cárdenas Baja California Mexico 31.24N 115.43W
115 G5 Lázaro Cárdenas, Presa res Durango Mexico
82 J7 Lazar Stanevo Bulgaria 43.06N 24.17E
121 E6 La Zauja Argentina 36.05S 62.50W
121 G4 Lazcano Uruguay 33.42S 54.12W
87 M5 Laz Daua Somalia 10.26N 49.07E
46 E3 Lazdijai Lithuania U.S.S.R. 54.12N 23.30E
32 E7 Lāzeh Iran 26.48N 53.24E
72 J1 Lazenay France 47.04N 2.03E
80 E4 Lazio prov Italy
79 J3 Lazise Italy 45.31N 10.44E
64 O3 Lázně Kynžvart Czechoslovakia 50.00N 12.43E
121 F4 Lazo Argentina 32.55S 59.27W
39 F6 Lazo Kamchatka U.S.S.R. 55.32N 159.45E
40 F10 Lazo Primor'ye U.S.S.R. 43.26N 133.49E
39 E3 Lazo, Imeni U.S.S.R. 63.12N 152.13E
57 H3 Lazonby Cumbria Eng 54.46N 2.41W
45 D6 Lazorki Ukraine U.S.S.R. 50.07N 32.40E
56 G4 Lea Hereford & Worcs Eng 51.54N 2.30W
57 M6 Lea Lincs Eng 53.22N 0.45W
90 B7 Leaba Nigeria 9.40N 4.35E
110 C5 Leaburg Oregon 44.06N 122.41W
25 G6 Leach Cambodia 12.18N 103.51E
75 H2 Leache Spain 42.36N 1.25W
99 F5 Leach I Ontario 47.28N 84.57W
107 F6 Leachville Arkansas 35.56N 90.17W
103 B6 Leacock Pennsylvania 40.05N 76.12W
108 G5 Lead S Dakota 44.21N 103.48W
58 K7 Leadburn Lothian Scotland 55.47N 3.14W
57 M6 Leadenham Lincs Eng 53.04N 0.35W
56 M4 Leaden Roding Essex Eng 51.48N 0.18E
100 H8 Leader Saskatchewan 50.55N 109.31W
57 F2 Leadhills Strathclyde Scotland 55.25N 3.47W
110 M5 Leadore Idaho 44.40N 113.23W
109 D2 Leadville Colorado 39.14N 106.18W
12 J4 Leadville New S Wales 32.01S 149.35E
97 M6 Leaf R Quebec
100 P5 Leaf L Saskatchewan 53.00N 102.10W
100 R2 Leaf Rapids Manitoba 56.30N 100.02W
106 E7 Leaf River Illinois 42.09N 89.24W
112 M6 League City Texas 29.30N 95.08E
123 J11 Leahy, C Antarctica
14 C7 Leake, Mt W Australia 25.50S 119.10E
14 F4 Leake, Mt W Australia 17.36S 126.03E
107 H10 Leakesville Mississippi 31.09N 88.34W
112 H6 Leakey Texas 29.44N 99.48W
108 M2 Leal N Dakota 47.08N 98.19W
107 G10 Leal R Mississippi
15 J8 Lea Lea Papua New Guinea 9.19S 146.50E
121 D1 Leales Argentina 27.13S 65.15W
14 B5 Leal, Mt W Australia 21.34S 117.19E
92 A9 Lealui Zambia 15.12S 22.59E
11 K4 Leamington New Zealand 37.54S 175.30E
99 H10 Leamington Ontario 42.03N 82.35W
111 M2 Leamington Utah 39.31N 112.17W
Leamington Spa, Royal see Royal Leamington Spa
56 J3 Leam,R Warwicks Eng
99 C8 Leamy Creek Quebec
99 C8 Leamy L Quebec
23 G5 Le 'An Jiangxi China 27.18N 115.42E
112 K5 Leander Texas 30.35N 97.54W
14 A8 Leander Pt W Australia 29.18S 114.53E
117 F7 Leandro Brazil 6.00S 44.55W
121 G1 Leandro N.Alem Argentina 27.34S 55.15W
59 C7 Leane,L Kerry Irish Rep 52.03N 9.33W
23 H4 Le'an Jiang R Jiangxi China
59 D8 Leap Cork Irish Rep 51.35N 9.08W
55 G3 Lea, R London/Essex/Herts England
14 A5 Learmonth W Australia 22.13S 114.04E
105 C6 Leary Georgia 31.30N 84.30W
57 N6 Leasingham Lincs Eng 53.01N 0.26W
100 L5 Leask Saskatchewan 53.02N 106.44W
56 L5 Leatherhead Surrey Eng 51.18N 0.20W
110 M5 Leatherman Pk Idaho 44.04N 113.44W
61 H6 L'Eau d'Heure res Belgium
107 K3 Leavenworth Indiana 38.13N 86.20W
109 Q2 Leavenworth Kansas 39.19N 94.55W
110 E2 Leavenworth Washington 47.36N 120.39W
111 E3 Leavitt Pk California 38.17N 119.39W
62 K1 Łeba Poland 54.45N 17.32E
62 K1 Łeba R Poland
64 B5 Lebach W Germany 49.25N 6.55E
18 G9 Lebak Java Indonesia 6.32S 106.10E
19 M8 Lebak Mindanao Philippines 6.30N 124.02E
110 B3 Lebam Washington 46.34N 123.31W
91 B5 Lébamba Gabon 2.18S 11.20E
82 G8 Lebane Yugoslavia 42.56N 21.45E
91 D3 Lebango Congo 0.24N 14.44E
103 K3 Lebanon Connecticut 41.38N 72.14W
107 G3 Lebanon Illinois 38.37N 84.49W
106 H9 Lebanon Indiana 40.02N 87.28W
109 M2 Lebanon Kansas 39.49N 98.33W
107 L4 Lebanon Kentucky 37.33N 85.15W
107 D4 Lebanon Missouri 37.40N 92.40W
108 K9 Lebanon Nebraska 40.05N 100.15W
104 N3 Lebanon New Hampshire 43.40N 72.15W
103 E5 Lebanon New Jersey 40.38N 74.50W
104 A7 Lebanon Ohio 39.26N 84.12W
110 C5 Lebanon Oregon 44.32N 122.54W
103 B6 Lebanon Pennsylvania 40.20N 76.25W
108 L4 Lebanon S Dakota 45.05N 99.43W
107 K5 Lebanon Tennessee 36.11N 86.19W
104 C10 Lebanon Virginia 36.52N 82.07W
103 A6 Lebanon co Pennsylvania
34 C4 Lebanon rep S W Asia
107 L4 Lebanon Junc Kentucky 37.50N 85.45W
103 H2 Lebanon Springs New York 42.29N 73.23W
105 E8 Lebanon Station Florida 29.10N 82.39W
43 F6 Lebap Uzbekistan U.S.S.R. 41.03N 61.52E
61 G3 Lebbeke Belgium 51.00N 4.08E
111 F7 Lebec California 34.51N 118.54W
42 D2 Lebed' U.S.S.R. 62.05N 89.15E
45 T5 Lebedevka Saratov U.S.S.R. 51.05N 47.09E
47 K7 Lebedevka Tyumen U.S.S.R. 56.49N 66.55E
45 C8 Lebedin Cherkassy, Ukraine U.S.S.R. 48.57N 31.31E
45 F6 Lebedin Sumy, Ukraine U.S.S.R. 50.36N 34.30E
45 L3 Lebedyan' U.S.S.R. 53.01N 39.07E
89 B2 Lebeira Mauritania 19.30N 14.05W
99 O3 Lebel sur Quévillon Quebec 49.01N 76.56W
88 S4 Leben,el watercourse Tunisia
62 K8 Lébény Hungary 47.44N 17.26E
66 G2 Lebern mts Switzerland
51 N1 Lebesby Norway 70.34N 27.00E
93 G7 Lebetero Hills Kenya
118 J10 Leblon Brazil 22.59S 43.14W
109 P3 Lebo Kansas 38.27N 95.53W
91 H1 Lebo Zaïre 4.30N 23.58E
95 O8 Lebomboberge mts S Africa
94 L4 Lebombo Mts Mozambique etc
25 B2 Lebon Burma 20.52N 93.57E
29 L4 Lebong W Bengal India 27.03N 88.25E
62 K1 Lębórk Poland 54.32N 17.43E
19 D8 Lebos Timor Indonesia 9.09S 125.14E
91 C5 Leboulou Congo 3.06S 12.24E
98 H6 Le Bouthillier New Brunswick 47.48N 64.56W
94 K5 Lebowa Bantu Homeland S Africa
100 O8 Lebret Saskatchewan 50.46N 103.42W
119 D4 Lebrija Colombia 7.09N 73.14W
77 D7 Lebrija Spain 36.55N 6.10W
62 K1 Łebsko,Jezioro L Poland
Lebtar,Jebel el mts see Abtar,Jebel el mts
121 A6 Lebu Chile 37.38S 73.43W
76 E5 Lebução Portugal 41.45N 7.15W
63 S9 Lebusa E Germany 51.48N 13.26E
53 E7 Leby Denmark 54.55N 10.17E
44 B2 Lebyazhiy,Liman lagoon U.S.S.R.
43 N2 Lebyazh'ye Kazakhstan U.S.S.R. 51.30N 77.45E
46 P2 Lebyazh'ye Kirov U.S.S.R. 57.28N 49.28E
47 K7 Lebyazh'ye Kurgan U.S.S.R. 55.18N 66.30E
47 L7 Lebyazhye Omsk U.S.S.R. 55.13N 71.00E
19 E8 Leça Indonesia 8.48S 126.34E
76 C6 Leça R Portugal
76 B6 Leça da Palmeira Portugal 41.12N 8.43W
116 L3 Le Carbet Martinique W I 14.43N 61.11W

81 R12 Lecce Italy 40.21N 18.11E
81 R12 Lecce prov Italy
79 F3 Lecco Italy 45.51N 9.23E
79 F3 Lecco, L. di Italy
108 R5 Le Center Minnesota 44.24N 93.45W
75 J5 Lécera Spain 41.11N 0.43W
80 O1 Lečevica Yugoslavia 43.38N 16.21E
65 B7 Lech Austria 47.13N 10.09E
64 K6 Lech R W Germany
23 F6 Lechang Guangdong China 25.11N 113.16E
66 D7 Le Châtelard Switzerland 46.04N 6.57E
64 K8 Lechbruck W Germany 47.42N 10.48E
69 E6 Léchelle France 48.35N 3.25E
72 E6 Lèches, les France 44.58N 0.25E
64 K7 Lechfeld W Germany 48.10N 10.51E
64 K7 Lechfeld plain W Germany
82 J3 Lechința Romania 47.01N 24.20E
44 E5 Lechkhumskiy Khrebet mts Georgia U.S.S.R.
56 H4 Lechlade Glos Eng 51.43N 1.41W
98 H4 L'Echouerie Quebec 49.04N 64.32W
65 B7 Lech Tal V Austria
65 B7 Lechtaler Alpen mts Austria
58 K4 Lecht Road Grampian Scotland
75 J4 Leciñena Spain 41.47N 0.37W
63 J3 Leck W Germany 54.47N 8.58E
64 Q5 Lecker mt Czechoslovakia 49.03N 13.39E
123 B5 Leckie Ra Antarctica
106 D8 Le Claire Iowa 41.35N 90.23W
69 E3 Lecluse France 50.16N 3.02E
107 D10 Lecompte Louisiana 31.04N 92.23W
61 L5 Le Condroz plat Belgium
57 N5 Leconfield Humberside Eng 53.53N 0.28W
Le Coq see De Haan
72 F8 Lectoure France 43.56N 0.38E
75 G1 Lecumberri Spain 43.00N 1.54W
62 O4 Łęczna Poland 51.20N 22.52E
62 L3 Łęczyca Poland 52.04N 19.10E
47 E5 Led R U.S.S.R.
63 G6 Leda R W Germany
77 N2 Ledaña Spain 39.21N 1.44W
75 E6 Ledanca Spain 40.52N 2.51W
18 C9 Ledang, Gunong mt Pen Malaysia 2.22N 102.36E
56 G3 Ledbury Hereford & Worcs Eng 52.02N 2.25W
61 F3 Lede Belgium 50.58N 3.59E
61 F2 Ledeberg Belgium 51.02N 3.46E
65 M2 Ledeč nad Sázava Czechoslovakia 49.42N 15.17E
61 C3 Ledegem Belgium 50.51N 3.07E
65 L4 Ledenice Czechoslovakia 48.57N 14.38E
72 J7 Lédergues France 44.06N 2.25E
Ledesma Argentina see Libertador General San Martin
76 H6 Ledesma Spain 41.05N 6.00W
14 C10 Ledge Pt W Australia 34.28S 119.13E
110 O1 Ledger Montana 48.16N 111.50W
93 N2 Ledi Kenya 3.46N 41.42E
116 L4 Le Diamant Martinique W I 14.29N 61.02W
91 E5 Lediba Zaïre 3.01S 16.34E
71 E9 Lédignan France 43.59N 4.06E
47 G3 Ledkovo U.S.S.R. 67.14N 50.30E
58 G2 Ledmore Highland Scotland 58.03N 4.58W
65 P4 Lednice Czechoslovakia 48.48N 16.48E
41 C2 Ledniki Nordenshel'da ice field Novaya Zemlya U.S.S.R.
18 H5 Ledo Borneo Indon 0.59N 109.35E
91 C8 Ledo,C Angola 9.43S 13.12E
23 E9 Ledong Guangdong China 18.43N 109.09E
79 J3 Ledro,L.di Italy 45.53N 10.45E
22 F8 Ledu Gansu China 36.31N 102.24E
100 D5 Leduc Alberta 53.17N 113.30W
18 C4 Ledung Sumatra Indonesia 2.45N 99.58E
41 D2 Ledyanaya Gavan' Bukhta B Novaya Zemlya U.S.S.R.
39 J4 Ledyanaya,Gora mt U.S.S.R. 61.49N 171.39E
103 K4 Ledyard Connecticut 41.27N 72.01W
62 K2 Lędyczek Poland 53.31N 17.01E
111 P10 Lee Arizona 31.27N 109.28W
53 D4 Lee Denmark 56.26N 9.43E
105 D7 Lee Florida 30.24N 83.20W
106 F8 Lee Illinois 41.48N 88.57W
103 H2 Lee Massachusetts 42.19N 73.15W
104 F6 Leechburg Pennsylvania 40.38N 79.37W
108 Q2 Leech L Minnesota
100 P7 Leech L Saskatchewan
64 K8 Leeder W Germany 47.56N 10.50E
14 B1 Leederville dist Perth, W Aust
109 L6 Leedey Oklahoma 35.53N 99.23W
107 K8 Leeds Alabama 33.32N 86.31W
103 J2 Leeds Massachusetts 42.22N 72.42W
108 L1 Leeds N Dakota 48.19N 99.28W
103 G2 Leeds New York 42.15N 73.54W
111 L4 Leeds Utah 37.14N 113.23W
57 K5 Leeds W Yorks Eng 53.50N 1.35W
104 P2 Leeds Junction Maine 44.12N 70.05W
56 T9 Leedstown Cornwall Eng 50.09N 5.22W
60 O7 Leek Netherlands 53.10N 6.24E
57 J6 Leek Staffs Eng 53.06N 2.01W
60 O7 Leekstermeer L Netherlands
58 L5 Lee,L Tayside Scotland 56.54N 2.56W
106 J5 Leelanau L Michigan
57 K4 Leeming N Yorks Eng 54.18N 1.33W
14 F2 Leeming,Mt W Australia 14.33S 126.38E
59 C4 Leenaun Galway Irish Rep 53.36N 9.41W
60 L14 Leende Netherlands 51.21N 5.34E
60 O6 Leens Netherlands 53.22N 6.22E
56 J6 Lee-on-the-Solent Hants Eng 50.48N 1.12W
107 F4 Leeper Missouri 37.03N 90.40W
104 F5 Leeper Pennsylvania 41.23N 79.17W
59 D8 Lee,R Cork Irish Rep
63 F6 Leer W Germany 53.14N 7.27E
88 M6 Lé Er airport Algeria 31.30N 2.13W
61 G3 Leerbeek Belgium 50.47N 4.07E
60 J12 Leerdam Netherlands 51.54N 5.06E
60 Q6 Leermens Netherlands 53.21N 6.48E
61 H5 Leernes Belgium 50.24N 4.20E
61 H5 Leers-et-Fosteau Belgium 50.18N 4.15E
61 D4 Leers-Nord Belgium 50.42N 3.16E
60 K11 Leersum Netherlands 52.01N 5.26E
72 C10 Lées-Athas France 42.58N 0.38W
105 F9 Leesburg Florida 28.49N 81.54W
105 C6 Leesburg Georgia 31.44N 84.11W
110 L4 Leesburg Idaho 45.15N 114.06W
103 E8 Leesburg New Jersey 39.15N 74.59W
104 B7 Leesburg Ohio 39.21N 83.30W
112 M3 Leesburg Texas 32.59N 95.06W
104 H7 Leesburg Virginia 39.09N 77.34W
63 K7 Leese W Germany 52.32N 9.07E
107 B3 Lees Summit Missouri 38.54N 94.22W
61 H2 Leest Belgium 51.02N 4.25E
14 D7 Lee Steere Ra W Australia
11 G10 Leeston New Zealand 43.46S 172.18E
107 C10 Leesville Louisiana 31.10N 93.19W
105 F4 Leesville S Carolina 33.56N 81.30W
112 K6 Leesville Texas 29.24N 97.45W
104 F9 Leesville Lake res Virginia
104 D6 Leesville Res Ohio 40.30N 81.11W
12 H5 Leeton New S Wales 34.33S 146.24E
104 E6 Leetonia Ohio 40.54N 80.46W
106 J5 Leetsville Michigan 44.47N 85.07W
95 F8 Leeu R S Africa
95 J8 Leeu R S Africa
95 G5 Leeuberg S Africa 29.31S 23.39E
95 K3 Leeudoringstad S Africa 27.14S 26.15E
94 G9 Leeugamka Cape Prov S Africa 32.45S 21.59E
94 P11 Leeukop hill Cape Town S Africa 33.56S 18.23E
95 J4 Leeukop mt S Africa 28.15S 25.16E
95 M2 Leeupan salt pan S Africa 26.34S 28.59E
60 M7 Leeuwarden Netherlands 53.12N 5.48E
60 L12 Leeuwen Gelderland Netherlands 51.53N 5.31E
60 M15 Leeuwen Netherlands 51.12N 6.00E
61 F3 Leeuwergem Belgium 50.53N 3.50E
14 B10 Leeuwin,C W Australia 34.24S 115.09E
26 K9 Leeuwin Sill Indian Oc
107 F12 Leeville Louisiana 29.15N 90.14W
111 E4 Lee Vining California 37.58N 119.09W
11 K13 Leeward I Antipodes Is Pacific Oc 49.43S 178.51E
116 N5 Leewards Is West Indies
63 M5 Leezen W Germany 53.53N 10.15E
70 E4 Leff R France
61 B2 Leffinge Belgium 51.11N 2.53E
71 G1 Leffond France 47.40N 5.27E
91 D5 Léfini R Congo
84 Q14 Lefka Cyprus 35.06N 32.52E
84 R15 Lefkara Cyprus 34.51N 33.19E
84 S14 Lefkoniko Cyprus 35.15N 33.45E
112 D8 Lefors Texas 35.26N 100.48W
116 L4 Le François Martinique W I 14.36N 60.59W
99 L8 Lefroy Ontario 44.15N 79.34W
14 D9 Lefroy,L W Australia
100 T2 Leftrook L Manitoba
59 H3 Legakelly Fermanagh N Ireland 54.07N 7.20W
100 D5 Legal Alberta 53.58N 113.40W
9 B3 Legan islet Marshall Is Pacific Oc 8.58N 167.34E
75 C7 Leganés Spain 40.20N 3.46W
75 E7 Leganiel Spain 40.10N 2.58W
99 E2 Legarde R Ontario
99 R6 Légaré, L Quebec 46.58N 73.58W
19 L5 Legaspi Luzon Philippines 13.10N 123.45E
64 J8 Legau W Germany 47.51N 10.08E
57 O6 Legbourne Lincs Eng 53.21N 0.03E
63 F8 Legden W Germany 52.01N 7.08E
72 B6 Lège Gironde France 44.49N 1.09W
72 A2 Légé Loire-Atlantique France 46.52N 1.36W
14 B5 Legendre I W Australia 20.25S 116.55E
60 M10 Legerplaats-bij-Oldebroek Netherlands 52.23N 5.55E
12 J8 Legges Tor mt Tasmania 41.32S 147.41E
50 F5 Leggjabrjótur mt Iceland 64.40N 19.50W
Leghorn see Livorno
99 T4 Le Gîte Quebec 48.05N 71.34W
89 D2 Legleia Mauritania 19.10N 11.52W
61 N7 Léglise Belgium 49.48N 5.32E
79 K4 Legnago Italy 45.12N 11.18E
79 E3 Legnano Italy 45.36N 8.54E
79 L4 Legnaro Italy 45.21N 11.58E
62 J4 Legnica Poland 51.12N 16.10E
79 F2 Legnone,Monte Italy 46.06N 9.25E
59 L2 Legoniel Antrim Irish Rep 54.37N 5.59W
42 C5 Legostayevo U.S.S.R. 54.40N 83.47E
82 D4 Legrad Yugoslavia 46.17N 16.51E
111 D4 Le Grand California 37.13N 120.15W
14 E10 Le Grand,C W Australia 33.58S 122.05E
117 A1 Leguan I Guyana 6.57N 58.25W
120 E9 Leguena Chile 21.39S 68.40W
70 D4 Léguer R France
72 G8 Léguevin France 43.36N 1.13E
13 A3 Legune N Terr Australia 15.10S 129.30E
31 J3 Leh Kashmir 34.09N 77.35E
30 K6 Lehara Bihar India 26.09N 86.07E
35 D4 Lehavot Haviva Israel 32.24N 35.01E
70 L3 Le Havre France 49.30N 0.06E
87 L9 Lehel,El Somalia 2.55N 46.30E
64 L3 Lehesten E Germany 50.28N 11.28E
110 O9 Lehi Utah 40.25N 111.51W
108 Q7 Lehigh Iowa 42.21N 94.03W
109 O7 Lehigh Oklahoma 34.28N 96.15W
103 C5 Lehigh co Pennsylvania
103 C5 Lehigh R Pennsylvania
105 F11 Lehigh Acres Florida 26.37N 81.39W
103 C5 Lehighton Pennsylvania 40.50N 75.42W
82 K6 Lehliu Romania 44.27N 26.55E
110 G4 Lehman Oregon 45.10N 118.40W
103 B4 Lehman Pennsylvania 41.19N 76.02W
112 E2 Lehman Texas 33.36N 102.47W
95 K7 Lehmansdrif S Africa 31.55S 26.38E
63 R8 Lehnin E Germany 52.20N 12.45E
70 F5 Lehon France 48.27N 2.03W
90 K8 Léhou Cent Afr Rep 6.25N 21.22E
108 L3 Lehr N Dakota 46.20N 99.25W
64 K5 Lehrberg W Germany 49.21N 10.32E
63 N8 Lehre W Germany 52.20N 10.41E
63 L8 Lehrte W Germany 52.22N 9.59E
63 O5 Lehsen E Germany 53.30N 11.02E
51 K9 Lehtimäki Finland 62.47N 23.55E
23 G4 Lehua Jiangxi China 28.50N 115.53E
114 D3 Lehua I Hawaiian Is 22.01N 160.06W
94 F4 Lehututu Botswana 23.58S 21.51E
31 F5 Leiah Pakistan 30.59N 70.58E
64 O6 Leiblfing W Germany 48.46N 12.31E
65 N8 Leibnitz Austria 46.48N 15.33E
65 N8 Leibnitzer Feld reg Austria
23 C4 Leibo Sichuan China 28.19N 103.35E
63 T8 Leibsch E Germany 52.05N 13.54E
66 J1 Leibstadt Switzerland 47.36N 8.11E
56 J2 Leicester Leics Eng 52.38N 1.05W
103 L2 Leicester Massachusetts 42.15N 71.54W
56 J2 Leicester co England
12 M7 Leichhardt dist Sydney, N S W
13 E4 Leichhardt R Queensland
13 E4 Leichhardt Falls Queensland 18.10S 139.50E
13 G5 Leichhardt,Mt Queensland 22.28S 144.25E
13 H5 Leichhardt Ra Queensland
64 C1 Leichlingen W Germany 51.07N 7.01E
60 G11 Leiden Netherlands 52.10N 4.30E
60 G11 Leiderdorp Netherlands 52.08N 4.32E
50 D3 Leidharöxl mt Iceland 65.35N 21.39W
50 G7 Leidholfsfell mt Iceland 63.53N 18.27W
50 G7 Leidhvöllur Iceland 63.36N 18.20W
60 F11 Leidschendam Netherlands 52.05N 4.24E
61 D3 Leie R Belgium
63 M8 Leiferde W Germany 52.26N 10.28E
48 V13 Leifs Ø isld Greenland 65.50N 36.30W
57 H5 Leigh Greater Manchester Eng 53.30N 2.33W
56 M5 Leigh Kent Eng 51.12N 0.13E
11 J3 Leigh New Zealand 36.18S 174.49E
12 E4 Leigh R S Australia
12 E4 Leigh Cr S Australia 30.31S 138.25E
59 J6 Leighlinbridge Carlow Irish Rep 52.44N 6.59W
56 N4 Leigh-on-Sea Essex Eng 51.33N 0.40E
107 J7 Leighton Alabama 34.42N 87.31W
14 A2 Leighton Beach dist Perth, W Aust
56 K4 Leighton Buzzard Bucks Eng 51.55N 0.41W
13 D6 Leighton,Mt N Terr Australia 22.52S 136.04E
72 F3 Leignes-sur-Fontaine France 46.30N 0.46E
72 E2 Leigne-sur-Usseau France 46.54N 0.29E
61 L5 Leignon Belgium 50.17N 5.07E
53 T14 Leikanger Möre og Romsdal Norway 62.15N 5.47E
53 S14 Leikanger Sogn og Fjordane Norway 62.07N 5.20E
53 V16 Leikanger Sogn og Fjordane Norway 61.11N 6.50E
25 D3 Leiktho Burma 19.15N 96.35E
13 F5 Leila Vale Queensland 20.40S 141.08E
53 D3 Leille Binderup Denmark 56.48N 9.36E
63 O9 Leimbach E Germany 51.37N 11.28E
66 F2 Leimen France 47.30N 7.29E
64 D5 Leimen W Germany 49.16N 7.45E
60 G11 Leimuiden Netherlands 52.14N 4.40E
64 K2 Leina R E Germany
100 K8 Leinan Saskatchewan 50.31N 107.48W
63 L7 Leine R W Germany/E Germany
63 M10 Leinefelde E Germany 51.23N 10.19E
93 M6 Lein,El Kenya 0.21S 40.37E
64 G6 Leinfelden W Germany 48.40N 9.07E
79 C4 Leini Italy 45.11N 7.43E
53 T14 Leinøy Norway 62.21N 5.44E
53 T14 Leinøy isld Norway 62.21N 5.44E
59 H5 Leinster prov Irish Rep
59 J6 Leinster,Mt Carlow Irish Rep 52.37N 6.47W
64 J7 Leipheim W Germany 48.25N 10.13E
Lei-p'ing see Taiping
51 J4 Leipojärvi Sweden 67.03N 21.15E
103 C8 Leipsic Delaware 39.14N 75.31W
104 B5 Leipsic Ohio 41.06N 83.59W
63 Q10 Leipzig E Germany 51.20N 12.25E
100 J6 Leipzig Saskatchewan 52.13N 108.40W
64 N1 Leipzig reg E Germany 51.20N 12.20E
50 D6 Leirá Iceland 64.25N 21.51W
50 F6 Leirá R Iceland
51 D4 Leiranger Norway 67.45N 14.50E
50 C6 Leirárvogur B Iceland
51 K1 Leirbotn Norway 70.07N 23.20E
53 W16 Leirdal Norway 61.28N 7.15E
53 Y15 Leirdalen V Norway 61.40N 8.15E
50 J2 Leirhafnarfjöll mt Iceland 66.24N 16.23W
50 J3 Leirhnúkshraun lava field Iceland
50 J3 Leirhnúkur mt Iceland 65.43N 16.49W
50 J2 Leirhöfn Iceland 66.22N 16.28W
76 B9 Leiria Portugal 39.45N 8.49W
76 B9 Leiria dist Portugal
76 C4 Leiro Spain 42.23N 8.08W
53 X18 Leiro R Norway
51 M1 Leirpollen Norway 70.23N 25.31E
51 O1 Leirpollskogen Norway 70.26N 28.30E
53 Z15 Leirungsvatn L Norway 61.58N 8.32E
53 Y15 Leirvassbu Norway 61.33N 8.15E
53 T19 Leirvik Hordaland Norway 59.47N 5.31E
53 S16 Leirvik Sogn og Fjordane Norway 61.08N 5.20E
50 D6 Leirvogsa R Iceland
50 D6 Leirvogsvatn L Iceland 64.12N 21.27W
65 G8 Leisach Austria 46.49N 12.45E
61 A3 Leisele Belgium 50.59N 2.37E
65 O4 Leiser Berge mts Austria
23 E5 Leishan Guizhou China 26.15N 108.20E
23 F5 Lei Shui R Hunan China
12 B3 Leisler Hills S Australia
13 A6 Leisler,Mt N Terr Australia 23.21S 129.20E
64 O1 Leisnig E Germany 51.10N 12.56E
66 H5 Leissigen Switzerland 46.39N 7.46E
66 N3 Leistkamm mt Switzerland 47.08N 9.13E
56 P3 Leiston Suffolk Eng 52.13N 1.34E
105 B11 Leisure City Florida 25.27N 80.28W
76 G2 Leitariegos Spain 43.00N 6.25W
107 K4 Leitchfield Kentucky 37.28N 86.19W
108 D5 Leiter Wyoming 44.44N 106.18W
58 K7 Leith Lothian Scotland 55.59N 3.10W
108 J3 Leith N Dakota 46.23N 101.40W
65 P5 Leitha R Austria
65 P6 Leithagebirge mts Austria
65 O6 Leitha Kanal canal Austria
11 G10 Leithfield New Zealand 43.13S 172.47E
121 G8 Leith Harbour S Georgia 54.09S 36.50W
56 L5 Leith Hill Surrey Eng 51.11N 0.23W
58 K7 Leith,Water of R Lothian Scotland
11 M13 Leith,Water of R New Zealand
15 F5 Leitre Papua New Guinea 2.52S 141.42E
59 F4 Leitrim Leitrim Irish Rep 54.00N 8.04W
59 F3 Leitrim co Irish Rep
63 P8 Leitzkau E Germany 52.04N 11.58E
23 B9 Lei U Mun str Hong Kong
119 D6 Leiva,Cerro mt Colombia 2.55N 74.47W
66 O6 Lei,Valle di Italy/Switz
51 M10 Leivonmäki Finland 61.53N 26.05E
Lei-wan see Je-wang
Leix co see Laois
59 K5 Leixlip Kildare Irish Rep 53.22N 6.30W
23 F5 Leiyang Hunan China 26.26N 112.45E
75 G1 Leiza Spain 43.05N 1.55W
Leizhou see Haikang
23 E8 Leizhou Bandao Guangdong China
23 E8 Leizhou Wan B Guangdong China
23 E8 Leizhou Wan inlet Guangdong China
34 D6 Leja,El lava reg Syria
21 C13 Le Jima isld Okinawa Guntō Japan
Lejnum see Stykket
60 H12 Lek R Netherlands
51 B6 Leka isld Norway 65.05N 11.35E
91 D5 Lékana Congo 2.19S 14.35E
83 G3 Lekáni Greece 41.10N 24.35E
91 H4 Lekatero Zaïre 0.43S 23.56E
Le Kathe see Ban Le Kathe
61 B2 Leke Belgium 51.06N 2.54E
9 T12 Lekeleka islet Tonga, Pacific Oc 20.05S 174.35W
Lekemti see Nak'amet
91 C4 Lékey Gabon 1.30S 13.57E
30 E2 Lekh pass Xizang Zizhiqu 30.13N 81.02E
84 B6 Lekhainá Greece 37.56N 21.16E
84 F3 Lekhónia Greece 39.20N 23.03E
45 B1 Lekhovo U.S.S.R. 55.53N 30.25E
83 E4 Lékhovon Greece 40.35N 21.30E
91 C4 Lekila Gabon 0.55S 13.55E
18 A7 Lekir Pen Malaysia 4.08N 100.43E
19 D4 Lekitobi Moluccas Indon 1.58S 124.33E
90 B8 Lekki Nigeria 6.22N 4.10E
90 B8 Lekki Lagoon Nigeria
88 L4 Lekkous R Morocco
51 D3 Leknes Norway 68.07N 13.34E
53 S16 Leknes Norway 61.28N 5.25E
91 D4 Lékona R Congo
91 D4 Lékoni Gabon 1.34S 14.13E
91 C4 Lékoni R Gabon
89 H5 Lékoui Upper Volta 12.37N 3.40W
91 C5 Lékoumou div Congo
42 B2 Lekrisovo U.S.S.R. 60.54N 76.09E
52 H6 Leksand Sweden 60.44N 15.00E
47 D5 Lekshmozero U.S.S.R. 61.47N 37.45E
47 C4 Leksozero,Ozero L U.S.S.R.
88 J7 Lekst, Jbel mt Morocco 29.55N 8.56W
19 E5 Leksula Moluccas Indon 3.46S 126.35E
52 F3 Leksvik Norway 63.40N 10.40E
94 G5 Lekuru Botswana 24.49S 22.03E
93 F6 Lela Kenya 0.02S 34.37E
116 L3 Le Lamentin Martinique W I 14.37N 61.01W
108 R6 Leland Iowa 43.21N 93.38W
106 J4 Leland Michigan 45.01N 85.44W
107 F8 Leland Mississippi 33.25N 90.55W
89 C6 Lela Ndonde Guinea 11.37N 13.42W
52 F7 Lelången L Sweden
93 J9 Lelatema Mts Tanzania
46 G4 Lel'chitsy Belorussiya U.S.S.R. 51.48N 28.20E
114 D7 Leleiwi Pt Hawaiian Is 19.42N 155.00W
45 D8 Lelekovka Ukraine U.S.S.R. 48.34N 32.13E
121 B9 Leleque Argentina 42.28S 71.06W
19 B5 Lelewau Celebes Indonesia 3.02S 121.03E
Leli see Tianlin
112 G1 Lelia Lake Texas 34.54N 100.47W
15 M3 Leli I Solomon Is 8.45S 161.04E
82 E7 Lelija mt Yugoslavia 43.27N 18.29E
22 L8 Leling Shandong China 37.47N 117.15E
53 J6 Lellinge Denmark 55.28N 12.08E
19 C8 Lelogama Timor Indon 9.48S 123.59E
19 M4 Lelom Pass Truk Is Pacific Oc 7.25N 151.31E
116 L3 Le Lorrain Martinique W I 14.49N 61.04W
117 B2 Lely Gebergte mts Surinam
60 K9 Lelystad Netherlands 52.30N 5.26E
39 H1 Lelyuveem R U.S.S.R.
53 A4 Lem Ringkøbing Denmark 56.02N 8.24E
53 B3 Lem Viborg Denmark 56.36N 8.48E
90 B5 Lema Nigeria 12.53N 4.16E
93 G9 Lemagrut mt Tanzania 3.10S 35.33E
121 M10 Le Maire,Estrecho de str Arg
54 M9 Leman Bank oil field North Sea 53.03N 2.14E
15 J1 Lemankoa Papua New Guinea 5.06S 154.23E
66 B6 Léman, L Switzerland
70 L5 Le Mans France 48.00N 0.12E
116 L4 Le Marin Martinique W I 14.28N 60.53W
108 O7 Le Mars Iowa 42.48N 96.10W
119 H4 Lema,Sa.de mts Venezuela
104 H7 Lemasters Pennsylvania 39.53N 77.53W
65 J4 Lembach Austria 48.30N 13.55E
69 O5 Lembach France 49.00N 7.48E
18 M5 Lembak Borneo Indon 0.54N 117.35E
61 G4 Lembeek Belgium 50.43N 4.14E
19 D3 Lembeh isld Celebes Indonesia 1.25N 125.17E
90 F9 Lembé I Cameroon 4.16N 12.16E
61 E2 Lembeke Belgium 51.12N 3.38E
93 J9 Lembeni Tanzania 3.47S 37.35E
69 N5 Lemberg France 49.01N 7.23E
100 O8 Lemberg Saskatchewan 50.44N 103.10W
Lemberg Ukraine see L'vov
64 D5 Lemberg W Germany 49.09N 7.40E
72 D9 Lembeye France 43.27N 0.06W
72 G7 Lemboulas R France
63 H7 Lembruch W Germany 52.32N 8.23E
18 B3 Lembu, Gunung mt Sumatra Indon 4.05N 97.29E
43 N8 Lembur Uzbekistan U.S.S.R. 40.05N 71.08E
118 J9 Leme Rio de Janeiro Brazil 22.58S 43.11W
118 F8 Leme São Paulo Brazil 22.10S 47.23W
60 O10 Lemele Netherlands 52.27N 6.25E
60 O10 Lemelerberg mt Netherlands 52.28N 6.25E
60 O10 Lemelerveld Netherlands 52.27N 6.20E
118 K10 Leme,Ponta do C Brazil 22.58S 43.09W
92 D3 Lemera Zaïre 3.01S 29.00E
19 K5 Lemery Luzon Philippines 13.51N 120.55E
45 Q5 Lemeshkino U.S.S.R. 51.02N 44.29E
93 G7 Lemesikio Kenya/Tanzania 1.58S 35.43E
61 J6 Le Mesnil Belgium 50.02N 4.40E
63 H8 Lemförde W Germany 52.29N 8.23E
91 D6 Lemfu Zaïre 5.18S 15.13E
63 J8 Lemgo W Germany 52.02N 8.54E
110 M5 Lemhi Idaho 44.52N 113.37W
110 M5 Lemhi R Idaho
110 M5 Lemhi Ra Idaho
79 B4 Lemie Italy 45.13N 7.17E
60 U17 Lemiers Netherlands 50.47N 6.00E
99 S6 Lemieux Quebec 46.17N 72.07W
97 N5 Lemieux Is N W Terr
109 D7 Lemitar New Mexico 34.09N 106.56W
63 K7 Lemke W Germany 52.40N 9.09E
88 G9 Lemluia Morocco 25.52N 12.19W
51 M3 Lemmenjoki R Finland
60 L8 Lemmer, De Netherlands 52.50N 5.43E
53 D4 Lemming Denmark 56.15N 9.34E
108 H4 Lemmon S Dakota 45.56N 102.10W
111 O9 Lemmon, Mt Arizona 32.27N 110.48W
Lemnos see Límnos
95 D9 Lemoenshoek S Africa 33.50S 20.50E
103 C3 Lemon Pennsylvania 41.36N 75.56W
75 E1 Lemona Spain 43.13N 2.46W
111 E5 Lemoore California 36.17N 119.49W
116 L3 Le Morne Rouge Martinique W I 14.46N 61.09W
19 B4 Lemoro Celebes Indonesia 1.28S 121.08E
19 M4 Lemotol B Truk Is Pacific Oc
108 J8 Lemoyne Nebraska 41.18N 101.48W
99 T9 Lemoyne Quebec 45.30N 73.32W
115 P11 Lempa R Hond/El Salvador
51 K10 Lempäälä Finland 61.17N 23.45E
71 C6 Lempdes France 45.23N 3.16E
47 L5 Lempiny U.S.S.R. 60.54N 71.10E
101 O9 Lempriere Br Col 52.27N 119.08W
100 H8 Lemsford Saskatchewan 50.51N 109.04W
60 L8 Lemstervaart canal Netherlands
47 H4 Lemtybozh U.S.S.R. 63.48N 56.57E
18 H5 Lemukutan isld Borneo Indon 0.49N 108.40E
18 L4 Lemutan Borneo Indon 3.02N 115.50E
47 J3 Lemva R U.S.S.R.
53 A3 Lemvig Denmark 56.33N 8.20E
63 J6 Lemwerder W Germany 53.10N 8.36E
25 C4 Lemyethna Burma 17.36N 95.08E
47 G4 Lem'yu U.S.S.R. 64.04N 54.38E
47 H4 Lem'yu R U.S.S.R.
Len see Ban Len
18 L5 Len R Borneo Indon
106 E7 Lena Illinois 42.23N 89.50W
107 D10 Lena Louisiana 31.27N 92.48W
107 G9 Lena Mississippi 32.35N 89.38W
110 F4 Lena Oregon 45.25N 119.15W
52 K6 Lena Sweden 60.03N 17.43E
106 F5 Lena Wisconsin 44.57N 87.03W
38 M2 Lena R U.S.S.R.
16 N1 Lena,Delta of the U.S.S.R.
12 F8 Lenah Valley dist Hobart, Tasmania
9 D12 Lénakel New Hebrides 19.32S 169.16E
110 Q9 Lena, Mt Utah 40.46N 109.25W
109 P5 Lenapah Oklahoma 36.53N 95.37W
65 N8 Lenart Yugoslavia 46.35N 15.50E
71 D4 Lenax France 46.18N 3.48E
75 D2 Lences Spain 42.37N 3.30W
24 D9 Lenchung Tso L Xizang Zizhiqu China 33.20N 83.05E
72 E2 Lencloître France 46.49N 0.20E
118 H3 Lencóis Brazil 12.36S 41.24W
72 D7 Lencouacq France 44.05N 0.23W
65 H7 Lend Austria 47.18N 13.04E
92 D1 Lenda R Zaïre
57 D2 Lendalfoot Strathclyde Scotland 55.10N 4.55W
93 J10 Lendanai Tanzania 4.05S 37.06E
65 O8 Lendava Yugoslavia 46.34N 16.28E
65 O8 Lendava R Yugoslavia/Austria
32 D5 Lendeh Iran 30.59N 50.26E
61 C3 Lendelede Belgium 50.53N 3.15E
51 P8 Lendery Karelia U.S.S.R. 63.24N 31.04E
47 C4 Lendery U.S.S.R. 63.21N 31.12E
79 L4 Lendinara Italy 45.05N 11.36E
65 K8 Lendorf Austria 46.41N 14.17E
53 E2 Lendum Denmark 57.25N 10.19E
59 H4 Lene,L W Meath Irish Rep 53.40N 7.14W
47 N4 Lenevskoye U.S.S.R. 57.36N 61.21E
100 K6 Leney Saskatchewan 52.03N 107.35W
67 P14 Lenezzi, I Corsica 41.20N 9.15E
18 C9 Lenga Pen Malaysia 2.16N 102.49E
65 H5 Lengau Austria 48.01N 13.13E
65 G7 Lengau Salzburg Austria 47.23N 12.32E
32 H6 Lengbarūt Iran 29.19N 59.23E
108 P2 Lengby Minnesota 47.30N 95.45W
63 M8 Lengede W Germany 52.12N 10.19E
63 P2 Lengefeld E Germany 50.44N 13.12E
65 N5 Lengenfeld Austria 48.29N 15.37E
64 N2 Lengenfeld E Germany 50.34N 12.22E
43 J6 Lenger Kazakhstan U.S.S.R. 42.10N 69.54E
63 G7 Lengerich Niedersachsen W Germany 52.33N 7.31E
63 G8 Lengerich Nordrhein-Westfalen W Germany 52.12N 7.52E
18 A6 Lenggong Pen Malaysia 5.05N 100.58E
18 D9 Lenggor R Pen Malaysia
64 M8 Lenggries W Germany 47.41N 11.35E
22 C7 Lenghu Qinghai China 38.50N 93.30E
22 E8 Lenglong Ling mt ra Qinghai China
66 F3 Lengnau Switzerland 47.12N 7.23E
91 D3 Lengoue R Congo
23 F5 Lengshuijiang Hunan China 27.40N 111.26E
121 B3 Lengua de Vaca,Pta C Chile 30.15S 71.40W
21 B7 Lengzipu Liaoning China 41.42N 122.50E
56 N5 Lenham Kent Eng 51.15N 0.43E
103 C5 Lenhartsville Pennsylvania 40.34N 75.53W
52 J10 Lenhovda Sweden 57.00N 15.20E
81 B5 Leni R Sardinia
44 G7 Lenin Azerbaydzhan U.S.S.R. 40.48N 46.08E
46 D8 Lenin dist Moscow U.S.S.R.
43 J6 Leninabad Tadzhikistan U.S.S.R. 40.14N 69.40E
43 G5 Lenina, Im Kazakhstan U.S.S.R. 45.00N 63.30E
40 C2 Lenina, Im U.S.S.R. 59.10N 125.47E
44 F7 Leninakan Armenia U.S.S.R. 40.47N 43.49E
44 F4 Lenina,Kanal U.S.S.R.
43 L7 Lenina,Pik mt Tadzhikistan/Kirgiziya U.S.S.R. 39.21N 73.01E
41 G3 Lenina,Proliv str U.S.S.R.
45 S3 Lenina,V.I U.S.S.R. 53.34N 46.58E
43 O7 Lenindzhol Kirgiziya U.S.S.R. 41.05N 72.37E
69 M6 Léning France 48.58N 6.48E
44 F5 Leningori Georgia U.S.S.R. 42.11N 44.30E
47 C6 Leningrad U.S.S.R. 59.55N 30.25E
44 C1 Leningradskaya U.S.S.R. 46.19N 39.24E
123 K5 Leningradskaya U.S.S.R. Base Antarctica 69.30S 159.23E
46 H1 Leningradskaya Oblast' prov U.S.S.R.
41 H3 Leningradskaya,R U.S.S.R.
43 K7 Leningradskiy Tadzhikistan U.S.S.R. 38.06N 70.03E
39 K1 Leningradskiy U.S.S.R. 69.50N 179.14E
46 C8 Lenin Heights Moscow U.S.S.R.
Lenin,I.V.Kanal canal see Volgo-Balt Kanal
46 H4 Lenino Gomel', Belorussiya U.S.S.R. 52.10N 31.36E
46 H3 Lenino Mogilev, Belorussiya U.S.S.R. 54.21N 31.02E
40 F9 Lenino Primor'ye U.S.S.R. 44.15N 134.21E
44 D9 Lenino Ukraine U.S.S.R. 45.17N 35.46E
43 P2 Leninogorsk Kazakhstan U.S.S.R. 50.23N 83.32E
46 Q3 Leninogorsk U.S.S.R. 54.39N 52.30E
43 K6 Leninpol' Kirgiziya U.S.S.R. 42.29N 71.52E
47 M2 Leninport Leningrad U.S.S.R. 59.54N 30.12E
47 L6 Leninsk Chelyabinsk U.S.S.R. 54.52N 59.51E
44 F1 Leninsk Kalmyk A.S.S.R. U.S.S.R. 46.10N 43.46E
43 G4 Leninsk Kazakhstan U.S.S.R. 45.38N 63.16E
43 E6 Leninsk Turkmeniya U.S.S.R. 42.03N 59.22E
43 K6 Leninsk Uzbekistan U.S.S.R. 40.37N 72.15E
45 R8 Leninsk Volgograd U.S.S.R. 48.42N 45.14E
45 Q1 Leninskaya Sloboda U.S.S.R. 56.05N 44.26E
43 D3 Leninskiy Aktyubinsk, Kazakhstan U.S.S.R. 49.00N 57.14E
43 P3 Leninskiy Kazakhstan U.S.S.R. 48.57N 83.55E
46 O2 Leninskiy Mariy A.S.S.R. U.S.S.R. 56.32N 46.02E
45 J2 Leninskiy Tula U.S.S.R. 54.19N 37.25E
40 C2 Leninskiy Yakutsk U.S.S.R. 58.36N 125.29E
Leninskiye Gory see Lenin Heights
42 D5 Leninsk-Kuznetskiy U.S.S.R. 54.44N 86.13E
43 J6 Leninskoye Kazakhstan U.S.S.R. 41.44N 69.23E
47 K8 Leninskoye Kazakhstan U.S.S.R. 54.03N 65.16E
43 L6 Leninskoye Kirgiziya U.S.S.R. 40.45N 73.10E
46 O1 Leninskoye Kirov U.S.S.R. 58.20N 47.08E
40 F8 Leninskoye Yevreysk U.S.S.R. 47.58N 132.37E
41 F4 Lenivaya R U.S.S.R.
95 O3 Lenjanedrif S Africa 27.55S 30.59E
92 C9 Lenje tribe Zambia
66 F6 Lenk Switzerland 46.28N 7.27E
42 C5 Len'ki U.S.S.R. 53.00N 80.20E
44 J9 Lenkoran' Azerbaydzhan U.S.S.R. 38.45N 48.50E
15 A4 Len Malaäs Misoöl I, Irian Jaya 1.43S 130.20E
79 G3 Lenna Italy 45.57N 9.41E
14 E3 Lennard,R W Australia
52 F7 Lennartsfors Sweden 59.20N 11.55E
64 D1 Lenne R W Germany
110 P3 Lennep Montana 46.25N 110.31W
63 F10 Lennep W Germany 51.11N 7.16E
64 E1 Lennestadt W Germany 51.09N 8.01E
61 Q8 Lenningen Luxembourg 49.36N 6.23E
14 F7 Lennis Hills W Australia
66 N8 Lenno Italy 45.59N 9.13E
14 C8 Lennonville W Australia 27.59S 117.50E
108 O6 Lennox S Dakota 43.20N 96.52W
121 L10 Lennox,I Arg/Chile 55.19S 67.00W
58 H7 Lennoxtown Strathclyde Scotland 55.59N 4.12W
99 T7 Lennoxville Quebec 45.22N 71.51W
79 H4 Leno Italy 45.22N 10.13E
105 F2 Lenoir N Carolina 35.56N 81.31W
107 M6 Lenoir City Tennessee 35.48N 84.18W
109 K2 Lenora Kansas 39.38N 100.03W
112 F3 Lenorah Texas 32.19N 101.52W
100 R9 Lenore Manitoba 49.56N 100.49W
100 M6 Lenore L Saskatchewan
110 F2 Lenore, L Washington 47.30N 119.30W
105 D6 Lenox Georgia 31.16N 83.29W
108 Q9 Lenox Iowa 40.54N 94.32W
103 H2 Lenox Massachusetts 42.21N 73.17W
103 C3 Lenox Pennsylvania 41.42N 75.41W
103 C3 Lenoxville Pennsylvania 41.39N 75.39W
61 F4 Lens Belgium 50.33N 3.54E
69 D3 Lens France 50.26N 2.50E
66 F6 Lens Switzerland 46.18N 7.28E
63 N4 Lensahn W Germany 54.14N 10.52E
42 J2 Lensk U.S.S.R. 60.48N 114.55E
45 G2 Lenskoye Kaluga U.S.S.R. 54.36N 35.07E
47 J6 Lenskoye Sverdlovsk U.S.S.R. 58.10N 63.10E
61 L4 Lens-St.Remy Belgium 50.39N 5.08E
61 L4 Lens-St.Servais Belgium 50.40N 5.10E
52 E3 Lensvik Norway 63.31N 9.48E
71 G4 Lent France 46.08N 5.11E
60 M12 Lent Netherlands 51.52N 5.53E
79 D3 Lenta Italy 45.33N 8.23E
79 F3 Lentate sul Seveso Italy 45.40N 9.07E
71 G7 Lente,Forêt de France
44 E5 Lentekhi Georgia U.S.S.R. 42.46N 42.45E
65 P8 Lenti Hungary 46.37N 16.33E
79 M2 Lentiai Italy 46.03N 12.01E
66 E4 Lentigny Switzerland 46.46N 7.01E
51 O7 Lentiira Finland 64.23N 29.52E
64 L6 Lenting W Germany 48.48N 11.28E
81 K9 Lentini Sicily 37.17N 15.00E
81 K9 Lentini R Sicily
51 G2 Lenvik Norway 69.22N 18.10E
25 E7 Lenya Burma 11.27N 98.58E
25 E7 Lenya R Burma
58 H6 Leny, Pass of Central Scotland
95 L2 Lenz S Africa 26.20S 27.50E
Lenz Switzerland see Lantsch
66 J2 Lenzburg Switzerland 47.23N 8.11E
63 O6 Lenzen an der Elbe E Germany 53.07N 11.29E
66 P5 Lenzerheide Switzerland 46.44N 9.34E
66 P5 Lenzer Horn mt Switzerland 46.43N 9.36E
64 E8 Lenzkirch W Germany 47.52N 8.13E
89 H6 Leo Upper Volta 11.07N 2.08W
65 J8 Leoben Kärnten Austria 46.57N 13.38E
65 M7 Leoben Steiermark Austria 47.23N 15.06E
65 O6 Leobersdorf Austria 47.55N 16.13E
116 H5 Léogane Haiti 18.32N 72.37W
65 G7 Leogang Austria 47.27N 12.47E
65 G7 Leoganger Steinberge mts Austria
72 C6 Léognan France 44.43N 0.36W
107 D7 Leola Arkansas 34.09N 92.38W
108 M4 Leola S Dakota 45.43N 98.56W
56 F3 Leominster Hereford & Worcs Eng 52.14N 2.45W
104 O4 Leominster Massachusetts 42.31N 71.45W
72 B8 Léon France 43.53N 1.18W
108 R9 Leon Iowa 40.43N 93.46W
109 O4 Leon Kansas 37.43N 96.47W
115 J7 León Mexico 21.10N 101.42W
115 L3 León Nicaragua 12.24N 86.52W
76 H3 León Spain 42.35N 5.34W
104 D8 Leon W Virginia 38.46N 81.57W
74 C2 León prov Spain
119 C4 León R Colombia
112 K4 Leon R Texas
70 A5 Léon reg France
74 C4 León reg Spain
112 M4 Leona Texas 31.11N 95.59W
121 J7 Leona R Argentina
112 H7 Leona R Texas
106 L7 Leonard Michigan 42.52N 83.08W
107 D2 Leonard Missouri 39.54N 92.10W
108 N3 Leonard N Dakota 46.39N 97.15W
112 L2 Leonard Texas 33.22N 96.18W
15 D6 Leonard Darwin,Geb mt Irian Jaya 4.02S 136.45E
15 G7 Leonard Murray Mts Papua New Guinea
80 F5 Leonardo da Vinci airport Italy 41.47N 12.15E
15 G6 Leonard Schultze R Papua New Guinea
109 O2 Leonardville Kansas 39.22N 96.53W
84 T14 Leonarisso Cyprus 35.27N 34.09E
115 Q7 Leona Vicario Mexico 20.59N 87.12W
64 G6 Leonberg W Germany 48.48N 9.01E
64 F5 Leonbronn W Germany 49.03N 8.53E
71 G7 Léoncel France 44.55N 5.13E
118 A7 León,Cerro hill Paraguay 20.25S 60.30W
121 C1 Leoncito,L Argentina
112 E4 Leon Cr Texas
84 D3 Leondári Greece 39.11N 22.08E
84 D7 Leondárion Greece 37.19N 22.08E
122 D1 Leone Amer Samoa Pacific Oc 14.21S 170.47W
66 J6 Leone Monte mt Italy/Switz 46.15N 8.07E
121 L5 Leones,I Argentina
80 G3 Leonessa Italy 42.34N 12.58E
72 B8 Léon,Etang de L France 43.54N 1.19W
65 K4 Leonfelden Austria 48.32N 14.18E
81 H8 Leonforte Sicily 37.38N 14.23E
12 H7 Leongatha Victoria 38.39S 145.55E
77 D8 León,I.de Spain 36.25N 6.14W
84 E7 Leonídhion Greece 37.10N 22.51E
76 G3 León, Montañas de mts Spain
14 D8 Leonora W Australia 28.54S 121.20E
45 B2 Leonovka Belorussiya U.S.S.R. 54.24N 30.38E
121 L8 León, Pta C Argentina 50.26S 68.54W
112 J6 Leon Springs Texas 29.40N 98.39W
65 K6 Leonstein Austria 47.54N 14.14E
76 C5 Leonte Portugal 41.46N 8.09W
113 F9 Leontovitch,C Alaska 55.40N 162.20W
39 G1 Leont'yeva,O isld U.S.S.R. 70.45N 161.30E
Leopold & Astrid Coast see King Leopold & Queen Astrid Coast
14 F4 Leopold Downs W Australia 18.00S 125.25E
118 G7 Leopoldina Brazil 21.30S 42.38W
118 E5 Leopoldo de Bulhões Brazil 16.37S 48.45W
14 F4 Leopold R W Australia
61 M2 Léopoldsburg Belgium 51.07N 5.16E
65 P5 Leopoldsdorf Austria 48.14N 16.41E
63 T5 Leopoldshagen E Germany 53.47N 13.54E
64 D7 Leopoldskanal W Germany
Leopoldville see Kinshasa
109 J3 Leoti Kansas 38.28N 101.22W
100 K5 Leoville Saskatchewan 53.39N 107.33W
46 G6 Leovo Moldavia U.S.S.R. 46.29N 28.12E
107 F6 Lepanto Arkansas 35.36N 90.20W
115 M5 Lepanto Costa Rica 9.58N 85.01W
18 G7 Lepar isld Indonesia
18 D8 Lepar R Pen Malaysia
115 L2 Lepaterique Honduras 14.05N 87.25W
72 J3 Lépaud France 46.15N 2.23E
Lepaya see Liepāja
77 B6 Lepe Spain 37.15N 7.12W
45 S6 Lepekhinka U.S.S.R. 50.40N 46.56E
46 G3 Lepel' Belorussiya U.S.S.R. 54.48N 28.40E
60 F13 Lepelstraat Netherlands 51.33N 4.16E
84 B4 Lepenoú Greece 38.43N 21.17E
17 O2 Le Pérouse Str Japan/Sakhalin, U.S.S.R
94 H4 Lephepe Botswana 23.20S 25.50E
28 K3 Lephori Nagaland India 25.35N 94.40E
91 D10 Lepi Angola 12.51S 15.20E
121 A8 Lepihue Chile 41.34S 73.35W
69 G6 Lépine France 48.58N 4.27E
23 H4 Leping Jiangxi China 28.57N 117.07E
80 H5 Lepini,Monti Italy
99 R7 L'Epiphanie Quebec 45.50N 73.29W
41 N8 Lepiske R U.S.S.R.
47 J5 Leplya R U.S.S.R.
45 C7 Leplyavo Ukraine U.S.S.R. 49.48N 31.32E
19 C6 Lepolepo Celebes Indon 4.06S 122.31E
66 J6 Lepontine, Alpi mts Switz/Italy
81 P12 Leporano Italy 40.23N 17.20E
51 N9 Leppävirta Finland 62.30N 27.50E
11 J6 Lepperton New Zealand 39.03S 174.13E
50 F5 Leppir,mt Iceland 64.31N 19.20W
98 F8 Lepreau New Brunswick 45.10N 66.31W
98 F8 Lepreau,Pt New Brunswick 45.04N 66.28W
116 K3 Le Prêcheur Martinique W I 14.48N 61.14W
84 C7 Lépreon Greece 37.26N 21.43E
43 N4 Lepsa R Kazakhstan U.S.S.R.
62 L8 Lepsény Hungary 47.00N 18.14E
43 O4 Lepsinsk Kazakhstan U.S.S.R. 45.31N 80.35E
53 U13 Lepsøya isld Norway 62.37N 6.10E
43 N4 Lepsy Kazakhstan U.S.S.R. 46.14N 78.56E
Leptis Magna ruins see Labdah
84 E1 Leptokariá Greece 40.02N 22.32E
66 D1 Lepuix France 47.46N 6.50E
71 D6 Le Puy France 45.03N 3.53E
44 H9 Leqalān Iran 38.55N 47.25E
75 F1 Lequeitio Spain 43.21N 2.30W
87 C6 Ler Sudan 8.17N 30.06E
89 G6 Leraba Ivory Coast 10.05N 4.48W
116 N3 Le Raizet airport Guadeloupe W I 16.17N 61.33W
72 H10 Léran France 42.59N 1.54E
103 B3 Le Raysville Pennsylvania 41.51N 76.11W
63 M9 Lerbach W Germany 51.46N 10.18E
52 J8 Lerbäck Sweden 58.56N 15.02E
53 K4 Lerberget Sweden 56.11N 12.35E
53 D4 Lerbjerg Denmark 56.20N 9.59E
81 G8 Lercara Friddi Sicily 37.45N 13.37E
115 H5 Lerdo,Ciudad Mexico 25.34N 103.30W
90 G7 Léré Chad 9.41N 14.17E
71 B2 Léré France 47.28N 2.52E
90 D6 Lere Nigeria 10.23N 8.35E
90 D7 Lere Nigeria 9.42N 9.20E
18 C8 Lerek mt Pen Malaysia 3.45N 102.45E
99 T5 Le Relais Quebec 47.31N 71.17W
76 B3 Lerez R Spain
72 A10 Lerga Spain 42.35N 1.32W
53 K4 Lerhamn Sweden 56.16N 12.33E
95 M4 Leribe Lesotho 28.52S 28.03E
95 M4 Leribe dist Lesotho
79 G6 Lérici Italy 44.04N 9.55E
13 G5 Lerida Queensland 22.02S 143.55E
75 M4 Lérida Spain 41.37N 0.38E
119 D5 Lérida Tolima Colombia 5.05N 74.57W
119 E8 Lerida Vaupés Colombia 0.11S 70.43W
74 H3 Lérida prov Spain
44 J9 Lerik Azerbaydzhan U.S.S.R. 38.45N 48.24E
75 G3 Lerin Spain 42.29N 1.59W
71 L9 Lerins,Iles de France 43.31N 7.03E
75 G3 Lerin,Valle de Spain
53 C3 Lerkenfeld Å R Denmark
115 O8 Lerma Mexico 19.49N 90.38W
75 C3 Lerma Spain 42.02N 3.46W
72 D7 Lerm-et-Musset France 44.20N 0.08W
44 E3 Lermontov U.S.S.R. 44.05N 43.00E
40 F8 Lermontovka U.S.S.R. 47.14N 134.17E
45 P3 Lermontovo U.S.S.R. 53.00N 43.41E
65 C7 Lermoos Austria 47.24N 10.53E
107 H2 Lerna Illinois 39.25N 88.18W
72 E1 Lerné France 47.08N 0.07E
81 C2 Lerno,Mte Sardinia 40.37N 9.10E
116 L3 Le Robert Martinique W I 14.41N 60.57W
83 H7 Léros isld Greece
100 O7 Leross Saskatchewan 51.17N 103.53W
69 K6 Lérouville France 48.47N 5.33E
95 H5 Le Roux Dam, P.K res S Africa 29.59S 24.43E
106 F9 Le Roy Illinois 40.22N 88.47W
108 R9 Le Roy Iowa 40.53N 93.33W
109 P3 Le Roy Kansas 38.04N 95.37W
106 J5 Le Roy Michigan 44.03N 85.29W
108 S6 Le Roy Minnesota 43.30N 92.20W
104 G4 Le Roy New York 42.59N 78.01W
103 A3 Le Roy Pennsylvania 41.41N 76.43W
100 N7 Leroy Saskatchewan 52.00N 104.45W
110 P8 Le Roy Wyoming 41.20N 110.37W
53 S18 Lerøy isld Norway 60.14N 5.11E
69 L7 Lerrain France 48.08N 6.10E
52 G9 Lerum Sweden 57.46N 12.12E
53 N9 Lervig Faeroes 62.14N 6.32W
58 Q9 Lerwick Shetland Scotland 60.09N 1.09W
70 N3 Léry France 49.17N 1.12E
107 G12 Lery,L Louisiana 29.48N 89.51W
82 G4 Leș Romania 46.59N 21.49E
82 G4 Leș Romania 46.05N 21.43E
75 M2 Lés Spain 42.48N 0.42E
79 E3 Lesa Italy 45.49N 8.33E
75 G1 Lesaca Spain 43.14N 1.43W
65 G8 Lesachtal V Austria
116 L4 Le St. Esprit Martinique W I 14.34N 60.57W
116 L4 Les Anses d'Arlets Martinique W I 14.29N 61.05W
93 H6 Lesatima mt Kenya 0.17S 36.37E
61 M5 Les Avins Belgium 50.25N 5.18E
66 C4 Les Bayards Switzerland 46.55N 6.32E
Lesbos isld see Lésvos
61 M8 Les Bulles Belgium 49.42N 52.25E
57 K2 Lesbury Northumb Eng 55.24N 1.36W
61 H7 L'Escaillère Belgium 49.57N 4.26E
72 D9 Lescar France 43.20N 0.25W
14 B9 Leschenault, C W Australia 31.50S 115.23E
72 J8 Lescure-d'Albigeois France 43.58N 2.10E
61 D4 Lesdain Belgium 50.32N 3.23E
91 H2 Lese R Zaïre
98 B6 Les Éboulements Quebec 47.29N 70.16W
79 C6 Lésegno Italy 44.24N 7.58E
93 G5 Leseru Kenya 0.36N 35.11E
98 C5 Les Escoumins Quebec 48.21N 69.26W
98 D6 Les Étroits Quebec 47.24N 68.54W
23 C4 Leshan Sichuan China 29.34N 103.42E
70 E3 Les Hanois Lt.Ho English Chan 49.27N 2.43W
61 L7 Les Hayons Belgium 49.48N 5.09E
45 H5 Leshchinskaya Plota U.S.S.R. 51.31N 36.59E
47 F4 Leshukonskoye U.S.S.R. 64.55N 45.50E
87 B8 Lesi watercourse Sudan
9 S5 Lesiatheva Pt Vanua Levu Fiji 16.50S 179.17E
79 H5 Lesignano de Palmia Italy 44.37N 10.07E
79 F5 Lésima,Monte Italy 44.42N 9.15E
80 M5 Lesina Italy 41.52N 15.22E
80 M5 Lésina,Lago di Italy
52 D4 Lesja Norway 62.07N 8.51E
53 Y14 Lesjaskog Norway 62.15N 8.20E
53 Y14 Lesjaskogsvatn L Norway 62.14N 8.25E
53 Z14 Lesjaverk Norway 62.12N 8.34E
52 H7 Lesjöfors Sweden 59.57N 14.12E

62 N6 Lesko Poland 49.29N 22.20E
82 G7 Leskovac Yugoslavia 43.00N 21.57E
123 A14 Leskov I S Sandwich Is Atl Oc 56.46S 28.10W
83 D4 Leskovik Albania 40.10N 20.34E
107 D6 Leslie Arkansas 35.50N 92.34W
58 K6 Leslie Fife Scotland 56.13N 3.13W
105 C6 Leslie Georgia 31.57N 84.06W
110 M6 Leslie Idaho 43.53N 113.27W
106 K7 Leslie Michigan 42.26N 85.27W
95 M2 Leslie S Africa 26.22S 28.55E
100 O7 Leslie Saskatchewan 51.43N 103.44W
100 C6 Leslieville Alberta 52.25N 114.41W
58 J7 Lesmahagow Strathclyde Scotland 55.39N 3.55W
116 N3 Les Mangles Guadeloupe W I 16.24N 61.27W
98 F5 Les Mechins Quebec 48.59N 67.00W
69 G7 Lesmont France 48.26N 4.25E
46 E4 Lesna R Belorussiya U.S.S.R.
39 G5 Lesnaya U.S.S.R. 59.24N 160.35E
70 B4 Lesneven France 48.35N 4.20W
82 E6 Lešnica Yugoslavia 44.40N 19.20E
47 C3 Lesnoy Murmansk U.S.S.R. 66.40N 34.20E
47 K7 Lesnoy Tyumen U.S.S.R. 56.58N 67.10E
47 G6 Lesnoy U.S.S.R. 59.47N 52.08E
46 K1 Lesnoye U.S.S.R. 58.15N 35.31E
45 N2 Lesnoye-Konobeyevo U.S.S.R. 54.02N 41.56E
95 M5 Lesobeng Lesotho 29.45S 28.24E
45 P1 Lesogorsk Gor'kiy U.S.S.R. 55.06N 43.58E
40 J7 Lesogorsk Sakhalin U.S.S.R. 49.24N 142.10E
47 B5 Lesogorskiy U.S.S.R. 61.03N 28.57E
44 G5 Lesogorye U.S.S.R. 42.57N 45.02E
18 D9 Lesong hill Pen Malaysia 2.42N 103.14E
40 F8 Lesopil'noye U.S.S.R. 46.45N 134.19E
95 L5 Lesotho kingdom S E Africa
40 F9 Lesozavodsk U.S.S.R. 45.30N 133.29E
51 Q5 Lesozavodskiy U.S.S.R. 66.41N 32.53E
72 C5 Lesparre-Médoc France 45.19N 0.56W
26 S14 L'Espérance Mahé I Ind Oc 4.43S 55.29E
10 R8 L'Espérance Rock Kermadec Is Pacific Oc 31.26S 178.54W
72 B8 Lespéron France 43.58N 1.06W
71 C10 Lespignan France 43.16N 3.10E
72 K9 Lespinassière France 43.23N 2.31E
69 F4 Lesquielles-St.Germain France 49.56N 3.38E
72 F3 Lessac France 46.04N 0.40E
65 J7 Lessach Austria 47.12N 13.49E
70 G3 Lessay France 49.13N 1.32W
63 M8 Lesse W Germany 52.09N 10.16E
61 K6 Lesse R Belgium
52 J10 Lessebo Sweden 56.45N 15.20E
123 F10 Lesser Antarctica Antarctica
116 M6 Lesser Antilles islds West Indies
Lesser Khingan Range see Xiao Hinggan Ling
100 C3 Lesser Slave Lake Prov. Park Alberta
101 Q8 Lesser Slave Lake Prov. Park Alberta
122 C9 Lesser Sunda Is Indonesia
61 F4 Lessines Belgium 50.43N 3.50E
95 K5 Lessingskop mt S Africa 29.50S 26.35E
79 J3 Lessini,Monti mts Italy
61 L6 Lessive Belgium 50.08N 5.09E
66 E5 Lessoe Switzerland 46.31N 7.04E
79 C4 Lessolo Italy 45.28N 7.49E
108 O6 Lester Iowa 43.27N 96.20W
108 M9 Lester Nebraska 40.05N 98.26W
104 D9 Lester W Virginia 37.43N 81.20W
61 M6 Lesterny Belgium 50.07N 5.17E
108 Q5 Lester Prairie Minnesota 44.54N 94.02W
72 F3 Lesterps France 46.00N 0.47E
108 N6 Lesterville S Dakota 43.04N 97.34W
51 L8 Lestijärvi Finland 63.32N 24.40E
65 M2 Leština Czechoslovakia 49.47N 15.24E
79 O3 Lestizza Italy 45.58N 13.08E
100 N7 Lestock Saskatchewan 51.19N 104.01W
72 K7 Lestrade-et-Thouels France 44.04N 2.39E
116 L4 Les Trois-Ilets Martinique W I 14.32N 61.02W
108 R5 Le Sueur Minnesota 44.28N 93.52W
14 F2 Lesueur I W Australia 13.47S 127.10E
14 B9 Lesueur, Mt W Australia 30.15S 115.11E
18 L5 Lesung,Bukit mt Borneo Indon 0.37N 114.35E
61 K5 Lesve Belgium 50.23N 4.47E
83 H5 Lésvos isld Greece
61 L4 Les-Waleffes Belgium 50.38N 5.13E
57 C3 Leswalt Dumfries & Galloway Scotland 54.56N 5.05W
62 K4 Leszno Poland 51.51N 16.35E
94 L4 Letaba R S Africa
108 M6 Letcher S Dakota 43.54N 98.08W
56 L4 Letchworth Herts Eng 51.58N 0.14W
100 U9 Letellier Manitoba 49.09N 97.19W
65 P9 Letenye Hungary 46.25N 16.44E
110 J6 Letha Idaho 43.54N 116.38W
25 L9 Letha Ra Burma
100 E9 Lethbridge Alberta 49.43N 112.48W
98 T5 Lethbridge Newfoundland 48.21N 53.55W
119 J6 Lethem Guyana 3.18N 59.46W
56 O2 Letheringsett Norfolk Eng 52.55N 1.04E
19 E8 Leti isld Indon 8.10S 127.40E
46 G5 Letichev Ukraine U.S.S.R. 49.21N 27.32E
119 E8 Leticia Colombia 4.09S 69.57W
19 E8 Leti, Kep islds Indonesia
22 L7 Leting Hebei China 39.21N 118.56E
64 P4 Letiny Czechoslovakia 49.32N 13.28E
95 F8 Letjiesbos S Africa 32.34S 22.16E
47 F6 Letka R U.S.S.R.
25 C1 Letkokpin Burma 22.49N 95.54E
25 M10 Letkokpin Kyaukmyaung Burma 22.50N 95.59E
94 H3 Letlhakane Botswana 21.26S 25.36E
94 H5 Letlhakeng Botswana 24.05S 25.03E
63 G10 Letmathe W Germany 51.22N 7.36E
47 C4 Letnerechenskiy U.S.S.R. 64.17N 34.27E
82 J7 Letnitsa Bulgaria 43.19N 25.06E
47 D3 Letniy Bereg coast U.S.S.R.
39 E2 Letnya'ya R U.S.S.R.
47 C3 Letnyaya-Reka U.S.S.R. 65.08N 34.42E
44 E2 Letnyaya Stavka U.S.S.R. 45.24N 43.27E
47 D4 Letnyaya Zolotitsa U.S.S.R. 64.55N 36.58E
107 K9 Letohatchee Alabama 32.08N 86.30W
81 K8 Letoianni Sicily 37.53N 15.19E
18 F4 Letong Anambas Indonesia 2.55N 105.42E
69 B2 Le Touquet-Paris Plage France 50.31N 1.36E
65 P2 Letovice Czechoslovakia 49.34N 16.36E
41 F5 Letov'ye U.S.S.R. 71.23N 94.14E
25 C4 Letpadan Burma 17.46N 94.45E
69 L6 Létricourt France 48.52N 6.18E
95 H8 Letskraal S Africa 32.05S 24.49E
25 E7 Letsôk-aw Kyun isld Burma
12 G5 Lette New S Wales 34.22S 143.15E
63 F9 Lette W Germany 51.53N 7.12E
60 O7 Lettelbert Netherlands 53.11N 6.25E
60 O10 Lettele Netherlands 52.17N 6.16E
59 G2 Letter Donegal Irish Rep 54.32N 7.52W
59 D5 Lettercraffroe L Galway Irish Rep 53.23N 9.25W
59 C4 Letterfrack Galway Irish Rep 53.33N 9.57W
61 F3 Letterhouten Belgium 50.55N 3.53E
59 G2 Letterkenny Donegal Irish Rep 54.57N 7.44W
59 C5 Lettermore I Galway Irish Rep 53.18N 9.40W
56 B4 Letterston Dyfed Wales 51.56N 5.00W
107 L2 Letts Indiana 39.16N 85.34W
77 M4 Letur Spain 28.22N 2.06W
75 J5 Letux Spain 41.15N 0.48W
46 N4 Letyazhevka U.S.S.R. 51.51N 43.20E
63 O8 Letzlingen E Germany 52.27N 11.30E
82 J6 Leu Romania 44.10N 24.01E
91 G9 Leua Angola 11.40S 20.29E
Leuaniua I see Luaniua I
64 N2 Leubnitz E Germany 50.43N 12.22E
Leubringen see Evilard
72 J9 Leuc France 43.08N 2.19E
81 R13 Léuca Italy 39.47N 18.22E
72 L10 Leucate France 42.54N 3.02E
72 L10 Leucate, Cap C France 42.55N 3.04E
72 K10 Leucate, Etang de L France 42.50N 3.00E
121 A10 Leucaye, I Chile 44.00S 73.40W
58 L6 Leuchars Fife Scotland 56.23N 2.53W
64 N4 Leuchtenberg W Germany 49.36N 12.16E
64 M2 Leuchtenburg E Germany 50.48N 11.37E
111 G8 Leucidia California 33.07N 117.21W
61 P8 Leudelange Luxembourg 49.33N 6.04E
63 T7 Leuenberg E Germany 52.43N 13.53E
69 H8 Leuglay France 47.49N 4.47E
61 G6 Leugnies Belgium 50.13N 4.12E
70 C5 Leuhan France 48.05N 3.49W
66 G6 Leuk Switzerland 46.19N 7.39E
65 F6 Leuken-tal V Austria
66 G6 Leukerbad Switzerland 46.23N 7.38E
64 E2 Leun W Germany 50.32N 8.22E
63 Q10 Leuna E Germany 51.21N 12.00E
60 M13 Leunen Netherlands 51.30N 5.59E
47 E4 Leunovo U.S.S.R. 64.17N 42.43E
64 M3 Leupoldsdorf W Germany 50.01N 11.56E
66 Q1 Leupolz W Germany 47.44N 9.49E
60 G13 Leur Netherlands 51.35N 4.39E
13 J6 Leura Queensland 23.08S 149.34E
58 D2 Leurbost Lewis, W Isles Scotland 58.08N 6.28W
60 K11 Leusbroek Netherlands 52.07N 5.25E
18 B4 Leuser,Gunung mt Sumatra Indon 3.46N 97.12E
47 K6 Leushinskiy Tuman, Oz L U.S.S.R.
63 O6 Leussow E Germany 53.17N 11.18E
61 N3 Leut Belgium 50.59N 5.44E
65 D7 Leutasch Austria 47.23N 11.09E
64 L2 Leutenberg E Germany 50.33N 11.27E
64 J5 Leutershausen W Germany 49.18N 10.26E
69 N3 Leutesdorf W Germany 50.27N 7.23E
60 M12 Leuth Netherlands 51.50N 6.00E
64 J8 Leutkirch W Germany 47.50N 10.02E
65 M8 Leutschach Austria 46.41N 15.28E
61 J3 Leuven Belgium 50.53N 4.42E
60 N11 Leuvenheim Netherlands 52.05N 6.09E
72 C8 Leuy, le France 43.50N 0.38W
61 E4 Leuze Hainaut Belgium 50.36N 3.37E
61 K4 Leuze Namur Belgium 50.33N 4.55E
66 F3 Leuzigen Switzerland 47.11N 7.28E
99 J6 Levack Ontario 46.39N 81.24W
84 E5 Levádhia Greece 38.26N 22.53E
61 G6 Leval-Chaudeville Belgium 50.14N 4.13E
68 E3 Levallois-Perret France 48.54N 2.17E
59 D4 Levally L Mayo Irish Rep 53.59N 9.18W
61 G5 Leval-Trahegnies Belgium 50.26N 4.13E
83 C4 Levan Albania 40.40N 19.29E
111 N2 Levan Utah 39.34N 111.52W
52 F3 Levanger Norway 63.44N 11.20E
71 L6 Levanna, Mt France 45.24N 7.11E
79 B4 Levanne, Monte mt Italy 45.25N 7.10E
109 J2 Levant Kansas 39.22N 101.12W
71 J10 Levant,I.du France 43.02N 6.28E
79 G6 Lévanto Italy 44.10N 9.37E
81 E8 Lévanzo Egadi Is Italy 37.59N 12.22E
81 E6 Lévanzo isld Egadi Is Italy
70 J5 Levare France 48.25N 0.55W
45 V1 Levashevo U.S.S.R. 55.09N 49.55E
44 H5 Levashi U.S.S.R. 42.24N 47.17E
116 L4 Le Vauclin Martinique W I 14.32N 60.51W
47 L4 Levaya Khetta R U.S.S.R.
45 L5 Levaya Rossosh' U.S.S.R. 51.20N 39.25E
47 K2 Levdiyev, Os isld U.S.S.R. 68.45N 67.28E
47 K5 Levdym U.S.S.R. 60.26N 66.15E
87 L9 Leve,El Somalia 3.05N 46.20E
53 Z17 Leveld Norway 60.42N 8.30E
121 A10 Level, I Chile 44.30S 74.30W
112 E2 Levelland Texas 33.35N 102.23W
113 J7 Levelock Alaska 59.05N 156.59W
11 F11 Levels New Zealand 44.17S 171.13E
58 K6 Leven Fife Scotland 56.12N 3.00W
57 N5 Leven Humberside Eng 53.54N 0.19W
95 C2 Leven, Banc du Madagascar
58 A1 Levenish isld W Isles Scotland 57.47N 8.30W
58 F5 Leven,L Highland Scotland
58 K6 Leven,L Tayside Scotland 56.13N 3.23W
57 H4 Levens Cumbria Eng 54.16N 2.47W
71 L9 Levens France 43.51N 7.14E
63 M4 Levensau W Germany 54.22N 10.05E
37 D7 Levent Turkey 38.27N 37.51E
37 K1 Levent Turkey 41.04N 29.01E
66 M6 Leventina, Valle Switzerland
58 Q10 Levenwick Shetland Scotland 59.58N 1.17W
11 J11 L'Eveque,C Chatham Is Pacific Oc 44.06S 176.36W
14 E3 Lévêque,C W Australia 16.25S 122.55E
81 R12 Leverano Italy 40.17N 18.01E
58 B3 Leverburgh Harris, W Isles Scotland 57.46N 7.00W
103 J2 Leverett Massachusetts 42.27N 72.31W
108 F6 Leverett Wyoming 43.18N 104.48W
123 G8 Leverett Glacier Antarctica
106 K4 Levering Michigan 45.39N 84.47W
64 B1 Leverkusen W Germany 51.02N 6.59E
101 P3 Lever L N W Terr 65.25N 117.17W
63 H8 Levern W Germany 52.23N 8.27E
60 M15 Leveroij Netherlands 51.15N 5.51E
91 F6 Leverville Zaïre 4.50S 18.43E
70 N5 Lèves France 48.29N 1.29E
72 J2 Levet France 46.55N 2.24E
72 K7 Levezou mts France
62 L7 Levice Czechoslovakia 48.14N 18.35E
123 J6 Levick, Mt Antarctica
79 K2 Levico Italy 46.02N 11.18E
84 D6 Levídhi Greece 37.41N 22.17E
67 P13 Levie Corsica 41.42N 9.07E
71 J3 Levier France 46.57N 6.06E
72 G8 Lévignac France 43.40N 1.11E
72 E6 Lévignac de-Guyenne France 44.37N 0.12E
72 B7 Lévignacq France 44.01N 1.10W
47 H6 Levikha U.S.S.R. 57.38N 59.49E
11 K7 Levin New Zealand 40.37S 175.18E
46 M1 Levinskoye U.S.S.R. 58.32N 41.20E
13 B6 Levi Ra N Terr Australia
98 A7 Levis Quebec 46.47N 71.12W
104 C9 Levisa Fork R Kentucky
98 S8 Lévis,Pte Quebec 46.50N 71.10W
83 H7 Levítha isld Greece 37.01N 26.28E
103 N7 Levittown Long I, N Y 40.44N 73.32W
103 E6 Levittown New Jersey 40.02N 74.55W
103 E6 Levittown Pennsylvania 40.10N 74.50W
84 J11 Lévka Ori mts Crete
84 C4 Levkás Fthiótis Greece 38.55N 22.00E
84 A4 Levkás Greece 38.50N 20.42E
84 A4 Levkás isld Greece
84 C7 Lévki Greece 37.02N 21.40E
84 W23 Levkímmi Corfu 39.26N 20.05E
84 F4 Levkonisia islds Greece 38.57N 23.26E
45 J7 Levkovka Ukraine U.S.S.R. 49.17N 37.08E
84 F5 Lévktra Greece 38.15N 23.10E
66 K8 Levo Italy 45.53N 8.30E
44 F3 Levoberezhnyy,Kanal U.S.S.R.
62 M6 Levoča Czechoslovakia 49.01N 20.35E
44 F3 Levokumskoye U.S.S.R. 44.50N 44.40E
89 A1 Lévrier,B.du Mauritania
53 C4 Levring Denmark 56.18N 9.30E
72 H2 Levroux France 46.59N 1.36E
82 J7 Levski Bulgaria 43.21N 25.11E
45 L3 Lev Tolstoy U.S.S.R. 53.11N 39.28E
9 T7 Levuka Ovalau Fiji 17.42S 178.50E
109 F5 Levy New Mexico 36.05N 104.44W
70 H2 Levy,C France 49.42N 1.28W
105 E8 Levy,L Florida 29.33N 82.20W
108 K7 Lewanna Nebraska 42.16N 100.27W
103 E3 Lewbeach New York 42.00N 74.48W
25 D3 Lewe Burma 19.40N 96.04E
108 H8 Lewellen Nebraska 41.21N 102.10W
104 K8 Lewes Delaware 38.45N 75.09W
56 M6 Lewes E Sussex Eng 50.52N 0.01E
14 D6 Lewin,Mt W Australia 22.31S 120.18E
108 P8 Lewis Iowa 41.17N 95.06W
109 L4 Lewis Kansas 37.57N 99.16W
58 C2 Lewis div W Isles Scotland
110 D3 Lewis R Washington
12 D3 Lewis B S Australia
107 K5 Lewisburg Kentucky 37.00N 86.59W
104 A7 Lewisburg Ohio 39.51N 84.33W
104 J6 Lewisburg Pennsylvania 40.58N 76.55W
107 K6 Lewisburg Tennessee 35.29N 86.49W
104 E9 Lewisburg W Virginia 37.49N 80.28W
58 D1 Lewis,Butt of prom Lewis, W Isles Scotland 58.31N 6.15W
108 N7 Lewis & Clark Lake S Dakota
55 G4 Lewisham London Eng 51.27N 0.01W
94 S13 Lewisham S Africa 26.08S 27.48E
55 G4 Lewisham bor London England
98 O5 Lewis Hills Newfoundland 48.48N 58.33W
123 H3 Lewis I Antarctica 66.00S 134.15E
28 G7 Lewis Inlet Andaman Is
110 P5 Lewis L Wyoming 44.19N 110.38W
11 G9 Lewis Pass New Zealand 42.22S 172.27E
98 R4 Lewisporte Newfoundland 49.15N 55.04W
110 M1 Lewis Ra Montana
14 G5 Lewis Ra W Australia
104 G5 Lewis Run Pennsylvania 41.53N 78.40W
107 J7 Lewis Smith Lake res Alabama
111 O10 Lewis Springs Arizona 31.36N 110.09W
110 J3 Lewiston Idaho 46.25N 117.00W
104 P2 Lewiston Maine 44.08N 70.14W
106 K5 Lewiston Michigan 44.54N 84.18W
107 E1 Lewiston Missouri 40.04N 91.49W
105 K1 Lewiston N Carolina 36.07N 77.24W
104 F3 Lewiston New York 43.11N 79.03W
110 O8 Lewiston Utah 41.59N 111.51W
106 D9 Lewistown Illinois 40.25N 90.10W
110 Q2 Lewistown Montana 47.04N 109.26W
104 H6 Lewistown Pennsylvania 40.37N 77.36W
107 C8 Lewisville Arkansas 33.21N 93.38W
103 C7 Lewisville Chester, Pennsylvania 39.44N 75.53W
110 N6 Lewisville Idaho 43.42N 112.00W
108 Q6 Lewisville Minnesota 43.56N 94.26W
104 H5 Lewisville Potter Co, Penn 41.54N 77.47W
112 K2 Lewisville Texas 33.03N 96.59W
63 P6 Lewitz reg E Germany
56 K4 Lewknor Oxon Eng 51.41N 1.00W
19 C8 Lewotobi vol Indonesia 8.33S 122.48E
100 N8 Lewvan Saskatchewan 50.01N 104.08W
107 F7 Lexa Arkansas 34.36N 90.45W
56 N4 Lexden Essex Eng 51.54N 0.51E
106 F9 Lexington Illinois 40.39N 88.48W
107 L3 Lexington Indiana 38.40N 85.38W
107 M3 Lexington Kentucky 38.02N 84.30W
106 M6 Lexington Michigan 43.16N 82.32W
107 F8 Lexington Mississippi 33.07N 90.04W
107 C2 Lexington Missouri 39.11N 93.52W
105 G2 Lexington N Carolina 35.50N 80.27W
108 L9 Lexington Nebraska 40.46N 99.48W
103 F2 Lexington New York 42.15N 74.24W
109 N6 Lexington Oklahoma 35.02N 97.20W
110 F4 Lexington Oregon 45.27N 119.40W
105 F4 Lexington S Carolina 33.59N 81.15W
107 H6 Lexington Tennessee 35.39N 88.24W
112 L5 Lexington Texas 30.25N 97.01W
104 F9 Lexington Virginia 37.47N 79.27W
104 O8 Lexington dist Boston, Mass
104 J8 Lexington Park Maryland 38.15N 76.28W
60 J12 Lexmond Netherlands 51.58N 5.02E
72 H7 Lexos France 44.09N 1.52E
57 K4 Leyburn N Yorks Eng 54.19N 1.49W
108 N1 Leyden N Dakota 48.53N 97.49W
94 L4 Leydsdorp S Africa 23.59S 30.30E
23 D6 Leye Guangxi China 24.55N 106.28E
87 G9 Ley,El Ethiopia 3.45N 39.15E
64 L4 Leyerberg mt W Germany 49.38N 11.10E
26 Q14 Leygues Is Kerguelen Indian Ocean 48.40S 69.30E
32 B2 Leyla Dagh mt Iran 37.15N 46.21E
57 H5 Leyland Lancs Eng 53.42N 2.42W
37 E7 Leylek Turkey 38.02N 40.04E
71 L2 Leymen France 47.30N 7.30E
50 E6 Leynifoss Iceland 64.29N 20.17W
72 C6 Leyre R France
75 H2 Leyre,Monasterio de hist ruins Spain 42.38N 1.09W
72 C7 Leyre,Petite R France
56 N5 Leysdown Kent Eng 51.24N 0.55E
66 E6 Leysin Switzerland 46.21N 7.01E
19 M6 Leyte isld Philippines
19 M6 Leyte G Philippines
41 P2 Leyter,Mys C Franz Josef Land U.S.S.R. 80.39N 63.15E
55 G3 Leyton London Eng 51.34N 0.01W
55 G3 Leytonstone London England 51.34N 00.000
66 E7 Leytron Switzerland 46.12N 7.13E
71 F8 Lez R France
75 E2 Leza Spain 42.34N 2.38W
75 F3 Leza R Spain
62 N5 Leżajsk Poland 50.16N 22.26E
75 E1 Lezama Alava Spain 43.02N 2.59W
121 F5 Lezama Argentina 35.55S 57.54W
119 F3 Lezama Venezuela 9.44N 66.27W
75 E1 Lezama Viscaya Spain 43.17N 2.52W
71 E8 Lézan France 44.01N 4.03E
70 D4 Lèzardrieux France 48.47N 3.07W
72 G9 Lézat-sur-Lèze France 43.17N 1.21E
72 G9 Lèze R France
46 M1 Lezha U.S.S.R. 59.00N 40.32E
82 F9 Lezhë Albania 41.47N 19.39E
23 D3 Lezhi Sichuan China 30.16N 105.01E
46 M2 Lezhnevo U.S.S.R. 56.47N 40.59E
72 K9 Lézignan-Corbières France 43.12N 2.46E
69 G8 Lézinnes France 47.48N 4.05E
71 C5 Lezoux France 45.50N 3.23E
77 M3 Lezuza Spain 38.57N 2.22W
77 M3 Lezuza R Spain
66 N8 Lezzeno Italy 45.57N 9.11E
93 G8 Lgarya, L Tanzania 2.59S 35.02E
40 H3 L'gotnyy Mys C U.S.S.R. 56.27N 138.10E
45 G5 L'gov U.S.S.R. 51.41N 35.16E
45 G5 L'govskiy U.S.S.R. 51.39N 35.15E
24 G10 Lhachen La pass Xizang Zizhiqu 30.40N 91.05E
28 J1 Lhagyari Dzong Xizang Zizhiqu 29.00N 92.12E
23 B3 Lhakang Sichuan China 30.15N 101.30E
30 K2 Lhakpa La pass Xizang Zizhiqu 28.03N 86.59E
58 K3 Lhanbryde Grampian Scotland 57.38N 3.14W
24 G10 Lhanji La pass Xizang Zizhiqu 30.27N 91.25E
28 J1 Lhapso Xizang Zizhiqu 29.07N 92.30E
24 H10 Lhari Xizang Zizhiqu China 30.50N 93.24E
24 D9 Lhari mt pk Xizang Zizhiqu China 33.29N 81.43E
14 A7 Lharidon Bight W Australia
Lhariguo see Lhari Xizang Zizhiqu
24 G11 Lhasa Xizang Zizhiqu China 29.41N 91.10E
24 G11 Lhasa He R Xizang Zizhiqu China
24 G10 Lhasa Shi reg Xizang Zizhiqu China
Lhatse Dzong see Lhazê
24 F11 Lhazê Xizang Zizhiqu China 29.08N 87.43E
24 E9 Lhazhong Xizang Zizhiqu China 32.02N 86.34E
65 K4 Lhenice Czechoslovakia 48.59N 14.09E
72 G9 Lherm France 43.26N 1.13E
18 A3 Lhokkruet Sumatra Indon 4.51N 95.26E
18 A3 Lhoknga Sumatra Indon 5.25N 95.15E
18 B3 Lhokseumawe Sumatra Indon 5.09N 97.09E
18 B3 Lhoksukon Sumatra Indon 5.04N 97.19E
30 J2 Lho La pass Xizang Zizhiqu/Nepal 28.01N 86.53E
72 F3 Lhommaizé France 46.27N 0.36E
18 A3 Lhong Sumatra Indon 5.10N 95.18E
24 H10 Lhorong Xizang Zizhiqu China 30.45N 95.49E
72 G7 L'Hospitalet France 44.21N 1.24E
30 K2 Lhotse mt Xizang Zizhiqu/Nepal 27.58N 86.57E
30 J3 Lhotse Glacier Nepal
30 K2 Lhotse Shar mt Xizang Zizhiqu/Nepal 27.58N 86.57E
24 G11 Lhozhag Xizang Zizhiqu China 28.24N 90.49E
71 H5 Lhuis France 45.45N 5.32E
69 G6 Lhuître France 48.35N 4.16E
Lhuntse Dzong see Lhünzê
24 G11 Lhünzê Xizang Zizhiqu China 28.25N 92.30E
24 G10 Lhünzhub Xizang Zizhiqu China 30.15N 91.22E
90 H8 Lia Cent Afr Rep 6.50N 16.13E
53 X15 Liabre glacier Norway 61.37N 7.51E
53 W14 Liabygda Norway 62.19N 7.05E
44 F5 Liakhvi R Georgia U.S.S.R.
31 J3 Liakzun Kashmir 34.35N 77.40E
67 O12 Liamone R Corsica
Liancheng see Qinglong
23 H2 Liancheng Anhui China 33.13N 117.23E
23 G6 Liancheng Fujian China 25.43N 116.42E
69 C5 Liancourt France 49.20N 2.28E
Liancourt Rocks see Take-shima rocks
69 B2 Liane R France
23 C5 Lianfeng Yunnan China 27.52N 103.38E
19 F5 Liang Moluccas Indon 3.32S 128.16E
18 B8 Liang R Pen Malaysia
19 N7 Lianga Mindanao Philippines 8.38N 126.05E
19 N7 Lianga B Mindanao Philippines
21 D6 Liangbingtai Jilin China 43.12N 128.43E
18 M5 Liangbuaya Borneo Indon 0.04N 116.47E
22 J6 Liangcheng Nei Monggol Zizhiqu China 40.25N 112.20E
23 H1 Liangcheng Shandong China 35.30N 119.39E
23 D2 Liangdang Gansu China 33.52N 106.18E
22 G6 Lianggejing Nei Monggol Zizhiqu China 40.12N 105.10E
23 A6 Lianghe Yunnan China 24.50N 98.20E
23 C2 Lianghekou Gansu China 33.34N 104.27E
23 C3 Lianghekou Sichuan China 31.50N 104.54E
23 E4 Lianghekou Sichuan China 29.07N 108.45E
Liangjiayoufang see Youyu
Liangshizhen see Shaodong
25 K1 Liangtian Guangxi China 22.02N 110.06E
23 F6 Liangtian Hunan China 25.34N 112.58E
18 D4 Liang Timur, Gunong mt Pen Malaysia 3.47N 101.34E
23 C6 Liangwang Shan mts Yunnan China
23 G3 Liangze Hu L Hubei China
22 H8 Liangzhen Shaanxi China 37.32N 108.21E
Liangzhou see Wuwei
23 G3 Liangzi Hu L Hubei China
23 C1 Lianhua Gansu China 35.47N 103.00E
23 F5 Lianhua Jiangxi China 27.04N 113.54E
23 D1 Lianhuacheng Gansu China 35.05N 105.48E
23 G7 Lianhua Shan mts Guangdong China
23 H5 Lianjiang Fujian China 26.14N 119.33E
23 E8 Lianjiang Guangdong China 21.40N 110.16E
23 D6 Lian Jiang R Guizhou China
21 E4 Lianjiangkou Heilongjiang China 46.53N 130.16E
23 F6 Liannan Guangdong China 24.45N 112.20E
84 D4 Lianokládhion Greece 38.55N 22.18E
23 G6 Lianping Guangdong China 24.18N 114.27E
23 D3 Lianping Sichuan China 30.44N 107.50E
23 F6 Lianshan Guangdong China 24.33N 112.08E
21 C7 Lianshanguan Liaoning China 40.57N 123.46E
23 H2 Lianshui Jiangsu China 33.46N 119.15E
23 F5 Lian Shui R Hunan China
23 F7 Liantan Guangdong China 22.59N 111.44E
Liantang see Nanchang
25 F6 Liant, C Thailand 12.33N 100.55E
23 F3 Liantuo Hubei China 30.52N 111.09E
23 F6 Lian Xian Guangdong China 24.48N 112.26E
23 F5 Lianyuan Hunan China 27.42N 111.41E
23 H1 Lianyungang Jiangsu China 34.30N 117.22E
23 H1 Lianyungang city Jiangsu China 34.37N 119.10E
23 H1 Lianyungang port Jiangsu China 34.42N 119.28E
22 K8 Lianzhen Hebei China 37.51N 116.29E
Lianzhou see Hepu
21 E5 Lianzhushan Heilongjiang China 45.30N 131.43E
22 K8 Liaocheng Shandong China 36.29N 115.55E
21 B7 Liaodong Bandao pen Liaoning China
21 B7 Liaodong Wan gulf Liaoning China
24 G4 L'iaodun Xinjiang Uygur Zizhiqu China 43.15N 92.16E
21 C6 Liao He R Liaoning China
Liao-hsien see Zouquan
21 B7 Liaoning prov China
Liaotung, Gulf of see Liaodong Wan
21 C7 Liaoyang Liaoning China 41.16N 123.12E
21 C6 Liaoyangwopu Liaoning China 43.01N 123.28E
21 C6 Liaoyuan Jilin China 42.53N 125.10E
21 B7 Liaozhong Liaoning China 41.31N 122.43E
84 W22 Liapádhes Corfu 39.40N 19.45E
75 L2 Lia,Pico de mt Spain 42.43N 0.16E
31 F4 Liaqatabad Pakistan 32.17N 71.24E
101 M5 Liard R N W Terr/Yukon/Br Col
101 K6 Liard River Br Columbia 59.23N 126.02W
31 D8 Liari Pakistan 25.41N 66.30E
69 G4 Liart France 49.46N 4.21E
84 D8 Liasínova Greece 36.55N 22.14E
18 G7 Liat isld Indonesia
53 X15 Liavatn L Opland Norway 61.50N 7.45E
53 X17 Liavatn L Sogn og Fjordane Norway 60.52N 7.40E
30 F4 Libanggon Nepal 28.17N 82.38E
34 C5 Liban, Jebel mts Lebanon
119 C5 Libano Colombia 4.55N 75.02W
77 F7 Libar, Sierra de mts Spain
93 L6 Libat Kenya 0.52S 39.51E
58 J7 Libberton Strathclyde Scotland 55.41N 3.37W
110 K1 Libby Montana 48.25N 115.33W
101 P1 Libby L N W Terr 68.17N 117.29W
110 K1 Libby Res Montana
94 F2 Libebe Namibia 18.01S 21.29E
80 B3 Libeccio, Pta Italy 42.35N 10.03E
91 F2 Libenge Zaïre 3.39N 18.39E
109 K4 Liberal Kansas 37.03N 100.56W
107 B4 Liberal Missouri 37.33N 94.32W
113 H2 Liberator L Alaska 68.52N 158.20W
120 D3 Liberdade Acre Brazil 9.22S 71.09W
118 G8 Liberdade Minas Gerais Brazil 22.01S 44.22W
118 G10 Liberdade dist São Paulo Brazil
120 D2 Liberdade, R Amazonas Brazil
118 D2 Liberdade, R Mato Grosso Brazil
62 J5 Liberec Czechoslovakia 50.48N 15.05E
115 M4 Liberia Costa Rica 10.39N 85.28W
89 E8 Liberia rep W Africa
116 P4 Liberta Antigua W I 17.03N 61.48W
119 E3 Libertad Barinas Venez 8.21N 69.39W
119 F3 Libertad Cojedes Venez 9.15N 68.30W
119 D9 Libertad Peru 3.50S 74.07W
120 F10 Libertador General San Martin Jujuy Argentina 23.50S 64.45W
95 L4 Libertas S Africa 28.11S 27.44E
113 R4 Liberty Alaska 64.30N 141.15W
107 E2 Liberty Illinois 39.52N 91.07W
107 M2 Liberty Indiana 39.37N 84.56W
107 M4 Liberty Kentucky 37.19N 84.58W
107 F10 Liberty Mississippi 31.09N 90.50W
107 B2 Liberty Missouri 39.14N 94.25W
105 H2 Liberty N Carolina 35.52N 79.36W
108 O9 Liberty Nebraska 40.05N 96.27W
103 E3 Liberty New York 41.47N 74.46W
104 H5 Liberty Pennsylvania 41.33N 77.06W
100 M7 Liberty Saskatchewan 51.06N 105.29W
105 E3 Liberty S Carolina 34.47N 82.41W
112 N5 Liberty Texas 30.03N 94.47W
110 E2 Liberty Washington 47.14N 120.41W
104 A5 Liberty Center Ohio 41.28N 84.01W
105 G3 Liberty Hill S Carolina 34.27N 80.48W
112 K5 Liberty Hill Texas 30.41N 97.57W
103 J8 Liberty I New York
104 H7 Libertytown Maryland 39.30N 77.16W
106 B9 Libertyville Iowa 40.57N 92.02W
103 F3 Libertyville New York 41.43N 74.08W
9 C2 Lib I atoll Marshall Is Pacific Oc 8.26N 167.21E
61 M7 Libin Belgium 49.58N 5.15E
64 Q4 Liblín Czechoslovakia 49.55N 13.33E
19 L5 Libmanan Luzon Philippines 13.43N 123.04E
86 L4 Libni, Gebel hill Egypt 30.44N 33.50E
23 D6 Libo Guizhou China 25.25N 107.50E
19 F4 Libobo, Tanjung C Halmahera Indon 0.54S 128.28E
95 N7 Libode S Africa 31.33S 29.01E
83 D4 Libohovë Albania 40.02N 20.25E
93 M5 Liboi Kenya 0.23N 40.58E
91 E4 Liboka Congo 0.55S 16.01E
91 E4 Liboko watercourse Congo
92 A9 Libonda Zambia 14.50S 22.57E
95 M4 Libono Lesotho 28.38S 28.35E
72 F7 Libos France 44.29N 0.57E
91 C3 Liboumba R Gabon 0.38N 12.47E
72 D6 Libourne France 44.55N 0.14W
14 F5 Libral Well W Australia 22.09S 125.24E
61 M7 Libramont Belgium 49.55N 5.23E
83 D3 Librazhd Albania 41.12N 20.20E
115 L8 Libres Mexico 19.29N 97.42W
91 A3 Libreville Gabon 0.30N 9.25E
77 O5 Librilla Spain 37.54N 1.20W
75 H7 Libros Spain 40.10N 1.14W
19 M8 Libuganon R Mindanao Philippines
73 F3 Libya rep N Africa
85 F6 Libyan Desert Libya
85 H4 Libyan Plateau Egypt
37 G2 Libyssa anc site Turkey 40.48N 29.38E
120 E10 Licancabur vol Bolivia/Chile 22.51S 67.58W
121 A5 Licantén Chile 35.00S 72.00W
121 B5 Licantén Chile 35.00S 72.00W
81 G9 Licata Sicily 37.07N 13.57E
79 H6 Licciana Italy 44.16N 10.02E
37 F7 Lice Turkey 38.29N 40.39E
64 F2 Lich W Germany 50.31N 8.50E
Licheng see Jinhu
22 L8 Licheng Shandong China 36.41N 117.05E
22 J8 Licheng Shanxi China 36.25N 113.30E
11 K5 Lichfield New Zealand 38.08S 175.48E
56 H2 Lichfield Staffs Eng 52.42N 1.48W
92 G8 Lichinga Mozambique 13.19S 35.13E
61 K2 Lichtaart Belgium 51.13N 4.55E
64 E6 Lichtenau Baden-Württemberg W Germany 48.43N 8.00E
64 K5 Lichtenau Bayern W Germany 49.16N 10.42E
63 J9 Lichtenau Nordrhein-Westfalen W Germany 51.37N 8.53E
64 P2 Lichtenberg E Germany 50.51N 13.25E
64 M3 Lichtenberg W Germany 50.23N 11.41E
95 K2 Lichtenburg S Africa 26.09S 26.11E
64 L3 Lichtenfels W Germany 50.09N 11.04E
66 N2 Lichtensteig Switzerland 47.20N 9.06E
64 O2 Lichtenstein E Germany 50.46N 12.38E
64 G7 Lichtenstein W Germany 48.25N 9.17E
64 N2 Lichtentanne W Germany 50.40N 12.26E
60 P12 Lichtenvoorde Netherlands 51.59N 6.34E
61 C2 Lichtervelde Belgium 51.02N 3.09E
23 C1 Lichuan Gansu China 34.10N 104.23E
23 E3 Lichuan Hubei China 30.20N 108.57E
23 G5 Lichuan Jiangxi China 27.17N 116.46E
92 H10 Liciro Mozambique 16.27S 36.03E
103 A6 Lickdale Pennsylvania 40.28N 76.31W
107 E4 Licking Missouri 37.31N 91.51W
104 B8 Licking R Kentucky
82 C6 Ličko Petrovo Selo Yugoslavia 44.52N 15.44E
81 J9 Licodia Eubea Sicily 37.10N 14.42E
91 H12 Licoma Angola 17.17S 22.31E
81 J3 Licosa, Pta Italy 40.15N 14.55E
72 C9 Licq-Athérey France 43.04N 0.52W
69 B2 Licques France 50.47N 1.56E
46 F3 Lida Belorussiya U.S.S.R. 53.50N 25.19E
111 G4 Lida Nevada 37.29N 117.29W
21 B9 Lidao Shandong China 37.13N 122.31E
12 K7 Lidcombe dist Sydney, N S W
57 H2 Liddel Water R Borders etc Scotland
108 Q7 Lidderdale Iowa 42.05N 94.45W
66 E8 Liddes Switzerland 45.59N 7.12E
57 H2 Liddisdale V Borders etc Scotland
52 M2 Liden Västerbotten Sweden 64.40N 20.35E
52 K4 Liden Västernorrland Sweden 62.40N 16.55E
90 J4 Lidey Chad 15.40N 19.55E
10 E11 Lidgbird, Mt Lord Howe I Pacific Oc 31.35S 159.06E
108 N3 Lidgerwood N Dakota 46.06N 97.10W
95 O5 Lidgetton S Africa 29.27S 30.07E
52 G10 Lidhult Sweden 56.49N 13.25E
90 G7 Lidi R Cameroon
52 L7 Lidingö Sweden 59.22N 18.10E
91 E2 Lidjombo Cent Afr Rep 2.38N 16.03E
52 G8 Lidköping Sweden 58.30N 13.10E
79 M4 Lido Italy 45.25N 12.23E
79 N3 Lido di Iésolo Italy 45.30N 12.38E
80 F5 Lido di Ostia Italy 41.43N 12.17E
80 E4 Lido di Tarquinia Italy 42.20N 11.42E
72 D6 Lidoire R France
84 D4 Lidokhoríkion Greece 38.32N 22.12E
75 H6 Lidón Spain 40.43N 1.07W
62 M2 Lidzbark Poland 53.15N 19.49E
62 M1 Lidzbark Warmiński Poland 54.08N 20.35E
70 E5 Lié R France
65 M8 Liebach Austria 46.59N 15.20E
65 L4 Liebenau Austria 48.33N 14.48E
63 K9 Liebenau Hessen W Germany 51.30N 9.18E
63 K7 Liebenau Niedersachsen W Ger 52.37N 9.06E
95 M3 Liebenbergsvlei R S Africa
64 M2 Liebengrün E Germany 50.33N 11.38E
Liebenstein see Bad Liebenstein
100 H8 Liebenthal Saskatchewan 50.41N 109.32W
63 S7 Liebenwalde E Germany 52.53N 13.25E
63 S9 Liebenwerda E Germany 51.31N 13.23E
64 N1 Liebertwolkwitz E Germany 51.17N 12.28E
13 B6 Liebig, Mt N Terr Australia 23.16S 131.18E
11 E10 Liebig Ra New Zealand
63 S4 Liebitz isld E Germany 54.24N 13.13E
82 G5 Liebling Romania 45.33N 21.20E
66 P3 Liechtenstein principality Europe
51 J3 Liedakka Sweden 68.23N 21.35E
61 G3 Liedekerke Belgium 50.52N 4.05E
75 H2 Liédena Spain 42.37N 1.16W
61 G3 Lieferinge Belgium 50.47N 4.04E
61 N4 Liège Belgium 50.38N 5.35E
61 L4 Liège prov Belgium
72 G1 Liège, le France 47.13N 1.05E
Liegnitz see Legnica
91 J3 Lieki Zaïre 0.42N 24.12E
51 P8 Lieksa Finland 63.20N 30.00E
46 E2 Lielupe R Latvia U.S.S.R.
60 K13 Liempde Netherlands 51.35N 5.23E
91 J2 Lienart Zaïre 3.00N 25.35E
65 H6 Lienbach Austria 47.39N 13.26E
60 L12 Lienden Netherlands 51.57N 5.31E
75 F7 Liendre R Spain
66 F6 Liene R Switzerland
52 G2 Liene reg Norway
63 G8 Lienen W Germany 52.09N 7.59E
Lien-shan see Jinxi
65 G8 Lienz Austria 46.51N 12.50E
46 D2 Liepāja Latvia U.S.S.R. 56.30N 21.00E
63 S5 Liepen E Germany 53.54N 13.29E
69 N7 Lièpvre France 48.16N 7.17E
61 J2 Lier Belgium 51.08N 4.35E
52 F6 Lier Opland Norway 60.09N 11.59E
52 E7 Lierbyen Norway 59.57N 10.14E
60 E12 Lier, de Netherlands 51.58N 4.15E
75 C1 Liérganes Spain 43.20N 3.44W
79 F3 Lierna Italy 45.58N 9.18E
71 E2 Liernais France 47.12N 4.17E
61 O5 Lierneux Belgium 50.17N 5.48E
61 K4 Liernu Belgium 50.35N 4.50E
60 L14 Lierop Netherlands 51.25N 5.41E
61 N4 Liers Belgium 50.42N 5.34E
69 B5 Lierville France 49.11N 1.53E
65 J8 Liesar R Austria
64 B3 Lieser R W Germany
65 H8 Lieserhofen Austria 46.52N 13.30E
60 L13 Lieshout Netherlands 51.31N 5.36E
65 O5 Liesing Austria 48.09N 16.18E
65 L7 Liesingtal V Austria
71 H2 Liesle France 47.04N 5.50E
69 F4 Liesse France 49.36N 3.49E
60 M14 Liessel Netherlands 51.25N 5.49E
66 G2 Liestal Switzerland 47.29N 7.43E
82 L5 Liești Romania 45.36N 27.35E
87 C6 Liet Sudan 8.42N 30.40E
77 N3 Liétor Spain 38.33N 1.58W
66 B5 Lieu, le Switzerland 46.39N 6.17E
70 M3 Lieurey France 49.13N 0.30E
69 D6 Lieusaint France 48.38N 2.33E
70 L3 Lieuvin France 49.08N 0.21E
60 P11 Lievelde Netherlands 52.01N 6.35E
60 O7 Lieveren Netherlands 53.07N 6.27E
69 D3 Liévin France 50.25N 2.48E
99 P7 Lièvre R Quebec
98 C6 Lièvres, I. aux Quebec 47.50N 69.43W
61 H2 Liezele Belgium 51.04N 4.17E
65 K6 Liezen Austria 47.35N 14.15E
69 J8 Liez, Res. de France 47.52N 5.25E
19 E4 Lifamatola isld Moluccas Indon 1.49S 126.25E
59 K5 Liffey, R Dublin Irish Rep
69 K7 Liffol-le-Grand France 48.19N 5.35E
59 H2 Lifford Donegal Irish Rep 54.50N 7.29W
59 H2 Lifford Bridge Donegal Irish Rep 54.49N 7.29W
70 H5 Liffre France 48.13N 1.30W
121 C8 Lifi Mahuida mt Argentina 40.58S 68.46W
121 B8 Lifi Mahuida pk Argentina 41.47S 68.47W
34 L8 Lifiyah, Al Saudi Arabia 30.23N 43.04E
53 S16 Lifjorden inlet Norway 61.09N 5.12E
9 C13 Lifou isld Loyalty Is Pacific Oc
56 C6 Lifton Devon Eng 50.39N 4.17W
9 U12 Lifuka isld Tonga, Pacific Oc 19.50S 174.22W
91 C8 Lifune R Angola
80 K7 Li Galli Italy 40.35N 14.26E
19 L5 Ligao Luzon Philippines 13.14N 123.33E
72 E7 Ligardes France 44.01N 0.28E
84 C3 Ligariá Greece 39.29N 21.41E
91 H3 Ligasa Zaïre 0.44N 23.49E
88 H10 Ligdam reg Mauritania
Ligen-i Shkodrës L see Skadarsko Jezero lake
66 E3 Ligerz Switzerland 47.05N 7.08E
23 F1 Ligeta Shanxi China 35.23N 112.05E
23 F1 Ligeta Shanxi China 35.25N 112.07E
23 J1 Ligezhuang Shandong China 36.22N 120.12E
51 H5 Ligga Sweden 66.47N 19.55E
112 H7 Light Texas 28.21N 99.30W
14 E8 Lightfoot, L W Australia 29.02S 123.30E
105 B9 Lighthouse Point Florida 26.08N 80.06W
105 C8 Lighthouse Pt Florida 29.54N 84.21W
115 Q9 Lighthouse Reef Belize
14 F4 Lightjack Hill W Australia 19.10S 125.55E
12 J3 Lightning Ridge New S Wales 29.25S 147.59E
103 B4 Light Street Pennsylvania 41.03N 76.25W
72 J5 Liginiac France 45.25N 2.19E
65 M8 Ligist Austria 46.59N 15.12E
72 G2 Liglet France 46.31N 1.05E
72 G3 Lignac France 46.27N 1.14E
79 O3 Lignano Pineta Italy 45.41N 13.07E
79 O3 Lignano Sabbiadoro Italy 45.42N 13.08E
61 E4 Ligne Belgium 50.37N 3.43E
70 H7 Ligne France 47.25N 1.22W
66 B4 Lignerolle Switzerland 46.46N 6.27E
70 K4 Lignieres France 48.32N 0.13W
72 J2 Lignières France 46.45N 2.10E
70 K4 Lignières-Orgères France 48.32N 0.12W
108 H1 Lignite N Dakota 48.53N 102.32W
70 D5 Lignol France 48.02N 3.16W
71 E6 Lignon R France
71 E5 Lignon-du-Nord R France
104 H8 Lignum Virginia 38.25N 77.51W
61 J4 Ligny Belgium 50.31N 4.35E
69 J6 Ligny-en-Barrois France 48.41N 5.20E
69 F8 Ligny-le-Châtel France 47.54N 3.45E
70 O6 Ligny-le-Ribault France 47.42N 1.47E
79 H6 Ligonchio Italy 44.19N 10.20E
66 P7 Ligoncio, Passo Italy 46.14N 9.34E
92 J9 Ligonha R Mozambique
106 J8 Ligonier Indiana 41.27N 85.37W
104 F6 Ligonier Pennsylvania 40.14N 79.14W
84 F6 Ligoúrion Greece 37.37N 23.02E
121 B4 Ligua, B. de la Chile
72 F1 Ligueil France 47.03N 0.49E
72 E2 Ligugé France 46.31N 0.20E
115 D5 Ligui Mexico 25.48N 111.19W
23 H1 Liguoyi Jiangsu China 34.30N 117.22E
79 D6 Liguria Italy
78 B5 Ligurian Sea Italy
111 K9 Ligurta Arizona 32.40N 114.18W
86 M9 Lig, Wâdi watercourse Egypt
92 H7 Ligwera Tanzania 10.27S 37.51E
33 G3 Lihābah, Al Saudi Arabia 27.14N 47.00E
15 M5 Lihir Group islds Bismarck Arch
15 M5 Lihir I Bismarck Arch
53 B3 Lihme Denmark 56.36N 8.44E
69 D4 Lihons France 49.50N 2.46E
13 K3 Lihou Reef & Cays Gt Barrier Reef Aust
Li-hua see Litang
114 F4 Lihue Hawaiian Is 21.59N 159.23W
114 F3 Lihue dist Hawaiian Is
46 E1 Lihula Estonia U.S.S.R. 58.40N 23.58E
51 J3 Liiakero mt Sweden 68.28N 21.15E
84 Y20 Lija Malta 35.54N 14.27E
77 M6 Lijar Spain 37.18N 2.12W
23 B5 Lijiang Naxizu Zizhixian Yunnan China 26.51N 100.16E
22 L8 Lijin Shandong China 37.32N 118.16E
22 G8 Lijunbu Ningxia China 36.14N 105.52E
37 D6 Lik R Turkey
84 C7 Líkaion Oros mt Greece 37.27N 21.58E
91 K2 Likandi Zaïre 3.23N 26.09E
50 L5 Likárvatn L Iceland 64.48N 14.50W
91 K9 Likasi Zaïre 10.58S 26.47E
91 H2 Likati Zaïre 3.20N 23.56E
91 H2 Likati R Zaïre
101 N9 Likely Br Col 52.36N 121.31W
110 E8 Likely California 41.14N 120.30W
91 G4 Likete Zaïre 0.48S 21.31E
84 E4 Likhás pen Greece
46 K2 Likhoslavl' U.S.S.R. 57.10N 35.30E
45 M8 Likhovskoy U.S.S.R. 48.08N 40.11E
15 E4 Liki isld Irian Jaya 1.35S 138.40E
9 C2 Likiep atoll Marshall Is Pacific Oc 10.00N 169.08E
91 G2 Likimi Zaïre 2.44N 20.47E
45 K1 Likino-Dulevo U.S.S.R. 55.42N 38.58E
90 J6 Likkine Chad 11.20N 18.10E
29 H7 Likma Madhya Prad India 20.12N 82.02E
83 D3 Likmetaj Albania 41.33N 19.34E
84 C8 Likódhimos mt Greece 36.56N 21.49E
84 D7 Likókhia Greece 37.30N 22.10E
93 M4 Likole Kenya 1.25N 40.33E
92 G8 Likoma I Malawi 12.03S 34.47E
90 C6 Likoro Nigeria 11.12N 7.45E
91 J4 Likoto Zaïre 1.13S 24.51E
91 E2 Likouala div Congo
91 D3 Likouala R Congo
91 E3 Likouala aux Herbes R Congo
84 D6 Likoúri Greece 37.51N 22.12E
18 L3 Liku Sarawak Malaysia 4.30N 114.04E
19 D3 Likupang Celebes Indon 1.40N 125.05E
Likuri Harbour see Lomawai
92 G7 Likuyu Tanzania 10.41S 35.30E
92 H7 Likuyu Tanzania 10.20S 36.15E
87 D7 Likwangoli Sudan 7.04N 33.00E
84 D4 Lilaía Greece 38.37N 22.30E
93 C2 Lilak mt Uganda 3.03N 31.58E
91 H4 Lilanga Zaïre 0.34S 23.56E
68 G3 Lilas, les France 48.53N 2.25E
92 D9 Lilayi Zambia 15.31S 28.20E
107 G5 Lilbourn Mississippi 36.33N 89.32W
53 B2 Lildstrand Denmark 57.09N 8.58E
67 O11 L'Ile Rousse Corsica 42.37N 8.56E
9 D4 Lilian Pt Ocean I Pacific Oc 0.53S 169.35E
14 F8 Lilian, Pt W Australia 27.39S 126.00E
65 N5 Lilienfeld Austria 48.01N 15.36E
63 J6 Lilienthal W Germany 53.09N 8.54E
23 F5 Liling Hunan China 27.42N 113.29E
89 H6 Lilixia Ghana 10.48N 10.05W
31 G4 Lilla Pakistan 32.31N 72.50E
13 C7 Lilla Creek N Terr Australia 25.35S 134.05E
61 K2 Lille Belgium 51.14N 4.50E
69 E2 Lille France 50.39N 3.05E
53 E4 Lilleå R Århus Denmark
53 A4 Lilleå R Ringkøbing Denmark
53 D6 Lille Bælt str Denmark
70 M2 Lillebonne France 49.31N 0.32E
53 N10 Lille Dimon isld Faeroes 61.38N 6.43W
53 G5 Lille Fuglede Denmark 55.36N 11.17E
52 E5 Lillehammer Norway 61.06N 10.27E
48 R11 Lille Hellefiskebanke Greenland
53 K6 Lilleklint cliffs Denmark 55.01N 12.32E
53 G7 Lilleø isld Denmark 54.55N 11.29E
53 J5 Lillerød Denmark 55.53N 12.22E
69 C2 Lillers France 50.34N 2.29E
52 D8 Lillesand Norway 58.15N 8.23E

53 J5 Lille Skensved Denmark 55.31N 12.09E
53 S18 Lille Sotra isld Norway 60.23N 5.08E
52 F7 Lillestrøm Norway 59.58N 11.05E
53 E3 Lille Vildmose moor Denmark 56.52N 10.14E
52 H5 Lillhärdal Sweden 61.51N 14.05E
52 H3 Lillholmsjön Sweden 63.39N 14.20E
51 G6 Lillholmträsk Sweden 65.01N 19.10E
98 L2 Lillian L Quebec
107 D9 Lillie Louisiana 32.57N 92.39W
57 H1 Lilliesleaf Borders Scotland 55.31N 2.44W
105 J2 Lillington N Carolina 35.25N 78.50W
103 H3 Lillinonah, L Connecticut
109 O2 Lillis Kansas 39.35N 96.18W
61 H1 Lillo Belgium 51.18N 4.18E
76 F3 Lillo León Spain 42.47N 6.37W
75 D8 Lillo Toledo Spain 39.43N 3.19W
75 D8 Lillo, Altos de hills Spain
61 H4 Lillois-Witterzée Belgium 50.39N 4.22E
101 N10 Lillooet Br Columbia 50.41N 121.59W
101 M10 Lillooet R Br Columbia
104 G6 Lilly Pennsylvania 40.26N 78.38W
92 F8 Lilongwe Malawi 13.58S 33.49E
92 F8 Lilongwe R Malawi
120 F12 Lilo Viejo Argentina 26.54N 63.00W
19 L7 Liloy Mindanao Philippines 8.07N 122.41E
108 N4 Lily S Dakota 45.10N 97.41W
12 E4 Lilydale S Australia 32.58S 139.59E
12 H8 Lilydale Tasmania 41.14S 147.14E
82 F7 Lim R Yugoslavia
106 C9 Lima Illinois 40.11N 91.22W
19 E5 Lima Moluccas Indon 3.41S 127.56E
110 N5 Lima Montana 44.39N 112.37W
104 H4 Lima New York 42.54N 77.37W
104 A6 Lima Ohio 40.43N 84.06W
109 O6 Lima Oklahoma 35.12N 96.35W
33 M4 Limā Oman 25.57N 56.28E
118 C8 Lima Paraguay 23.53S 56.30W
103 D7 Lima Pennsylvania 39.55N 75.26W
120 B5 Lima Peru 12.06S 77.03W
52 G6 Lima Sweden 60.55N 13.20E
120 B4 Lima dept Peru
76 B5 Lima R Portugal
92 C8 Lima tribe Zambia
121 B4 Limache Chile 33.00S 71.16W
118 G7 Lima Duarte Brazil 21.50S 43.48W
72 L4 Limagne reg France

61 J4 Limal Belgium 50.42N 4.34E
72 E3 Limalonges France 46.08N 0.10E
35 D1 Liman Israel 33.03N 35.07E
46 K5 Liman Ukraine U.S.S.R. 49.32N 36.25E
40 J5 Liman U.S.S.R. 52.41N 141.10E
44 H2 Liman U.S.S.R. 45.45N 47.12E
79 M2 Limana Italy 46.06N 12.09E
44 F1 Liman Beren L U.S.S.R.
37 E2 Liman Burun C Turkey 40.58N 27.58E
18 J9 Liman, Gunung mt Java Indon 7.48S 111.45E
62 M6 Limanowa Poland 49.43N 20.25E
119 H6 Limão Brazil 3.55N 60.24W
118 F9 Limao dist São Paulo Brazil
110 N5 Lima Res Montana 44.38N 112.16W
24 D9 Lima Ringma Tso L Xizang Zizhiqu China 32.25N 82.25E
121 B3 Limarí, R Chile
18 F5 Limas Indonesia 0.12N 104.31E
76 D13 Limas R Portugal
19 M7 Limasawa isld Philippines 9.58N 125.05E
84 R15 Limassol Cyprus 34.40N 33.03E
18 E7 Limau Jerigi Sumatra Indon 3.34S 104.00E
18 H5 Limaumanis Borneo Indon 1.35N 109.20E
59 J1 Limavady Londonderry N Ireland 55.03N 6.57W
69 B6 Limay France 49.00N 1.44E
19 G1 Limay Luzon Philippines 14.34N 120.36E
121 C6 Limay Mahuida Argentina 37.20S 66.40W
121 C7 Limay, R Argentina
64 C5 Limbach W Germany 49.19N 7.17E
64 O2 Limbach-Oberfrohna E Germany 50.52N 12.46E
81 L6 Limbadi Italy 38.34N 15.58E
18 L3 Limbang Sarawak Malaysia 4.50N 115.00E
18 L3 Limbang R Sarawak Malaysia
120 D6 Limbani Peru 14.07S 69.41W
81 C2 Limbara, Monti Sardinia
46 E2 Limbaži Latvia U.S.S.R. 57.30N 24.40E
29 B7 Limbda Gujarat India 21.49N 71.43E
29 B6 Limbdi Gujarat India 22.36N 72.00E
116 H5 Limbé Haiti 19.44N 72.25W
92 G9 Limbe Malawi 15.50S 35.03E
84 D8 Limberdhon Greece 36.47N 22.29E
19 G2 Limbones Cove Luzon Philippines
19 C3 Limbotto Celebes Indon 0.39N 122.59E
19 C3 Limbotto, Danau L Celebes Indon 0.35N 122.58E
61 O4 Limbourg Belgium 50.37N 5.56E
60 T16 Limbricht Netherlands 51.01N 5.50E
91 F10 Limbueta Angola 12.30S 18.44E
18 H6 Limbung Borneo Indon 0.15S 109.50E
19 A6 Limbung Celebes Indon 5.22S 119.29E
13 A3 Limbunya N Terr Australia 17.12S 129.48E
64 E3 Limburg W Germany 50.23N 8.04E
61 L3 Limburg prov Belgium
60 M15 Limburg prov Netherlands
18 G2 Lim Chu Kang dist Singapore
110 H5 Lime Oregon 44.24N 117.18W
52 G6 Limedsforsen Sweden 60.52N 13.25E
113 K6 Lime Hills Alaska
11 C13 Limehills New Zealand 46.03S 168.20E
68 G5 Limeil-Brévannes France 48.45N 2.28E
118 F8 Limeira Brazil 22.34S 47.25W
61 J4 Limelette Belgium 50.41N 4.34E
79 L4 Limena Italy 45.29N 11.51E
83 G4 Limenária Greece 40.39N 24.34E
83 H7 Limén Vathéos Greece 37.45N 26.58E
59 E6 Limerick Limerick Irish Rep 52.40N 8.38W
104 P3 Limerick Maine 43.42N 70.48W
100 L9 Limerick Saskatchewan 49.39N 106.13W
59 D7 Limerick co Irish Rep
59 F7 Limerick Junction Tipperary Irish Rep 52.29N 8.12W
103 B4 Lime Ridge Pennsylvania 41.02N 76.20W
61 O6 Limerlé Belgium 50.10N 5.55E
103 H3 Lime Rock Connecticut 41.56N 73.27W
70 F6 Limerzel France 47.38N 2.20W
108 S6 Lime Springs Iowa 43.28N 92.18W
105 F10 Limestone Florida 27.22N 81.54W
104 R7 Limestone Maine 46.55N 67.50W
104 G4 Limestone New York 42.02N 78.39W
100 W2 Limestone L Manitoba
100 T5 Limestone Pt C Manitoba 53.45N 98.55W
70 M2 Limésy France 49.36N 0.56E
113 K6 Lime Village Alaska 61.20N 155.37W
53 B3 Limfjorden str Denmark
53 K5 Limhamn Sweden 55.34N 12.57E
76 D4 Limia R Spain
79 E2 Limidario, Monte mt Italy/Switz 46.08N 8.37E
Limín see Thásos
81 K8 Limina Sicily 37.57N 15.17E
52 H2 Limingen L Norway 64.50N 13.40E
51 L7 Liminka Finland 64.50N 25.20E
Limir see Lomir
66 K2 Limmat R Switzerland
60 G9 Limmen Netherlands 52.34N 4.41E
13 D2 Limmen Bight N Terr Australia
13 D3 Limmen Bight R N Terr Australia
66 N4 Limmernsee L Switzerland
84 E6 Limnes Greece 37.43N 22.52E
84 P14 Limni Cyprus 35.02N 32.28E
84 F4 Límni Greece 38.46N 23.20E
84 S14 Limnia Cyprus 35.11N 33.53E
84 E2 Límni Voïvi̇̈ís L Greece
84 A4 Límni Voulkariá L Greece
84 D3 Límni Xiniás L Greece
83 G5 Límnos isld Greece
84 B4 Límnos Amvrakia L Greece
84 A3 Limnothálassa Tsoukalió lagoon Greece
40 F4 Limnu R U.S.S.R.
117 J8 Limoeiro Brazil 7.51S 35.29W
117 H7 Limoeiro do Norte Brazil 5.08S 38.06W
84 E4 Limogárdhi Greece 38.57N 22.31E
72 G4 Limoges France 45.50N 1.15E
99 P7 Limoges Ontario 45.20N 75.17W
72 H7 Limogne, Causse de plat France
72 H7 Limogne-en-Quércey France 44.23N 1.46E
72 L2 Limoise France 46.41N 3.03E
109 G2 Limon Colorado 39.16N 103.40W
115 N5 Limón Costa Rica 10.00N 83.01W
115 M2 Limón Honduras 15.50N 85.31W
115 E9 Limon B Panama Canal Zone
79 C6 Limone Piemonte Italy 44.12N 7.34E
71 F5 Limonest France 45.51N 4.45E
79 J3 Limone sul Garda Italy 45.49N 10.47E
77 C3 Limonetes R Spain
26 B12 Limon, Mt Rodriguez I Ind Oc 19.42S 63.27E
61 M4 Limont Belgium 50.39N 5.19E
120 F6 Limoquije Bolivia 15.24S 64.46W
80 L5 Limosano Italy 41.40N 14.37E
68 B6 Limours France 48.39N 2.05E
67 F7 Limousin prov France
72 J9 Limoux France 43.03N 2.13E
112 D5 Limpia Cr Texas
75 D1 Limpias Spain 43.22N 3.25W
56 G5 Limpley Stoke Wilts Eng 51.21N 2.19W
94 L4 Limpopo R S E Africa
56 M5 Limpsfield Surrey Eng 51.16N 0.01E
79 P4 Limski Zaliv B Yugoslavia
23 E6 Limu Guangxi China 25.10N 110.44E
9 U12 Limu atoll Tonga, Pacific Oc 20.02S 174.29W
93 H7 Limuru Kenya 1.07S 36.38E
53 D4 Linå Denmark 56.09N 9.42E
51 H4 Linaälv Sweden 67.16N 20.15E
51 J5 Lina älv R Sweden
15 B4 Lina, Gunung mt Irian Jaya 1.26S 133.50E
33 E2 Līnah Saudi Arabia 28.47N 43.45E
34 L10 Linah Saudi Arabia 28.48N 43.47E
95 M5 Linakeng Lesotho 29.31S 28.47E
51 P2 Linakhamari U.S.S.R. 69.34N 31.28E
23 H3 Lin'an Jiangsu China 30.16N 119.43E
19 M8 Linao B Mindanao Philippines 6.45N 124.01E
19 J6 Linapacan isld Philippines
19 J6 Linapacan Str Philippines
66 R4 Linard, Piz mt Switzerland 46.48N 10.04E
72 H4 Linards France 45.42N 1.32E
121 B5 Linares Chile 35.47S 71.40W
119 C7 Linares Colombia 1.24N 77.30W
115 K5 Linares Mexico 24.54N 99.38W
77 J4 Linares Spain 38.05N 3.38W
121 B6 Linares prov Chile
75 J7 Linares R Spain
75 C4 Linares del Arroyo, Embalse de res Spain 41.31N 3.33W
75 J7 Linares de Mora Spain 40.19N 0.35W
76 H7 Linares de Ríofrío Spain 40.35N 5.55W
84 H4 Linariá Greece 38.50N 24.32E
80 E4 Linaro, C Italy 42.01N 11.52E
69 C6 Linas France 48.38N 2.16E
81 B5 Linas, Mte Sardinia 39.27N 8.37E
79 F8 Linate dist Milan Italy
39 L2 Linatkhyrvuvaam R U.S.S.R.
18 L4 Linau Balui Plat Sarawak Malaysia
23 B7 Lincang Yunnan China 23.54N 100.01E
120 B10 Lince dist Lima Peru
61 L4 Lincent Belgium 50.42N 5.02E
56 K5 Linch W Sussex Eng 51.02N 0.47W
22 K8 Lincheng Hebei China 37.30N 114.28E
Lin-chiang Yunnan China see Menghun
Lin-ch'uan see Fuzhou
23 G5 Linchuan Jiangxi China 27.55N 116.16E

94 J4 Linchwe Botswana 23.56S 26.20E
107 K8 Lincoln Alabama 33.35N 86.09W
121 E5 Lincoln Argentina 34.54S 61.30W
111 C3 Lincoln California 38.53N 121.18W
106 E9 Lincoln Illinois 40.10N 89.21W
109 M2 Lincoln Kansas 39.04N 98.12W
57 M6 Lincoln Lincs Eng 53.14N 0.33W
104 R1 Lincoln Maine 45.24N 68.29W
106 L5 Lincoln Michigan 44.41N 83.25W
108 Q3 Lincoln Minnesota 46.12N 94.40W
110 N3 Lincoln Montana 46.57N 112.40W
108 O9 Lincoln Nebraska 40.49N 96.41W
104 O2 Lincoln New Hampshire 44.03N 71.40W
109 E8 Lincoln New Mexico 33.30N 105.23W
11 G10 Lincoln New Zealand 43.38S 172.30E
103 B6 Lincoln Pennsylvania 40.12N 76.13W
57 N6 Lincoln co England
107 K3 Lincoln City Indiana 38.08N 87.00W
110 A5 Lincoln City Oregon 44.56N 124.00W
108 N9 Lincoln Cr Nebraska
12 D5 Lincoln Gap S Australia 32.45S 137.18E
48 R1 Lincoln Hav sea Greenland
25 M4 Lincoln I Paracel Islands S China Sea
103 F5 Lincoln Park New Jersey 40.56N 74.18W
106 L3 Lincoln Park dist Detroit, Michigan
97 N1 Lincoln Sea Greenland
105 E4 Lincolnton Georgia 33.47N 82.29W
105 F2 Lincolnton N Carolina 35.27N 81.16W
104 Q2 Lincolnville Maine 44.16N 69.03W
98 L8 Lincolnville Nova Scotia 45.30N 61.33W
57 N6 Lincoln Wolds hills Lincs Eng
65 H8 Lind Austria 46.47N 13.22E
110 G3 Lind Washington 46.59N 118.38W
46 N2 Linda U.S.S.R. 56.30N 44.08E
13 E6 Linda R Queensland
46 N2 Linda R U.S.S.R.
105 B3 Lindale Georgia 34.09N 85.10W
57 H4 Lindale Lancs Eng 54.13N 2.54W
112 M3 Lindale Texas 32.31N 95.26W
53 S17 Lindås Norway 60.44N 5.10E
118 H4 Linda, Serra mts Brazil
63 Q8 Lindau E Germany 52.02N 12.06E
64 H8 Lindau (Bodensee) W Germany 47.33N 9.41E
120 G1 Linda Vista Brazil 5.30S 62.55W
100 G5 Lindbergh Alberta 53.53N 110.40W
108 F8 Lindbergh Wyoming 41.20N 104.08W
110 M2 Lindbergh, L Montana 47.21N 113.49W
53 B4 Linde Denmark 56.25N 8.31E
60 N7 Linde canal Netherlands
41 M7 Linde R U.S.S.R.
53 F7 Lindelse Denmark 54.52N 10.44E
13 J5 Lindeman I Queensland 20.26S 149.03E
107 J9 Linden Alabama 32.19N 87.49W
64 K4 Linden Bayern W Germany 49.30N 10.36E
61 K3 Linden Belgium 50.54N 4.46E
117 A2 Linden Guyana 5.59N 58.19W
106 H9 Linden Indiana 40.11N 86.54W
105 J2 Linden N Carolina 35.13N 78.48W
60 M13 Linden Netherlands 51.45N 5.50E
103 J8 Linden New Jersey 40.37N 74.15W
104 G4 Linden New York 42.53N 78.10W
11 D4 Linden New Zealand 41.09S 174.51E
63 L8 Linden Niedersachsen W Ger 52.22N 9.42E
94 S13 Linden S Africa 26.08S 27.59E
107 J6 Linden Tennessee 35.38N 87.50W
112 N2 Linden Texas 33.01N 94.22W
64 K3 Lindenau Friedrichshall E Germany 50.14N 10.48E
63 U8 Lindenberg Frankfurt E Germany 52.12N 14.07E
63 Q6 Lindenberg Potsdam E Germany 53.04N 12.08E
66 K3 Linden-Berg mts Switzerland
65 A6 Lindenberg im Allgäu W Germany 47.36N 9.54E
53 D3 Lindenborg Denmark 56.57N 10.00E
53 D3 Lindenborg Å R Denmark
64 F4 Lindenfels W Germany 49.41N 8.47E
63 T6 Lindenhagen E Germany 53.15N 13.46E
63 R9 Lindenhayn E Germany 51.31N 12.30E
103 H5 Lindenhurst Long I, N Y 40.41N 73.22W
48 V16 Lindenow Fjord Greenland 60.30N 43.00W
63 Q10 Lindenthal E Germany 51.24N 12.19E
103 D7 Lindenwold New Jersey 39.50N 75.00W
65 C6 Linderhof W Germany 47.34N 10.58E
63 G7 Lindern W Germany 52.51N 7.47E
12 L3 Lindesay, Mt New S Wales 28.20S 152.45E
14 B10 Lindesay, Mt W Australia 34.49S 117.16E
52 J7 Lindesberg Sweden 59.36N 15.15E
52 C8 Lindesnes Lt Ho Norway 58.00N 7.05E
56 L5 Lindfield W Sussex Eng 51.01N 0.05W
12 L6 Lindfield dist Sydney, N S W
52 H7 Lindfors Sweden 59.36N 13.50E
53 D2 Lindholm Denmark 57.05N 9.54E
63 J3 Lindholm W Germany 54.46N 8.52E
53 F5 Lindholm isld Denmark 55.56N 10.43E
92 J6 Lindi Tanzania 10.00S 39.41E
91 J3 Lindi R Zaïre
92 D2 Lindi R Zaïre
21 C4 Lindian Heilongjiang China 47.15N 124.51E
Lindisfarne see Holy Island Northumb
12 F8 Lindisfarne Tasmania 42.51S 147.22E
11 D11 Lindis Pass New Zealand 44.33S 169.43E
11 D11 Lindis Valley New Zealand 44.43S 169.31E
53 C5 Lindknud Denmark 55.34N 9.02E
109 D1 Lindland Colorado 40.34N 106.04W
64 C1 Lindlar W Germany 51.02N 7.23E
95 L3 Lindley S Africa 27.52S 27.55E
63 K8 Lindnorst W Germany 52.22N 9.18E
109 G2 Lindon Colorado 39.45N 103.26W
Lindong see Bairin Zuoqi

58 K6 Lindores Fife Scotland 56.20N 3.12W
58 K6 Lindores Abbey Fife Scotland 56.22N 3.14W
84 V17 Lindos Rhodes Greece 36.05N 28.05E
76 C5 Lindoso Portugal 41.52N 8.12W
63 R7 Lindow (Mark) E Germany 52.59N 12.59E
69 M6 Lindre, Étang de L France 48.48N 6.46E
111 E5 Lindsay California 36.11N 119.05W
108 E2 Lindsay Montana 47.14N 105.09W
108 N8 Lindsay Nebraska 41.42N 97.41W
109 N7 Lindsay Oklahoma 34.51N 97.36W
99 M8 Lindsay Ontario 44.21N 78.44W
14 D7 Lindsay Gordon, L W Australia 26.15S 121.29E
13 A6 Lindsay, Mt N Terr Australia 23.00S 129.03E
109 N3 Lindsborg Kansas 38.36N 97.41W
104 B5 Lindsey Ohio 41.24N 83.13W
57 N6 Lindsey div Lincs Eng
63 P7 Lindstedt E Germany 52.36N 11.33E
26 S8 Lindula Sri Lanka 6.56N 80.41E
53 D3 Lindum Denmark 56.34N 9.42E
53 D5 Lindved Denmark 55.48N 9.35E
64 P4 Linĕ Czechoslovakia 49.42N 13.15E
89 D3 Liné Mauritania 16.25N 10.07W
77 F8 Línea de la Concepción, La Spain 36.10N 5.21W
122 L7 Line Is Pacific Oc
104 E5 Linesville Pennsylvania 41.40N 80.26W
107 L8 Lineville Alabama 33.19N 85.47W
108 R9 Lineville Iowa 40.37N 93.30W
45 Q6 Linevo U.S.S.R. 50.54N 44.50E
44 H1 Lineynoye U.S.S.R. 46.15N 47.24E
23 F1 Linfen Shanxi China 36.08N 111.34E
23 F1 Linfen Shanxi China 36.05N 111.30E
28 D2 Lingagiri Andhra Prad India 16.53N 79.53E
58 T11 Linga Holm isld Orkney Scotland 59.08N 2.40W
94 N4 Linga Linga,Pta.da Mozambique 23.45S 35.27E
28 F2 Lingamparti Andhra Prad India 17.20N 82.11E
28 D1 Lingampet Andhra Prad India 18.13N 78.05E
28 B3 Linganamakki res Karnataka India
23 E9 Lingao Guangdong China 19.59N 109.41E
28 L1 Lingar Xizang Zizhiqu 29.45N 97.28E
19 K3 Lingayen Luzon Philippines 16.02N 120.14E
19 K3 Lingayen G Luzon Philippines
23 E1 Lingbao Henan China 34.29N 110.50E
Ling Barut see Lengbarūt
23 H2 Lingbi Anhui China 33.33N 117.32E
52 K5 Lingbo Sweden 61.04N 16.45E
23 H2 Lingcheng Jiangsu China 33.48N 118.08E
23 E6 Lingchuan Guangxi China 25.25N 110.21E
23 F1 Lingchuan Shanxi China 35.46N 113.26E
57 M3 Lingdale Cleveland Eng 54.32N 0.58W
72 G2 Lingé France 46.46N 1.06E
60 L12 Linge R Netherlands
Lingeh see Bandar-e Lengeh
56 F3 Lingen Hereford & Worcs Eng 52.18N 2.56W
63 F7 Lingen W Germany 52.32N 7.19E
18 F6 Lingga Indonesia 0.14S 104.37E
18 J5 Lingga Sarawak Malaysia 1.22N 111.14E
18 F6 Lingga isld Indonesia
18 F6 Lingga, Kep islds Indonesia
52 J6 Linghed Sweden 60.48N 15.55E
57 M4 Ling Hill Lt. Ho N Yorks Eng 54.28N 0.34W
19 N7 Lingig Mindanao Philippines 8.02N 126.22E
23 J4 Ling Jiang R Zhejiang China
18 M4 Lingkas Borneo Indon 3.16N 117.40E
108 F7 Lingle Wyoming 42.08N 104.20W
23 F5 Lingling Hunan China 26.15N 111.33E

91 H3 Lingomo Zaïre 0.38N 22.03E
84 B2 Lingos mts Greece
22 K7 Lingqiu Shanxi China 39.25N 114.04E
58 F4 Ling, River Highland Scotland
23 E7 Lingshan Guangxi China 22.23N 109.10E
23 J1 Lingshan Dao isld Shandong China 35.45N 120.08E
28 G2 Lingshi Bhutan 27.54N 89.34E
22 J8 Lingshi Shanxi China 36.25N 111.46E
110 O3 Lingshire Montana 46.50N 111.24W
22 K7 Lingshou Hebei China 38.20N 114.24E
23 E9 Lingshui Guangdong China 18.36N 110.03E
22 J8 Lingshui Shanxi China 36.52N 111.46E
28 C2 Lingsugur Karnataka India 16.11N 76.33E
23 D1 Lingtai Gansu China 35.05N 107.46E
23 E9 Lingtou Guangdong China 18.40N 108.42E
30 J2 Lingtren mt Xizang Zizhiqu 28.02N 86.52E
30 H2 Lingtren Nup Xizang Zizhiqu 28.02N 86.48E
81 K8 Linguaglossa Sicily 37.51N 15.09E
89 B4 Linguère Senegal 15.22N 15.11W
23 E6 Lingui Guangxi China 25.12N 110.02E
91 G3 Lingunda Zaïre 0.49N 21.08E
22 G7 Lingwu Ningxia China 38.04N 106.21E
Lingxi see Yongshun

23 F5 Ling Xian Hunan China 26.45N 113.45E
22 K8 Ling Xian Shandong China 37.21N 116.31E
23 D6 Lingyang Guizhou China 25.28N 106.58E
22 L6 Lingyuan Liaoning China 41.12N 119.16E
23 D6 Lingyun Guangxi China 24.25N 106.29E
24 J11 Lingzê Xizang Zizhiqu China 29.51N 96.10E
31 J1 Lingzi Thang Plains Kashmir
21 C2 Linhai Heilongjiang China 51.35N 124.28E
23 J4 Linhai Zhejiang China 28.54N 121.08E
118 H6 Linhares Brazil 19.22S 40.04W
76 E7 Linhares Portugal 40.32N 7.28W
25 H3 Linh Cam Vietnam 18.31N 105.35E
22 G6 Linhe Nei Monggol Zizhiqu China 40.45N 107.26E
76 B15 Linhó Portugal 38.46N 9.24W
23 H1 Linhong Kou estuary Jiangsu China
76 B8 Linhos, L. dos Portugal 40.02N 8.52W
23 H2 Linhuaiguan Anhui China 32.53N 117.45E
23 G2 Linhuanji Anhui China 33.40N 116.35E

98 B7 Linière Quebec 46.04N 70.30W
121 J4 Liniers dist Buenos Aires Arg
72 H1 Liniez France 47.03N 1.46E
32 D4 Linj Iran 32.20N 51.34E
21 D7 Linjiang Jilin China 41.45N 126.56E
23 B5 Linjiang Yunnan China 26.14N 100.34E
21 C7 Linjiatai Liaoning China 40.39N 123.56E
23 E1 Linjin Shanxi China 35.05N 110.39E
61 H3 Linkebeek Belgium 50.47N 4.20E
64 E5 Linkenheim W Germany 49.07N 8.25E
61 L3 Linkhout Belgium 50.58N 5.08E
37 H8 Linkī mt Iraq 37.04N 43.46E
52 J8 Linköping Sweden 58.25N 15.35E
21 E5 Linkou Heilongjiang China 45.18N 130.17E
23 C5 Linkou Yunnan China 27.30N 104.32E
46 E2 Linkuva Lithuania U.S.S.R. 56.02N 23.58E
23 F4 Linli Hunan China 29.25N 111.30E
103 G2 Linlithgo New York 42.11N 73.54W
58 J7 Linlithgow Lothian Scotland 55.59N 3.37W
Linmingguan see Yongnian
109 N2 Linn Kansas 39.41N 97.06W
107 E3 Linn Missouri 38.29N 91.51W
112 J9 Linn Texas 26.35N 98.09W
63 E10 Linn W Germany 51.20N 6.37E
60 T16 Linne Netherlands 51.09N 5.56E
50 S14 Linné, Kapp Spitsbergen 78.02N 13.40E
104 R7 Linneus Maine 46.02N 67.58W
107 C2 Linneus Missouri 39.52N 93.11W
56 A4 Linney Hd Dyfed Wales 51.38N 5.04W
58 F5 Linnhe, L Highland Scotland
64 A2 Linnich W Germany 50.59N 6.15E
110 C9 Linn, Mt California 40.04N 122.50W
91 E3 Lino tribe Congo
75 M4 Liñola Spain 41.42N 0.54E
91 F11 Linongo Angola 15.20S 18.49E
81 E10 Linosa Linosa, I di Italy 35.53N 12.52E
81 E10 Linosa, I. di Pelagie, Is Italy 35.53N 12.23E
45 D6 Linovitsa Ukraine U.S.S.R. 50.27N 32.23E
45 F5 Linovo Ukraine U.S.S.R. 51.20N 34.03E
63 R6 Linow E Germany 53.07N 12.50E
25 M8 Linpha Burma 25.49N 95.34E
Linping see Yuhang
23 F1 Linqi Henan China 35.42N 113.46E
22 K8 Linqing Shandong China 36.51N 115.42E
22 L8 Linqu Shandong China 36.32N 118.29E
23 F1 Linru Henan China 34.14N 112.45E
118 E7 Lins Brazil 21.40S 49.44W
89 C6 Linsan Guinea 10.18N 12.29W
63 K7 Linsburg W Germany 52.35N 9.18E
60 H11 Linschoten Netherlands 52.04N 4.55E
52 H4 Linsell Sweden 62.10N 13.50E
23 D4 Linshizhen Sichuan China 29.41N 107.15E
23 H1 Linshu Shandong China 34.55N 118.38E
23 D3 Linshui Sichuan China 30.24N 106.54E

61 K4 Linsmeau Belgium 50.44N 5.00E
116 K2 Linstead Jamaica, W I 18.08N 77.02W
61 J2 Lint Belgium 51.08N 4.30E
19 A8 Lintah, Selat str Indonesia

23 C1 Lintan Gansu China 34.43N 101.27E
23 C1 Lintao Gansu China 35.19N 103.50E
60 P12 Lintelo Netherlands 51.55N 6.31E
61 L3 Linter Belgium 50.51N 5.02E
61 P8 Lintgen Luxembourg 49.43N 6.08E
66 M4 Linthal Switzerland 46.55N 9.00E
103 A8 Linthicum Maryland 39.13N 76.39W
104 E3 Linthicum Heights Maryland 39.12N 76.38W
66 M3 Linth Kanal Switzerland
100 O6 Lintlaw Saskatchewan 52.05N 103.15W
58 L3 Lintmill Grampian Scotland 57.40N 2.49W
56 M3 Linton Cambs Eng 52.06N 0.17E
107 J2 Linton Indiana 39.01N 87.10W
108 K3 Linton N Dakota 46.17N 100.14W
11 K7 Linton New Zealand 40.24S 175.33E
99 S5 Linton Quebec 47.16N 72.15W
23 E1 Lintong Shaanxi China 34.25N 109.10E
63 E10 Lintorf W Germany 51.21N 6.50E
58 K5 Lintrathen Tayside Scotland 56.40N 3.10W

63 R7 Linum E Germany 52.46N 12.53E
105 F1 Linville N Carolina 36.03N 81.52W
104 G8 Linville Virginia 38.32N 78.52W
109 P2 Linwood Kansas 39.00N 95.03W
106 L6 Linwood Michigan 43.44N 83.56W
108 O8 Linwood Nebraska 41.26N 96.58W
11 M9 Linwood dist Christchurch New Zealand
23 F6 Linwu Hunan China 24.16N 112.27E
72 B8 Linxe France 43.55N 1.14W
22 K8 Linxi Hebei China 36.50N 115.30E
22 L5 Linxi Nei Monggol Zizhiqu China 43.40N 117.37E
23 C1 Linxia Gansu China 35.31N 103.08E
23 F1 Lin Xian Henan China 36.01N 113.50E
22 H8 Lin Xian Shanxi China 37.58N 110.55E
23 F4 Linxiang Hunan China 29.30N 113.28E
94 H2 Linyanti Namibia 18.03S 24.02E
Linyanti R see Chobe R
22 K8 Linyi Shandong China 37.12N 116.54E
23 H1 Linyi Shandong China 35.10N 118.18E
23 E1 Linyi Shanxi China 35.11N 110.47E
23 F2 Linying Henan China 33.48N 113.55E
23 D1 Linyou Shaanxi China 34.45N 107.51E
65 K5 Linz Austria 48.19N 14.18E
64 C2 Linz am Rhein W Germany 50.34N 7.18E
22 E7 Linze Gansu China 39.10N 100.10E
22 K8 Linzhang Hebei China 36.19N 114.33E
22 L8 Linzi Shandong China 36.55N 118.20E
91 D6 Linzolo Congo 4.25S 15.06E
91 H3 Lioko Zaïre 0.03N 22.07E
92 H9 Lioma Mozambique 15.10S 36.49E
18 L4 Lio Matoh Sarawak Malaysia 3.08N 115.09E
70 J6 Lion-d' Angers, le France 47.37N 0.42W
91 H4 Liondo Zaïre 0.57S 22.44E
116 K2 Lionel Town Jamaica, W I 17.49N 77.14W
67 H9 Lion, G. du France
93 A3 Liongo Zaïre 2.02N 29.44E
80 M7 Lioni Italy 40.53N 15.11E
12 M5 Lion I New S Wales 33.34S 151.17E
110 Q8 Lionkol Wyoming 41.38N 109.10W
92 E10 Lions Den Zimbabwe 17.14S 30.01E
94 K1 Lion's Den Zimbabwe 17.15S 30.05E
99 J8 Lions Head Ontario 44.59N 81.16W
70 K3 Lion-sur-Mer France 49.17N 0.18W
11 B11 Lion, The mt New Zealand 44.37S 167.54E
103 C6 Lionville Pennsylvania 40.04N 75.40W
84 S15 Liopetri Cyprus 34.59N 33.54E
19 E7 Lioppa Indon 7.41S 126.01E
72 F6 Liorac France 44.54N 0.40E
15 H4 Liot I Bismarck Arch 1.23S 144.31E
91 D3 Liouesso Congo 1.09N 15.40E
Lioyang see Lüeh-yang
45 B1 Liozno Belorussiya U.S.S.R. 55.02N 30.50E
19 K5 Lipa Luzon Philippines 13.57N 121.10E
82 C6 Lipa Yugoslavia 44.42N 16.03E
92 G9 Lipale Mozambique 15.49S 35.51E
112 J3 Lipan Texas 32.32N 98.04W
19 D2 Lipang isld Indonesia 3.56N 125.23E
65 L1 Lipany Czechoslovakia 50.02N 14.55E
81 J7 Lipari Lipari Is Italy 38.27N 14.58E
81 J7 Lipari isld Lipari Is Italy
81 H6 Lipari Is Italy
18 D6 Lipatkain Sumatra Indonesia 0.02S 101.16E
91 E2 Lipéité Congo 3.02N 17.17E
65 K4 Lipenska nádrž res Czechoslovakia
51 O9 Liperi Finland 62.33N 29.29E
45 L4 Lipetsk U.S.S.R. 52.37N 39.36E
46 L3 Lipetskaya Oblast' prov U.S.S.R.
120 E9 Lipez, Cord. de mts Bolivia
56 K5 Liphook Hants Eng 51.05N 0.49W
62 H2 Lipiany Poland 53.00N 14.56E
47 D5 Lipin Bor U.S.S.R. 60.15N 37.59E
23 E5 Liping Guizhou China 26.16N 109.08E
18 B7 Lipis R Pen Malaysia
45 J3 Lipitsy U.S.S.R. 53.21N 37.19E
46 F5 Lipkany Moldavia U.S.S.R. 48.18N 26.48E
46 L3 Lipki U.S.S.R. 53.50N 37.51E
82 G8 Lipljan Yugoslavia 42.30N 21.06E
65 M2 Lipnice nad Sázavu Czechoslovakia 49.36N 15.25E
62 K6 Lipník Czechoslovakia 49.31N 17.30E
82 L6 Lipniţa Romania 44.06N 27.38E
62 L3 Lipno Poland 52.52N 19.10E
65 K4 Lipno nad Vitava Czechoslovakia 48.38N 14.16E
114 D5 Lipoa Pt Hawaiian Is 21.03N 156.39W
65 M3 Lipolec Czechoslovakia 49.06N 15.22E
72 C7 Liposthey France 44.20N 0.52W
45 E6 Lipovaya-Dolina Ukraine U.S.S.R. 50.34N 33.49E
46 G5 Lipovets Ukraine U.S.S.R. 49.11N 29.01E
45 U4 Lipovka Saratov U.S.S.R. 52.24N 48.24E
46 N5 Lipovka Volgograd U.S.S.R. 49.40N 44.58E
47 N4 Lipovskoye U.S.S.R. 57.28N 61.10E
40 E9 Lipovtsy U.S.S.R. 44.15N 131.42E
63 F9 Lippe R W Germany
61 H2 Lippelo Belgium 51.03N 4.16E
60 N7 Lippenhuizen Netherlands 53.01N 6.06E
63 H9 Lipperode W Germany 51.42N 8.22E
63 H9 Lippetal W Germany 51.39N 8.08E
63 H9 Lippstadt W Germany 51.41N 8.20E
112 D7 Lipscomb Texas 36.14N 100.16W
62 O2 Lipsk Poland 53.48N 23.23E
83 H7 Lipsói isld Greece 37.19N 26.50E
84 B3 Lipsón Greece 39.23N 21.12E
100 O8 Lipton Saskatchewan 50.55N 103.49W
89 K5 Liptougou Upper Volta 13.18N 0.18E
62 M6 Liptovský Mikuláš Czechoslovakia 49.06N 19.35E
12 H7 Liptrap, C Victoria 38.56S 145.56E
45 H6 Liptsy Ukraine U.S.S.R. 50.12N 36.25E
23 E6 Lipu Guangxi China 24.25N 110.15E
92 G7 Lipumba Tanzania 10.49S 35.05E
62 K1 Lipusz Poland 54.07N 17.45E
Liqen-i Shkodrës see Skadarsko Jez
84 E8 Líra Greece 36.39N 22.58E
93 D3 Lira Uganda 2.15N 32.55E
19 D7 Liran isld Indon 8.00S 125.45E
91 E4 Liranga Congo 0.43S 17.32E
87 B8 Li Rangu Sudan 4.45N 28.20E
120 C5 Lircay Peru 12.59S 74.44W
70 H7 Liré France 47.21N 1.09W
80 H5 Liri R Italy
75 J8 Liria Spain 39.38N 0.37W
93 D1 Liria Sudan 4.38N 32.05E
76 D9 Liria R Portugal
87 C5 Liri, Jeb. el hills Sudan
18 E6 Lirik Ukui Sumatra Indon 0.12S 102.15E
84 E6 Lirkía Greece 37.42N 22.23E
84 D6 Lírkion Óros mts Greece
79 F2 Liro R Italy
19 E2 Lirung Indonesia 3.57N 126.40E
19 F5 Lisabata Moluccas Indon 2.51S 128.58E
91 F4 Lisafa Zaïre 0.09S 19.43E
33 G3 Lişāfah,Al Saudi Arabia 27.52N 46.52E
90 G7 Lisaka R Cameroon
43 H2 Lisakovsk Kazakhstan U.S.S.R. 52.32N 62.32E
91 G2 Lisala Zaïre 2.08N 21.37E
95 B7 L 'Isalo, Massif de mts Madagascar
35 E8 Lisan, El pen Jordan
116 O2 Lisas B Trinidad & Tobago
59 G3 Lisbellaw Fermanagh N Ireland 54.19N 7.32W
76 A11 Lisboa Portugal 38.44N 9.08W
76 A11 Lisboa dist Portugal
106 F8 Lisbon Illinois 41.29N 88.28W
108 N3 Lisbon N Dakota 46.28N 97.40W
104 O2 Lisbon New Hampshire 44.13N 71.56W
104 K2 Lisbon New York 44.44N 75.22W
Lisbon Portugal see Lisboa
104 P3 Lisbon Falls Maine 44.00N 70.05W
59 K2 Lisburn Antrim N Ireland 54.31N 6.03W
113 D2 Lisburne, C Alaska 68.54N 166.18W
59 D6 Liscannor Clare Irish Rep 52.57N 9.23W
59 D6 Liscannor B Clare Irish Rep 52.55N 9.25W
59 E7 Liscarroll Cork Irish Rep 52.15N 8.48W
66 S4 Lischanna, Piz mt Switzerland 46.47N 10.22E
81 C1 Liscia R Sardinia
81 C1 Liscia, L. di Sardinia 41.00N 9.16E
80 F2 Lisciano Niccone Italy 43.14N 12.08E
108 H8 Lisco Nebraska 41.30N 102.37W
81 C3 Liscoi R Sardinia
98 K8 Liscomb Nova Scotia 45.02N 62.00W
59 D5 Lisdoonvarna Clare Irish Rep 53.02N 9.17W
53 H4 Liseleje Denmark 56.01N 11.59E
65 P3 Lišeň Czechoslovakia 49.13N 16.42E
39 H7 Lisennova Komandorskiye O-va U.S.S.R. 54.49N 166.32E
23 F3 Lishan Hubei China 31.53N 113.19E
23 F1 Li Shan mt Shanxi China 35.26N 111.58E
23 B6 Lishe Jiang R Yunnan China
22 J8 Lishi Shanxi China 37.29N 111.08E
Lishtar see Līshtar-e Bālā
32 D5 Līshtar-e Bālā Iran 30.25N 50.35E
21 C6 Lishu Jilin China 43.20N 124.20E

23 H3 Lishui Jiangsu China 31.43N 119.01E
23 H4 Lishui Zhejiang China 28.30N 119.59E
23 E4 Li Shui R Hunan China

86 F7 Lishyâb, Wâdi watercourse Egypt
114 B1 Lisianski I Hawaiian Is 26.04N 173.58W
45 K8 Lisichansk Ukraine U.S.S.R. 48.53N 38.25E
70 L3 Lisieux France 49.09N 0.14E
100 M9 Lisieux Saskatchewan 49.17N 105.59W
84 B4 Lisimákhia, Limni L Greece 38.34N 21.22E
51 P12 Lisino U.S.S.R. 59.25N 30.36E
39 H7 Lisinskaya Bukhta B Komandorskiye O-va U.S.S.R.
42 D3 Lisitsa R U.S.S.R.
56 C7 Liskeard Cornwall Eng 50.28N 4.28W
29 F3 Liskot Uttar Prad India 29.48N 79.10E
72 F5 Lisle France 45.16N 0.34E
103 B2 Lisle New York 42.21N 76.00W
69 J6 Lisle-en-Barrois France 48.54N 5.08E
72 H8 Lisle-sur-Tarn France 43.52N 1.48E
56 V11 L'Islet Chan Is 49.29N 2.33W
98 B6 L'Islet Quebec 47.08N 70.23W
98 C5 L'Isle Verte Quebec 48.00N 69.20W
107 H9 Lisman Alabama 32.10N 88.19W
42 B2 Lismanovy U.S.S.R. 61.13N 75.18E
12 L3 Lismore New S Wales 28.48S 153.17E
98 K8 Lismore Nova Scotia 45.42N 62.16W
12 G7 Lismore Victoria 37.58S 143.22E
59 G7 Lismore Waterford Irish Rep 52.08N 7.55W
58 E6 Lismore isld Strathclyde Scotland
59 K3 Lisnacree Down N Ireland 54.05N 6.05W
59 H3 Lisnaskea Fermanagh N Ireland 54.15N 7.26W
61 K5 Lisogne Belgium 50.17N 4.58E
70 H3 Lison France 49.15N 1.03W
70 N3 Lisors France 49.21N 1.28E
59 H4 Lisryan Longford Irish Rep 53.44N 7.30W
56 K5 Liss Hants Eng 51.03N 0.55W
34 F7 Liss mt Saudi Arabia 31.14N 38.32E
72 H6 Lissac-et-Mouret France 44.37N 1.57E
14 G3 Lissadell W Australia 16.34S 128.38E
Lissar see Khūshāvar
84 C6 Lissaréa Greece 37.39N 21.56E
60 G10 Lisse Netherlands 52.15N 4.33E
88 S5 Lisseri watercourse Tunisia
57 N5 Lissett Humberside Eng 54.00N 0.15W
61 C1 Lissewege Belgium 51.18N 3.12E
63 H3 List W Germany 55.01N 8.26E
52 C8 Listafjord inlet Norway
53 Q12 Listed Bornholm Denmark 55.09N 15.07E
13 E7 Listore R Queensland
59 D7 Listowel Kerry Irish Rep 52.27N 9.29W
99 K9 Listowel Ontario 43.44N 80.57W
13 H7 Listowel Downs Queensland 25.10S 145.11E
72 C5 Listrac-Médoc France 45.04N 0.48W
42 D7 Listvyaga, Khrebet mts U.S.S.R.
42 G6 Listvyanka U.S.S.R. 51.55N 104.50E
42 C5 Listvyanskiy U.S.S.R. 54.27N 83.27E
39 D5 Lisyanskogo, Poluostrov pen U.S.S.R.
52 H3 Lit Sweden 63.20N 14.50E
23 E7 Litang Guangxi China 23.09N 109.08E
18 N3 Litang Sabah Malaysia 5.25N 118.30E
23 B3 Litang Sichuan China 30.02N 100.18E
23 B4 Litang Qu R Sichuan China
34 C5 Lītāni R Lebanon
117 B3 Litani R Surinam
65 P3 Litava R Czechoslovakia
56 N2 Litcham Norfolk Eng 52.44N 0.47E
110 E9 Litchfield California 40.24N 120.24W
103 H3 Litchfield Connecticut 41.45N 73.11W
56 J5 Litchfield Hants Eng 51.18N 1.20W
107 G2 Litchfield Illinois 39.11N 89.40W
106 K7 Litchfield Michigan 42.03N 84.43W
108 Q4 Litchfield Minnesota 45.09N 94.31W
108 L8 Litchfield Nebraska 41.09N 99.10W
103 H3 Litchfield co Connecticut
111 M8 Litchfield Park Arizona 33.32N 112.20W
108 M3 Litchville N Dakota 46.39N 98.10W
58 G7 Lit Cumbrae I Strathclyde Scotland 55.43N 4.57W
65 K2 Liteň Czechoslovakia 49.54N 14.10E
82 K3 Liteni Romania 47.30N 26.34E
75 L4 Litera, La plain Spain
72 B7 Lit-et-Mixte France 44.02N 1.15W
60 K12 Lith Netherlands 51.48N 5.26E
84 C2 Lithaíos R Greece
84 A6 Lithakiá Greece 37.43N 20.50E
33 D6 Lith,Al Saudi Arabia 20.10N 40.16E
12 K5 Lithgow New S Wales 33.30S 150.09E
103 G3 Lithgow New York 41.50N 73.37W
60 K12 Lithoijen Netherlands 51.48N 5.29E
Lithuania see Litva S.S.R.
33 D6 Lith, Wādi Al watercourse Saudi Arabia
64 P4 Litice Czechoslovakia 49.42N 13.22E
82 B4 Litija Yugoslavia 46.03N 14.50E
46 G5 Litin Ukraine U.S.S.R. 49.20N 28.01E
103 B6 Lititz Pennsylvania 40.09N 76.19W
46 J4 Litizh U.S.S.R. 52.18N 34.50E
40 H4 Litke Khabarovsk U.S.S.R. 54.00N 140.14E
41 B3 Litke Novaya Zemlya U.S.S.R. 72.24N 55.30E
41 A3 Litke, Mys C Novaya Zemlya U.S.S.R. 74.01N 54.35E
39 M1 Litke, Mys C Vrangelya, Ostrov U.S.S.R. 71.16N 177.17W
41 C2 Litke, P-ov pen Novaya Zemlya U.S.S.R.
39 G5 Litke, Proliv str U.S.S.R.
41 B3 Litke, Zaliv B Novaya Zemlya U.S.S.R.
53 S19 Litlabø Norway 59.47N 5.25E
Lítla Dímun see Lille Dimon
53 U19 Litledalen Norway 59.40N 6.05E
53 Z13 Litledalen R Norway 62.36N 8.32E
53 Y14 Litlevatn L Norway 62.27N 8.15E
50 G6 Litlisjór L Iceland 64.10N 18.40W
53 W18 Litloshytta Norway 60.06N 7.09E
84 E1 Litókhoron Greece 40.06N 22.30E
62 H5 Litoměřice Czechoslovakia 50.33N 14.10E
65 O2 Litomyšl Czechoslovakia 49.54N 16.18E
65 N2 Litošice Czechoslovakia 49.59N 15.32E
65 Q2 Litovel Czechoslovakia 49.42N 17.05E
40 G7 Litovko U.S.S.R. 49.19N 135.11E
38 B3 Litovskaya S.S.R U.S.S.R.
65 M4 Litschau Austria 48.58N 15.04E
52 K7 Litslena Sweden 59.39N 17.17E
66 K3 Littau Switzerland 47.03N 8.16E
107 J5 Little R Kentucky
107 D10 Little R Louisiana
109 O6 Little R Oklahoma
99 J2 Little Abitibi R Ontario
99 K3 Little Abitibi L Ontario 49.25N 80.33W
33 F10 Little Aden S Yemen 12.44N 44.53E
28 G8 Little Andaman isld Andaman Is
11 K3 Little Barrier I New Zealand 36.12S 175.07E
26 U9 Little Basses isld Sri Lanka 6.26N 81.43E
106 G4 Little Bay de Noc Michigan
98 R4 Little Bay Is Newfoundland 49.38N 55.48W
100 N4 Little Bear L Saskatchewan 54.23N 104.35W
100 V1 Little Beaver R Manitoba
110 P3 Little Belt Mts Montana
113 Q3 Little Black R Alaska 67.02N 142.43W
57 J5 Littleborough Greater Manchester Eng 53.39N 2.05W
56 O5 Littlebourne Kent Eng 51.17N 1.10E
100 E8 Little Bow Prov. Park Alberta
100 D8 Little Bow R Alberta
98 R2 Little Brehat Newfoundland 51.27N 55.30W
101 R5 Little Buffalo R N W Terr
100 V7 Little Bullhead Manitoba 51.42N 96.51W
98 R4 Little Burnt Bay Newfoundland 49.20N 55.05W
56 M3 Littlebury Essex Eng 52.02N 0.13E
110 K6 Little Camas Res Idaho 43.20N 115.22W
106 F5 Little Chute Wisconsin 44.18N 88.19W
28 G6 Little Coco I Andaman Is 13.59N 93.12E
111 N6 Little Colorado R Arizona
103 M3 Little Compton Rhode I 41.31N 71.10W
103 D8 Little Creek Delaware 39.10N 75.26W
111 M4 Little Creek Pk Utah 37.54N 112.37W
99 J7 Little Current Ontario 45.57N 81.56W
99 D2 Little Current R Ontario
113 C4 Little Diomede I Alaska Bering Strait 65.47N 169.00W
108 D2 Little Dry Cr Montana
103 F7 Little Egg Harb New Jersey
103 F8 Little Egg Inlet New Jersey
108 Q4 Little Falls Minnesota 45.58N 94.20W
103 H6 Little Falls New Jersey 40.53N 74.14W
104 L3 Little Falls New York 43.03N 74.52W
111 L5 Littlefield Arizona 36.52N 113.55W
112 E2 Littlefield Texas 33.56N 102.20W
100 E7 Little Fish Lake Prov. Park Alberta 51.22N 112.12W
108 R1 Little Fork Minnesota 48.26N 93.33W
108 R1 Little Fork R Minnesota
101 N10 Little Fort Br Columbia 51.26N 120.12W
30 G6 Little Gandak R Uttar Prad Ind
103 C5 Little Gap Pennsylvania 40.49N 75.32W
107 G4 Little Grassy L Illinois 37.38N 89.08W
54 K4 Little Halibut Bank North Sea
56 K6 Littlehampton W Sussex Eng 50.48N 0.33W
105 K11 Little Harb Bahamas
98 Q3 Little Harbour Deep Newfoundland 50.16N 56.30W
56 F3 Little Hereford Hereford & Worcs Eng 52.19N 2.39W
23 B9 Little Hong Kong Hong Kong 22.14N 114.10E
95 E9 Little Karroo reg S Africa
113 N10 Little Kiska I Aleutian Is 51.59N 177.40E
113 H9 Little Koniuji I Alaska 55.00N 159.25W
107 F12 Little L Louisiana 29.30N 90.13W
111 G6 Little Lake California 35.58N 117.53W
116 G1 Little London Jamaica, W I 18.15N 78.13W
110 M5 Little Lost R Idaho
110 N7 Little Malad R Idaho
98 E2 Little Manicouagan L Quebec
103 B3 Little Meadow Pennsylvania 41.59N 76.08W
104 J5 Little Meadows Pennsylvania 41.59N 76.06W
108 D7 Little Medicine Wyoming 42.25N 106.00W
108 G3 Little Missouri R N Dakota
Little Mt.Ararat see Ağrı Dağı, Küçük mt
103 L7 Little Neck B New York
28 J7 Little Nicobar isld Nicobar Is
107 B4 Little Osage R Kansas/Missouri
57 L4 Little Ouseburn N Yorks Eng 54.02N 1.20W
31 H2 Little Pamir mts Afghanistan
12 A7 Little Para R S Australia
105 H3 Little Pee Dee R S Carolina
56 B6 Little Petherick Cornwall Eng 50.31N 4.56W
100 U4 Little Playgreen L Manitoba
57 H5 Little Plumpton Lancs Eng 53.48N 2.57W
56 M3 Littleport Cambs Eng 52.28N 0.19E
108 E5 Little Powder R Montana/Wyoming
105 D6 Little, R Georgia
105 E4 Little, R Georgia
105 H2 Little, R N Carolina
105 J2 Little, R N Carolina
98 P6 Little, R Newfoundland
101 H6 Little Rancheria R Br Col/Yukon Terr
107 D6 Little Red R Arkansas
107 J10 Little River Alabama 31.16N 87.54W
109 M3 Little River Kansas 38.24N 98.01W
11 G10 Little River New Zealand 43.46S 172.47E
105 J4 Little River S Carolina 33.53N 78.40W
105 J4 Little River Inlet S Carolina 33.52N 78.34W
107 D7 Little Rock Arkansas 34.42N 92.17W
111 G7 Littlerock California 34.31N 117.59W
57 E3 Little Ross I Dumfries & Galloway Scotland 54.46N 4.05W
92 G6 Little Ruaha R Tanzania
101 F4 Little Salmon Yukon Terr 62.15N 134.28W
101 F4 Little Salmon L Yukon Terr 62.10N 134.40W
111 M4 Little Salt L Utah 37.55N 112.53W
111 H8 Little San Bernardino Mts California
110 Q7 Little Sandy Cr Wyoming
105 E6 Little Satilla, R Georgia
103 F6 Little Silver New Jersey 40.20N 74.03W
108 P7 Little Sioux R Iowa
113 O10 Little Sitkin I Aleutian Is 51.58N 178.30E
101 P8 Little Smoky Alberta 54.43N 117.10W
101 P8 Little Smoky R Alberta
109 B1 Little Snake R Colorado
96 A2 Little Sound B Bermuda
56 N6 Littlestone-on-Sea Kent Eng 50.59N 0.58E
104 H7 Littlestown Pennsylvania 39.45N 77.06W
56 L3 Little Stukeley Cambs Eng 52.22N 0.14W
106 F5 Little Suamico Wisconsin 44.43N 88.00W
113 Q10 Little Tanaga I Aleutian Is 51.50N 176.10W
56 M3 Little Thurlow Suffolk Eng 52.08N 0.26E
Little Tibet see Ladakh
109 E2 Littleton Colorado 39.36N 105.02W
106 D9 Littleton Illinois 40.13N 90.37W
105 K1 Littleton N Carolina 36.26N 77.56W
104 O2 Littleton New Hampshire 44.18N 71.46W
55 B5 Littleton Surrey Eng 51.24N 0.27W
59 G6 Littleton Tipperary Irish Rep 52.38N 7.44W
104 E7 Littleton W Virginia 39.42N 80.31W
104 G4 Little Valley New York 42.15N 78.47W
110 J7 Little Valley Cr Idaho
107 J7 Littleville Alabama 34.35N 87.39W
56 M4 Little Waltham Essex Eng 51.48N 0.28E
108 K6 Little White R S Dakota
56 G2 Littleworth Staffs Eng 52.49N 2.19W
103 D5 Little York New Jersey 40.37N 75.05W
112 F8 Little York dist Houston, Texas
90 D9 Littoral reg Cameroon

92 G7 Lituhi Tanzania 10.50S 34.45E
92 G8 Litunde Mozambique 13.19S 35.48E
113 T7 Lituya B Alaska
46 E2 Litva S.S.R U.S.S.R.
64 Q2 Litvínov Czechoslovakia 50.37N 13.36E
45 M8 Litvinovka U.S.S.R. 48.25N 40.54E
66 Q3 Litz R Austria
66 R4 Litzner, Great mt Austria/Switz 46.54N 10.03E
23 D2 Liuba Shaanxi China 33.35N 106.58E
23 E6 Liucheng Guangxi China 24.38N 109.16E
23 C5 Liuchong He R Guizhou China
23 D5 Liuchong He R Guizhou China
Liuchuan see Jianhe
23 D4 Liudu Guizhou China 28.17N 107.43E
23 D5 Liuguang Guizhou China 27.00N 106.28E
21 C6 Liuhe Jilin China 42.18N 125.44E
21 B6 Liu He R Liaoning China
21 C6 Liu He R Liaoning China
23 D3 Liuhechang Sichuan China 31.30N 106.47E
23 J4 Liuheng Dao isld Zhejiang China
21 B5 Liuhu Nei Monggol Zizhiqu China 45.39N 121.17E
23 F3 Liujiachang Hubei China 30.05N 111.29E
23 E6 Liujiang Guangxi China 24.26N 109.11E
23 E6 Liu Jiang R Guangxi China
21 D4 Liukesong Heilongjiang China 47.40N 127.48E
92 G7 Liuli Tanzania 11.05S 34.40E
22 K7 Liulihezhen Beijing Shi China 40.38N 116.40E
22 H8 Liulin Shanxi China 37.27N 110.53E
23 J2 Liulishe Jiangsu China 32.45N 120.48E
23 D6 Liuma Guizhou China 25.31N 105.57E
Liupai see Tian'e
23 D1 Liupan Shan mts Gansu China
92 K9 Liupo Mozambique 15.34S 40.00E
115 L3 Liure Honduras 13.31N 87.07W
23 F3 Liushuigou Hubei China 31.35N 112.29E
24 G4 Liushuquan Xinjiang Uygur Zizhiqu China 43.00N 92.58E
51 Q9 Liusvara Karelia U.S.S.R. 62.40N 32.09E
23 E6 Liutang Guangxi China 25.06N 110.10E
92 A9 Liuwa Plain Nat. Park Zambia
22 C6 Liuyan Gansu China 41.05N 95.30E
23 F4 Liuyang Hunan China 28.12N 113.36E
23 F4 Liuyang He R Hunan China
23 D6 Liuzhai Guangxi China 25.15N 107.23E
Liuzhangzhen see Yuanqu
23 E6 Liuzhou Guangxi China 24.17N 109.15E
23 J2 Liuzhuang Jiangsu China 33.08N 120.16E
23 G1 Liuzhuang Shandong China 35.23N 115.14E
82 H3 Livada Romania 47.52N 23.04E
84 C1 Livadherón Greece 40.02N 21.57E
84 D1 Livádhion Greece 40.07N 22.09E
44 C10 Livadiya Ukraine U.S.S.R. 44.28N 34.06E
84 F4 Livanátais Greece 38.43N 23.03E
46 F2 Livāni Latvia U.S.S.R. 56.20N 26.12E
84 C6 Livárji Greece 37.55N 21.55E
70 L3 Livarot France 49.01N 0.10E
100 J5 Livelong Saskatchewan 53.28N 108.41W
121 E10 Lively I Falkland Is
113 N4 Livengood Alaska 65.31N 148.40W
79 N3 Livenza R Italy
111 C2 Live Oak California 39.16N 121.40W
105 E7 Live Oak Florida 30.19N 82.59W
84 Q14 Liveras Cyprus 35.23N 32.58E
69 L6 Liverdun France 48.46N 6.05E
14 E4 Liveringa W Australia 18.05S 124.13E
111 C4 Livermore California 37.40N 121.46W
108 Q7 Livermore Iowa 42.52N 94.10W
107 J4 Livermore Kentucky 37.30N 87.11W
104 P2 Livermore Falls Maine 44.28N 70.11W
112 C5 Livermore, Mt Texas 30.39N 104.11W
72 H6 Livernon France 44.39N 1.50E
57 H6 Liverpool Merseyside Eng 53.25N 2.55W
12 K5 Liverpool New S Wales 33.57S 150.52E
104 J3 Liverpool New York 43.12N 76.02W
98 H9 Liverpool Nova Scotia 44.03N 64.43W
13 C1 Liverpool R N Terr Australia
57 G6 Liverpool B England
101 H1 Liverpool B N W Terr
97 M3 Liverpool, C N W Terr 73.38N 78.05W
48 V11 Liverpool Land Greenland
12 J4 Liverpool Plains New S Wales
12 J4 Liverpool Ra New S Wales
57 K5 Liversedge W Yorks Eng 53.43N 1.41W
14 F7 Livesey Ra W Australia
71 H6 Livet-et-Gavet France 45.06N 5.56E
80 D4 Livdónia, Pta Italy 42.27N 11.07E
79 H1 Livigno Italy 46.33N 10.08E
79 L2 Livinallongo Italy 46.29N 11.58E
107 H9 Livingston Alabama 32.35N 88.12W
115 P10 Livingston Guatemala 15.50N 88.44W
107 M4 Livingston Kentucky 37.18N 84.11W
58 J7 Livingston Lothian Scotland 55.51N 3.31W
107 F11 Livingston Louisiana 30.31N 90.45W
110 P4 Livingston Montana 45.40N 110.33W
103 G2 Livingston New York 42.09N 73.46W
107 L5 Livingston Tennessee 36.22N 85.20W
112 N5 Livingston Texas 30.42N 94.58W
106 D7 Livingston Wisconsin 42.54N 90.27W
103 F5 Livingstone New Jersey 40.47N 74.18W
92 B10 Livingstone Zambia 17.50S 25.53E
101 F5 Livingstone Creek Yukon Terr 61.20N 134.21W
92 E8 Livingstone Memorial Zambia 12.20S 30.19E
11 C12 Livingstone Mts New Zealand
92 G6 Livingstone Mts Tanzania
100 C8 Livingstone Ra Alberta
123 E15 Livingston I S Shetland Is Antarctica 62.38S 60.30W
92 G7 Livingstonia Malawi 10.35S 34.10E
112 M5 Livingston, L Texas
103 E3 Livingston Manor New York 41.54N 74.50W
103 F2 Livingstonville New York 42.29N 74.17W
71 B10 Livinière, La France 43.19N 2.38E
93 H9 Liviseki Tanzania 3.32S 36.26E
82 D7 Livno Yugoslavia 43.50N 17.00E
45 J4 Livny U.S.S.R. 52.25N 37.35E
53 C3 Livø Bredning B Denmark 56.52N 9.00E
51 M6 Livojoki R Finland
107 E11 Livonia Louisiana 30.34N 91.35W
106 L7 Livonia Michigan 42.25N 83.23W
107 D1 Livonia Missouri 40.28N 92.42W
79 H7 Livorno Italy 43.33N 10.18E
80 B2 Livorno prov Italy
79 D4 Livorno Ferraris Italy 45.17N 8.05E
71 D6 Livradois, Massif du mts France
96 T1 Livramento Azores 37.30N 25.36W
117 B6 Livramento Pará Brazil 3.18S 55.19W
118 H3 Livramento do Brumado Brazil 13.43S 41.51W
70 H5 Livré France 48.13N 1.20W
71 F7 Livron-sur-Drôme France 44.46N 4.51E
69 D6 Livry France 48.56N 2.34E
68 H2 Livry-Gargan France 48.55N 2.33E
33 M4 Liwā Oman 24.32N 56.38E
34 D5 Liwa watercourse Syria
33 K5 Liwā', Al oasis U.A.E.
92 H6 Liwale Tanzania 9.47S 38.00E
22 G8 Liwangbu Ningxia China 36.42N 106.05E
62 N3 Liwiec R Poland
92 G9 Liwonde Malawi 15.01S 35.15E
18 G3 Liwung, Ci R Indonesia
69 N6 Lixheim France 48.47N 7.09E
23 G4 Lixi Jiangxi China 29.15N 114.55E
23 D1 Li Xian Gansu China 34.05N 105.00E
22 K7 Li Xian Hebei China 38.50N 115.32E
23 F4 Li Xian Hunan China 29.35N 111.40E
23 C3 Li Xian Sichuan China 31.22N 103.10E
23 G2 Lixin Anhui China 33.07N 116.13E
69 M5 Lixing-lès-St. Avold France 49.02N 6.45E
59 C7 Lixnaw Kerry Irish Rep 52.25N 9.37W
83 D6 Lixoúrion Greece 38.14N 20.24E
23 H3 Liyang Jiangsu China 31.26N 119.27E
26 T8 Liyangolla Sri Lanka 6.54N 81.25E
23 E6 Liyong Guangxi China 24.10N 109.35E
87 A8 Li Yubu Sudan 5.26N 27.15E
37 G7 Liz Turkey 39.00N 42.04E
76 B9 Liz R Portugal
117 E9 Lizarda Brazil 9.33S 46.38W
110 Q7 Lizard Head Pk Wyoming 42.48N 109.13W
13 H2 Lizard I Gt Barrier Reef Australia 14.40S 145.30E
56 T10 Lizard Pt Cornwall Eng 49.56N 5.13W
56 T10 Lizard Town Cornwall Eng 49.57N 5.13W
75 F2 Lizarraga Spain 42.53N 2.03W
105 D5 Lizella Georgia 32.48N 83.50W
104 D8 Lizemores W Virginia 38.20N 81.12W
66 E6 Lizerne R Switzerland
47 C5 Lizhma U.S.S.R. 62.16N 34.25E
99 S4 Lizotte Quebec 48.07N 72.12W
107 K2 Lizton Indiana 39.53N 86.31W
69 E5 Lizy-sur-Ourcq France 49.02N 3.02E
81 R12 Lizzanello Italy 40.18N 18.14E
81 P12 Lizzano Italy 40.23N 17.27E
79 J6 Lizzano in Belvedere Italy 44.09N 10.54E
53 V14 Ljøen Norway 62.07N 6.55E
52 G5 Ljøra R Norway
53 W20 Ljosådalen V Norway 59.15N 7.10E
50 D6 Ljósafoss Iceland 64.05N 21.00W
50 L3 Ljósaland Iceland 65.53N 14.41W
50 H3 Ljósavatn Iceland 65.42N 17.35W
50 H3 Ljosavatnskardh pass Iceland
50 C5 Ljosufjöll mt Snæfellsnessýsla Iceland 64.54N 22.34W
50 G6 Ljósuföll mt Iceland 64.16N 18.25W
65 K9 Ljubelj P pass Yugoslavia/Austria 46.25N 14.15E
82 D6 Ljubija Yugoslavia 44.55N 16.35E
82 E8 Ljubinje Yugoslavia 42.57N 18.05E
82 E7 Ljubišnja mts Yugoslavia
82 B4 Ljubljana Yugoslavia 46.04N 14.30E
82 G8 Ljuboten mt Yugoslavia 42.11N 21.09E
82 E6 Ljubovija Yugoslavia 44.11N 19.22E
82 D7 Ljubuški Yugoslavia 43.12N 17.34E
52 L9 Ljugarn Sweden 57.20N 18.45E
52 J4 Ljunga Sweden 62.46N 16.20E
52 J4 Ljungan R Sweden
52 J4 Ljungaverk Sweden 62.30N 16.05E
52 H10 Ljungby Sweden 56.49N 13.55E
52 G4 Ljungdalen Sweden 62.54N 12.45E
52 J5 Ljüsda Sweden 61.50N 16.10E
52 J4 Ljusnan R Sweden
52 K5 Ljusne Sweden 61.14N 17.12E
52 L7 Ljusterö Sweden 59.32N 18.40E
82 C4 Ljutomer Yugoslavia 46.31N 16.11E
75 O5 Llacuna, La Spain 41.28N 1.32E
75 Q3 Lladó Spain 42.14N 2.48E
75 R4 Llafranch Spain 41.53N 3.11E
72 J10 Llagonne, La France 42.32N 2.08E
75 Q4 Llagostera Spain 41.50N 2.54E
121 B7 Llaima, V Chile 38.40S 71.46W
120 D9 Llamara, Salar de salt pan Chile
76 H3 Llamas de la Ribera Spain 42.38N 5.50W
56 C2 Llanaber Gwynedd Wales 52.45N 4.05W
57 E7 Llanaelhaiarn Gwynedd Wales 52.59N 4.24W
57 E6 Llanallgo Gwynedd Wales 53.21N 4.15W
56 E2 Llanarmon Dyffryn Ceiriog Clwyd Wales 52.53N 3.16W
56 C3 Llanarth Dyfed Wales 52.12N 4.18W
56 C4 Llanarthne Dyfed Wales 51.52N 4.09W
76 K2 Llanaves de la Reina Spain 43.04N 4.49W
57 G6 Llanbedr Clwyd Wales 53.07N 3.17W
56 C2 Llanbedr Gwynedd Wales 52.49N 4.06W
56 C2 Llanbedrog Gwynedd Wales 52.52N 4.29W
57 E6 Llanberis Gwynedd Wales 53.07N 4.06W
57 E6 Llanberis, Pass of Gwynedd Wales 53.06N 4.04W
56 E3 Llanbister Powys Wales 52.21N 3.19W
56 B4 Llanboidy Dyfed Wales 51.54N 4.36W
56 D2 Llanbrynmair Powys Wales 52.37N 3.37W
121 A9 Llancahue isld Chile 42.10S 72.30W
121 B5 Llancanelo, L Argentina
121 B5 Llancanelo, Salina salt pan Arg
56 E4 Llandaff S Glam Wales 51.30N 3.14W
56 C4 Llanddarog Dyfed Wales 51.51N 4.11W
56 C4 Llanddewi W Glam Wales 51.35N 4.13W
56 C4 Llandefaelog Dyfed Wales 51.48N 4.18W
56 D4 Llandeilo Dyfed Wales 51.53N 3.59W
56 E3 Llandinam Powys Wales 52.29N 3.26W
56 D4 Llandovery Dyfed Wales 51.59N 3.48W
56 B4 Llandowror Dyfed Wales 51.49N 4.32W
57 G7 Llandrillo Clwyd Wales 52.55N 3.25W
57 F6 Llandrillo Gwynedd Wales 53.19N 3.46W
56 E3 Llandrindod Wells Powys Wales 52.15N 3.23W
94 P12 Llandudno Cape Town S Africa 34.01S 18.21E
57 F6 Llandudno Gwynedd Wales 53.19N 3.49W
94 P12 Llandudno B Cape Town S Africa
56 C4 Llandybie Dyfed Wales 51.50N 4.00W
56 B4 Llandysilio Dyfed Wales 51.53N 4.44W
56 C3 Llandysul Dyfed Wales 52.02N 4.19W
56 C4 Llanegwad Dyfed Wales 51.53N 4.09W
56 C4 Llanelli Dyfed Wales 51.42N 4.10W
56 D2 Llanelltud Gwynedd Wales 52.45N 3.54W
57 E6 Llanerchymedd Gwynedd Wales 53.20N 4.22W
76 K2 Llanes Spain 43.25N 4.45W
57 E6 Llanfaelog Gwynedd Wales 53.14N 4.30W
57 D6 Llanfaethlu Gwynedd Wales 53.22N 4.31W
56 E2 Llanfair Caereinion Powys Wales 52.39N 3.20W
57 F6 Llanfairfechan Gwynedd Wales 53.15N 3.58W
57 E6 Llanfairpwllgwyngyll Gwynedd Wales 53.13N 4.12W
57 F6 Llanfair Talhaiarn Clwyd Wales 53.13N 3.36W
56 C3 Llanfihangel Ystrad Dyfed Wales 52.11N 4.11W
56 E4 Llanfrynach Powys Wales 51.56N 3.21W
56 E2 Llanfyllin Powys Wales 52.46N 3.17W
56 E2 Llangadfan Powys Wales 52.41N 3.28W
56 D4 Llangadog Dyfed Wales 51.57N 3.53W
56 D3 Llangammarch Wells Powys Wales 52.07N 3.34W
57 E6 Llangefni Gwynedd Wales 53.16N 4.18W
56 C3 Llangeler Dyfed Wales 52.01N 4.24W
56 C2 Llangelynnin Gwynedd Wales 52.38N 4.06W
56 C4 Llangennith W Glam Wales 51.36N 4.16W
57 F6 Llangerniew Clwyd Wales 53.12N 3.41W
57 E6 Llangoed Gwynedd Wales 53.18N 4.05W
57 G7 Llangollen Clwyd Wales 52.58N 3.10W
56 E4 Llangorse Powys Wales 51.57N 3.16W
56 D3 Llangurig Powys Wales 52.25N 3.36W
56 B2 Llangwnadl Gwynedd Wales 52.52N 4.41W
56 C3 Llangybi Dyfed Wales 52.10N 4.02W
56 E2 Llangynog Powys Wales 52.50N 3.25W
56 D3 Llanidloes Powys Wales 52.27N 3.32W
56 C3 Llanilar Dyfed Wales 52.21N 4.01W
57 E6 Llanllyfni Gwynedd Wales 53.03N 4.17W
56 C4 Llanmadog W Glam Wales 51.37N 4.15W
56 C4 Llannon Dyfed Wales 51.46N 4.07W
115 D2 Llano Mexico 30.24N 111.08W
112 J5 Llano Texas 30.49N 98.42W
112 H5 Llano R Texas
109 G8 Llano Estacado plat New Mex/Texas
115 G6 Llano Grande Mexico 23.52N 105.12W
77 L7 Llanos de Almería plain Spain
120 F6 Llanos de Mojos plain Bolivia
121 C3 Llanos, Sa. de los mts Argentina
121 A8 Llanquihue prov Chile
121 A8 Llanquihue, L Chile
13 F5 Llanrheidol Queensland 22.16S 141.33E
56 C3 Llanrhystud Dyfed Wales 52.18N 4.09W
57 F6 Llanrwst Clwyd Wales 53.08N 3.48W
75 R3 Llansá Spain 42.21N 3.09E
57 F6 Llansannan Clwyd Wales 53.11N 3.35W
56 C3 Llansantffraid Dyfed Wales 52.17N 4.10W
56 F4 Llansoy Gwent Wales 51.44N 2.47W
56 C4 Llanstephan Dyfed Wales 51.47N 4.24W
56 E4 Llanthony Gwent Wales 51.57N 3.03W
56 E4 Llantrisant Mid Glam Wales 51.33N 3.23W
56 E5 Llantwit Maj S Glam Wales 51.25N 3.30W
56 D2 Llanuwchllyn Gwynedd Wales 52.52N 3.41W
56 F4 Llanvetherin Gwent Wales 51.52N 2.55W
56 F4 Llanvihangel Crucorney Gwent Wales 51.53N 2.59W
56 E2 Llanwddyn Powys Wales 52.46N 3.27W
56 C3 Llanwnnen Dyfed Wales 52.06N 4.09W
56 D4 Llanwrda Dyfed Wales 51.58N 3.53W
56 D3 Llanwrtyd Wells Powys Wales 52.07N 3.38W
56 C3 Llanybydder Dyfed Wales 52.04N 4.09W
56 E2 Llanymynech Shropshire Eng 52.47N 3.05W
56 E3 Llanyre Powys Wales 52.16N 3.25W
75 M5 Llardecáns Spain 41.22N 0.33E
120 B3 Llata Peru 9.26S 76.46W
77 Q2 Llauri Spain 39.10N 0.20W
75 M5 Llaveria, Sierra de mts Spain
75 N3 Llavorsí Spain 42.30N 1.12E
77 V15 Llebeche, C Balearic Is 39.10N 2.55E
56 B3 Llechryd Dyfed Wales 52.04N 4.36W
56 D3 Lledrod Dyfed Wales 52.19N 3.59W
75 M5 Llena, Sierra de la mts Spain
77 S12 Llentrisca, C Balearic Is 38.51N 1.15E
77 D4 Llera Spain 38.27N 6.03W
77 D4 Llerena Spain 38.14N 6.00W
75 Q3 Llers Spain 42.17N 2.55E
75 O3 Llés Spain 42.23N 1.41E
103 B5 Llewellyn Pennsylvania 40.41N 76.16W
56 B2 LLeyn pen Gwynedd Wales
77 T12 Llibrell, C Balearic Is 38.56N 1.32E
120 E8 Llica Bolivia 19.52S 68.16W
121 A5 Llico Chile 34.46S 72.10W
121 A8 Llico, R Chile
75 O3 Llivia Spain 42.28N 1.59E
75 O4 Llobregat R Spain
75 N4 Llobregós R Spain
75 E1 Llodio Spain 43.08N 2.58W
121 B4 Llolleo Chile 33.38S 71.40W
77 P2 Llombay Spain 39.18N 0.34W
75 Q4 Lloret de Mar Spain 41.42N 2.51E
77 P2 Llosa de Ranes Spain 39.02N 0.32W
77 V14 Lloseta Balearic Is 39.43N 2.51E
75 N4 Llovera Spain 41.57N 1.28E
110 Q1 Lloyd Montana 48.18N 109.22W
13 G2 Lloyd B Queensland
101 L7 Lloyd George, Mt Br Col 57.53N 124.59W
103 H5 Lloyd Harbor Long I, N Y 40.54N 73.27W
101 T7 Lloyd L Saskatchewan 57.23N 109.00W
100 H5 Lloydminster Alberta/Sask 53.18N 110.00W
77 W14 Llubí Balearic Is 39.42N 3.00E
77 V15 Lluchmayor Balearic Is 39.29N 2.53E
116 K2 Lluidas Vale Jamaica, W I 18.08N 77.10W
120 E11 Llullaillaco vol Arg/Chile 24.43S 68.30W
75 P4 Llusanés R Spain
56 C2 Llwyngwril Gwynedd Wales 52.40N 4.05W
56 D3 Llyn Brianne Res Dyfed Wales
57 F6 Llyn Ogwen L Gwynedd Wales 53.08N 4.00W
57 E6 Llyn Padarn L Gwynedd Wales 53.08N 4.07W
56 E3 Llyswen Powys Wales 52.02N 3.17W
65 J3 Lnáře Czechoslovakia 49.28N 13.47E
61 B3 Lo Belgium 50.59N 2.45E
93 C2 Loa Sudan 3.48N 31.58E
111 N3 Loa Utah 38.24N 111.40W
103 C6 Loag Pennsylvania 40.07N 75.48W
18 M6 Loakulu Borneo Indon 0.31S 117.00E
107 G2 Loami Illinois 39.41N 89.51W
Loanda Angola see Luanda
118 D8 Loanda Brazil 22.53S 53.10W
91 B6 Loandjili Congo 4.44S 11.52E
91 G6 Loange R Zaïre
91 B6 Loango Congo 4.38S 11.50E
91 C6 Loango Zaïre 5.09S 13.01E
91 C6 Loango tribe Angola/Zaïre
58 K7 Loanhead Lothian Scotland 55.53N 3.09W
79 D6 Loano Italy 44.07N 8.16E
57 D1 Loans Strathclyde Scotland 55.33N 4.38W
120 D9 Loa, R Chile
75 J3 Loarre Spain 42.19N 0.37W
19 M7 Loay Philippines 9.37N 124.02E
46 K2 Lob R U.S.S.R.
46 Q1 Loban' R U.S.S.R.
25 K8 Lobang Assam India 25.29N 92.39E
Lobanggu see Lavanggu
45 K3 Lobanovo U.S.S.R. 53.03N 38.12E
76 D2 Loba, Sierra de la mts Spain
77 H6 Lobatejo mt Spain 37.30N 4.20W
94 H5 Lobatsi Botswana 25.11S 25.40E
62 H4 Löbau E Germany 51.06N 14.42E
90 H9 Lobaye dist Cent Afr Rep
90 H9 Lobaye R Cent Afr Rep
61 H5 Lobbes Belgium 50.21N 4.16E
90 D9 Lobe Cameroon 5.09N 9.11E
64 M2 Lobeda Jena E Germany 50.53N 11.36E
63 P9 Löbejün E Germany 51.38N 11.55E
93 G2 Lobeloik watercourse Kenya
64 M3 Lobenstein E Germany 50.27N 11.38E
76 C5 Lobera Spain 41.59N 8.03W
121 F7 Loberia Argentina 38.08S 58.48W
62 J2 Łobez Poland 53.38N 15.39E
89 H6 Lobi tribe Upper Volta
60 N12 Lobith Netherlands 51.53N 6.07E
91 C10 Lobito Angola 12.20S 13.34E
91 C10 Lobito B Angola
119 A10 Lobitos Peru 4.30S 81.15W
63 R4 Löbnitz E Germany 54.18N 12.43E
45 J1 Lobnya U.S.S.R. 56.01N 37.30E
89 F8 Lobo R Ivory Coast
90 H1 Lobogue Chad 20.31N 16.34E
91 E4 Loboko Congo 0.45S 16.38E
77 C3 Lobón Spain 38.51N 6.38W
52 J5 Lobonäs Sweden 61.33N 15.20E
121 F5 Lobos Argentina 35.11S 59.08W
96 U9 Lobos isld Canary Is 28.44N 13.49W
115 D4 Lobos isld Mexico 27.20N 110.30W
77 M5 Lobos mt Spain 37.56N 2.27W
120 D8 Lobos, C Chile 18.48S 70.25W
115 C3 Lobos, C Mexico 29.55N 112.41W
116 F3 Lobos Cay isld Cuba 22.22N 77.36W
120 A7 Lobos de Afuera, Islas Peru
119 B11 Lobos de Tierra, I Peru 6.30S 80.55W
121 G5 Lobos, I Uruguay
115 L7 Lobos, I. de Mexico 21.30N 97.10W
111 A8 Lobos, Pt San Francisco, Cal
121 D9 Lobos, Pta C Argentina 43.46S 65.20W
120 D9 Lobos, Pta C Chubut Chile 21.07S 70.10W
121 A5 Lobos, Pta C Colchagua Chile 34.27S 72.05W
53 N11 Lobra Faeroes 61.27N 6.46W
56 H5 Lobscombe Corner Wilts Eng 51.07N 1.38W
64 N1 Lobstadt E Germany 51.08N 12.27E
97 N7 Lobstick L Labrador, Nfld 54.00N 65.00W
30 H2 Lobujya Nepal 27.57N 86.49E
30 H2 Lobujya East mt Nepal 27.57N 86.47E
30 H2 Lobujya Glacier Nepal
30 H2 Lobujya West mt Nepal 27.58N 86.47E
93 G1 Loburet Kenya 4.14N 35.10E
63 Q8 Loburg E Germany 52.07N 12.05E
47 J6 Lobva U.S.S.R. 59.14N 60.28E
47 J6 Lobva R U.S.S.R.
62 K2 Łobżenica Poland 53.17N 17.14E
79 B4 Locana Italy 45.25N 7.28E
66 M7 Locarno Switzerland 46.10N 8.48E
108 E3 Locate Montana 46.27N 105.20W
79 F4 Locate Triulzi Italy 45.22N 9.13E
25 J2 Loc Binh Vietnam 21.45N 106.57E
63 K8 Loccum W Germany 52.27N 9.09E
58 G5 Lochaber dist Highland Scotland
98 K8 Lochaber Mines Nova Scotia 45.02N 62.32W
58 E5 Lochailort Highland Scotland 56.53N 5.40W
58 E5 Lochaline Highland Scotland 56.32N 5.47W
58 E4 Lochalsh Highland Scotland 57.17N 5.35W
99 F4 Lochalsh Ontario 48.21N 84.17W
58 F3 Lochan Fada Highland Scotland 57.41N 5.20W
57 F2 Locharbriggs Dumfries & Galloway Scotland 55.06N 3.35W
92 D11 Lochard Zimbabwe 19.57S 29.03E
Lo Chau see Beaufort I
66 Q1 Lochau Austria 47.32N 9.46E
58 G6 Lochay, R Central Scotland
58 B4 Lochboisdale S Uist, W Isles Scotland 57.09N 7.19W
58 E6 Lochbuie Mull, Strathclyde Scotland 56.21N 5.52W
58 F4 Lochcarron Highland Scotland 57.23N 5.00W
58 E6 Lochdonhead Mull, Strathclyde Scotland 56.26N 5.41W
58 H6 Lochearnhead Central Scotland 56.23N 4.18W
100 H2 Loche, L la Saskatchewan
60 O11 Lochem Netherlands 52.10N 6.25E
60 O11 Lochemerberg mt Netherlands 52.08N 6.26E
93 F3 Lochemon R Uganda
72 F1 Loches France 47.08N 1.00E
72 G1 Loché-sur-Indrois France 47.05N 1.12E
58 F6 Lochgair Strathclyde Scotland 56.04N 5.21W
58 K6 Lochgelly Fife Scotland 56.08N 3.19W
58 F6 Lochgilphead Strathclyde Scotland 56.03N 5.26W
58 G6 Lochgoilhead Strathclyde Scotland 56.10N 4.54W
11 C13 Lochiel New Zealand 46.12S 168.20E
95 O2 Lochiel S Africa 26.09S 30.47E
58 J4 Lochindorb L Highland Scotland 57.24N 3.43W
92 C9 Lochinvar Nat. Park Zambia
58 F2 Lochinver Highland Scotland 58.09N 5.15W
58 L5 Lochlee Church Tayside Scotland 56.55N 2.55W
57 G2 Lochmaben Dumfries & Galloway Scotland 55.08N 3.27W
58 B3 Lochmaddy N Uist, W Isles Scotland 57.36N 7.10W
58 K5 Lochnagar mt Grampian Scotland 56.57N 3.15W
11 C11 Lochnagar L New Zealand
65 J2 Lochovice Czechoslovakia 49.52N 13.58E
58 F7 Lochranza Arran, Strathclyde Scotland 55.42N 5.18W
103 A8 Loch Raven Res Maryland 39.27N 76.34W
61 F2 Lochristi Belgium 51.06N 3.50E
110 K3 Lochsa R Idaho
58 K1 Lochside Highland Scotland 58.34N 3.22W
60 U17 Locht Netherlands 50.51N 6.00E
25 J2 Lo Chuc San isld Vietnam 21.13N 107.55E
58 G7 Lochwinnoch Strathclyde Scotland 55.48N 4.39W
58 G5 Lochy, L Highland Scotland
58 F5 Lochy, R Highland Scotland
12 D5 Lock S Australia 33.33S 135.45E
104 J4 Locke New York 42.39N 76.26W
110 H1 Locke Washington 48.25N 117.19W
98 G10 Lockeport Nova Scotia 43.42N 65.08W
112 J4 Locker Texas 31.23N 98.54W
57 G2 Lockerbie Dumfries & Galloway Scotland 55.07N 3.22W
101 Q1 Locker Pt N W Terr 68.25N 114.00W
14 A5 Locker Pt W Australia 21.45S 114.50E
111 J3 Lockes Nevada 38.33N 115.47W
107 B8 Lockesburg Arkansas 33.59N 94.11W
112 H1 Lockett Texas 34.06N 99.14W
107 K10 Lockhart Alabama 31.02N 86.22W
108 O2 Lockhart Minnesota 47.26N 96.32W
12 H6 Lockhart New S Wales 35.16S 146.42E
105 F3 Lockhart S Carolina 34.46N 81.29W
112 K6 Lockhart Texas 29.54N 97.41W
101 T4 Lockhart R N W Terr
13 G2 Lockhart River Mission Queensland 12.56S 143.30E
104 H5 Lock Haven Pennsylvania 41.09N 77.28W
14 B6 Lockier Ra W Australia
56 F5 Locking Avon Eng 51.21N 2.55W
112 F1 Lockney Texas 34.06N 101.25W
63 U6 Löcknitz E Germany 53.28N 14.13E
63 P6 Löcknitz R E Germany
106 F8 Lockport Illinois 41.34N 88.03W
107 F12 Lockport Louisiana 29.40N 90.34W
100 U8 Lockport Manitoba 50.04N 97.00W
104 G3 Lockport New York 43.11N 78.39W
106 C9 Lockridge Iowa 40.59N 91.45W
107 C4 Lockwood Missouri 37.21N 93.58W
103 A2 Lockwood New York 42.05N 76.34W
100 N7 Lockwood Saskatchewan 51.39N 105.00W
113 J3 Lockwood Hills Alaska
48 S1 Lockwood Ø isld Greenland 83.15N 40.30N
66 C3 Locle, le Switzerland 47.04N 6.45E
70 D7 Locmaria Belle Isle, Nfld France 47.18N 3.04W
70 E6 Locmaria Morbihan France 47.46N 2.47W
70 E6 Locmariaquer France 47.34N 2.57W
70 E6 Locminé France 47.53N 2.50W
25 J7 Loc Ninh Vietnam 11.51N 106.35E
109 N7 Loco Oklahoma 34.21N 97.42W
66 L7 Loco Switzerland 46.13N 8.41E
110 P3 Loco Mt Montana 46.15N 110.20W
80 O6 Locone R Italy
81 P11 Locorotondo Italy 40.45N 17.20E
70 C4 Locquirec France 48.41N 3.40W
81 M7 Locri Italy 38.14N 16.15E
120 C5 Locroja Peru 12.39S 74.23W
70 B5 Locronan France 48.06N 4.13W
70 B6 Loctudy France 47.50N 4.11W
120 D7 Locumba Peru 17.35S 70.46W
120 D7 Locumba R Peru
121 G8 Lo Curro dist Santiago Chile
107 C1 Locust Cr Missouri
107 K7 Locust Fork R Alabama
103 C8 Locust Grove Maryland 39.20N 75.57W
104 B8 Locust Grove Ohio 38.59N 83.21W
109 P5 Locust Grove Oklahoma 36.12N 95.12W
35 C6 Lod Israel 31.57N 34.54E
106 F9 Loda Illinois 40.32N 88.05W
86 L9 Lo'da, Gebel hill Egypt 28.27N 33.56E
53 W15 Lodalskåpa mt Norway 61.47N 7.13E
93 G2 Lodapalinga Hills Kenya
Lödar see Lawdar
56 O2 Loddon Norfolk Eng 52.32N 1.29E
12 G6 Loddon R Victoria
81 D2 Lodè Sardinia 40.36N 9.32E
61 H5 Lodelinsart Belgium 50.26N 4.27E
65 K1 Lodĕnice Czechoslovakia 50.01N 14.11E
63 P10 Lodersleben E Germany 51.24N 11.32E
71 C9 Lodève France 43.44N 3.19E
47 C5 Lodeynoye Pole U.S.S.R. 60.43N 33.30E
110 Q1 Lodge Cr Montana/Sask
108 C4 Lodge Grass Montana 45.20N 107.20W
113 T7 Lodge, Mt Alaska/Br Col 59.05N 137.35W
108 H8 Lodgepole Nebraska 41.09N 102.38W
108 F8 Lodgepole Cr Wyoming
29 B6 Lodhika Gujarat India 22.05N 70.41E
29 F7 Lodhikheda Madhya Prad India 21.35N 78.56E
50 M4 Lodhmundarfjördhur B Iceland
50 F6 Lodhmundur mt Iceland 64.05N 19.16W
31 F6 Lodhran Pakistan 29.32N 71.40E
111 C3 Lodi California 38.07N 121.18W
79 F4 Lodi Italy 45.19N 9.30E
103 L6 Lodi New Jersey 40.53N 74.05W
104 C5 Lodi Ohio 41.02N 82.01W
37 F8 Lodi Turkey 37.44N 41.55E
106 E6 Lodi Wisconsin 43.18N 89.32W
51 E3 Lødingen Norway 68.25N 16.00E
93 D1 Lodio, Jeb mt Sudan 4.38N 32.54E
79 F4 Lodi Vecchio Italy 45.18N 9.25E
91 H5 Lodja Zaïre 3.30S 23.33E
75 F3 Lodosa Spain 42.26N 2.05W
75 G3 Lodosa, Canal de Spain
29 B6 Lodrani Gujarat India 23.52N 70.40E
66 M6 Lodrino Switzerland 46.18N 8.59E
79 J3 Lodrone Italy 45.50N 10.32E
71 J2 Lods France 47.03N 6.14E
93 G2 Lodwar Kenya 3.06N 35.38E
62 L4 Łódź Poland 51.49N 19.28E
75 D7 Loeches Spain 40.23N 3.25W
31 F3 Loe Dakha Afghanistan 34.15N 71.05E
Loei see Muang Loei
87 E8 Loelli Sudan 5.10N 34.39E
91 C6 Loemé R Congo
53 V15 Loen Norway 61.52N 6.51E
60 N11 Loenen Gelderland Netherlands 52.07N 6.01E
60 J11 Loenen Netherlands 52.13N 5.01E
91 K6 Loengo Zaïre 4.49S 26.30E
61 J1 Loenhout Belgium 51.24N 4.39E
95 J9 Loerie S Africa 33.52S 25.02E
94 E8 Loeriesfontein S Africa 30.59S 19.29E
69 C4 Loeuilly France 49.46N 2.10E
89 D8 Lofa R Liberia
53 U18 Løfallstrand Norway 60.01N 6.00E
9 T12 Lofanga atoll Tonga, Pacific Oc 19.50S 174.35W
65 G6 Lofer Austria 47.36N 12.42E
65 G6 Loferer Steinberge mts Austria
66 Q2 Löffel Spitze mt Austria 47.16N 9.50E
64 E6 Loffenau W Germany 48.46N 8.23E
64 E8 Löffingen W Germany 47.54N 8.20E
91 K9 Lofoi, Chutes rapids Zaïre 10.14S 27.30E
51 C3 Lofoten islds Norway
52 G4 Lofsdalen Sweden 62.07N 13.20E
53 B5 Loft Denmark 55.46N 8.53E
52 K9 Loftahammar Sweden 57.55N 16.45E
95 J6 Lofter S Africa 30.10S 25.44E
53 Y14 Lofthøene glacier Norway 62.06N 8.05E
57 K4 Lofthouse N Yorks Eng 54.09N 1.49W
53 V18 Lofthus Norway 60.20N 6.40E
57 M3 Loftus Cleveland Eng 54.33N 0.53W
14 C6 Lofty Ra W Australia
93 E2 Lofusa Sudan 3.51N 33.13E
45 P7 Log U.S.S.R. 49.28N 43.51E
79 P2 Log Yugoslavia 46.24N 13.36E
89 L5 Loga Niger 13.40N 3.15E
30 L8 Logai Bihar India 24.56N 87.35E
108 P8 Logan Iowa 41.38N 95.49W
109 L2 Logan Kansas 39.40N 99.35W
108 K8 Logan Nebraska 41.31N 100.28W
109 G6 Logan New Mexico 35.23N 103.24W
104 C7 Logan Ohio 39.32N 82.24W
110 O8 Logan Utah 41.45N 111.50W
104 D9 Logan W Virginia 37.52N 82.00W
13 H5 Logan R Queensland
13 L8 Logan R Queensland
108 O8 Logan Cr Nebraska
111 K5 Logandale Nevada 36.37N 114.33W
13 J5 Logan Downs Queensland 22.25S 147.55E
113 R6 Logan Glacier Alaska/Yukon Terr 60.55N 141.20W
104 Q9 Logan International Airport Boston, Mass 42.22N 71.01W
100 F3 Logan L Alberta
98 F5 Logan, Mt Quebec 48.54N 66.43W
110 E1 Logan, Mt Washington 48.33N 120.55W
101 C5 Logan, Mt Yukon Terr 60.31N 140.22W
101 J5 Logan Mts Yukon/N W Terr
110 M1 Logan Pass Montana 48.42N 113.40W
56 S9 Logan Rock Cornwall Eng 50.02N 5.39W
106 H9 Logansport Indiana 40.45N 86.25W
107 B10 Logansport Louisiana 31.59N 94.01W
104 H5 Loganton Pennsylvania 41.03N 77.18W
103 A7 Loganville Pennsylvania 39.51N 76.43W
106 D6 Loganville Wisconsin 43.27N 90.01W
31 E3 Logar prov Afghanistan
31 E3 Logar R Afghanistan
47 K3 Logas'yegan R U.S.S.R.
41 G4 Logata R U.S.S.R.
109 E1 Logcabin Colorado 40.45N 105.29W
52 L3 Lögde älv R Sweden
110 F5 Logdell Oregon 44.13N 119.09W
91 C7 Loge R Angola
70 L2 Loges, les France 49.42N 0.17E
58 J5 Logierait Tayside Scotland 56.39N 3.42W
47 N5 Loginovo U.S.S.R. 56.39N 61.18E
93 H3 Logipi, L Kenya 2.13N 36.35E
71 K9 Logis-du-Pin, le France 43.46N 6.39E
53 Y19 Lognvikvatn L Norway 59.42N 8.08E
93 B3 Logo Zaïre 2.09N 30.55E
93 E2 Logoforok Sudan 3.58N 33.07E
90 G7 Logone div Chad
90 G6 Logone R Chad
90 G6 Logone Birni Chad 11.50N 15.00E
90 G6 Logone Gana Chad 11.36N 15.04E
90 H7 Logone Oriental R Chad
89 D6 Logorombo Guinea 10.59N 10.41W
89 F8 Logoualé Ivory Coast 7.12N 7.35W
45 P8 Logovskiy Volgograd U.S.S.R. 48.27N 43.22E
46 G3 Logoysk Belorussiya U.S.S.R. 54.08N 27.42E
90 G1 Logozonou Niger 20.34N 15.21E
79 H4 Lograto Italy 45.28N 10.03E
70 N5 Logron France 48.08N 1.17E
75 F3 Logroño Spain 42.28N 2.26W
74 F2 Logroño prov Spain
76 J10 Logrosán Spain 39.21N 5.29W
53 C3 Løgstør Denmark 56.59N 9.16E
53 C3 Løgstør Bredning B Denmark 56.59N 9.05E
53 C3 Løgstrup Denmark 56.31N 9.21E
28 J3 Logtak L Manipur India
53 E4 Løgten Denmark 56.17N 10.20E
81 B2 Logudoro reg Sardinia
70 D4 Loguivy-Plougras France 48.32N 3.30W
53 B6 Løgumkloster Denmark 55.04N 8.58E
Lögurinn R see Lagarfljót R
9 C9 Loh isld New Hebrides 13.22S 166.36E
53 F6 Lohals Denmark 55.08N 10.55E
35 D2 Lohame HaGeta 'ot Israel 32.57N 35.06E
29 J6 Lohardaga Bihar India 23.27N 84.42E
29 D3 Loharu Haryana India 28.28N 75.50E
95 G4 Lohatlha S Africa 28.03S 23.03E
64 B1 Lohausen airport W Germany 51.15N 6.46E
29 C4 Lohawat Rajasthan India 26.57N 72.30E
30 C2 Lohba Uttar Prad India 30.05N 79.18E
70 G6 Lohéac France 47.52N 1.53W
121 G10 Lo Hermida dist Santiago Chile
64 M7 Lohhof W Germany 48.16N 11.35E
51 L5 Lohijärvi Finland 66.29N 24.20E
28 L2 Lohit R Assam India
28 K1 Lohit Frontier Div Assam India
51 L11 Lohja Finland 60.12N 24.10E
64 G1 Löhlbach W Germany 51.04N 9.00E
110 Q1 Lohman Montana 48.35N 109.25W
69 N2 Lohmar W Germany 50.49N 7.13E
63 T3 Lohme E Germany 54.35N 13.36E
63 Q5 Lohmen E Germany 53.42N 12.05E
112 H4 Lohn Texas 31.20N 99.26W
64 E3 Löhnberg W Germany 50.30N 8.16E
Lohne see Schepsdorf-Lohne
63 H7 Lohne Niedersachsen W Ger 52.40N 8.15E
63 J8 Löhne Nordrhein-Westfalen W Germany 52.12N 8.41E
66 G6 Lohner mt Switzerland 46.28N 7.37E
65 H5 Lohnsburg Austria 48.08N 13.23E
64 D4 Lohnsfeld W Germany 49.33N 7.52E
19 B5 Loholoho Celebes Indon 3.12S 121.06E
64 H4 Lohr W Germany 50.00N 9.35E
30 D7 Lohra Uttar Prad India 25.29N 80.58E
64 F2 Lohra W Germany 50.44N 8.39E
108 Q7 Lohrville Iowa 42.17N 94.31W
51 K7 Lohtaja Finland 64.01N 23.30E
92 F3 Lohumbo Tanzania 3.43S 33.06E
23 B8 Loi R Burma
25 D2 Loi-ai Burma 20.21N 96.42E
79 K6 Loiano Italy 44.17N 11.20E
82 B4 Loibl Pass Austria/Yugoslavia 46.25N 14.17E
93 H9 Loiborsoit Tanzania 3.54S 36.26E
70 J6 Loigne France 47.52N 0.45W
25 D3 Loikaw Burma 19.40N 97.17E
25 D3 Loi Lan mt Burma 19.38N 97.52E
91 G4 Loile R Zaïre
25 D2 Loi-lem Burma 20.57N 97.31E
25 E1 Loi Lun Burma 22.28N 99.12E
51 K11 Loimaa Finland 60.50N 23.05E
23 B8 Loi Mwe Burma 21.07N 99.45E
71 C1 Loing R France
70 L6 Loir R France
72 D4 Loiré Charente-Maritime France 45.58N 0.16W
70 J6 Loiré Maine-et-Loire France 47.37N 0.58W
67 H7 Loire dept France
70 K7 Loire R France
67 D5 Loire-Atlantique dept France
67 G5 Loiret dept France
67 F5 Loir-et-Cher dept France
70 J5 Loiron France 48.03N 0.56W
64 L8 Loisach R W Germany
25 D2 Loi Sang mt Burma 21.34N 97.24E
69 J5 Loison R France
71 G3 Loisy Saône-et-Loire France 46.35N 5.02E
69 H6 Loisy-sur-Marne France 48.46N 4.33E
93 G7 Loita Plains Kenya
63 S5 Loitz E Germany 53.58N 13.09E
93 G3 Loiya Kenya 2.40N 35.05E
93 G3 Loiya Puya Kenya 2.27N 35.25E
119 B9 Loja Ecuador 3.59S 79.16W
77 H6 Loja Spain 37.10N 4.09W
119 B10 Loja prov Ecuador
30 E2 Lojandak Xizang Zizhiqu 30.55N 81.08E
19 E4 Loji Moluccas Indon 1.23S 127.26E
25 L2 Lo Jiang R China
53 C6 Løjt Kirkeby Denmark 55.06N 9.29E
93 C1 Loka Sudan 4.15N 31.01E
91 F3 Loka Zaïre 0.22N 18.02E
93 D2 Lokai Sudan 3.49N 32.07E
91 G5 Lokak Zaïre 2.22S 21.39E
94 J4 Lokala Drift Botswana 23.59S 26.39E
51 J11 Lokalahti Finland 60.41N 21.30E
91 C6 Lokandu Zaïre 5.47S 13.03E
91 J5 Lokandu Zaïre 2.34S 25.44E
51 N4 Lokan tekorjärvi Finland 67.49N 27.45E
30 A2 Lokar Uttar Prad India 30.50N 77.57E
91 G5 Lokaw Zaïre 2.40S 20.12E
44 K7 Lokbatan Azerbaydzhan U.S.S.R. 40.19N 49.47E
18 L7 Lokbatu Borneo Indon 2.25S 115.26E
47 G5 Lokchim R U.S.S.R.
52 F7 Løken Norway 59.48N 11.27E
61 B3 Loker Belgium 50.47N 2.47E
61 F2 Lokeren Belgium 51.06N 3.59E
64 O3 Loket Czechoslovakia 50.12N 12.45E
94 F5 Lokgwabe Botswana 24.10S 21.50E
47 K3 Lokhpodgort U.S.S.R. 66.02N 65.30E
45 E6 Lokhvitsa Ukraine U.S.S.R. 50.22N 33.16E
93 G3 Lokichar Kenya 2.23N 35.40E
93 G3 Lokichar watercourse Kenya
93 F1 Lokichokio Kenya 4.16N 34.22E
19 B4 Lokilalaki, Gunung mt Celebes Indon 1.16S 120.18E
50 B3 Lokinhamrar Iceland 65.50N 23.49W
93 F3 Lokiriama Kenya 2.48N 35.00E
93 G1 Lokitaung Kenya 4.15N 35.45E
53 U19 Løkjelsvatn L Norway 59.40N 6.10E
51 N4 Lokka Finland 67.55N 27.30E
51 N4 Lokka L Finland
53 D2 Løkken Denmark 57.22N 9.44E
52 E3 Løkken Norway 63.06N 9.43E
46 G2 Loknya U.S.S.R. 56.49N 30.00E
90 C7 Loko Nigeria 8.01N 7.53E
91 H4 Lokofe Zaïre 1.08S 23.23E
90 C8 Lokoja Nigeria 7.49N 6.44E
91 F5 Lokolama Zaïre 2.34S 19.53E
91 H3 Lokolenge Zaïre 1.12N 22.38E
91 G4 Lokolia Zaïre 0.34S 20.38E
91 F4 Lokolo R Zaïre
95 C7 Lokomby Madagascar 22.10S 47.45E
91 H4 Lokona Zaïre 1.29S 23.12E
93 H4 Lokori Kenya 1.56N 36.03E
91 G5 Lokoro R Zaïre
42 A2 Lokosovo U.S.S.R. 61.07N 74.50E
42 C6 Lokot' Altay U.S.S.R. 51.13N 81.13E
45 F4 Lokot' Bryansk U.S.S.R. 52.34N 34.35E
91 B2 Lokoundjé R Cameroon
46 F1 Loksa Estonia U.S.S.R. 59.32N 25.42E
61 L3 Loksbergen Belgium 50.57N 5.04E
40 E4 Lokshak U.S.S.R. 54.46N 130.28E
97 N5 Loks Land N W Terr
Loktak L see Logtak L
93 D2 Lokung Uganda 3.37N 32.43E
93 H3 Lokurakwa Kenya 2.12N 36.08E
15 K3 Lokuru Solomon Is 8.36S 157.18E
93 G1 Lokwanamoru Ra Kenya/Sudan
18 H3 Lokyang Singapore 1.19N 103.41E
87 A6 Lol watercourse Sudan
91 C11 Lola Angola 14.19S 13.37E
89 E8 Lola Guinea 7.52N 8.29W
93 J3 Lolajonga mt Kenya 2.08N 37.45E
91 H4 Lolaka R Zaïre
111 D2 Lola, Mt California 39.27N 120.22W
93 E10 Lolanguru Tanzania 4.37S 33.48E
93 J9 Lolbene Tanzania 3.52S 37.08E
93 G6 Loldiani mt Kenya 0.07S 35.45E
110 A9 Loleta California 40.40N 124.15W
93 F7 Lolgorien Kenya 1.14S 34.49E
15 K4 Loliang Bismarck Arch 1.32S 148.36E
70 H4 Lolif France 48.43N 1.23W
93 G8 Loliondo Tanzania 2.03S 35.40E
53 H7 Lolland isld Denmark
64 F2 Lollar W Germany 50.39N 8.43E
87 C6 Lolle,R Sudan
89 L6 Lollo Nigeria 11.35N 3.30E
60 L7 Lollum Netherlands 53.08N 5.32E
93 J10 Lolmuryoi Tanzania 4.26S 37.05E
110 L3 Lolo Montana 46.45N 114.06W
91 H2 Lolo Zaïre 2.15N 23.03E
91 K5 Lolo Zaïre 2.15S 27.40E
91 C4 Lolo R Gabon
15 L6 Lolobau I New Britain 4.55S 151.10E
19 E3 Loloda Halmahera Indonesia 1.39N 127.37E
19 E3 Loloda, Teluk B Halmahera Indon 1.35N 127.30E
19 E2 Loloda Utara, Kep islds Moluccas Indon
91 B2 Lolodorf Cameroon 3.17N 10.50E
47 G6 Lolog R U.S.S.R.
121 B8 Lolog, L Argentina
110 L3 Lolo Hot Springs Montana 46.45N 114.34W
9 T13 Lolona atoll Tonga, Pacific Oc 20.17S 174.30W
110 L3 Lolo Pass Idaho/Montana 46.39N 114.34W
15 J8 Lolorua Papua New Guinea 9.00S 146.57E
19 D8 Lolotoe Indonesia 9.09S 125.16E
18 B5 Lolowau Indonesia 0.55N 97.32E
93 E6 Lolui I Uganda 0.08S 33.43E
93 A4 Lolwa Zaïre 1.26N 29.31E
95 G2 Lolwane S Africa 26.57S 23.49E
82 H7 Lom Bulgaria 43.50N 23.12E
64 O4 Lom Czechoslovakia 49.50N 12.40E
53 Z15 Lom Norway 61.51N 8.32E
64 P4 Lom mt Czechoslovakia 49.55N 13.10E
90 G9 Lom R Cameroon
109 B2 Loma Colorado 39.11N 108.49W
89 D8 Loma Liberia 7.43N 10.05W
110 P2 Loma Montana 47.57N 110.30W
108 M1 Loma N Dakota 48.39N 98.31W
120 E4 Loma Alta Bolivia 10.48S 66.10W
72 F7 Lomagne reg France
50 H7 Lómagnupúr pk Iceland 63.59N 17.25W
92 D10 Lomagundi dist Zimbabwe
43 J6 Lomakino Uzbekistan U.S.S.R. 40.04N 68.05E
91 G3 Lomako R Zaïre
9 U2 Lomaloma Vanua Mbalavu Fiji 17.46S 179.00W
91 H4 Lomami Zaïre 1.53S 22.42E
91 J3 Lomami R Zaïre
108 R1 Loman Minnesota 48.32N 93.50W
121 D6 Loma Negra, Planicie de la plain Argentina
77 M7 Loma Pelada, Pta de pt Spain 36.47N 2.03W
31 D4 Lomar Pass Afghanistan 33.18N 67.41E
120 C6 Lomas Peru 15.33S 74.50W
Lomas R see Acari, R. de
121 K9 Lomas, B. de Chile
115 B10 Lomas Chapultepec dist Mexico City Mexico
121 C9 Lomas Coloradas mts Argentina
115 L6 Lomas del Real Mexico 22.33N 97.52W
121 F1 Lomas de Vallejos Argentina 27.44S 57.51W
9 S8 Lomawai Viti Levu Fiji 18.00S 177.16E
62 O4 Łomazy Poland 51.51N 23.09E
91 G11 Lomba R Angola
96 U1 Lomba da Maia Azores 37.35N 25.22W
19 D3 Lombagin Celebes Indon 0.56N 124.05E
110 O3 Lombard Montana 46.06N 111.25W
79 B6 Lombarda, Col du Italy/France 44.13N 7.07E
117 C3 Lombarda, Sa mts Brazil
79 F4 Lombardia reg Italy
14 E3 Lombardina Mission W Australia 16.50S 122.55E
61 B2 Lombardsijde Belgium 51.09N 2.46E
91 E8 Lombe Angola 9.27S 16.13E
72 J8 Lombers France 43.49N 2.09E
72 F9 Lombez France 43.29N 0.54E
61 F4 Lombise Belgium 50.36N 3.56E
19 C8 Lomblen isld Indonesia
18 M10 Lombok Indonesia 8.29S 116.40E
18 M10 Lombok isld Indonesia
18 L10 Lombok, Selat str Indonesia
18 D10 Lombong Pen Malaysia 1.46N 103.51E
53 A3 Lomborg Denmark 56.30N 8.17E
76 L2 Lombrana Spain 43.06N 4.25W
70 L5 Lombron France 48.05N 0.25E
121 F5 Lomde Argentina 34.45S 58.26W
89 K8 Lomé Togo 6.10N 1.21E
93 E2 Lomej Uganda 3.45N 33.50E
91 H5 Lomela Zaïre 2.19S 23.15E
91 G4 Lomela R Zaïre
79 E4 Lomello Italy 45.07N 8.48E
93 G4 Lomelo Kenya 1.28N 35.55E
112 J4 Lometa Texas 31.14N 98.24W
91 C2 Lomié Cameroon 3.09N 13.35E
32 C1 Lomir Iran 38.19N 48.54E
106 F6 Lomira Wisconsin 43.36N 88.27W
111 D10 Lomita California 33.48N 118.19W

120 F10 Lomitas Argentina 22.36S 3.55W
60 N14 Lomm Netherlands 51.27N 6.11E
53 K5 Lomma Sweden 55.41N 13.06E
53 K5 Lommabukten *B* Sweden 55.40N 13.00E
64 P1 Lommatzsch E Germany 51.12N 13.19E
69 D2 Lomme France 50.38N 2.59E
61 M2 Lommel Belgium 51.14N 5.19E
61 P6 Lommersweiler Belgium 50.14N 6.10E
30 K4 Lomnang Nepal 28.01N 86.10E
65 K3 Lomnice *R* Czechoslovakia
65 L3 Lomnice nad Lužnice Czechoslovakia 49.05N 14.44E
96 R14 Lomo de Arico Tenerife Canary Is 28.10N 16.30W
100 E8 Lomond Alberta 50.24N 112.36W
98 P4 Lomond Newfoundland 49.26N 57.46W
54 M5 Lomond *oil field* North Sea 57.14N 2.03E
58 K6 Lomond Hills Fife Scotland
98 M8 Lomond, Loch C Breton I, Nova Scotia
58 G6 Lomond, Loch Central/Strathclyde Scotland
51 O12 Lomonosov U.S.S.R. 59.50N 29.48E
41 D2 Lomonosova, Gory *mts* Novaya Zemlya U.S.S.R.
45 D1 Lomonosovo U.S.S.R. 55.47N 32.20E
48 J8 Lomonosov Ridge Arctic Oc
43 H1 Lomonosovskaya Kazakhstan U.S.S.R. 52.49N 66.23E
71 K2 Lomont, Mtgne du France
96 R13 Lomo Román Tenerife Canary Is 28.26N 16.30W
45 P1 Lomovka Gor'kiy U.S.S.R. 55.34N 43.49E
45 Q3 Lomovka Penza U.S.S.R. 53.29N 44.20E
47 E4 Lomovoye U.S.S.R. 64.05N 40.47E
111 D7 Lompac California 34.38N 120.27W
25 J6 Lomphat Cambodia 13.30N 107.00E
19 A6 Lompobattang, Gunung *mt* Celebes Indon 5.22S 119.58E
61 H6 Lompret Belgium 50.04N 4.23E
61 L6 Lomprez Belgium 50.05N 5.05E
53 Y15 Lomsegga *mt* Norway 61.50N 8.20E
51 F6 Lomsele Sweden 65.18N 17.40E
53 Y15 Lomshurrungen *mt* Norway 61.57N 8.27E
52 K2 Lomsjö Sweden 64.11N 17.00E
42 K6 Lomy U.S.S.R. 52.23N 118.08E
62 N2 Łomża Poland 53.11N 22.04E
50 J2 Lón Iceland 66.06N 16.54W
109 E7 Lon New Mexico 34.08N 105.08W
91 J6 Lona Zaïre 5.28S 25.25E
104 G7 Lonaconing Maryland 39.32N 78.59W
50 C2 Lónafjördhur *B* Ísafjardharsýsla, Nordhur Iceland
50 K2 Lónafjördhur *B* Thingeyjarsýsla, Nordhur Iceland
53 U17 Lønahorg *mt* Norway 60.41N 6.25E
28 K2 Lo Nakpo *dist* Assam India
50 G6 Lónakvísl *R* Iceland
29 E8 Lonar Maharashtra India 19.59N 76.38E
79 E3 Lonate Pozzolo Italy 45.36N 8.44E
79 H4 Lonato Italy 45.28N 10.29E
28 A1 Lonaula Maharashtra India 18.45N 73.27E
53 U17 Lønavatn *L* Norway 60.41N 6.29E
53 A5 Lønborg Denmark 55.54N 8.27E
61 N4 Loncin Belgium 50.40N 5.30E
121 A7 Loncoche Chile 39.23S 72.44W
121 B7 Loncopue Argentina 38.04S 70.43W
50 M5 Lönd Iceland 64.51N 13.50W
31 H10 Londa Bangladesh 22.06N 90.23E
28 B3 Londa Karnataka India 15.31N 74.32E
18 A7 Londang, Tanjong *C* Pen Malaysia 4.40N 100.34E
71 J10 Londe-les-Maures, la France 43.08N 6.14E
61 H2 Londerzeel Belgium 51.00N 4.19E
99 J9 Londesborough Ontario 43.41N 81.29W
93 G6 Londiani Kenya 0.10S 35.36E
70 N2 Londinières France 49.50N 1.25E
40 F7 Londoko U.S.S.R. 49.00N 132.02E
107 C6 London Arkansas 35.20N 93.15W
122 U9 London Christmas I Pacific Oc 2.00N 157.28W
56 L4 London England 51.30N 0.10W
107 M4 London Kentucky 37.07N 84.05W
104 B7 London Ohio 39.52N 83.27W
99 J10 London Ontario 42.58N 81.15W
112 H5 London Texas 30.42N 99.36W
56 L5 London Airport(Gatwick) W Sussex Eng 51.08N 0.11W
London Airport(Heathrow) *see* Heathrow
56 M4 London Airport(Stansted) Essex Eng 51.54N 0.14E
56 L4 London Colney Herts Eng 51.44N 0.18W
59 H2 Londonderry Londonderry N Ireland 55.00N 7.19W
104 O4 Londonderry New Hampshire 42.54N 71.22W
98 J8 Londonderry Nova Scotia 45.28N 63.38W
104 N3 Londonderry Vermont 43.13N 72.37W
59 H2 Londonderry *co* N Ireland
14 F2 Londonderry, C W Australia 13.45S 126.56E
121 K10 Londonderry I Chile 55.00S 70.40W
9 T7 Londoni Viti Levu Fiji 17.43S 178.33E
Londorf *see* Rabenau
50 B5 Lóndrangar *beach* Iceland 64.45N 23.45W
121 C1 Londres Argentina 27.45S 67.05W
118 D8 Londrina Brazil 23.18S 51.13W
93 H8 Londurot Hills Kenya
109 N7 Lone Grove Oklahoma 34.12N 97.16W
99 J7 Lonely I Ontario 45.34N 81.29W
92 D11 Lonely Mine Zimbabwe 19.30S 28.49E
111 G3 Lone Mt Nevada 38.01N 117.30W
112 M3 Lone Oak Texas 32.59N 95.55W
111 F5 Lone Pine California 36.35N 118.04W
110 L2 Lonepine Montana 47.44N 114.39W
110 F4 Lonerock Oregon 45.06N 119.52W
100 H5 Lone Rock Saskatchewan 53.04N 109.53W
106 D6 Lone Rock Wisconsin 43.11N 90.14W
110 P1 Lonesome Lake Res Montana 48.15N 110.15W
110 P8 Lonetree Wyoming 41.04N 110.10W
109 L7 Lone Wolf Oklahoma 34.59N 99.16W
113 K4 Long Alaska 64.25N 155.39W
Long Thailand*see* Muang Long
91 F11 Longa Angola 14.44S 18.36E
84 C8 Longá Greece 36.52N 21.55E
91 F4 Longa Zaïre 0.12S 18.52E
91 D9 Longa *R* Angola
91 F11 Longa *R* Angola
72 G9 Longages France 43.21N 1.14E
18 L4 Long Akah Sarawak Malaysia 3.16N 114.50E
23 D7 Long'an Guangxi China 23.11N 107.38E
84 D7 Longaníkos Greece 37.14N 22.15E
48 O6 Longa, Ostrova de *islds* Arctic Oc
91 C9 Longa, Ponta *pt* Angola 10.15S 13.27E
39 K1 Longa, Proliv *str* U.S.S.R.
75 H5 Longares Spain 41.24N 1.10W
79 M2 Longarone Italy 46.17N 12.18E
84 D7 Longástra Greece 37.07N 22.20E
121 B5 Longavi Chile 35.57N 71.45W
121 B6 Longavi *pk* Chile 36.12S 71.16W
116 G1 Long B Jamaica, W I 18.20N 78.20W
116 J2 Long B Jamaica, W I 17.50N 77.20W
12 M8 Long B New S Wales
105 J4 Long B S Carolina
18 L5 Longbangun Borneo Indon 0.35N 115.10E
116 M2 Long Bay Jamaica, W I 18.06N 76.20W
111 F8 Long Beach California 33.47N 118.15W
103 M8 Long Beach Long I, N Y 40.35N 73.40W
107 G11 Long Beach Mississippi 30.21N 89.11W
11 F11 Longbeach New Zealand 44.05S 171.42E
11 N11 Long Beach New Zealand 45.45S 170.40E
110 A3 Long Beach Washington 46.26N 124.02W
103 F7 Long Beach I New Jersey
57 M7 Long Bennington Lincs Eng 52.59N 0.46W
18 M5 Longbleh Borneo Indon 0.15N 116.15E
105 E10 Longboat Key *isld* Florida 27.23N 82.38W
103 G6 Long Branch New Jersey 40.17N 73.59W
56 G5 Longbridge Deverill Wilts Eng 51.10N 2.12W
11 K7 Longburn New Zealand 40.22S 175.34E
56 F6 Long Burton Dorset Eng 50.55N 2.30W
116 G3 Long Cay *isld* Bahamas 22.37N 74.21W
69 J7 Longchamp France 48.08N 5.27E
61 N6 Longchamps Luxembourg Belgium 50.03N 5.41E
61 K4 Longchamps Namur Belgium 50.35N 4.54E
23 D4 Longchang Sichuan China 29.20N 105.16E
71 H4 Longchaumois France 46.27N 5.55E
23 G6 Longchuan Guangdong China 24.03N 115.14E
23 A6 Longchuan Yunnan China 24.21N 97.50E
23 A6 Longchuan Jiang *R* Yunnan China
56 H4 Long Compton Warwicks Eng 52.00N 1.35W
108 G1 Long Cr N Dakota
100 O9 Long Cr Saskatchewan
12 C3 Long Cr S Australia
110 F5 Long Creek Oregon 44.43N 119.06W
56 J4 Long Crendon Bucks Eng 51.47N 1.01W
25 J4 Long Dai Vietnam 17.22N 106.35E
109 M5 Longdale Oklahoma 36.09N 98.33W
23 D1 Longde Gansu China 35.38N 106.06E
55 C5 Long Ditton Surrey Eng 51.23N 0.20W
56 G3 Longdon Hereford & Worcs Eng 52.01N 2.14W
56 H2 Longdon Staffs Eng 52.44N 1.51W
57 L7 Long Eaton Derbys Eng 52.54N 1.15W
71 G2 Longecourt-en-Plaine France 47.11N 5.10E
103 D3 Long Eddy New York 41.51N 75.08W
Longemer *see* Xonrupt-Longemer
64 B1 Longerich Nordrhein-Westfalen W Germany 51.00N 6.54E
71 K7 Longet, Col de *pass* France/Italy 44.39N 6.58E
72 B3 Longeville France 46.26N 1.29W
104 P1 Long Falls Dam Maine 45.14N 70.12W
112 E5 Longfellow Texas 30.09N 102.38W
11 G9 Longfellow, Mt New Zealand 42.41S 172.19E
21 D5 Longfengshan Sk *L* Heilongjiang China
109 N2 Longford Kansas 39.12N 97.20W
59 G4 Longford Longford Irish Rep 53.44N 7.47W
11 G8 Longford New Zealand 41.48S 172.22E
59 G5 Longford Offaly Irish Rep 53.04N 7.44E
12 H8 Longford Tasmania 41.25S 147.02E
59 G4 Longford *co* Irish Rep
58 K6 Longforgan Tayside Scotland 56.28N 3.08W
58 M7 Longformacus Borders Scotland 55.49N 2.29W
54 K5 Long Forties *sea bank* North Sea
21 D6 Longgang Shan *mts* Jilin China
18 M5 Longgi *R* Borneo Indon
18 M4 Longglat Borneo Indon 2.50N 116.58E
22 K6 Longguan Hebei China 40.45N 115.43E
23 G1 Longguji Shandong China 35.17N 115.53E
23 E9 Longgun Guangdong China 19.12N 110.31E
18 K5 Longguntur Borneo Indon 0.12N 112.09E
23 H6 Longhai Fujian China 24.25N 117.46E
56 H6 Longham Dorset Eng 50.47N 1.55W
98 T6 Long Harbour Newfoundland 47.27N 53.48W
21 C1 Longhe Heilongjiang China 53.17N 123.43E
103 H4 Long Hill Connecticut 41.17N 73.14W
57 K2 Longhirst Northumb Eng 55.12N 1.39W
95 J8 Long Hope S Africa 32.50S 25.48E
57 K2 Long Horsley Northumb Eng 55.15N 1.46W
57 K2 Longhoughton Northumb Eng 55.26N 1.36W
22 L6 Longhua Hebei China 41.17N 117.37E
23 F5 Longhui Hunan China 27.11N 111.05E
105 J1 Longhurst N Carolina 36.25N 78.58W
28 G7 Long I Andaman Is 12.25N 92.55E
116 G3 Long I Bahamas
97 M7 Long I Hudson B, N W Terr 54.55N 79.30W
109 L2 Long I Kansas 39.57N 99.33W
26 S14 Long I Mahé I Seychelles, Ind Oc 4.37S 55.31E
116 L4 Long, I Martinique W I 14.37N 60.52W
104 R10 Long I Massachusetts 42.20N 70.58W
12 L4 Long I New S Wales 33.33S 151.13E
103 G5 Long I New York
11 A12 Long I New Zealand
98 F9 Long I Nova Scotia 44.20N 66.15W
15 J6 Long I Papua New Guinea 5.20S 147.05E
13 J5 Long I Queensland
110 A3 Long I Washington
103 K7 Long I. City New York 40.46N 73.55W
93 H8 Longido Tanzania 2.44S 36.39E
93 H8 Longido *mt* Tanzania 2.41S 36.41E
93 H3 Longippi *hill* Kenya
18 L6 Longiram Borneo Indon 0.02S 115.40E
103 H4 Long I. Sd Conn/New York
91 A2 Longji Cameroon 3.04N 9.59E
21 C4 Longjiang Heilongjiang China 47.24N 123.08E
23 D6 Long Jiang *R* Guangxi China
23 E6 Long Jiang *R* Guangxi China
23 B6 Longjie Yunnan China 25.17N 99.52E
Longjing *see* Yanji (Longjing)
69 C6 Longjumeau France 48.42N 2.18E
Longjuzhai *see* Danfeng
25 K8 Longka Assam India 25.42N 92.48E
64 C4 Longkamp W Germany 49.53N 7.08E
22 M8 Longkou Shandong China 37.41N 120.18E
113 K6 Long L Alaska 60.10N 155.00W
58 F4 Long, L Highland Scotland 57.18N 5.29W
104 Q6 Long L Maine
106 L4 Long L Michigan 45.13N 83.29W
108 Q3 Long L Minnesota
108 K3 Long L N Dakota
98 F6 Long L New Brunswick
104 L2 Long L New York
99 D3 Long L Ontario
98 J1 Long, L Quebec
58 G6 Long,L Strathclyde Scotland
99 D3 Longlac Ontario 49.47N 86.34W
106 J5 Long Lake Michigan
104 L3 Long Lake New York 43.57N 74.26W
106 F4 Long Lake Wisconsin 45.52N 88.40W
100 E4 Long Lake Prov. Park Alberta 54.27N 112.45W
110 F2 Long Lake Res Washington 47.30N 119.12W
18 L4 Long Lama Sarawak Malaysia 3.46N 114.28E
95 H4 Longlands S Africa 28.27S 24.22E
96 A13 Long Ledge *rock* St Helena 15.57S 5.46W
18 M4 Longleju Borneo Indon 2.50N 116.40E
28 K1 Longlep Xizang Zizhiqu 29.45N 95.21E
23 D5 Longli Guizhou China 26.26N 106.56E
61 M7 Longlier Belgium 49.52N 5.27E
23 D6 Longlin Guangxi China 24.44N 105.27E
23 A6 Longling Yunnan China 24.33N 98.40E
58 M3 Longmanhill Grampian Scotland 57.39N 2.26W
103 J2 Longmeadow Massachusetts 42.04N 72.35W
56 N3 Long Melford Suffolk Eng 52.05N 0.43E
23 E8 Longmen Guangdong China 20.42N 110.02E
23 G7 Longmen Guangdong China 23.43N 114.05E
23 E1 Longmen Shan *mt* Shanxi China
23 C2 Longmen Shan *mts* Sichuan China
109 E1 Longmont Colorado 40.11N 105.06W
26 U12 Long Mt Mauritius, Indian Oc 20.09S 57.34E
56 E2 Long Mt Powys Wales 53.39N 3.04W
18 L4 Long Murum Sarawak Malaysia 2.45N 114.04E
23 G6 Longnan Jiangxi China 24.45N 114.32E
18 L5 Longnawan Borneo Indon 1.51N 114.49E
69 B6 Longnes France 48.55N 1.35E
57 L3 Long Newton Cleveland Eng 54.32N 1.25W
58 L7 Longniddry Lothian Scotland 55.58N 2.53W
57 K6 Longnor Staffs Eng 53.11N 1.51W
70 M4 Longny France 48.32N 0.45E
81 M5 Longobardi Italy 39.12N 16.05E
91 B6 Longobonde Congo 4.20S 11.36E
81 N5 Longobucco Italy 39.27N 16.37E
93 H2 Longondoti *mts* Kenya
91 D10 Longonjo Angola 12.54S 15.15E
93 H6 Longonot Kenya 0.53S 36.30E
93 H6 Longonot *crater* Kenya 0.55S 36.25E
89 J7 Longoro Ghana 8.14N 1.49W
121 B4 Longotoma Chile 32.20S 71.19W
23 C7 Longpeng Yunnan China 23.53N 102.40E
25 J8 Long Phu Vietnam 9.37N 106.09E
72 E10 Long, Pic *mt* France 42.49N 0.06E
108 L7 Long Pine Nebraska 42.32N 99.41W
Longping *see* Luodian
106 F8 Long Point Illinois 41.01N 88.55W
98 O5 Long Point Newfoundland 48.47N 58.46W
100 T5 Long Point *pen* Manitoba
99 K10 Long Point B Ontario
99 K10 Long Point Prov. Park Ontario
98 T6 Long Pond Newfoundland 47.31N 52.58W
103 N3 Long Pond *L* Massachusetts
69 E5 Longpont France 49.16N 3.14E
108 Q4 Long Prairie Minnesota 45.58N 94.51W
108 Q3 Long Prairie *R* Minnesota
69 B3 Longpré-les-Corps-Saints France 50.01N 1.59E
57 J4 Long Preston N Yorks Eng 54.02N 2.15W
105 L9 Long Pt New Providence I Bahamas 25.01N 77.18W
11 M6 Long Pt North I New Zealand 39.10S 177.50E
99 K10 Long Pt Ontario 42.33N 80.04W
19 J7 Long Pt Philippines 9.37N 118.20E
11 B13 Long Pt South I New Zealand 46.16S 167.08E
11 D13 Long Pt South I New Zealand 46.35S 169.38E
14 A7 Long Pt W Australia 25.28S 113.59E
Longquan *see* Fenggang
Longquan *see* Danzhai
23 H4 Longquan Zhejiang China 28.09N 119.14E
23 C3 Longquan Shan *mt ra* Sichuan China
23 H4 Longquan Xi *R* Zhejiang China
96 B14 Long Range *mts* St Helena
98 N6 Long Range Mts Newfoundland
98 P4 Long Range Mts Newfoundland
13 G6 Longreach Queensland 23.30S 144.15E
15 L9 Long Reef Louisiade Arch
15 G9 Long Reef Torres Str, Qnsld 10.17S 142.14E
14 F2 Long Reef W Australia 13.53S 125.43E
12 N6 Long Reef *pt* New S Wales 33.45S 151.20E
11 B11 Long Reef *pt* New Zealand 44.19S 168.00E
57 H5 Longridge Lancs Eng 53.51N 2.36W
11 C11 Longridge Pt New Zealand 44.12S 168.10E
57 N5 Long Riston Humberside Eng 53.52N 0.17W
76 E7 Longroiva Portugal 40.58N 7.12W
105 J4 Longs S Carolina 33.46N 78.46W
99 S2 Long Sault Ontario 45.02N 74.54W
99 S2 Long Sault Dam Ontario 45.00N 74.53W
11 A13 Long Sd South I New Zealand
18 M4 Longsegah Borneo Indon 2.16N 116.45E
23 E4 Longshan Hunan China 29.27N 109.27E
23 F7 Longsheng Guangdong China 22.32N 112.28E
23 E6 Longsheng Guangxi China 25.51N 109.54E
Longshi *see* Ninggang
56 S9 Longships Lt. Ho Cornwall Eng 50.03N 5.45W
22 E7 Longshou Shan *mts* Gansu China
58 N3 Longside Grampian Scotland 57.31N 1.56W
109 E1 Longs Peak Colorado 40.16N 105.37W
13 B6 Longs Ra N Terr Australia
Long Str *see* Longa, Proliv *str*
56 O3 Long Stratton Norfolk Eng 52.29N 1.14E
56 M2 Long Sutton Lincs Eng 52.47N 0.08E
56 F5 Long Sutton Somerset Eng 51.02N 2.46W
87 C6 Longtam Sudan 8.58N 30.45E
23 D4 Longtan Sichuan China 29.27N 107.14E
23 E4 Longtan Sichuan China 28.44N 108.58E
18 L4 Long Teru Sarawak Malaysia 3.50N 114.13E
23 E5 Longtian Guizhou China 27.20N 108.29E
101 P3 Longtom L N W Terr 65.09N 117.45W
110 K6 Long Tom Res Idaho 43.17N 115.35W
109 O4 Longton Kansas 37.24N 96.05W
57 H5 Longton Lancs Eng 53.44N 2.48W
13 H5 Longton Queensland 20.58S 145.53E
57 J7 Longton Staffs Eng 52.59N 2.08W
57 H2 Longtown Cumbria Eng 55.01N 2.58W
107 G4 Longtown Missouri 37.39N 89.47W
69 C4 Longueau France 49.52N 2.22E
26 R16 Longue, I Kerguelen Indian Ocean 49.32S 69.52E
69 D5 Longueil-St. Marie France 49.22N 2.43E
70 K7 Longué-Jumelles France 47.22N 0.06W
76 C2 Longuelles *R* Spain
99 T9 Longueuil Quebec 45.32N 73.31W
69 D3 Longueval France 50.02N 2.49E
61 J4 Longueville Belgium 50.42N 4.45E
69 E6 Longueville Seine-et-Marne France 48.31N 3.15E
70 N2 Longueville Seine-Inférieure France 49.48N 1.07E
18 L5 Longuro Borneo Indon 1.45N 114.51E
69 K5 Longuyon France 49.27N 5.36E
53 U13 Longva Norway 62.40N 6.18E
103 E5 Long Valley New Jersey 40.47N 74.47W
108 J6 Longvalley S Dakota 43.28N 101.29W
Long Valley Res *see* Crowley, L
71 G2 Longvic France 47.17N 5.05E
100 C8 Longview Alberta 50.34N 114.14W
112 N3 Longview Texas 32.30N 94.45W
110 C3 Longview Washington 46.08N 122.56W
107 C11 Longville Louisiana 30.35N 93.15W
61 O6 Longvilly Belgium 50.02N 5.50E
18 M5 Longwai Borneo Indon 0.42N 116.40E
21 F5 Longwangmiao Heilongjiang China 45.05N 132.48E
21 C8 Longwangmiao Liaoning China 40.00N 124.00E
23 G7 Longwo Guangdong China 23.25N 115.18E
105 F9 Longwood Florida 28.42N 81.20W
59 J5 Longwood Meath Irish Rep 53.27N 6.55W
107 E8 Longwood Mississippi 33.10N 91.03W
96 B13 Longwood St Helena 15.57S 5.42W
103 B9 Longwoods Maryland 38.52N 76.05W
112 G3 Longworth Texas 32.39N 100.22W
23 C6 Longwu Yunnan China 24.01N 102.24E
69 K4 Longwy France 49.32N 5.46E
23 C1 Longxi Gansu China 34.59N 104.46E
Longxian *see* Wengyuan
23 D1 Long Xian Shaanxi China 34.51N 106.57E
23 D4 Longxing Guizhou China 28.42N 107.44E
Longxu *see* Cangwu
25 H7 Long Xuyen Vietnam 10.23N 105.25E
23 G6 Longyan Fujian China 25.10N 117.00E
23 H6 Longyan Fujian China 25.06N 117.02E
22 K8 Longyao Hebei China 37.23N 114.40E
50 T14 Longyearbyen Spitsbergen 78.12N 15.40E
23 H4 Longyou Zhejiang China 29.00N 119.10E
21 D3 Longzhen Heilongjiang China 48.43N 126.45E
23 D7 Longzhou Guangxi China 22.24N 106.59E
25 K6 Lon, Hon *isld* Vietnam 12.35N 109.23E
30 D6 Loni *R* Uttar Prad India
79 K4 Lonigo Italy 45.23N 11.23E
63 G7 Löningen W Germany 52.44N 7.46E
93 H3 Lonjemn Kenya 2.21N 36.50E
25 M8 Lonkin Burma 25.40N 96.21E
95 D4 Lonkintsy Madagascar 16.51S 49.55E
70 J4 Lonlay-L'Abbaye France 48.39N 0.42W
60 Q10 Lonneker Netherlands 52.15N 6.55E
64 P1 Lonnewitz E Germany 51.17N 13.09E
69 H4 Lonny France 49.48N 4.36E
53 V19 Lono Norway 59.45N 6.45E
107 E7 Lonoke Arkansas 34.46N 91.56W
121 B7 Lonquimay Chile 38.25S 71.23W
51 E5 Lønsdal Norway 66.46N 15.26E
108 R5 Lonsdale Minnesota 44.28N 93.24W
103 M3 Lonsdale Rhode I 41.55N 71.24W
12 G6 Lonsdale, L Victoria 37.05S 142.15E
64 H6 Lonsee W Germany 48.31N 9.56E
52 E4 Lønset Norway 62.35N 9.23E
50 L6 Lónsfjördhur *B* Iceland
50 L6 Lónsheidhi *heath* Iceland
71 H3 Lons-le-Saunier France 46.41N 5.33E
53 D2 Lønstrup Denmark 57.29N 9.50E
50 L6 Lónsvik *B* Iceland
25 M8 Lonton Burma 25.04N 96.17E
117 C7 Lontra Brazil 4.25S 51.55W
117 D8 Lontra *R* Pará Brazil
118 D7 Lontra, R Mato Grosso do Sul Brazil
87 H8 Lontullo Ethiopia 5.30N 41.04E
61 P4 Lontzen Belgium 50.41N 6.01E
19 B3 Lonu Celebes Indon 1.04N 121.34E
66 G6 Lonza *R* Switzerland
72 H5 Lonzac, la France 45.28N 1.44E
61 J4 Lonzée Belgium 50.33N 4.44E
60 M12 Loo Netherlands 51.57N 5.59E
44 C4 Loo U.S.S.R. 43.42N 39.40E
69 C2 Looberghe France 50.55N 2.16E
19 L5 Looc Philippines 12.17N 122.01E
107 K3 Loogootee Indiana 38.41N 86.57W
109 M6 Lookeba Oklahoma 35.23N 98.23W
106 K7 Lookingglass, R Michigan
110 D8 Lookout California 41.12N 121.10W
103 D3 Lookout Pennsylvania 41.46N 75.10W
105 L3 Lookout, C N Carolina 34.34N 76.34W
105 B3 Lookout Mt Alabama/Georgia
113 H5 Lookout Mt Alaska 62.05N 158.31W
111 F5 Lookout Mt California 36.05N 118.24W
109 B6 Lookout Mt New Mexico 35.13N 108.17W
110 K2 Lookout Pass Montana/Idaho 47.28N 115.40W
106 L5 Lookout, Pt Michigan 44.03N 83.34W
13 H2 Lookout Pt Queensland 14.48S 145.12E
13 L7 Lookout, Pt Queensland 27.28S 153.29E
110 C6 Lookout Pt. Res Oregon
113 H2 Lookout Ridge Alaska
105 F2 Lookout Shoals L N Carolina 35.47N 81.08W
93 G9 Loolmalasin Tanzania 3.03S 35.49E
100 D5 Looma Alberta 53.23N 113.12W
108 L9 Loomis Nebraska 40.30N 99.30W
100 J9 Loomis Saskatchewan 49.12N 108.45W
110 F1 Loomis Washington 48.50N 119.39W
60 P7 Loon Netherlands 53.00N 6.37E
99 B4 Loon Ontario 48.38N 88.46W
101 Q7 Loon *R* Alberta
98 S4 Loon Bay Newfoundland 49.16N 54.50W
61 J3 Loonbeek Belgium 50.48N 4.36E
14 F9 Loongana W Australia 30.54S 127.01E
104 P7 Loon L Maine 46.10N 69.39W
100 H4 Loon Lake Saskatchewan 54.02N 109.10W
60 J13 Loon op Zand Netherlands 51.38N 5.05E
69 C2 Loon-Plage France 51.00N 2.13E
100 Q2 Loon R Manitoba
59 C6 Loop Head *pt* Clare Irish Rep 52.34N 9.56W
95 L2 Loopspruit S Africa 26.39S 27.18E
101 N9 Loos Br Columbia 53.36N 120.43W
107 G6 Loosahatchie *R* Tennessee
60 L13 Loosbroek Netherlands 51.42N 5.33E
65 M5 Loosdorf Austria 48.13N 15.25E
60 E11 Loosduinen Netherlands 52.03N 4.15E
69 D3 Loos-en-Gohelle France 50.27N 2.48E
24 C7 Lop Xinjiang Uygur Zizhiqu China 37.03N 80.15E
45 F4 Lopandino U.S.S.R. 52.25N 34.50E
91 G3 Lopari *R* Zaïre
95 C7 Lopary Madagascar 23.11S 47.40E
44 H4 Lopatin U.S.S.R. 43.52N 47.40E
40 J6 Lopatina, Gory *mt* Sakhalin U.S.S.R. 50.47N 143.10E
45 R4 Lopatino Penza U.S.S.R. 52.38N 45.46E
40 J7 Lopatino Sakhalin U.S.S.R. 48.25N 142.15E
39 E8 Lopatka U.S.S.R. 50.56N 156.35E
39 E8 Lopatka, Mys *C* Kamchatka U.S.S.R. 50.50N 156.33E
41 R5 Lopatka, Mys *C* Yakutsk U.S.S.R. 71.45N 149.39E
41 R5 Lopatka, Poluostrov *pen* U.S.S.R.
47 K7 Lopatki U.S.S.R. 55.00N 66.35E
25 F5 Lop Buri Thailand 14.49N 100.37E
40 B4 Lopcha U.S.S.R. 55.44N 122.38E
77 H5 Lopera Spain 37.56N 4.12W
93 G3 Loperot Kenya 2.20N 35.52E
9 C11 Lopevi *isld* New Hebrides 16.30S 168.21E
121 F6 López Argentina 37.33S 59.40W
119 B8 López Ecuador 1.37S 80.48W
19 L5 Lopez Luzon Philippines 13.51N 122.15E
103 B4 Lopez Pennsylvania 41.27N 76.20W
91 A4 Lopez, C Gabon 0.36S 8.45E
115 E9 Lopez I Panama 9.18N 79.50W
121 E7 López Lecube Argentina 38.08S 62.45W
91 E2 Lopi Congo 2.57N 16.47E
60 H12 Lopik Netherlands 51.58N 4.57E
60 J12 Lopikerkapel Netherlands 52.00N 5.03E
Lop Nor *L see* Lop Nur
Lopnur *see* Yuli
24 G5 Lop Nur *L* Xinjiang Uygur Zizhiqu China 40.15N 90.20E
93 H4 Lopokino *crater* Kenya 1.09N 36.13E
45 H1 Lopotovo U.S.S.R. 56.05N 36.51E
51 J1 Loppa Norway 70.21N 21.25E
61 C2 Loppem Belgium 51.09N 3.12E
60 Q6 Loppersum Netherlands 53.20N 6.45E
51 J1 Lopphavet *channel* Norway
47 F4 Loptyuga Komi U.S.S.R. 63.13N 47.58E
47 F4 Loptyuga Komi U.S.S.R. 62.54N 49.41E
45 Q5 Lopukhovka Saratov U.S.S.R. 52.00N 44.44E
45 Q6 Lopukhovka Volgograd U.S.S.R. 50.39N 44.30E
46 J3 Lopush U.S.S.R. 53.04N 34.00E
62 M5 Łopuszno Poland 50.58N 20.17E
47 G5 Lopydino U.S.S.R. 61.10N 52.02E
70 C5 Loqueffret France 48.19N 3.51W
76 E3 Lor *R* Spain
31 C7 Lora Pakistan 27.51N 65.05E
12 C3 Lora *R* S Australia
77 E5 Lora del Río Spain 37.39N 5.32W
104 C5 Lorain Ohio 41.28N 82.11W
106 C9 Loraine Illinois 40.09N 91.13W
108 J1 Loraine N Dakota 48.52N 101.32W
112 G3 Loraine Texas 32.23N 100.44W
76 L3 Lora, La *tableland* Spain
31 E5 Loralai Pakistan 30.20N 68.41E
31 E5 Loralai *dist* Pakistan
31 E5 Loralai R Pakistan
26 P14 Loranchet, Presqu'ile *pen* Kerguelen Ind Oc
121 A5 Lora, Pta *C* Chile 34.33S 72.07W
31 D5 Lora R Afghanistan
119 D3 Lora, R Venezuela
77 N5 Lorca Spain 37.40N 1.41W
61 N5 Lorcé Belgium 50.25N 5.44E
64 H6 Lorch Baden-Württemberg W Ger 48.48N 9.42E
64 D3 Lorch Hessen W Ger 50.03N 7.49E
77 Q3 Lorcha Spain 38.51N 0.19W
69 C7 Lorcy France 48.04N 2.30E
53 Y14 Lordalen *V* Norway 62.05N 8.30E
19 H6 Lord Auckland *bank* Philippines 10.18N 117.22E
32 D5 Lordegān Iran 31.30N 50.51E
10 M8 Lord Howe I Pacific Oc 31.28S 159.09E
10 N7 Lord Howe Rise *sea feature* Pacific Oc
10 M8 Lord Howe Seamounts Pacific Oc
25 D7 Lord Loughborough I Burma
97 K4 Lord Mayor B N W Terr
109 B9 Lordsburg New Mexico 32.22N 108.43W
11 C13 Lords R Stewart I New Zealand
103 D4 Lords Valley Pennsylvania 41.22N 75.04W
103 D3 Lordville New York 41.52N 75.13W
19 E8 Loré Indonesia 8.39S 127.02E
100 L7 Loreburn Saskatchewan 51.15N 106.38W
79 L3 Loreggia Italy 45.35N 11.57E
64 D3 Loreley *cliffs* W Germany 50.08N 7.45E
118 F8 Lorena Brazil 22.44S 45.07W
112 K4 Lorena Texas 31.24N 97.14W
15 J5 Lorengau Admiralty Is 2.01S 147.15E
15 E6 Lorentz *R* Irian Jaya
79 M2 Lorenzago Italy 46.29N 12.28E
Lorenzana *see* Villanueva Spain
76 E2 Lorenzana, Sierra de *mts* Spain
63 S10 Lorenzkirch E Germany 51.22N 13.16E
110 O6 Lorenzo Idaho 43.45N 111.52W
108 G8 Lorenzo Nebraska 41.03N 103.04W
112 F2 Lorenzo Texas 33.41N 101.33W
121 F4 Lorenzo Geyres Uruguay 32.05S 57.53W
61 P8 Lorenzweiler Luxembourg 49.42N 6.09E
79 M4 Loreo Italy 45.04N 12.11E
76 K3 Lores Spain 43.00N 4.32W
32 B4 Lorestān *prov* Iran
115 D4 Loreto Baja Cal Mexico 26.00N 111.20W
120 F6 Loreto Bolivia 15.13S 64.44W
117 E8 Loreto Brazil 7.01S 45.10W
121 F1 Loreto Corrientes Arg 27.45S 57.15W
80 J2 Loreto Italy 43.26N 13.36E
115 J6 Loreto Mexico 22.15N 102.00W
118 B8 Loreto Paraguay 23.11S 57.26W
19 M6 Loreto Philippines 10.21N 125.37E
121 D2 Loreto Santiago del Estero Arg 28.15S 64.12W
119 C9 Loreto *dept* Peru
80 J4 Loreto Aprutino Italy 42.26N 13.59E
119 E9 Loreto Yacu Colombia 3.48S 70.16W
106 D4 Loretta Wisconsin 45.54N 90.51W
100 V9 Lorette Manitoba 49.44N 96.52W
98 A7 Loretteville Quebec 46.52N 71.24W
107 L4 Loretto Kentucky 37.37N 85.25W
107 J6 Loretto Tennessee 35.05N 87.28W
71 J10 Lorgues France 43.30N 6.21E
89 H6 Lorhosso Upper Volta 10.17N 3.38W
37 E5 Lori *R* Turkey
79 L3 Loria Italy 45.43N 11.52E
119 C3 Lorica Colombia 9.14N 75.50W
87 E8 Lorienatom *mts* Sudan
70 D6 Lorient France 47.45N 3.21W
76 D8 Loriga Portugal 40.19N 7.42W
72 C5 Lorignac France 45.27N 0.41W
99 Q7 L'Orignal Ontario 45.37N 74.43W
75 J8 Loriguilla, Embalse de *res* Spain
108 Q8 Lorimor Iowa 41.06N 94.04W
13 F2 Lorim Point Queensland 12.35S 141.51E
66 N6 Lorina *R* Switzerland
110 S1 Loring Montana 48.48N 107.52W
39 M2 Lorino U.S.S.R. 65.30N 171.56W
71 F7 Loriol-sur-Drôme France 44.45N 4.49E
105 J3 Loris S Carolina 34.05N 78.54W
120 D7 Loriscota, L Peru
93 H4 Loriu Plat Kenya
93 H3 Loriu Ra Kenya
100 O8 Lorlie Saskatchewan 50.51N 103.15W
107 E10 Lorman Mississippi 31.50N 91.04W
71 D2 Lormes France 47.17N 3.49E
58 F6 Lorn *dist* Strathclyde Scotland
14 D7 Lorna Glen W Australia 26.12S 121.31E
98 F6 Lorne New Brunswick 47.53N 66.10W
13 H6 Lorne Queensland 24.50S 145.20E
12 G7 Lorne Victoria 38.34S 144.01E
13 D4 Lorne *R* N Terr Australia
122 L11 L'Orne Bank Pacific Oc 27.42S 157.44W
69 B2 Lornel, Pte de France 50.33N 1.35E
58 E6 Lorn, Firth of Strathclyde Scotland
119 E6 Loro Colombia 2.16N 69.28W
79 L7 Loro Ciuffenna Italy 43.35N 11.38E
93 H5 Lorogi Plat Kenya
87 D8 Loronyo Sudan 4.45N 32.40E
121 B1 Loros Chile 27.50S 70.05W
93 H3 Lorot Kenya 2.15N 36.27E
72 B1 Loroux-Bottereau, le France 47.15N 1.20W
77 O4 Lorqui Spain 38.05N 1.14W
69 M6 Lorquin France 48.40N 7.00E
64 D8 Lörrach W Germany 47.37N 7.40E
109 M3 Lorraine Kansas 38.33N 98.19W
13 E4 Lorraine Queensland 19.08S 139.53E
67 J3 Lorraine *prov* France
99 L5 Lorrainville Quebec 47.21N 79.23W
69 D7 Lorrez-le-Bocage France 48.14N 2.55E
69 D8 Lorris France 47.54N 2.31E
64 F4 Lorsch W Germany 49.39N 8.35E
53 E2 Lørslev Nordjylland Denmark 57.26N 10.07E
53 B3 Lørslev Viborg Denmark 56.45N 8.48E
53 Y14 Lortjøen *L* Norway 62.00N 8.09E
57 G3 Lorton Cumbria Eng 54.38N 3.15W
14 D10 Lort, R W Australia
93 H5 Loruk Kenya 0.44N 36.01E
93 G3 Lorukumu Kenya 2.53N 35.16E
63 G7 Lorup W Germany 52.56N 7.38E
76 C8 Lorvão Portugal 40.16N 8.19W
66 K3 Lorze *R* Switzerland
52 J5 Los Sweden 61.44N 15.15E
77 N3 Losa *mt* Spain 38.35N 1.51W
75 D2 Losa *R* Spain
76 G5 Losacino Spain 41.41N 6.05W
119 D6 Losada, R Colombia
75 J8 Losa del Obispo Spain 39.41N 0.53W
111 E10 Los Alamitos California 33.48N 118.05W
111 D7 Los Alamos California 34.45N 120.16W
121 A6 Los Alamos Chile 37.40S 73.30W
109 D6 Los Alamos New Mexico 35.52N 106.19W
77 P5 Los Alcázares Spain 37.45N 0.51W
115 K4 Los Aldamas Mexico 26.02N 99.12W
115 P10 Los Amates Guatemala 15.14N 89.06W
121 E2 Los Amores Argentina 28.05S 60.00W
121 B4 Los Andes Chile 32.53S 70.32W
111 F7 Los Angeles California 34.00N 118.15W
121 A6 Los Angeles Chile 37.28S 72.23W
112 H7 Los Angeles Texas 28.27N 99.01W
111 F6 Los Angeles Aqueduct California
111 E9 Los Angeles R California
29 E1 Losar Himachal Prad India 32.25N 77.50E
116 D3 Los Arabos Cuba 22.44N 80.43W
75 F2 Los Arcos Spain 42.34N 2.11W
76 H8 Losar de la Vera Spain 40.08N 5.36W
75 F7 Losares *mt* Spain 40.13N 2.13W
18 H9 Losari Java Indon 6.52S 108.47E
76 L4 Los Balbases Spain 42.13N 4.05W
121 B2 Los Bañitas, Paso de Arg/Chile 29.44S 69.55W
111 D4 Los Banos California 37.04N 120.51W
115 F4 Los Baños Mexico 26.48N 106.19W
77 F8 Los Barrios Spain 36.11N 5.30W
76 H3 Los Barrios de Luna Spain 42.50N 5.52W
76 F3 Los Barrios de Salas Spain 42.30N 6.33W
76 G3 Los Bayos Spain 42.54N 6.12W
96 U15 Los Berrazales Gran Canaria Canary Is 28.05N 15.40W
120 G10 Los Blancos Argentina 23.36S 62.35W
77 P5 Los Blancos Spain 37.37N 0.48W
115 D5 Los Burros Mexico 25.01N 110.52W
116 L9 Los Caracas Venezuela 10.37N 66.35W
115 E10 Los Cedros Panama 9.02N 80.04W
77 M5 Los Cerricos Spain 37.32N 2.11W
121 D3 Los Cerrillos Argentina 31.55S 65.35W
121 F10 Los Cerrillos, Aeropuerto Santiago Chile
115 M4 Los Chiles Costa Rica 11.04N 84.44W
121 C2 Los Colorados La Rioja Arg 29.55S 67.11W
111 G9 Los Coronados *islds* Mexico
77 G6 Los Corrales Spain 37.05N 4.59W
76 L2 Los Corrales de Buelna Spain 43.15N 4.04W
76 L10 Los Cortijos Spain 39.19N 4.05W
120 F6 Los Cusis Bolivia 15.30S 64.03W
77 O5 Los Dolores Spain 37.39N 1.01W
95 K3 Losdorings S Africa 27.45S 26.29E
112 J9 Los Ebanos Texas 26.15N 98.36W
65 K6 Losenstein Austria 47.56N 14.27E
81 L3 Lo Serrone *mt* Italy 40.19N 15.42E
45 M6 Losevo U.S.S.R. 50.41N 40.02E
119 G2 Los Frailes *islds* Venezuela 11.15N 63.48W
112 K9 Los Fresnos Texas 26.04N 97.30W
111 C4 Los Gatos California 37.13N 121.59W
77 N5 Los Gázquez Spain 37.34N 1.56W
96 Q14 Los Giganxes Tenerife Canary Is 28.15N 16.50W
121 J8 Los Glaciares,Parque Nacionale Arg
61 Q5 Losheim W Germany 50.21N 6.22E
64 B5 Losheim W Germany 49.30N 6.45E
119 G2 Los Hermanos, Islas Venezuela 11.45N 66.28W
112 H10 Los Herreras Mexico 25.55N 99.22W
75 E8 Los Hinojosos Spain 39.36N 2.50W
39 D3 Loshkalakh U.S.S.R. 62.35N 147.16E
45 F9 Loshkarevka Ukraine U.S.S.R. 47.55N 34.10E
115 E2 Los Hoyos Mexico 30.08N 109.48W
52 H10 Loshult Sweden 56.30N 14.10E
62 O3 Łosice Poland 52.14N 22.41E
115 N8 Los Idolos Mexico 18.20N 92.40W
89 C7 Los, Iles de Guinea 9.30N 13.50W
93 H9 Losimingor *mt* Tanzania 3.24S 36.03E
112 K9 Los Indios Texas 26.02N 97.44W
82 B6 Lošinj *isld* Yugoslavia 44.35N 14.25E
42 D3 Losinoborskaya U.S.S.R. 58.28N 89.27E
45 C6 Losinovka Ukraine U.S.S.R. 50.50N 31.57E
42 B4 Losinskiy U.S.S.R. 56.24N 79.14E
47 N4 Losinyy U.S.S.R. 57.14N 61.01E
77 O2 Los Isidros Spain 39.24N 1.17W
121 E2 Los Juríes Argentina 28.14S 62.06W
95 N4 Loskop S Africa 28.56S 29.37E
94 K5 Loskop Dam S Africa 25.23S 29.20E
121 A7 Los Lagos Chile 39.50S 72.50W
96 P10 Los Llanos de Aridane La Palma Canary Is 28.39N 17.54W
96 T10 Los Llanos de la Concepción Fuerteventura Canary Is 28.27N 14.02W
77 N6 Los Lobos Spain 37.19N 1.45W
109 D7 Los Lúnas New Mexico 34.48N 106.46W
112 A4 Los Médanos Mexico 31.10N 106.32W
121 C8 Los Menucos Argentina 40.52S 68.07W
45 F1 Los'mino U.S.S.R. 55.04N 34.22E
115 E5 Los Mochis Mexico 25.48N 109.00W
110 C9 Los Molinos California 40.01N 122.07W
77 P5 Los Molinos Spain 37.37N 0.59W
121 B3 Los Molles, R Chile
75 K5 Los Monegros *reg* Spain
119 E1 Los Monjes *islds* Venezuela 12.29N 70.58W
52 E5 Losna Opland Norway 61.23N 10.13E
76 K9 Los Navalmorales Spain 39.43N 4.38W
76 K9 Los Navalucillos Spain 39.40N 4.39W
53 S16 Losnegard Sogn og Fjordane Norway 61.07N 5.05E
53 D5 Løsning Denmark 55.48N 9.43E
76 E3 Los Nogales Spain 42.48N 7.06W
111 D7 Los Olivos California 34.40N 120.06W
75 K6 Los Olmos Spain 40.52N 0.29W
91 F3 Losombo Zaïre 1.02N 19.04E
116 C3 Los Palacios Cuba 22.35N 83.16W
77 E6 Los Palacios y Villafranca Spain 37.10N 5.55W
19 E8 Lospalos Indonesia 8.34S 127.01E
76 D4 Los Peares Spain 42.27N 7.45W
96 U15 Los Pechos *mt* Gran Canaria Canary Is 27.56N 15.34W
77 F3 Los Pedroches *reg* Spain
77 O2 Los Pedrones de Abajo Spain 39.21N 1.05W
88 F9 Los Pilones *pt* Morocco 25.48N 14.40W
115 D3 Los Pocitos Mexico 28.30N 111.08W
120 D12 Los Pozos Chile 26.35S 69.20W
75 F4 Los Rábanos Spain 41.42N 2.28W
120 F12 Los Ralos Argentina 26.50S 64.58W
115 K5 Los Ramones Mexico 25.42N 99.34W
115 H8 Los Reyes Mexico 19.34N 102.30W
15 K4 Los Reyes Is Admiralty Is 1.59S 148.02E
119 B8 Los Ríos *prov* Ecuador
96 S13 Los Rodeos *airport* Tenerife Canary Is 28.27N 16.20W
116 L9 Los Roques, Islas Lesser Antilles
116 L8 Los Roques Trench Caribbean Sea
77 E5 Los Rosales Spain 37.35N 5.44W
64 L1 Lossa E Germany 51.14N 11.26E
115 O6 Los Santos Panama 7.56N 80.23W
76 H7 Los Santos Spain 40.33N 5.48W
77 D4 Los Santos de Maimona Spain 38.27N 6.22W
121 A6 Los Sauces Chile 37.59S 72.50W
96 P9 Los Sauces La Palma Canary Is 28.48N 17.46W
64 E7 Lossburg W Germany 48.25N 8.27E
72 D7 Losse France 44.06N 0.07W
60 R10 Losser Netherlands 52.16N 7.01E
58 K3 Lossiemouth Grampian Scotland 57.43N 3.18W
58 K3 Lossie R Grampian Scotland
96 Q14 Los Silos Tenerife Canary Is 28.22N 16.49W
64 O2 Lössnitz E Germany 50.37N 12.44E
66 N6 Lostallo Switzerland 46.18N 9.12E
119 E2 Los Taques Venezuela 11.50N 70.16W
108 C6 Lost Cabin Wyoming 43.19N 107.36W
104 G8 Lost City W Virginia 38.55N 78.51W
108 B7 Lost Cr Wyoming
121 D2 Los Telares Argentina 29.01S 63.26W
119 F2 Los Teques Venezuela 10.25N 67.01W
116 N9 Los Testigos *islds* W I 11.24N 63.07W
111 E6 Lost Hills California 35.37N 119.41W
65 P2 Lostice Czechoslovakia 49.45N 16.56E
120 G11 Los Tigres Argentina 25.53S 62.35W
110 H4 Lostine Oregon 45.30N 117.25W
107 E12 Lost L Louisiana 29.20N 91.05W
106 D8 Lost Nation Iowa 41.58N 90.49W
76 L2 Los Tojos Spain 43.10N 4.15W
66 H2 Lostorf Switzerland 47.23N 7.57E
104 G8 Lost River W Virginia 38.57N 78.50W
110 L5 Lost River Ra Idaho
109 O3 Lost Springs Kansas 38.36N 96.57W
108 F7 Lost Springs Wyoming 42.47N 104.55W
110 M4 Lost Trail Pass Idaho/Montana 45.43N 113.56W
56 B7 Lostwithiel Cornwall Eng 50.25N 4.40W
108 H1 Lostwood N Dakota 48.30N 102.25W
15 L8 Losuia Trobriand Is Papua New Guinea 8.29S 151.03E
19 F2 Losuwo Moluccas Indon 2.33N 128.38E
120 D11 Los Vientos Chile 24.38S 69.45W
77 J5 Los Villares Spain 37.41N 3.49W
121 B3 Los Vilos Chile 31.56S 71.35W
75 C8 Los Yébenes Spain 39.35N 3.52W
61 H3 Lot Belgium 50.46N 4.17E
67 G8 Lot *dept* France
96 B14 Lot *mt* St Helena 15.59S 5.44W
72 F7 Lot *R* France
35 E9 Lot *watercourse* Israel
121 A6 Lota Chile 37.07S 73.10W
87 E8 Lotagipi Swamp Sudan/Kenya
18 L6 Lotak Borneo Indon 0.10S 115.51E
45 C3 Lotaki U.S.S.R. 53.07N 31.35E
53 U15 Lote Norway 61.52N 6.05E
61 D2 Lotenhulle Belgium 51.03N 3.28E
67 F8 Lot-et-Garonne *dept* France
32 H2 Lotfābād Iran 37.32N 59.17E
87 E8 Lothagum Hill Sudan 5.25N 34.21E
110 O1 Lothair Montana 48.29N 111.14W
95 O2 Lothair S Africa 26.23S 30.26E
58 K7 Lothian *reg* Scotland
72 H2 Lothiers France 46.42N 1.34E
92 B12 Lothlekane Botswana 21.20S 25.32E
93 F1 Lotikipi Plain Kenya
87 D8 Lotillt *watercourse* Sudan
94 G4 Lotlhake Pan Botswana 23.52S 22.27E
91 H5 Loto Zaïre 2.48S 22.30E
90 M8 Loto *R* Cent Afr Rep
122 C2 Lotofaga W Samoa, Pacific Oc 14.01S 171.33W
91 F4 Lotoi *R* Zaïre
93 F3 Lotome Uganda 2.21N 34.36E
45 G1 Lotoshino U.S.S.R. 56.14N 35.44E
94 J4 Lotsane *R* Botswana
66 G6 Lotschenpass Switzerland 46.26N 7.43E
66 H6 Lotschental *V* Switzerland
45 G8 Lotsmano-Kamenka Ukraine U.S.S.R. 48.21N 35.04E
96 A14 Lot's Wife *hill* St Helena 16.01S 5.44W
Lot's Wife *rock* Japan*see* Sōfu-gan
112 K4 Lott Texas 31.14N 97.04W
47 B2 Lotta *R* U.S.S.R.
64 N3 Lottengrün E Germany 50.27N 12.15E
66 M6 Lottigna Switzerland 46.28N 8.58E
105 F5 Lotts Cr Georgia
64 F8 Lottstetten W Germany 47.37N 8.35E
60 N14 Lottum Netherlands 51.28N 6.10E
87 D8 Lotuke *mt* Sudan 4.10N 33.46E
93 E1 Lotuke, Jeb Sudan 4.06N 33.47E
91 F4 Lotumbe Zaïre 0.32S 19.21E
23 J6 Lo-tung Taiwan 24.40N 121.45E
110 J2 Lotus Idaho 47.15N 116.39W
106 F9 Lotus Illinois 40.20N 88.27W
Lotus Vale *see* Myra Vale
Lötzen *see* Gizycko
81 D4 Lotzorai Sardinia 39.58N 9.40E
66 H3 Lotzwil Switzerland 47.12N 7.48E
70 K6 Louailles France 47.47N 0.15W
107 D8 Louann Arkansas 33.23N 92.48W
70 D4 Louannec France 48.47N 3.24W
72 F1 Louans France 47.11N 0.44E
70 D4 Louargat France 48.34N 3.20W
90 K2 Loubayed Chad 19.11N 20.57E
Loubbein *see* Lubba'ain
72 D3 Loubillé France 46.04N 0.03W
65 N1 Loučná *R* Czechoslovakia
70 E5 Loudéac France 48.11N 2.45W
72 E10 Loudenvielle France 42.47N 0.25E
71 D6 Loudes France 45.05N 3.46E
83 E4 Loudhías *R* Greece
91 C6 Loudima Congo 4.06S 13.05E
92 F8 Loudon Malawi 12.09S 33.27E
104 O3 Loudon New Hampshire 43.16N 71.28W
107 M6 Loudon Tennessee 35.44N 84.20W
104 C6 Loudonville Ohio 40.39N 82.14W
72 E1 Loudun France 47.01N 0.05E
56 K4 Loudwater Bucks Eng 51.37N 0.43W
70 K6 Loué France 48.00N 0.09W
71 H2 Loue *R* France
61 K7 Louette-St.-Denis Belgium 49.58N 4.57E
61 K7 Louette-St.-Pierre Belgium 49.58N 4.55E
89 D6 Loufa Guinea 11.24N 11.04W
22 J7 Loufan Shanxi China 38.04N 111.46E
89 A4 Louga Senegal 15.37N 16.13W
72 G9 Louge *R* France
56 J2 Loughborough Leics Eng 52.47N 1.11W
59 K3 Loughbrickland Down N Ireland 54.19N 6.18W
100 F6 Lougheed Alberta 52.44N 111.29W
97 J2 Lougheed I N W Terr 77.30N 105.00W

59 E4 Loughglinn Roscommon Irish Rep 53.50N 8.34W
56 C4 Loughor Dyfed Wales 51.40N 4.04W
56 C4 Loughor, R Dyfed/W Glam Wales
59 E5 Loughrea Galway Irish Rep 53.12N 8.34W
59 E2 Loughros More B Donegal Irish Rep 54.47N 8.35W
59 K4 Loughshinny Dublin Irish Rep 53.33N 6.05W
55 H2 Loughton Essex Eng 51.39N 0.03E
89 L6 Lougou Benin 11.09N 3.21E
72 F6 Lougratte France 44.35N 0.38E
71 G3 Louhans France 46.37N 5.13E
72 B9 Louhossoa France 43.19N 1.21W
15 J5 Lou I Admiralty Is 2.25S 147.23E
107 G9 Louin Mississippi 32.05N 89.17W
104 C8 Louisa Kentucky 38.06N 82.37W
104 G8 Louisa Virginia 38.02N 78.02W
14 E3 Louisa, L W Australia 17.04S 122.55E
17 H10 Louisa Reef S China Sea 6.15N 113.15E
98 N8 Louisbourg C Breton I, Nova Scotia 45.56N 59.58W
109 Q3 Louisburg Kansas 38.36N 94.42W
105 J1 Louisburg N Carolina 36.06N 78.17W
59 C4 Louisburgh Mayo Irish Rep 53.46N 9.48W
98 M8 Louisburg Nat. Hist. Park C Breton I, Nova Scotia 45.57N 59.56W
98 L8 Louisdale C Breton I, Nova Scotia 45.38N 61.04W
112 L6 Louise Texas 29.06N 96.26W
101 P5 Louise Falls waterfall N W Terr 60.30N 116.13W
101 H9 Louise I Queen Charlotte Is, Br Col 52.59N 131.50W
113 O5 Louise, L Alaska 62.20N 146.30W
101 P10 Louise, L Alberta 51.18N 116.18W
99 S6 Louiseville Quebec 46.16N 72.56W
15 M9 Louisiade Arch Papua New Guinea
10 M4 Louisiade Rise sea feature Coral Sea
107 E2 Louisiana Missouri 39.27N 91.02W
102 H4 Louisiana state U.S.A.
107 C12 Louisiana Pt Louisiana 29.40N 93.50W
94 K4 Louis Trichardt S Africa 23.01S 29.43E
107 L10 Louisville Alabama 31.47N 85.35W
109 E2 Louisville Colorado 39.58N 105.09W
105 E5 Louisville Georgia 33.00N 82.24W
107 L3 Louisville Kentucky 38.13N 85.48W
107 G8 Louisville Mississippi 33.06N 89.03W
108 O9 Louisville Nebraska 41.00N 96.10W
99 R2 Louisville New York 44.55N 75.02W
104 D6 Louisville Ohio 40.51N 81.16W
97 M7 Louis XIV, Pte Quebec 54.35N 79.50W
84 D6 Louká Greece 37.34N 22.27E
51 R5 Loukhi Karelia U.S.S.R. 66.05N 33.04E
47 C3 Loukhi U.S.S.R. 66.04N 33.09E
91 E4 Loukolela Congo 1.04S 17.10E
74 D10 Loukos R Morocco
91 D5 Loukouo Congo 3.38S 14.39E
66 A2 Loulans France 47.27N 6.12E
24 F5 Loulan Yiji anc site Xinjiang Uygur Zizhiqu China 40.30N 89.44E
72 D3 Loulay France 46.03N 0.30W
76 C14 Loulé Portugal 37.08N 8.02W
89 G6 Loulouni Mali 10.50N 5.30W
91 A1 Loum Cameroon 4.46N 9.43E
89 A2 Loumoila Mauritania 19.55N 16.05W
91 D5 Louna R Congo
91 B4 Loungouagou Gabon 0.38S 11.48E
103 B2 Lounsberry New York 42.03N 76.20W
64 Q3 Louny Czechoslovakia 50.22N 13.47E
71 L9 Loup R France
108 M8 Loup R Nebraska
108 M8 Loup City Nebraska 41.18N 98.59W
70 N5 Loupe, la France 48.29N 1.01E
72 D6 Loupiac France 44.37N 0.18W
61 H4 Loupoigne Belgium 50.36N 4.26E
69 J5 Louppy-sur-Loison France 49.27N 5.21E
59 J2 Loup, The Londonderry N Ireland 54.42N 6.36W
69 E3 Lourches France 50.19N 3.22E
72 D9 Lourdes France 43.06N 0.02W
98 N5 Lourdes Newfoundland 48.30N 59.00W
75 K2 Lourdes, Pic de mt Spain 42.46N 0.09W
72 H3 Lourdoueix St. Michel France 46.26N 1.45E
72 H3 Lourdoueix St. Pierre France 46.24N 1.49E
76 C15 Lourel Portugal 38.48N 9.22W
117 C3 Lourenço Brazil 2.30N 51.37W
118 B5 Lourenço R Brazil
Lourenço Marques see Maputo
94 M5 Lourenço Marques, B. de Mozambique
76 A11 Loures Portugal 38.50N 9.10W
72 F9 Loures-Barousse France 43.02N 0.36E
76 B8 Louriçal Portugal 40.01N 8.44W
76 A10 Lourinhã Portugal 39.14N 9.19W
76 B6 Louro Portugal 41.26N 8.33W
84 A3 Louros R Greece
76 B7 Lourosa Portugal 41.00N 8.32W
70 J6 Louroux-Beconnais, le France 47.32N 0.53W
66 F7 Lourtier Switzerland 46.03N 7.17E
69 C7 Loury France 48.00N 2.05E
76 A11 Lousa Portugal 38.53N 9.12W
76 C8 Lousã Portugal 40.07N 8.15W
76 C6 Lousada Portugal 41.17N 8.17W
76 B3 Lousame Spain 42.46N 8.51W
100 D6 Lousana Alberta 52.09N 113.11W
76 C8 Lousã, Serra da mts Portugal
84 C5 Lousiká Greece 38.06N 21.35E
89 H5 Louta Upper Volta 13.29N 3.09W
57 N6 Louth Lincs Eng 53.22N 0.01W
59 J4 Louth Louth Irish Rep 53.57N 6.33W
12 H4 Louth New S Wales 30.34S 145.09E
59 J4 Louth co Irish Rep
84 F5 Loutoúfi Greece 38.16N 23.16E
84 F4 Loutrá Aidhipsoú Greece 38.51N 23.03E
84 D4 Loutrá Ipátis Greece 38.53N 22.16E
84 E6 Loutráki Greece 37.58N 22.58E
84 B6 Loutrá Killínis Greece 37.51N 21.06E
84 B4 Loutron Greece 38.57N 21.13E
84 D3 Loutroplyí Greece 39.08N 22.00E
84 G6 Loútsa Greece 37.59N 24.00E
84 W22 Loútsai Corfu 39.48N 19.52E
Louvain see Leuven
61 N4 Louveigné Belgium 50.32N 5.43E
69 C3 Louvencourt France 50.06N 2.29E
70 J5 Louverne France 48.07N 0.43W
72 D9 Louvie Juzon France 43.05N 0.24W
61 G5 Louvière, La Belgium 50.29N 4.12E
109 E2 Louviers Colorado 39.30N 105.03W
70 N3 Louviers France 49.13N 1.11E
70 H5 Louvigné-de-Bais France 48.03N 1.20W
70 H5 Louvigné-du-Désert France 48.29N 1.07W
69 D5 Louvres France 49.03N 2.31E
95 O9 Louwsburg S Africa 27.35S 31.19E
69 H7 Louze France 48.26N 4.43E
53 H6 Lov Denmark 55.10N 11.52E
52 N2 Lövånger Sweden 64.21N 21.15E
62 L8 Lovasberény Hungary 47.19N 18.31E
65 P8 Lovászi Hungary 46.33N 16.35E
62 K8 Lovászpatona Hungary 47.26N 17.39E
46 H1 Lovat' R U.S.S.R.
58 H4 Lovat Bridge Highland Scotland 57.28N 4.29W
53 V15 Lovatn L Norway 61.50N 6.56E
51 G6 Lövberg Sweden 65.06N 18.50E
52 J3 Lövberga Sweden 63.57N 15.50E
82 E8 Lovćen mt Yugoslavia 42.23N 18.49E
53 G6 Løve Denmark 55.29N 11.18E
100 N5 Love Saskatchewan 53.30N 104.12W
25 G6 Lovea Cambodia 13.19N 102.57E
25 H6 Lovea Cambodia 13.47N 104.01E
82 J7 Lovech Bulgaria 43.08N 24.45E
112 O9 Love Field Airport Texas 32.48N 96.51W
53 C3 Løvel Denmark 56.32N 9.29E
112 M4 Lovelady Texas 31.09N 95.28W
109 E1 Loveland Colorado 40.24N 105.06W
104 A7 Loveland Ohio 39.16N 84.14W
109 E2 Loveland Pass Colorado 39.40N 105.53W
108 B5 Lovell Wyoming 44.50N 108.15W
106 K5 Lovells Michigan 44.50N 84.30W
110 G9 Lovelock Nevada 40.12N 118.28W
103 B3 Lovelton Pennsylvania 41.32N 76.12W
61 E2 Lovendegem Belgium 51.06N 3.36E
110 P9 Lovenia, Mt Utah 40.45N 110.36W
69 M2 Lövenich W Germany 50.56N 6.49E
61 K3 Lovenjoel Belgium 50.52N 4.47E
103 B8 Love Point Maryland 39.03N 76.18W
79 H3 Lóvere Italy 45.49N 10.04E
100 H7 Loverna Saskatchewan 51.40N 109.59W
11 N13 Lovers Leap New Zealand 45.54S 170.40E
61 H5 Loverval Belgium 50.23N 4.28E
13 C6 Loves Creek N Terr Australia 23.34S 134.28E
105 D7 Lovett Florida 30.37N 83.37E
26 B16 Lovett, C Heard I Antarctica 53.12S 73.30E
52 G5 Lövhögen Sweden 61.54N 13.25E
Loviisa see Lovisa
51 K4 Lovikka Sweden 67.20N 22.35E
108 S8 Lovilia Iowa 41.06N 92.55W
109 F9 Loving New Mexico 32.17N 104.06W
112 J2 Loving Texas 33.16N 98.32W
104 G9 Lovingston Virginia 37.46N 78.54W
107 H2 Lovington Illinois 39.42N 88.39W
109 G9 Lovington New Mexico 32.58N 103.21W
76 C5 Lovíos Spain 41.55N 8.05W
51 M11 Lovisa Finland 60.27N 26.15E
52 G5 Lövnäs Kopparberg Sweden 61.21N 13.20E
51 F5 Lövnäs Norrbotten Sweden 66.21N 17.50E
53 C3 Lovns Bredning B Denmark 56.38N 9.15E
65 P6 Lövö Hungary 47.30N 16.48E
91 J8 Lovoi R Zaïre
62 H5 Lovosice Czechoslovakia 50.31N 14.02E
47 D2 Lovozero U.S.S.R. 68.01N 35.08E
47 D2 Lovozero, Oz L U.S.S.R.
53 U20 Lovra Norway 59.22N 6.10E
79 P4 Lovrečica Yugoslavia 45.23N 13.32E
65 M8 Lovrenc na Pohorju Yugoslavia 46.33N 15.22E
82 F5 Lovrin Romania 45.58N 20.49E
52 J2 Lövsjön Sweden 64.46N 15.20E
91 G7 Lóvua Lunda Angola 7.19S 20.12E
91 H9 Lóvua Moxico Angola 11.33S 23.33E
51 C5 Lovunden isld Norway 66.21N 12.20E
40 N7 Lovushki Ostrova islds Kuril Is U.S.S.R.
99 P7 Low Quebec 45.48N 75.56W
110 M9 Low Utah 40.45N 113.01W
91 J4 Lowa Zaïre 1.23S 25.50E
92 C2 Lowa R Zaïre
93 B2 Lowa R Zaïre
31 F3 Lowarai Pass Pakistan 35.22N 71.48E
11 D11 Lowburn New Zealand 45.00S 169.13E
99 K4 Low Bush River Ontario 48.57N 80.09W
97 L5 Low, C N W Terr 63.05N 85.30W
106 D8 Lowden Iowa 41.51N 90.57W
110 E6 Low Des Oregon
57 L6 Lowdham Notts Eng 53.01N 1.00W
111 P10 Lowell Arizona 31.26N 109.54W
107 B5 Lowell Arkansas 36.15N 94.09W
110 K3 Lowell Idaho 46.09N 115.35W
106 G8 Lowell Indiana 41.16N 87.25W
104 O4 Lowell Massachusetts 42.38N 71.19W
106 J7 Lowell Michigan 42.54N 85.22W
104 D7 Lowell Ohio 39.32N 81.32W
110 C6 Lowell Oregon 43.56N 122.45W
110 J6 Lowell, L Idaho 43.34N 116.40W
63 S7 Löwenberg E Germany 52.54N 13.10E
66 E4 Löwenberg Switzerland 46.57N 7.09E
64 G5 Löwenstein W Germany 49.06N 9.24E
95 K7 Lower Adamson S Africa 31.08S 26.18E
101 O11 Lower Arrow Lake Br Col
108 L5 Lower Brule S Dakota 44.05N 99.32W
Lower California see Baja California
58 E3 Lower Diabaig Highland Scotland 57.35N 5.42W
95 F3 Lower Dikgatlhong S Africa 27.06S 22.56E
110 P5 Lower Falls waterfall Wyoming 44.43N 110.30W
100 V8 Lower Fort Garry Manitoba 50.07N 96.48W
111 L6 Lower Granite Gorge Arizona
11 J8 Lower Hutt New Zealand 41.12S 174.54E
95 K7 Lower Incline S Africa 31.30S 26.31E
98 T6 Lower Island Cove Newfoundland 48.00N 53.00W
110 D8 Lower Klamath L California 41.55N 121.41W
110 E8 Lower L California 41.15N 120.02W
101 F5 Lower Laberge Yukon Terr 61.24N 135.13W
111 B3 Lower Lake California 38.54N 122.37W
95 N5 Lower Loteni S Africa 29.32S 29.36E
97 K4 Lower Macdougall L N W Terr
98 G6 Lower Neguac New Brunswick 47.15N 65.06W
98 G10 Lower Ohio Nova Scotia 43.52N 65.22W
114 E6 Lower Paia Hawaiian Is 20.56N 156.22W
57 J6 Lower Peover Cheshire Eng 53.16N 2.24W
101 J6 Lower Post Br Columbia 59.56N 128.29W
110 O5 Lower Red Rock L Montana 44.40N 111.50W
110 M1 Lower St. Mary L Montana 48.50N 113.25W
97 N5 Lower Savage Is N W Terr
97 M6 Lower Seal L Quebec
56 J6 Lower Upham Hants Eng 50.59N 1.15W
98 G10 Lower West Pubnico Nova Scotia 43.38N 65.49W
58 T11 Lower Whitehall Orkney Scotland 59.09N 2.36W
98 G10 Lower Woods Harbour Nova Scotia 43.31N 65.44W
Lower Zaïre prov see Bas Zaïre
107 H5 Lowes Kentucky 36.54N 88.47W
56 P3 Lowestoft Suffolk Eng 52.29N 1.45E
12 H8 Low Hd Tasmania 40.58S 146.50E
90 D6 Lowi Nigeria 10.37N 10.00E
58 N7 Lowick Northumb Eng 55.38N 1.58W
62 M3 Łowicz Poland 52.06N 19.55E
13 H3 Low Is Queensland 16.18S 145.35E
95 N5 Lowlands S Africa 29.07S 29.55E
110 K5 Lowman Idaho 44.05N 115.36W
103 A2 Lowman New York 42.02N 76.44W
107 K9 Lowndesboro Alabama 32.15N 86.35W
26 V3 Low Pt Christmas I Ind Oc 10.27S 105.46E
12 H9 Low Rocky Pt Tasmania 42.59S 145.31E
11 D5 Lowry B New Zealand 41.15S 174.55E
107 C3 Lowry City Missouri 38.09N 93.45W
105 F3 Lowrys S Carolina 34.47N 81.13W
57 H3 Lowther Cumbria Eng 54.37N 2.43W
97 K3 Lowther I N W Terr 74.35N 97.58W
104 K3 Lowville New York 43.47N 75.30W
115 L9 Loxicha Mexico 16.01N 96.38W
107 J11 Loxley Alabama 30.38N 87.45W
63 J6 Loxstedt W Germany 53.28N 8.38E
95 F7 Loxton S Africa 31.29S 22.21E
12 F5 Loxton S Australia 34.38S 140.38E
23 B2 Loxur Sichuan China 32.31N 100.40E
56 K5 Loxwood W Sussex Eng 51.04N 0.32W
91 K4 Loya R Zaïre
87 J5 Loyada Somalia 11.27N 43.18E
106 D5 Loyal Wisconsin 44.43N 90.29W
100 F7 Loyalist Alberta 52.00N 111.00W
58 H2 Loyal, L Highland Scotland 58.23N 4.21W
105 D1 Loyall Kentucky 36.51N 83.23W
103 A4 Loyalsock Cr Pennsylvania
111 D2 Loyalton California 39.41N 120.15W
108 L4 Loyalton S Dakota 45.16N 99.17W
Loyalty Is see Loyauté, Is
Loyang see Luoyang
9 C13 Loyauté, Is Pacific Oc
71 H2 Loye, la France 47.02N 5.32E
61 K5 Loyers Belgium 50.28N 4.57E
72 J2 Loye-sur-Arnon France 46.40N 2.23E
71 G5 Loyettes France 45.47N 5.12E
45 B5 Loyev Belorussiya U.S.S.R. 51.55N 30.47E
47 F5 Loyma U.S.S.R. 60.39N 48.49E
51 Q10 Loymola Karelia U.S.S.R. 61.59N 31.44E
58 F4 Loyne, L Highland Scotland 57.06N 5.01W
47 G6 Loyno U.S.S.R. 59.45N 52.32E
121 K8 Loyola, Pta Argentina 51.38S 69.00W
93 F2 Loyoro Uganda 3.22N 34.16E
71 F5 Lozanne France 45.52N 4.41E
82 K8 Lozarevo Bulgaria 42.45N 26.54E
67 H8 Lozère dept France
71 D8 Lozere, Mt France
92 A9 Lozi tribe Zambia
Löz, Jabal al mt see Lawz, Jabal al
82 E6 Loznica Yugoslavia 44.31N 19.14E
45 K7 Lozno-Alexandrovka Ukraine U.S.S.R. 49.51N 38.46E
45 J7 Lozovaya Donetsk, Ukraine U.S.S.R. 49.12N 37.35E
43 N1 Lozovaya Kazakhstan U.S.S.R. 53.21N 77.45E
45 H8 Lozovaya Khar'kov, Ukraine U.S.S.R. 48.54N 36.20E
75 C6 Lozoya Spain 40.56N 3.49W
75 C6 Lozoya R Spain
75 C6 Lozoya, Can. de Spain
75 C6 Lozoyuela Spain 40.55N 3.36W
47 J6 Loz'va R U.S.S.R.
79 L4 Lozzo Atestino Italy 45.18N 11.38E
79 M2 Lozzo Cadore Italy 46.29N 12.26E
52 J2 Lsngseleân R Sweden
79 D4 Lu Italy 45.00N 8.29E
92 H9 Lua Mozambique 15.46S 37.03E
91 F2 Lua R Zaïre
9 R13 Lua'afuleheu islet Tonga, Pacific Oc 18.49S 174.05W
93 A10 Luaba R Burundi
94 O2 Luabo Mozambique 18.30S 36.10E
91 J8 Luabo Zaïre 9.05S 25.10E
91 G9 Luacano Angola 11.13S 21.40E
91 G7 Luachimo Angola 7.23S 20.48E
91 G8 Luachimo R Angola
91 G7 Luaco Angola 7.59S 21.12E
91 F2 Lua Dekere R Zaïre
18 C6 Luahasibuka Indonesia 0.31S 98.29E
9 R13 Luahiapu islet Tonga, Pacific Oc 18.49S 174.04W
9 U12 Lua Hoko atoll Tonga, Pacific Oc 19.40S 174.24W
91 K7 Luala Zaïre 6.28S 27.26E
92 H10 Luala R Mozambique
91 J9 Lualaba Zaïre 10.29S 25.36E
91 J4 Lualaba R Zaïre
114 E6 Lualailua Hills Hawaiian Is
91 C6 Luali Angola 4.35S 12.42E
114 A5 Lualualei Hawaiian Is 21.24N 158.09W
92 D4 Luama R Zaïre
114 D6 Lua Makika mt Hawaiian Is 20.33N 156.34W
92 G8 Luambala R Mozambique
92 F8 Luambe Nat. Park Zambia
91 H9 Luambo R Angola
92 B9 Luampa Zambia 15.02S 24.21E
92 B9 Luampa R Zambia
91 H9 Luan Angola 10.44S 22.11E
23 G3 Lu'an Anhui China 31.48N 116.30E
116 H2 Luana Pt Jamaica, W I 18.02N 77.56W
25 G2 Luan Chau Vietnam 21.42N 103.20E
23 E7 Luancheng Guangxi China 22.47N 108.54E
22 K8 Luancheng Hebei China 37.55N 114.41E
23 F2 Luanchuan Henan China 33.48N 111.38E
76 H1 Luanco Spain 43.36N 5.48W
91 C8 Luanda Angola 8.50S 13.15E
91 C8 Luanda dist Angola
91 C8 Luanda, I. de Angola 8.48S 13.12E
91 F9 Luando Angola 11.32S 18.27E
91 E9 Luando R Angola
19 F8 Luang isld Indon 8.11S 128.43E
25 G4 Luang, Huai R Thailand
91 G10 Luanginga R Angola
25 E8 Luang, Khao mt Thailand 8.31N 99.44E
25 G3 Luang Prabang Laos 19.53N 102.10E
91 F7 Luangue Angola 7.17S 19.41E
91 F8 Luangue Angola 9.28S 19.36E
91 F8 Luangue R Angola
91 G12 Luangundo, R Angola
92 E9 Luangwa Zambia 14.59S 30.14E
92 E6 Luangwa R Zambia
92 F7 Luangwa R Zambia
24 G8 Luanhaizi Qinghai China 34.43N 92.45E
91 G11 Luanhica Angola 14.56S 20.31E
91 J7 Luania Bubi Zaïre 7.28S 24.49E
91 D6 Luanika Zaïre 5.36S 14.22E
15 L1 Luaniua I Solomon Is 5.30S 159.43E
22 G8 Luanjing Nei Monggol Zizhiqu China 37.59N 105.15E
22 L7 Luannan Hebei China 39.29N 118.39E
92 D9 Luano tribe Zambia
117 B7 Lua Nova Brazil 5.00S 56.37W
22 L6 Luanping Hebei China 40.56N 117.14E
92 D8 Luanshya Zambia 13.09S 28.24E
121 D6 Luan Toro Argentina 36.14S 65.05W
22 L7 Luan Xian Hebei China 39.46N 118.46E
92 D6 Luanza Zaïre 8.40S 28.42E
92 D7 Luapula prov Zambia
92 D7 Luapula R Zaïre
Luar see Horsburgh I
76 F1 Luarca Spain 43.33N 6.31W
18 K5 Luar, Danau L Borneo Indon
15 J7 Luard Is Papua New Guinea 7.41S 147.39E
91 H9 Luashi Zaïre 10.57S 23.34E
91 H9 Luashi R Zaïre
91 F11 Luassinga R Angola
9 R13 Luatafito islet Tonga, Pacific Oc 18.49S 173.58W
91 G10 Luatamba Angola 12.06S 20.19E
91 G11 Luate R Angola
92 H8 Luatize R Mozambique
19 L1 Luayao Guam Pacific Oc 13.28N 144.49E
91 A2 Luba Fernando Póo Eq Guinea 3.27N 8.33E
115 P9 Lubaantum ruins Belize 16.21N 88.58W
87 H4 Lubacdebot Ethiopia 13.50N 40.49E
62 O5 Lúbaczów Poland 50.11N 23.08E
91 J6 Lubala Zaïre 5.33S 25.01E
91 F8 Lubalo Angola 9.13S 19.21E
91 F8 Lubalo R Angola
91 E5 Lubamiti Zaïre 2.28S 17.47E
62 J4 Lubań Poland 51.07N 15.17E
46 F2 Lubāna Latvia U.S.S.R. 56.54N 26.42E
46 F2 Lubānas ezers L Latvia U.S.S.R.
19 K5 Lubang Philippines 13.51N 120.08E
19 K5 Lubang isld Philippines 13.45N 120.10E
19 K5 Lubang Is Philippines
Lubango see Sá da Bandeira
91 C11 Lubango Angola 14.55S 13.30E
92 E7 Lubansenshi R Zambia
63 Q8 Lübars E Germany 52.11N 12.08E
62 O4 Lubartów Poland 51.29N 22.38E
62 M2 Lubawa Poland 53.31N 19.44E
35 J2 Lubba'ain Syria 32.55N 36.24E
35 G6 Lubban, El Jordan 31.50N 35.58E
35 D5 Lubban Sharqiya Jordan 32.04N 35.15E
63 J8 Lübbecke W Germany 52.19N 8.37E
61 K3 Lubbeek Belgium 50.53N 4.50E
63 T9 Lübben E Germany 51.57N 13.54E
63 T9 Lübbenau E Germany 51.52N 13.58E
112 F2 Lubbock Texas 33.35N 101.53W
104 S2 Lubec Maine 44.50N 67.00W
12 G6 Lubeck Victoria 36.47S 142.38E
63 N5 Lübeck W Germany 53.52N 10.40E
63 N4 Lübecker Bucht B Germany
91 J6 Lubefu Zaïre 4.43S 24.25E
91 H6 Lubefu R Zaïre
Lubei see Jarud Qi
64 P3 Lubenec Czechoslovakia 50.08N 13.20E
56 K3 Lubenham Leics Eng 52.29N 0.58W
43 C2 Lubenka Kazakhstan U.S.S.R. 50.22N 54.13E
93 A6 Lubero Zaïre 0.10S 29.12E
71 G9 Lubéron, Mtgne. du France
72 G5 Lubersac France 45.26N 1.24E
92 E8 Lubi R Zambia
91 E9 Lubia Angola 11.01S 17.06E
76 F4 Lubián Spain 42.02N 6.55W
19 K6 Lubic isld Philippines 10.58N 120.45E
100 B2 Lubicon L Alberta 56.22N 115.45W
62 J2 Lubie, Jezioro L Poland
62 L3 Lubień Bydgoszcz Poland 52.23N 19.09E
62 K5 Lubień Opole Poland 50.46N 17.36E
92 D5 Lubika Zaïre 7.48S 29.18E
91 J8 Lubilash R Zaïre
91 K5 Lubile Zaïre 2.47S 26.54E
91 K3 Lubilo R Zaïre
62 J4 Lubiń Poland 51.23N 16.10E
63 U5 Lubin Poland 53.52N 14.30E
62 O4 Lublin Poland 51.18N 22.31E
106 D4 Lublin Wisconsin 45.06N 90.44W
62 L5 Lubliniec Poland 50.40N 18.40E
63 T4 Lubmin E Germany 54.08N 13.37E
64 Q3 Lubná Czechoslovakia 50.05N 13.43E
58 H6 Lubnaig, L Central Scotland 56.17N 4.18W
45 D6 Lubny Ukraine U.S.S.R. 50.01N 33.00E
18 J5 Lubok Antu Sarawak Malaysia 1.01N 111.49E
18 C9 Lubok China Pen Malaysia 2.26N 102.04E
92 C9 Lubombo Zambia 15.51S 27.51E
91 K8 Lubondaie Zaïre 8.01S 26.32E
92 C3 Lubongola Zaïre 2.35S 27.53E
45 N2 Lubonos U.S.S.R. 54.34N 41.22E
47 C4 Lubosalma U.S.S.R. 63.02N 31.50E
77 M6 Lubrín Spain 37.13N 2.04W
62 H4 Lubsko Poland 51.49N 14.59E
63 O6 Lübtheen E Germany 53.19N 11.05E
92 F7 Lubu R Zambia
19 K3 Lubuagan Luzon Philippines 17.22N 121.08E
91 G7 Lubudi Zaïre 6.51S 21.18E
91 J8 Lubudi Zaïre 9.57S 25.59E
91 G6 Lubudi R Zaïre
91 J8 Lubudi R Zaïre
91 F6 Lubue R Zaïre
18 F7 Lubukbatang Sumatra Indon 4.00S 104.15E
18 E5 Lubukbertubung Sumatra Indonesia 0.01N 102.08E
18 E7 Lubuklinggau Sumatra Indon 3.24S 102.56E
18 C4 Lubukpakam Sumatra Indon 3.35N 98.54E
18 D5 Lubuksikaping Sumatra Indon 0.02N 100.09E
92 D6 Lubule R Zaïre
91 K9 Lubumbashi Zaïre 11.41S 27.29E
92 C4 Lubunda Zaïre 5.12S 26.41E
92 D7 Lubunda Zambia 10.18S 28.40E
91 K4 Lubutu Zaïre 0.48S 26.39E
91 K4 Lubutu R Zaïre
92 D7 Lubwe Zambia 11.06S 29.38E
64 N3 Luby Czechoslovakia 50.15N 12.25E
63 Q6 Lübz E Germany 53.28N 12.03E
70 K3 Luc Calvados France 49.18N 0.21W
71 D7 Luc Lozère France 44.39N 3.53E
77 M6 Lucainena de las Torres Spain 37.03N 2.11W
91 D8 Lucala Angola 9.16S 15.17E
91 D8 Lucala R Angola
59 K5 Lucan Dublin Irish Rep 53.22N 6.27W
99 J9 Lucan Ontario 43.11N 81.24W
120 C6 Lucanas Peru 14.37S 74.15W
25 H1 Luc An Chau Vietnam 22.05N 104.45E
81 K3 Lucania reg Italy
101 C5 Lucania, Mt Yukon Terr 60.48N 140.25W
22 C8 Lücaoshan Qinghai China 37.38N 95.45E
77 M6 Lúcar Spain 37.24N 2.25W
77 L6 Lúcar, Sierra de mts Spain
118 C3 Lucas Brazil 13.09S 55.48W
108 R8 Lucas Iowa 41.03N 93.27W
109 M2 Lucas Kansas 39.04N 98.33W
104 C6 Lucas Ohio 40.43N 82.26W
121 F4 Lucas González Argentina 32.25S 59.33W
14 G5 Lucas, L W Australia
105 J11 Lucaya Bahamas 26.32N 78.40W
72 G1 Luçay-le-Mâle France 47.08N 1.26E
19 K4 Lucban Luzon Philippines 14.08N 121.36E
79 J7 Lucca Italy 43.50N 10.30E
108 N3 Lucca N Dakota 46.42N 97.42W
79 H6 Lucca prov Italy
81 F8 Lucca Sicula Sicily 37.35N 13.18E
116 H1 Lucea Jamaica, W I 18.26N 78.11W
57 D3 Luce B Dumfries & Galloway Scotland
107 H11 Lucedale Mississippi 30.55N 88.36W
76 E11 Lucefeci R Portugal
118 E7 Lucélia Brazil 21.45S 51.00W
66 F2 Lucelle Switzerland 47.26N 7.16E
19 K5 Lucena Luzon Philippines 13.57N 121.36E
77 H6 Lucena Spain 37.25N 4.29W
75 H4 Lucena de Jalón Spain 41.32N 1.18W
75 K7 Lucena del Cid Spain 40.09N 0.17W
77 C6 Lucena del Puerto Spain 37.18N 6.44W
77 J5 Lucena, Sierra de mts Spain
71 C3 Lucenay les Aix France 46.43N 3.27E
71 E2 Lucenay-l'Evêque France 47.05N 4.15E
71 G7 Luc-en-Diois France 44.36N 5.28E
66 L5 Lucendro, Piz mt Switzerland 46.34N 8.32E
62 M7 Lučenec Czechoslovakia 48.20N 19.40E
75 H4 Luceni Spain 41.49N 1.14W
66 D5 Lucens Switzerland 46.43N 6.51E
91 E12 Luceque Angola 16.39S 17.59E
80 M5 Lucera Italy 41.30N 15.20E
120 D5 Lucerna Peru 12.05S 69.29W
111 B2 Lucerne California 39.05N 122.48W
107 C1 Lucerne Missouri 40.27N 93.20W
95 K1 Lucerne S Africa 25.39S 26.05E
Lucerne Switzerland see Luzern
110 E1 Lucerne Washington 48.12N 120.36W
108 B6 Lucerne Wyoming 43.44N 108.10W
111 H7 Lucerne L California 34.30N 116.55W
Lucerne, Lake of see Vierwaldstätter See
111 H7 Lucerne Valley California 34.25N 116.58W
115 F2 Lucero Mexico 30.50N 106.30W
98 D5 Luceville Quebec 48.32N 68.22W
57 D3 Luce, Water of R Dumfries & Galloway Scotland
69 K6 Lucey Meurthe-et-Moselle France 48.43N 5.52E
71 H5 Lucey Savoie France 45.45N 5.47E
40 E4 Lucha R U.S.S.R.
72 F3 Luchapt France 46.10N 0.48E
91 F10 Luchazi tribe Angola
40 F8 Luchegorsk U.S.S.R. 46.30N 134.19E
44 H6 Luchek U.S.S.R. 41.38N 47.17E
23 D6 Lucheng Guangxi China 24.29N 106.03E
22 J8 Lucheng Shanxi China 36.14N 113.20E
92 G9 Luchenza Malawi 16.00S 35.15E
70 L6 Luché-Pringé France 47.40N 0.04E
45 B2 Luchesa R Belorussiya U.S.S.R.
69 C3 Lucheux France 50.11N 2.25E
23 J6 Lu-chiang Taiwan 24.04N 120.23E
91 F7 Luchico Angola 7.13S 19.56E
66 P2 Lüchingen Switzerland 47.22N 9.33E
63 O7 Lüchow W Germany 52.58N 11.11E
66 N4 Luchsingen Switzerland 46.58N 9.02E
23 E7 Luchuan Guangxi China 22.24N 110.15E
92 G8 Luchulingo R Mozambique
23 C7 Lüchun Yunnan China 22.54N 102.13E
69 C4 Luchy France 49.33N 2.07E
18 J7 Luci Borneo Indon 2.59S 111.14E
111 C5 Lucia California 36.02N 121.34W
77 H3 Luciana Spain 38.59N 4.17W
117 A3 Lucie R Surinam
99 M2 Lucie, L Quebec 50.24N 78.25W
80 E2 Lucignano Italy 43.17N 11.44E
110 J4 Lucile Idaho 45.34N 116.17W
76 G4 Lucillo Spain 42.24N 6.18W
110 M8 Lucin Utah 41.22N 113.55W
104 F5 Lucinda Pennsylvania 41.19N 79.23W
13 H4 Lucinda Queensland 18.30S 146.20E
12 F6 Lucindale S Australia 36.59S 140.25E
76 L3 Lucio R Spain
91 C10 Lucira Angola 13.51S 12.31E
94 M2 Lucite R Mozambique
80 L5 Lucito Italy 41.43N 14.42E
106 B4 Luck Wisconsin 45.35N 92.29W
64 N1 Lucka E Germany 51.06N 12.20E
63 T9 Luckau E Germany 51.51N 13.43E
30 K7 Luckeesarai Bihar India 25.12N 86.06E
63 S8 Luckenwalde E Germany 52.05N 13.11E
57 K1 Lucker Northumb Eng 55.34N 1.45W
95 H5 Luckhoff S Africa 29.45S 24.48E
14 E8 Luck, Mt W Australia 28.48S 123.31E
99 J9 Lucknow Ontario 43.58N 81.31W
13 F6 Lucknow Queensland 22.40S 140.55E
30 D6 Lucknow Uttar Prad India 26.50N 80.54E
30 D5 Lucknow Faizabad div Uttar Prad India
100 K8 Lucky Lake Saskatchewan 50.59N 107.10W
110 K6 Lucky Peak Res Idaho 43.34N 116.00W
100 F9 Lucky Strike Alberta 49.18N 111.36W
71 J10 Luc, le France 43.24N 6.19E
120 A2 Lucma Peru 7.38S 78.34W
72 D7 Lucmau France 44.20N 0.18W
75 K6 Luco de Bordón Spain 40.42N 0.18W
75 H6 Luco de Jiloca Spain 40.59N 1.18W
66 M5 Lucomagno, Piz mt Switzerland 46.32N 8.46E
79 K1 Luco, Monte Italy 46.32N 11.05E
72 B3 Luçon France 46.28N 1.10W
80 H5 Luco ne Marsi Italy 41.58N 13.29E
91 C7 Luconge Angola 6.59S 13.10E
72 C9 Lucq-de-Béarn France 43.17N 0.39W
69 G4 Lucquy France 49.32N 4.29E
116 G4 Lucrecia, C Cuba 21.05N 75.36W
72 B2 Lucs-sur-Boulogne, les France 46.50N 1.29W
91 G10 Lucula R Angola
91 E6 Lucula R Zaïre
91 D7 Lucunga Angola 6.50S 14.42E
91 C7 Lucunga R Angola
91 G10 Lucusse Angola 12.38S 20.52E
109 E7 Lucy New Mexico 34.40N 105.51W
13 D5 Lucy Cr N Terr Australia
13 D5 Lucy Creek N Terr Australia 22.20S 136.18E
71 D1 Lucy-le-Bois France 47.33N 3.53E
13 C6 Lucy, Mt N Terr Australia 22.32S 133.30E
21 B8 Luda Liaoning China 38.53N 121.37E
21 B8 Lüda Liaoning China 38.53N 121.37E
82 K8 Luda Kamchiya R Bulgaria
57 N6 Ludborough Lincs Eng 53.27N 0.03W
82 D4 Ludbreg Yugoslavia 46.15N 16.33E
108 M3 Ludden N Dakota 46.01N 98.08W
70 L6 Lude, le France 47.39N 0.09E
109 K2 Ludell Kansas 39.53N 100.57W
64 D1 Lüdenscheid W Germany 51.13N 7.38E
63 P7 Lüderitz E Germany 51.31N 11.44E
94 C6 Lüderitz Namibia 26.38S 15.10E
63 U7 Lüdersdorf E Germany 52.56N 14.05E
69 G5 Ludes France 49.10N 4.05E
66 Q3 Ludesch Austria 47.13N 9.48E
99 K7 Ludgate Ontario 45.54N 80.32W
56 H5 Ludgershall Wilts Eng 51.16N 1.37W
29 D2 Ludhiana Punjab India 30.56N 75.52E
29 D2 Ludhiana dist Punjab India
23 C5 Ludian Yunnan China 27.08N 103.26E
66 M6 Ludiano Switzerland 46.25N 8.58E
75 K7 Ludiente Spain 40.05N 0.23W
91 J6 Ludimbi R Zaïre
23 C4 Luding Sichuan China 29.54N 102.19E
63 F9 Lüdinghausen W Germany 51.46N 7.27E
106 H6 Ludington Michigan 43.58N 86.27W
111 H7 Ludlow California 34.43N 116.11W
109 F4 Ludlow Colorado 37.20N 104.37W
106 F9 Ludlow Illinois 40.23N 88.09W
103 K2 Ludlow Massachusetts 42.10N 72.28W
98 F7 Ludlow New Brunswick 46.30N 66.20W
104 G5 Ludlow Pennsylvania 41.45N 78.55W
108 G4 Ludlow S Dakota 45.49N 103.21W
56 F3 Ludlow Shropshire Eng 52.22N 2.43W
104 N3 Ludlow Vermont 43.22N 72.39W
103 A1 Ludlowville New York 42.33N 76.33W
82 K7 Ludogorie hills Bulgaria
46 G1 Ludoni U.S.S.R. 58.15N 29.29E
72 C6 Ludon-Médoc France 44.59N 0.36W
105 F6 Ludowici Georgia 31.42N 81.45W
64 E5 Ludswigshöhe W Germany 49.16N 8.05E
82 J4 Luduş Romania 46.28N 24.05E
52 J6 Ludvika Sweden 60.08N 15.14E
64 H2 Ludwigsau W Germany 50.56N 9.40E
64 G6 Ludwigsburg W Germany 48.54N 9.12E
64 M3 Ludwigschorgast W Germany 50.08N 11.34E
63 S8 Ludwigsfelde E Germany 52.18N 13.16E
64 G8 Ludwigshafen Baden-Württemberg W Germany 47.50N 9.04E
64 E5 Ludwigshafen am Rhein W Germany 49.29N 8.27E
64 L5 Ludwigskanal canal W Germany
63 P6 Ludwigslust E Germany 53.20N 11.30E
64 L3 Ludwigsstadt W Germany 50.29N 11.24E
64 P5 Ludwigsthal W Germany 49.04N 13.15E
46 G2 Ludza Latvia U.S.S.R. 56.30N 27.41E
72 C7 Lüe France 44.14N 0.59W
91 G6 Luebo Zaïre 5.20S 21.23E
91 G6 Luebo R Zaïre
112 H3 Lueders Texas 32.47N 99.37W
91 J5 Lueki Zaïre 3.25S 25.50E
91 G8 Luele R Angola
76 G6 Luelmo Spain 41.26N 6.09W
92 D3 Luemba Zaïre 3.42S 28.39E
91 J7 Luembe R Zaïre
91 F9 Luena Angola 11.48S 19.55E
91 J8 Luena Zaïre 9.28S 25.45E
92 E7 Luena Zambia 10.40S 30.21E
91 G9 Luena R Angola
92 B9 Luena R Zambia
92 A9 Luena Flats marsh Zambia
91 G12 Luengue R Angola
92 F10 Luenha R Mozambique
91 H8 Lueo R Zaïre
119 H5 Luepa Venezuela 5.44N 61.31W
75 H3 Luesia Spain 42.22N 1.01W
91 H7 Lueta Zaïre 7.20S 22.05E
91 G8 Luete Angola 9.58S 20.02E
23 D2 Lüeyang Gansu China 33.20N 105.58E
75 F3 Luezas Spain 42.17N 2.29W
15 H7 Lufa Papua New Guinea 6.22S 145.19E
23 G7 Lufeng Guangdong China 22.59N 115.40E
23 C6 Lufeng Yunnan China 25.07N 102.10E
15 H4 Luf I Bismarck Arch 1.30S 145.06E
91 C7 Lufico Angola 6.29S 13.26E
92 F6 Lufilya R Malawi
91 K8 Lufira R Zaïre
91 K8 Lufira, Chutesde la rapids Zaïre 9.33S 27.02E
112 N4 Lufkin Texas 31.21N 94.47W
91 C6 Lufu Zaïre 5.52S 13.53E
91 D6 Lufu R Zaïre
91 H8 Lufu R Zaïre
92 D6 Lufubu Zambia 9.58S 28.50E
92 E6 Lufubu R Zambia
91 D7 Lufunde R Angola
92 B8 Lufupa R Zambia
95 L7 Lufuta S Africa 31.40S 27.40E
92 D10 Lufya R Zambia
82 F6 Lug R Yugoslavia
46 G1 Luga U.S.S.R. 58.42N 29.49E
46 G1 Luga R U.S.S.R.
93 C6 Lugaga Uganda 0.48S 31.04E
79 G5 Lugagnano Val d'Arda Italy 44.49N 9.39E
93 E5 Lugala Uganda 0.13N 33.55E
92 D4 Lugamba Zaïre 5.32S 29.10E
76 J3 Lugan Spain 42.46N 5.21W
66 M7 Lugano Switzerland 46.01N 8.57E
79 E3 Lugano, L. di Italy/Switz
Lugansk Ukraine U.S.S.R. see Voroshilovgrad
45 R5 Lugansk U.S.S.R. 51.10N 45.39E
45 L8 Luganskaya Oblast' prov Ukraine U.S.S.R.
45 K8 Luganskoye Ukraine U.S.S.R. 48.25N 38.16E
9 C10 Luganville New Hebrides 15.31S 167.10E
93 K9 Lugard's Falls Kenya 3.04S 38.42E
116 F4 Lugareño Cuba 21.32N 77.28W
93 F5 Lugari Kenya 0.39N 34.53E
30 C7 Lugasi Madhya Prad India 25.05N 79.35E
64 O2 Lugau E Germany 50.45N 12.45E
93 D5 Lugazi Uganda 0.23N 32.57E
63 K9 Lügde W Germany 51.58N 9.15E
92 H10 Lugela Mozambique 16.25S 36.42E
92 H10 Lugela R Mozambique
92 H8 Lugenda Mozambique 12.26S 37.40E
92 H8 Lugenda R Mozambique
93 B9 Lugeti Hills Tanzania
11 D11 Luggate New Zealand 44.46S 169.16E
87 J5 Lughaya Somalia 10.46N 43.55E
87 J9 Lugh Ganana Somalia 2.52N 42.34E
46 G4 Luginy Ukraine U.S.S.R. 51.05N 28.21E
72 C7 Luglon France 44.05N 0.43W
80 F3 Lugnano in Teverina Italy 42.34N 12.20E
59 K6 Lugnaquillia Mt Wicklow Irish Rep 52.58N 6.27W
66 N5 Lugnezer Tal V Switzerland
71 F4 Lugny France 46.28N 4.49E
71 E4 Lugny-les-Charolles France 46.25N 4.12E
76 D2 Lugo Spain 43.00N 7.33W
74 B1 Lugo prov Spain
92 J5 Lugoba Tanzania 6.30S 38.21E
93 D4 Lugogo R Uganda
82 G5 Lugoj Romania 45.41N 21.57E
76 H2 Lugones Spain 43.24N 5.49W
72 C7 Lugos France 44.29N 0.52W
42 D3 Lugovatka U.S.S.R. 59.11N 89.03E
45 R7 Lugovaya-Proleyka U.S.S.R. 49.21N 45.04E
47 K6 Lugovaya Subbota U.S.S.R. 59.54N 69.49E
43 L5 Lugovoy Kazakhstan U.S.S.R. 42.54N 72.45E
47 K5 Lugovoy Tyumen U.S.S.R. 61.05N 68.29E
42 J3 Lugovskiy U.S.S.R. 58.05N 112.55E
66 C6 Lugrin France 46.24N 6.40E
77 K6 Lugros Spain 37.15N 3.14W
58 G7 Lugton Strathclyde Scotland 55.45N 4.32W
58 G7 Lugton Water R Strathclyde Scotland
24 E9 Lugu Xizang Zizhiqu China 33.09N 84.10E
71 B6 Luguet, Mt. du France 45.19N 2.59E
92 E4 Lugufu Tanzania 5.01S 30.10E
92 E4 Lugufu R Tanzania
29 J1 Lugu Hill Bihar India 23.46N 85.40E
91 K5 Lugulu R Zaïre
93 E8 Luguru Tanzania 2.56S 33.55E
19 K9 Lugus isld Philippines 5.42N 120.50E
19 B5 Luha isld Celebes Indon 2.47S 121.34E
Luhaiya see Luḥayyah, Al
51 M10 Luhanka Finland 61.46N 25.40E
33 E9 Luḥayyah, Al Yemen 15.44N 42.42E
23 H2 Luhe Jiangsu China 32.20N 118.52E
64 N4 Luhe W Germany 49.35N 12.09E
63 M6 Luhe R W Germany
34 D6 Luhfi, Wādī watercourse Jordan
22 L3 Luhin Sum Nei Monggol Zizhiqu China 46.42N 118.43E
93 A7 Luhiza Uganda 1.03S 29.48E
63 T4 Lühmannsdorf E Germany 54.01N 13.40E
Lu-hsi see Mang-shih
Lu-hsi see Luxi
23 B3 Luhuo Sichuan China 31.18N 100.39E
91 E8 Lui R Angola
92 A9 Lui R Zambia
91 G8 Luia Angola 8.10S 21.32E
91 G8 Luia R Angola
92 F10 Luia R Mozambique
91 H12 Luiana Angola 17.15S 22.50E
91 H12 Luiana R Angola
58 H6 Luib Central Scotland 56.25N 4.26W
58 D4 Luib Skye, Highland Scotland 57.16N 6.03W
58 G3 Luichart, L Highland Scotland 57.36N 4.45W
23 D5 Luichong He R Guizhou China
94 N3 Luido Mozambique 21.31S 34.41E
41 N2 Luidzhi, Ostrov isld Franz Josef Land U.S.S.R.
91 E6 Luie R Zaïre
60 K14 Luijksgestel Netherlands 51.17N 5.19E
91 K6 Luika R Zaïre
91 H10 Luila Angola 12.35S 23.33E
91 G4 Luilaka R Zaïre
91 H7 Luilu R Zaïre
91 D10 Luimbale Angola 12.13S 15.19E
91 E9 Luimbe tribe Angola
Luimneach see Limerick Irish Rep
58 E6 Luing isld Strathclyde Scotland 56.13N 5.39W
61 C4 Luingne Belgium 50.44N 3.14E
79 E2 Luino Italy 46.00N 8.44E
91 G10 Luio R Angola
Luiri Hill see Myooye
51 N4 Luirojoki R Finland
118 E10 Luís Alves Brazil 26.44S 48.58W
117 G6 Luís Correia Brazil 2.54S 41.39W
117 H8 Luís Gomes Brazil 6.23S 38.23W
91 K9 Luishia Zaïre 11.10S 27.04E
77 F5 Luisiana, La Spain 37.32N 5.14W
115 H5 Luis Moya Durango Mexico 24.36N 103.59W
115 H6 Luis Moya Zacatecas Mexico 22.28N 102.17W
117 G9 Luís Viana Brazil 8.44S 41.19W
91 F8 Luita Angola 8.02S 19.27E
123 D10 Luitpold Coast Antarctica
91 H7 Luiza Zaïre 7.11S 22.27E
91 K7 Luizi Zaïre 6.01S 27.30E
92 C5 Luizi R Zaïre
121 C4 Luján Argentina 33.05S 68.53W
121 F5 Lujan Argentina 34.41S 59.05W
121 F5 Lujan R Argentina
77 K7 Lújar Spain 36.47N 3.24W
23 H3 Lujiang Anhui China 31.16N 117.14E
23 E7 Lujing Guangxi China 22.15N 110.31E
22 E6 Lu Jing well Nei Monggol Zizhiqu China 41.51N 99.26E
64 P3 Luka Czechoslovakia 50.10N 13.09E
80 N1 Luka Yugoslavia 43.44N 15.48E
91 K5 Lukabia Zaïre 2.52S 27.10E
40 F5 Lukachek U.S.S.R. 53.10N 132.15E
65 P7 Lukacshaza Hungary 47.20N 16.34E
91 K9 Lukafu Zaïre 10.28S 27.32E
65 N3 Luka nad Jihlavou Czech 49.23N 15.43E
92 D8 Lukanga R Zambia
92 C9 Lukanga Swamp Zambia
45 G5 Lukashevka U.S.S.R. 51.38N 35.36E
42 B2 Lukashkin Yar U.S.S.R. 60.26N 78.24E
23 B10 Luk Chau Hong Kong 22.12N 114.07E
Lukchun see Lükqün
14 B7 Luke, Mt W Australia 27.13S 116.50E
91 F5 Lukenie R Zaïre
91 J6 Lukeshi R Zaïre
46 M2 Lukh U.S.S.R. 56.59N 42.19E
46 M2 Lukh R U.S.S.R.
31 B3 Lukh-i-Surkh Afghanistan 35.14N 63.28E
45 L2 Lukhovitsy U.S.S.R. 54.58N 39.02E
42 G5 Lukinovo U.S.S.R. 54.10N 104.40E
85 H4 Lukk Libya 31.57N 24.46E
66 M5 Lukmanier Pass Switzerland 46.34N 8.48E
45 N1 Luknovo U.S.S.R. 56.10N 42.00E
91 E4 Lukolela Zaïre 1.10S 17.11E
91 J6 Lukolela Zaïre 5.23S 24.32E
93 D5 Lukoma Uganda 0.30N 32.16E
92 G7 Lukoma B Tanzania
46 G3 Lukom'skoye, Ozero L Belorussiya U.S.S.R.
91 K8 Lukonde Zaïre 9.55S 27.28E
92 H6 Lukongole Tanzania 9.05S 37.30E
92 D6 Lukonzolwa Zaïre 8.45S 28.40E
91 H9 Lukoshi R Zaïre
92 C11 Lukosi Zimbabwe 18.30S 26.25E
Lukou see Zhuzhou
82 F9 Lukova Yugoslavia 41.20N 20.38E
45 H4 Lukovets U.S.S.R. 52.19N 36.40E
82 J7 Lukovit Bulgaria 43.11N 24.10E
47 M3 Lukovka U.S.S.R. 58.04N 59.02E
62 N4 Łuków Poland 51.57N 22.21E
45 Q1 Lukoyanov U.S.S.R. 55.03N 44.29E
24 F4 Lükqün Xinjiang Uygur Zizhiqu China 42.49N 89.40E
91 C6 Lukt Zaïre 5.38S 13.04E
93 E7 Lukuba I Tanzania 1.25S 33.42E
91 K6 Lukuga R Zaïre
Lukuk see Luwu
91 C6 Lukula Zaïre 5.21S 13.02E
91 J7 Lukuledi R Tanzania
44 C10 Lukull, Mys C Ukraine U.S.S.R. 44.51N 33.33E
92 A9 Lukulu Zambia 14.28S 23.12E
92 E8 Lukulu R Zambia
92 G6 Lukumburu Tanzania 9.42S 35.07E
91 D6 Lukunga Zaïre 5.00S 14.17E
91 E6 Lukuni Zaïre 5.50S 17.16E
41 H4 Lukunskiy U.S.S.R. 72.32N 104.46E
18 B3 Lukup Sumatra Indon 4.24N 97.33E
92 D8 Lukusashi R Zaïre
92 E9 Lukusashi R Zambia
92 F8 Lukusuzi Nat. Park Zambia
92 F8 Lukuzye R Zambia
30 A7 Lukwasa Madhya Prad India 25.07N 77.36E
92 J7 Lukwika Tanzania 11.10S 38.35E
105 D3 Lula Georgia 34.22N 83.40W
107 F7 Lula Mississippi 34.28N 90.29W
81 C3 Lula Sardinia 40.28N 9.30E
91 G5 Lula R Zaïre
51 J6 Luleå Sweden 65.35N 22.10E
51 J6 Lule älv R Sweden
36 C1 Luleburgaz Turkey 41.25N 27.22E
91 G7 Lulemba Zaïre 6.38S 21.14E
120 F12 Lules Argentina 26.54S 65.25W
Luli R see Lurio R
23 C6 Luliang Yunnan China 25.05N 103.39E
22 J8 Lüliang Shan mt ra Shanxi China
107 F12 Luling Louisiana 29.56N 90.24W
112 K6 Luling Texas 29.40N 97.40W
66 C6 Lullin France 46.17N 6.31E
66 B6 Lully France 46.17N 6.25E
91 F8 Lulo R Angola
22 L7 Lulong Hebei China 39.52N 118.50E
91 F3 Lulonga Zaïre 0.32N 18.25E
91 F3 Lulonga R Zaïre
56 F5 Lulsgate airport Avon Eng 51.24N 2.44W
105 E7 Lulu Florida 30.06N 82.30W
32 C6 Lulu oil well The Gulf 28.43N 49.30E
33 H2 Lulu oil field The Gulf 28.42N 49.27E
91 H3 Lulu R Zaïre
91 G6 Lulua R Zaïre
Luluabourg see Kananga
101 G11 Lulu I Br Col
24 E11 Lülung Xizang Zizhiqu China 29.02N 85.57E
Luluvato see Chirovanga
56 G6 Lulworth Cove Dorset Eng 50.37N 2.15W
14 C7 Lulworth, Mt W Australia 26.57N 117.43E
122 F1 Luma Amer Samoa Pacific Oc 14.15S 169.30W
93 B3 Luma Zaïre 2.34N 30.38E
91 F9 Luma-Cassai Angola 11.17S 19.50E

91 G10 Lumai Angola 13.13S 21.13E
18 K10 Lumajang Java Indon 8.06S 113.13E
24 D8 Lumajangdong Co *L* Xizang Zizhiqu China 34.02N 81.40E
18 L3 Lumaku, Gunong *mt* Sabah Malaysia 4.48N 115.43E
30 F1 Luma Nakpo Xizang Zizhiqu 31.10N 82.13E
91 G11 Lumbala Angola 14.08S 21.25E
91 H10 Lumbala Angola 12.37S 22.33E
91 G10 Lumbala *R* Angola
119 C8 Lumbaqui Ecuador 0.02S 77.33W
92 A10 Lumbe *R* Zambia
105 E6 Lumber City Georgia 31.56N 82.41W
104 G6 Lumber City Pennsylvania 40.56N 78.37W
104 E7 Lumberport W Virginia 39.22N 80.23W
105 H3 Lumber, R N Carolina
107 G10 Lumberton Mississippi 31.01N 89.27W
105 H3 Lumberton N Carolina 34.37N 79.03W
109 D5 Lumberton New Mexico 36.55N 106.56W
91 E6 Lumbi Zaïre 4.59S 17.58E
75 H2 Lumbier Spain 42.39N 1.19W
18 M3 Lumbis Borneo Indon 4.17N 116.15E
92 K9 Lumbo Mozambique 15.00S 40.40E
47 E2 Lumbovka U.S.S.R. 67.42N 40.35E
76 F7 Lumbrales Spain 40.56N 6.44W
75 E3 Lumbreras Spain 42.06N 2.38W
69 C2 Lumbres France 50.43N 2.07E
Lumbur Ringmo Tso *L see* Lu-pu-erh-ho-mu Hu
93 G6 Lumbwa Kenya 0.12S 35.30E
53 E6 Lumby Denmark 55.28N 10.23E
28 J3 Lumding Assam India 25.46N 93.10E
91 G9 Lumeje Angola 11.34S 20.50E
91 E6 Lumeme *R* Zaïre
65 J7 Lumgau *reg* Austria
15 G5 Lumi Papua New Guinea 3.30S 142.02E
76 A11 Lumiar Portugal 38.46N 9.09W
51 L7 Lumijoki Finland 64.51N 25.10E
92 F8 Lumimba *R* Zambia
67 O11 Lumio Corsica 42.34N 8.49E
61 L3 Lummen Belgium 50.58N 5.11E
51 H11 Lumparland Finland 60.06N 20.15E
91 H5 Lumpeto Zaïre 2.59S 23.08E
58 L4 Lumphanan Grampian Scotland 57.08N 2.42W
75 H4 Lumpiaque Spain 41.37N 1.18W
105 C5 Lumpkin Georgia 32.03N 84.49W
53 H5 Lumsås Denmark 55.58N 11.32E
58 L4 Lumsden Grampian Scotland 57.17N 2.53W
98 T4 Lumsden Newfoundland 49.18N 53.39W
11 C12 Lumsden New Zealand 45.45S 168.27E
100 N8 Lumsden Saskatchewan 50.39N 104.52W
19 A5 Lumu Celebes Indon 2.12S 119.12E
91 K5 Lumuna Zaïre 3.47S 26.30E
91 G12 Lumuna *R* Angola
18 A7 Lumut Pen Malaysia 4.13N 100.37E
18 L6 Lumut, Gunung *mt* Borneo Indon 1.23S 115.57E
18 B9 Lumut, Pulau *isld* Pen Malaysia
18 F7 Lumut, Tanjung *C* Sumatra Indonesia 3.50S 105.57E
22 F3 Lün Mongolia 47.20N 102.50E
22 G3 Lün Mongolia 47.52N 105.19E
19 K3 Luna Luzon Philippines 16.52N 120.24E
109 B8 Luna New Mexico 33.49N 108.57W
75 J3 Luna Spain 42.10N 0.56W
45 H10 Lunacharskoye Ukraine U.S.S.R. 46.50N 36.41E
91 H10 Lunache Angola 12.09S 22.42E
69 D7 Lunain *R* France
30 F2 Lunak Glacier Nepal
121 G2 Luna, L Argentina
81 B4 Lunamatrona Sardinia 39.38N 8.54E
23 C6 Lunan Yunnan China 24.47N 103.17E
58 L5 Lunan B Tayside Scotland 56.38N 2.30W
23 C5 Lunan Shan *mt ra* Sichuan China
120 G1 Luna, R Brazil
71 C9 Lunas France 43.42N 3.12E
29 C6 Lunavada Gujarat India 23.08N 73.40E
18 D10 Lunchoo *hill* Pen Malaysia 1.30N 103.52E
101 L10 Lund Br Columbia 50.01N 124.46W
53 D5 Lund Denmark 55.53N 9.47E
111 J3 Lund Nevada 38.50N 115.01W
31 E7 Lund Pakistan 27.24N 69.22E
52 G11 Lund Sweden 55.42N 13.10E
111 L3 Lund Utah 38.01N 113.25W
52 K8 Lunda Sweden 58.44N 16.45E
91 F8 Lunda *dist* Angola
92 B8 Lunda *tribe* Zambia
92 D7 Lunda *tribe* Zambia
53 Y15 Lundadalsvatnet *L* Norway 61.46N 8.02E
53 K5 Lundåkrabukten *B* Sweden 55.48N 12.50E
100 T8 Lundar Manitoba 50.41N 98.01W
50 H4 Lundarbrekka Iceland 65.28N 17.25W
50 D5 Lundarreykjadalur *V* Iceland
92 F8 Lundazi Zambia 12.19S 33.11E
92 F8 Lundazi *R* Zambia
100 C9 Lundbreck Alberta 49.35N 114.04W
53 C3 Lundby Nordjylland Denmark 56.57N 9.28E
53 H6 Lundby Storstrøm Denmark 55.07N 11.53E
53 E6 Lunde Fyn Denmark 55.29N 10.22E
53 V15 Lunde Norway 61.31N 6.38E
53 A5 Lunde Ribe Denmark 55.46N 8.23E
53 F6 Lundeborg Denmark 55.08N 10.47E
63 K4 Lunden W Germany 54.20N 9.02E
53 C6 Lunderskov Denmark 55.28N 9.18E
50 H2 Lundey *isld* Iceland 66.08N 17.20W
92 E12 Lundi *R* Zimbabwe
53 C3 Lundø Denmark 56.38N 9.09E
31 H4 Lundra Kashmir 33.07N 75.10E
18 H5 Lundu Sarawak Malaysia 1.40N 109.52E
53 D5 Lundum Denmark 55.56N 9.47E
50 D5 Lundur Iceland 64.33N 21.19W
56 B5 Lundy *isld* Devon Eng 51.11N 4.40W
63 M6 Lüne W Germany 53.16N 10.26E
63 J6 Lüne *R* W Germany
64 A3 Lünebach W Germany 50.08N 6.21E
63 M6 Lüneburg W Germany 53.15N 10.24E
63 L6 Lüneburger Heide *reg* W Germany
71 E9 Lunel France 43.40N 4.08E
63 G9 Lünen W Germany 51.37N 7.31E
98 H9 Lunenburg Nova Scotia 44.23N 64.21W
99 S1 Lunenburg Ontario 45.04N 74.58W
104 O2 Lunenburg Vermont 44.28N 71.39W
57 H4 Lune, R Lancs Eng
70 M2 Luneray France 49.50N 0.55E
65 A7 Lüner See *L* Austria 47.04N 9.45E
72 J2 Lunery France 46.56N 2.15E
69 L6 Lunéville France 48.35N 6.30E
92 K9 Lunga Mozambique 15.12S 40.32E
91 C6 Lunga Zaïre 5.46S 12.14E
92 C8 Lunga *R* Zambia
93 N6 Lungana Somalia 0.53S 41.14E
30 G3 Lungare Nepal 27.56N 86.40E
79 F4 Lungavilla Italy 45.02N 9.04E
24 D9 Lungdo Xizang Zizhiqu China 33.45N 82.09E
91 E10 Lunge Angola 12.13S 16.07E
66 J4 Lungern Switzerland 46.48N 8.10E
66 J4 Lungern-see *L* Switzerland
15 L3 Lungga Guadalcanal I Solomon Is 9.25S 160.02E
24 E10 Lunggar Xizang Zizhiqu China 31.10N 84.01E
Lung-hui *see* Longhui
89 C7 Lungi Sierra Leone 8.40N 13.17W
41 N8 Lungkha *R* U.S.S.R.
28 J1 Lung La *pass* Xizang Zizhiqu 29.24N 92.32E
28 J4 Lungleh Mizoram India 22.55N 92.49E
25 E8 Lung, Mae *R* Thailand
D8 Lungnak Pass *pass* Xizang Zizhiqu China 34.27N 81.09E
79 L1 Lungo, Sasso il *mt* Italy 46.32N 11.44E
81 M4 Lungro Italy 39.44N 16.07E
30 G2 Lungsampa Glacier Nepal
24 F11 Lungsang Xizang Zizhiqu China 29.50N 88.27E
Lungshan *see* Mashan Guangxi
52 J3 Lungsjön Sweden 63.28N 16.20E
52 H7 Lungsund Sweden 59.32N 14.13E
Lungtan *see* Longtan
30 L5 Lungthung Nepal 27.34N 87.48E
92 E6 Lungu *tribe* Zambia
91 G10 Lungue-Bungo *R* Angola
91 F8 Lunguena Angola 9.04S 19.44E
93 D9 Lunguya Tanzania 3.23S 32.25E
29 C4 Luni Rajasthan India 26.02N 73.09E
79 G6 Lunigiana *dist* Italy
46 F4 Luninets Belorussiya U.S.S.R. 52.18N 26.50E
111 F3 Luning Nevada 38.30N 118.10W
23 B4 Luning Sichuan China 28.22N 101.56E
45 R3 Lunino U.S.S.R. 53.37N 45.15E
31 E5 Luni R Pakistan
29 B5 Luni R Rajasthan India
91 G9 Lunjata Angola 10.04S 20.20E
29 C3 Lunkaransar Rajasthan India 28.32N 73.50E
Lunkar Gompa *see* Lunggar
24 D10 Lunkar La *pass* Xizang Zizhiqu China 31.05N 83.55E
Lunkar Ra *see* Kan-shu-erh-la Shan *mts*
29 C3 Lunkha Rajasthan India 28.42N 72.56E
31 G2 Lunkho *mt* Afghanistan 36.49N 72.30E
58 Q9 Lunna Shetland Scotland 60.24N 1.07W
58 Q9 Lunna Ness *prom* Shetland Scotland 60.27N 1.03W
63 F8 Lünne W Germany 52.26N 7.26E
15 L9 Lunn I Louisiade Arch 10.47S 151.59E
58 Q9 Lunning Shetland Scotland 60.23N 1.05W
39 G4 Lunovayam U.S.S.R. 60.05N 164.40E
92 D9 Lunsemfwa *R* Zambia
92 D9 Lunsemfwa Wonder Gorge Zambia 14.30S 29.06E
94 K5 Lunsklip S Africa 24.02S 29.02E
64 M1 Lunstädt E Germany 51.15N 11.55E
24 E5 Luntai Xinjiang Uygur Zizhiqu China 41.45N 84.10E
60 L11 Lunteren Netherlands 52.05N 5.38E
26 T7 Lunugala Sri Lanka 7.05N 81.13E
18 M10 Lunyuk Indonesia 9.00S 117.16E
65 M6 Lunz am See *L* Austria 47.52N 15.02E
64 O2 Lunzenau E Germany 50.57N 12.45E
92 F7 Lunzi *R* Zambia
21 E4 Luobei Heilongjiang China 47.35N 130.56E
91 C6 Luobomo Congo 4.09S 12.47E
24 F6 Luobuzhuang Xinjiang Uygur Zizhiqu China 39.28N 88.17E
22 E7 Luocheng Gansu China 39.40N 99.32E
23 E6 Luocheng Guangxi China 24.45N 108.52E
23 E1 Luochuan Shaanxi China 35.55N 109.28E
23 C6 Luoci Yunnan China 25.15N 102.20E
23 D6 Luodian Guizhou China 25.25N 106.49E
23 F7 Luoding Guangdong China 22.40N 111.32E
25 L2 Luodou Sha *isld* Guangdong China
92 D2 Luofu Zaïre 0.38S 29.08E
21 B1 Luoguhe Heilongjiang China 53.24N 121.31E
23 G2 Luohe Henan China 33.33N 114.00E
23 F1 Luo He *R* Henan China
22 H8 Luo He *R* Shaanxi China
23 E1 Luo He *R* Shaanxi China
23 C3 Luojiang Sichuan China 31.20N 104.31E
23 F7 Luojing Guangdong China 22.32N 111.13E
23 D4 Luolong Guizhou China 29.04N 107.44E
23 E1 Luonan Shaanxi China 34.09N 110.04E
51 J4 Luongastunturu *mt* Sweden 67.38N 21.10E
92 D7 Luongo *R* Zambia
23 F1 Luoning Henan China 34.21N 111.37E
23 C6 Luoping Yunnan China 24.58N 104.20E
23 E6 Luoqing Jiang *R* Guangxi China
23 E6 Luorong Guangxi China 24.26N 109.32E
23 G2 Luoshan Henan China 32.12N 114.30E
23 F4 Luoshan Hubei China 29.40N 113.17E
23 G3 Luotian Hubei China 30.55N 115.28E
Luoto *see* Larsmo
21 B4 Luotuobozi Heilongjiang China 47.11N 122.09E
23 D3 Luowenba Sichuan China 31.47N 107.50E
23 F1 Luoyang Henan China 34.47N 112.26E
23 H5 Luoyuan Fujian China 26.25N 119.33E
91 D6 Luozi Zaïre 4.56S 14.14E
92 F6 Lupa *R* Tanzania
94 E1 Lupala Namibia 17.50S 19.05E
92 F6 Lupa Market Tanzania 8.40S 33.16E
92 C11 Lupane Zimbabwe 18.54S 27.44E
92 D11 Lupane *dist* Zimbabwe
92 D11 Lupani *R* Zimbabwe
18 J5 Lupar *R* Sarawak Malaysia
62 K1 Łupawa *R* Poland
64 M5 Lupburg W Germany 49.09N 11.46E
92 G6 Lupembe Tanzania 9.12S 35.10E
82 H5 Lupeni Romania 45.20N 23.10E
116 J5 Luperón Dominican Rep 19.54N 70.57W
64 F7 Lupfen *mt* W Germany 48.02N 8.40E
66 J2 Lupfig Switzerland 47.26N 8.15E
72 E8 Lupiac France 43.41N 0.12E
92 G7 Lupilichi Mozambique 11.45S 35.15E
23 D5 Luping Guizhou China 26.47N 107.38E
91 F11 Lupire Angola 14.35S 19.31E
92 H6 Lupiro Tanzania 8.25S 36.39E
45 B3 Lupolovo Belorussiya U.S.S.R. 53.53N 30.21E
92 F5 Lupombelo Tanzania 7.50S 33.00E
19 N8 Lupon Mindanao Philippines 6.53N 126.02E
91 K9 Lupoto Zaïre 11.16S 26.55E
63 R10 Luppa E Germany 51.21N 12.58E
69 L6 Luppy France 48.59N 6.21E
57 H4 Lupton Cumbria Eng 54.14N 2.42W
24 E9 Lu-pu-erh-ho-mu Hu *L* Xizang Zizhiqu China 33.04N 84.03E
107 D3 Lupus Missouri 38.50N 92.27W
91 H7 Luputa Zaïre 7.07S 23.43E
91 J8 Lupweji *R* Zaïre
47 F5 Lup'ya *R* Arkhangel'sk U.S.S.R.
47 G5 Lup'ya *R* Komi U.S.S.R.
84 Y20 Luqa Malta 35.52N 14.30E
84 Y20 Luqa International Airport Malta
Lu Qu *see* Tao He
23 C1 Luqu Gansu China 34.33N 102.24E
23 C6 Luquan Yunnan China 25.35N 102.28E
118 B9 Luque Paraguay 25.12S 57.38W
77 H5 Luque Spain 37.35N 4.16W
91 E9 Luquembo Angola 10.44S 17.43E
105 K7 Luquillo Puerto Rico 18.23N 65.44W
93 H3 Lurachi Kenya 2.46N 36.50E
81 C2 Luras Sardinia 40.57N 9.11E
32 A2 Lūrā Shīrīn Iran 37.57N 44.32E
109 M2 Luray Kansas 39.07N 98.41W
104 G8 Luray Virginia 38.40N 78.28W
72 C9 Lurbe France 43.07N 0.36W
72 K2 Lurcy-Lévis France 46.44N 2.55E
Lurdagan *see* Lordegān
71 J1 Lure France 47.42N 6.30E
92 H8 Lureco *R* Mozambique
105 E2 Lure, L N Carolina
91 E8 Luremo Angola 8.31S 17.50E
71 H8 Lure, Mtgne. de France 44.06N 5.46E
58 F2 Lurgain, L Highland Scotland 58.01N 5.12W
59 K3 Lurgan Armagh N Ireland 54.28N 6.20W
32 H4 Lūrg-e-Shotorān *salt marsh* Iran 32.00N 60.00E
Lurg-i-Shurturan *see* Lūrg-e-Shotorān
65 M7 Lurgrotte Austria 47.15N 15.23E
67 P11 Luri Corsica 42.53N 9.23E
87 C8 Luri *watercourse* Sudan
120 E7 Luribay Bolivia 17.05S 67.37W
120 B5 Lurín Peru 12.16S 76.53W
92 K8 Lurio Mozambique 13.32S 40.30E
92 J8 Lurio *R* Mozambique
92 K8 Lurio, B. de Mozambique
34 O5 Luristan *reg* Iran
51 C5 Lurøy Norway 66.25N 12.50E
71 H9 Lurs France 43.58N 5.52E
93 L5 Lurt, El Kenya 0.19N 39.03E
107 C6 Lurton Arkansas 35.48N 93.05W
72 J1 Lury sur-Arnon France 47.08N 2.03E
30 F8 Lusa Uttar Prad India 24.56N 82.49E
93 C8 Lusahanga Tanzania 2.55S 31.12E
91 J7 Lusaka Zaïre 6.54S 25.19E
92 D9 Lusaka Zambia 15.26S 28.20E
91 H6 Lusambo Zaïre 4.59S 23.26E
15 K8 Lusancay Is & Reefs Trobriand Is Papua New Guinea
91 F3 Lusangania Zaïre 0.09N 19.29E
92 E8 Lusangazi Zambia 13.28S 31.32E
70 G6 Lusanger France 47.41N 1.35W
91 K6 Lusangi Zaïre 4.39S 27.10E
101 P9 Luscar Alberta 53.05N 117.26W
100 H6 Luseland Saskatchewan 52.06N 109.24W
64 Q6 Lusen *mt* W Germany 48.56N 13.32E
79 C3 Luseney *mt* Italy 45.52N 7.30E
91 K5 Lusenge Zaïre 3.39S 27.08E
91 F3 Lusengo Zaïre 1.47N 19.31E
79 B5 Luserna San Giovanni Italy 44.48N 7.15E
79 O2 Lusévera Italy 46.17N 13.16E
23 F2 Lushan Henan China 33.44N 112.55E
23 C3 Lushan Sichuan China 30.14N 102.59E
22 L8 Lu Shan *mts* Shandong China 36.20N 117.10E
23 F1 Lushi Henan China 34.02N 111.03E
14 F3 Lush, Mt W Australia 17.03S 127.25E
83 D4 Lushnje Albania 40.57N 19.41E
92 J4 Lushoto Tanzania 4.48S 38.20E
23 A6 Lushui Yunnan China 25.57N 98.49E
23 G5 Lu Shui *R* Jiangxi China
22 M7 Lushun Liaoning China 38.46N 121.15E
21 B8 Lüshun Liaoning China 38.46N 121.15E
92 C8 Lushwishi *R* Zambia
23 J2 Lüsi Jiangsu China 32.02N 121.40E
18 J9 Lusi *R* Java Indon
91 H8 Lusia *R* Zaïre
72 E3 Lusignan France 46.26N 0.08E
71 C3 Lusigny Allier France 46.35N 3.28E
69 G7 Lusigny-sur-Barse Aube France 48.16N 4.16E
92 D2 Lusika Zaïre 0.20S 28.06E
95 N7 Lusikisiki S Africa 31.22S 29.35E
10 B11 Lusitania B Macquarie I Pacific Oc
92 D10 Lusitu *R* Zambia
92 E8 Lusiwasi, L Zambia 13.00S 30.50E
59 K4 Lusk Dublin Irish Rep 53.32N 6.10W
108 F7 Lusk Wyoming 42.47N 104.26W
58 C3 Luskentyre Harris, W Isles Scotland 57.53N 6.57W
71 H7 Lus-la-Croix-Haute France 44.40N 5.42E
76 C8 Luso Portugal 40.23N 8.22W
Luso Angola *see* Luena
79 L1 Lusón Italy 46.45N 11.47E
91 K7 Lusonde Zaïre 7.09S 26.48E
51 H4 Luspebryggan Sweden 67.02N 19.50E
58 G6 Luss Strathclyde Scotland 56.07N 4.38W
72 D6 Lussac France 44.56N 0.06W
72 F3 Lussac-les Châteaux France 46.24N 0.44E
72 G3 Lussac-les-Églises France 46.21N 1.11E
71 E8 Lussan France 44.08N 4.22E
118 D7 Lussanvira Brazil 20.42S 51.08W
34 L7 Lussuf, Al Iraq 31.31N 43.12E
13 J7 Lussvale Queensland 27.09S 147.34E
64 E5 Lustadt W Germany 49.15N 8.16E
65 A7 Lustenau Austria 47.26N 9.42E
64 J5 Lustenau W Germany 49.08N 10.16E
53 W16 Luster Norway 61.27N 7.28E
53 W16 Lusterfjorden *inlet* Norway
61 K5 Lustin Belgium 50.23N 4.54E
76 C6 Lustosa Portugal 41.20N 8.20W
108 E1 Lustre Montana 48.26N 105.54W
91 K8 Luswaka Zaïre 9.53S 26.30E
79 L1 Lutago Italy 46.57N 11.56E
Lutai *see* Ninghe
107 F11 Lutcher Louisiana 30.02N 90.43W
91 G10 Lutembo Angola 13.28S 21.23E
66 G3 Luterbach Switzerland 47.13N 7.35E
107 G4 Lutesville Missouri 37.16N 89.59W
91 D8 Lutete *R* Angola
Lutfabad *see* Lotfābād
109 N6 Luther Oklahoma 35.40N 97.13W
66 H3 Luthern Switzerland 47.04N 7.55E
66 H3 Luthernbad Switzerland 47.02N 7.56E
103 A8 Lutherville Maryland 39.26N 76.37W
112 D8 Lutie Texas 35.02N 100.13W
Lu-tien *see* Ludian
66 N2 Lütisburg Switzerland 47.24N 9.05E
66 O3 Lütispitz *mt* Switzerland 47.14N 9.17E
63 O4 Lütjenbrode W Germany 54.22N 11.02E
63 N4 Lütjenburg W Germany 54.17N 10.36E
93 B6 Lutoma Uganda 0.22S 30.35E
56 L4 Luton Beds Eng 51.53N 0.25W
18 K3 Lutong Sarawak 4.30N 113.59E
66 C5 Lutry Switzerland 46.31N 6.42E
45 E6 Lutsenki Ukraine U.S.S.R. 50.27N 33.04E
91 F6 Lutshima Zaïre 5.27S 19.03E
91 G6 Lutshwadi *R* Zaïre
46 F4 Lutsk Ukraine U.S.S.R. 50.42N 25.15E
60 Q10 Lutte, De Netherlands 52.19N 7.00E
60 M8 Luttelgeest Netherlands 52.45N 5.52E
60 P9 Lutten Netherlands 52.37N 6.34E
60 O10 Luttenberg Netherlands 52.24N 6.22E
63 M9 Lutter am Barenberge W Germany 51.59N 10.15E
66 F1 Lutterbach France 47.46N 7.17E
63 M7 Lutterloh W Germany 52.49N 10.12E
56 J3 Lutterworth Leics Eng 52.28N 1.10W
95 F8 Luttig S Africa 32.39S 22.07E
61 H4 Luttre Belgium 50.31N 4.24E
105 D1 Luttrel Tennessee 36.13N 83.44W
64 C1 Lüttringhausen W Germany 51.13N 7.22E
91 G10 Lutuai Angola 12.39S 20.12E
45 L8 Lutugino Ukraine U.S.S.R. 48.24N 39.15E
93 G3 Luturere Hills Kenya
105 E9 Lutz Florida 28.10N 82.29W
66 Q3 Lutz *R* Austria
69 N6 Lutzelbourg France 48.45N 7.15E
66 G3 Lützelflüh Switzerland 47.01N 7.42E
69 N6 Lutzelhouse France 48.32N 7.18E
64 N1 Lützen E Germany 51.15N 12.09E
64 C3 Lutzerath W Germany 50.08N 7.01E
65 P7 Lutzmannsburg Austria 47.28N 16.37E
63 O5 Lützow E Germany 53.39N 11.11E
123 A6 Lützow-Holmbukta *B* Antarctica
94 E8 Lutzville Cape Prov S Africa 31.46S 18.21E
51 N11 Luumäki Finland 60.54N 27.40E
22 G4 Luus Mongolia 45.23N 105.40E
51 N5 Luusua Finland 66.29N 27.17E
92 A8 Luvale *tribe* Zambia
66 N4 Luven Switzerland 46.46N 9.12E
107 K10 Luverne Alabama 31.43N 86.18W
108 Q7 Luverne Iowa 42.55N 94.05W
108 O6 Luverne Minnesota 43.39N 96.11W
108 N2 Luverne N Dakota 47.17N 97.56W
51 J10 Luvia Finland 61.23N 21.35E
91 K7 Luvidjo *R* Zaïre
93 A9 Luvironza *R* Burundi
91 D6 Luvo Angola 5.52S 14.10E
51 G5 Luvos Sweden 66.40N 18.50E
51 P7 Luvozero Karelia U.S.S.R. 64.29N 30.46E
91 J8 Luvua Zaïre 8.49S 25.19E
92 D5 Luvua *R* Zaïre
91 G10 Luvuei Angola 13.06S 21.11E
92 D3 Luvungi Zaïre 2.51S 28.58E
92 E8 Luvushi Manda Nat. Park Zambia
92 H6 Luwegu *R* Tanzania
93 D5 Luwero Uganda 0.51N 32.30E
92 D7 Luwingu Zambia 10.13S 29.58E
19 F3 Luwo *isld* Moluccas Indon 0.27N 128.55E
23 E7 Luwu Guangxi China 22.16N 108.55E
19 C4 Luwuk Celebes Indon 0.56S 122.47E
92 F7 Luwumbu *R* Zambia
71 G2 Lux France 47.30N 5.13E
107 J8 Luxapalila *R* Alabama
61 P8 Luxembourg Luxembourg 49.37N 6.08E
61 L7 Luxembourg *prov* Belgium
61 O7 Luxembourg, Grand Duchy of Europe
106 C7 Luxemburg Iowa 42.35N 91.04W
72 B9 Luxe-Sumberraute France 43.21N 1.03W
69 L8 Luxeuil-les-Bains France 47.49N 6.24E
72 C7 Luxey France 44.16N 0.30W
23 E4 Luxi Hunan China 28.16N 110.03E
23 A6 Luxi Yunnan China 24.25N 98.35E
23 C6 Luxi Yunnan China 24.32N 103.43E
23 D4 Lu Xian Sichuan China 28.56N 105.27E
85 M7 Luxor Egypt 25.41N 32.24E
60 M8 Luxwoude Netherlands 53.00N 5.59E
72 B8 Luy *R* France
91 K5 Luyamba Zaïre 3.27S 26.26E
72 D8 Luy-de-Béarn *R* France
76 G4 Luyego Spain 42.22N 6.15W
95 P2 Luyengo Swaziland 26.35S 31.10E
95 M6 Luyengweni S Africa 30.38S 28.48E
23 G2 Luyi Henan China 33.51N 115.29E
70 M7 Luynes France 47.23N 0.34E
96 R2 Luz Azores 39.02N 27.59W
76 B14 Luz Portugal 37.05N 8.44W
76 E12 Luz Portugal 38.20N 7.24W
121 J5 Luz *isld* Chile 45.30S 74.00W
47 F5 Luza U.S.S.R. 60.41N 47.12E
47 F5 Luza *R* Kirov etc U.S.S.R.
47 H3 Luza *R* Komi U.S.S.R.
75 F6 Luzaga Spain 40.59N 2.26W
69 C5 Luzarches France 49.07N 2.26E
65 O2 Luže Czechoslovakia 49.54N 16.03E
23 C2 Luzê Gansu China 33.45N 104.00E
72 G7 Luzech France 44.28N 1.17E
72 J5 Luzège *R* France
117 A6 Luzeia Brazil 3.15S 57.37W
72 H10 Luzenac France 42.44N 1.46E
72 G2 Luzeret France 46.33N 1.24E
66 K3 Luzern Switzerland 47.03N 8.17E
66 J3 Luzern *canton* Switzerland
106 K5 Luzerne Michigan 44.37N 84.16W
104 M3 Luzerne New York 43.19N 73.53W
103 C4 Luzerne Pennsylvania 41.17N 75.52W
103 C4 Luzerne *co* Pennsylvania
23 E6 Luzhai Guangxi China 24.30N 109.35E
Luzhangjie *see* Lushui
23 D5 Luzhi Guizhou China 26.21N 105.16E
45 F5 Luzhki Ukraine U.S.S.R. 51.47N 34.10E
23 D4 Luzhou Sichuan China 28.55N 105.25E
91 G10 Luzi *R* Angola
118 F5 Luziânia Brazil 16.16S 47.57W
66 P3 Luziensteig Switzerland 47.03N 9.32E
117 F6 Luzilândia Brazil 3.29S 42.23W
71 C5 Luzillat France 45.57N 3.23E
72 G1 Luzillé France 47.16N 1.03E
66 C1 Luzine *R* France
93 E5 Luzinga Uganda 0.42N 33.13E
41 E6 Luzino U.S.S.R. 69.00N 85.46E
35 C7 Luzit Israel 31.42N 34.53E
65 J1 Lužná Czechoslovakia 50.11N 13.47E
65 L4 Luznice *R* Czechoslovakia
75 F5 Luzón Spain 41.01N 2.16W
19 L3 Luzon *isld* Philippines
19 F2 Luzon Pt Luzon Philippines 14.28N 120.24E
19 K1 Luzon Str Philippines
72 D10 Luz-St. Sauveur France 42.52N 0.01W
71 D3 Luzy France 46.47N 3.58E
79 J5 Luzzara Italy 44.58N 10.41E
81 M5 Luzzi Italy 39.27N 16.17E
66 M5 Luzzone-see *L* Switzerland
45 H2 L'va Tolstoga U.S.S.R. 54.38N 36.02E
46 E5 L'vov Ukraine U.S.S.R. 49.50N 24.00E
42 B4 L'vovka U.S.S.R. 57.10N 78.40E
46 E5 L'vovskaya Oblast' *prov* Ukraine U.S.S.R.
93 E4 Lwala Uganda 1.52N 33.15E
92 D7 Lwela *R* Zambia
93 C5 Lwemiyaga Uganda 0.07N 31.07E
93 B7 Lwentobo Uganda 1.06S 30.12E
92 E7 Lwitikila *R* Zambia
62 J3 Lwówek Poland 52.28N 16.10E
62 J4 Lwówek Śląski Poland 51.06N 15.36E
53 Z17 Lya *R* Norway
47 D5 Lyadiny U.S.S.R. 61.34N 38.21E
82 L2 Lyadova *R* U.S.S.R.
45 C2 Lyady Belorussiya U.S.S.R. 54.36N 31.09E
43 O8 Lyaglan Kirgiziya U.S.S.R. 40.03N 73.06E
44 F2 Lyagushevskiy U.S.S.R. 45.40N 43.44E
43 N8 Lyakan Tadzhikistan U.S.S.R. 40.12N 70.53E
41 P4 Lyakhovshiye Ostrova *islds* U.S.S.R.
44 H7 Lyaki Azerbaydzhan U.S.S.R. 40.33N 47.25E
11 C6 Lyall B Wellington New Zealand
11 C6 Lyall Bay *dist* Wellington New Zealand
11 B8 Lyall, Mt Campbell I Pacific Oc 52.32S 169.10E
11 B12 Lyall, Mt New Zealand 45.18S 167.38E
31 G5 Lyallpur Pakistan 31.25N 73.09E
31 G5 Lyallpur *dist* Pakistan
43 J7 Lyal'-Mikar Uzbekistan U.S.S.R. 37.38N 67.43E
47 J6 Lyalya *R* U.S.S.R.
45 R2 Lyambir' U.S.S.R. 54.17N 45.09E
47 H2 Lyamchina, Guba *gulf* U.S.S.R.
47 L5 Lyamin *R* U.S.S.R.
47 D4 Lyamtsa U.S.S.R. 64.25N 37.10E
43 O8 Lyangar Kirgiziya U.S.S.R. 40.24N 73.06E
43 H6 Lyangar Samarkand, Uzbekistan U.S.S.R. 40.27N 66.00E
43 H7 Lyangar Surkhan-Dar'inskaya, Uzbekistan U.S.S.R. 38.41N 66.45E
31 F1 Lyangar Tadzhikistan U.S.S.R. 38.54N 70.50E
93 C6 Lyantonde Uganda 0.24S 31.12E
47 J4 Lyapin *R* U.S.S.R.
45 F7 Lyashkovka Ukraine U.S.S.R. 49.01N 34.25E
51 P10 Lyaskelya Karelia U.S.S.R. 61.47N 31.00E
82 K7 Lyaskovets Bulgaria 43.05N 25.42E
66 C6 Lyaud France 46.20N 6.31E
43 M8 Lyaylyak Kirgiziya U.S.S.R. 39.54N 69.55E
31 E1 Lyaylyak Tadzhikistan U.S.S.R. 39.52N 69.54E
109 C5 Lybrook New Mexico 36.13N 107.36W
58 K2 Lybster Highland Scotland 58.18N 3.18W
53 C3 Lyby Denmark 56.39N 9.02E
109 H4 Lycan Colorado 37.33N 102.09W
36 F4 Lycaonia *reg* Turkey
63 S6 Lychen E Germany 53.13N 13.19E
46 H1 Lychkovo U.S.S.R. 58.00N 32.30E
36 D6 Lycia *reg* Turkey
Lyck *see* Ełk
52 L2 Lycksele Sweden 64.34N 18.40E
103 A4 Lycoming *co* Pennsylvania
56 N6 Lydd Kent Eng 50.57N 0.55E
Lydda *see* Lod
100 T3 Lyddal Manitoba 55.02N 98.25W
94 L5 Lydenburg S Africa 25.10S 30.29E
53 J6 Lyderslev Denmark 55.17N 12.18E
56 C6 Lydford Devon Eng 50.39N 4.06W
105 G3 Lydia S Carolina 34.19N 80.08W
100 V9 Lydiatt Manitoba 50.03N 96.27W
56 F4 Lydney Glos Eng 51.44N 2.32W
53 A5 Lydum Denmark 55.48N 8.22E
53 A5 Lydum Å *R* Denmark
72 G1 Lye France 47.13N 1.28E
56 G3 Lye W Midlands Eng 52.27N 2.07W
11 G8 Lyell New Zealand 41.48S 172.03E
13 B6 Lyell Brown, Mt N Terr Australia 23.22S 130.25E
101 H9 Lyell I Queen Charlotte Is, Br Col
111 E4 Lyell, Mt California 37.45N 119.18W
12 H8 Lyell, Mt Tasmania 41.59S 145.35E
11 G8 Lyell Ra New Zealand
48 U10 Lyells Land Greenland
105 B3 Lyerly Georgia 34.22N 85.26W
51 G2 Lyfjord Norway 69.48N 18.45E
112 K9 Lyford Texas 26.25N 97.49W
105 K9 Lyford Cay New Providence I Bahamas 25.02N 77.33W
39 D1 Lygka U.S.S.R. 67.59N 146.31E
52 C8 Lygna *R* Norway
53 S17 Lygra Norway 60.42N 5.06E
41 L4 Lygyy, Mys *C* U.S.S.R. 73.44N 116.14E
103 A5 Lykens Pennsylvania 40.40N 76.45W
53 T15 Lykkjebøvatn *L* Norway 61.37N 5.36E
50 F5 Lyklafell *mt* Iceland 64.55N 19.48W
53 S19 Lykling Norway 59.42N 5.12E
46 J1 Lykoshino U.S.S.R. 58.08N 33.48E
95 H3 Lykso S Africa 27.13S 24.05E
108 S6 Lyle Minnesota 43.30N 92.58W
110 D4 Lyle Washington 45.42N 121.15W
107 J6 Lyles Tennessee 35.56N 87.21W
100 Q9 Lyleton Manitoba 49.04N 101.10W
107 G11 Lyman Mississippi 30.30N 89.09W
108 F8 Lyman Nebraska 41.57N 104.02W
109 O5 Lyman Oklahoma 36.51N 96.51W
105 E3 Lyman S Carolina 34.57N 82.07W
110 P8 Lyman Wyoming 41.20N 110.16W
101 O8 Lymburn Alberta 55.21N 119.51W
104 N3 Lyme New Hampshire 43.49N 72.10W
56 F6 Lyme B S W England
56 F6 Lyme Regis Dorset Eng 50.44N 2.57W
56 O5 Lyminge Kent Eng 51.08N 1.05E
56 H6 Lymington Hants Eng 50.46N 1.33W
57 J6 Lymm Cheshire Eng 53.23N 2.28W
56 O5 Lympne Kent Eng 51.05N 1.02E
47 G5 Lymva U.S.S.R. 62.10N 53.10E
62 M1 Łyna *R* Poland
53 H5 Lynæs Denmark 55.57N 11.53E
57 E6 Lynas, Pt Gwynedd Wales 53.25N 4.17W
121 J4 Lynch Buenos Aires Argentina 34.35S 58.32W
104 C10 Lynch Kentucky 36.56N 82.56W
103 B8 Lynch Maryland 39.18N 76.04W
108 M7 Lynch Nebraska 42.50N 98.28W
104 B7 Lynchburg Ohio 39.13N 83.46W
107 K6 Lynchburg Tennessee 35.17N 86.22W
104 F9 Lynchburg Virginia 37.24N 79.09W
105 H4 Lynches, R S Carolina
99 P10 Lynch, I Quebec 45.24N 73.51W
104 P2 Lynchville Maine 44.15N 70.47W
13 G4 Lynd Queensland 18.50S 144.27E
13 G3 Lynd *R* Queensland
53 H5 Lyndby Denmark 55.41N 11.57E
103 C6 Lyndell Pennsylvania 40.04N 75.45W
99 K9 Lynden Ontario 43.14N 80.10W
110 C1 Lynden Washington 48.56N 122.28W
56 H6 Lyndhurst Hants Eng 50.52N 1.34W
103 H7 Lyndhurst New Jersey 40.49N 74.07W
11 F10 Lyndhurst New Zealand 43.40S 171.42E
13 G4 Lyndhurst Queensland 19.10S 144.21E
94 T13 Lyndhurst S Africa 26.08S 28.06E
12 E4 Lyndhurst S Australia 30.19S 138.24E
109 P3 Lyndon Kansas 38.36N 95.40W
104 N2 Lyndon Vermont 44.32N 72.03W
14 B6 Lyndon W Australia 23.40S 115.12E
112 J5 Lyndon B. Johnson, L Texas 30.35N 98.25W
14 A6 Lyndon, R W Australia
104 G3 Lyndonville New York 43.20N 78.23W
104 N2 Lyndonville Vermont 44.33N 72.00W
58 K7 Lyne Borders Scotland 55.40N 3.18W
53 A5 Lyne Denmark 55.48N 8.30E
56 H4 Lyneham Wilts Eng 51.31N 1.58W
12 A6 Lyneham *dist* Canberra Australia
57 H2 Lyne, R Cumbria Eng
58 S12 Lyness Orkney Scotland 58.49N 3.12W
53 F4 Lyngby Århus Denmark 56.22N 10.45E
53 E3 Lyngby Nordjylland Denmark 55.46N 10.04E
53 A3 Lyngby Viborg Denmark 56.53N 8.20E
53 D4 Lyngbygd Å *R* Denmark
52 C8 Lyngdal Norway 58.10N 7.08E
50 E6 Lyngdalsheidhi *heath* Iceland
53 H6 Lynge Denmark 55.24N 11.35E
51 H2 Lyngen Norway 69.36N 20.10E
51 H2 Lyngen *inlet* Norway 69.35N 20.20E
52 E8 Lyngør Norway 58.38N 9.10E
53 A3 Lyngs Denmark 56.40N 8.29E
53 F2 Lyngså Denmark 57.15N 10.32E
51 H2 Lyngseidet Norway 69.36N 20.15E
53 V20 Lyngsvatn *L* Norway 59.06N 6.30E
53 W20 Lyngtveit Norway 59.22N 7.17E
14 D3 Lynher Reef W Australia 15.28S 121.55E
56 D5 Lynmouth Devon Eng 51.15N 3.50W
107 J7 Lynn Alabama 34.02N 87.32W
106 K9 Lynn Indiana 40.03N 84.55W
104 P4 Lynn Massachusetts 42.29N 70.57W
103 C3 Lynn Pennsylvania 41.39N 75.56W
110 M8 Lynn Utah 41.54N 113.45W
113 U7 Lynn Canal Alaska
111 M2 Lynndyl Utah 39.31N 112.25W
104 R8 Lynn Harb Massachusetts
105 B7 Lynn Haven Florida 30.14N 85.40W
100 Q2 Lynn Lake Manitoba 56.51N 101.01W
101 H11 Lynnmour Br Columbia 49.19N 123.02W
103 C5 Lynnport Pennsylvania 40.41N 75.48W
108 S8 Lynnville Iowa 41.33N 92.45W
107 J6 Lynnville Tennessee 35.24N 87.00W
56 D5 Lynton Devon Eng 51.15N 3.50W
14 A8 Lynton W Australia 28.14S 114.20E
111 E9 Lynwood *dist* Los Angeles, California
101 U4 Lynx L N W Terr
53 E6 Lyø Denmark 55.03N 10.08E
53 E6 Lyø *isld* Denmark 55.03N 10.08E
71 F5 Lyon France 45.46N 4.50E
58 G5 Lyon, L Tayside Scotland 56.32N 4.36W
106 K5 Lyon Manor Michigan 44.28N 84.45W
104 M2 Lyon Mountain New York 44.44N 73.56W
67 H7 Lyonnais *prov* France
71 E5 Lyonnais, Mts. du France
96 C15 Lyon Pt Tristan da Cunha 37.06S 12.13W
58 H5 Lyon, R Tayside Scotland
109 E1 Lyons Colorado 40.14N 105.17W
Lyons France*see* Lyon
105 E5 Lyons Georgia 32.12N 82.19W
107 J3 Lyons Indiana 38.59N 87.05W
109 M3 Lyons Kansas 38.22N 98.13W
106 K7 Lyons Michigan 42.58N 84.54W
108 O8 Lyons Nebraska 41.57N 96.29W
104 J3 Lyons New York 43.04N 76.59W
104 A5 Lyons Ohio 41.42N 84.04W
110 C5 Lyons Oregon 44.45N 122.40W
103 C6 Lyons Pennsylvania 40.29N 75.45W
12 C4 Lyons S Australia 30.34S 133.50E
108 O6 Lyons S Dakota 43.42N 96.51W
112 L5 Lyons Texas 30.23N 96.34W
106 F7 Lyons Wisconsin 42.39N 88.21W
12 A6 Lyons *dist* Canberra Australia
104 K3 Lyons Falls New York 43.36N 75.22W
56 F3 Lyonshall Hereford & Worcs Eng 52.12N 2.59W
70 N3 Lyons-la-Forêt France 49.24N 1.28E
14 B6 Lyons, R W Australia
10 L2 Lyra Reef Pacific Oc
69 D2 Lys *R* France
79 C3 Lys *R* Italy
62 H5 Lysá Czechoslovakia 50.12N 14.50E
45 B7 Lysanka Ukraine U.S.S.R. 49.20N 30.50E
45 C8 Lysaya-Gora Ukraine U.S.S.R. 48.09N 31.06E
66 E5 Lys, Dent de *mt* Switzerland 46.31N 7.01E
53 V20 Lysebotn Norway 59.04N 6.39E
53 V20 Lysebu Norway 59.10N 6.55E
53 U21 Lysefjorden *inlet* Norway
53 V20 Lyseheiene *moor* Norway 59.05N 6.50E
53 V20 Lysekammen *mt* Norway 59.07N 6.44E
52 F8 Lysekil Sweden 58.16N 11.26E
53 S18 Lysekloster Norway 60.13N 5.25E
53 V20 Lysestølene Norway 59.06N 6.38E
45 D4 Lyshchichi U.S.S.R. 52.44N 32.34E
84 S14 Lysi Cyprus 35.06N 33.41E
65 P3 Lysice Czechoslovakia 49.28N 16.31E
37 C2 Lysimachia *anc site* Turkey 40.36N 26.52E
108 C6 Lysite Wyoming 43.16N 107.40W
66 H8 Lyskamm *mt* Italy/Switz 45.55N 7.51E
45 R1 Lyskovo U.S.S.R. 56.02N 45.01E
45 L9 Lysogorka U.S.S.R. 47.41N 39.13E
39 G1 Lysova, Ostrov *isld* U.S.S.R. 70.40N 161.40E
52 E3 Lysøysund Norway 63.53N 9.53E
66 F3 Lyss Switzerland 47.04N 7.19E
66 G3 Lyssach Switzerland 47.04N 7.35E
99 T6 Lyster Quebec 46.22N 71.38W
36 F5 Lystra *anc site* Turkey 37.36N 32.17E
53 E4 Lystrup Århus Denmark 56.14N 10.14E
47 H6 Lys'va U.S.S.R. 58.07N 57.49E
52 G6 Lysvik Sweden 60.01N 13.09E
46 H5 Lysyanka Ukraine U.S.S.R. 49.16N 30.49E
45 Q5 Lysyye Gory Saratov U.S.S.R. 51.32N 44.48E
45 N4 Lysyye Gory Tambov U.S.S.R. 52.52N 41.14E
56 G6 Lytchett Minster Dorset Eng 50.44N 2.04W
57 G5 Lytham St. Annes Lancs Eng 53.45N 3.01W
84 R15 Lythrodhonda Cyprus 34.56N 33.20E
50 F4 Lytingstadhir Iceland 65.24N 19.09W
112 J6 Lytle Texas 29.13N 98.50W
11 G10 Lyttelton New Zealand 43.36S 172.42E
95 M1 Lyttelton S Africa 25.51S 28.13E
11 N10 Lyttelton Harb *inlet* New Zealand
101 N10 Lytton Br Columbia 50.12N 121.34W
111 B3 Lytton California 38.40N 122.54W
99 O6 Lytton Quebec 46.36N 76.02W
46 H1 Lyuban' U.S.S.R. 59.20N 31.20E
46 G5 Lyubar Ukraine U.S.S.R. 49.58N 27.41E
82 N3 Lyubashevka U.S.S.R. 47.50N 30.16E
46 F3 Lyubcha Belorussiya U.S.S.R. 53.46N 26.01E
45 B5 Lyubech Ukraine U.S.S.R. 51.42N 30.41E
45 J1 Lyubertsy U.S.S.R. 55.38N 37.58E
46 F4 Lyubeshov Ukraine U.S.S.R. 51.42N 25.32E
46 M1 Lyubim U.S.S.R. 58.21N 40.39E
82 K9 Lyubimets Bulgaria 41.50N 26.05E
47 H6 Lyubimova U.S.S.R. 57.30N 57.02E
45 G5 Lyubimovka Kursk U.S.S.R. 51.30N 35.39E
45 K3 Lyubimovka Tula U.S.S.R. 53.27N 38.16E
47 L7 Lyubinskiy U.S.S.R. 55.09N 72.45E
46 H2 Lyublino Novgorod U.S.S.R. 57.28N 31.30E
45 F3 Lyubokhna U.S.S.R. 53.30N 34.24E
47 L8 Lyubomirovka U.S.S.R. 54.27N 73.31E
45 G7 Lyubotin Ukraine U.S.S.R. 49.57N 35.57E
42 F2 Lyucha U.S.S.R. 60.10N 97.24E
45 F3 Lyudinovo U.S.S.R. 53.51N 34.25E
45 F2 Lyudkovo U.S.S.R. 54.37N 34.44E
46 R2 Lyuk U.S.S.R. 56.56N 52.45E
46 O2 Lyunda *R* U.S.S.R.
39 J4 Lyuri U.S.S.R. 60.29N 170.55E
46 F4 Lyushcha Belorussiya U.S.S.R. 52.28N 26.41E
47 H3 Lyzha *R* U.S.S.R.
25 E1 Ma *R* Burma
85 L6 Ma'âbda, El Egypt 27.26N 30.59E
35 F3 Ma'ad Jordan 32.36N 35.37E
Maadan *see* Ma'dan
74 J8 Maad, Djebel bou *mt* Algeria 36.26N 2.08E
86 F6 Ma'âdi, El Egypt 29.58N 31.15E
35 F6 Ma'agan Israel 32.42N 35.36E
35 C3 Ma'agan Mikha'el Israel 32.33N 34.55E
92 K9 Maaia Mozambique 14.29S 40.42E
114 E5 Maalaea Hawaiian Is 20.49N 156.31W
114 E5 Maalaea Bay Hawaiian Is
60 N15 Maalbroek Netherlands 51.12N 6.03E
35 D10 Ma'ale Aqrabbim *pass* Israel 30.56N 35.08E
35 E5 Ma'ale Efrayim Jordan 32.04N 35.23E
35 D6 Ma'ale HaHamisha Israel 31.49N 35.07E
35 E4 Ma'aleh Hagilboa Israel 34.27N 35.25E
33 C10 Ma'allā S Yemen 12.48N 45.01E
27 L8 Maalosmadulu Atoll Maldives, Ind Oc 5.30N 72.33E
35 E1 Ma'alot-Tarshiḥa Israel 33.01N 35.16E
Maaloula, Jebel *mts see* Ma'lūla, Jebel
59 C4 Maam Bridge Galway Irish Rep 53.31N 9.34W
59 C5 Maam Cross Galway Irish Rep 53.27N 9.33W
34 Q8 Ma'amīr Iraq 30.03N 48.24E
Maan *see* Nusratiye
91 B2 Ma'an Cameroon 2.23N 10.47E
86 P5 Ma'ān Jordan 30.11N 35.45E
51 N8 Maaninka Finland 63.10N 27.20E
35 D4 Ma'anit Israel 32.27N 35.02E
33 E1 Ma'ānīyah, Al Saudi Arabia 30.42N 43.01E
51 O8 Maanselkä Finland 63.49N 28.30E
23 H3 Ma'anshan Anhui China 31.49N 118.32E
85 O2 Ma'aret-en-Nu'man Syria 35.37N 36.41E
60 L14 Maarheeze Netherlands 51.19N 5.37E
Maarianhamina *see* Mariehamn
61 E3 Maarke Kerkem Belgium 50.49N 3.39E
60 K11 Maarn Netherlands 52.04N 5.21E
34 D2 Ma'arra, El Syria 36.02N 36.50E
Maarret enn Naamâne *see* Ma'arret en Nu'mān
34 D3 Ma'arret en Nu'mān Syria 35.40N 36.40E
60 K11 Maarsbergen Netherlands 52.04N 5.25E
60 J11 Maarssen Netherlands 52.08N 5.03E
60 J11 Maartensdijk Netherlands 52.10N 5.10E
59 F2 Maas Donegal Irish Rep 54.49N 8.22W
87 L8 Maas Somalia 4.25N 46.05E
60 K12 Maas *R* Netherlands
60 T16 Maasbracht Netherlands 51.08N 5.54E
60 N14 Maasbree Netherlands 51.22N 6.03E
60 G12 Maasdam Netherlands 51.47N 4.34E
60 E12 Maasdijk Netherlands 51.57N 4.13E
61 O2 Maaseik Belgium 51.05N 5.48E
60 N13 Maashees Netherlands 51.34N 6.02E
19 M6 Maasin Leyte Philippines 10.08N 124.51E
34 F8 Ma'āṣir, Al *salt marsh* Saudi Arabia 30.43N 38.18E
60 F12 Maasland Netherlands 51.56N 4.16E
61 N3 Maasmechelen Belgium 50.58N 5.42E
60 N15 Maasniel Netherlands 51.12N 6.01E
60 E12 Maassluis Netherlands 51.55N 4.15E
60 S17 Maastricht Netherlands 50.51N 5.42E
60 M12 Maas-Waalkanaal *canal* Netherlands
85 E5 Ma'aṭan Jufar Libya 29.59N 19.16E
12 H9 Maatsuyker Is Tasmania
71 G1 Maâtz France 47.43N 5.27E
92 G12 Maave Mozambique 21.06S 34.48E
Ma'ayan *see* Ma'yan Ẕevi
86 K4 Ma'aza, Gebel el *hill* Egypt 30.38N 33.27E
85 L6 Maaza Plateau Egypt
Maba *see* Qujiang
19 F3 Maba Halmahera Indonesia 0.46N 128.08E
94 J5 Mabaalstad S Africa 25.51N 26.38E
94 G2 Mababe Depression Botswana
91 D7 Mabaia Angola 7.12S 14.02E
19 K4 Mabalacat Luzon Philippines 15.15N 120.29E
94 M4 Mabalane Mozambique 23.51S 32.38E
93 C6 Mabale *mt* Uganda 0.59S 31.36E
112 L3 Mabank Texas 32.22N 96.06W
33 F9 Ma'bar Yemen 14.52N 44.17E
30 A2 Mabarakpur Haryana India 30.37N 76.53E
35 C4 Ma'barot Israel 32.22N 34.54E
119 J3 Mabaruma Guyana 8.09N 59.51W
20 F1 Mabashi Japan 35.48N 139.55E
18 J7 Mabau Borneo Indon 2.15S 111.51E
19 F1 Mabayo Luzon Philippines 14.43N 120.17E
20 P1 Mabechi-gawa *R* Japan
25 M9 Mabein Burma 23.30N 96.39E
106 C6 Mabel Minnesota 43.32N 91.45W
12 C3 Mabel Creek S Australia 28.50S 134.15E
14 G3 Mabel Downs W Australia 17.18S 128.00E
100 N2 Mabella Ontario 48.37N 89.59W
112 H2 Mabelle Texas 33.37N 99.08W
104 D9 Maben W Virginia 37.38N 81.25W
90 F8 Mabéré Cameroon 6.54N 13.54E
99 O8 Maberly Ontario 44.50N 76.36W
57 D2 Maberry, L Dumfries & Galloway Scotland 55.02N 4.41W
23 C4 Mabian Sichuan China 28.50N 103.10E
87 F5 Mabil Ethiopia 10.21N 36.46E
98 K2 Mabille, L Quebec 51.59N 62.51W
93 B7 Mabira Tanzania 1.14S 30.57E
91 D4 Mabirou Congo 1.03S 15.42E
53 B4 Måbjerg Denmark 56.23N 8.38E
57 O6 Mablethorpe Lincs Eng 53.21N 0.15E
90 M8 Mabo Cent Afr Rep 6.26N 25.23E
53 W18 Måbødalen *V* Norway 60.26N 7.10E
93 C10 Mabogwe Tanzania 4.05S 31.10E
89 C7 Mabole *R* Sierra Leone
61 N6 Mabompré Belgium 50.06N 5.44E
89 D7 Mabonto Sierra Leone 8.53N 11.49W
94 N4 Mabote Mozambique 22.03S 34.09E
98 L7 Mabou C Breton I, Nova Scotia 46.04N 61.22W
86 O7 Mabrak, Wādī el *watercourse* Saudi Arabia
88 N12 Mabrouk Mali 19.30N 1.14W
90 F1 Mabrous Niger 21.14N 13.35E
85 D5 Mabruk Libya 29.50N 17.20E
110 E3 Mabton Washington 46.14N 120.01W
94 G5 Mabuasehube Game Reserve Botswana 25.02S 22.09E
91 C8 Mabubas Angola 8.34S 13.38E
19 K1 Mabudis *isld* Philippines 20.55N 121.55E
92 F3 Mabuki Tanzania 2.54S 33.06E
94 H5 Mabuli Botswana 25.53S 24.33E
87 J10 Mabungo Somalia 0.48N 42.31E
20 P10 Mabuni Okinawa Japan 26.02N 127.42E
15 E7 Mabur *R* Irian Jaya
85 F7 Ma'bus Yūsuf Libya 25.38N 21.04E
91 K8 Mabwe Zaïre 8.41S 26.33E
120 B8 Macabi, I Peru 7.50S 79.28W
121 D6 Macachin Argentina 37.10S 63.43W
120 F3 Macacos, Cachoeira dos *rapids* Brazil 8.53S 64.04W
117 D5 Macacos, I. dos Brazil
98 E8 McAdam New Brunswick 45.34N 67.20W
14 B7 Macadam Plains W Australia
13 A2 Macadam Ra N Terr Australia
103 B5 McAdoo Pennsylvania 40.53N 76.00W
112 F2 McAdoo Texas 33.44N 101.02W
118 H8 Macaé Brazil 22.21S 41.48W
77 M6 Macael Spain 37.20N 2.18W
91 G10 Macafuma Angola 13.13S 21.42E
119 E4 Macaguan Colombia 6.36N 71.41W
37 F4 Maçahel Turkey 41.31N 41.54E
117 J7 Macaíba Brazil 5.50S 35.20W
76 E8 Maçainhas Portugal 40.23N 7.18W
19 M7 Macajalar B Mindanao Philippines

118 H3 Macajuba Brazil 12.09S 40.23W
109 P7 McAlester Oklahoma 34.56N 95.46W
109 P6 McAlester, L Oklahoma 35.03N 95.50W
92 H9 Macalia Mozambique 14.41S 37.27E
109 G7 McAlister New Mexico 34.43N 103.45W
12 J5 McAlister *mt* New S Wales 34.28S 149.45E
12 H7 Macalister *R* Victoria
112 J9 McAllen Texas 26.13N 98.15W
110 O4 McAllister Montana 45.27N 111.44W
92 G8 Macaloge Mozambique 12.27S 35.25E
105 E7 McAlpin Florida 30.09N 82.58W
101 W2 MacAlpine L N W Terr
121 G2 Macambará Brazil 29.06S 56.00W
117 G7 Macambira Brazil 4.47S 41.08W
99 L4 Macamic Quebec 48.46N 79.02W
121 J5 Macá, Mt Chile 45.10S 73.12W
119 F6 Macanacape, L Venezuela 2.38N 66.47W
11 N12 Macandrew Bay New Zealand 45.52S 170.36E
94 M4 Macandze Mozambique 23.33S 33.50E
19 B7 Macan, Pulau Pulau *islds* Indonesia
Macao China*see* Macau
76 D9 Mação Portugal 39.33N 8.00W
117 C4 Macapá Amapá Brazil 0.04N 51.04W
120 E3 Macapá Amazonas Brazil 9.30S 67.29W
Macar *see* Gebiz
119 B10 Macará Ecuador 4.25S 79.57W
115 O6 Macaracas Panama 7.46N 80.31W
118 H4 Macarani Brazil 15.34S 40.21W
119 B10 Macará, R Peru/Ecuador
119 D6 Macarena, Cord *mts* Colombia
119 H3 Macareo, Caño *crater* Venezuela
117 D4 Macari *R* Brazil
13 F3 Macaroni Queensland 16.36S 141.30E
94 M5 Macarretane Mozambique 24.22S 32.50E
110 D8 McArthur California 41.03N 121.25W
104 C7 McArthur Ohio 39.14N 82.29W
12 F7 Macarthur Victoria 38.02S 142.00E
13 D3 McArthur R N Terr Australia 16.37S 135.49E
13 D3 McArthur River N Terr Aust 16.20S 136.00E
119 B9 Macas Ecuador 2.22S 78.08W
76 F5 Macas *R* Portugal
76 C9 Maçãs de Dona Maria Portugal 39.52N 8.20W
87 J10 Macasi Somalia 0.24N 43.17E
94 Q12 Macassar Cape Town S Africa 34.05S 18.45E
Macassar Indonesia*see* Ujung Pandang
92 H10 Macatanja Mozambique 16.36S 36.18E
106 H7 Macatawa Michigan 42.45N 86.12W
117 H7 Macau Brazil 5.05S 36.37W
72 C5 Macau France 45.01N 0.36W
120 D4 Macauã, R Brazil
118 E2 Macaúba Brazil 10.26S 50.25W
118 G3 Macaúbas Brazil 13.00S 42.41W
100 Q8 McAuley Manitoba 50.17N 101.23W
10 R8 Macauley *isld* Kermadec Is Pacific Oc 30.13S 178.33W
119 D7 Macaya, R Colombia
119 D7 Macayari Colombia 1.00N 72.12W
106 J5 McBain Michigan 44.12N 85.12W
107 D3 McBaine Missouri 38.53N 92.25W
105 F4 McBean Georgia 33.15N 81.58W
105 G3 McBee S Carolina 34.27N 80.17W
100 U6 McBeth Pt *C* Manitoba 52.08N 97.30W
101 N9 McBride Br Columbia 53.21N 120.19W
121 E9 Macbride Hd Falkland Is 51.25S 57.55W
79 E2 Maccagno Italy 46.03N 8.45E
110 J5 McCall Idaho 44.55N 116.06W
112 E4 McCamey Texas 31.09N 102.14W
110 N7 McCammon Idaho 42.39N 112.12W
98 H8 Maccan Nova Scotia 45.45N 64.16W
108 N1 McCanna N Dakota 48.00N 97.42W
101 U5 McCann L N W Terr 61.10N 106.32W
80 F5 Maccarese Italy 41.53N 12.13E
80 F5 Maccarese, Bonifica di *reg* Italy
113 Q6 McCarthy Alaska 61.25N 142.59W
101 H9 McCauley I Br Columbia
110 B2 McCleary Washington 47.03N 123.17W
105 H4 McClellanville S Carolina 33.06N 79.30W
105 E7 Macclenny Florida 30.16N 82.07W
57 J6 Macclesfield Cheshire Eng 53.16N 2.07W
25 N5 Macclesfield Bank S China Sea
98 S5 Maccles L Newfoundland
97 J3 McClintock Chan N W Terr
McClintock I *see* Mak-Klintoka, Ostrov
123 H6 McClintock, Mt Antarctica 80.05S 156.50E
14 F4 McClintock Ra W Australia
110 C8 McCloud California 41.16N 122.09W
110 C8 McCloud *R* California
MacCluer Gulf *see* Berau, Teluk
13 C1 McCluer I N Terr Australia 11.08S 133.02E
103 C2 McClure New York 42.03N 75.30W
104 B5 McClure Ohio 41.23N 83.57W
104 H6 McClure Pennsylvania 40.42N 77.20W
104 C9 McClure Virginia 37.04N 82.22W
111 D4 McClure, L California 37.38N 120.16W
97 H3 McClure Strait N W Terr
108 K2 McClusky N Dakota 47.29N 100.29W
105 H3 McColl S Carolina 34.41N 79.33W
107 F10 McComb Mississippi 31.13N 90.29W
104 B5 McComb Ohio 41.07N 83.48W
108 H8 McConaughy, L Nebraska
101 M3 McConnell Ra N W Terr
104 G7 McConnellsburg Pennsylvania 39.56N 78.00W
108 K9 McCook Nebraska 40.13N 100.35W
107 G8 McCool Mississippi 33.10N 89.22W
108 N9 McCool Junction Nebraska 40.47N 97.35W
100 L9 McCord Saskatchewan 49.24N 106.50W
105 E4 McCormick S Carolina 33.55N 82.19W
109 D2 McCoy Colorado 39.55N 106.44W
109 L3 McCracken Kansas 38.34N 99.34W
100 S8 McCreary Manitoba 50.46N 99.30W
107 E3 McCredie Missouri 38.57N 91.56W
107 E6 McCrory Arkansas 35.13N 91.11W
97 M3 Macculloch, C N W Terr 72.30N 75.00W
107 J10 McCullough Alabama 31.10N 87.31W
111 J6 Mccullough Ridge Nevada
109 Q6 McCurtain Oklahoma 35.09N 94.58W
100 J3 McCusker R Saskatchewan
112 K5 McDade Texas 30.18N 97.15W
101 J6 McDame Br Columbia 59.15N 129.15W
107 J11 McDavid Florida 30.51N 87.20W
110 H8 McDermitt Nevada 42.00N 117.43W
104 B8 McDermott Ohio 38.50N 83.03W
99 B3 Macdiarmid Ontario 49.27N 88.08W
110 C8 Macdoel California 41.50N 122.00W
109 J2 McDonald Kansas 39.47N 101.23W
104 E6 McDonald Pennsylvania 40.23N 80.24W
13 D5 MacDonald Downs N Terr Australia 22.25S 135.08E
26 G10 Macdonald Is Indian Oc 52.50N 72.29E
110 M1 McDonald, L Montana 48.36N 113.55W
14 G6 Macdonald, L W Australia
110 E9 McDonald Pk California 40.57N 120.25W
110 M2 McDonald Pk Montana 47.22N 113.54W
110 L1 Macdonald Ra Br Columbia
14 E3 Macdonald Ra W Australia
11 M2 Macdonald Rock Kermadec Is Pacific Oc 30.12S 178.31W
12 E3 McDonnell *R* S Australia
105 C4 McDonough Georgia 33.25N 84.09W
103 C1 McDonough New York 42.30N 75.47W
12 C3 McDouall Peak S Australia 29.52S 134.56E
13 C4 McDouall Ra N Terr Australia
113 M6 McDougall Alaska 61.54N 150.52W
94 D7 Mc. Dougall Bay S Africa 29.19S 16.50E
97 K7 MacDowell L Ontario
111 N8 McDowell Pk *mt* Arizona 33.41N 111.48W
58 M3 Macduff Grampian Scotland 57.40N 2.29W
99 L4 Mace Ontario 48.57N 79.56W
76 D4 Maceda Spain 42.16N 7.39W
121 F6 Macedo Argentina 37.15S 57.05W
76 F5 Macedo de Cavaleiros Portugal 41.31N 6.57W
104 H3 Macedon New York 43.04N 77.19W
12 G6 Macedon *mt* Victoria 37.27S 144.34E
Macedonia *see* Makedonija Yugoslavia
108 P8 Macedonia Iowa 41.11N 95.23W
103 H3 Macedonia Brook State Park Connecticut
117 J9 Maceió Alagoas Brazil 9.40S 35.44W
117 H7 Maceio, Pta. da *C* Brazil 4.27S 37.46W
76 B9 Maceira Portugal 39.41N 8.53W
89 E7 Macenta Guinea 8.31N 9.32W
80 H2 Macerata Italy 43.18N 13.27E
80 G2 Macerata *prov* Italy
79 M7 Macerata Feltria Italy 43.48N 12.26E
107 J5 McEwan Tennessee 36.04N 87.39W
110 G5 McEwen Oregon 44.42N 118.05W
108 D8 McFadden Wyoming 41.38N 106.09W
107 B1 McFall Missouri 40.06N 94.14W
109 O2 McFarland Kansas 39.03N 96.14W
15 K9 McFarlane Harb Papua New Guinea
12 D4 Macfarlane, L S Australia
11 D10 Macfarlane, Mt New Zealand 43.56N 169.23E
109 B6 McGaffey New Mexico 35.22N 108.32W
100 J7 McGee Saskatchewan 51.30N 108.15W
107 E8 McGehee Arkansas 33.37N 91.24W
105 D2 McGhee-Tyson *airport* Tennessee 35.50N 83.59W
111 K2 McGill Nevada 39.24N 114.47W
59 C7 Macgillicuddy's Reeks *mts* Kerry Irish Rep
110 K1 McGillvray Ra Br Columbia
113 K5 McGrath Alaska 62.58N 155.40W
108 R3 McGrath Minnesota 46.14N 93.16W
104 J4 McGraw New York 42.36N 76.04W
100 T9 MacGregor Manitoba 49.57N 98.48W
106 M6 McGregor Michigan 43.28N 82.46W
108 R3 McGregor Minnesota 46.36N 93.19W
95 C9 McGregor S Africa 33.56S 19.50E
112 K4 McGregor Texas 31.27N 97.25W
100 E8 McGregor L Alberta
101 N8 McGregor R Br Columbia
13 F7 McGregor Ra Queensland
108 G8 McGrew Nebraska 41.46N 103.26W
110 L4 McGuire, Mt Idaho 45.11N 114.36W
31 D6 Mach Pakistan 29.52N 67.20E
40 A2 Macha U.S.S.R. 59.55N 117.30E
92 C10 Macha Zambia 16.29S 26.44E
119 B8 Machachi Ecuador 0.33S 78.34W
117 D5 Machadinho, I Brazil 0.10S 48.45W
120 G3 Machadinho, R Brazil
118 F7 Machado Brazil 21.39S 45.53W
Machado *R see* Jiparaná
95 O1 Machadodorp S Africa 25.41S 30.15E
76 E12 Machados *sta* Portugal 38.05N 7.25W
41 O6 Machakh U.S.S.R. 67.33N 132.55E
93 J7 Machakos Kenya 1.32S 27.16E
93 J7 Machakos *dist* Kenya
119 B9 Machala Ecuador 3.20S 79.57W
18 K5 Machan Sarawak Malaysia 1.56N 112.02E
19 M1 Machanao *mt* Guam Pacific Oc 13.38N 144.52E
94 N3 Machanga Mozambique 20.58S 35.01E
23 D5 Machangping Guizhou China 26.36N 107.28E
120 E8 Macharamarca Bolivia 18.10S 67.02W
60 L12 Macharen Netherlands 51.48N 5.33E
120 F9 Macharetí Bolivia 20.46S 63.22W
87 D6 Machar Marshes Sudan
57 D3 Machars, The *dist* Dumfries & Galloway Scotland
13 E6 Machattie L Queensland
94 M5 Machatuine Mozambique 25.10S 32.03E
69 G5 Machault France 49.21N 4.30E
94 M3 Machaze Mozambique 20.51S 33.26E
30 C6 Machchand Madhya Prad India 26.20N 79.03E
94 N2 Machece Mozambique 19.17S 35.33E
92 D9 Machechete *mt* Zambia 14.58S 29.55E
72 A2 Machecoul France 46.59N 1.49W
92 E11 Macheke Zimbabwe 18.05S 31.51E
45 P6 Machekha U.S.S.R. 50.49N 43.17E
45 F7 Machekhi Ukraine U.S.S.R. 49.30N 34.25E
61 H3 Machelen Brabant Belgium 50.55N 4.26E
61 D3 Machelen Oost Vlaanderen Belgium 50.57N 3.30E
105 D4 Machen Georgia 33.24N 83.35W
56 E4 Machen Gwent Wales 51.35N 3.07W
23 G3 Macheng Hubei China 31.13N 115.06E
106 F7 McHenry Illinois 42.21N 88.16W
107 G11 McHenry Mississippi 30.41N 89.09W
108 M2 McHenry N Dakota 47.35N 98.37W
Macheri *see* Malakhera
28 D2 Macherla Andhra Prad India 16.29N 79.25E
63 R10 Machern E Germany 51.23N 12.38E
76 L10 Machero *mt* Spain 39.21N 4.20W
39 J4 Machevna U.S.S.R. 60.46N 171.40E
39 J4 Machevna, Bukhta *gulf* U.S.S.R.
29 K7 Machgaon Orissa India 20.02N 86.05E
34 C5 Machgharah Lebanon 33.33N 35.38E
30 H3 Machherma Nepal 27.54N 86.43E
30 F7 Machhlishahr Uttar Prad India 25.42N 82.24E
29 B6 Machhu R Gujarat India
87 F4 Machia Ethiopia 12.31N 37.50E
104 S2 Machias Maine 44.44N 67.28W
104 Q7 Machias *R* Maine
104 S2 Machias B Maine
98 E9 Machias Seal I Maine/New Bruns 44.30N 67.08W
75 E1 Machichaco, C Spain 43.27N 2.45W
96 Q7 Machico Madeira Is 32.43N 16.47W
20 B4 Machida Kanagawa Japan 35.33N 139.28E
28 E2 Machilipatnam Andhra Prad India 16.12N 81.11E
71 J4 Machilly France 46.15N 6.20E
30 A6 Machilpur Rajasthan India 26.38N 77.13E
71 C3 Machine, la France 46.53N 3.28E
119 D2 Machiques Venezuela 10.04N 72.37W
58 D7 Machir B Islay, Strathclyde Scotland 55.47N 6.29W
92 B10 Machiti *R* Zambia
29 E2 Machiwara Punjab India 30.55N 76.15E
32 J8 Māch Kowr Iran 25.47N 61.29E
28 F1 Machkund Dam Andhra Prad/Orissa India 18.32N 82.34E
34 K7 Machmi, Al Iraq 31.32N 42.28E
57 C1 Machrie Arran, Strathclyde Scotland 55.33N 5.20W
57 B2 Machrihanish Strathclyde Scotland 55.26N 5.44W
94 N4 Machunguele Mozambique 22.46S 35.17E
120 C5 Machupicchu *ruins* Peru 13.08S 72.30W
120 F5 Machupo, R Bolivia
56 D2 Machynlleth Powys Wales 52.35N 3.51W
94 M5 Macia Mozambique 25.02S 33.08E
91 A2 Macias Nguema Biyogo / Equat Guinea
92 E10 McIlwaine, L Zimbabwe 17.53S 30.58E
13 G2 McIlwraith Ra Queensland
82 L5 Măcin Romania 45.15N 28.09E
99 J3 McInnes Ontario 49.34N 81.20W
108 S6 McIntire Iowa 43.28N 92.34W
108 P2 McIntosh Minnesota 47.36N 95.52W
100 J1 McIntosh Ontario 49.58N 93.36W
108 J4 McIntosh S Dakota 45.56N 101.21W
99 B3 McIntyre B Ontario
13 K8 Macintyre Brook Queensland
100 O2 McIntyre, N Ontario 48.30N 89.17W
12 K3 Macintyre R New S Wales
120 C5 Macizo de Tocate *hill ridge* Peru
109 B2 Mack Colorado 39.13N 108.54W
37 E5 Maçka Turkey 40.50N 39.39E
37 J2 Maçka *dist* İstanbul Turkey 41.03N 28.59E
100 O6 McKague Saskatchewan 52.38N 103.58W
110 M6 Mackay Idaho 43.56N 113.37W
13 J5 Mackay Queensland 21.10S 149.10E
14 G6 Mackay, L N Terr/W Aust
101 S4 MacKay L N W Terr
99 D3 McKay L Ontario 49.35N 86.25W
14 D5 Mackay, Mt W Australia 22.27S 120.05E
101 R7 McKay R Alberta
14 D6 McKay Ra W Australia
110 M6 Mackay Res Idaho 43.57N 113.42W
10 S2 McKean I Phoenix Is Pacific Oc 3.40S 174.10W
104 F6 McKeesport Pennsylvania 40.21N 79.52W
104 E6 McKees Rocks Pennsylvania 40.29N 80.09W
63 N9 Mackenrode E Germany 51.33N 10.35E
107 K10 McKenzie Alabama 31.32N 86.43W
101 M8 Mackenzie Br Columbia 55.18N 123.09W
Mackenzie Guyana*see* Linden Guyana
108 K3 McKenzie N Dakota 46.49N 100.25W
99 B4 Mackenzie Ontario 48.34N 88.59W
107 H5 McKenzie Tennessee 36.09N 88.31W
97 G5 Mackenzie *dist* N W Terr
110 C5 McKenzie *R* Oregon
13 J6 Mackenzie *R* Queensland
123 C4 Mackenzie B Antarctica
48 V9 Mackenzie B Greenland
101 E1 Mackenzie B Yukon Terr
110 C5 McKenzie Bridge Oregon 44.11N 122.11W
101 K3 Mackenzie, District of N W Terr
101 P6 Mackenzie Highway N W Terr/Alberta
97 H2 Mackenzie King I N W Terr 77.50N 112.00W
100 L2 McKenzie L Ontario 48.30N 91.00W
100 P4 McKenzie L Saskatchewan
101 F3 Mackenzie Mts Yukon/N W Terr
110 D5 McKenzie Pass Oregon 44.15N 121.45W
11 E11 Mackenzie Plains New Zealand
101 G2 Mackenzie, R N W Terr
100 S1 MacKerracher L Manitoba
11 C11 McKerrow, L New Zealand
103 F2 Mackey New York 42.27N 74.25W
Mackillop, L *see* Yamma Yamma, L
106 K4 Mackinac I Michigan 45.52N 84.37W
106 K4 Mackinac, Str. of Michigan
106 E9 Mackinaw Illinois 40.32N 89.21W
106 K4 Mackinaw City Michigan 45.47N 84.43W
106 E9 Mackinaw, R Illinois
13 F5 McKinlay Queensland 21.14S 141.13E
13 F5 McKinlay *R* Queensland
113 M5 McKinley, Mt Alaska 63.02N 151.01W
113 N5 McKinley Park Alaska 63.41N 149.00W
123 J9 McKinley Pk Antarctica 77.55S 148.03W
107 M4 McKinney Kentucky 37.25N 84.45W
112 L2 McKinney Texas 33.14N 96.37W
109 J3 McKinney, L Kansas 38.00N 101.13W
107 J5 McKinnon Tennessee 36.19N 87.55W
11 B11 McKinnon Pass New Zealand 44.50S 167.48E
93 L9 Mackinnon Road Kenya 3.44S 39.03E
14 F7 Mackintosh Ra W Australia
99 B3 McKirdy Ontario 49.16N 88.09W
111 E6 McKitrrick California 35.17N 119.38W
100 H6 Macklin Saskatchewan 52.20N 109.58W
95 N1 Mackmaar S Africa 25.37S 29.01E
100 Q2 McKnight L Manitoba 56.05N 101.10W
104 D7 Macksburg Ohio 39.37N 81.26W
110 O5 Macks Inn Idaho 44.30N 111.20W
109 M4 Macksville Kansas 37.57N 98.57W
12 L4 Macksville New S Wales 30.45S 152.54E
13 F6 Mackunda *R* Queensland
57 K7 Mackworth Derbys Eng 52.56N 1.32W
107 H10 McLain Mississippi 31.05N 88.50W
113 O5 Maclaren *R* Alaska
14 E4 McLarty Hills W Australia
14 D5 McLarty, Mt W Australia 22.24S 120.49E
71 F6 Maclas France 45.22N 4.40E
100 G6 McLaughlin Alberta 52.59N 110.12W
108 K4 McLaughlin S Dakota 45.50N 100.50W
100 U5 McLaughlin R Manitoba
106 E9 McLean Illinois 40.20N 89.10W
12 L3 Maclean New S Wales 29.27S 153.14E
103 B1 McLean New York 42.32N 76.18W
100 N8 McLean Saskatchewan 50.31N 104.01W
112 D8 McLean Texas 35.15N 100.36W
104 H8 McLean Virginia 38.57N 77.13W
100 H2 McLean L Saskatchewan 56.30N 109.15W
107 H3 McLeansboro Illinois 38.07N 88.32W
95 L8 Macleantown S Africa 32.47S 27.45E
95 M7 Maclear S Africa 31.05S 28.22E
92 G9 Maclear, C Malawi 14.01S 34.55E
12 K4 Macleay *R* New S Wales
101 P8 McLennan Alberta 55.42N 116.50W
100 N3 McLennan L Saskatchewan 55.57N 104.20W
108 N3 McLeod N Dakota 46.26N 97.18W
101 S4 McLeod B N W Terr
14 A6 McLeod, L W Australia 24.00S 113.30E
101 M8 McLeod Lake Br Columbia 55.00N 123.00W
100 B5 McLeod R Alberta
25 E7 McLeods I Burma
101 Y2 McLoughlin B N W Terr
110 C7 McLoughlin, Mt Oregon 42.27N 122.19W
109 P2 McLouth Kansas 39.13N 95.13W
100 K8 McMahon Saskatchewan 50.05N 107.32W
104 E7 McMechen W Virginia 39.00N 80.43W
103 D5 McMichaels Pennsylvania 41.00N 75.23W
26 V3 McMicken Pt Christmas I Ind Oc 10.30S 105.43E
106 J3 McMillan Michigan 46.21N 85.41W
13 G1 Macmillan *R* Queensland
101 F4 Macmillan *R* Yukon Terr
109 F9 McMillan, L New Mexico
13 C6 McMinns Cr N Terr Australia
110 B4 McMinnville Oregon 45.14N 123.12W
107 L6 McMinnville Tennessee 35.40N 85.49W
100 J7 McMorran Saskatchewan 51.19N 108.42W
100 F1 McMunn Manitoba 49.40N 95.45W
123 H6 McMurdo *U.S.A. Base* Antarctica 77.51S 166.37E
123 H6 McMurdo Sd Antarctica
101 O10 McMurphy Br Columbia 51.40N 119.25W
100 F2 McMurray Alberta 56.41N 111.23W
110 C1 McMurray Washington 48.19N 122.16W
26 B14 McMurray's Kop *hill* Marion I Ind Oc 46.53S 37.50E
107 E10 McNair Mississippi 31.38N 91.03W
111 P7 McNary Arizona 34.05N 109.51W
112 B4 McNary Texas 31.13N 105.53W
110 F4 McNary Dam Wash/Oregon 45.55N 119.17W
101 O9 McNaughton L *res* Br Columbia
111 P10 McNeal Arizona 31.36N 109.41W
59 G3 Macnean Lower, L Fermanagh N Ireland 54.17N 7.50W
59 G3 Macnean Upper, L Cavan etc Irish Rep 54.18N 7.55W
107 C8 McNeil Arkansas 33.22N 93.12W
112 K5 McNeil Texas 30.28N 97.45W
107 G11 McNeill Mississippi 30.40N 89.38W
100 Q7 MacNutt Saskatchewan 51.05N 101.34W
98 G10 McNutt I Nova Scotia 43.38N 65.18W
94 M3 Macobere Mozambique 21.13S 32.47E
91 E7 Macocola Angola 7.00S 16.10E
66 E3 Macolin Switzerland 47.09N 7.13E
91 E7 Macolo Angola 7.05S 16.42E
81 R13 Macolone, Pta Italy 39.51N 18.10E
106 D9 Macomb Illinois 40.29N 90.40W
109 N6 Macomb Oklahoma 35.08N 97.01W
81 B3 Macomer Sardinia 40.16N 8.47E
92 K8 Macomia Mozambique 12.15S 40.06E
61 G6 Macon Belgium 50.03N 4.13E
71 F4 Mâcon France 46.18N 4.50E
105 D5 Macon Georgia 32.49N 83.37W
107 H2 Macon Illinois 39.42N 88.59W
107 H8 Macon Mississippi 33.05N 88.35W
107 D2 Macon Missouri 39.44N 92.27W
108 M9 Macon Nebraska 40.12N 98.58W
91 H10 Macondo Angola 12.36S 23.48E
92 J7 Maconge Mozambique 11.38S 38.26E
59 J1 Macosquin Londonderry N Ireland 55.06N 6.43W
92 F10 Macossa Mozambique 17.52S 33.56E
76 J7 Macotera Spain 40.50N 5.17W
71 K5 Mâcot-la-Plagne France 45.33N 6.45E
100 O9 Macoun Saskatchewan 49.19N 103.15W
101 W7 Macoun L Saskatchewan 56.35N 103.40W
94 N3 Macovane Mozambique 21.28S 35.04E
109 N3 McPherson Kansas 38.22N 97.41W
14 D5 Macpherson, Mt W Australia 21.49S 121.32E
13 L8 Macpherson Ra N S W/Qnsld
28 G7 Macpherson's Str Andaman Is
12 A6 Macquarie *dist* Canberra Australia
12 J5 Macquarie *R* New S Wales
12 H8 Macquarie *R* Tasmania
12 H8 Macquarie Harb Tasmania
9 M12 Macquarie Is S Pacific Oc 54.29S 158.58E
12 K5 Macquarie, L New S Wales
12 H4 Macquarie Marshes New S Wales
12 J5 Macquarie Mt New S Wales 33.42S 149.13E
122 H14 Macquarie Ridge Pacific Oc
61 G7 Macquenoise Belgium 49.58N 4.11E
101 E4 McQuesten Yukon Terr 63.35N 137.20W
101 E4 Mc.Questen *R* Yukon Terr
72 D4 Macqueville France 45.48N 0.14W
105 E5 MacRae Georgia 32.02N 82.55W
11 H9 McRae, L New Zealand 42.11S 173.20E
14 C5 McRae, Mt W Australia 22.20S 117.34E
11 E12 Macraes Flat New Zealand 45.23S 170.26E
18 J3 Mac Ritchie Res Singapore
104 C9 McRoberts Kentucky 37.13N 82.41W
123 B5 Mac Robertson Land Antarctica
59 E8 Macroom Cork Irish Rep 51.54N 8.57W
100 K7 Macrorie Saskatchewan 51.22N 107.08W
13 H4 Macrossan Queensland 20.00S 146.30E
59 F2 McSwynes B Donegal Irish Rep 54.35N 8.28W
100 N9 McTaggart Saskatchewan 49.44N 104.01W
19 L6 Mactan *isld* Philippines 10.16N 123.58E
100 U9 McTavish Manitoba 49.28N 97.21W
101 O2 McTavish Arm *inlet* Great Bear L, N W Terr
99 L7 MacTier Ontario 45.09N 79.47W
119 E7 Macú Brazil 0.27N 69.16W
92 H10 Macúbi Mozambique 16.14S 36.59E
79 C3 Macugnaga Italy 45.58N 7.59E
119 D7 Macuje Colombia 0.20N 73.10W
121 G10 Macul *dist* Santiago Chile
119 C9 Macuma, R Ecuador
12 D2 Macumba *R* S Australia
104 K6 Macungie Pennsylvania 40.31N 75.33W
117 G9 Macururé Brazil 9.10S 39.02W
120 D6 Macusani Peru 14.05S 70.24W
115 N9 Macuspana Mexico 17.46N 92.36W
115 E4 Macuzari, Presa *res* Mexico
92 H10 Macuze Mozambique 17.42S 37.10E
104 C9 McVeigh Kentucky 37.32N 82.17W
100 Q2 McVeigh Manitoba 56.41N 101.16W
101 N3 McVicar Arm *inlet* Great Bear L, N W Terr
108 M2 McVille N Dakota 47.47N 98.09W
104 Q8 Macwahoc Maine 45.35N 68.14W
99 M4 McWatters Quebec 48.14N 79.56W
107 J10 McWilliams Alabama 31.50N 87.08W
90 F1 Mada Adziha Niger 22.04N 13.58E
35 G7 Madaba Jordan 31.44N 35.48E
92 H6 Madaba Tanzania 8.40S 37.48E
92 G12 Madade Mozambique 21.54S 34.13E
33 B2 Madāfi, Al *area* Saudi Arabia
90 F6 Madagali Nigeria 10.56N 13.36E
31 C6 Madagan Pakistan 28.28N 65.27E
73 J8 Madagascar *isld* Indian Oc
73 J8 Madagascar *rep* Indian Oc
26 E8 Madagascar Basin Indian Oc
44 H7 Madagiz Azerbaydzhan U.S.S.R. 40.17N 46.43E
87 H5 Madahtou Djibouti 11.05N 41.52E
33 B3 Madā'in Şālih Saudi Arabia 26.51N 37.58E
28 C4 Madakasira Andhra Prad India 13.56N 77.15E
92 D10 Madakwe *mt* Zimbabwe 17.59S 29.50E
19 N2 Madalai Palau Is Pacific Oc 7.20N 134.29E
96 P4 Madalena Azores 38.32N 28.32W
117 G7 Madalena Brazil 4.45S 39.38W
103 G2 Madalin New York 42.04N 73.54W
18 M2 Madalon, Gunong *mt* Sabah Malaysia 6.22N 116.44W
90 F1 Madama Niger 21.58N 13.40E
98 M8 Madame I C Breton I, Nova Scotia 45.30N 60.58W
72 B4 Madame, Ile *isld* France 45.58N 1.06W
26 S9 Madampe Sabaragamuwa Sri Lanka 6.32N 80.35E
26 Q6 Madampe Sri Lanka 7.55N 79.50E
32 H2 Ma'dan Iran 36.25N 58.20E
34 G3 Ma'dan Syria 35.46N 39.37E
90 J2 Madana Chad 18.49N 19.27E
28 D4 Madanapalle Andhra Prad India 13.34N 78.28E
85 B3 Ma'Dan, El Libya 32.04N 13.43E
15 H6 Madang Papua New Guinea 5.14S 145.45E
34 N9 Ma'daniyāt, Al Arabia/Iraq 29.15N 45.34E
30 L6 Madanpur Bihar India 26.12N 87.31E
30 B8 Madanpur Uttar Prad India 24.16N 78.41E
35 H3 Madan Zeidi *watercourse* Syria
23 D2 Madao Shaanxi China 33.25N 106.57E
30 B8 Madaora Uttar Prad India 24.23N 78.48E
89 M4 Madaoua Niger 14.02N 5.59E
33 F9 Madārī Yemen 14.28N 44.08E
29 L4 Madarihat W Bengal India 26.38N 89.20E
31 H9 Madaripur Bangladesh 23.09N 90.11E
Madar-i-Shāh *see* Mādar Shāh
89 N5 Madarounfa Niger 13.20N 7.11E
32 D4 Mādar Shāh Iran 33.01N 51.31E
44 F6 Madatapa, Ozero *L* Georgia U.S.S.R.
26 S6 Madatugama Sri Lanka 7.56N 80.39E
43 C7 Madau Turkmeniya U.S.S.R. 38.00N 49.50E
15 M8 Madau I Papua New Guinea 9.00S 152.27E
39 E4 Madaun U.S.S.R. 60.37N 150.46E
29 D6 Madawari Madhya Prad India 22.14N 75.08E
104 Q6 Madawaska Maine 47.21N 68.21W
99 N7 Madawaska Ontario 45.31N 77.59W
99 N7 Madawaska *R* Ontario
98 D6 Madawaska R Quebec/New Bruns
25 D1 Madaya Burma 22.12N 96.05E
33 E8 Madāyā, Al Saudi Arabia 16.46N 42.45E
33 E7 Maddah, Al Saudi Arabia 18.35N 42.39E
103 O4 Maddaket Massachusetts 41.16N 70.12W
79 B5 Maddalena Italy 44.37N 7.01E
Maddalena, Col de *pass see* Larche, Col de
81 C1 Maddalena, I., di Sardinia
81 C1 Maddalena, La Sardinia 41.13N 9.25E
81 C5 Maddalena, La Sardinia 39.09N 9.02E
81 K9 Maddalena, Pen. di Sicily 37.02N 15.20E
80 K6 Maddaloni Italy 41.03N 14.23E
28 E1 Maddar Madhya Prad India 18.45N 80.39E
115 F9 Madden Dam Panama Canal Zone 9.13N 79.37W
115 F9 Madden L Panama 9.20N 79.37W
14 C10 Madden, Mt W Australia 33.18S 119.59E
14 C2 Maddington *dist* Perth, W Aust
87 J7 Maddiso *watercourse* Ethiopia
108 L2 Maddock N Dakota 47.58N 99.31W
93 K4 Maddo Koni Kenya 1.21N 38.02E
30 G8 Maddupur Uttar Prad India 24.51N 83.03E
28 C4 Maddur Karnataka India 12.36N 77.00E
60 H13 Made Netherlands 51.41N 4.48E
Madehvan *see* Mādevān
76 C9 Madeira Portugal 39.57N 8.02W
96 P7 Madeira *isld* Madeira Is 32.45N 17.00W
117 G2 Madeira *R* Brazil
96 O7 Madeira Is Atlantic Oc 32.45N 17.00W
120 F3 Madeira, R Brazil
120 G3 Madeirinha, R Brazil
65 B7 Madelegabel *mt* W Germany 47.16N 10.12E
66 D1 Madeleine *R* France
70 M5 Madeleine-Bouvet, la France 48.28N 0.55E
98 G4 Madeleine, C. de la Quebec 49.14N 65.20W
98 L6 Madeleine, Is. de la Quebec
71 D4 Madeleine, Mtgnes, de la France
56 G2 Madeley Shropshire Eng 52.39N 2.28W
108 Q5 Madelia Minnesota 44.04N 94.26W
110 E8 Madeline California 41.04N 120.29W
106 D3 Madeline I Wisconsin 46.50N 90.42W
37 E7 Maden Elâzığ Turkey 38.24N 39.42E
37 E5 Maden Gümüşane Turkey 40.08N 40.22E
37 D6 Maden *R* Turkey
23 B5 Madeng Yunnan China 26.26N 99.35E
43 N3 Madeniyet Kazakhstan U.S.S.R. 47.51N 78.37E
43 E5 Madeniyet Uzbekistan U.S.S.R. 42.52N 58.55E
66 P2 Mäder Austria 47.22N 9.37E
111 D5 Madera California 36.57N 120.04W
115 E3 Madera Mexico 29.10N 108.10W
104 G6 Madera Pennsylvania 40.48N 78.27W
77 L4 Madera *R* Spain
112 E5 Madera Mt Texas 30.36N 102.54W
66 L4 Maderaner Tal *V* Switzerland
115 L6 Madero, Ciudad Mexico 22.19N 97.50W
Madero, Gustavo A *see* Villa de Guadalupe
75 F4 Madero, Sierra del *mts* Spain
75 C5 Maderuelo Spain 41.29N 3.31W
32 F6 Mādevān Iran 28.45N 54.17E
63 J10 Madfeld W Germany 51.26N 8.43E
100 Q7 Madge L Saskatchewan
26 Q12 Madge Rocks Seychelles, Ind Oc 4.25S 55.32E
87 J4 Madgoul Djibouti 12.20N 42.28E
28 B1 Madha Maharashtra India 18.03N 75.35E
30 D8 Madhagarh Madhya Prad India 24.34N 80.54E
34 M6 Madhatīyah, Al Iraq 32.25N 44.41E
29 B7 Madhavpur Gujarat India 21.18N 70.01E
30 K6 Madhepur Bihar India 26.11N 86.23E
84 C8 Madhia Greece 36.55N 21.53E
30 K7 Madhipura Bihar India 25.56N 86.48E
30 D5 Madhoganj Uttar Prad India 27.07N 80.08E
30 C6 Madhogarh Uttar Prad India 26.17N 79.11E
29 D1 Madhopur Punjab India 32.22N 75.40E
30 A6 Mādho Sāgar *res* Madhya Prad India 26.14N 77.59E
28 E2 Madhra Andhra Prad India 16.58N 80.25E
30 J6 Madhuban Bihar India 26.27N 85.08E
30 K6 Madhubani Bihar India 26.21N 86.05E
28 C4 Madhugiri Karnataka India 13.41N 77.14E
30 K8 Madhupur Bihar India 24.17N 86.38E
31 H9 Madhupur Jungle Bangladesh
30 L6 Madhura Bihar India 26.20N 87.06E
26 R4 Madhu Road Sri Lanka 8.46N 80.11E
30 C2 Madhyamaheshwar Uttar Prad India 30.37N 79.12E
29 F6 Madhya Pradesh *state* India
33 H9 Ma'di S Yemen 14.59N 49.24E
29 J3 Madi *R* Nepal
95 J1 Madiba S Africa 26.00S 25.33E
92 G6 Madibira Tanzania 8.12S 34.50E
95 J2 Madibogo S Africa 26.25S 25.12E
21 E6 Madida Jilin China 42.57N 130.43E
18 K5 Madi, Dataran Tinggi *high plat* Borneo Indon
120 E5 Madidi, R Bolivia
12 E3 Madigan G S Australia
123 J3 Madigan Nunatak *pk* Antarctica 67.12S 143.25E
109 O7 Madill Oklahoma 34.06N 96.46W
91 D7 Madimba Angola 6.33S 14.25E
91 D6 Madimba Zaïre 5.00s 15.08E
89 B6 Madina Guinea-Bissau 11.47N 14.11W
89 C6 Madina Bové Guinea 11.30N 13.21W
34 P8 Madīnah, Al Iraq 30.56N 47.16E
Madīnah, Al Saudi Arabia*see* Medina
94 J3 Madinare Botswana 21.57S 27.42E
33 E9 Madīnat al 'Abīd Yemen 14.40N 43.58E
34 F3 Madīnat al-Thawra Syria 35.50N 38.36E
33 B9 Madīnat ash Sha'b S Yemen 12.50N 44.56E
33 K5 Madīnat Zāyid U.A.E. 23.34N 53.48E
86 R12 Madinet Nasr *dist* Cairo Egypt
26 E5 Madingley Rise Indian Ocean
91 B6 Madingo Congo 4.05S 11.24E
91 B6 Madingo-Kayes Congo 4.27S 11.43E
91 C6 Madingou Congo 4.10S 13.33E
93 E2 Madi Opei Uganda 3.38N 33.06E
95 H3 Madipelesa S Africa 27.54S 24.25E
29 A1 Madipūr Delhi India 28.40N 77.08E
86 L10 Madîq Gûbâl *channel* Egypt
86 M10 Madîq Tîrân *channel* Egypt/Arabia
72 D8 Madiran France 43.33N 0.03W
90 F6 Madiri Nigeria 11.54N 13.51E
95 C4 Madirovalo Madagascar 16.25S 46.31E
107 K7 Madison Alabama 34.41N 86.45W
107 F6 Madison Arkansas 35.01N 90.42W
103 J4 Madison Connecticut 41.17N 72.36W
105 D7 Madison Florida 30.29N 83.39W
105 D4 Madison Georgia 33.33N 83.30W
107 L3 Madison Indiana 38.46N 85.22W
109 O3 Madison Kansas 38.09N 96.10W
104 Q2 Madison Maine 44.48N 69.53W
108 O4 Madison Minnesota 45.01N 96.11W
107 D2 Madison Missouri 39.27N 92.13W
105 H1 Madison N Carolina 36.24N 79.59W
108 N8 Madison Nebraska 41.50N 97.28W
103 F5 Madison New Jersey 40.45N 74.25W
104 D5 Madison Ohio 41.47N 81.04W
100 J7 Madison Saskatchewan 51.12N 109.00W
108 N5 Madison S Dakota 44.01N 97.08W
107 K5 Madison Tennessee 36.16N 86.44W
104 G8 Madison Virginia 38.23N 78.16W
106 E6 Madison Wisconsin 43.04N 89.22W
104 D8 Madison W Virginia 38.03N 81.50W
107 M12 Madison *dist* St Louis, Ill
110 O4 Madison *R* Montana
104 F9 Madison Heights Virginia 37.26N 79.08W
110 P5 Madison Junct Wyoming 44.39N 110.51W
110 O4 Madison Ra Montana
107 J4 Madisonville Kentucky 37.20N 87.30W
107 F11 Madisonville Louisiana 30.25N 90.09W
107 M6 Madisonville Tennessee 35.31N 84.21W
112 M5 Madisonville Texas 30.58N 95.56W
66 H3 Madiswil Switzerland 47.11N 7.48E
93 K7 Maditha *mt* Kenya 1.06S 38.42E
94 H3 Maditsenyane Botswana 20.59S 25.10E
18 J9 Madiun Java Indon 7.37S 111.33E
90 L6 Madjia Cent Afr Rep 10.01N 22.25E
91 D3 Madjingo Gabon 1.20N 14.04E
53 T21 Madla Norway 58.57N 5.40E
56 F3 Madley Hereford & Worcs Eng 52.03N 2.51W
14 E6 Madley, Mt W Australia 24.30S 123.55E
59 L2 Madman's Window Antrim N Ireland 54.58N 5.57W
30 C5 Madnapur Uttar Prad India 27.52N 79.40E
Madniskhevi *see* Uchkulan
93 L3 Mado Kenya 2.10N 39.42E
108 E1 Madoc Montana 48.50N 105.20W
99 N8 Madoc Ontario 44.30N 77.29W
93 K4 Mado Delbek Kenya 1.37N 38.20E
93 L5 Mado Gashi Kenya 0.45N 39.11E
23 A1 Madoi Qinghai China 34.53N 98.35E
91 C5 Madoko Congo 3.21S 13.13E
87 A6 Madol Sudan 9.03N 27.45E
69 L7 Madon *R* France
46 F2 Madona Latvia U.S.S.R. 56.54N 26.10E
66 M6 Madone-grosso *mt* Switzerland 46.22N 8.51E
95 N6 Madonela S Africa 30.15S 29.58E
81 G8 Madonie, le *mts* Sicily
79 J1 Madonna Italy 46.43N 10.51E
66 M7 Madonna del Sasso Switzerland 46.11N 8.48E
79 J2 Madonna di Campiglio Italy 46.13N 10.49E
93 K5 Mado Yaka Kenya 0.43N 38.21E
29 B5 Madpura Rajasthan India 25.55N 71.32E
110 B9 Mad R California
36 C3 Madra Dağı *mt* Turkey 39.23N 27.13E
33 C6 Madrakah Saudi Arabia 21.57N 39.59E
33 M7 Madrakah, Ra's *C* Oman 19.00N 57.52E
36 C5 Madran Baba Dağı *mt* Turkey
110 D5 Madras Oregon 44.39N 121.08W
28 C7 Madras Tamil Nadu India 13.05N 80.18E
Madras *state see* Tamil Nadu
120 D5 Madre de Dios Peru 12.35S 70.06W
120 D4 Madre de Dios *dept* Peru
121 H8 Madre de Dios, I Chile
120 E4 Madre de Dios, R Bolivia/Peru
77 D6 Madre de las Marismas *R* Spain
102 G7 Madre del Sur, Sierra *ra* Mexico
115 L5 Madre, L Mexico
112 K9 Madre, L Texas
109 C7 Madre Mt New Mexico 34.18N 107.55W
102 E5 Madre Occidental, Sierra *ra* Mexico
102 G6 Madre Oriental, Sierra *ra* Mexico
19 L3 Madre, Sa Luzon Philippines
115 N10 Madre, Sa *ra* Mexico/Guatemala
72 J10 Madrès, Pic de *mt* France 42.38N 2.11E
108 R8 Madrid Iowa 41.52N 93.49W
19 M7 Madrid Mindanao Philippines 9.15N 125.59E
108 J9 Madrid Nebraska 40.52N 101.32W
109 D6 Madrid New Mexico 35.23N 106.11W
104 K2 Madrid New York 44.46N 75.10W
75 C7 Madrid Spain 40.25N 3.43W
74 E4 Madrid *prov* Spain
19 L6 Madridejos Philippines 11.16N 123.45E
77 J2 Madridejos Spain 39.29N 3.32W
75 Q7 Madrid Moderno *dist* Madrid Spain
120 D8 Madrid, Pta *C* Chile 19.05S 70.20W
76 J6 Madrigal de las Altas Torres Spain 41.05N 5.00W
76 J8 Madrigal de la Vera Spain 40.09N 5.22W
77 E2 Madrigalejo Spain 39.09N 5.37W
75 C3 Madrigalejo del Monte Spain 42.07N 3.44W
75 D5 Madriguera Spain 41.18N 3.20W
77 N2 Madrigueras Spain 39.15N 1.49W
66 Q4 Madrisahorn *mt* Switzerland 46.56N 9.53E
77 H4 Madrona, Sierra *mts* Spain
76 H10 Madroñera Spain 39.26N 5.45W
77 N3 Madroño *mt* Spain 38.39N 1.32W
116 D3 Madruga Cuba 22.55N 81.50W
85 C7 Madrūsah Libya 24.48N 14.32E
86 L8 Madsûs, Gebel *hill* Egypt 28.31N 33.50E
86 M10 Madsûs, Gebel *hill* Egypt 27.55N 34.11E
90 N4 Madu Sudan 14.37N 26.04E
93 C5 Madu Uganda 0.14N 31.41E
19 B7 Madu *isld* Indonesia 7.31S 121.47E
19 K6 Maducang *isld* Philippines 10.41N 120.15E
91 C6 Maduda Zaïre 4.53S 13.04E
93 C5 Madudu Uganda 0.42N 31.30E
28 F2 Madugula Andhra Prad India 17.53N 82.54E
93 G9 Madukani Tanzania 3.55S 35.47E
26 T7 Madulsima Sri Lanka 7.06N 81.09E
53 A4 Madum Denmark 56.14N 8.18E
53 D3 Madum Sø *L* Denmark 56.48N 9.58E
35 H6 Maduna *watercourse* Jordan
Madura India*see* Madurai
14 F9 Madura W Australia 31.58N 127.00E
18 K9 Madura *isld* Indonesia
28 D6 Madurai Tamil Nadu India 9.55N 78.07E
28 C5 Madurai *dist* Tamil Nadu India
26 Q6 Madurankuli Sri Lanka 7.54N 79.50E
28 D4 Madurantakam Tamil Nadu India 12.31N 79.54E
18 K9 Madura, Selat *str* Java/Madura Indon
26 T6 Maduru Oya *R* Sri Lanka
31 F2 Madut Pass Afghanistan 38.00N 71.03E
35 G4 Madwar, El Jordan 32.17N 36.00E
31 G3 Madyan Pakistan 35.10N 72.30E
47 G5 Madzha U.S.S.R. 61.51N 51.21E
44 H5 Madzhalis U.S.S.R. 42.08N 47.50E
92 F8 Madzimoyo Zambia 13.42S 32.34E
20 D8 Maebaru Japan 33.34N 130.10E
20 N5 Maebashi Japan 36.24N 139.04E
25 E3 Mae Hong Son Thailand 19.18N 98.01E
20 O9 Mae-jima *isld* Okinawa Japan
53 V16 Mæl Sogn og Fjordane Norway 61.20N 6.34E
52 D7 Mæl Telemark Norway 59.55N 8.50E
88 J9 Ma, el *watercourse* Mauritania
70 D5 Maël-Carhaix France 48.17N 3.25W
25 E3 Mae Li *R* Thailand
50 F4 Mælifell Iceland 65.26N 19.21W
50 F4 Mælifellshnjukur *mt* Iceland 65.24N 19.22W
75 L5 Maella Spain 41.07N 0.09E
76 K7 Maello Spain 40.48N 4.31W
70 D5 Maël-Pestivien France 48.24N 3.17W
Mae Mo *see* Ban Mae Mo
25 F3 Mae Nam Ing *R* Thailand
25 G5 Mae Nam Mun *R* Thailand
25 F3 Mae Nam Nan *R* Thailand
25 F4 Mae Nam Pa Sak *R* Thailand
25 G4 Mae Nam Song Khram *R* Thailand
25 E4 Mae Nam Wang *R* Thailand
25 F3 Mae Nam Yam *R* Thailand
25 E4 Mae Nam Yom *R* Thailand
20 D2 Maeno *dist* Tōkyō Japan
57 F7 Maentwrog Gwynedd Wales 52.57N 3.59W
Mae Ranat *see* Ban Mae Ranat
56 E4 Maerdy Mid Glam Wales 51.41N 3.28W
15 H8 Maer I Torres Str, Qnsld 9.55S 144.04E
25 E3 Mae Rim Thailand 18.54N 98.58E
82 J5 Măeruş Romania 45.53N 25.30E
Mae Sariang *see* Ban Mae Sariang
20 P2 Maesawa Japan 39.02N 141.04E
110 Q9 Maeser Utah 40.27N 109.38W
Mae Sot *see* Ban Mae Sot
56 D4 Maesteg Mid Glam Wales 51.37N 3.40W
79 N5 Maestra, Pta *pt* Italy 44.59N 12.31E
116 F4 Maestra, Sa *mts* Cuba
75 K7 Maestrazgo, El *reg* Spain
77 F6 Maestre *mt* Spain 37.15N 5.13W
19 K5 Maestre de Campo *isld* Philippines 12.54N 121.44E
80 E2 Maestro di Chiana, Canale Italy
75 F2 Maestu Spain 42.44N 2.25W
Mae Suai *see* Ban Mae Suai
Mae Thalop *see* Ban Mae Thalop
95 C4 Maevatanana Madagascar 16.57S 46.50E
9 C10 Maewo *isld* New Hebrides
25 D3 Mae Yuam *R* Thailand
50 H7 Mafabót *isld* Iceland 63.43N 17.45W
50 J6 Máfabyggdhir *mt* Iceland 64.10N 16.38W
50 B5 Máfahlidh Iceland 64.55N 23.30W
92 K10 Mafamede, I Mozambique 16.19S 40.00E
26 T15 Mafate, Cirque de Réunion Ind Oc
100 Q6 Mafeking Manitoba 52.43N 101.06W
95 J1 Mafeking S Africa 25.53S 25.39E
95 L5 Mafeteng Lesotho 29.49S 27.14E
95 L5 Mafeteng *dist* Lesotho
61 M5 Maffe Belgium 50.22N 5.18E
61 F4 Maffle Belgium 50.37N 3.48E
12 H7 Maffra Victoria 37.58N 146.59E
92 J5 Mafia Channel East Africa
92 J5 Mafia I E Africa
92 H6 Mafingi Tanzania 8.35S 36.20E
92 G8 Mafinto *tribe* Mozambique
118 E10 Mafra Brazil 26.08S 49.47W
76 A11 Mafra Portugal 38.57N 9.19W
35 H4 Mafraq Jordan 32.20N 36.12E
117 G9 Mafrense Brazil 8.21S 41.04W
91 G10 Mafuca Angola 13.03S 21.48E
92 D11 Mafungabusi Plat Zimbabwe
77 E3 Magacela Spain 38.54N 5.44W
39 E5 Magadan U.S.S.R. 59.38N 150.50E
38 P2 Magadanskaya Oblast' *prov* U.S.S.R.
93 H7 Magadi Kenya 1.53S 36.18E
93 H7 Magadi, L (Soda) Kenya
66 M7 Magadino Switzerland 46.09N 8.52E
92 G5 Magaga Tanzania 6.29S 35.23E
98 E8 Magaguadavic L New Brunswick
94 M4 Magaiza Mozambique 23.42S 33.57E
90 J2 Magala Chad 18.19N 19.27E
87 F3 Magala Ethiopia 14.33N 36.54E
71 C10 Magalas France 43.28N 3.13E
95 L1 Magaliesberg *mts* S Africa
95 L2 Magaliesburg S Africa 26.00S 27.33E
Magallanes Chile*see* Punta Arenas
19 L5 Magallanes Luzon Philippines 12.49N 123.52E
121 J8 Magallanes *prov* Chile
116 F4 Magallanes Bank Gt Bahama Bank
121 K9 Magallanes, Estrecho de *str* Chile
75 H4 Magallón Spain 41.50N 1.27W
87 H7 Magalo Ethiopia 6.51N 40.48E
93 E5 Magamaga Uganda 0.31N 33.23E
90 C6 Magami Nigeria 11.44N 6.31E
15 A4 Magamo Irian Jaya 0.54S 131.49E
75 F4 Magaña Spain 41.54N 2.10W
92 G8 Maganga Malawi 13.50S 34.37E
119 D3 Magangué Colombia 9.14N 74.46W
42 E4 Magansk U.S.S.R. 55.52N 93.14E
37 F6 Mağara Erzincan Turkey 39.39N 40.43E
Mağara İçel Turkey*see* Kırobası
44 J6 Magaramkent U.S.S.R. 41.36N 48.21E
90 D5 Magaria Niger 13.00N 8.59E
15 K9 Magarida Papua New Guinea 10.10S 149.21E
20 Q8 Magari-zaki *C* Okinawa Japan 26.36N 128.09E
Magaro *see* El'brusskiy
Magas *see* Zābolī
19 K3 Magat *R* Luzon Philippines
94 L4 Magato Mts S Africa
19 G2 Magay *R* Luzon Philippines
76 L5 Magaz Spain 41.59N 4.26W
76 G3 Magaz de Cepeda Spain 42.33N 6.05W
107 C6 Magazine Mt Arkansas 35.11N 93.38W
81 F9 Magazzolo *R* Sicily
91 B1 Magba Cameroon 5.58N 11.09E
89 D7 Magburaka Sierra Leone 8.44N 11.57W
40 C5 Magdagachi U.S.S.R. 53.27N 125.44E
64 L2 Magdala E Germany 50.55N 11.25E
87 G5 Magdala Ethiopia 11.25N 39.18E
121 F5 Magdalena Argentina 35.05S 57.30W
115 C4 Magdalena Baja Cal Mexico 27.04N 112.09W
120 F5 Magdalena Bolivia 13.22S 64.07W
109 C7 Magdalena New Mexico 34.06N 107.14W
115 D2 Magdalena Sonora Mexico 30.38N 110.59W
119 D3 Magdalena *div* Colombia
119 C5 Magdalena, B Colombia 4.00N 77.16W
120 B10 Magdalena del Mar *dist* Lima Peru
121 A10 Magdalena, I Aisén Chile
115 C5 Magdalena, I Mexico
76 H3 Magdalena, La Spain 42.47N 5.48W
18 M3 Magdalena, Mt Sabah Malaysia 4.29N 117.56E
119 D3 Magdalena, R Colombia
Magdalen Is *see* Madeleine, Is. de la
45 F8 Magdalinovka Ukraine U.S.S.R. 48.54N 34.56E

63 P8 Magdeburg E Germany 52.08N 11.37E
63 O8 Magdeburg reg E Germany
63 Q8 Magdeburgerforth E Germany 52.15N 12.12E
13 K3 Magdelaine Cays islds Gt Barrier Reef Australia
66 H1 Magden Switzerland 47.32N 7.49E
63 O9 Mägdesprung E Germany 51.41N 11.09E
35 C5 Magdi'el Israel 32.11N 34.53E
107 G10 Magee Mississippi 31.52N 89.44W
59 L2 Magee, I Antrim N Ireland 54.50N 5.45W
113 K7 Mageik Vol Alaska 58.10N 155.25W
18 J9 Magelang Java Indon 7.28S 110.11E
122 F6 Magellan Seamounts Pacific Oc
Magellan, Straits of see Magallanes, Estrecho de
35 A8 Magen Israel 31.19N 34.25E
79 E4 Magenta Italy 45.28N 8.52E
14 C10 Magenta, L W Australia 33.30S 119.02E
53 V14 Magerholm Norway 62.27N 6.31E
51 M1 Magerøya isld Norway 71.00N 25.40E
66 N3 Magerrain mt Switzerland 47.02N 9.14E
72 B8 Magescq France 43.46N 1.13W
21 E12 Mageshima isld Japan 30.45N 130.52E
93 F6 Mageta I Kenya 0.08S 34.00E
40 G3 Magey R U.S.S.R.
35 D4 Maggal Israel 32.23N 35.02E
66 L7 Maggia Switzerland 46.15N 8.42E
66 L6 Maggia R Switzerland
66 L7 Maggia, Valle Switzerland
79 F5 Maggiorasca, Monte Italy 44.33N 9.29E
80 F2 Maggiore I Italy 43.10N 12.05E
79 E3 Maggiore, Lago L Italy
78 F7 Maggiore, Mte Italy 41.15N 14.10E
80 G3 Maggiore, Mte Italy 42.49N 12.52E
Magglingen see Macolin
116 J2 Maggotty Jamaica, W I 18.09N 77.46W
86 E8 Maghâgha Egypt 28.39N 30.50E
89 C4 Maghama Mauritania 15.32N 12.57W
35 E2 Maghār Israel 32.53N 35.24E
30 G6 Maghar Uttar Prad India 26.45N 83.08E
86 K4 Maghâra, Gebel hill Egypt 30.44N 33.25E
33 G2 Magharah Kuwait 29.19N 47.45E
59 B7 Magharee Is Kerry Irish Rep 52.20N 10.03W
35 H6 Maghayir watercourse Jordan
34 B10 Maghayir Shu'ayb anc site Saudi Arabia 28.28N 34.59E
59 J2 Maghera Londonderry N Ireland 54.51N 6.40W
59 J2 Magherafelt Londonderry N Ireland 54.45N 6.36W
59 K3 Magheralin Down N Ireland 54.28N 6.16W
59 J2 Maghery Armagh N Ireland 54.31N 6.35W
88 N4 Maghnia Algeria 34.50N 1.45W
31 B3 Maghor Afghanistan 35.02N 63.15E
86 A5 Maghra, El reg Egypt
57 H5 Maghull Merseyside Eng 55.32N 2.57W
43 J7 Magian Tadzhikistan U.S.S.R. 39.17N 67.33E
110 L6 Magic Res Idaho 43.19N 114.25W
15 H6 Magila Papua New Guinea 4.57S 145.31E
77 K5 Magina mt Spain 37.44N 3.28W
77 K5 Mágina, Sierra de mts Spain
95 D3 Magindrano Madagascar 14.15S 48.58E
20 D3 Maginu Kanagawa Japan
80 F2 Magione Italy 43.08N 12.12E
81 N5 Magisano Italy 39.01N 16.38E
115 K6 Magiscatzín Mexico 22.48N 98.41W
82 E6 Maglaj Yugoslavia 44.33N 18.09E
71 K4 Magland France 46.01N 6.38E
53 J7 Magleby Møn, Storstrøm Denmark 54.59N 11.59E
53 J6 Magleby Storstrøm Denmark 55.23N 12.22E
53 F7 Magleby Svendborg Denmark 54.47N 10.43E
53 G7 Maglehöjstrand Denmark 54.45N 11.08E
65 J8 Maglern Austria 46.34N 13.40E
80 F5 Magliana Italy 41.49N 12.26E
79 C6 Magliano Alpi Italy 44.27N 7.47E
80 H4 Magliano de Marsi Italy 42.06N 13.22E
80 D3 Magliano in Toscana Italy 42.36N 11.18E
80 F4 Magliano Sabino Italy 42.22N 12.29E
82 E7 Maglič mt Yugoslavia 43.15N 18.42E
81 R12 Maglie Italy 40.07N 18.18E
39 E2 Maglyy U.S.S.R. 67.08N 150.09E
111 N8 Magma Arizona 33.10N 111.29W
34 B10 Magnā Saudi Arabia 28.26N 34.44E
110 N9 Magna Utah 40.43N 112.06W
72 G4 Magnac Bourg France 45.37N 1.25E
72 G3 Magnac-Laval France 46.13N 1.10E
72 J4 Magnat l'Etrange France 45.47N 2.15E
Magnesia ad Sipylum see Manisa
108 N7 Magnet Nebraska 42.28N 97.28W
99 L7 Magnetawan Ontario 45.40N 79.38W
123 A5 Magnet B Antarctica
13 H4 Magnetic I Queensland
13 H4 Magnetic Pass Gt Barrier Reef Australia 18.10S 147.18E
69 M7 Magnières France 48.27N 6.34E
84 E3 Magnisía prov Greece
81 K9 Magnisi, Pen. di Sicily 37.09N 15.14E
47 L5 Magnitka U.S.S.R. 55.20N 59.44E
43 E1 Magnitogorsk U.S.S.R. 53.28N 59.06E
107 C8 Magnolia Arkansas 33.17N 93.16W
103 D8 Magnolia Delaware 39.04N 75.29W
108 O6 Magnolia Minnesota 43.38N 96.05W
107 F10 Magnolia Mississippi 31.08N 90.30W
105 J3 Magnolia N Carolina 34.55N 78.04W
112 M5 Magnolia Texas 30.11N 95.47W
52 G7 Magnon Norway 59.56N 12.15E
66 B1 Magny France 47.40N 6.29E
71 C3 Magny-Cours France 46.54N 3.08E
69 B5 Magny-en-Vexin France 49.09N 1.47E
70 K3 Magny-la-Campagne France 49.03N 0.06W
40 H5 Mago U.S.S.R. 53.15N 140.06E
92 E9 Magoe Mozambique 15.50S 31.42E
99 S7 Magog Quebec 45.16N 72.09W
95 H3 Magogong S Africa 27.40S 24.47E
20 G2 Magome Chiba Japan
56 F4 Magor Gwent Wales 51.35N 2.50W
29 C6 Magori Gujarat India 23.17N 73.23E
93 F4 Magoro Uganda 1.43N 34.07E
115 L7 Magosal Mexico 21.40N 97.59W
103 B8 Magothy R Maryland
84 W22 Magouládhes Corfu 39.46N 19.41E
84 D6 Magoúliana Greece 37.40N 22.07E
84 C3 Magoulítsa Greece 39.27N 21.45E
88 N4 Magoura Algeria 34.15N 1.38W
92 C10 Magoye Zambia 16.00S 27.34E
99 F4 Magpie Ontario 48.07N 84.41W
98 H3 Magpie Quebec 50.18N 64.31W
99 F4 Magpie R Ontario
98 H3 Magpie L Quebec
99 F4 Magpie Mine Ontario 48.17N 84.41W
98 H3 Magpie R Quebec
98 G2 Magpie, R., West Quebec
29 M6 Magra W Bengal India 22.59N 88.24E
79 G6 Magra R Italy
100 E9 Magrath Alberta 49.27N 112.52W
79 K2 Magrè all' Adige Italy 46.17N 11.13E
77 O2 Magro R Spain
88 O3 Magroua, C Algeria 36.25N 0.49E
111 G4 Magruder Mt Nevada 37.26N 117.33W
88 H7 Magruna, El Morocco 28.03N 11.48W
87 A3 Magrur,Wadi Sudan
19 K3 Magsingal Luzon Philippines 17.40N 120.25E
53 C6 Magstrup Denmark 55.18N 9.21E
89 C3 Magta Lahjar Mauritania 17.28N 13.17W
93 E8 Magu Tanzania 2.31S 33.28E
23 C7 Maguan Yunnan China 23.02N 104.20E
117 D5 Maguarinho, C Brazil 0.15S 48.23W
94 M5 Magude Mozambique 25.02S 32.40E
95 O9 Magudu S Africa 27.32S 31.40E
71 D9 Maguelonne France 43.30N 3.54E
96 V7 Maguez Lanzarote Canary Is 29.10N 13.30W
23 F7 Magui Guangdong China 22.10N 111.18E
77 E4 Maguilla Spain 38.22N 5.50W
59 H3 Maguire'sbridge Fermanagh N Ireland 54.18N 7.27W
94 M4 Maguje Mozambique 23.38S 32.30E
40 G5 Magu, Khrebet mts U.S.S.R.
90 F5 Magumeri Nigeria 12.10N 12.50E
19 E1 Magupu isld Indonesia 4.42N 127.08E
17 Q10 Magur Caroline Is Pacific Oc 8.59N 150.07E
31 H9 Magura Bangladesh 23.29N 89.25E
95 N6 Magusheni S Africa 30.51S 29.37E
33 M10 Magwa oil field Kuwait
25 C2 Magwe Burma 20.08N 94.55E
93 D1 Magwe Sudan 4.08N 32.19E
65 O8 Magyarszombatfa Hungary 46.46N 16.22E
25 B2 Magyichaung Burma 20.18N 92.42E
93 E5 Magyo Uganda 0.12N 33.18E
31 D5 Magzai Bedawan Pass Afghan/Pakistan 30.22N 66.21E
32 A2 Mahābād Iran 36.44N 45.44E
28 A2 Mahabaleshwar Maharashtra India 17.56N 73.42E
28 E4 Mahabalipuram Tamil Nadu India 12.37N 80.13E
30 A5 Mahaban Uttar Prad India 27.27N 77.46E
95 B4 Mahabe Madagascar 17.02S 45.20E
29 J4 Mahabharat Ra Nepal
95 B6 Mahabo Madagascar 20.22S 44.39E
95 C7 Mahabo Madagascar 23.40S 46.09E
95 B7 Mahaboboka Madagascar 22.52N 44.19E
28 A1 Mahad Maharashtra India 18.05N 73.29E
87 K9 Mahaddei Uen Somalia 2.58N 45.32E
29 E6 Mahadeo Hills Madhya Prad India
28 E1 Mahadeopur Andhra Prad India 18.44N 80.04E
87 F5 Mahadera Mariam Ethiopia 11.42N 37.54E
Mahadha see Maḩdah
26 T6 Mahaella Sri Lanka 7.37N 81.05E
122 C11 Mahaena Tahiti Pacific Oc 17.33S 149.19W
104 G6 Mahaffey Pennsylvania 40.53N 78.46W
28 C2 Mahagaon Karnataka India 17.33N 76.53E
93 B3 Mahagi Zaïre 2.16N 30.59E
93 C3 Mahagi-Port Zaïre 2.08N 31.15E
22 C7 Mahai Qinghai China 38.04N 94.15E
117 A1 Mahaicony Guyana 6.34N 57.50W
95 C5 Mahaiza Madagascar 19.55S 46.49E
95 C3 Mahajamba R Madagascar
29 C3 Mahajan Rajasthan Ind 28.47N 73.58E
95 C3 Mahajanga Madagascar 15.40S 46.20E
18 L5 Mahakam R Borneo Indon
33 J5 Maḩākik,Al sand area Saudi Arabia
94 J4 Mahalapye Botswana 23.05S 26.51E
84 B4 Mahalás Greece 38.41N 21.11E
95 D3 Mahalevona Madagascar 15.22S 49.55E
86 F4 Maḩalla El Kubra, El Egypt 30.59N 31.10E
32 D4 Maḩallat Iran 33.54N 50.28E
Mahallat Bala see Mahallat
86 D4 Mahallet Keil Egypt 31.00N 30.17E
95 C8 Mahaly Madagascar 24.10S 46.20E
29 E3 Maham Haryana India 29.00N 76.20E
95 P3 Mahamba S Africa 27.06S 31.04E
32 G5 Mahān Iran 30.05N 57.18E
30 E8 Mahana R Madhya Prad India
29 J7 Mahanadi R Madhya Prad/Orissa India
30 M6 Mahananda R Bihar/W Bengal India
19 M6 Mahanay isld Philippines 10.12N 124.15E
35 F2 Maḩanayim Israel 32.59N 33.34E
35 B1 Maḩane Yehuda sub Jerusalem
18 A6 Mahang Pen Malaysia 5.18N 100.44E
95 D5 Mahanoro Madagascar 19.53S 48.48E
103 B5 Mahanoy City Pennsylvania 40.48N 76.08W
103 A5 Mahanoy Cr Pennsylvania
21 D6 Mahao Jilin China 43.10N 128.00E
26 T6 Maha-Oya Sri Lanka 7.31N 81.22E
26 Q7 Maha Oya R Sri Lanka
Maharadh, Al reg see Mihrād, Al
89 A2 Mahara, El Mauritania 19.08N 16.12W
Maharah see Mahrah
30 H6 Maharajganj Bihar India 26.07N 84.31E
30 G5 Maharajganj Gorakhpur, Uttar Prad India 27.09N 83.34E
30 F5 Maharajganj Nepal 27.41N 82.48E
30 E6 Maharajganj Rae Bareli, Uttar Prad India 26.23N 81.17E
30 D5 Maharajnagar Uttar Prad India 27.34N 80.56E
30 L7 Maharajpur Bihar India 25.13N 87.44E
30 D6 Maharajpur Uttar Prad India 26.20N 80.27E
29 D7 Maharashtra state India
95 C5 Maharidaza Madagascar 18.15S 47.20E
85 L7 Mahâriq, El Egypt 25.36N 30.37E
86 H10 Mahârîq, Wâdi watercourse Egypt
33 A3 Mahārish, Ra's C Saudi Arabia 27.28N 35.34E
32 E6 Mahārlū, Daryācheh-ye salt L Iran
86 F6 Maḩarraqa, El Egypt 29.33N 31.14E
85 M8 Maḩarraqa Temple, El ruins Egypt 23.03N 32.41E
29 H7 Mahasamund Madhya Prad India 21.10N 82.10E
25 G4 Maha Sarakham Thailand 16.08N 102.16E
86 M6 Mahasham, Wâdî el watercourse Egypt
95 O9 Mahashini S Africa 27.53S 31.33E
86 L9 Maḩash, Wâdî watercourse Egypt
109 N2 Mahaska Kansas 39.58N 97.23W
95 C5 Mahasolo Madagascar 19.04S 46.21E
31 H8 Mahasthan Bangladesh 24.59N 89.24E
30 A1 Mahasu dist Himachal Prad India
95 C8 Mahatalaky Madagascar 24.48S 47.05E
95 B8 Mahatsanary Madagascar 25.14S 44.29E
95 B6 Mahatsinjo Madagascar 21.27S 45.50E
95 C4 Mahatsinjo Madagascar 17.44S 47.00E
35 H2 Mahattat Isra' Syria 32.51N 36.14E
95 D2 Mahavanona Madagascar 12.30S 49.23E
95 C4 Mahavavy R Madagascar
95 D4 Mahavelona Madagascar 17.40S 49.30E
30 B4 Mahawa R Uttar Prad India
26 S6 Mahaweli Ganga R Sri Lanka
33 D6 Maḩāwiyah,Al Saudi Arabia 20.15N 41.19E
25 H4 Mahaxay Laos 17.28N 105.18E
95 C7 Mahazoarivo Madagascar 22.40S 47.19E
87 B4 Mahbub Sudan 13.20N 29.12E
28 E2 Mahbubabad Andhra Prad India 17.40N 80.02E
28 C2 Mahbubnagar Andhra Prad India 16.45N 77.57E
28 C2 Mahbubnagar dist Andhra Prad India
33 D5 Mahd adh Dhahab Saudi Arabia 23.29N 40.50E
33 L4 Maḩdah Oman 24.25N 55.59E
33 D6 Maḩdam, Al Saudi Arabia 21.02N 40.45E
119 J5 Mahdia Guyana 5.10N 59.12W
88 T4 Mahdia Tunisia 35.29N 11.03E
28 B5 Mahé Kerala India 11.41N 75.31E
26 V13 Mahebourg Mauritius, Indian Oc 20.24S 57.42E
26 Q13 Mahé I Seychelles, Ind Oc
Mahelleh see Mo'alla
29 E3 Mahendragarh Haryana India 28.17N 76.14E
29 H6 Mahendragarh Madhya Prad Ind 23.21N 82.21E
29 J8 Mahendragiri mt Orissa India 19.00N 84.19E
92 H6 Mahenge Tanzania 8.41S 36.41E
11 E12 Maheno New Zealand 45.11S 170.51E
99 J3 Maher Ontario 49.28N 81.09W
30 L8 Maheshpur Bihar India 24.29N 87.45E
29 D6 Maheshwar Madhya Prad India 22.11N 75.40E
95 E3 Maheva Madagascar 14.22S 50.10E
30 D8 Mahewa Madhya Prad India 24.23N 80.09E
33 G9 Mahfidh, Al S Yemen 14.02N 46.57E
33 K10 Maḩfirhin Socotra Ind Oc 12.28N 54.14E
34 G8 Maḩfūr Saudi Arabia 30.38N 39.22E
30 C6 Mahgalpur Uttar Prad India 26.31N 79.41E
30 B6 Mahgawan Madhya Prad India 26.30N 78.36E
32 H6 Māhī Iran
11 M6 Mahia New Zealand 39.05S 177.56E
33 C3 Maḩiā, Al reg Saudi Arabia
88 M10 Maḩia, El reg Mali
11 M6 Mahia Pen New Zealand
76 G5 Mahide Spain 41.52N 6.23W
29 C8 Mahim Maharashtra India 19.40N 72.46E
28 A7 Mahim dist Bombay India
28 A7 Mahim Bay Bombay India
28 B7 Mahim R Bombay India
90 B8 Mahin Nigeria 6.05N 4.51E
122 C11 Mahina Tahiti Pacific Oc 17.29S 149.27W
11 D5 Mahina B New Zealand 41.16S 174.54E
11 E9 Mahinapua, L New Zealand 42.47S 170.55E
11 D12 Mahinerangi, L New Zealand 45.55S 169.58E
29 A3 Mahipalpur Delhi India 28.32N 77.08E
29 C6 Mahi R Rajasthan etc India
35 G6 Mahis Jordan 31.59N 35.46E
95 C5 Mahitsy Madagascar 18.42S 47.20E
31 K4 Mahiya Kashmir 33.18N 78.32E
26 T7 Mahiyangana Sri Lanka 7.19N 81.00E
35 F2 Mahjar, El Syria 32.54N 35.38E
95 O9 Mahlabatini S Africa 28.15S 31.28E
25 C2 Mahlaing Burma 21.03N 95.44E
95 O9 Mahlangasi S Africa 27.38S 31.44E
63 S8 Mahlow E Germany 52.22N 13.24E
63 P8 Mahlwinkel E Germany 52.24N 11.46E
86 E4 Mah Minûf Egypt 30.54N 30.58E
87 D2 Mahmiya Sudan 17.12N 33.43E
31 C9 Mahmoodabad Pakistan 24.51N 67.04E
34 O2 Mahmūdābād Kordestān Iran 36.14N 46.31E
32 E2 Mahmudabad Māzandarān Iran 36.35N 52.14E
30 E5 Mahmudabad Uttar Prad India 27.18N 81.07E
31 E3 Mahmūd-e 'Erāqī Afghanistan 35.01N 69.20E
82 M5 Mahmudia Romania 45.05N 29.05E
86 E3 Maḩmudiya, El Egypt 31.11N 30.31E
34 M5 Maḩmūdīyah, Al Iraq 33.04N 44.22E
36 E3 Mahmudiye Turkey 39.29N 30.57E
37 G1 Mahmutşevketpaşa Turkey 41.05N 29.19E
34 P2 Māhneshān Iran 36.43N 47.41E
32 C3 Mahniān Iran 35.34N 49.10E
108 P2 Mahnomen Minnesota 47.19N 95.58W
26 R6 Maho Sri Lanka 7.49N 80.17E
30 C7 Mahoba Uttar Prad India 25.18N 79.53E
11 J5 Mahoenui New Zealand 38.32S 174.52E
110 F8 Mahogany Pk Nevada 41.01N 119.35W
30 D5 Maholi Uttar Prad India 27.39N 80.28E
106 F9 Mahomet Illinois 40.13N 88.26W
77 Y14 Mahón Balearic Is 39.54N 4.15E
89 F9 Mahon Ivory Coast 5.08N 6.20W
92 J11 Mahonda Zanzibar 6.00S 39.15E
98 H9 Mahone B Nova Scotia
98 H9 Mahone Bay Nova Scotia 44.27N 64.24W
77 Y14 Mahón, Pto. de Balearic Is
101 L3 Mahony L N W Terr
59 E7 Mahoonagh Limerick Irish Rep 52.26N 9.00W
103 G4 Mahopac New York 41.22N 73.44W
103 G4 Mahopac Falls New York 41.22N 73.45W
77 N2 Mahora Spain 39.13N 1.44W
90 J6 Mahoua Chad 11.49N 18.26E
33 J8 Mahrah state S Yemen
33 J9 Mahrah tribe S Yemen
33 J8 Mahrah, Al dist S Yemen
86 E10 Mahraş, El Egypt 27.50N 30.47E
33 J8 Mahrāt,Jabal mts S Yemen
33 J8 Mahrāt, Wādī watercourse S Yemen
88 T4 Mahrès Tunisia 34.35N 10.30E
64 O4 Mähring W Germany 49.55N 12.33E
30 B8 Mahroni Uttar Prad India 24.36N 78.43E
35 E1 Mahroûné Lebanon 33.13N 35.20E
30 F6 Mahrua Uttar Prad India 26.23N 82.23E
32 J4 Māhrūd Iran 32.12N 60.39E
86 H4 Maḩsama, El Egypt 30.34N 32.01E
29 C6 Mahsana Gujarat India 23.37N 72.28E
29 B6 Mahsana dist Gujarat India
30 F6 Mahson Uttar Prad India 26.44N 82.47E
108 K4 Mahto S Dakota 45.46N 100.41W
22 C8 Mahuanggou Qinghai China 37.24N 95.28E
22 G8 Mahuangshan Ningxia China 37.12N 107.06E
114 B6 Mahukona Hawaiian Is 20.11N 155.55W
114 B6 Mahukona Harbor Hawaiian Is 20.11N 155.55W
30 F6 Mahul Uttar Prad India 26.09N 82.49E
28 B7 Mahul dist Bombay India 19.00N 72.53E
30 F6 Mahuli Uttar Prad India 26.38N 83.00E
29 K2 Mahulia Bihar India 22.40N 86.25E
94 G5 Mahulitlhake Botswana 24.09S 22.27E
Mahun see Mahān
93 J9 Mahunga mt Tanzania 3.58S 37.41E
28 J3 Mahur Assam India 25.11N 93.07E
29 E8 Mahur Maharashtra India 19.50N 77.59E
15 M5 Mahur I Bismarck Arch 2.50S 152.40E
92 J7 Mahuta Tanzania 10.52S 39.24E
29 B7 Mahuva Gujarat India 21.03N 71.50E
30 J7 Mahuwa Bihar India 25.49N 85.25E
103 F4 Mahwah New Jersey 41.06N 74.09W
32 D4 Mahyār Iran 32.16N 51.49E
19 E6 Mai isld Moluccas Indon 5.24S 127.48E
122 F1 Maia Amer Samoa Pacific Oc 14.14S 169.25W
96 U1 Maia Azores 37.35N 25.23W
76 B6 Maia Portugal 41.14N 8.38W
88 O5 Maïa, El Algeria 33.25N 1.59E
93 C2 Maia, Jeb mt Sudan 3.54N 31.16E
Maiamai see Mayamey
9 B5 Maiana atoll Kiribati, Pac Oc 1.00N 173.00E
79 O2 Maiano Italy 46.12N 13.04E
122 A15 Maïao isld Society Is Pacific Oc 17.23S 150.37W
117 D5 Maiauatá Brazil 1.50S 49.00W
28 J3 Maibang Assam India 25.16N 93.10E
19 D8 Maibang Indonesia 8.08S 124.33E
20 K6 Maibara Japan 35.20N 136.18E
Maibud see Meybod
82 L5 Măicănești Romania 45.30N 27.30E
116 H9 Maicao Colombia 11.23N 72.16W
71 K2 Maîche France 47.15N 6.47E
25 K2 Maichen Guangxi China 20.19N 109.59E
Maichew see Maych'ew
Maichîyé Jnainé see Janīn
120 G2 Maicimirim, R Brazil
120 G2 Maici, R Brazil
117 B4 Maicuru, R Brazil
81 M6 Maida Italy 38.51N 16.22E
Maidān see Maydān
Maidan-i-Gil see Meydān-e Gel salt flat
Maidan-i-Naftun see Meydān-e Naftūn
14 C1 Maida Vale W Australia 31.57S 116.00E
35 D1 Maidel Zoûn Lebanon 33.09N 35.14E
105 F2 Maiden N Carolina 35.34N 81.12W
56 G5 Maiden Bradley Wilts Eng 51.09N 2.17W
103 C5 Maiden Cr Pennsylvania
56 K4 Maidenhead Berks Eng 51.32N 0.44W
56 F6 Maiden Newton Dorset Eng 50.46N 2.35W
106 B5 Maiden Rock Wisconsin 44.34N 92.18W
57 D2 Maidens Strathclyde Scotland 55.20N 4.49W
59 L2 Maidens Lt.Ho.,The Antrim N Ireland 54.56N 5.45W
88 L6 Maider watercourse Morocco
19 E3 Maidi Halmahera Indon 0.08N 127.43E
Maidi Yemensee Maydī
56 N5 Maidstone Kent Eng 51.17N 0.32E
95 P5 Maidstone S Africa 29.33S 31.09E
100 H5 Maidstone Saskatchewan 53.06N 109.18W
90 F6 Maiduguri Nigeria 11.53N 13.16E
86 F7 Maidûm Egypt 29.23N 31.10E
93 B3 Maie Zaïre 2.47N 30.34E
88 O4 Maï, El Algeria 34.26N 0.24E
80 K4 Maiella, Montagna della Italy
66 P3 Maienfeld Switzerland 47.01N 9.32E
81 M6 Maierato Italy 38.44N 16.10E
77 P3 Maigmó mt Spain 38.30N 0.38E
69 D4 Maignelay France 49.33N 2.32E
119 G5 Maigualida, Sa mts Venezuela
87 F7 Maigudo mt Ethiopia 7.27N 37.15E
59 E6 Maigue, R Limerick Irish Rep
30 D8 Maihar Madhya Prad India 24.18N 80.46E
30 C7 Maihgawan Tank Uttar Prad India 25.11N 79.33E
31 J9 Maijdi Bangladesh 22.52N 91.06E
29 G6 Maikala Ra Madhya Prad India
64 E5 Maikammer W Germany 49.18N 8.09E
87 G4 Mai Keneta Ethiopia 13.58N 39.00E
43 J7 Maikhoura Tadzhikistan U.S.S.R. 39.07N 68.25E
91 K4 Maiko R Zaïre
93 J3 Maikona Kenya 2.56N 37.35E
90 C7 Maikonkele Nigeria 9.42N 6.30E
15 C7 Maikoor isld Moluccas Indon
114 A5 Maila Hawaiian Is 21.24N 158.13W
29 H6 Mailan Hill Madhya Prad India 23.30N 83.40E
30 D4 Mailani Uttar Prad India 28.17N 80.20E
65 O4 Mailberg Austria 48.41N 16.12E
71 C7 Mailhebiau mt France 44.34N 3.05E
101 H11 Maillardville Br Col 49.16N 122.52W
70 N4 Maillebois France 48.38N 1.09E
61 K5 Maillen Belgium 50.23N 4.58E
70 M3 Mailleraye-sur-Seine, la France 49.28N 0.46E
72 K3 Maillet France 46.29N 2.39E
66 A1 Mailley France 47.32N 6.03E
72 C3 Maillezais France 46.22N 0.44W
76 G7 Maillo, El Spain 40.34N 6.11W
74 K8 Maillot Algeria 36.22N 4.19E
69 G6 Mailly, Camp de France
69 G5 Mailly-Champagne France 49.09N 4.07E
71 D1 Mailly-la-Ville France 47.36N 3.39E
69 G6 Mailly-le-Camp France 48.41N 4.12E
69 D3 Mailly-Maillet France 50.05N 2.37E
31 G6 Mailsi Pakistan 29.46N 72.15E
11 F9 Maimai New Zealand 42.08S 171.45E
31 C3 Maimana Afghanistan 35.54N 64.43E
87 G3 Mai Mefales Ethiopia 15.00N 38.12E
39 G6 Maimlya R U.S.S.R.
116 J5 Maimon, Bahia de Dominican Rep
81 A4 Maimoni, Pta Sardinia 39.55N 8.23E
86 F7 Maimûn, El Egypt 29.14N 31.12E
91 G7 Mai Munene Zaïre 6.32S 21.00E
35 F7 Ma'in Jordan 31.41N 35.44E
33 F8 Ma'in anc site Yemen 16.06N 44.55E
64 G4 Main R W Germany
98 N8 Main-à-Dieu C Breton I, Nova Scotia 46.00N 59.50W
84 D6 Maínalon Oros mts Greece
30 L7 Mainanagar Bihar India 25.28N 87.43E
75 H5 Mainar Spain 41.11N 1.18W
30 H5 Mainatanr Bihar India 27.07N 84.39E
64 G8 Mainau isld Bodensee W Germany 47.42N 9.12E
66 N1 Mainau I W Germany 47.42N 9.12E
12 F4 Main Barrier Ra New S Wales
64 J4 Mainbernheim W Germany 49.42N 10.15E
98 Q2 Main Brook Newfoundland 51.10N 56.00W
64 M6 Mainburg W Germany 48.38N 11.48E
122 V9 Main Camp Christmas I Pacific Oc 2.00N 157.25W
100 K8 Main Centre Saskatchewan 50.38N 107.20W
99 J7 Main Chan Ontario
69 D6 Maincy France 48.32N 2.43E
28 C2 Maindargi Maharashtra India 17.26N 76.15E
91 F5 Mai-Ndombe, Lac Zaïre 2.00S 18.20E
Maindong see Coqên
99 O9 Main Duck I Ontario 43.56N 76.37W
111 N6 Maine Arizona 35.15N 111.56W
103 B2 Maine New York 42.12N 76.04W
67 E4 Maine prov France
70 J7 Maine R France
102 M1 Maine state U.S.A.
67 E5 Maine-et-Loire dept France
119 D8 Mainé Hanari, Cerro mt Colombia 0.43S 73.06W
59 C7 Maine, R Kerry Irish Rep
90 E5 Maïné Soroa Niger 13.14N 12.00E
104 A7 Maineville Ohio 39.19N 84.13W
25 M8 Maingkaing Burma 24.50N 95.22E
25 M8 Maingkwan Burma 26.20N 96.37E
25 E6 Maingy I Burma
64 H5 Mainhardt W Germany 49.05N 9.33E
19 M7 Mainit Mindanao Philippines 9.34N 125.31E
19 M7 Mainit L Mindanao Philippines 9.29N 125.30E
23 A4 Mainkung Xizang Zizhiqu China 28.30N 98.20E
24 H11 Mainling Xizang Zizhiqu China 29.14N 94.10E
13 C2 Mainoru N Terr Aust 14.00S 134.06E
29 H6 Mainpat hills Madhya Prad India
30 C5 Mainpuri Uttar Prad India 27.14N 79.01E
30 B5 Mainpuri dist Uttar Prad India
59 K2 Main, R Antrim N Ireland
72 J3 Mainsat France 46.04N 2.22E
57 F3 Mainsriddle Dumfries & Galloway Scotland 54.54N 3.39W
18 D10 Main Str Singapore
64 F3 Maintal W Germany 50.07N 8.45E
70 O4 Maintenon France 48.35N 1.35E
95 B5 Maintirano Madagascar 18.01S 44.03E
98 Q4 Main Topsail pk Newfoundland 49.09N 56.32W
51 N7 Mainua Finland 64.05N 27.27E
61 E4 Mainvault Belgium 50.39N 3.43E
103 B5 Mainville Pennsylvania 40.58N 76.22W
25 L9 Mainyaung Burma 23.55N 94.50E
64 E3 Mainz W Germany 50.00N 8.16E
89 P11 Maio isld Cape Verde
80 H2 Maiolati Italy 43.28N 13.07E
76 B8 Maiorca Portugal 40.09N 8.50W
80 L7 Maiori Italy 40.38N 14.38E
15 J8 Maipa Papua New Guinea 8.16S 146.32E
121 B4 Maipo R Chile
121 B5 Maipó, Volcan pk Arg/Chile 34.10S 69.52W
121 F6 Maipú Buenos Aires Arg 36.52S 57.52W
121 B4 Maipú Chile 33.30S 70.52W
121 C4 Maipu Mendoza Arg 33.00S 68.46W
119 F5 Maipures Colombia 5.17N 67.51W
117 A2 Maipuri Landing Guyana 4.31N 58.30W
Maiqan see Mighān
119 F2 Maiquetía Venezuela 10.38N 66.59W
79 B6 Máira R Italy
28 J2 Mairabari Assam India 26.28N 92.22E
79 G4 Mairago Italy 45.15N 9.35E
77 E6 Mairena del Alcor Spain 37.23N 5.44W
118 H2 Mairi Brazil 11.45S 40.09W
30 H6 Mairwa Bihar India 26.13N 84.10E
64 L7 Maisach W Germany 48.12N 11.16E
72 B1 Maisdon-sur-Sèvre France 47.06N 1.23W
19 E6 Maisel, Pulau Pulau islds Indonesia
116 G4 Maisí Cuba 20.16N 74.09W
116 G4 Maisí, C Cuba 20.16N 74.10W
61 F5 Maisières Belgium 50.29N 3.58E
31 J10 Maiskhal Chan Bangladesh
31 J10 Maiskhal I Bangladesh
93 D8 Maisome I Tanzania
Maison Carrée see Harrach, El
67 O12 Maison Forestière de Bonifato Corsica 42.26N 8.50E
98 G6 Maisonnette New Brunswick 47.45N 65.00W
99 S9 Maisonneuve Quebec 45.34N 73.33W
69 E6 Maison-Rouge France 48.33N 3.10E
68 G4 Maisons-Alfort France 48.48N 2.27E
69 C6 Maisons-Laffitte France 48.57N 2.08E
66 H1 Maisprach Switzerland 47.32N 7.52E
65 N4 Maissau Austria 48.35N 15.51E
69 C7 Maisse France 48.23N 2.22E
61 L7 Maissin Belgium 49.58N 5.11E
87 L5 Mait Somalia 10.58N 47.05E
87 F3 Mai Teb Ethiopia 14.26N 36.51E
121 B3 Maitencillo Chile 30.58S 71.43W
94 J3 Maitengwe Botswana 20.07S 27.05E
29 K1 Maithon Res Bihar India
87 L5 Mait I Somalia 11.13N 47.12E
88 M8 Maitigat Barani Algeria 27.39N 3.37W
94 P11 Maitland Cape Town S Africa 33.55S 18.30E
107 A1 Maitland Missouri 40.11N 95.06W
12 K5 Maitland New S Wales 32.33S 151.33E
98 J8 Maitland Nova Scotia 45.19N 63.30W
12 E5 Maitland S Australia 34.21S 137.42E
98 G9 Maitland Bridge Nova Scotia 44.23N 65.15W
14 D7 Maitland, L W Australia
14 C7 Maitland, Mt W Australia 25.50S 117.59E
101 J1 Maitland Pt N W Terr 70.08N 128.24W
14 B5 Maitland, R W Australia
18 M3 Maitland Ra Sabah Malaysia
93 A3 Maituru Zaïre 2.43N 29.49E
26 Q12 Mai, Vallée de V Seychelles, Indian Oc 4.17S 55.44E
13 C2 Maiwok R N Terr Australia
20 P3 Maiya Japan 38.43N 141.18E
13 A4 Maiyu, Mt N Terr Australia 17.39S 129.25E
31 E4 Maizar Pakistan 32.52N 69.43E
115 K6 Maíz, Ciudad del Mexico 22.25N 99.38W
95 N2 Maizefield S Africa 26.39S 29.34E
61 K5 Maizeret Belgium 50.27N 4.59E
24 G11 Maizhokunggar Xizang Zizhiqu China 29.49N 91.48E
Maizi see Mayzī
69 L5 Maizières-lès-Metz France 49.12N 6.11E
69 M6 Maizières-lès-Vic France 48.43N 6.47E
115 N3 Maíz, Is. del Caribbean Sea
20 J6 Maizuru Japan 35.30N 135.20E
77 E7 Majaceite R Spain
76 H9 Majadas Spain 39.57N 5.45W
33 E8 Majadh Yemen 17.07N 43.31E
35 F10 Majadil Jordan 30.53N 35.38E
119 D3 Majagual Colombia 8.36N 74.39W
18 H9 Majalengka Java Indon 6.50S 108.11E
15 A4 Majalibit, Teluk B Irian Jaya
94 F5 Majana Pan Botswana 24.20S 21.48E
92 K7 Majapa, B. de Mozambique
119 H6 Majari, R Brazil
34 L6 Majarrah Canal Iraq
34 P7 Majarr Al Kabir, Al Iraq 31.34N 47.09E
51 C6 Majavatn, L Norway 65.10N 13.20E
33 M6 Majāyiz, Jabal mt Oman 21.37N 56.22E
53 H7 Majbølle Denmark 54.51N 11.45E
33 H10 Majdaḩah S Yemen 14.00N 48.28E
Majdal see Ashqelon
35 E5 Majdal Bani-Fadil Jordan 32.05N 35.22E
35 F8 Majdalein anc site Jordan 31.20N 35.43E
35 G5 Majdal, El Jordan 32.13N 35.50E
35 G1 Majdal Shams Syria 33.16N 35.46E
62 N5 Majdan Poland 50.25N 21.45E
82 G6 Majdanpek Yugoslavia 44.24N 21.54E
35 C8 Majd, El Jordan 31.29N 34.57E
Majdel Chams see Majdal Shams
35 E2 Majd el Kurum Israel 32.55N 35.15E
85 C7 Majdūl Libya 25.51N 15.07E
35 G1 Majduliye Syria 33.05N 35.55E
118 G8 Majé Brazil 22.37S 43.03W
19 A5 Majene Celebes Indon 3.33S 118.59E
87 H5 Majenta Ra Ethiopia
82 E6 Majevica mts Yugoslavia
30 H7 Majhaua Uttar Prad India 25.48N 84.24E
30 K7 Majhaul Bihar India 25.34N 86.08E
30 G6 Majhauli Uttar Prad India 26.18N 83.57E
30 D8 Majhgawan Madhya Prad India 24.55N 80.48E
30 G8 Majhiaon Kalan Bihar India 24.20N 83.49E
30 F6 Majhoi R Uttar Prad India
33 J5 Majḩud Saudi Arabia 22.53N 51.32E
87 E7 Maji Ethiopia 6.12N 35.32E
23 F7 Majiang Guangxi China 23.51N 111.01E
23 D5 Majiang Guizhou China 26.25N 107.32E
23 C6 Majie Yunnan China 24.56N 103.47E
92 E5 Maji Moto Tanzania 7.15S 31.25E
23 H4 Majin Zhejiang China 29.19N 118.26E
23 F4 Majitang Hunan China 28.32N 111.45E
29 D2 Majitha Punjab India 31.45N 75.02E
93 L9 Maji ya Chumvi Kenya 3.49S 39.22E
33 E8 Majma Saudi Arabia 17.58N 43.34E
33 F4 Majma'ah, Al Saudi Arabia 25.52N 45.26E
30 B8 Majna Madhya Prad India 24.49N 79.00E
32 E5 Majnavā Iran 30.23N 52.11E
96 P15 Majona, Pta pt Gomera Canary Is 28.09N 17.07W
100 H7 Major Saskatchewan 51.52N 109.33W
Majorca isld see Mallorca
10 B11 Major L Macquarie I Pacific Oc 54.41S 158.52E
30 L7 Majra Bihar India 25.43N 87.22E
35 F9 Majra Jordan 31.02N 35.41E
28 J2 Majuli I Assam India
92 H8 Majune Mozambique 13.26S 36.11E
Majunga see Mahajanga
12 B5 Majura, Mt A.C.Terr Australia 35.15S 149.11E
120 F2 Majuriã Brazil 7.30S 64.55W
9 D3 Majuro atoll Marshall Is Pacific Oc 7.05N 171.08E
15 M3 Maka Malaita I Solomon Is 9.33S 161.22E
89 B5 Maka Senegal 13.40N 14.12W
89 C5 Maka Senegal 13.12N 12.02W
90 F9 Maka tribe Cameroon
114 E6 Makaalae Pt Hawaiian Is 20.42N 156.01W
114 B8 Makaalia mt Hawaiian Is 19.11N 155.36W
91 C5 Makabana Congo 3.25S 12.41E
20 P10 Makabe Okinawa Japan 26.04N 127.40E
114 A5 Makaha Hawaiian Is 21.28N 158.14W
92 F10 Makaha Zimbabwe 17.20S 32.39E
9 S10 Makaha'a islet Tonga, Pacific Oc 21.07S 175.09W
114 E3 Makaha Pt Hawaiian Is 22.08N 159.44W
114 F4 Makahuena Pt Hawaiian Is 21.52N 159.26W
Makai see Majie
30 H5 Makaising Nepal 27.53N 84.40E
91 B2 Makak Cameroon 3.32N 11.05E
87 J4 Makaka Ethiopia 13.02N 42.41E
92 C2 Makalado Zaïre 0.02S 26.59E
94 G3 Makalamabedi Botswana 20.19S 23.51E
19 A5 Makale Celebes Indon 3.06S 119.53E
87 G4 Mak'alē Ethiopia 13.32N 39.33E
19 D2 Makalehi isld Indonesia 2.45N 125.12E
114 A7 Makalewena Hawaiian Is 19.47N 156.02W
18 D7 Makalo Indonesia 2.52S 100.16E
30 L3 Makalu mt Xizang Zizhiqu/Nepal 27.54N 87.06E
30 L3 Makalu Col pass Nep/Xizang Zizhiqu 27.55N 87.05E
30 L3 Makalu II mt Xizang Zizhiqu/Nepal 27.56N 87.05E
93 A10 Makamba Burundi 4.08S 29.48E
92 G6 Makambako Tanzania 8.49S 34.47E
90 D6 Makami Nigeria 10.36N 8.05E
93 H10 Makami Tanzania 4.36S 36.45E
Ma-k'a-mu Ts'o L see Markham L
43 O4 Makanchi Kazakhstan U.S.S.R. 46.47N 82.00E
92 H6 Makanda Tanzania 8.51S 37.50E
90 H9 Makandjia Cent Afr Rep 4.10N 16.49E
92 G5 Makangwa Tanzania 6.21S 35.50E
92 G8 Makanjila Malawi 13.41S 35.01E
30 C6 Makanpur Uttar Prad India 26.54N 79.59E
40 N7 Makanrushi, O isld Kuril Is U.S.S.R. 49.50N 154.26E
93 J10 Makanya Tanzania 4.21S 37.48E
114 C8 Makaopuhi Crater Hawaiian Is 19.22N 155.11W
114 B6 Makapala Hawaiian Is 20.11N 155.43W
122 S16 Maka-Pu isld Gambier Is Pacific Oc 23.12S 134.55W
114 B5 Makapuu Hd C Hawaiian Is 21.18N 157.40W
11 B5 Makara New Zealand 41.16S 174.43E
11 B5 Makara Beach New Zealand 41.13S 174.42E
95 B4 Makaraingo Madagascar 17.59S 45.35E
42 D4 Makarakskiy U.S.S.R. 55.39N 88.05E
117 A2 Makarapan Mt Guyana 4.02N 58.50W
11 B5 Makara R New Zealand
11 J3 Makarau New Zealand 36.37S 174.30E
11 C13 Makarewa New Zealand 46.19S 168.20E
90 G5 Makari Cameroon 12.35N 10.27E
47 F4 Makar Ib U.S.S.R. 63.39N 49.30E
Makarikari Pan see Makgadikgadi Pan
47 H3 Makarikha U.S.S.R. 66.17N 58.28E
11 D11 Makarora R New Zealand
41 P5 Makar, Ostrov isld U.S.S.R. 71.55N 138.31E
122 S16 Makarou isld Gambier Is Pacific Oc 23.13S 134.57W
40 J7 Makarov Sakhalin U.S.S.R. 48.39N 142.45E
41 E4 Makarova U.S.S.R. 73.37N 85.03E
42 H4 Makarovo Irkutsk U.S.S.R. 57.28N 107.45E
45 P4 Makarovo Saratov U.S.S.R. 52.17N 43.19E
82 D7 Makarska Yugoslavia 43.19N 17.01E
31 F4 Makarwal Pakistan 32.53N 71.10E
46 P1 Makar'ye U.S.S.R. 58.38N 48.01E
46 N1 Makaryev U.S.S.R. 57.52N 43.40E
42 G5 Makar'yevo U.S.S.R. 53.08N 103.20E
45 R1 Makar'yevo hill U.S.S.R. 56.05N 45.10E
39 G5 Makar'yevskoye Kamchatka U.S.S.R. 58.50N 162.50E
92 E6 Makasa Zambia 9.44S 31.24E
Makassar see Ujung Pandang
86 M4 Makassar el Fanâgîl hill Egypt 30.52N 34.14E
18 M7 Makassar Strait Kalimantan/Celebes S E Asia
43 C3 Makat Kazakhstan U.S.S.R. 47.38N 53.16E
122 B14 Makatéa isld Tuamotu Is Pacific Oc 16.10S 148.14W
19 H1 Makati Luzon Philippines 14.34N 121.01E
95 P8 Makatini Flats physical reg S Africa
92 G4 Makatupora Tanzania 5.45S 35.08E
25 M8 Makaw Burma 26.28N 96.40E
91 F5 Makaw Zaïre 3.29S 18.20E
114 E6 Makawa dist Hawaiian Is
114 E6 Makawao Hawaiian Is 20.51N 156.19W
114 D6 Makawao dist Hawaiian Is
114 E4 Makaweli Landing Hawaiian Is 21.56N 159.38W
91 F5 Makaya Zaïre 3.21S 18.01E
95 B6 Makay, Massif du mts Madagascar
15 A4 Makbon Irian Jaya 0.47S 131.33E
87 G5 Makdala Ethiopia 11.30N 38.18E
15 A4 Makebon Irian Jaya 0.18S 131.30E
93 A9 Makebuko Burundi 3.36S 29.59E
83 E4 Makedhonia div Greece
82 F9 Makedonija rep Yugoslavia
19 N2 Makelulu mt Palau Is Pacific Oc 7.34N 134.35E
122 D14 Makemo atoll Tuamotu Is Pacific Oc 16.30S 143.45W
114 E6 Makena Hawaiian Is 20.39N 156.26W
89 C7 Makeni Sierra Leone 8.57N 12.02W
93 B10 Makere Tanzania 4.17S 30.26E
31 G9 Makespur Bangladesh 23.21N 88.58E
11 L4 Maketu New Zealand 37.46S 176.29E
45 K8 Makeyevka Ukraine U.S.S.R. 48.01N 38.00E
94 H3 Makgadikgadi salt pan Botswana
44 H5 Makhachkala U.S.S.R. 42.59N 47.30E
31 F4 Makhad Pakistan 33.07N 71.51E
84 B4 Makhaira Greece 38.38N 21.08E
84 A6 Makhairádhon Greece 37.45N 20.48E
46 Q5 Makhambet Kazakhstan U.S.S.R. 47.40N 51.35E
33 E4 Makhāmir,Jabal al mt Saudi Arabia 25.06N 43.14E
44 E6 Makharadze Georgia U.S.S.R. 41.55N 42.02E
74 D9 Makhazen R Morocco
95 N5 Makheka mt Lesotho 29.14S 29.17E
84 R15 Makheras Monastery Cyprus 34.57N 33.11E
30 D6 Makhi Uttar Prad India 26.39N 80.29E
43 F8 Makhmaldepe Turkmeniya U.S.S.R. 37.01N 60.12E
44 G3 Makhmud Mekteb U.S.S.R. 44.27N 45.14E
34 L3 Makhmūr Iraq 35.47N 43.32E
47 J6 Makhnevo U.S.S.R. 58.30N 61.46E
40 B3 Makhochen, Porog falls U.S.S.R. 57.25N 121.30E
43 J1 Makhorovka Kazakhstan U.S.S.R. 54.14N 69.40E
95 O9 Makhowe S Africa 27.58S 32.08E
35 F3 Makhraba Jordan 32.35N 35.39E
35 F5 Makhrūk, El Jordan 32.08N 35.31E
41 O5 Makhsogol, Mys C U.S.S.R. 71.45N 133.00E
28 C2 Makhtal Andhra Prad India 16.30N 77.28E
86 N4 Makhtesh Ramon canyon Israel
95 G2 Makhubareeks mts S Africa
34 L3 Makḩūl, Jabal hills Iraq
Makḩwan see Marwah, Al
33 H8 Makhyah, Wādī watercourse S Yemen
15 C5 Maki Irian Jaya 3.18S 134.13E
20 M4 Maki Japan 37.47N 138.55E
19 E3 Makian isld Moluccas Indon 0.20N 127.22E
11 F11 Makikihi New Zealand 44.38S 171.10E
85 G3 Makīlī, Al Libya 32.07N 22.16E
92 D5 Makimba Zaïre 6.21S 28.03E
92 H6 Makimguwira Tanzania 10.00S 37.32E
9 B4 Makin atoll Kiribati, Pac Oc 3.10N 172.45E
100 S8 Makinak Manitoba 50.59N 99.40W
93 J8 Makindu Kenya 2.18S 37.50E
9 B4 Makin Meang isld Kiribati, Pac Oc 3.14N 172.57E
43 K1 Makinsk Kazakhstan U.S.S.R. 52.40N 70.28E
97 M2 Makinson Inlet N W Terr
Makkah see Mecca
51 P1 Makkaur Norway 70.40N 30.03E
42 J6 Makkaveyevo U.S.S.R. 51.48N 114.00E
60 N8 Makkinga Netherlands 52.59N 6.14E
41 O2 Mak-Klintoka, Ostrov isld Franz Josef Ld U.S.S.R.
97 O6 Makkovik Labrador, Nfld 55.00N 59.10W
Makku see Mākū
35 E6 Makkuk watercourse Jordan
60 K7 Makkum Netherlands 53.03N 5.25E
42 E3 Maklakovo U.S.S.R. 58.13N 92.30E
94 K4 Maklautsi Botswana 22.01S 28.26E
39 C4 Maklikhan, Gora mt U.S.S.R. 60.15N 141.19E
88 S4 Maknassy Tunisia 34.37N 9.39E
62 M9 Makó Hungary 46.11N 20.30E
117 A4 Makoa, Sa mts Brazil
93 B3 Makofi Zaïre 2.18N 30.08E
91 J5 Makoka Zaïre 2.36S 25.30E
99 C1 Makokibatan L Ontario
90 D5 Makokiya Niger 13.19N 8.56E
91 C3 Makokou Gabon 0.38N 12.47E
95 K2 Makokskraal S Africa 26.21S 26.38E
92 C10 Makoli Zambia 17.29S 26.08E
92 J7 Makondi Plat Tanzania
9 U7 Makondronga islet Fiji 17.24S 179.01E
92 A8 Makondu R Zambia
9 U7 Makongai isld Fiji 17.26S 178.59E
89 J7 Makongo Ghana 8.27N 0.40W
91 K2 Makongo R Zaïre
92 F6 Makongolosi Tanzania 8.25S 33.19E
92 E11 Makoni dist Zimbabwe
94 G5 Makopong Botswana 25.18S 23.01E
44 C4 Makopse U.S.S.R. 43.59N 39.18E
11 L6 Makorako mt New Zealand 39.08S 176.03E
94 J4 Makoro Botswana 22.45S 27.05E
93 A2 Makoro Zaïre 3.10N 29.58E
45 D5 Makoshino Ukraine U.S.S.R. 51.25N 32.21E
108 J2 Makoti N Dakota 47.58N 101.49W
11 L7 Makotuku New Zealand 40.08S 176.16E
23 C5 Makou Yunnan China 27.40N 103.25E
91 D4 Makoua Congo 0.01S 15.40E
62 L6 Makov Czechoslovakia 49.23N 18.25E
41 D7 Makovskaya R U.S.S.R.
41 E7 Makovskoye Krasnoyarsk U.S.S.R. 66.58N 85.05E
42 E3 Makovskoye Krasnoyarsk U.S.S.R. 58.12N 90.54E
41 E7 Makovskoye, Ozero L U.S.S.R.
62 M6 Maków Poland 49.43N 19.40E
62 N3 Maków Mazowiecki Poland 52.52N 21.02E
35 D2 Makr Israel 32.56N 35.08E
83 H8 Makrá isld Greece 36.15N 25.54E
29 E6 Makrai Madhya Prad India 22.04N 77.08E
84 G5 Makrakómi Attikí Greece 38.07N 23.48E
84 D4 Makrakómi Fthiótis Greece 38.57N 22.06E
31 B7 Makran dist Pakistan
32 H7 Makran reg Iran/Pakistan
29 D4 Makrana Rajasthan India 27.02N 74.44E
31 C8 Makran Coast Ra Pakistan
84 D7 Mákri Arkadhía Greece 37.28N 22.19E
29 G8 Makri Madhya Prad India 19.46N 81.58E
83 H4 Mákri Thraki Greece 40.52N 25.44E
84 G4 Makrikáppa Greece 38.37N 23.45E
84 D2 Makrikhóri Greece 39.48N 22.29E
84 E3 Makrinítsa Greece 39.24N 22.59E
84 D3 Makrirrákhi Greece 39.05N 22.09E
84 C6 Makrísia Greece 37.37N 21.36E
84 G4 Makrokhóri Greece 38.32N 23.59E
84 H6 Makrónisos isld Greece
84 H6 Makronísou, Dhíavlos str Greece
34 Q7 Makşar Iran 31.11N 48.28E
46 K1 Maksatikha U.S.S.R. 57.48N 35.51E
85 L7 Maks el Bahari, El Egypt 24.35N 30.37E
85 L7 Maks el Qibli, El Egypt 24.34N 30.38E
29 E6 Maksi Madhya Prad India 23.20N 76.36E
47 H4 Maksim U.S.S.R. 62.40N 57.12E
43 J5 Maksima Gor'kogo, im Kazakhstan U.S.S.R. 43.01N 67.44E
42 H5 Maksimikha U.S.S.R. 53.18N 108.40E
42 D3 Maksimkiy Yar U.S.S.R. 58.44N 86.50E
45 S4 Maksimovka Saratov U.S.S.R. 52.03N 46.34E
42 C4 Maksimovka Tomsk U.S.S.R. 57.18N 83.02E
40 G8 Maksimovka U.S.S.R. 46.04N 135.18E
32 K6 Maksotag Iran 28.06N 62.42E

29 D5 **Maksudangarh** Madhya Prad India 24.15N 75.30E
29 E5 **Maksudangarh** Madhya Prad India 24.00N 77.10E
44 H7 **Maksudlu** Azerbaydzhan U.S.S.R. 40.06N 46.54E
37 C1 **Maksutlu** Turkey 41.07N 26.41E
88 S4 **Maktar** Tunisia 35.50N 9.12E
93 K9 **Maktau** Kenya 3.25S 38.08E
88 H11 **Makteir** *reg* Mauritania
32 A1 **Mākū** Āzārbāījān-e Bākhtarī Iran 39.18N 44.34E
32 E6 **Mākū** Fārs Iran 28.11N 53.05E
92 K9 **Makua** *tribe* Mozambique
20 H2 **Makuhari** Chiba Japan 35.39N 140.03E
28 K2 **Makum** Assam India 27.28N 95.28E
91 G6 **Makumbi** Zaïre 5.50S 20.41E
92 K12 **Makunduchi** Zanzibar 6.26S 39.32E
92 D4 **Makungu** Burundi 4.58S 28.51E
91 J8 **Makunza** Zaïre 8.52S 24.19E
18 K5 **Makup, Bukit** *hill* Kalimantan/Sarawak 1.24N 112.08E
20 D10 **Makurazaki** Japan 31.16N 130.18E
90 D8 **Makurdi** Nigeria 7.44N 8.35E
11 K7 **Makuri** New Zealand 40.32S 176.00E
113 D10 **Makushin B** Aleutian Is
47 K7 **Makushino** U.S.S.R. 55.12N 67.15E
113 D10 **Makushin Vol** Aleutian Is 53.52N 166.55W
93 J7 **Makutano** Kenya 1.25S 37.28E
92 G4 **Makutapora** Tanzania 5.59S 35.41E
92 F7 **Makutu Mts** Zambia
32 E6 **Makūyeh** Iran 28.06N 53.08E
93 H9 **Makuyuni** Tanzania 3.34S 36.05E
9 A9 **Makwa** Nauru, Pacific Oc 0.32S 166.55E
100 H4 **Makwa L** Saskatchewan 54.03N 109.18W
30 J5 **Makwanpur Garhi** Nepal 27.25N 85.09E
95 J3 **Makwassie** S Africa 27.19S 25.59E
92 D5 **Makwende** Zaïre 7.08S 28.05E
92 E10 **Makwiro** Zimbabwe 17.58S 30.25E
89 C3 **Mal** Mauritania 16.59N 13.25W
30 D5 **Mal** Uttar Prad India 27.02N 80.44E
114 D6 **Mala** Hawaiian Is 20.53N 156.41W
120 B5 **Mala** Peru 12.40S 76.36W
77 J6 **Mala** Spain 37.06N 3.43W
120 B5 **Mala** *R* Peru
30 A4 **Malab** Haryana India 28.02N 77.00E
93 F5 **Malaba** Kenya 0.38N 34.17E
19 M8 **Malabang** Mindanao Philippines 7.35N 124.04E
105 G9 **Malabar** Florida 28.01N 80.36W
10 E11 **Malabar** Lord Howe I Pacific Oc 31.31S 159.05E
28 B4 **Malabar Coast** Kerala India
18 G9 **Malabar, Gunung** *mt* Java Indon 7.10S 107.35E
28 A8 **Malabar Hill** *dist* Bombay India
28 A8 **Malabar Pt** Bombay India 18.57N 72.48E
91 A2 **Malabo** Fernando Póo Eq Guinea 3.45N 8.48E
19 H1 **Malabon** Luzon Philippines 14.40N 120.57E
121 F2 **Malabrigo** Argentina 29.22S 59.55W
121 G5 **Mal Abrigo** Uruguay 34.10S 56.55W
90 F7 **Malabu** Nigeria 9.32N 12.48E
15 M6 **Malabunga** New Britain 4.27S 152.06E
19 H7 **Malabuñgan** Philippines 9.02N 117.37E
118 G5 **Malacacheta** Brazil 17.50S 42.07W
28 H6 **Malacca** Nicobar Is 9.12N 92.46E
Malacca Pen Malaysia *see* **Melaka**
Malacca *state see* **Melaka** *state*
18 D4 **Malacca, Str. of** Pen Malaysia/Sumatra S E Asia
100 G1 **Malachi** Ontario 49.56N 94.58W
65 Q5 **Malacky** Czechoslovakia 48.26N 17.01E
28 A1 **Malad** Maharashtra India 19.20N 72.55E
110 N7 **Malad City** Idaho 42.12N 112.15W
75 M2 **Maladeta, Pico de la** *mt* Spain 42.39N 0.39E
87 H5 **Malafaburi** Ethiopia 10.37N 40.30E
62 L6 **Malá Fatra** *mts* Czechoslovakia
119 D4 **Málaga** Colombia 6.44N 72.45W
103 D7 **Malaga** New Jersey 39.34N 75.03W
109 F9 **Malaga** New Mexico 32.13N 104.04W
77 H7 **Málaga** Spain 36.43N 4.25W
110 E2 **Malaga** Washington 47.23N 120.16W
74 D8 **Málaga** *prov* Spain
77 H7 **Málaga, Mtes de** Spain
93 B10 **Malagarasi** *R* Tanzania/Burundi
95 D10 **Malagas** S Africa 34.19S 20.35E
Malagasy Rep *see* **Madagascar**
77 J2 **Malagón** Spain 39.10N 3.50W
77 B5 **Malagón** *R* Spain
76 L7 **Malagón, Sierra de** *mts* Spain
75 D6 **Malaguilla** Spain 40.49N 3.15W
30 C7 **Malahar** Madhya Prad India 25.02N 79.41E
59 K5 **Malahide** Dublin Irish Rep 53.27N 6.09W
15 J6 **Malai I** Bismarck Arch 5.53S 147.55E
95 B6 **Malaimbandy** Madagascar 20.20S 45.35E
71 F2 **Mâlain** France 47.20N 4.48E
15 M3 **Malaita I** Solomon Is
18 N10 **Malaka** *mt* Indonesia 8.39S 118.34E
19 N2 **Malakal** Palau Is Pacific Oc 7.20N 134.28E
87 C6 **Malakal** Sudan 9.31N 31.40E
19 N2 **Malakal Harb** Palau Is Pacific Oc
19 N2 **Malakal Pass** Palau Is Pacific Oc
28 E1 **Malakanagiri** Orissa India 18.22N 81.57E
31 F3 **Malakand** Pakistan 34.35N 71.55E
31 F3 **Malakand** *dist* Pakistan
31 F3 **Malakand Pass** Pakistan 34.35N 71.55E
82 C6 **Mala Kapela** *mts* Yugoslavia
84 B2 **Malakási** Greece 39.47N 21.18E
9 S7 **Malake** *isld* Fiji 17.20S 178.09E
29 E4 **Malakhera** Rajasthan India 27.16N 76.38E
68 E4 **Malakoff** France 48.49N 2.18E
112 L3 **Malakoff** Texas 32.10N 96.01W
82 F6 **Mala Krsna** Yugoslavia 44.34N 21.00E
41 P3 **Malaktyn-Tas, Gora** *mt* U.S.S.R. 75.05N 139.55E
31 G4 **Malakwal** Pakistan 32.32N 73.18E
15 J6 **Malala** Papua New Guinea 5.15S 147.10E
15 J6 **Malalamai** Papua New Guinea 5.49S 146.44E
15 J8 **Malalaua** Papua New Guinea 8.05S 146.09E
79 L5 **Malalbergo** Italy 44.43N 11.32E
117 A2 **Malali** Guyana 5.40N 58.23W
119 J5 **Malali Rapids** Guyana 5.36N 58.21W
19 G1 **Malalos** Luzon Philippines 14.50N 120.54E
15 G8 **Malam** Papua New Guinea 8.45S 142.46E
19 B5 **Malamala** Celebes Indon 3.21S 120.58E
19 E4 **Malamala** *isld* Moluccas Indon 1.30S 127.23E
89 H9 **Malamalasso** Ivory Coast 5.48N 3.25W
19 K8 **Malamaui** *isld* Philippines 6.43N 121.59E
79 M4 **Malamocco** Italy 45.22N 12.20E
93 E9 **Malampaka** Tanzania 3.07S 33.16E
19 J6 **Malampaya Sd** Philippines
19 J7 **Malanao** *isld* Philippines 9.25N 118.38E
31 H10 **Malancha R** Bangladesh
69 J5 **Malancourt** France 49.14N 5.11E
13 H3 **Malanda** Queensland 17.20S 145.35E
77 D7 **Malandar, Pta.de** *pt* Spain 36.48N 6.22W
29 L2 **Malandighi** W Bengal India 23.33N 87.25E
91 H6 **Malandji** Zaïre 5.55S 22.19E
84 E6 **Malandríni** Greece 37.43N 22.38E
84 D5 **Malandrínon** Greece 38.27N 22.14E
18 K9 **Malang** Java Indon 7.59S 112.45E
92 G6 **Malangali** Tanzania 8.37S 34.55E
90 L9 **Malangamba** Cent Afr Rep 4.32N 22.40E
18 H9 **Malangbong** Java Indon 7.10S 108.10E
51 G2 **Malangen** Norway 69.24N 18.40E
51 G2 **Malangen** *inlet* Norway 69.30N 18.10E
51 F2 **Malangsgrunnen** *shoal* Norway
30 J6 **Malangwa** Nepal 26.52N 85.33E
30 J6 **Malangwa** Nepal 26.55N 85.37E
82 K3 **Mălani** Romania 47.26N 26.07E
19 L8 **Malanipa** *isld* Philippines 6.55N 122.10E
91 E8 **Malanje** Angola 9.36S 16.21E
91 E8 **Malanje** *dist* Angola
75 G4 **Malanquilla** Spain 41.33N 1.52W
31 C8 **Malan, Ras** *C* Pakistan 25.17N 65.15E
66 P4 **Malans** Switzerland 46.58N 9.34E
70 F6 **Malansac** France 47.41N 2.16W
19 J7 **Malanut B** Philippines
89 L6 **Malanville** Benin 11.50N 3.23E
22 L6 **Malanyu** Hebei China 40.11N 117.42E
121 C3 **Malanzán** Argentina 30.50S 66.32W
121 C3 **Malanzán, Sa. de** *ra* Argentina
30 G6 **Malaon** Uttar Prad India 26.35N 83.26E
115 O6 **Mala, Pta** *C* Panama 7.30N 80.00W
34 L3 **Malā Qara** Iraq 35.57N 43.40E
85 D6 **Malāqī, al** Libya 26.56N 17.00E
52 K7 **Mälaren** *L* Sweden
121 B5 **Malargue** Argentina 35.32S 69.35W
121 B5 **Malargue** *R* Argentina
117 B4 **Malaripo** Brazil 0.45N 54.17W
50 B5 **Malarrif** *Lt Ho* Iceland 64.44N 23.49W
99 M4 **Malartic** Quebec 48.09N 78.09W
99 M4 **Malartic, L** Quebec
19 A6 **Malasoro,Teluk** *B* Celebes Indon 5.40S 119.38E
121 C10 **Malaspina** Argentina 44.56S 66.55W
113 R7 **Malaspina Glacier** Alaska 59.50N 140.40W
11 B12 **Malaspina Reach** New Zealand
101 L11 **Malaspina Str** Br Col
18 K7 **Malatayur, Tanjung** *C* Borneo Indon 3.27S 113.38E
37 B2 **Maláthria, Ákra** *C* Samothráki Greece 40.23N 25.34E
84 H4 **Malatiánoi** Greece 38.38N 24.04E
51 G6 **Malåträsk** Sweden 65.12N 18.45E
94 F5 **Malatswane Pan** Botswana 24.34S 20.21E
37 D7 **Malatya** Turkey 38.22N 38.18E
9 S5 **Malau** Vanua Levu Fiji 16.24S 179.23E
71 G8 **Malaucène** France 44.10N 5.08E
70 N2 **Malaunay** France 49.31N 1.03E
72 D8 **Malaussanne** France 43.34N 0.29W
29 D2 **Malaut** Punjab India 30.12N 74.40E
23 C9 **Ma Lau Tong** Hong Kong 22.19N 114.14E
28 C4 **Malavalli** Karnataka India 12.23N 77.03E
117 B3 **Malavate** Fr Guiana 3.15N 54.08W
32 B4 **Mālavi** Iran 33.16N 47.50E
18 M2 **Malawali** *isld* Sabah Malaysia
30 B5 **Malawan** Uttar Prad India 27.29N 78.49E
73 H7 **Malawi** *rep* Cent Africa
Malawi,L *see* **Nyasa,L**
87 F3 **Malawiya** Sudan 15.12N 36.12E
51 J9 **Malax** Finland 62.55N 21.30E
39 E1 **Malaya** U.S.S.R. 68.10N 152.28E
Malaya *federation see* **Peninsular Malaysia**
39 H1 **Malaya Baranikha** U.S.S.R. 69.38N 165.03E
45 D1 **Malaya Beresnevo** U.S.S.R. 55.22N 32.20E
45 T5 **Malaya Bykovka** U.S.S.R. 51.54N 47.45E
42 J3 **Malaya Chuya** *R* U.S.S.R.
45 D6 **Malaya Devitsa** Ukraine U.S.S.R. 50.40N 32.10E
45 U4 **Malaya Fedorovka** U.S.S.R. 52.37N 48.11E
29 J7 **Malayagiri Mt** Orissa India 21.26N 85.24E
39 G4 **Malaya Itkana** U.S.S.R. 61.40N 162.19E
45 V2 **Malaya Kandala** U.S.S.R. 54.30N 49.22E
47 G1 **Malaya Karmakuly** U.S.S.R. 72.25N 52.48E
41 D6 **Malaya Kheta** *R* U.S.S.R.
46 P2 **Malaya Kokshaga** *R* U.S.S.R.
41 K5 **Malaya Kuonamka** *R* U.S.S.R.
39 F1 **Malaya Kuropatoch'ya** *R* U.S.S.R.
45 G5 **Malaya Loknya** U.S.S.R. 51.20N 35.17E
47 M2 **Malaya Neva** *R* Leningrad U.S.S.R.
47 J3 **Malaya Ob'** *R* U.S.S.R.
45 Q4 **Malaya Serdoba** U.S.S.R. 52.28N 44.56E
40 G7 **Malaya Sidima** U.S.S.R. 48.10N 136.05E
47 J5 **Malaya Sos'va** *R* U.S.S.R.
45 U7 **Malaya Uzen'** *R* U.S.S.R.
42 K3 **Malaya Valyukhta** U.S.S.R. 59.30N 117.15E
46 H1 **Malaya Vishera** U.S.S.R. 58.53N 32.08E
45 C8 **Malaya Viska** Ukraine U.S.S.R. 48.39N 31.36E
45 Q5 **Malaya Vorontsovka** U.S.S.R. 51.20N 44.15E
39 D1 **Malaya Yercha** U.S.S.R. 69.50N 148.40E
19 M7 **Malaybalay** Mindanao Philippines 8.09N 125.07E
32 C3 **Malāyer** Iran 34.19N 48.51E
34 Q4 **Malāyer** *R* Iran
41 Q4 **Malaye Zimov'ye** U.S.S.R. 73.22N 141.15E
23 A1 **Malayiwan** Qinghai China 34.56N 98.25E
69 E7 **Mâlay-le-Grand** France 48.11N 3.20E
13 J4 **Malay Reef** Gt Barrier Reef Australia 17.59S 149.17E
43 N5 **Malay-Sary** Kazakhstan U.S.S.R. 44.16N 77.41E
17 F11 **Malaysia** S E Asia
Malaysia, East *div see* **Sabah and Sarawak** *states*
Malaysia, West *div see* **Peninsular Malaysia**
37 G6 **Malazgirt** Turkey 39.09N 42.30E
59 D6 **Mal B** Clare Irish Rep 52.50N 9.28W
98 H5 **Mal B** Quebec
98 B6 **Malbaie** *R* Quebec
121 B6 **Malbarco** *L* Argentina
89 M5 **Malbaza-Usine** Niger 13.59N 5.38E
13 F5 **Malbon** Queensland 21.05S 140.20E
12 C4 **Malbooma** S Australia 30.40S 134.14E
79 O1 **Malborghetto** Italy 46.31N 13.26E
62 L1 **Malbork** Poland 54.02N 19.01E
56 D7 **Malborough** Devon Eng 50.14N 3.48W
66 C1 **Malbouhans** France 47.44N 6.35E
71 C7 **Malbouzon** France 44.43N 3.08E
121 E2 **Malbrán** Argentina 29.23S 62.26W
87 H9 **Malca Rie** Somalia 3.58N 41.57E
76 E8 **Malcata.Sa da** *mts* Portugal
79 J3 **Malcésine** Italy 45.46N 10.49E
45 M7 **Mal'chevskaya** U.S.S.R. 49.04N 40.22E
63 R5 **Malchin** E Germany 53.45N 12.45E
22 C2 **Malchin** Mongolia 49.40N 93.12E
63 R5 **Malchiner See** *L* E Germany
63 Q6 **Malchow** Neubrandenburg E Germany 53.29N 12.25E
63 T6 **Malchow** Neubrandenburg E Germany 53.27N 13.57E
77 E4 **Malcocinado** Spain 38.08N 5.40W
14 D8 **Malcolm** W Australia 28.59S 121.33E
101 C1 **Malcolm** *R* Yukon Terr
25 E7 **Malcolm I** Burma
14 E10 **Malcolm,Pt** W Australia 33.47S 123.44E
108 S8 **Malcom** Iowa 41.42N 92.34W
29 L5 **Malda** W Bengal India 25.03N 88.12E
29 L5 **Malda** *dist* W Bengal India
61 D2 **Maldegem** Belgium 51.12N 3.27E
55 D5 **Malden** London Eng 51.23N 0.15W
107 G5 **Malden** Missouri 36.34N 89.58W
60 M12 **Malden** Netherlands 51.47N 5.51E
110 H2 **Malden** Washington 47.15N 117.28W
104 D8 **Malden** W Virginia 38.19N 81.34W
104 Q8 **Malden** *dist* Boston
103 G2 **Malden Bridge** New York 42.28N 73.35W
122 L8 **Malden I** Line Is Pacific Oc 4.00S 155.00W
37 E3 **Maldere Burun** *C* Turkey 40.19N 27.43E
61 G2 **Malderen** Belgium 51.01N 4.15E
75 M2 **Malditos,Mtes** Spain
81 A4 **Mal di Ventre.I.di** Sardinia 39.59N 8.18E
26 G6 **Maldive Ridge** Indian Ocean
27 L9 **Maldives** *islds* Indian Ocean
56 N4 **Maldon** Essex Eng 51.45N 0.40E
121 G5 **Maldonado** Uruguay 34.57S 54.59W
121 G5 **Maldonado** *dept* Uruguay
115 K9 **Maldonado,Pta** *C* Mexico 16.19N 98.35W
39 D3 **Mal'dyak** U.S.S.R. 62.57N 148.18E
25 M9 **Male** Burma 23.06N 96.01E
79 J2 **Malé** Italy 46.21N 10.55E
27 L9 **Male** Maldives, Ind Oc 4.00N 73.28E
36 B3 **Maléa,Ákra** *C* Lésvos Greece 39.02N 26.38E
27 L9 **Male Atoll** Maldives, Ind Oc 4.45N 73.15E
29 D7 **Malegaon** Nasik, Maharashtra India 20.32N 74.38E
30 C8 **Malehra** Madhya Prad India 24.34N 79.18E
92 H10 **Malei** Mozambique 17.11S 37.00E
87 A6 **Malek** Sudan 8.34N 27.32E
87 C7 **Malek** Sudan 6.09N 31.38E
37 J9 **Malek** *mt* Iran 36.41N 45.52E
32 C3 **Malekābād** Iran 34.06N 49.55E
90 J5 **Malekandji** Chad 12.24N 18.59E
62 K7 **Malé Karpaty** *mts* Czechoslovakia
32 B2 **Malek Kandī** Iran 37.06N 46.05E
87 G5 **Malek Sanka** Ethiopia 11.00N 38.42E
32 J6 **Malek Siāh, Kūh-e** *mt* Iran 29.51N 60.55E
9 C11 **Malekula** *isld* New Hebrides
91 C6 **Malela** Zaïre 6.00S 12.40E
91 K5 **Malela** Zaïre 2.23S 26.09E
91 K6 **Malela** Zaïre 4.23S 26.10E
99 P4 **Mâle,Lac du** Quebec
94 L5 **Malelane** S Africa 25.30S 31.28E
92 H9 **Malema** Mozambique 14.57S 37.25E
91 K8 **Malemba Nkulu** Zaïre 8.01S 26.48E
91 C6 **Malembo** Angola 5.21S 12.14E
91 C6 **Malembo, Pte. de** *pt* Angola 5.17S 12.11E
84 J10 **Máleme** Crete 35.31N 23.46E
89 B4 **Malème Hodar** Senegal 14.03N 15.18W
72 H5 **Malemort-sur-Corrèze** France 45.10N 1.34E
61 N5 **Malempré** Belgium 50.17N 5.43E
15 M5 **Malendok I** Bismarck Arch 3.30S 153.15E
71 C8 **Malène, la** France 44.18N 3.19E
47 D4 **Malen'ga** U.S.S.R. 63.50N 36.50E
95 N6 **Malenge** S Africa 30.10S 29.38E
91 E10 **Malengue** Angola 13.57S 16.49E
93 E10 **Malengya** *watercourse* Tanzania
63 N4 **Malente** W Germany 54.10N 10.33E
30 K8 **Malepur** Bihar India 24.59N 86.15E
93 F4 **Malera** Uganda 1.26N 34.05E
52 J10 **Målerås** Sweden 56.55N 15.35E
29 D2 **Maler Kotla** Punjab India 30.34N 75.56E
84 N11 **Máles** Crete 35.05N 25.35E
79 D2 **Malesco** Italy 46.08N 8.30E
69 C7 **Malesherbes** France 48.17N 2.25E
84 B4 **Malesiádha** Greece 38.54N 21.20E
84 F4 **Malesína** Greece 38.37N 23.15E
65 M2 **Malešov** Czechoslovakia 49.55N 15.14E
31 D4 **Mālestān** Afghanistan 33.18N 67.10E
70 F6 **Malestroit** France 47.49N 2.23W
42 H6 **Maleta** U.S.S.R. 50.50N 108.28E
95 M5 **Maletsunyane Falls** Lesotho 29.52S 28.04E
81 J8 **Maletto** Sicily 37.49N 14.52E
15 J2 **Malevangga** Choiseul I Solomon Is 6.40S 156.28E
61 K4 **Malèves-Ste.-Marie-Wastines** Belgium 50.39N 4.47E
45 K3 **Malevka** U.S.S.R. 53.36N 38.16E
89 E6 **Maleya** Guinea 11.42N 9.43W
46 J6 **Maleyevka** Ukraine U.S.S.R. 47.29N 32.42E
85 C4 **Malfa** Libya 31.57N 15.20E
81 J6 **Malfa** Lipari Is Italy 38.35N 14.50E
81 B6 **Malfatano,C** Sardinia 38.53N 8.48E
79 J2 **Malga Bissina,L.di** *L* Italy
90 J7 **Malgaze** Cent Afr Rep 8.15N 19.28E
Mal Gazol *see* **Malgazūl**
32 J5 **Malgazūl** Iran 30.20N 60.02E
64 O6 **Malgersdorf** W Germany 48.31N 12.46E
44 F4 **Malgobek** U.S.S.R. 42.33N 44.36E
52 J2 **Malgomaj** *L* Sweden 64.45N 16.00E
52 J2 **Malgovik** Sweden 64.37N 16.25E
75 Q4 **Malgrat** Spain 41.39N 2.45E
77 U15 **Malgrats, I** Balearic Is 39.29N 2.27E
90 N5 **Malha** Sudan 15.02N 26.03E
118 G4 **Malhada** Brazil 14.20S 43.45W
76 G5 **Malhadas** Portugal 41.32N 6.20W
76 F7 **Malhada Sorda** Portugal 40.32N 6.55W
57 J4 **Malham** N Yorks Eng 54.04N 2.09W
33 G4 **Malham** Saudi Arabia 25.08N 46.18E
76 D14 **Malhão, Sa do** *mts* Portugal
86 M9 **Malhaq, Wâdi** *watercourse* Egypt
30 B8 **Malhargarh** Bhilsa, Madhya Prad India 24.17N 78.04E
29 D5 **Malhargarh** Mandasor, Madhya Prad India 24.18N 75.02E
34 K4 **Malhāt** Iraq 34.41N 42.44E
35 D9 **Malhata** *watercourse* Israel
86 J7 **Malha, Wâdi** *watercourse* Egypt
110 H5 **Malheur** Oregon 44.26N 117.43W
110 H6 **Malheur** *R* Oregon
26 S14 **Malheureux,C** Mahé I Seychelles, Ind Oc 4.48S 55.32E
26 U11 **Malheureux,C** Mauritius, Indian Oc 19.58S 57.36E
110 G6 **Malheur L** Oregon 43.20N 118.45W
15 H4 **Mal I** Bismarck Arch 1.23S 144.15E
89 C5 **Mali** Guinea 12.08N 12.19W
91 K5 **Mali** Zaïre 2.47S 26.11E
9 S4 **Mali** *isld* Fiji 16.28S 179.21E
89 G4 **Mali** *rep* W Africa
84 E4 **Maliakós,Kólpos** *gulf* Greece
19 D8 **Maliana** Indonesia 8.04S 125.15E
92 D2 **Malianga** Zaïre 1.00S 29.02E
23 E1 **Malian He** *R* Gansu China
22 E7 **Malianjing** Gansu China 38.43N 101.20E
22 C6 **Malian Jing** *well* Gansu China 41.34N 95.22E
93 K10 **Malibui** Tanzania 4.44S 38.24E
70 K6 **Malicorne-sur-Sarthe** France 47.48N 0.05W
19 L8 **Maligay B** Mindanao Philippines 7.31N 123.15E
98 K8 **Malignant Cove** Nova Scotia 45.46N 62.06W
69 F8 **Maligny** France 47.52N 3.46E
35 F4 **Malih** *R* Jordan
86 C4 **Maliha** *oil well* Egypt 30.49N 29.33E
30 D6 **Malihabad** Uttar Prad India 26.54N 80.42E
35 J3 **Malihah el Gharbiyah** Syria 32.45N 36.21E
35 J2 **Malihah esh Sharqiyah** Syria 32.45N 36.22E
Māliha,Tell el *see* **Tel Milha**
25 N7 **Mali Hka** *R* Burma
71 J8 **Malijai** France 44.03N 6.02E
19 C4 **Malik** Celebes Indon 0.36S 123.15E
Malik *R see* **Zippori** *R*
31 E4 **Malikdin** Afghanistan 32.27N 68.06E
31 B6 **Malik Dokand** *mt* Afghanistan 29.38N 63.33E
31 B4 **Mali Khan** Afghanistan 32.39N 62.15E
Malikiya *see* **Malkiyya** Israel
33 B8 **Mālikīyah,Al** Bahrain, The Gulf 26.06N 50.30E
Malikkandi *see* **Malek Kandī**
31 B6 **Malik Naro** *mt* Pakistan 29.23N 63.28E
36 F3 **Malıköy** Turkey 39.47N 32.26E
Malik Siah,Kuh-i- *see* **Malek Siāh, Kūh-e** *mt*
25 E6 **Mali Kyun** *isld* Burma
19 B5 **Malili** Celebes Indon 2.38S 121.06E
52 J9 **Målilla** Sweden 57.24N 15.50E
9 U6 **Malima** *islets* Fiji 17.07S 179.13W
91 B5 **Malimba** Gabon 2.09S 10.41E
92 D5 **Malimba,Mts** Zaïre
18 B7 **Malim Nawar** Pen Malaysia 4.20N 101.06E
65 M2 **Malin** Czechoslovakia 49.58N 15.20E
59 H1 **Malin** Donegal Irish Rep 55.18N 7.15W
110 D7 **Malin** Oregon 42.02N 121.26W
46 G4 **Malin** Ukraine U.S.S.R. 50.48N 29.08E
30 B3 **Malin** *R* Uttar Prad India
19 M6 **Malinao Inlet** Philippines 10.16N 125.38E
18 M4 **Malinau** Borneo Indon 3.35N 116.40E
19 L7 **Malindang, Mt** Mindanao Philippines 8.12N 123.40E
93 M9 **Malindi** Kenya 3.14S 40.05E
93 K10 **Malindi** Tanzania 4.39S 38.18E
92 C11 **Malindi** Zimbabwe 18.45S 27.00E
62 M7 **Málinec** Czechoslovakia 48.32N 19.40E
Malines *see* **Mechelen** Belgium
91 C5 **Malinga** Congo 2.30S 12.14E
92 E3 **Malingara** Tanzania 3.59S 31.04E
19 B3 **Maling, Gunung** *mt* Celebes Indon 0.45N 120.46E
18 G9 **Malingping** Java Indon 6.45S 106.01E
52 J7 **Malingsbo** Sweden 59.56N 15.25E
59 H1 **Malin Hd** Donegal Irish Rep 55.23N 7.24W
59 E2 **Malin More** Donegal Irish Rep 54.41N 8.46W
19 A6 **Malino** Celebes Indonesia 5.18S 119.45E
45 K1 **Malino** U.S.S.R. 55.07N 38.13E
9 S10 **Malinoa** *islet* Tonga, Pacific Oc 21.01S 175.08W
45 P5 **Malinovka** Saratov U.S.S.R. 51.45N 43.24E
45 N3 **Malinovka** Tambov U.S.S.R. 53.03N 41.30E
42 D4 **Malinovka** Tomsk U.S.S.R. 57.03N 87.10E
45 H7 **Malinovka** Ukraine U.S.S.R. 49.47N 36.44E
40 F9 **Malinovka** *R* U.S.S.R.
42 B5 **Malinovoye Ozero** U.S.S.R. 51.38N 79.44E
53 M9 **Malinstindur** *mt* Faeroes 62.05N 7.08W
18 D6 **Malintang, Gunung** *mt* Sumatra Indon 0.23S 100.38E
92 H6 **Malinyi** Tanzania 8.55S 36.00E
15 M6 **Maliom** New Ireland 4.32S 153.02E
23 C7 **Malipo** Yunnan China 23.06N 104.53E
30 F6 **Malipur** Uttar Prad India 26.17N 82.39E
31 C10 **Malir R** Pakistan
19 M8 **Malita** Mindanao Philippines 6.23N 125.37E
19 M6 **Malitbog** Philippines 10.10N 124.59E
26 Q3 **Malivadi** Sri Lanka 9.01N 79.52E
25 E7 **Maliwun** Burma 10.16N 98.32E
66 P4 **Malix** Switzerland 46.49N 9.32E
29 B6 **Maliya** Gujarat India 23.03N 70.48E
109 G9 **Maljamar** New Mexico 32.50N 103.46W
71 K7 **Maljasser-Maurin** France 44.36N 6.51E
82 F6 **Maljen** *mt* Yugoslavia 44.09N 20.01E
35 F3 **Malka** Jordan 32.40N 35.45E
39 F7 **Malka** U.S.S.R. 53.18N 157.28E
44 E4 **Malka** *R* U.S.S.R.
39 E5 **Malkachan** U.S.S.R. 59.52N 154.11E
32 B4 **Malkaili** Iran 33.45N 47.25E
30 D5 **Malkalganj** Uttar Prad India 27.42N 80.22E
93 M1 **Malka Mari** Kenya 4.16N 40.45E
29 E7 **Malkapur** Buldana, Maharashtra India 20.52N 76.18E
28 A2 **Malkapur** Kolhapur, Maharashtra India 16.57N 74.00E
37 C2 **Malkara** Turkey 40.54N 26.54E
19 N3 **Malk,Eil** *isld* Palau Is Pacific Oc 7.09N 134.23E
53 T18 **Malkenes** Norway 60.05N 5.42E
42 H6 **Malkhanskiy Khrebet** *mts* U.S.S.R.
62 N3 **Małkinia** Poland 52.41N 22.01E
35 F1 **Malkiyya** Israel 33.06N 35.31E
82 L9 **Malko Tŭrnovo** Bulgaria 42.00N 27.31E
87 K9 **Mallable** Somalia 2.10N 45.35E
12 J7 **Mallacoota** Victoria 37.34S 149.43E
12 J7 **Mallacoota Inlet** Victoria 37.32S 149.42E
86 K9 **Mallâha,El** *marsh reg* Egypt
85 A3 **Mallāḥat Al Burayqā** *dist* Libya
100 F4 **Mallaig** Alberta 54.13N 111.20W
58 E4 **Mallaig** Highland Scotland 57.00N 5.50W
12 E5 **Mallala** S Australia 34.23S 138.25E
90 L2 **Mallanga** Chad 18.32N 22.59E
29 B5 **Mallani** *reg* Rajasthan India
30 E5 **Mallanpur** Uttar Prad India 27.42N 81.15E
30 D5 **Mallanwan** Uttar Prad India 27.02N 80.08E
108 Q7 **Mallard** Iowa 42.57N 94.42W
86 E10 **Mallawi** Egypt 27.44N 30.50E
121 A7 **Malleco** *prov* Chile
71 G9 **Mallemort** France 43.43N 5.10E
75 H4 **Mallén** Spain 41.53N 1.25W
66 F3 **Malleray** Switzerland 47.14N 7.16E
64 N6 **Mallersdorf** W Germany 48.47N 12.17E
101 Y4 **Mallery L** N W Terr
79 J1 **Malles Venosta** Italy 46.42N 10.32E
118 E9 **Mallét** Brazil 25.53S 50.57W
58 H7 **Malletsheugh** Strathclyde Scotland 55.46N 4.20W
84 M11 **Mállia** Crete 35.17N 25.27E
84 Q15 **Mallia** Cyprus 34.49N 32.47E
Mallicolo *isld see* **Malekula**
14 C5 **Mallina** W Australia 20.58S 118.01E
53 E4 **Malling** Denmark 56.02N 10.12E
84 M11 **Mallión, Kólpos** *gulf* Crete
65 H8 **Mallnitz** Austria 46.59N 13.11E
121 B5 **Malloa** Chile 34.28S 70.51W
74 J5 **Mallorca** *isld* Balearic Is Spain
104 D9 **Mallory** W Virginia 37.44N 81.51W
99 P8 **Mallorytown** Ontario 44.28N 75.54W
59 E7 **Mallow** Cork Irish Rep 52.08N 8.39W
14 E5 **Mallowa Well** W Australia 22.30S 124.26E
56 D2 **Mallwyd** Gwynedd Wales 52.42N 3.41W
52 F2 **Malm** Norway 64.04N 11.12E
69 L5 **Malmaison** France 49.08N 6.02E
69 F4 **Malmaison,la** France 49.30N 4.00E
Malmal *see* **Pal Malmal**
117 C2 **Malmanoury** Fr Guiana 5.20N 52.50W
31 B4 **Malman Rud** *R* Afghanistan
52 H9 **Malmbäck** Sweden 57.35N 14.30E
51 H4 **Malmberget** Sweden 67.11N 20.40E
61 P5 **Malmédy** Belgium 50.26N 6.02E
95 B9 **Malmesbury** S Africa 33.28S 18.43E
56 G4 **Malmesbury** Wilts Eng 51.36N 2.06W
51 G6 **Malmesjaure** *L* Sweden 65.54N 19.20E
50 F2 **Málmey** *isld* Iceland 66.01N 19.33W
39 G1 **Malmikha** U.S.S.R. 68.16N 160.36E
52 K7 **Malmköping** Sweden 59.08N 16.49E
52 G11 **Malmö** Sweden 55.35N 13.00E
52 G11 **Malmöhus** *dist* Sweden
116 K8 **Malmok** *hill* Bonaire W I 12.16N 68.24W
46 Q2 **Malmyzh** U.S.S.R. 56.34N 50.41E
79 E3 **Malnate** Italy 45.48N 8.52E
51 D3 **Malnes** Norway 68.45N 14.35E
79 K3 **Malo** Italy 45.39N 11.25E
19 E1 **Malo** *isld* Indonesia 4.35N 127.09E
9 C11 **Malo** *isld* New Hebrides 15.40S 167.10E
45 H4 **Maloarchangelsk** U.S.S.R. 52.23N 36.30E
91 K7 **Maloba** Zaïre 7.22S 26.36E
92 C5 **Maloba** Zaïre 6.19S 27.39E
120 D4 **Maloca** Acre Brazil 10.49S 70.11W
119 G9 **Maloca** Amazonas Brazil 3.19S 63.33W
117 B4 **Maloca** Pará Brazil 0.43N 55.55W
120 F3 **Maloca de Indios** Brazil 9.43S 65.00W
120 G5 **Maloca Salamaim** Brazil 12.15S 61.08W
9 D2 **Maloelap** *atoll* Marshall Is Pacific Oc 8.45N 171.00E
Maloggia *see* **Maloja**
66 P6 **Maloja** Switzerland 46.25N 9.43E
66 P6 **Maloja Pass** Switzerland 46.24N 9.43E
Malokuril'skoye Kuril Is *see* **Shikotan**
15 G5 **Malol** Papua New Guinea 3.08S 142.09E
92 E7 **Malole** Zambia 10.06S 31.37E
15 J7 **Malolo** Papua New Guinea 7.01S 147.00E
9 R7 **Malolo** *isld* Fiji 17.45S 177.10E
9 R7 **Malolo Barrier Reef** Fiji
19 L1 **Malolos** Guam Pacific Oc 13.18N 144.46E
94 G1 **Malombe** Namibia 17.46S 23.10E
92 G9 **Malombe, L** Malawi 14.40S 35.15E
82 K8 **Malomir** Bulgaria 42.16N 26.30E
75 G4 **Malón** Spain 41.57N 1.40W
84 V17 **Malóna** Rhodes Greece 36.12N 28.05E
105 B7 **Malone** Florida 30.56N 85.11W
104 L2 **Malone** New York 44.52N 74.19W
99 N8 **Malone** Ontario 44.34N 77.36W
112 L4 **Malone** Texas 31.56N 96.55W
108 K8 **Maloney, Lake** *res* Nebraska
23 C6 **Malong** Yunnan China 25.27N 103.40E
91 H9 **Malonga** Zaïre 10.26S 23.10E
61 K5 **Malonné** Belgium 50.27N 4.48E
79 H2 **Malonno** Italy 46.07N 10.18E
66 L6 **Malora,Pizzo** *mt* Switzerland 46.23N 8.36E
51 K6 **Malören** *Lt Ho* Sweden 65.31N 23.30E
46 E4 **Malorita** Belorussiya U.S.S.R. 51.50N 24.08E
47 D4 **Maloshuyka** U.S.S.R. 63.42N 37.29E
45 F8 **Malosofiyevka** Ukraine U.S.S.R. 48.10N 34.09E
95 L5 **Maloti Mts** Lesotho
110 F1 **Malott** Washington 48.19N 119.39W
47 H8 **Malouchalinskiy** U.S.S.R. 54.18N 59.28E
84 R14 **Malounda** Cyprus 35.00N 33.10E
45 T6 **Malouzensk** U.S.S.R. 50.31N 47.39E
94 N4 **Malova** Mozambique 23.25S 35.25E
53 S15 **Måløy** Norway 61.57N 5.06E
45 H2 **Maloyaroslavets** U.S.S.R. 55.00N 36.28E
47 H7 **Maloyaz** U.S.S.R. 55.14N 58.09E
44 G5 **Maloye** U.S.S.R. 42.57N 45.42E
45 G4 **Maloye Bobrovo** U.S.S.R. 52.25N 35.13E
45 H3 **Maloye Dumchino** U.S.S.R. 53.15N 36.27E
42 H6 **Maloye Goloustnoye** U.S.S.R. 52.20N 105.18E
47 K6 **Maloye Gorodishche** U.S.S.R. 58.00N 65.30E
45 G9 **Maloyekaterinovka** Ukraine U.S.S.R. 47.40N 35.16E
45 P1 **Maloye Kozino** U.S.S.R. 56.26N 43.41E
42 H5 **Maloye More, Proliv** *str* Baykal, Oz U.S.S.R.
42 J5 **Maloye Yeravnoye,Ozero** *L* U.S.S.R. 52.40N 111.40E
47 F3 **Malozemel'skaya Tundra** *plain* U.S.S.R.
109 C10 **Malpais** New Mexico 31.48N 107.16W
115 L3 **Malpaisillo** Nicaragua 12.38N 86.36W
76 F7 **Malpartida** Portugal 40.45N 6.51W
76 F10 **Malpartida de Cáceres** Spain 39.26N 6.30W
77 E3 **Malpartida de la Serena** Spain 38.40N 5.38W
76 G9 **Malpartida Plasencia** Spain 39.59N 6.03W
57 H6 **Malpas** Cheshire Eng 53.01N 2.46W
12 F5 **Malpas** S Australia 34.44S 140.43E
77 G6 **Malpasillo,Embalse de** *res* Spain 37.15N 4.37W
115 H6 **Malpaso** Mexico 22.40N 102.49W
96 P12 **Malpaso,Pico** *hill* Hierro Canary Is 27.44N 18.02W
119 A6 **Malpelo,I.de** Pacific Oc 4.00N 81.35W
98 J7 **Malpeque B** Prince Edward I
76 E9 **Malpica** Portugal 39.41N 7.24W
74 D5 **Malpica** Spain 39.55N 4.31W
75 H3 **Malpica de Arba** Spain 42.19N 1.07W
76 B2 **Malpica de Bergantiños** Spain 43.19N 8.50W
28 B3 **Malprabha R** Karnataka India
29 D4 **Malpura** Rajasthan India 26.19N 75.24E
41 D4 **Mal-Pura** *R* U.S.S.R.
64 E6 **Malsch** W Germany 48.52N 8.20E
62 H7 **Malše** *R* Austria/Czech
51 G2 **Målselv** Norway 69.12N 18.35E
51 G2 **Målselv** *R* Norway
64 H1 **Malsfeld** W Germany 51.06N 9.33E
40 G4 **Mal Shantar, Ostrov** *isld* U.S.S.R. 54.30N 137.32E
65 L3 **Malšice** Czechoslovakia 49.22N 14.35E
28 B2 **Malsiras** Maharashtra India 17.53N 74.55E
33 H4 **Malsūnīyah Al** *escarp* Saudi Arabia
65 J8 **Malta** Austria 46.58N 13.31E
109 D2 **Malta** Colorado 39.13N 106.23W
110 M7 **Malta** Idaho 42.19N 113.25W
110 S1 **Malta** Montana 48.22N 107.51W
104 D7 **Malta** Ohio 39.39N 81.52W
76 E7 **Malta** Portugal 40.45N 7.06W
42 G5 **Mal'ta** U.S.S.R. 52.52N 103.30E
84 Y20 **Malta** *rep* Mediterranean Sea
78 F12 **Malta Chan** Medit Sea
94 D5 **Maltahöhe** Namibia 24.50S 17.00E
41 O8 **Maltakhan** U.S.S.R. 63.15N 131.14E
39 E4 **Maltan** *R* U.S.S.R.
65 H7 **Maltatal** *V* Austria
57 L6 **Maltby** S Yorks Eng 53.26N 1.11W
11 E10 **Malte Brun** *mt* New Zealand 43.34S 170.19E
37 G2 **Maltepe** Turkey 40.56N 29.08E
66 J3 **Malters** Switzerland 47.03N 8.11E
30 B8 **Malthon** Madhya Prad India 24.18N 78.32E
57 M4 **Malton** N Yorks Eng 54.08N 0.48W
99 L9 **Malton** *airport* Ontario 43.42N 79.39W
82 K6 **Malu** Romania 44.38N 26.51E
81 B4 **Malu** *R* Sardinia
87 E5 **Malua** Sudan 11.39N 34.26E
122 B1 **Malua** W Samoa, Pacific Oc 13.46S 171.54W
19 J6 **Malubutglubut** *isld* Philippines 11.30N 119.42E
75 G5 **Maluenda** Spain 41.18N 1.37W
Maluku *islds see* **Moluccas** *Is*
34 D5 **Ma'lūla, Jebel** *mts* Syria 33.50N 36.33E
90 C6 **Malumfashi** Nigeria 11.48N 7.39E
90 L6 **Malumn** Sudan 11.31N 23.48E
19 A5 **Malunda** Celebes Indonesia 2.58S 118.52E
91 G11 **Malundo** Angola 14.51S 22.00E
52 H6 **Malung** Sweden 60.40N 13.45E
52 H6 **Malungsfors** Sweden 60.44N 13.35E
31 C3 **Malur Pass** Afghanistan 35.26N 64.46E
15 M3 **Maluu** Malaita I Solomon Is 8.20S 160.35E
66 M6 **Malvaglia** Switzerland 46.25N 8.59E
28 A2 **Malvan** Maharashtra India 16.05N 73.30E
76 A11 **Malveira** Portugal 38.56N 9.16W
76 B15 **Malveira** Portugal 38.45N 9.27W
107 D7 **Malvern** Arkansas 34.21N 92.50W
108 P9 **Malvern** Iowa 41.00N 95.42W
116 J2 **Malvern** Jamaica, W I 17.59N 77.42W
104 D6 **Malvern** Ohio 40.42N 81.11W
103 C6 **Malvern** Pennsylvania 40.02N 75.32W
12 D8 **Malvern** *dist* Melbourne, Vic
116 J2 **Malvern** *hill* Jamaica, W I 17.58N 77.47W
56 G3 **Malvern Hills** Hereford & Worcs England
13 H6 **Malvern Hills** Queensland 24.30S 145.07E
56 G3 **Malvern Link** Hereford & Worcs Eng 52.08N 2.18W
56 G3 **Malvern Wells** Hereford & Worcs Eng 52.05N 2.20W
70 G7 **Malville** France 47.22N 1.50W
Malvinas, Islas *see* **Falkland Is**
61 K6 **Malvoisin** Belgium 50.01N 4.58E
29 D6 **Malwa** *reg* Madhya Prad India
30 D6 **Malwan** Uttar Prad India 26.02N 80.42E
26 R4 **Malwatu Oya** *R* Sri Lanka
93 E8 **Malya** Tanzania 2.59S 33.32E
41 B4 **Malygina,Proliv** *str* U.S.S.R.
41 L8 **Malykay** U.S.S.R. 63.29N 117.09E
39 D3 **Malyk,Ozero** *L* U.S.S.R. 63.36N 147.50E
41 D6 **Malyshevka** U.S.S.R. 69.47N 84.46E
42 B3 **Mal-Yugan** *R* U.S.S.R.
40 E5 **Malyutka** U.S.S.R. 53.50N 130.18E
42 F2 **Malyy Aim** *R* U.S.S.R.
39 G1 **Malyy Anyuy** *R* U.S.S.R.
42 D6 **Malyy Anzas** U.S.S.R. 52.26N 89.49E
43 O5 **Malyy Ashinakho** Kazakhstan U.S.S.R. 43.31N 80.29E
47 K5 **Malyy Atlym** U.S.S.R. 62.20N 66.59E
43 C7 **Malyy Balkhan** *mts* Turkmeniya U.S.S.R.
42 A2 **Malyy Balyk** *R* U.S.S.R.
39 J1 **Malyy Chaun** *R* U.S.S.R.
39 H1 **Malyy Chaunskiy Proliv** *str* U.S.S.R.
43 M1 **Malyye Chany,Ozero** *L* U.S.S.R. 54.34N 77.15E
45 Q9 **Malyye Derbety** U.S.S.R. 47.57N 44.41E
41 A3 **Malyye Karmakuly** Novaya Zemlya U.S.S.R. 72.20N 52.46E
45 U4 **Malyy Irgiz** *R* U.S.S.R.
44 E6 **Malyy Kavkaz** *mts* U.S.S.R.
42 G6 **Malyy Khamar-Daban,Khrebet,mts** U.S.S.R.
42 H6 **Malyy Kunaley** U.S.S.R. 50.35N 107.50E
46 P2 **Malyy Kundysh** *R* U.S.S.R.
41 Q4 **Malyy Lyakhovskiy, Os** *isld* U.S.S.R.
40 C2 **Malyy Nimnyr** *R* U.S.S.R.
39 F1 **Malyy Oler, Ozero** *L* U.S.S.R. 69.30N 156.30E
39 G2 **Malyy Oloy** *R* U.S.S.R.
39 F7 **Malyy Semlyachik** *vol* Kamchatka U.S.S.R. 54.07N 159.39E
41 J2 **Malyy Taymyr,Ostrov** *isld* Severnaya Zemlya U.S.S.R.
46 R3 **Malyy Uran** *R* U.S.S.R.
46 P4 **Malyy Uzen'** *R* U.S.S.R.
41 Q4 **Malyy Van'kin,Mys** *C* U.S.S.R. 73.53N 142.00E
42 E6 **Malyy Yenisey** *R* U.S.S.R.
46 M7 **Malyy Zelenchuk** *R* U.S.S.R.
71 C7 **Malzieu-Ville,le** France 44.51N 3.21E
42 J3 **Mama** U.S.S.R. 58.20N 112.55E
37 D2 **Mama** *isld* Turkey 40.32N 27.36E
42 J3 **Mama** *R* U.S.S.R.
46 Q2 **Mamadysh** U.S.S.R. 55.43N 51.20E
15 J2 **Mamagota** Bougainville I Papua New Guinea 6.45S 155.21E
82 M6 **Mamaia** Romania 44.17N 28.39E
99 F5 **Mamainse Pt** Ontario 47.04N 84.43W
42 J3 **Mamakan** U.S.S.R. 57.48N 114.00E
42 J4 **Mamakan** *R* U.S.S.R.
103 F3 **Mamakating** New York 41.35N 74.27W
31 E3 **Māmā Kheyl** Afghanistan 34.15N 69.59E
11 L5 **Mamaku** New Zealand 38.06S 176.05E
92 J9 **Mamala** Mozambique 15.52S 38.40E
114 E9 **Mamala B** Hawaiian Is
114 E6 **Mamalu B** Hawaiian Is
9 R7 **Mamanutha Grp** *islds* Fiji
11 H2 **Mamaranui** New Zealand 35.50S 173.47E
103 G5 **Mamaroneck** New York 40.57N 73.44W
86 J5 **Mamarr Mitla** *pass* Egypt 30.02N 32.58E
76 B8 **Mamarrosa** Portugal 40.28N 8.35W
19 A5 **Mamasa** Celebes Indon 2.57S 119.24E
Mamatain *oil bore see* **Māmātīn**
31 D5 **Mamatan Nawar** *L* Afghanistan 30.36N 66.01E
32 C5 **Māmātīn** Iran 31.18N 49.46E
92 H8 **Mamauela** Mozambique 13.24S 37.23E
92 E5 **Mamba** Tanzania 7.24S 31.23E
66 H1 **Mambach** W Germany 47.44N 7.53E
19 J8 **Mambahenauhan** *isld* Philippines 6.29N 118.31E
118 F4 **Mambai** Brazil 14.27S 46.05W
19 M7 **Mambajao** Philippines 9.14N 124.41E
92 D12 **Mambala Cave** Zimbabwe 20.33S 28.15E
93 D10 **Mambali** Tanzania 4.31S 32.39E
84 B4 **Mambalioú** Greece 38.49N 21.20E
92 C11 **Mambanje** Zimbabwe 18.35S 26.43E
15 J8 **Mambare** *R* Papua New Guinea
92 D1 **Mambasa** Zaïre 1.20N 29.05E
28 C5 **Mambat** Kerala India 11.15N 76.11E
18 B9 **Mambau** Pen Malaysia 2.39N 101.54E
87 B8 **Mambe** Sudan 4.51N 29.50E
Mamberamo *see* **Teba** W Irian
15 E5 **Mamberamo** *R* Irian Jaya
90 G9 **Mambéré** *R* Cent Afr Rep
91 D3 **Mambili** *R* Congo
92 D7 **Mambilima Falls** Zambia 10.32S 28.39E
56 G3 **Mamble** Hereford & Worcs Eng 52.21N 2.27W
89 C7 **Mambolo** Sierra Leone 8.57N 13.01W
15 C5 **Mamboor, Kepulauan** *islds* Irian Jaya 3.05S 135.36E
89 C5 **Mamboya** Senegal 12.59N 13.59W
93 M9 **Mambrui** Kenya 3.08S 40.08E
91 F11 **Mambua** Angola 14.42S 19.47E
19 K5 **Mamburao** Philippines 13.13N 120.39E
29 D2 **Mamdot** Punjab India 30.52N 74.30E
39 G4 **Mamechinskiy Zaliv** *B* U.S.S.R.
76 B2 **Mamed de Silva** Spain 43.09N 8.32W
44 J5 **Mamedkala** U.S.S.R. 42.11N 48.05E
18 L5 **Mamehaktebo** Borneo Indon 0.09N 115.30E
100 L1 **Mameigwess L** Ontario 49.30N 91.50W
60 T17 **Mamelis** Netherlands 50.48N 5.58E
26 Q12 **Mamelle I** Seychelles, Ind Oc 4.29S 55.31E
37 G8 **Mamemusa Dağ** *mt* Turkey 37.46N 43.10E
100 D6 **Ma-Me-O Beach** Alberta 52.59N 113.58W
100 D5 **Ma-Me-O Beach Prov. Park** Alberta
61 P8 **Mamer** Luxembourg 49.37N 6.01E
70 L5 **Mamers** France 48.21N 0.22E
90 D9 **Mamfe** Cameroon 5.46N 9.18E
120 G1 **Mamiá** Brazil 4.03S 62.52W
120 F1 **Mamiá, L** Brazil
20 E9 **Mamihara** Japan 32.42N 131.11E
120 D9 **Mamiña** Chile 20.01S 69.15W
47 N5 **Maminskoye** U.S.S.R. 56.26N 61.24E
71 J2 **Mamirolle** France 47.11N 6.09E
44 F5 **Mamisonskiy Pereval** *pass* Georgia U.S.S.R. 42.43N 43.48E
43 J1 **Mamlyutka** Kazakhstan U.S.S.R. 54.54N 68.36E
99 F2 **Mammamattawa** Ontario 50.25N 84.23W
84 R14 **Mammari** Cyprus 35.10N 33.15E
53 D4 **Mammen** Denmark 56.25N 9.38E
64 L7 **Mammendorf** W Germany 48.12N 11.10E
64 O6 **Mamming** W Germany 48.39N 12.38E
81 M7 **Mammola** Italy 38.22N 16.15E
111 O9 **Mammoth** Arizona 32.43N 110.40W
104 D8 **Mammoth** W Virginia 38.17N 81.22W
107 K4 **Mammoth Cave** Kentucky 37.10N 86.08W
107 K4 **Mammoth Cave Nat.Park** Kentucky
110 P5 **Mammoth Hot Springs** Wyoming 44.58N 110.41W
107 E5 **Mammoth Spring** Arkansas 36.29N 91.31W
81 C3 **Mamoiada** Sardinia 40.13N 9.17E
119 C2 **Mamonal** Colombia 10.20N 75.30W
118 G4 **Mamonas** Brazil 15.05S 42.55W
46 C3 **Mamonovo** U.S.S.R. 54.30N 19.59E
41 F3 **Mamonta** *R* U.S.S.R.
41 C5 **Mamonta,Poluostrov** *pen* U.S.S.R.
42 C5 **Mamontovo** U.S.S.R. 52.44N 81.40E
88 K4 **Mamora,Forêt de** Morocco
120 F4 **Mamore** *R* Brazil/Bolivia
58 G5 **Mamore Forest** Highland Scotland
59 H1 **Mamore,Gap of** *pass* Donegal Irish Rep 55.14N 7.28W
120 F6 **Mamoré,R** Brazil/Bolivia
119 F8 **Mamori** Brazil 1.37S 67.41W
120 E2 **Mamoriá** Brazil 7.31S 66.16W
119 H9 **Mamori, L** Brazil
89 C6 **Mamou** Guinea 10.24N 12.05W
107 D11 **Mamou** Louisiana 30.37N 92.25W
90 K6 **Mamoun** Cent Afr Rep 10.05N 21.55E
89 J2 **Mamoun,El** Mali 18.45N 1.52W
95 B2 **Mamoutsou** Comoros, Ind Oc 12.47S 45.14E
95 C4 **Mampikony** Madagascar 16.03S 47.39E
76 J2 **Mampodre** *mt* Spain 43.02N 5.11W
91 F3 **Mampoko** Zaïre 0.51N 18.42E
89 J8 **Mampong** Ghana 7.06N 1.20W
26 Q6 **Mampuri** Sri Lanka 8.00N 79.43E
95 B9 **Mamre** S Africa 33.30S 18.28E
62 N1 **Mamry,Jezioro** *L* Poland
35 D9 **Mamshit** *anc site* Israel
35 D9 **Mamshit** *watercourse* Israel
58 F4 **Mam Soul** *mt* Highland Scotland 57.17N 5.08W
37 C6 **Mamuga** Turkey 39.42N 37.18E
121 B7 **Mamuil Malal Paso** *pass* Arg/Chile 39.34S 71.38W
Mamuji *see* **Yucheng**
19 A5 **Mamuju** Celebes Indon 2.41S 118.55E
33 L7 **Ma'mūl** *oil bore* Oman 18.11N 55.14E
32 D3 **Māmūnīyeh** Iran 35.18N 50.35E
94 E4 **Mamuno** Namibia 22.19S 20.00E
89 C7 **Mamunta** Sierra Leone 8.37N 12.00W
86 D3 **Ma'mûra,El** Egypt 31.18N 30.03E
33 M5 **Ma'mūrah** Oman 22.36N 57.21E
37 G2 **Mamure** Bursa Turkey 40.24N 29.23E
36 H2 **Mamure** Yozgat Turkey 40.08N 35.17E
37 G2 **Mamurıye** Turkey 40.32N 29.35E
117 B6 **Mamurú,R** Brazil
45 W2 **Mamykovo** U.S.S.R. 54.39N 50.34E
40 E5 **Mamyn** *R* U.S.S.R.
43 E2 **Mamyt** Kazakhstan U.S.S.R. 50.35N 58.44E
89 F8 **Man** Ivory Coast 7.31N 7.37W
28 B2 **Man** Maharashtra India 17.49N 74.32E
104 D9 **Man** W Virginia 37.45N 81.54W
117 C2 **Mana** Fr Guiana 5.40N 53.49W
84 E6 **Mána** Greece 37.58N 22.30E
114 E3 **Mana** Hawaiian Is 22.03N 159.46W
50 H2 **Maná** Iceland 66.12N 17.04W
30 C2 **Mana** Uttar Prad India 30.45N 79.32E
9 R7 **Mana** *I* Fiji 17.40S 177.09E
117 C2 **Mana** *R* Fr Guiana
52 D7 **Måna** *R* Norway
42 E4 **Mana** *R* U.S.S.R.
95 P8 **Manaba** S Africa 27.16S 32.26E
119 D3 **Mana Bárbara** Venezuela 9.39N 72.14W
119 B8 **Manabi** *prov* Ecuador
119 D6 **Manacacías, R** Colombia
119 H9 **Manacapuru** Brazil 3.16S 60.37W
119 H9 **Manacapuru, L.Grande de** Brazil
77 W14 **Manacor** Balearic Is 39.35N 3.12E
33 L5 **Manadir, Al** *des area* Oman
19 D3 **Manado** Celebes Indon 1.32N 124.55E
19 D3 **Manadotua** *isld* Indonesia 1.38N 124.43E
93 F5 **Manafwa** Uganda 0.56N 34.09E
61 H4 **Manage** Belgium 50.30N 4.14E
13 D3 **Managoora** N Terr Australia 16.02S 136.50E
115 L3 **Managua** Nicaragua 12.06N 86.18W
115 L3 **Managua, L.de** Nicaragua
33 M5 **Manaḩ** Oman 22.44N 57.36E
103 F7 **Manahawkin** New Jersey 39.42N 74.15W
33 H8 **Manahil** *tribe* S Yemen
36 G3 **Manahoz** *R* Turkey
11 J8 **Mana I** New Zealand 41.03S 174.45E
11 J6 **Manaia** New Zealand 39.33S 174.07E
95 D4 **Manakambahiny** Madagascar 17.44S 48.41E
95 D7 **Manakara** Madagascar 22.09S 48.00E
11 K7 **Manakau** New Zealand 40.42S 175.12E
11 H9 **Manakau** *mt* New Zealand 42.14S 173.38E
33 E9 **Manākhah** Yemen 15.00N 43.44E
104 H9 **Manakin** Virginia 37.36N 77.41W
Mana La *pass see* **Mana Shankou** *pass*
29 E1 **Manali** Himachal Prad India 32.12N 77.06E
28 D6 **Manamadurai** Tamil Nadu India 9.40N 78.27E
33 J3 **Manāmah,Al** Bahrain, The Gulf 26.12N 50.38E
95 B4 **Manambaho** *R* Madagascar
95 D2 **Manambato** Madagascar 13.43S 49.05E
95 D2 **Manambato** *R* Madagascar
95 B5 **Manambolo** *R* Madagascar
95 D3 **Manambolosy** Madagascar 16.01S 49.40E
95 D5 **Manambonitra** Madagascar 18.58S 48.57E
28 D5 **Manamelkudi** Tamil Nadu India 10.03N 79.15E
15 H6 **Manam I** Papua New Guinea 4.08S 145.05E
24 H9 **Manam La** *pass* Qinghai China
24 J9 **Manam La** *pass* Xizang Zizhiqu 32.08N 96.05E
19 K6 **Manamoc** *isld* Philippines 11.18N 120.43E
119 H3 **Manamo, Caño** *crater* Venezuela
114 B5 **Manana** *isld* Hawaiian Is 21.20N 157.40W
95 D4 **Mananara** Madagascar 16.10S 49.46E
95 C7 **Mananara** *R* Madagascar
95 D4 **Mananara** *R* Madagascar
95 B5 **Manandaza** Madagascar 19.19S 45.23E
95 C6 **Manandona** Madagascar 20.03S 47.03E
95 B7 **Manandréa** Madagascar 22.04S 44.50E
12 G6 **Manangatang** Victoria 35.03S 142.53E

95 D6 Mananjary Madagascar 21.13S 48.20E
95 C8 Manantenina Madagascar 24.17S 47.20E
28 C5 Manantoddy Kerala India 11.49N 76.01E
15 M3 Manaoba I Solomon Is 8.18S 160.45E
119 F3 Manapire, R Venezuela
11 B12 Manapouri New Zealand 45.35S 167.38E
11 B12 Manapouri, L New Zealand
28 D5 Manapparai Tamil Nadu India 10.34N 78.27E
87 D3 Manaqil, El Sudan 14.12N 33.01E
86 D7 Manâqîr el Ruwayân *hill* Egypt 29.02N 30.19E
87 H8 Mana,R Ethiopia
35 F1 Manara Israel 33.12N 35.32E
95 B7 Manaravolo Madagascar 23.59S 45.38E
50 H2 Mánáreyjar *islds* Iceland
84 D7 Mánari Greece 37.24N 22.19E
87 K3 Manar, Jeb *mt* Yemen 14.01N 44.23E
44 H5 Manas U.S.S.R. 42.44N 47.41E
24 E3 Manas Xinjiang Uygur Zizhiqu China 44.16N 86.02E
Manasarowar *L see* Mapam Yumco *L*
34 H3 Manasef, El *reg* Syria
24 C10 Mana Shankou *pass* Xizang Zizhiqu China 31.03N 79.30E
24 E3 Manas He *R* Xinjiang Uygur Zizhiqu China
24 E4 Manas He *R* Xinjiang Uygur Zizhiqu China
24 E3 Manas Hu *L* Xinjiang Uygur Zizhiqu China
29 J3 Manaslu Nepal 28.33N 84.33E
87 J9 Manaso Somalia 2.55N 43.25E
103 F6 Manasquan New Jersey 40.07N 74.02W
103 F6 Manasquan *R* New Jersey
28 H2 Manas R Assam/Bhutan
109 E4 Manassa Colorado 37.11N 105.56W
104 H8 Manassas Virginia 38.45N 77.39W
Manâssif, El *see* Manasef, El
37 F3 Manastır *isld* Turkey 40.10N 28.38E
Manastırbüku *see* Harşit
19 D8 Manatang Indonesia 8.26S 124.27E
103 C6 Manatawny Pennsylvania 40.22N 75.44W
96 A14 Manati Bay St Helena
35 F10 Manatir, Jeb.el *mt* Jordan 30.56N 35.35E
15 K8 Manau Papua New Guinea 8.02S 148.00E
119 H9 Manaus Brazil 3.06S 60.00W
36 E6 Manavgat Turkey 36.47N 31.28E
106 F5 Manawa Wisconsin 44.28N 88.56W
100 O3 Manawan L Saskatchewan
Manawar *see* Madawari
11 K4 Manawaru New Zealand 37.38S 175.46E
11 K7 Manawatu Gorge New Zealand
11 K7 Manawatu R New Zealand
19 G6 Manawoka *isld* Moluccas Indon 4.06S 131.21E
19 N8 Manay Mindanao Philippines 7.12N 126.32E
104 B1 Manayunk *dist* Philadelphia, Penn
29 K2 Manbazar W Bengal India 23.04N 86.41E
13 B2 Manbulla N Terr Australia 14.31S 132.12E
57 D4 Man, Calf of *islet* Isle of Man U.K. 54.03N 4.49W
106 J5 Mancelona Michigan 44.54N 85.03W
76 J7 Mancera de Abajo Spain 40.50N 5.12W
77 K3 Mancha, La *reg* Spain
28 A1 Manchar Maharashtra India 19.00N 73.56E
77 J5 Mancha Real Spain 37.47N 3.37W
103 L2 Manchaug Massachusetts 42.06N 71.45W
103 L2 Manchaug Pond *L* Massachusetts 42.06N 71.47W
67 E3 Manche *dept* France
69 C7 Manchecourt France 48.14N 2.20E
Manche, La *see* English Chan
22 K7 Mancheng Hebei China 38.56N 115.17E
120 E4 Manchester Bolivia 11.33S 68.04W
111 A3 Manchester California 38.58N 123.41W
103 J3 Manchester Connecticut 41.47N 72.31W
105 C5 Manchester Georgia 32.52N 84.34W
57 J5 Manchester Greater Manchester Eng 53.30N 2.15W
107 F2 Manchester Illinois 39.32N 90.20W
106 C7 Manchester Iowa 42.29N 91.28W
109 N2 Manchester Kansas 39.06N 97.21W
104 B9 Manchester Kentucky 37.09N 83.46W
106 K7 Manchester Michigan 42.10N 84.01W
104 O4 Manchester New Hampshire 42.59N 71.28W
104 H4 Manchester New York 42.58N 77.16W
104 B8 Manchester Ohio 38.42N 83.38W
109 M5 Manchester Oklahoma 37.00N 98.03W
103 A6 Manchester Pennsylvania 40.03N 76.43W
107 K6 Manchester Tennessee 35.29N 86.04W
104 M3 Manchester Vermont 43.09N 73.03W
116 J2 Manchester *parish* Jamaica, W I
103 G3 Manchester Bridge New York 41.41N 73.51W
31 D7 Manchhar L Pakistan
64 M6 Manching W Germany 48.43N 11.31E
116 M2 Manchioneal Jamaica, W I 18.02N 76.18W
77 D3 Manchita Spain 38.49N 6.01W
26 N15 Manchots, Falaises des *cliffs* St Paul I Ind Oc 38.44S 77.30E
26 N14 Manchots, Terrasses des *escarp* Amsterdam I Ind Oc
21 B4 Manchuria *reg* China
80 E3 Manciano Italy 42.35N 11.31E
72 E8 Manciet France 43.48N 0.04E
109 B4 Mancos Colorado 37.21N 108.19W
109 B4 Mancos *R* Colorado
31 B7 Mand Pakistan 26.05N 62.04E
32 D6 Mand *R* Iran
31 G8 Manda Bangladesh 24.45N 88.46E
29 B4 Manda Rajasthan India 27.19N 70.59E
92 F5 Manda Tanzania 7.59S 32.25E
92 F6 Manda Tanzania 8.31S 32.45E
92 G7 Manda Tanzania 10.30S 34.37E
30 F7 Manda Uttar Prad India 25.06N 82.15E
33 E10 Mandab, Bāb al *str* Arabia/Africa
95 B6 Mandabe Madagascar 21.02S 44.56E
95 B7 Mandabe Madagascar 22.30S 45.10E
90 H7 Man Dadji *R* Chad
Mandagay *see* Myndagayy
118 D8 Mandaguari Brazil 23.33S 51.41W
35 F3 Mandah Jordan 32.33N 35.40E
22 H4 Mandah Mongolia 44.24N 108.02E
92 F7 Manda Hill Zambia 11.38S 33.15E
93 M8 Manda I Kenya 2.16S 40.58E
18 H2 Mandai *dist* Singapore
18 H2 Mandai *hill* Singapore 1.24N 103.46E
26 Q2 Mandaitivu *isld* Sri Lanka 9.39E 79.59E
90 M7 Manda, Jebel *mt* Sudan 8.51N 24.20E
31 A4 Mandal Afghanistan 33.14N 61.50E
22 E3 Mandal Mongolia 46.51N 100.01E
52 D8 Mandal Norway 58.02N 7.30E
29 D5 Mandal Rajasthan India 25.29N 74.38E
15 F6 Mandala, Pk Irian Jaya 4.39S 140.18E
25 D2 Mandalay Burma 21.57N 96.04E
25 C2 Mandalay *dist* Burma
29 D5 Mandalgarh Rajasthan India 25.16N 75.09E
22 G4 Mandalgovĭ Mongolia 45.40N 106.10E
34 N5 Mandalī Iraq 33.43N 45.33E
90 H6 Mandaloigne Chad 10.59N 16.44E
22 F4 Mandal-Ovoo Mongolia 44.39N 104.03E
31 F3 Mandal P Afghanistan 36.00N 71.10E
52 C8 Mandalselva *R* Norway
Mandalt *see* Sonid Zuoqi
19 H1 Mandaluyong Luzon Philippines 14.36N 121.02E
36 C5 Mandalya Körfezi *gulf* Turkey
108 K3 Mandan N Dakota 46.50N 100.54W
81 K7 Mandanici Sicily 38.01N 15.20E
19 L5 Mandaon Philippines 12.15N 123.18E
28 D6 Mandapam Tamil Nadu India 9.18N 79.08E
90 F6 Mandara Mts Cameroon/Nigeria
30 L8 Mandargiri Hill Bihar India 24.51N 87.03E
87 C8 Mandari *tribe* Sudan
19 A5 Mandar, Tanjung *C* Celebes Indonesia 3.35S 118.56E
19 A5 Mandar, Teluk *B* Celebes Indon
81 C4 Mandas Sardinia 39.39N 9.08E
29 J8 Mandasa Andhra Prad India 18.53N 84.31E
84 D3 Mandasiá Greece 39.07N 22.27E
29 D5 Mandasor Madhya Prad India 24.03N 75.10E
29 D5 Mandasor *dist* Madhya Prad India
81 N5 Mandatoriccio Italy 39.28N 16.51E
18 D5 Mandau *R* Sumatra Indon
29 B6 Mandav Hills Gujarat India
29 D3 Mandawa Rajasthan India 28.02N 75.13E
92 J6 Mandawa Tanzania 9.20S 39.25E
29 E4 Mandawar Rajasthan India 27.52N 76.36E
75 E6 Mandayona Spain 40.58N 2.45W
26 R3 Mandekal Aru *R* Sri Lanka
64 C5 Mandelbachtal W Germany 49.08N 7.14E
79 F3 Mandello del Lario Italy 45.55N 9.19E
63 L7 Mandelsloh in der Wiek W Germany 52.36N 9.34E
76 D2 Mandeo *R* Spain
93 N2 Mandera Kenya 3.56N 41.53E
92 J5 Mandera Tanzania 6.13S 38.26E
93 M2 Mandera *dist* Kenya
61 Q5 Manderfeld Belgium 50.20N 6.20E
111 M3 Manderfield Utah 38.21N 112.38W
64 B3 Manderscheid W Germany 50.05N 6.49E
108 C5 Manderson Wyoming 44.18N 107.56W
18 D6 Manderubiah, Gunung *mt* Sumatra Indon 1.18S 100.49E
71 K2 Mandeure France 47.27N 6.48E
116 J2 Mandeville Jamaica, W I 18.02N 77.31W
107 F11 Mandeville Louisiana 30.21N 90.04W
11 C13 Mandeville New Zealand 46.00S 168.50E
30 D6 Mandhana Uttar Prad India 26.34N 80.14E
29 E6 Mandhata Madhya Prad India 22.14N 76.11E
29 E2 Mandi Himachal Prad India 31.40N 76.59E
30 D2 Mandi Xizang Zizhiqu 30.49N 80.45E
29 E2 Mandi *dist* Himachal Prad India
89 E6 Mandiana Guinea 10.37N 8.39W
90 K9 Mandiao Cent Afr Rep 4.54N 21.35E
31 G4 Mandi Bahauddin Pakistan 32.33N 73.31E
31 G5 Mandi Burewala Pakistan 30.05N 72.47E
92 F10 Mandie Mozambique 16.30S 33.31E
31 C5 Mandi Hisar Afghanistan 31.33N 65.47E
92 G9 Mandimba Mozambique 14.21S 35.40E
89 E5 Manding *reg* Guinea/Mali
119 B3 Mandinga Panama 9.33N 79.07W
95 P5 Mandini S Africa 29.09S 31.25E
19 E4 Mandioli *isld* Moluccas Indon
118 B6 Mandioré, L Bolivia/Brazil
37 E3 Mandıra Turkey 40.04N 28.10E
29 J6 Mandira Dam Madhya Prad India 22.17N 84.44E
86 N9 Mandisha, Jebel *mt* Saudi Arabia 28.25N 34.52E
91 C4 Mandja Gabon 1.56S 13.24E
90 G6 Mandjafa Chad 11.11N 15.20E
95 P8 Mandjene, L Mozambique 26.45S 32.21E
91 B4 Mandji Gabon 1.43S 10.19E
90 H9 Mandjia *tribe* Cent Afr Rep
29 G6 Mandla Madhya Prad India 22.35N 80.28E
29 D6 Mandleshawar Madhya Prad India 22.15N 75.45E
65 J7 Mandling Austria 47.25N 13.35E
65 J7 Mandling *pass* Austria 47.26N 13.34E
53 B6 Mandø Denmark 55.17N 8.33E
53 B6 Mandø *isld* Denmark 55.17N 8.33E
18 H5 Mandor Borneo Indon 0.16N 109.15E
29 C4 Mandor Rajasthan India 26.25N 73.07E
14 D4 Mandora W Australia 19.45S 120.50E
Mandori *see* Alizai
95 C5 Mandoto Madagascar 19.33S 46.17E
84 F4 Mandoúdhion Greece 38.48N 23.29E
84 F5 Mándra Attikí Greece 38.04N 23.30E
84 C7 Mándra Messinía Greece 37.18N 21.55E
31 G4 Mandra Pakistan 33.24N 73.16E
30 A6 Mandrael Rajasthan India 26.19N 77.14E
84 S14 Mandres Cyprus 35.19N 33.48E
69 J7 Mandres-en-Barrois France 48.30N 5.24E
84 Q15 Mandria Cyprus 34.51N 32.50E
79 L7 Mandrioli, Passo dei *pass* Italy 43.48N 11.54E
95 D3 Mandritsara Madagascar 15.49S 48.50E
30 L7 Mandro Bihar India 25.13N 87.30E
79 J2 Mandrone, Monte Italy 46.11N 10.32E
95 B6 Mandrosonoro Madagascar 20.34S 46.00E
45 K6 Mandrovo U.S.S.R. 50.18N 38.16E
29 J1 Mandu Bihar India 23.48N 85.29E
29 D6 Mandu Madhya Prad India 22.22N 75.24E
71 E9 Manduel France 43.49N 4.29E
18 M4 Mandul *isld* Borneo Indon
26 U7 Mandur Sri Lanka 7.30N 81.45E
14 B10 Mandurah W Australia 32.31S 115.41E
81 Q12 Manduria Italy 40.24N 17.38E
29 A6 Mandvi Kutch, Gujarat India 22.50N 69.25E
29 C7 Mandvi Surat, Gujarat India 21.16N 73.22E
28 C4 Mandya Karnataka India 12.34N 76.55E
28 C4 Mandya *dist* Karnataka India
44 F2 Mandzhikiny U.S.S.R. 45.39N 44.40E
71 H9 Mane Alpes de Haute Provence France 43.56N 5.45E
72 F9 Mane Haute-Garonne France 43.05N 0.57E
89 J5 Mané Upper Volta 12.58N 1.23W
30 K5 Manebhanjyang Nepal 27.12N 86.26E
32 G2 Maneh Iran 37.40N 57.09E
92 H10 Maneia Mozambique 16.46S 37.35E
29 B7 Manekwara Gujarat India 21.28N 70.56E
114 D6 Manele Bay Hawaiian Is
19 L1 Manell Pt Guam Pacific Oc 13.15N 144.41E
29 H6 Manendragarh Madhya Prad India 23.20N 82.22E
30 H7 Maner Bihar India 25.38N 84.53E
79 J3 Manerba Italy 45.33N 10.33E
79 H4 Manerbio Italy 45.22N 10.09E
48 S9 Manermiut Greenland 68.35N 53.05W
92 J5 Maneromango Tanzania 7.10S 38.51E
28 D1 Maner R Andhra Prad India
75 G2 Mañeru Spain 42.40N 1.52W
64 P4 Manětin Czechoslovakia 49.59N 13.15E
46 F4 Manevichi Ukraine U.S.S.R. 51.19N 25.35E
85 L6 Manfalût Egypt 27.23N 30.58E
108 L2 Manfred N Dakota 47.42N 99.43W
12 G5 Manfred New S Wales 33.21S 143.50E
80 N5 Manfredonia Italy 41.37N 15.55E
80 O5 Manfredónia, Golfo di Italy
90 K5 Manga Chad 13.00N 21.07E
91 E4 Manga Congo 0.13S 16.05E
118 G4 Manga Minas Gerais Brazil 14.48S 43.55W
92 G11 Manga Mozambique 19.46S 34.53E
89 J6 Manga Upper Volta 11.41N 1.04W
90 E5 Manga *reg* Chad/Niger
95 D4 Mangabe Madagascar 17.44S 49.13E
117 E9 Mangabeiras, Chapada das *mts* Brazil
11 K7 Mangahao *H E Station* New Zealand 40.35S 175.31E
11 K7 Mangahao R New Zealand
28 E1 Mangahpett Andhra Prad India 18.16N 80.33E
15 L5 Mangai New Ireland 2.49S 151.09E
91 F6 Mangai Zaïre 4.02S 19.33E
122 L10 Mangaia *isld* Cook Is Pacific Oc 21.56S 157.56W
87 E6 Manga,Jeb *mt* Ethiopia 9.32N 34.10E
11 K5 Mangakino New Zealand 38.23S 175.47E
28 E2 Mangalagiri Andhra Prad India 16.29N 80.35E
82 M7 Mangalia Romania 43.48N 28.36E
90 J5 Mangalmé Chad 12.26N 19.37E
28 B4 Mangalore Karnataka India 12.54N 74.51E
13 H7 Mangalore Queensland 26.42S 146.08E
31 E3 Mangalpur Afghanistan 35.08N 69.50E
28 B2 Mangalvedha Maharashtra India 17.32N 75.32E
11 K7 Mangamahoe New Zealand 40.43S 175.42E
11 K6 Mangamahu New Zealand 39.49S 175.23E
11 H9 Mangamaunu New Zealand 42.18S 173.47E
95 C5 Mangamila Madagascar 18.30S 47.51E
11 H2 Mangamuka New Zealand 35.13S 173.36E
29 L4 Mangan India 27.29N 88.40E
91 E8 Mangando Angola 8.02S 17.08E
76 H5 Manganeses de la Lampreana Spain 41.45N 5.43W
91 G3 Mangania Zaïre 0.30N 21.12E
81 K8 Mangano Sicily 37.41N 15.11E
28 A1 Mangaon Maharashtra India 18.18N 73.22E
11 K5 Mangapehi New Zealand 38.29S 175.19E
92 J11 Mangapwani Zanzibar 6.00S 39.11E
118 G8 Mangaratiba Brazil 22.54S 43.59W
122 S15 Mangaréva *isld* Gambier Is Pacific Oc 23.07S 134.57W
19 K5 Mangarin B Philippines 12.16N 121.05E
109 B7 Mangas New Mexico 34.09N 108.19W
58 Q9 Mangaster Shetland Scotland 60.25N 1.25W
95 C6 Mangataboahangy Madagascar 20.15S 46.10E
11 K7 Mangatainoka New Zealand 40.24S 175.52E
30 E8 Mangawan Madhya Prad India 24.39N 81.33E
11 K6 Mangaweka New Zealand 39.48S 175.48E
11 L6 Mangaweka *mt* New Zealand 39.48S 176.05E
11 J3 Mangawhai New Zealand 36.08S 174.36E
11 J3 Mangawhai Harb *inlet* New Zealand
28 H2 Mangde *R* Bhutan
89 C7 Mange Sierra Leone 8.57N 12.51W
91 G3 Mange Zaïre 0.50N 20.33E
91 D6 Mangembo Zaïre 4.36S 14.18E
29 L4 Mangen Sikkim India 27.30N 88.33E
95 O4 Mangeni S Africa 28.28S 30.49E
53 S17 Manger Norway 60.39N 5.02E
11 C3 Mangere New Zealand 36.58S 174.47E
11 D3 Mangere East New Zealand 36.58S 174.49E
11 K11 Mangere I Chatham Is Pacific Oc 44.16S 176.17W
11 C3 Mangere, Mt *hill* New Zealand 36.57S 174.47E
59 D8 Mangerton Mt Kerry Irish Rep 51.58N 9.29W
87 F5 Mangestu *mts* Ethiopia
64 M8 Mangfall *R* W Germany
64 M8 Mangfall Gebirge *mts* W Germany
18 H7 Manggar Belitung Indonesia 2.52S 108.13E
15 L4 Manggautu Solomon Is 11.38S 159.58E
15 B6 Manggawitu Irian Jaya 4.13S 133.30E
107 E9 Mangham Louisiana 32.19N 91.48W
23 F1 Mang He *R* Henan China
69 K5 Mangiennes France 49.22N 5.31E
43 F6 Mangit Uzbekistan U.S.S.R. 42.08N 60.02E
18 N5 Mangkalihat, Tanjung *C* Borneo Indon 1.00N 119.01E
19 B9 Mangkudu *isld* Indonesia 10.19S 120.14E
23 C9 Mang Kung Uk Hong Kong 22.18N 114.16E
18 L6 Mangkutup *R* Borneo Indon
25 N8 Mangkyi Burma 26.16N 98.19E
31 G4 Mangla Pakistan 33.09N 73.44E
119 B8 Manglar Alto Ecuador 1.55S 80.43W
119 B7 Manglares, Pta Colombia 1.34N 79.04W
30 A3 Manglaur Uttar Prad India 29.45N 77.52E
14 A4 Mangles B W Australia
71 C5 Manglieu France 45.37N 3.21E
44 F6 Manglisi Georgia U.S.S.R. 41.43N 44.25E
28 G7 Manglutan Andaman Is 11.35N 92.36E
22 B8 Mangnai Qinghai China 37.52N 91.26E
24 G6 Mangnai Zhen Xinjiang Uygur Zizhiqu China 38.21N 90.05E
30 C1 Mangnang Xizang Zizhiqu 31.21N 79.50E
30 C1 Mangnang *R* Xizang Zizhiqu
9 U6 Mango *isld* Fiji 17.28S 179.09W
9 T13 Mango *isld* Tonga, Pacific Oc 20.20S 174.53W
95 D2 Mangoaka Madagascar 12.20S 49.07E
89 J9 Mangoasi Ghana 5.58N 0.15W
92 G9 Mangoche Malawi 14.30S 35.15E
95 B6 Mangoky *R* Madagascar
19 D4 Mangole *isld* Moluccas Indon
19 D4 Mangole, Selat *str* Moluccas Indon
28 B2 Mangoli Karnataka India 16.44N 75.54E
92 G4 Mangoloma Tanzania 4.54S 35.34E
95 A6 Mangolovolo Madagascar 21.42S 43.30E
91 K4 Mangombe Zaïre 1.23S 26.50E
11 H2 Mangonui New Zealand 35.00S 173.34E
95 D5 Mangoro *R* Madagascar
29 B7 Mangrol Gujarat India 21.10N 70.11E
30 A6 Mangrol Madhya Prad India 26.15N 77.20E
29 E5 Mangrol Rajasthan India 25.22N 76.32E
116 F2 Mangrove Cay Andros Bahamas 24.16N 77.40W
105 J11 Mangrove Cay Bahamas 26.55N 78.40W
29 E7 Mangrul Maharashtra India 20.36N 77.52E
29 E7 Mangrul Pir Maharashtra India 20.20N 77.24E
18 E7 Mangsang Sumatra Indon 2.10S 103.58E
Mangshi *see* Luxi
117 J9 Manguaba, L Brazil
76 D7 Mangualde Portugal 40.36N 7.46W
119 E8 Manguari Brazil 1.40N 69.08W
31 D6 Manguchar Pakistan 29.21N 66.38E
91 C7 Mangue Angola 6.40S 12.36E
90 K6 Mangueigne Chad 10.30N 21.15E
121 H4 Mangueira, L Brazil
118 D9 Mangueirinha Brazil 25.59S 52.15W
118 E2 Mangues *R* Brazil
21 B1 Mangui Nei Monggol Zizhiqu China 52.05N 122.17E
118 J2 Manguinha, Pontal do *pt* Brazil 10.31S 36.22W
118 J9 Manguinhos, Aeroporto Brazil 22.52S 43.14W
92 H5 Mangula Tanzania 7.49S 37.10E
92 E10 Mangula Zimbabwe 16.51S 30.13E
87 E7 Mangum Ethiopia 7.30N 34.29E
109 L7 Mangum Oklahoma 34.54N 99.31W
117 F5 Mangunça, I Brazil 1.37S 44.40W
91 F6 Mangungu Zaïre 5.16S 19.36E
94 N4 Mangunhana Mozambique 23.58S 34.21E
18 E7 Mangunjaya Sumatra Indon 2.44S 103.35E
42 J7 Mangut U.S.S.R. 49.45N 112.40E
91 J7 Mangwa Zaïre 6.53S 24.14E
92 D12 Mangwe *R* Zimbabwe
43 B5 Mangyshlak Kazakhstan U.S.S.R. 43.42N 51.15E
44 L4 Mangyshlak U.S.S.R. 43.40N 51.15E
43 C5 Mangyshlak A.S.S.R. U.S.S.R.
44 L4 Mangyshlak, Poluostrov *pen* Kazakhstan U.S.S.R.
44 K3 Mangyshlaksiy Zaliv *gulf* Kazakhstan U.S.S.R.
118 F3 Manhã Brazil 12.43S 46.25W
22 B3 Manhan Mongolia 47.24N 92.10E
103 J2 Manhan *R* Massachusetts
23 C7 Manhao Yunnan China 23.02N 103.14E
88 G9 Manhar, El *reg* Morocco
65 N4 Manharts Berg *mt* Austria 48.34N 15.45E
103 M7 Manhasset New York
103 M6 Manhasset B New York
106 G8 Manhattan Illinois 41.26N 87.59W
109 O2 Manhattan Kansas 39.11N 96.35W
110 O4 Manhattan Montana 45.52N 111.20W
111 G3 Manhattan Nevada 38.31N 117.05W
103 M7 Manhattan *bor* New York
111 D9 Manhattan Beach California 33.53N 118.24W
103 B6 Manheim Pennsylvania 40.10N 76.24W
90 J3 Manherté Chad 17.14N 18.08E
69 K5 Manheulles France 49.07N 5.36E
94 M5 Manhica Mozambique 25.25S 32.49E
95 P8 Manhoca Mozambique 26.49S 32.36E
118 G7 Manhuaçu Brazil 20.16S 42.01W
118 H6 Manhuaçu, R Brazil
118 H7 Manhumirim Brazil 20.22S 41.57W
105 L12 Man I Bahamas 25.34N 76.37W
119 D5 Mani Colombia 4.50N 72.15W
Mani Irian Jaya *see* Wami
91 J7 Mani Zaïre 6.30S 25.19E
84 D8 Máni *mts* Greece
30 A6 Mania Rajasthan India 26.49N 77.55E
79 N2 Maniago Italy 46.10N 12.42E
92 G8 Maniamba Mozambique 12.49S 35.00E
89 E7 Manianko Guinea 10.01N 8.20W
29 G6 Maniari *res* Madhya Prad India 22.25N 81.40E
30 E6 Maniari Aliganj Uttar Prad India 26.20N 81.51E
92 F11 Manica Mozambique 18.56S 32.52E
92 F11 Manicaland *prov* Zimbabwe
19 M6 Manicani *isld* Philippines 10.59N 125.37E
94 M1 Manica Sofala *dist* Mozambique
97 N7 Manic-Cinq Quebec 50.40N 68.54W
98 D4 Manic Deux Dam Quebec 49.20N 68.25W
120 G1 Manicoré Brazil 5.48S 61.16W
120 G2 Manicoré, R Brazil
98 D3 Manicouagan Quebec 50.40N 68.46W
98 D4 Manicouagan Pen Quebec 49.05N 68.18W
98 D4 Manicouagan R Quebec
98 D2 Manicouagan Res Quebec
98 D4 Manic Trois Dam Quebec 49.45N 68.40W
33 H3 Manifa *oil well* Saudi Arabia 27.44N 49.02E
33 H3 Manīfah Saudi Arabia 27.35N 48.55E
13 K6 Manifold, C Queensland 22.42S 150.50E
30 K6 Manigachi Bihar India 26.13N 86.08E
66 B8 Manigod France 45.52N 6.22E
100 V7 Manigotagan Manitoba 51.06N 96.18W
30 L7 Manihari Bihar India 25.21N 87.37E
Manihari Ghat *see* Manihari
122 C14 Manihi *atoll* Tuamotu Is Pacific Oc 14.20S 145.58W
122 L9 Manihiki *atoll* Cook Is Pacific Oc 10.24S 161.01W
31 C8 Maniji R Pakistan
91 J9 Manika, Plat. de la Zaïre
31 H9 Manikganj Bangladesh 23.52N 90.00E
Manikgarh *see* Rajura Chanda, Maharashtra
92 F5 Manikonde Tanzania 7.26S 32.27E
30 E7 Manikpur Uttar Prad India 25.04N 81.06E
107 F6 Manila Arkansas 35.53N 90.11W
19 H1 Manila Luzon Philippines 14.37N 120.58E
110 Q9 Manila Utah 40.59N 109.44W
19 G1 Manila Bay Luzon Philippines
12 J5 Manildra New S Wales 33.12S 148.41E
108 P8 Manilla Iowa 41.54N 95.14W
12 K4 Manilla New S Wales 30.45S 150.45E
77 N5 Manilla *mt* Spain 37.45N 1.37W
77 F8 Manilva Spain 36.23N 5.15W
39 H3 Manily U.S.S.R. 62.31N 165.45E
30 A2 Mani Majra Punjab India 30.42N 76.50E
19 A4 Manimbaya, Tanjung *C* Celebes Indonesia 0.01S 119.38E
95 D4 Maningory *R* Madagascar
13 C1 Maningrida N Terr Australia 12.04S 134.14E
89 F6 Maninian Ivory Coast 10.03N 7.52W
9 R13 Maninita *islet* Tonga, Pacific Oc 18.51S 174.00W
18 D6 Maninjau, Danau *L* Sumatra Indon
45 N6 Manino U.S.S.R. 50.29N 41.22E
19 E5 Manipa *isld* Moluccas Indon 3.18S 127.33E
19 E5 Manipa, Selat *str* Moluccas Indon
Manipur *see* Imphal
25 L9 Manipur *R* Burma
28 J3 Manipur *state* India
28 J3 Manipur R Burma/India
76 C16 Manique de Baixo Portugal 38.44N 9.22W
36 C4 Manisa Turkey 38.36N 27.29E
75 K9 Manises Spain 39.30N 0.28W
58 C3 Manish Harris, W Isles Scotland 57.48N 6.53W
32 B4 Manisht Kūh *mt* Iran 33.42N 46.27E
85 M10 Manisir *reg* Sudan
57 E4 Man, Isle of Irish Sea
28 J7 Man, Isle of Nicobar Is 8.22N 93.37E
118 C2 Manissauá Missu, R Brazil
106 H5 Manistee Michigan 44.14N 86.20W
106 J5 Manistee, R Michigan
106 H4 Manistique Michigan 45.58N 86.17W
106 J3 Manistique L Michigan 46.15N 85.45W
106 H3 Manistique, R Michigan
106 E9 Manito Illinois 40.25N 89.49W
97 J6 Manitoba *prov* Canada
100 T8 Manitoba, L Manitoba
100 H6 Manito L Saskatchewan
100 T9 Manitou Manitoba 49.15N 98.32W
103 G4 Manitou New York 41.20N 73.58W
109 M7 Manitou Oklahoma 34.31N 98.57W
100 M7 Manitou Beach Saskatchewan 51.43N 105.30W
106 G2 Manitou I Michigan 47.25N 87.36W
106 H4 Manitou Island, North Michigan 45.07N 86.01W
106 H4 Manitou Island, South Michigan 45.02N 86.07W
99 J7 Manitou L Ontario
98 G3 Manitou L Quebec
99 H7 Manitoulin I Ontario
100 K1 Manitou L.,Lower Ontario 49.15N 93.00W
100 J2 Manitou L.,Upper Ontario 49.25N 92.45W
98 G2 Manitou R Quebec
109 F3 Manitou Springs Colorado 38.51N 104.55W
99 E3 Manitouwadge Ontario 49.14N 85.51W
99 E3 Manitouwadge L Ontario 49.13N 85.49W
99 J7 Manitowaning Ontario 45.44N 81.50W
99 F4 Manitowik L Ontario
106 G5 Manitowoc Wisconsin 44.04N 87.40W
Manîtsoq *see* Sukkertoppen
121 J5 Mañiuales, R Chile
34 H5 Mānī, Wādī al *watercourse* Iraq
99 P6 Maniwaki Quebec 46.22N 75.58W
28 C6 Maniyachi Tamil Nadu India 8.51N 77.56E
34 K8 Ma'nīyah, Al Saudi Arabia 30.44N 42.57E
119 C5 Manizales Colombia 5.03N 75.32W
32 D5 Manj Iran 31.31N 50.50E
35 G6 Manja Jordan 31.45N 35.51E
95 B6 Manja Madagascar 21.26S 44.20E
94 M5 Manjacaze Mozambique 24.47S 33.50E
95 C5 Manjak Madagascar 18.54S 47.48E
28 B4 Manjarabad Karnataka India 12.56N 75.41E
28 C5 Manjeri Kerala India 11.06N 76.06E
31 E8 Manjhand Pakistan 25.54N 68.16E
30 E7 Manjhanpur Uttar Prad India 25.32N 81.22E
30 H7 Manjhi Bihar India 25.50N 84.34E
32 C2 Manjil Iran 36.44N 49.29E
14 B10 Manjimup W Australia 34.14S 116.06E
28 C1 Manjlegaon Maharashtra India 19.09N 76.14E
91 A1 Manjo Cameroon 4.40N 9.44E
28 C1 Manjra *R* Andhra Prad India
28 C1 Manjra R Maharashtra India
87 K5 Manjr Asseh Somalia 10.06N 45.10E
33 F5 Manjūr, Al Saudi Arabia 23.00N 45.39E
65 M5 Mank Austria 48.08N 15.21E
25 N7 Man Kabat Burma 27.39N 97.22E
28 G3 Mankachar Assam India 25.35N 89.54E
95 P2 Mankaiana Swaziland 26.40S 31.03E
30 F5 Mankapur Uttar Prad India 27.03N 82.12E
29 J7 Mankarnacha *mt* Orissa India 21.46N 85.16E
109 M2 Mankato Kansas 39.48N 98.13W
108 R5 Mankato Minnesota 44.10N 94.00W
26 T5 Mankeni Sri Lanka 8.01N 81.28E
31 F5 Mankera Pakistan 31.24N 71.30E
29 J6 Mankheri Bihar India 23.41N 84.32E
91 C1 Mankim Cameroon 5.06N 12.03E
112 J2 Mankins Texas 33.47N 98.49W
89 F7 Mankono Ivory Coast 8.01N 6.09W
100 K9 Mankota Saskatchewan 49.25N 107.05W
82 N2 Mankovka U.S.S.R. 48.59N 30.19E
Mankoya *see* Kaoma
26 R3 Mankulam Sri Lanka 9.07N 80.27E
89 H7 Mankuma Ghana 9.13N 2.24W
71 E2 Manlay France 47.08N 4.21E
22 G4 Manlay Mongolia 44.05N 107.00E
113 M4 Manley Hot Springs Alaska 65.00N 150.49W
75 P4 Manlleu Spain 42.00N 2.17E
23 B8 Man-lu Ho *R* China/Burma
104 K3 Manluis New York 43.01N 75.59W
108 R6 Manly Iowa 43.19N 93.11W
12 K5 Manly New S Wales 33.47S 151.17E
12 M6 Manly Beach *dist* Sydney, N S W 33.48S 151.17E
30 E3 Manma Nepal 29.08N 81.37E
29 D7 Manmad Maharashtra India 20.15N 74.29E
9 B3 Mann *islet* Marshall Is Pacific Oc 8.53N 167.34E
13 C2 Mann *R* N Terr Australia
25 N9 Man Na Burma 23.30N 97.13E
18 E8 Manna Sumatra Indonesia 4.29S 102.55E
12 E4 Mannahill S Australia 32.27S 139.58E
89 C8 Manna Pt Sierra Leone 7.23N 12.30W
26 Q3 Mannar Sri Lanka 8.58N 79.54E
28 D6 Mannar G.of Tamil Nadu/Sri Lanka
28 D5 Mannargudi Tamil Nadu India 10.41N 79.28E
26 Q3 Mannar I Sri Lanka
66 L3 Männedorf Switzerland 47.15N 8.43E
61 B2 Mannekensvere Belgium 51.08N 2.50E
66 N1 Mannenbach Switzerland 47.40N 9.03E
13 D5 Manners *R* N Terr Australia
65 P6 Mannersdorf Austria 47.59N 16.36E
28 D3 Manneru R Andhra Prad India
64 F5 Mannheim W Germany 49.30N 8.28E
59 B5 Mannin B Galway Irish Rep 53.27N 10.04W
101 P7 Manning Alberta 56.53N 117.39W
107 D7 Manning Arkansas 34.01N 92.49W
108 P8 Manning Iowa 41.56N 95.04W
108 H2 Manning N Dakota 47.15N 102.48W
105 G4 Manning S Carolina 33.42N 80.12W
112 N4 Manning Texas 31.10N 94.33W
12 K4 Manning *R* New S Wales
103 D4 Manning Junction Pennsylvania 41.28N 75.23W
101 N11 Manning Prov.Park Br Col 49.09N 120.50W
15 K2 Manning Str Solomon Is
104 E7 Mannington W Virginia 39.32N 80.22W
56 O4 Manningtree Essex Eng 51.57N 1.04E
59 E4 Mannin L Mayo Irish Rep 53.49N 8.49W
66 H5 Männlichen *mt* Switzerland 46.38N 7.56E
66 G5 Männlifluh *mt* Switzerland 46.33N 7.33E
13 A7 Mann, Mt N Terr Australia 25.58S 129.39E
13 A7 Mann Ranges N Terr/S Aust
105 M2 Manns Harbor N Carolina 35.55N 75.54W
88 N8 Mannsour, El Algeria 27.34N 0.19W
35 D1 Mannsoûri, El Lebanon 33.10N 35.12E
104 J3 Mannsville New York 43.44N 76.04W
81 B4 Mannu *R* Cagliari, Sardinia
81 D2 Mannu *R* Nuoro, Sardinia
81 C3 Mannu *R* Sassari/Nuoro, Sardinia
81 A2 Mannu *R* Sassari, Sardinia
81 B2 Mannu *R* Sassari, Sardinia
81 A3 Mannu, C Cagliari, Sardinia 40.02N 8.22E
81 A2 Mannu, C Sassari, Sardinia 40.48N 8.10E
12 E5 Mannum S Australia 34.50S 139.20E
81 A3 Mannu, Mte Sardinia 40.23N 8.25E
100 F5 Mannville Alberta 53.20N 111.10W
89 C7 Mano Sierra Leone 8.04N 12.02W
89 D8 Mano *R* Liberia
120 F3 Manoa Bolivia 9.43S 65.24W
35 B8 Manoah *watercourse* Israel
116 M1 Man of War B Tobago W I
29 D4 Manoharpur Rajasthan India 27.19N 76.00E
29 E5 Manohar Thana Rajasthan India 24.18N 76.46E
113 H7 Manokotak Alaska 58.59N 159.06W
15 C4 Manokwari Irian Jaya 0.53S 134.05E
75 Q3 Manol *R* Spain
84 B5 Manolás Greece 38.03N 21.21E
95 A7 Manombo Madagascar 22.56S 43.29E
95 D4 Manompana Madagascar 16.40S 49.45E
18 A7 Manong Pen Malaysia 4.35N 100.52E
93 E9 Manonga *R* Tanzania
91 K7 Manono Zaïre 7.18S 27.24E
122 B2 Manono / W Samoa, Pacific Oc 13.50S 172.06W
91 J6 Manonwa Zaïre 4.54S 25.00E
80 K4 Manoppello Italy 42.16N 14.04E
105 E6 Manor Georgia 31.06N 82.34W
100 P9 Manor Saskatchewan 49.36N 102.01W
112 K5 Manor Texas 30.21N 97.34W
31 B10 Manora Pakistan 24.48N 66.59E
31 D8 Manora Hd Pakistan 24.46N 67.00E
56 B4 Manorbier Dyfed Wales 51.39N 4.48W
11 D12 Manorburn Res New Zealand 45.24S 169.39E
59 F3 Manorhamilton Leitrim Irish Rep 54.18N 8.10W
103 F2 Manorkill New York 42.23N 74.20W
25 E7 Manoron Burma 11.36N 99.02E
103 J5 Manorville Long I, N Y 40.53N 72.49W
71 H9 Manosque France 43.50N 5.47E
72 F4 Manot France 45.56N 0.39E
70 M4 Manou France 48.31N 1.00E
98 B3 Manouame L Quebec
99 Q5 Manouane Quebec 47.14N 74.25W
99 Q5 Manouane *R* Quebec
99 Q5 Manouane L Quebec
98 B3 Manouane R Quebec
20 M4 Mano-wan *B* Japan
45 O7 Manoylin U.S.S.R. 49.02N 42.54E
25 D1 Man Pan Burma 22.15N 97.46E
110 D4 Manpin Oregon 45.10N 121.05W
21 D7 Manpojin N Korea 41.06N 126.24E
30 J8 Manpur Bihar India 24.49N 85.02E
30 A5 Manpur Haryana India 27.58N 77.17E
29 D6 Manpur Madhya Prad India 22.23N 75.38E
28 B2 Man R Maharashtra India
75 O4 Manresa Spain 41.43N 1.50E
75 N4 Manresana Spain 41.43N 1.21E
37 E6 Mans Turkey 39.47N 40.00E
29 C6 Mansa Gujarat India 23.24N 72.42E
29 D2 Mansa Punjab India 30.00N 75.25E
92 D7 Mansa Zambia 11.10S 28.52E
121 A8 Mansa *R* Chile
93 M3 Mansa Guda Kenya 2.31N 40.18E
89 B5 Mansa Konko The Gambia 13.20N 15.30W
19 K5 Mansalay B Philippines 12.25N 121.28E
25 D1 Man Sam Burma 22.57N 97.25E
29 F7 Mansar Maharashtra India 21.27N 79.24E
89 G5 Mansara Mali 13.20N 4.37W
25 N9 Man-Sawn Burma 23.54N 97.35E
14 G4 Mansbridge, Mt W Australia 19.09S 128.29E
99 T6 Manseau Quebec 46.22N 72.00W
31 G3 Mansehra Pakistan 34.23N 73.18E
97 L5 Mansel I N W Terr 62.00N 80.00W
63 O9 Mansfeld E Germany 51.36N 11.28E
107 B6 Mansfield Arkansas 35.03N 94.17W
103 K3 Mansfield Connecticut 41.50N 72.16W
105 D4 Mansfield Georgia 33.31N 83.44W
106 F9 Mansfield Illinois 40.13N 88.31W
107 C9 Mansfield Louisiana 32.02N 93.41W
103 M2 Mansfield Massachusetts 42.02N 71.12W
107 D4 Mansfield Missouri 37.04N 92.36W
57 L6 Mansfield Notts Eng 53.09N 1.11W
104 C6 Mansfield Ohio 40.46N 82.31W
104 H5 Mansfield Pennsylvania 41.47N 77.05W
108 M4 Mansfield S Dakota 45.14N 98.33W
112 K3 Mansfield Texas 32.34N 97.09W
12 H6 Mansfield Victoria 37.04S 146.04E
110 F2 Mansfield Washington 47.49N 119.39W
104 N2 Mansfield, Mt Vermont 44.33N 72.49W
85 L6 Manshâh, El Egypt 26.29N 31.50E
35 H4 Manshiya, El Jordan 32.22N 36.05E
25 M9 Man Si Burma 24.07N 97.16E
25 M9 Mansi Burma 24.48N 95.52E
118 G2 Mansidão Brazil 10.48S 44.04W
70 L6 Mansigne France 47.45N 0.08E
121 F4 Mansilla Argentina 32.32S 59.22W
75 E3 Mansilla Spain 42.09N 2.57W
76 J4 Mansilla de las Mulas Spain 42.30N 5.25W
42 E5 Manskoye Belogor'ye *mts* U.S.S.R.
72 E4 Mansle France 45.52N 0.11E
89 J9 Manso Ghana 5.08N 1.50W
89 B5 Mansôa Guinea-Bissau 12.08N 15.18W
89 B5 Mansôa *R* Guinea-Bissau
108 Q7 Manson Iowa 42.33N 94.31W
110 E2 Manson Washington 47.53N 120.09W
101 L8 Manson Creek Br Col 55.40N 124.32W
72 F7 Mansonville France 44.01N 0.51E
118 C4 Manso, R Brazil
76 C7 Mansores Portugal 40.57N 8.22W
88 Q3 Mansoura Algeria 36.02N 4.30E
56 G6 Manston Dorset Eng 50.57N 2.16W
19 G4 Mansuar *isld* Irian Jaya 0.37S 130.36E
79 N3 Mansuè Italy 45.49N 12.32E
87 J9 Mansur Somalia 2.10N 42.12E
107 D10 Mansura Louisiana 31.03N 92.02W
86 F3 Mansûra, El Egypt 31.03N 31.23E
35 G1 Mansurah Syria 33.08N 35.47E
32 C5 Manşūrī Iran 30.57N 48.53E
32 C5 Mansuri *oil well* Iran 30.32N 48.51E
86 F5 Manşûrîya, El Egypt 30.08N 31.04E
34 M4 Manşūrīyah, Al Iraq 34.05N 44.52E
36 H5 Mansurlu Turkey 37.51N 35.40E
45 J5 Mansurovo U.S.S.R. 51.43N 37.28E
17 O9 Mansyu Depth *trough* Pacific Oc 11.08N 141.48W
119 B8 Manta Ecuador 0.59S 80.44W
79 B5 Manta Italy 44.37N 7.29E
119 B8 Manta, B.de Ecuador
19 H7 Mantalingajan, Mt Philippines 8.50N 117.43E
18 M2 Mantanani Besar *isld* Sabah Malaysia 6.46N 116.18E
91 G5 Mantantale Zaïre 2.10S 20.11E
116 D3 Mantanzas *prov* Cuba
21 E7 Mantap-san *mt* N Korea 41.16N 129.11E
19 D4 Mantarara Moluccas Indon 1.50S 125.03E
93 E8 Mantare Tanzania 2.43S 33.13E
19 D3 Mantarewu *isld* Indonesia 1.45N 124.45E
100 H7 Mantario Saskatchewan 51.16N 109.40W
120 C5 Mantaro *R* Peru
111 C4 Manteca California 37.49N 121.15W
119 E4 Mantecal Venezuela 7.34N 69.09W
115 K6 Mante, Ciudad Mexico 22.44N 98.59W
107 G8 Mantee Mississippi 33.44N 89.03W
76 D8 Manteigas Portugal 40.24N 7.32W
64 N4 Mantel W Germany 49.39N 12.03E
118 H6 Mantena Brazil 18.50S 40.56W
106 G8 Manteno Illinois 41.14N 87.50W
105 M2 Manteo N Carolina 35.54N 75.42W
109 J4 Manter Kansas 37.32N 101.53W
61 Q8 Manternach Luxembourg 49.42N 6.25E
69 B6 Mantes-la-Jolie France 48.59N 1.43E
29 L2 Manteswar W Bengal India 23.25N 88.08E
60 L7 Mantgum Netherlands 53.07N 5.43E
28 D1 Manthani Andhra Prad India 18.40N 79.40E
72 F1 Manthelan France 47.08N 0.47E
84 D7 Manthiréa Greece 37.25N 22.24E
111 N2 Manti Utah 39.16N 111.38W
75 E6 Mantiel Spain 40.37N 2.39W
18 B9 Mantin Pen Malaysia 2.48N 101.53E
84 D6 Mantinea *ruins* Greece 37.38N 22.23E
60 P8 Mantinge Netherlands 52.47N 6.36E
89 E4 Mantiouga Mali 15.30N 8.10W
118 F8 Mantiqueira, Sa.da *mts* Brazil
115 L2 Manto Honduras 14.58N 86.20W
71 H2 Mantoche France 47.26N 5.32E
103 F6 Mantoloking New Jersey 40.02N 74.03W
25 M9 Man Ton Burma 23.16N 97.07E
110 D9 Manton California 40.26N 121.53W
106 J5 Manton Michigan 44.25N 85.24W
72 C9 Mantory France 43.06N 0.49W
120 D10 Mantos Blancos Chile 23.27S 70.03W
22 J7 Mantou Shan *mt* Shanxi China 39.16N 112.57E
79 J4 Mantova Italy 45.10N 10.47E
79 J4 Mantova *prov* Italy
51 L11 Mäntsälä Finland 60.39N 25.15E
51 L10 Mänttä Finland 62.00N 24.40E
116 B3 Mantua Cuba 22.18N 84.18W
Mantua Italy*see* Mantova
103 D7 Mantua New Jersey 39.47N 75.11W
104 D5 Mantua Ohio 41.17N 81.16W
13 H6 Mantuan Downs Queensland 24.25S 147.15E
46 N1 Manturovo Kostroma U.S.S.R. 58.20N 44.42E
45 J5 Manturovo Kursk U.S.S.R. 51.25N 37.09E
51 M10 Mäntyharju Finland 61.26N 26.50E
51 J10 Mäntyluoto Finland 61.36N 21.28E
Manu *see* Ataa
120 D5 Manú Peru 12.14S 70.51W
122 F1 Manua Is Amer Samoa Pacific Oc
98 B3 Manuanis L Quebec
77 Q2 Manuel Spain 39.03N 0.30W
117 E8 Manuel Alves Grande *R* Brazil
117 E9 Manuel Alves Pequeno *R* Brazil
118 E2 Manuel Alves, R Brazil
120 F5 Manuel Correia, R Brazil
109 B6 Manuelito New Mexico 35.25N 109.00W
118 D9 Manuel Ribas Brazil 24.25S 51.35W
121 J9 Manuel Rodriguez, I Chile 52.33S 74.05W
120 D3 Manuel Urbano Brazil 8.53S 69.17W
117 B8 Manuelzinho Brazil 7.13S 54.50W
122 E16 Manuhangi *atoll* Tuamotu Is Pacific Oc 19.09S 141.17W
15 G4 Manu I Bismarck Arch 1.15S 143.30E
122 S16 Manui *isld* Gambier Is Pacific Oc 23.14S 134.56W
19 C5 Manui *isld* Indonesia 3.35S 123.09E
32 G7 Manūjān Iran 27.27N 57.31E
19 G6 Manuk *isld* Moluccas Indon 5.34S 130.18E
19 L7 Manukan Mindanao Philippines 8.30N 123.06E
11 J3 Manukau New Zealand 36.59S 174.53E
11 J4 Manukau Ent New Zealand 37.03S 174.32E
11 B3 Manukau Harb *inlet* New Zealand
11 K11 Manukau Pt Chatham Is Pacific Oc 44.01S 176.19W
19 J9 Manuk Manka *isld* Philippines 4.49N 119.50E
59 D4 Manulla Mayo Irish Rep 53.50N 9.10W
12 E5 Manunda *R* S Australia
11 K5 Manunui New Zealand 38.53S 175.20E
120 E5 Manupari, R Bolivia
Manu, R Bolivia*see* Mapiri *R*
120 D4 Manú, R Peru
19 G3 Manuran *isld* Irian Jaya 0.01N 131.05E
11 E3 Manurewa New Zealand 37.03S 174.55E
120 E5 Manurimi, R Bolivia
120 D4 Manuripe, R Peru
120 E4 Manuripi, R Bolivia
15 J5 Manus I Admiralty Is
122 E8 Manus I Bismarck Arch 2.00S 147.00E
30 J6 Manusmar, R Nepal
11 J6 Manutahi New Zealand 39.41S 174.26E
12 E3 Manuwalkaninna S Australia 29.00S 139.08E
108 N1 Manvel N Dakota 48.06N 97.12W
28 C3 Manvi Karnataka India 15.57N 76.59E
103 E5 Manville New Jersey 40.32N 74.35W
103 M3 Manville Rhode I 41.58N 71.28W
108 F7 Manville Wyoming 42.48N 104.36W
30 F6 Manwar *R* Uttar Prad India
29 E8 Manwat Maharashtra India 19.20N 76.32E
107 C10 Many Louisiana 31.34N 93.29W
47 J5 Man'ya U.S.S.R. 62.20N 60.08E
91 D6 Manyanga Zaïre 4.53S 14.23E
92 D10 Manyangau *mt* Zimbabwe 16.26S 29.38E
93 K9 Manyani Kenya 3.04S 38.30E
93 G9 Manyara, L (Soda) Tanzania
36 C2 Manyas Turkey 40.03N 27.57E
Manyas Gölü *L see* Kuş Gölü
100 G9 Manyberries Alberta 49.26N 110.41W
45 M9 Manych *R* U.S.S.R.
44 E1 Manych Gudilo, Ozero *L* U.S.S.R.
44 E1 Manychskaya Vpadina *depression* U.S.S.R.
92 B8 Manyinga Zambia 32.27S 24.23E
92 B8 Manyinga *R* Zambia
100 G8 Many Island L Alberta 50.10N 110.05W
92 G4 Manyoni Tanzania 5.46S 34.50E
93 A10 Manyovu Tanzania 4.28S 29.49E
13 K6 Many Peaks Queensland 24.32S 151.20E
14 C10 Many Peaks, Mt W Australia 34.48S 118.15E
23 A6 Manyunjie Yunnan China 24.28N 97.39E
72 F5 Manzac-sur-Vern France 45.06N 0.35E
31 F4 Manzai Pakistan 32.12N 70.15E
86 G3 Manzala, El Egypt 31.10N 31.56E
92 C11 Manzamnyama *R* Zimbabwe
76 G5 Manzanal de Arriba Spain 41.59N 6.26W
76 G3 Manzanal, Puerto de *pass* Spain 42.35N 6.14W
77 K2 Manzanares Spain 39.00N 3.23W
75 C6 Manzanares el Real Spain 40.43N 3.52W
76 E4 Manzaneda Spain 42.18N 7.14W
75 C2 Manzanedo Spain 42.53N 3.41W
75 C8 Manzaneque Spain 39.37N 3.48W
75 J7 Manzanera Spain 40.04N 0.50W
75 C7 Manzaneres *R* Spain
116 P2 Manzanilla B Trinidad & Tobago
116 P2 Manzanilla Pt Trinidad & Tobago 10.31N 61.01W
116 F4 Manzanillo Cuba 20.21N 77.21W
115 G8 Manzanillo Mexico 19.00N 104.20W
119 B3 Manzanillo, Pta Panama 9.37N 79.36W
79 O3 Manzano Italy 45.59N 13.23E
109 D7 Manzano New Mexico 34.38N 106.22W
121 A8 Manzano, B.del Chile
109 G3 Manzanola Colorado 38.06N 103.53W
109 D7 Manzano Mts New Mexico
92 D4 Manzanza Zaïre 5.03S 28.51E
32 D3 Manzārīyeh Iran 34.53N 50.52E
71 B5 Manzat France 45.57N 2.56E
90 J8 Manze Cent Afr Rep 6.41N 18.38E
45 E7 Manzheliya Ukraine U.S.S.R. 49.19N 33.39E
22 L2 Manzhouli Nei Monggol Zizhiqu China 49.36N 117.28E
92 D2 Manzia Zaïre 0.20S 29.00E
80 F4 Manziana Italy 42.08N 12.08E
71 F4 Manziat France 46.22N 4.54E
34 D7 Manzil Jordan 31.04N 36.02E
85 O4 Manzil, El Jordan 31.06N 36.00E
35 H9 Manzil Sta Jordan 31.03N 36.00E
95 P2 Manzini Swaziland 26.30S 31.22E
42 H5 Manzurka U.S.S.R. 53.30N 106.02E
42 F3 Manzya U.S.S.R. 58.30N 96.17E
90 G4 Mao Chad 14.06N 15.17E

116 J5 Mao Dominican Rep 19.37N 71.04W
21 D5 Mao 'ershan Heilongjiang China 45.18N 127.34E
15 D5 Maoke, Pegunungan *mts* Irian Jaya
21 C7 Maokui Shan *mt* Liaoning China 40.34N 123.46E
21 C6 Maolin Jilin China 43.57N 123.27E
22 F8 Maomao Shan *mt pk* Gansu China
23 E8 Maoming Guangdong China 21.50N 110.56E
22 D8 Maoniushan Qinghai China 36.50N 97.55E
23 E3 Maoping Hubei China 30.49N 110.58E
23 J8 Mao-pi T'ou *C* Taiwan 21.56N 120.43E
11 M13 Maori Hd New Zealand 45.55S 170.34E
11 L12 Maori Hill *dist* Dunedin New Zealand
23 D5 Maotai Guizhou China 27.55N 106.18E
23 B6 Maotou Shan *mt pk* Yunnan China 24.27N 100.43E
91 C5 Maouilla Congo 3.38S 13.59E
88 T3 Maouin Pena *pen* Tunisia
23 C3 Maowen Qiangzu Zizhixian Sichuan China 31.46N 103.54E
21 C5 Maoxing Heilongjiang China 45.31N 124.32E
35 F4 Ma'oz Hayyim Israel 32.29N 35.33E
19 A4 Mapaga Celebes Indon 0.06S 119.50E
94 L4 Mapai Mozambique 22.51S 31.59E
91 J2 Mapalma Zaïre 2.03N 24.30E
24 D10 Mapam Yumco *L* Xizang Zizhiqu China 30.40N 81.20E
18 J7 Mapan Borneo Indon 2.20S 111.10E
19 B4 Mapane Celebes Indonesia 1.25S 120.39E
92 C10 Mapanza Zambia 16.16S 26.54E
119 E2 Maparari Venezuela 10.52N 69.27W
93 H8 Maparasha Hills Kenya 2.13S 36.53E
117 C4 Mapari *R* Brazil
115 N10 Mapastepec Mexico 15.28N 93.00W
15 J5 Mapei Admiralty Is 2.08S 147.13E
87 B7 Maper Sudan 7.41N 29.41E
15 E7 Mapi Irian Jaya 7.06S 139.23E
15 E7 Mapi *R* Irian Jaya
15 C3 Mapia, Pulau Pulau *islds* Irian Jaya
19 A4 Mapida Celebes Indonesia 0.38S 119.51E
19 A5 Mapili Celebes Indon 3.25S 119.10E
115 H5 Mapimí Mexico 25.51N 103.50W
23 F3 Maping Hubei China 31.36N 113.36E
94 N4 Mapinhane Mozambique 22.19S 35.03E
119 G4 Mapire Venezuela 7.46N 64.41W
117 B4 Mapireme Brazil 0.32N 54.05W
120 E6 Mapiri Bolivia 15.17S 68.05W
120 E6 Mapiri *R* La Paz Bolivia
119 E6 Mapiripán, L Colombia 2.58N 71.45W
119 E6 Mapiripán, R Colombia
120 E4 Mapiri, R Pando Bolivia
119 G9 Mapixari, I Brazil 2.10S 65.10W
108 P7 Maple *R* Iowa
100 H9 Maple Creek Saskatchewan 49.55N 109.28W
108 R6 Maple Island Minnesota 43.46N 93.08W
106 K6 Maple, R Michigan
103 E7 Maple Shade New Jersey 39.57N 75.00W
107 K9 Maplesville Alabama 32.47N 86.53W
108 P7 Mapleton Iowa 42.09N 95.49W
104 Q7 Mapleton Maine 46.41N 68.11W
108 R6 Mapleton Minnesota 43.56N 93.57W
98 H8 Mapleton Nova Scotia 45.32N 64.11W
110 B5 Mapleton Oregon 44.02N 123.52W
94 U14 Mapleton S Africa 26.21S 28.15E
110 C2 Maple Valley Washington 47.24N 122.02W
104 J3 Maple View New York 43.26N 76.06W
103 G7 Maplewood New Jersey 40.44N 74.17W
103 D4 Maplewood Pennsylvania 41.26N 75.27W
121 F9 Mapocho, R Chile
21 J1 Map'o-gu *dist* Seoul S Korea
13 F1 Mapoon Queensland 12.00S 141.55E
11 E10 Mapourika, L New Zealand 43.19S 170.11E
15 E7 Mappi Irian Jaya 7.02S 139.12E
57 N5 Mappleton Humberside Eng 53.53N 0.08W
15 G5 Maprik Papua New Guinea 3.38S 143.02E
28 A3 Mapuca Goa India 15.37N 73.50E
117 A5 Mapuera, R Brazil
94 M5 Mapulanguene Mozambique 24.29S 32.06E
119 G7 Mapulau, R Brazil
95 P5 Mapumulo S Africa 29.10S 31.05E
18 F5 Mapur *isld* Indonesia 0.58N 104.45E
19 A3 Maputi *isld* Celebes Indonesia 0.33N 119.54E
94 M5 Maputo Mozambique 25.58S 32.35E
94 M6 Maputo *R* Mozambique
Maqainama *see* Muqaynimah
Ma'qalā' *see* Shumlūl, Ash
35 F8 Maqam en Nabi Yusha *tomb* Jordan 31.20N 35.39E
34 H7 Maqar an Na'am Arabia/Iraq 31.57N 40.26E
35 G3 Maqarin Sta Syria 32.43N 35.52E
33 D7 Ma'qas, Al Saudi Arabia 19.31N 41.43E
83 D3 Maqellarë Albania 41.34N 20.27E
23 B1 Maqên Qinghai China 34.25N 100.06E
24 E3 Maqiao Xinjiang Uygur Zizhiqu China 44.45N 85.30E
21 E5 Maqiaohe Heilongjiang China 44.40N 130.36E
34 P8 Ma'qil, Al Iraq 30.33N 47.49E
34 C10 Maqla, Jabal al *mt* Saudi Arabia 28.36N 35.20E
86 N9 Maqna Saudi Arabia 28.25N 34.45E
86 N9 Maqna, Wādī el *watercourse* Saudi Arabia
85 M10 Maqran, Jeb *mt* Sudan 19.42N 33.13E
85 F4 Maqrūn, Al Libya 31.24N 20.10E
Ma Qu *see* Huang He
23 C1 Maqu Gansu China 34.04N 102.04E
24 D11 Maquan He *R* Xizang Zizhiqu China
76 L8 Maqueda Spain 40.04N 4.22W
19 M5 Maqueda Chan Philippines
121 L6 Maqueda, Pta *C* Argentina 46.00S 67.32W
91 D7 Maquela do Zombo Angola 6.06S 15.12E
98 H5 Maquereau, Pte.au *C* Quebec 48.12N 64.48W
19 J2 Maquiling, Mt Luzon Philippines 14.08N 121.12E
121 C8 Maquinchao Argentina 41.19S 68.47W
121 B8 Maquinchao, R Argentina
106 D7 Maquoketa Iowa 42.03N 90.41W
106 C7 Maquoketa R Iowa
106 D9 Maquon Illinois 40.49N 90.09W
33 M9 Maqwa', Al Kuwait 29.10N 47.58E
76 B5 Mar Portugal 41.34N 8.48W
28 K1 Mara Assam India 28.07N 94.14E
18 M4 Mara Borneo Indon 2.45N 117.14E
117 A1 Mara Guyana 6.00N 57.39W
Mara Madhya Prad India*see* Muri
120 C6 Mara Peru 14.07S 72.10W
93 F7 Mara Tanzania 1.29S 34.34E
119 E2 Mara Venezuela 10.53N 71.53W
101 T2 Mara *R* N W Terr
93 F7 Mara *R* Tanzania
92 G3 Mara *reg* Tanzania
119 G8 Maraã Brazil 1.52S 65.21W
122 B12 Maraa Tahiti Pacific Oc 17.44S 149.34W
93 E7 Mara B Tanzania
117 D7 Marabá Brazil 5.23S 49.10W
89 G7 Marabadiassa Ivory Coast 8.11N 5.19W
18 L7 Marabahan Borneo Indon 2.59S 114.46E
94 K4 Marabastad S Africa 24.00S 29.18E
119 F7 Marabitanas Brazil 0.57N 66.55W
88 L8 Maraboutia Algeria 27.02N 5.31W
93 G7 Mara Bridge Kenya 1.09S 35.07E
90 C6 Marabu Nigeria 11.24N 6.35E
69 J8 Marac France 47.56N 5.11E
117 E6 Maracaçumé Brazil 2.03S 45.54W
117 E6 Maracaçumé, R Brazil
119 H6 Maracá, I Roraima Brazil
119 E2 Maracaibo Venezuela 10.44N 71.37W
119 E3 Maracaibo, Lago de *B* Venezuela
117 D3 Maracá, I.de Amapá Brazil
119 G8 Maracaí, L de Brazil 1.31S 65.46W
118 C7 Maracaju Brazil 21.38S 55.10W
118 C9 Maracaju, Sa. de Paraguay/Brazil
118 C7 Maracaju, Serra de *mts* Brazil/Paraguay
117 E5 Maracanã Brazil 0.46S 47.28W
117 C5 Maracanaquará, Planalto *plat* Brazil
117 C4 Maracá, R Brazil
118 H3 Maracás Brazil 13.22S 40.18W
116 O1 Maracas B Trinidad & Tobago 10.45N 61.34W
118 H3 Maracás, Chapada de *hills* Brazil
119 F2 Maracay Venezuela 10.20N 67.28W
77 J6 Maracena Spain 37.12N 3.38W
93 B2 Maracha Uganda 3.17N 30.58E
66 D5 Maracon Switzerland 46.33N 6.52E
85 E5 Marādah Libya 29.15N 19.14E
26 S5 Maradankadawala Sri Lanka 8.07N 80.33E
89 N5 Maradi Niger 13.29N 7.10E
31 E4 Maradin Pakistan 32.44N 69.36E
21 D11 Mara do *isld* Japan 33.08N 126.17E
90 C5 Maradun Nigeria 12.35N 6.18E
11 K5 Maraetai New Zealand 38.20S 175.43E
26 R5 Maragahawewa Sri Lanka 8.14N 80.08E
76 G4 Maragateria, La *reg* Spain
32 F7 Marāgh Iran 26.51N 54.19E
85 L6 Marâgha, El Egypt 26.33N 31.37E
85 O2 Maragha, Sabkha *salt marsh* Syria
37 J8 Marāgheh Iran 37.25N 46.13E
117 J9 Maragogi Brazil 8.59S 35.14W
118 J3 Maragogipe Brazil 12.48S 38.59W
19 K4 Maragondon Luzon Philippines 14.17N 120.45E
93 K9 Marago ya Ngasha Kenya 3.37S 38.42E
93 J6 Maragua Kenya 0.48S 37.08E
33 F4 Marah Saudi Arabia 25.04N 45.27E
87 H4 Maraha Bad *salt L* Ethiopia 13.30N 40.30E
33 H4 Marāh, Al Saudi Arabia 25.40N 49.38E
30 B5 Marahra Uttar Prad India 27.44N 78.33E
119 G6 Marahuaca, Cerro *mt* Venezuela 3.37N 65.25W
21 B5 Marain Sum Nei Monggol Zizhiqu China 44.03N 120.54E
95 H8 Marais S Africa 32.37S 24.25E
94 S13 Maraisburg S Africa 26.11S 27.56E
109 P3 Marais des Cygnes *R* Kansas
70 L3 Marais-Vernier France 49.25N 0.27E
117 D5 Marajó, B. de Brazil
117 D5 Marajó, I.de Brazil
53 W14 Maråk Norway 62.07N 7.13E
95 M5 Marakabeis Lesotho 29.32S 28.09E
32 A1 Marakand Iran 38.50N 45.16E
9 B4 Marakei *atoll* Kiribati, Pac Oc 2.00N 173.25E
28 D4 Marakkanam Tamil Nadu India 12.15N 79.59E
93 H4 Maralal Kenya 1.05N 36.42E
94 G5 Maralaleng Botswana 25.47S 22.45E
31 H4 Marala Weir Pakistan 32.37N 74.28E
Maral Bashi *see* Bachu
43 N2 Maraldy Kazakhstan U.S.S.R. 52.24N 77.45E
43 N2 Maraldy, Ozero *L* Kazakhstan U.S.S.R. 52.17N 77.45E
90 J9 Marali Cent Afr Rep 6.00N 18.24E
44 F7 Maralik Armenia U.S.S.R. 40.34N 43.50E
42 C6 Maralikha U.S.S.R. 51.34N 82.58E
12 B4 Maralinga S Australia 30.13S 131.32E
Maralwexi *see* Bachu
25 L8 Maram Manipur India 25.27N 94.09E
93 F5 Maramas Kenya 0.12N 34.31E
15 M3 Maramasike I Solomon Is 9.30S 161.30E
33 G6 Marāmik, Jabal al *mt* Saudi Arabia 21.37N 46.53E
89 C7 Marampa Sierra Leone 8.44N 12.28W
15 G6 Maramuni *R* Papua New Guinea
82 H3 Maramureș *old prov* Romania
31 C6 Maran Pakistan 29.28N 64.32E
18 C8 Maran Pen Malaysia 3.36N 102.42E
66 P4 Maran Switzerland 46.48N 9.42E
111 N9 Marana Arizona 32.29N 111.12W
34 N3 Marāna Iraq 35.50N 45.37E
13 C2 Maranboy N Terr Australia 14.30S 132.45E
75 F5 Maranchón Spain 41.02N 2.11W
32 A1 Marand Iran 38.25N 45.50E
92 E11 Marandellas Zimbabwe 18.10S 31.36E
92 E11 Marandellas *dist* Zimbabwe
79 J5 Maranello Italy 44.31N 10.51E
25 E7 Marang Burma 10.30N 98.45E
18 E3 Marang Pen Malaysia 5.07N 103.11E
29 J6 Marang Buru *mt* Bihar India 23.32N 85.30E
94 N5 Marangua, L Mozambique 24.44S 34.15E
117 H6 Maranguape Brazil 3.55S 38.45W
117 E7 Maranhão *state* Brazil
76 D10 Maranhão, Barragem do *res* Portugal 39.02N 7.55W
117 B7 Maranhão Grande, Cachoeira *rapids* Brazil 4.26S 56.05W
118 E4 Maranhão, R Brazil
13 J7 Maranoa *R* Queensland
80 K7 Marano di Napoli Italy 40.53N 14.12E
79 O3 Marano Lagunare Italy 45.46N 13.10E
79 O3 Marano, L.di *lagoon* Italy
117 G2 Marañon *R* Brazil/Peru
120 C1 Marañón, R Peru
79 K3 Marano Vicentino Italy 45.42N 11.26E
72 B3 Marans France 46.19N 1.01W
61 H4 Maransart Belgium 50.40N 4.28E
69 H7 Maranville France 48.08N 4.52E
76 D6 Marão, Sa.de Portugal
15 M3 Marapa I Solomon Is 9.51S 160.53E
117 E5 Marapanim Brazil 0.42S 47.40W
118 C3 Marape Brazil 13.03S 56.41W
118 H10 Marapendi, L.de Brazil
18 D6 Marapi, Gunung *mt* Sumatra Indon 0.20S 100.26E
117 B4 Marapi, R Brazil
95 G1 Marapo-a-bathopan *salt pan* S Africa 25.40S 23.06E
93 N7 Mararani Kenya 1.34S 41.15E
120 E1 Marari Brazil 5.45S 67.45W
119 G7 Marari, R Brazil
11 B12 Mararoa, R New Zealand
93 N7 Mararui Kenya 1.57S 41.18E
18 N8 Marasende *isld* Indonesia 5.10S 118.10E
82 L5 Mărășești Romania 45.53N 27.14E
71 D5 Marat France 45.40N 3.41E
81 L4 Maratea Italy 40.00N 15.44E
76 B11 Marateca Portugal 38.34N 8.40W
76 B11 Marateca *R* Portugal
105 F13 Marathon Florida 24.43N 81.06W
84 G5 Marathón Greece 38.09N 23.57E
108 P7 Marathon Iowa 42.51N 95.00W
103 B2 Marathon New York 42.25N 76.04W
99 D4 Marathon Ontario 48.44N 86.23W
13 G5 Marathon Queensland 20.50S 143.36E
112 D5 Marathon Texas 30.13N 103.16W
106 E5 Marathon Wisconsin 44.58N 89.36W
84 G5 Marathónos *L* Greece 38.10N 23.54E
84 C7 Marathópolis Greece 37.03N 21.35E
84 C4 Márathos Greece 38.53N 21.49E
18 N4 Maratua *isld* Indonesia
118 J4 Maraú Brazil 14.07S 39.00W
119 F9 Marauá Brazil 3.25S 66.16W
119 G7 Marauiá, R Brazil
11 N5 Marau Pt New Zealand 38.18S 178.23E
30 A1 Maraur Himachal Prad India 31.48N 77.32E
81 E8 Marausa Sicily 37.55N 12.31E
71 C10 Maraussan France 43.22N 3.09E
15 K2 Maravae Solomon Is 7.50S 156.40E
116 O1 Maraval Trinidad & Tobago 10.42N 61.31W
115 J8 Maravatío Mexico 19.53N 100.30W
Maravilla *L see* Toro, L. del
112 D6 Maravillas Cr Texas
31 E6 Marav L Pakistan
15 L3 Maravovo Guadalcanal I Solomon Is 9.21S 159.37E
85 F3 Marāwah Libya 32.24N 21.27E
19 M8 Marawi Mindanao Philippines 7.59N 124.16E
33 E9 Marāwi'ah, Al Yemen 14.49N 43.08E
33 D7 Marāyā *isld* Saudi Arabia 18.04N 41.19E
69 F7 Maraye-en-Othe France 48.09N 3.52E
121 C3 Marayes Argentina 31.28S 67.23W
47 K7 Marayskoye U.S.S.R. 55.45N 66.05E
44 J7 Maraza Azerbaydzhan U.S.S.R. 40.32N 48.55E
56 T9 Marazion Cornwall Eng 50.07N 5.29W
65 M5 Marbach Austria 48.13N 15.08E
64 E7 Marbach Baden-Württemberg W Germany 48.02N 8.28E
64 G6 Marbach Baden-Württemberg W Germany 48.56N 9.16E
66 H4 Marbach Luzern Switzerland 46.52N 7.55E
66 P2 Marbach St Gallen Switzerland 47.23N 9.34E
64 F2 Marbach W Germany 50.50N 8.45E
69 L6 Marbache France 48.48N 6.06E
61 J4 Marbais Belgium 50.32N 4.32E
61 H5 Marbaix Belgium 50.20N 4.22E
Marbat *see* Mirbāt
77 G7 Marbella Spain 36.31N 4.53W
109 C2 Marble Colorado 39.04N 107.13W
110 H1 Marble Washington 48.51N 117.55W
85 E4 Marble Arch Libya 30.27N 18.29E
14 C5 Marble Bar W Australia 21.16S 119.45E
111 N5 Marble Canyon Arizona 36.50N 111.38W
111 N5 Marble Canyon *gorge* Arizona
109 Q6 Marble City Oklahoma 35.36N 94.47W
112 J5 Marble Falls Texas 30.34N 98.16W
94 K5 Marble Hall S Africa 24.57S 29.13E
107 E2 Marblehead Illinois 39.50N 91.21W
104 P4 Marblehead Massachusetts 42.30N 70.50W
104 C5 Marblehead Ohio 41.33N 82.45W
108 S7 Marble Rock Iowa 42.58N 92.50W
29 F6 Marble Rocks Madhya Prad India 23.08N 79.52E
99 T7 Marbleton Quebec 45.39N 71.37W
110 P7 Marbleton Wyoming 42.35N 110.05W
74 J9 Marbot Algeria 36.00N 2.09E
71 G4 Marboz France 46.20N 5.15E
53 Y18 Mårbu Norway 60.11N 8.10E
31 H4 Marbul Pass Kashmir 33.33N 75.27E
95 O6 Marburg S Africa 30.45S 30.25E
64 F2 Marburg an der Lahn W Germany 50.49N 8.36E
104 H8 Marbury Maryland 38.34N 77.10W
52 H3 Marby Sweden 63.08N 14.20E
72 G10 Marc France 42.42N 1.27E
120 B4 Marca Peru 10.02S 77.32W
62 K8 Marcal *R* Hungary
115 L2 Marcala Honduras 14.11N 88.00W
36 C5 Marçal Dağı *mt* Turkey 37.09N 28.04E
62 K9 Marcali Hungary 46.33N 17.29E
120 D5 Marcapata Peru 13.31S 70.52W
91 B12 Marca, Pta.da *pt* Angola 16.33S 11.43E
79 J4 Marcaria Italy 45.07N 10.32E
72 E3 Marçay France 46.28N 0.13E
76 K2 Mar, C.de Spain 43.28N 4.55W
98 F2 Marceau, L Quebec
81 N5 Marcedusa Italy 39.02N 16.50E
100 L6 Marcelin Saskatchewan 52.56N 106.49W
107 D2 Marceline Missouri 39.42N 92.58W
119 F8 Marcelino Brazil 1.52S 66.21W
121 H1 Marcelino Ramos Brazil 27.14S 51.56W
107 E6 Marcella Arkansas 35.47N 91.54W
106 J7 Marcellus Michigan 42.03N 85.49W
110 G2 Marcellus Washington 47.14N 118.25W
117 C6 Marcelo Brazil 2.13S 51.25W
72 D5 Marcenais France 45.04N 0.21W
72 K5 Marcenat France 45.18N 2.49E
80 H4 Marcetelli Italy 42.14N 13.03E
56 M2 March Cambs Eng 52.33N 0.06E
64 D7 March W Germany 48.03N 7.50E
65 P4 March *R* Austria
30 D2 Marcha Uttar Prad India 30.18N 80.29E
70 M4 Marchainville France 48.34N 0.49E
66 B5 Marchairuz, Col du *pass* Switz 46.33N 6.16E
69 E8 Marchais-Beton France 47.50N 3.03E
91 D6 Marchal Zaïre 5.17S 15.01E
75 D6 Marchamalo Spain 40.40N 3.13W
100 F1 Marchand Manitoba 49.25N 96.19W
12 E4 Marchant Hill S Australia 32.16S 138.49E
71 J2 Marchaux France 47.19N 6.07E
67 G6 Marche *prov* France
79 M7 Marche *reg* Italy
61 M6 Marche-en-Famenne Belgium 50.13N 5.21E
65 P5 Marchegg Austria 48.17N 16.55E
71 C2 Marche, la France 47.07N 3.02E
61 K5 Marche-les-Dames Belgium 50.29N 4.58E
61 G4 Marche-lez-Ecaussines Belgium 50.33N 4.11E
77 F6 Marchena Spain 37.20N 5.24W
119 B5 Marchena, I Galápagos Is 0.20N 90.30W
70 N6 Marchenoir France 47.49N 1.24E
72 G3 Marche, Plateaux de la France
72 C6 Marcheprime France 44.43N 0.52W
18 M2 Marchesa, Telok *B* Sabah Malaysia
81 N5 Marchesato *physical reg* Italy
80 B3 Marchese, Pta.del Italy 42.37N 10.05E
70 H3 Marchésieux France 49.10N 1.18W
71 H5 Marches, les France 45.30N 6.00E
65 P5 Marchfeld *reg* Austria
116 P6 Marchfield Barbados 13.07N 59.29W
61 H5 Marchienne-au-Pont Belgium 50.24N 4.24E
69 E3 Marchiennes-Ville France 50.24N 3.17E
121 B5 Marchigüe Chile 34.21S 71.45W
61 L5 Marchin Belgium 50.28N 5.14E
13 D1 Marchinbar I N Terr Australia
61 E5 Marchipont Belgium 50.23N 3.40E
121 F6 Mar Chiquita, L Argentina
121 E3 Mar Chiquita, L Córdoba Argentina
61 K4 Marchovelette Belgium 50.32N 4.56E
65 K5 Marchtrenk Austria 48.12N 14.06E
46 M3 Marchuki U.S.S.R. 53.34N 40.10E
Marchun *see* Marshūn
57 H6 Marchwiel Clwyd Wales 53.01N 2.58W
72 E8 Marciac France 43.32N 0.10E
80 B3 Marciana Italy 42.48N 10.10E
80 B3 Marciana Marina Italy 42.49N 10.12E
80 K6 Marcianise Italy 41.02N 14.18E
80 E2 Marciano Italy 43.18N 11.47E
71 E4 Marcigny France 46.17N 4.03E
72 H6 Marcilhac-sur-Célé France 44.33N 1.46E
75 G3 Marcilla Spain 42.20N 1.45W
72 C5 Marcillac France 45.16N 0.32W
72 J5 Marcillac-la-Croizille France 45.17N 2.02E
72 J7 Marcillac Vallon France 44.29N 2.27E
72 K3 Marcillat-en-Combraille France 46.10N 2.37E
70 J5 Marcille-la-Ville France 48.18N 0.31W
70 H4 Marcilly Manche France 48.39N 1.15W
70 O7 Marcilly-en-Gault France 47.28N 1.52E
70 P6 Marcilly-en-Villette France 47.46N 2.01E
69 F7 Marcilly-le-Hayer France 48.21N 3.40E
70 N4 Marcilly-sur-Eure France 48.49N 1.21E
61 H5 Marcinelle Belgium 50.24N 4.27E
69 B2 Marck France 50.57N 1.57E
69 O7 Marckolsheim France 48.10N 7.34E
98 J1 Marc, L Labrador, Nfld
105 F12 Marco Florida 26.57N 81.46W
107 J3 Marco Indiana 38.54N 87.10W
79 K3 Marco Italy 45.51N 11.01E
76 C6 Marco de Canavezes Portugal 41.11N 8.09W
69 E3 Marcoing France 50.07N 3.10E
110 C5 Marcola Oregon 44.11N 122.51W
72 J6 Marcolès France 44.47N 2.20E
118 B2 Marcolina, R Brazil
71 E7 Marcols-les-Eaux France 44.48N 4.25E
70 M6 Marçon France 47.42N 0.31E
120 B6 Marcona Peru 15.10S 75.02W
100 C1 Marconi Manitoba 49.55N 97.04W
121 E4 Marcos Juárez Argentina 32.42S 62.05W
121 F5 Marcos Paz Argentina 34.51S 58.50W
61 N6 Marcourt Belgium 50.13N 5.32E
71 J8 Marcoux France 44.07N 6.16E
61 G4 Marcq Belgium 50.42N 4.01E
108 P7 Marcus Iowa 42.49N 95.48W
110 G1 Marcus Washington 48.40N 118.05W
113 O6 Marcus Baker, Mt Alaska 61.28N 147.49W
103 D7 Marcus Hook Pennsylvania 39.50N 75.25W
122 G5 Marcus I Pacific Oc
122 G6 Marcus-Wake Seamounts Pacific Oc
104 K3 Marcy New York 43.12N 75.19W
104 M2 Marcy, Mt New York 44.07N 73.56W
35 D5 Marda Jordan 32.07N 35.12E
44 H7 Mardakert Azerbaydzhan U.S.S.R. 40.14N 46.46E
31 G3 Mardan Pakistan 34.14N 72.05E
31 F3 Mardan *dist* Pakistan
121 F6 Mar del Plata Argentina 38.00S 57.32W
121 F7 Mar del Sur Argentina 38.20S 58.01W
56 M5 Marden Kent Eng 51.11N 0.30E
29 J2 Mardhan Bihar India 23.00N 85.46E
14 B5 Mardie W Australia 21.14S 115.57E
37 F8 Mardin Turkey 37.19N 40.43E
51 J5 Mårdsel Sweden 66.17N 21.25E
52 L2 Mårdsele Sweden 64.39N 19.15E
52 K2 Mårdsjö Sweden 64.17N 16.35E
52 J3 Mårdsjön Sweden 63.18N 15.40E
19 B6 Mare Celebes Indonesia 4.48S 120.20E
9 C13 Maré *isld* Loyalty Is Pacific Oc
19 E3 Mare *isld* Moluccas Indon 0.35N 127.24E
26 U13 Mare aux Vacoas Res Mauritius, Indian Oc
87 G3 Mareb *watercourse* Ethiopia
79 M6 Marecchia *R* Italy
117 J9 Marechal Deodoro Brazil 9.44S 35.51W
89 D4 Mare de Magui *L* Mali
13 H3 Mareeba Queensland 17.00S 145.28E
58 E3 Maree, L Highland Scotland
95 J2 Mareetsane S Africa 26.09S 25.25E
95 J2 Mareetsane *watercourse* S Africa
72 J5 Marèges, Barrage de France 45.25N 2.20E
81 P12 Mare Grande *isld* Italy 40.26N 17.11E
57 N6 Mareham le Fen Lincs Eng 53.08N 0.05W
87 L8 Marehan *tribe* Somalia
80 D3 Maremma *dist* Italy
53 U16 Måren Norway 61.09N 6.05E
89 F5 Maréna Mali 13.55N 7.20W
92 J6 Marendego Tanzania 8.20S 39.15E
79 C5 Marene Italy 44.40N 7.43E
106 F7 Marengo Illinois 42.16N 88.36W
107 K3 Marengo Indiana 38.22N 86.22W
106 B8 Marengo Iowa 41.47N 92.05W
104 C6 Marengo Ohio 40.24N 82.49W
100 H7 Marengo Saskatchewan 51.28N 109.44W
110 G2 Marengo Washington 47.02N 118.11W
106 D3 Marengo Wisconsin 46.25N 90.49W
106 E3 Marenisco Michigan 46.23N 89.42W
61 M6 Marenne Belgium 50.14N 5.25E
72 B4 Marennes France 45.50N 1.06W
81 P12 Mare Piccolo Italy 40.28N 17.14E
95 B6 Marerano Madagascar 21.21S 44.50E
11 J3 Mareretu New Zealand 36.02S 174.16E
56 M6 Maresfield E Sussex Eng 51.00N 0.05E
88 T5 Mareth Tunisia 33.37N 10.12E
14 E2 Maret Is W Australia 14.27S 124.58E
81 E6 Marettimo Egadi Is Italy 37.58N 12.05E
81 E6 Marettimo *isld* Egadi Is Italy
69 E3 Maretz France 50.03N 3.26E
72 E5 Mareuil Dordogne France 45.27N 0.28E
72 J2 Mareuil-sur-Arnon France 46.53N 2.09E
69 G5 Mareuil-sur-Ay France 49.03N 4.09E
72 B2 Mareuil-sur-Lay France 46.32N 1.13W
69 E5 Mareuil-sur-Ourcq France 49.09N 3.05E
46 H2 Marevo U.S.S.R. 57.18N 32.10E
71 G1 Marey-sur-Tille France 47.35N 5.07E
79 P4 Marezige Yugoslavia 45.30N 13.48E
112 C5 Marfa Texas 30.19N 104.03W
84 X20 Marfa Pt Malta 35.59N 14.20E
84 Y20 Marfa Ridge Malta
34 J10 Marfi Saudi Arabia 28.17N 41.47E
44 J1 Marfino Astrakhan' U.S.S.R. 46.24N 48.45E
45 R5 Marfino Saratov U.S.S.R. 51.52N 45.14E
44 E9 Marfovka Ukraine U.S.S.R. 45.12N 36.04E
24 E8 Margai Caka *L* Xizang Zizhiqu China 35.00N 87.00E
56 D4 Margam W Glam Wales 51.34N 3.44W
43 H3 Marganets Kazakhstan U.S.S.R. 48.02N 67.03E
45 F9 Marganets Ukraine U.S.S.R. 47.35N 34.37E
28 A3 Margao Goa India 15.15N 73.59E
98 L7 Margaree Harbour C Breton I, Nova Scotia 46.26N 61.08W
98 L7 Margaree I Nova Scotia 46.21N 61.17W
98 M7 Margaree V C Breton I, Nova Scotia 46.24N 60.59W
60 C3 Margaret Netherlands 51.17N 3.54E
112 H1 Margaret Texas 34.03N 99.40W
12 D3 Margaret *R* S Australia
101 K10 Margaret Bay Br Col 51.19N 126.35W
13 G1 Margaret Bay Queensland
101 Q6 Margaret L Alberta
101 P3 Margaret L N W Terr
14 C5 Margaret, Mt W Australia 22.03S 117.53E
14 B10 Margaret R W Australia 33.57S 115.04E
14 F4 Margaret R W Australia
103 E2 Margaretville New York 42.09N 74.39W
118 C7 Margarida Brazil 21.40S 56.30W
15 G6 Margarima Papua New Guinea 6.00S 143.23E
121 E2 Margarita Argentina 29.45S 60.12W
119 D3 Margarita, I Colombia
119 G2 Margarita, I.de Venezuela
115 N10 Margaritas Mexico 15.32N 93.08W
84 L11 Margarites Crete 35.20N 24.40E
83 D5 Margarítion Greece 39.23N 20.26E
40 F10 Margaritovo U.S.S.R. 43.25N 134.46E
Margat *castle see* Qal'at el Marqab
105 B9 Margate Florida 26.14N 80.08W
56 O5 Margate Kent Eng 51.24N 1.24E
95 O6 Margate S Africa 30.51S 30.22E
12 H9 Margate Tasmania 42.58S 147.25E
103 E8 Margate City New Jersey 39.20N 74.31W
72 C5 Margaux France 45.03N 0.40W
86 F5 Marg, El Egypt 30.09N 31.20E
43 K6 Margelan Uzbekistan U.S.S.R. 40.30N 71.45E
71 C7 Margeride, Montagnes de la France
69 H6 Margerie-Hancourt France 48.34N 4.32E
Marghak *see* Morghak
28 K2 Margherita Assam India 27.17N 95.40E
80 O6 Margherita di Savoia Italy 41.23N 16.09E
Margherita, L *see* Abaya, L
93 A5 Margherita, Pk Uganda/Zaïre 0.23N 29.54E
81 B3 Marghine, Catena del *mts* Sardinia
82 G3 Marghita Romania 47.20N 22.20E
100 F3 Margie Alberta 55.27N 111.19W
108 R1 Margie Minnesota 48.06N 93.55W
82 G5 Mărgina Romania 45.50N 22.16E
82 G5 Margita Yugoslavia 45.12N 21.05E
100 O7 Margo Saskatchewan 51.50N 103.20W
120 B4 Margos Peru 10.04S 76.29W
19 L8 Margosatubig Mindanao Philippines 7.34N 123.12E
29 K5 Margram W Bengal India 24.06N 87.52E
60 T17 Margraten Netherlands 50.49N 5.49E
106 K5 Margrethe L Michigan 44.40N 84.48W
101 M9 Marguerite Br Col 52.27N 122.22W
123 F13 Marguerite B Antarctica
71 E9 Marguerittes France 43.52N 4.26E
69 J4 Margut France 49.36N 5.16E
24 G11 Margyang Xizang Zizhiqu China 29.46N 90.00E
35 F3 Marhaba Jordan 32.31N 35.40E
34 O6 Marhaj Khalil Iraq 32.13N 46.42E
30 H7 Marhaura Bihar India 25.58N 84.52E
88 N4 Marhoum Algeria 34.26N 0.05W
88 M6 Marhouma Algeria 30.01N 2.06W
90 M4 Marhum Sudan 14.59N 25.06E
21 D8 Marhwi-ri N Korea 38.50N 127.55E
25 N7 Mari Burma 27.29N 98.31E
84 R15 Mari Cyprus 34.44N 33.20E
84 E7 Marí Greece 37.02N 22.50E
15 F8 Mari Papua New Guinea 9.16S 141.40E
98 F5 Maria Quebec 48.12N 66.01W
77 M5 María Spain 37.43N 2.09W
26 K7 Maria Augustina Bank Indian Oc 14.10S 106.00E
71 E7 Mariac France 44.52N 4.23E
115 F7 María Cleofas, I Mexico
75 K7 Maria Cristina, Embalse de *res* Spain 40.02N 0.11W
77 L6 María, Da Spain 37.09N 2.41W
77 W14 María de la Salud Balearic Is 39.40N 3.04E
76 C15 Maria Dias *mt* Portugal 38.49N 9.19W
29 F5 Mariadoh Madhya Prad India 24.17N 79.41E
120 D10 María Elena Chile 22.18S 69.40W
115 G10 María Enrique Panama 9.07N 79.33W
53 D3 Mariager Denmark 56.39N 9.59E
53 E3 Mariager Fjord *inlet* Denmark 56.42N 10.15E
63 M7 Mariaglück W Germany 52.42N 10.15E
121 F3 María Grande Argentina 31.45S 59.55W
30 F8 Mariahan Uttar Prad India 24.56N 82.41E
96 B2 Maria Hill Bermuda 32.19N 64.52W
30 F7 Mariahu Uttar Prad India 25.37N 82.37E
25 D7 Maria I Burma 11.27N 98.00E
13 D2 Maria I N Terr Australia
12 J9 Maria I Tasmania
122 M10 Maria, Is Tubuai Is Pacific Oc 21.48S 154.41W
93 L9 Mariakani Kenya 3.52S 39.29E
61 E2 Mariakerke Belgium 51.04N 3.40E
64 C3 Maria Laach *abbey* W Germany 50.25N 7.17E
65 G8 Maria Luggau Austria 46.43N 12.45E
76 E7 Marialva Portugal 40.55N 7.14W
115 F7 María Madre, I Mexico
115 F7 María Magdelena, I Mexico
111 K8 Maria Mts California
50 O10 Maria Muschbukta *B* Jan Mayen I 71.00N 8.35W
13 J5 Marian Queensland 21.10S 148.52E
118 G7 Mariana Brazil 20.23S 43.23W
100 E3 Mariana L Alberta 55.56N 112.02W
116 C3 Marianao Cuba 23.03N 82.29W
17 O9 Marianas *islds* Pacific Oc
122 E6 Marianas Ridge Pacific Oc
122 E7 Marianas Trench Pacific Oc
28 K2 Mariani Assam India 26.39N 94.18E
101 P4 Marian L N W Terr
101 P4 Marian Lake N W Terr 63.02N 116.15W
107 F7 Marianna Arkansas 34.46N 90.49W
105 B7 Marianna Florida 30.45N 85.15W
52 J9 Mariannelund Sweden 57.37N 15.33E
95 O5 Mariannhill S Africa 29.52S 30.50E
79 F3 Mariano Comense Italy 45.42N 9.10E
91 D10 Mariano Machado Angola 13.01S 14.39E
81 G8 Marianopoli Sicily 37.36N 13.55E
64 O4 Mariánské Lázně Czechoslovakia 49.48N 12.45E
119 E6 Mariapirí, Mesa de *plat* Colombia
100 T9 Mariapolis Manitoba 49.22N 98.59W
110 P1 Marias *R* Montana
65 K8 Maria Saal Austria 46.42N 14.22E
77 M5 María, Sierra de *mts* Spain
110 M1 Marias Pass Montana 48.18N 113.29W
65 F6 Mariastein Austria 47.33N 12.03E
66 F2 Mariastein Switzerland 47.29N 7.30E
122 M12 Maria Theresa Reef Pacific Oc 37.00S 151.10W
115 O6 Mariato, Pta *C* Panama 7.12N 80.52W
11 G1 Maria van Diemen, C New Zealand 34.29S 172.39E
65 K8 Maria Wörth Austria 46.38N 14.10E
65 M6 Mariazell Austria 47.47N 15.20E
33 F9 Ma'rib Yemen 15.30N 45.30E
106 G5 Maribel Wisconsin 44.17N 87.48W
53 H7 Maribo Denmark 54.47N 11.30E
Maribo *co see* Storstrøm
65 N8 Maribor Yugoslavia 46.34N 15.38E
12 C7 Maribyrnong R Victoria
19 K5 Maricaban *isld* Philippines 13.39N 120.50E
26 Q4 Marichchukkaddi Sri Lanka 8.36N 79.57E
94 J5 Marico *R* S Africa/Botswana
111 M8 Maricopa Arizona 33.04N 112.02W
111 E6 Maricopa California 35.04N 119.25W
111 M8 Maricopa Mts Arizona
97 M5 Maricourt Quebec 61.35N 72.00W
121 B1 Maricunga, Sa.de *mts* Chile
87 B8 Maridi Sudan 4.55N 29.30E
87 B8 Maridi *watercourse* Sudan
19 D1 Marie *isld* Indonesia 4.38N 125.34E
26 R12 Marie Anne I Seychelles, Ind Oc 4.18S 55.56E
Marie Byrd Land *see* Byrd Land
52 J8 Mariedam Sweden 58.51N 15.05E
52 K7 Mariefred Sweden 59.05N 17.15E
116 N4 Marie Galante *isld* Guadeloupe W I
51 H11 Mariehamn Finland 60.05N 19.55E
61 G2 Mariekerke Belgium 51.04N 4.12E
100 G4 Marie L Alberta 54.40N 110.20W
116 C3 Mariel Cuba 23.02N 82.44W
118 D3 Mariembero, R Brazil
61 J6 Mariembourg Belgium 50.06N 4.31E
Marienbad *see* Mariánské Lázně
Marienberg *see* Bad Marienberg
64 P2 Marienberg E Germany 50.38N 13.11E
60 P9 Mariënberg Netherlands 52.31N 6.34E
15 H5 Marienberg Papua New Guinea 3.56S 144.14E
63 O8 Marienborn E Germany 52.12N 11.07E
63 L8 Marienburg Niedersachsen W Germany 52.11N 9.46E
64 B2 Marienburg Nordrhein-Westfalen W Germany 50.54N 6.59E
Marienburg Poland*see* Malbork
64 N3 Marieney E Germany 50.22N 12.16E
63 F5 Marienhafe W Germany 53.32N 7.18E
64 C1 Marienheide W Germany 41.05N 7.33E
63 O4 Marienleuchte W Germany 54.30N 11.15E
94 D5 Mariental Namibia 24.36S 17.59E
109 J3 Marienthal Kansas 38.28N 101.14W
104 F5 Marienville Pennsylvania 41.28N 79.09W
Marienwerder *see* Kwidzyn
119 F8 Marié, R Brazil
13 B1 Marie Shoal N Terr Australia 10.57S 130.03E
52 H8 Mariestad Sweden 58.44N 13.50E
119 F5 Marieta, R Venezuela
105 C4 Marietta Georgia 33.57N 84.34W
104 D7 Marietta Ohio 39.26N 81.27W
109 N8 Marietta Oklahoma 33.57N 97.08W
103 A6 Marietta Pennsylvania 40.04N 76.33W
105 E2 Marietta S Carolina 35.02N 82.30W
48 V6 Marie Valdemar, Kap *C* Greenland 77.20N 18.30W
99 R7 Marieville Quebec 45.26N 73.11W
53 W16 Marifjøra Norway 61.23N 7.18E
90 B6 Mariga *R* Nigeria
93 G5 Marigat Kenya 0.29N 35.59E
72 D4 Marignac France 45.32N 0.29E
67 O12 Marignana Corsica 42.14N 8.48E
71 G10 Marignane France 43.25N 5.12E
70 J6 Marigné Maine-et-Loire France 47.43N 0.37W
70 L6 Marigné Sarthe France 47.49N 0.21E
66 C7 Marignier France 46.06N 6.30E
70 H3 Marigny France 49.06N 1.14W
69 F7 Marigny le Châtel France 48.24N 3.45E
71 D2 Marigny-l'Eglise France 47.21N 3.56E
116 O7 Marigot Dominica, W I 15.32N 61.18W
116 L3 Marigot Martinique W I 14.49N 61.02W
116 N5 Marigot Saint Martin I W I 18.06N 63.06W
40 J4 Marii, Mys *C* Sakhalin U.S.S.R. 54.20N 142.16E
42 D4 Mariinsk Kemerovo U.S.S.R. 56.14N 87.45E
47 M4 Mariinskiy U.S.S.R. 56.38N 59.51E
45 T1 Mariinskiy Posad U.S.S.R. 56.06N 47.42E
43 F2 Mariinskoye Chelyabinsk U.S.S.R. 52.20N 61.00E
40 H6 Mariinskoye Khabarovsk U.S.S.R. 51.42N 140.10E
41 K3 Marii Pronchishchevoy, Bukhta *gulf* U.S.S.R.
95 L1 Marikana S Africa 25.42S 27.30E
19 D4 Marikasu, Tanjung *C* Moluccas Indon 1.40S 124.23E
30 F4 Mari Khola *R* Nepal
19 J1 Marikina Luzon Philippines 14.38N 121.05E
118 D8 Marila Brazil 23.30S 52.20W
118 E8 Marília Brazil 22.13S 49.58W
14 C6 Marillana W Australia 22.33S 119.16E
61 K4 Marilles Belgium 50.42N 4.57E
117 A7 Marimari, R Brazil
91 E8 Marimba Angola 8.22S 17.02E
118 E7 Marimbondo Cachoeira do *rapids* Brazil 20.15S 49.15W
115 K5 Marin Mexico 25.55N 100.00W
76 B4 Marín Spain 42.23N 8.42W
80 O1 Marina Yugoslavia 43.30N 16.07E
Marína *isld see* Espíritu Santo
95 O6 Marina Beach S Africa 30.57S 30.18E
79 H6 Marina di Carrara Italy 44.02N 10.03E
81 N6 Marina di Catanzaro Italy 38.49N 16.37E
81 N3 Marina di Ginosa Italy 40.26N 16.53E
80 C3 Marina di Grosseto Italy 42.43N 10.58E
79 H6 Marina di Massa Italy 44.01N 10.06E
81 N7 Marina di Monasterace Italy 38.26N 16.34E
81 G9 Marina di Palma Sicily 37.11N 13.44E
79 H7 Marina di Pisa Italy 43.40N 10.16E
81 J10 Marina di Ragusa Sicily 36.50N 14.33E
79 M6 Marina di Ravenna Italy 44.29N 12.17E
80 B3 Marina in Campo Italy 42.44N 10.15E
77 G6 Marinaleda Spain 37.23N 4.57W
81 N4 Marina Schiavonia Italy 39.39N 16.34E
19 K5 Marinduque *isld* Philippines 13.20N 122.00E
107 G3 Marine Illinois 38.49N 89.48W
106 M7 Marine City Michigan 42.45N 82.31W
105 F8 Marineland Florida 29.39N 81.13W
81 E8 Marinella Sicily 37.35N 12.51E
81 D1 Marinella, G.di Sardinia 41.01N 9.35E
93 M9 Marine Nat. Park Kenya
81 F8 Marineo Sicily 37.57N 13.24E
69 C5 Marines France 49.07N 2.00E
75 J8 Marines Spain 39.45N 0.33W
106 G4 Marinette Wisconsin 45.06N 87.38W
118 D8 Maringá Brazil 23.26S 52.02W
92 J8 Maringa Mozambique 12.59S 38.24E
91 G3 Maringa *R* Zaïre
107 E11 Maringouin Louisiana 30.29N 91.31W
71 C5 Maringues France 45.55N 3.20E
76 B9 Marinha Grande Portugal 39.45N 8.55W
119 C4 Marinilla Colombia 6.09N 75.20W
111 A8 Marin Is California
32 D3 Marinjab Iran 34.20N 51.55E
18 J7 Marinjahan Borneo Indon 2.37S 111.20E
45 J9 Mar'inka Ukraine U.S.S.R. 47.56N 37.31E
80 G5 Marino Italy 41.46N 12.40E
44 C4 Mar'ino Krasnodar U.S.S.R. 43.57N 39.33E
111 A8 Marin Pen California
18 H5 Marintu Borneo Indon 0.17N 109.56E
39 D4 Mariny, Imeni U.S.S.R. 62.04N 146.30E
77 P3 Mariola, Sierra *mts* Spain
107 J9 Marion Alabama 32.37N 87.20W
107 F6 Marion Arkansas 35.12N 90.12W
107 H4 Marion Illinois 37.42N 88.58W
106 C7 Marion Iowa 42.02N 91.36W
109 N3 Marion Kansas 38.22N 97.02W
107 H4 Marion Kentucky 37.19N 88.06W
107 D9 Marion Louisiana 32.53N 92.16W
104 S2 Marion Maine 44.54N 67.20W
103 N3 Marion Massachusetts 41.43N 70.45W
106 J5 Marion Michigan 44.07N 85.08W
107 H9 Marion Mississippi 32.24N 88.39W
110 L1 Marion Montana 48.06N 114.40W
105 E2 Marion N Carolina 35.43N 82.00W
108 M3 Marion N Dakota 46.37N 98.19W
108 K9 Marion Nebraska 40.01N 100.28W
104 B6 Marion Ohio 40.35N 83.08W
105 H3 Marion S Carolina 34.11N 79.23W
108 N6 Marion S Dakota 43.26N 97.16W
112 J6 Marion Texas 29.35N 98.09W
104 D10 Marion Virginia 36.51N 81.30W
106 F5 Marion Wisconsin 44.41N 88.55W
12 A9 Marion *dist* Adelaide, S Aust
12 J9 Marion B Tasmania
13 E6 Marion Downs Queensland 23.20S 139.36E
26 A14 Marion I Prince Edward I Indian Oc 46.55S 37.45E
107 J9 Marion Junction Alabama 32.26N 87.16W
105 G4 Marion, L S Carolina
109 N3 Marion Lake *res* Kansas
13 K4 Marion Reef Gt Barrier Reef Australia
107 C4 Marionville Missouri 37.01N 93.36W
81 N1 Mariotto Italy 41.03N 16.34E
119 G4 Maripa Venezuela 7.24N 65.10W
117 B3 Maripasoula Fr Guiana 3.43N 54.04W
19 M6 Maripipi *isld* Philippines 11.48N 124.19E
111 E4 Mariposa California 37.30N 119.58W
111 D4 Mariposa *R* California
111 D4 Mariposa Res California 37.20N 120.04W
19 J1 Mariquina *R* Luzon Philippines
119 D5 Mariquita Colombia 5.11N 74.54W
120 F2 Mari, R Brazil
19 B3 Marisa Celebes Indon 0.28N 121.57E
115 K9 Mariscala Mexico 17.51N 98.08W
120 F9 Mariscal Braun Bolivia 20.05S 64.35W
118 A8 Mariscal Estigarribia Paraguay 22.03S 60.35W
115 N10 Mariscal Suchiate Mexico 14.40N 92.11W
119 B8 Mariscal Sucre *airport* Ecuador 0.15S 78.30W
118 J10 Marisco, Pta.do Brazil 23.01S 43.18W
26 P15 Marisny, C Kerguelen Ind Oc 49.02S 68.42E
107 G3 Marissa Illinois 38.14N 89.46W
53 Y16 Maristuen Norway 61.06N 8.02E
71 K8 Maritimes, Alpes *mts* France
82 K8 Maritsa Bulgaria 42.01N 25.50E
84 V17 Marítsa Rhodes Greece 36.21N 28.08E
Maritsa *R see* Évros
82 J8 Maritsa *R* Bulgaria
79 A6 Marittime, Alpi *mts* Italy/France
46 P2 Mari Turek U.S.S.R. 56.50N 49.38E
42 G6 Marituy U.S.S.R. 51.50N 104.10E
15 F8 Mariu Irian Jaya 8.40S 140.37E
Mariupol *see* Zhdanov
119 H3 Mariusa, Caño *crater* Venezuela
119 H3 Mariusa, I Venezuela 9.44N 61.23W
19 G2 Mariveles Luzon Philippines 14.26N 120.29E
19 G1 Mariveles Mts Luzon Philippines 14.32N 120.30E
Mariyan *see* Dezh Shāhpūr
38 D3 Mariyskaya A.S.S.R U.S.S.R.
33 K5 Mārīyyah, Al U.A.E. 23.10N 53.42E
71 E3 Marizy France 46.34N 4.19E
85 F3 Marj, Al Libya 32.30N 20.50E
75 C8 Marjaliza Spain 39.34N 3.56W
Marjan Afghanistan*see* Wazi Khwa
32 C6 Marjan *oil well* The Gulf 28.20N 49.41E
35 J1 Marjanah Syria 33.14N 36.22E
34 C5 Marjayoûn Lebanon 33.22N 35.34E
66 J6 Marjelen See *L* Switzerland 46.27N 8.07E
101 Y3 Marjorie L N W Terr
56 F5 Mark Somerset Eng 51.14N 2.54W
35 G6 Marka Jordan 31.58N 35.58E
30 D7 Marka Uttar Prad India 25.40N 80.53E
33 D7 Markā *isld* Saudi Arabia 18.14N 41.19E
35 F1 Markabe Lebanon 33.14N 35.31E
52 F3 Markabygd Norway 63.37N 11.16E
34 H3 Markada Syria 35.44N 40.48E
43 Q3 Markakol', Ozero *L* Kazakhstan U.S.S.R.
89 G5 Markala R Mali
47 H5 Markalasta U.S.S.R. 62.26N 56.15E
50 K5 Markalda *mt* Iceland 64.41N 15.11W
23 A4 Markam Xizang Zizhiqu China 29.40N 98.30E
28 D3 Markapur Andhra Prad India 15.46N 79.14E
50 F7 Markarfljot *R* Iceland
52 G10 Markaryd Sweden 56.26N 13.35E
84 G4 Markátes Greece 38.42N 23.35E
Markaz al Halfāya *see* Halfāyah, Al
Markaz Hajr *see* Hajr, Al
33 M7 Markaz, Ra's *C* Oman 19.10N 57.50E
Markaz Thamarīd *see* Thamarīt
99 K8 Markdale Ontario 44.19N 80.39W
64 G8 Markdorf W Germany 47.43N 9.24E
61 C3 Marke Belgium 50.48N 3.14E
107 F6 Marked Tree Arkansas 35.32N 90.25W
61 D3 Markegem Belgium 50.57N 3.25E
66 N1 Markelfingen W Germany 47.44N 9.01E
60 P11 Markelo Netherlands 52.15N 6.30E
63 O3 Markelsdorfer Huk *pt* W Germany 54.32N 11.05E
60 J10 Marken Netherlands 52.27N 5.06E
60 J9 Markerwaard *sea* Netherlands
106 E6 Markesan Wisconsin 43.42N 89.00W
56 L2 Market Deeping Lincs Eng 52.41N 0.19W
57 J7 Market Drayton Shropshire England 52.54N 2.29W
56 K3 Market Harborough Leics Eng 52.29N 0.55W
59 J3 Markethill Armagh N Ireland 54.18N 6.31W
58 L4 Market Inn Grampian Scotland 57.27N 2.57W
56 H5 Market Lavington Wilts Eng 51.18N 1.59W
57 N6 Market Rasen Lincs Eng 53.24N 0.21W
57 L6 Market Warsop Notts Eng 53.13N 1.08W
57 M5 Market Weighton Humberside Eng 53.52N 0.40W
56 J2 Markfield Leics Eng 52.42N 1.16W
65 P5 Markgrafneusiedl Austria 48.17N 16.38E
64 G6 Markgröningen W Germany 48.53N 9.05E
42 L2 Markha U.S.S.R. 60.38N 123.15E
42 L2 Markha *R* U.S.S.R.
41 N9 Markha, Bol'shaya U.S.S.R. 62.11N 129.51E
99 L9 Markham Ontario 43.54N 79.16W
112 L7 Markham Texas 28.57N 96.07W
104 G8 Markham Virginia 38.55N 78.01W
110 B3 Markham Washington 46.55N 123.59W
24 D8 Markham *L* Xizang Zizhiqu China
15 J7 Markham *R* Papua New Guinea
43 O8 Markhamat Uzbekistan U.S.S.R. 40.29N 72.20E
Markham Ferry Res *see* Hudson, L
101 W4 Markham L N W Terr 62.30N 102.35W

57 M6 Markham Moor Notts Eng 53.16N 0.56W
123 G7 Markham, Mt Antarctica 82.45S 160.25E
41 K7 Markhara R U.S.S.R.
39 G1 Markhayanovskiy, Ostrov isld U.S.S.R. 69.10N 161.15E
45 L6 Marki U.S.S.R. 50.48N 39.40E
58 K6 Markinch Fife Scotland 56.12N 3.09W
100 N8 Markinch Saskatchewan 50.57N 104.21W
63 T8 Märkisch Buchholz E Germany 52.07N 13.46E
24 B6 Markit Xinjiang Uygur Zizhiqu China 38.52N 77.35E
51 J4 Markitta Sweden 67.10N 21.35E
63 Q10 Markkleeberg E Germany 51.18N 12.21E
111 E3 Markleeville California 38.41N 119.46W
64 O6 Marklkofen W Germany 48.32N 12.35E
60 M9 Marknesse Netherlands 52.43N 5.52E
64 N3 Markneukirchen E Germany 50.18N 12.20E
84 D3 Márkon Greece 39.26N 22.02E
84 G6 Markópoulon Greece 37.53N 23.55E
51 F4 Markotjåkko mt Sweden 67.57N 17.15E
90 H8 Markounda Cent Afr Rep 7.39N 16.55E
45 L7 Markovka Ukraine U.S.S.R. 49.30N 39.35E
41 E8 Markovo Krasnoyarsk U.S.S.R. 64.02N 87.29E
45 F5 Markovo Kursk U.S.S.R. 51.25N 34.21E
39 J3 Markovo Magadan U.S.S.R. 64.40N 170.24E
39 E1 Markovo Yakutsk U.S.S.R. 70.51N 150.38E
89 K4 Markoy Upper Volta 14.39N 0.02E
107 F7 Marks Mississippi 35.16N 90.19W
45 S5 Marks U.S.S.R. 51.43N 46.45E
103 E5 Marksboro New Jersey 41.00N 74.55W
56 G5 Marksbury Avon Eng 51.23N 2.29W
99 K6 Markstay Ontario 46.29N 80.33W
56 N4 Mark's Tey Essex Eng 51.53N 0.46E
64 J2 Marksuhl E Germany 50.55N 10.12E
107 D10 Marksville Louisiana 31.09N 92.05W
64 N1 Marktanstädt E Germany 51.18N 12.14E
64 J5 Marktbergel W Germany 49.26N 10.24E
64 J4 Markt Bibart W Germany 49.39N 10.28E
64 J4 Marktbreit W Germany 49.40N 10.10E
64 K5 Markt Erlbach W Germany 49.29N 10.40E
64 L3 Marktgraitz W Germany 50.11N 11.12E
64 H4 Marktheidenfeld W Germany 49.50N 9.37E
65 O7 Markthodis Austria 47.18N 16.23E
64 L7 Markt Indersdorf W Germany 48.21N 11.22E
65 N5 Marktl Austria 48.02N 15.36E
64 O7 Marktl W Germany 48.14N 12.52E
64 M3 Marktleugast W Germany 50.09N 11.41E
64 N3 Marktleuthen W Germany 50.08N 12.00E
64 K8 Marktoberdorf W Germany 47.47N 10.37E
64 J6 Marktoffingen W Germany 48.56N 10.30E
64 N3 Marktredwitz W Germany 50.00N 12.06E
64 J8 Markt Rettenbach W Germany 47.57N 10.24E
65 K5 Markt St.Florian Austria 48.13N 14.23E
64 P8 Marktschellenberg W Germany 47.41N 13.05E
64 M3 Marktschorgast W Germany 50.06N 11.40E
64 M7 Markt Schwaben W Germany 48.10N 11.53E
64 J4 Marktsteft W Germany 49.41N 10.10E
64 K7 Markt Wald W Germany 48.08N 10.35E
64 L3 Marktzeuln W Germany 50.10N 11.10E
108 S3 Markville Minnesota 46.04N 92.23W
87 C7 Markwoit Sudan 6.30N 31.10E
56 L4 Markyate Street Herts Eng 52.51N 0.28W
63 F9 Marl W Germany 51.38N 7.06E
109 N5 Marland Oklahoma 36.34N 97.11W
14 B8 Marlandy Hill W Australia 28.12S 116.25E
99 N8 Marlbank Ontario 44.24N 77.06W
103 L2 Marlboro Massachusetts 42.21N 71.33W
104 N4 Marlboro New Hampshire 42.54N 72.13W
103 F6 Marlboro New Jersey 40.19N 74.15W
103 G3 Marlboro New York 41.36N 73.58W
103 K3 Marlborough Connecticut 41.37N 72.27W
117 A1 Marlborough Guyana 7.31N 58.38W
13 J6 Marlborough Queensland 22.51S 149.50E
56 H5 Marlborough Wilts Eng 51.26N 1.43W
11 H8 Marlborough stat area New Zealand
69 F4 Marle France 49.44N 3.47E
66 B8 Marlens France 45.47N 6.21E
106 L6 Marlette Michigan 43.20N 83.04W
71 E6 Marlhes France 45.17N 4.23E
71 G4 Marlieux France 46.05N 5.05E
112 L4 Marlin Texas 31.20N 96.55W
104 E8 Marlington W Virginia 38.14N 80.06W
71 J4 Marlioz France 46.03N 6.00E
12 J7 Marlo Victoria 37.50S 148.35E
56 K4 Marlow Bucks Eng 51.35N 0.48W
63 R4 Marlow E Germany 54.10N 12.35E
104 N3 Marlow New Hampshire 43.07N 72.14W
109 N7 Marlow Oklahoma 34.39N 97.57W
13 H5 Marlow Queensland 20.00S 146.23E
103 E7 Marlton New Jersey 39.55N 74.55W
30 G3 Marlung Nepal 27.54N 86.40E
69 F4 Marly France 49.54N 3.48E
66 E4 Marly Switzerland 46.47N 7.10E
68 B3 Marly, Forêt de France
69 C6 Marly-le-Roi France 48.52N 2.05E
52 K5 Marma Sweden 61.17N 16.50E
29 C7 Marmada R India
107 F5 Marmaduke Arkansas 36.10N 90.23W
28 A3 Marmagao Goa India 15.26N 73.50E
72 J1 Marmagne Cher France 47.06N 2.16E
71 E3 Marmagne Saône-et-Loire France 46.51N 4.22E
72 E6 Marmande France 44.30N 0.10E
33 C7 Marmar isld Saudi Arabia 19.50N 39.56E
84 D4 Mármara Greece 38.48N 22.06E
37 D2 Marmara Marmara I Turkey 40.36N 27.34E
37 D2 Marmara isld Turkey
37 E2 Marmara Denizi sea Turkey
37 E2 Marmaraereğlisi Turkey 40.59N 27.57E
36 C4 Marmara Gölü L Turkey
Marmara, Sea of see Marmara Denizi
84 H5 Marmári Greece 38.03N 24.19E
85 G4 Marmarica reg Libya
36 C6 Marmaris Turkey 36.52N 28.17E
79 M1 Marmarole, Gruppo delle mts Italy 46.33N 12.24E
108 G3 Marmarth N Dakota 46.18N 103.55W
51 G3 Mårmatjåkko mt Sweden 68.06N 18.40E
76 D12 Marmelar Portugal 38.10N 7.39W
76 B14 Marmelete Portugal 37.18N 8.40W
120 G2 Marmelos, R Brazil
77 P5 Mar Menor L Spain
104 D8 Marmet W Virginia 38.14N 81.37W
99 Q4 Marmette, L Quebec
72 G6 Marminiac France 44.40N 1.11E
100 L2 Marmion L res Ontario
14 C8 Marmion, Mt W Australia 29.20S 119.50E
79 J4 Marmirolo Italy 45.13N 10.45E
79 L2 Marmolada, Gruppo della mts Italy
77 L5 Marmolance, Sierra de mts Spain
77 H4 Marmolejo Spain 38.03N 4.10W
94 C6 Marmora Namibia 27.50S 15.30E
99 N8 Marmora Ontario 44.29N 77.40W
81 C4 Marmora, Pta. la pk Sardinia 39.59N 9.20E
66 G8 Marmore R Italy
66 P6 Marmorera Switzerland 46.30N 9.39E
66 P5 Marmorerasee L Switzerland
48 T7 Mârmorilik fjord Greenland
113 L7 Marmot B Alaska
113 M7 Marmot I Alaska 58.15N 151.50W
69 N6 Marmoutier France 48.42N 7.23E
115 M9 Mar Muerto inlet Mexico 16.15N 94.15W
120 D10 Mar Muerto, Salar salt pan Chile
46 L4 Marmyzhi U.S.S.R. 51.50N 37.31E
71 H2 Marnay Haute-Saône France 47.17N 5.46E
72 E3 Marnay Vienne France 46.24N 0.20E
66 C7 Marnaz France 46.04N 6.31E
106 J6 Marne Michigan 43.02N 85.51W
63 K5 Marne W Germany 53.57N 9.02E
67 H4 Marne dept France
69 F5 Marne R France
69 M6 Marne, Can.de la France
61 L4 Marneffe Belgium 50.35N 5.09E
68 J3 Marne-la-Vallée France 48.50N 2.39E
44 F6 Marneuli Georgia U.S.S.R. 41.30N 44.48E
64 E4 Marnheim W Germany 49.38N 8.03E
63 P6 Marnitz E Germany 53.20N 11.56E
28 K2 Marniu Assam India 27.54N 94.26E
12 G6 Marnoo Victoria 36.40S 142.55E
66 N7 Marnotto, Monte Italy 46.07N 9.10E
42 F5 Marnya U.S.S.R. 54.21N 98.50E
24 D10 Marnyak La pass Xizang Zizhiqu China 30.29N 82.19E
90 J7 Maro Chad 8.23N 18.36E
90 H2 Maro watercourse Chad
106 F9 Maroa Illinois 40.02N 88.57W
11 L5 Maroa New Zealand 38.30S 176.04E
95 C3 Maroala Madagascar 15.20S 48.00E
95 D3 Maroantsetra Madagascar 15.23S 49.44E
85 O9 Mar'ob, Marsa inlet Sudan 21.50N 36.48E
Maroc see Morocco
69 D3 Maroeuil France 50.19N 2.43E
81 H9 Maroglio R Sicily
69 F3 Maroilles France 50.09N 3.46E
122 E15 Marokau atoll Tuamotu Is Pacific Oc 18.00S 142.15W
11 J5 Marokopa R New Zealand
31 J3 Marol Kashmir 34.43N 76.18E
95 D6 Marolambo Madagascar 20.03S 48.08E
64 K3 Maroldsweisach W Germany 50.12N 10.41E
70 L5 Marolles-les-Braults France 48.14N 0.19E
69 E7 Marolles-sur-Seine France 48.23N 3.02E
95 D3 Maromandia Madagascar 14.10S 48.06E
95 E3 Maromandia Madagascar 15.00S 50.08E
95 C8 Maromby Madagascar 24.20S 46.35E
95 B4 Maromena Madagascar 16.57S 44.40E
70 N3 Maromme France 49.29N 1.02E
72 H2 Mâron Indre France 46.49N 1.50E
69 L6 Maron Meurthe-et-Moselle France 48.39N 6.03E
79 H3 Marone Italy 45.44N 10.06E
15 H4 Maron I Bismarck Arch 1.35S 145.00E
93 M7 Maroni Kenya 1.50S 40.05E
117 B2 Maroni R Fr Guiana
83 H4 Marónia Greece 40.56N 25.32E
72 J5 Maronne R France
13 G7 Maroo Queensland 25.42S 143.00E
14 B6 Maroonah W Australia 23.29S 115.30E
116 H1 Maroon Town Jamaica, W I 18.21N 77.49W
95 C7 Maropaika Madagascar 22.41S 47.00E
19 D1 Marore isld Indonesia 4.43N 125.29E
114 B1 Maro Reef Hawaiian Is
19 A6 Maros Celebes Indon 4.59S 119.35E
19 A6 Maros R Celebes Indon
95 D6 Marosangy Madagascar 20.58S 48.18E
95 D5 Maroseranana Madagascar 18.30S 48.50E
79 L3 Marostica Italy 45.45N 11.40E
31 G6 Marot Pakistan 29.10N 72.23E
95 D4 Marotandrano Madagascar 16.10S 48.50E
95 C7 Maroteza Madagascar 22.18S 47.10E
29 D4 Maroth Rajasthan India 27.06N 75.10E
11 J2 Marotiri Is New Zealand 35.52S 174.49E
90 G6 Maroua Cameroon 10.35N 14.20E
12 M8 Maroubra dist Sydney, N S W
12 M8 Maroubra B New S Wales
70 E5 Maroué France 48.26N 2.32W
99 L4 Marouf Junction Quebec 48.31N 79.01W
117 C3 Marouini R Fr Guiana
119 H8 Marova Brazil 1.13S 62.36W
95 D3 Marovato Madagascar 15.47S 48.05E
95 D4 Marovato Madagascar 16.26S 48.26E
95 B4 Marovoay Madagascar 16.57S 44.33E
95 C4 Marovoay Madagascar 16.05S 46.40E
117 B2 Marowijne dist Surinam
117 B2 Marowijne R Surinam
57 J6 Marple Greater Manchester Eng 53.24N 2.03W
Marqab see Qal'at el Marqab
34 K5 Marqab al Khubbāz hill Iraq 33.40N 42.12E
61 D4 Marquain Belgium 50.37N 3.20E
107 F4 Marquano Missouri 37.25N 90.10W
95 L4 Marquard S Africa 28.40S 27.25E
64 N8 Marquartstein W Germany 47.45N 12.29E
72 G6 Marquay France 44.57N 1.09E
122 R16 Marquesas Is Pacific Oc
105 E13 Marquesas Keys islds Florida 24.34N 82.07W
118 G8 Marquês de Valença Brazil 22.14S 43.45W
106 C6 Marquette Iowa 43.02N 91.11W
109 N3 Marquette Kansas 38.33N 97.50W
100 U8 Marquette Manitoba 50.04N 97.43W
106 G3 Marquette Michigan 46.33N 87.23W
108 N9 Marquette Nebraska 41.00N 98.00W
109 C6 Marquez New Mexico 35.18N 107.19W
112 L4 Marquez Texas 31.16N 96.17W
75 F1 Marquina Spain 43.16N 2.29W
75 E2 Marquinez Spain 42.42N 2.34W
69 E3 Marquion France 50.12N 3.06E
100 M8 Marquis Saskatchewan 50.37N 105.41W
69 B2 Marquise France 50.48N 1.42E
Marquises, Is see Marquesas Is
72 K10 Marquixanes France 42.39N 2.31E
31 C8 Mar R Pakistan
57 L5 Marr S Yorks Eng 53.33N 1.13W
12 G4 Marra New S Wales 31.11S 144.03E
12 H4 Marra R New S Wales
79 L6 Marradi Italy 44.05N 11.37E
14 B10 Marradong W Australia 32.49S 116.27E
90 M5 Marra, Jebel mts Sudan
33 D8 Marrāk Farasān Is Red Sea 16.23N 41.55E
13 B2 Marrakai N Terr Australia 12.48S 131.32E
88 K6 Marrakech Morocco 31.49N 8.00W
Marrakesh see Marrakech
33 D7 Marrān Saudi Arabia 19.37N 41.45E
12 H5 Marrar New S Wales 34.49S 147.21E
81 A3 Marrargiu, C Sardinia 40.21N 8.23E
51 L5 Marraskoski Finland 66.48N 25.25E
86 M8 Marra, Wâdi watercourse Egypt
12 G8 Marrawah Tasmania 40.57S 144.44E
53 H7 Marrebæk Denmark 54.41N 11.55E
12 E3 Marree S Australia 29.40S 138.04E
107 J13 Marrero dist New Orleans, Louisiana
47 K2 Marresale U.S.S.R. 69.45N 66.46E
47 K2 Marresal'skiye isld U.S.S.R.
31 E6 Marri reg Pakistan
12 L7 Marrickville dist Sydney, N S W
94 M4 Marrimane Mozambique 22.57S 33.40E
81 L7 Marro R Italy
94 N2 Marromeu Mozambique 18.20S 35.56E
75 D1 Marrón Spain 43.20N 3.25W
77 E8 Marroqui, Pta pt Spain 36.00N 5.36W
76 D3 Marrube Spain 42.35N 7.40W
81 B4 Marrubiu Sardinia 39.45N 8.38E
60 M6 Marrum Netherlands 53.19N 5.48E
92 H8 Marrupa Mozambique 13.10S 37.30E
12 C2 Marryat R S Australia
104 E6 Mars Pennsylvania 40.42N 80.01W
72 J5 Mars R France
72 J10 Marsa France 42.49N 2.08E
85 N7 Marsa Alam Egypt 25.03N 33.44E
85 G3 Marsa al Hariga Libya 32.00N 23.59E
86 M10 Marsa Bareika inlet Egypt
88 M4 Marsa ben Mehidi Algeria 35.05N 2.13W
93 J3 Marsabit Kenya 2.20N 37.59E
93 H3 Marsabit dist Kenya
71 D6 Marsac-en-Livradois France 45.28N 3.43E
70 G6 Marsac-sur-Don France 47.36N 1.40W
87 G2 Marsa Deresa inlet Ethiopia 17.18N 38.59E
117 H3 Mar, Sa.do mts Brazil
Marsa el Brega see Qasr al Burayqah
86 F5 Marṣafa Egypt 30.25N 31.15E
Marsa Fatma see Mersa Fatma
85 N7 Marsa'Igla inlet Egypt
72 C3 Marsais France 46.07N 0.35W
69 M6 Marsal France 48.47N 6.36E
95 M3 Marsala S Africa 27.29S 28.33E
81 E8 Marsala Sicily 37.48N 12.27E
84 X19 Marsalforn Gozo Medit Sea 36.04N 14.16E
85 J4 Marsa Matrûh Egypt 31.22N 27.15E
87 G2 Marsa Mubarek inlet Ethiopia 16.35N 39.11E
84 Z20 Marsamxett Harbour Malta 35.54N 14.31E
72 F5 Marsaneix France 45.06N 0.47E
71 F2 Marsannay-la-Côte France 47.17N 5.00E
71 F7 Marsanne France 44.39N 4.53E
85 N8 Marsa Sha'b Egypt 22.52N 35.47E
85 O9 Marsa Shin'ab inlet Sudan 21.20N 37.03E
84 Z20 Marsaskala Malta 35.52N 14.34E
84 Z20 Marsaskala B Malta 35.52N 14.34E
89 B5 Marsassoum Senegal 12.49N 16.00W
85 F3 Marsá Sūsah Libya 32.52N 21.59E
87 G2 Marsa Taklai inlet Ethiopia 17.38N 38.50E
85 N7 Marsa Tundaba inlet Egypt
84 Z20 Marsaxlokk Malta 35.51N 14.33E
84 Z21 Marsaxlokk B Malta
86 L10 Marsa Zaraba inlet Egypt
96 A12 Mars B Ascension I 7.59S 14.25W
80 F3 Marsciano Italy 42.52N 12.20E
12 J5 Marsden New S Wales 33.46S 147.35E
100 H6 Marsden Saskatchewan 52.51N 109.50W
57 L3 Marsden Tyne and Wear Eng 54.58N 1.21W
57 K5 Marsden W Yorks Eng 53.36N 1.55W
11 J2 Marsden Pt New Zealand 35.50S 174.30E
60 G8 Marsdiep channel Netherlands
71 D10 Marseillan France 43.22N 3.32E
71 G10 Marseille France 43.18N 5.22E
69 B4 Marseille-en-Beauvaisis France 49.34N 1.58E
71 F10 Marseille-Rhône, Can France
Marseilles France see Marseille
106 F8 Marseilles Illinois 41.20N 88.42W
104 B6 Marseilles Ohio 40.43N 83.23W
95 L5 Marseilles S Africa 29.10S 27.17E
120 F5 Marsella Bolivia 13.51S 65.22W
Marsengdi see Madi
56 E6 Marsh Devon Eng 50.54N 3.05W
108 F3 Marsh Montana 46.55N 104.55W
33 C10 Marshag, Ra's C S Yemen 12.46N 45.04E
34 B10 Marshah, Jabal mt Saudi Arabia 28.38N 34.52E
113 F6 Marshall Alaska 61.52N 162.04W
107 D6 Marshall Arkansas 35.54N 92.40W
107 J2 Marshall Illinois 39.24N 87.40W
89 D8 Marshall Liberia 6.10N 10.23W
106 K7 Marshall Michigan 42.16N 84.57W
108 P5 Marshall Minnesota 44.26N 95.46W
107 C2 Marshall Missouri 39.06N 93.11W
105 E2 Marshall N Carolina 35.48N 82.43W
108 H2 Marshall N Dakota 47.09N 102.20W
109 N5 Marshall Oklahoma 36.11N 97.38W
100 H5 Marshall Saskatchewan 53.12N 109.46W
112 N3 Marshall Texas 32.33N 94.22W
104 H8 Marshall Virginia 38.53N 77.52W
108 E7 Marshall Wyoming 42.18N 105.52W
13 D6 Marshall R N Terr Australia
12 J7 Marshall Bay Tasmania
15 L8 Marshall Bennett Is Papua New Guinea
9 A2 Marshall Is island grp Pacific Oc
99 C2 Marshall L Ontario
103 D4 Marshalls Creek Pennsylvania 41.03N 75.08W
103 C7 Marshallton Delaware 39.45N 75.38W
103 C7 Marshallton Pennsylvania 39.57N 75.41W
108 S7 Marshalltown Iowa 42.05N 92.54W
39 C3 Marshal'skiy U.S.S.R. 64.24N 142.01E
56 O2 Marsham Norfolk Eng 52.46N 1.15E
103 C3 Marshbrook Pennsylvania 41.38N 75.40W
56 F2 Marshbrook Shropshire Eng 52.30N 2.50W
92 E11 Marshbrook Zimbabwe 18.33S 31.09E
56 G5 Marshfield Avon Eng 51.28N 2.19W
103 N2 Marshfield Massachusetts 42.06N 70.43W
107 D4 Marshfield Missouri 37.20N 92.55W
106 D5 Marshfield Wisconsin 44.40N 90.11W
103 N2 Marshfield Hills Massachusetts 42.09N 70.44W
105 K11 Marsh Harbour Great Abaco I Bahamas 26.31N 77.05W
104 J5 Marsh Hill Pennsylvania 41.28N 76.57W
107 D12 Marsh I Louisiana
104 R7 Mars Hill Maine 46.32N 67.53W
108 O4 Marsh L Minnesota
101 F5 Marsh L Yukon Terr 60.30N 134.19W
11 M9 Marshland New Zealand 43.29S 172.39E
110 Q9 Marsh Pk Utah 40.43N 109.50W
32 C2 Marshūn Iran 36.22N 49.25E
105 G3 Marshville N Carolina 35.00N 80.22W
80 J5 Marsica mts Italy
81 L3 Marsico Nuovo Italy 40.25N 15.44E
81 L3 Marsico Vetere Italy 40.22N 15.50E
80 D3 Marsiliana Italy 42.32N 11.21E
71 E9 Marsillargues France 43.39N 4.11E
19 G5 Marsimang, Tanjung C Moluccas Indon 3.27S 130.49E
110 J6 Marsing Idaho 43.33N 116.48W
57 L3 Marske Cleveland Eng 54.36N 1.01W
108 G7 Marsland Nebraska 42.28N 103.18W
69 K5 Mars-la-Tour France 49.06N 5.54E
53 E4 Mårslet Denmark 56.04N 10.10E
53 F6 Marslev Denmark 55.23N 10.32E
69 H6 Marson France 48.55N 4.32E
65 L2 Maršovice Czechoslovakia 49.43N 14.33E
72 J8 Marssac-sur-Tarn France 43.55N 2.02E
60 L7 Marssum Netherlands 53.13N 5.44E
71 C3 Mars-sur-Allier France 46.52N 3.05E
52 K7 Märsta Sweden 59.37N 17.52E
53 F7 Marstal Denmark 54.52N 10.32E
53 F7 Marstal Bugt B Denmark 54.50N 10.30E
53 X14 Marstein Norway 62.27N 7.50E
53 S18 Marsteinen Lt Ho Norway 60.08N 5.02E
66 N1 Märstetten Switzerland 47.36N 9.04E
110 Q8 Marston Wyoming 41.38N 109.48W
56 F4 Marstow Hereford & Worcs Eng 51.53N 2.39W
52 F9 Marstrand Sweden 57.54N 11.31W
53 C6 Marstrup Denmark 55.12N 9.28E
47 J5 Marsyaty U.S.S.R. 60.00N 60.30E
112 L4 Mart Texas 31.33N 96.50W
80 E3 Marta Italy 42.32N 11.55E
80 E4 Marta R Italy
25 D4 Martaban Burma 16.32N 97.35E
25 D4 Martaban, G.of Burma
72 E2 Martaizé France 46.55N 0.05E
81 R12 Martano Italy 40.12N 18.19E
80 G3 Martano, Monte Italy 42.48N 12.35E
90 F8 Martap Cameroon 6.56N 13.00E
18 L7 Martapura Borneo Indon 3.25S 114.47E
18 F8 Martapura Sumatra Indon 4.20S 104.22E
90 F5 Marte Nigeria 12.23N 13.46E
50 H5 Marteinsflædha Iceland 64.52N 17.42W
50 E7 Marteinstunga Iceland 63.56N 20.25W
72 H6 Martel France 44.56N 1.35E
61 N7 Martelange Belgium 49.50N 5.44E
79 J1 Martello Plima, Val di V Italy
82 K7 Marten Bulgaria 43.54N 26.05E
108 R8 Martensdale Iowa 41.22N 93.44W
77 P2 Martés mt Spain 39.20N 0.57W
77 P2 Martés, Sierra mts Spain
12 J4 Marthaguy R New S Wales
66 L1 Marthalen Switzerland 47.39N 8.39E
56 P2 Martham Norfolk Eng 52.42N 1.38E
29 G8 Marthapal Madhya Prad India 19.24N 81.37E
107 E3 Marthasville Missouri 38.39N 91.05W
103 N4 Martha's Vineyard isld Massachusetts
69 M6 Marthille France 48.55N 6.32E
72 E4 Marthon France 45.37N 0.27E
116 F4 Martí Cuba 21.09N 77.29W
76 G8 Martiago Spain 40.27N 6.30W
72 H7 Martiel France 44.23N 1.54E
41 G2 Marti, F'yord inlet U.S.S.R.
80 F4 Martignano, Lago di Italy
72 C6 Martignas-sur-Jalle France 44.50N 0.49W
70 J5 Martigné France 48.11N 0.40W
72 D1 Martigné Briand France 47.14N 0.25W
70 H6 Martigné-Ferchaud France 47.50N 1.18W
66 E7 Martigny Bourg Switzerland 46.06N 7.04E
71 E3 Martigny-le-Comte France 46.32N 4.20E
69 K7 Martigny-les-Bains France 48.07N 5.50E
69 K7 Martigny-les-Gerbonvaux France 48.26N 5.48E
66 E7 Martigny-Ville Switzerland 46.07N 7.05E
71 G10 Martigues France 43.24N 5.03E
88 L4 Martil Morocco 35.37N 5.17W
77 F9 Martil R Morocco
76 B5 Martim Portugal 41.32N 8.30W
76 D14 Martim Longo Portugal 37.26N 7.46W
113 N4 Martin Alaska 64.55N 148.20W
62 L6 Martin Czechoslovakia 49.05N 18.55E
104 C9 Martin Kentucky 37.34N 82.46W
57 N6 Martin Lincs Eng 53.08N 0.20W
106 J7 Martin Michigan 42.31N 85.37W
108 J6 Martin S Dakota 43.10N 101.44W
107 H5 Martin Tennessee 36.20N 88.50W
75 J5 Martín R Spain
66 S4 Martina Switzerland 46.53N 10.28E
81 P11 Martina Franca Italy 40.42N 17.20E
96 U9 Martina, Pta pt Lobos Canary Is 28.45N 13.49W
11 K8 Martinborough New Zealand 41.12S 175.28E
71 L9 Martin, C France 43.45N 7.29E
95 K9 Martindale S Africa 33.22S 26.49E
112 K6 Martindale Texas 29.52N 97.52W
103 G2 Martindale Depot New York 42.12N 73.37W
77 G6 Martín de la Jara Spain 37.06N 4.58W
121 C5 Martín de Loyola Argentina 35.40S 66.15W
75 J6 Martín del Río Spain 40.50N 0.54W
26 O13 Martin-de-Viviès Amsterdam I Ind Oc 37.48S 77.34E
76 G7 Martín de Yeltes Spain 40.46N 6.17W
79 G3 Martinengo Italy 45.34N 9.45E
71 E8 Martinet, le France 44.15N 4.05E
111 B3 Martinez California 38.00N 122.12W
115 L7 Martínez Mexico 20.05N 97.02W
76 J7 Martínez Spain 40.38N 5.21W
64 J1 Martinfeld E Germany 51.17N 10.10E
76 B9 Martingança Portugal 39.41N 8.59W
121 F5 Martín García I Argentina 34.13S 58.16W
118 F6 Martinho Campos Brazil 19.22S 45.14W
56 G3 Martin Hussingtree Hereford & Worcs Eng 52.14N 2.10W
44 H8 Martini Azerbaydzhan U.S.S.R. 39.46N 47.06E
79 B5 Martiniana Po Italy 44.37N 7.21E
116 L4 Martinique isld Lesser Antilles
116 O7 Martinique Passage Lesser Antilles
107 L9 Martin L Alabama
76 K7 Martín Muñoz de las Posadas Spain 41.00N 4.36W
84 F4 Martínon Greece 38.34N 23.13E
117 G6 Martinópole Brazil 3.12S 40.44W
118 D8 Martinópolis Brazil 22.10S 51.09W
123 H11 Martin Pen Antarctica
113 Q1 Martin Pt Alaska 70.08N 143.20W
11 B11 Martin's B New Zealand
65 M5 Martinsberg Austria 48.23N 15.10E
Martinsbrück see Martina
107 E2 Martinsburg Missouri 39.05N 91.38W
104 K3 Martinsburg New York 43.44N 75.27W
104 C6 Martinsburg Ohio 40.18N 82.20W
104 G6 Martinsburg Pennsylvania 40.19N 78.21W
104 H7 Martinsburg W Virginia 39.28N 77.59W
103 D5 Martins Creek Pennsylvania 40.47N 75.12W
103 D5 Martins Creek Junc Pennsylvania 40.49N 75.13W
110 P3 Martinsdale Montana 46.28N 110.20W
104 E6 Martins Ferry Ohio 40.07N 80.45W
56 F6 Martinstown Dorset Eng 50.42N 2.31W
107 J2 Martinsville Illinois 39.20N 87.53W
107 K2 Martinsville Indiana 39.25N 86.25W
104 F10 Martinsville Virginia 36.43N 79.53W
117 F2 Martin Vas, Is Atlantic Oc
70 G2 Martinvast France 49.35N 1.40W
81 M5 Martirano Italy 39.04N 16.14E
81 B2 Martis Sardinia 40.47N 8.49E
72 G2 Martizay France 46.49N 1.03E
65 O8 Martjanci Yugoslavia 46.42N 16.12E
56 G3 Martley Hereford & Worcs Eng 52.15N 2.21W
56 F6 Martock Somerset Eng 50.59N 2.46W
53 F5 Martofte Denmark 55.33N 10.40E
30 D2 Martoli Uttar Prad India 30.18N 80.11E
57 L3 Marton Cleveland Eng 54.32N 1.12W
57 M6 Marton Lincs Eng 53.20N 0.44W
11 K7 Marton New Zealand 40.04S 175.25E
56 E2 Marton Shropshire Eng 52.37N 3.04W
56 J3 Marton Warwicks Eng 52.19N 1.23W
75 O5 Martorell Spain 41.29N 1.55E
77 J5 Martos Spain 37.44N 3.58W
61 L6 Martouzin-Neuville Belgium 50.07N 5.00E
45 H7 Martovaya Ukraine U.S.S.R. 49.58N 36.59E
101 O4 Martre, L.la N W Terr
71 C5 Martres-de-Veyre France 45.41N 3.11E
72 G9 Martres Tolosane France 43.13N 1.00E
72 D5 Martron Charente-Maritime France 45.16N 0.06W
51 N4 Martti Finland 67.28N 28.20E
51 K11 Marttila Finland 60.35N 22.55E
85 G3 Martūbah Libya 32.30N 22.46E
43 D2 Martuk Kazakhstan U.S.S.R. 50.45N 56.30E
44 G7 Martuni Armenia U.S.S.R. 40.08N 45.16E
47 H3 Martyn U.S.S.R. 67.22N 58.22E
42 H3 Martynova U.S.S.R. 59.36N 108.01E
72 J9 Martys, les France 43.24N 2.19E
23 C1 Maru Gansu China 34.40N 103.12E
35 G3 Maru Jordan 32.36N 35.53E
31 H4 Maru Kashmir 33.40N 75.46E
28 H7 Maru Nicobar Is 8.07N 93.27E
90 C5 Maru Nigeria 12.23N 6.23E
15 A7 Maru isld Moluccas Indon 6.53S 131.30E
15 K8 Marua Point Papua New Guinea 9.32S 149.18E
31 B3 Maruchak Afghanistan 35.50N 63.08E
18 L3 Marudi Sarawak Malaysia 4.15N 114.19E
18 M2 Marudu, Telok B Sabah Malaysia
31 D5 Maruf Afghanistan 31.34N 67.06E
85 E7 Ma'rūf, al Libya 25.10N 18.30E
20 G7 Marugame Japan 34.17N 133.46E
81 Q12 Maruggio Italy 40.19N 17.34E
11 G9 Maruia New Zealand 42.12S 172.17E
11 G9 Maruia R New Zealand
118 J2 Maruim Brazil 10.44S 37.06W
44 D4 Marukhskiy Perevel pass U.S.S.R. 43.23N 41.26E
92 D12 Marula Zimbabwe 20.26S 28.06E
53 J4 Mårum Denmark 56.02N 12.18E
60 O7 Marum Netherlands 53.08N 6.16E
11 M5 Marumaru New Zealand 38.55S 177.26E
92 H7 Marumba Tanzania 11.19S 36.53E
13 C2 Marumba Mt N Terr Australia 13.38S 134.26E
9 C11 Marum, Mt New Hebrides 16.15S 168.08E
32 C5 Marun oil well Iran 30.42N 48.56E
32 C5 Mārūn R Iran
91 G12 Marunga Angola 17.28S 20.04E
15 M6 Marunga New Britain 4.58S 152.13E
92 E3 Marungu Tanzania 3.45S 30.50E
92 D6 Marungu mts Zaïre
20 K5 Maruoka Japan 36.08N 136.17E
42 D5 Marushka U.S.S.R. 52.52N 85.30E
29 C4 Marusthali reg Rajasthan India
122 D15 Marutéa atoll Tuamotu Is Pacific Oc 17.00S 143.10W
87 D7 Maruwa Hills Sudan
76 E10 Marvão Portugal 39.23N 7.23W
Marvas see Marvast
32 F5 Marvast Iran 30.30N 54.14E
53 Y18 Mårvatn L Norway 60.08N 8.14E
71 C7 Marvejols France 44.33N 3.18E
107 F7 Marvell Arkansas 34.34N 90.58W
14 C9 Marvel Loch W Australia 31.31S 119.30E
53 U20 Marvik Norway 59.24N 6.05E
52 K8 Marviken Sweden 58.29N 16.52E
69 J5 Marville France 49.27N 5.28E
108 O4 Marvin S Dakota 45.15N 96.54W
109 C1 Marvine Colorado 40.03N 107.30W
111 N3 Marvine, Mt Utah 38.40N 111.39W
33 D7 Marwah, Al Saudi Arabia 19.53N 41.26E
29 C5 Marwar Junction Rajasthan India 25.41N 73.42E
29 G5 Marwas Madhya Prad India 24.05N 81.47E
100 G5 Marwayne Alberta 53.32N 110.20W
58 S11 Marwick Hd Orkney Scotland 59.06N 3.21W
66 N1 Märwil Switzerland 47.32N 9.05E
Marx U.S.S.R. see Marks U.S.S.R.
63 G6 Marx W Germany 53.27N 7.52E
63 S9 Marxdorf E Germany 51.32N 13.17E
64 M3 Marxgrün W Germany 50.21N 11.42E
43 F7 Mary Turkmeniya U.S.S.R. 37.42N 61.54E
87 A6 Maryal Bai Sudan 9.08N 26.47E
14 B5 Mary Ann Pt W Australia 21.36S 115.13E
47 L8 Mar'yanovka U.S.S.R. 54.57N 72.38E
58 G3 Marybank Highland Scotland 57.33N 4.33W
13 L7 Maryborough Queensland 25.32S 152.36E
12 G6 Maryborough Victoria 37.05S 143.47E
95 F5 Marydale S Africa 29.25S 22.06E
103 C8 Marydel Maryland 39.06N 75.45W
43 H1 Mar'yevka Kazakhstan U.S.S.R. 53.48N 67.54E
45 V4 Mar'yevka U.S.S.R. 52.30N 49.26E
100 Q9 Maryfield Saskatchewan 49.50N 101.30W
58 Q9 Maryfield Shetland Scotland 60.10N 1.08W
101 U4 Mary Frances, L N W Terr
101 L6 Mary Henry, Mt Br Col 58.31N 124.22W
13 F5 Mary Kathleen Queensland 20.44S 140.01E
58 L5 Marykirk Tayside Scotland 56.46N 2.31W
107 E10 Mary, L Mississippi 31.10N 91.32W
101 W4 Mary L N W Terr
103 E1 Maryland New York 42.32N 74.53W
92 E10 Maryland Zimbabwe 17.39S 30.30E
102 L3 Maryland state U.S.A.
103 A7 Maryland Line Maryland 39.43N 76.39W
112 G3 Maryneal Texas 32.14N 100.26W
57 G3 Maryport Cumbria Eng 54.43N 3.30W
72 K5 Mary, Puy mt France 45.06N 2.39E
13 B2 Mary R N Terr Australia
13 K7 Mary R Queensland
14 F4 Mary R W Australia
98 R1 Mary's Harbour Labrador, Nfld 52.18N 55.51W
110 K8 Marys R Nevada
98 R6 Marystown Newfoundland 47.10N 55.10W
111 M3 Marysvale Utah 38.28N 112.14W
111 C2 Marysville California 39.10N 121.34W
110 O5 Marysville Idaho 44.04N 111.25W
109 O2 Marysville Kansas 39.50N 96.49W
106 M7 Marysville Michigan 42.55N 82.29W
98 F8 Marysville New Brunswick 45.58N 66.35W
104 B6 Marysville Ohio 40.13N 83.22W
110 C1 Marysville Washington 48.03N 122.10W
13 H4 Maryvale Queensland 19.30S 145.17E
13 K8 Maryvale Queensland 28.04S 152.12E
107 B1 Maryville Missouri 40.20N 94.53W
105 D2 Maryville Tennessee 35.45N 83.59W
58 L4 Marywell Grampian Scotland 57.03N 2.42W
58 L5 Marywell Tayside Scotland 56.35N 2.34W
79 K6 Marzabotto Italy 44.21N 11.12E
89 J3 Marzafal Mali 17.57N 0.57W
118 E5 Marzagão Brazil 17.59S 48.41W
63 R8 Marzahna E Germany 52.01N 12.45E
63 R7 Marzahne E Germany 52.32N 12.32E
81 K10 Marzamemi Sicily 36.45N 15.07E
70 F6 Marzan France 47.33N 2.19W
80 M7 Marzano, Monte Italy 40.44N 15.18E
81 M5 Marzi Italy 39.10N 16.18E
119 C4 Marzo, C Colombia 6.49N 77.44W
79 C3 Marzo, Monte Italy 45.34N 7.37E
85 B7 Marzūq Libya 25.56N 13.57E
71 C3 Marzy France 46.59N 3.06E
79 M2 Mas Italy 46.09N 12.08E
18 K9 Mas R Java Indon
75 C2 Masa Spain 42.39N 3.43W
18 C6 Masa isld Indonesia 0.02S 98.31E
86 G2 Masabb Dumyât estuary Egypt
86 D2 Masabb Rashîd estuary Egypt
93 M7 Masabubu Kenya 1.12S 40.01E
115 L4 Masachapa Nicaragua 11.47N 86.31W
35 F1 Mas'ada Syria 33.14N 35.45E
Masada anc site see Mezada
75 R3 Masa de Oro, I Spain 42.19N 3.20E
93 F5 Masafu Uganda 0.25N 34.03E
Más Afuera isld see Alejandro Selkirk
93 G10 Masagaloda Tanzania 4.23S 35.34E
115 O10 Masagua Guatemala 14.11N 90.50W
115 Q10 Masaguara Honduras 14.22N 87.59W
92 J7 Masaguru Tanzania 11.20S 38.36E
15 M5 Masahet I Bismarck Arch 2.59S 152.40E
Masahim, Kuh-i see Masāhūn, Kūh-e mt
32 F5 Masāhūn, Kūh-e mt Iran 30.42N 55.19E
18 D10 Masai Pen Malaysia 1.26N 103.54E
18 J2 Masai R Pen Malaysia
92 G2 Masai tribe Tanzania
93 G8 Masai tribal area Tanzania
81 B5 Masainas Sardinia 39.03N 8.37E
93 H10 Masai Steppe Tanzania
93 C6 Masaka Uganda 0.20S 31.46E
77 P2 Masalavés Spain 39.09N 0.31W
87 M5 Mas Aled Somalia 10.59N 48.19E
30 L7 Masalhada Bazar W Bengal India 25.20N 87.55E
44 J8 Masally Azerbaydzhan U.S.S.R. 39.03N 48.40E
19 L1 Masalog Guam Pacific Oc 13.26N 144.47E
75 K8 Masamagrell Spain 39.35N 0.20W
19 B5 Masamba Celebes Indon 2.33S 120.20E
92 C4 Masamba Zaïre 5.45S 27.59E
21 D10 Masan S Korea 35.10N 128.35E
33 M5 Masana'a, Al Oman 23.45N 57.37E
77 Q2 Masanasa Spain 39.25N 0.25W
91 F2 Masanga Congo 3.19N 18.34E
21 D9 Masan-ni S Korea 37.12N 126.40E
19 E7 Masapun Indon 7.46S 126.39E
33 E8 Masāqif isld Farasān Is Red Sea 16.35N 42.20E
30 H7 Masar Bihar India 25.33N 84.35E
86 E10 Masâra Egypt 27.30N 30.50E
86 E10 Ma'ṣara, El Egypt 27.42N 30.52E
104 Q7 Masardis Maine 46.31N 68.22W
86 E9 Ma'saret Samâlût Egypt 28.19N 30.42E
84 R14 Masari Cyprus 35.10N 33.05E
35 G5 Masarra, El Jordan 32.10N 35.56E
105 E9 Masaryktown Florida 28.27N 82.28W
92 J7 Masasi Tanzania 10.43S 38.48E
115 L4 Masatepe Nicaragua 11.55N 86.09W
Más á Tierra isld see Robinson Crusoe
120 F8 Masavi Bolivia 19.20S 63.16W
115 L4 Masaya Nicaragua 11.59N 86.03W
19 L5 Masbate Philippines 12.21N 123.36E
19 L5 Masbate isld Philippines
63 F9 Masbeck W Germany 51.58N 7.27E
61 M6 Masbourg Belgium 50.07N 5.19E
72 J9 Mas Cabardès France 43.22N 2.23E
81 K8 Mascali Sicily 37.46N 15.12E
81 K8 Mascalucia Sicily 37.34N 15.04E
88 O4 Mascara Algeria 35.20N 0.09E
75 C8 Mascaraque Spain 39.43N 3.49W
26 D6 Mascarene Basin Indian Oc
26 E7 Mascarene Is Indian Oc
26 E6 Mascarene Ridge Indian Oc
76 E5 Mascarenhas Portugal 41.34N 7.09W
80 N7 Maschito Italy 40.54N 15.50E
66 K3 Maschwanden Switzerland 47.14N 8.26E
72 G6 Masclat France 44.50N 1.22E
108 L9 Mascot Nebraska 40.17N 99.34W
105 D1 Mascot Tennessee 36.03N 83.45W
12 M7 Mascot dist Sydney, N S W
115 G7 Mascota Mexico 20.34N 104.49W
118 H4 Mascote Brazil 15.35S 39.18W
107 G3 Mascoutah Illinois 38.28N 89.47W
72 E7 Mas d'Agenais, le France 44.25N 0.14E
72 G9 Mas d'Azil, le France 43.05N 1.20E
75 L6 Mas de Barberans Spain 40.44N 0.22E
75 K6 Mas de las Matas Spain 40.50N 0.15W
100 K9 Masefield Saskatchewan 49.09N 107.50W
77 M3 Masegoso Spain 38.44N 2.19W
75 E6 Masegoso de Tajuña Spain 40.49N 2.40W
25 L9 Masein Burma 23.25N 94.21E
18 M4 Ma Sekatok B Borneo Indon
19 F8 Masela Indon 8.06S 129.50E
19 F8 Masela isld Indon 8.07S 129.51E
95 G5 Maselsfontein S Africa 29.04S 23.38E
65 N7 Masenberg mt Austria 47.22N 15.54E
93 F5 Maseno Kenya 0.01N 34.35E
93 F6 Maseno Kenya 0.02S 34.33E
19 C5 Masepe isld Indonesia 2.02S 123.46E
79 L3 Masèr Italy 45.48N 11.58E
79 D2 Masera Italy 46.08N 8.19E
79 M3 Maserada sul Piave Italy 45.45N 12.19E
79 L4 Masera di Padova Italy 45.19N 11.52E
99 P4 Masères, L Quebec
Maserti see Omerli Mardin Turkey
95 L5 Maseru Lesotho 29.19S 27.29E
95 L5 Maseru dist Lesotho
92 B10 Masese Zambia 17.18S 24.40E
69 N8 Masevaux France 47.47N 7.00E
35 G10 Masfara, Jeb.el mts Jordan
87 F4 Masfinto Ethiopia 13.30N 37.22E
53 S17 Masfjorden Norway 60.48N 5.18E
53 S17 Masfjorden inlet Norway 60.49N 5.19E
72 G8 Mas-Grenier France 43.53N 1.12E
35 D5 Mas-ha Jordan 32.06N 35.03E
92 E12 Mashaba Zimbabwe 20.02S 30.29E
35 C9 Mash'abbe Sade Israel 31.00N 34.47E
33 B4 Mashābih isld Saudi Arabia 25.37N 36.33E
43 J8 Mashad Afghanistan 36.50N 69.50E
31 E4 Mashaki Afghanistan 33.15N 68.13E
86 F4 Mashala Egypt 30.44N 31.08E
91 H6 Mashala Zaïre 5.07S 22.57E
57 K4 Masham N Yorks Eng 54.13N 1.40W
23 E7 Mashan Guangxi China 23.49N 108.15E
21 E5 Mashan Heilongjiang China 45.14N 130.39E
87 A6 Mashar Sudan 9.16N 26.51E
35 G1 Masharah Syria 33.08N 35.58E
35 E7 Mashash watercourse Jordan
86 F7 Mashâsh Atfîh Egypt 29.21N 31.24E
33 A2 Mashāsh, El Egypt 29.26N 34.27E
44 F6 Mashavra R Georgia U.S.S.R.
90 B7 Mashegu Nigeria 10.00N 5.35E
35 B7 Mash'en Israel 31.40N 34.37E
31 J3 Masherbrum mt Kashmir 35.35N 76.20E
45 F7 Mashevka Ukraine U.S.S.R. 49.25N 34.52E
45 D4 Mashevo Ukraine U.S.S.R. 52.05N 32.49E
92 J4 Mashewa Tanzania 4.48S 38.43E
35 F2 Mashfa' Syria 32.55N 35.38E
32 H2 Mashhad Iran 36.16N 59.34E
35 E3 Mash-had Israel 32.44N 35.19E
90 C5 Mashi Nigeria 13.00N 7.54E
41 B2 Mashigina,Guba gulf Novaya Zemlya U.S.S.R.
20 L1 Mashike Japan 43.52N 141.32E
Mashileh see Hājjābād-e Māsileh
29 D4 Mashi R Rajasthan India
32 B1 Mashīrān Iran 38.39N 47.36E
32 G6 Mashīz Iran 29.54N 56.35E
Mashjān see Maskān
31 B6 Mashkel R Pakistan
31 B6 Mashki Chah Pakistan 29.00N 62.28E
32 K7 Māshkīd R Iran
99 F5 Mashkode Ontario 47.02N 84.07W
92 E10 Mashonaland, North prov Zimbabwe
92 E11 Mashonaland, South prov Zimbabwe
94 J3 Mashoro Botswana 21.59S 26.25E
95 F2 Mashowing watercourse S Africa
103 O3 Mashpee Massachusetts 41.39N 70.28W
44 K7 Mashtagi Azerbaydzhan U.S.S.R. 40.33N 50.00E
85 N9 Mashushenai, Jebel mt Sudan 21.44N 34.37E
44 F7 Masi Armenia U.S.S.R. 40.04N 44.26E
51 K2 Masi Norway 69.26N 23.40E
115 E4 Masiáca Mexico 26.46N 109.19W
94 G1 Masida Namibia 17.50S 23.40E
76 C4 Maside Spain 42.25N 8.02W
87 D3 Masid, El Sudan 15.18N 32.59E
33 J9 Masīlah, Wādī al R S Yemen
93 J10 Masimani Tanzania 4.15S 37.35E
91 E6 Masi-Manimba Zaïre 4.47S 17.54E
89 A4 Masimbu Celebes Indon 1.37S 119.23E
89 C7 Masimera Sierra Leone 8.41N 12.28W
15 E7 Masin Irian Jaya 6.09S 139.25E
93 C4 Masindi Uganda 1.41N 31.45E
93 D4 Masindi Port Uganda 1.41N 32.05E
19 J4 Masinloc Luzon Philippines 15.32N 119.58E
79 G2 Másino, Val Italy
33 N6 Maṣīrah isld Oman
33 N6 Maṣīrah Channel Oman
33 N7 Maṣīrah, G. of Oman
44 F7 Masis Armenia U.S.S.R. 40.04N 44.26E
120 C3 Masisea Peru 8.35S 74.22W
92 D2 Masisi Zaïre 1.25S 28.50E
94 L5 Masitonto R S Africa/Moz
19 G5 Masiwang R Moluccas Indon
32 C5 Masjed Soleymān Iran 31.59N 49.18E
Masjid-i-Sulaiman see Masjed Soleymān
29 B3 Masjid Moth Delhi India 28.33N 77.13E
18 C9 Masjid Tanah Pen Malaysia 2.20N 102.06E
31 D4 Maska Afghanistan 33.10N 66.52E
90 C6 Maska Nigeria 11.23N 7.18E
87 G4 Maskalo mt reg Ethiopia
33 N9 Maskān isld Kuwait 29.29N 48.15E
26 S8 Maskeliya Sri Lanka 6.50N 80.35E
88 L5 Masker, Jbel mt Morocco 32.25N 5.19W
Mask Hutan see Maskūtān
99 R6 Maskinongé Quebec 46.14N 73.01W
59 D4 Mask, L Mayo Irish Rep 53.35N 9.20W
51 J11 Masku Finland 60.34N 22.10E
32 H7 Maskūtān Iran 26.50N 59.50E
72 C9 Maslacq France 43.26N 0.41W
82 L8 Maslen Nos C Bulgaria 42.16N 27.48E
80 O2 Maslinica Yugoslavia 43.24N 16.13E
45 L5 Maslovka U.S.S.R. 51.33N 39.17E
47 J5 Maslovo U.S.S.R. 60.10N 60.30E
51 Q8 Maslozero L Karelia U.S.S.R.
31 C6 Maslti Pakistan 28.39N 64.50E
35 B8 Maslul Israel 31.19N 34.35E
42 C5 Maslyanino U.S.S.R. 54.22N 84.15E
47 L7 Maslyanskoye U.S.S.R. 55.58N 70.08E
Masmiyah see Mesmīye
66 M8 Masnago Italy 45.50N 8.48E
33 F9 Maṣna, Jabal mts Yemen
72 K8 Masnau-Massuguiès, le France 43.47N 2.32E
53 H7 Masnedsund Denmark 55.00N 11.54E
69 E3 Masnières France 50.07N 3.13E
75 P5 Masnou Spain 41.29N 2.19E
61 F4 Masnuy-St.Jean Belgium 50.32N 3.56E
61 F4 Masnuy-St.Pierre Belgium 50.32N 3.57E
89 H8 Maso Ghana 7.19N 2.45W
79 L2 Maso R Italy
95 E3 Masoala.C Madagascar 15.59S 50.13E
95 B5 Masoarivo Madagascar 19.02S 44.20E
92 F6 Masoko Tanzania 9.19S 33.45E
95 D6 Masomeloka Madagascar 20.18S 48.40E
107 H3 Mason Illinois 38.57N 88.39W
106 K7 Mason Michigan 85.27N 85.27W
111 E3 Mason Nevada 38.58N 119.12W
104 A7 Mason Ohio 39.19N 84.18W
108 G4 Mason S Dakota 45.10N 103.25W
107 G6 Mason Tennessee 35.25N 89.31W
112 H5 Mason Texas 30.45N 99.15W
106 C3 Mason Wisconsin 46.24N 91.03W
104 C7 Mason W Virginia 39.02N 82.02W
110 P7 Mason Wyoming 42.39N 110.17W
11 B13 Mason B Stewart I New Zealand
106 E9 Mason City Illinois 40.12N 89.43W
108 R6 Mason City Iowa 43.10N 93.10W
108 L8 Mason City Nebraska 41.15N 99.18W
101 M7 Mason Creek Br Col 57.18N 122.42W
79 E5 Masone Italy 44.30N 8.43E
93 K8 Masongaleni Kenya 2.29S 38.03E
11 B13 Mason Hd Stewart I New Zealand 46.53S 167.46E
19 D4 Masoni isld Moluccas Indonesia 1.46S 124.10E
14 C8 Mason, L W Australia 27.40S 119.30E
104 F7 Masontown Pennsylvania 39.51N 79.54W
104 F7 Masontown W Virginia 39.33N 79.49W
103 D2 Masonville New York 42.14N 75.23W
51 L1 Måsøya isld Norway 71.01N 24.56E
96 V16 Maspalomas Gran Canaria Canary Is 27.42N 15.34W
96 V16 Maspalomas, Pta pt Gran Canaria Canary Is 27.42N 15.34W
Masqaṭ see Muscat
75 O5 Masquefa Spain 41.30N 1.49E
86 F3 Masraf el Gharbîya el Ra'îsi canal Egypt
30 H6 Masrakh Bihar India 26.06N 84.49E
85 M8 Masrar, Gebel mt Egypt 23.24N 33.54E
75 M5 Masroig Spain 41.07N 0.43E
33 L5 Masrūq Oman 22.38N 55.58E
106 E3 Mass Michigan 46.44N 89.04W
79 H6 Massa Italy 44.02N 10.09E
88 J7 Massa R Morocco
102 M2 Massachusetts state U.S.A.
103 N2 Massachusetts B Massachusetts
79 H7 Massaciuccoli, L.di L Italy 43.49N 10.19E
110 F8 Massacre L Nevada 41.40N 119.35W
35 F3 Massada Israel 32.41N 35.36E
109 B1 Massadona Colorado 40.15N 108.39W
79 G6 Massa e Carrara prov Italy
79 M5 Massa Fiscáglia Italy 44.48N 12.01E
81 O2 Massafra Italy 40.35N 17.08E
71 C8 Mas-St. Chély France 44.20N 3.23E
90 G5 Massakori Chad 13.02N 15.43E
79 L6 Massa Lombarda Italy 44.27N 11.50E
80 K7 Massa Lubrense Italy 40.36N 14.20E
80 C2 Massa Marittima Italy 43.03N 10.53E
80 G3 Massa Martana Italy 42.47N 12.31E
31 F4 Massan Pakistan 32.54N 71.42E
75 Q3 Massanet de Cabrenys Spain 42.23N 2.45E
75 Q4 Massanet de la Selva Spain 41.47N 2.44E
92 F10 Massanga Mozambique 17.16S 33.05E
91 D8 Massangano Angola 9.40S 14.13E
94 M3 Massangena Mozambique 21.31S 33.03E
91 E8 Massango Angola 8.01S 16.10E
92 G8 Massangulo Mozambique 13.55S 35.30E
104 G8 Massanutten Mt Virginia
117 G6 Massapê Brazil 3.33S 40.18W
104 H8 Massaponax Virginia 38.12N 77.31W
94 N2 Massara Mozambique 18.20S 34.09E

66 L6 **Massari, Pizzo** *mt* Switzerland 46.29N 8.42E
117 G9 **Massaroca** Brazil 9.50S 40.18W
79 H7 **Massarosa** Italy 43.52N 10.20E
72 G10 **Massat** France 42.54N 1.20E
47 J5 **Massava** U.S.S.R. 60.33N 62.15E
Massawa *see* **Mits'iwa**
87 G3 **Massawa Chan** Ethiopia
87 D2 **Massawarat es Sufra** *ruins* Sudan 16.29N 33.20E
72 H1 **Massay** France 47.09N 1.59E
64 J3 **Massbach** W Germany 50.11N 10.17E
71 C8 **Massegros,le** France 44.19N 3.10E
61 F3 **Massemen** Belgium 50.59N 3.53E
108 O8 **Massena** Iowa 41.15N 94.46W
104 L2 **Massena** New York 44.56N 74.57W
99 S2 **Massena Center** New York 44.58N 74.50W
61 J2 **Massenhoven** Belgium 51.12N 4.38E
90 H6 **Massénya** Chad 11.21N 16.09E
70 G6 **Masserac** France 47.41N 1.55W
79 D3 **Masserano** Italy 45.36N 8.13E
72 H4 **Masseret** France 45.32N 1.30E
101 G9 **Masset** Graham I, Br Col 54.00N 132.09W
101 G9 **Masset Inlet** Graham I, Br Col
72 F9 **Masseube** France 43.26N 0.35E
103 C8 **Massey** Maryland 39.18N 75.50W
99 H6 **Massey** Ontario 46.13N 82.06W
72 L5 **Massiac** France 45.15N 3.11E
Massiâf *see* **Masyâf**
91 H9 **Massibi** Angola 11.06S 22.40E
80 J6 **Massico, Monte** Italy 41.10N 13.55E
104 F9 **Massies Mill** Virginia 37.48N 79.01W
67 H7 **Massif Central** *mts* France
90 F8 **Massif de l'Adamoua** *mts* Cameroon
88 O4 **Massif de l'Ouarsenis** *mts* Algeria
90 L7 **Massif des Mongos** *mts* Cent Afr Rep
90 E3 **Massif de Termit** *mts* Niger
91 C4 **Massif du Chaillu** *mts* Gabon
72 F4 **Massignac** France 45.47N 0.40E
89 F6 **Massigui** Mali 11.48N 6.50W
104 D6 **Massillon** Ohio 40.48N 81.32W
94 N4 **Massinga** Mozambique 23.20S 35.25E
94 L4 **Massingir** Mozambique 23.51S 31.58E
66 L8 **Massino** Italy 45.49N 8.33E
87 G7 **Masslo** Ethiopia 6.22N 39.48E
99 P7 **Masson** Quebec 45.33N 75.26W
80 B3 **Massoncello, Monte** Italy 42.58N 10.30E
66 K8 **Massone, Monte** Italy 45.57N 8.20E
66 D7 **Massongex** Switzerland 46.15N 6.59E
123 E2 **Masson I** Antarctica 66.20S 97.00E
35 C7 **Massu'a** Israel 31.41N 34.54E
35 E5 **Massu'a** Jordan 32.07N 35.29E
15 L6 **Massua** New Britain 5.59S 151.03E
76 E7 **Massueime** *R* Portugal
35 B7 **Mass'uot Yizhaq** Israel 31.42N 34.42E
68 E5 **Massy** France 48.44N 2.17E
35 G5 **Mastaba, El** Jordan 32.11N 35.51E
33 C6 **Mastâbah** Saudi Arabia 20.54N 39.25E
86 D7 **Mastabet el Ruwayân** *hill* Egypt 29.06N 30.08E
41 M8 **Mastakh** U.S.S.R. 64.29N 122.45E
94 P12 **Mast B** Cape Town S Africa
44 L3 **Mastek** Kazakhstan U.S.S.R. 44.46N 52.25E
43 B3 **Masteksay** Kazakhstan U.S.S.R. 48.57N 49.55E
60 M9 **Mastenbroek** *polder* Netherlands
52 L9 **Mästerby** Sweden 57.29N 18.19E
11 K7 **Masterton** New Zealand 40.57S 175.39E
60 E13 **Mastgat** *waterway* Netherlands
103 J5 **Mastic Beach** Long I, N Y 40.45N 72.50W
116 E2 **Mastic Point** Andros Bahamas 25.02N 78.00W
99 R6 **Mastigouche, Parc** Quebec
36 B4 **Mástikho, Ákra** *C* Khíos Greece 38.08N 26.01E
81 D4 **Mastixi, Pta** Sardinia 39.52N 9.43E
64 P3 **Maštov** Czechoslovakia 50.16N 13.16E
66 P4 **Mastrils** Switzerland 46.59N 9.33E
31 G2 **Mastuj** Pakistan 36.15N 72.35E
31 D6 **Mastung** Pakistan 29.44N 66.56E
33 C5 **Mastûrah** Saudi Arabia 23.09N 38.51E
79 H2 **Masúccio, Monte** Italy 46.16N 10.11E
20 E7 **Masuda** Japan 34.42N 131.51E
86 O5 **Mas'uda, Jebel** *mt* Jordan 30.10N 35.21E
92 B11 **Masue** Zimbabwe 18.05S 25.50E
51 J4 **Masugnsbyn** Sweden 67.28N 22.01E
91 H7 **Masuika** Zaïre 7.35S 22.33E
32 C2 **Masuleh** Iran 37.10N 49.00E
18 D7 **Masurai, Bukit** *mt* Sumatra Indon 2.29S 101.52E
50 H3 **Másvatn** *L* Iceland 65.38N 17.14W
Maswa Tanzania*see* **Nyalikungu**
93 E9 **Maswa** *tribe* Tanzania
34 D3 **Masyâf** Syria 35.04N 36.21E
30 A5 **Mat** Uttar Prad India 27.39N 77.43E
83 D3 **Mat** *R* Albania
121 K7 **Mata Amarilla** Argentina 49.34S 71.15W
35 H6 **Matabba** *watercourse* Jordan
92 C11 **Matabeleland** *prov* Zimbabwe
29 L4 **Matabhanga** W Bengal India 26.18N 89.20E
75 C5 **Matabuena** Spain 41.06N 3.45W
19 C3 **Matabulawa, Gunung** *mt* Celebes Indon 0.33N 123.33E
92 H8 **Mataca** Mozambique 12.26S 36.05E
77 D3 **Matachel** *R* Spain
99 K5 **Matachewan** Ontario 47.58N 80.37W
115 F3 **Matachic** Mexico 28.54N 107.42W
119 G6 **Matacuni, R** Venezuela
22 K3 **Matad** Mongolia 47.12N 115.30E
76 F9 **Mata de Alcántara** Spain 39.44N 6.49W
76 F7 **Mata de Lobos** Portugal 40.55N 6.55W
75 P4 **Matadepera** Spain 41.36N 2.01E
118 J3 **Mata de São João** Brazil 12.34S 38.12W
91 C6 **Matadi** Zaïre 5.50S 13.32E
117 E6 **Mata do Boi** Brazil 3.58S 45.22W
100 K8 **Matador** Saskatchewan 50.49N 107.56W
112 G1 **Matador** Texas 34.01N 100.50W
75 P4 **Matagalls** *mt* Spain 41.48N 2.24E
115 M3 **Matagalpa** Nicaragua 12.52N 85.58W
99 N3 **Matagami** Quebec 49.47N 77.38W
99 N3 **Matagami, L** Quebec
61 J6 **Matagne-la-Grande** Belgium 50.07N 4.38E
61 J6 **Matagne-la-Petite** Belgium 50.07N 4.39E
87 J10 **Matagoi** Somalia 1.59N 43.05E
112 M7 **Matagorda** Texas 28.42N 95.59W
112 L7 **Matagorda B** Texas
112 L7 **Matagorda I** Texas
112 M7 **Matagorda Pen** Texas
92 G7 **Matagoro Mt** Tanzania 10.49S 35.40E
117 H9 **Mata Grande** Brazil 9.05S 37.45W
116 C3 **Matahambre** Cuba 22.35N 83.56W
11 L5 **Matahina** New Zealand 38.10S 176.46E
86 E9 **Maṭâi** Egypt 28.25N 30.46E
122 C12 **Mataiea** Tahiti Pacific Oc 17.47S 149.24W
11 L7 **Mataikona** New Zealand 40.45S 176.18E
11 J6 **Mataimoana** *mt* New Zealand 39.32S 174.59E
Mataiqou *see* **Taole**
79 P2 **Mataiur, Monte** Italy/Yugoslavia 46.13N 13.32E
122 B14 **Mataiva** *atoll* Tuamotu Is Pacific Oc 14.49S 148.34W
12 H5 **Matakana** New S Wales 32.59S 145.53E
11 J3 **Matakana** New Zealand 36.21S 174.45E
11 L4 **Matakana I** New Zealand
11 N4 **Matakaoa Pt** New Zealand 37.34S 178.20E
11 G9 **Matakitaki R** New Zealand
11 J3 **Matakohe** New Zealand 36.08S 174.12E
91 D11 **Matala** Angola 14.45S 15.02E
84 L12 **Mátala** Crete 34.59N 24.45E
76 L9 **Mata, La** Spain 39.56N 4.27W
93 K3 **Mata Lama** *locality* Kenya 2.08N 38.10E
26 S7 **Matale** Sri Lanka 7.28N 80.37E
92 H5 **Matale** Tanzania 6.10S 37.23E
75 F4 **Matalebreras** Spain 41.50N 2.03W
33 D3 **Maṭâli', Jabal** *mts* Saudi Arabia
86 L5 **Maṭalla, El** *hill* Egypt 30.09N 33.59E
76 H3 **Matallana** León Spain 42.52N 5.31W
76 J4 **Matallana** León Spain 42.21N 5.20W
89 C4 **Matam** Senegal 15.40N 13.18W
87 F4 **Matamā** Ethiopia 12.56N 36.13E
75 E4 **Matamala de Almazán** Spain 41.30N 2.39W
11 K4 **Matamata** New Zealand 37.49S 175.48E
11 L7 **Matamau** New Zealand 40.08S 176.11E
92 F6 **Matamba** Tanzania 9.00S 33.59E
90 D5 **Matameye** Niger 13.21N 8.27E
103 E4 **Matamoras** Pennsylvania 41.23N 74.41W
115 O8 **Matamoros** Campeche Mexico 18.38N 90.39W
115 H5 **Matamoros** Coahuila Mexico 25.33N 103.15W
115 L5 **Matamoros** Tamaulipas Mexico 25.50N 97.31W
76 L3 **Matamorosa** Spain 42.59N 4.09W
76 B9 **Mata Mourisca** Portugal 39.57N 8.44W
18 J6 **Matan** Borneo Indonesia 1.55S 110.01E
93 A9 **Matana** Burundi 3.45S 29.40E
19 L8 **Matanal Pt** Philippines 6.35N 122.20E
85 F9 **Ma'tan as Sarra** Libya 21.44N 21.58E
85 G8 **Ma'ṭan Bishārah** Libya 23.00N 22.32E
76 D7 **Matança** Portugal 40.42N 7.32W
92 J6 **Matandu** *R* Tanzania
98 E5 **Matane** Quebec 48.50N 67.31W
119 H3 **Mata Negra** Venezuela 9.01N 62.46W
98 E5 **Matane, Parc de** Quebec
98 E5 **Matane R** Quebec
18 A7 **Matang** Pen Malaysia 4.47N 100.39E
11 K4 **Matangi** New Zealand 37.49S 175.25E
105 J10 **Matanilla Reef** Bahamas
89 L5 **Matankari** Niger 13.47N 4.00E
31 F4 **Matanui** Pakistan 33.54N 71.36E
113 N6 **Matanuska** Alaska 61.31N 149.19W
113 N6 **Matanuska** *R* Alaska
119 D4 **Matanza** Colombia 7.22N 73.02W
76 J4 **Matanza** Spain 42.14N 5.23W
116 D3 **Matanzas** Cuba 23.04N 81.35W
105 F8 **Matanzas Inlet** Florida 29.42N 81.13W
121 C6 **Matanzilla, Pampa de la** Argentina
117 D9 **Matão, Sa.do** *mts* Brazil
94 H4 **Matapa** Botswana 23.11S 24.39E
115 N5 **Matapalo, C** Costa Rica 8.24N 83.20W
Matapán, Cape *see* **Akra Taínaron** *cape*
98 F6 **Matapedia** Quebec 47.59N 66.58W
98 E5 **Matapedia L** Quebec
98 E5 **Matapedia R** Quebec
76 L3 **Mataporquera** Spain 42.53N 4.10W
76 K6 **Matapozuelos** Spain 41.24N 4.48W
92 J6 **Matapwa** Tanzania 9.40S 39.24E
121 B5 **Mataquito** *R* Chile
33 G3 **Maṭār** Saudi Arabia 26.06N 47.41E
121 D2 **Matará** Argentina 28.07S 63.12W
26 S10 **Matara** Sri Lanka 5.57N 80.32E
18 M10 **Mataram** Indonesia 8.36S 116.07E
84 B4 **Matarángа** Greece 38.32N 21.28E
84 D3 **Matarángа** Greece 39.24N 22.04E
120 C7 **Matarani** Peru 17.00S 72.07W
13 C2 **Mataranka** N Terr Australia 14.56S 133.04E
19 C5 **Matarape, Teluk** *B* Celebes Indon
19 M6 **Matarinao B** Philippines 11.15N 125.33E
118 J3 **Mataripe** Brazil 12.51S 38.22W
86 R11 **Matarîya, El** Cairo Egypt
86 H3 **Matarîya, El** Egypt 31.12N 32.02E
88 M5 **Matarka** Morocco 33.14N 2.41W
75 P4 **Mataró** Spain 41.32N 2.27E
11 K6 **Mataroa** New Zealand 39.38S 175.43E
20 C2 **Mataroku** Saitama Japan
75 L6 **Matarraña** *R* Spain
75 D6 **Matarrubia** Spain 40.52N 3.18W
19 D8 **Mataru** Indonesia 8.22S 124.38E
93 K4 **Matasade** *hill* Kenya 1.31N 38.37E
119 G4 **Mata, Sa.de** *mts* Venezuela
77 P4 **Mata, Salinas de la** *salt pan* Spain 38.03N 0.40W
75 F5 **Mata, Sierra de la** *mts* Spain
115 M9 **Matás Romero** Mexico 16.52N 95.04W
11 L4 **Matata** New Zealand 37.54S 176.48E
9 R6 **Matathawa Levu** *isld* Fiji 16.59S 177.20E
93 H7 **Matathia** Kenya 1.02S 36.37E
95 M6 **Matatiele** S Africa 30.20S 28.49E
30 B7 **Matatila Dam** Madhya Prad India 25.05N 78.20E
122 E1 **Matatula, C** Amer Samoa Pacific Oc 14.15S 170.35W
30 D7 **Mataundh** Uttar Prad India 25.26N 80.09E
11 C13 **Mataura** New Zealand 46.10S 168.53E
120 G2 **Mataurá, R** Brazil
11 C13 **Mataura R** New Zealand
122 B2 **Matautu** W Samoa, Pacific Oc 13.57S 171.55W
9 S12 **Mata'utuliki** *C* Tonga, Pacific Oc 18.34S 173.56W
122 B11 **Matavai B** Tahiti Pacific Oc 17.30S 149.30W
122 B1 **Matavanu Crater** W Samoa, Pacific Oc 13.30S 172.23W
85 F5 **Ma'tav Bū at Tifl** Libya 29.00N 21.40E
119 F5 **Mataveni, R** Colombia
122 B10 **Matavera** Rarotonga Pacific Oc 21.13S 159.44W
122 U16 **Mataveri** Easter I Pacific Oc 27.10S 109.27W
11 M5 **Matawai** New Zealand 38.22S 177.32E
103 F6 **Matawan** New Jersey 40.25N 74.15W
99 R6 **Matawin** *R* Quebec
43 N4 **Matay** Kazakhstan U.S.S.R. 45.53N 78.45E
33 J4 **Matbakh, Ra's al** *C* Qatar, The Gulf 25.41N 51.36E
86 F3 **Matbûl** Egypt 31.05N 31.02E
43 J7 **Matcha** Tadzhikistan U.S.S.R. 39.30N 69.41E
99 N5 **Matchi-manitou, L** Quebec 48.00N 77.05W
115 L3 **Mateare** Nicaragua 12.11N 86.25W
76 J4 **Matedeón** *mt* Spain 42.20N 5.23W
120 G5 **Mategua** Bolivia 13.02S 62.47W
115 J6 **Matehuala** Mexico 23.40N 100.40W
92 E12 **Mateke Hills** Zimbabwe
80 H2 **Matelica** Italy 43.15N 13.01E
71 D9 **Matelles, les** France 43.43N 3.49E
116 P1 **Matelot** Trinidad & Tobago 10.49N 61.07W
11 J6 **Matemateaonga Ra** New Zealand
92 K8 **Matemo, I** Mozambique 12.12S 40.38E
60 R8 **Maten** Netherlands 52.52N 7.04E
92 G9 **Matende** Mozambique 14.05S 35.48E
61 E3 **Mater** Belgium 50.51N 3.40E
81 N2 **Matera** Italy 40.40N 16.37E
80 O7 **Matera** *prov* Italy
30 E5 **Matera Bazar** Uttar Prad India 27.46N 81.33E
80 K6 **Matese, Lago del** Italy
80 L6 **Matese, Monti del** *mts* Italy
62 N8 **Mátészalka** Hungary 47.58N 22.20E
75 K8 **Matet** Spain 39.56N 0.29W
92 B11 **Matetsi** Zimbabwe 18.14S 25.59E
88 S3 **Mateur** Tunisia 37.03N 9.40E
76 D6 **Mateus** Portugal 41.17N 7.43W
104 C9 **Matewan** W Virginia 37.38N 82.09W
109 O3 **Matfield Green** Kansas 38.10N 96.35W
52 K4 **Matfors** Sweden 62.21N 17.02E
72 D4 **Matha** France 45.52N 0.18W
29 B4 **Mathaji** Rajasthan India 26.30N 71.15E
123 F14 **Matha Str** Antarctica
66 D2 **Mathay** France 47.26N 6.47E
122 Q6 **Mathematicians Seamounts** Pacific Oc
111 E4 **Mather** California 37.53N 119.51W
104 E7 **Mather** Pennsylvania 39.56N 80.06W
28 A1 **Matheran** Maharashtra India 18.59N 73.28E
106 D8 **Matherville** Illinois 41.15N 90.37W
109 G2 **Matheson** Colorado 39.10N 103.59W
99 K4 **Matheson** Ontario 48.33N 80.28W
100 V7 **Matheson Island** Manitoba 51.45N 96.56W
117 D7 **Matheus** Brazil 5.38S 48.14W
107 K9 **Mathews** Alabama 32.16N 86.02W
104 J9 **Mathews** Virginia 37.26N 76.20W
79 C4 **Mathi** Italy 45.16N 7.32E
11 F10 **Mathias Pass** New Zealand 43.07S 171.06E
30 H7 **Mathila** Bihar India 25.28N 84.09E
112 K7 **Mathis** Texas 28.07N 97.50W
112 G4 **Mathis Field** *airport* Texas 31.20N 100.30W
107 G8 **Mathiston** Mississippi 33.32N 89.08W
35 F8 **Mathlutha** Jordan 31.29N 35.45E
70 N2 **Mathonville** France 49.37N 1.23E
12 G6 **Mathoura** New S Wales 35.49S 144.54E
56 A4 **Mathry** Dyfed Wales 51.57N 5.05W
9 R5 **Mathuata-i-Wai** *isld* Fiji 16.25S 179.05E
30 F5 **Mathura** Gonda, Uttar Prad India 27.35N 82.04E
30 A5 **Mathura** Mathura, Uttar Prad India 27.30N 77.42E
30 A5 **Mathura** *dist* Uttar Prad India
30 H8 **Mathurapur** Bihar India 24.38N 84.47E
26 B12 **Mathurin B** Rodriguez I Ind Oc
29 D6 **Mathwar** Madhya Prad India 22.01N 74.10E
84 D6 **Máti** Korinthía Greece 37.49N 22.20E
19 N8 **Mati** Mindanao Philippines 6.59N 126.12E
39 B5 **Mati** *R* U.S.S.R.
93 K7 **Matia** *watercourse* Kenya
89 K5 **Matiacoali** Upper Volta 12.28N 1.02E
29 L4 **Matiali** W Bengal India 26.54N 88.56E
30 A1 **Matiana** Himachal Prad India 31.12N 77.24E
31 E8 **Matiari** Pakistan 25.38N 68.29E
118 G4 **Matias Cardoso** Brazil 14.55S 43.48W
92 K9 **Matibane** Mozambique 14.49S 40.43E
86 K3 **Mât Iblîs** *C* Egypt
119 E2 **Maticora, R** Venezuela
75 C1 **Matienzo** Spain 43.18N 3.35W
11 K5 **Matiere** New Zealand 38.47S 175.06E
30 M6 **Matigara** W Bengal India 26.44N 88.24E
70 F4 **Matignon** France 48.36N 2.17W
69 E4 **Matigny** France 49.48N 3.01E
115 M3 **Matiguás** Nicaragua 12.52N 85.22W
76 H7 **Matilla de los Caños del Río** Spain 40.50N 5.56W
75 C5 **Matilla, La** Spain 41.12N 3.47W
92 G7 **Matimbuka** Tanzania 11.10S 35.56E
29 H6 **Matin** Madhya Prad India 22.45N 82.29E
115 N4 **Matina** Costa Rica 10.06N 83.18W
99 G6 **Matinenda L** Ontario
117 E6 **Matinha** Brazil 3.07S 45.02W
104 R3 **Matinicus I** Maine 43.52N 68.54W
93 B5 **Matiri** Uganda 0.34N 30.47E
86 E7 **Maṭir Ṭâris** Egypt 29.22N 30.54E
18 L8 **Matisiri** *isld* Indonesia
122 C13 **Matiti** Tahiti Pacific Oc 17.49S 149.17W
95 D9 **Matjiesfontein** S Africa 33.14S 20.35E
95 F9 **Matjiesrivier** S Africa 33.24S 22.04E
84 J5 **Matlabas** *R* S Africa
29 L7 **Matla R** W Bengal India
95 G3 **Matlaring** *watercourse* S Africa
31 E8 **Matli** Pakistan 25.06N 68.37E
57 K6 **Matlock** Derbys Eng 53.08N 1.32W
100 V8 **Matlock** Manitoba 50.28N 96.59W
110 B2 **Matlock** Washington 47.13N 123.25W
57 K6 **Matlock Bank** Derbys Eng 53.09N 1.32W
57 K6 **Matlock Bath** Derbys Eng 53.07N 1.34W
88 S5 **Matmata** Tunisia 33.37N 9.54E
87 E4 **Matna** Sudan 13.49N 35.10E
91 J8 **Mato** Zaïre 8.01S 24.24E
91 H5 **Mato** *tribe* Zaïre
104 D9 **Matoaka** W Virginia 37.26N 81.16W
92 D12 **Matobo** *dist* Zimbabwe
119 G4 **Mato, Cerro** *mt* Venezuela 7.15N 65.22W
41 B3 **Matochkin Shar** Novaya Zemlya U.S.S.R. 73.15N 56.35E
41 B3 **Matochkin Shar, Proliv** *str* Novaya Zemlya U.S.S.R.
118 B4 **Mato Grosso** Brazil 15.05S 59.57W
118 C3 **Mato Grosso** *state* Brazil
118 D4 **Mato Grosso, Chapada de** *hills* Brazil
118 C6 **Mato Grosso do Sul** *state* Brazil
118 C4 **Mato Grosso, Planalto de** *plat* Brazil
81 K3 **Matola, Monte** Italy 40.22N 15.27E
94 M5 **Matola Rio** Mozambique 25.57S 32.27E
91 B2 **Matomb** Cameroon 3.47N 11.05E
92 H5 **Matombo** Tanzania 7.07S 37.49E
92 B7 **Matonchi** Zambia 11.39S 24.06E
15 L6 **Matong** New Britain 5.35S 151.46E
98 C2 **Matonipi L** Quebec
98 C2 **Matonipis L** Quebec
92 G9 **Matope** Malawi 15.20S 35.01E
92 D12 **Matopo Hills** Zimbabwe
92 D12 **Matopos** Zimbabwe 20.27S 28.30E
119 G4 **Mato, R** Venezuela
96 S12 **Matorral, Pta.del** *pt* Fuerteventura Canary Is 28.02N 14.19W
118 D10 **Matos Costa** Brazil 26.20S 51.04W
76 B6 **Matosinhos** Portugal 41.11N 8.42W
53 U14 **Matøskja** *mt* Norway 62.03N 6.10E
118 J8 **Matoso, Pta.da** Brazil 22.51S 43.11W
120 E6 **Matos, R** Bolivia
89 D7 **Matotaka** Sierra Leone 8.40N 11.49W
Matou *see* **Qiu Xian**
71 E4 **Matour** France 46.19N 4.29E
118 E2 **Mato Verde** Mato Grosso Brazil 11.25S 50.41W
118 G4 **Mato Verde** Minas Gerais Brazil 15.23S 42.52W
121 F10 **Matpó** *dist* Santiago Chile
67 P12 **Matra** Corsica 42.16N 9.22E
62 M8 **Mátra** *mts* Hungary
33 N5 **Maṭraḥ** Oman 23.37N 58.34E
66 E4 **Matran** Switzerland 46.48N 7.06E
52 G6 **Matrand** Norway 60.01N 12.08E
12 M8 **Matraville** *dist* Sydney, N S W
31 F1 **Matravn** Tadzhikistan U.S.S.R. 38.11N 71.25E
26 U14 **Mât, R.du** Réunion Ind Oc
53 T17 **Matre** Norway 60.52N 5.35E
65 D7 **Matrei am Brenner** Austria 47.08N 11.28E
65 G7 **Matrei in Osttirol** Austria 47.01N 12.32E
53 U19 **Matre, Indre** Norway 59.51N 6.00E
53 T19 **Matresfjord** *inlet* Norway 59.48N 5.58E
53 U19 **Matre, Ytre** Norway 59.49N 6.00E
88 O8 **Matriouene** Algeria 27.50N 1.20E
95 C9 **Matroosberg** S Africa 33.25S 19.50E
95 C9 **Matroosberg** *mt* S Africa 33.23S 19.40E
94 Q11 **Matroosfontein** Cape Town S Africa 3.356 18.35E
40 J7 **Matrosovo** Sakhalin U.S.S.R. 49.24N 142.51E
89 C8 **Matru** Sierra Leone 7.37N 12.08W
85 J4 **Matrûh** Egypt 31.21N 27.15E
95 B2 **Matsamudu** Anjouan Comoros, Ind Oc 12.05S 44.30E
Matsang Tsangpo *R* *see* **Maquan He**
95 F4 **Matsap** S Africa 28.44S 22.44E
90 E5 **Matsena** Nigeria 13.10N 10.02E
44 C4 **Matsesta** U.S.S.R. 43.34N 39.51E
95 L5 **Matsieng** Lesotho 29.36S 27.32E
94 J3 **Matsitama** Botswana 20.59S 26.39E
Matsova *see* **Mazzuva**
21 D12 **Matsubara** Amami Guntō Japan 27.59N 128.59E
20 D2 **Matsudo** Japan 35.48N 139.54E
20 G6 **Matsue** Japan 35.29N 133.04E
20 J3 **Matsumae** Japan 41.28N 140.06E
20 L5 **Matsumoto** Japan 36.18N 137.58E
20 G7 **Matsunaga** Japan 34.28N 133.15E
Matsusaki *see* **Matsuzaka**
20 M5 **Matsushiro** Japan 36.35N 138.12E
44 F5 **Matsuta** U.S.S.R. 42.56N 43.46E
20 K5 **Matsuto** Japan 36.33N 136.34E
20 C8 **Matsuura** Japan 33.21N 129.44E
20 F8 **Matsuyama** Shikoku Japan 33.50N 132.47E
20 K7 **Matsuzaka** Japan 34.33N 136.31E
20 M7 **Matsuzaki** Japan 34.44N 138.45E
66 N4 **Matt** Switzerland 46.58N 9.10E
35 D7 **Matta** Israel 31.43N 35.04E
41 O9 **Matta** U.S.S.R. 62.28N 130.50E
99 J4 **Mattagami Heights** Ontario 48.28N 81.22W
99 J5 **Mattagami L** Ontario
99 H2 **Mattagami, R** Ontario
69 L7 **Mattaincourt** France 48.17N 6.08E
121 D5 **Mattaldi** Argentina 34.26S 64.14W
105 L2 **Mattamuskeet L** N Carolina 35.29N 76.12W
28 C6 **Mattancheri** Kerala India 9.51N 76.16E
103 N3 **Mattapoisett** Massachusetts 41.40N 70.48W
104 J9 **Mattaponi** *R* Virginia
79 K2 **Mattarello** Italy 46.01N 11.08E
99 M6 **Mattawa** Ontario 46.19N 78.42W
104 R1 **Mattawamkeag** Maine 45.32N 68.21W
99 S6 **Mattawin** Quebec 46.55N 72.55W
66 G8 **Matterhorn** *mt* Italy/Switz 45.59N 7.39E
110 K8 **Matterhorn** *mt* Nevada 41.50N 115.22W
110 H4 **Matterhorn** *pk* Oregon 45.16N 117.17W
65 O6 **Mattersburg** Austria 47.45N 16.24E
66 H7 **Mattervisp** *R* Switzerland
10 P6 **Matthew** *isld* Pacific Oc 22.29S 171.15E
93 J4 **Matthews Peak** Kenya 1.18N 37.20E
93 J4 **Matthews Range** Kenya
119 H4 **Matthews Ridge** Guyana 7.30N 60.08W
116 H4 **Matthew Town** Great Inagua Bahamas 20.58N 73.40W
111 M7 **Matthie** Arizona 34.00N 112.49W
99 G3 **Mattice** Ontario 49.36N 83.16W
65 H5 **Mattighofen** Austria 48.07N 13.09E
103 J5 **Mattituck** Long I, N Y 40.59N 72.33W
52 H3 **Mattmar** Sweden 63.19N 13.45E
66 H7 **Mattmark** Switzerland 46.03N 7.58E
110 A9 **Mattole** *R* California
107 H2 **Mattoon** Illinois 39.29N 88.21W
107 H4 **Mattoon** Kentucky 37.24N 88.02W
106 E4 **Mattoon** Wisconsin 45.01N 89.02W
105 E7 **Mattox** Georgia 30.56N 82.06W
65 H6 **Mattsee** Austria 47.58N 13.07E
66 N3 **Mattstock** *mt* Switzerland 47.11N 9.08E
18 J4 **Matu** Sarawak Malaysia 2.44N 111.26E
18 J7 **Matua** Borneo Indon 2.58S 110.46E
40 N7 **Matua, O** *isld* Kuril Is U.S.S.R. 48.06N 153.12E
120 B4 **Matucana** Peru 11.54S 76.25W
93 D5 **Matuga** Uganda 0.27N 32.32E
26 R9 **Matugama** Sri Lanka 6.32N 80.06E
11 C11 **Matukituki, R** New Zealand
9 T12 **Matuku** *atoll* Tonga, Pacific Oc 19.59S 174.50W
9 T3 **Matuku** *isld* Fiji 19.11S 179.45E
31 F4 **Matun** Afghanistan 33.22N 70.01E
91 G11 **Matungo** *R* Angola
103 L4 **Matunuck** Rhode I 41.23N 71.32W
15 J2 **Matupena Pt** Bougainville I Papua New Guinea 6.31S 155.08E
87 D3 **Matuq** Sudan 14.10N 32.32E
116 P1 **Matura** Trinidad & Tobago 10.40N 61.04W
116 P1 **Matura B** Trinidad & Tobago
119 G3 **Maturín** Venezuela 9.45N 63.10W
119 H5 **Maturuca** Brazil 4.25N 60.07W
41 G1 **Matusevicha, F'yord** U.S.S.R.
75 F4 **Matúte** *mt* Spain 41.50N 2.12W
19 D1 **Matutuang** *isld* Indonesia 4.25N 125.38E
46 R3 **Matveyevka** U.S.S.R. 53.32N 53.30E
45 K9 **Matveyev-Kurgan** U.S.S.R. 47.35N 38.55E
47 H2 **Matveyev, Os** *isld* U.S.S.R. 69.28N 58.30E
39 F5 **Matykyl', Ostrov** *isld* U.S.S.R. 59.17N 155.27E
41 E8 **Matyl'ka** U.S.S.R. 63.24N 85.45E
46 N4 **Matyshevo** U.S.S.R. 50.46N 44.20E
42 B3 **Matyushkinskaya** U.S.S.R. 59.59N 76.59E
84 E6 **Mátzani** Greece 37.57N 22.38E
65 P5 **Matzen** Austria 48.24N 16.42E
66 M1 **Matzingen** Switzerland 47.33N 8.56E
30 G7 **Mau** Azamgarh, Uttar Prad India 25.57N 83.33E
29 G6 **Mau** Balaghat, Madhya Prad India 22.14N 80.11E
30 D7 **Mau** Banda, Uttar Prad India 25.37N 80.53E
30 E7 **Mau** Banda, Uttar Prad India 25.16N 81.22E
30 B6 **Mau** Bhind, Madhya Prad India 26.16N 78.40E
30 H7 **Mau** Bihar India 25.01N 84.49E
93 G6 **Mau** Kenya 0.10S 35.42E
93 G6 **Mau** *mt* Kenya 0.29S 35.55E
93 J5 **Maua** Kenya 0.12N 37.57E
92 H8 **Maua** Mozambique 13.53S 37.10E
30 E7 **Mau Aimma** Uttar Prad India 25.42N 81.55E
19 F1 **Mauban** Luzon Philippines 14.38N 120.18E
19 D8 **Maubara** Indonesia 8.39S 125.19E
72 F10 **Mauberme, Pic de** *mt* France 42.48N 0.54E
69 G4 **Maubert-Fontaine** France 49.52N 4.26E
69 F3 **Maubeuge** France 50.17N 3.58E
25 C4 **Maubin** Burma 16.44N 95.37E
25 N9 **Ma-ubin** Burma 24.22N 97.27E
72 E9 **Maubourguet** France 43.28N 0.03E
61 E4 **Maubray** Belgium 50.33N 3.30E
57 E1 **Mauchline** Strathclyde Scotland 55.31N 4.24W
107 K3 **Mauckport** Indiana 38.02N 86.11W
58 M3 **Maud** Grampian Scotland 57.31N 2.08W
109 O6 **Maud** Oklahoma 35.08N 96.47W
112 N2 **Maud** Texas 33.20N 94.20W
30 D7 **Maudaha** Uttar Prad India 25.41N 80.07E
12 G5 **Maude** New S Wales 34.27S 144.21E
123 B10 **Maudheim** Antarctica 71.08S 10.56W
123 B10 **Maudheim Vidda** *ra* Antarctica
66 D8 **Maudit, Mont** France/Italy 45.51N 6.53E
110 O3 **Maudlow** Montana 46.07N 111.10W
14 A6 **Maud, Pt** W Australia 23.12S 113.45E
96 J15 **Maud Seamount** S Atlantic Oc
94 N5 **Mau-e-ele** Mozambique 24.22S 34.07E
66 J3 **Mauensee** Switzerland 47.10N 8.04E
65 H5 **Mauerkirchen** Austria 48.11N 13.08E
117 A6 **Maués** Brazil 3.22S 57.38W
93 G6 **Mau Escarpment** Kenya
117 A6 **Maués, R** Brazil
122 A1 **Maugaafi** *pk* W Samoa, Pacific Oc 13.33S 172.29W
28 J2 **Maugaldai** Assam India 26.28N 92.02E
30 E8 **Mauganj** Madhya Prad India 24.40N 81.53E
104 H7 **Maugansville** Maryland 39.41N 77.46W
70 H7 **Mauges, Les** *reg* France
57 E4 **Maughold** Isle of Man U.K. 54.18N 4.19W
17 P7 **Maug Is** Marianas Pacific Oc 20.02N 145.19E
71 E9 **Mauguio** France 43.37N 4.01E
71 D9 **Maugulo, Etang de** *L* France 43.33N 4.00E
114 E6 **Maui** *isld* Hawaiian Is
114 C5 **Maui County** *div* Hawaiian Is
47 M5 **Mauk** U.S.S.R. 55.56N 60.30E
25 L9 **Maukkadaw** Burma 22.59N 94.38E
51 L6 **Maula** Finland 65.55N 24.41E
88 K4 **Maulâya bou Selham** Morocco 34.57N 6.18W
64 F6 **Maulbronn** W Germany 49.00N 8.50E
66 H1 **Maulburg** W Germany 47.38N 7.46E
61 E4 **Maulde** Belgium 50.37N 3.33E
69 E3 **Maulde** France 50.29N 3.26E
121 B5 **Maule** Chile 35.32S 71.43W
69 B6 **Maule** France 48.55N 1.51E
121 A5 **Maule** *prov* Chile
121 B5 **Maule** *R* Chile
121 B6 **Maule, L. del** Chile
72 C2 **Mauléon** France 46.56N 0.45W
72 F10 **Mauléon-Barousse** France 42.58N 0.34E
72 D8 **Mauléon d'Armagnac** France 43.55N 0.12W
72 C9 **Mauléon-Licharre** France 43.14N 0.53W
72 C1 **Maulévrier** France 47.00N 0.44W
26 T6 **Maulilwala** Sri Lanka 7.47N 81.14E
121 A8 **Maullín** Chile 41.38S 73.35W
121 A8 **Maullín** *R* Chile
31 J9 **Maulvi-Bazar** Bangladesh 24.30N 91.48E
104 B5 **Maumee** Ohio 41.34N 83.41W
104 B5 **Maumee** *R* Ohio
106 L8 **Maumee Bay** Michigan/Ohio
107 D7 **Maumelle, L** Arkansas 34.56N 92.30W
19 C8 **Maumere** Indonesia 8.35S 122.13E
59 C4 **Maumturk Mts** Galway Irish Rep
70 H7 **Maumusson** France 47.29N 1.06W
72 B4 **Maumusson, Pertuis de** *str* France 45.48N 1.14W
94 G3 **Maun** Botswana 20.00S 23.25E
114 C7 **Mauna Kea** *pk* Hawaiian Is 19.50N 155.25W
114 C5 **Maunaloa** Hawaiian Is 21.09N 157.12W
114 C5 **Mauna Loa** *mt* Hawaiian Is 21.08N 157.10W
114 B8 **Mauna Loa** *vol* Hawaiian Is 19.28N 155.35W
114 B5 **Maunalua B** Hawaiian Is
93 G6 **Mau Narok** Kenya 0.37S 35.59E
29 F7 **Maunda** Maharashtra India 21.10N 79.30E
113 J3 **Mauneluk** *R* Alaska
11 M5 **Maungahaumi** *mt* New Zealand 38.18S 177.41E
11 J5 **Maungamangero** *mt* New Zealand 38.22S 174.48E
11 H2 **Maunganui Bluff** New Zealand 35.43S 173.32E
11 M5 **Maungapohatu** New Zealand 38.33S 177.04E
11 L5 **Maungataniwha** *mt* New Zealand 38.48S 176.49E
11 J2 **Maungatapere** New Zealand 35.45S 174.13E
11 J3 **Maungaturoto** New Zealand 36.08S 174.27E
11 D11 **Maungawera** New Zealand 44.39S 169.14E
25 B2 **Maungdaw** Burma 20.50N 92.35E
25 M9 **Maungkan** Burma 25.04N 95.03E
25 E5 **Maungmagan** Burma 14.06N 98.06E
25 D5 **Maungmagan Is** Burma
93 K9 **Maungu** Kenya 3.34S 38.46E
101 L2 **Maunoir, L** N W Terr
69 E6 **Mauperthuis** France 48.46N 3.02E
12 D6 **Maupertius B** S Australia
122 A15 **Maupiti** *isld* Society Is Pacific Oc 16.27S 152.15W
Mauqaq *see* **Mawqaq**
66 L2 **Maur** Switzerland 47.21N 8.40E
87 J3 **Maur** *watercourse* Yemen
65 E7 **Maurach** Austria 47.26N 11.47E
61 G5 **Maurage** Belgium 50.27N 4.06E
53 U18 **Maurangerfjord** *inlet* Norway 60.06N 6.10E
30 C7 **Mau Ranipur** Uttar Prad India 25.14N 79.07E
30 D6 **Maurawan** Uttar Prad India 26.26N 80.53E
71 J8 **Maure, Col de** *pass* France 44.20N 6.23E
70 G6 **Maure-de-Bretagne** France 47.54N 1.59W
54 M4 **Maureen** *oil field* North Sea 58.06N 1.39E
72 K10 **Maureillas-las-Illas** France 42.30N 2.49E
66 P3 **Mauren** Liechtenstein 47.13N 9.33E
72 E6 **Maurens** France 44.55N 0.29E
107 F11 **Maurepas, L** Louisiana
71 J10 **Maures, Massif des** *mts* France
72 J5 **Mauriac** Cantal France 45.13N 2.19E
72 D6 **Mauriac** Gironde France 44.45N 0.02W
103 D8 **Maurice** *R* New Jersey
12 B3 **Maurice, L** S Australia
103 D8 **Mauricetown** New Jersey 39.17N 75.00W
11 K7 **Mauriceville** New Zealand 40.48S 175.42E
112 O5 **Mauriceville** Texas 30.12N 93.53W
99 R6 **Mauricie, Parc Nat. de la** Quebec
71 J6 **Maurienne** *V* France
60 K12 **Maurik** Netherlands 51.57N 5.25E
Maurin *see* **Maljasser-Maurin**
108 H4 **Maurine** S Dakota 45.01N 102.35W
120 E7 **Mauri R** Bolivia
89 B1 **Mauritania** *rep* W Africa
26 E7 **Mauritius** *isld* Indian Oc
26 E8 **Mauritius Basin** Indian Oc
80 L5 **Mauro, Monte** Italy 41.49N 14.42E
70 F5 **Mauron** France 48.05N 2.17W
72 G7 **Mauroux** France 44.28N 1.03E
72 J6 **Maurs** France 44.43N 2.12E
53 S15 **Maurstadeidet** Norway 62.00N 5.30E
92 J4 **Maurui** Tanzania 5.10S 38.23E
72 K10 **Maury** France 42.49N 2.34E
123 H2 **Maury B** Antarctica
Maushij *see* **Mawshij**
77 V15 **Mausoleo** Balearic Is 39.08N 2.56E
71 F9 **Maussane-les Alpilles** France 43.43N 4.48E
106 D6 **Mauston** Wisconsin 43.46N 90.06W
35 F9 **Mauta** Jordan 31.05N 35.41E
65 N5 **Mautern** Nieder-Österreich Austria 48.23N 15.37E
65 L7 **Mautern** Steiermark Austria 47.24N 14.50E
65 J7 **Mauterndorf** Austria 47.09N 13.41E
72 J4 **Mautes** France 45.56N 2.22E
64 Q6 **Mauth** W Germany 48.54N 13.36E
65 L5 **Mauthausen** Austria 48.15N 14.31E
65 G8 **Mauthen** Austria 46.40N 13.00E
69 K6 **Mauvages** France 48.35N 5.33E
71 F6 **Mauves** France 45.02N 4.50E
72 F8 **Mauvezin** Gers France 43.44N 0.53E
72 F9 **Mauvezin-de-Prat** France 43.02N 0.59E
66 F7 **Mauvoisin** Switzerland 46.01N 7.21E
66 F8 **Mauvoisin, Lac de** Switzerland
87 J4 **Mauza** Yemen 13.19N 43.34E
72 C3 **Mauzé-sur-le-Mignon** France 46.12N 0.40W
72 D2 **Mauzé Thouarsais** France 46.58N 0.17W
119 G6 **Mavaca, R** Venezuela
94 M5 **Mavalane** *airport* Mozambique 25.50S 32.30E
Mavamba *see* **Livingstone** Zambia
32 G4 **Mavan, Kūh-e** *mt* Iran 32.22N 57.50E
28 C6 **Mavelikara** Kerala India 9.14N 76.33E
26 Q2 **Mavelitural** Sri Lanka 9.31N 79.42E
91 F12 **Mavengue** Angola 17.00S 19.28E
70 N6 **Maves-Pontijou** France 47.44N 1.21E
92 J7 **Mavia, Planalto do** *plat* Mozambique
91 G11 **Mavinga** Angola 15.44S 20.21E
116 L2 **Mavis Bank** Jamaica, W I 18.02N 76.42W
94 M2 **Mavita** Mozambique 19.33S 33.10E
92 F11 **Mavonde** Mozambique 18.32S 33.02E
35 B7 **Mavqi'im** Israel 31.37N 34.34E
84 B1 **Mavranaíoi** Greece 40.02N 21.22E
84 A5 **Mavráta** Greece 38.04N 20.44E
84 C2 **Mavréli** Greece 39.50N 21.52E
84 D5 **Mavríkion** Greece 38.12N 22.04E
84 C3 **Mavrommáti** Kardhítsa Greece 39.25N 21.42E
84 F5 **Mavrommáti** Voiotía Greece 38.20N 23.08E
84 E4 **Mavronéri** Greece 38.32N 22.47E
84 Q14 **Mavrorouni** Cyprus 35.06N 32.51E
84 D2 **Mavrovoúni** Greece 39.32N 22.16E
84 E2 **Mavrovoúni** *mts* Greece
84 F6 **Mavrovoúni** *mt* Greece 37.32N 23.05E
82 F9 **Mavrovsko Jezero** *L* Yugoslavia 41.42N 20.49E
37 C2 **Mavroz** Turkey 40.48N 26.40E
92 F9 **Mavudzi** *R* Mozambique
94 M3 **Mavue** Mozambique 21.20S 32.26E
94 N4 **Mavume** Mozambique 23.28S 34.34E
92 E10 **Mavuradonha Mts** Zimbabwe
91 K2 **Mawa** Zaïre 2.45N 26.40E
33 L7 **Mawaafaq** Oman 18.21N 55.06E
18 K5 **Mawa, Bukit** *mt* Borneo Indon 0.27N 113.44E
18 D10 **Mawai** Pen Malaysia 1.52N 103.58E
23 A9 **Ma Wan** *isld* Hong Kong 22.21N 114.03E
30 A3 **Mawana** Uttar Prad India 29.06N 77.54E
26 R7 **Mawanella** Sri Lanka 7.16N 80.27E
91 E7 **Mawanga** Zaïre 6.25S 17.23E
24 C8 **Mawang Kangri** *mt pk* Xizang Zizhiqu China
Mawan, Kuh-i- *see* **Mavan, Kūh-e** *mt*
11 N5 **Mawa R** New Zealand
19 C6 **Mawasangka** Indonesia 5.18S 122.20E
34 N3 **Māwat** Iraq 35.53N 45.25E
25 D3 **Mawchi** Burma 18.48N 97.11E
25 E7 **Mawdaung Pass** Burma/Thailand 11.45N 99.37E
100 R4 **Mawdesley L** Manitoba 54.00N 100.45W
93 J9 **Mawenzi** *mt* Tanzania 3.05S 37.27E
100 L8 **Mawer** Saskatchewan 50.46N 106.22W
11 N5 **Mawhai Pt** New Zealand 38.12S 178.23E
25 K8 **Mawhati** Assam India 25.51N 92.07E
11 F9 **Mawheraiti** New Zealand 42.10S 171.44E
25 M9 **Mawhun** Burma 24.35N 96.11E
33 F10 **Māwiyah** Yemen 13.38N 44.23E
25 E4 **Mawkhi** Burma 16.17N 98.53E
25 D2 **Mawkmai** Burma 20.12N 97.37E
25 L9 **Mawlaik** Burma 23.40N 94.26E
33 H9 **Mawlá Maṭar** S Yemen 14.49N 48.44E
89 J7 **Mawli** *R* Ghana
92 F6 **Mawoga** Tanzania 8.22S 33.05E
28 H3 **Mawphlang** Meghalaya India 25.26N 91.42E
33 D3 **Mawqaq** Saudi Arabia 27.22N 41.08E
33 E10 **Mawshij** Yemen 13.46N 43.15E
Mawṣil, Al *see* **Mosul**
123 B4 **Mawson** *Aust Base* Antarctica 67.36S 62.53E
12 A6 **Mawson** *dist* Canberra Australia
123 B4 **Mawson Coast** Antarctica
123 C5 **Mawson Escarpt** Antarctica
123 K4 **Mawson Pen** Antarctica
26 B16 **Mawson Pk** *vol* Heard I Antarctica 53.06S 73.31E
10 B10 **Mawson Pt** Macquarie I Pacific Oc 54.33S 158.53E
25 E7 **Maw Taung** *mt* Burma 11.47N 99.10E
18 G9 **Mawuk** Java Indonesia 6.02S 106.31E
108 J2 **Max** N Dakota 47.49N 101.20W
108 J9 **Max** Nebraska 40.07N 101.24W
94 M4 **Maxaila** Mozambique 22.15S 32.55E
121 C2 **Maxán** Argentina 28.42S 66.30W
108 J1 **Maxbass** N Dakota 48.45N 101.09W
115 O7 **Maxcanú** Mexico 20.35N 90.00W
70 F6 **Maxent** France 47.59N 2.02W
105 D4 **Maxeys** Georgia 33.43N 83.10W
69 K6 **Maxey-sur-Vaise** France 48.32N 5.41E
64 O8 **Maxglan** *airport* Austria 47.46N 12.57E
101 M6 **Maxhamish L** Br Col 59.52N 123.20W
64 N5 **Maxhütte-Haidhof** W Germany 49.12N 12.05E
76 A10 **Maxial** Portugal 39.07N 9.10W
23 G2 **Maxiang** Henan China 32.45N 114.22E
81 B5 **Maxia, Pta** Sardinia 39.05N 8.51E
43 N4 **Maxima Gor'kogo, im** Kazakhstan U.S.S.R. 46.04N 79.34E
64 E5 **Maximiliansau** W Germany 49.02N 8.18E
91 F8 **Maxinje** *tribe* Angola
94 N4 **Maxixe** Mozambique 23.51S 35.21E
104 E10 **Max Meadows** Virginia 36.57N 80.57W
51 J8 **Maxmo** Finland 63.14N 22.05E
100 L9 **Maxstone** Saskatchewan 49.28N 106.02W
57 H1 **Maxton** Borders Scotland 55.34N 2.37W
105 H3 **Maxton** N Carolina 34.43N 79.20W
105 E7 **Maxville** Florida 30.14N 82.01W
110 M3 **Maxville** Montana 46.28N 113.14W
99 Q7 **Maxville** Ontario 45.17N 74.51W
111 B2 **Maxwell** California 39.16N 122.11W
108 R8 **Maxwell** Iowa 41.53N 93.21W
108 K8 **Maxwell** Nebraska 41.05N 100.31W
109 F5 **Maxwell** New Mexico 36.32N 104.33W
57 F2 **Maxwelltown** Dumfries & Galloway Scotland 55.04N 3.38W
13 G5 **Maxwelton** Queensland 20.48S 142.44E
110 M5 **May** Idaho 44.37N 113.54W
109 L5 **May** Oklahoma 36.37N 99.46W
112 J4 **May** Texas 31.58N 98.51W
18 H6 **Maya** *isld* Borneo Indon
40 F2 **Maya** *R* Khabarovsk U.S.S.R.
40 F4 **Maya** *R* Khabarovsk U.S.S.R.
40 H2 **Maya** *R* Khabarovsk U.S.S.R.
30 F6 **Maya Bhikhi** Uttar Prad India 26.40N 82.19E
20 L1 **Mayachi** Japan 42.58N 142.04E
43 D1 **Mayachnyy** Bashkir U.S.S.R. 52.45N 55.43E
39 F7 **Mayachnyy, Mys** *C* U.S.S.R. 52.51N 158.42E
75 H1 **Maya del Baztán** Spain 43.12N 1.29W
Mayâdine *see* **Meyadin**
116 H3 **Mayaguana** *isld* Bahamas
116 H3 **Mayaguana Passage** Bahamas
105 J7 **Mayagüez** Puerto Rico 18.13N 67.09W
89 N5 **Mayahi** Niger 13.59N 7.45E
43 D2 **Mayak** U.S.S.R. 51.23N 55.14E
39 E4 **Mayakan** U.S.S.R. 60.03N 151.36E
89 L5 **Mayaki Koara** Niger 13.31N 3.33E
62 M1 **Mayak Lt.Ho** U.S.S.R. 54.57N 20.02E
31 F2 **Mayakovskogo** U.S.S.R. 37.05N 71.42E
43 K8 **Mayakovskogo, Pik** *mt* Tadzhikistan U.S.S.R. 37.00N 71.46E
75 L5 **Mayals** Spain 41.22N 0.30E
91 D5 **Mayama** Congo 3.50S 14.52E
91 D6 **Maya-Maya** *airport* Congo 4.10S 15.12E
91 E6 **Mayamba** Zaïre 4.49S 16.53E
32 F2 **Mayamey** Iran 36.27N 55.40E
35 D3 **May 'Ami** Israel 32.30N 35.09E
115 P9 **Maya Mts** Belize/Guatemala
35 F1 **Ma'yan Barukh** Israel 33.15N 35.36E
23 E5 **Mayang** Hunan China 27.46N 109.57E
93 C4 **Mayanja** *R* Uganda
35 C3 **Ma'yan Zevi** Israel 32.34N 34.57E
116 G4 **Mayarí** Cuba 20.41N 75.42W
116 P2 **Mayaro** *co* Trinidad & Tobago
116 P2 **Mayaro B** Trinidad & Tobago
20 N3 **Maya-san** *mt* Honshu Japan 38.31N 139.45E
Mayaveram *see* **Mayuram**
106 L7 **Maybee** Michigan 42.01N 83.30W
109 B1 **Maybell** Colorado 40.32N 108.05W
57 D2 **Maybole** Strathclyde Scotland 55.21N 4.41W
103 F4 **Maybrook** New York 41.29N 74.13W
87 G4 **Maych'ew** Ethiopia 12.46N 39.31E
34 N4 **Maydān** Iraq 34.55N 45.38E
43 O8 **Maydan** Kirgiziya U.S.S.R. 40.04N 72.05E
32 E8 **Maydan Mahzam** *oil well* The Gulf 25.37N 52.39E
116 J2 **May Day Mts** Jamaica, W I
112 M4 **Maydelle** Texas 31.48N 95.19W
12 H9 **Maydena** Tasmania 42.48S 146.30E
Maydos *see* **Eceabat**
64 C3 **Mayen** W Germany 50.19N 7.14E
69 E5 **May-en-Multien** France 49.04N 3.02E
20 D5 **Mayenne** France
70 J5 **Mayenne** France 48.18N 0.37W
67 E4 **Mayenne** *dept* France
70 J5 **Mayenne** *R* France
111 M7 **Mayer** Arizona 34.25N 112.14W
121 J7 **Mayer** *R* Argentina
100 B5 **Mayerthorpe** Alberta 53.59N 115.06W
105 G4 **Mayesville** S Carolina 34.00N 80.12W
70 L6 **Mayet** France 47.45N 0.16E
71 D4 **Mayet-de-Montagne, le** France 46.05N 3.40E
109 P2 **Mayetta** Kansas 39.21N 95.44W
33 G9 **Mayfa'ah** S Yemen 14.17N 47.35E
100 K5 **Mayfair** Saskatchewan 53.00N 107.37W
56 M5 **Mayfield** E Sussex Eng 51.01N 0.16E
110 K6 **Mayfield** Idaho 43.24N 115.59W
107 H5 **Mayfield** Kentucky 36.45N 88.40W
11 F10 **Mayfield** New Zealand 43.49S 171.26E
109 L6 **Mayfield** Oklahoma 35.22N 99.54W
103 C3 **Mayfield** Pennsylvania 41.32N 75.32W
13 G7 **Mayfield** Queensland 25.42S 142.38E
57 K6 **Mayfield** Staffs Eng 53.01N 1.45W
111 N2 **Mayfield** Utah 39.06N 111.44W
107 H5 **Mayfield** *R* Kentucky
107 D7 **Mayflower** Arkansas 34.57N 92.25W
56 K5 **Mayford** Surrey Eng 51.18N 0.35W
107 H8 **Mayhew** Mississippi 33.30N 88.39W
109 E9 **Mayhill** New Mexico 32.54N 105.29W
93 J3 **Mayidahad** Kenya 2.48N 37.45E
21 D5 **Mayi He** *R* Heilongjiang China
23 D1 **Maying** Gansu China 35.22N 105.06E
58 L6 **May, I. of** Scotland 56.12N 2.32W
43 M2 **Maykain** Kazakhstan U.S.S.R. 51.28N 75.46E
44 C3 **Maykop** U.S.S.R. 44.37N 40.48E
47 H6 **Maykor** U.S.S.R. 59.01N 55.50E
107 L5 **Mayland** Tennessee 36.02N 85.11W
14 B1 **Maylands** *dist* Perth, W Aust
43 G4 **Maylibash** Kazakhstan U.S.S.R. 45.48N 62.40E
43 P4 **Mayli, Khrebet** *mts* Xinjiang Uygur Zizhiqu China
43 K6 **Mayli-Say** Kirgiziya U.S.S.R. 41.14N 72.27E
43 O7 **Maylisu** *R* Kirgiziya U.S.S.R.
43 H4 **Maylykum** Kazakhstan U.S.S.R. 45.04N 65.12E
43 K5 **Maymak** Kirgiziya U.S.S.R. 42.37N 71.10E
40 G3 **Maymakan** U.S.S.R. 56.22N 135.30E
40 F3 **Maymakan** *R* U.S.S.R.
39 E4 **Maymandzhinskiy Khrebet** *mts* U.S.S.R.
41 G5 **Maymecha** *R* U.S.S.R.
100 K6 **Maymont** Saskatchewan 52.36N 107.46W
25 D1 **Maymyo** Burma 22.05N 96.33E
39 J2 **Mayn** *R* U.S.S.R.
42 E5 **Mayna** Khakass U.S.S.R. 53.02N 91.29E
45 T2 **Mayna** Ul'yanovsk U.S.S.R. 54.07N 47.37E
106 C7 **Maynard** Iowa 42.46N 91.53W
103 M2 **Maynard** Massachusetts 42.26N 71.28W
14 C8 **Maynard Hills** W Australia
13 F6 **Mayne** *R* Queensland
39 K3 **Maynel'vegyrgyrgyn** *R* U.S.S.R.
28 B2 **Mayni** Maharashtra India 17.26N 74.35E
39 K3 **Mayno-Amamkut** U.S.S.R. 62.55N 179.27E
59 J5 **Maynooth** Kildare Irish Rep 53.23N 6.35W
99 N7 **Maynooth** Ontario 45.13N 77.57W
39 K3 **Maynopyl'gin** U.S.S.R. 62.35N 177.26E
105 D7 **Mayo** Florida 30.03N 83.11W
104 J8 **Mayo** Maryland 38.54N 76.31W
101 F4 **Mayo** Yukon Terr 63.34N 135.52W
59 D4 **Mayo** *co* Irish Rep
19 N8 **Mayo B** Mindanao Philippines
90 F7 **Mayo Belwa** Nigeria 8.58N 12.05E
90 E8 **Mayo Daga** Nigeria 6.59N 11.25E
105 H1 **Mayodan** N Carolina 36.27N 79.58W
90 G7 **Mayo Kebi** *div* Chad
91 C5 **Mayoko** Congo 2.19S 12.47E
91 H4 **Mayoko** Zaïre 1.06S 23.50E
101 F4 **Mayo L** Yukon Terr 63.45N 135.00W
120 F5 **Mayo Mayo** Bolivia 12.18S 65.13W
91 C6 **Mayombe** *tribe* Zaïre
19 L5 **Mayon** *mt* Luzon Philippines 13.15N 123.42E
121 K5 **Mayo, R** Argentina
120 B2 **Mayo, R** Peru
75 E7 **Mayor** *R* Spain

75 F3 Mayor R Spain
121 E7 Mayor Buratovich Argentina 39.15S 62.35W
75 C1 Mayor, C Spain 43.29N 3.47W
76 J4 Mayorga Spain 42.10N 5.16W
11 L4 Mayor I New Zealand 37.17S 176.17E
77 D6 Mayor, I Spain 37.05N 6.10W
77 P5 Mayor, I Spain 37.42N 0.45W
39 C1 Mayor-Krest U.S.S.R. 67.36N 144.51E
101 F5 Mayo Road Yukon Terr
118 A6 Mayor Pablo Lagerenza Paraguay 19.55S 60.46W
39 E4 Mayorych U.S.S.R. 62.29N 150.35E
72 B7 Mayotte France 44.27N 1.08W
95 B2 Mayotte isld Comoros, Ind Oc
116 K2 May Pen Jamaica, W I 17.58N 77.15W
105 F7 Mayport Florida 30.13N 81.23W
15 F6 May, R Papua New Guinea
14 E3 May R W Australia
19 K2 Mayraira Pt Luzon Philippines 18.37N 120.50E
71 E7 Mayres France 44.40N 4.07E
72 H9 Mayreville France 43.13N 1.51E
65 E7 Mayrhofen Austria 47.10N 11.52E
15 F6 May River Papua New Guinea 4.24S 141.52E
34 C4 Mayrouba Lebanon 34.00N 35.44E
33 C1 Maysarī, Al Saudi Arabia 30.23N 38.10E
42 B3 Maysk Tomsk U.S.S.R. 57.50N 77.04E
40 E5 Mayskiy Amur U.S.S.R. 52.19N 129.40E
44 F4 Mayskiy Kabardino-Balkar A.S.S.R. U.S.S.R. 43.37N 44.06E
40 H7 Mayskiy Khabarovsk U.S.S.R. 48.57N 140.14E
40 F4 Mayskiy, Khrebet mts U.S.S.R.
43 N2 Mayskoye Kazakhstan U.S.S.R. 50.53N 78.13E
103 E8 Mays Landing New Jersey 39.27N 74.44W
101 U7 Mayson L Saskatchewan 57.55N 107.10W
72 C1 May-sur-Evre, le France 47.09N 0.54W
105 D3 Maysville Georgia 34.15N 83.33W
104 B8 Maysville Kentucky 38.38N 83.46W
107 B2 Maysville Missouri 39.53N 94.22W
105 K3 Maysville N Carolina 34.54N 77.15W
109 N7 Maysville Oklahoma 34.50N 97.25W
Maytag see Dushanzi
19 J6 Maytiguid isld Philippines 11.05N 119.35E
103 A6 Maytown Pennsylvania 40.04N 76.34W
13 G3 Maytown Queensland 16.00S 144.15E
19 E3 Mayu isld Moluccas Indon 1.29N 126.23E
25 B2 Mayu R Burma
91 B5 Mayumba Gabon 3.23S 10.38E
24 D10 Mayum La pass Xizang Zizhiqu China 30.34N 82.27E
91 J4 Mayunga Zaïre 1.18S 25.36E
28 D5 Mayuram Tamil Nadu India 11.08N 79.40E
29 K7 Mayurbhanj dist Orissa India
12 H2 Mayvale Queensland 27.57S 146.08E
13 H8 Mayvale Queensland 27.57S 146.08E
106 L6 Mayville Michigan 43.21N 83.22W
108 N2 Mayville N Dakota 47.30N 97.20W
104 F4 Mayville New York 42.15N 79.32W
110 E4 Mayville Oregon 45.07N 120.12W
106 F6 Mayville Wisconsin 43.30N 88.33W
108 K9 Maywood Nebraska 40.41N 100.36W
103 D2 Maywood New York 42.17N 75.15W
106 P2 Maywood dist Chicago, Illinois
111 E9 Maywood dist Los Angeles, California
41 O9 Mayya U.S.S.R. 61.50N 130.15E
33 E3 Mayyâh, Al Saudi Arabia 27.44N 42.55E
34 M1 Mayzi Iraq 37.13N 44.05E
121 D6 Maza Argentina 36.55S 63.16W
108 L1 Maza N Dakota 48.23N 99.12W
92 C9 Mazabuka Zambia 15.50S 27.47E
117 C5 Mazagão Brazil 0.07S 51.16W
28 B8 Mazagaon dist Bombay India
117 C5 Mazagão Velho Brazil 0.14S 51.28W
69 H5 Mazagran France 49.24N 4.36E
33 G4 Mazāhimiyah,Al Saudi Arabia 24.26N 46.20E
34 H3 Māza, Jebel hill Syria 35.49N 40.39E
82 J8 Mazalat mt Bulgaria 42.43N 25.07E
75 L5 Mazaleón Spain 41.03N 0.05E
90 D3 Mazalet Niger 16.20N 9.01E
33 H4 Mazalij oil field Saudi Arabia 24.20N 48.10E
110 E1 Mazama Washington 48.37N 120.25W
120 C4 Mazamari Peru 11.21S 74.36W
94 N2 Mazamba Mozambique 18.32S 34.50E
72 J9 Mazamet France 43.29N 2.22E
119 D9 Mazán Peru 3.30S 73.04W
71 G8 Mazan Vaucluse France 44.03N 5.03E
32 D2 Māzandarān prov Iran
70 M6 Mazange France 47.50N 0.57E
71 E7 Mazan-l'Abbaye France 44.43N 4.05E
119 D9 Mazán, R Peru
115 J5 Mazapil Mexico 24.40N 101.35W
35 F9 Mazar Jordan 31.04N 35.42E
43 N7 Mazar Uzbekistan U.S.S.R. 41.04N 70.44E
24 B7 Mazar Xinjiang Uygur Zizhiqu China 36.28N 77.00E
24 D4 Mazar Xinjiang Uygur Zizhiqu China 43.50N 81.59E
88 O5 Mazar watercourse Algeria
33 N5 Mazāra' Oman 23.08N 58.52E
81 E8 Mazara del Vallo Sicily 37.39N 12.36E
84 C5 Mazaráki Greece 38.04N 21.39E
81 F8 Mazara, Val di Sicily
86 K3 Mazâr, El Egypt 31.03N 33.24E
35 G4 Mazar, El Jordan 32.28N 35.47E
75 F5 Mazarete Spain 41.00N 2.09W
74 D9 Mazari,C Morocco 35.33N 5.09W
88 L4 Mazari, C C Morocco 35.33N 5.02W
76 A3 Mazaricos Spain 42.58N 9.00W
31 D2 Mazar-i-Sharif Afghanistan 36.43N 67.05E
31 D4 Mazar, Koh-i- mt Afghanistan 32.30N 66.23E
81 E8 Mazaro R Sicily
121 L6 Mazarredo Argentina 47.00S 66.45W
77 O5 Mazarrón Spain 37.36N 1.19W
77 O6 Mazarrón, G.de Spain
35 F8 Mazar Saiyidna Suleiman tomb Jordan 31.21N 35.37E
43 L6 Mazarsu Kirgiziya U.S.S.R. 41.55N 72.34E
24 C6 Mazar Tagh ruins Xinjiang Uygur Zizhiqu China 38.35N 80.14E
75 E7 Mazarulleque Spain 40.11N 2.45W
119 H4 Mazaruni, R Guyana
35 J1 Mazar Zaghbar Syria 33.16N 36.20E
115 D3 Mazatán Mexico 29.00N 110.10W
115 O10 Mazatenango Guatemala 14.31N 91.30W
115 F6 Mazatlán Mexico 23.11N 106.25W
111 N7 Mazatzal Pk mt Arizona 34.05N 111.28W
32 G7 Mazāvī R Iran
32 D4 Mazdaj Iran 32.15N 50.28E
61 J6 Mazée Belgium 50.06N 4.42E
46 D2 Mazeikiai Lithuania U.S.S.R. 56.19N 22.21E
61 G3 Mazenzele Belgium 50.57N 4.10E
100 D8 Mazeppa Alberta 50.42N 113.46W
95 M8 Mazeppa Bay S Africa 32.28S 28.39E
93 L9 Mazeras Kenya 3.58S 39.33E
72 H9 Mazères Ariège France 43.16N 1.40E
72 F9 Mazères-sur-Salat France 43.09N 0.58E
72 D9 Mazerolles France 43.27N 0.28E
71 E6 Mazet-St.-Voy France 45.03N 4.15E
72 E6 Mazeyrolles France 44.40N 1.01E
84 A2 Mázia Greece 39.40N 20.57E
32 C2 Mazīdābād Iran 36.11N 48.38E
37 E8 Mazı Dağ mt Turkey 37.20N 40.17E
37 E8 Mazıdağı Turkey 37.29N 40.29E
70 L7 Mazières Touraine France 47.23N 0.25E
72 D2 Mazières-en-Gâtine France 46.32N 0.19W
87 E5 Mazila Ethiopia 10.40N 34.33E
33 M5 Mazim Oman 23.26N 56.15E
Mazinan see Kalāteh-ye Mazinan
91 E6 Mazingu Zaïre 5.55S 16.39E
46 D1 Mazirbe Latvia U.S.S.R. 57.40N 22.21E
95 K1 Mazista S Africa 25.44S 26.45E
35 C6 Mazkeret Batya Israel 31.51N 34.50E
37 E6 Mazkirt Turkey 39.03N 39.35E
35 C6 Mazliaḥ Israel 31.54N 34.53E
87 D4 Mazmum,Jeb mt Sudan 12.18N 33.31E
96 P10 Mazo La Palma Canary Is 28.36N 17.46W
115 D3 Mazocahui Mexico 29.32N 110.09W
92 G7 Mazoco Mozambique 11.40S 35.48E
120 D7 Mazocruz Peru 16.45S 69.44W
92 E10 Mazoe Zimbabwe 17.30S 31.03E
92 E10 Mazoe dist Zimbabwe
92 E10 Mazoe R Zimbabwe
92 F10 Mazoi Mozambique 16.38S 33.07E
106 E6 Mazomanie Wisconsin 43.11N 89.49W
92 G5 Mazombe Tanzania 7.41S 35.53E
91 K6 Mazomeno Zaïre 4.54S 27.13E
106 F8 Mazon Illinois 41.14N 88.26W
22 D6 Mazong Shan mts Gansu China
35 C5 Mazor Israel 32.03N 34.55E
120 B4 Mazorca Lt Ho Peru 11.25S 77.46W
84 R15 Mazotos Cyprus 34.47N 33.30E
35 D6 Mazra'a Jordan 31.57N 35.09E
35 E5 Mazra'a Jordan 32.00N 35.16E
35 F8 Mazra'a Jordan 31.18N 35.32E
35 G2 Mazra'a Syria 32.54N 35.55E
86 O1 Mazraa esh Sharqiya Jordan 32.00N 35.16E
32 C2 Mazra'eh Iran 37.25N 48.16E
44 G9 Mazra'eh Mazāre Iran 38.38N 46.29E
35 F2 Mazra 'et Kanif Syria 32.52N 35.41E
87 B4 Mazrub Sudan 13.56N 29.20E
32 C4 Māzū Iran 32.45N 48.34E
23 J5 Mazu Dao isld Fujian China
23 J5 Mazu Liedao isld Fujian China 26.10N 119.59E
42 E4 Mazul'skiy U.S.S.R. 56.16N 90.22E
92 D12 Mazunga Zimbabwe 21.45S 29.52E
69 H4 Mazures,les France 49.54N 4.38E
62 M2 Mazury reg Poland
61 J4 Mazy Belgium 50.31N 4.40E
81 H9 Mazzarino Sicily 37.18N 14.13E
81 K7 Mazzarrà Sant' Andrea Sicily 38.06N 15.07E
81 J9 Mazzarrone R Sicily
88 M6 Mazzer Algeria 30.20N 2.18W
35 D1 Mazzuva Israel 33.04N 35.09E

9 S7 Mba Viti Levu Fiji 17.34S 177.40E
9 S7 Mba R Viti Levu Fiji
95 P2 Mbabane Swaziland 26.20S 31.08E
90 D9 Mbabon Cameroon 5.39N 9.01E
15 K2 Mbagha I Solomon Is 7.50S 156.31E
89 G8 Mbahiakro Ivory Coast 7.33N 4.19W
90 J10 Mbaiki Cent Afr Rep 3.53N 18.01E
90 F8 M'bakaou res Cameroon
89 B4 Mbaké Senegal 14.47N 15.54W
91 E3 M'Bako Congo 1.17N 16.27E
90 K8 M'Bala Cent Afr Rep 7.50N 20.50E
91 E3 Mbala Congo 0.40N 17.52E
92 E6 Mbala Zambia 8.50S 31.24E
92 G3 Mbalageti R Tanzania
93 F8 Mbalageti watercourse Tanzania
93 L6 Mbalambala Kenya 0.02S 39.03E
93 F4 Mbale Uganda 1.04N 34.12E
90 J9 M'Bali R Cent Afr Rep
90 E10 Mbalmayo Cameroon 3.30N 11.31E
90 E10 M'Balmayo R Cameroon
15 M3 Mbalo Guadalcanal I Solomon Is 9.55S 160.37E
90 E9 Mbam R Cameroon
91 D4 Mbama Congo 0.31S 15.03E
92 G7 Mbamba Bay Tanzania 11.18S 34.50E
91 D6 M'Bamou, I Congo 4.12S 15.25E
91 F3 Mbandaka Zaïre 0.03N 18.28E
91 B1 Mbandjok Cameroon 4.28N 11.58E
90 D9 Mbanga Cameroon 4.32N 9.31E
92 H6 Mbangala Tanzania 8.37S 36.31E
90 F8 Mbang,Mts Cameroon
91 B5 M'Banio,Lag Gabon
91 D7 M 'Banza Congo 6.18S 14.16E
91 D6 Mbanza-Ngungu Zaïre 5.17S 14.51E
93 B6 Mbarara Uganda 0.36S 30.40E
90 L9 M'Bari R Cent Afr Rep
92 H6 Mbarika mt Tanzania 9.20S 36.25E
15 L3 Mbarukua I Solomon Is 9.01S 158.15E
90 G8 Mbassai Chad 7.40N 15.35E
92 J6 Mbate Tanzania 8.55S 39.10E
9 U8 Mbatiki isld Fiji 17.47S 179.10E
9 T8 Mbau islet Fiji 17.55S 178.37E
91 D5 Mbé Congo 3.14S 15.50E
91 E2 M'Beï Cent Afr Rep 2.33N 17.09E
91 B3 Mbéi R Gabon
92 J7 Mbemba Tanzania 10.02S 38.31E
92 J6 Mbemkuru R Tanzania
91 D3 Mbèndza Congo 0.35N 14.18E
9 S8 Mbengga isld Viti Levu Fiji 18.24S 178.09E
9 T9 Mbengga Barrier Reef Fiji
91 A1 Mbengwi Cameroon 5.58N 9.56E
90 G8 Mbere R Cameroon etc
92 D6 Mbereshi Zambia 9.45S 28.50E
92 F7 Mbesuma Zambia 10.02S 32.08E
92 G10 Mbewe Malawi 16.10S 35.00E
92 F6 Mbeya Tanzania 8.54S 33.29E
92 F6 Mbeya mt Tanzania 8.50S 33.20E
92 F6 Mbeya reg Tanzania
90 H9 M'Bi R Cent Afr Rep
91 A2 Mbia R Equat Guinea
91 B4 Mbigou Gabon 1.54S 12.00E
87 B7 Mbili Sudan 7.35N 28.15E
91 C5 Mbinda Congo 2.11S 12.59E
92 H6 Mbindera Tanzania 9.35S 37.23E
92 G7 Mbinga Tanzania 10.56S 35.02E
92 H6 Mbinga Tanzania 8.51S 36.47E
91 A3 Mbini Equat Guinea 1.34N 9.38E
91 B3 Mbini, R Equat Guinea
93 B10 Mbirira Tanzania 4.20S 30.12E
93 C6 Mbirizi Uganda 0.24S 31.28E
15 M3 Mbita'ami Malaita I Solomon Is 8.20S 160.42E
92 E12 Mbizi Zimbabwe 21.23S 30.54E
91 G7 M'Boi Zaïre 6.57S 21.54E
90 N9 Mbokou R Cent Afr Rep
91 F4 Mbole tribe Zaïre
91 H1 M'Boli Zaïre 4.01N 23.17E
91 D3 Mbomo Congo 0.25N 14.42E
90 L9 Mbomou dist Cent Afr Rep
93 J7 Mbooni Hills Kenya
90 L9 Mbori Cent Afr Rep 5.05N 23.00E
89 A4 Mboro Senegal 15.09N 16.53W
87 A7 Mboro Sudan 7.39N 27.40E
91 E3 Mbou tribe Congo
91 D4 M'Boubou Congo 1.45S 15.10E
91 B1 Mbouda Cameroon 5.32N 10.12E
90 F8 Mboum tribe Cameroon
89 A4 M'Bour Senegal 14.22N 16.54W
89 C3 Mbout Mauritania 16.02N 12.38W
90 J8 M'Bres Cent Afr Rep 6.40N 19.46E
9 R5 Mbua Vanua Levu Fiji 16.49S 178.39E
91 E6 Mbudi Zaïre 5.42S 16.15E
91 H7 Mbuji Mayi Zaïre 6.10S 23.39E
93 E5 Mbulamuti Uganda 0.50N 33.05E
93 G9 Mbulu Tanzania 3.50S 35.32E
91 G11 Mbunda tribe Angola
92 G7 Mbunga Tanzania 10.10S 35.50E
92 G6 Mbungu tribe Tanzania
87 A8 Mbungu watercourse Sudan
121 F2 Mburucuyá Argentina 28.03S 58.15W
92 C2 Mbusi Zaïre 1.40S 27.51E
92 G3 Mbusi R Tanzania
15 C5 Mbuta,Danau L Irian Jaya 3.54S 134.33E
9 T5 Mbutha Vanua Levu Fiji 16.39S 179.51E
93 J9 Mbuyuni Kenya 3.25S 37.56E
92 J5 Mbwawa Tanzania 6.40S 38.47E
91 F11 Mbwela tribe Angola
92 J5 Mbwewe Tanzania 6.09S 38.20E
88 L8 Mcherrah tribe Algeria
92 J6 Mchinja Tanzania 9.44S 39.45E
92 F8 Mchinji Malawi 13.48S 32.55E
88 Q4 M'Chounèche Algeria 34.57N 5.59E
101 F5 M'Clintock Yukon Terr 60.33N 134.25W
97 M1 M'Clintock, C N-W Terr 80.05N 70.50W
97 M1 M'Clintock Inlet N W Terr
48 H3 M'Clure Str N W Terr Canada
92 F5 Mdabulo Tanzania 7.00S 33.19E
92 G5 Mdaburo Tanzania 6.14S 34.49E
92 G6 Mdandu Tanzania 9.09S 34.40E
78 B12 M'Daourouch Algeria 36.05N 7.50E
88 K10 Mdennah reg Mali/Mauritania
84 Y20 Mdina Malta 35.53N 14.15E
77 F9 Mdiq Morocco 35.41N 5.20W
88 Q4 M'Doukal Algeria 35.09N 5.05E
25 K6 Mdrak Vietnam 12.40N 108.48E
19 G4 Me isld Irian Jaya 0.05S 130.05E
110 G4 Meacham Oregon 45.31N 118.26W
100 M6 Meacham Saskatchewan 52.07N 105.47W
112 M9 Meacham Airport airport Fort Worth, Texas 32.47N 97.23W
99 G3 Mead Ontario 49.26N 83.53W
110 H2 Mead Washington 47.45N 117.20W
109 K4 Meade Kansas 37.17N 100.21W
113 J1 Meade R Alaska
110 O7 Meade Pk Idaho 42.30N 111.15W
Meade River see Atkasuk
58 G2 Meadie,L Highland Scotland 58.20N 4.34W
111 K5 Mead, L Nevada/Arizona
108 H4 Meadow S Dakota 45.30N 102.13W
112 E2 Meadow Texas 33.21N 102.14W
111 M3 Meadow Utah 38.52N 112.25W
14 A7 Meadow W Australia 26.40S 114.33E
101 Z3 Meadowbank R N W Terr
104 E9 Meadow Bridge W Virginia 37.53N 80.52W
112 M9 Meadowbrook Fort Worth, Texas 32.45N 97.13W
104 E9 Meadow Cr W Virginia 37.49N 80.55W
104 J8 Meadow Creek Maryland 38.42N 76.33W
100 J4 Meadow Lake Saskatchewan 54.09N 108.26W
100 H4 Meadow Lake Prov. Park Saskatchewan
108 S2 Meadowlands Minnesota 47.04N 92.42W
94 S13 Meadowlands S Africa 26.13S 27.54E
100 S7 Meadow Portage Manitoba 51.42N 99.37W
94 P12 Meadowridge Cape Town S Africa 34.01S 18.27E
110 J5 Meadows Idaho 44.58N 116.15W
95 K5 Meadows S Africa 29.30S 26.41E
108 F7 Meadowvale Wyoming 42.34N 104.42W
111 K4 Meadow Valley Mts Nevada
111 K5 Meadow Valley Wash R Nevada
107 F10 Meadville Mississippi 31.30N 90.55W
107 C2 Meadville Missouri 39.46N 93.20W
108 L7 Meadville Nebraska 42.46N 99.50W
104 E5 Meadville Pennsylvania 41.38N 80.10W
99 K8 Meaford Ontario 44.36N 80.35W
98 J9 Meaghers Grant Nova Scotia 44.57N 63.15W
21 K6 Me-akan dake mt Japan 43.24N 144.01E
76 C8 Mealhada Portugal 40.22N 8.27W
58 B2 Mealisval mt Lewis, W Isles Scotland 58.08N 7.05W
57 G3 Mealsgate Cumbria Eng 54.46N 3.14W
97 O7 Mealy Mts Labrador, Nfld
9 T12 Meama atoll Tonga, Pacific Oc 19.45S 174.35W
61 M5 Méan Belgium 50.22N 5.20E
43 F8 Meana Turkmeniya U.S.S.R. 36.55N 60.23E
81 C4 Meana Sardo Sardinia 39.57N 9.05E
13 J7 Meandarra Queensland 27.20S 149.55E
Meander R see Büyük Menderes R
101 P6 Meander River Alberta 59.02N 117.42W
76 B4 Meano Spain 42.26N 8.47W
110 B4 Meares,C Oregon 45.34N 123.56W
117 E7 Mearim, R Brazil
35 C3 Me'arot Karmel anc site Israel 32.41N 34.58E
106 H6 Mears Michigan 43.41N 86.25W
58 F3 Measach,Falls of Highland Scotland 57.45N 5.01W
56 J2 Measham Leics Eng 52.43N 1.29W
35 B1 Mea Shearim sub Jerusalem
72 H3 Méasnes France 46.25N 1.47E
59 J4 Meath co Irish Rep
59 G4 Meathas Troim Longford Irish Rep 53.42N 7.36W
100 M5 Meath Park Saskatchewan 53.27N 105.22W
72 K2 Meaulne France 46.36N 2.36E
69 D6 Meaux France 48.58N 2.54E
72 G7 Meauzac France 44.06N 1.14E

58 C2 Meavig Lewis, W Isles Scotland 58.12N 6.58W
105 H1 Mebane N Carolina 36.05N 79.16W
89 F3 Mebdoua Mauritania 17.29N 7.14W
91 C7 Mebridege, R Angola
74 G9 Mebtoub R Algeria
28 K1 Mebu Assam India 28.09N 95.26E
18 L10 Mebulu,Tandjung C Bali Indon 8.50S 115.04E
77 B5 Meca R Spain
110 S2 Mecaha Montana 47.20N 107.54W
92 G9 Mecanhelas Mozambique 15.10S 35.50E
98 O3 Mecatina I.,Gt Quebec 50.50N 58.52W
98 N3 Mecatina I.,Little Quebec 50.35N 59.20W
119 C7 Mecaya,R Colombia
111 H8 Mecca California 33.35N 116.03W
89 D8 Mecca Liberia 6.49N 10.37W
33 C6 Mecca Saudi Arabia 21.26N 39.49E
87 H6 Mecciara Ethiopia 8.36N 40.20E
104 P2 Mechanic Falls Maine 44.06N 70.24W
104 B6 Mechanicsburg Ohio 40.04N 83.34W
104 H6 Mechanicsburg Pennsylvania 40.13N 77.01W
103 B7 Mechanics Grove Pennsylvania 39.51N 76.10W
104 J8 Mechanicsville Maryland 38.25N 76.46W
104 M4 Mechanicville New York 42.55N 73.42W
107 F12 Mechant, L Louisiana 29.20N 90.55W
45 H7 Mechebilovo Ukraine U.S.S.R. 49.04N 36.42E
61 H2 Mechelen Belgium 51.02N 4.29E
60 T17 Mechelen Limburg Netherlands 50.47N 5.55E
Mechelen-aan-de Maas see Maasmechelen
90 L3 Mechera Chad 16.30N 22.27E
61 O7 Mecher-Dunkrodt Luxembourg 49.55N 5.53E
88 N5 Mecheria Algeria 33.31N 0.20W
64 B2 Mechernich W Germany 50.35N 6.39E
44 C1 Mechetinskaya U.S.S.R. 46.46N 40.29E
44 C1 Mechetka R U.S.S.R.
39 M2 Mechigmen U.S.S.R. 65.33N 172.02W
39 M2 Mechigmenskiy,Zaliv gulf U.S.S.R.
88 T6 Mechiguig Tunisia 30.58N 10.18E
64 Q3 Měcholupy Czechoslovakia 50.16N 13.32E
88 L4 Mechra bel Ksiri Morocco 34.38N 5.58W
88 K5 Mechra Benabbou Morocco 32.38N 7.48W
74 F10 Mechra-Saf-Saf Morocco 34.59N 2.40W
63 M6 Mechtersen W Germany 53.17N 10.19E
37 C2 Mecidiye Turkey 40.39N 26.33E
37 J1 Mecidiyeköyü Turkey 41.04N 29.00E
64 P5 Měčín Czechoslovakia 49.29N 13.25E
77 K7 Mecina Bombarón Spain 36.59N 3.09W
36 H2 Meçitözü Turkey 40.31N 35.17E
9 B3 Meck islet Marshall Is Pacific Oc 8.59N 167.44E
64 H8 Meckenbeuren W Germany 47.42N 9.35E
64 C2 Meckenheim Nordrhein-Westfalen W Germany 50.37N 7.02E
64 E5 Meckenheim Rheinland-Pfalz W Germany 49.25N 8.15E
64 F5 Meckesheim W Germany 49.20N 8.50E
103 C5 Meckesville Pennsylvania 41.00N 75.33W
63 O5 Mecklenburg E Germany 53.52N 11.27E
103 A2 Mecklenburg New York 42.27N 76.43W
63 O4 Mecklenburger Bucht B E Germany/W Germany
75 D6 Meco Spain 40.33N 3.20W
92 J9 Meconta Mozambique 15.00S 39.50E
106 J6 Mecosta Michigan 43.37N 85.14W
62 L9 Mecsek mts Hungary
92 J9 Mecuburi Mozambique 14.39S 38.54E
92 J9 Mecuburi R Mozambique
92 K8 Mecufi Mozambique 13.20S 40.32E
92 H8 Mecula Mozambique 12.05S 37.39E
92 E10 Mecumbura Mozambique 16.05S 31.35E
76 E7 Meda Portugal 40.58N 7.15W
26 T8 Medagama Sri Lanka 7.02N 81.17E
88 P5 Medaguine Algeria 33.39N 3.20E
28 D1 Medak Andhra Prad India 18.03N 78.15E
82 C6 Medak Yugoslavia 44.26N 15.31E
28 D2 Medak dist Andhra Prad India
18 C4 Medan Sumatra Indon 3.35N 98.39E
18 M10 Medang isld Indonesia 8.10S 117.25E
18 B9 Medang,Tandjung C Sumatra Indon 2.07N 101.39E
121 D3 Medano Argentina 31.20S 65.52W
96 R15 Médano,El Tenerife Canary Is 28.03N 16.32W
121 E7 Medanos Buenos Aires Arg 38.52S 62.45W
121 F4 Médanos Corrientes Arg 33.28S 59.07W
121 M7 Medanosa, Pta C Argentina 48.08S 65.55W
119 E2 Médanos,Istmo de isthmus Venezuela 11.37N 69.45W
14 E3 Meda,R W Australia
79 D2 Medaro,Pizzo pk Italy/Switz 46.14N 8.28E
106 H8 Medaryville Indiana 41.04N 86.53W
75 R3 Medas, I Spain 42.03N 3.14E
26 R4 Medawachchiya Sri Lanka 8.32N 80.30E
11 G9 Medbury New Zealand 42.53S 172.42E
28 D2 Medchal Andhra Prad India 17.41N 78.27E
60 P11 Meddo Netherlands 52.01N 6.42E
104 S1 Meddybemps L Maine
79 E4 Mede Italy 45.06N 8.44E
88 P3 Médéa Algeria 36.15N 2.48E
64 F1 Medebach W Germany 51.12N 8.44E
36 H5 Mededsiz mt Turkey 37.22N 34.36E
91 B3 Médegue Gabon 0.37N 10.08E
76 E8 Medelim Portugal 40.03N 7.11W
119 C4 Medellín Colombia 6.15N 75.36W
77 E3 Medellin Spain 38.58N 5.58W
66 M5 Medel, Piz Switzerland 46.37N 8.55E
66 M5 Medelserrhein R Switzerland
66 M5 Medel, Val Switzerland
63 J5 Medem R W Germany
60 J8 Medemblik Netherlands 52.47N 5.06E
88 T5 Medenine Tunisia 33.24N 10.25E
87 H3 Méder Ethiopia 14.42N 40.44E
89 B3 Mederdra Senegal 16.56N 15.40W
61 P7 Medernach Luxembourg 49.48N 6.13E
79 H5 Medesano Italy 44.45N 10.09E
103 M2 Medfield Massachusetts 42.12N 71.19W
103 H5 Medford Long I, N Y 40.49N 73.00W
103 M2 Medford Massachusetts 42.25N 71.05W
103 E7 Medford New Jersey 39.54N 74.50W
109 N5 Medford Oklahoma 36.48N 97.45W
110 C7 Medford Oregon 42.20N 122.52W
106 D4 Medford Wisconsin 45.08N 90.22W
104 P8 Medford dist Boston, Mass
113 K5 Medfra Alaska 63.05N 154.52W
82 L6 Medgidia Romania 44.15N 28.16E
50 G7 Medhalland dist Iceland
50 G8 Medhallandsfjörur coast Iceland
50 G8 Medhallandssandur sand reg Iceland
32 B3 Medhīkhan Iran 35.29N 47.46E
103 D7 Media Pennsylvania 39.56N 75.23W
121 C3 Media Agua Argentina 31.58S 68.25W
121 C5 Media Luna Argentina 34.45S 66.44W
75 J5 Mediana Spain 41.27N 0.43W
76 K7 Mediana Spain 40.41N 4.35W
75 L3 Mediano,Embalse de res Spain 42.21N 0.10E
106 C8 Mediapolis Iowa 41.00N 91.10W
82 J4 Mediaş Romania 46.10N 24.21E
110 H2 Medical Lake Washington 47.35N 117.39W
79 L6 Medicina Italy 44.28N 11.38E
108 D8 Medicine Bow Wyoming 41.53N 106.14W
108 D8 Medicine Bow R Wyoming
108 D8 Medicine Bow Mts Wyoming/Colorado
108 D8 Medicine Bow Pk Wyoming 41.22N 106.20W
100 G8 Medicine Hat Alberta 50.03N 110.41W
110 D8 Medicine L California 41.35N 121.36W
108 F1 Medicine L Montana
108 F1 Medicine L Montana 48.31N 104.30W
109 M4 Medicine Lodge Kansas 37.18N 98.35W
109 L4 Medicine Lodge R Kansas
112 H1 Medicine Mound Texas 34.12N 99.36W
100 C6 Medicine R Alberta
108 F4 Medicine Rocks Montana 45.59N 104.32W
66 C2 Médiere France 47.27N 6.36E
42 D6 Medigan U.S.S.R. 51.11N 86.15E
90 J2 Medimi Chad 19.04N 18.26E
118 H5 Medina Brazil 16.15S 41.32W
119 D5 Medina Colombia 4.31N 73.21W
108 L3 Medina N Dakota 46.56N 99.18W
104 G3 Medina New York 43.14N 78.23W
104 D5 Medina Ohio 41.07N 81.51W
33 C4 Medina Saudi Arabia 24.30N 39.35E
89 B5 Medina Senegal 13.35N 15.39W
75 Q3 Medina Spain 42.03N 2.52E
107 H6 Medina Tennessee 35.48N 88.48W
112 H6 Medina Texas 29.49N 99.18W
14 A4 Medina W Australia 32.14S 115.48E
112 H6 Medina R Texas
75 F5 Medinaceli Spain 41.10N 2.26W
77 D4 Medina de las Torres Spain 38.20N 6.25W
76 K6 Medina del Campo Spain 41.18N 4.55W
75 D2 Medina de Pomar Spain 42.55N 3.29W
76 J5 Medina de Rioseco Spain 41.53N 5.03W
89 C5 Médina Kouta Guinea 12.14N 12.11W
121 F2 Medina,L Argentina
112 H6 Medina L Texas 29.35N 98.58W
77 D7 Medina,L.de Spain 36.37N 6.03W
77 E8 Medina Sidonia Spain 36.28N 5.55W
89 D4 Médine Mali 14.20N 11.20W
26 T12 Medine Mauritius, Indian Oc 20.16S 57.22E
63 N6 Medingen W Germany 53.06N 10.33E
72 E10 Mediodia, P. del mt Spain 42.37N 0.13E
75 O5 Mediona Spain 41.29N 1.37E
88 K5 Mediouna Morocco 33.29N 7.29W
72 C4 Médis France 45.39N 0.58W
87 L5 Medishe Somalia 10.44N 47.39E
73 E2 Mediterranean Sea Europe/Africa
88 Q3 Medjana Algeria 36.09N 4.42E
87 A9 Medje Zaïre 2.25N 27.18E
88 P4 Medjedel Algeria 35.10N 3.42E
88 R3 Medjerda,Monts de la Algeria

82 H7 Medkovets Bulgaria 43.37N 23.10E
100 G4 Medley Alberta 54.25N 110.15W
101 S8 Medley Alberta 54.25N 110.17W
30 H7 Mednipur Bihar India 25.06N 84.24E
43 E2 Mednogorsk U.S.S.R. 51.23N 57.36E
41 F2 Mednyy,Mys C U.S.S.R. 79.02N 94.55E
39 H7 Mednyy,Ostrov isld Komandorskiye O-va U.S.S.R.
72 C5 Médoc reg France
24 H11 Mêdog Xizang Zizhiqu China 29.16N 95.18E
79 J4 Médole Italy 45.20N 10.30E
107 H6 Medon Tennessee 35.27N 88.51W
107 F2 Medora Illinois 39.11N 90.09W
109 N3 Medora Kansas 38.09N 97.52W
100 R9 Medora Manitoba 49.15N 100.41W
108 G3 Medora N Dakota 46.56N 103.40W
91 B3 Medouneu Gabon 0.58N 10.50E
70 F5 Médréac France 48.16N 2.05W
89 D3 Médroun Mauritania 17.10N 10.24W
100 J5 Medstead Saskatchewan 53.19N 108.05W
98 E7 Meductic New Brunswick 46.00N 67.30W
Medu Kongkar Dzong see Maizhokunggar
24 G9 Medu Kun mt pk Qinghai China
65 O9 Medumurje mts Yugoslavia
79 N3 Meduna R Italy
79 N2 Meduno Italy 46.13N 12.47E
103 F2 Medusa New York 42.26N 74.07W
82 G8 Medveda Yugoslavia 42.50N 21.32E
47 K6 Medvedchikovo U.S.S.R. 58.25N 68.21E
47 L5 Medvedevka U.S.S.R. 55.13N 59.31E
45 O7 Medveditsa R Volgograd U.S.S.R.
Medveditskoye see Linevo
46 Q2 Medvedok U.S.S.R. 57.22N 50.00E
44 C2 Medvedovskaya U.S.S.R. 45.27N 39.03E
45 H5 Medvenka U.S.S.R. 51.24N 36.08E
39 G1 Medvezh'i,Ostrova islds U.S.S.R.
41 C2 Medvezhiy,Mys C Novaya Zemlya U.S.S.R. 75.18N 62.21E
41 D2 Medvezhiy,Mys C Novaya Zemlya U.S.S.R. 76.47N 65.49E
41 P4 Medvezhiy,Mys C U.S.S.R. 74.39N 139.18E
39 G1 Medvezhiy Mys C Yakutsk U.S.S.R. 69.40N 162.58E
40 G4 Medvezhiy,Ostrov isld U.S.S.R. 54.40N 136.15E
41 F5 Medvezhiy Yar U.S.S.R. 70.32N 91.14E
41 B3 Medvezhiy,Zaliv gulf Novaya Zemlya U.S.S.R.
41 H5 Medvezh'ya R U.S.S.R.
40 G8 Medvezh'ya,Gora mt U.S.S.R. 47.26N 137.56E
40 L9 Medvezh'ye Kuril Is U.S.S.R. 45.20N 148.52E
47 L7 Medvezh'ye Omsk U.S.S.R. 55.06N 71.25E
47 C4 Medvezh'yegorsk U.S.S.R. 62.56N 34.28E
45 B7 Medvin Ukraine U.S.S.R. 49.25N 30.48E
46 H5 Medvin Ukraine U.S.S.R. 49.24N 30.49E
46 K2 Medvyeditsa R Kalinin U.S.S.R.
104 R1 Medway Maine 45.37N 68.32W
103 M2 Medway Massachusetts 42.09N 71.24W
103 G2 Medway New York 42.24N 73.53W
56 M5 Medway,R Kent Eng
26 V4 Medwin Pt Christmas I Ind Oc 10.32S 105.43E
45 G2 Medyn U.S.S.R. 54.59N 35.51E
46 F5 Medzhibozh Ukraine U.S.S.R. 49.29N 27.28E
62 N6 Medzilaborce Czechoslovakia 49.17N 21.50E
13 L1 Meeandah dist Brisbane, Qnsld 27.27S 153.07E
14 B7 Meeberrie W Australia 26.58S 115.51E
39 L2 Meechkyn Kosa sand spit U.S.S.R.
60 Q7 Meeden Netherlands 53.08N 6.56E
64 K3 Meeder W Germany 50.19N 10.56E
60 Q6 Meedhuizen Netherlands 53.17N 6.55E
61 L4 Meeffe Belgium 50.37N 5.01E
14 C7 Meekatharra W Australia 26.30S 118.30E
109 C1 Meeker Colorado 40.03N 107.56W
109 O6 Meeker Oklahoma 35.31N 96.56W
95 G8 Meelberg mt S Africa 32.11S 23.59E
61 K3 Meensel-Kiezegem Belgium 50.53N 4.55E
61 J1 Meer Belgium 51.27N 4.45E
60 M8 Meer Netherlands 52.58N 5.56E
64 N2 Meerane E Germany 50.50N 12.28E
61 G3 Meerbeke Belgium 50.49N 4.03E
63 E10 Meerbusch W Germany 51.20N 6.43E
69 M1 Meerbusch W Germany 51.15N 6.41E
61 G1 Meerdonk Belgium 51.16N 4.09E
64 B3 Meerfeld W Germany 50.05N 6.45E
64 G3 Meerholz W Germany 50.11N 9.12E
61 L2 Meerhout Belgium 51.08N 5.05E
60 H12 Meerkerk Netherlands 51.55N 5.00E
61 K1 Meerle Belgium 51.29N 4.48E
60 N13 Meerlo Netherlands 51.31N 6.06E
64 G8 Meersburg W Germany 47.42N 9.17E
60 T17 Meerssen Netherlands 50.53N 5.45E
30 A3 Meerut Uttar Prad India 29.00N 77.42E
30 A3 Meerut div Uttar Prad India
30 A4 Meerut dist Uttar Prad India
15 D5 Meervlakte river basin Irian Jaya
71 H8 Mées,les France 44.01N 5.58E
61 N3 Meeswijk Belgium 51.00N 5.45E
110 R5 Meeteetse Wyoming 44.10N 108.53W
100 E6 Meeting Creek Alberta 52.40N 112.42W
59 K6 Meeting-of-the-waters Wicklow Irish Rep 52.54N 6.13W
61 C2 Meetkerke Belgium 51.14N 3.09E
100 K5 Meetoos Saskatchewan 53.54N 107.55W
63 R5 Meetschow E Germany 53.50N 12.58E
61 N2 Meeuwen Belgium 51.06N 5.31E
60 H13 Meeuwen Netherlands 51.44N 5.00E
35 B7 Mefallesim Israel 31.30N 34.33E
87 G8 Mega Ethiopia 4.02N 38.19E
15 A4 Mega Irian Jaya 0.41S 131.53E
18 D7 Mega isld Indonesia 3.53S 100.57E
35 C3 Megadim Israel 32.43N 34.57E
84 C4 Méga Khorió Greece 38.50N 21.44E
84 C2 Megála Kalívia Greece 39.30N 21.48E
84 C2 Megáli Poliána Greece 39.31N 21.42E
83 J8 Megálo Khorió Greece 36.26N 27.24E
84 C2 Megálo Khorió Greece 39.33N 21.50E
84 D7 Megalópolis Greece 37.24N 22.08E
84 A4 Meganísi isld Greece
44 D10 Meganom,Mys C Ukraine U.S.S.R. 44.48N 35.06E
98 B8 Mégantic Quebec 45.34N 70.53W
84 B2 Méga Peristéri Greece 39.43N 21.04E
84 C5 Méga Pondiás Greece 38.04N 21.57E
84 F5 Mégara Greece 38.00N 23.20E
112 J2 Megargel Texas 33.27N 98.56W
84 C2 Megárkhi Greece 39.37N 21.39E
84 B1 Mégaron Greece 40.07N 21.17E
29 K7 Megasani Hill Orissa India 21.38N 86.26E
84 D5 Megaspílaion monastery Greece 38.05N 22.10E
60 O12 Megchelen Gelderland Netherlands 51.50N 6.24E
84 C4 Mégdhova R Greece
60 L12 Megen Netherlands 51.49N 5.35E
42 G6 Meget U.S.S.R. 52.25N 104.00E
71 K5 Megève France 45.51N 6.37E
66 C7 Mégevette France 46.13N 6.31E
66 K3 Meggen Switzerland 47.03N 8.24E
64 E1 Meggen W Germany 51.08N 8.05E
105 G5 Meggett S Carolina 32.43N 80.15W
88 Q5 Meghaier, El Algeria 33.58N 5.56E
28 H3 Meghalaya state India
30 J8 Meghatari Bihar India 24.35N 85.36E
31 H9 Meghna R Bangladesh
32 G1 Megin Turkmeniya U.S.S.R. 38.20N 57.40E
42 B2 Megion U.S.S.R. 61.03N 76.06E
99 P4 Mégiscane,L Quebec
83 K8 Megísti isld Greece 36.08N 29.35E
110 B3 Megler Washington 46.15N 123.52W
47 E3 Megra Arkhangel'sk U.S.S.R. 66.11N 41.38E
47 D5 Megra Vologda U.S.S.R. 60.11N 37.10E
47 D5 Megra Vologda U.S.S.R. 60.55N 36.02E
47 E3 Megra R U.S.S.R.
44 G9 Megri Armenia U.S.S.R. 38.54N 46.13E
88 M7 Megsem Drâa Algeria 29.33N 3.30W
90 H6 Méguédi Chad 11.34N 17.30E
88 O7 Meguidene reg Algeria
20 E3 Meguro dist Tōkyō Japan
82 G6 Mehadia Romania 44.53N 22.20E
61 K4 Mehaigne Belgium 50.36N 4.53E
61 K4 Mehaigne R Belgium
88 P5 Méhaïguène watercourse Algeria
88 K4 Mehaiya Morocco 34.20N 6.41W
18 L7 Mehakit Borneo Indon 2.50S 115.56E
51 N1 Mehamn Norway 71.00N 27.50E
31 D7 Mehar Pakistan 27.12N 67.51E
88 O6 Mehareg,El reg Algeria
30 B6 Mehda Madhya Prad India 26.25N 78.56E
30 G6 Mehdia Uttar Prad India 26.26N 83.27E
34 P1 Mehdikhān Iran 37.09N 47.12E
82 H6 Mehedinţi div Romania
85 M10 Meheisa Sudan 19.36N 32.57E
31 G9 Meherpur Bangladesh 23.47N 88.40E
104 G9 Meherrin Virginia 37.05N 78.23W
104 G10 Meherrin R Virginia
122 B15 Méhétia isld Society Is Pacific Oc 17.55S 148.02W
29 D6 Mehidpur Madhya Prad India 23.30N 75.42E
29 E7 Mehkar Maharashtra India 20.11N 76.39E
95 O6 Mehlomnyama S Africa 30.36S 30.22E
64 N2 Mehltheuer E Germany 50.32N 12.01E
29 C6 Mehmadabad Gujarat India 22.51N 72.46E
30 G7 Mehnajpur Khas Uttar Prad India 25.41N 83.07E
30 J7 Mehnar Bihar India 25.37N 85.29E
30 G6 Mehndawal Uttar Prad India 26.59N 83.06E
35 F4 Mehola Jordan 32.22N 35.30E
103 B3 Mehoopany Pennsylvania 41.34N 76.04W
30 J3 Mehra mt Nepal 27.57N 86.50E
32 E5 Mehrābād Fārs Iran 31.02N 53.20E
32 B2 Mehrābād Gīlān Iran 36.55N 47.58E
32 B1 Mehrābān Iran 38.03N 47.09E

32 F7 Mehrakān salt marsh Iran
32 B4 Mehrān Iran 33.07N 46.10E
32 F7 Mehrān R Iran
30 F7 Mehrawan Uttar Prad India 25.53N 82.41E
64 B3 Mehren W Germany 50.10N 6.54E
Mehrevan see Mehrābān
64 B4 Mehring W Germany 49.48N 6.49E
32 F5 Mehriz Iran 31.32N 54.28E
32 F4 Mehr Jān Iran 33.30N 55.08E
31 F3 Mehtar Lam Afghanistan 34.39N 70.10E
72 J1 Mehun-sur-Yèvre France 47.09N 2.13E
92 G4 Meia Meia Tanzania 5.50S 35.48E
118 E5 Meia Ponte, R Brazil
79 B6 Meia, Rocca la mt Italy 44.23N 7.04E
23 F4 Meichengzhen Hunan China 28.13N 111.39E
23 C1 Meichuan Gansu China 34.30N 104.05E
23 G3 Meichuan Hubei China 30.09N 115.35E
34 D2 Meidan Ekbes Syria 36.48N 36.41E
66 G7 Meiden Switzerland 46.13N 7.43E
87 A3 Meidob Hills Sudan
53 W19 Meien reg Norway
66 L5 Meien Tal V Switzerland
118 J9 Meier Brazil 22.55S 43.18W
Meifa'a see Mayfa'ah
56 E2 Meifod Powys Wales 52.43N 3.16W
90 G8 Meiganga Cameroon 6.30N 14.25E
61 E2 Meigem Belgium 51.01N 3.33E
97 K1 Meighen I N W Terr 80.00N 99.00W
58 K5 Meigle Tayside Scotland 56.35N 3.10W
58 G3 Meig, R Highland Scotland
105 C6 Meigs Georgia 31.04N 84.05W
106 S2 Meigs Field Airport Chicago, Illinois
23 C4 Meigu Sichuan China 28.16N 103.20E
Meihekou see Hailong
76 D3 Meijaboy Spain 42.53N 7.44W
60 M14 Meijel Netherlands 51.22N 5.53E
71 J6 Meije,la mt France 45.00N 6.18E
23 G7 Mei Jiang R Guangdong China
101 O7 Meikle R Alberta
58 K5 Meikleour Tayside Scotland 56.33N 3.24W
58 G4 Meiklie L Highland Scotland 57.19N 4.36W
25 C2 Meiktila Burma 20.53N 95.54E
66 L2 Meilen Switzerland 47.17N 8.39E
72 C8 Meilhan Landes France 43.51N 0.42W
72 E6 Meilhan-sur-Garonne France 44.31N 0.02E
72 H4 Meilhards France 45.34N 1.38E
Meili see Warzhong
Meilin see Gan Xian
70 G5 Meillac France 48.25N 1.49W
72 K2 Meillant France 46.47N 2.30E
70 H6 Meilleraye-de-Bretagne,la France 47.34N 1.24W
71 K4 Meillerie France 46.24N 6.43E
101 L5 Meilleur Cr N W Terr
72 D9 Meillon France 43.16N 0.18W
Meilü see Wuchuan
76 E8 Meimão Portugal 40.17N 7.07W
Meimeh see Meymeh
76 E8 Meimôa Portugal 40.14N 7.11W
79 E3 Meina Italy 45.47N 8.31E
63 N8 Meine W Germany 52.23N 10.32E
35 A1 Mei Neftoah sub Jerusalem
63 M8 Meinersen W Germany 52.28N 10.22E
64 D1 Meinerzhagen W Germany 51.07N 7.40E
64 J1 Meinhard W Germany 51.12N 10.00E
65 A7 Meiningen Austria 47.18N 9.37E
64 J2 Meiningen E Germany 50.34N 10.25E
66 F3 Meinisberg Switzerland 47.10N 7.21E
118 J10 Meio,I.do Brazil 23.02S 43.17W
57 J7 Meir Staffs Eng 52.59N 2.06W
76 E2 Meira Spain 43.13N 7.17W
76 E2 Meira,Sierra de mts Spain
66 J5 Meiringen Switzerland 46.44N 8.12E
35 C3 Me'ir Shefeya Israel 32.36N 34.58E
76 B4 Meis Spain 42.29N 8.44W
61 H3 Meise Belgium 50.56N 4.20E
64 D4 Meisenheim W Germany 49.42N 7.40E
Meishan see Jinzhai
23 C3 Meishan Sichuan China 30.02N 103.23E
23 G3 Meishan Sk res Anhui China 31.51N 115.57E
35 F1 Meiss ej Jebel Lebanon 33.10N 35.31E
64 P1 Meissen E Germany 51.10N 13.28E
63 L7 Meissendorf W Germany 52.44N 9.50E
64 H1 Meissner mt W Germany 51.14N 9.52E
66 J2 Meisterschwanden Switzerland 47.18N 8.14E
23 D5 Meitan Guizhou China 27.46N 107.25E
35 E4 Meithalun Jordan 32.21N 35.16E
64 K6 Meitingen W Germany 48.32N 10.52E
61 M8 Meix-devant-Virton Belgium 49.37N 5.29E
23 G6 Mei Xian Guangdong China 24.19N 116.13E
23 D1 Mei Xian Shaanxi China 34.12N 107.50E
61 N8 Meix-le-Tige Belgium 49.37N 5.43E
21 B5 Meiyao Jilin China 45.46N 121.48E
29 D5 Mej R Rajasthan India
30 F7 Meja Uttar Prad India 25.09N 82.06E
Mejanodas see Meyanobab
88 K10 Méjaouda Mauritania 22.33N 7.07W
9 A3 Mejatta islet Marshall Is Pacific Oc 9.05N 166.55E
78 C12 Mejaz el-Bab Tunisia 36.39N 9.40E
71 C8 Méjean,Causse plat France
78 C12 Mejerda R Tunisia
88 S3 Mejerda R Tunisia
88 S3 Mejez el Bab Tunisia 36.40N 9.35E
121 C2 Mejicana pk Argentina 29.00S 67.50W
120 D10 Mejillones Chile 23.03S 70.25W
120 D10 Mejillones del Sur,B.de Chile
9 D1 Mejit atoll Marshall Is Pacific Oc 10.19N 170.40E
76 K8 Mejorada Spain 40.01N 4.54W
53 B4 Mejrup Denmark 56.22N 8.42E
88 N5 Mékalis Algeria 33.01N 0.30W
91 C3 Mekambo Gabon 1.03N 13.50E
99 F5 Mekatina Ontario 47.05N 84.07W
46 P8 Mekege U.S.S.R. 42.19N 47.33E
88 N4 Mekerra R Algeria
87 G4 Meketoa Ethiopia 12.04N 38.28E
89 A4 Mekhé Senegal 15.02N 16.40W
44 H5 Mekhel'ta U.S.S.R. 42.47N 46.34E
47 J7 Mekhonskoye U.S.S.R. 56.12N 64.30E
31 E5 Mekhtar Pakistan 30.28N 69.26E
108 N1 Mekinock N Dakota 48.02N 97.23W
122 S15 Mekiro isld Gambier Is Pacific Oc 23.11S 134.54W
88 L5 Meknès Morocco 33.53N 5.37W
90 A8 Meko Nigeria 7.28N 2.55E
Mekoahe isld see Balontohe
Mekong R see Lancang Jiang
25 F3 Mekong R Laos
19 B5 Mekongga, Gunung mt Celebes Indon 3.39S 121.15E
19 B6 Mekongga,Teluk B Celebes Indon
25 J8 Mekong,Mouths of the Vietnam
91 B3 Mekongo Gabon 0.57N 11.39E
35 E5 Mekora Jordan 32.10N 35.25E
113 D6 Mekoryuk Alaska 60.20N 166.20W
89 L6 Mekrou R Benin etc
79 M2 Mel Italy 46.04N 12.05E
90 L7 Mela,Djebel mt Cent Afr Rep 8.27N 23.20E
28 C4 Melagiri Hills Tamil Nadu India
88 Q4 Melah watercourse Algeria
88 N5 Melah,Djebel mt Morocco 32.23N 1.33W
88 O5 Melah,el R Algeria
85 A3 Melah,Sebkha el salt marsh Tunisia
18 C10 Melaka Pen Malaysia 2.14N 102.14E
18 C9 Melaka state Pen Malaysia
18 L3 Melalap Sabah Malaysia 5.14N 115.59E
18 F6 Melala, Tanjung C Indon 1.31S 105.36E
84 L11 Mélambes Crete 35.08N 24.40E
53 S17 Meland Norway 60.33N 5.10E
9 L8 Melanesia ethnic reg Pacific Oc
10 P4 Melanesian Border Plat Pacific Oc
66 M8 Melano Switzerland 45.55N 8.59E
50 C6 Melar Borgarfjardharsýsla Iceland 64.25N 22.02W
50 D4 Melar Strandasýsla Iceland 65.07N 21.05W
87 F4 Melau mt Ethiopia 13.38N 37.28E
18 M3 Melaut R Sabah Malaysia
100 L9 Melaval Saskatchewan 49.42N 106.22W
18 K6 Melawi R Borneo Indon
69 K8 Melay Haute-Marne France 47.54N 5.49E
72 C1 Melay Maine-et-Loire France 47.12N 0.41W
71 E4 Melay Saône-et-Loire France 46.13N 4.00E
18 F2 Melayu R Pen Malaysia
79 D5 Melazzo Italy 44.38N 8.26E
110 J6 Melba Idaho 43.24N 116.33W
87 G9 Melbana,El Ethiopia 3.50N 38.30E
63 M6 Melbeck W Germany 53.10N 10.24E
58 D2 Melbost Lewis, W Isles Scotland 58.13N 6.20W
56 M3 Melbourn Cambs Eng 52.05N 0.01E
56 J2 Melbourne Derbys Eng 52.49N 1.25W
105 G9 Melbourne Florida 28.04N 80.38W
108 R8 Melbourne Iowa 41.56N 93.03W
12 G7 Melbourne Victoria 37.45S 144.58E
105 G9 Melbourne Beach Florida 28.04N 80.33W
101 V1 Melbourne I N W Terr 68.34N 104.40W
51 D3 Melbu Norway 68.31N 14.50E
56 G6 Melbury Abbas Dorset Eng 50.59N 2.10W
53 H5 Melby Denmark 55.59N 11.59E
58 P9 Melby Shetland Scotland 60.18N 1.40W
53 K3 Melbystrand Sweden 56.30N 13.00E
108 R8 Melcher Iowa 41.14N 93.15W
50 U15 Melchers,Kapp Spitsbergen 77.53N 24.15E
99 D2 Melchett L Ontario 50.43N 87.34W
30 F3 Melchham Nepal 29.47N 82.01E
66 H3 Melchnau Switzerland 47.11N 7.52E
115 P9 Melchor de Mencos Guatemala 17.03N 89.12W
121 J5 Melchor, I Chile 45.10S 74.00W
115 J5 Melchor Ocampo Coahuila Mexico 24.52N 101.40W
66 K4 Melch Tal V Switzerland
66 K4 Melchthal Switzerland 46.51N 8.18E
52 E3 Meldal Norway 63.03N 9.45E
61 E3 Melden Belgium 50.49N 3.34E
53 U19 Melderskin mt Norway 60.00N 6.05E
51 J6 Melderstein Sweden 65.56N 22.14E
61 L2 Meldert Limburg Belgium 51.00N 5.09E

61 G3 Meldert Oost Vlaanderen Belgium 50.56N 4.08E
79 M6 Méldola Italy 44.07N 12.03E
63 K4 Meldorf W Germany 54.06N 9.04E
105 F5 Meldrim Georgia 32.09N 81.23W
99 G7 Meldrum Bay Ontario 45.55N 83.09W
100 U8 Meleb Manitoba 50.43N 97.12W
79 D7 Mele,Capo C Italy 43.58N 8.11E
76 C15 Meleças Portugal 38.48N 9.18W
87 M5 Meleden Somalia 10.27N 49.50E
79 F4 Melegnano Italy 45.22N 9.19E
19 N2 Melekeiok Palau Is Pacific Oc 7.30N 134.39E
45 V2 Melekess U.S.S.R. 54.14N 49.37E
47 H6 Melekhina U.S.S.R. 59.18N 55.01E
45 N1 Melekhovo U.S.S.R. 56.16N 41.19E
18 K10 Meleman Java Indon 8.18S 113.22E
87 B6 Melemm,El Sudan 9.51N 28.45E
61 N4 Melen Belgium 50.38N 5.44E
36 E2 Melen R Turkey
96 V15 Melenara Gran Canaria Canary Is 28.00N 15.22W
36 G4 Melendiz Dağları mts Turkey
81 R12 Melendugno Italy 40.16N 18.21E
45 N1 Melenki U.S.S.R. 55.20N 41.40E
47 M6 Melent'yevskoye U.S.S.R. 55.04N 60.04E
70 G5 Melesse France 48.13N 1.40W
70 L4 Mêle-sur-Sarthe,le France 48.31N 0.22E
Melet see Mesudiye Ordu Turkey
42 E4 Meletsk U.S.S.R. 57.27N 90.14E
43 D1 Meleuz Bashkir U.S.S.R. 52.58N 55.56E
88 H10 Melezem Mauritania 22.19N 11.25W
66 L7 Melezza R Switzerland
104 K9 Melfa Virginia 37.38N 75.47W
80 J5 Melfa R Italy
90 H6 Melfi Chad 11.05N 17.57E
80 N7 Melfi Italy 41.00N 15.33E
100 N6 Melfort Saskatchewan 52.52N 104.38W
92 E10 Melfort Zimbabwe 18.00S 31.25E
117 D5 Melgaço Brazil 1.45S 50.45W
76 C4 Melgaço Portugal 42.07N 8.15W
76 J4 Melgar de Arriba Spain 42.15N 5.06W
76 L4 Melgar de Fernamental Spain 42.24N 4.15W
29 E7 Melghat Maharashtra India 21.44N 77.12E
50 C2 Melgraseyri Iceland 66.02N 22.26W
45 M4 Mel'guny U.S.S.R. 52.09N 40.50E
70 C6 Melgven France 47.55N 3.50W
89 C2 Melhes,El Mauritania 18.18N 13.51W
59 K4 Melhfont Abbey Louth Irish Rep 53.45N 6.27W
53 E2 Melholt Denmark 57.07N 10.23E
52 E3 Melhus Norway 63.17N 10.18E
89 D7 Meli R Sierra Leone
84 E2 Melía Greece 39.34N 22.37E
75 K8 Meliana Spain 39.32N 0.21W
18 J6 Meliau Borneo Indonesia 0.07S 110.17E
64 F4 Melibocus mt W Germany 49.44N 8.41E
60 U16 Melick Netherlands 51.09N 6.00E
70 M4 Melicourt France 48.54N 0.31E
75 G3 Mélida Spain 42.22N 1.33W
66 M8 Melide Switzerland 45.57N 8.57E
76 B12 Melides Portugal 38.08N 8.43W
118 E9 Mel,I.do Brazil 25.32S 48.23W
84 C7 Meligalá Greece 37.13N 21.58E
37 G5 Melik Turkey 40.40N 43.05E
45 M9 Melikhovskaya U.S.S.R. 47.30N 40.30E
93 H6 Melili mt Kenya 0.44S 36.06E
19 C4 Melilis isld Indonesia 1.53S 123.24E
88 M4 Melilla Spain 35.20N 3.00W
81 K9 Melilli Sicily 37.12N 15.08E
35 B8 Melilot Israel 31.23N 34.36E
37 D2 Melima Burun C Marmara I Turkey 40.37N 27.32E
121 A10 Melimoyu,Monte pk Chile 44.05S 72.55W
61 K4 Mélin Belgium 50.44N 4.50E
11 D11 Melina,Mt New Zealand 44.26S 169.35E
82 H6 Melineşti Romania 44.33N 23.42E
18 M6 Melintang,Danau L Borneo Indon
121 B4 Melipilla Chile 33.42S 71.15W
69 M8 Mélisey France 47.46N 6.35E
60 B2 Meliskerke Netherlands 51.31N 3.31E
81 O5 Melissa Italy 39.18N 17.02E
60 E12 Melissant Netherlands 51.46N 4.03E
84 E5 Melissi Korinthía Greece 38.03N 22.41E
84 C2 Melíssi Kozáni Greece 39.58N 21.30E
84 E2 Melissokhóri Greece 39.38N 22.30E
100 R9 Melita Manitoba 49.16N 100.59W
Melitene anc site see Malatya
81 L8 Melito di Porto Salvo Italy 37.56N 15.47E
45 G10 Melitopol' Ukraine U.S.S.R. 46.51N 35.22E
103 B8 Melitota Maryland 39.17N 76.10W
65 M5 Melk Austria 48.14N 15.21E
95 H8 Melk R S Africa
93 K5 Melka Lorni Kenya 0.11N 38.29E
31 D5 Mel Karez Afghanistan 31.12N 66.10E
95 B9 Melkbosstrand S Africa 33.44S 18.26E
95 E10 Melkhoutfontein S Africa 34.20S 21.25E
56 G5 Melksham Wilts Eng 51.23N 2.09W
61 L3 Melkwezer Belgium 50.49N 5.03E
79 H4 Mella R Italy
88 K5 Mellah R Morocco
77 F9 Mellaliyne,El Morocco 35.38N 5.21W
52 J4 Mellansjö Sweden 62.19N 15.40E
66 Q2 Mellau Austria 47.22N 9.53E
61 F2 Melle Belgium 51.00N 3.48E
72 D3 Melle France 46.13N 0.08W
79 B5 Melle Italy 44.33N 7.19E
63 H8 Melle W Germany 52.13N 8.20E
88 S3 Mellégue R Tunisia
106 D3 Mellen Wisconsin 46.21N 90.40W
66 Q2 Mellen R Austria
63 L7 Mellendorf W Germany 52.33N 9.44E
103 G2 Mellenville New York 42.15N 73.40W
59 G7 Melleray Monastery Waterford Irish Rep 52.13N 7.51W
52 G8 Mellerud Sweden 58.42N 12.27E
53 E3 Mellerup Denmark 56.32N 10.13E
61 D4 Melles Belgium 50.39N 3.30E
61 H4 Mellet Belgium 50.30N 4.28E
108 M4 Mellette S Dakota 45.09N 98.30W
36 E5 Melli Turkey 37.19N 30.45E
76 C3 Mellid Spain 42.55N 8.01W
84 Y20 Mellieha Malta 35.58N 14.22E
84 Y20 Mellieha B Malta
61 N7 Mellier Belgium 49.47N 5.32E
64 L2 Mellingen E Germany 50.56N 11.22E
66 K2 Mellingen Switzerland 47.25N 8.16E
87 H5 Melli,R Ethiopia
122 J4 Mellish Bank Pacific Oc 34.00N 178.12E
10 M5 Mellish Reef Coral Sea 17.28S 155.55E
10 L5 Mellish Rise Coral Sea
90 M4 Mellit Sudan 14.07N 25.34E
121 J7 Mellizo Sur,Cerro pk Chile 48.35N 73.45W
87 J5 Mello Ethiopia 10.03N 42.00E
57 H5 Mellor Brook Lancs Eng 53.47N 2.33W
88 P9 Mellouline Algeria 24.45N 3.09E
77 E9 Melloussa Morocco 35.45N 5.39W
64 J3 Mellrichstadt W Germany 50.26N 10.19E
9 B2 Mellu islet Marshall Is Pacific Oc 9.20N 167.26E
63 H5 Mellum isld W Germany
95 P5 Mellville S Africa 29.22S 31.15E
107 F7 Mellwood Arkansas 34.13N 90.59W
57 H3 Melmerby Cumbria Eng 54.44N 2.35W
95 P4 Melmoth S Africa 28.35S 31.25E
58 H1 Melness Highland Scotland 58.31N 4.26W
41 E7 Mel'nichnaya U.S.S.R. 65.29N 88.08E
82 H9 Melnik Bulgaria 41.30N 23.22E
43 M8 Mel'nikovo Tadzhikistan U.S.S.R. 40.20N 70.24E
42 C4 Mel'nikovo U.S.S.R. 56.39N 84.11E
82 K2 Melnitsa Podolskaya U.S.S.R. 48.37N 26.11E
121 D5 Melo Argentina 34.27S 63.25W
76 D7 Melo Portugal 40.31N 7.32W
121 G4 Melo Uruguay 32.22S 54.10W
92 J8 Melôco Mozambique 13.30S 39.13E
47 F3 Melogorskoye U.S.S.R. 65.25N 45.10E
19 B8 Melolo Indonesia 9.55S 120.41E
76 C4 Melón Spain 42.15N 8.13W
77 K7 Melonar,Pta pt Spain 36.44N 3.21W
111 D4 Melones Res California 37.58N 120.30W
91 A1 Mélong Cameroon 5.03N 9.56E
79 H7 Meloria,Torre della isld Italy 43.32N 10.10E
44 L4 Melovay,Mys C Kazakhstan U.S.S.R. 43.37N 51.12E
45 M7 Melovoye U.S.S.R. 49.21N 40.08E
51 C5 Meløy Norway 66.50N 13.25E
113 K4 Melozitna R Alaska
50 L5 Melrakkanes Iceland 64.36N 14.29W
50 K2 Melrakkanès C Iceland 66.24N 15.40W
50 J2 Melrakkaslétta pen Iceland
70 D6 Melrand France 47.58N 3.07W
76 C9 Melrica mt Portugal 39.43N 8.08W
74 G9 Melrir R Algeria
57 H1 Melrose Borders Scotland 53.36N 2.44W
110 J3 Melrose Idaho 46.26N 116.26W
108 Q4 Melrose Minnesota 45.40N 94.46W
110 N4 Melrose Montana 45.37N 112.41W
109 G7 Melrose New Mexico 34.26N 103.38W
98 K8 Melrose Nova Scotia 45.15N 62.03W
110 B6 Melrose Oregon 43.16N 123.29W
14 D8 Melrose W Australia 27.57S 121.16E
106 C5 Melrose Wisconsin 44.07N 91.01W
104 Q8 Melrose dist Boston
66 O3 Mels Switzerland 47.03N 9.26E
61 H3 Melsbroek Belgium 50.55N 4.29E
61 H2 Melsele Belgium 51.13N 4.17E
61 E3 Melsen Belgium 50.57N 3.42E
58 S12 Melsetter Orkney Scotland 58.47N 3.16W
92 F11 Melsetter Zimbabwe 19.48S 32.50E
92 F11 Melsetter dist Zimbabwe
53 V16 Melsnipa mt Norway 61.21N 6.36E
57 K4 Melsonby N Yorks Eng 54.28N 1.41W
50 E4 Melstadhur Iceland 65.20N 20.55W
53 P12 Melsted Bornholm Denmark 55.13N 14.59E
110 S3 Melstone Montana 46.36N 107.50W
106 H3 Melstrand Michigan 46.28N 86.25W
64 H1 Melsungen W Germany 51.08N 9.32E
18 M3 Melta mt Sabah Malaysia 5.40N 117.17E
51 L5 Meltaus Finland 66.55N 25.20E
57 K5 Meltham W Yorks Eng 53.36N 1.52W
56 O3 Melton Suffolk Eng 52.06N 1.20E
56 K2 Melton Mowbray Leics Eng 52.46N 0.53W
51 L5 Meltosjärvi Finland 66.29N 24.34E
45 Q2 Mel'tsan U.S.S.R. 54.27N 44.44E
18 J5 Meluan Sarawak Malaysia 1.54N 111.55E
92 J8 Meluco Mozambique 12.31S 39.39E
92 J10 Meluli R Mozambique
25 B2 Melun Burma 20.15N 93.25E
69 D6 Melun France 48.32N 2.40E
30 K5 Melung Nepal 27.32N 86.02E
91 E12 Melunga Angola 17.17S 16.27E
28 D5 Melur Tamil Nadu India 10.04N 78.23E
87 D5 Melut Sudan 10.27N 32.13E
58 E3 Melvaig Highland Scotland 57.48N 5.49W
109 P3 Melvern Kansas 38.31N 95.38W
109 P3 Melvern, Lake Kansas
58 J1 Melvich Highland Scotland 58.33N 3.55W
103 H5 Melville Long I, N Y 40.48N 73.25W
107 E11 Melville Louisiana 30.41N 91.48W
110 Q3 Melville Montana 46.06N 109.58W
108 L2 Melville N Dakota 47.21N 99.02W
100 P8 Melville Saskatchewan 50.57N 102.49W
13 D1 Melville B N Terr Australia
48 T4 Melville Bugt B Greenland
13 G2 Melville, C Queensland 14.08S 144.31E
19 H8 Melville,Cape Philippines 7.56N 117.01E
101 N1 Melville Hills N W Terr
13 B1 Melville I N Terr Australia
97 H2 Melville I N W Terr 75.30N 112.00W
48 T4 Melville,Kap C Greenland 76.08N 63.30W
97 O7 Melville,L Labrador, Nfld 53.30N 60.00W
48 T2 Melville Land Greenland
97 L4 Melville Pen N W Terr
101 T1 Melville Sd N W Terr
14 A1 Melville Water B Perth, W Aust
112 H4 Melvin Texas 31.12N 99.36W
106 L3 Melvindale dist Detroit, Michigan
107 L6 Melvine Tennessee 35.44N 85.04W
59 F3 Melvin L Irish Rep 54.25N 8.10W
100 R1 Melvin L Manitoba
62 L9 Mélykút Hungary 46.11N 19.23E
39 J4 Melyuveyem U.S.S.R. 61.59N 174.44E
79 F4 Melzo Italy 45.30N 9.25E
18 K6 Memala Borneo Indon 1.42S 112.40E
25 J6 Meman Cambodia 13.05N 106.54E
15 H4 Meman I Bismarck Arch 1.12S 144.20E
19 D1 Memanuk isld Indonesia 4.34N 125.35E
24 D8 Mêmar Co L Xizang Zizhiqu China 34.10N 82.15E
29 L2 Memari W Bengal India 23.10N 88.07E
Memar Tsaka L see Mêmar Co
92 K9 Memba Mozambique 14.10S 40.30E
92 K9 Memba,B.de Mozambique
34 E2 Membij Syria 36.32N 37.55E
19 A8 Memboro Indonesia 9.25S 119.34E
61 K7 Membre Belgium 49.52N 4.54E
71 H1 Membrey France 47.36N 5.44E
77 K3 Membrilla Spain 38.59N 3.21W
76 K3 Membrillar Spain 42.33N 4.42W
75 E6 Membrillera Spain 40.57N 3.00W
76 E9 Membrio Spain 39.31N 7.03W
70 M7 Membrolle,la France 47.26N 0.39E
61 N3 Membruggen Belgium 50.49N 5.32E
90 D9 Meme R Cameroon
Memel see Klaipėda
95 N3 Memel S Africa 27.41S 29.35E
89 H6 Méméré Upper Volta 11.12N 2.52W
63 E5 Memmert isld W Germany
64 J8 Memmingen W Germany 47.59N 10.11E
18 L3 Mempakul Sabah Malaysia 5.20N 115.24E
18 H5 Mempawah Borneo Indonesia 0.23N 108.56E
107 D1 Memphis Missouri 40.28N 92.11W
107 G6 Memphis Tennessee 35.10N 90.00W
112 G1 Memphis Texas 34.43N 100.34W
86 F6 Memphis ruins Egypt 29.52N 31.12E
99 T7 Memphrémagog,L Quebec/New York
98 H7 Memramcook New Brunswick 46.00N 64.34W
20 M2 Memuro Japan 42.55N 143.02E
20 M2 Memuro-dake mt Japan 42.53N 142.44E
53 Y15 Memurubre glacier Norway 61.34N 8.30E
53 Z16 Memurubu Norway 61.30N 8.35E
107 B7 Mena Arkansas 34.40N 94.15W
19 D8 Mena Timor Indonesia 9.12S 124.36E
45 D5 Mena Ukraine U.S.S.R. 51.30N 32.15E
121 F4 Menafra Uruguay 32.33S 57.30W
79 F2 Menaggio Italy 46.02N 9.14E
95 D5 Menagisy Madagascar 19.59S 48.40E
Menahamiya see Menaḥemya
35 A2 Menahat sub Jerusalem
35 F3 Menaḥemya Israel 32.40N 35.33E
108 P3 Menahga Minnesota 46.45N 95.05W
57 E6 Menai Bridge Gwynedd Wales 53.14N 4.10W
57 E6 Menai Str Gwynedd Wales 53.14N 4.10W
89 L4 Ménaka Mali 15.54N 2.18E
90 K3 Ménakin Chad 17.40N 21.54E
60 L7 Menaldum Netherlands 53.13N 5.40E
89 G5 Menamba Mali 12.25N 4.42W
19 D4 Menanga Moluccas Indon 1.41S 124.52E
110 O4 Menard Montana 45.59N 111.10W
112 H5 Menard Texas 30.56N 99.48W
76 L9 Menasalbas Spain 39.39N 4.17W
106 F5 Menasha Wisconsin 44.12N 8.27W
98 L2 Menaskwagama,L Quebec
71 B4 Menat France 46.06N 2.53E
72 K3 Menat France 46.07N 2.54E
18 K6 Menate Borneo Indon 0.14S 113.03E
79 L5 Menate Italy 44.36N 12.00E
69 J6 Menaucourt France 48.39N 5.22E
90 M5 Menawashei Sudan 12.41N 24.59E
77 K5 Mencal mt Spain 37.30N 3.11W
121 B8 Mencue Argentina 40.20S 69.36W
18 G7 Mendanau isld Indonesia
118 G6 Mendanha Brazil 18.06S 43.30W
29 B7 Mendarda Gujarat India 21.19N 70.26E
18 G5 Mendarik isld Indonesia 1.19N 107.05E
79 C6 Mendática Italy 44.05N 7.48E
75 F3 Mendavia Spain 42.27N 2.11W
18 K7 Mendawai Borneo Indonesia 3.00S 113.17E
18 K7 Mendawai R Borneo Indon
71 C7 Mende France 44.32N 3.30E
30 G3 Mende Nepal 27.50N 86.42E
87 G7 Mendebo Mts Ethiopia
32 C2 Mendejīn Iran 37.22N 48.08E
42 E3 Mendel' R U.S.S.R.
41 C2 Mendeleyeva,Gory mts Novaya Zemlya U.S.S.R.
40 K10 Mendeleyevka vol Kuril Is U.S.S.R. 43.59N 145.42E
46 Q2 Mendeleyevsk U.S.S.R. 55.54N 52.20E
63 G10 Menden W Germany 51.26N 7.47E
107 G10 Mendenhall Mississippi 31.58N 89.54W
113 D7 Mendenhall C Alaska 59.45N 166.10W
113 U7 Mendenhall Glacier Alaska 58.27N 134.11W
83 J7 Menderes Büyük R Turkey
83 H5 Menderes,Kanal R Turkey
83 J6 Menderes Küçük R Turkey
43 J2 Mendesh Kazakhstan U.S.S.R. 51.00N 67.45E
119 B9 Mendez Ecuador 2.44S 78.19W
115 K5 Méndez Mexico 25.05N 98.32W
19 H2 Mendez-Nuñez Luzon Philippines 14.07N 120.54E
103 E5 Mendham New Jersey 40.47N 74.37W
100 H8 Mendham Saskatchewan 50.46N 109.38W
87 E6 Mendi Ethiopia 9.47N 35.04E
15 G7 Mendi Papua New Guinea 6.13S 143.39E
64 C3 Mendig W Germany 50.22N 7.17E
76 B9 Mendiga Portugal 39.30N 8.50W
75 G2 Mendigorria Spain 42.37N 1.50W
56 F5 Mendip Hills Avon/Somerset Eng
72 C9 Menditte France 43.10N 0.54W
14 D8 Mendleyarri W Australia 29.40S 121.40E
111 A2 Mendocino California 39.20N 123.46W
110 A9 Mendocino,C California 40.26N 124.24W
122 M4 Mendocino Seascarp Pacific Oc
79 K2 Mendola Italy 46.25N 11.13E
81 F8 Mendola R Sicily
103 L2 Mendon Massachusetts 42.07N 71.33W
106 J7 Mendon Michigan 42.02N 85.28W
104 A6 Mendon Ohio 40.40N 84.31W
Mendong Gompa see Coqên
12 J4 Mendooran New S Wales 31.50S 149.08E
111 D5 Mendota California 36.44N 120.24W
106 E8 Mendota Illinois 41.33N 89.09W
112 D8 Mendota Texas 35.49N 100.30W
106 E6 Mendota,L Wisconsin 43.05N 89.23W
121 C4 Mendoza Argentina 32.48S 68.52W
120 F7 Mendoza Bolivia 16.55S 65.53W
120 B2 Mendoza Peru 6.19S 77.28W
120 B10 Mendoza dist Lima Peru
121 C5 Mendoza prov Argentina
121 C4 Mendoza R Argentina
115 L8 Mendoza, Ciudad Mexico 18.49N 97.14W
66 M8 Mendrisio Switzerland 45.53N 8.59E
76 D12 Mendro,Sa.de mts Portugal
18 E5 Mendung Sumatra Indon 0.31N 103.12E
91 E2 Mêné Congo 2.02N 16.36E
70 F5 Ménéac France 48.08N 2.27W
116 J9 Mene de Mauroa Venezuela 10.39N 71.04W
79 G5 Menegosa,Monte Italy 44.42N 9.40E
119 E3 Mene Grande Venezuela 9.51N 70.57W
87 G6 Menelik Falls Ethiopia 8.29N 39.00E
36 C4 Menemen Turkey 38.34N 27.03E
61 C3 Menen Belgium 50.48N 3.07E
121 B9 Menéndez,L Argentina
93 H6 Menengai crater Kenya 0.12S 36.05E
9 B9 Menen Pt Nauru, Pacific Oc 0.32S 166.57E
75 L2 Méné, Pic mt France 42.44N 0.02E
75 G6 Menera,Sierra mts Spain
77 M2 Meneses mt Spain 39.26N 2.13W
71 E2 Menessaire France 47.08N 4.08E
70 P6 Ménestreau France 47.42N 2.00E
72 K5 Menet France 45.18N 2.35E
83 J9 Menetai Greece 35.29N 27.10E
71 B2 Menetou-Ratel France 47.21N 2.45E
72 J1 Menetou Salon France 47.13N 2.29E
70 P7 Ménétréol-sous-Sancerre France 47.27N 2.18E
71 H3 Ménétrux-en-Joux France 46.38N 5.51E
70 B5 Ménez Hom mt France 48.13N 4.16W
70 F5 Menez, Landes du reg France
81 E8 Menfi Sicily 37.36N 12.59E
90 F8 Meng R Cameroon
77 E3 Mengabril Spain 38.56N 5.56W
18 L2 Mengalum isld S China Sea 6.16N 115.14E
81 B6 Menga,Pta Sardinia 38.58N 8.34E
80 G2 Mengara Italy 43.17N 12.34E
23 B7 Mengban Yunnan China 23.10N 100.23E
23 G2 Mengcheng Anhui China 33.15N 116.33E
Meng-chiang Jilin see Jingyu Jilin
22 L7 Mengcun Huizu Zizhixian Hebei China 38.04N 117.06E
23 B7 Mengdingjie Yunnan China 23.30N 99.03E
36 F2 Mengen Turkey 40.56N 32.11E
64 G7 Mengen W Germany 48.03N 9.20E
37 H7 Mengene Dağ mt Turkey 38.14N 44.03E
63 J10 Mengeringhausen W Germany 51.22N 8.59E
64 E2 Mengerskirchen W Germany 50.34N 8.10E
18 F8 Menggala Sumatra Indon 4.30S 105.19E
23 B8 Menghai Yunnan China 21.59N 100.35E
Meng-hua see Weishan
23 B8 Menghun Yunnan China 21.43N 100.23E
77 J5 Mengibar Spain 37.58N 3.48W
47 K8 Mengiser,Oz L Kazakhstan U.S.S.R. 54.31N 68.00E
21 E4 Mengjiagang Heilongjiang China 46.25N 130.35E
23 E7 Mengjiang Guangxi China 23.26N 110.43E
22 H7 Mengjiawan Shaanxi China 38.37N 109.40E
23 F1 Mengjin Henan China 34.52N 112.40E
18 J5 Mengkiang R Borneo Indon
18 D10 Mengkibol Pen Malaysia 1.58N 103.19E
64 N6 Mengkofen W Germany 48.43N 12.28E
18 C8 Mengkuang Pen Malaysia 3.11N 102.24E
23 B8 Mengla Yunnan China 31.30N 101.36E
Menglangba see Lancang
23 B7 Menglian Yunnan China 22.19N 99.33E
23 B7 Mengman Yunnan China 22.05N 100.10E
91 B2 Mengong Cameroon 3.00N 11.29E
88 M5 Mengoub Morocco 32.15N 2.21W
23 E6 Mengshan Guangxi China 24.07N 110.55E
23 E7 Mengshan Guangxi China 23.26N 110.43E
22 L9 Meng Shan mts Shandong China
23 B7 Mengsheng Yunnan China 23.20N 99.29E
91 B2 Menguemé Cameroon 3.19N 11.30E
23 B7 Mengwang Yunnan China 22.17N 100.33E
23 F1 Meng Xian Henan China 34.57N 112.43E
23 H1 Mengyin Shandong China 35.45N 117.56E
23 B8 Mengyuan Yunnan China 21.40N 101.32E
23 C7 Mengzi Yunnan China 23.20N 103.21E
88 P5 Menia,El Algeria 33.10N 2.05E
88 Q9 Meniet Algeria 25.00N 4.19E
72 D3 Ménigoute France 46.30N 0.03W
97 N7 Menihek, Lac L Nfld/Labrador
26 T8 Menik Ganga R Sri Lanka
69 K6 Ménil-la-Tour France 48.46N 5.53E
70 N3 Menilles France 49.02N 1.22E
68 F3 Menilmontant dist Paris France
69 M7 Ménil-sur-Bélvitte France 48.24N 6.41E
Menin see Menen
12 F4 Menindee New S Wales 32.23S 142.30E
12 F4 Menindee L New S Wales
12 E6 Meningie S Australia 35.35S 139.00E
70 K7 Ménitre,la France 47.24N 0.15W
32 C3 Menjān Iran 34.26N 48.20E
99 P5 Menjo Quebec 47.12N 75.08W
41 M6 Menkere U.S.S.R. 68.00N 123.31E
41 M6 Menkere R U.S.S.R.
47 J4 Menk'ya U.S.S.R. 63.00N 61.30E
39 B3 Menkyule R U.S.S.R.
105 B3 Menlo Georgia 34.30N 85.25W
108 Q8 Menlo Iowa 41.31N 94.24W
109 K2 Menlo Kansas 39.21N 100.44W
111 B4 Menlo Park California 37.27N 122.11W
59 E5 Menlough Galway Irish Rep 53.25N 8.35W
30 F2 Menlung La pass Nepal/China 27.58N 86.33N
87 G4 Menna watercourse Ethiopia
Mennbidj see Membij
69 C6 Mennecy France 48.34N 2.26E
72 H1 Mennetou-sur-Cher France 47.16N 1.52E
108 N6 Menno S Dakota 43.14N 97.34W
57 F2 Mennock Dumfries & Galloway Scotland 55.21N 3.53W
57 F2 Mennock Pass Dumfries & Galloway Scotland 55.22N 3.48W
118 A8 Mennonite Colony Paraguay
109 M5 Meno Oklahoma 36.25N 98.12W
66 B7 Menoge R France
106 G4 Menomminee Michigan 45.07N 87.37W
106 G4 Menomminee R Michigan
106 F6 Menomonee Falls Wisconsin 43.11N 88.09W
106 C5 Menomonie Wisconsin 44.52N 91.55W
91 E11 Menongue Angola 14.40S 17.41E
74 K4 Menorca isld Balearic Is Spain
77 W14 Menorca,C.de Balearic Is 39.51N 3.11E
77 D6 Menor, I Spain 37.09N 6.04W
71 C2 Menou France 47.22N 3.16E
88 M6 Menouarar Algeria 31.10N 2.15W
71 H7 Mens France 44.48N 5.45E
37 G1 Menşar Turkey 41.05N 29.46E
47 M7 Men'shchikovo U.S.S.R. 55.56N 76:42E
41 B4 Men'shikova,Mys C Novaya Zemlya U.S.S.R. 70.38N 57.35E
40 H4 Men'shikova, Ostrov isld U.S.S.R. 54.42N 139.15E
60 O6 Mensingemeer Netherlands 53.22N 6.28E
95 B10 Menskoppunt pt S Africa 34.16S 18.23E
63 G7 Menslage W Germany 52.41N 7.49E
58 J6 Menstrie Central Scotland 56.09N 3.52W
53 H6 Menstrup Denmark 55.13N 11.36E
18 C8 Mentakab Pen Malaysia 3.28N 102.20E
80 G4 Mentana Italy 42.02N 12.39E
18 M3 Mentapok mt Sabah Malaysia 5.50N 117.06E
113 Q5 Mentasta Lake Alaska 62.55N 143.59W
113 Q5 Mentasta Mts Alaska
18 C7 Mentawai,Kep islds Indonesia
26 J5 Mentawai Ridge Indian Oc
18 C6 Mentawi,Selat str Sumatra Indon
18 K6 Mentaya R Borneo Indon
58 H6 Menteith,L.of Central Scotland 56.10N 4.18W
14 B10 Mentelle,C W Australia 33.56S 114.59E
71 J5 Menthon-St. Bernard France 45.50N 6.12E
76 E12 Mentiras mt Portugal 38.14N 7.10W
77 M4 Mentiras mt Spain 38.20N 2.28W
18 F7 Mentok Indonesia 2.04S 105.12E
121 A10 Mentolat, Mt Chile 44.42S 73.08W
71 M9 Menton France 43.47N 7.30E
106 H8 Mentone Indiana 41.11N 86.02W
112 D4 Mentone Texas 31.42N 103.36W
108 O2 Mentor Minnesota 47.41N 96.06W
104 D5 Mentor Ohio 41.42N 81.22W
18 M4 Mentorang R Borneo Indon
76 L8 Méntrida Spain 40.14N 4.12W
18 K6 Mentubar R Borneo Indon
66 C5 Mentue R Switzerland
95 J9 Mentz,L S Africa 33.10S 25.08E
15 H7 Menyamya Papua New Guinea 7.07S 145.59E
18 M5 Menyapa, Gunung mt Borneo Indon 0.59N 116.06E
22 E8 Menyuan Huizu Zizhixian Qinghai China 37.30N 101.33E
42 H6 Menza R U.S.S.R.
66 H3 Menzberg Switzerland 47.03N 7.59E
Menze see Moincêr
87 E5 Menze Sudan 11.32N 35.05E
24 C10 Menze Xizang Zizhiqu 31.10N 80.50E
88 S3 Menzel Bourguiba Tunisia 37.10N 9.49E
63 E9 Menzelen W Germany 51.37N 6.32E
46 R2 Menzelinsk U.S.S.R. 55.45N 53.00E
78 D12 Menzel Temime Tunisia 36.45N 11.00E
14 D8 Menzies W Australia 29.42S 121.03E
123 C5 Menzies,Mt Antarctica 73.30S 62.00E
66 J3 Menziken Switzerland 47.15N 8.12E
Menzingen see Kraichtal
66 L3 Menzingen Switzerland 47.11N 8.36E
42 H7 Menzinskaya U.S.S.R. 49.26N 108.52E
66 J3 Menznau Switzerland 47.05N 8.03E
66 L6 Menzonio Switzerland 46.22N 8.38E
72 G2 Méobecq France 46.44N 1.54E
79 M3 Méolo Italy 45.38N 12.27E
35 E1 Me'ona Israel 33.01N 35.16E
56 J6 Meon,R Hants Eng
56 M5 Meopham Kent Eng 51.23N 0.22E
115 G3 Meoqui Mexico 28.18N 105.30W
100 J5 Meota Saskatchewan 53.03N 108.28W
71 H10 Méounes-les-Montrieux France 43.17N 5.58E
44 E6 Mepistskaro mt Georgia U.S.S.R. 41.50N 42.40E
92 G8 Meponda Mozambique 13.20S 34.53E
60 N9 Meppel Netherlands 52.42N 6.12E
60 N10 Meppeler diep canal Netherlands
60 P8 Meppen Netherlands 52.47N 6.42E
63 F7 Meppen W Germany 52.41N 7.18E
94 M4 Mepuze Mozambique 23.07S 32.16E
35 B2 Meqor Haiyim sub Jerusalem
120 G5 Mequéns R Brazil
75 L5 Mequinenza Spain 41.22N 0.17E
75 K5 Mequinenza,Embalse de res Spain
75 L5 Mequinenza,Sierra de mts Spain
70 O6 Mer France 47.43N 1.30E
76 D1 Mera Spain 43.39N 7.54W
79 F2 Mera R Italy
76 D1 Mera R Spain
46 M1 Mera R U.S.S.R.
87 K7 Meraa,El Ethiopia 7.39N 45.20E
84 N11 Merabéllou,Kólpos gulf Crete
72 D8 Meracq France 43.30N 0.22W
88 M4 Merada Morocco 34.21N 3.15W
18 L9 Merafi, Gunung mt Java Indon 7.52S 114.21E
18 M5 Merah Borneo Indon 0.50N 116.49E
15 M6 Merai New Britain 4.49S 152.20E
18 F8 Merak Java Indon 5.55S 106.00E
52 F3 Meråker Norway 63.26N 11.48E
30 J3 Mera La pass Nepal 27.50N 86.53E
9 C10 Mera Lava isld New Hebrides 14.28S 168.00E
12 B3 Meramangye, L S Australia
19 E1 Merampi isld Indonesia 4.45N 127.07E
Meran see Merano
18 J6 Meranggau Borneo Indon 0.13S 110.12E
79 K1 Merano Italy 46.41N 11.10E
18 J9 Merapi,Gunung mt Java Indon 7.32S 110.26E
18 C7 Merapoh Pen Malaysia 4.40N 102.00E
119 H5 Merari,Sa mt Brazil 4.20N 60.54W
98 S6 Merasheen Newfoundland 47.24N 54.20W
98 S6 Merasheen I Newfoundland
79 F3 Merate Italy 45.42N 9.25E
18 L7 Meratus,Pegunungan mts Borneo Indon
15 F8 Merauke Irian Jaya 8.30S 140.22E
15 F8 Merauke R Irian Jaya
33 K4 Merawwah isld U.A.E.
66 Q1 Merazhofen W Germany 47.44N 9.58E
84 E6 Merbakas Greece 37.38N 22.48E
18 E5 Merbau Sumatra Indon 1.05N 102.31E
12 F5 Merbein Victoria 34.11S 142.05E
61 G5 Merbes-le-Château Belgium 50.19N 4.10E
61 G5 Merbes-Ste.-Marie Belgium 50.22N 4.10E
18 A6 Merbok R Pen Malaysia
18 L10 Merbuk,Gunung mt Bali Indon 8.15S 114.41E
87 K10 Merca Somalia 1.42N 44.47E
77 Y14 Mercadel Balearic Is 39.59N 4.05E
119 C7 Mercaderes Colombia 1.46N 77.09W
75 D1 Mercadillo Spain 43.15N 3.09W
76 D4 Merca,La Spain 42.13N 7.54W
66 L9 Mercallo Italy 45.45N 8.40E
37 E6 Mercan Dağ mt Turkey 39.32N 39.31E
28 B4 Mercara Karnataka India 12.29N 75.40E
80 L7 Mercato San Sever Italy 40.47N 14.46E
79 M7 Mercato Saraceno Italy 43.57N 12.12E
111 D4 Merced California 37.17N 120.29W
111 D4 Merced R California
121 B3 Mercedario,Cerro mt Argentina 31.59S 70.10W
121 F5 Mercedes Buenos Aires Arg 34.42S 59.30W
121 F2 Mercedes Corrientes Arg 29.15S 58.05W
121 D4 Mercedes San Luis Argentina 33.41S 65.28W
112 K9 Mercedes Texas 26.09N 97.55W
121 F4 Mercedes Uruguay 34.15S 58.02W
96 S13 Mercedes, Mt. de las Tenerife Canary Is
121 B2 Merceditas Chile 28.25S 70.30W
111 A9 Merced, L. de la San Francisco, Cal
107 C1 Mercer Missouri 40.32N 93.33W
108 K2 Mercer N Dakota 47.29N 100.42W
11 K4 Mercer New Zealand 37.17S 175.04E
104 E5 Mercer Pennsylvania 41.14N 80.14W
107 G6 Mercer Tennessee 35.29N 89.02W
106 D3 Mercer Wisconsin 46.09N 90.06W
103 E6 Mercer co New Jersey
104 H7 Mercersburg Pennsylvania 39.51N 77.53W
120 E3 Mercês Acre Brazil 9.25S 68.46W
118 G7 Mercés Minas Gerais Brazil 21.13S 43.23W
76 C15 Mercês Portugal 38.48N 9.19W
18 D8 Merchong R Pen Malaysia
61 G3 Merchtem Belgium 50.57N 4.14E
Merciantaira,Punta see Grand Glaiza, Pic du
120 E4 Mercier Bolivia 10.48S 68.07W
99 P6 Mercier Dam Quebec 46.43N 75.59W
Mercier Lacombe see Sfisef
36 H5 Mercimek Turkey 37.07N 35.45E
101 P9 Mercoal Alberta 53.10N 117.06W
72 H5 Mercœur France 45.01N 1.56E
80 L7 Mercogliano Italy 40.54N 14.44E
72 G6 Mercuès France 44.30N 1.22E
110 N9 Mercur Utah 40.20N 112.13W
66 L9 Mercurago Italy 45.44N 8.33E
82 H5 Mercurea Romania 45.51N 23.43E
71 J5 Mercury France 45.40N 6.19E
112 H4 Mercury Texas 31.24N 99.10W
11 K3 Mercury B New Zealand
11 K3 Mercury Is New Zealand
97 G3 Mercy B N W Terr
97 N5 Mercy,C N W Terr 65.00N 63.30W
66 D8 Mer de Glace glacier France
Merdenik see Göle
70 H3 Merderet R France
88 K4 Merdja Zerga salt L Morocco
61 K4 Merdorp Belgium 50.38N 5.00E
70 F5 Merdrignac France 48.11N 2.24W
46 M3 Merdushinskiy U.S.S.R. 54.51N 42.11E
61 F3 Mere Belgium 50.55N 3.58E
57 J6 Mere Cheshire Eng 53.20N 2.25W
56 G5 Mere Wilts Eng 51.06N 2.16W
72 J1 Méreau France 47.10N 2.02E
104 O3 Meredith New Hampshire 43.38N 71.30W
121 D10 Meredith,C Falkland Is 52.15S 60.40W
112 C8 Meredith, L Texas 35.40N 101.34W
107 F2 Meredosia Illinois 39.49N 90.32W
88 O9 Meredoua Algeria 25.12N 1.49E
45 H7 Merefa Ukraine U.S.S.R. 49.49N 36.05E
87 L9 Meregh Somalia 3.46N 47.15E
37 G4 Merehevi R Turkey
88 K12 Mereié,El reg Mauritania
89 F2 Mereié, El reg Mauritania
90 M6 Mereigha Sudan 11.11N 25.34E
33 A2 Mereighat Egypt 29.00N 33.13E
90 L8 Mereke Cent Afr Rep 7.34N 23.09E
117 C2 Mére,la isld Fr Guiana 4.55N 51.57W
61 F3 Merelbeke Belgium 51.00N 3.45E
64 E2 Merenberg W Germany 50.30N 8.11E
61 E2 Merendree Belgium 51.05N 3.35E
39 F4 Merenga U.S.S.R. 61.52N 156.05E
66 K2 Merenschwand Switzerland 47.15N 8.23E
72 H10 Mérens-les-Vals France 42.39N 1.49E
87 L8 Merergur Somalia 5.43N 46.22E
79 O2 Mereto Italy 46.04N 13.02E
42 C5 Meret'y U.S.S.R. 53.33N 82.28E
69 C7 Méréville France 48.18N 2.05E
56 M5 Mereworth Kent Eng 51.16N 0.24E
Merga see Nukheila
46 Q5 Mergenevo Kazakhstan U.S.S.R. 49.59N 51.19E
66 M7 Mergoscia Switzerland 46.13N 8.51E
79 D3 Mergozzo Italy 45.58N 8.27E
88 P4 Mergueb R Algeria
25 E6 Mergui Burma 12.26N 98.34E
25 D7 Mergui Arch Burma
36 G1 Mergüze Turkey 41.12N 33.32E
35 E3 Merḥavya Israel 32.36N 35.18E
81 K7 Merì Sicily 38.10N 15.17E
87 G4 Meri watercourse Ethiopia
67 P11 Méria Corsica 42.55N 9.27E
15 J8 Meriani Papua New Guinea 9.27S 147.27E
12 F5 Meribah S Australia 34.42S 140.53E
71 K6 Méribel-les-Allues France 45.23N 6.35E
37 C1 Meriç Turkey 41.12N 26.24E
37 C1 Meriç R Turkey/Greece
100 H7 Merid Saskatchewan 51.25N 109.55W
115 P7 Mérida Mexico 20.59N 89.39W
77 D3 Mérida Spain 38.55N 6.20W
119 E3 Mérida Venezuela 8.24N 71.08W
119 E3 Mérida state Venezuela
119 E3 Mérida,Cord.do mts Venezuela
103 E2 Meridale New York 42.22N 74.57W
103 J3 Meriden Connecticut 41.32N 72.48W
109 P2 Meriden Kansas 39.12N 95.33W
104 N3 Meriden New Hampshire 43.33N 72.17W
56 H3 Meriden W Midlands Eng 52.26N 1.37W
108 F8 Meriden Wyoming 41.34N 104.19W
111 C2 Meridian California 39.09N 121.55W
110 J6 Meridian Idaho 43.37N 116.24W
107 H9 Meridian Mississippi 32.21N 88.42W
104 J3 Meridian New York 43.10N 76.32W
112 K4 Meridian Texas 31.56N 97.40W
121 D5 Meridiano Argentina 35.34S 63.20W
88 M6 Meridja Algeria 31.30N 2.58W
10 O4 Merig isld New Hebrides 14.18S 167.47E
72 D4 Mérignac Charente France 45.42N 0.06W
72 C6 Mérignac Gironde France 44.50N 0.36W
72 F2 Merigny France 46.38N 0.56E
51 J10 Merikarvia Finland 61.51N 21.30E
41 M2 Meri Kharmsuort, Mys C Franz Josef Land U.S.S.R. 80.38N 45.00E
65 N3 Měřín Czechoslovakia 49.24N 15.54E
89 B4 Merinaghen Senegal 15.57N 15.55W
13 J4 Merinda Queensland 20.00S 148.09E
71 G9 Mérindol France 43.46N 5.12E
64 L7 Mering W Germany 48.15N 11.00E
12 F5 Meringur Victoria 34.24S 141.29E
109 G1 Merino Colorado 40.29N 103.23W
12 F7 Merino Victoria 37.45S 141.35E
121 J6 Merino Jarpa isld Chile 47.50S 74.15W
Merioneth co see Gwynedd co
17 M11 Merir isld Caroline Is Pacific Oc 4.19N 132.18E
117 B4 Merirumã Brazil 1.15N 54.50W
66 L1 Merishausen Switzerland 47.45N 8.37E
18 K4 Merit Sarawak Malaysia 2.18N 113.10E
13 J7 Merivale R Queensland
107 J6 Meriwether Lewis Nat. Mon Tennessee 35.32N 87.28W
19 L1 Merizo Guam Pacific Oc 13.16N 144.40E
Merjâné see Marjanah
43 L5 Merke Kazakhstan U.S.S.R. 42.48N 73.10E
112 G3 Merkel Texas 32.29N 100.02W
61 B3 Merkem Belgium 50.57N 2.51E
64 K5 Merkendorf W Germany 49.12N 10.44E
51 E5 Merkenes Sweden 66.41N 16.10E
Merket see Markit
62 P1 Merkine Lithuania U.S.S.R. 54.10N 24.10E
58 G2 Merkland,L Highland Scotland 58.14N 4.45W
64 O3 Merklín Karlovy Vary Czech 50.20N 12.51E
64 P4 Merklín Plzeň Czech 49.35N 13.12E
89 E5 Merkoya Mali 13.58N 8.11W
61 K1 Merkplas Belgium 51.22N 4.52E
61 H2 Merksem Belgium 51.14N 4.29E
64 A2 Merkstein W Germany 50.54N 6.09E
41 R5 Merkushina Strelka spit U.S.S.R.
47 K6 Merkushino U.S.S.R. 59.29N 69.54E
64 C3 Merl W Germany 50.03N 7.10E
79 K4 Merlara Italy 45.10N 11.26E
71 G9 Merle,le France 43.39N 5.00E
61 J6 Merlemont Belgium 50.10N 4.36E
70 L4 Merlerault,le France 48.42N 0.16E
66 G5 Merligen Switzerland 46.42N 7.44E
18 H3 Merlimau,Pulau isld Singapore
69 B3 Merlimont France 50.28N 1.37E
99 H10 Merlin Ontario 42.15N 82.13W
110 B7 Merlin Oregon 42.31N 123.25W
72 J4 Merlines France 45.39N 2.26E
121 F5 Merlo Argentina 34.38S 58.45W
13 F2 Merluna Queensland 13.00S 142.30E
14 C3 Mermaid Reef Indian Oc 17.10S 119.37E
107 D11 Mermentau Louisiana 30.11N 92.35W
107 D12 Mermentau R Louisiana
37 E7 Mermer Turkey 38.07N 40.25E
53 J6 Mern Denmark 55.03N 12.04E
79 P3 Merna Italy 45.53N 13.36E
108 L8 Merna Nebraska 41.30N 99.46W
110 P7 Merna Wyoming 42.57N 110.20W
12 E4 Mernemerna S Australia 31.45S 138.21E
76 C2 Mero R Spain
91 H7 Mérode Zaïre 6.20S 23.12E
28 H7 Meroe isld Nicobar Is India 7.30N 93.29E
87 E3 Meroë reg Sudan
14 D8 Merolia W Australia 28.49S 122.07E
35 G1 Merom Golan Syria 33.08N 35.46E
35 E2 Meron Israel 32.59N 35.26E
66 N8 Merone Italy 45.47N 9.15E
35 E2 Meron,Har mt Israel 33.00N 35.25E
84 C7 Merópi Greece 37.15N 22.00E
88 Q4 Merouana Algeria 35.38N 55.55E
66 D1 Meroux France 47.36N 6.55E
87 C1 Merowe Sudan 18.30N 31.49E
90 M3 Merowe reg Sudan
29 G8 Merpatti Maharashtra India 19.08N 80.11E
14 C9 Merredin W Australia 31.31S 118.14E
69 K7 Merrey France 48.03N 5.36E
109 Q2 Merriam Kansas 39.02N 94.42W
103 N8 Merrick New York
57 E2 Merrick mt Dumfries & Galloway Scotland 55.08N 4.29W
103 D2 Merrickville New York 42.17N 75.12W
99 P8 Merrickville Ontario 44.54N 75.50W
108 M3 Merricourt N Dakota 46.12N 98.46W
12 D6 Merri Cr Victoria
108 O7 Merrill Iowa 42.43N 96.14W
106 K6 Merrill Michigan 43.25N 84.19W
107 H11 Merrill Mississippi 30.58N 88.44W
110 D7 Merrill Oregon 42.02N 121.37W
106 E4 Merrill Wisconsin 45.12N 89.43W
106 D5 Merrillan Wisconsin 44.27N 90.50W
106 E6 Merrimac Wisconsin 43.23N 89.37W
104 O3 Merrimack R New Hampshire
108 J7 Merriman Nebraska 42.57N 101.42W
95 G7 Merriman S Africa 31.13S 23.37E
103 F3 Merriman Dam New York 41.48N 74.26W
12 J6 Merrimbula New S Wales 36.58S 149.58E
101 N10 Merritt Br Col 50.09N 120.49W
105 G9 Merritt I Florida 28.30N 80.30W
111 B8 Merritt,L Oakland, Cal
108 K7 Merritt Res Nebraska
56 C6 Merrivale Devon Eng 50.33N 4.03W
95 O5 Merrivale S Africa 29.31S 30.15E
12 K4 Merriwa New S Wales 32.08S 150.20E
107 E9 Mer Rouge Louisiana 32.49N 91.49W
56 K5 Merrow Surrey Eng 51.15N 0.32W
12 J4 Merrygoen New S Wales 31.51S 149.16E
12 K7 Merrylands dist Sydney, N S W
107 C11 Merryville Louisiana 30.44N 93.32W
87 H3 Mersa Fatma Ethiopia 14.57N 40.17E
86 J7 Mersa Thilmet B Egypt
61 P7 Mersch Luxembourg 49.45N 6.06E
80 D2 Merse R Italy
56 N4 Mersea I Essex Eng 51.48N 0.55E
63 Q10 Merseburg E Germany 51.22N 12.00E
88 N4 Mers el Kébir Algeria 35.48N 0.43W
58 M7 Merse,The div Borders Scotland
57 H6 Mersey,R Merseyside etc Eng
57 H6 Merseyside co Eng
87 K7 Mersi Ethiopia 7.36N 44.58E
89 J4 Mersi L Mali 15.42N 0.10W
36 H6 Mersin Turkey 36.47N 34.37E
18 D9 Mersing Pen Malaysia 2.25N 103.50E
69 A3 Mers-les-Bains France 50.04N 1.24E
46 E2 Mērsrags Latvia U.S.S.R. 57.20N 23.10E
72 H2 Mers-sur-Indre France 46.39N 1.52E
93 F2 Mersuk Hills Kenya
29 D4 Merta Rajasthan India 26.40N 74.07E
29 C4 Merta Road Rajasthan India 26.42N 73.54E
61 Q8 Mertert Luxembourg 49.42N 6.29E
56 E4 Merthyr Tydfil Mid Glam Wales 51.46N 3.23W
93 K4 Merti Kenya 1.01N 38.39E
64 K6 Mertingen W Germany 48.38N 10.49E
93 K4 Merti Plat Kenya
76 D13 Mértola Portugal 37.38N 7.40W
87 G5 Mertola Maryam Ethiopia 10.46N 38.13E
56 C6 Merton Devon Eng 50.54N 4.05W
55 E5 Merton bor London Eng 51.25N 0.12W
14 D8 Mertondale W Australia 28.40S 121.34E
43 C4 Mertvyy Kultuk,Sor mud flat Kazakhstan U.S.S.R.
123 J4 Mertz Glacier Antarctica
61 P7 Mertzig Luxembourg 49.50N 6.00E
112 G4 Mertzon Texas 31.16N 100.50W
69 C5 Méru France 49.15N 2.08E
93 J5 Meru Kenya 0.03N 37.38E
93 H9 Meru vol Tanzania 3.14S 36.45E
93 J8 Meruesh Kenya 2.22S 37.33E
76 C4 Merufe Portugal 42.01N 8.24W
31 B6 Merui Pakistan 28.56N 63.46E
119 H5 Merume Mts Guyana
93 K5 Meru Nat. Park Kenya
18 M3 Merutai Sabah Malaysia 4.20N 117.46E
Merv see Mary U.S.S.R.
71 G3 Mervans France 46.48N 5.11E
66 F2 Mervelier Switzerland 47.21N 7.30E
72 C2 Mervent France 46.31N 0.45W
72 G8 Merville Haute-Garonne France 43.44N 1.17E
69 D2 Merville Nord France 50.39N 2.39E
100 J5 Mervin Saskatchewan 53.20N 108.52W
95 E8 Merweville S Africa 32.40S 21.31E
110 C4 Merwin,L Washington 45.59N 122.30W
37 G4 Merya Turkey 41.18N 42.25E
10 D1 Meryapa, Gunong mt Borneo Indonesia 0.59N 116.06E
72 J1 Méry-lès-Bois France 47.19N 2.20E
69 F6 Méry-sur-Seine France 48.31N 3.55E
36 H2 Merzifon Turkey 40.52N 35.28E
64 B5 Merzig W Germany 49.26N 6.39E
111 N8 Mesa Arizona 33.25N 115.50W
19 F3 Mesa Halmahera Indon 0.27N 128.19E
110 J5 Mesa Idaho 44.38N 116.27W
109 F8 Mesa New Mexico 33.59N 104.42W
95 K2 Mesa S Africa 26.29S 26.59E
75 G5 Mesa R Spain
108 S2 Mesabi Range mts Minnesota
119 E3 Mesa Bolívar Venezuela 8.30N 71.38W
96 R13 Mesa del Mar Tenerife Canary Is 28.31N 16.25W
77 N7 Mesa de Roldán, Pta. de la pt Spain 36.56N 1.54W
81 Q11 Mesagne Italy 40.33N 17.49E
87 C5 Mesakin,Jeb mt Sudan 10.37N 30.20E
99 L1 Mesakonan Pt Quebec 51.34N 79.33W
101 Q3 Mesa L N W Terr 64.50N 115.10W
89 E8 Mésampleu Ivory Coast 7.13N 8.20W
113 K6 Mesa Mt Alaska 60.23N 155.13W
84 U17 Mesanagrós Rhodes Greece 36.01N 27.50E
18 F5 Mesanak isld Indonesia 0.25N 104.32E
70 H7 Mésanger France 47.26N 1.13W
76 D6 Mesão Frio Portugal 41.10N 7.54W
84 R14 Mesaöria Plain Cyprus
18 L3 Mesapol Sabah Malaysia 5.06N 115.34E
84 L11 Mesarás,Kólpos gulf Crete
76 H9 Mesas de Ibor Spain 39.46N 5.33W
109 B4 Mesa Verde Nat.Park Colorado
119 D7 Mesay,R Colombia
111 O10 Mescal Arizona 31.59N 110.29W
109 E8 Mescalero New Mexico 33.07N 105.44W
60 S17 Mesch Netherlands 50.46N 5.45E
63 H10 Meschede W Germany 51.21N 8.16E
72 C4 Meschers-sur-Gironde France 45.34N 0.57W
37 F5 Mescit Dağı mt Turkey 40.22N 41.16E
37 D6 Mesçitli R Turkey
25 D3 Mese Burma 18.39N 97.37E
19 N5 Mesegon isld Truk Is Pacific Oc 7.09N 151.55E
52 K2 Meselefors Sweden 64.27N 16.50E
87 D3 Mesellemiya,El Sudan 14.33N 33.21E
61 B3 Mesen Belgium 50.46N 2.53E
84 C3 Mesenikólas Greece 39.20N 21.45E
66 M8 Mesenzana Italy 45.57N 8.46E
82 H3 Meseşului, Munţii mts Romania
36 G1 Meset Turkey 41.59N 33.27E
69 F7 Mesgrigny France 48.29N 3.54E
46 P2 Mesha R U.S.S.R.
56 D6 Meshaw Devon Eng 50.58N 3.45W
45 L1 Meshchera lowland U.S.S.R.
45 G2 Meshchovsk U.S.S.R. 54.20N 35.16E
47 G4 Meshchura U.S.S.R. 63.18N 51.52E
Meshed see Mashhad
Meshed-i-Sar see Bābol Sar
43 F6 Meshekli Uzbekistan U.S.S.R. 41.16N 61.44E
113 H8 Meshik Alaska 57.00N 158.40W
32 H2 Meshkān Iran 36.35N 58.05E
32 F1 Meshkhed Turkmeniya U.S.S.R. 38.20N 54.38E
32 B1 Meshkinshahr Iran 38.24N 47.40E
103 B3 Meshoppen Pennsylvania 41.36N 76.03W
103 C3 Meshoppen Cr Pennsylvania
87 B6 Meshra'er Req Sudan 8.21N 29.19E
76 C2 Mesia Spain 43.07N 8.15W
88 G9 Mesiah,El reg Morocco

106 J5 **Mesick** Michigan 44.24N 85.43W
101 L7 **Mesilinka** *R* Br Col
109 D9 **Mesilla** New Mexico 32.16N 106.47W
35 D6 **Mesillat Ziyyon** Israel 31.48N 35.01E
81 M6 **Mesima** *R* Italy
53 F6 **Mesinge** Denmark 55.30N 10.39E
34 F2 **Mesken** Syria 36.02N 38.04E
88 L6 **Meski** Morocco 31.53N 4.18W
88 R4 **Meskiana** Algeria 35.34N 7.34E
37 E8 **Meşkinan** Turkey 37.17N 40.22E
84 J11 **Mesklá** Crete 35.24N 23.57E
90 J2 **Meskou** Chad 19.17N 18.09E
18 C10 **Meskum** Sumatra Indon 1.32N 102.02E
70 J6 **Meslay-du-Maine** France 47.57N 0.33W
66 D2 **Meslières** France 47.25N 6.54E
61 F4 **Meslin-l'Evêque** Belgium 50.39N 3.51E
34 D5 **Mesmīye** Syria 33.08N 36.24E
52 F5 **Mesna** *L* Norway 61.25N 10.45E
71 H3 **Mesnay** France 46.55N 5.48E
70 N2 **Mesnières-en-Béthune** France 49.45N 1.25E
70 J4 **Mesnil-Auzouf,le** France 48.58N 0.46W
61 K6 **Mesnil-Église** Belgium 50.10N 4.58E
61 K6 **Mesnil-St.-Blaise** Belgium 50.10N 4.53E
69 C4 **Mesnil-St.Firmin,le** France 49.38N 2.25E
69 G6 **Mesnil-sur-Oger,le** France 48.56N 4.02E
70 H3 **Mesnil-Vigot,le** France 49.08N 1.17W
70 K4 **Mesnil-Villement,le** France 48.51N 0.22W
66 N6 **Mesocco** Switzerland 46.23N 9.15E
84 B3 **Mesokhóra** Greece 39.28N 21.20E
84 C8 **Mesokhóri** Greece 36.53N 21.43E
79 M5 **Mésola** Italy 44.55N 12.14E
66 N6 **Mesolcina, Valle** Switzerland
84 B5 **Mesolóngion** Greece 38.21N 21.26E
76 C2 **Mesón del Viento** Spain 43.09N 8.23W
75 D6 **Mesones** Spain 40.46N 3.25W
34 H3 **Mesopotamia** *reg* Iraq/Syria
84 C8 **Mesopótamos** Greece 36.58N 21.50E
81 N5 **Mesoraca** Italy 39.05N 16.47E
84 E7 **Mesorrákhi** Greece 37.23N 22.32E
61 G3 **Mespelare** Belgium 50.59N 4.05E
70 F7 **Mesquer** France 47.24N 2.29W
118 G6 **Mesquita** Brazil 19.15S 42.32W
76 C14 **Mesquita, Sa da** *mts* Portugal
111 K5 **Mesquite** Nevada 36.48N 114.05W
109 D9 **Mesquite** New Mexico 32.09N 106.41W
112 O9 **Mesquite** Texas 32.46N 96.37W
111 J6 **Mesquite L** California 35.41N 115.35W
88 P4 **Mesrane,El** Algeria 34.57N 3.04E
89 E3 **Messa** Mauritania 17.57N 9.21W
88 P4 **Messaad** Algeria 34.11N 3.31E
70 G6 **Messac** France 47.49N 1.48W
85 A7 **Messak Mellet** *hills* Libya
85 A7 **Messak Set't'afed** *hills* Libya
Messalo *R see* **Mualo** *R*
90 F10 **Messaména** Cameroon 3.48N 12.49E
61 O8 **Messancy** Belgium 49.35N 5.49E
Messandaluz *see* **Muze**
72 B8 **Messanges** France 43.49N 1.23W
88 N7 **Messaoud** *watercourse* Algeria
63 P7 **Messdorf** E Germany 52.44N 11.34E
70 J4 **Messei** France 48.42N 0.32W
88 H8 **Messeied** Morocco 28.00N 10.50W
71 B5 **Messeix** France 45.37N 2.32E
76 C13 **Messejana** Portugal 37.50N 8.14W
65 M7 **Messendorf** Austria 47.03N 15.30E
103 B2 **Messengerville** New York 42.29N 76.05W
43 C7 **Messerian** *anc site* Turkmeniya **U.S.S.R.** 38.15N 54.35E
71 J4 **Messery** France 46.20N 6.17E
Messick *see* **Poquoson**
121 J7 **Messier,Canal** *str* Chile
71 F2 **Messigny-et-Vantoux** France 47.25N 5.00E
94 K4 **Messina** S Africa 22.23S 30.00E
81 L7 **Messina** Sicily 38.13N 15.33E
81 J7 **Messina** *prov* Sicily
81 L7 **Messina,Str.di** Italy/Sicily
69 J4 **Messincourt** France 49.40N 5.10E
99 O6 **Messines** Quebec 46.14N 76.01W
57 M5 **Messingham** Humberside **Eng** 53.32N 0.39W
84 C7 **Messíni** Greece 37.03N 22.00E
84 C7 **Messinía** *prov* Greece
84 D8 **Messiniakós Kólpos** *gulf* Greece
64 G8 **Messkirch** W Germany 48.00N 9.07E
41 C6 **Messo** U.S.S.R. 67.59N 78.31E
91 B2 **Messondo** Cameroon 3.40N 10.30E
41 C6 **Messoyakha** *R* U.S.S.R.
94 C3 **Messum Berg** *mt* Namibia 21.32S 14.06E
94 B3 **Messum Mts** Namibia
Mesta *R see* **Néstos** *R*
82 H9 **Mesta** *R* Bulgaria etc
77 H3 **Mestanza** Spain 38.35N 4.04W
65 P2 **Městečko Trnávka** Czechoslovakia 49.43N 16.43E
48 U10 **Mesters Vig** Greenland 72.15N 24.00W
44 E4 **Mestiya** Georgia **U.S.S.R.** 43.04N 42.46E
63 P5 **Mestlin** E Germany 53.36N 11.56E
64 P4 **Město-Touškov** Czechoslovakia 49.47N 13.15E
79 M4 **Mestre** Italy 45.30N 12.14E
79 L4 **Mestrino** Italy 45.27N 11.46E
37 H2 **Mesudiye** Kocaeli **Turkey** 40.35N 29.51E
37 D5 **Mesudiye** Ordu **Turkey** 40.28N 37.45E
18 F7 **Mesuji** *R* Sumatra **Indon**
89 D8 **Mesurado,C** Liberia 6.20N 10.50W
72 L1 **Mésves-sur-Loire** France 47.15N 3.00E
61 F5 **Mesvin** Belgium 50.26N 3.58E
71 E3 **Mesvres** France 46.51N 4.15E
80 K7 **Meta** Italy 40.38N 14.25E
107 D3 **Meta** Missouri 38.19N 92.10W
119 D6 **Meta** *div* Colombia
99 J5 **Metagama** Ontario 47.05N 81.57W
Metahara *see* **Metehara**
97 N5 **Meta Incognita Pen** N W Terr
107 H2 **Metairie** *dist* New Orleans, Louisiana
122 S15 **Metaiutea,Pte** *C* Mangaréva **Pacific Oc** 23.06S 134.55W
99 C2 **Meta L** Ontario
80 J5 **Meta,La** *mt* Italy 41.41N 13.57E
82 H4 **Metalici, Munţii** *mts* Romania
110 H1 **Metaline Falls** Washington 48.52N 117.20W
80 C2 **Metallifere,Colline** *mts* Italy
84 D3 **Metallíon** Greece 39.05N 22.19E
88 S11 **Métal,Mt.du** Algeria 21.49N 8.24E
121 A9 **Metalqui,C** Chile 42.15S 74.14W
88 T5 **Metameur** Tunisia 33.28N 10.20E
106 E9 **Metamora** Illinois 40.48N 89.23W
120 F11 **Metań** Argentina 25.30S 65.00W
92 G8 **Metangula** Mozambique 12.41S 34.50E
115 P10 **Metapán** El Salvador 14.20N 89.28W
98 S5 **Meta Pond** Newfoundland 48.00N 54.38W
81 N3 **Metaponto** Italy 40.22N 16.49E
81 N3 **Metapontum** *ruins* Italy 40.23N 16.50E
119 F4 **Meta,R** Venez/Colombia
92 H9 **Metarica** Mozambique 14.20S 36.49E
79 N7 **Metauro** *R* Italy
84 C7 **Metaxádha** Greece 37.06N 21.45E
98 F9 **Meteghan** Nova Scotia 44.12N 66.10W
98 F9 **Meteghan Sta** Nova Scotia 44.13N 66.06W
87 G6 **Metehara** Ethiopia 8.58N 39.57E
91 F6 **Meteke** Zaïre 4.01S 18.53E
63 F8 **Metelen** W Germany 52.09N 7.13E
Metemma Ethiopia*see* **Matamā**
87 D3 **Metemma** Sudan 15.05N 33.15E
92 G9 **Metende** Mozambique 14.07S 35.44E
92 G9 **Metengobalame** Mozambique 14.49S 34.34E
13 J6 **Meteor** *R* Queensland
84 C2 **Metéora,Monasteries of** Greece 39.44N 21.38E
111 N6 **Meteor Crater** *depression* Arizona 35.01N 111.03W
96 H14 **Meteor Depth** Atlantic Oc
96 L14 **Meteor Seamount** S Atlantic Oc 47.49S 9.02E
15 L5 **Meteran** Bismarck Arch 2.40S 150.12E
69 D2 **Météren** France 50.44N 2.41E
60 K12 **Meteren** Netherlands 51.52N 5.17E
60 N14 **Meterik** Netherlands 51.28N 6.02E
84 F6 **Méthana** Greece 37.35N 23.23E
84 F6 **Methánon,Stenon Ton** *str* Greece
58 K6 **Methil** Fife **Scotland** 56.12N 3.01W
58 M4 **Methlick** Grampian **Scotland** 57.25N 2.15W
84 C8 **Methóni** Greece 36.49N 21.42E
110 E1 **Methow** *R* Washington
104 O4 **Methuen** Massachusetts 42.43N 71.13W
14 E3 **Methuen,Mt** W Australia 15.57S 124.50E
Me Thuot *see* **Ban Me Thuot**
11 F10 **Methven** New Zealand 43.38S 171.40E
58 J6 **Methven** Tayside **Scotland** 56.25N 3.37W
14 D7 **Methwin,Mt** W Australia 25.05S 120.39E
56 N2 **Methwold** Norfolk **Eng** 52.31N 0.33E
92 J10 **Metil** Mozambique 16.25S 39.00E
121 D5 **Metileo** Argentina 35.45S 63.54W
100 N1 **Metionga L** Ontario
100 G6 **Metiskow** Alberta 52.25N 110.38W
98 E5 **Métis sur Mer** Quebec 48.40N 67.58W
82 D7 **Metković** Yugoslavia 43.02N 17.39E
113 W9 **Metlakatla** Alaska 55.09N 131.35W
88 S4 **Metlaoui** Tunisia 34.20N 8.22E
82 C5 **Metlika** Yugoslavia 45.39N 15.19E
88 P5 **Metlili Chaamba** Algeria 32.18N 3.40E
88 Q4 **Metlili,Djebel** *mts* Algeria
47 M5 **Metlino** U.S.S.R. 55.44N 60.56E
65 K8 **Metnitz** Austria 46.59N 14.13E
82 F8 **Metohija** Yugoslavia 42.37N 20.34E
110 D5 **Metolins** *R* Oregon
110 D5 **Metolius** Oregon 44.36N 121.10W
92 G10 **Metolola** Mozambique 16.36S 35.44E
92 J8 **Metoro** Mozambique 13.06S 39.52E
88 T5 **Metouia** Tunisia 33.58N 10.04E
82 G7 **Metovnica** Yugoslavia 43.58N 22.10E
81 M7 **Metramo** *R* Italy
18 F8 **Metro** Sumatra **Indonesia** 5.08S 105.15E
107 H4 **Metropolis** Illinois 37.10N 88.46W
51 N6 **Metsäkylä** Finland 65.22N 28.25E
44 F7 **Metsamor** Armenia U.S.S.R. 40.04N 44.16E
94 H5 **Metsebotlhoko Pan** Botswana 24.02S 24.52E
94 H5 **Metsematluku** Botswana 24.01S 24.40E
60 N6 **Metslawier** Netherlands 53.22N 6.04E
84 B2 **Métsovon** Greece 39.46N 21.11E
66 G7 **Mettelhorn** *mt* Switzerland 46.03N 7.45E
64 O6 **Metten** W Germany 48.52N 12.56E
64 A4 **Mettendorf** W Germany 49.56N 6.20E
105 E5 **Metter** Georgia 32.24N 82.06W
61 J5 **Mettet** Belgium 50.19N 4.40E
63 G8 **Mettingen** W Germany 52.19N 7.46E
56 O3 **Mettingham** Suffolk **Eng** 52.28N 1.29E
64 B4 **Mettlach** W Germany 49.30N 6.36E
66 H4 **Mettlen** Switzerland 46.59N 7.57E
66 N1 **Mettlen** Thurgau **Switzerland** 47.32N 9.07E
65 H5 **Mettmach** Austria 48.10N 13.21E
64 B1 **Mettmann** W Germany 51.15N 6.58E
66 K3 **Mettmenstetten** Switzerland 47.15N 8.28E
64 B4 **Mettnich** W Germany 49.32N 6.59E
70 M7 **Mettray** France 47.27N 0.39E
28 C5 **Mettuppalaiyam** Tamil Nadu **India** 11.18N 76.57E
28 C5 **Mettur** Tamil Nadu **India** 11.53N 77.51E
87 E6 **Metu** Ethiopia 8.20N 35.35E
103 F5 **Metuchen** New Jersey 40.33N 74.23W
92 K7 **Metudo, I** Mozambique 11.10S 40.41E
92 K8 **Metuge** Mozambique 12.58S 40.23E
35 F1 **Metulla** Israel 33.17N 35.34E
69 L5 **Metz** France 49.07N 6.11E
69 N7 **Metzeral** France 48.00N 7.02E
69 L5 **Metzervisse** France 49.19N 6.17E
64 G6 **Metzingen** W Germany 48.32N 9.18E
69 M1 **Metz-Kausen** W Germany 51.16N 6.57E
70 F5 **Meu** *R* France
68 D4 **Meudon** France 48.49N 2.15E
68 D4 **Meudon, Bois de** *wood* France
64 D3 **Meudt** W Germany 50.29N 7.54E
18 B3 **Meulaboh** Sumatra Indon 4.10N 96.09E
69 B5 **Meulan** France 49.00N 1.55E
61 D3 **Meulebeke** Belgium 50.57N 3.18E
70 L4 **Meulles** France 48.57N 0.20E
70 O6 **Meung-sur-Loire** France 47.50N 1.42E
18 B3 **Meureudu** Sumatra Indon 5.14N 96.14E
72 C4 **Meursac** France 45.39N 0.48W
71 F3 **Meursault** France 46.59N 4.47E
69 M7 **Meurthe** *R* France
67 J4 **Meurthe-et-Moselle** *dept* France
69 K8 **Meuse** France 48.00N 5.33E
67 J4 **Meuse** *dept* France
69 J4 **Meuse** *R* Belgium/France
69 J5 **Meuse,Côtes de** *hills* France
64 N1 **Meuselwitz** E Germany 51.03N 12.18E
72 H1 **Meusnes** France 47.15N 1.30E
61 K4 **Meux** Belgium 50.33N 4.48E
72 G4 **Meuzac** France 45.33N 1.26E
56 B7 **Mevagissey** Cornwall **Eng** 50.16N 4.48W
61 F4 **Mévergnies-les-Lens** Belgium 50.36N 3.51E
35 D7 **Mevo Betar** Israel 31.43N 35.06E
35 F3 **Mevo Hamma** Syria 32.44N 35.39E
23 C2 **Mêwa** Sichuan **China** 33.02N 102.45E
59 L2 **Mew I** Down **N Ireland** 54.42N 5.32W
57 L5 **Mexborough** S Yorks **Eng** 53.30N 1.17W
115 K9 **Mexcala** Mexico 17.56N 99.36W
115 N9 **Mexcalapa** *R* Mexico
86 C3 **Mex, El** Egypt 31.08N 29.51E
112 L4 **Mexia** Texas 31.41N 96.30W
117 D4 **Mexiana, I** Brazil
84 D4 **Mexiátais** Greece 38.53N 22.19E
111 J9 **Mexicali** Mexico 32.38N 115.27W
115 B1 **Mexicali** Mexico 32.36N 115.30W
111 P4 **Mexican Hat** Utah 37.10N 109.54W
115 F3 **Mexicanos, L de los** Mexico
111 P5 **Mexican Water** Arizona 36.59N 109.40W
106 H9 **Mexico** Indiana 40.51N 86.07W
104 P2 **Mexico** Maine 44.34N 70.33W
115 K8 **México** Mexico 19.25N 99.10W
107 E2 **Mexico** Missouri 39.10N 91.53W
104 J3 **Mexico** New York 43.26N 76.15W
102 E5 **Mexico** *rep* N America
115 K8 **México** *state* Mexico
102 H6 **Mexico,G.of** Mexico/U.S.A.
76 B14 **Mexilhoeira Grande** Portugal 37.10N 8.36W
71 G5 **Meximieux** France 45.54N 5.11E
58 K1 **Mey** Highland **Scotland** 53.38N 3.14W
34 H3 **Meyadīn** Syria 35.01N 40.28E
15 A7 **Meyanobab** Moluccas **Indon** 7.38S 131.38E
32 E4 **Meybod** Iran 32.18N 53.59E
Meycauayan *see* **Valenzuela**
37 G4 **Meydancık** Turkey 41.28N 42.12E
32 F6 **Meydān-e Gel** *salt flat* Iran 29.00N 55.15E
32 C5 **Meydān-e Naftūn** Iran 31.56N 49.19E
32 H8 **Meydanī, Ra's-e** *C* Iran 25.24N 59.06E
88 F10 **Meyeihido** Mauritania 22.52N 15.53W
63 Q6 **Meyenburg** E Germany 53.20N 12.14E
61 P5 **Meyerode** Belgium 50.20N 6.11E
101 G8 **Meyers Chuck** Alaska 55.40N 132.12W
104 F7 **Meyersdale** Pennsylvania 39.48N 79.04W
95 M2 **Meyerton** S Africa 26.33S 28.01E
56 B2 **Meyllteyrn** Gwynedd **Wales** 52.52N 4.37W
72 J4 **Meymac** France 45.32N 2.08E
32 D4 **Meymeh** Iran 33.26N 51.08E
32 B4 **Meymeh** *R* Iraq/Iran
91 B2 **Méyo-Centre** Cameroon 2.17N 11.03E
71 H9 **Meyrargues** France 43.38N 5.32E
71 E7 **Meyras** France 44.41N 4.17E
66 A7 **Meyrin** Switzerland 46.14N 6.05E
100 L9 **Meyronne** Saskatchewan 49.40N 106.50W
71 C8 **Meyrueis** France 44.11N 3.26E
72 H5 **Meyssac** France 45.03N 1.40E
71 F7 **Meysse** France 44.37N 4.43E
72 G4 **Meyze,la** France 45.37N 1.12E
71 G5 **Meyzieu** France 45.46N 5.00E
25 M9 **Meza** Burma 24.07N 96.03E
35 E8 **Mezada** *anc site* Israel 31.19N 35.21E
35 E9 **Mezad Boqeq** *anc site* Israel 31.12N 35.22E
35 E9 **Mezad Zohar** *anc site* Israel 31.09N 35.21E
75 H5 **Mezalocha,Embalse de** *res* Spain 41.24N 1.04W
37 G3 **Mezar** *mt* Turkey 40.06N 29.11E
37 C2 **Mezar** *R* Turkey
88 N6 **Mézarif,Djebel** *mt* Algeria 31.35N 1.34W
76 F8 **Mezas** *mt* Spain 40.16N 6.51W
82 H7 **Mezdra** Bulgaria 43.08N 23.42E
71 D10 **Méze** France 43.26N 3.37E
71 J9 **Mézel** France 44.00N 6.12E
47 E3 **Mezen'** U.S.S.R. 65.50N 44.20E
47 F3 **Mezen'** *R* U.S.S.R.
71 E7 **Mezenc,Mt** France 44.54N 4.11E
47 E3 **Mezenskaya Guba** *gulf* U.S.S.R.
41 G5 **Mezenskiy** U.S.S.R. 71.16N 98.27E
35 D4 **Mezer** Israel 32.27N 35.03E
71 G4 **Mezeriat** France 46.14N 5.02E
45 B1 **Mezha** Belorussiya **U.S.S.R.** 55.39N 30.25E
45 C1 **Mezha** *R* U.S.S.R.
42 D5 **Mezhdurechensk** U.S.S.R. 53.43N 88.11E
47 K6 **Mezhdurechenskiy** U.S.S.R. 59.38N 65.48E
Mezhdurech'ye *see* **Shali**
62 N1 **Mezhdurech'ye** U.S.S.R. 54.36N 21.31E
41 A4 **Mezhdusharskiy, Ostrov** *isld* Novaya Zemlya **U.S.S.R.**
45 H8 **Mezhevaya** Ukraine **U.S.S.R.** 48.16N 36.47E
45 C7 **Mezhirich** Ukraine **U.S.S.R.** 49.37N 31.25E
42 F4 **Mezhovo** U.S.S.R. 55.34N 95.03E
47 H8 **Mezhozernyy** U.S.S.R. 54.09N 59.22E
44 B9 **Mezhvodnoye** Ukraine **U.S.S.R.** 45.35N 32.51E
82 B4 **Mežica** Yugoslavia 46.30N 14.52E
70 K3 **Mézidon-Canon** France 49.04N 0.03W
69 H4 **Mézières** Ardennes **France** 49.46N 4.44E
66 D5 **Mézières** Switzerland 46.36N 6.46E
72 G2 **Mézières-en-Brenne** France 46.50N 1.12E
72 F3 **Mézières-sur-Issoire** France 46.07N 0.55E
69 B6 **Mézières-sur-Seine** France 48.58N 1.47E
71 E7 **Mézilhac** France 44.48N 4.22E
71 C1 **Mézilles** France 47.42N 3.09E
65 L3 **Mezimostí** Czechoslovakia 49.12N 14.44E
72 E7 **Mézin** France 44.04N 0.16E
45 M1 **Mezinovskiy** U.S.S.R. 55.30N 40.22E
76 D7 **Mézio** Portugal 40.58N 7.54W
66 D1 **Meziré** France 47.32N 6.55E
62 N9 **Mezőberény** Hungary 46.50N 21.00E
62 M8 **Mezőcsát** Hungary 47.50N 20.55E
62 M9 **Mezőhegyes** Hungary 46.20N 20.48E
62 M9 **Mezőkovacsháza** Hungary 46.24N 20.52E
62 M8 **Mezőkövesd** Hungary 47.49N 20.32E
72 B7 **Mézos** France 44.05N 1.10W
62 M8 **Mezőtúr** Hungary 47.00N 20.37E
115 G6 **Mezquital** Mexico 23.31N 104.19W
115 G6 **Mezquital** *R* Mexico
76 E4 **Mezquita,La** Spain 42.01N 7.04W
115 H6 **Mezquitic** Mexico 22.22N 103.42W
36 H1 **Mezraa** Turkey 41.13N 35.07E
79 J2 **Mezzana** Italy 46.19N 10.48E
79 F6 **Mezzánego** Italy 44.23N 9.22E
79 M6 **Mezzano** Emilia **Italy** 44.28N 12.04E
79 L2 **Mezzano** Trento **Italy** 46.09N 11.49E
79 L1 **Mezzaselva** Italy 46.49N 11.35E
79 B4 **Mezzenilé** Italy 45.17N 7.23E
79 K2 **Mezzocorona** Italy 46.13N 11.08E
80 C4 **Mezzo Franco,Pta.di** Italy 42.22N 10.52E
79 M5 **Mezzogoro** Italy 44.54N 12.06E
81 J10 **Mezzo Gregorio,Mte** Sicily 36.58N 14.58E
81 F8 **Mezzoiuso** Sicily 37.52N 13.28E
79 F2 **Mezzola,L.di** *L* Italy 46.13N 9.26E
79 K2 **Mezzolombardo** Italy 46.13N 11.06E
88 S4 **Mezzouna, El** Tunisia 34.34N 9.50E
93 F6 **Mfanganu I** Kenya 0.27S 34.03E
91 D5 **M'Fia** Congo 3.25S 14.52E
91 B2 **Mfou** Cameroon 3.47N 11.41E
91 C6 **Mfouati** Congo 4.26S 13.48E
Mfumbiro *mts see* **Virunga** *mts*
46 H1 **Mga** U.S.S.R. 59.30N 31.00E
40 J6 **Mgachi** Sakhalin **U.S.S.R.** 51.03N 142.20E
89 C4 **Mgallou,Mt** Mauritania 14.59N 12.08W
84 X19 **Mġarr** Gozo **Mediterranean Sea** 36.01N 14.18E
84 Y20 **Mġarr** Malta 35.56N 14.22E
93 C10 **Mgende** Tanzania 4.37S 31.12E
92 G4 **Mgeni** Tanzania 4.49S 34.45E
92 H4 **Mgera** Tanzania 5.24S 37.34E
92 H6 **Mgeta** Tanzania 8.19S 36.04E
85 F5 **M. Ghayzal** Libya 29.45N 20.04E
45 D3 **Mglin** U.S.S.R. 53.03N 32.50E
92 G4 **Mgori** Tanzania 4.50S 35.00E
95 L7 **Mgwali** *R* S Africa
88 L7 **M'Hamid** Morocco 29.50N 5.40W
93 D9 **Mhandu Hills** Tanzania
77 E9 **Mharhar** *R* Morocco
28 B2 **Mhasvad** Maharashtra **India** 17.40N 74.50E
60 T17 **Mheer** Netherlands 50.47N 5.47E
95 O4 **Mhlangana** S Africa 28.50S 30.20E
95 O10 **Mhlatuze** *R* S Africa
95 O9 **Mhlosinga** S Africa 27.54S 32.13E
92 H5 **Mhonda** Tanzania 6.07S 37.36E
58 H4 **Mhor,L** Highland **Scotland** 57.14N 4.25W
29 D6 **Mhow** Madhya Prad **India** 22.32N 75.49E
93 E9 **Mhunze** Tanzania 3.36S 33.50E
25 B2 **Mi** *R* Burma
53 V13 **Mia** *isld* Norway 62.39N 6.36E
115 L9 **Miahuatlán** Mexico 16.21N 96.36W
76 H10 **Miajadas** Spain 39.10N 5.54W
29 B4 **Miajlar** Rajasthan **India** 26.16N 70.21E
111 O8 **Miami** Arizona 33.24N 110.54W
105 G12 **Miami** Florida 25.45N 80.15W
100 T9 **Miami** Manitoba 49.22N 98.16W
109 Q5 **Miami** Oklahoma 36.53N 94.54W
112 D8 **Miami** Texas 35.42N 100.37W
92 D10 **Miami** Zimbabwe 16.40S 29.49E
104 A7 **Miami** *R* Ohio
105 B11 **Miami Airport** Florida 25.45N 80.16W
23 B5 **Miamian Shan** *mt ra* Sichuan **China**
105 G12 **Miami Beach** Florida 25.47N 80.07W
105 G11 **Miami Canal** Florida
104 A7 **Miami, Gt** *R* Ohio
84 R14 **Mia Milea** Cyprus 35.12N 33.26E
104 A7 **Miami, Little** *R* Ohio
104 A7 **Miamisburg** Ohio 39.37N 84.16W
105 G12 **Miami Shores** Florida 25.52N 80.11W
105 G12 **Miami Springs** Florida 25.48N 80.18W
32 H7 **Miām Kand** Iran 26.15N 59.23E
30 A8 **Miana** Madhya Prad **India** 24.50N 77.28E
32 C5 **Miān Ab** Iran 31.59N 48.29E
32 G2 **Miānābad** Iran 37.03N 57.26E
31 B7 **Mianaz** Pakistan 26.19N 63.08E
23 B1 **Miancaowan** Qinghai **China** 35.15N 98.46E
31 G5 **Mian Channun** Pakistan 30.24N 72.27E
23 F1 **Mianchi** Henan **China** 34.45N 111.47E
32 E3 **Miāndarreh** Iran 35.33N 53.44E
32 G2 **Miāndasht** Iran 36.25N 56.05E
32 H3 **Miāndehi** Iran 34.51N 58.37E
32 B2 **Miāndowāb** Iran 36.57N 46.06E
95 C5 **Miandrarivo** Madagascar 19.25S 46.44E
95 B5 **Miandrivazo** Madagascar 19.31S 45.29E
21 B3 **Mianduhe** Nei Monggol Zizhiqu **China** 49.10N 121.02E
32 B2 **Miāneh** Iran 37.23N 47.45E
34 O3 **Miāneh, Kūreh-ye** *mt* Iran 35.20N 46.26E
19 E1 **Miangas** *isld* Indonesia 5.32N 126.37E
25 F4 **Miang,Phukao** *mt* Thailand 16.52N 101.01E
29 A7 **Miani** Gujarat **India** 21.50N 69.26E
29 D2 **Miani** Punjab **India** 31.42N 75.39E
31 G4 **Miani** Rawalpindi **Pakistan** 32.31N 73.08E
31 D8 **Miani Hor** *lagoon* Pakistan
31 C4 **Mianjoi** Afghanistan 32.30N 64.14E
31 F3 **Mian Kalai** Pakistan 34.49N 71.40E
32 E2 **Mian Kaleh, Shebh-e Jazīreh-ye** *pen* Iran
23 B5 **Mianmian Shan** *mt ra* Yunnan **China**
23 C4 **Mianning** Sichuan **China** 28.33N 102.09E
23 G6 **Mian Shui** *R* Jiangxi **China**
31 F4 **Mianwali** Pakistan 32.32N 71.33E
31 F5 **Mianwali** *dist* Pakistan
23 D2 **Mian Xian** Shaanxi **China** 33.12N 106.36E
23 F3 **Mianyang** Hubei **China** 30.20N 113.31E
23 C3 **Mianyang** Sichuan **China** 31.25N 104.45E
23 C3 **Mianzhu** Sichuan **China** 31.22N 104.11E
22 M7 **Miaodao Qundao** *isld* Liaoning **China**
24 D3 **Miao'ergou** Xinjiang Uygur Zizhiqu **China** 45.30N 83.50E
23 J6 **Miao-li** Taiwan 24.33N 120.48E
21 E6 **Miaoling** Jilin **China** 43.30N 129.39E
23 D5 **Miao Ling** *mt ra* Guizhou **China**
23 E6 **Miaoping** Guangxi **China** 25.38N 110.03E
91 G11 **Mia Pulo** Angola 15.34S 20.31E
95 C5 **Miarinarivo** Madagascar 18.56S 46.55E
95 D4 **Miarinarivo** Madagascar 16.35S 48.15E
95 C6 **Miarinavaratra** Madagascar 20.12S 47.30E
15 J8 **Miaru** Papua New Guinea 8.21S 146.08E
95 A7 **Miary** Madagascar 23.20S 43.45E
87 E1 **Mias** Sudan 18.15N 35.47E
66 K8 **Miasino** Italy 45.48N 8.26E
47 M6 **Miass** U.S.S.R. 55.00N 60.08E
47 M6 **Miass** *R* U.S.S.R.
62 K1 **Miastko** Poland 54.00N 16.58E
119 C9 **Miazal** Ecuador 2.37S 77.50W
91 F5 **Mibenge** Zaïre 3.58S 19.10E
93 A8 **Mibirizi** Rwanda 2.36S 28.57E
85 N11 **Mib,Jebel** *mt* Sudan 17.51N 35.49E
15 G8 **Mibu I** Papua New Guinea 8.42S 143.26E
120 D9 **Mica,Cerro de** *pk* Chile 21.43S 69.55W
101 O9 **Mica Creek** *dam site* Br Col 52.00N 118.28W
111 O9 **Mica Mt** Arizona 32.13N 110.34W
91 E8 **Micanda** Angola 8.31S 16.25E
23 D2 **Micang Shan** *mts* Shaanxi **China**
105 E8 **Micanopy** Florida 29.29N 82.18W
94 O2 **Micaune** Mozambique 18.18S 36.35E
105 C7 **Miccosukee** Florida 30.35N 84.02W
105 D7 **Miccosukee L** Florida 30.35N 83.59W
15 H7 **Michael, Mt** Papua New Guinea 6.25S 145.20E
47 G4 **Michaichmon'** U.S.S.R. 64.12N 50.02E
62 N7 **Michal'any** Czechoslovakia 48.33N 21.40E
62 N7 **Michalovce** Czechoslovakia 48.45N 21.55E
100 H3 **Michel** Saskatchewan 55.59N 109.06W
65 N5 **Michelbach** Austria 48.06N 15.47E
61 F3 **Michelbeke** Belgium 50.50N 3.46E
56 J5 **Micheldever** Hants **Eng** 51.09N 1.15W
74 K8 **Michelet** Algeria 36.34N 4.20E
113 P2 **Michelson,Mt** Alaska 69.19N 144.20W
64 G4 **Michelstadt** W Germany 49.40N 9.00E
63 S8 **Michendorf** E Germany 52.19N 13.02E
61 N4 **Micheroux** Belgium 50.37N 5.43E
116 K5 **Miches** Dominican Rep 19.00N 69.00W
100 E7 **Michichi** Alberta 51.35N 112.28W
105 J1 **Michie,L** N Carolina 36.10N 78.51W
11 M11 **Michies Crossing** New Zealand 45.45S 170.35E
106 F3 **Michigamme** Michigan 46.32N 88.08W
106 F3 **Michigamme, L** Michigan 43.30N 88.04W
106 F3 **Michigamme Res** Michigan 46.11N 88.12W
108 M1 **Michigan** N Dakota 48.02N 98.08W
102 J1 **Michigan** *state* U.S.A.
106 K7 **Michigan Center** Michigan 42.14N 84.20W
106 H8 **Michigan City** Indiana 41.43N 86.54W
106 G6 **Michigan,L** U.S.A.
106 H9 **Michigantown** Indiana 40.22N 86.21W
90 F6 **Michika** Nigeria 10.36N 13.23E
29 G8 **Michinberi** Madhya Prad **India** 19.32N 81.08E
99 F5 **Michipicoten** Ontario 47.57N 84.55W
99 E5 **Michipicoten B** Ontario
99 E5 **Michipicoten I** Ontario
99 F5 **Michipicoten River** Ontario 47.56N 84.50W
Michkap *see* **Muchkapskiy**
115 H8 **Michoacan** *state* Mexico
62 N4 **Michów** Poland 51.32N 22.17E
82 L8 **Michurin** Bulgaria 42.09N 27.51E
45 M4 **Michurinsk** U.S.S.R. 52.54N 40.30E
37 G7 **Micinger** *R* Turkey
57 J3 **Mickle Fell** *mt* Durham **Eng** 54.38N 2.18W
56 L5 **Mickleham** Surrey **Eng** 51.16N 0.20W
56 H3 **Mickleton** Glos **Eng** 52.06N 1.45W
91 C6 **Miconje** Angola 4.26S 12.48E
115 K6 **Micos** Mexico 22.10N 99.11W
116 O8 **Micoud** St Lucia, W I 13.50N 60.55W
9 L7 **Micronesia** *ethnic reg* **Pacific Oc**
120 F8 **Miculpaya** Bolivia 19.45S 65.32W
18 G4 **Midai** *isld* Indonesia 3.00N 107.46E
100 O9 **Midale** Saskatchewan 49.23N 103.21W
74 E10 **Midar** Morocco 34.57N 3.33W
110 J8 **Midas** Nevada 41.15N 116.48W
96 F7 **Mid-Atlantic Ridge** Atlantic Oc
86 D7 **Midawara,El** *hill* Egypt 29.11N 30.21E
58 T11 **Midbea** Orkney **Scotland** 59.17N 2.59W
58 K7 **Mid Calder** Lothian **Scotland** 55.54N 3.29W
53 W19 **Middagsrusti** *mt* Norway 59.52N 7.04E
53 W14 **Middagstind** *mt* Norway 62.27N 7.28E
60 M13 **Middelaar** Netherlands 51.44N 5.55E
60 K14 **Middelbeers** Netherlands 51.28N 5.15E
61 D1 **Middelburg** Belgium 51.15N 3.25E
95 H7 **Middelburg** Cape Province **S Africa** 31.28S 25.01E
60 B2 **Middelburg** Netherlands 51.30N 3.36E
95 N1 **Middelburg** Transvaal **S Africa** 25.47S 29.28E
53 D6 **Middelfart** Denmark 55.30N 9.44E
60 C3 **Middelgat** *channel* Netherlands
63 T4 **Middelhagen** E Germany 54.20N 13.43E
60 E12 **Middelharnis** Netherlands 51.45N 4.10E
60 J9 **Middelie** Netherlands 52.32N 5.01E
61 B2 **Middelkerke** Belgium 51.11N 2.50E
95 G8 **Middelkraal** S Africa 32.47S 23.04E
94 F8 **Middelpos** S Africa 31.55S 20.18E
60 F13 **Middelsluis** Netherlands 51.44N 4.26E
60 P6 **Middelstum** Netherlands 53.21N 6.39E
94 R13 **Middelvlei** S Africa 26.14S 27.38E
94 J5 **Middelwit** S Africa 24.58S 27.00E
60 H9 **Midden Beemster** Netherlands 52.33N 4.55E
41 D2 **Middendorfa,Mys** *C* Novaya Zemlya U.S.S.R. 76.03N 67.01E
41 F3 **Middendorfa,Zaliv** *gulf* U.S.S.R.
95 M3 **Middenin** S Africa 27.44S 28.02E
60 H8 **Middenmeer** Netherlands 52.48N 4.59E
35 F9 **Middin** Jordan 31.07N 35.44E
108 O1 **Middle** *R* Minnesota
96 A7 **Middle America Trench** Pacific Oc
122 R6 **Middle America Trench** Pacific Oc
28 G7 **Middle Andaman** *isld* Andaman Is
10 E11 **Middle B** Lord Howe I **Pacific Oc**
12 D5 **Middleback,Mt** S Australia 33.13S 136.06E
103 N3 **Middleboro** Massachusetts 41.54N 70.55W
104 E7 **Middlebourne** W Virginia 39.30N 80.53W
100 G1 **Middlebro** Manitoba 49.01N 95.24W
104 L4 **Middleburg** New York 42.36N 74.20W
104 H6 **Middleburg** Pennsylvania 40.47N 77.03W
104 H8 **Middleburg** Virginia 38.58N 77.46W
103 H3 **Middlebury** Connecticut 41.32N 73.08W
106 J8 **Middlebury** Indiana 41.41N 85.42W
104 M2 **Middlebury** Vermont 44.02N 73.11W
101 F1 **Middle Chan.** N W Terr
28 G7 **Middle Coral Bank** Andaman Is
13 C3 **Middle Cr** N Terr **Australia**
13 F3 **Middle Creek** Queensland
95 L8 **Middledrift** S Africa 32.50S 26.59E
103 J3 **Middlefield** Connecticut 41.30N 72.44W
103 H2 **Middlefield** Massachusetts 42.21N 73.01W
11 B12 **Middle Fiord** New Zealand
108 D6 **Middle Fork** *R* Wyoming
122 U1 **Middle Ground** *bank* Midway Is **Pacific Oc** 28.15N 177.24W
28 B8 **Middle Ground** *isld* Maharashtra **India** 18.56N 72.51E
57 K4 **Middleham** N Yorks **Eng** 54.17N 1.49W
12 M7 **Middle Harb** *inlet* New S Wales
23 B10 **Middle I** Hong Kong 22.13N 114.10E
106 L4 **Middle I** Michigan 45.12N 83.20W
25 D8 **Middle I** Thailand 9.04N 97.50E
96 B16 **Middle I** Tristan da Cunha 37.27S 12.31W
14 E10 **Middle I** W Australia 34.07S 123.10E
103 J5 **Middle Island** Long I, N Y 40.53N 72.57W
110 E8 **Middle L** California 41.25N 120.05W
110 F8 **Middle L** Nevada 41.38N 119.37W
100 M6 **Middle Lake** Saskatchewan 52.31N 105.20W
56 K6 **Middle Lavant** W Sussex **Eng** 50.52N 0.48W
108 L8 **Middle Loup** *R* Nebraska
11 E12 **Middlemarch** New Zealand 45.30S 170.10E
56 G6 **Middlemarsh** Dorset **Eng** 50.52N 2.29W
103 E2 **Middle Mt** New York 42.03N 74.48W
104 A6 **Middle Point** Ohio 40.52N 84.37W
104 G3 **Middleport** New York 43.13N 78.28W
104 C7 **Middleport** Ohio 39.00N 82.05W
103 B5 **Middleport** Pennsylvania 40.45N 76.05W
26 V3 **Middle Pt** Christmas I **Ind Oc** 10.29S 105.38E
98 R5 **Middle Ridge** *hills* Newfoundland
101 L8 **Middle River** Br Columbia 54.53N 125.07W
103 B8 **Middle River** Maryland 39.20N 76.26W
108 O1 **Middle River** Minnesota 48.25N 96.10W
100 G8 **Middle Sand Hills, The** Alberta
105 D1 **Middlesbro** Kentucky 36.37N 83.43W
57 L3 **Middlesbrough** Cleveland **Eng** 54.35N 1.14W
115 P9 **Middlesex** Belize 17.01N 88.30W
104 H4 **Middlesex** New York 42.42N 77.17W
103 J4 **Middlesex** *co* Connecticut
103 M2 **Middlesex** *co* Massachusetts
103 F6 **Middlesex** *co* New Jersey
104 P8 **Middlesex Fells** *hills* Massachusetts
57 K5 **Middlestown** W Yorks **Eng** 53.39N 1.36W
57 H4 **Middleton** Cumbria **Eng** 54.16N 2.35W
57 J5 **Middleton** Greater Manchester **Eng** 53.33N 2.12W
110 J6 **Middleton** Idaho 43.43N 116.37W
106 K6 **Middleton** Michigan 43.12N 84.40W
103 F4 **Middleton** New York 41.26N 74.26W
56 M2 **Middleton** Norfolk **Eng** 52.43N 0.28E
98 G9 **Middleton** Nova Scotia 44.56N 65.04W
57 M4 **Middleton** N Yorks **Eng** 54.15N 0.48W
13 F5 **Middleton** Queensland 22.20S 141.32E
95 J8 **Middleton** S Africa 32.57S 25.50E
107 H6 **Middleton** Tennessee 35.03N 88.53W
106 E6 **Middleton** Wisconsin 43.06N 89.31W
113 P7 **Middleton I** Alaska 59.29N 146.28W
57 J3 **Middleton in Teesdale** Durham **Eng** 54.38N 2.04W
57 M5 **Middleton on the Wolds** Humberside **Eng** 53.56N 0.33W
10 M7 **Middleton Reef** Pacific Oc 29.30S 159.12E
56 J4 **Middleton Stoney** Oxon **Eng** 51.55N 1.13W
59 J3 **Middletown** Armagh **N Ireland** 54.18N 6.50W
103 J3 **Middletown** Connecticut 41.34N 72.39W
103 C8 **Middletown** Delaware 39.27N 75.44W
106 J9 **Middletown** Indiana 40.02N 85.31W
104 H7 **Middletown** Maryland 39.27N 77.33W
103 F6 **Middletown** New Jersey 40.23N 74.08W
104 L5 **Middletown** New York 41.26N 74.26W
104 A7 **Middletown** Ohio 39.31N 84.22W
103 A6 **Middletown** Pennsylvania 40.12N 76.45W
56 E2 **Middletown** Powys **Wales** 52.43N 3.03E
103 M3 **Middletown** Rhode I 41.33N 71.18W
103 E5 **Middle Valley** New Jersey 40.45N 74.49W
106 J7 **Middleville** Michigan 42.42N 85.30W
104 L3 **Middleville** New York 43.09N 75.00W
112 B8 **Middle Water** Texas 35.51N 102.48W
57 J6 **Middlewich** Cheshire **Eng** 53.11N 2.27W
98 H9 **Middlewood** Nova Scotia 44.14N 64.33W
87 C8 **Mide** Sudan 5.05N 30.45E
88 L5 **Midelt** Morocco 32.41N 4.43W
112 L7 **Midfield** Texas 28.56N 96.15W
57 H3 **Midgeholme** Cumbria **Eng** 54.56N 2.34W
56 E4 **Mid Glamorgan** *co* Wales
35 E10 **Midhbah,Jeb.el** *mt* Jordan 30.52N 35.28E
50 E6 **Midhdalsfjall** *mt* Iceland 64.19N 20.40W
50 K3 **Midhdalsvatn** *L* Iceland 65.55N 15.29W
50 E6 **Midhdalur** Iceland 64.15N 20.40W
84 E6 **Midhéa** Greece 37.40N 22.50E
50 E7 **Midhey** Iceland 63.36N 20.08W
50 D4 **Midhfjall** *mt* Iceland 65.18N 21.49W
50 E4 **Midhfjardhará** *R* Iceland
50 K3 **Midhfjardhará** *R* Iceland
50 K2 **Midhfjördhur** Múlasýsla, Nordhur **Iceland** 66.03N 15.06W
50 E4 **Midhfjördhur** *B* Húnavatnssýsla, Vestur Iceland
50 K2 **Midhfjördhur** *B* Múlasýsla, Nordhur **Iceland** 66.03N 15.05W
50 G1 **Midhgardhar** Iceland 66.32N 18.00W
50 E4 **Midhhop** Iceland 65.30N 20.25W
33 F4 **Midhnab,Al** Saudi Arabia 25.55N 44.15E
50 C7 **Midhnes** *pen* Iceland
Midhnib *see* **Midhnab, Al**
50 D6 **Midhsandur** Iceland 64.24N 21.28W
11 J6 **Midhurst** New Zealand 39.16S 174.18E
99 L8 **Midhurst** Ontario 44.26N 79.45W
56 K6 **Midhurst** W Sussex **Eng** 50.59N 0.45W
33 E8 **Midī** Yemen 16.18N 42.47E
Midian *reg see* **Midyan** *region*
72 K9 **Midi,Can.du** France
72 E10 **Midi de Bigorre,Pic du** *mt* France 42.57N 0.08E
72 D10 **Midi d'Ossau, Pic du** *mt* France 42.50N 0.26W
95 O5 **Mid Illovo** S Africa 29.58S 30.31E
26 G6 **Mid-Indian Basin** Indian Oc
26 F6 **Mid-Indian Ridge** Indian Oc
107 B6 **Midland** Arkansas 35.06N 94.23W
111 K8 **Midland** California 33.52N 114.46W
104 G7 **Midland** Maryland 39.34N 78.59W
106 K6 **Midland** Michigan 43.38N 84.14W
99 L8 **Midland** Ontario 44.45N 79.53W
108 J5 **Midland** S Dakota 44.04N 101.10W
112 E4 **Midland** Texas 32.00N 102.09W
107 L10 **Midland City** Alabama 31.20N 85.31W
14 B9 **Midland Junc** W Australia 31.54S 115.57E
103 F5 **Midland Park** New Jersey 40.59N 74.09W
92 D10 **Midlands** *prov* Zimbabwe
72 F4 **Midlet** France 45.34N 0.54E
59 F8 **Midleton** Cork **Irish Rep** 51.55N 8.10W
114 E8 **Mid Lock** Hawaiian Is
112 L3 **Midlothian** Texas 32.30N 97.01W
104 H9 **Midlothian** Virginia 37.31N 77.39W
Midlothian *co see* **Lothian and Borders** *regions*
63 J5 **Midlum** W Germany 53.44N 8.38E
95 O5 **Midmar Dam** *res* Natal **S Africa** 29.32S 30.06E
29 K6 **Midnapore** W Bengal **India** 22.25N 87.24E
29 K6 **Midnapore** *dist* W Bengal **India**
107 F8 **Midnight** Mississippi 33.02N 90.35W
76 D8 **Midões** Portugal 40.23N 7.57W
95 C7 **Midongy Atsimo** Madagascar 23.35S 47.01E
95 C6 **Midongy Ouest** Madagascar 20.40S 46.11E
20 D3 **Midori** Kanagawa **Japan**
20 D9 **Midori-kawa** *R* Japan
72 D8 **Midou** *R* France
72 C8 **Midouze** *R* France
122 G6 **Mid-Pacific Mountains** Pacific Oc
122 J6 **Mid-Pacific Mts** Pacific Oc
35 D3 **Midrakh Oz** Israel 32.36N 35.10E
19 M8 **Midsayap** Mindanao **Philippines** 7.14N 124.33E
60 K6 **Midsland** Terschelling **Netherlands** 53.23N 5.17E
53 T15 **Midtbø** Norway 61.40N 5.28E
53 X19 **Midtfjell** *mt* Norway 59.37N 7.40E
53 S15 **Midtgulen** Norway 61.44N 5.11E
23 B6 **Midu** Yunnan **China** 25.22N 100.33E
110 J5 **Midvale** Idaho 44.29N 116.45W
110 O9 **Midvale** Utah 40.37N 111.55W
105 E5 **Midville** Georgia 32.50N 82.13W
107 L9 **Midway** Alabama 32.04N 85.32W
101 O11 **Midway** Br Col 49.02N 118.45W
105 F6 **Midway** Georgia 31.48N 81.27W
107 M3 **Midway** Kentucky 38.09N 84.40W
Midway Oman*see* **Thamarīt**
94 S14 **Midway** S Africa 26.18S 27.51E
112 F3 **Midway** Texas 32.42N 101.46W
112 M4 **Midway** Texas 31.02N 95.48W
106 Q3 **Midway Airport** Chicago, Illinois 41.47N 87.45W
113 O1 **Midway Is** Alaska
122 U2 **Midway Is** Pacific Oc 28.12N 177.24W
114 A1 **Midway Is** *atoll* Hawaiian Is 28.15N 177.25W
98 E1 **Midway L** Quebec 52.28N 67.05W
11 N4 **Midway Pt** New Zealand 37.33S 178.14E
14 E6 **Midway Well** W Australia 23.27S 123.45E
108 D6 **Midwest** Wyoming 43.26N 106.19W
109 N6 **Midwest City** Oklahoma 35.28N 98.24W
89 M8 **Mid-Western** *reg* Nigeria
60 Q7 **Midwolda** Netherlands 53.12N 7.00E
60 J9 **Midwoud** Netherlands 52.43N 5.05E
33 A3 **Midyan** *reg* Saudi Arabia
37 F8 **Midyat** Turkey 37.25N 41.20E
37 F8 **Midyat Dağları** *mts* Turkey
36 C1 **Midye** Turkey 41.36N 28.06E
58 Q8 **Mid Yell** Shetland **Scotland** 60.36N 1.05W
82 H7 **Midžor** *mt* Yugoslavia 43.24N 22.40E
20 K7 **Mie** *prefect* Japan
62 M5 **Miechów** Poland 50.20N 20.00E
61 L5 **Miécret** Belgium 50.22N 5.15E
65 D7 **Mieders** Austria 47.10N 11.23E
75 H5 **Miedes** Spain 41.15N 1.30W
62 H2 **Miedwie, L** Poland
62 J3 **Międzychód** Poland 52.36N 15.53E
62 K5 **Międzylesie** Poland 50.10N 16.40E
62 O4 **Międzyrzec** Poland 52.00N 22.48E
62 J3 **Międzyrzecz** Poland 52.27N 15.34E
62 K4 **Miejska Gorka** Poland 51.40N 16.59E
51 L5 **Miekojärvi** *L* Finland 66.35N 24.20E
72 E9 **Miélan** France 43.26N 0.19E
62 N5 **Mielec** Poland 50.18N 21.25E
61 L3 **Mielen-boven-Aalst** Belgium 50.45N 5.13E
65 C7 **Mieminger Kette** *mts* Austria
52 H10 **Mien** *L* Sweden 56.25N 14.55E
89 G5 **Miéna** Mali 12.37N 5.57W
12 H8 **Miena** Tasmania 41.58S 146.11E
91 F12 **Mienga** Angola 17.16S 19.50E
23 J6 **Mien-hua Hsü** *isld* Taiwan
Mien-ning *see* **Lincang**
109 D7 **Miera** New Mexico 34.57N 106.18W
75 C1 **Miera** *R* Spain
75 Q3 **Mieras** Spain 42.07N 2.39E
115 K4 **Mier,Ciudad** Mexico 26.28N 99.10W
82 K4 **Miercurea Ciuc** Romania 46.21N 25.48E
76 H2 **Mieres** Spain 43.15N 5.46W
60 L14 **Mierlo** Netherlands 51.27N 5.37E
51 K2 **Mieron** Norway 69.08N 23.20E
72 H6 **Miers** France 44.51N 1.41E
115 J6 **Miery Noriaga** Mexico 23.28N 100.10W
64 M8 **Miesbach** W Germany 47.47N 11.50E
87 H6 **Mieso** Ethiopia 9.15N 40.43E
Miesso *see* **Mieso**
63 O8 **Mieste** E Germany 52.29N 11.12E
62 H3 **Mieszkowice** Poland 52.48N 14.31E
71 K4 **Mieussy** France 46.08N 6.32E
76 F6 **Mieza** Spain 41.10N 6.42W
33 D7 **Mifah** Saudi Arabia 18.54N 41.57E
104 H6 **Mifflin** Pennsylvania 40.33N 77.26W
104 H6 **Mifflinburg** Pennsylvania 40.56N 77.03W
104 H6 **Mifflintown** Pennsylvania 40.34N 77.24W
103 B4 **Mifflinville** Pennsylvania 41.02N 76.17W
Mifjir *R see* **Hadera** *R*
53 V13 **Mifjord** *inlet* Norway 62.38N 6.35E
87 D2 **Miga,El** Sudan 16.26N 32.59E
92 C3 **Migamba** Zaïre 3.00S 27.59E
26 T5 **Migaswewa** Sri Lanka 8.12N 81.05E
35 F1 **Migav 'Am** Israel 33.15N 35.33E
44 H5 **Mig Bolyu** U.S.S.R. 42.15N 47.26E
35 F2 **Migda** Israel 32.50N 35.30E
35 D3 **Migdal Ha'Emeq** Israel 32.40N 35.13E
95 J2 **Migdol** S Africa 26.53S 25.27E
69 F8 **Migennes** France 47.58N 3.31E
92 J6 **Migeregere** Tanzania 8.50S 39.15E
32 H5 **Mighān** Iran 31.49N 59.29E
66 K8 **Migiandone** Italy 45.58N 8.22E
33 A4 **Migif,Gebel** *mt* Egypt 24.46N 34.29E
28 K1 **Miging** Assam India 28.49N 94.42E
87 E5 **Migin,Jeb** *mt* Sudan 11.51N 34.54E
36 J6 **Mığır** *mt* Turkey 36.50N 36.22E
87 M5 **Migiurtinia** *prov* Somalia
67 P13 **Migliacciaro** Corsica 42.00N 9.24E
79 L5 **Migliarino** Italy 44.46N 11.56E
81 N2 **Migliónico** Italy 40.34N 16.30E
72 E2 **Mignaloux Beauvoir** France 46.33N 0.26E
80 J6 **Mignano** Italy 41.24N 13.28E
79 G5 **Mignano,L.di** *L* Italy
61 G4 **Mignault** Belgium 50.32N 4.10E
72 G2 **Migné** Indre France 46.43N 1.19E
72 E2 **Migné-Auxances** Vienne France 46.37N 0.19E
80 E4 **Mignone** *R* Italy
71 J3 **Mignovillard-Petit-Villard** France 46.47N 6.03E
93 F7 **Migori** Kenya 1.03S 34.28E
87 E3 **Migreh** Sudan 14.01N 34.35E
72 D4 **Migron** France 45.48N 0.23W
115 L8 **Miguel Alemán, Preso** *res* Mexico
117 F7 **Miguel Alves** Brazil 4.11S 42.55W
115 H5 **Miguel Auza** Mexico 24.20N 103.30W
118 H2 **Miguel Calmon** Brazil 11.23S 40.36W
119 B3 **Miguel de la Borda** Panama 9.09N 80.20W
75 D8 **Miguel Esteban** Spain 39.31N 3.05W
77 J3 **Miguelturra** Spain 38.58N 3.53W
45 N7 **Migulinskaya** U.S.S.R. 49.42N 41.15E
93 K7 **Migwani** Kenya 1.10S 38.01E
25 E5 **Migyaunglaung** Burma 14.42N 98.07E
25 C3 **Migyaunye** Burma 19.51N 95.07E
82 K3 **Mihăileni** Romania 47.58N 26.09E
36 E2 **Mihalgazi** Turkey 40.02N 30.33E
36 F3 **Mihalıççık** Turkey 39.52N 31.30E
20 G7 **Mihara** Japan 34.24N 133.04E
20 N7 **Mihara-yama** *vol* Japan 34.43N 139.23E
20 O4 **Miharu** Japan 37.25N 140.29E
26 R5 **Mihintale** Sri Lanka 8.20N 80.30E
11 M12 **Mihiwaka** *mt* New Zealand 45.47S 170.36E
64 J1 **Mihla** E Germany 51.05N 10.20E
36 H6 **Mihmandar** Turkey 36.52N 35.20E
31 H2 **Mihman Yoli Davan** *pass* Afghanistan/China 37.17N 74.45E
35 F9 **Mihna** Jordan 31.07N 35.42E
35 G4 **Mihna** Jordan 32.22N 35.45E
20 G6 **Miho-wan** *B* Japan
33 K6 **Mihrād,Al** *des reg* Saudi Arabia
Mihrakan *see* **Mehrakān** *salt marsh*
Mihran *R see* **Mehrān** *R*
37 F5 **Mihrap Dağı** *mt* Turkey 40.37N 41.26E
Mihrjan *see* **Mehr Jān**
92 H7 **Mihuru** Tanzania 10.10S 36.55E
21 E11 **Miike** Japan 33.07N 130.36E
35 E1 **Mi'ilya** Israel 33.02N 35.15E
33 J4 **Mijann, Al** *area* Saudi Arabia/U.A.E.
76 K8 **Mijares** Spain 40.18N 4.50W
75 J7 **Mijares** *R* Spain
77 G7 **Mijas** Spain 36.36N 4.38W
77 G7 **Mijas, Sierra de** *mts* Spain
60 H11 **Mijdrecht** Netherlands 52.12N 4.52E
87 M6 **Mijjarten** *tribe* Somalia
Mijnabad *see* **Mozhnābād**
71 J4 **Mijoux** France 46.22N 6.00E
106 L5 **Mikado** Michigan 44.37N 83.27W
100 P7 **Mikado** Saskatchewan 51.36N 102.15W
20 B1 **Mikajima-Shinden** Saitama **Japan**
20 G1 **Mikasa** Japan 43.15N 141.57E
46 F4 **Mikashevichi** Belorussiya **U.S.S.R.** 52.16N 27.20E
20 K5 **Mikawa** Japan 36.30N 136.30E
92 B6 **Mikengere** Zaïre 9.51S 25.30E
92 H5 **Mikese** Tanzania 6.49S 37.51E
82 L1 **Mikhailovka** U.S.S.R. 49.14N 27.10E
39 G1 **Mikhalkino** U.S.S.R. 69.28N 161.30E
44 D5 **Mikha Tskhakaya** Georgia **U.S.S.R.** 42.16N 41.59E
45 L2 **Mikhaylov** U.S.S.R. 54.14N 39.00E
41 E3 **Mikhaylova** U.S.S.R. 75.07N 87.00E
82 H7 **Mikhaylovgrad** Bulgaria 43.25N 23.11E
123 C3 **Mikhaylov I** Antarctica
42 B5 **Mikhaylovka** Altay **U.S.S.R.** 51.48N 79.45E
40 E7 **Mikhaylovka** Amur **U.S.S.R.** 49.10N 129.55E
46 O5 **Mikhaylovka** Astrakhan' **U.S.S.R.** 47.37N 46.59E
42 J6 **Mikhaylovka** Buryat **U.S.S.R.** 51.58N 110.30E
42 K6 **Mikhaylovka** Chita **U.S.S.R.** 51.08N 119.29E
45 E9 **Mikhaylovka** Dnepropetrovsk, Ukraine **U.S.S.R.** 47.46N 33.45E
43 K5 **Mikhaylovka** Dzhambul, Kazakhstan U.S.S.R. 43.01N 71.32E
43 M1 **Mikhaylovka** Pavlodar, Kazakhstan **U.S.S.R.** 53.52N 76.31E
40 F10 **Mikhaylovka** Primor'ye **U.S.S.R.** 43.58N 132.01E
45 G9 **Mikhaylovka** Ukraine **U.S.S.R.** 47.34N 35.16E
45 P6 **Mikhaylovka** Volgograd **U.S.S.R.** 50.05N 43.15E
82 K8 **Mikhaylovo** Bulgaria 42.13N 25.30E
45 M7 **Mikhaylovo-Aleksandrovskiy** U.S.S.R. 49.12N 40.15E
47 L4 **Mikhaylovsk** Sverdlovsk **U.S.S.R.** 56.29N 59.05E
45 N6 **Mikhaylovskaya** Volgograd **U.S.S.R.** 50.58N 41.54E
42 B5 **Mikhaylovskiy** Altay **U.S.S.R.** 51.41N 79.47E
44 C4 **Mikhel'ripshi** Georgia **U.S.S.R.** 46.31N 40.06E
42 H4 **Mikheyevo** U.S.S.R. 57.10N 104.55E
35 C4 **Mikhmoret** Israel 32.24N 34.52E
45 J1 **Mikhnevo** U.S.S.R. 55.07N 37.59E
84 C6 **Mikhói** Greece 37.58N 21.30E
41 E3 **Mikhoylova,Bukhta** *gulf* U.S.S.R.
34 B9 **Mikhrot Timna** Israel 29.46N 34.58E
33 D7 **Mikhwa** Saudi Arabia 19.48N 41.28E
20 H7 **Miki** Japan 34.50N 134.59E
92 K7 **Mikindani** Tanzania 10.16S 40.05E
39 G3 **Mikino** U.S.S.R. 62.44N 163.50E
28 J3 **Mikir and North Cachar Hills, United Dists.of** Assam India
28 J2 **Mikir Hills** Assam India
113 D6 **Mikisagimiut** Alaska 60.12N 167.20W
110 E4 **Mikkalo** Oregon 45.29N 120.13W
51 N10 **Mikkeli** Finland 61.44N 27.15E

51 M10 **Mikkeli** *dist* Finland
101 Q7 **Mikkwa** *R* Alberta
50 F2 **Miklavatn** *L* Skagafjardharsýsla **Iceland** 66.05N 19.08W
50 F3 **Miklavatn** *L* Skagafjardharsýsla **Iceland** 65.42N 19.34W
50 F3 **Miklibær** Iceland 65.30N 19.18W
50 G3 **Mikligardhur** Iceland 65.30N 18.10W
62 N2 **Mikołajki** Poland 53.50N 21.33E
62 L5 **Mikołów** Poland 50.10N 18.50E
91 B2 **Mikomeseng** Equat Guinea 2.08N 10.41E
83 G7 **Míkonos** *isld* Greece
91 G6 **Mikope** Zaïre 4.58S 20.43E
Mikoyan *see* **Yekhegnadzor**
Mikoyana, im *see* **Oktyabr'skiy** Kamchatka U.S.S.R
Mikoyanovka *see* **Oktyabr'skiy** Belgorod U.S.S.R
82 J7 **Mikre** Bulgaria 43.01N 24.31E
83 E4 **Mikrí Préspa L** Greece
84 D7 **Mikrománi** Greece 37.05N 22.02E
84 C5 **Mikrón Pondiás** Greece 38.04N 21.56E
84 E3 **Mikrothívai** Greece 39.15N 22.45E
84 C1 **Mikróvalton** Greece 40.04N 21.53E
45 C1 **Mikulino** U.S.S.R. 55.02N 31.05E
47 F2 **Mikulkin,Mys** *C* U.S.S.R. 67.47N 46.41E
65 P4 **Mikulov** Czechoslovakia 48.48N 16.38E
64 Q2 **Mikulov** Karlovy Vary **Czech** 50.44N 13.44E
92 H5 **Mikumi** Tanzania 7.22S 37.00E
92 H5 **Mikumi Nat.Park** Tanzania
47 G5 **Mikun'** U.S.S.R. 62.20N 50.01E
20 K5 **Mikuni** Japan 36.14N 136.09E
20 M5 **Mikuni-sammyaku** *mts* Japan
20 N8 **Mikura-jima** *isld* Japan 33.53N 139.35E
40 F2 **Mil'** *R* U.S.S.R.
88 R3 **Mila** Algeria 36.18N 6.16E
108 R4 **Milaca** Minnesota 45.46N 93.38W
27 L8 **Miladunmadulu Atoll** Maldives, Ind Oc 5.50N 73.00E
117 H8 **Milagres** Brazil 7.19S 38.50W
76 B9 **Milagres** Portugal 39.47N 8.47W
121 D3 **Milagro** Argentina 30.59S 65.59W
119 B9 **Milagro** Ecuador 2.11S 79.36W
75 G3 **Milagro** Spain 42.15N 1.45W
76 L10 **Milagro** *R* Spain
86 K10 **Milâha,Gebel** *hill* Egypt 27.31N 33.02E
86 K10 **Milâha,Wâdi** *watercourse* Egypt
30 C4 **Milak** Uttar Prad **India** 28.37N 79.11E
30 D2 **Milam** Uttar Prad **India** 30.26N 80.08E
107 L2 **Milan** Indiana 39.08N 85.09W
Milan Italy*see* **Milano**
109 N4 **Milan** Kansas 37.16N 97.41W
106 L7 **Milan** Michigan 42.04N 83.40W
108 P4 **Milan** Minnesota 45.06N 95.54W
107 C1 **Milan** Missouri 40.12N 93.08W
104 C5 **Milan** Ohio 41.17N 82.37W
103 A3 **Milan** Pennsylvania 41.55N 76.31W
98 A8 **Milan** Quebec 45.35N 71.09W
107 H6 **Milan** Tennessee 35.55N 88.47W
110 H2 **Milan** Washington 47.58N 117.20W
91 E8 **Milando** Angola 8.45S 17.36E
12 E6 **Milang** S Australia 35.24S 138.57E
92 G10 **Milange** Mozambique 16.09S 35.44E
19 B3 **Milango** *R* Celebes **Indonesia**
79 F4 **Milano** Italy 45.28N 9.12E
76 F6 **Milano** Spain 41.05N 6.35W
112 L5 **Milano** Texas 30.44N 96.53W
79 F4 **Milano** *prov* Italy
95 D2 **Milanoa** Madagascar 13.34S 49.46E
103 D3 **Milanville** Pennsylvania 41.40N 75.04W
36 C5 **Milâs** Turkey 37.19N 27.48E
84 N11 **Milatos** Crete 35.19N 25.34E
81 K7 **Milazzo** Sicily 38.13N 15.15E
81 K7 **Milazzo, C. di** Sicily 38.16N 15.13E
81 K7 **Milazzo,Golfo di** Sicily
108 O4 **Milbank** S Dakota 45.14N 96.38W
56 G6 **Milborne St.Andrew** Dorset **Eng** 50.47N 2.17W
104 F9 **Milboro** Virginia 37.58N 79.37W
20 K5 **Milboro Dam** Japan 36.12N 136.55E
106 H7 **Milburg** Michigan 42.07N 86.20W
11 E13 **Milburn** New Zealand 46.08S 170.00E
53 S18 **Milde** Norway 60.14N 5.18E
100 K7 **Milden** Saskatchewan 51.29N 107.32W
56 N3 **Mildenhall** Suffolk **Eng** 52.21N 0.30E
65 D7 **Milders** Austria 47.07N 11.17E
99 J8 **Mildmay** Ontario 44.03N 81.08W
108 E3 **Mildred** Montana 46.40N 105.00W
103 B4 **Mildred** Pennsylvania 41.28N 76.24W
100 K5 **Mildred** Saskatchewan 53.22N 107.24W
101 S7 **Mildred L** Alberta 57.04N 111.33W
63 K4 **Mildstedt** W Germany 54.28N 9.06E
12 F5 **Mildura** Victoria 34.14S 142.13E
23 C6 **Mile** Yunnan **China** 24.23N 103.22E
84 F3 **Miléai** Greece 39.20N 23.09E
84 F4 **Miléai** Greece 38.57N 23.17E
116 J2 **Mile Gully** Jamaica, W I 18.13N 77.33W
32 B4 **Mileh, Kūh-e** *mt* Iran 33.16N 47.38E
34 L5 **Mileh Tharthār** *flood basin* Iraq
33 L4 **Mileihah, Jabal** U.A.E. 25.06N 55.50E
86 K5 **Mileiz, Wâdi el** *watercourse* Egypt
92 H7 **Milepa** Mozambique 11.42S 36.17E
111 A8 **Mile Rocks** *islds* California 37.47N 122.31W
13 K7 **Miles** Queensland 26.40S 150.09E
112 G4 **Miles** Texas 31.36N 100.12W
110 G2 **Miles** Washington 47.54N 118.19W
108 E3 **Miles City** Montana 46.24N 105.48W
84 G5 **Milesi** Greece 38.18N 23.45E
70 L5 **Milesse,la** France 48.04N 0.08E
100 N9 **Milestone** Saskatchewan 49.59N 104.31W
59 F6 **Milestone** Tipperary **Irish Rep** 52.40N 8.05W
81 M6 **Mileto** Italy 38.36N 16.04E
80 K6 **Miletto,Monte** Italy 41.27N 14.23E
36 C5 **Miletus** *anc site* **Turkey** 37.30N 27.18E
14 B7 **Mileura** W Australia 26.23S 117.24E
65 K3 **Milevsko** Czechoslovakia 49.27N 14.22E
45 D2 **Mileyevo** U.S.S.R. 54.48N 32.51E
110 E9 **Milford** California 40.11N 120.26W
103 H4 **Milford** Connecticut 41.13N 73.04W
59 E7 **Milford** Cork **Irish Rep** 52.20N 8.51W
103 D9 **Milford** Delaware 38.54N 75.25W
106 G9 **Milford** Illinois 40.39N 87.42W
106 J8 **Milford** Indiana 41.23N 85.51W
108 P6 **Milford** Iowa 43.19N 95.10W
109 O2 **Milford** Kansas 39.10N 96.55W
104 R2 **Milford** Maine 44.57N 68.39W
103 L2 **Milford** Massachusetts 42.09N 71.31W
106 L7 **Milford** Michigan 42.37N 83.36W
108 N9 **Milford** Nebraska 40.45N 97.03W
104 O4 **Milford** New Hampshire 42.50N 71.40W
103 D5 **Milford** New Jersey 40.34N 75.06W
104 L4 **Milford** New York 42.35N 74.57W
107 M2 **Milford** Ohio 39.11N 84.16W
103 E4 **Milford** Pennsylvania 41.20N 74.48W
56 K5 **Milford** Surrey **Eng** 51.10N 0.40W
112 L3 **Milford** Texas 32.06N 96.56W
111 L3 **Milford** Utah 38.22N 113.00W
104 H8 **Milford** Virginia 38.01N 77.23W
104 B6 **Milford Center** Ohio 40.10N 83.27W
56 A4 **Milford Haven** Dyfed **Wales** 51.44N 5.02W
56 A4 **Milford Haven** *inlet* Dyfed **Wales**
109 N2 **Milford Res** Kansas
11 B11 **Milford Sd New Zealand**
11 B11 **Milford Sound New Zealand** 44.41S 167.56E
11 B11 **Milford Track** *mt path* **New Zealand**
13 F4 **Milgarra** Queensland 18.10S 140.55E
93 J4 **Milgis** *watercourse* **Kenya**
14 C8 **Milgoo, Mt** W Australia 29.00S 118.15E
14 C7 **Milgun** W Australia 25.04S 118.19E
39 J1 **Mil'guveem** *R* **U.S.S.R.**
76 F5 **Milhão** Portugal 41.46N 6.38W
72 H7 **Milhars** France 44.07N 1.52E
34 K3 **Milhat Ash'qar** *salt marsh* Iraq
34 L6 **Milḥ, Bahr al** *L* Iraq
88 K9 **Milhéas** Mauritania 25.24N 6.54W
60 M13 **Milheeze** Netherlands 51.30N 5.46E
85 H4 **Milḥ, Ra's al** *C* **Libya** 31.54N 25.06E
34 M6 **Milḥ, Wādī al** *watercourse* Iraq
9 D3 **Mili** *atoll* Marshall Is **Pacific Oc** 6.08N 171.59E
84 D5 **Miliá** Greece 38.26N 22.09E
88 R3 **Milia,El** Algeria 36.48N 6.14E
84 C6 **Miliaís** Greece 37.44N 21.41E
88 P3 **Miliana** Algeria 36.20N 2.15E
88 P8 **Miliana** Algeria 27.24N 2.28E
78 C12 **Miliane** *R* **Tunisia**
65 L2 **Miličín** Czechoslovakia 49.34N 14.40E
62 K4 **Milicz** Poland 51.32N 17.15E
Milid *anc site see* **Malatya**
93 M7 **Milimani** Kenya 1.48S 40.58E
65 K2 **Milín** Czechoslovakia 49.38N 14.03E
14 B9 **Miling** W Australia 30.27S 116.20E
13 C1 **Milingimbi** N Terr **Australia** 12.02S 134.50E
81 B3 **Milis** Sardinia 40.03N 8.38E
81 J9 **Militello in Val di Catania** Sicily 37.17N 14.47E
84 C8 **Milítsa** Greece 36.52N 21.50E
26 N15 **Miliue.I.du** St Paul I **Ind Oc** 38.42S 77.31E
70 A5 **Milizac** France 48.29N 4.34W
108 D1 **Milk** *R* Montana
40 F4 **Mil'kan** U.S.S.R. 54.10N 133.59E
87 B2 **Milk,El** *watercourse* **Sudan**
30 E6 **Milkipur** Uttar Prad **India** 26.36N 81.54E
39 F7 **Milkovo** U.S.S.R. 54.44N 158.36E
110 N1 **Milk R** Alberta/Mont
100 E9 **Milk River** Alberta 49.10N 112.06W
116 J2 **Milk River Bath** Jamaica, W I 17.51N 77.22W
100 E9 **Milk River Ridge** Alberta
57 G2 **Milk,Water of** *R* Dumfries & Galloway **Scotland**
60 M13 **Mill** Netherlands 51.42N 5.47E
103 J2 **Mill** *R* Massachusetts
13 H4 **Millaa Millaa** Queensland 17.30S 145.36E
72 F3 **Millac** France 46.11N 0.42E
75 E6 **Millana** Spain 40.31N 2.35W
70 O7 **Millançay** France 47.27N 1.45E
14 F8 **Millar Breakaways** W Australia 27.54S 125.22E
107 D1 **Millard** Missouri 40.05N 92.33W
77 P2 **Millares** Spain 39.15N 0.46W
13 H4 **Millaroo** Queensland 19.45S 147.15E
105 L9 **Millars** New Providence I **Bahamas** 25.00N 77.26W
108 M3 **Millarton** N Dakota 46.40N 98.45W
72 K10 **Millas** France 42.42N 2.42E
72 L7 **Millau** France 44.06N 3.05E
71 E3 **Millay** France 46.51N 4.00E
111 B9 **Millbrae** California 37.34N 122.23W
103 G3 **Millbrook** New York 41.47N 73.42W
99 M8 **Millbrook** Ontario 44.09N 78.28W
103 L2 **Millbury** Massachusetts 42.12N 71.45W
110 G9 **Mill City** Nevada 40.42N 118.03W
110 C5 **Mill City** Oregon 44.45N 122.29W
110 D9 **Mill Cr** California
110 D9 **Mill Creek** California 40.20N 121.34W
109 O7 **Mill Creek** Oklahoma 34.24N 96.50W
104 E8 **Mill Creek** W Virginia 38.45N 80.00W
103 J3 **Milldale** Connecticut 41.34N 72.54W
105 D4 **Milledgeville** Georgia 33.04N 83.13W
106 E8 **Milledgeville** Illinois 41.58N 89.46W
110 O2 **Millegan** Montana 47.04N 111.24W
108 R3 **Mille Lacs** *L* Minnesota
100 M2 **Mille Lacs,L.des** Ontario
61 N3 **Millen** Belgium 50.47N 5.34E
105 F5 **Millen** Georgia 32.48N 81.58W
77 Q3 **Millena** Spain 38.45N 0.22W
107 C4 **Miller** Missouri 37.12N 93.51W
108 L9 **Miller** Nebraska 40.56N 99.24W
95 G9 **Miller** S Africa 33.05S 23.55E
108 M5 **Miller** S Dakota 44.31N 98.58W
12 D3 **Miller** *R* S Australia
113 Q6 **Miller,Mt** Alaska 60.29N 142.20W
45 M8 **Millerovo** U.S.S.R. 48.55N 40.25E
111 O10 **Miller Pk** *mt* Arizona 31.24N 110.20W
111 G3 **Millers** Nevada 38.07N 117.28W
106 J8 **Millersburg** Indiana 41.32N 85.43W
107 M3 **Millersburg** Kentucky 38.18N 84.09W
106 K4 **Millersburg** Michigan 45.21N 84.02W
104 D6 **Millersburg** Ohio 40.33N 81.56W
104 J6 **Millersburg** Pennsylvania 40.32N 76.57W
101 C3 **Millers Camp** Alaska 65.01N 141.20W
12 D4 **Millers Creek** S Australia 30.00S 136.02E
104 N4 **Millers Falls** Massachusetts 42.34N 72.30W
107 J9 **Millers Ferry** Alabama 32.05N 87.24W
11 D12 **Miller's Flat New Zealand** 45.40S 169.28E
104 F6 **Millerstown** Pennsylvania 40.57N 79.45W
112 H4 **Millersview** Texas 31.25N 99.46W
103 A8 **Millersville** Maryland 39.03N 76.39W
103 B6 **Millersville** Pennsylvania 40.01N 76.21W
98 G7 **Millerton** New Brunswick 46.55N 65.40W
103 G3 **Millerton** New York 41.57N 73.31W
11 F8 **Millerton New Zealand** 41.40S 171.54E
111 E4 **Millerton L** California 37.00N 119.40W
98 Q5 **Millertown** Newfoundland 48.49N 56.31W
98 Q4 **Millertown Junc** Newfoundland 49.00N 56.20W
79 D6 **Millesimo** Italy 44.22N 8.12E
100 D5 **Millet** Alberta 53.05N 113.24W
104 C9 **Millet** W Virginia 37.57N 82.29W
111 G2 **Millett** Nevada 39.01N 117.10W
112 H7 **Millett** Texas 28.36N 99.14W
72 J4 **Millevaches** France 45.38N 2.04E
59 G1 **Millford** Donegal **Irish Rep** 55.07N 7.43W
103 B5 **Millgrove** Pennsylvania 40.53N 76.21W
104 H5 **Mill Hall** Pennsylvania 41.06N 77.31W
104 H6 **Millheim** Pennsylvania 40.54N 77.30W
55 E2 **Mill Hill** London **Eng** 51.37N 0.14W
123 E2 **Mill I** Antarctica 65.42S 101.00E
97 M5 **Mill I** N W Terr 64.00N 77.50W
110 E6 **Millican** Oregon 43.54N 120.55W
112 L5 **Millican** Texas 30.28N 96.14W
100 F8 **Millicent** Alberta 50.44N 111.45W
12 F6 **Millicent** S Australia 37.29S 140.01E
12 F7 **Millicent** S Australia 37.36S 140.22E
14 D8 **Millicent,Mt** W Australia 29.29S 122.25E
69 J7 **Millières** France 48.08N 5.25E
107 K11 **Milligan** Florida 30.43N 86.40W
108 N9 **Milligan** Nebraska 40.31N 97.21W
109 F1 **Milliken** Colorado 40.21N 104.53W
60 N12 **Millingen** Netherlands 51.52N 6.02E
104 K7 **Millington** Delaware 39.15N 75.50W
106 L6 **Millington** Michigan 43.16N 83.31W
103 E5 **Millington** New Jersey 40.40N 74.32W
104 Q8 **Millinocket** Maine 45.42N 68.43W
104 Q8 **Millinocket L** Maine
40 D4 **Millionnyy** U.S.S.R. 54.33N 126.15E
120 E9 **Milliri,Cerro** *pk* **Chile** 20.38S 68.28W
103 M2 **Millis** Massachusetts 42.10N 71.22W
59 L2 **Mill Isle** Down **N Ireland** 54.37N 5.32W
56 G2 **Millmeece** Staffs **Eng** 52.54N 2.15W
13 K8 **Millmerran** Queensland 27.53S 151.15E
57 G4 **Millom** Cumbria **Eng** 54.13N 3.18W
107 H8 **Millport** Alabama 33.33N 88.07W
104 J4 **Millport** New York 42.16N 76.51W
58 G7 **Millport** Strathclyde **Scotland** 55.46N 4.55W
103 H2 **Mill River** Massachusetts 42.07N 73.16W
107 H10 **Millry** Alabama 31.38N 88.20W
108 L7 **Mills** Nebraska 42.57N 99.20W
109 F5 **Mills** New Mexico 36.05N 104.16W
108 D7 **Mills** Wyoming 42.50N 106.24W
13 G5 **Mills** *R* Queensland
112 J3 **Millsap** Texas 32.46N 98.01W
111 B2 **Millsaps** California 39.45N 122.34W
104 K8 **Millsboro** Delaware 38.34N 75.19W
104 E7 **Millsboro** Pennsylvania 40.00N 80.01W
101 O5 **Mills L** N W Terr
65 J8 **Millstatt** Austria 46.49N 13.34E
65 J8 **Millstätter See** *L* Austria
106 D5 **Millston** Wisconsin 44.12N 90.40W
103 E6 **Millstone** New Jersey 40.30N 74.36W
103 F6 **Millstone R** New Jersey
14 B5 **Millstream** W Australia 21.41S 117.10E
59 D7 **Millstreet** Cork **Irish Rep** 52.03N 9.04W
59 H3 **Milltown** Cavan **Irish Rep** 54.04N 7.28W
59 E4 **Milltown** Galway **Irish Rep** 53.37N 8.54W
59 B7 **Milltown** Kerry **Irish Rep** 52.09N 10.17W
59 C7 **Milltown** Kerry **Irish Rep** 52.08N 9.43W
59 J5 **Milltown** Kildare **Irish Rep** 53.12N 6.52W
98 E8 **Milltown** New Brunswick 45.10N 67.19W
98 R6 **Milltown** Newfoundland 47.55N 55.47W
103 F6 **Milltown** New Jersey 40.27N 74.27W
13 F4 **Millungera** Queensland 19.50S 141.30E
98 H9 **Mill Village** Nova Scotia 44.08N 64.40W
103 L2 **Millville** Massachusetts 42.02N 71.35W
98 E7 **Millville** New Brunswick 46.08N 67.12W
103 D8 **Millville** New Jersey 39.24N 75.02W
104 A7 **Millville** Ohio 39.22N 84.41W
103 A4 **Millville** Pennsylvania 41.08N 76.32W
55 G4 **Millwall** London **Eng** 51.30N 0.01W
107 B8 **Millwood Lake** *res* Arkansas
69 C7 **Milly-la-Forêt** France 48.24N 2.28E
14 B7 **Milly Milly** W Australia 26.08S 116.51E
69 C5 **Milly-sur Thérain** France 49.30N 2.01E
75 G5 **Milmarcos** Spain 41.05N 1.54W
103 E8 **Milmay** New Jersey 39.27N 74.52W
63 T6 **Milmersdorf** E Germany 53.07N 13.39E
87 J6 **Milmil** Ethiopia 8.20N 43.50E
61 N4 **Milmort** Belgium 50.42N 5.36E
80 O2 **Milna** Yugoslavia 43.20N 16.28E
58 K6 **Milnathort** Tayside **Scotland** 56.14N 3.26W
13 D5 **Milne** *R* N Terr **Australia**
15 L9 **Milne B** Papua New Guinea
105 C4 **Milner** Georgia 33.07N 84.12W
110 L7 **Milner** Idaho 42.31N 114.00W
100 F1 **Milner Ridge** Manitoba 50.10N 96.12W
94 P11 **Milnerton** Cape Town **S Africa** 33.53S 18.29E
109 G8 **Milnesand** New Mexico 33.38N 103.20W
103 C5 **Milnesville** Pennsylvania 40.59N 75.58W
99 K6 **Milnet** Ontario 46.49N 80.59W
58 H7 **Milngavie** Strathclyde **Scotland** 55.57N 4.19W
108 N3 **Milnor** N Dakota 46.17N 97.27W
57 J5 **Milnrow** Greater Manchester **Eng** 53.37N 2.06W
57 H4 **Milnthorpe** Cumbria **Eng** 54.14N 2.46W
100 E8 **Milo** Alberta 50.35N 112.50W
108 R8 **Milo** Iowa 41.18N 93.27W
104 Q1 **Milo** Maine 45.15N 69.01W
110 B7 **Milo** Oregon 42.56N 123.03W
13 G7 **Milo** Queensland 25.38S 144.30E
92 G6 **Milo** Tanzania 9.50S 34.39E
89 E6 **Milo** *R* Guinea
40 F10 **Milogradovo** U.S.S.R. 43.15N 134.31E
84 E6 **Míloi** Greece 37.33N 22.43E
114 B8 **Milolii** Hawaiian Is 19.11N 155.54W
62 M2 **Miłomłyn** Poland 53.46N 19.50E
84 H8 **Mílos** Greece 36.44N 24.25E
84 H8 **Mílos** *isld* Greece
82 F5 **Miloševo** Yugoslavia 45.42N 20.20E
45 L3 **Miloskavskoye** U.S.S.R. 53.35N 39.29E
62 K3 **Miłosław** Poland 52.12N 17.30E
88 L8 **Miloud** Algeria 27.26N 5.37W
58 C4 **Milovaig** Skye, Highland **Scotland** 57.27N 6.45W
63 Q7 **Milow** E Germany 52.32N 12.20E
12 F3 **Milparinka** New S Wales 29.45S 141.55E
12 K8 **Milperra** *dist* Sydney, N S W
111 C4 **Milpitas** California 37.25N 121.54W
107 L2 **Milroy** Indiana 39.30N 85.28W
104 H6 **Milroy** Pennsylvania 40.44N 77.35W
29 H7 **Milsika** Orissa **India** 20.19N 83.50E
44 H8 **Mil'skaya Step** Azerbaydzhan **U.S.S.R.**
64 O5 **Miltach** W Germany 49.10N 12.47E
64 G4 **Miltenberg** W Germany 49.42N 9.16E
104 K8 **Milton** Delaware 38.46N 75.20W
56 H6 **Milton** Dorset **Eng** 50.45N 1.39W
107 J11 **Milton** Florida 30.36N 87.03W
107 F2 **Milton** Illinois 39.33N 90.39W
106 B9 **Milton** Iowa 40.40N 92.11W
109 N4 **Milton** Kansas 37.26N 97.46W
103 M2 **Milton** Massachusetts 42.16N 71.05W
105 H1 **Milton** N Carolina 36.32N 79.14W
108 M1 **Milton** N Dakota 48.39N 98.03W
104 P3 **Milton** New Hampshire 43.23N 70.59W
12 K6 **Milton** New S Wales 35.19S 150.24E
103 G3 **Milton** New York 41.40N 73.57W
11 D13 **Milton New Zealand** 46.08S 169.59E
98 H9 **Milton** Nova Scotia 44.04N 64.44W
99 L9 **Milton** Ontario 43.31N 79.53W
104 J5 **Milton** Pennsylvania 41.01N 76.52W
104 M2 **Milton** Vermont 44.38N 73.08W
106 F7 **Milton** Wisconsin 42.47N 88.56W
104 C8 **Milton** W Virginia 38.26N 82.07W
104 Q10 **Milton** *dist* Boston, Mass
56 C6 **Milton Abbot** Devon **Eng** 50.35N 4.15W
12 J3 **Milton Downs** New S Wales 29.49S 149.34E
56 K3 **Milton Ernest** Beds **Eng** 52.12N 0.31W
110 G4 **Milton-Freewater** Oregon 45.57N 118.24W
57 D2 **Miltonise** Dumfries & Galloway **Scotland** 55.01N 4.50W
56 K3 **Milton Keynes** Bucks **England** 52.02N 0.42W
109 N2 **Miltonvale** Kansas 39.22N 97.27W
90 H6 **Miltou** Chad 10.10N 17.30E
59 D6 **Miltown Malbay** Clare **Irish Rep** 52.52N 9.23W
63 S4 **Miltzow** E Germany 54.12N 13.14E
23 F4 **Miluo** Hunan **China** 29.00N 112.59E
99 K9 **Milverton** Ontario 43.34N 80.55W
56 E5 **Milverton** Somerset **Eng** 51.02N 3.16W
106 G6 **Milwaukee** Wisconsin 43.03N 87.56W
96 D6 **Milwaukee Depth** Atlantic Oc 19.50N 65.30W
45 F2 **Milyatino** U.S.S.R. 54.30N 34.20E
45 N8 **Milyutinskaya** U.S.S.R. 48.39N 41.41E
89 H8 **Mim** Ghana 6.57N 2.33W
72 C8 **Mimbaste** France 43.38N 0.57W
15 M6 **Mimias,C** New Ireland 4.23S 153.08E
15 D6 **Mimiko** Irian Jaya 4.43S 136.28E
28 D6 **Mimisal** Tamil Nadu **India** 9.55N 79.09E
20 E9 **Mimitsu** Japan 32.20N 131.34E
72 B7 **Mimizan** France 44.12N 1.14W
72 B7 **Mimizan-les-Bains** France 44.13N 1.18W
66 O1 **Mimmenhausen** W Germany 47.45N 9.17E
62 H5 **Mimoň** Czechoslovakia 50.40N 14.45E
91 B4 **Mimongo** Gabon 1.36S 11.44E
91 B4 **Mimongo** Gabon 1.12S 11.34E
95 G4 **Mimosa** S Africa 28.12S 23.19E
95 J9 **Mimosa** S Africa 33.26S 25.52E
118 H7 **Mimoso do Sul** Brazil 21.01S 41.19W
25 J7 **Mimot** Cambodia 11.49N 106.11E
20 H6 **Mimuro-yama** *mt* Japan 35.16N 134.25E
111 A2 **Mina** California 39.59N 123.21W
115 J4 **Mina** Mexico 26.00N 100.33W
111 F3 **Mina** Nevada 38.25N 118.06W
42 E5 **Mina** U.S.S.R. 54.59N 94.15E
74 H9 **Mina** *R* Algeria
33 N10 **Mīnā' 'Abd Allāh** Kuwait 29.01N 48.10E
33 N5 **Mina al Fahal** Oman 23.38N 58.31E
32 G7 **Mīnāb** Iran 27.07N 57.06E
32 G7 **Mīnāb** *R* Iran
31 E5 **Mina Bazar** Pakistan 31.06N 69.20E
20 J8 **Minabe** Japan 33.47N 135.20E
115 F3 **Miñaca** Mexico 28.28N 107.26W
76 D13 **Mina de São Domingos** Portugal 37.40N 7.30W
86 M8 **Minâdir,Gebel** *hill* Egypt 28.44N 34.02E
34 C4 **Mina,El** Lebanon 34.28N 35.47E
33 M10 **Minagish** *oil field* Kuwait 29.03N 47.32E
93 A9 **Minago** Burundi 3.47S 29.21E
100 T4 **Minago R** Manitoba
19 B3 **Minahassa Pen** Celebes Indon
100 G1 **Minaki** Ontario 50.00N 94.40W
20 K7 **Minakuchi** Japan 35.00N 136.10E
110 H4 **Minam** Oregon 45.39N 117.42W
110 H4 **Minam** *R* Oregon
20 D9 **Minamata** Japan 32.13N 130.23E
20 D5 **Minami** *dist* Yokohama **Japan**
20 B3 **Minamidaira** Tōkyō **Japan**
21 J13 **Minami-iō-jima** *isld* Kazan-Rettō **Pacific Oc** 24.12N 141.26E
20 B1 **Minami-Iriso** Saitama **Japan**
20 E10 **Minamikata** Japan 31.16N 131.04E
20 A1 **Minamimine** Saitama **Japan**
Minami-tori-shima *see* **Marcus I**
89 G6 **Mina,Mt** Mali 11.00N 5.48W
75 F4 **Miñana** Spain 41.32N 2.07W
120 D6 **Mina,Nev** *mt* Peru 15.24S 70.40W
37 F7 **Minar** Turkey 38.04N 41.47E
120 B4 **Mina Ragra** Peru 10.52S 76.33W
76 A3 **Miñarzo,Pta** *pt* Spain 42.48N 9.09W
116 F4 **Minas** Cuba 21.30N 77.38W
18 D5 **Minas** Sumatra **Indon** 0.40N 101.26E
121 G5 **Minas** Uruguay 34.20S 55.15W
33 N10 **Mīnā' Sa'ūd** Saudi Arabia 28.44N 48.28E
98 H8 **Minas Basin** Nova Scotia
98 H8 **Minas Chan** Nova Scotia
118 B8 **Minas Cué** Paraguay 22.03S 59.35W
121 G3 **Minas de Corrales** Uruguay 31.35S 55.20W
115 M3 **Minas de Pis Pis** *mines* **Nicaragua** 13.55N 84.31W
77 C5 **Minas de Riotinto** Spain 37.42N 6.35W
118 F5 **Minas Gerais** *state* **Brazil**
118 G5 **Minas Novas** Brazil 17.16S 42.34W
115 P10 **Minas, Sa. de las** *ra* **Guatemala**
108 G8 **Minatare** Nebraska 41.50N 103.30W
99 B2 **Minataree** Ontario 50.14N 88.05W
77 N4 **Minateda** Spain 38.28N 1.35W
115 M9 **Minatitlán** Mexico 17.59N 94.32W
20 E3 **Minato** *dist* Tōkyō **Japan**
77 M2 **Minaya** Spain 39.17N 2.20W
25 C2 **Minbu** Burma 20.09N 94.52E
100 F5 **Minburn** Alberta 53.20N 111.20W
108 Q8 **Minburn** Iowa 41.45N 94.01W
25 B2 **Minbya** Burma 20.22N 93.18E
121 B3 **Mincha** Chile 31.38S 71.26W
31 G5 **Minchinabad** Pakistan 30.10N 73.40E
121 A9 **Minchinmavida** *pk* **Chile** 42.48S 72.30W
58 C3 **Minch,Lit** *channel* W Isles/Highland **Scotland**
58 D2 **Minch,N** *channel* **Scotland**
113 L5 **Minchumina,L** Alaska 63.55N 152.10W
79 J4 **Mincio** *R* Italy
109 N6 **Minco** Oklahoma 35.19N 97.57W
62 M6 **Minčol** *mt* Czechoslovakia 49.14N 21.00E
Mindajin *see* **Mendejin**
33 D6 **Mindak,Al** Saudi Arabia 20.08N 41.14E
24 D9 **Mindam Tso** *L* Xizang Zizhiqu **China** 33.07N 81.35E
19 L8 **Mindanao** *isld* **Philippines**
19 M8 **Mindanao** *R* Mindanao **Philippines**
12 F5 **Mindarie** S Australia 34.51S 140.12E
25 B2 **Mindat Sakan** Burma 21.21N 93.58E
76 B9 **Minde** Portugal 39.31N 8.41W
64 J7 **Mindel** *R* **W Germany**
64 J7 **Mindelheim** W Germany 48.03N 10.30E
89 O10 **Mindelo** Cape Verde 16.54N 25.00W
76 B6 **Mindelo** Portugal 41.18N 8.44W
66 N1 **Mindel See** *L* **W Germany** 47.45N 9.01E
108 P8 **Minden** Iowa 41.27N 95.32W
107 C9 **Minden** Louisiana 32.36N 93.17W
108 M9 **Minden** Nebraska 40.30N 98.59W
111 E3 **Minden** Nevada 38.58N 119.47W
99 M8 **Minden** Ontario 44.56N 78.44W
63 J8 **Minden** W Germany 52.18N 8.54E
104 D9 **Minden** W Virginia 37.58N 81.08W
106 M6 **Minden City** Michigan 43.41N 82.48W
61 K1 **Minderhout** Belgium 51.25N 4.46E
14 B5 **Minderoo** W Australia 21.59S 115.04E
37 D5 **Mindeval** Turkey 40.08N 38.44E
115 E9 **Mindi Dyke** Panama Canal Zone 9.16N 79.56W
90 G6 **Mindif** Cameroon 10.25N 14.23E
84 C5 **Mindilógli** Greece 38.11N 21.41E
15 F6 **Mindiptanah** Irian Jaya 5.55S 140.25E
25 C3 **Mindon** Burma 19.20N 94.44E
12 F5 **Mindona L** New S Wales 33.09S 142.09E
19 K5 **Mindoro** *isld* **Philippines**
19 K5 **Mindoro Str Philippines**
91 D6 **Mindouli** Congo 4.14S 14.23E
91 C2 **Mindourou** Cameroon 3.29N 13.26E
82 H5 **Mindra** *mt* Romania 45.19N 23.33E
62 M9 **Mindszent** Hungary 46.30N 20.11E
47 H8 **Mindyak** U.S.S.R. 54.02N 58.51E
44 H8 **Mindzhevan** Azerbaydzhan **U.S.S.R.** 39.02N 46.41E
20 E7 **Mine** Japan 34.10N 131.13E
100 K2 **Mine Centre** Ontario 48.48N 92.37W
82 K5 **Mîneci-Ungureni** Romania 45.19N 25.59E
59 G8 **Mine Hd** Waterford **Irish Rep** 52.00N 7.35W
56 E5 **Minehead** Somerset **Eng** 51.13N 3.29W
85 N8 **Mineiga, Gebel** *mts* **Sudan**
118 D5 **Mineiros** Brazil 17.34S 52.33W
70 J3 **Mine,la** France 49.14N 0.53W
81 J9 **Mineo** Sicily 37.17N 14.42E
108 P8 **Mineola** Iowa 41.08N 95.40W
103 G5 **Mineola** Long I, N Y 40.45N 73.38W
112 M3 **Mineola** Texas 32.41N 95.30W
110 P4 **Miner** Montana 45.09N 110.59W
110 D9 **Mineral** California 40.23N 121.36W
112 K7 **Mineral** Texas 28.34N 97.54W
104 H8 **Mineral** Virginia 38.01N 77.55W
110 C3 **Mineral** Washington 46.43N 122.11W
115 K7 **Mineral del Monte** Mexico 20.10N 98.40W
121 D7 **Minerales de la Pampa** Argentina 38.13S 65.41W
111 M3 **Mineral Mts** Utah
40 F10 **Mineral'naya** U.S.S.R. 43.55N 134.55E
44 E3 **Mineral'nyye Vody** U.S.S.R. 44.14N 43.10E
106 D7 **Mineral Point** Wisconsin 42.52N 90.12W
107 C8 **Mineral Springs** Arkansas 33.54N 93.54W
112 J3 **Mineral Wells** Texas 32.49N 98.07W
79 K5 **Minerbio** Italy 44.38N 11.29E
103 B5 **Minersville** Pennsylvania 40.11N 76.15W
111 M3 **Minersville** Utah 38.14N 112.55W
104 D6 **Minerva** Ohio 40.43N 81.07W
13 J6 **Minerva** Queensland 24.00S 148.05E
10 R6 **Minerva Reefs** Pacific Oc
80 O6 **Minervino Murge** Italy 41.06N 16.05E
71 B10 **Minervois,Mts.du** France
104 J3 **Minetto** New York 43.23N 76.30W
24 D7 **Minfeng** Xinjiang Uygur Zizhiqu **China** 37.02N 82.47E
104 C8 **Minford** Ohio 38.52N 82.52W
91 J6 **Minga** Zaïre 4.42S 24.19E
92 C7 **Minga** Zaïre 11.06S 27.57E
92 E9 **Minga** Zambia 14.21S 31.07E
25 D4 **Mingaladon** Burma 16.55N 96.09E
98 H3 **Mingan** Quebec 50.19N 64.02W
98 H3 **Mingan Chan** Quebec
98 H3 **Mingan I** Quebec 50.13N 64.08W
98 H3 **Mingan Is** Quebec
98 J3 **Mingan R** Quebec
Mingāora *see* **Mongora**
12 F4 **Mingary** S Australia 32.09S 140.46E
30 J3 **Mingbo** Nepal 27.51N 86.49E
30 J3 **Mingbo La** *pass* **Nepal** 27.54N 86.53N
23 F7 **Mingcheng** Guangdong **China** 22.54N 112.39E
44 H7 **Mingechaur** Azerbaydzhan **U.S.S.R.** 40.45N 47.03E
44 H7 **Mingechaurskoye Vdkhr** *res* Azerbaydzhan U.S.S.R.
13 H4 **Mingela** Queensland 19.53S 146.40E
14 B8 **Mingenew** W Australia 29.15S 115.27E
13 E5 **Mingera** *R* Queensland
23 G2 **Minggang** Henan **China** 32.27N 114.04E
Mingguang *see* **Jiashan**
25 C1 **Mingin** Burma 22.51N 94.30E
25 M9 **Mingin Ra** Burma
23 D7 **Mingjiang** Guangxi **China** 22.08N 107.10E
75 G8 **Minglanilla** Spain 39.32N 1.36W
23 E6 **Minglun** Guangxi **China** 25.13N 108.23E
108 R8 **Mingo** Iowa 41.45N 93.18W
109 K2 **Mingo** Kansas 39.16N 100.58W
104 E6 **Mingo Junction** Ohio 40.18N 80.39W
Mingolsheim *see* **Bad Schönborn**
25 M9 **Mingon** Burma 23.21N 96.02E
76 K7 **Mingorría** Spain 40.45N 4.40W
92 J7 **Mingoyo** Tanzania 10.02S 39.38E
44 B2 **Mingrel'skaya** U.S.S.R. 45.00N 38.21E
23 C3 **Mingshan** Sichuan **China** 30.06N 103.10E
Mingshui *see* **Zhangqiu**
22 D5 **Mingshui** Gansu **China** 42.03N 96.12E
21 C4 **Mingshui** Heilongjiang **China** 47.10N 125.25E
24 A7 **Mingteke** Xinjiang Uygur Zizhiqu **China** 37.12N 74.46E
24 A7 **Mingteke Daban** *pass* **China/India** 37.02N 74.46E
58 A5 **Mingulay** *isld* W Isles **Scotland** 56.48N 7.37W
112 J3 **Mingus** Texas 32.33N 98.26W
23 H5 **Mingxi** Fujian **China** 26.20N 117.11E
23 B5 **Mingyin** Yunnan **China** 27.14N 100.20E
23 D3 **Mingyue Shan** *mt ra* Sichuan **China**
22 F8 **Minhe** Gansu **China** 36.16N 102.58E
25 H7 **Minh Hoa,Hon** *isld* **Vietnam** 10.03N 104.33E
25 C3 **Minhla** Burma 19.58N 95.03E
25 C4 **Minhla** Burma 17.59N 95.41E
76 B5 **Minho** *hist reg* **Portugal**
74 B3 **Minho** *prov* **Portugal**
76 B4 **Minho** *R* **Spain/Portugal**
116 K2 **Minho,Rio** Jamaica, W I
70 G4 **Miniac Morvan** France 48.31N 1.55W
82 G7 **Minićevo** Yugoslavia 43.42N 22.18E
27 L8 **Minicoy I** Laccadive Is **Ind Oc** 8.29N 73.01E
110 M7 **Minidoka** Idaho 42.46N 113.30W
106 E9 **Minier** Illinois 40.26N 89.20W
14 E8 **Minigwal,L** W Australia
77 D5 **Minilla,Embalse de la** *res* **Spain** 37.40N 6.15W
14 A6 **Minilya** W Australia 23.52S 114.00E
14 A6 **Minilya R** W Australia
120 D8 **Miñimiñe** Chile 19.16S 69.45W
65 H5 **Mining** Austria 48.17N 13.10E
100 Q8 **Miniota** Manitoba 50.10N 101.02W
26 S7 **Minipe** Sri Lanka 7.13N 80.59E
98 M1 **Minipi L** Labrador, Nfld
103 E4 **Minisink Ford** New York 41.28N 74.58W
100 H4 **Ministikwan L** Saskatchewan 54.00N 109.40W
75 E5 **Ministra,Sierra** *mts* **Spain**
100 Q6 **Minitonas** Manitoba 52.04N 101.02W
15 H6 **Minj** Papua New Guinea 5.55S 144.37E
Minjāp *see* **Menjān**
14 B8 **Minjar** *hill* W Australia 28.50S 117.01E
23 H5 **Min Jiang** *R* Fujian **China**
23 C2 **Min Jiang** *R* Sichuan **China**
23 C4 **Min Jiang** *R* Sichuan **China**
Minjūr,Al *see* **Manjūr,Al**
91 C3 **Minkébé** Gabon 1.45N 12.45E
44 G8 **Minkend** Azerbaydzhan **U.S.S.R.** 39.42N 46.16E
111 E5 **Minkler** California 36.42N 119.26W
82 L2 **Minkovtsy** U.S.S.R. 48.50N 27.03E
43 L6 **Min-Kush** Kirgiziya **U.S.S.R.** 41.41N 74.20E
12 E5 **Minlaton** S Australia 34.40S 137.35E
22 E7 **Minle** Gansu **China** 38.26N 100.54E
20 O1 **Minmaya** Japan 41.10N 140.25E
90 C7 **Minna** Nigeria 9.39N 6.32E
95 N2 **Minnaar** S Africa 26.02S 29.05E
123 H7 **Minna Bluff** *pt* **Antarctica** 78.40S 167.10E
20 P8 **Minna-jima** *isld* Okinawa **Japan** 26.39N 127.49E
87 H6 **Minne** Ethiopia 8.19N 40.02E
109 N2 **Minneapolis** Kansas 39.08N 97.43W
108 R4 **Minneapolis** Minnesota 45.00N 93.15W
100 S8 **Minnedosa** Manitoba 50.14N 99.50W
108 G6 **Minnekahta** S Dakota 43.26N 103.41W
109 K4 **Minneola** Kansas 37.27N 100.01W
108 P5 **Minneota** Minnesota 44.34N 95.59W
26 S5 **Minneriya** Sri Lanka 8.04N 80.53E
60 L6 **Minnertsga** Netherlands 53.15N 5.35E
108 Q5 **Minnesota** *R* Minnesota
102 G1 **Minnesota** *state* **U.S.A.**
106 C5 **Minnesota City** Minnesota 44.06N 91.46W
108 R6 **Minnesota Lake** Minnesota 43.50N 93.48W
52 F6 **Minnesund** Norway 60.23N 11.14E
15 G7 **Minnetonka I** Papua New Guinea
100 B7 **Minnewanka,L** Alberta 51.18N 115.20W
108 P4 **Minnewaska L** Minnesota
108 L1 **Minnewaukan** N Dakota 48.04N 99.14W
25 E6 **Min-ngaw** Burma 13.22N 99.02E
14 B6 **Minnie Creek** W Australia 23.57S 115.46E
13 H7 **Minnie Downs** Queensland 25.05S 145.53E
14 B5 **Minnie,Mt** W Australia 22.08S 115.33E
34 E2 **Minnik** Syria 36.32N 37.03E
12 D5 **Minnipa** S Australia 32.48S 135.08E
99 G4 **Minnipuka** Ontario 48.54N 83.50W
100 K1 **Minnitaki L** Ontario 49.55N 92.10W
120 E9 **Miño** Chile 21.12S 68.41W
20 K6 **Mino** Japan 35.34N 136.56E
76 C2 **Miño** Spain 43.21N 8.12W
Miño *R see* **Minho** *R*
20 M6 **Minobu** Japan 35.23N 138.23E
20 L6 **Mino-kamo** Japan 35.29N 137.01E
106 C3 **Minong** Wisconsin 46.04N 91.49W
106 E9 **Minonk** Illinois 40.54N 89.02W
106 F8 **Minooka** Illinois 41.26N 88.17W
106 E4 **Minoqua** Wisconsin 45.51N 89.43W
Minorca *isld see* **Menorca** *I*
71 F1 **Minot** France 47.39N 4.52E
108 J1 **Minot** N Dakota 48.16N 101.19W
20 H1 **Minowa** Chiba **Japan**
86 C4 **Minqâr'Anfigla** *hill* **Egypt** 30.39N 29.55E
86 C5 **Minqâr el Magâbra** Egypt 30.16N 29.49E
86 D7 **Minqâr el Ruwayân** *hill* **Egypt** 29.07N 30.18E
86 D8 **Minqâr Khurayif** *hill* **Egypt** 28.56N 30.26E
86 E8 **Minqâr Shinnâra** *hill* **Egypt** 28.51N 30.38E
22 F7 **Minqin** Gansu **China** 38.41N 103.11E
23 H5 **Minqing** Fujian **China** 26.12N 118.49E
23 G1 **Minquan** Henan **China** 34.41N 115.10E
70 F4 **Minquiers,les** English Chan 48.58N 2.08W
66 R4 **Minschun,Piz** *mt* **Switzerland** 46.50N 10.14E
63 G5 **Minsen** W Germany 53.43N 7.59E
23 C2 **Min Shan** *mt ra* Sichuan **China**
86 L5 **Minshara,El** *hill* **Egypt** 30.19N 33.43E
86 E3 **Minshât el Kubra,El** Egypt 31.03N 30.54E
22 H6 **Minsheng Canal** *canal* Nei Monggol Zizhiqu **China**
25 L9 **Minsin** Burma 25.35N 95.25E
46 G3 **Minsk** Belorussiya **U.S.S.R.** 53.51N 27.30E
46 G3 **Minskaya Oblast'** *prov* Belorussiya U.S.S.R.
62 N3 **Mińsk Mazowiecki** Poland 52.10N 21.31E
56 P3 **Minsmere Cliffs** Suffolk **Eng** 52.14N 1.36E
56 N5 **Minster** Kent **Eng** 51.26N 0.49E
56 O5 **Minster** Kent **Eng** 51.20N 1.19E
104 A6 **Minster** Ohio 40.23N 84.24W
56 F2 **Minsterley** Shropshire **Eng** 52.39N 2.55W
91 C1 **Minta** Cameroon 4.34N 12.54E
31 H2 **Mintaka Pass** Kashmir 36.58N 74.54E
107 J9 **Minter** Alabama 32.03N 87.00W
107 F8 **Minter City** Mississippi 33.45N 90.20W
25 M8 **Mintha** Burma 24.24N 94.26E
84 C7 **Mínthis Óros** *mts* **Greece**
33 N5 **Mintirib,Al** Oman 22.24N 58.47E
58 M3 **Mintlaw** Grampian **Scotland** 57.31N 2.00W
113 N4 **Minto** Alaska 64.55N 149.19W
100 R9 **Minto** Manitoba 49.24N 100.00W
98 F7 **Minto** New Brunswick 46.05N 66.05W
101 E4 **Minto** Yukon Terr 62.34N 136.50W
97 J3 **Minto Hd** N W Terr 73.00N 102.40W
101 O1 **Minto Inlet** Victoria I, N W Terr
97 M6 **Minto,L** Quebec 57.30N 75.00W
100 N9 **Minton** Saskatchewan 49.11N 104.38W
109 D2 **Minturn** Colorado 39.35N 106.24W
80 J6 **Minturno** Italy 41.16N 13.45E
32 F2 **Minūdasht** Iran 37.11N 55.21E
86 E5 **Minûf** Egypt 30.28N 30.56E
86 E4 **Minûfîya** *div* **Egypt**
91 F9 **Minungu** *tribe* **Angola**
42 E5 **Minusinsk** U.S.S.R. 53.43N 91.45E
28 L1 **Minutang** Assam **India** 28.14N 96.30E
26 Q7 **Minuwangoda** Sri Lanka 7.10N 79.57E
91 C2 **Minvoul** Gabon 2.08N 12.12E
33 H8 **Minwakh** S Yemen 16.57N 48.06E
23 C1 **Min Xian** Gansu **China** 34.20N 104.09E
86 E9 **Minya** *div* **Egypt**
86 E7 **Minya,El** Egypt 29.13N 30.44E
86 E9 **Minya,El** Egypt 28.06N 30.45E
86 F6 **Minya,El** Egypt 29.44N 31.18E
86 F4 **Minya el Qamh** Egypt 30.31N 31.21E
Minya Konka *mt see* **Gongga Shan**
47 H7 **Min'yar** U.S.S.R. 55.06N 57.29E
93 K7 **Minyau** Kenya 1.43S 38.44E
86 R11 **Minyet el Sîrig** Cairo **Egypt**
86 F3 **Minyet Sandûb** Egypt 31.00N 31.23E
12 G6 **Minyip** Victoria 36.28S 142.39E
25 C2 **Minywa** Burma 22.02N 94.04E
93 C7 **Minziro** Tanzania 1.04S 31.34E
28 L2 **Minzong** Assam **India** 27.57N 96.58E
106 K5 **Mio** Michigan 44.40N 84.09W
Mio New Britain *see* **Waku**
71 F5 **Mionnay** France 45.54N 4.56E
72 C6 **Mios** France 44.37N 0.56W
Mios Num *I see* **Num**
15 C5 **Mios Waar** *isld* Irian Jaya 2.05S 134.15E
26 Q6 **Mi Oya** *R* Sri Lanka
92 K8 **Mipande** Mozambique 12.13S 40.26E
34 M5 **Miqdādiyah,Al** Iraq 33.58N 44.58E
24 F4 **Miquan** Xinjiang Uygur Zizhiqu **China** 44.00N 87.44E
98 Q6 **Miquelon** Miquelon I **Atlantic Oc** 47.08N 56.23W
99 O3 **Miquelon** Quebec 49.25N 76.32W
98 Q6 **Miquelon** *isld* **Atl Oc**
98 Q6 **Miquelon, C** Miquelon I **Atl Oc** 47.08N 56.22W
100 E5 **Miquelon Prov.Park** Alberta 53.13N 112.48W
115 K6 **Miquihuana** Mexico 23.35N 99.46W
98 N7 **Mira** C Breton I, Nova Scotia 46.04N 59.59W
84 E3 **Míra** Greece 39.27N 22.33E
79 M4 **Mira** Italy 45.26N 12.07E
76 B8 **Mira** Portugal 40.26N 8.44W
76 B9 **Mira** Portugal 39.32N 8.43W
75 H8 **Mira** Spain 39.43N 1.26W
76 B13 **Mira** *R* **Portugal**
31 A5 **Mirabad** Afghanistan 30.25N 61.53E
71 H9 **Mirabeau** France 43.42N 5.38E
72 G7 **Mirabel** France 44.10N 1.25E
76 G9 **Mirabel** Spain 39.51N 6.14W
118 G5 **Mirabela** Brazil 16.17S 44.07W
80 L6 **Mirabella Eclano** Italy 41.03N 14.59E
81 H9 **Mirabella Imbaccari** Sicily 37.19N 14.27E
79 E4 **Mirabello Monferrato** Italy 45.02N 8.31E
118 G7 **Miracema** Brazil 21.22S 42.09W
117 D9 **Miracema do Norte** Brazil 9.30S 48.23W
121 A9 **Mirador,Pta** *C* **Chile** 43.05S 74.20W
72 F8 **Miradoux** France 44.00N 0.46E
120 D11 **Miraflores** Chile 25.28S 69.46W
119 D5 **Miraflores** Colombia 5.10N 73.15W
115 E6 **Miraflores** Mexico 23.20N 109.45W
119 D7 **Miraflores** Vaupés **Colombia** 1.24N 72.06W
75 C6 **Miraflores de la Sierra** Spain 40.48N 3.45W
115 F10 **Miraflores Locks** Panama Canal Zone 8.59N 79.36W
95 K3 **Mirage** S Africa 27.15S 26.41E
111 G7 **Mirage L** California 34.39N 117.35W
34 J6 **Mirah, Wādī al** *watercourse* **Arabia/Iraq**
118 G7 **Miraí** Brazil 21.09S 42.39W
28 B2 **Miraj** Maharashtra **India** 16.51N 74.42E
118 G5 **Miralta** Brazil 16.32S 43.55W
121 F7 **Miramar** Argentina 38.15S 57.50W
105 B10 **Miramar** Florida 25.59N 80.12W
11 C6 **Miramar** *dist* Wellington **New Zealand**
121 H7 **Miramar,Canal** *str* **Chile**
79 P3 **Miramare** Italy 45.42N 13.43E
115 O9 **Miramar,L** Mexico 16.17N 91.16W
71 G9 **Miramas** France 43.33N 5.02E
72 C5 **Mirambeau** France 45.23N 0.34W
75 K6 **Mirambel** Spain 40.35N 0.21W
92 G7 **Mirambo** Tanzania 11.23S 35.24E
98 G6 **Miramichi B** New Brunswick
98 F7 **Miramichi R.,Little S.W** New Brunswick
98 F7 **Miramichi R, Main SW** New Brunswick
98 F6 **Miramichi R.,N.W** New Brunswick
72 E6 **Miramont-de-Guyenne** France 44.36N 0.22E
72 D8 **Miramont Sensacq** France 43.37N 0.20W
31 F4 **Miram Shah** Pakistan 33.00N 70.05E
24 F6 **Miran** Xinjiang Uygur Zizhiqu **China** 39.15N 88.47E
119 E8 **Miraña** Colombia 1.17S 70.22W
121 F6 **Miranda** Argentina 36.33S 59.10W
118 C7 **Miranda** Brazil 20.10S 56.19W
11 K4 **Miranda** New Zealand 37.11S 175.20E
119 F2 **Miranda** *state* **Venezuela**
75 G3 **Miranda de Arga** Spain 42.29N 1.50W
75 E2 **Miranda de Ebro** Spain 42.41N 2.57W
76 G8 **Miranda del Castañar** Spain 40.29N 6.00W
76 C8 **Miranda do Corvo** Portugal 40.05N 8.20W
76 G6 **Miranda do Douro** Portugal 41.30N 6.16W
13 F3 **Miranda Downs** Queensland 17.17S 141.50E
118 C6 **Miranda,R** Brazil
72 E8 **Mirande** France 43.31N 0.25E
76 E6 **Mirandela** Portugal 41.28N 7.10W
77 D2 **Mirandilla** Spain 39.00N 6.18W
112 J8 **Mirando City** Texas 27.26N 99.00W
79 K5 **Mirandola** Italy 44.53N 11.04E
118 D7 **Mirandópolis** Brazil 21.08S 51.08W
79 M4 **Mirano** Italy 45.29N 12.06E
30 A3 **Miranpur** Uttar Prad **India** 29.18N 77.56E
Miranshah *see* **Īrānshāh**
118 H4 **Mirante** Brazil 14.15S 40.47W
118 E8 **Mirante,Serra do** *mts* **Brazil**
121 D5 **Mira Pampa** Argentina 35.55S 63.20W
119 H9 **Mirapinima** Brazil 2.10S 61.09W
119 B7 **Mira,R** Colombia/Ecuador
20 F7 **Mirasaka** Japan 34.46N 132.56E
75 H8 **Mira,Sierra de** *mts* **Spain**
118 E7 **Mirassol** Brazil 20.47S 49.28W
75 E1 **Miravalles** Spain 43.10N 2.54W
76 F3 **Miravalles** *mt* **Spain** 42.53N 6.46W
82 G9 **Miravci** Yugoslavia 41.18N 22.26E
75 M5 **Miravet** Spain 41.02N 0.35E
75 J6 **Miravete** Spain 40.34N 0.42W
31 E3 **Mīr Bachcheh Kūt** Afghanistan 34.45N 69.08E
33 K5 **Mirban** *oil bore* **U.A.E.** 23.58N 53.40E
44 H7 **Mir Bashir** Azerbaydzhan **U.S.S.R.** 40.20N 46.56E
33 L8 **Mirbāṭ** Oman 16.58N 54.43E
33 L8 **Mirbāṭ, Ra's** *C* **Oman** 16.55N 54.47E
30 F8 **Mirchaduri** Madhya Prad **India** 24.18N 82.46E
31 D2 **Mirdshi** Afghanistan 36.36N 67.46E
70 K6 **Miré** France 47.46N 0.28W
85 N8 **Mirear I** Egypt 23.15N 35.41E
116 H5 **Mirebalais** Haiti 18.51N 72.08W
71 G2 **Mirebeau** Côte d'Or **France** 47.24N 5.20E
72 E2 **Mirebeau** Vienne **France** 46.47N 0.12E
69 L7 **Mirecourt** France 48.18N 6.08E
36 F2 **Mire Dağı** *mt* **Turkey**
72 G9 **Miremont** France 43.22N 1.24E
72 H9 **Mirepoix** France 43.05N 1.51E
33 K4 **Mirfa, Al** U.A.E. 24.05N 53.32E
87 K7 **Mirgadudu** Ethiopia 7.48N 44.03E
Mirgah *see* **Marga**
34 N2 **Mirgah** Iraq 36.03N 45.06E
30 H6 **Mirganj** Bihar **India** 26.22N 84.21E
31 G6 **Mirgarh** Pakistan 29.09N 72.40E
45 E7 **Mirgorod** Ukraine **U.S.S.R.** 49.58N 33.37E
Mirhaj Khalil *see* **Marhaj Khalil**
31 E4 **Mir Hasan** Afghanistan 32.38N 69.13E
30 D8 **Mirhasan** *R* Madhya Prad **India**
18 K3 **Miri** Sarawak **Malaysia** 4.28N 114.00E
31 B6 **Miri** *mt* **Pakistan** 29.10N 62.50E
28 D2 **Mirialguda** Andhra Prad **India** 16.52N 79.35E
13 K6 **Miriam Vale** Queensland 24.17S 151.34E
71 F5 **Miribel** France 45.49N 4.56E
26 R7 **Mirigama** Sri Lanka 7.15N 80.08E
24 H12 **Miri Hills** Assam **India**
87 B5 **Miri,Jeb** *hills* **Sudan**
119 F2 **Mirimere** Venezuela 11.14N 68.39W
121 H4 **Mirim,L** Brazil/Uruguay
121 J2 **Mirim,L.do** Brazil 28.24S 48.50W
121 F2 **Miriñay, R** Argentina
13 G8 **Mirintu** *R* Queensland
28 K2 **Miris** *tribe* Assam **India**
93 L10 **Miritini** Kenya 4.00S 39.35E
119 E8 **Miritiparaná,R** Colombia
28 B3 **Mirjan** Karnataka **India** 14.33N 74.26E
32 J6 **Mīrjāveh** Iran 29.01N 61.30E
Mirjawa *see* **Mīrjāveh**
32 H7 **Mīr Kūh** Iran 26.20N 58.55E
33 G9 **Mirmal,Jabal** *mt* **S Yemen** 14.07N 46.12E
31 B3 **Mir Manna** Afghanistan 34.10N 62.20E
30 E6 **Mirmau** Uttar Prad **India** 26.41N 81.40E
79 P4 **Mirna** *R* **Italy**
82 B5 **Mirna** *R* **Yugoslavia**
42 D2 **Mirnoye** U.S.S.R. 62.19N 89.02E
42 B3 **Mirnoye Ozero** U.S.S.R. 57.46N 78.55E
123 D3 **Mirny** *U.S.S.R. Base* **Antarctica** 66.33S 93.01E
42 J1 **Mirnyy** U.S.S.R. 62.30N 113.58E
87 K7 **Miro** Ethiopia 7.03N 44.50E
41 E7 **Miroedikha** U.S.S.R. 65.38N 88.08E
93 F6 **Mirogi** Kenya 0.42S 34.23E
71 K2 **Miroir,Mt** France 47.15N 6.50E
92 H7 **Mirola** Tanzania 10.08S 37.21E
11 G9 **Miromiro** *mt* **New Zealand** 42.28S 172.42E
100 P3 **Mirond L** Saskatchewan
45 H7 **Mironovka** Khar'kov, Ukraine **U.S.S.R.** 49.14N 36.05E
45 B7 **Mironovka** Kiyev, Ukraine **U.S.S.R.** 49.40N 30.59E
42 H3 **Mironovo** Irkutsk **U.S.S.R.** 58.22N 109.32E
47 N4 **Mironovo** Sverdlovsk **U.S.S.R.** 57.31N 61.41E
45 G5 **Miropol'ye** Ukraine **U.S.S.R.** 51.01N 35.16E
82 J6 **Miroşi** Romania 44.25N 24.58E
65 O4 **Miroslav** Czechoslovakia 48.58N 16.19E
62 J2 **Mirosławiec** Poland 53.20N 16.05E
64 Q4 **Mirošov** Czechoslovakia 49.41N 13.40E
65 K3 **Mirotice** Czechoslovakia 49.27N 14.02E
65 P2 **Mírov** Czechoslovakia 49.48N 16.52E
65 K2 **Mirovice** Czechoslovakia 49.32N 14.03E

45 E8 **Mirovskoye** Ukraine U.S.S.R. 48.05N 33.25E
63 R6 **Mirow** E Germany 53.17N 12.49E
31 G4 **Mirpur** Kashmir 33.32N 73.56E
31 E8 **Mirpur Batoro** Pakistan 24.40N 68.15E
31 E8 **Mirpur Khas** Pakistan 25.33N 69.05E
31 D8 **Mirpur Sakro** Pakistan 24.32N 67.38E
13 D7 **Mirranponga Pongunna L** N Terr Australia 25.58S 137.38E
100 D6 **Mirror** Alberta 52.28N 113.07W
92 J8 **Mirrote** Mozambique 13.50S 39.34E
87 L8 **Mirsale** Somalia 5.57N 47.47E
82 J6 **Mîrşani** Romania 44.00N 24.01E
43 J7 **Mirshade** Tadzhikistan U.S.S.R. 38.09N 67.43E
32 H7 **Mīr Shahdād** Iran 26.15N 58.29E
84 B6 **Mirsíni** Greece 37.55N 21.15E
39 E4 **Mirskaya** U.S.S.R. 61.09N 152.59E
42 E6 **Mirskoy Khrebet** *mts* U.S.S.R.
Mirtağ *see* Mutki
84 C4 **Mirtiá** Aitolía Greece 38.35N 21.36E
84 B6 **Mirtiá** Ilía Greece 37.43N 21.21E
13 H5 **Mirtna** Queensland 21.16S 146.15E
83 F7 **Mirtoan Sea** Greece
Mirvan *see* Karabegân
86 L9 **Mi'r, Wâdi** *watercourse* Egypt
31 G2 **Mir Wali** Kashmir 36.33N 73.25E
61 M6 **Mirwart** Belgium 50.03N 5.16E
35 F9 **Mirwid** Jordan 31.06N 35.43E
21 D10 **Miryang** S Korea 35.31N 128.45E
46 G6 **Miryeny** Moldavia U.S.S.R. 47.00N 29.06E
42 F2 **Miryuginskiy,Porog** *falls* U.S.S.R. 60.23N 99.20E
44 G6 **Mirzaani** Georgia U.S.S.R. 41.22N 46.10E
43 F6 **Mirzachirla** Turkmeniya U.S.S.R. 39.37N 60.02E
30 F7 **Mirzapur** Mirzapur, Uttar Prad India 25.09N 82.34E
30 C5 **Mirzapur** Shahjahanpur, Uttar Prad India 27.41N 79.33E
30 F8 **Mirzapur** *dist* Uttar Prad India
29 C3 **Mirzawal** Rajasthan India 29.54N 73.49E
93 B1 **Misa** Zaïre 4.03N 30.10E
79 O7 **Misa** *R* Italy
89 K8 **Misahöhe** Togo 6.59N 0.40E
20 F8 **Misaki** Japan 33.23N 132.08E
20 G7 **Mi-saki** *C* Shikoku Japan 34.15N 133.33E
20 L6 **Misakubo** Japan 35.11N 137.52E
91 C5 **Misa Misonié** Congo 3.40S 12.50E
79 N7 **Misano Monte** Italy 43.58N 12.39E
115 L8 **Misantla** Mexico 19.56N 96.51W
30 B2 **Misarwala** Uttar Prad India 30.10N 78.08E
20 P9 **Misato** Okinawa Japan 26.19N 127.47E
20 F1 **Misato** Saitama Japan
90 E6 **Misau** Nigeria 11.21N 12.09E
20 P1 **Misawa** Japan 40.42N 141.26E
101 W6 **Misaw L** Saskatchewan
63 L8 **Misburg** W Germany 52.24N 9.51E
87 F2 **Misced** *mt* Ethiopia 16.15N 36.59E
66 H7 **Mischabel** *mts* Switzerland
98 H6 **Miscou Centre** New Brunswick 47.58N 64.35W
98 J7 **Miscouche** Prince Edward I 46.26N 63.52W
98 H6 **Miscou I** New Brunswick
98 H5 **Miscou Pt** New Brunswick 48.02N 64.33W
86 N9 **Miseir, Wādī el** *watercourse* Saudi Arabia
80 K7 **Miseno,C** Italy 40.46N 14.06E
71 H2 **Miserey-Salines** France 47.17N 5.58E
50 R11 **Miseryfjellet** *mt* Spitsbergen 74.25N 19.12E
116 P3 **Misery,Mt** St Kitts W I 17.23N 62.49W
86 K3 **Mişfaq** Egypt 31.02N 33.09E
31 H2 **Misgar** Kashmir 36.48N 74.50E
95 G9 **Misgund** S Africa 33.46S 23.30E
28 H7 **Misha** Nicobar Is 8.00N 93.22E
33 H2 **Mish'āb,Al** Saudi Arabia 28.07N 48.37E
44 G9 **Mishāb, Kuh-e** *mts* Iran
120 C4 **Mishahua, R** Peru
33 F10 **Mishāl, Am** S Yemen 13.39N 45.48E
21 E5 **Mishan** Heilongjiang China 45.33N 131.57E
33 H4 **Mishāsh al Ashāwī** Saudi Arabia 24.20N 48.58E
33 H3 **Mishāsh al Hādī** Saudi Arabia 26.05N 48.26E
33 H4 **Mishāsh az Zu'ayyinī** Saudi Arabia 25.35N 48.07E
33 H4 **Mishāsh Banī Wuţayfān** Saudi Arabia 24.28N 49.14E
34 D10 **Mishāsh Dabl** Saudi Arabia 28.45N 36.52E
34 F10 **Mishāsh Muḑayyān** Saudi Arabia 28.56N 38.39E
33 H4 **Mishāsh 'Uwayr** Saudi Arabia 25.09N 49.04E
106 H8 **Mishawaka** Indiana 41.38N 86.10W
113 G2 **Misheguk Mt** Alaska 68.15N 161.09W
86 M6 **Misheiti,Gebel el** *hill* Egypt 29.46N 34.17E
42 G5 **Mishelevka** U.S.S.R. 52.52N 103.10E
Mishgin *see* Khīyāv
99 E4 **Mishibishu L** Ontario 48.05N 85.25W
106 G5 **Mishicot** Wisconsin 44.14N 87.38W
20 M6 **Mishima** Japan 35.08N 138.54E
20 E7 **Mi-shima** *isld* Japan
86 D7 **Mishîqeiqa,El** *hill* Egypt 29.08N 30.27E
34 M7 **Mishkhab** Iraq 31.47N 44.29E
47 H7 **Mishkino** Bashkir U.S.S.R. 55.34N 56.00E
47 J7 **Mishkino** Kurgan U.S.S.R. 55.22N 63.50E
32 G3 **Mīsh,Kūh-e** *mt* Iran 35.54N 57.41E
35 F7 **Mishmaqa** *anc site* Jordan 31.34N 35.37E
35 E8 **Mishmar** *watercourse* Israel
35 C6 **Mishmar 'Ayyalon** Israel 31.52N 34.57E
35 D3 **Mishmar Ha'Emeq** Israel 32.37N 35.09E
35 B8 **Mishmar HaNegev** Israel 31.22N 34.42E
35 E1 **Mishmar HaYarden** Israel 33.00N 35.30E
90 L7 **Mishmira** *mt* Cent Afr Rep 9.40N 23.40E
28 K1 **Mishmis** *tribe* Assam India
99 P5 **Mishomis** Quebec 47.11N 75.40W
47 H3 **Mishvan'** U.S.S.R. 66.59N 55.51E
33 F10 **Mishyāf,Jabal al** *mt* S Yemen 13.37N 45.19E
15 G7 **Misiki** Papua New Guinea 7.40S 143.53E
81 F7 **Misilmeri** Sicily 38.03N 13.27E
15 M9 **Misima I** Louisiade Arch 10.38S 152.45E
118 B10 **Misiones** *dept* Paraguay
118 C10 **Misiones** *prov* Argentina
118 C10 **Misiones,Sa.de** *ra* Argentina
121 L10 **Misión Fagnano** Argentina 54.32S 67.16W
36 H6 **Misis** Turkey 36.57N 35.35E
36 H6 **Misis Dağ** *mt* Turkey
92 D4 **Misisi** Zaïre 4.45S 28.39E
37 G7 **Misk** Turkey 38.48N 42.17E
33 E4 **Miskah** Saudi Arabia 24.53N 42.58E
90 M4 **Miski** Sudan 14.50N 24.15E
33 M5 **Miskin** Oman 23.30N 56.53E
115 N2 **Miskito,Cayos** *islds* Nicaragua
62 M7 **Miskolc** Hungary 48.07N 20.47E
79 M2 **Mis,L.di** *L* Italy
36 H4 **Misli** Turkey 38.14N 34.46E
33 D3 **Mismá,Jibāl** *mts* Saudi Arabia
34 E6 **Misma,Tal** *mt* Jordan 32.42N 37.40E
15 A4 **Misoöl** *isld* Irian Jaya
85 C3 **Misrātah** Libya 32.24N 15.04E
85 C3 **Misratah, C** Libya 32.30N 15.10E
Misriç *see* Kurtalan
30 D5 **Misrikh** Uttar Prad India 27.25N 80.30E
91 K8 **Missa** Zaïre 8.50S 26.22E
79 F3 **Missaglia** Italy 45.43N 9.20E
99 F4 **Missanabie** Ontario 48.20N 84.06W
91 G9 **Missão de Boma** Angola 11.48S 20.06E
117 G8 **Miss 6ao Velha** Brazil 7.13S 39.07W
87 K9 **Missarole** Somalia 3.29N 45.00E
14 D4 **Missiessy,C** W Australia 19.01S 121.38E
70 F7 **Missillac** France 47.30N 2.09W
99 G4 **Missinaibi L** Ontario
99 H2 **Missinaibi R** Ontario
108 K6 **Mission** S Dakota 43.18N 100.40W
112 J9 **Mission** Texas 26.14N 98.20W
11 D2 **Mission Bay** Auckland New Zealand 36.51S 174.50E
101 M11 **Mission City** Br Col 49.17N 122.21W
108 N7 **Mission Hill** S Dakota 42.56N 97.17W
13 F2 **Mission R** Queensland
110 M2 **Mission Ra** Montana
89 C5 **Missira** Senegal 13.41N 13.32W
89 D5 **Missira** Senegal 13.11N 11.42W
89 A5 **Missirah** Senegal 13.40N 16.32W
99 L1 **Missisicabi** *R* Quebec
99 H6 **Mississagi Prov. Park** Ontario
99 G6 **Mississaqi** *R* Ontario
99 L9 **Mississauga** Ontario 43.38N 79.36W
106 J9 **Mississinewa Reservoir** Indiana
102 H4 **Mississippi** *R* U.S.A.
102 H4 **Mississippi** *state* U.S.A.
107 G12 **Mississippi Delta** Louisiana
99 O7 **Mississippi L** Ontario
107 G11 **Mississippi Sd** Mississippi
Missolonghi *see* Mesolóngion
99 H4 **Missonga** Ontario 48.25N 82.44W
110 L3 **Missoula** Montana 46.52N 114.00W
88 M5 **Missour** Morocco 33.04N 3.59W
102 G2 **Missouri** *R* U.S.A.
102 H3 **Missouri** *state* U.S.A.
112 F9 **Missouri City** Texas 29.32N 95.31W
107 C8 **Missouri, Little** *R* Arkansas
108 P8 **Missouri Valley** Iowa 41.32N 95.54W
13 H5 **Mistake Cr** Queensland
13 A3 **Mistake Creek** N Terr Australia 17.08S 129.04E
91 E5 **Mistandunga** Zaïre 2.05S 16.24E
98 K2 **Mistanipisipou R** Quebec
99 M3 **Mistaouak, L** Quebec
99 S3 **Mistassibi** *R* Quebec
98 A3 **Mistassibi,R.,N.E** Quebec
99 S4 **Mistassini** Quebec 48.54N 72.13W
99 S3 **Mistassini** *R* Quebec
97 M7 **Mistassini, L** Quebec 51.00N 73.30W
100 O6 **Mistatim** Saskatchewan 52.52N 103.26W
65 P4 **Mistelbach** Austria 48.35N 16.35E
81 K8 **Misterbianco** Sicily 37.31N 15.01E
52 K9 **Misterhult** Sweden 57.28N 16.35E
116 C5 **Misteriosa Bank** Caribbean Sea
57 M6 **Misterton** Notts Eng 53.27N 0.51W
56 F6 **Misterton** Somerset Eng 50.52N 2.47W
98 D5 **Mistigougèche L** Quebec 48.15N 68.00W
95 H9 **Mistkraal,De** S Africa 33.45S 24.45E
64 P3 **Misto** Czechoslovakia 50.27N 13.15E
121 D3 **Mistolar, L** Argentina
52 F5 **Mistra** *R* Norway
84 D7 **Mistrás** *ruins* Greece 37.04N 22.22E
81 H8 **Mistretta** Sicily 37.56N 14.22E
84 G4 **Místros** Greece 38.32N 23.51E
91 G6 **Misumba** Zaïre 4.20S 21.51E
20 E7 **Misumi** Honshu Japan 34.49N 131.59E
20 D9 **Misumiura** Kyūshū Japan 32.37N 130.28E
93 E8 **Misungwi** Tanzania 2.51S 33.06E
Misurata *see* Misrātah
93 E7 **Misuri Pt** Tanzania 1.20S 33.49E
93 J7 **Mitaboni** Kenya 1.24S 37.16E
86 G3 **Mît Abu Ghâlib** Egypt 31.19N 31.41E
86 O8 **Mitaha, Wādī el** *watercourse* Saudi Arabia
92 D9 **Mita Hills Dam** *res* Zambia
20 E9 **Mitai** Japan 32.42N 131.19E
20 C2 **Mitaka** *dist* Tōkyō Japan 35.42N 139.34E
86 P4 **Mi'ţan** Jordan 30.46N 35.35E
116 P2 **Mitan** Trinidad & Tobago 10.28N 61.07W
92 J6 **Mitandawala** Tanzania 9.08S 39.08E
115 G7 **Mita,Pta.de** *C* Mexico 20.46N 105.33W
117 B3 **Mitaraca** *pk* Fr Guiana/Surinam 2.18N 54.31W
119 E2 **Mitare** Venezuela 11.23N 70.04W
87 F3 **Mitatib** Sudan 15.59N 36.12E
55 F5 **Mitcham** London Eng 51.24N 0.09W
12 B8 **Mitcham** *dist* Adelaide, S Aust
56 G4 **Mitcheldean** Glos Eng 51.53N 2.30W
56 U9 **Mitchell** Cornwall Eng 50.21N 5.00W
107 K3 **Mitchell** Indiana 38.43N 86.29W
108 G8 **Mitchell** Nebraska 41.56N 103.48W
99 J9 **Mitchell** Ontario 43.27N 81.13W
110 E5 **Mitchell** Oregon 44.34N 120.08W
13 J7 **Mitchell** Queensland 26.30S 147.56E
108 M6 **Mitchell** S Dakota 43.40N 98.01W
12 K3 **Mitchell** *R* New S Wales
13 F3 **Mitchell** *R* Queensland
12 H7 **Mitchell** *R* Victoria
107 K9 **Mitchell L** Alabama
106 J5 **Mitchell,L** Michigan 44.14N 85.30W
105 E2 **Mitchell,Mt** N Carolina 35.47N 82.16W
13 A1 **Mitchell Pt** N Terr Australia 11.50S 130.00E
13 F3 **Mitchell River** Queensland 15.30S 141.40E
56 F4 **Mitchell Troy** Gwent Wales 51.47N 2.44W
59 F7 **Mitchelstown** Cork Irish Rep 52.16N 8.16W
99 P5 **Mitchinamécus, L** Quebec
92 J7 **Miteda** Mozambique 11.49S 39.40E
92 J6 **Miteja** Tanzania 8.36S 39.14E
86 F4 **Mît el Âmil** Egypt 30.54N 31.21E
86 G3 **Mît el Nasâra** Egypt 31.08N 31.39E
86 G3 **Mît Fâris** Egypt 31.03N 31.36E
57 K2 **Mitford** Northumb Eng 55.10N 1.44W
86 F4 **Mît Ghamr** Egypt 30.43N 31.16E
33 G9 **Mitḩāf** S Yemen 14.04N 47.18E
86 G5 **Mît Hamal** Egypt 30.26N 31.32E
31 F6 **Mithankot** Pakistan 28.53N 70.25E
31 G4 **Mitha Tiwana** Pakistan 32.18N 72.08E
31 E8 **Mithi** Pakistan 24.43N 69.53E
83 H5 **Míthimna** Greece 39.20N 26.12E
31 E7 **Mithrau** Pakistan 27.30N 69.40E
31 E7 **Mithrau Can** Pakistan
31 D6 **Mithri** Pakistan 29.22N 67.51E
19 F3 **Miti** *isld* Moluccas Indon 1.31N 128.04E
74 J8 **Mitidja** *plain* Algeria
85 M6 **Mitig, Gebel** *mts* Egypt
84 G5 **Mitikas** Greece 38.26N 23.39E
83 H5 **Mitilíni** Greece 39.06N 26.34E
47 F3 **Mitina** U.S.S.R. 65.43N 49.29E
100 S4 **Mitishto R** Manitoba
98 E5 **Mitis L** Quebec
101 G7 **Mitkof I** Alaska 56.40N 132.50W
115 L9 **Mitla** Mexico 16.56N 96.19W
86 L5 **Mitmitni** *reg* Egypt
20 O5 **Mito** Japan 36.22N 140.29E
91 J6 **Mitombe** Zaïre 5.20S 24.52E
92 G7 **Mitomoni** Tanzania 11.34S 35.19E
91 A3 **Mitra** *mt* Equat Guinea 1.21N 9.59E
50 S13 **Mitra K** *C* Spitsbergen
10 P4 **Mitre** *isld* Santa Cruz Is Pacific Oc 11.55S 170.12E
11 K7 **Mitre** *mt* North I New Zealand 40.48S 175.28E
121 M10 **Mitre,Pen** Argentina
11 B11 **Mitre Pk** *mt* South I New Zealand 44.37S 167.47E
113 H9 **Mitrofania I** Alaska 55.53N 158.50W
45 L7 **Mitrofanovka** U.S.S.R. 49.58N 39.41E
47 H4 **Mitrofanovskaya** U.S.S.R. 63.12N 56.00E
84 C3 **Mitrópolis** Greece 39.20N 21.50E
68 J2 **Mitry-Mory** France 48.59N 2.37E
95 A1 **Mitsamiouli** Comoros, Ind Oc 11.22S 43.21E
84 A2 **Mitsikéli,Óros** *mts* Greece
95 B4 **Mitsinjo** Madagascar 16.00S 45.52E
87 G3 **Mits'iwa** Ethiopia 15.37N 39.28E
Mitspa *see* Mizpa
20 F7 **Mitsu** Japan 34.19N 132.48E
20 F8 **Mitsuhama** Japan 33.50N 132.42E
20 M2 **Mitsuishi** Hokkaido Japan 42.15N 142.33E
20 H7 **Mitsuishi** Honshu Japan 34.50N 134.15E
20 O5 **Mitsukaidō** Japan 36.03N 140.01E
20 M4 **Mitsuke** Japan 37.30N 138.54E
20 M1 **Mitsumata** Japan 43.31N 143.07E
88 R4 **Mitta,el** *watercourse* Algeria
12 K5 **Mittagong** New S Wales 34.27S 150.25E
13 F4 **Mittagong** Queensland 18.32S 142.30E
65 J9 **Mittagskogel** *mt* Yugoslavia/Austria 46.30N 13.57E
65 A7 **Mittag-Spitze** *mt* Austria 47.18N 9.53E
12 H6 **Mitta Mitta** Victoria 36.35S 147.28E
63 B1 **Mitte** *dist* E Berlin E Germany
65 C8 **Mittelberg** Tirol Austria 46.58N 10.53E
65 B7 **Mittelberg** Vorarlberg Austria 47.20N 10.10E
64 J5 **Mittelfranken** *dist* Bayern W Germany
66 F4 **Mittelland** *reg* Switzerland
63 H8 **Mittellandkanal** W Germany
63 R8 **Mittelmark** *reg* E Germany
64 H3 **Mittelsinn** W Germany 50.12N 9.37E
66 N1 **Mittel-Zell** W Germany 47.42N 9.03E
65 D7 **Mittenwald** W Germany 47.27N 11.17E
63 T8 **Mittenwalde** E Germany 52.16N 13.33E
65 M6 **Mitterbach** Austria 47.49N 15.18E
65 H7 **Mitterberg** Austria 47.26N 13.07E
65 H5 **Mitterding** Austria 48.22N 13.28E
64 O6 **Mitterfels** W Germany 48.58N 12.42E
65 H7 **Mitter Klein Arl** Austria 47.18N 13.20E
65 J6 **Mitterndorf** Austria 47.34N 13.56E
65 G7 **Mitter Pinzgau** *V* Austria
69 M6 **Mittersheim** France 48.51N 6.57E
65 F7 **Mittersill** Austria 47.18N 12.29E
64 N4 **Mitterteich** W Germany 49.57N 12.15E
65 J6 **Mitter Weissenbach** Austria 47.46N 13.40E
65 G8 **Mittewald** Austria 46.47N 12.35E
13 D4 **Mittiebah** *R* N Terr Australia
64 O2 **Mittweida** E Germany 50.59N 12.59E
119 E7 **Mitú** Colombia 1.07N 70.05W
119 F6 **Mituas** Colombia 3.53N 68.48W
93 J6 **Mitubiri** Kenya 0.59S 37.09E
91 J4 **Mituku** *tribe* Zaïre
92 E5 **Mitumba** Tanzania 7.08S 31.02E
92 C5 **Mitumba** *tribe* Zaïre
93 J6 **Mitunguu** Kenya 0.04S 37.47E
91 K8 **Mitwaba** Zaïre 8.37S 27.20E
93 D5 **Mityana** Uganda 0.25N 32.04E
47 J5 **Mityayevo** U.S.S.R. 60.16N 61.05E
86 F4 **Mît Yazîd** Egypt 30.51N 31.07E
41 A3 **Mityushikha, Guba** *gulf* Novaya Zemlya U.S.S.R.
91 B3 **Mitzic** Gabon 0.48N 11.30E
9 S10 **Miu Hopohoponga** *pt* Tonga, Pacific Oc 21.09S 175.02W
20 B5 **Miura** Japan 35.08N 139.37E
45 K9 **Mius** *R* U.S.S.R.
45 K9 **Miusskiy Liman** *lagoon* U.S.S.R.
35 A9 **Mivtaḩim** Israel 31.15N 34.24E
93 F6 **Miwani** Kenya 0.04S 34.59E
115 B10 **Mixcoac** *dist* Mexico City Mexico
23 F1 **Mi Xian** Henan China 34.31N 113.15E
65 M7 **Mixnitz** Austria 47.20N 15.24E
20 K7 **Miya-gawa** *R* Japan
20 Q8 **Miyagi** Okinawa Japan 26.37N 128.10E
20 O3 **Miyagi** *prefect* Japan
20 P9 **Miyagusuku-jima** *I* Okinawa Japan 26.20N 128.00E
33 A4 **Miyah,Wâdi** *watercourse* Egypt
34 G4 **Miyāh, Wādī** *watercourse* Syria
33 E4 **Miyah, Wādī al** *watercourse* Saudi Arabia
20 E9 **Miyaji** Japan 32.57N 131.08E
20 F7 **Miyajima** Japan 34.18N 132.18E
20 B3 **Miyakami** Kanagawa Japan
20 N7 **Miyake-jima** *isld* Japan
20 P2 **Miyako** Honshu Japan 39.38N 141.59E
17 L7 **Miyako** *isld* Ryūkyū Retto Japan 24.45N 125.25E
20 E10 **Miyakonojō** Japan 31.43N 131.02E
20 P2 **Miyako-wan** *B* Japan
43 C3 **Miyaly** Kazakhstan U.S.S.R. 48.55N 53.56E
Miyanabad *see* Miānābād
Miyandasht *see* Miāndasht
Miyandeh *see* Miāndehī
Mi-yang *see* Biyang
21 E12 **Miyanoura dake** *mt* Japan 30.22N 130.35E
20 E10 **Miyazaki** Japan 31.56N 131.27E
20 E10 **Miyazaki** *prefect* Japan
20 J6 **Miyazu** Japan 35.33N 135.12E
88 G10 **Miyec** Morocco 23.28N 10.42W
23 C5 **Miyi** Sichuan China 26.50N 102.04E
20 C1 **Miyoshi** Saitama Japan
20 F7 **Miyoshi** Hiroshima Japan 34.51N 132.49E
22 K6 **Miyun** Beijing China 40.20N 116.51E
22 L6 **Miyun Sk** *L* Beijing China
21 E12 **Mi-zaki** *C* Tanega Japan 30.51N 131.03E
86 P9 **Mizannad, Wādī el** *watercourse* Saudi Arabia
87 E7 **Mizan Teferi** Ethiopia 6.57N 35.03E
Mizar *see* Karakeçi
85 B4 **Mizdah** Libya 31.25N 13.02E
107 G10 **Mize** Mississippi 31.51N 89.35W
59 C9 **Mizen Hd** Cork Irish Rep 51.27N 9.49W
59 K6 **Mizen Hd** Wicklow Irish Rep 52.52N 6.03W
22 H8 **Mizhi** Shaanxi China 37.50N 110.03E
82 K6 **Mizil** Romania 45.00N 26.29E
46 F4 **Mizoch** Ukraine U.S.S.R. 50.30N 25.50E
20 G6 **Mizogu chi** Japan 35.23N 133.27E
20 D3 **Mizonokuchi** Japan 35.36N 139.37E
28 J4 **Mizoram** *Union Terr* India
35 F2 **Mizpa** Israel 32.47N 35.30E
108 Q2 **Mizpah** Minnesota 47.54N 94.11W
103 E8 **Mizpah** New Jersey 39.29N 74.50W
86 N4 **Mizpe Ramon** Israel 30.36N 34.48E
35 E7 **Mizpe Shalem** Jordan 31.35N 35.24E
120 F7 **Mizque** Bolivia 17.57S 65.17W
120 F7 **Mizque** *R* Bolivia 17.57S 65.17W
35 E3 **Mizra** Israel 32.39N 35.17E
37 D1 **Mızraplı** *R* Turkey
20 F2 **Mizue** *dist* Tōkyō Japan
20 A2 **Mizuho** Tōkyō Japan
123 B6 **Mizuho** *Jap. Base* Antarctica 70.43S 40.20E
20 L6 **Mizunami** Japan 35.25N 137.16E
44 F5 **Mizurskiy** U.S.S.R. 42.52N 44.09E
20 P2 **Mizusawa** Japan 39.10N 141.07E
35 E1 **Mjâdel, El** Lebanon 33.14N 35.21E
93 E5 **Mjanji** Uganda 0.16N 34.00E
95 M7 **Mjanyama** S Africa 31.50S 28.10E
88 J10 **Mjebir** Mauritania 22.12N 8.04W
53 U16 **Mjell** Norway 61.21N 6.20E
95 M7 **Mjika** S Africa 31.25S 28.41E
52 G9 **Mjöbäck** Sweden 57.18N 12.53E
50 H4 **Mjóidalur** *V* Iceland
50 C3 **Mjóifjördhur** *B* Ísafjardharsýsla, Nordhur Iceland
50 M4 **Mjóifjördhur** *B* Múlasýsla, Sudhur Iceland
52 J8 **Mjölby** Sweden 58.19N 15.10E
53 B6 **Mjolden** Denmark 55.07N 8.46E
53 V17 **Mjølfjell** Norway 60.42N 6.50E
53 Y16 **Mjølkedalsvatn** *L* Norway 61.25N 8.15E
53 R17 **Mjømna** Norway 60.55N 4.55E
52 G9 **Mjörn** *L* Sweden 57.55N 12.25E
52 F6 **Mjøsa** *L* Norway
53 N9 **Mjóvanes** *C* Faeroes 62.08N 6.35W
93 F10 **Mkalama** Tanzania 4.09S 34.35E
95 N7 **Mkambati** S Africa 31.17S 29.58E
92 H6 **Mkangira** Tanzania 9.00S 37.30E
92 G6 **Mkasu** Tanzania 9.05S 35.51E
92 H5 **Mkata** Tanzania 6.41S 37.20E
92 J4 **Mkoani** Pemba I 5.21S 39.40E
92 E9 **Mkokomo** *mt* Zambia 14.49S 30.30E
92 J11 **Mkokotoni** Zanzibar 5.53S 39.15E
92 J7 **Mkoma** Tanzania 10.50S 39.14E
93 K10 **Mkomazi** Tanzania 4.38S 38.05E
93 N7 **Mkondoni** Kenya 1.36S 41.21E
93 E4 **Mkongoro** Uganda 1.22N 33.52E
95 O4 **Mkonjane** S Africa 28.09S 30.35E
92 D8 **Mkuku** Zambia 12.05S 29.54E
92 F6 **Mkulwe** Tanzania 8.35S 32.19E
93 M8 **Mkunumbi** Kenya 2.18S 40.44E
92 J5 **Mkuranga** Tanzania 7.05S 39.10E
92 D8 **Mkushi** Zambia 13.40S 29.26E
92 D8 **Mkushi** *R* Zambia
92 J11 **Mkuuni** Zanzibar 5.54S 39.20E
92 H5 **Mkuyuni** Tanzania 6.58S 37.49E
92 J11 **Mkuyuni Pwani** Zanzibar 5.55S 39.21E
95 O9 **Mkuze** S Africa 27.37S 32.03E
95 O9 **Mkuze** *R* S Africa
92 J4 **Mkwaja** Tanzania 5.49S 38.50E
92 J11 **Mkwajuni** Zanzibar 5.53S 39.17E
92 J7 **Mkwaya** Tanzania 10.06S 39.39E
92 G7 **Mkwera** Tanzania 10.45S 35.49E
62 H5 **Mladá Boleslav** Czechoslovakia 50.26N 14.55E
65 L2 **Mladá Vožice** Czechoslovakia 49.32N 14.48E
65 Q2 **Mladeč** Czechoslovakia 49.42N 17.01E
82 F6 **Mladenovac** Yugoslavia 44.29N 20.41E
64 P4 **Mladotice** Czechoslovakia 49.59N 13.22E
92 E5 **Mlala Hills** Tanzania
93 H5 **Mlali** Tanzania 6.19S 36.48E
93 K10 **Mlalo** Tanzania 4.34S 38.21E
92 G6 **Mlangali** Tanzania 9.47S 34.32E
82 G6 **Mlava** *R* Yugoslavia
62 M2 **Mława** Poland 53.08N 20.20E
88 K10 **Mléhas,El** Mauritania 23.38N 6.51W
88 K10 **Mleihas** Mauritania 22.39N 6.55W
92 J10 **M'lela** *R* Mozambique
44 F5 **Mleti** Georgia U.S.S.R. 42.30N 44.34E
92 J4 **Mligasi** *R* Tanzania
82 D8 **Mljet** *isld* Yugoslavia
92 J4 **Mlola** Tanzania 4.39S 38.25E
92 G7 **Mlowe** Malawi 10.46S 34.13E
Mlusi,Wadi al *watercourse see* **Mulūşī, Wādī al** *watercourse*
95 J1 **Mmabatho** S Africa 25.51S 25.37E
94 J3 **Mmadinare** Botswana 21.52S 27.45E
94 J4 **Mmamabula** Botswana 23.35S 26.32E
93 K10 **Mnazi** Tanzania 4.25S 38.17E
93 M7 **Mnazini** Kenya 1.57S 40.18E
95 N8 **Mncwasa Pt** S Africa 32.05S 29.05E
92 J7 **Mnero** Tanzania 10.09S 38.40E
64 O3 **Mnichov** Czechoslovakia 50.02N 12.47E
65 L2 **Mnichovice** Czechoslovakia 49.57N 14.43E
62 H5 **Mnichovo Hradiště** Czech 50.32N 15.00E
62 M7 **Mníšek** Czechoslovakia 48.49N 20.50E
65 K2 **Mníšek p.Brdy** Czechoslovakia 49.52N 14.17E
53 T17 **Mo** Hordaland Norway 60.48N 5.50E
52 L3 **Mo** Sweden 63.24N 18.30E
53 X20 **Mo** Telemark Norway 59.29N 7.51E
89 K7 **Mo** *R* Togo
116 G4 **Moa** Cuba 20.42N 74.57W
92 J4 **Moa** Tanzania 4.49S 39.10E
19 E8 **Moa** *isld* Indon
120 C2 **Moa** *R* Brazil
89 D8 **Moa** *R* Sierra Leone
111 P3 **Moab** Utah 38.35N 109.34W
35 F5 **Moab** *reg* Jordan
91 B5 **Moabi** Gabon 2.20S 11.00E
63 A1 **Moabit** *dist* W Berlin W Germany
120 D3 **Moaco,R** Brazil
100 U3 **Moak L** Manitoba 55.55N 97.30W
9 T3 **Moala** *isld* Fiji 18.34S 179.56E
32 E4 **Mo'alla** Iran 33.27N 53.51E
32 F3 **Mo'allemān** Iran 35.10N 54.38E
12 G6 **Moama** New S Wales 36.05S 144.50E
94 M5 **Moamba** Mozambique 25.35S 32.13E
11 F9 **Moana** New Zealand 42.34S 171.29E
76 B4 **Moaña** Spain 42.17N 8.44W
11 J6 **Moana** *mt* New Zealand 39.33S 174.34E
12 E3 **Moanba,L** S Australia
91 C4 **Moanda** Gabon 1.32S 13.17E
91 C6 **Moanda** Zaïre 5.55S 12.24E
111 K5 **Moapa** Nevada 36.40N 114.39W
19 E7 **Moapora** *isld* Indon 7.35S 127.37E
59 G5 **Moate** W Meath Irish Rep 53.24N 7.58W
92 F10 **Moatize** Mozambique 16.04S 33.43E
11 K6 **Moawhango** New Zealand 39.35S 175.53E
92 D5 **Moba** Zaïre 7.04S 29.45E
91 K6 **Mobanga** Zaïre 4.20S 26.34E
20 O6 **Mobara** Japan 35.26N 140.20E
32 E6 **Mobārakābād** Iran 28.24N 53.19E
32 D4 **Mobārakeh** Iran 32.18N 51.31E
90 K9 **Mobaye** Cent Afr Rep 4.21N 21.10E
92 G1 **Mobayi** Zaïre 4.18N 21.12E
57 J6 **Mobberley** Cheshire Eng 53.19N 2.18W
112 D8 **Mobeetie** Texas 35.32N 100.26W
91 F3 **Mobeka** Zaïre 1.52N 19.49E
12 C4 **Mobella** S Australia 30.45S 133.09E
91 E3 **Mobenzélé** Congo 0.56N 17.50E
107 D2 **Moberly** Missouri 39.25N 92.25W
101 N8 **Moberly Lake** Br Col 55.50N 121.48W
99 E4 **Mobert** Ontario 48.41N 85.40W
29 C6 **Mobha** Gujarat India 22.05N 73.00E
107 H11 **Mobile** Alabama 30.40N 88.05W
111 M8 **Mobile** Arizona 33.05N 112.13W
107 H11 **Mobile** *R* Alabama
107 H11 **Mobile B** Alabama
107 J11 **Mobile Pt** Alabama 30.12N 88.00W
12 B8 **Mobiltown** *dist* Melbourne, Vic
104 J9 **Mobjack** *B* Virginia
13 G7 **Moble** *R* Queensland
19 L5 **Mobo** Philippines 12.18N 123.38E
53 A4 **Møborg** Denmark 56.23N 8.22E
108 K4 **Mobridge** S Dakota 45.31N 100.25W
91 J2 **Mobula** Zaïre 2.02N 25.50E
94 G5 **Mobutsane** Botswana 24.24S 23.35E
Mobutu Sese Seko *L see* Albert, L
91 H2 **Mobwasa** Zaïre 2.42N 23.06E
116 J5 **Moca** Dominican Rep 19.26N 70.33W
117 D6 **Mocajuba** Brazil 2.36S 49.29W
Moçambique *see* Mozambique
92 K9 **Moçambique** Mozambique 15.00S 40.44E
92 K9 **Moçambo,Porto** *B* Mozambique 15.09S 40.34E
91 C11 **Moçâmedes** Angola 15.10S 12.10E
91 C11 **Moçâmedes** *dist* Angola
96 P11 **Mocanal** Hierro Canary Is 27.49N 17.57W
103 B4 **Mocanaqua** Pennsylvania 41.39N 76.07W
119 F3 **Mocapra,R** Venezuela
111 M5 **Moccasin** Arizona 36.55N 112.46W
110 Q2 **Moccasin** Montana 47.04N 109.55W
25 H2 **Moc Chau** Vietnam 20.49N 104.38E
115 Q7 **Mocche** Mexico 20.36N 87.04W
75 C8 **Mocejón** Spain 39.56N 3.55W
Mocha *see* Mukhā,Al
121 A7 **Mocha I** Chile
75 F5 **Mochales** Spain 41.06N 2.01W
93 M5 **Mochesa** Kenya 0.55N 40.23E
115 E5 **Mochicahui** Mexico 25.56N 108.55W
116 J2 **Mocho Mts** Jamaica, W I
57 D3 **Mochrum L** Dumfries & Galloway Scotland 54.51N 4.39W
94 J5 **Mochudi** Botswana 24.28S 26.05E
119 H7 **Mocidade,Sa.da** *hills* Brazil
92 K7 **Mocímboa, B.de** Mozambique
92 K7 **Mocímboa da Praia** Mozambique 11.19S 40.19E
92 J7 **Mocimboa do Rovuma** Mozambique 11.05S 39.15E
82 H4 **Mociu** Romania 46.49N 24.00E
52 H10 **Möckeln** Sweden 56.40N 14.15E
63 P8 **Möckern** E Germany 52.09N 11.57E
104 K9 **Mockhorn** *I* Virginia
64 G5 **Möckmühl** W Germany 49.20N 9.22E
63 R9 **Mockrehna** E Germany 51.31N 12.50E
105 G2 **Mocksville** N Carolina 35.55N 80.35W
77 J6 **Moclin** Spain 37.21N 3.47W
110 A2 **Moclips** Washington 47.14N 124.11W
119 C7 **Mocoa** Colombia 1.07N 76.38W
118 F7 **Mococa** Brazil 21.28S 47.00W
94 N4 **Mocodoene** Mozambique 23.39S 35.10E
120 E6 **Mocomoco** Bolivia 15.22S 68.56W
119 F9 **Mocó,R** Brazil
121 F3 **Mocoretá** *R* Argentina
115 F5 **Mocorito** Mexico 25.30N 107.53W
115 F2 **Moctezuma** Chihuahua Mexico 30.10N 106.28W
115 J6 **Moctezuma** San Luis Potosí Mexico 22.46N 101.06W
115 E3 **Moctezuma** Sonora Mexico 29.50N 109.40W
92 H10 **Mocuba** Mozambique 16.52S 36.57E
37 K3 **Moda** Turkey 40.59N 29.02E
87 H5 **Modahtou** Djibouti 11.04N 41.55E
53 T17 **Modalen** *V* Norway 60.49N 5.51E
15 B5 **Modan** Irian Jaya 2.23S 133.55E
71 K6 **Modane** France 45.12N 6.40E
26 Q4 **Modaragam Aru** *R* Sri Lanka
29 C6 **Modasa** Gujarat India 23.28N 73.20E
61 M5 **Modave** Belgium 50.27N 5.18E
41 J2 **Mod,Bukhta** *B* U.S.S.R.
56 D7 **Modbury** Devon Eng 50.21N 3.53W
95 J4 **Modder** *R* S Africa
94 U13 **Modderbee** S Africa 26.11S 28.24E
95 L2 **Modderfontein** S Africa 26.05S 28.10E
95 L5 **Modderpoort** S Africa 29.06S 27.27E
95 H5 **Modderrivier** S Africa 29.01S 24.38E
109 F4 **Model** Colorado 37.23N 104.15W
31 H5 **Model Town** Pakistan 31.30N 74.21E
79 J5 **Modena** Italy 44.39N 10.55E
103 F3 **Modena** New York 41.40N 74.06W
103 C7 **Modena** Pennsylvania 39.58N 75.47W
111 L4 **Modena** Utah 37.48N 113.57W
79 J6 **Modena** *prov* Italy
69 O6 **Moder** *R* France
65 K7 **Möderbrugg** Austria 47.18N 14.29E
111 C4 **Modesto** California 37.37N 121.00W
84 E4 **Módhion** Greece 38.40N 22.40E
50 K4 **Mödhrudalur** Iceland 65.22N 15.51W
50 G3 **Mödhruvellir** Iceland 65.47N 18.13W
50 G4 **Mödhruvellir** Iceland 65.28N 18.08W
50 K4 **Mödhurdalsfjallgardhar** *mts* Iceland
50 K3 **Mödhurdalsheidhi** *heath* Iceland
93 B1 **Modi** Sudan 4.03N 30.38E
81 J10 **Modica** Sicily 36.52N 14.46E
79 L6 **Modigliana** Italy 44.09N 11.48E
35 C6 **Modi'im** *anc site* Israel 31.55N 34.59E
90 J2 **Modiounga** Chad 19.55N 19.12E
76 B6 **Modivas** Portugal 41.18N 8.42W
91 H2 **Modjamboli** Zaïre 2.27N 22.09E
65 O5 **Mödling** Austria 48.06N 16.18E
106 J9 **Modoc** Indiana 40.02N 85.04W
109 J3 **Modoc** Kansas 38.28N 101.06W
105 E4 **Modoc** S Carolina 33.45N 82.13W
110 D7 **Modoc Point** Oregon 42.26N 121.52W
22 G6 **Modol Hure** Nei Monggol Zizhiqu China 40.29N 106.16E
15 C6 **Modowi** Irian Jaya 4.06S 134.38E
90 H1 **Modra** Chad 20.41N 17.42E
65 K1 **Modřany** Czechoslovakia 50.01N 14.26E
94 U13 **Modrea** S Africa 26.12S 28.22E
82 E6 **Modriča** Yugoslavia 44.56N 18.14E
62 L7 **Modrý Kameň** Czechoslovakia 48.16N 19.17E
81 N1 **Modugno** Italy 41.05N 16.47E
87 J9 **Modu Modi** Somalia 3.04N 43.56E
41 N8 **Modut** U.S.S.R. 64.22N 125.45E
91 D3 **Modzanghi** Congo 0.52N 15.36E
88 O4 **Modzbah** Algeria 34.22N 0.07E
12 H7 **Moe** Victoria 38.11S 146.18E
92 J10 **Moebase** Mozambique 17.04S 38.41E
76 D1 **Moeche** Spain 43.33N 7.59W
95 O1 **Moedig** S Africa 25.55S 30.11E
70 C6 **Moelan** France 47.49N 3.38W
57 E6 **Moelfre** Gwynedd Wales 53.21N 4.12W
57 E6 **Moel Hebog** *mt* Gwynedd Wales 53.00N 4.09W
15 E7 **Moeli** *str* Irian Jaya
50 G7 **Mœlifell** *mt* Iceland 63.47N 18.55W
50 K3 **Mœlifell** *mt* Iceland 65.42N 15.21W
50 F7 **Mœlifellssandur** *sand reg* Iceland
61 N3 **Moelingen** Belgium 50.45N 5.42E
52 F6 **Moelv** Norway 60.56N 10.44E
92 C4 **Moemba** Zaïre 4.52S 27.38E
61 D3 **Moen** Belgium 50.46N 3.25E
19 N4 **Moen** *isld* Truk Is Pacific Oc
79 L2 **Moéna** Italy 46.23N 11.40E
91 H2 **Moenge** Zaïre 2.02N 22.55E
60 J13 **Moengestel** Netherlands 51.33N 5.11E
117 B2 **Moengo** Surinam 5.36N 54.25W
111 N5 **Moenkopi** Arizona 36.06N 111.16W
11 D10 **Moeraki,L** New Zealand 43.43S 169.18E
11 E12 **Moeraki Pt** New Zealand 45.23S 170.52E
61 F2 **Moerbeke** Belgium 51.10N 3.57E
61 F4 **Moerbeke** Belgium 50.45N 3.55E
60 G13 **Moerdijk** Netherlands 51.42N 4.38E
61 B2 **Moere** Belgium 51.07N 2.58E
70 G7 **Moëre,la** France 47.23N 1.55W
11 J2 **Moerewa** New Zealand 35.23S 174.02E
61 D2 **Moerkerke** Belgium 51.14N 3.20E
66 F1 **Mœrnach** France 47.30N 7.15E
11 J6 **Moeroa** New Zealand 39.22S 174.39E
Moero, Lac *see* Mweru, Lake
63 E10 **Moers** W Germany 51.27N 6.36E
61 G2 **Moerzeke** Belgium 51.04N 4.09E
66 N7 **Moësa** *R* Switzerland
66 C1 **Moffans** France 47.38N 6.33E
109 E3 **Moffat** Colorado 38.00N 105.55W
57 G2 **Moffat** Dumfries & Galloway Scotland 55.20N 3.27W
11 C12 **Moffat Pk** *mt* New Zealand 45.02S 168.10E
109 E2 **Moffat Tunnel** Colorado 39.54N 105.44W
57 G2 **Moffat Water** *R* Dumfries & Galloway Scotland
50 S12 **Moffen** *isld* Spitsbergen 80.00N 15.00E
113 Q10 **Moffett,Mt** Aleutian Is 51.55N 176.45W
108 K3 **Moffit** N Dakota 46.40N 100.18W
76 J2 **Mofrecho** *mt* Spain 43.24N 5.01W
29 D2 **Moga** Punjab India 30.49N 75.13E
91 K5 **Moga** Zaïre 2.22S 26.50E
87 K9 **Mogadiscio** Somalia 2.02N 45.21E
Mogadishu *see* Mogadiscio
Mogador *see* Essaouira
104 D5 **Mogadore** Ohio 41.03N 81.24W
76 F6 **Mogadouro** Portugal 41.20N 6.43W
76 F6 **Mogadouro,Cimas de** *mts* Portugal
94 K4 **Mogalakwena** *R* S Africa
91 F2 **Mogalo** Zaïre 3.14N 19.06E
28 E2 **Mogalturru** Andhra Prad India 16.24N 81.42E
20 N3 **Mogami-gawa** *R* Japan
96 U16 **Mogán** Gran Canaria Canary Is 27.51N 15.44W
91 J3 **Mogandjo** Zaïre 1.23N 24.15E
23 H3 **Mogan Shan** *mt* Zhejiang China 30.39N 119.48E
87 F3 **Mogareb** *watercourse* Ethiopia
25 M8 **Mogaung** Burma 25.20N 96.54E
40 F6 **Mogdy** U.S.S.R. 50.34N 133.43E
66 N2 **Mogelsberg** Switzerland 47.22N 9.08E
53 B7 **Møgeltønder** Denmark 54.57N 8.49E
53 X18 **Mogen** Norway 60.01N 7.55E
77 P3 **Mogente** Spain 38.53N 0.45W
88 R5 **Moggar** Algeria 33.21N 6.01E
66 Q1 **Möggers** Austria 47.33N 9.48E
79 F3 **Móggio** Italy 45.56N 9.30E
79 O2 **Móggio Udinese** Italy 46.25N 13.12E
64 H6 **Mögglingen** W Germany 48.50N 9.56E
88 N5 **Moghar Faukani** Algeria 32.32N 0.40W
20 C9 **Mogi** Japan 32.42N 129.55E
62 M4 **Mogielnica** Poland 51.42N 20.41E
118 F8 **Mogi Guaçu** *R* Brazil
93 F1 **Mogila** *mt* Kenya 4.30N 34.24E
45 H9 **Mogila-Bel'mak,Gora** *mt* Ukraine U.S.S.R. 47.19N 36.35E
45 B3 **Mogilev** Belorussiya U.S.S.R. 53.54N 30.20E
45 F8 **Mogilev** Ukraine U.S.S.R. 48.51N 34.32E
46 G5 **Mogilev Podol'skiy** Ukraine U.S.S.R. 48.29N 27.49E
45 B3 **Mogilevskaya Oblast'** *prov* Belorussiya U.S.S.R.
12 J3 **Mogil-Mogil** New S Wales 29.21S 148.44E
62 K3 **Mogilno** Poland 52.39N 17.58E
118 F8 **Mogi Mirim** Brazil 22.29S 46.55W
92 K9 **Mogincual** Mozambique 15.33S 40.29E
118 J5 **Mogiquiçaba** Brazil 16.05S 38.58W
79 J5 **Móglia** Italy 44.56N 10.54E
80 H2 **Mogliano** Italy 43.11N 13.29E
79 M3 **Mogliano Véneto** Italy 45.34N 12.14E
83 D4 **Moglicë** Albania 40.44N 20.24E
71 F4 **Mogneneins** France 46.09N 4.49E
Mogno *see* Moquina
40 A5 **Mogocha** U.S.S.R. 53.44N 119.45E
42 C3 **Mogochin** U.S.S.R. 57.45N 83.30E
87 L8 **Mogocori** Somalia 4.04N 46.09E
88 S3 **Mogod** *tribe* Tunisia
76 C8 **Mogofores** Portugal 40.27N 8.28W
15 B4 **Mogoi** Irian Jaya 1.48S 133.08E
25 D1 **Mogok** Burma 22.55N 96.29E
94 J4 **Mogol** *R* S Africa
109 B8 **Mogollon** New Mexico 33.23N 108.48W
109 B8 **Mogollon Mts** New Mexico
111 O7 **Mogollon Rim** *tableland* Arizona
87 F3 **Mogolo** Ethiopia 15.19N 37.39E
77 K4 **Mogón** Spain 38.04N 3.02W
87 M5 **Mogor Hal** Somalia 10.53N 49.52E
81 B4 **Mogoro** Sardinia 39.41N 8.17E
81 B4 **Mogoro** *R* Sardinia
109 D4 **Mogote** Colorado 37.03N 106.06W
121 F7 **Mogotes,Pta** *C* Argentina 38.07S 57.33W
41 R5 **Mogotoyevo,Ozero** *L* U.S.S.R.
22 C2 **Mogoyn** Mongolia 49.54N 95.45E
42 J6 **Mogoytuy** U.S.S.R. 51.18N 114.58E
85 M10 **Mograt I** Sudan 19.28N 33.16E
87 H8 **Mogu** Ethiopia 4.52N 40.15E
77 C6 **Moguer** Spain 37.16N 6.50W
14 B9 **Mogumber** W Australia 31.01S 116.02E
42 J6 **Mogzon** U.S.S.R. 51.48N 112.00E
61 L4 **Moha** Belgium 50.33N 5.11E
29 C7 **Moha** Gujarat India 21.02N 73.13E
90 D4 **Moha** Niger 14.19N 9.44E
62 L9 **Mohács** Hungary 46.00N 18.40E
Mohadjé *see* Muhajjah
11 M6 **Mohaka** New Zealand 39.07S 177.07E
11 L6 **Mohaka R** New Zealand
29 G7 **Mohala** Madhya Prad India 20.34N 80.46E
95 L6 **Mohales Hoek** Lesotho 30.09S 27.29E
95 L6 **Mohales Hoek** *dist* Lesotho
108 J1 **Mohall** N Dakota 48.47N 101.31W
88 H8 **Mohamd el Quenti, S** Morocco 27.34N 10.30W
30 G5 **Mohami** Nepal 27.53N 83.57E
Moḩammadābād *see* Darreh Gaz
32 J5 **Moḩammadabad** Iran 30.50N 61.28E
88 O4 **Mohammadia** Algeria 35.35N 0.05E
31 C2 **Mohammad-Tashi** Afghanistan 37.03N 64.48E
88 K5 **Mohammedia** Morocco 33.43N 7.20W
30 A2 **Mohan** Uttar Prad India 30.11N 77.54E
30 D4 **Mohan** *R* Nepal/India
Mohana Madhya Prad India*see* Mohona
31 J8 **Mohanganj** Bangladesh 24.52N 91.00E
30 B8 **Mohangarh** Madhya Prad India 24.59N 78.41E
30 G7 **Mohania** Bihar India 25.11N 83.37E
30 D6 **Mohanlalganj** Uttar Prad India 26.41N 80.58E
30 K8 **Mohanpur** Bihar India 24.39N 86.37E
29 F7 **Mohari** Maharashtra India 21.19N 79.42E
30 A8 **Mohasa** Madhya Prad India 24.23N 77.40E
111 K6 **Mohave, L** Nevada 35.25N 114.38W
111 K7 **Mohave Mts** Arizona
111 L9 **Mohawk** Arizona 32.41N 113.47W
106 F2 **Mohawk** Michigan 47.29N 88.22W
104 L4 **Mohawk** New York 43.00N 74.59W
104 L4 **Mohawk** *R* New York
103 E4 **Mohawk,L** New Jersey 41.01N 74.39W
111 L9 **Mohawk Mts** Arizona
21 B1 **Mohe** Heilongjiang China 53.26N 122.19E
28 H7 **Mohean** Nicobar Is 7.59N 93.16E
52 H9 **Moheda** Sweden 57.00N 14.35E
76 G8 **Mohedas** Spain 40.16N 6.13W
76 F10 **Mohedas** *R* Spain
76 J9 **Mohedas de la Jara** Spain 39.37N 5.09W
23 B7 **Mohei** Yunnan China 23.10N 101.12E
95 A2 **Moheli** *isld* Comoros, Ind Oc
65 P2 **Mohelnice** Czechoslovakia 49.47N 16.56E
92 D4 **Mohemba** Zaïre 4.58S 28.46E
28 G3 **Mohendraganj** Meghalaya India 25.19N 89.51E
31 E7 **Mohenjo Daro** *anc site* Pakistan 27.17N 68.14E
59 D6 **Moher,Cliffs of** Clare Irish Rep 52.58N 9.27W
59 C4 **Moher,L** Mayo Irish Rep 53.44N 9.33W
29 F7 **Mohgaon** Madhya Prad India 21.40N 78.48E
113 D6 **Mohican,C** Alaska 60.11N 167.28W
59 G4 **Mohill** Leitrim Irish Rep 53.55N 7.52W
Mohindergarh *see* Mahendragarh
30 J7 **Mohiuddinnagar** Bihar India 25.35N 85.40E
61 L5 **Mohiville** Belgium 50.19N 5.12E
110 J3 **Mohler** Idaho 46.17N 116.20W
66 H1 **Möhlin** Switzerland 47.34N 7.51E
31 F3 **Mohmand** *reg* Pakistan/Afghan
63 H10 **Möhne** *R* W Germany
63 H9 **Möhnesee** W Germany 51.31N 8.07E
63 H10 **Möhnestausee** *L* W Germany
50 V13 **Mohn,Kapp** Spitsbergen 79.16N 25.00E
25 M9 **Mohnyin** Burma 24.49N 96.23E
120 D6 **Moho** Peru 15.10S 69.30W
28 B2 **Mohol** Maharashtra India 17.53N 75.38E
52 H8 **Moholm** Sweden 58.37N 14.05E
18 K10 **Mohomeru,Gunung** *mt* Java Indon 8.04S 112.53E
70 E5 **Mohon** France 48.03N 2.31W
30 A7 **Mohona** Madhya Prad India 25.55N 77.46E
111 L7 **Mohon Pk** *mt* Arizona 34.58N 113.18W
92 J6 **Mohoro** Tanzania 8.09S 39.10E
75 F7 **Mohorte** Spain 40.01N 2.04W
115 H4 **Mohovano Ranch** Mexico 26.42N 103.39W
29 F6 **Mohpani** Madhya Prad India 22.43N 78.52E
64 J2 **Möhra** E Germany 50.52N 10.15E
64 F8 **Möhringen** W Germany 47.58N 8.46E
64 G6 **Möhringen** W Germany 48.45N 9.10E
103 C6 **Mohrsville** Pennsylvania 40.28N 75.59W
29 J1 **Mohuda** Bihar India 23.45N 86.15E
24 E2 **Mohurtay** Xinjiang Uygur Zizhiqu China 46.10N 85.10E
93 L2 **Moiale** Ethiopia 3.34N 39.04E
58 E5 **Moidart** *dist* Highland Scotland
61 J5 **Moignelée** Belgium 50.27N 4.35E
25 L8 **Moi Len** *mt* Nagaland India 25.30N 94.46E
52 C8 **Moi Lunde-vatn** *L* Norway 58.25N 6.35E
15 G6 **Moim** Papua New Guinea 4.09S 143.55E
76 F5 **Moimenta** Portugal 41.57N 6.58W
76 D7 **Moimenta da Beira** Portugal 40.59N 7.36W
88 H12 **Moïnane,el** Mauritania 19.12N 11.26W
89 D2 **Moinane, El** Mauritania 19.12N 11.20W
24 C10 **Moincêr** Xizang Zizhiqu China 31.10N 80.52E
91 B5 **Moindi** Gabon 3.24S 11.43E
94 M5 **Moine** Mozambique 24.52S 32.31E
72 B1 **Moine** *R* France
67 O14 **Moines,les** *islds* Corsica 41.27N 8.54E
82 K4 **Moineşti** Romania 46.27N 26.31E
71 E5 **Moingt** France 45.35N 4.04E
43 L5 **Moinkum** Kazakhstan U.S.S.R. 43.47N 73.39E
43 J4 **Moinkum,Peski** *sand des* Kazakhstan U.S.S.R.
43 L4 **Mointy** Kazakhstan U.S.S.R. 47.10N 73.18E
59 K3 **Moira** Down N Ireland 54.29N 6.14W
104 L2 **Moira** New York 44.50N 74.34W
117 D6 **Moiraba** Brazil 2.26S 49.25W
51 D5 **Moi Rana** Norway 66.19N 14.10E
28 J3 **Moirang** Manipur India 24.29N 93.45E
71 H6 **Moirans** Isère France 45.20N 5.34E
71 H4 **Moirans-en-Montagne** France 46.26N 5.43E
72 F7 **Moirax** France 44.09N 0.36E
61 M7 **Moircy** Belgium 49.59N 5.28E
84 L11 **Moíres** Crete 35.02N 24.52E
84 C3 **Moírous** Greece 39.25N 21.58E
46 F1 **Mõisaküla** Estonia U.S.S.R. 58.02N 25.12E
93 G5 **Moi's Bridge** Kenya 0.53N 35.08E
70 H6 **Moisdon** France 47.37N 1.22W
121 E3 **Moisés Ville** Argentina 30.45S 61.25W
47 M6 **Moiseyevka** U.S.S.R. 58.02N 76.04E
98 F3 **Moisie** Quebec 50.12N 66.06W
98 G3 **Moisie B** Quebec
98 F3 **Moisie, R** Quebec
72 G7 **Moissac** Tarn-et-Garonne France 44.07N 1.05E
71 J9 **Moissac-Bellevue** France 43.39N 6.10E
90 H7 **Moïssala** Chad 8.20N 17.40E
71 C5 **Moissat** France 45.47N 3.21E
71 H2 **Moissey** France 47.12N 5.32E
69 B5 **Moisson** France 49.04N 1.40E
69 D6 **Moissy-Cramayel** France 48.38N 2.36E
70 N6 **Moisy** France 47.56N 1.20E
67 P12 **Moita** Corsica 42.16N 9.23E
76 B11 **Moita** Portugal 38.38N 8.59W
76 E8 **Moita** Portugal 40.18N 7.12W
119 G4 **Moitaco** Venezuela 8.00N 64.22W
87 G6 **Moja** Ethiopia 8.42N 39.05E
52 L7 **Möja** Sweden 59.25N 18.55E
77 N6 **Mojácar** Spain 37.09N 1.50W
76 K6 **Mojados** Spain 41.26N 4.40W
77 M4 **Mojantes** *mt* Spain 38.01N 2.06W
111 F6 **Mojave** California 35.02N 118.11W
111 G7 **Mojave** *R* California
111 G7 **Mojave Des** California
32 F2 **Mojen,Rūde** *R* Iran
20 D8 **Moji** Japan 33.57N 130.58E
23 B7 **Mojiang** Yunnan China 23.27N 101.40E
118 F8 **Moji das Cruzes** Brazil 23.33S 46.14W
99 B2 **Mojikit L** Ontario
77 J3 **Mojina** *mt* Spain 38.40N 3.53W
Mojjo *see* Moja
120 F9 **Mojo** Bolivia 21.51S 65.35W
120 F8 **Mojocoya** Bolivia 18.45S 64.35W
18 K9 **Mojokerto** Java Indon 7.25S 112.31E
75 F8 **Mojón Alto** *mt* Spain 39.41N 2.28W
120 E11 **Mojones,Cerro** *pk* Argentina 25.42S 67.22W
87 H6 **Mojo,R** Ethiopia
120 F8 **Mojotoro** Bolivia 18.55S 65.05W
117 D5 **Moju** Brazil 1.52S 48.45W
117 D6 **Moju,R** Brazil
20 O5 **Mōka** Japan 36.26N 140.02E
26 U12 **Moka** Mauritius, Indian Oc 20.13S 57.30E
91 K8 **Mokabe Kasari** Zaïre 9.59S 26.17E
87 G3 **Mokada** *mt* Ethiopia 14.18N 38.03E
11 K5 **Mokai** New Zealand 38.31S 175.54E
92 D8 **Mokambo** Zaïre 12.26S 28.22E
30 J7 **Mokameh** Bihar India 25.24N 85.55E
107 E3 **Mokane** Missouri 38.42N 91.53W
114 B5 **Mokapu Pen** Hawaiian Is
91 H3 **Mokaria** Zaïre 1.59N 23.19E
90 K9 **Mokassa** Cent Afr Rep 4.57N 21.05E
90 H7 **Mokassa** Chad 8.04N 17.17E
91 E6 **Mokata** Zaïre 5.19S 17.20E
11 J5 **Mokau** New Zealand 38.40S 174.38E
11 J5 **Mokau R** New Zealand
111 D3 **Mokelumne** *R* California
111 D3 **Mokelumne Hill** California 38.16N 120.43W
30 G6 **Mokhlispur** Uttar Prad India 26.36N 83.02E
84 M11 **Mokhós** Crete 35.16N 25.25E

95 N5 Mokhotlong Lesotho 29.18S 29.05E
95 M5 Mokhotlong dist Lesotho
42 F4 Mokhovaya U.S.S.R. 56.28N 95.36E
41 D5 Mokhovaya R U.S.S.R.
39 F7 Mokhovaya Rybachiy Kamchatka U.S.S.R. 52.54N 158.30E
45 H4 Mokhovoye U.S.S.R. 52.55N 36.35E
47 L7 Mokhovoy Prival U.S.S.R. 56.05N 74.55E
41 N9 Mokhsogollokh U.S.S.R. 61.18N 129.00E
32 H4 Mokhtārān Iran 32.30N 59.24E
91 E6 Mokila Zaïre 5.04S 17.04E
114 C5 Mokio Pt Hawaiian Is 21.13N 157.14W
29 K3 Mok Kyong mt Xizang Zizhiqu 29.14N 87.16E
40 B4 Mokla R U.S.S.R.
40 A4 Moklakan U.S.S.R. 54.51N 118.49E
52 K6 Möklinta Sweden 60.05N 16.35E
15 D4 Mokmer Irian Jaya 1.13S 136.08E
88 T4 Moknine Tunisia 35.39N 10.53E
11 J6 Mokoia New Zealand 39.38S 174.24E
28 K2 Mokokchung Nagaland India 26.20N 94.30E
28 K2 Mokokchung dist Nagaland India
90 F6 Mokolo Cameroon 10.49N 13.54E
91 F3 Mokolo Zaïre 1.55N 18.06E
11 D13 Mokoreta New Zealand 46.26S 169.04E
11 C13 Mokotua New Zealand 46.28S 168.36E
21 D10 Mokpo S Korea 34.50N 126.25E
82 F8 Mokra Planina mts Yugoslavia
44 E2 Mokraya Buyvola,R U.S.S.R.
45 C8 Mokraya Kaligorka Ukraine U.S.S.R. 48.50N 31.14E
45 Q6 Mokraya-Ol'khovka U.S.S.R. 50.27N 44.59E
30 G7 Mokri Bihar India 25.02N 83.34E
82 F5 Mokrin Yugoslavia 45.56N 20.26E
45 T5 Mokrous U.S.S.R. 51.15N 47.30E
47 K7 Mokrousova U.S.S.R. 55.51N 66.50E
45 H3 Mokroye U.S.S.R. 53.37N 36.53E
44 E1 Mokryy Gashun U.S.S.R. 46.53N 42.46E
45 O2 Moksha R U.S.S.R.
45 Q3 Mokshan U.S.S.R. 53.27N 44.35E
53 S18 Møkster Norway 60.01N 5.05E
51 L8 Möksy Finland 63.03N 24.15E
114 D5 Moku Hawaiian Is 21.04N 156.03W
93 A3 Moku Zaïre 2.58N 29.23E
114 B4 Mokuauia I Hawaiian Is 21.39N 157.55W
114 B8 Mokuaweoweo Crater Hawaiian Is 19.28N 155.35W
114 D5 Mokuhooniki islds Hawaiian Is 21.08N 156.42W
114 A4 Mokuleia Hawaiian Is 21.35N 158.11W
114 B5 Mokulua Is Hawaiian Is
Mokundurra see Mukandwara
114 D7 Mokuopihi Hawaiian Is 19.34N 154.55W
114 B6 Mokupuku I Hawaiian Is 20.11N 155.42W
90 B7 Mokwa Nigeria 9.19N 5.00E
61 L2 Mol Belgium 51.11N 5.07E
70 F6 Molac France 47.44N 2.26W
77 U14 Mola,C.de la Balearic Is 39.31N 2.22E
81 O1 Mola di Bari Italy 41.03N 17.05E
77 T12 Mola,La mt Balearic Is 38.40N 1.34E
77 Y14 Mola,La pt Balearic Is 39.53N 4.19E
87 G5 Molale Ethiopia 10.10N 39.41E
110 C4 Molalla Oregon 45.09N 122.36W
72 H9 Molandier France 43.15N 1.43E
39 G3 Molandzha R U.S.S.R.
115 K7 Molango Mexico 20.48N 98.44W
100 M4 Molanosa Saskatchewan 54.30N 105.34W
84 E8 Moláoi Greece 36.48N 22.51E
81 D2 Molara I Sardinia 40.53N 9.45E
79 E5 Molare Italy 44.37N 8.36E
75 C6 Molar,El Spain 40.43N 3.35W
66 M6 Molare,Pizzo mt Switzerland 46.30N 8.53E
115 Q7 Molas, Pta C Mexico 20.50N 86.45W
82 B6 Molat isld Yugoslavia 44.13N 14.50E
77 O3 Molatón mt Spain 39.00N 1.25W
71 H1 Molay France 47.44N 5.43E
70 J3 Molay-Littry, le France 49.15N 0.54W
63 G7 Molbergen W Germany 52.52N 7.54E
42 C3 Molchanovo U.S.S.R. 57.39N 83.45E
57 G6 Mold Clwyd Wales 53.10N 3.08W
43 N2 Moldary Kazakhstan U.S.S.R. 50.47N 78.47E
64 Q2 Moldava Czechoslovakia 50.44N 13.40E
62 N7 Moldava nad Bodvou Czech 48.38N 21.00E
82 K4 Moldavia old prov Romania
Moldavian S.S.R. see Moldavskaya S.S.R.
38 B4 Moldavskaya S.S.R U.S.S.R.
52 C4 Molde Norway 62.44N 7.08E
121 D4 Moldes Argentina 33.35S 64.38W
82 K3 Moldova R Romania
82 G6 Moldova Nouă Romania 44.45N 21.39E
82 J5 Moldoveanu mt Romania 45.37N 24.49E
82 K3 Moldovita Romania 47.41N 25.33E
53 D3 Møldrup Denmark 56.37N 9.32E
71 J4 Môle mt France 46.07N 6.27E
25 N9 Mole Chaung R Burma
76 B5 Moledo Portugal 41.51N 8.51W
76 D7 Moledo Portugal 40.49N 7.52W
91 G1 Molegbe Zaïre 4.12N 20.53E
15 J5 Mole I Bismarck Arch 2.53S 146.25E
96 O6 Mole I Madeira Is 32.52N 17.11W
91 E5 Moleke Zaïre 2.59S 17.14E
71 J10 Môle,la France 43.13N 6.27E
60 H12 Molenaarsgraaf Netherlands 51.53N 4.50E
61 D4 Molenbaix Belgium 50.42N 3.27E
61 R9 Molenbeek dist Bruxelles
60 M14 Molenbeek R Netherlands
61 K3 Molenbeek-Wersbeek Belgium 50.55N 4.56E
61 N2 Molenbeersel Belgium 51.10N 5.44E
70 A5 Molène isld France 48.24N 4.58W
60 G7 Molengat channel Netherlands
66 M6 Móleno Switzerland 46.17N 9.00E
61 L2 Molenstede Belgium 51.00N 5.01E
94 H5 Molepolole Botswana 24.25S 25.30E
55 C5 Mole, R Surrey England
116 H5 Môle St. Nicolas, Le Haiti 19.48N 73.30W
69 G8 Molesmes France 47.56N 4.22E
66 E5 Moléson mt Switzerland 46.33N 7.01E
56 L3 Molesworth Cambs Eng 52.22N 0.26W
11 H9 Molesworth New Zealand 42.04S 173.20E
81 N1 Molfetta Italy 41.12N 16.36E
74 J9 Molière Algeria 35.50N 1.36E
72 H6 Molières Lot France 44.48N 1.54E
72 G7 Molières Tarn-et-Garonne France 44.12N 1.22E
72 B8 Moliets-et-Maa France 43.51N 1.22W
121 C4 Molina Argentina 32.09S 68.05W
121 B5 Molina Chile 35.06S 71.18W
75 G6 Molina de Aragón Spain 40.50N 1.54W
77 O4 Molina de Segura Spain 38.03N 1.11W
75 O3 Molina, La Spain 42.21N 1.59E
76 F3 Molinaseca Spain 42.32N 6.31W
75 G7 Molina, Sierra de mts Spain
81 E9 Molinazzo, Pta Pantelleria I Italy 36.45N 11.59E
106 D8 Moline Illinois 41.30N 90.30W
109 O4 Moline Kansas 37.22N 96.18W
106 J7 Moline Michigan 42.43N 85.40W
13 B2 Moline N Terr Australia 13.30S 132.10E
79 L5 Molinella Italy 44.37N 11.40E
81 K9 Molinello R Sicily
71 D4 Molinet France 46.28N 3.55E
71 H4 Molinges France 46.21N 5.45E
81 K8 Molini, C Sicily 37.34N 15.11E
77 M4 Molinicos Spain 38.28N 2.14W
79 L1 Molini di Tures Italy 46.54N 11.57E
107 J11 Molino Florida 30.41N 87.20W
115 D3 Molino Mexico 29.07N 110.51W
120 B2 Molinopampa Peru 6.09S 77.38W
120 E11 Molinos Argentina 25.28S 66.15W
75 K6 Molinos Spain 40.49N 0.27W
75 P5 Molins de Rey Spain 41.25N 2.01E
92 E6 Moliro Zaïre 8.11S 30.31E
80 K5 Molise prov Italy
93 D4 Molitar Uganda 1.38N 32.50E
81 L3 Moliterno Italy 40.14N 15.52E
72 J10 Molitg-les-Bains France 42.39N 2.23E
60 K8 Molkwerum Netherlands 52.53N 5.24E
32 C3 Mollā Bodāgh Iran 35.34N 48.40E
81 A1 Molla C Sardinia 41.07N 8.17E
37 G2 Mollafeneri Turkey 40.55N 29.28E
43 C7 Mollakara Turkmeniya U.S.S.R. 39.37N 54.12E
44 J7 Mollakend Azerbaydzhan U.S.S.R. 40.07N 48.07E
37 E7 Mollakendi Turkey 38.37N 39.20E
37 J9 Mollālar Iran 36.41N 46.08E
71 J1 Mollans Haute-Saône France 47.39N 6.23E
71 G8 Mollans-sur-Ouvèze France 44.14N 5.10E
65 H8 Möllbrücke Austria 46.51N 13.23E
52 G10 Mölle Sweden 56.15N 12.20E
53 J4 Mölle Sweden 56.16N 12.30E
53 C5 Møllebjerg mt Denmark 55.46N 9.16E
76 L2 Molledo Spain 43.10N 4.03W
61 G3 Mollem Belgium 50.56N 4.14E
63 S6 Möllenbeck E Germany 53.24N 13.21E
120 C7 Mollendo Peru 17.00S 72.00W
63 R5 Möllenhagen E Germany 53.32N 12.56E
41 A3 Mollera, Zaliv B Novaya Zemlya U.S.S.R.
14 C9 Mollerin, L W Australia 30.35S 117.30E
53 D4 Mollerup Denmark 56.09N 9.44E
75 M4 Mollerusa Spain 41.37N 0.53E
71 D4 Molles France 46.07N 3.32E
75 P4 Mollet Spain 41.32N 2.13E
66 J8 Mollia Italy 45.49N 8.02E
69 C4 Molliens-Dreuil France 49.53N 2.01E
51 J2 Mollijus mt Norway 69.24N 22.15E
77 G6 Mollina Spain 37.06N 4.39W
58 H7 Mollinsburn Strathclyde Scotland 55.56N 4.03W
66 N3 Mollis Switzerland 47.06N 9.04E
51 L2 Mollisjok Norway 69.34N 24.25E
63 S5 Mölln E Germany 53.36N 13.06E
63 N5 Mölln W Germany 53.37N 10.42E
75 P3 Molló Spain 42.21N 2.24E
65 G7 Mölltal V Austria
53 Y14 Mølmen Norway 62.15N 8.20E
52 G9 Mölndal Sweden 57.40N 12.00E
52 G9 Mölnlycke Sweden 57.42N 12.20E
25 L9 Molnom Manipur India 24.10N 93.22E
Mo-lo see Gonjo
25 M9 Molo Burma 23.23N 96.52E
93 G6 Molo Kenya 0.15S 35.45E
93 F5 Molo Uganda 0.49N 34.12E
114 F3 Moloaa Hawaiian Is 22.12N 159.20W
89 G5 Molobala Mali 12.05N 5.15W
93 J2 Molobot Kenya 3.12N 37.04E
45 G9 Molochansk Ukraine U.S.S.R. 47.11N 35.35E
44 D7 Molochnaya R Ukraine U.S.S.R.
44 D8 Molochnoye, Ozero L Ukraine U.S.S.R.
46 K6 Molochnyy Liman lagoon Ukraine U.S.S.R.
92 J10 Molocue R Mozambique
46 F3 Molodechnenskaya Oblast' prov Belorussiya U.S.S.R.
46 F3 Molodechno Belorussiya U.S.S.R. 54.16N 26.50E
123 A6 Molodezhnaya U.S.S.R. Base Antarctica 67.40S 45.51E
89 F4 Molodo Mali 14.18N 6.04W
41 M6 Molodo U.S.S.R. 69.09N 122.33E
41 M6 Molodo R U.S.S.R.
43 K1 Molodogvardeyskaya Kazakhstan U.S.S.R. 54.06N 70.54E
46 J2 Molodoy-Tud U.S.S.R. 56.25N 33.39E
46 K1 Mologa R U.S.S.R.
114 C5 Molokai dist Hawaiian Is
114 C5 Molokai isld Hawaiian Is
122 M5 Molokai Fracture Zone Pacific Oc
114 D6 Molokini isld Hawaiian Is 20.36N 156.33W
46 K1 Molokovo U.S.S.R. 58.10N 36.41E
47 F6 Moloma R U.S.S.R.
72 L5 Molompize France 45.14N 3.08E
12 J5 Molong New S Wales 33.08S 148.53E
12 B6 Molonglo R A.C.Terr Australia
94 F6 Molopo R Botswana etc
95 H1 Molopo R S Africa
94 F6 Molopo, Old Course of watercourse S Africa
84 E4 Mólos Greece 38.48N 22.39E
Molotov see Perm
Molotovabad see Uch-Korgon
Molotova, Im V.M see Oktyabr'skiy Gor'kiy U.S.S.R
Molotovo see Oktyabr'skoye Lipetsk U.S.S.R
46 N8 Molotovo Georgia U.S.S.R. 41.30N 44.00E
Molotovo Uzbekistan see Uchkupryuk
Molotovsk Arkhangel'sk see Severodvinsk
Molotovsk Kirgiziya see Kainda
Molotovsk Kirov see Nolinsk
Molotovskoye see Krasnogvardeyskoye
91 D2 Moloundou Cameroon 2.03N 15.14E
91 H6 Molowaie Zaïre 5.47S 23.18E
71 F1 Moloy France 47.33N 4.56E
51 J9 Molpe Finland 62.52N 21.18E
66 O3 Mols Switzerland 47.07N 9.17E
53 F4 Mols Bjerge mt Denmark 56.19N 10.33E
94 K5 Molsgat S Africa 24.21S 29.35E
69 O6 Molsheim France 48.33N 7.30E
100 E1 Molson Manitoba 50.02N 96.19W
100 V4 Molson L Manitoba
53 S19 Mølstrevåg Norway 59.32N 5.16E
110 R4 Molt Montana 45.52N 108.56W
95 K7 Molteno S Africa 31.24S 26.22E
67 P12 Moltifao Corsica 42.29N 9.07E
66 N8 Moltrasio Italy 45.52N 9.06E
Moltsog see Naran
15 A7 Molu isld Moluccas Indon
Moluccas islds see Malaku
17 L12 Moluccas islds Indonesia
19 D4 Molucca Sea Indonesia
77 O2 Moluengo mt Spain 39.29N 1.26W
92 H9 Molumbo Mozambique 15.30S 36.19E
79 J2 Molveno Italy 46.08N 10.58E
79 J2 Molveno, L. di Italy 46.07N 10.57E
77 J7 Molvizar Spain 36.47N 3.36W
40 A2 Molvo R U.S.S.R.
45 C3 Molyatichi Belorussiya U.S.S.R. 53.52N 31.34E
Molyneux R see Clutha R
92 J10 Moma Mozambique 16.46S 39.10E
91 H4 Moma Zaïre 1.35S 23.57E
39 D3 Moma R U.S.S.R.
61 M4 Momalle Belgium 50.41N 5.23E
12 G4 Momba New S Wales 30.57S 143.32E
92 F6 Momba R Tanzania
117 G7 Mombaça Brazil 5.45S 39.39W
79 N7 Mombaroccio Italy 43.48N 12.51E
79 D5 Mombaruzzo Italy 44.46N 8.27E
93 L10 Mombasa Kenya 4.04S 39.40E
91 E2 Mombellé Congo 2.23N 17.34E
66 L8 Mombello Italy 45.54N 8.37E
79 D4 Mombello Monferrato Italy 45.08N 8.15E
76 J8 Mombeltrán Spain 40.15N 5.00W
79 D5 Mombercelli Italy 44.49N 8.17E
Mombetsu see Monbetsu
25 L9 Mombi Manipur India 24.02N 93.59E
28 J3 Mombi New Manipur India 24.05N 93.53E
53 B4 Mombjerge hill Denmark 56.04N 8.52E
92 J4 Mombo Tanzania 4.54S 38.18E
91 G9 Mombo R Angola
91 F4 Momboyo R Zaïre
118 D6 Mombuca, Serra da mts Brazil
76 G4 Mombuey Spain 42.01N 6.19W
82 J9 Momchilgrad Bulgaria 41.32N 25.24E
33 D8 Momed isld Farasān Is Red Sea 17.04N 41.45E
106 G8 Momence Illinois 41.11N 87.39W
91 K4 Momi Zaïre 1.42S 27.03E
77 E8 Momia, Sierra mts Spain
61 G6 Momignies Belgium 50.02N 4.10E
119 C3 Momil Colombia 9.15N 75.40W
33 K10 Momi, Ra's pen Socotra Ind Oc 12.05N 54.29E
53 E7 Mommark Denmark 54.55N 10.03E
69 O6 Mommenheim France 48.46N 7.39E
79 E3 Momo Italy 45.34N 8.32E
39 D3 Momontay, Ozero L U.S.S.R. 63.48N 148.09E
15 J5 Momote airport Admiralty Is 2.00S 147.28E
115 L3 Momotombo pk Nicaragua 12.26N 86.31W
61 Q7 Mompach Luxembourg 49.45N 6.28E
19 L5 Mompog Pass Luzon Philippines
91 F4 Mompoma Zaïre 0.48S 19.17E
91 G3 Mompono Zaïre 0.06N 21.50E
119 D3 Mompós Colombia 9.15N 74.29W
91 E2 Mompoutou Congo 2.58N 17.24E
53 Y20 Momrak Norway 59.08N 8.08E
39 C2 Momskiy Khrebet ra U.S.S.R.
72 C8 Momuy France 43.37N 0.37W
25 D3 Mon Burma 18.32N 96.36E
53 J7 Møn isld Denmark
25 C2 Mon R Burma
116 L2 Mona Jamaica, W I 18.01N 76.46W
111 N2 Mona Utah 39.49N 111.52W
104 E6 Monaca Pennsylvania 40.42N 80.19W
91 F8 Mona Caia Angola 8.47S 18.26E
67 P13 Monaccia Corsica 41.31N 9.01E
77 J6 Monachil Spain 37.08N 3.32W
58 A3 Monach Is W Isles Scotland 57.32N 7.36W
58 A3 Monach, Sound of W Isles Scotland
71 L9 Monaco principality Mediterranean Sea
58 H4 Monadhliath Mts Highland Scotland
51 J8 Monåfjard inlet Finland 63.20N 22.20E
119 G3 Monagas state Venezuela
59 J3 Monaghan Monaghan Irish Rep 54.15N 6.58W
59 H3 Monaghan co Irish Rep
115 O5 Monagrillo Panama 8.00N 80.28W
112 E4 Monahans Texas 31.35N 102.54W
116 L5 Mona, I Puerto Rico 18.06N 67.54W
59 J4 Monalty L Monaghan Irish Rep 53.58N 6.40W
59 K6 Monamolin Wexford Irish Rep 52.33N 6.20W
108 M3 Monango N Dakota 46.11N 98.34W
116 K5 Mona Passage Dominican Rep/Puerto Rico
92 K9 Monapo Mozambique 14.56S 40.19E
77 J7 Mona, Pta de la pt Spain 36.44N 3.43W
91 F8 Mona Quimbundo Angola 9.51S 19.58E
26 T8 Monaragala Sri Lanka 6.52N 81.22E
100 D9 Monarch Alberta 49.51N 113.04W
109 D3 Monarch Colorado 38.32N 106.19W
110 P2 Monarch Montana 47.05N 110.50W
101 L10 Monarch Mt Br Columbia 51.55N 125.57W
111 N2 Mona Res Utah 39.52N 111.54W
58 F4 Monar, L Highland Scotland 57.25N 5.05W
101 O10 Monashee Mts Br Col
59 H5 Monasterevin Kildare Irish Rep 53.08N 7.03W
77 V14 Monasterio de Lluch ruin Balearic Is 39.49N 2.52E
75 G5 Monasterio de Piedra Spain 41.11N 1.46W
79 D5 Monastero Bormida Italy 44.39N 8.19E
71 C7 Monastier, le France 44.31N 3.15E
71 E7 Monastier-sur-Gazeille, le France 44.56N 4.00E
81 C5 Monastir Sardinia 39.23N 9.03E
88 T4 Monastir Tunisia 35.46N 10.59E
Monastir Yugoslavia see Bitola
84 A4 Monastiráki Akarnanía Greece 38.51N 20.56E
84 C6 Monastiráki Arkadhía Greece 37.46N 21.50E
84 D6 Monástra Greece 37.45N 22.05E
45 D6 Monastyrishche Ukraine U.S.S.R. 50.50N 32.10E
82 J1 Monastyriska U.S.S.R. 49.05N 25.10E
45 C2 Monastyrshchina U.S.S.R. 54.22N 31.51E
47 J6 Monastyrskoye Sverdlovsk U.S.S.R. 58.01N 62.01E
45 U1 Monastyrskoye Tatar A.S.S.R. U.S.S.R. 55.02N 48.50E
66 L8 Monate, L. di Italy 45.48N 8.40E
91 B1 Monatélé Cameroon 5.50N 11.16E
39 H7 Monati, Mys C Komandorskiye O-va U.S.S.R. 54.42N 166.44E
12 M5 Mona Vale New S Wales 33.41S 151.19E
9 S8 Monavatu mt Viti Levu Fiji 17.54S 178.00E
59 G7 Monavullagh Mts Waterford Irish Rep
72 F6 Monbahus France 44.33N 0.32E
72 G8 Monbéqui France 43.54N 1.14E
20 L2 Monbetsu Japan 42.28N 142.10E
21 J5 Monbetsu Japan 44.23N 143.22E
72 G8 Monbrun France 43.40N 1.02E
75 K8 Moncada Spain 39.33N 0.24W
75 P5 Moncada Spain 41.29N 2.12E
79 C4 Moncalieri Italy 45.00N 7.41E
79 D4 Moncalvo Italy 45.03N 8.16E
76 F4 Moncalvo mt Spain 42.12N 6.48W
117 E6 Monção Brazil 3.30S 45.15W
76 C4 Monção Portugal 42.04N 8.29W
76 D14 Moncarapacho Portugal 37.05N 7.47W
72 F7 Moncaut France 44.09N 0.31E
75 G4 Moncayo mt Spain 41.47N 1.50W
75 G4 Moncayo, Sierra del mts Spain
61 K7 Monceau-en-Ardenne Belgium 49.55N 4.59E
61 G6 Monceau-Imbrechies Belgium 50.02N 4.14E
69 F4 Monceau-le-Neuf-et-Faucouzy France 49.47N 3.38E
61 H5 Monceau-sur-Sambre Belgium 50.25N 4.23E
69 L6 Moncel-sur-Seille France 48.46N 6.25E
66 A2 Moncey France 47.22N 6.07E
66 J5 Mönch mt Switzerland 46.33N 8.01E
66 L2 Mönchaltorf Switzerland 47.18N 8.44E
65 L5 Mönchdorf Austria 48.22N 14.49E
47 C2 Monchegorsk U.S.S.R. 67.55N 33.01E
64 A1 Mönchengladbach W Germany 51.12N 6.25E
63 T4 Mönchgut pen E Germany
79 H6 Monchio Italy 44.25N 10.07E
76 B14 Monchique Portugal 37.19N 8.33W
76 B14 Monchique, Sa. de mts Portugal
69 P7 Mönchweiler W Germany 48.06N 8.25E
105 G4 Moncks Corner S Carolina 33.12N 80.03W
72 F7 Monclar France 44.27N 0.33E
72 H8 Monclar-de-Quercy France 43.58N 1.34E
115 J4 Monclova Mexico 26.55N 101.25W
19 A6 Moncobalang Celebes Indon 5.20S 119.26E
75 K8 Moncófar Spain 39.49N 0.10W
19 A6 Monconglowe Celebes Indon 5.09S 119.36E
70 E5 Moncontour Côtes-du-Nord France 48.22N 2.38W
72 D2 Moncontour Vienne France 46.53N 0.01W
98 B5 Moncouche, L Quebec 48.46N 70.41W
72 C2 Moncoutant France 46.43N 0.35W
72 E7 Moncrabeau France 44.03N 0.24E
98 H7 Moncton New Brunswick 46.04N 64.50W
66 J7 Moncucco mt Italy 46.06N 8.14E
79 C4 Moncucco Torinese Italy 45.04N 7.56E
105 H2 Moncure N Carolina 35.38N 79.06W
77 G7 Monda Spain 36.38N 4.50W
91 A3 Mondah estuary Gabon
118 D10 Mondai Brazil 27.07S 53.25W
108 O8 Mondamin Iowa 41.42N 96.01W
76 C4 Mondariz Spain 42.14N 8.27W
72 G9 Mondavezan France 43.15N 1.02E
79 N7 Mondavio Italy 43.41N 12.59E
118 C9 Monday, R Paraguay
76 B8 Mondego R Portugal
76 D7 Mondego R Portugal
76 B8 Mondego, C Portugal 40.11N 8.54W
75 D7 Mondéjar Spain 40.19N 3.07W
81 F7 Mondello Sicily 38.12N 13.19E
19 C5 Mondeodo Celebes Indon 3.34S 122.12E
61 O8 Mondercange Luxembourg 49.32N 5.59E
70 K3 Mondeville France 49.10N 0.18W
92 E12 Mondi R Zimbabwe
91 H3 Mondimbi Zaïre 1.48N 22.46E
76 D6 Mondim de Basto Portugal 41.24N 7.57W
91 F3 Mondjoie Zaïre 1.06N 18.05E
91 G4 Mondjuku Zaïre 1.41S 21.12E
90 G5 Mondo Chad 13.50N 15.38E
92 G4 Mondo Tanzania 5.00S 35.55E
20 C5 Mondobun Kanagawa Japan
79 O7 Mondolfo Italy 43.45N 13.06E
91 H4 Mondombe Zaïre 0.55S 22.52E
76 E2 Mondoñedo Spain 43.26N 7.22W
61 Q8 Mondorf-les-Bains Luxembourg 49.30N 6.16E
70 M6 Mondoubleau France 47.59N 0.54E
79 C6 Mondovì Italy 44.23N 7.49E
106 C5 Mondovi Wisconsin 44.34N 91.41W
71 F8 Mondragon France 44.14N 4.43E
75 E1 Mondragón Spain 43.04N 2.30W
80 J6 Mondragone Italy 41.07N 13.53E
14 E10 Mondrain I W Australia 34.09S 122.15E
65 E7 Mondschein, Spitze mt Austria 47.28N 11.37E
65 H6 Mondsee Austria 47.52N 13.21E
65 H6 Mondsee L Austria
77 Q2 Monduber mt Spain 39.01N 0.17W
93 H9 Monduli Tanzania 3.18S 36.26E
87 H8 Mondulle, Mt Ethiopia 5.38N 41.25E
42 G6 Mondy U.S.S.R. 51.45N 101.00E
58 M5 Mondynes, Bri of Grampian Scotland 55.54N 2.22W
116 K1 Moneague Jamaica, W I 18.16N 77.07W
72 H5 Monédières, Mts de France
79 F6 Moneglia Italy 44.14N 9.30E
75 K4 Monegrillo Spain 41.38N 0.25W
72 C9 Monein France 43.19N 0.34W
84 F8 Monemvasía Greece 36.41N 23.03E
40 J8 Moneron, Ostrov isld U.S.S.R. 46.14N 141.12E
79 D6 Monesiglio Italy 44.28N 8.07E
104 F6 Monessen Pennsylvania 40.08N 79.54W
77 D4 Monesterio Spain 38.05N 6.16W
71 H7 Monestier-de-Clermont France 44.55N 5.38E
72 J4 Monestier-Port Dieu France 45.31N 2.30E
72 J7 Monestiés France 44.05N 2.05E
99 P4 Monet Quebec 48.10N 75.40W
104 F9 Moneta Virginia 37.11N 79.37W
108 C6 Moneta Wyoming 43.10N 107.42W
71 K7 Monêtier-les-Bains, le France 44.58N 6.30E
47 M4 Monetnyy U.S.S.R. 57.04N 60.53E
107 C5 Monett Missouri 36.55N 93.56W
107 F6 Monette Arkansas 35.52N 90.20W
75 J5 Moneva Spain 41.07N 0.50W
75 J5 Moneva, Embalse de res Spain 41.10N 0.50W
59 G6 Moneygall Offaly Irish Rep 52.53N 7.57W
25 L4 Money Island Paracel Islands S China Sea
59 J2 Moneymore Londonderry N Ireland 54.42N 6.40W
59 J2 Moneyneany Londonderry N Ireland 54.49N 6.50W
79 P3 Monfalcone Italy 45.49N 13.32E
79 M2 Monfalcone, Cima mt Italy 46.25N 12.29E
76 C2 Monfero Spain 43.19N 8.03W
72 F8 Monferran-Saves France 43.36N 0.59E
79 C5 Monferrato dist Italy
72 F6 Monflanquin France 44.32N 0.46E
119 E7 Monfort Colombia 0.37N 69.45W
72 F8 Monfort France 43.48N 0.51E
76 E9 Monforte Portugal 39.45N 7.18W
76 E10 Monforte Portugal 39.03N 7.26W
79 C5 Monforte d'Alba Italy 44.35N 7.58E
77 P4 Monforte del Cid Spain 38.23N 0.44W
76 D3 Monforte de Lemos Spain 42.32N 7.30W
76 F8 Monfortinho Portugal 40.01N 6.55W
76 C11 Monfurado, Sa. de mts Portugal
92 H6 Monga Tanzania 9.05S 37.49E
91 H1 Monga Zaïre 4.05N 22.56E
92 C5 Monga Zaïre 7.56S 28.00E
91 F2 Mongala R Zaïre
87 C8 Mongalla Sudan 5.12N 31.42E
91 E3 Mongandia Congo 0.45N 17.11E
28 H2 Mongar Bhutan 27.16N 91.09E
103 E4 Mongaup New York 41.26N 74.45W
103 E3 Mongaup R New York
103 E3 Mongaup Valley New York 41.40N 74.45W
93 B4 Mongbwalu Zaïre 1.56N 30.03E
25 J2 Mong Cai Vietnam 21.31N 108.00E
14 A1 Monger L Perth, W Aust
14 B8 Monger, L W Australia
71 J8 Monges, les mt France 44.17N 6.11E
15 K2 Mongga Solomon Is 7.52S 157.00E
15 B4 Mongge Irian Jaya 1.43S 132.44E
Monggolküre see Zhaosu
22 F6 Monggon Bulag Nei Monggol Zizhiqu China 40.03N 103.43E
21 A3 Monggon Qulu Nei Monggol Zizhiqu China 48.38N 119.44E
21 C8 Monggŭmp'o-ri N Korea 38.10N 124.55E
25 E2 Mong Hai Burma 20.49N 99.51E
25 E2 Mong Hang Burma 20.07N 98.57E
79 K6 Monghidoro Italy 44.13N 11.19E
25 F2 Mong Hkan Burma 21.28N 100.52E
25 E2 Mong Hkok Burma 20.45N 99.26E
25 E2 Mong Hpayak Burma 20.32N 99.57E
25 E2 Mong Hsat Burma 20.35N 99.17E
25 D2 Mong Hsawk Burma 20.35N 96.59E
25 E2 Mong Hsu Burma 21.15N 98.20E
30 K7 Monghur Ghat Bihar India 25.25N 86.25E
30 K7 Monghyr Bihar India 25.24N 86.29E
30 K7 Monghyr dist Bihar India
15 J7 Mongi R Papua New Guinea
79 F5 Mongiardino Ligure Italy 44.38N 9.04E
79 C6 Mongioie mt Italy 44.10N 7.47E
25 G6 Mongkol Borey Cambodia 13.29N 103.04E
Mongkong see Mengshan
25 D2 Mong Kung Burma 21.37N 97.31E
25 E3 Mong Kyawt Burma 19.56N 98.46E
25 F2 Mong La Burma 21.40N 100.01E
25 D2 Mong Lang Burma 21.28N 97.20E
25 N9 Mong Li Burma 23.12N 97.52E
25 F2 Mong Lin Burma 20.48N 100.22E
25 F2 Mong Loi Burma 21.20N 100.34E
25 D1 Mong Long Burma 22.47N 96.35E
25 E2 Mong Ma Burma 21.35N 99.56E
23 B7 Mongmau Burma 23.01N 99.01E
25 D3 Mong Mau Burma 19.42N 97.59E
25 M9 Mong Mit Burma 23.05N 96.45E
25 D2 Mong Nai Burma 20.30N 97.46E
25 E2 Mong Nawng Burma 21.40N 98.09E
25 N9 Mong Nawng Burma 23.01N 98.31E
90 J5 Mongo Chad 12.14N 18.45E
106 J8 Mongo Indiana 41.43N 85.16W
77 R3 Mongo mt Spain 38.49N 0.08E
89 C7 Mongo R Sierra Leone
91 G3 Mongo tribe Zaïre
91 E5 Mongobele Zaïre 2.46S 17.50E
75 R3 Mongo, C Spain 42.07N 3.10E
41 C5 Mongocheyakha R U.S.S.R.
92 G10 Môngoè Mozambique 16.24S 35.33E
17 D2 Mongolia rep Asia
41 J6 Mongolo U.S.S.R. 69.11N 109.45E
22 H2 Möngönmorit Mongolia 48.07N 108.30E
91 B3 Mongono Equat Guinea 1.40N 11.15E
90 F5 Mongonu Nigeria 12.43N 13.34E
91 B5 Mongo Nyanga Gabon 2.50S 10.28E
31 G3 Mongora Pakistan 34.47N 72.22E
90 L5 Mongororo Chad 12.03N 22.28E
90 L7 Mongos, Massif des mts Cent Afr Rep
25 D3 Mong Pai Burma 19.42N 97.04E
25 E2 Mong Pan Burma 20.20N 93.22E
25 E1 Mong Pat Burma 22.32N 98.05E
25 E1 Mong Pawk Burma 22.01N 99.39E
25 D2 Mong Pawn Burma 20.46N 97.29E
25 E2 Mong Ping Burma 21.26N 99.01E
25 E2 Mong Pu Burma 20.59N 98.42E
25 E2 Mong Pu-awn Burma 21.12N 99.04E
79 D3 Mongrando Italy 45.31N 8.00E
81 M4 Mongrassano Italy 39.32N 16.07E
115 H9 Mongrove, Pta C Mexico 17.55N 102.10W
25 N9 Mong Si Burma 23.40N 98.22E
25 E2 Mong Ton Burma 20.17N 98.54E
25 E2 Mong Tum Burma 20.28N 99.34E
25 D1 Mong Tung Burma 22.02N 97.45E
92 A9 Mongu Zambia 15.13S 23.09E
91 D12 Mongua Angola 16.43S 15.22E
79 M1 Monguelfo Italy 46.46N 12.07E
90 J10 Mongumba Cent Afr Rep 3.40N 18.35E
25 F2 Mong Un Burma 21.39N 100.54E
25 N9 Mong Wi Burma 23.35N 97.35E
25 E1 Mong Yai Burma 22.21N 98.02E
25 E2 Mong Yang Burma 21.50N 99.42E
25 N9 Mong Yaw Burma 23.05N 98.08E
25 E2 Mong Yawn Burma 20.11N 99.27E
25 F2 Mong Yawng Burma 21.07N 100.24E
25 N9 Mong Yu Burma 24.00N 97.59E
104 Q3 Monhegan I Maine 43.47N 69.19W
64 K6 Monheim Bayern W Germany 48.51N 10.52E
64 B1 Monheim Nordrhein-Westfalen W Germany 51.06N 6.54E
22 J3 Mönhhaan Mongolia 46.58N 112.00E
22 B3 Mönh Hayrhan Üul Mongolia 47.03N 91.35E
84 R15 Moni Cyprus 34.43N 33.13E
105 E7 Moniac Georgia 30.32N 82.13W
57 F2 Moniaive Dumfries & Galloway Scotland 55.12N 3.55W
91 F2 Monianga Zaïre 2.09N 19.06E
106 E4 Monico Wisconsin 45.35N 89.10W
71 G8 Monieux France 44.04N 5.21E
58 L6 Monifieth Tayside Scotland 56.29N 2.50W
121 E3 Monigotes Argentina 30.30S 61.37W
89 G4 Monimpebougou Mali 14.02N 5.33W
119 D5 Moniquirá Colombia 5.54N 73.35W
75 O4 Monistrol Spain 41.37N 1.50E
71 D7 Monistrol-d'Allier France 44.58N 3.38E
75 P4 Monistrol de Calders Spain 41.46N 2.01E
71 E6 Monistrol-sur-Loire France 45.17N 4.10E
100 G7 Monitor Alberta 51.58N 110.32W
111 H3 Monitor mt Nevada 38.50N 116.35W
111 H3 Monitor Ra Nevada
59 E5 Monivea Galway Irish Rep 53.23N 8.43W
32 E5 Monj Iran 30.22N 53.57E
76 B15 Monje mt Portugal 38.46N 9.27W
30 H4 Monjo Nepal 27.47N 86.44E
63 J3 Mönkebüll W Germany 54.42N 8.57E
55 E2 Monken Hadley London Eng 51.40N 0.11E
92 G8 Monkey Bay Malawi
Monkey Pt see Mono, Punta del
87 B6 Monkien Sudan 9.02N 29.08E
13 F6 Monkira Queensland 24.48S 140.30E
56 C6 Monkleigh Devon Eng 50.58N 4.12W
91 G4 Monkoto Zaïre 1.39S 20.41E
56 N3 Monks Eleigh Suffolk Eng 52.05N 0.52E
103 A7 Monkton Maryland 39.35N 79.36W
99 J9 Monkton Ontario 43.35N 81.06W
57 D1 Monkton Strathclyde Scotland 55.31N 4.36W
29 K3 Mon La pass Xizang Zizhiqu China
72 F9 Monléon France 43.15N 0.30E
76 G6 Monleras Spain 41.11N 6.15W
71 D6 Monlet France 45.15N 3.43E
75 K7 Monlleó R Spain
56 F4 Monmouth Gwent Wales 51.50N 2.43W
106 D9 Monmouth Illinois 40.54N 90.39W
104 P2 Monmouth Maine 44.14N 70.02W
Monmouth co see Gwent Wales
103 F6 Monmouth co New Jersey
103 E6 Monmouth Junction New Jersey 40.22N 74.33W
101 M10 Monmouth, Mt Br Col 51.01N 123.43W
70 L4 Monnai France 48.53N 0.24E
70 M7 Monnaie France 47.30N 0.46E
69 L5 Monneren France 49.22N 6.27E
66 A7 Monnetier France 46.10N 6.12E
60 J10 Monnickendam Netherlands 52.28N 5.02E
56 F4 Monnow, R Hereford & Worcs etc Eng
89 K7 Mono R Togo
71 D8 Monoblet France 44.01N 3.53E
40 E2 Mon'obut U.S.S.R. 59.01N 131.19E
84 H4 Monódhri Greece 38.33N 24.05E
15 J2 Mono I Solomon Is 7.23S 155.32E
111 F3 Mono L California 38.00N 119.00W
84 U17 Monólithos Rhodes 36.08N 27.45E
103 O3 Monomoy Beach Massachusetts
103 O3 Monomoy Pt Massachusetts 41.33N 70.00W
106 H9 Monon Indiana 40.52N 86.53W
106 C6 Monona Iowa 43.02N 91.23W
94 F4 Monong Botswana 23.40S 21.35E
104 F6 Monongahela Pennsylvania 40.12N 79.58W
104 F7 Monongahela R Pennsylvania
104 E7 Monongali W Virginia 39.27N 80.16W
81 P11 Monopoli Italy 40.57N 17.18E
115 N4 Mono, Pta. del C Nicaragua 11.36N 83.37W
62 L8 Monor Hungary 47.21N 18.27E
116 N1 Monos I Trinidad & Tobago 10.42N 61.42W
90 L3 Monou Chad 16.21N 22.18E
41 D5 Monouchi U.S.S.R. 71.31N 80.40E
77 P4 Monóvar Spain 38.26N 0.50W
11 B12 Monowai New Zealand 45.50S 167.31E
11 B12 Monowai, L New Zealand
108 M7 Monowi Nebraska 42.50N 98.20W
72 F6 Monpazier France 44.41N 0.54E
72 E6 Monpon-Ménestrol sur-l'Isle France 45.00N 0.10E
58 M4 Monquich Mill Grampian Scotland 57.03N 2.15W
86 K10 Monqûl, Gebel hill Egypt 27.52N 33.03E
75 G2 Monreal Spain 42.42N 1.31W
64 C3 Monreal W Germany 50.18N 7.10E
75 H6 Monreal del Campo Spain 40.47N 1.20W
81 F7 Monreale Sicily 38.05N 13.17E
111 A2 Monroe California 39.50N 123.46W
103 H4 Monroe Connecticut 41.21N 73.12W
105 D4 Monroe Georgia 33.47N 83.43W
106 K9 Monroe Indiana 40.45N 84.57W
108 R8 Monroe Iowa 41.32N 93.09W
107 D9 Monroe Louisiana 32.31N 92.06W
106 L8 Monroe Michigan 41.56N 83.21W
105 G3 Monroe N Carolina 35.00N 80.35W
103 F4 Monroe New York 41.20N 74.12W
110 B5 Monroe Oregon 44.19N 123.19W
104 J5 Monroe Pennsylvania 41.43N 76.29W
108 N6 Monroe S Dakota 43.30N 97.14W
111 M3 Monroe Utah 38.38N 112.06W
104 F9 Monroe Virginia 37.31N 79.09W
110 D2 Monroe Washington 47.51N 121.59W
106 E7 Monroe Wisconsin 42.35N 89.39W
103 D4 Monroe co Pennsylvania
107 E2 Monroe City Missouri 39.38N 91.43W
105 F9 Monroe, L Florida 28.50N 81.17W
107 K2 Monroe Res Indiana
103 B3 Monroeton Pennsylvania 41.43N 76.29W
107 J10 Monroeville Alabama 31.32N 87.21W
106 K9 Monroeville Indiana 40.59N 84.52W
104 C5 Monroeville Ohio 41.14N 82.42W
111 F7 Monrovia California 34.09N 118.00W
89 D8 Monrovia Liberia 6.20N 10.46W
76 G9 Monroy Spain 39.38N 6.13W
75 K6 Monroyo Spain 40.47N 0.03W
61 F5 Mons Hainaut Belgium 50.28N 3.58E
71 B9 Mons Hérault France 43.34N 2.58E
66 P5 Mons Switzerland 46.39N 9.34E
71 K9 Mons Var France 43.41N 6.42E
76 G7 Monsagro Spain 40.30N 6.17W
76 B10 Monsanto Portugal 39.27N 8.43W
76 E8 Monsanto Portugal 40.02N 7.07W
118 H6 Monsarás, Pta. de Brazil 19.32S 39.50W
76 E12 Monsaraz Portugal 38.26N 7.22W
64 A2 Monschau W Germany 50.33N 6.15E
19 C6 Monse Indonesia 4.05S 123.15E
72 F5 Monsec France 45.24N 0.32E
72 E6 Monségur Gironde France 44.39N 0.06E
72 D9 Monsegur Pyrénées Atlantiques France 43.25N 0.01W
79 L4 Monselice Italy 45.14N 11.46E
72 F6 Monsempron-Libos France 44.31N 0.57E
77 P2 Monserrat Spain 39.21N 0.36W
81 C5 Monserrato Sardinia 39.16N 9.09E
64 E4 Monsheim W Germany 49.38N 8.13E
53 K7 Møns Klint cliffs Denmark 54.59N 12.03E
61 M4 Mons-lez-Liège Belgium 50.37N 5.28E
71 F4 Monsols France 46.13N 4.31E
98 C8 Monson Maine 45.18N 69.31W
103 K2 Monson Massachusetts 42.06N 72.19W
53 C4 Mønsted Denmark 56.27N 9.12E
66 Q5 Monstein Switzerland 46.43N 9.46E
60 E11 Monster Netherlands 52.01N 4.10E
52 J9 Mönsterås Sweden 57.04N 16.25E
61 H4 Monstreux Belgium 50.36N 4.18E
79 J7 Monsummano Italy 43.52N 10.48E
61 O6 Mont Luxembourg Belgium 50.09N 5.46E
79 C5 Montà Italy 44.48N 7.58E
64 D3 Montabaur W Germany 50.26N 7.50E
79 D5 Montafia Italy 44.59N 8.02E
65 A7 Montafon tal V Austria
80 L5 Montágano Italy 41.38N 14.40E
Montagnac Algeria see Remchi
71 C10 Montagnac France 43.29N 3.29E
79 K4 Montagnana Italy 45.14N 11.28E
66 B4 Montagne du Larmont mts France
66 B4 Montagne du Laveron mts France
26 U14 Montagne, La Réunion Indian Oc 20.53S 55.26E
71 H2 Montagney France 47.17N 5.40E
72 L8 Montagnol France 43.50N 3.01E
80 D2 Montagnola mt Italy 43.18N 11.10E
81 G8 Montagnola, La mt Sicily 37.37N 13.50E
71 E4 Montagny France 46.03N 4.18E
66 C4 Montagny Switzerland 46.47N 6.37E
72 E5 Montagrier France 45.16N 0.30E
95 D9 Montagu S Africa 33.47S 20.07E
12 G8 Montagu Tasmania 40.46S 144.58E
110 C8 Montague California 41.44N 122.32W
106 H6 Montague Michigan 43.26N 86.22W
103 E4 Montague New Jersey 41.19N 74.47W
98 K7 Montague Prince Edward I 46.10N 62.39W
112 K2 Montague Texas 33.40N 97.44W
113 O6 Montague I Alaska
111 K10 Montague, I Mexico 31.44N 114.45W
12 K6 Montague I New S Wales 36.16S 150.12E
14 C7 Montague Ra W Australia
14 F2 Montague Sd W Australia
113 N7 Montague Str Alaska
15 L7 Montagu Harb New Britain 6.05S 150.46E
123 A14 Montagu I S Sandwich Is Atl Oc 58.27S 26.20W
72 B2 Montaigu France 46.58N 1.18W
72 G7 Montaigu-de-Quercy France 44.21N 1.01E
71 D4 Montaiguët-en-Forez France 46.17N 3.48E
72 K3 Montaigut France 46.41N 2.48E
71 B4 Montaigut Puy-de-Dôme France 46.10N 2.48E
72 K3 Montaigut-en-Combraille France 46.11N 2.49E
72 G8 Montaigut-sur-Save France 43.42N 1.14E
71 J6 Montaimont France 45.22N 6.21E
79 J7 Montaione Italy 43.33N 10.55E
71 H6 Monta, la France 45.15N 5.43E
18 L6 Montalat R Borneo Indon
19 J1 Montalban Luzon Philippines 14.44N 121.08E
75 J6 Montalbán Spain 40.50N 0.48W
77 G5 Montalbán de Córdoba Spain 37.35N 4.45W
75 E8 Montalbanejo Spain 39.44N 2.30W
81 K7 Montalbano di Elicona Sicily 38.02N 15.01E
81 N3 Montalbano Iónico Italy 40.17N 16.34E
75 E8 Montalbo Spain 39.52N 2.40W
77 M2 Montalbos Spain 39.10N 2.02W
80 D2 Montalcino Italy 43.03N 11.29E
79 K7 Montale Italy 43.56N 11.01E
91 E8 Montalegre Angola 8.54S 17.04E
76 D5 Montalegre Portugal 41.49N 7.48W
71 G5 Montalieu-Vercieu France 45.49N 5.24E
72 B5 Montalivet-les-Bains France 45.24N 1.10W
81 F9 Montallegro Sicily 37.24N 13.22E
81 L7 Montalto mt Italy 38.10N 15.55E
80 J3 Montalto delle Marche Italy 43.00N 13.36E
80 E4 Montalto di Castro Italy 42.22N 11.36E
81 M5 Montalto Uffugo Italy 39.24N 16.10E
76 D9 Montalvão Portugal 39.36N 7.31W
119 C9 Montalvo Ecuador 2.06S 76.59W
76 B12 Montalvo Portugal 38.24N 8.38W
76 H5 Montamarta Spain 41.39N 5.49W
72 E2 Montamise France 46.38N 0.25E
75 J7 Montan Spain 40.03N 0.34W
113 N5 Montana Alaska 62.08N 150.06W
66 F6 Montana Switzerland 46.19N 7.29E
102 D1 Montana state U.S.A.
96 V6 Montaña Clara isld Canary Is 29.18N 13.33W
79 C4 Montanaro Italy 45.14N 7.51E
76 G10 Montánchez Spain 39.14N 6.09W
76 H10 Montánchez, Sierra de mts Spain
75 J7 Montanejos, Embalse de res Spain
79 C6 Montanera Italy 44.28N 7.40E
72 E10 Montañesa, Peña mt Spain 42.30N 0.14E
121 J8 Montanes, Pen. de las Chile
119 C7 Montañita Colombia 1.22N 75.25W
72 H8 Montans France 43.51N 1.52E
99 T5 Mont-Apica Quebec 47.59N 71.20W
111 A10 Montara California 37.32N 122.31W
111 A10 Montara Mts California
76 C10 Montargil Portugal 39.05N 8.10W
76 C10 Montargil mt Portugal 39.04N 8.11W
76 C10 Montargil, Barragem de res Portugal 39.07N 8.08W
69 D8 Montargis France 48.00N 2.44E
75 M2 Montarto mt Spain 42.38N 0.52E
79 O2 Montasio mts Italy 46.27N 13.25E
72 H8 Montastruc-la-Conseillère France 43.43N 1.34E
70 P3 Montataire France 49.16N 2.24E
72 G7 Montauban France 44.01N 1.20E
70 F5 Montauban-de-Bretagne France 48.12N 2.03W
70 J5 Montaudin France 48.22N 0.59W
103 L4 Montauk Long I, N Y 41.02N 71.57W
103 L4 Montauk Pt Long I, N Y 41.04N 71.51W
72 F6 Montauriol France 44.36N 0.35E
72 H9 Montaut Ariège France 43.10N 1.37E
72 C8 Montaut Landes France 43.44N 0.39W
72 D9 Montaut Pyrénées Atlantiques France 43.07N 0.12W
72 F8 Montaut-les-Créneaux France 43.42N 0.40E
80 K5 Montazzoli Italy 41.57N 14.26E
71 E1 Montbard France 47.38N 4.20E
71 H2 Montbarrey France 47.01N 5.37E
66 E5 Montbarry Switzerland 46.36N 7.03E
72 G8 Montbartier France 43.55N 1.16E
72 J7 Montbazens France 44.28N 2.13E
71 D9 Montbazin France 43.31N 3.43E
72 F1 Montbazon France 47.17N 0.42E
71 K1 Montbéliard France 47.31N 6.48E
112 N6 Mont Belvieu Texas 29.51N 94.55W
71 J3 Montbenoît France 47.00N 6.25E
72 F9 Montbernard France 43.18N 0.46E
70 B1 Montbert France 47.04N 1.29W
72 G7 Montbeton France 44.01N 1.16E
71 C10 Montblanc France 43.24N 3.22E
71 K5 Mont Blanc mt France/Italy 45.50N 6.52E
75 N5 Montblanch Spain 41.23N 1.10E
26 U12 Mont Blanche Mauritius, Indian Oc 20.17S 57.39E
61 G6 Montbliart Belgium 50.08N 4.14E
66 E6 Montbovon Switzerland 46.30N 7.03E
72 E5 Montboyer France 45.20N 0.04E
71 J2 Montbozon France 47.28N 6.15E
70 H4 Montbray France 48.53N 1.06W
71 E5 Montbrison France 45.37N 4.04E
72 F4 Montbron France 45.40N 0.30E
72 H6 Montbrun France 44.30N 1.53E
71 G8 Montbrun-les-Bains France 44.10N 5.27E
Montcalm, L see Dogai Coring
72 G10 Montcalm, Pic de mt France 42.41N 1.24E
71 E3 Montceau-les-Mines France 46.40N 4.23E
69 E6 Montceaux-lès-Provins France 48.42N 3.27E
71 E3 Montcenis France 46.47N 4.23E
71 K6 Mont Cenis, Col du pass France 45.15N 6.55E
79 A4 Mont Cenis, L. du res France
71 K6 Mont Cenis, Tunnel du France 45.08N 6.41E
98 M2 Montcevelles, L Quebec
70 J4 Montchamp France 48.54N 0.47W
71 E3 Montchanin France 46.46N 4.30E
72 H3 Montchevrier France 46.28N 1.44E
103 K6 Montclair New Jersey 40.49N 74.13W
103 D6 Mont Clare Pennsylvania 40.08N 75.30W
71 K5 Mont, Col du pass France/Italy 45.36N 7.00E
69 G4 Montcornet France 49.42N 4.01E
69 D8 Montcresson France 47.54N 2.49E
72 G7 Montcuq France 44.21N 1.14E
71 D9 Montdardier France 43.56N 3.35E
71 K7 Mont-Dauphin France 44.40N 6.38E
72 D8 Mont-de-Marsan France 43.54N 0.30W
69 D4 Montdidier France 49.39N 2.35E
71 B5 Mont-Dore, le France 45.35N 2.48E
81 L4 Montea mt Italy 39.40N 15.57E
107 L6 Monteagle Tennessee 35.11N 85.31W
121 G1 Monteagudo Argentina 27.13S 54.04W
120 F8 Monteagudo Bolivia 19.50S 64.00W
75 G4 Monteagudo Spain 41.58N 1.42W
75 G8 Monteagudo de las Salinas Spain 39.48N 1.54W
75 F5 Monteagudo de las Vicarías Spain 41.21N 2.10W
75 J7 Monteagudo del Castillo Spain 40.28N 0.50W
75 F5 Monteagudo, Embalse de res Spain 41.23N 2.10W
117 B5 Monte Alegre Brazil 2.00S 54.04W
118 F3 Monte Alegre de Goiás Brazil 13.18S 47.15W
77 O3 Montealegre del Castillo Spain 38.47N 1.20W
118 E6 Monte Alegre de Minas Brazil 18.53S 48.53W
80 D3 Monte Antico Italy 42.59N 11.22E
74 F9 Monte Arruit Morocco 35.03N 2.59W
118 G4 Monte Azul Brazil 15.13S 42.53W
118 E7 Monte Azul Paulista Brazil 20.49S 48.39W
111 E9 Montebello California 34.01N 118.07W
120 B2 Monte Bello Peru 6.09S 75.13W
99 Q7 Montebello Quebec 45.40N 74.56W
81 L8 Montebello Ionico Italy 37.58N 15.46E

14 B5 **Monte Bello Is** W Australia 20.30S 115.30E
79 K4 **Montebello Vicentino** Italy 45.28N 11.23E
79 M3 **Montebelluna** Italy 45.46N 12.03E
70 H3 **Montebourg** France 49.29N 1.22W
76 B13 **Monte Branco** Portugal 37.46N 8.33W
79 F5 **Montebruno** Italy 44.31N 9.15E
80 F2 **Monte Buono** Italy 43.05N 12.11E
79 N7 **Montecalvo in Foglia** Italy 43.48N 12.38E
80 M6 **Montecalvo Irpino** Italy 41.12N 15.03E
118 C10 **Montecarlo** Argentina 26.38S 54.45W
71 L9 **Monte Carlo** Monaco 43.44N 7.25E
118 F6 **Monte Carmelo** Brazil 18.45S 47.30W
79 O7 **Montecarotto** Italy 43.32N 13.04E
121 F3 **Monte Caseros** Argentina 30.15S 57.41W
80 H2 **Montecassiano** Italy 43.21N 13.26E
80 F3 **Montecastello di Vibio** Italy 42.50N 12.21E
79 J7 **Montecatini Terme** Italy 43.53N 10.46E
80 C2 **Montecatini Val di Cecina** Italy 43.23N 10.45E
79 K3 **Montécchio Maggiore** Italy 45.31N 11.24E
79 H5 **Montécchio nell'Emilia** Italy 44.42N 10.27E
80 G4 **Montecélio** Italy 42.02N 12.45E
66 M7 **Monte Ceneri** Switzerland 46.08N 8.55E
72 G8 **Montech** France 43.58N 1.14E
66 D2 **Montecheroux** France 47.21N 6.47E
79 D4 **Montechiaro d'Asti** Italy 45.01N 8.07E
80 L5 **Montecilfone** Italy 41.54N 14.50E
105 H3 **Monte Clare** S Carolina 34.26N 79.49W
96 V15 **Monte Coello** Gran Canaria **Canary Is** 28.05N 15.25W
121 C5 **Monte Comán** Argentina 34.35S 67.53W
80 G5 **Monte Compatri** Italy 41.48N 12.44E
80 L7 **Montecorvino Rovella** Italy 40.43N 14.57E
66 K7 **Montecrestese** Italy 46.10N 8.19E
79 J6 **Montecreto** Italy 44.15N 10.42E
116 J5 **Monte Cristi** Dominican Rep 19.52N 71.39W
119 B8 **Montecristi** Ecuador 1.05S 80.39W
120 G6 **Monte Cristo** Bolivia 14.45S 61.20W
80 B4 **Montecristo, I.di** Italy
79 K1 **Montecroce** mt Italy 46.52N 11.13E
79 M1 **Monte Croce di Comelico, Passo** pass Italy 46.39N 12.26E
76 D10 **Monte da Pedra** Portugal 39.22N 7.45W
76 C13 **Monte da Rocha, Barragem do** res Portugal 37.42N 8.17W
76 D11 **Monte das Flores** sta Portugal 38.31N 7.57W
76 E4 **Montederramo** Spain 42.16N 7.30W
76 D12 **Monte de Triego** Portugal 38.23N 7.43W
121 L9 **Monte Dinero** Argentina 52.15S 68.30W
80 K7 **Monte di Procida** Italy 40.47N 14.03E
76 B5 **Montedor** Portugal 41.45N 8.53W
81 G9 **Montedoro** Sicily 37.28N 13.49E
115 H6 **Monte Escobedo** Mexico 22.20N 103.30W
76 B16 **Monte Estoril** Portugal 38.42N 9.23W
80 G3 **Montefalco** Italy 42.53N 12.39E
80 L5 **Montefalcone nel Sannio** Italy 41.52N 14.39E
80 H2 **Montefano** Italy 43.24N 13.27E
79 M7 **Montefeltro** mts Italy
80 F3 **Montefiascone** Italy 42.32N 12.03E
76 D14 **Monte Figo, Sa de** mts Portugal
79 J6 **Montefiorino** Italy 44.22N 10.37E
80 L7 **Monteforte Irpina** Italy 40.53N 14.43E
80 H3 **Montefortino** Italy 42.56N 13.21E
77 H6 **Montefrío** Spain 37.19N 4.00W
80 H3 **Montegallo** Italy 42.51N 13.20E
81 N3 **Montegiordano** Italy 40.02N 16.32E
80 J2 **Montegiorgio** Italy 43.08N 13.33E
61 N4 **Montegnée** Belgium 50.38N 5.31E
116 H1 **Montego Bay** Jamaica, W I 18.27N 77.56W
116 H1 **Montego Bay** B Jamaica, W I
80 J2 **Montegranaro** Italy 43.13N 13.38E
79 M7 **Monte Grimano** Italy 43.52N 12.28E
107 F12 **Montegut** Louisiana 29.29N 90.33W
72 E9 **Montégut-Arros** France 43.22N 0.14E
72 H9 **Montégut-Lauragais** France 43.29N 1.54E
121 E7 **Monte Hermoso** Argentina 38.56S 61.21W
76 G8 **Montehermoso** Spain 40.05N 6.20W
72 H4 **Monteil-au-Vicomte, le** France 45.54N 1.54E
72 H7 **Monteils** France 44.16N 1.56E
117 H8 **Monteiro** Paraíba Brazil 7.51S 37.05W
77 F7 **Montejaque** Spain 36.45N 5.15W
77 K5 **Montejícar** Spain 37.34N 3.29W
13 B3 **Montejinnie** N Terr Australia 16.36S 131.38E
75 C2 **Montejo de Bricia** Spain 42.57N 3.55W
75 D2 **Montejo de Cevas** Spain 42.45N 3.16W
75 C5 **Montejo de la Sierra** Spain 41.04N 3.32W
75 D5 **Montejo de Liceras** Spain 41.23N 3.12W
80 H5 **Montelanico** Italy 41.38N 13.03E
76 A11 **Montelavar** Portugal 38.51N 9.19W
71 B5 **Montel-de-Gelat** France 45.56N 2.35E
121 E6 **Monte, L. del** Argentina
121 K8 **Monte León** Argentina 50.15S 69.00W
80 M6 **Monteleone di Puglia** Italy 41.10N 15.16E
80 G3 **Monteleone di Spoleto** Italy 42.39N 12.58E
80 F3 **Monteleone d'Orvieto** Italy 42.54N 12.03E
81 B3 **Monteleone Rocca Doria** Sardinia 40.28N 8.34E
81 F7 **Montelepre** Sicily 38.06N 13.10E
71 F7 **Montélimar** France 44.33N 4.45E
118 B8 **Monte Lindo** R Paraguay
118 B9 **Monte Lindo, R** Argentina
115 E9 **Monte Lirio** Panama Canal Zone 9.14N 79.51W
112 G6 **Montell** Texas 29.33N 100.03W
80 M7 **Montella** Italy 40.50N 15.02E
77 E6 **Montellano** Spain 37.00N 5.34W
119 C3 **Montel Libano** Colombia 8.04N 75.28W
110 L8 **Montello** Nevada 41.16N 114.11W
106 E6 **Montello** Wisconsin 43.47N 89.20W
79 M3 **Montello, il** hill Italy
67 P13 **Montellucio, Mt** Corsica 41.56N 9.02E
72 G9 **Montels** France 43.00N 1.28E
79 D5 **Montelupo Albese** Italy 44.37N 8.03E
79 K7 **Montelupo Fiorentino** Italy 43.43N 11.01E
81 G8 **Montemaggiore Belsito** Sicily 37.51N 13.47E
79 D5 **Montemagno** Italy 44.59N 8.19E
79 B6 **Montemale di Cúneo** Italy 44.27N 7.22E
80 L7 **Montemarano** Italy 40.54N 14.59E
79 O7 **Montemarciano** Italy 43.38N 13.18E
80 D3 **Montemassi** Italy 42.59N 11.04E
77 G5 **Montemayor** Spain 37.39N 4.43W
76 H8 **Montemayor del Rio** Spain 40.21N 5.54W
76 L5 **Montemayor de Pililla** Spain 41.30N 4.28W
121 C9 **Montemayor, Meseta de** plat Arg
76 B2 **Montemayor, Sierra de** mts Spain
72 F4 **Montembœuf** France 45.46N 0.34E
80 D3 **Montemerano** Italy 42.37N 11.29E
81 P11 **Montemesola** Italy 40.34N 17.20E
79 L7 **Montemignaio** Italy 43.44N 11.38E
80 L6 **Montemiletto** Italy 41.01N 14.54E
80 N6 **Montemilone** Italy 41.03N 15.58E
77 D4 **Montemolin** Spain 38.10N 6.13W
80 H3 **Montemonaco** Italy 42.54N 13.20E
115 K5 **Montemorelos** Mexico 25.12N 99.50W
76 C11 **Montemor-o-Novo** Portugal 38.38N 8.13W
66 H8 **Monte Moro Pass** Italy/Switz 45.59N 7.59E
76 B8 **Montemor-o-Vélho** Portugal 40.11N 8.41W
79 K7 **Montemurlo** Italy 43.56N 11.03E
76 D7 **Montemuro** mt Portugal 40.59N 7.59W
81 L3 **Montemurro** Italy 40.17N 15.59E
70 J5 **Montenay** France 48.16N 0.54W
72 D5 **Montendre** France 45.18N 0.25W
121 H2 **Montenegro** Brazil 29.39S 51.29W
82 E8 **Montenegro** reg Yugoslavia
75 E3 **Montenegro de Cameros** Spain 42.06N 2.45W
80 B2 **Montenero** Italy 43.29N 10.21E
81 N5 **Montenero** mt Italy 39.13N 16.36E
80 L5 **Montenero di Bisaccia** Italy 41.57N 14.47E
70 F6 **Monteneuf** France 47.52N 2.13W
91 F2 **Monteng-Boma** Zaïre 3.12N 18.40E
71 C2 **Montenoison** France 47.12N 3.24E
72 L1 **Montenoison** France 47.12N 3.24E
88 O3 **Montenotte** Algeria 36.30N 1.17E
72 L3 **Montent, le** France 46.25N 3.03E
71 K5 **Montenvers** France 45.55N 6.55E
80 J3 **Montepagano** Italy 42.40N 13.59E
121 B3 **Monte Patria** Chile 30.40S 71.00W
80 D3 **Montepescali** Italy 42.53N 11.05E
116 K5 **Monte Plata** Dominican Republic 18.50N 69.47W
79 O7 **Monteporzio** Italy 43.42N 13.03E
80 J3 **Monteprandone** Italy 42.55N 13.51E
81 B5 **Monte Pranu, L.di** Sardinia 39.05N 8.36E
92 J8 **Montepuez** Mozambique 13.09S 39.00E
92 J8 **Montepuez** R Mozambique
92 K8 **Montepuezi, B. de** Mozambique
80 E2 **Montepulciano** Italy 43.05N 11.46E
80 E2 **Montepulciano, Lago di** Italy 43.04N 11.55E
120 G11 **Monte Quemado** Argentina 25.48S 62.45W
18 H5 **Monterado** Borneo Indon 0.46N 109.05E
80 F2 **Monterchi** Italy 43.29N 12.06E
75 H6 **Monterde de Albarracin** Spain 40.30N 1.28W
76 B9 **Monte Real** Portugal 39.50N 8.52W
80 H3 **Montereale** Italy 42.32N 13.15E
79 N2 **Montereale Val Cellina** Italy 46.10N 12.39E
69 D8 **Montereau** France 47.51N 2.34E
69 D7 **Montereau-faut-Yonne** France 48.23N 2.57E
76 B9 **Monte Redondo** Portugal 39.53N 8.50W
79 K6 **Monterenzio** Italy 44.19N 11.26E
111 C5 **Monterey** California 36.35N 121.55W
106 H8 **Monterey** Indiana 41.08N 86.30W
103 H2 **Monterey** Massachusetts 42.11N 73.13W
107 L5 **Monterey** Tennessee 36.10N 85.16W
104 F8 **Monterey** Virginia 38.24N 79.36W
111 B5 **Monterey B** California
119 C3 **Montería** Colombia 8.45N 75.54W
80 D2 **Monteriggioni** Italy 43.23N 11.14E
120 F7 **Montero** Bolivia 17.20S 63.15W
70 N2 **Montérolier** France 49.38N 1.20E
80 E4 **Monte Romano** Italy 42.16N 11.54E
80 D2 **Monteroni d'Arbia** Italy 43.14N 11.25E
81 R12 **Monteroni di Lecce** Italy 40.19N 18.06E
121 D1 **Monteros** Argentina 27.12S 65.30W
66 H8 **Monte Rosa** mt Italy/Switz 45.57N 7.53E
80 F4 **Monterosi** Italy 42.12N 12.18E
80 F4 **Monterosi, Lago** Italy 42.13N 12.18E
79 G6 **Monterosso al Mare** Italy 44.08N 9.39E
81 J9 **Monterosso Almo** Sicily 37.06N 14.46E
81 M6 **Monterosso Cálabro** Italy 38.43N 16.17E
80 C2 **Monterotondo** Italy 43.08N 10.51E
80 G4 **Monterotondo** Italy 42.03N 12.38E
115 J5 **Monterrey** Mexico 25.40N 100.20W
76 E5 **Monterrey** Spain 41.56N 7.27W
76 D3 **Monterroso** Spain 42.47N 7.50W
75 D3 **Monterrubio de Demanda** Spain 42.08N 3.06W
77 F3 **Monterrubio de la Serena** Spain 38.36N 5.26W
80 J2 **Monterubbiano** Italy 43.05N 13.43E
77 P3 **Montesa** Spain 38.57N 0.39W
117 E7 **Montes Altos** Brazil 5.52S 47.02W
80 H6 **Monte San Biagio** Italy 41.22N 13.22E
80 J5 **Monte San Giovanni Campano** Italy 41.38N 13.32E
110 B3 **Montesano** Washington 46.58N 123.36W
81 L3 **Montesano sulla Marcellana** Italy 40.16N 15.42E
80 J2 **Monte San Pietrangeli** Italy 43.12N 13.34E
80 E2 **Monte San Savino** Italy 43.19N 11.43E
80 F2 **Monte Santa Maria Tiberina** Italy 43.26N 12.09E
80 N5 **Monte Sant'Angelo** Italy 41.43N 15.58E
118 H2 **Monte Santo** Brazil 10.24S 39.23W
118 F7 **Monte Santo de Minas** Brazil 21.10S 46.59W
81 D3 **Monte Santu, C. di** Sardinia 40.06N 9.45E
80 L6 **Montesarchio** Italy 41.04N 14.38E
81 N2 **Montescaglioso** Italy 40.33N 16.40E
118 G5 **Montes Claros** Brazil 16.45S 43.52W
76 K8 **Montesclaros** Spain 40.06N 4.56W
79 J6 **Montese** Italy 44.16N 10.56E
75 Q4 **Montes Gabarras** mts Spain
79 O7 **Montesicuro** Italy 43.33N 13.28E
80 K4 **Montesilvano** Italy 42.29N 14.08E
79 K7 **Montespértoli** Italy 43.38N 11.04E
Montesquieu Algeria see **Dourouche**
72 G7 **Montesquieu** France 44.11N 1.05E
72 G9 **Montesquieu Volvestre** France 43.13N 1.13E
72 E8 **Montesquiou** France 43.35N 0.20E
68 C3 **Montesson** France 48.55N 2.09E
72 F8 **Montestruc-sur-Gers** France 43.48N 0.38E
71 K4 **Montets, Col. des** pass France 46.00N 6.56E
71 G8 **Monteux** France 44.02N 5.00E
81 E8 **Montevago** Sicily 37.42N 12.59E
107 K8 **Montevallo** Alabama 33.04N 86.51W
79 L7 **Montevarchi** Italy 43.32N 11.34E
81 B4 **Montevecchio** Sardinia 39.34N 8.34E
81 A4 **Montevecchio Marina** Sardinia 39.37N 8.27E
79 K6 **Monteveglio** Italy 44.28N 11.06E
80 N7 **Monteverde** Italy 41.00N 15.32E
80 C2 **Monteverdi Marittimo** Italy 43.11N 10.43E
108 P5 **Montevideo** Minnesota 44.58N 95.45W
121 G5 **Montevideo** Uruguay 34.55S 56.10W
110 N6 **Monteview** Idaho 43.59N 112.32W
109 D4 **Monte Vista** Colorado 37.34N 106.11W
111 L8 **Montezuma** Arizona 33.06N 113.10W
105 C5 **Montezuma** Georgia 32.17N 84.02W
107 J2 **Montezuma** Indiana 39.45N 87.15W
108 S8 **Montezuma** Iowa 41.34N 92.30W
109 K4 **Montezuma** Kansas 37.35N 100.27W
111 N7 **Montezuma Castle Nat. Mon** Arizona 34.39N 111.48W
111 G4 **Montezuma Pk** mt Nevada 37.41N 117.24W
70 H2 **Montfarville** France 49.39N 1.16W
66 A3 **Montfaucon** France 47.14N 6.05E
72 H6 **Montfaucon** Lot France 44.41N 1.33E
72 B1 **Montfaucon** Maine-et-Loire **France** 47.06N 1.08W
69 J5 **Montfaucon** Meuse France 49.16N 5.08E
66 E2 **Montfaucon** Switzerland 47.17N 7.04E
71 E6 **Montfaucon-en-Velay** Haute-Loire **France** 45.11N 4.19E
68 H3 **Montfermeil** France 48.54N 2.34E
72 F6 **Montferrand-du-Périgord** France 44.44N 0.54E
71 H6 **Montferrat** Isère France 45.29N 5.35E
71 J9 **Montferrat** Var France 43.37N 6.29E
72 H10 **Montferrier** France 42.53N 1.46E
71 G4 **Montfleur** France 46.19N 5.26E
60 H11 **Montfoort** Netherlands 52.03N 4.57E
71 H6 **Montfort** Isère France 45.18N 5.55E
60 T16 **Montfort** Netherlands 51.07N 5.56E
72 C9 **Montfort** Pyrénées Atlantiques **France** 43.22N 0.51W
106 D7 **Montfort** Wisconsin 42.58N 90.26W
35 D1 **Montfort** anc site Israel 33.03N 35.13E
72 C8 **Montfort-en-Chalosse** France 43.43N 0.50W
69 B6 **Montfort-l'Amaury** France 48.47N 1.49E
70 L5 **Montfort-le-Rotrou** France 48.03N 0.25E
70 G5 **Montfort-sur-Meu** France 48.08N 1.57W
70 M3 **Montfort-sur-Risle** France 49.17N 0.40E
71 F9 **Montfrin** France 43.52N 4.35E
72 H10 **Montgaillard** Ariège **France** 42.56N 1.38E
72 E9 **Montgaillard** Hautes-Pyrénées **France** 43.08N 0.07E
72 F8 **Montgaillard** Tarn-et-Garonne **France** 43.55N 0.52E
61 L6 **Mont-Gauthier** Belgium 50.12N 5.08E
71 K7 **Mont Genèvre, Col de** pass France 44.56N 6.45E
68 G5 **Montgeron** France 48.42N 2.27E
72 H9 **Montgiscard** France 43.27N 1.33E
74 H9 **Montgolfier** Algeria 35.34N 1.00E
107 K9 **Montgomery** Alabama 32.22N 86.20W
107 D10 **Montgomery** Louisiana 31.40N 92.53W
103 J2 **Montgomery** Massachusetts 42.13N 72.48W
106 K8 **Montgomery** Michigan 41.47N 84.49W
108 R5 **Montgomery** Minnesota 44.26N 93.32W
103 F3 **Montgomery** New York 41.32N 74.15W
104 J5 **Montgomery** Pennsylvania 41.09N 76.54W
56 E2 **Montgomery** Powys **Wales** 52.34N 3.10W
112 M5 **Montgomery** Texas 30.24N 95.44W
104 D8 **Montgomery** W Virginia 38.10N 81.21W
103 D6 **Montgomery** co Pennsylvania
Montgomery co Wales see **Powys** co
107 E3 **Montgomery City** Missouri 38.57N 91.27W
110 D9 **Montgomery Creek** California 40.52N 121.55W
14 E3 **Montgomery I** W Australia 15.58S 124.12E
103 D6 **Montgomeryville** Pennsylvania 40.15N 75.15W
72 D5 **Montguyon** France 45.13N 0.12W
69 H4 **Monthermé** France 49.53N 4.44E
66 C5 **Montheron** Switzerland 46.36N 6.40E
66 D6 **Monthey** Switzerland 46.16N 6.57E
69 H5 **Monthois** France 49.18N 4.43E
69 K7 **Monthureux-sur-Saône** France 48.02N 5.59E
81 C2 **Monti** Sardinia 40.49N 9.20E
80 D3 **Montiano** Italy 42.38N 11.13E
79 M3 **Monticano** R Italy
79 G4 **Monticelli d'Ongina** Italy 45.05N 9.55E
107 E8 **Monticello** Arkansas 33.38N 91.49W
105 D7 **Monticello** Florida 30.34N 83.54W
105 D4 **Monticello** Georgia 33.19N 83.41W
106 F9 **Monticello** Illinois 40.02N 88.34W
106 H9 **Monticello** Indiana 40.45N 86.46W
106 C7 **Monticello** Iowa 42.14N 91.12W
107 M5 **Monticello** Kentucky 36.50N 84.50W
104 R7 **Monticello** Maine 46.19N 67.51W
108 R4 **Monticello** Minnesota 45.17N 93.44W
107 F10 **Monticello** Mississippi 31.33N 90.08W
107 E1 **Monticello** Missouri 40.06N 91.41W
109 C8 **Monticello** New Mexico 33.24N 107.27W
103 E3 **Monticello** New York 41.39N 74.41W
111 P4 **Monticello** Utah 37.53N 109.22W
106 E7 **Monticello** Wisconsin 42.43N 89.36W
79 C5 **Monticello Alba** Italy 44.43N 7.56E
79 H4 **Montichiari** Italy 45.24N 10.23E
80 D2 **Monticiano** Italy 43.08N 11.11E
77 L3 **Montiel** Spain 38.42N 2.52W
121 F3 **Montiel, Cuchilla de** mts Arg
72 H2 **Montierchaume** France 46.53N 1.47E
69 H7 **Montiér-en-Der** France 48.29N 44.46E
80 D2 **Montieri** Italy 43.08N 11.08E
69 D4 **Montiers** France 49.30N 2.35E
69 J6 **Montiers-sur-Saulx** France 48.32N 5.17E
79 D4 **Montiglio** Italy 45.04N 8.06E
72 G5 **Montignac** France 45.04N 1.10E
61 H5 **Montignies-le-Tilleul** Belgium 50.22N 4.23E
61 F4 **Montignies-lez-Lens** Belgium 50.34N 3.56E
61 G5 **Montignies-St.-Christophe** Belgium 50.17N 4.12E
61 E5 **Montignies-sur-Roc** Belgium 50.22N 3.44E
61 H5 **Montignies-sur-Sambre** Belgium 50.24N 4.29E
72 K1 **Montigny** Cher France 47.14N 2.40E
70 H4 **Montigny** Manche France 48.39N 1.07W
69 M6 **Montigny** Meurthe-et-Moselle **France** 48.31N 6.48E
71 D2 **Montigny-en-Morvand** France 47.08N 3.50E
69 F8 **Montigny-la-Resle** France 47.52N 3.41E
69 E7 **Montigny-Lencoup** France 48.27N 3.04E
69 K8 **Montigny-le-Roi** France 48.00N 5.30E
68 D2 **Montigny-les-Cormeilles** France 48.59N 2.12E
71 G1 **Montigny-Mornay-Villeneuve-sur-Vingeanne** France 47.34N 5.27E
69 H8 **Montigny-sur-Aube** France 47.57N 4.46E
115 O6 **Montijo** Panama 7.59N 80.58W
76 B11 **Montijo** Portugal 38.42N 8.59W
77 C3 **Montijo** Spain 38.55N 6.38W
115 O6 **Montijo, G. de** Panama
77 G5 **Montilla** Spain 37.36N 4.39W
77 J5 **Montillana** Spain 37.30N 3.40W
77 G5 **Montilla, Sierra de** mts Spain
72 C4 **Montils** France 45.39N 0.31W
91 C11 **Montipa** Angola 14.39S 13.14E
72 H2 **Montipouret** France 46.39N 1.52E
72 J7 **Montirat** France 44.10N 2.06E
118 D5 **Montividiu** Brazil 17.33S 51.08W
70 L2 **Montivilliers** France 49.32N 0.11E
77 K4 **Montizón** Spain 38.21N 3.06W
77 K4 **Montizón** R Spain
72 K7 **Montjaux** France 44.07N 2.54E
72 E3 **Montjean** Charente **France** 46.04N 0.07E
70 J7 **Montjean** Maine-et-Loire **France** 47.23N 0.51W
70 J5 **Montjean** Mayenne **France** 48.00N 0.57W
71 C8 **Montjézieu** France 44.29N 3.12E
70 H4 **Montjoie** France 48.46N 1.01W
98 D5 **Mont Joli** Quebec 48.36N 68.14W
79 C3 **Montjovet** Italy 45.43N 7.41E
12 F2 **Montkeleary** R S Australia
70 N5 **Montlandon** France 48.23N 1.00E
72 K9 **Montlaur** Aude **France** 43.07N 2.34E
72 K8 **Montlaur** Aveyron **France** 43.52N 2.49E
99 P6 **Mont Laurier** Quebec 46.33N 75.31W
66 B5 **Mont la Ville** Switzerland 46.39N 6.25E
71 E2 **Montlay-en-Auxois** France 47.20N 4.17E
66 C5 **Mont, le** Switzerland 46.33N 6.39E
61 O6 **Montleban** Belgium 50.12N 5.50E
71 K2 **Montlebon** France 47.02N 6.36E
69 C6 **Montlhéry** France 48.39N 2.17E
72 D5 **Montlieu la Garde** France 45.15N 0.16W
66 P2 **Montlingen** Switzerland 47.21N 9.36E
72 J10 **Mont Louis** France 42.30N 2.08E
98 G4 **Mont Louis** Quebec 49.15N 65.46W
72 K3 **Montluçon** France 46.20N 2.36E
71 G5 **Montluel** France 45.51N 5.03E
98 B7 **Montmagny** Quebec 46.58N 70.33W
75 P4 **Montmany** Spain 41.42N 2.15E
72 K3 **Montmarault** France 46.19N 2.56E
70 G4 **Montmartin-sur-Mer** France 48.59N 1.32W
68 E3 **Montmartre** Paris **France** 48.53N 2.20E
100 O8 **Montmartre** Saskatchewan 50.14N 103.24W
69 J4 **Montmédy** France 49.31N 5.21E
71 J5 **Montmélian** France 45.30N 6.04E
71 F4 **Montmerle-sur-Saône** France 46.05N 4.45E
71 J9 **Montmeyan** France 43.39N 6.04E
71 F7 **Montmeyran** France 44.50N 4.59E
66 B8 **Montmin** France 45.48N 6.15E
98 B7 **Montminy** Quebec 46.44N 70.20W
69 F6 **Montmirail** Marne **France** 48.52N 3.34E
70 M5 **Montmirail** Sarthe **France** 48.06N 0.48E
71 G8 **Montmirail** Vaucluse **France** 44.08N 5.00E
71 G6 **Montmiral** France 45.10N 5.08E
71 H2 **Montmirey-le-Château** France 47.13N 5.32E
72 E5 **Montmoreau-St. Cybard** France 45.24N 0.08E
68 E2 **Montmorency** France 48.59N 2.19E
98 A7 **Montmorency** Quebec 46.55N 71.10W
68 E1 **Montmorency, Forêt de** France
98 A6 **Montmorency, R** Quebec
72 F3 **Montmorillon** France 46.26N 0.52E
71 H8 **Montmorin** France 44.22N 5.33E
69 F6 **Montmort-Lucy** France 48.56N 3.50E
75 Q4 **Montnegre, Sierra** mts Spain
66 A5 **Mont Noir, le** mt France 46.38N 6.05E
13 K6 **Monto** Queensland 24.53S 151.06E
70 F7 **Montoir-de-Bretagne** France 47.20N 2.08W
70 M6 **Montoire-sur-le-Loir** France 47.45N 0.52E
76 D11 **Montoito** Portugal 38.30N 7.36W
72 J9 **Montolieu** France 43.18N 2.13E
75 H5 **Montón** Spain 41.12N 1.30W
80 F2 **Montone** Italy 43.22N 12.19E
79 M6 **Montone** R Italy
66 N8 **Montorfano** Italy 45.47N 9.09E
80 D3 **Montorgiali** Italy 42.44N 11.18E
80 J3 **Montorio al Vomano** Italy 42.36N 13.38E
80 L5 **Montorio nei Frentani** Italy 41.45N 14.56E
77 H4 **Montoro** Spain 38.02N 4.23W
77 H3 **Montoro** R Spain
75 J6 **Montoro de Mezquita** Spain 40.40N 0.36W
108 S8 **Montour** Iowa 41.59N 92.45W
103 A4 **Montour** co Pennsylvania
104 J4 **Montour Falls** New York 42.22N 76.53W
72 C2 **Montournais** France 46.45N 0.46W
104 J5 **Montoursville** Pennsylvania 41.15N 76.55W
76 E4 **Montouto, Mtes** mts Spain
109 F6 **Montoya** New Mexico 35.05N 104.04W
66 F3 **Montoz** mt Switzerland 47.13N 7.17E
72 L8 **Montpaon** France 43.52N 3.06E
95 N3 **Mont Pelaan** S Africa 27.55S 29.32E
110 O7 **Montpelier** Idaho 42.20N 111.20W
106 J9 **Montpelier** Indiana 40.34N 85.16W
116 H1 **Montpelier** Jamaica, W I 18.22N 77.56W
108 M3 **Montpelier** N Dakota 46.42N 98.35W
104 A5 **Montpelier** Ohio 41.35N 84.35W
104 N2 **Montpelier** Vermont 44.16N 72.34W
71 D9 **Montpellier** France 43.36N 3.53E
99 P7 **Montpellier** Quebec 45.50N 75.11W
72 L7 **Montpellier-le-Vieux** France 44.08N 3.13E
71 C4 **Montpensier** France 46.03N 3.13E
48 V5 **Montpensier, Kap** C Greenland 77.40N 18.00W
72 K6 **Montpeyroux** France 44.39N 2.48E
72 F9 **Montpezat** Gers France 43.24N 0.58E
72 F7 **Montpezat** Lot-et-Garonne **France** 44.21N 0.32E
72 G7 **Montpezat-de-Quercy** France 44.15N 1.28E
71 E7 **Montpezat-sous-Bauzon** France 44.43N 4.22E
71 G3 **Montpont** France 46.33N 5.09E
72 H8 **Montrabé** France 43.38N 1.31E
75 R4 **Montrás** Spain 41.55N 3.09E
72 J9 **Montréal** Aude France 43.11N 2.08E
72 E8 **Montréal** Gers France 43.57N 0.13E
106 D3 **Montreal** Wisconsin 46.24N 90.19W
99 F5 **Montreal** R Ontario
99 K5 **Montreal** R Ontario
99 T8 **Montreal Est** Quebec 45.38N 73.33W
99 F5 **Montreal I** Ontario 47.19N 84.45W
100 M4 **Montreal L** Saskatchewan
100 M4 **Montreal Lake** Saskatchewan 54.03N 105.49W
99 R8 **Montréal Nord** Montreal, Quebec 45.36N 73.38W
99 R10 **Montréal-Ouest** Montreal, Que 45.28N 73.39W
100 M4 **Montreal R** Saskatchewan
99 F5 **Montreal River** Ontario 47.13N 84.40W
71 D2 **Montrecon** mt France 47.15N 3.53E
72 J8 **Montredon Labessonie** France 44.45N 2.18E
99 R7 **Montreéal** Quebec 45.30N 73.36W
71 E6 **Montregard** France 45.10N 4.21E
72 F9 **Montrejeau** France 43.05N 0.33E
72 G1 **Montrésor** France 47.09N 1.12E
81 A3 **Montresta** Sardinia 40.23N 8.30E
71 G3 **Montret** France 46.40N 5.06E
68 G3 **Montreuil** France 48.52N 2.28E
69 B3 **Montreuil** Pas de Calais France 50.28N 1.46E
69 E5 **Montreuil-aux-Lions** France 49.01N 3.11E
72 D1 **Montreuil Bellay** France 47.08N 0.10W
70 K5 **Montreuil-le-Chetif** France 48.14N 0.03W
70 G5 **Montreuil-sur-Ille** France 48.18N 1.40W
66 E1 **Montreux** France 47.37N 7.01E
66 D6 **Montreux** Switzerland 46.27N 6.55E
72 B1 **Montrevault** France 47.15N 1.03W
71 G4 **Montrevel-en-Bresse** France 46.20N 5.07E
70 N7 **Montrichard** France 47.21N 1.11E
66 B5 **Montricher** Switzerland 46.37N 6.23E
72 H7 **Montricoux** France 44.05N 1.36E
71 H10 **Montrieux-le-Vieux** France 43.15N 5.58E
71 K4 **Montriond** France 46.13N 6.40E
71 C7 **Montrodat** France 44.33N 3.20E
61 E4 **Montrœul-au-Bois** Belgium 50.38N 3.35E
61 E5 **Montrœul-sur-Haine** Belgium 50.27N 3.43E
75 M5 **Montroig** Spain 41.05N 0.58E
71 H3 **Montrond** France 46.48N 5.50E
71 E5 **Montrond-les-Bains** France 45.39N 4.14E
107 E8 **Montrose** Arkansas 33.18N 91.30W
109 C3 **Montrose** Colorado 38.29N 107.53W
107 H2 **Montrose** Illinois 39.10N 88.21W
106 C9 **Montrose** Iowa 40.32N 91.26W
108 G7 **Montrose** Nebraska 42.57N 103.44W
103 C3 **Montrose** Pennsylvania 41.49N 75.53W
94 L5 **Montrose** S Africa 25.55S 30.58E
108 N6 **Montrose** S Dakota 43.42N 97.12W
58 M5 **Montrose** Tayside **Scotland** 56.43N 2.29W
54 L5 **Montrose** oil field North Sea 57.25N 1.24E
104 J8 **Montross** Virginia 38.04N 76.51W
68 E4 **Montrouge** France 48.49N 2.19E
77 P2 **Montroy** Spain 39.20N 0.37W
99 R9 **Mont Royal** dist Montreal, Quebec 45.32N 73.38W
72 K7 **Montrozier** France 44.25N 2.44E
61 G5 **Mont-Ste.-Aldegonde** Belgium 50.26N 4.14E
61 D4 **Mont-St.-Aubert** Belgium 50.39N 3.24E
71 D10 **Mont St. Clair** Lt Ho France 43.25N 3.45E
61 G5 **Mont-Ste.-Geneviève** Belgium 50.22N 4.14E
61 J4 **Mont-St.Guibert** Belgium 50.38N 4.37E
71 E2 **Mont-St.Jean** France 47.18N 4.24W
69 K4 **Mont-St.-Martin** France 49.33N 5.47E
70 G4 **Mont-St. Michel, B. du** France
70 G4 **Mont-St.Michel, le** France 48.38N 1.30W
69 F8 **Mont-St.Sulpice** France 47.57N 3.38E
71 E3 **Mont-St.Vincent** France 46.38N 4.30E
66 E5 **Montsalvens, L. de** Switzerland 46.38N 7.10E
72 J6 **Montsalvy** France 44.42N 2.30E
75 M5 **Montsant** R Spain
75 M5 **Montsant, Sierra de** mts Spain
71 E2 **Montsauche** France 47.13N 4.01E
72 F9 **Montsaunés** France 43.07N 0.56E
72 F4 **Monts de Blond** mts France
88 P4 **Monts Des Ouled Nail** mts Algeria
72 F4 **Monts du Limousin** mts France
75 M3 **Montsech** mt Spain 42.03N 0.45E
75 M3 **Montsech, Sierra de** mts Spain
70 J4 **Montsecret** France 48.48N 0.40W
72 H10 **Montségur** France 42.51N 1.49E
75 P4 **Montseny** Spain 41.45N 2.25E
75 N3 **Montseny** mt Spain 42.30N 1.01E
75 P4 **Montseny, Sierra de** mts Spain
116 N6 **Montserrat** isld Leeward Is **W I** 16.45N 62.14W
75 O4 **Montserrat** mt Spain 41.36N 1.48E
75 M6 **Montsiá** mt Spain 40.36N 0.31E
117 C2 **Montsinéry** Fr Guiana 4.54N 52.36W
72 E1 **Montsoreau** France 47.13N 0.03E
72 C8 **Montsoué** France 43.43N 0.30W
69 C5 **Montsoult** France 49.04N 2.19E
71 H3 **Mont-sous-Vaudrey** France 46.59N 5.36E
97 N8 **Monts, Pte. des** Quebec
72 E2 **Mont-sur-Guesnes** France 46.55N 0.14E
61 H5 **Mont-sur-Marchienne** Belgium 50.23N 4.25E
70 J5 **Montsûrs** France 48.08N 0.33W
99 Q6 **Mont-Tremblant** Quebec 46.12N 74.36W
99 Q6 **Mont-Tremblant, Parc du** Quebec
75 A5 **Montuenga** Spain 41.03N 4.38W
76 K6 **Montuenga** Spain 41.04N 4.38W
77 V14 **Montuiri** Balearic Is 39.34N 3.00E
119 A4 **Montuosa, I** Panama 7.26N 82.19W
77 G6 **Monturque** Spain 37.28N 4.35W
77 G6 **Monturque** R Spain
72 H6 **Montvalent** France 44.53N 1.36E
72 K3 **Montvicq** France 46.19N 2.48E
70 L4 **Montviette** France 49.00N 0.05E
103 K4 **Montville** Connecticut 41.27N 72.07W
61 O4 **Montzen** Belgium 50.42N 5.58E
109 F2 **Monument** Colorado 39.05N 104.53W
109 J2 **Monument** Kansas 39.06N 101.09W
60 J8 **Monument** Netherlands
109 G9 **Monument** New Mexico 32.38N 103.16W
110 F5 **Monument** Oregon 44.50N 119.26W
11 B8 **Monument Harb** inlet Campbell I Pacific Oc
113 F4 **Monument Mt** Alaska 65.36N 162.15W
111 O4 **Monument Val** Utah/Arizona
66 L8 **Monvalle** Italy 45.52N 8.38E
91 G2 **Monveda** Zaïre 2.56N 21.33E
70 N2 **Monville** France 49.33N 1.04E
57 K6 **Monyash** Derbys Eng 53.12N 1.46W
58 L4 **Monymusk** Grampian **Scotland** 57.14N 2.32W
28 H2 **Mon Yul** reg Assam/Xizang Zizhiqu
25 C1 **Monywa** Burma 22.05N 95.12E
79 F3 **Monza** Italy 45.35N 9.16E
92 C10 **Monze** Zambia 16.16S 27.28E
31 D8 **Monze, C** Pakistan 24.45N 66.40E
43 D7 **Monzhukly** Turkmeniya **U.S.S.R.** 38.13N 55.55E
58 J6 **Monzie** Tayside **Scotland** 56.24N 3.50W
91 F6 **Monzomo** Zaïre 4.14S 19.40E
120 B3 **Monzón** Peru 9.06S 76.24W
75 L4 **Monzón** Spain 41.54N 0.12E
120 B3 **Monzón** R Peru
76 L4 **Monzón de Campos** Spain 42.07N 4.29W
79 K6 **Monzuno** Italy 44.17N 11.16E
92 F12 **Moodie's Drift** Zimbabwe 20.01S 32.20E
103 K3 **Moodus** Connecticut 41.30N 72.27W
103 K3 **Moodus Res** Connecticut
112 K4 **Moody** Texas 31.19N 97.23W
104 M2 **Mooers** New York 44.57N 73.37W
95 O4 **Mooi** R S Africa
95 M8 **Mooiplaas** S Africa 32.44S 28.02E
95 O5 **Mooirivier** S Africa 29.13S 30.00E
60 M12 **Mook** Netherlands 51.45N 5.53E
12 B2 **Moolalpinna Hill** S Australia 27.08S 131.04E
12 E3 **Moolawatana** S Australia 29.56S 139.45E
12 E2 **Moolionburrinna, L** S Australia
95 O3 **Moolman** S Africa 27.09S 30.52E
13 B3 **Moolooloo** N Terr **Australia** 16.16S 131.36E
12 F3 **Moomba** S Australia 28.10S 140.15E
12 J3 **Moomin** R New S Wales
13 E5 **Moonah** R Queensland
12 F8 **Moonah, dist** Hobart, Tasmania
12 D4 **Moonaree** S Australia 31.58S 135.49E
99 H3 **Moonbeam** Ontario 49.20N 82.09W
12 K4 **Moonbi Ra** New S Wales
13 F7 **Moonda L** Queensland
59 J6 **Moone** Kildare **Irish Rep** 52.58N 6.49W
13 K8 **Moonie** Queensland 27.40S 150.19E
13 J8 **Moonie** R Queensland
110 P9 **Moon L** Utah 40.34N 110.28W
122 N5 **Moonless Mts** seamounts **Pacific Oc**
12 E5 **Moonta** S Australia 34.04S 137.37E
14 B9 **Moora** W Australia 30.40S 116.01E
12 D8 **Moorabbin** dist Melbourne, Vic
12 D8 **Moorabbin airport** Melbourne, Vic
13 F7 **Mooraberree** Queensland 25.12S 140.57E
108 F5 **Moorcroft** Wyoming 44.15N 104.58W
94 K5 **Moorddrift** S Africa 24.20S 28.50E
95 C9 **Moordkuil** S Africa 33.46S 19.28E
60 G12 **Moordrecht** Netherlands 51.59N 4.40E
110 M6 **Moore** Idaho 43.44N 113.22W
110 Q3 **Moore** Montana 46.59N 109.40W
109 N6 **Moore** Oklahoma 35.21N 97.30W
112 H6 **Moore** Texas 29.03N 99.03W
122 A11 **Moorea** isld Society Is **Pacific Oc** 17.30S 149.50W
123 H6 **Moore B** Antarctica
59 C6 **Moore B** Clare **Irish Rep** 52.41N 9.38W
113 J5 **Moore Creek** Alaska 62.37N 157.19W
108 K9 **Moorefield** Nebraska 40.44N 100.23W
104 G7 **Moorefield** W Virginia 39.04N 78.59W
105 F11 **Moore Haven** Florida 26.50N 81.08W
14 C8 **Moore, L** W Australia
109 L5 **Mooreland** Oklahoma 36.27N 99.13W
13 D2 **Moore, Mt** N Terr **Australia** 14.36S 135.15E
14 C9 **Moore, Mt** W Australia 31.13S 118.16E
14 E7 **Moore, Mt** W Australia 25.27S 122.36E
14 G7 **Moore, Mt** W Australia 26.29S 128.40E
14 B9 **Moore, R** W Australia
104 O2 **Moore Res** Vermont 44.21N 71.50W
121 E5 **Moores** Argentina 34.55S 62.55W
103 A5 **Mooresburg** Pennsylvania 40.58N 76.52W
105 J3 **Moores Cr. Nat. Mil. Park** N Carolina 34.26N 78.06W
98 E8 **Moore's Mills** New Brunswick 45.17N 67.18W
103 E7 **Moorestown** New Jersey 39.58N 74.54W
107 K2 **Mooresville** Indiana 39.36N 86.22W
105 G2 **Mooresville** N Carolina 35.34N 80.50W
108 O3 **Mooreton** N Dakota 46.20N 96.52W
116 M2 **Moore Town** Jamaica, W I 18.05N 76.26W
59 K2 **Moorfields** Antrim **N Ireland** 54.50N 6.09W
58 K7 **Moorfoot Hills** Lothian/Borders **Scotland**
108 O3 **Moorhead** Minnesota 46.51N 96.44W
107 F8 **Moorhead** Mississippi 33.27N 90.31W
108 E4 **Moorhead** Montana 45.03N 105.52W
107 C9 **Mooringsport** Louisiana 32.41N 93.58W
15 C5 **Moor, Kepulauan** islds Irian Jaya 2.55S 135.44E
99 N6 **Moorlake** Ontario 46.09N 77.42W
108 Q7 **Moorland** Iowa 42.27N 94.20W
12 E6 **Moorlands** S Australia 35.20S 139.40E
107 J4 **Moorman** Kentucky 37.22N 87.09W
12 C4 **Moornaba Rock** mt S Australia 31.33S 133.11E
12 G5 **Moornanyah L** New S Wales 33.04S 144.00E
13 K2 **Moorooka** dist Brisbane, Qnsld
13 D1 **Mooroongga I** N Terr **Australia** 11.54S 135.02E
12 H6 **Mooroopna** Victoria 36.24S 145.22E
111 F7 **Moorpark** California 34.16N 118.54W
95 B9 **Moorreesburg** S Africa 33.10S 18.40E
61 G3 **Moorsel** Belgium 50.57N 4.06E
61 C3 **Moorsele** West Vlaanderen **Belgium** 50.50N 3.10E
61 C3 **Moorslede** Belgium 50.53N 3.04E
57 D3 **Moors, The** dist Dumfries & Galloway Scotland
61 F3 **Moortsele** Oost Vlaanderen **Belgium** 50.57N 3.47E
94 K5 **Moos** R S Africa
64 N4 **Moosbach** W Germany 49.35N 12.25E
63 L9 **Moosberg** mt W Germany 51.46N 9.32E
64 M7 **Moosburg** W Germany 48.27N 11.57E
110 P6 **Moose** Wyoming 43.40N 110.43W
97 L7 **Moose** R Ontario
99 K1 **Moose Factory** Ontario 51.16N 80.32W
104 P8 **Moosehead L** Maine
104 Q1 **Moosehead L.**Maine 45.34N 69.45W
100 N2 **Moose Hill** Ontario 48.14N 89.26W
100 T7 **Moosehorn** Manitoba 51.18N 98.25W
100 U7 **Moose I** Manitoba
100 M8 **Moose Jaw** Saskatchewan 50.23N 105.35W
100 N8 **Moosejaw Cr** Saskatchewan
100 R5 **Moose L** Manitoba
100 R5 **Moose Lake** Manitoba 53.45N 100.20W
108 S3 **Moose Lake** Minnesota 46.26N 92.47W
104 P2 **Mooselookmeguntic L** Maine
100 P9 **Moose Mt. Prov. Park** Saskatchewan
100 W2 **Moose Nose L** Manitoba
113 N6 **Moose Pass** Alaska 60.29N 149.27W
99 J2 **Moose R** Ontario
65 G7 **Mooserboden** L Austria 47.09N 12.41E
99 J2 **Moose River** Ontario 50.48N 81.18W
64 N6 **Moosham** W Germany 48.55N 12.17E
103 C4 **Moosic** Pennsylvania 41.21N 75.44W
103 C4 **Moosic Mts** Pennsylvania
65 M8 **Mooskirchen** Austria 46.59N 15.17E
66 J2 **Moosleerau** Switzerland 47.16N 8.04E
100 Q8 **Moosomin** Saskatchewan 50.09N 101.41W
99 K1 **Moosonee** Ontario 51.18N 80.40W
103 L3 **Moosup** Connecticut 41.43N 71.53W
87 H10 **Mooti** Somalia 0.31N 41.58E
12 F4 **Mootwingee** New S Wales 31.52S 141.14E
91 G6 **Mopangu** Zaïre 5.12S 21.23E
92 G10 **Mopêia Velha** Mozambique 17.58S 35.42E
61 N3 **Mopertingen** Belgium 50.52N 5.35E
94 H3 **Mopipi** Botswana 21.07S 24.55E
90 N9 **Mopoi** Cent Afr Rep 5.05N 26.50E
Moppo see **Mokpo**
89 G4 **Mopti** Mali 14.29N 4.10W
87 E3 **Moqatta** Sudan 14.40N 35.51E
106 C3 **Moquah** Wisconsin 46.34N 91.04W
120 D7 **Moquegua** Peru 17.07S 70.55W
120 D7 **Moquegua** dept Peru
120 D7 **Moquegua** R Peru
121 C3 **Moquina** Argentina 30.44S 68.18W
62 L8 **Mór** Hungary 47.21N 18.12E
19 N4 **Mor** isld Truk Is **Pacific Oc** 7.31N 151.58E
30 L8 **Mor** R Bihar India
90 G6 **Mora** Cameroon 11.02N 14.07E
84 S14 **Mora** Cyprus 35.10N 33.33E
110 J6 **Mora** Idaho 43.27N 116.19W
108 R4 **Mora** Minnesota 45.51N 93.18W
109 E6 **Mora** New Mexico 35.58N 105.20W
76 C11 **Mora** Portugal 38.56N 8.10W
75 C8 **Mora** Spain 39.40N 3.46W
52 H5 **Mora** Sweden 61.00N 14.30E
109 F6 **Mora** R New Mexico
37 E2 **Mora Burun** C Turkey 40.24N 28.24E
13 J7 **Moraby** Queensland 26.54S 149.45E
82 E8 **Morača** R Yugoslavia
121 B5 **Mora, Cerro** pk Arg/Chile 35.35S 70.29W
32 D3 **Morādābād** Iran 34.39N 51.01E
30 B4 **Moradabad** Uttar Prad **India** 28.50N 78.45E
30 B4 **Moradabad** dist Uttar Prad **India**
76 D9 **Moradal, Sa. do** mts Portugal
117 H7 **Morada Nova** Brazil 5.06S 38.25W
120 D2 **Morada Nova** Brazil 7.25S 69.40W
118 F6 **Morada Nova de Minas** Brazil 18.36S 45.21W
75 M5 **Mora de Ebro** Spain 41.05N 0.38E
75 J7 **Mora de Rubielos** Spain 40.15N 0.45W
31 D6 **Morad R** Pakistan
76 F6 **Moraes** Portugal 41.29N 6.47W
95 B4 **Morafenobe** Madagascar 17.49S 44.54E
62 M2 **Morąg** Poland 53.55N 19.56E
111 C8 **Moraga** California 37.49N 122.08W
26 R9 **Moragala** Sri Lanka 6.27N 80.11E
90 A7 **Morai** Nigeria 9.16N 3.43E
101 V3 **Moraine L** N W Terr 64.10N 106.00W
69 G6 **Morains** France 48.49N 4.00E
77 R3 **Moraira, C. de** Spain 38.41N 0.09E
117 G8 **Morais** Brazil 7.34S 40.26W
87 J7 **Morala** Ethiopia 7.42N 43.23E
12 E4 **Moralana** S Australia 31.40S 138.27E
75 M5 **Mora la Nueva** Spain 41.06N 0.39E
77 J3 **Moral de Calatrava** Spain 38.50N 3.34W
76 J5 **Moral de la Reina** Spain 41.59N 5.05W
121 A10 **Moraleda, Canal** str Chile
77 J6 **Moraleda de Zafayona** Spain 37.10N 3.57W
76 F8 **Moraleja** Spain 40.04N 6.39W
76 H6 **Moraleja del Vino** Spain 41.28N 5.39W
76 H6 **Moraleja de Sayago** Spain 41.10N 6.00W
77 M5 **Moral, El** Spain 38.00N 2.13W
119 D3 **Morales** Bolívar **Colombia** 8.21N 74.00W
119 C6 **Morales** Cauca **Colombia** 2.46N 76.44W
115 P10 **Morales** Guatemala 15.28N 88.46W
112 L6 **Morales** Texas 29.08N 96.46W
76 J5 **Morales de Campos** Spain 41.51N 5.10W
76 H6 **Morales del Vino** Spain 41.27N 5.44W
76 J5 **Morales de Toro** Spain 41.32N 5.19W
76 G6 **Moralina** Spain 41.29N 6.09W
75 C6 **Moralzarzal** Spain 40.40N 3.59W
28 C2 **Moram** Maharashtra **India** 17.46N 76.32E
95 D5 **Moramanga** Madagascar 18.57S 48.13E
109 P4 **Moran** Kansas 37.56N 95.11W
106 K4 **Moran** Michigan 46.00N 84.50W
112 H3 **Moran** Texas 32.33N 99.11W
110 P6 **Moran** Wyoming 43.52N 110.35W
76 B3 **Moraña** Spain 42.35N 8.36W
76 K7 **Moraña, La** V Spain
13 J5 **Moranbah** Queensland 22.01S 148.08E
70 K6 **Morannes** France 47.45N 0.25W
81 M4 **Morano Cálabro** Italy 39.50N 16.08E
79 D4 **Morano Po** Italy 45.10N 8.22E
116 M2 **Morant Bay** Jamaica, W I 17.53N 76.25W
116 G6 **Morant Cays** islds Jamaica, W I
77 C5 **Morante** mt Spain 37.39N 6.53W
116 M2 **Morant Pt** Jamaica, W I 17.55N 76.12W
28 D4 **Morappur** Tamil Nadu **India** 12.09N 78.23E
58 E5 **Morar** Highland **Scotland** 56.58N 5.49W
30 B6 **Morar** Madhya Prad **India** 26.15N 78.14E
30 B6 **Morar** R Madhya Prad **India**
95 C5 **Morarano** Madagascar 18.40S 47.02E
Morarha, Sabkhat see **Sabkha Marâgha**
58 E5 **Morar, Loch** Highland **Scotland**
53 K4 **Mörarp** Sweden 56.04N 12.54E
71 G6 **Moras** France 45.18N 5.00E
76 E1 **Morás, C** Spain 43.43N 7.27W
76 G7 **Morasverdes** Spain 40.36N 6.16W
Morat see **Murten**
77 N5 **Morata** Spain 37.35N 1.30W
75 H5 **Morata de Jalón** Spain 41.28N 1.28W
75 D7 **Morata de Tajuña** Spain 40.12N 3.26W
77 N4 **Moratalla** Spain 38.11N 1.53W
77 N4 **Moratalla** R Spain
26 Q8 **Moratuwa** Sri Lanka 6.47N 79.53E
Morava R Austria see **March** R
62 K6 **Morava** R Czechoslovakia
82 G6 **Morava** R Yugoslavia
66 S5 **Mora, Val** Switzerland
65 N1 **Moravany** Czechoslovakia 50.01N 15.55E
32 F2 **Moraveh Tappeh** Iran 37.52N 55.40E
108 S9 **Moravia** Iowa 40.54N 92.49W
104 J4 **Moravia** New York 42.43N 76.26W
95 B8 **Moravia** S Africa 32.56S 18.41E
62 J6 **Moravia** old prov Czech
82 F7 **Moravica** R Yugoslavia
62 K6 **Moravice** R Czechoslovakia
65 N3 **Moravské Budějovice** Czechoslovakia 49.04N 15.49E
65 P2 **Moravská Třebová** Czechoslovakia 49.47N 16.40E
65 O3 **Moravský Krumlov** Czech 49.03N 16.18E
14 B8 **Morawa** W Australia 29.16S 116.00E
119 J3 **Morawhanna** Guyana 8.14N 59.45W
Moray co see **Grampian** reg
13 H5 **Moray Downs** Queensland 21.58S 146.40E
58 J3 **Moray Firth** inlet Scotland
13 B3 **Moray Ra** N Terr **Australia**
115 L2 **Morazán** Honduras 15.15N 87.36W
66 M8 **Morazzone** Italy 45.46N 8.50E
64 C4 **Morbach** W Germany 49.48N 7.08E
69 D2 **Morbecque** France 50.42N 2.31E
79 G2 **Morbegno** Italy 46.08N 9.34E
Morbi see **Morvi**
71 J3 **Morbier** France 46.32N 6.01E
67 D5 **Morbihan** dept France
26 R15 **Morbihan, B. du** Kerguelen **Indian Oc**
70 E6 **Morbihan, le** B France
52 J10 **Mörbylånga** Sweden 56.31N 16.25E
72 C7 **Morcenx** France 44.02N 0.55W
81 R13 **Morciano di Léuca** Italy 39.51N 18.19E
79 N7 **Morciano di Romagna** Italy 43.55N 12.38E
115 G5 **Morcillo** Mexico 24.11N 104.40W
76 G8 **Morcillo** Spain 40.00N 6.24W
66 E7 **Morcles, Dent de** mt Switzerland 46.13N 7.05E
80 L6 **Morcone** Italy 41.20N 14.40E
66 M8 **Morcote** Switzerland 45.55N 8.55E
56 K2 **Morcott** Leics Eng 52.36N 0.38W
75 D5 **Morcuera** Spain 41.28N 3.13W
32 C2 **Mordāb** lagoon Iran
37 H8 **Mor Dağ** mt Turkey 37.45N 44.19E
21 B2 **Mordaga** Nei Monggol Zizhiqu **China** 51.11N 120.48E
70 G5 **Mordelles** France 48.04N 1.50W
56 G6 **Morden** Dorset Eng 50.46N 2.08W
55 E5 **Morden** London Eng 51.23N 0.12W
100 T9 **Morden** Manitoba 49.12N 98.05W
12 F4 **Morden** New S Wales 30.30S 142.23E
98 H8 **Morden** Nova Scotia 45.05N 64.58W
37 J8 **Mordī** R Iran
12 H7 **Mordialloc** Victoria 38.00S 145.07E
56 F3 **Mordiford** Hereford & Worcs **Eng** 52.02N 2.37W
47 G5 **Mordino** U.S.S.R. 61.20N 51.55E
36 B4 **Mordoğan** Turkey 38.30N 26.35E
Mordovian A.S.S.R see **Mordovskaya A.S.S.R**
45 M4 **Mordovo** U.S.S.R. 52.06N 40.45E
Mordovshchikovo see **Navashino**
38 D3 **Mordovskaya A.S.S.R** U.S.S.R.
46 R3 **Mordovskaya Bokla** U.S.S.R. 53.49N 53.00E
45 K2 **Mordves** U.S.S.R. 54.35N 38.14E
113 E9 **Mordvinof, C** Aleutian Is 54.55N 164.39W
62 N3 **Mordy** Poland 52.14N 22.30E
65 M3 **Mor Dyje** R Czechoslovakia
70 E6 **Moréac** France 47.56N 2.49W
108 J4 **Moreau** R S Dakota
107 E10 **Moreauville** Louisiana 31.03N 91.58W
57 J1 **Morebattle** Borders **Scotland** 55.31N 2.22W
57 H4 **Morecambe** Lancs Eng 54.04N 2.53W
57 G4 **Morecambe B** Cumbria **Eng**
89 C7 **Morecania** Guinea 9.06N 13.10W
77 K6 **Moreda** Spain 37.26N 3.20W
70 N6 **Morée** France 47.55N 1.15E
12 J3 **Moree** New S Wales 29.29S 149.53E
104 B8 **Morehead** Kentucky 38.11N 83.27W
15 F8 **Morehead** Papua New Guinea 8.40S 141.36E
15 F8 **Morehead** R Papua New Guinea
13 G2 **Morehead** R Queensland
105 L3 **Morehead City** N Carolina 34.43N 76.44W
107 G5 **Morehouse** Missouri 36.51N 89.41W
119 G8 **Moreira** Brazil 0.37S 63.28W
76 B6 **Moreira** Portugal 41.15N 8.40W
76 E7 **Moreira de Rei** Portugal 40.50N 7.20W
76 C6 **Moreira do Rei** Portugal 41.28N 8.08W
47 J2 **More-Iz, Gora** mt U.S.S.R. 69.28N 62.10E
53 Y17 **Mørekvam** Norway 60.59N 8.21E
58 G2 **More, L** Highland **Scotland** 58.17N 4.51W

58 J2 More, L Highland Scotland 58.23N 3.35W
66 J6 Mörel Switzerland 46.22N 8.03E
110 N6 Moreland Idaho 43.14N 112.27W
119 C7 Morelia Colombia 1.30N 75.43W
115 J8 Morelia Mexico 19.40N 101.11W
75 N5 Morell Spain 41.11N 1.12E
13 G6 Morella Queensland 22.59S 143.50E
75 K6 Morella Spain 40.37N 0.06W
75 O5 Morella mt Spain 41.17N 1.55E
115 O8 Morelos Campeche Mexico 19.10N 90.40W
115 H6 Morelos Zacatecas Mexico 22.51N 102.31W
115 K8 Morelos state Mexico
29 E4 Morel R Rajasthan India
92 A11 Moremi Game Res Botswana
30 B6 Morena Madhya Prad India 26.30N 78.04E
30 A6 Morena dist Madhya Prad India
111 H9 Morena Res California 32.40N 116.30W
77 F4 Morena, Sierra mts Spain
111 P8 Morenci Arizona 33.05N 109.22W
106 K8 Morenci Michigan 41.44N 84.12W
82 K6 Moreni Romania 44.59N 25.39E
120 E4 Moreno Bolivia 11.06S 66.10W
115 D3 Moreno Mexico 28.29N 110.41W
120 D10 Moreno, B Chile
71 B5 Moreno, Col de la pass France 45.44N 2.56E
75 K5 Moreno, Puig mt Spain 41.08N 0.15W
75 F2 Morentin Spain 42.36N 2.01W
52 D4 Møre og Romsdal co Norway
77 C3 Morera, La Spain 38.33N 6.40W
11 M5 Morere New Zealand 38.59S 177.50E
118 B2 Morerú, R Brazil
81 B2 Mores Sardinia 40.33N 8.51E
75 G5 Morés mt Spain 41.27N 1.37W
57 F3 Moresby Cumbria Eng 54.35N 3.34W
101 G9 Moresby I Br Col
Moresby I Papua New Guinea see Basilaki I
15 L8 Moresby Str D'Entrecasteaux Is Papua New Guinea
105 K11 Mores I Bahamas 26.19N 77.35W
61 O4 Moresnet Belgium 50.43N 5.59E
56 J5 Morestead Hants Eng 51.02N 1.16W
71 G5 Morestel France 45.40N 5.28E
56 G6 Moreton Dorset Eng 50.42N 2.18W
56 F3 Moreton Hereford & Worcs Eng 52.06N 2.44W
13 G1 Moreton Queensland 12.24S 142.40E
13 L7 Moreton B Queensland
13 L7 Moreton, C Queensland 27.02S 153.25E
56 D6 Moreton Hampstead Devon Eng 50.40N 3.45W
13 L7 Moreton I Queensland
56 H4 Moreton-in-Marsh Glos Eng 51.59N 1.42W
104 N2 Moretown Vermont 44.16N 72.47W
69 D7 Moret-sur-Loing France 48.22N 2.49E
79 C5 Moretta Italy 44.46N 7.32E
69 C4 Moreuil France 49.46N 2.30E
77 W14 Morey mt Balearic Is 39.45N 3.20E
71 F2 Morey-St.Denis France 47.12N 4.57E
47 H2 Moreyu R U.S.S.R.
71 J3 Morez France 46.31N 6.02E
79 G5 Morfasso Italy 44.43N 9.42E
64 F4 Mörfelden W Germany 49.58N 8.35E
84 C3 Morfovoúni Greece 39.21N 21.45E
51 M3 Morgam Viibus mt Finland 68.38N 25.55E
105 C6 Morgan Georgia 31.33N 84.35W
12 E5 Morgan S Australia 34.02S 139.40E
112 K3 Morgan Texas 32.02N 97.37W
110 O8 Morgan Utah 41.02N 111.40W
41 P2 Morgana, Proliv str Franz Josef Land U.S.S.R.
107 E12 Morgan City Louisiana 29.41N 91.13W
86 K9 Morgan, El oil well Egypt 28.13N 33.28E
107 J4 Morganfield Kentucky 37.41N 87.55W
111 C4 Morgan Hill California 37.08N 121.39W
26 B16 Morgan I Heard I Antarctica 53.01S 73.34E
112 J3 Morgan Mill Texas 32.24N 98.10W
111 F4 Morgan, Mt California 37.25N 118.44W
13 D4 Morgan, Mt N Terr Australia 18.52S 137.04E
95 M8 Morgan's Bay S Africa 32.42S 28.20E
105 J12 Morgans Bluff Bahamas 25.11N 78.02W
105 F2 Morganton N Carolina 35.44N 81.43W
107 K2 Morgantown Indiana 39.22N 86.16W
107 K4 Morgantown Kentucky 37.12N 86.42W
107 G10 Morgantown Mississippi 31.19N 89.59W
103 C6 Morgantown Pennsylvania 40.09N 75.53W
104 F7 Morgantown W Virginia 39.38N 79.57W
103 F6 Morganville New Jersey 40.23N 74.15W
13 K7 Morganville Queensland 25.16S 151.50E
107 E11 Morganza Louisiana 30.42N 91.38W
66 L3 Morgarten Switzerland 47.06N 8.39E
70 A5 Morgat France 48.14N 4.31W
45 S1 Morgaushi U.S.S.R. 55.57N 46.46E
76 B13 Morgável Portugal 37.55N 8.46W
71 C5 Morge R France
66 F6 Morge R Switzerland
53 Y20 Morgedal V Norway 59.29N 8.25E
95 N2 Morgenzon S Africa 26.44S 29.37E
66 B5 Morges Switzerland 46.31N 6.30E
79 B3 Morgex Italy 45.45N 7.03E
32 E5 Morghāb Iran 30.19N 53.15E
32 G6 Morghak Iran 29.09N 57.55E
66 D7 Morgins Switzerland 46.15N 6.52E
66 D7 Morgins, Pas de France/Switz 46.16N 6.50E
66 D7 Morgins, V. de Switzerland
70 O3 Morgny France 49.23N 1.35E
69 M6 Morhange France 48.56N 6.38E
30 H8 Morhar R Bihar India
61 N7 Morhet Belgium 49.58N 5.35E
98 K2 Morhiban, L. de Quebec
20 F4 Mori Hokkaido Japan 42.07N 140.33E
79 J3 Mori Italy 45.52N 10.59E
15 K8 Mori R Papua New Guinea
92 G2 Mori R Tanzania
104 M2 Moriah New York 44.02N 73.31W
116 M1 Moriah Tobago W I 11.15N 60.43W
111 K2 Moriah, Mt Nevada 39.17N 114.11W
61 J5 Morialmé Belgium 50.17N 4.34E
76 D13 Morianes Portugal 37.38N 7.34W
109 D7 Moriarty New Mexico 34.59N 106.03W
13 H8 Moriarty's Ra Queensland
18 B9 Morib Pen Malaysia 2.44N 101.26E
57 G3 Moricambe B Cumbria Eng
12 D2 Morice Hill S Australia 26.55S 136.31E
101 K8 Morice L Br Col
119 E6 Morichal Colombia 2.09N 70.35W
119 G3 Morichal Largo, R Venezuela
103 J5 Moriches B Long I, N Y
80 G4 Moricone Italy 42.07N 12.46E
58 H3 Morie, L Highland Scotland 57.44N 4.27W
15 G7 Morigio I Papua New Guinea 7.45S 143.53E
95 L5 Morija Lesotho 29.36S 27.31E
24 G4 Mori Kazak Zizhixian Xinjiang Uygur Zizhiqu China 43.52N 90.19E
77 G6 Moriles Spain 37.26N 4.36W
75 F6 Morillejo Spain 40.41N 2.28W
75 L3 Morillo de Monclús Spain 42.21N 0.17E
100 J4 Morin Creek Saskatchewan 54.04N 108.42W
21 C3 Morin Dawa Daurzu Zizhiqi Heilongjiang China 48.30N 124.33E
63 L9 Moringen W Germany 51.42N 9.52E
69 E6 Morin, Grand R France
46 H1 Morino U.S.S.R. 57.50N 30.24E
100 D5 Morinville Alberta 53.48N 113.38W
20 P2 Morioka Japan 39.43N 141.08E
115 E3 Moris Mexico 28.08N 108.35W
12 K5 Morisset New S Wales 33.07S 151.28E
98 B7 Morisset Station Quebec 46.16N 70.33W
89 C5 Morissou Senegal 13.38N 12.09W
58 G4 Moriston, R Highland Scotland
63 L8 Moritzberg W Germany 52.09N 9.55E
64 L5 Moritzberg mt W Germany 49.27N 11.20E
64 Q1 Moritzburg E Germany 51.10N 13.41E
20 O2 Moriyoshi-zan mt Japan 39.58N 140.32E
51 K5 Morjärv Sweden 66.04N 22.45E
31 B6 Morjen R Pakistan
53 X15 Mork Norway 61.53N 7.54E
12 F5 Morkalla New S Wales 34.22S 141.10E
53 E4 Mørke Denmark 56.21N 10.23E
61 K2 Morkhoven Belgium 51.07N 4.49E
46 P2 Morki U.S.S.R. 56.29N 49.00E
41 K7 Morkoka R U.S.S.R.
53 H5 Mørkøv Denmark 55.39N 11.31E
53 X15 Mørkri Norway 61.32N 7.37E
76 G4 Morla Spain 42.14N 6.16W
72 D9 Morlaàs France 43.21N 0.15W
70 C4 Morlaix France 48.35N 3.50W
109 K2 Morland Kansas 39.22N 100.05W
72 C8 Morlanne France 43.31N 0.31W
61 G5 Morlanwelz-Mariemont Belgium 50.27N 4.15E
77 Q2 Morla, Sierra de la mts Spain
64 F4 Mörlenbach W Germany 49.36N 8.45E
100 C7 Morley Alberta 51.12N 114.50W
109 F4 Morley Colorado 37.02N 104.30W
69 J6 Morley France 48.35N 5.15E
107 G4 Morley Missouri 37.02N 89.36W
57 K5 Morley W Yorks Eng 53.46N 1.36W
101 G5 Morley R Yukon Terr 60.02N 132.12W
58 J4 Morlich, L Highland Scotland 57.09N 3.43W
52 J9 Mörlunda Sweden 57.19N 15.53E
80 G4 Morlupo Italy 42.08N 12.30E
45 A4 Mormal' Belorussiya U.S.S.R. 52.46N 29.54E
81 L4 Mormanno Italy 39.53N 15.59E
69 D6 Mormant France 48.36N 2.54E
71 G8 Mormoiron France 44.04N 5.11E
111 N7 Mormon L Arizona 34.57N 111.27W
110 L4 Mormon Mt Idaho 45.01N 114.53W
111 K5 Mormon Mts Nevada
61 N5 Mormont Belgium 50.20N 5.36E
72 B4 Mornac-sur-Seudre France 45.42N 1.00W
66 L9 Mornago Italy 45.45N 8.44E
71 E5 Mornand France 45.41N 4.07E
71 F5 Mornant France 45.37N 4.39E
71 F8 Mornas France 44.12N 4.43E
72 K1 Mornay Berry France 47.03N 2.52E
116 N3 Morne-à-l'Eau Guadeloupe W I 16.20N 61.31W
26 T13 Morne Brabant, Le pen Mauritius, Indian Oc
116 N4 Morne Constant mt Marie Galente, Guadeloupe W I 15.58N 61.15W
116 O7 Morne Diablotin mt Dominica, W I 15.31N 61.25W
26 T13 Morne I Mauritius, Indian Oc 20.25S 57.20E
26 R15 Morne, Pte Kerguelen Ind Oc 49.21S 70.28E
26 R14 Morne Seychellois mt Mahé I Seychelles, Ind Oc 4.38S 55.27E
13 F7 Morney Queensland 25.21S 141.22E
13 F7 Morney R Queensland
13 F4 Morning Inlet R Queensland
94 T13 Morningside S Africa 26.04S 28.04E
13 K1 Morningside dist Brisbane, Qnsld
106 C8 Morning Sun Iowa 41.04N 91.15W
59 K4 Mornington Meath Irish Rep 53.43N 6.17W
12 H7 Mornington Victoria 38.12S 145.05E
11 L13 Mornington dist Dunedin New Zealand
121 H7 Mornington, I Chile
13 E3 Mornington I Queensland
13 E3 Mornington Mission Queensland 16.40S 139.10E
84 C4 Mórnos R Greece
69 E6 Morn, Petit R France
64 F2 Mornshausen W Germany 50.50N 8.33E
64 L6 Mörnsheim W Germany 48.53N 11.02E
107 F7 Moro Arkansas 34.49N 91.00W
110 E4 Moro Oregon 45.30N 120.46W
31 D7 Moro Pakistan 26.36N 67.59E
87 C5 Moro Sudan 10.51N 30.06E
89 D8 Moro R Sierra Leone/Liberia
66 N7 Morobbia, Val Switzerland
15 J7 Morobe Papua New Guinea 7.45S 147.37E
106 G9 Morocco Indiana 40.56N 87.27W
73 D2 Morocco kingdom N Africa
120 E8 Morococala pk Bolivia 18.10S 66.42W
120 B4 Morococha Peru 11.39S 76.07W
19 L8 Moro G Philippines
92 H5 Morogoro Tanzania 6.49S 37.40E
92 H6 Morogoro reg Tanzania
87 C5 Moro,Jeb hills Sudan
94 S14 Moroka S Africa 26.16S 27.53E
39 J2 Morokovo U.S.S.R. 65.10N 171.55E
95 G2 Morokweng S Africa 26.08S 23.45E
115 J7 Moroleón Mexico 20.08N 101.15W
80 H5 Morolo Italy 41.38N 13.12E
19 D7 Moromaho Indonesia 6.08S 124.38E
95 A6 Morombe Madagascar 21.47S 43.21E
120 F8 Moromoro Bolivia 18.23S 64.17W
121 D8 Moron Argentina 41.08S 63.22W
116 E3 Morón Cuba 22.08N 78.39W
22 E2 Mörön Mongolia 49.36N 100.08E
22 H3 Mörön Mongolia 47.24N 110.15E
119 F2 Moron Venezuela 10.34N 68.16W
66 F2 Moron mt Switzerland 47.16N 7.16E
119 C9 Morona Ecuador 2.57S 77.38W
119 C9 Morona, R Peru
119 B9 Morona Santiago prov Ecuador
95 B6 Morondava Madagascar 20.19S 44.17E
75 F5 Morón de Almazán Spain 41.25N 2.24W
77 F6 Morón de la Frontera Spain 37.07N 5.27W
89 F7 Morondo Ivory Coast 9.00N 6.42W
95 A1 Moroni Comoros, Ind Oc 11.40S 43.16E
111 N2 Moroni Utah 39.33N 111.35W
24 G9 Moron Us He R Qinghai China
24 H8 Moron Us He R Qinghai China
20 A2 Morooka Tōkyō Japan
77 L7 Moro, Pta, del pt Spain 36.42N 2.50W
75 G5 Moros Spain 41.24N 1.50W
76 L7 Moros R Spain
67 P12 Morosaglia Corsica 42.26N 9.18E
20 K7 Morosaki Japan 34.41N 136.58E
39 F6 Moroshechnaya R U.S.S.R.
39 F6 Moroshechnoye U.S.S.R. 56.23N 156.12E
19 F2 Morotai isld Moluccas Indon
19 F2 Morotai, Selat str Moluccas Indon
93 F3 Moroto Uganda 2.32N 34.41E
93 F3 Moroto Mt Uganda 2.35N 34.46E
90 K8 Moroubas Cent Afr Rep 6.13N 20.16E
82 E5 Morovič Yugoslavia 45.00N 19.13E
45 B5 Morovsk Ukraine U.S.S.R. 51.02N 30.50E
19 B4 Morowali Celebes Indon 1.53S 121.33E
47 K1 Moroyyakha R U.S.S.R.
47 J6 Morozkovo U.S.S.R. 59.27N 60.58E
41 J2 Morozova, Mys C U.S.S.R. 78.31N 105.31E
45 M3 Morozovi Borki U.S.S.R. 53.57N 40.56E
45 N8 Morozovsk U.S.S.R. 48.21N 41.50E
79 C6 Morozzo Italy 44.26N 7.42E
118 G2 Morpara Brazil 11.36S 43.15W
57 K2 Morpeth Northumb Eng 55.10N 1.41W
99 J10 Morpeth Ontario 42.23N 81.50W
36 F7 Morphou Cyprus 35.12N 32.59E
84 Q14 Morphou B Cyprus
39 J1 Morport U.S.S.R. 70.03N 171.05E
92 J9 Morra Mozambique 15.13S 39.24E
60 K8 Morra L Netherlands 52.54N 5.26E
104 B6 Morral Ohio 40.41N 83.13W
79 C5 Morra, La Italy 44.38N 7.56E
31 H10 Morrelganj Bangladesh 22.28N 89.51E
118 E9 Morretes Brazil 25.29S 48.49W
106 K7 Morrice Michigan 42.52N 84.09W
109 P2 Morrill Kansas 39.55N 95.43W
108 G8 Morrill Nebraska 41.57N 103.55W
107 D6 Morrilton Arkansas 35.09N 92.45W
100 E7 Morrin Alberta 51.40N 112.44W
118 E5 Morrinhos Brazil 17.45S 49.07W
11 K4 Morrinsville New Zealand 37.40S 175.33E
103 H3 Morris Connecticut 41.41N 73.12W
106 F8 Morris Illinois 41.22N 88.25W
100 U9 Morris Manitoba 49.22N 97.21W
108 P4 Morris Minnesota 45.32N 95.53W
103 D1 Morris New York 42.33N 75.14W
109 P6 Morris Oklahoma 35.37N 95.53W
104 H5 Morris Pennsylvania 41.36N 77.18W
103 E5 Morris co New Jersey
99 P8 Morrisburg Ontario 44.54N 75.14W
105 H5 Morris I S Carolina 32.43N 79.54W
48 T1 Morris Jesup, Kap C Greenland 83.20N 33.00W
12 B2 Morris, Mt S Australia 26.09S 131.04E
14 D4 Morris, Mt W Australia 19.55S 121.55E
106 E8 Morrison Illinois 41.48N 89.58W
109 N5 Morrison Oklahoma 36.17N 97.00W
107 L6 Morrison Tennessee 35.37N 85.54W
11 E12 Morrisons New Zealand 45.16S 170.29E
107 G2 Morrisonville Illinois 39.26N 89.25W
103 F5 Morris Plains New Jersey 40.50N 74.29W
104 H5 Morris Run Pennsylvania 41.41N 77.02W
105 E8 Morriston Florida 29.16N 82.27W
56 D4 Morriston W Glam Wales 51.40N 3.55W
111 M8 Morristown Arizona 33.51N 112.35W
108 R5 Morristown Minnesota 44.14N 93.22W
103 F5 Morristown New Jersey 40.48N 74.29W
104 K2 Morristown New York 44.35N 75.40W
95 L7 Morristown S Africa 31.19S 27.21E
108 J4 Morristown S Dakota 45.55N 101.42W
105 D1 Morristown Tennessee 36.13N 83.18W
103 E5 Morristown Nat. Hist. Park New Jersey
104 K4 Morrisville New York 42.54N 75.40W
103 E6 Morrisville Pennsylvania 40.13N 74.47W
104 N2 Morrisville Vermont 44.34N 72.36W
104 H8 Morrisville Virginia 38.31N 77.43W
118 G4 Morro Brazil 15.59S 44.45W
118 E7 Morro Agudo Brazil 20.43S 48.07W
111 D6 Morro Bay California 35.24N 120.50W
121 A7 Morro Bonifacio C Chile 39.42S 73.30W
119 B9 Morro, Can. de Ecuador
118 H6 Morro d'Anta Brazil 18.14S 39.56W
118 H10 Morro da Taquara mt Brazil 22.58S 43.18W
118 K9 Morro da Viração mts Brazil 22.57S 43.07W
77 W14 Morro de Cataluña headland Balearic Is 39.58N 3.10E
96 S12 Morro de Jable Fuerteventura Canary Is 28.02N 14.18W
88 F9 Morro del Ancla Norte pt Morocco
77 V14 Morro de la Vaca headland Balearic Is 39.51N 2.46E
121 A8 Morro del Compas C Chile 40.41S 73.55W
115 J9 Morro de Papanoa prom Mexico 17.16N 101.05W
115 J9 Morro de Petatlán prom Mexico 17.32N 101.30W
118 H9 Morro do Caricó mt Brazil 22.52S 43.18W
118 H2 Morro do Chapéu Brazil 11.35S 41.13W
118 J10 Morro do Cócrane Brazil 22.59S 43.16W
118 J8 Morro do Dende mt Brazil 22.49S 43.12W
118 H9 Morro do Inácio Dias mt Brazil 22.55S 43.20W
118 C2 Morro do Sinal hills Brazil
96 O2 Morro Grande mt Azores 39.28N 31.14W
117 B5 Morro Grande pk Brazil 1.15S 54.45W
96 S12 Morro Jable Fuerteventura Canary Is 28.02N 14.19W
80 L5 Morrone del Sannio Italy 41.43N 14.47E
80 J4 Morrone, Monte Italy 42.07N 13.58E
119 B10 Morropón Peru 5.15S 79.57W
121 B1 Morro, Pta C Chile 27.06S 71.00W
121 D4 Morro, Sa.del mts Argentina
119 C3 Morrosquillo, G.de Colombia
80 J2 Morrovalle Italy 43.18N 13.34E
107 D11 Morrow Louisiana 30.50N 92.04W
104 A7 Morrow Ohio 39.21N 84.08W
92 G10 Morrumbala Mozambique 17.17S 35.35E
94 N4 Morrumbene Mozambique 23.41S 35.25E
53 B3 Mors isld Denmark 56.47N 8.45E
69 F6 Morsains France 48.47N 3.33E
70 H2 Morsalines France 49.35N 1.19W
68 F6 Morsang-sur-Orge France 48.40N 2.22E
79 N3 Morsanó al Tagliamento Italy 45.52N 12.55E
50 J6 Morsarjökull ice cap Iceland 64.06N 16.55W
64 D2 Morsbach W Germany 50.52N 7.44E
64 E6 Mörsch W Germany 48.57N 8.18E
66 L4 Morschach Switzerland 46.58N 8.38E
64 M2 Mörsdorf E Germany 50.52N 11.48E
107 D11 Morse Louisiana 30.09N 92.30W
100 K8 Morse Saskatchewan 50.24N 107.00W
112 C7 Morse Texas 36.03N 101.30W
45 N3 Morshansk U.S.S.R. 53.26N 41.48E
29 F7 Morsi Maharashtra India 21.21N 78.04E
67 P11 Morsiglia Corsica 42.57N 9.22E
39 K3 Morskaya U.S.S.R. 64.26N 178.17E
47 C4 Morskaya Masel'ga U.S.S.R. 63.03N 34.45E
52 F6 Morskogen Norway 60.28N 11.15E
44 H3 Morskoy Biryuchek, Os isld U.S.S.R. 44.43N 47.02E
100 H1 Morson Ontario 49.06N 94.16W
88 S4 Morsott Algeria 35.38N 8.00E
13 E4 Morstone Queensland 19.29S 138.25E
63 H3 Morsum W Germany 54.52N 8.28E
51 E4 Morsvik Norway 67.44N 15.50E
13 F5 Mort R Queensland
69 M7 Mortagne R France
70 M4 Mortagne-au-Perche France 48.32N 0.33E
72 C5 Mortagne-sur-Gironde France 45.27N 0.48W
72 C2 Mortagne-sur-Sèvre France 47.00N 0.57W
76 C8 Mortágua Portugal 40.24N 8.14W
70 J4 Mortain France 48.39N 0.56W
12 C5 Mortana S Australia 33.02S 134.29E
79 E4 Mortara Italy 45.15N 8.44E
69 D6 Mortcerf France 48.46N 2.55E
71 K2 Morteau France 47.03N 6.35E
70 K4 Morteaux-Coulibœuf France 48.55N 0.04W
56 C5 Morte B Devon Eng 51.10N 4.15W
79 O3 Mortegliano Italy 45.57N 13.10E
56 C5 Mortehoe Devon Eng 51.12N 4.12W
71 H6 Morte, la France 45.02N 5.45E
72 F3 Mortemart France 46.02N 0.57E
66 Q6 Morteratsch, Piz mt Switzerland 46.24N 9.54E
121 E3 Morteros Argentina 30.45S 62.00W
118 G7 Mortes R Brazil
118 D3 Mortes, R. das Brazil
61 N4 Mortier Belgium 50.41N 5.45E
69 F4 Mortiers France 49.42N 3.41E
95 J8 Mortimer S Africa 32.22S 25.41E
14 B6 Mortimer, Mt W Australia 23.09S 116.35E
56 F3 Mortimers Cross Hereford & Worcs Eng 52.16N 2.50W
100 L8 Mortlach Saskatchewan 50.29N 106.01W
55 D4 Mortlake London Eng 51.28N 0.16W
12 G7 Mortlake Victoria 38.06S 142.52E
101 S4 Mort, L. du N W Terr 63.02N 111.09W
Mortlock Is see Tauu Is
111 J8 Mortmar California 33.32N 115.56W
79 M2 Morto, Lago L 46.05N 12.20E
106 E9 Morton Illinois 40.37N 89.28W
108 Q5 Morton Minnesota 44.34N 94.59W
107 G9 Morton Mississippi 32.21N 89.40W
112 E2 Morton Texas 33.43N 102.46W
110 C3 Morton Washington 46.35N 122.16W
106 Q1 Morton Grove dist Chicago, Illinois
107 J4 Mortons Gap Kentucky 37.12N 87.29W
81 D1 Mortorio, I Sardinia 41.05N 9.37E
70 L4 Mortrée France 48.38N 0.05E
61 O4 Mortroux Belgium 50.43N 5.45E
61 H2 Mortsel Belgium 51.10N 4.28E
45 T5 Mortsy U.S.S.R. 51.17N 47.50E
53 E6 Morud Denmark 55.26N 10.12E
116 O2 Moruga Trinidad & Tobago 10.06N 61.17W
116 O2 Moruga Pt Trinidad & Tobago 10.05N 61.16W
93 F4 Moruita Uganda 1.54N 34.46E
12 H5 Morundah New S Wales 34.56S 146.18E
93 F2 Morungole mt Uganda 3.48N 34.03E
95 L5 Morunyaneng Lesotho 29.50S 27.32E
12 K6 Moruya New S Wales 35.56S 150.06E
56 S9 Morvah Cornwall Eng 50.09N 5.39W
71 E2 Morvan, Mts. du France
105 D7 Morven Georgia 30.56N 83.31W
105 G3 Morven N Carolina 34.53N 80.01W
11 F11 Morven New Zealand 44.49S 171.07E
13 H7 Morven Queensland 26.25S 147.05E
58 K4 Morven mt Grampian Scotland 57.07N 3.02W
58 J2 Morven mt Highland Scotland 58.13N 3.42W
58 E5 Morvern dist Highland Scotland
29 B6 Morvi Gujarat India 22.50N 70.52E
66 D1 Morvillars France 47.33N 6.56E
61 J6 Morville Belgium 50.14N 4.45E
56 G2 Morville Shropshire Eng 52.33N 2.29W
29 B5 Morwara Gujarat India 24.02N 71.30E
12 H7 Morwell Victoria 38.14S 146.25E
42 C4 Moryakovskiy Zaton U.S.S.R. 56.46N 84.40E
76 C12 Morzela Portugal 38.17N 8.17W
66 Q2 Morzelspitze mt Austria 47.22N 9.47E
39 K3 Morzhovaya, Gora mt U.S.S.R. 62.38N 178.04E
47 E3 Morzhovets, Ostrov isld U.S.S.R. 66.45N 42.30E
113 F9 Morzhovoi B Alaska
71 K4 Morzine France 46.11N 6.43E
89 A1 Morzouba Mauritania 20.58N 16.28W
76 B4 Mos Spain 42.12N 8.37W
45 F2 Mosal'sk U.S.S.R. 54.30N 35.00E
64 G5 Mosbach W Germany 49.21N 9.10E
53 E1 Mosbjerg Denmark 57.31N 10.18E
110 S2 Mosby Montana 47.00N 107.52W
75 G7 Moscardón Spain 40.20N 1.33W
76 E15 Moscavide Portugal 38.47N 9.06W
65 O7 Moschendorf Austria 47.05N 16.28E
80 J3 Mosciano Sant'Angelo Italy 42.45N 13.54E
110 J3 Moscow Idaho 46.44N 117.00W
109 J4 Moscow Kansas 37.21N 101.12W
104 A8 Moscow Ohio 38.52N 84.14W
103 C4 Moscow Pennsylvania 41.20N 75.31W
107 G6 Moscow Tennessee 35.04N 89.25W
Moscow U.S.S.R. see Moskva
107 F3 Moscow Mills Missouri 38.58N 90.54W
50 B3 Mosdalur Iceland 65.44N 23.21W
123 H3 Mose, C Antarctica 66.00S 130.12E
64 N2 Mosel E Germany 50.47N 12.28E
64 C3 Mosel R W Germany
103 C6 Moselem Springs Pennsylvania 40.30N 75.51W
104 H9 Moseley Virginia 37.28N 77.47W
64 C3 Moselkern W Germany 50.12N 7.22E
107 G10 Moselle Mississippi 31.31N 89.18W
67 K3 Moselle dept France
69 L7 Moselle R France/Luxembourg
69 M8 Moselotte R France
98 K9 Mosers River Nova Scotia 44.58N 62.18W
109 G5 Moses New Mexico 36.43N 103.04W
110 F2 Moses Coulee canyon Washington
110 F2 Moses Coulee R Washington
110 F2 Moses L Washington 47.08N 119.20W
110 F2 Moses Lake Washington 47.09N 119.18W
110 H9 Moses, Mt Nevada 40.10N 117.25W
113 F4 Moses Pt Alaska 64.41N 162.10W
94 J3 Mosetse Botswana 20.40S 26.38E
20 L1 Moseushi Japan 43.42N 141.58E
47 F3 Moseyevo U.S.S.R. 65.45N 46.22E
50 E6 Mosfell Iceland 64.07N 20.36W
50 D6 Mosfellsheidhi heath Iceland
11 E12 Mosgiel New Zealand 45.54S 170.21E
47 C3 Mosha U.S.S.R. 66.31N 31.59E
47 E5 Mosha U.S.S.R. 61.41N 40.50E
47 E5 Mosha R U.S.S.R.
51 N12 Moshchnyy, Ostrov islds U.S.S.R. 60.00N 27.50E
105 E1 Mosheim Tennessee 36.11N 82.59W
99 F4 Mosher Ontario 48.43N 84.13W
93 J9 Moshi Tanzania 3.21S 37.19E
90 A7 Moshi watercourse Nigeria
42 C4 Moshkovo U.S.S.R. 55.16N 83.35E
45 C7 Moshny Ukraine U.S.S.R. 49.32N 31.45E
46 M2 Moshok U.S.S.R. 55.45N 41.10E
94 H5 Moshupa Botswana 24.57S 25.20E
47 G4 Mosh'yuga U.S.S.R. 64.50N 53.40E
95 P8 Mosi S Africa 26.54S 32.36E
63 Q9 Mosigkau E Germany 51.49N 12.10E
62 K3 Mosina Poland 52.15N 16.50E
47 N5 Mosina U.S.S.R. 56.34N 61.42E
106 E5 Mosinee Wisconsin 44.47N 89.44W
Mosi-Oa-Toenja see Victoria Falls
93 H7 Mosiro Kenya 1.28S 36.06E
95 H2 Mosito S Africa 26.09S 24.45E
51 C6 Mosjøen Norway 65.50N 13.10E
47 L8 Moskalenki U.S.S.R. 54.58N 71.58E
40 J5 Moskal'vo Sakhalin U.S.S.R. 53.37N 142.32E
108 F5 Moskee Wyoming 44.16N 104.10W
51 C4 Moskenes Norway 67.55N 13.00E
51 C4 Moskenesøya isld Norway 67.55N 13.00E
51 C4 Moskenstraumen isld Norway 67.47N 12.45E
84 D4 Moskhokariá Greece 39.00N 22.16E
84 D4 Moskhokhórion Greece 38.50N 22.27E
53 T16 Moskog Sogn og Fjordane Norway 61.26N 6.00E
51 J4 Moskojärvi Sweden 67.24N 21.05E
51 H6 Moskosel Sweden 65.52N 19.30E
46 S2 Moskovo U.S.S.R. 55.18N 55.02E
46 K2 Moskovskaya Oblast' prov U.S.S.R.
43 J7 Moskovskiy Tadzhikistan U.S.S.R. 37.36N 69.44E
44 D2 Moskovskoye Stavropol' U.S.S.R. 45.16N 41.57E
45 L5 Moskovskoye Voronezh U.S.S.R. 51.25N 39.35E
51 M4 Moskuvaara Finland 67.34N 26.57E
46 K2 Moskva U.S.S.R. 55.45N 37.42E
45 K1 Moskva R U.S.S.R.
42 E5 Moskva, Gora mt U.S.S.R. 54.23N 93.50E
46 K2 Moskva-Volga Kanal U.S.S.R.
46 E8 Moskvoretskiy dist Moscow U.S.S.R.
45 J1 Moskvy, Kanal imeni U.S.S.R.
82 D5 Moslavacka Gora mts Yugoslavia
12 M7 Mosman dist Sydney, N S W
66 N2 Mosnang Switzerland 47.23N 9.03E
70 N7 Mosnes France 47.27N 1.06E
45 M2 Mosolovo U.S.S.R. 54.17N 40.33E
94 J5 Mosomane Botswana 24.04S 26.15E
62 K8 Mosonmagyaróvár Hungary 47.51N 17.18E
45 K9 Mospino Ukraine U.S.S.R. 47.54N 38.04E
117 D5 Mosqueiro Brazil 1.08S 48.28W
119 B6 Mosquera Colombia 2.32N 78.24W
109 G6 Mosquero New Mexico 35.45N 103.56W
75 K7 Mosqueruela Spain 40.21N 0.27W
115 M2 Mosquitia reg Honduras
118 H4 Mosquito R Brazil
104 E5 Mosquito Creek Res Ohio
101 W4 Mosquito L N W Terr
105 G9 Mosquito Lagoon Florida
119 C3 Mosquito, Pta C Panama 9.08N 77.53W
115 N3 Mosquitos, Costa de reg Nic
115 O5 Mosquitos, G. de los Panama
52 F7 Moss Norway 59.26N 10.41E
85 E8 Mossadem watercourse Libya
91 E4 Mossaka div Congo
Mossâmedes Angola see Moçâmedes
118 E5 Mossâmedes Brazil 16.05S 50.09W
58 L4 Mossat Grampian Scotland 57.15N 2.53W
100 M9 Mossbank Saskatchewan 49.56N 105.59W
58 Q9 Mossbank Shetland Scotland 60.27N 1.10W
111 A10 Moss Beach California 37.31N 122.31W
11 C12 Mossburn New Zealand 45.40S 168.15E
94 P12 Mosselbaai B Cape Town S Africa
95 C10 Mosselrivier S Africa 34.25S 19.17E
91 C5 Mossendjo Congo 2.55S 12.48E
117 H7 Mosseró Brazil 5.10S 37.18W
66 E6 Mosses, les pass Switzerland 46.25N 7.07E
72 J10 Mosset France 42.41N 2.21E
12 G5 Mossgiel New S Wales 33.18S 144.05E
89 H5 Mossi reg Upper Volta
64 G7 Mössingen W Germany 48.25N 9.04E
100 T1 Moss L Manitoba
13 H3 Mossman Queensland 16.21S 145.15E
53 D4 Mossø L Denmark 56.03N 9.50E
79 D3 Mosso Santa Maria Italy 45.39N 8.08E
107 H11 Moss Point Mississippi 30.25N 88.31W
59 K1 Moss-side Antrim N Ireland 55.09N 6.25W
58 K3 Mosstodlock Grampian Scotland 57.37N 3.09W
53 Y19 Møsstrand Norway 59.52N 8.04E
92 K9 Mossuril Mozambique 14.55S 40.41E
12 K5 Moss Vale New S Wales 34.33S 150.20E
107 K11 Mossy Head Florida 30.43N 86.19W
100 U6 Mossy Pt Manitoba 52.38N 97.12W
100 O4 Mossy R Saskatchewan
110 C3 Mossyrock Washington 46.33N 122.29W
82 K9 Most Bulgaria 41.45N 25.31E
64 Q2 Most Czechoslovakia 50.31N 13.39E
84 Y20 Mosta Malta 35.55N 14.26E
45 O1 Mosta U.S.S.R. 56.31N 42.10E
32 F4 Mostafaabad Iran 33.40N 54.54E
88 O4 Mostaganem Algeria 35.54N 0.05E
82 D7 Mostar Yugoslavia 43.20N 17.50E
121 J3 Mostardas Brazil 31.02S 50.51W
121 J3 Mostardas, Pta. de C Brazil 31.17S 50.52W
76 D9 Mosteiro Portugal 39.53N 7.58W
76 D13 Mosteiro Portugal 37.47N 7.44W
96 T1 Mosteiros Azores 37.37N 25.49W
53 S19 Moster Norway 59.43N 5.20E
53 S19 Mosterhamn Norway 59.42N 5.24E
53 T20 Mosterøy Norway 59.05N 5.42E
53 T20 Mosterøy isld Norway 59.05N 5.42E
56 F6 Mosterton Dorset Eng 50.51N 2.47W
46 E5 Mostiska Ukraine U.S.S.R. 49.48N 23.05E
45 K7 Mostki Ukraine U.S.S.R. 49.20N 38.30E
79 P2 Most na Soči Yugoslavia 46.09N 13.45E
53 V19 Mostøl Norway 59.34N 6.50E
75 C7 Móstoles Spain 40.19N 3.53W
101 T8 Mostoos Hills Saskatchewan
47 H7 Mostovaya U.S.S.R. 57.01N 57.24E
44 D3 Mostovoye Krasnodar U.S.S.R. 44.26N 40.48E
45 B9 Mostovoye Ukraine U.S.S.R. 47.27N 30.59E
47 K7 Mostovskoy Kurgan U.S.S.R. 55.45N 66.05E
47 M4 Mostovskoye Sverdlovsk U.S.S.R. 57.10N 60.40E
62 P2 Mosty Belorussiya U.S.S.R. 53.25N 24.32E
57 G6 Mostyn Clwyd Wales 53.19N 3.16W
18 N3 Mostyn Sabah Malaysia 4.37N 118.09E
34 L2 Mosul Iraq 36.21N 43.08E
21 D11 Mosŭlpo S Korea 33.20N 126.17E
Mosun see Wuxuan
23 C5 Mosuoying Sichuan China 27.00N 102.11E
53 Y19 Møsvatn L Norway
87 F5 Mot'a Ethiopia 11.06N 37.50E
9 C10 Mota isld New Hebrides 13.51S 167.37E
91 E2 Motaba R Congo
120 G7 Motacucito Bolivia 17.32S 61.32W
75 E8 Mota del Cuervo Spain 39.30N 2.52W
76 J5 Mota del Marqués Spain 41.38N 5.11W
115 O10 Motagua R Guatemala
25 N9 Motai Burma 24.06N 98.48E
89 B6 Mô Tairou Guinea 11.38N 14.16W
52 J8 Motala Sweden 58.34N 15.05E
122 V14 Motane I Marquesas Is Pacific Oc 10.00S 138.55W
119 E3 Motatán, R Venezuela
94 M5 Motaze Mozambique 24.48S 32.52E
20 O5 Motegi Japan 36.33N 140.12E
11 K5 Motere mt New Zealand 38.44S 175.32E
30 B7 Moth Uttar Prad India 25.44N 78.56E
9 U3 Mothe isld Fiji 18.39S 178.32W
72 A2 Mothe-Achard, la France 46.37N 1.39W
72 E6 Mothe Montravel, la France 44.51N 0.02E
57 H3 Motherby Cumbria Eng 54.39N 2.52W
113 J8 Mother Goose L Alaska 57.15N 157.20W
15 M6 Mother, The vol New Britain 4.15S 152.14E
58 J7 Motherwell Strathclyde Scotland 55.48N 4.00W
72 D3 Mothe St. Héraye, la France 46.21N 0.06W
19 E3 Moti isld Moluccas Indon 0.26N 127.24E
66 C4 Môtiers Switzerland 46.55N 6.37E
30 H6 Motihari Bihar India 26.40N 84.55E
77 F3 Motilla mt Spain 38.57N 5.03W
75 G8 Motilla del Palancar Spain 39.34N 1.55W
77 N2 Motilleja Spain 39.11N 1.49W
30 E4 Motipur Uttar Prad India 28.01N 81.21E
11 L4 Motiti I New Zealand 37.58S 176.26E
52 H7 Motjärnshyttan Sweden 59.56N 13.59E
108 Q3 Motley Minnesota 46.20N 94.38W
94 K3 Motloutse R Botswana
119 G5 Motocurunya Venezuela 4.23N 64.07W
94 G5 Motokwe Botswana 24.04S 23.18E
46 F4 Motol Belorussiya U.S.S.R. 52.25N 25.05E
20 K3 Motomachi Japan 41.35N 140.26E
41 M6 Motorchuna R U.S.S.R.
15 M9 Motorina I Louisiade Arch 11.06S 152.34E
42 E5 Motorskoye U.S.S.R. 53.24N 92.57E
75 G6 Motos Spain 40.35N 1.37W
66 F7 Motôt Switzerland 46.06N 7.25E
47 C2 Motovskiy Zaliv gulf U.S.S.R.
82 B5 Motovun Yugoslavia 45.20N 13.50E
20 G8 Motoyama Japan 33.45N 133.36E
20 N9 Moto-yama hill Iwo Jima Pacific Oc 24.47N 141.19E
20 P3 Motoyoshi Japan 38.46N 141.32E
115 N10 Motozintla Mexico 15.21N 92.14W
75 F1 Motrico Spain 43.18N 2.22W
77 J7 Motril Spain 36.45N 3.31W
Motsa see Moza
108 H3 Mott N Dakota 46.22N 102.29W
79 H4 Motta Baluffi Italy 45.03N 10.15E
79 N3 Motta di Livenza Italy 45.46N 12.37E
66 K8 Mottarone, Monte Italy 45.53N 8.28E
81 L7 Motta San Giovanni Italy 38.00N 15.41E
79 E4 Motta Visconti Italy 45.18N 8.59E
71 G8 Motte-Chalançon, la France 44.29N 5.23E
71 H7 Motte-d'Aveillans, la France 44.57N 5.44E
71 J8 Motte-du-Caire, la France 44.20N 6.02E
79 J4 Motteggiana Italy 45.02N 10.46E
70 E5 Motte, la France 48.14N 2.45W
69 K7 Motte, Mt. de la France 48.13N 5.40E
64 H3 Motten W Germany 50.25N 9.47E
71 H5 Motte-Servolex, la France 45.36N 5.52E
70 M2 Motteville France 49.37N 0.52E
55 H4 Mottingham London Eng 51.26N 0.03E
121 D2 Motto Botello Argentina 28.30S 65.38W
81 O2 Mottola Italy 40.38N 17.02E
57 J6 Mottram Greater Manchester Eng 53.28N 2.01W
101 Z1 Motty I N W Terr
11 M5 Motu New Zealand 38.15S 177.33E
11 N5 Motu Ahiauru isld New Zealand 38.04S 178.26E
122 R15 Motu-Ari isld Gambier Is Pacific Oc 23.09S 135.00W
11 H8 Motueka New Zealand 41.08S 173.01E
11 G8 Motueka R New Zealand
11 L4 Motuhora isld New Zealand 37.51S 177.00E
122 A14 Motu Iti atoll Society Is Pacific Oc 16.15S 151.50W
122 T16 Motu Iti isld Easter I Pacific Oc 27.11S 109.28W
122 T13 Motu Iti isld Marquesas Is Pacific Oc 8.40S 140.42W
11 G10 Motukarara New Zealand 43.47S 172.40E
11 H1 Motukawanui I New Zealand 35.00S 173.58E
Motukorea see Browns I
11 D1 Motukorea Chan New Zealand
115 P7 Motul Mexico 21.09N 89.19W
11 H10 Motunau I New Zealand 43.04S 173.06E
122 T16 Motu Nui isld Easter I Pacific Oc 27.12S 109.28W
122 L10 Motu One I Society Is Pacific Oc 15.48S 154.33W
11 N5 Motuoroi I New Zealand 38.17S 178.22E
119 B11 Motupe Peru 6.09S 79.45W
11 G1 Motupia I New Zealand 34.37S 172.49E
11 G8 Motupiko New Zealand 41.28S 172.52E
11 M4 Motu R New Zealand
9 T8 Moturiki I Fiji 17.46S 178.45E
11 H1 Moturoa Is New Zealand
11 K5 Mototaiko I New Zealand 38.52S 175.58E
11 H1 Motutangi New Zealand 34.54S 173.10E
11 J3 Motutapu isld New Zealand 36.47S 174.57E
122 B10 Motutapu isld Rarotonga Pacific Oc 21.15S 159.43W
9 S10 Motu Tapu islet Tonga, Pacific Oc 21.05S 175.04W
122 U15 Motu Tautara isld Easter I Pacific Oc 27.06S 109.26W
122 S16 Motu-Teiko isld Gambier Is Pacific Oc 23.12S 134.58W
122 D15 Motutunga atoll Tuamotu Is Pacific Oc 17.00S 144.20W
42 E3 Motygino U.S.S.R. 58.15N 94.43E
39 D5 Motykleyka U.S.S.R. 59.28N 148.40E
53 E3 Mou Denmark 56.59N 10.15E
91 D3 Mouali Congo 0.10N 15.33E
88 L8 Mouat el Fehed Algeria 27.42N 5.37W
123 K6 Moubray B Antarctica
87 J5 Moucha,I Djibouti 11.44N 43.15E
97 M7 Mouchalagane, Lac Quebec
98 C1 Mouchalagane, R Quebec
72 B2 Mouchamps France 46.47N 1.04W
72 E8 Mouchan France 43.54N 0.18E
71 H3 Mouchard France 46.58N 5.48E
69 E2 Mouchin France 50.31N 3.18E
116 J4 Mouchoir Bank West Indies
116 J4 Mouchoir Passage West Indies
83 G5 Moúdhros Greece 39.53N 25.19E
23 B6 Mouding Yunnan China 25.20N 101.33E
74 K10 Moudjbara Algeria 34.30N 3.26E
74 J10 Moudjehaf Algeria 34.39N 1.43E
89 C3 Moudjéria Mauritania 17.51N 12.28W
66 D5 Moudon Switzerland 46.41N 6.48E
71 K9 Mougins France 43.36N 6.59E
72 D3 Mougon France 46.17N 0.16W
90 J4 Mougran Chad 14.16N 19.41E
72 B9 Mouguerre France 43.28N 1.24W
Mouhassane see Muhasan
72 G3 Mouhet France 46.23N 1.26E
Moûh, Sabkhet see Sabkhat Mūh
88 N9 Mouila Algeria 25.56N 0.25W
91 B4 Mouila Gabon 1.50S 11.02E
72 C2 Mouilleron-en-Pareds France 46.41N 0.51W
89 C3 Mouit Mauritania 16.37N 13.11W
90 K8 Mouka Cent Afr Rep 7.16N 21.52E
91 B4 Moukandé, Mts Gabon
91 C5 Moukani Gabon/Congo 2.00S 12.58E
91 C5 Moukassa Congo 3.00S 13.36E
90 F4 Moul Niger 15.05N 13.11E
12 G6 Moulamein New S Wales 35.03S 144.05E
12 G6 Moulamein R New S Wales
89 A1 Moulaouitgat Mauritania 20.15N 16.00W
72 J7 Moularès France 44.04N 2.17E
88 K4 Moulay Bouselham Morocco 35.00N 6.22W
88 L4 Moulay Idriss Morocco 34.04N 5.32W
61 E4 Moulbaix Belgium 50.37N 3.43E
97 H2 Mould Bay N W Terr 76.15N 119.30W
116 N3 Moule Guadeloupe W I 16.20N 61.21W
72 F6 Mouleydier France 44.51N 0.36E
87 J4 Moulhoule Djibouti 12.36N 43.10E
70 M4 Moulicent France 48.33N 0.46E
70 L7 Mouliherne France 47.28N 0.01E
58 J5 Moulin Tayside Scotland 56.43N 3.45W
72 L2 Moulins Allier France 46.34N 3.20E
70 K5 Moulins Sarthe France 48.22N 0.01W
71 D3 Moulins-Engilbert France 47.00N 3.48E
70 L4 Moulins-la-Marche France 48.39N 0.29E
72 H1 Moulins-sur-Cephons France 47.01N 1.33E
72 G10 Moulis Ariège France 42.58N 1.05E
72 C5 Moulis-en-Médoc France 45.03N 0.47W
72 F3 Moulismes France 46.20N 0.48E
72 B6 Moulleau, le France 44.38N 1.12W
72 D9 Moulle, Pic de mt France 43.02N 0.20W
25 D4 Moulmein Burma 16.30N 97.39E
25 C4 Moulmeingyun Burma 16.24N 95.15E
88 M5 Moulouya R Morocco
107 J7 Moulton Alabama 34.28N 87.18W
110 M7 Moulton Idaho 42.01N 113.46W
108 S9 Moulton Iowa 40.40N 92.40W
112 K6 Moulton Texas 29.33N 97.10W
105 D6 Moultrie Georgia 31.11N 83.47W
105 G4 Moultrie, L S Carolina
91 C4 Mounana Gabon 1.18S 13.13E
107 F8 Mound Bayou Mississippi 33.53N 90.45W
107 G4 Mound City Illinois 37.06N 89.09W
109 Q3 Mound City Kansas 38.07N 94.49W
107 A1 Mound City Missouri 40.09N 95.14W
108 K4 Mound City S Dakota 45.44N 100.03W
104 B7 Mound City Nat. Mon Ohio 39.23N 83.01W
90 H7 Moundou Chad 8.35N 16.01E
109 N3 Mound Ridge Kansas 38.12N 97.33W
84 K11 Moúndros Crete 35.17N 24.22E
107 G4 Mounds Illinois 37.07N 89.10W
109 O6 Mounds Oklahoma 35.53N 96.04W
104 E7 Moundsville W Virginia 39.54N 80.44W
109 P4 Mound Valley Kansas 37.12N 95.25W
107 J9 Moundville Alabama 33.00N 87.38W
25 G6 Moung Cambodia 12.47N 103.28E
9 T12 Mo'unga'one atoll Tonga, Pacific Oc 19.44S 174.30W
71 K8 Mounier, Mt France 44.09N 6.59E
15 G9 Mount Adolphus I Torres Str, Qnsld 10.40S 142.38E
103 B6 Mount Aetna Pennsylvania 40.25N 76.18W
108 N1 Mountain N Dakota 48.44N 97.51W
106 F4 Mountain Wisconsin 45.12N 88.28W
104 E7 Mountain W Virginia 39.22N 80.56W
101 J3 Mountain R N W Terr
109 D7 Mountainair New Mexico 34.32N 106.16W
56 E4 Mountain Ash Mid Glam Wales 51.42N 3.24W
110 K8 Mountain City Nevada 41.50N 115.57W
105 F1 Mountain City Tennessee 39.29N 81.49W
112 N9 Mountain Creek L Texas
103 E3 Mountain Dale New York 41.42N 74.32W
109 Q7 Mountain Fork R Oklahoma
107 D4 Mountain Grove Missouri 37.07N 92.18W
107 D5 Mountain Home Arkansas 36.21N 92.23W
110 K6 Mountain Home Idaho 43.09N 115.42W
103 D4 Mountainhome Pennsylvania 41.10N 75.16W
112 H5 Mountain Home Texas 30.11N 99.24W
110 P9 Mountain Home Utah 40.25N 110.24W
105 G2 Mountain Island L N Carolina 35.22N 80.58W
108 Q6 Mountain Lake Minnesota 43.57N 94.55W
103 F5 Mountain Lakes New Jersey 40.53N 74.26W
101 P9 Mountain Park Alberta 52.57N 117.19W
109 M7 Mountain Park Oklahoma 34.44N 98.57W
107 C7 Mountain Pine Arkansas 34.34N 93.11W
103 C4 Mountain Top Pennsylvania 41.10N 75.53W
100 D9 Mountain View Alberta 49.07N 113.33W
107 D6 Mountain View Arkansas 35.51N 92.08W
114 C7 Mountain View Hawaiian Is 19.32N 155.03W
107 E5 Mountain View Missouri 37.00N 91.43W
109 M6 Mountain View Oklahoma 35.06N 98.46W
110 P8 Mountainview Wyoming 41.16N 110.20W
113 F5 Mountain Village Alaska 62.09N 163.49W
103 F4 Mountainville New York 41.24N 74.05W
104 H7 Mount Airy Maryland 39.22N 77.09W
105 G1 Mount Airy N Carolina 36.31N 80.38W
11 C2 Mount Albert bor Auckland New Zealand
95 O5 Mount Alida S Africa 29.10S 30.21E
110 C4 Mount Angel Oregon 45.05N 122.48W
89 E4 Mountan Kagoro Mali 14.11N 9.19W
11 C11 Mount Aspiring Nat. Park New Zealand
100 B8 Mount Assiniboine Prov. Park Alberta/Br Col
Mount Athos see Áyion Óros
107 G2 Mount Auburn Illinois 39.46N 89.12W
14 B6 Mount Augustus W Australia 24.18S 116.55E
95 N6 Mount Ayliff S Africa 30.48S 29.23E
108 Q9 Mount Ayr Iowa 40.43N 94.16W
12 E6 Mount Barker S Australia 35.06S 138.52E
14 C10 Mount Barker W Australia 34.36S 117.37E
14 F3 Mount Barnett W Australia 16.47S 125.51E
12 H6 Mount Beauty Victoria 36.40S 147.10E
59 F5 Mount Bellew Galway Irish Rep 53.28N 8.30W
12 F3 Mount Browne New S Wales 29.45S 141.52E
11 K7 Mount Bruce New Zealand 40.45S 175.36E
99 J10 Mount Brydges Ontario 42.54N 81.30W
13 B2 Mount Bundey N Terr Australia 12.54S 131.40E
112 L4 Mount Calm Texas 31.45N 96.54W
106 F6 Mount Calvary Wisconsin 43.52N 88.16W
13 H3 Mount Carbine Queensland 16.31S 145.07E
98 F6 Mount Carleton Prov. Park New Brunswick
103 J4 Mount Carmel Connecticut 41.24N 72.55W
107 J3 Mount Carmel Illinois 38.25N 87.48W
98 T6 Mount Carmel Newfoundland 47.08N 53.31W
103 B5 Mount Carmel Pennsylvania 40.48N 76.25W
105 E3 Mount Carmel S Carolina 34.01N 82.32W
111 M4 Mount Carmel Utah 37.13N 112.41W
106 E7 Mount Carroll Illinois 42.05N 89.59W
13 C7 Mount Cavenagh N Terr Australia 25.58S 133.12E
14 D8 Mount Celia W Australia 29.25S 122.30E
12 C4 Mount Christie S Australia 30.32S 133.10E
108 M9 Mount Clare Nebraska 40.12N 98.15W
104 E7 Mount Clare W Virginia 39.13N 80.22W
106 M7 Mount Clemens Michigan 42.35N 82.55W
14 C7 Mount Clere W Australia 25.03S 117.33E

12 L5 Mount Colah New S Wales 33.41S 151.07E
11 E10 Mount Cook Nat. Park New Zealand
13 H5 Mount Coolon Queensland 21.26S 147.24E
12 C5 Mount Cooper S Australia 33.05S 134.42E
92 E10 Mount Darwin Zimbabwe 16.45S 31.39E
13 B5 Mount Denison N Terr Australia 22.08S 132.02E
104 R2 Mount Desert I Maine
104 R3 Mount Desert Rock Maine 43.58N 68.08W
105 F9 Mount Dora Florida 28.48N 81.39W
109 G5 Mount Dora New Mexico 36.31N 103.30W
13 B5 Mount Doreen N Terr Australia 22.10S 131.20E
13 H5 Mount Douglas Queensland 21.31S 146.50E
12 D3 Mount Dutton S Australia 27.45S 135.38E
12 D4 Mount Eba S Australia 30.12S 135.33E
13 C7 Mount Ebenezer N Terr Australia 25.14S 132.40E
111 C9 Mount Eden California 37.38N 122.09W
11 C2 Mount Eden bor Auckland New Zealand
113 U8 Mount Edgecumbe Alaska 57.00N 135.24W
101 H7 Mount Edziza Prov. Park Br Col
Mount Elliot see Selwyn
110 P9 Mount Emmons Utah 40.22N 110.16W
13 G5 Mount Emu Plains Queensland 20.05S 143.30E
112 N4 Mount Enterprise Texas 31.56N 94.42W
15 G9 Mount Ernest I Torres Str, Qnsld 10.16S 142.29E
13 C6 Mount Ertwa N Terr Australia 23.45S 133.50E
95 M6 Mount Fletcher S Africa 30.41S 28.30E
99 K9 Mount Forest Ontario 43.58N 80.44W
95 N6 Mount Frere S Africa 30.54S 29.00E
12 F7 Mount Gambier S Australia 37.51S 140.50E
13 H4 Mount Garnet Queensland 17.39S 145.08E
105 G2 Mount Gilead N Carolina 35.13N 80.00W
104 C6 Mount Gilead Ohio 40.33N 82.49W
13 L2 Mount Gravatt dist Brisbane, Qnsld
58 L5 Mounth dist Tayside/Grampian Scotland
15 H6 Mount Hagen Papua New Guinea 5.54S 144.13E
59 H2 Mount Hamilton Tyrone N Ireland 54.47N 7.01W
109 C1 Mount Harris Colorado 40.28N 107.09W
104 F1 Mount Hays dist Baltimore, Md
110 C8 Mount Hebron California 41.47N 122.01W
13 G4 Mount Hogan Queensland 19.09S 143.48E
103 E6 Mount Holly New Jersey 40.00N 74.47W
104 H6 Mount Holly Springs Penn 40.06N 77.14W
109 N4 Mount Hope Kansas 37.52N 97.41W
103 E5 Mount Hope New Jersey 40.56N 74.32W
12 D5 Mount Hope S Australia 34.03S 136.22E
104 D9 Mount Hope W Virginia 37.54N 81.11W
103 M3 Mount Hope B Massachusetts/Rhode I
106 E6 Mount Horeb Wisconsin 43.01N 89.46W
14 F3 Mount House W Australia 17.00S 125.30E
13 F7 Mount Howitt Queensland 26.32S 142.15E
11 F10 Mount Hutt New Zealand 43.31S 171.36E
107 C7 Mount Ida Arkansas 34.32N 93.38W
14 D8 Mount Ida W Australia 29.03S 120.31E
110 J4 Mount Idaho Idaho 45.54N 116.04W
13 E5 Mount Isa Queensland 20.50S 139.29E
104 G8 Mount Jackson Virginia 38.45N 78.40W
104 G5 Mount Jewett Pennsylvania 41.44N 78.38W
103 B6 Mount Joy Pennsylvania 40.07N 76.30W
93 J6 Mount Kenya Nat. Park Kenya
103 G4 Mount Kisco New York 41.13N 73.44W
12 L5 Mount Ku-ring-gai New S Wales 33.40S 151.08E
99 H6 Mount L Ontario 46.41N 82.44W
103 E7 Mount Laurel New Jersey 39.57N 74.57W
26 Q8 Mount Lavinia Sri Lanka 6.50N 79.52E
14 B1 Mount Lawley dist Perth, W Aust
12 E6 Mount Lofty Ra S Australia
13 J5 Mount Lookout Queensland 21.19S 147.49E
13 H5 Mount McConnell Queensland 20.48S 147.00E
113 M5 Mount McKinley Nat. Park Alaska
14 C8 Mount Magnet W Australia 28.06N 117.50E
12 G4 Mount Manara New S Wales 32.28S 143.59E
13 G6 Mount Marlow Queensland 25.00S 143.45E
11 L4 Mount Maunganui New Zealand 37.38S 176.12E
110 E9 Mount Meadows Res California 40.18N 120.58W
59 H5 Mountmellick Leix Irish Rep 53.07N 7.20W
13 H3 Mount Molloy Queensland 16.37S 145.23E
111 F4 Mount Montgomery Nevada 37.59N 118.20W
13 K6 Mount Morgan Queensland 23.40S 150.25E
107 C1 Mount Moriah Missouri 40.20N 93.48W
106 E7 Mount Morris Illinois 42.03N 89.26W
104 H4 Mount Morris New York 42.44N 77.51W
104 H4 Mount Morris Res New York
13 G3 Mount Mulligan Queensland 16.50S 144.56E
12 G4 Mount Murchison New S Wales 31.23S 143.42E
103 B7 Mount Nebo Pennsylvania 39.53N 76.19W
12 F8 Mount Nelson dist Hobart, Tasmania
14 C6 Mount Newman W Australia 23.20S 119.39E
13 C1 Mount Norris B N Terr Australia
107 G2 Mount Olive Illinois 39.04N 89.44W
107 G10 Mount Olive Mississippi 31.46N 89.40W
105 J2 Mount Olive N Carolina 35.12N 78.08W
107 M3 Mount Olivet Kentucky 38.32N 84.01W
104 B7 Mount Orab Ohio 39.03N 83.56W
99 S7 Mount Orford, Parc de Quebec
13 C5 Mount Peake N Terr Australia 21.45S 132.45E
103 C6 Mount Penn Pennsylvania 40.19N 75.53W
13 K7 Mount Perry Queensland 25.11S 151.40E
13 E5 Mount Philip Queensland 21.10S 139.47E
106 C9 Mount Pleasant Iowa 40.58N 91.34W
106 K6 Mount Pleasant Michigan 43.36N 84.46W
105 K9 Mount Pleasant New Providence I Bahamas 25.02N 77.31W
104 F6 Mount Pleasant Pennsylvania 40.09N 79.33W
12 E5 Mount Pleasant S Australia 34.47S 139.01E
105 H5 Mount Pleasant S Carolina 32.48N 79.54W
107 J6 Mount Pleasant Tennessee 35.32N 87.11W
112 N2 Mount Pleasant Texas 33.10N 94.59W
111 N2 Mount Pleasant Utah 39.33N 111.29W
11 N10 Mount Pleasant dist Christchurch New Zealand
103 D4 Mount Pocono Pennsylvania 41.08N 75.22W
95 N3 Mount Prospect S Africa 27.30S 29.52E
106 E9 Mount Pulaski Illinois 40.01N 89.19W
104 N8 Mount Rainier Maryland 38.57N 76.58W
110 D3 Mount Rainier Nat. Park Washington
59 H5 Mountrath Leix Irish Rep 53.00N 7.28W
101 O10 Mount Revelstoke Nat. Park Br Columbia
103 G3 Mount Riga New York 41.59N 73.31W
109 C10 Mount Riley New Mexico 31.50N 107.06W
11 C2 Mount Roskill bor Auckland New Zealand
103 D7 Mount Royal New Jersey 39.48N 75.13W
95 H4 Mount Rupert S Africa 28.10S 24.29E
108 G6 Mount Rushmore Nat. Mem S Dakota 43.52N 103.41W
13 B3 Mount Sanford N Terr Australia 17.00S 130.34E
104 G7 Mount Savage Maryland 39.41N 78.53W
56 T9 Mount's B Cornwall Eng
112 M3 Mount Selman Texas 32.03N 95.17W
101 H10 Mount Seymour Prov. Park Br Columbia
59 F6 Mountshannon Clare Irish Rep 52.56N 8.26W
110 C8 Mount Shasta California 41.19N 122.20W
11 F10 Mount Somers New Zealand 43.43S 171.24E
56 J2 Mountsorrel Leics Eng 52.44N 1.07W
13 C7 Mount Squires N Terr Australia 25.10S 134.28E
107 F2 Mount Sterling Illinois 39.59N 90.49W
104 B8 Mount Sterling Kentucky 38.03N 83.56W
104 B7 Mount Sterling Ohio 39.43N 83.17W
98 K7 Mount Stewart Prince Edward I 46.22N 62.52W
95 H9 Mount Stewart S Africa 33.10S 24.26E
104 F7 Mount Storm W Virginia 39.16N 79.15W
13 G5 Mount Sturgeon Queensland 20.08S 144.00E
13 G4 Mount Surprise Queensland 18.10S 144.20E
13 D6 Mount Swan N Terr Australia 22.31S 135.00E
103 F2 Mount Tremper New York 42.02N 74.17W
111 L5 Mount Trumbull Arizona 36.26N 113.20W
98 J9 Mount Uniacke Nova Scotia 44.54N 63.50W
106 C8 Mount Union Iowa 41.02N 91.23W
104 H6 Mount Union Pennsylvania 40.23N 77.54W
103 D2 Mount Upton New York 42.25N 72.54W
107 J10 Mount Vernon Alabama 31.05N 88.00W
107 D6 Mount Vernon Arkansas 35.12N 92.07W
105 E5 Mount Vernon Georgia 32.11N 82.56W
107 H3 Mount Vernon Illinois 38.19N 88.52W
107 J4 Mount Vernon Indiana 37.55N 87.55W
106 C8 Mount Vernon Iowa 41.56N 91.26W
107 M4 Mount Vernon Kentucky 37.20N 84.20W
107 C4 Mount Vernon Missouri 37.05N 93.49W
103 N6 Mount Vernon New York 40.54N 73.50W
110 F5 Mount Vernon Oregon 44.26N 119.06W
108 M6 Mount Vernon S Dakota 43.42N 98.15W
112 M2 Mount Vernon Texas 33.12N 95.15W
104 H8 Mount Vernon Virginia 38.43N 77.07W
110 C1 Mount Vernon Washington 48.25N 122.20W
14 C6 Mount Vernon W Australia 24.09S 118.10E
104 B6 Mount Victory Ohio 40.32N 83.32W
103 B6 Mountville Pennsylvania 40.02N 76.26W
12 D4 Mount Vivian S Australia 30.38S 135.40E
103 H2 Mount Washington Massachusetts 42.07N 73.28W
12 E8 Mount Waverley dist Melbourne, Vic
12 D5 Mount Wedge S Australia 33.30S 135.08E
11 D2 Mount Wellington bor Auckland New Zealand
107 K9 Mount Willing Alabama 32.03N 86.41W
12 C3 Mount Willoughby S Australia 27.55S 134.06E
103 A6 Mount Wolf Pennsylvania 40.04N 76.42W
14 B1 Mount Yokine dist Perth, W Aust
107 H2 Mount Zion Illinois 39.46N 88.52W
106 C9 Mount Zion Iowa 40.46N 91.55W
35 B1 Mount Zion dist Jerusalem
119 H8 Moura Brazil 1.32S 61.38W
76 E12 Moura Portugal 38.08N 7.27W
13 J6 Moura Queensland 24.35S 149.57E
76 E12 Mourão Portugal 38.22N 7.20W
120 C2 Moura, R Brazil
61 D4 Mourcourt Belgium 50.39N 3.27E
89 F4 Mourdiah Mali 14.35N 7.25W
90 L2 Mourdi, Dépression du Chad
76 B15 Mourelinho Portugal 38.49N 9.25W
72 C9 Mourenx France 43.26N 0.39W
Mourhr see Mughur
Mourhr Chebaâ see Mughur Shab'a
90 G9 Mouri Cent Afr Rep 5.30N 14.40E
71 F9 Mouriès France 43.41N 4.52E
84 F5 Mourikion Greece 38.25N 23.21E
76 D5 Mourilhe Portugal 41.50N 7.50W
13 H4 Mourilyan Harbour Queensland 17.32S 146.07E
72 H3 Mourioux France 46.05N 1.37E
76 B11 Mourisca Portugal 38.32N 8.48W
76 C10 Mouriscas Portugal 39.30N 8.06W
69 G5 Mourmelon, Camp de France
69 G5 Mourmelon-le-Grand France 49.08N 4.21E
90 L5 Mournei Sudan 12.59N 22.55E
59 G2 Mourne, L Donegal Irish Rep 54.45N 7.54W
59 K3 Mourne Mts Down N Ireland
59 H2 Mourne, R Tyrone N Ireland
84 K11 Mourniés Crete 35.29N 24.00E
75 C1 Mouro isld Spain 43.29N 3.45W
76 C8 Mouronho Portugal 40.17N 8.03W
26 V15 Mourouvin, Forêt Réunion Ind Oc
90 K5 Mourra Chad 13.47N 21.13E
89 G4 Mourrari Mali 14.21N 4.40W
71 J9 Mourre-de-Chanier mt France 43.50N 6.22E
58 Q9 Mousa isld Shetland Scotland 60.00N 1.10W
88 L5 Mousaaou Salah, Jbel mt Morocco 33.50N 4.06W
61 C4 Mouscron Belgium 50.44N 3.14E
108 J1 Mouse R N Dakota
56 S9 Mousehole Cornwall Eng 50.05N 5.33W
15 J5 Mouse I Bismarck Arch 2.53S 146.24E
90 G6 Mousgoum Chad 10.59N 15.00E
Mouslimiyé see Muslimiya
90 H3 Moussa Chad 16.51N 16.49E
71 E9 Moussac France 43.59N 4.14E
72 F3 Moussac Vienne France 46.17N 0.42E
91 C5 Moussanga Congo 3.54S 12.58E
Mousseifré see Museifre
85 A8 Mousselimi, Er Roui mts Niger
69 M6 Moussey Moselle France 48.40N 6.47E
69 N7 Moussey Vosges France 48.25N 7.00E
90 J3 Mousso Chad 17.59N 19.54E
90 H5 Moussoro Chad 13.41N 16.31E
72 J9 Moussoulens France 43.17N 2.14E
70 D4 Mousterus France 48.32N 3.14W
72 C7 Moustey France 44.22N 0.45W
61 E4 Moustier Hainaut Belgium 50.39N 3.37E
61 J5 Moustier Namur Belgium 50.28N 4.42E
71 J9 Moustiers-Ste.Marie France 43.50N 6.13E
57 G2 Mouswold Dumfries & Galloway Scotland 55.02N 3.28W
91 C5 Moutamba Congo 3.10S 12.59E
Moutbîne see Mutbin
69 N6 Mouterhouse France 48.59N 7.27E
71 J3 Mouthe France 46.44N 6.14E
71 G3 Mouthier-en-Bresse France 46.51N 5.22E
71 J2 Mouthier-Haute-Pierre France 47.03N 6.16E
72 E4 Mouthiers-sur-Boëme France 45.34N 0.08E
72 K10 Mouthoumet France 42.57N 2.32E
66 F2 Moutier Switzerland 47.18N 7.23E
72 H3 Moutier Malcard France 46.23N 1.56E
72 J4 Moutier-Rozeille France 45.56N 2.11E
71 K6 Moûtiers France 45.29N 6.32E
70 M5 Moutiers-au-Perche France 48.29N 0.51E
72 B3 Moutiers-les-Mauxfaits France 46.30N 1.26W
11 M5 Moutohora New Zealand 38.18S 177.32E
19 B3 Moutong Celebes Indon 0.30N 121.15E
98 H10 Mouton I Nova Scotia 43.55N 64.46W
84 Q15 Moutoullas Cyprus 35.00N 32.50E
72 K9 Moux Aude France 43.11N 2.39E
71 E2 Moux Nièvre France 47.10N 4.08E
69 C5 Mouy France 49.19N 2.20E
88 P9 Mouydir reg Algeria
89 B4 Mouye Senegal 15.31N 15.38W
91 D6 Mouyondzi Congo 4.01S 13.59E
84 C6 Mouzáki Ilía Greece 37.47N 21.34E
84 C3 Mouzáki Kardhítsa Greece 39.25N 21.40E
84 A6 Mouzáki Zákinthos Greece 37.44N 20.49E
69 J5 Mouzay France 49.28N 5.13E
72 F6 Mouzens France 44.51N 1.00E
69 J4 Mouzon France 49.36N 5.05E
115 E3 Movas Mexico 28.10N 109.27W
53 U15 Movatn L Norway 61.59N 6.12E
66 F2 Movelier Switzerland 47.25N 7.20E
53 R18 Movik Norway 60.19N 5.00E
59 H1 Moville Donegal Irish Rep 55.11N 7.03W
108 O7 Moville Iowa 42.30N 96.05W
29 F7 Mowar Maharashtra India 21.27N 78.31E
13 K7 Mowbullan, Mt Queensland 26.55S 151.33E
107 H2 Moweaqua Illinois 39.38N 89.00W
11 J6 Mowhanau New Zealand 39.52S 174.52E
110 D6 Mowich Oregon 43.23N 121.49W
34 O3 Mowlānābād Iran 35.58N 46.29E
58 M5 Mowtie Grampian Scotland 56.59N 2.16W
110 E3 Moxee City Washington 46.35N 120.23W
61 L4 Moxhe Belgium 50.37N 5.05E
91 G9 Moxico Angola 11.50S 20.03E
91 F10 Moxico dist Angola
117 H9 Moxotó, R Brazil
58 H4 Moy Highland Scotland 57.23N 4.04W
59 J3 Moy Monaghan Irish Rep 54.24N 6.59W
59 J3 Moy Tyrone N Ireland 54.27N 6.42W
75 P4 Moya Barcelona Spain 41.48N 2.06E
75 H8 Moya Cuenca Spain 39.58N 1.23W
96 U15 Moya Gran Canaria Canary Is 28.07N 15.34W
14 C8 Moyagee W Australia 27.27S 117.53E
115 H7 Moyahua Mexico 21.18N 103.09W
93 L2 Moyale Kenya 3.31N 39.04E
93 L2 Moyale dist Kenya
89 C7 Moyamba Sierra Leone 8.04N 12.30W
28 C5 Moyar R Tamil Nadu India
59 C6 Moyasta Clare Irish Rep 52.40N 9.34W
70 L3 Moyaux France 49.11N 0.21E
58 G3 Moy Bridge Highland Scotland 57.33N 4.34W
59 D5 Moycullen Galway Irish Rep 53.20N 9.10W
47 E3 Moyda U.S.S.R. 66.18N 41.45E
69 E4 Moy-de-l'Aisne France 49.46N 3.22E
21 B9 Moye Dao isld Shandong China
88 K5 Moyen Atlas mts Morocco
90 J7 Moyen Chari dist Chad
69 M7 Moyenmoutier France 48.23N 6.55E
26 S13 Moyenne I Mahé I Seychelles, Ind Oc 4.36S 55.30E
69 B3 Moyenneville France 50.05N 1.45E
91 A4 Moyen-Ogooué reg Gabon
69 M6 Moyenvic France 48.47N 6.34E
41 H6 Moyero R U.S.S.R.
69 L5 Moyeuvre-Grande France 49.15N 6.03E
42 G6 Moygoty U.S.S.R. 51.40N 101.15E
101 Q11 Moyie Br Col 49.15N 115.50W
110 K1 Moyie R Br Columbia
110 J1 Moyie Springs Idaho 48.43N 116.11W
59 E5 Moylough Galway Irish Rep 53.30N 8.34W
59 J4 Moynalty Meath Irish Rep 53.48N 6.53W
42 F6 Moynalyk U.S.S.R. 51.21N 95.32E
59 G4 Moyne Longford Irish Rep 53.55N 7.38W
59 D3 Moyne Abbey Mayo Irish Rep 54.14N 9.12W
93 C2 Moyo Uganda 3.38N 31.43E
91 K5 Moyo Zaïre 3.20S 26.28E
18 M10 Moyo isld Indonesia
120 B2 Moyobamba Peru 6.04S 76.56W
93 C9 Moyowosi R Tanzania
41 J7 Moypere, Ozero L U.S.S.R. 65.30N 109.55E
59 D3 Moy,R Mayo Irish Rep
90 H5 Moyto Chad 12.35N 16.33E
24 C7 Moyu Xinjiang Uygur Zizhiqu China 37.17N 79.43E
75 J5 Moyuéla Spain 41.07N 0.55W
59 J5 Moyvalley Kildare Irish Rep 53.26N 6.55W
59 G4 Moyvore W Meath Irish Rep 53.33N 7.39W
59 G5 Moyvoughly W Meath Irish Rep 53.26N 7.42W
41 O7 Moy-Yuryakh U.S.S.R. 65.56N 131.19E
35 A1 Moza sub Jerusalem
73 H8 Mozambique terr S E Africa
73 J7 Mozambique Channel Madagascar/Mozambique
26 C9 Mozambique Ridge Indian Oc
76 H7 Mozárbez Spain 40.50N 5.40W
44 F4 Mozdok U.S.S.R. 43.45N 44.43E
32 J2 Mozdūrān Iran 36.15N 60.34E
61 K5 Mozet Belgium 50.27N 4.59E
99 H6 Mozhabong L Ontario 46.56N 82.05W
42 E5 Mozharka U.S.S.R. 54.01N 93.20E
45 N3 Mozhary U.S.S.R. 53.53N 41.02E
45 L8 Mozhayevka U.S.S.R. 48.43N 39.45E
45 H1 Mozhaysk U.S.S.R. 55.29N 36.02E
46 Q2 Mozhga U.S.S.R. 56.25N 52.10E
32 J3 Mozhnābād Iran 34.05N 60.09E
25 C1 Mozo Burma 22.34N 94.08E
76 L6 Mozoncillo Spain 41.09N 4.10W
46 G4 Mozyr' Belorussiya U.S.S.R. 52.02N 29.10E
79 E3 Mozzate Italy 45.41N 8.52E
79 J4 Mozzecane Italy 45.19N 10.49E
92 J5 Mpakani Tanzania 7.10S 39.30E
92 D5 Mpala Zaïre 6.46S 29.30E
93 B7 Mpalo Uganda 1.08S 30.03E
91 D4 Mpama R Congo
92 E5 Mpanda Tanzania 6.21S 31.01E
92 J5 Mpanganya Tanzania 7.57S 38.41E
93 C5 Mparo Uganda 0.24N 31.02E
91 D5 Mpé Congo 2.58S 14.38E
93 M8 Mpekatoni Kenya 2.27S 40.42E
28 L2 Mpen Assam India 27.30N 96.16E
93 D5 Mpenja Uganda 0.14N 32.04E
91 D6 Mpese Zaïre 5.16S 15.30E
95 M8 Mpetu S Africa 32.39S 28.09E
92 C12 Mphoengs Zimbabwe 21.10S 27.51E
29 F7 Mphpa Maharashtra India 21.21N 78.49E
29 K6 Mphuda Bihar India 23.42N 86.18E
93 D5 Mpigi Uganda 0.14N 32.19E
92 E7 Mpika Zambia 11.50S 31.30E
92 G7 Mpitimbi Tanzania 10.55S 35.31E
91 F5 Mpoko Zaïre 3.35S 18.03E
90 J9 M'Poko R Cent Afr Rep
92 F8 Mponela Malawi 13.32S 33.45E
92 E6 Mporokoso Zambia 9.22S 30.06E
95 O10 Mposa S Africa 28.38S 32.04E
91 E5 Mpouya Congo 2.38S 16.13E
89 J8 Mpraeso Ghana 6.36N 0.43W
93 C6 Mpugwe Uganda 0.14S 31.51E
92 E6 Mpui Tanzania 8.20S 31.50E
92 E6 Mpulungu Zambia 8.50S 31.06E
95 M8 Mpuluswa S Africa 32.14S 28.14E
92 H7 Mpurukasese Tanzania 10.11S 36.30E
91 J9 Mputu Zaïre 10.12S 24.22E
92 H5 Mpwapwa Tanzania 6.23S 36.38E
84 Y20 Mqabba Malta 35.51N 14.28E
95 M7 Mqanduli S Africa 31.49S 28.45E
62 N2 Mragowo Poland 53.53N 21.19E
89 H2 Mraiti, El Mali 19.15N 2.20W
43 D1 Mrakovo Bashkir U.S.S.R. 52.45N 56.38E
47 M5 Mramorskiy U.S.S.R. 56.34N 60.26E
42 D5 Mras-Su R U.S.S.R.
34 C5 Mreffi, Harfel mt Lebanon 33.57N 35.54E
86 E4 Mreir, Gebel hill Egypt 30.31N 30.37E
88 K10 Mreiti, El Mauritania 23.29N 7.53W
92 E10 Mrewa Zimbabwe 17.38S 31.46E
92 E10 Mrewa dist Zimbabwe
88 J11 Mreyer, El Mauritania 21.35N 8.05W
89 J2 Mrezzig Mali 18.29N 1.52W
115 K4 M. R. Gómez, Presa res Mexico
88 M6 Mrheimine Morocco 31.09N 3.36W
92 H4 Mrijo Tanzania 5.10S 36.17E
93 L10 Mrima Kenya 4.28S 39.17E
88 L5 Mrirt Morocco 33.10N 5.38W
82 D6 Mrkonjič Grad Yugoslavia 44.26N 17.04E
62 J5 Mrlina R Czechoslovakia
62 K2 Mrocza Poland 53.16N 17.34E
62 D4 Mruvila Tanzania 4.54S 29.55E
62 J1 Mrzeżyno Poland 54.07N 15.17E
92 H5 Msagali Tanzania 6.25S 36.21E
88 T4 Msaken Tunisia 35.45N 10.33E
92 G4 Msalalo Tanzania 5.57S 34.24E
92 H5 Msanga Tanzania 6.01S 36.04E
92 J4 Msangasi R Tanzania
95 P8 Mseleni S Africa 27.23S 32.32E
62 H5 Mšeno Czechoslovakia 50.27N 14.40E
84 Y20 Msida Malta 35.54N 14.30E
84 Y20 Msierah Malta 35.54N 14.29E
88 Q4 M'Sila Algeria 35.40N 4.31E
92 J5 Msindaji Tanzania 7.38S 39.16E
95 O6 Msinsini S Africa 30.30S 30.32E
88 L6 Msissi Morocco 31.12N 4.50W
92 E10 Msonedi Zimbabwe 17.08S 30.57E
92 E8 Msoro Zambia 13.35S 31.53E
88 M4 Msoun Morocco 34.21N 3.43W
92 H5 Msowero Tanzania 6.33S 37.13E
46 H1 Msta R U.S.S.R.
45 N1 Mstera U.S.S.R. 56.22N 41.56E
45 C2 Mstislavl' Belorussiya U.S.S.R. 54.02N 31.44E
92 J4 Msuka B Pemba I
62 M4 Mszczonów Poland 51.59N 20.32E
93 K10 Mtai Tanzania 4.30S 38.14E
Mtaié see Muta'iyah
92 G9 Mtakataka Malawi 14.14S 34.32E
92 E5 Mtakuja Tanzania 7.21S 30.37E
94 L6 Mtambama Mt Swaziland 26.50S 31.29E
92 E5 Mtambo R Tanzania
95 N6 Mtamvuna R S Africa
92 J6 Mtandi Tanzania 9.29S 39.25E
92 H5 Mtandika Tanzania 7.32S 36.25E
92 J6 Mtandura Tanzania 9.10S 39.32E
93 C10 Mtani watercourse Tanzania
92 F11 Mtarazi Falls Zimbabwe 18.36S 32.42E
95 M7 Mtata R S Africa
92 H5 Mtegere Tanzania 7.39S 37.35E
88 T3 M. Temime Tunisia 36.47N 10.58E
92 K12 Mtende Zanzibar 6.27S 39.32E
77 G10 M'ter R Morocco
92 G5 Mtera Tanzania 7.06S 35.56E
92 E12 Mtilikwe R Zimbabwe
93 K8 Mtito Andei Kenya 2.41S 38.10E
13 G6 Mt Marlow Queensland 24.59S 143.30E
92 F10 Mtoko Zimbabwe 17.25S 32.14E
92 F10 Mtoko dist Zimbabwe
93 L9 Mtondia Kenya 3.34S 39.52E
92 J6 Mtondo Tanzania 9.30S 38.20E
93 G8 Mtowabaga Tanzania 2.32S 35.53E
59 G6 Mt St Joseph Abbey Offaly Irish Rep 52.58N 7.45W
45 H3 Mtsensk U.S.S.R. 53.18N 36.35E
44 F6 Mtskheta Georgia U.S.S.R. 41.50N 44.43E
92 J7 Mtua Tanzania 10.12S 39.30E
95 P9 Mtubatuba S Africa 28.25S 32.11E
92 D8 Mtuga Zambia 13.52S 29.10E
95 O10 Mtunzini S Africa 28.58S 31.46E
95 O6 Mtwalume S Africa 30.30S 30.38E
93 L9 Mtwapa Kenya 3.56S 39.44E
93 L9 Mtwapa Creek Kenya
92 K7 Mtwara Tanzania 10.17S 40.11E
92 H6 Mtwara reg Tanzania
104 E1 Mt. Washington dist Baltimore, Md
76 C14 Mu mt Portugal 37.22N 8.05W
25 M9 Mu R Burma
9 S10 Mu'a Tonga, Pacific Oc 21.11S 175.07W
92 J8 Muaguide Mozambique 12.25S 40.00E
93 J7 Mua Hills Kenya
92 J10 Mualama Mozambique 16.53S 38.16E
18 J5 Mualang Borneo Indon 0.44N 111.19E
35 G2 Mu'allagah Syria 32.55N 35.53E
92 J7 Mualo R Mozambique
92 E8 Muamadzi R Zambia
117 D5 Muana Brazil 1.30S 49.15W
70 K3 Muance R France
92 G10 Muandiua Mozambique 17.05S 35.43E
25 G6 Muang Cambodia 13.46N 103.33E
91 F10 Muangai Angola 12.32S 19.55E
91 F10 Muangangia Angola 13.33S 18.04E
25 F4 Muang Botene Thailand 17.34N 101.09E
25 H5 Muang Bua Thailand 14.32N 104.19E
25 F5 Muang Chainat Thailand 15.20N 100.21E
25 F3 Muang Chaiyaphum Thailand 19.02N 100.48E
25 G5 Muang Cha Tao Thailand 15.48N 103.35E
25 F4 Muang Chiang Khan Thailand 17.53N 101.34E
25 E3 Muang Chiang Rai Thailand 19.56N 99.51E
Muang Fang see Fang
25 G4 Muang Kalasin Thailand 16.21N 103.32E
Muang Kansin see Muang Kalasin
25 G4 Muang Khon Kaen Thailand 16.25N 102.50E
25 E4 Muang Kosamphi Thailand 16.50N 99.28E
25 G4 Muang Kuk Thailand 17.47N 102.38E
25 E3 Muang Lampang Thailand 18.16N 99.30E
25 E3 Muang Lamphun Thailand 18.36N 99.02E
25 F4 Muang Loei Thailand 17.32N 101.40E
25 F4 Muang Lom Sak Thailand 16.47N 101.13E
25 E3 Muang Long Thailand 18.05N 99.50E
25 H5 Muang Mai Thailand 15.17N 105.22E
25 H4 Muang Nakhon Phanom Thailand 17.22N 104.45E
25 F5 Muang Nakhon Sawan Thailand 15.42N 100.04E
25 F3 Muang Nan Thailand 18.47N 100.50E
25 E3 Muang Ngao Thailand 18.45N 99.58E
25 F3 Muang Oi Thailand 19.14N 100.20E
25 H4 Muang Phaluka Thailand 16.40N 104.45E
25 E3 Muang Phan Thailand 19.34N 99.44E
25 G4 Muang Phannanikhom Thailand 17.20N 103.48E
25 E3 Muang Phayao Thailand 19.10N 99.55E
25 F4 Muang Phetchabun Thailand 16.25N 101.08E
25 F4 Muang Phichai Thailand 17.18N 100.04E
25 F4 Muang Phichit Thailand 16.29N 100.21E
25 F4 Muang Phitsanulok Thailand 16.50N 100.15E
Muang Phon see Ban Muang Phon
25 F3 Muang Phrae Thailand 18.07N 100.09E
25 H4 Muang Renu Nakhon Thailand 17.05N 104.32E
25 G4 Muang Roi Et Thailand 16.05N 103.38E
25 H4 Muang Sakon Nakhon Thailand 17.10N 104.08E
25 H5 Muang Sam Sip Thailand 15.32N 104.43E
25 F6 Muang Samut Prakan Thailand 13.32N 100.35E
25 G5 Muang Si Chalalai Thailand 15.25N 103.59E
25 G4 Muang Song Badan Thailand 16.48N 103.40E
25 E4 Muang Thoen Thailand 17.43N 99.12E
25 F3 Muang Thong Laos 18.25N 101.10E
Muang Ubon see Ubon Ratchathani
25 F5 Muang Uthai Thani Thailand 15.22N 100.03E
25 H5 Muang Yasothon Thailand 15.45N 104.08E
92 G11 Muanza Mozambique 18.50S 34.50E
94 N2 Muanza Mozambique 18.45S 34.55E
18 C10 Muar Pen Malaysia 2.01N 102.35E
18 C10 Muar R Pen Malaysia
18 L3 Muara Brunei Malaysia 5.01N 115.01E
18 D6 Muara Sumatra Indon 0.42S 101.00E
18 E7 Muaraäman Sumatra Indon 3.01S 102.12E
18 M5 Muara Ancalung Borneo Indon 0.25N 116.39E
18 M5 Muaraätan Borneo Indon 0.50N 116.30E
18 E7 Muarabeliti Sumatra Indon 3.17S 103.02E
18 L6 Muarabenangin Borneo Indon 0.58S 115.18E
18 F9 Muarabinuangeun Java Indon 6.49S 105.52E
18 E6 Muarabungo Sumatra Indonesia 1.28S 102.06E
18 F8 Muaradua Sumatra Indon 4.32S 104.09E
18 E7 Muaraenim Sumatra Indon 3.40S 103.48E
18 M5 Muaragusung Borneo Indon 1.30N 117.13E
18 L6 Muarajuloi Borneo Indon 0.13S 114.02E
18 F6 Muarakumpe Sumatra Indon 1.21S 104.01E
18 D6 Muaralabuh Sumatra Indon 1.32S 101.05E
18 E7 Muaralakitan Sumatra Indon 2.46S 103.22E
18 M5 Muaralasan Kalimantan Indonesia 1.37N 117.10E
18 M5 Muaramawai Borneo Indon 0.31N 116.47E
18 M4 Muarapangean Borneo Indon 2.42N 116.44E
18 L6 Muarapayang Borneo Indon 1.32S 115.47E
18 L7 Muarapulau Borneo Indon 2.46S 114.43E
18 E7 Muararupit Sumatra Indon 2.44S 102.58E
18 E6 Muarasabak Sumatra Indon 1.08S 103.48E
18 C6 Muarasiberut Indonesia 1.36S 99.12E
18 C5 Muarasoma Sumatra Indon 0.44N 99.16E
18 N5 Muaras Reef Indonesia
18 B4 Muarasukon Sumatra Indon 3.34N 96.58E
18 E6 Muaratebo Sumatra Indon 1.28S 102.28E
18 E6 Muaratembesi Sumatra Indon 1.40S 103.08E
18 L6 Muarateweh Borneo Indon 0.58S 114.52E
18 J5 Muara Tuang Sarawak Malaysia 1.25N 110.30E
18 L6 Muaratuhup Borneo Indon 0.36S 114.47E
18 M6 Muaratunan Borneo Indon 1.24S 116.37E
18 M5 Muarawahau Borneo Indon 1.02N 116.49E
19 E4 Muari isld Moluccas Indon 0.14S 127.06E
31 D8 Muari, Ras C Pakistan 24.45N 66.40E
86 F8 Muathîl, Wâdi watercourse Egypt
92 J9 Muatua Mozambique 15.41S 39.40E
34 L4 Muayjir Iraq 34.18N 43.50E
33 C2 Mu'ayzilah, Al Saudi Arabia 29.46N 38.08E
34 F9 Mu'ayzilah, Al hill Saudi Arabia 29.47N 38.07E
29 D2 Muazzam Punjab India 30.30N 74.00E
Mubarabad see Moradabad
Mubarakabad see Mobārakābād
86 O7 Mubārak, Jabal mt Jordan/Saudi Arabia 29.19N 35.13E
30 G6 Mubarakpur Uttar Prad India 26.06N 83.18E
33 A4 Mubarak, Wâdi watercourse Egypt
33 D2 Mubarraz Saudi Arabia 29.43N 40.32E
33 H4 Mubarraz, Al Saudi Arabia 25.26N 49.37E
33 K4 Mubarraz, Al oil field The Gulf 23.34N 53.40E
93 C5 Mubende Uganda 0.35N 31.24E
90 F6 Mubi Nigeria 10.16N 13.17E
35 G5 Mubis Jordan 32.06N 35.53E
34 C8 Mubrak, Jebel mt Jordan 30.12N 35.27E
15 B4 Mubrani Irian Jaya 0.45S 133.25E
80 O1 Muc Yugoslavia 43.43N 16.30E
92 J8 Mucacata Mozambique 13.23S 39.47E
117 A6 Mucajá Brazil 3.54S 57.29W
119 H6 Mucajaí, R Brazil
119 H6 Mucajaí, Sa. do hills Brazil
91 E10 Mucandombe Angola 12.02S 17.50E
91 E8 Mucanona Angola 8.13S 17.39E
14 C5 Muccan W Australia 20.40S 120.00E
80 H2 Muccia Italy 43.05N 13.02E
64 C2 Much W Germany 50.55N 7.25E
58 M4 Muchalls Grampian Scotland 57.02N 2.10W
77 Q4 Muchamiel Spain 38.25N 0.26W
56 F4 Much Birch Hereford & Worcs Eng 51.59N 2.44W
14 B9 Muchea W Australia 31.36S 115.57E
64 M1 Mücheln E Germany 51.18N 11.48E
92 F9 Muchena Mozambique 15.40S 33.44E
56 M4 Much Hadham Herts Eng 51.52N 0.04E
91 C7 Muchicongo tribe Angola
40 B5 Muchikan U.S.S.R. 53.08N 120.25E
92 E8 Muchinga Escarpment Zambia
120 F8 Muchiri Bolivia 19.05S 63.25W
45 O5 Muchkapskiy U.S.S.R. 51.51N 42.29E
47 F4 Muchkas U.S.S.R. 64.04N 48.30E
31 F4 Much Pai Khel Pakistan 32.43N 71.35E
23 C4 Muchuan Sichuan China 28.57N 103.55E
56 F2 Much Wenlock Shropshire Eng 52.36N 2.34W
76 K5 Mucientes Spain 41.44N 4.46W
76 B15 Mucifal Portugal 38.48N 9.27W
58 D5 Muck isld Highland Scotland 56.50N 6.14W
13 J7 Muckadilla Queensland 26.35S 148.20E
64 F2 Mücke W Germany 50.35N 9.00E
63 T10 Mückenberg E Germany 51.28N 13.45E
59 G1 Muckish Mt Donegal Irish Rep 55.06N 7.49W
58 R8 Muckle Flugga isld Shetland Scotland 60.51N 0.54W
58 Q9 Muckle Roe isld Shetland Scotland 60.22N 1.26W
59 J3 Muckno L Monaghan Irish Rep 54.06N 6.41W
59 E2 Muckros Hd Donegal Irish Rep 54.36N 8.35W
92 K8 Mucojo Mozambique 12.05S 40.30E
95 P8 Mucomaze Mozambique 26.45S 32.50E
81 M5 Mucone R Italy
91 G8 Mucongola Angola 9.59S 21.33E
91 D12 Mucope Angola 16.24S 14.52E
94 N3 Mucoque Mozambique 21.59S 35.20E
119 E5 Muco, R Colombia
92 H10 Mucubela Mozambique 16.53S 37.49E
119 E3 Mucuchíes Venezuela 8.50N 70.58W
119 H7 Mucucuaú, R Brazil
118 H3 Mucugê Brazil 12.59S 41.22W
120 F2 Mucuim, R Brazil
117 F6 Mucunambiba, I Brazil 2.23S 43.35W
26 Q4 Mucunkan Sri Lanka 8.47N 80.02E
94 O2 Mucupia Mozambique 18.00S 36.42E
36 G3 Mucur Turkey 39.05N 34.25E
119 H9 Mucura Brazil 2.30S 62.41W
118 H6 Mucuri Brazil 18.05S 39.36W
119 E9 Mucuripe Brazil 2.51N 69.27W
117 H6 Mucuripe, Pta de C Brazil 3.43S 38.31W
118 H6 Mucuri, R Brazil
91 G12 Mucusso Angola 18.00S 21.24E
91 G12 Mucusso tribe Angola
91 G9 Mucussueje Angola 10.58S 21.58E
93 E2 Mucwini Uganda 3.26N 33.02E
Mud see Mūd-e-Dahanāb
92 G11 Muda Mozambique 19.23S 34.24E
18 E5 Muda isld Sumatra Indon 0.15N 120.50E
96 T9 Muda mt Fuerteventura Canary Is 28.34N 13.52W
18 D3 Muda R Pen Malaysia
33 N5 Mudaibi, Al Oman 22.35N 58.08E
33 N5 Mudairib, Al Oman 22.36N 58.38E
35 G7 Mudaiyina anc site Jordan 31.35N 35.54E
21 E5 Mudanjiang Heilongjiang China 44.36N 129.42E
21 E5 Mudan Jiang R Heilongjiang China
37 F2 Mudanya Turkey 40.23N 28.53E
37 G1 Mudarlı Turkey 41.01N 29.32E
33 C4 Mudarraj, Al Saudi Arabia 25.41N 38.40E
64 G4 Mudau W Germany 49.32N 9.13E
34 C9 Mudawwara, Al Jordan 29.20N 36.00E
33 M9 Mudayrah Kuwait 29.30N 47.50E
101 H12 Mud Bay Br Col
28 B4 Mudbidri Karnataka India 13.05N 74.57E
108 H4 Mud Butte S Dakota 45.01N 102.55W
108 L8 Mud Cr Nebraska
28 C2 Muddebihal Karnataka India 16.22N 76.09E
69 M2 Müddersheim W Germany 50.41N 6.39E
56 L6 Muddleswood W Sussex Eng 50.55N 0.12W
93 H2 Muddo Segunti Kenya 3.12N 36.45E
109 O7 Muddy Boggy Cr Oklahoma
111 N3 Muddy Cr Utah
108 B6 Muddy Cr Wyoming
108 C8 Muddy Cr Wyoming
108 D7 Muddy Cr Wyoming
110 P8 Muddy Cr Wyoming
108 C7 Muddy Gap Wyoming 42.23N 107.25W
100 H6 Muddy L Saskatchewan 52.20N 109.08W
111 K5 Muddy Pk mt Nevada 36.18N 114.42W
32 H4 Mūd-e Dahanāb Iran 32.41N 59.30E
35 G9 Mudeibi anc site Jordan 31.02N 35.51E
34 D7 Mudeisisat, Jebel mt Jordan 31.38N 36.18E
35 H7 Mudeisisat, Jebel mt Jordan 31.38N 36.15E
95 O4 Muden S Africa 28.59S 30.23E
63 M7 Müden W Germany 52.52N 10.07E
63 M7 Müden W Germany 52.32N 10.22E
110 F9 Mud Flat reg Nevada
28 C2 Mudgal Karnataka India 16.01N 76.27E
12 J5 Mudgee New S Wales 32.37S 149.36E
13 H6 Mudge, Mt Queensland 24.08S 147.15E
33 K8 Mudhai Oman 17.31N 53.18E
28 C1 Mudhol Andhra Prad India 19.00N 77.54E
28 B2 Mudhol Karnataka India 16.21N 75.18E
28 B4 Mudigere Karnataka India 13.11N 75.36E
86 D4 Mudiriyat al-Tahrir div Egypt
35 G1 Mudiriye Syria 33.07N 35.50E
92 H10 Mudirra Mozambique 16.53S 36.36E
33 G10 Mū'diyah S Yemen 13.49N 46.08E
101 U7 Mudjatik R Saskatchewan
28 C1 Mudkhed Maharashtra India 19.08N 77.32E
29 D2 Mudki Punjab India 30.46N 74.53E
110 N6 Mud L Idaho 43.53N 112.25W
108 P1 Mud L Minnesota
110 Q1 Mud L Montana 48.50N 109.40W
110 F8 Mud L Nevada 41.50N 119.41W
111 G4 Mud L Nevada 37.51N 117.05W
108 M4 Mud Lake Res S Dakota 45.50N 98.10W
25 D4 Mudon Burma 16.17N 97.40E
29 L7 Mud Pt W Bengal Ind 21.52N 88.09E
30 A8 Mudra Madhya Prad India 24.43N 77.35E
87 L7 Mudugh prov Somalia
87 L7 Mudugh reg Somalia
36 E2 Mudurnu Turkey 40.27N 31.12E
36 E2 Mudurnu R Turkey
41 D6 Muduyyakha R U.S.S.R.
47 D4 Mud'yuga U.S.S.R. 63.45N 39.29E
92 F10 Mudzi R Zimbabwe
93 B4 Mudzi Maria Zaïre 1.37N 30.16E
70 K3 Mue R France
92 J9 Muecate Mozambique 14.55S 39.40E
92 J7 Mueda Mozambique 11.40S 39.31E
70 F5 Muel France 48.07N 2.09W
75 H5 Muel Spain 41.28N 1.04W
75 H4 Muela, La Spain 41.34N 1.07W
75 H4 Muela, Sierra de la mts Spain
115 M3 Muelle Real Nicaragua 13.05N 84.19W
14 G4 Mueller, Mt W Australia 19.51S 127.50E
14 F4 Mueller Ra W Australia
13 F6 Muellers Ra Queensland
92 G8 Muembe Mozambique 13.05S 35.39E
92 F9 Muende Mozambique 14.24S 32.59E
91 H9 Muene Zaïre 10.43S 23.20E
91 F9 Muene Quibau Angola 11.27S 19.14E
92 H8 Muenheher Mozambique 13.50S 36.06E
100 N6 Muenster Saskatchewan 52.12N 104.59W
112 K2 Muenster Texas 33.39N 97.23W
91 H9 Muentamba Angola 11.42S 22.21E
9 B13 Muéo New Caledonia 21.15S 165.03E
115 N2 Muerto, Cayo isld Nicaragua
116 D2 Muertos Cays islds Cay Sal Bank Bahamas 24.03N 80.03W
92 H9 Muetetere Mozambique 14.40S 37.51E
51 Q8 Muezerka R Karelia U.S.S.R.
59 H1 Muff Donegal Irish Rep 55.04N 7.16W
47 F4 Muftyuga U.S.S.R. 64.04N 47.00E
92 D8 Mufulira Zambia 12.30S 28.12E
92 D8 Mufulwe Hills Zambia
23 G4 Mufu Shan mt ra Jiangxi China
75 Q3 Muga R Spain
76 G6 Muga de Sayago Spain 41.24N 6.18W
75 G1 Mugaire Spain 43.07N 1.38W
93 B5 Mugalike Uganda 1.00N 30.52E
23 D7 Mugang Yunnan China 23.27N 105.19E
44 G6 Muganly Azerbaydzhan U.S.S.R. 41.29N 46.29E
44 J8 Muganskaya Step' Azerbaydzhan U.S.S.R.
93 A10 Mugara Burundi 4.03S 29.30E
76 C2 Mugardos Spain 43.27N 8.15W
90 M4 Mugarib, Wadi watercourse Sudan
24 F9 Mugarripug Xizang Zizhiqu China 32.18N 87.41E
47 N4 Mugayskiy U.S.S.R. 58.12N 61.35E
76 B10 Muge Portugal 39.06N 8.42W
76 C10 Muge R Portugal
92 H10 Mugeba Mozambique 16.35S 37.11E
79 K7 Mugello V Italy
64 P1 Mügeln E Germany 51.14N 13.04E
87 G6 Muger,R Ethiopia
93 B8 Mugesera, L Rwanda
12 A6 Mugga Mugga mt A.C.Terr Australia 35.22S 149.08E
64 L4 Muggendorf W Germany 49.48N 11.16E
79 P3 Muggia Italy 45.36N 13.46E
Mughaira see Mughayrā', Al
35 E4 Mughaiyir Jordan 32.25N 35.23E
35 E5 Mughaiyir Jordan 32.01N 35.21E
35 G3 Mughaiyir, El Jordan 32.37N 35.56E
Mughalbhin see Jati
31 E5 Mughal Kot Pakistan 31.54N 69.46E
30 G7 Mughal Sarai Uttar Prad India 25.18N 83.07E
32 E4 Mūghār Iran 33.33N 52.10E
33 F4 Mughayrā' Saudi Arabia 24.26N 45.03E
33 B2 Mughayrā', Al Saudi Arabia 29.15N 37.39E
33 K5 Mughrib, Al des area U.A.E.
Mughu see Band-e Moghūyeh
35 F1 Mughur Syria 33.05N 35.44E
35 F1 Mughur Shab'a Syria 33.16N 35.40E
20 H8 Mugi Japan 33.38N 134.23E
76 A2 Mugia Spain 43.06N 9.10W
75 E1 Mugica Spain 43.18N 2.43W
92 D5 Mugila, Mts Zaïre
36 C5 Muğla Turkey 37.13N 28.22E
87 A5 Muglad, El Sudan 11.01N 27.50E
43 E3 Mugodzharskaya Kazakhstan U.S.S.R. 48.33N 58.27E
43 E3 Mugodzhary mts Kazakhstan U.S.S.R.
92 E4 Mugombazi Tanzania 5.52S 30.06E
24 H9 Mug Qu R Qinghai China
72 C8 Mugron France 43.45N 0.44W
77 O3 Mugrón, El mt Spain 38.54N 1.12W
90 E5 Mugrum Nigeria 12.18N 11.07E
Mugshin see Muqshin
29 H3 Mugu Nepal 29.42N 82.33E
93 H7 Muguga Kenya 1.14S 36.40E
92 J8 Muguia Mozambique 12.22S 39.06E
29 H3 Mugu Karnali R Nepal
42 E6 Mugur-Aksy U.S.S.R. 50.24N 90.24E
15 B4 Mugutira Irian Jaya 1.57S 133.12E
90 M6 Muhagiriya Sudan 12.00N 25.40E
35 G10 Muhai Jordan 30.59N 35.51E
Muhaiwir see Muhaywir
35 H2 Muhajjah Syria 32.57N 36.14E
30 D5 Muhamdi Uttar Prad India 27.57N 80.12E
30 G6 Muhammadabad Banaras, Uttar Prad India 26.02N 83.22E
30 C5 Muhammadabad Farukhabad, Uttar Prad India 27.19N 79.26E
30 G7 Muhammadabad Gorakhpur, Uttar Prad India 25.38N 83.47E
Muhammadabad Iransee Darreh Gaz
31 E7 Muhammad Ashraf Pakistan 26.12N 69.31E
30 G8 Muhammadganj Bihar India 24.26N 83.52E
29 F6 Muhammadgarh Madhya Prad India 23.40N 78.12E
31 D4 Muhammad Gul Afghanistan 32.03N 67.33E
31 H9 Muhammadpur Bangladesh 23.25N 89.35E
30 H7 Muhammadpur Bihar India 25.58N 84.26E
30 G7 Muhammadpur Uttar Prad India 25.59N 83.01E
85 O9 Muhammad Qol Sudan 20.53N 37.09E
33 A3 Muhammad, Râs C Egypt 27.42N 34.13E
30 J6 Muhammedpur Balmi Bihar India 26.16N 85.09E
22 E8 Muhar Qinghai China 36.50N 99.00E
34 M7 Muhārī, Sh'ib al watercourse Iraq
33 J3 Muharraq, Al Bahrain, The Gulf 26.15N 50.39E
33 B7 Muharraq, Jazīrat isld Bahrain, The Gulf
34 G2 Muhasan Syria 36.39N 39.17E
93 A7 Muhavura mt Rwanda/Uganda 1.24S 29.39E
33 K8 Muhayfif S Yemen 16.12N 52.15E
33 F5 Muhayriqah Saudi Arabia 24.00N 45.04E
34 J5 Muhaywir Iraq 33.33N 41.07E
34 C9 Muheish watercourse Jordan
66 J2 Muhen Switzerland 47.21N 8.03E
92 J4 Muheza Tanzania 5.11S 38.50E
30 G5 Muhjung Nepal 27.53N 83.23E
64 F6 Mühlacker W Germany 48.57N 8.51E
66 K3 Mühlau Switzerland 47.14N 8.23E
64 H2 Mühlbach W Germany 50.56N 9.35E
63 S10 Mühlberg Cottbus E Germany 51.26N 13.13E
64 K2 Mühlberg Thüringen E Germany 50.52N 10.50E
64 O7 Mühldorf W Germany 48.14N 12.33E
66 N3 Mühlehorn Switzerland 47.08N 9.11E
63 S7 Mühlenbeck E Germany 52.40N 13.23E
103 B4 Mühlenburg Pennsylvania 41.14N 76.10W
63 O5 Mühlen Eichsen E Germany 53.46N 11.15E
64 K4 Mühlhausen W Germany 49.45N 10.47E
64 J1 Mühlhausen in Thüringen E Germany 51.13N 10.28E
64 F7 Mühlheim Baden-Württemberg W Germany 48.01N 8.55E
66 O1 Mühlhofen W Germany 47.44N 9.16E
64 M2 Mühltroff E Germany 50.32N 12.55E
51 M7 Muhos Finland 64.49N 26.00E
65 H7 Muhr Austria 47.07N 13.29E
Muhrabad see Mehrābād
35 D3 Muhraqa Israel 32.40N 35.05E
64 F7 Mühringen W Germany 48.25N 8.45E
33 B2 Muhtatab, Al area Saudi Arabia
46 E1 Muhu Estonia U.S.S.R. 58.32N 23.20E
92 G7 Muhukuru Tanzania 11.04S 35.29E
91 K4 Muhulu Zaïre 1.03S 27.16E
92 J7 Muhumbika Tanzania 10.09S 39.33E
37 E7 Muhundu Turkey 38.59N 39.50E
93 C7 Muhutwe Tanzania 1.31S 31.41E
92 H7 Muhuwesi R Tanzania
25 H8 Mui Bai Bung C Vietnam 8.38N 104.42E
25 K5 Mui Batangan C Vietnam 15.10N 108.58E
25 K4 Mui Chon May Dong C Vietnam 16.20N 108.03E
58 K5 Muick, L Grampian Scotland 56.55N 3.10W
58 K5 Muick, R Grampian Scotland
25 K7 Mui da Vaich C Vietnam 11.44N 109.14E
60 J10 Muiden Netherlands 52.20N 5.05E

60 J10 **Muiderberg** Netherlands 52.20N 5.07E
70 O6 **Muides-sur-Loire** France 47.40N 1.32E
25 K7 **Mui Dinh** C Vietnam 11.22N 109.02E
70 N3 **Muids** France 49.13N 1.18E
92 J7 **Muidumbe** Mozambique 11.49S 39.51E
91 G11 **Muié** Angola 14.23S 20.25E
92 H11 **Muiembe** Mozambique 18.38S 36.17E
20 M4 **Muikamachi** Japan 37.04N 138.52E
25 K7 **Mui Ke Ga** C Vietnam 10.40N 108.02E
19 F4 **Muiliyk** isld Moluccas Indon 0.34S 128.23E
25 K7 **Mui Ne** Vietnam 10.55N 108.17E
Muine Bheag see **Bagenalstown**
76 D5 **Muiños** Spain 41.57N 7.59W
106 K6 **Muir** Michigan 43.01N 84.56W
92 F10 **Muira** R Mozambique
58 L5 **Muirdrum** Tayside Scotland 56.32N 2.44W
113 T7 **Muir Glacier** Alaska 59.05N 136.20W
57 E1 **Muirkirk** Strathclyde Scotland 55.31N 4.04W
14 B10 **Muir, L** W Australia 34.28S 116.35E
14 G7 **Muir, Mt** W Australia 25.29S 128.04E
58 L4 **Muir of Fowlis** Grampian Scotland 57.12N 2.44W
58 H3 **Muir of Ord** Highland Scotland 57.31N 4.28W
14 A5 **Muiron I., N** W Australia 21.38S 114.26E
14 A5 **Muiron I., S** W Australia 21.44S 114.21E
25 J3 **Mui Ron Ma** C Vietnam 18.07N 106.27E
111 B4 **Muir Woods Nat. Mon** California 37.54N 122.34W
95 E9 **Muiskraal** S Africa 33.55S 21.12E
119 B7 **Muisne** Ecuador 0.35N 79.58W
92 J9 **Muite** Mozambique 14.01S 39.00E
9 R12 **Muitoulo** pt Tonga, Pacific Oc 18.38S 174.04W
25 K6 **Mui Yen** C Vietnam 13.43N 109.13E
61 J2 **Muizen** Belgium 51.01N 4.31E
94 P12 **Muizenberg** Cape Town S Africa 34.06S 18.28E
87 G4 **Muja** Ethiopia 12.02N 39.30E
33 H8 **Mujaza'ah, Al** S Yemen 17.25N 49.40E
33 F4 **Mujazzal, Jabal** mts Saudi Arabia
35 J2 **Mujeidil, El** Syria 32.58N 36.15E
35 F2 **Mujeiniye, El** Syria 32.49N 35.42E
115 Q7 **Mujeres, I** Mexico
24 C7 **Muji** Xinjiang Uygur Zizhiqu China 37.30N 78.28E
35 F8 **Mujib** R Jordan
30 E3 **Mujigaon** Nepal 29.27N 81.07E
92 B8 **Mujimbeji** Zambia 12.11S 24.58E
18 K4 **Mujong** R Sarawak Malaysia
32 B1 **Mujūmbar** Iran 38.22N 46.11E
25 E9 **Muk** isld Thailand 7.20N 99.00E
46 E5 **Mukachevo** Ukraine U.S.S.R. 48.26N 22.45E
20 H4 **Mukaeda** Chiba Japan
93 B8 **Mukafigere** Tanzania 2.36S 30.32E
18 K4 **Mukah** Sarawak Malaysia 2.56N 112.02E
18 K4 **Mukah** R Sarawak Malaysia
93 L8 **Mukale** Kenya 2.34S 39.46E
33 A11 **Mukaliab Hādī, Ra's** C S Yemen 12.43N 44.53E
33 H9 **Mukallā,Al** S Yemen 14.34N 49.07E
35 E6 **Mukallik** watercourse Jordan
91 H6 **Mukamba, L** Zaïre 5.41S 23.03E
91 K8 **Mukana** Zaïre 9.18S 27.11E
29 E5 **Mukandwara** Rajasthan India 24.49N 76.02E
24 F11 **Mükangsar** Xizang Zizhiqu China 29.28N 87.38E
94 H1 **Mukassa** Namibia 17.57S 24.29E
91 K6 **Mukatano** Zaïre 5.12S 27.31E
20 L2 **Mukawa** Japan 42.35N 141.55E
20 L2 **Mu-Kawa** R Japan
35 F7 **Mukawir** anc site Jordan 31.34N 35.38E see **Machaerus** Anc Site Jordan
85 O9 **Mukawwar I** Sudan 20.50N 37.17E
25 H4 **Mukdahan** Thailand 16.31N 104.43E
Mukden see **Shenyang**
91 G6 **Mukeba** Zaïre 5.10S 21.15E
92 D5 **Mukebo** Zaïre 6.49S 28.02E
91 F6 **Mukedi** Zaïre 5.40S 19.48E
57 J4 **Muker** N Yorks Eng 54.23N 2.08W
19 N2 **Mukeru** Palau Is Pacific Oc 7.25N 134.31E
29 D2 **Mukerum** Punjab India 31.56N 75.40E
33 E10 **Mukhā, Al** Yemen 13.20N 43.16E
35 F3 **Mukheiba** Jordan 32.42N 35.40E
28 C1 **Mukher** Maharashtra India 18.42N 77.24E
40 D5 **Mukhino** U.S.S.R. 52.18N 127.09E
35 E6 **Mukhmas** Jordan 31.52N 35.17E
39 J2 **Mukhomornoye** U.S.S.R. 66.24N 173.16E
42 J6 **Mukhor-Konduy** U.S.S.R. 52.28N 113.15E
42 H6 **Mukhor-Shibir'** U.S.S.R. 51.03N 107.50E
30 G7 **Mukhrawan** Bihar India 25.20N 83.51E
44 J6 **Mukhtadir** Azerbaydzhan U.S.S.R. 41.40N 48.46E
Mukhtaran see **Mokhtārān**
45 P1 **Mukhtolovo** U.S.S.R. 55.28N 43.11E
91 D6 **Mukimbungu** Zaïre 5.07S 14.04E
14 C9 **Mukinbudin** W Australia 30.52S 118.08E
92 D8 **Mukinga** Zaïre 12.30S 29.30E
92 B8 **Mukinge Hill** Zambia 13.30S 25.51E
91 G6 **Mukishi** Zaïre 5.39S 21.03E
91 J8 **Mukishi** Zaïre 8.31S 24.41E
28 K1 **Mukki** Assam India 28.04N 94.16E
91 G7 **Mukoba** Zaïre 6.50S 20.50E
21 J11 **Muko jima rettō** islds Ogasawara-Guntō Pacific Oc
93 C6 **Mukoko** Uganda 0.11S 31.53E
18 D7 **Mukomuko** Sumatra Indon 2.30S 101.05E
91 H7 **Mukongo** Zaïre 6.32S 23.30E
93 D5 **Mukono** Uganda 0.22N 32.46E
63 P9 **Mukrena** E Germany 51.43N 11.41E
43 H7 **Mukry** Turkmeniya U.S.S.R. 37.37N 65.50E
43 K7 **Muksu** R Tadzhikistan U.S.S.R.
31 H8 **Muktagacha** Bangladesh 24.46N 90.16E
30 C3 **Mukteswar** Uttar Prad India 29.27N 79.41E
29 H3 **Muktinath** Nepal 28.50N 83.52E
29 D2 **Muktsar** Punjab India 30.30N 74.34E
93 F5 **Mukuju** Uganda 0.43N 34.15E
91 J8 **Mukulakulu** Zaïre 9.38S 25.48E
91 J9 **Mukuleshi** R Zaïre
92 E10 **Mukumbura** R Mozambique/Zimbabwe
92 D6 **Mukunsa** Zambia 9.25S 29.50E
31 D4 **Mukur** Afghanistan 32.52N 67.42E
43 C3 **Mukur** Kazakhstan U.S.S.R. 48.03N 45.31E
93 E4 **Mukura** Uganda 1.34N 33.53E
90 D8 **Mukuru** Cameroon 6.20N 9.56E
37 G7 **Müküs** Turkey 38.05N 42.52E
93 H5 **Mukutan** Kenya 0.38N 36.17E
100 U5 **Mukutawa R** Manitoba
92 D5 **Mukuy** Zaïre 7.28S 28.37E
92 C10 **Mukwela** Zambia 17.01S 26.39E
106 F7 **Mukwonago** Wisconsin 42.52N 88.20W
29 F7 **Mul** Maharashtra India 20.04N 79.42E
23 B4 **Mula** Sichuan China 29.39N 100.38E
77 O4 **Mula** Spain 38.02N 1.29W
29 C8 **Mula** R Maharashtra India
33 M5 **Muladdah** Oman 23.45N 57.34E
50 D6 **Mulafjall** mt Iceland 64.23N 21.20W
50 F7 **Múlakot** Iceland 63.43N 19.53W
27 L9 **Mulaku Atol** Maldives, Ind Oc 2.57N 73.34E
50 G7 **Múlakvísl** R Iceland
92 D4 **Mulala** Zaïre 5.51S 29.11E
119 B8 **Mulaló** Ecuador 0.47S 78.35W
43 N4 **Mulaly** Kazakhstan U.S.S.R. 45.25N 78.16E
91 G7 **Mulamba** Zaïre 6.21S 21.13E
21 D5 **Mulan** Heilongjiang China 45.57N 128.03E
30 A2 **Mulana** Haryana India 30.16N 77.02E
19 L5 **Mulanay** Luzon Philippines 13.31N 122.25E
92 G10 **Mulanje** Malawi 16.05S 35.29E
92 G9 **Mulanje, Mt** Malawi 16.00S 35.37E
31 D6 **Mula R** Pakistan
50 H4 **Múlar** ridge Iceland 65.04N 17.35W
81 C4 **Mulárgia, L** Sardinia 39.37N 9.15E
50 K4 **Múlasýsla, Nordhur** co Iceland
50 L5 **Múlasýsla, Sudhur** co Iceland
117 C5 **Mulata** Brazil 1.45S 54.00W
34 N6 **Mūlat al Mashkhūr** Iraq 32.52N 45.58E
87 H6 **Mulata Mts** Ethiopia
26 S9 **Mulatiyana** Sri Lanka 6.10N 80.35E
115 E3 **Mulatos** Mexico 28.39N 108.50W
115 Q5 **Mulatupo Sasardí** Panama 8.59N 77.45W
33 F3 **Mulayh** Saudi Arabia 26.08N 44.56E
Mulayhah, Jabal see **Mileihah, Jabal**
33 F5 **Mulayh, Al** Saudi Arabia 22.37N 45.50E
33 H3 **Mulayjah** Saudi Arabia 27.16N 48.29E
79 G6 **Mulazzo** Italy 44.18N 9.53E
28 D4 **Mulbagal** Karnataka India 13.11N 78.23E
31 J3 **Mulbekh** Kashmir 34.22N 76.22E
107 B6 **Mulberry** Arkansas 35.29N 94.05W
105 F10 **Mulberry** Florida 27.53N 81.59W
106 H9 **Mulberry** Indiana 40.22N 86.40W
109 Q4 **Mulberry** Kansas 37.32N 94.37W
107 C6 **Mulberry** R Arkansas
107 J8 **Mulberry Fork** R Alabama
107 G3 **Mulberry Grove** Illinois 38.56N 89.12W
53 E3 **Mulbjerge** mt Denmark 56.55N 10.17E
113 K6 **Mulchatna** R Alaska
121 A6 **Mulchén** Chile 37.43S 72.20W
64 P2 **Mulda** E Germany 50.49N 13.25E
47 J3 **Mul'da** U.S.S.R. 67.29N 63.52E
53 W14 **Muldal** Norway 62.15N 7.25E
47 L6 **Muldashevo** U.S.S.R. 54.50N 59.47E
53 A4 **Muldbjerg** Denmark 56.09N 8.29E
64 O2 **Mulde** R E Germany
95 L2 **Muldersdrif** S Africa 26.03S 27.51E
58 B5 **Muldoanich** isld W Isles Scotland 56.55N 7.27W
110 M6 **Muldoon** Idaho 43.32N 113.56W
53 N9 **Mule** Faeroes 62.22N 6.34W
112 E5 **Mule Cr** Texas
109 B8 **Mule Creek** New Mexico 33.08N 108.57W
108 F6 **Mule Creek** Wyoming 43.23N 104.08W
115 D4 **Mulegé** Mexico 26.54N 112.00W
66 P5 **Mulegns** Switzerland 46.32N 9.38E
35 G7 **Muleih** Jordan 31.35N 35.49E
86 P4 **Muleih, Jebel** mt Jordan 30.56N 35.34E
92 E2 **Mulemba** Tanzania 1.49S 31.40E
93 C7 **Mulemba** Tanzania 1.49S 31.40E
92 E8 **Mulembo** R Zambia
92 E4 **Mulenbera** Tanzania 4.21S 30.21E
66 G5 **Mülenen** Switzerland 46.38N 7.42E
79 L1 **Mules** Italy 46.52N 11.32E
19 B8 **Mules** isld Indonesia 8.54S 120.18E
112 E1 **Muleshoe** Texas 34.14N 102.44W
92 H10 **Mulevala** Mozambique 16.25S 37.35E
64 H5 **Mulfingen** W Germany 49.20N 9.49E
14 C5 **Mulga Downs** W Australia 22.12S 118.25E
13 B7 **Mulga Park** N Terr Australia 25.50S 131.45E
14 C8 **Mulgar Pk** W Australia 29.15S 118.57E
12 C4 **Mulgathing** S Australia 30.20S 134.08E
12 C4 **Mulgathing Rocks** mt S Aust 30.12S 134.00E
13 K6 **Mulgildie** Queensland 25.00S 151.10E
98 L8 **Mulgrave** Nova Scotia 45.36N 61.25W
113 F3 **Mulgrave Hills** Alaska
13 F1 **Mulgrave I** Queensland
14 C6 **Mulgul** W Australia 24.45S 118.32E
77 K6 **Mulhacén, Cerro de** mt Spain 37.04N 3.19W
109 N5 **Mulhall** Oklahoma 36.05N 97.26W
69 O3 **Mülheim** W Germany 50.23N 7.30E
63 E10 **Mülheim an der Ruhr** W Germany 51.25N 6.50E
69 N8 **Mulhouse** France 47.45N 7.21E
29 B6 **Muli** Gujarat India 22.40N 71.34E
50 H3 **Múli** Iceland 65.47N 17.16W
122 B2 **Mulifanua** W Samoa, Pacific Oc 13.50S 172.00W
47 J4 **Muligort** U.S.S.R. 63.07N 64.40E
92 J10 **Muligudje** Mozambique 16.30S 38.54E
29 B6 **Mulila** Gujarat India 22.05N 70.21E
Mu-ling see **Muling**
21 E5 **Muling** Heilongjiang China 44.32N 130.14E
21 E5 **Muling** Heilongjiang China 44.56N 130.32E
22 L8 **Muling Guan** pass Shandong China 36.09N 118.41E
21 E5 **Muling He** R Heilongjiang China
21 F5 **Muling He** R Heilongjiang China
Mu-lin Ho see **Xi He**
Mu-lin Ho R see **Hsi Ho**
Mulin'u see **Apia** W.Samoa
122 B2 **Mulitapuili, C** W Samoa, Pacific Oc 13.55S 171.58W
23 B5 **Muli Zangzu Zizhixian** Sichuan China 27.50N 101.18E
58 E6 **Mull** isld Strathclyde Scotland
24 D4 **Mulla Akchi Dawan** pass Xinjiang Uygur Zizhiqu China 42.27N 83.12E
32 C2 **Mulla Ali** Iran 36.30N 49.34E
Mulla Badaq see **Mollā Bodāgh**
59 K6 **Mullacor** Wicklow Irish Rep 52.59N 6.22W
26 T7 **Mullagama** Sri Lanka 7.20N 81.28E
59 J4 **Mullagh** Cavan Irish Rep 53.49N 6.47W
59 C8 **Mullaghanattin** mt Kerry Irish Rep 51.56N 9.51W
59 D8 **Mullaghanish** mt Cork Irish Rep 51.59N 9.09W
59 D7 **Mullaghareirk** mt Cork Irish Rep 52.19N 9.05W
59 D7 **Mullaghareirk Mts** Irish Rep
59 B8 **Mullaghbeg** mt Kerry Irish Rep 51.49N 10.05W
59 H2 **Mullaghcarn** mt Tyrone N Ireland 54.40N 7.13W
59 K5 **Mullaghcleevaun** mt Wicklow Irish Rep 53.06N 6.25W
59 F3 **Mullaghmore** Sligo Irish Rep 54.28N 8.27W
26 S3 **Mullaittivu** Sri Lanka 9.15N 80.48E
12 J4 **Mullaley** New S Wales 31.06S 149.55E
59 G3 **Mullan** Fermanagh N Ireland 54.13N 7.42W
110 K2 **Mullan** Idaho 47.27N 115.47W
Mulla Qara see **Malā Qara**
58 F4 **Mullardoch, L** Highland Scotland
108 J7 **Mullen** Nebraska 42.03N 101.02W
59 H2 **Mullenan** Londonderry Irish Rep 54.57N 7.24W
12 H4 **Mullengudgery** New S Wales 31.40S 147.23E
104 D9 **Mullens** W Virginia 37.35N 81.25W
13 C6 **Muller** R N Terr Australia
18 K5 **Muller, Pegunungan** mts Borneo Indonesia
15 G6 **Muller Ra** Papua New Guinea
91 B4 **Mullèrville** Gabon 1.15S 11.40E
105 E10 **Mullet Key** isld Florida 27.37N 82.44W
59 B3 **Mullet, The** isld Mayo Irish Rep 54.15N 10.04W
106 K4 **Mullett L** Michigan
14 B8 **Mullewa** W Australia 28.32S 115.30E
58 T11 **Mull Hd** Orkney Scotland 59.23N 2.53W
58 T12 **Mull Hd** Orkney Scotland 58.58N 2.42W
66 N1 **Müllheim** Switzerland 47.36N 9.01E
64 D8 **Müllheim** W Germany 47.48N 7.37E
103 E7 **Mullica** R New Jersey
103 D7 **Mullica Hill** New Jersey 39.45N 75.14W
13 E6 **Mulligan** R Queensland
112 J4 **Mullin** Texas 31.34N 98.41W
59 G6 **Mullinahone** Tipperary Irish Rep 52.30N 7.30W
59 H7 **Mullinavat** Kilkenny Irish Rep 52.22N 7.10W
59 H4 **Mullingar** W Meath Irish Rep 53.32N 7.20W
105 H3 **Mullins** S Carolina 34.13N 79.16W
15 K9 **Mullins Harb** Papua New Guinea 10.28S 149.58E
109 L4 **Mullinville** Kansas 37.35N 99.29W
56 T9 **Mullion** Cornwall Eng 50.01N 5.14W
56 T9 **Mullion Cove** Cornwall Eng 50.00N 5.16W
12 J5 **Mullion Creek** New S Wales 33.09S 149.09E
26 S3 **Mulliyavalai** Sri Lanka 9.13N 80.46E
87 H6 **Mullo** Ethiopia 9.20N 40.52E
57 D3 **Mull of Galloway** prom Dumfries & Galloway Scot 54.38N 4.52W
57 B2 **Mull of Kintyre** prom Strathclyde Scotland 55.18N 5.45W
45 V2 **Mullovka** U.S.S.R. 54.12N 49.26E
58 E5 **Mull, Sd. of** Highland/Strathclyde Scotland
52 H9 **Mullsjö** Sweden 57.56N 13.55E
12 L3 **Mullumbimby** New S Wales 28.32S 153.30E
40 D4 **Mulmuga** R U.S.S.R.
92 D2 **Mulo** Zaïre 0.07S 29.15E
92 B10 **Mulobezi** Zambia 16.48S 25.11E
91 D11 **Mulondo** Angola 15.41S 15.12E
91 D11 **Mulondo** tribe Angola
91 K7 **Mulongo** Zaïre 7.47S 27.00E
12 E3 **Muloorina** S Australia 29.10S 137.51E
92 B7 **Mulopwa** Zaïre 10.59S 24.44E
59 C4 **Mulrany** Co Mayo Irish Rep 53.55N 9.47W
59 C4 **Mulrany** Mayo Irish Rep 53.55N 9.46W
59 G1 **Mulroy B** Donegal Irish Rep 55.15N 7.46W
70 L6 **Mulsanne** France 47.53N 0.15E
28 A1 **Mulshi L** Bombay India 18.25N 73.48E
63 P5 **Mulsow** E Germany 53.58N 11.41E
29 F7 **Multai** Madhya Prad India 21.46N 78.21E
32 J7 **Multān** Iran 26.58N 61.33E
31 F5 **Multan** Pakistan 30.10N 71.36E
31 F6 **Multan** dist Pakistan
42 A2 **Multanovy** U.S.S.R. 60.03N 73.15E
51 L9 **Multia** Finland 62.27N 24.50E
52 K3 **Multrå** Sweden 63.10N 17.25E
28 D1 **Mulug** Andhra Prad India 18.14N 79.57E
18 L3 **Mulu, Gunung** mt Sarawak Malaysia 4.02N 114.54E
91 J6 **Mulumbu** Zaïre 5.50S 25.39E
91 G7 **Mulundu** Zaïre 6.40S 20.33E
117 J8 **Mulungu** Brazil 7.00S 35.20W
92 D9 **Mulungushi Dam** Zambia 14.43S 28.50E
91 K9 **Mulungwishi** Zaïre 10.44S 26.38E
34 G5 **Mulūşi, Wādī al** Iraq
109 N4 **Mulvane** Kansas 37.31N 97.15W
100 T8 **Mulvihill** Manitoba 50.58N 98.11W
91 F8 **Mulvulege** Angola 9.06S 18.51E
12 G4 **Mulyah Mt** New S Wales 30.37S 144.35E
47 J5 **Mulym'ya** U.S.S.R. 60.34N 64.35E
47 J5 **Mulym'ya** R U.S.S.R.
12 F4 **Mulyungarie** S Australia 31.30S 140.45E
91 H2 **Muma** Zaïre 3.25N 23.21E
90 M6 **Mumallah** Sudan 10.50N 25.30E
32 J8 **Mūman** Iran 25.35N 60.30E
56 D4 **Mumbles** W Glam Wales 51.35N 3.59W
91 D9 **Mumbondo** Angola 10.11S 14.09E
92 D8 **Mumbotuta Falls** Zambia 12.21S 29.16E
91 E10 **Mumbué** Angola 13.54S 17.18E
92 C9 **Mumbwa** Zambia 15.00S 27.01E
57 O6 **Mumby** Lincs Eng 53.16N 0.16E
Mumcular see **Karaova**
91 K9 **Mumena** Zaïre 11.44S 26.31E
15 J7 **Mumeng** Papua New Guinea 6.57S 146.34E
112 L5 **Mumford** Texas 30.45N 96.35W
93 F5 **Mumias** Kenya 0.20N 34.29E
31 F1 **Muminabad** Tadzhikistan U.S.S.R. 38.11N 70.02E
35 G1 **Mumisiye** Syria 33.05N 35.50E
66 G2 **Mümliswil** Switzerland 47.21N 7.42E
25 E9 **Mum Nauk, Laem** C Thailand 7.44N 98.17E
76 E8 **Mumoa** R Portugal
91 H7 **Mumoma** Zaïre 7.14S 22.34E
66 H1 **Mumpf** Switzerland 47.33N 7.55E
44 H2 **Mumra** U.S.S.R. 45.46N 47.41E
Mumtrak see **Goodnews Bay**
81 A5 **Mumullonis, pta** Sardinia 39.28N 8.24E
15 G8 **Mumuni** Papua New Guinea 8.00S 142.38E
31 J2 **Mun** Kashmir 33.50N 78.32E
15 B6 **Mun** Moluccas Indon 5.25S 133.04E
115 P7 **Muna** Mexico 20.29N 89.41W
39 E2 **Muna** U.S.S.R. 65.57N 150.50E
19 C6 **Muna** isld Indonesia
41 M6 **Muna** R U.S.S.R.
29 B5 **Munabao** Rajasthan India 25.46N 70.19E
50 D2 **Munadharnes** C Iceland 66.05N 21.35W
28 D2 **Munagala** Andhra Prad India 17.04N 79.54E
86 H4 **Munâgât el Kubra, El** Egypt 30.51N 32.00E
33 J6 **Munajjar, Al** des area Saudi Arabia
41 L7 **Munakan** R U.S.S.R.
20 D8 **Munakata** Japan 33.49N 130.33E
24 D9 **Munak Thok** Xizang Zizhiqu China 33.09N 81.21E
76 J7 **Muñana** Spain 40.35N 5.03W
23 D7 **Munankwan Lin** pass Vietnam/China 22.06N 106.46E
43 C4 **Munayly** Kazakhstan U.S.S.R. 46.46N 54.33E
33 H5 **Munbaţih,Al** area of sand & gravel Saudi Arabia
14 B8 **Munbinia** W Australia 28.15S 117.25E
13 G2 **Munburra** Queensland 14.54S 145.00E
64 M3 **Münchberg** W Germany 50.12N 11.48E
63 U7 **Müncheberg** E Germany 52.31N 14.08E
64 M7 **München** W Germany 48.08N 11.35E
64 M2 **Münchenbernsdorf** E Germany 50.49N 11.56E
66 F3 **Münchenbuchsee** Switzerland 47.02N 7.28E
66 G1 **Münchenstein** Switzerland 47.31N 7.38E
66 E4 **Münchenwiler** Switzerland 46.55N 7.08E
64 F2 **Münchhausen** W Germany 50.57N 8.44E
119 C6 **Munchique, Cerro** mt Colombia 2.32N 76.59W
101 L6 **Muncho Lake** Br Columbia 59.00N 125.46W
101 L6 **Muncho Lake Prov. Park** Br Columbia
21 D8 **Munch'ŏn** N Korea 39.14N 127.19E
64 O6 **Münchshofen** Nieder-Bayern W Germany 48.47N 12.42E
64 N5 **Münchshofen** Oberpfalz, Bayern W Germany 49.15N 12.05E
64 M6 **Münchsmünster** W Germany 48.46N 11.43E
66 M2 **Münchwilen** Switzerland 47.28N 8.59E
106 J9 **Muncie** Indiana 40.11N 85.22W
13 E7 **Muncoonie, L** Queensland
36 H4 **Muncusun** Turkey 38.54N 35.37E
103 A4 **Muncy** Pennsylvania 41.12N 76.47W
103 A4 **Muncy Cr** Pennsylvania
103 A4 **Muncy Cr., Little** Pennsylvania
103 A4 **Muncy Valley** Pennsylvania 41.21N 76.35W
66 H6 **Mund** Switzerland 46.19N 7.56E
91 C12 **Munda** Angola 16.01S 13.06E
15 K3 **Munda** New Georgia I Solomon Is 8.18S 157.15E
31 F5 **Munda** Pakistan 30.33N 71.14E
91 G3 **Munda** Zaïre 1.28N 20.30E
33 F7 **Mundafan, Al** des area Saudi Arabia
29 H7 **Mundagor** Orissa India 20.01N 83.30E
53 V16 **Mundal** Norway 61.24N 6.45E
26 Q6 **Mundal L** Sri Lanka
90 D9 **Mundame** Cameroon 4.35N 9.31E
93 N7 **Mundane Ra** Kenya
39 D2 **Mundar** U.S.S.R. 66.59N 145.21E
100 E5 **Mundare** Alberta 53.36N 112.20W
28 B3 **Mundargi** Karnataka India 15.16N 75.53E
30 C6 **Mundarwa** Uttar Prad India 26.57N 79.47E
117 G6 **Mundaú** Brazil 3.15S 39.24W
66 N5 **Mundaun, Piz** mt Switzerland 46.44N 9.09E
112 H2 **Munday** Texas 33.27N 99.38W
106 F7 **Mundelein** Illinois 42.16N 88.00W
109 N2 **Munden** Kansas 39.54N 97.34W
63 L10 **Münden** W Germany 51.25N 9.39E
65 H5 **Munderfing** Austria 48.04N 13.11E
64 H7 **Munderkingen** W Germany 48.14N 9.40E
56 O2 **Mundesley** Norfolk Eng 52.53N 1.26E
56 N2 **Mundford** Norfolk Eng 52.31N 0.39E
53 T18 **Mundheim** Norway 60.10N 5.55E
92 H10 **Mundimo** Mozambique 18.00S 37.00E
14 D6 **Mundiwindi** W Australia 23.50S 120.07E
13 F4 **Mundjuro** R Queensland
77 M3 **Mundo** R Spain
91 J8 **Mundoi** Zaïre 8.03S 24.21E
118 H2 **Mundo Novo** Brazil 11.52S 40.34W
96 P9 **Mundo, Pta. del** pt La Palma Canary Is 28.52N 17.55W
29 A6 **Mundra** Gujarat India 22.50N 69.48E
14 G9 **Mundrabilla** W Australia 31.51S 127.51E
15 K6 **Mundua I** Bismarck Arch 4.38S 149.23E
13 K7 **Mundubbera** Queensland 25.35S 151.18E
117 G9 **Munduri** Brazil 8.10S 40.36W
40 E1 **Munduruchchu** U.S.S.R. 60.04N 129.01E
40 D1 **Munduruchchu** R U.S.S.R.
29 C4 **Mundwa** Rajasthan India 27.02N 73.49E
42 D5 **Mundybash** U.S.S.R. 53.14N 87.20E
75 G5 **Munébrega** Spain 41.15N 1.42W
83 D3 **Munella** mt Albania 41.57N 20.04E
91 D9 **Munenga** Angola 10.03S 14.40E
77 M2 **Munera** Spain 39.03N 2.29W
28 E2 **Munera R** Andhra Prad India
58 P9 **Mu Ness** prom Shetland Scotland 60.15N 1.42W
58 R8 **Mu Ness** prom Shetland Scotland 60.41N 0.50W
107 L4 **Munfordville** Kentucky 37.17N 85.55W
Mung see **Monj**
30 L5 **Munga** Nepal 27.02N 87.13E
13 J7 **Mungallala** Queensland 26.25S 147.35E
13 H8 **Mungallala** R Queensland
13 G3 **Mungana** Queensland 17.05S 144.24E
29 F5 **Mungaoli** Madhya Prad India 24.25N 78.06E
13 L7 **Mungar** Queensland 25.40S 152.32E
92 F10 **Mungari** Mozambique 17.10S 33.30E
14 C5 **Mungaroona Ra** W Australia
42 E6 **Mungash-Kul', Gora** mt U.S.S.R. 51.46N 90.11E
87 B9 **Mungbere** Zaïre 2.40N 28.25E
30 H4 **Munge** Nepal 28.06N 84.33E
29 G6 **Mungeli** Madhya Prad India 22.04N 81.42E
106 L6 **Munger** Michigan 43.32N 83.45W
12 E3 **Mungerannie** S Australia 28.00S 138.36E
112 E3 **Mungerville** Texas 32.46N 102.06W
75 E1 **Mungía** Spain 43.21N 2.51W
13 J8 **Mungindi** Queensland 28.58S 148.56E
31 H10 **Mungla** Bangladesh 22.18N 89.34E
91 E9 **Mungo** Angola 11.49S 16.16E
90 D9 **Mungo** R Nigeria/Cameroon
30 F7 **Mungra Budshah Pur** Uttar Prad India 25.39N 82.12E
30 E7 **Mungri Tal** L Uttar Prad India 25.35N 81.15E
21 D9 **Mung'yŏng** S Korea 36.46N 128.01E
34 L10 **Munhadar Linah** plat Saudi Arabia
34 M10 **Munhadar Umm ar Ruḍumah** plat Saudi Arabia
92 H10 **Munhamade** Mozambique 16.39S 36.55E
91 F10 **Munhango** Angola 12.10S 18.36E
91 C11 **Munhino** Angola 14.56S 12.58E
94 M5 **Munhuana** Mozambique 25.55S 32.37E
75 L2 **Munia, Pico de la** mt Spain 42.43N 0.07E
108 M1 **Munich** N Dakota 48.49N 98.42W
Munich W Germany see **München**
92 D8 **Muniengashi** R Zaïre
Munier see **Aïn-Kerma**
75 J5 **Muniesa** Spain 41.02N 0.49W
75 F3 **Munilla** Spain 42.12N 2.18W
117 F6 **Munim** R Brazil
92 H5 **Munisagara** Tanzania 6.45S 36.54E
106 H3 **Munising** Michigan 46.24N 86.40W
118 H7 **Muniz Freire** Brazil 20.25S 41.23W
29 B6 **Munjpur** Gujarat India 23.34N 71.57E
50 G3 **Munkathverá** Iceland 65.33N 18.02W
53 H5 **Munke-Bjergby** Denmark 55.31N 11.32E
53 F6 **Munkebo** Denmark 55.28N 10.34E
52 F8 **Munkedal** Sweden 58.28N 11.38E
53 U16 **Munkegga** mt Norway 61.11N 6.25E
53 N11 **Munken** isld Faeroes 61.21N 6.40W
52 H3 **Munkflohögen** Sweden 63.32N 15.00E
52 H7 **Munkfors** Sweden 59.50N 13.35E
Munkhafaḍ ath Tharthār see **Mileh Tharthār** flood basin
52 N1 **Munksund** Sweden 65.17N 21.29E
42 G6 **Munku-Sardyk, Gora** mt U.S.S.R./Mongolia 51.48N 100.30E
61 E3 **Munkzwalm** Belgium 50.52N 3.44E
58 H3 **Munlochy** Highland Scotland 57.33N 4.16W
60 M8 **Munnekeburen** Netherlands 52.50N 5.54E
60 O6 **Munnekezijl** Netherlands 53.18N 6.16E
64 J3 **Münnerstadt** W Germany 50.15N 10.12E
94 K4 **Munnik** S Africa 23.35S 29.55E
11 K11 **Munning Pt** Chatham Is Pacific Oc 43.33S 176.10W
41 N8 **Munniyskiy Khrebet** mts U.S.S.R.
61 L8 **Muno** Belgium 49.43N 5.11E
76 K7 **Muñogalindo** Spain 40.36N 4.54W
19 K4 **Muñoz** Luzon Philippines 15.40N 120.51E
121 J9 **Muñoz Gamero, Pen. de** Chile
30 H7 **Munriar** Bihar India 25.01N 84.14E
12 J8 **Munro, Mt** C Barren I , Tasmania 40.23S 148.07E
21 D9 **Munsan** S Korea 37.56N 126.42E
61 P6 **Munshausen** Luxembourg 50.02N 6.02E
31 H9 **Munshiganj** Bangladesh 23.32N 90.32E
66 G4 **Münsingen** Switzerland 46.53N 7.34E
64 H7 **Münsingen** W Germany 48.25N 9.30E
56 F3 **Munslow** Shropshire Eng 52.29N 2.42W
100 E7 **Munson** Alberta 51.32N 112.41W
107 K11 **Munson** Florida 30.51N 86.53W
69 N7 **Munster** France 48.03N 7.09E
63 M7 **Munster** Niedersachsen W Germany 52.59N 10.05E
63 G9 **Münster** Nordrhein-Westfalen W Germany 51.58N 7.37E
66 K6 **Münster** Switzerland 46.30N 8.17E
59 D7 **Munster** prov Irish Rep
61 N3 **Munsterbilzen** Belgium 50.53N 5.32E
Münstereifel see **Bad Münstereifel**
60 T17 **Munstergeleen** Netherlands 50.58N 5.52E
63 F9 **Münsterland** reg W Germany
66 N1 **Münsterlingen** Switzerland 47.38N 9.14E
64 C3 **Münstermaifeld** W Germany 50.15N 7.23E
69 O4 **Münster-Sarmsheim** W Germany 49.57N 7.53E
69 O8 **Münstertal** W Germany 47.52N 7.49E
75 P5 **Muntadas** airport Spain 41.18N 2.10W
14 C9 **Muntadgin** W Australia 31.41S 118.32E
18 D10 **Muntahak** hill Pen Malaysia 1.50N 103.48E
65 G7 **Muntanitz** mt Austria 47.06N 12.35E
86 D3 **Muntazah, El** Egypt 31.16N 30.01E
61 F3 **Munte** Belgium 50.57N 3.45E
19 A3 **Munte** Celebes Indon 0.30N 119.57E
82 H4 **Muntelui Mare** mt Romania 46.30N 23.12E
93 C4 **Munteme** Uganda 1.20N 31.13E
60 Q7 **Muntendam** Netherlands 53.07N 6.53E
82 K6 **Muntenia** dist Romania
59 C8 **Muntervary Hd** Cork Irish Rep 51.33N 9.51W
66 E4 **Müntschemier** Switzerland 46.59N 7.08E
93 D4 **Muntu** Uganda 1.35N 32.52E
91 F5 **Muntu** Zaïre 2.51S 18.30E
39 G3 **Munugudzhak** U.S.S.R. 63.50N 160.00E
106 K3 **Munuscong L** Michigan 46.14N 84.15W
84 X19 **Munxar** Gozo Mediterranean Sea 36.02N 14.14E
84 Z20 **Munxar Pt** Malta 35.51N 14.35E
93 F3 **Munyen** watercourse Kenya 2.46N 34.54E
93 K7 **Munyoni** watercourse Kenya
95 M7 **Munyu** S Africa 31.58S 28.19E
64 F3 **Münzenberg** W Germany 50.27N 8.47E
37 D6 **Munzur Dağ** Turkey 39.18N 38.43E
37 D6 **Munzur Silsilesi** mts Turkey
51 O6 **Muojärvi** Finland 65.56N 29.40E
114 E6 **Muolea Pt** Hawaiian Is 20.41N 156.02W
25 H3 **Muone, Nam** R Laos
25 G1 **Muong Boum** Vietnam 22.23N 102.53E
25 H2 **Muong Et** Laos 20.47N 104.02E
25 H2 **Muong Ham** Laos 20.19N 104.01E
25 G1 **Muong Hat Hin** Laos 22.05N 102.13E
25 G2 **Muong Hiem** Laos 20.07N 103.23E
Muong Hou see **Phong Saly**
25 G2 **Muong Hun Xieng Hung** Laos 21.37N 102.20E
25 G3 **Muong Khao** Laos 19.38N 103.32E
25 G2 **Muong Khoua** Laos 21.04N 102.28E
25 H1 **Muong Khuong** Vietnam 22.48N 104.09E
25 F3 **Muong Ki** Laos 18.25N 101.50E
25 H3 **Muong Lam** Vietnam 19.27N 104.42E
25 F3 **Muong Liep** Laos 18.29N 101.40E
25 F2 **Muong Luong Nam Tha** Laos 21.01N 101.27E
25 K7 **Muong Man** Vietnam 10.59N 108.02E
25 G3 **Muong May** Laos 18.30N 103.39E
25 G3 **Muong Moc** Laos 18.55N 103.59E
25 G2 **Muong Ngoi** Laos 20.43N 102.42E
25 G1 **Muong Nhie** Vietnam 22.11N 102.28E
25 J4 **Muong Nong** Laos 16.23N 106.31E
25 F3 **Muong Oua** Laos 18.19N 101.18E
25 F1 **Muong Ou Neua** Laos 22.20N 101.47E
25 F1 **Muong Ou Tay** Laos 22.06N 101.46E
25 F3 **Muong Pa** Laos 18.32N 101.36E
25 H4 **Muong Phalane** Laos 16.39N 105.36E
25 F3 **Muong Phieng** Laos 19.06N 101.32E
25 F2 **Muong Sai** Laos 20.44N 101.59E
25 F3 **Muong Saiapoun** Laos 18.34N 101.31E
25 H3 **Muong Sen** Vietnam 19.24N 104.10E
25 F2 **Muong Sing** Laos 21.10N 101.06E
25 G2 **Muong Son** Laos 20.27N 103.20E
25 H4 **Muong Song Khone** Laos 16.17N 105.18E
25 G3 **Muong Soui** Laos 19.32N 102.54E
25 G3 **Muong Soum** Laos 18.46N 102.36E
25 G1 **Muong Te** Vietnam 22.28N 102.38E
25 F3 **Muong Tha Deua** Laos 19.24N 101.49E
25 G2 **Muong Va** Laos 21.51N 102.19E
51 K4 **Muonio** Finland 67.58N 23.40E
51 K4 **Muonionalusta** Sweden 67.55N 23.35E
51 K3 **Muonionjoki** R Sweden/Finland
19 F3 **Muor** isld Moluccas Indon 0.12N 128.58E
41 N5 **Muostakh, Mys** C U.S.S.R. 71.45N 129.30E
66 L4 **Muota Tal** V Switzerland
66 M4 **Muotathal** Switzerland 46.58N 8.46E
66 Q5 **Muottas** Switzerland 46.32N 9.54E
91 D12 **Mupa** Angola 16.07S 15.45E
92 D9 **Mupata Gorge** Zambia/Zimbabwe 15.35S 30.05E
21 B9 **Muping** Shandong China 37.23N 121.35E
87 A8 **Mupoi** Sudan 5.30N 27.36E
21 D7 **Mupyŏng-ni** N Korea 40.40N 126.30E
35 G6 **Muqabalein, El** Jordan 31.54N 35.54E
87 C2 **Muqaddam** watercourse Sudan
86 P4 **Muqārī'iya** Jordan 30.34N 35.34E
86 R12 **Muqattam City** dist Cairo Egypt
86 R12 **Muqaṭṭam, Gebel el** ra Cairo Egypt
33 H5 **Muqaynimah** Saudi Arabia 22.10N 48.50E
35 G4 **Muqbilla** Jordan 32.19N 35.52E
Muqdadiyah see **Miqdādiyah, Al**
Muqdisho see **Mogadiscio**
35 E3 **Muqeibila** Israel 32.31N 35.18E
33 M5 **Muqnīyāt** Oman 23.26N 56.51E
33 L7 **Muqshin** Oman 19.40N 54.57E
33 L7 **Muqshin, Wādī** watercourse Oman
118 E4 **Muquem** Brazil 14.39S 48.07W
118 H7 **Muqui** Brazil 20.53S 41.20W
65 K7 **Mur** R Austria
42 F3 **Mura** R U.S.S.R.
82 C4 **Mura** R Yugoslavia
35 G1 **Murabba 'at** Syria 33.05N 35.57E
36 C4 **Muradiye** Manisa Turkey 38.38N 27.21E
37 H7 **Muradiye** Van Turkey 39.00N 43.44E
30 A4 **Muradnagar** Uttar Prad India 28.47N 77.29E
Murāghā, Sabkhat see **Sabkha Marāgha**
79 L7 **Muraglione, Passo di** pass Italy 43.56N 11.40E
18 M6 **Murakaman** Borneo Indon 0.10S 116.45E
20 N3 **Murakami** Japan 38.13N 139.28E
62 K9 **Murakeresztúr** Hungary 46.21N 16.52E
121 J7 **Murallón, Cerro** pk Arg/Chile 49.48S 73.26W
66 M7 **Muralto** Switzerland 46.11N 8.49E
20 N4 **Muramatsu** Japan 37.40N 139.12E
93 A7 **Muramba** Rwanda 1.45S 29.36E
93 A8 **Muramba** Rwanda 2.10S 29.15E
93 B9 **Muramba** mt Tanzania 3.48S 30.31E
93 A9 **Muramvya** Burundi 3.14S 29.36E
15 B5 **Murana** Irian Jaya 3.33S 133.48E
53 X16 **Murane** Norway 61.23N 7.44E
30 B1 **Murang** Himachal Prad India 31.36N 78.28E
93 J6 **Murang'a** Kenya 0.43S 37.10E
34 P5 **Mūrānī** Iran 33.15N 47.46E
79 M4 **Murano** Italy 45.27N 12.22E
20 H6 **Muraoka** Japan 35.31N 134.34E
34 G8 **Murayr, Al** Saudi Arabia 30.04N 39.56E
76 D2 **Muras** Spain 43.28N 7.43W
47 F6 **Murashi** U.S.S.R. 59.20N 48.59E
18 C5 **Murasipongi** Sumatra Indon 0.34N 99.48E
72 K8 **Murasson** France 43.45N 2.44E
72 K5 **Murat** France 45.06N 2.51E
37 F7 **Murat** R Bingöl etc Turkey
36 J1 **Murat** R Samsun etc Turkey
37 G6 **Muratbası** mt Turkey 39.25N 43.20E
36 D4 **Murat Dağı** mt Turkey 38.56N 29.43E
37 C2 **Muratkorusu** R Turkey
37 D1 **Muratlı** Turkey 41.12N 27.30E
37 F4 **Muratli** Turkey 41.29N 41.39E
67 P11 **Murato** Corsica 42.35N 9.19E
72 K8 **Murat-sur-Vèbre** France 43.41N 2.50E
65 K7 **Murau** Austria 47.08N 14.10E
15 D6 **Muraukwa** Irian Jaya 4.50S 136.43E
66 M5 **Muraun, Piz** mt Switzerland 46.41N 8.55E
81 D5 **Muravera** Sardinia 39.25N 9.36E
45 N3 **Muravlyanka** U.S.S.R. 53.40N 41.12E
20 O3 **Murayama** Japan 38.29N 140.21E
33 D4 **Murayr, Jabal** mts Saudi Arabia
33 J8 **Mur'ayt** S Yemen 16.24N 51.16E
66 A7 **Muraz, la** France 46.08N 6.12E
79 D6 **Murazzano** Italy 44.28N 8.01E
Murbat see **Mirbāţ**
76 E6 **Murça** Portugal 41.24N 7.28W
76 E6 **Murça** Portugal 41.06N 7.14W
75 G3 **Murchante** Spain 42.02N 1.40W
Murcheh Khurt see **Mūrcheh Khvort**
32 D4 **Mūrcheh Khvort** Iran 33.06N 51.32E
77 J7 **Murches** Spain 36.57N 3.34W
63 T5 **Murchin** E Germany 53.55N 13.45E
11 G8 **Murchison** New Zealand 41.50S 172.20E
12 H6 **Murchison** Victoria 36.40S 145.14E
93 C3 **Murchison Falls Nat. Park** Uganda
93 C3 **Murchison (Kabalega) Falls** Uganda 2.17N 31.41E
11 F10 **Murchison, Mt** New Zealand 43.02S 171.24E
11 G8 **Murchison, Mt** New Zealand 41.45S 172.31E
14 B7 **Murchison, Mt** W Australia 26.45S 116.25E
11 B12 **Murchison Mts** New Zealand
14 A8 **Murchison, R** W Australia
13 C5 **Murchison Ra** N Terr Australia
94 L4 **Murchison Range** mts S Africa
48 R3 **Murchison, Sd** Greenland
80 D3 **Murci** Italy 42.44N 11.25E
77 O5 **Murcia** Spain 37.59N 1.08W
74 F7 **Murcia** prov Spain
74 F6 **Murcia** reg Spain
19 L7 **Murcielagos B** Mindanao Philippines
Murdab see **Mordāb**
14 E10 **Murdarbilla** W Australia 32.49S 123.49E
72 K6 **Mur-de-Barrez** France 44.50N 2.39E
70 E5 **Mur-de-Bretagne** France 48.12N 2.59W
70 O7 **Mur-de-Sologne** France 47.25N 1.36E
108 K6 **Murdo** S Dakota 43.54N 100.42W
13 G2 **Murdoch Pt** Queensland 14.37S 144.55E
98 G5 **Murdochville** Quebec 48.57N 65.30W
105 E10 **Murdock** Florida 27.02N 82.08W
108 O9 **Murdock** Nebraska 40.58N 96.17W
70 O4 **Mureaux, Les** France 48.59N 1.55E
65 N8 **Mureck** Austria 46.43N 15.47E
37 D2 **Mürefte** Turkey 40.41N 27.15E
92 D3 **Murehe** Burundi 2.42S 30.00E
20 M5 **Murei** Japan 36.46N 138.12E
35 G7 **Mureijimat Ibn Hamid** Jordan 31.40N 35.47E
90 B7 **Mureji** Nigeria 8.47N 5.45E
71 H7 **Mure, la** France 44.53N 5.47E
30 G6 **Murera** Uttar Prad India 26.39N 83.36E
82 G4 **Muresul** R Romania
72 G9 **Muret** France 43.28N 1.19E
72 C7 **Muret, le** France 44.24N 0.50W
66 P6 **Muretto, Passo del** Italy/Switz 46.22N 9.43E
107 C7 **Murfreesboro** Arkansas 34.04N 93.42W
105 K1 **Murfreesboro** N Carolina 36.28N 77.08W
107 K6 **Murfreesboro** Tennessee 35.50N 86.25W
66 N3 **Murg** Switzerland 47.08N 9.13E
64 E8 **Murg** W Germany 47.34N 8.01E
66 M1 **Murg** R Switzerland
66 N3 **Murg** R Switzerland
64 E6 **Murg** R W Germany
66 H1 **Murg** R W Germany
43 L7 **Murgab** Tadzhikistan U.S.S.R. 38.12N 74.01E
43 F7 **Murgab** U.S.S.R. 37.43N 62.00E
43 L7 **Murgab** R Tadzhikistan U.S.S.R.
43 F8 **Murgab** R Turkmeniya U.S.S.R.
83 D5 **Murgana** mt Greece/Albania 39.46N 20.24E
82 H8 **Murgash** mt Bulgaria 42.50N 23.40E
81 N2 **Murge, Le** physical reg Italy
13 C1 **Murgenella Cr** N Terr Australia
82 L4 **Murgeni** Romania 46.12N 28.04E
66 H2 **Mürgenthal** Switzerland 47.16N 7.50E
Murghab see **Morghāb**
31 B3 **Murghab** reg Afghanistan
31 B3 **Murghab R** Afghanistan
31 E5 **Murgha Kibzai** Pakistan 30.48N 69.25E
31 D5 **Murgha Mehterzai** Pakistan 30.42N 67.34E
31 E3 **Murgh Pass** Afghanistan 35.48N 69.17E
Murghun see **Mūrjān**
81 N2 **Murgia Sant'Elia** Italy 40.52N 16.34E
81 M2 **Murgia Serraficaia** mt Italy 40.57N 16.21E
82 K4 **Murgociu** mt Romania 46.45N 26.20E
13 K7 **Murgon** Queensland 26.14S 151.54E
14 B7 **Murgoo** W Australia 27.20S 116.27E
90 F6 **Murguba** Nigeria 11.43N 12.40E
75 E2 **Murguía** Spain 42.57N 2.49W
44 G7 **Murguz** Armenia U.S.S.R. 40.44N 45.15E
66 K2 **Muri** Aargau Switzerland 47.16N 8.21E
66 F4 **Muri** Bern Switzerland 46.56N 7.29E
32 G2 **Mūrī** Iran 37.11N 56.50E
29 H6 **Muri** Madhya Prad India 23.51N 82.34E
90 E7 **Muri** Nigeria 9.08N 10.50E
22 E7 **Muri** Qinghai China 38.06N 98.58E
122 B10 **Muri** Rarotonga Pacific Oc 21.15S 159.44W
118 G7 **Muriaé** Brazil 21.08S 42.23W
79 D6 **Murialdo** Italy 44.19N 8.09E
76 G3 **Murias de Paredes** Spain 42.51N 6.11W
117 J9 **Muricí** Brazil 9.16S 35.57W
31 D6 **Murid** Pakistan 29.14N 66.12E
31 H5 **Muridke** Pakistan 31.46N 74.21E
91 G8 **Muriege** Angola 9.58S 21.13E
100 G4 **Muriel L** Alberta 54.10N 110.40W
20 M1 **Murii-dake** mt Japan 43.43N 143.12E
Muri Kuh see **Mīr Kūh**
100 O2 **Murillo** Ontario 48.26N 89.31W
75 J3 **Murillo de Gállego** Spain 42.20N 0.45W
75 F3 **Murillo de Rio Leza** Spain 42.24N 2.19W
75 H3 **Murillo el Fruto** Spain 42.24N 1.28W
70 G6 **Murin, L. de** France 47.40N 1.56W
42 G6 **Murino** U.S.S.R. 51.28N 104.25E
42 H5 **Murin'ya** U.S.S.R. 54.45N 107.20E
11 D6 **Muritai** New Zealand 41.18S 174.53E
37 E6 **Mürit Dağları** mts Turkey 39.43N 39.56E
63 R6 **Müritz** L E Germany
11 M5 **Muriwai** New Zealand 38.45S 177.56E
32 E6 **Mūrjān** Iran 29.10N 52.10E
51 H5 **Murjek** Sweden 66.29N 20.50E
25 M7 **Murkong Selek** Assam India 26.47N 95.12E
31 H2 **Murkushi** Kashmir 36.55N 74.49E
87 F8 **Murle** Ethiopia 5.11N 36.09E
64 B3 **Mürlenbach** W Germany 50.08N 6.35E
30 K7 **Murliganj** Bihar India 25.54N 87.00E
80 D2 **Murlo** Italy 43.09N 11.23E
47 C2 **Murmansk** U.S.S.R. 68.59N 33.08E
47 C2 **Murmanskaya Oblast'** prov U.S.S.R.
47 C2 **Murmanskiy Bereg** coast U.S.S.R.
41 D2 **Murmantsa, Bukhta** B Novaya Zemlya U.S.S.R.
47 C2 **Murmashi** U.S.S.R. 68.50N 32.51E
60 M6 **Murmerwoude** Netherlands 53.18N 6.00E
45 M2 **Murmino** U.S.S.R. 54.37N 40.04E
64 L8 **Murnau** W Germany 47.40N 11.13E
77 W14 **Muro** Balearic Is 39.45N 3.03E
67 O11 **Muro** Corsica 42.32N 8.55E
67 O13 **Muro, C. di** Corsica 41.45N 8.40E
Muroc L see **Rogers L**
77 Q3 **Muro de Alcoy** Spain 38.47N 0.26W
71 B5 **Murol** France 45.35N 2.56E
81 R12 **Muro Leccese** Italy 40.06N 18.21E
80 M7 **Muro Lucano** Italy 40.45N 15.29E
45 O1 **Murom** U.S.S.R. 55.34N 42.04E
47 M7 **Muromtsevo** U.S.S.R. 56.24N 75.10E
72 C3 **Muron** France 46.03N 0.50W
92 E2 **Murongo** Tanzania 1.05S 30.41E
20 K2 **Muroran** Japan 42.21N 140.59E
93 B9 **Murore** Burundi 3.11S 30.42E
76 A3 **Muros** Spain 42.47N 9.04W
76 G1 **Muros de Nalón** Spain 43.32N 6.06W
76 A3 **Muros y Noya, Ría de** B Spain
20 H8 **Muroto** Japan 33.16N 134.10E
20 H8 **Muroto-misaki** C Japan 33.13N 134.11E
82 L2 **Murovano Kurilovtsy** U.S.S.R. 48.45N 27.30E
62 K3 **Murowana Goslina** Poland 52.34N 16.59E
20 E8 **Murozumi** Japan 33.56N 131.58E
110 J6 **Murphy** Idaho 43.14N 116.32W
105 C2 **Murphy** N Carolina 35.05N 84.02W
110 B7 **Murphy** Oregon 42.23N 123.20W
107 G4 **Murphy, Lake** res Illinois
123 H11 **Murphy, Mt** Antarctica 74.55S 148.00W
111 D3 **Murphys** California 38.07N 120.28W
107 G4 **Murphysboro** Illinois 37.45N 89.20W
33 H5 **Murrah** tribe Saudi Arabia
13 H8 **Murra Murra** Queensland 28.18S 146.48E
108 R8 **Murray** Iowa 41.04N 93.56W
107 H5 **Murray** Kentucky 36.35N 88.20W
108 P9 **Murray** Nebraska 40.58N 95.56W
110 O9 **Murray** Utah 40.40N 111.53W
12 F5 **Murray** R New S Wales/S Australia
12 E6 **Murray Bridge** S Australia 35.10S 139.17E
104 C7 **Murray City** Ohio 39.30N 82.10W
122 L5 **Murray Deep** Pacific Oc 28.00N 156.00W
13 C5 **Murray Downs** N Terr Australia 21.03S 134.42E
98 K7 **Murray Harbour** Prince Edward I 46.00N 62.32W
98 K8 **Murray Head** C Prince Edward I 46.00N 62.28W
26 V3 **Murray Hill** Christmas I Ind Oc 10.28S 105.37E
15 H8 **Murray Is** Torres Str, Qnsld 9.55S 144.05E
109 N7 **Murray L** Oklahoma 34.03N 97.04W
15 F7 **Murray,L** Papua New Guinea
105 F3 **Murray L** South Carolina
123 B4 **Murray Monolith** Antarctica
15 G7 **Murray, Mt** Papua New Guinea 6.50S 144.00E
101 S1 **Murray Pt** Victoria I, N W Terr 68.35N 110.17W
101 N8 **Murray R** Br Columbia
14 B10 **Murray, R** W Australia
14 G7 **Murray Ra** W Australia
26 E3 **Murray Ridge** Arabian Sea
98 K8 **Murray River** Prince Edward I 46.00N 62.38W
96 C1 **Murray's Anchorage** Bermuda
95 G7 **Murraysburg** S Africa 31.58S 23.45E
122 M5 **Murray Seascarp** Pacific Oc
101 K11 **Murrayville** Br Col 49.05N 122.37W
107 F2 **Murrayville** Illinois 39.35N 90.16W
12 F6 **Murrayville** Victoria 35.16S 141.14E
31 G4 **Murree** Pakistan 33.55N 73.26E
105 H4 **Murrells Inlet** S Carolina 33.34N 79.03W
66 H5 **Mürren** Switzerland 46.33N 7.54E
64 H6 **Murrhardt** W Germany 48.59N 9.35E
87 H8 **Murri** Ethiopia 4.18N 40.47E
93 M1 **Murri** Kenya 4.11N 40.42E
12 J5 **Murringo** New S Wales 34.19S 148.36E
14 D8 **Murrin Murrin** W Australia 28.58S 121.33E
119 C4 **Murrí, R** Colombia
59 C4 **Murrisk, mts** Mayo Irish Rep
81 K9 **Murro di Porco, C** Sicily 37.01N 15.21E
12 G5 **Murrumbidgee** R New S Wales
12 J5 **Murrumburrah** New S Wales 34.35S 148.25E
92 J9 **Murrupula** Mozambique 15.26S 38.41E
12 K4 **Murrurundi** New S Wales 31.47S 150.51E
71 G9 **Murs** France 43.57N 5.17E
30 A5 **Mursan** Uttar Prad India 27.35N 77.55E
33 N6 **Murşays** Oman 20.28N 58.50E
37 D2 **Mürselli** Turkey 40.42N 27.21E
29 L5 **Murshidabad** W Bengal India 24.11N 88.19E
29 L5 **Murshidabad** dist W Bengal India
35 G5 **Mursi** Jordan 32.08N 35.52E
84 N11 **Mursín** Crete 35.10N 25.57E
37 D9 **Mürşitpınar** Turkey 36.55N 38.20E
82 C4 **Murska Sobota** Yugoslavia 46.40N 16.11E
42 F3 **Murskiy, Porog** falls U.S.S.R. 58.28N 98.30E
82 C4 **Mursko Središće** Yugoslavia 46.30N 16.28E
32 K7 **Murt** Iran 27.09N 62.44E
65 K7 **Mur-tal** V Austria
66 S5 **Murtaröl, Piz** mt Italy/Switz 46.34N 10.18E
77 K7 **Murtas** Spain 36.53N 3.06W
110 L7 **Murtaugh** Idaho 42.30N 114.10W
29 E7 **Murtazapur** Maharashtra India 20.43N 77.28E
12 G4 **Murtee** New S Wales 31.05S 143.35E
66 E4 **Murten** Switzerland 46.56N 7.07E
66 E4 **Murtensee** L Switzerland
82 C7 **Murter** isld Yugoslavia 43.49N 15.37E
12 F3 **Murteree, L** S Australia
30 A3 **Murthal** Haryana India 29.02N 77.05E

58 K5 Murthly Tayside Scotland 56.32N 3.30W
76 E12 Murtigão R Portugal
101 O9 Murtle L Br Columbia 52.09N 119.40W
12 G6 Murtoa Victoria 36.40S 142.31E
76 B7 Murtosa Portugal 40.45N 8.39W
51 O6 Murtovaara Finland 65.40N 29.25E
66 N3 Mürtschenstock mt Switzerland 47.05N 9.09E
Murua I see Woodlark I
93 F2 Murua Ngithigerr mts Kenya
117 D5 Murucupi Brazil 1.32S 48.45W
28 A1 Murud Maharashtra India 18.20N 73.00E
18 L4 Murud mt Sarawak Malaysia 3.54N 115.45E
75 E1 Murueta Spain 43.21N 2.41W
93 B8 Murugwanza Tanzania 2.28S 30.39E
18 L6 Murui R Borneo Indon
21 B6 Muruin Sum Sk L Nei Monggol Zizhiqu China
41 H6 Murukta U.S.S.R. 67.48N 102.02E
92 D2 Murunda Rwanda 1.56S 29.30E
18 L5 Murung R Borneo Indon
93 C10 Murungu Tanzania 4.15S 31.11E
11 L5 Murupara New Zealand 38.27S 176.41E
120 D3 Muru, R Brazil
122 N10 Mururoa atoll Pacific Oc 22.00S 140.00W
33 C2 Murūt, Al Saudi Arabia 29.14N 39.52E
119 J9 Murutinga Brazil 3.29S 59.13W
92 F3 Murutunguru Tanzania 2.01S 33.05E
112 N3 Murvaul Res Texas 32.02N 94.30W
37 E3 Mürvetler R Turkey
71 C10 Murviel-lès-Béziers France 43.27N 3.09E
69 K5 Murville France 49.20N 5.50E
30 D7 Murwal Uttar Prad India 25.31N 80.34E
33 C5 Murwāni, Wādī watercourse Saudi Arabia
29 G6 Murwara Madhya Prad India 23.49N 80.28E
12 L3 Murwillumba New S Wales 28.20S 153.24E
46 P1 Murygino U.S.S.R. 58.48N 49.25E
18 J9 Muryo, Gunung mt Java Indon 6.39S 110.51E
65 M7 Mürz R Austria
44 M4 Murzair Kazakhstan U.S.S.R. 43.50N 52.32E
47 N4 Murzinka U.S.S.R. 57.42N 61.00E
65 M6 Mürzsteg Austria 47.42N 15.29E
65 M7 Mürz-tal V Austria
Murzuk see Marzūq
65 N6 Mürzzuschlag Austria 47.37N 15.41E
37 F7 Muş Turkey 38.45N 41.30E
90 F6 Musa Nigeria 10.42N 13.10E
91 F2 Musa Zaïre 2.39N 19.22E
46 E2 Mūša R Lithuania U.S.S.R.
15 K8 Musa R Papua New Guinea
36 J6 Musabeyli Gaziantep Turkey 36.54N 36.54E
33 E7 Muşābih Saudi Arabia 18.45N 42.00E
34 G6 Musad ar Raggas watercourse Iraq
91 H5 Musadi Zaïre 2.31S 22.50E
35 F2 Musadiye Syria 32.53N 35.38E
30 E6 Musafirkhana Uttar Prad India 26.23N 81.48E
86 L8 Mûsa, Gebel hill Egypt 28.32N 33.59E
89 D7 Musaia Sierra Leone 9.49N 11.39W
Musaiyib see Musayyib, Al
31 E5 Musa Khel Bazar Pakistan 30.53N 69.52E
32 C5 Mūsā, Khowr-e inlet Iran
37 G1 Musaköyalçaği Burun C Turkey 41.10N 29.45E
18 C5 Musala isld Sumatra Indon
82 H8 Musala mt Bulgaria 42.10N 23.35E
92 C9 Musale Zambia 15.25S 26.48E
34 F7 Muşallá, Aqran al mt Saudi Arabia 31.32N 38.17E
34 O7 Musallam Iraq 31.53N 46.57E
33 M6 Muşallam, Wādī watercourse Oman
26 P3 Musaltivu isld Tamil Nadu India 9.12N 79.05E
21 E6 Musan N Korea 42.12N 129.15E
33 M3 Musandam Pen U.A.E./Oman
91 J8 Musangoi Zaïre 9.29S 24.33E
33 G2 Musannāh, Al ridge Saudi Arabia
91 K7 Musao Zaïre 7.43S 26.19E
31 C4 Musa Qala Afghanistan 32.23N 64.49E
31 C4 Musa Qala, R-i- Afghanistan
37 D7 Muşar Turkey 38.44N 38.32E
Musara see Rabaraba
75 N5 Musara mt Spain 41.16N 1.03E
Musaras see Mushorah
20 A2 Musashi-Murayama Tōkyō Japan
20 D2 Musashino dist Tōkyō Japan 35.43N 139.35E
90 C5 Musawa Nigeria 12.11N 7.40E
86 O5 Mūsā, Wādī watercourse Jordan
36 H3 Musaybeli Yozgat Turkey 39.51N 34.34E
Musay'id see Umm Sa'id
33 C4 Musayjīd, Al Saudi Arabia 24.04N 39.03E
33 F10 Musaymir S Yemen 13.26N 44.37E
33 J9 Muşayna'ah S Yemen 15.05N 50.37E
87 L3 Musaynūm S Yemen 15.16N 47.14E
33 G6 Muşayqirah mt Saudi Arabia 21.08N 46.15E
34 M6 Musayyib, Al Iraq 32.47N 44.20E
93 B8 Musaza mt Rwanda 2.19S 30.40E
Musazade see Arhavi
90 M4 Musbat Sudan 15.15N 24.15E
33 N5 Muscat Oman 23.37N 58.38E
33 M4 Muscat prov Oman
106 C8 Muscatine Iowa 41.25N 91.03W
Muscat & Oman see Oman
107 J7 Muscle Shoals Alabama 34.45N 87.38W
106 D6 Muscoda Wisconsin 43.11N 90.27W
103 E5 Musconetcong R New Jersey
104 Q3 Muscongus B Maine
92 E9 Muse R Mozambique
35 J3 Museifre Syria 32.38N 36.20E
Museimir see Musaymir
Museina'a see Muşayna'ah
35 G8 Museitiba anc site Jordan 31.29N 35.58E
91 H9 Musela Zaïre 10.13S 22.53E
76 H1 Musel, El Spain 43.34N 5.41W
93 A9 Musema Burundi 3.03S 29.44E
93 B8 Musenyi Burundi 2.58S 30.03E
91 G6 Musese Zaïre 5.28S 21.30E
36 C5 Müsgebi Turkey 37.02N 27.22E
13 G2 Musgrave Queensland 14.47S 143.36E
12 B2 Musgrave Ranges S Australia
98 T5 Musgravetown Newfoundland 48.24N 53.56W
92 E12 Mushandike Dam Zimbabwe 20.10S 30.40E
35 G6 Mushaqqar, El Jordan 31.48N 35.47E
35 H6 Mushash watercourse Jordan
34 D7 Mushâsh Hudruj Jordan 31.29N 36.47E
86 M7 Mushâsh Sirtabba Egypt 29.22N 34.20E
33 F8 Mushaynīqah Yemen 16.30N 45.58E
Musheirib, Ras see Mushayrib, Ra's
35 F9 Musheirifa Jordan 31.08N 35.43E
35 G8 Musheirifa anc site Jordan 31.30N 35.52E
35 H10 Musheish watercourse Jordan
91 G6 Mushenge Zaïre 4.30S 21.20E
59 E7 Musheramore mt Cork Irish Rep 52.00N 8.58W
91 E5 Mushie Zaïre 2.59S 16.55E
92 C8 Mushingashi R Zambia
31 D6 Mushkaf Pakistan 29.30N 67.45E
53 G6 Musholm isld Denmark 55.28N 11.05E
53 G6 Musholm Bugt B Denmark 55.27N 11.05E
34 K2 Mushorah Iraq 36.57N 42.18E
86 M4 Mushraq, Gebel hill Egypt 30.40N 34.16E
15 G5 Mushu I Papua New Guinea 3.28S 143.35E
91 E6 Mushuni Zaïre 4.18S 17.55E
18 F7 Musi R Sumatra Indon
32 B4 Musian Iran 32.35N 47.21E
34 P6 Mūsiān Iran 32.27N 47.24E
11 E2 Musick Pt New Zealand 36.51S 174.54E
111 L6 Music Mt Arizona 35.33N 113.40W
93 A5 Musienene Zaïre 0.03N 29.17E
30 G4 Musikot Nepal 28.10N 83.15E
79 N3 Musile di Piave Italy 45.38N 12.33E
111 N2 Musinia Pk mt Utah 39.03N 111.34W
28 D2 Musi R Andhra Prad India
28 D5 Musiri Tamil Nadu India 10.58N 78.26E
33 D7 Muskah isld Saudi Arabia 18.52N 40.40E
101 M5 Muskeg R N W Terr
108 P1 Muskeg B Minnesota
103 O4 Muskeget Chan Massachusetts
103 O4 Muskeget I Massachusetts 41.20N 70.19W
100 N1 Muskeg L Ontario
106 H6 Muskegon Michigan 43.13N 86.15W
106 H6 Muskegon Heights Michigan 43.13N 86.16W
106 H6 Muskegon, R Michigan
51 E4 Musken Norway 67.54N 16.15E
86 R12 Muski dist Cairo Egypt
104 D7 Muskingum R Ohio
30 C7 Muskira Uttar Prad India 25.40N 79.48E
52 L8 Muskö Sweden 58.59N 18.10E
109 P6 Muskogee Oklahoma 35.45N 95.21W
99 L7 Muskoka, L Ontario
108 C6 Muskrat Cr Wyoming
101 M6 Muskwa Br Columbia 58.45N 122.48W
100 C2 Muskwa L Alberta
100 C2 Muskwa R Alberta
53 T20 Muslandsvåg Norway 59.21N 5.45E
34 E2 Muslimīya Syria 36.20N 37.10E
47 M5 Muslyumovo Chelyabinsk U.S.S.R. 55.36N 61.39E
46 R2 Muslyumovo Tatar A.S.S.R. U.S.S.R. 55.20N 53.10E
87 E1 Musmar Sudan 18.13N 35.40E
35 D3 Musmus Israel 32.33N 35.09E
79 E7 Musocco dist Milan Italy
92 D8 Musofu Zambia 13.31S 29.02E
91 J9 Musokantanda Zaïre 10.56S 25.07E
93 E7 Musoma Tanzania 1.31S 33.49E
79 M3 Musone R Italy
80 H2 Musone R Italy
45 V3 Musorka U.S.S.R. 53.45N 49.44E
92 C7 Musoshi Zaïre 11.54S 27.45E
65 P4 Mušov Czechoslovakia 48.54N 16.37E
93 C5 Musozi Uganda 0.22N 31.36E
98 L3 Musquanus L Quebec
98 L3 Musquaro Quebec 50.14N 61.03W
98 L3 Musquaro, L Quebec
98 F8 Musquash New Brunswick 45.11N 66.21W
98 J8 Musquodoboit Nova Scotia 45.03N 63.10W
98 J9 Musquodoboit Harb Nova Scotia 44.48N 63.10W
87 D4 Musran I Sudan 12.50N 32.47E
87 J4 Mussa Ali mt Ethiopia 12.30N 42.25E
91 E10 Mussari Angola 13.07S 17.56E
15 K4 Mussau I Bismarck Arch
53 H7 Musse Denmark 54.44N 11.40E
60 R8 Mussel Netherlands 52.57N 7.02E
60 R8 Mussel A-Kanaal canal Netherlands
58 K7 Musselburgh Lothian Scotland 55.57N 3.04W
60 R8 Musselkanaal Netherlands 52.55N 7.01E
110 R3 Musselshell Montana 46.30N 108.05W
110 S3 Musselshell R Montana
91 E9 Mussende Angola 10.33S 16.02E
91 C7 Musserra Angola 7.31S 13.02E
69 J6 Mussey France 48.48N 5.04E
72 E5 Mussidan France 45.02N 0.22E
37 F7 Muş Sira Dağları mts Turkey
66 O7 Musso Italy 46.07N 9.17E
91 E9 Mussolo Angola 10.01S 17.20E
81 G8 Mussomeli Sicily 37.35N 13.45E
61 N8 Musson Belgium 49.33N 5.43E
30 B2 Mussoorie Uttar Prad India 30.26N 78.04E
91 C7 Mussorongo tribe Angola
91 G11 Mussuma Angola 14.13S 21.57E
91 G11 Mussuma R Angola
61 N8 Mussy-la-Ville Belgium 49.34N 5.40E
69 H8 Mussy-sur-Seine France 47.58N 4.30E
39 B4 Mustafa U.S.S.R. 61.43N 138.21E
Mustafaabad see Moştafaabad
30 E7 Mustafabad Rae Bareli, Uttar Prad India 25.54N 81.17E
30 B5 Mustafabad Agra Agra, Uttar Prad India 27.18N 78.35E
36 C2 Mustafa Kemalpaşa Turkey 40.03N 28.25E
Mustafa Kemalpaşa R see Kirmasti R
87 K8 Mustahil Ethiopia 5.13N 44.44E
86 F4 Mustâi Egypt 30.37N 31.09E
66 S5 Müstair Switzerland 46.38N 10.28E
66 S5 Müstair, Val Italy/Switz
29 H3 Mustang Nepal 29.10N 83.55E
109 N6 Mustang Oklahoma 35.24N 97.45W
112 E3 Mustang Cr Texas
112 K8 Mustang I Texas
43 C2 Mustayevo U.S.S.R. 51.49N 53.30E
Müstecip see Balli
Muster see Disentis Muster
121 K5 Musterl, L Argentina
108 O4 Mustinka R Minnesota
51 K11 Mustio Finland 60.08N 23.55E
116 O8 Mustique isld Grenadines W I 12.52N 61.11W
46 F1 Mustla Estonia U.S.S.R. 58.12N 25.50E
51 N3 Mustola Finland 68.47N 28.10E
57 N4 Muston N Yorks Eng 54.11N 0.19W
46 F1 Mustvee Estonia U.S.S.R. 58.51N 26.59E
15 F5 Musu Papua New Guinea 2.40S 140.10E
21 E7 Musu-dan C N Korea 40.52N 129.45E
37 H6 Musun Turkey 39.41N 43.50E
12 K4 Muswellbrook New S Wales 32.17S 150.55E
62 M6 Muszyna Poland 49.21N 20.51E
85 K7 Mut Egypt 25.28N 28.58E
36 G6 Mut Turkey 36.38N 33.27E
65 M8 Muta Yugoslavia 46.37N 15.10E
35 J4 Muta'iyah Syria 32.29N 36.17E
Mutaiyin see Mutayyin
92 H9 Mutala Mozambique 15.54S 37.51E
79 J1 Muta, L.della L Italy 46.46N 10.32E
94 L4 Mutale R S Africa
33 B3 Mutalla', Al Saudi Arabia 27.10N 37.50E
86 F3 Mu'tamadīya, El Egypt 31.02N 31.05E
92 C8 Mutanda Zambia 12.24S 26.13E
118 J3 Mutá, Pta.do C Brazil 13.54S 38.54W
35 H9 Mutarammil, Jeb.el mts Jordan
92 G10 Mutarara Mozambique 17.30S 35.06E
33 F3 Mutayr tribe Saudi Arabia
33 E9 Mutayyin Yemen 16.00N 43.03E
35 J1 Mutbin Syria 33.08N 36.15E
91 J7 Mutengwa Zaïre 6.34S 25.13E
65 Q4 Mutěnice Czechoslovakia 48.54N 17.02E
64 O4 Mutěnín Czechoslovakia 49.33N 12.45E
29 F2 Muth Himachal Prad India 31.58N 78.02E
93 K7 Mutha Kenya 1.47S 38.26E
58 J6 Muthill Tayside Scotland 56.20N 3.51W
33 M5 Muti Oman 23.01N 57.45E
92 G11 Mutiambamba Mozambique 19.00S 34.07E
92 D2 Mutiko Zaïre 1.40S 28.11E
15 F7 Muting Irian Jaya 7.23S 140.19E
91 K6 Mutingwa Zaïre 4.30S 27.19E
93 C3 Mutir Uganda 2.45N 31.26E
19 D8 Mutis mt Timor Indon 9.35S 124.15E
117 C5 Mutiti, I Brazil
37 F7 Mutki Turkey 38.25N 41.54E
37 D7 Mutmur Turkey 38.52N 38.32E
39 F8 Mutnovskaya Sopka vol Kamchatka U.S.S.R. 52.27N 158.12E
47 H3 Mutnyy-Materik U.S.S.R. 66.00N 55.02E
91 H7 Mutombo Zaïre 6.16S 22.17E
91 H7 Mutombo-Mukulu Zaïre 7.42S 24.00E
93 K7 Mutomo Kenya 1.50S 38.13E
92 D2 Mutongo Zaïre 1.10S 28.40E
12 F4 Mutooroo S Australia 32.30S 140.58E
42 G2 Mutoray U.S.S.R. 61.20N 100.32E
91 H6 Mutoto Zaïre 5.45S 22.39E
22 L6 Mutoudeng Hebei China 40.30N 119.27E
22 L5 Mutougou Nei Monggol Zizhiqu China 42.25N 118.55E
80 L6 Mutria, Monte Italy 41.23N 14.33E
33 G2 Mutriba oil field Kuwait 29.45N 47.27E
95 B2 Mutsamudu Comoro Is Indian Oc 12.10S 44.25E
91 J9 Mutshatsha Zaïre 10.40S 24.26E
20 P1 Mutsu Japan 41.18N 141.15E
20 O1 Mutsu-wan B Japan
13 G6 Muttaburra Queensland 22.33S 144.31E
66 G1 Muttenz Switzerland 47.31N 7.39E
69 O7 Muttersholtz France 48.16N 7.32E
64 E5 Mutterstadt W Germany 49.26N 8.22E
Mutti, Sabkhat see Sabkhat Maţţi salt marsh
66 S4 Muttler mt Switzerland 46.54N 10.23E
98 N3 Mutton Bay Quebec 50.47N 59.02W
10 E11 Mutton Bird I Lord Howe I Pacific Oc 31.33S 159.08E
11 B13 Muttonbird Is New Zealand
11 C13 Muttonbird Is New Zealand 46.50S 168.15E
59 C6 Mutton,I Clare Irish Rep 52.49N 9.31W
Muttra see Mathura
28 E3 Muttukuru Andhra Prad India 14.21N 80.09E
28 D5 Muttupet Tamil Nadu India 10.24N 79.32E
109 L5 Mutual Oklahoma 36.14N 99.12W
92 H9 Mutuáli Mozambique 14.54S 37.00E
90 F6 Mutube Nigeria 11.14N 13.20E
86 E3 Mutûbis Egypt 31.18N 30.32E
81 D2 Mutucrone, Pta su pk Sardinia 40.32N 9.37E
93 K6 Mutukya mt Kenya 0.56S 38.22E
120 G2 Mutum Amazonas Brazil 6.45S 60.19W
118 H6 Mutum Minas Gerais Brazil 19.45S 41.23W
120 F3 Mutum Rondônia Brazil 8.33S 63.45W
90 E7 Mutum Biyu Nigeria 8.40N 10.50E
91 E10 Mutumbo Angola 13.12S 17.21E
92 C9 Mutumbwe mt Zambia 14.41S 26.39E
90 C6 Mutumji Nigeria 11.24N 6.26E
120 F3 Mutumparaná Brazil 9.37S 64.56W
120 E1 Mutum R Brazil
118 E3 Mutunópolis Brazil 13.38S 49.20W
26 T5 Mutur Sri Lanka 8.27N 81.15E
15 B5 Muturi R Irian Jaya
93 A5 Mutwanga Zaïre 0.22N 29.46E
90 E6 Mutwe Nigeria 11.15N 11.45E
69 N6 Mutzig France 48.33N 7.27E
64 O1 Mutzschen E Germany 51.15N 12.54E
51 M9 Muurame Finland 62.07N 25.40E
51 L5 Muurola Finland 66.23N 25.24E
22 H7 Mu Us Shamo des Nei Monggol Zizhiqu China
34 N6 Muwaffaqīyah, Al Iraq 32.16N 45.57E
Muwai Hakran see Muwayh, Al
Muwailih, El see Muwaylih, Al
92 F5 Muwale Tanzania 6.21S 33.46E
35 H6 Muwaqqar, El anc site Jordan 31.49N 36.06E
33 D5 Muwayh, Al Saudi Arabia 22.41N 41.37E
33 A3 Muwaylih,Al Saudi Arabia 27.41N 35.31E
86 D8 Muweilih, Wâdi V Egypt
15 L8 Muwo I Trobriand Is Papua New Guinea 8.44S 150.59E
76 E6 Muxagata Portugal 41.02N 7.10W
91 C8 Muxima Angola 9.33S 13.58E
42 K4 Muya U.S.S.R. 56.28N 115.50E
42 J4 Muya R U.S.S.R.
93 B9 Muyaga Burundi 3.15S 30.33E
90 C7 Muye Nigeria 8.12N 6.31E
92 C5 Muyela Zaïre 7.41S 27.50E
50 O9 Muyen, Kapp C Jan Mayen I Arctic Oc 71.06N 8.22W
51 P8 Muyezero Karelia U.S.S.R. 63.51N 31.29E
47 C4 Muyezerskiy U.S.S.R. 63.56N 32.01E
93 B8 Muyinga Burundi 2.50S 30.20E
71 K10 Muy, le France 43.28N 6.31E
115 M3 Muy Muy Nicaragua 12.43N 85.35W
43 E5 Muynak Uzbekistan U.S.S.R. 43.46N 59.00E
91 K7 Muyumba Zaïre 7.12S 27.03E
92 J11 Muyuni Zanzibar 5.49S 39.21E
43 K5 Muyunkum, Peski sand des Kazakhstan U.S.S.R.
23 E3 Muyuping Hubei China 31.26N 110.25E
120 E6 Muyuri Bolivia 15.13S 67.06W
31 G3 Muzaffarabad Kashmir 34.23N 73.34E
31 G3 Muzaffarabad dist Kashmir
31 F5 Muzaffargarh Pakistan 30.04N 71.15E
31 F6 Muzaffargarh dist Pakistan
30 A3 Muzaffarnagar Uttar Prad India 29.28N 77.42E
30 A3 Muzaffarnagar dist Uttar Prad India
30 J6 Muzaffarpur Bihar India 26.07N 85.23E
30 J6 Muzaffarpur dist Bihar India
Muzaira, Al see Muzayri'ah, Al
33 A10 Muzalkam mt S Yemen 12.46N 44.53E
118 F7 Muzambinho Brazil 21.22S 46.31W
Muzart R see Muzat He
24 C4 Muzart Davan pass Xinjiang Uygur Zizhiqu China 42.22N 80.54E
24 D5 Muzat He R Xinjiang Uygur Zizhiqu China
34 P7 Muzayri'ah, Al Iraq 31.00N 47.29E
Muzduran see Mozdūrān
92 E9 Muze Mozambique 14.58S 31.22E
35 H3 Muzeirib, El Syria 32.43N 36.02E
47 J3 Muzhi U.S.S.R. 65.25N 64.40E
45 N6 Muzhichye U.S.S.R. 50.45N 41.06E
31 F2 Muzik Dasht Pass Afghanistan 37.21N 70.18E
70 F6 Muzillac France 47.34N 2.28W
32 J7 Mūzin Iran 27.58N 61.35E
71 F2 Muzin R France
93 B5 Muzizi R Uganda
43 L7 Muzkol Khr ra Tadzhikistan U.S.S.R.
40 J5 Muz'ma Sakhalin U.S.S.R. 53.55N 142.45E
119 D5 Muzo Colombia 5.34N 74.07W
92 C10 Muzoka Zambia 16.39S 27.18E
113 V9 Muzon, C Alaska 54.41N 132.40W
115 J4 Múzquiz Mexico 27.54N 101.30W
24 C8 Muztag mt pk Xinjiang Uygur Zizhiqu China 35.57N 80.14E
24 F7 Muztag mt pk Xinjiang/Xizang China 36.28N 87.29E
24 B6 Muztagata mt pk Xinjiang Uygur Zizhiqu China 38.15N 75.05E
Muz Tagh mt see Muztag
Muztagh Ata mt see Muxtagata mt
86 E8 Muzûra Egypt 28.53N 30.48E
45 D10 Muzykovka Ukraine U.S.S.R. 46.45N 32.35E
79 O3 Muzzana Turgnano Italy 45.49N 13.07E
91 B2 Mvangan Cameroon 2.17N 11.43E
92 G9 Mvela Malawi 14.46S 35.15E
91 B2 Mvengué Cameroon 3.17N 11.02E
92 G8 Mvera Malawi 13.41S 34.10E
87 B7 Mvolo Sudan 6.02N 29.53E
92 H5 Mvomero Tanzania 6.20S 37.25E
91 C3 Mvoung R Gabon
91 C6 Mvouti Congo 4.14S 12.31E
92 H5 Mvuha Tanzania 7.15S 37.56E
91 F7 Mwadi-Kalumbu Zaïre 7.53S 18.43E
91 K9 Mwadingusha Zaïre 10.43S 27.14E
93 E9 Mwadui Tanzania 3.26S 33.32E
91 J6 Mwaka Zaïre 5.43S 25.13E
92 K7 Mwambo Tanzania 10.30S 40.24E
92 F7 Mwambwa R Zambia
93 M8 Mwanamundia Kenya 2.15S 40.10E
92 J11 Mwana Mwana C Zanzibar 5.46S 39.13E
92 J11 Mwanda Zanzibar 5.44S 39.18E
92 B10 Mwandi Zambia 17.30S 24.51E
92 C7 Mwangalala Zaïre 11.27S 27.40E
93 E10 Mwanhala Tanzania 4.24S 33.09E
15 M4 Mwaniwowo Solomon Is 10.50S 162.12E
93 E9 Mwantine mt Tanzania 3.38S 33.22E
92 F8 Mwanya Zambia 12.43S 32.15E
92 G9 Mwanza Malawi 15.40S 34.34E
93 D8 Mwanza Tanzania 2.31S 32.56E
91 K7 Mwanza Zaïre 7.51S 26.43E
93 D8 Mwanza reg Tanzania
92 G4 Mwaru Tanzania 4.53S 34.10E
93 K9 Mwatate Kenya 3.30S 38.23E
92 F6 Mwaya Tanzania 9.33S 33.56E
92 H6 Mwaya Tanzania 8.56S 36.50E
93 J6 Mwea Kenya 0.41S 37.28E
59 C4 Mweelrea mt Mayo Irish Rep 53.38N 9.50W
91 K6 Mweho Zaïre 4.58S 26.44E
93 H6 Mweiga Kenya 0.19S 36.54E
91 G6 Mweka Zaïre 4.51S 21.34E
93 J10 Mwemba Tanzania 4.10S 37.49E
93 G9 Mwembe mt Tanzania 3.48S 35.54E
92 D7 Mwenda Zambia 10.30S 29.10E
92 A6 Mwene Biji Zaïre 8.29S 22.09E
91 H7 Mwene Ditu Zaïre 7.01S 23.27E
92 D3 Mwenga Zaïre 3.00S 28.28E
92 J4 Mwera Tanzania 5.31S 38.58E
93 D5 Mwera Uganda 0.19N 32.09E
92 J6 Mwera tribe Tanzania
93 L10 Mwereni Kenya 4.22S 39.05E
92 E11 Mwerihari R Zimbabwe
92 D6 Mweru, Lake Zaïre/Zambia 9.00S 28.40E
92 D6 Mweru Wantipa L Zambia 8.50S 29.40E
92 D6 Mweru Wantipa Nat. Park Zambia
91 H6 Mwetshi Zaïre 4.50S 22.38E
92 D12 Mwewe R Zimbabwe
93 A6 Mweya Uganda 0.12S 29.53E
91 F6 Mwilambongo Zaïre 4.59S 19.50E
92 A6 Mwimba Zaïre 9.12S 22.44E
93 M8 Mwina Kenya 2.04S 40.11E
93 K6 Mwingi Kenya 0.56S 38.05E
92 B7 Mwinilunga Zambia 11.44S 24.24E
93 B6 Mwirasandu Uganda 0.58S 30.23E
92 G5 Mwitikira Tanzania 6.29S 35.40E
92 B8 Mwombezhi R Zambia
87 D6 Mwot Tot Sudan 8.12N 32.03E
61 N5 My Belgium 50.24N 5.34E
88 P7 Mya watercourse Algeria
25 M9 Myadaung Burma 23.43N 96.14E
47 L5 Myagkiy-Tupik U.S.S.R. 55.55N 59.26E
25 C2 Myaing Burma 21.35N 94.50E
39 E4 Myakit U.S.S.R. 61.25N 154.04E
105 E10 Myakka Florida 27.19N 82.16W
105 E10 Myakka R Florida
105 E10 Myakka City Florida 27.22N 82.10W
46 L1 Myaksa U.S.S.R. 58.52N 38.12E
12 K4 Myall L New S Wales
25 C3 Myanaung Burma 18.17N 95.19E
47 C4 Myanduselga U.S.S.R. 62.51N 33.45E
93 F5 Myanga Kenya 0.33N 34.25E
93 C5 Myanzi Uganda 0.27N 31.53E
39 D2 Myatis R U.S.S.R.
45 G2 Myatlevo U.S.S.R. 54.51N 35.41E
39 D3 Myaundzha U.S.S.R. 63.02N 147.04E
25 B2 Myaungbwe Burma 20.29N 93.16E
25 C4 Myaungmya Burma 16.33N 94.55E
88 Q6 Mya, Wadi Algeria
25 E4 Myawadi Burma 16.42N 98.30E
58 K2 Mybster Highland Scotland 58.27N 3.25W
84 E6 Mycenae ruins Greece 37.44N 22.45E
25 B2 Myebon Burma 20.04N 93.23E
25 M9 Myedu Burma 23.11N 95.25E
71 B2 Myennes France 47.27N 2.55E
103 A1 Myers New York 42.32N 76.33W
113 V9 Myers Chuck Alaska 55.44N 132.11W
103 B6 Myerstown Pennsylvania 40.23N 76.18W
48 V9 Myggbukta Greenland 73.30N 21.25W
53 L9 Myggenæs Faeroes 62.07N 7.38W
53 L9 Myggenæs isld Faeroes 62.08N 7.38W
53 N9 Mygledal Faeroes 62.21N 6.46W
45 J2 Myhega U.S.S.R. 54.31N 37.01E
25 C2 Myingyan Burma 21.25N 95.20E
25 D2 Myinkyado Burma 20.56N 96.42E
25 E6 Myinmoletkat mt Burma 13.28N 98.50E
25 C2 Myinmu Burma 21.58N 95.34E
25 C2 Myitche Burma 21.15N 94.52E
25 N8 Myitkyina Burma 25.24N 97.25E
25 D2 Myitnge R Burma
25 M9 Myitson Burma 23.19N 96.36E
25 E5 Myitta Burma 14.10N 98.31E
25 D2 Myittha Burma 21.21N 96.06E
25 C1 Myittha R Burma
62 K7 Myjava Czechoslovakia 48.45N 17.35E
112 G9 Mykawa Houston, Texas 29.36N 95.20W
51 C5 Myken Lt Ho Norway 66.45N 12.25E
Mykines see Myggenæs
53 S17 Myking Norway 60.42N 5.19E
53 W15 Myklemyr Norway 61.32N 7.17E
53 U17 Mykletveitveten mt Norway 60.36N 6.05E
47 G3 Myla U.S.S.R. 65.25N 50.45E
47 G3 Myla R U.S.S.R.
28 C8 Mylapore dist Madras, Tamil Nadu India
Mylasa anc site see Milâs
64 N2 Mylau E Germany 50.36N 12.15E
42 B3 Myl'dzhino U.S.S.R. 59.05N 78.29E
39 D3 Mylga U.S.S.R. 62.55N 149.45E
39 D3 Mylga R U.S.S.R.
48 T3 Mylius Erichsens Land Greenland
51 M11 Myllykoski Finland 60.47N 26.45E
108 L1 Mylo N Dakota 48.40N 99.30W
31 H9 Mymensingh Bangladesh 24.45N 90.23E
31 H8 Mymensingh dist Bangladesh
51 J11 Mynämäki Finland 60.41N 22.00E
43 L4 Myn-Aral Kazakhstan U.S.S.R. 45.24N 73.40E
100 S2 Mynarski Lakes Manitoba
43 G6 Mynbulak Uzbekistan U.S.S.R. 42.16N 62.55E
43 G6 Mynbulak, Kotlovina depression Uzbekistan U.S.S.R.
41 O9 Myndagayy U.S.S.R. 61.42N 133.10E
95 G6 Mynfontein S Africa 30.55S 23.56E
50 J3 Mynnisvötn L Iceland
56 C3 Mynydd Bach ra Dyfed Wales
56 D3 Mynydd Eppynt ra Powys Wales
25 B2 Myohaung Burma 20.35N 93.12E
25 D2 Myohla Burma 20.18N 96.02E
17 N5 Myojin isld Pacific Oc 32.00N 139.55E
20 M5 Myōkō-san mt Japan 36.56N 138.05E
71 H2 Myon France 47.02N 5.57E
92 C9 Myooye Zambia 15.11S 27.10E
25 C2 Myotha Burma 21.42N 95.44E
25 C2 Myothit Burma 20.09N 95.26E
112 K2 Myra Texas 33.37N 97.19W
36 D6 Myra anc site Turkey 36.17N 29.58E
50 B3 Mýrar Isafjardharsýsla, Vestur Iceland 65.54N 23.27W
50 G7 Myrar Skaftafellssýsla, Vestur Iceland 63.32N 18.20W
50 C5 Mýrasýsla co Iceland
13 F3 Myra Vale Queensland 17.02S 141.20E
53 W17 Myrdal Norway 60.44N 7.08E
50 F7 Mýrdalsjökull Rangárvallasýsla Iceland 63.36N 20.00W
50 F7 Mýrdalsjökull ice cap Iceland 63.40N 19.00W
50 G8 Mýrdalssandur sand reg Iceland
50 F7 Mýrdalur reg Iceland
50 F8 Mýrdalur V Iceland
52 H9 Myresjö Sweden 57.25N 14.55E
52 M1 Myrheden Sweden 65.19N 20.15E
50 H4 Mýri Iceland 65.23N 17.25W
103 M3 Myricks Massachusetts 41.50N 71.02W
53 U17 Myrkdalen R Norway 60.50N 6.29E
53 Y17 Myrkedalen V Norway 60.53N 8.15E
100 F5 Myrnam Alberta 53.40N 111.18W
90 D5 Myrria Niger 13.41N 9.10E
110 J3 Myrtle Idaho 46.30N 116.45W
100 U9 Myrtle Manitoba 49.22N 97.48W
107 G7 Myrtle Mississippi 34.33N 89.07W
99 M8 Myrtle Ontario 44.02N 78.59W
105 J4 Myrtle Beach S Carolina 33.42N 78.54W
110 B6 Myrtle Creek Oregon 43.02N 123.16W
12 H6 Myrtleford Victoria 36.35S 146.44E
110 A6 Myrtle Point Oregon 43.04N 124.08W
12 E4 Myrtle Springs S Australia 30.20S 138.00E
13 L1 Myrtletown Queensland 27.24S 153.07E
84 R14 Myrtou Cyprus 35.18N 33.05E
39 F1 Mys U.S.S.R. 68.48N 159.00E
52 F7 Mysen Norway 59.33N 11.20E
59 J6 Myshall Carlow Irish Rep 52.41N 6.47W
46 L1 Myshkino U.S.S.R. 57.45N 38.25E
42 D5 Myski U.S.S.R. 53.43N 87.50E
62 M6 Myślenice Poland 49.50N 19.55E
65 N3 Myšlibořice Czechoslovakia 49.07N 15.58E
62 H3 Myślibórz Poland 52.55N 14.51E
28 C4 Mysore Karnataka India 12.18N 76.37E
28 C4 Mysore dist Karnataka India
Mysore state see Karnataka state
39 F1 Mysovaya U.S.S.R. 67.40N 156.11E
44 D9 Mysovoye Ukraine U.S.S.R. 45.27N 35.51E
48 Q4 Mys Shelagskiy C U.S.S.R. 70.05N 170.05W
52 H4 Myssjö Sweden 62.56N 14.20E
100 U3 Mystery L Manitoba 55.50N 97.45W
103 L4 Mystic Connecticut 41.21N 71.58W
105 D6 Mystic Georgia 31.39N 83.19W
108 S9 Mystic Iowa 40.48N 92.57W
108 G5 Mystic S Dakota 44.05N 103.40W
53 X15 Mysubyttseter Norway 61.49N 7.35E
41 E4 Mys-Vkhodnoy U.S.S.R. 73.51N 86.32E
47 G5 Mysy U.S.S.R. 60.35N 54.00E
41 D2 Mys Zhelaniya Novaya Zemlya U.S.S.R. 77.00N 68.31E
62 N2 Myszyniec Poland 53.23N 21.20E
46 M2 Myt U.S.S.R. 56.49N 42.20E
25 J7 My Tho Vietnam 10.21N 106.21E
45 J1 Mytishchi U.S.S.R. 55.54N 37.47E
113 V8 Mytkof I Alaska 56.40N 132.45W
64 Q4 Mýto Czechoslovakia 49.48N 13.44E
110 P9 Myton Utah 40.11N 110.03W
25 K6 My Trach Vietnam 13.39N 108.01E
41 O8 Myuru, Ozero L U.S.S.R. 62.45N 130.20E
39 C2 Myuryule R U.S.S.R.
44 H7 Myusyuslyu Azerbaydzhan U.S.S.R. 40.24N 47.59E
50 J3 Mývatn L Iceland 65.36N 17.00W
50 J3 Myvatns Oræfi des Iceland
47 G5 Myyeldino U.S.S.R. 61.45N 54.51E
43 M3 Myylybulak Kazakhstan U.S.S.R. 48.30N 75.02E
88 P5 M'zab tribe Algeria
88 Q5 M'zab watercourse Algeria
Mzar Zarhbar see Mazar Zaghbar
64 O4 Mže Czechoslovakia 49.46N 12.54E
65 J2 Mže R Czechoslovakia
92 J5 Mzenga Tanzania 7.00S 38.44E
88 K9 Mzereb el Mali 24.44N 6.20W
Mzérib see Muzeirib, El
88 F12 M'Zérif Mauritania 19.08N 14.38W
89 J1 Mzerif, El Mali 21.50N 0.17W
88 P5 Mzi R Algeria
88 N5 Mzi, Djebel mt Algeria 32.22N 0.55W
92 H4 Mziha Tanzania 5.55S 37.45E
93 K8 Mzima Kenya 2.58S 38.02E
92 F7 Mzimba Malawi 11.55S 33.39E
Mzisa see Nizhnyaya Teberda
92 F7 Mzuzu Malawi 11.31S 34.00E
44 C4 Mzyinta R U.S.S.R.
Na see Ban Na
53 V18 Nå Norway 60.14N 6.35E
64 M5 Naab R W Germany
66 P3 Naaf Kopf mt Switz/Austria/Liech 47.04N 9.37E
85 M8 Na'ag, Gebel mt Egypt 23.32N 33.47E
60 E12 Naaldwijk Netherlands 52.00N 4.13E
114 B8 Naalehu Hawaiian Is 19.04N 155.36W
86 E7 Na'âlûn, Gebel, el hill Egypt 29.12N 30.53E
Na'am R Sudansee Era R
88 N5 Naama Algeria 33.18N 0.20W
86 M10 Na'ama Egypt 27.55N 34.19E
35 D2 Na'aman R Israel
15 F7 Naamloos, Danau L Irian Jaya
35 C6 Na'an Israel 31.53N 34.51E
87 A8 Naandi Sudan 5.00N 27.43E
51 J11 Naantali Finland 60.28N 22.05E
35 E6 Na'aram Jordan 31.57N 35.25E
60 J10 Naarden Netherlands 52.18N 5.10E
60 J10 Naarder Meer L Netherlands 52.18N 5.07E
59 J5 Naas Kildare Irish Rep 53.13N 6.39W
95 P7 Naas Naas Pt S Africa 29.50S 17.00E
61 G4 Naast Belgium 50.33N 4.06E
51 N2 Näätämöjoki R Finland
94 F8 Naauwte, De S Africa 30.06S 21.41E
25 M9 Naba Burma 24.17N 96.12E
94 D7 Nababiep S Africa 29.36S 17.46E
29 L6 Nabadwip W Bengal India 23.24N 88.23E
Na Baek see Ban Na Baek
93 C5 Nabakazi R Uganda
Naband see Nay Band
76 C9 Nabão R Portugal
20 H8 Nabari Japan 33.25N 134.01E
20 K7 Nabari Japan 34.37N 136.05E
86 F3 Nabarôh Egypt 31.06N 31.18E
19 L6 Nabas Philippines 11.50N 122.05E
85 M10 Nabati, Jeb. el mt Sudan 18.21N 33.29E
34 C5 Nabatīyet Ett Tahta Lebanon 33.24N 35.27E
14 D7 Nabberu, L W Australia
64 N5 Nabburg W Germany 49.27N 12.11E
93 H10 Naberera Tanzania 4.13S 36.55E
46 Q2 Naberezhnyye Chelny U.S.S.R. 55.42N 52.20E
113 Q5 Nabesna Alaska 62.20N 143.10W
113 Q5 Nabesna R Alaska
113 Q5 Nabesna Glacier Alaska 62.00N 143.00W
113 Q5 Nabesna Village Alaska 63.00N 142.05W
35 G1 Nab' es Sakhr Syria 33.05N 35.57E
88 T3 Nabeul Tunisia 36.30N 10.44E
29 E2 Nabha Punjab India 30.22N 76.12E
33 E4 Nabhānīyah, An Saudi Arabia 25.54N 43.03E
12 K4 Nabiac New S Wales 32.05S 152.17E
32 G6 Nabīd Iran 29.41N 57.37E
93 D4 Nabieso Uganda 1.52N 32.46E
35 G4 Nabi Hud, En Jordan 32.15N 35.54E
93 F3 Nabilatuk Uganda 2.04N 34.35E
118 B7 Nabileque, R Brazil
40 J6 Nabil'skiy, Zaliv gulf Sakhalin U.S.S.R.
35 E6 Nabi Musa tomb Jordan 31.47N 35.26E
30 H8 Nabinagar Bihar India 24.38N 84.08E
93 C5 Nabingora Uganda 0.31N 31.12E
15 C5 Nabire Irian Jaya 3.23S 135.31E
35 D5 Nabi Salih Jordan 32.01N 35.08E
98 K3 Nabisipi R Quebec
93 D4 Nabiswera Uganda 1.28N 32.17E
93 C6 Nabitanga Uganda 0.01S 31.10E
33 E10 Nābiyah, Am S Yemen 12.46N 43.43E
35 F5 Nabi Yusha tomb Jordan 32.04N 35.42E
33 C1 Nabk Abū Qaşr, An Saudi Arabia 30.11N 38.36E
34 E7 Nabk, An Saudi Arabia 31.21N 37.20E
Nabk, An Syriasee Nebk, En
35 E5 Nablus Jordan 32.13N 35.16E
76 E6 Nabo Portugal 41.16N 7.08W
89 H6 Nabon Upper Volta 11.28N 2.26W
94 K5 Naboomspruit S Africa 24.32S 28.36E
89 E5 Nabou Guinea 12.01N 9.32W
89 H6 Nabou Upper Volta 11.25N 2.50W
86 M9 Nabq Egypt 28.04N 34.26E
93 L3 Nabsid hill Kenya 2.37N 39.25E
93 C6 Nabugabo, L Uganda 0.20S 31.55E
19 L7 Nabulao B Philippines 9.38N 122.27E
25 E5 Nabule Burma 14.24N 98.02E
93 D5 Nabusanke Uganda 0.03N 32.03E
93 D7 Nabuyongo I Tanzania 1.28S 32.36E
115 N8 Nacajuca Mexico 18.12N 93.01W
92 K9 Nacala Mozambique 14.30S 40.37E
115 L3 Nacaome Honduras 13.30N 87.31W
92 J9 Nacarôa Mozambique 14.22S 39.55E
92 J9 Nacavala Mozambique 15.00S 39.40E
120 E4 Nacebe Bolivia 11.00S 67.22W
65 L2 Načeradec Czechoslovakia 49.36N 14.55E
25 J1 Na Cham Vietnam 22.04N 106.36E
29 B4 Nachana India 27.30N 71.40E
30 A1 Nachar Himachal Prad India 31.33N 77.59E
110 E3 Naches Washington 46.45N 120.41W
110 E3 Naches R Washington
110 D2 Naches Pass Washington 47.06N 121.24W
39 G4 Nachgaty U.S.S.R. 62.20N 163.20E
39 F7 Nachiki U.S.S.R. 53.06N 157.44E
39 G5 Nachiki R U.S.S.R.
39 G5 Nachikinskaya, Gora mt U.S.S.R. 57.50N 162.40E
39 G5 Nachikinskiy, Mys C U.S.S.R. 57.57N 162.42E
31 H4 Nachiland Kashmir 33.23N 75.15E
39 F7 Nachilevo U.S.S.R. 52.55N 156.30E
92 J7 Nachingwea Tanzania 10.21S 38.46E
91 G9 Nachiungo Angola 11.52S 21.22E
62 J5 Náchod Czechoslovakia 50.26N 16.10E
Na Ch'ü R see Salween
28 G8 Nachuge Andaman Is 10.43N 92.21E
121 A6 Nacimiento Chile 37.32S 72.43W
77 L6 Nacimiento Spain 37.06N 2.38W
111 C6 Nacimiento R California
77 L6 Nacimiento R Spain
111 C6 Nacimiento Res California 35.42N 121.00E
12 E5 Nackara S Australia 32.51S 139.13E
63 R7 Nackel E Germany 52.50N 12.35E
63 J4 Nackhorn pt W Germany 54.21N 8.37E
100 E7 Nacmine Alberta 51.27N 112.43W
111 P10 Naco Arizona 31.20N 109.56W
115 E2 Naco Mexico 31.20N 109.53W
112 N4 Nacogdoches Texas 31.36N 94.40W
59 C4 Nacorra,L Mayo Irish Rep 53.44N 9.41W
59 D4 Nacorralea, L Mayo Irish Rep 53.44N 9.20W
115 E2 Nacozari de García Mexico 30.22N 109.32W
121 C5 Nacuñan Argentina 34.05S 67.58W
59 F1 Nacung, L Donegal Irish Rep 55.02N 8.10W
Nada see Dan Xian
111 L3 Nada Utah 38.07N 113.19W
20 M4 Nadachi Japan 37.10N 138.08E
115 J4 Nadadores Mexico 27.02N 101.38W
23 D8 Nadang Guangxi China 21.58N 107.57E
30 B7 Nadanwara Tal L Madhya Prad India 25.05N 78.46E
65 P8 Nadasd Hungary 46.57N 16.36E
41 H4 Nadaturku, Ozero L U.S.S.R. 73.35N 100.00E
30 J7 Nadaul Bihar India 25.18N 85.02E
30 A5 Nadbai Rajasthan India 27.12N 77.11E
53 X16 Naddvik Norway 61.11N 7.38E
106 G4 Nadeau Michigan 45.38N 87.33W
65 K2 Nadějkov Czechoslovakia 49.31N 14.28E
66 N5 Nadels, Piz mt Switzerland 46.42N 9.02E
Nädendal see Naantali
43 G1 Nadezhdinskiy Kazakhstan U.S.S.R. 53.46N 63.44E
40 F7 Nadezhdinskoye U.S.S.R. 48.18N 133.10E
40 M8 Nadezhdy, Proliv str Kuril Is U.S.S.R.
41 R4 Nadezhnyy, Mys C U.S.S.R. 74.45N 149.50E
34 H5 Nadhara, An hill Iraq 33.14N 40.18E
85 M10 Nadi Sudan 18.40N 33.41E
9 R8 Nadi Viti Levu Fiji 17.47S 177.29E
Nadia see Krishnanagar
29 L6 Nadia dist W Bengal India
29 C6 Nadiad Gujarat India 22.42N 72.55E
30 C6 Nadigaon Uttar Prad India 26.07N 79.02E
32 F5 Nadik Iran 30.21N 55.01E
86 E4 Nâdir Egypt 30.33N 30.51E
35 G4 Nadira Jordan 32.19N 35.58E
90 G9 Nadjiboro Cent Afr Rep 5.09N 15.19E
82 F4 Nădlac Romania 46.10N 20.44E
29 C5 Nadol Rajasthan India 25.30N 73.38E
88 M4 Nador Morocco 35.10N 3.00W
61 N6 Nadrin Belgium 50.09N 5.41E
44 G4 Nadterechnaya U.S.S.R. 43.38N 45.22E
41 D4 Nadudoturku, Ozero L U.S.S.R. 72.45N 84.10E
62 N8 Nádudvar Hungary 47.26N 21.09E
84 X19 Nadur Gozo Mediterranean Sea 36.02N 14.18E
84 Y20 Nadur Tower mt Malta 35.54N 14.22E
32 E4 Nadūshan Iran 32.02N 53.36E
47 K1 Naduyyakha R U.S.S.R.
47 C4 Nadvoitsy U.S.S.R. 63.56N 34.20E
46 E5 Nadvornaya Ukraine U.S.S.R. 48.37N 24.30E
30 J7 Nadwan Bihar India 25.24N 85.02E
47 L3 Nadym U.S.S.R. 65.25N 72.40E
47 L3 Nadym R U.S.S.R.
15 J7 Nadzab Papua New Guinea 6.36S 146.46E
44 H7 Nadzhafkulubeyli Azerbaydzhan U.S.S.R. 40.07N 47.32E
11 E5 Naenae New Zealand
29 D5 Naenwa Rajasthan India 25.46N 75.56E
53 W14 Næremstindane mt Norway 62.30N 7.02E
52 F2 Nærøy Nord-Tröndelag Norway 64.48N 11.17E
53 V17 Nærøy Sogn og Fjordane Norway 60.54N 6.52E
53 V17 Nærøydalen V Norway 60.50N 6.45E
53 V17 Nærøyfjord inlet Norway 60.58N 6.59E
53 K5 Nærum Denmark 55.50N 12.33E
53 N9 Næs Faeroes 62.05N 6.43W
53 N10 Næs Faeroes 61.36N 6.55W
53 B5 Næsbjerg Denmark 55.38N 8.37E
53 C3 Næsborg Denmark 56.59N 9.21E
53 H6 Næsby Storstrøm Denmark 55.23N 11.38E
53 E6 Næsbyhoved Broby Denmark 55.26N 10.19E
53 G6 Næsby ved Stranden Denmark 55.24N 11.16E
53 H6 Næstelsø Denmark 55.13N 11.52E
53 H6 Næstved Denmark 55.14N 11.47E
110 M7 Naf Idaho 42.01N 113.18W
25 B2 Naf R Burma
90 E6 Nafada Nigeria 11.08N 11.20E
89 E7 Nafadie Guinea 9.42N 9.40W
34 L5 Nafatah oil bore Iraq 33.30N 43.05E
88 S8 Nafeg Algeria 26.10N 8.39E
66 N3 Näfels Switzerland 47.06N 9.04E
57 N4 Nafferton Humberside Eng 54.01N 0.24W
34 B8 Nafha, Har mt Israel 30.42N 34.45E
35 G2 Nafi'ah Syria 32.48N 35.54E
59 C4 Nafooey, L Galway Irish Rep 53.35N 9.33W
85 F5 Nafoora Libya 29.15N 21.30E
61 K7 Nafraiture Belgium 49.55N 4.55E
32 A4 Naft R Iraq
44 H7 Naftalan Azerbaydzhan U.S.S.R. 40.31N 46.51E
32 C5 Naft-e-Safid oil field Iran 31.38N 49.19E
32 A3 Naft-e Shāh oil field Iran 34.02N 45.30E
34 N4 Naft Khaneh Iraq 34.03N 45.27E
Naft Shah see Naft-e Shāh oil field
33 F5 Nafūd ad Dahl sand dunes Saudi Arabia
33 F3 Nafūd al Jur'ā sand dunes Saudi Arabia
33 E4 Nafūd al 'Urayq des Saudi Arabia
33 D2 Nafūd, An des Saudi Arabia
33 F4 Nafūd as Sirr sand dunes Saudi Arabia
33 E5 Nafūd as Surrah des area Saudi Arabia
33 F4 Nafūd Qunayfidhah sand dunes Saudi Arabia
33 M7 Nafūn Oman 19.50N 57.41E
85 A4 Nafūsa, Jabal mts Libya
33 E4 Nafy Saudi Arabia 25.03N 43.51E
32 J7 Nāg Iran 27.08N 61.44E
19 A8 Naga Indonesia 8.41S 119.56E
19 L5 Naga Luzon Philippines 13.36N 123.12E
92 J7 Nagaga Tanzania 10.55S 39.09E
99 F3 Nagagami Ontario 49.52N 84.45W
99 F3 Nagagami R Ontario
99 E3 Nagagami L Ontario 49.25N 85.00W
99 F3 Nagagamisis L Ontario 49.29N 84.38W
99 F3 Nagagamisis Prov. Park Ontario
20 K6 Nagahama Honshu Japan 35.25N 136.16E
20 F8 Nagahama Shikoku Japan 33.37N 132.30E
28 K2 Naga Hills Assam/Nagaland India
20 N3 Nagai Japan 38.08N 140.00E
113 G9 Nagai I Alaska 55.10N 160.00W
30 A3 Nagal Uttar Prad India 29.50N 77.37E
87 M6 Nagal watercourse Somalia
28 K2 Nagaland state India
28 C4 Nagamangala Karnataka India 12.50N 76.45E
12 H6 Nagambie Victoria 36.48S 145.12E
20 O9 Nagannu-jima isld Okinawa Japan 26.14N 127.33E
20 M5 Nagano Japan 36.39N 138.10E
20 L5 Nagano prefect Japan
20 M5 Naganohara Japan 36.34N 138.38E
20 H2 Naganuma Chiba Japan
20 M4 Nagaoka Japan 37.27N 138.50E
28 D5 Nagappattinam Tamil Nadu India 10.45N 79.50E
29 E1 Nagar Himachal Prad India 32.12N 77.00E
28 B4 Nagar Karnataka India 13.49N 74.59E
30 A5 Nagar Rajasthan India 27.25N 77.06E
28 D4 Nagari Hills Andhra Prad India
28 D2 Nagarjunasagar Dam Andhra Prad India 16.35N 79.17E
28 D2 Nagar Karnul Andhra Prad India 16.29N 78.20E
115 L3 Nagarote Nicaragua 12.15N 86.35W
31 F8 Nagar Parkar Pakistan 24.20N 70.44E
31 G8 Nagar R Bangladesh etc
Nagartse Dzong see Nagarzê Xizang Zizhiqu China
Nagar Untari see Untari
24 G11 Nagarzê Xizang Zizhiqu China 28.57N 90.26E
20 C9 Nagasaki Japan 32.45N 129.52E
20 C8 Nagasaki prefect Japan
20 D9 Naga-shima isld Japan
20 F8 Naga-shima isld Japan 33.50N 132.05E
20 E8 Nagasu Kyūshū Japan 33.34N 131.23E
20 E7 Nagato Japan 34.22N 131.11E
20 C4 Nagatsuda Kanagawa Japan
29 C4 Nagaur Rajasthan India 27.12N 73.48E
29 C4 Nagaur dist Rajasthan India
20 G4 Nagaura Chiba Japan
28 E2 Nagavaram Andhra Prad India 17.16N 81.22E
39 E5 Nagayeva, Bukhta gulf U.S.S.R.
29 F7 Nagbhir Maharashtra India 20.33N 79.55E
Nagchu Dzong Xizang Zizhiqu see Nagqu
29 D6 Nagda Madhya Prad India 23.30N 75.29E
87 G8 Nagēlē Ethiopia 5.20N 39.35E
60 L9 Nagele Netherlands 52.38N 5.43E
28 C6 Nagercoil Tamil Nadu India 8.11N 77.30E
52 J4 Naggen Sweden 62.25N 16.00E

31 C7 Nagha Kalat Pakistan 27.24N 65.12E
85 M6 Nag'Hammâdi Egypt 26.04N 32.13E
75 F5 Nágima R Spain
30 B3 Nagina Uttar Prad India 29.26N 78.27E
32 G3 Nagineh Iran 34.14N 57.20E
28 K2 Naginimora Nagaland India 26.44N 94.51E
Naginu see Nagineh
31 H2 Nagir Kashmir 36.15N 74.46E
93 E1 Nagishot Sudan 4.16N 33.34E
59 F7 Nagles Mts Cork Irish Rep
39 H1 Nagloynyn, Gora mt U.S.S.R. 69.08N 168.33E
30 E3 Nagma Nepal 29.12N 81.53E
79 J3 Nago Italy 45.53N 10.53E
20 P8 Nago Okinawa Japan 26.36N 127.59E
30 D8 Nagod Madhya Prad India 24.34N 80.34E
64 F6 Nagold W Germany 48.33N 8.44E
64 F6 Nagold R W Germany
69 P6 Nagold res W Germany
45 L9 Nagol'no-Tarasovka Ukraine U.S.S.R. 48.00N 39.30E
28 L1 Nagong Chu R Xizang Zizhiqu
93 F5 Nagongera Uganda 0.45N 34.03E
75 H2 Nagore Spain 42.52N 1.22W
28 D5 Nagore Tamil Nadu India 10.49N 79.50E
44 H8 Nagorno-Karabakhskaya Aut.Oblast' Azerbaydzhan U.S.S.R.
42 E4 Nagornovo U.S.S.R. 56.25N 90.21E
47 H6 Nagornskiy U.S.S.R. 58.48N 57.30E
39 K3 Nagornyy U.S.S.R. 63.10N 179.29E
40 C4 Nagornyy U.S.S.R. 55.57N 124.54E
47 G6 Nagorsk U.S.S.R. 59.18N 50.50E
20 P9 Nago-wan B Okinawa Japan
20 K6 Nagoya Japan 35.08N 136.53E
29 F7 Nagpur Maharashtra India 21.10N 79.12E
29 F7 Nagpur dist Maharashtra India
24 G10 Nagqu Xizang Zizhiqu China 31.30N 91.57E
30 E6 Nagram Uttar Prad India 26.37N 81.08E
30 H7 Nagri Bihar India 25.21N 84.28E
29 E1 Nagrota Himachal Prad India 32.03N 76.24E
51 J11 Nagu Finland 60.12N 21.55E
116 K5 Nagua Dominican Rep 19.25N 69.49W
105 K7 Naguabo Puerto Rico 18.12N 65.47W
19 K3 Naguilian Luzon Philippines 17.04N 121.48E
19 M5 Nagumbuaya Pt Philippines 13.34N 124.20E
41 M2 Nagurskoye Franz Josef Land U.S.S.R. 80.51N 47.30E
44 E3 Nagutskoye U.S.S.R. 44.27N 42.55E
62 K9 Nagybajom Hungary 46.25N 17.31E
65 P6 Nagycenk Hungary 47.37N 16.41E
62 N8 Nagyecsed Hungary 47.52N 22.24E
62 N8 Nagykálló Hungary 47.51N 21.51E
62 K9 Nagykanizsa Hungary 46.27N 17.00E
62 M8 Nagykáta Hungary 47.25N 19.45E
62 M8 Nagykőrös Hungary 47.01N 19.47E
62 N8 Nagyleta Hungary 47.21N 21.54E
Nagyvárad see Oradea
20 O9 Naha Okinawa Japan 26.10N 127.40E
18 L5 Nahabuan Borneo Indon 0.51N 114.03E
24 D11 Nahaisum pass Xizang Zizhiqu China 29.30N 83.41E
35 C7 Nahala Israel 31.40N 34.48E
35 D3 Nahalal Israel 32.41N 35.12E
35 C6 Nahalat Yehuda Israel 31.58N 34.48E
35 G2 Nahal Geshure Syria 32.57N 35.47E
35 A8 Nahal 'Oz Israel 31.29N 34.30E
86 O2 Naham Israel 31.46N 35.00E
30 A2 Nahan Himachal Prad India 30.33N 77.18E
31 B7 Nahang R Iran/Pakistan
101 M5 Nahanni Butte N W Terr 61.03N 123.31W
101 K5 Nahanni National Park N-W Terr
101 M5 Nahanni Ra N W Terr
35 D1 Nahariyya Israel 33.01N 35.05E
88 O4 Nahar Ouassel R Algeria
75 F7 Naharros Spain 40.04N 2.30W
32 C3 Nahāvand Iran 34.13N 48.21E
15 L6 Nahavio New Britain 5.38S 150.20E
64 C4 Nahbollenbach W Germany 49.43N 7.23E
37 G5 Nahcivan Turkey 40.17N 43.29E
86 R12 Nahdein, Wâdî el watercourse Cairo Egypt
64 C4 Nahe R W Germany
87 H2 Nahelej I Ethiopia 16.10N 40.10E
35 E2 Nahf Israel 32.56N 35.19E
35 D7 Nahhalin Jordan 31.41N 35.07E
114 E6 Nahiku Hawaiian Is 20.49N 156.06W
35 J2 Nahitah Syria 32.47N 36.21E
34 J4 Nāhiyah, An Iraq 34.26N 41.33E
86 G8 Nahîya, Wâdî watercourse Egypt
35 G4 Nahla Jordan 32.16N 35.50E
106 H4 Nahma Michigan 45.51N 86.40W
30 A2 Nahna Himachal Prad India 30.48N 77.06E
85 M9 Nahoganet, Jebel mt Sudan 21.15N 32.29E
72 H1 Nahon R France 47.11N 1.36E
34 M5 Nahrawān Canal Iraq
33 C3 Nahr, Jabal mts Saudi Arabia
34 P8 Nahr 'Umr oil well Iraq 30.46N 47.39E
34 O6 Nahr Wādi R Iraq
35 C3 Nahsholim Israel 32.37N 34.55E
35 C6 Nahshon Israel 31.50N 34.57E
35 C5 Nahshonim Israel 32.04N 34.57E
87 B4 Nahud, En Sudan 12.41N 28.28E
121 B8 Nahuel Huapí Argentina 41.03S 71.12W
121 B8 Nahuel Huapí, L Argentina
121 B8 Nahuel Huapí, Parque Nacionale Argentina
121 C5 Nahuel Mapa Argentina 34.50S 66.15W
121 C8 Nahuel Niyeu Argentina 40.31S 66.31W
32 K7 Nāhūg Iran 27.37N 62.21E
105 F6 Nahunta Georgia 31.12N 82.00W
15 K4 Nai Bismarck Arch 1.34S 149.49E
28 H1 Nai Xizang Zizhiqu 29.45N 90.45E
31 D3 Naiak Afghanistan 34.44N 66.58E
31 D2 Naibabad Afghanistan 36.48N 67.30E
Naibandan see Nāy Band
19 G2 Naic Luzon Philippines 14.18N 120.46E
115 G4 Naica Mexico 27.51N 105.30W
100 N6 Naicam Saskatchewan 52.26N 104.31W
Naichi see Nai-chi-kuo-le Ho
Naifa see Nayfah
25 N7 Nai Ga Burma 27.48N 97.30E
30 A7 Naigaon Madhya Prad India 25.54N 77.09E
30 E8 Naigarhi Madhya Prad India 24.48N 81.46E
93 E5 Naigobia Uganda 0.49N 33.22E
29 L6 Naihati W Bengal India 22.54N 88.26E
24 H8 Naij Gol He R Qinghai China
24 H8 Naij Tal Qinghai China 35.53N 94.35E
19 C8 Naikliu Timor Indon 9.32S 123.48E
31 G8 Naik Murad Bangladesh 25.58N 88.20E
64 M3 Naila W Germany 50.20N 11.43E
22 L6 Nailin Nei Monggol Zizhiqu China 41.55N 119.17E
72 H9 Nailloux France 43.21N 1.36E
9 T4 Nailotha Pk Vanua Levu Fiji 16.24S 179.38E
56 G4 Nailsworth Glos Eng 51.42N 2.14W
87 D3 Na'ima Sudan 14.36N 32.15E
Nai-man-ch'i see Naiman Qi
21 B6 Naiman Qi Nei Monggol Zizhiqu China 42.50N 120.43E
Naimé see Nu'aiyimah
35 C9 Na'im, Har hill Israel 31.10N 34.47E
24 G3 Naimin Bulak spring Xinjiang Uygur Zizhiqu China 45.00N 90.30E
32 E4 Nā'īn Iran 32.52N 53.05E
97 N6 Nain Labrador, Nfld 56.30N 61.45W
26 Q2 Nainativu isld Sri Lanka 9.36N 79.46E
9 S5 Naindi Vanua Levu Fiji 16.47S 179.21E
9 T7 Naingani isld Fiji 17.36S 178.40E
30 H7 Naini Bihar India 25.50N 84.44E
30 E7 Naini Uttar Prad India 25.24N 81.51E
30 C3 Naini Tal Uttar Prad India 29.22N 79.26E
30 C3 Naini Tal dist Uttar Prad India
29 G6 Nainpur Madhya Prad India 22.26N 80.10E
72 E2 Naintré France 46.46N 0.29E
Nainwa see Naenwa
37 D2 Naip Turkey 40.53N 27.26E
37 D5 Naipli Turkey 40.19N 38.10E
9 U8 Nairai isld Fiji 17.50S 179.26E
122 C12 Nairiri Tahiti Pacific Oc 17.47S 149.25W
58 J3 Nairn Highland Scotland 57.35N 3.53W
99 J6 Nairn Ontario 46.21N 81.36W
Nairn co see Highland reg
14 B7 Nairn, Mt W Australia 25.56S 116.33E
58 H4 Nairn, R Highland Scotland
93 H7 Nairobi Kenya 1.17S 36.50E
93 H7 Nairobi Nat.Park Kenya
30 A8 Nai Sarai Madhya Prad India 24.48N 77.36E
66 A3 Naisey France 47.12N 6.15E
51 L12 Naissaar isld Estonia U.S.S.R. 59.36N 24.30E
Naistanak see Neyestānak
87 E8 Naita mt Ethiopia 5.31N 35.18E
9 U5 Naitamba isld Fiji 17.01S 179.19W
9 S5 Naituamba isld Fiji 17.08S 179.07E
30 E6 Naiva R Uttar Prad India
93 H6 Naivasha Kenya 0.44S 36.26E
93 H6 Naivasha, L Kenya
69 J6 Naives-devant Bar France 48.48N 5.14E
70 E6 Naizin France 48.00N 2.49W
72 H7 Najac France 44.13N 1.59E
32 D4 Najafābād Esfahān Iran 32.38N 51.23E
32 F5 Najafābād Kermān Iran 30.19N 55.55E
34 M7 Najaf, An Iraq 31.59N 44.19E
34 M7 Najaf, Bahr an L Iraq
30 A4 Najafgarh Delhi India 28.37N 76.59E
29 A2 Najafgarh Jhil Cut R Delhi India
33 G4 Na'jān Saudi Arabia 24.05N 47.08E
116 F4 Najasa R Cuba
33 C3 Najd prov Saudi Arabia
75 E3 Nájera Spain 42.25N 2.45W
75 E3 Najerilla R Spain
Naji'ah see Nāqī', An
30 B3 Najibabad Uttar Prad India 29.37N 78.19E
35 J2 Najih, En Syria 32.56N 36.15E
21 E6 Najin N Korea 42.10N 130.20E
21 D2 Najinkouzi Heilongjiang China 50.24N 127.00E
Najitun see Arun Qi
34 L3 Najmah Iraq 35.55N 43.08E
33 J3 Najmah Saudi Arabia 26.45N 50.05E
33 F8 Najrān Saudi Arabia 17.31N 44.19E
33 F8 Najrān,Wādī watercourse Saudi Arabia
20 H6 Naka Japan 35.03N 134.55E
20 D5 Naka dist Yokohama Japan
20 C9 Nakadōri-shima isld Japan
20 H8 Naka-gawa R Japan
20 O5 Naka-gawa R Japan
20 C8 Nakagumi Japan 33.04N 129.52E
20 P9 Nakagusuku-wan B Okinawa Japan
20 D3 Nakahara dist Kanagawa Japan
20 F8 Naka-jima isld Japan 33.54N 132.44E
20 G5 Naka-jima isld Japan 36.10N 133.05E
20 N3 Nakajō Japan 38.02N 139.22E
20 C10 Naka-Koshiki-jima isld Japan
114 D5 Nakalele Pt Hawaiian Is 21.02N 156.36W
93 B5 Nakaliro Uganda 0.09N 30.57E
93 B5 Nakalongo Uganda 0.57N 30.40E
20 D8 Nakama Japan 33.53N 130.48E
20 P9 Nakama Okinawa Japan 26.12N 127.43E
87 F6 Nak'amet Ethiopia 9.04N 36.30E
20 O5 Nakaminato Japan 36.21N 140.38E
Nakamti see Nak'amet
20 E10 Nakamura Japan 31.32N 131.21E
20 F8 Nakamura Japan 33.02N 132.58E
42 H1 Nakanno U.S.S.R. 62.52N 108.28E
20 G4 Nakano Chiba Japan
20 M5 Nakano Japan 36.43N 138.23E
20 D2 Nakano Tōkyō Japan
20 E3 Nakanobu dist Tōkyō Japan
20 M5 Nakanojō Japan 36.35N 138.50E
23 K6 Nakanokami isld Japan 24.12N 123.35E
20 F5 Nakano-shima I Japan
20 A4 Naka-Ogino Kanagawa Japan
20 Q8 Nakaoshi Okinawa Japan 26.37N 128.02E
92 H7 Nakapanya Tanzania 10.58S 37.51E
31 E4 Naka Pass Afghanistan 33.25N 69.17E
20 O1 Nakasato Japan 40.58N 140.26E
20 M2 Naka-Satsunai Hokkaido Japan 42.38N 143.09E
20 B4 Naka-Shinden Kanagawa Japan
93 D4 Nakasongola Uganda 1.19N 32.28E
47 J6 Nakatay U.S.S.R. 59.56N 63.29E
20 B1 Naka-Tomi Saitama Japan
20 E8 Nakatsu Japan 33.37N 131.11E
20 A4 Nakatsu Kanagawa Japan
20 L6 Nakatsugawa Japan 35.32N 137.30E
20 G6 Naka-umi Japan
93 D5 Nakawuka Uganda 0.12N 32.27E
20 D3 Nakayama Kanagawa Japan
30 F1 Nakchail La pass Xizang Zizhiqu 31.27N 82.02E
113 J8 Nakchamik I Alaska 56.21N 157.50W
113 O6 Naked I Alaska
87 G2 Nakfa Ethiopia 16.40N 38.30E
39 C2 Nakhatta R U.S.S.R.
44 G8 Nakhichevan' Nakhichevan' U.S.S.R. 39.12N 45.24E
44 G8 Nakhichevan' A.S.S.R Azerbaydzhan U.S.S.R.
Nakhili see Bīr Nakhili
Nakhilu see Band-e Nakhīlū
86 L6 Nakhl Egypt 29.55N 33.45E
33 M5 Nakhl Oman 23.26N 57.52E
35 H1 Nakhl, En Syria 33.01N 36.08E
32 E7 Nakhl-e Taqī Iran 27.28N 52.39E
33 M5 Nakhl, Jibal mts Oman
40 F10 Nakhodka Primor'ye U.S.S.R. 42.53N 132.54E
47 L3 Nakhodka Tyumen U.S.S.R. 67.19N 72.05E
41 C6 Nakhodka U.S.S.R. 67.45N 77.31E
39 M1 Nakhodka, O isld Vrangelya, Ostrov U.S.S.R. 71.10N 179.05N
28 J2 Nakhola Assam India 26.05N 92.12E
25 F5 Nakhon Nayok Thailand 14.15N 101.12E
25 F6 Nakhon Pathom Thailand 13.50N 100.01E
25 G5 Nakhon Ratchasima Thailand 15.00N 102.06E
25 E8 Nakhon Si Thammarat Thailand 8.24N 99.58E
25 F4 Nakhon Thai Thailand 17.04N 100.41E
29 A6 Nakhtarana Gujarat India 23.26N 69.18E
101 G6 Nakina Br Col 59.12N 132.48W
99 D2 Nakina Ontario 50.11N 86.43W
101 G6 Nakina R Br Col
93 D4 Nakitoma Uganda 1.33N 32.05E
93 B6 Nakivale, L Uganda 0.48S 30.53E
51 K3 Näkkälä Finland 68.37N 23.35E
37 F1 Nakkaş Turkey 41.12N 28.34E
51 J10 Nakkila Finland 61.21N 22.00E
53 N10 Nakkur C Faeroes 61.46N 6.40W
33 D6 Nakl an Nīlah Saudi Arabia 20.30N 40.30E
62 K2 Nakło Poland 53.08N 17.35E
113 J7 Naknek Alaska 58.45N 157.00W
113 J7 Naknek L Alaska 58.40N 156.20W
89 H6 Nako Upper Volta 10.39N 3.04W
29 D2 Nakodar Punjab India 31.06N 75.31E
24 C9 Na-k'o Hu L Xizang Zizhiqu 33.26N 79.55E
92 F6 Nakonde Zambia 9.22S 32.47E
20 O5 Nakoso Japan 36.52N 140.48E
23 H5 Nakou Fujian China 27.12N 117.38E
89 J6 Nakpanduri Ghana 10.38N 0.11W
30 M6 Naksalbari W Bengal India 26.42N 88.12E
Naksho Biru see Biru
53 G7 Nakskov Denmark 54.50N 11.10E
53 F8 Nakskov Fjord inlet Denmark 54.50N 11.05E
52 H4 Näkten L Sweden 62.50N 14.35E
21 D10 Naktong R S Korea
30 D1 Nak-tsok Xizang Zizhiqu 31.04N 80.18E
15 L1 Naku Dabu I Nukumanu Is Papua New Guinea 4.37S 159.30E
30 A3 Nakur Uttar Prad India 29.55N 77.18E
93 H6 Nakuru Kenya 0.16S 36.04E
93 H6 Nakuru, L Kenya 0.22S 36.05E
101 P10 Nakusp Br Col 50.15N 117.48W
31 D7 Nal Pakistan 27.40N 66.18E
87 A9 Nala Zaïre 2.55N 27.40E
29 E2 Nalagarh Himachal Prad India 31.03N 76.48E
30 J7 Nalanda Bihar India 25.07N 85.25E
26 S6 Nalanda Sri Lanka 7.39N 80.38E
26 S6 Nalanda Res Sri Lanka
25 D1 Na-lang Burma 22.41N 97.55E
51 M8 Näläntö Finland 63.51N 26.25E
22 G3 Nalayh Mongolia 47.40N 107.12E
94 M5 Nalázi Mozambique 24.03S 33.20E
44 F7 Nalband Armenia U.S.S.R. 40.52N 44.11E
28 H2 Nalbari Assam India 26.26N 91.30E
44 F4 Nal'chik U.S.S.R. 43.31N 43.38E
31 H10 Nalchiti Bangladesh 22.36N 90.15E
29 E2 Naldera Himachal Prad India 31.12N 77.10E
28 C2 Naldrug Maharashtra India 17.49N 76.20E
89 J6 Nalerigu Ghana 10.35N 0.16W
39 H3 Nalgimskaya U.S.S.R. 63.48N 168.58E
28 D2 Nalgonda Andhra Prad India 17.04N 79.15E
28 D2 Nalgonda dist Andhra Prad India
29 K5 Nalhati W Bengal India 24.19N 87.53E
30 F6 Nalhiapur Uttar Prad India 26.46N 82.24E
114 C8 Naliikakani Pt Hawaiian Is 19.17N 155.20W
41 E8 Nalim'ye Ozero U.S.S.R. 63.54N 85.52E
41 E7 Nalim'ye, Ozero L U.S.S.R. 66.30N 85.35E
87 D8 Nalingaru Sudan 4.47N 33.37E
Na-lin Ho see Dong He
61 H5 Nalinnes Belgium 50.19N 4.27E
31 H8 Nalitabari Bangladesh 25.06N 90.11E
29 A6 Naliya Gujarat India 23.19N 68.51E
28 D3 Nallamala Ra mts Andhra Prad India
104 E8 Nallen W Virginia 38.06N 80.53W
79 K1 Nálles Italy 46.33N 11.12E
72 B3 Nalliers Vendée France 46.28N 1.02W
72 F2 Nalliers Vienne France 46.37N 0.50E
36 E2 Nallıhan Turkey 40.12N 31.22E
47 K7 Nalobino U.S.S.R. 55.15N 68.45E
92 A9 Nalolo Zambia 15.31S 23.06E
76 G2 Nalón R Spain
31 C7 Nal R Pakistan
29 K7 Naltigiri Hill Orissa India 21.36N 86.20E
85 A4 Nālūt Libya 31.53N 10.59E
93 C4 Nalweyo Uganda 1.09N 31.18E
39 F7 Nalychevo U.S.S.R. 53.10N 159.14E
64 Q5 Nalžovské Hory Czechoslovakia 49.20N 13.34E
28 H1 Nam Xizang Zizhiqu 29.28N 90.52E
21 D8 Nam R N Korea
120 D8 Nama Chile 19.12S 69.25W
20 C8 Nama Japan 33.02N 129.03E
94 M5 Namaacha Mozambique 25.58S 32.05E
19 F5 Namaa, Tanjung C Moluccas Indon 2.48S 129.03E
92 J9 Namacala Mozambique 14.34S 38.17E
91 D12 Namacunde Angola 17.18S 15.50E
92 H10 Namacurra Mozambique 17.30S 37.00E
30 F5 Namai Nepal 27.51N 82.32E
19 N2 Namai B Palau Is Pacific Oc
100 D8 Namaka Alberta 50.58N 113.12W
108 S1 Namakan L Minnesota/Ontario
32 C3 Namak-e Mīqhān, Kavīr-e salt L Iran
32 F5 Namakī R Iran
28 D5 Namakkal Tamil Nadu India 11.12N 78.10E
32 G3 Namak, Kavir-i- salt waste Iran
31 A4 Namakzar Afghanistan 34.00N 60.55E
32 H5 Namakzar-e Shadad salt marsh Iran
42 L2 Namana R U.S.S.R.
33 A3 Na'mān, An isld Saudi Arabia 27.02N 35.45E
18 G7 Namang Indonesia 2.17S 106.13E
93 H8 Namanga Kenya 2.33S 36.48E
93 H8 Namanga watercourse Kenya/Tanzania
43 K6 Namangan Uzbekistan U.S.S.R. 40.59N 71.41E
N'amānīyah see Nu'mānīyah, An
92 E5 Namanyere Tanzania 7.31S 31.04E
92 J8 Namapa Mozambique 13.42S 39.50E
92 J9 Namaponda Mozambique 15.51S 39.52E
94 C5 Namaqualand reg Namibia
94 D7 Namaqualand reg S Africa
15 C6 Namaripi, Tg C Irian Jaya 4.27S 135.10E
92 H9 Namarroi Mozambique 15.57S 36.51E
93 D4 Namasagali Uganda 1.02N 32.58E
93 D4 Namasale Uganda 1.31N 32.38E
35 F10 Namata Jordan 30.50N 35.33E
15 M5 Namatanai New Ireland 3.40S 152.26E
9 S6 Namathu Koro Fiji 17.21S 179.24E
92 J7 Namaua Mozambique 11.35S 39.40E
91 D9 Namba Angola 11.32S 15.33E
93 K5 Nambala Kenya 0.23N 38.27E
92 C9 Nambala Zambia 15.04S 26.56E
9 S5 Nambavetu Viti Levu Fiji 16.38S 178.56E
14 D4 Nambeet Well W Australia 19.32S 121.14E
15 C4 Namber Numfoor I, Irian Jaya 1.06S 134.49E
89 K7 Nambiri Ghana 9.53N 0.25E
Nambling see Kalip
92 J6 Nambondo Tanzania 8.40S 39.09E
13 L7 Nambour Queensland 26.40S 152.52E
9 S8 Namboutini Viti Levu Fiji 18.16S 177.50E
9 R5 Nambouwalu Vanua Levu Fiji 17.00S 178.43E
12 L4 Nambucca Heads New S Wales 30.38S 152.59E
25 H3 Nam Ca Dinh R Laos
25 H8 Nam Can Vietnam 8.46N 104.59E
30 H4 Namche Bazar Nepal 27.49N 86.44E
21 D8 Namch'ŏnjom N Korea 38.15N 126.26E
24 G10 Namco Xizang Zizhiqu China 30.53N 91.06E
24 F10 Nam Co L Xizang Zizhiqu China
32 D5 Namdagun Iran 31.03N 51.36E
52 F2 Namdalen V Norway
52 F2 Namdalseid Norway 64.13N 11.13E
25 J2 Nam Dinh Vietnam 20.25N 106.12E
92 J8 Namecala Mozambique 12.50S 39.38E
61 K5 Namêche Belgium 50.28N 5.00E
92 H9 Namecuna Mozambique 14.55S 37.38E
18 M4 Nameh Borneo Indon 2.34N 116.22E
106 C3 Namekagon, R Wisconsin
19 N2 Namelakl Pass Palau Is Pacific Oc 7.25N 134.36E
9 S5 Namena Barrier Reef Fiji
89 K4 Namenga Niger 14.12N 1.04E
42 K4 Namenga U.S.S.R. 56.36N 118.22E
20 L5 Namerikawa Japan 36.46N 137.18E
65 O3 Náměšť nad Oslavou Czech 49.13N 16.10E
62 L6 Námestovo Czechoslovakia 49.24N 19.25E
92 J9 Nametil Mozambique 15.41S 39.20E
100 P4 Namew L Saskatchewan
30 B1 Namgia Himachal Prad India 31.48N 78.40E
25 G2 Nam Het R Laos
25 E2 Nam Hka R Burma
25 N9 Namhkam Burma 23.49N 97.43E
25 M9 Namhsan Burma 23.01N 97.09E
25 E2 Nam Hsin R Burma
34 C10 Na'mi, An Saudi Arabia 28.15N 35.42E
94 B2 Namib Des Namibia
Namibia see South West Africa
73 F8 Namibia rep Africa
92 H9 Namicunde Mozambique 14.12S 36.54E
20 O4 Namie Japan 37.28N 140.58E
32 C1 Namīn Iran 38.25N 48.35E
92 J9 Namina Mozambique 14.56S 38.41E
20 O1 Namioka Japan 40.42N 140.36E
35 H1 Namir Syria 33.02N 36.01E
35 H2 Namir Syria 32.47N 36.13E
34 O4 Nāmīvand Iran 34.23N 46.46E
94 D6 Namiziz mt Namibia 27.08S 16.51E
24 F10 Namka Tso L Xizang Zizhiqu 31.58N 89.50E
25 D1 Namlan Burma 22.16N 97.25E
25 D2 Namlang R Burma
19 E5 Namlea Moluccas Indon 3.15S 127.07E
25 G3 Nam Lik R Laos
24 F11 Namling Xizang Zizhiqu China 29.40N 89.00E
25 F2 Nam Loi R Burma
25 M7 Nam Long R Burma
25 F2 Nam Ma R Laos
25 N9 Nam Mao R Burma
25 G3 Nam Mat R Laos
25 D3 Nammekon Burma 19.40N 97.08E
25 H3 Nam Muone R Laos
25 G1 Nam Na R Vietnam
25 H4 Nam One R Laos
25 H3 Nam Neun R Laos
25 F2 Nam Ngaov R Laos
25 G3 Nam Ngum R Laos
25 G3 Nam Nhiep R Laos
25 G2 Nam Noua R Laos
19 A4 Namo Celebes Indonesia 1.26S 119.59E
Namob see Namutoni
30 D1 Namochina Xizang Zizhiqu 31.36N 80.22E
12 J4 Namoi R New S Wales
114 E3 Namolokama Mts Hawaiian Is
9 C3 Namorik atoll Marshall Is Pacific Oc 5.40N 168.05E
95 D6 Namorona Madagascar 21.40S 48.10E
88 N6 Namous watercourse Algeria
92 C4 Namoya Zaïre 4.01S 27.36E
101 P7 Nampa Alberta 56.02N 117.07W
51 M5 Nampa Finland 66.49N 26.10E
110 J6 Nampa Idaho 43.35N 116.34W
30 E2 Nampa mt Nepal 30.01N 87.00E
89 G4 Nampala Mali 15.19N 5.31W
25 E1 Nam Pang R Burma
25 F4 Nam Pat Thailand 17.40N 100.37E
25 G4 Nam Phong Thailand 16.44N 102.51E
28 L5 Nam Pilu R Burma
92 H6 Nampinga Tanzania 9.39S 37.10E
Nam Pong see Ban Nam Pong
69 B3 Nampont France 50.21N 1.45E
25 F3 Nam Poui R Laos
92 J9 Nampuio Mozambique 15.20S 38.52E
24 H12 Nampuk R Burma
92 J9 Nampula Mozambique 15.09S 39.14E
92 H9 Nampula dist Mozambique
25 G4 Nam Pung Res Thailand
92 H7 Nampungu Tanzania 11.00S 37.05E
19 E5 Namrole Moluccas Indon 3.50S 126.43E
36 H5 Namrun Turkey 37.03N 34.46E
28 K2 Namrup Assam India 27.12N 95.20E
24 F9 Namru Tso L Xizang Zizhiqu China 32.04N 90.29E
25 N8 Namsai Burma 24.44N 97.26E
25 H2 Nam Sam R Laos
25 G3 Nam Sane R Laos
25 D2 Namsang Burma 20.53N 97.45E
52 G2 Namsen R Norway
25 G2 Nam Seng R Laos
24 D11 Namsê Shankou pass Xizang Zizhiqu China 30.00N 82.40E
32 A2 Namshir Iran 36.04N 45.52E
28 H1 Namsi La pass Bhutan 28.01N 90.07E
42 J2 Namskiy U.S.S.R. 60.35N 113.40E
52 F2 Namsos Norway 64.28N 11.30E
25 G2 Nam Suong R Laos
51 D6 Namsvatn L Norway 65.00N 13.40E
25 N9 Nam Tabet R Burma
25 N7 Nam Tamai R Burma
90 F7 Namtari Nigeria 9.18N 12.19E
25 D2 Nam Teng R Burma
25 F2 Nam Tha R Laos
25 H3 Nam Theun R Laos
25 G3 Nam Thon R Laos
25 M8 Namti Burma 25.21N 97.00E
25 D3 Namtok Burma 19.59N 97.00E
25 E5 Nam Tok Thailand 14.18N 98.58E
25 E1 Namton Burma 22.01N 99.31E
Nam Tso L see Nam Co
41 N8 Namtsy U.S.S.R. 62.45N 129.45E
25 N9 Namtu Burma 23.04N 97.26E
101 K10 Namu Br Col 51.52N 127.52W
9 C2 Namu atoll Marshall Is Pacific Oc 8.00N 168.08E
25 G1 Nam Ou R Laos
9 U3 Namuka-i-Lau atoll Fiji 18.50S 178.41W
92 H9 Namuli mt Mozambique 15.25S 37.00E
Na-mu-lin see Namling
26 T8 Namunakuli mt Sri Lanka 6.56N 81.07E
92 J8 Namuno Mozambique 13.39S 38.50E
26 T8 Namunukula Sri Lanka 6.53N 81.07E
61 K5 Namur Belgium 50.28N 4.52E
99 Q7 Namur Quebec 45.54N 74.58W
61 J5 Namur prov Belgium
101 R7 Namur L Alberta 57.27N 112.40W
93 G1 Namuruputh Kenya 4.35N 35.56E
94 D2 Namutoni Namibia 18.49S 16.55E
93 E5 Namutumba Uganda 0.50N 33.42E
15 A7 Namwaän isld Moluccas Indon 7.08S 131.28E
23 C8 Nam Wai Hong Kong 22.21N 114.15E
92 C9 Namwala Zambia 15.44S 26.25E
93 E5 Namwendwa Uganda 0.55N 33.16E
92 G9 Namwera Malawi 14.23S 35.30E
93 E4 Namwiwa Uganda 1.06N 33.33E
21 D10 Namwŏn S Korea 35.23N 127.23E
41 O6 Namy U.S.S.R. 69.31N 132.04E
25 M7 Namya Ra Burma 27.02N 96.15E
25 N10 Nam Yi Tu R Burma
25 M8 Namyla Chaung R Burma
62 L4 Namysłaki Poland 51.34N 18.02E
62 K4 Namysłów Poland 51.03N 17.41E
Nan see Muang Nan
29 C5 Nana Rajasthan India 25.00N 73.13E
90 G9 Nana R Cent Afr Rep
85 C5 Nānā watercourse Libya
90 H8 Nana Barya R Cent Afr Rep
91 H9 Nana Candundo Angola 11.30S 23.00E
101 M11 Nanaimo Vancouver I, Br Col 49.08N 123.58W
89 E9 Nana Kru Liberia 4.54N 8.46W
114 A5 Nanakuli Hawaiian Is 21.23N 158.10W
21 E7 Nanam N Korea 41.44N 129.40E
90 G9 Nana-Mambéré dist Cent Afr Rep
14 E10 Nanambinia W Australia 32.40S 123.32E
23 H6 Nan 'An Fujian China 24.57N 118.25E
23 D8 Nanan Guangxi China 21.53N 107.26E
13 K7 Nanango Queensland 26.42S 151.58E
94 D5 Nananib Plateau Namibia
9 T7 Nananu-i-Ra isld Fiji 17.17S 178.18E
23 H7 Nan'ao Guangdong China 23.25N 117.06E
20 K4 Nanao Japan 37.03N 136.58E
23 H7 Nan'ao Dao isld Guangdong China 23.14N 117.18E
20 L4 Nanao-wan B Japan
18 K2 Nanas Chan Pen Malaysia/Singapore
15 G7 Nanase Papua New Guinea 7.32S 143.22E
20 K4 Nanatsu-jima isld Japan
30 A3 Nanauta Uttar Prad India 29.42N 77.25E
43 N7 Nanay Uzbekistan U.S.S.R. 41.30N 71.41E
119 D9 Nanay, R Peru
Nanbai see Zunyi (Nanbai)
22 C7 Nanbaxian Qinghai China 37.59N 94.20E
23 D3 Nanbazhen Sichuan China 31.28N 107.58E
23 D3 Nanbu Sichuan China 31.24N 106.06E
121 B5 Nancagua Chile 34.35S 71.15W
70 P7 Nançay France 47.21N 2.11E
94 S14 Nancefield S Africa 26.17S 27.53E
94 S14 Nancefield sta S Africa 26.15S 27.54E
21 E4 Nancha Heilongjiang China 47.09N 129.21E
23 G4 Nanchang Jiangxi China 28.33N 115.58E
23 G4 Nanchang Jiangxi China 28.42N 115.55E
22 M8 Nanchangshan Dao isld Shandong China 37.55N 120.45E
Nan-cheng see Nanzheng
23 G5 Nancheng Jiangxi China 27.36N 116.35E
23 D3 Nanchong Sichuan China 30.54N 106.06E
23 D4 Nanchuan Sichuan China 29.06N 107.13E
75 E2 Nanclares de Oca Spain 42.49N 2.49W
69 J6 Nançois-sur-Ornain France 48.43N 5.18E
120 F9 Nancorainza Bolivia 20.39S 63.20W
28 J7 Nancowry isld Nicobar Is
66 A3 Nancray France 47.15N 6.11E
69 L6 Nancy France 48.42N 6.12E
11 A12 Nancy Sd New Zealand
30 C2 Nanda Devi mt Uttar Prad India 30.21N 79.58E
115 L4 Nandaime Nicaragua 11.45N 86.02W
30 D2 Nanda Kot mt Uttar Prad India 30.14N 80.05E
23 D6 Nandan Guangxi China 24.58N 107.33E
28 F1 Nandapur Orissa India 18.32N 82.52E
Nandaran see Qingyuan
9 S7 Nandarivatu Viti Levu Fiji 17.35S 177.58E
29 E8 Nander Maharashtra India 19.11N 77.21E
29 E8 Nander dist Maharashtra India
12 K4 Nandewar Ra New S Wales
29 D7 Nandgaon Maharashtra India 20.17N 74.43E
92 E12 Nandi Zimbabwe 20.56S 31.43E
93 G5 Nandi tribe Kenya
9 R8 Nandi B Viti Levu Fiji
28 C4 Nandi Drug Karnataka India 13.28N 77.40E
28 E2 Nandigama Andhra Prad India 16.48N 80.19E
28 D3 Nandikanama Pass Andhra Prad India 15.26N 78.45E
28 D3 Nandikotkur Andhra Prad India 15.54N 78.17E
23 B7 Nanding He R Yunnan China
28 E1 Nandiraj mt Madhya Prad India 18.46N 81.16E
64 M6 Nandlstadt W Germany 48.31N 11.49E
29 C7 Nandod Gujarat India 21.52N 73.32E
89 H6 Nandom Ghana 10.57N 2.43W
89 H4 Nandouli Mali 14.30N 3.24W
9 S7 Nandrau Plateau Viti Levu Fiji
61 M4 Nandrin Belgium 50.31N 5.25E
121 E3 Nanducita Argentina 30.24S 61.06W
23 E9 Nandu Jiang R Guangdong China
29 E7 Nandura Maharashtra India 20.50N 76.31E
29 D7 Nandurbar Maharashtra India 21.22N 74.18E
9 S5 Nanduri Vanua Levu Fiji 16.26S 179.08E
28 D3 Nandyal Andhra Prad India 15.30N 78.28E
64 D4 Nane R W Germany
21 C7 Nanfen Liaoning China 41.00N 123.44E
23 F7 Nanfeng Guangdong China 23.41N 111.38E
23 G5 Nanfeng Jiangxi China 27.15N 116.20E
30 H3 Nang Nepal 27.55N 86.44E
18 K5 Nangabadau Borneo Indon 1.05N 112.00E
92 J7 Nangade Mozambique 11.05S 39.37E
90 F9 Nanga Eboko Cameroon 4.38N 12.21E
19 C8 Nangahale Indonesia 8.35S 122.33E
18 K5 Nangakelawit Borneo Indon 0.24N 112.30E
91 B6 Nanga, L Congo 4.13S 11.52E
18 J6 Nangalanki Kalimantan Indonesia 1.16S 111.34E
19 K6 Nangalao isld Philippines 11.27N 120.11E
29 E2 Nangal Dam Punjab India 31.19N 76.26E
18 J6 Nangamau Borneo Indon 0.09S 111.51E
18 K6 Nangamuntatai Borneo Indon 0.20S 112.22E
18 K5 Nangaobat Borneo Indon 1.00N 113.15E
30 K5 Nangaon Nepal 27.52N 86.26E
31 H3 Nanga Parbat mt Kashmir 35.15N 74.36E
18 J6 Nangapinoh Borneo Indon 0.21S 111.44E
28 E1 Nangaram Andhra Prad India 18.20N 80.30E
18 K5 Nangaraun Borneo Indon 0.39N 113.12E
31 F3 Nangarhar prov Afghanistan
18 K5 Nangasuruk Borneo Indon 0.35N 112.44E
92 K9 Nangata, Pta Mozambique 14.11S 40.41E
18 J6 Nangatayap Borneo Indon 1.30S 110.33E
24 H9 Nangchen Japo mt pk Qinghai China 32.59N 94.14E
93 E2 Nangeya Mts Uganda/Sudan
25 E7 Nangin Burma 10.31N 98.31E
69 E6 Nangis France 48.34N 3.01E
30 D2 Nangling Uttar Prad India 30.11N 80.34E
21 D8 Nangnim Sanmaek mts N Korea
89 F5 Nango Mali 13.18N 6.35W
21 F11 Nangoku Japan 33.38N 133.42E
89 F5 Nangola Mali 12.41N 6.35W
22 K8 Nangong Hebei China 37.22N 115.20E
30 G1 Nangpa Glacier Nepal
30 G1 Nangpai Gosum mt Nepal/Xizang Zizhiqu 28.04N 86.37E
30 G2 Nangpai Gotaya mt Nepal 28.03N 86.36E
30 G1 Nangpa La pass Nepal/Xizang Zizhiqu 28.06N 86.36E
Nangpoh see Nongpoh
24 J9 Nangqên Qinghai China 32.15N 96.29E
28 C6 Nanguneri Tamil Nadu India 8.29N 77.42E
24 H11 Nang Xian Xizang Zizhiqu China 29.02N 93.05E
Nan Hai see South China Sea
Nan-hai see Fosnan
23 F7 Nanhai Guangdong China 23.00N 113.03E
23 G9 Nan Hai sea China
Nanhaoqian see Shangyi
22 J6 Nanhaoqian Hebei China 41.05N 113.58E
22 K8 Nanhe Hebei China 37.00N 114.42E
23 F2 Nan He R Hubei China
23 F2 Nanhedian Henan China 33.23N 112.24E
22 C7 Nanhu Gansu China 39.55N 94.09E
23 D1 Nanhu Gansu China 35.23N 105.58E
23 B6 Nanhua Yunnan China 25.15N 101.15E
21 B12 Nanhui Shanghai China 31.03N 121.45E
22 D8 Nan Hulsan Hu L Qinghai China
31 E4 Nani Afghanistan 33.23N 68.23E
89 D5 Nanifara Mali 13.02N 10.49W
61 K5 Naninne Belgium 50.25N 4.55E
28 C4 Nanjangud Karnataka India 12.07N 76.40E
23 B6 Nanjian Yunnan China 25.04N 100.37E
23 D2 Nanjiang Sichuan China 32.22N 106.53E
23 G4 Nanjiangqiao Hunan China 28.59N 113.47E
23 H6 Nanjing Fujian China 24.26N 117.20E
23 H2 Nanjing Jiangsu China 32.03N 118.47E
23 E8 Nankang Guangxi China 21.29N 109.30E
23 G6 Nankang Jiangxi China 25.42N 114.45E
Nanking see Nanjing
20 G8 Nankoku Japan 33.33N 133.37E
22 K6 Nankouzhen Beijing China 40.16N 116.05E
23 B8 Nanlan He R Yunnan China
23 G1 Nanle Henan China 36.05N 115.13E
92 H8 Nanlicha Mozambique 12.53S 37.42E
23 H3 Nanling Anhui China 30.55N 118.18E
25 K2 Nanliu Jiang R China
Nanma see Yiyuan
23 J4 Nanma Zhejiang China 29.05N 120.15E
23 G5 Nanmiao Jiangxi China 27.40N 114.28E
64 L7 Nannhofen W Germany 48.13N 11.10E
14 C7 Nannine W Australia 26.53S 118.20E
23 E7 Nanning Guangxi China 22.50N 108.19E
28 D5 Nanntlam Tamil Nadu India 10.55N 79.34E
14 B10 Nannup W Australia 33.57S 115.42E
71 K6 Nanoise mts France
Nanomana isld see Nanumanga
Nanomea Is see Nanumea Is
48 U16 Nanortalik Greenland 60.09N 45.15W
121 J9 Naños, I Chile 53.35S 73.48W
41 Q3 Nanosnyy, Ostrov isld U.S.S.R. 76.27N 140.29E
23 D6 Nanpan Jiang R Guizhou China
23 C6 Nanpan Jiang R Yunnan China
30 E5 Nanpara Uttar Prad India 27.51N 81.30E
23 H7 Nanpeng Liedao isld Guangdong China
22 K7 Nanpi Hebei China 38.06N 116.41E
23 H5 Nanping Fujian China 26.40N 118.07E
21 E6 Nanping Jilin China 42.18N 129.11E
23 C2 Nanping Sichuan China 33.15N 104.15E
22 L7 Nanpu Hebei China 39.15N 118.05E
23 H5 Nanpu Xi R Fujian China
Nanqiao see Fengxian
23 H6 Nanri Dao isld Fujian China 25.13N 119.29E
92 J9 Nanripo Mozambique 14.08S 38.52E
76 L2 Nansa R Spain
Nansei Trench see Ryukyu Trench
41 N2 Nansena, Ostrov I Franz Josef Land U.S.S.R.
41 F3 Nansena, Ostrov isld U.S.S.R.
Nansen I see Nansena, Ostrov Franz Josef Land U.S.S.R
121 J6 Nansen, L Argentina
97 K1 Nansen Sd N W Terr
48 S1 Nansens Land Greenland
17 J9 Nanshan islds S China Sea
17 E4 Nan Shan mts China
40 H3 Nansikan Ostrov isld U.S.S.R. 57.25N 139.51E
93 E8 Nansio Tanzania 2.06S 33.03E
71 H10 Nans-les-Pins France 43.22N 5.47E
14 A8 Nanson W Australia 28.34S 114.44E
72 L7 Nant France 44.01N 3.18E
29 D5 Nanta Rajasthan India 25.12N 75.52E
105 D2 Nantahala L N Carolina 35.10N 83.40W
97 M5 Nantais, L Quebec 61.00N 74.00W
20 H7 Nantan Japan 34.16N 134.42E
103 N2 Nantasket Beach Massachusetts 42.17N 70.52W
92 H10 Nante Mozambique 17.25S 37.20E
68 D3 Nanterre France 48.53N 2.13E
72 A1 Nantes France 47.14N 1.35W
98 A8 Nantes Quebec 45.38N 71.01W
72 E3 Nanteuil-en-Vallée France 46.01N 0.20E
69 D5 Nanteuil-le-Haudouin France 49.08N 2.49E
56 E4 Nantgarw Mid Glam Wales 51.34N 3.17W
26 S3 Nanthi Kadal L Sri Lanka
23 J4 Nantian Zhejiang China 29.07N 121.57E
72 G3 Nantiat France 46.01N 1.11E
18 E8 Nanti, Bukit mt Sumatra Indon 4.14S 103.51E
103 B2 Nanticoke New York 42.17N 76.04W
104 K5 Nanticoke Pennsylvania 41.13N 76.00W
104 K8 Nanticoke R Maryland
100 D8 Nanton Alberta 50.21N 113.47W
23 J2 Nantong Jiangsu China 32.05N 120.51E
23 J2 Nantong Jiangsu China 32.06N 121.04E
25 M1 Nantou Guangdong China 22.35N 113.58E
23 J7 Nan-t'ou Taiwan 23.54N 120.42E
71 H4 Nantua France 46.09N 5.36E
103 O4 Nantucket Massachusetts 41.17N 70.05W
103 O4 Nantucket co Massachusetts
103 O4 Nantucket I Massachusetts
123 E12 Nantucket Inlet Antarctica
103 O3 Nantucket Sd Massachusetts
92 J8 Nantulo Mozambique 12.34S 39.00E
Nantun see Ewenkizu Zizhiqi
57 H6 Nantwich Cheshire Eng 53.04N 2.32W
104 G6 Nanty Glo Pennsylvania 40.28N 78.50W
56 D3 Nant-y-Moch Reservoir Dyfed Wales
56 D4 Nant-y-moel Mid Glam Wales 51.38N 3.33W
56 D3 Nant-y-mwyn Dyfed Wales 52.04N 3.46W
103 F4 Nanuet New York 41.06N 74.01W
9 T7 Nanukuloa Viti Levu Fiji 17.29S 178.14E
9 U5 Nanuku Passage Fiji
9 U5 Nanuku Reef Fiji 16.40S 179.25W
9 C7 Nanumanga isld Tuvalu, Pacific Oc 6.20S 176.25E
9 C7 Nanumea Is Tuvalu, Pacific Oc 5.40S 176.10E
118 H5 Nanuque Brazil 17.49S 40.21W
29 L1 Nanur W Bengal India 23.42N 87.53E
113 M2 Nanushuk R Alaska
22 J8 Nanweiquan Shaanxi China 36.42N 113.22E
21 C2 Nanweng He R Nei Monggol Zizhiqu China
23 E2 Nanwutai mt pk Shaanxi China 33.59N 108.58E
23 C4 Nanxi Sichuan China 28.54N 104.59E
23 F4 Nan Xian Hunan China 29.21N 112.22E
23 E7 Nanxiang Guangxi China 22.31N 109.10E
23 D2 Nanxing Shaanxi China 33.46N 106.43E
23 G6 Nanxiong Guangdong China 25.14N 114.20E
13 J6 Nanya Queensland 22.58S 147.51E
92 J7 Nanyamba Tanzania 10.41S 39.50E
23 F2 Nanyang Henan China 33.06N 112.31E
23 E4 Nanyaojie Sichuan China 28.42N 108.22E
23 H1 Nanyi Shandong China 35.52N 117.11E
23 H3 Nanyi Hu L Anhui China
20 O3 Nanyō Japan 38.04N 140.06E
22 K7 Nanyuan Beijing China 39.47N 116.22E
93 J5 Nanyuki Kenya 0.01N 37.05E
21 C7 Nanzamu Liaoning China 41.56N 124.36E
23 E3 Nanzhang Hubei China 31.51N 111.45E
23 F2 Nanzhao Henan China 33.30N 112.27E
23 J5 Nanzhen Fujian China 27.07N 120.25E
23 D2 Nanzheng Shaanxi China 33.00N 106.55E
92 C10 Nanzhila Zambia 16.04S 26.06E
31 F3 Nao Afghanistan 35.54N 70.44E
77 R3 Nao, C. de la Spain 38.44N 0.14E
Nao-chou Tao isld see P'ao Chou Tao
97 M7 Naococane, L Quebec 52.50N 70.45W
20 M4 Naoetsu Japan 37.10N 138.15E
31 G8 Naogaon Bangladesh 24.49N 88.59E
31 E8 Naokot Pakistan 24.52N 69.27E
21 F4 Naoli He R Heilongjiang China
32 J4 Naomid, Dasht-e des Iran
110 O8 Naomi Pk Utah 41.56N 111.40W
29 J6 Naomundi Bihar India 22.10N 85.30E
24 C6 Naor Hu L Xinjiang Uygur Zizhiqu China
115 G10 Naos I Panama Canal Zone
96 P12 Naos, Pto B Hierro Canary Is
Naoua see Nawa
83 E4 Náousa Greece 40.38N 22.04E
23 E8 Naozhou Dao isld Guangdong China 20.55N 110.35E
111 B3 Napa California 38.19N 122.18W
92 J8 Napa Mozambique 13.20S 38.59E
19 C6 Napabalana Indonesia 4.38S 122.44E
98 F7 Napadogan New Brunswick 46.25N 66.56W
Napaimiut see Napamute
113 G6 Napaiskak Alaska 60.41N 161.46W
93 F3 Napak Mt Uganda 2.03N 34.16E
18 L4 Napaku Borneo Indon 2.30N 115.59E
47 L1 Napalkovo U.S.S.R. 70.03N 73.50E
113 H6 Napamute Alaska 61.31N 158.45W
39 F5 Napana U.S.S.R. 57.49N 158.21E
39 F6 Napana R U.S.S.R.
99 O8 Napanee Ontario 44.15N 74.57W
93 E3 Napano mt Uganda 2.56N 33.35E
103 F3 Napanoch New York 41.44N 74.22W
44 G5 Napareuli Georgia U.S.S.R. 42.02N 45.33E
Napari see Whaler Anchorage
42 C3 Napas U.S.S.R. 59.51N 82.00E
93 F2 Napass watercourse Kenya
48 S12 Napassoq Greenland 65.05N 52.20W
110 C3 Napavine Washington 46.35N 122.56W
19 L5 Napayauan isld Philippines 12.23N 123.15E
25 H3 Nape Laos 18.18N 105.07E
103 K4 Napeague B Long I, N Y
103 K5 Napeague Beach Long I, N Y
15 L5 Napekur Bismarck Arch 2.41S 152.00E
53 V20 Napen mt Norway 59.25N 6.41E
106 F8 Naperville Illinois 41.46N 88.08W
98 O2 Napetipi R Quebec
53 Y20 Napevatn L Norway 59.10N 8.15E
66 H3 Napf mt Switzerland 47.01N 7.56E
50 B4 Napi mt Iceland 65.26N 23.51W
15 C4 Napido Biak I, Irian Jaya 0.39S 135.27E
107 A1 Napier Missouri 40.02N 95.15W
11 L6 Napier New Zealand 39.29S 176.58E
95 C10 Napier S Africa 34.28S 19.54E
14 F2 Napier Broome B W Australia
13 A4 Napier, Mt N Terr Australia 17.33S 129.09E
123 A5 Napier Mts Antarctica
13 D1 Napier Pen N Terr Australia
14 E3 Napier Ra W Australia
99 R7 Napierville Quebec 45.11N 73.25W
100 R9 Napinka Manitoba 49.19N 100.50W
105 F11 Naples Florida 26.09N 81.48W
Naples Italysee Napoli
104 H4 Naples New York 42.36N 77.25W
112 N2 Naples Texas 33.13N 94.40W
23 D7 Napo Guangxi China 23.26N 105.50E
23 D7 Napo Guangxi China 23.50N 106.52E
119 C8 Napo prov Ecuador
81 E8 Napola Sicily 37.59N 12.38E
107 L2 Napoleon Indiana 39.12N 85.20W
108 L3 Napoleon N Dakota 46.31N 99.45W
104 A5 Napoleon Ohio 41.24N 84.09W
96 B13 Napoleon's Tomb St Helena 15.58S 5.42W
107 E12 Napoleonville Louisiana 29.58N 91.02W
80 M6 Napoletano, Appennino mts Italy
80 K7 Napoli Italy 40.50N 14.15E
80 K7 Napoli prov Italy
80 K7 Napoli, G. di Italy
108 L9 Naponee Nebraska 40.04N 99.10W
114 B8 Napoopoo Hawaiian Is 19.29N 155.55W
87 B8 Napopo Zaïre 4.14N 28.02E
119 D9 Napo, R Peru
121 E7 Naposta Argentina 38.25S 62.12W
121 E7 Naposta R Argentina
71 K9 Napoule, G.de la France 43.32N 6.58E
71 K9 Napoule, la France 43.32N 6.56E
13 F8 Nappamerry Queensland 27.35S 141.00E
106 H8 Nappanee Indiana 41.27N 86.01W
13 C6 Napperby N Terr Australia 22.30S 132.41E
107 C2 Napton Missouri 39.03N 93.06W
122 E14 Napuka atoll Tuamotu Is Pacific Oc 14.05S 141.20W
114 B7 Na Puukulua mt Hawaiian Is 19.43N 155.39W
87 D2 Naqa Sudan 16.17N 33.16E
85 M7 Naqâda Egypt 25.52N 32.41E
32 A2 Naqadeh Iran 36.57N 45.24E
86 F8 Naqb el Daqîq hill Egypt 28.34N 31.01E
86 G6 Naqb Ghûl hill Egypt 29.31N 31.56E
86 P6 Naqb Ishtar Jordan 30.00N 35.30E
86 L8 Naqb Watia pass Egypt 28.41N 33.59E
33 E6 Nāqī', An Saudi Arabia 20.12N 42.41E
33 H3 Naqīrah, An Saudi Arabia 27.50N 48.14E
35 D1 Nâqoûra, Enn Lebanon 33.07N 35.08E
32 C3 Naqqash Iran 35.37N 48.45E
33 F9 Naqūb S Yemen 15.01N 45.50E
75 K8 Náquera Spain 39.40N 0.26W
29 A6 Nara Gujarat India 23.40N 69.10E
20 J7 Nara Japan 34.41N 135.49E
89 F4 Nara Mali 15.13N 7.20W
Nara des reg see Indian Desert
20 J7 Nara prefect Japan

12 J4 **Narabri West** New S Wales 30.22S 149.47E
37 C3 **Nara Burun** *C* **Turkey** 40.13N 26.25E
12 G7 **Naracoopa** King I, Tasmania 39.56S 144.11E
12 F6 **Naracoorte** S Australia 36.57S 140.50E
12 H5 **Naradhan** New S Wales 33.39S 146.20E
15 K6 **Narage I** Bismarck Arch 4.34S 149.06E
90 D7 **Naraguta Nigeria** 9.59N 8.54E
20 B2 **Narahashi** Tōkyō **Japan**
30 K6 **Narahia** Bihar **India** 26.21N 86.32E
29 A2 **Naraina** Delhi **India** 28.37N 77.08E
29 D4 **Naraina** Rajasthan **India** 26.48N 75.13E
29 J4 **Narainghat Nepal** 27.42N 84.08E
30 D7 **Naraini** Uttar Prad **India** 25.12N 80.30E
29 G8 **Narainpur** Madhya Prad **India** 19.42N 81.18E
29 J7 **Naraj Dam** Orissa **India** 20.25N 85.46E
Narak *see* **Naraq**
31 H9 **Naral** Bangladesh 23.10N 89.30E
14 A8 **Naraling** W Australia 28.25S 114.49E
101 O11 **Naramata** Br Col 49.35N 119.35W
26 R7 **Narammale Sri Lanka** 7.25N 80.13E
93 J8 **Naramuru Kenya** 2.45S 37.43E
22 D3 **Naran** Govĭaltay **Mongolia** 46.02N 96.44E
22 J4 **Naran** Sühbaatar **Mongolia** 45.20N 113.41E
22 K4 **Naran Bulag** Nei Monggol Zizhiqu **China** 44.30N 114.19E
31 F3 **Narang Afghanistan** 34.47N 71.05E
105 G12 **Naranja** Florida 25.31N 80.27W
119 B9 **Naranjal Ecuador** 2.43S 79.38W
120 B1 **Naranjal Peru** 5.01S 75.48W
119 B9 **Naranjal, R Ecuador**
115 P10 **Naranjito Honduras** 14.58N 88.36W
115 E5 **Naranjo** Sinaloa **Mexico** 25.48N 108.30W
115 K6 **Naranjo** Tamaulipas **Mexico** 22.30N 98.40W
Naran Mandaha *see* **Mandah**
32 D4 **Naraq** Iran 34.00N 50.49E
29 J8 **Narasannapeta** Andhra Pradesh **India** 18.21N 84.11E
Narasapatnam *see* **Narasapur**
28 E2 **Narasapatnam Pt** Andhra Prad **India** 16.20N 81.47E
28 E2 **Narasapur** Godavari, Andhra Prad **India** 16.27N 81.45E
28 E2 **Narasaraopet** Andhra Prad **India** 16.17N 80.03E
20 H2 **Narashinō** Chiba **Japan** 35.41N 140.02E
42 J6 **Narasun U.S.S.R.** 50.05N 112.58E
24 E4 **Narat** Xinjiang Uygur Zizhiqu **China** 43.20N 84.02E
25 F9 **Narathiwat Thailand** 6.30N 101.50E
42 G4 **Naratoy U.S.S.R.** 56.00N 102.20E
30 B8 **Naravan** *R* Uttar Prad **India**
109 G6 **Nara Visa** New Mexico 35.36N 103.06W
31 H9 **Narayanganj Bangladesh** 23.36N 90.28E
28 B1 **Narayangaon** Maharashtra **India** 19.10N 74.00E
30 A2 **Narayangarh** Haryana **India** 30.28N 77.07E
30 H5 **Narayani** *R* **Nepal**
28 C2 **Narayanpet** Andhra Prad **India** 16.46N 77.27E
43 G7 **Narazym** Turkmeniya **U.S.S.R.** 38.53N 64.00E
56 B4 **Narberth** Dyfed **Wales** 51.48N 4.45W
104 A2 **Narberth** *dist* Philadelphia, Penn
81 B3 **Narbolia** Sardinia 40.03N 8.34E
75 H8 **Narboneta Spain** 39.45N 1.29W
72 L9 **Narbonne France** 43.11N 3.00E
71 C10 **Narbonne-Plage France** 43.11N 3.10E
56 J2 **Narborough** Leics **Eng** 52.35N 1.11W
56 N2 **Narborough** Norfolk **Eng** 52.42N 0.35E
Narborough I *see* **Fernandina, I**
81 B5 **Narcao** Sardinia 39.10N 8.40E
76 G2 **Narcea** *R* **Spain**
32 F2 **Nardin** Iran 37.03N 55.55E
29 G6 **Nardinganj** Madhya Prad **India** 22.50N 80.19E
81 R12 **Nardó** Italy 40.11N 18.02E
95 H8 **Nardousberg** *mt* **S Africa** 32.14S 24.54E
121 E3 **Nare** Argentina 30.50S 60.25W
31 E5 **Narechi R** Pakistan
28 B3 **Naregal** Karnataka **India** 15.40N 75.53E
30 A4 **Narela** Delhi **India** 28.50N 77.05E
30 A4 **Narela Mahrauli** Delhi **India** 28.31N 77.11E
14 C9 **Narembeen** W Australia 32.04S 118.23E
89 D5 **Naréna Mali** 12.59N 11.10W
30 B2 **Narendranagar** Uttar Prad **India** 30.10N 78.21E
56 U9 **Nare Pt** Cornwall **Eng** 50.11N 4.55W
96 E6 **Nares Deep Atlantic Oc**
48 R1 **Nares Land** Greenland
97 M2 **Nares Str Canada/Greenland**
14 E9 **Naretha** W Australia 31.01S 124.50E
66 L6 **Naret, Passo di Switzerland** 46.29N 8.33E
62 O3 **Narew Poland** 52.55N 23.29E
62 N2 **Narew** *R* **Poland/U.S.S.R.**
50 C4 **Narfeyri** Iceland 65.01N 22.37W
30 K8 **Narganjo** Bihar **India** 24.44N 86.30E
69 D7 **Nargis France** 48.07N 2.45E
29 C7 **Nargol** Dadra & Nagar Haveli **India** 20.12N 72.48E
30 K6 **Narhi** Bihar **India** 26.12N 86.39E
21 D6 **Narhong** Jilin **China** 42.22N 127.04E
31 H9 **Naria** Bangladesh 23.19N 90.24E
94 D5 **Narib** Namibia 24.11S 17.46E
43 O8 **Nariman** Kirgiziya **U.S.S.R.** 40.35N 72.46E
44 J9 **Narimanabad** Azerbaydzhan **U.S.S.R.** 38.53N 48.50E
31 E2 **Narin Afghanistan** 36.06N 69.03E
59 F2 **Narin** Donegal **Irish Rep** 54.50N 8.27W
22 H7 **Narin** Nei Monggol Zizhiqu **China** 39.51N 110.50E
31 E2 **Narin** *reg* **Afghanistan**
37 D8 **Narınca Turkey** 37.53N 38.44E
22 B8 **Narin Gol** *R* Qinghai **China**
119 C7 **Nariño** *div* **Colombia**
Narīn Tēli *see* **Nariynteel**
31 D6 **Nari R Pakistan**
20 O6 **Narita Japan** 35.46N 140.20E
116 O2 **Nariva** *co* **Trinidad & Tobago**
116 P2 **Nariva Swamp Trinidad & Tobago**
20 G7 **Nariwa Japan** 34.48N 133.30E
22 E4 **Nariynteel Mongolia** 45.58N 101.31E
115 D4 **Narizon, Pta Mexico** 27.50N 110.52W
109 N2 **Narka** Kansas 39.56N 97.28W
29 E2 **Narkanda** Himachal Prad **India** 31.14N 77.27E
30 A1 **Narkanda** Himachal Prad **India** 31.15N 77.38E
30 H5 **Narkatiaganj** Bihar **India** 27.06N 84.29E
51 M5 **Narkaus Finland** 66.17N 26.10E
51 K5 **Narken Sweden** 66.55N 22.45E
29 F7 **Narkher** Maharashtra **India** 21.30N 78.34E
30 B5 **Narki** Uttar Prad **India** 27.18N 78.24E
37 C8 **Narlı** Maraş **Turkey** 37.24N 37.05E
37 G8 **Narlı** Van **Turkey** 37.54N 43.04E
37 F5 **Narman Turkey** 40.22N 41.50E
29 E7 **Narnala** Maharashtra **India** 21.16N 77.06E
29 E3 **Narnaul** Haryana **India** 28.04N 76.10E
80 G3 **Narni Italy** 42.31N 12.31E
81 G9 **Naro** Sicily 37.18N 13.48E
19 L6 **Naro** *isld* **Philippines** 11.55N 123.40E
81 G9 **Naro** *R* Sicily
46 G4 **Narodichi** Ukraine **U.S.S.R.** 51.11N 29.01E
47 J3 **Narodnaya, Gora** *mt* **U.S.S.R.** 65.02N 60.01E
45 N5 **Narodnoye U.S.S.R.** 51.36N 41.52E
45 H1 **Naro-Fominsk U.S.S.R.** 55.22N 36.45E
93 G7 **Narok Kenya** 1.04S 35.54E
93 G7 **Narok** *dist* **Kenya**
93 J6 **Naro Moru Kenya** 0.10S 37.01E
76 C1 **Narón Spain** 43.31N 8.09W
12 K6 **Narooma** New S Wales 36.15S 150.06E
94 D5 **Narop** *watercourse* **Namibia**
45 P3 **Narovchat U.S.S.R.** 53.54N 43.40E
31 H4 **Narowal Pakistan** 32.04N 74.54E
51 J9 **Närpes Finland** 62.28N 21.19E
56 N2 **Nar, R** Norfolk **Eng**
12 M6 **Narrabeen** New S Wales 33.43S 151.19E
12 M6 **Narrabeen L** New S Wales
12 J4 **Narrabri** New S Wales 30.20S 149.49E
12 B6 **Narrabundah** *dist* Canberra **Australia**
103 M3 **Narragansett B** Rhode I
103 M4 **Narragansett Pier** Rhode I 41.26N 71.27W
59 J5 **Narraghmore** Kildare **Irish Rep** 53.03N 6.50W
12 J3 **Narran** *R* New S Wales
12 H5 **Narrandera** New S Wales 34.36S 146.34E
12 H3 **Narran L** New S Wales
14 E8 **Narra Spring** W Australia 29.10S 124.36E
101 N8 **Narraway** *R* Br Col/Alberta
13 H6 **Narrien Ra** Queensland
14 B10 **Narrogin** W Australia 32.57S 117.07E
12 J4 **Narromine** New S Wales 32.17S 148.20E
76 J7 **Narros del Castillo Spain** 40.51N 5.04W
110 G6 **Narrows** Oregon 43.16N 118.56W
104 E9 **Narrows** Virginia 37.20N 80.50W
103 D3 **Narrowsburg** New York 41.36N 75.03W
96 C2 **Narrows, The** *channel* Bermuda
103 J8 **Narrows, The** *str* New York
14 B1 **Narrows, The** *str* Perth, W Aust 31.57S 115.51E
116 P3 **Narrows, The** *str* St Kitts/Nevis **W I**
14 B7 **Narryer, Mt** W Australia 26.34S 116.20E
28 D1 **Narsapur** Andhra Prad **India** 19.03N 78.10E
64 O1 **Narsdorf E Germany** 51.01N 12.43E
29 F6 **Narsimhapur** Madhya Prad **India** 22.58N 79.15E
29 F6 **Narsimhapur** *dist* Madhya Prad **India**
31 H9 **Narsingdi Bangladesh** 23.56N 90.40E
29 F6 **Narsinghgarh** Damoh, Madhya Prad **India** 24.00N 79.27E
29 E6 **Narsinghgarh** Rajgarh, Madhya Prad **India** 23.42N 77.08E
29 J7 **Narsinghpur** Orissa **India** 20.28N 85.08E
28 F2 **Narsipatnam** Vishakhapatnam, Andhra Prad **India** 17.44N 82.39E
48 S15 **Narssalik Greenland** 61.35N 49.20W
48 S13 **Narssaq Greenland** 64.00N 51.10W
48 U15 **Narssaq Greenland** 61.00N 46.00W
48 U15 **Narssarssuaq Greenland** 61.10N 45.19W
22 K5 **Nart** Nei Monggol Zizhiqu **China** 42.52N 115.47E
83 C4 **Nartës,Gjol i** *L* **Albania**
84 D3 **Narthákion** *hills* **Greece**
44 F4 **Nartkala U.S.S.R.** 43.33N 43.51E
94 E6 **Narubis** Namibia 27.10S 18.36E
94 E7 **Narugas** S Africa 29.39S 19.11E
119 D7 **Naruje, R Colombia**
20 O3 **Naruko** Japan 38.44N 140.43E
45 Q2 **Naruksovo** U.S.S.R. 54.27N 44.32E
92 J6 **Narungombe** Tanzania 9.20S 38.39E
121 F2 **Narunjito, L** Argentina
20 B9 **Naru-shima** *isld* Japan 32.52N 128.53E
20 H7 **Naruto** Japan 34.11N 134.37E
20 O6 **Narutō** Japan 35.37N 140.25E
20 H7 **Naruto-kaikyō** *str* Japan
46 G1 **Narva** Estonia **U.S.S.R.** 59.22N 28.17E
42 E4 **Narva** U.S.S.R. 55.23N 93.33E
46 G1 **Narva** *R* Estonia **U.S.S.R.**
19 K3 **Narvacan** Luzon **Philippines** 17.29N 120.28E
46 G1 **Narva-Jõesuu** Estonia **U.S.S.R.** 59.28N 28.01E
Narva laht *see* **Narvskiy Zaliv**
51 F3 **Narvik Norway** 68.26N 17.25E
46 G1 **Narvskiy Zaliv** *gulf* Estonia **U.S.S.R.**
51 N12 **Narvskoye Vdkhr** *res* **U.S.S.R.**
30 A7 **Narwai** Madhya Prad **India** 25.51N 77.42E
30 D6 **Narwal** Uttar Prad **India** 26.15N 80.25E
29 E3 **Narwana** Haryana **India** 29.36N 76.11E
30 A7 **Narwar** Madhya Prad **India** 25.39N 77.54E
13 C6 **Narwietooma** N Terr **Australia** 23.10S 132.30E
47 G2 **Nar'yan Mar U.S.S.R.** 67.37N 53.02E
13 F8 **Naryilco** Queensland 28.41S 141.50E
42 C3 **Narym U.S.S.R.** 59.00N 81.30E
43 P3 **Narymskiy Khrebet** *mts* Kazakhstan **U.S.S.R.**
43 M6 **Naryn** Kirgiziya **U.S.S.R.** 41.24N 76.00E
42 F6 **Naryn U.S.S.R.** 50.16N 96.17E
43 K6 **Naryn** Uzbekistan **U.S.S.R.** 40.54N 72.06E
43 L6 **Naryn** *R* Kirgiziya **U.S.S.R.**
43 O5 **Narynkol'** Kazakhstan **U.S.S.R.** 42.45N 80.12E
24 C4 **Narynkol** Xinjiang Uygur Zizhiqu **China** 42.45N 80.14E
45 G4 **Naryshkino U.S.S.R.** 52.55N 35.44E
79 C5 **Narzole** Italy 44.35N 7.52E
52 H6 **Nås Sweden** 60.28N 14.30E
51 F8 **Näsåker Sweden** 63.27N 16.55E
25 E8 **Na San Thailand** 8.45N 99.21E
90 C7 **Nasarawa Nigeria** 8.35N 7.44E
82 J3 **Năsăud Romania** 47.16N 24.24E
65 N2 **Nasavrky Czechoslovakia** 49.52N 15.48E
85 M10 **Nasb el Hidem, Jebel** *mt* **Sudan** 19.49N 32.09E
85 M10 **Nasb el Husan, Jebel** *mt* **Sudan** 19.33N 32.12E
51 J5 **Näsberg Sweden** 66.22N 21.00E
71 C7 **Nasbinals France** 44.40N 3.03E
86 P6 **Naşb, Jebel** *mt* **Jordan** 29.32N 35.33E
86 M8 **Naşb, Wâdî** *watercourse* **Egypt**
122 S11 **Nasca Ridge Pacific Oc**
11 E12 **Naseby New Zealand** 45.02S 170.10E
109 M5 **Nash** Oklahoma 36.41N 98.04W
56 E5 **Nash** S Glam **Wales** 51.28N 3.30W
112 N2 **Nash** Texas 33.28N 94.09W
103 N4 **Nashawena I** Massachusetts 41.26N 70.53W
98 F6 **Nash Creek** New Brunswick 47.56N 66.06W
113 D6 **Nash Harbor** Alaska 60.10N 167.00W
13 E5 **Nash, L** Queensland 21.05S 138.00E
56 D5 **Nash Pt** S Glam **Wales** 51.25N 3.34W
108 S7 **Nashua** Iowa 42.58N 92.31W
107 B2 **Nashua** Missouri 39.18N 94.34W
108 D1 **Nashua** Montana 48.09N 106.22W
104 O4 **Nashua** New Hampshire 42.44N 71.28W
107 C8 **Nashville** Arkansas 33.57N 93.50W
105 D6 **Nashville** Georgia 31.03N 83.16W
107 G3 **Nashville** Illinois 38.21N 89.25W
107 K2 **Nashville** Indiana 39.13N 86.15W
109 M4 **Nashville** Kansas 37.27N 98.25W
106 J7 **Nashville** Michigan 42.36N 85.05W
105 K2 **Nashville** N Carolina 35.58N 78.00W
104 C6 **Nashville** Ohio 40.34N 82.08W
107 K5 **Nashville** Tennessee 36.10N 86.50W
107 K6 **Nashville Basin** *reg* Tennessee
98 F8 **Nashwaaksis** New Brunswick 45.58N 66.40W
108 R2 **Nashwauk** Minnesota 47.23N 93.10W
89 J6 **Nasia** *R* **Ghana**
35 H3 **Nasib Syria** 32.33N 36.11E
82 E5 **Našice Yugoslavia** 45.29N 18.04E
62 M3 **Nasielsk Poland** 52.35N 20.46E
51 K10 **Näsijärvi** *L* **Finland**
Nasik Iran*see* **Nazik**
29 C7 **Nasik** Maharashtra **India** 20.00N 73.52E
29 C7 **Nasik** *dist* Maharashtra **India**
9 T8 **Nasilai** *reef* **Fiji** 18.09S 178.41E
87 E6 **Nasi, Mt Ethiopia** 9.42N 35.31E
34 O7 **Nasir Iraq** 31.33N 46.08E
31 E6 **Nasir Pakistan** 29.46N 69.30E
87 D6 **Nasir Sudan** 8.37N 33.06E
Nasirabad Bangladesh*see* **Mymensingh**
29 D7 **Nasirabad** Maharashtra **India** 21.00N 75.43E
31 E6 **Nasirabad Pakistan** 28.25N 68.29E
29 D4 **Nasirabad** Rajasthan **India** 26.16N 74.42E
30 E6 **Nasirabad** Uttar Prad **India** 26.12N 81.32E
31 E6 **Nasirabad** *dist* **Pakistan**
34 O7 **Nāşirīyah, An Iraq** 31.04N 46.17E
81 J7 **Naso** Sicily 38.07N 14.47E
91 J9 **Nasondoye Zaïre** 10.22S 25.03E
9 S5 **Nasorolevu** *mt* Vanua Levu **Fiji** 16.44S 179.23E
44 K7 **Nasosnyy** Azerbaydzhan **U.S.S.R.** 40.37N 49.33E
32 G4 **Nasqenj** Iran 33.56N 56.39E
86 D4 **Nasr** Egypt 30.36N 30.23E
32 H3 **Naşrābād** Khorāsān **Iran** 34.47N 59.49E
32 D3 **Naşrābād** Tehrān **India** 34.08N 51.24E
31 F4 **Nasral Khan Pakistan** 32.31N 71.15E
88 S4 **Nasr Allah Tunisia** 35.16N 9.50E
34 E4 **Naşrānī, Jebel an** *mts* **Syria**
Nasratabad *see* **Zābol**
Nasratabad Sipi *see* **Noşratābād**
32 B4 **Nasrīān-e-Pā'īn** Iran 32.52N 46.53E
30 H7 **Nasriganj** Bihar **India** 25.04N 84.20E
101 J8 **Nass** *R* Br Col
108 O4 **Nassau** Minnesota 45.05N 96.28W
105 L9 **Nassau** New Providence I **Bahamas** 25.05N 77.20W
103 G1 **Nassau** New York 42.31N 73.36W
64 D3 **Nassau W Germany** 50.18N 7.49E
103 G5 **Nassau** *co* Long I, N Y
122 K9 **Nassau** *isld* Cook Is **Pacific Oc** 11.33S 165.25W
13 F3 **Nassau** *R* Queensland
105 K9 **Nassau Airport** New Providence I Bahamas 25.03N 77.29W
121 L10 **Nassau, B.de Chile**
105 F7 **Nassau Sd** Florida 30.31N 81.27W
105 L9 **Nassau Village** New Providence I Bahamas 25.03N 77.20W
104 K9 **Nassawadox** Virginia 37.28N 75.52W
63 T10 **Nassebōhla E Germany** 51.20N 13.33E
64 L6 **Nassenfels W Germany** 48.48N 11.14E
63 S7 **Nassenheide E Germany** 52.49N 13.13E
85 M7 **Nasser City Egypt** 24.26N 32.57E
65 C7 **Nassereith Austria** 47.19N 10.51E
85 M8 **Nasser, Lake Egypt**
89 H7 **Nassian** Ivory Coast 8.28N 3.28W
52 H9 **Nässjö Sweden** 57.39N 14.40E
61 M6 **Nassogne Belgium** 50.08N 5.20E
65 N6 **Nasswald Austria** 47.45N 15.42E
Nastānj *see* **Nasqenj**
97 M6 **Nastapoka Is** Hudson B, N W Terr
64 D3 **Nastätten W Germany** 50.11N 7.52E
20 N4 **Nasu-dake** *mt* Honshu **Japan** 37.07N 139.58E
19 G2 **Nasugbu** Luzon **Philippines** 14.04N 120.37E
20 N4 **Nasu-Yumoto Japan** 37.06N 140.00E
46 H2 **Nasva U.S.S.R.** 56.32N 30.08E
52 K5 **Näsviken Sweden** 61.46N 16.55E
94 J3 **Nata** Botswana 20.11S 26.10E
115 O5 **Natá** Panama 8.20N 80.30W
93 F8 **Nata** Tanzania 2.01S 34.25E
94 J3 **Nata** *R* Botswana
119 C6 **Natagaima Colombia** 3.38N 75.07W
120 G2 **Natal** Amazonas **Brazil** 6.59S 60.16W
100 C9 **Natal** Br Col 49.45N 114.50W
117 F7 **Natal** Piauí **Brazil** 5.35S 42.37W
117 J7 **Natal** Rio Grande do Norte **Brazil** 5.46S 35.15W
18 C5 **Natal** Sumatra **Indon** 0.35N 99.07E
95 O4 **Natal** *prov* **S Africa**
13 H5 **Natal** *R* Queensland
26 B14 **Natal Bank** Indian Oc 46.48S 38.00E
26 D10 **Natal Basin** Indian Oc
13 H5 **Natal Downs** Queensland 21.05S 146.10E
112 J6 **Natalia** Texas 29.12N 98.53W
39 J4 **Natalii, Bukhta** *gulf* **U.S.S.R.**
47 H7 **Natal'insk U.S.S.R.** 56.30N 57.59E
26 C9 **Natal Ridge** Indian Oc
95 O3 **Natal Spa** S Africa 27.31S 30.52E
94 T14 **Natalspruit** S Africa 26.18S 28.08E
Natanya *see* **Netanya**
32 D4 **Natanz** Iran 33.29N 51.57E
41 M6 **Natara U.S.S.R.** 68.26N 124.02E
98 L3 **Natashquan** Quebec 50.10N 61.50W
98 K1 **Natashquan R** Labrador/Quebec
33 A4 **Natash, Wâdi** *watercourse* **Egypt**
30 J7 **Nataul** Bihar **India** 25.17N 85.04E
113 R6 **Natazhat, Mt** Alaska 61.32N 141.10W
107 E10 **Natchez** Mississippi 31.35N 91.25W
107 C10 **Natchitoches** Louisiana 31.46N 93.06W
92 B10 **Natebe Zambia** 17.44S 25.53E
57 J4 **Nateby** Cumbria **Eng** 54.27N 2.20W
66 H6 **Naters Switzerland** 46.20N 8.00E
9 S5 **Natewa B** Vanua Levu **Fiji**
12 H6 **Nathalia** Victoria 36.06S 145.13E
29 D2 **Nathana** Punjab **India** 30.22N 75.06E
Nathania *see* **Netanya**
104 R9 **Nathant Bay** Massachusetts
29 C5 **Nathdwara** Rajasthan **India** 24.55N 73.52E
31 G3 **Nathia Gali Pakistan** 34.05N 73.26E
9 S7 **Nathilau Pt** Viti Levu **Fiji** 17.30S 177.30E
50 T15 **Nathorst Land** *reg* Spitsbergen
48 U10 **Nathorsts Land Greenland**
109 D3 **Nathrop** Colorado 38.45N 106.06W
19 F1 **Natib, Mt** Luzon **Philippines** 14.43N 120.25E
103 M2 **Natick** Massachusetts 42.17N 71.21W
103 M3 **Natick** Rhode I 41.46N 71.30W
35 G3 **Natifa Jordan** 32.31N 35.49E
86 K6 **Natila, Wâdi el** *watercourse* **Egypt**
115 J5 **Natillas Mexico** 25.06N 101.25W
12 F6 **Natimuk** Victoria 36.45S 142.00E
113 R4 **Nation** Alaska 65.11N 141.50W
113 R4 **Nation** *R* Alaska
110 L2 **National Bison Range** Montana 47.20N 114.15W
111 G9 **National City** California 32.39N 117.06W
11 K6 **National Park New Zealand** 39.11S 175.25E
101 L8 **Nation R** Br Col
77 X13 **Nati, Pta** *pt* Balearic Is 40.03N 3.49E
98 K4 **Natiskotek B** Anticosti I, Que
79 O2 **Natisone** *R* **Italy**
89 K6 **Natitingou Benin** 10.17N 1.29E
13 H6 **Native Companion Cr** Queensland
120 E5 **Natividad Bolivia** 12.21S 66.05W
115 B4 **Natividad** *isld* **Mexico** 27.50N 115.10W
118 F2 **Natividade Brazil** 11.39S 47.49W
25 D5 **Natkyizin Burma** 14.55N 97.57E
25 C2 **Natmauk Burma** 20.26N 95.21E
109 L2 **Natoma** Kansas 39.13N 99.02W
31 H9 **Nator Bangladesh** 24.25N 89.04E
115 E3 **Nátora Mexico** 29.00N 108.50W
20 O3 **Natori Japan** 38.12N 140.51E
61 L5 **Natoye Belgium** 50.20N 5.04E
52 L3 **Nätra Sweden** 63.12N 18.35E
108 D6 **Natrona** Wyoming 43.03N 106.48W
93 G8 **Natron, L (Soda) Tanzania**
86 D5 **Natrûn, Wâdi el** *watercourse* **Egypt**
25 C3 **Nattalin Burma** 18.25N 95.34E
28 D5 **Nattam** Tamil Nadu **India** 10.14N 78.11E
26 Q7 **Nattandiya Sri Lanka** 7.24N 79.52E
51 N3 **Nattaset** *mt* **Finland** 68.10N 27.30E
25 D3 **Nattaung** *mt* **Burma** 19.48N 97.00E
51 H5 **Nattavaara Sweden** 66.45N 20.56E
64 O6 **Natternberg W Germany** 48.41N 12.55E
50 H2 **Náttfaravikur** *coast* Iceland
64 J6 **Nattheim W Germany** 48.41N 10.15E
52 J10 **Nättraby Sweden** 56.12N 15.30E
32 J3 **Na'tū** Iran 35.52N 60.43E
Natu La *pass see* **Jelep La**
Natuna Besar *isld see* **Bunguran**
104 K2 **Natural Bridge** New York 44.02N 75.30W
104 F9 **Natural Bridge** Virginia 37.37N 79.33W
111 O4 **Natural Bridges Nat.Mon** Utah 37.37N 110.00W
112 F3 **Natural Dam Lake** Texas 32.14N 101.39W
14 B10 **Naturaliste, C** W Australia 33.32S 115.01E
14 A7 **Naturaliste Chan** W Australia
26 K9 **Naturaliste Plateau Indian Ocean**
109 B3 **Naturita** Colorado 38.12N 108.36W
79 J1 **Naturno Italy** 46.39N 11.00E
113 K3 **Natuvukti L** Alaska 67.00N 154.45W
Nau Iran*see* **Now**
43 J6 **Nau** Tadzhikistan **U.S.S.R.** 40.09N 69.24E
30 H7 **Naubatpur** Bihar **India** 25.30N 84.54E
106 J3 **Naubinway** Michigan 46.05N 85.27W
115 B9 **Naucalpan de Júarez** *dist* Mexico City Mexico
72 J7 **Naucelle France** 44.12N 2.20E
72 J6 **Naucelles-Reilhac France** 44.58N 2.25E
94 D4 **Nauchas Namibia** 23.40S 16.19E
Nauche *see* **Namche Bazar**
20 H1 **Nauchi** Chiba **Japan**
44 C10 **Nauchnyy** Ukraine **U.S.S.R.** 44.43N 34.00E
Naudeh Pasang *see* **Now Deh-e Pashang**
65 C8 **Nauders Austria** 46.54N 10.31E
99 T4 **Naudville** Quebec 48.35N 71.42W
92 H9 **Nauela Mozambique** 15.27S 37.25E
63 R7 **Nauen E Germany** 52.37N 12.53E
46 E2 **Naueyi-Akmyane** Lithuania **U.S.S.R.** 56.20N 22.50E
121 J1 **Naufragados, Pta.dos** *C* Brazil 27.52S 48.35W
30 L7 **Naugachhia** Bihar **India** 25.24N 87.06E
30 G8 **Naugarh** Uttar Prad **India** 24.51N 83.15E
103 H4 **Naugatuck** Connecticut 41.30N 73.04W
Nau Gumbad *see* **Now Gombad**
30 K7 **Nauhata** Bihar **India** 25.59N 86.29E
69 P4 **Nauheim W Germany** 49.57N 8.27E
31 D5 **Nau Hissar Pakistan** 30.15N 66.54E
72 B5 **Naujac-sur-Mer France** 45.16N 1.02W
19 K5 **Naujan Philippines** 13.21N 121.15E
19 K5 **Naujan, L Philippines** 13.10N 121.22E
46 F3 **Naujoji Vilnia** Lithuania **U.S.S.R.** 54.44N 25.24E
Naukot *see* **Naokot**
59 K4 **Naul** Dublin **Irish Rep** 53.35N 6.17W
26 S6 **Naula Sri Lanka** 7.42N 80.40E
51 N8 **Naulavaara** *mt* **Finland** 63.50N 28.15E
91 D12 **Naulila Angola** 17.13S 14.39E
64 M1 **Naumburg E Germany** 51.09N 11.48E
64 G1 **Naumburg W Germany** 51.15N 9.10E
86 D4 **Na'um, Gebel** *hill* **Egypt** 30.37N 30.20E
15 K5 **Nauna I** Admiralty Is 2.12S 148.11E
25 M9 **Naungkan Burma** 24.33N 95.32E
25 D4 **Naunglon Burma** 16.47N 97.41E
25 D3 **Naungpale Burma** 19.32N 97.10E
64 O1 **Naunhof E Germany** 51.16N 12.35E
29 J8 **Naupada** Andhra Prad **India** 18.33N 84.14E
Nauplia *see* **Návplion**
35 G6 **Na'ur Jordan** 31.52N 35.50E
35 E3 **Na'ura** Israel 32.37N 35.23E
15 L8 **Nauria I** Trobriand Is **Papua New Guinea** 8.35S 150.17E
64 D2 **Nauroth W Germany** 50.41N 7.53E
31 C6 **Nauroz Kalat Pakistan** 28.46N 65.40E
44 G4 **Naurskaya U.S.S.R.** 43.41N 45.18E
9 A8 **Nauru** *isld rep* **Pacific Oc**
43 G2 **Naurzum** Kazakhstan **U.S.S.R.** 51.30N 64.30E
Nau Shahr *see* **Now Shahr**
31 H4 **Naushahra** Kashmir 33.12N 74.17E
31 E7 **Naushahro Firoz Pakistan** 26.51N 68.11E
31 E7 **Naushara Pakistan** 27.10N 96.06E
42 H6 **Naushki U.S.S.R.** 50.22N 106.10E
103 N3 **Naushon I** Massachusetts
Naushshro *see* **Naushahro Firoz**
9 T8 **Nausori** Viti Levu **Fiji** 18.01S 178.31E
53 T15 **Naustdal Norway** 61.31N 5.43E
53 T15 **Naustdal Norway** 61.55N 5.52E
52 D4 **Nauste Norway** 63.42N 8.08E
50 D3 **Naustvik** Iceland 65.59N 21.28W
120 C1 **Nauta Peru** 4.31S 73.36W
30 G5 **Nautanwa** Uttar Prad **India** 27.26N 83.25E
94 E6 **Naute Dam** *res* **Namibia** 26.55S 18.02E
50 C3 **Nauteyri** Iceland 65.55N 22.19W
15 B6 **Nautilus, Selat** *str* Irian Jaya
115 L7 **Nautla Mexico** 20.15N 96.45W
47 B2 **Nautsi U.S.S.R.** 69.00N 29.01E
53 S16 **Nautsund Norway** 61.15N 5.24E
Nauvo *see* **Nagu**
107 J8 **Nauvoo** Alabama 34.00N 87.29W
106 C9 **Nauvoo** Illinois 40.33N 91.23W
95 C8 **Nauwte, De** S Africa 32.51S 19.27E
61 G1 **Nauw van Bath** *inlet* **Netherlands**
31 C4 **Nauzad Afghanistan** 32.22N 64.32E
115 J3 **Nava Mexico** 28.28N 100.45W
76 H2 **Nava Spain** 43.21N 5.30W
76 J8 **Navacepeda de Tormes Spain** 40.21N 5.15W
76 L7 **Navacerrada Spain** 40.43N 4.01W
75 B6 **Navacerrada, Pto. de** *pass* **Spain** 40.49N 4.01W
77 J7 **Navachica** *mt* **Spain** 36.50N 3.49W
79 C6 **Nava, Colle di** *pass* **Italy** 44.05N 7.52E
76 H8 **Navaconcejo Spain** 40.10N 5.50W
76 K7 **Nava de Arévalo Spain** 40.58N 4.47W
76 H8 **Nava de Béjar Spain** 40.29N 5.40W
76 L6 **Nava de la Asunción Spain** 41.09N 4.30W
76 J6 **Nava del Rey Spain** 41.19N 5.05W
76 K9 **Nava de Ricomalillo, La Spain** 39.40N 4.59W
75 C4 **Nava de Roa Spain** 41.37N 3.58W
77 C2 **Nava de Santiago, La Spain** 39.04N 6.31W
75 C5 **Navafría Spain** 41.03N 3.50W
76 L9 **Navahermosa Spain** 39.38N 4.28W
76 L8 **Navahondilla Spain** 40.19N 4.29W
75 J8 **Navajas Spain** 39.53N 0.30W
75 D6 **Navajeras, Presa de** *res* **Spain** 40.53N 3.27W
111 P6 **Navajo** Arizona 35.08N 109.33W
111 M4 **Navajo L** Utah 37.31N 112.46W
111 O4 **Navajo Mt** Utah 37.01N 110.51W
111 O5 **Navajo Nat.Mon** Arizona 36.45N 110.36W
111 N5 **Navajo Point** Arizona 36.05N 111.45W
109 C5 **Navajo Res** Colo/New Mex
76 J4 **Navajos** *mt* **Spain** 42.09N 5.05W
19 M6 **Naval Philippines** 11.34N 124.28E
75 L3 **Naval Spain** 42.12N 0.09E
77 C5 **Nava, La Spain** 37.58N 6.44W
76 K8 **Navalacruz Spain** 40.27N 4.56W
76 L8 **Navalagamella Spain** 40.28N 4.08W
77 H2 **Navalagrulla, Sierra de** *mts* **Spain**
75 A3 **Nava, Laguna de** *res* **Spain**
75 E4 **Navalcaballo Spain** 41.41N 2.31W
76 J8 **Navalcán Spain** 40.04N 5.05W
76 L8 **Navalcarnero Spain** 40.17N 4.01W
76 K4 **Nava, L de Spain** 42.03N 4.35W
75 D4 **Navaleno Spain** 41.50N 3.00W
95 N4 **Naval Hill** S Africa 28.46S 29.49E
76 L6 **Navalmanzano Spain** 41.12N 4.16W
76 K8 **Navalmoral Spain** 40.27N 4.45W
76 H9 **Navalmoral de la Mata Spain** 39.54N 5.33W
76 J8 **Navalonguilla Spain** 40.16N 5.30W
76 L7 **Navalpera de Pinares Spain** 40.35N 4.27W
75 B6 **Navalperal de Pinares Spain** 40.35N 4.25W
76 J8 **Navalperal de Tormes Spain** 40.21N 5.19W
76 K10 **Navalpino Spain** 39.13N 4.35W
76 K8 **Navaluenga Spain** 40.24N 4.42W
76 J9 **Navalvillar de Ibor Spain** 39.35N 5.24W
77 F2 **Navalvillar del Pela Spain** 39.05N 5.28W
76 K8 **Navamorcuende Spain** 40.10N 4.48W
Navan *see* **An Uaimh**
Navangar *see* **Jamnagar**
87 A9 **Nava,R** Zaïre
75 O4 **Navarclés Spain** 41.45N 1.55E
75 H2 **Navardún Spain** 42.30N 1.09W
39 K4 **Navarin, Mys** *C* **U.S.S.R.** 62.17N 179.13E
121 L10 **Navarino, I Chile**
84 E6 **Navaríti Greece** 37.59N 22.32E
74 F2 **Navarra** *prov* **Spain**
74 F2 **Navarra** *reg* **Spain**
104 D6 **Navarre** Ohio 40.44N 81.32W
12 G6 **Navarre** Victoria 36.50S 142.00E
76 J8 **Navarredonda de la Sierra Spain** 40.21N 5.08W
72 C9 **Navarrenx France** 43.20N 0.45W
77 P2 **Navarrés Spain** 39.06N 0.42W
75 E3 **Navarrete Spain** 42.26N 2.34W
121 F5 **Navarro Argentina** 35.00S 59.15W
111 A2 **Navarro** California 39.10N 123.34W
120 B2 **Navarro Peru** 6.23S 75.43W
111 A2 **Navarro** *R* California
112 L4 **Navarro Mills Res** Texas
75 O4 **Navas Spain** 41.54N 1.47E
75 K2 **Navasa Spain** 42.32N 0.29W
75 H2 **Navascués Spain** 42.43N 1.07W
76 K10 **Navas de Estena Spain** 39.30N 4.31W
77 F5 **Navas de la Concepción, Las Spain** 37.56N 5.28W
76 F9 **Navas del Madroño Spain** 39.37N 6.39W
76 L8 **Navas del Rey Spain** 40.23N 4.15W
76 L6 **Navas de Oro Spain** 41.12N 4.27W
77 K4 **Navas de San Juan Spain** 38.11N 3.19W
77 J4 **Navas de Tolosa Spain** 38.17N 3.35W
76 F8 **Navasfrías Spain** 40.18N 6.49W
47 E7 **Navashino U.S.S.R.** 55.33N 42.11E
112 L5 **Navasota** Texas 30.24N 96.06W
112 L5 **Navasota** *R* Texas
116 G5 **Navassa I Caribbean Sea** 18.25N 75.00W
75 Q3 **Navata Spain** 42.13N 2.52E
76 K8 **Navatalgordo Spain** 40.25N 4.53W
79 H3 **Nave Italy** 45.35N 10.17E
76 E4 **Navea** *R* **Spain**
76 F7 **Nave de Haver Portugal** 40.31N 6.50W
Naveh *see* **Anveh**
76 F2 **Navelgas Spain** 43.24N 6.32W
80 J4 **Navelli Italy** 42.14N 13.44E
57 M6 **Navenby** Lincs **Eng** 53.06N 0.32W
58 H2 **Naver, L** Highland **Scotland** 58.17N 4.20W
58 H2 **Naver, R** Highland **Scotland**
103 F6 **Navesink** New Jersey 40.23N 74.02W
45 J4 **Navesnoye U.S.S.R.** 52.18N 37.58E
55 K2 **Navestock** Essex **Eng** 51.39N 0.12E
76 F1 **Navia Spain** 43.33N 6.43W
76 F2 **Navia** *R* **Spain**
76 E3 **Navia de Suarna Spain** 42.58N 7.00W
76 F1 **Navia, Ría de** *B* **Spain**
29 A7 **Navibandar** Gujarat **India** 21.29N 69.52E
121 B4 **Navidad Chile** 33.56S 71.52W
112 L6 **Navidad** *R* Texas
116 K4 **Navidad Bank Atlantic Oc**
66 G6 **Navigenze** *R* **Switzerland**
71 G3 **Navilly France** 46.56N 5.09E
117 H9 **Navio** *R* **Brazil**
9 R7 **Naviti** *isld* **Fiji** 17.08S 177.15E
15 G8 **Naviu I Papua New Guinea** 8.10S 143.40E
29 B6 **Navlakhi** Gujarat **India** 22.56N 70.30E
45 F4 **Navlya U.S.S.R.** 52.51N 34.30E
45 F4 **Navlya** *R* **U.S.S.R.**
43 H6 **Navoi** Uzbekistan **U.S.S.R.** 40.04N 65.20E
115 E4 **Navojoa Mexico** 27.04N 109.28W
115 F5 **Navolato Mexico** 24.46N 107.42W
46 M2 **Navoloki U.S.S.R.** 57.28N 41.58E
9 R5 **Navotuvotu** *mt* Vanua Levu **Fiji** 16.52S 178.45E
84 C5 **Návpaktos Greece** 38.23N 21.50E
84 E6 **Návplion Greece** 37.34N 22.48E
53 B4 **Navr Denmark** 56.23N 8.32E
89 J6 **Navrongo Ghana** 10.51N 1.03W
44 J10 **Nāvrūd** Iran 37.43N 48.58E
Navşar *see* **Şemdinli**
29 C7 **Navsari** Gujarat **India** 20.58N 73.01E
44 F6 **Navtlug** Georgia **U.S.S.R.** 41.41N 44.53E
9 S8 **Navua** Viti Levu **Fiji** 18.15S 178.10E
9 S8 **Navua** *R* Viti Levu **Fiji** 18.15S 178.10E
9 R8 **Navula** *reef* **Fiji** 17.56S 177.14E
113 L9 **Navy Town** Aleutian Is 52.50N 173.09E
29 D4 **Nawa** Rajasthan **India** 27.01N 75.04E
87 C4 **Nawa Sudan** 12.53N 30.29E
35 H2 **Nawa Syria** 32.53N 36.03E
29 F6 **Nawab Basoda** Madhya Prad **Ind** 23.38N 78.15E
31 G9 **Nawabganj Bangladesh** 24.35N 88.21E
30 E6 **Nawabganj** Bara Banki, Uttar Prad **India** 26.56N 81.13E
30 C4 **Nawabganj** Bareilly, Uttar Prad **India** 28.32N 79.37E
30 C5 **Nawabganj** Farukhabad, Uttar Prad **India** 27.26N 79.24E
30 F6 **Nawabganj** Gonda, Uttar Prad **India** 26.52N 82.09E
31 E7 **Nawabshah Pakistan** 26.15N 68.26E
31 E7 **Nawabshah** *dist* **Pakistan**
30 J8 **Nawada** Bihar **India** 24.54N 85.33E
30 D6 **Nawada** Uttar Prad **India** 27.00N 80.04E
31 F3 **Nawagai Pakistan** 34.41N 71.20E
31 D4 **Nāwah Afghanistan** 32.19N 67.53E
29 D4 **Nawai** Rajasthan **India** 26.25N 75.98E
93 E4 **Nawaikoke Uganda** 1.06N 33.25E
31 D4 **Nawa-i-Murgha Afghanistan** 32.13N 67.30E
30 J5 **Nawakot Nepal** 27.56N 85.11E
31 F6 **Nawakot Pakistan** 28.20N 71.24E
26 S7 **Nawalapitiya Sri Lanka** 7.03N 80.32E
29 D4 **Nawalgarli** Rajasthan **India** 27.48N 75.21E
30 G6 **Nawanagur** Uttar Prad **India** 26.04N 84.00E
31 F5 **Nawan Kot Pakistan** 31.05N 71.30E
29 H7 **Nawāpāra** Orissa **India** 20.46N 82.33E
Nawa Rojhan *see* **Rojhan**
31 G3 **Nawashahr Pakistan** 34.13N 73.20E
29 E2 **Nawashahr** Punjab **India** 31.06N 76.09E
30 H8 **Nawatanr** Bihar **India** 24.17N 84.18E
85 D4 **Nawfalīyah, An Libya** 30.47N 17.50E
9 T5 **Nawi** Vanua Levu **Fiji** 16.42S 179.56E
114 F4 **Nawiliwili** Hawaiian Is 21.58N 159.20W
25 C3 **Nawin** *R* **Burma**
12 F5 **Nawingi** Victoria 34.36S 142.15E
25 E1 **Nawng Hpa Burma** 22.30N 98.30E
25 D1 **Nawngkio Burma** 22.17N 96.50E
25 E1 **Nawngleng Burma** 22.40N 98.18E
33 L8 **Naws, Ra's** *C* **Oman** 17.12N 55.18E
57 M4 **Nawton** N Yorks **Eng** 54.15N 1.00W
66 F7 **Nax Switzerland** 46.14N 7.25E
23 D4 **Naxi** Sichuan **China** 28.50N 105.20E
83 G7 **Náxos Greece** 37.06N 25.24E
83 G7 **Náxos** *I* **Greece** 37.06N 25.24E
84 Y20 **Naxxar Malta** 35.55N 14.27E
18 H5 **Naya** Borneo **Indon** 0.08N 109.45E
119 C6 **Naya Colombia** 3.22N 77.23W
29 J7 **Nayagarh** Orissa **India** 20.10N 85.08E
39 F4 **Nayakhan U.S.S.R.** 61.56N 158.57E
39 F3 **Nayakhan** *R* **U.S.S.R.**
119 C6 **Naya, R Colombia**
115 G6 **Nayar Mexico** 22.18N 104.30W
115 G6 **Nayarit** *state* **Mexico**
9 U2 **Nayau** *isld* **Fiji** 18.00S 179.05W
32 E7 **Nāy Band** Banāder va Jazāyer-e Khalīj-e Fārs **Iran** 27.22N 52.38E
32 G4 **Nāy Band** Khorāsān **Iran** 32.20N 57.34E
32 G4 **Nāy Band,Kūh-e** *mt* **Iran** 32.25N 57.30E
72 D9 **Nay-Bourdettes France** 43.10N 0.16W
33 J7 **Nayfah Saudi Arabia** 19.59N 50.46E
35 G9 **Nayim, Jeb. en** *mt* **Jordan** 31.04N 35.54E
31 A4 **Nayi Nawak Afghanistan** 33.40N 61.07E
40 G7 **Naykhin U.S.S.R.** 49.14N 136.29E
56 N4 **Nayland** Suffolk **Eng** 51.59N 0.52E
105 D7 **Naylor** Georgia 30.55N 83.05W
107 F5 **Naylor** Missouri 36.34N 90.36W
23 D5 **Nayong** Guizhou **China** 26.50N 105.24E
21 J5 **Nayoro Japan** 44.21N 142.30E
28 D4 **Nayudapeta** Andhra Prad **India** 13.56N 80.00E
33 C2 **Nayyāl,Wādī** *watercourse* **Saudi Arabia**
120 E7 **Nazacara Bolivia** 16.50S 68.44W
37 H7 **Nazar Beg Pass Turkey** 38.41N 44.18E
117 D4 **Nazaré** Amapá **Brazil** 1.15N 50.52W
119 F7 **Nazaré** Amazonas **Brazil** 1.16N 67.52W
118 J3 **Nazaré** Bahia **Brazil** 13.00S 39.00W
117 C8 **Nazaré** Pará **Brazil** 6.25S 52.29W
117 E5 **Nazaré** Pará **Brazil** 0.45S 47.15W
117 F8 **Nazaré** Piauí **Brazil** 6.58S 42.44W
76 A9 **Nazaré Portugal** 39.36N 9.04W
91 A4 **Nazare,B de Gabon** 0.47S 9.05E
117 J8 **Nazaré da Mata Brazil** 7.44S 35.14W
115 H5 **Nazareno Mexico** 25.27N 103.26W
119 F6 **Nazaret Colombia** 2.14N 67.37W
61 E3 **Nazareth Belgium** 50.57N 3.36E
Nazareth Ethiopia*see* **Nazaret**
35 E3 **Nazareth** Israel 32.42N 35.18E
103 D5 **Nazareth** Pennsylvania 40.44N 75.18W
28 C6 **Nazareth** Tamil Nadu **India** 8.34N 77.58E
112 E1 **Nazareth** Texas 34.32N 102.06W
26 E6 **Nazareth Bank** Indian Oc
26 F7 **Nazareth Trough** Indian Ocean
118 E5 **Nazário Brazil** 16.38S 49.42W
45 N2 **Nazarovka U.S.S.R.** 54.19N 41.20E
42 E4 **Nazarovo** Krasnoyarsk **U.S.S.R.** 56.02N 90.30E
47 L7 **Nazarovo** Tyumen **U.S.S.R.** 56.36N 70.50E
45 M7 **Nazarovskiy U.S.S.R.** 49.34N 40.59E
115 G5 **Nazas Mexico** 25.15N 104.06W
115 G5 **Nazas** *R* **Mexico**
120 C6 **Nazca Peru** 14.53S 74.54W
21 D12 **Naze** Japan 28.21N 129.30E
35 E3 **Nazerat 'Illit** Israel 32.42N 35.19E
56 O4 **Naze,The** *headland* Essex **Eng** 51.53N 1.16E
32 C4 **Nazian** Iran 33.17N 48.30E
32 A1 **Nazik** Iran 39.03N 45.05E
37 G7 **Nazik Gölü** *L* Turkey
32 J6 **Nāzil** Iran 28.45N 60.39E
36 C5 **Nazilli** Turkey 37.55N 28.20E
31 D8 **Nazimabad** Karachi **Pakistan** 24.56N 67.02E
37 E6 **Nazimiye** Turkey 39.12N 39.51E
42 E3 **Nazimovo** U.S.S.R. 59.31N 90.59E
42 B2 **Nazina** U.S.S.R. 60.09N 79.00E
42 B2 **Nazinskaya** *R* U.S.S.R.
28 K2 **Nazira** Assam **India** 26.51N 94.42E
31 J10 **Nazir Hat** Bangladesh 22.40N 91.49E
101 M9 **Nazko** Br Col 53.00N 123.37W
101 M9 **Nazko** *R* Br Col
35 A7 **Nazla** Gaza Strip 31.32N 34.29E
Nazla Jordan*see* **Nazlat**
86 E7 **Nazla,El Egypt** 29.19N 30.39E
35 D4 **Nazlat Jordan** 32.24N 35.06E
86 E9 **Nazlet el 'Amûdein Egypt** 28.14N 30.41E
86 E10 **Nazlet el Badramân Egypt** 27.40N 30.44E
86 E9 **Nazlet Tâbit Egypt** 28.25N 30.47E
32 A2 **Nāzlū** *R* Iran
92 J7 **Nazombe** Mozambique 11.21S 38.50E
44 F4 **Nazran'** U.S.S.R. 43.14N 44.47E
87 G6 **Nazret** Ethiopia 8.39N 39.19E
23 D6 **Nazuo** Guangxi **China** 24.12N 105.24E
47 K5 **Nazym** *R* U.S.S.R.
47 L7 **Nazyvayevsk** U.S.S.R. 55.34N 71.20E
67 P12 **Nazza** Corsica 42.04N 9.16E
64 J1 **Nazza** E Germany 51.07N 10.21E
92 C8 **Nchanga** Zambia 12.30S 27.53E
92 D6 **Nchelenge** Zambia 9.20S 28.50E
92 G9 **Ncheu** Malawi 14.50S 34.45E
91 B2 **Ncue** Equat Guinea 2.01N 10.38E
95 M8 **Ndabakazi** S Africa 32.21S 28.03E
92 J12 **Ndagaa** Zanzibar 6.04S 39.18E
15 M2 **Ndai I** Solomon Is 7.54S 160.36E
93 E10 **Ndala** Tanzania 4.45S 33.15E
91 D8 **Ndalatando** Angola 9.15S 14.53E
89 L7 **Ndali** Benin 9.50N 2.46E
91 B4 **Ndamba** Gabon 0.59S 11.22E
92 J7 **Ndanda** Tanzania 10.08S 38.50E
92 J6 **Ndandawala** Tanzania 9.44S 39.04E
89 A4 **N'Dandé** Senegal 15.18N 16.27W
90 L9 **N'Danga** Cent Afr Rep 5.06N 22.29E
92 E12 **Ndanga** Zimbabwe 20.10S 31.19E
92 E12 **Ndanga** *dist* Zimbabwe
91 C4 **Ndangui** Gabon 0.32S 12.56E
19 C9 **Ndao** *isld* Indonesia 10.50S 122.43E
93 K9 **Ndara** Kenya 3.29S 38.42E
93 G10 **Ndareda** Tanzania 4.13S 35.33E
93 G7 **Ndasegera** *mt* Tanzania 1.59S 35.43E
90 L8 **Ndékéti** Cent Afr Rep 6.21N 22.16E
9 R5 **Ndelanathau Pk** Vanua Levu **Fiji** 16.43S 178.55E
90 K7 **Ndélé** Cent Afr Rep 8.25N 20.38E
91 B5 **Ndendé** Gabon 2.22S 11.23E
10 O4 **Ndeni** *isld* Santa Cruz Is **Pacific Oc** 10.42S 165.50E
93 K6 **Ndeyini** Kenya 0.45S 38.56E
93 K9 **Ndi** Kenya 3.15S 38.31E
89 A4 **Ndiagne** Senegal 15.27N 16.05W
89 A3 **N'Diago** Mauritania 16.12N 16.31W
89 B3 **Ndiayène** Senegal 16.28N 15.00W
91 K4 **Ndigida** Zaïre 0.40S 26.44E
9 S5 **Ndikeva** *mt* Vanua Levu **Fiji** 16.35S 179.30E
90 E9 **Ndikiniméki** Cameroon 4.46N 10.50E
91 B5 **Ndindi** Gabon 3.47S 11.06E
89 C4 **Ndiot** Senegal 14.52N 12.58W
89 B3 **Ndioum** Senegal 16.27N 14.39W
92 J11 **Ndizi Matemwe** Zanzibar 5.53S 39.21E
90 G5 **N'Djamena** Chad 12.10N 14.59E
90 E9 **Ndjim** *watercourse* Cameroon
91 B4 **Ndjolé** Gabon 0.07S 10.45E
91 E4 **Ndjoundou** Congo 0.27S 17.41E
91 B5 **Ndogo, L** Gabon
90 E9 **Ndogongi** Cameroon 4.22N 10.25E
92 D8 **Ndola** Zambia 13.00S 28.39E
91 D6 **N'dola** *airport* Zaïre 4.15S 15.25E
91 D5 **N'Dolo** Congo
93 B2 **Ndolomo** Zaïre 3.03N 30.02E
93 J7 **Ndolo's Corner** Kenya 1.11S 37.57E
93 E4 **Ndolwa** Uganda 1.14N 33.05E
19 B8 **Ndona** Indonesia 8.48S 121.39E
90 C9 **Ndoni,Nigeria** 5.33N 6.34E
93 A8 **Ndora** Burundi 2.54S 29.24E
90 G7 **Ndori** Cameroon 8.52N 14.10E
91 C4 **Ndoro** Gabon 0.24S 12.34E
93 J4 **Ndoto Mts** Kenya
90 F8 **Ndoumbi** Cameroon 6.10N 13.41E
9 T4 **Ndrua Ndrua** *isld* **Fiji** 16.13S 179.36E
91 H1 **Ndu** Zaïre 4.36N 22.49E
93 F10 **Nduguti** Tanzania 4.19S 34.40E
15 L3 **Nduindui** Guadalcanal I **Solomon Is** 9.48S 159.55E
93 H7 **Ndulele** Kenya 1.04S 36.06E
92 J7 **Ndumbwe** Tanzania 10.15S 39.57E
95 O8 **Ndumo** S Africa 26.56S 32.16E
93 J4 **Ndumoteserem** Kenya 1.31N 37.10E
92 J5 **Ndundu** Tanzania 8.00S 39.02E
93 K10 **Ndungu** Tanzania 4.25S 38.04E
95 O5 **Ndwedwe** S Africa 29.31S 30.57E
72 D4 **Né** *R* France
52 F3 **Nea** *R* Norway
84 L11 **Néa Amari** Crete 35.14N 24.38E
84 E3 **Néa Ankhíalos** Greece 39.16N 22.49E
84 G4 **Néa Artáki** Greece 38.31N 23.39E
15 G7 **Neabo I** Papua New Guinea 7.50S 143.46E
13 J8 **Neabul** *R* Queensland
84 Q14 **Nea Dhimmata** Cyprus 35.08N 32.31E
84 F6 **Néa Epidhavros** Greece 37.40N 23.07E
84 D2 **Néa Filippoúpolis** Greece 39.38N 22.23E
84 A3 **Néa Fillippiás** Greece 39.12N 20.53E
59 K2 **Neagh,L** N Ireland 54.40N 6.25W
110 A1 **Neah Bay** Washington 48.22N 124.36W
84 D2 **Néai Kariaí** Greece 39.31N 22.28E
84 E6 **Néa Kíos** Greece 37.35N 22.44E
84 C8 **Néa Koróni** Greece 36.51N 21.55E
109 O4 **Neal** Kansas 37.50N 96.08W
59 D4 **Neale** Mayo **Irish Rep** 53.34N 9.14W
13 B6 **Neale,L** N Terr **Australia**
12 D3 **Neales** *R* S Australia
12 D2 **Neales, N.Branch** *R* S Australia
12 D3 **Neales, S. Branch** *R* S Australia
84 E2 **Néa Lévki** Greece 39.32N 22.30E
83 F4 **Néa Moudhaniá** Greece 40.14N 23.17E
70 F5 **Néant** France 48.01N 2.19W
70 O6 **Néant** *R* France
58 Q9 **Neap** Shetland **Scotland** 60.19N 1.05W
84 G5 **Néa Palátia** Greece 38.19N 23.48E
84 N11 **Neápolis** Crete 35.15N 25.36E
84 F8 **Neápolis** Lakonía **Greece** 36.31N 23.03E
83 E4 **Neápolis** Makedhonia **Greece** 40.20N 21.24E
84 G5 **Néa Psará** Greece 38.23N 23.47E
113 L9 **Near Is** Aleutian Is
103 B3 **Neath** Pennsylvania 41.52N 76.09W
56 D4 **Neath** W Glam **Wales** 51.40N 3.48W
56 D4 **Neath, R** Powys/W Glam **Wales**
69 B6 **Neauphle-le-Château** France 48.49N 1.54E
83 H3 **Néa Víssi** Greece 41.34N 26.33E
30 H7 **Neazipur** Bihar **India** 25.39N 84.10E
84 G5 **Néa Zoryiáni** Greece 38.08N 23.51E
88 L10 **Neba** Mali 23.33N 5.36W
89 J5 **Nebba** *R* Upper Volta
93 C3 **Nebbi** Uganda 2.30N 31.05E
47 F4 **Nebdino** U.S.S.R. 64.10N 48.09E
Nebek *see* **Nebk,En**
63 H3 **Nebel** W Germany 54.37N 8.22E
63 Q5 **Nebel** *R* E Germany
65 B7 **Nebelhorn** *mt* W Germany 47.26N 10.22E
88 S3 **Nebeur** Tunisia 36.21N 8.45E
88 S4 **Nebhana** *R* Tunisia
72 J10 **Nébias** France 42.53N 2.07E
66 H3 **Nebikon** Switzerland 47.12N 7.59E
13 H8 **Nebine** *R* Queensland
43 C7 **Nebit-Dag** Turkmeniya **U.S.S.R.** 39.31N 54.24E
88 M8 **Nebka** Algeria 27.28N 3.12W
34 D4 **Nebk,En** Syria 34.02N 36.43E
119 F7 **Neblina, Pico da** *mt* Venezuela 0.45N 66.01W
13 J5 **Nebo** Queensland 21.40S 148.39E
26 R8 **Neboda** Sri Lanka 6.36N 80.06E
46 J1 **Nebolchi** U.S.S.R. 59.10N 33.25E
35 F6 **Nebo,Mt** Jordan 31.46N 35.44E
111 N2 **Nebo, Mt** Utah 39.49N 111.48W
89 J6 **Nébou** Upper Volta 11.19N 1.51W
71 B5 **Nébouzat** France 45.43N 2.54E
64 M1 **Nebra** E Germany 51.17N 11.35E
102 F2 **Nebraska** *state* U.S.A.
108 P9 **Nebraska City** Nebraska 40.41N 95.50W
75 C4 **Nebreda** Spain 41.57N 3.32W
81 J8 **Nebrodi,Monti** Sicily
45 L1 **Nebyloye** U.S.S.R. 56.22N 40.00E
106 D5 **Necedah** Wisconsin 44.02N 90.05W
101 L9 **Nechako,R** Br Col
44 B8 **Nechayannoye** U.S.S.R. 46.59N 31.31E
45 Q3 **Nechayevka** U.S.S.R. 53.16N 44.28E
45 M1 **Nechayevskaya** U.S.S.R. 55.30N 40.38E
108 N1 **Neche** N Dakota 48.59N 97.34W
112 M4 **Neches** Texas 31.51N 95.32W
112 M4 **Neches** *R* Texas
61 D4 **Néchin** Belgium 50.40N 3.16E
119 D4 **Nechí,R** Colombia
63 T6 **Nechlin** E Germany 53.27N 13.53E
88 R3 **Nechmeya** Algeria 36.33N 7.30E
64 F5 **Neckar** *R* W Germany
64 F5 **Neckarbischofsheim** W Germany 49.18N 8.59E
64 G5 **Neckarelz** W Germany 49.21N 9.07E
64 F5 **Neckargemünd** W Germany 49.24N 8.50E
64 F5 **Neckarsteinach** W Germany 49.25N 8.50E
64 G5 **Neckarsulm** W Germany 49.11N 9.14E
64 G6 **Neckartailfingen** W Germany 48.37N 9.16E
65 P6 **Neckenmarkt** Austria 47.37N 16.33E
66 N2 **Necker** *R* Switzerland
114 D2 **Necker I** Hawaiian Is 23.35N 164.42W

105 M7 Necker I Virgin Is 18.30N 64.26W
11 C13 Neck, The pen Stewart I New Zealand 46.57S 168.11E
121 F7 Necochea Argentina 38.31S 58.46W
119 C3 Necoclí Colombia 8.29N 76.45W
81 K9 Necropoli Pantalica ruins Sicily 37.08N 15.01E
77 E6 Necrópolis Romana ruins Spain 37.28N 5.39W
64 P4 Nečtiny Czechoslovakia 49.58N 13.10E
56 N2 Necton Norfolk Eng 52.39N 0.46E
91 C6 Necuto Angola 4.57S 12.38E
70 K4 Nécy France 48.50N 0.12W
76 C2 Neda Spain 43.29N 8.09W
52 G4 Nedalshytta Norway 62.59N 12.06E
72 H4 Nedde France 45.43N 1.50E
63 S5 Neddemin E Germany 53.39N 13.17E
99 L5 Nédelec Quebec 47.43N 79.26W
90 J4 Nédélèy Chad 15.35N 18.12E
65 O9 Nedelišće Yugoslavia 46.21N 16.23E
52 D8 Nedenes reg Norway
60 M12 Nederasselt Netherlands 51.47N 5.45E
61 F3 Nederboelare Belgium 50.47N 3.53E
61 F3 Nederbrakel Belgium 50.48N 3.46E
61 F3 Nederhasselt Belgium 50.51N 3.58E
61 S9 Neder Heembeek vill Bruxelles Belgium
60 J12 Nederhemert Netherlands 51.46N 5.10E
60 J10 Nederhorst den Berg Netherlands 52.16N 5.02E
109 E2 Nederland Colorado 39.58N 105.30W
112 N6 Nederland Texas 29.59N 94.00W
60 L12 Neder Rijn R Netherlands
60 H12 Neder Slingeland Netherlands 51.53N 4.55E
60 L14 Nederweert Netherlands 51.17N 5.45E
61 E3 Nederzwalm Hermelgem Belgium 50.53N 3.41E
84 C7 Nédha Greece 37.25N 21.58E
84 D7 Nédhousa Greece 37.08N 22.14E
14 A2 Nedlands dist Perth, W Aust
63 Q8 Nedlitz E Germany 52.05N 12.15E
24 G11 Nêdong Xizang Zizhiqu China 29.12N 91.47E
Nedong Dzong see Nêdong
45 E6 Nedrigaylov Ukraine U.S.S.R. 50.51N 33.54E
88 N4 Nedroma Algeria 35.00N 1.44W
10 E11 Ned's Beach Lord Howe I Pacific Oc 31.31S 159.05E
26 B14 Ned's Kop hill Marion I Ind Oc 46.53S 37.46E
53 T20 Nedstrand Norway 59.21N 5.53E
65 O3 Nedvědice Czechoslovakia 49.28N 16.20E
62 L5 Nedza Poland 50.10N 18.14E
106 K3 Neebish I Michigan 46.16N 84.09W
60 P11 Neede Netherlands 52.08N 6.36E
103 M2 Needham Massachusetts 42.17N 71.14W
104 O10 Needham dist Boston, Mass
56 O3 Needham Market Suffolk Eng 52.09N 1.03E
110 Q5 Needle Mt Wyoming 44.04N 109.34W
11 A12 Needle Pk New Zealand 45.56S 166.51E
111 K7 Needles California 34.51N 114.36W
56 H6 Needles Lt.Ho I of Wight Eng 50.39N 1.35W
11 K3 Needles Pt New Zealand 36.04S 175.25E
105 E7 Needmore Georgia 30.41N 82.44W
112 E1 Needmore Texas 34.02N 102.44W
112 M6 Needville Texas 29.23N 95.51W
100 S9 Neelin Manitoba 49.15N 99.20W
110 N7 Neely Idaho 42.45N 112.55W
107 F5 Neelyville Missouri 36.33N 90.31W
118 B10 Neembucú dept Paraguay
106 F5 Neenah Wisconsin 44.10N 88.29W
100 S8 Neepawa Manitoba 50.14N 99.29W
60 M14 Neer Netherlands 51.16N 5.59E
66 K1 Neerach Switzerland 47.31N 8.29E
60 J12 Neer Andel Netherlands 51.47N 5.03E
14 B8 Neereno hill W Australia 29.28S 115.59E
109 H3 Nee Res Colorado
97 L3 Neergaard L N W Terr 70.10N 80.00W
61 N2 Neerglabbeek Belgium 51.05N 5.37E
61 N3 Neerharen Belgium 50.54N 5.41E
61 J3 Neerijse Belgium 50.49N 5.38E
60 T16 Neeritter Netherlands 51.10N 5.48E
60 M14 Neerkant Netherlands 51.22N 5.52E
61 N2 Neeroeteren Belgium 51.05N 5.42E
61 M2 Neerpelt Belgium 51.13N 5.26E
64 A1 Neersen W Germany 51.15N 6.28E
53 A4 Nees Denmark 56.24N 8.15E
105 F4 Neeses S Carolina 33.32N 81.08W
18 D10 Nee Soon Singapore 1.24N 103.49E
53 B3 Nees Sund sound Denmark 56.44N 8.30E
47 L6 Nefedovo U.S.S.R. 58.45N 72.28E
103 C5 Neffs Pennsylvania 40.42N 75.38W
88 R5 Nefta Tunisia 33.53N 7.50E
43 K6 Nefteabad Tadzhikistan U.S.S.R. 40.15N 70.36E
Neftechala see Bakinskikh Komissarov, Im 26 Azerbaydzhan U.S.S.R
44 J8 Neftechala Azerbaydzhan U.S.S.R. 39.23N 49.14E
40 J5 Neftegorsk Sakhalin U.S.S.R. 53.00N 143.07E
43 B1 Neftegorsk U.S.S.R. 52.40N 51.13E
44 C3 Neftegorsk U.S.S.R. 44.21N 39.44E
44 F3 Neftekumsk U.S.S.R. 44.46N 44.50E
42 H4 Neftelensk Irkutsk U.S.S.R. 57.18N 107.02E
66 L1 Neftenbach Switzerland 47.32N 8.41E
42 A2 Nefteyugansk U.S.S.R. 61.05N 72.42E
43 G7 Neftezavodsk Turkmeniya U.S.S.R. 39.24N 62.54E
Neft Sefid see Naft-e Safīd oil field
41 K4 Neftyanoy,Mys C U.S.S.R. 74.00N 111.30E
44 K7 Neftyanyye Kamni oil well Azerbaydzhan U.S.S.R. 40.13N 50.48E
78 C12 Nefza Tunisia 36.58N 9.06E
91 D7 Negage Angola 7.47S 15.27E
89 E5 Negala Mali 12.52N 8.30W
26 R6 Negama Sri Lanka 7.59N 80.29E
92 D9 Nega Nega Zambia 15.49S 28.02E
89 L6 Negansi Benin 10.34N 3.50E
32 G6 Negār Iran 29.51N 56.47E
18 L10 Negara Bali Indon 8.21S 114.35E
18 L7 Negara Borneo Indon 2.40S 115.05E
18 L7 Negara R Borneo Indon
106 G3 Negaunee Michigan 46.31N 87.37W
35 B7 Negba Israel 31.40N 34.41E
Negelli see Nagélé
18 C9 Negeri Sembilan state Pen Malaysia
34 B8 Negev reg Israel
20 B3 Negishi Tōkyō Japan
118 C8 Negla R Paraguay
82 J5 Negoiu mt Romania 45.35N 24.31E
91 D11 Negola Angola 14.10S 14.29E
91 D8 Negolome, L Angola 9.31S 14.10E
92 J7 Negomano Mozambique 11.26S 38.30E
26 Q7 Negombo Sri Lanka 7.13N 79.51E
93 F7 Negoti Tanzania 1.58S 34.40E
82 H6 Negotin Yugoslavia 44.14N 22.32E
82 G9 Negotino Yugoslavia 41.29N 22.07E
42 C3 Negotka U.S.S.R. 59.43N 80.39E
120 B3 Negra,Cord mts Peru
25 C5 Negrais,C Burma 15.57N 94.12E
119 A11 Negra,Pta C Peru 6.06S 81.09W
88 E10 Negra,Pta pt Mauritania 22.54N 16.18W
77 K7 Negra,Pta pt Spain 36.45N 3.11W
14 D7 Negrara,R W Australia
118 G6 Negra,Serra mts Brazil
118 A3 Negra,Serrania mts Bolivia
75 E5 Negredo Spain 41.02N 2.52W
76 B3 Negreira Spain 42.54N 8.45W
120 D8 Negreiros Chile 19.53S 69.50W
72 G7 Nègrepelisse France 44.05N 1.30E
75 O3 Nègre,Pic mt Andorra/Spain 42.27N 1.33E
72 A9 Negresse, la France 42.28N 1.32W
82 L4 Negreşti Romania 46.50N 27.28E
77 P5 Negrete,C Spain 37.35N 0.48W
13 A3 Negri R N Terr Australia
50 T14 Negribreen glacier Spitsbergen 78.30N 18.30E
116 G1 Negril Jamaica, W I 18.16N 78.21W
120 E8 Negrillos Bolivia 18.45S 68.42W
116 G1 Negril Pt.,North Jamaica, W I 18.22N 78.20W
116 G1 Negril Pt.,South Jamaica, W I 18.16N 78.22W
13 F7 Negri Mts Queensland
88 R4 Négrine Algeria 34.27N 7.32E
74 E9 Negri,Pta pt Morocco 35.17N 3.07W
119 A10 Negritos Peru 4.42S 81.18W
118 E9 Negro R Paraná Brazil
76 G4 Negro R Spain
87 M7 Negro,B.del Somalia 7.50N 49.48E
91 C11 Negro,C Angola 15.39S 11.58E
77 F9 Negro,C Morocco 35.41N 5.17W
81 K10 Negro,C Sicily 36.55N 15.11E
77 Y14 Negro, C C Balearic Is 39.54N 4.18E
104 F7 Negro Mt Maryland
121 D7 Negro Muerto Argentina 39.45S 65.18W
119 H8 Negro,R Amazonas Brazil
118 B10 Negro,R Chaco Argentina
118 C6 Negro,R Mato Grosso do Sul Brazil
120 F4 Negro,R Pando Bolivia
118 B9 Negro,R Paraguay
121 C7 Negro,R Rio Negro Arg
120 G6 Negro,R Santa Cruz Bolivia
121 F4 Negro,R Uruguay
119 D3 Negro,R Venezuela
19 L7 Negros isld Philippines
91 C11 Negros,Mts Angola
82 L7 Negru Vadă Romania 43.45N 28.21E
40 D2 Neguchay R U.S.S.R.
42 B2 Negus'yaun R U.S.S.R.
Neh see Nehbandān
110 B4 Nehalem Oregon 45.44N 123.54W
110 B4 Nehalem R Oregon
32 C3 Nehāvand Iran 35.54N 49.32E
32 J5 Nehbandān Iran 31.32N 60.04E
21 C3 Nehe Heilongjiang China 48.30N 124.50E
63 G10 Neheim-Hüsten W Germany 51.26N 7.58E
37 H8 Nehil R Turkey
82 K5 Nehoiaşu Romania 45.47N 25.50E
82 K5 Nehoissu Romania 45.24N 26.20E
91 E12 Nehone Angola 16.37S 16.04E
35 B7 Nehora Israel 31.37N 34.42E
70 G3 Néhou France 49.25N 1.33W
63 R4 Nehringen E Germany 54.00N 12.50E
65 L1 Nehvizdy Czechoslovakia 50.08N 14.44E
9 R12 Neiafu Tonga, Pacific Oc 18.44S 174.00W
116 J5 Neiba Dominican Rep 18.31N 71.25W
63 R10 Neichen E Germany 51.18N 12.47E
51 O2 Neiden Norway 69.42N 29.25E
100 K8 Neidpath Saskatchewan 50.15N 107.18W
58 K7 Neidpath Castle Borders Scotland 55.39N 3.12W
71 H4 Neige,Crêt-de-la mt France 46.17N 6.00E
61 G3 Neigem Belgium 50.48N 4.04E
26 U15 Neiges,Piton des pk Réunion Ind Oc 21.05S 55.28E
23 C1 Neiguanying Gansu China 35.31N 104.21E
110 P3 Neihart Montana 46.56N 110.44W
23 G1 Neihuang Henan China 35.54N 114.53E
23 D4 Neijiang Sichuan China 29.32N 105.03E
75 E3 Neila Spain 42.03N 3.00W
75 D3 Neila,Sierra de mts Spain
100 H6 Neilburg Saskatchewan 52.50N 109.38W
28 G7 Neill I Andaman Is 11.50N 93.02E
106 D5 Neillsville Wisconsin 44.34N 90.36W
98 M7 Neil's Harbour C Breton I, Nova Scotia 46.48N 60.20W
98 P10 Neilsonville Quebec 46.46N 71.17W
58 H7 Neilston Strathclyde Scotland 55.47N 4.27W
110 B2 Neilton Washington 47.23N 123.52W
Neimengku see Nei Monggol Zizhiqu
17 F3 Nei Monggol Zizhiqu aut reg China
35 E3 Nein Israel 32.38N 35.21E
63 N8 Neindorf W Germany 52.20N 10.50E
15 L5 Neinga Bismarck Arch 2.31S 150.22E
64 G5 Neipperg W Germany 49.07N 9.04E
22 K8 Neiqiu Hebei China 37.17N 114.31E
76 E3 Neira R Spain
Neira de Jusa see Baralla
79 F6 Neirone Italy 44.27N 9.11E
Neisse see Nysa
62 H4 Neisse R Europe
65 M5 Neiten Austria 48.18N 15.17E
94 E2 Neitsas Namibia 19.18S 18.45E
119 C6 Neiva Colombia 2.58N 75.15W
23 F2 Neixiang Henan China 33.08N 111.50E
Nejafabad see Najafābād
115 M9 Nejapa Mexico 16.38N 95.59W
Nejd prov see Najd
64 O3 Nejdek Czechoslovakia 50.20N 12.44E
87 E6 Nejo Ethiopia 9.30N 35.29E
32 E2 Neka Iran 36.36N 53.19E
32 E2 Neka R Iran
45 N6 Nekhayevskiy U.S.S.R. 50.25N 41.45E
88 M4 Nekhila Morocco 34.31N 3.13W
45 F7 Nekhvoroshcha Ukraine U.S.S.R. 49.10N 34.45E
45 P1 Neklyudovo Gor'kiy U.S.S.R. 56.25N 43.58E
45 M1 Neklyudovo Vladimir U.S.S.R. 55.50N 40.32E
108 M1 Nekoma N Dakota 48.37N 98.21W
106 E5 Nekoosa Wisconsin 44.19N 89.55W
40 G9 Nekrasovka U.S.S.R. 44.56N 136.32E
45 R5 Nekrasovo U.S.S.R. 51.10N 45.19E
53 G5 Nekselø isld Denmark 55.48N 11.18E
39 D3 Neksikan U.S.S.R. 62.42N 147.49E
53 Q12 Neksø Bornholm Denmark 55.04N 15.09E
41 L5 Nekyukyuy R U.S.S.R.
75 D2 Nela R Spain
28 C4 Nelamangala Karnataka India 13.04N 77.24E
76 D7 Nelas Portugal 40.32N 7.52W
52 D8 Nelaug Norway 58.39N 8.40E
89 C4 Nelbi Senegal 15.13N 13.52W
41 O9 Neleger U.S.S.R. 61.38N 130.55E
39 E2 Nelemnoye U.S.S.R. 65.20N 151.00E
39 A2 Nel'gese R U.S.S.R.
44 E7 Nel'govka Ukraine U.S.S.R. 47.03N 36.16E
13 F5 Nelia Queensland 20.40S 142.11E
45 D1 Nelidovo U.S.S.R. 56.13N 32.46E
108 M7 Neligh Nebraska 42.08N 98.02W
28 D5 Nelikkuppam Tamil Nadu India 11.46N 79.40E
39 C3 Nel'kan U.S.S.R. 64.12N 142.46E
40 G3 Nel'kan U.S.S.R. 57.40N 136.04E
41 M7 Nel'keskan U.S.S.R. 67.24N 122.03E
39 B3 Nelkuchan,Gora mt U.S.S.R. 64.54N 135.12E
9 A3 Nell islet Marshall Is Pacific Oc 9.05N 167.20E
14 E3 Nellie,Mt W Australia 16.34S 124.04E
12 K6 Nelligen New S Wales 35.39S 150.06E
51 N3 Nellimo Finland 68.49N 28.18E
28 D3 Nellore Andhra Prad India 14.29N 80.00E
28 D3 Nellore dist Andhra Prad India
37 E9 Nelluz watercourse Turkey
40 H8 Nel'ma U.S.S.R. 47.39N 139.05E
46 N1 Nel'sha R U.S.S.R.
121 E3 Nelson Argentina 31.16S 60.45W
111 L6 Nelson Arizona 35.30N 113.16W
101 P11 Nelson Br Col 49.29N 117.17W
111 C2 Nelson California 39.35N 121.47W
57 J5 Nelson Lancs Eng 53.51N 2.13W
56 E4 Nelson Mid Glam Wales 51.40N 3.18W
107 C2 Nelson Missouri 39.00N 93.02W
105 J2 Nelson N Carolina 35.53N 78.51W
108 M9 Nelson Nebraska 40.12N 98.04W
111 K6 Nelson Nevada 35.44N 114.48W
11 H8 Nelson New Zealand 41.18S 173.17E
104 H5 Nelson Pennsylvania 41.58N 77.14W
12 F7 Nelson Victoria 38.04S 141.05E
106 B5 Nelson Wisconsin 44.25N 92.01W
97 K6 Nelson R Manitoba
11 G8 Nelson stat area New Zealand
12 K4 Nelson Bay New S Wales 32.48S 152.10E
15 K8 Nelson,C Papua New Guinea
12 F7 Nelson,C Victoria 38.27S 141.35E
11 F9 Nelson Creek New Zealand 42.26S 171.31E
121 H8 Nelson,Estrecho str Chile
101 M6 Nelson Forks Br Col 59.30N 124.00W
101 M1 Nelson Hd N W Terr 71.05N 122.50W
100 T3 Nelson House Manitoba 55.49N 98.51W
113 E6 Nelson I Alaska 60.40N 164.40W
123 E15 Nelson I South Shetland Is Antarctica 62.15S 59.00W
11 G8 Nelson Lakes Nat.Park New Zealand
12 F8 Nelson,Mt Tasmania 42.56S 147.21E
100 V3 Nelson R Manitoba
110 S1 Nelson Res Montana 48.30N 107.35W
103 G4 Nelsonville New York 41.26N 73.56W
104 C7 Nelsonville Ohio 39.27N 82.14W
95 G8 Nelspoort S Africa 32.07S 23.01E
95 O1 Nelspruit S Africa 25.28S 30.58E
95 O5 Nelsrus S Africa 29.46S 30.22E
41 N6 Nëlu R U.S.S.R.
42 K4 Nelyaty U.S.S.R. 56.31N 115.50E
47 H5 Nem R U.S.S.R.
89 F3 Néma Mauritania 16.32N 7.12W
46 Q2 Nema U.S.S.R. 57.30N 50.30E
108 S3 Nemadji R Minnesota
108 P9 Nemaha Nebraska 40.21N 95.41W
46 E2 Neman R Lithuania U.S.S.R.
40 E1 Nemanka U.S.S.R. 61.06N 130.00E
29 E6 Nemawar Madhya Prad India 22.30N 77.02E
65 L4 Něm Benešov nad Cernou Czechoslovakia 48.44N 14.38E
19 C9 Nembrala Indonesia 10.54S 122.52E
65 P4 Němčice Czechoslovakia 48.59N 16.41E
46 N1 Nemda R U.S.S.R.
84 E6 Neméa Greece 37.49N 22.40E
65 O2 Německe Czechoslovakia 49.39N 16.07E
47 G4 Nemed U.S.S.R. 63.10N 54.20E
99 G5 Nemegos Ontario 47.43N 83.12W
99 G4 Nemegosenda L Ontario 48.00N 83.07W
100 M3 Nemeiben L Saskatchewan
88 R4 Nementcha, Mts des Algeria
83 D4 Nëmerçkë mts Albania
34 Q1 Nemhel Iran 37.15N 48.27E
80 G5 Nemi,Lago di Italy 41.43N 12.43E
40 G5 Nemilen R U.S.S.R.
82 K4 Nemira mt Romania 46.12N 26.21E
82 M2 Nemirov U.S.S.R. 48.58N 28.50E
97 M7 Némiscau Quebec 51.20N 77.01W
40 N7 Nemo vol Kuril Is U.S.S.R. 49.34N 154.49E
21 C3 Nemor He R Heilongjiang China
Nemours Algeria see Ghazaouet
69 D7 Nemours France 48.16N 2.41E
37 G7 Nemrut Dağ mt Turkey
37 G7 Nemrut Gölü L Turkey
40 G7 Nemta R U.S.S.R.
Nemunas R see Neman R
21 K6 Nemuro Japan 43.22N 145.36E
20 L2 Nemuro-kaikyō str Japan/U.S.S.R
40 G4 Nemuy U.S.S.R. 55.36N 136.09E
59 F6 Nenagh Tipperary Irish Rep 52.52N 8.12W
113 N4 Nenana Alaska 64.35N 149.20W
113 N4 Nenana R Alaska
45 J2 Nenashevo U.S.S.R. 54.36N 37.30E
18 D8 Nenasi Pen Malaysia 3.08N 103.25E
21 C2 Nen Chiang R Nei Monggol Zizhiqu China
66 F7 Nendaz Switzerland 46.12N 7.19E
66 F7 Nendaz, Val de Switzerland
66 P3 Nendeln Liechtenstein 47.13N 9.33E
56 L3 Nene, R Northants etc Eng
47 G2 Nenetskiy Nats.Okrug dist U.S.S.R.
18 B7 Nenggiri R Pen Malaysia
122 E15 Nengonengo atoll Tuamotu Is Pacific Oc 18.42S 141.46W
21 C3 Nenjiang Heilongjiang China 49.10N 125.15E
21 C3 Nen Jiang R Heilongjiang China
Nenndorf see Bad Nenndorf
36 E5 Nenni R Turkey
64 A4 Nennig W Germany 49.32N 6.23E
92 G9 Neno Malawi 15.26S 34.41E
64 H1 Nentershausen W Germany 51.02N 9.56E
57 J3 Nenthead Cumbria Eng 54.48N 2.20W
58 L7 Nenthorn Borders Scotland 55.38N 2.30W
19 E1 Nenusa,Kep islds Indonesia
40 B4 Nenyuga R U.S.S.R.
108 J7 Nenzel Nebraska 42.57N 101.06W
65 A7 Nenzing Austria 47.12N 9.44E
109 P4 Neodesha Kansas 37.26N 95.42W
109 P4 Neodesha Res Kansas
107 H2 Neoga Illinois 39.19N 88.26W
84 B6 Neokhór Greece 37.54N 21.11E
84 B5 Neokhóri Aitolía Greece 38.24N 21.16E
84 F3 Neokhóri Magnisía Greece 39.18N 23.13E
84 P14 Neokhorio Cyprus 35.01N 32.22E
84 C3 Neokhórion Greece 39.17N 21.44E
108 P8 Neola Iowa 41.26N 95.38W
110 P9 Neola Utah 40.27N 110.03W
81 B3 Neoneli Sardinia 40.04N 8.57E
83 H7 Néon Karlóvasi Greece 37.47N 26.40E
83 F3 Neon Petrítsi Greece 41.16N 23.15E
106 F5 Neopit Wisconsin 44.59N 88.49W
118 J2 Neópolis Brazil 10.20S 36.36W
30 C4 Neoria Husainpur Uttar Prad India 28.44N 79.53E
107 B5 Neosho Missouri 36.53N 94.24W
106 F6 Neosho Wisconsin 43.18N 88.30W
109 P4 Neosho R Kansas/Okla
84 G1 Néos Marmarás Greece 40.06N 23.47E
35 F2 Ne'ot Golan Syria 32.47N 35.42E
35 E10 Ne'ot HaKikar Israel 30.57N 35.22E
35 F1 Ne'ot Mordekhay Israel 33.09N 35.36E
86 L3 Ne'ot Sinay Egypt 31.08N 33.51E
72 E10 Neouvieille,Pic de mt France 42.51N 0.07E
90 K6 Néouya Chad 11.44N 21.08E
42 H3 Nepa U.S.S.R. 59.15N 108.20E
42 H3 Nepa R U.S.S.R.
27 N4 Nepal kingdom S Asia
29 K4 Nepalganj Nepal 26.38N 86.10E
30 E4 Nepalganj Nepal 28.02N 81.38E
103 J3 Nepaug Res Connecticut 41.48N 72.57W
10 V11 Nepean I Norfolk I Pacific Oc 29.05S 167.58E
111 N2 Nephi Utah 39.43N 111.50W
59 D3 Nephin mt Mayo Irish Rep 54.01N 9.22W
59 C3 Nephin Beg mt Mayo Irish Rep 54.02N 9.37W
99 N8 Nephton Ontario 44.38N 77.59W
80 F4 Nepi Italy 42.14N 12.21E
89 F9 Nepi Liberia 5.36N 7.45W
87 A9 Nepoko,R Zaïre
64 Q5 Nepomuk Czechoslovakia 49.29N 13.35E
64 P3 Nepomyšl Czechoslovakia 50.12N 13.20E
104 P10 Neponset R Massachusetts
100 N9 Neptune Saskatchewan 49.22N 104.03W
105 F7 Neptune Beach Florida 30.19N 81.23W
12 D6 Neptune Is S Australia 35.20S 136.05E
123 F10 Neptune Ra Antarctica
62 L4 Ner R Poland
80 F4 Nera R Italy
82 G6 Nera R Romania
72 E7 Nérac France 44.08N 0.21E
113 D6 Neragon I Alaska 61.45N 166.10W
28 L1 Nera Gönsar Xizang Zizhiqu 30.05N 96.55E
84 C3 Neráidha Greece 39.08N 21.47E
41 G6 Neranda,Ozero L U.S.S.R.
80 B3 Nera,Pta Italy 42.46N 10.06E
85 F7 Nerastro,Serir gravel des Libya
39 C5 Nerat U.S.S.R. 59.45N 143.05E
28 J1 Nera Tso L Xizang Zizhiqu 28.20N 92.04E
42 K5 Nercha R U.S.S.R.
64 O1 Nerchau E Germany 51.16N 12.48E
42 K6 Nerchinsk U.S.S.R. 52.02N 116.38E
42 K6 Nerchinskiy Khrebet mts U.S.S.R.
42 K6 Nerchinskiy Zavod U.S.S.R. 51.20N 119.40E
25 D7 Nerchus Pass Burma
72 D4 Nercillac France 45.43N 0.16W
81 D3 Nercone,Mte.su Sardinia 40.09N 9.31E
47 H6 Nerdva U.S.S.R. 58.45N 55.02E
72 D4 Néré France 45.58N 0.14W
89 C3 Néré Mauritania 16.13N 13.38W
89 G4 Néré Mauritania 15.36N 5.36W
39 E4 Nerega U.S.S.R. 62.00N 151.49E
39 E4 Nerega R U.S.S.R.
46 M1 Nerekhta U.S.S.R. 57.30N 40.40E
89 F5 Nérékoro Mali 13.32N 6.10W
64 J6 Neresheim W Germany 48.46N 10.22E
46 F2 Nereta Latvia U.S.S.R. 56.10N 25.12E
80 J3 Nereto Italy 42.48N 13.50E
82 D7 Neretva R Yugoslavia
117 B7 Nergulhão, Cachoeira falls Brazil 4.40S 56.20W
29 F7 Neri Maharashtra India 20.28N 79.31E
48 T15 Neria Greenland 61.45N 49.10W
20 D2 Nerima dist Tōkyō Japan
46 D2 Neringa Lithuania U.S.S.R. 55.30N 21.00E
91 G11 Neriquinha Angola 15.45S 21.32E
Neris R see Vilnya R
72 K3 Néris-les-Bains France 46.18N 2.38E
77 J7 Nerja Spain 36.45N 3.53W
113 H7 Nerka,L Alaska 59.35N 159.05W
42 F5 Nerkha U.S.S.R. 53.53N 98.15E
46 L2 Nerl' U.S.S.R. 57.01N 38.00E
46 M2 Nerl' U.S.S.R. 56.38N 40.22E
46 L2 Nerl' R U.S.S.R.
53 T14 Nerlandsøy isld Norway 62.21N 5.35E
119 A10 Nermete,Pta C Peru 5.10S 81.13W
66 B6 Nernier France 46.22N 6.18E
17 P9 Nero Deep trough Pacific Oc 12.40N 145.50E
84 K11 Nerokoúrou Crete 35.29N 24.02E
80 G4 Nerola Italy 42.10N 12.47E
71 E5 Néronde France 45.50N 4.14E
72 K1 Nérondes France 47.00N 2.48E
79 N7 Nerone,Monte Italy 43.33N 12.31E
118 E5 Nerópolis Brazil 16.24S 49.12W
79 L1 Nero,Sasso mt Italy/Austria 47.03N 11.57E
45 L6 Nerovnovka U.S.S.R. 50.09N 39.15E
42 F5 Neroy U.S.S.R. 54.30N 97.47E
47 H4 Neroyka,Gora mt U.S.S.R. 64.35N 59.44E
41 Q3 Nerpichiy,Mys C U.S.S.R. 75.51N 143.35E
39 G6 Nerpich'ye,Oz L Kamchatka U.S.S.R.
39 G1 Nerpich'ye,Oz L Yakutsk U.S.S.R.
29 F7 Ner Pinglai Maharashtra India 21.14N 78.03E
77 M4 Nerpio Spain 38.09N 2.18W
12 K6 Nerriga New S Wales 35.10S 150.03E
14 E4 Nerrima W Australia 18.28S 124.33E
72 E4 Nersac France 45.37N 0.04E
39 D3 Nerskoye Ploskogor'ye tableland U.S.S.R.
45 E4 Nerussa R U.S.S.R.
77 C5 Nerva Spain 37.41N 6.33W
34 L1 Nērva Zhūr Iraq 37.12N 43.41E
79 M3 Nervesa d.Battăglia Italy 45.50N 12.12E
79 F6 Nervi Italy 44.23N 9.03E
71 E5 Nervieux France 45.48N 4.09E
75 E1 Nervión R Spain
29 C7 Nerwal Maharashtra India 20.05N 73.20E
40 C3 Neryungri U.S.S.R. 56.39N 124.38E
47 J3 Neryuvom U.S.S.R. 67.06N 60.12E
60 M6 Nes Ameland Netherlands 53.27N 5.46E
50 D7 Nes Árnessýsla Iceland 63.50N 21.40W
60 N6 Nes Friesland Netherlands 53.24N 6.03E
53 U15 Nes Sogn og Fjordane Norway 61.36N 6.00E
53 W16 Nes Sogn og Fjordane Norway 61.23N 7.23E
53 W16 Nes Sogn og Fjordane Norway 61.28N 7.02E
52 E3 Nes Sör-Tröndelag Norway 63.48N 9.39E
50 H3 Nes Thingeyjarsýsla, Sudhur Iceland 65.53N 17.20W
47 E3 Nes' U.S.S.R. 66.39N 44.45E
47 E3 Nes' R U.S.S.R.
32 D2 Nesa' Iran 36.05N 51.21E
52 E6 Nesbyen Norway 60.36N 9.35E
103 B4 Nescopeck Pennsylvania 41.33N 76.14W
82 L8 Nesebŭr Bulgaria 42.39N 27.43E
53 V19 Nesflaten Norway 59.38N 6.48E
103 D6 Neshaminy Pennsylvania 40.14N 75.08W
103 D6 Neshaminy R Pennsylvania
35 D7 Nes Harim Israel 31.44N 35.04E
46 G2 Neshcherdo Oz L Belorussiya U.S.S.R.
53 U17 Nesheim Norway 60.48N 6.09E
35 D2 Nesher Israel 32.46N 35.03E
113 A3 Neshkan U.S.S.R. 67.04N 173.00W
39 M2 Neshkanpil'gyn,Laguna lagoon U.S.S.R.
106 E6 Neshkoro Wisconsin 43.57N 89.12W
107 G9 Neshoba Mississippi 32.38N 89.09W
50 M4 Neskaupstadhur Iceland 65.10N 13.43W
53 X19 Nesland Norway 59.31N 7.59E
52 E8 Neslandsvatn Norway 58.57N 9.10E
69 D4 Nesle France 49.45N 2.55E
69 G8 Nesle-et-Massoult France 47.48N 4.27E
98 N3 Nesle,L Quebec
51 C5 Nesna Norway 66.13N 13.04E
51 C5 Nesøya isld Norway 66.35N 12.40E
110 G1 Nespelem Washington 48.10N 118.58W
76 C6 Nespereira Portugal 41.01N 8.10W
80 H4 Nespolo Italy 42.09N 13.04E
72 G5 Nespouls France 45.02N 1.30E
71 G8 Nesque R France
103 C5 Nesquehoning Pennsylvania 40.52N 75.48W
28 B2 Nesri Maharashtra India 16.02N 74.25E
43 E7 Nessa anc site Turkmeniya U.S.S.R. 37.55N 58.08E
53 U16 Nessane Norway 61.08N 6.17E
109 L3 Ness City Kansas 38.27N 99.54W
56 F2 Nesscliff Shropshire Eng 52.46N 2.54W
63 F5 Nesse W Germany 53.40N 7.22E
64 K1 Nesse R E Germany
51 O1 Nesseby Norway 70.09N 28.56E
101 F6 Nesselrode,Mt Br Col/Alaska 58.55N 134.20W
64 K8 Nesselwang W Germany 47.38N 10.30E
58 G4 Ness,L Highland Scotland
66 N3 Nesslau Switzerland 47.14N 9.13E
66 N8 Nesso Italy 45.55N 9.10E
61 N4 Nessonvaux Belgium 50.34N 5.44E
58 H4 Ness,R Highland Scotland
34 N2 Nestān Dāgh mt Iran 36.18N 45.42E
84 D6 Nestáni Greece 37.37N 22.28E
76 L3 Nestar Spain 42.50N 4.15W
72 E10 Neste R France
46 E4 Nesterov Ukraine U.S.S.R. 50.04N 24.00E
62 O1 Nesterov U.S.S.R. 54.38N 22.34E
42 H6 Nesterovo U.S.S.R. 52.25N 107.55E
99 G6 Nesterville Ontario 46.17N 83.37W
66 H6 Nesthorn mt Switzerland 46.25N 7.56E
46 O2 Nestiary U.S.S.R. 56.32N 45.20E
39 F1 Nestka,Ozero L U.S.S.R. 69.58N 156.30E
57 G6 Neston Cheshire Eng 53.18N 3.04W
116 P2 Nestor Trinidad & Tobago 10.31N 61.09W
80 F2 Nestore R Italy
80 F3 Nestore R Italy
100 H1 Nestor Falls Ontario 49.06N 93.55W
106 F3 Nestoria Michigan 46.34N 88.15W
83 E4 Nestórion Greece 40.24N 21.02E
83 G3 Néstos R Greece
Nes Tsiyona see Nes Ziyyona
53 S18 Nesttun Norway 60.18N 5.23E
53 Y20 Nesvatn L Norway 59.02N 8.04E
46 F3 Nesvizh Belorussiya U.S.S.R. 53.16N 26.40E
35 C6 Nes Ziyyona Israel 31.56N 34.46E
40 H2 Nët R U.S.S.R.
35 C6 Neta'im Israel 31.57N 34.46E
20 G4 Netanai Japan 41.48N 141.08E
35 C4 Netanya Israel 32.20N 34.51E
109 P2 Netawaka Kansas 39.35N 95.44W
103 E5 Netcong New Jersey 40.54N 74.43W
60 J14 Netersel Netherlands 51.24N 5.12E
28 H1 Ne-thang Xizang Zizhiqu 29.31N 90.54E
63 K9 Nethe R W Germany
61 J3 Nethen Belgium 50.47N 4.40E
56 H5 Nether Avon Wilts Eng 51.15N 1.48W
13 J5 Netherdale Queensland 21.11S 148.31E
100 J7 Netherhill Saskatchewan 51.28N 108.51W
49 E6 Netherlands kingdom W Europe
Netherlands Antilles islds see Curaçao, Bonaire, Aruba islds
Netherlands Guiana see Surinam
56 E5 Nether Stowey Somerset Eng 51.09N 3.10W
11 K4 Netherton New Zealand 37.19S 175.38E
57 K2 Netherwitton Northumb Eng 55.12N 1.50W
58 J4 Nethybridge Highland Scotland 57.16N 3.40W
92 J9 Nétia Mozambique 14.41S 39.56E
35 C6 Netiva Israel 31.48N 34.49E
35 C7 Netiv HaLamed He Israel 31.41N 34.58E
35 B8 Netivot Israel 31.26N 34.36E
45 Q6 Netkachevo U.S.S.R. 50.32N 44.55E
81 O5 Neto R Italy
65 K3 Netolice Czechoslovakia 49.03N 14.12E
64 E2 Netphen W Germany 50.55N 8.06E
64 J1 Netra W Germany 51.05N 10.07E
31 H8 Netrakona Bangladesh 24.52N 90.46E
29 C7 Netrang Gujarat India 21.34N 73.18E
94 Q11 Netreg Cape Town S Africa 33.57S 18.33E
66 N3 Netstal Switzerland 47.05N 9.04E
69 H6 Nettancourt France 48.52N 4.57E
63 M8 Nette R W Germany
64 C3 Nette R W Germany
60 O12 Netterden Netherlands 51.52N 6.20E
64 B3 Nettersheim W Germany 50.29N 6.38E
69 M3 Nettersheim W Germany 50.30N 6.38E
63 D10 Nettetal W Germany 51.20N 6.14E
97 M4 Nettilling L N W Terr 66.30N 70.30W
61 M5 Nettinne Belgium 50.18N 5.15E
108 R1 Nett L Minnesota
56 K4 Nettlebed Oxon Eng 51.35N 1.00W
99 K4 Nettle Lakes Prov. Park Ontario
107 F6 Nettleton Arkansas 35.49N 90.49W
107 H7 Nettleton Mississippi 34.05N 88.37W
80 G6 Nettuno Italy 41.27N 12.40E
35 E1 Netu'a Israel 33.04N 35.20E
115 N9 Netzahualcóyotl, Presa res Mexico
64 N2 Netzschkau E Germany 50.36N 12.15E
64 H1 Neu W Germany 51.04N 9.36E
63 G7 Neu Arenberg W Germany 52.59N 7.46E
87 E7 Neubari watercourse Sudan
64 N5 Neubäu W Germany 49.14N 12.25E
63 H9 Neubeckum W Germany 51.47N 8.00E
65 N6 Neuberg Austria 47.40N 15.35E
64 N8 Neubeuern W Germany 47.46N 12.10E
70 M3 Neuborg,le France 49.09N 0.55E
63 S5 Neubrandenburg E Germany 53.33N 13.16E
63 S5 Neubrandenburg reg E Germany
63 J7 Neubruchhausen W Germany 52.51N 8.51E
64 H4 Neubrunn W Germany 49.44N 9.42E
63 P4 Neubukow E Germany 54.01N 11.39E
63 P5 Neuburg E Germany 53.58N 11.36E
64 L6 Neuburg an der Donau W Germany 48.44N 11.12E
66 D4 Neuchâtel Switzerland 46.59N 6.55E
66 D3 Neuchâtel canton Switzerland
66 D4 Neuchâtel,Lac de Switzerland
63 M9 Neuckrug W Germany 51.57N 10.14E
65 O7 Neudau Austria 47.11N 16.07E
Neudorf see Graben-Neudorf
65 O4 Neudorf Austria 48.43N 16.30E
100 P8 Neudorf Saskatchewan 50.43N 103.00W
66 J3 Neudorf Switzerland 47.11N 8.13E
65 O6 Neudörfl Austria 47.48N 16.18E
64 M3 Neudrossenfeld W Germany 50.01N 11.31E
63 L10 Neu-Eichenberg W Germany 51.23N 9.54E
64 D8 Neuenburg Baden-Württemberg W Germany 47.48N 7.34E
64 F6 Neuenbürg Baden-Württemberg W Germany 48.51N 8.36E
63 G6 Neuenburg Niedersachsen W Germany 53.23N 7.58E
Neuenburg Switzerland see Neuchâtel
66 H2 Neuendorf Switzerland 47.18N 7.47E
66 F4 Neuenegg Switzerland 46.54N 7.18E
63 T7 Neuenhagen E Germany 52.33N 13.43E
63 E7 Neuenhaus W Germany 52.30N 6.58E
63 S3 Neuenkirchen E Germany 54.33N 13.20E
63 J6 Neuenkirchen Niedersachsen W Germany 53.14N 8.31E
63 L6 Neuenkirchen Niedersachsen W Germany 53.02N 9.41E
63 F8 Neuenkirchen Nordrhein-Westfalen W Germany 52.15N 7.23E
64 M3 Neuenmarkt W Germany 50.06N 11.40E
64 O2 Neuen Morbitz E Germany 50.59N 12.36E
64 D1 Neuenrade W Germany 51.17N 7.48E
64 G5 Neuenstadt W Germany 49.15N 9.20E
64 H5 Neuenstein W Germany 49.12N 9.35E
64 G2 Neuental W Germany 51.00N 9.15E
63 J5 Neuenwalde W Germany 53.41N 8.42E
64 A3 Neuerburg W Germany 50.01N 6.18E
64 N6 Neufahrn Nieder-Bayern W Germany 48.45N 12.13E
64 M7 Neufahrn Ober-Bayern W Germany 48.18N 11.40E
69 O7 Neuf-Brisach France 48.01N 7.33E
61 M7 Neufchâteau Belgium 49.51N 5.26E
69 K7 Neufchâteau France 48.21N 5.42E
70 L5 Neufchâtel Sarthe France 48.23N 0.14E
70 N2 Neufchâtel-en-Bray France 49.44N 1.26E
69 B2 Neufchâtel-Hardelot France 50.37N 1.39E
69 G5 Neufchâtel-sur-Aisne France 49.27N 4.02E
65 K5 Neufelden Austria 48.29N 14.00E
64 G6 Neuffen W Germany 48.33N 9.22E
61 F4 Neufmaison Belgium 50.32N 3.48E
70 O3 Neuf-Marché France 49.26N 1.44E
64 G7 Neufra W Germany 48.15N 9.11E
66 B4 Neufs France 46.47N 6.23E
61 G4 Neufvilles Belgium 50.34N 4.00E
64 K8 Neugablonz W Germany 47.50N 10.36E
63 S6 Neuglobsow E Germany 53.08N 13.03E
63 U7 Neu Hardenberg E Germany 52.36N 14.15E
63 G5 Neuharlingersiel W Germany 53.42N 7.43E
65 M6 Neuhaus Austria 47.48N 15.12E
64 M4 Neuhaus Bayern W Germany 49.37N 11.33E
64 P7 Neuhaus Nieder-Bayern W Germany 48.28N 13.26E
63 K5 Neuhaus Niedersachsen W Germany 53.48N 9.03E
63 N6 Neuhaus Schwerin E Germany 53.18N 10.57E
64 L2 Neuhaus Suhl E Germany 50.30N 11.08E
64 L3 Neuhaus am Rennweg Suhl E Germany 50.19N 11.15E
Neuhausen see Filderstadt
64 P2 Neuhausen Karl-Marx-Stadt E Germany 50.41N 13.29E
66 L1 Neuhausen Switzerland 47.42N 8.37E
94 D4 Neu Heusis Namibia 22.33S 16.48E
64 K5 Neuhof Bayern W Germany 49.27N 10.39E
63 S8 Neuhof E Germany 52.08N 13.29E
64 E3 Neuhof Hessen W Germany 50.10N 8.14E
64 H3 Neuhof Hessen W Germany 50.28N 9.38E
65 K5 Neuhofen Austria 48.07N 14.14E
64 G5 Neuhütten W Germany 49.07N 9.29E
72 G2 Neuillay-les-Bois France 46.46N 1.29E
72 L1 Neuilly Nièvre France 47.14N 3.29E
70 M4 Neuilly Orne France 48.33N 0.55E
71 D4 Neuilly-en-Donjon France 46.20N 3.53E
69 C5 Neuilly-en-Thelle France 49.14N 2.17E
70 H3 Neuilly-la-Forêt France 49.16N 1.05W
71 C4 Neuilly-le-Réal France 46.28N 3.21E
69 J8 Neuilly-l'Évêque France 47.55N 5.27E
68 H3 Neuilly-Plaisance France 48.52N 2.31E
69 E5 Neuilly-St.Front France 49.10N 3.16E
68 H3 Neuilly-sur-Marne France 48.52N 2.33E
68 E3 Neuilly-sur-Seine France 48.53N 2.16E
64 F3 Neu-Isenburg W Germany 50.02N 8.42E
63 R5 Neukalen E Germany 53.50N 12.47E
63 O6 Neu Kaliss E Germany 53.11N 11.19E
66 N1 Neukirch Switzerland 47.31N 9.11E
66 O1 Neukirch Switzerland 47.32N 9.23E
66 P1 Neukirch W Germany 47.39N 9.42E
64 M4 Neukirchen Bayern W Germany 49.31N 11.40E
64 O2 Neukirchen E Germany 50.46N 12.51E
Neukirchen Hessen W Germany see Haunetal
64 G2 Neukirchen Hessen W Germany 50.52N 9.21E
65 H5 Neukirchen Ober-Österreich Austria 48.10N 13.02E
65 J5 Neukirchen Ober-Österreich Austria 48.24N 13.48E
65 F7 Neukirchen Salzburg Austria 47.16N 12.17E
63 L3 Neukirchen Schleswig Holstein W Germany 54.47N 9.46E
63 O4 Neukirchen Schleswig Holstein W Germany 54.19N 11.02E
64 N5 Neukirchen Balbini W Germany 49.17N 12.26E
63 E10 Neukirchen-Vluyn W Germany 51.26N 6.31E
63 P5 Neukloster E Germany 53.53N 11.40E
63 L6 Neukloster W Germany 53.28N 9.39E
63 C2 Neukölln dist W Berlin W Germany
63 K5 Neuland W Germany 53.45N 9.19E
65 N5 Neulengbach Austria 48.12N 15.55E
71 E5 Neulise France 45.54N 4.11E
70 M6 Neullé-Pont-Pierre France 47.33N 0.33E
70 E5 Neulliac France 48.07N 2.59W
87 E7 Neum Ethiopia 7.22N 34.03E
69 M4 Neumagen-Dhron W Germany 49.51N 6.55E
64 L1 Neumark Erfurt E Germany 51.05N 11.15E
64 N2 Neumark Karl-Marx-Stadt E Germany 50.39N 12.21E
65 O8 Neumark-an-der-Raab Austria 46.56N 16.09E
65 K5 Neumarkt Ober-Österreich Austria 48.27N 14.30E
65 H6 Neumarkt Salzburg Austria 47.56N 13.14E
65 K7 Neumarkt Steiermark Austria 47.05N 14.26E
64 M5 Neumarkt W Germany 49.17N 11.29E
65 J5 Neumarkt-Kallheim Austria 48.17N 13.44E
64 O7 Neumarkt-St. Veit W Germany 48.21N 12.32E
61 P4 Neu-Moresnet Belgium 50.43N 6.01E
64 H1 Neumorschen W Germany 51.03N 9.33E
63 L4 Neumünster W Germany 54.05N 9.59E
64 N5 Neunburg vorm Wald W Germany 49.21N 12.23E
70 O6 Neung-sur-Beuvron France 47.33N 1.48E
61 O7 Neunhausen Luxembourg 49.52N 5.53E
66 L1 Neunkirch Switzerland 47.42N 8.30E
65 O6 Neunkirchen Austria 47.44N 16.05E
64 L4 Neunkirchen Bayern W Germany 49.36N 11.08E
64 D2 Neunkirchen Nordrhein-Westfalen W Germany 50.47N 8.00E
64 E2 Neunkirchen Rheinland-Pfalz W Germany 50.32N 8.07E
64 C5 Neunkirchen Saarland W Germany 49.21N 7.12E
64 C2 Neunkirchen W Germany 50.50N 7.20E
25 H3 Neun,Nam R Laos
64 O7 Neuötting W Germany 48.13N 12.45E
41 G2 Neupokoyeva,Mys C U.S.S.R. 77.57N 99.17E
41 C4 Neupokoyeva,Ostrov isld U.S.S.R.
65 M4 Neu Pölla Austria 48.39N 15.28E
121 C7 Neuquén Argentina 38.55S 68.05W
121 B7 Neuquén terr Argentina
121 B7 Neuquén, R Argentina
69 P5 Neureut W Germany 49.03N 8.22E
66 A1 Neurey-en-Vaux France 47.45N 6.11E
63 R7 Neuruppin E Germany 52.56N 12.49E
66 N3 Neu St. Johann Switzerland 47.14N 9.13E
64 K7 Neusäss W Germany 48.24N 10.50E
66 F5 Neuschels Pass Switzerland 46.38N 7.17E
64 Q6 Neu Schönau W Germany 48.53N 13.30E
105 K2 Neuse,R N Carolina
65 P6 Neusiedl am See Austria 47.58N 16.51E
65 P6 Neusiedler See L Austria
64 B1 Neuss W Germany 51.12N 6.42E
72 K5 Neussargues Moissac France 45.08N 2.59E
Neustadt Baden-Württemberg see Titisee-Neustadt
64 G2 Neustadt Hessen W Germany 50.52N 9.08E
64 G4 Neustadt Hessen W Germany 49.50N 9.03E
64 K2 Neustadt Suhl E Germany 50.35N 10.57E
64 M4 Neustadt am Kulm Bayern W Germany 49.49N 11.51E
63 K7 Neustadt-am-Rübenberge W Germany 52.31N 9.28E
64 K4 Neustadt an der Aisch W Germany 49.35N 10.38E
64 M6 Neustadt an der Donau W Germany 48.49N 11.47E
64 M2 Neustadt an der Orla E Germany 50.45N 11.44E
64 N4 Neustadt an der Waldnaab W Germany 49.43N 12.11E
64 E5 Neustadt an der Weinstrasse W Germany 49.21N 8.09E
64 L3 Neustadt bei Coburg W Germany 50.20N 11.08E
63 Q7 Neustadt (Dosse) E Germany 52.52N 12.25E
63 P6 Neustadt-Glewe E Germany 53.23N 11.35E
63 G6 Neustadtgödens W Germany 53.28N 8.00E
63 N9 Neustadt (Harz) E Germany 51.34N 10.51E
64 C2 Neustadt/Wied W Germany 50.37N 7.27E
Neustettin see Szczecinek
65 D7 Neustift Austria 47.08N 11.19E
64 M7 Neustift W Germany 48.24N 11.46E
63 S6 Neustrelitz E Germany 53.22N 13.05E
63 U7 Neu Tornow E Germany 52.49N 14.05E
64 J7 Neu-Ulm W Germany 48.23N 10.01E
69 D2 Neuve-Chapelle France 50.35N 2.47E
72 K6 Neuvéglise France 44.57N 2.58E
70 M4 Neuve-Lyre,la France 48.54N 0.45E
69 L6 Neuves-Maisons France 48.37N 6.07E
66 E3 Neuveville Switzerland 47.04N 7.06E
72 E5 Neuvic France 45.06N 0.29E
72 J5 Neuvic France 45.23N 2.16E
72 J5 Neuvic,Barrage de France 45.23N 2.17E
61 J6 Neuville Belgium 50.11N 4.32E
72 H5 Neuville Corrèze France 45.06N 1.49E
112 N4 Neuville Texas 31.42N 94.10W
69 C7 Neuville-aux-Bois France 48.04N 2.02E
72 E2 Neuville-de-Poitou Vienne France 46.41N 0.15E
61 M4 Neuville-en-Condroz Belgium 50.33N 5.27E
69 G5 Neuville-en-Tourne-à-Fuy, La France 49.21N 4.22E
71 G4 Neuville-les-Dames France 46.10N 5.00E
70 N2 Neuville-les-Dieppe France 49.56N 1.08E
71 F5 Neuville-sur-Saône France 45.53N 4.48E
69 J5 Neuvilly-en-Argonne France 49.10N 5.04E
120 E4 Neuvo Mundo Bolivia 10.25S 66.42W
72 D2 Neuvy Bouin France 46.41N 0.28W
71 D3 Neuvy-Grandchamp France 46.35N 3.56E
70 M6 Neuvy-le-Roi France 47.36N 0.36E
72 H2 Neuvy Pailloux France 46.53N 1.52E
72 H2 Neuvy St. Sépulchre France 46.36N 1.48E
69 F7 Neuvy-Sautour France 48.02N 3.48E
72 J1 Neuvy-sur-Barangeon France 47.19N 2.15E
71 B1 Neuvy-sur-Loire Cher France 47.32N 2.52E
63 O8 Neuwegersleben E Germany 52.03N 11.07E
64 E6 Neuweier W Germany 48.42N 8.11E
63 H5 Neuwerk isld W Germany
64 C3 Neuwied W Germany 50.26N 7.28E
69 N6 Neuwiller-lès-Saverne France 48.49N 7.24E
63 L6 Neu-Wulmstorf W Germany 53.28N 9.46E
63 U9 Neu Zauche E Germany 51.56N 14.07E
63 T8 Neu Zittau E Germany 52.24N 13.45E
40 J7 Neva Sakhalin U.S.S.R. 49.16N 143.44E
52 H6 Neva Sweden 60.13N 14.09E
106 E4 Neva Wisconsin 45.14N 89.07W
47 C6 Neva R U.S.S.R.
51 P12 Neva R U.S.S.R.
71 K6 Névache France 45.01N 6.36E
108 R7 Nevada Iowa 42.01N 93.26W
107 B4 Nevada Missouri 37.51N 94.22W
95 K5 Nevada S Africa 29.38S 26.50E
112 L2 Nevada Texas 33.03N 96.22W
102 C3 Nevada state U.S.A.
111 D2 Nevada City California 39.16N 121.00W
119 D4 Nevada del Cocuy, Sa mt Colombia 6.30N 72.21W
102 C3 Nevada,Sa mts U.S.A.
120 E12 Nevada,Sa pk Argentina 26.30S 68.30W
77 K6 Nevada,Sierra mts Spain
121 C5 Nevado,Cerro pk Argentina 35.35S 68.32W
115 H8 Nevado de Colima pk Mexico 19.32N 103.36W
115 K8 Nevado de Toluca pk Mexico 19.09N 99.46W
121 C5 Nevado,Sierra del ra Argentina
77 F4 Névalo R Spain
42 F4 Nevanka U.S.S.R. 56.31N 98.57E
29 D8 Nevasa Maharashtra India 19.38N 74.58E
114 B1 Neva Shoal Hawaiian Is
35 C9 Nevatim Israel 31.13N 34.52E
65 L2 Neveklov Czechoslovakia 49.45N 14.32E
46 G2 Nevel' U.S.S.R. 56.00N 29.59E
61 E2 Nevele Belgium 51.02N 3.33E
40 J8 Nevel'sk Sakhalin U.S.S.R. 46.41N 141.55E
40 J5 Nevel'skogo Proliv str U.S.S.R.
56 N4 Nevendon Essex Eng 51.36N 0.30E
40 C5 Never U.S.S.R. 54.00N 124.09E
45 S4 Neverkino U.S.S.R. 52.48N 46.45E
51 C6 Nevernes Norway 65.25N 12.36E
72 L1 Nevers France 47.00N 3.09E
103 E3 Neversink New York 41.49N 74.38W
103 E3 Neversink R New York
103 E3 Neversink Res New York
12 H4 Nevertire New S Wales 31.52S 147.47E
118 K8 Neves Brazil 22.52S 43.06W

76 D12 Neves Portugal 38.01N 7.51W
75 O4 Nevés Spain 42.00N 1.37E
91 C10 Neve,Sa.da mts Angola
82 E7 Nevesinje Yugoslavia 43.15N 18.07E
70 C6 Névez France 47.49N 3.47W
79 H5 Neviano d'Arduini Italy 44.34N 10.19E
63 F10 Neviges W Germany 51.18N 7.06E
70 M2 Neville France 49.50N 0.43E
105 F5 Nevils Georgia 32.17N 81.45W
57 D7 Nevin Gwynedd Wales 52.57N 4.31W
44 D3 Nevinnomyssk U.S.S.R. 44.38N 41.59E
86 N7 Neviot Egypt 29.02N 34.40E
100 D6 Nevis Alberta 52.22N 113.01W
108 Q3 Nevis Minnesota 46.56N 94.50W
116 P4 Nevis I Leeward Is W I 17.11N 62.35W
58 E5 Nevis,L Highland Scotland
116 P4 Nevis Pk Nevis I W I 17.09N 62.34W
11 C12 Nevis,R New Zealand
42 G3 Nevon U.S.S.R. 58.05N 102.40E
Nevrokop see Gotse Delchev
36 H4 Nevşehir Turkey 38.38N 34.43E
40 F9 Nevskoye U.S.S.R. 45.42N 133.44E
47 M4 Nev'yansk U.S.S.R. 57.34N 60.10E
111 J9 New R U.S.A./Mexico
57 F3 New Abbey Dumfries & Galloway Scotland 54.59N 3.38W
58 M3 New Aberdour Grampian Scotland 57.39N 2.11W
89 J8 New Adawso Ghana 6.40N 0.40W
55 G5 New Addington London Eng 51.21N 0.01W
94 L4 New Agatha S Africa 23.58S 30.08E
104 Q3 Newagen Maine 43.47N 69.40W
92 J7 Newala Tanzania 10.59S 39.18E
107 L3 New Albany Indiana 38.17N 85.50W
107 G7 New Albany Mississippi 34.30N 89.01W
103 B3 New Albany Pennsylvania 41.36N 76.56W
106 C6 New Albin Iowa 43.29N 91.20W
106 F4 Newald Wisconsin 45.46N 88.42W
95 N6 New Amalfi S Africa 30.17S 29.10E
117 A1 New Amsterdam Guyana 6.18N 57.30W
13 J8 New Angledool New S Wales 29.06S 147.57E
107 E6 Newark Arkansas 35.41N 91.28W
111 B4 Newark California 37.31N 122.03W
103 C7 Newark Delaware 39.42N 75.45W
106 F8 Newark Illinois 41.32N 88.34W
108 M9 Newark Nebraska 40.29N 98.59W
103 K7 Newark New Jersey 40.44N 74.12W
104 H3 Newark New York 43.03N 77.06W
104 C6 Newark Ohio 40.03N 82.25W
95 P5 Newark S Africa 29.13S 31.25E
103 H8 Newark Airport New Jersey 40.42N 74.11W
103 H8 Newark B New Jersey
57 M6 Newark-on-Trent Notts Eng 53.05N 0.49W
103 B2 Newark Valley New York 42.13N 76.10W
92 J7 Newata Tanzania 10.36S 39.59E
107 G3 New Athens Illinois 38.19N 89.53W
106 C4 New Auburn Wisconsin 45.13N 91.34W
107 G10 New Augusta Mississippi 31.12N 89.05W
106 J6 Newaygo Michigan 43.23N 85.48W
57 M5 Newbald Humberside Eng 53.49N 0.36W
106 M7 New Baltimore Michigan 42.37N 82.46W
103 G2 New Baltimore New York 42.26N 73.47W
104 G7 New Baltimore Pennsylvania 39.59N 78.46W
55 E2 New Barnet London England 51.39N 0.10W
103 N3 New Bedford Massachusetts 41.38N 70.55W
123 E12 New Bedford Inlet Antarctica
56 M2 New Bedford R Norf/Cambs
110 C4 Newberg Oregon 45.19N 122.59W
107 G2 New Berlin Illinois 39.43N 89.54W
104 K4 New Berlin New York 42.37N 75.22W
103 C6 New Berlinville Pennsylvania 40.21N 75.38W
107 J9 Newbern Alabama 32.36N 87.31W
105 K2 New Bern N Carolina 35.05N 77.04W
107 G5 Newbern Tennessee 36.07N 89.17W
111 H7 Newberry California 34.50N 116.40W
105 E8 Newberry Florida 29.40N 82.38W
107 J3 Newberry Indiana 38.56N 87.01W
106 J3 Newberry Michigan 46.22N 85.30W
105 F3 Newberry S Carolina 34.17N 81.39W
104 F5 New Bethlehem Pennsylvania 41.01N 79.21W
57 J4 Newbiggin Cumbria Eng 54.27N 2.27W
57 J3 Newbiggin Durham Eng 54.39N 2.07W
57 L2 Newbiggin by the Sea Northumb Eng 55.11N 1.30W
59 H3 Newbliss Monaghan Irish Rep 54.09N 7.08W
107 D3 New Bloomfield Missouri 38.44N 92.06W
106 E4 Newbold Wisconsin 45.43N 89.32W
99 O8 Newboro Ontario 44.39N 76.20W
57 E6 Newborough Gwynedd Wales 53.09N 4.22W
106 D8 New Boston Illinois 41.11N 90.59W
103 H2 New Boston Massachusetts 42.05N 73.05W
112 N2 New Boston Texas 33.29N 94.25W
112 J6 New Braunfels Texas 29.43N 98.09W
104 A6 New Bremen Ohio 40.33N 84.24W
56 E4 Newbridge Gwent Wales 51.41N 3.09W
56 E3 Newbridge-on-Wye Powys Wales 52.13N 3.27W
100 G7 New Brigden Alberta 51.41N 110.34W
57 G6 New Brighton Merseyside Eng 53.27N 3.03W
11 N9 New Brighton New Zealand 43.31S 172.44E
103 J8 New Brighton Staten I, N Y 40.39N 74.07W
103 J3 New Britain Connecticut 41.40N 72.47W
15 K6 New Britain isld Bismarck Arch
10 K3 New Britain Trench Solomon Sea
107 L10 New Brockton Alabama 31.24N 85.59W
100 E4 Newbrook Alberta 54.24N 112.57W
116 G1 New Broughton Jamaica, W I 18.13N 78.13W
103 F6 New Brunswick New Jersey 40.29N 74.27W
97 N8 New Brunswick prov Canada
56 O3 New Buckenham Norfolk Eng 52.28N 1.05E
106 H8 New Buffalo Michigan 41.48N 86.44W
108 S8 Newburg Iowa 41.49N 92.43W
107 E4 Newburg Missouri 37.55N 91.55W
104 H6 Newburg Pennsylvania 40.09N 77.34W
104 F7 Newburg W Virginia 39.24N 79.52W
58 K6 Newburgh Fife Scotland 56.21N 3.15W
58 M4 Newburgh Grampian Scotland 57.19N 2.01W
107 J4 Newburgh Indiana 37.55N 87.25W
103 F3 Newburgh New York 41.30N 74.00W
99 O8 Newburgh Ontario 44.20N 76.54W
New Burnt Cove see Burgoyne's Cove
56 J5 Newbury Berks Eng 51.25N 1.20W
104 P4 Newburyport Massachusetts 42.47N 70.53W
90 B7 New Bussa Nigeria 9.57N 4.26E
57 H4 Newby Lancs Eng 54.16N 2.58W
58 M3 Newbyth Grampian Scotland 57.34N 2.19W
90 C9 New Calabar R Nigeria
10 N6 New Caledonia isld Pacific Oc
103 G4 New Canaan Connecticut 41.09N 73.30W
94 S13 New Canada S Africa 26.13S 27.56E
29 A2 New Cantomnet dist Delhi India
107 E2 New Canton Illinois 39.38N 91.05W
104 A7 New Carlisle Ohio 39.56N 84.02W
98 G6 New Carlisle Quebec 48.00N 65.22W
111 C3 Newcastle California 38.51N 121.08W
109 C2 New Castle Colorado 39.34N 107.33W
103 C7 New Castle Delaware 39.40N 75.34W
59 L3 Newcastle Down N Ireland 54.12N 5.54W
59 K5 Newcastle Dublin Irish Rep 53.18N 6.30W
107 L2 New Castle Indiana 39.56N 85.21W
116 L2 Newcastle Jamaica, W I 18.05N 76.44W
107 L3 New Castle Kentucky 38.28N 85.10W
108 O7 Newcastle Nebraska 42.38N 96.52W
116 P3 Newcastle Nevis I W I 17.12N 62.34W
98 G6 Newcastle New Brunswick 47.01N 65.36W
12 K5 Newcastle New S Wales 32.55S 151.46E
109 N6 Newcastle Oklahoma 35.16N 97.37W
99 M9 Newcastle Ontario 43.55N 78.35W
104 E6 New Castle Pennsylvania 41.00N 80.22W
95 N3 Newcastle S Africa 27.45S 29.55E
112 J2 Newcastle Texas 33.12N 98.45W
111 L4 Newcastle Utah 37.40N 113.34W
104 E9 New Castle Virginia 37.31N 80.09W
59 K5 Newcastle Wicklow Irish Rep 53.04N 6.04W
108 F6 Newcastle Wyoming 43.52N 104.14W
103 C7 New Castle co Delaware
13 G1 Newcastle B Queensland
98 F7 Newcastle Bridge New Brunswick 46.06N 66.02W
103 C7 Newcastle County airport Delaware 39.40N 75.35W
13 C3 Newcastle Cr N Terr Australia
56 C3 Newcastle Emlyn Dyfed Wales 52.02N 4.28W
100 E7 Newcastle Mine Alberta 51.26N 112.40W
13 G4 Newcastle Ra Queensland
57 H2 New Castleton Borders Scotland 55.11N 2.49W
57 J6 Newcastle under Lyme Staffs Eng 53.00N 2.14W
57 K3 Newcastle upon Tyne Tyne and Wear Eng 54.59N 1.35W
13 C3 Newcastle Waters N Terr Australia 17.20S 133.21E
59 D7 Newcastle West Limerick Irish Rep 52.25N 9.04W
56 L5 New Chapel Surrey Eng 51.10N 0.03W
57 J5 Newchurch Lancs Eng 53.42N 2.15W
103 G4 New City New York 41.08N 74.00W
109 B5 Newcomb New Mexico 36.16N 108.43W
104 D6 Newcomerstown Ohio 40.17N 81.37W
104 D7 New Concord Ohio 40.00N 81.46W
57 E2 New Coylton Strathclyde Scotland 55.27N 4.29W
103 G4 New Croton Res New York
57 E2 New Cumnock Strathclyde Scotland 55.24N 4.12W
57 D2 New Dailly Strathclyde Scotland 55.17N 4.44W
110 O6 Newdale Idaho 43.54N 111.36W
100 R8 Newdale Manitoba 50.22N 100.12W
100 E9 New Dayton Alberta 49.28N 112.22W
58 M3 New Deer Grampian Scotland 57.31N 2.11W
14 C10 Newdegate W Australia 33.06S 118.59E
29 B2 New Delhi Delhi India 28.37N 77.13E
95 N5 New Dell S Africa 29.09S 29.56E
98 E7 New Denmark New Brunswick 46.59N 67.36W
95 N2 New Denmark S Africa 26.43S 29.17E
101 P11 New Denver Br Col 49.59N 117.21W
103 H9 New Dorp Staten I, N Y 40.35N 74.07W
105 C3 New Echota Nat.Mon Georgia 34.32N 84.55W
107 D8 New Edinburg Arkansas 33.46N 92.16W
99 D8 New Edinburgh dist Ottawa/Ontario 45.28N 75.42W
35 F4 Newe Etan Israel 32.29N 35.32E
103 E6 New Egypt New Jersey 40.04N 74.32W
58 K3 New Elgin Grampian Scotland 57.38N 3.19W
105 E7 Newell Georgia 30.57N 82.02W
108 P7 Newell Iowa 42.36N 95.00W
105 G2 Newell N Carolina 35.14N 80.45W
108 G5 Newell S Dakota 44.44N 103.26W
105 F4 New Ellenton S Carolina 33.25N 81.43W
100 F8 Newell L Alberta 50.25N 111.55W
14 F6 Newell,L W Australia 24.50S 126.08E
107 E9 Newellton Louisiana 32.04N 91.15W
35 D7 Newe Mikh'ael Israel 31.41N 35.00E
108 H3 New England N Dakota 46.34N 102.52W
95 L6 New England S Africa 30.51S 27.30E
12 K4 New England Ra New S Wales
96 E4 New England Seamount Chain Atlantic Oc
113 F7 Newenham,C Alaska 58.40N 162.10W
103 K3 Newent Connecticut 41.37N 72.01W
56 G4 Newent Glos Eng 51.56N 2.24W
106 H6 New Era Michigan 43.33N 86.21W
94 U14 New Era S Africa 26.16S 28.24E
95 O2 New Ermelo S Africa 26.32S 30.03E
35 F3 Newe Ur Israel 32.35N 35.33E
35 C3 Newe Yam Israel 32.41N 34.56E
35 E9 Newe Zohar Israel 31.08N 35.22E
103 H4 New Fairfield Connecticut 41.28N 73.29W
104 G3 Newfane New York 43.17N 78.42W
104 N4 Newfane Vermont 42.59N 72.40W
13 K1 New Farm dist Brisbane, Qnsld
57 G6 New Ferry Merseyside Eng 53.22N 3.00W
104 P3 Newfield Maine 43.38N 70.53W
103 D7 Newfield New Jersey 39.33N 75.01W
103 A2 Newfield New York 42.22N 76.36W
101 P8 New Fish Creek Alberta 55.20N 117.20W
107 E3 New Florence Missouri 38.54N 91.26W
108 O1 Newfolden Minnesota 48.22N 96.18W
56 H6 New Forest Hants Eng
95 N5 New Formosa S Africa 29.02S 29.53E
104 O3 Newfound L New Hampshire
103 F4 Newfoundland New Jersey 41.02N 74.26W
103 D4 Newfoundland Pennsylvania 41.17N 75.21W
98 P5 Newfoundland isld Newfoundland
97 O7 Newfoundland prov Canada
96 G4 Newfoundland Basin Atlantic Oc
97 O7 Newfoundland, Island of Canada
96 F4 Newfoundland Rise Atlantic Oc
107 D2 New Franklin Missouri 39.02N 92.43W
103 A7 New Freedom Pennsylvania 39.44N 76.43W
56 A4 Newgale Dyfed Wales 51.53N 5.07W
57 E2 New Galloway Dumfries & Galloway Scotland 55.05N 4.10W
100 B9 Newgate Br Col 49.01N 115.08W
15 K3 New Georgia Grp islds Solomon Is
15 K3 New Georgia I Solomon Is
New Georgia Sd see Slot,The
98 H9 New Germany Nova Scotia 44.34N 64.44W
106 E7 New Glarus Wisconsin 42.49N 89.39W
98 K8 New Glasgow Nova Scotia 45.36N 62.38W
104 P3 New Gloucester Maine 43.57N 70.17W
116 O2 New Grant Trinidad 10.17N 61.19W
103 F7 New Gretna New Jersey 39.35N 74.28W
95 P5 New Guelderland S Africa 29.20S 31.20E
10 H2 New Guinea isld Pacific Oc
112 M6 Newgulf Texas 29.15N 95.56W
110 D1 Newhalem Washington 48.41N 121.15W
113 K7 Newhalen Alaska 59.41N 155.00W
87 E3 New Halfa Sudan 15.37N 35.36E
111 F7 Newhall California 34.23N 118.33W
55 H3 Newham bor London Eng
103 G3 New Hamburg New York 41.35N 73.56W
99 K9 New Hamburg Ontario 43.23N 80.43W
113 F5 New Hamilton Alaska 62.45N 164.00W
102 M2 New Hampshire state U.S.A.
108 S6 New Hampton Iowa 43.05N 92.19W
107 B1 New Hampton Missouri 40.17N 94.11W
103 F4 New Hampton New York 41.25N 74.24W
95 O5 New Hanover S Africa 29.21S 30.33E
15 L5 New Hanover isld Bismarck Arch
104 Q3 New Harbor Maine 43.53N 69.33W
107 J3 New Harmony Indiana 38.08N 87.57W
103 J3 New Hartford Connecticut 41.52N 72.58W
103 J4 New Haven Connecticut 41.18N 72.55W
56 M6 Newhaven E Sussex Eng 50.47N 0.03E
106 J8 New Haven Indiana 41.04N 85.01W
107 E3 New Haven Missouri 38.37N 91.15W
104 D8 New Haven W Virginia 38.59N 81.58W
108 F5 New Haven Wyoming 44.45N 104.51W
103 H4 New Haven co Connecticut
101 K8 New Hazelton Br Col 55.15N 127.30W
9 B10 New Hebrides condominium Pacific Oc
10 N4 New Hebrides Basin Pacific Oc
122 H9 New Hebrides Ridge Pacific Oc
10 O5 New Hebrides Trench Pacific Oc
57 J5 New Hey Greater Manchester Eng 53.36N 2.05W
57 N5 New Holland Humberside Eng 53.42N 0.22W
106 E9 New Holland Illinois 40.12N 89.34W
103 B6 New Holland Pennsylvania 40.06N 76.36W
106 F6 New Holstein Wisconsin 43.57N 88.06W
107 C7 Newhope Arkansas 34.13N 93.55W
103 E6 New Hope Pennsylvania 40.22N 74.56W
58 J7 Newhouse Strathclyde Scotland 55.50N 3.56W
57 O7 New Hunstanton Norfolk Eng 52.56N 0.30E
121 D10 New I Falkland Is 51.43N 61.16W
107 E12 New Iberia Louisiana 30.00N 91.51W
103 J3 Newington Connecticut 41.43N 72.45W
105 F5 Newington Georgia 32.35N 81.30W
56 N5 Newington Kent Eng 51.22N 0.40E
94 L4 Newington S Africa 24.50S 31.17E
59 F5 New Inn Galway Irish Rep 53.18N 8.30W
59 G7 Newinn Tipperary Irish Rep 52.26N 7.53W
56 O5 New Inn Green Kent Eng 51.06N 1.03E
15 L5 New Ireland isld Bismarck Arch
102 M2 New Jersey state U.S.A.
29 B6 New Kandla Gujarat India 23.00N 70.11E
104 F6 New Kensington Pennsylvania 40.34N 79.46W
104 J9 New Kent Virginia 37.32N 76.59W
109 F6 Newkirk New Mexico 35.03N 104.18W
109 N5 Newkirk Oklahoma 36.54N 97.03W
113 E5 New Knockhock Alaska 62.10N 165.00W
105 L2 New L N Carolina 35.39N 76.21W
14 E8 Newland Ra W Australia
11 D5 Newlands dist Wellington New Zealand
103 H2 New Lebanon New York 42.27N 73.24W
58 M3 New Leeds Grampian Scotland 57.34N 2.00W
95 N5 Newleigh S Africa 29.11S 29.59E
108 J3 New Leipzig N Dakota 46.23N 101.57W
103 H2 New Lenox Massachusetts 42.23N 73.15W
104 C7 New Lexington Ohio 39.43N 82.13W
112 G1 Newlin Texas 34.37N 100.26W
106 D6 New Lisbon Wisconsin 43.52N 90.11W
99 L5 New Liskeard Ontario 47.31N 79.41W
98 P10 New Liverpool Quebec 46.45N 71.16W
103 K4 New London Connecticut 41.21N 72.06W
106 C9 New London Iowa 40.54N 91.23W
108 Q4 New London Minnesota 45.18N 94.55W
107 E2 New London Missouri 39.34N 91.24W
104 C5 New London Ohio 41.05N 82.24W
103 C7 New London Pennsylvania 39.47N 75.53W
106 F5 New London Wisconsin 44.23N 88.43W
103 K4 New London co Connecticut
57 D3 New Luce Dumfries & Galloway Scotland 54.57N 4.51W
56 S9 Newlyn Cornwall Eng 50.06N 5.34W
58 M4 New Machar Grampian Scotland 57.15N 2.11W
95 K2 New Machavie S Africa 26.47S 26.55E
107 G5 New Madrid Missouri 36.34N 89.32W
58 J7 Newmains Strathclyde Scotland 55.47N 3.53W
55 D5 New Malden London Eng 51.25N 0.15W
111 C4 Newman California 37.20N 121.04W
107 J2 Newman Illinois 39.50N 88.00W
109 D9 Newman New Mexico 32.01N 106.20W
11 K7 Newman New Zealand 40.36S 175.42E
108 N8 Newman Grove Nebraska 41.46N 97.46W
14 C6 Newman,Mt W Australia 23.20S 119.34E
98 T5 Newman's Cove Newfoundland 48.35N 53.12W
103 B6 Newmanstown Pennsylvania 40.21N 76.13W
107 K7 New Market Alabama 34.56N 86.25W
59 E7 Newmarket Cork Irish Rep 52.13N 9.00W
108 Q9 New Market Iowa 40.44N 94.55W
116 H1 Newmarket Jamaica, W I 18.09N 77.55W
104 P3 Newmarket New Hampshire 43.04N 70.57W
12 G5 Newmarket New S Wales 34.43S 144.31E
99 L8 Newmarket Ontario 44.03N 79.27W
95 N6 Newmarket S Africa 30.22S 29.28E
56 M3 Newmarket Suffolk Eng 52.15N 0.25E
104 G8 New Market Virginia 38.39N 78.41W
11 C2 Newmarket dist Auckland New Zealand
13 K1 Newmarket dist Brisbane, Qnsld
59 E6 Newmarket-on-Fergus Clare Irish Rep 52.46N 8.54W
103 H2 New Marlborough Massachusetts 42.08N 73.14W
104 C7 New Marshfield Ohio 39.20N 82.15W
104 E7 New Martinsville W Virginia 39.39N 80.52W
104 D7 New Matamoras Ohio 39.31N 81.06W
110 J5 New Meadows Idaho 44.59N 116.16W
102 E4 New Mexico state U.S.A.
104 A7 New Miami Ohio 39.25N 84.33W
103 H3 New Milford Connecticut 41.35N 73.25W
103 J6 New Milford New Jersey 40.56N 74.01W
103 F4 New Milford New York 41.14N 74.25W
103 C3 New Milford Pennsylvania 41.52N 75.44W
57 K5 New Mill W Yorks Eng 53.35N 1.44W
57 J6 New Mills Derbys Eng 53.23N 2.00W
57 E1 Newmilns Strathclyde Scotland 55.37N 4.20W
112 E2 New Moore Texas 33.01N 102.04W
57 K2 New Moor House Northumb Eng 55.21N 1.50W
105 C4 Newnan Georgia 33.23N 84.48W
105 E8 Newnan L Florida 29.38N 82.15W
12 K5 Newnes New S Wales 33.10S 150.12E
56 G4 Newnham Glos Eng 51.49N 2.27W
56 N5 Newnham Kent Eng 51.18N 0.49E
14 B9 New Norcia W Australia 30.58S 116.15E
12 H9 New Norfolk Tasmania 42.46S 147.02E
100 E6 New Norway Alberta 52.54N 112.58W
107 F11 New Orleans Louisiana 30.00N 90.03W
100 O6 New Osgoode Saskatchewan 52.58N 103.49W
104 H7 New Oxford Pennsylvania 39.52N 77.04W
103 F3 New Paltz New York 41.45N 74.05W
104 A7 New Paris Ohio 39.52N 84.46W
103 A7 New Park Pennsylvania 39.44N 76.30W
107 K3 New Pekin Indiana 38.31N 86.01W
104 D6 New Philadelphia Ohio 40.31N 81.28W
110 E7 New Pine Creek Oregon 42.00N 120.19W
58 M3 New Pitsligo Grampian Scotland 57.35N 2.12W
110 J6 New Plymouth Idaho 43.58N 116.48W
11 J6 New Plymouth New Zealand 39.03S 174.04E
107 E6 Newport Arkansas 35.35N 91.16W
116 B2 New Port Curaçao W I 12.08N 68.50W
103 C7 Newport Delaware 39.43N 75.36W
56 B3 Newport Dyfed Wales 52.01N 4.50W
56 M4 Newport Essex Eng 51.58N 0.13E
56 F4 Newport Gwent Wales 51.35N 3.00W
107 J2 Newport Indiana 39.52N 87.24W
56 J6 Newport I of Wight Eng 50.42N 1.18W
116 J2 Newport Jamaica, W I 17.57N 77.30W
107 M2 Newport Kentucky 39.05N 84.27W
104 Q2 Newport Maine 44.50N 69.17W
59 C4 Newport Mayo Irish Rep 53.53N 9.32W
106 L7 Newport Michigan 42.00N 83.18W
108 S5 Newport Minnesota 44.52N 93.00W
105 L3 Newport N Carolina 34.47N 76.03W
108 L7 Newport Nebraska 42.38N 99.19W
104 N3 Newport New Hampshire 43.22N 72.11W
103 D8 Newport New Jersey 39.18N 75.10W
12 M5 Newport New S Wales 33.40S 151.19E
104 A7 Newport Ohio 39.07N 84.26W
110 A5 Newport Oregon 44.39N 124.04W
104 H6 Newport Pennsylvania 40.29N 77.09W
98 H5 Newport Quebec 48.16N 64.46W
103 M3 Newport Rhode I 41.30N 71.19W
56 G2 Newport Shropshire Eng 52.47N 2.22W
105 D2 Newport Tennessee 35.58N 83.13W
112 J2 Newport Texas 33.28N 98.02W
59 F6 Newport Tipperary Irish Rep 52.43N 8.25W
104 N2 Newport Vermont 44.56N 72.13W
110 H1 Newport Washington 48.11N 117.03W
103 M3 Newport co Rhode I
12 B7 Newport dist Melbourne, Vic
103 M4 Newport B Rhode I
111 G8 Newport Beach California 33.38N 117.55W
104 J10 Newport News Virginia 36.59N 76.26W
58 L6 Newport-on-Tay Fife Scotland 56.27N 2.56W
56 K3 Newport Pagnell Bucks Eng 52.05N 0.44W
105 E9 New Port Richey Florida 28.15N 82.44W
59 J2 Newport Trench Tyrone N Ireland 54.38N 6.31W
108 R5 New Prague Minnesota 44.34N 93.32W
103 H3 New Preston Connecticut 41.41N 73.22W
116 F2 New Providence isld Bahamas 25.03N 77.25W
56 A7 Newquay Cornwall Eng 50.25N 5.05W
56 C3 New Quay Dyfed Wales 52.13N 4.22W
105 E8 New R Florida
117 A3 New R Guyana
105 K3 New,R N Carolina
104 E10 New,R N Car/Virginia
56 E3 New Radnor Powys Wales 52.15N 3.10W
59 K5 Newrath Bridge Wicklow Irish Rep 53.00N 6.05W
109 G1 New Raymer Colorado 40.36N 103.51W
108 R6 New Richland Minnesota 43.53N 93.30W
104 A8 New Richmond Ohio 38.57N 84.16W
98 G5 New Richmond Quebec 48.12N 65.52W
106 B4 New Richmond Wisconsin 45.08N 92.33W
103 C5 New Ringgold Pennsylvania 40.42N 76.00W
107 M5 New River Tennessee 36.23N 84.32W
11 C13 New River Harb inlet New Zealand
105 K3 New River Inlet N Carolina
107 E11 New Roads Louisiana 30.40N 91.28W
103 N6 New Rochelle New York 40.54N 73.47W
108 L2 New Rockford N Dakota 47.40N 99.09W
56 N6 New Romney Kent Eng 50.59N 0.57E
107 K2 New Ross Indiana 39.58N 86.42W
59 J7 New Ross Wexford Irish Rep 52.24N 6.56W
59 K3 Newry Down N Ireland 54.11N 6.20W
104 P2 Newry Maine 44.31N 70.48W
13 A3 Newry N Terr Australia 16.01S 129.14E
104 G6 Newry Pennsylvania 40.24N 78.27W
59 K3 Newry Canal Down N Ireland 54.15N 6.22W
108 J3 New Salem N Dakota 46.51N 101.24W
103 A7 New Salem Pennsylvania 39.54N 76.46W
104 F7 New Salem Pennsylvania 39.55N 79.49W
58 K6 New Scone Tayside Scotland 56.25N 3.25W
57 L3 New Seaham Durham Eng 54.50N 1.22W
108 S8 New Sharon Iowa 41.26N 92.40W
New Siberian Is see Novosibirskiye Ostrova
105 G8 New Smyrna Beach Florida 29.01N 80.56W
10 J8 New South Wales state Australia
13 J5 Newstead Queensland 21.52S 148.50E
104 C7 New Straitsville Ohio 39.34N 82.16W
113 J7 New Stuyahok Alaska 59.30N 157.22W
89 J7 New Tamale Ghana 9.09N 1.07W
105 D1 New Tazewell Tennessee 36.25N 83.37W
95 O3 New Tendeka S Africa 27.43S 30.51E
113 E6 Newtok Alaska 60.59N 164.40W
107 L10 Newton Alabama 31.20N 85.39W
56 M3 Newton Cambs Eng 52.07N 0.06E
57 L3 Newton Cleveland Eng 54.30N 1.07W
57 G2 Newton Dumfries & Galloway Scotland 55.15N 3.25W
107 H3 Newton Illinois 38.59N 88.10W
108 R8 Newton Iowa 41.41N 93.02W
109 N3 Newton Kansas 38.02N 97.22W
57 J5 Newton Lancs England 53.58N 2.27W
103 M2 Newton Massachusetts 42.20N 71.13W
107 G9 Newton Mississippi 32.20N 89.10W
105 F2 Newton N Carolina 35.42N 81.14W
103 E4 Newton New Jersey 41.03N 74.45W
56 N2 Newton Norfolk Eng 52.42N 0.42E
58 F6 Newton Strathclyde Scotland 56.08N 5.09W
112 O5 Newton Texas 30.51N 93.45W
110 O8 Newton Utah 41.52N 111.59W
104 O9 Newton dist Boston, Mass
56 D6 Newton Abbot Devon Eng 50.32N 3.36W
57 G3 Newton Arlosh Cumbria Eng 54.53N 3.15W
57 K3 Newton Aycliffe Durham Eng 54.37N 1.34W
104 L2 Newton Falls New York 44.13N 74.58W
104 E5 Newton Falls Ohio 41.13N 80.57W
56 C7 Newton Ferrers Devon Eng 50.18N 4.02W
58 K7 Newtongranqe Lothian Scotland 55.52N 3.04W
105 J2 Newton Grove N Carolina 35.14N 78.21W
104 H6 Newton Hamilton Pennsylvania 40.24N 77.52W
58 H4 Newtonmore Highland Scotland 57.04N 4.08W
57 K2 Newton on the Moor Northumb Eng 55.21N 1.44W
56 E6 Newton Poppleford Devon Eng 50.42N 3.19W
57 H3 Newton Reigny Cumbria Eng 54.41N 2.48W
110 O8 Newton Res Utah 41.54N 111.53W
57 E3 Newton Stewart Dumfries & Galloway Scotland 54.57N 4.29W
50 T13 Newtontoppen mt Spitsbergen 79.00N 17.45E
103 E6 Newtown Bucks, Pennsylvania 40.13N 74.56W
103 H4 Newtown Connecticut 41.25N 73.19W
57 H3 Newtown Cumbria Eng 53.58N 2.46W
89 H9 Newtown Ghana 5.05N 3.05W
56 J5 Newtown Hants Eng 51.23N 1.19W
56 F3 Newtown Hereford & Worcs Eng 52.06N 2.34W
107 C1 Newtown Missouri 40.23N 93.20W
98 T4 Newtown Newfoundland 49.12N 53.33W
56 E2 Newtown Powys Wales 52.32N 3.19W
95 B9 Newtown S Africa 33.42S 19.00E
103 B5 Newtown Schuylkill, Pennsylvania 40.40N 76.21W
108 H2 New Town S Dakota 47.59N 102.32W
104 H9 Newtown Virginia 37.55N 77.08W
12 F8 New Town dist Hobart, Tasmania
12 M7 Newtown dist Sydney, N S W
11 C6 Newtown dist Wellington New Zealand
59 L2 Newtownabbey Antrim N Ireland 54.40N 5.57W
59 L2 Newtownards Down N Ireland 54.36N 5.41W
12 F8 New Town B Tasmania
Newtownbarry see Bunclody
Newtown Bellew see Moylough
59 H3 Newtown Butler Fermanagh N Ireland 54.11N 7.21W
12 F8 New Town Cr Tasmania
59 K2 Newtown Crommelin Antrim N Ireland 55.00N 6.13W
59 G2 Newtown Cunningham Donegal Irish Rep 54.59N 7.31W
59 J3 Newtownhamilton Armagh N Ireland 54.12N 6.35W
59 K4 Newtown Monasterboice Louth Irish Rep 53.47N 6.24W
59 K5 Newtown Mount Kennedy Wicklow Irish Rep 53.06N 6.07W
57 H1 Newtown St.Boswells Borders Scotland 55.34N 2.40W
59 D6 Newtown Sandes Kerry Irish Rep 52.30N 9.22W
103 D7 Newtown Square Pennsylvania 39.59N 75.24W
59 H2 Newtownstewart Tyrone N Ireland 54.43N 7.22W
103 C5 New Tripoli Pennsylvania 40.41N 75.45W
58 K5 Newtyle Tayside Scotland 56.34N 3.09W
108 Q5 New Ulm Minnesota 44.19N 94.28W
112 L6 New Ulm Texas 29.53N 96.30W
108 H5 New Underwood S Dakota 44.07N 102.50W
107 L10 Newville Alabama 31.25N 85.21W
111 B2 Newville California 39.49N 122.32W
104 H6 Newville Pennsylvania 40.10N 77.23W
108 R8 New Virginia Iowa 41.09N 93.45W
104 C6 New Washington Ohio 40.57N 82.52W
98 M7 New Waterford C Breton I, Nova Scotia 46.17N 60.05W
112 M5 New Waverly Texas 30.33N 95.30W
101 M11 New Westminster Br Col 49.10N 122.58W
107 K2 New Whiteland Indiana 39.32N 86.05W
104 H7 New Windsor Maryland 39.33N 77.08W
103 F4 New Windsor New York 41.28N 74.03W
98 S4 New World I Newfoundland
110 F8 New Year L Nevada 41.50N 119.50W
57 N6 New York Lincs Eng 53.05N 0.09W
103 M9 New York New York
102 L2 New York state U.S.A.
103 J8 New York B.,Lower New York
103 J8 New York B.,Upper New York/New Jersey
111 J6 New York Mts California
10 Q10 New Zealand dominion Australasia
10 O11 New Zealand Plat sea feature Pacific Oc
72 G4 Nexon France 45.40N 1.12E
104 A5 Ney Ohio 41.24N 84.33W
46 N1 Neya U.S.S.R. 58.18N 43.40E
46 N1 Neya R U.S.S.R.
31 A4 Neybasteh Afghanistan 32.57N 60.54E
41 N5 Neyelova, Zaliv B U.S.S.R.
32 E4 Neyestānak Iran 32.59N 52.50E
56 B4 Neyland Dyfed Wales 51.43N 4.57W
32 F6 Neyrīz Iran 29.14N 54.18E
66 E4 Neyruz Switzerland 46.47N 7.04E
32 G6 Neyseh Iran 28.04N 56.25E
32 H2 Neyshābūr Iran 36.13N 58.49E
47 L1 Neyto,Oz L U.S.S.R.
47 N4 Neyva R U.S.S.R.
28 D5 Neyveli Tamil Nadu India 11.36N 79.26E
47 M4 Neyvo Rudyanka U.S.S.R. 57.21N 60.10E
47 N4 Neyvo Shaytanskiy U.S.S.R. 57.48N 61.12E
28 C6 Neyyattinkara Kerala India 8.26N 77.06E
44 C1 Nezamayevskaya U.S.S.R. 46.09N 40.19E
65 L3 Nežárka R Czechoslovakia
26 U15 Nez de Bœuf mt Réunion Ind Oc 21.11S 55.38E
45 C5 Nezhin Ukraine U.S.S.R. 51.03N 31.54E
44 E3 Nezlobnaya U.S.S.R. 44.09N 43.23E
41 B3 Neznayemyy,Zaliv gulf Novaya Zemlya U.S.S.R.
110 J3 Nezperce Idaho 46.15N 116.14W
107 D11 Nezpique R Louisiana
20 N3 Nezugaseki Japan 38.32N 139.32E
64 Q4 Nezvěstice Czechoslovakia 49.39N 13.32E
85 M7 Nezzi,Gebel mt Egypt 25.35N 32.58E
88 J6 N'fiss R Morocco
18 H5 Ngabang Borneo Indon 0.15N 109.54E
91 E5 Ngabé Congo 3.12S 16.12E
15 C7 Ngabordamlu,Tg C Moluccas Indon 6.58S 134.13E
92 G10 Ngabu Malawi 16.27S 34.55E
25 E5 Nga Chong,Khao mt Thailand 14.47N 98.18E
90 F5 Ngadda, R Nigeria
90 K9 Ngadza Cent Afr Rep 5.08N 20.07E
92 J7 Ngaga Tanzania 10.50S 38.40E
25 M8 Ngagahtawng Burma 25.58N 96.40E
95 N3 Ngagane S Africa 27.51S 29.59E
25 B2 Ngahan Burma 21.22N 92.29E
11 F9 Ngahere New Zealand 42.23S 171.28E
11 C5 Ngaio dist Wellington New Zealand
19 N1 Ngajangel isld Palau Is Pacific Oc 8.05N 134.45E
92 G5 Ngajira Tanzania 7.40S 34.54E
90 G5 Ngala Nigeria 12.20N 14.11E
91 G2 Ngale Zaïre 2.27N 21.33E
87 F8 Ngalibong mt Ethiopia 5.40N 36.05E
Ngaliema, Mt see Stanley, Mt
19 D2 Ngalipaëng Indonesia 3.25N 125.37E
9 S3 Ngaloa Harb Kandavu Fiji
90 H6 N'Gama Chad 11.45N 17.06E
91 D6 Ngamaba Congo 4.06S 15.05E
11 L6 Ngamatea Swamp New Zealand
92 B10 Ngambwe Rapids Zambia 17.15S 24.10E
23 A3 Ngamda Xizang Zizhiqu China 31.00N 96.44E
24 J10 Ngamda Xizang Zizhiqu China 31.00N 9 .44E
19 N1 Ngamegei Passage Palau Is Pacific Oc
94 G3 Ngami, Lake Botswana
94 G2 Ngamiland dist Botswana
92 C11 Ngamo Zimbabwe 19.08S 27.32E
24 F11 Ngamring Xizang Zizhiqu China 29.15N 87.15E
Ngan Chau see Round I Hong Kong
89 B5 Nganda Senegal 13.48N 15.26W
87 C8 Ngangala Sudan 4.46N 31.54E
30 E2 Ngang Chhu R Xizang Zizhiqu
93 M7 Ngangerabeli Plain Kenya
24 D10 Ngangla Ringco L Xizang Zizhiqu China 31.40N 83.00E
Nganglaring Tso L see Ngangla Ringco
24 C9 Nganglong Kangri mt ra Xizang Zizhiqu China
92 H6 Ngangora Tanzania 9.50S 37.56E
Ngangtse Tso L see Ngangzê Co
24 E10 Ngangzê Co L Xizang Zizhiqu China 31.00N 87.00E
18 J9 Nganjuk Java Indon 7.36S 111.56E
25 H3 Ngan Pha R Vietnam
25 H3 Ngan Sau R Vietnam
25 H1 Ngan Son Vietnam 22.25N 106.00E
Ngao see Muang Ngao
90 F8 N'Gaoundéré Cameroon 7.20N 13.35E
11 E11 Ngapara New Zealand 44.58S 170.45E
25 C2 Ngape Burma 20.04N 94.30E
93 G2 Ngapoi Hills Kenya
11 L6 Ngapuketurua mt New Zealand 39.04S 176.03E
11 E12 Ngapuna New Zealand 45.27S 170.10E
25 C4 Ngaputaw Burma 16.31N 94.41E
92 G7 Ngara Malawi 10.14S 34.06E
93 B8 Ngara Tanzania 2.30S 30.40E
89 B4 Ngaraf Senegal 15.21N 15.20W
92 J6 Ngarambi Tanzania 8.28S 38.40E
90 K7 Ngardiam Cent Afr Rep 9.00N 20.58E
19 N2 Ngardmau Palau Is Pacific Oc 7.37N 134.36E
19 N2 Ngardmau B Palau Is Pacific Oc
19 M3 Ngardololok Palau Is Pacific Oc 7.01N 134.16E
19 N1 Ngaregur isld Palau Is Pacific Oc 7.45N 134.38E
19 N1 Ngariungs isld Palau Is Pacific Oc 8.04N 134.44E
47 L3 Ngarka Pyryayakha R U.S.S.R.
11 K5 Ngaroma New Zealand 38.16S 175.41E
11 K4 Ngaruawahia New Zealand 37.41S 175.10E
11 L6 Ngaruroro R New Zealand
90 B6 N'Gaski Nigeria 10.24N 4.42E
93 J10 Ngasumet Tanzania 4.29S 37.10E
11 H1 Ngataki New Zealand 34.43S 173.03E
122 B10 Ngatangiia Rarotonga Pacific Oc 21.14S 159.44W
11 M5 Ngatapa New Zealand 38.35S 177.49E
11 K4 Ngatea New Zealand 37.14S 175.33E
19 N2 Ngateguil,Pt Palau Is Pacific Oc 7.27N 134.37E
25 C4 Ngathainggyaung Burma 17.22N 95.04E
11 K5 Ngatira New Zealand 38.05S 175.58E
93 M8 Ngau Kenya 2.24S 40.12E
9 U8 Ngau isld Fiji 18.00S 179.16E
23 C8 Ngau Mei Hoi B Hong Kong
11 C5 Ngauranga New Zealand 41.15S 174.49E
11 K6 Ngauruhoe Vol New Zealand 39.10S 175.40E
Ngawa see Aba
11 L4 Ngawaro New Zealand 37.57S 176.12E
18 J9 Ngawi Java Indon 7.23S 111.22E
25 E7 Ngawun Chaung R Burma
90 L7 Ngaya R Cent Afr Rep
90 L7 Ngaya,Djebel mt Cent Afr Rep 9.15N 23.29E
25 C4 Ngayok B Burma
91 G4 Ngele Zaïre 0.30S 20.22E
90 F5 Ngelewa Nigeria 12.31N 13.43E
19 M3 Ngemelis Is Palau Is Pacific Oc
19 N3 Ngeregong isld Palau Is Pacific Oc 7.07N 134.22E
92 J5 Ngerengere Tanzania 6.45S 38.06E
19 M3 Ngergoi isld Palau Is Pacific Oc 7.06N 134.17E
19 M3 Ngesebus isld Palau Is Pacific Oc 7.04N 134.16E
92 E11 Ngezi R Zimbabwe
92 E12 Ngezi R Zimbabwe
92 E11 Ngezi Dam Zimbabwe 18.38S 30.25E
9 T5 Nggamea isld Fiji 16.46S 179.46W
15 L3 Nggatokae I Solomon Is
15 L3 Nggela I Solomon Is 9.05S 160.15E
9 U4 Nggele Levu isld Fiji 16.08S 179.10W
9 T5 Nggeleni Taveuni Fiji 16.45S 179.53W
94 G2 Ng-gokha R Botswana
94 G3 Nghabe R Botswana
Nghia Hung see Phu Qui
91 E6 Ngi Zaïre 4.27S 17.17E
91 D6 Ngidinga Zaïre 5.46S 15.17E
93 K7 Ngien mt Kenya 1.02S 38.19E
18 K9 Ngimbang Java Indon 7.17S 112.14E
92 H6 Ngindo tribe Tanzania
91 D12 N 'Giva Angola 17.03S 15.41E
91 D5 Ngo Congo 2.28S 15.43E
19 N2 Ngobasangel isld Palau Is Pacific Oc 7.17N 134.21E
95 P3 Ngobeni S Africa 27.40S 31.10E
91 C9 N'Goende Angola 10.19S 13.33E
19 E3 Ngofakiaha Moluccas Indon 0.23N 127.24E
90 F6 Ngohi Nigeria 10.44N 12.45E
91 C2 Ngoïla Cameroon 2.36N 13.58E
30 H2 Ngojumba Glacier Nepal
25 J5 Ngok Linh mt Vietnam 15.04N 107.59E
91 D4 Ngoko Congo 0.31S 15.19E
91 D3 Ngoko R Congo 1.58N 15.32E
22 E9 Ngola Shankou pass Qinghai China
90 E7 Ngol Bembal Nigeria 8.31N 10.42E
90 L7 Ngolo Cent Afr Rep 9.57N 22.13E
93 D4 Ngoma Uganda 1.11N 32.02E
92 F6 Ngomba Tanzania 8.26S 32.59E
91 E3 N'Gombe Congo 0.12N 17.06E
95 O9 Ngome S Africa 27.48S 31.28E
Ngome Zambiasee Nanzhila
91 B2 Ngomedzap Cameroon 3.18N 11.13E
93 M8 Ngomeni,Ras pt Kenya 2.59S 40.14E
24 H9 Ngom Qu R Qinghai China
24 J10 Ngom Qu R Qinghai China
23 A3 Ngom Qu R Xizang Zizhiqu China
Ngon see Ban Ngon
93 H7 Ngong Kenya 1.22S 36.40E
93 H7 Ngong Hills Kenya
92 E5 Ngongo Tanzania 7.50S 31.47E
91 F10 Ngongola Angola 13.57S 18.08E
11 L5 Ngongotaha New Zealand 38.04S 176.14E
92 F7 Ngoni tribe Malawi
Ngon Shun Chau see Stonecutters I
92 A10 Ngonya Falls Zambia 16.40S 23.39E
93 E4 Ngora Uganda 1.28N 33.47E
Ngoré see Iguela, Lag.
93 G7 Ngorengore Kenya 1.03S 35.30E
23 A1 Ngoring Qinghai China 35.01N 96.43E
24 J8 Ngoring Qinghai China 35.00N 96.45E
23 A1 Ngoring Hu L Qinghai China
24 J8 Ngoring Hu L Qinghai China
89 G6 Ngorolaba Upper Volta 11.51N 4.59W
93 G9 Ngorongoro crater Tanzania
93 A8 Ngosi Burundi 2.54S 29.48E
91 F6 Ngoso Zaïre 4.46S 19.18E
90 H10 Ngoto Cent Afr Rep 3.59N 17.19E
93 E3 Ngotokwe Uganda 2.25N 33.27E
90 M8 Ngoua mt Cent Afr Rep 7.59N 24.40E
91 B2 Ngoulemakong Cameroon 3.06N 11.24E
91 B4 N'Goumé R Gabon
91 C5 Ngoungi Congo 3.46S 12.07E
91 B4 N'Gounié reg Gabon
90 H5 Ngoura Chad 12.44N 16.21E
90 G5 N'Gouri Chad 13.42N 15.19E
90 L7 Ngourou Cent Afr Rep 9.45N 22.37E
90 F4 Ngourti Niger 15.21N 13.10E
88 Q5 Ngoussa Algeria 32.10N 5.16E
91 E6 Ngoyo Zaïre 5.36S 17.10E
92 F4 Ngoywa Tanzania 5.55S 32.49E
92 D3 Ngozi Burundi 2.54S 29.49E
95 N7 Ngqeleni S Africa 31.40S 29.02E
93 E8 Ngudu Tanzania 2.57S 33.21E
90 F9 Nguélémendouka Cameroon 4.19N 13.01E
89 C4 Nguigilore Mauritania 16.00N 13.20W
90 F4 Nguigmi Niger 14.19N 13.06E
90 E9 N'Guila Cameroon 4.41N 11.43E
93 K7 Ngula Kenya 1.02S 38.22E
92 J5 Ngulakula Tanzania 7.45S 38.49E
93 K9 Ngulia mt Kenya 3.01S 38.10E
17 N10 Ngulu atoll Caroline Is Pacific Oc 8.30N 137.30E
87 M10 Ngumi I Somalia 0.47S 42.18E
25 G3 Ngum,Nam R Laos
9 C11 Nguna isld New Hebrides 17.29S 168.23E
93 E9 Ngunga Tanzania 3.40S 33.35E
11 J2 Ngunguru New Zealand 35.38S 174.31E
93 K6 Nguni Kenya 0.48S 38.19E
93 K6 Nguni mt Kenya 0.50S 38.25E
92 G7 Nguni tribe Tanzania
19 B9 Ngunju, Tanjung C Indon 10.19S 120.29E
18 J10 Ngunut Java Indonesia 8.06S 111.59E
93 H9 Ngurdoto Crater Tanzania 3.17S 36.55E
93 H9 Ngurdoto Crater Nat.Park Tanzania
90 E5 Nguru Nigeria 12.53N 10.30E
92 H4 Nguru tribe Tanzania
93 F7 Nguruimi tribal area Tanzania
92 E4 Nguruka Tanzania 5.09S 31.03E
92 D3 Ngusa Zaïre 3.18S 28.30E
25 H1 Nguyen Binh Vietnam 22.41N 105.55E
94 H5 Ngwaketse dist Botswana
92 H7 Ngwale Tanzania 10.05S 37.56E
92 C11 Ngwasha Pan Zimbabwe 19.28S 26.12E
92 H6 Ngwasi Tanzania 8.30S 37.29E
Ngwavuma S Africasee Ingwavuma
95 O8 Ngwavuma R Swaziland
95 P2 Ngwempisi R Swaziland
92 B10 Ngweze Namibia 17.27S 24.10E
94 H2 Ngwezumba Botswana 18.22S 24.52E
94 N4 Nhachengue Mozambique 22.51S 35.11E
94 N5 Nhacoongo Mozambique 24.18S 35.14E
92 F10 Nhamassonge Mozambique 16.49S 33.32E
118 B3 Nhambiquara Brazil 12.50S 59.49W
117 B6 Nhamundá Brazil 2.15S 56.41W
117 A5 Nhamundá, R Brazil
92 F11 Nhandugue R Mozambique
94 N5 Nhangulaze, L Mozambique 24.00S 34.28E
91 E9 Nharea Angola 11.38S 16.58E
91 G10 Nhaseque Angola 13.27S 21.10E
25 K6 Nha Trang Vietnam 12.15N 109.10E
118 C6 Nhecolândia Brazil 19.17S 56.58W
91 E12 Nhenha watercourse Angola
91 D9 Nhia R Angola
25 G3 Nhiep,Nam R Laos
12 F6 Nhill Victoria 36.20S 141.40E
25 K7 Nhim,Da R Vietnam
95 P3 Nhlangano Swaziland 27.06S 31.12E
95 O6 Nhlavini S Africa 30.05S 30.17E
25 H4 Nhommarath Laos 17.39N 105.12E
13 D1 Nhulunbuy N Terr Australia 12.30S 136.56E
91 G11 Nhundo Angola 14.24S 21.24E
91 G10 Nhungo Angola 13.17S 20.06E
25 H3 Nhu Xuan Vietnam 19.35N 105.38E
92 C3 Niabembe Zaïre 2.10S 27.42E
89 H8 Niablé Ivory Coast 6.40N 3.15W
30 E1 Niacharphu Xizang Zizhiqu 31.44N 81.12E
91 F6 Niadi Zaïre 4.25S 18.53E
89 G4 Niafounke Mali 15.59N 4.00W
89 E4 Niagané Mali 14.15N 9.32W
108 N1 Niagara N Dakota 48.00N 97.55W
11 D13 Niagara New Zealand 46.37S 169.10E
106 F4 Niagara Wisconsin 45.47N 88.00W
104 F3 Niagara Falls New York 43.06N 79.04W
99 L9 Niagara Falls Ontario 43.05N 79.06W
99 L9 Niagara-on-the-Lake Ontario 43.14N 79.06W
104 F3 Niagara R New York
89 E5 Niagassola Guinea 12.24N 9.03W
31 J2 Niagzu Kashmir 34.03N 78.55E
18 K4 Niah Sarawak Malaysia 3.54N 113.41E
29 J3 Niak Nepal 28.30N 84.48E
89 G7 Niakaramandougou Ivory Coast 8.32N 5.10W
89 A4 Niakhar Senegal 14.28N 16.24W
89 L5 Niamey Niger 13.32N 2.05E
89 K4 Niamey reg Niger
89 F5 Niaming Mali 13.21N 6.58W
19 E1 Niampak Indonesia 4.04N 126.43E
89 K7 Niamtougou Togo 9.50N 1.08E
91 G6 Nianga Zaïre 5.58S 20.27E
87 A9 Niangara Zaïre 3.45N 27.54E
89 H4 Niangaye,L Mali 15.50N 2.50W
89 G7 Niangbo Ivory Coast 8.49N 5.09W
89 G7 Niangbo,Pic de mt Ivory Coast 9.00N 5.20W
23 D1 Niangniangba Gansu China 34.19N 105.49E
107 D4 Niangua R Missouri
Niangxi see Xinshao
92 C1 Nia-Nia Zaïre 1.30N 27.41E
89 E5 Niantankoura Mali 13.38N 9.31W
103 K4 Niantic Connecticut 41.20N 72.12W
21 B4 Nianzishan Heilongjiang China 47.31N 122.53E
84 F3 Niáou Greece 39.17N 23.10E
91 K2 Niapu Zaïre 2.25N 26.31E
48 S9 Niaqornârssuk Greenland 68.15N 52.50W
48 S7 Niaqornat Greenland 70.50N 53.45W
48 S12 Niaqúngunaq fjord Greenland
15 F6 Niar R Papua New Guinea
110 L2 Niarada Montana 47.49N 114.38W

91 C5 Niari div Congo
91 C5 Niari R Congo
69 C12 Nias isld Indonesia
90 H7 Niassa Chad 8.50N 16.45E
92 H8 Niassa dist Mozambique
Niassa, L see Nyasa, L
84 E8 Niáta Greece 36.54N 22.50E
122 C14 Niau atoll Tuamotu Is Pacific Oc 16.09S 146.20W
32 J3 Niāzābād Iran 34.14N 60.11E
33 J4 Nibāk Saudi Arabia 24.24N 50.51E
20 B2 Niban Tōkyō Japan
110 R4 Nibbe Montana 45.59N 108.02W
79 F5 Nibbiano Italy 44.55N 9.19E
60 J9 Nibbixwoud Netherlands 52.41N 5.03E
53 D3 Nibe Denmark 56.59N 9.39E
53 D2 Nibe Bredning B Denmark 57.00N 9.37E
95 P9 Nibela S Africa 27.52S 32.25E
14 E5 Nibil Well W Australia 22.20S 124.50E
66 O9 Nibionno Italy 45.45N 9.17E
18 A6 Nibong Tebal Pen Malaysia 5.12N 100.28E
99 Q3 Nicabau Quebec 49.22N 74.01W
Nicaea anc site see Iznik
82 F8 Nicaj Shale Albania 42.18N 19.45E
102 J8 Nicaragua rep Central America
115 M4 Nicaragua,L.de Nicaragua
116 G4 Nicaro Cuba 20.44N 75.33W
81 N6 Nicastro Italy 38.59N 16.20E
104 R1 Nicatous L Maine
80 F2 Niccone R Italy
111 B2 Nice California 39.07N 122.50W
71 L9 Nice France 43.42N 7.16E
107 K11 Niceville Florida 30.31N 86.30W
39 D1 Nichalakh U.S.S.R. 70.05N 145.51E
40 A3 Nichatka,Ozero L U.S.S.R.
79 C5 Nichelino Italy 45.00N 7.39E
31 D6 Nichera Pakistan 28.49N 66.44E
97 M7 Nichicun, L Quebec 53.00N 71.00W
20 E7 Nichihara Japan 34.36N 131.50E
20 E10 Nichinan Japan 31.36N 131.23E
30 G5 Nichlaul Uttar Prad India 27.19N 83.43E
116 D3 Nicholas Chan Cuba/Bahamas
107 M4 Nicholasville Kentucky 37.52N 84.34W
105 E6 Nicholls Georgia 31.31N 82.39W
105 K12 Nicholl's Town Bahamas 25.08N 77.59W
103 H4 Nichols Connecticut 41.14N 73.10W
106 C8 Nichols Iowa 41.28N 91.18W
103 B2 Nichols New York 42.01N 76.22W
105 H3 Nichols South Carolina 34.14N 79.10W
99 G5 Nicholson Ontario 47.58N 83.47W
103 C3 Nicholson Pennsylvania 41.37N 75.47W
14 G4 Nicholson W Australia 18.01S 128.55E
13 E4 Nicholson R Queensland
101 W4 Nicholson L N W Terr 62.40N 102.35W
14 B7 Nicholson Ra W Australia
104 L2 Nicholville New York 44.43N 74.42W
117 B2 Nickerie dist Surinam
117 B2 Nickerie R Surinam
109 M3 Nickerson Kansas 38.09N 98.05W
14 B5 Nickol B W Australia
98 G3 Nicman Quebec 50.32N 66.00W
27 P8 Nicobar Is Bay of Bengal
118 C3 Nicocli Colombia 8.26N 76.33W
101 N10 Nicola Br Col 50.10N 120.38W
115 K8 Nicolas Mexico 19.40N 99.52W
99 S6 Nicolet Quebec 46.14N 72.36W
106 K3 Nicolet,L Michigan
26 U12 Nicoliere, L Mauritius, Indian Oc 20.09S 57.37E
108 Q5 Nicollet Minnesota 44.18N 94.10W
105 K12 Nicolls Town Andros Bahamas 25.06N 78.00W
81 K8 Nicolosi Sicily 37.36N 15.02E
Nicomedia anc site see Izmit
101 J12 Nicomeki R Br Col
121 G4 Nico Pérez Uruguay 33.30S 55.10W
92 J8 Nicoque Mozambique 12.44S 39.03E
84 R15 Nicosia Cyprus 35.09N 33.21E
81 K8 Nicosia Sicily 37.45N 14.24E
81 L6 Nicotera Italy 38.33N 15.56E
115 M4 Nicoya Costa Rica 10.09N 85.26W
115 M5 Nicoya,G.de Costa Rica
115 M5 Nicoya,Pen de Costa Rica
98 E6 Nictau New Brunswick 47.16N 67.11W
98 G9 Nictaux Falls Nova Scotia 44.54N 65.03W
92 H10 Nicuadala Mozambique 17.40S 36.50E
62 M5 Nida R Poland
28 E2 Nidadavolu Andhra Prad India 16.56N 81.42E
28 D2 Nidagunda Andhra Prad India 17.46N 79.15E
Nid à l'Aigle, C. du see Miquelon, C
66 F3 Nidau Switzerland 47.07N 7.15E
64 G3 Nidda W Germany 50.25N 9.02E
64 F3 Nidda R W Germany
64 F3 Niddatal W Germany 50.16N 8.50E
57 L5 Nidd,R N Yorks Eng
64 D4 Nideggen W Germany 50.41N 6.30E
92 D4 Nideiba Egypt 30.59N 30.22E
52 D8 Nidelv R Aust Agder Norway
52 E3 Nidelva R Sör-Tröndelag Norway
66 K4 Nidwalden canton Switzerland
41 G8 Nidym U.S.S.R. 64.11N 99.55E
41 H8 Nidym R U.S.S.R.
44 H7 Nidzh Azerbaydzhan U.S.S.R. 40.55N 47.36E
62 M2 Nidzica Poland 53.22N 20.27E
77 C6 Niebla Spain 37.22N 6.40W
63 J3 Niebüll W Germany 54.47N 8.50E
69 L5 Nied R France
81 A3 Nieddu,C Sardinia 40.09N 8.27E
81 C5 Nieddu, Mte Cagliari, Sardinia 39.11N 9.26E
81 D2 Nieddu,Mte Sassari, Sardinia 40.44N 9.35E
64 G1 Niedenstein W Germany 51.13N 9.17E
64 N6 Niederaichbach W Germany 48.36N 12.21E
61 Q8 Niederanven Luxembourg 49.39N 6.15E
64 L6 Niederarnbach W Germany 48.38N 11.20E
64 H2 Nieder Aula W Germany 50.48N 9.37E
64 N6 Nieder-Bayern dist Bayern W Germany
64 G6 Niederbieber W Germany 50.28N 7.29E
66 G2 Nieder Bipp Switzerland 47.16N 7.42E
69 O6 Niederbronn-les-Bains France 48.58N 7.39E
64 K2 Nieder Dietendorf E Germany 50.55N 10.55E
63 O6 Nieder Elde R E Germany
65 H7 Niedere Tauern mts Austria
66 J1 Nieder Fellabrunn Austria 48.28N 16.17E
61 P7 Niederfeulen Luxembourg 49.52N 6.03E
64 G2 Nieder Gemünden W Germany 50.42N 9.04E
66 L2 Niederglatt Switzerland 47.29N 8.31E
63 P5 Niedergörsdorf E Germany 51.59N 12.59E
66 H2 Nieder Gösgen Switzerland 47.23N 7.59E
Nieder Hohe see Meinhard
66 F5 Niederhorn mt Switzerland 46.36N 7.26E
65 H2 Nieder Kreuzstetten Austria 48.30N 16.29E
64 A1 Niederkrüchten W Germany 51.12N 6.12E
63 J10 Nieder Marsberg W Germany 51.28N 8.52E
63 M6 Nieder Marschacht W Germany 53.24N 10.20E
67 F6 Niederndorf Austria 47.39N 12.14E
64 H5 Niedernhall W Germany 49.18N 9.35E
64 E3 Niedernhausen W Germany 50.09N 8.20E
64 F2 Nieder-Olm W Germany 49.55N 8.13E
65 M4 Nieder-Österreich prov Austria
69 P3 Niederquembach W Germany 50.28N 8.28E
66 H5 Niederried Switzerland 46.44N 7.56E
62 D3 Niedersachsen land W Germany
64 G2 Nieder Scheiden W Germany 50.50N 7.58E
66 H1 Nieder Schwörstadt W Germany 47.36N 7.53E
64 E3 Niederselters W Germany 50.20N 8.14E
64 F1 Niedersfeld W Germany 51.17N 8.32E
66 F5 Nieder-Simmen-Tal V Switz
64 H6 Niederstetten W Germany 49.25N 9.57E
64 H6 Niederstotzingen W Germany 48.31N 10.15E
66 J6 Niederwald Switzerland 46.26N 8.12E
64 D4 Niederwald W Germany 49.58N 7.53E
66 Q1 Nieder-Wangen W Germany 47.40N 9.48E
69 P2 Niederweidbach W Germany 50.42N 8.30E
64 F2 Nieder Weimar W Germany 50.45N 8.44E
66 K1 Niederweningen Switzerland 47.31N 8.22E
64 P2 Niederwiesa E Germany 50.52N 13.03E
66 K2 Niederwil Switzerland 47.23N 8.18E
64 F3 Nieder-Wöllstadt W Germany 50.16N 8.45E
65 K7 Niederwolz Austria 47.10N 14.23E
69 N3 Niederzissen W Germany 50.27N 7.14E
83 B1 Niefang Equat Guinea 1.55N 10.08E
63 K9 Nieheim W Germany 51.48N 9.05E
60 O6 Niekerk Netherlands 53.20N 6.20E
60 D7 Niekerk Netherlands 53.13N 6.21E
95 F5 Niekerkshoop S Africa 29.20S 22.50E
61 B2 Niel Belgium 51.07N 4.20E
61 H2 Niel-bij-As Belgium 51.01N 5.36E
89 G6 Niellé Ivory Coast 10.05N 5.28W
108 O2 Nielsville Minnesota 47.31N 96.50W
92 D4 Niemba Zaïre 5.58S 28.24E
92 D5 Niemba R Zaïre
62 L3 Niemberg E Germany 51.33N 12.06E
62 K5 Niemcza Poland 50.43N 16.50E
63 R8 Niemegk E Germany 52.04N 12.42E
92 C2 Niemilane Mauritania 19.37N 12.23W
51 K5 Niemis Sweden 66.17N 23.40E
61 N2 Niemodlin Poland 50.39N 17.36E
89 F5 Niempena Mali 13.55N 6.16W
63 N7 Nienbergen W Germany 52.52N 10.58E
63 F8 Nienburg W Germany 52.08N 7.06E
63 K6 Nienburg E Germany 51.51N 11.45E
63 F7 Nienburg (Weser) W Germany 52.38N 9.13E
63 N5 Niendorf W Germany 53.49N 10.36E
Nienhagen see Ostseebad Nienhagen
62 M5 Niepołomice Poland 50.02N 20.13E
69 D2 Nieppe France 50.42N 2.50E
63 D9 Niers R W Germany
64 E4 Nierstein W Germany 49.53N 8.20E
66 G5 Niesen mt Switzerland 46.39N 7.38E
62 L3 Nieszawa Poland 52.50N 18.51E
89 E9 Niete Mts Liberia
95 H7 Nieu Bethesda S Africa 31.52S 24.34E
72 F4 Nieuil France 45.53N 0.31E
72 G4 Nieuil France 45.56N 1.10E
72 B2 Nieul le Dolent France 46.34N 1.30W
72 B4 Nieulle-sur-Seudre France 45.45N 1.00W
72 C3 Nieul-sur-l'Autize France 46.25N 0.39W
72 B3 Nieul-sur-Mer France 46.12N 1.10W
25 N7 Nieumaton Xizang Zizhiqu 28.12N 98.40E
Nieuport see Nieuwpoort
60 Q9 Nieuw Amsterdam Netherlands 52.43N 6.52E
117 B2 Nieuw Amsterdam Surinam 5.53N 55.05W
60 P8 Nieuw-Balinge Netherlands 52.45N 6.36E
60 M7 Nieuw-Beerta Netherlands 53.12N 7.10E
60 P8 Nieuw-Beijerland Netherlands 51.48N 4.20E
60 Q8 Nieuw-Buinen Netherlands 52.57N 6.55E
60 Q9 Nieuw-Dordrecht Netherlands 52.45N 6.59E
60 B3 Nieuwdorp Netherlands 51.28N 3.45E
60 F12 Nieuwe Maas R Netherlands
60 G12 Nieuwe Merwede R Netherlands
60 H12 Nieuwendijk Netherlands 51.46N 4.55E
60 E12 Nieuwenhoorn Netherlands 51.51N 4.09E
61 E1 Nieuwenhove Belgium 50.47N 4.00E
60 H9 Nieuwe-Niedorp Netherlands 52.44N 4.54E
61 H3 Nieuwerode Belgium 50.58N 4.21E
61 F3 Nieuwe-Pekela Netherlands 53.04N 6.58E
60 C2 Nieuwerkerk Netherlands 51.39N 4.00E
60 G12 Nieuwerkerk Zuid Holland Netherlands 51.58N 4.35E
61 L3 Nieuwerkerken Limburg Belgium 50.52N 5.12E
61 G3 Nieuwerkerken Oost Vlaanderen Belgium 50.55N 4.00E
60 H11 Nieuwer-Ter Aa Netherlands 52.12N 4.59E
60 R7 Nieuwe-Schans Netherlands 53.11N 7.11E
60 E13 Nieuwe-Tonge Netherlands 51.42N 4.10E
60 E12 Nieuwe Vaart canal Netherlands
60 E12 Nieuwe Waterweg estuary Netherlands
60 G11 Nieuwe Wetering Netherlands 52.13N 4.36E
60 E12 Nieuw-Helvoet Netherlands 51.50N 4.07E
60 O10 Nieuw-Heten Netherlands 52.19N 6.21E
117 B2 Nieuw Jacobkondre Surinam 5.00N 55.35W
61 B4 Nieuwkerke Belgium 50.44N 2.49E
61 G2 Nieuwkerken-Waas Belgium 51.12N 4.11E
60 H12 Nieuwkoop Netherlands 52.09N 4.46E
60 B3 Nieuwland Zuid Holland Netherlands 51.29N 3.40E
Nieuwland Zuid Holland Netherlands see Vierpolders
60 J12 Nieuwland Zuid Holland Netherlands 51.54N 5.00E
60 G12 Nieuw Lekkerland Netherlands 51.53N 4.41E
60 O9 Nieuw-Leusen Netherlands 52.34N 6.17E
60 J11 Nieuw-Loosdrecht Netherlands 52.12N 5.08E
Nieuw Meerzorg see Alliance Surinam
60 M11 Nieuw Milligen Netherlands 52.14N 5.47E
61 C1 Nieuwmunster Belgium 51.16N 3.06E
60 E14 Nieuwnamen Netherlands 51.18N 4.10E
117 B2 Nieuw Nickerie Surinam 5.52N 57.00W
60 Q7 Nieuwolda Netherlands 53.15N 6.58E
94 E8 Nieuwoudtville Cape Prov S Africa 31.24S 19.06E
61 A2 Nieuwpoort Belgium 51.08N 2.45E
60 H12 Nieuwpoort Netherlands 51.56N 4.53E
61 K3 Nieuwrode Belgium 50.57N 4.50E
60 Q7 Nieuw Scheemda Netherlands 53.08N 6.24E
60 Q7 Nieuw Scheemda Netherlands 53.13N 6.57E
60 Q9 Nieuw-Schoonebeek Netherlands 52.38N 6.59E
60 T16 Nieuwstadt Netherlands 51.02N 5.51E
60 H11 Nieuw-Vennep Netherlands 52.12N 4.45E
60 G11 Nieuw-Vennep Netherlands 52.16N 4.38E
60 G10 Nieuwvliet Netherlands 51.22N 3.29E
60 E13 Nieuw Vossemeer Netherlands 51.35N 4.14E
60 O8 Nieuw Weerdinge Netherlands 52.51N 7.00E
120 A1 Nieva,R Peru
76 C4 Nieves Spain 42.05N 8.25W
Nieves, Pozo de las mt see Los Pechos
76 U15 Nieves,Pto de las B Gran Canaria Canary Is
67 H5 Nièvre dept France
71 C2 Nièvre R France 47.07N 3.11E
19 G5 Nif Moluccas Indon 3.17S 130.36E
71 M1 Niffer France 47.43N 7.31E
88 N8 Nifil Algeria 27.03N 0.47W
72 N8 Niftrik Netherlands 51.48N 5.41E
89 G5 Niga Mali 13.38N 5.27W
98 G6 Nigadoo New Brunswick 47.44N 65.46W
29 L2 Nigan W Bengal Ind 23.30N 88.00E
Nigar see Negar
36 H5 Nigde Turkey 37.58N 34.42E
86 P8 Nigeili, Wādi en watercourse Saudi Arabia
85 N10 Nigeim,Jebel mt Sudan 19.29N 34.19E
95 M2 Nigel S Africa 26.25S 28.28E
90 B7 Niger R W Africa
73 E4 Niger rep W Africa
73 E5 Niger,R W Africa
90 C10 Niger,R.Mouths of the Nigeria
58 H3 Nigg Highland Scotland 57.42N 4.01W
58 M4 Nigg B Grampian Scotland 57.08N 2.03W
58 H3 Nigg Bay Highland Scotland
30 G8 Nighasan Uttar Prad India 28.13N 80.51E
11 C12 Nightcaps New Zealand 45.58S 168.02E
110 F1 Nighthawk Washington 48.58N 119.38W
99 M4 Night Hawk L Ontario
13 G2 Night I Gt Barrier Reef Australia
Nightingale isld Vietnamsee Bach long Vi
96 B16 Nightingale I Tristan da Cunha 37.28S 12.32W
113 E6 Nightmute Alaska 60.28N 164.50W
30 E6 Nigohan Uttar Prad India 26.34N 81.02E
76 B4 Nigrán Spain 42.09N 8.48W
83 F8 Nigrita Greece 40.54N 23.29E
33 A5 Nigrūb-el-Fuqani,Gebel mts Egypt
60 Q10 Nigtevecht Netherlands 52.16N 5.01E
113 K2 Niguanak R Alaska
79 F7 Niguarda dist Milan Italy
77 J7 Niguelas Spain 36.59N 3.31W
86 H10 Nigeidat el Sūd,Gebel el hill Egypt 27.59N 32.22E
72 H2 Nihérne France 46.50N 1.33E
31 C6 Nihing Pakistan 28.15N 65.42E
122 E15 Nihiru atoll Tuamotu Is Pacific Oc 16.40S 142.50W
86 G7 Nihiya, Wādi el watercourse Egypt
114 D2 Nihoa isld Hawaiian Is 23.03N 161.56W
20 H4 Nihommatsu Japan 37.34N 140.25E
20 O4 Nihongi Saitama Japan
20 B3 Nihtaur Uttar Prad India 29.20N 78.22E
121 C5 Nihuil, Embalse del res Argentina 35.00S 68.42W
20 N4 Niigata Japan 37.58N 139.02E
20 N4 Niigata prefect Japan
20 G8 Niihama Japan 33.57N 133.15E
114 D4 Niihau isld Hawaiian Is 21.50N 160.11W
20 N7 Nii-jima isld Japan
20 P3 Niikappu-gawa R Japan
20 D10 Niitomi Japan 31.20N 130.52E
20 N4 Niitsu Japan 37.48N 139.09E
20 N2 Niiza Saitama Japan
77 M7 Nijar Spain 36.58N 2.11W
60 L10 Nij-Beets Netherlands 53.04N 6.00E
60 H8 Nijega Netherlands 52.55N 5.32E
60 M8 Nijemirdum Netherlands 52.52N 5.37E
60 M9 Nijeholtwolde Netherlands 52.54N 5.59E
60 L8 Nijemirdum Netherlands 52.51N 5.34E
60 N9 Nijeveen Netherlands 52.44N 6.11E
Nijgarh Orissa Indiasee Keonjhargarh
86 P4 Nijil Jordan 30.32N 35.03E
33 G4 Nijil,Wādi watercourse Jordan
60 C11 Nijkerk Gelderland Netherlands 52.13N 5.29E
60 K11 Nijkerkerveen Netherlands 52.12N 5.28E
60 L7 Nijlân Netherlands 53.03N 5.35E
61 J2 Nijlen Belgium 51.10N 4.40E
60 M12 Nijmegen Netherlands 51.50N 5.52E
60 O10 Nijverdal Netherlands 52.22N 6.28E
60 T17 Nijswiller Netherlands 50.48N 5.58E
60 O10 Nijverdal Netherlands 52.22N 6.28E
Nika see Neka
113 K6 Nikabuna Lakes Alaska
84 G6 Nikaia Attiki Greece 37.58N 23.37E
83 F8 Nikaia Lárisa Greece 39.34N 22.28E
Nikaria isld see Ikaria
26 R6 Nikaweratiya Sri Lanka 7.45N 80.08E
26 R6 Nikawewa N Central Sri Lanka 8.24N 80.17E
26 R6 Nikawewa N Western Sri Lanka 7.52N 80.24E
90 C8 Nike Nigeria 6.28N 7.29E
85 N8 Nikeiba,Gebel mt Egypt 23.53N 34.20E
87 K2 Nikel' U.S.S.R. 69.24N 30.12E
45 E2 Nikel'tau Kazakhstan U.S.S.R. 50.24N 58.09E
113 F8 Nikhb Saudi Arabia 21.13N 40.28E
35 L6 Nikheila,El Egypt 27.06N 31.17E
19 D8 Nikiboi Timor Indon 9.49S 124.29E
84 Q14 Nikitari Cyprus 35.05N 33.00E
72 F4 Nikitas Greece 40.14N 23.39E
43 K1 Nikitinka Kazakhstan U.S.S.R. 49.34N 82.27E
46 J2 Nikitinka U.S.S.R. 55.33N 33.12E
47 N3 Nikitino U.S.S.R. 57.57N 60.30E
46 J5 Nikitovka Ukraine U.S.S.R. 48.21N 38.03E
45 K6 Nikitovka U.S.S.R. 50.22N 38.25E
89 L7 Nikki Benin 9.55N 3.18E
20 N5 Nikkō Japan 36.45N 139.37E
20 N5 Nikkō Nat.Park Japan
86 E4 Nikla el'Inab Egypt 30.55N 30.45E
31 H9 Nikli Bangladesh 24.19N 90.58E
82 H1 Nikolaev U.S.S.R. 49.32N 23.59E
113 K5 Nikolai Alaska 63.00N 154.19W
66 H7 Nikolaital V Switzerland
41 B2 Nikolaya,Mys C Novaya Zemlya U.S.S.R. 75.14N 55.45E
40 H5 Nikolaya,Zaliv gulf U.S.S.R.
45 D10 Nikolayev Ukraine U.S.S.R. 46.57N 32.00E
45 K6 Nikolayevka Belgorod U.S.S.R. 50.25N 38.20E
47 M5 Nikolayevka Chelyabinsk U.S.S.R. 56.16N 59.36E
44 C10 Nikolayevka Crimea, Ukraine U.S.S.R. 44.36N 33.37E
45 E9 Nikolayevka Dnepropetrovsk, Ukraine U.S.S.R. 47.38N 33.14E
42 F4 Nikolayevka Irkutsk U.S.S.R. 55.46N 98.10E
43 J1 Nikolayevka Kazakhstan U.S.S.R. 54.13N 67.46E
42 F4 Nikolayevka Krasnoyarsk U.S.S.R. 56.30N 95.10E
44 A7 Nikolayevka Nikolayev, Ukraine U.S.S.R. 47.33N 30.47E
47 M8 Nikolayevka Novosibirsk U.S.S.R. 54.51N 75.45E
45 K9 Nikolayevka Rostov U.S.S.R. 47.20N 38.53E
45 U4 Nikolayevka Saratov U.S.S.R. 52.10N 48.05E
44 C7 Nikolayevka Ukraine U.S.S.R. 47.50N 33.15E
45 T3 Nikolayevka Ul'yanovsk U.S.S.R. 53.07N 47.12E
40 F7 Nikolayevka Yevreysk U.S.S.R. 48.35N 134.40E
44 F3 Nikolayevo Aleksandrovskoye U.S.S.R. 44.56N 44.32E
46 O4 Nikolayevsk U.S.S.R. 50.05N 45.32E
45 C10 Nikolayevskaya Oblast prov Ukraine U.S.S.R.
40 E4 Nikolayevskiy Amur U.S.S.R. 54.55N 129.18E
43 F1 Nikolayevskiy Chelyabinsk U.S.S.R. 53.04N 61.59E
45 R6 Nikolayevskiy Volgograd U.S.S.R. 50.05N 45.32E
40 H5 Nikolayevsk-na-Amure U.S.S.R. 53.10N 140.44E
45 N1 Nikologory U.S.S.R. 56.07N 42.00E
47 M4 Nikolopavlovskoye U.S.S.R. 57.48N 60.05E
42 E4 Nikol'sk Krasnoyarsk U.S.S.R. 57.20N 92.08E
46 O3 Nikol'sk Penza U.S.S.R. 53.41N 46.01E
47 F6 Nikol'sk Vologda U.S.S.R. 59.33N 45.30E
113 C10 Nikolski Aleutian Is 53.00N 168.50W
43 H3 Nikol'skiy Kazakhstan U.S.S.R. 47.54N 67.25E
45 S9 Nikol'skoye Astrakhan' U.S.S.R. 47.46N 46.22E
39 H6 Nikol'skoye Komandorskiye O-va U.S.S.R. 55.14N 166.04E
43 D2 Nikol'skoye Orenburg U.S.S.R. 52.04N 55.44E
46 R4 Nikol'skoye Orenburg U.S.S.R. 51.40N 54.30E
47 M5 Nikol'skoye Sverdlovsk U.S.S.R. 56.17N 60.56E
42 C4 Nikol'skoye Tomsk U.S.S.R. 57.12N 84.17E
47 E6 Nikolskoye Vologda U.S.S.R. 59.31N 42.28E
45 V2 Nikol'skoye-na-Cheremshame U.S.S.R. 54.03N 49.14E
92 E3 Nikonga R Tanzania
93 C9 Nikonga watercourse Tanzania
85 G2 Nikopol Bulgaria 43.41N 24.55E
82 J7 Nikopol' Ukraine U.S.S.R. 47.34N 34.25E
45 G9 Nik Pey Iran 36.50N 48.10E
32 C2 Niksar Turkey 40.35N 36.59E
36 J2 Nikshahr Iran 26.12N 60.14E
32 H7 Nikšić Yugoslavia 42.48N 18.56E
82 E8 Nikulino U.S.S.R. 60.24N 90.00E
42 D2 Nikunau isld Kiribati, Pacific Oc 1.20S 176.25E
9 C6
31 G4 Nila Pakistan 33.14N 72.46E
19 F7 Nila isld Indon 6.45S 129.30E
18 B9 Nilai Pen Malaysia 2.46N 101.47E
28 D5 Nilakkottai Tamil Nadu India 10.07N 77.53E
28 C5 Nilambur Kerala India 11.17N 76.15E
111 J8 Niland California 33.16N 115.30W
27 L9 Nilande Atoll Maldives, Ind Oc 3.00N 72.55E
30 E8 Nilang Uttar Prad India 31.05N 79.00E
28 C1 Nilanga Maharashtra India 18.07N 76.45E
26 T4 Nilaveli Sri Lanka 8.41N 81.11E
93 C2 Nile dist Uganda
86 D4 Nile prov Sudan
85 M10 Nile R N Africa
73 H3 Nile R NE Africa
32 F5 Nileh Iran 31.31N 54.07E
37 D7 Nilek Daǵ mt Turkey 38.54N 37.46E
111 C4 Niles California 37.35N 121.59W
109 N3 Niles Kansas 38.58N 97.28W
106 H8 Niles Michigan 41.51N 86.15W
104 E5 Niles Ohio 41.11N 80.46W
106 Q1 Niles dist Chicago, Illinois
93 A9 Nile,Source of the Burundi 3.44S 29.47E
28 B4 Nileswaram Kerala India 12.18N 75.07E
30 D5 Nilgaon Uttar Prad India 27.14N 80.57E
99 N6 Nilgaut L Quebec 46.35N 77.15W
28 C5 Nilgiris dist Tamil Nadu India
39 C4 Nilgiysy R U.S.S.R.
88 P5 Nili Algeria 33.22N 3.03E
113 E6 Nilikluguk Alaska 60.39N 165.00W
35 D6 Nil'in Jordan 31.57N 35.01E
24 D4 Nilka Xinjiang Uygur Zizhiqu China 43.46N 82.52E
Nilki see Nilka
39 D4 Nil'kobe U.S.S.R. 61.13N 148.51E
31 D3 Nil Pass Afghanistan 34.52N 67.11E
31 J8 Nilphamari Bangladesh 28.58N 88.57E
53 V20 Nil-St-Vincent Belgium 50.38N 4.40E
123 B4 Nilsebu Norway 59.11N 6.40E
51 N8 Nilsen B Antarctica 87.36S 64.40E
119 N9 Nilsiä Finland 63.13N 28.00E
115 K8 Nilson Mexico 16.32N 94.36W
37 B2 Nilüfer R Turkey
26 R10 Nilwala R Sri Lanka
53 D5 Nim Denmark 55.56N 9.42E
30 D6 Nimach Madhya Prad India 24.27N 74.56E
40 F5 Niman R U.S.S.R.
33 E7 Nimas, in Saudi Arabia 19.08N 42.10E
34 N2 Nimāvar Iran 36.09N 45.44E
Nimavar see Binab
29 D5 Nimbahera Rajasthan India 24.38N 74.45E
28 B2 Nimbal Karnataka India 17.07N 75.56E
89 E8 Nimba,Mts Guinea/Liberia/Ivory Coast 7.39N 8.30W
14 E6 Nimbera Well W Australia 23.10S 123.13E
90 C9 Nimbi Nigeria 4.31N 6.25E
12 L3 Nimbin New S Wales 28.35S 153.12E
71 E9 Nîmes France 43.50N 4.21E
84 W22 Nimfai Corfu 39.48N 19.47E
Nimfaion see Ákr. Pinnes
20 G6 Nimi Japan 35.00N 133.27E
14 O4 Nimiu Italy 46.13N 13.16E
29 E5 Nimka Thana Rajasthan India 27.42N 75.50E
12 J6 Nimmitabel New S Wales 36.32S 149.19E
40 C3 Nimnyrskiy U.S.S.R. 57.50N 125.12E
110 M3 Nimrod Montana 46.42N 113.26W
Nimrod Bay see Xiangshan Gang
123 G7 Nimrod Glacier Antarctica 82.30S 160.00E
107 C7 Nimrod L Arkansas 34.57N 93.15W
11 E11 Nimrod,Mt New Zealand 44.25S 170.46E
34 E2 Nimrud anc site Iraq 36.08N 43.19E
35 F1 Nimrud, Qirba hist ruin Syria 33.15N 35.40E
31 B5 Nimrūz prov Afghanistan
53 F4 Nimtofte Denmark 56.24N 10.35E
31 F4 Nimu Kashmir 34.12N 77.21E
33 H4 Nimule Sudan 3.35N 32.03E
53 G5 Nimy Belgium 50.28N 3.58E
82 C6 Nin Yugoslavia 44.14N 15.10E
18 B8 Ninakumbulu Nyasaland 12.12N 123.15E
61 F5 Ninakumbulu 12.12N 123.15E
19 F8 Ninati W Irian 5.43S 140.49E
91 G11 Ninda R Angola
13 F8 Nindigully Queensland 28.20S 148.47E
61 H11 Nindiri Nicaragua 12.00N 86.06W
13 J8 Nindigully
115 L3 Nine Degree Chan Laccadive Is Indian Oc
17 D4 Ninemile Alaska 56.00N 130.07W
113 W8 Ninemilehouse Tipperary Irish Rep 52.27N 7.27W
59 H7 Ninemilehouse
12 G4 Nine Mile L New S Wales 31.07S 143.33E
11 H2 Ninemile Pk mt Nevada 39.10N 116.15W
25 F2 Nine Pin Hong Kong 22.15N 114.20E
14 F2 Nine Point Mesa mt Texas 29.39N 103.29W
100 S9 Ninette Manitoba 49.24N 99.40W
26 H8 Ninety-East Ridge Indian Oc
11 G1 Ninety Mile Beach New Zealand
11 G1 Ninety Mile Beach Victoria
105 E3 Ninety Six S Carolina 34.10N 82.01W
104 E7 Nineveh Pennsylvania 39.57N 80.20W
103 E7 Nineveh New York 42.12N 75.37W
34 E2 Nineveh anc site Iraq 36.24N 43.08E
121 D9 Ninfas,Pta C Argentina 42.56S 63.22W
56 M6 Ninfield E Sussex Eng 50.53N 0.25E
14 A6 Ningaloo W Australia 22.41S 113.41E
13 L2 Ning'an Heilongjiang China 44.24N 129.38E
Ning-an-pu see Xuanhepu
23 J4 Ningbo Zhejiang China 29.54N 121.33E
22 L6 Ningcheng Liaoning China 41.38N 119.19E
Ning-chiang Yunnan see Mengwang
23 H5 Ningde Fujian China 26.40N 119.30E
23 G5 Ningdu Jiangxi China 26.23N 115.49E
23 F6 Ninggang Jiangxi China 26.43N 113.55E
23 H3 Ningguo Anhui China 30.36N 118.55E
23 J4 Ninghai Zhejiang China 29.18N 121.26E
Ninghan see Singleton,Mt W Australia
22 L7 Ninghe Tianjin China 39.21N 117.50E
Ning-hsia see Yinchuan
23 G5 Ninghua Fujian China 26.14N 116.31E
90 D6 Ningi Nigeria 10.55N 9.30E
28 F1 Ninging Assam India 28.58N 94.49E
22 K8 Ningjin Hebei China 37.40N 114.55E
22 K8 Ningjin Shandong China 37.40N 116.41E
23 A3 Ningjing Shan mts Xizang Zizhiqu China
23 B5 Ninglang Yizu Zizhixian Yunnan China 27.12N 100.59E
23 G1 Ningling Henan China 34.27N 115.24E
23 D7 Ningming Guangxi China 22.08N 107.06E
23 C5 Ningnan Sichuan China 27.04N 102.47E
28 H1 Ningong Xizang Zizhiqu 29.25N 91.26E
23 D2 Ningqiang Shaanxi China 32.54N 106.12E
23 E2 Ningshan Shaanxi China 33.19N 108.18E
Ningsia aut reg Chinasee Ningxia prov China
22 G8 Ningxia prov China
28 G3 Ning Ting Shan mts Xizang Zizhiqu
29 H6 Ninguani Madhya Prad India 23.18N 82.03E
22 J7 Ningwu Shanxi China 39.00N 112.19E
23 F4 Ning Xian Gansu China 35.30N 108.05E
22 D4 Ningxiang Hunan China 28.18N 112.30E
23 E1 Ningyang Shandong China 35.49N 116.51E
23 F6 Ningyuan Hunan China 25.36N 111.50E
25 H2 Ninh Binh Vietnam 20.14N 106.00E
23 F6 Ninh Hoa Vietnam 12.28N 109.07E
121 A6 Ninhue Chile 36.25S 72.29W
54 L2 Ninian oil field North Sea 60.48N 1.28E
16 C2 Ninigo Grp islds Bismarck Arch
15 G4 Ninigo Is atolls Bismarck Arch
103 L4 Ninigret Pond Rhode I
113 M6 Ninilchik Alaska 60.04N 151.44W
15 D5 Niningarra W Australia 20.35S 119.58E
14 C5 Ninios Papua New Guinea 4.39S 144.32E
16 D5 Ninios
9 T12 Niniva atoll Tonga, Pacific Oc 19.46S 174.39W
109 N8 Ninnekah Oklahoma 34.56N 97.56W
109 N4 Ninnescah R Kansas
123 J4 Ninnis Glacier Antarctica
107 C9 Ninock Louisiana 32.15N 93.28W
20 E10 Ninokata Japan 31.38N 131.02E
114 C7 Ninole Hawaiian Is 19.56N 155.09W
20 A2 Ninomiya Tōkyō Japan
77 E8 Niño,Sierra del mts Spain
61 E3 Ninove Belgium 50.50N 4.02E
92 H9 Nintulo Mozambique 15.05S 37.06E
121 A10 Ninualac,Canal str Chile
44 F3 Niny U.S.S.R. 44.30N 43.56E
41 C5 Ninyako-Vogumma U.S.S.R. 70.11N 79.32W
118 C7 Nioaque Brazil 21.05S 55.50W
114 F4 Niobe New York 42.01N 79.28W
108 M7 Niobrara Nebraska 42.46N 98.02W
108 J7 Niobrara R Nebraska
48 V4 Nioghalvfjerdsfjorden B Greenland
91 H7 Nioka Zaïre 7.41S 23.40E
93 B7 Nioka Zaïre 2.10N 30.40E
84 C2 Niokhóri Greece 39.51N 20.46E
91 E5 Nioki Zaïre 2.45S 17.42E
28 K2 Niokso Assam India 27.54N 94.07E
89 C6 Niokolo Koba,Parc Nat.du Senegal
89 F4 Niono Mali 14.18N 5.59W
89 B5 Nioro Senegal 13.45N 15.48W
89 E4 Nioro du Sahel Mali 15.12N 9.35W
72 D3 Niort France 46.19N 0.27W
Nios see Ios
106 C9 Niota Illinois 40.36N 91.17W
107 M6 Niota Tennessee 35.31N 84.33W
89 J5 Niou Upper Volta 12.50N 1.59W
89 F3 Niout Mauritania 16.01N 6.49W
53 U19 Nip Norway 59.41N 6.21E
53 T17 Nipa Norway 60.46N 5.38E
15 G7 Nipa Papua New Guinea 6.11S 143.27E
119 G3 Nipa Venezuela 9.06N 64.08W
53 W17 Nipane mt Norway 60.37N 7.05E
28 B2 Nipani Karnataka India 16.27N 74.28E
19 C5 Nipanipa, Tanjung C Celebes Indon 3.55S 122.40E
100 N5 Nipawin Saskatchewan 53.23N 104.01W
100 N4 Nipawin Prov.Park Saskatchewan
92 H9 Nipepe Mozambique 14.02S 37.51E
29 D7 Niphad Maharashtra India 20.04N 74.10E
99 B3 Nipigon Ontario 49.02N 88.15W
99 B3 Nipigon R Ontario
99 B4 Nipigon B Ontario
99 B3 Nipigon,L Ontario
100 H3 Nipin R Saskatchewan
48 S8 Nipisat Greenland 69.25N 54.15W
98 G6 Nipisiguit B New Brunswick
98 F6 Nipisiguit R New Brunswick
100 C3 Nipisi R Alberta
99 L6 Nipissing Junction Ontario 46.16N 79.25W
99 L6 Nipissing,L Ontario
98 F3 Nipissis L Quebec
98 F3 Nipissis R Quebec
98 G3 Nipissis L Quebec
111 D7 Nipomo California 35.04N 120.27W
34 N6 Nippur anc site Iraq 32.10N 45.11E
111 J6 Nipton California 35.27N 115.16W
85 N8 Niqrūb el-Fuqāni,Gebel mts Egypt
118 E4 Niquelândia Brazil 14.33S 48.23W
121 B6 Niquén Chile 36.18S 71.58W
116 F4 Niquero Cuba 20.03N 77.34W
32 C1 Nir Azarbāijān-e Khāvarī Iran 38.03N 48.00E
35 F5 Nir Esfahān Iran 31.20N 54.11E
35 B7 Nir'am Israel 31.32N 34.35E
28 B1 Nira R Maharashtra India
20 M6 Nirasaki Japan 35.45N 138.27E
35 E7 Nir Dawid Israel 32.31N 35.27E
121 A6 Nirgua,R Chile
35 C3 Nir 'Ezyon Israel 32.42N 35.00E
35 B6 Nir Galim Israel 31.50N 34.41E
35 B7 Nir Hen Israel 31.36N 34.42E
35 A8 Nirim Israel 31.20N 34.23E
Niriz see Neyriz
33 E4 Nir,Jabal an mts Saudi Arabia
Nirji see Morin Dawa Daurzu Zizhiqi
28 D1 Nirmal Andhra Prad India 19.04N 78.21E
29 E4 Nirmali Bihar India 26.18N 86.35E
29 E6 Nirmal Ra Maharashtra India
35 B8 Nir Moshe Israel 31.28N 34.37E
35 A8 Nir 'Oz Israel 31.19N 34.24E
29 K1 Nirsa Bihar India 23.46N 86.44E
106 J8 Nirvana Michigan 43.54N 85.41W
35 B8 Nir Yafe Israel 32.34N 35.15E
35 B7 Nir Yisra'el Israel 31.41N 34.38E
35 B7 Nir Yizhaq Israel 31.14N 34.24E
82 G7 Niš Yugoslavia 43.20N 21.54E
Nisa Iransee Neyseh
76 D9 Nisa Portugal 39.31N 7.39W
78 E9 Nisa R Portugal
34 M9 Nisāb Saudi Arabia 29.14N 44.42E
33 G8 Nisāb S Yemen 14.31N 46.30E
33 E4 Nisah,Wādi watercourse Saudi Arabia
34 D6 Nisarpur Madhya Prad India 22.05N 74.52E
82 H7 Nišava R Yugoslavia
104 H5 Nisbet Pennsylvania 41.13N 77.09W
81 J8 Niscemi Sicily 37.09N 14.23E
31 G8 Nischintapur Bangladesh 25.04N 88.35E
20 K2 Niseko Japan 42.49N 140.40E
45 K6 Nishan Uzbekistan U.S.S.R. 38.34N 65.40E
31 C1 Nishāpūr see Neyshābūr
20 E4 Nishi Hunan China 29.57N 110.43E
Nishi dist Yokohama Japan
20 N4 Nishi-azuma-yama mt Japan 37.43N 140.12E
20 P1 Nishi-Hoji Japan 40.12N 141.20E
20 F6 Nishi-jima Japan 36.05N 133.00E
20 N5 Nishi-jima isld Japan 34.45N 134.30E
20 D10 Nishikata Japan 31.54N 130.13E
20 F5 Nishi Nomi jima isld Japan
20 G7 Nishinomiya Japan 34.44N 135.22E
21 E12 Nishinoomote Japan 30.46N 131.02E
25 D3 Nishino-shima isld Japan
21 J11 Nishino-shima isld Ogasawara-Guntō Pacific Oc 27.15N 140.54E
20 C7 Nishio Japan 34.52N 137.02E
20 L7 Nishi-Sonogi-hantō pen Japan
20 B3 Nishi-suido str Japan/S Korea
20 A5 Nishi-Sunagawa Tōkyō Japan
20 A2 Nishi-Tomioka Kanagawa Japan
20 H3 Nishitsugaru Japan 34.59N 134.58E
20 R6 Nishlik L Alaska 60.29N 159.00W
86 F4 Nishwa Egypt 30.30N 31.28E
117 J8 Nisia Floresta Brazil 6.05S 35.10W
Nisibis anc site see Nusaybin
83 J8 Nisiros isld Greece 36.35N 27.13E
33 G9 Nisiyin,Jibal an plat S Yemen
62 N8 Nisko Poland 50.31N 22.08E
95 B3 Nisland S Dakota 44.40N 103.34W
81 H5 Nisling R Yukon Terr
61 J6 Nismes Belgium 50.04N 4.33E
84 R14 Nisou Cyprus 35.01N 33.24E
60 F14 Nispen Netherlands 51.28N 4.28E
53 N4 Nisporeny U.S.S.R. 47.04N 28.12E
53 B4 Nisqually R Washington
52 G10 Nissan France 43.18N 3.08E
52 G10 Nissan R Sweden
15 H4 Nissan I Papua New Guinea
53 N4 Nisse Netherlands 51.27N 3.52E
52 D7 Nissedal Norway 59.15N 8.30E
53 Y20 Nisser L Norway
81 J8 Nissoria Sicily 37.39N 14.28E
53 B4 Nissum Bredning B Denmark 56.10N 8.18E
53 A3 Nissumby Denmark 56.34N 8.25E
53 A4 Nissum Fjord inlet Denmark 56.22N 8.10E
60 L13 Nistelrode Netherlands 51.42N 5.34E
101 G5 Nisutlin R Yukon Terr
33 H3 Nitā Saudi Arabia 27.14N 48.25E
97 M7 Nitchequon Quebec 53.10N 70.58W
86 O9 Niteish, Wādi watercourse Saudi Arabia
118 K9 Niterói Brazil 22.54S 43.06W
Nithpur see Nischintapur
57 F2 Nith, R Dumfries & Galloway Scot
57 F2 Nithsdale V Dumfries & Galloway Scotland
19 D8 Nitibe Indonesia 9.21S 124.12E
35 G7 Nitil Jordan 31.39N 35.51E
110 A1 Nitinat L Vancouver I, Br Col
30 C2 Niti Pass Xizang Zizhiqu/Uttar Prad India 30.57N 79.53E
40 G2 Nitiya mt U.S.S.R. 58.26N 136.50E
56 J6 Niton I of Wight Eng 50.35N 1.16W
62 L7 Nitra Czechoslovakia 48.19N 18.04E
62 L7 Nitra R Czechoslovakia
104 D8 Nitro W Virginia 38.26N 81.51W
71 D1 Nitry France 47.41N 3.52E
47 J6 Nitsa R U.S.S.R.
Nitsana Israelsee Nizzana
86 N4 Nitsana watercourse Israel
51 N2 Nitsijärvi L Finland 69.14N 28.05E
64 N5 Nittenau W Germany 49.11N 12.17E
64 M5 Nittendorf W Germany 49.03N 11.58E
10 R5 Niuafo'ou isld Pacific Oc 15.36S 175.39W
10 S5 Niuatoputapu isld Pacific Oc 15.59S 173.58W
9 R10 Niu Aunofo cliff Tonga, Pacific Oc 21.03S 175.19W
22 B7 Niubiziliang Qinghai China 38.42N 92.11E
122 K10 Niue isld Cook Is Pacific Oc 19.02S 169.55W
Niu'erhe Nei Monggol Zizhiqu China 51.35N 121.57E
21 B9
9 D9 Niulakita atoll Tuvalu, Pacific Oc 10.30S 179.20E
23 C5 Niulan Jiang R Yunnan/Guizhou China
114 B6 Niuli Hawaiian Is 20.13N 155.45W
21 C7 Niumowu Liaoning China 41.00N 125.03E
Niushan see Donghai
9 C7 Niutao isld Tuvalu, Pacific Oc 6.06S 177.16E
18 J5 Niut,Gunung mt Borneo Indon 0.58N 110.10E
25 J5 Nui Ti On mt Vietnam 15.13N 107.46E
21 F5 Niuzhuang Liaoning China 40.56N 122.32E
53 K5 Nivå Denmark 55.56N 12.32E
51 L8 Nivala Finland 63.56N 25.00E
30 B7 Nivari Madhya Prad India 25.21N 78.48E
72 B9 Nive R France
13 H7 Nive R Queensland
13 H7 Nive Downs Queensland 25.35S 146.32E
61 H4 Nivelles Belgium 50.36N 4.20E
61 J6 Niverlée Belgium 50.07N 4.42E
67 H5 Nivernais prov France
71 C2 Nivernais,Côtes du reg France
100 U9 Niverville Manitoba 49.36N 97.03W
103 G2 Niverville New York 42.27N 73.39W
69 C5 Nivillers France 49.28N 2.09E
53 X16 Nivla R Norway
111 G4 Nivloc Nevada 37.45N 117.45W
41 D4 Nivnoye U.S.S.R. 53.10N 32.35E
71 G5 Nivolas-Vermelle France 45.34N 5.18E
47 G5 Nivshera U.S.S.R. 62.23N 52.50E
47 S3 Nivskiy U.S.S.R. 67.15N 32.30E
30 A4 Niwari Uttar Prad India 28.52N 77.32E
111 E2 Nixon Nevada 39.50N 119.22W
112 K6 Nixon Texas 29.17N 97.47W
Niya see Minfeng
Niya Bazar see Minfeng
Niya Darya R see Niya He
24 D7 Niya He R Xinjiang Uygur Zizhiqu China
37 F2 Niyandros isld Turkey 40.49N 29.07E
18 D9 Niyor Pen Malaysia 2.05N 103.15E
28 D1 Nizamabad Andhra Prad India 18.40N 78.05E
28 C1 Nizamabad dist Andhra Prad India
28 E3 Nizampatnam Andhra Prad India 15.56N 80.44E
28 C1 Nizam Sagar L Andhra Prad India 18.05N 78.00E
72 D7 Nizan, le France 44.28N 0.17W
65 K1 Nižbor Czechoslovakia 50.01N 14.01E
31 B4 Nizgan Afghanistan 33.09N 63.31E
47 K6 Nizh. Aremzyan U.S.S.R. 58.20N 68.38E
44 E4 Nizh Chegem U.S.S.R. 43.29N 43.20E
44 D4 Nizhmozero U.S.S.R. 64.21N 38.00E
41 H6 Nizhnaya Nele R U.S.S.R.
42 H4 Nizhnaya Pojma U.S.S.R. 55.48N 109.35E
42 C4 Nizhnebakanskiy U.S.S.R. 44.52N 37.52E
45 K5 Nizhnedevitsk U.S.S.R. 51.34N 38.22E
45 L9 Nizhne Gnilovskoy U.S.S.R. 47.12N 39.43E
44 D9 Nizhnegorskiy Ukraine U.S.S.R. 45.26N 34.44E
42 G4 Nizhneilimsk U.S.S.R. 57.12N 103.10E
41 E8 Nizhneimbatskoye U.S.S.R. 63.53N 87.37E
39 G6 Nizhne-Kamchatsk U.S.S.R. 56.15N 162.02E
47 G3 Nizhne Kamenka U.S.S.R. 67.27N 51.50E
39 G1 Nizhnekolymsk U.S.S.R. 68.34N 160.58E
39 G6 Nizhne-Ozernaya U.S.S.R. 57.17N 162.40E
45 F8 Nizhne Pirengskoye Ozero L U.S.S.R.
51 Q4 Nizhne Pirengskoye Ozero L U.S.S.R. 67.37N 31.50E
42 E3 Nizhneshadrino U.S.S.R. 59.55N 90.40E
40 H6 Nizhnetambovskoye U.S.S.R. 50.56N 138.10E
43 C1 Nizhnetroitskiy U.S.S.R. 54.22N 53.45E
42 F5 Nizhneudinsk U.S.S.R. 54.55N 99.00E
42 B2 Nizhnevartovskiy U.S.S.R. 60.57N 76.40E
42 B2 Nizhne Vodyanoy U.S.S.R. 46.34N 42.49E
44 E1 Nizhnevolzhsk U.S.S.R. 46.40N 47.50E
45 T10 Nizhneyansk U.S.S.R. 71.33N 136.15E
41 P5 Nizhnevyazovsk U.S.S.R. 71.33N 136.15E
39 E4 Nizhniye Ustriki U.S.S.R.
45 D4 Nizhniye Ustriki U.S.S.R. 52.32N 32.31E
47 G3 Nizhneye Bugayevo U.S.S.R. 66.00N 52.31E
42 K6 Nizhneye Giryunino U.S.S.R. 51.18N 116.58E
43 C1 Nizhneye Il'yasovo U.S.S.R. 52.54N 53.13E
42 H3 Nizhneye Karelina U.S.S.R. 57.52N 107.42E
47 C4 Nizhneye Kuyto,Oz L U.S.S.R.
45 V3 Nizhneye Sancheleyevo U.S.S.R. 53.41N 49.27E
47 M4 Nizhneye Selo U.S.S.R. 57.05N 59.30E
46 S2 Nizhni Irga U.S.S.R. 56.45N 57.00E
47 H7 Nizhni Irginski U.S.S.R. 56.50N 57.20E
42 C5 Nizhniy Artas U.S.S.R. 52.34N 90.12E
45 S8 Nizhniy Baskunchak U.S.S.R. 48.13N 46.50E
42 F5 Nizhniy Chir U.S.S.R. 48.22N 43.05E
42 B5 Nizhniy Chulym U.S.S.R. 54.35N 78.58E
46 R5 Nizhniy Dolgovskiy U.S.S.R. 50.33N 41.42E
45 P9 Nizhniye Cherni U.S.S.R. 47.44N 43.29E
47 J4 Nizhniye Narykary U.S.S.R. 63.15N 64.51E
47 M4 Nizhniye Sergi U.S.S.R. 56.40N 59.19E
45 F10 Nizhniye Serogozy Ukraine U.S.S.R. 46.51N 34.24E
47 M4 Nizhniye Tavolgi U.S.S.R. 57.36N 60.25E
42 E3 Nizhniye Tugiyany U.S.S.R. 63.27N 65.41E
45 U1 Nizhniye Vyazovye U.S.S.R. 55.46N 48.30E
39 H2 Nizhniy Iirneygytkhyn,Oz L U.S.S.R.
47 K2 Nizhniy Ingash U.S.S.R. 56.13N 96.33E
42 G6 Nizhniy Kholtoson U.S.S.R. 50.18N 103.38E
45 M6 Nizhniy Kislyay U.S.S.R. 50.54N 40.10E
40 C2 Nizhniy Kuranakh U.S.S.R. 58.51N 125.37E
45 P3 Nizhniy Lomov U.S.S.R. 53.33N 43.40E
47 L6 Nizhniy Nagol'chik Ukraine U.S.S.R. 48.02N 39.04E
47 G4 Nizhniy Odes U.S.S.R. 63.39N 54.51E
47 N6 Nizhniy Ol'shan U.S.S.R. 50.46N 39.31E
43 J8 Nizhniy Oserodok,Ostrov isld U.S.S.R.
43 J8 Nizhniy Pyandzh Tadzhikistan U.S.S.R. 37.14N 68.35E
47 N4 Nizhniy Shkaft U.S.S.R. 53.37N 45.40E
47 M3 Nizhniy Tagil U.S.S.R. 58.00N 59.58E
42 K6 Nizhniy Tsasuchey U.S.S.R. 50.30N 115.08E
47 M5 Nizhniy Ufaley U.S.S.R. 55.58N 60.00E
47 K5 Nizhniy Vyalozerskiy U.S.S.R. 66.54N 35.10E
47 F6 Nizhniy Yenangsk U.S.S.R. 59.59N 46.21E
42 E5 Nizhnyaya Baikha U.S.S.R. 64.45N 86.46E
45 N1 Nizhnyaya Bereya U.S.S.R. 55.14N 41.58E
45 T4 Nizhnyaya Chernavka U.S.S.R. 52.17N 47.12E
45 Q6 Nizhnyaya Dobrinka Volgograd U.S.S.R. 50.51N 44.45E
45 R5 Nizhnyaya Dobrinka Volgograd U.S.S.R. 50.21N 45.41E
45 K7 Nizhnyaya Duvanka Ukraine U.S.S.R. 49.35N 38.11E
42 G5 Nizhnyaya Iret' U.S.S.R. 53.00N 102.30E
47 L3 Nizhnyaya Khareuta U.S.S.R. 66.50N 73.30E
45 K8 Nizhnyaya Krynka Ukraine U.S.S.R. 48.07N 38.10E
40 C4 Nizhnyaya Larba R U.S.S.R.
42 E5 Nizhnyaya Mgla U.S.S.R. 66.29N 44.28E
45 L8 Nizhnyaya Ol'khovaya Ukraine U.S.S.R. 48.44N 39.35E
47 L7 Nizhnyaya Omka U.S.S.R. 55.28N 74.58E
42 M7 Nizhnyaya Omra U.S.S.R. 62.45N 55.48E
47 F3 Nizhnyaya Pesha U.S.S.R. 66.47N 47.40E
42 F4 Nizhnyaya Poyma U.S.S.R. 56.12N 97.14E
47 N3 Nizhnyaya Salda U.S.S.R. 58.09N 60.45E
43 K5 Nizhnyaya Savina U.S.S.R. 59.12N 91.25E
42 K6 Nizhnyaya Shakhtama U.S.S.R. 51.26N 117.45E
42 G5 Nizhnyaya Sloboda U.S.S.R. 54.43N 104.58E
45 J3 Nizhnyaya Suyetka U.S.S.R. 53.12N 79.53E
47 K6 Nizhnyaya Tavda U.S.S.R. 57.42N 66.08E
41 G3 Nizhnyaya Taymyra R U.S.S.R.
44 D4 Nizhnyaya Teberda U.S.S.R. 43.40N 41.56E
47 E4 Nizhnyaya Toyma R U.S.S.R.
38 J2 Nizhnyaya Tunguska R U.S.S.R.
47 M2 Nizhnyaya Tura U.S.S.R. 58.40N 59.48E
47 G5 Nizhnyaya Voch' U.S.S.R. 61.14N 54.06E
42 F4 Nizhnyaya Zaimka U.S.S.R. 56.09N 98.14E
47 N3 Nizhnyaya Zolotitsa U.S.S.R. 65.42N 40.10E
45 N9 Nizh. Paramonov U.S.S.R. 47.57N 41.57E
84 B3 Nizh Fatre 1.45N 30.18E
113 Q6 Nizina Alaska 61.17N 142.44W

113 Q6 Nizina R Alaska
37 D8 Nizip Turkey 37.02N 37.47E
37 P8 Nizip Turkey 37.02N 37.47E
37 D8 Nizip R Turkey
62 L7 Nízké Tatry mts Czechoslovakia
113 M9 Nizki I Aleutian Is 52.45N 174.00E
39 J4 Nizkiy,Mys C Kamchatka U.S.S.R. 61.39N 173.47E
39 K3 Nizkiy,Mys C Magadan U.S.S.R. 64.45N 179.32E
65 N2 Nížkov Czechoslovakia 49.32N 15.48E
40 G10 Nizmennyy,Mys C U.S.S.R. 43.32N 135.12E
62 M7 Nižní Medzev Czechoslovakia 48.43N 20.55E
72 E5 Nizonne R France
44 J6 Nizovaya Azerbaydzhan U.S.S.R. 41.31N 48.55E
33 M5 Nizwá Oman 22.56N 57.33E
46 J4 Nizy Ukraine U.S.S.R. 50.46N 34.42E
69 G4 Nizy-le-Comte France 49.35N 4.04E
81 K8 Nizza di Sicilia Sicily 37.59N 15.25E
79 D5 Nizza Monferrato Italy 44.47N 8.21E
35 A10 Nizzana ruins Israel 30.52N 34.26E
35 A10 Nizzana watercourse Israel
35 D4 Nizzane 'Oz Israel 32.18N 35.01E
35 B7 Nizzanim Israel 31.43N 34.38E
58 P10 Nizz,The pt Shetland Scotland 59.33N 1.36W
Njaän, Bukit see Nyaän, Bukit
50 M3 Njardhvík Iceland 65.34N 13.54W
50 C7 Njardhvikur Iceland 63.58N 22.33W
82 E8 Njegoš mt Yugoslavia 42.55N 18.42E
93 E5 Njeru Uganda 0.27N 33.11E
92 F6 Njila Tanzania 8.19S 32.46E
92 J6 Njinjo Tanzania 8.50S 38.52E
92 B10 Njoko R Zambia
91 G10 N'jomanca Angola 13.35S 20.58E
92 G6 Njombe Tanzania 9.20S 34.47E
92 G5 Njombe R Tanzania
93 G6 Njoro Kenya 0.20S 35.57E
92 H4 Njoro Tanzania 5.16S 36.30E
92 J10 Njoro, I Mozambique 16.26S 39.40E
92 H4 Njoro Neganga Tanzania 5.31S 36.41E
52 K4 Njurunda Sweden 62.15N 17.25E
52 K5 Njutånger Sweden 61.38N 17.05E
92 D11 Nkai Zimbabwe 19.00S 28.58E
90 C8 Nkalagu Nigeria 6.22N 7.48E
92 E5 Nkamba Tanzania 6.49S 30.50E
90 E8 Nkambe Cameroon 6.35N 10.44E
91 B3 Nkan R Gabon/Equat Guinea
95 P4 Nkandla S Africa 28.38S 31.06E
95 N7 Nkanga S Africa 31.28S 29.10E
92 F7 Nkanka R Zambia
94 E1 Nkarapamwe Namibia 17.52S 19.49E
93 M7 Nkashati Kenya 1.39S 40.55E
91 C6 N'Kayi Congo 4.07S 13.17E
92 G7 Nkhata Bay Malawi 11.37S 34.20E
92 G8 Nkhotakota Malawi 12.55S 34.19E
93 H8 Nkito Hills Kenya
91 B4 Nkogo Gabon 0.20S 10.28E
91 B3 Nkolabona Gabon 1.12N 11.33E
91 A4 N'Komi, Lag Gabon
92 E5 Nkonde Tanzania 6.20S 30.21E
91 H4 Nkone Zaïre 1.00S 22.15E
93 C5 Nkonge Uganda 0.14N 31.10E
90 D9 N'kongsamba Cameroon 4.59N 9.53E
89 J8 Nkoranza Ghana 7.39N 1.42W
93 D6 Nkose I Uganda 0.44S 32.19E
91 E3 Nkouda Congo 0.01N 16.25E
92 A9 Nkoya tribe Zambia
93 J6 Nkubu Kenya 0.03S 37.44E
92 F5 Nkululu R Tanzania
91 B3 Nkumekie Equat Guinea 1.40N 10.19E
93 B4 Nkusi R Uganda
95 O10 Nkwalini S Africa 28.45S 31.33E
25 N8 Nmai Hka R Burma
53 A4 No Denmark 56.07N 8.19E
28 L2 Noa Dihing R Assam India
72 D7 Noaillan France 44.30N 0.22W
69 C5 Noailles France 49.20N 2.12E
75 G2 Noain Spain 42.45N 1.38W
31 H9 Noakhali Bangladesh
31 H9 Noakhali dist Bangladesh
55 K2 Noak Hill London Eng 51.38N 0.14E
79 M3 Noale Italy 45.33N 12.04E
77 J5 Noalejo Spain 37.33N 3.39W
103 L4 Noank Connecticut 41.19N 72.00W
51 L3 Noarvas mt Norway 68.48N 24.44E
94 E4 Noasanabis Namibia 23.26S 18.46E
79 B4 Noasca Italy 45.27N 7.19E
113 F3 Noatak Alaska 67.33N 163.10W
113 F3 Noatak R Alaska
59 J4 Nobber Meath Irish Rep 53.49N 6.45W
99 K7 Nobel Ontario 45.26N 80.07W
20 E9 Nobeoka Japan 32.36N 131.40E
89 J6 Nobéré Upper Volta 11.37N 1.18W
20 C1 Nobidome Saitama Japan
107 H3 Noble Illinois 38.42N 88.15W
109 N6 Noble Oklahoma 35.10N 97.24W
100 D9 Nobleford Alberta 49.56N 113.03W
75 D8 Noblejas Spain 39.58N 3.26W
107 E7 Noble Lake Arkansas 34.10N 91.51W
95 G7 Noblesfontein S Africa 31.48S 23.10E
106 J9 Noblesville Indiana 40.03N 86.00W
19 C8 Nobo Indonesia 8.30S 122.49E
20 K2 Noboribetsu Japan 42.29N 141.10E
118 C4 Nobres Brazil 14.44S 56.16W
61 N8 Nobressart Belgium 49.44N 5.43E
103 N3 Nobska Pt C Massachusetts 41.31N 70.39W
20 M2 Nobuka Japan 42.16N 142.45E
81 M3 Nocara Italy 40.06N 16.29E
106 H4 Noc,Big Bay de Michigan
13 G8 Noccundra Queensland 27.45S 142.30E
70 M5 Noce France 48.23N 0.42E
79 J2 Noce R Italy
76 G3 Noceda Spain 42.43N 6.24W
80 L7 Nocera Inferiore Italy 40.43N 14.38E
81 M5 Nocera Terinese Italy 39.02N 16.10E
80 G2 Nocera Umbra Italy 43.06N 12.47E
79 H5 Noceto Italy 44.48N 10.11E
115 H7 Nochistlán Mexico 21.22N 102.51W
115 L9 Nochixtlán Mexico 17.29N 97.17W
81 O2 Noci Italy 40.47N 17.08E
81 R12 Nociglia Italy 40.02N 18.20E
13 G8 Nockatunga Queensland 27.40S 142.40E
71 D3 Nocle-Maulaix,la France 46.46N 3.48E
112 K2 Nocona Texas 33.48N 97.45W
82 J5 Nocrich Romania 45.55N 24.26E
20 P1 Noda Japan 40.05N 141.50E
20 A1 Noda Saitama Japan
121 M7 Nodales,B de los Argentina
108 Q9 Nodaway Iowa 40.58N 94.52W
108 Q8 Nodaway R Iowa
108 F7 Node Wyoming 42.44N 104.16W
Nodoa see Na-ta
71 J2 Nods France 47.06N 6.20E
66 E3 Nods Switzerland 47.07N 7.05E
61 K4 Noduwez Belgium 50.43N 4.58E
72 G9 Noé France 43.22N 1.16E
70 G6 Noé-Blanche France 47.48N 1.44W
118 D4 Noedori R Brazil
76 E8 Noeime R Portugal
107 B5 Noel Missouri 36.32N 94.29W
98 Q5 Noel Paul's Brook Newfoundland
99 K6 Noelville Ontario 46.09N 80.26W
89 K8 Noépé Togo 6.18N 1.08E
81 M3 Noepoli Italy 40.05N 16.20E
27 G11 Noeufs I Amirante Is Seychelles, Ind Oc 6.18S 53.02E
69 D3 Noeux les Mines France 50.29N 2.39E
76 L9 Noez mt Spain 39.45N 4.11W
66 P2 Nofels Austria 47.16N 9.35E
Nofilia,El see Nawfalīyah, An
75 D2 Nofuentes Spain 42.50N 3.25W
35 B7 Nogah Israel 31.38N 34.41E
111 O10 Nogales Arizona 31.20N 110.56W
115 D2 Nogales Sonora Mexico 31.20N 111.00W
77 C3 Nogales Spain 38.35N 6.45W
115 L8 Nogales Veracruz Mexico 18.50N 97.12W
87 L6 Nogal Valley reg Somalia
113 J6 Nogamut Alaska 61.00N 157.45W
79 K4 Nógara Italy 45.11N 11.04E
72 D8 Nogaro France 43.46N 0.02W
62 L1 Nogat R Poland
20 D8 Nōgata Japan 33.46N 130.42E
20 C3 Nōgaya Tōkyō Japan
44 G3 Nogayskiye Step' U.S.S.R.
43 D3 Nogayty Kazakhstan U.S.S.R. 48.23N 55.01E
39 C1 Nogdondzha R U.S.S.R.
69 J7 Nogent-en-Bassigny France 48.02N 5.22E
69 E6 Nogent-l'Artaud France 48.58N 3.20E
70 L5 Nogent-le-Bernard France 48.14N 0.30E
70 O4 Nogent-le-Roi France 48.39N 1.32E
70 M5 Nogent-le-Rotrou France 48.19N 0.50E
69 G7 Nogent-sur-Aube France 48.30N 4.19E
69 D6 Nogent-sur-Marne France 48.50N 2.30E
69 C5 Nogent-sur-Oise France 49.30N 2.28E
69 F7 Nogent-sur-Seine France 48.30N 3.31E
69 D8 Nogent-sur-Vernisson France 47.51N 2.45E
45 K1 Noginsk U.S.S.R. 55.52N 38.29E
41 F8 Noginskiy U.S.S.R. 64.30N 91.15E
40 J6 Nogliki Sakhalin U.S.S.R. 51.50N 143.10E
71 H3 Nogna France 46.36N 5.39E
13 K7 Nogo R Queensland
13 J6 Nogoa R Queensland
20 K6 Nōgōhoku san mt Japan 35.47N 136.30E
22 G7 Nogon Toli Nei Monggol Zizhiqu China 39.18N 105.35E
121 F4 Nogoyá Argentina 32.25S 59.50W
121 F4 Nogoya R Argentina
82 E3 Nográd co Hungary
75 E5 Nograles Spain 41.23N 2.59W
20 B2 Noguchi Tōkyō Japan
76 D4 Nogueira de Ramuin Spain 42.24N 7.42W
76 F5 Nogueira,Sa.de Portugal
75 G7 Noguera Spain 40.28N 1.36W
75 N2 Noguera de Cardós R Spain
75 M3 Noguera de Tor R Spain
75 M4 Noguera,La plain Spain
74 H2 Noguera Pallaresa R Spain
75 M3 Noguera Ribagorzana R Spain
75 J7 Nogueruelas Spain 40.14N 0.38W
Noh see Wüjang
31 K2 Noh Xizang Zizhiqu 33.30N 79.55E
72 H2 Nohant Vicq France 46.38N 1.58E
29 D3 Nohar Rajasthan India 29.11N 74.43E
20 P1 Noheji Japan 40.51N 141.09E
64 C4 Nohfelden W Germany 49.35N 7.09E
114 E3 Nohili Pt Hawaiian Is 22.04N 159.47W
30 A5 Nohjhil Uttar Prad India 27.52N 77.39E
64 B3 Nohn W Germany 50.20N 6.48E
Noi see Ban Noi
25 F5 Noi R Thailand
81 N1 Noicattaro Italy 41.02N 17.00E
71 H1 Noidans-le-Ferroux France 47.34N 5.57E
72 F8 Noilhan France 43.33N 0.56E
72 L7 Noir,Causse plat France
61 F5 Noirchain Belgium 50.24N 3.56E
99 N6 Noire R Quebec
25 H2 Noire R Vietnam
61 L7 Noirefontaine Belgium 49.49N 5.05E
72 J9 Noire, Montagne mts France
70 C5 Noires,Mtgnes France
71 D5 Noirétable France 45.49N 3.45E
121 J10 Noir,I Chile 54.30S 73.02W
66 A6 Noirmont mt Switzerland 46.30N 6.08E
66 D3 Noirmont,le Switzerland 47.14N 6.58E
70 F7 Noirmoutier France 47.01N 2.15W
70 F8 Noirmoutier,Ile de France 47.00N 2.15W
66 B5 Noir Mt France 46.43N 6.16E
70 C5 Noir,Mt France 48.11N 3.32W
72 D2 Noirterre France 46.52N 0.23W
76 E1 Nois Spain 43.36N 7.20W
25 H4 Noi,Se R Laos
61 M5 Noiseux Belgium 50.18N 5.23E
69 L5 Noisseville France 49.08N 6.16E
68 H3 Noisy-le-Grand France 48.51N 2.33E
74 H9 Noisy les Bains Algeria 35.47N 0.03E
68 G3 Noisy-le-Sec France 48.54N 2.27E
94 F4 Nojane Botswana 23.10S 20.10E
20 N7 Nojima-zaki C Japan 34.54N 139.54E
20 M5 Nojiri-ko L Japan
94 G2 Nokaneng Botswana 19.40S 22.12E
61 E3 Nokere Belgium 50.53N 3.31E
29 C4 Nokh Rajasthan India 27.33N 72.20E
31 B8 Nokhbur Pakistan 25.29N 63.01E
32 J7 Nokhowch,Kūh-e mt Iran 26.34N 60.24E
42 K3 Nokhtuysk U.S.S.R. 59.55N 117.45E
43 D7 Nokhur Turkmeniya U.S.S.R. 38.29N 57.00E
91 D6 Noki Zaïre 5.07S 14.49E
51 K10 Nokia Finland 61.29N 23.31E
31 B6 Nok Kundi Pakistan 28.49N 62.50E
11 C12 Nokomai New Zealand 45.33S 168.41E
107 G2 Nokomis Illinois 39.18N 89.18W
100 N7 Nokomis Saskatchewan 51.30N 105.00W
101 W7 Nokomis L Saskatchewan 57.00N 103.10W
90 G4 Nokou Chad 14.36N 14.45E
87 G3 Nokra Ethiopia 15.40N 39.55E
28 H3 Nokrek Pk Meghalaya India 25.29N 90.19E
87 C6 No,L Sudan 9.30N 30.30E
90 H10 Nola Cent Afr Rep 3.28N 16.08E
80 L7 Nola Italy 40.55N 14.32E
100 N2 Nolalu Ontario 48.19N 89.49W
108 N2 Nolan N Dakota 47.09N 97.32W
112 G3 Nolan Texas 32.16N 100.15W
13 G3 Nolan R Queensland
71 F3 Nolay France 46.57N 4.38E
39 J1 Nol'de Guba gulf U.S.S.R.
53 E5 Nølev Denmark 56.00N 10.13E
93 L5 Noleye Kenya 0.30N 39.12E
79 D6 Noli Italy 44.12N 8.25E
92 J7 Noli Tanzania 10.18S 38.18E
105 E1 Nolichucky R Tennessee
105 E1 Nolichucky Dam Tennessee 36.03N 82.54W
46 P1 Nolinsk U.S.S.R. 57.38N 49.52E
95 F9 Noll S Africa 33.46S 22.54E
66 O5 Nolla R Switzerland
70 N3 Nolléval France 49.29N 1.29E
61 L7 Nollevaux Belgium 49.52N 5.07E
53 N10 Nolsø isld Faeroes 61.58N 6.37W
Nólsoy isld see Nolsø
51 E6 Nolvik Sweden 65.41N 15.50E
66 B8 Nom R France
105 B7 Noma Florida 30.59N 85.39W
94 F2 Noma Namibia 19.15S 20.12E
94 F2 Nomab watercourse Namibia
20 L4 Nōmachi Japan 37.08N 137.59E
15 G7 Nomad Papua New Guinea 6.18S 142.13E
15 G7 Nomad R Papua New Guinea
20 D10 Noma-misaki C Japan 31.27N 130.06E
39 C5 Nomankur,Ozero L U.S.S.R. 59.55N 142.38E
103 N4 No Mans Land isld Massachusetts 41.15N 70.49W
33 B8 Noma, Ra's C Bahrain, The Gulf 25.59N 50.29E
90 G7 Nomatchi Cameroon 8.32N 15.04E
76 K8 Nombela Spain 40.10N 4.30W
115 P5 Nombre de Dios Panama 9.34N 79.26W
113 E4 Nome Alaska 64.30N 165.30W
113 E4 Nome, C Alaska 64.26N 164.58W
22 L3 Nomenkan Mongolia 47.54N 118.32E
69 L6 Nomény France 48.54N 6.14E
69 L7 Nomexy France 48.19N 6.22E
22 G5 Nomgon Mongolia 42.50N 105.13E
22 D8 Nomhon Qinghai China 36.23N 96.30E
22 D8 Nomhon He R Qinghai China
99 P6 Nominingue Quebec 46.24N 75.03W
9 T8 Nomosi Pks Viti Levu Fiji 18.00S 178.05E
20 C9 Nomo-zaki C Japan 32.33N 129.44E
42 G6 Nomto U.S.S.R. 50.44N 104.50E
9 T13 Nomuka isld Tonga, Pacific Oc 20.15S 174.46W
9 T13 Nomuka Grp islds Tonga, Pacific Oc
9 T13 Nomuka Iki isld Tonga, Pacific Oc 20.16S 174.46W
30 D6 Non R Uttar Prad India
72 E5 Nonac France 45.24N 0.03E
101 T5 Nonacho L N W Terr
70 N4 Nonancourt France 48.46N 1.13E
70 J3 Nonant France 49.14N 0.38W
70 L4 Nonant-le-Pin France 48.42N 0.13E
79 K5 Nonántola Italy 44.41N 11.03E
30 C8 Nonapanji Madhya Prad India 24.38N 79.51E
72 H5 Nonards France 45.01N 1.47E
75 L5 Nonaspe Spain 41.13N 0.14E
47 G3 Nonburg U.S.S.R. 65.32N 50.37E
113 K7 Nondalton Alaska 60.00N 154.52W
15 H6 Nondugl Papua New Guinea 5.53S 144.45E
95 O4 Nondweni S Africa 28.11S 30.49E
79 C5 None Italy 44.56N 7.33E
21 C5 Nong 'an Jilin China 44.25N 125.10E
25 H3 Nong Het Laos 19.29N 104.01E
25 N7 Nonghkai Burma 27.16N 97.32E
25 G5 Nong Hong Thailand 14.16N 102.45E
21 F4 Nong Jiang R Heilongjiang China
25 G4 Nong Khai Thailand 17.52N 102.44E
28 H3 Nongkhlao Meghalaya India 25.40N 91.40E
Nong Makha see Ban Nong Makha
95 O9 Nongoma S Africa 27.54S 31.40E
28 H3 Nongpoh Meghalaya India 25.54N 91.54E
28 H3 Nongstoin Meghalaya India 25.30N 91.16E
94 C4 Nonidas Namibia 22.36S 14.40E
71 E7 Nonières France 44.55N 4.30E
66 P1 Nonnenhorn W Germany 47.34N 9.37E
12 D5 Nonning S Australia 32.31S 136.29E
12 D4 Nonning,Mt S Australia 32.25S 136.57E
Nonni River see Nen Jiang
87 F6 Nonno Ethiopia 8.31N 37.28E
64 B4 Nonnweiler W Germany 49.36N 6.59E
119 B8 Nono Ecuador 0.01S 78.28W
121 H1 Nonoaí Brazil 27.25S 52.46W
115 F4 Nonoava Mexico 27.30N 106.41W
77 S11 Nonó,C Balearic Is 39.02N 1.18E
19 M7 Nonoc isld Philippines 9.52N 125.37E
114 E4 Nonopahu Ridge Hawaiian Is
114 D4 Nonopapa Hawaiian Is 21.52N 160.14W
9 B5 Nonouti atoll Kiribati, Pacific Oc 0.44S 174.28E
21 D9 Nonsan S Korea 36.10N 127.02E
100 W2 Nonsuch Manitoba 56.10N 95.30W
96 D1 Nonsuch I Bermuda 32.21N 64.40W
25 F6 Nonthaburi Thailand 13.48N 100.11E
72 F4 Nontron France 45.32N 0.40E
79 K2 Non,Val di V Italy
113 K7 Nonvianuk L Alaska 59.02N 155.20W
67 P11 Nonza Corsica 42.47N 9.20E
95 O1 Nooitgedacht Dam res Transvaal S Africa 25.57S 30.05E
12 H7 Noojee Victoria 37.57S 146.00E
14 B7 Nookawarra W Australia 26.19S 116.54E
12 D3 Noolyeanna L S Australia
108 G1 Noonan N Dakota 48.54N 103.00W
14 C9 Noongaar W Australia 31.21S 118.55E
14 B8 Noongal W Australia 28.11S 116.42E
14 E4 Noonkanbah W Australia 18.33S 124.51E
13 H8 Noorama R Queensland
60 T17 Noorbeek Netherlands 50.46N 5.48E
60 H9 Noord Beemster Netherlands 52.35N 4.55E
60 B2 Noord Beveland isld Netherlands
60 G13 Noord Brabant prov Netherlands
60 Q7 Noordbroek Netherlands 53.12N 6.52E
60 P7 Noorddijk Netherlands 53.15N 6.37E
60 H11 Noorden Netherlands 52.10N 4.50E
60 M14 Noordenvaart canal Netherlands
61 K2 Noorderwijk Belgium 51.08N 4.50E
60 C2 Noordgouwe Netherlands 51.42N 3.56E
60 H10 Noord Holland prov Netherlands
60 G8 Noord Hollandsch Kanaal canal Netherlands
60 O6 Noordhorn Netherlands 53.16N 6.24E
95 P1 Noordkaap S Africa 25.42S 31.05E
60 P7 Noordlaren Netherlands 53.07N 6.40E
60 G12 Noord Merwede R Netherlands
94 D7 Noordoewer Namibia 28.46S 17.37E
60 L9 Noord-Oost-Polder polder Netherlands
116 B1 Noord Pt Curaçao W I 12.28N 69.08W
60 H9 Noord Scharwoude Netherlands 52.42N 4.48E
61 B3 Noordschote Belgium 50.57N 2.49E
60 P9 Noordse Schut Netherlands 52.43N 6.32E
60 Q8 Noordsleen Netherlands 52.47N 6.47E
60 C2 Noordwelle Netherlands 51.43N 3.47E
60 F11 Noordwijk aan Zee Netherlands 52.15N 4.25E
60 F11 Noordwijk-Binnen Netherlands 52.14N 4.26E
60 F10 Noordwijkerhout Netherlands 52.16N 4.30E
60 P7 Noord Willems Kanaal canal Netherlands
60 N8 Noordwolde Netherlands 52.54N 6.10E
60 G10 Noordzeekanaal canal Netherlands
51 J10 Noormarkku Finland 61.35N 21.50E
113 G3 Noorvik Alaska 66.50N 161.14W
13 L7 Noosa Hd Queensland 26.25S 153.03E
13 L7 Noosaville Queensland 26.25S 153.02E
103 L3 Nooseneck Rhode I 41.38N 71.35W
101 K11 Nootka Vancouver I, Br Col 49.34N 126.39W
101 K11 Nootka I Vancouver I, Br Col 49.45N 126.50W
101 K11 Nootka Sd Vancouver I, Br Col
86 H6 No'oz, Wâdî watercourse Egypt
111 H5 Nopah Ra California
115 K7 Nopala pk Mexico 20.26N 99.40W
115 L9 Nopola Mexico 16.08N 97.11W
106 G4 Noquebay,L Wisconsin 45.15N 87.54W
91 C6 Noqui Angola 5.54S 13.30E
53 U15 Nor-Norway 61.54N 6.07E
108 N9 Nora Nebraska 40.12N 97.58W
52 H7 Nora Ørebro Sweden 59.32N 15.02E
100 O6 Nora Saskatchewan 52.23N 103.50W
52 L4 Nora Västernorrland Sweden 62.53N 18.05E
52 K6 Nora Västmanland Sweden 60.10N 16.57E
81 C6 Nora anc site Sardinia 39.00N 9.01E
76 H2 Nora R Spain
40 E5 Nora R U.S.S.R.
53 D3 Nørager Denmark 56.43N 9.38E
81 B3 Noragugume Sardinia 40.13N 8.55E
87 H2 Nora I Ethiopia 16.00N 40.04E
19 M8 Norala Mindanao Philippines 6.32N 124.34E
99 L4 Noranda Quebec 48.16N 79.03W
13 F5 Noranside Queensland 22.10S 140.04E
108 S6 Nora Springs Iowa 43.09N 93.00W
108 L4 Norbeck S Dakota 45.11N 99.12W
52 J6 Norberg Sweden 60.04N 15.34E
107 C2 Norborne Missouri 39.17N 93.41W
109 K2 Norcatur Kansas 39.51N 100.13W
80 H3 Norcia Italy 42.47N 13.05E
107 F12 Norco Louisiana 29.58N 90.24W
14 D9 Norcott,Mt W Australia 32.07S 122.00E
105 C4 Norcross Georgia 33.56N 84.12W
48 V2 Nord Greenland 81.30N 17.30W
67 H2 Nord dept France
89 F7 Nord dept Ivory Coast
90 F7 Nord reg Cameroon
52 E7 Nordagutu Norway 59.14N 9.17E
52 L2 Nordanåso Sweden 64.16N 18.10E
48 H9 Nordaustlandet C Greenland 81.30N 12.00W
50 U13 Nordaustlandet isld Spitsbergen
53 Y15 Nordberg Norway 61.54N 8.10E
53 Y20 Nordbø Norway 59.20N 8.29E
53 D6 Nordborg Denmark 55.04N 9.41E
41 N2 Nordbruk,Ostrov isld Franz Josef Land U.S.S.R.
53 A6 Nordby Ribe Denmark 55.27N 8.25E
53 F5 Nordby Vestjælland Denmark 55.58N 10.33E
Nord Cap see Horn,C Iceland
53 S15 Norddal Norway 61.39N 5.24E
53 W14 Norddal Norway 62.15N 7.15E
53 S15 Norddal inlet Norway 61.38N 5.15E
53 W14 Norddalsfjorden inlet Norway 62.16N 7.10E
53 N9 Norddeble Faeroes 62.18N 6.31W
63 F5 Norddeich W Germany 53.37N 7.10E
63 H3 Norddorf W Germany 54.41N 8.20E
63 L7 Norddrebber W Germany 52.42N 9.35E
Nordegg see Brazeau
100 B6 Nordegg R Alberta
53 U16 Nordeide Norway 61.10N 6.00E
56 M2 Nordelph Norfolk Eng 52.35N 0.18E
63 F5 Norden W Germany 53.36N 7.13E
64 K6 Nordendorf W Germany 48.35N 10.50E
63 H5 Nordenham W Germany 53.30N 8.29E
41 F3 Nordenshel'da,Arkhipelag arch U.S.S.R.
41 B2 Nordenshel'da,Zaliv B Novaya Zemlya U.S.S.R.
50 S15 Nordenskiøld Spitsbergen
101 E5 Nordenskiold R Yukon Terr
53 B5 Nordenskov Denmark 55.39N 8.41E
63 H3 Norderaue inlet W Germany
63 J5 Nordergründe sandbank W Germany
63 J4 Norderhever inlet W Germany
63 F5 Norderney W Germany 53.43N 7.09E
63 F5 Norderney isld W Germany
53 N9 Norderøerne island grp Faeroes
63 J3 Norderoog isld W Germany
63 L5 Norderstedt W Germany 53.43N 8.59E
89 L6 Nord-Est dept Benin
96 V1 Nordeste Azores 37.35N 25.10W
96 V1 Nordestinho Azores 37.36N 25.12W
53 T15 Nordfjord inlet Norway
53 T15 Nordfjord reg Norway
53 U15 Nordfjordeid Norway 61.54N 6.01E
50 S14 Nordfjorden inlet Spitsbergen
51 E4 Nordfold Norway 67.48N 15.20E
63 H3 Nord-friesische Inseln islds W Germany
63 J3 Nordfriesland reg W Germany
53 Y14 Nord Grøna R Norway
64 M3 Nordhalben W Germany 50.22N 11.31E
63 N9 Nordhausen E Germany 51.31N 10.48E
112 K7 Nordheim Texas 28.57N 97.37W
50 M4 Nordhfjördhur B Iceland
50 E5 Nordhlingafljót R Iceland
63 J5 Nordholz W Germany 53.47N 8.38E
63 F8 Nordhorn W Germany 52.27N 7.05E
50 D5 Nordhtunga Iceland 64.44N 21.22W
50 D5 Nordhurá R Iceland
50 B3 Nordhurbotn Iceland 65.36N 23.45W
50 K5 Nordhurdalur V Iceland
50 J3 Nordhur Fjoll mts Iceland
50 D2 Nordhurfjördhur Iceland 66.03N 21.32W
50 F5 Nordhurjökull ice cap Iceland 64.40N 19.57W
26 N15 Nord,I.du St Paul I Ind Oc 38.42S 77.30E
52 L4 Nordingrå Sweden 62.56N 18.20E
35 C4 Nordiyya Israel 32.19N 34.54E
50 O9 Nord-Jan Jan Mayen I
53 C3 Nordjylland co Denmark
50 P9 Nordkapp Jan Mayen I 71.10N 7.56W
51 M1 Nordkapp C Norway 71.11N 25.40E
50 R11 Nordkapp C Spitsbergen 74.31N 19.20E
50 U12 Nordkapp C Spitsbergen 80.30N 20.00E
51 N1 Nordkinn Norway 71.07N 27.40E
51 H2 Nordkjosbotn Norway 69.14N 19.34E
48 T1 Nordkronen pk Greenland 82.50N 33.30W
53 S17 Nord Kvingo Norway 60.45N 5.23E
51 C6 Nordland co Norway
52 H2 Nordli Norway 64.37N 13.36E
64 K6 Nördlingen W Germany 48.51N 10.31E
52 L3 Nordmaling Sweden 63.35N 19.30E
110 J1 Nordman Idaho 48.37N 116.56W
53 W18 Nordmannslågen L Norway 60.11N 7.26E
52 H7 Nordmark Sweden 59.52N 14.05E
52 E6 Nordmarka reg Norway
103 B4 Nordmont Pennsylvania 41.23N 76.29W
52 C4 Nordmøre reg Norway
52 F6 Nord-Odal Norway 60.23N 11.31E
108 K7 Nordon Nebraska 42.53N 100.03W
53 O9 Nordöre Faeroes 62.12N 6.30W
41 G3 Nord,Os isld U.S.S.R.
48 V2 Nordostrundingen pt Greenland 82.00N 12.30W
63 K4 Nord-Ostsee-Kanal W Germany
53 S15 Nordpollen Norway 61.58N 5.19E
26 N15 Nord,Pte C St Paul I Ind Oc 38.42S 77.29E
51 J2 Nordreisa Norway 69.46N 21.00E
48 R10 Nordre Isortoq fjord Greenland
53 Y16 Nordre Knipen mt Norway 61.19N 8.05E
53 F2 Nordre Rønner rocks Denmark 57.25N 10.57E
48 R10 Nordre Strømfjord fjord Greenland
62 C4 Nordrhein-Westfalen land W Germany
53 H6 Nordrupøster Denmark 55.25N 11.54E
53 U20 Nord Skår Norway 59.09N 6.05E
53 Y18 Nord Skarvsvatn L Norway
53 F5 Nordskov Denmark 55.36N 10.38E
53 B6 Nord Slesvig reg Denmark
53 X15 Nørdstedalsseter Norway 61.39N 7.48E
53 L8 Nord-stemmen W Germany 52.10N 9.47E
63 J4 Nordstrand isld W Germany
63 J3 Nordstrandischmoor isld W Germany
53 T16 Nordstrandsvatn L Norway 61.11N 5.29E
52 F2 Nord-Trøndelag co Norway
37 G8 Norduz Turkey 37.55N 43.59E
37 G7 Norduz R Turkey
Nord Vågsöy see Raudeberg
48 U11 Nordvestfjord inlet Greenland
53 W13 Nordvik Norway 62.35N 7.29E
41 K4 Nordvik U.S.S.R. 74.01N 111.30E
41 K4 Nordvik,Bukhta gulf U.S.S.R.
41 K4 Nordvik, Mys C U.S.S.R. 74.00N 112.58E
63 F8 Nordwalde W Germany 52.05N 7.30E
52 D6 Nore Norway 60.13N 8.59E
52 E6 Norefjell mt Norway 60.19N 9.36E
98 E1 Noré,L Quebec 52.04N 67.40W
56 N5 Nore Lt Kent Eng 51.29N 0.49E
99 K4 Norembega Ontario 48.59N 80.44W
76 H2 Noreña Spain 43.24N 5.43W
72 J9 Nore,Pic de mt France 43.25N 2.27E
59 H6 Nore,R Kilkenny Irish Rep
75 R3 Norfeo,C Spain 42.14N 3.16E
103 H3 Norfolk Connecticut 41.59N 73.10W
103 M2 Norfolk Massachusetts 42.08N 71.20W
108 N7 Norfolk Nebraska 42.01N 97.25W
99 Q2 Norfolk New York 44.48N 74.59W
104 J10 Norfolk Virginia 36.54N 76.18W
56 N2 Norfolk co England
103 M2 Norfolk co Massachusetts
10 O7 Norfolk I Pacific Oc 29.05S 167.59E
10 O6 Norfolk Island Ridge Pacific Oc
10 O6 Norfolk Island Trough Pacific Oc
107 D5 Norfork Arkansas 36.11N 92.17W
107 D5 Norfork L Arkansas
52 D3 Nor Frøya Norway 63.47N 8.51E
60 O7 Norg Netherlands 53.04N 6.28E
37 F5 Norgâh Turkey 40.26N 40.47E
60 O7 Norgervaart Netherlands 53.02N 6.29E
71 G2 Norges-la-Ville France 47.25N 5.06E
53 A3 Nørhå Denmark 56.54N 8.27E
58 M7 Norham Northumb Eng 55.43N 2.10W
53 U18 Norheimsund Norway 60.22N 6.09E
53 D2 Nørholm Denmark 57.02N 9.45E
47 L3 Nori U.S.S.R. 66.12N 72.21E
120 D9 Noria Chile 20.24S 69.50W
112 K9 Norias Texas 26.47N 97.48W
20 L5 Norikura-dake pk Japan 36.09N 137.32E
41 E6 Noril'sk U.S.S.R. 69.21N 88.02E
18 B6 Noring, Gunong mt Pen Malaysia 5.24N 101.43E
18 B6 Noring Timur mt Pen Malaysia 5.20N 101.46E
46 O4 Norka U.S.S.R. 51.12N 45.18E
44 F7 Nor Kharberd Armenia U.S.S.R. 40.06N 44.28E
13 G8 Norley Queensland 27.46S 143.50E
Norlim see Buxton
105 J1 Norlina N Carolina 36.27N 78.13W
80 G5 Norma Italy 41.34N 12.59E
103 C5 Normal Pennsylvania 40.47N 75.49W
107 C7 Norman Arkansas 34.28N 93.40W
108 M9 Norman Nebraska 40.30N 98.48W
109 N6 Norman Oklahoma 35.14N 97.27W
13 F4 Norman R Queensland
11 J6 Normanby New Zealand 39.32S 174.18E
11 M12 Normanby dist Dunedin New Zealand
13 G2 Normanby R Queensland
15 L8 Normanby I D'Entrecasteaux Is Papua New Guinea
13 K5 Normanby Ra Queensland
56 L2 Norman Cross Cambs Eng 52.30N 0.17W
11 D5 Normandale New Zealand 41.12S 174.54E
Normandes,Iles see Channel Is
119 J5 Normandia Brazil 4.22N 59.52W
67 E4 Normandie prov France
95 N3 Normandien S Africa 27.59S 29.47E
99 S4 Normandin Quebec 48.49N 72.31W
107 K6 Normandy Tennessee 35.27N 86.18W
112 L4 Normangee Texas 31.02N 96.06W
12 K6 Normanhurst New S Wales 33.44S 151.06E
14 E7 Norman Hurst,Mt W Australia 25.03S 122.33E
105 L7 Norman I Virgin Is 18.21N 64.39W
11 B7 Norman Inlet Auckland Is Pacific Oc
105 F2 Norman L N Carolina 35.40N 81.00W
112 K7 Normanna Texas 28.33N 97.49W
13 K2 Norman Park dist Brisbane, Qnsld
103 B9 Normans Maryland 38.56N 76.21W
13 F4 Normanton Queensland 17.40S 141.05E
101 K3 Norman Wells N W Terr 65.18N 126.42W
69 G6 Normée France 48.48N 4.04E
99 L4 Normétal Quebec 48.59N 79.23W
14 B10 Nornalup W Australia 34.58S 116.14E
115 F4 Norogachic Mexico 27.16N 107.09W
26 P15 Noroît, B du Kerguelen Indian Oc
118 B3 Noronha,R Brazil
71 J1 Noroy-le-Bourg France 47.37N 6.18E
107 D8 Norphlet Arkansas 33.18N 92.40W
100 Q7 Norquay Saskatchewan 51.52N 101.59W
121 B8 Ñorquinco Argentina 41.51S 70.55W
51 G5 Norra Bergnäs Sweden 66.24N 18.10E
52 H9 Norra Hestra Sweden 57.28N 13.35E
52 J2 Norråker Sweden 64.25N 15.40E
51 H8 Norra Kvarken channel Finland/Sweden
52 K5 Norrala Sweden 61.23N 17.05E
52 K10 Norra Möckleby Sweden 56.38N 16.40E
52 G6 Norra Ny Sweden 60.24N 13.15E
52 H10 Norraryd Sweden 56.28N 14.45E
52 H9 Norra Sandsjö Sweden 57.28N 14.45E
51 E6 Norra Storfjället mt Sweden 65.54N 15.10E
52 G8 Norra Vånga Sweden 58.16N 13.20E
52 J9 Norra Vi Sweden 57.53N 15.20E
52 K5 Norrbo Sweden 61.51N 16.45E
51 F4 Norrbotten dist Sweden
53 B4 Nørreå R Denmark
53 D4 Nørreå R Denmark
53 D6 Nørre Åby Denmark 55.28N 9.53E
53 H7 Nørre Alslev Denmark 54.54N 11.53E
53 B2 Nørre Arup Denmark 57.01N 8.56E
53 H5 Nørre Asmindrup Denmark 55.53N 11.38E
53 E1 Nørre Bindslev Denmark 57.33N 10.13E
53 D5 Nørre Bjert Denmark 55.31N 9.33E
53 A5 Nørre Bork Denmark 55.51N 8.19E
53 E6 Nørre Broby Denmark 55.16N 10.15E
53 B4 Nørre Felding Denmark 56.19N 8.37E
53 A5 Nørre Havrvig Denmark 55.57N 8.10E
53 J5 Nørre Herlev Denmark 55.54N 12.18E
53 H7 Nørre Kirkeby Denmark 54.53N 11.53E
53 E3 Nørre Kongerslev Denmark 56.54N 10.09E
53 D2 Nørre Lyngby Denmark 57.25N 9.46E
53 A4 Nørre Lyngvig Denmark 56.03N 8.08E
53 E5 Nørre Nærå Denmark 55.34N 10.18E
53 A5 Nørre Nebel Denmark 55.47N 8.18E
69 C2 Norrent Fontès France 50.35N 2.25E
53 C3 Nørre Ørum Denmark 56.34N 9.14E
53 D2 Nørre Saltum Denmark 57.17N 9.43E
53 C5 Nørre Snede Denmark 55.58N 9.24E
53 E6 Nørre Søby Denmark 55.17N 10.23E
53 D2 Nørresundby Denmark 57.04N 9.56E
53 D6 Nørre Vilstrup Denmark 55.13N 9.32E
53 B4 Nørre Vium Denmark 56.02N 8.44E
53 A3 Nørre Vorupør Denmark 56.58N 8.23E
51 J6 Norrfjärden Sweden 65.25N 21.30E
52 L3 Norrfors Sweden 63.48N 19.00E
106 Q1 Norridge dist Chicago, Illinois
104 Q2 Norridgewock Maine 44.43N 69.48W
106 D9 Norris Illinois 40.38N 90.03W
110 O4 Norris Montana 45.35N 111.40W
108 J6 Norris S Dakota 43.29N 101.11W
107 M5 Norris Tennessee 36.11N 84.05W
110 P5 Norris Wyoming 44.44N 110.41W
98 R4 Norris Arm Newfoundland 49.06N 55.18W
107 H4 Norris City Illinois 37.59N 88.20W
107 M5 Norris Dam Tennessee 36.13N 84.06W
105 D1 Norris L Tennessee
98 P4 Norris Point Newfoundland 49.32N 57.55W
103 D6 Norristown Pennsylvania 40.07N 75.20W
103 A7 Norrisville Maryland 39.43N 76.32W
52 J8 Norrköping Sweden 58.35N 16.10E
51 H8 Norrskär Lt.Ho Finland 63.07N 20.40E
52 K6 Norrsundet Sweden 60.57N 17.10E
52 L7 Norrtälje Sweden 59.46N 18.43E
53 B2 Nors Denmark 57.02N 8.41E
52 G7 Norsälven R Sweden
14 D9 Norseman W Australia 32.15S 121.47E
11 L7 Norsewood New Zealand 40.04S 176.15E
52 J8 Norsholm Sweden 58.30N 16.00E
Norşin see Çukur
52 M2 Norsjö Sweden 64.55N 19.30E
52 E7 Norsjø L Norway
40 E5 Norsk U.S.S.R. 52.22N 129.57E
48 V4 Norske Øer islds Greenland
51 N1 Norskholmen Norway 70.22N 28.11E
53 E4 Norsminde Denmark 56.02N 10.17E
53 B2 Nors Sø L Denmark 57.02N 8.37E
120 A12 Norte,C Alejandro Selkirk, I Pacific Oc 33.44S 80.46W
117 D4 Norte,C Brazil 1.43N 49.55W
122 U15 Norte,C Easter I Pacific Oc 27.03S 109.24W
117 D4 Norte, Canal do channel Brazil
121 J7 Norte,Cerro pk Argentina 49.45S 73.05W
119 D3 Norte de Santander div Colombia
117 F2 Norte, I. do Martin Vaz Atlantic Oc
118 C4 Nortelândia Brazil 14.25S 56.50W
63 L9 Nörten Hardenburg W Germany 51.37N 9.57E
121 G6 Norte,Pta C Buenos Aires Argentina 36.20S 56.45W
121 A9 Norte,Pta C Chile 43.32S 74.50W
121 D9 Norte,Pta C Chubut Arg 42.05S 63.46W
121 L8 Norte,Pta C Santa Cruz Arg 50.06S 68.05W
96 P11 Norte, Pta. del Hierro Canary Is 27.51N 17.51W
96 V4 Norte,Pta.do Azores 37.01N 25.04W
121 D3 Norte,Sa.de ra Argentina
118 B1 Norte,Sa.do mts Brazil
105 F4 North S Carolina 33.37N 81.06W
104 M4 North Adams Massachusetts 42.42N 73.07W
106 K8 North Adams Michigan 41.58N 84.31W
57 L4 Northallerton N Yorks Eng 54.20N 1.26W
94 J5 Northam S Africa 25.03S 27.11E
14 B9 Northam W Australia 31.40S 116.40E
96 D6 North American Basin Atlantic Oc
103 J2 North Amherst Massachusetts 42.25N 72.31W
103 J2 Northampton Massachusetts 42.19N 72.38W
56 K3 Northampton Northants Eng 52.14N 0.54W
103 D5 Northampton Pennsylvania 40.40N 75.29W
14 A8 Northampton W Australia 28.27S 114.37E
56 K3 Northampton co England
103 D5 Northampton co Pennsylvania
114 B1 Northampton Banks Hawaiian Is
13 H6 Northampton Downs Queensland 24.33S 145.46E
28 G6 North Andaman isld Andaman Is
104 H9 North Anna R Virginia
104 Q2 North Anson Maine 44.53N 69.54W
103 H7 North Arlington New Jersey 40.47N 74.08W
101 Q4 North Arm inlet Great Slave L, N W Terr
9 S3 North Astrolabe Reef Fiji 18.40S 178.30E
103 M3 North Attleboro Massachusetts 41.59N 71.20W
105 F4 North Augusta S Carolina 33.30N 81.58W
97 N6 North Aulatsivik I Labrador, Nfld 59.50N 64.00W
26 L7 North Australian Basin Indian Oc
19 H7 North Balabac Str Philippines
58 F5 North Ballachulish Highland Scotland 56.42N 5.11W
104 B5 North Baltimore Ohio 41.12N 83.43W
100 J6 North Battleford Saskatchewan 52.47N 108.19W
98 O6 North Bay Newfoundland 47.48N 58.20W
99 L6 North Bay Ontario 46.20N 79.28W
108 O8 North Bend Nebraska 41.29N 96.48W
110 A6 North Bend Oregon 43.26N 124.14W
104 M4 North Bennington Vermont 42.56N 73.14W
103 J7 North Bergen New Jersey 40.48N 74.03W
56 K6 North Bersted W Sussex Eng 50.48N 0.42W
58 L6 North Berwick Lothian Scotland 56.04N 2.44W
104 P3 North Berwick Maine 43.18N 70.44W
103 F2 North Blenheim New York 42.28N 74.28W
North Borneo see Sabah
108 P9 Northboro Iowa 40.37N 95.20W
103 L2 Northborough Massachusetts 42.19N 71.38W
12 H4 North Bourke New S Wales 30.01S 145.59E
106 L6 North Branch Michigan 43.14N 83.11W
103 E5 North Branch New Jersey 40.36N 74.40W
100 H2 North Branch Ontario 48.53N 94.09W
103 J4 North Branford Connecticut 41.20N 72.46W
122 U1 North Breakers reefs Midway Is Pacific Oc 28.14N 177.25W
103 L2 Northbridge Massachusetts 42.10N 71.39W
99 N8 Northbrook Ontario 44.45N 77.10W
103 K2 North Brookfield Massachusetts 42.16N 72.05W
Northbrook I see Nordbruk,Ostrov
93 C5 North Buganda dist Uganda
57 N4 North Burton Humberside Eng 54.08N 0.20W
113 R9 North C Aleutian Is 52.25N 174.10W
11 K13 North C Antipodes Is Pacific Oc 49.39S 178.50E
98 M6 North, C C Breton I, Nova Scotia 47.03N 60.24W
11 H1 North C New Zealand 34.23S 173.04E
North C Norway see Nordkapp
98 H6 North C Prince Edward I 47.03N 64.00W
121 G8 North C S Georgia 53.57S 37.45W
116 J4 North Caicos isld Caicos Is W I 21.54N 72.00W
109 L5 North Canadian R Oklahoma
104 D6 North Canton Ohio 40.54N 81.24W
122 U8 North Cape Fanning I Pacific Oc 3.53N 159.22W
10 P7 North Cape Rise sea feature Pacific Oc
97 K7 North Caribou L Ontario 52.50N 90.50W
102 K3 North Carolina state U.S.A.
103 N3 North Carver Massachusetts 41.55N 70.48W
110 D1 North Cascades National Park Washington
105 H12 North Cat Cay Bahamas 25.33N 79.16W
57 M5 North Cave Humberside Eng 53.47N 0.39W
26 R5 North Central prov Sri Lanka
90 C6 North Central state Nigeria
19 G2 North Chan Luzon Philippines
99 G6 North Chan Ontario
54 G7 North Channel N Ireland/Scotland
105 H5 North Charleston S Carolina 32.53N 79.59W
57 K1 North Charlton Northumb Eng 55.31N 1.44W
106 G7 North Chicago Illinois 42.18N 87.52W
94 S13 Northcliff S Africa 26.09S 27.58E
14 B10 Northcliffe W Australia 34.36S 116.04E
57 O6 North Coates Lincs Eng 53.30N 0.01E
103 H2 North Colebrook Connecticut 42.01N 73.08W
103 C2 North Colesville New York 42.14N 75.43W
104 G4 North Collins New York 42.36N 78.57W
104 O2 North Conway New Hampshire 44.03N 71.09W
11 M9 Northcote New Zealand 43.29S 172.37E
11 C2 Northcote bor Auckland New Zealand
12 D7 Northcote dist Melbourne, Vic
110 A3 North Cove Washington 46.43N 124.03W
55 J4 North Cray London Eng 51.26N 0.09E
104 L3 North Creek New York 43.42N 74.00W
102 F1 North Dakota state U.S.A.
57 M5 North Dalton Humberside Eng 53.58N 0.34W
North Devon New Brunswick see Nashwaaksis
103 M3 North Dighton Massachusetts 41.52N 71.07W
56 L5 North Downs chalk hills Kent etc Eng
11 M12 North Dunedin dist Dunedin New Zealand
103 C7 North East Maryland 39.37N 75.56W
104 F4 North East Pennsylvania 42.13N 79.51W
94 J3 North East dist Botswana
87 L6 North East reg Somalia
96 B11 North East B Ascension I 7.55S 14.21W
26 B13 North East C Prince Edward I Ind Oc 46.37S 37.59E
113 C5 Northeast C St Lawrence I Bering Sea 63.17N 168.42W
105 K3 North East Cape Fear R N Carolina
104 P8 North East Carry Maine 45.54N 69.40W
13 L5 North-East Cay isld Gt Barrier Reef Australia 21.35S 152.40E
93 L5 North Eastern prov Kenya
90 E6 North Eastern state Nigeria
96 H3 North-Eastern Atlantic Basin Atlantic Oc
North Eastern Frontier Agency (N.E.F.A) see Mizoram and Arunachal Pradesh Union Territories
11 B8 North East Harb inlet Campbell I Pacific Oc
104 R2 North East Harbor Maine 44.18N 68.17W
11 B9 North East I Snares Is Pacific Oc 48.01S 166.34E
13 D2 North East Is N Terr Australia
19 N4 Northeast Is Truk Is Pacific Oc 7.36N 151.57E
103 M2 North Easton Massachusetts 42.04N 71.06W
19 N4 Northeast Pass Truk Is Pacific Oc 7.31N 151.59E
105 K12 Northeast Providence Chan Bahamas
116 H3 Northeast Pt Acklins I Bahamas 22.46N 73.50W
98 R1 Northeast Pt Belle Isle, Nfld 52.01N 55.16W
26 V3 North-East Pt Christmas I Ind Oc 10.23S 105.45E
116 H4 Northeast Pt Great Inagua Bahamas 21.22N 72.59W
116 M2 Northeast Pt Jamaica, W I 18.09N 76.21W
11 M12 North East Valley dist Dunedin New Zealand
63 L9 Northeim W Germany 51.43N 9.59E
56 N2 North Elmham Norfolk Eng 52.45N 0.56E
57 L5 North Emsall W Yorks Eng 53.37N 1.16W
116 G2 North End Pt Cat I Bahamas 24.42N 75.46W
106 B8 North English Iowa 41.31N 92.04W
19 N1 North Entrance str Palau Is Pacific Oc
15 G8 North Entrance str Papua New Guinea
93 C3 Northern dist Uganda
92 F6 Northern prov Malawi
26 R3 Northern prov Sri Lanka
85 K10 Northern prov Sudan
92 E7 Northern prov Zambia
89 J7 Northern reg Ghana
98 T5 Northern Bight Newfoundland 48.02N 53.58W
90 M3 Northern Darfur prov Sudan
105 L12 Northern Eleuthera dist Eleuthera I Bahamas
98 F9 Northern Head New Brunswick 44.49N 66.46W
54 F8 Northern Ireland British Isles
87 B3 Northern Kordofan prov Sudan
100 M2 Northern Light L Ontario
26 V3 Northern Plateau Christmas I Ind Oc
89 C7 Northern Prov Sierra Leone
116 O1 Northern Ra Trinidad & Tobago
Northern Rhodesia see Zambia
10 G5 Northern Territory terr Australia
31 F4 Northern Waziristan reg Pakistan
12 H8 North Esk R Tasmania
58 L5 North Esk, R Tayside/Grampian Scotland
99 C10 North Fairbank Ontario 43.42N 79.28W
103 C2 North Felton New York 42.14N 75.48W
57 M5 North Ferriby Humberside Eng 53.44N 0.31W
104 N4 Northfield Massachusetts 42.42N 72.27W
108 R5 Northfield Minnesota 44.28N 93.10W
103 E8 Northfield New Jersey 39.22N 74.33W
103 D2 Northfield New York 42.15N 75.10W
104 N2 Northfield Vermont 44.08N 72.41W
56 H3 Northfield W Midlands Eng 52.25N 1.58W
12 B7 Northfield dist Adelaide, S Aust
95 J5 Northfield Farm S Africa 29.15S 25.48E
122 H10 North Fiji Basin Pacific Oc
11 B12 North Fiord New Zealand
106 F6 North Fond du Lac Wisconsin 43.50N 88.30W
103 J4 Northford Connecticut 41.25N 72.47W
56 O5 North Foreland headland Kent Eng 51.23N 1.27E
111 E4 North Fork California 37.13N 119.31W
110 M4 North Fork Idaho 45.25N 113.59W
110 K8 North Fork Nevada 41.29N 115.50W
111 D2 North Fork American R California
111 C2 North Fork Feather R California
109 H2 North Fork Smoky Hill R Colorado/Kansas

32 C3 Nowbarān Iran 35.10N 49.45E
32 H4 Now Deh Iran 32.35N 59.53E
32 H3 Now Deh-e Pashang Iran 34.26N 59.06E
34 O3 Nowdesheh Iran 35.10N 46.15E
32 D3 Now Dezh Iran 34.53N 50.37E
32 C2 Nowdī Iran 37.51N 48.30E
62 L2 Nowe Poland 53.39N 18.40E
62 M4 Nowe Miasto Łódź Poland 51.37N 20.32E
62 M2 Nowe Miasto Olsztyn Poland 53.25N 19.35E
12 K4 Nowendoc New S Wales 31.35S 151.45E
62 H2 Nowe Warpno Poland 53.43N 14.20E
32 H4 Nowghāb Iran 33.49N 59.04E
32 E4 Now Gombad Iran 32.44N 53.20E
28 J2 Nowgong Assam India 26.20N 92.41E
30 C7 Nowgong Madhya Prad India 25.03N 79.27E
28 J2 Nowgong dist Assam India
113 K4 Nowitna R Alaska
32 C1 Nowjeh Deh Iran 38.24N 48.25E
101 X4 Nowleye L N W Terr
108 J5 Nowlin S Dakota 44.02N 101.16W
62 J2 Nowógard* Poland 53.40N 15.08E
62 N2 Nowogród Poland 53.12N 21.53E
62 J4 Nowogrodziec Poland 51.11N 15.23E
108 C5 Nowood Cr Wyoming
12 K5 Nowra New S Wales 34.54S 150.36E
28 F1 Nowrangapur Orissa India 19.15N 82.39E
32 C1 Nowshahr Āzarbāījān-e Khāvarī Iran 38.07N 48.25E
32 D2 Now Shahr Māzandarān Iran 36.38N 51.30E
31 G3 Nowshera Pakistan 34.00N 72.00E
62 O2 Nowy Dwór Białystok Poland 53.37N 23.36E
62 M3 Nowy Dwór Warszawa Poland 52.27N 20.41E
62 L1 Nowy Dwór Gdański Poland 54.13N 19.08E
62 M5 Nowy Korczyn Poland 50.20N 20.50E
62 M6 Nowy Sącz Poland 49.39N 20.40E
62 M6 Nowy Targ Poland 49.28N 20.00E
62 J3 Nowy Tomysl Poland 52.20N 16.09E
107 G9 Noxapater Mississippi 32.59N 89.03W
103 B4 Noxen Pennsylvania 41.25N 76.04W
110 K2 Noxon Montana 47.59N 115.43W
110 K2 Noxon Res Montana 47.56N 115.45W
107 H8 Noxubee R Miss/Ala
76 B3 Noya Spain 42.47N 8.53W
91 A3 Noya R Gabon
75 O5 Noya R Spain
70 F6 Noyal Muzillac France 47.36N 2.27W
70 E6 Noyalo France 47.36N 2.40W
70 E5 Noyal-Pontivy France 48.04N 2.53W
70 G5 Noyal-sur-Vilaine France 48.07N 1.30W
70 J6 Noyant-la-Gravoyère France 47.42N 0.57W
72 D1 Noyant-la-Plaine France 47.16N 0.22W
70 L6 Noyant-sous-le-Lude France 47.31N 0.07E
69 C4 Noye R France
32 F2 Noyek Iran 36.46N 54.52E
69 B3 Noyelles-sur-Mer France 50.11N 1.43E
37 J4 Noyemberyan Armenia U.S.S.R. 41.11N 45.01E
70 K6 Noyen France 47.52N 0.06W
71 D1 Noyers Yonne France 47.42N 3.59E
72 G1 Noyers-sur-Cher Loir-et-Cher France 47.17N 1.24E
71 H8 Noyers-sur-Jabron Alpes de Haute Provence France 44.10N 5.49E
113 V9 Noyes I Alaska 55.30N 133.40W
28 C5 Noyil R Tamil Nadu India
111 A2 Noyo California 39.27N 123.47W
69 E4 Noyon France 49.35N 3.00E
22 F5 Noyon Mongolia 43.09N 102.13E
42 F5 Noyon Khol', Oz L U.S.S.R. 52.46N 97.10E
98 O2 Noyrot, L Quebec
70 G6 Nozay France 47.34N 1.37W
71 J3 Nozeroy France 46.47N 6.03E
44 G4 Nozhay Yurt U.S.S.R. 43.07N 46.23E
71 E9 Nozières France 43.58N 4.13E
25 M7 Npawp Ga Burma 26.41N 96.42E
93 F2 Npitamaiong mt Kenya 3.09N 34.54E
90 C8 Npologu Nigeria 6.46N 7.19E
95 O6 Nqabeni S Africa 30.44S 30.02E
95 L8 Nqamakwe S Africa 32.12S 27.57E
95 O4 Nqutu S Africa 28.13S 30.40E
88 Q5 Nsa watercourse Algeria
92 F9 Nsadzu Zambia 14.04S 32.21E
90 L9 Nsakkara tribe Cent Afr Rep
92 G10 Nsanje Malawi 16.47S 35.15E
89 J9 Nsawam Ghana 5.47N 0.19W
92 F7 Nsenga tribe Zambia
93 B6 Nsika Uganda 0.21S 30.27E
91 B3 Nsok Equat Guinea 1.10N 11.19E
95 O8 Nsoko Swaziland 27.01S 31.57E
92 D7 Nsombo Zambia 10.49S 29.51E
93 B6 Nsongezi Uganda 0.59S 30.46E
91 E5 Nsontin Zaïre 3.07S 17.56E
23 A6 Nsopzup Burma 25.53N 97.28E
90 C8 Nsukka Nigeria 6.51N 7.29E
89 J9 Nsuta Ghana 5.16N 1.59W
Nta see Nata
95 N5 Ntabamhlope S Africa 29.06S 29.36E
92 G9 Ntaja Malawi 14.52S 35.33E
89 D3 N'Takat Mauritania 16.51N 11.44W
89 B1 Ntalfa Mauritania 20.40N 15.30W
91 C2 Ntam Congo 2.10N 13.36E
95 O10 Ntambanana S Africa 28.36S 31.45E
92 B8 Ntambu Zambia 12.21S 25.03E
93 D5 Ntanzi Uganda 0.13N 32.47E
91 A4 N'Tchonga Tchine lagoon Gabon
91 B2 Ntem Cameroon 2.20N 11.20E
91 B2 Ntem R Cameroon
91 C2 N'tem R Gabon
95 N6 Ntola S Africa 30.35S 29.05E
91 H7 Ntolo Zaïre 6.38S 22.40E
93 B6 Ntungamo Uganda 0.54S 30.16E
93 C5 Ntusi Uganda 0.05N 31.13E
93 C5 Ntwetwe Uganda 0.58N 31.35E
94 H3 Ntwetwe Pan salt pan Botswana
95 O3 Ntyele mt S Africa 27.23S 30.04E
95 M7 Ntywenka S Africa 31.10S 28.34E
26 P14 Nuageuses, Îs Kerguelen Ind Oc 48.35S 68.41E
88 J8 Nuaib Morocco 27.59N 9.40W
72 C1 Nuaillé Maine-et-Loire France 47.05N 0.47W
72 C3 Nuaillé-d'Aunis Charente-Maritime France 46.14N 0.56W
35 H3 Nu'aiyimah Syria 32.38N 36.10E
15 L9 Nuakata I Papua New Guinea 10.22S 151.00E
92 E12 Nuanetsi Zimbabwe 21.22S 30.45E
92 E12 Nuanetsi dist Zimbabwe
92 E12 Nuanetsi R Zimbabwe
18 B8 Nuang, Gunong mt Pen Malaysia 3.15N 101.53E
9 R12 Nuapapu isld Tonga, Pacific Oc 18.42S 174.05W
89 K8 Nuatja Togo 6.59N 1.17E
33 L5 Nu'aym tribe Oman
30 H3 Nub Nepal 27.53N 86.44E
86 G5 Nûba Egypt 30.29N 31.33E
35 D7 Nuba Jordan 31.37N 35.02E
87 C5 Nuba tribe Sudan
85 L9 Nuba, L Sudan
87 C5 Nuba Mts Sudan
15 M8 Nubara I Papua New Guinea 9.15S 153.06E
24 H10 Nubgang La pass Xizang Zizhiqu China 30.50N 93.51E
85 L9 Nubian Desert Sudan
110 D8 Nubieber California 41.06N 121.11W
121 B6 Nuble prov Chile
121 B6 Nuble R Chile
31 J3 Nubra R Kashmir
82 H4 Nucet Romania 46.28N 22.35E
79 D6 Nucetto Italy 44.20N 8.03E
41 P5 Nuchcha R U.S.S.R.
77 Q3 Nucia, La Spain 38.37N 0.08W
120 B1 Nucuray, R Peru
22 L4 Nudam Nei Monggol Zizhiqu China 44.57N 119.50E
13 K1 Nudgee dist Brisbane, Qnsld
120 C6 Nudo Coropuna pk Peru 15.31S 72.45W
120 D6 Nudo de Apolobamba pks Peru
66 L8 Nudo, Monte Italy 45.55N 8.41E
Nudushan see Nadūshan
40 H2 Nudymi R U.S.S.R.
112 J7 Nueces R Texas
88 F9 Nueifed Morocco 24.53N 14.50W
72 D1 Nueil France 47.07N 0.22W
72 C2 Nueil-sur-Argent France 46.56N 0.34W
72 D1 Nueil-sur-Layon France 47.08N 0.38W
35 E6 Nu'eima watercourse Jordan
35 G4 Nu'eiyima, En Jordan 32.25N 35.54E
97 K5 Nueltin L N W Terr 60.30N 99.30W
60 L14 Nuenen Netherlands 51.28N 5.33E
75 K3 Nueno Spain 42.16N 0.27W
87 B6 Nuer tribe Sudan
21 B7 Nü'erhe Liaoning China 41.04N 121.00E
76 D11 Nuestra Senhora de Machede Portugal 38.34N 7.46W
120 D11 Nuestra Señora, B.de Chile
77 T12 Nuestra Señora del Pilar Balearic Is 38.41N 1.35E
76 K2 Nueva Spain 43.27N 4.56W
120 C1 Nueva Alejandría Peru 5.58S 73.25W
119 E4 Nueva Antioquia Colombia 6.06N 69.24W
115 P10 Nueva Arcadia Honduras 15.02N 88.40W
115 L2 Nueva Armenia Honduras 15.50N 86.31W
118 A7 Nueva Asunción dept Paraguay
77 H5 Nueva Carteya Spain 37.35N 4.28W
115 P10 Nueva Concepción El Salvador 14.09N 89.19W
119 G2 Nueva Esparta state Venezuela
119 E3 Nueva Florida Venezuela 8.58N 69.01W
118 C8 Nueva Germania Paraguay 23.52S 56.44W
116 C4 Nueva Gerona Pinos, I de Cuba 21.53N 82.49W
121 L10 Nueva Harberton Argentina 54.08S 67.15W
121 F5 Nueva Helvecia Uruguay 34.16S 57.53W
121 L10 Nueva, I Arg/Chile 55.15S 66.32W
121 A7 Nueva Imperial Chile 38.45S 72.58W
121 B10 Nueva Lubecka Argentina 44.32S 70.22W
120 G11 Nueva Población Argentina 25.00S 61.42W
118 A9 Nueva Pompeya Argentina 24.59S 61.31W
115 J4 Nueva Rosita Mexico 27.58N 101.11W
115 P11 Nueva San Salvador El Salvador 13.40N 89.18W
121 E5 Nueve de Julio Argentina 35.28S 60.58W
116 F4 Nuevitas Cuba 21.34N 77.18W
75 D7 Nuevo Baztán Spain 40.22N 3.15W
121 F4 Nuevo Berlin Uruguay 33.00S 58.05W
115 F2 Nuevo Casas Grandes Mexico 30.22N 107.53W
115 N7 Nuevo, Cayo reef Gulf of Mexico 21.50N 92.05W
115 E9 Nuevo Chagres Panama 9.14N 80.05W
121 D9 Nuevo, Golfo Argentina
112 H9 Nuevo Guerrero Mexico 26.34N 99.15W
115 G5 Nuevo Ideal Mexico 24.53N 105.02W
115 K4 Nuevo Laredo Mexico 27.30N 99.30W
115 J4 Nuevo León state Mexico
119 G3 Nuevo Mamo Venezuela 8.29N 63.01W
115 K6 Nuevo-Morelos Mexico 22.34N 99.17W
121 F4 Nuevo Palmira Uruguay 33.55S 58.22W
119 C8 Nuevo Rocafuerte Ecuador 0.59S 75.27W
115 F9 Nuevo San Juan Panama Canal Zone 9.13N 79.40W
33 F5 Nufayyid Şabḩah mts Saudi Arabia
66 N5 Nufenen Switzerland 46.33N 9.15E
66 K6 Nufenen Pass Switzerland 46.29N 8.23E
Nūfi, Jabal al hills see Yanūfi, Jabal al
13 J6 Nuga Nuga, L Queensland 25.00S 148.40E
48 S6 Nûgâtsiaq Greenland 71.30N 53.00W
11 D13 Nugget Pt New Zealand 46.27S 169.50E
10 C10 Nuggets Pt Macquarie I Pacific Oc 54.31S 158.58E
86 M8 Nughaimish, Gebel hill Egypt 28.42N 34.22E
81 B3 Nughedu Sardinia 40.06N 8.57E
81 C2 Nughedu di San Nicolò Sardinia 40.33N 9.02E
33 A4 Nugrus, Gebel mt Egypt 24.47N 34.35E
48 S7 Nûgssuaq reg Greenland
28 E1 Nugur Andhra Prad India 18.20N 80.32E
28 C5 Nugu R Kerala India
10 L2 Nuguria Is Pacific Oc 3.28S 150.49E
30 A4 Nuh Haryana India 28.07N 77.00E
11 M6 Nuhaka New Zealand 39.02S 177.46E
31 B8 Nuh, Ras C Pakistan 25.06N 62.26E
85 N7 Nuhûd, El Egypt 24.37N 34.22E
9 C8 Nui atoll Tuvalu, Pacific Oc 7.12S 177.10E
71 E1 Nuits France 47.43N 4.12E
71 F2 Nuits-St.Georges France 47.08N 4.57E
23 A4 Nu Jiang R Xizang Zizhiqu China
24 H10 Nu Jiang R Xizang Zizhiqu China
23 A5 Nu Jiang R Yunnan China
23 A6 Nu Jiang R Yunnan China
24 H10 Nu Jiang (Salween) R Xizang Zizhiqu China
23 A5 Nu Jiang (Salween) R Yunnan China
113 M7 Nuka I Alaska 59.24N 150.40W
44 H5 Nukatl, Khrebet mts U.S.S.R.
53 W15 Nuken mt Norway 61.55N 7.17E
61 E3 Nukerke Belgium 50.47N 3.36E
12 D4 Nukey Bluff S Australia 32.26S 135.29E
34 K6 Nukhayb Iraq 32.03N 42.16E
85 J10 Nukheila Sudan 19.01N 26.21E
35 G8 Nukheila R Jordan
94 E2 Nukhuwis Namibia 19.07S 18.40E
15 J2 Nukiki Choiseul I Solomon Is 6.45S 156.30E
9 S12 Nukomalolo atoll Tonga, Pacific Oc 18.38S 173.45W
15 G5 Nuku Papua New Guinea 3.48S 142.23E
9 S10 Nuku islet Tonga, Pacific Oc 21.05S 175.01W
9 S10 Nuku'alofa Tonga, Pacific Oc 21.09S 175.14W
9 D8 Nukufetau atoll Tuvalu, Pacific Oc 8.00S 178.30E
122 U13 Nuku Hiva isld Marquesas Is Pacific Oc 8.56S 140.00W
15 K6 Nukuhu New Britain 5.36S 149.23E
9 D9 Nukulaelae atoll Tuvalu, Pacific Oc 9.20S 179.50E
9 S12 Nukumalolo pt Tonga, Pacific Oc 18.38S 173.55W
15 L1 Nukumanu Is Papua New Guinea
9 U4 Nukumbasanga islet Fiji 16.20S 179.15W
10 S3 Nukunona isld Tokelau Is Pacific Oc 9.10S 171.55W
122 K9 Nukunono atoll Tokelau Is Pacific Oc 9.10S 171.55W
43 E6 Nukus Uzbekistan U.S.S.R. 42.28N 59.07E
122 F16 Nukutavaké isld Tuamotu Is Pacific Oc 19.11S 138.42W
122 D16 Nukutipipi atoll Tuamotu Is Pacific Oc 20.40S 142.30W
60 K13 Nuland Netherlands 51.43N 5.26E
113 H4 Nulato Alaska 64.42N 158.10W
81 C3 Nule Sardinia 40.28N 9.12E
75 K8 Nules Spain 39.52N 0.10W
14 D5 Nullagine W Australia 21.56S 120.06E
14 D5 Nullagine R W Australia
12 B4 Nullarbor S Australia 31.25S 130.51E
14 F9 Nullarbor Plain S Aust/W Aust
13 F5 Nulloocha Queensland 22.15S 142.29E
28 C5 Nullur Karnataka India 11.54N 77.27E
69 H7 Nully France 48.22N 4.48E
22 L6 Nulu'erhu Shan mt ra Liaoning China
43 K7 Nul'vand Tadzhikistan U.S.S.R. 38.17N 70.33E
81 B2 Nulvi Sardinia 40.47N 8.45E
30 L5 Num Nepal 27.33N 87.17E
15 C4 Num isld Irian Jaya 1.30S 135.10E
20 L5 Numaho Japan 36.58N 137.36E
90 C8 Numai Nigeria 7.50N 6.49E
13 G8 Numalla, L Queensland
90 F7 Numan Nigeria 9.28N 12.03E
79 P7 Numana Italy 43.31N 13.37E
19 M7 Numancia Philippines 9.54N 126.00E
75 F4 Numancia hist ruins Spain 41.48N 2.26W
34 N6 Nu'māniyah, An Iraq 32.34N 45.23E
60 F13 Numansdorp Netherlands 51.44N 4.26E
20 L1 Numata Japan 43.50N 141.59E
20 N5 Numata Japan 36.38N 139.03E
87 A7 Numatinna watercourse Sudan
20 M6 Numazu Japan 35.08N 138.50E
93 J9 Numba Ya Munga Dam Tanzania 3.49S 37.28E
69 O2 Nümbrecht W Germany 50.54N 7.33E
13 D2 Numbulwar Mission N Terr Aust 14.20S 135.40E
91 A3 Nume Equat Guinea 1.31N 9.35E
52 E6 Numedal V Norway
52 E7 Numedalslågen R Norway
15 C4 Numfoor isld Irian Jaya
47 L3 Numgi U.S.S.R. 66.40N 73.00E
103 B5 Numidia Pennsylvania 40.53N 76.24W
94 E2 Numkaub Namibia 18.33S 19.45E
51 L11 Nummela Finland 60.21N 24.20E
51 K11 Nummi Finland 60.25N 23.51E
47 L4 Numto U.S.S.R. 63.30N 70.22E
12 H6 Numurkah Victoria 36.05S 145.26E
30 B7 Nun R Madhya Prad India
113 J7 Nunachuak Alaska 59.38N 157.05W
113 F6 Nunapitchuk Alaska 60.51N 162.35W
66 R5 Nuna, Piz mt Switzerland 46.44N 10.10E
48 T15 Nunarssuit Greenland 60.45N 48.00W
113 E6 Nunavakanuk L Alaska 62.03N 164.40W
113 F6 Nunavak Anukslak L Alaska 61.04N 162.39W
113 F6 Nunavakpak L Alaska 60.47N 162.40W
113 H7 Nunavaugaluk, L Alaska 59.15N 158.55W
12 E8 Nunawading dist Melbourne, Vic
119 D5 Nunchía Colombia 5.37N 72.13W
104 H4 Nunda New York 42.36N 77.57W
13 K1 Nundah dist Brisbane, Qnsld
12 K4 Nundle New S Wales 31.28S 151.08E
92 D3 Nundu Zaïre 3.49S 29.04E
92 J8 Nune Mozambique 12.00S 38.25E
56 J2 Nuneaton Warwicks Eng 52.32N 1.28W
56 J4 Nuneham Courtenay Oxon Eng 51.42N 1.13W
90 C9 Nun Entrance of R.Niger Nigeria 4.20S 6.04E
89 B6 Nunez B Guinea
28 C8 Nungambakkam dist Madras, Tamil Nadu India
14 C9 Nungarin W Australia 31.11S 118.06E
25 L9 Nungba Manipur India 24.46N 93.25E
22 L4 Nungnain Sum Nei Monggol Zizhiqu China 45.39N 119.03E
92 H8 Nungo Mozambique 13.25S 37.45E
92 F3 Nungwe B Tanzania
19 F5 Nuniali Moluccas Indon 2.51S 128.18E
30 L8 Nunihat Bihar India 24.30N 87.08E
66 G6 Nünihorn mt Switzerland 46.29N 7.38E
113 E7 Nunivak I Alaska 60.00N 166.00W
29 J7 Nunkāpasi* Orissa India 20.54N 84.50E
Nun Kiang R see Nen Chiang R
69 M5 Nunkirchen W Germany 49.29N 6.50E
31 J4 Nunkun mt Kashmir 33.59N 76.02E
39 L3 Nunligran U.S.S.R. 64.49N 175.25W
109 F1 Nunn Colorado 40.41N 104.47W
107 J6 Nunnelly Tennessee 35.51N 87.30W
56 G5 Nunney Somerset Eng 51.13N 2.24W
56 G5 Nunney Catch Somerset Eng 51.12N 2.23W
66 G2 Nunningen Switzerland 47.23N 7.38E
120 D6 Nuñoa Peru 14.29S 70.39W
121 G9 Nuñoa dist Santiago Chile
76 G8 Nuñomoral Spain 40.25N 6.15W
29 E4 Nunrana Rajasthan India 27.59N 76.24E
60 M10 Nunspeet Netherlands 52.22N 5.47E
12 F4 Nuntherungie New S Wales 30.55S 142.29E
57 L3 Nunthorpe Cleveland Eng 54.30N 1.10W
18 M4 Nunukan Timur isld Borneo Indon
39 M2 Nunyamo U.S.S.R. 65.38N 170.40W
39 M2 Nunyamo, Mys C U.S.S.R. 65.35N 170.41W
80 D4 Nunziatella Italy 42.25N 11.21E
21 B2 Nuomin Dashan mt pk Nei Monggol Zizhiqu China 50.18N 122.43E
21 C3 Nuomin He R Heilongjiang China
21 D4 Nuomin He R Nei Monggol Zizhiqu China
87 C7 Nuong,L Sudan 7.22N 30.31E
41 N8 Nuora R U.S.S.R.
81 C3 Nuoro Sardinia 40.20N 9.21E
81 C3 Nuoro prov Sardinia
51 H5 Nuortikon Sweden 66.53N 20.50E
30 L5 Nup Nepal 27.44N 87.51E
50 H6 Nupahraun lava field Iceland
10 O4 Nupani isld Santa Cruz Is Pacific Oc 10.11S 165.32E
30 H2 Nup La pass Nepal/Xizang Zizhiqu 28.04N 86.46E
53 W19 Nupsfonn mt Norway 59.53N 7.08E
50 H7 Nupsstadhur Iceland 63.57N 17.35W
50 L5 Nupstindur pk Iceland 64.45N 14.08W
50 H7 Núpsvötn rivers Iceland
30 J2 Nuptse mt Nepal 27.58N 86.54E
30 J3 Nuptse Glacier Nepal
50 B3 Núpur Iceland 65.56N 23.32W
33 J4 Nuqay'ah, An Qatar, The Gulf 25.47N 50.56E
85 E8 Nuqayy, Jabal mts Libya
33 N6 Nuqdah, Ra's an C Oman 20.45N 58.46E
35 F2 Nuqeib Israel 32.48N 35.38E
33 D4 Nuqrah Saudi Arabia 25.35N 41.28E
119 C5 Nuquí Colombia 5.44N 77.16W
32 D2 Nur Iran 36.32N 52.00E
24 D7 Nur Xinjiang Uygur Zizhiqu China 36.18N 81.03E
32 E2 Nur R Iran
43 L3 Nura Kazakhstan U.S.S.R. 48.32N 74.01E
43 K2 Nura R Kazakhstan U.S.S.R.
32 G7 Nūrābād Banāder va Jazāyer-e Baḩr-e Oman Iran 27.49N 57.11E
32 D5 Nūrābād Fārs Iran 30.14N 51.30E
32 C3 Nūrābād Gīlān Iran 35.55N 48.52E
30 B6 Nurabad Madhya Prad India 26.24N 78.04E
81 C4 Nuragus Sardinia 39.47N 9.03E
10 Q4 Nurakita isld Tuvalu, Pacific Oc 10.56S 179.29E
81 C5 Nuraminis Sardinia 39.28N 9.01E
43 H6 Nurata Uzbekistan U.S.S.R. 40.33N 65.44E
43 H6 Nuratau, Khrebet mts Uzbekistan U.S.S.R.
85 N9 Nurayet, Jebel mt Sudan 20.07N 34.47E
64 B3 Nürburg W Germany 50.20N 6.58E
64 B3 Nürburgring W Germany
Nur Dağları mts see Gâvur Dağları Hatay
79 G5 Nure R Italy
43 J7 Nurek Tadzhikistan U.S.S.R. 38.24N 69.15E
103 B5 Nuremberg Pennsylvania 40.57N 76.11W
Nuremberg W Germany see Nürnberg
72 G2 Nuret-le-Ferron France 46.41N 1.25E
37 G6 Nurettın Turkey 39.15N 42.29E
31 F3 Nür Gal Afghanistan 34.36N 70.45E
31 D6 Nur Gamma Pakistan 28.35N 66.46E
37 C8 Nurhak Turkey 37.57N 37.21E
37 C7 Nurhak Dağı mt Turkey 38.04N 37.28E
115 E3 Nurí Mexico 28.01N 109.25W
87 C1 Nuri ruins Sudan 18.32N 31.55E
31 J3 Nuria Kashmir 34.20N 76.59E
119 H4 Nuria, Altipianicie plat Venezuela
80 H4 Nuria, Monte Italy 42.22N 13.06E
14 F9 Nurina W Australia 30.56S 126.33E
12 E5 Nuriootpa S Australia 34.28S 139.00E
93 J2 Nuri Peak mt Kenya 3.20N 37.39E
31 F3 Nuristan reg Afghanistan
35 E3 Nurit Israel 32.32N 35.21E
18 H6 Nuri, Teluk B Borneo Indon
40 H3 Nurki Mys C U.S.S.R. 56.49N 138.30E
46 Q3 Nurlat U.S.S.R. 54.28N 50.48E
45 U1 Nurlaty U.S.S.R. 55.37N 48.16E
29 D2 Nurmahal Punjab India 31.05N 75.36E
51 O8 Nurmes Finland 63.31N 29.10E
51 K9 Nurmo Finland 62.50N 22.55E
64 L5 Nürnberg W Germany 49.27N 11.05E
59 J6 Nurney Carlow Irish Rep 52.45N 6.55W
29 D1 Nurpur Himachal Prad India 32.18N 75.56E
31 F5 Nurpur Pakistan 31.54N 71.55E
30 B3 Nurpur Uttar Prad India 29.09N 78.24E
81 A2 Nurra, La reg Sardinia
12 A3 Nurrari Lakes S Australia
81 C4 Nurri Sardinia 39.43N 9.15E
12 H4 Nurri, Mt New S Wales 31.44S 146.04E
30 J7 Nur Sarai Bihar India 25.17N 85.28E
64 G6 Nürtingen W Germany 48.37N 9.20E
62 O3 Nurzec R Poland
79 B3 Nus Italy 45.44N 7.28E
92 F11 Nusa mt Zimbabwe 18.45S 32.50E
19 F5 Nusa Laut isld Moluccas Indon 3.40S 128.47E
15 M8 Nusam I Papua New Guinea 9.08S 152.28E
19 A8 Nusa Tenggara island prov Indon
18 L10 Nusa Tenggara islds Indonesia
31 F1 Nusay Afghanistan 38.27N 70.48E
37 F8 Nusaybin Turkey 37.05N 41.11E
80 M7 Nusco Italy 40.53N 15.05E
35 A8 Nuseirat Gaza Strip 31.26N 34.22E
85 J6 Nusf, Gebel mt Egypt 26.56N 27.23E
113 J7 Nushagak R Alaska
113 H7 Nushagak B Alaska
113 H7 Nushagak Pen Alaska
23 B5 Nu Shan mt ra Yunnan China
Nushar see Nowshahr
20 H7 Nu-shima isld Japan 34.10N 134.49E
31 D6 Nushki Pakistan 29.33N 66.01E
64 F7 Nusplingen W Germany 48.07N 8.55E
Nus, Ras C see Naws, Ra's
37 D9 Nusratiye Turkey 36.51N 38.51E
66 M1 Nussbaumen Switzerland 47.38N 8.50E
63 N5 Nusse W Germany 53.39N 10.35E
53 C6 Nustrup Denmark 55.16N 9.12E
Nuswotar isld see Wotap isld
122 D12 Nutae Tahiti Pacific Oc 17.44S 149.14W
97 N6 Nutak Labrador, Nfld 57.30N 61.59W
39 L1 Nutauge, Laguna U.S.S.R.
60 T17 Nuth Netherlands 50.55N 5.53E
63 S8 Nuthe R E Germany
100 O6 Nut L Saskatchewan
56 M5 Nutley E Sussex Eng 51.02N 0.03E
103 K6 Nutley New Jersey 40.49N 74.09W
100 O6 Nut Mountain Saskatchewan 52.08N 103.21W
100 P6 Nut Mt ra Saskatchewan
109 C9 Nutt New Mexico 32.26N 107.27W
31 E6 Nuttal Pakistan 28.43N 68.10E
13 C3 Nutwood Downs N Terr Australia 15.48S 134.06E
113 Q5 Nutzotin Mts Alaska
93 K7 Nuu Kenya 1.04S 38.21E
86 F6 Nu'umiya, Wâdi el watercourse Egypt
51 M5 Nuupas Finland 66.01N 26.19E
122 A11 Nuupéré, Pt Society Is Pacific Oc 17.35S 149.47W
122 D1 Nuuúli Amer Samoa Pacific Oc 14.19S 170.42W
30 G4 Nuwakot Nepal 28.09N 83.52E
26 S8 Nuwara Eliya Sri Lanka 6.58N 80.46E
33 L4 Nuway Oman 24.30N 55.57E
94 D8 Nuwefontein S Africa 30.58S 17.50E
86 N8 Nuweiba' Egypt 28.58N 34.38E
86 O7 Nuweibi, Wâdi el watercourse Saudi Arabia
35 G6 Nuweijis Jordan 31.59N 35.57E
94 P11 Nuweland Cape Town S Africa 33.58S 18.28E
95 G9 Nuweplaas S Africa 33.46S 23.35E
94 E8 Nuwerus S Africa 31.09S 18.21E
94 K5 Nuwe Smitsdorp S Africa 24.08S 29.20E
95 E8 Nuweveldreeks mts S Africa
113 J7 Nuyakuk R Alaska
113 H7 Nuyakuk, L Alaska 59.55N 158.50W
12 C4 Nuyts Arch S Australia
12 B4 Nuyts, C S Australia 32.03S 132.17E
14 B11 Nuyts, Pt W Australia 35.02S 116.32E
32 A3 Nuzi anc site Iraq 35.22N 44.18E
66 Q3 Nüziders Austria 47.11N 9.48E
28 E2 Nuzvid Andhra Prad India 16.47N 80.53E
94 F4 Nwatle Pan salt pan Botswana 23.41S 21.08E
94 F2 Nxainxai Botswana 19.54S 21.06E
94 F2 Nxaunxau Botswana 18.57S 21.18E
90 H8 Nya watercourse Chad etc
18 L5 Nyaän, Bukit hill Borneo Indon 0.59N 114.59E
93 H2 Nyaber Kenya 3.36N 36.53E
91 B2 Nyabessan Cameroon 2.28N 10.24E
14 C10 Nyabing W Australia 33.31S 118.10E
93 A8 Nyabisindu Rwanda 2.20S 29.43E
113 H6 Nyac Alaska 61.00N 160.00W
93 K4 Nyachisa Kenya 1.06N 38.11E
39 B2 Nyachyky U.S.S.R. 67.09N 137.21E
110 M1 Nyack Montana 48.26N 113.49W
103 G4 Nyack New York 41.05N 73.55W
41 D6 Nyadayakha R U.S.S.R.
92 F10 Nyaderi R Zimbabwe
92 F10 Nyagadsi R Zimbabwe
41 E4 Nyagame, Ozero L U.S.S.R. 72.44N 88.10E
Nyagquka see Yajiang
Nyagrong see Xinlong
93 E8 Nyahanga Tanzania 2.22S 33.34E
92 F4 Nyahua Tanzania 5.25S 33.20E
93 H5 Nyahururu Falls Kenya 0.04N 36.22E
12 G6 Nyah West Victoria 35.18S 143.25E
95 P9 Nyaiazi River S Africa 28.13S 32.18E
24 G10 Nyainqêntanglha Feng mt pk Xizang Zizhiqu China 30.27N 90.33E
24 G10 Nyainqêntanglha Shan mt ra Xizang Zizhiqu China
24 G9 Nyainrong Xizang Zizhiqu China 32.02N 92.15E
93 E8 Nyakabindi Tanzania 2.36S 33.58E
93 C8 Nyakahura Tanzania 2.47S 31.04E
93 B10 Nyaka Kangaga Tanzania 4.10S 30.29E
93 C8 Nyakakiri Tanzania 2.16S 31.30E
93 D8 Nyakalilo Tanzania 2.28S 32.26E
24 H9 Nyakamarbola pass Qinghai China
24 H9 Nyakamarbola pass Xizang Zizhiqu 32.40N 93.25E
93 C9 Nyakanazi Tanzania 3.03S 31.13E
93 E7 Nyakanga Tanzania 1.35S 33.55E
93 C7 Nyakanyasi Tanzania 1.10S 31.15E
93 B9 Nyakasu Burundi 3.54S 30.07E
93 B7 Nyakatale Rwanda 1.18S 30.20E
93 D8 Nyakato Tanzania 2.33S 32.59E
93 B7 Nyakayaga Rwanda 1.39S 30.25E
52 L3 Nyåker Sweden 63.46N 19.20E
93 A6 Nyakisanju Uganda 0.36S 29.40E
93 B10 Nyakisogo Tanzania 4.08S 30.48E
47 J4 Nyaksimvol' U.S.S.R. 62.30N 60.52E
24 D9 Nyakten Tso L Xizang Zizhiqu China 32.50N 81.20E
24 C9 Nyak Tso L Xizang Zizhiqu China 33.26N 79.55E
93 A4 Nyakunde Zaïre 1.28N 29.59E
93 E3 Nyakwai mt Uganda 2.32N 33.54E
90 M5 Nyala Sudan 12.01N 24.50E
24 E11 Nyalam Xizang Zizhiqu China 28.15N 85.51E
18 C9 Nyalas Pen Malaysia 2.26N 102.28E
50 S14 Ny-Alesund Spitsbergen 78.55N 12.00E
93 L10 Nyali Kenya 4.02S 39.42E
93 E8 Nyalikungu Mwanza Tanzania 2.35S 33.28E
47 K5 Nyalino U.S.S.R. 61.16N 69.25E
39 D1 Nyalym U.S.S.R. 67.51N 145.19E
92 D9 Nyama Zambia 14.39S 28.21E
92 F10 Nyamahara mt Zimbabwe 16.55S 32.50E
92 D11 Nyamandhlovu Zimbabwe 19.50S 28.16E
92 C11 Nyamandhlovu dist Zimbabwe
92 E10 Nyamanji mt Zimbabwe 16.35S 30.50E
93 C8 Nyamanyama mt Tanzania 2.41S 31.20E
93 A7 Nyamaragira vol Zaïre 1.25S 29.12E
93 A8 Nyamasheke Rwanda 2.21S 29.03E
87 C8 Nyambara tribe Sudan
93 J5 Nyambeni Ra Kenya
93 E8 Nyambiti Tanzania 2.50S 33.25E
92 A9 Nyamboma Rapids Zambia 14.10S 23.11E
41 D7 Nyamboyto U.S.S.R. 66.57N 80.28E
93 C10 Nyamgalika Tanzania 4.28S 31.11E
93 C8 Nyamirembe Tanzania 2.32S 31.42E
87 A6 Nyamlell Sudan 9.07N 26.59E
92 F3 Nyamtukusa Tanzania 2.57S 33.19E
93 D9 Nyamtukusa Tanzania 3.02S 32.45E
92 H7 Nyamtumbo Tanzania 10.30S 36.06E
92 F4 Nyamwezi tribe Tanzania
30 E1 Nyandi Gompa Xizang Zizhiqu 31.02N 81.16E
87 D6 Nyanding,R Sudan
47 E5 Nyandoma U.S.S.R. 61.43N 40.11E
39 B1 Nyaneli R U.S.S.R.
Nyang R see Nyang Qu R
94 Q11 Nyanga Cape Town S Africa 33.59S 18.35E
91 B5 Nyanga Gabon 2.59S 10.16E
91 B5 Nyanga R Gabon
91 B5 Nyanga reg Gabon
14 F8 Nyanga, L W Australia
28 J1 Nyang Chu R Xizang Zizhiqu
93 B10 Nyange Tanzania 4.05S 30.20E
24 F11 Nyang Qu R Xizang Zizhiqu China
24 H11 Nyang Qu R Xizang Zizhiqu China
93 E8 Nyanguge Tanzania 2.32S 33.11E
41 D6 Nyangus'yakha R U.S.S.R.
92 C4 Nyangwe Zaïre 4.15S 26.14E
92 G10 Nyanja tribe Malawi
92 E9 Nyanji Zambia 14.22S 31.48E
93 C9 Nyantakara Tanzania 3.05S 31.23E
93 C9 Nyantwiga Tanzania 3.06S 31.06E
47 G5 Nyanyayel' U.S.S.R. 62.05N 51.28E
92 E9 Nyanyembe tribe Tanzania
93 F4 Nyanza prov Kenya
93 A10 Nyanza-Lac Burundi 4.20S 29.35E
18 M5 Nyapa, Gunung mt Borneo Indon 1.50N 117.22E
101 Q5 Nyarling R N W Terr
93 B9 Nyarwana mt Burundi 3.16S 30.29E
92 G7 Nyasa tribe Tanzania
92 G7 Nyasa, L Malawi
Nyasaland see Malawi
47 G3 Nyashabozh U.S.S.R. 65.28N 53.42E
92 G4 Nyaturu tribe Tanzania
25 C3 Nyaungbinzeik Burma 19.03N 95.10E
25 D4 Nyaunglebin Burma 17.59N 94.44E
25 C2 Nyaungu Burma 21.12N 94.55E
91 J9 Nyavikungu Zaïre 11.26S 25.56E
93 A7 Nyawarungu R Rwanda
92 C3 Nyawatu Zaïre 3.44S 27.44E
95 M7 Nyaweni S Africa 31.26S 28.23E
41 O5 Nyayba U.S.S.R. 70.46N 130.45E
47 J4 Nyays R U.S.S.R.
47 M5 Nyazepetrovsk U.S.S.R. 56.06N 59.30E
92 E11 Nyazvidzi R Zimbabwe
53 D7 Nybøl Denmark 54.56N 9.42E
53 F6 Nyborg Denmark 55.19N 10.48E
51 O1 Nyborg Norway 70.12N 28.40E
53 F6 Nyborg Fjord inlet Denmark 55.18N 10.48E
52 J10 Nybro Sweden 56.44N 15.55E
47 L3 Nyda U.S.S.R. 66.35N 72.58E
47 L3 Nyda R U.S.S.R.
52 H9 Nydala Sweden 57.19N 14.20E
91 B3 Nye R Gabon/Cameroon
97 O1 Nyeboes Land Greenland
28 J1 Nyeme Xizang Zizhiqu 28.25N 92.40E
24 G11 Nyêmo Xizang Zizhiqu China 29.25N 90.00E
Nyenchen Tangiha Range see Nyainqêntanglha Shan
93 C6 Nyendo Uganda 0.18S 31.48E
93 E5 Nyenga Uganda 0.22N 33.10E
92 A9 Nyengo Swamp Zambia
93 H6 Nyeri Kenya 0.25S 36.56E
87 D6 Nyerol Sudan 8.41N 32.01E
56 B3 Nyfer Dyfed Wales 52.02N 4.48W
50 T13 Ny Friesland reg Spitsbergen
53 X18 Nygårdsvatn L Norway 60.30N 7.48E
39 K3 Nygchekveem R U.S.S.R.
39 M2 Nygchigen, Mys C U.S.S.R. 65.05N 172.03W
52 H6 Nyhammar Sweden 60.20N 14.55E
53 K4 Nyhamn Sweden 56.15N 12.34E
52 J4 Nyhem Sweden 62.54N 15.40E
92 F6 Nyiha tribe Tanzania
92 F7 Nyika Plateau Malawi
23 B2 Nyikog Qu R Sichuan China
24 F10 Nyima Xizang Zizhiqu China 31.50N 87.48E
92 E9 Nyimba Zambia 14.33S 30.49E
93 D2 Nyimur watercourse Uganda
24 H11 Nyingchi Xizang Zizhiqu China 29.31N 94.30E
50 H7 Nýiós B Iceland 63.45N 17.27W
62 N8 Nyíradony Hungary 47.41N 21.57E
93 A7 Nyiragongo vol Zaïre 1.28S 29.15E
62 N8 Nyírbátor Hungary 47.50N 22.09E
62 N8 Nyíregyháza Hungary 47.57N 21.43E
93 J8 Nyiri Desert Kenya
93 J5 Nyiro R Kenya
93 H3 Nyiru, Mt Kenya 2.11N 36.49E
50 G4 Nýjabœjarfjall mt Iceland 65.16N 18.40W
51 K8 Nykarleby Finland 63.22N 22.30E
53 P12 Nyker Bornholm Denmark 55.09N 14.47E
52 J8 Nykil Sweden 58.16N 15.25E
53 H7 Nykøbing Storstrøm Denmark 54.47N 11.53E
53 H5 Nykøbing Vestjælland Denmark 55.56N 11.41E
53 B3 Nykøbing Viborg Denmark 56.48N 8.52E
52 K8 Nyköping Sweden 58.45N 17.03E
52 H7 Nykroppa Sweden 59.37N 14.18E
53 T16 Nyksvatn L Norway 61.15N 5.45E
94 K5 Nyl R S Africa
53 P12 Nylarsker Bornholm Denmark 55.04N 14.49E
23 B2 Nylkog Qu R Sichuan China
94 K5 Nylstroom S Africa 24.42S 28.20E
12 H4 Nymagee New S Wales 32.05S 146.20E
53 T18 Nymark Norway 60.01N 5.43E
12 L3 Nymboida New S Wales 29.58S 152.40E
12 L3 Nymboida R New S Wales
62 J5 Nymburk Czechoslovakia 50.12N 15.00E
53 A5 Nymindegab Denmark 55.49N 8.12E
54 F11 Nymphe Bank Atlantic Oc
52 K8 Nynäshamn Sweden 58.54N 17.55E
12 H4 Nyngan New S Wales 31.34S 147.14E
12 G4 Nyngynderry New S Wales 32.16S 143.27E
70 J6 Nyoiseau France 47.43N 0.55W
92 E11 Nyombi Zimbabwe 19.28S 30.40E
66 A6 Nyon Switzerland 46.23N 6.15E
93 A7 Nyondo Rwanda 1.41S 29.19E
95 P5 Nyoni S Africa 29.05S 31.27E
24 F11 Nyonni Ri mt Xizang Zizhiqu 28.13N 87.39E
71 G8 Nyons France 44.22N 5.08E
53 J6 Nyord isld Denmark 55.03N 12.13E
47 K5 Nyorkoy U.S.S.R. 60.18N 68.18E
50 L3 Nýpsfjördhur B Iceland
50 L3 Nýpur Iceland 65.49N 14.51W
53 H6 Nyraad Denmark 55.01N 11.59E
64 P4 Nýřany Czechoslovakia 49.43N 13.13E
50 G7 Nyrdhri Ófœra R Iceland
47 H5 Nyrob U.S.S.R. 60.45N 56.38E
64 P5 Nýrsko Czechoslovakia 49.18N 13.10E
53 H5 Nyrup Bugt B Denmark 55.58N 11.40E
62 K5 Nysa Poland 50.30N 17.20E
62 K5 Nysa Kłodzka R Poland
53 Y19 Nysetdalen V Norway 59.59N 8.30E
53 X16 Nysetelv R Norway
53 V14 Nyseter Möre og Romsdal Norway 62.22N 6.49E
53 Y14 Nyseter Opland Norway 62.04N 8.21E
40 J6 Nysh Sakhalin U.S.S.R. 51.30N 142.50E
52 G6 Nyskoga Sweden 60.28N 12.50E
Nyslott see Savonlinna
Nysogn see Kloster
110 H6 Nyssa Oregon 43.54N 117.00W
53 H7 Nysted Denmark 54.40N 11.45E
53 Y16 Nystuen Norway 61.11N 8.10E
46 S1 Nytva U.S.S.R. 57.58N 55.22E
87 C7 Nyubor,L Sudan 6.51N 30.17E
Nyuchcha R see Nuchcha R
41 O6 Nyuchcha-Siryame U.S.S.R. 69.15N 134.21E
47 G5 Nyuchpas U.S.S.R. 60.40N 51.30E
20 N1 Nyūdō-zaki C Japan 40.00N 139.42E
30 E2 Nyuk Xizang Zizhiqu 30.42N 82.00E
47 F4 Nyukhcha Arkhangel'sk U.S.S.R. 63.24N 46.31E
47 D4 Nyukhcha Karelia U.S.S.R. 63.57N 36.13E
47 C4 Nyuk, Ozero L U.S.S.R.
47 E5 Nyuksenitsa U.S.S.R. 60.24N 44.08E
40 B3 Nyukzha R U.S.S.R.
41 J3 Nyun'karakutari R U.S.S.R.
92 C4 Nyunzu Zaïre 5.55S 28.00E
41 L8 Nyurba U.S.S.R. 63.18N 118.28E
39 E5 Nyurchan U.S.S.R. 59.20N 152.10E
42 B3 Nyurol'ka R U.S.S.R.
42 B3 Nyurol'skiy U.S.S.R. 58.59N 78.02E
39 C4 Nyut R U.S.S.R.
47 G5 Nyuvchim U.S.S.R. 61.23N 50.44E
42 K2 Nyuya U.S.S.R. 60.35N 116.15E
42 J2 Nyuya R U.S.S.R.
40 J4 Nyvrovo Sakhalin U.S.S.R. 54.16N 142.43E
40 J6 Nyyskiy Zaliv gulf Sakhalin U.S.S.R.
34 G3 Nzaiza salt swamp Syria
91 B5 Nzambi Congo 3.59S 11.17E
87 B8 Nzara Sudan 4.40N 28.13E
93 J7 Nzaui mt Kenya 1.54S 37.32E
89 E7 Nzébéla Guinea 8.09N 9.07W
93 E10 Nzega Tanzania 4.13S 33.11E
91 C2 Nzem tribe Cameroon
89 E8 Nzérékoré Guinea 7.49N 8.48W
91 C7 N'Zeto Angola 7.13S 12.54E
90 L6 Nzili Pool Sudan 11.05N 22.59E
93 D9 Nzima Tanzania 3.17S 32.52E
92 G5 Nzinge Tanzania 6.09S 35.34E
92 C3 Nzingu Zaïre 3.35S 27.42E
93 K7 Nziu watercourse Kenya
89 E8 N'Zo Guinea 7.46N 8.19W
89 F8 N'Zo R Ivory Coast
93 F5 Nzoia R Kenya
93 A2 Nzoro Zaïre 3.21N 29.32E
93 A2 Nzoro R Zaïre
93 D10 Nzubuka Tanzania 4.44S 32.49E
108 L6 Oacoma S Dakota 43.48N 99.22W
56 J2 Oadby Leics Eng 52.36N 1.04W
108 K5 Oahe Dam S Dakota 44.25N 100.24W
108 K4 Oahe Res N Dakota/S Dakota
114 B4 Oahu isld Hawaiian Is
111 N7 Oak R Arizona
12 F5 Oakbank S Australia 33.07S 140.33E
98 E8 Oak Bay New Brunswick 45.11N 67.12W
103 H5 Oak Beach Long I, N Y 40.37N 73.18W
103 N4 Oak Bluffs Massachusetts 41.28N 70.33W
105 G2 Oakbore N Carolina 35.12N 80.21W
100 R8 Oakburn Manitoba 50.34N 100.35W
105 K2 Oak City N Carolina 35.58N 77.20W
111 M2 Oak City Utah 39.22N 112.21W
112 O9 Oak Cliff Dallas, Texas 32.45N 96.52W
109 D1 Oak Creek Colorado 40.17N 106.57W
112 G3 Oak Creek Reservoir Texas
111 D4 Oakdale California 37.45N 120.50W
107 D11 Oakdale Louisiana 30.49N 92.40W
103 L2 Oakdale Massachusetts 42.24N 71.48W
108 N7 Oakdale Nebraska 42.06N 97.59W
56 G2 Oakengates Shropshire Eng 52.42N 2.28W
108 M3 Oakes N Dakota 46.08N 98.07W
110 H2 Oakesdale Washington 47.07N 117.15W
13 F7 Oakes, Mt Queensland 25.55S 140.45E
13 K7 Oakey Queensland 27.25S 151.40E
106 F6 Oakfield Wisconsin 43.41N 88.34W
106 E9 Oakford Illinois 40.06N 89.59W
112 F8 Oak Forest Houston, Texas 29.48N 95.25W
107 E9 Oak Grove Louisiana 32.52N 91.23W
56 K2 Oakham Leics Eng 52.40N 0.43W
103 K2 Oakham Massachusetts 42.21N 72.03W
104 B5 Oak Harbor Ohio 41.31N 83.10W
110 C1 Oak Harbor Washington 48.17N 122.40W
105 G9 Oak Hill Florida 28.52N 80.52W
109 N2 Oak Hill Kansas 39.16N 97.22W
103 F2 Oak Hill New York 42.24N 74.10W
104 C8 Oak Hill Ohio 38.54N 82.34W
56 F5 Oakhill Somerset Eng 51.13N 2.32W
104 D9 Oak Hill W Virginia 37.58N 81.11W
13 H4 Oak Hills Queensland 18.30S 145.35E
106 D3 Oak I Wisconsin 46.55N 90.44W
100 R9 Oak Lake Manitoba 49.40N 100.45W
111 B4 Oakland California 37.50N 122.15W
107 H2 Oakland Illinois 39.39N 88.01W
108 P8 Oakland Iowa 41.18N 95.22W
104 Q2 Oakland Maine 44.33N 69.45W
104 F7 Oakland Maryland 39.24N 79.25W
107 G7 Oakland Mississippi 34.03N 89.57W
108 O8 Oakland Nebraska 41.50N 96.28W
110 B6 Oakland Oregon 43.25N 123.19W
103 C3 Oakland Pennsylvania 41.56N 75.42W
103 L3 Oakland Rhode I 41.58N 72.38W
107 G6 Oakland Tennessee 35.12N 89.31W
112 L6 Oakland Texas 29.36N 96.51W
107 J3 Oakland City Indiana 38.21N 87.19W
105 G11 Oakland Park Florida 26.12N 80.08W
12 H6 Oaklands New S Wales 35.34S 146.25E
11 L10 Oaklands New Zealand 43.34S 172.35E
104 B1 Oak Lane dist Philadelphia, Penn
106 Q4 Oak Lawn dist Chicago, Illinois
11 J2 Oakleigh New Zealand 35.50S 174.19E
12 D8 Oakleigh dist Melbourne, Vic
56 J4 Oakley Bucks Eng 51.49N 1.05W
111 C4 Oakley California 38.00N 121.44W
58 J6 Oakley Fife Scotland 56.05N 3.35W
110 M7 Oakley Idaho 42.15N 113.53W
109 K2 Oakley Kansas 39.08N 100.53W
106 K6 Oakley Michigan 43.08N 84.11W
105 C3 Oakman Georgia 34.32N 84.41W
104 F6 Oakmont Pennsylvania 40.33N 79.50W
100 R8 Oakner Manitoba 50.06N 100.38W
14 D5 Oakover, R W Australia
105 E5 Oakpark Georgia 32.21N 82.19W
13 G4 Oak Park Queensland 19.18S 144.10E
106 Q2 Oak Park dist Chicago, Illinois
106 L1 Oak Park dist Detroit, Michigan
100 T8 Oak Point Manitoba 50.30N 98.01W
107 E9 Oak Ridge Louisiana 32.38N 91.48W
107 G4 Oak Ridge Missouri 37.30N 89.43W
110 C6 Oakridge Oregon 43.45N 122.28W
107 M5 Oak Ridge Tennessee 36.02N 84.12W
100 R8 Oak River Manitoba 50.08N 100.26W
11 H6 Oakura New Zealand 39.06S 173.58E
12 F4 Oakvale S Australia 33.01S 140.41E
103 H3 Oakville Connecticut 41.35N 73.05W
100 T9 Oakville Manitoba 49.56N 98.00W
99 L9 Oakville Ontario 43.27N 79.41W
112 J7 Oakville Texas 28.27N 98.06W
107 J1 Oakwood Illinois 40.08N 87.47W
103 B7 Oakwood Maryland 39.43N 76.12W
107 E2 Oakwood Missouri 39.40N 91.24W
104 A5 Oakwood Ohio 41.06N 84.23W
109 M6 Oakwood Oklahoma 35.56N 98.43W
13 H7 Oakwood Queensland 25.48S 146.11E
112 M4 Oakwood Texas 31.36N 95.52W
57 K5 Oakworth W Yorks Eng 53.51N 1.56W
53 W14 Oaldsbygd Norway 62.10N 7.04E
11 E12 Oamaru New Zealand 45.07S 170.58E
20 O6 Oami Japan 35.32N 140.20E
58 D7 Oa, Mull of Islay, Strathclyde Scotland 55.36N 6.21W
53 U21 Oanes Norway 58.55N 6.05E
56 H5 Oare Wilts Eng 51.23N 1.46W
94 B1 Oarusib R Namibia
19 L5 Oas Luzon Philippines 13.16N 123.31E
94 E4 Oas Namibia 22.37S 19.22E
20 F7 Oasa Japan 34.46N 132.26E
111 G4 Oasis California 37.29N 117.56W
110 L8 Oasis Nevada 41.01N 114.27W
87 A1 Oasis Sudan 18.10N 26.35E
88 Q8 Oasis dept Algeria
123 J5 Oates Land Antarctica
95 H8 Oatlands S Africa 32.51S 24.17E
12 H8 Oatlands Tasmania 42.16S 147.20E
12 L8 Oatley dist Sydney, N S W
111 K6 Oatman Arizona 35.02N 114.25W
64 D4 Oau-Odernheim W Germany 49.46N 7.43E
115 L9 Oaxaca Mexico 17.05N 96.41W
115 L9 Oaxaca state Mexico
42 C4 Ob' U.S.S.R. 55.02N 82.45E
38 G2 Ob' R U.S.S.R.
90 B8 Oba Nigeria 7.29N 5.51E
99 F3 Oba Ontario 49.04N 84.07W
9 C10 Oba isld New Hebrides
61 H4 Obaix Belgium 50.32N 4.22E
99 E3 Obakamiga L Ontario 49.10N 85.08W
37 C3 Obaköy Turkey 40.08N 26.37E
99 F4 Oba L Ontario 48.40N 84.18W
90 E9 Obala Cameroon 4.09N 11.32E
99 Q3 Obalski Quebec 49.45N 74.24W
20 D9 Obama Japan 32.44N 130.11E
20 J6 Obama Japan 35.32N 135.45E
90 D9 Oban Nigeria 5.17N 8.33E
100 J6 Oban Saskatchewan 52.09N 108.09W
11 C13 Oban Stewart I New Zealand 46.54S 168.08E
58 F6 Oban Strathclyde Scotland 56.25N 5.29W
20 O3 Obanazawa Japan 38.37N 140.22E
109 G6 Obar New Mexico 35.32N 103.12W
75 D2 Obarenes, Mtes Spain
99 E4 Obatanga Prov. Park Ontario
99 Q3 Obatogamau, L Quebec

93 D2 Obb Sudan 3.59N 32.28E
58 C3 Obbe Harris, W Isles Scotland 57.46N 7.00W
53 B6 Obbekær Denmark 55.21N 8.53E
87 M8 Obbia Somalia 5.20N 48.30E
60 T16 Obbicht Netherlands 51.02N 5.47E
93 K2 Obbo Ethiopia 3.34N 38.52E
65 L7 Obdach Austria 47.04N 14.42E
60 H9 Obdam Netherlands 52.40N 4.55E
101 P9 Obed Alberta 53.33N 117.13W
31 B3 Obeh Afghanistan 34.23N 63.06E
87 C4 Obeid, El Sudan 13.11N 30.10E
31 B5 Obeit Afghanistan 31.34N 63.16E
36 G2 Obek Tepesi mt Turkey 40.50N 34.03E
90 D9 Obekum Nigeria 5.55N 8.53E
87 G3 Obel watercourse Ethiopia
66 H3 Ober-Aargau reg Switzerland
66 J5 Oberaarhorn mt Switzerland 46.32N 8.11E
66 L3 Ober-Ägeri Switzerland 47.08N 8.37E
66 L5 Oberalp-pass Switzerland 46.39N 8.35E
66 M5 Oberalpstock mt Switzerland 46.45N 8.47E
64 L8 Oberammergau W Germany 47.35N 11.07E
66 Q1 Ober Argen R W Germany
64 Q1 Oberau E Germany 51.11N 13.34E
65 D6 Oberau W Germany 47.34N 11.08E
64 N8 Oberaudorf W Germany 47.38N 12.10E
64 H2 Oberaula W Germany 50.52N 9.31E
64 H3 Oberbach W Germany 50.21N 9.54E
66 F4 Ober Balm Switzerland 46.52N 7.25E
64 L7 Ober-Bayern dist Bayern W Germany
69 L1 Oberbruch-Dremmen W Germany 51.02N 6.09E
69 O1 Oberbrügge W Germany 51.10N 7.35E
66 G3 Oberburg Switzerland 47.03N 7.38E
66 G4 Oberdiessbach Switzerland 46.51N 7.37E
64 H7 Oberdischingen W Germany 48.18N 9.50E
66 G2 Oberdorf Switzerland 47.24N 7.45E
66 G3 Oberdorf Switzerland 47.14N 7.31E
66 P1 Oberdorf W Germany 47.37N 9.35E
65 G8 Oberdrauburg Austria 46.46N 12.59E
65 G8 Ober-drau-tal V Austria
66 P2 Oberegg Switzerland 47.26N 9.33E
66 G1 Ober-Eggenen W Germany 47.46N 7.39E
66 H4 Oberei Switzerland 46.49N 7.46E
64 J4 Obereisenheim W Germany 49.54N 10.12E
64 J2 Oberellen E Germany 50.57N 10.11E
66 K1 Ober Endingen Switzerland 47.32N 8.18E
66 Q6 Ober Engadin V Switzerland
65 K7 Ober-enns-tal V Austria
64 H7 Ober-essendorf W Germany 48.00N 9.47E
64 K3 Oberessfeld W Germany 50.16N 10.34E
64 P1 Ober Eula E Germany 51.04N 13.20E
64 L4 Oberfranken dist Bayern W Germany
Oberfrohna see Limbach-Oberfrohna
65 H8 Obergailtal V Austria
66 K5 Obergesteln Switzerland 46.31N 8.19E
66 L2 Oberglatt Switzerland 47.28N 8.32E
65 N5 Ober Grafendorf Austria 48.09N 15.33E
65 K6 Ober Grünburg Austria 47.58N 14.16E
64 J8 Obergünzburg W Germany 47.51N 10.25E
65 D8 Obergurgl Austria 46.52N 11.02E
64 M7 Oberhaching W Germany 48.00N 11.36E
66 P5 Oberhalbstein V Switzerland
64 E7 Oberharmersbach W Germany 48.22N 8.07E
69 N6 Oberhaslach France 48.33N 7.19E
64 L8 Oberhausen Bayern W Germany 47.46N 11.09E
63 E10 Oberhausen Nordrhein-Westfalen W Germany 51.27N 6.50E
69 Q5 Oberhausen W Germany 49.15N 8.29E
69 N8 Oberhergheim France 47.58N 7.24E
64 E4 Ober Hilbersheim W Germany 49.55N 8.01E
64 K2 Oberhof E Germany 50.42N 10.44E
66 G5 Oberhofen Bern Switzerland 46.44N 7.41E
66 M3 Ober Iberg Switzerland 47.02N 8.47E
66 L2 Ober Illnau Switzerland 47.26N 8.43E
65 C7 Ober Inntal V Austria
66 G1 Ober-Inzlingen W Germany 47.35N 7.42E
65 B7 Oberjoch Pass Austria/West Germany 47.33N 10.27E
Ober-Kaufungen see Kaufungen
64 E6 Oberkirch W Germany 48.31N 8.06E
69 P1 Oberkirchen W Germany 51.10N 8.22E
64 F3 Oberkleen W Germany 50.28N 8.35E
64 J6 Ober-Kochen W Germany 48.47N 10.07E
64 M3 Ober Kotzau W Germany 50.15N 11.57E
66 M5 Oberland V Switzerland
66 K1 Ober-Lauchringen W Germany 47.37N 8.19E
64 J3 Ober Lauringen W Germany 50.13N 10.24E
64 G6 Oberlenningen W Germany 48.33N 9.29E
109 K2 Oberlin Kansas 39.49N 100.33W
107 D11 Oberlin Louisiana 30.38N 92.45W
104 C5 Oberlin Ohio 41.17N 82.14W
65 P7 Oberloisdorf Austria 47.27N 16.31E
64 H7 Ober Marchthal W Germany 48.14N 9.35E
63 J10 Ober Marsberg W Germany 51.27N 8.52E
64 J2 Obermassfeld-Grimmenthal E Germany 50.32N 10.27E
69 O4 Obermoschel W Germany 49.43N 7.46E
65 J5 Obermühl Austria 48.28N 13.57E
69 N7 Obernai France 48.28N 7.30E
65 H5 Obernberg Austria 48.19N 13.20E
64 G4 Obernburg W Germany 49.51N 9.09E
64 F7 Oberndorf Baden-Württemberg W Germany 48.17N 8.35E
63 K5 Oberndorf Niedersachsen W Germany 53.45N 9.09E
65 G6 Oberndorf bei Salzburg Austria 47.57N 12.57E
63 K8 Obernkirchen W Germany 52.16N 9.07E
64 Q6 Obernzell W Germany 48.34N 13.40E
108 L2 Oberon N Dakota 47.56N 99.12W
12 J5 Oberon New S Wales 33.40S 149.44E
65 H5 Ober-Österreich prov Austria
69 K4 Oberpallen Luxembourg 49.45N 5.50E
64 M5 Oberpfalz dist Bayern W Germany
64 N4 Oberpfalzer Wald forest W Germany
64 C2 Oberpleis W Germany 50.40N 7.16E
69 N2 Oberpleis W Germany 50.43N 7.17E
65 P7 Oberpullendorf Austria 47.30N 16.30E
64 F4 Ober Ramstadt W Germany 49.50N 8.45E
64 H8 Ober Reitnau W Germany 47.36N 9.41E
66 Q1 Ober Reute W Germany 47.34N 9.56E
66 F6 Oberried Switzerland 46.27N 7.29E
66 H5 Oberried Switzerland 46.45N 7.58E
66 P2 Oberriet Switzerland 47.19N 9.34E
64 O3 Ober Rittersgrün E Germany 50.27N 12.49E
63 O10 Ober Roblingen E Germany 51.27N 11.18E
63 P10 Ober Röblingen E Germany 51.28N 11.40E
64 F4 Ober-Roden W Germany 49.58N 8.50E
64 F3 Ober Rosbach W Germany 50.18N 8.41E
66 N4 Obersaxen Switzerland 46.46N 9.06E
64 G5 Ober Schefflenz W Germany 49.25N 9.18E
65 O7 Oberschutzen Austria 47.21N 16.12E
66 H1 Ober-Schwörstadt W Germany 47.36N 7.52E
66 F5 Ober-Simmen-Tal V Switz
64 H5 Obersontheim W Germany 49.03N 9.54E
64 K1 Oberspier E Germany 51.18N 10.53E
65 B6 Oberstaufen W Germany 47.34N 10.05E
65 B7 Oberstdorf W Germany 47.25N 10.18E
69 O5 Obersteinbach France 49.02N 7.41E
64 O8 Ober Teisendorf W Germany 47.51N 12.47E
64 G8 Oberteuringen W Germany 47.43N 9.28E
64 J3 Obertheres W Germany 50.02N 10.29E
64 N6 Obertraubling W Germany 48.57N 12.11E
64 O7 Ober Trennbach W Germany 48.28N 12.35E
65 H6 Obertrumer See L Austria
63 T6 Oberuecker-see L E Germany
66 N1 Ober Uhldingen W Germany 47.44N 9.15E
64 F3 Oberursell W Germany 50.12N 8.35E
66 P5 Obervaz reg Switzerland 46.43N 9.32E
65 H8 Ober Vellach Austria 46.57N 13.13E
64 N5 Oberviechtach W Germany 49.27N 12.25E
66 K5 Oberwald Switzerland 46.32N 8.21E
61 O6 Oberwampach Luxembourg 50.02N 5.52E
65 O7 Oberwart Austria 47.18N 16.12E
65 G6 Ober Weissbach Austria 47.31N 12.45E
64 L2 Oberweissbach E Germany 50.35N 11.08E
64 D3 Oberwesel W Germany 50.06N 7.44E
66 K1 Ober Wiesen Switzerland 47.44N 8.29E
64 O3 Oberwiesenthal E Germany 50.25N 12.58E
66 K2 Oberwil Aargau Switzerland 47.20N 8.23E
66 G1 Oberwil Baselland Switzerland 47.32N 7.33E
66 F5 Oberwil Bern Switzerland 46.40N 7.27E
64 C2 Oberwinter W Germany 50.37N 7.13E
65 K7 Oberwölz Austria 47.13N 14.17E
65 K7 Ober Zeiring Austria 47.15N 14.30E
66 P1 Oberzell W Germany 47.44N 9.34E
121 G1 Obesá Argentina 27.29S 55.08W
47 G4 Obesdino U.S.S.R. 63.26N 54.25E
107 L5 Obey R Tennessee
66 K3 Obfelden Switzerland 47.15N 8.26E
29 H5 Obhra Dam Uttar Prad India 24.26N 83.02E
20 E10 Obi Japan 31.38N 131.20E
19 E4 Obi isld Moluccas Indon
Obiat see Obbia
Obiat Pt see Diga Pt
117 B5 Obidos Brazil 1.52S 55.30W
76 A10 Obidos Portugal 39.21N 9.09W
76 A10 Óbidos, Lagoa L Portugal
63 N10 Obierspier E Germany 51.18N 10.52E
43 J7 Obigarm Tadzhikistan U.S.S.R. 38.45N 69.45E
61 D4 Obigies Belgium 50.40N 3.22E
20 M2 Obihiro Japan 42.56N 143.10E
19 E4 Obi, Kep islds Moluccas Indon
19 E4 Obilatu isld Moluccas Indon 1.24S 127.20E
46 N5 Obil'noye U.S.S.R. 47.32N 44.28E
64 N8 Obing W Germany 48.00N 12.25E
107 G5 Obion Tennessee 36.16N 89.11W
107 G5 Obion R Tennessee
71 H7 Obiou, l' mt France 44.47N 5.50E
19 E4 Obi, Selat str Moluccas Indon
75 E8 Obispalia, La reg Spain
119 E3 Obispos Venezuela 8.19N 70.05W
44 E8 Obitochnaya Kosa sand spit Ukraine U.S.S.R.
44 D8 Obitochnyy Zaliv B Ukraine U.S.S.R.
39 F1 Obiye-Kyuyel', Oz L U.S.S.R. 68.30N 155.15E
72 G5 Objat France 45.16N 1.24E
45 O8 Oblivskaya U.S.S.R. 48.32N 42.31E
107 J3 Oblong Illinois 39.00N 87.55W
40 E7 Obluch'ye U.S.S.R. 49.01N 131.04E
39 F6 Oblukovina R U.S.S.R.
39 F6 Oblukovino U.S.S.R. 55.12N 155.38E
45 H1 Obninsk U.S.S.R. 55.05N 36.37E
28 L4 Obo Burma 22.01N 96.04E
90 N9 Obo Cent Afr Rep 5.18N 26.28E
22 E8 Obo Qinghai China 37.58N 100.50E
85 O10 Obo Sudan 19.15N 36.58E
87 J5 Obock Djibouti 11.59N 43.20E
46 G5 Obodovka Ukraine U.S.S.R. 48.28N 29.10E
91 K4 Obokote Zaïre 0.51S 26.20E
21 E7 Obŏk-tong N Korea 40.50N 129.10E
45 A1 Obol' Belorussiya U.S.S.R. 55.22N 29.15E
46 G2 Obol' R Belorussiya U.S.S.R.
103 B6 Obold Pennsylvania 40.24N 76.04W
91 D4 Oboli Congo 1.50S 14.46E
22 B7 Obo Liang Qinghai China 38.45N 92.52E
90 C8 Obolo Nigeria 6.53N 7.33E
45 D7 Obolon' Ukraine U.S.S.R. 49.36N 32.53E
45 D5 Obolon'ye Ukraine U.S.S.R. 51.36N 32.57E
Obome see Jarona
75 J6 Obón Spain 40.54N 0.45W
20 O2 Obonai Japan 39.42N 140.42E
100 O1 Obonga L Ontario 50.00N 89.15W
18 L3 Obong, Gunong mt Sarawak Malaysia 4.10N 115.09E
93 C2 Obongi Uganda 3.15N 31.34E
62 K3 Oborniki Poland 52.40N 16.50E
47 E2 Obornyy, Mys C U.S.S.R. 67.47N 40.45E
61 G5 Obourg Belgium 50.28N 4.01E
91 D4 Obouya Congo 0.56S 15.41E
43 D7 Oboy Turkmeniya U.S.S.R. 39.14N 55.23E
45 H5 Oboyan' U.S.S.R. 51.13N 36.17E
47 E4 Obozerskiy U.S.S.R. 63.28N 40.29E
121 F2 Obrage Argentina 29.00S 58.10W
65 L3 Obrataň Czechoslovakia 49.27N 14.58E
44 J2 Obraztsovo Travino U.S.S.R. 45.57N 48.03E
15 K8 Obree, Mt Papua New Guinea 9.30S 148.04E
115 B10 Obregon dist Mexico City Mexico
115 E4 Obregón, Ciudad Mexico 27.28N 109.59W
115 E4 Obregón, Presa res Mexico
101 W5 Obre L N W Terr 60.21N 103.00W
82 F6 Obrenovac Yugoslavia 44.40N 20.11E
99 K5 O'Brien Ontario 47.43N 80.44W
59 E6 O'Briensbridge Clare Irish Rep 52.45N 8.30W
59 D6 O'Brien's Tower Clare Irish Rep 52.58N 9.29W
64 Q2 Obrnice Czechoslovakia 50.31N 13.42E
47 L8 Obrochnoye U.S.S.R. 53.33N 73.29E
82 C6 Obrovac Yugoslavia 44.11N 15.41E
43 J6 Obruchevo Uzbekistan U.S.S.R. 40.08N 68.31E
36 G4 Obruk Turkey 38.10N 33.12E
40 K7 Obryvistoye Sakhalin U.S.S.R. 48.45N 144.40E
41 G2 Obryvistyy, Mys C U.S.S.R. 78.23N 99.57E
10 M6 Observatoire, Caye del' isld Coral Sea 21.28S 158.56E
121 M10 Observatorio, I Argentina 54.40S 64.28W
101 J8 Observatory Inlet Br Col
10 F12 Observatory Rock Lord Howe I Pacific Oc 31.46S 159.15E
46 J2 Obsha R U.S.S.R.
45 U3 Obshaovka U.S.S.R. 53.07N 48.50E
43 B2 Obshchiy Syrt ridge U.S.S.R.
110 L5 Obsidian Idaho 44.01N 114.50W
47 L3 Obskaya Guba gulf U.S.S.R.
22 C8 Obson Jah Qinghai China 37.49N 94.20E
65 C7 Obsteig Austria 47.18N 10.55E
121 J9 Obstrucción, Estero inlet Chile
Obta see Ibta
26 J8 Ob Trench Indian Ocean
89 J8 Obuasi Ghana 6.15N 1.36W
90 D8 Obubra Nigeria 6.05N 8.20E
90 D8 Obudu Nigeria 6.38N 9.05E
46 H4 Obukhov Ukraine U.S.S.R. 50.05N 30.36E
47 K8 Obukhovo Kazakhstan U.S.S.R. 53.42N 69.22E
39 G6 Obukhovo U.S.S.R. 56.14N 161.50E
15 H7 Obura Papua New Guinea 6.32S 145.59E
47 H6 Obva R U.S.S.R.
47 M3 Obvodnyy Kanal Leningrad U.S.S.R.
66 J4 Obwalden canton Switzerland
47 F5 Ob'yachevo U.S.S.R. 60.10N 49.25E
74 E2 Oca R Spain
105 E8 Ocala Florida 29.11N 82.09W
75 C2 Oca, Montes de mts Spain
119 G6 Ocamo, R Venezuela
115 E3 Ocampo Chihuahua Mexico 28.12N 108.24W
115 H4 Ocampo Mexico 27.20N 102.24W
115 K6 Ocampo Tamaulipas Mexico 22.52N 99.20W
75 C2 Oca, Mtes de Spain
119 D3 Ocaña Colombia 8.16N 73.21W
120 C6 Ocaña Peru 14.24S 74.50W
75 D8 Ocaña Spain 39.57N 3.30W
75 D8 Ocaña, Mesa de plat Spain
109 E5 Ocate New Mexico 36.11N 105.03W
79 D3 Occhieppo Inferióre Italy 45.33N 8.01E
79 L5 Occhiobello Italy 44.56N 11.35E
120 E8 Occidental, Cord mts Bolivia/Chile
119 C7 Occidental, Cord mts Colombia
120 B3 Occidental, Cord mts Peru
79 E4 Occimiano Italy 45.04N 8.30E
58 K2 Occumster Highland Scotland 58.18N 3.15W
103 H5 Ocean Beach Long I, N Y 40.40N 73.10W
113 S7 Ocean Cape Alaska 59.30N 139.53W
104 K8 Ocean City Maryland 38.21N 75.06W
103 E8 Ocean City New Jersey 39.16N 74.35W
110 A2 Ocean City Washington 47.04N 124.10W
101 K9 Ocean Falls Br Col 52.24N 127.42W
103 F7 Ocean Gate New Jersey 39.56N 74.07W
103 F6 Ocean Grove New Jersey 40.13N 74.00W
Ocean I Hawaiian Is see Kure I
Ocean I Kiribati, Pacific Ocsee Banaba
108 B6 Ocean L Wyoming
111 D6 Oceano California 35.05N 120.36W
96 G5 Oceanographer Fracture Atlantic Oc
101 J12 Ocean Park Br Col 49.02N 122.53W
111 C9 Ocean Park Los Angeles, California
110 A3 Ocean Park Washington 46.28N 124.03W
111 G8 Oceanside California 33.12N 117.23W
110 B4 Oceanside Oregon 45.28N 123.57W
107 H11 Ocean Springs Mississippi 30.25N 88.50W
104 K8 Ocean View Delaware 38.32N 75.05W
103 E8 Ocean View New Jersey 39.11N 74.44W
103 F8 Oceanville New Jersey 39.28N 74.28W
75 D5 Ocejon mt Spain 41.06N 3.16W
75 F6 Ocentejo Spain 40.47N 2.24W
75 H2 Ochagavia Spain 42.55N 1.05W
45 C10 Ochakov Ukraine U.S.S.R. 46.37N 31.33E
44 D5 Ochamchire Georgia U.S.S.R. 42.44N 41.30E
61 M7 Ochamps Belgium 49.56N 5.17E
75 E1 Ochandiano Spain 43.02N 2.39W
42 J2 Ochchuguy Botuobuya R U.S.S.R.
81 A5 Oche, Pta. d Sardinia 39.11N 8.16E
46 R1 Ocher U.S.S.R. 57.56N 54.43E
69 K6 Ochey-Thuilley France 48.34N 5.58E
20 C8 Ochi Japan 33.21N 129.59E
20 F7 Ochi Japan 35.00N 132.32E
20 G8 Ochi Japan 33.32N 133.16E
20 D2 Ochiai dist Tōkyō Japan
21 K6 Ochiishi-misaki C Japan 43.09N 145.31E
58 J6 Ochil Hills Tayside Scotland
31 G2 Ochili Pass Pakistan/Afghan 36.53N 73.03E
57 E2 Ochiltree Strathclyde Scotland 55.28N 4.23W
105 C7 Ochlocknee Georgia 30.59N 84.03W
105 C7 Ochlockonee, R Florida
110 E5 Ochoco Res Oregon 44.19N 120.40W
63 G6 Ocholt W Germany 53.12N 7.53E
105 F12 Ochopee Florida 26.53N 81.18W
116 K1 Ocho Rios Jamaica, W I 18.24N 77.06W
100 S7 Ochre River Manitoba 51.04N 99.46W
64 J2 Ochsen E Germany 50.44N 10.03E
64 J4 Ochsenfurt W Germany 49.40N 10.04E
64 H7 Ochsenhausen W Germany 48.04N 9.58E
64 M3 Ochsenkopf mt W Germany 50.02N 11.50E
63 L5 Ochsenzoll W Germany 53.42N 10.00E
60 L12 Ochten Netherlands 51.55N 5.35E
64 C3 Ochtendung W Germany 50.21N 7.23E
63 O8 Ochtmersleben E Germany 52.10N 11.26E
63 F8 Ochtrup W Germany 52.13N 7.13E
105 D6 Ocilla Georgia 31.35N 83.16W
52 K6 Ockelbo Sweden 60.52N 16.45E
95 E9 Ockertskraal S Africa 33.41S 21.10E
63 J3 Ockholm W Germany 54.40N 8.50E
56 L5 Ockley Surrey Eng 51.09N 0.22W
82 J4 Ocland Romania 46.10N 25.26E
105 D5 Ocmulgee Nat. Mon Georgia 32.50N 83.34W
105 D4 Ocmulgee, R Georgia
82 J5 Ocna Sibiului Romania 45.52N 24.02E
82 H3 Ocna Şugătag Romania 47.48N 23.58E
82 J5 Ocnele Mari Romania 45.03N 24.18E
115 N9 Ococingo Mexico 17.04N 92.15W
105 F9 Ocoee Florida 28.34N 81.33W
107 M6 Ocoee Tennessee 35.08N 84.53W
107 M6 Ocoee Dams Tennessee
120 C7 Ocoña Peru 16.41S 73.17W
120 C7 Ocoña, R Peru
107 G2 Oconee Illinois 39.16N 89.06W
108 N8 Oconee Nebraska 41.30N 97.32W
105 E5 Oconee, R Georgia
13 G5 O'Connell R Queensland
12 A5 O'Connor dist Canberra Australia
108 L8 Oconto Nebraska 41.09N 99.47W
106 G5 Oconto Wisconsin 44.55N 87.52W
106 F5 Oconto Falls Wisconsin 44.53N 88.08W
115 E5 Ocoroni Mexico 25.56N 108.28W
120 D6 Ocoruro Peru 15.06S 71.07W
115 N10 Ocos Mexico 14.32N 92.12W
115 L3 Ocotal Nicaragua 13.38N 86.31W
115 M3 Ocotal Nicaragua 12.59N 84.18W
115 P10 Ocotepeque Honduras 14.25N 89.10W
115 H7 Ocotlán Jalisco Mexico 20.21N 102.42W
115 L9 Ocotlán Oaxaca Mexico 16.49N 96.49W
66 E2 Ocourt Switzerland 47.22N 7.06E
115 N9 Ocozocoautla Mexico 16.46N 93.22W
61 M5 Ocquier Belgium 50.23N 5.24E
105 M2 Ocracoke N Carolina 35.06N 75.59W
105 M2 Ocracoke I N Carolina 35.07N 75.57W
76 D9 Ocreza R Portugal
120 B4 Ocros Peru 10.24S 77.24W
62 L8 Ócsa Hungary 47.18N 19.13E
62 M9 Ócsöd Hungary 46.56N 20.23E
70 G2 Octeville Manche France 49.37N 1.39W
70 L2 Octeville Seine-Inférieure France 49.33N 0.07E
99 D3 Octopus Ontario 49.46N 86.41W
103 B7 Octoraro Cr Pennsylvania
115 O6 Ocú Panama 7.55N 80.43W
92 J8 Ocua Mozambique 13.40S 39.46E
119 F2 Ocumare del Tuy Venezuela 10.07N 66.47W
120 F8 Ocuri Bolivia 18.49S 65.48W
19 D8 Ocussi Indonesia 9.15S 124.23E
19 D8 Ocussi Ambeno terr Indonesia
52 G9 Od Sweden 57.56N 13.10E
Oda see Ōta
89 J9 Oda Ghana 5.55N 0.56W
20 F6 Ōda Shimane, Honshu Japan 35.10N 132.29E
89 J8 Oda R Ghana
50 H5 Ódádhahraun lava field Iceland
50 L5 Ódadhavötn L Iceland 64.50N 14.45W
21 E7 Ŏdaejin N Korea 41.22N 129.49E
20 K7 Odaigahara-zan mt Japan 34.12N 136.06E
87 B4 Odaiya, El Sudan 12.03N 28.16E
87 C8 Oda, Jeb mt Equatoria Sudan 5.10N 30.35E
85 O9 Oda, Jeb mt Kassala Sudan 20.24N 36.41E
20 O4 Odaka Japan 37.32N 140.59E
87 H7 Odala Ethiopia 7.40N 40.53E
106 D3 Odanah Wisconsin 46.36N 90.41W
72 H8 Odars France 43.32N 1.34E
87 F3 Odas Ethiopia 14.37N 37.45E
20 O1 Ōdate Japan 40.18N 140.32E
20 N6 Odawara Japan 35.15N 139.08E
53 B3 Odby Denmark 56.37N 8.33E
53 V18 Odda Norway 60.03N 6.34E
87 N5 Odda, Jeb mt Somalia 11.24N 50.19E
50 C5 Oddastadhavatn L Iceland 64.54N 22.15W
53 E3 Odde Denmark 56.43N 10.19E
53 G5 Odden Kirke Denmark 55.58N 11.25E
53 B3 Oddense Denmark 56.39N 8.57E
53 E5 Odder Denmark 55.59N 10.10E
52 D8 Oddernes Norway 58.09N 8.03E
53 B3 Odde Sund sound Denmark 56.35N 8.33E
53 B3 Oddesund Nørre Denmark 56.35N 8.33E
50 E7 Oddi Iceland 63.47N 20.24W
26 S3 Odduchuddan Sri Lanka 9.08N 80.38E
87 J8 Oddur Somalia 4.11N 43.52E
76 D12 Odearce R Portugal
108 P7 Odebolt Iowa 42.18N 95.14W
76 B14 Odeceixe Portugal 37.26N 8.46W
53 H6 Øde Førslev Denmark 55.22N 11.55E
61 N5 Odeigne Belgium 50.16N 5.41E
50 G4 Ódeila reg Iceland
76 E14 Odeleite Portugal 37.20N 7.29W
76 D14 Odeleite, R Portugal
106 F8 Odell Illinois 41.01N 88.31W
108 O9 Odell Nebraska 40.04N 96.48W
112 H1 Odell Texas 34.21N 99.26W
76 C14 Odelouca Portugal 37.13N 8.30W
76 C14 Odelouca R Portugal
64 L7 Odelzhausen W Germany 48.18N 11.12E
112 K8 Odem Texas 27.56N 97.37W
76 B13 Odemira Portugal 37.35N 8.38W
76 C13 Odemira Portugal 37.35N 8.29W
36 C4 Ödemiş Turkey 38.11N 27.58E
107 C7 Oden Arkansas 34.37N 93.46W
64 D4 Odenbach W Germany 49.41N 7.40E
63 J3 Odenbüll W Germany 54.30N 8.51E
95 K3 Odendaalsrus S Africa 27.52S 26.42E
64 F5 Odenheim W Germany 49.10N 8.46E
64 A1 Odenkirchen W Germany 51.08N 6.28E
53 E6 Odense Denmark 55.24N 10.25E
Odense co see Fyn
53 E6 Odense Å R Denmark
53 F6 Odense Fjord inlet Denmark 55.29N 10.33E
69 N1 Odenthal W Germany 51.02N 7.08E
103 A8 Odenton Maryland 39.05N 76.41W
64 F4 Odenwald mts W Germany
62 H3 Oder R E Germany/Poland
Oder R Poland/Czechsee Odra R
63 M9 Oder R W Germany
63 U7 Oderberg E Germany 52.52N 14.03E
63 T8 Oderin E Germany 52.04N 13.44E
Odernheim see Oau-Odernheim
63 T8 Oder-Spree-Kanal E Germany
79 M3 Oderzo Italy 45.47N 12.29E
52 H8 Ödeshög Sweden 58.13N 14.40E
103 C8 Odessa Delaware 39.27N 75.40W
107 C3 Odessa Missouri 38.59N 93.57W
104 J4 Odessa New York 42.21N 76.46W
99 O8 Odessa Ontario 44.17N 76.46W
100 O8 Odessa Saskatchewan 50.16N 103.48W
112 E4 Odessa Texas 31.50N 102.23W
46 H6 Odessa Ukraine U.S.S.R. 46.30N 30.46E
110 G2 Odessa Washington 47.19N 118.40W
45 B10 Odesskaya Oblast' prov Ukraine U.S.S.R.
47 L8 Odesskoye U.S.S.R. 54.12N 72.58E
70 C5 Odet R France
Odhan Hayrhan see Otgon
100 T3 Odhill Manitoba 55.08N 98.12W
84 R15 Odhu Cyprus 34.53N 33.10E
87 F2 Odi watercourse Sudan
77 C5 Odiel R Spain
89 F7 Odienné Ivory Coast 9.36N 7.32W
56 K5 Odiham Hants Eng 51.15N 0.57W
60 J11 Odijk Netherlands 52.03N 5.14E
60 L13 Odiliapeel Netherlands 51.36N 5.44E
107 G3 Odin Illinois 38.38N 89.01W
92 K8 Odinepa Mozambique 13.36S 40.01E
63 E9 Öding W Germany 51.55N 6.50E
45 J1 Odintsovo U.S.S.R. 55.39N 37.15E
93 B1 Odio Sudan 4.20N 30.30E
53 C6 Ødis Denmark 55.24N 9.23E
76 A11 Odivelas Portugal 38.47N 9.11W
76 C12 Odivelas Portugal 38.10N 8.09W
76 C12 Odivelas R Portugal
72 C12 Odivelas, Barragem de res Portugal 38.12N 8.04W
82 L5 Odobeşti Romania 45.46N 27.06E
90 J2 Odofou Chad 18.10N 19.21E
62 K4 Odolanów Poland 51.31N 17.39E
123 E12 Odom Inlet Antarctica
107 K3 Odon Indiana 38.50N 87.00W
75 G6 Odón Spain 40.53N 1.35W
70 J3 Odon R France
89 J8 Odonkawkrom Ghana 7.08N 0.02W
112 F3 O'Donnell Texas 32.58N 101.49W
60 Q8 Odoorn Netherlands 52.51N 6.51E
82 J4 Odorhei Romania 46.18N 25.19E
46 K3 Odoyev U.S.S.R. 53.58N 36.48E
62 J4 Odra R Poland/Czech
76 L3 Odra R Spain
90 J1 Odrou Chad 20.48N 18.59E
53 C5 Ødsted Denmark 55.39N 9.25E
105 E6 Odum Georgia 31.40N 82.02W
87 K6 Odweina Somalia 9.20N 45.02E
39 E5 Odyan, Zaliv B U.S.S.R.
82 E5 Odžaci Yugoslavia 45.30N 19.17E
91 D3 Odzala Congo 0.37N 14.37E
40 H3 Odzhan Mys C U.S.S.R. 57.27N 139.50E
92 F11 Odzi Zimbabwe 18.59S 32.29E
92 F11 Odzi R Zimbabwe
91 D5 Odziba Congo 3.41S 15.28E
63 O8 Oebisfelde E Germany 52.26N 11.00E
64 J2 Oechsen E Germany 50.37N 10.04E
61 D2 Oedelem Belgium 51.10N 3.20E
64 P2 Oederan E Germany 50.52N 13.10E
64 E1 Oedingen W Germany 51.11N 8.06E
60 M13 Oeffelt Netherlands 51.42N 5.56E
60 F11 Oegstgeest Netherlands 52.11N 4.28E
117 F8 Oeiras Brazil 7.00S 42.07W
76 A11 Oeiras Portugal 38.41N 9.18W
76 D13 Oeiras R Portugal
76 C16 Oeiras, R Portugal
61 C3 Oekene Belgium 50.55N 3.10E
63 H9 Oelde W Germany 51.49N 8.09E
61 J2 Oelegem Belgium 51.13N 4.36E
117 B3 Oelemari R Surinam
108 G6 Oelrichs S Dakota 43.10N 103.13W
64 N3 Oelsnitz E Germany 50.25N 12.11E
64 O2 Oelsnitz E Germany 50.43N 12.42E
106 C7 Oelwein Iowa 42.40N 91.54W
64 L2 Oelze E Germany 50.32N 11.02E
122 O11 Oeno atoll Pacific Oc 23.55S 130.45W
13 C1 Oenpelli N Terr Australia 12.19S 133.02E
66 G2 Oensingen Switzerland 47.18N 7.44E
22 L1 O-erh-ku-na Ho R China/U.S.S.R.
60 K14 Oerle Netherlands 51.25N 5.22E
63 J9 Oerlinghausen W Germany 51.58N 8.40E
61 D3 Oeselgem Belgium 50.56N 3.26E
64 L3 Oeslau W Germany 50.17N 11.03E
121 H8 Oeste, Canal str Chile
64 E3 Oestrich-Winkel W Germany 50.00N 8.01E
61 G3 Oetingen Belgium 50.47N 4.04E
121 E1 Oetling Argentina 27.26S 60.00W
64 K6 Oettingen W Germany 48.57N 10.38E
61 E4 Œudeghien Belgium 50.41N 3.43E
61 K2 Oevel Belgium 51.08N 4.54E
63 H10 Oeventrop W Germany 51.23N 8.08E
63 K3 Oeversee W Germany 54.42N 9.27E
37 E5 Of Turkey 40.57N 40.17E
107 G9 Ofahoma Mississippi 32.41N 89.41W
80 N6 Ofanto R Italy
35 B8 Ofaqim Israel 31.19N 34.37E
50 D2 Ófeigsfjördhur Iceland 66.03N 21.36W
50 D2 Ófeigsfjördhur B Iceland
80 J4 Ofena Italy 42.20N 13.45E
79 D2 Ofenhorn mt Italy/Switz 46.23N 8.19E
66 K6 Ofenhorn mt Italy/Switz 46.23N 8.18E
66 S5 Ofenpass Switzerland 46.38N 10.18E
35 C3 'Ofer Israel 32.38N 34.58E
90 B7 Offa Nigeria 8.10N 4.40E
61 L7 Offagne Belgium 49.53N 5.10E
59 G5 Offaly co Irish Rep
64 F3 Offenbach am Main W Germany 50.06N 8.46E
64 D7 Offenburg W Germany 48.29N 7.57E
35 B1 Offence, Mt.of Jerusalem 31.46N 35.14E
65 J6 Offen-see L Austria 47.46N 13.50E
52 H3 Offerdal Sweden 63.29N 14.00E
105 E6 Offerman Georgia 31.25N 82.57W
12 B2 Officer Cr., The S Australia
80 J3 Offida Italy 42.56N 13.41E
64 J7 Offingen W Germany 48.28N 10.23E
91 B4 Offoué R Gabon
70 N2 Offranville France 49.52N 1.03E
64 E4 Offstein W Germany 49.36N 8.16E
93 B2 Offude Uganda 3.13N 30.59E
119 G3 Oficina Venezuela 8.51N 64.19W
83 H8 Ofidhoúsa isld Greece 36.33N 26.08E
90 A7 Ofiki R Nigeria
89 J8 Ofin R Ghana
76 B5 Ofir Portugal 41.31N 8.47W
86 M10 Ofira Egypt 27.52N 34.17E
59 E4 O'Flyn, L Roscommon Irish Rep 53.46N 8.38W
9 U12 Ofolanga atoll Tonga, Pacific Oc 19.43S 174.29W
51 F3 Ofotfjord inlet Norway
53 X16 Ofredal Norway 61.13N 7.33E
53 Y19 Ofte Norway 59.30N 8.10E
66 K1 Ofteringen W Germany 47.41N 8.23E
122 F1 Ofu isld Amer Samoa Pacific Oc 14.11S 169.40W
9 R12 Ofu isld Tonga, Pacific Oc 18.42S 173.58W
20 D5 Ofuna Japan 35.21N 139.32E
90 D8 Ofun Atam Nigeria 6.11N 8.29E
20 P2 Ofunato Japan 39.04N 141.43E
20 L1 Ofuyu-misaki C Japan 43.44N 141.21E
20 N2 Oga Japan 39.56N 139.47E
20 N6 Ogachi Dam Japan 35.47N 139.07E
87 J7 Ogaden reg Ethiopia
87 K7 Ogaden tribe Ethiopia
88 J10 Og Aguelt Abd el Jebar Mauritania 22.44N 9.29W
99 E2 Ogahalla Ontario 50.06N 85.51W
20 N2 Oga-hantō pen Japan
20 K6 Ogaki Japan 35.22N 136.36E
109 L3 Ogallah Kansas 38.59N 99.43W
108 J8 Ogallala Nebraska 41.09N 101.44W
18 F7 Ogan R Sumatra Indon
45 J3 Ogarevka U.S.S.R. 53.54N 37.37E
21 J11 Ogasawara-guntō islds Japan
99 M5 Ogascanane, L Quebec
20 B2 Ogawa Tōkyō Japan
20 P1 Ogawara-ko L Japan
41 B2 Oga, Zaliv B Novaya Zemlya U.S.S.R.
90 B7 Ogbomosho Nigeria 8.05N 4.11E
56 H5 Ogbourne St.George Wilts Eng 51.29N 1.42W
37 F5 Ogdem Turkey 40.54N 41.35E
106 G9 Ogden Illinois 40.08N 87.59W
108 Q7 Ogden Iowa 42.02N 94.01W
109 O2 Ogden Kansas 39.06N 96.44W
98 L8 Ogden Nova Scotia 45.21N 61.39W
110 O8 Ogden Utah 41.14N 111.59W
101 G6 Ogden, Mt Br Col/Alaska 58.26N 133.31W
103 E4 Ogdensburg New Jersey 41.05N 74.36W
104 K2 Ogdensburg New York 44.42N 75.31W
88 J10 Ogdet el Biar Mauritania 23.21N 8.04W
105 E4 Ogeechee, R Georgia
108 P2 Ogema Minnesota 47.06N 96.56W
100 N9 Ogema Saskatchewan 49.35N 104.56W
63 G5 Ogenbargen W Germany 53.33N 7.37E
69 G6 Oger France 48.57N 4.01E
69 M6 Ogéviller France 48.33N 6.43E
66 L8 Oggebbio Italy 45.59N 8.39E
79 F3 Oggiono Italy 45.47N 9.21E
31 G3 Oghi Pakistan 34.32N 73.02E
29 C5 Oghna Rajasthan India 24.32N 73.29E
15 K2 Ogho Solomon Is 6.50S 156.50E
88 Q6 Oghroud, Région des Algeria
20 M4 Ogi Sado Shima Japan 37.50N 138.18E
99 F6 Ogidaki Ontario 46.58N 84.14W
95 N2 Ogies S Africa 26.04S 29.03E
111 K9 Ogilby California 32.49N 114.50W
93 E2 Ogili mt Uganda 3.11N 33.17E
108 R4 Ogilvie Minnesota 45.50N 93.25W
14 A8 Ogilvie W Australia 28.09S 114.38E
101 D3 Ogilvie Mts Yukon Terr
20 Q8 Ogimi Okinawa Japan 26.44N 128.08E
46 F4 Oginskiy, Kanal Belorussiya U.S.S.R.
108 H6 Oglala S Dakota 43.10N 102.44W
113 O10 Oglala Pass. Aleutian Is
43 C7 Oglanly Turkmeniya U.S.S.R. 39.50N 54.30E
88 L8 Oglat Abderrhamane Algeria 26.52N 4.25W
89 F1 Oglat Ahel Bella Mauritania 21.43N 6.30W
88 M6 Oglat Beraber Algeria 30.15N 3.34W
89 F1 Oglat el Fersig Mauritania 21.50N 6.21W
88 L9 Oglat Sbita Algeria 25.20N 4.48W
101 Z1 Ogle Pt N W Terr 68.19N 95.58W
106 E8 Oglesby Illinois 41.16N 89.02W
112 K4 Oglesby Texas 31.25N 97.31W
105 C5 Oglethorpe Georgia 32.18N 84.04W
88 L8 Oglet Oued Yacoub Algeria 26.38N 5.58W
81 D4 Ogliastra reg Sardinia
81 D4 Ogliastra, I.dell Sardinia 39.58N 9.43E
81 K3 Ogliastro Cilento Italy 40.21N 15.03E
79 G4 Oglio R Italy
113 P10 Ogliuga Is Aleutian Is
101 D3 Oglivie R Yukon Terr
40 H5 Oglongi U.S.S.R. 52.58N 138.50E
47 L7 Oglukhino U.S.S.R. 55.54N 71.50E
56 D5 Ogmore Mid Glam Wales 51.29N 3.37W
13 J6 Ogmore Queensland 22.37S 149.40E
47 M5 Ognevskoye U.S.S.R. 56.03N 61.21E
42 B3 Ognev Yar U.S.S.R. 58.20N 76.27E
42 C6 Ogni U.S.S.R. 51.52N 83.30E
81 K10 Ognina, C Sicily 36.58N 15.16E
71 J2 Ognon R France
Oğnut see Gönük
19 B3 Ogoamas, Gunung mt Celebes Indonesia 0.39N 120.16E
90 D8 Ogoja Nigeria 6.40N 8.45E
97 L7 Ogoki Ontario 51.35N 86.00W
99 C2 Ogoki L Ontario
99 D2 Ogoki, R Ontario
99 B2 Ogoki Res Ontario
40 H2 Ogonëk U.S.S.R. 59.50N 138.10E
91 C4 Ogooué R Gabon
91 B3 Ogooué-Ivindo reg Gabon
91 C4 Ogooué-Lolo reg Gabon
40 D5 Ogoron U.S.S.R. 54.00N 128.57E
82 H7 Ogosta R Bulgaria
19 B3 Ogotumubu Celebes Indon 0.32N 120.34E
89 K7 Ogou R Togo
90 J3 Ogouro Chad 17.35N 19.13E
20 K5 Ogoya Japan 36.18N 136.32E
Ogr see Sharafa
82 H9 Ograzden Planina mts Yugoslavia
46 E2 Ogre Latvia U.S.S.R. 56.50N 24.31E
87 E2 Ogrein Sudan 17.55N 34.50E
87 E2 Ogrein,Jeb mt Sudan 17.41N 34.51E
53 N11 Øgrum Faeroes 61.28N 6.45W
88 M10 Oguilet Aïb Allah Mali 22.49N 2.50W
88 L10 Oguilet el Diab Mali 23.27N 4.49W
88 M10 Oguilet el Hamra Mali 22.34N 2.54W
88 M10 Oguilet el Mahdi Mali 22.04N 3.15W
88 L10 Oguilet el Moktar Mali 23.48N 5.22W
82 C5 Ogulin Yugoslavia 45.16N 15.14E
90 C8 Oguma Nigeria 7.52N 7.03E
90 A7 Ogun R Nigeria
20 E8 Oguni Japan 33.11N 131.08E
104 P3 Ogunquit Maine 43.16N 70.37W
50 C2 Ögur Iceland 66.02N 22.43W
43 C7 Ogurchinskiy Turkmeniya U.S.S.R. 39.06N 53.06E
43 C7 Ogurchinskiy, Ostrov isld Turkmeniya U.S.S.R. 39.00N 53.06E
41 O9 Oguruottakh U.S.S.R. 62.30N 130.10E
90 C9 Oguta Nigeria 5.44N 6.47E
37 D6 Oğuz Turkey 39.32N 38.56E
37 C9 Oğuzeli Turkey 36.58N 37.00E
44 H3 Oguzer U.S.S.R. 44.04N 47.05E
90 C8 Ogwashi-Uku Nigeria 6.15N 6.30E
61 F4 Ogy Belgium 50.43N 3.47E
11 H2 Ohaeawai New Zealand 35.21S 173.53E
11 B12 Ohai New Zealand 45.56S 167.58E
61 H4 Ohain Belgium 50.42N 4.28E
69 G3 Ohain France 50.03N 4.07E
11 K6 Ohakune New Zealand 39.24S 175.25E
30 E7 Ohan R Uttar Prad India
77 L6 Ohanes Spain 37.03N 2.44W
88 S7 Ohanet Algeria 28.40N 8.50E
88 S7 Ohanet watercourse Algeria
20 O6 Ohara Japan 35.16N 140.22E
106 P1 O'Hare Field Internat. Airport Chicago, Illinois
11 C5 Ohariu New Zealand 41.12S 174.46E
11 B5 Ohariu B New Zealand
11 C5 Ohariu R New Zealand
20 P1 Ohata Japan 41.22N 141.11E
100 E6 Ohaton Alberta 52.58N 112.40W
11 K7 Ohau New Zealand 40.40S 175.16E
11 D11 Ohau, L New Zealand
11 K4 Ohaupo New Zealand 37.53S 175.18E
11 B5 Ohau Pt New Zealand 41.14S 174.39E
11 E11 Ohau R New Zealand
20 P2 Ohazama Japan 39.30N 141.17E
60 T16 Ohe Netherlands 51.07N 5.50E
64 Q6 Ohe R Bayern W Germany
63 G7 Ohe R Niedersachsen W Germany
11 K3 Ohena I New Zealand 36.45S 175.53E
61 L5 Ohey Belgium 50.26N 5.08E
114 C7 Ohia Hawaiian Is 19.34N 155.05W
120 D10 O'Higgins Chile 23.40S 70.15W
121 J7 O'Higgins L Chile 48.47S 73.10W
121 B5 O'Higgins prov Chile
122 V15 O'Higgins, C Easter I Pacific Oc 27.05S 109.15W
121 J7 O'Higgins, Cerro pk Chile 48.47S 73.12W
11 K4 Ohinewai New Zealand 37.29S 175.10E
11 K6 Ohingaiti New Zealand 39.51S 175.45E
106 E8 Ohio Illinois 41.33N 89.28W
102 J3 Ohio R U.S.A.
102 K2 Ohio state U.S.A.
104 A6 Ohio City Ohio 40.45N 84.36W
123 G9 Ohio Ra Antarctica
11 M4 Ohiwa Harb inlet New Zealand
64 D1 Ohle W Germany 51.14N 7.50E
64 F2 Ohm R W Germany
63 M8 Ohof W Germany 52.27N 10.19E
113 G6 Ohogamiut Alaska 61.34N 161.55W
15 B6 Ohoitom Moluccas Indon 5.55S 132.40E
9 S11 'Ohonua Tonga, Pacific Oc 21.22S 174.58W
105 E5 Ohoopee, R Georgia
94 B2 Ohopoho Namibia 18.03S 13.54E
63 U10 Ohorn E Germany 51.11N 14.04E
63 N7 Ohrdorf W Germany 52.42N 10.49E
64 K2 Ohrdruf E Germany 50.50N 10.45E
64 O3 Ohře R Czechoslovakia
63 O8 Ohre R E Germany
82 F9 Ohrid Yugoslavia 41.06N 20.49E
82 F9 Ohridsko Jezero L Yugoslavia/Albania
94 L5 Ohrigstad S Africa 24.49S 30.33E
64 H5 Öhringen W Germany 49.12N 9.30E
64 H5 Ohrnberg W Germany 49.15N 9.29E
63 K3 Ohrstedt W Germany 54.31N 9.14E
51 K5 Ohtanajärvi Sweden 66.56N 23.10E
91 C12 Ohungiarundu mt Angola 16.43S 13.38E
11 J5 Ohura New Zealand 38.50S 175.00E
11 J5 Ohura R New Zealand
76 B7 Oiã Portugal 40.33N 8.33W
117 C3 Oiapoque Brazil 3.54N 51.46W
117 C3 Oiapoque R Brazil
119 D4 Oiba Colombia 6.16N 73.18W
58 G4 Oich, L Highland Scotland 57.04N 4.46W
58 G4 Oich, R Highland Scotland
20 M6 Oi-gawa R Japan
61 J6 Oignies-en-Thiérache Belgium 50.02N 4.38E
51 M6 Oijärvi Finland 65.37N 25.56E
60 L12 Oijen Netherlands 51.50N 5.30E
84 C7 Oikhalá Greece 37.17N 22.00E
109 G9 Oil Center New Mexico 32.31N 103.16W
111 F6 Oil City California 35.27N 118.57W
107 C9 Oil City Louisiana 32.45N 93.58W
104 F5 Oil City Pennsylvania 41.27N 79.44W
111 E6 Oildale California 35.25N 119.00W
59 J7 Oilgate Wexford Irish Rep 52.25N 6.32W
113 L7 Oil Pt Alaska 59.40N 153.15W
99 H10 Oil Springs Ontario 42.46N 82.08W
109 O5 Oilton Oklahoma 36.05N 96.33W
112 J8 Oilton Texas 27.29N 98.59W
104 H9 Oilville Virginia 37.42N 77.48W
59 F2 Oily R Donegal Irish Rep
76 E5 Oimbra Spain 41.53N 7.28W
83 H6 Oinoúsa isld Greece 38.33N 26.14E
84 C8 Oinoúsai islds Greece
23 A4 Oi Qu R Xizang Zizhiqu China
20 P1 Oirase-gawa R Japan
60 N13 Oirlo Netherlands 51.31N 6.02E
72 D2 Oiron France 46.57N 0.05W
60 K13 Oirschot Netherlands 51.30N 5.18E
71 J6 Oisans dist France
19 C9 Oisau Timor Indon 10.08S 123.47E
67 G3 Oise dept France
69 E4 Oise R France
72 B6 Oiseaux, l. aux France 44.42N 1.12W
71 H2 Oiselay-et-Grachaux France 47.25N 5.56E
69 B4 Oisemont France 49.58N 1.47E
21 H8 Oishida Japan 38.35N 140.25E
61 G4 Oisquercq Belgium 50.40N 4.13E
70 J5 Oisseau France 48.21N 0.41W
70 N3 Oissel France 49.21N 1.06E
60 J13 Oisterwijk Netherlands 51.35N 5.12E
116 P6 Oistins Barbados 13.04N 59.33W
69 E3 Oisy-le-Verger France 50.14N 3.08E
20 E8 Oita Japan 33.15N 131.36E
20 E8 Oita prefect Japan
76 C4 Oitaven R Spain
76 B16 Oitavos Portugal 38.43N 9.28W
84 D4 Oíti mt Greece 38.48N 22.15E
117 G7 Oiticica Brazil 5.02S 41.04W
84 D8 Oítilon Greece 36.43N 22.23E
58 B4 Oitir Mhor B W Isles Scotland
82 K4 Oituz Pass Romania 46.05N 26.25E
85 E8 Oiuru Libya 22.28N 18.58E
20 L2 Oiwake Japan 42.54N 141.47E
24 F11 Oiyug Xizang Zizhiqu China 29.39N 89.34E
71 A2 Oizon France 47.28N 2.30E
61 L7 Oizy Belgium 49.53N 5.01E
111 E7 Ojai California 34.28N 119.14W
77 J3 Ojailén R Spain
52 H6 Öje Sweden 60.50N 13.54E
77 G7 Ojén Spain 36.35N 4.51W
77 E8 Ojén, Sierra de mts Spain
20 J7 Oji Japan 34.38N 135.43E
20 C8 Ojika-jima isld Japan 33.15N 129.05E
115 G3 Ojinaga Mexico 29.35N 104.26W
115 L8 Ojitlán Mexico 18.04N 96.22W
20 M4 Ojiya Japan 37.18N 138.49E
115 H6 Ojocaliente Mexico 22.35N 102.18W
109 B7 Ojo Caliente New Mexico 34.54N 108.58W
121 D2 Ojo de Agua Argentina 29.30S 63.44W
115 F3 Ojo de Laguna Mexico 29.30N 106.18W
115 B4 Ojo de Liebre, L Mexico
77 O4 Ojos Spain 38.09N 1.20W
76 K7 Ojos Albos Spain 40.41N 4.31W
77 J2 Ojos del Guadiana lakes Spain
121 C1 Ojos del Salado pk Arg/Chile 27.05S 68.30W
75 H8 Ojos de Moya R Spain
75 H6 Ojos Negros Spain 40.44N 1.30W
66 K7 Ojra Italy 46.11N 8.18E
115 J7 Ojuelos de Jalisco Mexico 21.52N 101.40W
105 G12 Ojus Florida 25.56N 80.09W
52 G5 Öjvallberget Sweden 61.30N 13.05E
50 E5 Ok mt Iceland 64.36N 20.54W
99 Q7 Oka Quebec 45.29N 74.06W
42 G5 Oka R Irkutsk U.S.S.R.
46 K3 Oka R U.S.S.R.
15 E8 Okaba Irian Jaya 8.06S 139.46E
94 C2 Okahakana Namibia 18.52S 15.34E
94 D3 Okahandja Namibia 21.59S 16.58E
11 J2 Okahu New Zealand 35.59S 174.06E
11 K5 Okahukura New Zealand 38.47S 175.15E
11 J6 Okaiawa New Zealand 39.32S 174.12E
11 H2 Okaihau New Zealand 35.18S 173.47E
90 A7 Okaka Nigeria 8.11N 3.30E
94 D3 Okakarara Namibia 20.33S 17.29E
97 N6 Okak Is Labrador, Nfld
105 F11 Okaloacoochee Slough swamp Florida
37 G5 Okam Turkey 40.52N 42.40E
101 O10 Okanagan Centre Br Col 50.02N 119.23W
101 O11 Okanagan Falls Br Col 49.21N 119.33W
101 O10 Okanagan L Br Col
101 O10 Okanagan Landing Br Col 50.12N 119.22W
26 U8 Okanda Sri Lanka 6.39N 81.46E
91 B4 Okande tribe Gabon
91 B3 Okano R Gabon
110 F1 Okanogan Washington 48.22N 119.35W
110 F1 Okanogan R Washington
110 E1 Okanogan Ra Br Col/Wash
15 H7 Okapa Papua New Guinea 6.32S 145.40E
94 D3 Okaputa Namibia 20.09S 16.56E
31 G5 Okara Pakistan 30.49N 73.31E
109 N6 Okarche Oklahoma 35.45N 97.59W
43 C7 Okarem Turkmeniya U.S.S.R. 38.05N 54.06E
11 E10 Okarito New Zealand 43.14S 170.07E
11 E10 Okarito Lagoon New Zealand
93 D1 Okaru Sudan 4.30N 32.10E
20 D10 Okasaki Japan 31.22N 130.57E
94 D3 Okasise Namibia 21.53S 16.30E
11 L5 Okataina L New Zealand
11 H6 Okato New Zealand 39.11S 173.50E
107 G10 Okatoma R Mississippi
94 B2 Okau Namibia 18.17S 12.01E
94 C2 Okaukuejo Namibia 19.10S 15.54E
94 G2 Okavango R Botswana
94 G2 Okavango Delta Botswana
20 D8 Okawa Japan 33.12N 130.21E
20 N4 O-kawa R Japan
33 A6 Oka, Wādi watercourse Sudan
11 K11 Okawa Pt Chatham Is Pacific Oc 43.35S 176.08W
20 O3 Okawara Japan 38.04N 140.45E
94 D3 Okawe Namibia 20.18S 16.49E
107 G3 Okawville Illinois 38.24N 89.31W
109 P6 Okay Oklahoma 35.53N 95.19W
20 L5 Okaya Japan 36.03N 138.00E
20 G7 Okayama Japan 34.40N 133.54E
20 G7 Okayama prefect Japan
20 L7 Okazaki Japan 34.58N 137.10E
37 C3 Okçılar Turkey 40.03N 26.28E
37 C3 Okçular R Turkey
40 N6 Okeanskoye Kuril Is U.S.S.R. 50.11N 155.38E
105 G10 Okeechobee Florida 27.14N 80.50W
105 G11 Okeechobee, L Florida
109 M5 Okeene Oklahoma 36.07N 98.20W
105 E7 Okefenokee Swamp Georgia
61 G3 Okegem Belgium 50.52N 4.03E
56 D6 Okehampton Devon Eng 50.44N 4.00W
90 B8 Oke Igbo Nigeria 7.09N 4.47E
90 A7 Oke-Iho Nigeria 8.01N 3.21E
109 O6 Okemah Oklahoma 35.25N 96.20W
56 C6 Okement, R Devon Eng
90 C8 Okene Nigeria 7.31N 6.14E

63 M9 Oker W Germany 51.54N 10.29E
63 N8 Oker R W Germany
93 E3 Okere R Uganda
21 J6 Oketo Japan 43.42N 143.35E
109 O2 Oketo Kansas 39.58N 96.37W
29 A6 Okha Gujarat India 22.29N 69.09E
40 J5 Okha Sakhalin U.S.S.R. 53.35N 143.01E
30 K5 Okhaldhunga Nepal 27.19N 86.30E
43 J8 Okhan Odar'ya R Tadzhikistan U.S.S.R.
46 S1 Okhansk U.S.S.R. 57.42N 55.20E
29 A6 Okha Rann flood area Gujarat India
84 H5 Okhi mt Greece 38.03N 24.28E
45 H5 Okhochevka U.S.S.R. 51.54N 36.45E
39 C5 Okhota R U.S.S.R.
39 C5 Okhotsk U.S.S.R. 59.20N 143.15E
41 P9 Okhotskiy Perevoz U.S.S.R. 61.55N 135.40E
40 K3 Okhotskoye More sea U.S.S.R.
Okhotsk, Sea of see Okhotskoye More
51 P6 Okhta Karelia U.S.S.R. 65.31N 30.50E
51 P6 Okhta, Ozero L Karelia U.S.S.R. 65.31N 30.35E
42 B2 Okhteur'ye U.S.S.R. 60.50N 79.05E
20 G6 Oki Japan 35.18N 133.48E
90 C9 Okigwi Nigeria 5.48N 7.20E
20 Q8 Okinawa isld Japan
21 C13 Okinawa Guntō arch Japan
21 C12 Okino erabu shima isld Japan
94 C1 Okinoko watercourse Namibia
20 D7 Okino-shima isld Japan 34.14N 130.05E
20 F9 Okino-shima isld Japan 32.43N 132.32E
42 F5 Okinskiy Khrebet mts U.S.S.R.
20 F5 Oki-shotō islds Japan 36.05N 133.00E
90 B8 Okitipupa Nigeria 6.31N 4.50E
25 C4 Okkan Burma 17.30N 95.52E
21 C7 Okkang-dong N Korea 40.20N 124.45E
53 X17 Okken mt Norway 60.59N 7.45E
60 O10 Okkenbroek Netherlands 52.18N 6.18E
102 G3 Oklahoma state U.S.A.
109 N6 Oklahoma City Oklahoma 35.28N 97.33W
39 G3 Oklan R U.S.S.R.
112 H1 Oklaunion Texas 34.09N 99.08W
105 F8 Oklawaha, R Florida
108 P2 Oklee Minnesota 47.50N 95.50W
87 E1 Okliss watercourse Sudan
113 C10 Okmok Vol Aleutian Is 53.30N 168.10W
109 P6 Okmulgee Oklahoma 35.38N 95.59W
82 K2 Okna U.S.S.R. 48.34N 25.58E
46 G5 Oknitsa Moldavia U.S.S.R. 48.22N 27.30E
108 P6 Okoboji L Iowa 43.22N 95.10W
108 K5 Okobojo S Dakota 44.39N 100.24W
87 B9 Okodongwe Zaïre 3.18N 28.12E
114 B8 Okoe B Hawaiian Is
11 K6 Okoia New Zealand 39.55S 175.07E
93 E3 Okok R Uganda
93 C3 Okollo Uganda 2.38N 31.10E
107 H7 Okolona Mississippi 34.01N 88.47W
94 C3 Okombahe Namibia 21.23S 15.22E
89 K8 Okomfukrom Ghana 7.26N 0.25E
91 C4 Okondja Gabon 0.30S 13.45E
62 K2 Okonek Poland 53.31N 16.50E
47 M8 Okoneshnikovo U.S.S.R. 54.51N 75.04E
21 J5 Okoppe Japan 44.29N 143.09E
11 K4 Okoroire New Zealand 37.56S 175.48E
94 D2 Okorussu Namibia 19.50S 17.25E
93 L1 Okoto mt Ethiopia 4.30N 39.25E
100 D8 Okotoks Alberta 50.46N 113.57W
94 E1 Okovango R Namibia
85 N9 Oko, Wadi watercourse Sudan
91 D4 Okoyo Congo 1.28S 15.00E
90 B9 Okpara Nigeria 5.48N 6.00E
89 L8 Okpara R Benin/Ghana
108 K6 Okreek S Dakota 43.21N 100.23W
90 C9 Okrika Nigeria 4.40N 7.10E
65 N3 Okříšky Czechoslovakia 49.15N 15.47E
15 G6 Oksapmin Papua New Guinea 5.20S 142.12E
53 D6 Oksbøl Denmark 55.03N 9.47E
53 A5 Oksbøl Ribe Denmark 55.38N 8.17E
53 A5 Oksby Denmark 55.33N 8.09E
53 V18 Oksen mt Norway 60.27N 6.41E
52 D4 Øksendal Norway 62.43N 8.27E
53 F6 Øksendrup Denmark 55.13N 10.45E
53 C6 Oksenvad Denmark 55.19N 9.17E
51 J1 Øksfjord Norway 70.14N 22.20E
51 J1 Øksfjord-jøkel mt Norway 70.09N 22.00E
47 G2 Oksino U.S.S.R. 67.31N 52.15E
45 M3 Oksko-Donskaya Ravnina plain U.S.S.R.
51 D3 Øksnes Norway 68.54N 15.00E
47 D4 Oksovskiy U.S.S.R. 62.39N 39.57E
51 D6 Okstindan mt Norway 66.00N 14.24E
31 H2 Oksu R Tadzhikistan U.S.S.R.
43 M8 Oksukon, Ozero L Tadzhikistan U.S.S.R. 40.31N 70.24E
45 M9 Oktabr'skiy Rostov U.S.S.R. 47.30N 40.05E
109 P6 Oktaha Oklahoma 35.35N 95.28W
44 F7 Oktemberyan Armenia U.S.S.R. 40.10N 44.00E
84 H4 Oktoniá Greece 38.32N 24.10E
43 C6 Oktumkum, Peski sand des Turkmeniya U.S.S.R.
25 D3 Oktwin Burma 18.47N 96.21E
43 M5 Oktyabr' Kazakhstan U.S.S.R. 43.39N 77.09E
43 J7 Oktyabr' Tadzhikistan U.S.S.R. 38.34N 68.20E
43 D3 Oktyabr'sk Kazakhstan U.S.S.R. 49.30N 57.22E
46 P3 Oktyabr'sk Kuybyshev U.S.S.R. 53.10N 48.39E
40 D4 Oktyabr'skiy Amur U.S.S.R. 55.24N 126.17E
46 R3 Oktyabr'skiy Bashkir A.S.S.R. U.S.S.R. 54.30N 53.30E
45 H6 Oktyabr'skiy Belgorod U.S.S.R. 50.27N 36.23E
46 G3 Oktyabr'skiy Belorussiya U.S.S.R. 52.35N 28.45E
47 M6 Oktyabr'skiy Chelyabinsk U.S.S.R. 55.05N 60.08E
45 Q1 Oktyabr'skiy Gor'kiy U.S.S.R. 56.16N 44.14E
42 F4 Oktyabr'skiy Irkutsk U.S.S.R. 56.03N 99.31E
39 F7 Oktyabr'skiy Kamchatka U.S.S.R. 52.43N 156.14E
46 N1 Oktyabr'skiy Kostroma U.S.S.R. 58.20N 44.19E
44 C1 Oktyabr'skiy Krasnodar U.S.S.R. 46.17N 39.49E
43 G1 Oktyabr'skiy Kustanay, Kazakhstan U.S.S.R. 53.44N 62.43E
43 H2 Oktyabr'skiy Kustanay, Kazakhstan U.S.S.R. 52.07N 65.37E
46 S2 Oktyabr'skiy Perm U.S.S.R. 56.15N 56.50E
46 M5 Oktyabr'skiy Rostov U.S.S.R. 47.30N 40.02E
45 K2 Oktyabr'skiy Ryazan' U.S.S.R. 54.13N 38.53E
45 L3 Oktyabr'skiy Ryazan' U.S.S.R. 53.48N 39.30E
40 J6 Oktyabr'skiy Sakhalin U.S.S.R. 50.45N 142.10E
43 O3 Oktyabr'skiy Semipalatinsk, Kazakhstan U.S.S.R. 49.47N 81.20E
42 D3 Oktyabr'skiy Tomsk U.S.S.R. 57.35N 87.07E
42 E5 Oktyabr'skiy Tuvinsk U.S.S.R. 53.07N 94.40E
47 K6 Oktyabr'skiy Tyumen U.S.S.R. 58.20N 68.42E
42 C7 Oktyabr'skiy U.S.S.R. 49.36N 83.41E
47 E5 Oktyabr'skiy U.S.S.R. 61.05N 43.10E
43 H7 Oktyabr'skiy Uzbekistan U.S.S.R. 39.07N 66.50E
45 P9 Oktyabr'skiy Volgograd U.S.S.R. 47.58N 43.38E
46 D8 Oktyabr'skiy dist Moscow U.S.S.R.
45 T1 Oktyabr'skoye Cheboksary U.S.S.R. 55.54N 47.50E
47 J8 Oktyabr'skoye Chelyabinsk U.S.S.R. 54.26N 62.46E
44 C9 Oktyabr'skoye Crimea, Ukraine U.S.S.R. 45.20N 34.06E
45 L4 Oktyabr'skoye Lipetsk U.S.S.R. 52.19N 39.44E
45 D10 Oktyabr'skoye Nikolayev, Ukraine U.S.S.R. 46.53N 32.02E
43 D2 Oktyabr'skoye Orenburg U.S.S.R. 52.22N 55.31E
47 K4 Oktyabr'skoye Tyumen U.S.S.R. 62.30N 66.00E
40 E8 Oktyabr'skoye Yevreysk U.S.S.R. 47.44N 131.38E
41 G2 Oktyabr'skoy Revolyutsii, Ostrov isld U.S.S.R.
40 A4 Oktyabrya,iméni 11 letnyaya U.S.S.R. 55.51N 119.38E
20 Q8 Oku Okinawa Japan 26.53N 128.16E
20 D9 Ōkuchi Japan 32.04N 130.36E
90 B7 Okuku Nigeria 8.02N 4.40E
11 G10 Okuku R New Zealand
46 J1 Okulovka U.S.S.R. 58.25N 33.19E
123 J8 Okuma B Antarctica
44 D5 Okumi Georgia U.S.S.R. 42.44N 41.44E
94 D2 Okumukanti Namibia 19.50S 17.38E
90 D9 Okuni Nigeria 5.57N 8.35E
20 C3 Ōkura Tōkyō Japan
39 E5 Okurchan U.S.S.R. 59.10N 152.12E
11 C10 Okuru New Zealand 43.56S 168.55E
20 D3 Okusawa dist Tōkyō Japan
20 J2 Okushiri-kaikyō str Japan
21 H6 Okushiri-tō isld Japan
90 A7 Okuta Nigeria 9.15N 3.17E
20 J6 Okutango-hantō pen Japan
90 C7 Okwa R Nigeria
94 F4 Okwa watercourse Botswana
94 F4 Okwa Pan salt pan Botswana 22.25S 21.55E
85 O10 Okwer, Jebel mt Sudan 18.41N 36.27E
90 C8 Okwoga Nigeria 7.03N 7.50E
90 C9 Okwuzi Nigeria 5.30N 6.45E
107 C6 Ola Arkansas 35.03N 93.13W
110 J5 Ola Idaho 44.11N 116.16W
39 E5 Ola U.S.S.R. 59.35N 151.15E
39 E5 Ola R U.S.S.R.
114 C7 Olaa Hawaiian Is 19.38N 155.02W
91 D3 Olaba Gabon 0.36N 14.17E
50 D4 Ólafsdalur Iceland 65.25N 21.45W
50 G2 Ólafsfjördhur B Iceland 66.05N 18.35W
50 G2 Ólafsjördhur Iceland 66.05N 18.30W
50 E6 Ólafsvellir Iceland 64.01N 20.34W
50 B5 Ólafsvík Iceland 64.53N 23.44W
75 G2 Olagüe Spain 42.58N 1.37W
28 D4 Olakur Tamil Nadu India 12.21N 79.46E
76 C9 Olalhas Portugal 39.38N 8.18W
75 H6 Olalla Spain 40.58N 1.10W
71 E2 Olamerey France 47.23N 4.25E
104 R1 Olamon Maine 45.07N 68.37W
111 G5 Olancha California 36.18N 118.00W
111 F5 Olancha Pk mt California 36.16N 118.07W
115 L2 Olanchito Honduras 15.30N 86.34W
52 K10 Öland isld Sweden
53 D2 Øland reg Denmark
47 C3 Olanga U.S.S.R. 66.10N 30.39E
51 P5 Olanga L Karelia U.S.S.R. 66.16N 30.10E
90 C8 Olangbecho Nigeria 7.10N 7.55E
71 J7 Olan, Pic d' France 44.51N 6.11E
105 H4 Olanta S Carolina 33.56N 79.58W
71 B9 Olargues France 43.33N 2.55E
118 J8 Olaria Brazil 22.51S 43.17W
12 C2 Olarinna R S Australia
120 E10 Olaroz, Salina salt pan Argentina
12 F4 Olary S Australia 32.18S 140.19E
12 F4 Olary R S Australia
121 E5 Olascoaga Argentina 35.16S 60.38W
87 K8 Olason Ethiopia 5.21N 45.02E
109 Q3 Olathe Kansas 38.52N 94.50W
28 C5 Olavakod Kerala India 10.49N 76.37E
121 E5 Olavarria Buenos Aires Arg 35.43S 62.59W
121 E6 Olavarría Buenos Aires Arg 36.57S 60.20W
75 G2 Olave Spain 42.53N 1.37W
50 T14 Olav V Land Spitsbergen
62 K5 Oława Poland 50.57N 17.18E
75 F2 Olazagutia Spain 42.52N 2.12W
75 J7 Olba Spain 40.09N 0.38W
41 O8 Olba U.S.S.R. 62.48N 133.40E
111 N8 Olberg Arizona 33.07N 111.39W
64 P2 Olbernhau E Germany 50.40N 13.20E
64 L1 Olbersleben E Germany 51.09N 11.20E
81 D2 Olbia Sardinia 40.56N 9.30E
81 D2 Olbia, G.di Sardinia
65 P7 Ölbö Hungary 47.18N 16.54E
93 H6 Ol Bolossat, L Kenya 0.10S 36.26E
65 N4 Olbramkostel Czechoslovakia 48.56N 15.58E
65 O4 Olbramovice Czechoslovakia 48.59N 16.25E
53 B4 Ølby Denmark 56.29N 8.33E
64 L7 Olching W Germany 48.11N 11.19E
66 O8 Olcio Italy 45.57N 9.20E
104 G3 Olcott New York 43.21N 78.43W
116 E3 Old Bahama Chan Cuba/Bahamas
28 E1 Old Bastar Madhya Prad India 19.12N 81.59E
56 M2 Old Bedford R Norf/Cambs
103 F6 Old Bridge New Jersey 40.27N 74.23W
56 G2 Oldbury W Midlands Eng 52.30N 2.00W
86 Q12 Old Cairo dist Cairo Egypt
59 H4 Oldcastle Meath Irish Rep 53.46N 7.10W
103 G2 Old Chatham New York 42.26N 73.34W
14 F4 Old Cherrabun W Australia 18.34S 125.23E
29 B2 Old City dist Delhi India
13 F6 Old Cork Queensland 22.57S 141.49E
101 D2 Old Crow Yukon Terr 67.34N 139.43W
101 C1 Old Crow R Yukon Terr
57 D2 Old Dailly Strathclyde Scotland 55.16N 4.47W
58 M3 Old Deer Grampian Scotland 57.31N 2.02W
87 C1 Old Dongola Sudan 18.11N 30.44E
92 G3 Oldeani Tanzania 3.21S 35.32E
93 G9 Oldeani mt Tanzania 3.16S 35.28E
60 N8 Oldeberkoop Netherlands 52.56N 6.08E
60 M7 Oldeboorn Netherlands 53.03N 5.53E
60 M10 Oldebroek Netherlands 52.27N 5.54E
60 N8 Oldeholtpade Netherlands 52.54N 6.04E
60 O6 Oldehove Netherlands 53.18N 6.24E
53 S15 Oldeide Norway 61.55N 5.05E
60 M8 Oldemarkt Netherlands 52.49N 5.59E
53 V15 Olden Norway 61.50N 6.50E
112 J3 Olden Texas 32.24N 98.45W
63 H6 Oldenbrok W Germany 53.18N 8.24E
63 H6 Oldenburg Niedersachsen W Germany 53.08N 8.13E
63 N4 Oldenburg Schleswig Holstein W Germany 54.17N 10.52E
63 N6 Oldendorf W Germany 53.09N 10.49E
66 E6 Oldenhorn mt Switzerland 46.20N 7.13E
63 N7 Oldenstadt W Germany 52.58N 10.36E
63 J4 Oldenswort W Germany 54.22N 8.56E
60 Q10 Oldenzaal Netherlands 52.19N 6.55E
63 F6 Oldersum W Germany 53.20N 7.21E
53 V15 Oldevatn L Norway 61.45N 6.49E
110 P5 Old Faithful Wyoming 44.27N 110.49W
103 H5 Old Field Pt Long I, N Y 40.58N 73.10W
14 D10 Oldfield, R W Australia
104 L3 Old Forge New York 43.44N 74.59W
103 C4 Old Forge Pennsylvania 41.21N 75.44W
105 E2 Old Fort N Carolina 35.29N 82.11W
98 P2 Old Fort Bay Quebec 51.27N 57.50W
105 K9 Old Fort Pt New Providence I Bahamas 25.03N 77.30W
14 C8 Old Gidgee W Australia 27.33S 119.32E
112 G2 Old Glory Texas 33.08N 100.03W
92 G7 Old Gumbiro Tanzania 10.00S 35.23E
57 J5 Oldham Greater Manchester Eng 53.33N 2.07W
108 N5 Oldham S Dakota 44.15N 97.19W
101 Q11 Oldham R Alberta
113 L8 Old Harbor Alaska 57.12N 153.15W
116 K2 Old Harbour Jamaica, W I 17.56N 77.07W
116 K2 Old Harbour Bay Jamaica, W I 17.54N 77.06W
58 T12 Old Hd Orkney Scotland 58.44N 2.55W
107 K5 Old Hickory Tennessee 36.15N 86.39W
56 G3 Old Hill W Midlands Eng 52.29N 2.04W
101 L8 Old Hogem Br Col 55.45N 125.28W
56 L3 Old Hurst Cambs Eng 52.23N 0.06W
64 L1 Oldisleben E Germany 51.18N 11.10E
113 P2 Old John L Alaska 68.05N 145.00W
59 J5 Old Kilcullen Kildare Irish Rep 53.07N 6.45W
58 H7 Old Kilpatrick Strathclyde Scotland 55.56N 4.28W
56 G5 Oldland Common Avon Eng 51.27N 2.28W
57 O6 Old Leake Lincs Eng 53.02N 0.06E
103 K4 Old Lyme Connecticut 41.19N 72.20W
57 M4 Old Malton N Yorks Eng 54.09N 0.47W
58 M4 Old Meldrum Grampian Scotland 57.20N 2.20W
92 D9 Old Mkushi Zambia 14.21S 29.21E
107 F3 Old Monroe Missouri 38.56N 90.45W
95 M7 Old Morley S Africa 31.55S 28.59E
103 L4 Old Mystic Connecticut 41.23N 71.58W
32 A4 Old Nahrawān Can Iraq
93 F4 Old Nariam Uganda 1.58N 34.07E
93 G8 Ol Doinyo Lengai vol Tanzania 2.45S 35.56E
93 H5 Ol Doinyo Ngiro mt Kenya 0.40N 36.59E
93 H8 Ol Doinyo Orok mt Kenya 2.29S 36.45E
93 J7 Ol Doinyo Sapuk mt Kenya 1.07S 37.15E
104 P3 Old Orchard Beach Maine 43.31N 70.23W
40 C4 Ol'doy U.S.S.R. 54.08N 123.24E
98 T5 Old Perlican Newfoundland 48.05N 53.00W
98 L3 Old Post Pt Quebec 50.08N 61.50W
113 R3 Old Rampart Alaska 67.10N 141.49W
105 G12 Old Rhodes Key isld Florida 25.21N 80.13W
116 O4 Old Road Antigua W I 17.02N 61.50W
116 P3 Old Road Town St Kitts W I 17.20N 62.48W
76 C6 Oldroës Portugal 41.08N 8.18W
100 C7 Olds Alberta 51.50N 114.06W
56 H5 Old Sarum hist site Wilts Eng 51.06N 1.49W
103 K4 Old Saybrook Connecticut 41.18N 72.22W
58 K6 Old Scone Tayside Scotland 56.26N 3.27W
87 D4 Old Sennar Sudan 13.40N 33.33E
93 E9 Old Shinyanga Tanzania 3.34S 33.24E
104 P2 Old Spekle Mt Maine 44.33N 70.57W
56 K3 Old Stratford Northants Eng 52.04N 0.53W
63 H3 Oldsum W Germany 54.44N 8.26E
105 E10 Old Tampa B Florida
94 J3 Old Tate Botswana 21.22S 27.46E
12 E4 Old Telichie S Australia 31.43S 139.54E
105 E8 Old Town Florida 29.37N 82.58W
104 R2 Old Town Maine 44.55N 68.41W
50 G7 Öldufell mt Iceland 63.46N 18.50W
50 J7 Ölduós B Iceland 63.55N 16.28W
50 F4 Öldur reg Iceland
93 G8 Olduvai Tanzania 2.44S 35.19E
93 G8 Olduvai Gorge Tanzania 2.50S 35.13E
100 M8 Old Wives Saskatchewan 50.13N 105.59W
100 L8 Old Wives Lake Saskatchewan
56 K5 Old Woking Surrey Eng 51.19N 0.33W
113 H5 Old Woman R Alaska
111 J7 Old Woman Mts California
Öldzeyte see Öldziyt
39 B1 Ol'dzho R U.S.S.R.
103 C6 Old Zionsville Pennsylvania 40.29N 75.31W
22 F3 Öldziyt Mongolia 46.39N 103.18E
104 G4 Olean New York 42.05N 78.26W
98 H7 O'Leary Prince Edward I 46.43N 64.15W
62 N1 Olecko Poland 54.02N 22.29E
76 E9 Oledo Portugal 39.58N 7.18W
18 A3 Oleeheue Sumatra Indon 5.34N 95.18E
79 E3 Oleggio Italy 45.36N 8.38E
76 A3 Oleiros Coruña Spain 42.36N 9.00W
76 C2 Oleiros Coruña Spain 43.20N 8.20W
76 D9 Oleiros Portugal 38.55N 7.55W
40 B1 Olekma R U.S.S.R.
42 K2 Olekminsk U.S.S.R. 60.25N 120.25E
42 K2 Olekminskaya U.S.S.R. 60.22N 120.05E
40 A4 Olekminskiy Stanovik mt area U.S.S.R.
65 O4 Oleksovice Czechoslovakia 48.55N 16.15E
47 F4 Olema U.S.S.R. 64.25N 46.15E
61 K2 Olen Belgium 51.09N 4.52E
53 T19 Ølen Norway 59.36N 5.50E
66 H8 Olen, Colle d' pass Italy 45.53N 7.53E
110 D7 Olene Oregon 42.11N 121.39W
47 C2 Olenegorsk U.S.S.R. 68.04N 33.15E
41 K6 Olenëk U.S.S.R. 68.28N 112.18E
41 L6 Olenëk R U.S.S.R.
41 M4 Olenekskaya Protoka canal U.S.S.R.
41 M4 Olenëkskiy Zaliv B U.S.S.R.
44 B9 Olenevka Ukraine U.S.S.R. 45.23N 32.34E
39 F6 Olenevod U.S.S.R. 56.53N 157.43E
93 H8 Olengarua mt Kenya 2.08S 36.06E
42 K2 Olëng-Sala U.S.S.R. 62.12N 119.50E
45 E1 Olenino U.S.S.R. 56.12N 33.30E
47 D3 Olenitsa U.S.S.R. 66.30N 35.19E
41 E4 Oleniy, Ostrov isld Krasnoyarsk U.S.S.R.
41 C5 Oleniy, Ostrov isld U.S.S.R.
41 C5 Oleniy, Poluostrov pen U.S.S.R.
53 T19 Ølensfjord inlet Norway 59.39N 5.47E
53 T19 Ølensvåg Norway 59.36N 5.46E
42 J6 Olentuy U.S.S.R. 51.38N 114.20E
43 B3 Olenty R Kazakhstan U.S.S.R.
43 L2 Olenty R Kazakhstan U.S.S.R.
39 C1 Olenyakh U.S.S.R. 67.50N 141.00E
42 E5 Olen'ya Rechka U.S.S.R. 52.51N 93.15E
93 H6 Oleolondo Kenya 0.25S 36.21E
39 F1 Oler R U.S.S.R.
48 U9 Ole Rømers Land Greenland
72 B4 Oléron, Ile d' France 45.55N 1.16W
39 B2 Olersyubyut U.S.S.R. 67.25N 138.58E
75 O4 Olesa de Montserrat Spain 41.32N 1.54E
45 C5 Oleshnya Chernigov, Ukraine U.S.S.R. 51.55N 31.11E
45 F6 Oleshnya Ukraine U.S.S.R. 50.25N 34.47E
82 J1 Olesko U.S.S.R. 49.58N 24.55E
62 K4 Oleśnica Poland 51.12N 17.21E
65 O2 Olešnice Czechoslovakia 49.33N 16.24E
62 L5 Olesno Poland 50.51N 18.26E
67 P11 Oletta Corsica 42.37N 9.20E
72 J10 Olette France 42.33N 2.16E
18 M10 Olet Tongo mt Indonesia 8.56S 116.55E
80 H5 Olevano Romano Italy 41.52N 13.03E
53 Z16 Olevatn L Norway 61.18N 8.37E
46 G4 Olevsk Ukraine U.S.S.R. 51.12N 27.35E
15 L3 Olevuga I Solomon Is 9.00S 160.05E
110 E4 Olex Oregon 45.31N 120.09W
103 C6 Oley Pennsylvania 40.23N 75.48W
61 M4 Oleye Belgium 50.43N 5.17E
44 H2 Oleynikovo U.S.S.R. 45.41N 46.54E
63 F9 Olfen W Germany 51.43N 7.23E
50 D7 Ölfusa R Iceland
105 F11 Olga Florida 26.43N 81.38W
108 M1 Olga N Dakota 48.51N 98.02W
40 G10 Ol'ga Primor'ye U.S.S.R. 43.46N 135.14E
113 K8 Olga B Alaska
99 N3 Olga L Quebec
13 B7 Olga, Mt N Terr Australia 25.15S 130.50E
39 G7 Olga, Mys C U.S.S.R. 54.30N 161.17E
50 U14 Olgastretet str Spitsbergen
66 M8 Olgiate Italy 45.47N 8.58E
79 E3 Olgiate Comasco Italy 45.47N 8.58E
79 E3 Olgiate Olona Italy 45.38N 8.52E
66 O8 Olginate Italy 45.48N 9.26E
45 J9 Ol'ginka Ukraine U.S.S.R. 47.42N 37.34E
40 F5 Ol'ginsk Amur U.S.S.R. 52.52N 133.24E
44 B2 Ol'ginskaya Krasnodar U.S.S.R. 45.57N 38.29E
45 L9 Ol'ginskaya Rostov U.S.S.R. 47.12N 39.56E
22 A2 Ölgiy Mongolia 48.54N 90.00E
53 B5 Ølgod Denmark 55.44N 8.37E
45 D9 Ol'gopol' Nikolayev, Ukraine U.S.S.R. 47.43N 32.09E
46 G5 Ol'gopol' Vinnitsa, Ukraine U.S.S.R. 48.10N 29.30E
39 E2 Olguya R U.S.S.R.
76 A10 Olhalvo Portugal 39.06N 9.04W
76 D14 Olhão Portugal 37.01N 7.50W
51 L6 Olhava Finland 65.28N 25.25E
53 D5 Ølholm Denmark 55.49N 9.32E
13 A7 Olia Chain mts N Terr Australia
81 C2 Olia, Mte Sardinia 40.45N 9.21E
75 N3 Oliana Spain 42.04N 1.19E
75 N3 Oliana, Embalse de res Spain 42.10N 1.20E
77 H7 Olias Spain 36.46N 4.19W
82 B6 Olib isld Yugoslavia 44.22N 14.48E
81 C3 Oliena Sardinia 40.16N 9.25E
81 C3 Oliena R Sardinia
75 J6 Oliete Spain 41.00N 0.41W
94 E8 Olifants R Cape Prov S Africa
95 F9 Olifants R Cape Province S Africa
94 L5 Olifants R Transvaal S Africa
94 E5 Olifants watercourse Namibia
94 P12 Olifantsbosbaai B Cape Town S Africa
95 M1 Olifantsfontein S Africa 25.58S 28.14E
95 F3 Olifantshoek S Africa 27.56S 22.45E
94 F4 Olifants Kloof Botswana 22.11S 20.05E
94 E9 Olifants River Berge mts S Africa
121 G4 Olimar R Uruguay
83 J9 Olimbos Greece 35.44N 27.11E
84 G5 Olimbos mt Évvoia Greece 38.28N 23.52E
84 D1 Olimbos mt Pieria Greece 40.05N 22.21E
118 E7 Olímpia Brazil 20.43S 48.55W
106 C7 Olin Iowa 42.01N 91.08W
Olín R see Olnie R
115 K9 Olinalá Mexico 17.48N 98.44W
117 J8 Olinda Brazil 8.00S 34.51W
110 C9 Olinda California 40.27N 122.26W
114 E6 Olinda Hawaiian Is 20.48N 156.16W
13 G1 Olinda Ent Gt Barrier Reef Australia
42 K6 Olinsk U.S.S.R. 52.25N 116.15E
13 G5 Olio Queensland 21.55S 143.11E
75 N4 Oliola Spain 41.52N 1.11E
45 C5 Olishevka Ukraine U.S.S.R. 51.13N 31.20E
75 G3 Olite Spain 42.29N 1.40W
121 D4 Oliva Argentina 32.01S 63.40W
77 Q3 Oliva Spain 38.55N 0.09W
77 O3 Oliva mt Albacete Spain 38.44N 1.02W
77 D3 Oliva mt Badajoz Spain 38.46N 6.09W
121 B2 Oliva, Cord.de mts Arg/Chile
77 C4 Oliva de la Frontera Spain 38.17N 6.54W
77 D3 Oliva de Mérida Spain 38.47N 6.08W
76 G8 Oliva de Plasencia Spain 40.06N 6.05W
76 E15 Olivais Portugal 38.46N 9.06W
76 B9 Olival Portugal 39.42N 8.36W
77 D6 Olivares Spain 37.25N 6.10W
77 J6 Olivares R Spain
121 B3 Olivares, C. del pk Arg/Chile 30.19S 69.50W
75 F8 Olivares de Júcar Spain 39.45N 2.21W
108 E4 Olive Montana 45.34N 105.30W
107 G7 Olive Branch Mississippi 34.58N 89.50W
103 F3 Olivebridge New York 41.55N 74.15W
104 B8 Olive Hill Kentucky 38.18N 83.12W
118 G7 Oliveira Brazil 20.39N 44.47W
76 C6 Oliveira Portugal 41.06N 8.03W
76 C7 Oliveira de Azemeis Portugal 40.49N 8.29W
76 C7 Oliveira de Frades Portugal 40.44N 8.11W
76 C7 Oliveira do Bairro Portugal 40.32N 8.30W
76 D8 Oliveira do Conde Portugal 40.26N 7.58W
76 D8 Oliveira do Hospital Portugal 40.21N 7.52W
118 G3 Oliveira dos Brejinhos Brazil 12.19S 42.53W
91 C11 Olivença-a-Nova Angola 14.58S 14.00E
77 B3 Olivenza Spain 38.41N 7.06W
77 B3 Olivenza R Spain
101 O11 Oliver Br Col 49.10N 119.37W
105 F5 Oliver Georgia 32.31N 81.31W
103 F2 Oliverea New York 42.04N 74.26W
35 C1 Olives, Mt. of Jerusalem 31.47N 35.15E
70 O6 Olivet France 47.52N 1.52E
106 K7 Olivet Michigan 42.26N 84.55W
103 D7 Olivet New Jersey 39.33N 75.10W
108 N6 Olivet S Dakota 43.14N 97.40W
80 M7 Oliveto Citra Italy 40.42N 15.15E
81 M2 Oliveto Lucano Italy 40.33N 16.11E
108 Q5 Olivia Minnesota 44.47N 94.58W
112 L7 Olivia Texas 28.37N 96.27W
95 N4 Oliviershoek S Africa 28.41S 29.10E
11 C11 Olivine Ra New Zealand
66 M5 Olivone Switzerland 46.32N 8.57E
121 J3 Olivos Buenos Aires Arg 34.31S 58.28W
62 L1 Oliwa Poland 54.24N 18.31E
84 D6 Olíyirtos Óros mts Greece
22 L5 Olji Moron He R Nei Monggol Zizhiqu China
93 H6 Ol Joro Orok Kenya 0.04S 36.22E
53 Y17 Øljusjøen L Norway 60.57N 8.04E
53 X17 Øljuvatn L Norway 60.48N 7.45E
93 H6 Ol Kalou Kenya 0.16S 36.22E
93 J5 Ol Kanjo mt Kenya 0.53N 37.47E
45 N3 Ol'khi U.S.S.R. 53.53N 41.30E
42 H5 Ol'khon, Ostrov isld Baykal, Oz U.S.S.R.
42 H5 Ol'khonskiye Vorota str Baykal, Oz U.S.S.R.
45 K8 Ol'khovatka Donetsk, Ukraine U.S.S.R. 48.15N 38.25E
45 J6 Ol'khovatka Khar'kov, Ukraine U.S.S.R. 50.10N 37.34E
45 L6 Ol'khovatka U.S.S.R. 50.19N 39.19E
45 L3 Ol'khovets U.S.S.R. 53.06N 39.11E
45 M7 Ol'khoviy Rog U.S.S.R. 49.01N 40.42E
47 J7 Ol'khovka Kurgan U.S.S.R. 56.23N 63.43E
45 Q7 Ol'khovka Volgograd U.S.S.R. 49.52N 44.35E
62 M5 Olkusz Poland 50.18N 19.33E
107 D10 Olla Louisiana 31.55N 92.12W
58 Q8 Ollaberry Shetland Scotland 60.31N 1.20W
120 D5 Ollachea Peru 13.36S 70.29W
120 E9 Ollagüe Chile 21.12S 68.15W
120 E9 Ollagüe vol Bolivia/Chile 21.20S 68.09W
93 G6 Ol Lalunga Kenya 0.59S 35.40E
19 M4 Ollan isld Truk Is Pacific Oc 7.14N 151.38E
120 C5 Ollantaytambo Peru 13.14S 72.17W
81 C5 Ollastu R Sardinia
77 P3 Ollería Spain 38.55N 0.33W
57 L6 Ollerton Notts Eng 53.12N 1.00W
108 F3 Ollie Montana 46.35N 104.03W
71 D5 Olliergues France 45.41N 3.38E
61 F4 Ollignies Belgium 50.42N 3.52E
51 N2 Ollila Finland 69.38N 27.05E
71 H10 Ollioules France 43.08N 5.50E
121 B3 Ollita, Cord, de mts Arg/Chile
121 B3 Ollitas pk Argentina 31.21S 70.12W
75 G2 Ollo Spain 42.53N 1.52W
66 F8 Ollomont Italy 45.52N 7.19E
66 D6 Ollon Switzerland 46.18N 6.59E
61 J6 Olloy-sur-Viroin Belgium 50.04N 4.37E
52 H7 Olme Sweden 59.22N 13.55E
75 C4 Olmedillo de Roa Spain 41.47N 3.56W
81 A2 Olmedo Sardinia 40.39N 8.24E
76 K6 Olmedo Spain 41.17N 4.41W
61 L2 Olmen Belgium 51.09N 5.10E
79 H4 Olmeneta Italy 45.15N 10.01E
67 O13 Olmeto Corsica 41.42N 8.55E
67 P11 Olmi Cappella Corsica 42.31N 9.01E
79 G3 Olmo al Brembo Italy 45.59N 9.39E
119 B10 Olmos Peru 6.00S 79.46W
76 L3 Olmos de Ojeda Spain 42.43N 4.25W
121 D4 Olmos, L Argentina
61 N4 Olne Belgium 50.36N 5.45E
56 K3 Olney Bucks Eng 52.09N 0.43W
107 H3 Olney Illinois 38.45N 88.05W
110 L1 Olney Montana 48.34N 114.35W
112 J2 Olney Texas 33.23N 98.46W
41 Q2 Ol'ney Mys C Franz Josef Land U.S.S.R. 80.48N 65.02E
109 G3 Olney Springs Colorado 38.10N 103.57W
121 K6 Olnie, R Argentina
93 H8 Olobolodi Plain Kenya
75 J8 Olocau Spain 39.42N 0.33W
42 K6 Olochi U.S.S.R. 51.24N 119.55E
89 F9 Olodio Ivory Coast 4.44N 7.29W
52 L3 Olofsfors Sweden 63.36N 19.25E
52 H10 Olofström Sweden 56.16N 14.33E
Ölögey see Ölgiy
93 J8 Oloitokitok Kenya 2.56S 37.32E
90 A8 Olokemeji Nigeria 7.26N 3.37E
89 C4 Ololdou Senegal 14.51N 12.30W
91 D4 Ololi Congo 0.15S 14.36E
93 H7 Ololkisalie mts Kenya 1.40S 36.26E
41 O7 Olom U.S.S.R. 66.50N 132.08E
98 M3 Olomane R Quebec
76 L6 Olombrada Spain 41.25N 4.10W
15 M3 Olomburi Malaita I Solomon Is 9.03S 161.10E
62 K6 Olomouc Czechoslovakia 49.38N 17.15E
79 E3 Olona R Italy
Olon Bulak see Uzunbulak
82 M4 Oloneshty U.S.S.R. 46.29N 29.25E
47 C5 Olonets U.S.S.R. 61.00N 32.59E
19 F1 Olongapo Luzon Philippines 14.49N 120.17E
91 C4 Olongo Gabon 0.32S 13.50E
40 C4 Olongro U.S.S.R. 55.36N 125.47E
42 G5 Olonki U.S.S.R. 52.58N 103.45E
72 A2 Olonne-sur-Mer France 46.33N 1.46W
71 B10 Olonzac France 43.17N 2.43E
72 C9 Oloron Ste. Marie France 43.12N 0.35W
122 F1 Olosega isld Amer Samoa Pacific Oc 14.12S 169.38W
75 P4 Olost Spain 41.59N 2.06E
75 P3 Olot Spain 42.11N 2.30E
64 O3 Olovi Czechoslovakia 50.15N 12.34E
82 E6 Olovo Yugoslavia 44.07N 18.35E
42 K6 Olovyannaya U.S.S.R. 50.58N 115.35E
114 D6 Olowalu Hawaiian Is 20.48N 156.37W
93 J5 Olowa Werikoi mt Kenya 0.47N 37.26E
39 G2 Oloyskiye Gory mts U.S.S.R.
29 C7 Olpad Gujarat India 21.20N 72.49E
109 O3 Olpe Kansas 38.18N 96.09W
64 D1 Olpe W Germany 51.02N 7.52E
65 E7 Olperer mt Austria 47.03N 11.40E
48 S3 Olriks Fd Greenland
53 D3 Øls Denmark 56.37N 9.45E
64 Q5 Olšany Czechoslovakia 49.24N 13.39E
109 O2 Olsburg Kansas 39.25N 96.37W
62 L6 Olše R Czech/Poland
53 J6 Ølsemagle Denmark 55.30N 12.11E
61 D3 Olsene Belgium 50.56N 3.28E
26 A15 Olsen, Mt Heard I Antarctica 53.00S 73.17E
45 C7 Ol'shana Cherkassy, Ukraine U.S.S.R. 49.13N 31.13E
46 L5 Ol'shana Khar'kov, Ukraine U.S.S.R. 49.43N 37.55E
46 J4 Ol'shana Sumy, Ukraine U.S.S.R. 50.50N 34.00E
46 H5 Ol'shanka Ukraine U.S.S.R. 48.12N 30.55E
45 J5 Ol'shanka U.S.S.R. 51.00N 37.41E
45 G6 Ol'shany Ukraine U.S.S.R. 50.03N 35.53E
50 T16 Olsokbreen glacier Spitsbergen 76.40N 16.30E
53 E4 Ølst Denmark 56.23N 10.07E
60 N10 Olst Netherlands 52.20N 6.06E
53 J5 Ølsted Denmark 55.56N 12.06E
53 A4 Ølstrup Denmark 56.07N 8.26E
53 J5 Ølstykke Denmark 55.49N 12.10E
62 M2 Olsztyn Poland 53.48N 20.29E
62 M2 Olsztynek Poland 53.34N 20.19E
82 J6 Olt div Romania
121 C3 Olta Argentina 30.38S 66.20W
66 H2 Olten Switzerland 47.22N 7.55E
82 H6 Oltenia reg Romania
82 K6 Oltenița Romania 44.05N 26.40E
121 B9 Olte, Sa.de ra Argentina
82 H6 Oltețul R Romania
66 H2 Oltingen Switzerland 47.26N 7.56E
66 F2 Oltingue France 47.29N 7.24E
112 E1 Olton Texas 34.12N 102.08W
87 H10 Oltre Giuba reg Somalia
37 F5 Oltu Turkey 40.34N 41.59E
37 F5 Oltu R Turkey
82 J7 Oltul R Romania
23 J8 O-luan-pi C Taiwan 21.54N 120.53E
94 D1 Olukonda Namibia 17.58S 16.01E
77 M6 Olula de Castro Spain 37.11N 2.28W
15 M4 Olu Malau Is Solomon Is
37 G5 Olur Turkey 40.49N 42.08E
36 C3 Olus Dağı mt Turkey 39.18N 28.22E
105 E7 Olustee Florida 30.12N 82.28W
109 L7 Olustee Oklahoma 34.34N 99.26W
19 L8 Olutanga isld Philippines 7.23N 122.50E
75 O3 Olván Spain 42.03N 1.55E
53 T19 Ølve Norway 59.59N 5.48E
75 G4 Ólvega Spain 41.47N 1.59W
75 L3 Olvena Spain 42.07N 0.15E
63 P8 Olvenstedt E Germany 52.09N 11.36E
77 F7 Olvera Spain 36.56N 5.15W
84 S14 Olymbos mt Kyrenia Cyprus 35.20N 33.45E
110 C2 Olympia Washington 47.03N 122.53W
84 C6 Olympia ruins Greece 37.38N 21.39E
110 B2 Olympic Mts Washington
110 B2 Olympic Nat.Park Washington
84 Q15 Olympus mt Cyprus 34.55N 32.52E
Olympus mt Greecesee Ólimbos mt Pieria Greece
110 B2 Olympus, Mt Washington 47.49N 123.42W
103 C4 Olyphant Pennsylvania 41.28N 75.35W
39 H4 Olyutorka U.S.S.R. 60.22N 166.25E
39 H4 Olyutorskiy U.S.S.R. 60.30N 169.30E
39 J4 Olyutorskiy Gory mts U.S.S.R.
39 J5 Olyutorskiy Mys C U.S.S.R. 59.58N 170.25E
39 J4 Olyutorskiy Poluostrov pen U.S.S.R.
39 H4 Olyutorskiy Zaliv B U.S.S.R.
75 G2 Olza Spain 42.49N 1.45W
81 C3 Olzai Sardinia 40.11N 9.09E
64 A3 Olzheim W Germany 50.16N 6.27E
42 H5 Ol'zony U.S.S.R. 52.59N 105.15E
15 G5 Om R Papua New Guinea
15 G6 Om R Papua New Guinea
42 C4 Om' R U.S.S.R.
20 O1 Ōma Japan 41.29N 140.55E
107 F10 Oma Mississippi 31.46N 90.09W
47 F3 Oma U.S.S.R. 66.37N 46.33E
24 D9 Oma Xizang Zizhiqu China 32.30N 83.14E
47 F3 Oma R U.S.S.R.
20 G2 Ōmachi Chiba Japan
20 L5 Ōmachi Japan 36.30N 137.51E
20 M7 Ōmae-zaki C Japan 34.35N 138.15E
20 O2 Ōmagari Japan 39.29N 140.29E
59 H2 Omagh Tyrone N Ireland 54.36N 7.18W
120 C1 Omaguas Peru 4.09S 73.22W
107 C5 Omaha Arkansas 36.27N 93.11W
105 B5 Omaha Georgia 32.07N 85.01W
108 O8 Omaha Nebraska 41.15N 96.00W
112 N2 Omaha Texas 33.12N 94.47W
117 A2 Omai Guyana 5.25N 58.45W
116 F4 Omaja Cuba 20.50N 76.43W
110 F1 Omak Washington 48.25N 119.30W
11 D12 Omakau New Zealand 45.06S 169.39E
11 L7 Omakere New Zealand 40.04S 176.50E
110 F1 Omak L Washington 48.17N 119.20W
40 G5 Omal R U.S.S.R.
84 J11 Omalós Crete 35.20N 23.55E
40 G5 Omal'skiy Khrebet ra U.S.S.R.
33 L7 Oman sultanate Arabian Peninsula
26 E3 Oman Basin Arabian Sea
27 H5 Oman, G. of Iran/Oman
26 R4 Omantai Sri Lanka 8.52N 80.30E
19 M3 Omaok Palau Is Pacific Oc 7.01N 134.15E
114 C7 Omaokorli mt Hawaiian Is 19.42N 155.30W
11 H2 Omapere, L New Zealand 35.22S 173.49E
19 J9 Omapoy isld Philippines 4.55N 119.25E
104 C9 Omar W Virginia 37.46N 82.01W
11 D11 Omarama New Zealand 44.29S 169.59E
31 F6 Omarkot Pakistan 28.46N 70.12E
93 H4 Omaro Kenya 1.42N 36.28E
94 C3 Omaruru Namibia 21.28S 15.56E
94 C3 Omaruru watercourse Namibia
120 B5 Omas Peru 12.31S 76.14W
94 D3 Omatako mt Namibia 21.07S 16.43E
94 E2 Omatako, Omuramba watercourse Namibia
120 D7 Omate Peru 16.44S 70.59W
94 B2 Omaua Namibia 19.37S 13.52E
20 O1 Ōma-zaki C Japan 41.31N 140.58E
15 C5 Omba R Irian Jaya
99 C2 Ombabika Ontario 50.14N 87.54W
99 B2 Ombabika B Ontario
19 D8 Ombai, Selat str Indonesia
18 B5 Ombalata Indonesia 1.05N 97.32E
20 N7 Ombase-jima isld Japan 34.10N 139.03E
90 J9 Ombella R Cent Afr Rep
90 J9 Ombella M'Boko dist Cent Afr Rep
94 B1 Ombepera Namibia 17.38S 12.56E
56 G3 Ombersley Hereford & Worcs Eng 52.17N 2.13W
21 J6 Ombetsu Japan 42.54N 143.57E
91 D5 Ombima Congo 2.14S 15.43E
53 T20 Ombo isld Norway 59.15N 6.00E
94 B2 Ombombo Namibia 18.43S 13.53E
91 A4 Omboué Gabon 1.38S 9.20E
61 M4 Ombret-Rawsa Belgium 50.32N 5.20E
79 J7 Ombrone R Italy
80 E2 Ombrone R Italy
24 E10 Ombu Xizang Zizhiqu China 31.20N 86.34E
94 F3 Ombuohakaru Namibia 21.51S 20.01E
94 D3 Omburo Namibia 21.20S 16.12E
91 J6 Ombwe Zaïre 4.24S 25.32E
39 D4 Omchak U.S.S.R. 61.35N 148.03E
43 C6 Omchali Turkmeniya U.S.S.R. 40.38N 53.44E
43 C6 Omchali, Mys C Turkmeniya U.S.S.R. 40.53N 53.36E
41 Q6 Omchikandya U.S.S.R. 69.33N 141.44E
39 B1 Omchuk U.S.S.R. 67.40N 139.30E
95 G6 Omdraaisvlei S Africa 30.07S 23.07E
87 D3 Omdurman Sudan 15.37N 32.29E
20 N6 Ōme Japan 35.48N 139.17E
59 K3 O'Meath Louth Irish Rep 54.06N 6.17W
107 L10 Omega Alabama 31.58N 85.50W
105 D6 Omega Georgia 31.19N 83.37W
109 B7 Omega New Mexico 34.19N 108.26W
109 M6 Omega Oklahoma 35.53N 98.14W
79 D3 Omegna Italy 45.52N 8.25E
87 J7 Omein Ethiopia 6.50N 43.17E
39 J4 Omeleut U.S.S.R. 61.31N 172.44E
45 E7 Omel'nik Ukraine U.S.S.R. 49.12N 33.33E
108 K1 Omemee N Dakota 48.45N 100.21W
99 M8 Omemee Ontario 44.19N 78.33W
106 J4 Omena Michigan 45.04N 85.36W
12 J6 Omeo Victoria 37.09S 147.38E
91 J5 Omeonga Zaïre 3.42S 24.22E
35 C8 'Omer Israel 31.16N 34.50E
106 L5 Omer Michigan 44.03N 83.52W
36 C3 Ömerköy Turkey 39.50N 28.04E
37 E3 Ömerköy Turkey 40.19N 28.04E
Omerli İstanbul Turkeysee Mahmutşevketpaşa
37 F8 Omerli Mardin Turkey 37.24N 40.57E
67 P12 Omessa Corsica 42.22N 9.11E
115 K9 Ometepec Mexico 16.39N 98.23W
115 M4 Ometepe, I.de Nicaragua
59 B4 Omey I Galway Irish Rep 53.32N 10.10W
61 J6 Omezée Belgium 50.12N 4.42E
87 F3 Om Hajer Ethiopia 14.20N 36.41E
Omi see Ōmi-Hachiman
20 L5 Ōmi Japan 37.00N 137.43E
69 D4 Omiécourt France 49.49N 2.51E
20 O6 Omigawa Japan 35.50N 140.36E
20 K6 Ōmi-Hachiman Japan 35.08N 136.04E
11 G10 Omihi New Zealand 43.02S 172.52E
44 G5 Omilo Georgia U.S.S.R. 42.21N 45.36E
20 P1 Ōminato Japan 41.15N 141.10E
101 L8 Omineca R Br Col
101 K7 Omineca Mts Br Col
20 J7 Ōmine-san mt Japan 34.13N 135.53E
82 D7 Omiš Yugoslavia 43.28N 16.40E
20 F7 Ōmi-shima isld Ehime Japan
20 E7 Ōmi-shima isld Yamaguchi Japan 34.25N 131.12E
94 E4 Omitara Namibia 22.18S 18.01E
20 B1 Ōmiya Japan 35.54N 139.39E
20 O5 Ōmiya Japan 36.34N 140.23E
113 U8 Ommaney, C Alaska 56.10N 134.40W
97 J3 Ommanney B N W Terr
53 B5 Omme Å R Denmark
53 E7 Ommel Denmark 54.53N 10.30E
60 O9 Ommen Netherlands 52.31N 6.25E
41 P8 Ommo U.S.S.R. 62.37N 135.25E
22 H3 Ömnödelger Mongolia 47.57N 109.58E
22 B2 Ömnögovĭ Mongolia 49.04N 91.48E
22 F5 Ömnögovĭ prov Mongolia
40 F2 Omnya R U.S.S.R.
53 G6 Omø Denmark 55.09N 11.10E
87 F7 Omo Ethiopia 7.28N 37.28E
90 C8 Omo Nigeria 6.28N 7.05E
53 G6 Omø isld Denmark 55.09N 11.10E
93 H1 Omo R Ethiopia
87 F7 Omo Bottego,R Ethiopia
39 K3 Omocha U.S.S.R. 64.45N 175.58E
81 B3 Omodeo, L Sardinia
84 Q15 Omodhos Cyprus 34.50N 32.49E
90 C9 Omoko Nigeria 5.19N 6.40E
84 E2 Omólion Greece 39.53N 22.40E
39 G3 Omolon U.S.S.R. 64.05N 161.02E
39 F2 Omolon R U.S.S.R.
42 H4 Omoloy U.S.S.R. 56.28N 106.05E
41 O5 Omoloy R U.S.S.R.
20 O2 Omono-gawa R Japan
41 L6 Omonos R U.S.S.R.
69 H4 Omont France 49.35N 4.44E
70 G2 Omonville-la Rogue France 49.43N 1.51W
87 E8 Omo,R Ethiopia
84 D2 Omorfokhóri Greece 39.41N 22.29E
20 O2 Ōmori Akita Japan 39.20N 140.19E
20 H1 ōmori Chiba Japan
20 F6 Ōmori Japan 35.06N 132.25E
20 E3 Ōmori dist Tōkyō Japan
93 E3 Omoro Uganda 2.15N 33.24E
20 P2 Omoto Japan 39.50N 141.58E
20 P2 Omoto-gawa R Japan
91 C5 Omoy Congo 2.56S 13.16E
91 C12 Ompupa Angola 16.16S 13.30E
106 F5 Omro Wisconsin 44.03N 88.44W
47 L7 Omsk U.S.S.R. 55.00N 73.22E
38 G3 Omskaya Oblast' prov U.S.S.R.
39 F3 Omsukchan U.S.S.R. 62.33N 155.45E
39 F4 Omsukchanskiy Gory mts U.S.S.R.
25 E1 O-mu Burma 22.59N 99.18E
21 J5 Ōmu Japan 44.34N 143.00E
93 C2 Omugo Uganda 3.16N 31.07E
39 E3 Omulëvka R U.S.S.R.
62 N2 Omulew R Poland
41 Q5 Omullyakhskaya Guba str U.S.S.R.
26 T6 Omuna Sri Lanka 7.37N 81.15E
20 C9 Ōmura Japan 32.56N 129.58E
20 C9 Ōmura-wan B Japan
82 K7 Omurtag Bulgaria 43.05N 26.27E
93 C5 Omurwera Uganda 0.31N 31.02E
20 D8 Ōmuta Japan 33.02N 130.26E
20 E10 Ōmuta Japan 31.52N 131.03E
47 K7 Omutinskiy U.S.S.R. 56.30N 67.40E
46 Q1 Omutninsk U.S.S.R. 58.35N 52.28E
84 D3 Omvriáki Greece 39.06N 22.16E
61 M6 On Belgium 50.10N 5.17E
53 S16 Øn Norway 61.13N 5.12E
105 F10 Ona Florida 27.30N 81.55W
75 D2 Oña Spain 42.43N 3.26W
52 C4 Ona isld Norway 62.53N 6.34E
Ona R Irkutsk U.S.S.R.see Biryusa R
42 D6 Ona R Khakass U.S.S.R.
91 J5 Ona Dikonde Zaïre 3.51S 24.11E
109 O2 Onaga Kansas 39.29N 96.11W
20 P3 Onagawahama Japan 38.27N 141.28E
20 P3 Onagawa-wan B Japan
20 O5 Onahama Japan 36.58N 140.53E
91 E12 Onai Angola 16.43S 17.33E
94 C2 Onaiso Namibia 18.48S 14.40E
108 L4 Onaka S Dakota 45.11N 99.28W
99 J2 Onakawana Ontario 50.36N 81.27W
99 J1 Onakwahegan R Ontario
110 C3 Onalaska Washington 46.35N 122.43W
106 C6 Onalaska Wisconsin 43.54N 91.13W
99 C2 Onaman L Ontario
108 R3 Onamia Minnesota 46.06N 93.38W
19 M4 Onamue isld Truk Is Pacific Oc 7.21N 151.31E
104 K9 Onancock Virginia 37.43N 75.46W
19 A5 Onang Celebes Indon 3.07S 118.49E
91 B4 Onangué, L Gabon
81 C3 Onani Sardinia 40.29N 9.27E
99 J5 Onaping L Ontario
106 F9 Onarga Illinois 40.43N 88.02W
53 T19 Onarheim Norway 59.57N 5.39E
98 A4 Onatchiway L Quebec
115 F2 Oñate Mexico 30.10N 107.38W
75 F1 Oñate Spain 43.02N 2.25W
115 E3 Onavas Mexico 28.29N 109.32W
108 O7 Onawa Iowa 42.01N 96.06W
106 K4 Onaway Michigan 45.23N 84.14W
25 D5 Onbingwin Burma 14.38N 97.59E
75 F4 Oncala Spain 41.58N 2.18W
121 D3 Oncativo Argentina 31.58N 63.40W
57 E4 Onchan Isle of Man U.K. 54.11N 4.27W
21 C8 Onch'ŏn-ni N Korea 38.13N 125.25E
91 C12 Oncocua Angola 16.30S 13.25E
75 K8 Onda Spain 39.58N 0.16W
29 K2 Onda W Bengal India 23.07N 87.12E
94 C1 Ondangua Namibia 17.52S 15.59E
77 R3 Ondara Spain 38.50N 0.01E
75 F1 Ondárroa Spain 43.19N 2.25W
118 F3 Ondas R Brazil
62 N6 Ondava R Czechoslovakia
94 D4 Ondekaremba Namibia 22.30S 17.25E
30 A8 Onder Madhya Prad India 24.18N 77.55E
60 P6 Onderdendam Netherlands 53.20N 6.35E
60 J8 Onderdijk Netherlands 52.45N 5.08E
94 F8 Onderste Doorn S Africa 30.11S 20.38E
21 F10 Ondo Japan 34.10N 132.36E
90 B8 Ondo Nigeria 7.05N 4.55E
22 H3 Öndörhaan Mongolia 47.20N 110.35E
21 B5 Ondor Had Nei Monggol Zizhiqu China 44.57N 120.30E
Öndör Hän see Öndörshireet
22 F3 Öndörsant Mongolia 47.10N 102.16E
22 H4 Öndörshil Mongolia 44.55N 108.05E
22 F3 Öndörshireet Mongolia 47.25N 104.52E
72 B8 Ondres France 43.34N 1.26W
50 A5 Öndverdharnes C Iceland 64.53N 24.03W
27 L9 One and Half Degree Chan Maldive Is, Indian Oc
9 U3 Oneata isld Fiji 18.27S 178.30W
105 E10 Oneco Florida 27.26N 82.32W
47 D4 Onega U.S.S.R. 63.57N 38.11E
Onega L see Onezhskoye, Ozero L

47 D5 Onega R U.S.S.R.
45 T7 Onege Kazakhstan U.S.S.R. 49.15N 47.25E
79 D7 Oneglia Italy 43.53N 8.02E
13 H2 One & Half Mile Opening str Gt Barrier Reef Australia
11 D2 Onehunga New Zealand 36.56S 174.48E
106 D8 Oneida Illinois 41.04N 90.13W
106 C7 Oneida Iowa 42.32N 91.22W
104 B9 Oneida Kentucky 37.14N 83.41W
104 K3 Oneida New York 43.04N 75.40W
107 M5 Oneida Tennessee 36.31N 84.30W
104 K3 Oneida L New York
108 M7 O'Neill Nebraska 42.28N 98.38W
11 G7 Onekaka New Zealand 40.47S 172.44E
106 H5 Onekama Michigan 44.22N 86.12W
41 F7 Oneka, Ozero L U.S.S.R.
40 N7 Onekotan Kuril Is U.S.S.R. 49.20N 154.41E
40 N7 Onekotan, O isld Kuril Is U.S.S.R.
9 B3 Onemak islet Marshall Is Pacific Oc 9.04N 167.29E
91 H5 Onema Okolo Zaïre 3.44S 23.57E
39 K3 Onemen Zaliv gulf U.S.S.R.
53 W17 Onen, mt Norway 60.32N 7.05E
107 K8 Oneonta Alabama 33.57N 86.29W
103 D2 Oneonta New York 42.56N 75.04W
11 M5 Onepoto New Zealand 38.48S 177.07E
11 J2 Onerahi New Zealand 35.47S 174.22E
122 B10 Oneroa isld Rarotonga Pacific Oc 21.15S 159.43W
100 J1 One Sided Lake Ontario 49.02N 93.55W
72 B7 Onesse-et-Laharie France 44.04N 1.04W
11 D2 One Tree Hill dist Auckland New Zealand
9 S10 Onevai islet Tonga, Pacific Oc 21.05S 175.08W
47 D4 Onezhskaya Guba gulf U.S.S.R.
47 D5 Onezhskoye, Oz L U.S.S.R.
91 D4 Ongali Gabon 1.17S 14.14E
11 L6 Ongaonga New Zealand 39.57S 176.25E
11 K5 Ongarue New Zealand 38.42S 175.17E
9 U3 Ongea Levu I Fiji 19.11S 178.28W
95 G6 Ongers R S Africa
14 C10 Ongerup W Australia 33.59S 118.28E
22 K5 Onggon Ul Nei Monggol Zizhiqu China 42.33N 114.06E
22 F4 Ongiyn Gol R Mongolia
21 C9 Ongjin N Korea 37.56N 125.21E
71 H8 Ongles France 44.01N 5.43E
22 L5 Ongniud Qi Nei Monggol Zizhiqu China 43.05N 118.49E
91 K4 Ongoka Zaïre 1.24S 26.03E
28 E3 Ongole Andhra Prad India 15.33N 80.03E
22 J4 Ongon Mongolia 45.42N 113.05E
29 H7 Ong R Orissa India
94 C3 Onguati Namibia 21.51S 15.48E
42 D6 Onguday U.S.S.R. 50.46N 86.13E
91 D12 Ongweduga Namibia 17.52S 15.49E
61 K6 Onhaye Belgium 50.14N 4.50E
44 E5 Oni Georgia U.S.S.R. 42.34N 43.26E
90 B8 Oni R Nigeria
84 E6 Onia Ori mts Argolís Greece
58 F5 Onich Highland Scotland 56.43N 5.14W
108 K5 Onida S Dakota 44.43N 100.04W
81 C3 Oniferi Sardinia 40.16N 9.11E
77 P3 Onil Spain 38.39N 0.40W
95 B7 Onilahy R Madagascar
15 A5 Onin Pen Irian Jaya
100 H5 Onion Lake Saskatchewan 53.46N 109.59W
76 K2 Onís Spain 43.20N 4.59W
21 J5 Onishibetsu Japan 45.21N 142.06E
21 J5 Onishika Japan 44.12N 141.40E
98 A3 Onistagan L Quebec
90 C8 Onitsha Nigeria 6.10N 6.47E
69 A3 Onival France 50.08N 1.28E
92 D1 Onjo tribe Zaïre
21 C7 Onjŏng N Korea 40.06N 125.52E
22 G3 Önjüül Mongolia 46.45N 105.31E
88 R4 Onk, Djebel mt Algeria 34.52N 7.57E
61 F3 Onkerzele Belgium 50.47N 3.55E
87 L5 Onkhor Somalia 10.46N 46.10E
87 L5 Onkhor Pk mt Somalia 10.35N 46.20E
51 N8 Onkivesi L Finland
41 K7 Onkuchakh U.S.S.R. 66.13N 114.36E
104 K9 Onley Virginia 37.39N 75.42W
20 B5 Onna Kanagawa Japan
20 P9 Onna Okinawa Japan 26.30N 127.51E
19 N4 Onna isld Truk Is Pacific Oc 7.20N 151.57E
20 P9 Onna-dake hill Okinawa Japan 26.28N 127.50E
69 F3 Onnaing France 50.23N 3.36E
19 N4 Onnaram isld Truk Is Pacific Oc 7.17N 151.57E
40 E2 Onne R U.S.S.R.
61 E5 Onnezies Belgium 50.22N 3.43E
66 O8 Onno Italy 45.55N 9.18E
90 J2 Onnour Chad 19.49N 18.10E
41 K7 Onnya-Tërdë U.S.S.R. 66.12N 114.05E
20 K6 Ono Fukui Japan 35.59N 136.30E
20 K3 Ono Hokkaido Japan 41.54N 140.38E
20 H7 Ono Hyōgo Japan 34.52N 134.55E
20 P1 Ono Iwate, Honshu Japan 40.18N 141.40E
20 O4 Ono Japan 37.18N 140.39E
20 A5 Ono Kanagawa Japan
103 A6 Ono Pennsylvania 40.23N 76.32W
9 S3 Ono isld Fiji 18.53S 178.30E
20 E7 Onoda Japan 34.00N 131.11E
20 N7 Onohara-jima isld Japan 34.03N 139.22E
20 E9 Onoichi Japan 32.52N 131.39E
10 R6 Ono-i-Lau isld Pacific Oc 20.48S 178.45W
20 B3 Onoji Tōkyō Japan
11 K8 Onoke L New Zealand 41.23S 175.07E
42 H6 Onokhoy U.S.S.R. 51.56N 108.00E
18 B5 Onolimbu Indonesia 1.00N 97.54E
94 C2 Onolongo Namibia 18.26S 15.41E
114 C7 Onomea Hawaiian Is 19.48N 155.08W
20 G7 Onomichi Japan 34.25N 133.11E
42 K6 Onon R U.S.S.R.
42 K6 Onon-Borzya U.S.S.R. 51.04N 117.22E
106 K7 Onondaga Michigan 42.26N 84.34W
22 J2 Onon Gol R Mongolia
20 O4 Ono-Niimachi Japan 37.18N 140.39E
42 J6 Ononskiy Khrebet mts U.S.S.R.
21 B3 Onor Nei Monggol Zizhiqu China 48.52N 121.10E
76 F5 Onor R Portugal
9 C6 Onotoa atoll Kiribati, Pacific Oc 1.55S 175.34E
103 H2 Onoto L Massachusetts 42.28N 73.18W
39 F6 Onovgay U.S.S.R. 56.10N 159.00E
100 C5 Onoway Alberta 53.44N 114.13W
91 C4 Onoy R Gabon
61 J5 Onoz Belgium 50.29N 4.40E
95 C10 Onrus S Africa 34.25S 19.10E
52 F9 Onsala Sweden 57.25N 12.00E
53 F5 Onsbjerg Denmark 55.52N 10.35E
94 E7 Onseepkans S Africa 28.48S 19.13E
75 H3 Onsella R Spain
66 L7 Onsernone, Val Italy/Switz
103 N3 Onset Massachusetts 41.45N 70.37W
76 B4 Ons, I.de Spain 42.23N 8.56W
53 H7 Ønslev Denmark 54.51N 11.52E
14 B5 Onslow W Australia 21.41S 115.12E
105 K3 Onslow B N Carolina
11 D12 Onslow, L New Zealand
21 E6 Onsong N Korea 42.55N 129.59E
106 K7 Onsted Michigan 42.01N 84.12W
64 G7 Onstmettingen W Germany 48.16N 9.00E
60 R7 Onstwedde Netherlands 53.02N 7.02E
20 L6 Ontake-san mt Japan 35.55N 137.29E
77 N3 Ontalafia L Spain 38.43N 1.46W
75 C1 Ontaneda Spain 43.12N 3.55W
101 H2 Ontaratue R N W Terr
111 G7 Ontario California 34.04N 117.38W
110 J5 Ontario Oregon 44.02N 116.58W
106 D6 Ontario Wisconsin 43.43N 90.36W
97 K7 Ontario prov Canada
106 Q6 Ontario, L U.S.A./Canada
103 C6 Ontelaunee L Pennsylvania 40.27N 75.55W
77 P3 Onteniente Spain 38.49N 0.37W
75 L4 Ontiñena Spain 41.40N 0.05E
106 E3 Ontonagon Michigan 46.52N 89.18W
15 L1 Ontong Java Atoll Solomon Is
10 M3 Ontong Java Rise sea feature Pacific Oc
52 H5 Ontorp Sweden 61.23N 14.30E
77 N3 Ontur Spain 38.37N 1.30W
20 K2 Onuma Japan 41.58N 140.41E
50 B2 Önundarfjördhur B Iceland
117 B2 Onverwacht Surinam 5.36N 55.12W
107 F9 Onward Mississippi 32.42N 90.57W
111 F6 Onyx California 35.42N 118.15W
70 N6 Onzain France 47.30N 1.11E
61 J2 Onze-Lieve-Vrouw-Waver Belgium 51.03N 4.35E
76 H3 Onzonilla Spain 42.31N 5.35W
12 D3 Oodnadatta S Australia 27.30S 135.27E
61 D3 Ooigem Belgium 50.53N 3.20E
60 N13 Ooijen Netherlands 51.30N 6.10E
61 E3 Ooike Belgium 50.52N 3.33E
114 C6 Ookala Hawaiian Is 20.00N 155.16W
94 D7 Ookiep S Africa 29.38S 17.54E
59 F6 Oola Limerick Irish Rep 52.33N 8.16W
109 P5 Oolagah Oklahoma 36.26N 95.43W
72 F10 Oo, L.d' France 42.44N 0.30E
12 B4 Ooldea S Australia 30.30S 131.45E
12 B4 Ooldea Ra S Australia
107 K3 Oolitic Indiana 38.54N 86.31W
109 P5 Oologah Res Oklahoma
60 F13 Ooltgensplaat Netherlands 51.41N 4.20E
9 D5 Ooma Ocean I Pacific Oc 0.53S 169.36E
61 F3 Oombergen Belgium 50.54N 3.50E
13 G5 Oondooroo Queensland 22.10S 143.00E
13 C6 Ooraminna Ra N Terr Australia
13 D5 Ooratippra R N Terr Australia
61 K3 Oorbeek Belgium 50.48N 4.53E
61 F3 Oordegem Belgium 50.57N 3.54E
13 F5 Oorindi Queensland 20.44S 141.00E
Oos see Baden Baden West
61 F2 Oostakker Belgium 51.06N 3.46E
105 B3 Oostanaula, R Georgia
60 A3 Oostburg Netherlands 51.20N 3.30E
69 D2 Oost-Cappel France 50.55N 2.35E
60 E14 Oostdijk Netherlands 51.26N 4.05E
61 A2 Oostduinkerke Belgium 51.07N 2.41E
61 E2 Oosteekloo Belgium 51.12N 3.41E
60 Q6 Oosteinde Groningen Netherlands 53.25N 6.48E
60 K14 Oostelbeers Netherlands 51.28N 5.16E
60 L10 Oostelijk-Flevoland polder Netherlands
61 B2 Oostende Belgium 51.13N 2.55E
60 M10 Oostendorp Netherlands 52.27N 5.51E
60 N14 Oostenrijk Netherlands 51.28N 6.03E
60 M12 Oosterbeek Netherlands 51.59N 5.51E
60 L7 Oosterbierum Netherlands 53.14N 5.30E
60 J9 Oosterblokker Netherlands 52.40N 5.07E
Oosterburen see Schiermonnikoog
60 J9 Oosterdijk Netherlands 52.45N 5.15E
60 L7 Oosterend Friesland Netherlands 53.06N 5.37E
60 K6 Oosterend Terschelling Netherlands 53.25N 5.24E
60 H7 Oosterend Texel Netherlands 53.05N 4.52E
60 P8 Oosterhesselen Netherlands 52.45N 6.44E
60 H13 Oosterhout Netherlands 51.39N 4.52E
60 M12 Oosterhout Netherlands 51.52N 5.50E
60 H8 Oosterland Noord-Holland Netherlands 52.56N 5.00E
60 E13 Oosterland Zeeland Netherlands 51.38N 4.01E
60 J9 Oosterleek Netherlands 52.38N 5.11E
60 L7 Oosterlittens Netherlands 53.08N 5.38E
60 N7 Oostermeer Netherlands 53.10N 6.04E
60 Q6 Oosternieland Netherlands 53.24N 6.45E
60 N6 Ooster-Nijkerk Friesland Netherlands 53.23N 6.04E
60 C2 Oosterschelde channel Netherlands
60 C2 Oosterscheldebrug channel Netherlands
60 L7 Oosterwierum Netherlands 53.07N 5.45E
60 O8 Oosterwolde Friesland Netherlands 52.59N 6.18E
60 M10 Oosterwolde Gelderland Netherlands 52.28N 5.54E
60 M8 Oosterzee Netherlands 52.52N 5.45E
61 F3 Oosterzele Belgium 50.57N 3.48E
61 L2 Oostham Belgium 51.06N 5.11E
60 J9 Oosthuizen Netherlands 52.35N 5.00E
95 L3 Oosthuizen S Africa 27.54N 27.32E
61 C2 Oostkamp Belgium 51.09N 3.15E
60 B2 Oostkapelle Netherlands 51.34N 3.32E
61 B2 Oostkerke Belgium 51.03N 2.48E
61 D1 Oostkerke Belgium 51.17N 3.18E
60 N6 Oostmahorn Netherlands 53.22N 6.10E
61 J1 Oostmalle Belgium 51.18N 4.45E
61 C3 Oostnieuwkerke Belgium 50.57N 3.04E
61 D3 Oostrozebeke Belgium 50.55N 3.21E
60 B3 Oost-Souburg Netherlands 51.28N 3.36E
60 K10 Oostvaardersdiep Netherlands
61 F2 Oost Vlaanderen prov Belgium
61 A3 Oostvleteren Belgium 50.56N 2.45E
60 J6 Oost-Vlieland Vlieland Netherlands 53.18N 5.04E
60 E12 Oostvoorne Netherlands 51.55N 4.06E
61 E2 Oostwinkel Belgium 51.09N 3.32E
60 Q7 Oostwold Netherlands 53.14N 6.54E
60 R7 Oostwold Netherlands 53.13N 7.03E
60 O7 Oostwolde Netherlands 53.12N 6.27E
60 H10 Oostzaan Netherlands 52.26N 4.52E
28 C5 Ootacamund Tamil Nadu India 11.28N 76.42E
60 Q10 Ootmarsum Netherlands 52.25N 6.55E
101 K9 Ootsa L Br Col
101 K9 Ootsa Lake Br Col 53.47N 126.02W
100 S2 Opachuanau L Manitoba
114 A4 Opaeula R Hawaiian Is
82 K7 Opaka Bulgaria 43.28N 26.10E
11 K7 Opaki New Zealand 40.53S 175.40E
100 D5 Opal Alberta 53.59N 113.12W
115 H5 Opal Mexico 24.18N 102.22W
110 P8 Opal Wyoming 41.46N 110.19W
39 E7 Opala U.S.S.R. 51.58N 156.30E
91 J4 Opala Zaïre 0.40S 24.20E
39 F8 Opala R U.S.S.R.
Opal Bazar see Shufu
62 J3 Opalenica Poland 52.19N 16.28E
105 G12 Opa-locka Florida 25.53N 80.16W
13 G6 Opalton Queensland 23.14S 142.46E
13 G6 Opalville Queensland 24.47S 142.37E
26 S8 Opanake Sri Lanka 6.37N 80.38E
65 K3 Opařany Czechoslovakia 49.18N 14.29E
93 D2 Opari Sudan 3.57N 32.05E
47 F6 Oparino U.S.S.R. 59.53N 48.10E
99 H3 Opasatika Ontario 49.32N 82.53W
99 H3 Opasatika R Ontario
99 G3 Opasatika L Ontario 49.05N 83.08W
82 B5 Opatija Yugoslavia 45.20N 14.18E
65 P2 Opatov Czechoslovakia 49.49N 16.30E
62 N5 Opatów Poland 50.49N 21.25E
62 L4 Opatówek Poland 51.44N 18.12E
62 K6 Opava Czechoslovakia 49.58N 17.55E
62 K5 Opava R Czech/Poland
99 P3 Opawica R Ontario
99 P3 Opawica L Quebec
61 G2 Opdorp Belgium 51.02N 4.13E
60 N7 Opeinde Netherlands 53.08N 6.03E
107 L9 Opelika Alabama 32.39N 85.26W
107 D11 Opelousas Louisiana 30.31N 92.07W
99 D2 Opemisha Ontario 50.09N 86.30W
15 L6 Open B New Britain
11 C10 Open Bay Is New Zealand
14 D8 Open L W Australia
99 M7 Opeongo L Ontario
93 F4 Opeta,L Uganda
66 Q1 Opfenbach W Germany 47.37N 9.50E
61 N2 Opglabbeek Belgium 51.02N 5.35E
61 H4 Ophain-Bois-Seigneur-Isaac Belgium 50.42N 4.21E
61 F3 Ophasselt Belgium 50.49N 3.54E
61 M4 Opheers Belgium 50.44N 5.17E
108 D1 Opheim Montana 48.54N 106.25W
60 K12 Ophemert Netherlands 51.51N 5.24E
60 L12 Opheusden Netherlands 51.56N 5.37E
61 K4 Opheylissem Belgium 50.45N 4.58E
113 J5 Ophir Alaska 63.09N 156.40W
110 A7 Ophir Oregon 42.35N 124.25W
110 N9 Ophir Utah 40.23N 112.15W
Ophir, Mt see Ledang, Gunong
61 O2 Ophoven Belgium 51.07N 5.48E
14 C6 Ophthalmia Ra W Australia
80 J5 Opi Italy 41.47N 13.50E
96 Q4 O Pico mt Azores 38.28N 28.24W
92 C1 Opienge Zaïre 0.19N 27.21E
114 D8 Opihikao Hawaiian Is 19.25N 154.53W
11 F11 Opihi R New Zealand
60 K12 Opijnen Netherlands 51.50N 5.19E
32 A4 Opis ruins Iraq 33.48N 44.16E
61 N2 Opitter Belgium 51.07N 5.39E
64 C1 Opladen W Germany 51.10N 7.00E
52 D5 Opland co Norway
61 K3 Oplinter Belgium 50.50N 4.59E
120 F9 Oploca Bolivia 21.18S 65.46W
60 M13 Oploo Netherlands 51.37N 5.53E
52 F2 Opløyfjord inlet Norway 64.46N 11.46E
60 H9 Opmeer Netherlands 52.43N 4.56E
90 C9 Opobo Nigeria 4.35N 7.34E
90 C9 Opobo R Nigeria
46 G2 Opochka U.S.S.R. 56.41N 28.42E
120 E8 Opoco Bolivia 19.52S 66.40W
98 F1 Opocopa L Quebec
62 M4 Opoczno Poland 51.24N 20.18E
115 D3 Opodepe Mexico 29.54N 110.38W
61 N2 Opoeteren Belgium 51.04N 5.39E
62 N4 Opole Lublin Poland 51.08N 22.00E
62 K5 Opole Opole Poland 50.40N 17.56E
11 M5 Oponae New Zealand 38.14S 177.20E
11 H2 Opononi New Zealand 35.31S 173.26E
61 L7 Opont Belgium 49.56N 5.07E
43 C4 Opornyy Kazakhstan U.S.S.R. 46.13N 54.27E
Oporto see Porto Portugal
45 F7 Oposhnya Ukraine U.S.S.R. 49.58N 34.37E
11 M5 Opotiki New Zealand 38.00S 177.18E
72 K10 Opoul-Périllos France 42.53N 2.41E
11 B3 Opou Pt New Zealand 36.57S 174.40E
11 K4 Opoutere New Zealand 37.07S 175.54E
107 K10 Opp Alabama 31.16N 86.18W
103 A4 Opp Pennsylvania 41.11N 76.40W
20 P3 Oppa-gawa R Japan
95 K2 Oppaslaagte S Africa 26.23S 26.14E
20 P3 Oppa-wan B Japan
52 E4 Oppdal Norway 62.36N 9.41E
79 K4 Oppeano Italy 45.19N 11.11E
53 T16 Oppedal Norway 61.03N 5.33E
63 T9 Oppelhain E Germany 51.33N 13.36E
Oppeln see Opole
64 E7 Oppenau W Germany 48.28N 8.10E
64 E4 Oppenheim W Germany 49.52N 8.22E
60 L7 Oppenhuizen Netherlands 53.01N 5.42E
64 G6 Oppenweiler W Germany 48.59N 9.28E
60 J8 Opperdoes Netherlands 52.46N 5.05E
60 G12 Opperduit Netherlands 51.54N 4.42E
53 J5 Oppe Sundby Denmark 55.50N 12.07E
53 V17 Oppheimsvatn L Norway 60.47N 6.35E
80 N7 Oppido Lucano Italy 40.46N 16.00E
81 L7 Oppido Mamertina Italy 38.17N 15.59E
53 Y15 Oppland co Norway
65 L6 Opponitz Austria 47.54N 14.49E
61 K4 Opprebais Belgium 50.41N 4.48E
53 W15 Oppstryn Norway 61.54N 7.04E
61 H2 Oppuurs Belgium 51.05N 4.15E
100 Q4 Optic Lake Manitoba 54.47N 101.15W
109 J5 Optima Oklahoma 36.45N 101.22W
109 F6 Optimo New Mexico 35.53N 104.47W
11 J2 Opua New Zealand 35.20S 174.08E
11 J2 Opuawhanga New Zealand 35.31S 174.24E
11 H6 Opunake New Zealand 39.27S 173.52E
122 A11 Opunohu B Society Is Pacific Oc
115 E2 Oputo Mexico 30.10N 109.26W
61 G3 Opwijk Belgium 50.58N 4.11E
Oqair see 'Uqayr, Al
106 D9 Oquawka Illinois 40.56N 90.56W
88 N7 Oquilet Mohammed Algeria 28.50N 2.00W
75 C4 Oquillas Spain 41.50N 3.41W
115 D2 Oquitoa Mexico 30.46N 111.42W
104 P2 Oquossoc Maine 44.58N 70.47W
52 H10 Ör Sweden 56.59N 14.40E
30 A8 Or R Madhya Prad India
43 E2 Or' R U.S.S.R.
84 R15 Ora Cyprus 34.51N 33.12E
35 D7 Ora Israel 31.45N 35.09E
79 K2 Ora Italy 46.21N 11.18E
85 E5 Ora Libya 28.36N 19.36E
93 C3 Ora R Uganda
72 C9 Oraas France 43.26N 0.58W
94 D5 Orab Namibia 24.47S 17.55E
93 B2 Oraba Uganda 3.31N 30.54E
14 D9 Ora Banda W Australia 30.27S 121.04E
116 K1 Oracabessa Jamaica, W I 18.24N 76.57W
111 O9 Oracle Arizona 32.36N 110.46W
82 G3 Oradea Romania 47.03N 21.55E
76 E11 Orado Portugal 38.52N 7.28W
72 G4 Oradour-sur-Glane France 45.56N 1.03E
50 J6 Öræfajökull ice cap Iceland 64.02N 16.41W
50 F6 Öræfi reg Iceland
82 F8 Orahovac Yugoslavia 42.24N 20.40E
30 C7 Orai Uttar Prad India 26.00N 79.26E
111 O6 Oraibi Arizona 35.53N 110.39W
111 O5 Oraibi Wash R Arizona
71 H9 Oraison France 43.55N 5.55E
51 L5 Orajärvi Finland 66.54N 24.05E
51 M4 Orajärvi L Finland 67.20N 26.50E
11 D2 Orakei dist Auckland New Zealand
108 G6 Oral S Dakota 43.25N 103.16W
37 H8 Oramar Turkey 37.23N 44.04E
88 N4 Oran Algeria 35.45N 0.38W
120 F10 Orán Argentina 23.07S 64.16W
107 G4 Oran Missouri 37.05N 89.39W
30 D7 Oran Uttar Prad India 25.22N 80.44E
72 F4 Orandour-sur-Vayres France 45.44N 0.52E
28 J2 Orang Assam India 26.41N 92.16E
103 H4 Orange Connecticut 41.17N 73.02W
71 F8 Orange France 44.08N 4.48E
104 N4 Orange Massachusetts 42.35N 72.20W
103 J7 Orange New Jersey 40.47N 74.15W
12 J5 Orange New S Wales 33.19S 149.10E
112 O5 Orange Texas 30.05N 93.43W
104 G8 Orange Virginia 38.14N 78.07W
103 E4 Orange co New York
Orange R see Oranje R
107 J11 Orange Beach Alabama 30.16N 87.38W
105 G4 Orangeburg S Carolina 33.28N 80.53W
117 C2 Orange C Brazil 4.25N 51.32W
116 E2 Orange Cay isld Bahamas 24.57N 79.08W
105 F9 Orange City Florida 28.57N 81.19W
108 O6 Orange City Iowa 43.00N 96.05W
98 L8 Orangedale C Breton I, Nova Scotia 45.56N 61.06W
105 F7 Orangedale Florida 30.02N 81.36W
95 J4 Orange Free State prov S Africa
112 K8 Orange Grove Texas 28.57N 97.57W
105 E8 Orange L Florida 29.25N 82.10W
Orange Mouth see Oranjemund
105 F7 Orange Park Florida 30.11N 81.43W
15 K9 Orangerie B Papua New Guinea
106 E7 Orangeville Illinois 42.29N 89.41W
99 K9 Orangeville Ontario 43.55N 80.06W
103 B4 Orangeville Pennsylvania 41.05N 76.25W
111 N2 Orangeville Utah 39.12N 111.02W
115 P8 Orange Walk Belize 18.06N 88.31W
11 J6 Orangimea New Zealand 39.40S 174.52E
89 A6 Orango,I.de Guinea-Bissau 11.05N 16.00W
19 G1 Orani Luzon Philippines 14.48N 120.32E
81 C3 Orani Sardinia 40.15N 9.11E
63 Q9 Oranienbaum E Germany 51.48N 12.25E
63 S7 Oranienburg E Germany 52.46N 13.15E
94 D7 Oranje R S Africa
94 J4 Oranjefontein S Africa 23.25S 27.41E
117 B3 Oranje Gebergte mts Surinam
60 P8 Oranje Kanaal canal Netherlands
94 D7 Oranjemund Namibia 28.33N 16.25E
95 H5 Oranjerivier S Africa 29.40S 24.13E
116 A1 Oranjestad Aruba W I 12.32N 70.02W
116 N6 Oranjestad Saint Eustatius Lesser Antilles 17.33N 63.00W
95 M2 Oranjeville S Africa 26.59S 28.12E
60 M8 Oranjewoud Netherlands 52.58N 5.58E
94 P11 Oranjezicht dist Cape Town S Africa
59 E5 Oranmore Galway Irish Rep 53.16N 8.56W
15 C4 Oransbari Irian Jaya 1.16S 134.18E
14 G6 Orantjugurr,L W Australia 23.53S 128.18E
44 H2 Oranzherei U.S.S.R. 45.51N 47.35E
94 H3 Orapa Botswana 21.18S 25.30E
35 C3 Or 'Aqiva Israel 32.31N 34.55E
77 C5 Oraque R Spain
11 F11 Orari New Zealand 44.08S 171.18E
11 F10 Orari R New Zealand
19 M5 Oras Philippines 12.10N 125.28E
19 M5 Oras B Philippines
82 E5 Orašje Yugoslavia 45.01N 18.42E
66 L7 Orasso Italy 46.06N 8.36E
82 H5 Orăștie Romania 45.50N 23.11E
82 H3 Orașu Nou Romania 47.50N 23.19E
11 B2 Oratia Auckland New Zealand 36.01S 174.37E
80 L5 Oratina Italy 41.35N 14.35E
59 B7 Oratory of Gallarus Kerry Irish Rep 52.12N 10.20W
82 M1 Oratovo U.S.S.R. 49.12N 29.32E
62 L6 Orava R Czechoslovakia
51 J8 Oravais Finland 63.18N 22.25E
82 G5 Oravița Romania 45.02N 21.43E
62 L6 Oravská Magura mts Czechoslovakia
82 E1 Oravskanádrz res Czechoslovakia
11 B13 Orawia New Zealand 46.04S 167.49E
39 B1 Orazno R U.S.S.R.
71 C9 Orb R France
79 E5 Orba R Italy
24 D8 Orba Co L Xizang Zizhiqu China 34.30N 81.05E
53 F6 Ørbæk Denmark 55.16N 10.41E
61 K4 Orbais Belgium 50.38N 4.46E
69 F6 Orbais France 48.57N 3.42E
75 H2 Orbara Spain 42.58N 1.14W
79 C4 Orbassano Italy 45.01N 7.32E
66 C5 Orbe Switzerland 46.45N 6.32E
66 A5 Orbe R France/Switz
70 L3 Orbec France 49.01N 0.25E
80 D4 Orbetello Italy 42.27N 11.07E
80 D4 Orbetello,Laguna di Italy
69 H5 Orbéval France 49.04N 4.48E
72 K9 Orbieu R France
72 G1 Orbigny France 47.12N 1.14E
76 H3 Órbigo R Spain
104 H6 Orbisonia Pennsylvania 40.15N 77.55W
67 P12 Orbo R Corsica
12 J7 Orbost Victoria 37.42S 148.30E
53 F5 Ørby Denmark 55.48N 10.37E
52 G9 Örby Sweden 57.30N 12.40E
52 K6 Örbyhus Sweden 60.15N 17.43E
76 E8 Orca Portugal 40.04N 7.21W
113 O6 Orca B Alaska
123 C14 Orcadas Arg Base S Orkney Is S Atlantic Oc 60.45S 44.43W
110 C1 Orcas I Washington 48.40N 122.55W
77 M5 Orce Spain 37.44N 2.28W
77 L4 Orcera Spain 38.19N 2.40W
77 M5 Orce,Sierra de mts Spain
71 K2 Orchamps-Vennes France 47.08N 6.32E
109 F1 Orchard Colorado 40.20N 104.07W
110 J6 Orchard Idaho 43.19N 116.02W
108 M7 Orchard Nebraska 42.20N 98.15W
99 J5 Orchard Ontario 47.47N 81.34W
104 G4 Orchard Park New York 42.46N 78.45W
72 E2 Orches France 46.53N 0.20E
77 Q3 Orcheta Spain 38.34N 0.16W
30 B7 Orchha Madhya Prad India 25.21N 78.38E
69 E3 Orchies France 50.28N 3.15E
116 L9 Orchila, Isla Lesser Antilles 11.49N 66.10W
96 O12 Orchilla,Pta Hierro Canary Is 27.42N 18.09W
61 K7 Orchimont Belgium 49.53N 4.55E
84 D6 Orchomenus ruins Greece 37.43N 22.18E
62 L3 Orchowo Poland 52.30N 18.00E
80 D3 Orcia R Italy
79 N7 Orciano di Pesaro Italy 43.42N 12.58E
80 C2 Orciano Pisano Italy 43.29N 10.30E
71 J7 Orcières France 44.41N 6.20E
79 B4 Orco R Italy
120 C6 Orcopampa Peru 15.20S 72.23W
71 F2 Or,Côte d' hills France
120 B4 Orcotuna Junín Peru 11.58S 75.25W
61 D4 Orcq Belgium 50.37N 3.21E
37 F1 Örcünlü Turkey 41.15N 28.33E
111 D7 Orcutt California 34.52N 120.25W
108 M8 Ord Nebraska 41.36N 98.56W
47 H7 Orda U.S.S.R. 57.11N 56.58E
72 E8 Ordan-Larroque France 43.41N 0.28E
Ordeklik see Ordeklik
24 B6 Ordeklik Xinjiang Uygur Zizhiqu China 39.42N 77.48E
76 C2 Ordenes Spain 43.05N 8.24W
111 M4 Orderville Utah 37.16N 112.38W
75 K2 Ordesa,Parque Nac.de Spain
72 C9 Ordiarp France 43.11N 0.56W
58 L4 Ordie Grampian Scotland 57.06N 2.55W
Ordi,el see Dongola
Ording see Sankt Peter-Ording
53 B3 Ørding Denmark 56.43N 8.47E
75 O2 Ordino Andorra 42.34N 1.31E
111 H7 Ord Mt California 34.42N 116.50W
14 F3 Ord,Mt W Australia 17.19S 125.30E
80 N6 Ordona Italy 41.18N 15.38E
75 F2 Ordoñana Spain 42.53N 2.22W
14 G3 Ord River W Australia 17.30S 128.48E
14 G3 Ord River Dam W Australia 16.10S 128.38E
53 G5 Ordrup Næs C Denmark 55.51N 11.22E
Ordu Hatay Turkey see Yayladağı
37 D5 Ordu Ordu Turkey 41.00N 37.52E
44 G9 Ordubad Nakhichevan' U.S.S.R. 38.54N 46.00E
75 D2 Orduña Spain 43.00N 3.00W
75 D1 Ordunte,Embalse de res Spain 43.08N 3.17W
109 G3 Ordway Colorado 38.13N 103.47W
108 M4 Ordway S Dakota 45.35N 98.26W
42 C5 Ordynskoye U.S.S.R. 54.25N 82.00E
44 D10 Ordzhonikidze Crimea, Ukraine U.S.S.R. 44.58N 35.22E
45 F9 Ordzhonikidze Dnepropetrovsk, Ukraine U.S.S.R. 47.39N 34.08E
44 E6 Ordzhonikidze Georgia U.S.S.R. 42.00N 43.16E
44 F4 Ordzhonikidze U.S.S.R. 43.02N 44.43E
43 J6 Ordzhonikidze Uzbekistan U.S.S.R. 41.19N 69.23E
43 J7 Ordzhonikidzeabad Tadzhikistan U.S.S.R. 38.36N 69.03E
44 G4 Ordzhonikidzevskaya U.S.S.R. 43.20N 45.02E
44 D4 Ordzhonikidzevskiy Karachay-Cherkess Aut O U.S.S.R. 43.50N 41.55E
42 D5 Ordzhonikidzevskiy Khakass U.S.S.R. 54.48N 88.55E
53 E5 Ore Denmark 55.30N 10.03E
56 N6 Ore E Sussex Eng 50.52N 0.37E
52 D4 Øre Norway 62.54N 7.58E
93 A2 Ore Zaïre 3.17N 29.34E
75 G6 Orea Spain 40.33N 1.44W
117 A2 Orealla Guyana 5.15N 57.23W
52 L2 Öre älv R Sweden
110 J6 Oreana Idaho 43.05N 116.23W
110 G9 Oreana Nevada 40.21N 118.19W
9 A2 Oreba islet Marshall Is Pacific Oc 9.19N 166.57E
52 J7 Örebro Sweden 59.18N 15.05E
52 H7 Örebro dist Sweden
53 H7 Oreby Denmark 54.50N 11.37E
79 J1 Orécchia, l' mt Italy 46.33N 10.52E
112 N3 Ore City Texas 32.49N 94.46W
51 P13 Oredezh U.S.S.R. 58.49N 30.20E
90 L8 Oreganza Cent Afr Rep 6.59N 22.55E
106 E7 Oregon Illinois 42.01N 89.21W
107 A2 Oregon Missouri 39.59N 95.08W
106 E7 Oregon Wisconsin 42.55N 89.23W
102 B2 Oregon state U.S.A.
110 B7 Oregon Caves Nat.Mon Oregon 42.05N 123.24W
110 C4 Oregon City Oregon 45.21N 122.36W
105 M2 Oregon Inlet N Carolina
52 L6 Oregrund Sweden 60.20N 18.30E
53 H7 Orehoved Denmark 54.58N 11.52E
75 C1 Orejo Spain 43.24N 3.43W
45 G9 Orekhov Ukraine U.S.S.R. 47.32N 35.48E
45 P1 Orekhovets U.S.S.R. 55.13N 43.38E
82 J7 Orekhovitsa Bulgaria 43.37N 24.27E
45 U4 Orekhovka U.S.S.R. 52.57N 48.12E
82 H7 Orekhovo Bulgaria 43.44N 23.56E
47 L8 Orekhovo Omsk U.S.S.R. 54.00N 72.29E
45 L1 Orekhovo-Zuyevo U.S.S.R. 55.47N 39.00E
45 B2 Orekhovsk Belorussiya U.S.S.R. 54.40N 30.30E
45 S1 Orekhov Yar U.S.S.R. 56.13N 46.50E
47 H6 Orël Perm U.S.S.R. 59.25N 56.31E
45 H4 Orël U.S.S.R. 52.58N 36.04E
45 F8 Orel' R Ukraine U.S.S.R.
51 P12 Orelezh R U.S.S.R.
108 G7 Orella Nebraska 42.55N 103.36W
120 A1 Orellana Peru 4.35S 78.10W
120 B2 Orellana Peru 6.53S 75.10W
77 F2 Orellana,Embalse de res Spain
77 F2 Orellana la Sierra Spain 39.02N 5.29W
77 E2 Orellana la Vieja Spain 39.00N 5.32W
40 H5 Orel', Oz L U.S.S.R. 53.30N 139.45E
110 O9 Orem Utah 40.20N 111.42W
36 C5 Ören Turkey 37.03N 27.56E
46 S4 Orenburg U.S.S.R. 51.50N 55.00E
38 E3 Orenburgskaya Oblast' prov U.S.S.R.
Örencık see Virancık
121 F7 Orense Argentina 38.37S 59.48W
76 D4 Orense Spain 42.20N 7.52W
74 B2 Orense prov Spain
84 F4 Oreoi Greece 38.57N 23.06E
84 E4 Oreón, Dhíavlos str Greece
11 B13 Orepuki New Zealand 46.19S 167.46E
75 J3 Ores Spain 42.16N 0.59W
46 G3 Oressa R Belorussiya U.S.S.R.
83 H3 Orestiás Greece 41.30N 26.33E
53 K5 Oresund str Denmark/Sweden
61 J5 Oret Belgium 50.18N 4.37E
11 M4 Orete Pt New Zealand 37.35S 177.55E
11 C13 Oreti R New Zealand
11 J3 Orewa New Zealand 36.34S 174.43E
61 M4 Oreye Belgium 50.43N 5.22E
104 N3 Orford New Hampshire 43.54N 72.10W
56 P3 Orford Suffolk Eng 52.06N 1.31E
12 J8 Orford Tasmania 42.30S 147.27E
13 G1 Orford B Queensland
13 G1 Orfordness Queensland 11.22S 142.50E
56 P3 Orfordness Lt.Ho Suffolk Eng 52.05N 1.34E
109 D9 Organ New Mexico 32.25N 106.36W
75 N3 Organá Spain 42.13N 1.20E
117 C2 Organabo Fr Guiana 5.32N 53.29W
96 O14 Organos,Pta.de los Gomera Canary Is 28.13N 17.15W
116 C3 Organos, Sa de los mts Cuba
111 M9 Organ Pipe Cactus Nat.Mon Arizona 32.05N 112.50W
75 C8 Orgaz Spain 39.39N 3.52W
69 C6 Orge R France
71 H3 Orgelet-le-Bourget France 46.31N 5.37E
61 M7 Orgeo Belgium 49.50N 5.18E
70 O5 Orgères-en-Beauce France 48.08N 1.41E
69 B6 Orgeval France 48.54N 1.59E
46 G6 Orgeyev Moldavia U.S.S.R. 47.24N 28.50E
79 K4 Orgiano Italy 45.22N 11.28E
77 K7 Órgiva Spain 36.54N 3.25W
71 E8 Orgnac-l'Aven France 44.18N 4.26E
37 H1 Örgök Burun C Turkey 41.09N 29.50E
71 G9 Orgon France 43.47N 5.02E
22 J5 Orgon Tal Nei Monggol Zizhiqu China 43.20N 112.42E
81 C3 Orgosolo Sardinia 40.13N 9.22E
44 G9 Orgotīn Iran 38.48N 46.26E
45 M1 Orgtrud U.S.S.R. 56.11N 40.39E
41 L8 Orgullakh U.S.S.R. 63.50N 118.49E
36 D3 Orhaneli Turkey 39.52N 28.59E
36 D3 Orhaneli R Turkey
35 B7 Or Ha Ner Israel 31.33N 34.36E
37 G2 Orhangazi Turkey 40.30N 29.18E
37 F3 Orhaniye Turkey 40.18N 28.46E
36 C3 Orhanlar Turkey 39.54N 27.37E
22 F2 Orhon Gol R Mongolia
72 B10 Orhy,Pic d' France 42.59N 1.00W
81 Q12 Oria Italy 40.30N 17.38E
77 M6 Oria Spain 37.30N 2.17W
93 B2 Oria Zaïre 3.17N 30.43E
75 F1 Oria R Spain
76 L2 Oriambre,C.de Spain 43.24N 4.24W
46 P1 Orichi U.S.S.R. 58.22N 49.00E
110 A8 Orick California 41.18N 124.05W
90 F1 Orida Niger 21.20N 12.15E
109 E3 Orient Colorado 38.12N 105.51W
108 Q8 Orient Iowa 41.12N 94.24W
103 K4 Orient Long I, N Y 41.09N 72.18W
104 R8 Orient Maine 45.50N 67.51W
13 G8 Orient Queensland 28.10S 142.50E
108 L5 Orient S Dakota 44.54N 99.05W
112 G4 Orient Texas 31.39N 100.20W
110 G1 Orient Washington 48.52N 118.14W
115 L8 Oriental Mexico 19.24N 97.40W
105 L2 Oriental N Carolina 35.03N 76.43W
89 C5 Oriental reg Senegal
11 C6 Oriental B Wellington New Zealand
120 E7 Oriental,Cord mts Bolivia/Peru
119 C7 Oriental,Cord mts Colombia
Orientale prov see Haut Zaïre
99 B3 Orient Bay Ontario 49.23N 88.08W
121 E7 Oriente Argentina 38.45S 60.37W
120 F3 Oriente Brazil 9.55S 64.05W
116 F4 Oriente prov Cuba
12 F3 Orientos New S Wales 28.00S 141.30E
13 F8 Orientos Queensland 27.40S 141.20E
103 K4 Orient Pt. Lt. Ho Long I, N Y 41.10N 72.13W
69 G4 Origny-en-Thiérache France 49.54N 4.02E
69 F7 Origny-le-Sec France 48.28N 3.48E
69 F4 Origny-Ste.Benoîte France 49.51N 3.30E
77 P4 Orihuela Spain 38.05N 0.56W
75 G6 Orihuela del Tremedal Spain 40.33N 1.39W
99 L8 Orillia Ontario 44.36N 79.26W
51 M11 Orimattila Finland 60.48N 25.40E
108 E7 Orin Wyoming 42.40N 105.13W
111 C8 Orinda California 37.54N 122.12W
119 H5 Orinduik Guyana 4.42N 60.01W
66 L8 Orino Italy 45.53N 8.44E
119 F6 Orinoco,R Venezuela
75 F1 Orio Spain 43.16N 2.07W
76 D12 Oriola Portugal 38.19N 7.51W
81 M3 Oriolo Italy 40.03N 16.27E
80 F4 Oriolo Romano Italy 42.09N 12.06E
100 G9 Orion Alberta 49.28N 110.49W
106 D8 Orion Illinois 41.21N 90.23W
19 G1 Orion Luzon Philippines 14.37N 120.35E
79 J1 Oris Italy 46.38N 10.38E
75 P3 Oris Spain 42.03N 2.14E
108 N3 Oriska N Dakota 46.58N 97.48W
104 K4 Oriskany Falls New York 42.56N 75.30W
29 H7 Orissa state India
75 P4 Oristá Spain 41.56N 2.04E
81 B4 Oristano Sardinia 39.54N 8.36E
81 A4 Oristano prov Sardinia
81 A4 Oristano,G.di Sardinia
65 O8 Őriszentpéter Hungary 46.51N 16.25E
119 C7 Orito Colombia 0.49N 76.57W
122 U16 Orito crater Easter I Pacific Oc 27.10S 109.24W
119 F3 Orituco,R Venezuela
51 L10 Orivesi Finland 61.42N 24.20E
51 O9 Orivesi L Finland 62.17N 29.30E
117 B5 Oriximiná Brazil 1.45S 55.50W
47 C3 Oriyarvi. Ozero L U.S.S.R.
115 L8 Orizaba Mexico 18.51N 97.08W
Orizaba,Pico de vol see Citlaltepetl Vol
82 L8 Orizare Bulgaria 42.44N 27.40E
118 E5 Orizona Brazil 17.01S 48.18W
53 K5 Orja Sweden 55.53N 12.54E
52 F7 Ørje Norway 59.28N 11.40E
82 E8 Orjen mt Yugoslavia 42.35N 18.34E
52 E3 Orkanger Norway 63.17N 9.52E
52 E3 Orkdalen V Norway
52 G10 Örkelljunga Sweden 56.17N 13.20E
52 H10 Örkened Sweden 56.24N 14.20E
52 E4 Orkla R Norway
95 K2 Orkney S Africa 26.58S 26.40E
100 K9 Orkney Saskatchewan 49.10N 107.55W
54 J4 Orkney islds Scotland
58 S11 Orkney isld area Scotland
112 D4 Orla Texas 31.48N 103.55W
64 M2 Orla R E Germany
62 K4 Orla R Poland
31 D2 Orlamish Afghanistan 36.13N 67.31E
64 M2 Orlamünde E Germany 50.47N 11.31E
111 B2 Orland California 39.45N 122.13W
106 J8 Orland Indiana 41.44N 85.09W
104 R2 Orland Maine 44.34N 68.44W
118 F7 Orlândia Brazil 20.55S 47.54W
105 F9 Orlando Florida 28.33N 81.21W
109 N5 Orlando Oklahoma 36.10N 97.24W
95 L2 Orlando S Africa 26.15S 27.55E
81 J7 Orlando,C.d' Sicily 38.10N 14.45E
76 J2 Orlé Spain 43.12N 5.19W
121 J2 Orleaes Brazil 28.20S 49.20W
42 B5 Orlean U.S.S.R. 52.43N 79.36E
67 F5 Orléanais prov France
110 B8 Orleans California 41.19N 123.34W
70 O6 Orléans France 47.54N 1.54E
107 K3 Orleans Indiana 38.40N 86.28W
103 O3 Orleans Massachusetts 41.47N 69.58W
108 O1 Orleans Minnesota 48.57N 96.54W
108 L9 Orleans Nebraska 40.08N 99.28W
104 N2 Orleans Vermont 44.49N 72.13W
69 D8 Orléans, Can. d' France
98 A7 Orléans, I. d' Quebec
Orléansville see Asnam,El
62 J5 Orlice R Czechoslovakia
65 K2 Orlická nádrž res Czechoslovakia
42 F5 Orlik U.S.S.R. 52.31N 99.55E
42 H4 Orlinga U.S.S.R. 56.04N 105.50E
44 C10 Orlinoye Ukraine U.S.S.R. 44.27N 33.45E
94 F3 Orlogsende Namibia 21.29S 20.09E
62 L6 Orlová Czechoslovakia 49.50N 18.20E
45 U6 Orlov-Gay U.S.S.R. 50.56N 48.14E
47 M7 Orlovka Novosibirsk U.S.S.R. 56.58N 76.20E
45 Q8 Orlovka Volgograd U.S.S.R. 48.50N 44.31E
39 H3 Orlovka R Magadan U.S.S.R.
42 D3 Orlovka R Tomsk U.S.S.R.
47 E3 Orlov,Mys C U.S.S.R. 67.11N 41.23E
47 L7 Orlovo Omsk U.S.S.R. 56.40N 74.02E
39 D1 Orlovo U.S.S.R. 69.13N 147.38E
45 L5 Orlovo Voronezh U.S.S.R. 51.46N 39.35E
39 E1 Orlovo Yakutsk U.S.S.R. 68.27N 152.58E
42 J6 Orlovsk U.S.S.R. 51.06N 114.47E
39 H3 Orlovskaya Magadan U.S.S.R. 64.07N 169.16E
44 E1 Orlovskaya Rostov U.S.S.R. 46.53N 42.04E
46 K3 Orlovskaya Oblast' prov U.S.S.R.
68 F5 Orly France 48.45N 2.24E
69 C6 Orly airport France 48.41N 2.23E
66 H2 Ormalingen Switzerland 47.28N 7.52E
34 D6 'Ormān Syria 32.32N 36.46E
31 C8 Ormara Pakistan 25.12N 64.39E
31 C8 Ormara,Ras C Pakistan 25.10N 64.34E
79 C6 Ormea Italy 44.08N 7.54E
61 F4 Ormeignies Belgium 50.36N 3.45E
57 L3 Ormesby Cleveland England 54.33N 1.10W
56 P2 Ormesby St.Margaret Norfolk Eng 52.40N 1.42E
64 C5 Ormesheim W Germany 49.11N 7.08E
72 F2 Ormes,les France 46.59N 0.36E
69 E7 Ormes-sur-Voulzie,les France 48.28N 3.14E
84 S15 Ormidhia Cyprus 34.59N 33.47E
58 L7 Ormiston Lothian Scotland 55.55N 2.58W
100 M9 Ormiston Saskatchewan 49.44N 105.22W
19 M6 Ormoc Philippines 11.01N 124.36E
11 M5 Ormond New Zealand 38.35S 177.58E
105 F8 Ormond Beach Florida 29.26N 81.03W
12 C8 Ormond, Pt Victoria 37.53S 144.59E
11 L7 Ormondville New Zealand 40.05S 176.18E
66 E6 Ormonts, les Switzerland 46.23N 7.08E
84 B8 Ormos Navarinou B Greece
84 F6 Ormos Sofikoú B Greece
42 M1 Ormo-Surt U.S.S.R. 62.47N 125.32E
69 D5 Ormoy-Villers France 49.12N 2.50E
82 C4 Ormož Yugoslavia 46.25N 16.10E
108 Q6 Ormsby Minnesota 43.51N 94.40W
99 N8 Ormsby Ontario 44.52N 77.45W
106 E4 Ormsby Wisconsin 45.16N 89.14W
52 J2 Ormsjö Sweden 64.26N 16.05E
57 H5 Ormskirk Lancs Eng 53.35N 2.54W
53 E4 Ormslev Denmark 56.08N 10.04E
99 R7 Ormstown Quebec 45.08N 73.59W
71 J3 Or, Mt. d' France 46.44N 6.20E
31 D7 Ornach Pakistan 27.00N 66.10E
75 K3 Orna de Gállego Spain 42.27N 0.25W
69 J6 Ornain R France
71 J2 Ornans France 47.07N 6.08E
79 D3 Ornavasso Italy 45.58N 8.25E
64 K5 Ornbau W Germany 49.11N 10.40E
67 E4 Orne dept France
69 K5 Orne R France
70 L5 Orne R France
51 D5 Ørnes Norway 66.52N 13.45E
62 M1 Orneta Poland 54.08N 20.09E
53 B4 Ørnhøj Denmark 56.12N 8.35E
52 L7 Orno Sweden 59.03N 18.29E
39 G3 Ornochek U.S.S.R. 62.36N 164.50E
52 L3 Örnsköldsvik Sweden 63.19N 18.45E
53 H5 Orø Denmark 55.47N 11.50E
53 H5 Orø isld Denmark 55.47N 11.50E
Oroba see Kmagha
120 F5 Orobayaya Bolivia 13.05S 63.48W
79 G2 Orobie,Alpi mts Italy
118 H3 Orobo,Serra do mts Brazil
40 C2 Orochen U.S.S.R. 58.34N 125.23E
117 G9 Orocó Brazil 8.35S 39.37W
119 E5 Orocué Colombia 4.51N 71.21W
89 G6 Orodara Upper Volta 11.00N 4.54W
75 J2 Oroel,Peñe de mt Spain 42.31N 0.32W
110 J3 Orofino Idaho 46.30N 116.15W
28 G1 Orog Xizang Zizhiqu 29.36N 88.32E
22 B1 Orog Nuur L Mongolia
22 E4 Orog Nuur L Mongolia
111 G7 Oro Grande California 34.37N 117.20W
110 K4 Orogrande Idaho 45.43N 115.32W
109 D9 Orogrande New Mexico 32.23N 106.06W
122 C12 Orohena pk Tahiti Pacific Oc 17.37S 149.27W
15 H7 Orokolo B Papua New Guinea
20 P9 Oroku Okinawa Japan 26.08N 127.40E
76 D1 Orol Spain 43.34N 7.39W
122 F7 Oroluk I Caroline Is Pacific Oc
98 F8 Oromocto New Brunswick 45.50N 66.28W
98 F8 Oromocto L New Brunswick
67 P12 Oro,Mt d' Corsica 42.08N 9.06E
81 K10 Oro,Mte.di Sicily 36.58N 15.09E
34 C8 Oron Israel 30.55N 35.01E
90 D9 Oron Nigeria 4.46N 8.13E
42 K4 Oron U.S.S.R. 57.15N 116.30E
122 T16 Orongo Easter I Pacific Oc 27.11S 109.27W
89 H6 Oronkua Upper Volta 11.24N 3.05W
66 D5 Oron-la-ville Switzerland 46.35N 6.50E
104 R2 Orono Maine 44.53N 68.43W
99 M9 Orono Ontario 43.59N 78.36W
107 B4 Oronogo Missouri 37.12N 94.29W
117 A3 Oronoque Guyana 2.45N 57.30W
117 A3 Oronoque R Guyana
42 K4 Oron,Ozero L U.S.S.R.
58 D6 Oronsay isld Strathclyde Scotland 56.01N 6.14W
Orontes R see 'Āsi R
79 C3 Oropa Italy 45.37N 7.59E
119 D3 Orope Venezuela 8.24N 72.23W
75 L7 Oropesa Castellón Spain 40.06N 0.07E
76 J9 Oropesa Toledo Spain 39.55N 5.10W
75 L7 Oropesa,C.de Spain 40.05N 0.09E
93 F2 Oropoi Kenya 3.45N 34.21E
84 G5 Oropoú Greece 38.17N 23.50E
116 P1 Oropuche R Trinidad & Tobago
21 C2 Oroqen Zizhiqi Nei Monggol Zizhiqu China 50.31N 123.45E
19 L7 Oroquieta Mindanao Philippines 8.31N 123.46E
118 B10 Oro,R.de Argentina
76 E1 Oro,R.del R Spain
90 J2 Orori Chad 18.42N 18.55E
117 H8 Orós Brazil 6.15S 38.52W
84 F6 Oros mt Greece 37.42N 23.30E
117 G8 Orós,Açude res Brazil
81 D3 Orosei Sardinia 40.22N 9.42E
81 D3 Orosei,G.di Sardinia
62 M9 Orosháza Hungary 46.33N 20.40E
76 C3 Oroso Spain 43.00N 8.25W
82 E3 Oroszlány Hungary 47.28N 18.16E
96 R13 Orotava,La Tenerife Canary Is 28.23N 16.32W
81 C3 Orotelli Sardinia 40.18N 9.07E
81 C3 Orotelli,Serra d' mt Sardinia 40.21N 9.07E
19 L1 Orote Pen Guam Pacific Oc
39 E4 Orotukan U.S.S.R. 62.16N 151.43E
11 K7 Oroua R New Zealand
110 H8 Orovada Nevada 41.34N 117.49W
111 C2 Oroville California 39.31N 121.34W
110 F1 Oroville Washington 48.57N 119.27W
39 E3 Oroyëk U.S.S.R. 64.49N 152.49E
75 E1 Orozco Spain 43.06N 2.55W
108 E7 Orpha Wyoming 42.51N 105.30W
13 H4 Orpheus I Queensland 18.40S 146.30E
69 B6 Orphin France 48.35N 1.46E
58 S12 Orphir Orkney Scotland 58.56N 3.08W
71 H8 Orpierre France 44.19N 5.41E
55 H5 Orpington London England 51.23N 0.05E
61 K4 Orp-le-Grand Belgium 50.42N 4.59E
108 S1 Orr Minnesota 48.03N 92.50W
108 N1 Orr N Dakota 48.07N 97.41W
109 N7 Orr Oklahoma 34.02N 97.34W
50 G4 Orravatn L Iceland 65.05N 18.35W
53 B4 Ørre Denmark 56.14N 8.53E
52 J10 Orrefors Sweden 56.48N 15.45E
71 K7 Orres,les France 44.30N 6.32E
81 B5 Orri,Mte Sardinia 39.14N 8.45E

108 K1 **Orrin** N Dakota 48.05N 100.10W
58 G3 **Orrin,R** Highland Scotland
75 J6 **Orrios** Spain 40.35N 1.00W
100 U2 **Orr L** Manitoba
52 H5 **Orrmosjön** *L* Sweden 61.48N 14.10E
9 A8 **Orro** Nauru, Pacific Oc 0.32S 166.54E
61 D4 **Orroir** Belgium 50.45N 3.29E
81 C4 **Orroli** Sardinia 39.42N 9.16E
12 E5 **Orroroo** S Australia 32.46S 138.39E
52 K6 **Orrskog** Sweden 60.24N 17.25E
104 H6 **Orrstown** Pennsylvania 40.03N 77.37W
104 D6 **Orrville** Ohio 40.50N 81.47W
52 H5 **Orsa** Sweden 61.07N 14.40E
66 B3 **Orsans** France 47.15N 6.24E
80 M6 **Orsara di Puglia** Italy 41.17N 15.16E
79 G6 **Orsaro,Monte** Italy 44.24N 9.59E
68 D5 **Orsay** France 48.42N 2.12E
72 H3 **Orsennes** France 46.29N 1.40E
56 M4 **Orsett** Essex Eng 51.31N 0.23E
45 B2 **Orsha** Belorussiya U.S.S.R. 54.30N 30.23E
46 P2 **Orshanka** U.S.S.R. 56.55N 47.49E
66 H8 **Orsia** Italy 45.51N 7.49E
79 B4 **Orsiera,Monte** Italy 45.03N 7.07E
66 E7 **Orsières** Switzerland 46.02N 7.09E
52 J10 **Orsjö** Sweden 56.40N 15.45E
43 E2 **Orsk** U.S.S.R. 51.13N 58.35E
53 V14 **Orskog** Norway 62.28N 6.50E
53 H6 **Ørslev** Storstrøm Denmark 55.03N 11.59E
53 H6 **Ørslev** Vestjælland Denmark 55.23N 11.58E
53 C3 **Ørslevkloster** Denmark 56.37N 9.13E
52 G8 **Orslösa** Sweden 58.31N 13.00E
61 L3 **Orsmaal** Belgium 50.48N 5.03E
53 E2 **Ørsø** Denmark 57.11N 10.20E
80 K4 **Orsogna** Italy 42.13N 14.17E
81 L4 **Orsomarso** Italy 39.47N 15.55E
103 D3 **Orson** Pennsylvania 41.48N 75.28W
82 G6 **Orşova** Romania 44.42N 22.22E
63 E9 **Orsoy** W Germany 51.31N 6.40E
53 U14 **Ørsta** Norway 62.12N 6.09E
53 U14 **Ørstafjord** *inlet* Norway 62.12N 6.04E
53 E4 **Ørsted** Århus Denmark 56.30N 10.20E
53 E6 **Ørsted** Fyn Denmark 55.20N 10.03E
52 K7 **Orsundsbro** Sweden 59.45N 17.20E
36 G2 **Orta** Turkey 40.37N 33.04E
44 G5 **Orta** U.S.S.R. 42.12N 46.22E
36 D6 **Ortaca** Turkey 36.49N 28.43E
36 C5 **Ortaklar** Turkey 37.53N 27.30E
36 H2 **Ortaköy** Çorum Turkey 40.17N 35.17E
37 K2 **Ortaköy** İstanbul Turkey 41.03N 29.03E
36 G4 **Ortaköy** Niğde Turkey 38.46N 34.01E
36 G5 **Ortaköy** Niğde Turkey 37.59N 34.24E
79 D3 **Orta,L.d'** *L* Italy
87 M7 **Ortalis** Somalia 6.00N 48.12E
80 N6 **Orta Nova** Italy 41.20N 15.43E
79 D3 **Orta San Giulio** Italy 45.48N 8.24E
44 G3 **Orta Tyube** U.S.S.R. 44.15N 45.16E
80 F4 **Orte** Italy 42.27N 12.23E
121 C8 **Ortega** Argentina 40.45S 68.45W
119 C6 **Ortega** Colombia 3.57N 75.11W
76 D1 **Ortegal,C** Spain 43.46N 7.54W
119 C7 **Orteguaza,R** Colombia
Ortelsburg *see* **Szczytno**
64 G3 **Ortenberg** W Germany 50.20N 9.05E
64 P6 **Ortenburg** W Germany 48.33N 13.15E
65 P5 **Orth** Austria 48.09N 16.42E
63 O4 **Orth** W Germany 54.27N 11.04E
72 C9 **Orthez** France 43.29N 0.46W
61 N6 **Ortho** Belgium 50.07N 5.37E
120 E4 **Ortho, R** Bolivia
79 F8 **Ortica** *dist* Milan Italy
77 E3 **Ortiga** *R* Spain
79 L7 **Ortignano Raggiolo** Italy 43.41N 11.45E
75 E3 **Ortigosa** Spain 42.11N 2.42W
76 L7 **Ortigosa del Monte** Spain 40.50N 4.10W
76 D1 **Ortigueira** Spain 43.41N 7.50W
75 J3 **Ortilla** Spain 42.10N 0.37W
53 E5 **Ørting** Denmark 55.56N 10.09E
110 C2 **Orting** Washington 47.05N 122.13W
79 L1 **Ortisei** Italy 46.34N 11.42E
48 U14 **Ortit** Greenland 65.15N 39.45W
121 B10 **Ortiz** Argentina 44.21S 70.17W
109 D4 **Ortiz** Colorado 37.01N 106.03W
115 D3 **Ortiz** Sonora Mexico 28.18N 110.46W
119 F3 **Ortiz** Venezuela 9.37N 67.20W
42 K2 **Ort-Kyuyel'** U.S.S.R. 62.18N 116.55E
79 J1 **Ortles** *mt* Italy 46.31N 10.33E
79 J2 **Ortles** *mts* Italy
64 O2 **Ortmannsdorf** E Germany 50.42N 12.38E
53 U16 **Ortnevik** Norway 61.06N 6.08E
41 N5 **Orto-Ayan** U.S.S.R. 72.22N 129.10E
89 F5 **Ortobila** Mali 14.01N 7.11W
116 O2 **Ortoire R** Trinidad & Tobago
39 B1 **Orto-Kyuyel'** U.S.S.R. 68.32N 135.59E
67 P13 **Ortolo** *R* Corsica
57 H4 **Orton** Cumbria Eng 54.28N 2.35W
80 K4 **Ortona** Italy 42.21N 14.24E
106 L7 **Ortonville** Michigan 42.53N 83.28W
108 O4 **Ortonville** Minnesota 45.18N 96.28W
43 M6 **Orto-Tokoy** Kirgiziya U.S.S.R. 42.21N 76.01E
63 T10 **Ortrand** E Germany 51.23N 13.46E
52 L2 **Orträsk** Sweden 64.10N 19.00E
75 D1 **Ortuella** Spain 43.19N 3.04W
81 B3 **Ortueri** Sardinia 40.02N 8.59E
Ortülü *see* **Senkaya**
63 M7 **Ortze** *R* W Germany
90 A8 **Oru** Nigeria 6.56N 3.59E
11 L5 **Oruanui** New Zealand 38.36S 176.03E
19 M3 **Orukuizu** *isld* Palau Is Pacific Oc 7.11N 134.17E
41 N6 **Orulgan,Khrebet** *mts* U.S.S.R.
53 F4 **Ørum** Århus Denmark 56.27N 10.42E
53 D5 **Ørum** Denmark 55.42N 9.45E
53 E2 **Ørum** Nordjylland Denmark 57.12N 10.07E
53 A3 **Ørum** Viborg Denmark 56.49N 8.20E
53 D4 **Ørum** Viborg Denmark 56.29N 9.38E
81 C3 **Orune** Sardinia 40.24N 9.23E
93 E3 **Orungo** Uganda 2.03N 33.28E
120 E7 **Oruro** Bolivia 17.59S 67.08W
120 E8 **Oruro** *dept* Bolivia
11 H2 **Oruru** New Zealand 35.02S 173.32E
75 D7 **Orusco** Spain 40.17N 3.13W
52 F8 **Orust** *isld* Sweden 58.15N 11.40E
76 D8 **Orvalho** Portugal 40.01N 7.46W
69 D7 **Orvanne** *R* France
72 A1 **Orvault** France 47.16N 1.36W
60 P8 **Orvelte** Netherlands 52.50N 6.40E
80 F3 **Orvieto** Italy 42.43N 12.06E
123 F11 **Orville Coast** Antarctica
69 B6 **Orvilliers** France 48.52N 1.38E
66 E3 **Orvin** Switzerland 47.10N 7.13E
80 G4 **Orvinio** Italy 42.09N 12.56E
104 H5 **Orviston** Pennsylvania 41.06N 77.43W
104 K3 **Orwell** New York 43.36N 76.00W
104 E5 **Orwell** Ohio 41.32N 80.52W
103 B3 **Orwell** Pennsylvania 41.53N 76.17W
104 M3 **Orwell** Vermont 43.47N 73.17W
56 O3 **Orwell,R** Suffolk Eng
103 B5 **Orwigsburg** Pennsylvania 40.40N 76.06W
22 L2 **Orxon Gol** *R* Nei Monggol Zizhiqu China
35 C5 **Or Yehud** Israel 32.02N 34.50E
40 B3 **Oryus-Miyellya** *R* U.S.S.R.
66 C5 **Orzens** Switzerland 46.44N 6.41E
45 D7 **Orzhitsa** Ukraine U.S.S.R. 49.49N 32.43E
79 G4 **Orzinuovi** Italy 45.24N 9.55E
96 V7 **Orzola** Lanzarote Canary Is 29.13N 13.26W
62 M2 **Orzyc** *R* Poland
62 N2 **Orzysz** Poland 53.50N 21.58E
52 F4 **Os** Hedmark Norway 62.31N 11.11E
53 S18 **Os** Hordaland Norway 60.11N 5.30E
50 E2 **Ós** Húnavatnssýsla, Austur Iceland 66.02N 20.25W
50 L5 **Ós** Múlasýsla, Sudhur Iceland 64.46N 14.05W
42 G5 **Osa** Irkutsk U.S.S.R. 53.24N 103.55E
52 F5 **Osa** *R* Norway
77 L2 **Osa** *R* Spain
75 E8 **Osa de la Vega** Spain 39.39N 2.46W
108 S6 **Osage** Iowa 43.18N 92.49W
109 O5 **Osage** Oklahoma 36.26N 96.26W
100 O9 **Osage** Saskatchewan 49.57N 103.38W
108 F6 **Osage** Wyoming 43.59N 104.16W
107 D3 **Osage** *R* Missouri
109 P3 **Osage City** Kansas 38.38N 95.50W
107 D4 **Osage Fork** *R* Missouri
20 L6 **Osaka** Gifu Japan 35.57N 137.17E
20 J7 **Ōsaka** Japan 34.40N 135.30E
20 J7 **Ōsaka** *prefect* Japan
43 L2 **Osakarovka** Kazakhstan U.S.S.R. 50.36N 72.32E
20 J7 **Ōsaka-wan** *B* Japan
20 P2 **Ō-saki** *C* Japan 39.14N 141.58E
108 P4 **Osakis** Minnesota 45.51N 95.10W
108 P4 **Osakis** *L* Minnesota
19 N4 **Osakura** *isld* Truk Is Pacific Oc 7.29N 151.54E
115 N5 **Osa,Pen.de** Costa Rica 8.30N 83.30W
50 E3 **Ósar** Iceland 65.37N 20.35E
50 C7 **Ósar** *B* Iceland
53 W17 **Osastølen** Norway 60.35N 7.02E
109 Q3 **Osawatomie** Kansas 38.29N 94.57W
99 E3 **Osawin** *R* Ontario
14 F2 **Osborne Is** W Australia 14.15S 126.00E
52 H9 **Os Bruck** Sweden 57.10N 14.20E
53 Y14 **Osbua** Norway 62.29N 8.30E
53 Z14 **Osbuvatn** *L* Norway 62.28N 8.32E
53 D6 **Øsby** Denmark 55.15N 9.39E
52 H10 **Osby** Sweden 56.24N 14.00E
117 C3 **Oscar** Fr Guiana 2.50N 52.25W
50 S14 **Oscar II Land** *reg* Spitsbergen
117 B9 **Oscar Miranda,Cachoeira** *falls* Brazil 9.20S 56.51W
14 F4 **Oscar Ra** W Australia
107 G6 **Osceola** Arkansas 35.43N 89.58W
108 R8 **Osceola** Iowa 41.02N 93.46W
107 C3 **Osceola** Missouri 38.01N 93.41W
108 N8 **Osceola** Nebraska 41.10N 97.32W
104 G6 **Osceola** Pennsylvania 40.52N 78.17W
106 B4 **Osceola** Wisconsin 45.18N 92.42W
64 P1 **Oschatz** E Germany 51.18N 13.07E
63 O8 **Oschersleben** E Germany 52.02N 11.15E
66 G5 **Oschinen See** *L* Switzerland 46.30N 7.44E
81 C2 **Oschiri** Sardinia 40.43N 9.06E
81 C2 **Oschiri,R.di** Sardinia
64 Q2 **Osck** Czechoslovakia 50.37N 13.42E
106 L5 **Oscoda** Michigan 44.26N 83.20W
109 D8 **Oscuro** New Mexico 33.30N 106.04W
53 U15 **Osdal** Norway 62.00N 6.23E
53 B5 **Øse** Denmark 55.39N 8.40E
53 X21 **Ose** Norway 58.57N 7.40E
85 O9 **Oseif,Marsa** *inlet* Sudan 21.47N 36.48E
76 J2 **Oseja de Sajambre** Spain 43.09N 5.02W
64 Q5 **Oselec** Czechoslovakia 49.26N 13.41E
39 J3 **Oselkino** U.S.S.R. 64.45N 170.08E
52 F2 **Osen** Nord-Tröndelag Norway 64.18N 10.32E
53 T16 **Osen** Sogn og Fjordane Norway 61.22N 5.12E
76 D3 **Osera** Orense Spain 42.33N 7.57W
75 J4 **Osera** Zaragoza Spain 41.32N 0.34W
45 K2 **Osetr** *R* U.S.S.R.
42 H4 **Osetrovo** U.S.S.R. 56.48N 105.53E
20 B9 **Ōse-zaki** *C* Japan 32.36N 128.38E
57 N6 **Osgodby** Lincs Eng 53.26N 0.23W
107 L2 **Osgood** Indiana 39.08N 85.19W
107 C1 **Osgood** Missouri 40.12N 93.21W
99 P7 **Osgoode** Ontario 45.08N 75.37W
110 H8 **Osgood Mts** Nevada
43 L6 **Osh** Kirgiziya U.S.S.R. 40.37N 72.49E
47 L7 **Osha** *R* U.S.S.R.
94 C1 **Oshakati** Namibia 17.47S 15.48E
20 K2 **Oshamanbe** Japan 42.33N 140.22E
13 E4 **O'Shanassy** *R* Queensland
99 M9 **Oshawa** Ontario 43.53N 78.51W
20 P3 **Oshika** Japan 38.16N 141.31E
20 P3 **Oshika-hantō** *pen* Japan 38.23N 141.28E
94 C1 **Oshikango** Namibia 17.25S 15.55E
20 A3 **Oshima** Kanagawa Japan
20 P3 **Ō-shima** *I* Miyagi Japan 38.49N 141.40E
20 G7 **Ō-shima** *isld* Ehime Japan 34.08N 133.05E
20 D8 **Ō-shima** *isld* Fukuoka Japan 33.56N 130.22E
20 N7 **Ō-shima** *isld* Izu-shotō Japan 34.45N 139.25E
20 C8 **Ō-shima** *isld* Nagasaki Japan 33.30N 129.30E
20 H8 **Ō-shima** *isld* Tokushima Japan 33.38N 134.29E
20 J8 **Ō-shima** *isld* Wakayama Japan 33.27N 135.49E
20 E7 **Ō-shima** *isld* Yamaguchi Japan 34.30N 131.24E
20 K2 **Oshima** *sub-prefect* Hokkaido Japan
108 H8 **Oshkosh** Nebraska 41.26N 102.22W
106 F5 **Oshkosh** Wisconsin 44.01N 88.32W
47 H3 **Oshkur'ya** U.S.S.R. 66.04N 56.40E
41 D5 **Oshmarino** U.S.S.R. 71.46N 82.50E
47 J5 **Oshmar'ye** U.S.S.R. 60.02N 63.20E
46 F3 **Oshmyany** Belorussiya U.S.S.R. 54.22N 25.52E
32 A2 **Oshnovīyeh** Iran 37.03N 45.05E
95 O2 **Oshoek** S Africa 26.14S 30.59E
90 B8 **Oshogbo** Nigeria 7.50N 4.35E
108 F5 **Oshoto** Wyoming 44.33N 104.56W
32 C4 **Oshtorān Kūh** *mt* Iran 33.19N 49.18E
32 C3 **Oshtorīnān** Iran 34.01N 48.40E
47 J3 **Oshvor** U.S.S.R. 66.59N 62.59E
91 F5 **Oshwe** Zaïre 3.24S 19.32E
29 C4 **Osian** Rajasthan India 26.46N 72.56E
82 J6 **Osica de Jos** Romania 44.14N 24.20E
81 C2 **Osidda** Sardinia 40.32N 9.14E
79 D6 **Osiglia** Italy 44.17N 8.12E
82 E5 **Osijek** Yugoslavia 45.33N 18.41E
81 B2 **Osilo** Sardinia 40.45N 8.41E
80 H2 **Osimo** Italy 43.28N 13.29E
45 V4 **Osinki** U.S.S.R. 52.52N 49.31E
42 D5 **Osinniki** U.S.S.R. 53.39N 87.22E
42 H6 **Osinovka** Chita U.S.S.R. 50.35N 109.30E
42 G4 **Osinovka** Irkutsk U.S.S.R. 56.08N 101.55E
43 P3 **Osinovka** Kazakhstan U.S.S.R. 49.52N 83.57E
42 D2 **Osinovo** U.S.S.R. 61.26N 89.44E
45 B2 **Osintorf** Belorussiya U.S.S.R. 54.40N 30.39E
46 G3 **Osipovichi** Belorussiya U.S.S.R. 53.19N 28.36E
87 J7 **Oska** Ethiopia 6.30N 42.01E
51 K3 **Oskal** Norway 68.52N 23.10E
108 S8 **Oskaloosa** Iowa 41.16N 92.40W
109 P2 **Oskaloosa** Kansas 39.14N 95.21W
41 G3 **Oskara,Mys** *C* U.S.S.R. 76.31N 99.01E
52 J9 **Oskarshamn** Sweden 57.16N 16.25E
52 G10 **Oskarström** Sweden 56.48N 13.00E
99 P4 **Oskélanéo** Quebec 48.07N 75.14W
50 J4 **Öskjuvatn** *L* Iceland 65.02N 16.46W
42 G2 **Oskoba** U.S.S.R. 60.20N 100.35E
45 J7 **Oskol** *R* Ukraine U.S.S.R.
65 O3 **Oslava** *R* Czechoslovakia
65 O3 **Oslavany** Czechoslovakia 49.08N 16.20E
100 L6 **Osler** Saskatchewan 52.24N 106.32W
108 N1 **Oslo** Minnesota 48.13N 97.08W
52 F7 **Oslo** Norway 59.56N 10.45E
19 L7 **Oslob** Philippines 9.30N 123.24E
52 E8 **Oslofjord** *inlet* Norway
53 C2 **Øsløs** Denmark 57.02N 9.02E
75 D2 **Osma** Spain 42.52N 3.03W
45 E2 **Os'ma** *R* U.S.S.R.
28 C1 **Osmānābād** Maharashtra India 18.09N 76.06E
28 C1 **Osmānābād** *dist* Maharashtra India
36 H2 **Osmancık** Turkey 40.58N 34.50E
37 H2 **Osmaneli** Turkey 40.22N 30.01E
34 E4 **Osmānīya** Syria 34.53N 37.05E
Osmaniye *see* **Ergani**
36 J5 **Osmaniye** Turkey 37.04N 36.15E
37 C3 **Osmanlar** Turkey 40.06N 26.41E
36 H3 **Osmanpaşa** Turkey 39.56N 34.42E
51 O12 **Os'mino** U.S.S.R. 59.02N 29.05E
52 K8 **Ösmo** Sweden 58.58N 17.55E
108 N7 **Osmond** Nebraska 42.20N 97.35W
12 B8 **Osmond,Mt** Australia 34.58S 138.40E
51 K12 **Osmussaar** *isld* Estonia 59.19N 23.25E
108 M1 **Osnabrock** N Dakota 48.41N 98.09W
63 H8 **Osnabrück** W Germany 52.17N 8.03E
99 R1 **Osnabruck Centre** Ontario 45.03N 75.01W
79 F3 **Osnago** Italy 45.41N 9.23E
62 H3 **Ośno** Poland 52.28N 14.51E
92 C2 **Oso** *R* Zaïre
66 M6 **Osogna** Switzerland 46.18N 8.59E
82 G8 **Osogovska Planina** *mts* Yugoslavia
94 D2 **Osohama** Namibia 18.32S 16.49E
50 G6 **Ósoldur** *mt* Iceland 64.20N 18.50W
94 D4 **Osona** Namibia 22.01S 16.56E
79 O2 **Osoppo** Italy 46.16N 13.05E
75 O4 **Osor** Spain 41.57N 2.34E
20 P1 **Osore-yama** *vol* Japan 41.17N 141.03E
121 J2 **Osório** Brazil 29.53S 50.17W
121 A8 **Osorno** Chile 40.35S 73.14W
76 L4 **Osorno** Spain 42.24N 4.22W
121 A8 **Osorno** *prov* Chile
121 A8 **Osorno** *vol* Chile 41.06S 72.28W
101 O11 **Osoyoos** Br Col 49.02N 119.31W
110 F1 **Osoyoos L** Br Columbia 49.00N 119.28W
53 R16 **Ospa** *isld* Norway 61.12N 4.45E
50 D4 **Ospakseyri** Iceland 65.28N 21.26W
67 P13 **Ospedale,Forêt d'** Corsica 41.40N 9.13E
79 C7 **Ospedaletti** Italy 43.48N 7.43E
79 L4 **Ospedaletto Euganeo** Italy 45.13N 11.37E
60 M14 **Ospel** Netherlands 51.18N 5.46E
53 W13 **Øspetind** *mt* Norway 62.31N 7.15E
101 M7 **Ospika** *R* Br Col
119 E3 **Ospino** Venezuela 9.17N 69.26W
79 M2 **Ospitale** Italy 46.20N 12.20E
79 H3 **Ospitaletto** Italy 45.33N 10.04E
105 E10 **Osprey** Florida 27.12N 82.28W
13 H2 **Osprey Reef** Gt Barrier Reef Australia
60 L12 **Oss** Netherlands 51.46N 5.31E
105 F6 **Ossabaw I** Georgia 31.46N 81.05W
105 F6 **Ossabaw Sd** Georgia 31.51N 81.03W
77 L3 **Ossa de Montiel** Spain 38.58N 2.45W
90 E10 **Ossa L** Cameroon 3.50N 10.07E
12 H8 **Ossa,Mt** Tasmania 41.52S 146.04E
84 E2 **Ossa,Óros** *mts* Greece
76 D11 **Ossa,Sa.d'** *mts* Portugal
90 B8 **Osse** *R* Nigeria
91 D11 **Osse** *watercourse* Angola
52 L7 **Össeby-Garn** Sweden 59.34N 18.15E
72 C10 **Osse-en-Aspe** France 42.59N 0.38W
72 H11 **Ossèja** France 42.25N 1.58E
91 D4 **Ossélé** Congo 1.21S 15.22E
60 F14 **Ossendrecht** Netherlands 51.24N 4.19E
60 C3 **Ossenisse** Netherlands 51.23N 3.59E
60 M8 **Ossenzijl** Netherlands 52.48N 5.55E
106 C5 **Osseo** Wisconsin 44.35N 91.13W
72 B9 **Ossès** France 43.14N 1.17W
57 K5 **Ossett** W Yorks Eng 53.41N 1.35W
81 B2 **Ossi** Sardinia 40.41N 8.36E
65 J8 **Ossiach** Austria 46.41N 13.59E
65 J8 **Ossiacher See** *L* Austria
106 C6 **Ossian** Iowa 43.08N 91.46W
58 G5 **Ossian,L** Highland Scotland 56.47N 4.38W
15 F5 **Ossima** Papua New Guinea 2.58S 141.20E
106 L5 **Ossineke** Michigan 44.55N 83.26W
66 L1 **Ossingen** Switzerland 47.37N 8.43E
57 M6 **Ossington** Notts Eng 53.11N 0.52W
103 G4 **Ossining** New York 41.10N 73.52W
104 O3 **Ossipee L** New Hampshire 43.48N 71.09W
53 Y18 **Ossjøen** *L* Buskerud Norway 60.23N 8.11E
52 F5 **Ossjøen** *L* Hedmark Norway 61.25N 11.55E
63 J8 **Ossning** *hills* W Germany
66 K7 **Ossola, V. d'** Italy
39 G5 **Ossora** U.S.S.R. 59.16N 163.08E
72 D9 **Ossun** France 43.11N 0.02W
91 C3 **Ossyeba** *tribe* Gabon
99 M5 **Ostaboningue,L** Quebec
41 G3 **Ostaro,Poluostrov** *pen* U.S.S.R.
46 J2 **Ostashkov** U.S.S.R. 57.09N 33.10E
45 G1 **Ostashovo** U.S.S.R. 55.52N 35.52E
52 J4 **Östavall** Sweden 62.27N 15.30E
63 G8 **Ost-bevern** W Germany 52.03N 7.51E
53 D5 **Østbirk** Denmark 55.58N 9.45E
52 G5 **Østby** Norway 61.15N 12.32E
63 K5 **Oste** *R* W Germany
53 H5 **Osted** Denmark 55.34N 11.54E
105 F9 **Osteen** Florida 28.51N 81.09W
79 L5 **Ostellato** Italy 44.44N 11.57E
63 K5 **Osten** W Germany 53.42N 9.12E
Ostend *see* **Oostende**
63 K4 **Ostenfeld** W Germany 54.29N 9.13E
63 L7 **Ostenholz** W Germany 52.47N 9.44E
66 N7 **Osteno** Italy 46.01N 9.04E
45 B6 **Oster** Ukraine U.S.S.R. 50.55N 30.53E
45 D2 **Ostër** U.S.S.R. 54.02N 32.49E
45 C6 **Oster** *R* Ukraine U.S.S.R.
45 D3 **Oster** *R* U.S.S.R.
53 B3 **Øster Assels** Denmark 56.43N 8.42E
53 X17 **Østerbø** Norway 60.50N 7.31E
53 C3 **Øster Bølle** Denmark 56.43N 9.28E
53 T16 **Østerbøvatn** *L* Norway 61.05N 5.54E
104 G6 **Osterburg** Pennsylvania 40.11N 78.32W
63 P7 **Osterburg (Altmark)** E Germany 52.48N 11.45E
64 G5 **Osterburken** W Germany 49.25N 9.26E
53 G2 **Østerby** Denmark 57.18N 11.09E
52 K6 **Österbybruk** Sweden 60.13N 17.55E
48 U16 **Østerbygd** *hist reg* Greenland
52 J9 **Österbymo** Sweden 57.49N 15.15E
63 H8 **Ostercappeln** W Germany 52.21N 8.14E
52 H5 **Öster Dalälven** *R* Sweden
52 F4 **Østerdalen** *V* Norway
63 E5 **Osterems** *estuary* W Germany
64 M1 **Osterfeld** E Germany 51.05N 11.57E
53 S17 **Osterfjorden** *inlet* Norway 60.34N 5.26E
53 B6 **Øster Gasse** Denmark 55.10N 8.50E
52 J8 **Östergotland** *dist* Sweden
53 E6 **Øster Hæsinge** Denmark 55.11N 10.19E
63 J4 **Osterhever** W Germany 54.23N 8.44E
64 P6 **Osterhofen** W Germany 48.42N 13.02E
52 G5 **Østerhogna** *mt* Norway 61.43N 12.08E
53 C6 **Øster Højst** Denmark 55.01N 9.03E
63 J6 **Osterholz-Scharmbeck** W Germany 53.14N 8.48E
65 H6 **Osterhorn Gruppe** *mts* Austria
53 D3 **Øster Hornum** Denmark 56.56N 9.46E
103 C4 **Osterhout** Pennsylvania 41.30N 75.54W
53 E3 **Øster-Hurup** Nordjylland Denmark 56.48N 10.17E
53 B2 **Østerild** Denmark 57.02N 8.52E
53 P12 **Østerlars** Bornholm Denmark 55.10N 14.58E
53 C6 **Øster Lindet** Denmark 55.18N 9.08E
53 C6 **Øster Løgum** Denmark 55.07N 9.23E
52 K6 **Österlövsta** Sweden 60.27N 17.45E
53 Q12 **Østermarie** Bornholm Denmark 55.09N 15.02E
64 N8 **Ostermünchen** W Germany 47.56N 12.03E
66 F4 **Ostermundigen** Switzerland 46.58N 7.30E
52 K2 **Öster Noret** Sweden 64.05N 17.20E
53 N9 **Østerø** *isld* Faeroes 62.14N 6.59W
Osterode Poland *see* **Ostróda**
63 M9 **Osterode am Harz** W Germany 51.44N 10.15E
53 T17 **Osterøya** *isld* Norway 60.32N 5.30E
53 C5 **Øster Starup** Denmark 55.37N 9.28E
52 H3 **Östersund** Sweden 63.10N 14.40E
53 C2 **Øster Svenstrup** Denmark 57.06N 9.29E
53 E3 **Øster Tørslev** Denmark 56.35N 10.12E
53 H7 **Øster Ulslev** Denmark 54.42N 11.38E
52 K6 **Östervåla** Sweden 60.11N 17.14E
53 B3 **Øster Vandet** Denmark 57.00N 8.38E
53 B6 **Øster Vedsted** Denmark 55.19N 8.44E
53 D4 **Øster Velling** Denmark 56.26N 9.53E
103 O3 **Osterville** Massachusetts 41.38N 70.23W
53 E2 **Øster Vrå** Denmark 57.21N 10.15E
63 N9 **Osterwieck** E Germany 51.59N 10.43E
64 G6 **Ostfildern** W Germany 48.43N 9.16E
52 F7 **Østfold** *co* Norway
63 E5 **Ostfriesische Inseln** *islds* W Germany
63 F6 **Ostfriesland** *reg* W Germany
63 G6 **Ostgrossefehn** W Germany 53.24N 7.36E
52 L6 **Östhammar** Sweden 60.15N 18.25E
69 N7 **Ostheim** France 48.10N 7.23E
64 J3 **Ostheim** W Germany 50.28N 10.14E
69 P4 **Osthofen** W Germany 49.42N 8.20E
79 G5 **Ostia** Parma Italy 44.31N 9.50E
80 F5 **Ostia** Roma Italy 41.46N 12.18E
79 H4 **Ostiano** Italy 45.13N 10.15E
61 F4 **Ostiches** Belgium 50.41N 3.46E
79 K4 **Ostiglia** Italy 45.04N 11.09E
75 G2 **Ostiz** Spain 42.55N 1.37W
52 G6 **Östmark** Sweden 60.15N 12.45E
53 G7 **Østofte** Denmark 54.48N 11.24E
63 R5 **Ost Peene** *R* E Germany
79 O7 **Ostra** Italy 43.37N 13.09E
64 G8 **Ostrach** W Germany 47.57N 9.24E
52 K8 **Östra Ed** Sweden 57.01N 16.40E
52 G11 **Östra Grevie** Sweden 55.28N 13.10E
52 G10 **Östra Ljungby** Sweden 56.11N 13.05E
104 B6 **Ostrander** Ohio 40.15N 93.14W
52 H10 **Östra Torsås** Sweden 56.45N 14.55E
64 P1 **Ostrau** E Germany 51.12N 13.09E
62 L6 **Ostrava** Czechoslovakia 49.50N 18.15E
79 O7 **Ostra Vetere** Italy 43.36N 13.04E
39 K3 **Ostraya Sopka** *vol* U.S.S.R. 64.36N 175.31E
69 P3 **Östrich-Geisenheim** W Germany 50.00N 8.01E
46 C3 **Ostróda** Poland 53.42N 19.59E
46 F4 **Ostrog** Ukraine U.S.S.R. 50.20N 26.29E
45 L6 **Ostrogozhsk** U.S.S.R. 50.52N 39.03E
45 G2 **Ostrokhnoye** U.S.S.R. 54.50N 35.45E
62 N2 **Ostrołęka** Poland 53.05N 21.32E
99 J5 **Ostrom** Ontario 47.29N 91.37W
64 O3 **Ostrov** Czechoslovakia 50.18N 12.56E
82 L6 **Ostrov** Romania 44.06N 27.24E
46 G2 **Ostrov** U.S.S.R. 57.22N 28.22E
39 F1 **Ostrov Bruseninskiy** U.S.S.R. 67.40N 155.55E
47 L7 **Ostrovnaya** U.S.S.R. 56.24N 72.05E
39 G5 **Ostrovnoy** U.S.S.R. 58.58N 163.57E
39 F7 **Ostrovnoye** Kamchatka U.S.S.R. 53.16N 159.34E
39 G1 **Ostrovnoye** Magadan U.S.S.R. 68.07N 164.13E
41 A3 **Ostrovnoy,Mys** *C* Novaya Zemlya U.S.S.R. 73.37N 53.55E
39 F4 **Ostrovnoy,Mys** *C* U.S.S.R. 60.44N 155.51E
45 Q6 **Ostrovskaya** U.S.S.R. 50.27N 44.26E
62 K4 **Ostrów** Poland 51.39N 17.50E
62 N5 **Ostrowiec** Poland 50.58N 21.22E
62 O4 **Ostrów Lubelski** Poland 51.30N 22.51E
62 N3 **Ostrów Mazowiecki** Poland 52.50N 21.51E
53 C3 **Østrup** Denmark 56.46N 9.30E
64 P5 **Ostrý** *mt* Czechoslovakia 49.12N 13.07E
39 J3 **Ostryak,Gora** *vol* U.S.S.R. 64.31N 171.58E
62 K4 **Ostrzeszów** Poland 51.25N 17.55E
63 Q4 **Ostseebad Ahrenshoop** E Germany 54.24N 12.26E
63 O5 **Ostseebad Boltenhagen** E Germany 54.00N 11.13E
63 Q4 **Ostseebad Dierhagen** E Germany 54.18N 12.22E
63 Q4 **Ostseebad Graal-Müritz** E Germany 54.17N 12.16E
63 P4 **Ostseebad Kühlungsborn** E Germany 54.09N 11.44E
63 P4 **Ostseebad Nienhagen** E Germany 54.10N 11.56E
63 P4 **Ostseebad Rerik** E Germany 54.07N 11.37E
63 Q4 **Ostseebad Wustrow** E Germany 54.22N 12.24E
65 F7 **Ost Tirol** *prov* Austria
81 Q11 **Ostuni** Italy 40.44N 17.35E
45 F1 **Osuga** U.S.S.R. 56.02N 34.17E
46 J2 **Osuga** *R* U.S.S.R.
110 F3 **O'Sullivan Dam** Washington 46.59N 119.17W
99 C2 **O'Sullivan L** Ontario
99 P5 **O'Sullivan L** Quebec 47.34N 75.59W
83 D4 **Osum** *R* Albania
82 J7 **Osŭm** *R* Bulgaria
20 D10 **Ōsumi-hantō** *pen* Japan
21 E12 **Ōsumi-Kaiky** *str* Japan
21 E12 **Ōsumi-shotō** *islds* Kagoshima Japan
77 F6 **Osuna** Spain 37.14N 5.06W
47 H3 **Osvan'** U.S.S.R. 66.02N 57.50E
46 G2 **Osveya** Belorussiya U.S.S.R. 55.59N 28.08E
46 G2 **Osveyskoye Oz** *L* Belorussiya U.S.S.R.
57 L4 **Oswaldkirk** N Yorks Eng 54.12N 1.03W
104 G5 **Oswayo** Pennsylvania 41.56N 78.03W
104 K2 **Oswegatchie** *R* New York
106 F8 **Oswego** Illinois 41.41N 88.21W
109 P4 **Oswego** Kansas 37.11N 95.10W
108 E1 **Oswego** Montana 48.04N 105.52W
104 J3 **Oswego** New York 43.27N 76.31W
104 J3 **Oswego** *R* New York
56 E2 **Oswestry** Shropshire Eng 52.52N 3.04W
62 L5 **Oświęcim** Poland 50.02N 19.11E
107 F10 **Osyka** Mississippi 31.01N 90.29W
20 N5 **Ōta** Gumma Japan 36.18N 139.20E
20 O5 **Ōta** Ibaraki, Honshu Japan 36.34N 140.30E
20 E3 **Ōta** *dist* Tōkyō Japan
20 F7 **Ōta** *R* Japan
20 F7 **Ōta-gawa** *R* Honshu Japan
11 D12 **Otago** *stat area* New Zealand
11 M12 **Otago Harb** *inlet* New Zealand
11 E12 **Otago Pen** New Zealand
11 D3 **Otahuhu** New Zealand 36.56S 174.52E
11 F11 **Otaio** New Zealand 44.36S 171.10E
20 F7 **Ōtake** Japan 34.14N 132.12E
11 J6 **Otakeho** New Zealand 39.31S 174.03E
20 M6 **Ōtaki** Japan 35.57N 138.52E
11 K7 **Otaki** New Zealand 40.45S 175.09E
20 O4 **Ōtakine-yama** *mt* Japan 37.22N 140.42E
11 O12 **Otakou** New Zealand 45.48S 170.43E
11 L6 **Otane** New Zealand 39.56S 176.39E
11 L4 **Otanewainuku** *mt* New Zealand 37.53S 176.12E
51 N7 **Otanmäki** Finland 64.07N 27.06E
26 R5 **Otappuwa** Sri Lanka 8.10N 80.15E
43 M5 **Otar** Kazakhstan U.S.S.R. 43.30N 75.13E
119 D7 **Otare,Cerro** *mt* Colombia 1.44N 72.44W
20 K1 **Otaru** Japan 43.14N 140.59E
11 C13 **Otatara** New Zealand 46.26S 168.18E
11 B13 **Otautau** New Zealand 46.10S 168.00E
65 K3 **Otava** *R* Czechoslovakia
119 B7 **Otavalo** Ecuador 0.13N 78.15W
94 D2 **Otavi** Namibia 19.39S 17.20E
20 O5 **Ōtawara** Japan 36.52N 140.01E
91 C12 **Otchinjau** Angola 16.30S 13.57E
39 G7 **Otdel'naya Gora** *mt* Kamchatka U.S.S.R. 54.50N 161.43E
13 D3 **O.T. Downs** N Terr Aust 16.28S 135.10E
39 D4 **Otechestvennyy** U.S.S.R. 61.50N 146.39E
61 D3 **Otegem** Belgium 50.48N 3.26E
103 D2 **Otego** New York 42.53N 75.10W
103 D1 **Otego Cr** New York
75 G2 **Oteiza** Spain 42.37N 1.57W
11 E11 **Otekaieke** New Zealand 44.50S 170.34E
82 F5 **Otelec** Romania 45.36N 20.50E
11 E11 **Otematata** New Zealand 44.37S 170.16E
66 F8 **Otemma,Glacier d'** Switzerland
75 D1 **Oteo** Spain 43.00N 3.19W
46 F1 **Otepää** Estonia U.S.S.R. 58.01N 26.30E
61 L4 **Oteppe** Belgium 50.35N 5.08E
11 B5 **Oteranga R** New Zealand
60 Q6 **Oterdum** Netherlands 53.18N 7.00E
60 H9 **Oterleek** Netherlands 52.38N 4.50E
76 E2 **Otero** Spain 43.15N 7.25W
76 G5 **Otero de Bodas** Spain 41.56N 6.09W
76 D2 **Otero de Rey** Spain 43.06N 7.36W
56 M5 **Otford** Kent Eng 51.19N 0.12E
22 D3 **Otgon** Mongolia 47.08N 97.34E
69 J5 **Othain** *R* France
61 M4 **Othée** Belgium 50.43N 5.28E
69 F7 **Othe,Forêt d'** France
110 F3 **Othello** Washington 46.50N 119.10W
52 L9 **Othem** Sweden 57.45N 18.45E
60 C3 **Othene** Netherlands 51.20N 3.52E
101 U6 **Otherside R** Saskatchewan
56 F5 **Othery** Somerset Eng 51.05N 2.53W
15 K6 **Othlien Reef** Bismarck Arch 4.31S 148.46E
66 J2 **Othmarsingen** Switzerland 47.24N 8.14E
83 C5 **Othonoí** *isld* Greece 39.52N 19.22E
84 E3 **Óthris, Óros** *mts* Greece
19 A4 **Oti** Celebes Indon 0.30S 119.47E
89 K7 **Oti** *R* Ghana
115 G5 **Otinapa** Mexico 24.02N 105.00W
11 F9 **Otira** New Zealand 42.49S 171.34E
109 H1 **Otis** Colorado 40.09N 102.58W
109 L3 **Otis** Kansas 38.32N 99.03W
103 H2 **Otis** Massachusetts 42.12N 73.07W
104 J4 **Otisco L** New York 42.52N 76.17W
98 B1 **Otish Mts** Quebec
103 H2 **Otis Res** Massachusetts 42.09N 73.03W
103 E4 **Otisville** New York 41.28N 74.33W
77 J7 **Otivar** Spain 36.49N 3.40W
94 B1 **Otjewise** Namibia 17.40S 13.26E
94 C2 **Otjikondo** Namibia 19.50S 15.23E
94 B2 **Otjikuju** Namibia 18.05S 13.34E
94 D4 **Otjimbingwe** Namibia 22.19S 16.10E
94 D3 **Otjisazu** Namibia 21.58S 17.09E
94 C2 **Otjitambi** Namibia 19.48S 15.10E
94 D3 **Otjitasu** Namibia 20.29S 16.36E
94 C2 **Otjitundua** Namibia 18.37S 14.08E
94 E2 **Otjituuo** Namibia 19.40S 18.32E
94 C2 **Otjiverongo** Namibia 18.58S 14.12E
94 D3 **Otjiwarongo** Namibia 20.29S 16.36E
94 C2 **Otjokavare** Namibia 19.05S 14.22E
94 E2 **Otjomavare** Namibia 19.54S 18.23E
94 D3 **Otjosundu** Namibia 21.19S 17.51E
94 E3 **Otjozonjou, Omuramba** *watercourse* Namibia
45 O4 **Otkhozheye** U.S.S.R. 52.05N 42.04E
40 C2 **Otkrytyy** U.S.S.R. 58.14N 124.53E
57 K5 **Otley** W Yorks Eng 53.54N 1.41W
40 G4 **Otlichitel'nyy,Mys** *C* U.S.S.R. 55.46N 137.04E
52 F5 **Otnes** Norway 61.46N 11.10E
20 K2 **Otobe-dake** *mt* Japan 42.02N 140.16E
91 K4 **Otobo** Zaïre 1.06S 27.14E
120 C6 **Otoca** Peru 14.30S 74.40W
82 C6 **Otočac** Yugoslavia 44.52N 15.12E
108 O9 **Otoe** Nebraska 40.46N 96.08W
20 N1 **Otofuke** Japan 43.02N 143.10E
20 M1 **Otofuke-gawa** *R* Japan
22 G7 **Otog Qi** Nei Monggol Zizhiqu China 38.54N 107.24E
20 H1 **Otoineppu** Japan 44.41N 142.15E
11 M5 **Otoko** New Zealand 38.28S 177.35E
121 E6 **Otoño** Argentina 37.00S 61.47W
119 B3 **Otoque,I** Panama 8.36N 79.39W
11 K5 **Otorohanga** New Zealand 38.10S 175.14E
87 C5 **Otoro,Jeb** *mt* Sudan 11.05N 30.30E
100 P5 **Otosquen** Saskatchewan 53.19N 102.00W
90 H1 **Otoui** Chad 20.46N 16.36E
44 L3 **Otpan** *mt* Kazakhstan U.S.S.R. 44.14N 51.54E
66 Q5 **Ot,Piz** *mt* Switzerland 46.33N 9.48E
Otpor *see* **Zabaykal'sk**
53 W19 **Otra** *R* Norway
116 B1 **Otrabanda** Curaçao W I 12.12N 68.57W
44 D3 **Otradnaya** U.S.S.R. 44.24N 41.34E
39 E7 **Otradnoye** U.S.S.R. 51.50N 156.31E
43 B1 **Otradnyy** U.S.S.R. 53.26N 51.30E
44 D2 **Otrado Kubanskoye** U.S.S.R. 45.15N 40.51E
81 R12 **Otranto** Italy 40.08N 18.30E
81 R12 **Otranto,C.d'** Italy 40.07N 18.32E
83 C4 **Otranto,Str.of** Italy/Albania
50 B3 **Otrardalur** Iceland 65.39N 23.34W
80 F4 **Otricoli** Italy 42.25N 12.29E
42 E5 **Otrok** U.S.S.R. 54.27N 92.30E
52 C4 **Otrøy** *isld* Norway 62.45N 6.50E
39 J2 **Otrozhnyy** U.S.S.R. 65.10N 173.00E
72 B9 **Otsando, Pto. de** *pass* Spain 43.01N 1.20W
65 M6 **Otscher** *mt* Austria 47.52N 15.13E
106 J7 **Otsego** Michigan 42.26N 85.42W
106 K5 **Otsego L** Michigan
104 L4 **Otsego L** New York
106 K5 **Otsego Lake** Michigan 44.55N 84.41W
94 F4 **Otshwe Pan** *salt pan* Botswana 23.11S 21.00E
41 M5 **Ot-Siyen** U.S.S.R. 71.35N 121.10E
21 J6 **Otsu** Japan 42.39N 143.39E
20 J6 **Ōtsu** Shiga Japan 35.00N 135.50E
20 P2 **Ōtsuchi** Japan 39.22N 141.54E
20 P2 **Ōtsuchi-wan** *B* Japan
20 M6 **Ōtsuki** Japan 35.38N 138.53E
15 E6 **Otsyanep** Irian Jaya 6.01S 138.17E
90 A8 **Otta** Nigeria 6.40N 3.20E
52 E5 **Otta** Norway 61.46N 9.33E
19 N5 **Otta** *isld* Truk Is Pacific Oc 7.10N 151.54E
53 Y15 **Otta** *R* Norway
Ottai Puduk *see* **Pudukkottai**
81 C3 **Ottana** Sardinia 40.14N 9.03E
69 L5 **Ottange** France 49.27N 6.02E
19 N5 **Otta Pass** Truk Is Pacific Oc 7.10N 151.53E
28 C5 **Ottappalam** Kerala India 10.46N 76.23E
28 D6 **Ottappidaram** Tamil Nadu India 8.55N 78.05E
52 G11 **Ottarp** Sweden 55.55N 12.55E
Ottarsstadhir *see* **Straumsvik**
53 Z15 **Ottavatn** *L* Norway 61.51N 8.32E
80 K7 **Ottaviano** Italy 40.51N 14.29E
106 F8 **Ottawa** Illinois 41.21N 88.51W
109 P3 **Ottawa** Kansas 38.35N 95.16W
104 A5 **Ottawa** Ohio 41.02N 84.03W
99 P7 **Ottawa** Ontario 45.25N 75.43W
95 P5 **Ottawa** S Africa 29.40S 31.03E
97 L6 **Ottawa Is** Hudson B, N W Terr
99 M6 **Ottawa R** Quebec/Ontario
99 C9 **Ottawa West** Ontario 45.25N 75.45W
63 K9 **Ottbergen** W Germany 51.43N 9.18E
66 K2 **Ottenbach** Switzerland 47.17N 8.25E
66 N1 **Otten Berg** *mt* Switzerland 47.34N 9.07E
61 J4 **Ottenburg** Belgium 50.45N 4.37E
52 K10 **Ottenby** Sweden 56.15N 16.30E
64 H5 **Ottendorf** W Germany 49.02N 9.45E
63 T10 **Ottendorf-Okrilla** Dresden E Germany 51.10N 13.50E
64 E6 **Ottenhöfen** W Germany 48.34N 8.10E
65 M5 **Ottenschlag** Austria 48.26N 15.14E
65 K5 **Ottensheim** Austria 48.21N 14.11E
63 K9 **Ottenstein** Niedersachsen W Germany 51.57N 9.25E
63 E8 **Ottenstein** Nordrhein-Westfalen W Germany 52.04N 6.55E
108 D4 **Otter** Montana 45.12N 106.10W
106 G9 **Otterbein** Indiana 40.30N 87.04W
64 D4 **Otterberg** W Germany 49.30N 7.47E
56 J5 **Otterbourne** Hants Eng 51.01N 1.21W
57 J2 **Otterburn** Northumb Eng 55.14N 2.10W
108 D4 **Otter Cr** Montana
105 E8 **Otter Creek** Florida 29.20N 82.48W
111 N3 **Otter Creek Res** Utah 38.14N 111.57W
58 F6 **Otter Ferry** Strathclyde Scotland 56.00N 5.20W
64 M8 **Otterfing** W Germany 47.54N 11.41E
99 D4 **Otter I** Ontario 48.06N 86.04W
113 B8 **Otter I** Pribilof Is Bering Sea 57.00N 170.30W
106 L6 **Otter L** Michigan 43.13N 83.27W
100 N3 **Otter L** Saskatchewan
99 L7 **Otter Lake** Ontario 45.19N 79.57W
60 M11 **Otterlo** Netherlands 52.06N 5.46E
63 J5 **Otterndorf** W Germany 53.49N 8.54E
52 F2 **Otterøy** Norway 64.32N 11.18E
95 F6 **Otterpan** *salt pan* S Africa 30.30S 22.51E
56 E6 **Otter,R** Devon Eng
99 J2 **Otter Rapids** Ontario 50.12N 81.40W
63 K6 **Ottersberg** W Germany 53.07N 9.08E
56 K5 **Ottershaw** Surrey Eng 51.22N 0.32W
63 P8 **Ottersleben** E Germany 52.06N 11.35E
58 Q8 **Otterswick** Shetland Scotland 60.33N 1.03W
58 T11 **Otters Wick** *B* Orkney Scotland 59.17N 2.32W
108 O3 **Otter Tail** *R* Minnesota
108 P3 **Otter Tail L** Minnesota
53 E5 **Otterup** Denmark 55.31N 10.25E
56 C6 **Ottery,R** Cornwall Eng
56 E6 **Ottery St.Mary** Devon Eng 50.45N 3.17W
100 P7 **Otthon** Saskatchewan 51.05N 102.38W
79 D4 **Ottiglio** Italy 45.03N 8.20E
61 J4 **Ottignies** Belgium 50.40N 4.34E
81 D2 **Ottiolo,Pta.d'** Sardinia 40.45N 9.44E
69 O8 **Ottmarsheim** France 47.47N 7.31E
112 L4 **Otto** Texas 31.27N 96.49W
108 B5 **Otto** Wyoming 44.25N 108.15W
92 D9 **Otto Beit** Zimbabwe/Zambia 15.59S 28.56E
64 J8 **Ottobeuren** W Germany 47.56N 10.19E
64 M7 **Ottobrunn** W Germany 48.03N 11.40E
97 L1 **Otto Fd** N W Terr
41 M8 **Ottokh** U.S.S.R. 64.38N 123.54E
60 H12 **Ottoland** Netherlands 51.53N 4.54E
15 H6 **Otto,Mt** Papua New Guinea 5.59S 145.28E
79 F5 **Ottone** Italy 44.38N 9.19E
95 K2 **Ottosdal** S Africa 26.48S 26.00E
95 K1 **Ottoshoop** S Africa 25.45S 25.59E
104 A6 **Ottoville** Ohio 40.57N 84.23W
69 N7 **Ottrott** France 48.27N 7.24E
43 M6 **Ottuk** Kirgiziya U.S.S.R. 41.38N 75.53E
108 S8 **Ottumwa** Iowa 41.02N 92.26W
108 J5 **Ottumwa** S Dakota 44.16N 101.21W
64 C5 **Ottweiler** W Germany 49.24N 7.10E
93 E4 **Otuboi** Uganda 1.55N 33.18E
100 K2 **Otukamamoan L** Ontario 48.58N 92.50W
121 E1 **Otumpa** Argentina 27.20S 62.16W
90 B7 **Otunbede** Nigeria 8.02N 5.55E
77 J6 **Otura** Spain 37.05N 3.38W
11 D12 **Oturehua** New Zealand 45.01S 169.55E
90 D8 **Oturkpo** Nigeria 7.16N 8.16E
9 U13 **Otu Tolu Grp** *islds* Tonga, Pacific Oc
120 F8 **Otuyo** Bolivia 19.28S 65.15W
120 A2 **Otuzco** Peru 7.54S 78.35W
104 B8 **Otway** Ohio 38.52N 83.12W
121 J9 **Otway,B** Chile
12 G7 **Otway,C** Victoria 38.51S 143.34E
121 K9 **Otway,Seno** *gulf* Chile
62 N3 **Otwock** Poland 52.05N 21.19E
91 C12 **Otyabikwa** *tribe* Angola
82 J2 **Otynya** U.S.S.R. 48.44N 24.51E
65 C7 **Ötz** Austria 47.13N 10.54E
64 A1 **Otzenrath** W Germany 51.05N 6.28E
65 C7 **Ötz tal** *V* Austria
65 C7 **Ötztaler Ache** *R* Austria
65 C8 **Ötztaler Alpen** *mts* Austria
89 E8 **Oua** Ivory Coast 7.31N 8.10W
9 T12 **O'ua** *atoll* Tonga, Pacific Oc 20.01S 174.44W
88 J7 **Oua Belli** Morocco 29.14N 8.38W
107 C7 **Ouachita** *R* Arkansas
107 D9 **Ouachita** *R* Louisiana
107 C7 **Ouachita,L** Arkansas 34.34N 93.25W
107 B7 **Ouachita Mts** Okla/Arkansas
89 D1 **Ouadane** Mauritania 20.58N 11.30W
90 L7 **Ouadda** Cent Afr Rep 8.09N 22.20E
90 K8 **Ouadda** *tribe* Cent Afr Rep
90 K5 **Ouaddai** *dist* Chad
35 E1 **Ouâdi Jilou** Lebanon 33.15N 38.18E
89 J5 **Ouagadougou** Upper Volta 12.20N 1.40W
89 H5 **Ouahigouya** Upper Volta 13.31N 2.20W
88 L8 **Ouahila** *tribe* Algeria
Ouahran *see* **Oran** Algeria
90 J9 **Ouaka** *dist* Cent Afr Rep
9 R12 **Ouaka** *isld* Tonga, Pacific Oc 18.44S 174.07W
90 K9 **Ouaka** *R* Cent Afr Rep
90 H9 **Ouakama** Cent Afr Rep 5.00N 17.06E
89 E5 **Ouakaro** Mali 13.20N 9.45W
89 L4 **Oualam** Niger 14.23N 2.09E
90 H1 **Oualaséna** Chad 22.06N 16.28E
89 F3 **Oualata** Mauritania 17.15N 6.55W
88 J5 **Oualidia** Morocco 32.44N 9.08W
88 O9 **Ouallene Bordj** Algeria 24.37N 1.13E
117 C2 **Ouanary** Fr Guiana 4.11N 51.40W
90 L9 **Ouanda** Cent Afr Rep 5.16N 23.00E
90 L7 **Ouanda-Djallé** Cent Afr Rep 8.55N 22.53E
90 M8 **Ouando** Cent Afr Rep 6.01N 26.00E
90 L8 **Ouango** Cent Afr Rep 6.06N 23.11E
90 L9 **Ouango** Cent Afr Rep 4.19N 22.30E
71 C1 **Ouanne** France 47.39N 3.24E
69 E8 **Ouanne** *R* France
88 S8 **Ouan Taredert** Algeria 27.38N 9.28E
90 G8 **Ouantonou** Cent Afr Rep 7.19N 15.18E
88 P9 **Oua-n-Tourna** Algeria 24.31N 2.50E
103 C2 **Ouaquaga** New York 42.08N 75.40W
117 C3 **Ouaqui** Fr Guiana 3.30N 53.58W
117 C3 **Ouaqui** *R* Fr Guiana
89 D1 **Ouarane** *reg* Mauritania
99 Q6 **Ouareau, L** Quebec 46.17N 74.10W
89 K6 **Ouargaye** Upper Volta 11.39N 0.04E
88 Q6 **Ouargla** Algeria 32.00N 5.16E
89 F4 **Ouarho** Mali 14.11N 7.36W
89 L7 **Ouari Maro** Benin 9.11N 2.11E
88 J7 **Ouarkziz,Jbel** *mts* Morocco
Ouar,Ouâdi el *see* **Wa'r,Wadi** *water course*
90 M9 **Ouarra** *R* Cent Afr Rep
70 O5 **Ouarville** France 48.21N 1.47E
88 K6 **Ouarzazate** Morocco 30.57N 6.50W
90 J2 **Ouassar** Chad 18.51N 19.56E
Ouâssett *see* **Wâsit**
89 C6 **Ouassou** Guinea 10.04N 13.40W
89 K3 **Ouassouas** Mali 16.09N 1.23E
89 C3 **Ouasta,El** Mauritania 17.42N 13.49W
90 D5 **Ouatcha** Niger 13.22N 9.18E
89 E6 **Oubala** Guinea 10.21N 8.17W
91 F1 **Oubangui** *R* Congo/Cent Afr Rep
71 G2 **Ouche** *R* France
66 C5 **Ouchy** Switzerland 46.31N 6.38E
70 N6 **Oucques** France 47.50N 1.19E
60 G12 **Oud-Alblas** Netherlands 51.52N 4.42E
60 O9 **Oud-Avereest** Netherlands 52.37N 6.24E
60 F12 **Oud-Beijerland** Netherlands 51.50N 4.25E
60 C1 **Ouddorp** Netherlands 51.49N 3.56E
60 L6 **Oude-Bildtzijl** Netherlands 53.18N 5.43E
60 L8 **Oudega** Netherlands 53.00N 5.33E
60 M7 **Oudega** Netherlands 53.07N 6.00E
61 G2 **Oudegem** Belgium 51.01N 4.04E
60 M8 **Oudehaske** Netherlands 52.57N 5.52E
63 D9 **Oude Ijssel** *R* Netherlands
89 J3 **Oudeïka** Mali 17.30N 1.40W
60 C3 **Oudelande** Netherlands 51.24N 3.51E
60 F12 **Oude Maas** *R* Netherlands
61 E3 **Oudenaarde** Belgium 50.50N 3.37E
61 G3 **Oudenaken** Belgium 50.47N 4.12E
60 G13 **Oudenbosch** Netherlands 51.35N 4.32E
61 C2 **Oudenburg** Belgium 51.11N 3.01E
60 R7 **Oude Pekela** Netherlands 53.06N 7.00E
60 G11 **Oude Rijn** *R* Netherlands
60 H10 **Ouderkerk** Netherlands 52.18N 4.54E
60 G12 **Ouderkerk aan den Ijssel** Netherlands 51.52N 4.38E
60 L8 **Oudermirdum** Netherlands 52.51N 5.31E
88 T5 **Ouderna** *tribe* Tunisia
60 R7 **Oudeschans** Netherlands 53.08N 7.08E
60 H7 **Oudeschild** Texel Netherlands 53.02N 4.51E
60 M8 **Oudeschoot** Netherlands 52.56N 5.57E
60 H8 **Oudesluis** Netherlands 52.50N 4.48E
60 E13 **Oude Tonge** Netherlands 51.41N 4.14E
60 H11 **Oudewater** Netherlands 52.02N 4.54E
60 G11 **Oude Wetering** Netherlands 52.13N 4.39E
60 F13 **Oud Gastel** Netherlands 51.35N 4.28E
61 J3 **Oud-Heverlee** Belgium 50.50N 4.40E
88 R6 **Oudje** *reg* Algeria
88 O11 **Oudjiechit** Mali 20.22N 1.02E
60 H9 **Oudkarspel** Netherlands 52.43N 4.47E
60 M6 **Oudkerk** Netherlands 53.17N 5.53E
60 K11 **Oud-Leusden** Netherlands 52.08N 5.22E
60 O9 **Oudleusen** Netherlands 52.32N 6.19E
60 J11 **Oud-Loosdrecht** Netherlands 52.13N 5.05E
70 H7 **Oudon** France 47.22N 1.15W
70 J6 **Oudon** *R* France
60 Q9 **Oud-Schoonebeck** Netherlands 52.40N 6.53E
95 F9 **Oudtshoorn** S Africa 33.35S 22.12E
61 K1 **Oud-Turnhout** Belgium 51.19N 4.59E
60 E13 **Oud Vossemeer** Netherlands 51.34N 4.12E
88 R3 **Oued Athménia** Algeria 36.14N 6.15E
88 R4 **Oued el Abiod, Canyon de l'** Algeria
77 F10 **Oued Laou** Morocco 35.27N 5.06W
88 O4 **Oued Rhiou** Algeria 35.55N 0.56E
88 O3 **Oued Sly** Algeria 36.05N 1.11E
74 H9 **Oued Taria** Algeria 35.06N 0.05E
88 N4 **Oued Tlélat** Algeria 35.34N 0.25W
88 K5 **Oued Zem** Morocco 32.55N 6.33W
88 R3 **Oued Zenati** Algeria 36.19N 7.10E
9 A13 **Ouegoa** New Caledonia 20.20S 164.35E
90 K3 **Oueïta** Chad 17.47N 20.39E
89 C7 **Ouelia** Guinea 9.47N 12.44W
89 G8 **Ouéllé** Ivory Coast 7.26N 4.01W
89 L7 **Ouémé** *R* Benin
9 C14 **Ouen** *isld* New Caledonia 22.25S 166.51E
74 J9 **Ouerk** *R* Algeria
88 L4 **Ouerrha** *R* Morocco
66 B1 **Ouers** France 47.44N 6.25E
70 A5 **Ouessant, I.d'** France 48.28N 5.05W
91 E3 **Ouesso** Congo 1.38N 16.03E
89 E8 **Ouest** *dept* Ivory Coast
90 E9 **Ouest** *reg* Cameroon
26 P15 **Ouest, I. de l'** Kerguelen Ind Oc 49.26S 68.40E
26 N15 **Ouest, Pte** *C* St Paul I Ind Oc 38.44S 77.30E
88 L4 **Ouezzane** Morocco 34.52N 5.35W
61 M5 **Ouffet** Belgium 50.27N 5.28E
89 B4 **Ouga** Senegal 15.48N 14.10W
89 K5 **Ougarou** Upper Volta 12.11N 0.58E
88 M7 **Ougarta** Algeria 29.40N 2.13W
59 D5 **Oughterard** Galway Irish Rep 53.26N 9.19W
59 H4 **Oughter, L** Cavan Irish Rep 54.00N 7.29W
88 L6 **Ougnate, Jbel** *mts* Morocco
71 H2 **Ougney** France 47.14N 5.41E
91 A4 **Ogooué-Maritime** *reg* Gabon
61 N4 **Ougrée** Belgium 50.36N 5.32E
90 H8 **Ouham** *dist* Cent Afr Rep
90 H8 **Ouham** *R* Cent Afr Rep
90 G8 **Ouham Pende** *div* Cent Afr Rep
66 B4 **Ouhans** France 47.00N 6.18E
90 H2 **Ouichi** Chad 18.54N 17.44E
89 L8 **Ouidah** Benin 6.23N 2.08E
90 F4 **Ouidi** Niger 14.10N 13.00E
100 P1 **Ouimet** Ontario 48.43N 88.35W
70 K3 **Ouistreham** France 49.16N 0.15W
88 L5 **Ouizert** Morocco 32.54N 4.04W
89 F3 **Oujaf** Mauritania 17.51N 7.51W
88 N4 **Oujda** Morocco 34.41N 1.45W
89 C1 **Oujeft** Mauritania 20.05N 13.00W
88 M5 **Oulad el Haj** *tribe* Morocco

88 P5 Oulad Nail *tribe* Algeria
88 P4 Oulad-Nail, Monts des Algeria
88 J7 Oulad Noumer Morocco 29.55N 9.45W
88 R5 Oulad Saia *tribe* Algeria
88 O7 Oulad Said Algeria 29.30N 0.14E
88 O5 Oulad Sidi Cheikh *tribe* Algeria
88 P9 Oulahoum Algeria 25.05N 3.05E
51 L7 Oulainen Finland 64.17N 24.50E
72 G2 Oulches France 46.36N 1.19E
69 E5 Oulchy-le-Château France 49.12N 3.22E
89 M3 Ouled Areres Niger 16.05N 5.00E
88 Q4 Ouled Djellal Algeria 34.25N 5.02E
88 O7 Ouled Mahmoud Algeria 28.36N 0.01E
88 R3 Ouled Rahmoun Algeria 36.12N 6.43E
88 K5 Oulmès Morocco 33.28N 6.02W
57 G3 Oulton Cumbria Eng 54.51N 3.10W
57 L5 Oulton W Yorks Eng 53.45N 1.27W
51 L6 Oulu Finland 65.00N 25.26E
51 M7 Oulu *dist* Finland
51 N7 Ouluјärvi *L* Finland
51 M6 Oulujoki Finland 65.01N 25.35E
51 M7 Oulujoki *R* Finland
51 L7 Oulunsalo Finland 64.56N 25.20E
79 A4 Oulx Italy 45.02N 6.50E
90 K3 Oum Arche *watercourse* Chad
88 H9 Oumat el Ham *hills* Mauritania
90 L3 Oum Bao *watercourse* Chad
90 K4 Oum Chalouba Chad 15.47N 20.40E
88 J7 Oum Chemel *plat* Algeria/Morocco
90 K3 Oum Dougouro *watercourse* Chad
88 T3 Oum Douil Tunisia 36.44N 10.50E
89 G8 Oumé Ivory Coast 6.25N 5.23W
Oum el Aamad *see* Umm el 'Amad
90 K3 Oum el Adam Chad 17.35N 21.00E
88 L10 Oum el Asell Mali 23.30N 4.45W
88 R4 Oum el Bouaghi Algeria 35.51N 7.09E
88 L8 Oum el Guedour Algeria 27.10N 5.34W
89 G1 Oum el Jeim Mali 21.32N 4.53W
88 J6 Oumenast Morocco 31.27N 8.05W
88 K5 Oum Er Rbia *R* Morocco
90 J5 Oum Hadjer Chad 13.13N 19.37E
90 K3 Oum Hadjer *watercourse* Chad
90 K4 Oum Hawach *watercourse* Chad
90 K3 Oum Kandor *watercourse* Chad
90 K3 Oum Kochili *watercourse* Chad
90 K3 Oum Kordi *watercourse* Chad
Oumm el Mayadine *see* Umm el Mayadin
Oumm el Qoussour *see* Umm el Qusur
88 H10 Oum Mouchiaf Mauritania 22.16N 10.34W
89 D2 Oumoulaoutigat Mauritania 18.31N 10.29W
85 D8 Oumr, El Niger 22.29N 12.29E
90 K3 Oum Sala *watercourse* Chad
25 G2 Ou, Nam *R* Laos
88 R9 Ounane, Djebel *mt* Algeria 25.02N 7.19E
88 J6 Ounara Morocco 31.27N 9.46W
51 K3 Ounasjärvi *L* Finland 68.24N 23.40E
51 L3 Ounasjoki *R* Finland
51 K3 Ounastunturi *mt* Finland 68.16N 23.50E
56 L3 Oundle Northants Eng 52.29N 0.29W
89 L6 Ouné Benin 11.09N 2.30E
90 J1 Ounga *watercourse* Chad
108 G1 Oungre Saskatchewan 49.09N 103.49W
90 K2 Ounianga *reg* Chad
90 K2 Ounianga Kébir Chad 19.05N 20.29E
90 K2 Ounianga Sérir Chad 18.54N 20.50E
90 K3 Ounissoui Baba Niger 17.34N 12.13E
89 F5 Ouo Mali 12.19N 6.22W
89 H6 Ouo Upper Volta 10.27N 3.51W
89 F6 Ouola Mali 11.40N 6.37W
89 E4 Ouosseboubou-Bambara Mali 14.47N 8.04W
89 G8 Ouossou Ivory Coast 6.16N 5.01W
61 N4 Oupeye Belgium 50.42N 5.39E
95 G8 Oupias S Africa 32.23S 23.48E
21 D1 Oupu Heilongjiang China 52.47N 126.01E
61 P7 Our *R* Luxembourg
76 D5 Oura Portugal 41.36N 7.33W
76 E3 Oural Spain 42.43N 7.27W
89 N2 Ourarene Niger 19.31N 7.11E
20 Q9 Oura-wan *B* Okinawa Japan 26.32N 128.04E
109 C3 Ouray Colorado 38.02N 107.40W
110 Q9 Ouray Utah 40.06N 109.40W
69 H8 Ource *R* France
69 E5 Ourcq *R* France
53 F6 Oure Denmark 55.08N 10.43E
117 E5 Ourém Brazil 1.31S 47.05W
90 J1 Ouri Chad 21.28N 19.17E
89 H6 Ouri Upper Volta 11.59N 3.01W
117 G8 Ouricuri Brazil 7.51S 40.05W
117 G9 Ouricuri *R* Brazil
77 G10 Ouringa *R* Morocco
118 E8 Ourinhos Brazil 23.00S 49.54W
76 C13 Ourique Portugal 37.38N 8.13W
88 Q4 Ourlal Algeria 34.38N 5.25E
117 E9 Ouro Brazil 8.15S 46.15W
118 F8 Ouro Fino Brazil 22.16S 46.25W
89 G4 Ouro Modi Mali 14.16N 4.38W
89 G4 Ouro Ndia Mali 15.08N 4.36W
76 D8 Ourondo Portugal 40.08N 7.41W
118 G7 Ouro Prêto Brazil 20.25S 43.30W
117 F4 Ouro Prêto, R Brazil
95 P8 Ouro, Pt do Mozambique 26.52S 32.55E
118 F2 Ouro, R Bahia Brazil
118 D3 Ouro, R Goiás Brazil
89 C4 Ouro Sagui Senegal 15.38N 13.18W
72 K2 Ourouer-le-Bourdelins France 46.56N 2.46E
Ouroum es Sorha *see* Urum es Sughra
91 A4 Ourougou *tribe* Gabon
71 D2 Ouroux-en-Morvan France 47.12N 3.56E
122 C12 Ourtara Tahiti Pacific Oc 17.46S 149.24W
61 N6 Ourthe *R* Belgium
70 M2 Ourville France 49.43N 0.31E
12 H8 Ouse Tasmania 42.38S 146.38E
56 N6 Ouse, R E Sussex Eng
56 M2 Ouse, R Norfolk etc Eng
57 L5 Ouse, R N Yorks Eng
56 M3 Ouse R., Little Norfolk etc Eng
Ousse *see* Idron-Lée-Ousse-Sendets
71 B1 Ousson-sur-Loire France 47.36N 2.46E
72 G10 Oust France 42.52N 1.13E
72 E5 Oust *R* France
60 J9 Oostwood Netherlands 52.44N 5.05E
76 B12 Outão Portugal 38.29N 8.57W
98 D4 Outardes Quatre Dam Quebec 49.38N 68.56W
98 D4 Outardes, R. aux Quebec
98 D4 Outardes Trois Dam Quebec 49.35N 68.50W
69 C7 Outarville France 48.13N 2.01E
88 M5 Outat-Oulad El Haj Morocco 33.11N 3.40W
117 F5 Outeiro Brazil 1.59S 44.31W
76 D5 Outeiro Portugal 41.47N 7.58W
76 F5 Outeiro Portugal 41.40N 6.37W
76 C5 Outeiro Sêco Portugal 41.46N 7.27W
95 F9 Outeniekwaberge *mts* S Africa
61 G3 Outer Belgium 50.51N 4.00E
54 B2 Outer Bailey or Lousy Bank N Atlantic Oc
12 A7 Outer Harbour *inlet* S Australia
58 A4 Outer Hebrides *islds* Scotland
98 O2 Outer I Quebec 51.10N 58.30W
106 D2 Outer I Wisconsin 47.03N 90.28W
111 F8 Outer Santa Barbara Chan California
54 M8 Outer Silver Pit North Sea
76 B3 Outes Spain 42.52N 8.55W
88 E9 Outfene Mauritania 17.25N 8.37W
61 K3 Outgaarden Belgium 50.46N 4.55E
57 J4 Outhgill Cumbria Eng 54.25N 2.19W
94 D3 Outjo Namibia 20.08S 16.08E
108 F1 Outlook Montana 48.55N 104.45W
100 K7 Outlook Saskatchewan 51.30N 107.03W
11 B6 Outlook Hill New Zealand 41.19S 174.39E
51 O9 Outokumpu Finland 62.43N 29.05E
88 Q10 Outoul Algeria 23.00N 5.27E
11 E12 Outram New Zealand 45.52S 170.14E
69 E5 Outreau France 50.42N 1.36E
61 M4 Outrelouxhe Belgium 50.30N 5.20E
99 S9 Outremont Quebec 45.32N 73.37W
61 G3 Outrijve Belgium 50.45N 3.26E
58 R9 Out Skerries *islds* Shetland Scotland 60.25N 0.46W
56 M2 Outwell Norfolk Eng 52.37N 0.14E
9 C13 Ouvéa / Loyalty Is Pacific Oc 20.25S 166.39E
72 K9 Ouveillan France 43.17N 2.59E
61 B8 Ouvèze *R* France
76 F2 Ouviaño Spain 43.07N 6.55W
61 E3 Ouwegem Belgium 50.55N 3.36E
60 C2 Ouwerkerk Netherlands 51.38N 3.59E
12 F6 Ouyen Victoria 35.06S 142.22E
113 L8 Ouzinkie Alaska 57.56N 152.30W
70 O6 Ouzouer-le-Marché France 47.55N 1.32E
69 C8 Ouzouer-sur-Loire France 47.46N 2.29E
71 B1 Ouzouer-sur-Trézée France 47.41N 2.41E
88 P12 Ouzzeine, Ad *hills* Mali
36 F2 Ova *R* Ankara Turkey
36 F1 Ova *R* Zonguldak Turkey
67 P13 Ovace, P. d' *mt* Corsica 41.44N 9.16E
37 F5 Ovacık Erzurum Turkey 40.13N 41.02E
36 G6 Ovacık Içel Turkey 36.10N 33.40E
36 H4 Ovacık Niğde Turkey 38.05N 34.51E
37 E6 Ovacık Tunceli Turkey 39.23N 39.13E
36 G6 Ovacık Burun *C* Turkey 36.07N 33.42E
75 E5 Ovada Italy 44.38N 8.38E
36 D6 Ova Gölü *L* Turkey
9 T7 Ovalau *isld* Fiji 17.40S 178.47E
121 B3 Ovalle Chile 30.33S 71.16W
112 H3 Ovalo Texas 32.10N 99.49W
94 C2 Ovamboland *reg* Namibia
110 M2 Ovando Montana 47.01N 113.07W
81 Q12 Ova, Pta. dell *pt* Italy 40.17N 17.31E
75 B7 Ovar Portugal 40.52N 8.38W
79 N2 Ovaro Italy 46.28N 12.02E
15 J2 Ovau I Solomon Is 6.50S 156.00E
45 D3 Ovchinets U.S.S.R. 53.03N 32.30E
53 D3 Ove Denmark 56.42N 9.59E
121 D4 Oveja *pk* Argentina 32.22S 64.52W
119 C3 Ovejas Colombia 9.32N 75.14W
77 G4 Ovejo Spain 38.09N 4.49W
64 D6 Ovelgönne W Germany 53.21N 8.26E
91 C2 Oveng Cameroon 2.20N 12.17E
12 H6 Ovens *R* Victoria
53 Y13 Overås Norway 62.37N 8.08E
60 M12 Overasselt Netherlands 51.46N 5.47E
64 C2 Overath W Germany 50.56N 7.18E
61 F3 Overboelare Belgium 50.46N 3.52E
109 P3 Overbrook Kansas 38.47N 95.34W
99 D8 Overbrook Ontario 45.26N 75.40W
55 G5 Overby Denmark 55.58N 11.25E
53 Y14 Øverdalen Norway 62.20N 8.04E
60 R11 Overdinkel Netherlands 52.14N 7.02E
103 D9 Overfalls Light Ship Delaware 38.49N 75.01W
53 B4 Over Feldborg Denmark 56.21N 8.57E
60 E13 Overflakkee *isld* Netherlands
100 Q5 Overflowing R Man/Sask
100 Q5 Overflowing River Manitoba 53.08N 101.07W
61 S9 Over Heembeek *vill* Bruxelles Belgium
61 P5 Overhespen Belgium 50.47N 5.02E
52 H4 Overhogdal Sweden 62.18N 14.50E
61 J3 Overijse Belgium 50.46N 4.32E
60 O10 Overijssel *prov* Netherlands
53 C6 Over Jerstal Denmark 55.12N 9.19E
51 K5 Överkalix Sweden 66.19N 22.50E
53 C5 Overlade Denmark 56.52N 9.16E
109 Q3 Overland Park Kansas 38.57N 94.41W
103 A8 Overlea Maryland 39.23N 76.31W
60 M13 Overloon Netherlands 51.34N 5.57E
53 C4 Overlund Viborg Denmark 56.27N 9.26E
108 K1 Overly N Dakota 48.41N 100.02W
51 J9 Övermark Finland 62.37N 21.26E
61 F2 Overmere Belgium 51.03N 3.57E
121 B5 Overo *vol* Argentina 34.32S 70.02W
53 W14 Övergya Norway 62.24N 7.13E
61 M2 Overpelt Belgium 51.12N 5.25E
58 G2 Overscaig Highland Scotland 58.10N 4.43W
60 C4 Overslag Netherlands 51.13N 3.54E
56 O2 Overstrand Norfolk Eng 52.56N 1.20E
57 H7 Overton Clwyd Wales 52.58N 2.56W
56 J5 Overton Hants Eng 51.15N 1.15W
108 L9 Overton Nebraska 40.44N 99.32W
111 K5 Overton Nevada 36.34N 114.27W
103 B3 Overton Pennsylvania 41.35N 76.30W
112 N3 Overton Texas 32.18N 94.59W
61 E13 Övertorneå Sweden 66.22N 23.40E
52 J9 Överum Sweden 57.58N 16.20E
51 D5 Över-uman *L* Sweden 66.06N 14.40E
95 O2 Over-Vaal S Africa 26.39S 30.11E
60 G10 Overveen Netherlands 52.23N 4.36E
56 H5 Over Wallop Hants Eng 51.09N 1.35W
56 H2 Over Whitacre Warwicks Eng 52.31N 1.36W
61 L3 Overwinden Belgium 50.45N 5.03E
66 J7 Ovesca *R* Italy
53 A3 Ovesø *L* Denmark 56.53N 8.25E
107 G10 Ovett Mississippi 31.28N 89.03W
60 O10 Ovezande Netherlands 51.26N 3.50E
61 C3 Ovgos *R* Cyprus
84 R14 Ovid Colorado 40.57N 102.24W
109 H1 Ovid Idaho 42.18N 111.23W
110 O7 Ovid Michigan 43.01N 84.21W
106 K6 Ovid New York 42.40N 76.49W
104 J4 Ovidiopol' Ukraine U.S.S.R. 46.18N 30.28E
46 H6 Oviedo Florida 28.41N 81.14W
105 F9 Oviedo Spain 43.21N 5.50W
76 H2 Oviglio Italy 44.52N 8.28E
74 C1 Ovigui *R* Gabon
91 B4 Oviken Sweden 63.00N 14.20E
52 H4 Ovindoli Italy 42.08N 13.31E
80 J4 Ovinishche U.S.S.R. 58.20N 37.00E
46 K1 Ovityimba *tribe* Namibia
94 B1 Ovlinnoy *isld* Azerbaydzhan U.S.S.R. 39.39N 49.26E
93 B3 Ovo Zaïre 2.29N 30.36E
81 C3 Ovodda Sardinia 40.06N 9.10E
22 F3 Ovorhangay *prov* Mongolia
53 X16 Øvre Årdal Norway 61.18N 7.48E
52 C8 Ovrebygd Norway 58.42N 6.10E
53 Y17 Övre Grundsel Sweden 65.42N 20.15E
53 X18 Övre Hein *L* Norway 60.22N 7.51E
53 V20 Øvremoen Norway 59.25N 6.46E
52 L3 Övre Nyland Sweden 63.57N 18.45E
51 J3 Övre Soppero Sweden 68.07N 21.40E
53 U20 Övre Tysdalsvatn *L* Norway 59.10N 6.20E
53 V16 Ovrisdalen *V* Norway 61.02N 6.33E
46 G4 Ovruch Ukraine U.S.S.R. 51.20N 28.50E
52 C8 Ovsdal Norway 58.58N 6.45E
52 G8 Ovsjöbyn Sweden 63.03N 15.55E
53 V17 Øvstedalen Norway 60.57N 6.45E
45 C8 Ovsyanka U.S.S.R. 53.36N 126.54E
53 D3 Ovtrup Denmark 55.43N 8.21E
41 C4 Ovtsyna, Proliv *str* U.S.S.R.
15 L7 Ovulwul New Britain 6.00S 151.00E
25 D5 Owa *R* Irian Jaya
20 H2 Owada Chiba Japan
11 L7 Owahanga New Zealand 40.40S 176.21E
11 D6 Owaka New Zealand 46.29S 169.42E
15 J8 Owalama Ra Papua New Guinea
91 H4 Owamo Zaïre 0.10S 23.32E
20 O1 Owani Japan 40.30N 140.32E
20 O1 Owasco *L* New York
20 K7 Owase Japan 34.03N 136.12E
109 P5 Owasso Oklahoma 36.15N 95.52W
103 D6 Owatonna Minnesota 44.06N 93.10W
104 J4 Owego New York 42.06N 76.16W
103 B2 Owego Cr New York
59 H4 Owel, L W Meath Irish Rep 53.35N 7.23W
64 G6 Owen W Germany 48.35N 9.28E
106 D5 Owen Wisconsin 44.57N 90.34W
14 A3 Owen Anchorage W Australia
91 A3 Owendo Gabon 0.21N 9.29E
59 C3 Owenduff R Mayo Irish Rep
59 F2 Owenea R Donegal Irish Rep
93 E5 Owen Falls Dam Uganda 0.29N 33.11E
26 E5 Owen Fracture Indian Ocean
11 K11 Owenga Chatham Is Pacific Oc 44.01S 176.20W
59 D8 Owen Hill Cork Irish Rep 51.43N 9.15W
25 D7 Owen I Burma
59 C3 Owenine R Mayo Irish Rep
59 C3 Owenmore R Mayo Irish Rep
11 G8 Owen, Mt New Zealand 41.33S 172.33E
11 G8 Owen River New Zealand 41.41S 172.29E
104 B8 Owens W Virginia 38.20N 81.37W
111 F4 Owens *R* California
104 A7 Owensboro Kentucky 37.45N 87.05W
111 G5 Owens L California 36.25N 117.56W
99 K8 Owen Sound Ontario 44.34N 80.56W
99 K8 Owen Sound Ontario
13 C6 Owen Springs N Terr Australia 23.58S 133.25E
15 J8 Owen Stanley Ra Papua New Guinea
106 H3 Owensville Indiana 38.17N 87.41W
107 E3 Owensville Missouri 38.20N 91.30W
107 M3 Owenton Kentucky 38.33N 84.50W
111 F5 Owenyo California 36.41N 118.02W
56 H6 Ower Hants Eng 50.57N 1.32W
89 N7 Owerri Nigeria 5.29N 7.02E
11 K5 Owhango New Zealand 39.00S 175.24E
101 K10 Owikeno L Br Col 51.40N 127.05W
104 B8 Owingsville Kentucky 38.09N 83.46W
64 F5 Owisheim W Germany 49.09N 8.40E
109 F1 Owl Canyon Colorado 40.46N 105.11W
110 O6 Owl Cr Wyoming
108 B6 Owl Creek Mts Wyoming
100 F4 Owl River Alberta 54.53N 111.46W
89 N7 Owo Nigeria 7.10N 5.39E
106 K7 Owosso Michigan 43.00N 84.11W
59 J7 Ow R Wicklow Irish Rep
36 K2 Owrāman *ran* 35.18N 46.12E
32 B3 Owrāman, Kūh-e *mts* Iran/Iraq
63 L4 Owschlag W Germany 54.24N 9.36E
110 J8 Owyhee Nevada 41.58N 116.06W
110 G6 Owyhee Oregon 43.40N 117.16W
110 H6 Owyhee *R* Oregon
110 H6 Owyhee Dam Oregon 43.40N 117.16W
110 G6 Owyhee, L Oregon 43.25N 117.20W
110 J7 Owyhee S. Fork *R* Idaho/Nevada
110 H7 Owyhee, W., Lit *R* Oregon
120 B4 Oxapampa Peru 10.36S 75.25W
50 K5 Oxarfellsjökull *ice cap* Iceland 64.36N 15.20W
52 H5 Oxberg Sweden 61.07N 14.10E
100 P9 Oxbow Saskatchewan 49.16N 102.12W
110 J5 Oxbow Dam Idaho/Oregon 44.58N 116.51W
107 F7 Oxbow *L* Arkansas 34.40N 90.30W
100 J1 Oxdrift Ontario 49.49N 92.59W
52 L8 Oxelösund Sweden 58.40N 17.10E
107 L8 Oxford Alabama 33.35N 85.50W
103 F3 Oxford Connecticut 41.26N 73.08W
110 L7 Oxford Idaho 42.16N 112.01W
106 G9 Oxford Indiana 40.32N 87.18W
106 C8 Oxford Iowa 41.43N 91.47W
109 N4 Oxford Kansas 37.17N 97.12W
107 M4 Oxford Kentucky 38.16N 84.33W
104 J2 Oxford Maine 44.08N 70.32W
104 J8 Oxford Maryland 38.41N 76.10W
103 F2 Oxford Massachusetts 42.08N 71.52W
106 L7 Oxford Michigan 42.50N 83.16W
107 G7 Oxford Mississippi 34.21N 89.31W
104 D10 Oxford N Carolina 36.22N 78.37W
108 L10 Oxford Nebraska 40.16N 99.40W
103 E5 Oxford New Jersey 40.48N 74.59W
103 C2 Oxford New York 42.26N 75.36W
11 G10 Oxford New Zealand 43.18S 172.11E
98 J8 Oxford Nova Scotia 45.43N 63.52W
104 A7 Oxford Ohio 39.30N 84.45W
56 J4 Oxford Oxon Eng 51.46N 1.15W
103 C7 Oxford Pennsylvania 39.47N 75.58W
106 E6 Oxford Wisconsin 43.46N 89.35W
56 J4 Oxford *co* England
13 J5 Oxford Downs Queensland 21.51S 148.45E
100 W4 Oxford House Manitoba 54.58N 95.17W
100 W4 Oxford L Manitoba
110 N7 Oxford Pk Idaho 42.18N 112.06W
103 D6 Oxford Valley Pennsylvania 40.10N 74.53W
55 C2 Oxhey Herts Eng 51.39N 0.22W
84 C3 Oxiá *isld* Greece 38.17N 21.06E
84 C4 Oxiá *mt* Aitolia Greece 38.47N 21.24E
84 C2 Oxiá *mt* Lárisa Greece 39.45N 21.56E
13 E4 Oxide, Mt Queensland 19.39S 139.10E
84 H4 Oxilithos Greece 38.35N 24.07E
84 B2 Oxiniá Greece 39.49N 21.30E
115 P7 Oxkutzcab Mexico 20.18N 89.26W
12 G5 Oxley New S Wales 34.11S 144.10E
13 K2 Oxley *sub* Brisbane, Qnsld
12 K4 Oxleys Pk New S Wales 31.48S 150.17E
59 E3 Ox Mts Mayo etc Irish Rep
50 G4 Oxnadalur *V* Iceland
111 E7 Oxnard California 34.11N 119.10W
Oxon *co see* Oxford *co*
58 L7 Oxton Borders Scotland 55.46N 2.49W
57 L6 Oxton Notts Eng 53.03N 1.04W
95 K8 Oxton S Africa 32.13S 26.43E
Oxus *R see* Amu-Dar'ya *R*
56 C4 Oxwich W Glam Wales 51.35N 4.13W
56 C4 Oxwich B W Glam Wales
86 E8 Oxyrhynchus *ruins* Egypt 28.33N 30.38E
Oy *see* Bad Oy
20 B4 Oya Kanagawa Japan
18 J4 Oya Sarawak Malaysia 2.53N 111.54E
76 B4 Oya Spain 42.00N 8.53W
18 K4 Oya *R* Sarawak Malaysia
42 K5 Oya *R* U.S.S.R.
20 K6 Oyabe Japan 36.42N 136.52E
20 M6 Oyama Shizuoka Japan 35.24N 139.00E
20 N5 Oyama Tochigi Japan 36.18N 139.48E
20 O5 Oyama Yamagata Japan 38.45N 139.46E
91 B3 Oyan Gabon 0.02N 10.20E
20 D9 Oyano-shima *isld* Japan
117 C3 Oyapock *R* Fr Guiana
117 C2 Oyapock, B.d' Fr Guiana
53 W21 Øyarvatn *L* Norway 59.00N 7.07E
75 G1 Oyarzun Spain 43.17N 1.52W
42 D4 Oyash U.S.S.R. 55.29N 83.50E
66 B4 Oye France 46.52N 6.20E
53 V14 Øye Möre og Romsdal Norway 62.12N 6.40E
53 Y16 Øye Opland Norway 61.10N 8.23E
53 T16 Øye Sogn og Fjordane Norway 61.19N 5.32E
42 G5 Oyek U.S.S.R. 52.38N 104.28E
91 B3 Oyem Gabon 1.34N 11.31E
80 G3 Oyen Alberta 51.20N 110.28W
69 C2 Oye Plage France 50.58N 2.05E
52 F7 Oyeren *L* Norway 59.50N 11.15E
42 C4 Oyesh *R* U.S.S.R.
53 Y19 Øyfjell Norway 59.35N 8.10E
53 Y18 Øygarden Norway 59.41N 8.13E
22 D2 Oygon Nuur *L* Mongolia
51 F3 Øyjord Norway 68.29N 17.30E
58 G3 Oykel Bridge Highland Scotland 57.57N 4.44W
58 G2 Oykel, R Highland Scotland
39 C3 Oymyakon Yakutsk U.S.S.R. 63.30N 142.44E
58 L4 Oyne Grampian Scotland 57.19N 2.33W
91 D4 Oyo Congo 1.17S 16.00E
90 A8 Oyo Nigeria 7.50N 3.55E
86 O9 Oyo Sudan 21.58N 36.07E
89 M7 Oyo *prov* Nigeria
120 C6 Oyolo Peru 15.10S 73.13W
120 B4 Oyón Peru 10.39S 76.44W
72 O4 Oyonnax France 46.15N 5.40E
71 H4 Oyonnax France 46.15N 5.40E
39 D1 Oyotung U.S.S.R. 70.45N 148.45E
87 D6 Oyouroum *watercourse* Libya
72 F2 Oyré France 46.51N 0.38E
53 X20 Øyrsa Norway 59.17N 7.46E
53 X20 Øysævatn *L* Norway 59.16N 7.49E
53 W15 Oyster Norway 61.44N 7.22E
81 E6 Oysha Zaïre 0.42N 29.34E
43 P3 Oyshilik Kazakhstan U.S.S.R. 47.33N 82.59E
12 J8 Oyster B Tasmania
103 N6 Oyster Bay Long I, N Y 40.53N 73.31W
103 N6 Oyster Bay Harb New York
112 M6 Oyster Cr Texas
25 D7 Oyster I Burma 20.10N 92.35E
14 C5 Oyster Inlet W Australia 20.23S 118.29E
28 B8 Oyster Rock Maharashtra India 18.54N 72.50E
28 B3 Oyster Rocks Karnataka India 14.52N 74.06E
31 B10 Oyster Rocks Pakistan 24.48N 67.00E
110 A3 Oysterville Washington 46.34N 124.03W
53 U18 Oystese Norway 60.23N 6.13E
39 E1 Oysurdakh U.S.S.R. 68.12N 154.31E
43 K4 Oytal Kazakhstan U.S.S.R. 42.53N 73.15E
43 L6 Oytal Kirgiziya U.S.S.R. 40.26N 74.09E
63 K6 Oyten W Germany 53.03N 9.00E
24 D7 Oytograk Xinjiang Uygur Zizhiqu China 36.46N 81.47E
93 F6 Oyugis Kenya 0.27S 34.43E
36 F6 Oyuklu Dağ *mt* Turkey 36.52N 32.52E
41 L4 Oyulakh-Tumus Mys *C* U.S.S.R. 73.38N 117.30E
39 B2 Oyun-Khomoto U.S.S.R. 67.17N 135.35E
39 B1 Oyun-Kyuyel' U.S.S.R. 69.05N 138.12E
41 O6 Oyun-Yurege U.S.S.R. 62.93N 134.44E
42 K1 Oyusut U.S.S.R. 62.52N 115.15E
76 C2 Oza de los Rios Spain 43.13N 8.11W
75 F3 Ozaeta Spain 42.55N 2.29W
37 H7 Özalp Turkey 38.39N 43.57E
19 J7 Ozamiz Mindanao Philippines 8.09N 123.51E
46 G4 Ozarichi Belorussiya U.S.S.R. 52.28N 29.12E
107 L10 Ozark Alabama 31.27N 85.40W
107 C6 Ozark Arkansas 35.30N 93.50W
106 K3 Ozark Michigan 46.09N 84.58W
107 C4 Ozark Missouri 37.01N 93.12W
107 B5 Ozark Plat Missouri etc
107 D3 Ozarks, L. of the Missouri
115 P11 Ozatlán El Salvador 13.22N 88.29W
32 G3 Ozbagi Iran 34.41N 56.59E
82 G2 Ózd Hungary 48.13N 20.15E
35 B7 'Ozem Israel 31.38N 34.42E
19 N4 Ozen *isld* Truk Is Pacific Oc 7.16N 151.57E
45 A3 Ozerany Belorussiya U.S.S.R. 53.14N 31.55E
45 E2 Ozerishche U.S.S.R. 54.48N 33.14E
42 E5 Ozerki Altay U.S.S.R. 53.41N 83.44E
42 D5 Ozerki Novosibirsk U.S.S.R. 54.39N 80.15E
45 J4 Ozerki Penza U.S.S.R. 53.29N 46.29E
45 R4 Ozerki Saratov U.S.S.R. 52.01N 45.29E
39 D3 Ozernaya U.S.S.R. 63.48N 146.10E
42 G3 Ozernaya *R* U.S.S.R.
39 E7 Ozernovskiy U.S.S.R. 51.23N 156.30E
39 G6 Ozernoy Zaliv *B* U.S.S.R.
46 Q4 Ozernoye Orenburg U.S.S.R. 51.45N 51.29E
47 L7 Ozernoye Tyumen U.S.S.R. 56.45N 71.15E
39 G5 Ozernoy, Mys *C* U.S.S.R. 57.45N 163.15E
37 D2 Ozernoy Poluostrov *pen* U.S.S.R.
43 G1 Ozernyy Kazakhstan U.S.S.R. 53.29N 63.14E
43 F2 Ozernyy Orenburg U.S.S.R. 51.05N 60.53E
47 N4 Ozernyy Sverdlovsk U.S.S.R. 57.20N 61.10E
39 L2 Ozernyy U.S.S.R. 66.26N 179.10W
17 K7 Ozernyy U.S.S.R. 55.36N 32.26E
15 B4 Ozero Karachi U.S.S.R. 55.21N 76.57E
42 B4 Ozero Khanka *L* China/U.S.S.R.
45 E4 Ozeros, Limni *L* Greece 38.40N 21.14E
84 B4 Ozerpakh U.S.S.R. 53.05N 141.05E
41 J3 Ozershchina Belorussiya U.S.S.R. 52.25N 30.20E
42 N3 Ozerskiy U.S.S.R. 54.26N 22.00E
40 D5 Ozerskiy Sakhalin U.S.S.R. 46.36N 143.09E
62 P2 Ozery Belorussiya U.S.S.R. 53.42N 24.11E
45 G2 Ozery U.S.S.R. 54.52N 38.35E
42 K2 Ozery *L* U.S.S.R. 50.38N 128.44E
45 D6 Ozeryany Ukraine U.S.S.R. 50.30N 32.56E
110 A1 Ozette Washington 48.10N 124.40W
110 A1 Ozette L Washington 48.07N 124.35W
45 K2 Ozherel'ye U.S.S.R. 54.50N 38.26E
39 D2 Ozhogina *R* U.S.S.R.
39 D1 Ozhogino U.S.S.R. 69.08N 147.39E
39 D1 Ozhogino, Ozero *L* U.S.S.R.
81 C2 Ozieri Sardinia 40.35N 9.01E
62 G2 Ozimek Poland 50.40N 18.10E
45 L2 Ozinki U.S.S.R. 51.11N 49.43E
112 J5 Oznachennoye U.S.S.R. 53.05N 91.25E
45 E6 Ozoir-la-Ferrière France 48.46N 2.40E
69 F2 Ozona Texas 30.43N 101.13W
112 F5 Ozora Hungary 46.45N 18.21E
62 L3 Ozorków Poland 52.00N 19.17E
43 D2 Ozorodnyy Kazakhstan U.S.S.R. 50.21N 63.30E
20 F8 Ōzu Japan 33.30N 132.33E
20 D9 Ōzu Kyūshū Japan 32.53N 130.50E
20 E7 Ozuki Japan 34.04N 131.02E
15 L7 Ozuluama Mexico 21.40N 97.54W
118 H4 Ozzano dell' Emilia Italy 44.27N 11.29E
79 D4 Ozzano Monferrato Italy 54.07N 8.22E
89 H6 Pa Upper Volta 11.33N 3.19W
119 B4 Paakai Pt Hawaiian Is 19.15N 155.55W
51 L6 Paakkola Finland 65.58N 27.39E
61 G2 Paal Belgium 51.02N 5.10E
60 E14 Paal Netherlands 51.21N 4.07E
9 C11 Paama *isld* New Hebrides 16.29S 168.15E
35 B8 Pa'ame Tashaz Israel 31.26N 34.41E
24 D4 Pa-an Burma 16.51N 97.37E
63 R7 Paaren E Germany 52.40N 12.58E
95 B9 Paarl S Africa 33.45S 18.58E
51 O3 Paatsjoki *R* Finland
114 C4 Pauhau Hawaiian Is 20.05N 155.26W
114 C6 Paauilo Hawaiian Is 20.05N 155.21W
114 C6 Paauilo Mill Hawaiian Is 20.03N 155.21W
51 L7 Paavola Finland 64.37N 25.14E
76 E5 Pabaçal *R* Portugal
58 B3 Pabbay *isld* W Isles Scotland 56.51N 7.35W
58 B3 Pabbay *isld* W Isles Scotland 57.47N 7.14W
58 A5 Pabbay, Sound of W Isles Scotland
121 B1 Pabellon Chile 27.41S 70.15W
81 B4 Pabillonis Sardinia 39.36N 8.43E
62 L4 Pabianice Poland 51.40N 19.20E
31 H9 Pabna Bangladesh 24.00N 89.15E
28 H9 Pabna *dist* Bangladesh
65 L5 Pabneukirchen Austria 48.19N 14.49E
93 D2 Pabo Uganda 3.01N 32.10E
98 H5 Pabos Quebec 48.22N 64.36W
31 D7 Pab Ra Pakistan
46 F2 Pabrade Lithuania U.S.S.R. 55.01N 25.48E
120 F4 Pacaás Novos, R Brazil
120 F4 Pacaás Novos, Serra dos *mts* Brazil
120 E4 Pacahuaras, R Bolivia
119 B10 Pacaipampa Peru 5.03S 79.39W
120 F4 Pacajai, I. Grande do Brazil
117 C5 Pacajus Brazil 4.07S 38.31W
77 N5 Paca, La Spain 37.52N 1.51W
120 C6 Pacapausa Peru 14.58S 73.22W
117 A2 Pacaraima, Sa *mts* Brazil/Venez
120 B5 Pacarán Peru 12.52S 75.59W
120 B5 Pacaraos Peru 11.12S 76.40W
117 H7 Pacatuba Brazil 4.00S 38.39W
71 D4 Pacaudière, la France 46.11N 3.52E
120 C4 Pacaya Peru 10.10S 74.06W
81 C4 Pacaya, R Peru
70 G5 Pace France 48.08N 1.45W
107 F8 Pace Mississippi 33.48N 90.51W
81 L7 Pace Sicily 38.14N 15.35E
81 E8 Paceco Sicily 37.58N 12.33E
84 J2 Pacentro Italy 42.03N 14.00E
120 C5 Pachachaca *R* Peru
28 D5 Pachaimalai Hills Tamil Nadu India
28 K1 Pachakshiri *tribe* Assam India
23 H7 Pa-chao Tao *isld* Taiwan 23.23N 119.30E
103 L3 Pachaug Connecticut 41.35N 71.56W
103 L3 Pachaug L Connecticut
29 C5 Pachbhadra Rajasthan India 25.58N 72.21E
29 C5 Pachbhadra Pits Rajasthan India 25.58N 72.13E
121 H3 Pacheca Brazil 31.12S 51.45W
115 E2 Pacheco Mexico 30.06N 108.21W
115 H5 Pacheco Mexico 24.01N 102.28W
121 J9 Pacheco, I Chile 52.16S 74.45W
45 P3 Pachel'ma U.S.S.R. 53.20N 43.20E
Pachen *see* Baqên
110 A1 Pachena Pt Vancouver I, Br Col 48.43N 125.07W
115 F3 Pachera Mexico 28.18N 107.25W
Pachhar *see* Ashoknagar
120 D7 Pachía Peru 17.55S 70.10W
Pa-ch'ing *see* Baqên
81 K10 Pachino Sicily 36.43N 15.06E
120 B3 Pachitea *R* Peru
120 C3 Pachiza Peru 7.19S 76.48W
30 D4 Pachkaria Nepal 28.41N 80.29E
29 F6 Pachmarhi Madhya Prad India 22.29N 78.26E
119 D5 Pacho Colombia 5.09N 74.08W
29 D7 Pachora Maharashtra India 20.42N 75.29E
29 D7 Pachpahar Rajasthan India 24.24N 75.52E
30 F5 Pachperwa Uttar Prad India 27.30N 82.42E
115 K6 Pachuca Mexico 20.10N 98.44W
21 D8 Pach'unjang N Korea 39.42N 127.30E
107 H9 Pachuta Mississippi 32.02N 88.55W
80 F2 Paciano Italy 43.02N 12.04E
119 F6 Paciba, L Venezuela 2.23N 66.30W
111 D3 Pacific California 38.44N 120.30W
107 F2 Pacific Missouri 38.28N 90.45W
111 A9 Pacifica *dist* San Francisco, Cal
122 L14 Pacific-Antarctic Ridge Pacific Oc
110 B2 Pacific Beach Washington 47.12N 124.10W
110 B4 Pacific City Oregon 45.14N 123.57W
110 Q7 Pacific Cr Wyoming
111 C5 Pacific Grove California 36.36N 121.56W
122 Pacific Ocean
19 M6 Pacijan *isld* Philippines 10.38N 124.20E
18 G9 Pacinan, Tanjung *C* Java Indon 7.35S 114.02E
18 J10 Pacitan Java Indon 8.12S 111.05E
65 L8 Pack Austria 46.59N 14.58E
65 L8 Pack Alpe *mts* Austria
66 L8 Packsattel *pass* Austria 46.58N 14.58E
107 B10 Packton Louisiana 31.49N 92.35W
106 B8 Packwood Iowa 41.07N 92.04W
110 D3 Packwood Washington 46.37N 121.40W
76 C16 Paço de Arcos Portugal 38.42N 9.17W
105 F3 Pacolet Mills South Carolina 34.54N 81.43W
105 E2 Pacolet R South Carolina
76 C6 Paços de Ferreira Portugal 41.17N 8.23W
76 B6 Paços de Sousa Portugal 41.10N 8.21W
117 G7 Pacoti Brazil 4.05S 39.00W
103 J3 Pacotopaug L Connecticut 41.35N 72.30W
62 C7 Pacov Czechoslovakia 49.29N 15.01E
117 B6 Pacoval Brazil 2.42S 54.09W
98 R1 Pacquet Newfoundland 50.00N 55.52W
122 Q15 Pactolus Bank Pacific Oc 56.35S 74.20W
117 E4 Pacuí *R* Brazil
70 K3 Pacy-sur-Eure France 49.01N 1.24E
62 K5 Paczków Poland 50.30N 17.00E
16 C6 Padaido *isld* Celebes Indonesia 0.01S 122.23E
19 M8 Padada Mindanao Philippines 6.38N 125.25E
40 G6 Padali U.S.S.R. 50.17N 136.45E
31 J4 Padam Kashmir 33.28N 76.54E
19 B6 Padamarang *isld* Celebes Indonesia 4.09S 121.25E
119 G6 Padamo, R Venezuela
18 B5 Padang *islnd* Singapore
18 H3 Padang *R* Singapore
29 A6 Padang Gujarat India 22.22N 69.54E
18 F4 Padang Anambas Indon 3.02N 105.42E
18 J9 Padang Kabia I Indon 6.15S 120.27E
19 B6 Padang Karimata, Kep Indon 1.38S 108.56E
18 D6 Padang Sumatra Indon 1.00S 100.21E
18 D9 Padang *isld* Sumatra Indon
18 D6 Padangpanjang Sumatra Indon 0.30S 100.26E
18 A7 Padang Rengas Pen Malaysia 4.46N 100.50E
18 C5 Padangsidempuan Sumatra Indon 1.23N 99.15E
18 D5 Padangtiji Sumatra Indon 5.20N 95.51E
18 H3 Padangtikar *isld* Borneo Indon
18 B7 Padang Tungku Pen Malaysia 4.14N 101.58E
42 D5 Padany U.S.S.R. 63.12N 33.20E
18 L3 Padas *R* Sabah Malaysia
37 J8 Padasjoki Finland 61.24N 25.20E
32 C4 Padatha, Kūh-e *mt* Iran 33.04N 48.09E
119 G7 Padauiri, R Brazil
28 E5 Padavedu Tamil Nadu India
25 C4 Padawiya Tank Sri Lanka
53 C7 Padborg Denmark 54.49N 9.22E
56 K4 Padbury Bucks Eng 51.58N 0.58W
121 D1 Padcaya Bolivia 21.52S 64.47W
96 L3 Padda Nigeria 8.40N 5.49E
99 B9 Paddafontein S Africa 33.09S 25.22E
121 B9 Paddington London Eng 51.31N 0.12W
55 C3 Paddington *dist* Brisbane, Qnsld
28 U6 Paddiruppu Sri Lanka 7.31N 81.47E
101 P7 Paddle Prairie Alberta 57.59N 117.42W
100 D4 Paddle R Alberta
95 O6 Paddock S Africa 30.45S 30.15E
50 M5 Paddock Wood Kent Eng 51.11N 0.23E
100 M5 Paddockwood Saskatchewan 53.32N 105.35W
19 C5 Padea *isld* Indonesia 3.32S 123.06E
25 A5 Padeaido, Kepulauan *islds* Irian Jaya
15 F4 Padej Yugoslavia 45.50N 20.11E
104 E7 Paden City W Virginia 39.35N 80.56W
63 J9 Paderborn W Germany 51.43N 8.44E
71 C14 Paderne Portugal 37.10N 8.12W
76 D4 Paderne Spain 43.18N 8.10W
75 L5 Padarne de Allariz Spain 42.16N 7.45W
18 D4 Padeniongan Borneo Indon 3.32N 115.50E
68 E4 Padeşu *mt* Romania 45.40N 22.18E
84 E4 Pádhes Greece 40.02N 20.55E
93 D2 Padibe Uganda 3.29N 32.51E
57 J5 Padiham Lancs Eng 53.49N 2.19W
120 F8 Padilla Bolivia 19.18S 64.20W
115 K5 Padilla Mexico 24.00N 98.47W
77 L6 Padilla de Abajo *see* Padilla
77 L6 Padilla *mt* Spain 37.17N 2.46W
82 L6 Padina Romania 44.50N 27.08E
Pading *see* Pending
66 O6 Padion, Pizzo di *mt* Switzerland 46.19N 9.17E
71 F4 Padirac France 44.50N 1.44E
51 F4 Padjalenta Sweden
97 K5 Padlei N W Terr 62.00N 96.50W
97 K5 Padloping I N W Terr 67.00N 62.50W
31 H9 Padma *R* Bangladesh
28 C6 Padmanabhapuram Tamil Nadu India 8.14N 77.23E
29 G7 Padmapur Maharashtra India 21.19N 80.28E
51 H3 Padnatjärro *mt* Sweden 68.39N 20.20E
99 E5 Padoue Quebec 48.36N 68.00W
79 L4 Padova Italy 45.24N 11.53E
79 L4 Padova *prov* Italy
91 C7 Padrão, Ponta *pt* Angola 6.09S 12.19E
29 C8 Padrauna Uttar Prad India 26.54N 83.59E
122 U12 Padre, B Juan Fernández, Is Pacific Oc 33.40S 78.58W
77 C5 Padre Caro *mt* Spain 37.44N 6.33W
112 K9 Padre I Texas
112 K9 Padre Island Nat. Seashore Texas
76 E6 Padrela, Sa *mts* Portugal
76 C4 Padrenda Spain 42.08N 8.11W
30 C2 Padri Bihar India 25.40N 86.21E
30 F6 Padri Uttar Prad India 26.42N 83.40E
81 B3 Padria Sardinia 40.24N 8.38E
81 D2 Padrogiano *R* Sardinia
67 O12 Padro, Mte Corsica 42.28N 9.00E
76 B3 Padrón Spain 42.44N 8.40W
95 K9 Padrone, C S Africa 33.46S 26.29E
81 D2 Padru Sardinia 40.46N 9.32E
56 B6 Padstow Cornwall Eng 50.33N 4.56W
56 B6 Padstow B Cornwall Eng 50.35N 4.57W
12 F6 Padthaway S Australia 36.37S 140.28E
Padua *Italy see* Padova
31 H4 Padua Kashmir 32.34N 75.34E
107 H4 Paducah Kentucky 37.03N 88.36W
112 G1 Paducah Texas 34.01N 100.18W
26 R8 Padukka Sri Lanka 6.51N 80.07E
77 J8 Padul Spain 37.02N 3.37W
81 L3 Padula Italy 40.20N 15.40E
80 L6 Paduli Italy 41.10N 14.53E
Padumi *see* Fadāmi
47 C2 Padun U.S.S.R. 68.37N 32.00E
28 F1 Padwa Orissa India 18.23N 82.47E
45 P5 Pady U.S.S.R. 51.45N 43.15E
122 B12 Paea Tahiti Pacific Oc 17.41S 149.35W
118 K10 Pae, I.do Brazil 23.00S 43.06W
11 J7 Paekakariki New Zealand 41.00S 174.58E
11 L4 Paengaroa New Zealand 37.49S 176.25E
21 C9 Paengnyong-do *isld* S Korea
11 K4 Paeroa New Zealand 37.21S 175.41E
79 B5 Paesana Italy 44.41N 7.16E
79 M3 Paese Italy 45.41N 12.10E
81 K3 Paestum *ruins* Italy 40.24N 15.00E
19 K4 Paete Luzon Philippines 14.21N 121.30E
119 C6 Páez Colombia 2.48N 76.02W
94 L4 Pafuri Mozambique 22.27S 31.21E
82 C6 Pag Yugoslavia 44.27N 15.05E
82 B6 Pag *isld* Yugoslavia
19 C8 Paga Indonesia 8.45S 122.04E
47 J3 Paga *R* U.S.S.R.
117 B7 Paga Conta Brazil 4.55S 54.33W
19 L8 Pagadian Mindanao Philippines 7.50N 123.30E
18 D7 Pagai, Pulau Pulau *islds* Indonesia
17 F12 Pagai Selatan *isld* Indonesia
17 F12 Pagai Utara *isld* Indonesia
25 C2 Pagan Burma 21.07N 94.53E
19 C3 Pagan *isld* Marianas Pacific Oc 18.08N 145.46E
79 K2 Paganella *mt* Italy 46.08N 11.03E
80 L7 Pagani Italy 40.43N 14.37E
80 H4 Paganica Italy 42.22N 13.29E
80 D3 Paganico Italy 42.56N 11.16E
18 E7 Pagaralam Sumatra Indonesia 3.59N 103.26E
84 E3 Pagasitikós Kólpos *gulf* Greece
25 D4 Pagat Burma 16.50N 97.33E
18 L7 Pagatan Borneo Indon 3.36S 115.58E
100 P2 Pagato R Saskatchewan
19 L5 Pagbulungan Pt Philippines 12.14N 123.14E
111 N5 Page Arizona 36.57N 111.30W
108 N2 Page N Dakota 47.11N 97.35W
108 M7 Page Nebraska 42.25N 98.24W
109 N5 Page Oklahoma 34.44N 94.33W
104 D8 Page W Virginia 38.03N 81.17W
12 A5 Page *dist* Canberra Australia
103 Q4 Page, C Massachusetts 41.25N 70.26W
46 D2 Pagėgiai Lithuania U.S.S.R. 55.08N 21.54E
15 F5 Pagei Papua New Guinea 3.03S 141.11E
105 G3 Pageland S Carolina 34.46N 80.25W
14 E3 Page, Mt W Australia 16.34S 124.43E
93 E2 Pager *watercourse* Uganda
18 F7 Pagerdewa Sumatra Indon 3.44S 105.15E
13 K4 Paget Cay *isld* Gt Barrier Reef Australia 19.18S 151.55E
28 G6 Paget I Andaman Is 13.26N 92.49E
121 G8 Paget Mt S Georgia 54.23S 36.45W
28 A2 Paghman Afghanistan 34.33N 68.55E
28 A1 Paghman Ra Afghanistan
80 E3 Paglia *R* Italy
67 O12 Paglia Orba *mt* Corsica 42.20N 8.52E
66 N7 Paglia, Sasso della *mt* Italy/Switz 46.13N 9.13E
80 L4 Paglieta Italy 42.10N 14.30E
69 K6 Pagny-sur-Meuse France 48.41N 5.43E
69 L6 Pagny-sur-Moselle France 48.59N 6.02E
19 L1 Pago B Guam Pacific Oc
109 C1 Pagoda Pk Colorado 40.10N 107.20W
18 C9 Pagoh Pen Malaysia 2.07N 102.46E
14 F2 Pago Mission W Australia 14.10S 126.42E
83 H6 Pagóndhas Greece 37.41N 26.50E
18 H7 Pagonprick, Gunong *mt* Sarawak Malaysia 4.20N 115.19E
122 D1 Pago Pago Amer Samoa Pacific Oc 14.16S 170.43W
109 C4 Pagosa Springs Colorado 37.16N 107.01W
19 K2 Pagouda Togo 9.46N 1.20E
24 F12 Pagri Xizang Zizhiu China 27.44N 89.09E
109 C6 Paguate New Mexico 35.09N 107.24W
77 U14 Paguera Balearic Is 39.32N 2.28E
17 C3 Paguyaman *R* Celebes Indon
99 D3 Pagwachuan Ontario 49.40N 86.17W
99 E3 Pagwachuan *R* Ontario
99 E2 Pagwa River Ontario 50.02N 85.14W
15 G6 Pagwi Papua New Guinea 4.03S 143.00E
113 K3 Pah *R* Alaska
17 F14 Pahala Hawaiian Is 19.12N 155.28W
18 K7 Pahandut Borneo Indon 2.15S 113.55E
18 C8 Pahang *state* Pen Malaysia
18 D9 Pahang, Sungei *R* Pen Malaysia
11 K8 Pahaoa N New Zealand
30 A6 Paharagarh Madhya Prad India 26.12N 77.38E
29 B2 Pahar Ganj *dist* Delhi India
30 B5 Pahari Rajasthan India 27.43N 77.06E
30 B6 Pahari Rajasthan India 26.49N 78.03E
30 D8 Pahari Khera Madhya Prad India 24.52N 80.31E
31 F4 Paharpur Pakistan 32.06N 71.00E
30 B4 Pahasu Uttar Prad India 28.10N 78.04E
114 D4 Pahau Pt Hawaiian Is 21.48N 160.15W
11 B13 Pahia Pt New Zealand 46.20S 167.42E
11 K7 Pahiatua New Zealand 40.26S 175.49E
32 B3 Pahlavideh Iran 35.56N 46.03E
34 O3 Pahlavi Dezh Kordestān Iran 35.51N 46.01E
32 F2 Pahlavi Dezh Māzandarān Iran 36.59N 54.03E
53 C8 Pahlen W Germany 54.17N 9.17E
Pahlevi Diz *see* Pahlavi Dezh
31 H3 Pahlgam Kashmir 34.01N 75.25E
18 D4 Pahoa Hawaiian Is 19.29N 154.56W
105 G11 Pahokee Florida 26.49N 80.40W
28 A2 Pahra Afghanistan 34.09N 61.54E
30 D7 Pahra Madhya Prad India 25.23N 80.14E
111 J4 Pahranagat Ra Nevada
111 J4 Pahranagat L Nevada 37.14N 115.08W
111 K4 Pahrock Ra Nevada
111 J5 Pahrump Nevada 36.11N 115.58W
10 M5 Pahsimeroi *R* Idaho
30 F7 Pahuj *R* Uttar Prad India
111 H5 Pahute Mesa *tableland* Nevada
111 H5 Pahute Pk Nevada 41.18N 119.04W
Pai *see* Baicheng
25 E3 Pai Thailand 19.24N 98.26E
89 N7 Pai *R* Nigeria
114 E6 Paia Hawaiian Is 20.55N 156.22W
118 B6 Paiaguás Brazil 18.23S 57.06W
76 C9 Paialvo Portugal 39.34N 8.29W
84 G6 Paiania Greece 37.57N 23.51E
76 B8 Paião Portugal 40.04N 8.43W
30 H7 Pai Bigha Bihar India 25.03N 84.55E
58 B3 Paible N Uist, W Isles Scotland 57.35N 7.27W
31 D4 Pai Boom Afghanistan 33.54N 66.33E
41 F4 Paide Estonia U.S.S.R. 58.58N 25.32E
93 B3 Paidha Uganda 2.25N 30.59E
112 K5 Paige Texas 30.13N 97.07W
56 D7 Paignton Devon Eng 50.26N 3.34W
11 J2 Paihia New Zealand 35.18S 174.05E
121 B3 Paihuano Chile 30.01S 70.29W
51 M10 Päijänne *L* Finland
30 F6 Paikaulia Uttar Prad India 26.51N 82.33E
89 M6 Paiko Nigeria 9.21N 6.35E
65 F6 Pai, Ko *isld* Thailand 12.57N 100.40E
29 C7 Pai Khari Gujarat India 21.13N 73.12E
24 E11 Paikü Co *L* Xizang Zizhiqu China 28.49N 85.39E
29 E2 Pail Punjab India 30.46N 76.03E
30 D7 Pailani Uttar Prad India 25.46N 80.52E
120 F7 Paila, R Bolivia
61 M5 Pailhe Belgium 50.26N 5.15E
72 C7 Pailhès France 43.07N 1.26E
25 G6 Pailin Cambodia 12.51N 102.34E
121 A8 Paillaco Chile 40.02S 72.49W
72 D6 Paillet France 44.40N 0.21W
114 D6 Pailolo Chan Hawaiian Is
56 H5 Pailton Warwicks Eng 52.26N 1.17W
57 F5 Paimboeuf France 47.17N 2.01W
113 G5 Paimiut Alaska 61.59N 160.20W
93 E3 Paimol Uganda 3.06N 33.28E
70 F2 Paimpol France 48.47N 3.03W
70 F2 Paimpont France 48.01N 2.10W
31 D3 Pai Mush Afghanistan 34.24N 67.38E
66 Q6 Painale, Cima *mt* Italy 46.16N 9.59E
18 D6 Painan Sumatra Indon 1.21S 100.34E
99 H10 Paincourt Ontario 42.24N 82.17W
121 B4 Paine Santiago Chile 33.50S 70.45W
121 J8 Paine, Cerro *pk* Chile 50.57S 73.04W
117 F5 Paineiras Brazil 27.58S 50.04W
55 K2 Paines Brook London England
106 F2 Painesdale Michigan 47.02N 88.40W
104 C5 Painesville Ohio 41.43N 81.15W
19 E1 Painis Indonesia 4.16N 126.56E
117 F8 Pains Brazil 20.23S 45.38W
56 G4 Painswick Glos Eng 51.48N 2.11W
111 N5 Painted Des Arizona
111 L8 Painted Rock Res Arizona 33.00N 112.46W
64 M6 Painten W Germany 49.00N 11.50E
12 A6 Painter *mt* A.C.Terr Australia 35.17S 149.04E
12 E4 Painter, Mt S Australia 30.33S 139.20E
73 E1 Paint L Manitoba
112 H4 Paint Rock Texas 31.32N 99.56W

104 C9 Paintsville Kentucky 37.48N 82.48W
76 A11 Paio Pires Portugal 38.36N 9.06W
119 D5 Paipa Colombia 5.46N 73.10W
91 H2 Paipaie Zaïre 2.24N 23.16E
121 B1 Paipote Chile 27.22S 70.16W
29 H7 Pairi R Madhya Prad India
76 A3 País del Jallas reg Spain
76 D6 Pais do Vinho V Portugal
99 J8 Paisley Ontario 44.17N 81.16W
110 E7 Paisley Oregon 42.40N 120.34W
58 H7 Paisley Strathclyde Scotland 55.50N 4.26W
26 C7 Paisley Seapeak Mozambique Chan 14.10S 41.28E
51 M2 Paistunturit mt Finland 69.38N 26.25E
30 D7 Paisuni R Uttar Prad India
9 B14 Paita New Caledonia 22.08S 166.28E
119 A10 Paita Peru 5.11S 81.09W
18 M2 Paitan, Telok B Sabah Malaysia
29 D8 Paithan Maharashtra India 19.29N 75.28E
115 G10 Paitilla Pt Panama Canal Zone 8.58N 79.31W
18 K9 Paiton Java Indon 7.42S 113.30E
21 D7 P'ai-t'ou-shan pk China/N Korea 42.00N 128.05E
51 G4 Paittasjaure L Sweden 67.52N 19.10E
76 C7 Paiva R Portugal
91 D11 Paiva Couceiro Angola 14.50S 14.32E
115 O9 Paixban Guatemala 17.47N 90.06W
90 B7 Paiye Nigeria 8.44N 4.19E
Paiyeh, Kuh mt see Kūhpāyeh
72 D3 Paizay-le-Chapt France 46.05N 0.11W
72 F2 Paizey-le-Sec France 46.35N 0.47E
115 F10 Paja Panama 9.00N 79.44W
51 K4 Pajala Sweden 67.12N 23.20E
119 B8 Paján Ecuador 1.37S 80.25W
115 M8 Pajapán Mexico 18.16N 94.41W
115 N10 Pajapita Guatemala 14.43N 92.01W
96 S10 Pajara Fuerteventura Canary Is 28.16N 14.09W
76 H2 Pajares Spain 43.02N 5.47W
76 H3 Pajares, Pto.de pass Spain 43.00N 5.46W
119 D5 Pajarito Colombia 5.18N 72.43W
109 D7 Pajarito New Mexico 34.59N 106.43W
75 G8 Pajarón Spain 39.57N 1.48W
75 G8 Pajaroncillo Spain 39.56N 1.45W
121 B2 Pajaros isld Chile 29.35S 71.33W
92 K12 Paje Zanzibar 6.16S 39.32E
19 B8 Pajeti Indonesia 9.40S 120.24E
117 H9 Pajeú, R Brazil
93 D3 Pajule Uganda 2.58N 32.57E
65 P8 Páka Hungary 46.36N 16.40E
18 E3 Paka Pen Malaysia 4.31N 103.26E
28 D4 Pakala Andhra Prad India 13.25N 79.05E
28 E1 Pakanar Madhya Prad India 18.54N 81.48E
25 C2 Pakangyi Burma 21.36N 95.10E
119 H5 Pakaraima Mts Guyana
100 N1 Pakashkan L Ontario
30 L8 Pakaur Bihar India 24.39N 87.50E
25 F3 Pak Beng Laos 19.57N 101.08E
Pak Bong see Ban Pak Bong
Pak Chan see Ban Pak Chan
56 P3 Pakefield Suffolk Eng 52.27N 1.43E
99 O7 Pakenham Ontario 45.20N 76.19W
18 M4 Pakerayan R Borneo Indon
39 H4 Pakhacha U.S.S.R. 60.36N 169.05E
39 H4 Pakhacha R U.S.S.R.
28 E2 Pakhal L Andhra Prad India 17.59N 80.02E
25 H4 Pak Hin Boun Laos 17.35N 104.36E
43 H6 Pakhtakor Uzbekistan U.S.S.R. 40.02N 65.41E
41 B2 Pakhtusova, Ostrov isld Novaya Zemlya U.S.S.R. 74.25N 59.15E
94 E9 Pakhuis S Africa 32.09S 19.05E
15 J5 Pak I Admiralty Is 2.05S 147.40E
90 D6 Paki Nigeria 11.31N 8.12E
84 E8 Pákia Greece 36.47N 22.51E
91 J5 Pakima Zaïre 3.21S 24.06E
27 K4 Pakistan rep Asia
Pakistan, East see Bangladesh
Pakistan, West see Pakistan
31 E4 Pakita prov Afghanistan
Pak Khlong see Ban Pak Khlong
25 F3 Pak Khop Laos 19.49N 100.32E
25 F3 Pak Lay Laos 18.10N 101.24E
80 O2 Pakleni Otoci Yugoslavia
Paklow see Beiliu
Pak Nam see Ban Pak Nam
Paknampho see Nakhon Sawan
Pak Neun see Ban Pak Neun
25 F3 Pak Niam Laos 18.48N 101.52E
87 E7 Pakodi Ethiopia 7.37N 34.54E
25 C2 Pakokku Burma 21.20N 95.05E
62 L3 Pakośó Poland 52.49N 18.01E
11 H2 Pakotai New Zealand 35.40S 173.53E
100 F9 Pakowki L Alberta 49.20N 111.00W
31 G5 Pakpattan Pakistan 30.20N 73.27E
Pak Phanang see Ban Pak Phanang
25 F9 Pak Phayun Thailand 7.20N 100.20E
82 D5 Pakrac Yugoslavia 45.27N 17.11E
30 J8 Pakribarawan Bihar India 24.58N 85.46E
62 L9 Paks Hungary 46.38N 18.51E
25 G3 Pak Sane Laos 18.22N 103.41E
25 H5 Pakse Laos 14.09N 105.50E
25 G2 Pak Seng Laos 20.12N 102.42E
23 B8 Pak Sha Wan Hong Kong 22.21N 114.14E
25 J5 Pak Song Laos 15.09N 106.12E
25 F2 Pak Tha Laos 20.05N 100.38E
23 B8 Pak Tin Pa Hong Kong 22.22N 114.06E
18 K4 Paku R Sarawak Malaysia
114 B8 Pakua mt Hawaiian Is 19.09N 155.34W
11 E2 Pakuranga New Zealand 36.54S 174.54E
30 L8 Pakuria Bihar India 24.21N 87.39E
18 G7 Paku, Tanjung C Indonesia 3.05S 106.30E
93 C3 Pakwach Uganda 2.17N 31.28E
100 S4 Pakwa L Manitoba 54.55N 99.00W
94 K4 Pakwe R Botswana
89 A4 Pal Senegal 15.54N 16.15W
31 J2 Pal Xizang Zizhiqu 33.40N 79.40E
25 E6 Pala Burma 12.50N 98.38E
111 G8 Pala California 33.22N 117.05W
90 K7 Pala Cent Afr Rep 8.31N 21.16E
90 G7 Pala Chad 9.23N 15.01E
76 C8 Pala Portugal 40.25N 8.16W
93 D2 Palabek Uganda 3.26N 32.35E
77 F8 Palacio de la Almoraima Spain 36.19N 5.25W
120 F5 Palacíos Bolivia 13.34S 65.19W
112 L7 Palacios Texas 28.42N 96.15W
119 F3 Palacios Venezuela 9.06N 66.35W
120 F7 Palacios R Bolivia
75 D4 Palacios de la Sierra Spain 41.58N 3.07W
76 G3 Palacios del Sil Spain 42.53N 6.26W
76 F4 Palacios de Sanabria Spain 42.04N 6.31W
121 B10 Palacios, L Argentina
71 H6 Paladru, L.d' France 45.27N 5.32E
75 R4 Palafrugell Spain 41.55N 3.10E
81 O2 Palagiano Italy 40.35N 17.02E
81 J9 Palagonia Sicily 37.20N 14.45E
82 C8 Palagruža isld Yugoslavia 42.20N 16.20E
80 O4 Palagruža Lt Ho Yugoslavia 42.24N 16.15E
79 J7 Paláia Italy 43.37N 10.46E
84 F6 Palaiá Epídhavros Greece 37.38N 23.09E
84 E6 Palaiá Kórinthos Greece 37.54N 22.53E
84 O11 Palaiókastron Crete 35.12N 26.15E
84 C4 Palaiókastron Greece 38.59N 21.54E
84 J11 Palaiokhóra Crete 35.13N 23.40E
84 F3 Palaio Tríkeri isld Greece 39.10N 23.05E
84 D4 Palaiovrákha Greece 38.53N 22.03E
81 B3 Palai, Pizzo mt Sardinia 40.20N 8.55E
84 A4 Pálairos Greece 38.47N 20.53E
69 C6 Palaiseau France 48.41N 2.14E
70 D7 Palais, le Belle Isle, Nfld France 47.21N 3.09W
72 G4 Palais-sur-Vienne, le France 45.52N 1.20E
29 E5 Palaita Rajasthan India 25.09N 76.17E
26 Q2 Palaitivu isld Sri Lanka 9.29N 80.00E
28 E2 Palakollu Andhra Prad India 16.34N 81.48E
94 K4 Palala R S Africa
28 G7 Palalankwe Andaman Is 10.51N 92.28E
28 C1 Palam Maharashtra India 19.01N 76.59E
84 D3 Palamás Fthiótis Greece 39.02N 22.25E
84 D3 Palamás Kardhítsa Greece 39.28N 22.05E
29 J6 Palamau Bihar India 23.53N 84.17E
29 H6 Palamau dist Bihar India
Palamcottah see Palayankottai
19 A8 Palamedo Indonesia 9.26S 119.46E
29 A3 Palam International Airport Delhi India 28.34N 77.07E
75 R4 Palamós Spain 41.51N 3.07E
29 E1 Palampur Himachal Prad India 32.04N 76.29E
36 C4 Palamut Turkey 38.59N 27.20E
29 C4 Palana Rajasthan India 27.52N 73.19E
39 F5 Palana U.S.S.R. 59.05N 159.59E
19 L3 Palanan Luzon Philippines 17.06N 122.28E
19 L3 Palanan Pt Luzon Philippines 17.08N 122.30E
76 G2 Palancas mt Spain 43.30N 6.20W
75 K8 Palancia R Spain
37 F6 Palandöken Dağı mt Turkey 39.48N 41.15E
29 G7 Palandur Maharashtra India 20.50N 80.20E
46 D2 Palanga Lithuania U.S.S.R. 55.52N 21.00E
Palangān see Yūzīdar
91 F7 Palanganene Zaïre 6.32S 18.52E
32 J5 Palangān, Kūh-e mts Iran
72 K7 Palanges reg France
34 O5 Palang Gerd Iran 33.57N 46.49E
18 K7 Palangkaraya Borneo Indonesia 2.06S 113.55E
Palang Kuh see Palangān, Kūh-e mts
29 C5 Palanpur Gujarat India 24.12N 72.29E
75 K6 Palanques Spain 40.44N 0.10W
76 H4 Palanquinos Spain 42.27N 5.30W
19 A6 Palanro Celebes Indon 4.11S 119.40E
31 C7 Palantak Pakistan 27.29N 64.10E
114 D6 Palaoa Pt Hawaiian Is 20.44N 156.56W
19 M5 Palapag Philippines 12.31N 125.08E
94 J4 Palapye Botswana 22.37S 27.06E
28 D4 Palar R Tamil Nadu etc India
31 G3 Palas Pakistan 35.06N 73.14E
28 H2 Palasbari Assam India 26.07N 91.30E
76 D3 Palas de Rey Spain 42.51N 7.52W
29 K1 Palastha Bihar India 23.50N 87.04E
29 J7 Palasuni Orissa India 21.08N 85.30E
74 H9 Palat Algeria 35.15N 1.15E
80 L5 Palata Italy 41.53N 14.47E
80 E7 Palatino, Monte hill Roma Italy
105 F8 Palatka Florida 29.38N 81.40W
39 E4 Palatka U.S.S.R. 60.04N 151.00E
40 G3 Palatkanda U.S.S.R. 57.25N 136.13E
43 P3 Palattsy Kazakhstan U.S.S.R. 49.11N 83.41E
26 T9 Palatupana Sri Lanka 6.16N 81.24E
81 C1 Palau Sardinia 41.11N 9.23E
19 L2 Palaui isld Luzon Philippines 18.34N 122.09E
19 J4 Palauig Luzon Philippines 15.27N 119.55E
19 J4 Palauig Pt Luzon Philippines 15.27N 119.54E
19 M1 Palau Islands island grp Pacific Oc
25 E6 Palauk Burma 13.15N 98.39E
122 B1 Palauli B W Samoa, Pacific Oc 13.43S 172.16W
75 R3 Palau Sabardera Spain 42.18N 3.09E
122 D7 Palau Trench Pacific Oc
71 D9 Palavas-les-Flots France 43.31N 3.56E
26 Q6 Palavi Sri Lanka 7.58N 79.51E
25 E6 Palaw Burma 12.57N 98.39E
114 D6 Palawai Basin Hawaiian Is
19 H7 Palawan isld Philippines
19 H7 Palawan Pass Philippines
19 K4 Palayan Luzon Philippines 15.35N 121.07E
28 C6 Palayankottai Tamil Nadu India 8.42N 77.46E
19 G2 Palay Palay, Mt Luzon Philippines 14.14N 120.39E
76 J5 Palazuelo de Vedija Spain 41.55N 5.10W
81 F8 Palazzo Adriano Sicily 37.42N 13.23E
80 E2 Palazzo del Pero Italy 43.25N 11.58E
79 G3 Palazzolo Italy 45.36N 9.52E
81 J9 Palazzolo Acreide Sicily 37.04N 14.54E
79 O3 Palazzolo dello Stella Italy 45.48N 13.04E
67 O12 Palazzo, Pta Corsica 42.23N 8.32E
80 N7 Palazzo San Gervasio Italy 40.55N 15.59E
80 E2 Palazzuolo Arezzo Italy 43.21N 11.38E
79 L6 Palazzuolo Firenze Italy 44.07N 11.33E
120 F8 Palca Bolivia 18.40S 65.41W
109 L2 Palco Kansas 39.15N 99.34W
46 E1 Paldiski Estonia U.S.S.R. 59.22N 24.08E
25 C2 Pale Burma 21.55N 94.50E
28 G1 Pale Xizang Zizhiqu 28.35N 89.10E
79 L2 Pale di San Martino, Gruppo delle mts Italy
28 K3 Palel Manipur India 24.28N 94.04E
19 B3 Paleleh Celebes Indon 1.05N 121.59E
114 B8 Palemano Pt Hawaiian Is 19.28N 155.56W
18 F7 Palembang Sumatra Indon 2.59S 104.45E
121 A9 Palena Chile 43.48S 72.59W
121 B9 Palena Chile 43.40S 71.50W
80 K5 Palena Italy 41.58N 14.08E
121 B9 Palena, L Arg/Chile
121 A9 Palena, R Chile
76 K4 Palencia Spain 41.01N 4.32W
74 D2 Palencia prov Spain
77 G6 Palenciana Spain 37.15N 4.35W
111 J8 Palen L California 33.48N 115.14W
115 O9 Palenque Mexico 17.32N 91.59W
119 F3 Palenque Venezuela 9.01N 66.54W
116 J5 Palenque, Pta Dominican Rep 18.15N 70.09W
65 K6 Palen Tal V Austria
103 F2 Palenville New York 42.10N 74.01W
76 L4 Palenzuela Spain 42.06N 4.08W
84 R15 Paleokhorio Cyprus 34.55N 33.06E
44 D5 Paleostomi, Oz L Georgia U.S.S.R.
81 N5 Paleparto, Mte Italy 39.29N 16.35E
30 C7 Palera Madhya Prad India 25.02N 79.14E
120 F11 Palermo Argentina 24.44S 64.15W
111 C2 Palermo California 39.27N 121.34W
119 C6 Palermo Colombia 2.55N 75.24W
108 H1 Palermo N Dakota 48.22N 102.13W
81 F7 Palermo Sicily 38.08N 13.23E
121 K3 Palermo dist Buenos Aires Arg
81 F8 Palermo prov Sicily
81 F7 Palermo, G.di Sicily
120 D10 Palestina Chile 23.50S 69.47W
107 J3 Palestine Illinois 39.00N 87.36W
104 A6 Palestine Ohio 40.03N 84.45W
112 M4 Palestine Texas 31.45N 95.39W
34 B7 Palestine reg Israel/Jordan
112 M3 Palestine, L Texas 32.10N 95.28W
80 G5 Palestrina Italy 41.50N 12.54E
Palestro Algeriasee Lakhedaria
79 E4 Palestro Italy 45.18N 8.31E
71 K6 Palet, Col du pass France 45.27N 6.52E
25 B2 Paletwa Burma 21.25N 92.49E
40 J6 Palevo Sakhalin U.S.S.R. 50.35N 142.45E
30 J7 Paleza Ghat Bihar India 25.40N 85.06E
31 E5 Palezgir Pakistan 31.28N 68.07E
66 D5 Palézieux Switzerland 46.34N 6.50E
65 L6 Palfau Austria 47.43N 14.48E
50 O9 Palffykrater vol Jan Mayen I 71.02N 8.20W
24 G5 Palgan Bulak well Xinjiang Uygur Zizhiqu China 41.21N 90.25E
29 C8 Palghar Maharashtra India 19.42N 72.50E
28 C5 Palghat Kerala India 10.46N 76.42E
28 C5 Palghat dist Kerala India
14 B6 Palgrave, Mt W Australia 23.21S 116.00E
76 B7 Palhaça Portugal 40.32N 8.37W
76 A11 Palhais Portugal 38.36N 9.02W
76 E16 Palha, Mar de B Portugal
30 E7 Palhana Uttar Prad India 25.33N 81.33E
96 P7 Palheiro Madeira Is 32.39N 16.54W
121 J1 Palhoca Brazil 27.43S 48.40W
28 A1 Pali Maharashtra India 18.34N 73.18E
90 E6 Pali Nigeria 10.05N 10.29E
29 C5 Pali Rajasthan India 25.46N 73.26E
30 B8 Pali Uttar Prad India 24.30N 78.24E
29 C5 Pali dist Rajasthan India
Palia see Pallia
30 D4 Palia Kalan Uttar Prad India 28.25N 80.35E
80 H5 Paliano Italy 41.48N 13.04E
26 R3 Pali Aru R Sri Lanka
18 L9 Paliat isld Indonesia
80 F5 Palidoro Italy 41.56N 12.11E
74 H9 Palikao Algeria 35.24N 0.20E
114 C8 Palima Pt Hawaiian Is 19.09N 150.26W
19 M8 Palimbang Mindanao Philippines 6.12N 124.12E
19 M8 Palimbang Pt Mindanao Philippines 6.13N 124.10E
89 K8 Palimé Togo 6.55N 0.44E
71 E3 Palinges France 46.33N 4.13E
95 K8 Palingkloof S Africa 32.08S 26.07E
18 M2 Palin, Mt Sabah Malaysia 6.20N 117.07E
81 K3 Palinuro Italy 40.02N 15.17E
81 K3 Palinuro, Capo Italy 40.02N 15.15E
84 B4 Paliománina Greece 38.33N 21.15E
84 C3 Paliomonastíri Greece 39.27N 21.39E
84 D8 Paliopanayiá Greece 36.59N 22.26E
84 C5 Paliópirgos Aitolía Greece 38.29N 21.50E
84 C2 Paliópirgos Tríkkala Greece 39.37N 21.49E
84 Q14 Palió Pyrgos Cyprus 35.08N 32.41E
84 D9 Páliros Greece 36.25N 22.29E
69 F7 Pâlis France 48.18N 3.43E
109 B2 Palisade Colorado 39.05N 108.23W
108 J9 Palisade Nebraska 40.21N 101.05W
110 J9 Palisade Nevada 40.38N 116.11W
103 F4 Palisades Internat.State Park New York
110 O6 Palisades Res Idaho 43.15N 111.10W
116 L2 Palisadoes airport Jamaica, W I 17.57N 76.48W
61 L7 Paliseul Belgium 49.54N 5.08E
29 B7 Palitana Gujarat India 21.30N 71.50E
83 C3 Palit, Kep i C Albania 41.23N 19.23E
112 J8 Palito Blanco Texas 27.36N 98.12W
29 B6 Paliyad Gujarat India 22.16N 71.39E
115 N8 Palizada Mexico 18.18N 92.08W
81 L8 Palizzi Italy 37.58N 15.59E
51 G5 Paljaape mt Sweden 66.12N 19.15E
51 L10 Pälkäne Finland 61.22N 24.15E
26 Q3 Palk B Sri Lanka
46 N1 Palkino U.S.S.R. 58.11N 42.59E
29 H8 Palkonda Andhra Prad India 18.38N 83.50E
28 D4 Palkonda Ra mts Andhra Prad India
29 J6 Palkot Bihar India 22.52N 84.42E
28 D6 Palk Str Tamil Nadu/Sri Lanka
79 J1 Palla Bianca mt Italy/Austria 46.48N 10.43E
28 C5 Palladam Tamil Nadu India 10.59N 77.18E
81 N5 Pallagorio Italy 39.18N 16.55E
29 J7 Pal Lahara Orissa India 21.25N 85.18E
26 R2 Pallai Sri Lanka 9.35N 80.20E
26 R3 Pallamadu Sri Lanka 8.59N 80.05E
84 D7 Pallándion Greece 37.37N 22.21E
Pallanza see Verbania
79 D2 Pallanzeno Italy 46.02N 8.15E
120 C6 Pallapalla mt Peru 14.56S 73.44W
77 D4 Pallares Spain 38.07N 6.09W
72 G10 Pallaresa R Spain
Palla Road see Dinokwe
75 N2 Pallars reg Spain
75 K4 Pallaruelo de Monegros Spain 41.42N 0.13W
40 M8 Pallasa vol Kuril Is U.S.S.R. 47.21N 152.29E
59 F6 Pallas Grean Limerick Irish Rep 52.33N 8.22W
59 E6 Pallaskenry Limerick Irish Rep 52.39N 8.52W
45 S6 Pallasovka U.S.S.R. 50.02N 46.54E
51 L3 Pallastunturi mt Finland 68.04N 24.01E
28 E4 Pallavaram Tamil Nadu India 12.56N 80.11E
26 S6 Pallegama Sri Lanka 7.31N 80.50E
75 O5 Pallejá Spain 41.25N 2.00E
51 G3 Pallentjåkko mt Sweden 68.16N 18.50E
28 D2 Palleru R Andhra Prad India
72 B1 Pallet, le France 47.08N 1.20E
29 D6 Pallia Madhya Prad India 22.49N 75.52E
72 B3 Pallice, la France 46.10N 1.13W
64 B4 Pallien W Germany 49.46N 6.38E
19 B6 Pallima Celebes Indonesia 4.19S 120.22E
56 P2 Palling Norfolk Eng 52.48N 1.36E
Pallíni pen see Kassándra pen
14 C10 Pallinup, R W Australia
93 E4 Pallisa Uganda 1.11N 33.43E
11 K8 Palliser B New Zealand
11 K8 Palliser, C New Zealand 41.37S 175.16E
122 C14 Palliser Is Tuamotu Is Pacific Oc
28 C6 Pallivasal Kerala India 9.55N 77.02E
29 D3 Pallu Rajasthan India 28.56N 74.15E
72 A2 Palluau France 46.48N 1.37W
72 G2 Palluau-sur-Indre France 46.57N 1.18E
103 C6 Palm Pennsylvania 40.26N 75.32W
92 K7 Palma Mozambique 10.48S 40.29E
109 E6 Palma New Mexico 35.01N 105.32W
76 B12 Palma Portugal 38.29N 8.36W
29 K6 Palma W Bengal India 23.16N 86.29E
77 V15 Palma, B.de Balearic Is
80 L7 Palma Campània Italy 40.52N 14.33E
75 E5 Palmaces, Embalse de res Spain 41.04N 2.55W
75 M5 Palma de Ebro, La Spain 41.17N 0.40E
77 C6 Palma del Condado, La Spain 37.23N 6.33W
77 F5 Palma del Río Spain 37.43N 5.17W
77 V14 Palma de Mallorca Balearic Is 39.35N 2.39E
81 G9 Palma di Montechiaro Sicily 37.12N 13.46E
35 B6 Palmahim Israel 31.56N 34.42E
80 B3 Palmaiola Lt.Ho Italy 42.52N 10.28E
77 P5 Palma, La Spain 37.42N 0.57W
96 P9 Palma, La I Canary Is 28.40N 17.50W
15 L6 Pal Malmal New Britain 5.39S 151.26E
28 D4 Palmaner Andhra Prad India 13.13N 78.44E
77 V14 Palma Nova Balearic Is 39.31N 2.32E
79 O3 Palmanova Italy 45.54N 13.19E
118 F3 Palma, R.da Brazil
77 O5 Palmar, El Spain 37.56N 1.10W
67 O12 Palmarella, Col de pass Corsica 42.22N 8.38E
120 E4 Palmares Acre Brazil 10.22S 67.43W
117 J9 Palmares Pernambuco Brazil 8.40S 35.28W
121 J3 Palmares do Sul Brazil 30.15S 50.28W
116 G4 Palmarito Cuba
119 E4 Palmarito Venezuela 7.36N 70.08W
121 E2 Palmar, L.del Argentina
80 G7 Palmarola isld Italy 40.57N 12.52E
121 H5 Palmar, Pta. del C Uruguay 34.05S 53.33W
119 D2 Palmar, R Venezuela
115 N5 Palmar Sur Costa Rica 8.57N 83.28W
118 D10 Palmas Brazil 26.29S 52.00W
81 B4 Palmas Arborea Sardinia 39.53N 8.39E
115 E10 Palmas Bellas Panama 9.16N 80.05W
89 F9 Palmas, C Liberia 4.25N 7.50W
118 D10 Palmas, Campos de plains Brazil
118 G4 Palmas de Monte Alto Brazil 14.19S 43.03W
81 A6 Palmas, G.di Sardinia
118 J10 Palmas, I.das Brazil 23.02S 43.13W
119 F2 Palma Sola Venezuela 10.41N 68.32W
116 G4 Palma Soriano Cuba 20.15N 75.59W
39 H3 Palmatkina R U.S.S.R.
105 G11 Palm Beach Florida 26.41N 80.02W
12 M5 Palm Beach New S Wales 33.37S 151.20E
14 A4 Palm Beach W Australia
111 H8 Palm Canyon Nat Mon California 33.44N 116.34W
111 F7 Palmdale California 34.35N 118.07W
105 F11 Palmdale Florida 26.57N 81.19W
118 E9 Palmeira Brazil 25.28S 50.00W
76 C5 Palmeira Portugal 41.35N 8.27W
117 H9 Palmeira dos Indios Brazil 9.25S 36.38W
117 F7 Palmeirais Brazil 5.58S 43.05W
118 H3 Palmeiras Brazil 12.35S 41.38W
118 E5 Palmeiras de Goiás Brazil 16.49S 49.53W
118 F2 Palmeiras, R Brazil
91 C8 Palmeirinhas, Farol das pt Angola 9.09S 12.58E
76 E10 Palmeiro Portugal 39.15N 7.17W
76 B11 Palmela Portugal 38.34N 8.54W
113 N6 Palmer Alaska 61.35N 149.10W
107 G2 Palmer Illinois 39.28N 89.22W
108 Q7 Palmer Iowa 42.38N 94.35W
103 K2 Palmer Massachusetts 42.10N 72.19W
106 G3 Palmer Michigan 46.26N 87.36W
108 M8 Palmer Nebraska 41.14N 98.14W
100 L9 Palmer Saskatchewan 49.52N 106.19W
107 L6 Palmer Tennessee 35.21N 85.32W
112 L3 Palmer Texas 32.26N 96.41W
15 F6 Palmer R Papua New Guinea
13 G3 Palmer R Queensland
123 E14 Palmer Arch Antarctica
123 H12 Palmer, C Antarctica 71.43S 96.55W
30 H8 Palmerganj Bihar India 24.51N 84.20E
11 C6 Palmer Hd Wellington New Zealand 41.21S 174.49E
109 F2 Palmer Lake Colorado 39.07N 104.56W
123 F13 Palmer Land Antarctica
13 C6 Palmer R N Terr Australia
123 E14 Palmer Station U.S.A. Base Antarctica 64.46S 64.05W
11 E12 Palmerston New Zealand 45.30S 170.42E
99 K9 Palmerston Ontario 43.50N 80.50W
13 J5 Palmerston, C Queensland 21.32S 149.30E
122 L10 Palmerston I Cook Is Pacific Oc 18.04S 163.10W
11 K7 Palmerston North New Zealand 40.20S 175.39E
103 C5 Palmerton Pennsylvania 40.46N 75.32W
13 C6 Palmer Valley N Terr Australia 24.42S 133.10E
13 G3 Palmerville Queensland 16.00S 144.03E
105 E10 Palmetto Florida 27.31N 82.32W
105 C4 Palmetto Georgia 33.31N 84.41W
116 O6 Palmetto Pt Barbuda W I 17.39N 61.53W
95 N3 Palmford S Africa 27.12S 29.41E
105 E9 Palm Harbor Florida 28.04N 82.46W
81 L7 Palmi Italy 38.21N 15.51E
121 H1 Palmiera das Missões Brazil 27.54S 53.20W
95 L6 Palmietfontein S Africa 30.25S 27.33E
115 K6 Palmillas Mexico 23.20N 99.32W
119 C6 Palmira Colombia 3.33N 76.17W
116 D3 Palmira Cuba 22.15N 80.22W
13 H4 Palm Is Queensland
118 E8 Palmital Brazil 22.45S 50.12W
115 G6 Palmito del Verde, I Mexico
96 Q15 Palm-Mar Tenerife Canary Is 28.02N 16.42W
80 L5 Palmoli Italy 41.56N 14.35E
77 E8 Palmones R Spain
106 M6 Palms Michigan 43.37N 82.46W
111 H8 Palm Springs California 33.49N 116.34W
13 J7 Palm Tree Cr Queensland
13 C6 Palm Valley N Terr Aust 24.10S 132.33E
107 G2 Palmyra Illinois 39.27N 89.59W
107 E2 Palmyra Missouri 39.48N 91.31W
108 O9 Palmyra Nebraska 40.35N 96.23W
103 D6 Palmyra New Jersey 40.00N 75.01W
104 H3 Palmyra New York 43.03N 77.14W
103 A6 Palmyra Pennsylvania 40.18N 76.36W
34 F4 Palmyra Syria 34.36N 38.15E
107 J5 Palmyra Tennessee 36.26N 87.30W
104 G9 Palmyra Virginia 37.53N 78.17W
106 F7 Palmyra Wisconsin 42.52N 88.36W
122 U7 Palmyra I atoll Line Is Pacific Oc 5.52N 162.05W
29 K7 Palmyras Pt Orissa India 20.46N 87.02E
57 F3 Palnackie Dumfries & Galloway Scotland 54.54N 3.51W
28 C5 Palni Tamil Nadu India 10.27N 77.31E
28 C5 Palni Hills Tamil Nadu India
47 H5 Pal'niki U.S.S.R. 60.15N 55.30E
106 C7 Palo Iowa 42.02N 91.48W
80 F5 Palo Italy 41.56N 12.06E
19 M6 Palo Philippines 11.10N 125.00E
111 B4 Palo Alto California 37.26N 122.10W
115 J4 Palo Blanco Nuevo León Mexico 26.17N 100.23W
81 N1 Palo del Colle Italy 41.04N 16.43E
84 R15 Palodhia Cyprus 34.45N 33.00E
112 F1 Paloduro Texas 34.50N 101.12W
112 B8 Palo Duro Cr Texas
112 C7 Paloduro Cr Texas
19 B8 Paloë isld Indonesia 8.19S 121.44E
117 B3 Paloemeu R Surinam
18 H5 Paloh Borneo Indon 1.46N 109.17E
18 D9 Paloh Pen Malaysia 2.10N 103.11E
18 J4 Paloh Sarawak Malaysia 2.26N 111.16E
87 D5 Paloich Sudan 10.29N 32.31E
51 K3 Palojärvi Finland 68.33N 22.47E
51 K3 Palojoensuu Finland 68.17N 23.05E
51 K3 Palojoki R Finland
120 D6 Palomani pk Peru/Bolivia 14.38S 69.14W
115 M9 Palomares Mexico 17.10N 95.04W
75 E8 Palomares del Campo Spain 39.56N 2.36W
111 H8 Palomar Mt California 33.22N 116.50W
111 L9 Palomas Arizona 32.54N 113.30W
77 D3 Palomas Spain 38.42N 6.08W
119 C3 Palomas, Serranía de las Colombia
80 G4 Palombara Sabina Italy 42.10N 12.46E
80 K4 Palombaro Italy 42.08N 14.15E
81 J10 Palombieri R Sicily
75 F7 Palomera Spain 40.05N 2.02W
75 H6 Palomera mt Spain 40.35N 1.13W
75 H6 Palomera, Sierra mts Spain
77 D3 Palomillas R Spain
119 D2 Palomino Colombia 11.15N 73.36W
120 F11 Palomitas Argentina 24.55S 65.00W
28 E2 Paloncha Andhra Prad India 17.35N 80.44E
112 J3 Palo Pinto Texas 32.46N 98.17W
19 B5 Palopo Celebes Indon 3.01S 120.12E
118 B9 Palo Santo Argentina 25.32S 59.20W
77 P5 Palos, C. de Spain 37.38N 0.40W
77 C6 Palos de la Frontera Spain 37.14N 6.53W
116 N2 Palo Seco Trinidad & Tobago 10.06N 61.36W
115 F11 Palo Seco leper col Panama Canal Zone 8.55N 79.34W
31 G3 Palosi Pakistan 34.30N 72.50E
111 D10 Palos Verdes Hills California
111 D10 Palos Verdes Pt California 33.46N 118.25W
87 D8 Palotaka Sudan 4.00N 32.30E
93 D1 Palotaka Sudan 4.01N 32.29E
110 H3 Palouse Washington 46.56N 117.06W
110 H3 Palouse R Washington
111 M8 Palo Verde Arizona 33.23N 112.40W
111 K8 Palo Verde California 33.26N 114.44W
120 B6 Palpa Ica Peru 14.35S 75.09W
120 B4 Palpa Lima Peru 11.31S 77.06W
39 H3 Pal-Pal, Gora mt U.S.S.R. 62.53N 169.44E
13 F6 Palparara Queensland 24.47S 141.28E
19 E5 Palpetu, Tanjung C Moluccas Indonesia 3.05S 126.06E
30 A7 Palpur Madhya Prad India 25.48N 77.10E
30 D7 Palra Uttar Prad India 25.42N 80.27E
75 R4 Pals Spain 41.57N 3.09E
29 C7 Palsana R Gujarat India
52 J7 Pålsboda Sweden 59.04N 15.21E
53 Z18 Pålsbufjord L Norway 60.27N 8.35E
29 E8 Palsi Maharashtra India 19.54N 77.05E
51 N7 Paltamo Finland 64.25N 27.50E
65 H5 Palting Austria 48.02N 13.08E
45 F3 Pal'tso U.S.S.R. 53.10N 34.50E
19 A4 Palu Celebes Indon 0.54S 119.52E
79 K2 Palù Italy 46.08N 11.22E
37 E7 Palu Turkey 38.43N 39.56E
19 A4 Palu R Celebes Indon
119 H3 Palúa Venezuela 8.21N 62.41W
19 K5 Paluan Philippines 13.26N 120.28E
19 K5 Paluan B Philippines 13.25N 120.25E
81 N4 Paludi Italy 39.32N 16.41E
71 J9 Palud-sur-Verdon, la France 43.47N 6.20E
26 R5 Palugassegama Sri Lanka 8.09N 90.05E
66 Q6 Palü, Piz di mt Italy/Switz 46.24N 9.58E
66 Q6 Palü, Vedretta di glacier Switzerland 46.23N 9.57E
79 O1 Paluzza Italy 46.32N 13.01E
43 K6 Palvantash Uzbekistan U.S.S.R. 40.34N 72.14E
43 G7 Pal'vart Turkmeniya U.S.S.R. 38.14N 64.35E
30 A4 Palwal Haryana India 28.08N 77.19E
87 C7 Palwal Sudan 6.50N 30.43E
39 J1 Palyavaam R U.S.S.R.
39 K1 Palyavaam Khrebet mts U.S.S.R.
89 K6 Pama Upper Volta 11.15N 0.45E
90 H9 Pama R Cent Afr Rep
18 M6 Pamaluan Borneo Indon 1.02S 116.42E
18 H5 Pamangkat Borneo Indon 1.08N 108.55E
18 G9 Pamanukan Java Indon 6.16S 107.46E
119 E8 Pamar Colombia 1.30S 71.30W
28 D6 Pamban Tamil Nadu India 9.18N 79.15E
28 D6 Pamban Chan Tamil Nadu India
91 D9 Pambangala Angola 11.44S 15.15E
26 P3 Pamban I Tamil Nadu India
19 A3 Pambero Celebes Indon 0.21N 119.54E
84 T13 Pamboulos mt Cyprus 35.31N 34.15E
100 K9 Pambrun Saskatchewan 49.56N 107.29W
65 M8 Pameče Yugoslavia 46.33N 15.05E
18 K9 Pamekasan Indonesia 7.11S 113.30E
18 G9 Pameungpeuk Java Indonesia 7.39S 107.40E
65 P6 Pamhagen Austria 47.42N 16.56E
28 C3 Pamidi Andhra Prad India 14.57N 77.34E
72 H9 Pamiers France 43.07N 1.36E
27 L2 Pamir ra U.S.S.R.
31 G2 Pamir R Afghan/U.S.S.R.
83 E7 Pámisos R Greece
Pâmiut see Frederickshåb
105 L2 Pamlico R N Carolina
105 L2 Pamlico Sound N Carolina
25 G3 Pamong Dam Thailand 18.01N 102.18E
120 D10 Pampa Chile 23.20S 70.22W
112 D8 Pampa Texas 35.32N 100.58W
120 E8 Pampa Aullagas Bolivia 19.13S 67.05W
121 K6 Pampa Chica Argentina 47.52S 69.40W
120 C6 Pampachiri Peru 14.13S 73.31W
120 C6 Pampacolca Peru 15.37S 72.44W
120 G12 Pampa de Infierno Argentina 26.28S 61.10W
120 F8 Pampa Grande Bolivia 18.06S 64.03W
19 G1 Pampanga B Luzon Philippines
19 B6 Pampanua Celebes Indon 4.16S 120.10E
79 C6 Pamparato Italy 44.15N 7.54E
120 C5 Pampas Peru 12.22S 74.53W
117 G4 Pampas plains Argentina
120 C5 Pampas R Peru
119 G2 Pampatar Venezuela 11.03N 63.51W
121 G3 Pampeiro Brazil 30.32S 55.14W
72 J7 Pampelonne France 44.07N 2.14E
36 E5 Pamphylia reg Turkey
66 B5 Pampigny Switzerland 46.35N 6.26E
76 C8 Pampilhosa Portugal 40.20N 8.25W
76 D8 Pampilhosa de Serra Portugal 40.03N 7.58W
26 U12 Pamplemousses Mauritius, Indian Oc 20.06S 57.34E
75 C3 Pampliega Spain 42.13N 3.59W
104 G9 Pamplin City Virginia 37.15N 78.43W
119 D4 Pamplona Colombia 7.24N 72.38W
19 L7 Pamplona Philippines 9.27N 123.07E
75 G2 Pamplona Spain 42.49N 1.39W
95 F7 Pampoenpoort S Africa 31.04S 22.40E
63 O5 Pampow E Germany 53.35N 11.23E
72 D3 Pamproux France 46.23N 0.04W
24 F11 Pa-mu Hu L Xizang Zizhiqu 28.10N 89.25E
36 H5 Pamuk R Turkey
18 M7 Pamukan, Teluk B Borneo Indon
36 D5 Pamukkale Turkey 37.57N 28.50E
36 E2 Pamukova Turkey 40.30N 30.08E
104 H9 Pamunkey R Virginia
42 E4 Pamyati 13 Bortsov U.S.S.R. 56.14N 92.18E
45 Q1 Pamyat' Parizhskoy Kommuny U.S.S.R. 56.07N 44.30E
31 J2 Pamzal Kashmir 34.17N 78.50E
95 N1 Pan S Africa 25.47S 29.40E
91 C4 Pana Gabon 1.40S 12.41E
107 G2 Pana Illinois 39.23N 89.02W
115 P7 Panabá Mexico 21.20N 88.16W
19 M8 Panabo Mindanao Philippines 7.18N 125.41E
19 L8 Panabutan B Mindanao Philippines 7.38N 122.08E
111 K4 Panaca Nevada 37.48N 114.23W
99 J6 Panache, L Ontario
75 N4 Panadella, La Spain 41.37N 1.24E
26 Q8 Panadura Sri Lanka 6.42N 79.55E
15 M9 Panaete I Louisiade Arch 10.40S 152.22E
29 G6 Panagar Madhya Prad India 23.16N 80.03E
28 D2 Panagiri Andhra Prad India 17.27N 79.30E
19 J7 Panagtaran Pt Philippines 9.39N 118.44E
82 J8 Panagyurishte Bulgaria 42.29N 24.10E
18 J6 Panahan Borneo Indon 1.45S 111.45E
30 F4 Panaio Toupa mt Nepal 27.48N 86.35E
18 F9 Panaitan isld Indonesia
84 C4 Panaitolikón Óros mts Greece
84 B4 Panaitolion Greece 38.35N 21.27E
84 C5 Panakhaïkón Óros mts Greece
104 F4 Panama New York 42.03N 79.43W
109 Q6 Panama Oklahoma 35.10N 94.40W
115 G10 Panamá Panama 8.57N 79.30W
26 U8 Panama Sri Lanka 6.46N 81.47E
102 K9 Panama rep Central America
115 P5 Panamá, B.de Panama
115 F10 Panama Canal Central America
115 P5 Panama Canal Zone Central America
105 B7 Panama City Florida 30.10N 85.41W
115 P6 Panamá, G.de Panama
115 G10 Panamá Vieja ruins Panama 9.01N 79.29W
31 J3 Panamik Kashmir 34.44N 77.36E
111 G5 Panamint Ra California
111 G5 Panamint Val California
119 G9 Pananim I Brazil 3.24S 64.35W
23 D1 Pan'anzhen Gansu China 34.44N 105.09E
120 B3 Panao Peru 9.53S 76.00W
19 M6 Panaon isld Philippines
15 M9 Panapompom I Louisiade Arch 10.47S 152.24E
30 L7 Panar R Bihar India
81 K6 Panarea isld Lipari Is Italy 38.38N 15.04E
79 K5 Panaro R Italy
18 K9 Panarukan Java Indonesia 7.40S 113.55E
76 C9 Panascosa Portugal 39.32N 8.03W
76 B14 Panasqueira Portugal 37.21N 8.36W
72 F9 Panassac France 43.23N 0.34E
15 M9 Pana Tinai I Louisiade Arch 11.15S 153.10E
119 G9 Panauã, L Brazil 2.11S 65.47W
15 M9 Pana Wina I Louisiade Arch 11.13S 153.00E
19 L6 Panay isld Philippines
19 M5 Panay isld Philippines 13.58N 124.20E
19 L6 Panay G Philippines
84 M11 Panayiá Crete 35.07N 25.20E
83 G4 Panayía Greece 40.33N 24.38E
95 O2 Panbult S Africa 26.48S 30.27E
111 H3 Pancake Ra Nevada
79 C5 Pancalieri Italy 44.50N 7.35E
70 G6 Pancé France 47.53N 1.38W
82 F6 Pančevo Yugoslavia 44.52N 20.40E
30 G8 Panchadumar Bihar India 24.31N 83.33E
29 F5 Panchamnagar Madhya Prad Ind 24.05N 79.12E
29 K1 Panchet Hill Res Bihar India
29 C6 Panch Mahals dist Gujarat India
18 C9 Panchor Pen Malaysia 2.08N 102.42E
30 J3 Panch Pokhari L Nepal
29 C4 Panchun Rajasthan India 27.30N 73.12E
82 L5 Panciu Romania 45.54N 27.08E
18 N10 Panco Indonesia 8.16S 118.28E
75 D2 Pancorbo Spain 42.37N 3.07W
75 H6 Pancrudo Spain 40.46N 1.02W
75 H6 Pancrudo R Spain
18 L5 Pancungapang, Bukit mt Borneo Indon 0.34N 114.22E
18 C4 Pancurbatu Sumatra Indonesia 3.27N 98.35E
94 N5 Panda Mozambique 24.02S 34.45E
29 G7 Pandada Madhya Prad India 21.22N 80.55E
112 F5 Pandale Texas 30.13N 101.34W
94 H2 Pandamatenga Botswana 18.33S 25.39E
19 L6 Pandan Philippines 11.45N 122.06E
19 M4 Pandan Philippines 14.02N 124.11E
18 K4 Pandan Sarawak Malaysia 3.14N 113.26E
18 G3 Pandan dist Singapore
18 G3 Pandan R Singapore
19 H7 Pandanan isld Philippines 8.17N 117.13E
19 L6 Pandan B Philippines
18 E8 Pandan, Bukit mt Sumatra Indon 4.33S 103.32E
13 F3 Pandanus R Queensland
29 G6 Pandaria Madhya Prad India 22.15N 81.28E
29 G6 Pandatarai Madhya Prad India 22.12N 81.21E
28 C4 Pandavapura Karnataka India 12.29N 76.40E
120 D12 Pan de Azúcar Atacamá Chile 26.07S 70.40W
121 B3 Pan de Azúcar Coquimbo Chile 30.00S 71.22W
121 G5 Pan de Azúcar Uruguay 34.45S 55.14W
19 L6 Pan de Azucar isld Philippines 11.17N 123.10E
18 G9 Pandeglang Java Indonesia 6.19S 106.05E
118 F4 Pandeiros R Brazil
29 E7 Pandhana Madhya Prad India 21.43N 76.15E
28 B2 Pandharpur Maharashtra India 17.42N 75.24E
29 F7 Pandhurna Madhya Prad India 21.35N 78.34E
12 E2 Pandie Pandie S Australia 26.08S 139.20E
79 G4 Pandino Italy 45.25N 9.33E
81 A5 Pan di Zucchero, Scoglio rock Sardinia 39.20N 8.24E
121 G5 Pando Uruguay 34.44S 55.58W
120 E4 Pando dept Bolivia
76 J3 Pando, El mts Spain
84 A6 Pandokrátor Greece 37.44N 20.50E
84 W22 Pandokrátor mt Corfu 39.45N 19.52E
30 A1 Pandon Himachal Prad India 31.40N 77.02E
115 N5 Pandora Costa Rica 9.49N 82.58W
10 P4 Pandora Bank Pacific Oc
Pandora Basin see Fiji Basin, N
13 G1 Pandora Ent Gt Barrier Reef Australia
31 D6 Pandran Pakistan 28.44N 66.49E
30 F7 Pandri Shivgarh Uttar Prad India 25.06N 82.44E
53 D2 Pandrup Denmark 57.14N 9.42E
30 C6 Pandu R Uttar Prad India
31 J8 Pandua Bangladesh 25.07N 91.44E
19 K8 Panducan isld Philippines 6.16N 120.38E
56 F4 Pandy Gwent Wales 51.54N 2.57W
81 J9 Panebianco R Sicily
15 L8 Panemote I Papua New Guinea 9.22S 151.58E
Panes see Peñamellera Baja
46 E2 Panevėžys Lithuania U.S.S.R. 55.44N 24.24E
12 D5 Paney S Australia 32.37S 135.21E
43 O5 Panfilov Kazakhstan U.S.S.R. 44.10N 80.01E
43 M5 Panfilova, im Kazakhstan U.S.S.R. 43.23N 77.05E
45 O6 Panfilovo U.S.S.R. 50.25N 42.53E
91 K3 Panga Zaïre 1.52N 26.23E
9 U12 Pangai Tonga, Pacific Oc 19.50S 174.23W
9 R12 Pangaimotu isld Tonga, Pacific Oc 18.40S 174.00W
83 G4 Pangaíon mts Greece
28 D2 Pangal Mahbubnagar, Andhra Prad India 16.17N 78.05E
28 D2 Pangal Nalgonda, Andhra Prad India 17.10N 79.18E
91 D5 Pangala Congo 3.16S 14.34E
95 D6 Pangalanes, Canal des Madagascar
18 H9 Pangandaran Java Indonesia 7.41S 108.40E
92 G6 Pangani Tanzania 9.30S 35.27E
92 J4 Pangani Tanzania 5.27S 39.00E
19 M5 Pañganiban Philippines 13.54N 124.18E
93 J9 Pangani, R Tanzania
19 L5 Panganiran Luzon Philippines 13.01N 123.30E
30 H3 Pangar Nepal 27.54N 86.43E
90 F9 Pangar R Cameroon
18 H5 Pangaujalayan Borneo Indon 1.31N 109.42E
56 J5 Pangbourne Berks Eng 51.29N 1.05W
30 F2 Pangbug mt Nepal 27.57N 86.31E
30 F2 Pangbuk Glacier Nepal
107 E6 Pangburn Arkansas 35.26N 91.50W
69 L5 Pange France 49.06N 6.21E
19 A4 Pangean Celebes Indon 1.06S 119.28E
15 K2 Panggoe Choiseul I Solomon Is 7.01S 157.05E
Panggok Tso L see Bangkog Co
18 J10 Panggul Java Indonesia 8.12S 111.28E
25 E1 Panghsang Burma 22.08N 99.10E
91 K5 Pangi Zaïre 3.12S 26.39E
15 H7 Pangia Papua New Guinea 6.18S 144.12E
28 K1 Pang-in Assam India 28.15N 95.00E
31 H3 Pangi Ra Kashmir
18 K9 Pangkah, Tanjung C Java Indonesia 6.52S 112.33E
19 A6 Pangkajene Celebes Indon 4.50S 119.33E
18 C3 Pangkalanberandan Sumatra Indonesia 4.00N 98.13E
18 J7 Pangkalanbuun Borneo Indon 2.43S 111.38E
18 G3 Pangkalanjati Jakarta Indonesia 6.15S 106.54E
18 C3 Pangkalansusu Sumatra Indon 4.05N 98.13E
18 G3 Pangkalanuringin Jakarta Indonesia 6.16S 106.55E
18 G7 Pangkalpinang Indonesia 2.05S 106.09E
19 C4 Pangkalsiang, Tanjung C Celebes Indonesia 0.39S 123.25E
18 A7 Pangkor isld Pen Malaysia
25 N8 Panglang Burma 25.44N 97.08E
19 L7 Panglao isld Philippines 9.35N 123.49E
25 D2 Panglong Burma 21.02N 97.35E
25 N9 Pang Long Burma 23.25N 98.50E
100 N9 Pangman Saskatchewan 49.39N 104.41W
97 N4 Pangnirtung N W Terr 66.05N 65.45W
91 D8 Pango Aluquem Angola 8.43S 14.33E
31 K4 Pangong Or L Kashmir
Pangong Tso L see Bangong Co
31 J2 Pangong Tso L Xizang Zizhiqu China
30 H3 Pangpoche Nepal 27.52N 86.48E
18 G9 Pangrango mt Java Indonesia 6.48S 106.56E
25 D2 Pangtara Burma 20.58N 96.41E
21 C1 Pangu He R Heilongjiang China
121 A7 Panguipulli Chile 39.38S 72.20W
121 A7 Panguipulli, L Chile
111 M4 Panguitch Utah 37.49N 112.27W
89 D7 Panguma Sierra Leone 8.18N 11.13W
15 J2 Panguna Bougainville I Papua New Guinea 6.22S 155.20E
18 C4 Pangururan Sumatra Indon 2.35N 98.44E
19 K8 Pangutaran isld Philippines 6.19N 120.33E
19 K8 Pangutaran Grp islds Philippines
19 K8 Pangutaran Pass Philippines
92 G7 Pangwa tribe Tanzania
25 E1 Pang Yang Burma 22.05N 99.05E
92 E9 Panhame Mozambique 15.38S 30.40E
112 C8 Panhandle Texas 35.21N 101.24W
23 E1 Panhe Henan China 34.05N 110.50E
60 T16 Panheel Netherlands 51.10N 5.52E
25 C3 Pani R Burma
15 D5 Panial, Donau L Irian Jaya
91 H6 Pania Mutombo Zaïre 5.12S 23.53E
114 D4 Paniau pk Hawaiian Is 21.56N 160.05W
80 F2 Panicale Italy 43.02N 12.06E
80 F2 Panicarola Italy 43.04N 12.05E
26 T5 Panichchankeni Sri Lanka 8.04N 81.27E
9 B13 Panié, Mt New Caledonia 20.36S 164.47E
29 M2 Panihari W Bengal India 22.45N 88.23E
26 R3 Panikkankulam Sri Lanka 9.11N 80.24E
Panikota isld see Simbor
121 B5 Panimávida Chile 35.46S 71.30W
42 E3 Panimba U.S.S.R. 59.32N 93.37E
29 C6 Pani Mines Gujarat India 22.26N 73.48E
115 J8 Panindícuaro Mexico 19.59N 101.45W
19 M6 Paninihian Pt Philippines 11.47N 125.28E
45 M5 Panino U.S.S.R. 51.40N 40.09E
30 A3 Panipat Haryana India 29.24N 76.58E
31 D6 Panir Pakistan 29.40N 67.35E
71 E5 Panissières France 45.48N 4.20E
19 J7 Panitan Philippines 9.05N 118.05E
84 D8 Pánitsa Greece 36.45N 22.27E
66 N4 Panix Switzerland 46.48N 9.07E
66 N4 Panixer Pass Switzerland 46.52N 9.07E
75 H5 Paniza Spain 41.17N 1.12W
75 H5 Paniza, Pto pass Spain 41.14N 1.15W
Panjab see Punjab State
18 C3 Panjang Sumatra Indon 4.07N 98.13E
18 F8 Panjang Sumatra Indon 5.30S 105.21E
Panjang isld see West I Cocos Is
18 N4 Panjang isld Borneo Indon 2.23N 118.14E
18 H4 Panjang isld Indonesia 2.45N 108.50E
19 G5 Panjang isld Moluccas Indon 4.00S 131.15E
18 E5 Panjang, Selat str Sumatra Indon
19 B3 Panjang, Tanjung C Celebes Indonesia 0.24N 121.06E
31 D3 Panjao Afghanistan 34.21N 67.00E
72 D8 Panjas France 43.50N 0.06W
32 B4 Panjbarār Iran 32.45N 47.40E
31 C7 Panjgur Pakistan 26.58N 64.06E
31 B7 Panjgur reg Pakistan

29 D7 Panjhra R Maharashtra India
18 B4 Panji Sumatra Indon 2.35N 97.53E
28 A3 Panjim Goa India 15.31N 73.52E
31 G3 Panjkora R Pakistan
31 F6 Panjnad Barrage Pakistan 29.18N 71.02E
31 F6 Panjnad R Pakistan
31 E3 Panjshir reg Afghanistan
39 G5 Pankara U.S.S.R. 58.36N 162.26E
20 H1 Panke yama mt Japan 44.50N 142.12E
113 F9 Pankof, C Aleutian Is 54.41N 163.05W
94 K5 Pankop S Africa 25.12S 28.24E
45 C1 Pan'kovo U.S.S.R. 55.13N 31.55E
41 B2 Pankrat'yeva, Ostrov isld Novaya Zemlya U.S.S.R. 76.10N 60.00E
41 B2 Pankrat'yeva, P-ov pen Novaya Zemlya U.S.S.R.
42 C5 Pankrushikha U.S.S.R. 53.47N 80.18E
90 D7 Pankshin Nigeria 9.16N 9.30E
36 G4 Panlı Turkey 38.52N 33.55E
21 E6 Pan Ling mts Jilin China
21 D9 Panmunjŏm N Korea 37.59N 126.38E
11 D2 Panmure dist Auckland New Zealand
30 D8 Panna Madhya Prad India 24.43N 80.11E
30 D8 Panna dist Madhya Prad India
31 E4 Pannah Afghanistan 33.02N 68.24E
26 Q7 Pannala Sri Lanka 7.19N 80.02E
70 H7 Pannecé France 47.30N 1.14W
60 N12 Pannerden Netherlands 51.52N 6.02E
69 D7 Pannes France 48.02N 2.39E
80 M6 Panni Italy 41.13N 15.17E
30 B6 Panniar Madhya Prad India 26.06N 78.02E
60 M14 Panningen Netherlands 51.20N 5.59E
87 B6 Pan Nyal Sudan 9.10N 28.02E
31 E7 Pano Aqil Pakistan 27.55N 69.18E
111 D5 Panoche California 36.36N 120.50W
18 J6 Panopah Borneo Indon 1.58S 111.10E
84 Q15 Pano Panayia Cyprus 34.55N 32.38E
84 Q15 Pano Platres Cyprus 34.53N 32.52E
108 Q8 Panora Iowa 41.40N 94.20W
118 D7 Panorama Brazil 21.22S 51.51W
13 J6 Panorama, Mt Queensland 24.31S 148.31E
84 L11 Pánormon Crete 35.25N 24.41E
42 G3 Panovo Krasnoyarsk U.S.S.R. 58.58N 101.55E
47 L7 Panovo Omsk U.S.S.R. 56.23N 70.55E
45 N4 Panovy Kusty U.S.S.R. 52.06N 41.36E
47 C3 Panozero U.S.S.R. 65.00N 32.57E
28 D5 Panruti Tamil Nadu India 11.49N 79.31E
29 D7 Pansemal Madhya Prad India 21.39N 74.45E
21 B7 Panshan Liaoning China 41.14N 122.02E
21 D6 Panshi Jilin China 42.56N 125.58E
93 D8 Pansiansi Tanzania 2.30S 32.55E
29 L3 Panskura W Bengal India 22.24N 87.43E
18 M7 Pantai Borneo Indon 3.06S 116.10E
18 B9 Pantai Pen Malaysia 2.47N 101.59E
81 B5 Pantaleo Sardinia 39.06N 8.48E
25 C4 Pantanaw Burma 16.56N 95.10E
51 J9 Päntäne Finland 62.22N 22.05E
111 O9 Pantano Arizona 32.00N 110.36W
19 D8 Pantar isld Indonesia
45 D8 Pantayevka Ukraine U.S.S.R. 48.44N 32.52E
105 L2 Pantego N Carolina 35.36N 76.40W
112 M9 Pantego Texas 32.43N 97.09W
39 G1 Panteleikha U.S.S.R. 68.34N 161.36E
81 E9 Pantelleria Pantelleria I Italy 36.50N 11.57E
81 E9 Pantelleria isld Italy
66 N4 Pantenbrücke Switzerland 46.52N 9.03E
25 L9 Pantha Burma 23.50N 94.35E
107 J4 Panther R Kentucky
29 D6 Panth Piploda Madhya Prad Ind 23.38N 75.29E
18 D10 Panti hill Pen Malaysia 1.50N 103.53E
75 K2 Panticosa Spain 42.43N 0.16W
72 D10 Panticosta, Balneario de Spain 42.47N 0.15W
68 F3 Pantin France 48.54N 2.25E
77 Y13 Pantinat, Pta pt Balearic Is 40.04N 4.10E
75 C7 Pantoja Spain 40.03N 3.50W
76 D3 Pantón Spain 42.31N 7.37W
18 B3 Pantonlabu Sumatra Indon 5.06N 97.26E
14 G4 Panton, R W Australia
19 M8 Pantukan Mindanao Philippines 7.08N 125.54E
91 F5 Panu Zaïre 3.50S 19.10E
115 G6 Pánuco Sinaloa Mexico 23.29N 105.53W
115 K6 Pánuco Vera Cruz Mexico 22.01N 98.13W
115 K7 Pánuco R Mexico
121 B3 Panulcillo Chile 30.25S 71.22W
46 J4 Panurovka U.S.S.R. 52.28N 32.48E
28 A1 Panvel Maharashtra India 18.59N 73.10E
30 C7 Panwari Uttar Prad India 25.26N 79.28E
23 C6 Pan Xian Guizhou China 25.45N 104.29E
66 Q4 Pany Switzerland 46.56N 9.47E
90 D7 Panyam Nigeria 9.21N 9.10E
15 B5 Panyang isld Irian Jaya 3.00S 132.15E
93 C3 Panyimur Uganda 2.17N 31.20E
23 F7 Panyu Guangdong China 22.54N 113.18E
45 H8 Panyutino Ukraine U.S.S.R. 48.56N 36.18E
91 F5 Panza Zaïre 2.05S 18.28E
92 J4 Panza isld Tanzania 5.28S 39.40E
79 P3 Panzano, G.di B Italy
91 F7 Panzi Zaïre 7.17S 18.01E
115 P10 Panzos Guatemala 15.21N 89.40W
114 B6 Paoakalani I Hawaiian Is 20.11N 155.41W
117 H9 Pão de Açúcar Brazil 9.44S 37.23W
118 J9 Pão de Açúcar mt Rio de Janeiro Brazil 22.57S 43.10W
103 D6 Paoh Pennsylvania 40.03N 75.30W
81 M5 Paola Italy 39.22N 16.02E
109 Q3 Paola Kansas 38.34N 94.54W
84 Z20 Paola Malta 35.53N 14.31E
109 H1 Paoli Colorado 40.36N 102.28W
107 K3 Paoli Indiana 38.35N 86.29W
109 N7 Paoli Oklahoma 34.51N 97.16W
23 B5 Paomaping Yunnan China 27.00N 101.07E
75 E5 Paones Spain 41.25N 2.53W
109 C3 Paonia Colorado 38.52N 107.35W
30 A2 Paonta Makasu, Himachal Prad India 30.54N 77.39E
30 A2 Paonta Sirmur, Himachal Prad India 30.27N 77.37E
122 A11 Paopao Tahiti Pacific Oc 17.28S 149.48W
119 G3 Pao, R Anzoátegui Venez
119 G4 Pao, R Bolívar Venez
119 F3 Pao, R Cojedes Venez
90 H8 Paoua Cent Afr Rep 7.09N 16.20E
89 L8 Paouignan Benin 7.41N 2.13E
87 C7 Pap Sudan 6.08N 31.15E
43 N7 Pap Uzbekistan U.S.S.R. 40.54N 71.05E
114 B8 Papa Hawaiian Is 19.12N 155.53W
62 K8 Pápa Hungary 47.20N 17.29E
30 F3 Papa mt Nepal 27.57N 86.35E
77 L6 Papa mt Spain 37.20N 2.50W
114 C7 Papaaloa Hawaiian Is 19.58N 155.13W
114 B8 Papa B Hawaiian Is
84 B4 Papadhátais Greece 38.32N 21.27E
84 A3 Papadhátes Greece 39.18N 20.48E
84 B4 Papadhátos Greece 38.43N 21.10E
84 E8 Papadhiánika Greece 36.43N 22.51E
50 L6 Papafjördhur B Iceland
117 E8 Papagaio Brazil 6.05S 45.20W
Papagaio R see Sauêruiná, R
119 H9 Papagaios, R Amazonas Brazil
120 F3 Papagaios Brazil 8.09S 63.06W
115 M4 Papagayo, G. de Costa Rica
96 U8 Papagayo, Pta. de Lanzarote Canary Is 28.50N 13.47W
121 C3 Papagayos Argentina 31.30S 67.20W
28 D4 Papagni R Andhra Prad India
114 C7 Papaikou Hawaiian Is 19.45N 155.06W
11 F11 Papakaio New Zealand 45.00S 171.00E
11 J4 Papakura New Zealand 37.04S 174.59E
Papal isld see Hei Ling Chau
19 D6 Papalia Indonesia 5.59S 124.01E
119 B8 Papallacta Ecuador 0.24S 78.07W
114 B7 Papaloa Hawaiian Is 19.30N 155.47W
115 M8 Papaloapán R Mexico
81 L3 Papa, Monte del Italy 40.08N 15.50E
28 D5 Papanasam Thanjavur, Tamil Nadu India 10.54N 79.12E
28 C6 Papanasam Tirunelveli, Tamil Nadu India 8.46N 77.23E
81 O5 Papanice Italy 39.04N 17.02E
115 J9 Papanoa Mexico 17.20N 101.01W
115 L7 Papantla Mexico 20.30N 97.21W
11 L9 Papanui dist Christchurch New Zealand
11 N12 Papanui Inlet New Zealand
119 C11 Papa Playa Peru 6.13S 75.54W
18 L3 Papar Sabah Malaysia 5.44N 115.55E
122 B12 Papara Tahiti Pacific Oc 17.45S 149.33W
11 M5 Paparatu New Zealand 38.53S 177.39E
11 J3 Paparoa New Zealand 36.05S 174.15E
11 F9 Paparoa Ra New Zealand
36 B5 Papas, Ákra C Ikaría Greece 37.30N 25.55E
81 L4 Papasidero Italy 39.52N 15.55E
58 P9 Papa Stour isld Shetland Scotland 60.20N 1.42W
58 T11 Papa Stronsay isld Orkney Scotland 59.09N 2.35W
11 J3 Papatoetoe New Zealand 36.59S 174.52E
122 B11 Papava Tahiti Pacific Oc 17.31S 149.31W
114 D6 Papawai Pt Hawaiian Is 20.46N 156.32W
58 T11 Papa Westray isld Orkney Scotland 59.22N 2.54W
122 B11 Papeete Tahiti Pacific Oc 17.32S 149.34W
77 K6 Papeles mt Spain 37.09N 3.19W
63 F6 Papenburg W Germany 53.05N 7.25E
60 G12 Papendrecht Netherlands 51.50N 4.42E
122 C11 Papenoo Tahiti Pacific Oc 17.29S 149.25W
122 C11 Papenoo, R Tahiti Pacific Oc
15 B6 Papesoi, Tg C Irian Jaya 4.06S 132.54E
122 A11 Papetoai Society Is Pacific Oc 17.29S 149.52W
50 L5 Papey isld Iceland 64.36N 14.11W
36 F1 Paphlagonia reg Turkey
84 P15 Paphos Cyprus 34.45N 32.25E
61 F4 Papignies Belgium 50.41N 3.49E
115 E3 Papigochic R Mexico
108 O8 Papillion Nebraska 41.09N 96.04W
31 F3 Papin Afghanistan 34.07N 70.23E
99 P7 Papineau, Parc Quebec
99 P7 Papineauville Quebec 45.37N 75.02W
87 C7 Papiu Sudan 6.38N 31.22E
89 C6 Papodara Guinea 11.21N 12.31W
114 C5 Papohaku Beach Hawaiian Is
120 D11 Paposo Chile 25.00S 70.30W
79 M5 Papozze Italy 44.59N 12.02E
29 H8 Pappadahandi Orissa India 19.22N 82.34E
84 F4 Pappádhes Évvoia Greece 38.56N 23.22E
64 J2 Pappenheim E Germany 50.48N 10.29E
64 L6 Pappenheim W Germany 48.56N 10.59E
30 D7 Paprenda Uttar Prad India 25.37N 80.24E
58 E7 Paps of Jura mt Strathclyde Scotland 55.55N 6.00W
59 D7 Paps, The mts Kerry Irish Rep 52.00N 9.16W
15 G7 Papua terr Papua New Guinea
15 H8 Papua, Gulf of Papua New Guinea
15 J6 Papua New Guinea terr Australasia
13 H3 Papuan Passage Gt Barrier Reef Australia 15.45S 145.45E
121 B4 Papudo Chile 32.32S 71.30W
82 D5 Papuk mts Yugoslavia
25 D3 Papun Burma 18.05N 97.26E
13 B6 Papunya N Terr Australia 23.12S 131.56E
122 S14 Papuri isld Gambier Is Pacific Oc 23.02S 134.58W
119 E7 Papurí, R Colombia
82 J5 Papusa mt Romania 45.30N 25.01E
32 F5 Pa Qal'eh Iran 30.16N 55.30E
115 M5 Paquera Costa Rica 9.52N 84.56W
118 K7 Paquetá, I.de Brazil 22.45S 43.07W
56 B7 Par Cornwall Eng 50.21N 4.43W
Pará Brazil see Belém
11 H8 Para New Zealand 41.22S 173.58E
30 G7 Para Uttar Prad India 25.40N 83.39E
19 D2 Para isld Indonesia 3.05N 125.30E
118 G7 Para R Brazil
45 M2 Para R U.S.S.R.
119 J7 Pará state Brazil
93 C3 Paraa Uganda 2.19N 31.37E
42 C3 Parabel' U.S.S.R. 58.44N 81.30E
42 C3 Parabel' R U.S.S.R.
79 E3 Parabiago Italy 45.34N 8.57E
81 R12 Parabita Italy 40.02N 18.08E
93 E2 Parabong mt Uganda 3.05N 33.20E
19 L4 Paracale Luzon Philippines 14.15N 122.46E
117 A7 Paracari, R Brazil
120 B5 Paracas Peru 13.49S 76.14W
120 B5 Paracas pen Peru 13.53S 76.22W
118 F5 Paracatu Brazil 17.14S 46.52W
118 F5 Paracatu, R Brazil
17 H8 Paracel Is S China Sea
12 E4 Parachilna S Australia 31.09S 138.24E
31 F4 Parachinar Pakistan 33.56N 70.04E
29 F1 Para Chu R Kashmir
82 G7 Paraćin Yugoslavia 43.51N 21.25E
75 G8 Paracuellos Spain 39.43N 1.48W
117 G6 Paracuru Brazil 3.27S 39.07W
76 D7 Parada de Gonta Portugal 40.35N 8.00W
76 D4 Parada del Sil Spain 42.24N 7.34W
76 D6 Parada de Pinhão Portugal 41.20N 7.36W
76 J6 Parada de Rubiales Spain 41.09N 5.26W
120 B6 Parada, Pta Peru 15.23S 75.10W
77 F6 Paradas Spain 37.18N 5.29W
76 F3 Paradaseca Spain 42.40N 6.48W
108 J4 Parade S Dakota 45.01N 101.06W
76 D5 Paradela Portugal 41.45N 7.56W
76 D3 Paradela Spain 42.45N 7.34W
118 G6 Pará de Minas Brazil 19.53S 44.35W
116 A1 Paradera Aruba W I 12.32N 70.01W
76 C7 Parades Portugal 40.34N 8.11W
84 D7 Paradhísia Greece 37.19N 22.05E
45 C3 Paradino Belorussiya U.S.S.R. 53.59N 31.51E
29 K7 Paradip Orissa India 20.17N 86.42E
99 O4 Paradis Quebec 48.14N 76.35W
111 C2 Paradise California 39.46N 121.38W
117 A2 Paradise Guyana 5.34N 57.57W
109 M2 Paradise Kansas 39.08N 98.57W
106 J3 Paradise Michigan 46.38N 85.03W
110 L2 Paradise Montana 47.24N 114.47W
11 C11 Paradise New Zealand 44.44S 168.22E
103 B6 Paradise Pennsylvania 40.02N 76.08W
95 H2 Paradise S Africa 26.53S 24.49E
112 K2 Paradise Texas 33.10N 97.42W
110 O8 Paradise Utah 41.35N 111.49W
12 B7 Paradise dist Adelaide, S Aust
113 G5 Paradise Hill Alaska 62.26N 160.05W
100 H5 Paradise Hill Saskatchewan 53.32N 109.26W
105 L9 Paradise I Bahamas
122 U7 Paradise I Palmyra I Pacific Oc 5.52N 162.05W
111 G3 Paradise Pk mt Nevada 38.47N 117.50W
100 G5 Paradise Valley Alberta 53.02N 110.20W
110 H8 Paradise Valley Nevada 41.30N 117.33W
66 M8 Paradiso Switzerland 45.59N 8.57E
18 N10 Parado Indonesia 8.45S 118.35E
76 J8 Parador de Gredos Spain 40.22N 5.06W
45 D6 Parafiyevka Ukraine U.S.S.R. 50.54N 32.40E
Parag see Pārk
44 G8 Paragachai Nakhichevan' U.S.S.R. 39.05N 45.57E
107 K2 Paragon Indiana 39.25N 86.36W
111 M4 Paragonah Utah 37.54N 112.46W
107 F5 Paragould Arkansas 36.02N 90.30W
118 E8 Paraguaçu Paulista Brazil 22.22S 50.35W
118 H3 Paraguaçu, R Brazil
118 B4 Paraguai R Brazil
119 E2 Paraguaipoa Venezuela 11.21N 71.58W
119 E2 Paraguaná, Pen.de Venezuela
120 G6 Paraguá, R Bolivia
119 G4 Paragua, R Venezuela
118 B9 Paraguarí Paraguay 25.36S 57.06W
118 B10 Paraguarí dept Paraguay
117 H3 Paraguay R Paraguay
117 H3 Paraguay rep S America
31 B7 Parahadab Pakistan 27.42N 63.08E
12 B8 Para Hills dist Adelaide, S Aust
117 H8 Paraíba R Paraíba Brazil
117 H8 Paraíba state Brazil
118 G8 Paraíba do Sul Brazil 22.08S 43.18W
118 H7 Paraíba, R Rio de Janeiro Brazil
118 F8 Paraibuna Brazil 23.29S 45.32W
Parainen see Pargas
19 B9 Paraingkareha Indonesia 10.01S 120.05E
115 N5 Paraíso* Costa Rica 9.51N 83.50W
118 D6 Paraiso Mato Grosso do Sul Brazil 18.53S 52.51W
115 N8 Paraiso Mexico 18.26N 93.10W
115 F10 Paraíso Panama Canal Zone 9.02N 79.38W
118 E2 Paraiso do Norte Brazil 10.18S 48.58W
118 F8 Paraisópolis Brazil 22.33S 45.48W
117 H7 Parajuru Brazil 4.24S 37.52W
32 E7 Parak Iran 27.41N 52.25E
89 L7 Parakou Benin 9.23N 2.40E
26 T6 Parakrama Samudra L Sri Lanka
32 H7 Parākūn Iran 26.30N 58.09E
12 D4 Parakylia S Australia 30.28S 136.23E
84 T14 Paralímni Cyprus 35.02N 34.00E
84 F5 Paralímni L Greece 38.27N 23.20E
84 E7 Parálion-Astrous Greece 37.25N 22.45E
58 G5 Parallel Roads ledges Highland Scotland
19 N4 Param isld Truk Is Pacific Oc 7.23N 151.47E
28 D6 Paramagudi Tamil Nadu India 9.32N 78.37E
15 G8 Parama I Papua New Guinea 9.00S 143.25E
117 B2 Paramaribo Surinam 5.52N 55.14W
70 G4 Paramé France 48.39N 1.59W
76 K8 Paramera de Avila, La V Spain
76 F5 Paramia Portugal 41.53N 6.52W
119 C4 Paramillo mt Colombia 7.05N 75.58W
121 B4 Paramillos, Sa. de los ra Argentina
118 G3 Paramirim Brazil 13.24S 42.16W
118 G3 Paramirim R Brazil
83 D5 Paramithiá Greece 39.38N 20.30E
76 D3 Páramo Spain 42.50N 7.30W
76 G3 Páramo del Sil Spain 42.49N 6.30W
76 E3 Páramo, El mt Spain 42.48N 7.29W
76 H4 Páramo, El reg Spain
119 C4 Paramo Frontino mt Colombia 6.28N 76.10W
120 B4 Paramonga Peru 10.42S 77.50W
45 J3 Paramonovo U.S.S.R. 53.09N 37.24E
103 J6 Paramus New Jersey
40 N6 Paramushir O isld Kuril Is U.S.S.R.
86 O5 Paran Israel 30.23N 35.09E
86 N5 Paran watercourse Israel
121 E3 Paraná Argentina 31.45S 60.30W
118 F3 Paranã Brazil 12.33S 47.48W
117 H3 Paraná R Brazil
118 D9 Paraná state Brazil
119 G9 Paraná, Copeá, R Brazil
119 J10 Parana de Madeirinha, R Brazil
120 D3 Paraná do Ouro, R Brazil
118 E9 Paranagua Brazil 25.32S 48.36W
118 D6 Paranaíba Brazil 19.44S 51.12W
118 E6 Paranaíba, R Brazil
121 F4 Paraná Ibicuy R Argentina
117 E8 Paranaidji Brazil 6.32S 47.28W
117 B9 Paranaita, R Brazil
121 F2 Paraná, L Argentina
117 B2 Paranam Surinam 5.35N 55.10W
119 F8 Paraná Mirim Pirajauana, R Brazil
118 D8 Paranapanema, R Brazil
118 E9 Paranapiacaba, Serra mts Brazil
Paraná Pixuna R see Ipixuna, R Amazonas Brazil
120 B1 Paranapura Peru 5.36S 76.38W
120 B1 Paranapura R Peru
19 H2 Parañaque Luzon Philippines 14.29N 120.59E
121 F3 Paraná, R Argentina
118 F4 Paranã, R Brazil
119 G8 Paranari Brazil 0.13S 65.53W
118 F4 Paranã, Serra do mts Brazil
120 E1 Paraná Tucumã Brazil
118 D8 Paranavaí Brazil 23.02S 52.36W
32 D3 Parandak Iran 35.19N 50.40E
31 E3 Parandev Pass Afghanistan 35.29N 69.28E
83 G3 Paranéstion Greece 41.16N 24.32E
19 K9 Parang Philippines 5.55N 120.56E
18 J8 Parang isld Indon 5.45S 110.15E
19 G5 Parang isld Moluccas Indon 3.20S 130.45E
93 D3 Paranga Uganda 2.38N 32.57E
26 R3 Parangi Aru R Sri Lanka
29 F1 Parang Pass Himachal Prad India 32.28N 78.01E
76 D8 Paranhos Portugal 40.28N 7.48W
26 R2 Parantan Sri Lanka 9.25N 80.24E
29 C6 Parantij Gujarat India 23.26N 72.55E
122 E16 Paraoa atoll Tuamotu Is Pacific Oc 19.08S 140.39W
118 G6 Paraopeba Brazil 19.17S 44.24W
118 G6 Paraopeba, R Brazil
77 J6 Parapanda, Sierra mts Spain
15 H5 Parapap Papua New Guinea 3.50S 144.17E
34 M4 Parapára Iraq 34.57N 44.30E
11 K7 Paraparaumu New Zealand 40.55S 175.00E
11 J7 Paraparaumu Beach New Zealand 40.53S 174.59E
120 G8 Parapeti, R Bolivia
84 F8 Parapóla isld Greece 36.55N 23.27E
39 G4 Parapol'skiy Dolina V U.S.S.R.
84 C3 Parapráštaina Greece 39.29N 21.54E
119 F5 Paraque, Cerro mt Venezuela 5.00N 67.29W
19 B5 Parara Celebes Indonesia 2.37S 120.14E
117 D5 Pará, R.do Pará Brazil
115 K4 Parás Mexico 26.30N 99.30W
31 G3 Paras Pakistan 34.38N 73.32E
19 M6 Parasan isld Philippines 11.44N 124.46E
31 J9 Parashuram Bangladesh 23.12N 91.25E
30 G5 Parasi Nepal 27.32N 83.40E
29 F6 Parasia Madhya Prad India 22.11N 78.50E
29 J1 Parasnath Hill Bihar India 23.56N 86.07E
30 E5 Paraspur Uttar Prad India 27.02N 81.47E
67 O13 Parata, la Corsica 41.54N 8.36E
81 N2 Parata, Mte. della Italy 40.45N 16.45E
118 G3 Parateca Brazil 13.52N 43.31W
118 G8 Parati Brazil 23.15S 44.42W
79 G3 Paratico Italy 45.39N 9.57E
118 G3 Paratinga Brazil 12.45S 43.11W
12 E5 Parātoo S Australia 32.46S 139.40E
12 H8 Parattah Tasmania 42.21S 147.23E
39 F7 Paratunka U.S.S.R. 52.58N 158.14E
29 E7 Paratwada Maharashtra India 21.21N 77.29E
11 B3 Parau New Zealand 36.58S 174.37E
117 D7 Parauapebas, R Brazil
117 C5 Parauaquara, Sa Brazil
117 A7 Parauari, R Brazil
118 E5 Paraúna Brazil 16.55S 50.30W
77 F7 Parauta Spain 36.40N 5.08W
44 F6 Paravani, Oz L Georgia U.S.S.R.
84 C4 Paravóla Greece 38.37N 21.31E
71 E4 Paray-le-Monial France 46.26N 4.07E
68 F5 Paray-Vieille-Poste France 48.43N 2.21E
30 A6 Parbati R Bharatpur, Rajasthan India
30 A7 Parbati R Madhya Prad India
29 E5 Parbati R Madhya Prad/Rajasthan India
30 F6 Parbati Tal L Uttar Prad India 26.56N 82.09E
29 D4 Parbatsar Rajasthan India 26.52N 74.49E
29 E8 Parbhani Maharashtra India 19.16N 76.51E
29 E8 Parbhani dist Maharashtra India
42 C4 Parbig U.S.S.R. 57.14N 81.26E
42 C4 Parbig R U.S.S.R.
70 L7 Parçay-les-Pins France 47.26N 0.09E
70 H5 Parcé Ille-et-Vilaine France 48.15N 1.12W
70 K6 Parcé Sarthe France 47.50N 0.12W
77 Q3 Parcent Spain 38.45N 0.05W
71 H2 Parcey France 47.03N 5.32E
30 F3 Parchamo mt Nepal 27.52N 86.33E
43 H2 Parchevka Kazakhstan U.S.S.R. 52.07N 67.30E
63 P6 Parchim E Germany 53.26N 11.51E
32 D3 Parchin Iran 35.35N 51.50E
79 B3 Parco Nazionale Italy
72 E5 Parcoul France 45.12N 0.02E
69 C3 Parcq, le France 50.23N 2.08E
89 L5 Parcs Nationaux du W Niger etc
62 O4 Parczew Poland 51.39N 22.53E
76 E11 Pardaes R Portugal
111 D3 Pardee Res California 38.15N 120.50W
106 E6 Pardeeville Wisconsin 43.32N 89.19W
35 C4 Pardes Hanna Israel 32.29N 34.58E
72 C9 Pardies France 43.22N 0.34W
75 C4 Pardilla Spain 41.33N 3.43W
24 F9 Parding Xizang Zizhiqu China 32.46N 88.38E
121 F6 Pardo Argentina 36.16S 59.24W
118 F4 Pardo R Minas Gerais Brazil
121 H2 Pardo R Rio Grande do Sul Brazil
75 C6 Pardo, El Spain 40.31N 3.47W
14 C5 Pardoo W Australia 20.06S 119.07E
118 H4 Pardo, R Bahia Brazil
118 D7 Pardo, R Mato Grosso do Sul Brazil
118 E7 Pardo, R São Paulo Brazil
65 N1 Pardubice Czechoslovakia 50.03N 15.45E
18 K9 Pare Java Indon 7.43S 112.13E
30 G3 Pare Nepal 27.50N 86.41E
17 N7 Parece Vela reef Pacific Oc 20.24N 136.02E
118 C4 Parecis Brazil 14.05S 56.54W
118 C3 Parecis, R Brazil
120 G5 Parecis, Serra dos mts Brazil
96 S12 Pared, Bahia de la Fuerteventura Canary Is
76 C16 Parede Portugal 38.41N 9.21W
75 E7 Paredes Cuenca Spain 40.04N 2.51W
75 E5 Paredes Guadalajara Spain 41.15N 2.44W
76 C6 Paredes Portugal 41.12N 8.20W
76 B5 Paredes de Coura Portugal 41.54N 8.34W
76 K4 Paredes de Nava Spain 42.09N 4.42W
121 B4 Pareditas Argentina 33.55S 69.05W
115 J5 Paredón Mexico 25.54N 100.58W
77 H5 Paredón mt Spain 37.45N 4.23W
121 B5 Paredones Chile 34.42S 71.57W
96 S11 Pared, Playa de la B Fuerteventura Canary Is 28.15N 14.13W
32 B2 Pāreh Iran 36.51N 46.15E
75 E6 Pareja Spain 40.33N 2.39W
117 H8 Parelhas Brazil 6.40S 36.34W
72 K7 Pareloup, Lac de France
11 D4 Paremata New Zealand 41.07S 174.53E
92 H3 Pare Mts Tanzania
39 G3 Paren' U.S.S.R. 62.30N 163.15E
39 G3 Paren' R U.S.S.R.
28 B1 Parenda Maharashtra India 18.14N 75.33E
11 H1 Parengarenga Harb inlet New Zealand 34.32S 173.02E
70 K5 Parennes France 48.07N 0.11W
39 G3 Paren'skoye Oz L U.S.S.R. 62.34N 162.25E
99 Q5 Parent Quebec 47.55N 74.36W
81 M5 Parenti Italy 39.09N 16.25E
72 C8 Parentis-de-Marsin France 43.58N 0.31W
72 B7 Parentis-en-Born France 44.21N 1.04W
99 O4 Parent, L Quebec
11 F11 Pareora New Zealand 44.30S 171.12E
19 A6 Parepare Celebes Indon 4.00S 119.40E
121 F4 Parera Entre Ríos Arg 32.49S 58.54W
121 D5 Parera La Pampa Arg 35.10S 64.31W
30 L8 Parerkola Bihar India 24.37N 87.36E
79 D5 Pareto Italy 44.31N 8.23E
63 P8 Parey E Germany 52.24N 12.00E
46 N1 Parfenyevo U.S.S.R. 58.29N 43.22E
83 D5 Párga Greece 39.18N 20.23E
76 D2 Parga Spain 43.09N 7.49W
76 D2 Parga R Spain
51 J11 Pargas Finland 60.18N 22.20E
28 A2 Parghat Pass Maharashtra India 17.56N 73.38E
81 L6 Parghelia Italy 38.40N 15.56E
28 C2 Pargi Andhra Prad India 17.12N 77.49E
47 C5 Pargolovo U.S.S.R. 60.08N 30.19E
96 O7 Pargo, Pta. do pt Madeira Is 32.48N 17.17W
116 P4 Parham Antigua W I 17.06N 61.46W
44 E4 Pari Georgia U.S.S.R. 43.05N 42.32E
80 D2 Pari Italy 43.03N 11.19E
118 G10 Pari dist São Paulo Brazil
120 E7 Paria Bolivia 17.52S 67.01W
111 N4 Paria R Utah/Arizona
119 H2 Paria, Golfo de Venezuela
119 G3 Pariaguán Venezuela 8.52N 64.34W
18 D6 Pariaman Sumatra Indon 0.36S 100.09E
119 H2 Paria, Pen de Venezuela
111 N5 Paria Plat Arizona
119 G8 Parica, L Brazil 1.55S 65.54W
120 G1 Paricatuba Brazil 4.24S 61.53W
30 B7 Parichha Uttar Prad India 25.31N 78.45E
46 G3 Parichi Belorussiya U.S.S.R. 52.48N 29.25E
115 H8 Paricutín, Vol Mexico 19.29N 102.17W
115 N5 Parida, I Panama 8.10N 82.18W
19 B4 Parigi Celebes Indonesia 0.49S 120.10E
70 L6 Parigné-l'Eveque France 47.56N 0.22E
117 A1 Parika Guyana 6.51N 58.25W
11 H9 Parikawa New Zealand 42.04S 173.58E
61 F3 Parike Belgium 50.47N 3.48E
11 K6 Parikino New Zealand 39.46S 175.10E
51 O10 Parikkala Finland 61.35N 29.30E
29 J8 Parikud Is Orissa India
Parima see Uatatás, R
119 G6 Parima, Sa mts Brazil
119 H6 Parimé, R Brazil
120 C6 Parinacocha, L Peru
120 C1 Parinari Peru 4.35S 74.24W
119 A10 Pariñas, Pta pt Peru 4.45S 81.22W
82 L4 Părincea Romania 46.27N 27.09E
12 F5 Paringa S Australia 34.10S 140.45E
11 D10 Paringa, L New Zealand
117 B6 Parintins Brazil 2.38S 56.45W
11 J5 Pariokariwa Pt New Zealand 38.52S 174.30E
107 C6 Paris Arkansas 35.17N 93.46W
122 U9 Paris Christmas I Pacific Oc 1.55N 157.30W
69 C6 Paris France 48.52N 2.20E
110 O7 Paris Idaho 42.15N 111.24W
107 J2 Paris Illinois 39.35N 87.41W
107 M3 Paris Kentucky 38.13N 84.15W
107 E2 Paris Missouri 39.27N 91.59W
99 K9 Paris Ontario 43.12N 80.25W
107 H5 Paris Tennessee 36.19N 88.20W
112 M2 Paris Texas 33.41N 95.33W
68 H1 Paris-Charles de Gaulle, Aéroport France 49.01N 2.31E
104 J3 Parish New York 43.24N 76.07W
99 F6 Parisienne, I Ontario 46.40N 84.44W
68 G2 Paris-Le Bourget, Aéroport de France 48.57N 2.26E
11 B8 Paris, Mt Campbell I Pacific Oc 52.32S 169.02E
68 F5 Paris-Orly, Aéroport de France 48.44N 2.23E
72 H8 Parisot Tarn France 43.48N 1.49E
72 H7 Parisot Tarn-et-Garonne France 44.16N 1.51E
115 O5 Parita Panama 8.01N 80.30W
115 O5 Paríta, G de Panama
18 C9 Parit Bunga Pen Malaysia 2.04N 102.32E
18 A6 Parit Buntar Pen Malaysia 5.07N 100.27E
19 C9 Pariti Timor Indon 10.01S 123.45E
115 O6 Paritilla Panama 7.41N 80.10W
18 C10 Parit Jawa Pen Malaysia 1.56N 102.38E
18 C10 Parit, Tanjung C Sumatra Indon 1.29N 102.31E
32 F6 Pārīz Iran 29.53N 55.46E
43 F1 Parizhskiy U.S.S.R. 53.18N 60.07E
31 B4 Parjuman Afghanistan 33.10N 63.50E
32 J8 Pārk Iran 25.30N 60.36E
87 A8 Parka Zaïre 4.29N 27.30E
32 H8 Parkā Bandar Iran 25.55N 59.34E
51 K4 Parkajoki Sweden 67.45N 23.25E
28 D1 Parkal Andhra Prad India 18.15N 79.42E
51 K9 Parkano Finland 62.03N 23.00E
100 L8 Parkbeg Saskatchewan 50.28N 106.18W
107 K4 Park City Kentucky 37.04N 86.04W
110 R4 Park City Montana 45.37N 108.55W
110 O9 Park City Utah 40.39N 111.30W
109 E3 Parkdale Colorado 38.29N 105.24W
110 D4 Parkdale Oregon 45.31N 121.36W
43 J6 Parkent Uzbekistan U.S.S.R. 41.14N 69.44E
111 K7 Parker Arizona 34.09N 114.18W
109 F2 Parker Colorado 39.33N 104.47W
110 O6 Parker Idaho 43.58N 111.46W
109 Q3 Parker Kansas 38.21N 94.59W
108 N6 Parker S Dakota 43.24N 97.09W
106 J9 Parker City Indiana 40.12N 85.12W
104 F5 Parker City Pennsylvania 41.05N 79.42W
111 K7 Parker Dam California 34.18N 114.10W
14 D9 Parker Hill W Australia 31.18S 121.56E
23 B9 Parker Mt Hong Kong 22.16N 114.13E
13 E3 Parker Pt Queensland 17.01S 139.09E
14 C9 Parker Range W Australia
108 S7 Parkersburg Iowa 42.35N 92.48W
104 D7 Parkersburg W Virginia 39.17N 81.33W
108 P3 Parkers Prairie Minnesota 46.09N 95.20W
100 O7 Parkerview Saskatchewan 51.20N 103.16W
12 J5 Parkes New S Wales 33.10S 148.13E
103 C7 Parkesburg Pennsylvania 39.58N 75.55W
56 O4 Parkeston Essex Eng 51.57N 1.15E
106 D4 Park Falls Wisconsin 45.57N 90.28W
111 D6 Parkfield California 35.55N 120.25W
57 F2 Parkgate Dumfries & Galloway Scotland 55.10N 3.33W
104 J8 Park Hall Maryland 38.14N 76.26W
43 J7 Parkhar Dushanbe, Tadzhikistan U.S.S.R. 37.31N 69.24E
31 F1 Parkhar Tadzhikistan U.S.S.R. 38.23N 71.05E
56 A6 Park Head Cornwall Eng 50.31N 5.03W
99 J9 Parkhill Ontario 43.10N 81.41W
56 H5 Park House Hants Eng 51.11N 1.40W
51 G5 Parkijaure / Sweden 66.38N 19.30E
51 G5 Parkijaure L Sweden 66.49N 19.05E
107 F6 Parkin Arkansas 35.16N 90.34W
100 E9 Park Lake Prov. Park Alberta 49.53N 112.52W
100 D8 Parkland Alberta 50.18N 113.43W
100 Q9 Parkman Saskatchewan 49.43N 101.56W
108 C5 Parkman Wyoming 44.58N 107.20W
59 C8 Parknasilla Kerry Irish Rep 51.49N 9.52W
109 D1 Park Ra Colorado
108 P3 Park Rapids Minnesota 46.54N 95.05W
106 G7 Park Ridge Illinois 42.01N 87.50W
103 F4 Park Ridge New Jersey 41.02N 74.02W
106 Q1 Park Ridge dist Chicago, Illinois
108 N1 Park River N Dakota 48.26N 97.43W
55 D3 Park Royal London Eng 51.32N 0.17W
95 O6 Park Rynie S Africa 30.20S 30.45E
111 N6 Parks Arizona 35.17N 111.55W
108 J9 Parks Nebraska 40.02N 101.42W
100 L5 Parkside Saskatchewan 53.12N 106.31W
104 K9 Parksley Virginia 37.48N 75.40W
13 C6 Parks, Mt N Terr Australia 24.03S 133.16E
112 K2 Park Springs Texas 33.24N 97.49W
64 N4 Parkstein W Germany 49.44N 12.05W
108 N6 Parkston S Dakota 43.24N 97.59W
103 E3 Parksville New York 41.51N 74.45W
103 A7 Parkton Maryland 39.38N 76.40W
105 H3 Parkton N Carolina 34.55N 79.01W
31 H3 Parkutta Kashmir 35.07N 76.00E
110 M8 Park Valley Utah 41.49N 113.20W
109 D5 Park View New Mexico 36.44N 106.34W
109 D1 Park View Mt Colorado 40.20N 106.07W
110 D3 Parkway Washington 46.59N 121.31W
75 C7 Parla Spain 40.14N 3.46W
75 R3 Parlabá Spain 42.01N 3.02E
29 J8 Parla Kimedi Orissa India 19.30N 84.38E
29 J8 Parlakimedi Orissa India 18.48N 84.10E
29 G8 Parlakote Madhya Prad India 19.45N 80.45E
51 G5 Pärlälven R Sweden 66.33N 19.20E
72 J6 Parlan France 44.50N 2.10E
116 M1 Parlatuvier Tobago W I 11.18N 60.39W
110 J6 Parma Idaho 43.49N 116.58W
79 H5 Parma Italy 44.48N 10.19E
106 K7 Parma Michigan 42.16N 84.36W
107 G5 Parma Missouri 36.36N 89.49W
104 D5 Parma Ohio 41.24N 81.44W
79 G5 Parma prov Italy
79 H5 Parma R Italy
119 G4 Parmana Venezuela 7.51N 65.51W
72 G3 Parnac France 46.27N 1.26E
118 G2 Parnaguá Brazil 10.17S 44.39W
117 G6 Parnaíba Brazil 2.58S 41.46W
117 F7 Parnaíba, R Maranhão Brazil
118 D3 Parnaíba, R Mato Grosso Brazil
117 E9 Parnaibinha R Brazil
117 G9 Parnamirim Brazil 8.05S 39.35W
117 F7 Parnarama Brazil 5.31S 43.10W
84 E4 Parnassós mts Greece
11 H9 Parnassus New Zealand 42.42S 173.19E
12 D6 Parndana S Australia 35.44S 137.14E
65 P6 Parndorf Austria 47.59N 16.52E
106 B8 Parnell Iowa 41.33N 92.00W
107 B1 Parnell Missouri 40.26N 94.38W
112 G1 Parnell Texas 34.31N 100.36W
28 B1 Parner Maharashtra India 19.01N 74.30E
84 G5 Párnis Óros mts Greece
84 E7 Párnon Óros mts Greece
69 K7 Parnot France 48.01N 5.39E
46 E1 Pärnu Estonia U.S.S.R. 58.28N 24.30E
46 E1 Pärnu laht gulf Estonia U.S.S.R.
28 G2 Paro Bhutan 27.23N 89.31E
30 J6 Paro Bihar India 26.05N 85.04E
11 F9 Paroa New Zealand 42.32S 171.10E
35 E2 Parod Israel 32.56N 35.26E
28 G2 Paro Dzong Bhutan 27.29N 89.26E
69 J5 Parois France 49.08N 5.08E
120 E9 Paroma pk Chile 20.48S 68.30W
40 J5 Paromay Sakhalin U.S.S.R. 52.52N 143.10E
93 C3 Parombo Uganda 2.19N 31.12E
45 Q8 Paromnaya U.S.S.R. 48.51N 44.43E
107 D7 Paron Arkansas 34.47N 92.45W
69 E7 Paron France 48.11N 3.16E
30 B8 Paron Uttar Prad India 24.56N 78.35E
Parona see Fındık
12 G4 Paroo R New S Wales/Queensland
12 G4 Paroo Channel New S Wales
31 A3 Paropamisus mts Afghanistan
19 A5 Paroreang, Bukit mt Celebes Indon 3.04S 119.30E
83 G7 Páros Greece 37.04N 25.06E
83 G7 Páros isld Greece 47.04N 25.06E
116 H2 Parottee Pt Jamaica, W I 17.56N 77.50W
95 B9 Parow S Africa 33.49S 18.30E
111 M4 Parowan Utah 37.50N 112.50W
71 K8 Parpaillon, Chaîne de mts France
66 P4 Parpan Switzerland 46.47N 9.34E
58 G1 Parph, The moor Highland Scotland
106 G8 Parr Indiana 41.02N 87.13W
105 F3 Parr S Carolina 34.15N 81.19W
14 B6 Parraburdoo W Australia 23.20S 117.28E
56 D5 Parracombe Devon Eng 51.12N 3.54W
75 F8 Parra de las Vegas, La Spain 39.52N 2.13W
121 B6 Parral Chile 36.08S 71.52W
77 K7 Parra, La Almería Spain 36.47N 3.05W
77 C3 Parra, La Badajoz Spain 38.31N 6.38W
12 K5 Parramatta New S Wales 33.50S 150.57E
12 K7 Parramatta R New S Wales
104 K9 Parramore I Virginia 37.33N 75.39W
77 J2 Parra, Mte Spain 39.21N 3.37W
115 H5 Parras Mexico 25.30N 102.11W
121 F6 Parravicini Argentina 36.29S 57.43W
79 G3 Parre Italy 45.53N 9.53E
60 K7 Parrega Netherlands 53.01N 5.29E
Parres see Arriondas
56 F5 Parrett, R Somerset Eng
76 J8 Parrillas Spain 40.04N 5.04W
107 J8 Parrish Alabama 33.42N 87.18W
105 E10 Parrish Florida 27.36N 82.24W
115 M5 Parrita Costa Rica 9.30N 84.20W
105 C6 Parrott Georgia 31.54N 84.31W
104 E9 Parrott Virginia 37.12N 80.39W
98 H8 Parrsboro Nova Scotia 45.25N 64.21W
100 N9 Parry Saskatchewan 49.47N 104.41W
97 L4 Parry B N W Terr
101 U1 Parry B N W Terr
101 L1 Parry, C N W Terr 70.10N 124.33W
99 K7 Parry I Ontario
Parry Is Bonin Is see Muko jima rettō
97 H2 Parry Is N W Terr
48 R3 Parry, Kap C Greenland 77.00N 71.20W
48 V10 Parry, Kap C Greenland
116 N2 Parrylands Trinidad & Tobago 10.11N 61.37W
101 L1 Parry Pen N W Terr
14 B5 Parry Ra W Australia
99 K7 Parry Sound Ontario 45.21N 80.03W
99 K7 Parry Sound B Ontario
30 J7 Parsa Bihar India 25.54N 85.02E
30 H5 Parsa Nepal 27.28N 84.18E
72 J3 Parsac France 46.13N 2.09E
30 H7 Parsadi Inglis Bihar India 25.18N 84.42E
30 G7 Parsathua Bihar India 25.13N 83.49E
63 N7 Parsau W Germany 52.33N 10.55E
64 M5 Parsberg W Germany 49.10N 11.44E
15 J7 Parsee Pt Papua New Guinea 7.00S 147.50E
65 B7 Parseier Spitze mt Austria 47.11N 10.29E
30 D5 Parsendi Uttar Prad India 27.36N 80.53E
62 J2 Parseta R Poland
30 E6 Parshadepur Uttar Prad India 26.04N 81.31E
108 H2 Parshall N Dakota 47.58N 102.09W
42 J3 Parshino U.S.S.R. 59.15N 111.50E
111 K3 Parsnip Pk mt Nevada 38.09N 114.20W
30 A8 Parsol Madhya Prad India 24.53N 77.58E
109 P4 Parsons Kansas 37.20N 95.17W
107 H6 Parsons Tennessee 35.40N 88.09W
104 F7 Parsons W Virginia 39.06N 79.43W
101 G1 Parsons L N W Terr 68.55N 133.39W
98 P3 Parson's Pond Newfoundland 50.02N 57.43N
Parsons Pt see Pygmalion Pt
63 T7 Parsteiner See L E Germany
28 A2 Partabgarh Maharashtra India 17.54N 73.36E
Partabgarh dist see Pratapgarh
29 G8 Partabpur Bastar, Madhya Prad India 19.59N 80.48E
30 H8 Partabpur Bihar India 24.19N 84.42E
29 H6 Partabpur Surguja, Madhya Prad India 23.28N 83.15E
77 M6 Partaloa Spain 37.25N 2.13W
81 E8 Partanna Sicily 37.43N 12.54E
51 F4 Pårtefjällen mt Sweden 67.11N 17.40E
64 E4 Partenheim W Germany 49.54N 8.05E
72 D2 Parthenay France 46.39N 0.14W
65 B8 Parthenen Austria 46.58N 10.05E
84 E7 Parthénion Greece 37.28N 22.30E
115 D5 Partida isld Mexico
52 G9 Partille Sweden 57.46N 12.10E
67 O12 Partinello Corsica 42.18N 8.40E
81 F7 Partinico Sicily 38.03N 13.07E
40 F10 Partizansk U.S.S.R. 43.03N 133.05E
42 E3 Partizanskiy U.S.S.R. 58.40N 94.19E
42 E4 Partizanskoye U.S.S.R. 55.31N 94.19E
57 O6 Partney Lincs Eng 53.12N 0.06E
41 J4 Partnyagino, Oz L U.S.S.R.
30 E3 Partol Nepal 29.30N 81.43E
57 E2 Parton Dumfries & Galloway Scotland 55.01N 4.03W
109 M4 Partridge Kansas 37.57N 98.08W
99 K2 Partridge R Ontario
98 R5 Partridgeberry Hills Newfoundland
100 U1 Partridge Breast L Manitoba
98 Q3 Partridge Pt Newfoundland 50.10N 56.10W
59 D4 Partry Mayo Irish Rep 53.42N 9.16W
59 C4 Partry Mts Mayo Irish Rep
11 J2 Parua Bay New Zealand 35.46S 174.29E
119 G5 Parucito R Venezuela
32 J7 Parūd Iran 26.20N 61.23E
117 B4 Paru de Oeste, R Brazil
28 C6 Parui Kerala India 8.48N 76.41E
53 C4 Pårup Denmark 56.09N 9.22E
117 C5 Paru, R Brazil
28 C5 Parur Kerala India 10.10N 76.13E
119 F5 Parú, R Venezuela
120 D5 Paruro Peru 13.46S 71.53W
119 G5 Parú, Serranía mts Venezuela
45 C10 Parutino Ukraine U.S.S.R. 46.41N 31.54E
32 G4 Parvāreh Iran 33.04N 57.11E
31 H8 Parvatipur Bangladesh 25.40N 89.01E
29 H8 Parvatipuram Andhra Prad India 18.48N 83.28E
31 E3 Parwan prov Afghanistan
29 E5 Parwan R Rajasthan etc India
30 G6 Parwarpar Uttar Prad India 26.49N 83.51E
24 D10 Paryang Xizang Zizhiqu China 30.04N 83.28E
52 J10 Påryd Sweden 56.33N 15.55E
95 L2 Parys S Africa 26.55S 27.28E
72 E10 Parzan Spain 42.40N 0.13E
75 C1 Pas R Spain
36 G3 Paşa Dağı mt Turkey 39.16N 33.12E
111 F7 Pasadena California 34.10N 118.09W
103 A8 Pasadena Maryland 39.07N 76.35W
112 G9 Pasadena Texas 29.42N 95.14W
119 B8 Pasado, C Ecuador 0.22S 80.30W
119 B9 Pasaje Ecuador 3.23S 79.50W
115 H5 Pasaje Mexico 24.56N 103.51W
120 F11 Pasaje, R Argentina
75 G1 Pasajes Spain 43.20N 1.55W
37 D2 Paşalimanı Turkey 40.30N 27.37E
37 D2 Paşalimanı isld Turkey
109 G5 Pasamonte New Mexico 36.18N 103.46W
44 F5 Pasanauri Georgia U.S.S.R. 42.21N 44.42E
19 A4 Pasangkayu Celebes Indon 1.10S 119.23E
32 E5 Pasargadae anc site Iran 30.15N 53.14E
18 F3 Pasarminggu Jakarta Indonesia 6.17S 106.51E
76 H8 Pasarón Spain 40.04N 5.49W
18 G3 Pasarrebo Jakarta Indonesia 6.18S 106.52E
19 C6 Pasarwajo Indonesia 5.31S 122.51E
25 D3 Pasawng Burma 18.54N 97.19E
19 H1 Pasay Luzon Philippines 14.33N 121.00E
37 C2 Pasayiğit Turkey 40.58N 26.37E
107 H11 Pascagoula Mississippi 30.21N 88.32W
107 H11 Pascagoula R Mississippi
99 N4 Pascalis Quebec 48.09N 77.29W
82 K3 Paşcani Romania 47.14N 26.46E
65 K5 Pasching Austria 48.16N 14.12E
110 F3 Pasco Washington 46.15N 119.07W
120 B4 Pasco dept Peru
103 L3 Pascoag Rhode I 41.57N 71.42W
118 H5 Pascoal, Mte Brazil 16.55S 39.25W
13 E3 Pascoe Inlet Queensland
13 G2 Pascoe, R Queensland
14 B5 Pasco I W Australia 20.58S 115.21E
99 A2 Pascopee Ontario 50.22N 89.03W
121 J7 Pascua R Chile
Pascua, I. de see Easter I. Pac. Oc.
67 G2 Pas-de-Calais dept France
119 D4 Pas del Rio Colombia 6.02N 72.40W
69 D3 Pas-en-Artois France 50.10N 2.30E
63 U5 Pasewalk E Germany 53.30N 14.00E
101 V6 Pasfield L Saskatchewan
31 F3 Pashat Afghanistan 34.42N 71.03E
31 F1 Pashimgar Tadzhikistan U.S.S.R. 38.56N 71.30E
42 C4 Pashino U.S.S.R. 55.12N 83.01E
47 H6 Pashiya U.S.S.R. 58.30N 58.18E
42 E5 Pashkino U.S.S.R. 52.40N 91.43E
40 E7 Pashkovo Amur U.S.S.R. 48.56N 130.41E
46 M4 Pashkovo Lipetsk U.S.S.R. 51.59N 40.00E
45 O3 Pashkovo Penza U.S.S.R. 53.39N 42.25E
Pashkovskaya see Pashkovskiy
44 C2 Pashkovskiy U.S.S.R. 45.01N 39.06E
47 H4 Pashnya U.S.S.R. 63.19N 56.30E
47 C5 Pashskiy-Perevoz U.S.S.R. 60.20N 33.00E
Pashu see Pashū'iyeh
32 H6 Pashū'iyeh Iran 29.56N 58.11E
79 O2 Pasian di Prato Italy 46.03N 13.11E
79 N3 Pasiano Italy 45.51N 12.38E
19 J1 Pasig Luzon Philippines 14.34N 121.04E
19 J1 Pasig R Luzon Philippines
25 N7 Pasi Ga Burma 26.50N 97.35E
19 D2 Pasige isld Indonesia 2.22N 125.20E
28 K1 Pasighat Assam India 28.01N 95.20E
37 F6 Pasinler Turkey 39.59N 41.41E
92 D12 Pasipasi Zimbabwe 20.05S 28.30E
18 B4 Pasiputih Sumatra Indon 3.58N 96.44E
18 K10 Pasirian Java Indon 8.13S 113.04E
18 E2 Pasir Mas Pen Malaysia 6.02N 102.06E
18 B9 Pasir Panjang Pen Malaysia 2.25N 101.56E
18 H3 Pasir Panjang Singapore 1.18N 103.46E
18 H3 Pasir Panjang dist Singapore
18 D5 Pasirpengarayan Sumatra Indon 0.45N 100.15E
18 E3 Pasir Puteh Pen Malaysia 5.45N 102.29E
Pas-i-Rudak see Pasrūdak
31 F2 Pasi Shah Afghanistan 37.57N 70.29E
52 J9 Påskallavik Sweden 57.10N 16.25E
111 B2 Paskenta California 39.55N 122.33W
43 F4 Paskevicha, Zaliv B Kazakhstan U.S.S.R.
84 D3 Paskhalítsa Greece 39.19N 22.12E
32 J7 Paskūh Iran 27.33N 61.40E
62 M1 Pasłęk Poland 54.04N 19.39E
62 M1 Pasłęka R Poland
14 E10 Pasley, C W Australia 33.55S 123.30E
37 G5 Paslı Turkey 40.17N 42.55E
51 L4 Pasmajärvi Finland 67.06N 24.20E
82 C7 Pasman isld Yugoslavia 43.58N 15.20E
12 E4 Pasmore R S Australia
31 B8 Pasni Pakistan 25.13N 63.30E
19 F5 Paso Moluccas Indon 3.36S 128.15E
115 O9 Paso Caballos Guatemala 17.16N 90.18W
121 C9 Paso de Indios Argentina 43.55S 68.55W
115 M4 Paso del Cascal pk Nicaragua 11.50N 84.42W
121 B8 Paso del Limay Argentina 40.30S 70.30W
115 L8 Paso del Macho Mexico 19.00N 96.41W
121 F2 Paso de los Libres Argentina 29.43S 57.09W
121 G4 Paso de los Toros Uruguay 32.45S 56.30W

118 B10 Paso de Patria Paraguay 27.14S 58.33W
96 P10 Paso, El La Palma Canary Is 28.40N 17.53W
25 C2 Pasok Burma 21.22N 94.11E
120 F8 Pasorapa Bolivia 18.13S 64.37W
115 M2 Paso Reál Honduras 15.32N 85.45W
115 O8 Paso Real Mexico 18.48N 91.32W
121 K5 Paso Río Mayo Argentina 45.45S 70.20W
111 D6 Paso Robels California 35.38N 120.43W
98 G5 Paspébiac Quebec 48.03N 65.17W
100 M8 Pasqua Saskatchewan 50.22N 105.22W
103 N4 Pasque I Massachusetts 41.27N 70.50W
100 O5 Pasquia Hills Saskatchewan
100 Q5 Pasquia R Man/Saskatchewan
105 L1 Pasquotank R N Carolina
30 K7 Pasraha Bihar India 25.25N 86.43E
32 E6 Pasrūdak Iran 28.06N 52.19E
31 H4 Pasrur Pakistan 32.12N 74.42E
19 D8 Passábe Indonesia 9.25S 124.20E
104 R1 Passadumkeag Maine 45.11N 68.37W
92 E10 Passaford Zimbabwe 17.30S 30.59E
70 F8 Passage du Gois France
28 G7 Passage I Andaman Is Ind Oc 11.12N 92.42E
106 F1 Passage I Michigan 48.14N 88.22W
72 F7 Passage, le France 44.12N 0.36E
117 F8 Passagem Franca Brazil 6.10S 43.46W
59 F8 Passage West Cork Irish Rep 51.52N 8.20W
105 E10 Pass-a-Grille Beach Florida 27.42N 82.45W
103 K6 Passaic New Jersey 40.52N 74.08W
103 F4 Passaic co New Jersey
103 F5 Passaic R New Jersey
65 N7 Passail Austria 47.18N 15.32E
70 J4 Passais France 48.30N 0.46W
15 G5 Passam Papua New Guinea 3.42S 143.40E
30 K1 Passang Fall Col pass Xizang Zizhiqu 27.08N 87.02N
118 G8 Passa Quatro Brazil 22.23S 44.59W
26 T8 Passara Sri Lanka 6.57N 81.09E
119 H6 Passarão Brazil 3.09N 60.41W
118 G7 Passa Tempo Brazil 20.38S 44.31W
64 P6 Passau W Germany 48.35N 13.28E
66 B2 Passavant France 47.16N 6.23E
69 L8 Passavant-la-Rochère France 47.59N 6.02E
107 G11 Pass Christian Mississippi 30.20N 89.17W
108 D8 Pass Cr Wyoming
61 C3 Passendale Belgium 50.54N 3.01E
122 R15 Passe-Ouest channel Gambier Is Pacific Oc
81 K10 Passero, C Sicily 36.42N 15.09E
122 S16 Passe Sud-Est channel Gambier Is Pacific Oc
122 R16 Passe Sud-Ouest channel Gambier Is Pacific Oc
19 L6 Passi Philippines 11.06N 122.40E
95 L3 Passie S Africa 27.22S 27.07E
80 F2 Passignano sul Trasimeno Italy 43.11N 12.08E
84 E6 Pássion Greece 37.58N 22.35E
79 K1 Passiria, Val V Italy
98 Q6 Pass Island Newfoundland 47.31N 56.13W
99 B4 Pass Lake Ontario 48.34N 88.44W
121 E5 Passo Argentina 35.52S 62.16W
117 J9 Passo de Camaragibe Brazil 9.15S 35.29W
121 H2 Passo Fundo Brazil 28.16S 52.20W
118 F7 Passos Brazil 20.45S 46.38W
76 E6 Passos Portugal 41.27N 7.16W
63 U6 Passow E Germany 53.08N 14.08E
66 P4 Passugg Switzerland 46.49N 9.33E
25 L4 Passu Keah Reef Paracel Islands S China Sea
Pa-ssu-k'o-wo Shan mt see Basudan Ula
66 G2 Passwang mt Switzerland 47.22N 7.41E
71 K5 Passy Haute-Savoie France 45.55N 6.42E
68 E3 Passy Paris France 48.52N 2.17E
39 E2 Pastakh U.S.S.R. 67.06N 152.27E
119 C8 Pastaza prov Ecuador
119 C9 Pastaza, R Ecuador/Peru
120 B1 Pastaza, R Peru
121 E5 Pasteur Argentina 35.10S 62.14W
98 F3 Pasteur, L Quebec
100 Q5 Pas, The Manitoba 53.50N 101.15W
31 E1 Pastigav Tadzhikistan U.S.S.R. 39.24N 69.12E
119 C7 Pasto Colombia 1.12N 77.17W
120 G2 Pasto Grande Brazil 7.55S 62.56W
113 F5 Pastol B Alaska
111 P5 Pastora Pk mt Arizona 36.48N 109.12W
76 E2 Pastoriza Spain 43.18N 7.21W
117 F8 Pastos Bons Brazil 6.33S 44.04W
120 E9 Pastos Grandes, L Bolivia
75 E7 Pastrana Spain 40.25N 2.56W
84 F5 Pástra Óros mts Greece
79 J4 Pastrengo Italy 45.29N 10.48E
31 H2 Pasu Kashmir 36.30N 74.52E
79 K3 Pasúbio, Monte Italy 45.48N 11.11E
19 K2 Pasuquin Luzon Philippines 18.25N 120.37E
Pasur see Kulp
18 K9 Pasuruan Java Indon 7.38S 112.44E
46 E2 Pasvalys Lithuania U.S.S.R. 56.02N 24.30E
51 O2 Pasvikelv R Norway
100 O6 Paswegin Saskatchewan 52.00N 103.59W
26 R7 Pasyala Sri Lanka 7.10N 80.07E
120 E6 Pata Bolivia 14.36S 68.43W
19 K9 Pata isld Philippines 5.49N 121.13E
90 K8 Pata R Cent Afr Rep
120 D9 Patache, Pta C Chile 20.52S 70.15W
111 O10 Patagonia Arizona 31.33N 110.46W
121 K7 Patagonia reg Argentina
110 H3 Pataha R Washington
18 E8 Patah, Gunung mt Sumatra Indon 4.15S 103.18E
76 B9 Pataias Portugal 39.40N 9.00W
28 H3 Patakata Assam India 25.50N 90.00E
31 D2 Pata Kesar Afghanistan 37.11N 67.13E
96 U16 Patalavaca Gran Canaria Canary Is 27.45N 15.41W
32 J6 Patambar Iran 29.50N 60.13E
117 G9 Patamuté Brazil 9.29S 39.29W
Patan see Somnath
29 C6 Patan Gujarat India 23.51N 72.11E
31 G3 Patan India 35.08N 72.59E
28 A2 Patan Maharashtra India 17.24N 73.57E
30 J5 Patan Nepal 27.40N 85.20E
29 E4 Patan Rajasthan India 27.48N 76.01E
28 D2 Patancheru Andhra Prad India 17.32N 78.21E
31 C7 Patandar, Koh-i- mt Pakistan 27.15N 65.37E
19 F3 Patani Halmahera Indon 0.20N 128.46E
29 F7 Patan Saongi Maharashtra India 21.20N 79.08E
120 A7 Patapo Peru 6.45S 79.37W
103 A8 Patapsco R Maryland
104 D2 Patapsco State Park Maryland
29 E3 Pataudi Haryana India 28.20N 76.49E
32 D5 Pātāveh Iran 30.58N 51.19E
120 F12 Patay Argentina 26.45S 63.00W
69 B7 Patay France 48.03N 1.42E
12 F6 Patchewollock Victoria 35.22S 142.11E
103 H5 Patchogue Long I, N Y 40.46N 73.01W
56 D5 Patchole Devon Eng 51.11N 3.59W
11 J6 Patea New Zealand 39.45S 174.29E
11 J6 Patea R New Zealand
11 E12 Patearoa New Zealand 45.17S 170.04E
19 B5 Patedong Celebes Indon 3.14S 120.21E
90 B7 Pategi Nigeria 8.43N 5.43E
57 K4 Pateley Bridge N Yorks Eng 54.05N 1.45W
30 L6 Patenga Bihar India 26.15N 87.27E
89 J7 Patenga Ghana 9.47N 0.14W
31 J10 Patenga Pt Bangladesh 22.14N 91.48E
95 H9 Patensie S Africa 33.46S 24.49E
29 F6 Patera Madhya Prad India 23.59N 79.42E
84 F5 Patéras Óros mts Greece
75 K8 Paterna Spain 39.30N 0.27W
77 D6 Paterna del Campo Spain 37.25N 6.24W
77 M3 Paterna del Madera Spain 38.36N 2.20W
77 L6 Paterna del Río Spain 37.01N 2.57W
77 E7 Paterna de Rivera Spain 36.32N 5.52W
65 J8 Paternion Austria 46.43N 13.39E
81 J8 Paternò Sicily 37.34N 14.55E
80 M7 Paternopoli Italy 40.58N 15.03E
95 A8 Paternoster S Africa 32.48S 17.55E
110 F1 Pateros Washington 48.03N 119.55W
103 K6 Paterson New Jersey 40.56N 74.09W
95 J9 Paterson S Africa 33.27S 25.59E
110 F4 Paterson Washington 45.56N 119.35W
13 H8 Paterson R Queensland
11 C13 Paterson Inlet Stewart I New Zealand
14 D5 Paterson Ra W Australia
Paterswolde see Eelde-Paterswolde
60 P7 Paterswoldermeer L Netherlands
30 B8 Patha Uttar Prad India 24.30N 78.40E
28 K2 Pathalipam Assam India 27.30N 94.22E
32 G7 Pathān Iran 27.44N 56.35E
29 D1 Pathankot Himachal Prad India 32.16N 75.43E
30 G6 Pathardewa Uttar Prad India 26.35N 83.55E
30 L8 Pathargama Bihar India 24.58N 87.17E
29 F6 Pathari Bhilsa, Madhya Prad Ind 23.56N 78.12E
29 E6 Pathari Indore, Madhya Prad Ind 22.48N 76.12E
30 J5 Patharkot Nepal 27.06N 85.40E
28 H2 Patharughat Assam India 26.21N 91.54E
30 A5 Pathena Rajasthan India 27.08N 77.01E
108 D7 Pathfinder Res Wyoming
58 L7 Pathhead Lothian Scotland 55.52N 2.58W
25 E7 Pathiu Thailand 10.41N 99.18E
100 N6 Pathlow Saskatchewan 52.44N 104.50W
29 E8 Pathri Maharashtra India 19.17N 76.30E
Pathuk see Pazūk
25 F5 Pathum Thani Thailand 14.03N 100.29E
18 J6 Pati Borneo Indon 0.35S 111.14E
19 E8 Pati Indon 8.11S 127.54E
18 J9 Pati Java Indon 6.45S 111.00E
29 D7 Pati Madhya Prad India 21.55N 74.46E
29 E2 Patiala Punjab India 30.21N 76.27E
29 E2 Patiala dist Punjab India
30 C5 Patiali Uttar Prad India 27.41N 79.00E
119 B7 Patía, R Colombia
29 J2 Patiatoli Bihar India 23.30N 85.25E
117 C3 Patience Fr Guiana 3.54N 53.24W
14 F6 Patience Well W Australia 23.22S 125.45E
61 K6 Patignies Belgium 50.00N 4.57E
93 D2 Patiko Uganda 3.02N 32.24E
89 C5 Patim Gouta Senegal 12.43N 13.47W
19 E4 Patinti, Selat str Halmahera Indon
19 M1 Pati Pt Guam Pacific Oc 13.36N 144.58E
119 F9 Pati, R Brazil
29 L5 Patiram W Bengal India 25.20N 88.50E
19 B6 Patiro, Tanjung C Celebes Indonesia 4.40S 120.27E
120 B4 Pativilca Peru 10.44S 77.45W
120 B4 Pativilca R Peru
30 H6 Patjilrwa Bihar India 26.49N 84.25E
28 K2 Patkai Hills Assam India
30 F6 Patkauli Uttar Prad India 26.14N 82.18E
30 J5 Patlaiya Nepal 27.11N 84.59E
107 C8 Patmos Arkansas 33.31N 93.34W
83 H7 Pátmos isld Greece
30 J7 Patna Bihar India 25.37N 85.12E
57 D2 Patna Strathclyde Scot 55.20N 4.30W
30 E5 Patna Uttar Prad India 27.49N 81.46E
30 G7 Patna div Bihar India
30 J7 Patna dist Bihar India
29 H7 Patnagarh Orissa India 20.42N 83.12E
19 L4 Patnanongan isld Philippines 14.50N 122.13E
31 G8 Patnitola Bangladesh 24.56N 88.48E
37 G6 Patnos Turkey 39.14N 42.52E
119 D4 Pato Colombia 7.28N 74.57W
30 J5 Pato Nepal 27.03N 85.56E
118 D10 Pato Branco Brazil 26.20S 52.40W
120 A3 Pato, Cañón del Peru 8.40S 78.05W
121 J6 Pato, Cerro pk Chile 46.04S 72.22W
28 B1 Patoda Maharashtra India 18.48N 75.32E
107 G3 Patoka Illinois 38.45N 89.04W
11 L6 Patoka New Zealand 39.22S 176.36E
107 K3 Patoka R Indiana
89 F9 Patokla Ivory Coast 5.28N 7.19W
120 E5 Pato, L Bolivia 13.04S 67.00W
42 K2 Patom U.S.S.R. 60.06N 116.59E
42 J3 Patomskoye Nagor'ye highland U.S.S.R.
108 Q7 Paton Iowa 42.08N 94.15W
30 D2 Paton Uttar Prad India 39.09N 80.16E
93 E3 Patonga Uganda 2.46N 33.19E
12 M4 Patonga Beach New S Wales 33.33S 151.16E
117 H8 Patos Paraíba Brazil 6.55S 37.15W
117 G8 Patos Piauí Brazil 7.41S 41.14W
118 F6 Patos de Minas Brazil 18.35S 46.32W
116 N1 Patos, I Venezuela 10.36N 61.54W
110 C1 Patos I Washington 48.48N 122.57W
121 H3 Patos, Lagoa dos lagoon Brazil
112 A5 Patos, L. de Mexico
120 G11 Patos, L. de los Chaco Arg 25.15S 61.02W
121 E3 Patos, L. de los Córdoba Argentina
121 B3 Patos, R. de los Argentina
19 K9 Patotol Philippines 5.59N 121.23E
Patpo see Pa-pu
121 C3 Patquía Argentina 30.02S 66.54W
84 C5 Pátrai Greece 38.14N 21.44E
84 B5 Patraikós Kólpos gulf Greece
Patras see Pátrai
29 L2 Patrasayar W Bengal India 23.22N 87.34E
47 J4 Patrasuy U.S.S.R. 63.35N 61.50E
Patreksfjördhur see Vatneyri
50 A3 Patreksfjördhur B Iceland
29 B6 Patri Gujarat India 23.10N 71.10E
80 K7 Patria, Lago di Italy
100 F8 Patricia Alberta 50.43N 111.35W
108 J6 Patricia S Dakota 43.20N 101.30W
112 E3 Patricia Texas 32.33N 102.03W
13 B5 Patricia, Mt N Terr Australia 21.28S 131.32E
121 H7 Patricio Lynch, I Chile
57 D4 Patrick Isle of Man U.K. 54.12N 4.42W
57 K4 Patrick Brompton N Yorks Eng 54.19N 1.40W
59 E6 Patrickswell Limerick Irish Rep 52.36N 8.42W
42 F4 Patrikha U.S.S.R. 55.20N 97.52E
118 E6 Patrimônio* Brazil 19.32S 48.34W
57 N5 Patrington Humberside Eng 53.41N 0.02W
107 M3 Patriot Indiana 38.51N 84.50W
118 F6 Patrocínio Brazil 18.59S 46.58W
84 G6 Patróklou isld Greece 37.39N 23.57E
32 H3 Patrū Iran 35.25N 59.40E
107 K10 Patsaliga R Alabama
65 D7 Patscherkofel mt Austria 47.13N 11.29E
47 B2 Patsoyoki R U.S.S.R.
93 N8 Patta Kenya 2.08S 41.02E
81 C2 Pattada Sardinia 40.34N 9.07E
43 H8 Patta-Gisar Uzbekistan U.S.S.R. 37.16N 67.17E
93 N8 Patta I Kenya 2.05S 41.05E
19 A6 Pattallassang Celebes Indon 5.29S 119.26E
25 F9 Pattan R Thailand
28 C6 Pattanapuram Kerala India 9.10N 76.46E
25 F9 Pattani Thailand 6.50N 101.20E
25 F6 Pattaya Thailand 12.57N 100.53E
104 Q8 Patten Maine 45.59N 68.26W
63 L8 Pattensen W Germany 52.16N 9.45E
57 H3 Patterdale Cumbria Eng 54.32N 2.56W
111 C4 Patterson California 37.29N 121.10W
105 E6 Patterson Georgia 31.23N 82.10W
110 M5 Patterson Idaho 44.31N 113.44W
107 E12 Patterson Louisiana 29.40N 91.20W
103 G3 Patterson New York 41.31N 73.37W
104 F7 Patterson Cr R W Virginia
111 E5 Patterson Mt California 36.57N 119.05W
101 F3 Patterson, Mt Yukon Terr 64.03N 134.38W
106 J4 Patterson, Pt Michigan 45.59N 85.39W
9 C10 Patteson Passage New Hebrides
25 F9 Patthalung Thailand 7.38N 100.05E
29 D2 Patti Punjab India 31.17N 74.51E
81 J7 Patti Sicily 38.08N 14.58E
30 F7 Patti Uttar Prad India 25.52N 82.12E
13 B4 Pattie Cr N Terr Australia
81 K7 Patti, G. di Sicily
28 C3 Pattikonda Andhra Prad India 15.24N 77.30E
35 B8 Pattish Israel 31.20N 34.33E
35 B8 Pattish watercourse Israel
107 F10 Pattison Mississippi 31.55N 90.55W
11 J11 Pattisson, C Chatham Is Pacific Oc 43.44S 176.47W
25 L4 Pattle I Paracel Islands S China Sea
104 G6 Patton Pennsylvania 40.38N 78.38W
107 B1 Pattonsburg Missouri 40.03N 94.10W
28 D5 Pattukkottai Tamil Nadu India 10.29N 79.20E
101 J7 Pattullo, Mt Br Columbia 56.15N 129.43W
117 H8 Patu Brazil 6.07S 37.37W
28 J7 Patua Nicobar Is 7.17N 93.40E
31 H10 Patuakhali Bangladesh 22.20N 90.20E
31 H10 Patuakhali dist Bangladesh
115 M2 Patuca R Honduras
115 M2 Patuca, Pta Honduras 15.50N 84.16W
18 G9 Patuha, Gunung mt Java Indon 7.12S 107.17E
82 H6 Pătulele Romania 44.20N 22.45E
30 F8 Patulki Madhya Prad India 24.28N 82.10E
115 O10 Patulul Guatemala 14.26N 91.09W
29 J5 Patun Bihar India 24.14N 84.12E
Patuna see Pathān
29 E7 Patur Maharashtra India 20.28N 77.02E
61 F5 Pâturages Belgium 50.25N 3.52E
11 G7 Paturau River New Zealand 40.39S 172.27E
11 M5 Patutahi New Zealand 38.38S 177.56E
11 K6 Patutu New Zealand 39.14S 175.48E
103 A8 Patuxent, Little R Maryland
115 J8 Pátzcuaro Mexico 19.30N 101.38W
115 J8 Pátzcuaro, L. de Mexico
115 O10 Patzicía Guatemala 14.38N 90.52W
115 O10 Patzún Guatemala 14.41N 90.58W
72 D9 Pau France 43.18N 0.22W
11 G1 Paua New Zealand 34.33S 172.58E
117 G9 Pau-a-Pique Brazil 9.40S 41.35W
11 E4 Pauatahanui New Zealand 41.07S 174.55E
120 C5 Paucarbamba Peru 12.24S 74.36W
120 D5 Paucartambo Cuzco Peru 13.19S 71.36W
120 B4 Paucartambo Pasco Peru 10.54S 75.51W
120 D5 Paucartambo R Peru
117 D8 Pau d'Arco Brazil 7.32S 49.15W
117 D8 Pau d'Arco, R Brazil
117 H8 Pau dos Ferros Brazil 6.05S 38.11W
72 H1 Paudy France 47.03N 1.55E
99 P7 Paugan Falls Quebec 45.48N 75.56W
72 F8 Pauilhac France 43.53N 0.37E
72 C5 Pauillac France 45.12N 0.44W
120 E2 Pauini Brazil 7.43S 67.00W
119 G8 Pauini, R Amazonas Brazil
120 E2 Pauiní, R Amazonas Brazil
25 C2 Pauk Burma 21.25N 94.30E
114 C7 Paukaa Hawaiian Is 19.45N 155.07W
25 C3 Paukkaung Burma 18.54N 95.32E
25 B2 Pauktaw Burma 20.12N 93.07E
76 D8 Paul Beira Baixa Portugal 40.12N 7.38W
110 M7 Paul Idaho 42.37N 113.48W
76 C10 Paul Ribatejo Portugal 39.12N 8.07W
79 O1 Paularo Italy 46.32N 13.07E
101 M1 Paulatuk N W Terr 69.23N 124.00W
Paul Block B see Block Bay
96 O7 Paul da Serra mts Madeira Is
111 M7 Paulden Arizona 34.55N 112.27W
104 A5 Paulding Ohio 41.10N 84.37W
123 G2 Paulding B Antarctica
96 O7 Paúl do Mar Madeira Is 32.45N 17.14W
72 K5 Paulhac France 45.00N 2.52E
71 D6 Paulhaguet France 45.13N 3.30E
71 C9 Paulhan France 43.30N 3.27E
113 H9 Paul I Alaska 55.50N 159.20W
97 N6 Paul I Labrador, Nfld 56.30N 61.20W
118 D7 Paulicéia Brazil 21.18S 51.50W
81 B3 Paulilatino Sardinia 40.05N 8.46E
110 F5 Paulina Oregon 44.09N 119.58W
63 R7 Paulinenaue E Germany 52.41N 12.43E
72 J8 Paulinet France 43.51N 2.25E
117 F6 Paulino Neves Brazil 2.41S 42.32W
103 E4 Paulins Kill R New Jersey
Paulis see Isiro
117 J8 Paulista Brazil 7.56S 34.50W
117 G9 Paulistana Brazil 8.09S 41.06W
108 P7 Paullina Iowa 42.58N 95.40W
79 F4 Paullo Italy 45.25N 9.24E
72 G2 Paulnay France 46.51N 1.07E
117 H9 Paulo Afonso, Cachoeira de falls Brazil 9.25S 38.15W
118 E7 Paulo de Faria Brazil 20.02S 49.23W
95 O3 Paulpietersburg S Africa 27.25S 30.50E
95 L4 Paul Roux S Africa 28.18S 27.57E
75 L6 Paúls Spain 40.55N 0.24E
94 P12 Paulsberg mt Cape Town S Africa 34.17S 18.28E
103 D7 Paulsboro New Jersey 39.51N 75.15W
Paulstown see Whitehall Kilkenny
109 N7 Pauls Valley Oklahoma 34.46N 97.14W
64 M5 Paulushofen W Germany 49.01N 11.31E
60 D3 Pauluspolder Netherlands 51.20N 4.01E
72 A2 Paulx France 46.58N 1.45W
25 D4 Paung Burma 16.39N 97.27E
25 L9 Paungbyin Burma 24.16N 94.51E
25 C3 Paungde Burma 18.30N 95.30E
29 F7 Pauni Maharashtra India 20.45N 79.42E
15 G5 Paup Papua New Guinea 3.17S 142.35E
103 D4 Paupack Pennsylvania 41.24N 75.14W
30 A7 Pauri Madhya Prad India 25.32N 77.22E
30 B2 Pauri Uttar Prad India 30.08N 78.48E
120 G7 Paurito Bolivia 17.55S 62.58W
64 N2 Pausa E Germany 50.35N 12.01E
120 C6 Pausa Peru 15.18S 73.23W
63 S7 Pausin E Germany 52.39N 13.04E
119 B9 Paute Ecuador 2.52S 78.46W
119 E5 Pauto, R Colombia
52 K2 Pautrask Sweden 64.49N 17.30E
69 G5 Pauvres France 49.25N 4.30E
90 C6 Pauwa Nigeria 11.58N 7.19E
114 D5 Pauwalu Hawaiian Is 21.06N 156.46W
114 E6 Pauwalu Pt Hawaiian Is 20.51N 156.08W
15 F5 Pauwasi R Irian Jaya
114 E6 Pauwela Hawaiian Is 20.56N 156.20W
114 E6 Pauwela pt Hawaiian Is 20.57N 156.18W
28 C3 Pavagada Karnataka India 14.06N 77.15E
111 M3 Pavant Ra Utah
118 H5 Pavão Brazil 17.23S 41.01W
119 C4 Pavarandocito Colombia 7.17N 76.34W
82 D2 Pavazsky Inovec mts Czechoslovakia
47 H6 Pavda U.S.S.R. 59.15N 59.29E
32 B3 Pāveh Iran 35.02N 46.15E
45 L3 Pavelets U.S.S.R. 53.51N 39.16E
79 F4 Pavia Italy 45.12N 9.09E
76 C11 Pavia Portugal 38.54N 8.01W
79 E4 Pavia prov Italy
79 O3 Pavia d'Udine Italy 45.59N 13.19E
75 K8 Pavías Spain 39.59N 0.29W
72 F8 Pavie France 43.36N 0.36E
101 N10 Pavilion Br Columbia 50.52N 121.50W
104 G4 Pavilion New York 42.53N 78.02W
108 B6 Pavillion Wyoming 43.16N 108.41W
69 F7 Pavillon-Ste. Julie, le France 48.22N 3.55E
68 G3 Pavillons-sous-Bois, les France 48.55N 2.30E
70 M2 Pavilly France 49.34N 0.58E
46 D2 Pāvilosta Latvia U.S.S.R. 56.51N 21.12E
46 O1 Pavino U.S.S.R. 59.07N 46.11E
79 L2 Pavione, Monte mt Italy 46.06N 11.50E
84 D4 Pávliani Greece 38.45N 22.20E
82 J7 Pavlikeni Bulgaria 43.14N 25.20E
45 E2 Pavlinovo U.S.S.R. 54.30N 33.46E
43 M2 Pavlodar Kazakhstan U.S.S.R. 52.21N 76.59E
47 L8 Pavlodarskaya Oblast' prov Kazakhstan U.S.S.R.
113 G9 Pavlof Alaska 55.30N 161.30W
113 G9 Pavlof B Alaska
113 F9 Pavlof Harbor Aleutian Is 54.26N 162.47W
113 G9 Pavlof Is Alaska
113 G9 Pavlof Vol Alaska 55.26N 161.55W
46 K5 Pavlograd Ukraine U.S.S.R. 48.34N 35.50E
47 L8 Pavlogradka U.S.S.R. 54.14N 73.31E
84 F4 Pávlon Greece 38.32N 23.05E
43 L2 Pavlovka Akmolinsk, Kazakhstan U.S.S.R. 51.24N 72.40E
47 H7 Pavlovka Bashkir U.S.S.R. 55.26N 56.35E
43 G1 Pavlovka Kustanay, Kazakhstan U.S.S.R. 52.34N 63.05E
46 R4 Pavlovka Orenburg U.S.S.R. 51.52N 54.42E
45 T4 Pavlovka Ul'yanovsk U.S.S.R. 52.42N 47.06E
45 P1 Pavlovo U.S.S.R. 55.58N 43.05E
42 C5 Pavlovsk Altay U.S.S.R. 53.19N 83.01E
46 H1 Pavlovsk Leningrad U.S.S.R. 59.41N 30.23E
45 M6 Pavlovsk Voronezh U.S.S.R. 50.28N 40.07E
44 C1 Pavlovskaya U.S.S.R. 46.18N 39.48E
43 G1 Pavlovskiy Kazakhstan U.S.S.R. 53.02N 63.01E
46 R1 Pavlovskiy U.S.S.R. 57.50N 54.50E
45 E8 Pavlysh Ukraine U.S.S.R. 48.55N 33.23E
105 D7 Pavo Georgia 30.56N 83.46W
119 D6 Pavon Colombia 3.38N 72.16W
79 C4 Pavone Canavese Italy 45.26N 7.51E
79 J6 Pavullo nel Frignano Italy 44.20N 10.49E
118 H8 Pavuna Brazil 22.49S 43.22W
118 H8 Pavuna, R Brazil
15 L3 Pavuvu I Solomon Is 9.10S 159.07E
15 M4 Pawa Solomon Is 10.17S 161.45E
Pawah see Pāveh
25 N8 Pawahku Burma 26.09N 98.39E
30 D8 Pawai Madhya Prad India 24.16N 80.09E
18 J6 Pawan R Kalimantan Indonesia
30 D4 Pawayan Uttar Prad India 28.03N 80.06E
103 L4 Pawcatuck Connecticut 41.22N 71.50W
25 E7 Pawe-gyi Kyun isld Burma
109 O5 Pawhuska Oklahoma 36.42N 96.21W
100 Q3 Pawistik Manitoba 55.41N 101.15W
104 M3 Pawlet Vermont 43.22N 73.12W
56 F5 Pawlett Somerset Eng 51.12N 3.00W
105 H4 Pawleys I S Carolina 33.27N 79.03W
103 G3 Pawling New York 41.34N 73.37W
25 D3 Pawn R Burma
107 G2 Pawnee Illinois 39.35N 89.35W
109 O5 Pawnee Oklahoma 36.21N 96.50W
112 J7 Pawnee Texas 28.40N 98.00W
109 L3 Pawnee R Kansas
108 O9 Pawnee City Nebraska 40.07N 96.10W
109 G1 Pawnee Cr Colorado
109 M3 Pawnee Rock Kansas 38.16N 98.59W
106 J7 Paw Paw Michigan 42.13N 85.55W
104 G7 Paw Paw W Virginia 39.32N 78.27W
89 J7 Pawta Ghana 8.38N 1.32W
103 M3 Pawtucket Rhode I 41.53N 71.23W
25 E6 Pawut Burma 12.30N 99.00E
91 E9 Paxe Angola 10.17S 17.57E
84 L11 Paximádhia isld Crete 35.00N 24.35E
103 A5 Paxinos Pennsylvania 40.50N 76.36W
83 D5 Paxoí isld Greece
113 P5 Paxson Alaska 63.02N 145.35W
113 P5 Paxson L Alaska 62.56N 145.30W
103 A6 Paxtang Pennsylvania 40.15N 76.50W
106 F9 Paxton Illinois 40.28N 88.07W
103 L2 Paxton Massachusetts 42.19N 71.55W
108 J8 Paxton Nebraska 41.08N 101.22W
103 A6 Paxtonia Pennsylvania 40.18N 76.47W
115 M2 Paya Honduras 15.44N 84.51W
18 D8 Paya Besar Pen Malaysia 3.46N 103.14E
30 E5 Payagpur Uttar Prad India 27.24N 81.48E
25 D4 Payagyi Burma 17.28N 96.32E
121 C10 Payahile, L Argentina
18 D6 Payakumbuh Sumatra Indon 0.10S 100.30E
18 J3 Paya Lebar Singapore 1.21N 103.53E
18 J3 Paya Lebar dist Singapore
37 D8 Payamlı Turkey 37.02N 38.38E
36 J6 Payas Turkey 36.46N 36.10E
28 B4 Payaswari R Karnataka/Kerala India
42 C3 Paydugina R U.S.S.R.
Pa-yen-wu-la see Xi Ujimqin Qi
Pa-yeo-kao-le see Dengkou
65 N6 Payerbach Austria 47.42N 15.53E
50 U14 Payer, Kapp Spitsbergen 78.50N 21.40E
66 D4 Payerne Switzerland 46.49N 6.57E
110 J5 Payette Idaho 44.04N 116.56W
110 J5 Payette R Idaho
110 J5 Payette L Idaho 44.58N 116.06W
40 E6 Paykan U.S.S.R. 50.13N 130.07E
47 J2 Pay-Khoy, Khrebet mts U.S.S.R.
53 T18 Payla Norway 60.19N 5.40E
77 B5 Paymogo Spain 37.44N 7.21W
105 D5 Payne Georgia 32.52N 83.43W
106 K8 Payne Ohio 41.09N 84.45W
12 B8 Payneham dist Adelaide, S Aust 34.54S 138.39E
97 M6 Payne, L Quebec 59.25N 74.00W
110 D9 Paynes Creek California 40.21N 121.57W
14 C8 Payne's Find W Australia 29.15S 117.43E
108 Q4 Paynesville Minnesota 45.22N 94.41W
14 C8 Paynesville W Australia 28.03S 118.30E
100 J5 Paynton Saskatchewan 53.01N 108.54W
76 F8 Payo, El Spain 40.17N 6.44W
18 B8 Payong, Bukit hill Pen Malaysia 3.04N 101.57E
18 K4 Payong, Tanjong C Sarawak Malaysia 3.47N 113.27E
72 G6 Payrac France 44.47N 1.28E
72 A3 Payré, Pte. du France 46.26N 1.40W
72 E3 Payroux France 46.12N 0.28E
121 F4 Paysandú Uruguay 32.21S 58.05W
121 F4 Paysandú dept Uruguay
72 A9 Pays Basque reg France
72 C8 Pays d'Albret reg France
70 K3 Pays-d'Auge reg France
72 B7 Pays de Born reg France
70 O2 Pays-de-Bray reg France
71 F5 Pays-de-Dombes reg France
66 E6 Pays d'Enhaut V Switzerland
111 N7 Payson Arizona 34.16N 111.20W
110 O9 Payson Utah 40.04N 111.45W
32 B3 Paytak Pass Iran 34.14N 46.49E
43 O7 Paytok Uzbekistan U.S.S.R. 40.55N 72.14E
41 F5 Payturma U.S.S.R. 71.33N 94.55E
121 B6 Payún Matru, Cerros hills Arg
121 B6 Payún, V Argentina 36.30S 69.20W
47 J3 Pay-Yer, Gora mt U.S.S.R. 66.43N 64.28E
72 G5 Payzac France 45.24N 1.14E
Payzawat see Jiashi
81 C3 Paza, Cuccuru mt Sardinia 40.11N 9.23E
32 C5 Pāzanān Iran 30.38N 49.59E
32 D5 Pazanan oil well Iran 30.25N 50.04E
118 J2 Paza, Pta Brazil 11.07S 37.08W
36 F2 Pazar Ankara Turkey 40.17N 32.47E
37 F4 Pazar Rize Turkey 41.12N 40.52E
36 J2 Pazar Tokat Turkey 40.18N 36.19E
36 D3 Pazarcık Bilecik Turkey 39.58N 29.52E
37 C8 Pazarcık Maraş Turkey 37.31N 37.19E
82 J8 Pazardzhik Bulgaria 42.10N 24.20E
36 F2 Pazarköy Bolu Turkey 40.56N 32.11E
36 C3 Pazarköy Turkey 39.51N 27.24E
37 C3 Pazarliköy Turkey 40.19N 26.30E
36 J3 Pazarsu Turkey 39.08N 36.37E
36 E1 Pazartaşi Burun C Turkey 41.14N 30.16E
36 J4 Pazarviran Turkey 38.42N 36.10E
115 D5 Paz, B. de la Mexico
119 D5 Paz de Ariporo Colombia 5.54N 71.52W
44 H9 Pāzh R Iran
82 B5 Pazin Yugoslavia 45.14N 13.56E
72 K10 Paziols France 42.51N 2.42E
120 E8 Pazna Bolivia 18.34S 66.56W
65 B7 Paznauntal V Austria
76 B4 Pazos de Borbén Spain 42.17N 8.31W
117 C9 Paz, R. da Brazil
62 M8 Pázstó Hungary 47.56N 19.40E
32 G3 Pazūk Iran 34.59N 57.03E
46 H1 Pchevzha U.S.S.R. 59.21N 32.20E
62 M6 Pcim Poland 49.47N 19.52E
82 G8 Pčinja R Yugoslavia
9 R10 Pea Tonga, Pacific Oc 21.10S 175.13W
107 L10 Pea R Alabama
104 P4 Peabody Massachusetts 42.33N 70.58W
103 L4 Peace Dale Rhode I 41.27N 71.30W
101 R6 Peace Point Alberta 59.07N 112.20W
101 Q6 Peace R Alberta
101 M7 Peace R Br Col
105 F10 Peace R Florida
101 P7 Peace River Alberta 56.15N 117.18W
101 O11 Peachland Br Col 49.49N 119.48W
111 L6 Peach Springs Arizona 35.31N 113.25W
106 J5 Peacock Michigan 44.03N 85.54W
112 G2 Peacock Texas 33.11N 100.24W
9 B7 Peacock Pt Wake I Pacific Oc 19.16N 166.38E
71 F6 Péage-de-Roussillon, la France 45.23N 4.48E
114 E6 Peah Hawaiian Is 20.55N 156.17W
119 H4 Peaima Falls Guyana 6.19N 60.33W
30 H4 "Peak 43" Nepal 27.45N 86.49E
30 J4 "Peak 41" Nepal 27.47N 86.55E
30 K3 "Peak 4" Nepal 27.50N 87.03E
30 L4 "Peak 6" Nepal 27.47N 87.07E
30 L4 "Peak 7" Nepal 27.45N 87.08N
30 K2 "Peak 38" Xizang Zizhiqu/Nepal 27.58N 86.58E
30 L3 "Peak 3" Xizang Zizhiqu/Nepal 27.51N 87.08E
13 J5 Peak Downs Queensland 22.14S 148.09E
12 D3 Peake R S Australia
19 J6 Peaked Pt Philippines 10.22N 118.59E
59 C8 Peakeen Mt Kerry Irish Rep 51.56N 9.37W
13 B3 Peake, Mt N Terr Australia 15.53S 131.21E
57 K6 Peak Forest Derbys Eng 53.19N 1.49W
12 J5 Peak Hill New S Wales 32.47S 148.13E
14 C7 Peak Hill W Australia 25.40S 118.41E
12 L8 Peakhurst dist Sydney, N S W
111 E7 Peak Mt California 34.55N 119.53W
13 J6 Peak Ra Queensland
96 B11 Peak, The mt Ascension I 7.58S 14.21W
57 K6 Peak, The mt Derbys Eng 53.24N 1.51W
77 K5 Peal de Becerro Spain 37.55N 3.08W
9 B6 Peale I Pacific Oc 19.19N 166.36E
123 H12 Peale Inlet Antarctica
111 P3 Peale, Mt Utah 38.26N 109.14W
110 B9 Peanut California 40.29N 123.11W
103 E5 Peapack Gladstone New Jersey 40.43N 74.40W
12 A6 Peara dist Canberra Australia
100 D9 Pearce Alberta 49.48N 113.18W
111 P10 Pearce Arizona 31.53N 109.50W
13 A2 Pearce Pt N Terr Australia 14.22S 129.20E
107 C7 Pearcy Arkansas 34.25N 93.15W
113 H1 Peard B Alaska
76 D3 Peares, Embalse de los res Spain
107 F2 Pearl Illinois 39.27N 90.38W
99 B4 Pearl Ontario 48.41N 88.39W
107 G11 Pearl R Miss/Ala
112 G10 Pearland Texas 29.32N 95.16W
114 A1 Pearl and Hermes Reef Hawaiian Is 27.48N 175.51W
12 M4 Pearl Beach New S Wales 33.33S 151.18E
114 B5 Pearl City Hawaiian Is 21.24N 157.58W
106 E7 Pearl City Illinois 42.16N 89.50W
114 B5 Pearl Harbor Hawaiian Is 21.22N 158.00W
107 G11 Pearl River Louisiana 30.21N 89.46W
103 F4 Pearl River New York 41.03N 74.02W
26 O13 Pearl, Rochers de la rocks Amsterdam I Ind Oc 37.49S 77.33E
116 P5 Pearls airport Grenada, W I 12.10N 61.36W
112 H7 Pearsall Texas 28.54N 99.07W
105 E6 Pearson Georgia 31.16N 82.54W
12 C5 Pearson Is S Australia 33.56S 134.20E
100 U2 Pearson L Manitoba
95 J8 Pearston S Africa 32.35S 25.09E
97 J2 Peary Chan N W Terr
48 S1 Peary Land reg Greenland
112 H1 Pease R Texas
58 M7 Pease Bridge Borders Scotland 55.55N 2.20W
56 O3 Peasenhall Suffolk Eng 52.16N 1.26E
56 N6 Peasmarsh E Sussex Eng 50.59N 0.41E
83 G5 Peathoúra isld Greece 39.28N 24.12E
58 L6 Peat Inn Fife Scotland 56.17N 2.53W
70 F6 Péaule France 47.35N 2.21W
106 F3 Peavy Falls Res Michigan 46.00N 88.12W
14 C5 Peawah, R W Australia
92 J10 Pebane Mozambique 17.14S 38.10E
119 E9 Pebas Peru 3.10S 71.46W
121 E9 Pebble I Falkland Is 51.20S 59.40W
91 G6 Pebeangu Zaïre 4.26S 20.59E
90 J7 Pebo Cent Afr Rep 8.08N 18.43E
71 D6 Pébrac France 45.02N 3.30E
82 F8 Peć Yugoslavia 42.40N 20.19E
95 F10 Pecaltsdorp S Africa 34.01S 22.27E
118 G6 Peçanha Brazil 18.32S 42.32W
107 D12 Pecan Island Louisiana 29.40N 92.27W
118 E9 Peças, I. das Brazil 25.24S 48.22W
106 E7 Pecatonica Illinois 42.18N 89.22W
106 E7 Pecatonica, R Illinois
66 L6 Peccia Switzerland 46.25N 8.39E
66 L6 Peccia, V Switzerland
79 J7 Péccioli Italy 43.33N 10.43E
47 C2 Pecha R U.S.S.R.
41 D8 Pechal' R U.S.S.R.
82 L5 Pechea Romania 45.36N 27.49E
82 J2 Pechenezhin U.S.S.R. 48.32N 24.54E
47 C2 Pechenga U.S.S.R. 69.28N 31.04E
47 J5 Pecherakh U.S.S.R. 60.54N 63.29E
45 U3 Pechersk U.S.S.R. 53.15N 49.00E
77 G10 Pêcheurs, Pte des pt Morocco 35.14N 4.40W
96 T8 Pechiguera, Pta pt Lanzarote Canary Is 28.51N 13.52W
77 M7 Pechina Spain 36.55N 2.25W
118 H9 Pechincha Brazil 22.56S 43.21W
47 H3 Pechora U.S.S.R. 65.14N 57.18E
47 G3 Pechora R U.S.S.R.
47 G2 Pechorskaya Guba gulf U.S.S.R.
47 G2 Pechorskoye More sea U.S.S.R.
46 G1 Pechory U.S.S.R. 57.42N 27.41E
50 U14 Pechuel Løsche, Kapp Spitsbergen 78.10N 23.30E
82 G4 Pecica Romania 46.09N 21.06E
89 A6 Pecixe,I Guinea-Bissau 11.50N 16.25W
110 B7 Peck Oregon 42.55N 123.34W
63 S6 Peckatel E Germany 53.27N 13.04E
63 K9 Peckelsheim W Germany 51.34N 9.07E
11 F9 Pecksniff, Mt New Zealand 42.10S 171.30E
103 D4 Pecks Pond Pennsylvania 41.16N 75.06W
65 M1 Pečky Czechoslovakia 50.07N 15.02E
103 K4 Peconic Long I, N Y 41.02N 72.28W
103 K5 Peconic Bay, Gt New York
103 K5 Peconic Bay, Lit New York
81 A5 Pecora, C Sardinia 39.28N 8.22E
81 M6 Pecoraro, Mte Italy 38.32N 16.21E
109 E6 Pecos New Mexico 35.34N 105.41W
112 D4 Pecos Texas 31.25N 103.30W
112 F5 Pecos R Texas etc
61 D4 Pecq Belgium 50.41N 3.21E
68 C3 Pecq, le France 48.54N 2.07E
62 L9 Pécs Hungary 46.04N 18.15E
Pécs co see Baranya co
62 L9 Pécsvárad Hungary 46.09N 18.26E
107 B3 Peculiar Missouri 38.45N 94.27W
81 R11 Pedagne, le islds Italy 40.39N 18.00E
18 C9 Pedas Pen Malaysia 2.38N 102.01E
76 D9 Pe da Serra Portugal 39.35N 7.37W
115 O6 Pedasí Panama 7.36N 80.04W
80 J2 Pedaso Italy 43.06N 13.51E
28 F2 Peddapuram Andhra Prad India 17.06N 82.13E
28 D2 Peddavagu R Andhra Prad India
12 H9 Pedder, L Tasmania 42.55S 146.07E
12 H8 Pedder, L res Tasmania 42.56S 146.08E
95 L9 Peddie S Africa 33.12S 27.07E
104 R10 Peddocks I Massachusetts 42.17N 70.55W
110 B5 Pedee Oregon 44.45N 123.26W
66 H8 Pedemonte Italy 45.52N 7.57E
116 J5 Pedernales Dominican Rep 18.02N 71.41W
119 B7 Pedernales Ecuador 0.03N 80.00W
115 F3 Pedernales Mexico 28.25N 107.09W
75 E1 Pedernales Spain 43.24N 2.42W
119 H3 Pedernales Venezuela 9.58N 62.15W
120 D12 Pedernales, Salar de salt pan Chile
77 L2 Pedernoso, El Spain 39.29N 2.45W
79 L3 Pederobba Italy 45.53N 11.57E
53 H6 Pedersborg Denmark 55.28N 11.34E
53 P12 Pedersker Bornholm Denmark 55.02N 15.00E
84 D6 Pedhiás Feneoú plain Greece
84 Q15 Pedhoulas Cyprus 34.58N 32.50E
84 R14 Pedieas R Cyprus
12 D2 Pedirka S Australia 26.40S 135.10E
95 L5 Pedlars Peak mt Lesotho 29.59S 27.44E
56 F3 Pedlar's Rest Shropshire Eng 52.27N 2.45W
76 C6 Pedorido Portugal 41.03N 8.23W
24 D11 Pêdo Shankou pass Xizang Zizhiqu China 29.16N 83.29E
118 H5 Pedra Azul Brazil 16.02S 41.17W
117 G7 Pedra Branca Brazil 5.25S 39.45W
118 G9 Pedra Branca mt Brazil 22.56S 43.29W
118 J10 Pedra da Gávea mt Brazil 23.00S 43.18W
118 F2 Pedra de Amolar Brazil 10.24S 46.25W
117 E9 Pedra de Amolar, Cachoeira da falls Brazil 9.22S 45.50W
91 C6 Pedra do Feitiç Angola 4.58S 13.01E
81 D2 Pedra e Cupa, Pta Sardinia 40.41N 9.46E
81 A3 Pedra Ettori, Mte Sardinia 40.28N 8.26E
76 B6 Pedra Furada Portugal 41.28N 8.39W
76 K6 Pedrajas de San Esteban Spain 41.20N 4.35W
75 J8 Pedralba Spain 39.36N 0.44W
89 P10 Pedra Lume Cape Verde 16.47N 22.54W
76 C5 Pedralva Portugal 41.34N 8.20W
118 E4 Pedra Preta, Sa. da mts Brazil
117 J8 Pedra, Pta. de C Brazil 7.34S 34.48W
118 H10 Pedra Rosilha pk Brazil 22.58S 43.25W
117 A6 Pedras Brazil 2.48S 57.16W
118 F3 Pedras R Brazil
118 G4 Pedras de Maria da Cruz Brazil 15.37S 44.24W
120 G5 Pedras Negras Brazil 12.51S 62.54W
117 C9 Pedras, R Brazil
76 B6 Pedras Rubras airport Portugal 41.14N 8.42W
76 D5 Pedras Salgadas Portugal 41.32N 7.35W
76 K5 Pedraza de Campos Spain 41.58N 4.45W
119 E4 Pedraza La Vieja Venezuela 7.56N 71.06W
115 G10 Pedregal Panama 9.04N 79.25W
115 N5 Pedregal Panama 8.22N 82.26W
119 E2 Pedregal Venezuela 11.04N 70.08W
96 R8 Pedregal, Pta. do pt Madeira Is 32.32N 16.32W
77 R3 Pedreguer Spain 38.48N 0.02E
118 F7 Pedregulho Brazil 20.15S 47.29W
117 D4 Pedreira R Brazil
117 F7 Pedreiras Brazil 4.32S 44.40W
77 G6 Pedrera Spain 37.14N 4.53W
115 H5 Pedriceña Mexico 25.05N 103.48W
103 D7 Pedricktown New Jersey 39.46N 75.24W
77 J6 Pedriza, La Spain 37.25N 3.57W
75 D5 Pedro R Spain
77 H5 Pedro Abad Spain 37.58N 4.27W
117 D9 Pedro Afonso Brazil 8.59S 48.12W
117 H7 Pedro Avelino Brazil 5.30S 36.24W
116 E6 Pedro Bank Caribbean Sea
113 K7 Pedro Bay Alaska 50.46N 154.10W
76 K8 Pedro Bernardo Spain 40.14N 4.55W
116 D3 Pedro Betancourt Cuba 22.42N 81.16W
116 F6 Pedro Cays islds Caribbean Sea
77 G4 Pedroche Spain 38.26N 4.46W
119 E7 Pedro Chico Colombia 1.05N 70.25W
117 D3 Pedro de Freitas Brazil 2.11N 50.54W
120 D10 Pedro de Valdivia Chile 22.33S 69.38W
76 D12 Pedrógão Baixo Alentejo Portugal 38.07N 7.38W
76 E8 Pedrógão Beira Baixa Portugal 40.05N 7.15W
76 B9 Pedrógão Beira Litoral Portugal 39.55N 8.57W
76 B9 Pedrógão Ribatejo Portugal 39.32N 8.35W
76 C9 Pedrógão Grande Portugal 39.55N 8.09W
76 C9 Pedrógão Pequeno Portugal 39.54N 8.07W
118 C5 Pedro Gomes Brazil 17.59S 54.35W
76 H10 Pedro Gómez mt Spain 39.24N 5.43W
119 B3 Pedro González isld Panama 8.23N 79.07W
117 G7 Pedro II Brazil 4.25S 41.28W
119 F7 Pedro II, Ilha plain Brazil/Venez
118 C8 Pedro Juan Cabellero Paraguay 22.30S 55.44W
75 H4 Pedrola Spain 41.47N 1.13W
118 G6 Pedro Leopoldo Brazil 19.39S 44.03W
121 E7 Pedro Luro Argentina 39.30S 62.38W
77 K5 Pedro Marín Embalse de res Spain
77 K5 Pedro Martínez Spain 37.30N 3.13W
115 F10 Pedro Miguel Panama Canal Zone 9.01N 79.36W
77 L2 Pedro Muñoz Spain 39.25N 2.56W
66 R6 Pedrona, Passo di Switz/Italy 46.18N 10.08E
116 G1 Pedro Pt Jamaica, W I 18.27N 78.13W
116 K2 Pedro, R Jamaica, W I
121 F2 Pedro R. Fernández Argentina 28.45S 58.40W
76 L4 Pedrosa del Principe Spain 42.15N 4.12W
75 C1 Pedrosa de Valdeporres Spain 43.01N 3.44W
76 H7 Pedrosillo de los Aires Spain 40.43N 5.42W
75 E3 Pedroso Spain 42.18N 2.43W
76 G9 Pedroso de Acim Spain 39.50N 6.25W
76 J6 Pedroso de la Armuña, El Spain 41.05N 5.24W
77 E5 Pedroso, El Spain 37.51N 5.45W
76 B3 Pedroso, Mte Spain 42.54N 8.34W
118 F9 Pedro Toledo Brazil 24.16S 47.14W
35 B8 Peduyyim Israel 31.20N 34.37E
47 H4 Pedy, Gora mt U.S.S.R. 64.06N 59.48E
12 F5 Peebinga S Australia 34.55S 140.57E
58 K7 Peebles Borders Scotland 55.39N 3.12W
104 B8 Peebles Ohio 38.57N 83.14W
100 P8 Peebles Saskatchewan 50.10N 102.58W
Peebles co see Borders reg
13 D7 Peebles, Mt N Terr Australia 25.37S 135.07E
14 B5 Peedamulla W Australia 21.45S 115.27E
105 H3 Pee Dee S Carolina 34.14N 79.33W
105 H4 Pee Dee R S Carolina
103 G4 Peekskill New York 41.18N 73.56W
57 D4 Peel Isle of Man U.K. 54.14N 4.42W
98 E7 Peel New Brunswick 46.21N 67.33W
110 B6 Peel Oregon 43.16N 123.01W
12 K4 Peel R New S Wales
101 F2 Peel R Yukon/N W Terr
60 M14 Peel, De reg Netherlands
121 J8 Peel, Est Chile
57 H2 Peel Fell mt Northumb Eng/Scot 55.17N 2.35W
14 B10 Peel Inlet W Australia
110 B3 Pe Ell Washington 46.35N 123.18W
11 F10 Peel, Mt New Zealand 43.51S 171.09E
97 H3 Peel Pt N W Terr 73.30N 114.50W
97 K3 Peel Sd N W Terr
63 S5 Peene R E Germany
63 T4 Peenemünde E Germany 54.09N 13.46E
111 M7 Peeples Valley Arizona 34.19N 112.43W
61 M2 Peer Belgium 51.08N 5.27E
12 E2 Peera Peera Poolanna L S Aust
108 E1 Peerless Montana 48.48N 105.50W
101 Q7 Peerless L Alberta 56.40N 114.40W
100 A5 Peers Alberta 53.40N 116.00W
12 G4 Peery L New S Wales
109 G1 Peetz Colorado 40.57N 104.07W
108 O4 Peever S Dakota 45.30N 96.59W
76 E8 Pega Portugal 40.25N 7.08W
71 C9 Pégairolles-de-l'Escalette France 43.48N 3.18E
77 J5 Pegalajar Spain 37.45N 3.39W
11 G10 Pegasus B New Zealand
64 N1 Pegau E Germany 51.10N 12.15E
65 M7 Peggau Austria 47.13N 15.22E
79 E6 Pegli Italy 44.25N 8.49E
80 F3 Peglia, Monte Italy 42.48N 12.12E
64 M4 Pegnitz W Germany 49.45N 11.33E
64 M4 Pegnitz R W Germany
76 C10 Pêgo Portugal 39.28N 8.09W
77 Q3 Pego Spain 38.51N 0.08W
76 C12 Pego do Altar, Barragem do res Portugal 38.25N 8.20W
76 B11 Pegões sta Portugal 38.40N 8.37W
76 B11 Pegões Velhos Portugal 38.41N 8.40W
79 J5 Pegognaga Italy 45.00N 10.51E
110 O7 Pegram Idaho 42.08N 111.09W
39 J1 Pegtymel' R U.S.S.R.
39 K1 Pegtymel'skiy, Khrebet mts U.S.S.R.
25 D4 Pegu Burma 17.18N 96.31E
25 D3 Pegu div Burma
72 G10 Peguera, P. de mt Spain 42.34N 1.00E
15 C3 Pegun isld Mapia Is, Irian Jaya 0.50N 134.16E
18 D6 Pegunungan Barisan mts Sumatra Indon
25 C3 Pegu Yoma mts Burma
56 O5 Pegwell Bay Kent Eng 51.19N 1.22E
47 G4 Pegysh U.S.S.R. 63.27N 50.30E
82 H9 Pehčevo Yugoslavia 41.45N 22.52E
29 E3 Pehowa Haryana India 29.57N 76.39E
23 J7 Pei-chiang Taiwan 23.36N 120.18E
60 T16 Peij Netherlands 51.05N 5.54E
23 D3 Peijiangchang Sichuan China 30.06N 107.32E
70 F6 Peillac France 47.43N 2.12W
71 L9 Peille France 43.49N 7.22E
66 B7 Peillonnex France 46.08N 6.22E
65 J4 Peilstein Austria 48.37N 13.54E
65 M5 Peilstein mt Austria 48.19N 15.07E
120 E10 Peine Chile 23.45S 68.08W
63 M8 Peine W Germany 52.19N 10.13E
121 J8 Peineta, Cerro pk Arg/Chile 50.15S 73.20W
29 C7 Peint Maharashtra India 20.18N 73.30E
25 C2 Peinwa Burma 20.06N 94.02E
79 J2 Peio Italy 46.22N 10.40E

71 H8 Peipin France 44.08N 5.57E
Peipus L see Chudskoye, Oz
71 L9 Peira-Cava France 43.57N 7.23E
113 G7 Peirce, C Alaska 58.35N 161.45W
18 J3 Peirce Res Singapore
71 K5 Peisey-Nancroix France 45.33N 6.47E
64 M8 Peiss W Germany 47.56N 11.48E
61 G5 Peissant Belgium 50.21N 4.07E
64 L8 Peissenberg W Germany 47.48N 11.04E
24 G3 Pei-t'a Shan mts Mongolia/Xinjiang Uygur Zizhiqu
64 K8 Peiting W Germany 43.48N 10.55E
118 E3 Peixe Brazil 12.02S 48.36W
121 H1 Peixe R Santa Catarina Brazil
118 D7 Peixe R São Paulo Brazil
118 C5 Peixe de Couro R Brazil
118 E4 Peixe, R Goiás Brazil
118 B2 Peixes, R Brazil
23 H1 Pei Xian Jiangsu China 34.30N 118.01E
23 H1 Pei Xian Shandong China 34.30N 118.01E
118 C2 Peixoto de Azevedo, R Brazil
60 O7 Peize Netherlands 53.08N 6.30E
60 O7 Peizer Diep R Netherlands
18 G5 Pejantan islds Indonesia 0.08N 107.15E
82 G6 Pek R Yugoslavia
95 L4 Peka Lesotho 28.58S 27.45E
18 H9 Pekalongan Java Indon 6.54S 109.37E
18 D8 Pekan Pen Malaysia 3.29N 103.23E
18 D5 Pekanbaru Sumatra Indon 0.33N 101.30E
45 M3 Pekhlets U.S.S.R. 53.56N 40.06E
Pekhu Tso L see Paikü Co
106 E9 Pekin Illinois 40.34N 89.40W
108 M2 Pekin N Dakota 47.47N 98.19W
Peking see Beijing
51 M5 Pekkala Finland 66.21N 26.50E
45 E3 Peklino U.S.S.R. 53.32N 33.32E
25 D3 Pekon Burma 19.53N 97.00E
39 K3 Pekulheyskoye Oz L U.S.S.R.
39 J2 Pekul'ney, Khrebet mts U.S.S.R.
39 K3 Pekul'veyem U.S.S.R. 62.54N 177.15E
18 M3 Pelabahan Cowie inlet Sabah Malaysia
18 G9 Pelabanratu, Teluk B Java Indon
18 B9 Pelabohan Kelang Pen Malaysia 2.57N 101.24E
18 G9 Pelabuanratu Java Indonesia 7.00S 106.32E
121 C10 Pelada, Pampa plain Argentina
77 B5 Pelada, Sierra mts Spain
75 H8 Pelado mt Spain 39.45N 1.23W
81 E10 Pelagie, Is Italy
79 L7 Pelago Italy 43.46N 11.30E
84 G3 Pélagonisou, Dhíavlos str Greece
84 D6 Pélagos Greece 37.31N 22.25E
84 H3 Pélagos isld Greece
107 G9 Pelahatchie Mississippi 32.19N 89.48W
76 K8 Pelahustán Spain 40.10N 4.36W
18 E5 Pelalawan Sumatra Indon 0.28N 102.08E
18 L7 Pelampai Borneo Indon 3.27S 114.21E
18 H6 Pelapis isld Indonesia 1.20S 109.10E
75 H5 Pelarda, Sierra mts Spain
76 B9 Pelariga Portugal 39.58N 8.37W
84 E4 Pelasyía Greece 38.57N 22.50E
71 K8 Pelat, Mt France 44.17N 6.41E
95 M4 Pelatsoeu mt Lesotho 28.58S 28.25E
81 D4 Pelau, F R Sardinia
15 L1 Pelau I Solomon Is 5.14S 159.28E
18 C9 Pelawan Pen Malaysia 2.46N 102.56E
26 R9 Pelawatta Sri Lanka 6.23N 80.12E
119 G3 Pelayo Venezuela 9.00N 63.46W
62 J2 Pełczyce Poland 53.03N 15.18E
82 H5 Peleaga mt Romania 45.22N 22.51E
120 D6 Pelechuco Bolivia 14.21S 69.05W
42 J2 Peleduy U.S.S.R. 59.35N 112.45E
42 J3 Peleduy R U.S.S.R.
99 H10 Pelee I Ontario 41.45N 82.39W
116 L3 Pelée, Montagne Martinique W I 14.48N 61.10W
120 B2 Pelejo Peru 6.10S 75.49W
84 W22 Pélekas Corfu 39.36N 19.50E
93 G2 Pelekech mt Kenya 3.48N 35.05E
114 D5 Pelekunu Bay Hawaiian Is
19 M3 Peleliu isld Palau Is Pacific Oc 7.02N 134.15E
19 C4 Peleng isld Indonesia
91 H5 Pelenge Zaïre 2.44S 22.39E
19 C4 Peleng, Selat str Indonesia
19 C4 Peleng, Teluk B Indonesia
46 G5 Peleniya Moldavia U.S.S.R. 47.58N 27.48E
66 D6 Pélerin, Mt Switzerland 46.30N 6.49E
51 R3 Pelesmozero, Ozero L U.S.S.R. 68.10N 33.20E
89 F8 Pélézi Ivory Coast 7.17N 6.54W
105 C6 Pelham Georgia 31.09N 84.10W
103 K2 Pelham Massachusetts 42.24N 72.24W
103 L6 Pelham Manor New York 40.53N 73.48W
65 M3 Pelhřimov Czechoslovakia 49.26N 15.13E
113 T8 Pelican Alaska 57.55N 136.10W
100 R6 Pelican B Manitoba
105 K11 Pelican Harb Bahamas
100 D3 Pelican L Alberta 55.48N 113.15W
100 R6 Pelican L Manitoba 52.30N 100.20W
100 S9 Pelican L Manitoba 49.20N 99.35W
108 Q3 Pelican L Minnesota
108 S1 Pelican L Minnesota
100 O3 Pelican L Saskatchewan
106 E4 Pelican L Wisconsin 45.30N 89.13W
106 E4 Pelican Lake Wisconsin 43.30N 89.09W
100 D3 Pelican Mts Alberta
100 P3 Pelican Narrows Saskatchewan 55.12N 102.55W
111 K10 Pelicano, I Mexico
100 E3 Pelican Portage Alberta 55.47N 112.35W
94 C4 Pelican Pt Namibia 22.54S 14.25E
13 G3 Pelican R Queensland
100 R6 Pelican Rapids Manitoba 52.45N 100.44W
108 O3 Pelican Rapids Minnesota 46.32N 96.06W
119 B8 Pelileo Ecuador 1.24S 78.30W
90 J9 Pélimandji Cent Afr Rep 5.06N 18.35E
105 F4 Pelion S Carolina 33.47N 81.14W
82 D8 Pelješac isld Yugoslavia
51 N4 Pelkosenniemi Finland 67.06N 27.30E
47 C4 Pelkula U.S.S.R. 63.39N 32.41E
63 G9 Pelkum W Germany 51.38N 7.44E
108 S8 Pella Iowa 41.28N 92.55W
79 D3 Pella Italy 45.48N 8.23E
90 F6 Pella Nigeria 10.10N 13.00E
94 E7 Pella S Africa 29.01S 19.06E
35 F4 Pella anc site Jordan 32.27N 35.37E
81 L7 Pellaro Italy 38.01N 15.40E
101 T3 Pellatt L N W Terr
107 K8 Pell City Alabama 33.33N 86.16W
99 H10 Pellee Pt Ontario 41.48N 82.30W
121 D6 Pellegrini Argentina 36.16S 63.07W
121 C7 Pellegrini, L Argentina
81 M4 Pellegrino Cozzo mt Italy 39.44N 16.01E
81 F7 Pellegrino, Mte Sicily 38.10N 13.21E
79 G5 Pellegrino Parmense Italy 44.44N 9.56E
81 B3 Pellegrinu, Mte Sardinia 40.28N 8.57E
72 E6 Pellegrue France 44.45N 0.06E
15 H4 Pelleluhu Is Bismarck Arch
61 K3 Pellenberg Belgium 50.52N 4.48E
70 H5 Pellerine, la France 48.18N 1.03W
79 M4 Pellestrina Italy 45.16N 12.18E
100 U2 Pelletier L Manitoba
72 G2 Pellevoisin France 46.59N 1.25E
13 D3 Pellew C N Terr Australia 15.29S 136.53E
66 F8 Pelline, Val Italy
64 B4 Pellingen W Germany 49.40N 6.41E
51 L5 Pello Finland 66.47N 24.00E
70 K6 Pellouailles France 47.32N 0.26W
106 K4 Pellston Michigan 45.32N 84.48W
121 A5 Pelluhue Chile 35.46S 72.38W
63 J3 Pellworm isld W Germany
100 Q7 Pelly Saskatchewan 51.52N 101.55W
101 E4 Pelly R Yukon Terr
97 L4 Pelly Bay N W Terr 68.38N 89.45W
101 E4 Pelly Crossing Yukon Terr 62.48N 136.30W
101 F1 Pelly I N W Terr 69.27N 135.24W
101 X3 Pelly L N W Terr
101 G5 Pelly Mts Yukon Terr
101 G12 Pelly, Pt Br Col 49.07N 123.12W
101 X1 Pelly Pt Victoria I, N W Terr 70.10N 100.55W
26 S8 Pelmadulla Sri Lanka 6.37N 80.33E
79 M2 Pelmo mt Italy 46.25N 12.09E
40 G5 Pelny Osipenko, Im U.S.S.R. 52.29N 136.30E
76 J10 Peloche Spain 39.12N 5.08W
18 N9 Pelokang isld Indonesia 7.14S 118.21E
84 C6 Pelópion Greece 37.41N 21.35E
83 E7 Pelopónnisos div Greece
81 K7 Peloritani, Monti Sicily
Peloro, C see Faro, Punta del Sicily
11 H8 Pelorus Sd New Zealand
84 E7 Pelotá Greece 37.03N 22.53E
121 H3 Pelotas Brazil 31.45S 52.20W
121 J2 Pelotas, R. das Brazil
82 J7 Pelovo Bulgaria 43.26N 24.17E
26 S6 Pelpendiyawa Sri Lanka 7.52N 80.33E
62 L2 Pelplin Poland 53.54N 18.40E
14 A8 Pelsart Group islds W Australia
63 T5 Pelsin E Germany 53.48N 12.41E
107 C6 Pelsor Arkansas 35.41N 93.06W
51 L3 Peltovuoma Finland 68.24N 24.10E
69 L5 Peltre-sur-Nied France 49.05N 6.14E
79 J2 Pelugo Italy 46.06N 10.43E
86 J3 Pelusium ruins Egypt 31.02N 32.32E
71 F6 Pélussin France 45.25N 4.40E
79 B5 Pelvo d'Elva mt Italy 44.33N 7.01E
71 J7 Pelvoux, Massif du mts France
71 J7 Pelvoux, Mt France 44.54N 6.22E
45 Q2 Pelya Khovanskaya U.S.S.R. 54.35N 44.57E
47 J6 Pelym U.S.S.R. 59.41N 63.06E
47 J5 Pelym R U.S.S.R.
47 J5 Pelymskiy Tuman, Oz L U.S.S.R. 60.00N 63.12E
56 B7 Pelynt Cornwall Eng 50.22N 4.32W
105 E3 Pelzer S Carolina 34.41N 82.29W
63 N4 Pelzerhaken pt W Germany 54.06N 10.54E
92 J4 Pema Channel East Africa
99 G5 Pemache, R Ontario
104 R1 Pemadumcook L Maine
18 H9 Pemalang Java Indon 6.53S 109.21E
18 H9 Pemalang, Udjung C Java Indon 6.50S 109.23E
19 C4 Pemali, Tanjung C Indonesia 1.17S 123.35E
18 E9 Pemanggil isld Pen Malaysia
18 K6 Pemarunan Borneo Indon 1.55S 113.55E
18 M6 Pemarung, Pulau isld Borneo Indon
18 E6 Pematang Sumatra Indon 0.12S 102.06E
18 C4 Pematangsiantar Sumatra Indon 2.59N 99.01E
Pemba see Porto Amelia
92 C10 Pemba Zambia 16.31S 27.20E
92 K8 Pemba, B.de Mozambique
92 J4 Pemba I E Africa
94 N4 Pembe Mozambique 23.43S 35.00E
101 M10 Pemberton Br Col 50.19N 122.49W
103 E7 Pemberton New Jersey 39.58N 74.41W
14 B10 Pemberton W Australia 34.27S 115.59E
108 N1 Pembina N Dakota 48.59N 97.16W
108 M1 Pembina R Manitoba/N Dakota
100 B5 Pembina Oil Fields Alberta 53.08N 115.25W
100 C5 Pembina Prov. Park Alberta
100 B5 Pembina R Alberta
106 G4 Pembine Wisconsin 45.38N 87.59W
56 C4 Pembrey Dyfed Wales 51.42N 4.16W
56 F3 Pembridge Hereford & Worcs Eng 52.14N 2.53W
56 B4 Pembroke Dyfed Wales 51.41N 4.55W
105 F5 Pembroke Georgia 32.09N 81.39W
107 J5 Pembroke Kentucky 36.45N 87.21W
103 N2 Pembroke Massachusetts 42.05N 70.48W
105 H3 Pembroke N Carolina 34.40N 79.23W
99 N7 Pembroke Ontario 45.49N 77.08W
104 E9 Pembroke Virginia 37.19N 80.39W
Pembroke co see Dyfed co
121 E10 Pembroke, C Falkland Is 51.42N 57.45W
56 B4 Pembroke Dock Dyfed Wales 51.42N 4.56W
96 B2 Pembroke Marsh Bermuda
11 B11 Pembroke, Mt New Zealand 44.34S 167.55E
18 K7 Pembuang Borneo Indon 2.25S 112.13E
18 F5 Pempang isld Indonesia
121 A6 Pemuco Chile 36.55S 72.12W
28 A1 Pen Maharashtra India 18.44N 73.08E
25 B2 Pen R Burma
116 J5 Peña Dominican Rep 19.33N 70.38W
76 C14 Pena Portugal 37.14N 8.06W
120 E10 Peña Barrosa Bolivia 22.10S 67.23W
121 B2 Peña Blanca Chile 28.42S 71.22W
109 D6 Penablanca* New Mexico 35.34N 106.20W
75 E2 Peñacerrada Spain 42.39N 2.42W
76 K2 Peña Cerredo mt Spain 43.13N 4.48W
104 O3 Penacook New Hampshire 43.15N 71.35W
76 C8 Penacova Portugal 40.16N 8.17W
76 G7 Peña de Francia, Sierra de la mts Spain
76 F10 Peña del Aguila, Embalse de la res Spain
77 M3 Peña del Roblo mt Spain 38.44N 2.05W
75 L6 Peña, Embalse de res Teruel Spain 40.49N 0.08E
75 J3 Peña, Embalse de la res Huesca Spain 42.24N 0.43W
76 C6 Penafiel Portugal 41.12N 8.17W
76 L5 Peñafiel Spain 41.36N 4.07W
77 F5 Peñaflor Sevilla Spain 37.43N 5.20W
75 J4 Peñaflor Zaragoza Spain 41.46N 0.48W
76 K5 Peñaflor de Hornija Spain 41.43N 4.59W
75 K7 Peñagolosa Spain 40.13N 0.21W
75 C1 Penagos Spain 43.21N 3.49W
116 O2 Penal Trinidad & Tobago 10.10N 61.28W
75 C6 Peñalara, Pico de mt Spain 40.51N 3.58W
75 K4 Peñalba Spain 41.30N 0.02W
75 D5 Peñalba de la Sierra Spain 41.09N 3.24W
75 F6 Peñalén Spain 40.40N 2.04W
56 B4 Penally Dyfed Wales 51.40N 4.44W
77 F3 Peñalsordo Spain 38.50N 5.07W
76 D7 Penalvo do Castelo Portugal 40.41N 7.42W
76 E8 Penamacor Portugal 40.10N 7.10W
118 G3 Penamar Brazil 12.44S 43.57W
18 L4 Penambo Ra Kalimantan/Sarawak
15 C7 Penambulai isld Moluccas Indon
76 H2 Peña Mea mt Spain 43.10N 5.31W
76 K2 Peñamellera Alta Spain 43.20N 4.42W
76 K2 Peñamellera Baja Spain 43.20N 4.36W
115 K7 Peñamiller Mexico 21.02N 99.51W
76 G5 Peña Mira mt Spain 41.55N 6.28W
18 M3 Penampang Sabah Malaysia 5.55N 116.07E
121 B2 Peña Negra, Paso de Arg/Chile 28.15S 69.25W
76 G4 Peña Negra, Sierra de mts Spain
115 K6 Peña Nevada, Cerro pk Mexico 23.49N 99.51W
Penang isld see Pinang
Penang state see Pinang state
76 E4 Peña Nofre mt Spain 42.02N 7.21W
76 B15 Pena Palace Portugal 38.47N 9.24W
76 F8 Peñaparda Spain 40.19N 6.40W
118 E7 Penápolis Brazil 21.23S 50.04W
76 J7 Peñaranda de Bracamonte Spain 40.54N 5.13W
75 D4 Peñaranda de Duero Spain 41.40N 3.29W
103 D5 Pen Argyl Pennsylvania 40.52N 75.15W
12 G5 Penarie New S Wales 34.21S 143.33E
75 J7 Peñarroya mt Spain 40.24N 0.40W
77 L2 Peñarroya, Embalse de res Spain 39.02N 3.00W
77 F4 Peñarroya-Pueblonuevo Spain 38.19N 5.16W
77 G7 Peñarrubia Spain 36.58N 4.50W
76 F4 Peñarrubia, Embalse de res Spain 42.30N 6.50W
56 E5 Penarth S Glam Wales 51.27N 3.11W
76 F3 Peña Rubia mt Spain 42.45N 6.54W
115 M4 Peñas Blancas Nicaragua 11.13N 85.42W
121 L9 Peñas, C Argentina 53.52S 67.32W
76 H1 Peñas, C. de Spain 43.39N 5.50W
109 E5 Peñasco New Mexico 36.11N 105.43W
109 F9 Peñasco, R New Mexico
77 M3 Peñascosa Spain 38.40N 2.25W
75 C4 Peñas de Cervera mts Spain
77 M3 Peñas de San Pedro Spain 38.45N 2.00W
121 H6 Penas, G. de Chile
75 D7 Peñas Gordas mt Spain 40.11N 3.19W
75 J2 Peña, Sierra de la mts Spain
119 H2 Peñas, Pta Venezuela 10.50N 61.53W
76 F4 Peña Trevinca mt Spain 42.14N 6.48W
76 H2 Peña Ubiña mt Spain 43.01N 5.57W
76 H6 Peñausende Spain 41.17N 5.52W
110 H3 Penawawa Washington 46.42N 117.43W
103 A6 Penbrook Pennsylvania 40.16N 76.51W
11 D6 Pencarrow Hd New Zealand 41.22S 174.51E
29 F7 Pench R Mad Prad/Maharashtra India
123 D3 Penck, C Antarctica 65.42S 87.45E
121 A6 Penco Chile 36.45S 73.00W
84 Q15 Pendaila Cyprus 34.51N 32.37E
83 E4 Pendálofon Greece 40.14N 21.09E
18 L6 Pendang Borneo Indonesia 1.30S 114.49E
100 G9 Pendant d'Oreille Alberta 49.15N 111.00W
84 Q14 Pendayia Cyprus 35.09N 32.54E
Pend d'Oreille R see Pend Oreille
90 H8 Pende R Cent Afr Rep
56 S9 Pendeen Lt Ho Cornwall Eng 50.09N 5.41W
84 G5 Pendelikón mt Greece 38.05N 23.53E
89 D7 Pendembu Sierra Leone 8.09N 10.42W
117 H7 Pendencia Brazil 5.15S 36.45W
84 D5 Pendeória Greece 38.25N 22.19E
108 O7 Pender Nebraska 42.08N 96.42W
14 E3 Pender W Australia 16.45S 122.45E
14 E3 Pender Bay W Australia 16.43S 122.35E
11 A12 Pender, Mt New Zealand 45.41S 166.56E
37 G2 Pendik Turkey 40.54N 29.15E
56 B4 Pendine Dyfed Wales 51.46N 4.34W
89 K6 Pendjari R Benin
89 K6 Pendjari, Parc Nat. de la Benin
57 J5 Pendlebury Greater Manchester Eng 53.32N 2.21W
106 J9 Pendleton Indiana 40.01N 85.44W
110 G4 Pendleton Oregon 45.40N 118.46W
105 E3 Pendleton S Carolina 34.38N 82.47W
101 L8 Pendleton Bay Br Columbia 54.29N 125.39W
101 J6 Pendleton, Mt Br Col 59.20N 129.45W
110 H1 Pend Oreille R Washington/Br Col
110 J1 Pend Oreille L Idaho 48.10N 116.20W
29 H6 Pendra Madhya Prad India 22.50N 82.02E
110 N1 Pendroy Montana 48.04N 112.20W
28 A2 Penduv Maharashtra India 16.04N 73.41E
43 J7 Pendzhikent Tadzhikistan U.S.S.R. 39.30N 67.08E
76 C5 Peneda Portugal 41.59N 8.14W
76 C5 Peneda, Sa. de Portugal
118 J2 Penedo Brazil 10.16S 36.33W
76 E7 Penedono Portugal 41.00N 7.25W
56 D2 Penegoes Powys Wales 52.36N 3.48W
42 C4 Penek U.S.S.R. 55.30N 81.30E
76 C8 Penela Portugal 40.02N 8.23W
18 H6 Penembagan isld Indonesia 1.14S 109.15E
92 D4 Pene Mende Zaïre 4.18S 28.11E
90 G8 Péné, Mt Cameroon 7.45N 14.32E
89 K7 Penessoulou Benin 9.15N 1.39E
70 F7 Penestin France 47.29N 2.28W
99 L8 Penetanguishene Ontario 44.47N 79.56W
66 C5 Peney le Jorat Switzerland 46.39N 6.45E
104 G5 Penfield Pennsylvania 41.13N 78.36W
23 D3 Peng'an Sichuan China 31.03N 106.20E
29 E7 Penganga R Maharashtra India
23 A9 Peng Chau isld Hong Kong 22.17N 114.02E
23 J6 P'eng-chia Hsü isld Taiwan
91 J6 Penge Kasai-Oriental Zaïre 5.32S 24.37E
92 D4 Penge Kivu Zaïre 4.26S 28.25E
55 G5 Penge London Eng 51.25N 0.04W
23 H7 P'eng-hu Lieh-tao islds Taiwan
23 H7 P'eng-hu Tao isld Taiwan 23.34N 119.35E
18 H5 Pengiki isld Borneo Indon 0.11N 108.04E
18 A7 Pengkalan Baharu Pen Malaysia 4.26N 100.38E
18 G3 Peng Kang dist Singapore
87 C7 Pengko Sudan 6.13N 31.56E
23 G6 Pengkou Fujian China 25.36N 116.35E
22 M8 Penglai Shandong China 37.50N 120.45E
23 C3 Pengshan Sichuan China 30.14N 103.58E
23 E4 Pengshui Sichuan China 29.15N 108.08E
12 H8 Penguin Tasmania 41.05S 146.01E
11 O12 Penguin Beach New Zealand 45.47S 170.45E
14 F2 Penguin Deeps Timor Sea
122 U7 Penguin Spit Palmyra I Pacific Oc 5.52N 162.06W
18 J7 Pengujan, Tanjung C Borneo Indon 3.01S 111.34E
23 D3 Pengxi Sichuan China 30.48N 105.40E
23 C3 Peng Xian Sichuan China 31.00N 103.58E
23 G4 Pengze Jiangxi China 29.56N 116.38E
118 J8 Penha Rio de Janeiro Brazil 22.51S 43.17W
118 E10 Penha Santa Catarina Brazil 26.47S 48.39W
118 G10 Penha de Franca dist São Paulo Brazil
76 E8 Penha Garcia Portugal 40.03N 7.01W
56 T9 Penhale Pt Cornwall Eng 50.23N 5.09W
92 F11 Penhalonga Zimbabwe 18.54S 32.40E
76 D8 Penhas da Saúde Portugal 40.19N 7.33W
70 A5 Penhir, Pte de France 48.15N 4.37W
100 D6 Penhold Alberta 52.11N 113.52W
56 F4 Penhow Gwent Wales 51.37N 2.50W
99 F3 Penhurst Ontario 49.13N 84.26W
79 F5 Penice, Monte Italy 44.47N 9.18E
76 A10 Peniche Portugal 39.21N 9.23W
58 K7 Penicuik Lothian Scotland 55.50N 3.14W
18 L10 Penida isld Indonesia
64 O2 Penig E Germany 50.56N 12.42E
76 D13 Penilhos Portugal 37.39N 7.50W
18 A7 Peninjau, Gunong mt Pen Malaysia 4.39N 100.58E
19 M6 Peninsula Pt Philippines 10.10N 125.40E
18 E4 Peninsular Malaysia div Malaysia
91 B5 Peni Nyoundou Gabon 2.42S 11.13E
75 L7 Peñíscola Spain 40.22N 0.24E
57 K5 Penistone S Yorks Eng 53.32N 1.37W
117 E9 Penitente, Sa. do mts Brazil
Penjireh see Panjbarār
15 C7 Penjuring I Moluccas Indonesia 6.45S 134.29E
34 N3 Pēnjwin Iraq 35.35N 45.57E
65 H8 Penk Austria 46.55N 13.17E
57 H6 Penketh Merseyside Eng 53.23N 2.40W
56 B2 Penkilan Hd Gwynedd Wales 52.47N 4.32W
56 G2 Penkridge Staffs Eng 52.44N 2.07W
63 U6 Penkun E Germany 53.18N 14.15E
57 F6 Penmaenmawr Gwynedd Wales 53.16N 3.54W
70 B6 Penmarc'h France 47.49N 4.20W
70 B6 Penmarc'h, Pte de France 47.48N 4.23W
100 K5 Penn Saskatchewan 53.42N 107.43W
79 M7 Pennabilli Italy 43.49N 12.16E
56 D2 Pennal Gwynedd Wales 52.35N 3.55W
79 L7 Penna, Monte Arezzo Italy 43.42N 11.56E
79 F6 Penna, Monte Parma Italy 44.28N 9.29E
80 G2 Penna, Monte Perugia Italy 43.12N 12.50E
58 M3 Pennan Grampian Scotland 57.41N 2.16W
100 J8 Pennant Saskatchewan 50.32N 108.16W
12 K6 Pennant Hills dist Sydney, New S Wales
98 J9 Pennant Pt Nova Scotia 44.27N 63.39W
80 K4 Pennapiedimonte Italy 42.09N 14.11E
80 L4 Penna, Punta della Italy 42.13N 14.43E
80 H2 Penna San Giovanni Italy 43.03N 13.26E
80 J4 Penne Italy 42.27N 13.56E
72 H7 Penne Tarn France 44.04N 1.43E
72 F7 Penne-d'Agenais France 44.23N 0.49E
13 F1 Pennefather R Queensland
71 K9 Penne, la France 43.55N 6.56E
123 J7 Pennell Bank sea feature Antarctica
28 D3 Penner R Andhra Prad India
12 E6 Penneshaw S Australia 35.42S 137.55E
71 G10 Pennes-Mirabeau, les France 43.25N 5.19E
98 F8 Pennfield New Brunswick 45.05N 66.44W
57 J3 Pennine Chain mts England
52 H2 Penningkeis mt Norway/Sweden 64.13N 14.10E
103 E6 Pennington New Jersey 40.19N 74.48W
112 M4 Pennington Texas 31.13N 95.15W
104 B10 Pennington Gap Virginia 36.44N 83.03W
80 G2 Pennino, Monte Italy 43.06N 12.54E
103 D7 Pennsauken New Jersey 39.58N 75.03W
104 E7 Pennsboro W Virginia 39.17N 80.59W
103 D6 Pennsburg Pennsylvania 40.23N 75.29W
103 A4 Pennsdale Pennsylvania 41.15N 76.48W
103 D7 Penns Grove New Jersey 39.43N 75.28W
103 C7 Pennsville New Jersey 39.39N 75.31W
102 L2 Pennsylvania state U.S.A.
104 H4 Penn Yan New York 42.41N 77.03W
101 P1 Penny B Victoria I, N W Terr
97 N4 Penny Ice Cap N W Terr 67.20N 66.30W
46 J2 Peno U.S.S.R. 56.59N 32.49E
104 R1 Penobscot R Maine
104 Q3 Penobscot B Maine
98 G8 Penobsquis New Brunswick 45.47N 65.26W
12 F6 Penola S Australia 37.23S 140.21E
12 C4 Penong S Australia 31.55S 133.02E
115 O5 Penonomé Panama 8.30N 80.20W
9 C11 Pénot, Mt New Hebrides 16.20S 167.32E
110 C8 Penoyar California 41.40N 122.05W
57 F2 Penpont Dumfries & Galloway Scotland 55.14N 3.49W
91 C6 Penra do Feitiço Angola 5.56S 12.59E
57 E7 Penrhyn Gwynedd Wales 52.56N 4.04W
57 H3 Penrith Cumbria Eng 54.40N 2.44W
12 K5 Penrith New S Wales 33.47S 150.44E
11 D2 Penrose New Zealand 36.55S 174.49E
11 D2 Penrose dist Auckland New Zealand
56 T9 Penryn Cornwall Eng 50.09N 5.06W
107 J11 Pensacola Florida 30.26N 87.12W
107 J11 Pensacola Bay Florida
105 K11 Pensacola Cay Bahamas 26.59N 77.41W
123 E10 Pensacola Mts Antarctica
120 G6 Pensamiento Bolivia 14.46S 61.37W
44 J9 Pensar Azerbaydzhan U.S.S.R. 38.39N 48.48E
100 N8 Pense Saskatchewan 50.26N 104.59W
39 G5 Pensepel', Mys C U.S.S.R. 59.35N 160.23E
56 F5 Pensford Avon Eng 51.23N 2.33W
56 M5 Penshurst Kent Eng 51.11N 0.11E
12 F7 Penshurst Victoria 37.52S 142.20E
18 M3 Pensiangan Sabah Malaysia 4.30N 116.20E
119 C5 Pensilvania Colombia 5.33N 75.03W
28 F2 Pentakota Andhra Prad India 17.20N 82.42E
117 G6 Pentecoste Brazil 3.49S 39.18W
9 C11 Pentecost I New Hebrides
14 G3 Pentecost, R W Australia
Pentecôte, I see Pentecost I
98 E4 Pentecôte, L Quebec
82 K5 Penteleu mt Romania 45.36N 26.26E
101 O11 Penticton Br Col 49.29N 119.38W
56 A6 Pentire Cornwall Eng 50.31N 5.02W
56 B6 Pentire Hd Cornwall Eng 50.36N 4.55W
13 H5 Pentland Queensland 20.31S 145.25E
58 K1 Pentland Firth Orkney Scotland
58 K7 Pentland Hills Lothian/Strathclyde/Borders Scotland
58 T12 Pentland Skerries isld Orkney Scotland 58.41N 2.55W
57 H2 Pentonbridge Cumbria Eng 55.05N 2.52W
57 E6 Pentraeth Gwynedd Wales 53.17N 4.12W
57 G6 Pentre Clwyd Wales 53.09N 3.22W
56 C3 Pentrebont Dyfed Wales 52.23N 4.05W
57 F6 Pentre-Foelas Clwyd Wales 53.03N 3.41W
106 H6 Pentwater Michigan 43.47N 86.25W
18 F6 Penuba Indonesia 0.18S 104.29E
18 F7 Penuguan Sumatra Indon 2.18S 104.30E
28 C3 Penukonda Andhra Prad India 14.05N 77.36E
18 E3 Penunjok, Tanjong C Pen Malaysia 4.20N 103.30E
70 D4 Penvénan France 48.48N 3.17W
25 D3 Penwegon Burma 18.14N 96.34E
112 E4 Penwell Texas 31.43N 102.37W
45 G5 Peny U.S.S.R. 51.06N 35.55E
56 E3 Penybont Powys Wales 52.16N 3.18W
57 J4 Pen-y-ghent mt N Yorks Eng 54.10N 2.14W
57 E6 Pen-y-groes Gwynedd Wales 53.04N 4.17W
57 F6 Pen-y-Gwryd Gwynedd Wales 53.05N 4.00W
101 U5 Penylan L N W Terr 61.50N 106.20W
19 E6 Penyu, Pulau Pulau islds Moluccas Indonesia
18 H9 Penyu, Teluk B Java Indon
45 Q3 Penza U.S.S.R. 53.11N 45.00E
56 S9 Penzance Cornwall Eng 50.07N 5.33W
100 M7 Penzance Saskatchewan 51.02N 105.28W
64 L8 Penzberg W Germany 47.45N 11.23E
91 F4 Penzele Zaïre 0.19S 18.14E
46 N3 Penzenskaya Oblast' prov U.S.S.R.
39 H4 Penzhina R U.S.S.R.
39 H3 Penzhino U.S.S.R. 63.31N 168.00E
39 G4 Penzhinskaya Guba gulf U.S.S.R.
39 G4 Penzhinskiy Khrebet mts U.S.S.R.
63 S5 Penzlin E Germany 53.30N 13.06E
110 H3 Peola Washington 46.18N 117.27W
89 F8 Péon Ivory Coast 6.57N 7.28W
71 K8 Péone France 46.08N 6.55E
110 R1 Peoples Cr Montana
111 M8 Peoria Arizona 33.38N 112.13W
106 E9 Peoria Illinois 40.43N 89.38W
106 G8 Peotone Illinois 41.20N 87.49W
92 D5 Pepa Zaïre 7.42S 29.46E
103 E2 Pepacton New York 42.04N 74.53W
103 E2 Pepacton Res New York
95 G2 Pepanilaagte watercourse S Africa
114 C7 Pepeekeo Hawaiian Is 19.49N 155.08W
114 C7 Pepeekeo Pt Hawaiian Is 19.50N 155.06W
89 C7 Pepel Sierra Leone 8.39N 13.04W
61 G3 Pepingen Belgium 50.46N 4.10E
11 H8 Pepin I New Zealand 41.08S 173.25E
106 B5 Pepin, L Wisconsin
61 O4 Pépinster Belgium 50.34N 5.49E
118 D10 Pepiri Guaçú, R Brazil/Argentina
71 L8 Peppiri, Mt France 44.07N 7.12E
95 N4 Pepworth S Africa 28.29S 29.51E
35 E2 Peqi'in Hadasha Israel 32.59N 35.20E
83 D3 Peqin Albania 41.04N 19.44E
103 B7 Pequea Pennsylvania 39.53N 76.19W
121 H3 Pequena, L Brazil
115 C4 Pequeña, Pta Mexico 26.13N 113.30W
110 L9 Pequop Mts Nevada
108 Q3 Pequot Lakes Minnesota 46.36N 94.18W
84 R14 Pera Cyprus 35.01N 33.16E
76 C14 Pera Portugal 37.07N 8.20W
18 F7 Perabumulih Sumatra Indon 3.29S 104.14E
75 H6 Peracense Spain 40.38N 1.29W
64 O7 Perach W Germany 48.15N 12.47E
26 S7 Peradeniya Sri Lanka 7.16N 80.37E
75 P3 Perafita Spain 42.03N 2.06E
13 F2 Pera Hd Queensland 12.57S 141.38E
18 A6 Perai Pen Malaysia 5.22N 100.17E
76 D9 Perais Portugal 39.40N 7.34W
119 H5 Peraitepuy Venezuela 4.35N 61.31W
18 C3 Perak isld Pen Malaysia 5.50N 99.15E
18 A7 Perak R Pen Malaysia
18 A7 Perak state Pen Malaysia
84 E5 Perakhóra Greece 38.02N 22.56E
84 R15 Pera Khorio Cyprus 35.00N 33.25E
18 A7 Perak, Kuala estuary Pen Malaysia
Peral see Los Molinos Spain
76 D9 Peral Portugal 39.42N 7.48W
79 N1 Peralba, Monte Italy 46.38N 12.43E
76 J9 Peraleda de la Mata Spain 39.51N 5.28W
76 J9 Peraleda de San Roman Spain 39.45N 5.23W
77 E4 Peraleda de Zaucejo Spain 38.29N 5.33W
75 E7 Peraleja, La Spain 40.14N 2.34W
75 H7 Peralejos Spain 40.29N 1.02W
76 G7 Peralejos de Abajo Spain 41.00N 6.23W
75 G6 Peralejos de las Truchas Spain 40.35N 1.55W
77 N2 Peral, El Cuenca Spain 39.30N 1.54W
75 H6 Perales del Alfambra Spain 40.38N 1.00W
76 F8 Perales del Puerto Spain 40.10N 6.40W
121 E7 Peralta Argentina 38.03S 61.42W
109 D7 Peralta New Mexico 34.51N 106.42W
75 G3 Peralta Spain 42.20N 1.48W
75 K4 Peralta de Alcofea Spain 41.56N 0.05W
75 L4 Peralta de la Sal Spain 42.00N 0.24E
76 D14 Peralva Portugal 37.17N 7.14W
75 F6 Peralveche Spain 40.36N 2.27W
84 L11 Pérama Crete 35.22N 24.42E
84 A2 Pérama Greece 39.42N 20.51E
28 D5 Perambalur Tamil Nadu India 11.15N 78.54E
28 E4 Perambur Tamil Nadu India 13.10N 80.16E
84 E7 Péra Mélana Greece 37.13N 22.52E
92 G7 Peramiho Tanzania 10.40S 35.29E
75 N3 Peramola Spain 42.04N 1.16E
76 F3 Peranzanes Spain 42.53N 6.38W
51 N5 Perä-Posio Finland 66.12N 27.58E
79 M2 Perarolo Italy 46.24N 12.22E
51 K9 Peräseinäjoki Finland 62.34N 23.05E
84 A4 Peratiá Greece 38.49N 20.44E
18 D5 Perawang Sumatra Indonesia 0.46N 101.35E
98 H5 Percé Quebec 48.32N 64.14W
71 K5 Percée mt France 45.52N 6.33E
70 J3 Percée, Pte. de la France 49.24N 0.56W
72 J11 Perche, Col de la pass France 42.30N 2.05E
70 M4 Perche, Coteaux du hills France
96 U16 Perchel, Pta pt Gran Canaria Canary Is 27.44N 15.39W
65 O5 Perchtoldsdorf Austria 48.08N 16.17E
81 H6 Perciato Lipari Is Italy 38.33N 14.22E
80 G4 Percile Italy 42.06N 12.55E
108 P9 Percival Iowa 40.45N 95.40W
14 E5 Percival Lakes W Australia
70 H4 Percy France 48.55N 1.10W
107 G3 Percy Illinois 38.01N 89.37W
108 R8 Percy Iowa 41.28N 93.11W
104 O2 Percy New Hampshire 44.37N 71.22W
13 K5 Percy Is Queensland
14 D9 Percy, L W Australia 31.50S 120.13E
13 G4 Percyville Queensland 19.00S 143.46E
81 C4 Perdasdefogu Sardinia 39.41N 9.27E
95 J4 Perdeberg S Africa 28.59S 25.05E
95 N3 Perdekop S Africa 27.10S 29.38E
84 F6 Pérdhika Greece 37.41N 23.27E
84 C4 Perdhikóvrisi Greece 38.40N 21.54E
75 F4 Perdices, Sierra de mts Spain
117 E9 Perdida, R Brazil
121 C9 Perdido R Argentina
107 J11 Perdido R Florida/Ala
107 J11 Perdido Bay Florida/Ala
75 L2 Perdido, Mte Spain 42.40N 0.02E
118 B7 Perdido, R Brazil
81 K3 Perdifumo Italy 40.15N 15.01E
76 D9 Perdigão, Sa. de mts Portugal
76 H6 Perdigón, El Spain 41.26N 5.46W
75 J4 Perdiguera Spain 41.45N 0.38W
77 P5 Perdiguera isld Spain 37.42N 0.47W
118 F6 Perdizes Brazil 19.23S 47.16W
118 F10 Perdizes dist São Paulo Brazil
100 K6 Perdue Saskatchewan 52.05N 107.33W
98 B3 Perdu, L Quebec
77 M5 Perea mt Spain 37.40N 2.29W
82 G2 Perechin U.S.S.R. 48.44N 22.29E
76 F6 Peredo Portugal 41.25N 6.52W
82 J2 Pereginsko U.S.S.R. 48.47N 24.11E
47 K4 Peregrebnoye U.S.S.R. 63.00N 65.01E
39 H7 Peregrednoy, Mys C Komandorskiye O-va U.S.S.R. 54.50N 166.44E
119 C5 Pereira Colombia 4.47N 75.46W
118 D7 Pereira Barreto Brazil 20.39S 51.07W
Pereira D 'Eça see N 'Giva
76 C14 Pereiras Portugal 37.24N 8.27W
117 H7 Pereiro Brazil 5.59S 38.30W
76 D14 Pereiro Portugal 37.27N 7.36W
76 D4 Pereiro de Aguiar Spain 42.21N 7.48W
75 G5 Perejil R Spain
77 F9 Perejil, I. del Morocco 35.55N 5.26W
92 F8 Perekezi Hill Malawi 12.00S 33.42E
44 C8 Perekop Ukraine U.S.S.R. 46.10N 33.42E
45 U5 Perekopnoye U.S.S.R. 51.13N 48.04E
44 C9 Perekopskiy Peresheyek isthmus Ukraine U.S.S.R.
45 O7 Perelazovskiy U.S.S.R. 49.08N 42.35E
45 C3 Perelazy U.S.S.R. 52.02N 31.29E
75 M6 Perelló Spain 40.53N 0.43E
77 Q2 Perelló, El Spain 39.17N 0.18W
45 D5 Perelyub Ukraine U.S.S.R. 51.59N 32.20E
46 Q4 Perelyub U.S.S.R. 51.50N 50.19E
106 H6 Pere Marquette, R Michigan
123 E2 Peremennyy, C Antarctica 66.25S 105.15E
45 C6 Peremoga Ukraine U.S.S.R. 50.30N 31.15E
45 H2 Peremyshl' U.S.S.R. 54.16N 36.09E
82 J1 Peremyshlyany U.S.S.R. 49.40N 24.33E
76 F6 Pereña Spain 41.14N 6.32W
120 B4 Perene Peru 10.55S 75.15W
120 C4 Perené R Peru
14 B8 Perenjori W Australia 29.28S 116.15E
113 L7 Perenosa B Alaska
89 L7 Péréré Benin 9.48N 3.04E
76 H6 Pereruela Spain 41.25N 5.53W
44 B7 Peresadovka Ukraine U.S.S.R. 47.07N 32.11E
45 G7 Pereshchepino Ukraine U.S.S.R. 49.02N 35.23E
46 L2 Pereslavl' Zalesskiy U.S.S.R. 56.40N 38.50E
46 N3 Peresypkino U.S.S.R. 52.52N 42.51E
80 H4 Pereto Italy 42.04N 13.06E
45 K8 Pereval'sk Kommuna Ukraine U.S.S.R. 48.25N 38.50E
82 H2 Pereval Veretski pass U.S.S.R. 48.45N 23.19E
45 G5 Pereverzevka U.S.S.R. 51.08N 35.45E
45 D6 Perevolochnaya Ukraine U.S.S.R. 50.37N 32.40E
39 E5 Perevolochnyy Zaliv B U.S.S.R.
46 R4 Perevolotskiy U.S.S.R. 51.50N 54.15E
47 L5 Perevoz Bashkir U.S.S.R. 56.07N 59.19E
42 K3 Perevoz Irkutsk U.S.S.R. 59.00N 116.58E
40 G8 Pereyaslavka U.S.S.R. 48.00N 135.04E
45 C6 Pereyaslav-Khmel'nitskiy Ukraine U.S.S.R. 50.05N 31.28E
110 D8 Perez California 41.40N 121.15W
120 D12 Pérez Chile 26.00S 69.55W
121 F1 Perez, L Argentina
42 G5 Perfilovo U.S.S.R. 54.26N 100.30E
25 D8 Perforated I Thailand 8.50N 97.48E
81 B2 Perfugas Sardinia 40.50N 8.53E
65 L5 Perg Austria 48.15N 14.38E
Pergamum anc site see Bergama
36 E6 Perge anc site Turkey 36.59N 30.46E
80 E2 Pérgine Valdarno Italy 43.28N 11.41E
79 K2 Pérgine Vals Italy 46.04N 11.14E
79 K2 Pérgine Valsugana Italy 46.04N 11.15E
79 N7 Pergola Italy 43.33N 12.50E
81 H8 Pergusa, L. di Sicily 37.31N 14.18E
108 P3 Perham Minnesota 46.36N 95.31W
Perhangök see Fahran
18 E3 Perhentian Besar isld Pen Malaysia
51 L8 Perho Finland 63.15N 24.25E
51 L8 Perhojoki R Finland
Peri see Çarsancak
79 J3 Peri Italy 45.39N 10.55E
37 E7 Perı R Turkey
82 F4 Periam Romania 46.02N 20.54E
77 H7 Periana Spain 36.55N 4.10W
99 S4 Péribonca Quebec 48.46N 72.03W
98 A3 Péribonca R Quebec
98 A3 Péribonca L Quebec
120 F11 Perico Argentina 24.20S 65.05W
112 B7 Perico Texas 36.17N 102.53W
115 F5 Pericos Mexico 25.03N 107.42W
120 F11 Pericote Argentina 24.31S 63.58W
72 H10 Péric, Pic mt France 42.37N 1.57E
71 H7 Périer, le France 44.56N 5.58E
70 H3 Périers France 49.11N 1.25W
72 D4 Pérignac France 45.38N 0.28W
72 D3 Périgne France 46.11N 0.16W
72 E5 Perigord reg France
117 D4 Perigoso, Can channel Brazil
72 F5 Périgueux France 45.12N 0.44E
119 D2 Perija, Sierra de mts Venezuela
72 K10 Périllou, Mt de France 42.55N 2.51E
98 P2 Peril Rock Quebec 51.20N 57.56W
101 F7 Peril Str Alaska
33 E10 Perim I Red Sea 12.40N 43.24E
41 C5 Periptaveto, Ozero L U.S.S.R.
120 G2 Periquito Brazil 7.18S 60.21W
117 H9 Períquito, Sa. do Brazil
82 K6 Periş Romania 44.43N 26.00E
84 G3 Peristéra isld Greece
84 B2 Peristéri mt Greece 39.40N 21.08E
84 R14 Peristerona Cyprus 35.07N 33.05E
84 R14 Peristerona R Cyprus
121 K6 Perito Moreno Argentina 46.35S 71.00W
121 J6 Perito Moreno, Nac. Parque Arg
117 F7 Peritoró Brazil 4.15S 44.17W
55 D3 Perivale London Eng 51.32N 0.19W
84 W23 Perivóli Corfu 39.25N 20.01E
84 D3 Perivóli Greece 39.04N 22.10E
84 D7 Perivólia Arkadhía Greece 37.23N 22.10E
84 J11 Perivólia Crete 35.29N 23.59E
84 L11 Perivólia Crete 35.22N 24.31E
28 C5 Periyakulam Tamil Nadu India 10.07N 77.33E
28 C6 Periyar L Kerala India 9.30N 77.20E
28 C5 Periyar R Kerala India
84 E6 Periyiáli Korinthía Greece 37.56N 22.50E
61 J3 Perk Belgium 50.56N 4.30E
103 D6 Perkasie Pennsylvania 40.22N 75.18W
46 M3 Perkino U.S.S.R. 53.08N 41.30E
105 F5 Perkins Georgia 32.54N 81.57W
107 C11 Perkins Louisiana 30.23N 93.27W
106 G4 Perkins Michigan 45.59N 87.04W
107 G11 Perkinston Mississippi 30.47N 89.09W
111 M7 Perkinsville Arizona 34.56N 112.10W
103 D6 Perkiomen Cr Pennsylvania
82 C7 Perkovic Yugoslavia 43.41N 16.08E
105 F13 Perky Florida 24.39N 81.34W
115 P5 Perlas, Arch. de las Panama
115 N3 Perlas, Laguna de Nicaragua
115 N3 Perlas, Pta. de C Nicaragua 12.23N 83.30W
61 O7 Perlé Luxembourg 49.48N 5.46E
63 P6 Perleberg E Germany 53.05N 11.52E
66 O7 Perledo Italy 46.02N 9.18E
64 P6 Perlesreut W Germany 48.47N 13.27E
45 K5 Perlevka U.S.S.R. 51.48N 38.53E
108 O2 Perley Minnesota 47.10N 96.50W
82 F5 Perlez Yugoslavia 45.11N 20.22E
18 C7 Perlis mt Pen Malaysia 4.43N 102.22E
18 D2 Perlis state Pen Malaysia
66 A7 Perly Switzerland 46.10N 6.06E
47 H6 Perm U.S.S.R. 58.01N 56.10E
110 L2 Perma Montana 47.21N 114.36W
18 C8 Permandang hill Pen Malaysia 3.10N 102.58E
47 F6 Permas U.S.S.R. 59.21N 45.33E
115 Q5 Permé Panama 8.46N 77.31W
83 D4 Përmet Albania 40.15N 20.21E
38 E3 Permskaya Oblast' prov U.S.S.R.
Pernambuco see Recife
117 H9 Pernambuco state Brazil
71 F2 Pernand-Vergelesses France 47.05N 4.51E
12 D4 Pernatty L S Australia
37 G5 Pernavut Turkey 40.06N 43.28E
65 N4 Pernegg Nieder-Österreich Austria 48.45N 15.38E
65 M7 Pernegg Steiermark Austria 47.22N 15.22E
109 N7 Pernell Oklahoma 34.35N 97.31W
69 C3 Pernes Pas de Calais France 50.29N 2.25E
76 B10 Pernes Portugal 39.23N 8.40W
71 G8 Pernes-les-Fontaines Vaucluse France 44.00N 5.03E
82 H8 Pernik Bulgaria 42.36N 23.03E
51 K11 Perniö Finland 60.13N 23.10E
60 F12 Pernis Netherlands 51.54N 4.23E
65 N6 Pernitz Austria 47.54N 15.58E
67 P12 Pero Casevecchio Corsica 42.24N 9.27E
76 C12 Peroguarda Portugal 38.06N 8.03W
76 D4 Peroja, La Spain 42.26N 7.48W
71 D9 Pérols France 43.33N 3.57E
71 H4 Péron France 46.12N 5.56E
14 A7 Peron, C W Australia 25.30S 113.33E
13 B2 Peron Is N Terr Australia
69 D4 Péronne France 49.56N 2.57E
61 D4 Péronnes Hainaut Belgium 50.33N 3.27E
61 G5 Péronnes Hainaut Belgium 50.27N 4.09E
14 A7 Peron Pen W Australia
14 A4 Peron, Pt W Australia 32.16S 115.42E
14 B9 Peron, Pt W Australia 32.18S 115.38E
70 O5 Péronville France 48.04N 1.32E
79 B5 Perosa Argentina Italy 44.58N 7.11E
27 L11 Peros Banhos isld Chagos Arch Br Indian Oc Terr 5.18S 72.00E
115 L8 Perote Mexico 19.32N 97.16W
120 F6 Perotó Bolivia 14.51S 64.33W
114 E6 Perouse Bay, la Hawaiian Is
12 M8 Perouse, La dist Sydney, N S W
21 J5 Pérouse Str., La Japan/Sakhalin, U.S.S.R
18 G2 Perpat R Pen Malaysia
18 F6 Perpat, Tanjung C Indonesia 0.40S 104.30E
11 F9 Perpendicular Pt New Zealand 42.03S 171.19E
72 K10 Perpignan France 42.42N 2.54E
121 A7 Perquenco Chile 38.26S 72.27W
105 L1 Perquimans R N Carolina
56 T9 Perranporth Cornwall Eng 50.20N 5.09W
69 B6 Perray-en-Yvelines, le France 48.42N 1.51E
71 E3 Perrecey-les-Forges France 46.37N 4.13E
79 B5 Perrero Italy 44.57N 7.07E
70 D5 Perret France 48.10N 3.10W
71 E4 Perreux Loire France 46.03N 4.07E
69 E8 Perreux Yonne France 47.51N 3.09E
68 G3 Perreux-sur-Marne, le France 48.51N 2.30E
66 G8 Perriase Italy 45.48N 7.43E
70 N3 Perriers-sur-Andelle France 49.24N 1.23E
66 B6 Perrignier France 46.19N 6.27E
112 J2 Perrin Texas 33.02N 98.05W
105 G12 Perrine Florida 25.36N 80.21W
103 F6 Perrineville New Jersey 40.14N 74.27W
111 G8 Perris California 33.48N 117.12W
69 J8 Perrogney-les-Fontaines France 47.49N 5.12E
109 E7 Perro, L. del New Mexico
99 N4 Perron Quebec 48.11N 77.34W
77 D7 Perro, Pta. del pt Spain 36.45N 6.26W
70 D4 Perros-Guirec France 48.49N 3.27W
107 D6 Perry Arkansas 35.02N 92.49W
105 D7 Perry Florida 30.08N 83.36W
105 D5 Perry Georgia 32.27N 83.45W
107 F2 Perry Illinois 39.48N 90.45W
108 Q8 Perry Iowa 41.50N 94.10W
106 K7 Perry Michigan 42.50N 84.13W
107 E2 Perry Missouri 39.26N 91.39W
104 G4 Perry New York 42.44N 78.01W
109 N5 Perry Oklahoma 36.17N 97.18W
99 F5 Perry Ontario 47.54N 84.33W
103 B8 Perry Hall Maryland 39.25N 76.27W
113 O6 Perry I Alaska 60.40N 147.59W
99 D2 Perry L Ontario 50.40N 86.35W
103 B8 Perryman Maryland 39.28N 76.12W
109 P2 Perry Res Kansas
101 W2 Perry River N W Terr 67.49N 102.19W
104 B5 Perrysburg Ohio 41.33N 83.39W
112 D7 Perryton Texas 36.23N 100.48W
100 D4 Perryvale Alberta 54.32N 113.20W
113 H9 Perryville Alaska 55.55N 159.11W
107 D7 Perryville Arkansas 35.00N 92.48W
103 B7 Perryville Maryland 39.34N 76.05W
107 G4 Perryville Missouri 37.43N 87.52W
66 B7 Pers France 46.06N 6.15E
72 J6 Pers France 44.53N 2.14E
72 F3 Persac France 46.21N 0.42E
69 C5 Persan France 49.09N 2.15E
37 D4 Perşembe Turkey 41.05N 37.46E
65 M5 Persenbeug Austria 48.12N 15.07E
32 E6 Persepolis anc site Iran 29.57N 52.59E
11 B8 Perseverance Harb inlet Campbell I Pacific Oc
120 G6 Perseverancia Bolivia 14.31S 62.46W
99 O4 Pershing Quebec 48.02N 76.58W
56 G3 Pershore Hereford & Worcs Eng 52.07N 2.05W
45 H8 Pershotravensk Ukraine U.S.S.R. 48.24N 36.22E
45 J9 Pershotravnevoye Ukraine U.S.S.R. 47.04N 37.20E
Persia see Iran
108 P8 Persia Iowa 41.34N 95.34W
27 F4 Persian Gulf S W Asia
94 E5 Persip Namibia 25.20S 18.59E
52 K9 Persnäs Sweden 57.04N 16.55E
18 C8 Pertang R Pen Malaysia
37 E7 Pertek Turkey 38.53N 39.19E
109 N4 Perth Kansas 37.11N 97.33W
108 L1 Perth N Dakota 48.44N 99.28W
98 E7 Perth New Brunswick 46.45N 67.42W
99 O8 Perth Ontario 44.54N 76.15W
58 T11 Perth Orkney Scotland 59.15N 2.52W
12 H8 Perth Tasmania 41.32S 147.09E
58 K6 Perth Tayside Scotland 56.24N 3.28W
14 B9 Perth W Australia 31.58S 115.49E
Perth co see Tayside and Central regions
58 H5 Perth co Scotland
103 J9 Perth Amboy New Jersey 40.31N 74.17W
69 G5 Perthes Ardennes France 49.27N 4.21E
69 H6 Perthes Haute-Marne France 48.39N 4.51E
69 D7 Perthes Seine-et-Marne France 48.28N 2.34E
72 K11 Perthus, le France 42.28N 2.52E
14 B2 Perth Water harb W Australia
65 E7 Pertisau Austria 47.26N 11.43E
47 D4 Pertominsk U.S.S.R. 64.46N 38.36E
70 H5 Pertre, le France 48.02N 1.02W
71 H9 Pertuis France 43.41N 5.30E

103 A4 **Picture Rocks** Pennsylvania 41.17N 76.40W
117 H8 **Picuí** Brazil 6.28S 36.20W
121 B7 **Picún-Leufú** Argentina 39.31S 69.09W
121 B7 **Picún-Leufú** *R* Argentina
66 P5 **Picuogl, Piz** *mt* Switzerland 46.32N 9.42E
31 B8 **Pidarak** Pakistan 25.50N 63.18E
56 G6 **Piddletrenthide** Dorset Eng 50.48N 2.25W
84 D7 **Pídhima** Greece 37.08N 22.03E
Pidile *see* **Podile**
64 O8 **Piding** W Germany 47.46N 12.55E
12 B4 **Pidinga** S Australia 30.48S 132.10E
26 S8 **Pidurutalagala** *mt* Sri Lanka 7.01N 80.45E
96 R4 **Piedade** Azores 38.27N 28.04W
118 H9 **Piedade** Rio de Janeiro Brazil 22.54S 43.19W
118 F8 **Piedade** São Paulo Brazil 23.42S 47.27W
76 B14 **Piedade, Pta. de** *C* Portugal 37.04N 8.44W
119 D4 **Piedecuesta** Colombia 6.59N 73.03W
121 C3 **Pie de Palo, Sa** *ra* Argentina
79 C3 **Piedicavallo** Italy 45.41N 7.57E
67 P12 **Piedicorte di Gaggio** Corsica 42.14N 9.19E
67 P12 **Piedicroce d'Orezza** Corsica 42.22N 9.22E
80 G3 **Piediluco** Italy 42.32N 12.46E
80 K6 **Piedimonte d'Alife** Italy 41.22N 14.22E
81 K8 **Piedimonte Etneo** Sicily 37.48N 15.12E
79 D2 **Piedimulera** Italy 46.01N 8.15E
107 L8 **Piedmont** Alabama 33.55N 85.39W
107 F4 **Piedmont** Missouri 37.09N 90.42W
105 E3 **Piedmont** S Carolina 34.43N 82.28W
108 G5 **Piedmont** S Dakota 44.14N 103.24W
104 F7 **Piedmont** W Virginia 39.27N 79.04W
111 B8 **Piedmont** *dist* Oakland, Cal 37.50N 122.14W
104 D6 **Piedmont Res** Ohio
111 E5 **Piedra** California 36.48N 119.20W
109 C4 **Piedra** *R* Colorado
75 G5 **Piedra** *R* Spain
77 H2 **Piedrabuena** Spain 39.02N 4.10W
121 B8 **Piedra de Aguilla** Argentina 40.03S 70.03W
119 F7 **Piedra de Cucuy** *mt* Venezuela 1.15N 66.51W
76 E3 **Piedrafita** Spain 42.44N 7.01W
76 E3 **Piedrafita, Puerto de** *pass* Spain 42.43N 7.00W
76 J8 **Piedrahita** Spain 40.27N 5.20W
76 K8 **Piedralaves** Spain 40.19N 4.42W
121 B3 **Piedra Lobos, Pta** Chile 30.50S 71.45W
119 B9 **Piedras** Ecuador 3.43S 79.56W
76 F9 **Piedras Albas** Spain 39.47N 6.55W
76 H1 **Piedras Blancas** Spain 43.33N 5.58W
111 C6 **Piedras Blancas, Pt** California 35.40N 121.17W
7 B6 **Piédras, Embalse de** *res* Spain
76 L2 **Piedrasluengas, Pto. de** *pass* Spain 43.04N 4.27W
115 J3 **Piedras Negras** Coahuila Mexico 28.40N 100.32W
115 O9 **Piedras Negras** Guatemala 17.11N 91.16W
115 L8 **Piedras Negras** Veracruz Mexico 18.48N 96.12W
121 G4 **Piedra Sola** Uruguay 32.05S 56.20W
19 J6 **Piedras Pt** Philippines 10.13N 118.50E
121 F5 **Piedras, Pta** *C* Argentina 35.28S 57.10W
120 D5 **Piedras, R. de las** Peru
80 F3 **Piegaro** Italy 42.58N 12.05E
72 F4 **Piégut-Pluviers** France 45.38N 0.42E
100 O2 **Pie I** Ontario 48.15N 89.05W
51 N9 **Pieksämäki** Finland 62.18N 27.10E
65 M5 **Pielach** *R* Austria
51 M8 **Pielavesi** *L* Finland 63.20N 26.30E
51 O8 **Pielinen** *L* Finland
51 O9 **Pielisjoki** *R* Finland
51 F5 **Pieljekaise Nat.Park** Sweden
12 G8 **Pieman R** Tasmania
79 C6 **Piemonte** *reg* Italy
94 K5 **Pienaar's River** S Africa 25.15S 28.18E
62 M1 **Pieniężno** Poland 54.15N 20.09E
69 K5 **Piennes** France 49.18N 5.47E
80 E2 **Pienza** Italy 43.04N 11.40E
64 A2 **Pier** W Germany 50.51N 6.23E
75 Q4 **Piera** Spain 41.31N 1.45E
80 F2 **Pierantonio** Italy 43.15N 12.23E
109 F1 **Pierce** Colorado 40.37N 104.45W
105 F10 **Pierce** Florida 27.50N 81.59W
110 K3 **Pierce** Idaho 46.30N 115.47W
108 N7 **Pierce** Nebraska 42.13N 97.34W
57 K3 **Piercebridge** Durham Eng 54.32N 1.41W
107 B5 **Pierce City** Missouri 36.56N 94.01W
112 F9 **Pierce Junction** Houston, Texas 29.40N 95.24W
106 J8 **Pierceton** Indiana 41.11N 85.42W
109 K4 **Pierceville** Kansas 37.54N 100.41W
111 A2 **Piercy** California 39.59N 123.47W
121 F7 **Pieres** Argentina 38.20S 58.41W
84 D1 **Pieria** *prov* Greece
83 E4 **Piéria Óri** *mts* Greece
103 G4 **Piermont** New York 41.02N 73.55W
58 T11 **Pierowall** Orkney Scotland 59.19N 3.00W
108 N4 **Pierpont** S Dakota 45.30N 97.50W
108 K5 **Pierre** S Dakota 44.23N 100.20W
66 E7 **Pierre à Voir** *mt* Switzerland 46.07N 7.13E
72 G4 **Pierre-Buffière** France 45.41N 1.22E
71 H7 **Pierre-Châtel** France 44.57N 5.46E
71 G3 **Pierre-de-Bresse** France 46.53N 5.16E
71 J10 **Pierrefeu-du-Var** France 43.13N 6.10E
72 D10 **Pierrefitte-Nestalas** France 42.57N 0.04W
69 J6 **Pierrefitte-sur-Aire** Meuse France 48.54N 5.20E
71 D3 **Pierrefitte-sur-Loire** Allier France 46.30N 3.50E
70 P6 **Pierrefitte-sur-Sauldre** France 47.31N 2.09E
68 F2 **Pierrefitte-sur-Seine** France 48.58N 2.23E
69 D5 **Pierrefonds** France 49.21N 2.59E
99 P10 **Pierrefonds** Quebec 45.28N 73.50W
66 C3 **Pierrefontaine** France 47.13N 6.33E
71 K2 **Pierrefontaine-les-Varans** France 47.13N 6.32E
72 K6 **Pierrefort** France 44.55N 2.50E
99 K3 **Pierre L** Ontario
71 F8 **Pierrelatte** France 44.22N 4.41E
68 C1 **Pierrelaye** France 49.01N 2.08E
79 A4 **Pierre Menue** *mt* Italy/France 45.09N 6.46E
69 K5 **Pierrepont** France 49.25N 5.44E
71 D5 **Pierre-sur-Haute** *mt* France 45.38N 3.50E
99 S6 **Pierreville** Quebec 46.04N 72.49W
116 P2 **Pierreville** Trinidad & Tobago 10.17N 61.01W
26 B12 **Pierrot I** Rodriguez I Ind Oc 19.46S 63.26E
72 C6 **Pierroton** France 44.45N 0.46W
69 F5 **Pierry** France 49.01N 3.56E
60 F12 **Piershil** Netherlands 51.47N 4.18E
105 F8 **Pierson** Florida 29.13N 81.29W
100 Q9 **Pierson** Manitoba 49.12N 101.15W
15 D5 **Piesapa** Irian Jaya 3.33S 137.18E
51 F5 **Pieskehaure** *L* Sweden 66.56N 16.40E
64 B4 **Piesport** W Germany 49.50N 6.56E
14 B10 **Piesseville** W Australia 33.11S 117.12E
62 K7 **Piešťany** Czechoslovakia 48.35N 17.50E
Pietarsaari *see* **Jakobstad**
26 U12 **Pieter Both** *mt* Mauritius, Indian Oc 20.12S 57.33E
60 O6 **Pieterburen** Netherlands 53.24N 6.27E
66 F3 **Pieterlen** Switzerland 47.11N 7.20E
95 O5 **Pietermaritzburg** S Africa 29.36S 30.24E
95 D9 **Pieter Meintjes** S Africa 33.15S 20.25E
95 N4 **Pieters** S Africa 28.40S 29.50E
94 K4 **Pietersburg** S Africa 23.54S 29.23E
109 B7 **Pie Town** New Mexico 34.18N 108.08W
80 K5 **Pietrabbondante** Italy 41.44N 14.25E
80 J3 **Pietracamela** Italy 42.32N 13.34E
67 P11 **Pietracorbara** Corsica 42.50N 9.25E
67 P12 **Pietradi-Verde** Corsica 42.17N 9.27E
80 N7 **Pietragalla** Italy 40.45N 15.53E
61 K4 **Piétrain** Belgium 50.43N 4.55E
79 D6 **Pietra Ligure** Italy 44.09N 88.17E
80 F2 **Pietralunga** Italy 43.26N 12.26E
80 M5 **Pietra Montecorvino** Italy 41.33N 15.09E
81 H9 **Pietraperzia** Sicily 37.25N 14.08E
67 P13 **Pietrapolo** Corsica 41.59N 9.16E
79 B6 **Pietra Porzio** Italy 44.20N 7.02E
79 H7 **Pietrasanta** Italy 43.57N 10.14E
80 K6 **Pietravairano** Italy 41.20N 14.10E
61 K4 **Piétrebais** Belgium 50.44N 4.47E
81 E9 **Pietre, Pta. tre** Pantelleria I Italy 36.47N 11.58E
95 O3 **Piet Retief** S Africa 27.00S 30.49E
80 K6 **Pietromelara** Italy 41.17N 14.12E
82 J5 **Pietroşiţa** Romania 45.11N 25.27E
82 J3 **Pietrosu** *mt* Romania 47.35N 24.39E
82 J3 **Pietrosul** *mt* Romania 47.07N 25.10E
51 P2 **Piets'yarvi, Ozero** *L* U.S.S.R. 69.03N 30.00E
70 G2 **Pieux, les** France 49.31N 1.48W
79 M2 **Pieve d'Alpago** Italy 46.10N 12.22E
79 E4 **Pieve del Cairo** Italy 45.03N 8.48E
79 J3 **Pieve di Bono** Italy 45.56N 10.38E
79 M2 **Pieve di Cadore** Italy 46.27N 12.23E
79 K5 **Pieve di Cento** Italy 44.43N 11.19E
79 J3 **Pieve di Ledro** Italy 45.53N 10.43E
79 C6 **Pieve di Teco** Italy 44.03N 7.55E
79 J6 **Pievepélago** Italy 44.12N 10.37E
79 F4 **Pieve Porto Morone** Italy 45.07N 9.26E
79 M7 **Pieve Santo Stefano** Italy 43.40N 12.02E
80 H2 **Pieve Torina** Italy 43.03N 13.03E
69 E7 **Piffonds** France 48.03N 3.07E
83 J9 **Pigádhia** Kárpathos Greece 35.30N 27.12E
84 D8 **Pigádhia** Messinía Greece 37.00N 22.15E
17 P10 **Pigailoe** *isld* Caroline Is Pacific Oc 8.08N 146.40E
45 V5 **Pigari** U.S.S.R. 51.26N 49.44E
92 F4 **Pigawasi** Tanzania 4.53S 33.08E
106 L6 **Pigeon** Michigan 43.50N 83.15W
99 H10 **Pigeon B** Ontario
107 K10 **Pigeon Cr** Alabama
13 B3 **Pigeon Hole** N Terr Australia 16.47S 131.14E
116 K2 **Pigeon I** Jamaica, W I 17.47N 77.05W
100 C5 **Pigeon L** Alberta 53.00N 114.00W
99 M8 **Pigeon L** Ontario
111 B4 **Pigeon Pt** California 37.10N 122.25W
116 M1 **Pigeon Pt** Tobago W I 11.10N 60.51W
100 V6 **Pigeon R** Manitoba
106 K4 **Pigeon R** Michigan
106 E1 **Pigeon River** Minnesota 48.01N 89.44W
100 N2 **Pigeon River** Ontario 48.01N 89.42W
14 C8 **Pigeon Rocks** W Australia 29.55S 119.12E
104 F10 **Pigg** *R* Virginia
107 F5 **Piggott** Arkansas 36.22N 90.11W
95 P1 **Pigg's Peak** Swaziland 25.58S 31.17E
11 C13 **Pig I** New Zealand 46.23N 167.58E
79 E7 **Pigino** *dist* Milan Italy
79 C7 **Pigna** Italy 43.57N 7.40E
71 D9 **Pignan** France 43.35N 3.47E
71 J10 **Pignans** France 43.19N 6.14E
80 J6 **Pignataro Interamna** Italy 41.26N 13.47E
80 K6 **Pignataro Maggiore** Italy 41.12N 14.11E
80 N7 **Pignola** Italy 40.34N 15.47E
Pigs, B. of *see* **Cochinos, B. de**
121 E6 **Pigüé** Argentina 37.38S 62.27W
76 G2 **Pigüeña** *R* Spain
115 K7 **Piguicas** *pk* Mexico 21.10N 99.41W
45 E1 **Pigulino** U.S.S.R. 55.25N 33.46E
11 H6 **Pihama** New Zealand 39.30S 173.56E
30 D5 **Pihani** Uttar Prad India 27.37N 80.12E
9 S10 **Piha Passage** Tonga, Pacific Oc
65 F7 **Pihapper Spitze** *mt* Austria 47.14N 12.28E
23 G3 **Pi He** *R* Anhui China
29 C6 **Pihij** Gujarat India 22.40N 72.52E
51 L9 **Pihlajavesi** Finland 62.21N 24.20E
51 M8 **Pihtipudas** Finland 63.24N 25.30E
115 H8 **Pihuamo** Mexico 19.20N 103.21W
15 H4 **Pihun I** Bismarck Arch 1.21S 144.20E
21 C8 **Pihyŏn** N Korea 40.00N 124.36E
45 C7 **Pii** Ukraine U.S.S.R. 49.53N 31.06E
114 C7 **Piihonua** Hawaiian Is 19.42N 155.09W
115 N10 **Pijijiapan** Mexico 15.42N 93.12W
60 F11 **Pijnacker** Netherlands 52.01N 4.26E
39 D4 **Pik Aborigen** *mt* U.S.S.R. 61.59N 149.21E
28 E1 **Pikaldadi** Maharashtra India 19.14N 80.05E
46 J1 **Pikalevo** U.S.S.R. 59.35N 34.07E
97 K7 **Pikangikum L** Ontario 51.50N 94.00W
103 D4 **Pike** *co* Pennsylvania
100 L7 **Pike Lake Prov. Park** Saskatchewan
109 E3 **Pikes Pk** Colorado 38.50N 105.03W
103 A8 **Pikesville** Maryland 39.23N 76.44W
95 B8 **Piketberg** S Africa 32.55S 18.45E
104 B7 **Piketon** Ohio 39.03N 83.01W
104 C9 **Pikeville** Kentucky 37.29N 82.33W
107 L6 **Pikeville** Tennessee 35.35N 85.11W
42 C4 **Pikhtovka** U.S.S.R. 56.00N 82.44E
97 P5 **Pikiutdleq** *dist* Greenland
113 F5 **Pikmiktalik** Alaska 63.11N 162.40W
91 E3 **Pikounda** Congo 0.30N 16.44E
24 C4 **Pik Pobedy** *mt pk* Xinjiang Uygur Zizhiqu China 42.02N 80.00E
100 U3 **Pikwitonei** Manitoba 55.35N 97.11W
121 F6 **Pila** Argentina 36.00S 58.05W
84 C8 **Píla** Greece 36.57N 21.44E
46 B3 **Piła** Poland 53.09N 16.44E
77 O4 **Pila** *mt* Spain 38.16N 1.11W
67 O13 **Pila Canale** Corsica 41.48N 8.55E
65 C6 **Pilach** Austria 47.31N 10.44E
118 B9 **Pilagá, R** Argentina
50 H4 **Pílagrímsfell** *mt* Iceland 65.24N 17.30W
25 D7 **Pila, Kyun** *isld* Burma
121 G6 **Pila, L. de** Argentina
84 C7 **Pilalístra** Greece 37.04N 21.57E
119 B8 **Pilaló** Ecuador 0.59S 79.02W
94 J5 **Pilanesberg** *mts* S Africa
18 L7 **Pilang** Borneo Indon 2.26S 114.11E
118 G2 **Pilão Arcado** Brazil 10.13S 42.30W
117 F9 **Pilão Arcado, R** Brazil
117 J9 **Pilar** Brazil 9.30S 35.52W
121 F5 **Pilar** Buenos Aires Arg 34.28S 58.55W
121 D3 **Pilar** Cordoba Argentina 31.44S 63.53W
118 B10 **Pilar** Paraguay 26.51S 58.20W
19 N7 **Pilar** Philippines 9.51N 126.07E
121 E3 **Pilar** Santa Fé Argentina 31.44S 61.16W
91 A12 **Pilar, B. do** São Tomé São Tomé & Principe, Gulf of Guinea
121 J9 **Pilar, C** Chile 52.43S 73.43W
111 B10 **Pilarcitos L** California 37.33N 122.26W
118 E4 **Pilar de Goiás** Brazil 14.50S 49.27W
77 P5 **Pilar de la Horadada** Spain 37.52N 0.48W
118 F8 **Pilar do Sul** Brazil 23.48S 47.45W
77 D6 **Pilas** Spain 37.18N 6.18W
19 K8 **Pilas** *isld* Philippines 6.35N 121.38E
19 K8 **Pilas Chan** Philippines
77 O4 **Pila, Sierra de la** *mts* Spain
71 F6 **Pilat, Mt** France 45.23N 4.34E
66 K4 **Pilatus** *mt* Switzerland 46.59N 8.16E
120 F9 **Pilaya, R** Bolivia
14 C5 **Pilbara** W Australia 21.20S 118.16E
121 B8 **Pilcaniyeu** Argentina 41.04S 70.40W
11 G7 **Pilch Pt** New Zealand 40.31S 172.40E
120 F9 **Pilcomaya, R** Paraguay/Bolivia
113 L7 **Pile Bay** Alaska 59.44N 154.00W
28 D4 **Piler** Andhra Prad India 13.39N 78.58E
Pileru *see* **Piler**
108 N7 **Pilger** Nebraska 42.00N 97.06W
100 M6 **Pilger** Saskatchewan 52.26N 105.18W
94 L5 **Pilgrims Rest** S Africa 24.55S 30.44E
39 L1 **Pil'gyn** U.S.S.R. 69.48N 179.20W
84 G5 **Píli** Attikí Greece 38.13N 23.30E
84 G4 **Píli** Évvoia Greece 38.45N 23.35E
19 L5 **Pili** Luzon Philippines 13.37N 123.17E
84 C3 **Píli** Tríkkala Greece 39.27N 21.37E
30 C4 **Pilibhit** Uttar Prad India 28.37N 79.48E
30 C4 **Pilibhit** *dist* Uttar Prad India
62 M5 **Pilica** Poland 50.28N 19.40E
62 M4 **Pilica** *R* Poland
84 F3 **Pílion** *mts* Greece
62 M8 **Pilis** Hungary 47.17N 19.33E
62 L8 **Pilisvörösvár** Hungary 47.38N 18.55E
30 A4 **Pilkhua** Uttar Prad India 28.42N 77.41E
56 F5 **Pill** Avon Eng 51.29N 2.41W
11 B12 **Pillans Pass** New Zealand 45.37S 167.11E
12 J9 **Pillar, C** Tasmania 43.10S 148.00E
23 B8 **Pillar I** Hong Kong 22.21N 114.06E
119 B8 **Pillaro** Ecuador 1.13S 78.36W
111 A10 **Pillar Pt** California 37.30N 122.30W
Pillau *see* **Baltiysk**
120 D5 **Pillcopata** Peru 13.01S 71.17W
98 R4 **Pilley's I** Newfoundland 49.30N 55.42W
12 J4 **Pilliga** New S Wales 30.23S 148.55E
57 H5 **Pilling** Lancs Eng 53.56N 2.54W
64 N6 **Pilling** W Germany 48.52N 12.29E
121 E4 **Pillo, I. del** Argentina
69 K5 **Pillon** France 49.22N 5.35E
66 E6 **Pillon, Col du** Switzerland 46.22N 7.13E
108 N2 **Pillsbury** N Dakota 47.14N 97.48W
111 B2 **Pillsbury, L** California 39.25N 122.57W
45 R1 **Pil'na** U.S.S.R. 55.34N 45.54E
47 H2 **Pil'nya Ostrov** *isld* U.S.S.R.
118 F5 **Pilões, Sa. dos** *mts* Brazil
116 F5 **Pilón** Cuba 19.53N 77.20W
Piloña *see* **Infiesto**
120 E10 **Pilo o Acamarachi, Cerro** *pk* Chile 23.18S 67.35W
84 C8 **Pílos** Greece 36.55N 21.42E
100 N8 **Pilot Butte** Saskatchewan 50.29N 104.28W
107 D3 **Pilot Grove** Missouri 38.53N 92.55W
101 S5 **Pilot L** N W Terr 60.19N 111.01W
100 T9 **Pilot Mound** Manitoba 49.13N 98.52W
105 G1 **Pilot Mt** N Carolina 36.31N 80.30W
110 L8 **Pilot Pk** Nevada 41.02N 114.05W
111 G3 **Pilot Pk** Nevada 38.17N 117.55W
110 Q5 **Pilot Pk** Wyoming 44.59N 109.55W
113 J8 **Pilot Point** Alaska 57.35N 157.37W
112 L2 **Pilot Point** Texas 33.25N 96.58W
110 G4 **Pilot Rock** Oregon 45.29N 118.50W
113 F6 **Pilot Station** Alaska 61.58N 162.59W
12 J6 **Pilot, The** *mt* New S Wales 36.45S 148.15E
107 G12 **Pilottown** Louisiana 29.10N 89.15W
64 M5 **Pilsach** W Germany 49.19N 11.32E
Pilsen Czechoslovakia *see* **Plzeň**
106 G5 **Pilsen** Wisconsin 44.27N 87.44W
64 L7 **Pilsensee** *L* W Germany 48.01N 11.12E
64 O6 **Pilsting** W Germany 48.42N 12.40E
42 A2 **Pil'tan-Lor, Ozero** *L* U.S.S.R.
46 D2 **Piltene** Latvia U.S.S.R. 57.09N 21.40E
56 F5 **Pilton** Somerset Eng 51.10N 2.35W
59 H7 **Piltown** Kilkenny Irish Rep 52.21N 7.25W
40 J5 **Pil'tun** Sakhalin U.S.S.R. 52.43N 143.19E
40 J5 **Pil'tun Zaliv** *gulf* Sakhalin U.S.S.R.
31 F8 **Pilu** Pakistan 24.43N 70.38E
47 H5 **Pil'va** *R* U.S.S.R.
40 J4 **Pil'vo** Sakhalin U.S.S.R. 54.04N 142.36E
30 B5 **Pilwa** Uttar Prad India 27.38N 78.34E
62 N5 **Pilzno** Poland 50.00N 21.16E
47 L5 **Pim** U.S.S.R. 61.35N 72.10E
47 L5 **Pim** *R* U.S.S.R.
111 P9 **Pima** Arizona 32.53N 109.50W
92 E5 **Pimbwe** *tribe* Tanzania
69 G8 **Pimelles** France 47.51N 4.10E
117 B7 **Pimenta** Brazil 4.30S 56.04W
120 G4 **Pimenta Bueno** Brazil 11.40S 61.14W
116 J5 **Pimental** Dominican Rep 19.12N 70.07W
Pimentas *see* **Barra do Turvo**
117 E6 **Pimentel** Maranhão Brazil 3.45S 45.28W
120 A8 **Pimentel** Peru 6.51S 79.53W
105 L12 **Pimlico I** Bahamas 25.20S 76.52W
29 D7 **Pimpalner** Maharashtra India 20.59N 74.09E
19 C3 **Pimpi** Celebes Indon 0.55N 123.30E
29 C7 **Pimpri** Gujarat India 20.54N 73.42E
91 G3 **Pimu** Zaïre 1.42N 20.58E
30 F3 **Pimu** *mt* Nepal 27.55N 86.34E
95 L2 **Pimville** S Africa 26.17S 27.53E
89 J6 **Pina** Ghana 10.54N 1.39W
115 E9 **Piña** Panama 9.16N 80.03W
75 J5 **Pina** Spain 41.29N 0.33W
75 J7 **Pina** *mt* Spain 40.02N 0.38W
111 L10 **Pinacate, Cerro** *mt* Mexico 31.48N 113.30W
115 C2 **Pinacate, Sa. del** *mt* Mexico
121 J8 **Pinacula, Cerro** *pk* Arg/Chile 50.46S 72.15W
76 L4 **Piña de Campos** Spain 42.13N 4.26W
76 L5 **Piña de Esgueva** Spain 41.44N 4.26W
30 B6 **Pinahat** Uttar Prad India 26.53N 78.23E
122 F16 **Pinaki** *isld* Tuamotu Is Pacific Oc 19.20S 138.40W
111 O9 **Pinaleno Mts** Arizona
19 K5 **Pinamalayan** Philippines 13.02N 121.29E
18 A6 **Pinang** Pen Malaysia 5.30N 100.28E
18 A6 **Pinang** *isld* Pen Malaysia
18 A6 **Pinang** *state* Pen Malaysia
18 M3 **Pinangah** Sabah Malaysia 5.09N 116.50E
18 G3 **Pinang, Ci** *R* Indonesia
77 K6 **Piñar** Spain 37.26N 3.26W
77 F7 **Pinar** *mt* Spain 36.46N 5.25W
36 G1 **Pınarbaşı** Kastamonu Turkey 41.45N 33.04E
36 J4 **Pınarbaşı** Kayseri Turkey 38.43N 36.23E
Pınarbaşı Konya Turkey *see* **Tömek**
77 W14 **Pinar, C. del** Balearic Is 39.54N 3.11E
116 C3 **Pinar del Río** Cuba 22.24N 83.42W
116 B3 **Pinar del Rio** *prov* Cuba
75 F8 **Pinarejo** Spain 39.37N 2.25W
36 C1 **Pınarhisar** Turkey 41.37N 27.32E
12 F3 **Pinaroo, L** New S Wales 29.06S 141.15E
121 D3 **Piñas** Argentina 31.10S 65.31W
119 B9 **Piñas** Ecuador 3.46S 79.45W
79 B5 **Pinasca** Italy 44.57N 7.13E
70 L4 **Pin-au-Haras, le** France 48.44N 0.08E
76 C11 **Pincaes** *R* Portugal
79 L5 **Pincara** Italy 44.59N 11.37E
56 L2 **Pinchbeck** Lincs Eng 52.49N 0.11W
100 D9 **Pincher** Alberta 49.33N 113.53W
100 D9 **Pincher Creek** Alberta 49.31N 113.53W
101 L8 **Pinchi** Br Columbia 54.34N 124.29W
106 L7 **Pinckney** Michigan 42.28N 83.57W
107 G3 **Pinckneyville** Illinois 38.05N 89.21W
70 J4 **Pinçon, Mt** France 48.58N 0.39W
106 L6 **Pinconning** Michigan 43.52N 83.59W
82 G4 **Pîncota** Romania 46.20N 21.45E
62 M5 **Pińczów** Poland 50.30N 20.30E
118 G4 **Pindaí** Brazil 14.30S 42.43W
118 D4 **Pindaíba** Brazil 15.01S 52.15W
107 D5 **Pindall** Arkansas 36.03N 92.55W
118 F8 **Pindamonhangaba** Brazil 22.54S 45.24W
14 B8 **Pindar** W Australia 28.27S 115.48E
30 C2 **Pindar** *R* Uttar Prad India
117 E6 **Pindaré Mirim** Brazil 3.38S 45.16W
117 E6 **Pindaré, R** Brazil
31 G4 **Pind Dadan Khan** Pakistan 32.36N 73.07E
Pinder Pt *see* **Southwest Pt** Bahama Is
84 B2 **Píndhos Óros** *mts* Greece
31 G5 **Pindi Bhattian** Pakistan 31.54N 73.20E
31 G4 **Pindi Gheb** Pakistan 33.16N 72.21E
15 J7 **Pindiu** Papua New Guinea 6.32S 147.39E
118 H2 **Pindobaçu** Brazil 10.38S 40.19W
117 D6 **Pindobal** Brazil 3.15S 48.25W
76 A3 **Pindo, Mte** Spain 42.53N 9.06W
119 C8 **Pindo, R** Ecuador
60 F14 **Pindorp** Netherlands 51.28N 4.23E
29 G6 **Pindrei** Madhya Prad India 22.32N 80.07E
53 E4 **Pindstrup** Denmark 56.24N 10.25E
47 C4 **Pindushi** U.S.S.R. 62.55N 34.37E
29 C5 **Pindwara** Rajasthan India 24.52N 73.14E
111 N7 **Pine** Arizona 34.25N 111.28W
110 K6 **Pine** Idaho 43.27N 115.19W
106 J5 **Pine** *R* Michigan
12 F4 **Pine** *R* New S Wales
107 K10 **Pine Apple** Alabama 31.52N 87.00W
107 D7 **Pine Bluff** Arkansas 34.13N 92.00W
100 P4 **Pinebluff L** Saskatchewan 54.05N 102.48W
108 F8 **Pine Bluffs** Wyoming 41.10N 104.06W
103 F3 **Pine Bush** New York 41.37N 74.18W
98 T7 **Pine, C** Newfoundland 46.38N 53.35W
105 F9 **Pine Castle** Florida 28.29N 81.22W
105 J12 **Pine Cay** *isld* Bahamas 25.12N 78.12W
107 E7 **Pine City** Arkansas 34.33N 91.06W
108 S4 **Pine City** Minnesota 45.49N 92.59W
110 J9 **Pine Cr** Nevada
104 H5 **Pine Cr** Pennsylvania
13 B2 **Pine Creek** N Terr Australia 13.51S 131.50E
109 P7 **Pine Creek Res** Oklahoma
111 E3 **Pinecrest** California 38.10N 119.59W
75 Q4 **Pineda** Spain 41.38N 2.42E
75 E7 **Pineda de Cigüela** Spain 40.05N 2.34W
75 D3 **Pineda de la Sierra** Spain 42.13N 3.17W
101 P9 **Pinedale** Alberta 53.35N 116.10W
111 E5 **Pinedale** California 36.50N 119.50W
110 Q7 **Pinedale** Wyoming 42.51N 109.50W
111 E5 **Pine Flat Res** California 36.50N 119.15W
110 G8 **Pine Forest Ra** Nevada
47 E4 **Pinega** U.S.S.R. 64.42N 43.28E
47 E4 **Pinega** *R* U.S.S.R.
103 B5 **Pine Grove** Pennsylvania 40.33N 76.22W
14 B8 **Pinegrove** W Australia 27.42S 115.40E
103 E2 **Pine Hill** New York 42.07N 74.30W
13 C5 **Pine Hill** N Terr Australia 23.20S 133.00E
13 H6 **Pinehill** Queensland 23.38S 146.57E
100 L3 **Pine House** Saskatchewan 55.31N 106.35W
100 L3 **Pine House L** Saskatchewan
105 H2 **Pinehurst** N Carolina 35.12N 79.29W
110 C2 **Pinehurst** Washington 47.56N 122.13W
100 F4 **Pinehurst L** Alberta
105 E11 **Pine I** Florida 26.35N 82.08W
105 F13 **Pine Is** Florida
108 S5 **Pine Island** Minnesota 44.12N 92.38W
103 F4 **Pine Island** New York 41.17N 74.28W
123 H11 **Pine Island B** Antarctica
106 F4 **Pine L** Wisconsin 45.41N 88.59W
112 O4 **Pineland** Texas 31.15N 93.59W
94 P11 **Pinelands** Cape Town S Africa 33.56S 18.30E
76 L5 **Piñel de Abajo** Spain 41.40N 4.09W
11 D12 **Pinelheugh** *mt* New Zealand 45.30S 169.30E
105 E10 **Pinellas** *airport* Florida 27.55N 82.45W
75 M5 **Pinell de Bray** Spain 41.01N 0.31E
76 F5 **Pinelo** Portugal 41.38N 6.34W
103 J3 **Pine Meadow** Connecticut 41.51N 72.57W
105 C5 **Pine Mountain** Georgia 32.52N 84.50W
111 C6 **Pine Mt** California 35.41N 121.06W
109 P7 **Pine Mt** Oklahoma
111 L7 **Pine Pk** Arizona 34.45N 113.51W
103 G3 **Pine Plains** New York 41.58N 73.38W
101 Q5 **Pine Point** N W Terr 60.52N 114.30W
99 B3 **Pine Portage** Ontario 49.19N 88.17W
105 D8 **Pine Pt** Florida 29.31N 83.24W
101 Q5 **Pine Pt** N W Terr 61.01N 114.17W
100 D4 **Pine R** Alberta
101 N8 **Pine R** Br Columbia
106 K6 **Pine, R** Michigan
106 D6 **Pine, R** Wisconsin
106 F4 **Pine, R** Wisconsin
121 F4 **Piñera** Uruguay 32.18S 57.03W
108 H6 **Pine Ridge** S Dakota 43.02N 102.33W
100 R7 **Pine River** Manitoba 51.46N 100.31W
108 Q3 **Pine River** Minnesota 46.40N 94.22W
100 K3 **Pine River** Saskatchewan 55.58N 107.24W
121 K4 **Pinero** Buenos Aires Argentina 34.39S 58.33W
79 B5 **Pinerolo** Italy 44.53N 7.19E
105 K7 **Pineros, I** Puerto Rico 18.18N 65.37W
45 P5 **Pinerovka** U.S.S.R. 51.35N 43.05E
99 J10 **Pinery Prov. Park** Ontario
112 N3 **Pines, L. O'The** Texas
112 C4 **Pine Springs** Texas 31.52N 104.50W
77 Q3 **Pinet** Spain 38.59N 0.20W
80 K3 **Pineto** Italy 42.36N 14.04E
95 O5 **Pinetown** S Africa 29.50S 30.53E
18 B8 **Pine Tree Hill** Pen Malaysia 3.41N 101.41E
109 Q7 **Pine Valley** Oklahoma 34.40N 94.45W
111 L4 **Pine Valley** Utah 37.25N 113.31W
111 L4 **Pine Valley Mts** Utah
105 D1 **Pineville** Kentucky 36.47N 83.43W
107 D10 **Pineville** Louisiana 31.20N 92.26W
107 B5 **Pineville** Missouri 36.36N 94.23W
105 G2 **Pineville** N Carolina 35.06N 80.53W
103 D6 **Pineville** Pennsylvania 40.17N 75.00W
104 D9 **Pineville** W Virginia 37.35N 81.34W
108 P2 **Pinewood** Minnesota 47.33N 95.08W
100 H2 **Pinewood** Ontario 48.44N 94.19W
105 G4 **Pinewood** S Carolina 33.46N 80.27W
69 G7 **Piney** France 48.22N 4.21E
100 F1 **Piney** Manitoba 49.05N 95.58W
108 D2 **Piney Buttes** *hills* Montana
107 C6 **Piney Cr** Arkansas
105 D8 **Piney Pt** Florida 29.46N 83.36W
92 D2 **Pinga** Zaïre 1.01S 28.41E
31 G2 **Pingal** Kashmir 36.09N 73.11E
21 C5 **Ping 'an** Jilin China 45.23N 123.40E
14 C10 **Pingaring** W Australia 32.45S 118.34E
23 D5 **Pingba** Guizhou China 26.26N 106.12E
23 C7 **Pingbian** Yunnan China 23.00N 103.45E
23 D3 **Pingchang** Sichuan China 31.36N 107.00E
23 B5 **Pingchuan** Sichuan China 27.39N 101.54E
22 L9 **Ping Dao** *isld* Shandong China
23 E5 **Pingdeng** Guangxi China 26.07N 109.58E
22 J8 **Pingding** Shanxi China 37.47N 113.31E
Pingdingbu *see* **Guyuan**
23 F2 **Pingdingshan** Henan China 33.50N 113.20E
21 C7 **Pingdingshan** Liaoning China 41.26N 124.46E
21 D4 **Pingding Shan** *mt pk* Heilongjiang China 46.37N 128.26E
22 L8 **Pingdu** Shandong China 36.50N 119.55E
14 B10 **Pingelly** W Australia 32.34S 117.04E
23 G1 **Pinggang** Henan China 34.15N 115.05E
21 C6 **Pinggang** Liaoning China 42.56N 124.48E
65 O7 **Pinggau** Austria 47.28N 16.05E
22 L6 **Pinggu** Beijing China 40.09N 117.06E
23 D7 **Pingguo** Guangxi China 23.24N 107.30E
23 H6 **Pinghai** Fujian China 25.12N 119.10E
25 N1 **Pinghai** Guangdong China 22.37N 114.48E
23 H6 **Pinghe** Fujian China 24.20N 117.22E
Pinghu *see* **Pingtang**
23 J3 **Pinghu** Zhejiang China 30.44N 121.02E
23 F4 **Pingjiang** Hunan China 28.45N 113.36E
60 K7 **Pingjum** Netherlands 53.07N 5.27E
23 E6 **Pingle** Guangxi China 24.36N 110.28E
23 E2 **Pingli** Shaanxi China 32.28N 109.28E
23 D1 **Pingliang** Gansu China 35.27N 106.31E
23 F3 **Pinglin** Hubei China 31.27N 113.40E
23 E6 **Pinglo** Guangxi China 24.36N 110.28E
22 J7 **Pinglu** Shanxi China 39.45N 112.19E
23 F1 **Pinglu** Shanxi China 34.49N 111.11E
22 G7 **Pingluo** Ningxia China 38.55N 106.31E
Pingma *see* **Tiandong**
25 E4 **Ping, Mae** *R* Thailand
23 E7 **Pingnah** Guangxi China 23.32N 110.22E
23 H5 **Pingnan** Fujian China 26.55N 118.54E
23 E7 **Pingnan** Guangxi China 23.32N 110.22E
43 K7 **Pingon** Tadzhikistan U.S.S.R. 39.10N 70.15E
26 N16 **Pingouins, Îs. des** Crozet Is Ind Oc 46.30S 50.20E
Pingqiao *see* **Xinyang**
23 D1 **Pingquan** Gansu China 35.36N 107.05E
22 L6 **Pingquan** Hebei China 41.02N 118.35E
110 N6 **Pingree** Idaho 43.08N 112.35W
108 M2 **Pingree** N Dakota 47.11N 98.54W
14 C10 **Pingrup** W Australia 33.33S 118.30E
14 C10 **Pingrup, L** W Australia 33.25S 118.59E
25 M1 **Pingsha** Guangdong China 22.04N 113.11E
Pingshan *see* **Huidong**
22 K7 **Pingshan** Hebei China 38.14N 114.06E
23 C4 **Pingshan** Sichuan China 28.39N 104.03E
23 H1 **Pingshang** Shandong China 35.11N 119.05E
23 F6 **Pingshi** Guangdong China 25.18N 112.59E
23 F2 **Pingshi** Henan China 32.32N 113.00E
23 G6 **Pingshi** Jiangxi China 25.17N 115.00E
23 F1 **Pingshun** Shanxi China 36.06N 113.32E
23 H6 **Pingtan** Fujian China 25.31N 119.45E
23 H6 **Pingtan Dao** *isld* Fujian China
23 D6 **Pingtang** Guizhou China 25.50N 107.20E
23 J7 **P'ing-tung** Taiwan 22.40N 120.30E
121 M6 **Pingüino, I** Argentina
92 K12 **Pingwe** Zanzibar 6.09S 39.31E
23 C2 **Pingwu** Sichuan China 32.25N 104.35E
23 D7 **Pingxiang** Guangxi China 22.06N 106.44E
22 K8 **Pingxiang** Hebei China 37.05N 115.02E
23 F5 **Pingxiang** Jiangxi China 27.35N 113.46E
21 C3 **Pingyang** Heilongjiang China 48.17N 124.20E
21 C4 **Pingyang** Heilongjiang China 46.37N 123.30E
23 J5 **Pingyang** Zhejiang China 27.43N 120.31E
22 J8 **Pingyao** Shanxi China 37.10N 112.08E
23 H1 **Pingyi** Shandong China 35.28N 117.45E
22 K8 **Pingyin** Shandong China 36.20N 116.30E
23 E5 **Pingyong** Guizhou China 26.05N 108.20E
23 G2 **Pingyu** Henan China 32.56N 114.32E
23 G6 **Pingyuan** Guangdong China 24.30N 115.56E
22 K8 **Pingyuan** Shandong China 37.11N 116.26E
23 C7 **Pingyuanjie** Yunnan China 23.43N 103.53E
Pin-hai *see* **Guannan**
Pin-hai *see* **Binhai**
118 F8 **Pinhal** Brazil 22.10S 46.46W
76 B11 **Pinhal Novo** Portugal 38.38N 8.55W
76 D6 **Pinhão** Portugal 41.12N 7.33W
118 J8 **Pinhão, Saco do** *gulf* Brazil 22.47S 43.10W
121 H3 **Pinheira Machado** Brazil 31.34S 53.22W
117 E6 **Pinheiro** Brazil 2.31S 45.05W
76 B12 **Pinheiro** Portugal 38.27N 8.41W
76 C10 **Pinheiro Grande** Portugal 39.23N 8.26W
118 F10 **Pinheiros** *dist* São Paulo Brazil
76 B9 **Pinhel** Portugal 39.39N 8.36W
76 E7 **Pinhel** Portugal 40.47N 7.03W
120 F2 **Pinhuã, R** Brazil
18 C5 **Pini** *isld* Indonesia
77 L3 **Pinilla** *R* Spain
75 G6 **Pinilla de Molina** Spain 40.40N 1.54W
119 D3 **Pinillos** Colombia 8.55N 74.26W
75 E3 **Pinillos** Spain 42.12N 2.35W
84 B6 **Piniós** *R* Ilía Greece
84 D2 **Piniós** *R* Lárisa Greece
15 H1 **Pinipel I** Papua New Guinea 4.25S 154.07E
19 B3 **Pinjang** Celebes Indon 1.18N 121.06E
14 B10 **Pinjarra** W Australia 32.36S 115.48E
30 A2 **Pinjaur** Himachal Prad India 30.43N 76.54E
14 E9 **Pinjin** W Australia 30.04S 122.42E
31 C9 **Pinjrāpur** Pakistan 24.54N 67.05E
65 O7 **Pinkafeld** Austria 47.23N 16.08E
65 P7 **Pinkamindszent** Hungary 47.03N 16.30E
65 O7 **Pinka, R** Austria
60 N6 **Pinke Gat** *channel* Netherlands
13 K1 **Pinkenba** *dist* Brisbane, Qnsld
100 H7 **Pinkham** Saskatchewan 51.27N 109.29W
105 K2 **Pink Hill** N Carolina 35.03N 77.46W
101 M7 **Pink Mountain** Br Col 57.10N 122.36W
99 B8 **Pinks L** Quebec 45.30N 75.50W
70 M5 **Pin-la-Garenne, le** France 48.27N 0.33E
25 D2 **Pinlaung** Burma 20.05N 96.50E
25 M9 **Pinlebu** Burma 24.05N 95.24E
107 D7 **Pinnacle** Arkansas 34.52N 92.30W
11 H8 **Pinnacle** *mt* New Zealand 41.48S 173.18E
113 A6 **Pinnacle I** Bering Sea 60.10N 172.50W
33 B10 **Pinnacle Rock** S Yemen 12.46N 44.56E
111 C5 **Pinnacles Nat. Mon** California 36.30N 121.13W
12 F5 **Pinnaroo** S Australia 35.18S 140.54E
63 L5 **Pinn Au** *R* W Germany
63 L5 **Pinneberg** W Germany 53.40N 9.49E
109 G1 **Pinneo** Colorado 40.12N 103.25W
55 C2 **Pinner** London England 51.36N 0.22W
63 U6 **Pinnow** Frankfurt E Germany 53.04N 14.05E
63 T5 **Pinnow** Neubrandenburg E Germany 53.55N 13.49E
67 P11 **Pino** Corsica 42.54N 9.20E
76 K3 **Pino del Rio** Spain 42.38N 4.49W
76 C3 **Pino, El** Spain 42.56N 8.20W
76 G8 **Pinofranqueado** Spain 40.19N 6.21W
115 Q5 **Pinogana** Panama 8.07N 77.39W
18 J6 **Pinoh** *R* Borneo Indon
107 G10 **Pinola** Mississippi 31.52N 89.59W
79 E2 **Pino Lago Maggiore** Italy 46.06N 8.45E
111 B7 **Pinole Cr** California
71 C6 **Pinols** France 45.02N 3.24E
109 F3 **Pinon** Colorado 38.24N 104.37W
109 E9 **Piñon** New Mexico 32.36N 105.24W
105 H4 **Pinopolis Dam** S Carolina 33.14N 80.00W
76 C3 **Piñor** Spain 42.30N 8.00W
115 J6 **Pinos** Mexico 22.18N 101.35W
115 Q5 **Pinos** Panama 9.01N 77.42W
75 O4 **Pinos** *mt* Spain 41.50N 1.31E
77 N5 **Pinosa** *mt* Spain 37.53N 1.59W
77 J7 **Pinos del Valle** Spain 36.54N 3.33W
116 C4 **Pinos, I. de** Cuba
111 E7 **Pinos, Mt** California 34.48N 119.09W
77 O4 **Pinoso** Spain 38.25N 1.02W
77 J6 **Pinos Puente** Spain 37.15N 3.45W
115 K9 **Pinotepa Nacional** Mexico 16.19N 98.03W
30 A1 **Pin Parbati** *pass* Himachal Prad India 31.47N 77.50E
29 F2 **Pin R** Punjab India
19 A5 **Pinrang** Celebes Indon 3.48S 119.41E
89 J5 **Pinsa** Upper Volta 13.39N 0.51W
72 H6 **Pinsac** France 44.51N 1.30E
26 S14 **Pins, Anse aux** *B* Mahé I Ind Oc
9 C14 **Pins, Î. des** New Caledonia 22.35S 167.30E
46 F4 **Pinsk** Belorussiya U.S.S.R. 52.08N 26.01E
107 K8 **Pinson** Alabama 33.42N 86.41W
107 H6 **Pinson** Tennessee 35.30N 88.45W
99 J10 **Pins, Pte., aux** Ontario 42.15N 81.51W
111 P6 **Pinta** Arizona 35.04N 109.40W
77 E4 **Pintado, Embalse del** *res* Spain 38.00N 5.55W
120 D9 **Pintados** Chile 20.35S 69.38W
120 D9 **Pintados, Salar de** *salt pan* Chile
119 B5 **Pinta, I** Galápagos Is 0.33N 90.45W
75 H2 **Pintano** Spain 42.32N 1.01W
18 M3 **Pintasan** Sabah Malaysia 5.25N 117.44E
111 L9 **Pinta, Sierra** *mts* Arizona
121 E2 **Pinto** Argentina 29.09S 62.38W
75 C7 **Pinto** Spain 40.15N 3.42W
77 J4 **Pinto** *R* Spain
100 K9 **Pinto Butte** *pk* Saskatchewan 49.21N 107.25W
111 J8 **Pinto Mts** California
119 D9 **Pintoyacu, R** Peru
18 B9 **Pintu Gedong, Pulau** *isld* Pen Malaysia
12 B4 **Pintumba** South Australia 31.30S 132.12E
111 L4 **Pintura** Utah 37.21N 113.17W
121 K6 **Pinturas, R** Argentina
111 J5 **Pintwater Ra** Nevada
81 C2 **Pinu, Mte** Sardinia 40.57N 9.23E
98 Q2 **Pinware B** Labrador, Nfld
98 Q2 **Pinware R** Labrador, Nfld
14 B8 **Pinyalling** *mt* W Australia 29.05S 117.21E
47 F5 **Pinyug** U.S.S.R. 60.10N 47.43E
79 N2 **Pinzano al Tagliamento** Italy 46.11N 12.57E
65 G7 **Pinzgau** *V* Austria
76 E7 **Pinzio** Portugal 40.37N 7.04W
79 J2 **Pinzolo** Italy 46.09N 10.46E
119 B5 **Pinzón, I** Galápagos Is 0.42S 90.42W
15 H7 **Pio** *R* Papua New Guinea
79 M7 **Piobbico** Italy 43.35N 12.30E
111 K4 **Pioche** Nevada 37.57N 114.30W
66 K7 **Pioda di Crana** *mt* Italy 46.12N 8.28E
66 J8 **Piode** Italy 45.47N 8.03E
117 G8 **Pio IX** Brazil 6.51S 40.31W
71 F8 **Piolence** France 44.10N 4.45E
80 J3 **Piomba** *R* Italy
80 C3 **Piombino** Italy 42.56N 10.32E
80 B3 **Piombino, Canale di** Italy
79 L3 **Piombino Dese** Italy 45.37N 12.00E
104 A5 **Pioneer** Ohio 41.42N 84.33W
112 H3 **Pioneer** Texas 32.07N 99.06W
114 B1 **Pioneer Bank** Hawaiian Is
110 M4 **Pioneer Mts** Montana
122 N4 **Pioneer Ridge** Pacific Oc
42 D4 **Pioner** U.S.S.R. 55.23N 86.00E
41 F2 **Pioner, Ostrov** *isld* U.S.S.R.
42 E5 **Pionersk** U.S.S.R. 54.22N 93.16E
46 D3 **Pionerskiy** U.S.S.R. 54.56N 20.11E
47 J5 **Pionerskiy** U.S.S.R. 61.15N 62.48E
15 D5 **Pionierbivak** Irian Jaya 2.04S 137.50E
72 K3 **Pionsat** France 46.08N 2.42E
11 K5 **Piopio** New Zealand 38.24S 175.03E
80 G2 **Pioraco** Italy 43.10N 12.59E
15 J7 **Piora, Mt** Papua New Guinea 6.45S 146.00E
66 L5 **Piora, Val** Switzerland
119 G9 **Piorini, L** Brazil 3.24N 63.15W
119 G9 **Piorini, R** Brazil
76 H8 **Piornal** Spain 40.07N 5.51W
77 L7 **Piorno** *mt* Spain 36.55N 2.39W
79 B5 **Piossasco** Italy 44.59N 7.28E
66 M7 **Piota, Poncione di** *mt* Switz 46.15N 8.56E
62 L3 **Piotrków** Bydgoszcz Poland 52.32N 18.28E
62 M4 **Piotrków** Łódź Poland 51.27N 19.40E
66 L5 **Piotta** Switzerland 46.31N 8.41E
79 M4 **Piove di Sacco** Italy 45.17N 12.02E
79 K3 **Piovene** Italy 45.46N 11.26E
79 E5 **Piovera** Italy 44.57N 8.44E
32 J7 **Pip** Iran 26.42N 60.10E
21 D6 **Pipa Dingzi** *mt pk* Jilin China 43.58N 128.30E
21 D6 **Pipa Dingzi** *mt pk* Jilin China 43.56N 128.14E
61 E4 **Pipaix** Belgium 50.35N 3.35E
121 C2 **Pipanaco, Salar de** *salt pan* Arg
75 E2 **Pipaón** Spain 42.37N 2.39W
29 C4 **Pipar** Rajasthan India 26.20N 73.36E
29 E5 **Piparda** Rajasthan India 25.28N 76.16E
29 C4 **Pipar Road** Rajasthan India 26.25N 73.29E
29 F7 **Piparwani** Madhya Prad India 21.40N 79.38E
54 L4 **Piper** *oil field* North Sea 58.29N 0.17E
84 H7 **Pipéri** *isld* Kikládhes Greece 37.20N 24.31E
83 G5 **Pipéri** *isld* Voríai Sporádhes Greece 39.20N 24.19E
111 G4 **Piper Pk** *mt* Nevada 37.41N 117.53W
56 C6 **Piperspool** Cornwall Eng 50.38N 4.28W
103 D6 **Pipersville** Pennsylvania 40.26N 75.09W
111 M5 **Pipe Springs Nat. Mon** Arizona 36.51N 112.44W
100 R9 **Pipestone** Manitoba 49.33N 100.57W
108 O6 **Pipestone** Minnesota 43.59N 96.19W
100 Q9 **Pipestone Cr** Manitoba/Sask
108 O5 **Pipestone Nat. Mon** Minnesota 44.00N 96.21W
90 L7 **Pipi** *R* Cent Afr Rep
11 C4 **Pipinui Pt** New Zealand 41.11S 174.44E
11 K6 **Pipipi** *mt* New Zealand 39.22S 175.11E
11 K6 **Pipiriki** New Zealand 39.26S 175.03E
11 J11 **Pipitarawai** *hill* Chatham Is Pacific Oc 44.01S 176.30W
29 D3 **Pipli** Haryana India 29.52N 74.45E
30 A2 **Pipli** Uttar Prad India 30.06N 77.25E
29 E7 **Piploda** Nimar, Madhya Prad India 21.39N 76.33E
29 D6 **Piploda** Ujjain, Madhya Prad India 23.37N 74.58E
98 B4 **Pipmuacan** *res* Quebec
20 M1 **Pippu** Japan 43.54N 142.31E
30 H6 **Pipra** Champaran, Bihar India 26.30N 84.59E
30 K6 **Pipra** Saharsa, Bihar India 26.09N 86.48E
30 G6 **Pipra** Uttar Prad India 26.46N 83.13E
29 H5 **Pipra Dam** Uttar Prad India 24.21N 83.02E
30 K7 **Pipra Dewas** Bihar India 25.28N 86.02E
30 A8 **Piprai** Madhya Prad India 24.30N 77.58E
30 G6 **Pipraich** Uttar Prad India 26.50N 83.33E
29 G7 **Pipraud** Madhya Prad India 20.25N 81.29E
70 G6 **Pipriac** France 47.49N 1.57W
30 A7 **Piproda** Madhya Prad India 25.05N 77.27E
Piqan *see* **Shanshan**
109 P4 **Piqua** Kansas 37.56N 95.33W
104 A6 **Piqua** Ohio 40.08N 84.14W
75 D4 **Piquera de San Esteban** Spain 41.30N 3.16W
75 G6 **Piqueras** Spain 40.40N 1.44W
75 E3 **Piqueras, Pto. de** *pass* Spain 42.04N 2.31W
92 J10 **Piquerra** Mozambique 16.06S 39.00E
117 G7 **Piquet Carneiro** Brazil 5.49S 39.28W
118 C5 **Piquiri, R** Mato Grosso Brazil
118 D9 **Piquiri, R** Paraná Brazil
89 K7 **Pira** Benin 8.28N 1.48E
75 N5 **Pira** Spain 41.25N 1.13E
118 F8 **Piracaia** Brazil 23.00S 46.22W
118 E5 **Piracanjuba** Brazil 17.18S 49.03W
118 F8 **Piracicaba** Brazil 22.45S 47.40W
118 G6 **Piracicaba** *R* Minas Gerais Brazil
118 F8 **Piracicaba** *R* São Paulo Brazil
118 F7 **Piraçununga** Brazil 21.59S 47.27W
117 G6 **Piracuruca** Brazil 3.56S 41.44W
89 B5 **Pirada** Guinea-Bissau 12.38N 14.09W
115 P10 **Piraera** Honduras 14.05N 88.24W
Piraeus *see* **Piraiévs**
118 E9 **Piraí do Sul** Brazil 24.30S 49.51W
84 G6 **Piraiévs** Greece 37.57N 23.42E
81 J7 **Piraino** Sicily 38.10N 14.52E
118 E8 **Piraju** Brazil 23.10S 49.21W
118 E7 **Pirajuí** Brazil 21.58S 49.25W
29 K3 **Pirakata** W Bengal India 22.35N 87.12E
29 C7 **Piram I** Gujarat India
42 F5 **Piramida, Gora** *mt* U.S.S.R. 54.14N 95.42E
Pirámide *see* **Lautaro, Cerro** *pk*
Piran Turkey *see* **Dicle** Diyarbakır
82 B5 **Piran** Yugoslavia 45.31N 13.36E
118 B9 **Pirané** Argentina 25.42S 59.06W
31 F5 **Piran Ghaib** Pakistan 30.15N 71.52E
117 H9 **Piranhas** Alagoas Brazil 9.35S 37.45W
120 F1 **Piranhas** Amazonas Brazil 5.35S 63.08W
118 H3 **Piranhas** Bahia Brazil 12.51S 41.09W
118 D5 **Piranhas** Mato Grosso Brazil 16.39S 51.50W
117 H7 **Piranhas** *R* Rio Grande do Norte Brazil
118 D5 **Piranhas, R** Goiás Brazil
117 H7 **Piranji, R** Brazil
32 A2 **Pirānshahr** Iran 36.41N 45.08E
119 E7 **Piraparaná, R** Colombia
117 F6 **Pirapemas** Brazil 3.46S 44.15W
120 G2 **Pirapetinga** Brazil 7.00S 62.52W
118 D8 **Pirapó, R** Paraná Brazil
118 G5 **Pirapora** Brazil 17.20S 44.54W
118 B6 **Piraputangas** Brazil 19.19S 57.34W
119 J6 **Pirara** Guyana 3.30N 50.45W
121 G4 **Pirarajá** Uruguay 33.44S 57.54W
30 H5 **Pirari** Nepal 27.12N 84.42E
81 B1 **Pirastru** *R* Sardinia
81 C3 **Pirastru, Cuccuru su** *mt* Sardinia 40.25N 9.21E
116 H3 **Pirates Well** Mayaguana Bahamas 22.26N 73.05W
121 H3 **Piratini** Brazil 31.26S 53.04W
121 H3 **Piratini** *R* Rio Grande do Sul Brazil
118 K9 **Piratininga, L. de** Brazil 22.57S 43.06W
117 D4 **Piratuba, L** Brazil
117 A6 **Piratucu** *R* Brazil
98 A3 **Piraube, L** Quebec
28 C6 **Piravam** Kerala India 9.49N 76.28E
29 E5 **Pirawa** Rajasthan India 24.20N 76.10E
65 P5 **Pirawarth** Austria 48.27N 16.36E
118 C10 **Piray** *R* Argentina
120 F7 **Piray, R** Bolivia
44 K10 **Pīr Bāzār** Iran 37.20N 49.33E
Pirdē *see* **Altin Köprü**
82 J8 **Pirdop** Bulgaria 42.40N 24.10E
70 H5 **Piré** France 48.00N 1.25W
121 C9 **Pire Mahuida, Sa** *ra* Argentina
118 E4 **Pirenópolis** Brazil 15.47S 48.58W
118 E5 **Pires do Rio** Brazil 17.19S 48.17W
31 G8 **Pirganj** Bangladesh 25.51N 88.25E
84 M11 **Pírgos** Crete 35.00N 25.10E
37 B3 **Pirgos** Gökçeada Turkey 40.06N 25.45E
84 B6 **Pírgos** Ilía Greece 37.40N 21.27E
84 C7 **Pírgos** Messinía Greece 37.05N 21.41E
84 D8 **Pírgos** Messinía Greece 36.50N 22.16E
84 D8 **Pírgos Dhiroú** Greece 36.38N 22.22E
32 G3 **Pir Haji** Iran 34.06N 56.29E
84 F5 **Pirí** Greece 38.19N 23.18E
117 D5 **Piriá** Brazil 1.42S 50.00W
70 E7 **Piriac** France 47.23N 2.32W
121 G5 **Piriápolis** Uruguay 34.51S 55.15W
117 E5 **Piriá, R** Brazil
118 B9 **Piribebuy** Paraguay 25.26S 57.02W
15 E7 **Pirimapuan** Irian Jaya 6.21S 138.24E
37 E8 **Pirinçlik** Turkey 37.54N 39.59E
74 G2 **Pirineos** *mts* Spain
11 K8 **Pirinoa** New Zealand 41.22S 175.11E
82 H9 **Pirin Planina** *mts* Bulgaria
11 M5 **Piripaua** New Zealand 38.51S 177.11E
117 G7 **Piripiri** Brazil 4.15S 41.46W
118 H2 **Piritiba** Brazil 11.46S 40.35W
119 E2 **Piritu** Falcón Venez 11.24N 69.08W
119 E3 **Píritu** Portuguesa Venez 9.21N 69.16W
118 F9 **Pirituba** *dist* São Paulo Brazil
119 G2 **Píritu, Is** Venezuela 10.09N 65.00W
118 C5 **Pirizal** Brazil 16.18S 56.14W
64 N3 **Pirk** E Germany 50.25N 12.04E
Pir Khan *see* **Parākūn**
51 K10 **Pirkkala** Finland 61.28N 23.30E
31 A5 **Pir Kundil** Afghanistan 31.50N 61.39E
Pirlerkondu *see* **Taşkent**
64 D5 **Pirmasens** W Germany 49.12N 7.37E
28 C6 **Pirmed** Kerala India 9.31N 77.02E
32 G4 **Pīr Morāl** Iran 32.45N 56.18E
Pīr Murāl *see* **Pīr Morāl**
62 H5 **Pirna** E Germany 50.58N 13.58E
Pirnak *see* **Pūrnāk**
58 F7 **Pirnmill** Arran, Strathclyde Scotland 55.39N 5.23W
45 E5 **Pirogovka** Ukraine U.S.S.R. 51.54N 33.16E
31 H10 **Pirojpur** Bangladesh 22.33N 89.56E
76 L6 **Pirón** *R* Spain
30 C7 **Pirona** Uttar Prad India 25.52N 79.09E
61 J5 **P'ironchamps** Belgium 50.26N 4.32E
11 K4 **Pirongia** New Zealand 37.59S 175.14E
11 K4 **Pirongia** *mt* New Zealand 37.59S 175.08E
15 M9 **Piron Lagoon** Louisiade Arch
82 H7 **Pirot** Yugoslavia 43.10N 22.32E
70 G3 **Pirou** France 49.11N 1.35W
121 E6 **Pirovano** Argentina 36.30S 61.30W
42 E3 **Pirovskoye** U.S.S.R. 57.36N 92.18E
30 L7 **Pirpainti** Bihar India 25.17N 87.25E
31 H4 **Pir Panjal Pass** Kashmir 33.38N 74.32E
31 G3 **Pir Panjal Ra** Kashmir
37 H7 **Pirrasıt Dağ** *mt* Turkey 38.54N 43.46E
93 F2 **Pirre** Uganda 3.50N 34.04E
119 C4 **Pirre, Cerro** *mt* Panama 7.57N 77.52W

44 J8 **Pirsagat** Azerbaydzhan U.S.S.R. 39.53N 49.25E
44 J7 **Pirsagat** *R* Azerbaydzhan U.S.S.R.
32 J6 **Pīr Shūrān, Selseleh-ye-** *mts* Iran
32 J8 **Pīr Sohrāb** Iran 25.45N 60.51E
Pir Surab *see* **Pīr Sohrāb**
30 A4 **Pirthala** Haryana India 28.14N 77.17E
30 B7 **Pirthipur** Madhya Prad India 25.13N 78.44E
51 N5 **Pirttikoski** Finland 66.21N 27.08E
111 F7 **Piru** California 34.25N 118.48W
19 F5 **Piru** Moluccas Indonesia 3.01S 128.10E
111 F7 **Piru Cr** California
19 F5 **Piru, Teluk** *B* Moluccas Indon
45 D6 **Piryatin** Ukraine U.S.S.R. 50.14N 32.31E
84 E2 **Piryetós** Greece 39.55N 22.35E
83 H6 **Piryí** Greece 38.13N 25.59E
31 C5 **Pirzada** Afghanistan 31.37N 65.05E
19 N3 **Pis** *isld* Truk Is Pacific Oc 7.41N 151.47E
79 H7 **Pisa** Italy 43.43N 10.24E
80 C2 **Pisa** *prov* Italy
120 D5 **Pisac** Peru 13.26S 71.49W
120 D8 **Pisagua** Chile 19.34S 70.14W
89 D8 **Pisa,L** Liberia 6.40N 11.15W
19 F4 **Pisang** *isld* Moluccas Indonesia 1.23S 128.55E
18 D10 **Pisang** *isld* Pen Malaysia 1.28N 103.17E
15 A5 **Pisang, Pulau Pulau** *islds* Irian Jaya
79 H6 **Pisanino, Monte** Italy 44.08N 10.13E
80 C1 **Pisano, Monte** Italy 43.45N 10.32E
72 C4 **Pisany** France 45.42N 0.47W
11 D11 **Pisa Ra** New Zealand
82 C5 **Pisarovina** Yugoslavia 45.35N 15.50E
18 M2 **Pisau, Tanjong** *C* Sabah Malaysia 6.05N 118.00E
30 A4 **Pisawa** Uttar Prad India 28.07N 77.45E
66 Q4 **Pischa Horn** *mt* Switzerland 46.49N 9.58E
65 N7 **Pischelsdorf** Austria 47.11N 15.48E
66 R6 **Pisciadello** Switzerland 46.23N 10.05E
67 O13 **Pisciatello** Corsica 41.54N 8.50E
79 B5 **Piscina** Italy 44.55N 7.25E
81 K3 **Pisciotta** Italy 40.06N 15.15E
120 B5 **Pisco** Peru 13.46S 76.12W
120 B5 **Pisco** *R* Peru
120 B5 **Pisco, B. de** Peru 13.51S 76.17W
Piscopi *isld see* **Tílos**
65 M4 **Pisečné** Czechoslovakia 48.58N 15.28E
104 L3 **Piseco** New York 43.26N 74.33W
104 L3 **Piseco L** New York 43.24N 74.33W
42 C4 **Pisega** U.S.S.R. 56.48N 80.57E
65 K3 **Písek** Czechoslovakia 49.18N 14.10E
108 N1 **Pisek** N Dakota 48.20N 97.41W
35 F6 **Pisga** *anc site* Jordan 31.46N 35.44E
108 P8 **Pisgah** Iowa 41.49N 95.55W
105 E2 **Pisgah, Mt** N Carolina 35.25N 82.48W
11 E12 **Pisgah, Mt** New Zealand 45.04S 170.25E
Pisha *see* **Puge**
24 C7 **Pishan** Xinjiang Uygur Zizhiqu China 37.37N 78.17E
32 F4 **Pīsh Gāzū** Iran 33.58N 54.40E
32 J7 **Pīshīn** Iran 26.04N 61.50E
31 D5 **Pishin** Pakistan 30.33N 67.01E
31 D5 **Pishin Lora R** Pakistan
32 F2 **Pīsh Kamar** Iran 37.30N 55.40E
31 B8 **Pishkan, Ras** *C* Pakistan 25.07N 62.09E
43 O7 **Pishkaran** Uzbekistan U.S.S.R. 41.19N 71.50E
51 P6 **Pishta** *R* Karelia U.S.S.R.
36 E5 **Pisidia** *reg* Turkey
19 B6 **Pising** Indonesia 5.04S 121.55E
111 M9 **Pisinimo** Arizona 32.01N 112.18W
111 D6 **Pismo Beach** California 35.10N 120.37W
66 S5 **Pisoc, Piz** *mt* Switzerland 46.45N 10.17E
120 G5 **Piso Firme** Bolivia 13.38S 61.53W
79 H3 **Pisogne** Italy 45.48N 10.07E
120 B2 **Pisqui** *R* Peru
66 D7 **Pissevache** Switzerland 46.08N 7.00E
89 J5 **Pissila** Upper Volta 13.07N 0.51W
121 C1 **Pissis, Cerro** *pk* Argentina 27.46S 68.48W
72 C7 **Pissos** France 44.19N 0.46W
84 Q15 **Pissouri** Cyprus 34.40N 32.42E
115 P7 **Pisté** Mexico 20.40N 88.34W
81 N3 **Pisticci** Italy 40.23N 16.33E
79 J7 **Pistoia** Italy 43.56N 10.55E
79 J7 **Pistoia** *prov* Italy
98 R2 **Pistolet Bay** Newfoundland
110 A7 **Pistol River** Oregon 42.17N 124.24W
46 M2 **Pistsovo** U.S.S.R. 57.08N 40.32E
75 C1 **Pisueña** *R* Spain
76 K5 **Pisuerga** *R* Spain
62 N2 **Pisz** Poland 53.38N 21.49E
110 D8 **Pit** *R* California
89 C6 **Pita** Guinea 11.05N 12.15W
98 G1 **Pitaga** Labrador, Nfld 52.27N 65.50W
115 O8 **Pital** Mexico 18.34N 91.08W
119 C7 **Pitalito** Colombia 1.51N 76.01W
118 D9 **Pitanga** Brazil 24.45S 51.43W
118 G6 **Pitangui** Brazil 19.40S 44.54W
18 L7 **Pitap** *R* Borneo Indon
29 B6 **Pitar** Gujarat India 22.42N 70.35E
12 G5 **Pitarpunga L** New S Wales 34.23S 143.32E
75 J6 **Pitarque** Spain 40.39N 0.36W
19 M8 **Pitas Pt** Mindanao Philippines 6.31N 124.03E
20 N2 **Pitatanunke** Japan 42.10N 143.17E
122 U11 **Pitcairn I** Pacific Oc 25.04S 130.06W
103 C1 **Pitcher** New York 42.34N 75.52W
110 Q5 **Pitchfork** Wyoming 44.06N 109.04W
116 N2 **Pitch L** Trinidad & Tobago 10.13N 61.38W
51 H6 **Pite** *R* Sweden
51 J6 **Piteå** Sweden 65.19N 21.30E
79 J6 **Piteglio** Italy 44.02N 10.46E
45 N2 **Pitelino** U.S.S.R. 54.35N 41.50E
45 T6 **Piterka** U.S.S.R. 50.41N 47.29E
82 J6 **Piteşti** Romania 44.51N 24.51E
42 E3 **Pit-Gorodok** U.S.S.R. 59.15N 93.48E
28 F2 **Pithapuram** Andhra Prad India 17.07N 82.20E
14 B9 **Pithara** W Australia 30.20S 116.39E
69 C7 **Pithiviers** France 48.10N 2.15E
30 D3 **Pithoragarh** Uttar Prad India 29.35N 80.12E
30 D2 **Pithoragarh** *dist* Uttar Prad India
29 F5 **Pithoria** Madhya Prad India 24.05N 78.31E
19 L1 **Piti** Guam Pacific Oc 13.28N 144.42E
31 D8 **Pitiani Cr** Pakistan
120 E10 **Piti, Co** *mt* Chile 23.15S 67.40W
80 E3 **Pitigliano** Italy 42.38N 11.40E
29 F6 **Pitihra** Madhya Prad India 23.04N 79.20E
75 G3 **Pitillas** Spain 42.26N 1.38W
115 C2 **Pitiquito** Mexico 30.40N 112.05W
109 D3 **Pitkin** Colorado 38.36N 106.32W
107 D11 **Pitkin** Louisiana 30.57N 92.58W
37 F5 **Pitkir** Turkey 40.26N 41.56E
47 C3 **Pitkul'** U.S.S.R. 67.28N 33.14E
47 C5 **Pitkyaranta** U.S.S.R. 61.33N 31.30E
58 J5 **Pitlochry** Tayside Scotland 56.43N 3.45W
47 K3 **Pitlyar** U.S.S.R. 65.50N 65.55E
47 K3 **Pitlyar** *R* U.S.S.R.
103 D7 **Pitman** New Jersey 39.44N 75.08W
103 A5 **Pitman** Pennsylvania 40.43N 76.31W
9 U5 **Pitman Reefs** Fiji 16.25S 179.25W
115 Q5 **Pito** Panama 8.43N 77.31W
76 D5 **Pitões** Portugal 41.49N 7.57W
101 X2 **Pitok** N W Terr
26 T13 **Piton de la Petite Rivière Noire** *mt* Mauritius, Indian Oc 20.24S 57.23E
26 T16 **Piton, Le** Réunion Ind Oc 21.12S 55.19E
115 L2 **Pito Solo** Honduras 14.50N 87.58W
107 G11 **Pitre, I. au** Louisiana 30.09N 89.17W
121 A7 **Pitrufquén** Chile 38.59S 72.40W
84 D5 **Pitsá** Greece 38.05N 22.29E
95 J1 **Pitsane** S Africa 25.45S 25.07E
58 L6 **Pitscottie** Fife Scotland 56.18N 2.57W
56 N4 **Pitsea** Essex Eng 51.34N 0.30E
95 M5 **Pitseng** Lesotho 29.02S 28.10E
56 K3 **Pitsford Res** Northants England 52.20N 0.51W
110 E8 **Pit South Fork** *R* California
44 C4 **Pitsunda** Georgia U.S.S.R. 43.10N 40.22E
44 C4 **Pitsunda, Mys** *C* Georgia U.S.S.R. 43.11N 40.21E
61 D3 **Pittem** Belgium 50.59N 3.17E
65 O6 **Pitten** Austria 47.43N 16.13E
58 H3 **Pittentrail** Highland Scotland 57.59N 4.09W
58 L6 **Pittenweem** Fife Scotland 56.13N 2.44W
101 J9 **Pitt I** Br Col
11 K11 **Pitt I** Chatham Is Pacific Oc 44.17S 176.10W
101 J11 **Pitt Meadows** Br Col 49.13N 122.42W
119 B6 **Pitt, Pta** *pt* Galápagos Is 0.44S 89.15W
101 J11 **Pitt R** Br Col
105 H2 **Pittsboro** N Carolina 35.46N 79.12W
111 C3 **Pittsburg** California 38.01N 121.55W
109 Q4 **Pittsburg** Kansas 37.25N 94.43W
107 M4 **Pittsburg** Kentucky 37.10N 84.05W
104 O1 **Pittsburg** New Hampshire 45.03N 71.26W
109 P7 **Pittsburg** Oklahoma 34.44N 95.54W
112 N3 **Pittsburg** Texas 33.00N 94.59W
104 F6 **Pittsburgh** Pennsylvania 40.26N 80.00W
107 F2 **Pittsfield** Illinois 39.37N 90.49W
104 Q2 **Pittsfield** Maine 44.46N 69.25W
103 H2 **Pittsfield** Massachusetts 42.27N 73.15W
104 O3 **Pittsfield** New Hampshire 43.18N 71.20W
104 H3 **Pittsford** New York 43.06N 77.33W
104 M3 **Pittsford** Vermont 43.43N 73.03W
103 C4 **Pittston** Pennsylvania 41.19N 75.45W
11 K11 **Pitt Str** Chatham Is Pacific Oc
107 L9 **Pittsview** Alabama 32.10N 85.10W
104 K8 **Pittsville** Maryland 38.23N 75.26W
107 C3 **Pittsville** Missouri 38.50N 93.59W
106 D5 **Pittsville** Wisconsin 44.27N 90.07W
13 K8 **Pittsworth** Queensland 27.43S 151.36E
110 D8 **Pittville** California 41.03N 121.20W
12 M5 **Pitt Water** *inlet* New S Wales
19 F2 **Pitu** Moluccas Indon 2.04N 128.19E
92 G6 **Pitu** *R* Tanzania
13 E6 **Pituri** *R* Queensland
28 E1 **Pitur Rani** *mt* Madhya Prad India 18.36N 81.21E
65 C7 **Pitztal** *V* Austria
79 J4 **Piúbega** Italy 45.13N 10.32E
121 A9 **Piuchue, Mts. de** Chile
118 F7 **Piũi** Brazil 20.28S 45.58W
15 J1 **Piuli I** Papua New Guinea 4.58S 155.27E
117 D10 **Pium** Brazil 10.19S 49.16W
119 B10 **Piura** Peru 5.15S 80.38W
119 B10 **Piura** *dept* Peru
119 B10 **Piura, R** Peru
66 O6 **Piuro** Italy 46.19N 9.28E
111 J7 **Piute Mts** California
111 F6 **Piute Pk** California 35.26N 118.25W
111 M3 **Piute Res** Utah 38.15N 112.12W
30 F4 **Piuthan** Nepal 28.05N 82.53E
82 E7 **Piva** *R* Yugoslavia
99 G2 **Pivabiska** *R* Ontario
40 G6 **Pivan'** U.S.S.R. 50.30N 137.03E
119 D2 **Pivijay** Colombia 10.31N 74.36W
82 B5 **Pivka** Yugoslavia 45.39N 14.12E
62 M6 **Piwniczna** Poland 49.27N 20.40E
24 C7 **Pixa** Xinjiang Uygur Zizhiqu China 36.18N 79.50E
84 G4 **Pixaná** *mt* Greece 38.41N 23.40E
23 C3 **Pi Xian** Sichuan China 30.49N 103.52E
111 E6 **Pixley** California 35.58N 119.20W
115 O8 **Pixoyal** Mexico 18.57N 90.38W
84 B3 **Piyaí** Greece 39.17N 21.25E
Piyanis *see* **Kaval**
84 S14 **Piyi** Cyprus 35.12N 33.47E
120 D7 **Pizacoma** Peru 16.54S 69.23W
77 G7 **Pizarra** Spain 36.46N 4.42W
98 Q9 **Pizeau, Pte** Quebec 46.46N 71.14W
46 P2 **Pizhanka** U.S.S.R. 57.30N 48.30E
46 O1 **Pizhma** U.S.S.R. 57.52N 47.12E
46 P1 **Pizhma** *R* U.S.S.R.
79 G4 **Pizzighettone** Italy 45.11N 9.47E
81 M6 **Pizzo** Italy 38.44N 16.10E
80 J5 **Pizzodeta, Monte** Italy 41.48N 13.32E
80 H4 **Pizzoli** Italy 42.27N 13.18E
81 Q13 **Pizzo, Torre del** *pt* Italy 40.00N 18.00E
81 F8 **Pizzuta, la** *mt* Sicily 38.00N 13.15E
80 G4 **Pizzuto, Monte** Italy 42.20N 12.44E
53 D5 **Pjedsted** Denmark 55.37N 9.38E
15 E5 **P Keten** *mts* Irian Jaya
19 N2 **Pkulagalid Pt** Palau Is Pacific Oc 7.36N 134.33E
19 N3 **Pkulagasemieg** *pt* Palau Is Pacific Oc 7.09N 134.24E
19 N2 **Pkulngri** *pt* Palau Is Pacific Oc 7.32N 134.31E
19 N2 **Pkurengel** *pt* Palau Is Pacific Oc 7.27N 134.28E
63 Q5 **Plaaz** E Germany 53.52N 12.22E
70 B4 **Plabennec** France 48.31N 4.26W
112 L7 **Placedo** Texas 28.41N 96.47W
98 T6 **Placentia** Newfoundland 47.15N 53.58W
98 S6 **Placentia B** Newfoundland
19 L6 **Placer** Masbate Philippines 11.56N 123.55E
19 M7 **Placer** Mindanao Philippines 9.37N 125.36E
110 G9 **Placeritos** Nevada 40.40N 118.40W
111 D3 **Placerville** California 38.43N 120.50W
109 B3 **Placerville** Colorado 38.02N 108.03W
116 E3 **Placetas** Cuba 22.18N 79.40W
105 E11 **Placida** Florida 26.51N 82.16W
105 F10 **Placid, L** Florida 27.14N 81.22W
120 E4 **Plácido de Castro** Brazil 10.20S 67.13W
109 D6 **Placitas** New Mexico 35.19N 106.27W
82 G9 **Plačkovica** *mts* Yugoslavia
57 C2 **Pladda** *isld* Strathclyde Scotland 55.26N 5.07W
75 N5 **Plá de Santa María** Spain 41.21N 1.18E
66 F5 **Plaffeien** Switzerland 46.45N 7.17E
88 H7 **Plage Blanche** *reg* Morocco
81 G7 **Plaia, C** Sicily 38.02N 13.57E
69 D5 **Plailly** France 49.06N 2.35E
72 J1 **Plaimpied-Givaudins** France 47.00N 2.26E
106 D6 **Plain** Wisconsin 43.16N 90.03W
104 B6 **Plain City** Ohio 40.06N 83.18W
110 N8 **Plain City** Utah 41.19N 112.06W
107 C9 **Plain Dealing** Louisiana 32.52N 93.42W
69 M8 **Plain-de-Corravillers, le** France 47.54N 6.38E
26 U16 **Plaine-des-Cafres, La** Réunion Indian Oc 21.12S 55.34E
71 K5 **Plaine Joux** *mt* France 45.57N 6.44E
72 C1 **Plaine, la** France 47.04N 0.37W
70 F7 **Plaine-sur-Mer, la** France 47.09N 2.10W
61 N4 **Plainevaux** Belgium 50.33N 5.31E
103 L3 **Plainfield** Connecticut 41.42N 71.55W
107 K2 **Plainfield** Indiana 39.43N 86.24W
108 S7 **Plainfield** Iowa 42.54N 92.29W
103 F5 **Plainfield** New Jersey 40.37N 74.25W
106 E5 **Plainfield** Wisconsin 44.13N 89.30W
105 C5 **Plains** Georgia 32.01N 84.24W
110 L2 **Plains** Montana 47.28N 114.51W
95 O6 **Plains** S Africa 30.45S 30.17E
112 E2 **Plains** Texas 33.12N 102.50W
104 H8 **Plains, The** Virginia 38.52N 77.47W
70 E5 **Plaintel** France 48.24N 2.50W
107 C7 **Plainview** Arkansas 35.00N 93.19W
108 S5 **Plainview** Minnesota 44.10N 92.10W
108 N7 **Plainview** Nebraska 42.21N 97.49W
112 F1 **Plainview** Texas 34.12N 101.43W
103 J3 **Plainville** Connecticut 41.40N 72.53W
107 E2 **Plainville** Illinois 39.47N 91.10W
109 L2 **Plainville** Kansas 39.15N 99.17W
103 M2 **Plainville** Massachusetts 42.01N 71.20W
106 J7 **Plainwell** Michigan 42.25N 85.38W
72 E8 **Plaisance** Gers France 43.36N 0.03E
116 H5 **Plaisance** Haiti 19.40N 72.27W
26 V13 **Plaisance** *airport* Mauritius, Indian Oc 20.25S 57.41E
72 G8 **Plaisance-du-Touch** France 43.34N 1.17E
55 H3 **Plaistow** London Eng 51.32N 0.02E
56 K5 **Plaistow** W Sussex Eng 51.04N 0.35W
18 F7 **Plaju** Sumatra Indonesia 2.59S 104.47E
36 A2 **Pláka, Ákra** *C* Límnos Greece 40.03N 25.26E
82 F9 **Plakenska Planina** *mts* Yugoslavia
41 E6 **Plakhino** U.S.S.R. 67.55N 86.22E
84 S14 **Plakos** *R* Cyprus
84 T13 **Plakoti, C** Cyprus 35.33N 34.11E
39 K1 **Plamennyy** U.S.S.R. 68.17N 176.29E
100 E4 **Plamondon** Alberta 54.52N 112.15W
18 M10 **Plampang** Indonesia 9.50S 117.48E
72 E10 **Plan** Spain 42.35N 0.19E
64 O4 **Planá** Czechoslovakia 49.53N 12.44E
66 D7 **Planachaux** Switzerland 46.11N 6.51E
71 K4 **Planachaux le Plenay** France 46.09N 6.42E
111 D4 **Planada** California 37.16N 120.18W
118 F4 **Planaltina** Brazil 15.39S 47.38W
65 L3 **Planá nad Lužnici** Czechoslovakia 49.22N 14.43E
65 M1 **Plaňany** Czechoslovakia 50.03N 15.03E
77 Q4 **Plana o Nueva Tabarca** *isld* Spain 38.10N 0.28W
61 H4 **Plancenoit** Belgium 50.40N 4.25E
66 C1 **Plancher Bas** France 47.43N 6.45E
69 M8 **Plancher-les-Mines** France 47.46N 6.45E
71 J3 **Planches-en-Montagne, les** France 46.39N 6.01E
71 E2 **Planchez** France 47.09N 4.02E
121 B5 **Planchón, Pasa de** Chile/Arg 35.15S 70.34W
70 F4 **Plancoët** France 48.32N 2.14W
69 F6 **Plancy-l'Abbaye** France 48.34N 3.58E
71 G7 **Plan-de-Baix** France 44.49N 5.11E
71 K10 **Plan-de-la-Tour** France 43.21N 6.33E
75 L2 **Plandescán, Embalse de** *L* Spain 42.34N 0.19E
71 F9 **Plan-d'Orgon** France 43.48N 5.00E
74 G9 **Plane** *isld* Algeria 35.46N 0.55W
63 R8 **Plane** *R* E Germany
81 C2 **Planedda, Monte sa** Sardinia 40.45N 9.28E
64 L7 **Planegg** W Germany 48.05N 11.25E
75 J5 **Planerón, Balsa de** *L* Spain 41.22N 0.39W
44 D10 **Planerskoye** Ukraine U.S.S.R. 44.58N 35.15E
72 J11 **Planès** France 42.29N 2.09E
77 Q3 **Planes** Spain 38.48N 0.21W
119 C3 **Planeta Rica** Colombia 8.24N 75.39W
26 K6 **Planet Deep** Indian Oc
10 L3 **Planet Deep** Solomon Sea
66 D8 **Planet, le** France 46.00N 6.56E
71 E6 **Planfoy** France 45.23N 4.26E
64 P5 **Plánice** Czechoslovakia 49.24N 13.29E
71 G10 **Planier, I. de** France 43.11N 5.13E
84 D6 **Planíteron** Greece 37.55N 22.10E
64 L4 **Plankenfels** W Germany 49.47N 11.20E
108 M6 **Plankinton** S Dakota 43.42N 98.29W
72 G9 **Plan, le** France 43.10N 1.07E
106 F8 **Plano** Illinois 41.40N 88.32W
112 L2 **Plano** Texas 33.00N 96.43W
65 C7 **Plan See** *L* Austria 47.29N 10.50E
66 E6 **Plans, les** Switzerland 46.16N 7.05E
116 M2 **Plantain Garden R** Jamaica, W I
105 E9 **Plant City** Florida 28.01N 82.08W
107 K9 **Plantersville** Alabama 32.40N 86.55W
103 J3 **Plantsville** Connecticut 41.35N 72.54W
107 E11 **Plaquemine** Louisiana 30.17N 91.16W
19 H1 **Plaridel** Luzon Philippines 14.53N 120.52E
76 G8 **Plasencia** Spain 40.02N 6.05W
75 J3 **Plasencia del Monte** Spain 42.14N 0.34W
76 G9 **Plasencia Empalme** Spain 39.55N 6.05W
75 H4 **Plasencia, Llano de** *plain* Spain
76 G10 **Plasenzuela** Spain 39.23N 6.03W
82 C5 **Plaški** Yugoslavia 45.04N 15.22E
Pla Soi *see* **Chon Buri**
66 F5 **Plasselb** Switzerland 46.45N 7.16E
52 G5 **Plassen** Norway 61.08N 12.31E
47 J8 **Plast** U.S.S.R. 54.24N 60.45E
63 R5 **Plasten** E Germany 53.33N 12.51E
111 J9 **Plaster City** California 32.46N 115.50W
98 E7 **Plaster Rock** New Brunswick 46.55N 67.24W
94 L5 **Plaston** S Africa 25.21S 31.06E
40 G9 **Plastun** U.S.S.R. 44.43N 136.15E
44 C4 **Plastunka** U.S.S.R. 43.43N 39.48E
64 P4 **Plasy** Czechoslovakia 49.56N 13.24E
79 K1 **Plata** Italy 46.49N 11.09E
84 F5 **Plataií** Greece 38.12N 23.16E
121 B10 **Plata, L. de la** Argentina
84 E7 **Platanákion** Greece 37.10N 22.40E
120 D7 **Platanal** Peru 17.25S 71.22W
81 G9 **Platani** *R* Sicily
84 F3 **Plataniá** Greece 39.10N 23.16E
81 M5 **Platania** Italy 39.01N 16.20E
84 H5 **Platanistós** Greece 38.01N 24.31E
84 D5 **Plátanos** Akhaïa Greece 38.10N 22.15E
84 C6 **Plátanos** Ilía Greece 37.40N 21.37E
84 E3 **Plátanos** Magnisía Greece 39.08N 22.46E
84 B3 **Platanoúsa** Greece 39.25N 21.01E
120 D11 **Plata, Pta** *C* Chile 24.45S 70.34W
121 F5 **Plata, Rio de la** Arg/Uruguay
77 E8 **Plata, Sierra de la** *mts* Spain
95 N4 **Platberg** *mt* Orange Free State S Africa 28.16S 29.12E
94 S14 **Platberg** *mt* Transvaal S Africa 26.24S 28.00E
94 P12 **Platboombaai** *B* Cape Town S Africa
93 G5 **Plateau** Kenya 0.26N 35.22E
30 K4 **"Plateau" Glacier** Nepal
Plateau Of Tibet *see* **Xizang Gaoyuan**
91 D5 **Plateaux, Région des** Congo
98 T5 **Plate Cove** Newfoundland 48.30N 53.31W
50 U12 **Platen, Kapp** Spitsbergen 80.29N 23.00E
115 H6 **Plateros** Mexico 23.15N 102.51W
83 F4 **Platí** Greece 40.38N 22.31E
84 D7 **Platí** Greece 37.09N 22.01E
81 M7 **Platì** Italy 38.13N 16.03E
84 E7 **Platía** *isld* Greece 37.29N 22.55E
84 C6 **Platiána** Greece 37.32N 21.45E
84 E2 **Platíkambos** Greece 39.37N 22.32E
110 C9 **Platina** California 40.24N 122.52W
113 G7 **Platinum** Alaska 59.00N 161.50W
84 D7 **Platí Pídhima** Greece 37.08N 22.00E
79 O2 **Platischis** Italy 46.14N 13.23E
39 F7 **Platnikova** *R* U.S.S.R.
119 D3 **Plato** Colombia 9.54N 74.46W
107 D4 **Plato** Missouri 37.31N 92.12W
100 J7 **Plato** Saskatchewan 51.10N 108.28W
45 N4 **Platonovka** U.S.S.R. 52.44N 41.59E
115 K7 **Platón Sánchez** Mexico 21.18N 98.21W
95 N3 **Platrand** S Africa 27.06S 29.28E
84 D8 **Plátsa** Greece 36.48N 22.18E
66 P6 **Platta, Piz** *mt* Switzerland 46.30N 9.35E
108 M6 **Platte** S Dakota 43.25N 98.50W
64 N4 **Platte** *mt* W Germany 49.54N 12.04E
108 L9 **Platte** *R* Nebraska
108 N8 **Platte Center** Nebraska 41.32N 97.31W
107 B2 **Platte City** Missouri 39.22N 94.47W
109 E2 **Platte Mt** Colorado 39.16N 105.06W
66 R4 **Platten Horn** *mt* Switzerland 46.48N 10.02E
109 F1 **Platteville** Colorado 40.13N 104.50W
106 D7 **Platteville** Wisconsin 42.44N 90.29W
27 H11 **Platt I** Seychelles, Ind Oc
64 O6 **Plattling** W Germany 48.46N 12.54E
109 O7 **Platt Nat Park** Oklahoma 34.30N 97.00W
107 B2 **Plattsburg** Missouri 39.33N 94.27W
104 M2 **Plattsburg** New York 44.42N 73.29W
108 P8 **Plattsmouth** Nebraska 41.00N 95.52W
63 Q6 **Plau** E Germany 53.28N 12.16E
64 K2 **Plaue** Erfurt E Germany 50.47N 10.54E
63 Q8 **Plaue an der Havel** Potsdam E Germany 52.25N 12.25E
64 N3 **Plauen** E Germany 50.29N 12.08E
63 Q6 **Plauer See** *L* E Germany
71 C5 **Plauzat** France 45.38N 3.08E
79 P2 **Plave** Yugoslavia 46.03N 13.35E
62 K7 **Plavecký Svätý Mikuláš** Czech 48.30N 17.20E
46 F2 **Plaviņas** Latvia U.S.S.R. 56.35N 25.46E
66 R5 **Plavnadadaint, Piz** *mt* Switzerland 46.44N 10.13E
82 E8 **Plavnica** Yugoslavia 42.17N 19.13E
41 D4 **Plavnikovye, Ostrova** *islds* U.S.S.R.
45 J3 **Plavsk** U.S.S.R. 53.40N 37.20E
96 S11 **Playa Amanay** *beach* Fuerteventura Canary Is
115 H9 **Playa Azul** Mexico 18.00N 102.24W
96 U8 **Playa Blanca** Lanzarote Canary Is 28.55N 13.37W
96 T10 **Playa Blanca** *beach* Fuerteventura Canary Is
75 R4 **Playa de Aro** Spain 41.49N 3.04E
96 S11 **Playa de Barlovento** *beach* Fuerteventura Canary Is
96 Q15 **Playa de Las Américas** Tenerife Canary Is 28.05N 16.43W
96 T10 **Playa del Castillo** *beach* Fuerteventura Canary Is
111 C9 **Playa del Rey** California 33.57N 118.27W
96 O15 **Playa de Santiago** Gomera Canary Is 28.02N 17.11W
96 S11 **Playa de Sotavento** *beach* Fuerteventura Canary Is
75 K5 **Playa, L.de** Spain 41.25N 0.12W
115 F11 **Playa Leona** Panama 8.47N 79.46W
115 D3 **Playa Noriega** *L* Mexico 29.05N 112.00W
96 T10 **Playa Pozo Negro** *beach* Fuerteventura Canary Is
119 B9 **Playas** Ecuador 2.38S 80.25W
109 B10 **Playas L** New Mexico
56 N6 **Playden** E Sussex Eng 50.58N 0.44E
13 D4 **Playford** *R* N Terr Australia
13 D6 **Playford Mt** N Terr Australia 22.34S 136.22E
100 T5 **Playgreen L** Manitoba
100 U4 **Playgreen L** Manitoba 54.15N 97.45W
115 E5 **Playón** Mexico 25.16N 108.10W
108 J1 **Plaza** N Dakota 48.02N 101.57W
72 G5 **Plazac** France 45.02N 1.02E
121 B7 **Plaza Huincul** Argentina 38.55S 69.14W
76 G2 **Plaza, La** Spain 43.10N 6.05W
58 J6 **Plean** Central Scotland 56.04N 3.52W
98 M7 **Pleasant Bay** C Breton I, Nova Scotia 46.50N 60.48W
103 O3 **Pleasant Bay** Massachusetts
104 D7 **Pleasant City** Ohio 39.54N 81.34W
100 N6 **Pleasantdale** Saskatchewan 52.36N 104.34W
104 H6 **Pleasant Gap** Pennsylvania 40.52N 77.46W
103 B7 **Pleasant Grove** Pennsylvania 39.45N 76.12W
110 O9 **Pleasant Grove** Utah 40.23N 111.45W
107 F2 **Pleasant Hill** Illinois 39.27N 90.52W
107 C10 **Pleasant Hill** Louisiana 31.51N 93.31W
107 B3 **Pleasant Hill** Missouri 38.47N 94.16W
104 A6 **Pleasant Hill** Ohio 40.03N 84.20W
106 M9 **Pleasant Hill Res** Ohio 40.35N 82.20W
111 M8 **Pleasant, L** Arizona 33.54N 112.17W
103 D3 **Pleasant Mount** Pennsylvania 41.44N 75.26W
98 F8 **Pleasant, Mt** New Brunswick 45.26N 66.50W
11 N10 **Pleasant, Mt** New Zealand 43.35S 172.44E
111 C4 **Pleasanton** California 37.39N 121.53W
109 Q3 **Pleasanton** Kansas 38.10N 94.42W
108 L9 **Pleasanton** Nebraska 40.58N 99.06W
112 J7 **Pleasanton** Texas 28.58N 98.31W
107 E6 **Pleasant Plains** Arkansas 35.31N 91.36W
103 F6 **Pleasant Plains** New Jersey 40.00N 74.13W
103 G3 **Pleasant Plains** New York 41.52N 73.53W
100 S9 **Pleasant Point** Manitoba 49.48N 99.10W
11 F11 **Pleasant Point** New Zealand 44.15S 171.08E
103 G3 **Pleasant Valley** New York 41.45N 73.49W
110 H5 **Pleasant Valley** Oregon 44.41N 117.38W
95 K8 **Pleasant View** S Africa 32.40S 26.54E
110 G3 **Pleasant View** Washington 46.29N 118.20W
108 R8 **Pleasantville** Iowa 41.25N 93.14W
103 E8 **Pleasantville** New Jersey 39.23N 74.32W
103 G4 **Pleasantville** New York 41.10N 73.47W
104 F5 **Pleasantville** Pennsylvania 41.35N 79.36W
57 L6 **Pleasley** Derbys Eng 53.11N 1.14W
107 L3 **Pleasureville** Kentucky 38.21N 85.07W
72 J5 **Pléaux** France 45.08N 2.13E
64 L4 **Plech** W Germany 49.39N 11.29E
70 F5 **Plédéliac** France 48.27N 2.25W
99 G2 **Pledger L** Ontario 50.54N 83.42W
70 E5 **Plédran** France 48.27N 2.45W
70 D4 **Pléhedel** France 48.42N 3.00W
66 D6 **Pléiades** *mt* Switzerland 46.30N 6.55E
18 L7 **Pleihari** Borneo Indonesia 3.47S 114.45E
25 K5 **Plei Herel** Vietnam 14.01N 108.16E
25 K6 **Plei Kly** Vietnam 13.32N 108.06E
25 K6 **Pleiku** Vietnam 13.57N 108.01E
70 G4 **Pleine Fougères** France 48.32N 1.33W
64 L5 **Pleinfeld** W Germany 49.07N 11.01E
70 E3 **Pleinmont Pt** Chan Is 49.26N 2.40W
64 P6 **Pleinting** W Germany 48.40N 13.08E
64 N1 **Pleisse** *R* E Germany
25 K5 **Plei Ta Uan** Vietnam 14.12N 108.01E
70 F5 **Plélan-le-Grand** France 48.00N 2.05W
70 F5 **Plélan-le-Petit** France 48.26N 2.14W
70 E5 **Plemet** France 48.11N 2.35W
75 E1 **Plencia** Spain 43.24N 2.56W
70 F5 **Plenée-Jugon** France 48.22N 2.25W
70 E4 **Pléneuf** France 48.35N 2.32W
82 H6 **Pleniţea** Romania 44.14N 23.10E
100 J7 **Plenty** Saskatchewan 51.47N 108.38W
11 M4 **Plenty, B. of** New Zealand
13 D6 **Plenty R** N Terr Australia
108 F1 **Plentywood** Montana 48.46N 104.32W
70 G4 **Plerguer** France 48.32N 1.51W
70 E4 **Plérin** France 48.33N 2.46W
70 E6 **Plescop** France 47.42N 2.48W
63 Q5 **Plesen-see** *L* E Germany 53.31N 12.30E
47 E4 **Plesetsk** U.S.S.R. 62.42N 40.21E
46 G3 **Pleshchenitsy** Belorussiya U.S.S.R. 54.24N 27.52E
45 B2 **Pleshchitsy** Belorussiya U.S.S.R. 54.07N 30.24E
47 K7 **Pleshkova** U.S.S.R. 56.05N 69.42E
70 D5 **Plésidy** France 48.27N 3.09W
62 M7 **Plešivec** Czechoslovakia 48.33N 20.25E
70 F4 **Pleslin-Trivagou** France 48.32N 2.03W
116 B1 **Plesman** *airport* Curaçao W I 12.18N 68.59W
70 G6 **Plessé** France 47.33N 1.53W
68 E4 **Plessis-Robinson, Le** France 48.47N 2.16E
99 T6 **Plessisville** Quebec 46.14N 71.46W
66 P4 **Plessur** *R* Switzerland
70 F5 **Plestan** France 48.26N 2.27W
70 C4 **Plestin-les-Greves** France 48.39N 3.38W
62 K4 **Pleszew** Poland 51.52N 17.47E
98 B2 **Pletipi L** Quebec
64 D1 **Plettenberg** W Germany 51.13N 7.50E
95 G10 **Plettenbergbaai** S Africa 34.05S 23.21E
70 D4 **Pleubian** France 48.50N 3.08W
70 G4 **Pleudihen-sur-Rance** France 48.31N 1.57W
70 G5 **Pleugueneuc** France 48.23N 1.53W
72 F2 **Pleumartin** France 46.45N 0.45E
70 C4 **Pleumeur** France 48.46N 3.32W
69 F6 **Pleurs** France 48.42N 3.53E
70 F4 **Pleurtuit** France 48.35N 2.03W
72 E3 **Pleuville** France 46.05N 0.29E
82 J7 **Pleven** Bulgaria 43.25N 24.40E
Plévenon *see* **Fréhel**
108 F3 **Plevna** Montana 46.26N 104.32W
70 C5 **Pleyben** France 48.13N 3.59W
70 C4 **Pleyber-Christ** France 48.30N 3.52W
64 N4 **Pleystein** W Germany 49.38N 12.25E
89 F9 **Plibo** Liberia 4.38N 7.41W
77 O5 **Pliego** Spain 37.59N 1.29W
64 M7 **Pliening** W Germany 48.11N 11.48E
18 L4 **Plieran** *R* Sarawak Malaysia
72 F8 **Plieux** France 43.57N 0.44E
11 J8 **Plimmerton** New Zealand 41.03S 174.52E
90 H6 **Plimouta** Chad 10.01N 16.56E
45 D5 **Pliski** Ukraine U.S.S.R. 51.07N 32.25E
82 M1 **Pliskov** U.S.S.R. 49.24N 29.18E
84 E8 **Plítra** Greece 36.42N 22.50E
82 C6 **Pljesivica** *mts* Yugoslavia
82 E7 **Pljevlja** Yugoslavia 43.21N 19.21E
81 B2 **Ploaghe** Sardinia 40.40N 8.45E
69 O7 **Plobsheim** France 48.28N 7.44E
82 D7 **Ploča** *Lt Ho* Yugoslavia 43.05N 16.46E
83 B1 **Ploče** Yugoslavia 43.02N 17.27E
64 G6 **Plochingen** W Germany 48.43N 9.25E
62 M3 **Płock** Poland 52.32N 19.40E
65 G8 **Plöcken Pass** Austria/Italy 46.37N 12.58E
65 J4 **Plöckenstein** *mt* Czechoslovakia 48.47N 13.52E
58 E4 **Plockton** Highland Scotland 57.20N 5.40W
70 E5 **Plœuc** France 48.21N 2.45W
61 B4 **Ploegsteert** Belgium 50.44N 2.53E
70 D6 **Ploemel** France 47.39N 3.05W
70 D6 **Ploemeur** France 47.44N 3.26W
70 D5 **Ploërdut** France 48.05N 3.16W
70 F6 **Ploërmel** France 47.56N 2.23W
70 B6 **Plogastel-St. Germain** France 47.59N 4.17W
70 A5 **Plogoff** France 48.02N 4.40W
70 B5 **Plogonnec** France 48.05N 4.12W
82 K6 **Ploieşti** Romania 44.57N 26.01E
83 H6 **Plomárion** Greece 38.58N 26.24E
69 L8 **Plombières-les-Bains** France 47.58N 6.28E
71 F2 **Plombières-les-Dijon** France 47.20N 4.58E
70 B6 **Plomelin** France 47.56N 4.10W
70 B6 **Plomeur** France 47.50N 4.17W
69 G4 **Plomion** France 49.48N 4.03E
121 B4 **Plomo, Nevado del** *pk* Chile 33.16S 70.15W
63 M4 **Plön** W Germany 54.10N 10.26E
62 J2 **Płona** *R* Poland
70 B5 **Plonéis** France 48.01N 4.13W
70 B6 **Plonéour-Lanvern** France 47.54N 4.18W
70 C5 **Plonévez-du-Faou** France 48.15N 3.50W
70 B5 **Plonévez-Porzay** France 48.08N 4.15W
100 K3 **Plonge, L. la** Saskatchewan
62 M3 **Płońsk** Poland 52.37N 20.21E
95 H5 **Plooysburg** S Africa 29.02S 24.14E
82 H6 **Plopi** Romania 44.31N 23.00E
39 J4 **Ploskaya, Gora** *mt* U.S.S.R. 61.53N 174.15E
40 H3 **Ploskiy Mys** *C* Khabarovsk U.S.S.R. 57.17N 139.30E
41 R3 **Ploskiy, Mys** *C* U.S.S.R. 75.25N 148.45E
46 H2 **Ploskosh'** U.S.S.R. 56.41N 31.11E
45 K4 **Ploskoye** U.S.S.R. 52.46N 38.20E
64 N4 **Plössberg** W Germany 49.46N 12.19E
62 J2 **Płoty** Poland 53.48N 15.14E
63 P8 **Plötzky** E Germany 52.03N 11.49E
75 J6 **Plou** Spain 41.00N 0.52W
70 D4 **Plouagat** France 48.32N 3.00W
70 D4 **Plouaret** France 48.37N 3.28W
70 A5 **Plouarzel** France 48.27N 4.44W
70 D6 **Plouay** France 47.55N 3.19W
70 F4 **Ploubalay** France 48.35N 2.09W
62 H5 **Ploučnice** *R* Czechoslovakia
70 A4 **Ploudalmézeau** France 48.33N 4.39W
70 B4 **Ploudaniel** France 48.33N 4.19W
70 B5 **Ploudiry** France 48.27N 4.10W
70 B4 **Plouénan** France 48.38N 4.00W
70 G4 **Plouër-Langrolay-sur-Rance** France 48.32N 2.00W
70 B4 **Plouescat** France 48.40N 4.12W
70 E4 **Plouézec** France 48.45N 2.59W
70 E4 **Plouézec, Pte.de** France 48.46N 2.57W
70 B5 **Plougastel-Daoulas** France 48.23N 4.23W
70 E5 **Plougenast** France 48.17N 2.43W
70 A5 **Plougonvelin** France 48.20N 4.43W
70 C4 **Plougonven** France 48.42N 3.47W
70 C4 **Plougonven** France 48.32N 3.43W
70 D5 **Plougonver** France 48.29N 3.23W
70 E6 **Plougoumelen** France 47.40N 2.55W
70 D4 **Plougrescant** France 48.51N 3.14W
70 A4 **Plouguerneau** France 48.37N 4.30W
70 D5 **Plouguernevel** France 48.15N 3.15W
70 E4 **Plouha** France 48.41N 2.55W
70 D6 **Plouharnel** France 47.36N 3.07W
70 A5 **Plouhinec** Finistère France 48.01N 4.30W
70 D6 **Plouhinec** Morbihan France 47.42N 3.14W
70 C4 **Plouigneau** France 48.34N 3.42W
70 C4 **Ploujean** France 48.37N 3.50W
70 D4 **Ploumanac'h** France 48.50N 3.28W
70 C4 **Ploumilliau** France 48.41N 3.31W
70 A5 **Ploumoguer** France 48.24N 4.43W
70 C5 **Plounëour-Ménez** France 48.27N 3.54W
70 B4 **Plouneour-Tréz** France 48.39N 4.19W
70 C4 **Plounérin** France 48.34N 3.33W
70 B4 **Plounévez-Lochrist** France 48.37N 4.14W
70 D5 **Plounevez-Quintin** France 48.17N 3.13W
70 C5 **Plourach** France 48.25N 3.33W
70 D5 **Plouray** France 48.08N 3.23W
70 A4 **Plourin** France 48.31N 4.40W
84 C6 **Ploutokhóri** Greece 37.37N 21.42E
70 B4 **Plouvien** France 48.32N 4.28W
70 B4 **Plouvorn** France 48.35N 4.03W
70 C5 **Plouyé** France 48.19N 3.44W
70 B4 **Plouzévéde** France 48.36N 4.08W
82 J8 **Plovdiv** Bulgaria 42.08N 24.45E
108 Q7 **Plover** Iowa 42.54N 94.39W
106 E5 **Plover** Wisconsin 44.27N 89.35W
113 K1 **Plover Is** Alaska
106 E5 **Plover, R** Wisconsin
70 B6 **Plozévet** France 47.59N 4.26W
56 N5 **Pluckley** Kent Eng 51.11N 0.46E
64 H6 **Plüderhausen** W Germany 48.49N 9.36E
115 L10 **Pluma Hidalgo** Mexico 15.56N 96.28W
100 S8 **Plumas** Manitoba 50.25N 99.05W
70 F5 **Plumaugat** France 48.16N 2.14W
59 H2 **Plumbridge** Tyrone N Ireland 54.46N 7.15W
106 B5 **Plum City** Wisconsin 44.38N 92.12W
100 U9 **Plum Coulee** Manitoba 49.12N 97.45W
70 E6 **Plumelec** France 47.51N 2.38W
70 E6 **Pluméliau** France 47.57N 2.57W
70 E6 **Plumelin** France 47.52N 2.52W
70 E6 **Plumergat** France 47.45N 2.55W
12 L4 **Plumer, Pt** New S Wales 31.21S 152.56E
107 D6 **Plumerville** Arkansas 35.09N 92.39W
103 K4 **Plum I** Long I, N Y 41.11N 72.10W
70 E5 **Plumieux** France 48.05N 2.34W
65 P3 **Plumlov** Czechoslovakia 49.28N 16.59E
110 J2 **Plummer** Idaho 47.19N 116.55W
108 O2 **Plummer** Minnesota 47.55N 96.02W
113 H6 **Plummer, Mt** Alaska 61.10N 159.49W
57 H3 **Plumpton Wall** Cumbria Eng 54.44N 2.46W
14 F8 **Plumridge Lakes** W Australia
94 P12 **Plumstead** Cape Town S Africa 34.01S 18.29E
92 C12 **Plumtree** Zimbabwe 20.30S 27.50E
70 E6 **Pluneret** France 47.42N 2.58W
46 D2 **Plunge** Lithuania U.S.S.R. 55.52N 21.49E
100 M7 **Plunkett** Saskatchewan 51.56N 105.29W
58 K3 **Pluscarden Abbey** Grampian Scotland 57.36N 3.28W
110 F7 **Plush** Oregon 42.25N 119.55W
70 D6 **Pluvigner** France 47.47N 3.00W
64 B4 **Pluwig** W Germany 49.42N 6.44E
70 D4 **Pluzunet** France 48.39N 3.21W
25 E4 **Ply Huey Wati, Khao** *mt* Burma 16.24N 98.52E
111 D3 **Plymouth** California 38.29N 120.52W
103 H3 **Plymouth** Connecticut 41.40N 73.05W
56 C7 **Plymouth** Devon Eng 50.23N 4.10W
106 D9 **Plymouth** Illinois 40.18N 90.56W
106 H8 **Plymouth** Indiana 41.20N 86.19W
108 R6 **Plymouth** Iowa 43.14N 93.06W
103 N3 **Plymouth** Massachusetts 41.58N 70.40W
116 N6 **Plymouth** Montserrat W I 16.44N 62.14W
105 L2 **Plymouth** N Carolina 35.53N 76.46W
108 O9 **Plymouth** Nebraska 40.16N 96.59W
104 O3 **Plymouth** New Hampshire 43.45N 71.43W
104 C6 **Plymouth** Ohio 41.00N 82.41W
103 C4 **Plymouth** Pennsylvania 41.14N 75.55W
116 M1 **Plymouth** Tobago W I 11.13N 60.47W
110 N8 **Plymouth** Utah 41.55N 112.09W
104 N3 **Plymouth** Vermont 43.32N 72.45W
106 G6 **Plymouth** Wisconsin 43.44N 87.58W
103 N3 **Plymouth** *co* Massachusetts
103 N3 **Plymouth B** Massachusetts
56 C7 **Plymouth Sd** Devon Eng
56 C7 **Plympton** Devon Eng 50.23N 4.03W
103 N3 **Plympton** Massachusetts 41.58N 70.48W
98 G9 **Plympton** Nova Scotia 44.30N 65.57W
12 A8 **Plympton** *dist* Adelaide, S Aust
56 D7 **Plym, R** Devon Eng
56 D3 **Plynlimon Fawr** *mt* Dyfed Wales 52.28N 3.47W
45 E4 **Plyuskovo** U.S.S.R. 52.45N 33.51E
46 G1 **Plyussa** U.S.S.R. 58.30N 29.28E
46 G1 **Plyussa** *R* U.S.S.R.
64 P4 **Plzeň** Czechoslovakia 49.45N 13.25E
95 B9 **Pniel** S Africa 33.54S 18.58E
62 J3 **Pniewy** Poland 52.31N 16.10E
89 J6 **Po** Upper Volta 11.11N 1.10W
28 L1 **Po** Xizang Zizhiqu 30.05N 97.16E
79 L5 **Po** *R* Italy
89 H5 **Poa** Upper Volta 12.15N 2.07W
12 H8 **Poatina** Tasmania 41.44S 146.58E
89 L8 **Pobé** Benin 7.00N 2.56E
89 J5 **Pobé** Upper Volta 13.53N 1.42W
39 C3 **Pobeda** U.S.S.R. 64.27N 144.59E
39 D2 **Pobeda, Gora** *mt* U.S.S.R. 65.10N 146.00E
40 J7 **Pobedino** Sakhalin U.S.S.R. 49.50N 142.52E
43 O6 **Pobedy, Pik** *mt* U.S.S.R./China 42.25N 80.15E
75 E2 **Pobes** Spain 42.48N 2.54W
64 O4 **Poběžovice** Czechoslovakia 49.30N 12.47E
62 K3 **Pobiedziska** Poland 52.29N 17.11E
75 O4 **Pobla de Claramunt, La** Spain 41.33N 1.40E
75 O3 **Pobla de Lillet, La** Spain 42.15N 1.58E
75 L5 **Pobla de Masaluca** Spain 41.11N 0.21E
75 M3 **Pobla de Segur** Spain 42.15N 0.58E
76 H4 **Pobladura del Valle** Spain 42.06N 5.44W
76 G4 **Pobladura, Sierra de la** *mts* Spain
77 J3 **Poblete** Spain 38.56N 3.59W
75 G6 **Pobo de Dueñas, El** Spain 40.46N 1.39W
75 J6 **Pobo, El** Spain 40.30N 0.52W
75 M5 **Poboleda** Spain 41.14N 0.50E
107 E5 **Pocahontas** Arkansas 36.15N 91.00W
108 Q7 **Pocahontas** Iowa 42.43N 94.40W
104 D9 **Pocahontas** Virginia 37.17N 81.22W
117 B6 **Pocáo, L. de** Brazil
118 B4 **Poca, R.da** Brazil
109 N6 **Pocasse** Oklahoma 35.13N 97.57W
103 N3 **Pocasset** Massachusetts 41.42N 70.37W
110 N7 **Pocatello** Idaho 42.53N 112.26W
65 M3 **Počátky** Czechoslovakia 49.16N 15.15E
76 B11 **Poceirão** *sta* Portugal 38.38N 8.45W
64 Q3 **Počerady** Czechoslovakia 50.25N 13.42E
87 E7 **Pochala** Sudan 7.10N 34.10E
30 F2 **Pochenkong La** *pass* Xizang Zizhiqu 30.41N 82.00E
45 E4 **Pochep** U.S.S.R. 52.55N 33.29E
42 F4 **Pochet** U.S.S.R. 57.09N 96.30E
45 Q2 **Pochinki** U.S.S.R. 54.43N 44.53E
45 D2 **Pochinok** Smolensk U.S.S.R. 54.24N 32.28E
47 M4 **Pochinok** Sverdlovsk U.S.S.R. 57.04N 59.58E
65 M5 **Pöchlarn** Austria 48.13N 15.13E
121 D3 **Pocho, Sa.de** *ra* Argentina
39 D3 **Pochtovaya** U.S.S.R. 63.25N 145.34E
115 L10 **Pochutla** Mexico 15.45N 96.30W
121 A6 **Pocillas** Chile 36.06S 72.15W
76 E6 **Pocinho** Portugal 41.07N 7.07W
64 P5 **Pocinovice** Czechoslovakia 49.20N 13.09E
76 L10 **Pocito, Sierra del** *mts* Spain
120 E11 **Pocitos, Salar de** *salt pan* Arg
64 P2 **Pockau** E Germany 50.42N 13.14E
64 P7 **Pocking** W Germany 48.24N 13.20E
57 M5 **Pocklington** Humberside Eng 53.56N 0.46W
95 M3 **Pocklington** S Africa 27.06S 28.48E
18 N3 **Pock, Mt** Sabah Malaysia 4.27N 118.22E
117 G9 **Poco** *R* Brazil
118 G2 **Poço** *R* Brazil
76 E16 **Poço do Bispo** Portugal 38.44N 9.06W
118 H4 **Poções** Brazil 14.33S 40.23W
91 C11 **Pocolo** Angola 15.43S 13.49E
19 B8 **Poco Mandasawu** *mt* Indonesia 8.38S 120.26E
56 D6 **Pocombe Bridge** Devon Eng 50.43N 3.34W
104 K8 **Pocomoke City** Maryland 38.04N 75.35W
104 K8 **Pocomoke, R** Maryland
104 K9 **Pocomoke Sd** Virginia
120 F7 **Pocona** Bolivia 17.36S 65.22W
118 C5 **Poconé** Brazil 16.16S 56.38W
103 D4 **Pocono L** Pennsylvania 41.07N 75.30W
103 C4 **Pocono Lake** Pennsylvania 41.06N 75.32W
103 D4 **Pocono Mts** Pennsylvania
103 D4 **Pocono Pines** Pennsylvania 41.07N 75.27W
19 B8 **Poco Ranakah** *mt* Indonesia 8.37S 120.32E
117 F9 **Poços** Brazil 9.35S 42.29W
118 F7 **Poços de Caldas** Brazil 21.48S 46.33W
115 O6 **Pocrí** Panama 7.44N 80.09W
111 L5 **Pocum Wash** *crater* Arizona
12 F4 **Podamacca** New S Wales 31.27S 141.31E
28 C5 **Podanur** Tamil Nadu India 10.57N 77.00E
64 P3 **Podbořany** Czechoslovakia 50.15N 13.25E
47 H4 **Podcher'ye** U.S.S.R. 63.55N 57.35E
47 H4 **Podcher'ye** *R* U.S.S.R.
43 D7 **Podchineniya** *dist* Turkmeniya U.S.S.R.
45 R6 **Podchinnyy** U.S.S.R. 50.52N 45.15E
62 L4 **Poddębice** Poland 51.54N 18.53E
46 H2 **Poddor'ye** U.S.S.R. 57.29N 31.11E
62 J5 **Poděbrady** Czechoslovakia 50.10N 15.05E
79 M5 **Po delle Tolle** *R* Italy
76 F5 **Podence** Portugal 41.35N 6.55W
72 D6 **Podensac** France 44.39N 0.21W
65 P6 **Podersdorf am See** Austria 47.51N 16.51E
46 F5 **Podgaytsy** Ukraine U.S.S.R. 49.19N 25.10E
45 L6 **Podgorenskiy** U.S.S.R. 50.25N 39.37E
Podgorica *see* **Titograd**
65 M9 **Podgorje** Yugoslavia 46.26N 15.05E
40 N6 **Podgornoye** Kuril Is U.S.S.R. 50.11N 155.23E
44 E1 **Podgornoye** Rostov U.S.S.R. 46.32N 43.09E
42 C3 **Podgornoye** Tomsk U.S.S.R. 57.45N 82.30E
Podgornoye Voronezh *see* **Podgorenskiy**
40 L9 **Podgornyy** Kuril Is U.S.S.R. 45.51N 149.45E
44 K3 **Podgornyy, Ostrov** *isld* Kazakhstan U.S.S.R. 44.49N 50.23E
45 H8 **Podgorodneye** Ukraine U.S.S.R. 48.07N 36.48E
45 G8 **Podgorodnoye** Ukraine U.S.S.R. 48.33N 35.05E
79 M5 **Po di Goro** *R* Italy
28 D3 **Podile** Andhra Prad India 15.37N 79.36E
65 P4 **Podivin** Czechoslovakia 48.50N 16.51E
79 L5 **Po di Volano** *R* Italy
39 G4 **Podkagernaya Bukhta** *gulf* U.S.S.R.
39 G4 **Podkagernoye** U.S.S.R. 60.20N 161.58E
41 J4 **Podkamennaya** *R* U.S.S.R.
42 E2 **Podkamennaya Tunguska** U.S.S.R. 61.45N 90.13E
42 E2 **Podkamennaya Tunguska** *R* U.S.S.R.
65 J9 **Podkoren** Yugoslavia 46.28N 13.45E
82 J9 **Podkova*** Bulgaria 41.24N 25.24E
45 T5 **Podlesnoye** U.S.S.R. 51.50N 47.00E
43 D2 **Podnikovskiy** Kazakhstan U.S.S.R. 50.37N 57.04E
62 M6 **Podolinec** Czechoslovakia 49.16N 20.30E
45 J1 **Podolsk** U.S.S.R. 55.23N 37.32E
45 H4 **Podolyan'** U.S.S.R. 52.23N 36.05E
89 B3 **Podor** Senegal 16.35N 15.02W
47 F5 **Podosinovets** U.S.S.R. 60.16N 47.02E
82 D6 **Podovi** Yugoslavia 44.15N 17.01E
47 C5 **Podporozh'ye** U.S.S.R. 60.55N 34.02E
42 E3 **Podtësovo** U.S.S.R. 58.37N 92.08E
65 P9 **Podturen** Yugoslavia 46.27N 16.32E
82 L3 **Podu Iloaiei** Romania 47.12N 27.20E
82 G8 **Podujevo** Yugoslavia 42.54N 21.10E
103 K2 **Podunk** Massachusetts 42.10N 72.02W
42 D4 **Podunskaya** U.S.S.R. 55.03N 85.01E
39 H6 **Podutesnaya** Komandorskiye O-va U.S.S.R. 55.04N 166.13E
82 L4 **Podu Turcului** Romania 46.11N 27.25E
42 G4 **Pod'yelanka** U.S.S.R. 57.01N 101.30E
42 H4 **Podymakhino** U.S.S.R. 56.59N 106.03E
47 E5 **Podyuga** U.S.S.R. 61.08N 40.43E
61 K2 **Poederlee** Belgium 51.13N 4.50E
60 J12 **Poederoijen** Netherlands 51.47N 5.05E
61 D2 **Poeke** Belgium 51.03N 3.27E
63 O4 **Poel** *isld* E Germany
60 E11 **Poeldijk** Netherlands 52.02N 4.14E
94 N5 **Poelela, L** Mozambique 24.36S 35.09E
61 B3 **Poelkapelle** Belgium 50.55N 2.57E
106 K4 **Poe Reef Lt. Ho** Michigan 45.43N 84.22W
11 F9 **Poerua** New Zealand 42.43S 171.32E
61 E2 **Poesele** Belgium 51.02N 3.31E
71 H8 **Poët, le** France 44.17N 5.53E
94 E7 **Pofadder** S Africa 29.09S 19.25E
80 H5 **Pofi** Italy 41.33N 13.26E
99 J6 **Pogamasing** Ontario 46.55N 81.46W
45 E4 **Pogar** U.S.S.R. 52.35N 33.15E
63 S4 **Poggendorf** E Germany 54.03N 13.08E
81 R12 **Poggiardo** Italy 40.03N 18.23E
80 D2 **Poggibonsi** Italy 43.28N 11.09E
79 K7 **Poggio a Caiano** Italy 43.48N 11.03E
80 C3 **Poggio Ballone** *mt* Italy 42.50N 10.53E
80 D4 **Poggio di Leccio** *mt* Italy 42.29N 11.17E
80 D2 **Poggio di Montieri** *mt* Italy 43.08N 11.00E
80 M5 **Poggio Imperiale** Italy 41.49N 15.22E
80 G4 **Poggio Mirteto** Italy 42.16N 12.42E
80 G4 **Poggio Moiano** Italy 42.13N 12.53E
80 C3 **Poggio Peroni** *mt* Italy 42.47N 10.48E
81 F8 **Poggioreale** Sicily 37.48N 13.02E
79 K5 **Póggio Renatico** Italy 44.46N 11.29E
81 M2 **Poggiorsini** Italy 40.55N 16.15E
79 K5 **Póggio Rusco** Italy 44.58N 11.07E
65 M5 **Pöggstall** Austria 48.20N 15.13E
31 C5 **Poghdar** Afghanistan 30.17N 64.44E
40 J5 **Pogibi** Sakhalin U.S.S.R. 52.13N 141.43E
81 A2 **Poglina, Pta.di** Sardinia 40.31N 8.20E
66 N8 **Pognana** Italy 45.53N 9.10E
66 K8 **Pogno** Italy 45.46N 8.23E
69 G6 **Pogny** France 48.52N 4.30E
82 K6 **Pogoanele** Romania 44.55N 27.00E
45 F1 **Pogoreloye** U.S.S.R. 56.08N 34.50E
91 E7 **Pogoso** Zaïre 6.45S 17.13E
83 D4 **Pogradec** Albania 40.55N 20.37E
79 M4 **Po Grande** *R* Italy
43 G8 **Pogranichnik** Türkmeniya U.S.S.R. 36.00N 62.50E
40 J6 **Pogranichnoye** Sakhalin U.S.S.R. 50.20N 143.45E

45 U6 Pogranichnoye Saratov U.S.S.R. 50.32N 48.37E
40 E9 Pogranichnyy U.S.S.R. 44.28N 131.28E
46 G5 Pogrebishche Ukraine U.S.S.R. 49.30N 29.15E
45 B6 Pogreby Ukraine U.S.S.R. 50.34N 30.37E
113 E9 Pogromni Vol Aleutian Is 54.36N 164.45W
63 F6 Pogum W Germany 53.19N 7.16E
39 G1 Pogynden U.S.S.R. 68.10N 164.00E
39 G1 Pogynden *R* U.S.S.R.
19 C4 Poh Celebes Indon 0.46S 122.50E
114 D6 Pohakuloa Pt Hawaiian Is 20.56N 156.58W
21 E10 P'ohang S Korea 36.00N 129.26E
11 K7 Pohangina New Zealand 40.08S 175.24E
11 G7 Pohara New Zealand 40.51S 172.53E
51 K11 Pohja Finland 60.07N 23.30E
51 O8 Pohjois-Karjala *dist* Finland
64 F2 Pohlheim W Germany 50.31N 8.44E
69 Q2 Pohlheim W Germany 50.31N 8.41E
114 D8 Pohoiki Hawaiian Is 19.27N 154.51W
11 J6 Pohokura New Zealand 39.10S 174.39E
11 L5 Pohokura *mt* New Zealand 38.57S 176.41E
62 M7 Pohorelá Czechoslovakia 48.52N 20.00E
65 P4 Pohořelice Czechoslovakia 48.59N 16.32E
65 L4 Pohoří Czechoslovakia 48.37N 14.43E
82 C4 Pohorje *mts* Yugoslavia
114 B8 Pohue B Hawaiian Is
28 K3 Poi Manipur India 25.20N 94.36E
79 K4 Poiana Maggiore Italy 45.17N 11.30E
82 H7 Poiana Mare Romania 43.55N 23.02E
82 K3 Poiana Teiului Romania 47.07N 25.59E
76 C8 Poiares Beira Litoral Portugal 40.12N 8.15W
76 D6 Poiares Trás os Montes e Alto Douro Portugal 41.11N 7.44W
19 D3 Poigar Celebes Indon 1.03N 124.19E
71 B1 Poilly-les-Gien France 47.41N 2.34E
69 F8 Poilly-sur-Serein France 47.46N 3.54E
45 P3 Poim U.S.S.R. 53.02N 43.10E
Poincaré, C Kerguelen *see* Marisny, C
98 O2 Poincaré, L Quebec
69 G8 Poinçon-lès-Larrey France 47.53N 4.27E
Poindo *see* Lhünzhub
123 F2 Poinsett, C Antarctica 65.35S 113.00E
105 G9 Poinsett, L Florida 28.20N 80.50W
Point Alcock *see* Sandy Point
111 A3 Point Arena California 38.54N 123.40W
107 E12 Point au Fer I Louisiana 29.17N 91.50W
113 V8 Point Baker Alaska 56.20N 133.35W
112 M5 Pointblank Texas 30.45N 95.14W
12 G7 Point Campbell Victoria 38.37S 143.04E
11 C2 Point Chevalier *dist* Auckland New Zealand
107 G12 Point Chicot I Louisiana 29.43N 89.18W
Point Cloates *see* Ningaloo
112 L7 Point Comfort Texas 28.40N 96.32W
107 G12 Pointe à la Hache Louisiana 29.35N 89.49W
98 N3 Pointe-à-Maurier Quebec 50.20N 59.49W
116 O2 Pointe-à-Pierre Trinidad & Tobago 10.18N 61.27W
116 N3 Pointe-à-Pitre Guadeloupe W I 16.14N 61.32W
99 K7 Pointe au Baril Station Ontario 45.36N 80.23W
98 B6 Pointe-au-Pic Quebec 47.38N 70.10W
99 R7 Pointe aux Trembles Quebec 45.40N 73.30W
99 S4 Pointe Bleue Quebec 48.34N 72.16W
99 R7 Pointe-Claire Quebec 45.27N 73.50W
66 B7 Pointe d'Andey *mt* France 46.03N 6.25E
98 H7 Pointe-du-Chêne New Brunswick 46.14N 64.32W
66 C8 Pointe du Colleney *mt* France 45.58N 6.41E
99 H9 Point Edward Ontario 43.00N 82.25W
98 D4 Pointe Le Bel Quebec 49.09N 68.12W
91 B6 Pointe Noire Congo 4.46S 11.53E
116 M3 Pointe Noire Guadeloupe W I 16.14N 61.47W
103 D7 Pointers New Jersey 39.37N 75.26W
98 G6 Pointe Verte New Brunswick 47.46N 65.48W
116 N2 Point Fortin Trinidad & Tobago 10.12N 61.41W
105 M1 Point Harbor N Carolina 36.05N 75.50W
113 D2 Point Hope Alaska 68.20N 166.50W
11 D5 Point Howard New Zealand 41.15S 174.54E
72 F9 Pointis-Inard France 43.06N 0.49E
103 M4 Point Judith Pond Rhode I
101 R3 Point L N W Terr
113 F2 Point Lay Alaska 69.45N 163.10W
26 S14 Point Lazare *C* Mahé I Seychelles, Ind Oc
98 R4 Point Leamington Newfoundland 49.20N 55.24W
104 J8 Point Lookout Maryland 38.06N 76.22W
12 K4 Point Lookout New S Wales 30.33S 152.20E
104 F7 Point Marion Pennsylvania 39.43N 79.54W
104 H7 Point of Rocks Maryland 39.16N 77.32W
110 R8 Point of Rocks Wyoming 41.41N 108.47W
28 J2 Pointong Assam India 27.33N 92.30E
26 R2 Point Pedro Sri Lanka 9.49N 80.14E
99 H10 Point Pelee Nat. Park Ontario 41.57N 82.31W
103 F6 Point Pleasant New Jersey 40.06N 74.02W
103 D6 Point Pleasant Pennsylvania 40.25N 75.05W
104 C8 Point Pleasant W Virginia 38.53N 82.07W
111 A3 Point Reyes National Seashore California 38.05N 122.58W
110 B1 Point Roberts Washington 49.00N 123.05W
14 B5 Point Samson W Australia 20.46S 117.10E
98 H7 Point Sapin New Brunswick 46.59N 64.50W
13 B1 Point Stuart N Terr Australia 12.19S 131.46E
12 D5 Point Turton S Australia 34.55S 137.20E
25 G6 Poipet Cambodia 13.41N 102.34E
72 A2 Poiré-sur-Vie, le France 46.46N 1.30W
79 C5 Poirino Italy 44.55N 7.50E
72 L1 Poiseux France 47.07N 3.13E
46 R2 Poisevo U.S.S.R. 55.30N 53.31E
96 P7 Poiso Madeira Is 32.43N 16.54W
108 C6 Poison Cr Wyoming
14 B1 Poison Gully *R* Perth, W Aust
99 P6 Poisson Blanc, L Quebec
14 C5 Poissonnier Pt W Australia 19.58S 119.15E
69 J7 Poissons France 48.26N 5.14E
69 C6 Poissy France 48.56N 2.02E
72 B3 Poitevin, Marais *marsh* France 46.22N 1.06W
72 E2 Poitiers France 46.35N 0.20E
67 E6 Poitou *prov* France
14 B5 Poivre, C W Australia 20.56S 115.21E
27 G11 Poivre I Amirante Is Seychelles, Ind Oc 5.50S 53.20E
69 B4 Poix-de-Picardie France 49.47N 2.00E
69 H4 Poix-Terron France 49.39N 4.39E
83 D4 Pojan Albania 40.43N 20.54E
120 F7 Pojo Bolivia 17.45S 64.48W
109 D6 Pojoaque New Mexico 35.54N 106.02W
118 J3 Pojuca Brazil 12.24S 38.16W
118 J3 Pojuca, R Brazil
42 A1 Pokacheva U.S.S.R. 62.43N 72.32E
114 A5 Pokai Bay Hawaiian Is
11 K6 Pokaka New Zealand 39.18S 175.25E
31 G3 Pokal Pakistan 34.52N 73.09E
30 J2 Pokalde *mt* Nepal 27.56N 86.51E
29 B4 Pokaran Rajasthan India 27.57N 71.56E
12 J3 Pokataroo New S Wales 29.37S 148.44E
42 F4 Pokateyeva U.S.S.R. 57.00N 97.21E
47 H4 Pokcha U.S.S.R. 62.55N 56.02E
91 H3 Poke *tribe* Zaïre
11 K4 Pokeno New Zealand 37.14S 175.02E
23 B9 Pok Fu Lam Hong Kong 22.15N 114.08E
30 G4 Pokhara Nepal 28.14N 83.58E
Pokharedanda *see* Khanchikot
30 J6 Pokharia Nepal 26.50N 85.15E
39 G1 Pokhodsk U.S.S.R. 69.06N 160.55E
30 B3 Pokhra Uttar Prad India 29.55N 78.54E
30 J6 Pokhraira Bihar India 26.03N 85.12E
39 D1 Pokhval'noye U.S.S.R. 69.25N 147.38E
46 Q3 Pokhvistnevo U.S.S.R. 53.36N 52.00E
117 B2 Pokigron Surinam 4.31N 55.23W
51 M3 Pokka Finland 68.11N 25.45E
21 D8 Pokkye-ri N Korea 38.25N 127.19E
Pok-lui Chau *see* Lamma I
87 A9 Poko Zaïre 3.08N 26.52E
90 M8 Poko *R* Cent Afr Rep
62 K5 Pokój Poland 50.56N 17.50E
42 C1 Pokol'ka *R* U.S.S.R.
113 F2 Poko Mt Alaska 68.50N 162.30W
42 C2 Pokontopugol U.S.S.R. 61.48N 81.55E
90 F7 Pokor Cameroon 8.06N 13.24E
Pokpak *see* Bobai
31 D8 Pokran Pakistan 25.49N 67.47E
47 H5 Pokrevsk-Ural'skiy U.S.S.R. 60.09N 59.48E
45 G2 Pokrov Kaluga U.S.S.R. 54.15N 35.15E
45 L1 Pokrov Vladimir U.S.S.R. 55.54N 39.13E
40 B5 Pokrovka Chita U.S.S.R. 53.23N 121.30E
43 J2 Pokrovka Kazakhstan U.S.S.R. 51.58N 68.31E
43 K5 Pokrovka Kirgiziya U.S.S.R. 42.45N 71.32E
43 N6 Pokrovka Kirgiziya U.S.S.R. 42.22N 78.00E
42 B4 Pokrovka Novosibirsk U.S.S.R. 55.34N 77.14E
46 R4 Pokrovka Orenburg U.S.S.R. 51.58N 54.00E
40 E10 Pokrovka Primor'ye U.S.S.R. 43.58N 131.37E
40 F9 Pokrovka Primor'ye U.S.S.R. 44.24N 133.31E
45 N4 Pokrovo-Marfino U.S.S.R. 52.24N 41.01E
41 N9 Pokrovsk U.S.S.R. 61.32N 129.12E
45 E7 Pokrovskaya Bagachka Ukraine U.S.S.R. 49.52N 33.08E
44 B8 Pokrovskiy Ukraine U.S.S.R. 46.33N 31.41E
45 H9 Pokrovskoye Dnepropetrovsk, Ukraine U.S.S.R. 47.58N 36.15E
45 V4 Pokrovskoye Kuybyshev U.S.S.R. 52.54N 49.37E
45 K7 Pokrovskoye Lugansk, Ukraine U.S.S.R. 49.45N 38.15E
45 H4 Pokrovskoye Orël U.S.S.R. 52.37N 36.50E
45 K9 Pokrovskoye Rostov U.S.S.R. 47.25N 38.55E
47 M3 Pokrovskoye Sverdlovsk U.S.S.R. 57.58N 60.16E
47 N4 Pokrovskoye Sverdlovsk U.S.S.R. 57.22N 61.41E
47 N5 Pokrovskoye Sverdlovsk U.S.S.R. 56.28N 61.38E
47 K7 Pokrovskoye Tyumen U.S.S.R. 57.16N 66.50E
39 C3 Pokryshkina, Imeni U.S.S.R. 64.10N 143.01E
47 E4 Pokshen'ga *R* U.S.S.R.
42 B2 Pokur U.S.S.R. 61.00N 75.30E
29 C6 Pol Gujarat India 24.00N 73.20E
76 E2 Pol Spain 43.09N 7.20W
19 K5 Pola Philippines 13.08N 121.25E
19 K5 Pola B Philippines 13.10N 121.30E
111 O6 Polacca Arizona 35.51N 110.24W
111 O6 Polacca Wash *R* Arizona
77 N7 Polacra, Pta.de la *pt* Spain 36.50N 2.00W
76 F2 Pola de Allande Spain 43.16N 6.37W
76 H3 Pola de Gordón, La Spain 42.51N 5.40W
76 H2 Pola de Laviana Spain 43.15N 5.33W
76 H2 Pola de Lena Spain 43.10N 5.49W
76 H2 Pola de Siero Spain 43.24N 5.39W
76 G2 Pola de Somiedo Spain 43.05N 6.15W
69 L8 Polaincourt-et-Clairefontaine France 47.52N 6.05E
32 J8 Polān Iran 25.35N 61.15E
76 L9 Polán Spain 39.47N 4.10W
62 L7 Polana *mt* Czechoslovakia 48.38N 19.30E
76 L2 Polanco Spain 43.23N 4.00W
104 K3 Poland New York 43.13N 75.05W
49 H6 Poland *rep* Cent Europe
62 K1 Polanow Poland 54.07N 16.40E
31 C3 Polanzar Gardneh *pass* Afghanistan 34.50N 65.00E
106 F4 Polar Wisconsin 45.11N 89.00W
110 M4 Polaris Montana 45.23N 113.06W
37 C9 Polateli Turkey 36.49N 37.06E
Polathane *see* Akçaabat
36 F3 Polatlı Turkey 39.34N 32.08E
28 E2 Polavaram Andhra Prad India 17.15N 81.43E
56 C7 Polbathick Cornwall Eng 50.23N 4.20W
79 M2 Polcenigo Italy 46.02N 12.30E
64 C3 Polch W Germany 50.18N 7.20E
62 J2 Połczyn Zdrój Poland 53.47N 16.07E
12 D5 Polda S Australia 33.30S 135.10E
32 A1 Poldasht Iran 39.24N 44.59E
60 H7 Polder Eierland *polder* Netherlands
47 M5 Poldnevaya U.S.S.R. 56.18N 60.18E
76 B14 Poldra *mt* Portugal 37.13N 8.47W
47 D4 Pole U.S.S.R. 63.36N 39.15E
91 H5 Pole Zaïre 2.51S 23.12E
19 B6 Poleang Celebes Indonesia 4.42S 121.48E
64 P5 Poledník *mt* Czechoslovakia 49.04N 13.25E
35 C5 Poleg *R* Israel
56 M6 Polegate E Sussex Eng 50.49N 0.15E
25 J5 Polei Monu Vietnam 14.04N 107.38E
25 J5 Polei Nong Vietnam 14.21N 107.29E
43 F8 Pole-Khatun Turkmeniya U.S.S.R. 36.00N 61.11E
84 R15 Polemidhia Cyprus 34.41N 33.00E
64 P5 Poleň Czechoslovakia 49.25N 13.11E
75 K4 Poleñino Spain 41.52N 0.18W
65 O9 Polenšak Yugoslavia 46.27N 16.01E
76 K3 Polentinos Spain 42.56N 4.32W
123 D7 Pole of Inaccessibility Antarctica 78.24S 87.35E
58 H3 Poles Highland Scotland 57.54N 4.04W
32 E2 Pol-e Safid Iran 36.05N 53.01E
79 L5 Polesella Italy 44.58N 11.46E
79 H4 Polesine Parmense Italy 45.01N 10.05E
46 D3 Polessk U.S.S.R. 54.51N 21.09E
46 F4 Poles'ye *marshy plain* Belorussiya/Ukraine U.S.S.R.
47 M6 Poletayevo Chelyabinsk U.S.S.R. 55.03N 61.07E
45 N5 Poletayevo Tambov U.S.S.R. 51.53N 41.05E
32 G4 Pol-e Tofangchi Iran 33.00N 56.56E
45 H5 Polevaya U.S.S.R. 51.37N 36.30E
47 M5 Polevskoy U.S.S.R. 56.28N 60.15E
19 A5 Polewali Celebes Indon 3.26S 119.23E
26 R7 Polgahawela Sri Lanka 7.20N 80.19E
62 N8 Polgár Hungary 47.53N 21.05E
62 L8 Polgárdi Hungary 47.03N 18.18E
47 K7 Polgovskoye U.S.S.R. 55.34N 67.42E
90 F7 Poli Cameroon 8.31N 13.10E
81 M6 Polia Italy 38.45N 16.19E
83 G8 Políaigos *isld* Greece 36.45N 24.38E
84 D7 Poliána Greece 37.09N 22.08E
121 M10 Policarpo Argentina 54.40S 65.40W
81 L3 Policastro Italy 40.04N 15.37E
81 K4 Policastro, G.di Italy
62 H2 Police Poland 53.34N 14.34E
26 Q13 Police, Pte *C* Mahé I Seychelles, Ind Oc 4.48S 55.31E
65 O2 Polička Czechoslovakia 49.44N 16.16E
81 N3 Policoro Italy 40.12N 16.40E
84 E4 Polídhroson Greece 38.38N 22.32E
75 C2 Polientes Spain 42.48N 3.56W
71 D6 Polignac France 45.04N 3.52E
81 O2 Polignano a Mare Italy 40.59N 17.13E
71 H3 Poligny France 46.50N 5.42E
42 E2 Poligus U.S.S.R. 62.03N 94.40E
83 F3 Políkastron Greece 41.01N 22.33E
83 H5 Políkhnitos Greece 39.04N 26.10E
19 K4 Polillo *isld* Philippines 14.50N 121.55E
19 L4 Polillo Is Philippines
19 K4 Polillo Str Luzon Philippines
79 J6 Polinago Italy 44.21N 10.43E
84 D3 Polinéri Greece 39.20N 22.15E
65 H8 Polinik *mt* Austria 46.54N 13.10E
116 K2 Polink Pt Jamaica, W I 17.50N 76.57W
84 P14 Polis Cyprus 35.02N 32.25E
46 H1 Polist' *R* U.S.S.R.
81 M7 Polistena Italy 38.25N 16.05E
69 G7 Polisy France 48.05N 4.23E
84 G4 Politiká Greece 38.36N 23.33E
45 R6 Polítotdel'skoye U.S.S.R. 50.13N 45.42E
47 F4 Politovo U.S.S.R. 64.05N 48.55E
83 F4 Políyiros Greece 40.23N 23.25E
81 H8 Polizzi Generosa Sicily 37.48N 14.01E
108 N8 Polk Nebraska 41.06N 97.45W
104 F5 Polk Pennsylvania 41.23N 79.56W
42 E2 Polkan, Gora *mt* U.S.S.R. 60.18N 91.34E
105 F9 Polk City Florida 28.11N 81.51W
63 P7 Polkritz E Germany 52.46N 11.58E
107 G9 Polkville Mississippi 32.09N 89.30W
41 G5 Pol'kyko U.S.S.R. 71.12N 99.28E
80 M7 Polla Italy 40.31N 15.27E
28 C5 Pollachi Tamil Nadu India 10.38N 77.00E
64 L5 Pollanten W Germany 49.09N 11.30E
59 K5 Pollaphuca Br Wicklow Irish Rep 53.08N 6.29W
107 F5 Pollard Arkansas 36.27N 90.17W
61 F3 Pollare Belgium 50.49N 4.00E
59 C3 Pollatomish Mayo Irish Rep 54.16N 9.48W
65 N7 Pöllau Austria 47.19N 15.50E
63 K9 Polle W Germany 51.54N 9.24E
66 M6 Pollegio Switzerland 46.23N 8.57E
60 P10 Pollen, De Netherlands 52.26N 6.40E
11 C2 Pollen I New Zealand 36.52S 174.41E
77 W14 Pollensa Balearic Is 39.52N 3.01E
77 W14 Pollensa, B.de Balearic Is
80 H2 Pollenza Italy 43.16N 13.21E
98 A1 Pollet, L Quebec
61 O4 Polleur Belgium 50.32N 5.53E
53 X15 Pollfoss Norway 61.58N 7.53E
71 G4 Polliat France 46.15N 5.08E
81 K3 Pollica Italy 40.11N 15.03E
81 H8 Pollina Sicily 37.59N 14.09E
61 A3 Pollinkhove Belgium 50.58N 2.44E
81 M4 Pollino, Mte Italy 39.54N 16.11E
63 P7 Pollitz E Germany 52.58N 11.38E
19 M8 Polloc Harb Mindanao Philippines 7.23N 124.14E
110 J4 Pollock Idaho 45.20N 116.21W
107 D10 Pollock Louisiana 31.31N 92.24W
108 K4 Pollock S Dakota 45.56N 100.18W
14 E10 Pollock Reef W Australia 34.35S 123.35E
100 F7 Pollockville Alberta 51.10N 111.36W
105 K3 Polloksville N Carolina 35.00N 77.15W
76 J6 Pollos Spain 41.25N 5.08W
11 C11 Pollux *mt* New Zealand 44.14S 168.53E
53 X15 Pollvatn *L* Norway 61.57N 7.55E
57 D2 Polmaddie Hill Strathclyde Scotland 55.11N 4.38W
51 N1 Polmak Norway 70.03N 28.00E
72 K6 Polminhac France 44.57N 2.34E
58 J7 Polmont Central Scotland 55.59N 3.44W
65 N3 Polná Czechoslovakia 49.29N 15.43E
46 G1 Polna U.S.S.R. 58.31N 28.03E
47 K4 Polnovat U.S.S.R. 63.47N 65.54E
106 E8 Polo Illinois 41.59N 89.35W
19 H1 Polo Luzon Philippines 14.43N 120.56E
107 B2 Polo Missouri 39.32N 94.02W
9 R10 Poloa *islet* Tonga, Pacific Oc 21.05S 175.15W
45 H9 Pologi Ukraine U.S.S.R. 47.30N 36.18E
41 D3 Pologiy, Ostrov *isld* U.S.S.R. 75.50N 82.00E
45 R8 Pologoye Zaymishche U.S.S.R. 48.28N 45.58E
47 M4 Pologrudino U.S.S.R. 57.39N 60.32E
19 M8 Polomoloc Mindanao Philippines 6.10N 125.01E
26 T6 Polonnaruwa Sri Lanka 7.56N 81.02E
46 F4 Polonnoye Ukraine U.S.S.R. 50.10N 27.30E
Polonskogo, Ostrov *isld see* Taraku-shima
77 K7 Polopos Spain 36.48N 3.17W
36 C1 Polos Turkey 41.50N 27.05E
45 G2 Polotnyanyy U.S.S.R. 54.44N 35.59E
46 G2 Polotsk Belorussiya U.S.S.R. 55.30N 28.43E
39 C1 Polousnyy, Kryazh *ridge* Yakutsk U.S.S.R.
40 E5 Polovinka Amur U.S.S.R. 52.47N 131.30E
42 K3 Polovinka Irkutsk U.S.S.R. 59.12N 116.30E
39 B2 Polovinka Yakutsk U.S.S.R. 66.57N 136.29E
42 J2 Polovinka Yakutsk U.S.S.R. 60.05N 113.50E
45 K7 Polovinkino Ukraine U.S.S.R. 49.13N 38.55E
47 J8 Polovinnoye Kurgan U.S.S.R. 54.40N 63.52E
47 K8 Polovinnoye Kurgan U.S.S.R. 54.50N 65.55E
41 E5 Polovinnoye, Oz *L* U.S.S.R. 70.14N 87.45E
47 G4 Polovniki U.S.S.R. 62.30N 50.45E
41 E7 Poloy U.S.S.R. 66.45N 86.30E
56 B7 Polperro Cornwall Eng 50.19N 4.31W
103 O4 Polpis Massachusetts 41.18N 70.00W
26 R6 Polpitigama Sri Lanka 7.48N 80.25E
65 L7 Pöls *R* Austria
60 H12 Polsbroek Netherlands 51.59N 4.51E
110 L2 Polson Montana 47.41N 114.10W
65 K7 Pöls-tal *V* Austria
47 E3 Polta *R* U.S.S.R.
62 M7 Poltár Czechoslovakia 48.27N 19.45E
45 F7 Poltava Ukraine U.S.S.R. 49.35N 34.35E
47 L8 Poltavka Omsk U.S.S.R. 54.24N 71.49E
40 E9 Poltavka Primor'ye U.S.S.R. 44.02N 131.24E
45 F7 Poltavskaya Oblast' *prov* Ukraine U.S.S.R.
99 P7 Poltimore Quebec 45.46N 75.44W
46 F1 Põltsamaa Estonia U.S.S.R. 58.40N 26.00E
47 M4 Poludennyy U.S.S.R. 56.29N 59.25E
39 H7 Poludennyy, Mys *C* Komandorskiye O-va U.S.S.R. 54.57N 166.15E
43 J1 Poludino Kazakhstan U.S.S.R. 54.51N 69.53E
47 J5 Polunochnoye U.S.S.R. 60.52N 60.28E
41 H3 Poluostrovnoy, Mys *C* U.S.S.R. 77.21N 102.00E
Polur *see* Pulu
28 D4 Polur Tamil Nadu India 12.31N 79.05E
65 K4 Poluška *mt* Czechoslovakia 48.46N 14.26E
47 K3 Poluy *R* U.S.S.R.
109 D7 Polvadera New Mexico 34.12N 106.56W
80 D3 Polveraia Italy 42.47N 11.19E
80 F2 Polvese, I Italy 43.07N 12.08E
51 O9 Polvijärvi Finland 62.53N 29.20E
115 O8 Polvoxal Mexico 18.38N 91.14W
58 M7 Polwarth Borders Scotland 55.45N 2.25W
100 L5 Polwarth Saskatchewan 53.27N 106.43W
62 L1 Półwysep Hel *pen* Poland
47 K5 Pol'yanovo U.S.S.R. 61.34N 66.50E
39 L2 Polyarnik U.S.S.R. 66.58N 178.52W
39 D1 Polyarnyy U.S.S.R. 71.15N 149.20E
47 C2 Polyarnyy Murmansk U.S.S.R. 69.14N 33.30E
39 C1 Polyarnyy U.S.S.R. 69.45N 141.48E
39 K1 Polyarnyy U.S.S.R. 69.10N 179.16E
41 Q6 Polyarnyy Yakutsk U.S.S.R. 69.42N 141.50E
41 R5 Polyarnyy Yakutsk U.S.S.R. 71.10N 149.30E
47 C3 Polyarnyye Zori U.S.S.R. 67.28N 32.25E
39 E3 Polyarnyy, Khrebet *ra* U.S.S.R.
47 J3 Polyarnyy Ural *mts* U.S.S.R.
113 N5 Polychrome Pass Alaska 63.30N 149.59W
122 K12 Polynesia *ethnic reg* Pacific Oc
45 S10 Polynnoye Kalmyk A.S.S.R. U.S.S.R. 46.54N 46.50E
42 D5 Polysayevo U.S.S.R. 54.39N 86.16E
56 B6 Polzeath Cornwall Eng 50.34N 4.54W
64 N2 Pölzig E Germany 50.57N 12.11E
115 N8 Pom Mexico 18.39N 92.12W
15 C4 Pom Yapen I, Irian Jaya 1.38S 135.40E
120 B3 Pomabamba Peru 8.48S 77.30W
120 D6 Pomacanchi Peru 14.05S 71.35W
11 D12 Pomahaka R New Zealand
119 B10 Pomahuaca Peru 5.59S 79.15W
121 C2 Pomán Argentina 28.26S 66.15W
19 C8 Pomana Besar *isld* Indonesia 8.21S 122.19E
75 L4 Pomar Spain 41.51N 0.07E
80 C2 Pomarance Italy 43.18N 10.52E
76 D13 Pomarão Portugal 37.33N 7.32W
76 L3 Pomar de Valdivia Spain 42.46N 4.10W
72 C8 Pomarez France 43.38N 0.49W
105 F3 Pomaria S Carolina 34.14N 81.26W
81 N2 Pomarico Italy 40.31N 16.33E
51 J10 Pomarkku Finland 61.40N 22.00E
120 D7 Pomata Peru 16.16S 69.16W
31 D5 Pomazai Afghanistan 31.55N 66.17E
118 G7 Pomba *R* Brazil
76 B9 Pombal Beira Litoral Portugal 39.55N 8.38W
117 C6 Pombal Pará Brazil 2.20S 52.00W
117 H8 Pombal Paraíba Brazil 6.45S 37.45W
76 E6 Pombal Portugal 41.16N 7.21W
117 C8 Pombal, R Brazil
120 G2 Pombas, R Brazil
76 C8 Pombeiro Portugal 40.13N 8.08W
84 L12 Pómbia Crete 35.00N 24.51E
118 D7 Pombo *R* Brazil
71 G10 Pomègues, Ile France 43.16N 5.17E
75 G4 Pomer Spain 41.38N 1.50W
62 G2 Pomerania *reg* Poland/E Ger
111 O9 Pomerene Arizona 32.01N 110.19W
117 A1 Pomeroon *R* Guyana
108 Q7 Pomeroy Iowa 42.34N 94.41W
104 C7 Pomeroy Ohio 39.03N 82.03W
95 O4 Pomeroy S Africa 28.34S 30.27E
59 J2 Pomeroy Tyrone N Ireland 54.36N 6.55W
110 H3 Pomeroy Washington 46.29N 117.36W
80 F5 Pomezia Italy 41.40N 12.29E
103 L3 Pomfret Connecticut 41.54N 71.56W
95 G1 Pomfret S Africa 25.50S 23.32E
103 L3 Pomfret Center Connecticut 41.53N 71.57W
80 K7 Pomigliano d'Arco Italy 40.55N 14.25E
15 L6 Pomio New Britain 5.31S 151.30E
71 F2 Pommard France 47.01N 4.48E
108 P4 Pomme de Terre *R* Minnesota
107 C4 Pomme de Terre *R* Missouri
107 C4 Pomme de Terre *res* Missouri
64 M4 Pommelsbrunn W Germany 49.30N 11.32E
70 D4 Pommerit-Jaudy France 48.44N 3.15W
70 D4 Pommerit-le-Vicomte France 48.37N 3.06W
61 E5 Pommerœul Belgium 50.28N 3.43E
72 H2 Pommiers France 46.32N 1.37E
25 M7 Pomna Assam India 27.57N 96.23E
115 P9 Pomona Belize 17.00N 88.20W
111 G7 Pomona California 34.04N 117.45W
109 P3 Pomona Kansas 38.37N 95.27W
103 B8 Pomona Maryland 39.10N 76.06W
107 E5 Pomona Missouri 36.52N 91.55W
94 C6 Pomona Namibia 27.09S 15.18E
103 E8 Pomona New Jersey 39.28N 74.34W
103 F4 Pomona New York 41.11N 74.03W
13 L7 Pomona Queensland 26.20S 152.47E
109 P3 Pomona Res Kansas
82 L8 Pomorie Bulgaria 42.32N 27.39E
47 D4 Pomorskiy Bereg *coast* U.S.S.R.
82 J1 Pomoryany U.S.S.R. 49.36N 24.56E
84 Q14 Pomos Cyprus 35.09N 32.33E
45 C8 Pomoshnaya Ukraine U.S.S.R. 48.13N 31.36E
84 Q14 Pomos Pt Cyprus 35.10N 32.34E
Pomo Tso *L see* Puma Yumco
66 B1 Pomoy France 47.40N 6.21E
47 G5 Pomozdino U.S.S.R. 62.12N 54.10E
72 D2 Pompaire France 46.37N 0.14W
105 G11 Pompano Beach Florida 26.14N 80.07W
26 Q4 Pomparippu Sri Lanka 8.22N 79.52E
80 K7 Pompei Italy 40.45N 14.27E
118 E8 Pompéia Brazil 22.07S 50.11W
118 G6 Pompéu Brazil 19.16S 44.58W
104 J4 Pompey New York 42.54N 76.01W
40 E7 Pompeyevka U.S.S.R. 48.22N 130.55E
110 S4 Pompeys Pillar Montana 45.59N 107.56W
79 G4 Pompiano Italy 45.26N 9.59E
71 D9 Pompignan France 43.54N 3.51E
94 G5 Pompom S Africa 25.50S 23.32E
103 F4 Pompton Lakes New Jersey 41.01N 74.16W
92 F10 Pompué *R* Mozambique
98 L8 Pomquet Nova Scotia 45.34N 61.50W
64 O1 Pomssen E Germany 51.14N 12.38E
66 C4 Pomy Switzerland 46.46N 6.40E
47 K4 Pomyt U.S.S.R. 63.30N 68.28E
47 K4 Pomyt *R* U.S.S.R.
24 H9 Pon *R* Xizang Zizhiqu
100 O6 Ponass L Saskatchewan
108 O7 Ponca Nebraska 42.35N 96.42W
109 N5 Ponca City Oklahoma 36.41N 97.04W
105 J7 Ponce Puerto Rico 18.01N 66.36W
105 B7 Ponce de Leon Florida 30.42N 85.58W
105 F12 Ponce de Leon B Florida
105 G8 Ponce de Leon Inlet Florida 29.04N 80.54W
107 F11 Ponchatoula Louisiana 30.26N 90.27W
71 G4 Poncin France 46.05N 5.25E
115 H7 Poncitlán Mexico 20.25N 102.54W
14 F2 Pond, C W Australia 14.44S 125.13E
109 N5 Pond Creek Oklahoma 36.41N 97.41W
103 E4 Pond Eddy New York 41.26N 74.49W
112 K2 Ponder Texas 33.12N 97.19W
56 L4 Ponders End London Eng 51.39N 0.03W
28 D5 Pondicherry India 11.59N 79.50E
84 J10 Pondikonísi *isld* Crete
97 M3 Pond Inlet N W Terr 72.40N 77.59W
15 L6 Pondo New Britain 4.30S 151.38E
18 A6 Pondok Tanjong Pen Malaysia 5.00N 100.43E
95 N7 Pondoland *reg* S Africa
110 D8 Pondosa California 41.13N 121.42W
110 H4 Pondosa Oregon 45.01N 117.39W
61 L6 Pondrome Belgium 50.06N 5.00E
115 L3 Poneloya Nicaragua 12.22N 87.01W
108 Q1 Ponemah Minnesota 48.02N 94.51W
81 E10 Ponente, C Lampedusa, I di Italy 35.31N 12.32E
9 B13 Ponérihuen New Caledonia 21.01S 165.21E
19 N5 Pones *isld* Truk Is Pacific Oc 7.13N 151.59E
106 J9 Poneto Indiana 40.38N 85.13W
44 C3 Ponezhukay U.S.S.R. 44.53N 39.25E
76 F3 Ponferrada Spain 42.33N 6.35W
Pong *see* Ban Pong
76 J2 Ponga Spain 43.11N 5.10W
91 A3 Pongara, Pte Gabon 0.23N 9.20E
11 L7 Pongaroa New Zealand 40.32S 176.14E
65 H7 Pongau *reg* Austria
28 K2 Pongchad Assam India 26.50N 95.18E
21 C9 Ponggang-ni N Korea 37.42N 125.25E
23 C1 Ponggartang Gansu China 35.10N 102.50E
24 G12 Pongkhua Bhutan 26.44N 90.05E
19 B6 Pongkolaero Indonesia 5.24S 121.56E
87 A7 Pongo *watercourse* Sudan
120 B1 Pongo de Manseriche *gorge* Peru 14.27S 77.37W
94 L6 Pongola Natal S Africa 27.22S 31.37E
95 O8 Pongola S Africa 27.23S 31.38E
95 O8 Pongola *R* S Africa
47 C3 Pon'goma U.S.S.R. 65.15N 34.21E
51 R6 Pongoma, Ozero *L* Karelia U.S.S.R. 65.20N 33.00E
92 J4 Pongwe Tanzania 5.10S 39.00E
92 K11 Pongwe Zanzibar 6.02S 39.24E
20 C6 Pŏngyŏng S Korea 35.34N 129.22E
98 H9 Ponhook L Nova Scotia
98 H9 Ponhook Lake Nova Scotia
63 T10 Ponickau E Germany 51.20N 13.48E
62 K4 Poniec Poland 51.48N 16.50E
19 C3 Poniki, Gunung *mt* Celebes Indon 0.27N 123.48E
19 B4 Ponindilisa, Tandjung *C* Celebes Indonesia 0.55S 120.25E
45 C1 Ponizovye U.S.S.R. 55.16N 31.06E
25 B2 Ponnagyun Burma 20.19N 93.02E
28 D4 Ponnaiyar R Karnataka/Tamil Nadu India
28 B4 Ponnampet Karnataka India 12.08N 75.58E
28 B5 Ponnani Kerala India 10.46N 75.57E
28 C5 Ponnani *R* Kerala India
28 E4 Ponneri Tamil Nadu India 13.21N 80.10E
25 C1 Ponnyadaung Ra Burma
15 C7 Pono Moluccas Indon 6.21S 134.37E
100 D6 Ponoka Alberta 52.42N 113.33W
46 R3 Ponomarevka U.S.S.R. 53.20N 54.01E
45 D5 Ponornitsa Ukraine U.S.S.R. 51.44N 32.52E
18 J9 Ponorogo Java Indon 7.51S 111.30E
47 E3 Ponoy U.S.S.R. 67.02N 41.03E
47 D3 Ponoy *R* U.S.S.R.
72 C4 Pons France 45.35N 0.32W
75 N4 Pons Spain 41.55N 1.12E
79 J7 Ponsacco Italy 43.37N 10.37E
19 M6 Ponson *isld* Philippines 10.45N 124.30E
11 C2 Ponsonby *dist* Auckland New Zealand
76 E9 Ponsul *R* Portugal
79 B3 Pont Italy 45.32N 7.12E
61 H4 Pont-à-Celles Belgium 50.31N 4.22E
72 D9 Pontacq France 43.11N 0.06W
96 V1 Ponta de Arnel Azores 37.36N 25.09W
96 U2 Ponta de Garça Azores 37.28N 25.23W
96 O2 Ponta Delgada Azores 39.21N 31.09W
96 T2 Ponta Delgada Azores 37.29N 25.40W
117 D5 Ponta de Pedras Brazil 1.23S 48.51W
117 C2 Ponta dos Indios Brazil 4.05N 51.34W
96 P7 Ponta do Sol Madeira Is 32.41N 17.07W
118 E9 Ponta Grossa Brazil 25.07S 50.09W
71 G2 Pontailler-sur-Saône France 47.18N 5.25E
71 G7 Pontaix France 44.45N 5.15E
118 E2 Pontal Goiás Brazil 10.42S 48.31W
118 E7 Pontal São Paulo Brazil 21.01S 48.06W
117 G9 Pontal *R* Pernambuco Brazil
118 E5 Pontalina Brazil 17.31S 49.27W
69 E2 Pont-à-Marcq France 50.31N 3.07E
69 L6 Pont-à-Mousson France 48.55N 6.03E
121 E6 Pontant Argentina 37.44S 61.22W
76 C9 Pontão Portugal 39.53N 8.23W
119 H9 Ponta Pelada *airport* Brazil 3.10S 60.05W
118 C8 Ponta Porã Brazil 22.27S 55.39W
56 D4 Pontardawe W Glam Wales 51.44N 3.51W
56 C4 Pontarddulais W Glam Wales 51.43N 4.02W
72 H3 Pontarion France 46.00N 1.50E
71 J3 Pontarlier France 46.54N 6.20E
79 K7 Pontassieve Italy 43.47N 11.27E
70 H4 Pontaubault France 48.38N 1.20W
70 M3 Pont Audemer France 49.22N 0.31E
68 J4 Pontault-Combault France 48.48N 2.37E
71 B5 Pontaumur France 45.52N 2.40E
70 C6 Pont-Aven France 47.51N 3.44W
69 F5 Pontavert France 49.25N 3.50E
99 M1 Pontax *R* Ontario
98 K3 Pontbriand B Quebec
79 C4 Pont Canavese Italy 45.25N 7.35E
71 J6 Pontcharra France 45.25N 6.01E
72 J4 Pontcharraud France 45.52N 2.15E
107 F11 Pontchartrain, L Louisiana
70 F7 Pont-Château France 47.27N 2.04W
70 B5 Pont-Croix France 48.03N 4.29W
71 J9 Pont-d'Aiguines France 43.47N 6.13E
71 G4 Pont-d'Ain France 46.03N 5.20E
75 N5 Pont de Armentera Spain 41.23N 1.21E
71 G7 Pont-de-Barret France 44.36N 5.02E
71 H5 Pont-de-Beauvoisin France 45.32N 5.40E
70 M6 Pont-de-Braye France 47.47N 0.42E
70 B5 Pont-de-Buis France 48.15N 4.04W
71 G5 Pont-de-Chéruy France 45.45N 5.10E
70 N3 Pont-de-l'Arche France 49.18N 1.10E
72 J8 Pont-de-Larn France 43.31N 2.24E
61 J5 Pont-de-Loup Belgium 50.25N 4.33E
75 Q3 Pont de Molins Spain 42.19N 2.55E
71 D8 Pont-de-Monvert, le France 44.22N 3.45E
71 H3 Pont-de-Poitte France 46.35N 5.42E
71 G7 Pont-de-Quart France 44.42N 5.25E
98 P10 Pont-de-Québec, Le Quebec 46.46N 71.18W
71 K2 Pont-de-Roide France 47.23N 6.46E
72 K7 Pont de Salars France 44.17N 24.42E
75 M3 Pont de Suert Spain 42.25N 0.44E
71 F4 Pont-de-Vaux France 46.26N 4.56E
71 F4 Pont-de-Veyle France 46.15N 4.53E
71 D8 Pont-d'Hérault France 44.00N 3.40E
56 E2 Pontdolgoch Powys Wales 52.32N 3.27W
71 F2 Pont-d'Ouche France 47.10N 4.42E
70 K4 Pont-d'Ouilly France 48.52N 0.24W
72 F7 Pont-du-Casse France 44.15N 0.43E
71 C5 Pont-du-Château France 45.48N 3.15E
88 O3 Pont du Cheliff Algeria 36.02N 0.18E
71 J7 Pont-du-Fossé France 44.40N 6.11E
71 F9 Pont-du-Gard France 43.57N 4.32E
71 H3 Pont-du-Navoy France 46.43N 5.47E
72 F10 Pont-du-Roi *pass* France 42.52N 0.44E
118 F2 Ponte Alta do Norte Brazil 10.50S 47.40W
79 O1 Pontebba Italy 46.31N 13.18E
80 L7 Pontecagnano Italy 40.38N 14.53E
80 J6 Pontecorvo Italy 41.27N 13.40E
79 E5 Pontecurone Italy 44.58N 8.55E
76 C5 Ponte da Barca Portugal 41.48N 8.25W
79 D7 Pontedassio Italy 43.57N 8.00E
79 E6 Pontedécimo Italy 44.30N 8.54E
76 B5 Ponte de Lima Portugal 41.46N 8.35W
79 G5 Ponte dell'Olio Italy 44.52N 9.39E
118 B3 Ponte de Pedra Mato Grosso Brazil 13.35S 57.21W
118 C5 Ponte de Pedra Mato Grosso Brazil 17.01S 54.32W
79 J7 Pontedera Italy 43.40N 10.38E
76 C10 Ponte de Sor Portugal 39.15N 8.01W
79 J2 Ponte di Legno Italy 46.15N 10.30E
79 M3 Ponte di Piave Italy 45.43N 12.28E
94 N2 Ponte do Pungue Mozambique 19.32S 34.32E
76 A10 Ponte do Rol Portugal 39.05N 9.19W
118 F6 Ponte Firme Brazil 18.03S 46.24W
81 M2 Ponte Fontanelle, L di Italy
57 L5 Pontefract W Yorks Eng 53.42N 1.18W
76 D15 Ponte Frielas Portugal 38.49N 9.09W
80 F5 Ponte Galeria Italy 41.49N 12.21E
79 L1 Ponte Gardena Italy 46.36N 11.33E
80 C2 Ponteginori Italy 43.21N 10.44E
79 G2 Ponte in Valtellina Italy 46.11N 9.58E
100 K9 Ponteix Saskatchewan 49.46N 107.29W
79 L5 Pontelagoscuro Italy 44.53N 11.37E
57 K2 Ponteland Northumb Eng 55.03N 1.44W
80 L6 Pontelandolfo Italy 41.18N 14.42E
67 P12 Ponte Leccia Corsica 42.28N 9.12E
79 M4 Pontelongo Italy 45.14N 12.01E
79 M2 Ponte nell' Alpi Italy 46.11N 12.17E
79 G3 Ponte Nossa Italy 45.52N 9.53E
118 G7 Ponte Nova Brazil 20.25S 42.54W
71 G6 Pont-en-Royans France 45.04N 5.20E
67 P12 Ponte Nuovo Corsica 42.29N 9.16E
79 G5 Pontenure Italy 45.00N 9.47E
72 B7 Pontenx-les-Forges France 44.14N 1.06W
79 G2 Ponteranica, Monte *mt* Italy 46.03N 9.36E
56 D3 Ponterwyd Dyfed Wales 52.25N 3.50W
80 F2 Ponte San Giovanni Italy 43.05N 12.26E
79 L4 Ponte San Nicolò Italy 45.22N 11.57E
79 G3 Ponte San Pietro Italy 45.42N 9.35E
118 B4 Pontes-e-Lacerda Brazil 15.14S 59.21W
79 D4 Pontestura Italy 45.08N 8.20E
98 Q10 Pont Etchemin Quebec 46.46N 71.13W
66 M8 Ponte Tresa Switzerland 45.58N 8.52E
66 M6 Ponte Valentino Switzerland 46.30N 8.57E
76 B4 Pontevedra Spain 42.25N 8.39W
74 B2 Pontevedra *prov* Spain
105 F7 Ponte Vedra Beach Florida 30.13N 81.23W
76 B4 Pontevedra, Ría de *B* Spain
76 B10 Pontével Portugal 39.09N 8.50W
71 F5 Pont-Evêque France 45.32N 4.54E
79 H4 Pontevico Italy 45.16N 10.06E
70 H4 Pontfarcy France 48.56N 1.02W
69 G5 Pont-Faverger France 49.18N 4.20E
72 K4 Pontgibaud France 45.50N 2.51E
70 N5 Pontgouin France 48.29N 1.10E
70 E5 Pont-Hamon France 48.00N 2.44W
70 H3 Pont-Hébert France 49.10N 1.08W
Ponthierville *see* Ubundu
79 D5 Ponti Italy 44.38N 8.22E
106 F9 Pontiac Illinois 40.54N 88.36W
106 L7 Pontiac Michigan 42.39N 83.18W
99 O6 Pontiac, Parc Quebec
18 D9 Pontian *R* Pen Malaysia
18 H6 Pontianak Borneo Indon 0.05S 109.16E
18 D10 Pontian Kechil Pen Malaysia 1.26N 103.24E
61 L4 Pontillas Belgium 50.32N 5.01E
80 H6 Pontinia Italy 41.24N 13.03E
66 N6 Pontirone Switzerland 46.23N 9.01E
70 E5 Pontivy France 48.04N 2.58W
70 B6 Pont-l'Abbé France 47.52N 4.14W
72 C4 Pont l'Abbé d'Arnoult France 45.50N 0.52W
98 H6 Pont Lafrance New Brunswick 47.27N 64.56W
69 H7 Pont-la-Ville France 48.04N 4.54E
66 B5 Pont, le Switzerland 46.41N 6.20E
70 L3 Pont-l'Evêque France 49.17N 0.11E
70 N7 Pontlevoy France 47.24N 1.15E
70 D5 Pont-Melvez France 48.27N 3.18W
117 B3 Pontoetoe Surinam 3.15N 55.20W
Pontoise *see* Cergy-Pontoise
100 S4 Ponton Manitoba 54.40N 99.06W
14 E9 Ponton, Cr W Australia
77 L4 Pontones Spain 38.06N 2.40W
76 J2 Pontón, Pto del *pass* Spain 43.07N 5.01W
75 O5 Pontons Spain 41.25N 1.30E
72 C8 Pontonx-sur-l'Adour France 43.47N 0.55W
59 D4 Pontoon Bridge Mayo Irish Rep 53.59N 9.15W
103 H2 Pontoosuc L Massachusetts 42.30N 73.16W
70 H4 Pontorson France 48.34N 1.30W
107 G7 Pontotoc Mississippi 34.15N 89.01W
112 J5 Pontotoc Texas 30.56N 98.59W
79 G6 Pontremoli Italy 44.23N 9.53E
66 Q6 Pontresina Switzerland 46.30N 9.54E
56 D3 Pontrhydfendigaid Dyfed Wales 52.17N 3.51W
70 D4 Pontrieux France 48.42N 3.09W
56 F4 Pontrilas Hereford & Worcs Eng 51.57N 2.53W
100 N5 Pontrilas Saskatchewan 53.14N 104.02W
99 T6 Pont Rouge Quebec 46.45N 71.43W
71 F8 Pont-St. Esprit France 44.15N 4.39E
69 G7 Pont-Ste. Marie France 48.20N 4.06E
79 C3 Pont St. Martin Italy 45.36N 7.47E
69 D5 Pont-Ste. Maxence France 49.18N 2.37E
70 D6 Pont-Scorff France 47.50N 3.23W
70 J7 Ponts-de-Cé, les France 47.26N 0.31W
66 C4 Ponts de Martel, les Switzerland 47.00N 6.44E
69 F3 Pont-sur-Sambre France 50.14N 3.50E
69 F6 Pont-sur-Seine France 48.31N 3.35E
69 E7 Pont-sur-Yonne France 48.17N 3.13E
118 J10 Pontuda, I Brazil 23.03S 43.19W
37 C5 Pontus *reg* Turkey
70 B4 Pontusval, Pte.de France 48.41N 4.21W
70 L6 Pontvallain France 47.45N 0.11E
99 R9 Pont Viau Quebec 45.34N 73.42W
56 C4 Pontyates Dyfed Wales 51.46N 4.13W
56 E4 Pontypool Gwent Wales 51.43N 3.02W
99 M8 Pontypool Ontario 44.06N 78.38W
56 E4 Pontypridd Mid Glam Wales 51.37N 3.22W
11 K3 Ponui I New Zealand 36.52S 175.12E
110 O4 Pony Montana 45.40N 111.54W
25 L8 Ponyo Burma 26.19N 95.09E
45 H4 Ponyri U.S.S.R. 52.20N 36.18E
80 G7 Ponza Italy 40.53N 12.58E
80 G7 Ponza, I. di Italy
46 M4 Ponzari U.S.S.R. 52.11N 41.39E
80 H7 Ponziane,Isole Italy
79 D5 Ponzone Italy 44.35N 8.27E
12 C5 Poochera S Australia 32.42S 134.52E
91 D5 Pool *div* Congo
11 D12 Poolburn Dam New Zealand 45.16S 169.46E
56 H6 Poole Dorset Eng 50.43N 1.59W
56 H6 Poole Harb Dorset Eng 50.42N 2.00W
12 F3 Poole,Mt New S Wales 29.40S 141.49E
105 F5 Pooler Georgia 32.09N 81.17W
103 B8 Pooles I Maryland 39.17N 76.16W
104 H7 Poolesville Maryland 39.10N 77.24W
58 E3 Poolewe Highland Scotland 57.45N 5.37W
57 H3 Pooley Bridge Cumbria Eng 54.38N 2.49W
91 D6 Pool Malebo *L* Zaïre/Congo 4.15S 15.25E
12 E2 Poolowanna L S Australia
55 G4 Pool, R London England
95 B8 Pools S Africa 32.49S 18.50E
112 K3 Poolville Texas 32.58N 97.53W
28 A1 Poona Maharashtra India 18.34N 73.58E
28 A1 Poona *dist* Maharashtra India
28 E4 Poonamallee Tamil Nadu India 13.02N 80.04E
12 G5 Pooncarie New S Wales 33.25S 142.38E
14 B8 Poondarrie,Mt W Australia 27.47S 116.20E
12 A2 Poondinna, Mt S Australia 27.25S 129.55E
26 R2 Pooneryn Sri Lanka 9.30N 80.13E
12 G4 Poopelloe,L New S Wales
120 E8 Poopó Bolivia 18.23S 66.58W
120 E8 Poopó, L. de Bolivia
12 B7 Pooraka *dist* Adelaide, S Aust
11 J2 Poor Knights Is New Zealand
113 K4 Poorman Alaska 64.06N 155.48W
95 F6 Poortjie S Africa 30.15S 22.46E
60 F12 Poortugaal Netherlands 51.52N 4.23E
119 A3 Popa, I Panama 9.10N 82.09W
45 K8 Popasnaya Ukraine U.S.S.R. 48.38N 38.24E
119 C6 Popayán Colombia 2.27N 76.32W
111 J8 Pope California 33.21N 115.41W
107 G7 Pope Mississippi 34.12N 89.59W
108 R7 Popejoy Iowa 42.36N 93.23W
42 J6 Poperechnoye U.S.S.R. 52.24N 110.45E
45 P9 Poperechnyy U.S.S.R. 47.32N 43.31E
39 J3 Poperechnyy Algan *R* U.S.S.R.
61 A3 Poperinge Belgium 50.52N 2.44E
104 J8 Popes Creek Maryland 38.24N 77.00W
104 Q3 Popham Beach Maine 43.44N 69.50W
41 K5 Popigay U.S.S.R. 72.01N 110.39E
41 J4 Popigay *R* U.S.S.R.
12 F5 Popiltah New S Wales 33.15S 141.49E
12 F5 Popiltah L New S Wales 33.09S 141.45E
45 Q6 Popki U.S.S.R. 50.11N 44.31E
55 G3 Poplar London Eng 51.31N 0.01W
108 E1 Poplar Montana 48.08N 105.12W
106 C3 Poplar Wisconsin 46.34N 91.48W
108 P2 Poplar *R* Minnesota
107 F5 Poplar Bluff Missouri 36.46N 90.25W
108 E1 Poplar Cr Montana
100 U8 Poplarfield Manitoba 50.52N 97.37W
100 U8 Poplar Point Manitoba 50.04N 97.57W
100 U6 Poplar Pt Manitoba 52.58N 97.28W
100 U6 Poplar R Manitoba
107 G11 Poplarville Mississippi 30.50N 89.32W
45 M3 Poplevino U.S.S.R. 53.46N 40.06E
45 L3 Poplevinskiy U.S.S.R. 53.42N 39.34E
115 K8 Popocatepetl *vol* Mexico 19.02N 98.38W
113 G9 Popof I Alaska 55.20N 160.30W
18 J10 Popoh Java Indon 8.15S 111.48E
91 E6 Popokabaka Zaïre 5.41S 16.40E
80 J4 Popoli Italy 42.10N 13.50E
15 L3 Popomanaseu, Mt Guadalcanal I Solomon Is 9.45S 160.03E
15 K8 Popondetta Papua New Guinea 8.45S 148.15E
Popovicheskaya *see* Kalininskaya
45 N7 Popovka U.S.S.R. 49.14N 41.14E
39 E3 Popovka *R* U.S.S.R.
82 K7 Popovo Bulgaria 43.20N 26.14E
64 M5 Poppberg *mt* W Germany 49.24N 11.35E
61 L1 Poppel Belgium 51.27N 5.02E
64 J3 Poppenhausen W Germany 50.05N 10.10E
79 L7 Poppi Italy 43.43N 11.46E
62 M6 Poprad Czechoslovakia 49.03N 20.12E
62 M6 Poprad *R* Czech/Poland
115 P9 Poptún Guatemala 16.23N 89.27W
76 E6 Pópulo Portugal 41.22N 7.30W
80 B3 Populónia Italy 42.59N 10.30E
120 E10 Poquis, Nevados de *pk* Bolivia/Chile 23.05S 67.02W
104 J9 Poquoson Virginia 37.08N 76.21W
29 J6 Porahat Bihar India 22.35N 85.27E
31 D7 Porali R Pakistan
11 L7 Porangahau New Zealand 40.18S 176.39E
11 L7 Porangahau R New Zealand
118 E3 Porangatu Brazil 13.28S 49.14W
29 A7 Porbandar Gujarat India 21.40N 69.40E
119 C4 Porce, R Colombia
61 L7 Porcheresse Luxembourg Belgium 49.58N 5.05E
61 L5 Porcheresse Namur Belgium 50.21N 5.14E
101 H9 Porcher I Br Columbia 54.00N 130.30W
76 C14 Porches Portugal 37.07N 8.25W
79 N3 Porcia Italy 45.58N 12.37E
120 E8 Porco Bolivia 19.50S 66.00W
118 F3 Porcos *R* Brazil
77 H5 Porcuna Spain 37.52N 4.11W
113 Q3 Porcupine *R* Alaska etc
13 G5 Porcupine *R* Queensland
101 D2 Porcupine *R* Yukon Terr
96 J3 Porcupine Bank Atlantic Oc
108 D1 Porcupine Creek Montana
100 C8 Porcupine Hills Alberta
100 Q6 Porcupine Hills Man/Sask
106 E3 Porcupine Mts Michigan
100 O6 Porcupine Plain Saskatchewan 52.36N 103.15W
79 N3 Pordenone Italy 45.58N 12.39E
82 J7 Pordim Bulgaria 43.23N 24.51E
79 L2 Pordoi, Passo di *pass* Italy 46.29N 11.50E
119 E5 Pore Colombia 5.42N 71.59W
82 B5 Poreč Yugoslavia 45.14N 13.36E
118 D8 Porecatu Brazil 22.43S 51.25W
45 B1 Porech'ye Pskov U.S.S.R. 56.06N 30.29E
47 J6 Porech'ye Sverdlovsk U.S.S.R. 58.04N 64.06E
45 S1 Poretskoye U.S.S.R. 55.12N 46.19E
67 P11 Poretta *airport* Corsica 42.33N 9.27E
11 K7 Porewa New Zealand 40.02S 175.28E
30 L8 Poreya Bihar India 24.41N 87.11E
121 D8 Pórfida, Pta *C* Argentina 41.45S 65.00W

72 B6 **Porge,le** France 44.53N 1.06W
15 G6 **Porgera** Papua New Guinea 5.32S 143.08E
51 J10 **Pori** Finland 61.28N 21.45E
65 L1 **Poříčany** Czechoslovakia 50.07N 14.55E
65 L2 **Poříčí nad Sázavou** Czechoslovakia 49.50N 14.41E
65 L3 **Pořin** Czechoslovakia 49.25N 14.54E
11 D4 **Porirua** New Zealand 41.08S 174.52E
11 D4 **Porirua East** New Zealand 41.08S 174.53E
11 J8 **Porirua Harb** *inlet* New Zealand
96 R15 **Poris de Abona** Tenerife Canary Is 28.09N 16.26W
35 F3 **Poriyya** Israel 32.44N 35.32E
51 H5 **Porjus** Sweden 66.57N 19.50E
53 N11 **Porkere** Faeroes 61.29N 6.45W
46 G1 **Porkhov** U.S.S.R. 57.43N 29.31E
51 L12 **Porkkala** Finland 60.00N 24.25E
119 G2 **Porlamar** Venezuela 11.01N 63.54W
79 F2 **Porlezza** Italy 46.02N 9.08E
56 D5 **Porlock** Somerset Eng 51.14N 3.36W
76 J3 **Porma** *R* Spain
76 J3 **Porma, Embalse de** *res* Spain
64 L6 **Pörnbach** W Germany 48.36N 11.28E
70 F7 **Pornic** France 47.07N 2.05W
70 F7 **Pornichet** France 47.17N 2.20W
19 M6 **Poro** *isld* Philippines 10.39N 124.27E
47 D4 **Porog** Arkhangel'sk U.S.S.R. 63.50N 38.32E
47 H5 **Porog** Komi U.S.S.R. 62.04N 56.40E
120 F8 **Poroma** Bolivia 18.30S 65.28W
40 J7 **Poronaysk** Sakhalin U.S.S.R. 49.13N 143.05E
11 K5 **Porootarao** New Zealand 38.34S 175.20E
84 F7 **Póros** Greece 37.30N 23.27E
84 F6 **Póros** *isld* Greece 37.31N 23.29E
47 C4 **Porosozero** U.S.S.R. 62.45N 32.48E
42 C4 **Porotnikovo** U.S.S.R. 57.05N 82.21E
47 G4 **Porozhsk** U.S.S.R. 63.55N 53.37E
42 G4 **Porozhskiy** U.S.S.R. 56.02N 101.50E
65 P7 **Porpac** Hungary 47.15N 16.49E
123 H3 **Porpoise B** Antarctica
11 D13 **Porpoise B** New Zealand
96 B11 **Porpoise Pt** Ascension I 7.54S 14.22W
76 D4 **Porquera** Spain 42.01N 7.50W
71 J10 **Porquerolles, I.de** France 43.00N 6.13E
99 K4 **Porquis Junction** Ontario 48.43N 80.46W
80 K5 **Porrara, Monte** Italy 41.58N 14.06E
66 E2 **Porrentruy** Switzerland 47.25N 7.06E
75 M5 **Porrera** Spain 41.11N 0.51E
77 W14 **Porreras** Balearic Is 39.30N 3.01E
79 J6 **Porretta Terme** Italy 44.09N 10.58E
81 J10 **Porri, Isole de'** Sicily 36.41N 14.57E
76 B4 **Porriño** Spain 42.10N 8.38W
77 N4 **Porrón** *mt* Spain 38.28N 1.52W
47 C3 **Porr'ya Guba** U.S.S.R. 66.50N 33.45E
30 B6 **Porsa** Madhya Prad India 26.40N 78.22E
51 K1 **Porsa** Norway 70.23N 23.37E
51 L1 **Porsangen** *inlet* Norway
52 E7 **Porsgrunn** Norway 59.10N 9.40E
53 U18 **Porsmyr** Norway 60.24N 6.15E
70 A4 **Porspoder** France 48.31N 4.45W
63 Q9 **Porst** E Germany 51.47N 12.00E
36 F3 **Porsuk** *R* Turkey
36 E3 **Porsuk Barajı** *dam* Turkey 39.39N 30.20E
47 L3 **Pors'yakha** U.S.S.R. 67.22N 71.00E
67 P12 **Porta** Corsica 42.25N 9.21E
72 H10 **Porta** France 42.31N 1.48E
84 E3 **Pórta** *mt* Greece 39.15N 22.40E
120 F7 **Portachuelo** Bolivia 17.20S 53.23W
77 Q1 **Porta Coeli** Spain 39.42N 0.28W
79 D5 **Portacomaro** Italy 44.58N 8.16E
12 E5 **Port Adelaide** S Australia 34.52S 138.30E
59 K3 **Portadown** Armagh N Ireland 54.26N 6.27W
11 C13 **Port Adventure** *inlet* Stewart I New Zealand
59 L3 **Portaferry** Down N Ireland 54.23N 5.33W
113 N6 **Portage** Alaska 60.50N 148.59W
104 Q7 **Portage** Maine 46.45N 68.30W
110 O2 **Portage** Montana 47.38N 111.09W
104 G6 **Portage** Pennsylvania 40.23N 78.41W
98 H7 **Portage** Prince Edward I 46.40N 64.05W
110 N8 **Portage** Utah 41.59N 112.16W
106 E6 **Portage** Wisconsin 43.33N 89.29W
104 B5 **Portage** *R* Ohio
107 F3 **Portage Des Sioux** Missouri 38.57N 90.21W
98 G6 **Portage I** New Brunswick 47.12N 65.03W
100 T9 **Portage la Prairie** Manitoba 49.58N 98.20W
107 G5 **Portageville** Missouri 36.26N 89.42W
104 G4 **Portageville** New York 42.33N 78.03W
76 F9 **Portaje** Spain 39.55N 6.34W
111 P10 **Portal** Arizona 31.55N 109.09W
105 F5 **Portal** Georgia 32.33N 81.58W
108 H1 **Portal** N Dakota 49.00N 102.32W
66 D4 **Portalban** Switzerland 46.56N 6.58E
101 L11 **Port Alberni** Vancouver I, Br Col 49.11N 124.49W
11 J3 **Port Albert** New Zealand 36.16S 174.28E
99 J9 **Port Albert** Ontario 43.53N 81.43W
12 H7 **Port Albert** Victoria 38.09S 146.40E
76 E10 **Portalegre** Portugal 39.17N 7.25W
76 E10 **Portalegre** *dist* Portugal
109 G7 **Portales** New Mexico 34.12N 103.20W
113 U8 **Port Alexander** Alaska 56.15N 134.50W
98 B5 **Port Alfred** Quebec 48.20N 70.54W
95 K9 **Port Alfred** S Africa 33.36S 26.54E
101 K10 **Port Alice** Vancouver I, Br Col 50.23N 127.24W
121 E2 **Portalis** Argentina 29.32S 61.40W
104 G5 **Port Allegany** Pennsylvania 41.48N 78.18W
107 E11 **Port Allen** Louisiana 30.28N 91.11W
13 K6 **Port Alma** Queensland 23.36S 150.51E
75 H6 **Portalrubio** Spain 40.49N 1.03W
77 V14 **Portals Nous** Balearic Is 39.32N 2.34E
110 B1 **Port Angeles** Washington 48.06N 123.26W
116 L2 **Port Antonio** Jamaica, W I 18.10N 76.27W
116 G5 **Port-à-Piment** Haiti 18.20N 74.11W
58 F5 **Port Appin** Strathclyde Scotland 56.33N 5.25W
112 K8 **Port Aransas** Texas 27.50N 97.05W
84 F3 **Portariá** Greece 39.23N 23.00E
59 H5 **Portarlington** Offaly Irish Rep 53.10N 7.11W
Port Arthur China *see* **Lüshun**
Port Arthur Ontario *see* **Thunder Bay**
12 J9 **Port Arthur** Tasmania 43.08S 147.50E
112 O6 **Port Arthur** Texas 29.55N 93.56W
76 B3 **Portas** Spain 42.35N 8.40W
58 D7 **Portaskaig** Islay, Strathclyde Scotland 55.51N 6.07W
77 S12 **Portas,Pta** *pt* Balearic Is 38.50N 1.25E
12 E4 **Port Augusta** S Australia 32.30S 137.27E
98 O5 **Port-au-Port** Newfoundland 48.33N 58.45W
98 O5 **Port-au-Port B** Newfoundland
98 N5 **Port-au-Port Pen** Newfoundland
116 H5 **Port-au-Prince** Haiti 18.33N 72.20W
106 M5 **Port Austin** Michigan 44.04N 82.59W
26 R15 **Port-aux-Français** Kerguelen Ind Oc 49.22S 70.14E
59 M3 **Portavogie** Down N Ireland 54.28N 5.27W
63 J8 **Porta Westfalica** *gap* W Germany
70 G3 **Portbail** France 49.20N 1.42W
59 J1 **Portballintrae** Antrim N Ireland 55.13N 6.32W
58 F7 **Port Bannatyne** Strathclyde Scotland 55.52N 5.05W
107 E11 **Port Barre** Louisiana 30.31N 91.58W
19 J6 **Port Barton** *B* Philippines 10.27N 119.08E
95 D10 **Port Beaufort** S Africa 34.24S 20.49E
93 D5 **Port Bell** Uganda 0.19N 32.38E
95 C3 **Port-Bergé** Madagascar 15.31S 47.40E
98 L8 **Port Bickerton** Nova Scotia 45.06N 61.44W
28 G7 **Port Blair** Andaman Is 11.40N 92.44E
98 S5 **Port Blandford** Newfoundland 48.21N 54.10W
112 N6 **Port Bolivar** Texas 29.22N 94.47W
75 R3 **Port-Bou** Spain 42.25N 3.09E
89 H9 **Port Bouet** Ivory Coast 5.14N 3.58W
13 D2 **Port Bradshaw** *inlet* N Terr Australia
13 B1 **Port Bremer** *inlet* N Terr Australia
70 J5 **Port Brillet** France 48.06N 0.58W
12 E5 **Port Broughton** S Australia 33.38S 137.55E
99 K10 **Port Bruce** Ontario 42.40N 81.00W
99 K10 **Port Burwell** Ontario 42.39N 80.47W
106 D8 **Port Byron** Illinois 41.35N 90.20W
104 J3 **Port Byron** New York 43.03N 76.38W
28 G7 **Port Campbell** *inlet* Andaman Is
29 L6 **Port Canning** W Bengal India 22.19N 88.40E
103 B5 **Port Carbon** Pennsylvania 40.42N 76.10W
99 L7 **Port Carling** Ontario 45.07N 79.36W
57 G3 **Port Carlisle** Cumbria England 54.57N 3.10W
98 F3 **Port Cartier** Quebec 50.03N 66.46W
98 F3 **Port-Cartier-Ouest** Quebec 50.01N 66.53W
11 E12 **Port Chalmers** New Zealand 45.48S 170.38E
11 K3 **Port Charles** New Zealand 36.31S 175.30E
105 E10 **Port Charlotte** Florida 27.00N 82.07W
58 D7 **Port Charlotte** Islay, Strathclyde Scotland 55.45N 6.23W
103 G5 **Port Chester** New York 41.00N 73.40W
113 U7 **Port Chilkoot** Alaska 59.09N 135.20W
113 D4 **Port Clarence** *inlet* Alaska 65.15N 166.40W
101 G9 **Port Clements** Graham I, Br Col 53.41N 132.11W
104 C5 **Port Clinton** Ohio 41.30N 82.58W
13 K5 **Port Clinton** *inlet* Queensland
104 Q3 **Port Clyde** Maine 43.56N 69.16W
99 L10 **Port Colborne** Ontario 42.53N 79.16W
101 M11 **Port Coquitlam** Br Col 49.12N 122.49W
28 G6 **Port Cornwallis** *inlet* Andaman Is
103 C2 **Port Crane** New York 42.09N 75.51W
99 L9 **Port Credit** Ontario 43.33N 79.36W
71 J10 **Port Cros,Ide** France 43.00N 6.23E
26 P15 **Port Curiouse** Kerguelen Ind Oc 49.22S 68.43E
13 K6 **Port Curtis** *inlet* Queensland
99 L9 **Port Dalhousie** Ontario 43.12N 79.16W
98 H5 **Port Daniel** Quebec 48.12N 65.00W
121 E10 **Port Darwin** Falkland Is 51.51S 58.55W
13 B1 **Port Darwin** *inlet* N Terr Australia
71 J1 **Port d'Atelier** France 47.45N 6.03E
12 H9 **Port Davey** *inlet* Tasmania
71 F10 **Port-de-Bouc** France 43.25N 4.58E
26 Q15 **Port Decaen** Kerguelen Ind Oc 49.02S 69.00E
72 C4 **Port d'Envaux** France 45.51N 0.41W
116 H5 **Port-de-Paix** Haiti 19.56N 72.52W
72 F1 **Port-de-Piles** France 47.01N 0.36W
103 B7 **Port Deposit** Maryland 39.37N 76.06W
72 G10 **Port-de-Salau** *pass* France 42.44N 1.07E
18 B9 **Port Dickson** Pen Malaysia 2.31N 101.48E
94 C4 **Port d'Ilheo B** Namibia 23.20S 14.29E
72 E10 **Port d'Oo** *mt* France 42.42N 0.29E
13 H3 **Port Douglas** Queensland 16.25S 145.29E
99 K10 **Port Dover** Ontario 42.47N 80.12W
98 K9 **Port Dufferin** Nova Scotia 44.55N 62.24W
95 O10 **Port Durnford** S Africa 28.55S 31.50E
79 B5 **Porte** Italy 44.54N 7.16E
25 J4 **Porte d'Annam** *pass* Vietnam 17.57N 106.28E
106 H4 **Porte des Morts** *str* Wisconsin
101 H8 **Port Edward** Br Col 54.11N 130.16W
95 O7 **Port Edward** S Africa 31.03S 30.14E
79 M3 **Portegrandi** Italy 45.34N 12.27E
56 C4 **Port Einon** W Glam Wales 51.33N 4.13W
118 G4 **Porteirinha** Brazil 15.44S 43.00W
117 D5 **Portel** Brazil 1.58S 50.45W
72 K9 **Portel** France 43.03N 2.55E
76 D12 **Portel** Portugal 38.18N 7.42W
118 H7 **Portela** Brazil 21.38S 41.59W
76 E15 **Portela** *airport* Portugal 38.46N 9.08W
98 H7 **Port Elgin** New Brunswick 46.03N 64.08W
99 J8 **Port Elgin** Ontario 44.25N 81.23W
116 O8 **Port Elizabeth** Bequia I W I 13.01N 61.15W
103 E8 **Port Elizabeth** New Jersey 39.19N 74.59W
95 J9 **Port Elizabeth** S Africa 33.58S 25.36E
75 L6 **Portellada,La** Spain 40.52N 0.03E
80 J4 **Portella, Passo d** *pass* Italy 42.29N 13.35E
75 K6 **Portell de Morella** Spain 40.32N 0.16W
69 B2 **Portel,le** France 50.42N 1.35E
58 D7 **Port Ellen** Islay, Strathclyde Scotland 55.39N 6.12W
121 E3 **Portena** Argentina 31.00S 62.03W
70 J3 **Port-en-Bessin-Huppain** France 49.21N 0.45W
118 B9 **Porteño** *R* Argentina
72 H10 **Porté-Puymorens** France 42.33N 1.49E
108 O5 **Porter** Minnesota 44.38N 96.10W
108 G7 **Porter** Nebraska 42.03N 103.58W
109 P6 **Porter** Oklahoma 35.53N 95.32W
77 O2 **Portera,La** Spain 39.25N 1.06W
77 Y14 **Porter, Cala en** *B* Balearic Is
80 D4 **Port'Ercole** Italy 42.23N 11.13E
105 D4 **Porterdale** Georgia 33.34N 83.55W
106 G4 **Porterfield** Wisconsin 45.10N 87.50W
57 D4 **Port Erin** Isle of Man U.K. 54.05N 4.45W
101 U5 **Porter L** N W Terr 61.40N 108.00W
101 U7 **Porter L** Saskatchewan 56.22N 107.20W
101 H6 **Porter Landing** Br Col 58.46N 130.05W
58 N4 **Port Erroll** Grampian Scotland 57.25N 1.51W
103 D4 **Porters L** Pennsylvania 41.14N 75.04W
111 E5 **Porterville** California 36.05N 119.02W
95 C9 **Porterville** S Africa 33.01S 19.00E
72 E7 **Porte Ste. Marie** France 44.15N 0.25E
91 K6 **Portes d'Enfer** *rapids* Zaïre 5.15S 26.59E
72 B3 **Portes,les** France 46.15N 1.30W
71 F7 **Portes-lès-Valence** France 44.53N 4.53E
116 K2 **Port Esquivel** Jamaica, W I 17.53N 77.08W
58 L3 **Portessie** Grampian Scotland 57.41N 2.56W
13 B1 **Port Essington** *inlet* N Terr Australia
Port Étienne *see* **Nouadhibou**
72 D6 **Portets** France 44.41N 0.25W
72 G8 **Portet-sur-Garonne** France 43.32N 1.24E
103 G3 **Port Ewen** New York 41.54N 73.58W
76 G9 **Portezuelo** Spain 39.49N 6.29W
12 F7 **Port Fairy** Victoria 38.23S 142.17E
98 L8 **Port Felix** Nova Scotia 45.15N 61.15W
11 K3 **Port Fitzroy** New Zealand 36.10S 175.23E
Port Francqui *see* **Ilebo**
91 A4 **Port Gentil** Gabon 0.40S 8.50E
98 G9 **Port George** Nova Scotia 45.00N 65.10W
12 E5 **Port Germein** S Australia 33.01S 138.00E
107 E10 **Port Gibson** Mississippi 31.58N 91.00W
58 G7 **Port Glasgow** Strathclyde Scotland 55.56N 4.41W
59 K2 **Portglenone** Antrim N Ireland 54.52N 6.29W
58 K3 **Portgordon** Grampian Scotland 57.40N 3.01W
11 J8 **Port Gore** *inlet* New Zealand
58 J2 **Portgower** Highland Scotland 58.06N 3.41W
113 M7 **Port Graham** Alaska 59.20N 151.51W
14 A8 **Port Gregory** *B* W Australia
98 H8 **Port Greville** Nova Scotia 45.25N 64.33W
95 N7 **Port Grosvenor** S Africa 31.23S 29.55E
Port Gueydon *see* **Azeffoun**
101 H12 **Port Guichon** Br Col 49.05N 123.06W
56 E4 **Porth** Mid Glam Wales 51.38N 3.25W
12 L9 **Port Hacking** *inlet* New S Wales
12 M9 **Port Hacking Pt** New S Wales 34.05S 151.11E
101 J11 **Port Hammond** Br Columbia
89 N9 **Port Harcourt** Nigeria 4.43N 7.10E
101 K10 **Port Hardy** Vancouver I, Br Col 50.41N 127.30W
11 H7 **Port Hardy** *inlet* New Zealand
97 M6 **Port Harrison** Quebec 58.25N 78.15W
98 L8 **Port Hastings** C Breton I, N S 45.40N 61.26W
98 L8 **Port Hawkesbury** C Breton I, Nova Scotia 45.36N 61.22W
56 D5 **Porthcawl** Mid Glam Wales 51.29N 3.43W
14 C5 **Port Hedland** W Australia 20.24S 118.36E
Port Heiden *see* **Meshik**
113 H8 **Port Heiden** *B* Alaska
116 L2 **Port Henderson** Jamaica, W I 17.57N 76.58W
104 M2 **Port Henry** New York 44.03N 73.28W
Port Herald Malawi *see* **Nsanje**
110 J1 **Porthill** Idaho 49.00N 116.30W
57 E7 **Porthmadog** Gwynedd Wales 52.55N 4.08W
83 G7 **Porthmós Kafiréos** *str* Greece
56 B2 **Porth Neigwl** *B* Gwynedd Wales 52.48N 4.35W
98 L8 **Port Hood** C Breton I, N S 46.00N 61.32W
106 M6 **Port Hope** Michigan 43.57N 82.43W
99 M9 **Port Hope** Ontario 43.58N 78.18W
98 Q1 **Port Hope Simpson** Labrador, Nfld 52.30N 56.18W
56 T9 **Porthtowan** Cornwall Eng 50.16N 5.14W
111 E7 **Port Hueneme** California 34.09N 119.13W
106 M7 **Port Huron** Michigan 42.59N 82.28W
56 C4 **Porth-y-Rhyd** Dyfed Wales 51.50N 4.09W
84 C3 **Portí** Greece 39.25N 21.37E
80 K7 **Portici** Italy 40.48N 14.20E
26 Q15 **Port, Î du** Kerguelen Ind Oc 49.10S 69.54E
69 L7 **Portieux** France 48.21N 6.20E
82 H6 **Portile de Fier** *gorge* Romania/Yugoslavia
44 J9 **Port Il'ich** Azerbaydzhan U.S.S.R. 38.55N 48.47E
75 F7 **Portilla** Spain 40.18N 2.05W
116 F5 **Portillo** Cuba 19.55N 77.19W
76 K6 **Portillo** Spain 41.28N 4.36W
76 L8 **Portillo de Toledo** Spain 40.04N 4.14W
76 B14 **Portimão** Portugal 37.08N 8.32W
51 M5 **Portimo** Finland 66.08N 26.25E
77 T11 **Portinatx,Cala** *B* Balearic Is
76 B12 **Portinho** Portugal 38.29N 8.59W
57 G3 **Portinscale** Cumbria Eng 54.37N 3.10W
109 M2 **Portis** Kansas 39.34N 98.41W
56 B6 **Port Isaac** Cornwall Eng 50.35N 4.49W
112 K9 **Port Isabel** Texas 26.04N 97.14W
56 F5 **Portishead** Avon Eng 51.30N 2.46W
11 K3 **Port Jackson** New Zealand 36.29S 175.22E
12 K5 **Port Jackson** *inlet* New S Wales
103 H5 **Port Jefferson** Long I, N Y 40.57N 73.04W
103 E4 **Port Jervis** New York 41.22N 74.40W
70 F8 **Port Joinville** France 46.44N 2.21W
116 J2 **Port Kaiser** Jamaica, W I 17.51N 77.37W
119 J4 **Port Kaituma** Guyana 7.44N 59.53W
46 L6 **Port Katon** U.S.S.R. 46.52N 38.49E
13 A2 **Port Keats** N Terr Australia 14.15S 129.35E
101 J11 **Port Kells** Br Col 49.10N 122.43W
12 K5 **Port Kembla** New S Wales 34.30S 150.54E
Port Kennedy *see* **Thursday I**
12 C5 **Port Kenny** S Australia 33.09S 134.42E
44 C8 **Port Khorly** Ukraine U.S.S.R. 46.04N 33.17E
58 L3 **Portknockie** Grampian Scotland 57.42N 2.52W
Port Láirge *see* **Waterford** Irish Rep
116 P6 **Portland** Barbados 13.16N 59.37W
109 E3 **Portland** Colorado 38.23N 105.03W
103 J3 **Portland** Connecticut 41.34N 72.37W
56 G6 **Portland** Dorset Eng 50.33N 2.27W
106 K9 **Portland** Indiana 40.25N 84.58W
104 P3 **Portland** Maine 43.41N 70.18W
106 K7 **Portland** Michigan 42.52N 84.53W
108 N2 **Portland** N Dakota 47.30N 97.22W
12 J5 **Portland** New S Wales 33.20S 150.00E
11 J2 **Portland** New Zealand 35.48S 174.20E
99 O8 **Portland** Ontario 44.41N 76.13W
110 C4 **Portland** Oregon 45.32N 122.40W
103 D5 **Portland** Pennsylvania 40.55N 75.07W
107 K5 **Portland** Tennessee 36.35N 86.31W
112 K8 **Portland** Texas 27.53N 97.21W
12 F7 **Portland** Victoria 38.21S 141.38E
Portland *Lt Ho* Iceland *see* **Dyrhólaey**
116 L2 **Portland** *parish* Jamaica, W I
116 K2 **Portland Bight** *B* Jamaica, W I
56 G6 **Portland Bill** *prom* Dorset Eng 50.31N 2.27W
12 J8 **Portland, C** Tasmania 40.43S 148.08E
101 H8 **Portland Can** *fjord* Alaska/Br Col
98 P3 **Portland Cr.Pond** Newfoundland
13 G6 **Portland Downs** Queensland 24.08S 144.33E
56 G6 **Portland Harb** Dorset Eng 50.35N 2.27W
11 M6 **Portland I** New Zealand 39.17S 177.52E
101 H8 **Portland Inlet** Br Col
96 A12 **Portland Pt** Ascension I 7.58S 14.26W
116 K2 **Portland Pt** Jamaica, W I 17.42N 77.11W
116 K2 **Portland Ridge** *hill* Jamaica, W I 17.44N 77.09W
13 G2 **Portland Roads** Queensland 12.32S 143.23E
116 F6 **Portland Rock** Caribbean Sea
103 E1 **Portlandville** New York 42.32N 74.57W
19 K9 **Port Languyan** Philippines 5.16N 12.05E
72 L9 **Port-la-Nouvelle** France 43.02N 3.03E
59 H5 **Port Laoise** Leix Irish Rep 53.02N 7.17W
12 H8 **Port Latta** Tasmania 40.50S 145.16E
112 L7 **Port Lavaca** Texas 28.36N 96.39W
59 H7 **Portlaw** Waterford Irish Rep 52.15N 7.23W
26 T14 **Port, Le** Réunion Ind Oc 20.55S 55.17E
58 M4 **Portlethen** Grampian Scotland 57.03N 2.07W
11 G10 **Port Levy** New Zealand 43.40S 172.51E
11 O10 **Port Levy** *inlet* New Zealand
104 K3 **Port Leyden** New York 43.34N 75.21W
12 D5 **Port Lincoln** S Australia 34.43S 135.49E
113 M7 **Portlock** Alaska 59.12N 151.45W
56 B7 **Portloe** Cornwall Eng 50.13N 4.54W
57 D3 **Port Logan** Dumfries & Galloway Scotland 54.43N 4.56W
89 C7 **Port Loko** Sierra Leone 8.50N 12.50W
99 L7 **Port Loring** Ontario 45.56N 79.58W
70 D6 **Port-Louis** France 47.42N 3.20W
116 N3 **Port Louis** Guadeloupe W I 16.25N 61.32W
26 U12 **Port Louis** Mauritius, Indian Oc 20.10S 57.30E
26 Q15 **Port Louise** Kerguelen Indian Ocean 49.10S 69.20E
Port Lyautey *see* **Kenitra**
13 D3 **Port McArthur** *B* N Terr Australia
12 F7 **Port Macdonnell** S Australia 38.00S 140.48E
99 L8 **Port McNicoll** Ontario 44.44N 79.49W
12 L4 **Port Macquarie** New S Wales 31.28S 152.25E
59 B8 **Portmagee** Kerry Irish Rep 51.53N 10.22W
58 J3 **Portmahomack** Highland Scotland 57.49N 3.50W
98 F10 **Port Maitland** Nova Scotia 43.59N 66.09W
99 L10 **Port Maitland** Ontario 42.50N 79.35W
77 P5 **Portman** Spain 37.35N 0.50W
28 G7 **Portman Bay** Andaman Is
112 K9 **Port Mansfield** Texas 26.35N 97.26W
97 N6 **Port Manvers** Labrador, Nfld 57.00N 61.20W
116 K1 **Port Maria** Jamaica, W I 18.22N 76.54W
59 K5 **Portmarnock** Dublin Irish Rep 53.26N 6.08W
123 J3 **Port Martin** Antarctica 66.50S 141.30E
26 B12 **Port Mathurin** Rodriguez I Ind Oc 19.41S 63.25E
104 G6 **Port Matilda** Pennsylvania 40.47N 78.04W
72 C5 **Port Maubert** France 45.26N 0.46W
105 G11 **Port Mayaca** Florida 26.59N 80.38W
98 H9 **Port Medway** Nova Scotia 44.07N 64.36W
12 C7 **Port Melbourne** *dist* Melbourne, Vic
101 M11 **Port Mellon** Br Col 49.32N 123.30W
98 H4 **Port Menier** Anticosti I, Que 49.50N 64.20W
89 A1 **Port Minéralier** Mauritania 20.46N 17.03W
113 G8 **Port Moller** Alaska 56.00N 160.40W
113 G8 **Port Moller** *B* Alaska
101 M11 **Port Moody** Br Col 49.13N 122.57W
101 H11 **Port Moody** *inlet* Br Col
101 J10 **Port Moody Conservation Res** Br Col
116 M2 **Port Morant** Jamaica, W I 17.53N 76.20W
59 K2 **Portmore L** Antrim N Ireland 54.33N 6.17W
15 J8 **Port Moresby** Papua New Guinea 9.30S 147.07E
98 N7 **Port Morien** C Breton I, Nova Scotia 46.08N 59.52W
70 N3 **Port-Mort** France 49.10N 1.26E
28 G7 **Port Mouat** Andaman Is
98 H10 **Port Mouton** Nova Scotia 43.58N 64.50W
103 E5 **Port Murray** New Jersey 40.47N 74.55W
13 F1 **Port Musgrave** *inlet* Queensland
58 F5 **Portnacroish** Strathclyde Scotland 56.35N 5.23W
58 D2 **Portnaguran** Lewis, W Isles Scotland 58.15N 6.10W
58 C7 **Portnahaven** Islay, Strathclyde Scotland 55.41N 6.31W
58 B3 **Port nan Long** N Uist, W Isles Scotland 57.42N 7.13W
9 D12 **Port Narevin** New Hebrides 18.39S 169.11E
70 E6 **Port Navalo** France 47.33N 2.55W
112 O6 **Port Neches** Texas 30.00N 93.59W
12 D5 **Port Neill** S Australia 34.07S 136.18E
113 N6 **Port Nellie Juan** Alaska 60.32N 148.10W
116 G3 **Port Nelson** Rum Cay Bahamas 23.41N 74.51W
110 N7 **Portneuf** Idaho 42.49N 112.23W
99 T6 **Portneuf** Quebec 46.42N 71.53W
110 N7 **Portneuf** *R* Idaho
98 B4 **Portneuf,L** Quebec
99 S5 **Portneuf, Parc** Quebec
98 C5 **Portneuf, R** Quebec
110 O7 **Portneuf Res** Idaho 42.55N 111.58W
Portneuf sur Mer *see* **Rivière Portneuf**
103 H8 **Port Newark** New Jersey
11 J8 **Port Nicholson** *inlet* New Zealand
12 E6 **Port Noarlunga** S Australia 35.18S 138.32E
94 D7 **Port Nolloth** S Africa 29.17S 16.51E
59 F2 **Portnoo** Donegal Irish Rep 54.51N 8.28W
103 D8 **Port Norris** New Jersey 39.15N 75.02W
97 N6 **Port-Noveau-Québec** Quebec 58.35N 65.59W
117 F6 **Pôrto** Brazil 3.54S 42.45W
67 O12 **Porto** Corsica 42.17N 8.42E
76 B6 **Porto** Portugal 41.09N 8.37W
76 F4 **Porto** Spain 42.10N 6.53W
76 B6 **Porto** *dist* Portugal
120 E3 **Pôrto Acre** Brazil 9.37S 67.32W
81 A3 **Porto Alabe** *B* Sardinia 40.15N 8.28E
120 E3 **Pôrto Alegre** Amazonas Brazil 8.58S 67.48W
118 H3 **Pôrto Alegre** Bahia Brazil 13.48S 40.46W
118 D7 **Pôrto Alegre** Mato Grosso do Sul Brazil 21.33S 53.31W
117 C7 **Pôrto Alegre** Pará Brazil 4.23S 52.45W
121 H3 **Pôrto Alegre** Rio Grande do Sul Brazil 30.03S 51.10W
91 C11 **Porto Alexandre** Angola 15.50S 11.51E
91 B12 **Porto Alexandre Nat. Park** Angola
118 A3 **Pôrto Amarante** Brazil 13.00S 60.14W
91 C9 **Porto Amboim** Angola 10.47S 13.43E
92 K8 **Porto Amelia** Mozambique 13.00S 40.30E
118 C3 **Pôrto Artur** Brazil 13.14S 55.06W
80 B3 **Porto Azzurro** Italy 42.46N 10.24E
118 D8 **Pôrto Barra do Ivinheima** Brazil 22.56S 53.40W
58 K7 **Portobello** Lothian Scotland 55.58N 3.07W
11 E12 **Portobello** New Zealand 45.51S 170.39E
118 E10 **Pôrto Belo** Brazil 27.10S 48.33W
115 P5 **Portobelo** Panama 9.33N 79.37W
81 B5 **Porto Botte** Sardinia 39.03N 8.33E
113 L8 **Port O'brien** Alaska 57.45N 153.20W
118 C9 **Pôrto Britânia** Brazil 24.33S 54.18W
79 O3 **Porto Buso** Italy 45.43N 13.14E
118 C2 **Pôrto Calueiro** Brazil 10.57S 55.59W
117 J9 **Pôrto Calvo** Brazil 9.02S 35.24W
118 D8 **Pôrto Camargo** Brazil 23.21S 53.44W
80 M5 **Portocannone** Italy 41.55N 15.01E
79 E3 **Porto Ceresio** Italy 45.54N 8.54E
81 D1 **Porto Cervo** Sardinia 41.08N 9.33E
81 Q12 **Porto Cesáreo** Italy 40.15N 17.54E
77 W15 **Porto Colóm** Balearic Is 39.26N 3.15E
118 B5 **Pôrto Conceicão** Brazil 17.11S 57.20W
112 L7 **Port O'Connor** Texas 28.27N 96.26W
81 A2 **Porto Conte** Sardinia 40.36N 8.12E
81 A2 **Porto Conte** *B* Sardinia
76 B13 **Porto Covo** Portugal 37.50N 8.47W
77 W14 **Porto Cristo** Balearic Is 39.32N 3.20E
96 Q7 **Porto da Cruz** Madeira Is 32.46N 16.51W
117 H9 **Pôrto da Fôlha** Brazil 9.50S 37.16W
117 C7 **Pôrto da Lontra** Brazil 4.46S 52.17W
80 J3 **Porto d'Ascoli** Italy 42.55N 13.54E
76 B14 **Porto de Lagos** Portugal 37.12N 8.32W
76 B6 **Porto de Leixões** Portugal 41.11N 8.44W
117 C5 **Pôrto de Mós** Brazil 1.45S 52.13W
76 B9 **Porto de Mós** Portugal 39.36N 8.49W
117 J9 **Pôrto de Pedras** Brazil 9.06S 35.16W
76 C12 **Porto de Rei** Portugal 38.17N 8.24W
118 H4 **Pôrto de Santa Cruz** Brazil 15.31S 41.16W
79 N3 **Porto di Falconera** Italy 45.37N 12.55E
81 A3 **Porto di Foghe** *B* Sardinia 40.12N 8.28E
79 O3 **Porto di San Andrea** Italy 45.43N 13.11E
117 C7 **Pôrto do Barka** Brazil 50.05S 52.06W
120 G5 **Pôrto do Massaca** Brazil 12.32S 61.00W
118 B2 **Porto dos Gauchos** Brazil 11.32S 57.16W
118 D3 **Pôrto dos Meinacos** Brazil 12.37S 53.18W
81 G9 **Porto Empedocle** Sicily 37.18N 13.32E
118 B6 **Pôrto Esperança** Brazil 19.36S 57.24W
118 B4 **Pôrto Esperidião** Brazil 15.50S 58.28W
118 B4 **Pôrto Estrêla** Brazil 15.18S 57.15W
118 F8 **Pôrto Feliz** Brazil 23.11S 47.32W
80 B3 **Portoferráio** Italy 42.49N 10.20E
81 A2 **Porto Ferro** *B* Sardinia 40.42N 8.12E
79 F6 **Portofino** Italy 44.18N 9.12E
58 H6 **Port of Menteith** Central Scotland 56.11N 4.18W
96 U1 **Porto Formoso** Azores 37.34N 25.26W
117 E8 **Pôrto Franco** Brazil 6.21S 47.25W
116 O1 **Port of Spain** Trinidad & Tobago 10.38N 61.31W
79 M5 **Porto Garibaldi** Italy 44.41N 12.14E
67 O12 **Porto, G.di** Corsica 42.15N 8.35E
117 C4 **Pôrto Grande** Brazil 0.43N 51.23W
79 N3 **Portogruaro** Italy 45.46N 12.50E
118 D8 **Pôrto Guareí** Brazil 22.38S 53.36W
118 C5 **Pôrto Jofre** Brazil 17.19S 56.46W
96 U3 **Porto Judeu** Azores 38.39N 27.08W
84 F7 **Pórto-Khéli** Greece 37.20N 23.08E
111 D2 **Portola** California 39.48N 120.28W
51 J9 **Pörtom** Finland 62.44N 21.35E
79 L5 **Portomaggiore** Italy 44.42N 11.49E
81 A3 **Porto Managu** *B* Sardinia 40.20N 8.26E
79 J4 **Porto Mantovano** Italy 45.12N 10.47E
118 C9 **Pôrto Mendes** Brazil 24.28S 54.19W
96 O6 **Porto Moniz** Madeira Is 32.52N 17.12W
76 B3 **Portomouro** Spain 42.58N 8.39W
118 B7 **Pôrto Murtinho** Brazil 21.42S 57.52W
118 E2 **Pôrto Nacional** Brazil 10.41S 48.19W
89 L8 **Porto Novo** Benin 6.30N 2.47E
89 O10 **Porto Novo** Cape Verde 17.04N 25.05W
28 D5 **Porto Novo** Tamil Nadu India 11.30N 79.45E
81 A4 **Porto Palma** *B* Sardinia 39.41N 8.27E
81 E8 **Porto Palo** Agrigento, Sicily 37.34N 12.54E
81 K10 **Portopalo** Siracusa, Sicily 36.41N 15.08E
77 W15 **Porto Petro** Balearic Is 39.21N 3.12E
81 B6 **Porto Pino** *B* Sardinia
67 O13 **Porto Pollo** Corsica 41.42N 8.47E
118 D7 **Pôrto Quinze de Novembro** Brazil 21.45S 52.14W
84 H6 **Pórto Ráfti** Greece 37.53N 24.00E
105 G8 **Port Orange** Florida 29.08N 81.00W
110 C2 **Port Orchard** Washington 47.32N 122.39W
118 J2 **Pôrto Real do Colégio** Brazil 10.09S 36.51W
80 J2 **Porto Recanati** Italy 43.26N 13.39E
110 A7 **Port Orford** Oregon 42.45N 124.30W
91 C7 **Porto Rico** Angola 6.10S 12.30E
89 P11 **Porto Rincão** Cape Verde 15.03N 23.48W
79 P3 **Portoroz** Yugoslavia 45.31N 13.35E
76 C16 **Porto Salvo** Portugal 38.43N 9.18W
80 J2 **Porto San Giórgio** Italy 43.11N 13.49E
80 D4 **Porto San Stéfano** Italy 42.26N 11.06E
118 C9 **Pôrto Santa Helena** Brazil 24.54S 54.23W
117 C5 **Pôrto Santaña** Brazil 0.02S 51.07W
96 R6 **Porto Santo** Madeira Is 33.04N 16.20W
96 R6 **Porto Santo** *isld* Madeira Is 33.04N 16.20W
118 D8 **Pôrto São José** Brazil 22.39S 53.08W
81 A5 **Portoscuso** Sardinia 39.13N 8.22E
118 H5 **Pôrto Seguro** Brazil 16.25S 39.07W
89 K8 **Porto Séguro** Togo 6.15N 1.35E
118 D8 **Pôrto Sete de Setembro** Brazil 22.09S 52.31W
81 A3 **Porto Tangone** *B* Sardinia 40.24N 8.23E
79 M5 **Porto Tolle** Italy 44.57N 12.20E
81 A2 **Porto Tórres** Sardinia 40.51N 8.24E
120 G5 **Pôrto Triunfo** Brazil 13.03S 60.54W
118 D10 **Pôrto União** Brazil 26.15S 51.04W
79 E3 **Porto Valtravaglia** Italy 45.58N 8.40E
67 P13 **Porto Vecchio** Corsica 41.35N 9.16E
67 P13 **Porto Vecchio, G. de** Corsica
120 F3 **Pôrto Velho** Brazil 8.45S 63.54W
79 G6 **Portovenere** Italy 44.03N 9.50E
81 A5 **Porto Vesme** Sardinia 39.12N 8.23E
119 B8 **Portoviejo** Ecuador 1.07S 80.28W
120 C3 **Pôrto Wálter** Brazil 8.13S 72.47W
57 C3 **Portpatrick** Dumfries & Galloway Scotland 54.51N 5.07W
13 B2 **Port Patterson** *inlet* N Terr Australia
11 B13 **Port Pegasus** *inlet* Stewart I New Zealand
103 C7 **Port Penn** Delaware 39.32N 75.35W
99 M8 **Port Perry** Ontario 44.06N 78.58W
12 G7 **Port Phillip B** Victoria
12 E5 **Port Pirie** S Australia 33.11S 138.01E
12 A8 **Port R** S Australia
Port Radium *see* **Echo Bay**
56 T9 **Portreath** Cornwall Eng 50.15N 5.17W
58 D4 **Portree** Skye, Highland Scotland 57.24N 6.12W
100 J8 **Portreeve** Saskatchewan 50.50N 108.58W
26 V2 **Port Refuge** Cocos Is Ind Oc 12.05S 96.51E
93 L10 **Port Reitz** *airport* Kenya 4.02S 39.30E
110 A1 **Port Renfrew** Vancouver I, Br Col 48.33N 124.25W
98 T5 **Port Rexton** Newfoundland 48.23N 53.21W
116 J1 **Port Rhoades** Jamaica, W I 18.27N 77.26W
103 K8 **Port Richmond** Staten I, N Y 40.38N 74.08W
104 C2 **Port Richmond** *dist* Philadelphia, Penn 39.59N 75.06W
11 H9 **Port Robinson** New Zealand 42.55S 173.19E
59 F6 **Portroe** Tipperary Irish Rep 52.53N 8.21W
13 D2 **Port Roper** *inlet* N Terr Australia
11 B7 **Port Ross** *inlet* Auckland Is Pacific Oc
99 K10 **Port Rowan** Ontario 42.38N 80.27W
116 L2 **Port Royal** Jamaica, W I 17.55N 76.52W
105 G5 **Port Royal** S Carolina 32.23N 80.41W
104 H8 **Port Royal** Virginia 38.10N 77.13W
98 G9 **Port Royal Nat Hist Park** Nova Scotia 44.42N 65.41W
105 G5 **Port Royal Sd** S Carolina
59 J1 **Portrush** Antrim N Ireland 55.12N 6.40W
113 E4 **Port Safety** Alaska 64.28N 164.45W
86 H3 **Port Said** Egypt 31.17N 32.18E
105 B8 **Port St.Joe** Florida 29.49N 85.19W
95 N7 **Port St.Johns** S Africa 31.37S 29.32E
71 F10 **Port-St. Louis-du-Rhône** France 43.23N 4.48E
57 D4 **Port St.Mary** Isle of Man U.K. 54.04N 4.44W
72 A1 **Port St.Père** France 47.09N 1.44W
105 G10 **Port Salerno** Florida 27.09N 80.13W
70 A4 **Portsall** France 48.33N 4.42W
59 G1 **Portsalon** Donegal Irish Rep 55.13N 7.37W
121 F9 **Port Salvador** Falkland Is 51.22S 58.15W
106 M6 **Port Sanilac** Michigan 43.25N 82.33W
111 D6 **Port San Luis** California 35.11N 120.45W
98 P3 **Port Saunders** Newfoundland 50.40N 57.18W
65 K8 **Pörtschach** Austria 46.39N 14.08E
58 L7 **Port Seton** Lothian Scotland 55.58N 2.58W
Port Shelter *B* *see* **Ngau Mei Hoi** *bay*
95 O6 **Port Shepstone** S Africa 30.44S 30.28E
101 H8 **Port Simpson** Br Col 54.32N 130.25W
14 D4 **Port Smith** *B* W Australia
116 O7 **Portsmouth** Dominica, W I 15.34N 61.27W
56 J6 **Portsmouth** Hants Eng 50.48N 1.05W
108 P8 **Portsmouth** Iowa 41.39N 95.31W
105 L2 **Portsmouth** N Carolina 35.03N 76.05W
104 P3 **Portsmouth** New Hampshire 43.03N 70.47W
104 C8 **Portsmouth** Ohio 38.45N 82.59W
99 O8 **Portsmouth** Ontario 44.14N 76.33W
103 M3 **Portsmouth** Rhode I 41.37N 71.15W
104 J10 **Portsmouth** Virginia 36.50N 76.20W
122 V7 **Portsmouth Pt** Palmyra I Pacific Oc 5.53N 162.04W
58 F6 **Portsonachan** Strathclyde Scotland 56.20N 5.10W
93 F6 **Port Southby** Kenya 0.12S 34.11E
26 B12 **Port South East** *inlet* Rodriguez I Ind Oc
58 L3 **Portsoy** Grampian Scotland 57.41N 2.41W
Port Stanley *see* **Stanley** Falkland Is
99 J10 **Port Stanley** Ontario 42.40N 81.14W
121 D10 **Port Stephens** Falkland Is 52.10S 61.00W
12 K5 **Port Stephens** *B* New S Wales
59 J1 **Portstewart** Londonderry N Ireland 55.11N 6.43W
13 G2 **Port Stewart** *inlet* Queensland 14.00S 143.50E
85 O10 **Port Sudan** Sudan 19.38N 37.07E
107 G12 **Port Sulphur** Louisiana 29.29N 89.43W
71 J1 **Port-sur-Saône** France 47.42N 6.03E
Port Swettenham *see* **Pelabohan Kelang**
56 D4 **Port Talbot** W Glam Wales 51.36N 3.47W
19 L5 **Port Tambang** *B* Luzon Philippines 13.57N 123.26E
51 M3 **Porttipahdan tekojärvi** *L* Finland
110 C1 **Port Townsend** Washington 48.09N 122.48W
49 C9 **Portugal** *rep* S Europe
26 Q4 **Portugal B** Sri Lanka
98 T6 **Portugal Cove** Newfoundland 47.38N 52.51W
75 D1 **Portugalete** Spain 43.19N 3.01W
91 G7 **Portugalia** Angola 7.22S 20.47E
119 E3 **Portuguesa** *state* Venezuela
119 F3 **Portuguesa R** Venezuela
Portuguese Guinea *see* **Guinea-Bissau**
59 F5 **Portumna** Galway Irish Rep 53.06N 8.13W
76 B8 **Portunhos** Portugal 40.18N 8.32W
98 T5 **Port Union** Newfoundland 48.29N 53.08W
59 C3 **Porturlin** Mayo Irish Rep 54.19N 9.43W
76 B5 **Portuzelo** Portugal 41.42N 8.46W
72 L10 **Port Vendres** France 42.31N 3.06E
93 F5 **Port Victoria** Kenya 0.07N 34.00E
12 E5 **Port Victoria** S Australia 34.30S 137.30E
104 G4 **Portville** New York 42.02N 78.22W
12 E5 **Port Vincent** S Australia 34.50S 137.48E
47 C2 **Port Vladimir** U.S.S.R. 69.25N 33.09E
11 J4 **Port Waikato** New Zealand 37.23S 174.45E
12 E5 **Port Wakefield** S Australia 34.12S 138.11E
14 F2 **Port Warrender** *inlet* W Australia
103 M6 **Port Washington** Long I, N Y 40.50N 73.42W
106 G6 **Port Washington** Wisconsin 43.23N 87.54W
18 A7 **Port Weld** Pen Malaysia 4.48N 100.35E
14 B5 **Port Weld** *B* W Australia 21.22S 115.40E
113 N6 **Port Wells** *inlet* Alaska
105 F5 **Port Wentworth** Georgia 32.09N 81.10W
57 D3 **Port William** Dumfries & Galloway Scotland 54.46N 4.35W
98 H8 **Port Williams** Nova Scotia 45.06N 64.25W
106 C3 **Port Wing** Wisconsin 46.47N 91.23W
45 A1 **Porub'ye** Belorussiya U.S.S.R. 55.44N 29.15E
109 P6 **Porum** Oklahoma 35.22N 95.16W
28 D3 **Porumamilla** Andhra Prad India 15.01N 79.00E
116 J2 **Porus** Jamaica, W I 18.02N 77.25W
37 G8 **Porva Dağ** *mt* Turkey 37.42N 42.31E
121 E5 **Porvenir** Argentina 34.57S 62.13W
121 K9 **Porvenir** Chile 53.15S 70.16W
119 E5 **Porvenir** Colombia 4.45N 71.24W
115 L2 **Porvenir** Honduras 15.45N 86.54W
120 E4 **Porvenir** Pando Bolivia 11.15S 68.43W
120 G5 **Porvenir** Santa Cruz Bolivia 13.58S 61.40W
112 C5 **Porvenir** Texas 30.26N 104.52W
121 F4 **Porvenir** Uruguay 32.22S 57.52W
Porvoo *see* **Borgå**
64 C2 **Porz am Rhein** W Germany 50.50N 7.06E
76 L10 **Porzuna** Spain 39.10N 4.10W
76 L10 **Porzuna, Sa de** *mts* Spain
81 D2 **Posada** Sardinia 40.38N 9.44E
76 K2 **Posada** Spain 43.24N 4.52W
81 D2 **Posada** *R* Sardinia
76 K2 **Posada de Valdeón** Spain 43.11N 4.55W
76 H2 **Posada Llanera** Spain 43.24N 5.52W
118 C10 **Posadas** Argentina 27.27S 55.50W
77 F5 **Posadas** Spain 37.48N 5.06W
77 F4 **Posadilla** Spain 38.11N 5.17W
123 D3 **Posadowsky Bay** Antarctica
66 R6 **Poschiavo** Switzerland 46.19N 10.04E
66 R6 **Poschiavo, L. di** Switzerland
66 R6 **Poschiavo, V** Switzerland
13 H7 **Poseidon** Queensland 25.40S 146.38E
106 L4 **Posen** Michigan 45.16N 83.42W
Posen Poland *see* **Poznań**
75 L2 **Posets, Pico** *mt* Spain
42 C5 **Poseynaya** U.S.S.R. 54.20N 83.25E
107 J3 **Poseyville** Indiana 38.10N 87.47W
Posgam *see* **Zepu**
46 L1 **Poshekhon'ye Volodarsk** U.S.S.R. 58.20N 39.05E
100 O1 **Poshkokagan L** Ontario 49.15N 89.20W
32 F4 **Posht-e Badam** Iran 33.01N 55.25E
32 B4 **Posht-e Kūh** *mts* Iran
32 C2 **Posht Kūh** *mt* Iran
80 K7 **Posillipo, C. di** Italy 40.46N 14.14E
79 K3 **Pósina** Italy 45.48N 11.16E
64 O5 **Pösing** W Germany 49.14N 12.35E
51 N5 **Posio** Finland 66.08N 28.08E
80 K7 **Positano** Italy 40.37N 14.28E
Poskam *see* **Zepu**
19 B4 **Poso** Celebes Indonesia 1.23S 120.45E
19 B4 **Poso** *R* Celebes Indonesia
19 B4 **Poso, Danau** *L* Celebes Indonesia
37 G4 **Posof** Turkey 41.30N 42.44E
21 D10 **Posŏng** S Korea 34.48N 127.05E
45 R2 **Posop** U.S.S.R. 54.10N 45.13E
119 B9 **Posorja** Ecuador 2.46S 80.20W
19 B4 **Poso, Teluk** *B* Celebes Indonesia
42 C6 **Pospelikha** U.S.S.R. 52.00N 81.48E
41 D2 **Pospelova, Bukhta** *B* Novaya Zemlya U.S.S.R.
47 K3 **Pos Poluy** U.S.S.R. 65.04N 69.04E
118 F4 **Posse** Brazil 14.03S 46.19W
64 N3 **Posseck** E Germany 50.19N 12.08E
64 Q2 **Possendorf** E Germany 50.56N 13.41E
64 L8 **Possenhofen** W Germany 47.57N 11.18E
69 H6 **Possesse** France 48.47N 4.46E
121 G8 **Possession B** S Georgia
26 O16 **Possession, Î. de la** Crozet Is Indian Ocean
123 K6 **Possession Is** Antarctica
64 M2 **Pössneck** E Germany 50.40N 11.33E
70 J7 **Possonnière, la** France 47.20N 0.43W
112 J3 **Possum Kingdom L** Texas
110 E5 **Post** Oregon 44.11N 120.28W
112 F2 **Post** Texas 33.14N 101.24W
80 H3 **Posta** Italy 42.33N 13.06E
79 K3 **Posta, Cima** *mt* Italy 45.44N 11.08E
64 N6 **Postau** W Germany 48.37N 12.20E
64 L5 **Postbauer-Heng** W Germany 49.22N 11.25E
56 D6 **Post Bridge** Devon Eng 50.37N 3.54W
25 J6 **Post Deshayes** Cambodia 12.48N 107.10E
26 V12 **Poste de Flacq** Mauritius, Indian Oc 20.09S 57.45E
97 M6 **Poste-de-la-Baleine** Quebec 55.20N 77.50W
61 L1 **Postel** Belgium 51.17N 5.12E
26 V12 **Poste, R. du** Mauritius, Indian Oc
60 U16 **Posterholt** Netherlands 51.07N 6.02E
88 O9 **Poste Weygand** Algeria 24.34N 0.40E
110 J2 **Post Falls** Idaho 47.42N 116.55W
80 M7 **Postiglione** Italy 40.34N 15.14E
18 N9 **Postilyon, Pulau Pulau** *islds* Indon
79 M3 **Postioma** Italy 45.43N 12.09E
65 K5 **Pöstlingberg** Austria 48.21N 14.15E
95 G4 **Postmasburg** S Africa 28.20S 23.05E
56 C3 **Post-Mawr** Dyfed Wales 52.10N 4.21W
118 C2 **Posto Alto Manissauá** Brazil 11.10S 54.46W
82 B5 **Postojna** Yugoslavia 45.46N 14.12E
46 G3 **Postoli** Belorussiya U.S.S.R. 52.30N 28.00E
64 Q3 **Postoloprty** Czechoslovakia 50.22N 13.42E
120 F8 **Postrervalle** Bolivia 18.29S 63.53W
106 C6 **Postville** Iowa 43.04N 91.34W
82 D7 **Posušje** Yugoslavia 43.29N 17.20E
40 E10 **Pos'yet** U.S.S.R. 42.39N 130.47E
19 B8 **Pota** Indonesia 8.21S 120.50E
106 L3 **Potagannissing Bay** Michigan
42 J1 **Potakuy,Porog** *falls* U.S.S.R. 62.55N 110.40E
115 D4 **Pótam** Mexico 27.38N 110.22W
84 C6 **Potamiá** Arkadhía Greece 37.27N 21.48E
84 D8 **Potamiá** Lakonía Greece 36.56N 22.28E
83 G3 **Potamoí** Greece 41.24N 24.09E
24 G10 **Potamolam** *mt* Xizang Zizhiqu 30.35N 91.58E
84 W22 **Potamós** Corfu 39.38N 19.53E
83 F8 **Potamós** Greece 36.18N 22.56E
47 M6 **Potanino** U.S.S.R. 55.10N 61.39E
18 J5 **Po, Tanjong** *C* Sarawak Malaysia 1.45N 110.30E
41 E6 **Potapovo** U.S.S.R. 68.43N 86.15E
119 J5 **Potaro Landing** Guyana 5.20N 59.05W
119 J5 **Potaro,R** Guyana
39 H4 **Potat-Gytkhyn,Oz** *L* U.S.S.R. 60.47N 167.30E
11 N11 **Potato Pt** New Zealand 45.44S 170.39E
95 L2 **Potchefstroom** S Africa 26.42S 27.06E
82 J6 **Potcoava** Romania 44.30N 24.39E
118 H5 **Poté** Brazil 17.48S 41.47W
109 Q6 **Poteau** Oklahoma 35.03N 94.36W
109 Q7 **Poteau** *R* Oklahoma
72 D7 **Poteau,le** France 44.11N 0.17W
115 M3 **Poteca** Honduras 13.52N 85.45W
112 J6 **Poteet** Texas 29.03N 98.36W
29 G8 **Potegaon** Maharashtra India 19.59N 80.12E
82 J7 **Potelu,Lacul** *L* Romania 43.44N 24.20E
46 O4 **Potemkino** U.S.S.R. 50.25N 45.58E
117 J7 **Potengi** *R* Brazil
80 N7 **Potenza** Italy 40.38N 15.48E
80 N7 **Potenza** *prov* Italy
80 H2 **Potenza** *R* Italy
80 J2 **Potenza Picena** Italy 43.22N 13.37E
11 B13 **Poteriteri, L** New Zealand
76 K2 **Potes** Spain 43.10N 4.41W
95 H6 **Potfontein** S Africa 30.12S 24.07E
94 K5 **Potgietersrus** S Africa 24.15S 28.55E
112 J6 **Poth** Texas 29.05N 98.05W
30 L7 **Pothia** Bihar India 25.33N 87.16E
110 F2 **Potholes Res** Washington
44 D5 **Poti** Georgia U.S.S.R. 42.11N 41.41E
80 E2 **Poti,Alpe di** Italy 43.28N 11.58E
70 K4 **Potigny** France 48.57N 0.13W
28 E1 **Potikal** Madhya Prad India 18.31N 80.58E
117 F7 **Poti, R** Brazil
118 H4 **Potiraguá** Brazil 15.37S 39.53W
90 E6 **Potiskum** Nigeria 11.40N 11.03E
110 J3 **Potlach** *R* Idaho
110 J3 **Potlatch** Idaho 46.56N 116.53W
94 F8 **Potloer** *mt* S Africa 31.01S 21.10E
82 K6 **Potlogi** Romania 44.34N 25.34E
120 D6 **Poto** Peru 14.43S 69.35W
23 C9 **Po To An** Hong Kong 22.16N 114.17E
23 C10 **Po Toi Group** *islds* Hong Kong
23 B10 **Po Toi I** Hong Kong 22.10N 114.15E
110 M3 **Potomac** Montana 46.53N 113.35W
104 H7 **Potomac** *R* Virginia/Maryland
104 G7 **Potomac, S.Branch** *R* W Virg
120 F8 **Potosi** Bolivia 19.34S 65.45W
107 F4 **Potosi** Missouri 37.57N 90.49W
120 E9 **Potosi** *dept* Bolivia
111 J6 **Potosi Mt** Nevada 35.58N 115.31W
19 L6 **Pototan** Philippines 10.54N 122.38E
57 F2 **Potrail Water** Strathclyde Scotland
121 B2 **Potrerillo,Paso de** Chile/Arg 29.28S 70.00W
120 D12 **Potrerillos** Chile 26.30S 69.25W
115 Q10 **Potrerillos** Honduras 15.10N 87.58W
115 N5 **Potrerillos** Panama 8.40N 82.29W
112 B7 **Potrero** Mexico 28.49N 105.27W
121 B2 **Potro,Cerro de** *pk* Chile 28.25S 69.40W
120 B1 **Potro R** Peru
63 S8 **Potsdam** E Germany 52.24N 13.04E
104 K2 **Potsdam** New York 44.40N 75.01W
95 L8 **Potsdam** S Africa 32.55S 27.40E
63 Q7 **Potsdam** *reg* E Germany
65 O1 **Potštejn** Czechoslovakia 50.05N 16.18E
13 G3 **Pottalah Cr** Queensland 15.09S 143.01E
28 F1 **Pottangi** Orissa India 18.35N 83.03E
61 E3 **Pottelberg** *mt* Belgium 50.46N 3.43E
65 N5 **Pottenbrunn** Austria 48.15N 15.42E
65 O6 **Pottendorf** Austria 47.55N 16.23E
65 O6 **Pottenstein** Austria 47.58N 16.07E
64 L4 **Pottenstein** W Germany 49.45N 11.26E
108 G8 **Potter** Nebraska 41.15N 103.20W
99 K4 **Potter** Ontario 48.52N 80.50W
103 F2 **Potter Hollow** New York 42.26N 74.15W
56 G5 **Potterne** Wilts Eng 51.20N 2.00W
56 L4 **Potters Bar** Herts Eng 51.42N 0.11W
56 M4 **Potter Street** Essex Eng 51.46N 0.08E
103 E5 **Pottersville** New Jersey 40.43N 74.44W
111 A2 **Potter Valley** California 39.20N 123.06W
106 K7 **Potterville** Michigan 42.37N 85.45W
103 B3 **Potterville** Pennsylvania 41.54N 76.15W
61 D4 **Pottes** Belgium 50.44N 3.25E
56 L3 **Potton** Beds Eng 52.08N 0.14W
111 H2 **Potts** Nevada 39.05N 116.39W

112 L2 **Pottsboro** Texas 33.46N 96.42W
107 G7 **Potts Camp** Mississippi 34.40N 89.19W
65 O6 **Pottschach** Austria 47.43N 16.01E
103 C6 **Pottstown** Pennsylvania 40.15N 75.38W
103 B5 **Pottsville** Pennsylvania 40.41N 76.11W
112 J4 **Pottsville** Texas 31.41N 98.20W
26 U8 **Pottuvil** Sri Lanka 6.53N 81.49E
31 G4 **Potwar** *reg* Pakistan
109 N4 **Potwin** Kansas 37.57N 97.03W
70 H6 **Pouancé** France 47.44N 1.10W
101 N8 **Pouce Coupé** Br Columbia 55.40N 120.08W
26 U12 **Pouce, Le** *mt* Mauritius, Indian Oc 20.12S 57.32E
61 L4 **Poucet** Belgium 50.41N 5.07E
98 T6 **Pouch Cove** Newfoundland 47.47N 52.46W
9 B13 **Pouébo** New Caledonia 20.25S 164.30E
70 J6 **Poueze la** France 47.33N 0.48W
71 D9 **Pouget,le** France 43.35N 3.32E
103 G3 **Poughkeepsie** New York 41.43N 73.56W
103 G3 **Poughquag** New York 41.36N 73.40W
71 C2 **Pougny** France 47.23N 3.01E
72 L1 **Pougues-les-Eaux** France 47.05N 3.06E
72 G1 **Pouillé** France 47.18N 1.17E
72 C8 **Pouillon** France 43.36N 1.00W
71 F2 **Pouilly-en-Auxois** France 47.16N 4.33E
71 E4 **Pouilly-sous-Charlieu** France 46.08N 4.06E
72 K1 **Pouilly-sur-Loire** France 47.17N 2.57E
71 G2 **Pouilly-sur-Saône** France 47.01N 5.07E
72 H1 **Poulaines** France 47.08N 1.40E
70 B5 **Pouldergat** France 48.03N 4.21W
70 B6 **Pouldreuzic** France 47.57N 4.21W
70 C6 **Pouldu,le** France 47.46N 3.32W
71 E4 **Poule-les-Echarmeaux** France 46.08N 4.28E
59 D8 **Poulgorm Bridge** Kerry Irish Rep 51.59N 9.18W
72 G2 **Pouligny St. Pierre** France 46.41N 1.03E
70 F7 **Pouliguen,le** France 47.17N 2.26W
98 B5 **Poulin-de-Courval,L** Quebec
84 E7 **Poulíthra** Greece 37.07N 22.53E
84 E6 **Poulitsa** Greece 37.57N 22.46E
70 C5 **Poullaouen** France 48.20N 3.39W
Poulo Canton,Is.de *see* **Re,Cu Lao**
25 H8 **Poulo Dama,Iles** Vietnam 9.40N 104.20E
25 K6 **Poulo Gambir,Cu Lao** *isld* Vietnam 13.36N 109.21E
61 N4 **Poulseur** Belgium 50.30N 5.35E
104 M3 **Poultney** Vermont 43.30N 73.14W
56 H4 **Poulton** Glos Eng 51.43N 1.51W
57 H5 **Poulton** Lancs Eng 53.51N 3.00W
106 F4 **Pound** Wisconsin 45.06N 88.02W
56 L5 **Pound Hill** W Sussex Eng 51.07N 0.09W
92 F11 **Pounsley** Zimbabwe 18.54S 32.21E
95 H6 **Poupan** S Africa 30.03S 24.09E
95 F2 **Poupan** *salt pan* S Africa 26.36S 22.29E
72 F8 **Poupas** France 43.58N 0.51E
61 L7 **Poupehan** Belgium 49.48N 5.00E
15 F6 **Pourami** Papua New Guinea 4.05S 141.45E
71 H10 **Pourcieux** France 43.28N 5.46E
11 L7 **Pourerere** New Zealand 40.05S 176.52E
11 N5 **Pourewa I** New Zealand 38.25S 178.22E
58 L6 **Pourie Castle** Tayside Scotland 56.30N 2.56W
84 D3 **Pournári** Greece 39.09N 22.19E
123 F13 **Pourquoi Pas I** Antarctica 67.30S 67.30W
69 E8 **Pourrain** France 47.45N 3.24E
71 H10 **Pourrières** France 43.30N 5.44E
71 K5 **Pourri,Mt** France 45.31N 6.52E
121 E6 **Pourtale** Argentina 37.03S 60.35W
72 D10 **Pourtalet,Col du** France 42.49N 0.24W
70 N2 **Pourville** France 49.55N 1.02E
118 B2 **Pouso Alegre** Mato Grosso Brazil 11.46S 57.16W
118 F8 **Pouso Alegre** Minas Gerais Brazil 22.13S 45.49W
71 D10 **Poussan** France 43.30N 3.40E
69 L7 **Poussay** France 48.19N 6.07E
90 G6 **Pousse** Cameroon 10.56N 15.00E
51 O6 **Poussu** Finland 65.48N 29.20E
89 A4 **Pout** Senegal 14.45N 17.00W
11 B13 **Poutama I** New Zealand 47.17S 167.23E
122 C2 **Poutasi** W Samoa, Pacific Oc 14.00S 171.43W
11 J3 **Pouto** New Zealand 36.22S 174.13E
99 Q3 **Poutrincourt,L** Quebec
69 M7 **Pouxeux** France 48.07N 6.33E
72 E9 **Pouyastruc** France 43.16N 0.11E
72 D8 **Pouydesseaux** France 43.59N 0.20W
72 G9 **Pouy-de-Touges** France 43.20N 1.01E
72 C2 **Pouzauges** France 46.47N 0.51W
72 F1 **Pouzay** France 47.05N 0.32E
71 F7 **Pouzin,le** France 44.45N 4.45E
62 L6 **Povář Bystrica** Czechoslovakia 49.08N 18.25E
62 K7 **Považsky Inovec** *mts* Czechoslovakia
75 F8 **Poveda de la Obispalia** Spain 39.56N 2.25W
75 F6 **Poveda de la Sierra** Spain 40.38N 2.02W
77 L3 **Povedilla** Spain 38.42N 2.36W
79 M3 **Povegliano** Italy 45.46N 12.12E
47 C4 **Povenets** U.S.S.R. 62.52N 34.50E
11 N5 **Poverty B** New Zealand
56 L5 **Povey Cross** Surrey Eng 51.10N 0.12W
79 J5 **Poviglio** Italy 44.50N 10.32E
45 K1 **Povlavskiy Posad** U.S.S.R. 55.45N 38.41E
82 F6 **Povlen** *mt* Yugoslavia 44.07N 19.44E
96 V1 **Povoação** Azores 37.30N 25.15W
76 C5 **Póvoa de Lanhoso** Portugal 41.35N 8.17W
76 D15 **Póvoa de Santo Adrião** Portugal 38.48N 9.10W
76 E12 **Póvoa de São Miguel** Portugal 38.13N 7.20W
76 B6 **Póvoa de Varzim** Portugal 41.22N 8.46W
76 D10 **Póvoa,Embalse de** *res* Portugal
76 D9 **Póvoa e Meadas** Portugal 39.31N 7.31W
79 O2 **Povoletto** Italy 46.08N 13.18E
45 O5 **Povorino** U.S.S.R. 51.12N 42.15E
40 B5 **Povorotnaya** U.S.S.R. 53.31N 121.01E
39 F8 **Povorotnyy,Mys** *C* Kamchatka U.S.S.R. 52.17N 158.35E
39 G4 **Povorotnyy,Mys** *C* Magadan U.S.S.R. 60.43N 160.45W
40 F10 **Povorotnyy,Mys** *C* Primor'ye U.S.S.R. 42.40N 133.05E
97 M5 **Povungnituk** Quebec 60.10N 77.20W
97 M5 **Povungnituk,R** Quebec
99 L6 **Powassan** Ontario 46.05N 79.21W
108 E4 **Powder** *R* Montana
109 C3 **Powderhorn** Colorado 38.18N 107.08W
110 H5 **Powder R** Oregon
108 D6 **Powder River** Wyoming 43.03N 106.58W
108 E4 **Powderville** Montana 45.43N 105.07W
105 K11 **Powel Cay** *isld* Bahamas 26.57N 77.33W
111 K7 **Powell** Arizona 34.46N 114.20W
103 A3 **Powell** Pennsylvania 41.41N 76.29W
108 J5 **Powell** S Dakota 44.03N 101.33W
106 E3 **Powell** Wisconsin 46.07N 89.59W
108 B5 **Powell** Wyoming 44.45N 108.46W
13 G7 **Powell** *R* Queensland
110 D5 **Powell Butte** Oregon 44.15N 121.00W
13 C4 **Powell Creek** N Terr Australia 18.03S 133.41E
123 C14 **Powell I** South Orkney Is S Atlantic Oc 60.43S 44.55W
111 O4 **Powell, L** Arizona/Utah
101 L10 **Powell L** Br Col 50.08N 124.26W
109 D2 **Powell, Mt** Colorado 39.46N 106.21W
111 F3 **Powell Mt** Nevada 38.19N 118.44W
116 F2 **Powell Pt** Eleuthera I Bahamas 24.54N 76.21W
96 B14 **Powell Pt** St Helena 16.01S 5.42W
105 D1 **Powell,R** Tennessee
101 L11 **Powell River** Br Col 49.54N 124.34W
104 D8 **Powellton** W Virginia 38.05N 81.21W
110 O2 **Power** Montana 47.44N 111.40W
106 G4 **Powers** Michigan 45.42N 87.31W
110 A7 **Powers** Oregon 42.54N 124.05W
108 H1 **Powers Lake** N Dakota 48.35N 102.39W
107 C1 **Powersville** Missouri 40.33N 93.19W
57 G3 **Powfoot** Dumfries & Galloway Scotland 54.59N 3.20W
107 C10 **Powhatan** Louisiana 31.52N 93.12W
104 H9 **Powhatan** Virginia 37.33N 77.56W
104 E7 **Powhatan Point** Ohio 39.52N 80.49W
109 P2 **Powhattan** Kansas 39.44N 95.38W
56 G3 **Powick** Hereford & Worcs Eng 52.10N 2.14W
56 E2 **Powis, Vale of** Powys Wales
13 H5 **Powlathanga** Queensland 20.12S 145.50E
104 M4 **Pownal** Vermont 42.46N 73.15W
23 B2 **Powo** Sichuan China 32.39N 99.42E
56 E3 **Powys** *co* Wales
118 C4 **Poxoréu** Brazil 15.56S 54.21W
118 C5 **Poxoréu** *R* Brazil
75 F3 **Poyales** Spain 42.08N 2.14W
76 J8 **Poyales del Hoyo** Spain 40.10N 5.09W
23 G4 **Poyang Hu** *L* Jiangxi China
40 D7 **Poyarkovo** U.S.S.R. 49.37N 128.43E
75 F7 **Poyatos** Spain 40.25N 2.03W
41 B4 **Poyelovo,Mys** *C* U.S.S.R. 72.39N 72.55E
107 D7 **Poyen** Arkansas 34.19N 92.39W
120 C4 **Poyeni** *R* Peru
106 F5 **Poygan L** Wisconsin
42 A2 **Poykovskiy** U.S.S.R. 61.00N 72.05E
44 G6 **Poylu** Azerbaydzhan U.S.S.R. 41.08N 46.15E
56 L6 **Poynings** W Sussex Eng 50.53N 0.13W
103 D3 **Poyntelle** Pennsylvania 41.49N 75.25W
57 J6 **Poynton** Cheshire Eng 53.21N 2.07W
59 K3 **Poyntzpass** Armagh N Ireland 54.18N 6.23W
76 B4 **Poyo** Spain 42.27N 8.40W
75 E7 **Poyos** Spain 40.26N 2.45W
92 H7 **Poyo's** Tanzania 10.09S 37.01E
37 E7 **Poyraz** Turkey 38.48N 39.05E
51 K3 **Pöyrisjärvi** *L* Finland 68.44N 23.50E
65 P4 **Poysdorf** Austria 48.40N 16.38E
51 K11 **Pöytyä** Finland 60.47N 22.40E
75 D2 **Poza de la Sal** Spain 42.40N 3.30W
76 K6 **Pozal de Gallinas** Spain 41.18N 4.50W
76 K6 **Pozaldez** Spain 41.22N 4.50W
118 B6 **Pozama** Bolivia 18.28S 58.31W
36 H5 **Pozantı** Turkey 37.24N 34.52E
36 H5 **Pozantı Dağı** *mt* Turkey 37.51N 34.53E
82 G6 **Požarevac** Yugoslavia 44.37N 21.12E
115 L7 **Poza Rica** Mexico 20.34N 97.26W
36 G6 **Pozat Dağ** *mts* Turkey
40 D6 **Pozdeyevka** U.S.S.R. 50.34N 128.50E
40 F8 **Pozharskoye** U.S.S.R. 46.15N 134.04E
47 H6 **Pozhva** U.S.S.R. 59.10N 56.01E
69 D3 **Pozières** France 50.03N 2.45E
13 D5 **Pozieres,Mt** N Terr Australia 22.30S 137.30E
62 K3 **Poznań** Poland 52.25N 16.53E
111 D6 **Pozo** California 35.18N 120.22W
77 L5 **Pozo Alcón** Spain 37.43N 2.55W
120 D9 **Pozo Almonte** Chile 20.16S 69.46W
77 M2 **Pozoamargo** Spain 39.22N 2.12W
77 F6 **Pozo-Amargo,Sierra de** *mts* Spain
76 J5 **Pozoantiguo** Spain 41.35N 5.26W
120 F12 **Pozo Betbeder** Argentina 26.23S 64.20W
77 G4 **Pozoblanco** Spain 38.23N 4.51W
77 N3 **Pozo Cañada** Spain 38.49N 1.45W
111 J9 **Pozo Cenizo** Mexico 32.10N 115.32W
118 B8 **Pozo Colorado** Paraguay 23.26S 58.51W
75 D7 **Pozo de Guadalajara** Spain 40.30N 3.10W
Pozo de las Nieves *mt see* **Los Pechos** *mt*
121 E4 **Pozo del Molle** Argentina 32.00S 62.55W
75 D5 **Pozo de los Ramos, Embalse de** *res* Spain 41.04N 3.15W
118 A9 **Pozo del Tigre** Argentina 24.52S 60.20W
121 D1 **Pozo Hondo** Argentina 27.10S 64.26W
77 N3 **Pozohondo** Spain 38.44N 1.55W
77 N2 **Pozo Lorente** Spain 39.05N 1.30W
75 H6 **Pozondón** Spain 40.34N 1.29W
75 E8 **Pozorrubio** Spain 39.48N 2.58W
111 J9 **Pozo Salado** Mexico 32.33N 115.46W
121 E1 **Pozo San Martín** Argentina 27.57S 61.46W
76 G7 **Pozos de Hinojo** Spain 40.55N 6.24W
77 N2 **Pozoseco** Spain 39.30N 1.59W
77 L5 **Pozo,Sierra del** *mts* Spain
121 M6 **Pozos,Pta** *C* Argentina 47.55S 65.46W
111 N10 **Pozo Verde** Mexico 31.29N 111.40W
47 G5 **Poztykeros** U.S.S.R. 61.36N 51.33E
75 G6 **Pozuel del Campo** Spain 40.46N 1.30W
77 M3 **Pozuelo** Spain 38.49N 2.06W
75 C7 **Pozuelo de Alarcón** Spain 40.26N 3.49W
75 H4 **Pozuelo de Aragón** Spain 41.46N 1.25W
77 J3 **Pozuelo de Calatrava** Spain 38.55N 3.50W
76 H4 **Pozuelo del Páramo** Spain 42.10N 5.46W
76 H5 **Pozuelo de Tábara** Spain 41.47N 5.54W
76 G8 **Pozuelo de Zarzon** Spain 40.09N 6.25W
77 H3 **Pozuelos de Calatrava** Spain 38.54N 4.09W
120 F10 **Pozuelos,L.de** Argentina
120 B4 **Pozuzo** Peru 10.04S 76.36W
81 J10 **Pozzallo** Sicily 36.44N 14.51E
81 J8 **Pozzillo,L.di** Sicily 37.40N 14.35E
81 K7 **Pozzo di Gotto** Sicily 38.10N 15.13E
79 J4 **Pozzolengo** Italy 45.24N 10.38E
79 E5 **Pozzolo Formigaro** Italy 44.48N 8.47E
81 B3 **Pozzomaggiore** Sardinia 40.24N 8.40E
80 H3 **Pozzoni,Monte** Italy 42.40N 13.10E
79 L4 **Pozzonuovo** Italy 45.12N 11.48E
80 K7 **Pozzuoli** Italy 40.49N 14.07E
79 O3 **Pozzuolo del Friuli** Italy 45.58N 13.12E
89 J8 **Pra** *R* Ghana
45 M2 **Pra** *R* U.S.S.R.
65 L6 **Präbichl Pass** Austria 47.32N 14.58E
62 L2 **Prabuty** Poland 53.46N 19.10E
76 D9 **Pracana** *R* Portugal
76 D9 **Pracana, Barragem de** *res* Portugal 39.34N 7.49W
79 J6 **Pracchia** Italy 44.03N 10.54E
25 E7 **Pracham Hiang,Laem** *C* Thailand 10.14N 99.14E
65 J3 **Prachatice** Czechoslovakia 49.01N 14.00E
25 F5 **Prachin Buri** Thailand 14.05N 101.23E
29 K7 **Prachi R** Orissa India
29 B7 **Prachi Road** Gujarat India 20.56N 70.55E
65 N2 **Prachovice** Czechoslovakia 49.54N 15.38E
25 E7 **Prachuap Kiri Khan** Thailand 11.50N 99.49E
117 C6 **Pracui** *R* Brazil
76 E4 **Prada, Embalse de** *res* Spain
76 E2 **Pradairo** *mt* Spain 43.05N 7.18W
75 C5 **Pradales** Spain 41.27N 3.42W
75 C5 **Pradales,Sierra** *mts* Spain
79 O2 **Pradamano** Italy 46.03N 13.18E
62 K5 **Praděd** *mt* Czechoslovakia 50.05N 17.15E
75 F3 **Pradejón** Spain 42.20N 2.04W
72 C6 **Prade,la** France 4.42N 0.30W
71 D7 **Pradelles** France 44.46N 3.53E
72 K9 **Pradelles-en-Val** France 43.08N 2.31E
75 C5 **Prádena** Spain 41.09N 3.41W
119 C6 **Pradera** Colombia 3.23N 76.11W
71 E7 **Prades** Ardèche France 44.38N 4.19E
72 H10 **Prades** Ariège France 42.47N 1.51E
72 J10 **Prades** Pyrénées Orientales France 42.38N 2.25E
75 M5 **Prades** Spain 41.19N 0.59E
72 K6 **Prades-d'Aubrac** France 44.31N 2.56E
75 E3 **Pradillo** Spain 42.11N 2.38W
79 B6 **Pradlèves** Italy 44.25N 7.16E
118 H5 **Prado** Brazil 17.21S 39.15W
119 D6 **Prado** Colombia 3.45N 74.55W
76 C5 **Prado** Portugal 41.36N 8.29W
76 J3 **Prado** Spain 42.46N 5.02W
77 E7 **Prado del Rey** Spain 36.48N 5.33W
75 D3 **Pradoluengo** Spain 42.20N 3.12W
76 L3 **Prádonos de Ojeda** Spain 42.42N 4.20W
71 J8 **Prads** France 44.13N 6.27E
53 E2 **Præstbro** Denmark 57.14N 10.24E
53 J6 **Præstø** Denmark 55.08N 12.03E
Præstø *co see* **Storstrøm and Roskilde** *counties*
53 J6 **Præstø Fjord** *inlet* Denmark 55.10N 12.03E
76 D16 **Pragal** Portugal 38.40N 9.10W
65 L5 **Prägarten** Austria 48.22N 14.32E
79 A4 **Pragelato** Italy 45.01N 6.56E
66 M4 **Pragel-Pass** Switzerland 46.59N 8.53E
65 N9 **Pragersko** Yugoslavia 46.23N 15.38E
65 F7 **Prägraten** Austria 47.02N 12.23E
Prague Czechoslovakia*see* **Praha**
109 O6 **Prague** Oklahoma 35.30N 96.41W
65 K1 **Praha** Czech 50.06N 14.26E
65 J2 **Praha** *mt* Czechoslovakia 49.39N 13.49E
72 D3 **Prahecq** France 46.16N 0.21W
82 K5 **Prahova** *div* Romania
82 K6 **Prahova** *R* Romania
82 H6 **Prahovo** Yugoslavia 44.17N 22.35E
12 D8 **Prahran** *dist* Melbourne, Vic
96 P4 **Praia** Azores 38.33N 28.37W
96 R1 **Praia** Azores 39.03N 27.59W
81 L4 **Praia a Mare** Italy 39.54N 15.47E
76 B14 **Praia da Rocha** Portugal 37.07N 8.32W
76 B15 **Praia das Maçãs** Portugal 38.50N 9.28W
96 U3 **Praia da Vitória** Azores 38.44N 27.04W
76 B16 **Praia do Guincho** Portugal 38.44N 9.29W
96 P3 **Praia do Norte** Azores 38.37N 28.46W
118 C4 **Praia Rica** Brazil 14.50S 55.15W
82 J4 **Praid** Romania 46.33N 25.06E
120 G2 **Prainha** Amazonas Brazil 7.15S 60.24W
96 Q4 **Prainha** Azores 38.28N 28.13W
117 C5 **Prainha** Pará Brazil 1.46S 53.29W
117 D6 **Prainha** Pará Brazil 2.36S 50.30W
112 K6 **Prairia Lea** Texas 29.44N 97.46W
110 K6 **Prairie** Idaho 43.31N 115.35W
13 G5 **Prairie** Queensland 20.51S 144.35E
106 D9 **Prairie City** Illinois 40.37N 90.27W
110 G5 **Prairie City** Oregon 44.27N 118.43W
109 K2 **Prairie Dog Cr** Kansas
112 F1 **Prairie Dog Town Fork** *R* Texas
106 C6 **Prairie du Chien** Wisconsin 43.02N 91.08W
106 E6 **Prairie du Sac** Wisconsin 43.19N 89.43W
107 B6 **Prairie Grove** Arkansas 35.58N 94.20W
112 L4 **Prairie Hill** Texas 31.40N 96.47W
100 P6 **Prairie River** Saskatchewan 52.52N 102.59W
98 B3 **Prairies,L.des** Quebec
99 R9 **Prairies,R.des** Quebec
107 J2 **Prairieton** Indiana 39.22N 87.28W
109 L2 **Prairie View** Kansas 39.51N 99.34W
107 F11 **Prairieville** Louisiana 30.20N 91.00W
104 C9 **Praise** Kentucky 37.20N 82.20W
18 K9 **Prajekan** Java Indon 7.45S 113.58E
25 G5 **Prakhon Chai** Thailand 14.35N 103.13E
71 K8 **Pra,le** France 44.19N 6.54E
71 K6 **Pralognan-la-Vanoise** France 45.23N 6.44E
79 C5 **Pralormo** Italy 44.52N 7.54E
65 J5 **Pram** Austria 48.14N 13.38E
79 N2 **Pramaggiore,Mont** Italy 46.22N 12.33E
84 B2 **Prámanda** Greece 39.32N 21.07E
18 J9 **Prambanan** Java Indon 7.44S 110.31E
64 O3 **Prameny** Czechoslovakia 50.03N 12.45E
65 H5 **Pramet** Austria 48.08N 13.30E
63 R4 **Pramort** E Germany 54.27N 12.54E
89 K9 **Prampram** Ghana 5.43N 0.08E
25 E6 **Pran** *R* Thailand
25 E6 **Pran Buri** Thailand 12.20N 99.58E
31 F3 **Prang** Pakistan 34.10N 71.48E
66 B6 **Prangins** Switzerland 46.24N 6.16E
51 L12 **Prangli** *isld* Estonia U.S.S.R. 59.38N 25.00E
29 G8 **Pranhita R** Andhra Prad/Maharashtra India
65 K7 **Prankerhöhe** *mt* Austria 47.02N 14.05E
18 C4 **Prapat** Sumatra Indonesia 2.43N 98.58E
44 F3 **Praskoveya** U.S.S.R. 44.47N 44.15E
69 J8 **Praslay** France 47.45N 5.06E
26 Q12 **Praslin I** Seychelles, Ind Oc 4.18S 55.45E
84 U18 **Prasonisi** *isld* Rhodes 35.53N 27.45E
84 H4 **Prasoúdha** *isld* Greece 38.40N 24.15E
84 S14 **Prastio** Cyprus 35.10N 33.45E
84 E7 **Prastós** Greece 37.16N 22.41E
62 L4 **Praszka** Poland 51.02N 18.28E
121 J7 **Prat** *isld* Chile 48.15S 75.00W
66 O6 **Prata** Lombardy Italy 46.18N 9.25E
118 E6 **Prata** Minas Gerais Brazil 19.20S 48.54W
117 E5 **Prata** Pará Brazil 1.16S 47.36W
66 K7 **Prata** Piemonte Italy 46.03N 8.18E
118 D6 **Prata** *R* Goiás Brazil
Pratabpur *see* **Partabpur**
79 N3 **Prata di Pordenone** Italy 45.54N 12.36E
29 D5 **Pratapgarh** Rajasthan India 24.03N 74.50E
30 E7 **Pratapgarh** *dist* Uttar Prad India
66 O6 **Prata,Pizzo** *mt* Italy 46.17N 9.28E
118 E6 **Prata, R** Minas Gerais Brazil
117 F8 **Prata, R** Piauí Brazil
Pratas *see* **Dongsha Qundao**
Pratas *isld see* **Dongsha Qundao**
63 R9 **Pratau** E Germany 51.51N 12.39E
75 P5 **Prat del Llobregat** Spain 41.20N 2.05E
75 M5 **Pratdip** Spain 41.03N 0.52E
72 G9 **Prat-et-Bonrepaux** France 43.02N 1.01E
79 K1 **Prati** Italy 46.54N 11.28E
66 P4 **Prätigau** *V* Switzerland
79 K7 **Prato** Italy 43.53N 11.06E
66 L6 **Prato** Switzerland 46.24N 8.40E
79 J1 **Prato allo Stelvio** Italy 46.37N 10.36E
80 J4 **Pratola Peligna** Italy 42.06N 13.52E
80 L7 **Prátola Serra** Italy 40.58N 14.51E
79 L7 **Pratomagno** *mts* Italy
79 H6 **Prato,Monte** Italy 44.15N 10.24E
79 L7 **Pratovecchio** Italy 43.47N 11.43E
75 P3 **Prats de Llusanes** Spain 42.00N 2.01E
75 O4 **Prats del Rey** Spain 41.42N 1.33E
72 J11 **Prats-de-Mollo-la-Preste** France 42.25N 2.28E
109 M4 **Pratt** Kansas 37.40N 98.45W
100 T9 **Pratt** Manitoba 49.49N 98.57W
66 G1 **Pratteln** Switzerland 47.32N 7.42E
103 F2 **Prattsville** New York 42.19N 74.27W
107 K9 **Prattville** Alabama 32.29N 86.30W
18 H9 **Prau, Gunung** *mt* Java Indon 7.14S 109.54E
71 G1 **Prauthoy** France 47.42N 5.18E
29 C8 **Pravara R** Maharashtra India
39 F7 **Pravaya Zhupanova** *R* U.S.S.R.
40 J8 **Pravda** Sakhalin U.S.S.R. 46.50N 142.00E
45 V3 **Pravda** Ul'yanovsk U.S.S.R. 53.57N 49.29E
45 P1 **Pravdinsk** U.S.S.R. 56.32N 43.32E
62 N1 **Pravdinsk** U.S.S.R. 54.27N 21.01E
45 J1 **Pravdinskiy** U.S.S.R. 56.05N 37.52E
76 G2 **Pravia** Spain 43.29N 6.07W
56 D7 **Prawle Pt** Devon Eng 50.12N 3.44W
18 M10 **Praya** Indonesia 8.38S 116.15E
72 G6 **Prayssac** France 44.31N 1.12E
72 E7 **Prayssas** France 44.17N 0.30E
66 C8 **Praz** France 45.50N 6.35E
66 O5 **Präz** Graubünden Switzerland 46.45N 9.25E
66 E4 **Praz** Switzerland 46.57N 7.06E
66 E8 **Praz de Fort** Switzerland 45.59N 7.08E
112 A4 **Prazedis G. Guerrero** Mexico 31.22N 106.00W
76 E11 **Prazeres** Portugal 39.00N 7.25W
79 B6 **Prazzo** Italy 44.29N 7.03E
72 G1 **Préaux** France 47.02N 1.17E
11 L10 **Prebbleton** New Zealand 43.35S 172.32E
65 L8 **Preblau** Austria 46.56N 14.49E
64 O3 **Přebuz** Czechoslovakia 50.22N 12.38E
70 H4 **Precey** France 48.36N 1.23W
72 D7 **Préchac** France 44.24N 0.21W
72 C8 **Préchacq-les-Bains** France 43.46N 0.55W
45 D1 **Prechistoye** U.S.S.R. 55.31N 32.24E
80 H3 **Preci** Italy 42.53N 13.03E
70 K6 **Précigné** France 47.46N 0.19W
71 E2 **Précy-sous-Thil** France 47.23N 4.19W
69 C5 **Précy-sur-Oise** France 49.12N 2.22E
66 Q5 **Preda** Switzerland 46.35N 9.47E
79 L6 **Predappio** Italy 44.06N 11.58E
79 L2 **Predazzo** Italy 46.19N 11.37E
82 K5 **Predeal** Romania 45.30N 25.31E
44 G4 **Predgornoye** U.S.S.R. 43.08N 45.45E
64 O5 **Predigtstuhl** *mt* Nieder-Bayern W Germany 49.00N 12.52E
64 O8 **Predigtstuhl** *mt* Ober-Bayern W Germany 47.41N 12.52E
79 P2 **Predil, Passo del** *pass* Italy 46.25N 13.35E
65 M8 **Preding** Austria 46.52N 15.25E
42 E4 **Predivinsk** U.S.S.R. 57.04N 93.29E
65 J7 **Predlitz** Austria 46.04N 13.55E
79 M1 **Predoi** Italy 47.03N 12.07E
79 E5 **Predosa** Italy 44.45N 8.40E
100 P7 **Preeceville** Saskatchewan 51.58N 102.40W
70 K5 **Pré-en-Pail** France 48.27N 0.12W
56 F2 **Prees** Shropshire Eng 52.54N 2.40W
57 H5 **Preesall** Lancs Eng 53.55N 2.57W
63 M4 **Preetz** W Germany 54.14N 10.17E
70 F7 **Préfailles** France 47.08N 2.12W
79 M3 **Preganziol** Italy 45.36N 12.14E
46 D3 **Pregel** *R* U.S.S.R.
66 K7 **Preglia** Italy 46.09N 8.18E
79 F3 **Pregnana Milanese** Italy 45.31N 9.00E
66 A7 **Pregny** Switzerland 46.15N 6.09E
77 Y13 **Pregonda,Cala** *B* Balearic Is
119 E3 **Pregonero** Venezuela 8.02N 71.35W
44 D4 **Pregradnaya** U.S.S.R. 43.57N 41.11E
44 D2 **Pregradnoye** U.S.S.R. 45.50N 41.46E
117 F6 **Preguiças,R** Brazil
72 D6 **Preignac** France 44.35N 0.18W
46 F2 **Preiļi** Latvia U.S.S.R. 56.16N 26.50E
99 M4 **Preissac** Quebec 48.25N 78.24W
99 M4 **Preissac, L** Quebec
72 J9 **Preixan** France 43.08N 2.17E
75 F3 **Préjano** Spain 42.11N 2.10W
25 J6 **Prek Chhlong** *R* Cambodia
53 U21 **Prekestolen** Norway 58.58N 6.05E
25 H6 **Prek Kak** Cambodia 12.14N 105.31E
65 O8 **Prekomurje** *mts* Yugoslavia
25 G7 **Prek Piphat** *R* Cambodia
25 J6 **Prek Preas** *R* Cambodia
25 H7 **Prek Sandek** Cambodia 11.50N 105.22E
25 G7 **Prek Taley** *R* Cambodia
25 J6 **Prek Te** *R* Cambodia
25 H7 **Prek Thnot** *R* Cambodia
25 H7 **Prek Thnot Res** Cambodia
100 H8 **Prelate** Saskatchewan 50.52N 109.22W
66 E3 **Prêles** Switzerland 47.07N 7.08E
65 N1 **Přelouč** Czechoslovakia 50.03N 15.33E
79 F2 **Premana** Italy 46.03N 9.26E
71 F2 **Prémeaux** France 47.06N 4.56E
66 L8 **Premeno** Italy 45.59N 8.36E
12 J4 **Premer** New S Wales 31.26S 149.54E
72 L1 **Prémery** France 47.10N 3.19E
79 D2 **Premia** Italy 46.17N 8.20E
75 P5 **Premiá de Mar** Spain 41.29N 2.20E
14 F9 **Premier Downs** W Australia
95 M1 **Premier Mine Dam** *res* S Africa 25.49S 28.51E
79 L7 **Premilcuore** Italy 43.58N 11.46E
98 G2 **Premio** Quebec 51.09N 65.44W
63 Q7 **Premnitz** E Germany 52.33N 12.20E
112 J8 **Premont** Texas 27.22N 98.09W
66 K7 **Premosello** Italy 46.00N 8.20E
65 M8 **Premstätten** Austria 46.58N 15.25E
82 B6 **Premuda** *isld* Yugoslavia 44.20N 14.37E
100 J4 **Prendergast** Saskatchewan 54.06N 108.04W
80 G5 **Prenestini,Monti** Italy
83 D3 **Prenjas** Albania 41.04N 20.32E
82 D7 **Prenj Planina** *mts* Yugoslavia
106 D4 **Prentice** Wisconsin 45.33N 90.17W
107 G10 **Prentiss** Mississippi 31.38N 89.52W
63 T6 **Prenzlau** E Germany 53.19N 13.52E
63 C1 **Prenzlauer Berg** *dist* E Berlin E Germany
42 H2 **Preobrazhenka** U.S.S.R. 60.02N 108.05E
39 H7 **Preobrazhenskoye** Komandorskiye O-va U.S.S.R. 54.52N 167.40E
44 F3 **Preobrazhenskoye** Stavropol' U.S.S.R. 44.41N 42.11E
28 H5 **Preparis I** Andaman Is 14.51N 93.38E
28 G6 **Preparis South Chan** Andaman Is
71 D3 **Préporché** France 46.56N 3.50E
79 O2 **Prepotto** Italy 46.03N 13.28E
62 K6 **Přerov** Czechoslovakia 49.28N 17.30E
63 R4 **Prerow** E Germany 54.27N 12.35E
71 E7 **Présailles** France 44.54N 4.03E
68 F3 **Pré-St.Gervais,le** France 48.53N 2.25E
115 L8 **Presa M. Alemán** *res* Mexico
79 A3 **Pré San Didier** Italy 45.45N 6.59E
79 J2 **Presanella** *mt* Italy 46.13N 10.40E
81 Q12 **Presciutto,Pta** Italy 40.17N 17.46E
57 H6 **Prescot** Merseyside Eng 53.26N 2.48W
111 M7 **Prescott** Arizona 34.34N 112.28W
107 C8 **Prescott** Arkansas 33.49N 93.25W
108 Q8 **Prescott** Iowa 41.03N 94.35W
106 L5 **Prescott** Michigan 44.12N 83.57W
99 P8 **Prescott** Ontario 44.43N 75.33W
110 G3 **Prescott** Washington 46.18N 118.17W
106 B5 **Prescott** Wisconsin 44.44N 92.46W
66 R6 **Prese,Le** Switzerland 46.18N 10.05E
80 K6 **Presenzano** Italy 41.23N 14.05E
11 A13 **Preservation Inlet** New Zealand
82 G8 **Preševo** Yugoslavia 42.16N 21.37E
61 H6 **Presgaux** Belgium 50.02N 4.25E
108 K6 **Presho** S Dakota 43.54N 100.03W
81 R13 **Presicce** Italy 39.53N 18.16E
121 F1 **Presidencia de la Plaza** Argentina 27.00S 59.50W
118 B10 **Presidencia Roca** Argentina 26.09S 59.38W
118 A10 **Presidencia Roque Saenz Peña** Argentina 26.45S 60.30W
118 D8 **Presidente Bernardes** Brazil 22.03S 51.36W
117 F7 **Presidente Dutra** Brazil 5.17S 44.30W
118 D7 **Presidente Epitácio** Brazil 21.56S 52.07W
123 D15 **Presidente Frei** *Chile Base* Antarctica 62.12S 58.55W
118 B8 **Presidente Hayes** *dept* Paraguay
120 G4 **Presidente Hermes** Brazil 11.17S 61.55W
118 D4 **Presidente Murtinho** Brazil 15.39S 53.55W
118 F6 **Presidente Olegário** Brazil 18.24S 46.23W
118 D8 **Presidente Prudente** Brazil 22.09S 51.24W
121 J6 **Presidente Rios,L** Chile
118 D7 **Presidente Venceslau** Brazil 21.52S 51.51W
122 N11 **Président Thiers, Récif** *reef* Tubuai Is Pacific Oc 24.30S 146.00W
112 C6 **Presidio** Texas 29.34N 104.23W
115 G5 **Presidio de San Nicolás** Mexico 25.20N 105.38W
82 K7 **Preslav** Bulgaria 43.09N 26.50E
61 J5 **Presles** Belgium 50.23N 4.35E
43 H1 **Presnogor'kovka** Kazakhstan U.S.S.R. 54.31N 65.45E
43 H1 **Presnovka** Kazakhstan U.S.S.R. 54.41N 67.09E
62 N6 **Prešov** Czechoslovakia 49.00N 21.10E
82 J9 **Prespa** *mt* Bulgaria 41.42N 24.52E
82 G10 **Prespansko Jezero** *L* Yugoslavia etc
106 L4 **Presque I** Michigan 45.18N 83.28W
106 G3 **Presque I.Pt** Michigan 46.35N 87.22W
104 R7 **Presque Isle** Maine 46.42N 68.01W
116 L3 **Presqu'île de la Caravelle** *pen* Martinique W I
99 N9 **Presqu'île Prov. Park** Ontario
99 O4 **Press** Quebec 48.14N 76.45W
72 F3 **Pressac** France 46.07N 0.34E
64 M4 **Pressath** W Germany 49.46N 11.57E
Pressburg *see* **Bratislava**
64 M3 **Presseck** W Germany 50.13N 11.34E
72 F4 **Pressignac** France 45.49N 0.44E
57 G6 **Prestatyn** Clwyd Wales 53.20N 3.24W
50 G7 **Prestbakki** Skaftafellssýsla, Vestur Iceland 63.50N 18.02W
50 D4 **Prestbakki** Strandasýsla Iceland 65.18N 21.11W
89 H9 **Prestea** Ghana 5.26N 2.07W
56 E3 **Presteigne** Powys Wales 52.17N 3.00W
72 J11 **Preste-les-Bains,la** France 42.25N 2.24E
50 J2 **Presthólar** Iceland 66.16N 16.23W
53 Y17 **Prestholtskarvet** *mt* Norway 60.34N 8.02E
64 P4 **Přeštice** Czechoslovakia 49.35N 13.21E
120 F8 **Presto** Bolivia 18.53S 64.51W
58 M7 **Preston** Borders Scotland 55.49N 2.20W
111 A3 **Preston** California 38.49N 123.00W
103 L3 **Preston** Connecticut 41.32N 71.58W
116 G4 **Preston** Cuba 20.45N 75.40W
56 G6 **Preston** Dorset Eng 50.39N 2.25W
105 C5 **Preston** Georgia 32.03N 84.32W
56 G3 **Preston** Glos Eng 52.01N 2.28W
57 N5 **Preston** Humberside Eng 53.46N 0.12W
110 O7 **Preston** Idaho 42.06N 111.53W
106 D7 **Preston** Iowa 42.03N 90.23W
109 M4 **Preston** Kansas 37.46N 98.34W
57 H5 **Preston** Lancs Eng 53.46N 2.42W
56 K2 **Preston** Leics Eng 52.37N 0.43W
104 K8 **Preston** Maryland 38.43N 75.55W
106 B6 **Preston** Minnesota 43.40N 92.04W
107 C4 **Preston** Missouri 37.59N 93.12W
111 J3 **Preston** Nevada 38.53N 115.05W
103 C1 **Preston** New York 42.32N 75.37W
109 P6 **Preston** Oklahoma 35.43N 96.00W
12 D7 **Preston** *dist* Melbourne, Vic
56 F2 **Preston Brockhurst** Shropshire Eng 52.49N 2.42W
14 B5 **Preston,C** W Australia 20.52S 116.10E
56 J5 **Preston Candover** Hants Eng 51.11N 1.08W
103 F2 **Preston Hollow** New York 42.27N 74.14W
112 O8 **Preston Hollow** Texas 32.53N 96.49W
58 L7 **Prestonpans** Lothian Scotland 55.57N 3.00W
103 D3 **Preston Park** Pennsylvania 41.53N 75.21W
104 C9 **Prestonsburg** Kentucky 37.41N 82.45W
57 D2 **Prestwick** Strathclyde Scotland 55.30N 4.37W
119 J9 **Prêtada Eva, R** Brazil
118 H3 **Prêto** *R* Bahia Brazil
120 G1 **Prêto do Igapó Acu, R** Brazil
119 G8 **Prêto,R** Amazonas Brazil
118 F2 **Prêto,R** Bahia Brazil
119 G7 **Prêto, R** Brazil
118 F5 **Prêto,R** Minas Gerais Brazil
120 G3 **Prêto,R** Rondônia Brazil
95 M1 **Pretoria** S Africa 25.45S 28.12E
95 M1 **Pretoria North** S Africa 25.41S 28.11E
118 J9 **Pretos Forros,Sa dos** *ra* Brazil
70 H3 **Prétot** France 49.19N 1.25W
63 R9 **Prettin** E Germany 51.41N 12.55E
103 A7 **Prettyboy Res** Maryland 39.38N 76.45W
109 M4 **Pretty Prairie** Kansas 37.47N 98.01W
63 O7 **Pretzier** E Germany 52.50N 11.16E
63 R9 **Pretzsch** E Germany 51.44N 12.49E
72 F2 **Preuilly-sur-Claise** France 46.51N 0.56E
63 H8 **Preussisch Oldendorf** W Germany 52.19N 8.29E
65 L8 **Prevalje** Yugoslavia 46.33N 14.54E
71 D7 **Prévenchères** France 44.31N 3.55E
72 J3 **Préveranges** France 46.26N 2.14E
84 A4 **Préveza** Greece 38.58N 20.45E
84 A3 **Préveza** *prov* Greece
99 T10 **Préville** Quebec 45.29N 73.29W
40 M8 **Prevo** *vol* Kuril Is U.S.S.R. 47.01N 152.07E
74 H9 **Prévost Paradol** Algeria 35.22N 1.04E
109 B6 **Prewitt** New Mexico 35.23N 108.04W
109 G1 **Prewitt Res** Colorado 40.25N 103.23W
70 N4 **Prey** France 48.58N 1.18E
25 H7 **Prey Lovea** Cambodia 11.10N 104.57E
25 H7 **Prey Veng** Cambodia 11.30N 105.20E
69 K7 **Prez-sous-Lafouche** France 48.18N 5.31E
66 E4 **Prez-vers-Noréaz** Switzerland 46.47N 7.00E
80 J4 **Prezza** Italy 42.03N 13.50E
80 O1 **Prgomet** Yugoslavia 43.37N 16.14E
43 F4 **Priaral'skiye Karakumy,Peski** *sand des* Kazakhstan U.S.S.R.
76 F3 **Priaranza del Bierzo** Spain 42.30N 6.40W
42 K6 **Priargunsk** U.S.S.R. 50.52N 119.10E
45 G9 **Priazovskaya Vozvyshennost'** *upland* Ukraine U.S.S.R.
44 D8 **Priazovskoye** Ukraine U.S.S.R. 46.44N 35.40E
40 G4 **Pribezhnyy, Khrebet** *mts* U.S.S.R.
113 B8 **Pribilov Is** Bering Sea
82 D6 **Pribinić** Yugoslavia 44.39N 17.39E
82 F7 **Priboj** Yugoslavia 43.35N 19.32E
65 K2 **Príbram** Czechoslovakia 49.42N 14.01E
65 N2 **Přibyslav** Czechoslovakia 49.34N 15.44E
103 C8 **Price** Maryland 39.06N 75.58W
108 K2 **Price** N Dakota 47.05N 100.57W
98 D5 **Price** Quebec 48.38N 68.10W
111 O2 **Price** Utah 39.35N 110.49W
13 B3 **Price** *R* N Terr Australia
111 O2 **Price** *R* Utah
28 G6 **Price,C** Andaman Is 13.35N 93.01E
109 B1 **Price Cr** Colorado 40.16N 108.04W
101 J9 **Price I** Br Col 52.25N 128.40W
103 C6 **Pricetown** Pennsylvania 40.25N 75.49W
45 Q8 **Prichal'naya** U.S.S.R. 48.52N 44.37E
107 H11 **Prichard** Alabama 30.46N 88.06W
110 K2 **Prichard** Idaho 47.39N 115.57W
46 H6 **Prichernomorskaya Nizmennost'** *lowland* Ukraine U.S.S.R.
64 J4 **Prichsenstadt** W Germany 49.50N 10.22E
116 P5 **Prickly Pt** Grenada, W I 11.59N 61.46W
56 F5 **Priddy** Somerset Eng 51.16N 2.41W
112 J4 **Priddy** Texas 31.40N 98.32W
45 B3 **Pridneprovskaya Nizmennost'** *lowland* U.S.S.R.
45 B8 **Pridneprovskaya Vozvyshennost'** *uplands* Ukraine U.S.S.R.
75 F7 **Priego** Spain 40.26N 2.19W
77 H6 **Priego de Córdoba** Spain 37.27N 4.12W
77 H6 **Priego,Sierra de** *mts* Spain
46 D2 **Priekule** Latvia U.S.S.R. 56.24N 21.39E
46 D2 **Priekulė** Lithuania U.S.S.R. 55.32N 21.19E
63 Q5 **Priemerburg** E Germany 53.48N 12.15E
64 N8 **Prien** W Germany 47.51N 12.21E
46 E3 **Prienai** Lithuania U.S.S.R. 54.37N 23.58E
36 C5 **Priene** *anc site* Turkey 37.38N 27.17E
79 D6 **Priero** Italy 44.23N 8.05E
95 F5 **Prieska** S Africa 29.40S 22.45E
64 M1 **Priessnitz** E Germany 51.06N 11.48E
64 Q1 **Priestewitz** E Germany 51.15N 13.30E
110 J1 **Priest L** Idaho 48.35N 116.55W
116 M2 **Priestman's River** Jamaica, W I 18.08N 76.20W
110 F3 **Priest Rapids** Washington 46.39N 119.55W
110 F3 **Priest Rapids Res** Washington
110 J1 **Priest River** Idaho 48.11N 116.55W
76 K2 **Prieta,Penña** *mt* Spain 43.02N 4.44W
77 G7 **Prieta,Sierra** *mts* Spain
77 J3 **Prieto** *mt* Spain 38.50N 3.30W
76 K2 **Prieto,C** Spain 43.27N 4.50W
115 G5 **Prieto,Cerro** *pk* Mexico 24.12N 105.20W
62 L7 **Prievidza** Czechoslovakia 48.47N 18.35E
63 P6 **Prignitz** *reg* E Germany
45 E3 **Prigory** U.S.S.R. 53.50N 33.08E
42 D5 **Priiskovyy** U.S.S.R. 54.42N 88.44E
82 D6 **Prijedor** Yugoslavia 45.00N 16.41E
82 F7 **Prijepolje** Yugoslavia 43.23N 19.39E
43 A4 **Prikaspiyskaya Nizm** Kazakhstan U.S.S.R.
44 G2 **Prikaspiyskaya Nizmennost'** *lowland* U.S.S.R.
44 H2 **Prikaspiyskiy** U.S.S.R. 45.19N 46.58E
89 H8 **Prikro** Ivory Coast 7.40N 00.359
44 B2 **Prikubanskaya Nizmennost'** *lowland* U.S.S.R.
82 G9 **Prilep** Yugoslavia 41.20N 21.32E
45 K5 **Prilepy** U.S.S.R. 51.04N 38.55E
66 C5 **Prilly** Switzerland 46.32N 6.38E
47 E4 **Priluki** Arkhangel'sk U.S.S.R. 62.59N 42.30E
45 C1 **Priluki** Pskov U.S.S.R. 56.07N 31.20E
45 D6 **Priluki** Ukraine U.S.S.R. 50.35N 32.24E
77 S12 **Prima,Pta** Balearic Is 38.44N 1.29E
77 P5 **Prima,Pta** *pt* Spain 37.56N 0.41W
71 G6 **Primarette** France 45.24N 5.02E
100 H6 **Primate** Saskatchewan 52.17N 109.50W
115 K6 **Primavera** Mexico 23.30N 98.49W
121 E4 **Primavera de Marzo** Argentina 33.05S 60.41W
64 O4 **Přimda** Czechoslovakia 49.40N 12.40E
117 F6 **Primeira Cruz** Brazil 2.30S 43.25W
70 C4 **Primel,Pte.de** France 48.43N 3.50W
121 D3 **Primero,R** Argentina
12 J8 **Prime Seal I** Tasmania 40.05S 147.45E
108 P6 **Primghar** Iowa 43.05N 95.36W
66 Q1 **Primisweiler** W Germany 47.39N 9.46E
79 L3 **Primolano** Italy 45.58N 11.43E
44 E8 **Primorsk** Ukraine U.S.S.R. 46.44N 36.19E
47 B5 **Primorsk** U.S.S.R. 60.18N 28.35E
45 R7 **Primorsk** Volgograd U.S.S.R. 49.15N 45.02E
44 D9 **Primorskiy** Ukraine U.S.S.R. 45.09N 35.30E
40 E10 **Primorskiy** U.S.S.R. 43.10N 131.40E
42 G5 **Primorskiy Khrebet** *mts* U.S.S.R.
38 N4 **Primorskiy Kray** *terr* U.S.S.R.
41 N5 **Primorskiy Kryazh** *ridge* U.S.S.R.
82 L8 **Primorsko** Bulgaria 42.16N 27.46E
44 B1 **Primorsko Akhtarsk** U.S.S.R. 46.03N 38.11E
45 J9 **Primorskoye** Ukraine U.S.S.R. 47.10N 37.38E
Primor'ye *reg see* **Primorskiy Kray** *terr*
80 N1 **Primošten** Yugoslavia 43.41N 15.57E
98 J7 **Prim Pt** Prince Edward I 46.06N 63.02W
94 T13 **Primrose** S Africa 26.11S 28.10E
101 F5 **Primrose** *R* Yukon/Br Col
100 H4 **Primrose L** Saskatchewan
64 B5 **Prims** *R* W Germany
64 C4 **Primstal** W Germany 49.35N 7.01E
100 J6 **Prince** Saskatchewan 52.58N 108.21W
95 F9 **Prince Albert** S Africa 33.13S 22.03E
100 M5 **Prince Albert** Saskatchewan 53.13N 105.45W
123 H6 **Prince Albert Mts** Antarctica
100 L4 **Prince Albert Nat.Park** Saskatchewan
97 H3 **Prince Albert Pen** N W Terr
95 E8 **Prince Albert Road** S Africa 32.59S 21.41E
101 P1 **Prince Albert Sd** Victoria I, N W Terr
97 G3 **Prince Alfred, C** N W Terr 74.30N 124.50W
95 C9 **Prince Alfred Hamlet** S Africa 33.18S 19.20E
97 M4 **Prince Charles I** N W Terr 68.00N 76.00W
123 C5 **Prince Charles Mts** Antarctica
123 D15 **Prince Charles Str** S Shetland Is Antarctica
99 O9 **Prince Edward B** Ontario
26 D11 **Prince Edward-Crozet Ridge** Indian Oc
26 B13 **Prince Edward I** Indian Oc 46.38S 37.55E
98 J7 **Prince Edward I** *prov* Canada
98 J7 **Prince Edward I.Nat.Park** Prince Edward I
26 D10 **Prince Edward Is** Indian Oc
99 O9 **Prince Edward Pt** Ontario 43.57N 76.54W
104 J8 **Prince Frederick** Maryland 38.32N 76.35W
14 F3 **Prince Frederick Harb** W Australia
101 M9 **Prince George** Br Col 53.55N 122.49W
103 A9 **Prince Georges** *co* Maryland
97 J2 **Prince Gustaf Adolf Sea** N W Terr
60 G13 **Princenhage** Netherlands 51.35N 4.45E
113 C4 **Prince of Wales, C** Alaska 65.35N 168.05W
113 V9 **Prince of Wales I** Alaska 55.40N 133.00W
97 J3 **Prince of Wales I** N W Terr 72.30N 99.00W
13 F1 **Prince of Wales I** Queensland
97 H2 **Prince of Wales Str** N W Terr 77.00N 120.00W
123 G8 **Prince Olav Mts** Antarctica
97 H2 **Prince Patrick I** N W Terr 77.00N 120.00W
97 K3 **Prince Regent Inlet** N W Terr
14 F3 **Prince Regent R** W Australia
101 H8 **Prince Rupert** Br Col 54.18N 130.17W
101 K8 **Prince Rupert Highway** Br Col
117 H8 **Princesa Isabel** Brazil 7.43S 37.56W
Princes Is *see* **Kızıl Adalar** *Is*
Princes Lake *see* **Wallace**
56 K4 **Princes Risborough** Bucks Eng 51.44N 0.51W
104 K8 **Princess Anne** Maryland 38.12N 75.42W
13 G2 **Princess Charlotte B** Queensland
123 D4 **Princess Elizabeth Land** Antarctica
14 F3 **Princess May Ra** W Australia
11 B12 **Princess Mts** New Zealand
14 D7 **Princess Ra** W Australia
101 J9 **Princess Royal I** Br Columbia
89 H9 **Prince's Town** Ghana 4.47N 2.08W
116 O2 **Prince's Town** Trinidad & Tobago 10.16N 61.23W
56 J3 **Princethorpe** Warwicks Eng 52.20N 1.24W
101 N11 **Princeton** Br Columbia 49.25N 120.35W
111 B2 **Princeton** California 39.25N 122.01W
105 B11 **Princeton** Florida 25.32N 80.26W
106 E8 **Princeton** Illinois 41.23N 89.27W
107 J3 **Princeton** Indiana 38.21N 87.33W
106 D8 **Princeton** Iowa 41.40N 90.22W
107 J4 **Princeton** Kentucky 37.06N 87.55W
104 S1 **Princeton** Maine 45.14N 67.34W
106 G3 **Princeton** Michigan 46.18N 87.28W
108 R4 **Princeton** Minnesota 45.33N 93.35W
107 C1 **Princeton** Missouri 40.22N 93.37W
105 J2 **Princeton** N Carolina 35.27N 78.11W
103 E6 **Princeton** New Jersey 40.21N 74.40W
106 E6 **Princeton** Wisconsin 43.52N 89.09W
104 D9 **Princeton** W Virginia 37.23N 81.06W
103 E6 **Princeton Junc** New Jersey 40.19N 74.37W
56 D6 **Princetown** Devon Eng 50.33N 3.59W
106 E9 **Princeville** Illinois 40.57N 89.47W
99 T6 **Princeville** Quebec 46.10N 71.52W
10 E11 **Prince William Henry B** Lord Howe I Pacific Oc
113 O6 **Prince William Sd** Alaska
13 J6 **Princhester** Queensland 22.56S 150.00E
96 M8 **Príncipe** *isld* G of Guinea 1.37N 7.27E
101 J9 **Principe Chan** Br Columbia
120 F5 **Príncipe da Beira** Brazil 12.23S 64.28W
110 E5 **Prineville** Oregon 44.19N 120.50W
110 E5 **Prineville Res** Oregon 44.10N 120.42W
108 G6 **Pringle** S Dakota 43.36N 103.36W
112 C8 **Pringle** Texas 35.56N 101.27W
121 D8 **Pringles** Argentina 40.22S 63.45W
71 J5 **Pringy** France 45.57N 6.08E
84 C2 **Prínos** Greece 39.34N 21.37E
48 V16 **Prins Christian Sd** Greenland 60.00N 42.30W
60 G13 **Prinsenbeek** Netherlands 51.36N 4.42E
60 M7 **Prinsenhof** *L* Netherlands
25 D6 **Prinsep I** Burma 12.02N 97.35E
60 M7 **Prinses Margriet Kanaal** *canal* Netherlands
123 A8 **Prinsesse Astrid Kyst** *coast* Antarctica
48 U2 **Prinsesse Dagmar Ø** *isld* Greenland 81.45N 19.00W
48 U2 **Prinsesse Margarethe Ø** *isld* Greenland 82.05N 19.30W
123 A7 **Prinsesse Ragnhild Kyst** *coast* Antarctica
48 U2 **Prinsesse Thyra Ø** *isld* Greenland 82.00N 20.30W
123 A7 **Prins Harald Kyst** *coast* Antarctica
50 S14 **Prins Karls Forland** *isld* Spitsbergen
48 V2 **Prins Knud,Kap** *C* Greenland 81.55N 15.00W
98 L4 **Prinsta B** Anticosti I, Que
45 J6 **Printsevka** U.S.S.R. 50.20N 37.57E
115 N3 **Prinzapolca** Nicaragua 13.19N 83.35W
18 G9 **Priok** Java Indonesia 6.07S 106.45E
45 L2 **Priokskiy** U.S.S.R. 54.42N 39.39E
79 D6 **Priola** Italy 44.14N 8.01E
84 D6 **Priólithos** Greece 37.55N 22.02E
81 K9 **Priolo** Sicily 37.10N 15.11E
10 C10 **Prion L** Macquarie I Pacific Oc 54.35S 158.55E
76 C1 **Prior,C** Spain 43.34N 8.19W
80 H3 **Priore,Monte** Italy 42.46N 13.15E
76 K3 **Prioro** Spain 42.53N 4.58W
95 J6 **Priors** S Africa 30.26S 25.35E
42 C7 **Priozernyy** U.S.S.R. 47.43N 84.12E
45 R9 **Priozernyy** U.S.S.R. 47.23N 45.16E
47 C5 **Priozersk** U.S.S.R. 61.01N 30.08E
44 F2 **Priozerskoye** U.S.S.R. 45.13N 44.50E
Pripet Marshes *see* **Poles'ye** *marshland*
28 J3 **Priphema** Nagaland India 25.45N 93.58E
47 J4 **Pripolyarnyy Ural** *mts* U.S.S.R.
46 G4 **Pripyat'** *R* Belorussiya U.S.S.R.
42 G4 **Prirechnyy** U.S.S.R. 55.08N 101.04E
47 C2 **Prirechnyy** U.S.S.R. 69.00N 30.20E
45 R9 **Prisarpinskiy** U.S.S.R. 47.34N 45.49E
64 P3 **Přisečnice** Czechoslovakia 50.29N 13.08E
82 C5 **Priseka** *mt* Yugoslavia 45.12N 16.19E
44 J8 **Prishib** Azerbaydzhan U.S.S.R. 39.09N 48.34E
82 J3 **Prislop Pass** Romania 47.36N 24.50E
72 G2 **Prissac** France 46.31N 1.18E
43 N5 **Pristan' Przheval'sk** Kirgiziya U.S.S.R. 42.37N 78.23E
45 H5 **Pristen'** U.S.S.R. 51.15N 36.44E
82 G8 **Priština** Yugoslavia 42.39N 21.10E
109 H4 **Pritchett** Colorado 37.22N 102.53W
63 Q7 **Pritzerbe** E Germany 52.31N 12.28E
63 O6 **Pritzier** E Germany 53.23N 11.05E
63 Q6 **Pritzwalk** E Germany 53.09N 12.11E
71 F7 **Privas** France 44.44N 4.36E
80 H6 **Priverno** Italy 41.28N 13.11E
80 H6 **Privernum** *ruins* Italy 41.29N 13.12E
44 D10 **Privetnoye** Ukraine U.S.S.R. 44.50N 34.42E
44 B1 **Privod'naya** U.S.S.R. 46.09N 38.42E
45 D9 **Privol'noye** Ukraine U.S.S.R. 47.29N 32.17E
45 S6 **Privol'noye** U.S.S.R. 50.55N 46.05E
44 E1 **Privol'nyy** U.S.S.R. 46.39N 43.26E
46 M2 **Privolzhsk** U.S.S.R. 57.21N 41.20E
45 Q7 **Privolzhskaya Vozvyshennost'** *uplands* U.S.S.R.
44 H1 **Privolzhskiy** Astrakhan' U.S.S.R. 46.24N 48.00E
45 S5 **Privolzhskiy** Saratov U.S.S.R. 51.25N 46.04E
45 R5 **Privolzhskoye** U.S.S.R. 51.05N 45.59E
45 U4 **Privolzhye** U.S.S.R. 52.51N 48.36E
44 E1 **Priyutnoye** U.S.S.R. 46.05N 43.30E
46 R3 **Priyutovo** U.S.S.R. 53.55N 53.59E
70 D5 **Priziac** France 48.03N 3.25W
82 F8 **Prizren** Yugoslavia 42.12N 20.43E
81 F8 **Prizzi** Sicily 37.44N 13.26E
82 D6 **Prnjavor** Yugoslavia 44.54N 17.40E
76 G2 **Proaza** Spain 43.15N 6.01W
82 K1 **Probezhna** U.S.S.R. 49.01N 25.59E
18 K9 **Probolinggo** Java Indon 7.45S 113.09E
63 M4 **Probstei** *reg* W Germany
64 L2 **Probstzella** E Germany 50.31N 11.23E
56 B7 **Probus** Cornwall Eng 50.17N 4.57W
80 E3 **Proceno** Italy 42.45N 11.50E
62 J4 **Prochowice** Poland 51.18N 16.21E
80 K7 **Procida** Italy 40.47N 14.02E

80 K7 Procida,I.di Italy
101 P11 Procter Br Col 49.37N 116.57W
109 H1 Proctor Colorado 40.49N 102.57W
112 J4 Proctor Texas 32.00N 98.26W
104 M3 Proctor Vermont 43.40N 73.03W
112 J3 Proctor Res Texas
104 N3 Proctorsville Vermont 43.23N 72.43W
28 D3 Proddatur Andhra Prad India 14.45N 78.34E
84 Q15 Prodhromos Cyprus 34.57N 32.50E
76 D9 Proença-a-Nova Portugal 39.45N 7.56W
76 E8 Proença-a-Velha Portugal 40.02N 7.15W
64 N1 Profen E Germany 51.07N 12.13E
61 K5 Profondeville Belgium 50.23N 4.52E
76 D3 Prógalo Spain 42.59N 7.40W
121 E3 Progreso Argentina 31.10S 61.00W
Progreso Ecuador see Gómez Rendón
115 O9 Progreso Guatemala 17.18N 90.56W
115 K7 Progreso Hidalgo Mexico 20.20N 99.12W
115 J4 Progreso Mexico 27.24N 100.59W
115 N5 Progreso Panama 8.29N 82.50W
115 P7 Progreso Yucatán Mexico 21.20N 89.40W
120 D3 Progresso Brazil 9.47S 71.41W
109 E7 Progresso New Mexico 34.28N 105.54W
63 S4 Prohn E Germany 54.23N 13.03E
63 S4 Prohner Wiek B E Germany
44 F4 Prokhladnyy U.S.S.R. 43.46N 44.03E
42 B3 Prokhorkino U.S.S.R. 59.36N 79.28E
46 K4 Prokhorofka U.S.S.R. 51.03N 36.45E
82 F8 Prokletije mts Yugoslavia
40 H4 Prokof'yeva,O isld U.S.S.R. 55.04N 138.20E
84 F4 Prokópion Greece 38.44N 23.30E
42 G3 Prokop'yevo U.S.S.R. 58.05N 100.45E
42 D5 Prokop'yevsk U.S.S.R. 53.55N 86.45E
82 G7 Prokuplje Yugoslavia 43.14N 21.35E
46 H1 Proletariy U.S.S.R. 58.22N 31.45E
43 M8 Proletarsk Tadzhikistan U.S.S.R. 40.12N 69.32E
45 K8 Proletarsk Ukraine U.S.S.R. 48.55N 38.22E
44 D1 Proletarskaya U.S.S.R. 46.43N 41.45E
45 G6 Proletarskiy Belgorod U.S.S.R. 50.47N 35.49E
45 J1 Proletarskiy Moscow U.S.S.R. 55.01N 37.22E
46 E8 Proletarskiy dist Moscow U.S.S.R.
64 K4 Prolsdorf W Germany 49.52N 10.39E
66 D5 Promasens Switzerland 46.37N 6.50E
25 C3 Prome Burma 18.50N 95.14E
84 F3 Promíri Greece 39.12N 23.18E
108 R9 Promise City Iowa 40.44N 93.09W
103 D4 Promised Land L Pennsylvania 41.18N 75.11W
118 C6 Promissão Mato Grosso do Sul Brazil 18.12S 55.40W
118 E7 Promissão São Paulo Brazil 21.31S 49.47W
110 N8 Promontory Utah 41.37N 112.35W
103 D3 Prompton Pennsylvania 41.35N 75.20W
42 D5 Promyshlennaya U.S.S.R. 54.55N 85.46E
47 J2 Promyshlennyy U.S.S.R. 67.34N 63.58E
47 M3 Promysla U.S.S.R. 58.35N 59.10E
44 H2 Promyslovka U.S.S.R. 45.42N 47.09E
41 K3 Pronchishcheva, Bereg coast U.S.S.R.
41 L4 Pronchishcheva,Kryazh ridge U.S.S.R.
41 J2 Pronchishcheva,Mys C U.S.S.R. 77.33N 106.00E
28 A8 Prongs Lt Ho Bombay India 18.54N 72.49E
45 O7 Pronin U.S.S.R. 49.12N 42.11E
46 M1 Pronino U.S.S.R. 58.11N 42.02E
64 A3 Pronsfeld W Germany 50.09N 6.20E
45 L2 Pronsk U.S.S.R. 54.07N 39.36E
110 G9 Pronto Nevada 40.56N 118.05W
45 M2 Pronya U.S.S.R. 54.18N 40.15E
45 C3 Pronya R Belorussiya U.S.S.R.
45 M2 Pronya R U.S.S.R.
101 M6 Prophet R Br Col
101 M6 Prophet River Br Columbia 58.05N 122.42W
106 E8 Prophetstown Illinois 41.40N 89.57W
71 G8 Propiac France 44.16N 5.12E
118 J2 Propriá Brazil 10.15S 36.51W
67 O13 Propriano Corsica 41.40N 8.54E
63 T4 Prorer Wiek B E Germany
43 C4 Prorva Kazakhstan U.S.S.R. 45.59N 53.16E
42 B3 Proryto U.S.S.R. 59.28N 79.46E
47 J8 Proryvnoye U.S.S.R. 54.25N 64.20E
66 L5 Prosa,Mt Switzerland 46.33N 8.36E
65 O2 Proseč Czechoslovakia 49.49N 16.08E
79 P3 Prosecco Italy 45.43N 13.43E
83 D3 Prosek Albania 41.43N 19.55E
63 T10 Prösen E Germany 51.25N 13.30E
13 J5 Proserpine Queensland 20.25S 148.33E
63 Q9 Prosigk E Germany 51.43N 12.04E
84 D8 Prosíli Greece 36.50N 22.28E
84 D4 Prosilion Greece 38.35N 22.20E
65 O4 Prosiměřice Czechoslovakia 48.55N 16.11E
62 K3 Prosna R Poland
46 Q1 Prosnitsa U.S.S.R. 58.29N 50.18E
83 F3 Prosotsáni Greece 41.11N 23.59E
103 J4 Prospect Connecticut 41.30N 73.00W
104 K3 Prospect New York 43.18N 75.09W
104 B6 Prospect Ohio 40.25N 83.11W
110 C7 Prospect Oregon 42.45N 122.30W
104 E6 Prospect Pennsylvania 40.55N 80.02W
12 A8 Prospect dist Adelaide, S Aust
12 K7 Prospect Cr Sydney, N S W
113 M3 Prospect Cr Camp Alaska 66.50N 150.30W
103 D7 Prospect Park Pennsylvania 39.53N 75.18W
103 F6 Prospect Plains New Jersey 40.20N 74.27W
116 M2 Prospect Pt Jamaica, W I 17.51N 76.21W
110 A6 Prosper Oregon 43.09N 124.24W
19 M7 Prosperidad Mindanao Philippines 8.38N 125.54E
75 Q7 Prosperidad, La dist Madrid Spain
105 F3 Prosperity S Carolina 34.12N 81.33W
59 J5 Prosperous Kildare Irish Rep 53.17N 6.45W
96 B13 Prosperous B St Helena
42 F3 Prospikhino U.S.S.R. 58.32N 99.10E
108 M9 Prosser Nebraska 40.42N 98.34W
110 F3 Prosser Washington 46.13N 119.46W
65 Q3 Prostějov Czechoslovakia 49.28N 17.07E
13 K7 Proston Queensland 26.08S 151.32E
43 L3 Prostornoye Kazakhstan U.S.S.R. 49.02N 72.33E
47 G3 Prosunduy U.S.S.R. 67.16N 53.11E
45 H8 Prosyanaya Ukraine U.S.S.R. 48.06N 36.23E
62 M5 Proszowice Poland 50.11N 20.19E
109 L4 Protection Kansas 37.13N 99.30W
95 D10 Protem S Africa 34.16S 20.05E
84 C7 Próti isld Greece 37.03N 21.33E
65 K3 Protivín Czechoslovakia 49.13N 14.13E
106 B6 Protivin Iowa 43.14N 92.05W
47 K4 Protochnyye U.S.S.R. 63.25N 65.12E
44 B2 Protoka R U.S.S.R.
45 J2 Protva R U.S.S.R.
63 T7 Prötzel E Germany 52.39N 14.00E
84 C3 Proussós Greece 38.45N 21.40E
82 L7 Provadiya Bulgaria 43.10N 27.29E
75 F8 Proveda De La Obispalia Spain 39.53N 3.36W
61 A3 Proven Belgium 50.53N 2.39E
48 S5 Prøven Greenland 72.20N 56.00W
76 B13 Provença Portugal 37.56N 8.47W
107 C10 Provencal Louisiana 31.40N 93.11W
67 J9 Provence prov France
71 J9 Provence,Alpes de France
69 N7 Provenchères-sur-Fave France 48.19N 7.04E
77 L2 Provencio, El Spain 39.23N 2.35W
79 K2 Provés Italy 46.29N 11.02E
116 P5 Providence Grenada, W I 12.04N 61.40W
107 J4 Providence Kentucky 37.22N 87.47W
103 C7 Providence Maryland 39.42N 75.53W
105 J1 Providence N Carolina 36.16N 78.41W
103 M3 Providence Rhode I 41.50N 71.28W
107 K3 Providence Tennessee 36.03N 86.47W
110 O8 Providence Utah 41.43N 111.47W
103 L3 Providence co Rhode I
99 H7 Providence Bay Ontario 45.41N 82.16W
113 J8 Providence,C Alaska 57.00N 156.35W
11 A13 Providence,C New Zealand 46.01S 166.28E
26 D6 Providence Is Seychelles, Ind Oc
111 J7 Providence Mts California
119 C8 Providencia Ecuador 0.29S 76.29W
121 G9 Providencia dist Santiago Chile
119 G8 Providência,I Brazil 0.21S 64.02W
115 O3 Providencia,I.de Caribbean Sea
116 H4 Providenciales isld Caicos Is W I 21.48N 72.18W
120 G4 Providência,Sa.de mts Brazil
39 M3 Provideniya U.S.S.R. 64.30N 173.11W
39 M3 Provideniya,Bukhta gulf U.S.S.R.
13 G2 Providential Chan Gt Barrier Reef Australia
103 O2 Provincetown Massachusetts 42.04N 70.11W
119 D4 Provincia Colombia 7.24N 73.27W
69 E6 Provins France 48.34N 3.18E
108 G6 Provo S Dakota 43.11N 103.50W
110 O9 Provo Utah 40.15N 111.40W
100 G6 Provost Alberta 52.24N 110.16W
69 D4 Proyart France 49.54N 2.43E
82 D7 Prozor Yugoslavia 43.50N 17.36E
47 G5 Prub R U.S.S.R.
103 M3 Prudence I Rhode I
118 E9 Prudentópolis Brazil 25.09S 50.58W
106 K5 Prudenville Michigan 44.18N 84.40W
57 K3 Prudhoe Northumb Eng 54.58N 1.51W
113 N1 Prudhoe B Alaska 70.20N 148.25W
13 J5 Prudhoe I Queensland 21.15S 149.40E
48 S3 Prudhoe Land Greenland
100 M6 Prud'homme Saskatchewan 52.21N 105.57W
62 K5 Prudnik Poland 50.20N 17.34E
45 H6 Prudyanka Ukraine U.S.S.R. 50.15N 36.11E
66 H1 Prug W Germany 47.47N 7.58E
64 A3 Prüm W Germany 50.12N 6.25E
64 A3 Prüm R W Germany
79 J3 Prun Italy 45.34N 10.57E
77 F7 Pruna Spain 36.58N 5.14W
70 M6 Prunay France 47.42N 0.56E
70 O5 Prunay-le-Gillon France 48.21N 1.40E
82 J3 Prundu Bîrgăului Romania 47.11N 24.42E
67 O13 Prunelli R Corsica
67 P12 Prunelli di Fiumorbo Corsica 42.01N 9.19E
72 J6 Prunet France 44.49N 2.26E
67 Q12 Prunete-Cervione Corsica 42.19N 9.32E
79 J6 Prunetta Italy 44.01N 10.48E
71 J7 Prunières France 44.32N 6.19E
72 J2 Pruniers Indre France 46.47N 2.03E
70 O7 Pruniers Loir-et-Cher France 47.20N 1.40E
80 C2 Pruno,Poggio al mt Italy 43.15N 10.40E
62 K2 Pruszcz Bydgoszcz Poland 53.28N 17.49E
62 L1 Pruszcz Gdańsk Poland 54.16N 18.36E
62 M3 Pruszków Poland 52.10N 20.47E
46 F5 Prut R Ukraine etc Romania/U.S.S.R.
82 L3 Prutul R Romania etc
65 C7 Prutz Austria 47.05N 10.40E
46 E3 Pruzhany Belorussiya U.S.S.R. 52.23N 24.28E
45 L4 Pruzhinki U.S.S.R. 52.43N 39.10E
79 P3 Prvačina Yugoslavia 45.53N 13.45E
61 H5 Pry Belgium 50.17N 4.26E
45 G5 Pryamitsyno U.S.S.R. 51.37N 35.58E
47 N3 Pryanichnikova U.S.S.R. 58.12N 60.32E
47 C5 Pryazha U.S.S.R. 61.42N 33.33E
123 C4 Prydz B Antarctica
109 F4 Pryor Colorado 37.30N 104.44W
110 R4 Pryor Montana 45.25N 108.32W
109 P5 Pryor Oklahoma 36.19N 95.19W
110 R4 Pryor Cr Montana
62 M2 Przasnysz Poland 53.01N 20.51E
62 K2 Przechlewo Poland 53.49N 17.15E
62 M4 Przedbórz Poland 51.05N 19.50E
62 O6 Przemyśl Poland 49.48N 22.48E
62 O5 Przeworsk Poland 50.04N 22.30E
62 H4 Przewóz Poland 51.30N 14.59E
43 N6 Przheval'sk Kirgiziya U.S.S.R. 42.31N 78.22E
62 M4 Przysucha Poland 51.22N 20.38E
84 G4 Psakhná Greece 38.35N 23.39E
83 H6 Psará isld Greece
84 B5 Psári Ilía Greece 38.01N 21.23E
84 E6 Psári Korinthía Greece 37.52N 22.31E
84 C7 Psári Messinía Greece 37.22N 21.53E
44 C4 Pseashko mt U.S.S.R. 43.45N 40.27E
44 D3 Psebay U.S.S.R. 44.07N 40.49E
44 F4 Psedakh U.S.S.R. 43.28N 44.36E
44 C3 Psekups R U.S.S.R.
45 E7 Psël R Ukraine U.S.S.R.
44 B3 Pshada U.S.S.R. 44.28N 38.26E
31 D5 Psha Pass Pakistan 31.03N 66.42E
44 C3 Pshekha R U.S.S.R.
44 C3 Pshish R U.S.S.R.
62 K4 Psie Pole Poland 51.10N 17.10E
84 V17 Psíndhos Rhodes 36.18N 28.06E
84 N11 Psira isld Crete 35.11N 25.51E
43 K6 Pskem Uzbekistan U.S.S.R. 41.53N 70.23E
43 J6 Pskent Uzbekistan U.S.S.R. 40.52N 69.24E
44 D4 Pskhu Georgia U.S.S.R. 43.24N 40.50E
46 G1 Pskov U.S.S.R. 57.48N 28.26E
46 G1 Pskovskaya Oblast' prov U.S.S.R.
46 G1 Pskovskoye,Oz U.S.S.R.
82 D5 Psunj mt Yugoslavia 45.21N 17.20E
62 L1 Pszczółki Poland 54.10N 18.40E
62 L6 Pszczyna Poland 49.59N 18.54E
84 E3 Pteleón Greece 39.03N 22.57E
65 P2 Pteni Czechoslovakia 49.31N 16.58E
46 G4 Ptich' Belorussiya U.S.S.R. 52.15N 28.49E
46 G3 Ptich' R Belorussiya U.S.S.R.
83 E4 Ptolemaïs Greece 40.32N 21.42E
82 C4 Ptuj Yugoslavia 46.27N 15.51E
121 A7 Púa Chile 38.21S 72.24W
114 C7 Pua Akala mt Hawaiian Is 19.46N 155.20W
19 C4 Puah isld Indonesia 0.30S 122.35E
114 B6 Puakea Pt Hawaiian Is 20.14N 155.54W
114 B7 Puako Hawaiian Is 19.58N 155.49W
114 B7 Puako B Hawaiian Is
113 K8 Puale B Alaska
121 E6 Puán Argentina 37.35S 62.45W
21 D10 Puan S Korea 35.44N 126.44E
122 B1 Puapua W Samoa, Pacific Oc 13.32S 172.09W
122 S14 Puaumu islds Gambier Is Pacific Oc 23.01S 134.55W
122 A1 Puava C W Samoa, Pacific Oc 13.24S 172.44W
23 E7 Pubei Guangxi China 22.17N 109.31E
66 C6 Publier France 46.24N 6.32E
98 G10 Pubnico Nova Scotia 43.42N 65.48W
120 B2 Pucacaca Peru 6.48S 76.13W
119 C9 Pucacuro Peru 2.15S 75.26W
119 C9 Pucacuro, R Peru
120 A7 Pucala Peru 6.49S 79.34W
120 C3 Pucallpa Peru 8.21S 74.33W
120 F8 Pucará Bolivia 18.40S 64.13W
120 D6 Pucará Peru 15.05S 70.24W
120 E7 Pucarani Bolivia 16.25S 68.29W
120 D6 Pucará,R Peru
119 E9 Puca Urco Peru 2.18S 71.53W
120 B3 Puccha R Peru
65 H6 Puch Austria 47.43N 13.06E
70 O3 Puchay France 49.21N 1.33E
23 H5 Pucheng Fujian China 27.59N 118.31E
23 G1 Pucheng Henan China 35.44N 115.24E
23 E1 Pucheng Shaanxi China 35.00N 109.34E
65 M6 Puchenstuben Austria 47.55N 15.18E
39 J1 Pucheveem R U.S.S.R.
46 N2 Puchezh U.S.S.R. 57.00N 43.00E
18 B8 Puchong Pen Malaysia 3.02N 101.37E
62 L6 Púchov Czechoslovakia 49.08N 18.15E
82 J5 Pucioasa Romania 45.04N 25.23E
19 K6 Pucio Pt Philippines 11.46N 121.51E
62 L1 Puck Poland 54.43N 18.21E
59 F6 Puckaun Tipperary Irish Rep 52.56N 8.14W
106 E6 Puckaway,L Wisconsin 43.45N 89.10W
62 L1 Pucka,Zatoka B Poland
56 M4 Puckeridge Herts Eng 51.53N 0.01E
107 G9 Puckett Mississippi 32.04N 89.47W
14 B7 Puckford,Mt W Australia 25.09S 116.30E
121 B7 Pucón Chile 39.15S 71.52W
31 B5 Pudai R Afghanistan
32 F4 Pūdanū Iran 32.05N 55.57E
51 M6 Pudasjärvi Finland 65.23N 27.00E
56 G6 Puddletown Dorset Eng 50.45N 2.21W
46 Q1 Pudem U.S.S.R. 58.17N 52.16E
95 H3 Pudimoe S Africa 27.24S 24.43E
23 D5 Puding Guizhou China 26.18N 105.43E
42 B3 Pudino U.S.S.R. 57.33N 79.25E
98 Q5 Pudops Dam Newfoundland 48.10N 56.40W
47 D5 Pudozh U.S.S.R. 61.50N 36.32E
47 D5 Pudozhgora U.S.S.R. 62.18N 35.54E
57 K5 Pudsey W Yorks Eng 53.48N 1.40W
18 E6 Pudu Sumatra Indon 0.27S 102.16E
Puduchcheri see Pondicherry
28 D5 Pudukkottai Tamil Nadu India 10.23N 78.47E
115 K8 Puebla Mexico 19.03N 98.10W
115 K8 Puebla state Mexico
121 E3 Puebla Brugo Argentina 31.26S 60.05W
75 J5 Puebla de Albortón Spain 41.23N 0.51W
77 F3 Puebla de Alcocer Spain 38.59N 5.14W
75 J4 Puebla de Alfindén Spain 41.38N 0.45W
75 E8 Puebla de Almenara Spain 39.47N 2.50W
75 D8 Puebla de Almoradiel,La Spain 39.36N 3.07W
75 J7 Puebla de Arenoso Spain 40.06N 0.35W
77 F6 Puebla de Cazalla,La Spain 37.14N 5.18W
77 M5 Puebla de Don Fadrique Spain 37.58N 2.25W
77 G2 Puebla de Don Rodrigo Spain 39.05N 4.37W
77 B5 Puebla de Guzmán Spain 37.37N 7.15W
75 K5 Puebla de Híjar Spain 41.13N 0.27W
77 C3 Puebla de la Calzada Spain 38.54N 6.38W
77 D3 Puebla de la Reina Spain 38.40N 6.06W
76 E3 Puebla del Brollón Spain 42.34N 7.23W
76 B3 Puebla del Caramiñal Spain 42.37N 8.56W
77 Q3 Puebla del Duc Spain 38.55N 0.25W
76 J2 Puebla de Lillo Spain 43.00N 5.16W
77 D4 Puebla del Maestre Spain 38.05N 6.05W
77 F5 Puebla de los Infantes,La Spain 37.47N 5.23W
77 L3 Puebla del Principe Spain 38.35N 2.55W
75 G8 Puebla del Salvador Spain 39.34N 1.41W
76 L9 Puebla de Montalbán,La Spain 39.52N 4.22W
76 F10 Puebla de Obardo Spain 39.10N 6.39W
76 F4 Puebla de Sanabria Spain 42.04N 6.38W
77 D4 Puebla de Sancho Pérez Spain 38.24N 6.24W
76 E3 Puebla de San Julián Spain 42.52N 7.25W
77 D6 Puebla des Río, La Spain 37.16N 6.04W
76 E4 Puebla de Trives Spain 42.20N 7.15W
76 K3 Puebla de Valdavia,La Spain 42.40N 4.36W
75 J7 Puebla de Valverde,La Spain 40.14N 0.56W
77 W14 Puebla,La Balearic Is 39.46N 3.01E
77 Q2 Puebla Larga Spain 39.05N 0.29W
76 K9 Puebla Nueva,La Spain 39.55N 4.40W
119 D2 Pueblito Colombia 10.15N 74.21W
109 F3 Pueblo Colorado 38.17N 104.38W
109 C5 Pueblo Bonito New Mexico 36.04N 107.58W
120 D12 Pueblo Hundido Chile 26.25S 70.02W
120 B10 Pueblo Libre dist Lima Peru
118 A9 Pueblo Maidana Argentina 25.35S 60.38W
121 E3 Pueblo Marini Argentina 31.01S 61.53W
110 G7 Pueblo Mts Oregon
115 G6 Pueblo Nuevo Durango Mexico 23.26N 105.22W
115 L3 Pueblo Nuevo Nicaragua 13.21N 86.30W
115 G10 Pueblo Nuevo Panama 9.01N 79.31W
119 E2 Pueblo Nuevo Venezuela 11.59N 69.57W
119 B8 Puebloviejo Ecuador 1.35S 79.32W
119 F6 Pueblo Viejo Guainia Colombia 3.36N 67.25W
115 N9 Pueblo Viejo ruins Mexico 17.24N 93.45W
115 L6 Pueblo Viejo, L. de Mexico
91 G8 Puege Angola 8.54S 21.32E
121 D7 Puelches Argentina 38.10S 65.51W
121 C6 Puelén Argentina 37.32S 67.38W
121 B9 Puelo,L Argentina
121 B4 Puente Alto Chile 33.32S 70.35W
76 C4 Puenteareas Spain 42.12N 8.30W
76 B4 Puente Caldelas Spain 42.23N 8.30W
76 B2 Puente Ceso Spain 43.15N 8.54W
76 B3 Puente Cesures Spain 42.43N 8.39W
76 F4 Puente de Domingo Flórez Spain 42.25N 6.49W
115 K8 Puente de Ixtla Mexico 18.32N 99.26W
75 G2 Puente de la Reina Spain 42.40N 1.49W
76 J9 Puente del Arzobispo,El Spain 39.48N 5.10W
76 H8 Puente del Congosto Spain 40.30N 5.31W
121 B4 Puente del Inca Argentina 32.46S 70.00W
76 A2 Puente del Puerto Spain 43.09N 9.07W
75 M3 Puente de Montañana Spain 42.10N 0.41E
76 C2 Puentedeume Spain 43.24N 8.10W
75 Q9 Puente de Vallecas dist Madrid Spain 40.24N 3.40W
77 G6 Puente Genil Spain 37.24N 4.46W
76 L2 Puentenansa Spain 43.15N 4.24W
77 G4 Puente Nuevo,Embalse de res Spain 38.05N 5.00W
76 B4 Puente Sampayo Spain 42.21N 8.36W
76 D2 Puentes de Garcia Rodriguez Spain 43.26N 7.51W
77 N5 Puentes,Embalse de res Spain 37.44N 1.50W
116 K9 Puente Torres Venezuela 10.12N 69.54W
75 C1 Puenteviesgo Spain 43.18N 3.58W
114 D4 Pueo Pt Hawaiian Is 21.53N 160.04W
23 B7 Pu'er Yunnan China 23.05N 101.06E
111 O7 Puerco R Arizona
109 C6 Puerco,R New Mexico
119 B4 Puercos,Morro de pt Panama 7.13N 80.27W
77 L4 Puerta de Segura,La Spain 38.21N 2.44W
75 E6 Puerta,La Spain 40.38N 2.35W
76 G6 Puertas Spain 41.06N 6.18W
76 A2 Puerto R Spain
120 D6 Puerto Acosta Bolivia 15.33S 69.15W
118 C9 Puerto Adela Paraguay 24.32S 54.23W
121 J5 Puerto Aisén Chile 45.27S 72.58W
120 G5 Puerto Alegre Bolivia 13.52S 61.37W
119 E9 Puerto Alfonso Colombia 2.09S 71.01W
121 F3 Puerto Algarrobo Argentina 30.35S 59.35W
120 B1 Puerto América Peru 4.45S 76.59W
115 L10 Puerto Angel Mexico 15.40N 96.32W
118 B9 Puerto Antequera Paraguay 24.09S 57.07W
115 N10 Puerto Arista Mexico 15.58N 93.46W
115 N5 Puerto Armuelles Panama 8.19N 82.51W
118 A4 Puerto Arturo Bolivia 15.09S 60.41W
119 C7 Puerto Asís Colombia 0.31N 76.31W
119 F5 Puerto Ayacucho Venezuela 5.39N 67.32W
119 B6 Puerto Ayora Galápagos Is 0.45S 90.19W
121 J6 Puerto Bajo Pisagua Chile 47.48S 73.40W
115 P10 Puerto Barrios Guatemala 15.41N 88.32W
121 E7 Puerto Belgrano Argentina 38.52S 62.08W
118 B10 Puerto Bermejo Argentina 26.55S 58.34W
120 C4 Puerto Bermudez Peru 10.14S 74.56W
119 D4 Puerto Berrío Colombia 6.28N 74.28W
121 J6 Puerto Bertrand Chile 47.00S 72.55W
121 B8 Puerto Blest Argentina 41.05S 71.55W
119 B9 Puerto Bolívar Ecuador 3.19S 79.59W
119 D5 Puerto Boyaca Colombia 5.58N 74.36W
119 F2 Puerto Cabello Venezuela 10.29N 68.02W
115 N2 Puerto Cabezas Nicaragua 14.02N 83.24W
115 N2 Puerto Cabo Gracias á Dios Honduras 15.00N 83.10W
115 F11 Puerto Caimito Panama 8.52N 79.43W
119 C6 Puerto Cali airport Colombia 3.25N 76.27W
120 C3 Puerto Callao Peru 8.55S 74.31W
88 G7 Puerto Cansado inlet Morocco 28.04N 12.15W
Puerto Capaz see Jebha, El
119 F4 Puerto Carreño Colombia 6.08N 69.27W
118 B8 Puerto Casado Paraguay 22.15S 57.55W
76 H8 Puerto Castilla Spain 40.18N 5.37W
119 D9 Puerto Cerpera Peru 3.01S 75.00W
120 D4 Puerto Ceticayo Peru 11.21S 71.08W
120 A8 Puerto Chicama Peru 7.48S 79.23W
115 G3 Puerto Chilicote Mexico 28.59N 104.50W
121 A10 Puerto Cisnes Chile 44.49S 72.37W
121 K8 Puerto Coig Argentina 50.54S 69.15W
119 D2 Puerto Colombia Colombia 11.00N 74.56W
121 F4 Puerto Constanza Argentina 33.55S 59.00W
118 B8 Puerto Cooper Paraguay 23.00S 57.45W
119 E8 Puerto Cordoba Colombia 1.15S 69.56W
115 N5 Puerto Cortés Costa Rica 9.00N 83.32W
115 Q10 Puerto Cortés Honduras 15.50N 87.55W
115 D5 Puerto Cortés Mexico 24.29N 111.50W
Puerto Coyle see Puerto Coig
119 D7 Puerto Cuba Colombia 0.40N 73.29W
119 D7 Puerto Cuemaní Colombia 0.03N 73.21W
119 E2 Puerto Cumarebo Venezuela 11.31N 69.30W
77 W14 Puerto de Alcudia Balearic Is 39.50N 3.07E
77 U14 Puerto de Andraitx,El Balearic Is 39.32N 2.24E
75 L6 Puerto de Beceite reg Spain
76 H8 Puerto de Béjar Spain 40.21N 5.50W
120 D5 Puerto Definitivo Peru 12.23S 70.54W
96 R14 Puerto de Güimar Tenerife Canary Is 28.18N 16.22W
119 H2 Puerto de Hierro Venezuela 10.40N 62.03W
96 R13 Puerto de la Cruz Tenerife Canary Is 28.24N 16.33W
96 P11 Puerto de la Estaca Hierro Canary Is 27.46N 17.54W
77 B5 Puerto de la Laja Spain 37.31N 7.29W
96 V14 Puerto de la Luz Gran Canaria Canary Is 28.10N 15.25W
96 S10 Puerto de la Peña Fuerteventura Canary Is 28.20N 14.10W
75 R3 Puerto de la Selva Spain 42.20N 3.12E
115 C2 Puerto de Lobos Mexico 30.16N 112.50W
76 M7 Puerto del Paular pass Spain 40.50N 3.57W
96 T10 Puerto del Rosario Fuerteventura Canary Is 28.29N 13.52W
115 P10 Puerto de Matás de Galvez Guatemala 15.39N 88.35W
77 O5 Puerto de Mazarrón Spain 37.34N 1.15W
96 U16 Puerto de Mogán Gran Canaria Canary Is 27.48N 15.47W
115 Q7 Puerto de Morelos Mexico 20.49N 86.52W
96 P10 Puerto de Naös La Palma Canary Is 28.35N 17.54W
119 E3 Puerto de Nutrias Venezuela 8.07N 69.18W
120 G7 Puerto de Pailas Bolivia 17.35S 62.46W
77 W14 Puerto de Pollensa Balearic Is 39.54N 3.05E
76 H10 Puerto de Santa Cruz Spain 39.19N 5.51W
77 D7 Puerto de Santa Maria Spain 36.36N 6.13W
96 Q14 Puerto de Santiago Tenerife Canary Is 28.14N 16.50W
76 J9 Puerto de San Vicente Spain 39.32N 5.06W
96 P10 Puerto de Tazacorte La Palma Canary Is 28.38N 17.56W
119 E1 Puerto Estrella Colombia 12.21N 71.18W
120 A8 Puerto Eten Peru 6.55S 79.50W
120 G6 Puerto Frey Bolivia 14.46S 61.13W
121 E7 Puerto Galvan Argentina 38.45S 62.20W
120 F7 Puerto Grether Bolivia 17.12S 64.48W
118 B7 Puerto Guaraní Paraguay 21.15S 57.53W
121 L10 Puerto Harberton Argentina 54.54S 67.20W
120 E5 Puerto Heath Peru 12.34S 68.39W
119 D7 Puerto Huitoto Colombia 0.16N 74.03W
121 F4 Puerto Ibicuy Argentina 33.44S 59.10W
118 C9 Puerto Iguazú Argentina 25.39S 54.35W
120 C3 Puerto Inca Peru 9.22S 74.54W
121 E7 Puerto Ingeniero White Arg 38.46S 62.16W
Puerto Iradier see Cogo
120 G10 Puerto Irigoyen Argentina 23.15S 61.46W
118 B6 Puerto Isabel Bolivia 18.13S 57.37W
115 N5 Puerto Jiménez Costa Rica 8.35N 83.20W
115 Q7 Puerto Juárez Mexico 21.10N 86.50W
119 G2 Puerto La Cruz Venezuela 10.14N 64.40W
96 T10 Puerto Lajas Fuerteventura Canary Is 28.32N 13.50W
120 G10 Puerto La Paz Argentina 22.30S 62.21W
77 K2 Puerto Lápiche Spain 39.20N 3.29W
75 L2 Puértolas Spain 42.33N 0.08E
119 D8 Puerto Leguízamo Colombia 0.14S 74.45W
115 N2 Puerto Lempira Honduras 15.12N 83.51W
115 C3 Puerto Libertad Mexico 29.55N 112.41W
119 D6 Puerto Limón Meta Colombia 3.24N 73.38W
115 G9 Puerto Limón Panama 9.15N 79.48W
119 C7 Puerto Limón Putumayo Colombia 1.02N 76.30W
77 H3 Puertollano Spain 38.41N 4.07W
121 D9 Puerto Lobos Argentina 42.02S 65.05W
119 E2 Puerto Lopez Guajira Colombia 11.58N 71.17W
119 D5 Puerto Lopéz Meta Colombia 4.06N 72.57W
77 J6 Puerto Lopez Spain 37.20N 3.50W
121 G1 Puerto Lucena Brazil 27.50S 54.59W
77 N5 Puerto Lumbreras Spain 37.35N 1.49W
115 N10 Puerto Madero Mexico 14.53N 92.23W
121 D9 Puerto Madryn Argentina 42.45S 65.02W
115 C5 Puerto Magdalena Mexico 24.39N 112.10W
120 D5 Puerto Maldonado Peru 12.37S 69.11W
116 F4 Puerto Manatí Cuba 21.24N 76.50W
119 A10 Puerto Máncora Peru 4.09S 81.01W
118 B7 Puerto María Auxiliadora Paraguay 21.44S 57.57W
76 D3 Puertomarín Spain 42.48N 7.37W
119 E8 Puerto Mariti Colombia 1.11S 70.02W
120 E6 Puerto Marquez Bolivia 15.46S 66.07W
121 A9 Puerto Melinka Chile 43.52S 73.47W
119 D7 Puerto Mercedes Colombia 1.10N 72.55W
Puerto México see Coatzacoalcos
118 B7 Puerto Mihanovich Paraguay 20.44S 57.56W
75 K7 Puertomingalvo Spain 40.16N 0.28W
119 F4 Puerto Miranda Venezuela 7.56N 67.29W
121 A8 Puerto Montt Chile 41.28S 73.00W
115 L3 Puerto Morazán Nicaragua 12.50N 87.12W
120 A3 Puerto Morín Peru 8.23S 78.52W
119 C4 Puerto Mutis Colombia 6.10N 77.24W
121 J8 Puerto Natales Chile 51.41S 72.15W
119 E5 Puerto Nuevo Colombia 5.46N 69.59W
118 B7 Puerto Nuevo Paraguay 20.28S 58.01W
121 A8 Puerto Octay Chile 40.58S 72.55W
119 D4 Puerto Olaya Colombia 6.29N 74.23W
119 H3 Puerto Ordaz Venezuela 8.17N 62.44W
119 C7 Puerto Ospina Colombia 0.08N 75.53W
116 F4 Puerto Padre Cuba 21.13N 76.35W
115 F11 Puerto Padre Panama 8.54N 79.43W
119 F4 Puerto Páez Venezuela 6.14N 67.26W
120 E6 Puerto Pando Bolivia 15.10S 67.41W
119 C9 Puerto Pardo Loreto Peru 3.45S 76.23W
120 E5 Puerto Pardo Madre de Dios Peru 12.31S 68.45W
120 D5 Puerto Pariamanu Peru 12.26S 69.12W
115 C2 Puerto Peñasco Mexico 31.20N 113.35W
115 F9 Puerto Pilón Panama 9.21N 79.48W
118 B8 Puerto Pinasco Paraguay 22.36S 57.53W
121 D9 Puerto Pirámides Argentina 42.34S 64.20W
118 C10 Puerto Piray Argentina 26.37S 54.44W
119 G2 Puerto Píritu Venezuela 10.04N 65.00W
119 D8 Puerto Pizarro Colombia 0.34S 73.25W
119 B9 Puerto Pizarro Peru 3.34S 80.24W
116 J5 Puerto Plata Dominican Rep 19.48N 70.41W
120 C3 Puerto Portillo Peru 9.44S 72.47W
96 T10 Puerto Pozo Negro Fuerteventura Canary Is 28.18N 13.54W
120 C4 Puerto Prado Peru 11.08S 74.21W
19 J7 Puerto Princesa Philippines 9.46N 118.45E
120 D4 Puerto Providencia Peru 11.40S 70.36W
121 A9 Puerto Quellón Chile 43.08S 73.40W
115 M5 Puerto Quepos Costa Rica 9.28N 84.10W
121 A9 Puerto Ramirez Chile 43.28S 72.11W
77 D7 Puerto Real Spain 36.32N 6.11W
119 C3 Puerto Rey Colombia 8.53N 76.25W
118 C10 Puerto Rico Argentina 26.50S 55.08W
120 E4 Puerto Rico Bolivia 11.07S 67.32W
119 C7 Puerto Rico Colombia 1.54N 75.13W
96 U16 Puerto Rico Gran Canaria Canary Is 27.47N 15.42W
116 L5 Puerto Rico isld W Indies
116 L5 Puerto Rico Trench West Indies
121 F4 Puerto Ruiz Argentina 33.14S 59.25W
121 A7 Puerto Saavedra Chile 38.45S 73.25W
119 D5 Puerto Salgar Colombia 5.30N 74.38W
116 G4 Puerto Samá Cuba 21.08N 75.48W
119 E9 Puerto San Agustin Peru 2.46S 71.17W
121 J6 Puerto San Carlos Chile 47.33S 73.01W
121 D9 Puerto San José Argentina 42.27S 64.07W
118 C10 Puerto San Lorenzo Paraguay 26.25S 54.44W
121 L8 Puerto Santa Cruz Argentina 50.03S 68.35W
121 L8 Puerto Santa Cruz inlet Argentina
118 B8 Puerto Sastre Paraguay 22.02S 58.00W
120 G5 Puerto Saucedo Bolivia 13.58S 62.51W
77 E7 Puerto Serrano Spain 36.55N 5.32W
77 O5 Puerto,Sierra del mts Spain
120 F5 Puerto Siles Bolivia 12.49S 65.04W
119 E9 Puerto Socorro Peru 2.46S 70.04W
77 V14 Puerto Sóller Balearic Is 39.48N 2.41E
115 L4 Puerto Somoza Nicaragua 12.12N 86.46W
118 C9 Puerto Strossner Paraguay 25.32S 54.34W
118 B6 Puerto Suárez Bolivia 18.59S 57.46W
Puerto Sucre Bolivia see Guayaramerin
119 G2 Puerto Sucre Venezuela 10.28N 64.11W
120 B4 Puerto Supe Peru 10.47S 77.46W
120 D5 Puerto Tahuantisuyo Peru 12.36S 70.21W
119 C6 Puerto Tejado Colombia 3.16N 76.22W
115 E10 Puerto Trinidad Panama 8.59N 79.58W
119 C9 Puerto Tunigrama Peru 2.47S 76.37W
119 C7 Puerto Umbría Colombia 0.52N 76.36W
121 D9 Puerto Valdés Argentina 42.28S 63.40W
115 G7 Puerto Vallarta Mexico 20.36N 105.15W
121 A8 Puerto Varas Chile 41.20S 73.00W
120 C3 Puerto Victoria Peru 9.54S 74.55W
121 B1 Puerto Viejo Chile 27.20S 70.58W
116 H10 Puerto Villamizar Colombia 8.18N 72.26W
120 G5 Puerto Villazon Bolivia 13.26S 61.55W
121 L5 Puerto Visser Argentina 45.23S 67.08W
119 D4 Puerto Wilches Colombia 7.22N 73.53W
121 L10 Puerto Williams Chile 54.57S 68.15W
121 K9 Puerto Yartou Chile 53.53S 70.09W
118 B8 Puerto Ybapobó Paraguay 23.36S 57.20W
121 F3 Puerto Yerua Argentina 31.35S 58.00W
119 D8 Puesto Arturo Peru 1.49S 73.19W
118 A7 Puesto Estrella Paraguay 21.04S 62.06W
121 C7 Puesto Sánchez Argentina 38.26S 67.05W
122 D12 Pueu Tahiti Pacific Oc 17.44S 149.12W
75 G2 Pueyo Spain 42.34N 1.40W
75 L4 Pueyo de Santa Cruz Spain 41.51N 0.10E
121 K6 Pueyrredón, L Argentina
64 A2 Puffendorf W Germany 50.56N 6.13E
57 E6 Puffin I Gwynedd Wales 53.19N 4.01W
118 B6 Puga Brazil 19.39S 57.31W
45 U4 Pugachev U.S.S.R. 52.02N 48.49E
40 J7 Pugachevo Sakhalin U.S.S.R. 48.10N 142.33E
46 R2 Pugachevo Udmurt A.S.S.R. U.S.S.R. 56.32N 52.59E
29 C3 Pugal Rajasthan India 28.32N 72.41E
92 J10 Puga Puga I Mozambique 16.25S 39.54E
23 C5 Puge Sichuan China 27.00N 102.48E
93 E10 Puge Tanzania 4.43S 33.06E
18 K10 Puger Java Indon 8.20S 113.29E
18 K10 Puger R Java Indonesia
110 C2 Puget Sd Washington
71 K9 Puget-Théniers France 43.57N 6.54E
71 J10 Puget-Ville France 43.17N 6.08E
103 C6 Pughtown Pennsylvania 40.10N 75.40W
71 H5 Pugieu France 45.49N 5.40E
78 G8 Puglia reg Italy
72 D5 Pugnac France 45.05N 0.30W
92 J5 Pugu Tanzania 6.55S 39.04E
19 B8 Pugubengo Indonesia 8.36S 121.14E
18 E8 Pugung,Gunung mt Sumatra Indon 4.59S 103.50E
32 H8 Pūgūnzī Iran 25.50N 59.05E
98 J8 Pugwash Nova Scotia 45.52N 63.40W
98 J8 Pugwash Harb Nova Scotia
98 J8 Pugwash Junction Nova Scotia 45.46N 63.39W
11 M5 Puha New Zealand 38.29S 177.52E
32 F7 Pūhāl-e-Khamir, Kūh-e mts Iran
23 D1 Pu He R Gansu China
114 F4 Puhi Hawaiian Is 21.57N 159.24W
122 U15 Puhi crater Easter I Pacific Oc 27.06S 109.20W
114 E6 Puhilele Pt Hawaiian Is 20.39N 156.04W
11 D3 Puhinui Cr New Zealand
11 J3 Puhoi New Zealand 36.30S 174.42E
Pu-hsi see Chahayang
Pu-hsien see Pucheng
82 H5 Pui Romania 45.30N 23.05E
48 V15 Puiagtoq fjord Greenland
18 B6 Puian R Pen Malaysia
66 D5 Puidoux Switzerland 46.31N 6.47E
82 L4 Puieşti Romania 46.25N 27.33E
60 L12 Puiflijk Netherlands 51.52N 5.36E
75 K8 Puig Spain 39.36N 0.19W
75 O3 Puigcerdá Spain 42.26N 1.55E
75 J3 Puig Chilibro mt Spain 42.21N 0.35W
75 O5 Puigdalba Spain 41.25N 1.42E
72 J11 Puigmal mt France 42.23N 2.07E
75 P3 Puigmale mt Spain 42.23N 2.07E
77 V14 Puig Mayor mt Balearic Is 39.49N 2.47E
77 V14 Puigpuñent Balearic Is 39.37N 2.31E
75 O4 Puigreig Spain 41.58N 1.53E
75 M4 Puigvert Spain 41.33N 0.43E
23 B10 Pui Kau Hong Kong 22.14N 114.06E
71 J9 Puimoisson France 43.52N 6.08E
120 C1 Puinahua,Can.de Peru
71 C1 Puisaye,Collines de la France 47.35N 3.18E
69 C7 Puiseaux France 48.12N 2.28E
72 D6 Puisseguin France 44.55N 0.04W
71 C10 Puisserguier France 43.22N 3.03E
31 H10 Puisur R Bangladesh
72 J10 Puivert France 42.55N 2.03E
19 N8 Pujada B Mindanao Philippines
71 F9 Pujaut France 44.00N 4.46E
89 D8 Pujehun Sierra Leone 7.23N 11.44W
77 F7 Pujerra Spain 36.37N 5.09W
Puji see Wugong
23 C3 Pujiang Sichuan China 30.14N 103.30E
23 H4 Pujiang Zhejiang China 29.29N 119.54E
119 B8 Pujili Ecuador 1.00S 78.54W
72 E9 Pujo France 43.21N 0.04E
72 D6 Pujols France 44.48N 0.02W
21 D7 Pujon Resr N Korea
18 L6 Pujun Borneo Indon 1.19S 114.19E
11 E11 Pukaki,L New Zealand
122 F14 Pukapuka atoll Tuamotu Is Pacific Oc 14.50S 138.50W
122 K9 Pukapuka I Cook Is Pacific Oc 10.53S 165.49W
122 G15 Pukarua atoll Tuamotu Is Pacific Oc 18.16S 137.00W
99 E4 Pukaskwa National Park Ontario
100 Q3 Pukatawagan Manitoba 55.46N 101.14W
100 Q3 Pukatawagan L Manitoba
21 C7 Pukchin N Korea 40.11N 125.46E
21 D7 Pukch'ŏng N Korea 40.12N 128.10E
83 D2 Pukë Albania 42.02N 19.53E
11 N4 Pukeamaru mt New Zealand 37.39S 178.18E
11 J5 Pukearuhe New Zealand 38.53S 174.31E
11 N13 Pukehiki New Zealand 45.53S 170.37E
11 L6 Pukehou New Zealand 39.51S 176.39E
11 J4 Pukekawa New Zealand 37.21S 174.59E
11 J4 Pukekohe New Zealand 37.12S 174.56E
11 E10 Pukekura New Zealand 43.02S 170.39E
11 K4 Pukemiro New Zealand 37.37S 175.03E
11 H1 Pukenui New Zealand 34.49S 173.06E
11 L6 Pukeokahu New Zealand 39.37S 176.01E
11 E12 Pukerangi New Zealand 45.38S 170.13E
11 D13 Pukerau New Zealand 46.07S 169.06E
11 K6 Pukeroa New Zealand 39.45S 175.32E
11 G10 Puketaraki Ra New Zealand
11 N5 Puketawai New Zealand 38.22S 178.20E
11 L6 Puketitiri New Zealand 39.17S 176.32E
11 M4 Puketoetoe mt New Zealand 37.58S 177.41E
11 L7 Puketoi Ra New Zealand
11 K5 Puketutu New Zealand 38.27S 175.17E
11 C3 Puketutu I New Zealand
11 F12 Pukeuri Junction New Zealand 45.03S 171.02E
46 G3 Pukhovichi Belorussiya U.S.S.R. 53.28N 28.18E
45 L6 Pukhovo U.S.S.R. 50.53N 39.24E
30 C6 Pukhrayan Uttar Prad India 26.14N 79.50E
51 M11 Pukkila Finland 60.38N 25.35E
114 D5 Pukoo Hawaiian Is 21.05N 156.47W
23 H2 Pukou Anhui China 32.05N 118.43E
47 E4 Puksa U.S.S.R. 62.35N 40.26E
47 E4 Puksoozero U.S.S.R. 62.42N 40.39E
47 G6 Puksub U.S.S.R. 59.48N 54.59E
108 L6 Pukwana S Dakota 43.47N 99.10W
81 B5 Pula Sardinia 39.01N 9.00E
82 B6 Pula Yugoslavia 44.52N 13.52E
120 E9 Pulacayo Bolivia 20.25S 66.41W
81 C6 Pula, C. di Sardinia 39.59N 9.02E
18 D10 Pulai,Gunong mt Pen Malaysia 1.35N 103.32E
31 B5 Pulalak Afghanistan 30.15N 62.54E
Pulandian see Xinjin
19 M7 Pulangi R Mindanao Philippines
18 L7 Pulangpisau Borneo Indon 2.45S 114.15E
30 E3 Pulanto Nepal 29.22N 81.45E
17 P10 Pulap atoll Caroline Is Pacific Oc 7.38N 149.25E
120 E11 Pular,Cerro pk Chile 24.12S 68.05W
18 F9 Pulasari mt Java Indon 6.20S 105.59E
106 B9 Pulaski Iowa 40.41N 92.17W
104 J3 Pulaski New York 43.34N 76.06W
107 J6 Pulaski Tennessee 35.11N 87.02W
104 E9 Pulaski Virginia 37.03N 80.47W
106 F5 Pulaski Wisconsin 44.40N 88.15W
37 D2 Pulat Marmara I Turkey 40.39N 27.40E
15 E6 Pulau R Irian Jaya
18 E6 Pulaukijang Sumatra Indon 0.43S 103.14E
18 J5 Pulaumajang Borneo Indon 0.57N 112.00E
18 F9 Pulau Seribu isld Sumatra Indonesia
18 C6 Pulautelo Indonesia 0.04S 98.17E
62 N4 Puławy Poland 51.26N 21.59E
56 K6 Pulborough W Sussex Eng 50.58N 0.30W
Pul Dashi see Poldasht
61 J2 Pulderbos Belgium 51.13N 4.42E
89 E9 Puleba R Liberia
114 E6 Pulehu Hawaiian Is 20.46N 156.18W
79 O2 Púlfero Italy 46.11N 13.29E
29 F7 Pulgaon Maharashtra India 20.40N 78.22E
76 L9 Pulgar Spain 39.41N 4.09W
56 O3 Pulham Norfolk Eng 52.26N 1.14E
69 M1 Pulheim W Germany 51.00N 6.48E
P'u-li see Taxkorgan
23 J7 Pu-li Taiwan 23.58N 120.55E
28 E4 Pulicat Tamil Nadu India 13.26N 80.20E
28 E4 Pulicat L Andhra Prad India
71 F3 Puligny-Montrachet France 46.57N 4.45E
31 E3 Pul-i-Khumri Afghanistan 35.55N 68.45E
Pul-i-Khvatun see Pole-Khatun
19 H1 Pulilan Luzon Philippines 14.54N 120.50E
Pul-i-Sefid see Pol-e Safid
Pul-i-Tufangchi see Pol-e Tofangchi
28 D3 Pulivendla Andhra Prad India 14.29N 78.13E
28 C6 Puliyangudi Tamil Nadu India 9.12N 77.29E
26 R3 Puliyankulam Sri Lanka 8.57N 80.13E
65 N4 Pulkau Austria 48.43N 15.52E
65 O4 Pulkau R Austria
34 M4 Pulkhana oil bore Iraq 34.48N 44.44E
51 M7 Pulkkila Finland 64.16N 25.50E
64 L7 Pullach W Germany 48.03N 11.33E
26 U7 Pulladiputti Sri Lanka 7.20N 81.51E
28 D3 Pullampet Andhra Prad India 14.10N 79.15E
61 J2 Pulle Belgium 51.12N 4.43E
110 H3 Pullman Washington 46.46N 117.09W
120 C6 Pullo Peru 15.13S 73.51W
66 C5 Pully Switzerland 46.31N 6.40E
26 S4 Pulmoddai Sri Lanka 8.57N 80.57E
17 M11 Pulo Anna isld Caroline Is Pacific Oc 4.40N 131.58E
18 G2 Pulogadung Jakarta Indonesia 6.11S 106.54E
19 K3 Pulog, Mt Luzon Philippines 16.37N 120.54E
26 R2 Puloli Sri Lanka 9.47N 80.14E
47 E3 Pulonga U.S.S.R. 66.19N 40.01E
47 C2 Pulozero U.S.S.R. 68.22N 33.15E
77 N6 Pulpí Spain 37.25N 1.44W
80 B3 Púlpito, Pta Italy 42.36N 10.03E
115 D4 Púlpito, Pta Mexico 26.31N 111.25W
120 F8 Pulquina Bolivia 18.07S 64.23W
81 P12 Pulsano Italy 40.23N 17.21E
63 U10 Pulsnitz E Germany 51.11N 14.01E
63 T10 Pulsnitz R E Germany
62 N3 Pułtusk Poland 52.42N 21.02E
24 D7 Pulu Xinjiang Uygur Zizhiqu China 36.10N 81.29E
37 E6 Pülümür Turkey 39.30N 39.51E
18 L10 Pulukan Bali Indon 8.25S 114.49E
26 U6 Pulukunava Sri Lanka 7.32N 81.38E
37 E5 Pulur Turkey 40.10N 39.45E
19 E1 Pulutan Indonesia 4.09N 126.50E
17 P10 Puluwat atoll Caroline Is Pacific Oc 7.21N 149.11E
Pulvar R see Shādkām R
92 G4 Puma Tanzania 5.00S 34.46E
120 C5 Pumasillo, Cerro mt Peru 13.11S 73.00W
24 G11 Puma Yumco L Xizang Zizhiqu China 28.30N 90.15E
Pumiao see Yongning
30 J2 Pumori mt Xizang Zizhiqu/Nepal 28.01N 86.50E
30 J2 Pumori Glacier Xizang Zizhiqu
104 E2 Pumphrey Maryland 39.13N 76.38W
108 E4 Pumpkin Cr Montana
108 G8 Pumpkin Cr Nebraska
112 F6 Pumpville Texas 29.57N 101.44W
56 D3 Pumsaint Dyfed Wales 52.03N 3.58W
121 E1 Puna Argentina 27.46S 62.30W
119 B9 Puná Ecuador 2.48S 79.55W
114 C7 Puna dist Hawaiian Is
19 B4 Puna R Celebes Indon
122 B12 Punaauia Tahiti Pacific Oc 17.38S 149.37W
122 B12 Punaauia, Pt Tahiti Pacific Oc 17.38S 149.37W
120 E11 Puna de Atacama mts Argentina
30 A5 Punahana Haryana India 27.52N 77.12E
119 B9 Puná, I Ecuador 2.52S 80.07W
11 F9 Punakaiki New Zealand 42.06S 171.20E
28 G2 Punakha Bhutan 27.38N 89.50E
11 H2 Punakitere, R New Zealand
114 B8 Punaluu Hawaiian Is 19.08N 155.30W
18 L5 Punan Borneo Indon 1.15N 115.29E
18 M4 Punan Borneo Indon 3.27N 116.17E
26 T6 Punanai Sri Lanka 7.58N 81.22E
122 U16 Punapau pk Easter I Pacific Oc 27.09S 109.24W
30 J7 Punarakh Bihar India 25.29N 85.50E
29 E6 Punasa Madhya Prad India 22.15N 76.29E
120 F7 Punata Bolivia 17.32S 65.50W
31 H4 Punch Kashmir 33.46N 74.08E
31 G4 Punch dist Kashmir
101 M9 Punchaw Br Col 53.30N 123.17W
65 N6 Punchberg Austria 47.48N 15.54E
24 F11 Püncogling Xizang Zizhiqu China 29.17N 88.00E
93 J6 Punda Milia Kenya 0.54S 37.10E
94 L4 Punda Milia Transvaal S Africa 22.43S 31.02E
29 E3 Pundri Haryana India 29.46N 76.38E
28 J1 Pundro Xizang Zizhiqu 28.38N 92.24E
18 K7 Pundu Borneo Indon 2.02S 113.11E
47 E5 Punduga U.S.S.R. 60.07N 40.10E
Pune see Poona
26 R4 Punewa Sri Lanka 8.35N 80.28E
47 J4 Punga R U.S.S.R.
43 N7 Pungan Uzbekistan U.S.S.R. 40.45N 70.50E
28 D4 Punganuru Andhra Prad India 13.23N 78.34E
82 L4 Pungeşti Romania 46.41N 27.24E
18 J2 Punggol dist Singapore
18 J2 Punggol R Singapore
18 J2 Punggol,Tanjong C Singapore 1.25N 103.55E
76 C4 Pungín Spain 42.23N 8.00W
105 L2 Pungo N Carolina 35.28N 76.35W
91 D8 Pungo Andongo Angola 9.44S 15.35E
105 L2 Pungo L N Carolina 35.43N 76.33W

105 L2 Pungo R N Carolina
25 M8 Pungra Bum mt Burma 26.32N 95.51E
21 D7 P'ungsan N Korea 40.50N 128.09E
92 F11 Pungue Mozambique 18.33S 33.15E
94 M2 Pungüe R Mozambique
92 K12 Pungume I Zanzibar 6.25S 39.20E
92 F11 Pungwe Falls Zimbabwe 18.27S 32.49E
91 K4 Punia Zaïre 1.28S 26.25E
18 M10 Punikan, Gunung mt Indonesia 8.28S 116.14E
121 B2 Punilla, Sa. de la mts Chile
23 G7 Puning Guangdong China 23.24N 116.14E
121 B3 Punitaqui Chile 30.50S 71.20W
29 D2 Punjab state India
31 F5 Punjab, The dist Pakistan
13 E4 Punjaub Queensland 18.09S 139.07E
Punkaharju see Puttiko
51 K10 Punkalaidun Finland 61.07N 23.05E
109 G3 Punkin Center Colorado 38.50N 103.39W
26 Q2 Punkudutivu isld Sri Lanka 9.35N 79.50E
104 G6 Punkxsutawney Pennsylvania 40.57N 78.59W
31 J3 Punmah Glacier Kashmir
100 N7 Punnichy Saskatchewan 51.22N 104.18W
120 D6 Puno Peru 15.53S 70.03W
120 D6 Puno dept Peru
30 H7 Punpun R Bihar India
120 B4 Punrrun, L Peru 10.51S 76.30W
19 J2 Punta Luzon Philippines 14.18N 121.18E
109 D7 Punta New Mexico 34.36N 106.17W
121 E7 Punta Alta Argentina 38.50S 62.00W
121 K9 Punta Arenas Chile 53.10S 70.56W
12 C4 Puntabie S Australia 32.15S 134.13E
119 E2 Punta Cardón Venezuela 11.24N 70.09W
81 C1 Puntaccia, Mte Sardinia 41.02N 9.05E
121 C5 Punta de Agua Argentina 35.54S 67.05W
112 B8 Punta de Agua R New Mexico/Texas
120 D7 Punta de Bombon Peru 17.12S 71.48W
121 B2 Punta de Diaz Chile 28.05S 70.38W
121 G5 Punta del Este Uruguay 34.59S 54.58W
121 D9 Punta Delgada Argentina 42.45S 63.40W
121 K9 Punta Delgada Chile 52.25S 69.44W
121 C3 Punta de los Llanos Argentina 30.10S 66.35W
119 G2 Punta de Piedras Venezuela 10.57N 64.06W
121 B4 Punta de Vacas Argentina 32.50S 69.45W
115 P9 Punta Gorda Belize 16.10N 88.45W
105 E11 Punta Gorda Florida 26.56N 82.01W
96 P9 Puntagorda La Palma Canary Is 28.47N 17.59W
115 N4 Punta Gorda Nicaragua 11.31N 83.46W
96 S13 Punta Hidalgo Tenerife Canary Is 28.35N 16.19W
75 M6 Punta, La pt Spain 40.48N 0.45E
96 P9 Puntallana La Palma Canary Is 28.44N 17.43W
120 D11 Punta Negra, Salar de salt pan Chile
121 D9 Punta Norte Argentina 42.05S 63.46W
115 B3 Punta Prieta Mexico 28.56N 114.11W
77 Y14 Punta Prima Balearic Is 39.49N 4.16E
105 E11 Punta Rassa Florida 26.29N 82.00W
115 M4 Puntarenas Costa Rica 10.00N 84.50W
120 E10 Puntas Negras, Cerro pk Chile 23.45S 67.35W
121 G6 Punta Sur C Argentina 36.55S 56.41W
77 C6 Punta Umbria Spain 37.10N 6.57W
60 P7 Punt, De Netherlands 53.07N 6.37E
66 Q5 Punt, La Switzerland 46.35N 9.56E
119 E2 Punto Fijo Venezuela 11.50N 70.16W
43 N7 Punuk Tadzhikistan U.S.S.R. 40.53N 70.37E
113 C5 Punuk Is Bering Sea
21 D9 Punwŏn-ni S Korea 37.31N 127.20E
25 G6 Puok Cambodia 13.26N 103.44E
51 N7 Puolanka Finland 64.50N 27.44E
114 E4 Puolo Pt Hawaiian Is 21.53N 159.36W
79 M2 Puos d'Alpago Italy 46.09N 12.23E
51 H5 Puottaure Sweden 66.11N 20.20E
15 A4 Puper Waigeo, Irian Jaya 0.10S 131.17E
121 B3 Pupio Chile 31.57S 71.12W
11 G7 Puponga New Zealand 40.31S 172.44E
30 J6 Pupri Bihar India 26.28N 85.42E
11 C1 Pupuke, L New Zealand
23 F4 Puqi Hubei China 29.45N 113.55E
120 D7 Puquina Peru 16.38S 71.10W
120 D8 Puquintica, Cerro pk Chile 18.45S 69.00W
120 C6 Puquio Peru 14.44S 74.07W
121 B1 Puquios Atacamá Chile 27.10S 69.53W
120 D8 Puquios Tarapacá Chile 18.10S 69.45W
32 G7 Pūr Iran 27.59N 56.50E
29 D5 Pur Rajasthan India 25.20N 74.34E
38 G2 Pur R Tyumen U.S.S.R.
41 L5 Pur R Yakutsk U.S.S.R.
41 E4 Pura U.S.S.R. 73.06N 86.45E
41 E4 Pura R U.S.S.R.
119 C6 Purace, Vol. de vol Colombia 2.22N 76.23W
30 C6 Puraha R Uttar Prad India
30 K7 Puraini Bihar India 25.08N 86.59E
11 N11 Purakanui New Zealand 45.45S 170.39E
30 E7 Pura Mufti Uttar Prad India 25.29N 81.41E
28 B1 Purandhar Maharashtra India 18.15N 74.04E
30 D4 Puranpur Uttar Prad India 28.30N 80.09E
15 H7 Purari R Papua New Guinea
28 C7 Purasawalkam dist Madras, Tamil Nadu India
11 N10 Purau New Zealand 43.39S 172.45E
11 N10 Purau B New Zealand
65 M4 Purbach Austria 48.46N 15.07E
56 G6 Purbeck Downs Dorset Eng
18 H9 Purbolinggo Java Indon 7.22S 109.15E
109 N6 Purcell Oklahoma 35.01N 97.23W
113 J3 Purcell Mt Alaska 66.16N 157.49W
101 P10 Purcell Mts Br Columbia
110 K1 Purcell Ra Montana
104 H7 Purcellville Virginia 39.08N 77.45W
77 M6 Purchena Spain 37.21N 2.21W
31 C4 Purdil Afghanistan 32.34N 65.56E
107 C2 Purdin Missouri 39.58N 93.10W
45 P2 Purdoshki U.S.S.R. 54.41N 43.35E
108 K7 Purdum Nebraska 42.04N 100.17W
107 C5 Purdy Missouri 36.50N 93.57W
15 J5 Purdy Is Bismarck Arch
103 G4 Purdys New York 41.19N 73.39W
121 A7 Purén Chile 38.03S 73.05W
11 K5 Pureora mt New Zealand 38.32S 175.38E
115 H8 Purépero Mexico 19.50N 102.00W
11 J1 Purerua New Zealand 35.08S 174.03E
55 K4 Purfleet Essex England 51.29N 0.14E
109 G4 Purgatoire R Colorado
65 M5 Purgstall Austria 48.03N 15.08E
Purhus see Misk
18 H5 Puri Borneo Indon 1.21N 109.49E
29 J8 Puri Orissa India 19.49N 85.54E
29 J7 Puri dist Orissa India
119 D6 Purificación Colombia 3.52N 74.57W
41 E5 Purinskoye, Ozero L U.S.S.R. 71.48N 88.30E
11 K4 Puriri New Zealand 37.12S 175.38E
65 O5 Purkersdorf Austria 48.13N 16.12E
91 D7 Purl Angola 7.45S 15.43E
55 F5 Purley London England 51.20N 0.07W
28 C1 Purli Maharashtra India 18.53N 76.36E
103 F2 Purling New York 42.16N 74.00W
60 H10 Purmer dist Netherlands
60 H9 Purmerend Netherlands 52.30N 4.56E
60 H10 Purmerland Netherlands 52.29N 4.56E
28 C1 Purna Maharashtra India 19.11N 77.05E
29 L5 Purnabhaba R India/Bangladesh
28 A2 Purnagad Maharashtra India 16.52N 73.19E
32 A1 Pūrnāk Iran 39.17N 44.58E
29 E7 Purna R Buldana, Maharashtra India
29 E8 Purna R Parbhani, Maharashtra India
12 B2 Purndu Saltpan S Australia 27.25S 131.50E
30 L7 Purnea Bihar India 25.47N 87.28E
30 L7 Purnea dist Bihar India
47 D4 Purnema U.S.S.R. 64.21N 37.30E
61 K5 Purnode Belgium 50.18N 4.57E
59 C7 Purple Mt Kerry Irish Rep 52.00N 9.37W
100 F9 Purple Springs Alberta 49.50N 111.54W
30 A3 Pur Qazi Uttar Prad India 29.38N 77.51E
121 A8 Purranque Chile 40.55S 73.14W
94 B2 Purros Namibia 18.50S 12.59E
25 G6 Pursat Cambodia 12.27N 103.40E
36 F3 Pürtek R Turkey
30 G4 Purti Ghat Nepal 28.03N 83.32E
56 H4 Purton Wilts Eng 51.36N 1.52W
115 J7 Puruandíro Mexico 20.06N 101.32W
119 F9 Puruê, R Amazonas Brazil
119 H6 Purue, R Brazil
75 G4 Purujosa Spain 41.41N 1.46W
18 L6 Purukcahu Borneo Indon 0.36S 114.35E
115 O10 Purulhá Guatemala 15.12N 90.11W
29 K2 Purulia W Bengal India 23.20N 86.24E
29 K6 Purulia dist W Bengal India
77 K6 Purullena Spain 37.20N 3.11W
119 J4 Puruni, R Guyana
117 G2 Purus R Brazil
15 G8 Purutu I Papua New Guinea 8.22S 143.25E
51 O10 Puruvesi L Finland 61.50N 29.30E
Purvadeh see Parvāreh
107 G10 Purvis Mississippi 31.09N 89.25W
82 J8 Pŭrvomay Bulgaria 42.08N 25.17E
30 D6 Purwa Uttar Prad India 26.27N 80.47E
18 G9 Purwakarta Java Indon 6.30S 107.25E
18 J9 Purwodadi Java Indon 7.05S 110.53E
18 H9 Purwokerto Java Indon 7.28S 109.09E
18 J9 Purworejo Java Indon 7.45S 110.04E
107 H5 Puryear Tennessee 36.26N 88.22W
21 E6 Puryŏng N Korea 42.04N 129.44E
30 J7 Pusa Bihar India 25.59N 85.40E
46 F2 Puša Latvia U.S.S.R. 56.15N 27.12E
18 J5 Pusa Sarawak Malaysia 1.35N 111.16E
24 C7 Pusa Xinjiang Uygur Zizhiqu China 36.23N 78.59E
76 K9 Pusa R Spain
29 E8 Pusad Maharashtra India 19.56N 77.38E
46 E2 Pušalotas Lithuania U.S.S.R. 55.52N 24.12E
21 E10 Pusan S Korea 35.05N 129.02E
94 H5 Pusani Botswana 25.30S 25.35E
19 N8 Pusan Pt Mindanao Philippines 7.19N 126.37E
66 A1 Pusey France 47.39N 6.08E
23 H1 Pushang Shandong China 36.12N 119.40E
104 R2 Pushaw L Maine
39 F7 Pushchino U.S.S.R. 54.10N 158.00E
29 D4 Pushkar Rajasthan India 26.28N 74.36E
39 G1 Pushkareva, Ostrov isld U.S.S.R. 70.55N 161.30E
46 H1 Pushkin U.S.S.R. 59.43N 30.22E
44 J8 Pushkino Azerbaydzhan U.S.S.R. 39.28N 48.34E
45 J1 Pushkino Moscow U.S.S.R. 56.01N 37.52E
45 S5 Pushkino U.S.S.R. 51.15N 47.00E
47 D4 Pushlakhta U.S.S.R. 64.47N 36.34E
Pushteh Jaghvir see Chaqvir, Poshteh-ye mt
98 Q6 Pushthrough Newfoundland 47.39N 56.10W
32 G3 Pusht-i-Āsmān Iran 35.34N 57.00E
Pusht-i-Kuh mts see Posht-e Kūh
31 B5 Pusht-i-Rud reg Afghanistan
66 O8 Pusiano Italy 45.49N 9.17E
66 O8 Pusiano, L. di Italy
53 W14 Puskensetrene Norway 62.25N 7.15E
28 E1 Puspal Madhya Prad India 18.36N 81.57E
62 N8 Püspökladány Hungary 47.20N 21.05E
29 E8 Pus R Maharashtra India
69 B7 Pussay France 48.21N 2.00E
61 K7 Pussemange Belgium 49.48N 4.52E
39 G4 Pustaya R U.S.S.R.
79 L1 Pusteria,Val V Italy
65 F8 Puster-tal V Austria
65 K7 Pusterwald Austria 47.19N 14.23E
99 O3 Pusticamica, L Quebec
39 G4 Pustoretsk U.S.S.R. 60.33N 163.15E
46 G2 Pustoshka U.S.S.R. 56.20N 28.50E
31 H10 Pusur R Bangladesh
115 P8 Put Mexico 19.40N 89.25W
44 K7 Puta Azerbaydzhan U.S.S.R. 40.19N 49.41E
121 B4 Putaendo Chile 32.35S 70.40W
23 J7 Pu-tai Taiwan 23.21N 120.11E
19 D8 Putain Timor Indon 9.46S 124.40E
70 K4 Putanges-Pont-Ecrepin France 48.45N 0.15W
25 N7 Putao Burma 27.22N 97.27E
23 D1 Putaoyuan Gansu China 34.41N 105.50E
120 G5 Putari,L Brazil 13.06S 61.31W
11 K5 Putaruru New Zealand 38.03S 175.48E
63 S4 Putbus E Germany 54.22N 13.29E
68 D3 Puteaux France 48.53N 2.15E
Pu-t'e-ha Ch'i see Butha Qi
18 L9 Puteran isld Indonesia
95 K2 Putfontein S Africa 26.14S 26.28E
63 S3 Putgarten E Germany 54.41N 13.26E
60 T17 Puth Netherlands 50.57N 5.52E
23 H6 Putian Fujian China 25.32N 119.02E
79 L1 Pútia, Sasso di mt Italy 46.39N 11.49E
81 A2 Putifigari Sardinia 40.34N 8.28E
81 O2 Putignano Italy 40.51N 17.08E
82 J3 Putila U.S.S.R. 47.59N 25.01E
47 E6 Putilovo U.S.S.R. 59.25N 44.40E
65 K3 Putim Czechoslovakia 49.16N 14.12E
120 D6 Putina Peru 14.52S 69.53W
18 J7 Puting, Tanjung C Borneo Indon 3.35S 111.52E
43 P3 Putintsevo Kazakhstan U.S.S.R. 49.53N 84.19E
45 E5 Putivl' Ukraine U.S.S.R. 51.21N 33.53E
115 L9 Putla Mexico 17.01N 97.56W
31 D5 Putla Khan Afghanistan 30.06N 66.10E
63 Q6 Putlitz E Germany 53.16N 12.03E
82 K3 Putna Romania 47.50N 25.33E
103 L3 Putnam Connecticut 41.55N 71.54W
109 M6 Putnam Oklahoma 35.51N 98.58W
112 H3 Putnam Texas 32.22N 99.12W
103 G4 Putnam co New York
103 G4 Putnam Junction New York 41.25N 73.36W
103 G4 Putnam Lake New York 41.27N 73.33W
105 C6 Putney Georgia 31.30N 84.08W
55 E4 Putney London Eng 51.28N 0.14W
108 M4 Putney S Dakota 45.34N 98.10W
104 N4 Putney Vermont 42.58N 72.35W
62 M7 Putnok Hungary 48.18N 20.25E
15 J1 Puto Bougainville I Papua New Guinea 5.41S 154.42E
41 G6 Putorana,Gory mts U.S.S.R.
11 L6 Putorino New Zealand 39.08S 177.00E
28 J1 Putrang La pass Xizang Zizhiqu 29.01N 92.19E
120 D8 Putre Chile 18.13S 69.35W
61 P7 Putscheid Luxembourg 49.58N 6.08E
56 E5 Putsham Somerset Eng 51.11N 3.13W
94 F7 Putsonderwater S Africa 29.14S 21.52E
26 Q4 Puttalam Sri Lanka 8.02N 79.50E
26 Q5 Puttalam Lagoon Sri Lanka
61 J2 Putte Belgium 51.03N 4.38E
60 F14 Putte Netherlands 51.21N 4.23E
69 M5 Puttelange France 49.03N 6.56E
63 O5 Püttelkow E Germany 53.33N 11.05E
60 L10 Putten Netherlands 52.15N 5.36E
60 E12 Putten isld Netherlands
60 G12 Puttershoek Netherlands 51.48N 4.33E
63 O4 Puttgarden W Germany 54.30N 11.13E
51 O10 Puttiko Finland 61.43N 29.25E
64 B5 Püttlingen W Germany 49.48N 6.51E
28 B4 Puttur Karnataka India 12.45N 75.11E
26 R2 Puttur Sri Lanka 9.44N 80.05E
121 A5 Putú Chile 35.10S 72.22W
91 F6 Putubumba Zaïre 4.45S 18.15E
26 S3 Putukkudiyirippu Sri Lanka 9.18N 80.41E
119 C7 Putumayo Ecuador 0.05N 75.54W
119 C7 Putumayo div Colombia
21 B12 Putuo Shan isld Zhejiang China
37 D7 Pütürge Turkey 38.12N 38.53E
18 K5 Putussibau Borneo Indon 0.50N 112.55E
40 F10 Putyatin U.S.S.R. 42.50N 132.29E
45 N2 Putyatino U.S.S.R. 54.10N 41.10E
63 T5 Putzar E Germany 53.44N 13.40E
114 B7 Puuanahula Hawaiian Is 19.48N 155.50W
114 E6 Puuene Hawaiian Is 20.52N 156.26W
114 B8 Puu Enuhe mt Hawaiian Is 19.10N 155.32W
114 B7 Puu Hualalei crater Hawaiian Is 19.41N 155.52W
114 E6 Puuiki Hawaiian Is 20.42N 156.01W
114 D6 Puukolii Hawaiian Is 20.56N 156.50W
114 D6 Puukukui mt Hawaiian Is 20.53N 156.35W
51 M10 Puulavesi L Finland 61.50N 26.48E
114 C7 Puu Makanaka mt Hawaiian Is 19.50N 155.25W
51 N10 Puumala Finland 61.34N 28.15E
114 D6 Puunoa Pt Hawaiian Is 20.53N 156.41W
114 B8 Puu o Keokeo mt Hawaiian Is 19.12N 155.45W
114 C7 Puu Oo mt Hawaiian Is 19.43N 155.24W
61 H2 Puurs Belgium 51.05N 4.17E
114 B7 Puu Waawaa Hawaiian Is 19.46N 15.50W
114 D4 Puuwai Hawaiian Is 21.54N 160.12W
26 R4 Puvarasankulam Sri Lanka 8.45N 80.22E
23 B7 Puwen Yunnan China 22.31N 101.06E
Puxian see Pucheng
22 H8 Pu Xian Shanxi China 36.19N 110.59E
47 E5 Puya R U.S.S.R.
110 C2 Puyallup Washington 47.12N 122.19W
23 G1 Puyang Henan China 35.40N 115.00E
72 H6 Puybrun France 44.55N 1.47E
72 F8 Puycasquier France 43.46N 0.46E
72 H8 Puycelci France 44.00N 1.42E
67 H7 Puy-de-Dôme dept France
71 B5 Puy-de-Dôme mt France 45.46N 2.56E
71 B5 Puy-de-Sancy mt France 45.32N 2.48E
121 A8 Puyehue Chile 40.39S 72.15W
121 A8 Puyehue, L de Chile
121 B8 Puyehue,Paso pass Arg/Chile 40.42S 71.50W
121 A8 Puyehue, P. de mt Chile 40.35S 72.10W
121 A8 Puyehue, V mt Chile 40.35S 72.10W
121 B9 Puyel Argentina 43.37S 71.02W
72 F2 Puye, La France 46.39N 0.45E
71 J6 Puy Gris mt France 45.18N 6.10E
71 C5 Puy-Guillaume France 45.57N 3.28E
47 K3 Puyko U.S.S.R. 66.48N 69.30E
72 H7 Puylaroque France 44.15N 1.36E
72 J8 Puylaurens France 43.34N 2.00E
72 G6 Puy l'Evêque France 44.30N 1.08E
72 F9 Puymaurin France 43.22N 0.46E
72 F7 Puymirol France 44.11N 0.48E
72 H10 Puymorens,Col de France 42.34N 1.47E
72 D1 Puy Notre Dame, le France 47.07N 0.14W
119 C8 Puyo Ecuador 1.30S 77.58W
72 C8 Puyôo France 43.32N 0.54W
70 N2 Puys France 49.57N 1.08E
71 G9 Puy-Ste.Réparade,le France 43.40N 5.24E
11 A13 Puysegur Pt New Zealand 46.10S 166.38E
121 J5 Puyuguapi canal Chile
121 A10 Puyuguapi str Chile
72 J10 Puyvalador France 42.39N 2.07E
Puzeh Gani see Gānī
47 G5 Puzla U.S.S.R. 62.28N 54.40E
32 J8 Pūzm Iran 25.12N 60.23E
75 K8 Puzol Spain 39.37N 0.19W
67 P12 Puzzichello Corsica 42.06N 9.24E
92 D6 Pweto Zaïre 8.28S 28.52E
25 C2 Pwinbyu Burma 20.20N 94.40E
57 E7 Pwllheli Gwynedd Wales 52.53N 4.25W
39 E5 Pyagina,Poluostrov pen U.S.S.R.
42 B1 Pyakupur R U.S.S.R.
42 A1 Pyaku-To, Ozero L U.S.S.R. 63.35N 73.58E
47 D3 Pyalitsa U.S.S.R. 66.12N 39.35E
47 D5 Pyal'ma U.S.S.R. 62.20N 35.47E
25 C3 Pyalo Burma 19.08N 95.10E
47 C4 Pyal'vozero U.S.S.R. 62.34N 33.00E
25 C5 Pyamalaw R Burma
45 R1 P'yana R U.S.S.R.
31 F2 Pyandzh R Tadzhikistan U.S.S.R. etc
45 Q1 P'yanskiy Perevoz U.S.S.R. 55.36N 44.30E
47 H5 Pyanteg U.S.S.R. 60.11N 56.12E
47 C3 Pyaozero,Oz L U.S.S.R.
28 C3 Pyapalli Andhra Prad India 15.16N 77.43E
25 C4 Pyapon Burma 16.15N 95.40E
41 E4 Pyasina R U.S.S.R.
41 C7 Pyasinado U.S.S.R. 67.24N 77.59E
41 E6 Pyasino,Oz L U.S.S.R.
41 D4 Pyasinskiy Zaliv B U.S.S.R.
44 E3 Pyatigorsk U.S.S.R. 44.04N 43.06E
47 G5 Pyatigory U.S.S.R. 60.11N 54.44E
45 E8 Pyatikhatki Ukraine U.S.S.R. 48.23N 33.43E
43 B3 Pyatimar Kazakhstan U.S.S.R. 49.33N 50.34E
39 G1 Pyatistennoye U.S.S.R. 68.00N 161.19E
39 F2 Pyatkovende,Gora mt U.S.S.R. 65.50N 158.59E
41 B3 Pyat' Paltsev, Mys C Novaya Zemlya U.S.S.R. 74.00N 58.25E
107 D5 Pyatt Arkansas 36.15N 92.50W
25 D2 Pyawbwe Burma 20.37N 96.05E
46 Q2 Pychas U.S.S.R. 56.29N 52.28E
56 L6 Pyecombe W Sussex England 50.54N 0.10W
113 M7 Pye Is Alaska
28 J8 Pygmalion Pt Nicobar Is 6.45N 93.50E
51 M8 Pyhäjärvi Finland 63.41N 25.58E
51 O10 Pyhäjärvi L Finland 61.50N 30.00E
51 J10 Pyhäjärvi L Turku Finland 61.00N 22.20E
51 L7 Pyhäjoki Finland 64.28N 24.15E
51 L7 Pyhäjoki R Finland
51 M7 Pyhäntä Finland 64.07N 26.20E
51 J11 Pyhäranta Finland 60.57N 21.30E
51 O9 Pyhäselkä Finland 62.25N 29.55E
51 O9 Pyhäselkä L Finland 62.30N 29.43E
65 N5 Pyhra Austria 48.09N 15.42E
65 L4 Pyhrabruck Austria 48.46N 14.49E
65 K6 Pyhrgas,Gross mt Austria 47.40N 14.24E
65 K6 Pyhrnpass Austria 47.38N 14.18E
25 L9 Pyingaing Burma 23.08N 94.50E
25 D3 Pyinmana Burma 19.45N 96.12E
84 S15 Pyla,C Cyprus 34.56N 33.53E
72 B6 Pyla-sur-Mer France 44.37N 1.13W
56 D4 Pyle W Glam Wales 51.32N 3.42W
39 H4 Pylgovayam R U.S.S.R.
42 C2 Pyl'karamo U.S.S.R. 60.10N 83.15E
51 L9 Pylkönmäki Finland 62.40N 24.50E
45 T5 Pylkovka U.S.S.R. 51.49N 47.50E
104 E5 Pymatuning Res Pennsylvania
12 L6 Pymble dist Sydney, N S W
39 F7 Pymta R U.S.S.R.
39 F7 Pymtinskiy U.S.S.R. 53.40N 156.01E
39 L2 Pyngopil'gyn,Laguna U.S.S.R.
21 C7 Pyoktong N Korea 40.50N 125.50E
21 E9 Pyŏnggok-tong S Korea 36.37N 129.24E
21 E9 P'yŏnghae-ri S Korea 36.42N 129.35E
21 D9 Pyŏngt'aeng-ni S Korea 37.01N 127.04E
21 C8 Pyŏngyang N Korea 39.00N 125.47E
21 D7 Pyorha-ri N Korea 40.47N 126.37E
112 D4 Pyote Texas 31.31N 103.08W
110 F9 Pyramid Nevada 40.05N 119.43W
95 M1 Pyramid S Africa 25.36S 28.14E
111 K6 Pyramid Canyon gorge Arizona/Nevada
12 G6 Pyramid Hill Victoria 36.03S 144.24E
11 K11 Pyramid I Chatham Is Pacific Oc 44.26S 176.14W
110 F9 Pyramid L Nevada 40.00N 119.35W
30 K4 "Pyramid Peak" mt Nepal 27.50N 87.01E
109 C1 Pyramid Pk mt Colorado 40.05N 107.07W
96 A11 Pyramid Pt Ascension I 7.54S 14.24W
106 J5 Pyramid Pt Michigan 44.58N 85.55W
111 E2 Pyramid Ra Nevada
Pyramids see Giza Pyramids
67 E9 Pyrénées mts France/Spain
67 E9 Pyrénées Atlantiques dept France
67 G10 Pyrénées-Orientales dept France
55 A6 Pyrford Surrey Eng 51.19N 0.30W
84 R14 Pyroi Cyprus 35.04N 33.30E
14 B5 Pyrton,Mt W Australia 22.00S 117.22E
62 H2 Pyrzyce Poland 53.09N 14.53E
65 L2 Pyšely Czechoslovakia 49.53N 14.40E
46 O1 Pyshchug U.S.S.R. 58.51N 45.40E
42 D4 Pyshkino-Troitskoye U.S.S.R. 57.08N 86.15E
47 J7 Pyshma U.S.S.R. 57.00N 63.10E
47 J7 Pyshma R U.S.S.R.
46 G2 Pytalovo U.S.S.R. 57.03N 27.57E
99 O6 Pythonga,L Quebec
53 X14 Pyttbua Norway 62.13N 7.50E
53 X14 Pyttegga mt Norway 62.13N 7.42E
25 D3 Pyu Burma 18.29N 96.28E
25 D3 Pyu R Burma
25 D4 Pyuntaza Burma 17.51N 96.44E
62 K3 Pyzdry Poland 52.10N 17.40E
85 O2 Qaa,El Lebanon 34.20N 36.30E
33 D6 Qā', Al Saudi Arabia 20.23N 41.08E
33 D7 Qā', Al Saudi Arabia 19.10N 41.11E
33 H7 Qa'āmīyāt, Al des reg Saudi Arabia
34 D9 Qa 'ash Shubyk, Wādī watercourse Jordan
35 E5 Qabalan Jordan 32.06N 35.17E
35 E4 Qabatiya Jordan 32.25N 35.17E
33 L5 Qābil Oman 23.55N 55.50E
24 H11 Qabnag Xizang Zizhiqu China 30.17N 94.31E
33 E1 Qabr Bandar anc site Saudi Arabia 30.13N 43.40E
33 H8 Qabr Hūd S Yemen 16.09N 49.36E
87 J5 Qabri Bahar Somalia 10.20N 43.42E
35 E1 Qabrikha Lebanon 33.15N 35.28E
35 G9 Qabr Madh-ha tomb Jordan 31.13N 35.52E
85 A4 Qabr Şāliḩ Libya 30.43N 11.24E
32 C1 Qachāghem Kūh mt Iran 38.12N 48.45E
95 M6 Qachas Nek Lesotho 30.08S 28.41E
95 M5 Qachas Nek dist Lesotho
33 A7 Qadaia Saudi Arabia 26.34N 49.59E
Qadaisa see Qadaysah
32 H2 Qadamgah Iran 36.07N 59.00E
33 M7 Qadaysah Oman 18.42N 56.45E
33 E7 Qaḑḑā Saudi Arabia 18.56N 42.55E
85 C4 Qaddāhiya, Al Libya 31.24N 15.12E
37 J9 Qāder R Iran
31 B3 Qādes Afghanistan 34.48N 63.26E
Qadhimah see Qaḑimah
87 O4 Qadhub Socotra S Yemen 12.39N 53.52E
33 K10 Qādib Socotra Ind Oc 12.37N 53.57E
86 M10 Qad Ibn Haddân B Egypt
35 C4 Qadima Israel 32.17N 34.55E
33 C5 Qaḑimah Saudi Arabia 22.22N 39.10E
30 C5 Qadirganj Uttar Prad India 27.48N 79.02E
35 F1 Qadiriye Syria 33.02N 35.44E
34 M3 Qādir Karam Iraq 35.12N 44.55E
34 D3 Qadmūs,El Syria 35.06N 36.10E
37 J9 Qa'eh-ye Pasveh Iran 36.48N 45.20E
86 L9 Qā', El reg Egypt
35 H9 Qa' el Hafira mud flats Jordan
32 J5 Qa'emabad Iran 31.44N 60.05E
48 S7 Qaersut Greenland 70.35N 52.30W
Qafarah see Jifārah, Al
33 J4 Qaffāy,Al isld U.A.E. 24.35N 51.46E
35 D4 Qaffin Jordan 32.26N 35.05E
33 E8 Qafl Yemen 16.01N 43.17E
86 D3 Qâfla Egypt 31.04N 30.16E
35 G4 Qafqafa Jordan 32.21N 35.56E
33 F9 Qafrah,Al Yemen 14.34N 45.19E
22 L2 Qagan Nei Monggol Zizhiqu China 49.16N 118.02E
22 G6 Qagan Ders Nei Monggol Zizhiqu China 40.25N 105.56E
Qagan Nur see Zhengxiangbai (Xulun Hobot Qagan) Qi
22 H7 Qagan Nur Nei Monggol Zizhiqu China 39.15N 108.04E
22 J5 Qagan Nur Nei Monggol Zizhiqu China 43.20N 112.52E
21 C5 Qagan Nur L Jilin China
22 J6 Qagan Nur L Nei Monggol Zizhiqu China
22 K5 Qagan Nur L Nei Monggol Zizhiqu China
22 H7 Qagan Nur L Nei Monggol Zizhiqu China
22 D5 Qagan Qonj well Gansu China 42.05N 96.45E
22 L3 Qagan Qulut Nei Monggol Zizhiqu China 46.10N 118.15E
Qagan Us see Dulan
22 L5 Qagan Us Nei Monggol Zizhiqu China 43.44N 118.55E
22 D8 Qagan Us He R Qinghai China
24 G10 Qagbasêrag Xizang Zizhiqu China 30.47N 92.40E
24 D9 Qagcaka Xizang Zizhiqu China 32.32N 81.52E
Qagchêng see Xiangcheng
48 T15 Qagssimiut Greenland 60.35N 47.15W
86 F5 Qaha Egypt 30.17N 31.11E
32 C2 Qahab Iran 36.58N 48.05E
22 J6 Qahar Youyi Houqi Nei Monggol Zizhiqu China 41.28N 113.14E
22 J6 Qahar Youyi Qianqi Nei Monggol Zizhiqu China 40.48N 113.14E
86 G4 Qahbûna Egypt 30.49N 31.55E
33 D3 Qahd, Wādī watercourse Saudi Arabia
Qâhira,El see Cairo Egypt
33 B9 Qāhirah,Al S Yemen 12.54N 44.59E
33 D7 Qaḩmah, Al Saudi Arabia 18.02N 41.41E
33 F7 Qahr,Jibāl al mts Saudi Arabia
33 E6 Qaḩtān tribe Saudi Arabia
22 D8 Qaidam He R Qinghai China
22 C8 Qaidam Pendi salt flat Qinghai China
22 D8 Qaidam Shan mts Qinghai China
Qā'īfah,Al see Qā'īyah, Al
34 J4 Qā'im, Al Iraq 34.23N 41.11E
Qain see Qāyen
Qairwan see Kairouan
Qais isld see Qeys
31 C3 Qaisar Afghanistan 35.43N 64.13E
31 C2 Qaisar R Afghanistan
31 B4 Qaisar,Koh-i- mt Afghanistan 33.00N 63.56E
33 E4 Qā'īyah,Al Saudi Arabia 24.16N 43.31E
33 F3 Qā'īyah,Al wells Saudi Arabia 26.25N 45.34E
86 E8 Qâiyât,El Egypt 28.40N 30.41E
34 Q7 Qajarīyeh Iran 31.02N 48.24E
24 C7 Qakar Xinjiang Uygur Zizhiqu China 36.30N 80.40E
34 D6 Qa Khanna salt marsh Jordan
84 X19 Qala Gozo Mediterranean Sea 36.02N 14.19E
31 B4 Qala Adras-Kand Afghanistan 33.35N 62.15E
Qala Ahangaran see Chakhcharan
Qalaat el Hosn see Qal'at al Husn
31 C3 Qala Chashmeh Afghanistan 34.32N 64.02E
31 E4 Qala Daulat Khan Afghanistan 33.30N 68.45E
34 N2 Qalā Diza Iraq 36.12N 45.08E
31 E3 Qala Doab Afghanistan 34.57N 68.39E
87 E4 Qala'en Nahl Sudan 13.36N 34.57E
31 E3 Qalagai Afghanistan 35.46N 68.48E
31 E4 Qala-i-Babakar Afghanistan 32.24N 68.43E
31 A5 Qala-i-Fateh Afghanistan 30.32N 61.52E
31 A5 Qala-i-Kang Afghanistan 31.05N 61.52E
31 B4 Qala Jamal Afghanistan 33.05N 62.10E
31 D3 Qala Khak Balak Afghanistan 35.44N 66.38E
31 D4 Qala Maidan Afghanistan 32.28N 66.45E
33 K6 Qalamat Abū Shafrah Saudi Arabia 21.13N 53.02E
33 J6 Qalamat āl Juḩaysh Saudi Arabia 20.32N 50.58E
33 K6 Qalamat aţ Ţawīl Saudi Arabia 20.38N 52.45E
33 J5 Qalamat Nadqān Saudi Arabia 23.09N 50.05E
33 K5 Qalamat Shutfah Saudi Arabia 22.49N 52.53E
86 E7 Qalamshâh Egypt 29.10N 30.50E
85 K7 Qalamun,El Egypt 25.31N 28.54E
33 J9 Qalana S Yemen 15.26N 50.58E
31 C3 Qala Nagshi Afghanistan 34.10N 65.05E
31 B3 Qala Nau Afghanistan 34.58N 63.04E
35 D6 Qalandiya Jordan 31.52N 35.12E
31 C3 Qala Nilinj Afghanistan 35.04N 65.10E
33 K10 Qalansīyah Socotra Ind Oc 12.40N 53.28E
35 C4 Qalansuwa Israel 32.17N 34.59E
31 G2 Qala Panja Afghanistan 36.59N 72.40E
Qal'a Salili see Qal'at Sālih
31 C3 Qala Shahar Afghanistan 35.33N 65.33E
31 D3 Qala Shinia Takht Afghanistan 34.14N 66.05E
Qala Sikar see Qal'at Sukkar
31 D4 Qalāt Afghanistan 32.07N 66.54E
32 E6 Qalat Iran 29.49N 52.18E
33 A7 Qal'at Saudi Arabia 26.34N 50.05E
34 O8 Qal'at Abū Ghar Iraq 30.26N 46.08E
33 A3 Qal'at al Azlam Saudi Arabia 27.01N 35.59E
34 D4 Qal'at al Husn Syria 34.46N 36.18E
Qal'at al Mu'adhdham see Qal'at al Mu'azzam
33 B3 Qal'at al Mu'azzam Saudi Arabia 27.47N 37.29E
Qal'at as Saura see Sawrah, As
33 E6 Qal'at Bīshah Saudi Arabia 20.01N 42.39E
33 A2 Qal'at el Al Mudawwarah Saudi Arabia 29.19N 35.59E
35 G10 Qal'at el Hasa anc site Jordan 30.50N 35.55E
34 C3 Qal'at el Marqab anc site Syria 35.11N 35.57E
Qal'at el Mudauwara see Mudawwara, Al
35 F4 Qal'at er Rabad anc site Jordan 32.20N 35.44E
34 H4 Qalat es Sālihīya Syria 34.46N 40.46E
85 O4 Qal'at et Dab'a Jordan 31.35N 36.07E
34 P7 Qal'at Sālih Iraq 31.32N 47.19E
34 O7 Qal'at Sukkar Iraq 31.52N 46.05E
31 B3 Qala Vali Afghanistan 35.48N 63.40E
Qal'eg Huma see Homā
Qal'eh Bikui see Bīkhū
32 A1 Qal'eh Dagh mt Iran 38.38N 45.26E
34 O5 Qal'eh Darreh Iran 33.22N 46.36E
34 O2 Qal'eh Gāh Iran 36.23N 46.28E
Qal'eh-i-Gulab see Qal'eh-ye Golāb
34 P5 Qal'eh Mashkara Iran 33.57N 47.11E
43 D8 Qal'eh Mūreh, Rūd-e R Iran
32 A8 Qal'eh Murgeh Tehrān Iran 35.38N 51.23E
32 B4 Qal'eh Safīd Iran 33.12N 47.23E
Qal'eh Tashan see Tashān
32 D5 Qal'eh-ye Golāb Iran 30.57N 50.42E
32 F2 Qal'eh-ye Mīr Iran 36.18N 54.57E
32 C4 Qal'eh-ye-Now Iran 33.44N 48.53E
32 F2 Qal'eh-ye Now Kharegan Iran 36.38N 55.10E
32 H4 Qal'eh ye Shūrak Iran 32.13N 58.31E
34 L2 Qalfan oil bore Iraq 36.07N 43.04E
33 N5 Qalhāt Oman 22.40N 59.21E
33 B2 Qalībah,Al Saudi Arabia 28.23N 37.43E
33 H5 Qalībah,Al Saudi Arabia 22.53N 49.00E
33 M10 Qalīb,Al area Kuwait
34 M9 Qalīb ar Rufayfāt Iraq 29.22N 44.48E
34 M9 Qalīb Bāqūr Iraq 29.43N 44.49E
86 E3 Qallîn Egypt 31.03N 30.51E
35 C5 Qalqiliya Jordan 32.11N 34.58E
86 N6 Qalt, Wâdî el watercourse Egypt
35 E6 Qalya Jordan 31.46N 35.30E
86 F5 Qalyûb Egypt 30.11N 31.12E
86 F5 Qalyûbîya div Egypt
37 J9 Qāmā Iran 36.54N 45.17E
23 B1 Qamalung Qinghai China 34.32N 99.20E
33 K8 Qamar B S Yemen
33 K8 Qamar,Jabal al mts Oman
95 L7 Qamata S Africa 31.58S 27.25E
31 E7 Qambar Pakistan 27.35N 68.03E
34 P2 Qamcheqāy R Iran
23 A3 Qamdo Xizang Zizhiqu China 31.11N 97.18E
85 F4 Qamīnis Libya 31.38N 20.01E
34 J1 Qamishliye,El Syria 37.03N 41.15E
31 E5 Qamruddin Karez Pakistan 31.39N 68.25E
32 D4 Qamşar Iran 33.43N 51.25E
35 E1 Qâna Lebanon 33.13N 35.18E
35 C5 Qana watercourse Israel/Jordan
35 F1 Qana'bah Syria 33.08N 35.41E
33 G8 Qanābīr hill Saudi Arabia/S Yemen 16.55N 47.15E
86 G3 Qanâ el Manzala canal Egypt
Qanâ el Suweis see Suez Can
Qanaker see Kanakir
Qanaouâte see Qanawāt, El
Qânâq see Thule
86 F5 Qanâtir Muhammad 'Alî Egypt 30.12N 31.08E
34 D6 Qanawāt,El Syria 32.44N 36.36E
86 F4 Qanâyat,El Egypt 30.38N 31.28E
35 H1 Qanaye Syria 33.01N 36.11E
32 B1 Qandarañbashi mt Iran 38.47N 46.49E
22 K5 Qangdin Gol R Nei Monggol Zizhiqu China
22 K5 Qangdin Sum Nei Monggol Zizhiqu China 43.33N 115.05E
94 F2 Qangwa Botswana 19.34S 21.12E
86 H4 Qantara, El Egypt 30.52N 32.20E
86 D5 Qanţara, Gebel hill Egypt 30.12N 30.08E
86 O5 Qantara, Wādī el watercourse Jordan
32 F2 Qapan Iran 37.37N 55.43E
24 D4 Qapqal Xinjiang Uygur Zizhiqu China 43.48N 81.15E
85 J5 Qara Egypt 29.38N 26.30E
Qara'a see Qar'ah,Al
Qara,Al see Qar'ah, Al
33 K8 Qarā' and Shahrah tribe Oman
31 A3 Qarabagh Herat Afghanistan 34.57N 61.49E
31 E3 Qarabagh Parwan Afghanistan 34.52N 69.11E
34 N4 Qara Bulaq Iraq 34.32N 45.12E
Qara Buran Köl see T'ai-t'e-ma Hu
32 D3 Qara Chai R Iran
Qara Chaok see Karakök Dagh
Qara Chauq,Jabal mts see Qarachōq,Jabal mts
34 L3 Qarachōq,Jabal mts Iraq
34 K1 Qarachuk Syria 37.00N 42.05E
34 N3 Qara Dagh Iraq 35.20N 45.22E
34 N3 Qara Dagh mts Iraq
85 L6 Qara,El Egypt 26.01N 31.52E
86 E4 Qar'a el Bâgûrîya canal Egypt
86 E8 Qar'a el Ibrâhîmîya canal Egypt
86 D3 Qar'a el Maḩmudîya canal Egypt
86 D4 Qar'a el Nûbârîya canal Egypt
33 G3 Qar'ah,Al Saudi Arabia 27.26N 46.56E
31 E4 Qarah Bāgh Afghanistan 33.12N 68.06E
Qarah Chauq,Jabal mts see Qarachōq, Jabal mts
33 E3 Qa'rah, Jabal al mts Saudi Arabia
33 F7 Qārah,Jabal al mt Saudi Arabia 18.27N 44.25E
Qarah Tapah see Qara Tepe Syria
34 M4 Qarah Tappah Iraq 34.25N 44.58E
35 F2 Qara'inah Syria 32.56N 35.40E
Qarā'in, Al wells see Quryān, Al
33 B8 Qarain,Ra's al C Bahrain, The Gulf 25.57N 50.37E
31 F2 Qaraja Afghanistan 37.11N 70.35E
33 L8 Qarā',Jabal mts Oman
24 B6 Qarak Xinjiang Uygur Zizhiqu China 38.20N 77.10E
Qarakuzi see Qara Qūzī
32 B2 Qaranqu R Iran
34 F3 Qaraqol Hamman Syria 35.52N 38.44E
32 F2 Qara Qūzī Iran 37.32N 55.30E
85 E6 Qarārat al 'Azzāzīyah Libya 27.06N 18.07E
85 E6 Qarārat an Nāqah depression Libya
31 E2 Qara Shahrakyar Afghanistan 36.30N 68.10E
Qara Su R see Qareh Sū R
Qaratagan see Qareh Tekān
44 F9 Qara Tappeh Pass Iran 38.21N 44.51E
31 C3 Qara Tarai mt Afghanistan 34.03N 65.27E
Qaratchôl Dârh see Karakök Dagh
Qara Tepe Iraq see Qarah Tappah
34 H2 Qara Tepe Syria 36.58N 40.57E
32 C2 Qara Tikan Iran 36.36N 49.37E
33 H2 Qārawah isld The Gulf 28.49N 48.54E
33 N6 Qarayyih al 'Qaţā Oman 21.18N 58.16E
34 D3 Qardāha Syria 35.28N 36.03E
87 C5 Qardud,El Sudan 11.01N 31.40E
32 B2 Qareh Aghaj Iran 37.08N 47.00E
32 B1 Qareh Dāgh mts Iran
44 F8 Qareh Dāgh mt Iran 39.12N 44.33E
32 B2 Qareh Dāsh, Kūh-e mt Iran 36.46N 46.51E
32 E3 Qareh Qāch, Kūh-e mts Iran
32 B1 Qareh Sū R Āzārbāījān-e Khāvarī Iran
32 B3 Qareh Sū R Kermānshāh Iran
43 D8 Qareh-Sū R Semnān Iran
32 J2 Qareh Tekān Iran 36.48N 60.10E
32 B2 Qareh Urgān,Kūh-e mt Iran 37.14N 47.08E
32 A1 Qareh Ziāed Din Iran 38.57N 45.01E
44 G9 Qareh Zīā'oddin Iran 38.52N 45.03E
86 D8 Qâret 'abd el Ḩafîz hill Egypt 28.53N 30.08E
85 J5 Qâret Agnes mt Egypt 29.28N 27.56E
86 D8 Qâret el Balad el Kharba hill Egypt 28.46N 30.21E
86 E6 Qâret el Gindi hill Egypt 29.38N 30.53E
86 E5 Qâret el Haddâdîn hill Egypt 30.04N 30.58E
86 A5 Qâret el Himeimât hill Egypt 30.27N 28.54E
86 A6 Qâret el Ided hill Egypt 29.55N 28.54E
86 B5 Qâret el Mashrûka hill Egypt 30.22N 29.30E
86 E5 Qâret el Raml hill Egypt 30.02N 30.39E
85 H7 Qaret es Segar mt Libya 24.46N 24.32E
86 D7 Qâret Gahannam hill Egypt 29.20N 30.10E
86 B5 Qâret Sumâra hill Egypt 30.21N 29.05E
34 J3 Qāret Tāris hill Syria 35.52N 41.08E
85 H4 Qâret Teira mt Egypt 30.09N 25.08E
35 H2 Qarfah Syria 32.49N 36.12E
33 E7 Qarḩah, Al Saudi Arabia 18.07N 42.52E
22 C8 Qarhan Qinghai China 36.48N 95.11E
Qariateine see Qaryatein,El
33 H3 Qariya, Jabal al mt Saudi Arabia 26.53N 48.05E
Qariyat al Gharab see Qaryat al Gharab
Qariya 'Ulya see Qaryat al Ulyā
Qarkilik see Ruoqiang
48 U16 Qarmat Greenland 60.40N 46.32W
Qarn R see Keziv R
33 G9 Qarn,Al S Yemen 14.44N 47.49E
Qarnaw anc site see Ma'īn anc site
33 D6 Qarnayţ,Jabal mt Saudi Arabia 21.01N 40.26E
33 K4 Qarnein isld The Gulf 24.58N 52.55E
85 M5 Qarne Kabsh,Gebel mt Egypt 28.40N 32.22E
35 H5 Qarnel Jabsh tomb Jordan 32.08N 36.08E
33 D7 Qarn Hadīl Saudi Arabia 19.16N 41.51E
Qarn,Jebel hill see Qeren,Har hill
24 D4 Qarqal Xinjiang Uygur Zizhiqu China 43.48N 81.15E
Qarqan see Qiemo
24 F6 Qarqan He R Xinjiang Uygur Zizhiqu China
32 F2 Qārqi Iran 37.01N 54.10E
24 E5 Qarqi Xinjiang Uygur Zizhiqu China 41.51N 85.25E
31 D2 Qarqīn Afghanistan 37.25N 66.03E
86 D7 Qârûn Egypt 29.25N 30.24E
85 B4 Qaryah ash Sharqīyah, Al Libya 30.26N 13.38E
33 F7 Qaryat al Faw ruin Saudi Arabia 18.27N 45.09E
34 M7 Qaryat al Gharab Iraq 31.28N 44.48E
33 G3 Qaryat al Ulyā Saudi Arabia 27.33N 47.42E
33 G3 Qaryat as Sufla Saudi Arabia 27.29N 47.46E
Qaryatayn see Qaryatein,El
34 E4 Qaryatein,El Syria 34.13N 37.13E
35 G7 Qaryat Falha Jordan 31.31N 35.48E
34 K4 Qaryat Ḩubayn al Gharbīyah Iraq 34.23N 42.06E
35 E5 Qaryut Jordan 32.04N 35.18E
34 L2 Qasab oil bore Iraq 36.00N 43.07E
33 F4 Qaşab, Al Saudi Arabia 25.19N 45.30E
33 H5 Qaşab, Al Saudi Arabia 22.45N 49.16E
85 B3 Qasabat,Al Libya 32.28N 14.00E
85 M7 Qasa, El Egypt 24.45N 32.56E
32 G4 Qasamī Iran 32.50N 56.45E
32 F2 Qāsam, Kūh-e mt Iran 36.46N 55.09E
31 B3 Qasa Murg mts Afghanistan
34 B10 Qaşbah, Ras al C Saudi Arabia 28.03N 34.37E
30 J7 Qasba Maker Bihar India 25.58N 85.03E
33 M4 Qaşbīyat al Burayk Oman 24.02N 57.04E
32 G3 Qāsemābād Khorāsān Iran 34.30N 57.54E
32 H2 Qāsemābād Khorāsān Iran 36.25N 59.30E
32 H3 Qāsemābād Khorāsān Iran 35.54N 58.33E
33 B2 Qā' Sharawrā' Saudi Arabia
32 D5 Qashqai tribe Iran
33 E3 Qaşim dist Saudi Arabia
32 H3 Qasimabad Iran 34.39N 58.05E
Qasimadbad see Qāsemābād
34 M6 Qāsim,Al Iraq 32.17N 44.43E
34 C5 Qasimiye,El R Lebanon
33 H8 Qasin S Yemen 16.10N 49.04E
35 F8 Qasr Jordan 31.19N 35.45E
35 G9 Qasr Abu Rukba anc site Jordan 31.07N 35.53E
33 D3 Qaşr, Al Saudi Arabia 27.21N 41.28E
85 E4 Qasr al Burayqah Libya 30.23N 19.37E
Qasr al Khubbaz see Marqab al Khubbāz
85 B3 Qasr al Qarahbulli Libya 32.48N 13.41E
34 J5 Qaşr 'Āmij Iraq 33.30N 41.50E
33 N9 Qaşr aş Şabīyah Kuwait 29.33N 48.09E
86 E4 Qasr Baghâd Egypt 30.44N 30.52E
34 O10 Qasr Balāl anc site Saudi Arabia 28.42N 46.13E
34 C8 Qasr ed Deir,Jebel mt Jordan 30.48N 35.34E
85 K7 Qasr,El Egypt 25.43N 28.54E
35 G8 Qasr el 'Al anc site Jordan 31.24N 35.58E
34 D7 Qasr el Azraq Jordan 31.54N 36.50E
34 E6 Qasr el Burqu anc site Jordan 32.36N 37.59E
Qasr el Hair see Qasr el Hayr
35 J5 Qasr el Hallabat anc site Jordan 32.06N 36.19E
35 H7 Qasr el Hammam anc site Jordan 31.32N 36.11E
34 E4 Qasr el Hayr anc site Syria 34.24N 37.36E
35 H7 Qasr el Mushatta anc site Syria 31.45N 36.00E
35 H10 Qasr el Musheish anc site Jordan 30.55N 36.09E
86 C4 Qaşr el Qatâgi ruins Egypt 30.32N 29.40E
35 F6 Qasr el Yahud monastery Jordan 31.50N 35.32E
32 J7 Qaşr-e-Qand Iran 26.14N 60.47E
34 N4 Qaşr-e-Shīrīn Iran 34.32N 45.36E
35 G8 Qasr eth Thuraiya anc site Jordan 31.26N 35.59E
35 G9 Qasr et Tamra anc site Jordan 31.06N 35.52E
35 H8 Qasr et Tirsa anc site Jordan 31.24N 36.02E
85 K6 Qasr Farafra Egypt 27.03N 28.00E
35 E10 Qasr Feifa anc site Jordan 30.57N 35.27E
35 J5 Qasr Hammam es Sarkh anc site Jordan 32.05N 36.21E
33 F6 Qaşr Ḩimām Saudi Arabia 20.51N 45.50E
85 H4 Qaşr Kunbūth Libya 31.48N 24.31E
35 G10 Qasr Muhai anc site Jordan 30.59N 35.51E
35 J6 Qasr Mushash anc site Jordan 31.49N 36.19E
Qasrqand see Qaşr-e-Qand
35 H5 Qasr Shabib anc site Jordan 32.04N 36.04E
Qasr Shagra see Qaşr Shaqrah
34 O8 Qaşr Shaqrah anc site Iraq 30.19N 46.26E
35 G10 Qasr Shuhar anc site Jordan 30.58N 35.54E
31 C2 Qassaba Qala Afghanistan 36.03N 64.32E
86 G4 Qassâsîn, El Egypt 30.34N 31.56E
35 G7 Qastal,El anc site Jordan 31.45N 35.57E
Qaşūmah, Al see Qayşūmah, Al
34 H3 Qatâa Syria 35.11N 40.21E
33 F10 Qa'ţabah Yemen 13.52N 44.30E
34 H4 Qatā, El Syria 34.40N 40.48E
34 E7 Qatafa,Wādī watercourse Jordan
34 D5 Qatana Syria 33.27N 36.04E
33 J4 Qatar sheikhdom The Gulf
32 C7 Qatif oil well Saudi Arabia 26.48N 49.54E
33 H3 Qatif oil field Saudi Arabia 26.47N 49.58E
33 J3 Qaţīf,Al Saudi Arabia 26.30N 50.00E
34 C9 Qatim,Jebel mt Jordan 29.53N 35.16E
Qatlish Afghanistansee Katlish
32 G2 Qatlish Iran 37.50N 57.19E
34 D2 Qatma Syria 36.36N 36.57E
33 H9 Qaţn,Al S Yemen 15.53N 48.28E
35 H9 Qatrana Sta Jordan 31.14N 36.03E
86 D6 Qaţrâni,Gebel hill Egypt 29.40N 30.36E
35 H6 Qattar watercourse Jordan
85 J5 Qattâra Depression Egypt
85 M6 Qattâr,Gebel mt Egypt 27.05N 33.20E
86 O6 Qattār,Jebel el mt Jordan 29.31N 35.23E
86 G4 Qattâwîya,El Egypt 30.34N 31.40E
85 C6 Qāţţusah, Sarīr al gravel des Libya
85 L6 Qâu el-Kebir Egypt 26.57N 31.33E
32 E5 Qavāmābād Iran 30.10N 52.59E
33 C3 Qā', Wādī al watercourse Saudi Arabia
33 G6 Qawnas,Al des area Saudi Arabia
32 H4 Qāyen Iran 33.43N 59.06E

Qay'īyah see Qā'īyah, Al
87 O4 Qaysah Socotra S Yemen 12.40N 53.29E
33 E2 Qayşūmah, Al Saudi Arabia 29.09N 43.00E
33 G2 Qayşūmah, Al Saudi Arabia 28.19N 46.10E
35 H1 Qaytah Syria 33.04N 36.08E
34 M3 Qaytūl-i-Kōn Iraq 35.25N 44.52E
24 G11 Qayü Xizang Zizhiqu China 28.18N 92.49E
31 E7 Qazi Ahmad Pakistan 26.19N 68.08E
32 D2 Qazvīn Iran 36.16N 50.00E
32 C3 Qazvīn reg Iran
Qdeim see Qudeim,El
35 C7 Qedma Israel 31.42N 34.46E
22 E5 Qeh Nei Monggol Zizhiqu China 42.20N 101.12E
87 D3 Qeili,Jeb mt Sudan 15.29N 33.49E
34 D7 Qeisiya,El flood area Jordan 31.49N 36.50E
87 E5 Qeissan Sudan 10.50N 34.48E
Qeita see Qaytah
85 M6 Qena Egypt 26.08N 32.42E
85 M6 Qena, Wâdi watercourse Egypt
86 G6 Qena, Wâdi watercourse Egypt
86 J10 Qena, Wâdi watercourse Egypt
48 T8 Qeqertaq Greenland 70.00N 51.28W
48 S6 Qeqertaq isld Greenland 71.55N 65.30W
Qeqertarrssuaq see Godhavn
Qerdâha see Qardāha
35 A10 Qeren,Har hill Israel 30.59N 34.29E
35 C3 Qesari,Har anc site Israel 32.30N 34.54E
32 B3 Qeshlaq Iran 34.56N 46.24E
32 B3 Qeshlaq R Iran
32 D3 Qeshlāq-e Ḩoseyn Iran 35.34N 50.29E
32 G7 Qeshm Iran 26.58N 56.17E
32 F7 Qeshm isld Iran
86 O6 Qetura Israel 29.57N 35.03E
32 C2 Qeydār Iran 36.05N 48.38E
32 D4 Qeydū Iran 33.40N 50.19E
23 B3 Qeyi Sichuan China 31.12N 100.10E
32 E7 Qeys isld Iran
44 F8 Qezel R Iran
44 G9 Qezel Dœzeh Iran 38.07N 45.55E
32 B2 Qezel Owzan R Iran
35 A10 Qezi'ot Israel 30.53N 34.28E
22 L6 Qian'an Hebei China 40.00N 118.42E
21 C5 Qian 'an Jilin China 45.05N 123.54E
23 E5 Qiancheng Hunan China 27.21N 110.11E
21 D4 Qianfeng Heilongjiang China 47.48N 126.12E
22 C6 Qianfodong Gansu China 40.03N 94.50E
21 C5 Qian Gorlos Jilin China 45.10N 124.93E
23 E5 Qiangu'ao Hunan China 27.29N 110.55E
Qianguozhen see Qian Gorlos
23 H1 Qiangwei He R Jiangsu China
23 E7 Qianjiang Guangxi China 23.36N 108.44E
23 F3 Qianjiang Hubei China 30.23N 112.58E
23 E4 Qianjiang Sichuan China 29.30N 108.20E
23 E7 Qian Jiang R Guangxi China
23 B3 Qianning Sichuan China 30.36N 101.35E
23 G3 Qianshan Anhui China 30.35N 116.38E
21 C7 Qian Shan pen Liaoning China
22 M6 Qianwei Liaoning China 40.10N 120.05E
23 C4 Qianwei Sichuan China 29.10N 103.55E
23 D5 Qianxi Guizhou China 27.04N 106.01E
22 L6 Qianxi Hebei China 40.08N 118.20E
23 E1 Qian Xian Shaanxi China 34.30N 108.15E
23 E5 Qianyang Hunan China 27.21N 110.11E
23 D1 Qianyang Shaanxi China 34.39N 107.20E
23 B5 Qiaohou Yunnan China 26.08N 99.50E
23 C5 Qiaojia Yunnan China 26.55N 102.51E
23 C5 Qiaomaidi Yunnan China 27.08N 103.03E
23 G5 Qiaotou Hunan China 26.09N 114.08E
22 L5 Qiaotou Nei Monggol Zizhiqu China 42.36N 118.56E
23 B5 Qiaotou Yunnan China 27.12N 100.05E
22 D6 Qiaowan Gansu China 40.37N 96.40E
32 A1 Qīās Iran 39.12N 45.01E
33 F3 Qibā' Saudi Arabia 27.21N 44.23E
33 M8 Qibiliya, Al isld Oman 17.30N 56.20E
35 D6 Qibya Jordan 31.58N 35.01E
23 G3 Qichun Hubei China 30.15N 115.26E
86 K4 Qideira,Gebel hill Egypt 30.35N 33.02E
86 M7 Qideira, Wâdi watercourse Egypt
23 F5 Qidong Hunan China 26.43N 112.03E
23 J3 Qidong Jiangsu China 31.50N 121.39E
35 C6 Qidron Israel 31.49N 34.47E
35 E7 Qidron watercourse Jordan
24 H8 Qidukou Qinghai China 34.23N 95.17E
24 E6 Qiemo Xinjiang Uygur Zizhiqu China 38.08N 85.33E
22 L7 Qigou Hebei China 41.00N 118.26E
22 K8 Qihe Shandong China 36.46N 116.49E
23 F1 Qi He R Henan China
22 J5 Qihreg Nei Monggol Zizhiqu China 43.10N 112.29E
23 D4 Qijiang Sichuan China 29.01N 106.40E
24 G4 Qijiaojing Xinjiang Uygur Zizhiqu China 43.29N 91.35E
Qike see Xunke
24 G4 Qiktim Xinjiang Uygur Zizhiqu China 43.00N 90.36E
31 D5 Qila Abdullah Pakistan 30.43N 66.40E
34 M4 Qilābāt Iraq 34.36N 44.52E
31 B7 Qila Ladgasht Pakistan 27.55N 62.59E
22 L6 Qilaotu Shan mts Hebei China
31 A6 Qila Safed Pakistan 29.01N 61.38E
31 E5 Qila Saifullah Pakistan 30.42N 68.30E
23 E4 Qileng Guan pass Hubei China
Qili see Shitai
22 F8 Qilian Gansu China 37.42N 102.23E
22 E7 Qilian Qinghai China 38.10N 100.17E
22 D7 Qilian Shan mt ra Qinghai China
21 B7 Qilihe Liaoning China 41.20N 121.12E
22 C6 Qilizhen Gansu China 40.09N 94.35E
24 D5 Qiman Xinjiang Uygur Zizhiqu China 41.10N 82.49E
86 N9 Qimeila, Wādī watercourse Saudi Arabia
23 H4 Qimen Anhui China 29.50N 117.31E
33 H8 Qināb, Wādī watercourse S Yemen
23 D1 Qin'an Gansu China 34.45N 105.49E
21 F3 Qindeli Heilongjiang China 48.07N 133.21E
22 L8 Qingcheng Shandong China 37.12N 117.40E
23 D2 Qingchuan Sichuan China 32.32N 105.10E
22 M8 Qingdao Shandong China 36.04N 120.22E
23 J1 Qingdao Shandong China 36.04N 120.22E
21 C8 Qingduizi Liaoning China 39.45N 123.12E
23 G1 Qingfeng Henan China 35.54N 115.06E
23 C4 Qingfu Sichuan China 28.30N 104.30E
21 D4 Qinggang Heilongjiang China 46.41N 126.05E
22 G6 Qinggel Nei Monggol Zizhiqu China 40.18N 105.52E
Qinggil see Qinghe
24 F5 Qinggir Xinjiang Uygur Zizhiqu China 41.27N 88.38E
21 B4 Qinggis Han Nei Monggol Zizhiqu China 47.46N 122.55E
23 G1 Qingguji Shandong China 34.42N 115.47E
22 D8 Qinghai prov China
22 E8 Qinghai Hu L Qinghai China
22 E8 Qinghai Nanshan mts Qinghai China
22 K8 Qinghe Hebei China 37.05N 115.35E
21 E4 Qinghe Heilongjiang China 46.10N 129.20E
24 G2 Qinghe Xinjiang Uygur Zizhiqu China 46.37N 90.25E
21 C7 Qinghecheng Liaoning China 41.28N 124.15E
21 B7 Qinghemen Liaoning China 41.45N 121.24E
21 C6 Qinghe Sk L Liaoning China
23 H4 Qinghu Zhejiang China 28.38N 118.34E
22 H8 Qingjian Shaanxi China 37.10N 110.03E
23 H2 Qingjiang Jiangsu China 33.35N 119.02E
23 G4 Qingjiang Jiangxi China 28.04N 115.31E
23 E3 Qing Jiang R Hubei China
23 E4 Qing Jiang R Hubei China
22 H8 Qingjian He R Shaanxi China
Qingkou see Ganyu
23 E9 Qinglan Guangdong China 19.35N 110.53E
23 E9 Qinglan Gang inlet Guangdong China
23 F6 Qinglian Guangdong China 24.19N 112.44E
23 G5 Qingliu Fujian China 26.14N 116.31E
23 D6 Qinglong Guizhou China 25.49N 105.10E
22 L6 Qinglong Hebei China 40.24N 119.00E
22 L6 Qinglong He R Hebei China
25 L2 Qingping Guangdong China 21.37N 109.55E
22 K8 Qingping Shandong China 36.46N 116.01E
23 J3 Qingpu Jiangsu China 31.10N 121.06E
Qingshan see Dedu
23 C4 Qingshen Sichuan China 29.48N 103.49E
22 E7 Qingshui Gansu China 39.23N 99.08E
23 D1 Qingshui Gansu China 34.40N 106.25E
22 J7 Qingshuihe Nei Monggol Zizhiqu China 39.56N 111.55E
23 A2 Qingshuihe Qinghai China 33.47N 97.10E
24 J9 Qingshuihe Qinghai China 33.47N 97.10E
22 G8 Qingshui He R Ningxia China
23 D5 Qingshui Jiang R Guizhou China
23 E5 Qingshui Jiang R Guizhou China
23 A5 Qingshuilang Shan mt ra Yunnan China
23 B5 Qingshuilang Shan mts Yunnan China
23 J4 Qingtian Zhejiang China 28.10N 120.17E
22 G7 Qingtongxia Ningxia China 38.03N 106.03E
22 G8 Qingtongxia Sk res Ningxia China 37.35N 105.40E
22 K7 Qing Xian Hebei China 38.37N 116.51E
22 J8 Qingxu Shanxi China 37.39N 112.20E
Qingyang see Jinjiang
23 H3 Qingyang Anhui China 30.41N 117.45E
22 G8 Qingyang Gansu China 36.05N 107.53E
23 C3 Qingyi Jiang R Sichuan China

Qingyuan see Yishan
23 F7 Qingyuan Guangdong China 23.46N 112.59E
22 K7 Qingyuan Hebei China 38.46N 115.30E
21 C6 Qingyuan Liaoning China 42.05N 124.45E
23 H5 Qingyuan Zhejiang China 27.38N 119.03E
22 L8 Qingyun Shandong China 37.50N 117.21E
23 D5 Qingzhen Guizhou China 26.33N 106.30E
23 F1 Qin He R Shanxi China
22 L7 Qinhuangdao Hebei China 39.55N 119.37E
24 B6 Qinjan Sanchang Xinjiang Uygur Zizhiqu China 38.55N 78.00E
23 E7 Qin Jiang R Guangxi China
23 D1 Qinling Shaanxi China 34.17N 106.52E
23 D2 Qin Ling mts Shaanxi China
23 F1 Qinshui Shanxi China 35.45N 112.15E
23 E7 Qintang Guangxi China 23.09N 109.25E
23 J2 Qintong Jiangsu China 32.38N 120.05E
22 J8 Qin Xian Shanxi China 36.40N 112.44E
23 F1 Qinyang Henan China 35.07N 112.51E
23 J5 Qinyu Fujian China 27.07N 120.16E
22 J8 Qinyuan Shanxi China 36.34N 112.19E
23 E8 Qinzhou Guangxi China 21.58N 108.34E
23 E8 Qinzhou Wan inlet Guangdong China
23 E9 Qionghai Guangdong China 19.17N 110.30E
23 C5 Qiong Hai L Sichuan China
23 C3 Qionglai Sichuan China 30.35N 103.30E
23 C2 Qionglai Shan mts Sichuan China
23 E9 Qiongshan Guangdong China 19.56N 110.30E
23 E9 Qiongzhong Guangdong China 19.02N 109.49E
Qiongzhou see Qiongshan
23 E8 Qiongzhou Haixia str Guangdong China
23 D3 Qiping Sichuan China 31.52N 106.09E
21 B1 Qiqian Nei Monggol Zizhiqu China 52.14N 120.42E
21 C4 Qiqihar Heilongjiang China 47.23N 124.00E
32 E6 Qīr Fārs Iran 28.27N 53.04E
32 C4 Qīr Lorestān Iran 33.42N 48.28E
24 C7 Qira Xinjiang Uygur Zizhiqu China 37.02N 80.54E
86 M5 Qiraîya, Wâdi watercourse Egypt
Qiran,Al see Karān
85 G5 Qirdābīyah reg Libya
33 H4 Qirdi oil field Saudi Arabia 24.50N 48.20E
35 D6 Qiryat 'Anavim Israel 31.49N 35.07E
35 D2 Qiryat Ata Israel 32.48N 35.06E
35 C7 Qiryat Gat Israel 31.37N 34.47E
35 B7 Qiryat Mal'akhi Israel 31.44N 34.45E
35 A2 Qiryat Menahem dist Jerusalem
35 A1 Qiryat Moshe sub Jerusalem
35 D2 Qiryat Motmkin Israel 32.49N 35.03E
35 C5 Qiryat Ono Israel 32.04N 34.51E
35 F1 Qiryat Shemona Israel 33.13N 35.35E
35 D3 Qiryat Tiv'on Israel 32.43N 35.08E
35 D2 Qiryat Yam Israel 32.51N 35.04E
35 A2 Qiryat Yovel sub Jerusalem
85 C4 Qirzah Libya 31.00N 14.39E
35 G3 Qisfa,El Jordan 32.38N 35.51E
23 E8 Qisha Guangxi China 21.35N 108.30E
23 D1 Qishan Shaanxi China 34.25N 107.40E
Qishlaq see Qeshlaq
Qishlaq R see Qeshlaq R
Qishlaq Hosain see Qeshlaq-E Ḩoseyn
Qishm see Qeshm
33 J9 Qishn S Yemen 15.25N 51.40E
Qishn & Socotra sultanate see Mahrah state
35 D3 Qishon watercourse Israel
33 C6 Qishrān I Saudi Arabia 20.14N 40.02E
24 F3 Qitai Xinjiang Uygur Zizhiqu China 44.02N 89.33E
21 E5 Qitaihe Heilongjiang China 45.47N 130.50E
33 L7 Qitbīt,Wādī watercourse Oman
35 D9 Qitmit watercourse Israel
23 C6 Qiubei Yunnan China 24.05N 104.10E
22 K8 Qiu Xian Hebei China 36.44N 115.09E
22 M8 Qixia Shandong China 37.17N 120.49E
23 G1 Qi Xian Henan China 35.35N 114.10E
22 J8 Qi Xian Shanxi China 37.20N 112.20E
22 J6 Qixiaying Nei Monggol Zizhiqu China 41.01N 112.09E
21 F4 Qixinggang Heilongjiang China 47.11N 132.44E
21 F4 Qixing He R Heilongjiang China
21 D3 Qixingpao Heilongjiang China 49.00N 126.02E
21 E4 Qixingpao Heilongjiang China 46.32N 131.45E
21 B1 Qiyahe Nei Monggol Zizhiqu China 52.14N 120.42E
23 F5 Qiyang Hunan China 26.40N 111.55E
22 G8 Qiying Ningxia China 37.00N 106.08E
Qizan see Jīzān
23 G3 Qizhou Hubei China 30.01N 115.23E
25 L3 Qizhou Liedao islds Guangdong China
31 C3 Qizil Afghanistan 34.28N 65.59E
31 A3 Qizil Bulak Afghanistan 35.19N 61.22E
31 E2 Qizil Qala Afghanistan 37.10N 68.50E
Qizil Ribat see Sa'dīyah, As
35 D1 Qlaiîîye Lebanon 33.12N 35.14E
Qnaïtra see Quneitra
95 M8 Qoboqobo S Africa 32.25S 28.15E
24 B8 Qogir Feng mt pk Xinjiang Uygur Zizhiqu China 35.47N 76.30E
22 G6 Qog Qi Nei Monggol Zizhiqu China 41.27N 106.55E
22 K4 Qog Ul Nei Monggol Zizhiqu China 44.48N 116.25E
32 B2 Qojūr Iran 36.16N 47.52E
95 M8 Qoloha S Africa 32.38S 28.25E
24 F4 Qoltag mts Xinjiang Uygur Zizhiqu China
32 D3 Qom Iran 34.39N 50.57E
24 H10 Qomdo Xizang Zizhiqu China 30.03N 95.41E
35 B7 Qomemiyyut Israel 31.40N 34.44E
Qomisheh see Shahrezā
24 H11 Qomo Xizang Zizhiqu China 29.40N 94.16E
Qomolangma Feng see Everest, Mt
24 E11 Qomolangma Feng mt pk Xizang Zizhiqu China 28.00N 86.58E
35 D9 Qomot,Har hills Israel
44 G9 Qom Tappeh Iran 38.12N 46.00E
32 D3 Qonāq, Kūh-e mt Iran 35.25N 50.38E
24 G11 Qonggyai Xizang Zizhiqu China 29.03N 91.40E
22 H6 Qongj Nei Monggol Zizhiqu China 41.55N 108.17E
24 E5 Qongkol Xinjiang Uygur Zizhiqu China 41.07N 86.26E
Qoqek see Tacheng
34 N4 Qōratū Iraq 34.36N 45.29E
35 B10 Qorha watercourse Israel
84 Y20 Qormi Malta 35.53N 14.28E
34 D4 Qornet es Saouda mt Lebanon 34.18N 36.07E
48 S12 Qôrnoq Greenland 64.35N 51.00W
32 B3 Qorveh Iran 35.09N 47.48E
34 L2 Qōsh,Al Iraq 36.45N 43.06E
32 A3 Qosh Ṭepe Iraq 36.00N 44.01E
32 G7 Qoṭbābād Iran 27.46N 56.05E
32 A1 Qotūr Iran 38.28N 44.25E
44 G9 Qoṭūr R Iran
32 A1 Qotūr Chai R Iran
34 D4 Qoubayat Lebanon 34.34N 36.16E
Qouiq R see Quweiq R
35 E1 Qouzah,El Lebanon 33.07N 35.20E
87 D2 Qoz Abu Dulu sand reg Sudan
Qoz Bal'Air see Qūz
15 F5 Q, Pegunungan mts Irian Jaya
84 Y20 Qrendi Malta 35.50N 14.28E
Qtaïfé see Quteifa
103 K2 Quabbin Res Massachusetts 42.25N 72.18W
103 K2 Quaboag R Massachusetts
98 G8 Quaco Hd New Brunswick 45.19N 65.33W
79 F2 Quadra, Pizzo mt Italy 46.23N 9.17E
69 M2 Quadrath-Ichendorf W Germany 50.56N 6.42E
80 K5 Quadri Italy 41.55N 14.17E
121 J2 Quadros, L. dos Brazil
31 F4 Quaidabad Pakistan 32.19N 71.59E
31 H9 Quaidabad dist Bangladesh
31 B9 Quaid-i-Azam's Mazar dist Karachi Pakistan
11 M10 Quail I New Zealand 43.37S 172.42E
111 H6 Quail Mts California
14 B9 Quairading W Australia 32.00S 117.22E
Qu'aiti see Qu'ayṭī sultanate
Quaiya see Quwayīyah, Al
63 G7 Quakenbrück W Germany 52.41N 7.57E
103 E5 Quakertown New Jersey 40.33N 74.56W
103 D6 Quakertown Pennsylvania 40.27N 75.20W
33 H3 Qual ay'ah, Ra's al C Saudi Arabia 26.52N 49.58E
80 K7 Qualiano Italy 40.55N 14.09E
12 G6 Quambatook Victoria 35.52S 143.36E
12 J4 Quambone New S Wales 30.54S 147.55E
13 F5 Quamby Queensland 20.22S 140.17E
12 H1 Quanah Texas 34.17N 99.46W
119 G9 Quanaru, I Brazil 2.55S 64.50W
23 F1 Quanbao Shan mt Henan China 34.18N 111.25E
25 K5 Quang Nam Vietnam 15.55N 108.14E
25 K5 Quang Ngai Vietnam 15.09N 108.50E
25 J4 Quang Tri Vietnam 16.46N 107.11E
25 J2 Quang Yen Vietnam 20.56N 106.49E
23 G2 Quan He R Anhui China
23 H2 Quanjiao Anhui China 32.05N 118.12E
25 H8 Quan Long Vietnam 9.15N 105.10E
23 G6 Quannan Jiangxi China 24.45N 114.24E
25 G7 Quan Phu Quoc isld Vietnam
24 C8 Quanshuigou Xinjiang Uygur Zizhiqu China 35.40N 79.28E
104 H8 Quantico Virginia 38.31N 77.20W
56 E5 Quantock Hills Somerset Eng
99 E1 Quantz L Ontario 51.10N 85.24W

23 H6 Quanzhou Fujian China 24.53N 118.36E
23 E6 Quanzhou Guangxi China 26.00N 110.57E
100 O8 Qu'Appelle Saskatchewan 50.33N 103.54W
100 P8 Qu'Appelle R Saskatchewan
100 L7 Qu'Appelle River Dam Saskatchewan 50.58N 106.28W
121 G3 Quaraí Brazil 30.28S 56.25W
121 G3 Quaraí,R Brazil
11 N12 Quarantine I New Zealand 45.50S 170.38E
80 E2 Quarata Italy 43.30N 11.49E
61 F5 Quaregnon Belgium 50.27N 3.52E
58 Q9 Quarff Shetland Scotland 60.06N 1.14W
63 L4 Quarnbek W Germany 54.20N 9.58E
79 D3 Quarona Italy 45.46N 8.16E
71 E2 Quarré-les-Tombes France 47.23N 4.00E
98 G7 Quarryville New Brunswick 46.50N 65.50W
103 G2 Quarryville New York 42.07N 73.59W
103 B7 Quarryville Pennsylvania 39.54N 76.10W
76 C14 Quarteira Portugal 37.04N 8.07W
66 N3 Quarten Switzerland 47.07N 9.15E
61 E4 Quartes Belgium 50.39N 3.31E
79 L5 Quartesana Italy 44.48N 11.44E
80 G5 Quartière Monte Sacro Italy 41.57N 12.32E
79 E8 Quartiere Zingone dist Milan Italy
26 U14 Quartier-Français Réunion Ind Oc 20.55S 55.38E
79 M3 Quarto d'Altino Italy 45.35N 12.21E
81 C5 Quartu,G.di Sardinia
81 C5 Quartu Sant'Elena Sardinia 39.15N 9.12E
79 B3 Quart Villefranche Italy 45.45N 7.23E
111 H4 Quartzite Mt Nevada 37.31N 116.21W
111 G2 Quartz Mount Nevada 39.03N 117.58W
110 G1 Quartz Mt Washington 48.33N 118.35W
111 K8 Quartzsite Arizona 33.41N 114.14W
106 C7 Quasqueton Iowa 42.23N 91.44W
118 E8 Quatá Brazil 22.15S 50.43W
117 E5 Quatipuru Brazil 0.50S 46.58W
26 U12 Quatre Bornes Mauritius, Indian Oc 20.15S 57.28E
69 G2 Quatre-Bras Belgium 50.34N 4.28E
69 H5 Quatre-Champs France 49.27N 4.46E
26 V12 Quatre Cocos,Pte Mauritius, Indian Oc 20.14S 57.47E
121 H1 Quatro Irmãos Brazil 27.47S 52.25W
96 U3 Quatro Ribeiras Azores 38.48N 27.14W
101 K10 Quatsino Vancouver I, Br Col 50.32N 127.36W
56 G3 Quatt Shropshire Eng 52.30N 2.22W
66 R5 Quattervals,Piz mt Switzerland 46.38N 10.06E
79 H5 Quattro Castella Italy 44.39N 10.28E
109 G7 Quay New Mexico 34.56N 103.47W
33 H9 Qu'ayṭī sultanate S Yemen
34 P7 Qubab,Al Iraq 31.22N 47.12E
86 F7 Qubâbât,El Egypt 29.28N 31.16E
86 R11 Qubba Cairo Egypt
85 G3 Qubbah,Al Libya 32.44N 22.15E
87 D3 Qubba Kadaro Sudan 15.47N 32.36E
85 L9 Qubbat Salim mt Sudan 20.34N 30.15E
35 D6 Qubeiba Jordan 31.51N 35.08E
85 C6 Qubūr as Sulṭān Libya 26.07N 15.13E
32 H2 Quchan Iran 37.04N 58.32E
Qudaym see Qudeim,El
34 F3 Qudeim,El Syria 35.04N 38.23E
Quds esh Sherif, El see Jerusalem
43 J8 Quduq Toba Afghanistan 37.01N 68.14E
91 D11 Qué Angola 14.26S 14.48E
110 P8 Quealy Wyoming 41.55N 110.32W
12 J6 Queanbeyan New S Wales 35.24S 149.17E
12 B6 Queanbeyan R New S Wales
72 F3 Queaux France 46.20N 0.40E
74 F10 Quebdana, Monts de Morocco
98 Q9 Québec Quebec 46.50N 71.15W
97 M7 Quebec prov Canada
118 F6 Quebra Anzol R Brazil
92 F9 Quebrabasa Rapids Mozambique 15.34S 33.00E
121 F3 Quebracho Uruguay 31.58S 57.53W
120 F12 Quebracho Coto Argentina 26.16S 64.29W
121 D2 Quebrachos Argentina 29.16S 63.41W
105 J7 Quebradillas Puerto Rico 18.28N 66.50W
120 D12 Quebrado de Salado gorge Chile
117 H9 Quebrangulo Brazil 9.17S 36.24W
121 A8 Quedal, C. de Chile 41.00S 73.56W
Quedas do Iguaçú falls see Iguazú, Cataratas del falls
91 D12 Quedas do Ruacaná waterfall Angola 17.22S 14.20E
63 O9 Quedlinburg E Germany 51.48N 11.09E
123 G7 Queen Alexandria Ra Antarctica
103 C9 Queen Anne Maryland 38.55N 75.57W
103 C8 Queen Annes co Maryland
101 L10 Queen Bess Mt Br Col 51.13N 124.35W
56 N5 Queenborough Kent Eng 51.26N 0.45E
97 M5 Queen,C N W Terr 64.45N 78.10W
101 G9 Queen Charlotte Graham I, Br Col 53.18N 132.04W
121 D9 Queen Charlotte B Falkland Is
101 G9 Queen Charlotte Is Br Col
11 J8 Queen Charlotte Sd New Zealand
101 J10 Queen Charlotte Sound Br Col
101 K10 Queen Charlotte Str Br Col
107 D1 Queen City Missouri 40.23N 92.34W
112 N2 Queen City Texas 33.10N 94.10W
97 J1 Queen Elizabeth Is N W Terr
55 C5 Queen Elizabeth 11 Res Surrey England
123 D3 Queen Mary Land Antarctica
101 D5 Queen Mary, Mt Yukon Terr 60.39N 139.43W
55 B4 Queen Mary Res Surrey Eng
96 B15 Queen Mary's Peak mt Tristan da Cunha 37.06S 12.17W
121 G8 Queen Maud B S Georgia
101 W1 Queen Maud G N W Terr
123 F8 Queen Maud Ra Antarctica
92 D11 Queens Zimbabwe 19.45S 28.49E
103 M7 Queens bor New York
57 K5 Queensbury W Yorks Eng 53.46N 1.50W
13 A2 Queens Chan N Terr Australia
97 K2 Queen's Chan N W Terr 76.50N 95.00W
12 G7 Queenscliff Victoria 38.17S 144.42E
57 G6 Queensferry Clwyd Wales 53.12N 3.01W
10 J6 Queensland state Australia
95 M6 Queen's Mercy S Africa 30.15S 28.34E
14 B2 Queens Park dist Perth, W Aust
98 L8 Queensport Nova Scotia 45.20N 61.16W
100 E8 Queenstown Alberta 50.39N 112.52W
103 B9 Queenstown Maryland 39.00N 76.10W
11 C12 Queenstown New Zealand 45.03S 168.41E
95 K7 Queenstown S Africa 31.54S 26.53E
18 J3 Queenstown Singapore 1.19N 103.48E
12 H8 Queenstown Tasmania 42.07S 145.33E
58 J5 Queen's View Tayside Scotland
14 E9 Queen Victoria Spring W Australia 30.25S 123.40E
110 A2 Queets Washington 47.32N 124.19W
110 B2 Queets R Washington
94 M5 Queguele Mozambique 24.07S 32.37E
120 E8 Quehua Bolivia 19.50S 66.56W
121 D6 Quehue Argentina 37.05S 64.30W
64 E5 Queich R W Germany
71 J5 Queige France 45.43N 6.28E
76 B5 Queijada Portugal 41.43N 8.33W
76 E4 Queija,Sierra de mts Spain
121 A9 Queilén Chile 42.50S 73.30W
75 G4 Queiles R Spain
120 G3 Queimada Rondônia Brazil 9.23S 62.25W
117 D5 Queimada ou Serraria, I Brazil
96 Q4 Queimada, Pta. da Azores 38.23N 28.15W
118 H2 Queimadas Brazil 10.59S 39.38W
96 T3 Queimado, Pta Azores 38.46N 27.22W
76 D7 Queiriga Portugal 40.49N 7.45W
121 A9 Queitao, I Chile 43.43S 73.31W
75 C1 Quejo,C Spain 43.30N 3.31W
75 F3 Quel Spain 42.14N 2.03W
91 E8 Quela Angola 9.18S 17.05E
70 J6 Quelaines France 47.56N 0.47W
76 D14 Quelfes Portugal 37.03N 7.49W
92 H10 Quelimane Mozambique 17.53S 36.51E
115 F6 Quelite Mexico 23.32N 106.28W
120 C5 Quellocochа Peru 12.22S 74.08W
91 C7 Quelo Angola 6.29S 12.36E
Quelpart I see Cheju Do
76 A11 Queluz Portugal 38.45N 9.15W
75 C4 Quemada Spain 41.41N 3.35W
118 F9 Quemada Grande,I Brazil 24.29S 46.40W
109 B7 Quemado New Mexico 34.21N 108.31W
112 G7 Quemado Texas 28.57N 100.37W
91 F10 Quembo R Angola
91 F8 Quembo tribe Angola
121 A9 Quemchi Chile 42.07S 73.30W
70 B5 Quéménéven France 48.07N 4.09W
Quemoy see Jinmen
121 D6 Quemu Quemu Argentina 36.03S 63.36W
120 D6 Quenamari,Nev.de pk Peru 14.11S 70.24W
61 G4 Quenast Belgium 50.40N 4.10E
120 C5 Quenco Peru 13.52S 74.53W
69 B3 Quend France 50.19N 1.39E
91 D10 Quenda Angola 12.42S 14.22E
58 Q10 Quendale Shetland Scotland 59.54N 1.20W
56 M4 Quendon Essex Eng 51.57N 0.12E
69 B3 Quend Plage France 50.19N 1.33E
109 P3 Quenemo Kansas 38.34N 95.34W
56 H4 Quenington Glos Eng 51.45N 1.47W
77 K6 Quéntar,Embalse de res Spain 37.14N 3.25W
107 F10 Quentin Mississippi 31.31N 90.45W
103 B6 Quentin Pennsylvania 40.17N 76.27W
28 B3 Quepem Goa India 15.13N 74.03E
121 F4 Quequay Grande R Uruguay
92 D11 Que Que Zimbabwe 18.55S 29.51E
121 F7 Quequén Argentina 38.30S 58.44W
120 D7 Quequeña Peru 16.35S 71.29W
121 F7 Quequén, R Argentina
69 C2 Quercamps France 50.45N 2.04E
80 B2 Quercianella Italy 43.27N 10.22E
79 H7 Querciolaia,Poggio mt Italy 43.31N 10.25E
72 G7 Quercy reg France

119 B10 Querecotillo Peru 4.53S 80.38W
76 D14 Querenca Portugal 37.11N 7.59W
118 D8 Querência do Norte Brazil 23.05S 53.30W
115 J7 Querétaro Mexico 20.38N 100.23W
115 J7 Querétaro state Mexico
63 P10 Querfurt E Germany 51.23N 11.36E
72 J10 Quérigut France 42.42N 2.07E
79 L3 Quero Italy 45.55N 11.56E
75 D8 Quero Spain 39.30N 3.15W
115 D2 Querobabi Mexico 30.02N 111.02W
119 B10 Querpon Peru 5.45S 79.54W
70 G2 Querqueville France 49.40N 1.42W
70 C6 Querrien France 47.57N 3.32W
69 C4 Querrieu France 49.57N 2.27E
77 P2 Quesa Spain 39.07N 0.45W
77 K5 Quesada Spain 37.51N 3.04W
23 G2 Queshan Henan China 32.48N 114.03E
101 M9 Quesnel Br Col 53.03N 122.31W
101 N9 Quesnel L Br Col
69 D4 Quesnoy, le France 49.45N 2.42E
69 F3 Quesnoy,le France 50.15N 3.39E
69 E2 Quesnoy-sur-Deûle France 50.43N 3.00E
70 E5 Quessoy France 48.25N 2.41W
109 E5 Questa New Mexico 36.43N 105.36W
70 F6 Questembert France 47.40N 2.26W
Quetena see Peña Barrosa
120 E9 Quetena, R Bolivia
100 M2 Quetico Ontario 48.45N 90.55W
100 L2 Quetico L Ontario 48.35N 91.58W
100 L2 Quetico Prov.Park Ontario
31 D4 Quetta Afghanistan 33.03N 66.09E
31 D5 Quetta Pakistan 30.15N 67.00E
31 D5 Quetta-Pishin dist Pakistan
70 H2 Quettehou France 49.36N 1.19W
70 L3 Quetteville France 49.20N 0.19E
70 H4 Quettreville France 48.58N 1.28W
121 B6 Queuco Chile 37.44S 71.30W
107 D11 Queue de Tortue R Louisiana
61 N4 Queue-du-Bois Belgium 50.38N 5.40E
69 B6 Queue-lèz-Yvelines,la France 48.49N 1.45E
121 A7 Queule Chile 39.20S 73.15W
121 C8 Queupán Argentina 41.23S 66.05W
61 E4 Quevaucamps Belgium 50.31N 3.41E
69 C4 Quevauvillers France 49.49N 2.05E
119 B8 Quevedo Ecuador 0.59S 79.27W
99 O3 Quévillon,L Quebec 49.04N 76.56W
61 F5 Quévy-le-Grand Belgium 50.22N 3.57E
61 F5 Quévy-le-Petit Belgium 50.22N 3.56E
72 C5 Queyrac France 45.23N 1.00W
71 K7 Queyras reg France
79 A5 Queyron,Gran mt Italy/France 44.51N 6.59E
72 J6 Quézac France 44.45N 2.10E
115 O10 Quezaltenango Guatemala 14.50N 91.30W
115 P11 Quezaltepeque El Salvador 13.50N 89.18W
19 L6 Quezon Negros Philippines 10.26N 123.19E
19 J7 Quezon Palawan Philippines 9.14N 118.02E
19 J1 Quezon City Luzon Philippines 14.39N 121.02E
33 D3 Qufār Saudi Arabia 27.25N 41.41E
33 D3 Qufayfah,Al Saudi Arabia 27.09N 40.55E
23 H1 Qufu Shandong China 35.40N 117.01E
Qufur see Qufār
76 B8 Quiaios Portugal 40.13N 8.51W
91 C7 Quibala Angola 7.25S 13.45E
91 D9 Quibala Angola 10.48S 14.59E
91 D8 Quibaxi Angola 8.34S 14.37E
119 C5 Quibdó Colombia 5.40N 76.38W
100 J1 Quibell Ontario 49.58N 93.24W
70 D7 Quiberon France 47.29N 3.07W
70 D6 Quiberon,B.de France
70 M2 Quiberville France 49.54N 0.54E
91 D7 Quibocolo Angola 6.20S 15.05E
119 E3 Quíbor Venezuela 9.55N 69.35W
12 M8 Quibray B New S Wales
91 C8 Quicabo Angola 8.17S 13.50E
91 C8 Quicama, Parque Nacional de Angola
25 H3 Qui Chau Vietnam 19.33N 105.07E
63 L5 Quickborn W Germany 53.44N 9.55E
91 C9 Quicombo Angola 11.23S 13.52E
91 C9 Quicombo,Pto pt Angola 11.18S 13.50E
91 D8 Quiculungo Angola 8.38S 15.19E
91 D9 Quienha Angola 10.15S 15.29E
64 C5 Quierschied W Germany 49.20N 7.04E
101 G5 Quiet L Yukon Terr 61.09N 133.05W
61 E5 Quiévrain Belgium 50.25N 3.41E
69 E3 Quiévy France 50.10N 3.25E
100 G2 Quigley Alberta 56.10N 110.51W
87 G4 Quiha Ethiopia 13.29N 39.32E
91 C11 Quihita Angola 15.23S 13.59E
91 E7 Quihuhu Angola 7.42S 16.33E
118 B9 Quiindy Paraguay 25.58S 57.14W
111 M9 Quijotoa Arizona 32.09N 112.06W
115 F5 Quilá Mexico 24.26N 107.11W
115 L3 Quilalí Nicaragua 13.31N 86.04W
121 A9 Quilán,C Chile 43.16S 74.27W
28 B5 Quilandi Kerala India 11.25N 75.41E
74 E9 Quilates,C Morocco 35.15N 3.39W
13 H7 Quilberry Queensland 27.04S 146.00E
120 C7 Quilca Peru 16.44S 72.26W
110 C2 Quilcene Washington 47.50N 122.54W
121 E6 Quilco Argentina 37.05S 61.15W
91 D9 Quilenda Angola 10.39S 14.23E
91 D11 Quilengues Huila Angola 14.09S 14.04E
121 B4 Quilimarí Chile 32.05S 70.30W
121 D3 Quilino Argentina 30.14S 64.29W
120 C5 Quillabamba Peru 12.49S 72.41W
120 E7 Quillacollo Bolivia 17.26S 66.16W
120 D9 Quillagua Chile 21.43S 69.30W
121 B3 Quillaicillo Chile 31.17S 71.40W
72 J10 Quillan France 42.52N 2.11E
120 D7 Quillaveco Peru 17.28S 70.17W
70 M3 Quillebeuf France 49.28N 0.32E
26 N15 Quille,la isld St Paul I Ind Oc 38.43S 77.31E
121 B7 Quillén,L Argentina
100 N6 Quill Lake Saskatchewan 52.03N 104.12W
100 N7 Quill Lakes Saskatchewan
121 B4 Quillota Chile 32.54S 71.16W
70 G7 Quilly France 47.28N 1.56W
121 F5 Quilmes Argentina 34.45S 58.15W
120 E12 Quilmes,Sa.del mts Argentina
91 D8 Quilombo dos Dembos Angola 8.56S 14.44E
28 C6 Quilon Kerala India 8.53N 76.38E
28 C6 Quilon dist Kerala India
13 G7 Quilpie Queensland 26.35S 144.14E
121 B4 Quilpué Chile 33.05S 71.33W
59 D6 Quilty Clare Irish Rep 52.50N 9.27W
119 C3 Quimari,Alto de mt Colombia 8.07N 76.23W
91 E9 Quimbango Angola 10.56S 17.34E
91 E7 Quimbele Angola 6.30S 16.25E
91 D7 Quimbianda Angola 7.03S 15.51E
91 F8 Quimbonge Angola 8.35S 18.31E
120 E7 Quime Bolivia 17.00S 67.27W
70 B5 Quimerch France 48.17N 4.07W
121 E1 Quimilí Argentina 27.35S 62.25W
120 G7 Quimome Bolivia 17.45S 61.15W
70 B6 Quimper France 48.00N 4.06W
70 C6 Quimperlé France 47.52N 3.33W
59 E6 Quin Clare Irish Rep 52.49N 8.52W
19 L4 Quinabucasan Pt Luzon Philippines 14.06N 123.18E
58 F2 Quinag mt Highland Scotland 58.13N 5.02W
19 L5 Quinalasag isld Luzon Philippines 13.57N 123.38E
110 B2 Quinault Washington 47.27N 123.50W
110 A2 Quinault R Washington
70 N2 Quincampoix France 49.31N 1.11E
72 E2 Quinçay France 46.36N 0.14E
120 D5 Quince Mil Peru 13.15S 70.41W
121 A9 Quinchao isld Chile 42.30S 73.30W
79 C3 Quincinetto Italy 45.34N 7.48E
75 D2 Quincoces de Yuso Spain 42.59N 3.15W
111 D2 Quincy California 39.56N 120.56W
105 C7 Quincy Florida 30.34N 84.35W
107 E2 Quincy Illinois 39.55N 91.22W
104 B8 Quincy Kentucky 38.38N 83.06W
106 K8 Quincy Michigan 41.58N 84.51W
104 B6 Quincy Ohio 40.18N 83.58W
110 B3 Quincy Oregon 46.07N 123.14W
110 F2 Quincy Washington 47.13N 119.51W
104 Q10 Quincy dist Boston, Mass
104 R10 Quincy Bay Massachusetts
69 D6 Quincy-Voisins France 48.54N 2.53E
119 C5 Quindio div Colombia
119 C5 Quindio Pass Colombia 4.25N 75.31W
103 K2 Quinebaug R Massachusetts
121 D4 Quines Argentina 32.15S 65.46W
70 H2 Quineville France 49.31N 1.18W
92 K9 Quinga Mozambique 15.50S 40.14E
91 D8 Quinge Angola 9.07S 15.43E
91 D10 Quingenge Angola 12.48S 14.54E
71 H2 Quingey France 47.06N 5.53E
91 C7 Quingombe Angola 6.38S 13.01E
Quinhagak see Kwinhagak
25 G2 Quinh Nhai Vietnam 21.53N 103.33E
25 K6 Qui Nhon Vietnam 13.47N 109.11E
119 G5 Quinigua, Cerro mts Venezuela
19 K6 Quiniluban isld Philippines 11.25N 120.51E
91 G10 Quinjama Angola 12.33S 21.28E
112 L3 Quinlan Texas 32.53N 96.09W
108 H6 Quinn S Dakota 44.00N 102.07W
110 G8 Quinn R Nevada
111 J4 Quinn Canyon Ra Nevada
13 C6 Quinn, Mt N Terr Australia 24.50S 133.01E
110 G8 Quinn R.Crossing Nevada 41.36N 118.26W
71 J9 Quinson France 43.42N 6.03E
72 J3 Quinssaines France 46.19N 2.28E
64 B4 Quint W Germany 49.49N 6.43E
121 B5 Quinta Chile 34.46S 71.08W
76 B11 Quinta Grande Portugal 38.56N 8.31W
77 E3 Quintana de la Serena Spain 38.45N 5.40W

76 G3 Quintana del Castillo Spain 42.39N 6.03W
76 L4 Quintana del Puente Spain 42.05N 4.12W
75 C3 Quintanalara Spain 42.10N 3.30W
75 C3 Quintanapalla Spain 42.25N 3.30W
75 D8 Quintanar de la Orden Spain 39.36N 3.03W
75 D4 Quintanar de la Sierra Spain 41.59N 3.02W
77 N2 Quintanar del Rey Spain 39.21N 1.56W
75 E4 Quintana Redonda Spain 41.38N 2.37W
115 P8 Quintana Roo state Mexico
75 E4 Quintanas de Gormaz Spain 41.30N 2.58W
75 D3 Quintanavides Spain 42.29N 3.25W
76 F5 Quintanilha Portugal 41.45N 6.35W
76 L9 Quintanilla mt Spain 39.48N 4.30W
76 G4 Quintanilla de Florez Spain 42.15N 6.06W
75 C3 Quintanilla del Agua Spain 42.02N 3.39W
75 D2 Quintanilla de la Ojeda Spain 42.55N 3.18W
76 L3 Quintanilla de las Torres Spain 42.49N 4.11W
76 L5 Quintanilla de Onésimo Spain 41.37N 4.22W
75 D2 Quintanilla San Garcia Spain 42.33N 3.11W
75 C2 Quintanilla Sobresierra Spain 42.34N 3.43W
121 F9 Quinta Normal dist Santiago Chile
76 D7 Quintela Portugal 40.52N 7.35W
76 E2 Quintela Spain 43.11N 7.28W
71 F6 Quintenas France 45.12N 4.40E
109 K2 Quinter Kansas 39.04N 100.15W
121 B4 Quintero Chile 32.47S 71.30W
70 E5 Quintin France 48.24N 2.55W
77 H3 Quintín, Minas des San mines Spain 38.48N 4.18W
75 J5 Quinto Spain 41.25N 0.30W
66 L5 Quinto Switzerland 46.31N 8.43E
121 D5 Quinto R Argentina
79 M3 Quinto di Treviso Italy 45.39N 12.10E
103 D7 Quinton New Jersey 39.32N 75.25E
109 P6 Quinton Oklahoma 35.09N 95.24W
100 N7 Quinton Saskatchewan 51.23N 104.27W
76 D13 Quintos Portugal 37.57N 7.43W
79 L3 Quinto Vicentino Italy 45.35N 11.38E
104 E8 Quinwood W Virginia 38.03N 80.43W
91 D7 Quinzala Angola 7.20S 15.29E
79 H4 Quinzano d'Oglio Italy 45.19N 10.00E
91 C7 Quinzau Angola 6.51S 12.44E
92 K7 Quionga Mozambique 10.37S 40.31E
115 L9 Quiotepec Mexico 17.55N 96.59W
117 J9 Quipapá Brazil 8.49S 35.54W
77 N4 Quipar R Spain
77 N4 Quipar,Embalse del L Spain 38.13N 1.36W
91 D7 Quipedro Angola 7.56S 14.27E
91 D10 Quipeio Angola 12.27S 15.30E
120 E6 Quiquive, R Bolivia
58 D3 Quirang mt Skye, Highland Scotland 57.38N 6.17W
115 E4 Quiriego Mexico 27.31N 109.12W
121 A6 Quiriguina I Chile 36.40S 73.05W
121 A6 Quirihue Chile 36.15S 72.35W
91 F9 Quirima Angola 10.47S 18.06E
91 D9 Quirimbo Angola 10.41S 14.16E
80 D7 Quirinale, Monte hill Roma Italy
12 K4 Quirindi New S Wales 31.32S 150.44E
118 E6 Quirinópolis Brazil 18.33S 50.30W
119 G3 Quiriquire Venezuela 9.59N 63.14W
99 H6 Quirke L Ontario 46.29N 82.33W
64 C5 Quirnbach W Germany 49.29N 7.25E
121 E5 Quiroga Argentina 35.18S 61.22W
120 F8 Quiroga Bolivia 18.25S 65.08W
76 E4 Quiroga Spain 42.28N 7.15W
121 K7 Quiroga,L Argentina
120 E11 Quirón, Salar de salt pan Arg
Quiros see Barzana Spain
76 E5 Quiroz Portugal 41.56N 7.10W
119 B10 Quiróz,R Peru
98 R2 Quirpon Newfoundland 51.35N 55.27W
98 R2 Quirpon,I Newfoundland 51.37N 55.25W
81 D4 Quirra,I.di Sardinia 39.32N 9.40E
120 A2 Quiruvilca Peru 7.59S 78.21W
35 D2 Quiryat Bialik Israel 32.50N 35.05E
75 C1 Quisicedo Spain 43.04N 3.40W
119 E2 Quisiro Venezuela 10.54N 71.17W
71 D9 Quissac France 43.54N 4.00E
91 C8 Quissama tribe Angola
92 K8 Quissanga Mozambique 12.24S 40.33E
94 N5 Quissico Mozambique 24.42S 34.44E
91 D9 Quissongo Angola 10.00S 15.08E
79 J4 Quistello Italy 45.01N 10.59E
70 D6 Quistinic France 47.56N 3.05W
91 F9 Quitapa Angola 10.10S 18.16E
112 F1 Quitaque Texas 34.23N 101.04W
116 D7 Quita Seuño Bank Caribbean Sea
92 K7 Quiterajo Mozambique 11.46S 40.25E
118 D6 Quitéria R Brazil
91 D12 Quiteve Angola 16.02S 15.10E
91 D7 Quitexe Angola 7.56S 15.03E
121 E1 Quitilipi Argentina 26.50S 60.15W
107 D6 Quitman Arkansas 35.22N 92.11W
105 D7 Quitman Georgia 30.57N 83.34W
107 D9 Quitman Louisiana 32.21N 92.41W
107 H9 Quitman Mississippi 32.02N 88.43W
112 M3 Quitman Texas 32.47N 95.26W
119 B8 Quito Ecuador 0.14S 78.30W
115 C2 Quitovac Mexico 31.30N 112.46W
70 N3 Quittebeuf France 49.06N 1.00E
111 M6 Quivero Arizona 35.30N 112.10W
118 G2 Quixaba Brazil 11.52S 43.11W
117 G7 Quixadá Brazil 4.57S 39.04W
92 K9 Quixaxe Mozambique 15.18S 40.06E
117 G7 Quixeramobim Brazil 5.16S 39.20W
91 D8 Quixinge Angola 9.51S 14.24E
58 M7 Quixwood Borders Scotland 55.52N 2.21W
23 F6 Qujiang Guangdong China 24.47N 113.17E
23 D3 Qu Jiang R Sichuan China
23 E8 Qujie Guangdong China 20.31N 110.20E
23 C6 Qujing Yunnan China 25.29N 103.47E
83 D3 Qūkes Shkumbin Albania 41.05N 20.27E
Qulansiyah see Qalansīyah
Qulashgird see Golāshkerd
33 N10 Qulay'ah, Ra's al C Kuwait 28.54N 48.19E
33 N10 Qulay'at al Ḩarār B Kuwait
34 K10 Qulayyabah,Al Saudi Arabia 28.11N 42.43E
34 K10 Qulayyibah,Al Saudi Arabia 28.08N 42.21E
34 O9 Qulbān Layyah Iraq 29.48N 46.02E
35 G6 Quleib watercourse Jordan
Quli Kush see Kowlī Kosh,Gardaneh-ye pass
86 E10 Qulubba Egypt 27.46N 30.49E
32 D4 Qūlūng Kūh-e mt Iran 33.19N 51.18E
86 E9 Qulûşna Egypt 28.21N 30.44E
95 L7 Qumanco S Africa 31.49S 27.53E
24 G8 Qumar He R Qinghai China
24 H8 Qumar Heyan Qinghai China 35.20N 93.20E
23 A1 Qumarlêb Qinghai China 34.33N 95.25E
24 H8 Qumarlêb Qinghai China 34.33N 95.25E
24 H8 Qumarrabdün Qinghai China 34.44N 94.51E
95 M7 Qumbu S Africa 31.10S 28.53E
24 E10 Qumigxung Xizang Zizhiqu China 30.53N 86.38E
35 E7 Qumran anc site Jordan 31.44N 35.27E
Qunagh,Kūh-i see Qonāq,Kūh-e mt
Qunaytirah see Quneitra
33 F5 Qunayy Saudi Arabia 23.16N 45.51E
35 H7 Quneitira,El anc site Jordan 31.40N 36.04E
35 G1 Quneitra Syria 33.08N 35.49E
33 D7 Qunfidhah,Al Saudi Arabia 19.09N 41.07E
33 H8 Qunfudh S Yemen 16.44N 49.32E
24 F10 Qungtag Xizang Zizhiqu China 30.00N 87.40E
23 A3 Qu'nyido Xizang Zizhiqu China 31.15N 98.06E
103 J5 Quogue Long I, N Y 40.48N 72.37W
19 N4 Quoi isld Truk Is Pacific Oc 7.32N 151.59E
58 F4 Quoich,L Highland Scotland
58 K4 Quoich, Linn of pool Grampian Scotland 57.00N 3.29W
59 L3 Quoile,R Down N Ireland
26 U11 Quoin Chan Mauritius, Indian Oc
14 A7 Quoin Hd W Australia 25.47S 113.00E
13 A2 Quoin I N Terr Australia 14.55S 129.30E
13 K6 Quoin I Queensland 23.50S 153.15E
11 E13 Quoin Pt New Zealand 46.09S 170.12E
95 C10 Quoin Pt S Africa 34.47S 19.38E
22 K6 Quojiatun Hebei China 41.40N 116.56E
103 L4 Quonochontaug Rhode I 41.20N 71.42W
100 M1 Quorn Ontario 49.25N 90.53W
12 E4 Quorn S Australia 32.20S 138.02E
56 J2 Quorndon Leics Eng 52.45N 1.09W
Qupan see Qapan
Quqên see Jinchuan
32 B2 Qurābeh Iran 36.18N 46.58E
33 D2 Qurāh Saudi Arabia 29.52N 40.11E
34 H9 Qurah Saudi Arabia 29.53N 40.12E
Quraitu see Qōratū
35 F7 Quraiyat Jordan 31.32N 35.41E
33 N5 Qurayāt Oman 23.20N 58.58E
33 E4 Qurayn,Al Saudi Arabia 24.43N 43.44E
33 H4 Qurayn,Al Saudi Arabia 25.30N 49.37E
33 K6 Qurayni,Al Saudi Arabia 21.58N 53.37E
33 E4 Qurayyah, Al Saudi Arabia 24.51N 43.18E
33 L4 Qurayyah, Al U.A.E. 25.15N 56.21E
33 B2 Qurayyah, 'Al anc site Saudi Arabia 28.48N 36.03E
33 A8 Qurayyah,Ra's al C Saudi Arabia 26.03N 50.09E
34 E7 Qurayyat al Milḩ oasis Saudi Arabia
35 G2 Qurayz el Wawi Syria 32.55N 35.50E
87 E4 Qurein Sudan 13.30N 34.50E
86 G4 Qurein,El Egypt 30.37N 31.44E
35 G6 Qureiyat Nafi Jordan 31.52N 35.57E
35 G6 Qureiyat Salim Jordan 31.51N 35.58E
85 J5 Qûr el Laban mts Egypt

86 A5 Qûr Laban *hill* Egypt 30.23N 28.59E
85 M7 Qurnâ, El Egypt 25.44N 32.34E
34 P7 Qurnah,Al Iraq 31.01N 47.27E
85 J5 Qûr Sawân *mt* Egypt 28.17N 27.53E
32 E4 Qūrtān Iran 32.27N 52.35E
Qurtun *see* Qūrtān
32 A1 Qūrū Gol Pass Iran 38.56N 44.28E
86 G9 Qurûn Harhash *hill* Egypt 28.09N 31.41E
32 D2 Quruq Pass Iran 36.18N 51.45E
Qurveh *see* Qorveh
34 M10 Quryān,Al *wells* Saudi Arabia
85 M7 Qus Egypt 25.53N 32.48E
34 H4 Quşaybah Iraq 34.25N 40.59E
33 J9 Quşay'ir S Yemen 14.55N 50.15E
Quşayr Syria*see* Quseir,El
34 K2 Quşayr *oil well* Iraq 36.34N 42.25E
85 H4 Quşayr ad Daffah Libya 30.06N 24.09E
34 N8 Qusayr,Al Iraq 30.37N 45.51E
33 G2 Quşayr Bilāl *anc site* Saudi Arabia 28.40N 46.14E
35 F2 Qusbiye Syria 32.58N 35.43E
33 A1 Quseima,El Egypt 30.39N 34.22E
86 M4 Quşeima, El Egypt 30.38N 34.21E
85 N6 Quseir Egypt 26.04N 34.15E
34 D4 Quseir,El Syria 34.32N 36.34E
34 N4 Qusha Chāwpān *R* Iraq
32 A2 Qūshchi Iran 37.59N 45.05E
32 B1 Qūsheh Dagh *mts* Iran
34 P6 Qū Sīāh *R* Iran
35 D5 Qusin Jordan 32.14N 35.10E
85 L6 Qûsîya, El Egypt 27.32N 30.48E
35 E5 Qusra Jordan 32.05N 35.20E
85 J6 Quss Abû Sa'îd, E1 *plat* Egypt
86 F8 Quss, Wâdî *watercourse* Egypt
24 G11 Qusum Xizang Zizhiqu China 29.03N 92.13E
33 F5 Qūşūrīyah, Al Saudi Arabia 23.40N 44.31E
23 E3 Qutang Xia *R* Sichuan China
Quţayfah *see* Quteifa
33 F9 Qūţbīn Yemen 15.57N 44.37E
48 S8 Qutdligssat Greenland 70.03N 53.00W
34 D5 Quteifa Syria 33.44N 36.36E
95 L6 Quthing Lesotho 30.25S 27.43E
95 L6 Quthing *dist* Lesotho
32 C3 Qūtīābād Iran 35.47N 48.31E
33 E3 Quţn, Jabal *mts* Saudi Arabia
85 C7 Quţrūn, Al Libya 24.55N 14.36E
33 D7 Quţu *isld* Saudi Arabia 18.30N 41.04E
86 E4 Qutûr Egypt 30.59N 30.57E
Qutur Iran*see* Qotūr
Qutur Chai *R see* Qotūr Chai *R*
Quwair *see* Guwer
33 E3 Quwārah,Al Saudi Arabia 26.52N 43.29E
85 F5 Quway'id, al Libya 29.36N 21.37E
33 F4 Quwayīyah,Al Saudi Arabia 24.05N 45.15E
Quwayr *see* Guwer
85 D4 Quwayrat al Marbaḩ Libya 30.09N 16.20E
35 F7 Quweijiya Jordan 31.44N 35.44E
34 E2 Quweiq *R* Syria
86 O6 Quweira, El Jordan 29.47N 35.18E
86 F4 Quweisna Egypt 30.34N 31.09E
33 L7 Qū' Wishām *reg* Oman
23 F1 Quwo Shanxi China 35.38N 111.29E
22 G8 Quwu Shan *mts* Gansu China
Quwwamabad *see* Qavāmābād
23 D3 Qu Xian Sichuan China 30.50N 106.58E
23 H4 Qu Xian Zhejiang China 28.55N 118.54E
24 G11 Qūxü Xizang Zizhiqu China 29.19N 90.45E
22 K7 Quyang Hebei China 38.40N 114.31E
23 G5 Quyang Jiangxi China 26.09N 115.31E
25 H3 Quynh Luu Vietnam 19.08N 105.40E
99 O7 Quyon Quebec 45.32N 76.16W
118 C10 Quyquyó Paraguay 26.13S 57.00W
32 A2 Qūyūn *isld* Iran 37.27N 45.37E
33 D7 Qūz Saudi Arabia 19.00N 41.21E
33 H9 Quzah,Al S Yemen 15.07N 49.06E
22 K8 Quzhou Hebei China 36.49N 114.55E
83 D4 Qyteti Stalin Albania 40.49N 19.56E
52 G11 Råå Sweden 55.59N 12.45E
65 J5 Raab Austria 48.22N 13.39E
Raab Hungary*see* Győr
65 N7 Raab *R* Austria
65 N4 Raabs Austria 48.52N 15.31E
65 N7 Raab-tal *V* Austria
51 L7 Raahe Finland 64.42N 24.30E
51 O9 Rääkkylä Finland 62.19N 29.40E
60 O10 Raalte Netherlands 52.23N 6.16E
60 H13 Raamsdonk Netherlands 51.42N 4.55E
60 H13 Raamsdonksveer Netherlands 51.42N 4.52E
35 C5 Ra'ananna Israel 32.11N 34.52E
97 L2 Raanes Pen N W Terr
51 L5 Raanujärvi Finland 66.39N 24.40E
18 L9 Raas *isld* Indonesia
58 D4 Raasay *isld* Highland Scotland
58 D4 Raasay, Sound of Highland Scotland
82 B6 Rab *isld* Yugoslavia 44.46N 14.44E
18 N10 Raba Indonesia 8.27S 118.45E
35 E4 Raba Jordan 32.23N 35.23E
90 B7 Raba Nigeria 9.14N 4.59E
62 K8 Rába *R* Hungary
62 M6 Raba *R* Poland
76 C8 Rabaçal Portugal 40.02N 8.28W
Rabad,Ar *see* Rubad, Ar
76 D2 Rábade Spain 43.07N 7.37W
24 F12 Rabagala Shankou *pass* Xizang Zizhiqu China 27.46N 87.32E
90 B5 Rabah Nigeria 13.05N 5.30E
65 P7 Rabahidvég Hungary 47.05N 16.45E
93 L9 Rabai Kenya 3.55S 39.34E
87 D4 Rabak Sudan 13.12N 32.44E
15 C7 Rabal Moluccas Indon 6.21S 134.52E
76 G4 Rabanal del Camino Spain 42.28N 6.17W
76 G5 Rabanales Spain 41.44N 6.15W
24 C9 Rabang Xizang Zizhiqu China 33.03N 80.29E
29 G1 Rabang Xizang Zizhiqu China 33.03N 80.29E
15 K8 Rabaraba Papua New Guinea 10.00S 149.50E
77 P4 Rabasa *airport* Spain 38.22N 0.31W
98 H4 Rabast,C.de Anticosti I, Que 49.57N 64.10W
72 H8 Rabastens Tarn France 43.49N 1.42E
72 E9 Rabastens-de-Bigorre France 43.23N 0.10E
Rabat Gozo Mediterranean*see* Victoria
84 Y20 Rabat Malta 35.53N 14.25E
88 K4 Rabat Morocco 34.02N 6.51W
32 H3 Rabāt-e Kamah Iran 34.48N 58.49E
72 H10 Rabat-les-Trois-Seigneurs France 42.51N 1.32E
15 M6 Rabaul New Britain 4.13S 152.11E
35 F8 Rabba Jordan 31.16N 35.44E
33 L5 Rabbād, Al *des area* U.A.E.
Rabbah *see* 'Amman
66 O7 Rabbi,Pizzo *mt* Italy 46.14N 9.18E
101 K6 Rabbit *R* Br Col
108 H4 Rabbit Cr S Dakota
109 D1 Rabbit Ears Pass Colorado 40.24N 106.39W
10 E11 Rabbit I Lord Howe I Pacific Oc 31.33S 159.05E
11 H8 Rabbit I New Zealand 41.17S 173.08E
100 K5 Rabbit Lake Saskatchewan 53.10N 107.46W
101 N5 Rabbitskin *R* N W Terr
Rabch *R see* Rapch
87 J8 Rabdurre Somalia 4.23N 43.09E
64 Q2 Rabenau E Germany 50.57N 13.39E
64 F2 Rabenau W Germany 50.40N 8.52E
65 N7 Rabenwald Kopf *mt* Austria 47.18N 15.44E
106 K3 Raber Michigan 46.04N 84.04W
64 Q5 Rábí Czechoslovakia 49.17N 13.39E
119 B5 Rabida, I Galápagos Is 0.25S 90.43W
33 C5 Rābigh Saudi Arabia 22.48N 39.01E
115 O10 Rabinal Guatemala 15.05N 90.26W
85 B3 Rābiţā Libya 32.12N 12.48E
77 H6 Rabita,La Spain 37.30N 4.03W
66 M5 Rabius Switzerland 46.44N 8.58E
66 O5 Rabiusa *R* Switzerland
62 M6 Rabka Poland 49.36N 19.55E
Rabkob *see* Dharmjaygarh
31 H10 Rabnabad Is Bangladesh
65 O6 Rabnitz *R* Austria
76 G2 Rabo *mt* Spain 43.06N 6.24W
42 B3 Rabochiy U.S.S.R. 59.07N 79.07E
96 T1 Rabo de Peixe Azores 37.33N 25.35W
18 C7 Rabong,Gunong *mt* Pen Malaysia 4.49N 102.07E
32 G6 Rābor Iran 29.19N 56.55E
45 Q1 Rabotki U.S.S.R. 56.02N 44.37E
64 P3 Rabštejn Czechoslovakia 50.03N 13.18E
88 F10 Rabt Sebeta *reg* Morocco
105 D3 Rabun, L Georgia 34.45N 83.27W
82 F6 Rača Yugoslavia 44.14N 20.59E
82 K4 Răcăciuni Romania 46.20N 27.00E
81 R13 Racale Italy 39.52N 18.06E
81 G9 Racalmuto Sicily 37.25N 13.44E
87 L7 Racan Somalia 6.03N 47.51E
82 G6 Răcăşdia Romania 44.58N 21.36E
79 C5 Racconigi Italy 44.46N 7.41E
108 Q8 Raccoon *R* Iowa
116 G3 Raccoon Cay *isld* Bahamas 22.22N 75.48W
104 C8 Raccoon Cr *R* Ohio
107 F7 Raccoon Pt Louisiana 29.04N 90.58W
81 J7 Raccuia Sicily 38.07N 14.55E
65 N9 Rače Yugoslavia 46.26N 15.40E
11 F10 Race *canal* New Zealand
98 T7 Race,C Newfoundland 46.38N 53.10W
104 C8 Raceland Kentucky 38.32N 82.45W
107 F12 Raceland Louisiana 29.43N 90.38W
105 E6 Racepond Georgia 31.01N 82.09W
103 O2 Race Pt Massachusetts 42.04N 70.14W
110 B1 Race Rocks Lt.Ho Br Columbia 48.18N 123.33W
110 N3 Race Track Montana 46.17N 112.47W
18 B9 Rachado *C* Pen Malaysia 2.24N 101.51E
112 J9 Rachal Texas 26.54N 98.09W
25 E9 Racha Noi,Ko *isld* Thailand 7.32N 98.18E
34 C5 Rāchaya Lebanon 33.30N 35.50E
25 E9 Racha Yai, Ko *isld* Thailand 7.34N 98.23E
61 N8 Rachecourt Belgium 49.35N 5.44E
69 J6 Rachecourt-sur-Marne France 48.31N 5.06E
35 D7 Rachel's Tomb *anc site* Jordan 31.43N 35.12E
25 H8 Rach Gia Vietnam 9.55N 105.05E
89 D2 Rachid Mauritania 18.45N 11.35W
35 D1 Rachidiye Lebanon 33.14N 35.13E
Rachîdîyé Syria*see* Rashidīya
44 E5 Rachinskiy Khrebet *mts* Georgia U.S.S.R.
87 J4 Rachmat *isld* Ethiopia 13.41N 42.12E
62 M3 Raciąż Poland 52.46N 20.05E
62 L5 Racibórz Poland 50.05N 18.10E
104 D8 Racine Ohio 38.59N 81.54W
106 G7 Racine Wisconsin 42.42N 87.50W
98 D1 Racine-de-Bouleau,R Quebec
99 G4 Racine L Ontario 48.02N 83.20W
64 P3 Račio Czechoslovakia 50.21N 13.23E
56 D6 Rackenford Devon Eng 50.57N 3.38W
62 L8 Ráckeve Hungary 47.10N 18.58E
58 S12 Rackwick Orkney Scotland 58.52N 3.23W
63 Q10 Rackwitz E Germany 51.27N 12.22E
106 K3 Raco Michigan 46.23N 84.43W
64 O4 Racovský *mt* Czechoslovakia 49.38N 12.51E
Racza *mt see* Vel'ke Raca *mt*
33 F9 Rada' Yemen 14.30N 44.56E
75 E8 Rada de Haro Spain 39.34N 2.38W
81 A1 Rada della Reale *B* Sardinia
82 G7 Radan *mt* Yugoslavia 43.00N 21.29E
30 A2 Radaur Haryana India 30.02N 77.08E
82 K3 Rădăuţi Romania 47.49N 25.58E
64 P4 Radbuza *R* Czechoslovakia
45 M7 Radchenskoye U.S.S.R. 49.48N 40.31E
57 J5 Radcliffe Greater Manchester Eng 53.34N 2.20W
108 R7 Radcliffe Iowa 42.20N 93.25W
57 L7 Radcliffe on Trent Notts Eng 52.57N 1.03W
80 D2 Radda in Chianti Italy 43.29N 11.23E
40 E7 Radde U.S.S.R. 48.37N 130.37E
81 J9 Raddusa Sicily 37.28N 14.32E
34 J2 Radd,Wādī er *R* Syria
52 F7 Råde Norway 59.21N 10.53E
62 H4 Radeberg E Germany 51.08N 13.56E
64 Q1 Radebeul E Germany 51.06N 13.41E
64 Q1 Radeburg E Germany 51.13N 13.44E
64 Q4 Radeč *mt* Czechoslovakia 49.50N 13.40E
63 Q9 Radegast E Germany 51.41N 12.07E
46 E4 Radekhov Ukraine U.S.S.R. 50.18N 24.35E
66 F3 Radelfingen Switzerland 47.02N 7.17E
65 M8 Radel Pass Austria/Yugoslavia 46.38N 15.13E
45 D10 Radensk Ukraine U.S.S.R. 46.35N 32.57E
65 J8 Radenthein Austria 46.48N 13.43E
64 C1 Radevormwald W Germany 51.12N 7.22E
104 E9 Radford Virginia 37.07N 80.34W
13 B1 Radford Pt N Terr Australia 11.18S 130.55E
Radhamat al Hiri *see* Rudhumat al Hiri
29 B6 Radhanpur Gujarat India 23.52N 71.49E
28 C6 Radhapuram Tamil Nadu India 8.16N 77.43E
Radhwa,Jabal *see* Radwá, Jabal *mt*
79 H6 Radici,Foce di *pass* Italy 44.12N 10.29E
80 E3 Radicofani Italy 42.54N 11.46E
80 D2 Radicóndoli Italy 43.16N 11.03E
14 D4 Radi Hills W Australia 19.57S 121.05E
33 D6 Rādi'ī,Ar Saudi Arabia 21.06N 40.30E
45 S5 Radishchevo Saratov U.S.S.R. 51.55N 46.10E
45 T4 Radishchevo Ul'yanovsk U.S.S.R. 52.51N 47.52E
100 K6 Radisson Saskatchewan 52.27N 107.24W
106 C4 Radisson Wisconsin 45.47N 91.12W
109 D2 Radium Colorado 39.58N 106.33W
108 O1 Radium Minnesota 48.14N 96.38W
64 N3 Radiumbad-Brambach E Germany 50.13N 12.19E
12 F4 Radium Hill *pk* S Australia 32.30S 140.32E
101 P10 Radium Hot Springs Br Col 50.39N 116.09W
109 D9 Radium Springs New Mexico 32.31N 106.56W
18 B4 Radja, Udjung *C* Sumatra Indonesia 3.42N 96.30E
32 H2 Rādkān Iran 36.54N 59.00E
65 N8 Radkersburg Austria 46.42N 16.00E
Radldorf *see* Bergsdorf
55 D1 Radlett Herts England 51.41N 0.19W
65 M8 Radlje ob Dravi Yugoslavia 46.37N 15.13E
65 L6 Radmer an dem Hasel Austria 47.33N 14.43E
82 G4 Radna Romania 46.05N 21.41E
82 K8 Radnevo Bulgaria 42.17N 25.58E
64 Q4 Radnice Czechoslovakia 49.52N 13.36E
Radnor *co see* Powys *co*
56 E3 Radnor Forest Powys Wales
119 B7 Rado de Tumaco Colombia
82 F5 Radojevo Yugoslavia 45.42N 20.46E
64 F8 Radolfzell W Germany 47.44N 8.59E
62 N4 Radom Poland 51.26N 21.10E
90 M7 Radom Sudan 9.58N 24.53E
82 H8 Radomir Bulgaria 42.32N 22.56E
62 L4 Radomsko Poland 51.04N 19.25E
75 F5 Radona Spain 41.16N 2.26W
64 P3 Radonice Czechoslovakia 50.18N 13.17E
62 K7 Radošina Czechoslovakia 48.32N 18.00E
62 M4 Radoszyce Poland 51.03N 20.15E
65 K2 Radotín Czechoslovakia 49.59N 14.22E
82 H9 Radoviš Yugoslavia 41.38N 22.28E
45 L1 Radovitsy U.S.S.R. 55.10N 39.36E
82 B4 Radovljica Yugoslavia 46.20N 14.10E
53 R17 Radøy *isld* Norway 60.42N 4.58E
53 R17 Radøy Fjord *inlet* Norway 60.37N 5.00E
53 S17 Radøysund *sound* Norway 60.37N 5.10E
65 H7 Radstadt Austria 47.23N 13.28E
65 H7 Radstädter Tauern *mts* Austria
65 J7 Radstädter Tauern *mt* Austria 47.15N 13.34E
56 G5 Radstock Avon Eng 51.18N 2.28W
12 C5 Radstock,C S Australia 33.11S 134.21E
65 L9 Raduha Yugoslavia 46.23N 14.44E
45 B5 Radul' Ukraine U.S.S.R. 51.50N 30.44E
82 D7 Radusa *mt* Yugoslavia 43.52N 17.28E
46 E2 Radviliškis Lithuania U.S.S.R. 55.49N 23.30E
100 N9 Radville Saskatchewan 49.28N 104.19W
33 C4 Radwá,Jabal *mt* Saudi Arabia 24.36N 38.18E
100 E4 Radway Alberta 54.05N 112.55W
56 M3 Radwinter Essex Eng 52.01N 0.20E
62 O6 Radymno Poland 49.57N 22.50E
62 M3 Radzanów Poland 52.56N 20.04E
62 L3 Radziejów Poland 52.39N 18.31E
62 N3 Radzymin Poland 52.25N 21.10E
62 O4 Radzyń Podlaski Poland 51.49N 22.38E
101 Q4 Rae N W Terr 62.50N 116.00W
101 P1 Rae *R* N W Terr
30 E6 Rae Bareli Uttar Prad India 26.14N 81.14E
30 D6 Rae Bareli *dist* Uttar Prad India
122 D15 Raeffsky, Is Tuamotu Is Pacific Oc
105 H3 Raeford N Carolina 34.59N 79.15W
53 B2 Rær Denmark 57.06N 8.40E
97 L4 Rae Isthmus N W Terr
97 H5 Rae L N W Terr
100 C8 Rae,Mt Alberta 50.41N 114.50W
61 P4 Raeren Belgium 50.41N 6.07E
63 E9 Raesfeld W Germany 51.46N 6.50E
14 D8 Raeside, L W Australia
101 Z1 Rae Str N W Terr
11 H2 Raetea *mt* New Zealand 35.13S 173.26E
11 K6 Raetihi New Zealand 39.24S 175.16E
34 G9 Rāf *hill* Saudi Arabia 29.13N 39.53E
33 C2 Rāf *pk* Saudi Arabia 29.06N 39.50E
121 E3 Rafaela Argentina 31.16S 61.30W
86 M3 Rafah Gaza Strip Egypt 31.18N 34.15E
35 A8 Rafah Sta Egypt 31.16N 34.14E
90 L9 Rafai Cent Afr Rep 4.56N 23.55E
75 L6 Ráfales Spain 40.51N 0.01E
35 D6 Rafat Jordan 31.53N 35.12E
75 K8 Rafelbuñol Spain 39.36N 0.20W
81 G9 Raffadali Sicily 37.25N 13.32E
87 B7 Raffili Rapids Sudan 6.50N 28.00E
92 E10 Raffingora Zimbabwe 17.00S 30.36E
18 D10 Raffles Lt.Ho Pen Malaysia 1.10N 103.45E
33 E2 Rafḩā Saudi Arabia 29.35N 43.31E
35 G2 Rafid Syria 32.57N 35.54E
35 G3 Rafid,Er Jordan 32.42N 35.49E
35 D5 Rafidiya Jordan 32.13N 35.14E
30 H8 Rafiganj Bihar India 24.50N 84.38E
32 G5 Rafsanjān Iran 30.25N 56.00E
110 M7 Raft *R* Idaho
100 Q3 Rafter Manitoba 55.37N 101.07W
110 M8 Raft River Mts Utah
51 E3 Raftsund Norway 68.20N 15.05E
66 L1 Rafz Switzerland 47.37N 8.32E
Raga *see* Raka
90 M7 Raga Sudan 8.26N 25.46E
Raga *isld see* Pentecost I
90 M7 Raga *watercourse* Sudan
90 M6 Ragag Sudan 10.59N 24.40E
26 S8 Ragala Sri Lanka 7.01N 80.51E
90 B6 Ragam Nigeria 11.40N 5.40E
76 J7 Ragama Spain 41.00N 5.08W
26 Q8 Ragama Sri Lanka 7.02N 79.56E
19 M8 Ragang, Mt Mindanao Philippines 7.39N 124.30E
19 L5 Ragay G Luzon Philippines
29 K2 Ragda W Bengal India 23.15N 86.40E
53 J4 Rågeleje Denmark 56.06N 12.11E
63 R6 Rägelin E Germany 53.01N 12.39E
64 O1 Ragewitz E Germany 51.14N 12.52E
116 G3 Ragged I Bahamas 22.13N 75.44W
104 R3 Ragged I Maine 43.47N 68.53W
14 E10 Ragged,Mt W Australia 33.27S 123.27E
116 P6 Ragged Pt Barbados 13.10N 59.26W
53 X17 Raggsteinhytta Norway 60.40N 7.50E
33 F4 Raghbah, Ar Saudi Arabia 25.09N 45.47E
30 A8 Raghugarh Madhya Prad India 24.26N 77.12E
30 E8 Raghunathganj Madhya Prad India 24.41N 81.39E
30 L7 Raghunathpur Bihar India 25.40N 87.55E
34 M10 Raghwah Saudi Arabia 28.38N 44.11E
33 F9 Raghwān,Wādī *watercourse* Yemen
56 F4 Raglan Gwent Wales 51.47N 2.51W
11 J4 Raglan New Zealand 37.48S 174.54E
107 K8 Ragland Alabama 33.42N 86.10W
109 G7 Ragland New Mexico 34.49N 103.45W
11 J4 Raglan Harb *inlet* New Zealand
11 G8 Raglan Ra New Zealand
107 C11 Ragley Louisiana 30.30N 93.11W
61 H5 Ragnies Belgium 50.18N 4.17E
109 M4 Rago Kansas 37.28N 98.05W
79 N2 Ragogna Italy 46.11N 12.59E
77 L6 Rágol Spain 37.00N 2.40W
79 G5 Ragola,Monte Italy 44.35N 9.32E
63 R8 Ragösen E Germany 52.15N 12.35E
53 G7 Rågø Sund Denmark 54.58N 11.18E
41 B4 Ragozina,Mys *C* Belyy, Ostrov U.S.S.R. 73.25N 70.01E
41 D4 Ragozinka U.S.S.R. 72.52N 80.59E
85 E5 Raguba Libya 29.04N 19.08E
87 L5 Raguda Somalia 10.41N 46.29E
63 Q9 Raguhn E Germany 51.44N 12.18E
44 F2 Raguli R U.S.S.R.
18 F3 Ragunan Jakarta Indonesia 6.17S 106.50E
52 J3 Ragunda Sweden 63.06N 16.25E
81 J10 Ragusa Sicily 36.56N 14.44E
Ragusa Yugoslavia*see* Dubrovnik
81 J10 Ragusa *prov* Sicily
23 B1 Ra'gyagoinba Qinghai China 34.44N 100.35E
Rah *see* Chāh-e Rāh
28 J2 Raha Assam India 26.19N 92.30E
19 C6 Raha Indonesia 4.50S 122.43E
90 B5 Raha Nigeria 12.06N 4.04E
34 G8 Rahá, Ar *hill* Saudi Arabia 30.51N 39.14E
Rahāb,Ar *see* Rihāb, Ar
90 L6 Rahad el Berdi Sudan 11.16N 23.51E
87 C4 Rahad,Er Sudan 12.42N 30.33E
87 E4 Rahad,R Sudan
Rahaeng *see* Tak
35 E8 Rahaf *watercourse* Israel
86 J6 Râha,Gebel el *ra* Egypt
52 K6 Råhällan Sweden 60.50N 17.00E
35 C10 Rahama, Har *hills* Israel
86 G3 Rahâmna,El Egypt 31.19N 31.45E
87 J9 Rahanuin *tribe* Somalia
59 H4 Raharney W Meath Irish Rep 53.32N 7.06W
36 D5 Rahat Dağ *mt* Turkey 37.08N 29.50E
29 E6 Rahatgaon Madhya Prad India 22.10N 77.12E
29 F6 Rahatgarh Madhya Prad India 23.47N 78.28E
86 J6 Râha,Wâdi el *watercourse* Egypt
86 O8 Râha, Wādī er *watercourse* Saudi Arabia
Rahbur *see* Rābor
63 J8 Rahden W Germany 52.27N 8.37E
Rahgird *see* Rāhjerd
34 L6 Raḩḩālīyah Iraq 32.46N 43.24E
87 A2 Rahib Darfur Sudan 17.34N 27.05E
90 M4 Rahib Darfur Sudan 15.35N 24.39E
61 O5 Rahier Belgium 50.23N 5.47E
33 J3 Raḩīmah Saudi Arabia 26.44N 50.02E
28 B2 Rahimatpur Maharashtra India 17.37N 74.17E
37 J9 Rahim Khān Iran 36.47N 46.11E
31 F6 Rahimyar Khan Pakistan 28.22N 70.20E
31 F6 Rahimyar Khan *dist* Pakistan
66 C1 Rahin *R* France
35 D8 Rahiya Jordan 31.28N 35.04E
32 D3 Rāhjerd Iran 34.24N 50.24E
86 E3 Rahmânîya,El Egypt 31.06N 30.38E
87 D4 Rahmaniya,Er Sudan 13.17N 32.37E
11 H6 Rahotu New Zealand 39.20S 173.49E
121 B7 Rahue *pk* Arg/Chile 38.44S 71.06W
29 D8 Rahuri Maharashtra India 19.26N 74.42E
103 J8 Rahway New Jersey 40.37N 74.17W
31 A3 Rahzanak Afghanistan 34.26N 61.28E
76 C11 Raia *R* Portugal
80 J4 Raiano Italy 42.06N 13.49E
122 A15 Raiatea *isld* Society Is Pacific Oc 16.50S 151.30W
121 F3 Raices Argentina 31.55S 59.20W
30 E1 Raichung Naga Xizang Zizhiqu 31.18N 81.50E
28 C2 Raichur Karnataka India 16.15N 77.20E
28 C3 Raichur *dist* Karnataka India
Raidat al Abdul Wadud *see* Raydat al 'Abd al Wadūd
Raidat al Johiyin *see* Raydat al Jūhīyīn
29 L5 Raiganj W Bengal India 25.38N 88.11E
29 H7 Raigarh Madhya Prad India 21.53N 83.28E
29 H8 Raigarh Orissa India 19.51N 82.06E
29 H6 Raigarh *dist* Madhya Prad India
9 R13 Raihifahifa *islet* Tonga, Pacific Oc 18.48S 174.00W
25 H8 Rai,Hon *isld* Vietnam 9.50N 104.38E
19 B9 Raijua *isld* Indonesia 10.38S 121.35E
29 D2 Raikot Punjab India 30.41N 75.42E
113 H5 Railroad City Alaska 62.12N 164.40W
111 G2 Railroad Pass Nevada 39.22N 117.24W
111 J4 Railroad Val Nevada
12 H8 Railton Tasmania 41.20S 146.24E
31 H10 Raimangal R Bangladesh/India
88 E10 Raimas, Pta de las Mauritania 23.03N 16.13W
66 F2 Raimeux,les *mts* Switzerland
64 N6 Rain Nieder-Bayern W Germany 48.55N 12.30E
64 K6 Rain Schwaben, Bayern W Germany 48.40N 10.56E
30 G5 Rainabas Nepal 27.42N 83.50E
29 L2 Rainaga W Bengal India 23.04N 87.54E
64 J6 Rainau W Germany 48.55N 10.10E
12 F6 Rainbow Victoria 35.56S 142.01E
111 O4 Rainbow Bridge Nat.Mon Utah 37.02N 110.56W
115 E9 Rainbow City Panama Canal Zone 9.20N 79.53W
101 O6 Rainbow Lake Alberta 58.30N 119.24W
69 D6 Raincy,le France 48.54N 2.32E
13 G1 Raine Ent Gt Barrier Reef Australia
13 G1 Raine I Gt Barrier Reef Australia
Rainer I *see* Raynera,O
57 H5 Rainford Merseyside Eng 53.30N 2.48W
56 N5 Rainham Kent Eng 51.23N 0.36E
55 K3 Rainham London England 51.31N 0.13E
110 C3 Rainier Oregon 46.05N 122.57W
110 C3 Rainier Washington 46.54N 122.41W
110 D3 Rainier,Mt Washington 46.52N 121.45W
31 E7 Raini N *R* Pakistan
110 B5 Rainrock Oregon 44.07N 123.52W
104 G7 Rainsburg Pennsylvania 39.54N 78.31W
108 Q1 Rainy *R* Minnesota/Ontario
108 S1 Rainy L Minnesota/Ontario
113 L5 Rainy Pass Alaska 62.13N 153.07W
110 E1 Rainy Pass Washington 48.36N 120.46W
113 L5 Rainy Pass Lodge Alaska 62.05N 152.40W
106 K4 Rainy,R Michigan
100 H2 Rainy River Ontario 48.44N 94.33W
51 H8 Raippaluoto *isld* Finland
31 H9 Raipur Bangladesh 23.03N 90.46E
29 G7 Raipur Raipur, Madhya Prad India 21.16N 81.42E
30 E8 Raipur Rewa, Madhya Prad India 24.34N 81.27E
29 K2 Raipur W Bengal India 22.47N 86.58E
29 G7 Raipur *dist* Madhya Prad India
30 E7 Raipura Uttar Prad India 25.14N 81.07E
Rairakhol *see* Rampur
86 E10 Rairamûn,El Egypt 27.45N 30.51E
76 D4 Rairiz de Veiga Spain 42.05N 7.50W
53 E8 Raisdorf W Germany 54.17N 10.15E
29 E6 Raisen Madhya Prad India 23.21N 77.49E
29 E6 Raisen *dist* Madhya Prad India
29 C3 Raisinghnagar Rajasthan India 29.32N 73.33E
51 J11 Raisio Finland 60.30N 22.10E
81 F7 Raisi,Pta Sicily 38.12N 13.04E
69 E3 Raismes France 50.23N 3.29E
51 N5 Raistakka Finland 66.03N 28.05E
31 G9 Raita Bangladesh 24.06N 88.54E
114 C1 Raita Bank Hawaiian Is
66 H1 Raitbach W Germany 47.41N 7.51E
100 N2 Raith Ontario 48.51N 89.56W
11 H8 Rai Valley New Zealand 41.13S 173.34E
122 M11 Raivavaé Tubuai Is Pacific Oc 23.52S 147.40W
31 H5 Raiwind Pakistan 31.14N 74.10E
93 L6 Raiya Kenya 0.41S 39.37E
86 E5 Raiyâh el Beḩeira *canal* Egypt
86 F5 Raiyâh el Taufîqi,El *canal* Egypt
Raiyan *see* Rayyān, Ar
18 K9 Raja *isld* Indonesia 7.14S 113.45E
18 F8 Rajabasa Sumatra Indon 5.28S 104.12E
18 F8 Rajabasa, Gunung *mt* Sumatra Indonesia 5.47S 105.38E
30 L8 Rajabhita Bihar India 24.57N 87.22E
117 G9 Rajada Brazil 8.49S 40.41W
75 O4 Rajadell Spain 41.44N 1.43E
29 G6 Rajadhar Madhya Prad India 22.12N 81.04E
28 E2 Rajahmundry Andhra Prad India 17.01N 81.52E
30 B6 Rajakhera Rajasthan India 26.54N 78.10E
26 P1 Rajamatam Tamil Nadu India 10.18N 79.21E
28 D3 Rajampet Andhra Prad India 14.11N 79.09E
18 B7 Raja Muda,Bukit *hill* Pen Malaysia 4.39N 101.56E
18 J4 Rajang Sarawak Malaysia 2.10N 111.16E
18 K4 Rajang Sarawak Malaysia 2.01N 112.50E
18 K4 Rajang R Sarawak Malaysia
31 F6 Rajanpur Bahawalpur Pakistan 28.30N 70.10E
31 F6 Rajanpur Bahawalpur Pakistan 29.05N 70.25E
30 J8 Rajanr Bihar India 24.45N 85.26E
28 C6 Rajapalaiyam Tamil Nadu India 9.26N 77.36E
30 E7 Rajapur Allahabad, Uttar Prad India 25.23N 81.09E
30 H6 Rajapur Bihar India 26.22N 84.53E
30 G7 Rajapur Ghazipur, Uttar Prad India 25.42N 83.51E
28 A2 Rajapur Maharashtra India 16.38N 73.32E
30 E4 Rajapur Nepal 28.25N 81.05E
29 B4 Rajasthan *state* India
29 C3 Rajasthan Can Rajasthan India
30 J8 Rajauli Bihar India 24.39N 85.30E
31 H9 Rajbari Bangladesh 23.47N 89.39E
83 D2 Rajë Albania 42.16N 20.01E
65 P3 Rájec Jestřebí Czechoslovakia 49.25N 16.39E
28 B1 Rajewadi Maharashtra India 18.22N 74.15E
30 L8 Rajgan W Bengal India 24.34N 87.51E
29 E4 Rajgarh Alwar, Rajasthan India 27.11N 76.37E
30 C8 Rajgarh Chhatarpur, Madhya Prad India 24.44N 79.58E
29 D3 Rajgarh Churu, Rajasthan India 28.38N 75.21E
28 A1 Rajgarh Maharashtra India 18.16N 73.46E
29 E5 Rajgarh Rajgarh, Madhya Prad India 24.01N 76.42E
30 A7 Rajgarh Shivpuri, Madhya Prad India 25.20N 77.30E
30 F8 Rajgarh Uttar Prad India 24.52N 82.53E
29 E6 Rajgarh *dist* Madhya Prad India
31 F5 Rajghat Pakistan 30.13N 71.28E
30 J7 Rajgir Bihar India 25.01N 85.26E
62 O2 Rajgród Poland 53.46N 22.41E
29 J5 Rajhara Bihar India 24.10N 84.00E
35 F5 Rajib Jordan 32.14N 35.42E
35 F5 Rajib *R* Jordan
35 G6 Rajib,Er Jordan 31.54N 35.59E
18 F7 Rajik Indonesia 2.32S 105.58E
29 G7 Rajim Madhya Prad India 20.57N 81.58E
82 B6 Rajinac *mt* Yugoslavia 44.49N 14.59E
96 O15 Rajita,La Gomera Canary Is 28.04N 17.18W
29 B6 Rajkot Gujarat India 22.18N 70.53E
29 B7 Rajkot *dist* Gujarat India
30 L7 Rajmahal Bihar India 25.03N 87.49E
29 D5 Raj Mahal Rajasthan India 25.56N 75.35E
30 K8 Rajmahal Hills Bihar India
30 K6 Rajnagar Bihar India 26.23N 86.10E
30 C8 Rajnagar Madhya Prad India 24.53N 79.54E
29 K6 Rajnagar W Bengal India 23.56N 87.25E
29 G7 Raj Nandgaon Madhya Prad Ind 21.06N 81.08E
29 K17 Rajnilgiri Orissa India 21.29N 86.49E
29 A2 Rajouri Garden *dist* Delhi India
29 C7 Rajpipla Gujarat India 21.49N 73.36E
29 D6 Rajpur Jhabua, Madhya Prad India 22.18N 74.22E
30 C6 Rajpur Uttar Prad India 26.18N 79.42E
29 M3 Rajpur W Bengal India 22.27N 88.26E
29 D7 Rajpur W Nimay, Madhya Prad India 21.58N 75.09E
29 E2 Rajpura Punjab India 30.29N 76.40E
31 G9 Rajshahi Bangladesh 24.24N 88.40E
31 G9 Rajshahi *dist* Bangladesh
29 B7 Rajula Gujarat India 21.01N 71.34E
29 F7 Rajur Maharashtra India 20.04N 79.00E
Rajura *see* Ahmadpur Maharashtra India
29 F8 Rajura Chanda, Maharashtra India 19.48N 79.25E
30 K8 Rajwara Bihar India 24.44N 86.44E
24 E11 Raka Xizang Zizhiqu China 29.26N 85.51E
122 L9 Rakahanga *atoll* Cook Is Pacific Oc 10.03S 161.06W
93 C6 Rakai Uganda 0.42S 31.25E
11 G10 Rakaia New Zealand 43.46S 172.02E
11 G10 Rakaia R New Zealand
33 J3 Rakan,Ra's *C* Qatar, The Gulf 26.13N 51.15E
24 A7 Rakaposhi *mt* Kashmir 36.06N 74.31E
Rakas Tal *L see* Lan'ga Co *L*
18 F9 Rakata *isld* Indonesia 6.11S 105.26E
11 M5 Rakauroa New Zealand 38.24S 177.32E
86 O9 Rāka,Wādī er *watercourse* Saudi Arabia
24 E11 Raka Zangbo *R* Xizang Zizhiqu China
33 D6 Rakbah,Sahl *plain* Saudi Arabia
108 R6 Rake Iowa 43.29N 93.55W
11 B13 Rakeahua *mt* Stewart I New Zealand 46.58S 167.54E
29 C5 Rakhab Dev Rajasthan India 24.05N 73.50E
30 L5 Rakha La *pass* Xizang Zizhiqu/Nepal 27.54N 87.35E
35 J3 Rakham Syria 32.43N 36.21E
33 M9 Rakhām,Ar *mt* Kuwait 29.41N 47.55E
33 J8 Rakhawt,Wādī *watercourse* S Yemen
84 E4 Rákhes Greece 38.53N 22.47E
42 D7 Rakhmanoviskoye Kazakhstan U.S.S.R. 49.34N 86.30E
31 B3 Rakhnat Afghanistan 34.20N 62.20E
31 E5 Rakhni Pakistan 30.03N 69.55E
84 C3 Rakhoúla Greece 39.14N 21.52E
46 E5 Rakhov Ukraine U.S.S.R. 48.02N 24.10E
33 K4 Rakhsh *oil field* The Gulf 25.57N 52.54E
31 C7 Rakhshan R Pakistan
Rakhya, Wādī *see* Rakya Wādī
33 G9 Rakhya,Wādī *watercourse* S Yemen
33 K8 Rakhyūt Oman 16.45N 53.30E
34 P8 Rākī Iraq 30.12N 47.00E
35 F9 Rakin Jordan 31.13N 35.42E
11 J3 Rakino I New Zealand 36.43S 174.58E
51 H3 Rakisvare *mt* Sweden 68.16N 20.20E
18 H8 Rakit *isld* Indonesia 5.56S 108.24E
18 M10 Rakit *isld* Indonesia 8.38S 117.58E
45 G6 Rakitnoye Belgorod U.S.S.R. 50.52N 35.51E
40 F9 Rakitnoye Primor'ye U.S.S.R. 45.35N 134.15E
46 F4 Rakitnoye Ukraine U.S.S.R. 51.18N 27.10E
11 K3 Rakitu I New Zealand 36.08S 175.31E
43 E2 Rakityanka U.S.S.R. 51.30N 57.39E
Raki-Ura *see* Stewart I New Zealand
86 O5 Rakīya, Wādī *watercourse* Jordan
50 B3 Raknadalar Iceland 65.34N 23.51W
31 E6 Rakni R Pakistan
94 G2 Rakoko Botswana 19.32S 23.51E
62 J3 Rakoniewice Poland 52.09N 16.12E
94 H3 Rakops Botswana 21.00S 24.32E
46 F3 Rakov Belorussiya U.S.S.R. 53.58N 26.59E
64 Q3 Rakovník Czechoslovakia 50.07N 13.44E
82 H8 Rakovo Bulgaria 42.04N 22.42E
63 S4 Rakow E Germany 54.02N 13.04E
45 N3 Raksha U.S.S.R. 53.34N 41.39E
37 E5 Raksik Turkey 40.19N 40.09E
47 E4 Rakula U.S.S.R. 63.48N 41.29E
47 F5 Rakulka U.S.S.R. 61.55N 46.28E
46 R6 Rakusha Kazakhstan U.S.S.R. 47.05N 52.45E
44 L5 Rakushechnyy,Mys *C* Kazakhstan U.S.S.R. 42.50N 51.56E
51 M12 Rakvere Estonia U.S.S.R. 59.21N 26.20E
26 S9 Rakwana Sri Lanka 6.30N 80.35E
30 H3 Rala Nepal 27.52N 86.49E
33 H6 Ralā,Ar *des area* Saudi Arabia
107 G9 Raleigh Mississippi 32.02N 89.31W
105 J2 Raleigh N Carolina 35.42N 78.40W
108 J3 Raleigh N Dakota 46.22N 101.19W
98 R2 Raleigh Newfoundland 51.35N 55.42W
105 L3 Raleigh B N Carolina
100 D9 Raley Alberta 49.20N 113.10W
9 A1 Ralik Chain *atolls* Marshall Is Pacific Oc
88 O11 Rali Salem Algeria 21.03N 1.09E
88 H9 Rall Amane *reg* Mauritania
88 H11 Rallaouïa Mauritania 21.32N 10.38W
89 D1 Rallaouia Mauritania 21.35N 12.35W
26 P16 Rallier du Baty, Presqu'ile *pen* Kerguelen Ind Oc
112 F2 Ralls Texas 33.41N 101.23W
106 G3 Ralph Michigan 46.06N 87.47W
108 G4 Ralph S Dakota 45.47N 103.03W
108 O8 Ralston Nebraska 41.11N 96.02W
109 O5 Ralston Oklahoma 36.30N 96.46W
104 J5 Ralston Pennsylvania 41.31N 76.56W
110 G3 Ralston Washington 46.59N 118.21W
110 R5 Ralston Wyoming 44.43N 108.53W
28 H1 Ralung Xizang Zizhiqu 28.50N 90.00E
86 O6 Ram Jordan 29.34N 35.24E
101 M5 Ram *R* N W Terr
87 H4 Rama Ethiopia 12.27N 40.03E
35 E2 Rāma Israel 32.56N 35.22E
35 D4 Rāma Jordan 32.22N 35.11E
93 M5 Rama Kenya 0.31N 40.03E
115 M3 Rama Nicaragua 12.09N 84.15W
100 P7 Rama Saskatchewan 51.45N 102.58W
76 J8 Ramacastañas Spain 40.11N 5.02W
81 J9 Ramacca Sicily 37.24N 14.42E
81 F7 Rama,C.di Sicily 38.08N 13.03E
28 F2 Ramachandrapuram Andhra Prad India 16.54N 82.03E
34 L5 Ramādī,Ar Iraq 33.27N 43.19E
34 L5 Ramadi Barrage Iraq 33.28N 43.20E
120 D9 Ramaditas Chile 21.01S 69.29W
29 J8 Ramagiri-Udayagiri Orissa India 19.10N 84.11E
109 F2 Ramah Colorado 39.07N 104.10W
109 B6 Ramah New Mexico 35.08N 108.30W
29 A3 Ramakrishnapuram Delhi India 28.33N 77.11E
75 D1 Ramales de la Victoria Spain 43.15N 3.28W
76 A10 Ramalhal Portugal 39.09N 9.14W
118 G3 Ramalho,Serra do *mts* Brazil
35 D6 Ramallah Jordan 31.55N 35.12E
28 D3 Ramallakota Andhra Prad India 15.37N 78.02E
121 E4 Ramallo Argentina 33.30S 60.01W
76 B4 Ramallosa Spain 42.07N 8.48W
37 F8 Raman Turkey 37.46N 41.10E
28 C4 Ramanagaram Karnataka India 12.45N 77.16E
28 D6 Ramanathapuram Tamil Nadu India 9.23N 78.53E
28 D6 Ramanathapuram *dist* Tamil Nadu India
37 F8 Raman Dağ *mt* Turkey
28 C3 Ramandrug Karnataka India 15.07N 76.25E
29 H6 Ramanuj Ganj Madhya Prad India 23.46N 82.44E
103 F4 Ramapo New York 41.08N 74.11W
103 F4 Ramapo *R* New York/New Jersey
17 O5 Ramapo Deep Pacific Oc 30.20N 142.21E
103 F4 Ramapo Mts New York/New Jersey
92 C12 Ramaquabane, R Zimbabwe
28 A3 Ramas,C Goa India 15.06N 73.56E
94 J4 Ramaselwana *mt* Botswana 23.41S 26.08E
45 E4 Ramasukha U.S.S.R. 52.45N 33.32E
35 F2 Ramat Syria 32.51N 35.39E
35 D3 Ramat Dawid Israel 32.40N 35.12E
35 B1 Ramat Eshkol *dist* Jerusalem
35 C5 Ramat HaKovesh Israel 32.13N 34.56E
35 C5 Ramat HaSharon Israel 32.08N 34.51E
35 D3 Ramat HasHofet Israel 32.36N 35.06E
95 J1 Ramatlabama S Africa 25.40S 25.35E
35 G2 Ramat Magshimim Syria 32.51N 35.49E
35 B2 Ramat Rahel Israel 31.44N 35.13E
35 D6 Ramat Razi'el Israel 31.46N 35.04E
Ramat Tsevi *see* Ramat Zevi
71 K10 Ramatuelle France 43.13N 6.37E
35 D3 Ramat Yishay Israel 32.42N 35.10E
35 D2 Ramat Yohanan Israel 32.47N 35.08E
35 E3 Ramat Zevi Israel 32.35N 35.25E
28 D1 Ramayampet Andhra Prad India 18.05N 78.25E
31 H4 Ramban Kashmir 33.15N 75.18E
26 R6 Rambe Sri Lanka 7.43N 80.26E
53 V16 Rambera *mt* Norway 61.03N 6.42E
64 E5 Ramberg W Germany 49.15N 8.01E
69 M7 Rambervillers France 48.21N 6.38E
26 R5 Rambewa Sri Lanka 8.25N 80.30E
29 D6 Rambhapur Madhya Prad India 22.56N 74.30E
9 T5 Rambi *isld* Fiji
63 S4 Rambin E Germany 54.22N 13.12E
77 M6 Rambla de Albox *R* Spain
77 M5 Rambla de Chirivel *R* Spain
77 G5 Rambla,La Spain 37.37N 4.45W
23 B8 Rambler Chan Hong Kong
121 D2 Ramblones Argentina 29.10S 65.26W
69 B6 Rambouillet France 48.39N 1.50E
63 P6 Rambow E Germany 53.09N 11.35E
93 A7 Rambura Rwanda 1.41S 29.32E
15 J5 Rambutyo I Admiralty Is 2.15S 147.50E
30 J4 Ramche Nepal 28.01N 85.12E
28 B3 Ramdurg Karnataka India 15.57N 75.24E
98 P6 Ramea Newfoundland 47.32N 57.24W
98 P6 Ramea Is Newfoundland 47.32N 57.22W
30 K5 Ramechhap Nepal 27.19N 86.05E
61 D4 Ramegnies-Chin Belgium 50.39N 3.20E
56 C7 Rame Hd Cornwall Eng 50.19N 4.13W
95 N7 Rame Hd S Africa 31.47S 29.22E
61 M5 Ramelot Belgium 50.28N 5.20E
45 C10 Ramenka Ukraine U.S.S.R. 46.48N 31.40E
45 K1 Ramenskoye U.S.S.R. 55.35N 38.15E
107 K9 Ramer Alabama 32.03N 86.12W
46 K2 Rameshki U.S.S.R. 57.22N 36.00E
28 D6 Rameswaram Tamil Nadu India 9.18N 79.19E
30 D3 Ramganga *R* Almora, Uttar Prad India
30 C4 Ramganga *R* Bareilly, Uttar Prad India
29 E4 Ramgarh Alwar, Rajasthan India 27.35N 76.48E
31 J9 Ramgarh Bangladesh 22.59N 91.43E
29 J1 Ramgarh Bihar India 23.37N 85.32E
29 D3 Ramgarh Churu, Rajasthan India 28.09N 75.00E
29 B4 Ramgarh Jaisalmer, Rajasthan Ind 27.29N 70.38E
29 G6 Ramgarh Madhya Prad India 22.49N 81.00E
30 D5 Ramgarh Uttar Prad India 27.14N 80.31E
29 K2 Ramgarh W Bengal India 22.42N 87.04E
30 H6 Ramgarhwa Bihar India 26.53N 84.48E
31 F3 Ramgul *reg* Afghanistan
31 F3 Ramgul Pass Afghanistan 35.43N 70.35E
12 J7 Ram Hd Victoria 37.49S 149.29E
32 C5 Rāmhormoz Iran 31.15N 49.38E
37 H2 Rami İstanbul Turkey 41.03N 28.49E
32 F2 Ramian Iran 37.01N 55.19E
79 A5 Ramière,Punta *mt* Italy/France 44.52N 6.56E
61 K4 Ramillies-Offus Belgium 50.38N 4.55E
Ramim *see* Manara
65 J7 Ramingstein Austria 47.04N 13.50E
96 T3 Raminho Azores 38.48N 27.21W
61 M4 Ramioulle Belgium 50.35N 5.26E
112 K10 Ramirez Mexico 25.57N 97.46W
112 J8 Ramirez Texas 27.22N 98.25W
121 H8 Ramírez,I Chile 51.45S 75.10W
112 J9 Ramirito Texas 26.49N 98.36W
120 D6 Ramis *R* Peru
79 H6 Ramiseto Italy 44.24N 10.16E
Ramishk *see* Remeshk
87 H6 Ramis,R Ethiopia
43 J7 Ramit Tadzhikistan U.S.S.R. 38.45N 69.16E
35 E1 Râmîyé Lebanon 33.07N 35.18E
86 O6 Ram, Jabal *mt* Jordan 29.35N 35.23E
29 K6 Ramjibanpur W Bengal India 22.49N 87.40E
29 H6 Ramkola Madhya Prad India 23.40N 83.00E
30 D5 Ramkot Uttar Prad India 27.31N 80.35E
52 H9 Ramkvilla Sweden 57.13N 14.55E
35 C6 Ramla Israel 31.56N 34.52E
85 C5 Ramlah al Kabīrah, ar *sand reg* Libya
34 C9 Ramlah, Ar Jordan 29.28N 35.58E
84 X19 Ramla l'Kbira *B* Gozo Medit Sea 36.04N 14.17E
33 L6 Ramlat al Ghāfah *sandy des* Saudi Arabia
85 D7 Ramlat al Wigh *sand reg* Libya
33 K7 Ramlat Amilḩayt *sandy des* Oman
33 L6 Ramlat as Saḩmah *sandy des* Oman
33 F8 Ramlat Dahm *sand dunes* Saudi Arabia/Yemen
33 K7 Ramlat Fasad *sandy des* Oman
33 L6 Ramlat Ibn Su'aydan *sandy des* Saudi Arabia
33 K7 Ramlat Mītan *sandy des* Oman
33 F9 Ramlat Sab'atayn *sand des* S Yemen/Yemen
Ramlat Sh'ait *see* Ramlat Shu'ayt *sandy des*
33 K7 Ramlat Shu'ayt *sandy des* S Yemen
33 F8 Ramlat Yām *sand dunes* Saudi Arabia
Ramle *see* Ramla
85 K4 Ramleh Egypt 31.15N 29.59E
53 J4 Ramløse Denmark 56.01N 12.08E
53 A4 Ramme Denmark 56.30N 8.13E
52 H6 Rämmen Sweden 60.02N 14.11E
35 E6 Rammun Jordan 31.55N 35.18E
Ramnad *see* Ramanathapuram
30 G7 Ramnagar Banaras, Uttar Prad India 25.18N 83.02E
30 E5 Ramnagar Bara Banki, Uttar Prad India 27.05N 81.24E
30 C4 Ramnagar Bareilly, Uttar Prad India 28.23N 79.06E
30 H5 Ramnagar Bihar India 27.10N 84.20E
30 F6 Ramnagar Faizabad, Uttar Prad India 26.27N 82.54E
31 H4 Ramnagar Kashmir 32.48N 75.21E
29 G6 Ramnagar Mandla, Madhya Prad India 22.36N 80.34E
30 C3 Ramnagar Naini Tal, Uttar Prad India 29.23N 79.07E
Ramnagar Pakistan*see* Rasulnagar
29 G5 Ramnagar Rewa, Madhya Prad India 24.12N 81.10E
52 J7 Ramnäs Sweden 59.16N 16.12E
53 V15 Ramnefjord *mt* Norway 61.47N 6.55E
82 J5 Râmnicu Vâlcea Romania 45.06N 24.21E
30 K8 Ramnitanr Bihar India 24.37N 86.13E
87 H7 Ramo Ethiopia 6.48N 41.20E
94 J3 Ramokgwebana Botswana 20.38S 27.40E
65 C8 Ramolkogl *mt* Austria 46.51N 10.58E
35 E3 Ram On Israel 32.32N 35.15E
45 L5 Ramon' U.S.S.R. 51.54N 39.19E
34 B8 Ramon *watercourse* Israel
111 H8 Ramona California 33.02N 116.52W
106 J6 Ramona Michigan 43.36N 85.49W
109 P5 Ramona Oklahoma 36.33N 95.56W
108 N5 Ramona S Dakota 44.08N 97.12W
115 P8 Ramonal Mexico 18.25N 88.30W
119 E10 Ramon Castilla Peru 4.14S 69.58W
121 L6 Ramón Lista Argentina 47.21S 66.50W
99 K4 Ramore Ontario 48.27N 80.20W
59 H4 Ramor,L Cavan Irish Rep 53.49N 7.05W
120 F10 Ramos Argentina 22.40S 64.07W
115 G5 Ramos Mexico 25.30N 105.08W
117 C5 Ramos Pará Brazil 1.20S 53.08W
118 J9 Ramos Rio de Janeiro Brazil 22.52S 43.16W
19 H7 Ramos *isld* Philippines 8.08N 117.03E
115 J5 Ramos Arizpe Mexico 25.35N 100.59W
15 L3 Ramos I Solomon Is 8.15S 160.10E
35 F1 Ramot Naftali Israel 33.06N 35.33E
94 G2 Ramotsaudi Botswana 19.49S 22.20E
94 H5 Ramotswa Botswana 24.56S 25.50E
113 M4 Rampart Alaska 65.29N 150.18W
101 C2 Rampart House Yukon Terr 67.25N 140.59W
101 H2 Ramparts *R* N W Terr
66 N8 Ramponio Italy 45.59N 9.04E
57 G4 Rampside Cumbria Eng 54.05N 3.10W
30 L6 Rampur Bihar India 26.04N 87.29E
29 A1 Rampūr Delhi India 28.40N 77.09E
30 G6 Rampur Deoria, Uttar Prad Ind 26.35N 83.49E

29 C6 Rampur Gujarat India 23.11N 73.56E
30 A8 Rampur Guna, Madhya Prad Ind 24.45N 77.09E
30 A8 Rampur Guna, Madhya Prad Ind 24.18N 77.27E
30 A1 Rampur Himachal Prad India 31.26N 77.37E
30 F7 Rampur Jaunpur, Uttar Prad Ind 25.29N 82.34E
30 A6 Rampur Morena, Madhya Prad Ind 26.09N 77.28E
29 J7 Rampur Orissa India 21.03N 84.23E
29 J7 Rampur Orissa India 21.48N 84.00E
30 C4 Rampur Rampur, Uttar Prad India 28.48N 79.03E
30 E8 Rampur Rewa, Madhya Prad Ind 24.21N 81.26E
30 A3 Rampur Saharanpur, Uttar Prad Ind 29.48N 77.27E
30 E8 Rampur Satna, Madhya Prad Ind 24.31N 81.02E
30 C4 Rampur *dist* Uttar Prad India
30 C6 Rampura Jalaum, Uttar Prad Ind 26.21N 79.10E
29 D5 Rampura Madhya Prad India 24.30N 75.32E
30 C4 Rampura Rampur, Uttar Prad India 28.57N 79.23E
Rampur Boalia *see* Rajshahi
29 K5 Rampur Hat W Bengal India 24.11N 87.51E
29 G1 Ramrajatala W Bengal India 22.35N 88.18E
25 B3 Ramree Burma 19.05N 93.54E
25 B3 Ramree I Burma
32 J5 Ramrod *ruins* Iran 30.17N 61.12E
33 M4 Rams U.A.E. 25.53N 56.02E
30 A6 Ram Sagar *L* Rajasthan India 26.36N 77.35E
30 E6 Ramsanehighat Uttar Prad India 26.48N 81.32E
32 D2 Rāmsar Iran 36.54N 50.41E
64 O8 Ramsau W Germany 47.36N 12.54E
99 H5 Ramsay Ontario 47.26N 82.19W
99 H5 Ramsay L Ontario
14 F4 Ramsay Ra W Australia
64 E1 Ramsbeck W Germany 51.23N 8.24E
52 J7 Ramsberg Sweden 59.46N 15.20E
57 J5 Ramsbottom Greater Manchester Eng 53.40N 2.19W
94 F3 Ramsden Botswana 21.45S 21.18E
61 H2 Ramsdonk Belgium 51.01N 4.20E
63 E9 Ramsdorf W Germany 51.53N 6.55E
61 K2 Ramsel Belgium 51.02N 4.50E
63 F7 Ramsel W Germany 52.31N 7.24E
52 J3 Ramsele Sweden 63.32N 16.30E
52 M2 Ramsele Sweden 64.03N 19.30E
66 M1 Ramsen Switzerland 47.43N 8.49E
105 H2 Ramseur N Carolina 35.46N 79.40W
56 L3 Ramsey Cambs Eng 52.27N 0.07W
107 G2 Ramsey Illinois 39.08N 89.06W
57 E4 Ramsey Isle of Man U.K. 54.19N 4.23W
103 F4 Ramsey New Jersey 41.03N 74.08W
57 E4 Ramsey B Isle of Man U.K.
56 A4 Ramsey I Dyfed Wales 51.53N 5.20W
56 O5 Ramsgate Kent Eng 51.20N 1.25E
95 O6 Ramsgate S Africa 30.55S 30.20E
12 L8 Ramsgate *dist* Sydney, N S W
57 K4 Ramsgill N Yorks Eng 54.08N 1.49W
Ramshai *see* Ramshai Hat
29 L4 Ramshai Hat W Bengal India 26.42N 88.56E
52 J6 Rämshyttan Sweden 60.17N 15.15E
28 K1 Ramsing Assam India 28.40N 94.58E
53 B3 Ramsing Denmark 56.37N 8.52E
52 J4 Ramsjö Sweden 62.10N 15.40E
61 B2 Ramskapelle Belgium 51.07N 2.46E
58 R8 Rams Ness *prom* Shetland Scotland 60.34N 0.52W
53 V14 Ramstad Norway 62.25N 6.50E
69 O5 Ramstein-Miesenbach W Germany 49.27N 7.33E
29 F7 Ramtek Maharashtra India 21.28N 79.28E
53 F4 Ramten Denmark 56.27N 10.38E
35 G3 Ramtha Jordan 32.34N 36.00E
31 J10 Ramu Bangladesh 21.26N 92.04E
93 N2 Ramu Kenya 3.54N 41.12E
18 N10 Ramu *mt* Indonesia 8.28S 118.13E
15 H6 Ramu *R* Papua New Guinea
116 L3 Ramville, I Martinique W I 14.41N 60.53W
46 E2 Ramygala Lithuania U.S.S.R. 55.30N 24.19E
45 O4 Ramza U.S.S.R. 52.30N 42.39E
45 Q3 Ramzay U.S.S.R. 53.19N 44.44E
51 C5 Rana *inlet* Norway 66.11N 13.10E
51 D5 Rana *R* Norway
51 D5 Rana *reg* Norway
119 F6 Rana,Cerro *mt* Colombia 3.37N 68.04W
76 F2 Rañadoiro,Sierra de *mts* Spain
52 G1 Ranafjord *inlet* Norway
29 M2 Ranaghat W Bengal India 23.10N 88.36E
Ranak *see* Hanak
65 D7 Ranalt Austria 47.02N 11.14E
29 D5 Rana Pratap Sagar *dam* Rajasthan India 24.58N 75.38E
52 L7 Rånäs Sweden 59.47N 18.17E
29 B5 Rānāsar Rajasthan India 25.49N 70.42E
52 F6 Rånåsfoss Norway 60.00N 11.20E
18 M3 Ranau Sabah Malaysia 5.56N 116.43E
18 E8 Ranau,Danu *L* Sumatra Indon
57 L6 Ranby Notts Eng 53.19N 1.00W
121 B5 Rancagua Chile 34.10S 70.45W
61 H6 Rance Belgium 50.08N 4.16E
72 K8 Rancé *R* Aveyron France
70 G4 Rance *R* Côtes-du-Nord France
66 C4 Rances Switzerland 46.46N 6.32E
118 E8 Rancharia Brazil 22.13S 50.55W
101 H5 Rancheria Yukon Terr 60.06N 130.40W
101 H5 Rancheria *R* Yukon Terr
119 D2 Rancheria,R Colombia
108 C5 Ranchester Wyoming 44.55N 107.10W
29 J6 Ranchi Bihar India 23.22N 85.20E
29 J6 Ranchi *dist* Bihar India
80 F2 Ranchi d.Nestore Italy 43.21N 12.13E
118 C2 Rancho de Caça dos Tapiúnas Brazil 10.43S 56.05W
115 H6 Rancho Grande Mexico 23.30N 102.56W
109 E5 Ranchos de Taos New Mexico 36.21N 105.37W
116 D3 Rancho Veloz Cuba 22.53N 80.23W
103 E6 Rancocas Cr New Jersey
121 A8 Ranco,L.de Chile
72 G3 Rancon France 46.07N 1.12E
109 D1 Rand Colorado 40.27N 106.11W
12 H6 Rand New S Wales 35.34S 146.35E
77 V14 Randa Balearic Is 39.31N 2.54E
87 J5 Randa Djibouti 11.52N 42.39E
66 H7 Randa Switzerland 46.07N 7.47E
53 T21 Randaberg Norway 59.00N 5.38E
53 U15 Randabygd Norway 61.52N 6.20E
112 J8 Randado Texas 27.04N 98.54W
108 R7 Randall Iowa 42.14N 93.36W
109 M2 Randall Kansas 39.40N 98.04W
108 Q3 Randall Minnesota 46.05N 94.29W
59 K2 Randalstown Antrim N Ireland 54.45N 6.19W
71 C4 Randan France 46.00N 3.26E
81 J8 Randazzo Sicily 37.52N 14.57E
53 C5 Randbøl Denmark 55.42N 9.15E
94 T13 Randburg Witwatersrand S Africa 26.07S 28.02E
65 L5 Randegg Austria 48.01N 14.59E
64 F8 Randegg W Germany 47.43N 8.45E
64 F8 Randen W Germany 47.49N 8.35E
66 L1 Randen *reg* Switzerland 47.45N 8.32E
29 C7 Rander Gujarat India 21.15N 72.50E
69 L1 Randerath W Germany 51.01N 6.10E
53 E4 Randers Denmark 56.28N 10.03E
Randers *co see* Århus
64 J4 Randersacker W Germany 49.44N 10.00E
53 E3 Randers Fjord *inlet* Denmark 56.35N 10.22E
53 B6 Randerup Denmark 55.06N 8.44E
95 L2 Randfontein S Africa 26.10S 27.43E
94 R13 Randgate S Africa 26.11S 27.41E
51 G5 Randijaure *L* Sweden 66.44N 19.20E
110 D3 Randle Washington 46.34N 121.58W
105 H2 Randleman N Carolina 35.51N 79.49W
109 M7 Randlett Oklahoma 34.12N 98.30W
110 Q9 Randlett Utah 40.14N 109.50W
53 E5 Randlev Denmark 55.58N 10.13E
108 P9 Randolph Iowa 40.52N 95.36W
109 O2 Randolph Kansas 39.27N 96.44W
104 Q2 Randolph Maine 44.14N 69.46W
103 M2 Randolph Massachusetts 42.11N 71.03W
107 G7 Randolph Mississippi 34.11N 89.10W
108 N7 Randolph Nebraska 42.22N 97.21W
104 G4 Randolph New York 42.10N 78.59W
110 O8 Randolph Utah 41.41N 111.10W
104 N3 Randolph Vermont 43.56N 72.42W
106 E6 Randolph Wisconsin 43.33N 89.00W
98 T5 Random I Newfoundland
106 G6 Random L Wisconsin 43.32N 87.58W
71 D7 Randon,Mt France 44.39N 3.32E
70 M4 Randonnai France 48.39N 0.41E
63 U6 Randow *R* E Germany
15 D4 Randowaya Yapen I, Irian Jaya 1.50S 136.30E
53 U20 Randøy I Norway 59.12N 6.02E
111 G6 Randsburg California 35.23N 117.38W
52 E6 Randsfjord Norway 60.15N 10.22E
52 E6 Randsfjord *L* Norway
12 M7 Randwick *dist* Sydney, N S W
60 L12 Randwijk Netherlands 51.57N 5.43E
63 E5 Randzel *sandbank* W Germany
51 J6 Råneå Sweden 65.51N 22.20E
70 K4 Rânes France 48.38N 0.12W
29 L1 Raneswar Bihar India 24.02N 87.26E
100 F5 Ranfurly Alberta 53.25N 111.40W
11 E12 Ranfurly New Zealand 45.08S 170.08E
66 C2 Rang France 47.25N 6.34E
50 L4 Rangá Iceland 65.22N 14.25W
50 L4 Rangá *R* Iceland
18 D2 Rangae Thailand 6.15N 101.45E
31 J10 Rangamati Bangladesh 22.40N 92.10E
30 K5 Rangang Nepal 27.39N 86.26E
18 K6 Rangantamiang Borneo Indon 0.41S 113.18E
28 J2 Rangapara North Assam India 26.50N 92.44E
28 J2 Ranga R Assam India
50 E7 Rangárvallasýsla *co* Iceland
50 E7 Rangárvellir *plains* Iceland
19 A5 Rangasa, Tanjung *C* Celebes Indonesia 2.38S 118.51E
11 K6 Rangataua New Zealand 39.27S 175.28E
11 K11 Rangatira I Chatham Is Pacific Oc 44.20S 176.09W
11 H1 Rangaunu Harb New Zealand
23 F2 Rangdong Henan China 31.51N 112.18E
107 J10 Range Alabama 31.19N 87.14W
104 P2 Rangeley Maine 44.58N 70.40W
104 P2 Rangeley L Maine
30 L6 Rangeli Nepal 26.28N 87.30E
109 B1 Rangely Colorado 40.04N 108.48W
112 J3 Ranger Texas 32.29N 98.42W
104 C8 Ranger W Virginia 38.07N 82.10W
99 G6 Ranger L Ontario
99 G6 Ranger Lake Ontario 46.54N 83.36W
29 G7 Rangi Maharashtra India 20.23N 80.16E
28 H2 Rangia Assam India 26.26N 91.38E
Rangiauria *isld* Chatham Is *see* Pitt I
11 K5 Ranginui *mt* New Zealand 38.21S 175.29E
11 G10 Rangiora New Zealand 43.18S 172.38E
122 B14 Rangiroa *isld* Tuamotu Is Pacific Oc 15.00S 147.40W
11 L5 Rangitaiki New Zealand 38.53S 176.22E
11 L5 Rangitaiki R New Zealand
11 F11 Rangitata New Zealand 44.04S 171.23E
11 E10 Rangitata R New Zealand
11 L6 Rangitikei R New Zealand
11 D1 Rangitoto Chan New Zealand
11 J3 Rangitoto I New Zealand 36.48S 174.53E
11 J7 Rangitoto Is New Zealand
11 K5 Rangitoto Ra New Zealand
11 N4 Rangitukia New Zealand 37.45S 178.30E
18 G9 Rangkasbitung Java Indon 6.21S 106.12E
28 K1 Rangku Assam India 28.20N 94.41E
43 L7 Rangkul' Tadzhikistan U.S.S.R. 38.30N 74.24E
25 D4 Rangoon Burma 16.47N 96.10E
25 D4 Rangoon *R* Burma
29 L4 Rangphu W Bengal India 27.10N 88.38E
31 H8 Rangpur Bangladesh 25.45N 89.21E
31 F5 Rangpur Pakistan 30.32N 71.37E
31 H8 Rangpur *dist* Bangladesh
31 F4 Rangpur Bhagut Pakistan 32.04N 71.52E
18 E5 Rangsang *isld* Sumatra Indon
63 S8 Rangsdorf E Germany 52.19N 13.26E
25 M8 Rangse Burma 26.35N 95.42E
53 C6 Rangstrup Denmark 55.09N 9.13E
23 C2 Rangtag Gansu 33.52N 103.53E
93 F6 Rangwe Kenya 0.37S 34.37E
76 C15 Ranholas Portugal 38.47N 9.22W
29 C5 Rani Rajasthan India 25.20N 73.26E
29 D3 Rania Haryana India 29.32N 74.54E
Rania Iraq*see* Rānya
28 B3 Ranibennur Karnataka India 14.35N 75.36E
108 R1 Ranier Minnesota 48.39N 93.20W
30 L6 Raniganj Bihar India 26.05N 87.14E
29 K1 Raniganj Birbhum, W Bengal Ind 23.35N 87.07E
30 F7 Raniganj Uttar Prad India 25.48N 82.01E
29 K5 Raniganj W Dinajpur, W Bengal India 25.56N 87.58E
30 L7 Raniganj West Bengal India 25.52N 87.53E
30 F6 Rani Jot Uttar Prad India 27.00N 82.21E
29 H6 Ranijula Pk Madhya Prad India 22.59N 83.40E
30 C3 Ranikhet Uttar Prad India 29.39N 79.25E
28 D4 Ranipet Tamil Nadu India 12.56N 79.17E
31 E7 Ranipur Pakistan 27.17N 68.34E
64 M2 Ranis E Germany 50.40N 11.33E
30 H7 Rani Sagar Bihar India 25.37N 84.22E
29 C5 Raniwari Rajasthan India 24.46N 72.20E
30 D8 Ranj *R* Madhya Prad India
29 L4 Ranjit R Sikkim India
29 H6 Ranka Bihar India 23.59N 83.50E
13 D5 Ranken *R* N Terr Australia
13 D4 Ranken Store N Terr Australia 19.35S 136.54E
106 G9 Rankin Illinois 40.28N 87.54W
112 F4 Rankin Texas 31.14N 101.56W
97 K5 Rankin Inlet N W Terr 62.52N 92.00W
12 H5 Rankin's Springs New S Wales 33.52S 146.18E
65 A7 Rankweil Austria 47.17N 9.40E
26 S10 Ranna Sri Lanka 6.05N 80.52E
35 B8 Rannen Israel 31.20N 34.36E
13 K6 Rannes Queensland 24.06S 150.09E
43 C2 Ranniy U.S.S.R. 51.30N 52.36E
58 H5 Rannoch,L Tayside Scotland
58 G5 Rannoch,Moor of Tayside/Highland/Strathclyde Scotland
58 G5 Rannoch Station Tayside Scotland 56.42N 4.34W
9 C11 Rannon New Hebrides 16.08S 168.08E
90 D6 Rano Nigeria 11.37N 8.34E
122 U15 Rano Aroi *crater* Easter I Pacific Oc 27.06S 109.22W
30 A7 Ranod Madhya Prad India 25.06N 77.53E
95 B7 Ranohira Madagascar 22.32S 45.27E
122 T16 Rano Kao *crater* Easter I Pacific Oc 27.11S 109.26W
99 J2 Ranoke Ontario 50.27N 81.36W
95 C8 Ranomafana Madagascar 24.32S 46.59E
95 D5 Ranomafana Madagascar 18.55S 48.50E
95 C8 Ranomainty Madagascar 24.30S 46.06E
95 C7 Ranomena Madagascar 23.25S 47.16E
25 E8 Ranong Thailand 9.58N 98.35E
95 C8 Ranopiso Madagascar 25.02S 46.40E
122 V16 Rano Raraku *crater* Easter I Pacific Oc 27.07S 109.18W
25 F9 Ranot Thailand 7.45N 100.20E
95 C7 Ranotsara-Nord Madagascar 22.48S 46.35E
95 C7 Ranotsara-Sud Madagascar 23.41S 46.39E
46 M3 Ranova *R* U.S.S.R.
29 J7 Ranpur Orissa India 20.04N 85.22E
31 E5 Ranrkan Pakistan 30.15N 69.55E
32 C4 Rānsa Iran 33.38N 48.21E
51 D6 Ransaren *L* Sweden 65.15N 15.00E
61 H5 Ransart Belgium 50.28N 4.29E
52 G7 Ransäter Sweden 59.46N 13.30E
64 D3 Ransbach-Baumbach W Germany 50.28N 7.44E
61 L3 Ransberg Belgium 50.52N 5.02E
64 D3 Ransel W Germany 50.07N 7.53E
15 C4 Ransiki Irian Jaya 1.27S 134.12E
106 F8 Ransom Illinois 41.10N 88.38W
109 L3 Ransom Kansas 38.37N 99.56W
104 H7 Ranson W Virginia 39.19N 77.53W
61 J2 Ranst Belgium 51.11N 4.34E
64 F3 Ranstadt W Germany 50.21N 8.59E
95 D3 Rantabe Madagascar 15.40S 49.40E
51 N9 Rantasalmi Finland 62.06N 28.20E
18 L7 Rantau Borneo Indon 3.02S 115.05E
18 B9 Rantau Pen Malaysia 2.35N 101.57E
18 D5 Rantaukampar Sumatra Indonesia 1.22N 101.01E
18 M4 Rantaupanjang Borneo Indon 2.05N 117.25E
18 C4 Rantauparapat Sumatra Indon 2.05N 99.46E
19 B5 Rantekombola,Bukit *mt* Celebes Indon 3.23S 120.02E
19 A5 Rantepao Celebes Indon 2.58S 119.58E
29 E4 Ranthambhor Rajasthan India 26.04N 76.32E
69 C5 Rantigny France 49.20N 2.26E
35 D5 Rantis Jordan 32.02N 35.01E
106 F9 Rantoul Illinois 40.18N 88.11W
51 M7 Rantsila Finland 64.31N 25.40E
51 M6 Ranua Finland 65.55N 26.34E
121 A8 Ranue,R Chile
53 C3 Ranum Denmark 56.54N 9.15E
34 M2 Rānya Iraq 36.15N 44.54E
33 E6 Ranyah *dist* Saudi Arabia
33 E6 Ranyah,Wādī *watercourse* Saudi Arabia
79 D6 Ranzo Italy 44.03N 8.01E
66 M7 Ranzo Switzerland 46.07N 8.47E
89 A4 Rao Senegal 15.58N 16.22W
25 H3 Rao Go *mt* Laos 18.10N 104.25E
21 F4 Raohe Heilongjiang China 46.53N 134.00E
31 J10 Raojan Bangladesh 22.30N 91.59E
30 B3 Raoli Uttar Prad India 29.27N 78.04E
69 M7 Raon-l'Etape France 48.25N 6.50E
69 N6 Raon-sur-Plaine France 48.31N 7.05E
23 H7 Raoping Guangdong China 23.42N 117.01E
Raoûda *see* Rōda
Râouîyé *see* Rawiye
11 N1 Raoul I Kermadec Is Pacific Oc 29.15S 177.52W
15 K6 Raoult,C New Britain 5.28S 148.59E
22 K7 Raoyang Hebei China 38.15N 115.44E
11 F9 Rapahoe New Zealand 42.23S 171.12E
122 N11 Rapa Iti *isld* Tubuai Is Pacific Oc 27.35S 144.20W
11 M10 Rapaki New Zealand 43.36S 172.41E
79 F6 Rapallo Italy 44.21N 9.13E
Rapa Nui *isld see* Easter I
122 V8 Rapa Passage Fanning I Pacific Oc 3.53N 159.19W
118 E10 Rapa,Pta.do Brazil 27.24S 48.28W
29 B6 Rapar Gujarat India 23.32N 70.40E
32 H8 Rapch *watercourse* Iran
121 B4 Rapel *R* Chile
110 Q4 Rapelje Montana 45.58N 109.16W
60 C3 Rapenburg Netherlands 51.19N 3.59E
121 H6 Raper,C Chile 46.50S 75.40W
97 N4 Raper,C N W Terr 69.45N 67.00W
104 F9 Raphine Virginia 37.57N 79.16W
59 G2 Raphoe Donegal Irish Rep 54.52N 7.36W
30 K2 Raphu La Xizang Zizhiqu 28.02N 87.58E
113 R3 Rapid *R* Alaska
108 Q1 Rapid *R* Minnesota
104 G8 Rapidan Virginia 38.18N 78.05W
104 H8 Rapidan *R* Virginia
12 E6 Rapid Bay S Australia 35.33S 138.09E
100 R8 Rapid City Manitoba 50.09N 100.03W
108 G5 Rapid City S Dakota 44.06N 103.14W
99 R5 Rapide Blanc Quebec 47.41N 73.03W
99 N6 Rapides des Joachims Quebec 46.13N 77.43W
13 H2 Rapid Horn *C* Gt Barrier Reef Australia 14.01S 146.40E
106 H4 Rapid R Michigan 45.57N 86.59W
100 J4 Rapid View Saskatchewan 54.09N 108.46W
46 F1 Räpina Estonia U.S.S.R. 58.01N 27.29E
120 E4 Rapirrān *R* Brazil
77 V15 Rápita,B.la Balearic Is
46 E1 Rapla Estonia U.S.S.R. 58.59N 24.49E
80 E2 Rapolano Terme Italy 43.17N 11.36E
80 N7 Rapolla Italy 40.58N 15.41E
76 B10 Raposa Portugal 39.06N 8.34W
76 B14 Raposeira Portugal 37.05N 8.54W
104 H8 Rappahannock *R* Virginia
19 A5 Rappang Celebes Indonesia 3.51S 119.53E
66 F3 Rapperswil Bern Switzerland 47.04N 7.26E
66 M3 Rapperswil Schwyz Switzerland 47.14N 8.50E
65 M4 Rappottenstein Austria 48.32N 15.05E
84 E2 Rapsáni Greece 39.54N 22.33E
30 G6 Rapti *R* Uttar Prad India
30 H5 Rapti Doon *R* Nepal
120 E6 Rapulo,R Bolivia
28 D3 Rapur Andhra Prad India 14.15N 79.30E
29 A6 Rapur Gujarat India 23.03N 68.50E
19 M5 Rapurapu *isld* Philippines 13.12N 124.09E
87 B6 Raqaba ez Zarqa *watercourse* Sudan
34 G3 Raqqa Syria 35.57N 39.03E
Raqqâdîye *see* Ruqqadiye
Raqqâd,Nahr *R see* Ruqqād
Raqqâd,Ouâdi er *R see* Ruqqād
104 L2 Raquette *R* New York
104 L3 Raquette L New York
104 L3 Raquette Lake New York 43.49N 74.41W
99 R2 Raquette R New York
99 S2 Raquette River New York 44.58N 74.48W
30 F3 Rara Nepal 29.33N 82.05E
30 F3 Rara Daha *L* Nepal 29.33N 82.06E
92 H10 Raraga *R* Mozambique
13 D1 Raragala I N Terr Australia 11.38S 136.06E
122 D14 Raraka *atoll* Tuamotu Is Pacific Oc 16.10S 144.50W
69 J5 Rarécourt France 49.05N 5.07E
103 E5 Raritan New Jersey 40.34N 74.39W
103 E5 Raritan *R* New Jersey
104 L6 Raritan B New Jersey
89 M3 Raro Niger 16.23N 5.48E
122 E14 Raroia *atoll* Tuamotu Is Pacific Oc 16.00S 142.25W
66 H6 Raron Switzerland 46.19N 7.48E
122 A10 Rarotonga *I* Cook Is Pacific Oc 21.15S 159.45W
39 J3 Rarytkin,Khrebet *mts* U.S.S.R.
29 D4 Ras Rajasthan India 26.16N 74.13E
87 H3 Rasa Ethiopia 14.58N 40.25E
18 B8 Rasa Pen Malaysia 3.30N 101.37E
82 B5 Raša Yugoslavia 45.05N 14.05E
19 J7 Rasa *isld* Philippines 9.13N 118.26E
86 J8 Râs Abu Bakr *C* Egypt 28.33N 32.56E
85 O8 Râs Abû Dâra *C* Egypt 22.40N 36.05E
86 J7 Râs Abu Darag *C* Egypt 29.22N 32.35E
86 N8 Râs Abu Galûm *C* Egypt 28.39N 34.35E
85 J4 Râs Abu Laho *C* Egypt 31.25N 27.00E
86 N9 Rās Abū Seif *C* Saudi Arabia 28.05N 34.50E
85 O9 Ras Abu Shagara *C* Sudan 21.04N 37.19E
86 L9 Râs Abu Suweira *C* Egypt 28.18N 33.33E
86 L6 Râs Abu Tileihat *hill* Egypt 29.51N 33.56E
86 J6 Râs Adabîya *C* Egypt 29.52N 32.30E
87 M5 Ras Adado *C* Somalia 10.20N 48.44E
33 M7 Ra's ad Daqm Oman 19.40N 57.45E
Rasafah,Ar *see* Risāfe
75 D4 Rasa,La Spain 41.31N 3.06W
85 J4 Râs 'Alam el Rûm *C* Egypt 31.24N 27.25E
33 N5 Ra's al Hadd Oman 22.31N 59.45E
87 M5 Ras al Hamar *C* Somalia 11.19N 49.18E
Ras-al-Khaima *see* Ra's al Khaymah
33 L4 Ra's al Khaymah U.A.E. 25.48N 55.56E
33 H2 Ra's al Mish'āb Saudi Arabia 28.12N 48.37E
86 N9 Rās al Qasbah *C* Saudi Arabia 28.02N 34.36E
18 D6 Rasam,Gunung *mt* Sumatra Indon 1.11S 100.46E
86 J8 Râs Amit *oil well* Egypt 28.35N 32.54E
87 H3 Ras Andadda *C* Ethiopia 14.59N 40.36E
33 E5 Raşan, Jabal *mts* Saudi Arabia
121 E8 Rasa,Pta *C* Argentina 40.55S 62.15W
86 N9 Ra's ash Shaykh Humayd *C* Saudi Arabia 28.06N 34.35E
Ras Asir *see* Guardfui, C
86 M9 Râs Atantûr *C* Egypt 28.14N 34.25E
85 G3 Ra's at Tīn *C* Libya 32.38N 23.05E
87 M8 Ras Awat *C* Somalia 5.52N 48.53E
15 C5 Rasawi Irian Jaya 2.03S 134.03E
33 N10 Ra's az Zawr Saudi Arabia 28.43N 48.22E
85 N8 Râs Banâs *C* Egypt
87 N5 Ras Binnah *C* Somalia 11.08N 51.10E
86 K8 Râs Budrân *C* Egypt 28.57N 33.10E
86 K3 Râs Burun *hill* Egypt 31.14N 33.04E
75 C6 Rascafría Spain 40.54N 3.53W
96 Q15 Rasca,Pta de la Tenerife Canary Is 28.01N 16.42W
87 G4 Rāsdajan *mt* Ethiopia 13.15N 38.27E
87 P4 Ras Darishah Socotra S Yemen 12.35N 54.29E
Ras Dashan *mt see* Rāsdajan *mt*
86 K9 Râs Dib *C* Egypt 28.02N 33.25E
87 J4 Ras Dormo *C* Ethiopia 13.14N 42.35E
87 N6 Ras Durdura *C* Somalia 9.03N 50.39E
Râs el Ahmar Israel*see* Kerem Ben Zimra
86 L4 Râs el Ahmar *hill* Egypt 30.59N 33.48E
34 H2 Ras el'Ain Syria 36.52N 40.05E
Râs el 'Anf *see* Râs Banâs
35 G4 Ras el Aqra *anc site* Jordan 32.16N 35.49E
86 L10 Râs el Bahr *C* Egypt 27.46N 33.33E
86 A5 Râs el Baqar *hill* Egypt 30.12N 28.58E
86 G2 Râs el Barr *C* Egypt 31.32N 31.50E
87 J4 Ras el Bir *C* Djibouti 12.00N 43.25E
87 M7 Ras el Cheil *C* Somalia 7.45N 49.50E
86 M5 Râs el Farûdi *hill* Egypt 30.27N 34.29E
86 M4 Râs el Ghagham *hill* Egypt 30.33N 34.16E
35 F8 Ras el Ghor *prom* Jordan 31.28N 35.34E
86 K5 Râs el Gifa *hill* Egypt 30.01N 33.04E
86 L7 Râs el Gineina *hill* Egypt 29.02N 33.58E
86 H3 Râs el 'Ish Egypt 31.09N 32.22E
85 J4 Râs el Kenâyis *C* Egypt 31.16N 27.53E
86 G3 Râs el Khalîg Egypt 31.16N 31.38E
88 M5 Ras el Ksar Morocco 33.58N 3.50W
88 N4 Ras el Ma Algeria 34.29N 0.48W
89 G3 Ras el Ma Mali 16.36N 4.40W
86 M7 Râs el Nafas *hill* Egypt 29.26N 34.11E
88 Q4 Ras el Oued Algeria 35.57N 5.03E
86 A4 Râs el Shaqîq *C* Egypt 30.57N 28.50E
86 J6 Râs el Sudr *C* Egypt 29.36N 32.41E
86 K9 Râs el Wa'ir *C* Egypt 28.21N 33.26E
Râs en Naqb *see* Naqb Ishtar
86 P6 Râs en Naqb *ra* Jordan
35 G1 Ras en Nuriye Syria 33.13N 35.54E
46 E2 Raseynyay Lithuania U.S.S.R. 55.28N 23.02E
Râs ez Zuweira *see* Rosh Zohar
87 N6 Ras Gabah *C* Somalia 8.08N 50.03E
86 L9 Râs Garra *C* Egypt 28.01N 33.45E
86 K9 Râs Ghârib Egypt 28.22N 33.04E
86 K9 Râs Ghârib *C* Egypt 28.21N 33.06E
87 N6 Ras Giog-Giog-ti *C* Somalia 8.30N 50.20E
87 N5 Ras Gubba *C* Somalia 10.00N 50.52E
87 C5 Rashad Sudan 11.55N 31.05E
35 G5 Rashada, Er Jordan 32.15N 35.54E
85 O8 Râs Hadarba *C* Egypt 22.04N 36.51E
34 C8 Rashādīya Jordan 30.42N 35.38E
87 C5 Rashad,Jeb *mt* Sudan 11.53N 31.05E
87 N5 Ras Hafun *C* Somalia 10.29N 51.20E
87 N6 Ras Haor *C* Somalia 8.45N 50.25E
59 K2 Rasharkin Antrim N Ireland 54.57N 6.29W
85 K7 Rashda,El Egypt 25.36N 28.57E
45 E6 Rashevka Ukraine U.S.S.R. 50.15N 33.54E
32 B5 Rashi *oil well* Iraq 30.17N 47.25E
86 D3 Rashîd Egypt 31.25N 30.25E
34 M5 Rashīd Iraq 33.19N 44.29E
33 J7 Rāshid *tribe* Saudi Arabia
33 K5 Rāshid *tribe* Saudi Arabia
34 H2 Rashīdīya Syria 36.08N 40.41E
31 D5 Rashid Qala Afghanistan 31.31N 67.34E
44 J10 Rashkasri Dāgh *mt* Iran 37.57N 48.48E
32 F3 Rashm Iran 35.16N 54.32E
33 G9 Rashshah S Yemen 15.20N 47.30E
32 C2 Rasht Iran 37.18N 49.38E
84 Y20 Ras Id-Dawwara *C* Malta 35.52N 14.21E
84 X19 Ras Id-Dwejra *C* Gozo Medit Sea 36.03N 14.11E
84 Y20 Ras I-Irqieqa *C* Malta 35.57N 14.29E
84 X19 Ras il Bajda *C* Gozo Medit Sea 36.02N 14.13E
84 Y20 Ras il-Griebeġ *C* Malta 35.58N 14.23E
84 Y21 Ras il-Hamrija *C* Malta 35.49N 14.27E
84 X19 Ras il-Heqqa *C* Gozo Medit Sea 36.05N 14.12E
75 E3 Rasillo,El Spain 42.12N 2.42W
84 Y19 Ras il-Qala *C* Gozo Medit Sea 36.02N 14.20E
84 X20 Ras il-Qammeh *C* Malta 35.58N 14.19E
84 Y20 Ras il-Qrejten *C* Malta 35.57N 14.27E
84 X20 Ras il-Wahx *C* Malta 35.57N 14.20E
84 X19 Ras il-Wardija *C* Gozo Medit Sea 36.02N 14.11E
75 D1 Rasines Spain 43.18N 3.25W
93 N8 Rasini Kenya 2.06S 41.07E
84 Y20 Ras in Niexfa *C* Malta 35.58N 14.21E
28 D5 Rasipur Tamil Nadu India 11.28N 78.13E
84 X20 Ras ir-Raheb *C* Malta 35.54N 14.20E
84 X19 Ras ir-Reqqa *C* Gozo Medit Sea 36.05N 14.14E
86 J8 Râs Issaran *C* Egypt 28.48N 32.48E
32 J7 Rāsk Iran 26.13N 61.28E
82 F7 Raška Yugoslavia 43.17N 20.37E
88 T4 Ras Kaboudia *C* Tunisia 35.12N 11.08E
86 L10 Râs Kanîsa *C* Egypt 27.56N 33.53E
87 O4 Ras Karma *C* Socotra S Yemen 12.39N 53.52E
87 G1 Ras Kasar *C* Sudan 18.02N 38.36E
87 K5 Ras Khanzira *C* Somalia 10.52N 45.50E
87 K5 Ras Khatib *C* Somalia 10.40N 45.20E
87 L5 Ras Khatib *C* Somalia 11.05N 47.07E
92 J4 Ras Kigomasha *C* Pemba I 4.49S 39.22E
92 J4 Ras Kiuyu *C* Pemba I 4.54S 39.51E
92 K12 Ras Kizimkazi *C* Zanzibar 6.29S 39.30E
53 D5 Raskmølle Denmark 55.53N 9.38E
31 C6 Raskoh *mts* Pakistan
31 C6 Ras Koh *mt* Pakistan 28.50N 65.12E
87 M5 Ras Koreh *C* Somalia 11.29N 49.40E
30 E3 Raskot Nepal 29.18N 81.38E
87 H3 Ras Kozar *C* Ethiopia 14.30N 41.19E
84 Z21 Ras L'Artal *C* Malta 35.48N 14.32E
62 N6 Raslavice Czechoslovakia 49.11N 21.15E
87 N6 Ras Mabber *C* Somalia 9.29N 50.50E
86 P10 Râs Mahârish *C* Saudi Arabia 27.30N 35.33E
86 J7 Râs Mal'ab *C* Egypt 29.12N 32.55E
87 J5 Ras Maskan *C* Somalia 11.10N 43.37E
86 J7 Râs Matarma *C* Egypt 29.29N 32.44E
86 J7 Ras Matarma *oil well* Egypt 29.28N 32.46E
92 K7 Ras Matunda *C* Tanzania 10.21S 40.28E
29 D5 Rasmi Rajasthan India 25.03N 74.24E
92 K12 Ras Michamwi Zanzibar 6.055 39.30E
86 J6 Râs Misalla *C* Egypt 29.50N 32.36E
92 J5 Ras Mkumbi *C* Mafia I E Africa 7.40S 39.55E
87 M10 Ras Mtoni *C* Somalia 0.30S 42.28E
86 M10 Râs Muhammad *C* Egypt 27.44N 34.15E
89 A1 Ras Nouadhibou Mauritania 20.44N 17.05W
92 J11 Ras Nungwi *C* Tanzania 5.43S 39.19E
86 M10 Râs Nuşrâni *C* Egypt 27.58N 34.25E
89 O10 Raso *isld* Cape Verde 16.39N 24.38W
75 G7 Raso *mt* Spain 40.30N 1.57W
121 D10 Raso,C Argentina 44.23S 65.15W
76 A11 Raso, Cabo Portugal 38.42N 9.30W
81 L7 Rasocolmo,C Sicily 38.17N 15.31E
117 H9 Raso da Catarina *reg* Brazil
76 K5 Raso del Portillo *plain* Spain
14 E8 Rason,L W Australia
82 H7 Rasovo Bulgaria 43.42N 23.17E
113 L7 Raspberry I Alaska 58.05N 153.20W
85 J4 Râs Qattâra Egypt 30.12N 27.13E
75 M5 Rasquera Spain 41.00N 0.35E
30 G7 Rasra Uttar Prad India 25.52N 83.50E
86 J8 Râs Ruahmi *C* Egypt 28.44N 32.50E
66 J8 Rassa Italy 45.47N 8.01E
84 X19 Ras San Dimitri *C* Gozo Medit Sea 36.04N 14.11E
33 B3 Ra's Sāq,Jabal *mts* Saudi Arabia
33 E4 Rass,Ar *oasis* Saudi Arabia 25.54N 43.30E
88 S3 Rass Ben Sekka *C* Tunisia 37.21N 9.41E
Râss el Bassîte *see* Basît, El Ras el
66 C4 Rasses,les Switzerland 46.51N 6.34E
87 H3 Ras Shaks *C* Ethiopia 14.37N 41.12E
86 K8 Râs Sharâtîb *C* Egypt 28.40N 33.12E
44 D2 Rasshevatskaya U.S.S.R. 45.35N 41.04E
40 M8 Rasshua *vol* Kuril Is U.S.S.R. 47.46N 152.59E
33 K10 Ra's Shu'ab *C* Socotra S Yemen
40 M8 Rasshua Ostrov *isld* Kuril Is U.S.S.R. 47.46N 152.59E
86 K9 Râs Shukheir *C* Egypt 28.08N 33.16E
86 K9 Râs Shukheir *oil well* Egypt 28.08N 33.15E
88 T3 Ras Si Ali Mekki *C* Tunisia 37.10N 10.14E
33 M6 Ra's Şirāb Oman
45 N4 Rasskazovo U.S.S.R. 52.39N 41.54E
87 K9 Rasso Somalia 3.38N 45.02E
41 J5 Rassokha *R* Krasnoyarsk U.S.S.R.
39 E2 Rassokha *R* U.S.S.R.
39 F2 Rassokha *R* U.S.S.R.
39 E1 Rassokha *R* Yakutsk U.S.S.R.
41 G5 Rassomashye U.S.S.R. 71.50N 99.44E
39 F6 Rassoshina *R* U.S.S.R.
87 L5 Ras Sura *C* Somalia 11.10N 47.30E
86 N8 Rās Suweihil *C* Saudi Arabia 28.40N 34.47E
39 C5 Rassvet U.S.S.R. 59.30N 143.20E
34 D4 Rastan,Er Syria 34.56N 36.44E
33 J3 Ras Tannūrah Saudi Arabia 26.41N 50.11E
51 J3 Råstätno *R* Sweden
64 E6 Rastatt W Germany 48.51N 8.13E
46 G5 Rastavitsa *R* Ukraine U.S.S.R.
53 D3 Råsted Nordjylland Denmark 56.30N 9.58E
53 A4 Råsted Ringkøbing Denmark 56.19N 8.29E
63 H6 Rastede W Germany 53.15N 8.12E
51 M1 Rastegaissa *mt* Norway 70.00N 26.16E
64 L1 Rastenberg E Germany 51.10N 11.25E
Rastenburg *see* Kętrzyn
65 M4 Rastenfeld Austria 48.34N 15.21E
51 O8 Rastinjärvi Finland 63.56N 29.40E
65 E7 Rastkogel *mt* Austria 47.13N 11.46E
51 H3 Råsto *reg* Sweden
51 H3 Råstojaure *L* Sweden 68.46N 20.30E
82 J4 Răstolița Romania 46.59N 24.59E
41 D4 Rastorgueva, Ostrov *isld* U.S.S.R. 73.59N 84.00E
30 J4 Rasua Garhi Nepal 28.18N 85.24E
Ras Uarc *see* Tres Forcas,C
76 J6 Rasueros Spain 41.02N 5.04W
31 G4 Rasul Pakistan 32.46N 73.40E
32 F7 Rasūl *R* Iran
30 C6 Rasulabad Kanpur, Uttar Prad India 26.39N 79.48E
30 D6 Rasulabad Unnao, Uttar Prad India 26.45N 80.29E
31 G4 Rasulnagar Pakistan 32.20N 73.51E
30 A8 Rasulpura Madhya Prad India 24.27N 77.24E
86 K7 Râs Umm Maghrab *hill* Egypt 29.18N 33.13E
86 H10 Râs Umm 'Omeiyid *hill* Egypt 27.50N 32.18E
86 O6 Râs Umm Seisabân *mt* Jordan 29.44N 35.09E
78 C8 Rasu,Mte Sardinia 40.29N 9.02E
35 G4 Rasun Jordan 32.24N 35.45E
92 J4 Ras Upembe *C* Pemba I 5.25S 39.42E
92 K12 Ras Uroa *C* Zanzibar 6.04S 39.26E
92 J11 Ras Uso wa Membe *C* Zanzibar 5.54S 39.11E
29 D3 Rasuwala Rajasthan India 29.54N 74.22E
86 O10 Rās Wādi Tiryām *C* Saudi Arabia 27.48N 35.21E
86 J7 Râs Za'farâna *C* Egypt 29.07N 32.40E
86 L10 Râs Zeit *C* Egypt 27.56N 33.32E
11 K6 Rata New Zealand 40.00S 175.31E
19 D3 Ratahan Celebes Indon 1.05N 124.49E
65 L2 Rataje nad Sázavou Czech 49.51N 14.58E
9 C1 Ratak Chain *atolls* Marshall Is Pacific Oc
46 F4 Ratalovka U.S.S.R. 51.19N 25.52E
52 H4 Rätan Jämtland Sweden 62.28N 14.35E
52 M3 Ratan Västerbotten Sweden 64.00N 20.50E
29 D3 Ratangarh Rajasthan India 28.02N 74.39E
29 C7 Ratanpur Gujarat India 21.43N 73.16E
29 H6 Ratanpur Madhya Prad India 22.18N 82.12E
34 P8 Raṭawī Iraq 30.34N 47.08E
65 M2 Ratbor Czechoslovakia 49.59N 15.12E
25 E6 Rat Buri Thailand 13.30N 99.50E
Ratcha Kram *see* Ban Ratcha Khram
45 L3 Ratchino Lipetsk U.S.S.R. 53.03N 39.54E
43 C1 Ratchino Orenburg U.S.S.R. 53.06N 54.29E
107 C6 Ratcliff Arkansas 35.19N 93.55W
112 M4 Ratcliff Texas 31.24N 95.10W
14 B10 Ratcliff B W Australia
63 N5 Ratekau W Germany 53.55N 10.43E
94 D7 Ratel Poort S Africa 29.29S 17.50E
59 G5 Rath Offaly Irish Rep 53.08N 7.48W
30 C7 Rath Uttar Prad India 25.36N 79.34E
59 J5 Rathangan Kildare Irish Rep 53.13N 7.00W
59 G4 Rathconrath W Meath Irish Rep 53.32N 7.31W
59 K5 Rathcoole Dublin Irish Rep 53.17N 6.28W
59 F7 Rathcormack Cork Irish Rep 52.05N 8.17W
59 J6 Rathdangan Wicklow Irish Rep 52.55N 6.32W
59 G6 Rathdowney Leix Irish Rep 52.51N 7.35W
110 J2 Rathdrum Idaho 47.49N 116.54W
59 K6 Rathdrum Wicklow Irish Rep 52.56N 6.13W
25 B2 Rathedaung Burma 20.30N 92.48E
58 M3 Rathen Grampian Scotland 57.38N 2.00W
63 Q7 Rathenow E Germany 52.37N 12.21E
59 K3 Rathfriland Down N Ireland 54.14N 6.10W
59 E6 Rathkeale Limerick Irish Rep 52.32N 8.56W
59 D3 Rathlackan Mayo Irish Rep 54.18N 9.15W
59 K1 Rathlin I Antrim N Ireland 55.17N 6.15W
59 E2 Rathlin O'Birne I Donegal Irish Rep 54.35N 8.49W
59 E7 Ráth Luirc Cork Irish Rep 52.21N 8.41W
59 G1 Rathmelton Donegal Irish Rep 55.02N 7.39W
59 J5 Rathmolyon Meath Irish Rep 53.29N 6.48W
59 D7 Rathmore Kerry Irish Rep 52.05N 9.13W
59 G1 Rathmullen Donegal Irish Rep 55.06N 7.32W
31 D8 Rath Nath Pakistan 25.48N 67.34E
59 K6 Rathnew Wicklow Irish Rep 53.00N 6.05W
59 J5 Rathoan Meath Irish Rep 53.26N 6.48W
59 G4 Rathowen W Meath Irish Rep 53.40N 7.31W
59 J6 Rathvilly Carlow Irish Rep 52.53N 6.41W
100 T9 Rathwell Manitoba 49.38N 98.31W
113 O10 Rat I Aleutian Is 51.48N 178.15E
15 J5 Rat I Bismarck Arch 2.55S 146.22E
29 D3 Ratia Haryana India 29.41N 75.38E
Ratibor *see* Racibórz
65 L3 Ratibořske Hory Czechoslovakia 49.28N 14.45E
63 E10 Ratingen W Germany 51.18N 6.50E
113 N10 Rat Is Aleutian Is
Ratisbon *see* Regensburg
34 D9 Ratiyah, Wādī *watercourse* Jordan
100 S2 Rat L Manitoba
29 D6 Ratlam Madhya Prad India 23.18N 75.06E
29 D6 Ratlam *dist* Madhya Prad India
56 F2 Ratlinghope Shropshire Eng 52.34N 2.54W
26 Q8 Ratmalana Sri Lanka 6.48N 79.54E
26 R5 Ratmale Sri Lanka 8.16N 80.22E
41 B4 Ratmanova,Mys *C* Novaya Zemlya U.S.S.R. 71.08N 56.27E
39 N2 Ratmanova,O *isld* U.S.S.R. 65.48N 169.02W
28 A2 Ratnagiri Maharashtra India 17.00N 73.20E
28 A2 Ratnagiri *dist* Maharashtra India
26 R8 Ratnapura Sri Lanka 6.41N 80.25E
100 N5 Ratner Saskatchewan 53.11N 104.21W
46 E4 Ratno Ukraine U.S.S.R. 51.40N 24.32E
59 K4 Ratoath Meath Irish Rep 53.31N 6.24W
31 E7 Rato Dero Pakistan 27.47N 68.22E
109 F5 Raton New Mexico 36.54N 104.27W
71 G10 Ratonneau *isld* France 43.17N 5.18E
109 F5 Raton Pass New Mexico 36.59N 104.29W
97 K7 Rat Rapids Ontario 51.10N 90.28W
101 R5 Rat River N W Terr 61.07N 112.35W
41 D8 Ratta U.S.S.R. 63.33N 83.55E
109 P7 Rattan Oklahoma 34.13N 95.24W
65 N7 Ratten Austria 47.29N 15.43E
65 E7 Rattenberg Austria 47.26N 11.54E
65 P7 Rattersdorf Austria 47.25N 16.31E
64 K3 Rattlesdorf W Germany 50.01N 10.54E
109 F4 Rattlesnake Buttes *mts* Colorado
109 L4 Rattlesnake Cr Kansas
110 H7 Rattlesnake Cr Oregon
108 C7 Rattlesnake Ra Wyoming
98 Q4 Rattling Brook Newfoundland 49.36N 56.11W
51 L5 Rattosjärvi Finland 66.50N 24.50E
26 S7 Rattota Sri Lanka 7.31N 80.41E
58 K5 Rattray Tayside Scotland 56.36N 3.20W
58 N3 Rattray Hd Grampian Scotland 57.37N 1.49W
52 J6 Rättvik Sweden 60.56N 15.10E
30 L7 Ratua W Bengal India 25.12N 87.56E
63 N5 Ratzeburg W Germany 53.42N 10.46E
63 N5 Ratzeburger See *L* W Germany
66 Q1 Ratzenried W Germany 47.43N 9.54E
101 G7 Ratz,Mt Br Col 57.22N 132.20W
28 L1 Rau Xizang Zizhiqu 29.30N 96.47E
19 F2 Rau *isld* Moluccas Indon 2.22N 128.05E
18 B8 Raub Pen Malaysia 3.54N 101.47E
53 Y17 Raubergnut *mt* Norway 60.53N 8.01E
53 X16 Raubergsnut *mt* Norway 61.12N 7.48E
103 D5 Raubsville Pennsylvania 40.38N 75.12W
121 F6 Rauch Argentina 36.45S 59.05W
119 F6 Rauchi Colombia 3.54N 67.53W
39 H1 Rauchua *R* U.S.S.R.
121 B5 Rauco Chile 34.55S 71.23W
69 L6 Raucourt Meurthe-et-Moselle France 48.56N 6.13E
69 H4 Raucourt-et-Flaba Ardennes France 49.35N 4.58E
53 Y16 Raudalstindan *mts* Norway 61.30N 8.15E
53 X15 Raudalsvatn *L* Norway 61.54N 7.38E
51 M4 Raudanjoki *R* Finland
53 S15 Raudeberg Norway 61.59N 5.08E
53 S15 Raudeberg Norway 61.59N 5.08E
Raudh *see* Rawḑ, Ar
Raudha,Ar *see* Rawḑah, Ar
50 K6 Raudhaberg Iceland 64.21N 15.27W
50 H6 Raudhabergsheidhi *heath* Iceland
50 B5 Raudhakúlur *mt* Iceland 64.52N 23.16W
50 C5 Raudhamelur Iceland 64.52N 22.21W
33 M9 Raudhatain *oil field* Kuwait 29.53N 47.44E
50 F6 Raudhfoss *waterfall* Iceland 64.01N 19.20W
50 F6 Raudhfossafjall *mt* Iceland 64.00N 19.22W
50 H6 Raudhholar *mt* Iceland 64.04N 17.57W
50 J1 Raudhinúpur *C* Iceland 66.30N 16.30W
50 A4 Raudhisandúr *sand spit* Iceland
50 C5 Raudhkollsstadhir Iceland 64.50N 22.30W
50 B4 Raudhsdalur Iceland 65.30N 23.14W
50 C4 Raudhseyjar *isld* Iceland 65.19N 22.35W
50 K2 Raufarhöfn Iceland 66.28N 15.55W
52 F6 Raufoss Norway 60.44N 10.39E
64 G7 Rauhe Alb *mts* W Germany
64 K4 Rauhe Ebrach *R* W Germany
53 X18 Rauhellern Norway 60.15N 7.50E
64 K4 Rauhenebrach W Germany 49.54N 10.34E
51 L7 Raukki Finland 64.38N 24.09E
11 M4 Raukokore New Zealand 37.38S 177.55E
11 N4 Raukumara *mt* New Zealand 37.45S 178.09E
11 M5 Raukumara Ra New Zealand
53 Y19 Rauland Norway 59.43N 8.00E
53 X19 Raulandsfjell *mt* Norway 59.46N 7.56E
72 K6 Raulhac France 44.54N 2.39E
29 H7 Raul R Orissa India
118 G7 Raul Soares Brazil 20.04S 42.27W
51 J10 Rauma Finland 61.09N 21.30E
53 Y14 Rauma *R* Norway 62.18N 8.05E
11 J7 Raumati New Zealand 40.55S 174.58E
64 E6 Raumünzach W Germany 48.38N 8.21E
53 Y14 Raumyrhø *mt* Norway 62.20N 8.11E
46 F2 Rauna Latvia U.S.S.R. 57.22N 25.40E
53 V17 Raundal Norway 60.40N 6.37E
53 V17 Raundalen *V* Norway
56 K3 Raunds Northants Eng 52.21N 0.33W
18 L10 Raung,Gunung *mt* Java Indon 8.07S 114.03E
103 L8 Raunt,The *B* New York
11 K6 Raurimu New Zealand 39.05S 175.25E
65 H7 Rauris Austria 47.14N 13.00E
29 J6 Raurkela Orissa India 22.16N 85.01E
53 K4 Raus Sweden 56.01N 12.48E
64 F2 Rauschenberg W Germany 50.53N 8.57E
103 C5 Rauschs Pennsylvania 40.40N 76.00W
Raushan *see* Rawshan,Ar
53 W17 Rausmesdalen Norway 60.47N 7.25E
21 K5 Rausu Japan 44.04N 145.12E
Rausu *vol see* Mendeleyevka *vol*
43 K7 Raut Tadzhikistan U.S.S.R. 39.50N 71.10E
51 M9 Rautalampi Finland 62.38N 26.21E
51 H3 Rautas Sweden 68.00N 19.55E
51 G3 Rautasjaure *L* Sweden 68.08N 19.10E
51 N8 Rautavaara Finland 63.30N 28.20E
66 N3 Rautispitz *mt* Switzerland 47.04N 9.01E
51 O10 Rautjärvi Finland 61.18N 29.10E
79 N2 Raut,Monte Italy 46.14N 12.39E
87 D2 Rauwiyan Sudan 16.10N 32.45E
Rauza *see* Khuldabad
31 B3 Rauzabagh Afghanistan 34.12N 62.13E
30 E6 Rauzagaon Uttar Prad India 26.48N 81.42E
72 D6 Rauzan France 44.46N 0.07W
122 E15 Ravahéré *atoll* Tuamotu Is Pacific Oc 18.10S 142.10W
110 L2 Ravalli Montana 47.16N 114.11W
32 G7 Rāvang Iran 27.03N 57.15E
32 B3 Ravānsar Iran 34.41N 46.40E
81 G9 Ravanusa Sicily 37.16N 13.59E
32 G5 Rāvar Iran 31.15N 56.51E
46 E4 Rava-Russkaya Ukraine U.S.S.R. 50.15N 23.36E
79 N1 Ravascletto Italy 46.32N 12.55E
43 M8 Ravat Kirgiziya U.S.S.R. 39.54N 70.18E
43 M8 Ravat Tadzhikistan U.S.S.R. 40.21N 70.34E
80 L7 Ravello Italy 40.38N 14.36E
120 F8 Ravelo Bolivia 18.48S 65.33W
61 K1 Ravels Belgium 51.22N 5.00E
104 D9 Raven Virginia 37.06N 81.42W
103 G2 Ravena New York 42.28N 73.48W
100 O5 Ravendal Saskatchewan 53.33N 103.25W
110 E9 Ravendale California 40.49N 120.23W
69 D4 Ravenel France 49.31N 2.30E
57 G4 Ravenglas Cumbria Eng 54.21N 3.24W
111 F7 Ravenna California 34.26N 118.15W
79 M6 Ravenna Italy 44.25N 12.12E
107 N4 Ravenna Kentucky 37.41N 84.00W
108 M8 Ravenna Nebraska 41.03N 98.53W
104 D5 Ravenna Ohio 41.10N 81.15W
79 L6 Ravenna *prov* Italy
70 H3 Ravenoville France 49.27N 1.16W
11 M13 Ravensbourne *dist* Dunedin New Zealand
13 H6 Ravensbourne *R* Queensland
63 S6 Ravensbrück E Germany 53.12N 13.10E
64 H8 Ravensburg W Germany 47.47N 9.37E
57 N4 Ravenscar N Yorks Eng 54.24N 0.30W
100 H9 Ravenscrag Saskatchewan 49.30N 109.08W
13 H4 Ravenshoe Queensland 17.38S 145.30E
60 L12 Ravenstein Netherlands 51.47N 5.39E
14 D10 Ravensthorpe W Australia 33.34S 120.01E
57 J4 Ravenstonedale Cumbria Eng 54.26N 2.25W
13 H5 Ravenswood Queensland 20.05S 146.52E
104 D8 Ravenswood W Virginia 38.56N 81.44W
99 L7 Ravensworth Ontario 45.36N 79.06W
29 E7 Raver Maharashtra India 21.15N 76.05E
109 O7 Ravia Oklahoma 34.15N 96.46W
71 E1 Ravières France 47.43N 4.13E
103 B5 Ravine Pennsylvania 40.35N 76.24W
31 H5 Ravi R Pakistan etc
36 G2 Ravlı Turkey 40.07N 33.05E
82 G7 Ravna Reka Yugoslavia 44.00N 21.35E
65 L8 Ravne na Koroškem Yugoslavia 46.32N 14.57E
43 G7 Ravnina Turkmeniya U.S.S.R. 37.59N 62.45E
97 R4 Ravn, Kap *C* Greenland 68.30N 27.50W
53 D3 Ravnkilde Denmark 56.46N 9.45E
82 D8 Ravno Yugoslavia 42.54N 17.58E
82 E6 Ravno *mt* Yugoslavia 44.12N 18.14E
48 S14 Ravns Storø Greenland 62.45N 50.33W
53 C4 Ravnstrup Denmark 56.28N 9.17E
53 C6 Ravsted Denmark 55.01N 9.08E
84 B3 Ravtópoulon Greece 39.09N 21.29E
34 J4 Rāwah Iraq 34.30N 41.55E
31 G4 Rawala Kot Kashmir 33.50N 73.48E
31 G4 Rawalpindi Pakistan 33.40N 73.08E
31 G4 Rawalpindi *dist* Pakistan
101 Q3 Rawalpindi L N W Terr 65.00N 114.40W
62 M4 Rawa Mazowiecka Poland 51.46N 20.12E
34 M2 Rawāndiz Iraq 36.38N 44.32E
37 H9 Rawānduz *R* Iraq

Rawang *see* **Rabang** Xizang Zizhiqu
18 B8 **Rawang** Pen Malaysia 3.20N 101.34E
15 B4 **Rawas** Irian Jaya 1.07S 132.12E
18 E7 **Rawas** *R* Sumatra Indon
Rawashid *tribe see* **Rāshid** *tribe*
29 D3 **Rawatsar** Rajasthan India 29.13N 74.21E
18 G9 **Rawauncal** Java Indon 7.25S 106.37E
86 O9 **Rāwa, Wādī** *watercourse* Saudi Arabia
57 M5 **Rawcliffe** Humberside Eng 53.42N 0.58W
33 F9 **Rawḑah** Yemen 15.26N 44.13E
33 D3 **Rawḑah, Ar** Saudi Arabia 26.08N 40.37E
33 E6 **Rawḑah, Ar** Saudi Arabia 21.18N 42.55E
33 G9 **Rawḑah, Ar** S Yemen 14.29N 47.15E
34 K9 **Rawḑ, Ar** Saudi Arabia 29.48N 42.35E
99 R6 **Rawdon** Quebec 46.03N 73.42W
100 R4 **Rawebb** Manitoba 54.18N 100.20W
11 H2 **Rawene** New Zealand 35.26S 173.32E
34 E10 **Rawghah** *watercourse* Saudi Arabia
108 F7 **Rawhide Cr** Wyoming
25 E9 **Rawi** *isld* Thailand
62 K4 **Rawicz** Poland 51.38N 16.51E
66 F6 **Rawil Pass** Switzerland 46.23N 7.28E
35 F1 **Rawiye** Syria 33.07N 35.41E
14 F9 **Rawlinna** W Australia 31.00S 125.21E
108 C8 **Rawlins** Wyoming 41.46N 107.16W
14 F7 **Rawlinson, Mt** W Australia 25.50S 127.30E
14 G7 **Rawlinson Ra** W Australia
103 B7 **Rawlinsville** Pennsylvania 39.53N 76.16W
33 E6 **Rawshan, Ar** Saudi Arabia 20.03N 42.38E
121 E5 **Rawson** Buenos Aires Arg 34.34S 60.05W
121 D9 **Rawson** Chubut Arg 43.15S 65.06W
104 B6 **Rawson** Ohio 40.57N 83.46W
95 C9 **Rawsonville** S Africa 33.41S 19.19E
57 J5 **Rawtenstall** Lancs Eng 53.42N 2.18W
23 A4 **Rawu** Xizang Zizhiqu China 29.40N 96.41E
24 J11 **Rawu** Xizang Zizhiqu China 29.30N 96.44E
33 H9 **Rāwuk, Ar** S Yemen 15.44N 48.51E
33 B3 **Rawwafah, Ar** *anc site* Saudi Arabia 27.51N 36.10E
84 C2 **Ráxa** Greece 39.37N 21.44E
65 N6 **Raxalpe** *mts* Austria
30 H6 **Raxaul** Bihar India 26.58N 84.51E
111 O8 **Ray** Arizona 33.11N 110.59W
108 R1 **Ray** Minnesota 48.25N 93.12W
108 G1 **Ray** N Dakota 48.22N 103.11W
113 M4 **Ray** *R* Alaska
18 N5 **Raya** Borneo Indon 1.04N 118.34E
18 J6 **Raya, Bukit** *mt* Borneo Indon 1.35S 111.06E
18 K6 **Raya, Bukit** *mt* Borneo Indon 0.31S 112.37E
28 D3 **Rayachoti** Andhra Prad India 14.04N 78.46E
28 C3 **Rayadrug** Andhra Prad India 14.42N 76.48E
29 H8 **Rayagada** Orissa India 19.10N 83.28E
34 D5 **Rayak** Lebanon 33.52N 36.02E
31 G2 **Rayan** Pakistan 36.27N 72.24E
34 M2 **Rāyat** Iraq 36.42N 44.59E
98 N6 **Ray, C** Newfoundland 47.38N 59.18W
40 E7 **Raychikhinsk** U.S.S.R. 49.47N 129.21E
105 D6 **Ray City** Georgia 31.04N 83.13W
33 G6 **Raydā'** *gravel plain* Saudi Arabia
33 J9 **Raydat al 'Abd al Wadūd** S Yemen 15.01N 50.22E
33 H9 **Raydat al Jūhīyīn** S Yemen 15.13N 48.51E
33 H9 **Raydat al Ma'arah** S Yemen 15.11N 49.09E
71 G7 **Raye, la** *mt* France 44.50N 5.05E
32 G6 **Rāyen** Iran 29.35N 57.28E
46 R3 **Rayevskiy** U.S.S.R. 54.04N 54.51E
33 E9 **Rayghah** Yemen 15.36N 43.06E
45 Q8 **Raygorod** U.S.S.R. 48.26N 44.55E
43 C3 **Raygorodok** Kazakhstan U.S.S.R. 48.47N 52.56E
45 J8 **Raygorodok** Ukraine U.S.S.R. 48.54N 37.45E
33 L5 **Rayḩānī, Ar** Oman 23.38N 55.59E
112 L3 **Ray Hubbard L** *res* Texas
Rayin *see* **Rāyen**
40 N7 **Raykoke** *vol* Kuril Is U.S.S.R. 48.15N 153.15E
40 N7 **Raykoke, O** *isld* Kuril Is U.S.S.R. 48.15N 153.15E
56 N4 **Rayleigh** Essex Eng 51.36N 0.36E
33 E9 **Raymah, Jabal** *hills* Yemen
34 C10 **Rayman** *isld* Saudi Arabia 28.05N 35.03E
100 E9 **Raymond** Alberta 49.30N 112.41W
111 E4 **Raymond** California 37.12N 119.55W
72 K2 **Raymond** France 46.58N 2.40E
107 G2 **Raymond** Illinois 39.20N 89.32W
107 F9 **Raymond** Mississippi 32.13N 90.30W
108 F1 **Raymond** Montana 48.55N 104.33W
104 O3 **Raymond** New Hampshire 43.02N 71.11W
108 N5 **Raymond** S Dakota 44.56N 97.57W
112 N3 **Raymond** Texas 32.21N 94.58W
110 B3 **Raymond** Washington 46.42N 123.44W
12 K5 **Raymond Terrace** New S Wales 32.47S 151.45E
99 R2 **Raymondville** New York 44.48N 74.59W
112 K9 **Raymondville** Texas 26.30N 97.48W
100 N7 **Raymore** Saskatchewan 51.24N 104.34W
113 M4 **Ray Mountains** Alaska
113 L4 **Ray Mts** Alaska
33 F5 **Rayn, Ar** Saudi Arabia 23.33N 45.35E
56 M4 **Rayne** Essex Eng 51.53N 0.30E
107 D11 **Rayne** Louisiana 30.13N 92.18W
41 O2 **Raynera, Ostrov** *isld* Franz Josef Land U.S.S.R.
110 P2 **Raynesford** Montana 47.16N 110.44W
103 M3 **Raynham** Massachusetts 41.57N 71.04W
109 D7 **Rayo** New Mexico 34.14N 106.26W
71 J10 **Rayol** France 43.10N 6.30E
71 J10 **Rayol-Canadel-sur-Mer, le** France 43.10N 6.29E
115 K7 **Rayón** Mexico 21.52N 99.40W
115 J5 **Rayones** Mexico 25.00N 100.08W
25 F6 **Rayong** Thailand 12.38N 101.17E
75 K7 **Rayo, Sierra del** *mts* Spain
33 K8 **Raysūt** Oman 16.56N 54.00E
34 E10 **Rayth al Khayl** *watercourse* Saudi Arabia
95 M1 **Rayton** S Africa 25.45S 28.32E
24 H10 **Rayü** Xizang Zizhiqu China 31.04N 95.12E
107 E9 **Rayville** Louisiana 32.28N 91.46W
Rayyānah, Ar *see* **Rayyān, Ar**
33 J4 **Rayyān, Ar** Qatar, The Gulf 25.18N 51.29E
33 C5 **Rayyān, Ar** Saudi Arabia 23.33N 39.45E
33 C6 **Rayyān, Ar** Saudi Arabia 21.40N 39.55E
33 G8 **Rayyān, Ar** *hills* Yemen 16.45N 46.19E
33 C5 **Rayyis** Saudi Arabia 23.36N 38.35E
72 F5 **Razac-sur-l'Isle** France 45.10N 0.37E
31 B5 **Razai** Afghanistan 31.27N 62.43E
29 H8 **Razam** Andhra Prad India 18.27N 83.48E
32 C3 **Razan** Iran 35.22N 49.01E
32 C4 **Rāzān** Iran 33.33N 48.51E
31 E4 **Razani** Pakistan 32.47N 69.58E
35 G2 **Razaniye, Er** Syria 32.53N 35.51E
Razazah *see* **Rozāzah**
44 F7 **Razdan** Armenia U.S.S.R. 40.29N 44.45E
44 F7 **Razdan** *R* Armenia U.S.S.R.
46 H6 **Razdel'naya** Ukraine U.S.S.R. 46.50N 30.02E
42 E3 **Razdolinsk** U.S.S.R. 58.25N 94.40E
39 E3 **Razdol'noye** Magadan U.S.S.R. 63.40N 153.08E
40 E10 **Razdol'noye** Primor'ye U.S.S.R. 43.36N 131.57E
44 C9 **Razdol'noye** Ukraine U.S.S.R. 45.46N 33.29E
42 G6 **Razdol'ye** U.S.S.R. 52.28N 103.15E
45 M9 **Razdorskaya** U.S.S.R. 47.33N 40.39E
45 G8 **Razdory** Ukraine U.S.S.R. 48.20N 35.43E
32 C4 **Razeh** Iran 32.48N 48.05E
82 M6 **Razelm, L** Romania
72 G3 **Razès** France 46.02N 1.22E
82 K7 **Razgrad** Bulgaria 43.31N 26.33E
65 K3 **Ražice** Czechoslovakia 49.14N 14.07E
82 H9 **Razlog** Bulgaria 41.53N 23.28E
31 E4 **Razmak** Pakistan 32.41N 69.56E
23 C9 **Razor Hill** Hong Kong 22.19N 114.14E
70 A5 **Raz, Pte.du** France 48.02N 4.44W
45 D3 **Razrytoye** U.S.S.R. 53.28N 32.52E
Razshevatskaya *see* **Rasshevatskaya**
45 H6 **Razumnoye** U.S.S.R. 50.33N 36.43E
44 D1 **Razvil'noye** U.S.S.R. 46.14N 41.19E
86 A4 **Razzaq, Al** *oil well* Egypt 30.37N 28.54E
81 C1 **Razzoli, I** Sardinia 41.18N 9.22E
66 L7 **Re** Italy 46.08N 8.33E
107 B1 **Rea** Missouri 40.04N 94.45W
14 A1 **Reabold Hill** W Australia 31.57S 115.47E
113 S7 **Reaburn, Mt** Alaska 59.23N 138.40W
107 C8 **Reader** Arkansas 33.44N 93.06W
100 Q5 **Reader L** Manitoba 53.55N 101.20W
56 K5 **Reading** Berks Eng 51.28N 0.59W
116 H1 **Reading** Jamaica, W I 18.26N 77.57W
109 P3 **Reading** Kansas 38.32N 95.58W
106 K8 **Reading** Michigan 41.51N 84.46W
108 P6 **Reading** Minnesota 43.42N 95.41W
103 C6 **Reading** Pennsylvania 40.20N 75.55W
103 E5 **Readington** New Jersey 40.34N 74.44W
100 M9 **Readlyn** Saskatchewan 49.35N 105.40W
104 N4 **Readsboro** Vermont 42.45N 72.58W
106 D6 **Readstown** Wisconsin 43.27N 90.48W
112 L4 **Reagan** Texas 31.15N 96.49W
59 E5 **Rea, L** Galway Irish Rep 53.11N 8.35W
120 E7 **Real, Cord** *mts* Bolivia
77 D5 **Real de la Jara, El** Spain 37.57N 6.09W
111 H10 **Real del Castillo** Mexico 31.59N 116.19W
121 C5 **Real de Padre** Argentina 34.52S 67.46W
76 K8 **Real de San Vicente, El** Spain 40.09N 4.42W
96 R14 **Realejo Alto** Tenerife Canary Is 28.22N 16.35W
96 R14 **Realejo Bajo** Tenerife Canary Is 28.23N 16.35W
118 H9 **Realengo** Brazil 22.53S 43.26W
77 F8 **Reales** *mt* Spain 36.30N 5.12W
121 D5 **Realíco** Argentina 35.02S 64.14W
112 J8 **Realitos** Texas 27.27N 98.33W
72 J8 **Réalmont** France 43.46N 2.11E
81 F9 **Realmonte** Sicily 37.18N 13.28E
66 L5 **Realp** Switzerland 46.36N 8.31E
118 J2 **Real, R** Brazil
77 G7 **Real,Sierra** *mts* Spain
72 G7 **Réalville** France 44.07N 1.29E
25 G7 **Ream** Cambodia 10.31N 103.33E
103 B6 **Reamstown** Pennsylvania 40.13N 76.08W
122 G15 **Réao** *atoll* Tuamotu Is Pacific Oc 18.30S 136.24W
30 F5 **Rear** Nepal 27.55N 82.20E
59 F6 **Rear Cross** Tipperary Irish Rep 52.42N 8.15W
110 H2 **Reardan** Washington 47.40N 117.52W
56 J2 **Rearsby** Leics Eng 52.44N 1.01W
115 J4 **Reata** Mexico 26.08N 101.05W
80 G3 **Reatini, Monti** Italy
72 E7 **Réaup** France 44.05N 0.11E
72 D5 **Réaux** France 45.28N 0.22W
103 E6 **Reaville** New Jersey 40.28N 74.49W
58 Q9 **Reawick** Shetland Scotland 60.11N 1.25W
58 J1 **Reay** Highland Scotland 58.33N 3.47W
58 J1 **Reay Bridge** Highland Scotland 58.33N 3.46W
58 G2 **Reay Forest** Highland Scotland
30 C7 **Rebai** Uttar Prad India 25.21N 79.28E
69 E6 **Rebais** France 48.51N 3.15E
61 F4 **Rebaix** Belgium 50.39N 3.47E
75 K8 **Rebalsadores** *mt* Spain 39.42N 0.28W
51 G1 **Rebbenesøy** *isld* Norway 70.04N 18.50E
118 A4 **Rebeca, L.da** Brazil 15.44S 60.02W
105 D6 **Rebecca** Georgia 31.48N 83.31W
14 D9 **Rebecca, L** W Australia
61 G4 **Rebecq-Rognon** Belgium 50.40N 4.08E
110 H8 **Rebel Creek** Nevada 41.37N 117.46W
63 T5 **Rebelow** E Germany 53.46N 13.31E
72 D9 **Rébénacq** France 43.09N 0.23W
101 P3 **Rebesca L** N W Terr
15 C7 **Rebi** Moluccas Indon 6.24S 134.08E
85 G7 **Rebiana** Libya 24.14N 22.00E
85 E7 **Rebiana Sand Sea** Libya
53 D3 **Rebild** Denmark 56.51N 9.53E
76 L3 **Rebolledo de la Torre** Spain 42.41N 4.14W
77 H4 **Rebollera** *mt* Spain 38.25N 4.02W
75 E5 **Rebollosa de Jadraque** Spain 41.05N 2.51W
47 C4 **Reboly** U.S.S.R. 63.50N 30.49E
76 F5 **Rebordãos** Portugal 41.44N 6.49W
76 E5 **Rebordelo** Portugal 41.43N 7.09W
42 C5 **Rebrikha** U.S.S.R. 53.05N 82.18E
82 H8 **Rebrovo** Bulgaria 42.52N 23.21E
66 P2 **Rebstein** Switzerland 47.24N 9.35E
21 H5 **Rebun-tō** *isld* Japan 45.25N 141.04E
121 E6 **Recalde** Argentina 36.40S 61.02W
80 J2 **Recanati** Italy 43.24N 13.32E
82 G5 **Recaş** Romania 45.46N 21.30E
88 T3 **Recas** *mt* Tunisia 36.39N 10.18E
79 F6 **Recco** Italy 44.22N 9.08E
82 H6 **Recea** Romania 44.20N 22.52E
59 C5 **Recess** Galway Irish Rep 52.28N 9.43W
69 H8 **Recey-sur-Ouree** France 47.47N 4.52E
14 D10 **Recherche, Arch.of the** W Australia
26 N13 **Recherche, Pte.de la** Amsterdam I Ind Oc 37.49S 77.30E
69 M6 **Réchicourt-le-Château** France 48.40N 6.50E
45 B4 **Rechitsa** Belorussiya U.S.S.R. 52.21N 30.24E
45 K1 **Rechitsy** U.S.S.R. 55.36N 38.28E
63 R6 **Rechlin** E Germany 53.22N 12.44E
31 G5 **Rechna Doab** *interfluve* Pakistan
40 J7 **Rechnaya** Sakhalin U.S.S.R. 49.15N 143.12E
65 O7 **Rechnitz** Austria 47.19N 16.26E
61 P5 **Recht** Belgium 50.20N 6.03E
82 C5 **Rečica** Yugoslavia 45.30N 15.40E
117 J9 **Recife** Brazil 8.06S 34.53W
95 J10 **Recife, C** S Africa 34.02S 25.42E
26 R12 **Recif I** Seychelles, Ind Oc 4.36S 55.42E
121 B6 **Recinto** Chile 36.50S 71.45W
61 P8 **Reckange** Luxembourg 49.34N 6.00E
63 G8 **Recke** W Germany 52.22N 7.44E
66 J6 **Reckingen** Switzerland 46.28N 8.15E
63 F9 **Recklinghausen** W Germany 51.37N 7.11E
63 R4 **Recknitz** *R* E Germany
71 K2 **Réclère** Switzerland 47.22N 6.57E
69 E3 **Récluse** France 50.16N 3.02E
108 E5 **Recluse** Wyoming 44.45N 105.42W
79 K3 **Recoaro Terme** Italy 45.42N 11.13E
61 M7 **Recogne** Belgium 49.55N 5.22E
121 G9 **Recoleta** *dist* Santiago Chile
121 F2 **Reconquista** Argentina 29.08S 59.38W
66 E3 **Reconvilier** Switzerland 47.14N 7.14E
71 G7 **Recoubeau** France 44.39N 5.24E
72 K7 **Recoules-Prévinquières** France 44.21N 2.57E
123 E10 **Recovery Glacier** Antarctica
117 A9 **Recreio** Brazil 8.10S 58.13W
121 D2 **Recreo** Catamarca Argentina 29.18S 65.05W
14 C8 **Recruit Flats** *salt pan* W Australia
107 F5 **Rector** Arkansas 36.15N 90.20W
75 F6 **Recuenco, El** Spain 40.36N 2.20W
75 E5 **Recuerda** Spain 41.28N 3.00W
25 K5 **Re, Cu Lao** *isld* Vietnam 15.22N 109.07E
88 S8 **Reculée, La** Algeria 28.00N 9.10E
56 O5 **Reculver** Kent Eng 51.23N 1.12E
62 J2 **Recz** Poland 53.17N 15.34E
97 K8 **Red** *R* Manitoba/N Dak
107 J5 **Red** *R* Tennessee
102 H4 **Red** *R* U.S.A.
95 L2 **Redan** S Africa 26.37S 27.58E
18 E3 **Redang** *isld* Pen Malaysia
61 O7 **Redange-sur-Attert** Luxembourg 49.46N 5.53E
18 A6 **Redang Panjang** Pen Malaysia 5.06N 100.45E
104 B3 **Red Bank** Camden, N J 39.52N 75.10W
103 F6 **Red Bank** Monmouth, New Jersey 40.21N 74.04W
98 G7 **Red Bank** New Brunswick 46.56N 65.51W
13 K7 **Redbank** Queensland 25.32S 150.36E
92 D11 **Redbank** Zimbabwe 19.58S 28.21E
Red Basin *see* **Sichuan Pendi**
107 H7 **Red Bay** Alabama 34.25N 86.08W
59 K1 **Red Bay** Antrim N Ireland 55.04N 6.02W
105 B7 **Redbay** Florida 30.34N 85.58W
98 Q2 **Red Bay** Labrador, Nfld 51.46N 56.24W
99 J8 **Red Bay** Ontario 44.47N 81.19W
100 K6 **Redberry L** Saskatchewan
108 F6 **Redbird** Wyoming 43.16N 104.19W
112 N9 **Red Bird Airfield** Texas 32.41N 96.55W
110 C9 **Red Bluff** California 40.11N 122.16W
13 G3 **Red Bluff** Queensland 15.40S 144.26E
14 C6 **Red Bluff** *mt* W Australia 24.39S 119.28E
14 A6 **Red Bluff** *pt* W Australia 24.03S 113.30E
112 D4 **Red Bluff Res** Texas 31.58N 103.56W
107 L5 **Red Boiling Springs** Tennessee 36.31N 85.51W
56 L4 **Redbourn** Herts Eng 51.48N 0.24W
57 M6 **Redbourne** Humberside Eng 53.30N 0.32W
55 H2 **Redbridge** *bor* London Eng
56 F4 **Redbrook** Glos Eng 51.48N 2.40W
107 G3 **Red Bud** Illinois 38.12N 90.00W
111 M6 **Red Butte** *mt* Arizona 35.50N 112.07W
108 E8 **Red Buttes** Wyoming 41.10N 105.35W
108 Q2 **Redby** Minnesota 47.52N 94.53W
57 L3 **Redcar** Cleveland Eng 54.37N 1.04W
58 H3 **Redcastle** Highland Scotland 57.31N 4.22W
100 G8 **Redcliff** Alberta 50.06N 110.48W
109 D2 **Red Cliff** Colorado 39.31N 106.22W
92 D11 **Redcliff** Zimbabwe 19.00S 29.49E
13 L7 **Redcliffe** Queensland 27.12S 153.03E
14 D8 **Redcliffe, Mt** W Australia 28.25S 121.38E
11 N10 **Redcliffs** New Zealand 43.34S 172.45E
12 F5 **Red Cliffs** Victoria 34.22S 142.13E
108 M9 **Red Cloud** Nebraska 40.04N 98.31W
107 H11 **Red Cr** Mississippi
108 B8 **Red Cr** Wyoming
104 J3 **Red Creek** New York 43.15N 76.44W
103 A5 **Red Cross** Pennsylvania 40.43N 76.46W
100 D6 **Red Deer** Alberta 52.15N 113.48W
100 Q6 **Red Deer L** Manitoba
100 E7 **Red Deer R** Alberta
100 P6 **Red Deer R** Saskatchewan
107 D11 **Reddell** Louisiana 30.41N 92.28W
95 K5 **Reddersburg** S Africa 29.40S 26.10E
113 J6 **Red Devil** Alaska 61.45N 157.19W
57 G3 **Red Dial** Cumbria Eng 54.48N 3.10W
105 E8 **Reddick** Florida 29.21N 82.12W
110 C9 **Redding** California 40.35N 122.24W
103 H4 **Redding** Connecticut 41.19N 73.22W
100 H1 **Reddit** Ontario 50.00N 94.20W
56 H3 **Redditch** Hereford & Worcs Eng 52.19N 1.56W
63 O6 **Redefin** E Germany 53.22N 11.13E
94 E9 **Redelinghuys** S Africa 32.30S 18.30E
108 J4 **Red Elm** S Dakota 45.05N 101.48W
117 H7 **Redencão** Ceará Brazil 4.14S 38.46W
117 F9 **Redenção** Piauí Brazil 9.30S 44.38W
70 D6 **Redené** France 47.51N 3.28W
57 J2 **Rede, R** Northumb Eng
71 F9 **Redessan** France 43.50N 4.31E
88 S4 **Redeyef** Tunisia 34.24N 8.10E
12 M7 **Redfern** *dist* Sydney, N S W
107 D7 **Redfield** Arkansas 34.25N 92.10W
108 Q8 **Redfield** Iowa 41.36N 94.10W
108 M5 **Redfield** S Dakota 44.51N 98.31W
110 L5 **Redfish L** Idaho 44.07N 114.56W
112 C6 **Redford** Texas 29.26N 104.12W
106 E5 **Redgranite** Wisconsin 44.02N 89.06W
116 P1 **Redhead** Trinidad & Tobago 10.44N 60.58W
11 B13 **Red Head Pt, South** Stewart I New Zealand 47.05S 167.34E
56 F5 **Redhill** Avon Eng 51.23N 2.43W
12 E5 **Red Hill** S Australia 33.34S 138.12E
56 L5 **Redhill** Surrey Eng 51.14N 0.11W
12 A6 **Red Hill** *dist* Canberra Australia
11 H8 **Red Hill** *mt* New Zealand 41.38S 173.03E
14 B7 **Red Hill** *pk* W Australia 25.15S 115.44E
96 B12 **Red Hill, Mt** Ascension I 7.58S 14.22W
107 K10 **Red Hills** Alabama
59 H3 **Redhills** Cavan Irish Rep 54.06N 7.19W
105 F4 **Red Hills** S Carolina
58 E4 **Red Hills** Skye, Highland Scotland
103 G3 **Red Hook** New York 41.59N 73.52W
110 H8 **Red House** Nevada 41.01N 117.16W
95 J9 **Redhouse** S Africa 33.50S 25.35E
26 A15 **Red I** Heard I Antarctica 52.57S 73.17E
98 S6 **Red I** Newfoundland 47.25N 54.10W
65 O8 **Rédics** Hungary 46.36N 16.28E
28 G1 **Red Idol Gorge** Xizang Zizhiqu 28.41N 89.33E
108 G4 **Redig** S Dakota 45.16N 103.32W
98 P5 **Red Indian L** Newfoundland
69 N6 **Réding** France 48.45N 7.05E
111 O9 **Redington** Arizona 32.26N 110.30W
108 G8 **Redington** Nebraska 41.36N 103.17W
76 B8 **Redinha** Portugal 40.01N 8.36W
79 O3 **Redipuglia** Italy 45.51N 13.29E
106 J9 **Redkey** Indiana 40.21N 85.08W
46 K2 **Redkino** U.S.S.R. 56.39N 36.18E
101 O5 **Redknife** *R* N W Terr
111 K6 **Red L** Arizona 35.40N 114.05W
12 D4 **Red L** S Australia 30.14S 136.53E
111 M6 **Red Lake** Arizona 35.24N 112.09W
97 K7 **Red Lake** Ontario 50.59N 93.40W
14 D10 **Red Lake** W Australia 33.10S 121.40E
108 P1 **Red Lake** *R* Minnesota
108 O2 **Red Lake Falls** Minnesota 47.52N 96.10W
105 B11 **Redland** Florida 25.32N 80.30W
111 G7 **Redlands** California 34.03N 117.10W
103 E7 **Red Lion** New Jersey 39.53N 74.43W
103 A7 **Red Lion** Pennsylvania 39.53N 76.37W
108 P2 **Red L., Lower** Minnesota
110 Q4 **Red Lodge** Montana 45.10N 109.15W
100 C7 **Red Lodge Prov.Park** Alberta 51.58N 114.12W
108 Q1 **Red L., Upper** Minnesota
11 K3 **Red Mercury I** New Zealand 36.40S 175.58E
57 K4 **Redmire** N Yorks Eng 54.19N 1.56W
107 J2 **Redmon** Illinois 39.39N 87.52W
110 D5 **Redmond** Oregon 44.16N 121.10W
111 N2 **Redmond** Utah 39.01N 111.52W
111 G6 **Red Mountain** California 35.22N 117.35W
110 B8 **Red Mt** California 41.34N 123.06W
64 L5 **Rednitz** *R* W Germany
93 L6 **Redo** Kenya 0.26S 39.20E
108 P8 **Red Oak** Iowa 41.01N 95.15W
109 P7 **Red Oak** Oklahoma 34.57N 95.06W
112 L3 **Red Oak** Texas 32.32N 96.47W
103 G3 **Red Oaks Mill** New York 41.39N 73.53W
70 F6 **Redon** France 47.39N 2.05W
116 N6 **Redonda** *I* Leeward Is W I 16.58N 62.19W
76 B4 **Redondela** Spain 42.17N 8.36W
76 D11 **Redondo** Portugal 38.38N 7.32W
76 L3 **Redondo-Areños** Spain 43.00N 4.28W
111 F8 **Redondo Beach** California 33.51N 118.24W
119 G6 **Redondo, Pico** *pk* Brazil 2.29N 63.27W
66 L6 **Redorta, Passo di** Switzerland 46.22N 8.44E
79 G2 **Redorta, Pizzo** *mt* Italy 46.04N 9.59E
113 L6 **Redoubt Vol** Alaska 60.30N 152.46W
101 O9 **Red Pass** Br Col 53.02N 119.08W
100 J6 **Red Pheasant** Saskatchewan 52.29N 108.17W
58 E3 **Redpoint** Highland Scotland 57.39N 5.49W
13 G2 **Red Pt** Queensland 14.32S 144.50E
101 J6 **Red R** Br Col
13 G3 **Red R** Queensland
Red R Vietnam*see* **Song Koi**
98 E7 **Red Rapids** New Brunswick 46.47N 67.30W
110 K4 **Red River Hot Springs** Idaho 45.49N 115.11W
25 J2 **Red R., Mouths of the** Vietnam
111 N9 **Redrock** Arizona 32.35N 111.19W
109 B9 **Red Rock** New Mexico 32.42N 108.44W
109 N5 **Red Rock** Oklahoma 36.27N 97.13W
99 B4 **Red Rock** Ontario 48.57N 88.18W
103 B4 **Red Rock** Pennsylvania 41.17N 76.18W
112 K6 **Red Rock** Texas 29.59N 97.28W
111 A8 **Red Rock** *isld* California 37.55N 122.26W
101 Q3 **Redrock L** N W Terr 65.22N 114.11W
14 G9 **Red Rocks Pt** W Australia 32.11S 127.31E
56 B4 **Red Roses** Dyfed Wales 51.47N 4.36W
56 T9 **Redruth** Cornwall Eng 50.13N 5.14W
27 D4 **Red Sea** Africa/Asia
85 N10 **Red Sea** *prov* Sudan
105 H3 **Red Springs** N Carolina 34.49N 79.11W
101 M9 **Redstone** Br Col 52.13N 123.50W
108 F1 **Redstone** Montana 48.50N 104.58W
101 K4 **Redstone** *R* N W Terr
99 J4 **Redstone** *R* Ontario
115 F10 **Red Tank** Panama Canal Zone 9.01N 79.36W
61 L6 **Redu** Belgium 50.00N 5.10E
46 Q6 **Redut** Kazakhstan U.S.S.R. 47.22N 51.49E
100 Q9 **Redvers** Saskatchewan 49.34N 101.42W
100 D5 **Redwater** Alberta 53.57N 113.06W
99 L6 **Redwater** Ontario 46.54N 79.40W
112 N2 **Redwater** Texas 33.22N 94.15W
108 E2 **Redwater Cr** Montana
14 C7 **Red Well** W Australia 26.32S 118.20E
57 E6 **Redwharf B** Gwynedd Wales 53.18N 4.10W
100 E6 **Red Willow** Alberta 52.29N 112.35W
109 H1 **Red Willow Cr** Colorado
108 J9 **Red Willow Cr** Nebraska
108 S5 **Red Wing** Minnesota 44.33N 92.31W
64 L3 **Redwitz** W Germany 50.11N 11.13E
107 F9 **Redwood** Mississippi 32.28N 90.48W
108 P5 **Redwood** *R* Minnesota
111 B4 **Redwood City** California 37.28N 122.15W
108 P5 **Redwood Falls** Minnesota 44.30N 95.06W
111 A2 **Redwood Valley** California 39.17N 123.12W
95 H6 **Reebokrand** S Africa 30.04S 24.57E
106 J6 **Reed City** Michigan 43.54N 85.31W
108 H3 **Reeder** N Dakota 46.07N 102.58W
56 P2 **Reedham** Norfolk Eng 52.34N 1.34E
100 R4 **Reed L** Manitoba 54.40N 100.30W
111 E5 **Reedley** California 36.35N 119.27W
110 Q4 **Reedpoint** Montana 45.42N 109.34W
106 E6 **Reedsburg** Wisconsin 43.30N 89.59W
109 C8 **Reeds Pk** New Mexico 33.09N 107.52W
110 A6 **Reedsport** Oregon 43.42N 124.05W
104 D7 **Reedsville** Ohio 39.07N 81.43W
104 D8 **Reedy** W Virginia 38.54N 81.26W
13 H5 **Reedy** *R* Queensland
12 D4 **Reedy L** S Australia 30.20S 136.04E
105 E3 **Reedy, R** S Carolina
13 G4 **Reedy Springs** Queensland 19.55S 144.30E
9 C10 **Reef Islets** New Hebrides 13.35S 167.30E
11 K13 **Reef Pt** Antipodes Is Pacific Oc 49.40S 178.51E
95 H10 **Reef Pt** S Africa 34.12S 24.36E
11 F9 **Reefton** New Zealand 42.05S 171.51E
108 L5 **Ree Heights** S Dakota 44.30N 99.14W
60 L13 **Reek** Netherlands 51.45N 5.41E
59 G4 **Ree, L** Roscommon Irish Rep 53.30N 8.00W
107 G5 **Reelfoot L** Tennessee
56 O2 **Reepham** Norfolk Eng 52.46N 1.07E
63 G6 **Reepsholt** W Germany 53.29N 7.51E
53 G5 **Reersø** Denmark 55.32N 11.08E
63 D9 **Rees** W Germany 51.45N 6.25E
106 L6 **Reese** Michigan 43.28N 83.41W
110 H9 **Reese** *R* Nevada
99 G3 **Reesor** Ontario 49.34N 83.06W
60 O9 **Reest** *R* Netherlands
61 H2 **Reet** Belgium 51.06N 4.25E
57 K4 **Reeth** N Yorks Eng 54.23N 1.56W
63 P6 **Reetz** E Germany 53.11N 11.53E
60 G11 **Reeuwijkdorp** Netherlands 52.03N 4.44E
123 J6 **Reeves Glacier** Antarctica 74.45S 162.00E
37 D6 **Refahiye** Turkey 39.54N 38.45E
34 D6 **Refa'i, Tell** *mt* Jordan 32.19N 36.46E
107 H8 **Reform** Alabama 33.22N 88.01W
115 N9 **Reforma** Mexico 17.52N 93.09W
120 D11 **Refresco** Chile 25.19S 69.50W
53 F6 **Refs** Denmark 55.17N 10.41E
47 N4 **Reft** *R* U.S.S.R.
52 H9 **Reftele** Sweden 57.11N 13.35E
47 N4 **Reftinskiy** U.S.S.R. 57.04N 61.40E
103 B7 **Refton** Pennsylvania 39.57N 76.14W
112 K7 **Refugio** Texas 28.19N 97.18W
121 A9 **Refugio** *isld* Chile 44.00S 73.10W
62 J2 **Rega** *R* Poland
81 J8 **Regalbuto** Sicily 37.38N 14.38E
108 K2 **Regan** N Dakota 47.10N 100.31W
99 E4 **Regan** Ontario 48.42N 85.37W
77 V15 **Regana, C** Balearic Is 39.25N 2.44E
43 J7 **Regar** Tadzhikistan U.S.S.R. 38.32N 68.15E
35 D3 **Regavim** Israel 32.32N 35.02E
35 D2 **Regba** Israel 32.59N 35.06E
89 B3 **Regba** Mauritania 16.40N 14.43W
88 K8 **Regbat** *tribe* Algeria
66 N3 **Regelstein** *mt* Switzerland 47.15N 9.05E
64 P6 **Regen** W Germany 48.58N 13.09E
64 N5 **Regen** *R* W Germany
118 H6 **Regência** Brazil 19.38S 39.53W
66 K2 **Regensberg** Switzerland 47.29N 8.26E
64 N5 **Regensburg** W Germany 49.01N 12.07E
66 K2 **Regensdorf** Switzerland 47.26N 8.28E
64 N5 **Regenstauf** W Germany 49.07N 12.09E
100 R9 **Regent** Manitoba 49.21N 100.20W
108 H3 **Regent** N Dakota 46.26N 102.31W
99 F5 **Regent** Ontario 47.14N 84.25W
12 K7 **Regents Park** *dist* Sydney, N S W
88 O8 **Reggane** Algeria 26.42N 0.13E
63 E8 **Regge** *R* Netherlands
79 L7 **Reggello** Italy 43.41N 11.32E
81 L7 **Réggio Calábria** Italy 38.06N 15.39E
79 J5 **Reggiolo** Italy 44.55N 10.48E
79 J5 **Reggio nell'Emilia** Italy 44.42N 10.37E
79 J5 **Reggio nell 'Emilia** *prov* Italy
82 J4 **Reghin** Romania 46.46N 24.41E
31 C4 **Regi** Afghanistan 32.13N 64.51E
117 C3 **Regina** Brazil 2.35N 51.43W
117 C2 **Régina** Fr Guiana 4.20N 52.07W
95 K3 **Regina** S Africa 27.04S 26.32E
100 N8 **Regina** Saskatchewan 50.30N 104.38W
100 N8 **Regina Beach** Saskatchewan 50.48N 104.59W
64 N1 **Regis** E Germany 51.05N 12.27E
31 C5 **Registan** *reg* Afghanistan
118 D4 **Registro do Araguaia** Brazil 15.45S 51.44W
52 J8 **Regna** Sweden 58.54N 15.42E
70 G3 **Regnéville** France 49.01N 1.33W
69 G4 **Régniowez** France 49.56N 4.26E
64 K4 **Regnitz** *R* W Germany
71 E5 **Regny** France 46.00N 4.12E
87 C8 **Rego** Sudan 5.30N 31.21E
66 O7 **Regoledo** Italy 46.02N 9.18E
28 K1 **Regong** Assam India 28.30N 94.25E
88 H8 **Regueibat** *tribe* Mauritania
76 A10 **Reguengo Grande** Portugal 39.17N 9.12W
76 D12 **Reguengos de Monsaraz** Portugal 38.25N 7.32W
70 E6 **Reguiny** France 47.58N 2.44W
88 J5 **Rehamna** *tribe* Morocco
64 N3 **Rehau** W Germany 50.14N 12.03E
35 B1 **Rehavya** *sub* Jerusalem
Rehberg *see* **Bad Rehberg**
64 D5 **Reh Berg** *mt* W Germany 49.11N 8.00E
63 H7 **Rehden** W Germany 52.37N 8.30E
66 O2 **Rehetobel** Switzerland 47.26N 9.29E
63 Q7 **Rehfeld** E Germany 52.57N 12.20E
87 G2 **Rehib** Ethiopia 17.30N 38.42E
29 F6 **Rehli** Madhya Prad India 23.38N 79.08E
63 J8 **Rehme** W Germany 52.13N 8.49E
63 O5 **Rehna** E Germany 53.47N 11.03E
103 M3 **Rehoboth** Massachusetts 41.51N 71.15W
94 C1 **Rehoboth** Namibia 17.54S 15.10E
94 D4 **Rehoboth** Namibia 23.18S 17.03E
104 K8 **Rehoboth B** Delaware
104 K8 **Rehoboth Beach** Delaware 38.42N 75.06W
35 E4 **Reḩov** Israel 32.27N 35.29E
35 C6 **Reḩovot** Israel 31.54N 34.49E
30 B4 **Rehra** Uttar Prad India 28.31N 78.19E
30 F5 **Rehra Bazar** Uttar Prad India 27.11N 82.16E
103 B6 **Rehrersburg** Pennsylvania 40.28N 76.15W
90 G7 **Rei** *R* Cameroon
15 K6 **Reibeck B** New Britain
Reibell *see* **Chellala**
90 G7 **Reï Bouba** Cameroon 8.37N 14.11E
64 F3 **Reichelshausen** W Germany 50.21N 8.52E
64 F4 **Reichelsheim** W Germany 49.43N 8.51E
64 G8 **Reichenau I** W Germany 47.42N 9.05E
Reichenbach *see* **Klosterreichenbach**
64 N2 **Reichenbach** E Germany 50.36N 12.18E
66 G5 **Reichenbach** Switzerland 46.38N 7.42E
69 Q4 **Reichenbach** W Germany 49.43N 8.41E
66 J5 **Reichenbach Fall** Switzerland 46.43N 8.12E
64 D4 **Reichenbach-Steegen** W Germany 49.30N 7.33E
66 M3 **Reichenburg** Switzerland 47.10N 8.58E
65 L7 **Reichenfels** Austria 47.01N 14.45E
64 J1 **Reichensachsen** W Germany 51.10N 10.00E
65 F7 **Reichen-Spitze** *mt* Austria 47.09N 12.07E
64 N7 **Reichertsheim** W Germany 48.12N 12.19E
64 L6 **Reichertshofen** W Germany 43.39N 11.30E
64 M6 **Reichertshofen** W Germany 48.35N 11.31E
110 N4 **Reichle** Montana 45.29N 112.40W
65 K6 **Reichraming** Austria 47.54N 14.28E
64 D2 **Reichshof** W Germany 50.59N 7.42E
69 O6 **Reichshoffen** France 48.56N 7.40E
14 G9 **Reid** W Australia 30.48S 128.17E
12 A6 **Reid** *dist* Canberra Australia
87 K9 **Reidabderei** Somalia 2.21N 44.30E
66 H3 **Reiden** Switzerland 47.14N 7.59E
66 F5 **Reidenbach** Switzerland 46.38N 7.23E
100 J8 **Reid L** Saskatchewan
61 O5 **Reid, La** Belgium 50.29N 5.47E
13 B4 **Reid, Mt** N Terr Australia 17.56S 130.36E
13 H4 **Reid R** Queensland 19.45S 146.48E
9 U2 **Reid Reef** Fiji 17.55S 178.20W
105 E5 **Reidsville** Georgia 32.04N 82.07W
105 H1 **Reidsville** N Carolina 36.21N 79.40W
56 L5 **Reigate** Surrey Eng 51.14N 0.13W
15 E6 **Reiger** *R* Irian Jaya
57 N4 **Reighton** N Yorks Eng 54.10N 0.16W
72 C5 **Reignac** Gironde France 45.14N 0.32W
72 F1 **Reignac-sur-Indre** Indre-et-Loire France 47.14N 0.54E
71 J4 **Reignier** France 46.08N 6.16E
64 G2 **Reigoldswil** Switzerland 47.24N 7.42E
72 B3 **Ré, Ile de** France 46.10N 1.26W
111 O9 **Reiley Pk** Arizona 32.24N 110.06W
72 G6 **Reilhaguet** France 44.46N 1.30E
64 F5 **Reilingen** W Germany 49.17N 8.35E
71 H9 **Reillanne** France 43.52N 5.39E
75 G8 **Reillo** Spain 39.54N 1.53W
35 A8 **Re'im** Israel 31.23N 34.27E
Reima, Jabal *see* **Raymah, Jabal** *hills*
53 V17 **Reimegrend** Norway 60.41N 6.44E
69 G5 **Reims** France 49.15N 4.02E
69 G5 **Reims, Mtgne de** France
35 G4 **Reimun** Jordan 32.17N 35.49E
35 E3 **Reina** Israel 32.43N 35.19E
77 E4 **Reina** Spain 38.11N 5.57W
121 J9 **Reina Adelaida, Arch.de la** Chile
66 J2 **Reinach** Aargau Switzerland 47.16N 8.12E
66 G2 **Reinach** Baselland Switzerland 47.30N 7.36E
108 S7 **Reinbeck** Iowa 42.20N 92.33W
63 M5 **Reinbek** W Germany 53.31N 10.15E
63 S4 **Reinberg** E Germany 54.13N 13.15E
53 X14 **Reindalsseter** Norway 62.12N 7.35E
101 W7 **Reindeer L** Manitoba/Sask
101 W8 **Reindeer R** Saskatchewan
51 C4 **Reine** Norway 67.57N 13.05E
13 D6 **Reinecke, Mt** N Terr Australia 23.01S 137.30E
100 U6 **Reineer I** Manitoba
103 A5 **Reinerton** Pennsylvania 40.36N 76.30W
53 Y17 **Reineskarvet** *mt* Norway 60.46N 8.12E
53 Y17 **Reinestølen** Buskerud Norway 60.45N 8.17E
63 M5 **Reinfeld** W Germany 53.49N 10.29E
11 G1 **Reinga, C** New Zealand 34.26S 172.41E
63 L10 **Reinhausen** W Germany 51.28N 9.59E
64 C5 **Reinheim** W Germany 49.08N 7.12E
64 F4 **Reinheim** W Germany 49.49N 8.50E
103 B6 **Reinholds** Pennsylvania 40.16N 76.07W
63 S7 **Reinickendorf** W Berlin W Germany 52.35N 13.22E
63 T7 **Reinickendorf** W Germany 52.38N 13.20E
66 E1 **Reiningue** France 47.45N 7.15E
76 L2 **Reinosa** Spain 43.01N 4.09W
51 H2 **Reinøy** *isld* Norway 69.55N 19.40E
64 P1 **Reinsberg** E Germany 51.00N 13.22E
63 B8 **Reinsbüttel** W Germany 54.12N 8.55E
64 B4 **Reinsfeld** W Germany 49.40N 6.53E
53 X19 **Reinshornnuten** *mt* Norway 59.57N 7.55E
53 V19 **Reinsnosvatn** *L* Norway 59.57N 6.41E
63 P5 **Reinstorf** E Germany 53.51N 11.38E
53 Y13 **Reinsvatn** *L* Norway 62.33N 8.23E
51 J2 **Reisa** *R* Norway
65 H8 **Reisach** Austria 46.39N 13.10E
64 O6 **Reisbach** W Germany 48.35N 12.39E
66 O5 **Reischen** Switzerland 46.38N 9.27E
61 Q7 **Reisdorf** Luxembourg 49.52N 6.16E
95 E10 **Reisiesbaan** S Africa 34.10S 21.22E
51 L8 **Reisjarvi** Finland 63.38N 24.55E
58 K2 **Reiss** Highland Scotland 58.28N 3.09W
65 H8 **Reisseck** *mt* Austria 46.58N 13.23E
104 J7 **Reisterstown** Maryland 39.27N 76.51W
53 Y14 **Reitan** Norway 62.28N 8.11E
81 H8 **Reitano** Sicily 37.58N 14.21E
65 G6 **Reiter Alpen** *mts* Austria
65 J7 **Reitereck** *mt* Austria 47.02N 13.32E
64 N8 **Reit-i-Winkl** W Germany 47.40N 12.30E
66 J2 **Reitnau** Switzerland 47.15N 8.03E
94 Q11 **Reitvlei** *pond* Cape Town S Africa 33.51S 18.30E
95 M3 **Reitz** S Africa 27.48S 28.26E
64 P2 **Reitzenhain** E Germany 50.34N 13.13E
95 H3 **Reivilo** S Africa 27.34S 24.11E
87 C8 **Rejaf** Sudan 4.47N 31.35E
90 B6 **Rejau** Nigeria 11.08N 5.16E
52 J8 **Rejmyra** Sweden 58.50N 15.55E
62 O4 **Rejowiec** Poland 51.06N 23.18E
53 B6 **Rejsby** Denmark 55.14N 8.43E
64 Q5 **Rejštejn** Czechoslovakia 49.09N 13.32E
119 G5 **Rejunya** Venezuela 4.44N 65.15W
28 E2 **Rekapalle** Andhra Prad India 17.33N 81.27E
122 E15 **Rékaréka** *atoll* Tuamotu Is Pacific Oc 16.45S 141.50W
52 J7 **Rekarne** Sweden 59.25N 16.05E
53 V13 **Rekdal** Norway 62.38N 6.45E
61 N3 **Rekem** Belgium 50.56N 5.42E
63 F9 **Reken** W Germany 51.47N 7.03E
31 D6 **Rekgwash** Pakistan 29.16N 67.18E
35 C9 **Rekhes Yeroham** *hills* Israel
20 M2 **Rekifune-gawa** *R* Japan
39 G4 **Rekinniki** U.S.S.R. 60.50N 163.40E
39 G4 **Rekinninskaya, Guba** *gulf* U.S.S.R.
61 C3 **Rekkem** Belgium 50.47N 3.10E
60 P11 **Rekken** Netherlands 52.07N 6.43E
112 N4 **Reklaw** Texas 31.52N 95.01W
Rekohua *isld see* **Chatham I.** Chatham Is
82 G7 **Rekovac** Yugoslavia 43.51N 21.03E
53 Y18 **Reksjåeggin** *mt* Norway 60.04N 8.08E
53 R15 **Reksta** *isld* Norway 61.34N 4.50E
53 S18 **Reksteren** *isld* Norway 60.03N 5.25E
50 O10 **Rekvedbukta** *B* Jan Mayen I 70.56N 8.30W
70 B5 **Relecq-Kerhoun,le** France 48.25N 4.25W
105 E6 **Relee** Georgia 31.44N 82.58W
Relegem *see* **Zellik**
101 T4 **Reliance** N W Terr 62.45N 109.08W
108 L6 **Reliance** S Dakota 43.54N 99.35W
110 Q8 **Reliance** Wyoming 41.40N 109.11W
81 J10 **Religione, Pta** Sicily 36.43N 14.47E
76 C13 **Relíquias** Portugal 37.42N 8.30W
88 O4 **Relizane** Algeria 35.44N 0.35E
115 G4 **Rellano** Mexico 26.54N 104.29W
77 Q3 **Relleu** Spain 38.36N 0.19W
28 F2 **Relli** Andhra Prad India 17.53N 83.17E
96 T1 **Relva** Azores 37.30N 25.44W
88 O5 **Remad** *watercourse* Algeria
88 T5 **Remada** Tunisia 32.22N 10.20E
64 C2 **Remagen** W Germany 50.34N 7.14E
61 M7 **Remagne** Belgium 49.58N 5.30E
70 M5 **Rémalard** France 48.26N 0.46E
117 D7 **Remansão** Brazil 4.21S 49.36W
117 F9 **Remanso** Brazil 9.40S 42.04W
79 O2 **Remanzacco** Italy 46.05N 13.19E
11 K13 **Remarkable Arch** Antipodes Is Pacific Oc
12 E5 **Remarkable, Mt** S Australia 32.50S 138.08E
11 C12 **Remarkables, The** *mts* New Zealand
18 J9 **Rembang** Java Indon 6.45S 111.22E
18 C9 **Rembau** Pen Malaysia 2.35N 102.05E
18 C9 **Rembau, Gunong** *mt* Pen Malaysia 2.35N 102.10E
53 W17 **Rembesdalseter** Norway 60.32N 7.18E
18 C9 **Rembia** Pen Malaysia 2.17N 102.13E
100 T9 **Rembina Mt** Manitoba
91 A4 **Rembo N'Komi** *R* Gabon
88 N4 **Remchi** Algeria 35.04N 1.27W
64 F6 **Remchingen** W Germany 48.56N 8.35E
64 L2 **Remda** E Germany 50.45N 11.14E
121 D6 **Remecó** Argentina 37.40S 63.43W
119 D4 **Remedios** Colombia 7.02N 74.42W
116 E3 **Remedios** Cuba 22.30N 79.32W
115 O5 **Remedios** Panama 8.13N 81.48W
115 P11 **Remedios, Pta** *C* El Salvador 13.30N 89.48W
115 C9 **Remedios, R. de los** Mexico
63 G6 **Remels** W Germany 53.18N 7.46E
45 R6 **Remennikovo** U.S.S.R. 50.19N 45.04E
87 B8 **Remenze** Sudan 4.40N 28.40E
108 R2 **Remer** Minnesota 47.02N 93.57W
93 A7 **Remera** Rwanda 1.46S 29.59E
61 Q9 **Remerschen** Luxembourg 49.29N 6.22E
61 O4 **Remersdaal** Belgium 50.43N 5.53E
32 H7 **Remeshk** Iran 26.53N 58.46E
61 Q8 **Remich** Luxembourg 49.33N 6.23E
61 M4 **Remicourt** Belgium 50.41N 5.20E
99 C8 **Remic Rapids** Quebec/Ontario 45.25N 75.45W
66 J1 **Remigen** Switzerland 47.31N 8.11E
99 L5 **Rémigny** Quebec 47.46N 79.14W
99 L5 **Rémigny, L** Quebec
99 H3 **Remi L** Ontario 49.25N 82.10W
69 L5 **Rémilly** France 49.01N 6.24E
69 H4 **Remilly-Aillicourt** France 49.39N 5.00E
106 G9 **Remington** Indiana 40.46N 87.09W
104 H8 **Remington** Virginia 38.33N 77.49W
117 C2 **Rémire** Fr Guiana 4.52N 52.16W
69 M7 **Remiremont** France 48.01N 6.35E
63 N8 **Remlingen** W Germany 52.05N 10.43E
31 J3 **Remo Glacier** Kashmir
69 L7 **Remoncourt** France 48.14N 6.04E
44 F1 **Remontnoye** U.S.S.R. 46.33N 43.42E
66 A4 **Remoray** France 46.47N 6.15E
110 B6 **Remote** Oregon 43.01N 123.54W
61 N5 **Remouchamps** Belgium 50.29N 5.43E
71 F9 **Remoulins** France 43.56N 4.34E
26 U16 **Remparts, R.des** Réunion Ind Oc
56 J2 **Rempstone** Notts Eng 52.49N 1.08W
64 H6 **Rems** *R* W Germany
64 C1 **Remscheid** W Germany 51.10N 7.11E
108 P7 **Remsen** Iowa 42.49N 95.59W
104 K3 **Remsen** New York 43.20N 75.12W
11 D2 **Remuera** *dist* Auckland New Zealand
81 D2 **Remule, Monti** *mts* Sardinia
29 K7 **Remuna** Orissa India 21.33N 86.57E
70 E6 **Remungol** France 47.56N 2.54W
106 J6 **Remus** Michigan 43.35N 85.09W
66 S4 **Remüs** Switzerland 46.51N 10.23E
71 G8 **Rémuzat** France 44.25N 5.22E
52 F5 **Rena** Norway 61.06N 11.20E
77 E2 **Rena** Spain 39.03N 5.49W
99 G4 **Renabie** Ontario 48.23N 83.56W
70 G6 **Renac** France 47.43N 2.00W
71 D4 **Renaison** *R* France
Renaix *see* **Ronse**
75 E6 **Renales** Spain 40.54N 2.32W
117 E6 **Renalva** Brazil 3.16S 45.10W
25 N7 **Renam** Burma 27.43N 98.05E
66 D3 **Renan** Switzerland 47.07N 6.56E
19 J3 **Rena Pt** Luzon Philippines 16.10N 119.46E
52 F5 **Rena, R** Norway
15 M9 **Renard Is** Louisiade Arch
119 F9 **Renascença** Brazil 3.47S 66.18W
70 H6 **Renazé** France 47.47N 1.04W
121 D4 **Renca** Argentina 32.47S 65.23W
121 F9 **Renca** *dist* Santiago Chile
64 E6 **Renchen** W Germany 48.35N 8.01E
92 E12 **Renco** Zimbabwe 20.39S 31.11E
98 R6 **Rencontre East** Newfoundland 47.40N 55.12W
87 G3 **Rendakoma** Ethiopia 14.30N 40.00E
52 F5 **Rendal** Norway 61.54N 11.05E
81 M5 **Rende** Italy 39.19N 16.11E
79 J2 **Rendena, Val** *V* Italy
53 A5 **Renderne** Denmark 55.59N 8.08E
61 M6 **Rendeux** Belgium 50.14N 5.30E
30 C6 **Rendhar** Uttar Prad India 26.09N 79.06E
84 C3 **Rendína** Greece 39.04N 21.58E
90 M9 **Rendji** Cent Afr Rep 5.09N 25.12E
107 G3 **Rend Lake** *res* Illinois
76 E8 **Rendo** Portugal 40.22N 7.03W
15 K3 **Rendova I** Solomon Is 8.30S 157.16E
28 C1 **Rendpur** Maharashtra India 18.31N 76.38E
63 L4 **Rendsburg** W Germany 54.19N 9.39E
99 L4 **Reneault** Quebec 48.29N 79.05W
75 C1 **Renedo** Santander Spain 43.22N 3.57W
76 K5 **Renedo** Valladolid Spain 41.39N 4.38W
76 K4 **Renedo de la Vega** Spain 42.26N 4.42W
76 K3 **Renedo de Valdetuéjar** Spain 42.49N 5.00W
66 C5 **Renens** Switzerland 46.32N 6.36E
60 C2 **Renesse** Netherlands 51.44N 3.46E
98 T7 **Renews** Newfoundland 46.56N 52.59W
99 O7 **Renfrew** Ontario 45.28N 76.44W
58 H7 **Renfrew** Strathclyde Scotland 55.53N 4.24W
Renfrew *co see* **Strathclyde** *reg*
18 D10 **Rengam** Pen Malaysia 1.54N 103.23E
18 E6 **Rengat** Sumatra Indon 0.26S 102.35E
84 E4 **Rengínion** Greece 38.43N 22.42E
18 D10 **Rengit** Pen Malaysia 1.40N 103.08E
28 J2 **Rengma Hills** Assam India
121 B5 **Rengo** Chile 34.24S 70.50W
76 F2 **Rengos** Spain 43.01N 6.37W
23 E2 **Ren He** *R* Shaanxi China
23 F6 **Renhua** Guangdong China 25.07N 113.40E
23 D5 **Renhuai** Guizhou China 27.47N 106.20E
46 G6 **Reni** Ukraine U.S.S.R. 45.30N 28.18E
104 E8 **Renick** W Virginia 38.01N 80.22W
28 D4 **Renigunta** Andhra Prad India 13.40N 79.31E
121 A9 **Reñihue, L** Chile
61 B3 **Reninge** Belgium 50.57N 2.48E
61 B3 **Reningelst** Belgium 50.49N 2.46E
58 C3 **Renish Pt** Harris, W Isles Scotland 57.43N 6.58W
99 J2 **Renison** Ontario 50.58N 81.09W
12 H8 **Renison Bell** Tasmania 41.50S 145.30E
87 D5 **Renk** Sudan 11.48N 32.49E
51 L11 **Renko** Finland 60.54N 24.10E
60 L12 **Renkum** Netherlands 51.58N 5.44E
48 U11 **Renland Milne Land** Greenland
61 H6 **Renlies** Belgium 50.12N 4.16E
12 F5 **Renmark** S Australia 34.10S 140.45E
21 C4 **Renmin** Heilongjiang China 46.35N 125.37E
52 E4 **Rennebu** Norway 62.53N 9.52E
15 L4 **Rennell I** Solomon Is 11.45S 160.15E
121 J9 **Rennell, Is** Chile 52.00S 74.18W
64 E2 **Rennerod** W Germany 50.36N 8.04E
13 C4 **Renner Springs** N Terr Australia 18.10S 133.42E
64 L6 **Rennertshofen** W Germany 48.46N 11.03E
70 G5 **Rennes** France 48.06N 1.40W
72 J10 **Rennes-les-Bains** France 42.55N 2.18E
53 T20 **Rennesøy** *isld* Norway 59.06N 5.43E
100 F1 **Rennie** Manitoba 49.53N 95.33W
101 V5 **Rennie L** N W Terr
65 J7 **Rennweg** Austria 47.01N 13.38E
111 E2 **Reno** Nevada 39.32N 119.49W
79 K5 **Reno** *R* Italy
71 K6 **Rénod, Pte** *mt* France 45.15N 6.37E
108 E6 **Reno Junction** Wyoming 43.45N 105.29W
108 P4 **Reno, L** Minnesota
67 P12 **Renoso, Mt** Corsica 42.03N 9.07E
95 H7 **Renosterberg** *mt* S Africa 31.42S 24.50E
95 F8 **Renosterkop** S Africa 32.13S 22.51E
95 M1 **Renosterkop** *mt* S Africa 25.36S 28.57E
95 K2 **Renostersprult** S Africa 26.55S 26.24E
98 G7 **Renous** New Brunswick 46.49N 65.50W
104 H5 **Renovo** Pennsylvania 41.20N 77.45W
100 M7 **Renown** Saskatchewan 51.36N 105.31W
30 A7 **Renpi** *R* Madhya Prad India
22 K7 **Renqiu** Hebei China 38.45N 116.04E
53 C7 **Rens** Denmark 54.54N 9.06E
95 M2 **Rensburgdorp** S Africa 26.32S 28.22E
23 G7 **Renshan** Guangdong China 22.45N 114.45E
23 C4 **Renshou** Sichuan China 30.02N 104.09E
106 G9 **Rensselaer** Indiana 40.57N 87.09W
104 M4 **Rensselaer** New York 42.37N 73.44W
103 F1 **Rensselaerville** New York 42.30N 74.07W
60 L11 **Renswoude** Netherlands 52.04N 5.32E
75 G1 **Rentería** Spain 43.19N 1.54W
110 C2 **Renton** Washington 47.29N 122.14W
64 K3 **Rentweinsdorf** W Germany 50.04N 10.49E
64 J3 **Rentwertshausen** E Germany 50.27N 10.28E
108 P5 **Renville** Minnesota 44.48N 95.12W
100 R6 **Renwer** Manitoba 52.06N 100.45W
69 H4 **Renwez** France 49.50N 4.36E
57 H3 **Renwick** Cumbria Eng 54.47N 2.37W
108 R7 **Renwick** Iowa 42.49N 93.59W
11 H8 **Renwick** New Zealand 41.31S 173.51E
22 K8 **Ren Xian** Hebei China 37.07N 114.41E
23 E9 **Renxing** Guangdong China 19.30N 109.50E
19 B8 **Reo** Indonesia 8.20S 120.29E
89 H5 **Réo** Upper Volta 12.20N 2.28W
76 L2 **Reocín** Spain 43.20N 4.05W
72 D6 **Réole, la** France 44.35N 0.02W
30 G7 **Reotipur** Uttar Prad India 25.32N 83.43E
28 E2 **Repalle** Andhra Prad India 16.03N 80.54E

117 F6 Reparticão Brazil 3.45S 42.40W
117 A6 Repartimento Brazil 3.43S 57.31W
120 E1 Repartimento, R Brazil
62 K8 Répcelak Hungary 47.24N 17.00E
94 N3 Repembe R Mozambique
71 K2 Repentir, Mt France 47.09N 6.40E
43 G7 Repetek Turkmeniya U.S.S.R. 38.36N 63.11E
45 C5 Repki Ukraine U.S.S.R. 51.47N 31.06E
51 J8 Replot Finland 63.15N 21.25E
47 K5 Repolovo U.S.S.R. 60.41N 69.50E
11 L5 Reporoa New Zealand 38.27S 176.21E
51 J10 Reposaari Finland 61.38N 21.25E
71 K5 Reposoir, Chaine de mts France
53 Y18 Reppehølåsen mt Norway 60.20N 8.10E
61 N2 Reppel Belgium 51.09N 5.34E
66 K2 Reppisch R Switzerland
107 J10 Repton Alabama 31.24N 87.15W
56 H2 Repton Derbys Eng 52.50N 1.32W
109 N2 Republic Kansas 39.55N 97.51W
106 G3 Republic Michigan 46.25N 87.59W
104 B5 Republic Ohio 41.07N 83.02W
110 G1 Republic Washington 48.39N 118.45W
109 M1 Republican R Kansas/Nebraska
97 L4 Repulse Bay N W Terr 66.35N 86.20W
13 J5 Repulse Bay Queensland
51 M1 Repvåg Norway 70.45N 25.40E
45 U3 Rep'yevka Ul'yanovsk U.S.S.R. 53.09N 48.05E
45 K5 Rep'yevka Voronezh U.S.S.R. 51.05N 38.40E
85 A3 Reqdalin Libya 32.57N 11.59E
110 A8 Requa California 41.34N 124.05W
76 F4 Requejo Spain 42.01N 6.45W
120 C1 Requena Peru 5.05S 73.52W
77 O2 Requena Spain 39.29N 1.08W
72 K7 Réquista France 44.02N 2.31E
30 F8 Rer R Uttar Prad India
87 J8 Rer Afgab tribe Ethiopia
87 J6 Rer Ali tribe Ethiopia
87 J7 Rer Amaden tribe Ethiopia
15 M3 Rere Guadalcanal I Solomon Is 9.43S 160.35E
70 P7 Rère R France
11 L5 Rerewhakaaitu L New Zealand
87 J8 Rer Hamar tribe Ethiopia
Rerik see Ostseebad Rerik
122 D15 Réritou atoll Tuamotu Is Pacific Oc 17.45S 143.05W
117 G7 Reriutaba Brazil 4.08S 40.35W
76 D7 Reriz Portugal 40.54N 8.00W
87 F8 Rerriba Laga watercourse Ethiopia
58 Q10 Rerwick Shetland Scotland 59.58N 1.20W
58 T12 Rerwick Hd Orkney Scotland 58.59N 2.48W
37 G7 Reşadiye Bitlis Turkey 38.25N 42.30E
Reşadiye Bolu Turkey see Yeniçağa
37 G2 Reşadiye Bursa Turkey 40.21N 29.35E
Reşadiye Muğla Turkey see Datça
37 C5 Reşadiye Tokat Turkey 40.24N 37.19E
36 C6 Reşadiye Yarımadası pen Turkey
18 F8 Resag, Gunung mt Sumatra Indon 4.55S 104.07E
18 D9 Resang, Tanjong C Pen Malaysia 2.34N 103.50E
79 J1 Reschen Scheideck Pass pass Italy/Austria 46.50N 10.30E
111 F7 Reseda California 34.13N 118.30W
52 K3 Resele Sweden 63.20N 17.10E
53 C3 Resen Denmark 56.36N 9.03E
53 C4 Resen Denmark 56.23N 9.06E
82 G9 Resen Yugoslavia 41.05N 21.01E
76 D6 Resende Portugal 41.06N 7.59W
81 J8 Re, Serra del mt Sicily 37.57N 14.47E
118 E9 Reserva Brazil 24.37S 50.51W
121 J3 Reserva, L.da Brazil
107 F11 Reserve Louisiana 30.05N 90.35W
108 F1 Reserve Montana 48.37N 104.28W
109 B8 Reserve New Mexico 33.43N 108.46W
100 P6 Reserve Saskatchewan 52.28N 102.40W
35 E4 Reshafim Israel 32.29N 35.28E
45 F7 Reshetilovka Ukraine U.S.S.R. 49.34N 34.05E
47 M4 Reshety U.S.S.R. 56.52N 60.15E
47 M4 Reshi U.S.S.R. 57.42N 60.22E
Resht see Rasht
44 H9 Reshteh-ye-Şalavât mts Iran
22 E8 Reshui Qinghai China 37.29N 100.29E
79 J1 Resia Italy 46.50N 10.31E
65 C8 Resia, Passo di Austria/Italy 46.52N 10.32E
80 K7 Resina Italy 40.48N 14.21E
121 F1 Resistencia Argentina 27.28S 59.00W
82 G5 Reşiţa Romania 45.16N 21.55E
79 O2 Resiutta Italy 46.24N 13.13E
37 H8 Resko Tepeler hills Turkey
76 K3 Resoba Spain 42.54N 4.34W
56 D4 Resolfen W Glam Wales 51.42N 3.42W
97 K3 Resolute N W Terr 74.40N 95.00W
11 A12 Resolution I New Zealand
97 N5 Resolution I N W Terr 61.30N 65.00W
97 N6 Resolution L Quebec 55.15N 65.30W
58 C2 Resort, L Lewis, W Isles Scotland 58.03N 6.56W
75 D1 Respaldiza Spain 43.04N 3.04W
76 K3 Respenda de la Peña Spain 42.45N 4.41W
118 H6 Resplendor Brazil 19.20S 41.13W
117 A6 Ressaca Brazil 2.50S 57.50W
Ressafé, Er see Risâfe
61 G5 Ressaix Belgium 50.26N 4.11E
94 M5 Ressano Garcia Mozambique 25.26S 32.00E
63 L8 Resse W Germany 52.30N 9.39E
61 F3 Ressegem Belgium 50.53N 3.55E
60 M12 Ressen Netherlands 51.53N 5.52E
69 C5 Ressons France 49.18N 2.06E
69 D4 Ressons-sur-Matz France 49.33N 2.45E
116 J2 Rest Jamaica, W I 17.53N 77.22W
120 C3 Restauração Brazil 9.14S 72.14W
58 G6 Rest & be Thankful Strathclyde Scotland 56.14N 4.47W
61 L6 Resteigne Belgium 50.05N 5.11E
94 P12 Resthaven Cape Town S Africa 34.04S 18.26E
76 G2 Restiello Spain 43.17N 6.11W
98 F5 Restigouche Quebec 48.02N 66.42W
98 E6 Restigouche, R New Brunswick
119 A10 Restin Peru 4.21S 81.15W
96 P12 Restinga Hierro Canary Is 27.39N 17.58W
77 F9 Restinga Morocco 35.47N 5.21W
88 L4 Restinga Morocco 35.47N 5.20W
96 P12 Reştinga, Pta Hierro Canary Is 27.38N 17.59W
121 H2 Restinga Seca Brazil 29.55S 53.25W
100 Q9 Reston Manitoba 49.33N 101.05W
99 L6 Restoule Ontario 46.02N 79.42W
119 D5 Restrepo Colombia 4.16N 73.33W
Resülayn see Ceylânpınar
81 H8 Resuttano Sicily 37.41N 14.02E
62 N1 Reszel Poland 54.04N 21.09E
115 O10 Retalhuleu Guatemala 14.31N 91.40W
77 E3 Retamal Spain 38.35N 5.50W
77 L2 Retamar, L.del Spain 39.26N 2.58W
121 C4 Retamito Argentina 32.06S 68.35W
121 G4 Retamosa Uruguay 33.32S 54.37W
72 C4 Rétaud France 45.41N 0.43W
82 H3 Reteag Romania 47.10N 24.00E
82 H5 Retezatului, Munţii mts Romania
69 G4 Rethel France 49.31N 4.22E
63 K7 Rethem W Germany 52.47N 9.23E
63 L8 Rethen W Germany 52.17N 9.50E
84 D5 Réthi Greece 38.01N 22.30E
84 K11 Réthimnon Crete 35.23N 24.28E
84 L11 Réthimnon prov Crete
31 E6 Reti Pakistan 28.02N 69.53E
61 L1 Retie Belgium 51.16N 5.05E
75 D6 Retiendas Spain 40.58N 3.16W
70 H6 Retiers France 47.55N 1.22W
77 D4 Retin R Spain
77 E8 Retín, Sierra de mts Spain
121 K4 Retiro dist Buenos Aires Arg
75 P8 Retiro, El park Madrid Spain
75 P9 Retiro-Mediodia dist Madrid Spain
39 J1 Retkucha U.S.S.R. 68.51N 170.48E
100 E8 Retlaw Alberta 50.05N 112.18W
77 F5 Retortillo R Spain
75 E5 Retortillo de Soria Spain 41.19N 2.59W
71 E6 Retournac France 45.13N 4.02E
60 A3 Retranchement Netherlands 51.21N 3.24E
94 P12 Retreat Cape Town S Africa 34.04S 18.29E
13 G7 Retreat Queensland 25.15S 143.18E
109 L6 Retrop Oklahoma 35.10N 99.24W
50 J3 Réttarfoss waterfall Iceland 65.52N 16.27W
50 E5 Rettarvatn L Iceland 64.57N 20.17W
56 N4 Rettendon Essex Eng 51.40N 0.33E
64 D3 Rettert W Germany 50.14N 7.57E
76 L10 Retuerta de Bullaque Spain 39.28N 4.24W
75 D3 Retuerto Spain 42.02N 3.30W
65 N4 Retz Austria 48.46N 15.58E
70 F7 Retz reg France
64 H4 Retzbach W Germany 49.55N 9.50E
66 A3 Reugney France 47.01N 6.09E
72 K3 Reugny Allier France 46.28N 2.37E
70 M7 Reugny Indre-et-Loire France 47.28N 0.53E
72 J1 Reuilly Indre France 47.05N 2.02E
68 F3 Reuilly Paris France 48.51N 2.24E
61 P6 Reuland Belgium 50.12N 6.08E
26 E7 Réunion isld Indian Oc
75 N5 Reus Spain 41.10N 1.06E
60 J14 Reusel Netherlands 51.21N 5.10E
60 J14 Reusel R Netherlands
66 K2 Reuss R Switzerland
66 L5 Reuss R Switzerland
63 Q9 Reussen E Germany 51.30N 12.09E
46 G5 Reut R Moldavia U.S.S.R.
63 R5 Reuterstadt Stavenhagen E Germany 53.42N 12.55E
64 M3 Reuth E Germany 50.28N 11.58E
64 N4 Reuth W Germany 49.50N 12.08E
66 Q2 Reuthe Austria 47.23N 9.53E
66 G5 Reutigen Switzerland 46.42N 7.38E
64 G7 Reutlingen W Germany 48.30N 9.13E
65 C7 Reutte Austria 47.30N 10.44E
60 Q10 Reutum Netherlands 52.24N 6.51E
60 N14 Reuver Netherlands 51.17N 6.05E
108 G4 Reva S Dakota 45.30N 103.04W
35 C6 Revadim Israel 31.46N 34.49E
31 F2 Revak Afghanistan 34.47N 71.30E
Reval see Tallinn
71 H5 Revard, Mt France 45.40N 6.00E
47 C2 Revda U.S.S.R. 67.56N 34.32E
47 M4 Revda U.S.S.R. 56.49N 59.58E
47 M5 Revda R U.S.S.R.
111 H4 Reveille Pk mt Nevada 37.51N 116.10W
Revel see Tallinn
72 H9 Revel France 43.27N 1.59E
14 G2 Reveley I W Australia 14.25S 127.49E
30 H7 Revelganj Bihar India 25.40N 84.38E
79 B5 Revello Italy 44.39N 7.23E
101 O10 Revelstoke Br Col 51.02N 118.12W
115 K6 Reventadero Mexico 22.10N 98.15W
119 A11 Reventazón Peru 6.10S 81.00W
81 M5 Reventino, Mte Italy 39.02N 16.18E
100 J6 Revenue Saskatchewan 52.16N 108.51W
79 K4 Revere Italy 45.04N 11.08E
104 Q9 Revere dist Boston, Mass
104 R9 Revere Beach Massachusetts
61 H4 Rêves Belgium 50.32N 4.25E
12 K8 Revesby dist Sydney, N S W
71 H8 Revest-du-Bion France 44.04N 5.32E
71 H10 Revest-les-Eaux, le France 43.10N 5.55E
92 H8 Révia Mozambique 13.20S 36.30E
69 H6 Révigny France 48.50N 5.00E
76 L3 Revilla de Collazos Spain 42.37N 4.30W
75 C3 Revilla del Campo Spain 42.13N 3.32W
113 W9 Revillagigedo I Alaska
115 B8 Revilla Gigedo, Is Mexico
75 C3 Revillarruz Spain 42.14N 3.39W
70 H2 Réville France 49.37N 1.15W
108 O4 Revillo S Dakota 45.00N 96.36W
69 H4 Revin France 49.57N 4.39E
79 M2 Revine Lago Italy 46.00N 12.15E
35 B9 Revivim Israel 31.02N 34.44E
35 B9 Revivim watercourse Israel
65 K2 Řevnice Czechoslovakia 49.55N 14.15E
53 F6 Revninge Denmark 55.25N 10.40E
79 K2 Revò Italy 46.24N 11.04E
77 M4 Revolcadores mt Spain 38.04N 2.15W
43 K7 Revolyutsii, Pik Tadzhikistan U.S.S.R. 38.32N 72.20E
51 L1 Revsbotn Norway 70.35N 24.36E
53 W16 Revsnes Norway 61.09N 7.16E
52 J4 Revsund Sweden 62.55N 15.05E
92 F9 Revubue R Mozambique
62 M7 Revúca Czechoslovakia 48.40N 20.10E
94 M2 Revue R Mozambique
92 F11 Revue Dam Mozambique 19.11S 33.07E
104 G5 Rew Pennsylvania 41.55N 78.32W
30 E8 Rewa Madhya Prad India 24.32N 81.18E
30 E8 Rewa dist Madhya Prad India
11 K8 Rewa mt New Zealand 41.03S 175.59E
9 T8 Rewa R Viti Levu Fiji
Rewah see Rewa
35 B7 Rewaha Israel 31.39N 34.44E
30 D7 Rewai R Uttar Prad India
100 H6 Reward Saskatchewan 52.20N 109.22W
29 E3 Rewari Haryana India 28.14N 76.38E
106 D7 Rewey Wisconsin 42.52N 90.23W
113 N4 Rex Alaska 64.10N 149.20W
110 O6 Rexburg Idaho 43.50N 111.48W
109 K2 Rexford Kansas 39.28N 100.46W
110 K1 Rexford Montana 48.54N 115.13W
69 D2 Rexpoëde France 50.57N 2.32E
98 H7 Rexton New Brunswick 46.41N 64.56W
87 K7 Reyd Abdair Ethiopia 7.22N 44.32E
53 N9 Reydafelstindur mt Faeroes 62.11N 6.51W
50 L6 Reydhara Iceland 64.25N 14.45W
50 L4 Reydharfjördhur Iceland 65.02N 14.13W
50 M4 Reydharfjördhur B Iceland
50 D6 Reydharvatn L Iceland 64.29N 21.01W
50 G4 Reydharvötn lakes Iceland
50 J3 Reydhur mt Iceland 65.52N 16.18W
109 L6 Reydon Oklahoma 35.40N 99.56W
56 P3 Reydon Suffolk Eng 52.21N 1.39E
120 E6 Reyes Bolivia 14.18S 67.23W
96 O12 Reyes, Bahia de los B Hierro Canary Is
111 E7 Reyes Pk California 34.38N 119.18W
111 A4 Reyes, Pt California 37.59N 123.01W
119 B6 Reyes, Pta C Colombia 2.44N 78.08W
120 D11 Reyes, Pta.dos C Chile 24.35S 70.35W
36 J6 Reyhanlı Turkey 36.16N 36.35E
115 P5 Rey, I.del Panama
50 C4 Reykhólar Iceland 65.27N 22.13W
50 D5 Reykholt Iceland 64.40N 21.15W
50 D5 Reykholtsdalur V Iceland
50 E3 Reykir Húnavatnssýsla, Austur Iceland 65.32N 20.12W
50 F3 Reykir Skagafjardharsýsla Iceland 65.39N 19.04W
50 F4 Reykir Skagafjardharsýsla Iceland 65.28N 19.21W
50 D4 Reykir Strandasýsla Iceland 65.15N 21.05W
50 C2 Reykjafjördhur B Iceland
50 H3 Reykjaheidhi heath Iceland
50 J3 Reykjahlidh Iceland 65.39N 16.55W
50 H3 Reykjakvisl R Iceland
48 A11 Reykjanes Ridge N Atlantic Oc
50 C7 Reykjanestá C Iceland 63.48N 22.43W
50 D3 Reykjarfjördhur Iceland 65.58N 21.35W
50 D3 Reykjarfjördhur inlet Iceland
50 D3 Reykjarneś C Iceland 66.00N 21.16W
Reykjasjóli see Reykir Strandasýsla Iceland
50 E5 Reykjavatn L Iceland 64.52N 20.20W
50 D6 Reykjavík Iceland 64.09N 21.58W
100 T7 Reykjavik Manitoba 51.11N 98.54W
100 M6 Reynaud Saskatchewan 52.38N 105.28W
40 H4 Reyneke,O isld U.S.S.R. 54.20N 139.50E
50 F3 Reynistadhur Iceland 65.39N 19.34W
50 D6 Reynivellir Kjósarsýsla Iceland 64.20N 21.31W
50 J6 Reynivellir Skaftafellssýsla, Austur Iceland 64.08N 16.05W
105 C5 Reynolds Georgia 32.33N 84.07W
110 J6 Reynolds Idaho 43.12N 116.46W
106 D8 Reynolds Illinois 41.20N 90.40W
106 H9 Reynolds Indiana 40.45N 86.53W
100 F1 Reynolds Manitoba 49.40N 95.54W
108 N9 Reynolds Nebraska 40.03N 97.22W
13 B2 Reynolds R N Terr Australia
12 D4 Reynolds, L S Australia 30.44S 136.05E
13 C5 Reynolds Ra N Terr Australia
104 G5 Reynoldsville Pennsylvania 41.06N 78.53W
115 K4 Reynosa Mexico 26.05N 98.18W
71 G4 Reyssouze R France
32 E4 Rezā Iran 33.18N 52.56E
32 E5 Rezāābād Iran 30.28N 52.34E
32 A2 Rezā'īyeh Iran 37.32N 45.02E
32 A2 Rezā'īyeh, Daryācheh-ye L Iran
32 D4 Rezā, Kūh-e mt Iran 33.46N 50.37E
64 K5 Rezat R W Germany
72 A1 Reze France 47.12N 1.34W
88 N8 Rezeg Allah Algeria 26.37N 0.44W
46 F2 Rēzekne Latvia U.S.S.R. 56.30N 27.22E
47 N4 Rezh U.S.S.R. 57.26N 61.20E
47 N4 Rezh R U.S.S.R.
39 C5 Rezidentsiya U.S.S.R. 59.24N 143.14E
82 M3 Rezina Moldavia U.S.S.R. 47.48N 28.55E
69 K5 Rezonville France 49.06N 6.00E
36 C1 Rezovo Bulgaria 41.59N 28.04E
32 J6 Rezvān Balūchestān va Sīstān Iran 28.48N 61.13E
32 G7 Rezvān Banāder va Jazāyer-e Baḩr-e Oman Iran 27.35N 56.05E
32 C2 Rezvāndeh Iran 37.32N 49.08E
36 C1 Rezvaya R Turkey/Bulgaria
79 H3 Rezzato Italy 45.31N 10.18E
79 C6 Rezzo Italy 44.02N 7.52E
79 F2 Rezzonico Italy 46.04N 9.16E
77 E9 R'gaia Morocco 35.38N 5.46W
25 J7 Rgna, Da R Vietnam
Rhabârheb see Ghabâghib
63 K6 Rhade W Germany 53.21N 9.07E
Rhadîr Motâtâ see Ghadir Minqâr
88 L4 Rhafsai Morocco 34.40N 4.55W
Rhages anc site see Shahr Rey
93 F6 Rhamba Kenya 0.05S 34.24E
29 J8 Rhambha Orissa India 19.31N 85.10E
108 G3 Rhame N Dakota 46.13N 103.40W
Rhanntor see Ghantūr
88 O6 Rharbi, El watercourse Algeria
88 Q9 Rharis reg Algeria
89 K2 Rharous Mali 18.32N 1.44E
66 P3 Rhätikon mts Switzerland
64 C4 Rhaunen W Germany 49.52N 7.21E
56 D3 Rhayader Powys Wales 52.18N 3.30W
34 C4 Rhazir Lebanon 34.02N 35.38E
66 O4 Rhäzüns Switzerland 46.48N 9.24E
63 H9 Rheda-Wiedenbrück W Germany 51.51N 8.17E
63 F6 Rhede Niedersachsen W Germany 53.04N 7.16E
63 E9 Rhede Nordrhein-Westfalen W Germany 51.50N 6.42E
60 N11 Rheden Netherlands 52.01N 6.02E
60 P9 Rheeze Netherlands 52.33N 6.35E
56 D3 Rheidol, R Dyfed Wales
100 P7 Rhein Saskatchewan 51.21N 102.11W
62 D5 Rhein R W Europe
66 L1 Rheinau Switzerland 47.37N 8.37E
64 D6 Rheinau W Germany 48.40N 7.56E
64 B2 Rheinbach W Germany 50.37N 6.57E
63 E9 Rheinberg W Germany 51.33N 6.35E
64 D3 Rheinböllen W Germany 50.00N 7.40E
64 C2 Rheinbrohl W Germany 50.30N 7.20E
64 A1 Rheindahlen W Germany 51.10N 6.22E
64 B1 Rheindorf Nordrhein-Westfalen W Germany 51.03N 6.56E
63 F8 Rheine W Germany 52.17N 7.26E
66 P2 Rheineck Switzerland 47.28N 9.36E
66 L1 Rheinfall falls Switzerland 47.40N 8.37E
66 H1 Rheinfelden Switzerland 47.33N 7.47E
66 H1 Rheinfelden W Germany 47.34N 7.47E
63 E10 Rheinhausen W Germany 51.23N 6.41E
64 E4 Rheinhessen dist W Germany
62 C5 Rheinland-Pfalz land W Germany
64 F3 Rhein-Main airport W Germany 50.01N 8.35E
64 E6 Rheinmünster Baden-Württemberg W Germany 48.44N 8.04E
63 R6 Rheinsberg E Germany 53.07N 12.55E
64 E6 Rheinstetten W Germany 48.58N 8.16E
66 N5 Rheinwald V Switzerland
66 N6 Rheinwaldhorn mt Switzerland 46.30N 9.03E
64 E5 Rheinzabern W Germany 49.07N 8.18E
79 B3 Rhême Notre Dame Italy 45.34N 7.07E
79 B3 Rhême St.Georges Italy 45.39N 7.09E
88 L7 Rhemilès Algeria 28.25N 4.20W
64 F1 Rhena W Germany 51.17N 8.47E
60 L12 Rhenen Netherlands 51.57N 5.34E
64 D3 Rhens W Germany 50.17N 7.37E
89 J3 Rhergo Mali 17.04N 1.49W
88 L6 Rheriss R Morocco
88 L8 Rhers, El Algeria 27.15N 5.14W
64 A1 Rheydt W Germany 51.10N 6.27E
58 G2 Rhiconich Highland Scotland 58.25N 4.59W
60 N11 Rhienderen Netherlands 52.06N 6.10E
115 K6 Rhil Field airport Mexico 22.19N 97.58W
63 R6 Rhin R E Germany
69 O7 Rhinau France 48.19N 7.43E
105 D6 Rhine Georgia 32.00N 83.13W
Rhine R see Rhein R
103 G3 Rhinebeck New York 41.57N 73.54W
103 G3 Rhinecliff New York 41.55N 73.57W
106 E4 Rhinelander Wisconsin 45.39N 89.23W
63 R7 Rhinkanal E Germany
58 D7 Rhinns Pt Islay, Strathclyde Scotland 55.41N 6.30W
93 C3 Rhino Camp Uganda 2.58N 31.24E
63 Q7 Rhinow E Germany 52.46N 12.21E
71 E5 Rhins R France
88 R5 Rhir R Algeria
88 J6 Rhir, C Morocco 30.40N 9.54W
74 E10 Rhis R Morocco
61 K4 Rhisnes Belgium 50.30N 4.48E
79 F3 Rho Italy 45.32N 9.02E
103 M3 Rhode I Rhode I 41.30N 71.20W
102 M2 Rhode I state U.S.A.
103 M3 Rhode Island State airport Rhode Island 41.42N 71.24W
104 D9 Rhodell W Virginia 37.37N 81.19W
63 K10 Rhoden W Germany 51.28N 9.01E
66 O2 Rhoden, Ausser demi-canton Switzerland
66 O2 Rhoden, Inner demi-canton Switzerland
Rhodes see Ródhos
106 K6 Rhodes Michigan 43.55N 84.10W
95 L6 Rhodes S Africa 30.48S 27.58E
84 U17 Rhodes isld Greece
26 Q15 Rhodes, B Kerguelen Ind Oc
94 K4 Rhodes Drift ford S Africa 22.12S 29.15E
Rhode's Grave see World's View
Rhodesia see Zimbabwe
73 G7 Rhodesia state Central Africa
105 F2 Rhodhiss L N Carolina
77 F10 Rhomara reg Morocco
112 K2 Rhome Texas 33.03N 97.29W
56 E4 Rhondda Mid Glam Wales 51.40N 3.30W
67 J7 Rhône dept France
71 F8 Rhône R France
66 K5 Rhône Glacier Switzerland
71 F10 Rhône, Grand R France
71 E9 Rhône, Petit R France
66 D1 Rhône-Rhein Canal France
60 F12 Rhoon Netherlands 51.52N 4.25E
56 E5 Rhoose airport S Glam Wales 51.26N 3.22W
56 C4 Rhosili W Glam Wales 51.34N 4.17W
57 G6 Rhosllanerchrugog Clwyd Wales 53.01N 3.04W
57 D6 Rhosneigr Gwynedd Wales 53.14N 4.31W
57 F6 Rhos-on-Sea Gwynedd Wales 53.19N 3.45W
Rhoubé see Ghuba, Al
88 R4 Rhoufi Algeria 35.03N 6.08E
88 R6 Rhourd el Baguel Algeria 31.14N 6.42E
58 G6 Rhu Strathclyde Scotland 56.01N 4.47W
57 G6 Rhuddlan Clwyd Wales 53.18N 3.27W
70 E6 Rhuis, Presqu'île de pen France
58 D5 Rhum isld Highland Scotland
63 M9 Rhume R W Germany
75 G1 Rhune, La mt France/Spain 43.18N 1.39W
18 J3 Rhu, Tanjong C Singapore 1.18N 103.52E
56 C3 Rhyd-Owen Dyfed Wales 52.05N 4.17W
57 G6 Rhyl Clwyd Wales 53.19N 3.29W
56 E4 Rhymney Gwent Wales 51.46N 3.18W
56 E4 Rhymney R Gwent/Mid Glam Wales
63 G9 Rhynern W Germany 51.38N 7.51E
58 L4 Rhynie Grampian Scotland 57.20N 2.50W
90 D10 Ri-Aba Fernando Póo Eq Guinea 3.30N 8.50E
Riabad see Ryābād
81 M7 Riace Italy 38.25N 16.30E
117 E8 Riachão Brazil 7.20S 46.35W
118 G2 Riachão das Neves Brazil 11.47S 44.58W
118 H2 Riachão do Jacuípe Brazil 11.48S 39.23W
118 H6 Riacho Brazil 19.46S 40.06W
118 G3 Riacho de Santana Brazil 13.36S 42.59W
117 F8 Riacho do Mendes Brazil 7.35S 43.38W
118 G4 Riacho dos Machados Brazil 15.59S 43.03W
117 G8 Riacho, R Brazil
121 E8 Riachos, Is.de los Argentina
121 K4 Riachuelo dist Buenos Aires Argentina
66 K6 Riale Italy 46.26N 8.25E
34 D10 Ri'al Fuhah hill Saudi Arabia 28.17N 36.12E
70 H6 Riallé France 47.32N 1.18W
118 E4 Rialma Brazil 15.23S 49.29W
75 N3 Rialp Spain 42.27N 1.08E
18 J6 Riam Borneo Indon 1.51S 111.50E
28 J2 Riang Assam India 27.36N 92.51E
87 C6 Riangnom Sudan 9.57N 30.02E
76 B3 Rianjo Spain 42.39N 8.49W
80 G4 Riano Italy 42.06N 12.31E
76 J3 Riaño Spain 42.59N 5.00W
118 E4 Rianópolis Brazil 15.31S 49.24W
76 K2 Riaño, Sierra de mts Spain
71 H9 Rians France 43.36N 5.45E
75 D8 Riánsares R Spain
70 D6 Riantec France 47.43N 3.17W
31 H4 Riasi Kashmir 33.03N 74.51E
31 H4 Riasi dist Kashmir
33 C1 Ri'atayn, Jabal ar mts Saudi Arabia
18 D5 Riau prov Sumatra Indonesia
66 E5 Riaz Switzerland 46.39N 7.05E
75 D5 Riaza Spain 41.16N 3.29W
75 C4 Riaza R Spain
76 C4 Ribadavia Spain 42.17N 8.08W
75 E5 Riba de Escalote, La Spain 41.21N 2.48W
76 E1 Ribadeo Spain 43.32N 7.04W
75 F6 Riba de Saelices Spain 40.55N 2.18W
76 J2 Ribadesella Spain 43.28N 5.04W
87 K8 Ribadleh Ethiopia 5.54N 45.30E
90 F7 Ribado Nigeria 9.16N 12.47E
76 B3 Ribadumia Spain 42.31N 8.45W
75 F3 Ribafrecha Spain 42.21N 2.23W
75 F7 Ribagorda Spain 40.20N 2.14W
75 L3 Ribagorza reg Spain
117 F6 Ribamar Brazil 2.34S 44.05W
90 E8 Ribao Cameroon 6.32N 11.30E
75 F6 Ribarredonda Spain 40.52N 2.19W
75 L5 Ribarroja de Ebro Spain 41.15N 0.29E
75 J8 Ribarroja del Turia Spain 39.33N 0.34W
75 L5 Ribarroja, Embalse de res Spain 41.16N 0.20E
75 P3 Ribas de Fresser Spain 42.18N 2.10E
Ribas del Sil see San Clodio
118 D7 Ribas do Rio Pardo Brazil 20.25S 53.39W
31 E2 Ribat Baghlan Afghanistan 36.09N 68.26E
31 B4 Ribat Farah Afghanistan 33.00N 63.47E
31 B4 Ribat Harat Afghanistan 33.46N 62.13E
Ribat Iran see Robāt
75 F7 Ribatajada Spain 40.20N 2.10W
33 F9 Ribāţ, Ar Yemen 14.22N 44.30E
75 D6 Ribatejada Spain 40.40N 3.24W
76 B10 Ribatejo hist reg Portugal
74 B5 Ribatejo prov Portugal
31 B3 Ribat Hashim Afghanistan 34.15N 62.59E
Ribat-i-Ab-i-Garm see Robat-e Ābgarm
Ribat-i-Chāh Gunbad see Ghebar Gumbad
Ribat-i-Pusht i Bādām see Posht-e Badam
32 G4 Ribat-i-Shur Iran 33.55N 57.49E
31 A3 Ribat-i-Surkh Afghanistan 35.02N 61.28E
31 A4 Ribat Shah Balucho Afghanistan 33.59N 60.59E
92 J9 Ribauè Mozambique 14.57S 38.19E
57 H5 Ribble, R Lancs/N Yorks Eng
53 B6 Ribe Denmark 55.20N 8.47E
93 L9 Ribe Kenya 3.52S 39.39E
53 B5 Ribe co Denmark
53 B6 Ribe Å R Denmark
69 N7 Ribeauvillé France 48.12N 7.20E
69 D4 Ribécourt France 49.31N 2.55E
86 G5 Ribeiqi, El Egypt 30.10N 31.46E
118 J8 Ribeira Rio de Janeiro Brazil 22.50S 43.10W
118 E9 Ribeira São Paulo Brazil 24.39S 49.00W
118 E9 Ribeira R Brazil
96 P7 Ribeira Brava Madeira Is 32.39N 17.04W
96 O3 Ribeira das Cabras, B. da Azores
96 U2 Ribeira das Tainhas Azores 37.28N 25.25W
76 D5 Ribeira de Pena Portugal 41.31N 7.47W
118 J2 Ribeira do Pombal Brazil 10.49S 38.34W
76 D2 Ribeira, Embalse de res Spain 43.28N 7.50W
96 U1 Ribeira Grande Azores 37.34N 25.32W
89 O10 Ribeira Grande Cape Verde 17.12N 25.03W
120 F4 Ribeirão Brazil 10.14S 65.59W
118 F7 Ribeirão Prêto Brazil 21.09S 47.48W
96 R4 Ribeiras Azores 38.24N 28.11W
96 U1 Ribeira Secca Azores 37.34N 25.33W
96 U3 Ribeirinha Azores 38.40N 27.12W
96 P4 Ribeirinha, Pta Azores 38.36N 28.36W
118 J2 Ribeiro do Amparo Brazil 11.02S 38.26W
117 E8 Ribeiro Goncalves Brazil 7.30S 45.13W
69 E4 Ribemont France 49.48N 3.28E
81 F8 Ribera Sicily 37.31N 13.16E
72 E5 Ribérac France 45.14N 0.22E
77 D3 Ribera del Fresno Spain 38.33N 6.15W
77 P5 Ribera, La Spain 37.48N 0.48W
75 C4 Ribera, La reg Burgos Spain
75 G3 Ribera, la reg Navarra Spain
120 E4 Riberalta Bolivia 10.59S 66.06W
75 K7 Ribesalbes Spain 40.01N 0.18W
71 H8 Ribiers France 44.13N 5.50E
99 L5 Rib Lake Ontario 47.12N 79.44W
106 D4 Rib Lake Wisconsin 45.19N 90.11W
106 E5 Rib Mt Wisconsin 44.55N 89.44W
82 B5 Ribnica Yugoslavia 45.44N 14.44E
63 Q4 Ribnitz-Damgarten E Germany 54.15N 12.26E
75 D5 Ribota Spain 41.22N 3.25W
75 G5 Ribota R Spain
100 G6 Ribstone Alberta 52.43N 110.18W
100 F6 Ribstone Cr Alberta
120 D9 Rica Aventura Chile 22.00S 69.35W
81 L6 Ricadi Italy 38.37N 15.52E
71 E6 Ricamarie France 45.24N 4.22E
65 L2 Říčany Czechoslovakia 49.59N 14.40E
112 K8 Ricardo Texas 27.26N 97.53W
115 F3 Ricardo Flores Magón Mexico 29.58N 106.58W
120 G4 Ricardo Franco, R Brazil
11 L9 Riccarton dist Christchurch New Zealand
57 H2 Riccarton Junc Borders Scotland 55.16N 2.44W
80 L6 Riccia Italy 41.24N 14.50E
80 F2 Riccio Italy 43.13N 12.01E
79 N6 Riccione Italy 44.00N 12.39E
79 G6 Ricco del Golfo della Spezia Italy 44.09N 9.46E
111 K7 Rice California 34.06N 114.50W
108 Q4 Rice Minnesota 45.46N 94.12W
112 L3 Rice Texas 32.15N 96.30W
105 F6 Riceboro Georgia 31.43N 81.27W
108 R3 Rice L Minnesota
99 H5 Rice L Ontario 47.44N 82.08W
99 M8 Rice, L Ontario 44.10N 78.15W
106 C4 Rice Lake Wisconsin 45.30N 91.43W
100 N8 Riceton Saskatchewan 50.08N 104.22W
108 S6 Riceville Iowa 43.25N 92.31W
69 G8 Riceys, les France 48.00N 4.22E
88 L5 Rich Morocco 32.16N 4.30W
100 K6 Richard Saskatchewan 52.42N 107.42W
98 P4 Richard A. Squires Mem. Park Newfoundland
Richard Black Coast see Black Coast
107 L6 Richard City Tennessee 35.00N 85.41W
97 H3 Richard Collinson Inlet N W Terr
107 B4 Richards Missouri 37.55N 94.34W
95 O10 Richard's B S Africa 28.48S 32.03E
95 O7 Richards Bay S Africa 31.01S 30.15E
95 O10 Richard's Bay S Africa 28.47S 32.05E
50 T15 Richardsbreen glacier Spitsbergen 77.40N 18.00E
120 D11 Richards Deep Pacific Oc
101 F1 Richards I N W Terr
99 F6 Richards Landing Ontario 46.16N 84.04W
11 A12 Richards, Mt New Zealand 45.32S 166.41E
113 O4 Richardson Alaska 64.19N 146.30W
112 O8 Richardson Texas 32.55N 96.44W
101 P2 Richardson R N W Terr
111 A8 Richardson B California
101 O3 Richardson I Gt Bear L, N W Terr 65.46N 118.20W
101 S1 Richardson Is N W Terr
104 P2 Richardson Lakes Maine
14 C8 Richardson, Mt W Australia 28.50S 119.55E
11 C11 Richardson Mts New Zealand
101 E1 Richardson Mts Yukon/N W Terr
101 S6 Richardson R Alberta
100 N8 Richardson Sta Saskatchewan 50.23N 104.28W
9 R13 Richards Patches coral shoals Tonga, Pacific Oc
89 B3 Richard Toll Senegal 16.25N 15.42W
108 H3 Richardton N Dakota 46.55N 102.20W
88 H11 Richat mt Mauritania 21.11N 11.23W
103 D6 Richboro Pennsylvania 40.13N 75.01W
56 O5 Richborough Kent Eng 51.18N 1.22E
104 G4 Richburg New York 42.05N 78.09W
100 F7 Richdale Alberta 51.37N 111.36W
14 C10 Riche, C W Australia 34.32S 118.43E
26 U13 Riche en Eau Mauritius, Indian Oc 20.23S 57.38E
60 J6 Richel isld Netherlands
72 E1 Richelieu France 47.01N 0.20E
99 R7 Richelieu R Quebec
61 N4 Richelle Belgium 50.43N 5.42E
70 O2 Richemont France 49.49N 1.38E
98 P3 Riche Pt Newfoundland 50.43N 57.25W
108 E2 Richey Montana 47.38N 106.04W
110 L6 Richfield Idaho 43.04N 114.10W
109 J4 Richfield Kansas 37.17N 101.48W
111 M3 Richfield Utah 38.45N 112.05W
104 K4 Richfield Springs New York 42.53N 75.00W
103 B2 Richford New York 42.21N 76.11W
104 N2 Richford Vermont 44.59N 72.41W
111 E6 Richgrove California 35.46N 119.08W
107 B3 Rich Hill Missouri 38.05N 94.22W
98 H7 Richibucto New Brunswick 46.42N 64.54W
66 M3 Richisau Switzerland 47.01N 8.55E
88 H7 Rich, Jbel mts Morocco
100 F4 Rich Lake Alberta 54.31N 111.36W
105 C5 Richland Georgia 32.04N 84.39W
106 C8 Richland Iowa 41.11N 91.59W
106 J7 Richland Michigan 42.23N 85.27W
107 D4 Richland Missouri 37.52N 92.27W
108 D1 Richland Montana 48.50N 106.06W
103 E7 Richland New Jersey 39.30N 74.52W
110 H5 Richland Oregon 44.47N 117.10W
103 B6 Richland Pennsylvania 40.22N 76.15W
112 L4 Richland Texas 31.55N 96.28W
110 F3 Richland Washington 46.17N 119.17W
105 E2 Richland Balsam N Carolina 35.23N 82.59W
106 D6 Richland Center Wisconsin 43.22N 90.24W
112 L4 Richland Cr Texas
112 M9 Richland Hills Texas 32.47N 97.14W
105 K3 Richlands N Carolina 34.55N 77.33W
104 D9 Richlands Virginia 37.07N 81.48W
112 J4 Richland Springs Texas 31.17N 98.57W
103 D6 Richlandtown Pennsylvania 40.29N 75.19W
100 J7 Richlea Saskatchewan 51.10N 108.38W
111 B4 Richmond California 37.56N 122.20W
95 G7 Richmond Cape Province S Africa 31.25S 23.57E
95 K9 Richmond Cape Province S Africa 33.45S 26.35E
107 M2 Richmond Indiana 39.50N 84.51W
116 K1 Richmond Jamaica, W I 18.14N 76.54W
109 P3 Richmond Kansas 38.24N 95.15W
107 M4 Richmond Kentucky 37.45N 84.19W
55 D4 Richmond London Eng 51.28N 0.19W
104 Q2 Richmond Maine 44.05N 69.50W
103 H2 Richmond Massachusetts 42.22N 73.22W
108 Q4 Richmond Minnesota 45.28N 94.37W
107 C2 Richmond Missouri 39.15N 93.59W
95 O5 Richmond Natal S Africa 29.53S 30.17E
12 K5 Richmond New S Wales 33.36S 150.44E
11 H8 Richmond New Zealand 41.20S 173.10E
57 K4 Richmond N Yorks Eng 54.24N 1.44W
99 P7 Richmond Ontario 45.11N 75.50W
110 F5 Richmond Oregon 44.44N 120.00W
98 H7 Richmond Prince Edward I 46.31N 64.00W
99 S7 Richmond Quebec 45.40N 72.08W
13 G5 Richmond Queensland 20.45S 143.05E
12 H9 Richmond Tasmania 42.45S 147.20E
112 M6 Richmond Texas 29.36N 95.48W
110 O8 Richmond Utah 41.57N 111.49W
104 N2 Richmond Vermont 44.23N 72.56W
104 H9 Richmond Virginia 37.34N 77.27W
103 F5 Richmond bor New York
101 G11 Richmond co Br Col
11 M9 Richmond dist Christchurch New Zealand
12 D7 Richmond dist Melbourne, Vic
105 B11 Richmond Heights Florida 25.38N 80.25W
105 F6 Richmond Hill Georgia 31.56N 81.19W
99 L9 Richmond Hill Ontario 43.53N 79.26W
14 A4 Richmond, L W Australia 32.17S 115.43E
11 H8 Richmond, Mt New Zealand 41.30S 173.21E
12 L3 Richmond R New S Wales
12 L3 Richmond Ra New S Wales
11 H8 Richmond Ra New Zealand
55 C4 Richmond upon Thames bor London Eng 51.27N 0.20W
104 L4 Richmondville New York 42.39N 74.34W
100 H8 Richmound Saskatchewan 50.29N 109.43W
107 B7 Rich Mt Arkansas 34.40N 94.20W
94 D6 Richtberg mt Namibia 27.30S 17.00E
63 R4 Richtenberg E Germany 54.13N 12.53E
66 L3 Richterswil Switzerland 47.13N 8.43E
107 H10 Richton Mississippi 31.20N 88.58W
108 P3 Richville Minnesota 46.29N 95.36W
104 B6 Richwood Ohio 40.25N 83.18W
106 F6 Richwood Wisconsin 43.15N 88.48W
104 E8 Richwood W Virginia 38.14N 80.33W
107 F3 Richwoods Missouri 38.08N 90.48W
80 M7 Ricigliano Italy 40.41N 15.27E
66 N2 Ricken Switzerland 47.16N 9.03E
66 N2 Rickenbach Switzerland 47.27N 9.03E
66 N3 Ricken Tunnel Switzerland
103 B4 Ricketts Glen State Park Pennsylvania
12 D9 Ricketts Pt Victoria 37.57S 145.02E
63 M4 Rickling W Germany 54.01N 10.10E
55 B2 Rickmansworth Herts England 51.38N 0.29W
75 H4 Ricla Spain 41.30N 1.24W
109 B4 Rico Colorado 37.41N 108.03W
76 H5 Ricobayo Spain 41.31N 5.59W
77 O4 Ricote Spain 38.10N 1.21W
60 G12 Ridderkerk Netherlands 51.52N 4.35E
66 E7 Riddes Switzerland 46.11N 7.14E
110 J7 Riddle Idaho 42.11N 116.05W
110 B7 Riddle Oregon 42.56N 123.24W
13 C6 Riddock, Mt N Terr Australia 23.04S 134.38E
58 F7 Riddon, L Strathclyde Scotland 55.58N 5.12W
99 P7 Rideau R Ontario
99 P8 Rideau Can Ontario
99 D8 Rideau Falls Ontario 45.27N 75.42W
99 O8 Rideau L Ontario
108 F4 Ridge Montana 45.03N 105.00W
99 F2 Ridge R Ontario
103 A3 Ridgebury Pennsylvania 41.58N 76.44W
110 N7 Ridgedale Idaho 42.02N 112.29W
100 N5 Ridgedale Saskatchewan 53.03N 104.10W
107 J2 Ridge Farm Illinois 39.55N 87.39W
103 H4 Ridgefield Connecticut 41.17N 73.30W
103 J6 Ridgefield New Jersey 40.50N 74.01W
103 J6 Ridgefield Park New Jersey 40.52N 74.02W
107 F9 Ridgeland Mississippi 32.27N 90.09W
105 G5 Ridgeland S Carolina 32.30N 80.59W
106 C4 Ridgeland Wisconsin 45.13N 91.53W
13 K6 Ridgelands Queensland 23.13S 150.12E
112 L9 Ridgelea Texas 32.44N 97.26W
104 G7 Ridgeley W Virginia 39.36N 78.47W
103 C9 Ridgely Maryland 38.57N 75.54W
99 C9 Ridgemont Ontario 45.24N 75.44W
105 F4 Ridge Spring S Carolina 33.51N 81.40W
99 J10 Ridgetown Ontario 42.26N 81.52W
108 K4 Ridgeview S Dakota 45.05N 100.49W
106 J9 Ridgeville Indiana 40.17N 85.02W
100 V9 Ridgeville Manitoba 49.05N 97.00W
105 G4 Ridgeville S Carolina 33.06N 80.20W
109 C3 Ridgeway Colorado 38.09N 107.44W
107 C1 Ridgeway Missouri 40.23N 93.56W
105 G3 Ridgeway S Carolina 34.19N 80.58W
106 D6 Ridgeway Wisconsin 43.01N 90.01W
12 F8 Ridgeway dist Hobart, Tasmania
56 N3 Ridgewell Essex Eng 52.02N 0.31E
103 F5 Ridgewood New Jersey 40.58N 74.08W
107 G5 Ridgley Tennessee 36.15N 89.30W
107 H4 Ridgway Illinois 37.47N 88.15W
108 F4 Ridgway Montana 45.30N 104.28W
104 G5 Ridgway Pennsylvania 41.25N 78.45W
82 E5 Ridica Yugoslavia 46.00N 19.03E
57 K3 Riding Mill Northumberland Eng 54.57N 1.59W
100 R8 Riding Mt ra Manitoba
100 R8 Riding Mt.Nat. Park Manitoba
85 M7 Ridisīya Bahari, Er Egypt 24.52N 32.54E
14 D10 Ridley, Mt W Australia 33.18S 122.10E
14 C5 Ridley, R W Australia
100 J7 Ridpath Saskatchewan 51.30N 108.05W
57 J2 Ridsdale Northumberland Eng 55.09N 2.08W
37 F8 Ridvan Turkey 37.52N 41.32E
95 B9 Riebeek-kasteel S Africa 33.22S 18.52E
95 K9 Riebeek-Oos S Africa 33.12S 26.10E
95 B9 Riebeek Wes S Africa 33.20S 18.51E
51 F5 Riebnesjaura L Sweden 66.35N 17.00E
70 C6 Riec France 47.50N 3.41W
119 F2 Riecito Venezuela 10.54N 68.46W
66 F5 Ried Bern Switzerland 46.32N 7.24E
60 L7 Ried Netherlands 53.13N 5.36E
65 C7 Ried Tirol Austria 47.03N 10.39E
65 E7 Ried Tirol Austria 47.18N 11.52E
66 H6 Ried Valais Switzerland 46.25N 7.48E
65 J5 Riedau Austria 48.18N 13.38E
64 M5 Rieden W Germany 49.19N 11.57E
64 M6 Riedenburg W Germany 48.57N 11.42E
65 H5 Ried im Innkreis Ober-Österreich Austria 48.13N 13.29E
64 G7 Riedlingen W Germany 48.09N 9.29E
69 O5 Riedseltz France 49.00N 7.57E
66 G3 Riedtwil Switzerland 47.08N 7.42E
65 A6 Riefensburg Austria 47.31N 9.58E
64 D7 Riegel W Germany 48.08N 7.45E
103 D5 Riegelsville Pennsylvania 40.36N 75.12W
65 N7 Riegersberg Austria 47.01N 15.57E
65 J8 Riegersdorf Austria 46.34N 13.47E
76 H4 Riego de la Vega Spain 42.23N 5.59W
66 G1 Riehen Switzerland 47.35N 7.39E
66 O5 Riein, Piz mt Switzerland 46.45N 9.17E
94 J5 Riekertsdam S Africa 25.27S 26.23E
100 B2 Riel Manitoba 49.49N 97.07W
60 J13 Riel Netherlands 51.32N 5.02E
64 F8 Rielasingen-Worblingen W Germany 47.44N 8.50E
76 H3 Riello Spain 42.46N 5.57W
76 L9 Rielves Spain 39.57N 4.12W
63 H8 Riemsloh W Germany 52.10N 8.24E
61 N3 Riemst Belgium 50.48N 5.36E
64 H3 Rieneck W Germany 50.05N 9.39E
61 K7 Rienne Belgium 49.59N 4.53E
79 L1 Rienza R Italy
107 H7 Rienzi Mississippi 34.47N 88.32W
51 F5 Riepentjåkkå mt Sweden 66.51N 17.30E
75 N5 Riera, La Spain 41.09N 1.21E
91 G10 Riero Angola 13.47S 20.59E
64 K6 Ries reg W Germany
64 P1 Riesa E Germany 51.18N 13.18E
121 J9 Riesco, I Chile
63 L3 Rieseby W Germany 54.32N 9.49E
79 L3 Riese Pio X Italy 45.43N 11.55E
81 H9 Riesi Sicily 37.17N 14.05E
63 O9 Riestedt E Germany 51.30N 11.21E
95 H4 Riet R S Africa
46 D2 Rietavas Lithuania U.S.S.R. 55.40N 22.00E
63 H9 Rietberg W Germany 51.48N 8.25E
95 G8 Rietbron S Africa 32.55S 23.10E
60 O6 Riet Diep R Netherlands
94 F3 Rietfontein Namibia 21.58S 20.58E
94 F6 Rietfontein S Africa 26.43S 20.03E
63 U5 Rieth E Germany 53.42N 14.16E
60 K14 Riethoven Netherlands 51.21N 5.23E
95 E10 Riethuiskraal S Africa 34.18S 21.20E
80 G4 Rieti Italy 42.24N 12.51E
80 G4 Rieti prov Italy
95 N3 Rietkuil S Africa 27.35S 29.04E
95 C10 Rietpoel S Africa 34.15S 19.45E
95 L4 Rietspruit S Africa 28.26S 27.18E
65 D7 Rietzer Grieskogel mt Austria 47.14N 11.03E
72 G9 Rieumes France 43.25N 1.07E
72 J7 Rieupeyroux France 44.18N 2.14E
71 C7 Rieutort-de-Random France 44.37N 3.29E
72 G9 Rieux Haute-Garonne France 43.16N 1.12E
70 F6 Rieux Morbihan France 47.36N 2.05W
57 L4 Rievaulx N Yorks Eng 54.15N 1.07W
71 J9 Riez France 43.49N 6.06E
61 H7 Rièzes Belgium 49.58N 4.22E
88 L4 Rif mts Morocco
74 D10 Rif reg Morocco
33 B8 Rifa, Ar Bahrain, The Gulf 26.07N 50.03E
85 L4 Rif, Er reg Egypt
66 H7 Riffelalp Switzerland 46.01N 7.46E
66 H8 Riffelberg mt Switzerland 45.59N 7.48E
77 F9 Riffien Morocco 35.50N 5.22W
79 K1 Rifiano Italy 46.43N 11.11E
109 C2 Rifle Colorado 39.32N 107.47W
106 K5 Rifle, R Michigan
50 E2 Rifsnes C Iceland 66.05N 20.26W
50 J2 Rifsœdharvötn lakes Iceland
50 J1 Rifstangi pt Iceland 66.32N 16.10W
103 F3 Rifton New York 41.50N 74.02W
93 H6 Rift Valley Kenya
93 G6 Rift Valley prov Kenya
28 K1 Riga Assam India 28.25N 95.05E
30 J6 Riga Bihar India 26.40N 85.27E
46 E2 Riga Latvia U.S.S.R. 56.53N 24.08E
42 H4 Riga U.S.S.R. 56.40N 106.10E
90 C6 Rigachikun Nigeria 10.39N 7.30E
46 E1 Riga, G.of Estonia/Latvia U.S.S.R.
79 L1 Rigais, Sass mt Italy 46.37N 11.47E
86 J4 Rigal el Khalla hill Egypt 30.43N 32.56E
84 C5 Rigáli mt Greece 38.27N 21.46E
14 B5 Riga, Mt W Australia 22.04S 116.30E
32 H6 Rigān Iran 28.40N 58.58E
84 C5 Rigánion Greece 38.28N 21.46E
71 K9 Rigaud France 44.00N 7.00E
99 Q7 Rigaud Quebec 45.29N 74.19W
93 C2 Rigbo Uganda 3.04N 31.26E
110 O6 Rigby Idaho 43.40N 111.55W
110 J4 Riggins Idaho 45.26N 116.20W
66 F4 Riggisberg Switzerland 46.47N 7.29E
107 F2 Riggston Illinois 39.41N 90.25W
66 K4 Rigidalstock mt Switzerland 46.52N 8.26E
64 M4 Riglasreuth W Germany 49.55N 11.58E
75 J3 Riglos Spain 42.21N 0.44W
32 H7 Rig Mati Iran 27.42N 58.10E
93 N7 Rigmio Kenya 1.08S 41.01E
72 J7 Rignac France 44.24N 2.16E
80 F4 Rignano Flaminio Italy 42.13N 12.29E
80 N5 Rignano Garganico Italy 41.40N 15.36E
79 K7 Rignano sull'Arno Italy 43.43N 11.27E
66 A2 Rigney France 47.23N 6.11E
69 F7 Rigny-le-Ferron France 48.12N 3.38E
71 E3 Rigny-sur-Arroux France 46.32N 4.02E
72 E1 Rigny-Ussé France 47.15N 0.18E
75 E1 Rigoitia Spain 43.19N 2.44W
79 N1 Rigolato Italy 46.33N 12.51E
97 O7 Rigolet Labrador, Nfld 54.10N 58.30W
79 H6 Rigoso Italy 44.22N 10.08E
90 G4 Rig-Rig Chad 14.20N 14.27E
32 G3 Rigū Iran 34.15N 57.23E
75 H3 Riguel R Spain
86 O8 Riha Saudi Arabia 28.51N 35.02E
35 G4 Rihaba Jordan 32.26N 35.47E
34 N7 Rihāb, Ar salt marsh Iraq
29 H5 Rihand Dam Uttar Prad India 24.09N 83.02E
29 H6 Rihand R Madhya Prad India
35 E1 Rihāniya Israel 33.03N 35.29E
51 L11 Riihimäki Finland 60.45N 24.45E
51 M4 Riipi Finland 67.22N 26.10E
123 A7 Riiser-Larsenhalvøya pen Antarctica
115 B1 Riito Mexico 32.10N 114.58W
33 F10 Rija,Am S Yemen 13.03N 44.34E

31 B4 **Rijai** Afghanistan 33.33N 62.54E
60 S17 **Rijckholt** Netherlands 50.48N 5.44E
82 B5 **Rijeka** Yugoslavia 45.20N 14.27E
60 H13 **Rijen** Netherlands 51.35N 4.55E
61 K1 **Rijkevorsel** Belgium 51.21N 4.46E
61 N3 **Rijkhoven** Belgium 50.50N 5.31E
34 G6 **Rijm al Mudhari** cairn Iraq
60 F11 **Rijnsburg** Netherlands 52.12N 4.27E
60 H9 **Rijp, De** Netherlands 52.33N 4.50E
50 U12 **Rijpfjorden** inlet Spitsbergen
60 G11 **Rijpwetering** Netherlands 52.12N 4.38E
60 G13 **Rijsbergen** Netherlands 51.31N 4.42E
Rijsenburg see **Driebergen-Rijsenburg**
60 P10 **Rijssen** Netherlands 52.18N 6.31E
60 K12 **Rijswijk** Gelderland Netherlands 51.58N 5.22E
60 F11 **Rijswijk** Zuid Holland Netherlands 52.03N 4.20E
82 H2 **Rika** R U.S.S.R.
33 F5 **Rikā, Wādī ar** watercourse Saudi Arabia
86 O9 **Rikeib, Wādi er** watercourse Saudi Arabia
103 K7 **Rikers I** New York 40.48N 73.53W
84 E8 **Rikhéa** Greece 36.51N 23.00E
Rikhikesh see **Rishikesh**
26 S7 **Rikiligaskada** Sri Lanka 7.07N 80.47E
122 S15 **Rikitéa** Mangaréva Pacific Oc 23.07S 134.57W
87 G5 **Rikkye** Ethiopia 10.48N 39.55E
28 K1 **Rikor** Assam India 28.50N 94.51E
40 K9 **Rikorda, Mys** C Kuril Is U.S.S.R. 44.25N 146.50E
40 M8 **Rikorda, Proliv** str Kuril Is U.S.S.R.
61 M3 **Riksingen** Belgium 50.48N 5.28E
20 Q2 **Rikuchū Kaigan Nat.Park** Japan
20 P2 **Rikuzen-Takata** Japan 39.03N 141.38E
82 H8 **Rila Planina** mts Bulgaria
107 J2 **Riley** Indiana 39.23N 87.18W
109 O2 **Riley** Kansas 39.17N 96.48W
109 C7 **Riley** New Mexico 34.24N 107.14W
110 F6 **Riley** Oregon 43.31N 119.28W
103 D3 **Rileyville** Pennsylvania 41.44N 75.15W
75 H6 **Rilla** Spain 40.43N 1.00W
61 K3 **Rillaar** Belgium 50.58N 4.53E
60 E14 **Rilland** Netherlands 51.25N 4.11E
70 L7 **Rillé** France 47.27N 0.15E
57 M4 **Rillington** N Yorks Eng 54.09N 0.42W
75 G6 **Rillo de Gallo** Spain 40.52N 1.56W
69 G5 **Rilly-la-Montagne** France 49.11N 4.03E
82 H8 **Rilski Manastir** Bulgaria 42.07N 23.19E
87 B3 **Ril,Wadi Er** Sudan
90 J6 **Rim** Chad 10.29N 18.30E
Rima see **Zayü**
79 D3 **Rima** Italy 45.53N 8.00E
120 B9 **Rimac** dist Lima Peru
120 B1 **Rimachi, L** Peru 4.13S 76.38W
33 E4 **Rimah, Wādī ar** watercourse Saudi Arabia
33 K6 **Rimāl, Ar** des reg Saudi Arabia
50 G3 **Rimar** mt Iceland 65.52N 18.26W
11 J2 **Rimariki I** New Zealand 35.27S 174.47E
79 D3 **Rimasco** Italy 45.52N 8.04E
122 M10 **Rimatara** Tubuai Is Pacific Oc 22.40S 152.45W
69 J7 **Rimaucourt** France 48.15N 5.20E
62 M7 **Rimava** R Czechoslovakia
62 M7 **Rimavská Sobota** Czechoslovakia 48.24N 20.00E
100 C6 **Rimbey** Alberta 52.39N 114.10W
52 L7 **Rimbo** Sweden 59.44N 18.21E
60 U17 **Rimburg** Netherlands 50.55N 6.05E
90 J5 **Rimé** watercourse Chad
66 J8 **Rimella** Italy 45.55N 8.11E
104 F5 **Rimersburg** Pennsylvania 41.03N 79.30W
52 J8 **Rimforsa** Sweden 58.06N 15.40E
86 L9 **Rimhân, Gebel** hill Egypt 28.20N 33.57E
120 A9 **Rimic, Rio** Peru
79 N6 **Rimini** Italy 44.03N 12.34E
82 K5 **Rîmnicul** R Romania
82 L5 **Rîmnicu Sărat** Romania 45.24N 27.06E
69 H4 **Rimogne** France 49.50N 4.33E
72 G9 **Rimont** France 43.01N 1.16E
98 D5 **Rimouski** Quebec 48.26N 68.32W
98 D5 **Rimouski, Parc de** Quebec
98 D5 **Rimouski R** Quebec
53 T14 **Rimøy** isld Norway 62.22N 5.40E
64 H4 **Rimpar** W Germany 49.52N 9.57E
66 H7 **Rimpfischhorn** mt Switzerland 46.02N 7.53E
110 D3 **Rimrock Lake** res Washington 46.38N 121.10W
45 U5 **Rimsko-Korsakovka** U.S.S.R. 51.35N 48.32E
24 F11 **Rinbung** Xizang Zizhiqu China 29.15N 89.47E
118 E7 **Rincão** Brazil 21.35S 48.06W
22 E1 **Rinchinlhümbe** Mongolia 51.05N 99.38E
64 P6 **Rinchnach** W Germany 48.57N 13.14E
120 E12 **Rincón** Argentina 27.05S 68.06W
115 N5 **Rincón** Costa Rica 8.42N 83.30W
109 C9 **Rincon** New Mexico 32.41N 107.03W
105 H7 **Rincon** Puerto Rico 30.22N 67.15W
120 E10 **Rinconada** Argentina 22.25S 66.12W
77 E6 **Rinconada, La** Spain 37.29N 5.58W
120 E10 **Rincon, Cerro del** pk Arg/Chile 24.00S 67.20W
77 H7 **Rincón de la Victoria** Spain 36.43N 4.18W
115 H6 **Rincón de Romos** Mexico 22.13N 102.20W
75 G3 **Rincón de Soto** Spain 42.15N 1.50W
75 H3 **Rincones** R Spain
120 E11 **Rincón, Salina del** salt pan Arg
30 B5 **Rind** R Uttar Prad India
23 B3 **Rinda** Sichuan China 31.14N 100.45E
52 E3 **Rindal** Norway 63.04N 9.13E
53 W15 **Rindalshorne** mt Norway 61.58N 7.06E
53 A6 **Rindby** Denmark 55.26N 8.25E
18 F8 **Rindingan, Bukit** mt Sumatra Indon 5.17S 104.35E
53 B4 **Rind Kirke** Denmark 56.06N 8.58E
53 A4 **Rindūm** Denmark 56.06N 8.17E
81 J6 **Rinella** Lipari Is Italy 38.33N 14.50E
12 J8 **Ringarooma** Tasmania 41.14S 147.44E
12 J8 **Ringarooma B** Tasmania
Ringdove see **Lamenu**
53 E6 **Ringe** Denmark 55.14N 10.30E
52 E5 **Ringebu** Norway 61.30N 10.12E
53 V18 **Ringedalsvatn** L Norway 60.08N 6.13E
66 O4 **Ringelspitz** mt Switzerland 46.54N 9.22E
63 E9 **Ringenberg** W Germany 51.44N 6.37E
63 T6 **Ringenwalde** E Germany 53.04N 13.44E
52 E6 **Ringerike** Norway 60.10N 10.16E
57 E3 **Ringford** Dumfries & Galloway Scotland 54.54N 4.03W
64 J1 **Ringgau** W Germany 51.06N 10.05E
66 H5 **Ringgenberg** Switzerland 46.43N 7.53E
107 C9 **Ringgold** Louisiana 32.20N 93.19W
108 K8 **Ringgold** Nebraska 41.31N 100.46W
112 K2 **Ringgold** Texas 33.50N 97.57W
9 U4 **Ringgold Is** Fiji
25 N7 **Ringhkung** Burma 26.45N 98.22E
90 D5 **Ringim** Nigeria 12.11N 9.13E
53 C5 **Ringive Kirke** Denmark 55.48N 9.11E
53 A4 **Ringkøbing** Denmark 56.06N 8.05E
53 B4 **Ringkøbing** co Denmark
53 A4 **Ringkøbing Fjord** inlet Denmark 56.00N 8.12E
84 W23 **Ringládhes** Corfu 39.26N 20.03E
18 B7 **Ringlet** Pen Malaysia 4.24N 101.22E
110 P3 **Ringling** Montana 46.16N 110.49W
109 N7 **Ringling** Oklahoma 34.12N 97.36W
56 M6 **Ringmer** E Sussex Eng 50.53N 0.04E
103 E6 **Ringoes** New Jersey 40.26N 74.52W
109 P7 **Ringold** Oklahoma 34.14N 95.10W
91 E10 **Ringoma** Angola 12.25S 17.32E
53 V18 **Ringøy** Norway 60.26N 6.45E
52 F6 **Ringsaker** Norway 60.54N 10.45E
59 J1 **Ringsend** Londonderry N Ireland 55.02N 6.45W
52 H11 **Ringsjön** L Sweden 55.55N 13.30E
53 H6 **Ringsted** Denmark 55.28N 11.48E
108 Q6 **Ringsted** Iowa 43.19N 94.30W
52 J8 **Ringstorp** Sweden 58.25N 15.01E
103 B5 **Ringtown** Pennsylvania 40.52N 76.14W
29 D4 **Ringus** Rajasthan India 27.18N 75.27E
51 G2 **Ringvassøy** isld Norway 69.55N 19.10E
59 G7 **Ringville** Waterford Irish Rep 52.03N 7.35W
57 J6 **Ringway** airport Greater Manchester Eng 53.21N 2.15W
56 H6 **Ringwood** Dorset Eng 50.51N 1.47W
103 F4 **Ringwood** New Jersey 41.07N 74.15W
13 C6 **Ringwood** N Terr Australia 23.50S 134.58E
109 M5 **Ringwood** Oklahoma 36.24N 98.16W
12 H7 **Ringwood** Victoria 37.51S 145.13E
83 G7 **Rinía** isld Greece 37.23N 25.13E
121 A7 **Riñihue** Chile 39.47S 72.30W
121 A7 **Riñihue, L** Chile
19 A8 **Rinja** isld Indonesia 8.43S 119.40E
18 M10 **Rinjani** mt Indonesia 8.25S 116.28E
53 D7 **Rinkenæs** Denmark 54.54N 9.35E
48 T6 **Rinks Isbræ** ice field Greenland
65 E7 **Rinn** Austria 47.15N 11.31E
59 G4 **Rinn L** Leitrim Irish Rep 53.53N 7.50W
59 G4 **Rinn R** Leitrim etc Irish Rep
57 D3 **Rinns of Galloway, The** reg Dumfries & Galloway Scotland
57 E2 **Rinns of Kells** reg Dumfries & Galloway Scotland
24 F11 **Rinqênzê** Xizang Zizhiqu China 29.26N 88.33E
60 M6 **Rinsumageest** Netherlands 53.18N 5.57E
63 K8 **Rinteln** W Germany 52.11N 9.04E
69 B2 **Rinxent** France 50.47N 1.43E
23 B4 **Rinzhubtang** Sichuan China 29.39N 101.44E
106 D8 **Rio** Illinois 41.06N 90.24W
107 G11 **Rio** Louisiana 30.41N 89.55W
103 E4 **Rio** New York 41.28N 74.45W
76 E4 **Rio** Spain 42.22N 7.18W
106 E6 **Rio** Wisconsin 43.26N 89.14W
115 G10 **Río Abajo** Panama 9.00N 79.28W
118 C5 **Rio Alegre** Brazil 16.52S 56.45W
121 F1 **Río Araza** Argentina 27.25S 59.05W
118 E9 **Rio Azul** Brazil 25.42S 50.49W
119 B8 **Riobamba** Ecuador 1.44S 78.40W
76 D1 **Riobarba** Spain 43.40N 7.40W
120 D7 **Río Blanco** Bolivia 17.53S 69.04W
115 L8 **Río Blanco** Mexico 18.49N 97.14W
118 G8 **Rio Bonito** Brazil 22.39S 42.37W
120 E3 **Rio Branco** Brazil 9.59S 67.49W
121 H4 **Río Branco** Uruguay 32.32S 53.28W
118 E9 **Rio Branco do Sul** Brazil 25.05S 49.31W
112 J10 **Río Bravo** Tamaulipas Mexico 25.59N 98.05W
115 K5 **Río Bravo, Ciudad** Mexico 25.58N 98.04W
118 C7 **Rio Brilhante** Brazil 21.48S 54.32W
121 A8 **Río Bueno** Chile 40.20S 72.55W
116 J1 **Rio Bueno** Jamaica, W I 18.28N 77.28W
76 C5 **Riocaldo** Spain 41.52N 8.07W
119 G2 **Río Caribe** Venezuela 10.43N 63.06W
118 G7 **Rio Casca** Brazil 20.13S 42.38W
121 D3 **Río Ceballos** Argentina 31.07S 64.18W
121 L7 **Río Chico** Argentina 49.50S 68.35W
119 G2 **Río Chico** Venezuela 10.22N 65.59W
118 F8 **Rio Claro** Brazil 22.19S 47.35W
116 O2 **Rio Claro** Trinidad & Tobago 10.18N 61.11W
119 E3 **Río Claro** Venezuela 9.54N 69.23W
121 D7 **Río Colorado** Argentina 38.58S 64.05W
118 J9 **Rio Comprido** Brazil 22.55S 43.13W
119 C9 **Río Corrientes** Ecuador 2.24S 76.27W
121 D4 **Río Cuarto** Argentina 33.08S 64.20W
118 F2 **Rio da Conceição** Brazil 11.22S 46.48W
118 H3 **Rio de Contas** Brazil 13.34S 41.46W
118 G7 **Rio de Janeiro** Brazil 22.53S 43.17W
118 G8 **Rio de Janeiro** state Brazil
115 O6 **Río de Jesús** Panama 7.58N 81.01W
110 A9 **Rio Dell Scotia** California 40.30N 124.07W
75 D2 **Río de Losa** Spain 42.57N 3.16W
90 D9 **Rio-del-Rey** Cameroon 4.44N 8.37E
76 E7 **Rio de Mel** Portugal 40.48N 7.24W
76 C12 **Rio de Moinhos** Baixo Alentejo Portugal 38.12N 8.20W
76 C13 **Rio de Moinhos** Baixo Alentejo Portugal 37.53N 8.13W
76 A11 **Rio de Mouro** Portugal 38.46N 9.19W
76 F5 **Rio de Onor** Portugal 41.56N 6.38W
88 F10 **Rio de Oro, B.de** Mauritania
79 L1 **Rio de Pusteria** Italy 46.48N 11.41E
75 H7 **Riodeva** Spain 40.07N 1.09W
121 J1 **Rio do Sul** Brazil 27.15S 49.37W
96 V7 **Rio, El** str Canary Is
117 J9 **Rio Formoso** Brazil 8.35S 35.04W
76 K7 **Riofrío** Spain 40.32N 4.47W
76 G5 **Riofrío de Aliste** Spain 41.49N 6.10W
75 D5 **Riofrio de Riaza** Spain 41.14N 3.27W
77 H7 **Ríogordo** Spain 36.55N 4.18W
121 L9 **Río Grande** Argentina 53.45S 67.46W
120 E9 **Río Grande** Bolivia 20.50S 67.16W
115 H6 **Río Grande** Mexico 23.50N 103.02W
103 E8 **Rio Grande** New Jersey 39.02N 74.51W
117 F8 **Rio Grande** Piauí Brazil 7.40S 43.04W
105 K7 **Rio Grande** Puerto Rico 18.23N 65.51W
121 H4 **Rio Grande** Rio Grande do Sul Brazil 32.03S 52.08W
116 M2 **Rio Grande** R Jamaica, W I
112 J9 **Rio Grande City** Texas 26.24N 98.50W
117 H7 **Rio Grande do Norte** state Brazil
121 H2 **Rio Grande do Sul** state Brazil
109 C4 **Rio Grande Res** Colorado 37.43N 107.19W
96 G12 **Rio Grande Rise** Atlantic Oc
120 E11 **Río Grande, Salar de** salt pan Arg
112 K10 **Rio Grande Valley** airport Texas 25.55N 97.24W
119 D2 **Ríohacha** Colombia 11.34N 72.58W
115 O5 **Río Hato** Panama 8.21N 80.10W
121 D1 **Río Hondo** Argentina 27.32S 64.57W
112 K9 **Rio Hondo** Texas 26.24N 97.36W
121 D1 **Río Hondo, Embalse** res Argentina
120 B2 **Rioja** Peru 6.02S 77.10W
77 M7 **Rioja** Spain 36.56N 2.26W
75 F3 **Rioja, La** reg Spain
115 P7 **Río Lagartos** Mexico 21.36N 88.08W
117 J9 **Rio Largo** Brazil 9.28S 35.50W
81 B4 **Riola Sardo** Sardinia 40.00N 8.32E
111 C3 **Rio Linda** California 38.41N 121.30W
79 L6 **Riolo** Italy 44.17N 11.43E
76 G9 **Riolobos** Spain 39.55N 6.19W
71 B9 **Riols** France 43.31N 2.47E
71 C5 **Riom** France 45.54N 3.07E
79 G6 **Riomaggiore** Italy 44.06N 9.44E
76 B10 **Rio Maior** Portugal 39.20N 8.55W
118 C4 **Rio Manso** Brazil 15.40S 55.15W
80 B3 **Rio Marina** Italy 42.49N 10.26E
112 J6 **Riomedina** Texas 29.26N 98.54W
72 K5 **Riom-lès-Montagnes** France 45.17N 2.39E
120 G12 **Río Muerto** Argentina 26.16S 61.40W
120 E8 **Río Mulatos** Bolivia 19.40S 66.46W
Rio Muni see **Mbini**
72 C8 **Rion-des-Landes** France 43.56N 0.55W
120 F3 **Río Negro** Bolivia 9.51S 65.39W
121 A8 **Río Negro** Chile 40.50S 73.14W
118 E10 **Rio Negro** Paraná Brazil 26.06S 49.46W
121 F4 **Río Negro** dept Uruguay
121 C8 **Río Negro** terr Argentina
121 G4 **Río Negro, Embalse del** res Uruguay
118 C6 **Rio Negro, Pantanal do** swamp Brazil
80 B3 **Rio nell'Elba** Italy 42.49N 10.24E
80 N7 **Rionero in Vulture** Italy 40.55N 15.40E
80 K5 **Rionero Sannitico** Italy 41.43N 14.09E
44 E5 **Rioni** R Georgia U.S.S.R.
118 J9 **Rio Niterói, Ponte** Brazil
118 G7 **Rio Novo** Minas Gerais Brazil 21.15S 43.09W
77 M3 **Riopar** Spain 38.30N 2.26W
121 H2 **Rio Pardo** Brazil 30.00S 52.20W
118 G4 **Rio Pardo de Minas** Brazil 15.38S 42.34W
120 F10 **Río Pescado** Argentina 22.55S 64.26W
120 F11 **Río Piedras** Argentina 25.18S 64.54W
118 G7 **Rio Pomba** Brazil 21.15S 43.12W
118 G8 **Rio Prêto** Brazil 22.06S 43.52W
118 E3 **Rio Prêto, Cachoeira do** rapids Brazil 13.39S 48.08W
118 F5 **Rio Prêto, Serra do** mts Brazil
121 D3 **Río Primero** Argentina 31.20S 63.40W
77 M7 **Río, Pta. del** Spain 36.49N 2.24W
109 D7 **Rio Puerco** New Mexico 34.48N 106.59W
118 J2 **Rio Real** Brazil 11.30S 37.56W
103 E3 **Rio Res** New York
76 E5 **Ríos** Spain 41.58N 7.16W
76 H2 **Riosa** Spain 43.14N 5.53W
79 J5 **Rio Saliceto** Italy 44.49N 10.48E
Rio Seco see **Ville de María**
76 H3 **Rioseco de Tapia** Spain 42.43N 5.47W
121 D3 **Río Segundo de Garay** Argentina 31.40S 63.59W
75 C6 **Río Sequillo, Embalse de** res Spain 40.58N 3.37W
117 D10 **Riosinho** R Brazil
119 C5 **Ríosucio** Caldas Colombia 5.26N 75.44W
119 C4 **Ríosucio** Choco Colombia 7.25N 77.05W
121 D4 **Río Tercero** Argentina 32.15S 64.08W
119 C9 **Río Tigre** Ecuador 2.07S 76.07W
117 J8 **Rio Tinto** Brazil 6.45S 35.07W
110 K8 **Rio Tinto** Nevada 41.49N 115.59W
76 B6 **Rio Tinto** Portugal 41.11N 8.34W
119 E2 **Río Tocuyo** Venezuela 10.18N 70.00W
76 E2 **Ríotorto** Spain 43.20N 7.15W
19 H7 **Rio Tuba** Philippines 8.30N 117.24E
121 J8 **Rio Turbio Mines** Argentina 51.41S 72.16W
74 H9 **Riou** R Algeria
71 G10 **Riou, I de** France 43.10N 5.23E
101 U6 **Riou L** Saskatchewan
118 E5 **Rio Verde** Brazil 17.50S 50.55W
121 K9 **Río Verde** Chile 52.38S 71.15W
119 B7 **Rioverde** Ecuador 1.03N 79.24W
115 J7 **Río Verde** Mexico 21.58N 100.00W
118 C6 **Rio Verdi de Mato Grosso** Brazil 18.54S 54.50W
115 F9 **Río Viejo** Panama 9.24N 79.48W
112 K3 **Rio Vista** Texas 32.15N 97.24W
71 J2 **Rioz** France 47.25N 6.05E
120 E3 **Riozinho** Amazonas Brazil 9.30S 66.48W
120 G4 **Riozinho** Rondônia Brazil 11.32S 61.18W
118 C6 **Riozinho** R Mato Grosso do Sul Brazil
117 B8 **Riozinho** R Pará Brazil
117 C8 **Riozinho** R Pará Brazil
119 F9 **Riozinho, R** Amazonas Brazil
50 F3 **Rip** Iceland 65.40N 19.30W
80 L5 **Ripabottoni** Italy 41.41N 14.49E
80 N7 **Ripacandida** Italy 40.54N 15.49E
80 B3 **Ripalti, Pta.dei** Italy 42.42N 10.26E
82 F6 **Ripanj** Yugoslavia 44.39N 20.30E
80 C2 **Riparbella** Italy 43.22N 10.36E
110 G3 **Riparia** Washington 46.36N 118.04W
80 J3 **Ripatransone** Italy 43.00N 13.46E
51 H5 **Ripats** Sweden 66.57N 20.45E
98 K2 **Ripault, L** Quebec
79 O7 **Ripe** Italy 43.40N 13.06E
80 H5 **Ripi** Italy 41.37N 13.26E
111 K8 **Ripley** California 33.30N 114.40W
57 L6 **Ripley** Derbys Eng 53.03N 1.24W
107 H7 **Ripley** Mississippi 34.43N 88.58W
104 F4 **Ripley** New York 42.16N 79.43W
57 K4 **Ripley** N Yorks Eng 54.03N 1.34W
104 B8 **Ripley** Ohio 38.45N 83.50W
109 O5 **Ripley** Oklahoma 36.01N 96.55W
99 J8 **Ripley** Ontario 44.04N 81.34W
56 L5 **Ripley** Surrey Eng 51.18N 0.29W
107 G6 **Ripley** Tennessee 35.43N 89.30W
104 D8 **Ripley** W Virginia 38.49N 81.44W
75 P3 **Ripoll** Spain 42.12N 2.12E
75 P5 **Ripollet** Spain 41.29N 2.10E
111 C4 **Ripon** California 37.44N 121.08W
57 K4 **Ripon** N Yorks Eng 54.08N 1.31W
99 P7 **Ripon** Quebec 45.45N 75.07W
106 F6 **Ripon** Wisconsin 43.51N 88.50W
81 K8 **Riposto** Sicily 37.44N 15.13E
108 Q8 **Rippey** Iowa 41.55N 94.10W
Rippoldsau see **Bad Rippoldsau**
57 K5 **Ripponden** W Yorks Eng 53.41N 1.57W
28 H2 **Ripu** Assam India 26.45N 90.09E
93 J2 **Ririba** watercourse Kenya/Ethiopia
30 G5 **Riri Bazar** Nepal 27.58N 83.26E
30 E3 **Ririkot** Nepal 29.13N 81.13E
90 D6 **Ririwai** Nigeria 10.43N 8.45E
53 C5 **Ris** Denmark 55.50N 9.19E
34 F3 **Risāfe** Syria 35.38N 38.43E
31 G3 **Risalpur** Pakistan 34.05N 72.02E
82 E8 **Risan** Yugoslavia 42.32N 18.42E
86 L4 **Risân 'Aneiza** hill Egypt 30.54N 33.44E
119 C5 **Risaralda** div Colombia
91 J4 **Risasi** Zaïre 0.30S 25.48E
52 J2 **Risbäck** Sweden 64.43N 15.35E
56 E4 **Risca** Gwent Wales 51.37N 3.07W
72 D8 **Riscle** France 43.40N 0.04W
77 F3 **Risco** Spain 38.55N 5.07W
96 U15 **Risco, El** Gran Canaria Canary Is 28.03N 15.45W
121 B5 **Risco Plateado** mt Argentina 34.55S 70.02W
12 F7 **Risdon** Hobart, Tasmania 42.49S 147.21E
12 F8 **Risdon Cove** Tasmania
12 F7 **Risdon Vale** Tasmania 42.49S 147.21E
53 C6 **Rise** Denmark 55.03N 9.22E
52 J2 **Risede** Sweden 64.24N 15.10E
56 L3 **Riseley** Beds Eng 52.15N 0.29W
56 K5 **Riseley** Berks Eng 51.22N 0.58W
53 S15 **Risevatn** L Norway 61.45N 5.19E
53 C3 **Risgårde Bredning** B Denmark 56.45N 9.12E
82 K8 **Rish** Bulgaria 42.57N 26.57E
32 D6 **Rishahr** Iran 28.52N 50.53E
86 N9 **Risha, Jabal** mt Saudi Arabia 28.18N 34.47E
33 F4 **Rishā', Wādī ar** watercourse Saudi Arabia
30 B2 **Rishikesh** Uttar Prad India 30.06N 78.16E
21 J5 **Rishiri-tō** isld Japan
Rishon Letsiyon see **Rishon le Zion**
35 C6 **Rishon le Zion** Israel 31.57N 34.48E
35 B6 **Rishon le Zion, Holot** sand dunes Israel
32 K7 **Rish Pish** Iran 26.48N 63.11E
35 C5 **Rishpon** Israel 32.12N 34.49E
86 G7 **Rishrâsh Wâdî** watercourse Egypt
57 J5 **Rishton** Lancs Eng 53.47N 2.24W
81 J9 **Risicone** R Sicily
105 B3 **Rising Fawn** Georgia 34.44N 85.32W
112 J3 **Rising Star** Texas 32.05N 98.58W
104 K7 **Rising Sun** Delaware 39.41N 75.48W
107 M3 **Rising Sun** Indiana 38.58N 84.53W
103 B7 **Rising Sun** Maryland 39.43N 76.04W
104 B5 **Rising Sun** Ohio 41.15N 83.26W
53 T21 **Riska** Norway 58.56N 5.52E
101 M10 **Riske Creek** Br Col 51.58N 122.31W
70 L3 **Risle** R France
57 H6 **Risley** Cheshire Eng 53.26N 2.32W
53 S16 **Risnes** Norway 61.09N 5.10E
82 B5 **Risnjak** mt Yugoslavia 45.24N 14.36E
82 J5 **Rîşnov** Romania 45.35N 25.27E
107 D8 **Rison** Arkansas 33.58N 92.11W
52 E8 **Risør** Norway 58.44N 9.15E
69 C6 **Ris-Orangis** France 48.39N 2.25E
71 J3 **Risoux, Mt** France 46.38N 6.12E
64 H7 **Riss** R W Germany
87 F2 **Rissai, Er** Sudan 16.40N 36.39E
88 L6 **Rissani** Morocco 31.23N 4.09W
11 L6 **Rissington** New Zealand 39.24S 176.42E
53 E4 **Risskov** Denmark 56.11N 10.15E
86 D6 **Rissu, Gebel** hill Egypt 29.54N 30.25E
46 E1 **Risti** Estonia U.S.S.R. 58.59N 24.01E
51 N10 **Ristiina** Finland 61.32N 27.15E
51 N7 **Ristijärvi** Finland 64.30N 28.15E
47 C2 **Ristikent** U.S.S.R. 68.40N 31.47E
53 F7 **Ristinge** Denmark 54.50N 10.38E
51 J5 **Risträsk** Sweden 66.32N 21.55E
Risūt see **Raysūt**
103 C4 **Rita** Pennsylvania 41.07N 75.52W
112 B8 **Rita Blanca Cr** R Texas
101 O2 **Ritch I** Gt Bear L, N W Terr 66.52N 119.18W
95 H5 **Ritchie** S Africa 29.02S 24.35E
14 B5 **Ritchie Reef** W Australia 20.18S 115.20E
28 G7 **Ritchie's Arch'** Andaman Is
48 T8 **Ritenbenk** Greenland 69.48N 51.30W
19 M1 **Ritidian Pt** Guam Pacific Oc 13.39N 144.51E
26 S5 **Ritigala** mt Sri Lanka 8.06N 80.40E
91 F12 **Rito** Angola 16.34S 19.04E
66 L5 **Ritom, L** Switzerland 46.33N 8.42E
44 D4 **Ritsa** Georgia U.S.S.R. 43.28N 40.34E
64 J3 **Ritschenhausen** E Germany 50.30N 10.27E
84 G5 **Ritsóna** Greece 38.24N 23.31E
110 F5 **Ritter** Oregon 44.55N 119.09W
63 J6 **Ritterhude** W Germany 53.10N 8.45E
111 E4 **Ritter, Mt** California 37.40N 119.15W
66 J6 **Ritter Pass** Italy/Switz 46.18N 8.10E
60 B3 **Ritthem** Netherlands 51.27N 3.38E
104 D6 **Rittman** Ohio 40.58N 81.47W
63 M10 **Rittmarshausen** W Germany 51.29N 10.05E
75 F4 **Rituerto** R Spain
66 J5 **Ritzlihorn** mt Switzerland 46.38N 8.16E
110 G2 **Ritzville** Washington 47.08N 118.23W
30 L4 **Riu** Xizang Zizhiqu 28.01N 87.39E
75 Q4 **Riudarenas** Spain 41.50N 2.42E
75 M5 **Riudecanas** Spain 41.08N 0.58E
75 M5 **Riudecols** Spain 41.10N 0.59E
75 N5 **Riudoms** Spain 41.08N 1.03E
25 E7 **Riu, Laem** C Thailand 10.04N 99.10E
19 B8 **Riung** Indonesia 8.25S 120.57E
66 O7 **Riva** Italy 46.14N 9.28E
79 J3 **Riva** Italy 45.53N 10.50E
79 M1 **Riva** R Italy
37 G1 **Riva** R Turkey
70 K3 **Riva Bella** France 49.17N 0.15W
121 E5 **Rivadavia** Buenos Aires Arg 35.29S 62.59W
121 B2 **Rivadavia** Chile 29.57S 70.35W
121 C4 **Rivadavia** Mendoza Arg 33.13S 68.30W
120 G11 **Rivadavia** Salta Arg 24.08S 62.54W
121 B9 **Rivadavia, L** Argentina
79 M1 **Riva di Tures** Italy 46.57N 12.04E
79 O3 **Rivagnano** Italy 45.53N 13.03E
37 G1 **Rivaköy** Turkey 41.14N 29.05E
71 F6 **Rival** R France
50 V14 **Rivalensundet** sound Spitsbergen
79 E5 **Rivalta Bormida** Italy 44.43N 8.33E
79 M2 **Rivamonte** Italy 46.15N 12.01E
79 F5 **Rivanazzano** Italy 44.56N 9.01E
115 F3 **Riva Palacio** Mexico 28.32N 106.30W
79 C5 **Riva presso Chieri** Italy 44.58N 7.52E
79 C4 **Rivarolo Canavese** Italy 45.20N 7.43E
115 M4 **Rivas** Nicaragua 11.26N 85.50W
66 M8 **Riva San Vitale** Switzerland 45.54N 8.58E
32 H3 **Rivash** Iran 35.25N 58.25E
79 C3 **Riva Valdobbia** Italy 45.50N 7.58E
79 O2 **Rive d'Arcano** Italy 46.08N 13.02E
71 F5 **Rive-de-Gier** France 45.32N 4.36E
72 B3 **Rivedoux-Plage** France 46.09N 1.16W
67 O11 **Rivellata, Pta di a** Corsica 42.35N 8.43E
81 L3 **Rivello** Italy 40.04N 15.46E
53 W16 **Rivenosa** mt Norway 61.22N 7.29E
53 X15 **Rivenoskulen** mt Norway 61.44N 7.32E
121 D6 **Rivera** Argentina 37.13S 63.14W
111 D4 **Riverbank** California 37.43N 120.56W
89 E9 **River Cess** Liberia 5.28N 9.32W
59 K6 **Riverchapel** Wexford Irish Rep 52.38N 6.13W
111 E5 **Riverdale** California 36.26N 119.53W
109 N4 **Riverdale** Kansas 37.23N 97.25W
110 O2 **Riverdale** Montana 47.21N 111.36W
108 J2 **Riverdale** N Dakota 47.31N 101.22W
108 L9 **Riverdale** Nebraska 40.47N 99.08W
103 F5 **Riverdale** New Jersey 40.59N 74.19W
98 L8 **River Denys** C Breton I, Nova Scotia 45.47N 61.12W
103 J6 **River Edge** New Jersey 40.57N 74.03W
107 K10 **River Falls** Alabama 31.21N 86.33W
106 B5 **River Falls** Wisconsin 44.51N 92.40W
106 Q2 **River Forest** dist Chicago, Illinois
79 G5 **Rivergaro** Italy 44.55N 9.36E
56 M5 **Riverhead** Kent Eng 51.17N 0.11E
103 J5 **Riverhead** Long I, N Y 40.55N 72.40W
98 T7 **Riverhead** Newfoundland 46.58N 53.32W
98 H8 **River Hébert** Nova Scotia 45.42N 64.25W
100 L8 **Riverhurst** Saskatchewan 50.55N 106.50W
14 D8 **Riverina** W Australia 29.44S 120.32E
12 G5 **Riverina** reg New S Wales
98 J8 **River John** Nova Scotia 45.44N 63.03W
55 G2 **River Lea Navigation** canal London England
75 D1 **Rivero** Spain 43.02N 3.29W
112 M9 **River Oaks** Fort Worth, Texas 32.46N 97.23W
112 F9 **River Oaks** Houston, Texas 29.44N 95.25W
98 P3 **River of Ponds** Newfoundland 50.32N 57.23W
121 J5 **Rivero, I** Chile 45.45S 74.15W
103 L3 **River Point** Rhode I 41.43N 71.32W
98 H9 **Riverport** Nova Scotia 44.18N 64.21W
106 M3 **River Rouge** dist Detroit, Michigan
100 R8 **Rivers** Manitoba 50.02N 100.14W
90 C9 **Rivers** state Nigeria
95 E10 **Riversdale** Cape Province S Africa 34.05S 21.15E
11 C12 **Riversdale** New Zealand 45.50S 168.47E
11 L8 **Riversdale** New Zealand 41.04S 176.06E
95 M2 **Riversdale** Transvaal S Africa 26.35S 28.03E
111 G8 **Riverside** California 33.59N 117.22W
104 H8 **Riverside** Maryland 38.24N 77.10W
103 E6 **Riverside** New Jersey 40.02N 74.58W
99 H10 **Riverside** Ontario 42.20N 82.56W
110 G6 **Riverside** Oregon 43.32N 118.08W
103 A5 **Riverside** Pennsylvania 40.57N 76.38W
103 M3 **Riverside** Rhode I 41.47N 71.22W
95 N6 **Riverside** S Africa 30.05S 29.42E
112 M5 **Riverside** Texas 30.52N 95.26W
110 N8 **Riverside** Utah 41.48N 112.10W
108 D8 **Riverside** Wyoming 41.13N 106.46W
109 F1 **Riverside Res** Colorado 40.20N 104.16W
101 K10 **Rivers Inlet** Br Columbia 51.42N 127.15W
106 K7 **Rivers Junction** Michigan 42.23N 85.28W
13 E4 **Riversleigh** Queensland 19.01S 138.40E
100 M9 **Rivers, L. of the** Saskatchewan
59 K4 **Riverstown** Louth Irish Rep 53.51N 6.26W
59 F3 **Riverstown** Sligo Irish Rep 54.08N 8.24W
107 G2 **Riverton** Illinois 39.51N 89.31W
108 P9 **Riverton** Iowa 40.42N 95.32W
100 U8 **Riverton** Manitoba 51.00N 97.00W
108 M9 **Riverton** Nebraska 40.04N 98.44W
103 E6 **Riverton** New Jersey 40.01N 75.00W
11 C13 **Riverton** New Zealand 46.21S 168.02E
95 H4 **Riverton** S Africa 28.30S 24.47E
12 E5 **Riverton** S Australia 34.08S 138.24E
104 G8 **Riverton** Virginia 38.58N 78.13W
108 B6 **Riverton** Wyoming 43.02N 108.22W
107 F6 **Rivervale** Arkansas 35.41N 90.21W
99 K6 **River Valley** Ontario 46.35N 80.10W
108 L7 **Riverview** Nebraska 42.44N 99.25W
71 G6 **Rives** France 45.21N 5.29E
107 G5 **Rives** Tennessee 36.21N 89.02W
72 K10 **Rivesaltes** France 42.46N 2.52E
104 E7 **Rivesville** W Virginia 39.33N 80.08W
12 A6 **Rivett** dist Canberra Australia
112 K8 **Riviera** Texas 27.20N 97.50W
105 G11 **Riviera Beach** Florida 26.46N 80.06W
79 F6 **Riviera di Levante** reg Italy
79 D7 **Riviera di Ponente** Italy
61 K5 **Rivière** Belgium 50.22N 4.52E
70 J4 **Rivière** Orne France 48.46N 0.40W
69 D3 **Rivière** Pas de Calais France 50.14N 2.42E
98 G4 **Rivière-à-Claude** Quebec 49.14N 65.56W
98 J4 **Rivière-à-la Loutre** Anticosti I, Que 49.38N 63.48W
99 S6 **Rivière à Pierre** Quebec 46.59N 72.11W
98 H5 **Rivière-au-Renard** Quebec 48.59N 64.26W
98 G3 **Rivière aux Graines** Quebec 50.18N 65.13W
99 S5 **Rivière-aux-Rats** Quebec 47.13N 72.54W
98 C6 **Rivière-Bleue** Quebec 47.26N 69.02W
26 U16 **Rivière d'Abord, Pte** Réunion Indian Oc 21.20S 55.29E
98 K4 **Rivière-de-la-Chaloupe** Anticosti I, Que 49.09N 62.31W
26 U13 **Rivière des Anguilles** Mauritius, Indian Oc 20.29S 57.33E
98 C6 **Rivière du Loup** Quebec 47.49N 69.32W
99 S5 **Rivière du Milieu** Quebec 47.07N 72.36W
98 B5 **Rivière du Moulin** Quebec 48.26N 71.00W
26 V11 **Rivière du Rempart** Mauritius, Indian Oc 20.06S 57.41E
99 M4 **Rivière Héva** Quebec 48.15N 78.15W
66 A4 **Rivière, la** France 46.52N 6.13E
26 U16 **Rivière, La** Réunion Ind Oc 21.15S 55.27E
98 G4 **Rivière-Madeleine** Quebec 49.15N 65.19W
98 B6 **Rivière Ouelle** Quebec 47.27N 70.02W
98 E4 **Rivière Pentecôte** Quebec 49.46N 67.12W
98 G3 **Rivière Pigou** Quebec 50.17N 65.37W
116 L4 **Rivière Pilote** Martinique W I 14.29N 60.54W
98 C5 **Rivière-Portneuf** Quebec 48.38N 69.08W
98 F4 **Rivière-Ste. Anne, Parc** Quebec
98 H3 **Rivière St. Jean** Quebec 50.19N 64.21W
70 L3 **Rivière-St. Sauveur, la** France 49.24N 0.17E
116 L4 **Rivière Salée** Martinique W I 14.32N 60.59W
99 S8 **Rivières des Prairies** Quebec 45.38N 73.35W
72 L7 **Rivière-sur-Tarn** France 44.12N 3.07E
98 D6 **Rivière-Verte** New Brunswick 47.19N 68.09W
98 C6 **Rivière-Verte** Quebec 47.47N 69.28W
95 C10 **Riviersonderend** S Africa 34.10S 19.55E
95 C10 **Riviersonderend** R S Africa
57 H5 **Rivington** Lancs Eng 53.38N 2.35W
80 G3 **Rivodutri** Italy 42.31N 12.52E
79 C4 **Rivoli** Italy 45.04N 7.31E
12 F7 **Rivoli B** S Australia
79 J3 **Rivoli Veronese** Italy 45.34N 10.48E
79 G4 **Rivolta d'Adda** Italy 45.28N 9.31E
94 T13 **Rivonia** S Africa 26.03S 28.02E
53 N9 **Rivtangi** C Faeroes 62.21N 6.58W
11 G8 **Riwaka** New Zealand 41.05S 173.00E
Riwoche see **Riwoqê**
23 A3 **Riwoqê** Xizang Zizhiqu China 31.28N 96.25E
24 J10 **Riwoqê** Xizang Zizhiqu China 31.13N 96.30E
61 J4 **Rixensart** Belgium 50.43N 4.32E
66 F1 **Rixheim** France 47.45N 7.25E
Riyāḍ, Ar see **Riyadh**
33 G4 **Riyadh** Saudi Arabia 24.39N 46.46E
29 C4 **Riyan** Rajasthan India 26.25N 73.32E
33 H9 **Riyan** S Yemen 14.38N 49.16E
32 F3 **Riza** Iran 35.34N 55.21E
84 D7 **Rizais** Greece 37.27N 22.27E
Rizaīyeh see **Rezā'īyeh**
Riza, Kuh-i see **Rezā, Kūh-e** mt
19 K4 **Rizal** Luzon Philippines 15.42N 121.05E
37 F4 **Rize** Turkey 41.03N 40.31E
85 M7 **Rizeiqât, El** Egypt 25.29N 32.28E
23 H1 **Rizhao** Shandong China 35.29N 119.29E
Rizhskiy Zaliv see **Riga, G. of**
84 T13 **Rizokarpaso** Cyprus 35.35N 34.24E
84 C2 **Rízoma** Greece 39.40N 21.44E
84 E3 **Rizómilos** Greece 39.26N 22.45E
32 G4 **Rīzū** Iran 32.21N 56.04E
32 G5 **Rīzū'īyeh** Iran 31.04N 56.21E
67 O13 **Rizzanèse** R Corsica
81 L7 **Rizziconi** Italy 38.25N 15.58E
81 B2 **Rizzolu** R Sardinia
81 O6 **Rizzuto, C** Italy 38.54N 17.06E
53 T14 **Rjånes** Norway 62.15N 5.59E
53 V17 **Rjoande** R Norway 60.44N 6.18E
53 Z19 **Rjukan** Norway 59.54N 8.33E
50 F5 **Rjúpnafell** mt Húnavatnssýsla, Austur Iceland 64.51N 19.28W
50 G7 **Rjúpnafell** mt Skaftafellssýsla, Vestur Iceland 63.38N 18.43W
50 D4 **Rjúpnafell** mt Strandasýsla Iceland 65.23N 21.29W
53 W20 **Rjuven** mts Norway
15 F6 **R Keten** mts Irian Jaya
89 B3 **Rkiz, L** Mauritania
35 E1 **Rmaïch** Lebanon 33.04N 35.22E
53 P12 **Rø** Bornholm Denmark 55.13N 14.55E
52 L7 **Rö** Sweden 59.42N 18.22E
25 J5 **Ro** Vietnam 15.34N 107.49E
37 F7 **Ro** R Turkey
11 F9 **Roa** New Zealand 42.21S 171.21E
52 F6 **Roa** Norway 60.17N 10.37E
75 C4 **Roa** Spain 41.42N 3.55W
107 K2 **Roachdale** Indiana 39.51N 86.49W
59 H5 **Road** Offaly Irish Rep 53.21N 7.12W
56 K3 **Roade** Northants Eng 52.10N 0.54W
59 D5 **Roadford** Clare Irish Rep 53.01N 9.22W
109 B9 **Road Forks** New Mexico 32.13N 108.56W
58 M5 **Roadside** Grampian Scotland 56.53N 2.15W
58 K1 **Roadside** Highland Scotland 58.32N 3.27W
58 T11 **Roadside** Orkney Scotland 59.15N 2.33W
95 M3 **Roadside** S Africa 27.31S 28.51E
105 L7 **Roadtown** Virgin Is 18.28N 64.39W
53 B6 **Roager** Denmark 55.16N 8.50E
58 C2 **Roag, L** Lewis, W Isles Scotland 58.08N 6.53W
58 C2 **Roag, W.L** Lewis, W Isles Scotland
72 D6 **Roaillan** France 44.30N 0.17W
53 U13 **Roald** Norway 62.35N 6.09E
53 V19 **Roaldkvam** Norway 59.39N 6.52E
58 H1 **Roan** isld Highland Scotland 58.33N 4.18W
92 D8 **Roan Antelope Mine** Zambia
111 P2 **Roan Cliffs** escarp Utah
109 B2 **Roan Cr** Colorado
90 K8 **Roandji** Cent Afr Rep 6.05N 20.45E
57 H2 **Roan Fell** mt Borders/Dumfries & Galloway Scotland 55.13N 2.52W
105 E1 **Roan Mt** N Carolina 36.06N 82.06W
71 E4 **Roanne** France 46.02N 4.05E
72 J6 **Roannes St. Mary** France 44.51N 2.23E
107 L8 **Roanoke** Alabama 33.09N 85.24W
106 E9 **Roanoke** Illinois 40.48N 89.12W
106 J9 **Roanoke** Indiana 40.58N 85.24W
112 K2 **Roanoke** Texas 33.00N 97.14W
104 F9 **Roanoke** Virginia 37.15N 79.58W
105 M2 **Roanoke I** N Carolina
105 K1 **Roanoke, R** N Carolina/Virginia
105 K1 **Roanoke Rapids** N Carolina 36.27N 77.40W
105 K1 **Roanoke Rapids L** N Car/Virginia
109 B2 **Roan Plateau** Colorado
111 P2 **Roan Plateau** Utah/Colorado
112 M5 **Roans Prairie** Texas 30.34N 95.57W
104 J5 **Roaring Branch** Pennsylvania 41.34N 76.57W
105 G1 **Roaring Gap** N Carolina 36.23N 80.59W
112 G2 **Roaring Springs** Texas 33.55N 100.52W
59 C9 **Roaringwater B** Cork Irish Rep
115 L1 **Roatán** Honduras 16.20N 86.30W
115 N5 **Robálo** Panama 9.02N 82.16W
Robarhacibey Suyu R see **Hājī Beg** R
32 F5 **Robāt** Kermān Iran 30.05N 54.50E
32 G5 **Robāṭ** Kermān Iran 30.15N 56.35E
34 O4 **Robāṭ** Kermānshāh Iran 34.17N 46.48E
32 G4 **Robāt-E Ābgarm** Iran 32.40N 57.22E
32 G4 **Robāṭ-e-Khān** Iran 33.21N 56.03E
32 D4 **Robāṭe-Tork** Iran 33.47N 50.53E
32 H2 **Robāṭ-e-Ṭoroq** Iran 36.10N 59.36E
32 D3 **Robāt Karīm** Iran 35.28N 51.05E
31 B6 **Robat R** Afghanistan
31 A6 **Robat Thana** Pakistan 29.48N 61.00E
88 R5 **Robbah** Algeria 33.12N 6.55E
95 B9 **Robbeneiland** Lt Ho S Africa 33.48S 18.22E
112 J9 **Robberson** Texas 26.42N 98.35W
103 B8 **Robbin Pt** Maryland 39.18N 76.18W
105 H2 **Robbins** N Carolina 35.26N 79.36W
12 G8 **Robbins I** Tasmania 40.44S 145.00E
105 D2 **Robbinsville** N Carolina 35.18N 83.49W
103 E6 **Robbinsville** New Jersey 40.13N 74.38W
79 E4 **Robbio** Italy 45.17N 8.35E
12 E6 **Robe** S Australia 37.13S 139.46E
79 H4 **Robecco d'Oglio** Italy 45.15N 10.05E
61 H6 **Robechies** Belgium 50.05N 4.17E
63 R6 **Röbel** E Germany 53.24N 12.37E
107 C10 **Robeline** Louisiana 31.41N 93.19W
61 N8 **Robelmont** Belgium 49.36N 5.30E
12 F4 **Robe, Mt** New S Wales 31.39S 141.16E
98 K3 **Robe Noire, L. de la** Quebec
59 D4 **Robe R** Mayo Irish Rep
14 B5 **Robe R** W Australia
105 K2 **Robersonville** N Carolina 35.49N 77.17W
105 C5 **Roberta** Georgia 32.44N 84.01W
Robert English Coast see **English Coast**
69 J6 **Robert-Espagne** France 48.45N 5.02E
123 E15 **Robert I** S Shetland Is Antarctica 62.28S 59.30W
112 G4 **Robert Lee** Texas 31.50N 100.30W
13 B7 **Robert, Mt** N Terr Australia 25.50S 131.30E
57 H2 **Roberton** Borders Scotland 55.25N 2.54W
57 F1 **Roberton** Strathclyde Scotland 55.32N 3.42W
110 N6 **Roberts** Idaho 43.44N 112.07W
110 Q4 **Roberts** Montana 45.21N 109.10W
110 E5 **Roberts** Oregon 44.04N 120.41W
98 R4 **Robert's Arm** Newfoundland 49.30N 55.49W
28 G6 **Roberts B** Andaman Is
56 M6 **Robertsbridge** E Sussex Eng 50.59N 0.29E
123 G8 **Robert Scott Glacier** Antarctica
111 H2 **Roberts Creek Mt** Nevada 39.53N 116.19W
107 J11 **Robertsdale** Alabama 30.32N 87.42W
95 N3 **Roberts Drift** S Africa 27.01S 29.01E
89 D8 **Robertsfield** airfield Liberia 6.12N 10.20W
52 M2 **Robertsfors** Sweden 64.12N 20.50E
30 G8 **Robertsganj** Uttar Prad India 24.42N 83.04E
109 P6 **Robert S Kerr Res** Oklahoma
13 K8 **Roberts, Mt** Queensland 28.12S 152.21E
110 Q7 **Roberts Mt** Wyoming 42.55N 109.18W
95 C9 **Robertson** S Africa 33.48S 19.53E
110 P8 **Robertson** Wyoming 41.11N 110.24W
13 G4 **Robertson** R Queensland
123 K6 **Robertson Bay** Antarctica
48 R3 **Robertson Fd** Greenland 77.45N 71.00W
123 E14 **Robertson I** Antarctica 65.15S 59.30W
98 N2 **Robertson L** Quebec
14 D6 **Robertson Ra** W Australia
98 A7 **Robertsonville** Quebec 46.08N 71.14W
99 T6 **Robertsonville** Quebec 46.08N 71.15W
89 D8 **Robertsport** Liberia 6.45N 11.15W
59 J5 **Robertstown** Kildare Irish Rep 53.16N 6.49W
12 E5 **Robertstown** S Australia 33.59S 139.03E
61 P5 **Robertville** Belgium 50.27N 6.08E
98 G6 **Robertville** New Brunswick 47.40N 65.46W
91 D10 **Robert Williams** Angola 12.51S 15.34E
99 S4 **Roberval** Quebec 48.31N 72.16W
97 N1 **Robeson Chan** N W Terr/Greenland
103 B6 **Robesonia** Pennsylvania 40.21N 76.08W
56 B4 **Robeston Wathen** Dyfed Wales 51.49N 4.46W
87 G7 **Robi** Ethiopia 7.54N 39.40E
71 E8 **Robiac** France 44.16N 4.08E
79 C6 **Robilante** Italy 44.18N 7.30E
110 N7 **Robin** Idaho 42.36N 112.16W
110 H5 **Robinette** Oregon 44.46N 117.01W
57 M4 **Robin Hood's Bay** N Yorks Eng 54.25N 0.33W
107 J2 **Robinson** Illinois 39.00N 87.43W
108 L2 **Robinson** N Dakota 47.10N 99.47W
94 R13 **Robinson** S Africa 26.09S 27.43E
13 D3 **Robinson** R N Terr Australia
13 J7 **Robinson** R Queensland
122 V12 **Robinson Crusoe** I Juan Fernández, Is Pacific Oc
12 D3 **Robinson, Mt** S Australia 27.49S 136.20E
14 C6 **Robinson, Mt** W Australia 23.13S 118.57E
113 Q6 **Robinson Mts** Alaska
14 E3 **Robinson R** W Australia
14 C7 **Robinson Ranges** W Australia
13 D3 **Robinson River** N Terr Australia 16.41S 136.56E
15 K9 **Robinson River** Papua New Guinea 10.08S 148.51E
98 O5 **Robinson's** Newfoundland 48.13N 58.50W
98 F6 **Robinsonville** New Brunswick 47.50N 66.57W
12 G5 **Robinvale** Victoria 34.37S 142.50E
76 H3 **Robla, La** Spain 42.48N 5.38W
100 R4 **Roblaytin** Manitoba 54.45N 100.59W
76 F8 **Robleda** Spain 40.23N 6.35W
76 G8 **Robledillo de Gata** Spain 40.20N 6.27W
76 H10 **Robledillo de Trujillo** Spain 39.16N 5.59W
77 M3 **Robledo** Spain 38.45N 2.27W
76 L8 **Robledo de Chavela** Spain 40.30N 4.14W
76 K9 **Robledo del Mazo** Spain 39.37N 4.54W
76 H9 **Robledollano** Spain 39.37N 5.30W
Robles del Rio see **Carmel Valley**
119 D2 **Robles La Paz** Colombia 10.24N 73.11W
111 N9 **Robles Pass** Arizona 32.10N 111.04W
111 N9 **Robles Ranch** Arizona 32.05N 111.19W
100 Q7 **Roblin** Manitoba 51.15N 101.20W
100 A1 **Roblin Park** Manitoba 49.53N 97.15W
76 H7 **Robliza de Cojos** Spain 40.52N 5.59W
118 B6 **Roboré** Bolivia 18.20S 59.45W
76 F6 **Roboredo, Sa. de** Portugal
56 C7 **Roborough** airport Devon Eng 50.27N 4.05W
75 C5 **Robregordo** Spain 41.06N 3.35W
75 K4 **Robres** Spain 41.52N 0.28W
15 K2 **Rob Roy I** Solomon Is 7.25S 157.30E
28 H1 **Robsang** Xizang Zizhiqu 28.31N 90.02E
100 H9 **Robsart** Saskatchewan 49.22N 109.18W
101 O9 **Robson, Mt** Br Columbia 53.08N 119.18W
112 K8 **Robstown** Texas 27.47N 97.42W
79 C6 **Roburent** Italy 44.18N 7.53E
112 G3 **Roby** Texas 32.44N 100.23W
76 A11 **Roca, Cabo da** Portugal 38.46N 9.30W
75 Q3 **Roca Corva** mt Spain 42.04N 2.41E
115 O7 **Roca Culebra** isld Mexico 21.28N 90.30W
91 D12 **Roçadas** Angola 16.44S 15.00E
77 C2 **Roca de la Sierra, La** Spain 39.06N 6.42W
75 N5 **Rocafort de Queralt** Spain 41.29N 1.18E
119 B8 **Rocafuerte** Ecuador 0.54S 80.26W
75 N5 **Rocallaura** Spain 41.30N 1.08E
72 H6 **Rocamadour** France 44.48N 1.36E
100 Q8 **Rocanville** Saskatchewan 50.24N 101.44W
115 C8 **Roca Partida, I** Mexico
115 M8 **Roca Partida, Pta** Mexico 18.43N 95.12W
119 A5 **Roca Redonda** isld Galápagos Is 0.16N 91.38W
115 B5 **Rocas Alijos** isld Mexico 24.58N 115.49W
117 E1 **Rocas, Atol das** isld Atlantic Oc 3.50S 33.50W
79 A4 **Rocca d'Ambin** mt Italy/France 45.10N 6.48E
81 K3 **Roccadaspide** Italy 40.25N 15.11E
80 J4 **Rocca di Mezzo** Italy 42.13N 13.32E
81 O5 **Rocca di Neto** Italy 39.11N 17.00E
80 G5 **Rocca di Papa** Italy 41.46N 12.42E
79 G4 **Roccafranca** Italy 45.28N 9.55E
81 K3 **Roccagloriosa** Italy 40.06N 15.26E
80 H5 **Roccagorga** Italy 41.32N 13.09E
81 N3 **Rocca Imperiale** Italy 40.07N 16.35E
80 E3 **Roccalbegna** Italy 42.48N 11.30E
81 K8 **Roccalumera** Sicily 37.58N 15.24E
81 F8 **Roccamena** Sicily 37.50N 13.09E
80 J6 **Roccamonfina** Italy 41.17N 13.59E
81 M3 **Roccanova** Italy 40.13N 16.12E
81 G8 **Roccapalumba** Sicily 37.48N 13.38E
79 L2 **Rocca Piétore** Italy 46.26N 11.59E
79 D3 **Rocca Pietra** Italy 45.47N 8.17E
67 O13 **Roccapina** Corsica 41.30N 8.55E
80 K5 **Roccaraso** Italy 41.51N 14.05E
79 L6 **Rocca San Casciano** Italy 44.03N 11.50E
80 J5 **Roccasecca** Italy 41.33N 13.40E
80 G4 **Rocca Sinibalda** Italy 42.17N 12.56E
80 D2 **Roccastrada** Italy 43.01N 11.10E
79 D5 **Roccaverano** Italy 44.36N 8.16E
79 B6 **Roccavione** Italy 44.18N 7.28E
81 M7 **Roccella Iónica** Italy 38.20N 16.24E
79 F5 **Rocchetta Ligure** Italy 44.43N 9.03E
80 M6 **Rocchetta San Antonio** Italy 41.07N 15.28E
71 L6 **Rocciamelone** mt France/Italy 45.13N 7.04E
79 C5 **Rocco d'Arazzo** Italy 44.53N 8.17E
79 C6 **Rocco de Baldi** Italy 44.25N 7.46E
71 K4 **Roc d'Enfer** mt France 46.11N 6.36E
57 K7 **Rocester** Staffs Eng 52.57N 1.49W
56 A4 **Roch** Dyfed Wales 51.52N 5.04W
121 G5 **Rocha** Uruguay 34.30S 54.22W
121 G4 **Rocha** dept Uruguay
121 G5 **Rocha, L** Uruguay
117 C2 **Rochambeau** airport Fr Guiana 4.45N 52.22W
70 K5 **Rochard, Mt** France 48.12N 0.21W
57 J5 **Rochdale** Greater Manchester Eng 53.38N 2.09W
103 L2 **Rochdale** Massachusetts 42.12N 71.54W
66 D6 **Roche** Switzerland 46.23N 6.56E
99 N4 **Rochebaucourt** Quebec 48.41N 77.33W
72 E5 **Rochebeaucourt-et-Argentine, la** France 45.29N 0.24E
70 F6 **Roche-Bernard, la** France 47.32N 2.17W
70 H7 **Roche Blanche, la** France 47.27N 1.04W
71 K5 **Rochebrune** mt France 45.50N 6.37E
71 K7 **Rochebrune, Pic. de** mt France 44.49N 6.47E
77 D8 **Roche, C** Spain 36.18N 6.09W
72 H5 **Roche Canillac, la** France 45.12N 1.58E
Roche-chalais, la see **Roche-de-St.Michel, la**
72 F4 **Rochechouart** France 45.49N 0.50E
66 C3 **Roche de Barchey** mt France 47.09N 6.31E
71 D9 **Roche-de-la-Tude** mt France 43.55N 3.36E
71 K7 **Roche-de-Rame, La** France 44.45N 6.35E
70 D4 **Roche-Derrien, la** France 48.45N 3.16W
72 E5 **Roche-de-St. Michel, la** France 45.09N 0.01E
71 H7 **Roche-des-Arnauds, la** France 44.34N 5.57E
118 C6 **Rochedo** Brazil 19.55S 54.50W
61 N6 **Roche-en-Ardenne, La** Belgium 50.11N 5.35E
71 E2 **Roche-en-Brenil, la** France 47.23N 4.10E
61 L6 **Rochefort** Belgium 50.10N 5.13E
72 C4 **Rochefort** France 45.57N 0.58W
71 F9 **Rochefort-du-Gard** France 43.58N 4.40E
70 F6 **Rochefort-en-Terre** France 47.42N 2.20W

71 B5 Rochefort-Montagne France 45.42N 2.48E
71 H2 Rochefort-sur-Nénon France 47.08N 5.33E
72 E4 Rochefoucauld, la France 45.44N 0.24E
47 E4 Rochegda U.S.S.R. 62.40N 43.24E
26 O13 Roche-Godon, La Amsterdam I Ind Oc 37.49S 77.33E
69 B5 Roche-Guyon, la France 49.05N 1.37E
61 L7 Rochehaut Belgium 49.50N 5.00E
66 B4 Rochejean France 46.45N 6.16E
66 E5 Roche, la Switzerland 46.43N 7.08E
71 J2 Roche-les-Beaupré France 47.16N 6.07E
105 E8 Rochelle Florida 29.34N 82.15W
105 D6 Rochelle Georgia 31.58N 83.28W
106 E8 Rochelle Illinois 41.55N 89.05W
107 D10 Rochelle Louisiana 31.48N 92.22W
112 H4 Rochelle Texas 31.14N 99.14W
71 F7 Rochemaure France 44.35N 4.42E
79 A4 Rochemolles Italy 45.07N 6.45E
100 P9 Roche Percée Saskatchewan 49.05N 102.49W
107 D3 Rocheport Missouri 38.59N 92.32W
72 F2 Roche-Posay, la France 46.47N 0.49E
71 F3 Rochepot, la France 46.58N 4.45E
61 Q5 Rocherath Belgium 50.27N 6.18E
66 B5 Rocheray Switzerland 46.38N 6.16E
72 B3 Rocher d'Antioche France 46.04N 1.24W
74 K10 Rocher de Sel Algeria 34.49N 3.08E
116 L4 Rocher du Diamant isld Martinique West Indies 14.27N 61.03W
98 O2 Rocher, L. du Quebec
101 R5 Rocher River N W Terr 61.23N 112.45W
66 D6 Rochers de Naye mt Switzerland 46.27N 6.59E
98 E3 Rochers, R. aux Quebec
69 J7 Roches-Bettaincourt France 48.18N 5.15E
71 K2 Roches, Col des pass France 47.03N 6.42E
70 E3 Roches Douvres islds English Chan 49.07N 2.50W
72 B2 Rocheservière France 46.56N 1.30W
26 V12 Roches, Plaine des Mauritius, Indian Oc
69 M7 Rochesson France 48.01N 6.47E
100 D4 Rochester Alberta 54.22N 113.28W
107 G2 Rochester Illinois 39.44N 89.31W
106 H8 Rochester Indiana 41.03N 86.13W
56 M5 Rochester Kent Eng 51.24N 0.30E
103 N3 Rochester Massachusetts 41.45N 70.48W
106 L7 Rochester Michigan 42.41N 83.08W
108 S5 Rochester Minnesota 44.01N 92.27W
104 P3 Rochester New Hampshire 43.18N 70.59W
104 H3 Rochester New York 43.12N 77.37W
57 J2 Rochester Northumb Eng 55.16N 2.16W
104 C5 Rochester Ohio 41.08N 82.19W
104 E6 Rochester Pennsylvania 40.43N 80.17W
112 H2 Rochester Texas 33.18N 99.53W
12 G6 Rochester Victoria 36.24S 144.42E
110 B3 Rochester Washington 46.49N 123.05W
106 C8 Rochester Res Iowa
71 J4 Roche-sur-Foron, la France 46.04N 6.19E
72 G4 Roche-sur l'Abeille, la France 45.35N 1.14E
72 B2 Roche-sur-Yon, La France 46.40N 1.25W
71 J6 Rochetaillée Isère France 45.07N 6.00E
69 J8 Rochetaillée-sur-Aujon Haute-Marne France 47.52N 5.06E
72 H4 Roche Talamie, Barrage de la France 46.00N 1.37E
71 J6 Rochette, la France 45.27N 6.07E
71 F4 Roche-Vineuse, la France 46.21N 4.43E
56 N4 Rochford Essex Eng 51.36N 0.43E
108 G5 Rochford S Dakota 44.09N 103.43W
100 B5 Rochfort Bridge Alberta 53.57N 115.00W
59 H5 Rochfortbridge W Meath Irish Rep 53.25N 7.18W
64 O1 Rochlitz E Germany 51.03N 12.49E
100 E6 Rochon Sands Prov. Park Alberta
76 E7 Rochoso Portugal 40.31N 7.05W
69 C5 Rochy-Condé France 49.25N 2.10E
77 C6 Rociana Spain 37.19N 6.35W
77 C6 Rocina, Arroyo de la R Spain
77 C6 Rocío, El Spain 37.07N 6.31W
109 N4 Rock Kansas 37.26N 97.02W
103 N3 Rock Massachusetts 41.51N 70.52W
106 G3 Rock Michigan 46.03N 87.10W
108 O6 Rock R Iowa
101 E2 Rock R Yukon Terr
101 K5 Rock R Yukon Terr
59 K4 Rockabill Lt. Ho Irish Sea 53.36N 6.00W
54 A5 Rockall isld N Atlantic Oc 57.40N 13.30W
96 J3 Rockall Bank Atlantic Oc
11 E12 Rock and Pillar Ra New Zealand
60 E12 Rockanje Netherlands 51.52N 4.05E
103 E5 Rockaway New Jersey 40.54N 74.31W
103 M8 Rockaway Beach New York
103 K9 Rockaway Inlet New York
103 N8 Rockaway Park New York 40.35N 73.49W
101 L10 Rock Bay Vancouver I, Br Col 50.18N 125.31W
103 G3 Rock City New York 41.58N 73.50W
57 F3 Rockcliffe Dumfries & Galloway Scotland 54.52N 3.48W
99 D8 Rockcliffe Airport Ontario 45.29N 75.39W
99 D8 Rockcliffe Park Ontario 45.27N 75.41W
59 H3 Rockcorry Monaghan Irish Rep 54.07N 7.01W
108 C1 Rock Cr Montana
110 M3 Rock Cr Montana
110 E4 Rock Cr Oregon
108 D8 Rock Cr Wyoming
110 L7 Rockcreek Idaho 42.25N 114.20W
104 E5 Rock Creek Ohio 41.40N 80.53W
110 E4 Rock Creek Oregon 45.35N 120.18W
101 D3 Rock Creek Yukon Terr 64.03N 139.05W
103 D2 Rockdale New York 42.22N 75.25W
112 L5 Rockdale Texas 30.40N 97.00W
12 L8 Rockdale dist Sydney, N S W
123 H9 Rockefeller Mts Antarctica
123 H9 Rockefeller Plat Antarctica
64 D4 Rockenhausen W Germany 49.37N 7.50E
103 J3 Rockfall Connecticut 41.32N 72.42W
106 E8 Rock Falls Illinois 41.46N 89.42W
57 G6 Rock Ferry Merseyside Eng 53.23N 3.01W
104 G9 Rockfish Virginia 37.49N 78.46W
107 K9 Rockford Alabama 32.54N 86.15W
110 N6 Rockford Idaho 43.11N 112.30W
106 E7 Rockford Illinois 42.16N 89.06W
106 J6 Rockford Michigan 43.08N 85.34W
108 R4 Rockford Minnesota 45.05N 93.42W
104 A6 Rockford Ohio 40.42N 84.40W
110 H2 Rockford Washington 47.28N 117.07W
103 B5 Rock Glen Pennsylvania 40.58N 76.12W
100 M9 Rockglen Saskatchewan 49.11N 105.57W
103 B8 Rock Hall Maryland 39.08N 76.14W
108 M5 Rockham S Dakota 44.55N 98.50W
13 K6 Rockhampton Queensland 23.22S 150.32E
13 D4 Rockhampton Downs N Terr Australia 19.00S 135.06E
106 F1 Rock Harbor Michigan 48.08N 88.30W
100 J6 Rockhaven Saskatchewan 52.43N 108.57W
59 E7 Rockhill Limerick Irish Rep 52.25N 8.42W
105 F3 Rock Hill S Carolina 34.55N 81.01W
110 E2 Rock I. Dam Washington 47.21N 120.07W
59 C5 Rock I. Lt. Ho Galway Irish Rep 53.09N 9.51W
105 H3 Rockingham N Carolina 34.56N 79.47W
56 K2 Rockingham Northants Eng 52.31N 0.43W
14 B9 Rockingham W Australia 32.16S 115.21E
13 H4 Rockingham B Queensland
106 D8 Rock Island Illinois 41.30N 90.34W
99 S7 Rock Island Quebec 45.02N 72.05W
112 L6 Rock Island Texas 29.32N 96.35W
110 E2 Rock Island Washington 47.23N 120.08W
108 L1 Rock L Manitoba 49.13N 99.10W
110 H2 Rock L Washington 47.10N 117.40W
108 L1 Rock Lake N Dakota 48.49N 99.16W
103 J4 Rockland Connecticut 41.25N 72.39W
110 N7 Rockland Idaho 42.35N 112.53W
104 Q2 Rockland Maine 44.06N 69.08W
103 N2 Rockland Massachusetts 42.08N 70.55W
106 E3 Rockland Michigan 46.44N 89.12W
103 E3 Rockland New York 41.57N 74.55W
99 P7 Rockland Ontario 45.32N 75.19W
112 N4 Rockland Texas 31.02N 94.28W
103 F4 Rockland co New York
103 G4 Rockland Lake New York 41.09N 73.55W
13 E4 Rocklands Queensland 19.50S 138.06E
12 F6 Rocklands Res Victoria
14 B6 Rocklea W Australia 23.00S 117.28E
13 K2 Rocklea dist Brisbane, Qnsld
110 G2 Rocklyn Washington 47.37N 118.16W
105 B3 Rockmart Georgia 34.01N 85.02W
101 Q3 Rocknest L N W Terr
63 R10 Röcknitz E Germany 51.27N 12.47E
104 J8 Rock Point Maryland 38.16N 76.52W
111 A2 Rockport California 39.45N 123.47W
107 E2 Rockport Illinois 39.32N 91.01W
107 J4 Rockport Indiana 37.53N 87.04W
104 Q2 Rockport Maine 44.12N 69.05W
104 P4 Rockport Massachusetts 42.40N 70.40W
107 A1 Rock Port Missouri 40.25N 95.30W
112 K7 Rockport Texas 28.02N 97.04W
110 D1 Rockport Washington 48.30N 121.38W
11 C4 Rock Pt New Zealand 41.08S 174.47E
106 E8 Rock, R Illinois
106 F6 Rock, R Wisconsin
108 O6 Rock Rapids Iowa 43.25N 96.10W
103 D2 Rock Rift New York 42.07N 75.13W
108 E8 Rock River Wyoming 41.46N 105.59W
103 D2 Rockroyal New York 42.10N 75.18W
103 B7 Rocks Maryland 39.38N 76.24W
105 L13 Rock Sound Bahamas 24.54N 76.11W
116 F2 Rock Sound Eleuthera I Bahamas 24.56N 76.11W
111 M7 Rock Springs Arizona 34.03N 112.09W
108 D3 Rock Springs Montana 46.50N 106.13W
112 G5 Rocksprings Texas 30.02N 100.14W
110 Q8 Rock Springs Wyoming 41.35N 109.13W
11 G7 Rocks Pt New Zealand 40.53S 172.08E
117 A1 Rockstone Guyana 6.00N 58.30W
12 H6 Rock, The New S Wales 35.18S 147.06E
106 E7 Rockton Illinois 42.27N 89.04W
108 O6 Rock Valley Iowa 43.12N 96.17W
103 K3 Rockville Connecticut 41.53N 72.27W
107 J2 Rockville Indiana 39.45N 87.15W
104 H7 Rockville Maryland 39.05N 77.10W
11 G7 Rockville New Zealand 40.43S 172.38E
110 H6 Rockville Oregon 43.18N 117.07W
105 G5 Rockville S Carolina 32.37N 80.12W
111 L4 Rockville Utah 37.09N 113.01W
103 M8 Rockville Centre Long I, N Y 40.40N 73.39W
112 L3 Rockwall Texas 32.56N 96.27W
108 R7 Rockwell Iowa 42.59N 93.10W
105 G2 Rockwell N Carolina 35.32N 80.23W
108 Q7 Rockwell City Iowa 42.24N 94.39W
109 C4 Rockwood Colorado 37.31N 107.49W
104 Q1 Rockwood Maine 45.41N 69.46W
99 K9 Rockwood Ontario 43.37N 80.10W
104 F7 Rockwood Pennsylvania 39.55N 79.08W
107 M6 Rockwood Tennessee 35.52N 84.40W
112 H4 Rockwood Texas 31.30N 99.24W
109 L6 Rocky Oklahoma 35.10N 99.04W
110 K6 Rocky Bar Idaho 43.42N 115.17W
100 D7 Rockyford Alberta 51.13N 113.10W
109 G3 Rocky Ford Colorado 38.03N 103.44W
105 F5 Rocky Ford Georgia 32.41N 81.50W
108 H6 Rockyford S Dakota 43.30N 102.30W
104 B7 Rocky Ford Res Ohio 39.12N 83.35W
104 F5 Rocky Grove Pennsylvania 41.25N 79.50W
14 B10 Rocky Gully W Australia 34.31S 117.01E
23 C8 Rocky Harbour Hong Kong
103 J3 Rocky Hill Connecticut 41.40N 72.38W
103 E6 Rocky Hill New Jersey 40.24N 74.38W
99 G6 Rocky Island L Ontario
100 Q4 Rocky L Manitoba
105 K2 Rocky Mount N Carolina 35.56N 77.48W
104 F10 Rocky Mount Virginia 37.00N 79.57W
100 C6 Rocky Mountain House Alta 52.24N 114.52W
109 E1 Rocky Mountain Nat. Park Colorado
110 N2 Rocky Mt Montana 47.49N 112.47W
102 D1 Rocky Mts N America
116 K2 Rocky Point Jamaica, W I 17.46N 77.16W
103 J5 Rocky Point Long I, N Y 40.57N 72.55W
108 E5 Rockypoint Wyoming 44.56N 105.07W
113 F4 Rocky Pt Alaska 64.25N 163.10W
105 K11 Rocky Pt Bahamas 26.01N 77.23W
116 K2 Rocky Pt Jamaica, W I 17.49N 77.09W
10 U11 Rocky Pt Norfolk I Pacific Oc 29.04S 167.55E
13 B1 Rocky Pt N Terr Australia 11.20S 130.12E
116 A2 Rocky Pt San Salvador I Bahamas 24.07N 74.30W
14 E10 Rocky Pt W Australia 33.30S 124.01E
105 G2 Rocky, R N Carolina
105 E3 Rocky R S Carolina
104 D5 Rocky River Ohio 41.29N 81.51W
61 N3 Roclenge-sur-Geer Belgium 50.46N 5.36E
103 G2 Roclif Jansen Kill R New York
61 N4 Rocourt Belgium 50.41N 5.33E
69 E5 Rocourt-St.Martin France 49.09N 3.24E
70 F3 Rocque Pt. La Channel Is 49.10N 2.02W
69 H4 Rocroi France 49.56N 4.31E
64 M2 Roda R E Germany
34 H3 Rōda salt swamp Syria
64 K3 Rodach W Germany 50.20N 10.48E
64 K3 Rodach R E Ger/W Ger
64 L3 Rodach R W Germany
77 G6 Roda de Andalucia, La Spain 37.12N 4.47W
76 L6 Roda de Eresma Spain 41.03N 4.11W
75 P4 Roda de Ter Spain 41.59N 2.19E
86 E10 Rôda, El Asyût Egypt 27.48N 30.51E
86 F7 Rôda, El Faiyûm Egypt 29.27N 31.00E
45 L8 Rodakovo Ukraine U.S.S.R. 48.34N 39.02E
77 M2 Roda, La Spain 39.13N 2.10W
64 D5 Rodalben W Germany 49.15N 7.38E
75 J8 Rodana mt Spain 39.33N 0.39W
105 M2 Rodanthe N Carolina 35.34N 75.28W
52 D6 Rødberg Norway 60.16N 8.57E
53 G7 Rødby Denmark 54.42N 11.24E
53 G7 Rødbyhavn Denmark 54.39N 11.24E
79 C5 Roddi Italy 44.41N 7.59E
98 Q3 Roddickton Newfoundland 50.51N 56.08W
53 C6 Rødding Sønderjylland Denmark 55.22N 9.04E
53 B3 Rødding Viborg Denmark 56.39N 8.49E
53 D4 Rødding Viborg Denmark 56.30N 9.32E
48 T8 Rodebay Greenland 69.20N 51.00W
52 J10 Rödeby Sweden 56.16N 15.35E
118 E10 Rodeio Brazil 26.54S 49.24W
76 D3 Rodeiro Spain 42.39N 7.58W
53 C6 Rødekro Denmark 55.04N 9.20E
58 C3 Rodel Harris, W Isles Scotland 57.44N 6.58W
86 Q11 Rôd el Farag Cairo Egypt
75 K3 Rodellar Spain 42.17N 0.05W
72 K7 Rodelle France 44.29N 2.37E
60 O7 Roden Netherlands 53.08N 6.26E
75 G6 Ródenas Spain 40.38N 1.31W
69 O5 Rodenbach W Germany 49.29N 7.39E
63 K8 Rodenberg W Germany 52.18N 9.22E
61 Q8 Rodenbourg Luxembourg 49.41N 6.18E
52 F7 Rødenes Norway 59.35N 11.34E
63 H6 Rodenkirchen W Germany 53.24N 8.27E
69 M2 Rodenkirchen W Germany 50.53N 7.00E
64 L3 Rödental W Germany 50.17N 11.03E
121 B3 Rodeo Argentina 30.11S 69.16W
115 G5 Rodeo Mexico 25.12N 104.35W
109 B10 Rodeo New Mexico 31.51N 109.02W
Rodeon see Swartruggens
63 S10 Röderau E Germany 51.19N 13.19E
14 B7 Roderick R W Australia
66 F2 Rodersdorf Switzerland 47.29N 7.28E
107 B9 Rodessa Louisiana 32.59N 94.00W
63 K7 Rodewald W Germany 52.38N 9.28E
64 N2 Rodewisch E Germany 50.32N 12.25E
72 K7 Rodez France 44.21N 2.34E
104 E1 Rodgers Forge Maryland 39.24N 76.37W
83 F4 Rodholívos Greece 40.55N 24.00E
84 J10 Rodhopoú Crete 35.33N 23.45E
84 V17 Ródhos Rhodes Greece 36.26N 28.14E
83 J8 Ródhos isld Greece
76 H3 Rodiezmo Spain 42.56N 5.41W
80 N5 Rodi Garganico Italy 41.55N 15.53E
76 E2 Rodil R Spain
42 F3 Rodina U.S.S.R. 57.48N 95.15E
64 O5 Roding W Germany 49.12N 12.33E
13 C6 Rodinga N Terr Australia 24.35S 134.09E
63 J8 Rödinghausen W Germany 52.16N 8.35E
55 H3 Roding, R London/Essex England
47 H3 Rodionovo U.S.S.R. 65.32N 57.00E
53 D4 Rødkærsbro Denmark 56.22N 9.32E
31 C7 Rodkhan Pakistan 26.05N 64.26E
53 S17 Rødland Norway 60.41N 5.24E
82 J3 Rodna Romania 47.25N 24.50E
45 D3 Rodnaya Belorussiya U.S.S.R. 53.30N 32.09E
82 J3 Rodnei, Munţii mts Romania
106 J6 Rodney Michigan 43.41N 85.22W
99 J10 Rodney Ontario 42.34N 81.41W
113 D4 Rodney, C Alaska 64.40N 166.30W
11 J3 Rodney, C New Zealand 36.18S 174.51E
15 K9 Rodney, C Papua New Guinea 10.05S 148.11E
13 G6 Rodney Downs Queensland 23.08S 144.50E
15 K9 Rodney Ent Papua New Guinea 10.20S 148.25E
45 O5 Rodnichok U.S.S.R. 51.25N 42.57E
46 M2 Rodniki U.S.S.R. 57.08N 41.46E
12 H7 Rodondo Victoria 39.14S 146.22E
83 C3 Rodonit, Kep i C Albania 41.34N 19.26E
82 H9 Rodopi Planina mts Bulgaria
75 P4 Rodos mt Spain 41.51N 2.08E
Rodosto see Tekirdağ
51 C5 Rødøy Norway 66.42N 13.05E
118 J10 Rodrigo de Freitas, L Brazil 22.59S 43.13W
120 C2 Rodrigues Brazil 6.33S 73.01W
26 E7 Rodrigues Fracture Indian Ocean
26 B12 Rodrigues I Indian Ocean 19.43S 63.26E
111 H9 Rodriguez, Presa res Mexico 32.26N 116.53W
53 H7 Rødsand sandbank Denmark 54.36N 11.40E
53 D3 Rød Sø L Denmark 46.33N 9.33E
53 Y17 Rødungen L Norway 60.42N 8.12E
53 Z17 Rødungen L Norway 60.32N 8.32E
53 W13 Rødven Norway 62.37N 7.30E
53 J6 Rødvig Denmark 55.16N 12.23E
39 M1 Rodzhersa, Bukhta gulf Vrangelya, Ostrov U.S.S.R.
107 E7 Roe Arkansas 34.39N 91.26W
103 E6 Roebling New Jersey 40.07N 74.46W
14 B5 Roebourne W Australia 20.48S 117.10E
14 D4 Roebuck B W Australia
14 E4 Roebuck Downs W Australia 18.19S 123.42E
94 K5 Roedtan S Africa 24.37S 29.05E
55 E4 Roehampton London Eng 51.27N 0.14W
14 E9 Roe, L W Australia
70 H6 Roë, la France 47.54N 1.06W
95 H2 Roelofskamp S Africa 26.09S 24.25E
79 K2 Roén mt Italy 46.22N 11.12E
14 G9 Roe Plains W Australia
59 J2 Roe, R Londonderry N Ireland
14 F3 Roe, R W Australia
60 N15 Roermond Netherlands 51.12N 6.00E
61 A3 Roesbrugge-Haringe Belgium 50.55N 2.38E
61 C3 Roeselare Belgium 50.57N 3.08E
61 P8 Roeser Luxembourg 49.33N 6.09E
15 G6 Roesicke Mt Papua New Guinea 5.00S 142.39E
97 L5 Roes Welcome Sd N W Terr
64 A2 Roetgen W Germany 50.38N 6.13E
69 L2 Roetgen W Germany 50.38N 6.13E
61 G4 Rœulx, Le Belgium 50.30N 4.07E
79 L5 Ro Ferrarese Italy 44.57N 11.46E
109 O7 Roff Oklahoma 34.38N 96.52W
81 K3 Rofrano Italy 40.13N 15.26E
45 B3 Rogachev Belorussiya U.S.S.R. 53.05N 30.02E
41 A4 Rogacheva R Novaya Zemlya U.S.S.R.
45 L5 Rogachevka U.S.S.R. 51.31N 39.32E
120 F5 Rogaguado,L Bolivia
120 E5 Rogagua, L Bolivia
53 U20 Rogaland co Norway
121 K8 Ró Gallegos Argentina 51.35S 69.15W
45 H7 Rogan' Ukraine U.S.S.R. 49.54N 36.29E
112 O5 Roganville Texas 30.49N 93.55W
58 H3 Rogart Highland Scotland 58.00N 4.08W
63 Q8 Rogäsen E Germany 52.20N 12.22E
82 C4 Rogaška Slatina Yugoslavia 46.15N 15.42E
56 K5 Rogate W Sussex Eng 51.00N 0.51W
82 J1 Rogatin U.S.S.R. 49.23N 24.36E
63 P8 Rogätz E Germany 52.20N 11.46E
84 M11 Rogdhía Crete 35.22N 25.01E
87 E1 Rogel, Er Sudan 18.10N 35.21E
35 D7 Rogelit Israel 31.41N 35.00E
52 G4 Rogen L Sweden 62.20N 12.25E
99 M5 Roger, L Quebec
107 B5 Rogers Arkansas 36.21N 94.08W
108 M2 Rogers N Dakota 47.05N 98.11W
112 K5 Rogers Texas 30.56N 97.15W
106 L4 Rogers City Michigan 45.24N 83.50W
26 A15 Rogers Head Heard I Antarctica 53.00S 73.24E
111 G7 Rogers L California 34.55N 117.50W
101 P10 Rogers, Mt Br Columbia 51.29N 117.56W
110 L7 Rogerson Idaho 42.14N 114.37W
107 J7 Rogersville Alabama 34.50N 87.19W
107 C4 Rogersville Missouri 37.07N 93.05W
98 G7 Rogersville New Brunswick 46.44N 65.28W
105 D1 Rogersville Tennessee 36.26N 83.01W
60 M14 Roggel Netherlands 51.16N 5.55E
109 F1 Roggen Colorado 40.10N 104.23W
63 O5 Roggendorf E Germany 53.42N 11.02E
66 Q1 Roggenzell W Germany 47.37N 9.45E
122 V16 Roggeveen, C Easter I Pacific Oc 27.06S 109.16W
94 E8 Roggeveld Berge mts S Africa
94 F9 Roggeveld, Middel reg S Africa
81 M4 Roggiano Gravina Italy 39.37N 16.09E
66 H3 Roggwil Bern Switzerland 47.15N 7.50E
66 O1 Roggwil Thurgau Switzerland 47.30N 9.24E
67 P11 Rogliano Corsica 42.57N 9.25E
81 M5 Rogliano Italy 39.11N 16.19E
71 G10 Rognac France 43.29N 5.15E
53 R15 Rognaldsvåg Norway 61.34N 4.49E
51 E4 Rognan Norway 67.07N 15.25E
45 E3 Rognedino U.S.S.R. 53.50N 33.44E
61 H5 Rognée Belgium 50.17N 4.23E
71 G9 Rognes France 43.39N 5.21E
66 E7 Rogneux, Mont Switzerland 46.01N 7.15E
63 O6 Rögnitz R E Germany
69 J7 Rognon R France
79 A5 Rognosa, Punta mt Italy 44.56N 6.56E
69 D8 Rogny France 47.46N 2.53E
90 C6 Rogo Nigeria 11.32N 7.50E
79 F8 Rogoredo dist Milan Italy
45 K5 Rogovatoye U.S.S.R. 51.13N 38.24E
44 B2 Rogovskaya U.S.S.R. 45.44N 38.45E
82 F7 Rogozna mts Yugoslavia
80 N1 Rogožnica Yugoslavia 43.32N 15.59E
62 K3 Rogoźno Poland 52.47N 17.00E
45 C6 Rogozov Ukraine U.S.S.R. 50.12N 31.03E
52 K5 Rogsta Sweden 61.49N 17.20E
110 A7 Rogue R Oregon
110 B7 Rogue River Oregon 42.28N 120.10W
72 L7 Rogue St. Marguerite, la France 44.08N 3.13E
65 P2 Roh mt Czechoslovakia 49.45N 16.33E
28 A1 Roha Maharashtra India 18.25N 73.08E
70 E5 Rohan France 48.04N 2.44W
31 G8 Rohanpur Bangladesh 24.49N 88.25E
99 Q3 Rohault, L Quebec
29 C5 Rohera Rajasthan India 24.43N 73.08E
30 B4 Rohilkhand div Uttar Prad Ind
29 F3 Rohilkhand reg Uttar Prad Ind
15 M3 Rohinari Malaita I Solomon Is 9.23S 161.15E
30 K8 Rohini Bihar India 24.29N 86.39E
63 P6 Rohlsdorf E Germany 53.07N 11.57E
53 J6 Roholte Denmark 55.12N 12.07E
64 J2 Rohr E Germany 50.35N 10.30E
65 N6 Rohr Nieder-Österreich Austria 47.54N 15.44E
65 K5 Rohr Ober-Österreich Austria 48.05N 14.12E
64 M6 Rohr W Germany 48.47N 11.59E
65 P5 Rohrau Austria 48.04N 16.52E
65 J4 Rohrbach Nieder-Österreich Austria 48.35N 13.59E
65 O7 Rohrbach Steiermark Austria 47.24N 16.01E
66 H3 Rohrbach Switzerland 47.08N 7.50E
64 O7 Rohrbach W Germany 48.16N 12.35E
69 N5 Rohrbach-lès-Bitche France 49.03N 7.16E
63 O7 Rohrberg E Germany 52.43N 11.03E
64 G4 Rohrbrunn W Germany 49.54N 9.22E
103 B6 Rohrerstown Pennsylvania 40.03N 76.22W
31 E7 Rohri Pakistan 27.39N 68.57E
64 L7 Röhrmoos W Germany 48.19N 11.28E
64 Q6 Röhrnbach W Germany 48.45N 13.32E
103 B4 Rohrsburg Pennsylvania 41.38N 76.25W
30 A1 Rohru Himachal Prad India 31.12N 77.45E
29 E3 Rohtak Haryana India 28.57N 76.38E
29 E3 Rohtak dist Haryana India
31 G4 Rohtas Pakistan 32.59N 73.40E
30 G8 Rohtasgarh Bihar India 24.40N 83.59E
107 E8 Rohwer Arkansas 33.46N 91.19W
9 B2 Roi islet Marshall Is Pacific Oc 9.23N 167.28E
66 S4 Roia R Bolzano Italy
79 C7 Roia R Imperia Italy
Roi Et see Muang Roi Et
72 E1 Roiffe France 47.07N 0.04E
77 T11 Roig, C Balearic Is 39.01N 1.37E
77 P5 Roig, C Spain 37.55N 0.43W
71 K5 Roignais, le mt France 45.39N 6.43E
28 K1 Roing Assam India 28.06N 95.46E
76 B3 Rois Spain 42.46N 8.42W
66 F8 Roisan Italy 45.47N 7.19E
69 E4 Roisel France 49.58N 3.06E
61 E5 Roisin Belgium 50.20N 3.42E
65 J5 Roitham Austria 48.02N 13.50E
63 Q9 Roitzsch Halle E Germany 51.35N 12.16E
63 R9 Roitzsch Leipzig E Germany 51.36N 12.50E
28 K1 Roiung Assam India 28.08N 95.10E
46 E1 Roja Latvia U.S.S.R. 57.30N 22.46E
77 P4 Rojales Spain 38.06N 0.43W
52 H4 Röjan Sweden 62.29N 14.20E
96 R15 Roja, Pta Tenerife Canary Is 28.02N 16.33W
121 E5 Rojas Argentina 34.10S 60.45W
31 E6 Rojhan Pakistan 28.39N 70.00E
116 J6 Rojo, C Dominican Rep 17.57N 71.40W
115 L7 Rojo, C Mexico 21.38N 97.18W
18 D5 Rokan R Sumatra Indon
13 G2 Rokeby Queensland 13.38S 142.39E
100 P7 Rokeby Saskatchewan 51.07N 102.20W
89 C7 Rokel R Sierra Leone
46 F2 Rokiškis Lithuania U.S.S.R. 55.59N 25.32E
20 P1 Rokkasho Japan 40.53N 141.22E
51 E5 Røkland Norway 67.00N 15.20E
51 J6 Roknäs Sweden 65.22N 21.14E
89 C7 Rokon Sierra Leone 8.38N 12.42W
61 C2 Roksem Belgium 51.10N 3.02E
53 S20 Røksund Norway 59.20N 5.25E
20 O2 Rokugō Japan 39.26N 140.32E
20 E4 Rokugō dist Tōkyō Japan
20 L4 Rokugō-saki C Japan 37.30N 137.19E
64 Q4 Rokycany Czechoslovakia 49.45N 13.36E
65 O3 Rokytná R Czechoslovakia
24 F8 Rola Co L Xizang Zizhiqu China
69 J8 Rolampont France 47.57N 5.17E
108 R7 Roland Iowa 42.09N 93.28W
100 U9 Roland Manitoba 49.23N 97.56W
26 P14 Roland isld Kerguelen Ind Oc 48.34S 68.49E
118 D8 Rolândia Brazil 23.18S 51.23W
104 E1 Roland, L Maryland 39.24N 76.38W
64 C2 Rolandseck W Germany 50.37N 7.13E
91 A13 Rôlas, I Das isld S Tomé São Tomé & Principe, Gulf Of Guinea
53 D3 Rold Denmark 56.47N 9.49E
53 V19 Røldal Norway 59.50N 6.50E
53 V19 Røldalsvatn L Norway 59.48N 6.47E
119 C5 Roldanillo Colombia 4.23N 76.08W
60 P8 Rolde Netherlands 52.59N 6.39E
108 L1 Rolette N Dakota 48.41N 99.50W
108 Q7 Rolfe Iowa 42.48N 94.32W
104 G5 Rolfe Pennsylvania 41.30N 78.42W
13 H6 Rolfes Queensland 24.30S 147.25E
76 A10 Roliça Portugal 39.18N 9.10W
111 L9 Roll Arizona 32.45N 113.59W
101 N8 Rolla Br Columbia 55.55N 120.11W
109 J4 Rolla Kansas 37.07N 101.38W
107 E4 Rolla Missouri 37.56N 91.47W
108 L1 Rolla N Dakota 48.52N 99.36W
52 E6 Rollag Norway 60.01N 9.18E
76 H7 Rollán Spain 40.58N 5.55W
66 B6 Rolle Switzerland 46.28N 6.21E
61 D3 Rollegem Belgium 50.46N 3.16E
61 C3 Rollegem-Kapelle Belgium 50.52N 3.09E
79 L2 Rolle, Passo di pass Italy 46.18N 11.48E
11 G10 Rolleston New Zealand 43.36S 172.24E
13 J6 Rolleston Queensland 24.25S 148.35E
11 F9 Rolleston, Mt New Zealand 42.56S 171.31E
99 L5 Rollet Quebec 47.55N 79.15W
70 L2 Rolleville France 49.35N 0.13E
116 G3 Rolleville Great Exuma Bahamas 23.41N 76.00W
107 F9 Rolling Fork Mississippi 32.55N 90.54W
107 L4 Rolling Fork R Kentucky
111 D10 Rolling Hills California
110 L2 Rollins Montana 47.55N 114.13W
79 J5 Rolo Italy 44.53N 10.51E
63 R4 Rolofshagen E Germany 54.08N 12.58E
99 N6 Rolphton Ontario 46.11N 77.41W
53 F6 Rolsted Denmark 55.19N 10.34E
25 H6 Roluos Cambodia 13.17N 104.01E
51 K1 Rolvsøya isld Norway 70.58N 24.00E
61 J6 Roly Belgium 50.08N 4.33E
63 P6 Rom E Germany 53.27N 11.57E
72 E3 Rom France 46.18N 0.06E
87 D6 Rom Sudan 9.52N 32.11E
93 E2 Rom mt Uganda 3.24N 33.36E
80 F5 Roma Italy 41.53N 12.30E
95 L5 Roma Lesotho 29.28S 27.44E
13 J7 Roma Queensland 26.32S 148.46E
52 L9 Roma Sweden 57.32N 18.28W
80 F5 Roma prov Italy
79 H6 Romagna reg Italy
79 D3 Romagnano Sesia Italy 45.38N 8.23E
70 H5 Romagné France 48.21N 1.17W
69 J5 Romagne-Gesnes France 49.19N 5.05E
79 F5 Romagnese Italy 44.51N 9.19E
11 D13 Romahapa New Zealand 46.22S 169.45E
105 H4 Romain, C S Carolina 33.01N 79.23W
98 J3 Romaine R Quebec
66 B5 Romainmôtier Switzerland 46.43N 6.28E
68 G3 Romainville France 48.53N 2.26E
112 H9 Roma-Los Saenz Texas 26.26N 99.01W
82 H7 Roman Bulgaria 43.08N 23.54E
82 K4 Roman Romania 46.56N 26.56E
81 B3 Romana Sardinia 40.29N 8.36E
77 P4 Romana, La Spain 38.22N 0.54W
115 G4 Román Arreola Mexico 26.04N 105.00W
71 H6 Romanche R France
96 J8 Romanche Gap Atlantic Oc 0.12S 18.22W
103 B9 Romancoke Maryland 38.53N 76.20W
71 F4 Romanèche-Thorins France 46.11N 4.43E
79 G4 Romanengo Italy 45.23N 9.47E
19 E7 Romang isld Indon 7.34S 127.27E
76 H9 Romangorda Spain 39.45N 5.42W
49 J7 Romania rep Cent Europe
75 E5 Romanillos de Atienza Spain 41.16N 2.54W
44 C10 Roman Kosh mt Ukraine U.S.S.R. 44.36N 34.15E
58 K7 Romanno Bridge Borders Scotland 55.44N 3.20W
105 F12 Romano, C Florida 26.50N 81.42W
116 E3 Romano, Cayo isld Cuba 22.04N 77.50W
79 G3 Romano di Lombardia Italy 45.32N 9.45E
75 E6 Romanones Spain 40.34N 2.59W
42 G4 Romanova Irkutsk U.S.S.R. 57.02N 103.25E
42 J5 Romanovka Buryat U.S.S.R. 53.15N 112.48E
45 O5 Romanovka Saratov U.S.S.R. 51.45N 42.45E
42 C5 Romanovo Altay U.S.S.R. 52.38N 81.16E
47 J6 Romanovo Sverdlovsk U.S.S.R. 59.10N 61.30E
45 O9 Romanovskaya U.S.S.R. 47.32N 42.01E
35 G7 Roman Res Jordan 31.42N 35.57E
66 O1 Romanshorn Switzerland 47.34N 9.23E
71 G6 Romans-sur-Isère France 45.03N 5.03E
69 N6 Romanswiller France 48.39N 7.25E
113 D6 Romanzof, C Alaska 61.49N 166.09W
113 Q2 Romanzof Mts Alaska
119 H8 Romão Brazil 0.24S 62.58W
53 T17 Romarheim Norway 60.44N 5.39E
45 S6 Romashki U.S.S.R. 50.12N 46.40E
70 H5 Romazy France 48.23N 1.29W
66 S5 Rom Bach R Italy/Switz
15 D4 Rombebai, Danau L Irian Jaya
53 T15 Rombergvatn L Norway 61.38N 5.54E
81 M6 Rombiolo Italy 38.36N 16.00E
19 L5 Romblon Philippines 12.33N 122.17E
19 L5 Romblon I Philippines
19 L5 Romblon Pass Philippines
89 O11 Rombo, Is. do Cape Verde 15.10N 24.40W
53 A3 Romby Denmark 56.32N 8.19E
105 B3 Rome Georgia 34.01N 85.02W
Rome Italy see Roma
104 K3 Rome New York 43.13N 75.28W
110 H7 Rome Oregon 42.50N 117.37W
103 B3 Rome Pennsylvania 41.51N 76.21W
107 K5 Rome Tennessee 36.15N 86.06W
61 J6 Romedenne Belgium 50.10N 4.42E
35 G1 Rom, El Syria 33.11N 35.46E
35 A1 Romema sub Jerusalem
35 A1 Romema Ilit dist Jerusalem
71 G4 Romenay France 46.30N 5.03E
109 E4 Romeo Colorado 37.11N 106.00W
106 L7 Romeo Michigan 42.47N 83.01W
75 D8 Romeral mt Spain 39.40N 3.25W
75 D8 Romeral, El Spain 39.42N 3.26W
64 E5 Römerberg W Germany 49.15N 8.22E
69 P5 Römerberg W Germany 49.17N 8.24E
61 J6 Romerée Belgium 50.08N 4.40E
52 E6 Romerike reg Norway
115 K8 Romero Mexico 19.39N 99.20W
112 B8 Romero Texas 35.44N 102.56W
109 E6 Romeroville New Mexico 35.32N 105.16W
64 H7 Römerstein W Germany 48.30N 9.32E
43 G7 Rometan Uzbekistan U.S.S.R. 39.55N 64.24E
81 K7 Rometta Sicily 38.10N 15.25E
71 H5 Romey, Val France
55 K3 Romford London England 51.35N 0.11E
62 L8 Romhany Hungary 47.55N 19.16E
64 K3 Römhild E Germany 50.24N 10.34E
72 F8 Romieu, la France 43.59N 0.30E
57 J6 Romiley Greater Manchester Eng 53.25N 2.05W
70 G5 Romille France 48.13N 1.54W
70 M3 Romilly Eure France 49.00N 0.50E
70 N3 Romilly-sur-Andelle France 49.20N 1.15E
69 F6 Romilly-sur-Seine Aube France 48.31N 3.44E
14 F5 Romily, Mt W Australia 20.27S 126.30E
88 K5 Rommani Morocco 33.34N 6.37W
64 B1 Rommerskirchen W Germany 51.02N 6.42E
104 G7 Romney W Virginia 39.21N 78.44W
56 N5 Romney Marsh dist Kent Eng
45 E6 Romny Ukraine U.S.S.R. 50.45N 33.30E
53 B6 Rømø isld Denmark 55.10N 8.30E
45 E6 Romodan Ukraine U.S.S.R. 50.00N 33.20E
45 W1 Romodan U.S.S.R. 55.04N 50.00E
45 R2 Romodanovo U.S.S.R. 54.26N 45.19E
66 D5 Romont Switzerland 46.42N 6.56E
66 J3 Romoos Switzerland 47.01N 8.03E
70 O7 Romorantin France 47.22N 1.44E
53 V16 Romøyri Norway 61.17N 6.43E
77 G7 Rompedizo, El airport Spain 36.41N 4.31W
Rompin see Kuala Rompin
18 C9 Rompin Pen Malaysia 2.43N 102.30E
18 D9 Rompin R Pen Malaysia
55 J2 Rom, R London/Essex England
64 G2 Romrod W Germany 50.43N 9.14E
52 C4 Romsdal V Norway
53 X14 Romsdalen V Norway
52 C4 Romsdalsfjord inlet Norway
53 W13 Romsdalsfjorden inlet Norway 62.37N 7.24E
53 X13 Romsdalshorn mt Norway 62.31N 7.37E
53 X14 Romsdalshorn mt Norway 62.29N 7.49E
61 N4 Romsée Belgium 50.37N 5.40E
56 J6 Romsey Hants Eng 59.59N 1.30W
53 F5 Romsø isld Denmark 55.31N 10.48E
106 L7 Romulus Michigan 42.14N 83.23W
28 B3 Ron Karnataka India 15.44N 75.47E
30 B6 Ron Madhya Prad India 26.21N 78.56E
23 D10 Ron Vietnam 17.55N 106.26E
87 C9 Rona Zaïre 2.21N 30.45E
58 E3 Rona isld Highland Scotland
11 D5 Rona Bay New Zealand 41.17S 174.54E
57 D4 Ronaldsway airport Isle of Man U.K. 54.04N 4.36W
110 L2 Ronan Montana 47.31N 114.06W
58 Q8 Ronas Hill Shetland Scotland 60.32N 1.26W
58 Q8 Ronas Voe B Shetland Scotland 60.31N 1.29W
9 B8 Ronawi Nauru, Pacific Oc 0.30S 166.57E
58 B4 Ronay isld W Isles Scotland 57.29N 7.11W
53 B3 Rønbjerg Denmark 56.32N 8.56E
76 D1 Roncadoira, Pta Spain 43.44N 7.31W
116 D8 Roncador Cay isld Caribbean Sea 13.33N 80.03W
15 L2 Roncador Reef Solomon Is 6.15S 159.23E
118 D3 Roncador, Serra do mts Brazil
75 J2 Roncal Spain 42.49N 0.57W
75 J2 Roncal, Valle de Spain
79 K2 Roncegno Italy 46.03N 11.25E
72 B4 Ronce-les-Bains France 45.48N 1.11W
75 H1 Roncesvalles Spain 43.00N 1.19W
75 H1 Roncesvalles, Pto. de pass Spain 43.01N 1.19W
104 E9 Ronceverte W Virginia 37.46N 80.30W
70 H4 Roncey France 48.59N 1.20W
71 K1 Ronchamp France 47.42N 6.38E
79 O3 Ronchi del Legionari Italy 45.49N 13.30E
80 F4 Ronciglione Italy 42.17N 12.13E
66 L7 Ronco Switzerland 46.09N 8.44E
79 M6 Ronco R Italy
79 C3 Ronco Canavese Italy 45.30N 7.32E
79 J4 Roncoferraro Italy 45.08N 10.57E
79 M6 Roncofreddo Italy 44.03N 12.18E
79 J3 Roncone Italy 45.59N 10.40E
79 E5 Ronco Scrivia Italy 44.37N 8.57E
69 E2 Roncq France 50.45N 3.07E
76 A2 Roncudo, Pta. del Spain 43.17N 9.00W
31 H3 Ronda Kashmir 35.35N 75.15E
77 F7 Ronda Spain 36.45N 5.10W
118 A4 Ronda das Salinas Brazil 15.44S 60.09W
52 E5 Rondane plat Norway
77 F7 Ronda, Serrania de mts Spain
53 E4 Rønde Denmark 56.18N 10.30E
116 O8 Ronde isld Windward Is W I 12.29N 61.36W
99 J10 Rondeau Prov. Park Ontario 42.17N 81.52W
94 P11 Rondebosch dist Cape Town S Africa
26 P16 Ronde, Is Kerguelen Ind Oc 49.49S 68.45E
72 C3 Ronde, la France 46.18N 0.48W
52 E5 Rondeslottet mt Norway 61.56N 9.52E
95 F10 Rondevlei S Africa 34.00S 22.42E
94 P12 Rondevlei pond Cape Town S Africa 34.03S 18.30E
118 D8 Rondon Brazil 23.18S 52.57W
119 E4 Rondón Colombia 6.18N 71.07W
120 G4 Rondônia Brazil 10.51S 61.56W
120 F4 Rondônia fed terr Brazil
118 C5 Rondonópolis Brazil 16.29S 54.37W
119 G7 Rondon, Pico pk Brazil 1.35N 63.10W
92 J7 Rondo Plat Tanzania
103 F3 Rondout Cr New York
103 F3 Rondout Res New York
52 L9 Ronehamn Sweden 57.11N 18.30E
53 U17 Rong Norway 60.31N 6.28E
93 G6 Rongai Kenya 0.11S 35.52E
23 E6 Rong'an Guangxi China 25.10N 109.17E
23 B3 Rongbaca Sichuan China 31.41N 99.39E
30 K4 Rongbuk Xizang Zizhiqu 28.13N 86.49E
30 J1 Rongbuk Glacier Xizang Zizhiqu
30 J1 Rongbuk Glacier, East Xizang Zizhiqu
30 J2 Rongbuk Glacier, West Xizang Zizhiqu
23 D4 Rongchang Sichuan China 29.25N 105.34E
22 K7 Rongcheng Hebei China 39.04N 115.52E
21 B9 Rongcheng Shandong China 37.10N 122.25E
28 G1 Rong Chu R Xizang Zizhiqu
9 B1 Rongelap atoll Marshall Is Pacific Oc 11.30N 166.45E
9 C1 Rongerik atoll Marshall Is Pacific Oc 11.22N 167.28E
23 E6 Rongjiang Guizhou China 25.53N 108.38E
23 E6 Rong Jiang R Guangxi China
25 B1 Rongklang Ra Burma
11 K7 Rongotea New Zealand 40.15S 175.27E
29 L4 Rongphu Sikkim India 27.09N 88.32E
28 H3 Rongrengiri Meghalaya India 25.41N 90.22E
30 F1 Rongshar Glacier Xizang Zizhiqu
23 E6 Rongshui Guangxi China 25.05N 109.09E
92 K7 Rongüi, I Mozambique 10.54S 40.39E
24 F11 Rongxar Xizang Zizhiqu China 28.15N 87.45E
23 E7 Rong Xian Guangxi China 22.54N 110.30E
23 C4 Rong Xian Sichuan China 29.29N 104.24E
61 D4 Rongy Belgium 50.31N 3.23E
Rongzhag see Danba
122 D13 Roniu mt Tahiti Pacific Oc 17.50S 149.10W
103 H5 Ronkonkoma Long I, N Y 40.48N 73.07W
53 A3 Rønland C Denmark 56.39N 8.14E
53 P12 Rønne Bornholm Denmark 55.07N 14.43E
52 G10 Rönnea R Sweden
64 N2 Ronneburg E Germany 50.51N 12.11E
52 J10 Ronneby Sweden 56.13N 15.15E
123 F12 Ronne Entrance Antarctica
123 F11 Ronne Ice Shelf Antarctica
63 L8 Ronnenberg W Germany 52.20N 9.35E
52 H3 Rönnöfors Sweden 63.39N 13.40E
93 B3 Rono Zaïre 2.20N 30.45E
61 G4 Ronquières Belgium 50.37N 4.13E
77 D5 Ronquillo, El Spain 37.44N 6.10W
14 A6 Ronsard, C W Australia 24.46S 113.13E
14 C5 Ronsard I W Australia 20.31S 117.52E
64 J8 Ronsberg W Germany 47.54N 10.25E
61 E3 Ronse Belgium 50.45N 3.36E
79 D4 Ronsecco Italy 45.15N 8.16E
61 E2 Ronsele Belgium 51.08N 3.34E
93 K1 Ronso, El Ethiopia 4.01N 38.15E
53 U13 Rønstad Norway 67.37N 6.10E
118 C3 Ronuro, R Brazil
95 N2 Roodebank S Africa 26.38S 29.02E
60 K8 Roode Klif cliffs Netherlands
95 L2 Roodepoort S Africa 26.10S 27.53E
94 S13 Roodepoort West S Africa 26.09S 27.52E
60 Q6 Roodeschool Netherlands 53.25N 6.46E
107 F2 Roodhouse Illinois 39.29N 90.21W
69 L4 Roodt-sur-Syre Luxembourg 49.40N 6.15E
94 K4 Rooiberg mt Transvaal S Africa 23.08S 28.24E
95 M4 Rooiberge mts S Africa
95 J1 Rooigrond S Africa 25.55S 25.49E
95 H7 Rooihoogte S Africa 31.46S 24.55E
95 K2 Rooijantjiesfontein S Africa 26.25S 26.06E
94 T14 Rooikon S Africa 26.18S 28.11E
95 H5 Rooipan S Africa 29.31S 24.35E
95 J7 Rooispruit S Africa 31.27S 25.20E
95 L3 Rooiwal S Africa 27.18S 27.32E
Rooke I see Umboi I
96 B15 Rookery Point C Tristan da Cunha 37.03S 12.15W
60 A2 Roompot channel Netherlands
15 C5 Roon isld Irian Jaya 2.24S 134.32E
59 C4 Roonah, L Mayo Irish Rep 53.44N 9.54W
60 M7 Roordahuizum Netherlands 53.08N 5.47E
30 A3 Roorkee Uttar Prad India 29.51N 77.54E
61 K3 Roosbeek Belgium 50.50N 4.51E
61 G3 Roosdaal Belgium 50.45N 4.05E
60 F13 Roosendaal Netherlands 51.32N 4.28E
111 N8 Roosevelt Arizona 33.42N 111.07W
108 P1 Roosevelt Minnesota 48.49N 95.06W
109 L7 Roosevelt Oklahoma 34.52N 99.02W
112 G5 Roosevelt Texas 30.30N 100.05W
110 Q9 Roosevelt Utah 40.14N 109.59W
110 E4 Roosevelt Washington 45.45N 120.12W
117 H2 Roosevelt R Brazil
111 N8 Roosevelt Dam Arizona 33.42N 111.10W
123 H8 Roosevelt I Antarctica
101 L6 Roosevelt, Mt Br Columbia 58.26N 125.20W
99 S2 Rooseveltown New York 44.58N 74.43W
59 G4 Roosky Roscommon Irish Rep 53.50N 7.55W
94 K5 Roossenekal S Africa 25.14S 29.53E
60 T16 Roosteren Netherlands 51.05N 5.49E
66 K3 Root Switzerland 47.07N 8.23E
101 L4 Root R N W Terr
95 E9 Rootberg mt Cape Province S Africa 33.39S 21.30E
113 E9 Rootok I Aleutian Is 54.04N 165.31W
106 B6 Root, R Minnesota
46 E2 Ropaži Latvia U.S.S.R. 57.02N 24.31E
47 G4 Ropcha U.S.S.R. 62.57N 52.10E
62 N5 Ropczyce Poland 50.04N 21.31E
53 U20 Ropeid Norway 59.29N 6.12E
105 L2 Roper N Carolina 35.53N 76.38W
13 C2 Roper R N Terr Australia
13 J6 Roper R Queensland
13 J7 Roper Pass Queensland 25.08S 149.30E
13 C2 Roper River N Terr Australia 14.44S 134.51E
13 C2 Roper Valley N Terr Australia 14.58S 134.02E
112 E2 Ropesville Texas 33.25N 102.09W
122 V11 Rope, The cliff Pitcairn I Pacific Oc 25.05S 130.05W
51 J3 Ropi mt Finland 68.50N 21.40E
56 J5 Ropley Hants Eng 51.05N 1.04W
90 D7 Ropp Nigeria 9.30N 8.56E
66 D1 Roppe France 47.40N 6.55E
69 P6 Roppenheim France 48.50N 8.03E
66 F1 Roppentzwiller France 47.33N 7.20E
20 E2 Roppongi dist Tōkyō Japan
115 F10 Roque Panama 9.08N 79.37W
71 L8 Roquebillière France 44.01N 7.19E
71 C9 Roquebrun France 43.30N 3.01E
71 L9 Roquebrune Alpes-Maritimes France 43.47N 7.27E
71 K10 Roquebrune-sur-Argens France 43.26N 6.38E
71 H10 Roquebrussanne, la France 43.20N 5.58E
72 F7 Roquecor France 44.20N 0.57E
72 J8 Roquecourbe France 43.40N 2.17E
71 G9 Roque-d'Antheran, la France 43.43N 5.20E
96 V6 Roque del Este isld Canary Is 29.16N 13.21W
96 V6 Roque del Oeste isld Canary Is 29.18N 13.32W
96 P9 Roque de los Muchachos mt La Palma Canary Is 28.45N 17.52W
72 D7 Roquefort Landes France 44.02N 0.18W
72 J10 Roquefort-de-Sault France 42.45N 2.12E
72 F9 Roquefort-sur-Garonne France 43.10N 0.58E
72 K8 Roquefort-sur-Soulzon France 43.59N 2.58E
71 F8 Roquemaure France 44.03N 4.47E
99 L4 Roquemaure Quebec 48.38N 79.26W
121 F5 Roque Pérez Argentina 35.25S 59.24W
71 L9 Roquesteron France 43.52N 7.01E
75 L6 Roquetas Spain 40.50N 0.30E
77 L7 Roquetas de Mar Spain 36.46N 2.35W
71 H10 Roquevaire France 43.20N 5.36E
58 S12 Rora Hd Orkney Scotland 58.52N 3.26W
119 H7 Roraima state Brazil
119 H5 Roraima, Mt Guyana 5.14N 60.44W
87 D5 Rora,Jeb mt Sudan 11.54N 33.40E
87 A6 Rorayai Sudan 8.50N 27.39E
52 G5 Rörbäcksnäs Sweden 61.08N 12.50E
53 D3 Rørbæk Denmark 56.43N 9.44E
66 L1 Rorbas Switzerland 47.32N 8.35E
53 G5 Rørby Denmark 55.39N 11.10E
79 B5 Roreto Chisone Italy 44.59N 7.08E
101 J2 Rorey L N W Terr
29 D3 Rori Haryana India 29.46N 75.15E
95 O4 Rorke's Drift S Africa 28.21S 30.33E
100 S7 Rorketon Manitoba 51.24N 99.35W
52 F4 Røros Norway 62.35N 11.23E
66 O2 Rorschach Switzerland 47.28N 9.30E
51 E4 Rørstad Norway 67.36N 15.16E
89 C7 Roruks Sierra Leone 8.27N 12.29W
53 H5 Rørvig Denmark 55.58N 11.47E
52 F2 Rørvik Norway 64.54N 11.15E
53 S16 Rørvik Norway 61.27N 5.27E
45 C7 Ros' R Ukraine U.S.S.R.
79 L3 Rosà Italy 45.43N 11.46E
92 E6 Rosa Zambia 9.41S 31.24E
66 F7 Rosablanche mt Switzerland 46.08N 7.22E
88 S3 Rosa, C Algeria 36.58N 8.10E
119 A6 Rosa, C Galápagos Is 1.05S 91.10W
98 B7 Rosaire Quebec 46.48N 70.24W
96 Q3 Rosais Azores 38.43N 28.15W
96 Q3 Rosais, Pta. dos Azores 38.46N 28.19W
76 B5 Rosal Spain 41.57N 8.51W
66 R6 Rosa, la Switzerland 46.24N 10.04E
77 B5 Rosal de la Frontera Spain 37.59N 7.13W
115 H6 Rosales, Calera Victor Mexico 22.57N 102.41W
109 O4 Rosalia Kansas 37.50N 96.40W
110 H2 Rosalia Washington 47.15N 117.20W
122 U15 Rosalia, Pta Easter I Pacific Oc 27.04S 109.19W
120 C5 Rosalina Peru 12.36S 72.37W
100 E6 Rosalind Alberta 52.44N 112.21W
116 D6 Rosalind Bank Caribbean Sea

111 F7 **Rosamond** California 34.52N 118.10W
111 F7 **Rosamond L** California 34.50N 118.05W
79 C3 **Rosa, Monte** Italy/Switz 45.56N 7.50E
115 G6 **Rosamorada** Mexico 22.09N 105.12W
112 K6 **Rosanky** Texas 29.57N 97.19W
65 B7 **Rosanna** *R* Austria
71 G8 **Rosans** France 44.23N 5.29E
59 G1 **Rosapenna** Donegal Irish Rep 55.12N 7.50W
77 S12 **Rosa, Pta** Balearic Is 38.42N 1.24E
115 E4 **Rosa, Pta** Mexico 26.40N 109.40W
120 D11 **Rosario** Antofagasta Chile 24.16S 69.59W
115 B2 **Rosário** Baja Cal Mexico 30.02N 115.46W
117 F6 **Rosário** Brazil 3.00S 44.15W
115 H4 **Rosario** Coahuila Mexico 26.58N 102.30W
120 E10 **Rosario** Jujuy Argentina 22.52S 66.41W
19 K3 **Rosario** Luzon Philippines 16.15N 120.30E
19 K5 **Rosario** Luzon Philippines 13.50N 121.10E
118 B9 **Rosario** Paraguay 24.28S 57.13W
76 C13 **Rosário** Portugal 37.36N 8.05W
76 E11 **Rosário** Portugal 38.37N 7.20W
121 E4 **Rosario** Santa Fé Argentina 33.00S 60.40W
115 G6 **Rosario** Sinaloa Mexico 23.00N 105.51W
115 E4 **Rosario** Sonora Mexico 27.50N 109.23W
120 D8 **Rosario** Tarapacá Chile 18.25S 70.08W
121 F5 **Rosario** Uruguay 34.20S 57.26W
119 D2 **Rosario** Venezuela 10.21N 72.21W
115 J5 **Rosario** Zacatecas Mexico 24.25N 101.40W
116 B5 **Rosario Bank** Caribbean Sea
116 D4 **Rosario, Cayo del** *isld* Cuba 21.38N 81.53W
121 C9 **Rosario, Cerro del** *pk* Arg 43.32S 68.33W
120 F11 **Rosario de la Frontera** Arg 25.45S 65.00W
120 F11 **Rosario de Lerma** Argentina 24.59S 65.35W
121 F4 **Rosario del Tala** Argentina 32.20S 59.10W
121 C3 **Rosario del Tama** Argentina 30.28S 66.38W
121 G3 **Rosário do Sul** Brazil 30.15S 54.55W
Rosario I *see* **Nishino-shima** Ogasawara-guntō Bonin Is
118 C4 **Rosário Oeste** Brazil 14.50S 56.25W
116 C3 **Rosario, Sa. del** *mts* Cuba
115 A1 **Rosarito** Baja Cal Mexico 32.19N 117.10W
115 B3 **Rosarito** Baja Cal Mexico 28.38N 114.02W
111 G9 **Rosarito** Mexico 32.20N 117.04W
115 D4 **Rosarito** Mexico 26.28N 111.41W
76 J8 **Rosarito, Embalse de** *res* Spain 40.05N 5.12W
81 L7 **Rosarno** Italy 38.29N 15.59E
75 R3 **Rosas** Spain 42.15N 3.11E
118 J8 **Rosa, Saco do** *gulf* Brazil
75 R3 **Rosas, G. de** Spain
96 O14 **Rosas, Las** Gomera Canary Is 28.12N 17.12W
79 F4 **Rosate** Italy 45.22N 9.02E
119 B7 **Rosa Zárate** Ecuador 0.14N 79.28W
59 J7 **Rosbercon** Kilkenny Irish Rep 52.24N 6.57W
70 A5 **Roscanvel** France 48.18N 4.34W
63 N7 **Rosche** W Germany 52.59N 10.47E
65 N4 **Röschitz** Austria 48.40N 15.55E
80 K4 **Rosciano** Italy 42.19N 14.03E
81 K3 **Roscigno** Italy 40.24N 15.20E
106 E7 **Roscoe** Illinois 42.27N 89.01W
110 Q4 **Roscoe** Montana 45.20N 109.30W
104 L5 **Roscoe** New York 41.56N 74.56W
108 L4 **Roscoe** S Dakota 45.26N 99.20W
112 G3 **Roscoe** Texas 32.26N 100.34W
70 C4 **Roscoff** France 48.43N 3.59W
106 K5 **Roscommon** Michigan 44.31N 84.37W
59 F4 **Roscommon** Roscommon Irish Rep 53.38N 8.11W
59 F4 **Roscommon** *co* Irish Rep
59 G6 **Roscrea** Tipperary Irish Rep 52.57N 7.47W
81 M5 **Rose** Italy 39.23N 16.17E
108 L7 **Rose** Nebraska 42.08N 99.27W
116 O7 **Roseau** Dominica, W I 15.18N 61.23W
108 P1 **Roseau** Minnesota 48.51N 95.46W
108 O1 **Roseau** *R* Minnesota
94 P11 **Rosebank** Cape Town S Africa 33.57S 18.28E
12 M7 **Rose Bay** *dist* Sydney, N S W
26 U13 **Rose Belle** Mauritius, Indian Oc 20.24S 57.36E
110 J5 **Roseberry** Idaho 44.44N 116.02W
13 E7 **Roseberth** Queensland Australia 25.48S 139.42E
12 H8 **Rosebery** Tasmania 41.46S 145.34E
12 M7 **Rosebery** *dist* Sydney, N S W
98 O6 **Rose Blanche** Newfoundland 47.38N 58.42W
105 J3 **Roseboro** N Carolina 34.57N 78.32W
100 E7 **Rosebud** Alberta 51.18N 112.57W
107 E3 **Rosebud** Missouri 38.23N 91.24W
108 D3 **Rosebud** Montana 46.15N 106.28W
109 G6 **Rosebud** New Mexico 35.50N 103.27W
108 K6 **Rosebud** S Dakota 43.12N 100.50W
112 L4 **Rosebud** Texas 31.06N 96.59W
108 D4 **Rosebud Cr** Montana
108 C4 **Rosebud Mts** Montana
100 D7 **Rosebud R** Alberta
110 B6 **Roseburg** Oregon 43.13N 123.21W
106 K6 **Rosebush** Michigan 43.42N 84.47W
106 K5 **Rose City** Michigan 44.25N 84.08W
110 H9 **Rose Creek** Nevada 40.54N 117.55W
100 E7 **Rosedale** Alberta 51.26N 112.37W
107 J2 **Rosedale** Indiana 39.38N 87.18W
107 E8 **Rosedale** Mississippi 33.51N 91.01W
13 K6 **Rosedale** Queensland 24.35S 151.51E
57 M4 **Rosedale Abbey** N Yorks Eng 54.20N 0.53W
95 F8 **Rosedene** S Africa 32.02S 22.25E
61 J6 **Rosée** Belgium 50.14N 4.41E
65 K8 **Rosegg** Austria 46.36N 14.02E
66 Q6 **Roseg, Piz** *mt* Switzerland 46.23N 9.53E
59 G7 **Rosegreen** Tipperary Irish Rep 52.28N 7.50W
66 Q6 **Roseg, Val** Switzerland
117 A1 **Rosehall** Guyana 6.13N 57.19W
58 G3 **Rosehall** Highland Scotland 57.58N 4.36W
116 H1 **Rose Hall** Jamaica, W I 18.31N 77.50W
58 M3 **Rosehearty** Grampian Scotland 57.42N 2.07W
99 M8 **Roseheath** Ontario 44.11N 78.04W
108 S8 **Rose Hill** Iowa 41.19N 92.29W
26 U12 **Rose Hill** Mauritius, Indian Oc 20.14S 57.27E
105 J3 **Rose Hill** N Carolina 34.49N 78.03W
11 B7 **Rose I** Auckland Is Pacific Oc 50.30S 166.15E
105 K12 **Rose I** Bahamas 25.05N 77.10W
101 G12 **Rose I** Br Col 49.07N 123.07W
122 K9 **Rose I** Samoa Pacific Oc 14.32S 168.11W
87 E5 **Roseires, Er** Sudan 11.52N 34.23E
107 F11 **Roseland** Louisiana 30.46N 90.30W
71 K5 **Roselend** France 45.42N 6.38E
61 J5 **Roselies** Belgium 50.26N 4.35E
75 L6 **Rosell** Spain 40.38N 0.13E
80 D3 **Roselle** Italy 42.45N 11.10E
103 J8 **Roselle** New Jersey 40.38N 74.17W
100 F7 **Rose Lynn** Alberta 51.26N 111.40W
58 H3 **Rosemarkie** Highland Scotland 57.35N 4.08W
100 E8 **Rosemary** Alberta 50.46N 112.05W
54 D3 **Rosemary Bank** N Atlantic Oc
14 B5 **Rosemary I** W Australia 20.31S 116.35E
111 F7 **Rosemead** California 34.03N 118.07W
108 R5 **Rosemount** Minnesota 44.44N 93.06W
111 E2 **Rose, Mt** Nevada 39.21N 119.56W
59 H5 **Rosenallis** Leix Irish Rep 53.08N 7.24W
65 K8 **Rosenbach** Austria 46.32N 14.03E
63 O5 **Rosenberg** E Germany 53.40N 11.14E
112 M6 **Rosenberg** Texas 29.34N 95.51W
64 G5 **Rosenberg** W Germany 49.27N 9.28E
69 C1 **Rosendaël** France 51.02N 2.25E
53 U19 **Rosendal** Norway 59.59N 6.01E
95 L4 **Rosendal** S Africa 28.30S 27.55E
107 B1 **Rosendale** Missouri 40.03N 94.45W
103 F3 **Rosendale** New York 41.50N 74.05W
11 M12 **Roseneath** New Zealand 45.50S 170.36E
58 T12 **Rose Ness** *prom* Orkney Scotland 58.53N 2.50W
64 F7 **Rosenfeld** W Germany 48.17N 8.44E
63 L6 **Rosengarten** W Germany 53.25N 9.55E
103 D8 **Rosenhayn** New Jersey 39.28N 75.08W
64 N8 **Rosenheim** W Germany 47.51N 12.09E
65 M8 **Rosen Kopf** *mt* Austria 46.54N 15.08E
66 J5 **Rosenlaui** Switzerland 46.51N 8.09E
65 J8 **Rosennock** *mt* Austria 46.53N 13.41E
65 K8 **Rosental** *V* Austria
64 F2 **Rosenthal** W Germany 50.59N 8.53E
107 C11 **Rosepine** Louisiana 30.55N 93.18W
101 H8 **Rose Pt** Graham I, Br Col 54.11N 131.39W
13 D2 **Rose R** N Terr Australia
100 J8 **Roseray** Saskatchewan 50.28N 108.30W
Rose River Mission *see* **Numbulwar Mission**
116 G3 **Roses** Long I Bahamas 23.00N 74.54W
81 N4 **Roseto Capo Spulico** Italy 39.59N 16.37E
80 K3 **Roseto degli Abruzzi** Italy 42.40N 14.02E
103 F3 **Roseton** New York 41.34N 74.00W
80 M6 **Roseto Val Fortore** Italy 41.22N 15.06E
100 K7 **Rosetown** Saskatchewan 51.34N 107.59W
Rosetta Egypt *see* **Rashîd**
95 N5 **Rosetta** S Africa 29.19S 29.59E
13 H5 **Rosetta** *R* Queensland
110 M8 **Rosette** Utah 41.49N 113.27W
94 T14 **Rosettenville** S Africa 26.15S 28.03E
100 O6 **Rose Valley** Saskatchewan 52.19N 103.49W
100 A5 **Rosevear** Alberta 53.41N 116.07W
111 C3 **Roseville** California 38.44N 121.19W
106 D9 **Roseville** Illinois 40.44N 90.40W
104 C7 **Roseville** Ohio 39.49N 82.04W
12 A7 **Rosewater** *dist* Port Adelaide, S Australia
58 K7 **Rosewell** Lothian Scotland 55.51N 3.08W
13 K8 **Rosewood** Queensland 27.39S 152.20E
110 L7 **Roseworth** Idaho 42.23N 114.56W
45 L1 **Roshal'** U.S.S.R. 55.39N 39.53E
30 H8 **Roshanganj** Bihar India 24.33N 84.42E
112 M6 **Rosharon** Texas 29.21N 95.28W
47 B5 **Roshchino** U.S.S.R. 60.20N 29.28E
69 N6 **Rosheim** France 48.31N 7.28E
35 C5 **Rosh Ha'Ayin** Israel 32.05N 34.57E
32 H3 **Roshkhvār** Iran 34.59N 59.37E
108 O4 **Rosholt** S Dakota 45.52N 96.44W
106 E5 **Rosholt** Wisconsin 44.38N 89.18W
35 F2 **Rosh Pinna** Israel 32.58N 35.32E
43 K8 **Roshtkala** Tadzhikistan U.S.S.R. 37.21N 71.46E
35 D9 **Rosh Zohar** Israel 31.13N 35.14E
80 D2 **Rosia** Italy 43.14N 11.13E
65 O3 **Rosice** Czechoslovakia 49.12N 16.23E
65 N1 **Rosice** Pardubice Czechoslovakia 50.03N 15.44E
107 H4 **Rosiclare** Illinois 37.25N 88.21W
61 J4 **Rosières** Belgium 50.44N 4.33E
71 D6 **Rosières** France 45.08N 4.00E
69 L6 **Rosières-aux-Salines** France 48.36N 6.20E
69 K6 **Rosières-en-Blois** France 48.34N 5.33E
69 D4 **Rosières-en-Santerre** France 49.49N 2.43E
98 H5 **Rosiers, C. des** Quebec 48.52N 64.13W
70 K7 **Rosiers, les** France 47.21N 0.13W
80 B2 **Rosignano Marittimo** Italy 43.24N 10.28E
117 A1 **Rosignol** Guyana 6.18N 57.34W
14 A5 **Rosily I** W Australia 21.16S 115.01E
82 J6 **Roşiorii de Vede** Romania 44.06N 25.00E
82 L7 **Rositsa** Bulgaria 43.57N 27.57E
82 J7 **Rositsa** *R* Bulgaria
64 N1 **Rositz** E Germany 51.01N 12.23E
58 C4 **Roskhill** Skye, Highland Scotland 57.25N 6.32W
53 J5 **Roskilde** Denmark 55.39N 12.07E
53 J6 **Roskilde** *co* Denmark
53 J5 **Roskilde Fjord** *inlet* Denmark
11 C2 **Roskill, Mt** *hill* Auckland New Zealand 36.55S 174.44E
63 R8 **Roskow** E Germany 52.29N 12.44E
111 N9 **Roskruge Mts** Arizona
64 M3 **Röslau** W Germany 50.05N 11.59E
45 D3 **Roslavl'** U.S.S.R. 53.55N 32.53E
59 H3 **Roslea** Fermanagh N Ireland 54.14N 7.10W
53 B3 **Roslev** Denmark 56.43N 8.59E
58 K7 **Roslin** Lothian Scotland 55.51N 3.11W
47 E6 **Roslyatino** U.S.S.R. 59.45N 44.14E
103 G5 **Roslyn** Long I, N Y 40.48N 73.38W
108 N4 **Roslyn** S Dakota 45.30N 97.30W
110 D2 **Roslyn** Washington 47.15N 121.01W
11 L13 **Roslyn** *dist* Dunedin New Zealand
99 C3 **Roslyn L** Ontario
60 K13 **Rosmalen** Netherlands 51.43N 5.21E
76 E9 **Rosmaninhal** Portugal 39.44N 7.05W
95 J7 **Rosmead** S Africa 31.28S 25.07E
61 N3 **Rosmeer** Belgium 50.51N 5.35E
53 F4 **Rosmus** Denmark 56.18N 10.47E
53 F5 **Røsnæs** *pen* Denmark 55.43N 10.54E
72 G2 **Rosnay** France 46.42N 1.12E
58 G6 **Rosneath** Strathclyde Scotland 56.01N 4.49W
70 B5 **Rosnoen** France 48.15N 4.13W
68 G3 **Rosny-sous-Bois** France 48.53N 2.29E
79 M4 **Rosolina** Italy 45.05N 12.15E
81 J10 **Rosolini** Sicily 36.49N 14.57E
61 L4 **Rosoux-Crenwick** Belgium 50.42N 5.12E
69 E7 **Rosoy** France 48.08N 3.20E
70 C6 **Rosporden** France 47.57N 3.50W
61 Q7 **Rosport** Luxembourg 49.48N 6.30E
58 F3 **Rosque, L** Highland Scotland 57.34N 5.07W
64 C2 **Rösrath** W Germany 50.54N 7.11E
59 E6 **Rosroe, L** Clare Irish Rep 52.46N 8.50W
56 F4 **Ross** Hereford & Worcs Eng 51.55N 2.35W
108 H1 **Ross** N Dakota 48.20N 102.32W
11 E9 **Ross** New Zealand 42.54S 170.48E
89 A3 **Ross** Senegal 16.15N 16.10W
12 J8 **Ross** Tasmania 42.01S 147.31E
108 E6 **Ross** Wyoming 43.28N 105.52W
101 H4 **Ross** *R* Yukon Terr
66 J8 **Rossa** Italy 45.50N 8.08E
66 N6 **Rossa** Switzerland 46.23N 9.08E
96 U7 **Rossa, C** Lanzarote Canary Is 29.02N 13.49W
64 K3 **Rossach** W Germany 50.10N 10.57E
79 M1 **Rossa, Croda, mt** Italy 46.38N 12.09E
51 D6 **Røssåga** *R* Norway
81 B1 **Rossa, I** Sardinia 41.02N 8.52E
57 G5 **Rossall Pt** Lancs Eng 53.56N 3.04W
81 N4 **Rossano** Italy 39.35N 16.38E
59 E2 **Rossan Pt** Donegal Irish Rep 54.42N 8.48W
80 O5 **Rossa, Pta** Foggia Italy 41.42N 16.04E
80 B4 **Rossa, Pta** Montecristo I Italy 42.18N 10.19E
76 C5 **Rossas** Minho Portugal 41.34N 8.05W
64 N3 **Rossbach** Czechoslovakia 50.18N 12.10E
64 M1 **Rossbach** E Germany 51.15N 11.52E
107 G9 **Ross Barnett Res** Mississippi
59 E2 **Rossbeg** Donegal Irish Rep 54.49N 8.31W
64 H8 **Rossberg** W Germany 47.51N 9.47E
66 L3 **Rossberg** *mt* Switzerland 47.06N 8.35E
100 R8 **Rossburn** Manitoba 50.40N 100.50W
59 D8 **Ross Carbery** Cork Irish Rep 51.35N 9.02W
59 C7 **Ross Castle** Kerry Irish Rep 52.03N 9.33W
112 F3 **Ross City** Texas 32.06N 101.17W
Ross & Cromarty *co see* **Highland** *reg*
123 J7 **Ross Dependency** Antarctica
64 J2 **Rossdorf** E Germany 50.42N 10.13E
99 L7 **Rosseau** Ontario 45.16N 79.38W
15 M9 **Rossel I** Louisiade Arch
15 M9 **Rossel Lagoon** Louisiade Arch
81 F9 **Rossello, C** Sicily 37.18N 13.27E
121 A10 **Rosselot, L** Chile
100 T9 **Rossendale** Manitoba 49.50N 98.38W
53 V16 **Røssenipa** *mt* Norway 61.28N 6.53E
112 L3 **Rosser** Texas 32.30N 96.27W
59 D3 **Rosserk Abbey** Mayo Irish Rep 54.12N 9.11W
59 F1 **Rosses B** Donegal Irish Rep 55.01N 8.29W
59 E3 **Rosses Point** Sligo Irish Rep 54.18N 8.33W
59 F1 **Rosses, The** *dist* Donegal Irish Rep 55.02N 8.20W
57 H6 **Rossett** Clwyd Wales 53.06N 2.58W
51 G2 **Rossfjord** Norway 69.24N 18.26E
64 K8 **Rosshaupten** W Germany 47.40N 10.43E
26 V3 **Ross Hill** Christmas I Ind Oc 10.28S 105.43E
123 J6 **Ross I** Antarctica 77.40S 168.00E
Ross I Burma *see* **Daung Kyun**
100 U4 **Ross I** Manitoba
123 H7 **Ross Ice Shelf** Antarctica
79 E5 **Rossiglione** Italy 44.34N 8.39E
61 M8 **Rossignol** Belgium 49.43N 5.29E
71 H5 **Rossillon** France 45.50N 5.35E
94 C4 **Rossing** Namibia 22.31S 14.52E
66 E6 **Rossinière** Switzerland 46.28N 7.06E
59 F3 **Rossinver** Leitrim Irish Rep 54.23N 8.06W
76 C10 **Rossio ao Sul do Tejo** Portugal 39.27N 8.12W
104 G6 **Rossiter** Pennsylvania 40.54N 78.57W
14 E10 **Rossiter B** W Australia
Rossiya *see* **Union of Soviet Socialist Republics**
38 F2 **Rossiyskaya S.F.S.R** U.S.S.R.
53 W20 **Rosskreppfjorden** *L* Norway 59.07N 7.10E
59 D5 **Ross L** Galway Irish Rep 53.23N 9.12W
110 D1 **Ross L** Washington
63 O10 **Rossla** E Germany 51.28N 11.06E
101 P11 **Rossland** Br Columbia 49.03N 117.49W
59 K7 **Rosslare** Wexford Irish Rep 52.17N 6.23W
63 Q9 **Rosslau** E Germany 51.54N 12.16E
64 L1 **Rossleben** E Germany 51.18N 11.27E
112 F8 **Rosslyn** Houston, Texas 29.51N 95.27W
26 Q16 **Ross, Mt** Kerguelen Ind Oc 49.35S 69.30E
11 K8 **Ross, Mt** New Zealand 41.28S 175.21E
59 F2 **Rossnowlagh** Donegal Irish Rep 54.33N 8.11W
89 B3 **Rosso** Mauritania 16.29N 15.53W
67 O12 **Rosso, C** Corsica 42.14N 8.32E
66 P6 **Rosso, Cima di** *mt* Italy/Switz 46.18N 9.43E
66 H8 **Rosso, Corno** *mt* Italy 45.46N 7.53E
81 J8 **Rosso, Mte** Sicily 37.44N 14.57E
79 J2 **Rosso, Sasso** *mt* Italy 46.17N 10.54E
46 L4 **Rossosh** Belgorod U.S.S.R. 51.05N 38.28E
45 L6 **Rossosh'** Voronezh U.S.S.R. 50.12N 39.35E
95 L7 **Rossouw** S Africa 31.10S 27.16E
94 P12 **Rossouwsbank** Cape Town S Africa 34.10S 18.19E
63 R6 **Rossow** E Germany 53.04N 12.35E
99 C4 **Rossport** Ontario 48.51N 87.31W
10 V11 **Ross, Pt** Norfolk I Pacific Oc 29.05S 167.56E
101 G4 **Ross River** Yukon Terr 62.02N 132.28W
26 B13 **Ross Rocks** Prince Edward I Ind Oc 46.36S 37.56E
123 J7 **Ross Sea** Antarctica
64 K5 **Rosstal** W Germany 49.24N 10.55E
66 L4 **Rosstock** *mt* Switzerland 46.55N 8.43E
109 L5 **Rosston** Oklahoma 36.50N 99.56W
63 O9 **Rosstrappe** *mt* E Germany 51.46N 11.00E
60 K12 **Rossum** Gelderland Netherlands 51.48N 5.20E
60 Q10 **Rossum** Overijssel Netherlands 52.22N 6.56E
107 J5 **Rossview Res** Tennessee
105 B3 **Rossville** Georgia 34.58N 85.18W
106 G9 **Rossville** Illinois 40.23N 87.40W
109 P2 **Rossville** Kansas 39.09N 95.57W
103 H9 **Rossville** Staten I, N Y 40.33N 74.13W
98 G9 **Rossway** Nova Scotia 44.35N 65.55W
64 P1 **Rosswein** E Germany 51.04N 13.11E
101 J8 **Rosswood** Br Columbia 54.49N 128.42W
34 M2 **Rōst** Iraq 36.43N 44.47E
51 C4 **Røst** *isld* Norway 67.33N 12.10E
51 H3 **Rosta** Norway 68.59N 19.40E
51 H3 **Rostaelv** *R* Norway 68.56N 20.00E
51 H2 **Rostafjeld** *mt* Norway 69.04N 19.40E
33 K4 **Rostam** *oil field* The Gulf 25.50N 52.54E
52 G11 **Röstånga** Sweden 56.00N 13.18E
32 E7 **Rostāq** Banāder va Jazāyer-e Baḩr-e Oman Iran 26.54N 53.52E
32 F6 **Rostāq** Fārs Iran 28.28N 55.06E
100 L6 **Rosthern** Saskatchewan 52.40N 106.20W
63 Q4 **Rostock** E Germany 54.06N 12.09E
63 Q4 **Rostock** *reg* E Germany
45 M5 **Rostoshi** U.S.S.R. 51.39N 40.59E
46 L2 **Rostov** U.S.S.R. 57.11N 39.23E
45 L9 **Rostov-na-Donu** U.S.S.R. 47.15N 39.45E
46 M6 **Rostovskaya Oblast'** *prov* U.S.S.R.
95 J2 **Rostrataville** S Africa 26.48S 25.39E
70 D5 **Rostrenen** France 48.14N 3.19W
59 K3 **Rostrevor** Down N Ireland 54.06N 6.12W
53 D3 **Rostrup** Denmark 56.44N 9.57E
82 F9 **Rostuša** Yugoslavia 41.35N 20.37E
52 E4 **Røstvangen** Norway 62.24N 10.24E
51 D6 **Røsvatn** *L* Norway
47 G3 **Rosvinskoye** U.S.S.R. 66.31N 52.30E
105 C3 **Roswell** Georgia 34.02N 84.21W
109 F8 **Roswell** New Mexico 33.24N 104.33W
58 K6 **Rosyth** Fife Scotland 56.03N 3.26W
52 H5 **Rot** Sweden 61.17N 14.05E
64 J7 **Rot** W Germany 48.01N 10.02E
66 O2 **Rot** *R* Switzerland
64 J7 **Rot** *R* W Germany
77 D7 **Rota** Spain 36.37N 6.21W
51 C5 **Rota** *C* Norway 66.57N 13.30E
17 P9 **Rota** *isld* Marianas Pacific Oc 14.10N 145.15E
64 J5 **Rot am See** W Germany 49.16N 10.04E
112 G3 **Rotan** Texas 32.52N 100.28W
92 F11 **Rotanda** Mozambique 19.33S 32.50E
64 N5 **Rot Buhl** *mt* W Germany 49.30N 12.01E
65 A8 **Rotbühlspitz** *mt* Austria 46.55N 9.58E
80 K5 **Rotella, Monte** Italy 41.56N 14.01E
80 M5 **Rotello** Italy 41.44N 15.01E
61 N2 **Rotem** Belgium 51.03N 5.45E
64 H2 **Rotenburg** Hessen W Germany 51.00N 9.44E
63 K6 **Rotenburg/Wümme** Niedersachsen W Germany 53.07N 9.24E
65 G8 **Roter Kopf** *mt* Austria 46.59N 12.45E
64 L3 **Roter Main** *R* W Germany
63 H5 **Roter Sand** *sandbank* W Germany
65 A7 **Rote Wand** *mt* Austria 47.12N 9.59E
64 D2 **Roth** Rheinland-Pfalz W Germany 50.46N 7.42E
64 N1 **Rötha** E Germany 51.12N 12.25E
64 E1 **Rothaargebirge** *mts* W Germany
69 N7 **Rothau** France 48.27N 7.12E
64 L5 **Roth bei Nürnberg** Bayern W Germany 49.15N 11.06E
106 H6 **Rothbury** Michigan 43.29N 86.21W
57 K2 **Rothbury** Northumb Eng 55.19N 1.55W
64 D2 **Rothemühle** W Germany 50.56N 7.50E
64 H8 **Röthenbach** Bayern W Germany 47.38N 9.59E
60 U16 **Röthenbach** Netherlands 51.08N 6.07E
64 A1 **Rothenbach** Nordrhein-Westfalen W Germany 51.08N 6.08E
66 G4 **Röthenbach** Switzerland 46.52N 7.45E
64 L5 **Röthenbach** W Germany 49.29N 11.15E
66 O4 **Rothenbrunnen** Switzerland 46.47N 9.27E
63 P9 **Rothenburg** E Germany 51.38N 11.45E
66 K3 **Rothenburg** Switzerland 47.06N 8.16E
64 J5 **Rothenburg ober der Tauber** W Germany 49.23N 10.13E
70 G4 **Rothéneuf** France 48.41N 1.58W
64 H4 **Rothenfels** Bayern W Germany 49.55N 9.36E
64 L3 **Rothenkirchen** W Germany 50.22N 11.19E
63 P10 **Rothenschirmbach** E Germany 51.28N 11.33E
66 L3 **Rothenthurm** Switzerland 47.06N 8.41E
11 G9 **Rotherham** New Zealand 42.41S 173.00E
57 L6 **Rotherham** S Yorks Eng 53.26N 1.20W
56 N5 **Rother, R** E Sussex/Kent Eng
98 G8 **Rothesay** New Brunswick 45.23N 66.00W
58 F7 **Rothesay** Strathclyde Scotland 55.51N 5.03W
58 K3 **Rothes-on-Spey** Grampian Scotland 57.31N 3.13W
61 M4 **Rotheux-Rimière** Belgium 50.32N 5.29E
58 M4 **Rothie** Grampian Scotland 57.25N 2.28W
66 K3 **Rothkreuz** Switzerland 47.09N 8.26E
66 H2 **Rothrist** Switzerland 47.18N 7.54E
108 O3 **Rothsay** Minnesota 46.27N 96.18W
123 F13 **Rothschild I** Antarctica 69.30S 73.00W
66 N3 **Roththor** *mt* Switzerland 47.02N 9.11E
57 N6 **Rothwell** Lincs Eng 53.29N 0.16W
56 K3 **Rothwell** Northants Eng 52.25N 0.48W
19 C9 **Roti** *isld* Indonesia
19 C9 **Roti, Selat** *str* Indonesia
77 T12 **Rotja, Pta** Balearic Is 38.40N 1.35E
45 C7 **Rotmistrovka** Ukraine U.S.S.R. 49.09N 31.44E
12 H5 **Roto** New S Wales 33.04S 145.27E
11 K6 **Rotoaira** *L* New Zealand 39.02S 175.43E
122 C14 **Rotoava** Tuamotu Is Pacific Oc 16.02S 145.36W
11 L5 **Rotoehu** *L* New Zealand
11 L5 **Rotoiti** *L* North I New Zealand
11 G8 **Rotoiti, L** South I New Zealand 41.51S 172.52E
11 L5 **Rotoma** *L* New Zealand
11 L5 **Rotomahana** *L* New Zealand
11 F9 **Rotomanu** New Zealand 42.40S 171.33E
81 M4 **Rotonda** Italy 39.57N 16.02E
81 N3 **Rotondella** Italy 40.10N 16.32E
81 N3 **Rotondella, Mte** Italy 40.02N 16.31E
80 H4 **Rotondo, Monte** Italy 42.12N 13.30E
67 P12 **Rotondo, Mt** Corsica 42.13N 9.03E
66 N6 **Rotondo, Pizzo** *mt* Graubünden Switzerland 46.28N 9.09E
66 K5 **Rotondo, Pizzo** *mt* Switz 46.32N 8.28E
11 G8 **Rotoroa, L** New Zealand 41.52E 172.38E
11 L5 **Rotorua** New Zealand 38.07S 176.17E
11 L5 **Rotorua** *L* New Zealand
77 Q3 **Rótova** Spain 38.57N 0.15W
11 K4 **Rotowaro** New Zealand 37.34S 175.05E
70 K3 **Rots** France 49.13N 0.27W
61 J3 **Rotselaar** Belgium 50.57N 4.43E
60 M8 **Rotster-Gaast** Netherlands 52.54N 5.54E
64 K8 **Rott** W Germany 47.55N 10.58E
64 O7 **Rott** *R* W Germany
63 R9 **Rotta** E Germany 51.46N 12.37E
64 M8 **Rottach-Egern** W Germany 47.41N 11.47E
64 N8 **Rott am Inn** W Germany 47.59N 12.09E
64 K8 **Rottenbuch** W Germany 47.44N 10.58E
64 F7 **Rottenburg** Baden-Württemberg W Germany 48.28N 8.55E
64 N6 **Rottenburg** Bayern W Germany 48.42N 12.03E
64 J4 **Rottendorf** W Germany 49.47N 10.02E
65 K6 **Rottenmann** Austria 47.32N 14.23E
65 K7 **Rottenmanner Tauern, mts** Austria
60 F12 **Rotterdam** Netherlands 51.55N 4.29E
60 N7 **Rottevalle** Netherlands 53.08N 6.07E
64 P7 **Rotthalmünster** W Germany 48.21N 13.13E
56 L6 **Rottingdean** E Sussex Eng 50.48N 0.04W
64 H4 **Rottingen** W Germany 49.31N 9.58E
63 N9 **Rottleberode** E Germany 51.32N 10.57E
52 J10 **Rottnen** *L* Sweden 56.45N 15.10E
14 B9 **Rottnest I** W Australia 32.01S 115.28E
15 K6 **Rottock B** New Britain
63 R8 **Rottstock** E Germany 52.10N 12.45E
60 P5 **Rottumeroog** *isld* Netherlands 53.32N 6.35E
60 O5 **Rottumerplaat** *isld* Netherlands 53.33N 6.30E
64 F7 **Rottweil** W Germany 48.10N 8.38E
10 Q4 **Rotuma** Pacific Oc 12.30S 177.08E
9 P10 **Rotuma** *isld* Pacific Oc 12.30S 177.05E
64 O5 **Rötz** W Germany 49.21N 12.33E
66 J1 **Rotzel** W Germany 47.36N 8.04E
79 K3 **Rotzo** Italy 45.52N 11.24E
Rouâd *see* **Arwad**
Rouaïda *see* **Rueida**
72 A1 **Rouans** France 47.12N 1.50W
69 E2 **Roubaix** France 50.42N 3.10E
71 F7 **Roubion** *R* France
65 O3 **Rouchovany** Czechoslovakia 49.05N 16.07E
61 E4 **Roucourt** Belgium 50.32N 3.35E
62 H5 **Roudnice** Czechoslovakia 50.26N 14.16E
70 C5 **Roudouallec** France 48.07N 3.43W
25 J6 **Rouei, Dak** *R* Cambodia
70 N3 **Rouen** France 49.26N 1.05E
69 N8 **Rouffach** France 47.57N 7.18E
72 J5 **Rouffiac** France 45.01N 2.08E
72 F5 **Rouffignac-St. Cernin-de-Reilhac** France 45.02N 0.59E
70 H6 **Rougé** France 47.47N 1.26W
25 H1 **Rouge, Fleuve** *R* Vietnam
71 J2 **Rougemont** France 47.29N 6.21E
66 E6 **Rougemont** Switzerland 46.30N 7.13E
71 K1 **Rougemont-le-Château** France 47.44N 6.59E
116 N2 **Rouge, Pt** Trinidad & Tobago 10.09N 61.47W
106 M3 **Rouge, R** Detroit, Michigan
57 J7 **Rough Close** Staffs Eng 52.57N 2.07W
57 F3 **Rough Firth** Dumfries & Galloway Scotland 54.50N 3.50W
59 C7 **Rough Pt** Kerry Irish Rep 52.18N 10.00W
107 K4 **Rough R** Kentucky
11 D12 **Rough Ridge** *mts* New Zealand
107 K4 **Rough River Res** Kentucky
56 O2 **Roughton** Norfolk Eng 52.54N 1.18E
59 C8 **Roughty, R** Kerry Irish Rep
71 H10 **Rougiers** France 43.24N 5.50E
72 E4 **Rougnac** France 45.32N 0.22E
72 J3 **Rougnat** France 46.03N 2.28E
71 J9 **Rougon** France 43.48N 6.24E
75 N2 **Rougt, Mt** Spain 42.43N 1.10E
72 D4 **Rouillac** France 45.46N 0.04W
72 E3 **Rouillé** France 46.25N 0.03E
88 Q6 **Rouissat** Algeria 31.58N 5.21E
71 C9 **Roujan** France 43.19N 3.19E
71 J2 **Roulans** France 47.19N 6.15E
100 N8 **Rouleau** Saskatchewan 50.12N 104.56W
Roulers *see* **Roeselare**
104 G5 **Roulette** Pennsylvania 41.45N 78.10W
99 L5 **Roulier** Quebec 47.47N 79.24W
72 E4 **Roullet-St. Estèphe** France 45.36N 0.04E
72 F4 **Roumazières-Loubert** France 45.52N 0.35E
72 J6 **Roumégoux** France 44.51N 2.12E
Roummâna *see* **Rummāna**
71 J9 **Roumoules** France 43.50N 6.08E
113 J4 **Roundabout Mt** Alaska 65.30N 156.32W
110 L2 **Round Butte** Montana 47.32N 114.18W
98 R4 **Round Harbour** Newfoundland 49.53N 55.40W
100 E5 **Round Hill** Alberta 53.10N 112.39W
13 K6 **Round Hill Hd** Queensland 24.10S 151.50E
13 J5 **Roundhill, Mt** Queensland 20.35S 148.19E
113 H7 **Round I** Alaska 58.39N 160.00W
23 B10 **Round I** Hong Kong 22.12N 114.10E
56 R8 **Round I** Is of Scilly Eng 49.59N 6.19W
26 V10 **Round I** Mauritius, Indian Oc 19.51S 57.47E
33 C10 **Round I** S Yemen 12.46N 45.01E
11 D4 **Round Knob** *mt* New Zealand 41.10S 174.53E
111 G3 **Round Mountain** Nevada 38.42N 117.05W
112 J5 **Round Mountain** Texas 30.27N 98.20W
12 K4 **Round Mt** New S Wales 30.26S 152.15E
104 Q3 **Round Pond** Maine 43.56N 69.28W
98 R5 **Round Pond** Newfoundland
112 K5 **Round Rock** Texas 30.32N 97.42W
101 R3 **Roundrock L** N W Terr
107 E4 **Round Spring** Missouri 37.18N 91.23W
59 C5 **Roundstone** Galway Irish Rep 53.24N 9.50W
59 K4 **Round Tower** Louth Irish Rep 53.48N 6.25W
110 R3 **Roundup** Montana 46.27N 108.34W
59 K5 **Roundwood** Wicklow Irish Rep 53.04N 6.13W
59 K5 **Roundwood Res** Wicklow Irish Rep 53.04N 6.12W
100 S9 **Rounthwaite** Manitoba 49.39N 99.47W
84 C6 **Roupakia** Greece 37.59N 21.40E
72 H7 **Rouquette, la** France 44.19N 1.58E
117 C2 **Roura** Fr Guiana 4.44N 52.16W
58 S11 **Rousay** *isld* Orkney Scotland 59.10N 3.02W
104 M2 **Rouses Pt** New York 44.59N 73.24W
104 F5 **Rouseville** Pennsylvania 41.28N 79.42W
14 A2 **Rous Hd** Perth, W Aust 32.04S 115.44E
65 P3 **Rousinov** Czechoslovakia 49.12N 16.53E
72 G3 **Roussac** Haute-Vienne France 46.03N 1.13E
71 J4 **Rousses, les** France 46.29N 6.03E
71 H10 **Rousset** France 43.29N 5.36E
71 G7 **Rousset, Col de** *pass* France 44.50N 5.24E
71 F6 **Roussillon** Isère France 45.23N 4.50E
71 G9 **Roussillon** Vaucluse France 43.54N 5.18E
67 G10 **Roussillon** *prov* France
72 K10 **Roussillon, Plaine du** France
72 F4 **Roussines** France 45.44N 0.37E
69 L5 **Roussy-le-Village** France 49.27N 6.10E
Routh Bank *see* **Seahorse Bank**
98 E5 **Routhierville** Quebec 48.10N 76.10W
70 M3 **Routot** France 49.23N 0.44E
90 E1 **Rout Sanihida, Er** Niger 21.56N 11.57E
60 N9 **Rouveen** Netherlands 52.37N 6.11E
61 G5 **Rouveroy** Belgium 50.22N 4.04E
71 E2 **Rouvray** France 47.26N 4.06E
98 B4 **Rouvray, L** Quebec
69 H8 **Rouvres-Arbot** France 47.52N 5.00E
61 N5 **Rouvreux** Belgium 50.29N 5.39E
69 H4 **Rouvroy-sur-Audry** France 49.47N 4.30E
61 H5 **Roux** Belgium 50.27N 4.24E
85 A8 **Roux Bayard** *mts* Niger
88 S3 **Roux, C** Tunisia 36.57N 8.47E
71 K10 **Roux, Cap** France 43.27N 6.55E
61 K4 **Roux-Miroir** Belgium 50.42N 4.47E
95 K6 **Rouxville** S Africa 30.25S 26.50E
71 D2 **Rouy** France 47.02N 3.32E
99 M4 **Rouyn** Quebec 48.15N 79.00W
Rouyuanchengzi *see* **Huachi**
82 L1 **Rov** *R* U.S.S.R.
53 S20 **Røvær** *Lt Ho* Norway 59.26N 5.05E
51 M5 **Rovaniemi** Finland 66.29N 25.40E
79 G3 **Rovato** Italy 45.34N 10.00E
53 T14 **Rovde** Norway 62.10N 5.45E
53 T14 **Rovdefjorden** *inlet* Norway
47 E5 **Rovdino** U.S.S.R. 61.37N 42.30E
79 F5 **Rovegno** Italy 44.34N 9.17E
66 K8 **Rovegro** Italy 45.58N 8.29E
45 L8 **Roven'ki** Ukraine U.S.S.R. 48.05N 39.20E
45 K7 **Roven'ki** U.S.S.R. 49.54N 38.55E
46 F4 **Rovenskaya Oblast'** *prov* Ukraine U.S.S.R.
79 J4 **Roverbella** Italy 45.16N 10.46E
66 N7 **Roveredo** Switzerland 46.14N 9.09E
79 N2 **Roveredo in Piano** Italy 46.01N 12.37E
79 K3 **Rovereto** Italy 45.53N 11.03E
63 Q4 **Röversbagen** E Germany 54.11N 12.15E
121 E1 **Roversi** Argentina 27.33S 61.55W
80 H5 **Roveto, Val** Italy
71 G10 **Rove, Tunnel du** France
84 F4 **Roviaís** Greece 38.48N 23.15E
25 G6 **Rovieng** Cambodia 12.27N 103.25E
25 H6 **Rovieng** Cambodia 13.20N 105.06E
79 L4 **Rovigo** Italy 45.04N 11.47E
79 L4 **Rovigo** *prov* Italy
82 B5 **Rovinj** Yugoslavia 45.05N 13.40E
79 P4 **Rovinjskoselo** Yugoslavia 45.07N 13.43E
119 C5 **Rovira** Colombia 4.15N 75.15W
46 F4 **Rovno** Ukraine U.S.S.R. 50.39N 26.10E
45 C8 **Rovnoye** Ukraine U.S.S.R. 48.14N 31.45E
46 O4 **Rovnoye** U.S.S.R. 50.42N 46.04E
39 G5 **Rovnyy, Mys** *C* U.S.S.R. 58.54N 164.34E
39 G4 **Rovnyy, O** *isld* U.S.S.R. 60.50N 163.15E
92 H7 **Rovuma** *R* Mozambique
108 R7 **Rowan** Iowa 42.44N 93.35W
32 C3 **Row'ān** Iran 35.06N 48.55E
57 H2 **Rowanburn** Dumfries & Galloway Scotland 55.05N 2.55W
100 J1 **Rowan L** Ontario 49.15N 93.25W
58 G6 **Rowardennan** Central Scotland 56.09N 4.38W
109 E6 **Rowe** New Mexico 35.30N 105.41W
12 J3 **Rowena** New S Wales 29.49S 148.55E
112 G4 **Rowena** Texas 31.39N 100.03W
105 G4 **Rowesville** S Carolina 33.23N 80.11W
105 H3 **Rowland** N Carolina 34.32N 79.19W
110 K8 **Rowland** Nevada 41.57N 115.40W
103 D4 **Rowland** Pennsylvania 41.28N 75.03W
104 F7 **Rowlesburg** W Virginia 39.21N 79.42W
100 E7 **Rowley** Alberta 51.46N 112.45W
97 M4 **Rowley I** N W Terr 69.00N 79.00W
14 C3 **Rowley Shoals** W Australia
111 M9 **Rowood** Arizona 32.23N 112.49W
57 K6 **Rowsley** Derbys Eng 53.12N 1.36W
57 H6 **Rowton** Cheshire Eng 53.10N 2.50W
111 K5 **Rox** Nevada 36.54N 114.39W
89 B6 **Roxa, I** Guinea-Bissau 11.15N 15.45W
115 N4 **Roxana** Costa Rica 10.16N 83.46W
19 K3 **Roxas** Luzon Philippines 17.08N 121.36E
19 L7 **Roxas** Mindanao Philippines 8.31N 123.16E
19 K5 **Roxas** Mindoro Philippines 12.34N 121.30E
19 J6 **Roxas** Palawan Philippines 10.12N 119.18E
19 L6 **Roxas** Panay Philippines 11.36N 122.45E
105 J1 **Roxboro** N Carolina 36.24N 79.00W
99 Q9 **Roxboro** Quebec 45.30N 73.47W
13 E6 **Roxborough Downs** Queensland 22.30S 138.47E
103 D5 **Roxburg** New Jersey 40.47N 75.06W
11 D12 **Roxburgh** New Zealand 45.34S 169.21E
Roxburgh *co see* **Borders** *reg*
103 H3 **Roxbury** Connecticut 41.33N 73.18W
103 E2 **Roxbury** New York 42.17N 74.35W
104 N2 **Roxbury** Vermont 44.04N 72.46W
104 P9 **Roxbury** *dist* Boston, Mass 42.19N 71.03W
52 J8 **Roxen** *L* Sweden 58.30N 15.40E
107 E10 **Roxie** Mississippi 31.31N 91.05W
76 C13 **Roxo** *R* Portugal
76 C13 **Roxo, Barragem do** *res* Portugal 37.55N 8.05W
89 A5 **Roxo, C** Guinea-Bissau 12.20N 16.45W
56 L3 **Roxton** Beds Eng 52.10N 0.20W
99 S7 **Roxton** Quebec 45.29N 72.36W
112 M2 **Roxton** Texas 33.34N 95.44W
61 M6 **Roy** Belgium 50.12N 5.24E
110 N7 **Roy** Idaho 42.22N 112.48W
110 R2 **Roy** Montana 47.20N 108.57W
109 F6 **Roy** New Mexico 35.56N 104.14W
110 C2 **Roy** Washington 47.00N 122.33W
71 K8 **Roya** France 44.12N 6.57E
71 M8 **Roya** *R* France
108 M7 **Royal** Nebraska 42.20N 98.06W
121 G8 **Royal B** S Georgia
59 G4 **Royal Canal** Longford etc Irish Rep
106 H9 **Royal Center** Indiana 40.52N 86.30W
26 R16 **Royale, Passe** Kerguelen Ind Oc
101 X1 **Royal Geographical Society Is** N W Terr
105 L12 **Royal I** Bahamas 25.32N 76.52W
56 H3 **Royal Leamington Spa** Warwicks Eng 52.18N 1.31W
56 N5 **Royal Military Canal** Kent Eng
99 B3 **Royal, Mt** Ontario 49.56N 50.49W
106 L7 **Royal Oak** Michigan 42.31N 83.08W
106 M1 **Royal Oak** *dist* Detroit, Michigan
105 F12 **Royal Palm Hammock** Florida 26.59N 81.35W
105 G12 **Royal Palm Visitor Center** Florida 25.22N 80.37W
123 H6 **Royal Society Ra** Antarctica
100 C8 **Royalties** Alberta 50.37N 114.12W
103 A6 **Royalton** Pennsylvania 40.11N 76.44W
56 M5 **Royal Tunbridge Wells** London Eng 51.08N 0.16E
112 E4 **Royalty** Texas 31.24N 102.54W
72 B4 **Royan** France 45.38N 1.02W
71 C5 **Royat** France 45.45N 3.03E
71 G6 **Roybon** France 45.15N 5.15E
58 G5 **Roy Bridge** Highland Scotland 56.53N 4.50W
56 M4 **Roydon** Essex Eng 51.46N 0.03E
69 D4 **Roye** France 49.42N 2.48E
72 H4 **Royère-de-Vassivière** France 45.50N 1.54E
103 C6 **Royersford** Pennsylvania 40.11N 75.32W
14 C6 **Roy Hill** W Australia 22.45S 120.00E
52 E6 **Røykenvik** Norway 60.25N 10.29E
59 C3 **Roy L** Mayo Irish Rep 54.05N 9.56W
98 C4 **Roy, L** Quebec
75 E4 **Royo, El** Spain 41.55N 2.39W
77 M5 **Royos de Arriba** Spain 37.55N 2.03W
52 H2 **Røyrvik** Norway 64.53N 13.32E
112 L3 **Royse City** Texas 32.59N 96.18W
53 Y15 **Røysheim** Norway 61.45N 8.23E
105 D3 **Royston** Georgia 34.16N 83.06W
56 L3 **Royston** Herts Eng 52.03N 0.01W
57 J5 **Royton** Greater Manchester Eng 53.34N 2.08W
51 L6 **Röyttä** Finland 65.45N 24.10E
75 G7 **Royuela** Spain 40.23N 1.31W
47 M6 **Roza** U.S.S.R. 54.56N 61.30E
75 E8 **Rozalén del Monte** Spain 39.59N 2.49W
62 N3 **Różan** Poland 52.54N 21.21E
69 D6 **Rozay-en-Brie** France 48.41N 2.58E
34 L6 **Rozāzah** Iraq 32.42N 43.56E
82 G9 **Rožden** Yugoslavia 41.10N 21.56E
70 F3 **Rozel** Channel Is 49.14N 2.03W
109 L3 **Rozel** Kansas 38.11N 99.25W
70 G3 **Rozel, Pte du** France 49.28N 1.51W
60 E12 **Rozenburg** Netherlands 51.55N 4.15E
60 M11 **Rozendaal** Netherlands 52.01N 5.58E
19 G6 **Rozengain, I** Moluccas Indon 4.35S 130.01E
108 E5 **Rozet** Wyoming 44.18N 105.12W
62 L1 **Rozewie** *C* Poland 54.50N 18.20E
45 Q1 **Rozhdestven** U.S.S.R. 55.42N 44.46E
43 K2 **Rozhdestvenka** Kazakhstan U.S.S.R. 50.51N 71.25E
45 H9 **Rozhdestvenka** Ukraine U.S.S.R. 47.48N 36.04E
46 O1 **Rozhdestvenskoye** U.S.S.R. 58.10N 45.29E
46 F4 **Rozhishche** Ukraine U.S.S.R. 50.58N 25.15E
44 D4 **Rozhkao** U.S.S.R. 43.49N 40.56E
45 D6 **Rozhnovka** Ukraine U.S.S.R. 50.56N 32.35E
65 P2 **Rozhraní** Czechoslovakia 49.36N 16.33E
72 L7 **Rozier le** France 44.12N 3.12E
65 K4 **Rožmberk nad Vltava** Czech 48.39N 14.23E
65 J2 **Rožmitál** Czechoslovakia 49.37N 13.52E
62 M7 **Rožňava** Czechoslovakia 48.40N 20.30E
82 K4 **Roznov** Romania 46.47N 26.33E
45 J9 **Rozovka** Ukraine U.S.S.R. 47.23N 37.04E
69 G4 **Rozoy** France 49.42N 4.08E
62 M4 **Rozprza** Poland 51.20N 19.38E
32 D4 **Rozveh** Iran 32.51N 50.37E
62 N5 **Rozwadów** Poland 50.37N 22.02E
Rozweh *see* **Rozveh**
41 G1 **Rozy Lyuksemburg, Mys** *C* U.S.S.R. 80.45N 98.16E
82 G7 **Rtanj** *mts* Yugoslavia
45 P4 **Rtishchevo** U.S.S.R. 52.16N 43.45E
82 B6 **Rt Kamenjak** *C* Yugoslavia 44.46N 13.55E
87 D4 **Rua'at, Er** Sudan 12.21N 32.17E
15 K8 **Ruaba** *R* Papua New Guinea
57 G7 **Ruabon** Clwyd Wales 52.59N 3.02W
19 N4 **Ruac** *isld* Truk Is Pacific Oc 7.40N 151.52E
Ruad *isld see* **Arwad**
86 M4 **Ruâfa, El** Egypt 30.50N 34.08E
92 H5 **Ruaha** Tanzania 7.23S 36.31E
92 G5 **Ruaha Nat. Park** Tanzania
11 L7 **Ruahine Ra** New Zealand
11 K4 **Ruakura Junction** New Zealand 37.45S 175.21E
76 E4 **Rúa, La** Spain 42.24N 7.06W
59 E6 **Ruan** Clare Irish Rep 52.56N 8.59W
76 G10 **Ruanes** Spain 39.20N 6.01W
19 D2 **Ruang** *isld* Indonesia 2.18N 125.23E
66 D7 **Ruan, Mont** France/Switzerland 46.07N 6.54E
11 K6 **Ruapehu Vol** New Zealand 39.18S 175.36E
11 C13 **Ruapuke I** New Zealand
86 L6 **Ruâq, Wâdi el** *watercourse* Egypt
92 G7 **Ruarwe** Malawi 11.08S 34.11E
11 L5 **Ruatahuna** New Zealand 38.35S 176.58E
19 A8 **Rua, Tanjung** *C* Indonesia 9.49S 119.25E
11 E9 **Ruatapu** New Zealand 42.48S 170.53E
11 M5 **Ruatoki** New Zealand 38.08S 177.02E
11 N4 **Ruatoria** New Zealand 37.53S 178.20E
11 J3 **Ruawai** New Zealand 36.08S 174.02E
33 C5 **Rubad, Ar** Saudi Arabia 23.10N 39.35E
93 C7 **Rubafu** Tanzania 1.03S 31.50E
33 G7 **Rub' al Khālī** *des* Saudi Arabia
44 C8 **Rubanovka** Ukraine U.S.S.R. 46.59N 34.11E
44 J6 **Rubas** *R* U.S.S.R.
33 G9 **Rubāţ, Ar** S Yemen 14.13N 46.25E
33 H4 **Rubaydā'** *area* Saudi Arabia
33 F3 **Rubay'iyah, Ar** Saudi Arabia 26.24N 44.15E
53 S19 **Rubbestadneset** Norway 59.49N 5.17E
53 S19 **Rubbestadneset** Norway 59.49N 5.17E
63 N9 **Rübeland** E Germany 51.46N 10.52E
75 C3 **Rubena** Spain 42.23N 3.33W
93 A8 **Rubengera** Rwanda 2.03S 29.24E
45 K7 **Rubezhnoye** Ukraine U.S.S.R. 49.01N 38.22E
58 B4 **Rubha Ardvule** *pt* S Uist, W Isles Scotland 57.15N 7.28W
58 F2 **Rubha Coigeach** *prom* Highland Scotland 58.06N 5.25W
58 D3 **Rubha Hunish** *pt* Skye, Highland Scotland 57.42N 6.21W
58 B4 **Rubha na Hordag** *pt* S Uist, W Isles Scotland 57.07N 7.13W
58 C3 **Rubha Quidnish** *pt* Harris, W Isles Scotland 57.47N 6.53W
58 E3 **Rubha Réidh** *pt* Highland Scotland 57.52N 5.49W
75 P5 **Rubí** Spain 41.29N 2.02E
91 J2 **Rubi** Zaïre 2.45N 25.18E
91 J2 **Rubi** *R* Zaïre
75 F4 **Rubia, La** Spain 41.53N 2.23W
75 H7 **Rubiales** Spain 40.16N 1.16W
77 O2 **Rubial, Sierra de** *mts* Spain
76 E3 **Rubián** Spain 42.39N 7.29W
76 F4 **Rubiana** Spain 42.26N 6.57W
111 D3 **Rubicon** *R* California
75 H6 **Rubielos de la Cérida** Spain 40.46N 1.14W
75 J7 **Rubielos de Mora** Spain 40.11N 0.40W
79 J5 **Rubiera** Italy 44.39N 10.47E
66 G4 **Rubigen** Switzerland 46.54N 7.33E
93 C3 **Rubi, L** Uganda 2.37N 31.26E
118 D7 **Rubinéia** Brazil 20.10S 51.01W
119 D4 **Rubio** Venezuela 7.42N 72.23W
74 E3 **Rubio** *mt* Spain 41.28N 3.45W
77 G6 **Rubio, El** Spain 37.22N 4.59W
75 O4 **Rubió, Sierra de** *mts* Spain
93 B6 **Rubirizi** Uganda 0.16S 30.07E
77 K7 **Rubite** Spain 36.49N 3.21W
53 D2 **Rubjerg Knude** *pt* Denmark 57.28N 9.48E
93 A8 **Rubona** Rwanda 2.27S 29.44E
93 C8 **Rubondo I** Tanzania
46 G4 **Rubryn'** Belorussiya U.S.S.R. 51.52N 27.30E
42 C6 **Rubtsovsk** U.S.S.R. 51.34N 81.11E
33 E7 **Rubūţ, Jabal ar** *mt* Saudi Arabia 19.20N 43.25E
113 K4 **Ruby** Alaska 64.41N 155.35W
111 N10 **Ruby** Arizona 31.29N 111.14W
103 F2 **Ruby** New York 42.01N 74.00W
110 H1 **Ruby** Washington 48.32N 117.19W
110 N4 **Ruby** *R* Montana
110 K9 **Ruby Dome** *pk* Nevada 40.37N 115.27W
110 K9 **Ruby L** Nevada 40.10N 115.29W
110 K9 **Ruby Mts** Nevada
110 K9 **Ruby Valley** Nevada 40.27N 115.21W
82 J5 **Rucăr** Romania 45.21N 25.10E
110 B7 **Ruch** Oregon 42.15N 123.03W
47 G5 **Ruch'** U.S.S.R. 61.51N 53.09E
23 F6 **Rucheng** Hunan China 25.35N 113.42E
47 E3 **Ruch'i** Arkhangel'sk U.S.S.R. 66.03N 41.20E
51 Q4 **Ruchi** Karelia U.S.S.R. 67.00N 32.10E
Ruchugi *see* **Uvinza**
93 B10 **Ruchugi** *R* Tanzania
60 G13 **Rucphen** Netherlands 51.32N 4.34E
53 Y17 **Rud** Norway 60.38N 8.12E
52 J9 **Ruda** Sweden 57.06N 16.10E
14 E6 **Rudall, R** W Australia
13 B6 **Rudalls** *R* N Terr Australia
32 G7 **Rudan** Iran 27.24N 57.20E
Rudan *R see* **Dozdān** *R*
30 G6 **Rudarpur** Uttar Prad India 26.27N 83.37E
30 E6 **Rudauli** Uttar Prad India 26.44N 81.44E
31 B5 **Rudbar** Afghanistan 30.10N 62.39E
32 E6 **Rūdbār** Fārs Iran 28.44N 52.38E
32 C2 **Rūdbār** Gīlān Iran 36.49N 49.29E
Rūdbar-i Barasgird *R see* **Barāzgīr** *R*
53 B7 **Rudbøl** Denmark 54.54N 8.46E
57 L4 **Rudby** N Yorks Eng 54.27N 1.16W
100 K6 **Ruddell** Saskatchewan 52.38N 107.52W
39 L2 **Rudder, Bukhta** *gulf* U.S.S.R.
61 C2 **Ruddervoorde** Belgium 51.06N 3.12E
100 R3 **Ruddock** Manitoba 55.18N 100.55W
113 P6 **Rude** *R* Alaska
65 L8 **Ruden** Austria 46.40N 14.47E
63 T4 **Ruden** *isld* E Germany 54.13N 13.47E
64 H6 **Rudersberg** W Germany 48.52N 9.33E
63 T8 **Rüdersdorf** E Germany 52.29N 13.50E
64 D4 **Rüdesheim** W Germany 49.59N 7.56E
92 H5 **Rudewa** Tanzania 6.38S 37.10E
30 F5 **Rudhauli** Uttar Prad India 27.02N 82.48E
34 G5 **Rudhumat al Hiri** *hill* Iraq
34 J6 **Rudhumiya, Ar** Iraq 32.15N 41.04E
92 H5 **Rudi** Tanzania 7.00S 36.14E
32 D5 **Rūdiān** Iran 30.04N 51.59E
15 K6 **Rudiger Pt** New Britain 5.29S 149.39E
65 N3 **Rudíkov** Czechoslovakia 49.18N 15.57E
75 H5 **Rudilla** Spain 41.00N 1.01W
32 G5 **Rud-i-Shūr** *stream* Iran
45 C5 **Rudka** Ukraine U.S.S.R. 51.35N 31.08E
46 E5 **Rudki** Ukraine U.S.S.R. 49.40N 23.28E
53 F7 **Rudkøbing** Denmark 54.57N 10.43E
65 K1 **Rudna** Czechoslovakia 50.03N 14.14E
62 J4 **Rudna** Poland 51.31N 16.17E
40 K9 **Rudnaya** Kuril Is U.S.S.R. 44.20N 146.00E
40 G9 **Rudnaya Pristan'** U.S.S.R. 44.18N 135.51E
43 N5 **Rudnichnyy** Kazakhstan U.S.S.R. 44.39N 79.01E
47 G6 **Rudnichnyy** U.S.S.R. 59.40N 52.28E
82 L8 **Rudnik** Bulgaria 42.36N 27.30E

62 N5 Rudnik Poland 50.26N 22.16E
82 F6 Rudnik *mt* Yugoslavia 44.07N 20.35E
82 M2 Rudnitsa U.S.S.R. 48.13N 28.56E
45 D1 Rudnya Kalinin U.S.S.R. 56.04N 32.06E
46 G2 Rudnya Pskov U.S.S.R. 56.09N 28.31E
45 Q6 Rudnya Saratov U.S.S.R. 50.49N 44.35E
45 C2 Rudnya Smolensk U.S.S.R. 54.55N 31.07E
43 G1 Rudnyy Kazakhstan U.S.S.R. 53.00N 63.05E
40 G9 Rudnyy U.S.S.R. 44.28N 135.00E
Rudok *see* Rutog
82 F9 Rudoka Planina *mts* Yugoslavia
41 O1 Rudol'fa, Os *isld* Franz Josef Land U.S.S.R.
Rudolf Island *see* Rudol'fa, Ostrov
93 H1 Rudolf,L Kenya
65 L4 Rudolfov Czechoslovakia 48.59N 14.32E
50 O10 Rudolftoppen *mt* Jan Mayen I 70.54N 8.51W
64 L2 Rudolstadt E Germany 50.44N 11.20E
65 P2 Rudoltice Czechoslovakia 49.54N 16.35E
23 J2 Rudong Jiangsu China 32.28N 121.03E
30 B2 Rudraprayag Uttar Prad India 30.16N 78.59E
32 D2 Rūd Sar Iran 37.05N 50.20E
57 N4 Rudston Humberside Eng 54.06N 0.20W
53 G5 Ruds Vedby Denmark 55.33N 11.23E
106 K3 Rudyard Michigan 46.14N 84.25W
110 P1 Rudyard Montana 48.34N 110.33W
69 B3 Rue France 50.16N 1.40E
66 D5 Rue Switzerland 46.38N 6.49E
76 J10 Ruecas *R* Spain
76 K6 Rueda Spain 41.24N 4.58W
75 H4 Rueda de Jalón Spain 41.37N 1.15W
66 F4 Rüeggisberg Switzerland 46.49N 7.27E
66 G3 Rüegsau-schachen Switzerland 47.02N 7.40E
34 E3 Rueida Syria 35.26N 37.02E
68 D3 Rueil-Malmaison France 48.52N 2.11E
99 J5 Ruel Ontario 47.16N 81.29W
72 E4 Ruelle France 45.40N 0.13E
66 L5 Ruèras Switzerland 46.41N 8.45E
69 C5 Rue St. Pierre, la France 49.24N 2.17E
34 L1 Rū-ē Shamdīnān *R* Iraq/Turkey
75 H2 Ruesta Spain 42.35N 1.04W
61 N8 Ruette Belgium 49.32N 5.35E
87 D3 Rufa'a Sudan 14.49N 33.21E
85 O5 Rufaiya *reg* Saudi Arabia
81 R13 Ruffano Italy 39.59N 18.15E
72 E3 Ruffec Charente France 46.02N 0.12E
72 G2 Ruffec Indre France 46.38N 1.11E
71 G2 Ruffey-les-Échirey France 47.22N 5.05E
71 G3 Ruffey-sur-Seille France 46.44N 5.29E
70 F6 Ruffiac France 47.48N 2.15W
71 H5 Ruffieu France 45.59N 5.40E
71 H5 Ruffieux France 45.51N 5.51E
70 H6 Ruffigne France 47.46N 1.29W
105 G4 Ruffin S Carolina 33.01N 80.48W
105 M8 Ruffling Pt Virgin Is 18.48N 64.28W
57 H5 Rufford Lancs Eng 53.39N 2.49W
66 N3 Rufi Switzerland 47.11N 9.03E
92 J5 Rufiji *R* Tanzania
79 L7 Rufina Italy 43.49N 11.30E
121 E5 Rufino Argentina 34.16S 62.45W
89 A4 Rufisque Senegal 14.43N 17.16W
92 D9 Rufunsa Zambia 15.02S 29.35E
92 E9 Rufunsa *R* Zambia
101 J1 Rufus L N W Terr 69.35N 130.00W
56 H6 Rufus Stone *mon* Hants Eng 50.55N 1.37W
110 F1 Rufus Woods L Washington
23 J2 Rugao Jiangsu China 32.27N 120.35E
93 B8 Rugari Burundi 2.42S 30.24E
93 A7 Rugari Zaïre 1.25S 29.22E
108 L1 Rugby N Dakota 48.24N 100.00W
56 J3 Rugby Warwicks Eng 52.23N 1.15W
56 H2 Rugeley Staffs Eng 52.46N 1.55W
63 S4 Rügen *isld* E Germany
93 E8 Rugezi Tanzania 2.06S 33.14E
11 B13 Rugged Is New Zealand
64 K5 Rügland W Germany 49.24N 10.36E
70 M4 Rugles France 48.49N 0.42E
52 F4 Ruglsjø Norway 62.43N 11.22E
47 C3 Rugozero Karelia U.S.S.R. 66.35N 30.48E
47 C4 Rugozero Karelia U.S.S.R. 64.01N 32.46E
51 P5 Rug Ozero *L* Karelia U.S.S.R. 66.30N 31.00E
53 S15 Rugsund Norway 61.53N 5.20E
53 S15 Rugsundøy *isld* Norway 61.53N 5.15E
Rugu *see* Rigū
75 E6 Ruguilla Spain 40.45N 2.35W
93 B8 Rugwero, L Burundi/Rwanda
31 C5 Ruhabad Afghanistan 31.26N 65.42E
35 B7 Ruhama Israel 31.30N 34.41E
93 D8 Ruhama Tanzania 2.22S 32.29E
35 G1 Ruhaniye Syria 33.05N 35.52E
33 G4 Ruḥayyat al Ḥamr'ā' *mt* Saudi Arabia 24.49N 47.15E
31 G8 Ruhea Bangladesh 26.05N 88.28E
63 N7 Rühen W Germany 52.30N 10.55E
93 A7 Ruhengeri Rwanda 1.30S 29.37E
64 J2 Ruhla E Germany 50.53N 10.23E
63 T10 Ruhland E Germany 51.27N 13.53E
63 F7 Rühlertwist W Germany 52.39N 7.06E
64 O6 Ruhmannsfelden W Germany 48.59N 12.59E
63 P5 Rühn E Germany 53.50N 11.56E
63 P6 Ruhner Berge *mt* E Germany 53.18N 11.55E
64 O8 Ruhpolding W Germany 47.45N 12.39E
64 F1 Ruhr *R* W Germany
Ruhrort *see* Duisburg
92 G6 Ruhudji *R* Tanzania
92 G7 Ruhuhu *R* Tanzania
31 D3 Rui Afghanistan 35.46N 67.50E
53 X19 Rui Norway 59.43N 7.48E
92 E10 Ruia *R* Zimbabwe
81 D2 Ruia, I Sardinia 40.32N 9.50E
23 J5 Rui 'An Zhejiang China 27.51N 120.39E
118 H3 Rui Barbosa Brazil 12.19S 40.26W
23 G4 Ruichang Jiangxi China 29.35N 115.45E
23 E1 Ruicheng Shanxi China 34.42N
77 L3 Ruidera Spain 38.59N 2.53W
77 L3 Ruidera,L.de Spain 38.55N 2.49W
109 E8 Ruidoso New Mexico 33.20N 105.42W
23 G6 Ruijin Jiangxi China 25.51N 115.57E
23 A6 Ruili Yunnan China 24.01N 97.52E
81 B4 Ruinas Sardinia 39.55N 8.54E
60 O8 Ruinen Netherlands 52.46N 6.21E
60 O9 Ruinerwold Netherlands 52.43N 6.15E
66 F8 Ruinette *mt* Switzerland 45.59N 7.24E
93 H7 Ruiru Kenya 1.09S 26.57E
66 N4 Ruis Switzerland 46.47N 9.09E
61 H2 Ruisbroek Antwerp Belgium 51.06N 4.20E
61 H3 Ruisbroek Brabant Belgium 50.47N 4.18E
61 D2 Ruiselede Belgium 51.03N 3.24E
Ru-i Shamsdinan *R* *see* Rū-ē Shamdīnān *R*
55 B3 Ruislip London Eng 51.35N 0.25W
55 B2 Ruislip Res London England 51.36N 0.26W
60 O9 Ruitenveen Netherlands 52.34N 6.15E
81 D2 Ruiu,Mte Sassari, Sardinia 40.50N 9.36E
76 B5 Ruivães Portugal 41.54N 8.37W
76 E15 Ruivo,C Portugal 38.46N 9.06W
96 P7 Ruivo,Pico *mt* Madeira Is 32.46N 16.57W
92 F6 Ruiwa Tanzania 8.48S 33.40E
115 G6 Ruiz Mexico 22.00N 105.09W
119 G3 Ruiz Venezuela 9.06N 65.58W
119 C5 Ruiz,Nevada del *vol* Colombia 4.53N 75.22W
77 F6 Ruiz Sanchez,L.de Spain 37.25N 5.05W
35 E5 Rujeib Jordan 32.11N 35.18E
34 E6 Rujeila,Harrat er *lava flow* Jordan
35 G7 Rujeim Salim Jordan 31.31N 35.51E
82 G8 Rujen *mt* Yugoslavia 42.09N 22.30E
46 F1 Rūjiena Latvia U.S.S.R. 57.51N 25.19E
35 G7 Rujm el Hiri *anc site* Jordan 31.37N 35.54E
35 G9 Rujm el Mahiri *mt* Jordan 31.05N 35.50E
35 J7 Rujm esh Shid *anc site* Jordan 31.32N 36.19E
35 F9 Rujm es Sakhri Jordan 31.02N 35.43E
35 H5 Rujm es Saqra *tomb* Jordan 32.07N 36.11E
86 P3 Rujm Madīnal er Ras *mt* Jordan 31.03N 35.35E
35 H5 Rujm Mamduh *mt* Jordan 32.14N 36.14E
35 G10 Rujm Qufeiqif *mt* Jordan 30.59N 35.50E
86 O5 Rujm Tal'at el Jamā'a *mt* Jordan 30.24N 35.30E
81 B2 Ruju, Mte Sardinia 40.54N 8.55E
31 E7 Ruk Pakistan 27.47N 68.42E
31 E3 Ruka Afghanistan 35.17N 69.28E
26 U6 Rukam Sri Lanka 7.38N 81.30E
31 G6 Rukanpur Pakistan 28.22N 72.08E
51 O5 Rukatunturi *mt* Finland 66.12N 29.10E
33 H3 Rukbah Saudi Arabia 27.56N 48.15E
35 J6 Rukbali *watercourse* Jordan
35 H6 Rukban *watercourse* Jordan
31 J4 Rukchen Kashmir 33.22N 77.52E
35 F3 Rukheim Jordan 32.32N 35.40E
92 E3 Rukira Rwanda 2.15S 30.31E
92 D10 Rukomeshe *R* Zimbabwe
45 U5 Rukopol' U.S.S.R. 51.40N 48.40E
93 C8 Rukora Tanzania 2.46S 31.32E
92 E10 Rukovakuona Mts Zimbabwe
30 F4 Rukumkot Nepal 28.36N 82.45E
93 A6 Rukungiri Uganda 0.49S 29.57E
9 R5 Rukuruku B Vanua Levu Fiji
92 E5 Rukwa *reg* Tanzania
92 F6 Rukwa, L Tanzania 8.00S 32.20E
33 M4 Rūl U.A.E. 25.37N 56.05E
30 F1 Ruldap Tso *L* Xizang Zizhiqu 31.40N 82.12E
112 H2 Rule Texas 33.12N 99.54W
109 J2 Ruleton Kansas 39.19N 101.54W
107 F8 Ruleville Mississippi 33.42N 90.32W
14 F2 Rulhieres,C W Australia 13.57S 127.24E
93 A7 Rulindo Rwanda 1.43S 29.55E
52 H5 Rullbo Sweden 61.48N 14.55E
61 N8 Rulles Belgium 49.43N 5.34E
53 V19 Rullestadsata *reg* Norway 59.49N 6.42E
71 F3 Rully France 46.53N 4.44E
108 P9 Rulo Nebraska 40.02N 95.28W
64 E5 Rülzheim W Germany 49.09N 8.18E
65 P7 Rum Hungary 47.07N 16.52E
32 H4 Rūm Iran 33.27N 59.09E
58 D5 Rum *isld* Scotland
82 F5 Ruma Yugoslavia 45.01N 19.50E
15 B6 Rumaat Moluccas Indon 5.51S 132.49E
33 E10 Rumādah Yemen 13.33N 43.54E
33 E4 Rumādīyat, Ar Saudi Arabia 24.16N 43.54E
33 G4 Rumāh Saudi Arabia 25.29N 47.10E
34 P8 Rumaila *oil field* Iraq 30.15N 47.27E
Rumaila,Ar *see* Rumaylah,Ar
Rumaitha *see* Rumaythah,Ar
34 L3 Rumānah Iraq 35.48N 43.17E
93 A7 Rumangabo Zaïre 1.20S 29.21E
Rumania *see* Romania
34 P8 Rumaylah,Ar Iraq 30.35N 47.21E
33 E8 Rumayn *isld* Farasān Is Red Sea 16.25N 42.15E
33 B8 Rumaythā,Ar Bahrain, The Gulf 25.55N 50.33E
34 N7 Rumaythah,Ar Iraq 31.31N 45.15E
13 C7 Rumbalara N Terr Australia 25.15S 134.29E
Rumbati *see* Tanisepata
87 B7 Rumbek Sudan 6.50N 29.42E
61 C3 Rumbeke Belgium 50.56N 3.10E
15 C4 Rumberpon *I* Irian Jaya
19 D3 Rumbiä Celebes Indon 1.03N 124.56E
77 J4 Rumblar *R* Spain
77 J4 Rumblar,Embalse del *L* Spain 38.10N 3.49W
58 J6 Rumbling Bridge Tayside Scotland 56.11N 3.36W
62 H5 Rumburk Czechoslovakia 50.58N 14.35E
116 G3 Rum Cay *isld* Bahamas 23.41N 74.53W
69 E3 Rumegies France 50.29N 3.21E
35 G5 Rumeimin,Er Jordan 32.07N 34.48E
61 P9 Rumelange Luxembourg 49.28N 6.02E
37 F1 Rumelifeneri Turkey 41.14N 29.07E
37 K1 Rumelihisarı Turkey 41.06N 29.08E
61 D4 Rumes Belgium 50.33N 3.18E
104 P2 Rumford Maine 44.33N 70.34W
33 G4 Rumḥiyah, Ar Saudi Arabia 25.35N 47.00E
66 K8 Rumianca Italy 45.59N 8.17E
69 G4 Rumigny France 49.49N 4.16E
61 D4 Rumillies Belgium 50.37N 3.27E
71 H5 Rumilly Haute-Savoie France 45.52N 5.57E
69 G7 Rumilly-lès-Vaudes Aube France 48.08N 4.12E
13 B2 Rum Jungle N Terr Australia 13.00S 130.58E
66 L2 Rümlang Switzerland 47.27N 8.32E
35 E2 Rummāna Israel 32.47N 35.18E
35 D3 Rummana Jordan 32.32N 35.12E
34 F5 Rummāna *mt* Syria 33.33N 38.02E
35 G5 Rumman,Er Jordan 32.10N 35.50E
33 D3 Rummān,Jabal ar *mts* Saudi Arabia
86 O6 Rummān,Wādī *watercourse* Jordan
Rummelsburg *see* Miastko
61 L3 Rummen Belgium 50.53N 5.10E
20 L1 Rumoi Japan 43.57N 141.40E
93 A9 Rumonge Burundi 3.58S 29.26E
69 J6 Rumont France 48.51N 5.17E
92 F7 Rumphi Malawi 10.59S 33.50E
60 J12 Rumptë Netherlands 51.53N 5.11E
100 E7 Rumsey Alberta 51.51N 112.48W
103 G6 Rumson New Jersey 40.22N 74.00W
58 D5 Rum, Sound of Highland Scotland
61 H2 Rumst Belgium 51.05N 4.25E
11 E9 Rumu New Zealand 42.45S 171.00E
13 H3 Rumula Queensland 16.33S 145.18E
93 H5 Rumuruti Kenya 0.16N 36.32E
19 F6 Run *isld* Moluccas Indon 4.34S 129.40E
76 A10 Runa Portugal 39.04N 9.12W
59 K1 Runabay Hd Antrim N Ireland 55.09N 6.02W
23 G2 Runan Henan China 33.00N 114.20E
11 F9 Runanga New Zealand 42.24S 171.12E
116 J1 Runaway Bay Jamaica, W I 18.27N 77.20W
57 H6 Runcorn Merseyside Eng 53.20N 2.44W
18 B4 Rundeng Sumatra Indon 2.40N 97.45E
64 C1 Ründeroth W Germany 51.00N 7.28E
53 T14 Rundøy *isld* Norway 62.24N 5.37E
53 Y16 Rundtum *mt* Norway 61.25N 8.30E
Rundu *see* Nkarapamwe
19 D6 Runduna *isld* Indonesia 5.20S 124.21E
93 E9 Runere Tanzania 3.06S 33.18E
19 D7 Rung *isld* Indon 7.40S 125.57E
18 K7 Rungan *R* Borneo Indon
112 K7 Runge Texas 28.44N 97.44W
Rungmar Thok *see* Lungdo
53 K5 Rungsted Denmark 55.54N 12.34E
87 A9 Rungu Zaïre 3.15N 27.57E
92 F5 Rungwa Tanzania 6.58S 33.31E
92 F5 Rungwa *R* Tanzania
92 E5 Rungwa East Tanzania 7.20S 31.41E
92 E5 Rungwa West Tanzania 7.20S 31.40E
92 F6 Rungwe Tanzania 9.10S 33.35E
92 F6 Rungwe Mt Tanzania 9.10S 33.40E
52 K6 Runhällen Sweden 60.03N 16.51E
30 J6 Runi Saiyadpur Bihar India 26.23N 85.30E
32 E6 Rūniz-e Bālā Iran 29.11N 53.43E
64 E3 Runkel W Germany 50.24N 8.11E
61 L3 Runkelen Belgium 50.51N 5.09E
52 J6 Runn *L* Sweden 60.35N 15.40E
108 R8 Runnells Iowa 41.30N 93.20W
103 D7 Runnemede New Jersey 39.52N 75.05W
112 E1 Running Water Cr New Mexico/Texas
100 Q7 Runnymede Saskatchewan 51.30N 101.42W
57 M3 Runswick B N Yorks Eng 54.31N 0.42W
14 E6 Runton Ra W Australia
92 J7 Ruo Tanzania 10.12S 39.32E
51 O10 Ruokolahti Finland 61.19N 28.55E
71 E8 Ruoms France 44.27N 4.20E
24 F6 Ruoqiang Xinjiang Uygur Zizhiqu China 39.02N 88.02E
22 E6 Ruo Shui *R* Nei Monggol Zizhiqu China
80 N7 Ruoti Italy 40.43N 15.41E
51 L10 Ruovesi Finland 61.59N 24.05E
28 J2 Rupa Assam India 27.19N 92.21E
30 J8 Rupah Bihar India 24.52N 85.46E
121 A8 Rupanco, L Chile
12 G6 Rupanyup Victoria 36.39S 142.41E
29 E2 Rupar Punjab India 30.59N 76.36E
92 F8 Rupashe *R* Malawi
18 B10 Rupat *isld* Sumatra Indon
30 A6 Rupbas Rajasthan India 27.00N 77.35E
61 H2 Rupelmonde Belgium 51.08N 4.17E
110 M7 Rupert Idaho 42.37N 113.40W
103 B5 Rupert Pennsylvania 40.59N 76.29W
104 M3 Rupert Vermont 43.16N 73.14W
104 E9 Rupert W Virginia 37.57N 80.42W
97 M7 Rupert *R* Quebec
13 F5 Rupert *R* Queensland
99 L1 Rupert B Quebec
99 N1 Rupert R Quebec
64 L6 Rupertsbuch W Germany 48.56N 11.09E
30 A1 Rupi Himachal Prad India 31.36N 77.50E
30 E4 Rupidiha Uttar Prad India 28.00N 81.36E
29 D4 Rupnagar Rajasthan India 26.47N 74.52E
92 J7 Ruponda Tanzania 10.12S 38.42W
66 J2 Rupperswil Switzerland 47.25N 8.08E
123 J9 Ruppert Coast Antarctica
64 G2 Ruppertenrod W Germany 50.37N 9.05E
64 F2 Ruppertsburg W Germany 50.30N 8.58E
64 C2 Ruppichteroth W Germany 50.50N 7.28E
63 S7 Ruppiner Kanal E Germany
31 J4 Rupshu *reg* Kashmir
69 M8 Rupt-sur-Moselle France 47.55N 6.40E
119 J6 Rupununi *R* Guyana
35 H1 Ruqays Syria 33.14N 36.10E
33 E6 Ruqayṭah Saudi Arabia 20.12N 42.41E
34 O9 Ruq'i, Ar Iraq 29.01N 46.34E
33 G2 Ruq'i,Ar Saudi Arabia 29.05N 46.38E
35 G2 Ruqqād *R* Syria
35 G1 Ruqqād *watercourse* Syria
35 G1 Ruqqadiye Syria 33.08N 35.51E
64 A1 Rur *R* W Germany
30 C6 Rura Uttar Prad India 26.29N 79.54E
105 G1 Rural Hall N Carolina 36.15N 80.20W
104 D10 Rural Retreat Virginia 36.54N 81.18W
120 E6 Rurrenabaque Bolivia 14.30S 67.32W
69 L2 Rurstausee *res* W Germany 50.37N 6.23E
53 C6 Rurup Denmark 55.10N 9.02E
122 M10 Rurutu Tubuai Is Pacific Oc 22.25S 151.20W
77 K4 Rus Spain 38.04N 3.28W
77 M2 Rus *R* Spain
92 J5 Rusako Tanzania 6.27S 38.39E
39 G5 Rusakovo U.S.S.R. 58.15N 162.02E
41 C2 Rusanova,Zaliv *B* Novaya Zemlya U.S.S.R.
41 B4 Rusanovo Novaya Zemlya U.S.S.R. 70.36N 56.22E
92 F11 Rusape Zimbabwe 18.31S 32.15E
Ruṣayfah,Ar *see* Ruseifa,Er
66 L7 Ruscada,Pizzo *mt* Switzerland 46.11N 8.36E
66 L2 Rüschlikon Switzerland 47.18N 8.34E
82 K7 Ruse Bulgaria 43.50N 25.59E
65 M8 Ruše Yugoslavia 46.32N 15.29E
35 H5 Ruseifa,Er Jordan 32.01N 36.02E
86 J9 Ruseis, Gebel *hill* Egypt 28.02N 32.56E
64 P6 Rusel W Germany 48.53N 13.05E
92 J5 Rusende Tanzania 7.57S 38.50E
93 B9 Rusengo Burundi 3.23S 30.20E
30 K7 Rusera Bihar India 25.45N 86.02E
109 F3 Rush Colorado 38.51N 104.05W
59 K4 Rush Dublin Irish Rep 53.32N 6.06W
103 B3 Rush Pennsylvania 41.47N 76.02W
56 H5 Rushall Wilts Eng 51.19N 1.49W
21 B9 Rushan Shandong China 36.55N 121.26E
43 K7 Rushan Tadzhikistan U.S.S.R. 37.59N 71.32E
43 K8 Rushanshiy Khrebet *mts* Tadzhikistan U.S.S.R.
103 B3 Rushboro Pennsylvania 41.44N 76.02W
109 L3 Rush Center Kansas 38.28N 99.20W
108 S4 Rush City Minnesota 45.40N 92.59W
109 G3 Rush Cr Colorado
56 K3 Rushden Northants Eng 52.17N 0.36W
106 C6 Rushford Minnesota 43.48N 91.46W
104 G4 Rushford New York 42.24N 78.17W
55 K3 Rush Green London Eng 51.34N 0.10E
Rushkar *see* Roshkhvār
100 K8 Rush Lake Saskatchewan 50.25N 107.24W
28 K1 Rushon Assam India 28.50N 95.59E
109 N7 Rush Springs Oklahoma 34.47N 97.57W
103 A5 Rushtown Pennsylvania 40.55N 76.38W
106 D9 Rushville Illinois 40.07N 90.34W
107 L2 Rushville Indiana 39.38N 85.27W
108 H7 Rushville Nebraska 42.45N 102.27W
93 B7 Rushwa, L Tanzania
12 H6 Rushworth Victoria 36.38S 145.02E
57 K3 Rushyford Durham Eng 54.39N 1.33W
93 F6 Rusinga I Kenya 0.25S 34.13E
112 M4 Rusk Texas 31.49N 95.11W
105 E10 Ruskin Florida 27.43N 82.25W
57 N6 Ruskington Lincs Eng 53.03N 0.24W
52 L2 Rusksele Sweden 64.49N 18.55E
52 L2 Ruskträsk Sweden 64.48N 18.45E
108 K2 Ruso N Dakota 47.50N 100.58W
65 Q5 Rusovce Czechoslovakia 48.03N 17.09E
94 K5 Rusplaas S Africa 24.16S 29.33E
117 H7 Russas Brazil 4.56S 38.02W
65 H6 Russbachsaag Austria 47.36N 13.29E
61 E4 Russeignies Belgium 50.45N 3.32E
105 L12 Russel I Bahamas 25.34N 76.45W
108 R9 Russell Iowa 40.59N 93.10W
109 M3 Russell Kansas 38.54N 98.51W
104 C8 Russell Kentucky 38.32N 82.42W
100 Q8 Russell Manitoba 50.47N 101.17W
103 J2 Russell Massachusetts 42.12N 72.52W
108 P5 Russell Minnesota 44.20N 95.53W
104 K2 Russell New York 44.26N 75.11W
11 J2 Russell New Zealand 35.16S 174.10E
99 P7 Russell Ontario 45.15N 75.23W
104 F5 Russell Pennsylvania 41.58N 79.11W
48 T10 Russell Gletscher *glacier* Greenland
14 E6 Russell Headland *mt* W Australia 23.58S 122.40E
97 K3 Russell I N W Terr 74.00N 98.30W
15 L3 Russell Is Solomon Is
Russellkonda *see* Bhanjanagar
100 Q2 Russell L Manitoba
101 Q4 Russell L N W Terr
101 V7 Russell L Saskatchewan 57.29N 105.20W
113 M5 Russell,Mt Alaska 62.49N 151.54W
14 C7 Russell,Mt W Australia 26.28S 119.47E
14 E10 Russell Ra W Australia
104 B6 Russells Point Ohio 40.28N 83.55W
107 L4 Russell Springs Kentucky 37.02N 85.08W
107 J7 Russellville Alabama 34.30N 87.42W
107 C6 Russellville Arkansas 35.17N 93.06W
107 K5 Russellville Kentucky 36.50N 86.54W
107 D3 Russellville Missouri 38.31N 92.28W
104 B8 Russellville Ohio 38.53N 83.46W
103 C7 Russellville Pennsylvania 39.51N 75.57W
64 E4 Rüsselsheim W Germany 50.00N 8.25E
51 L1 Russenes Norway 70.30N 25.03E
71 K2 Russey,le France 47.10N 6.43E
79 M6 Russi Italy 44.22N 12.02E
Russia *see* Union of Soviet Socialist Republics
113 G6 Russian Mission Alaska 61.45N 161.25W
113 H6 Russian Mts Alaska
Russian Soviet Federated Socialist Republic *see* Rossiyskaya S.F.S.R
26 U12 Russie,La Mauritius, Indian Oc 20.14S 57.35E
40 G9 Russkaya U.S.S.R. 45.14N 136.50E
41 D7 Russkaya *R* U.S.S.R.
41 C2 Russkaya Gavan' Novaya Zemlya U.S.S.R. 76.13N 62.40E
41 C2 Russkaya Gavan',Zaliv *B* Novaya Zemlya U.S.S.R.
47 M5 Russkaya-Karabolka U.S.S.R. 55.56N 61.03E
39 K3 Russkaya Koshka,Kosa *sand spit* U.S.S.R.
47 L8 Russkaya Polyana U.S.S.R. 53.48N 73.54E
45 V7 Russkaya Talovka Kazakhstan U.S.S.R. 49.58N 49.05E
47 J7 Russkaya Techa U.S.S.R. 55.49N 62.05E
45 M6 Russkaya-Zhuravka U.S.S.R. 50.21N 40.35E
46 Q3 Russkiy Aktash U.S.S.R. 55.00N 52.00E
45 J4 Russkiy Brod U.S.S.R. 52.35N 37.21E
45 S4 Russkiy-Kameshkir U.S.S.R. 52.51N 46.05E
42 D6 Russkiy-Kamlak U.S.S.R. 51.41N 85.42E
41 G3 Russkiy,Ostrov *isld* U.S.S.R.
47 G2 Russkiy Zavorot, Poluostrov *pen* U.S.S.R.
40 B1 Russkorechenskaya U.S.S.R. 60.34N 121.51E
39 D1 Russkoye Ust'ye U.S.S.R. 71.04N 149.00E
66 L7 Russo Switzerland 46.13N 8.38E
53 Z15 Russvatnet *L* Norway 61.32N 8.40E
65 P6 Rust Austria 47.48N 16.40E
Rust Iraq*see* Rōst
95 B9 Rust S Africa 33.16S 18.39E
31 E2 Rustak Afghanistan 37.07N 69.48E
Rustakh *see* Rostāq
33 M5 Rustāq, Ar Oman 23.25N 57.25E
44 G6 Rustavi Georgia U.S.S.R. 41.34N 45.03E
104 F9 Rustburg Virginia 37.17N 79.07W
95 F9 Rust,De S Africa 33.30S 22.32E
95 L1 Rustenburg S Africa 25.40S 27.15E
63 H5 Rustersiel W Germany 53.33N 8.07E
95 N3 Rusthof S Africa 27.09S 29.32E
95 L3 Rustig S Africa 27.25S 27.10E
107 D9 Ruston Louisiana 32.32N 92.39W
44 J6 Rustov Azerbaydzhan U.S.S.R. 41.16N 48.35E
53 V15 Rustøy Norway 61.42N 6.49E
66 J3 Ruswil Switzerland 47.05N 8.08E
35 A10 Rut *watercourse* Israel
93 A9 Rutana Burundi 3.56S 29.59E
18 B9 Ru, Tanjong *C* Pen Malaysia 2.49N 101.17E
34 H5 Ruṭbah, Ar Iraq 33.03N 40.18E
45 K9 Rutchenkovo Ukraine U.S.S.R. 47.55N 38.07E
77 H6 Rute Spain 37.20N 4.23W
52 L9 Rute Sweden 57.51N 18.55E
63 S6 Rutenberg E Germany 53.16N 13.19E
63 F7 Rütenbrock W Germany 52.51N 7.06E
19 B8 Ruteng Indonesia 8.35S 120.28E
92 E12 Rutenga Zimbabwe 21.18S 30.43E
110 B9 Ruth California 40.20N 123.23W
111 K2 Ruth Nevada 39.16N 114.59W
63 H10 Rüthen W Germany 51.29N 8.25E
103 L6 Rutherford New Jersey 40.50N 74.06W
105 F2 Rutherfordton N Carolina 35.23N 81.57W
99 L6 Rutherglen Ontario 46.16N 79.04W
58 H7 Rutherglen Strathclyde Scotland 55.50N 4.12W
104 H9 Ruther Glen Virginia 37.54N 77.29W
113 M5 Ruth Glacier Alaska 62.45N 150.40W
66 P2 Rüthi Switzerland 47.18N 9.32E
100 J7 Ruthilda Saskatchewan 51.52N 108.30W
57 G6 Ruthin Clwyd Wales 53.07N 3.18W
34 J7 Rūthīyah,Ar Saudi Arabia 31.14N 41.15E
29 E5 Ruthiyai Rajasthan India 24.32N 77.06E
103 C8 Ruthsburg Maryland 39.00N 75.58W
108 O5 Ruthton Minnesota 44.10N 96.08W
108 Q6 Ruthven Iowa 43.08N 94.52W
13 G6 Ruthven Queensland 24.20S 144.10E
58 K5 Ruthven Tayside Scotland 56.38N 3.10W
57 G3 Ruthwell Dumfries & Galloway Scotland 55.00N 3.26W
66 F3 Rüti Bern Switzerland 47.09N 7.25E
66 N4 Rüti Glarus Switzerland 46.56N 9.01E
66 M2 Rüti Zürich Switzerland 47.16N 8.51E
81 O1 Rutigliano Italy 41.01N 17.01E
92 G7 Rutikira *R* Tanzania
46 O2 Rutka *R* U.S.S.R.
106 E9 Rutland Illinois 40.58N 89.02W
103 L2 Rutland Massachusetts 42.23N 71.57W
108 N3 Rutland N Dakota 46.04N 97.31W
104 C7 Rutland Ohio 39.03N 82.10W
100 H6 Rutland Saskatchewan 52.33N 109.34W
104 N3 Rutland Vermont 43.37N 72.59W
Rutland *co see* Leicestershire
28 G7 Rutland I Andaman Is
13 F3 Rutland Plains Queensland 15.39S 141.43E
53 S16 Rutledal Norway 61.04N 5.10E
108 S3 Rutledge Minnesota 46.15N 93.52W
107 D1 Rutledge Missouri 40.19N 92.06W
101 S5 Rutledge L N W Terr
66 L4 Rütli Switzerland 46.58N 8.36E
24 C9 Rutog Xizang Zizhiqu China 33.27N 79.43E
79 B3 Rutor,Testa del *mt* Italy/France 45.38N 7.01E
34 H5 Rutqa,Wādī *watercourse* Iraq
93 A7 Rutshuru Zaïre 1.11S 29.28E
93 A6 Rutshuru *R* Zaïre
53 P12 Rutsker Bornholm Denmark 55.13N 14.46E
61 M3 Rutten Belgium 50.45N 5.27E
60 L8 Rutten Netherlands 52.48N 5.42E
60 R8 Rutten A-Kanaal *canal* Netherlands
100 S2 Rutten L Manitoba
99 K6 Rutter Ontario 46.06N 80.40W
44 H6 Rutul U.S.S.R. 41.34N 47.25E
92 E2 Rutunguru Tanzania 1.16S 31.05E
65 D7 Rutz *R* Austria
60 O11 Ruurlo Netherlands 52.05N 6.27E
33 M4 Ru'us al Jibāl *mts* U.A.E./Oman
80 N7 Ruvo de Monte Italy 40.51N 15.33E
81 M1 Ruvo di Puglia Italy 41.07N 16.29E
92 J5 Ruvu Tanzania 6.50S 38.40E
92 J6 Ruvu Tanzania 9.39S 39.43E
93 J10 Ruvu Tanzania 4.38S 37.47E
Ruvu *R* *see* Pangani, R
92 J5 Ruvu *R* Tanzania
92 J7 Ruvuma *R* Tanzania
92 G7 Ruvuma *reg* Tanzania
93 B9 Ruvuvu *R* Burundi/Tanzania
92 E10 Ruwa Zimbabwe 17.52S 31.22E
33 N5 Ruwahah *tribe* Oman
Ruwais *see* Ruways
Ruwais,Ras *see* Ruways, Ra's ar *cape*
93 F8 Ruwana *watercourse* Tanzania
Ruwāndiz *see* Rawāndiz
86 D7 Ruwayān,Wâdi el *V* Egypt
85 E6 Ruwaybāt,ar Libya 26.39N 18.05E
33 F4 Ruwaydah Saudi Arabia 25.46N 45.06E
33 F3 Ruwayḍah, Ar Saudi Arabia 26.26N 44.16E
33 F4 Ruwaydah,Ar Saudi Arabia 25.11N 45.55E
33 F5 Ruwayḍah, Ar Saudi Arabia 23.46N 44.45E
33 C6 Ruways Saudi Arabia 21.35N 39.07E
33 N6 Ruways, Ra's ar *C* Oman 20.56N 58.51E
91 J9 Ruwe Zaïre 10.35S 25.30E
87 B3 Ruweiba Sudan 15.37N 28.47E
35 G9 Ruweifa,Jeb.er *mt* Jordan 31.12N 35.59E
34 B9 Ruweijil *isld* Saudi Arabia 29.13N 34.55E
33 K4 Ruweis U.A.E. 24.05N 52.48E
86 B4 Ruweisât El Egypt 30.48N 29.18E
34 F6 Ruweishid,Wādī ar *watercourse* Jordan
34 D9 Ruweita,Wādī *watercourse* Jordan
93 A5 Ruwenzori *mts* Uganda/Zaïre
93 A6 Ruwenzori Nat. Park Uganda
64 B4 Ruwer W Germany 49.47N 6.43E
93 A9 Ruwintare Burundi 3.36S 29.46E
32 F2 Rūyān Iran 36.21N 55.02E
23 F1 Ruyang Henan China 34.12N 112.20E
93 B9 Ruyigi Burundi 3.28S 30.14E
72 L5 Ruynes-en-Margeride France 45.00N 3.13E
23 F6 Ruyuan Guangdong China 24.50N 113.03E
45 H1 Ruza U.S.S.R. 55.40N 36.12E
92 E11 Ruzawi *R* Zimbabwe
43 H1 Ruzayevka Kazakhstan U.S.S.R. 52.48N 66.55E
45 Q2 Ruzayevka U.S.S.R. 54.04N 44.55E
46 G5 Ruzhin Ukraine U.S.S.R. 49.42N 29.10E
82 M1 Ruzhin U.S.S.R. 49.43N 29.08E
39 F1 Ruzhnikova U.S.S.R. 67.50N 156.00E
47 J4 Ruzitgort U.S.S.R. 62.51N 64.52E
93 A8 Ruzizi *R* Rwanda/Burundi/Zaïre
62 L6 Ružomberok Czechoslovakia 49.04N 19.15E
66 D3 Ruz,Val de Switzerland
65 K1 Ruzyne *airport* Czechoslovakia 50.07N 14.16E
86 D5 Ruzza,Gebel *hill* Egypt 30.01N 30.26E
93 B7 Rwamagana Rwanda 1.57S 30.26E
92 D2 Rwanda *rep* Cent Africa
93 B6 Rwashamaire Uganda 0.50S 30.09E
93 A7 Rwaza Rwanda 1.32S 29.44E
93 A6 Rwese Zaïre 0.02S 29.19E
53 D4 Ry Vejle Denmark 56.06N 9.46E
53 D2 Ryå Denmark 57.09N 9.43E
53 D2 Ryå *R* Denmark
32 F2 Ryābād Iran 36.42N 55.50E
45 G1 Ryabiki U.S.S.R. 55.13N 35.22E
45 N6 Ryabovskiy U.S.S.R. 50.01N 41.55E
45 D2 Ryabtsevo U.S.S.R. 54.38N 32.22E
82 K7 Ryakhovo Bulgaria 44.00N 26.19E
106 C7 Ryan Iowa 42.21N 91.30W
109 N7 Ryan Oklahoma 34.01N 97.58W
57 C3 Ryan,L Dumfries & Galloway Scotland 54.58N 5.03W
108 D8 Ryan Park Wyoming 41.19N 106.30W
110 L6 Ryan Pk Idaho 43.56N 114.24W
45 C3 Ryasna Belorussiya U.S.S.R. 54.00N 31.14E
44 A7 Ryasnopol Ukraine U.S.S.R. 47.05N 31.15E
45 L2 Ryazan' U.S.S.R. 54.37N 39.43E
45 O4 Ryazanka U.S.S.R. 52.08N 42.58E
45 L2 Ryazan'-Pristan' U.S.S.R. 54.43N 39.43E
46 L3 Ryazanskaya Oblast' *prov* U.S.S.R.
45 M3 Ryazhsk U.S.S.R. 53.40N 40.07E
44 K3 Rybachiy Ostrov *isld* Kazakhstan U.S.S.R. 44.50N 50.23E
47 C2 Rybachiy, Polustrov *pen* U.S.S.R.
43 E4 Rybachiy Poselok Uzbekistan U.S.S.R. 45.05N 59.13E
43 O4 Rybachye Kazakhstan U.S.S.R. 46.27N 81.30E
43 M6 Rybach'ye Kirgiziya U.S.S.R. 42.28N 76.09E
64 O3 Rybáře Czechoslovakia 50.14N 12.50E
46 L1 Rybinsk U.S.S.R. 58.01N 38.52E
42 C3 Rybinskiy U.S.S.R. 58.26N 84.45E
46 L1 Rybinskoye Vdkhr *res* U.S.S.R.
45 P2 Rybkino U.S.S.R. 54.15N 43.45E
41 J5 Rybnaya U.S.S.R. 72.14N 105.18E
45 W1 Rybnaya Sloboda U.S.S.R. 55.29N 50.09E
65 K4 Rybnik Czechoslovakia 48.38N 14.27E
62 L5 Rybnik Poland 50.07N 18.30E
46 G5 Rybnitsa Moldavia U.S.S.R. 47.42N 29.00E
42 E3 Rybnoye Krasnoyarsk U.S.S.R. 58.11N 94.29E
45 L2 Rybnoye Ryazan' U.S.S.R. 54.44N 39.30E
40 J5 Rybnoye Sakhalin U.S.S.R. 53.26N 141.56E
47 J6 Rychkovo U.S.S.R. 58.12N 61.50E
62 J5 Rychnov Czechoslovakia 50.10N 16.17E
62 L3 Rychwał Poland 52.03N 18.09E
63 S4 Ryckgraben *R* E Germany
101 O8 Rycroft Alberta 55.46N 118.43W
57 H4 Rydal Cumbria Eng 54.27N 2.59W
99 G6 Rydal Bank Ontario 46.22N 83.46W
56 J6 Ryde I of Wight Eng 50.44N 1.10W
53 B4 Ryde Ringkøbing Denmark 56.26N 8.48E
53 G7 Ryde Storstrøm Denmark 54.48N 11.18E
12 L7 Ryde *dist* Sydney, N S W
108 J2 Ryder N Dakota 47.57N 101.41W
110 B3 Ryderwood Washington 46.20N 123.05W
109 F4 Rye Colorado 37.55N 104.57W
56 N6 Rye E Sussex Eng 50.57N 0.44E
104 P4 Rye New Hampshire 43.00N 70.47W
103 G5 Rye New York 40.59N 73.42W
53 H5 Rye Roskilde Denmark 55.40N 11.54E
112 N5 Rye Texas 30.26N 94.48W
110 Q3 Ryegate Montana 46.19N 109.16W
110 G9 Rye Patch Nevada 40.27N 118.16W
110 G9 Rye Patch Res Nevada 40.40N 118.20W
57 M4 Rye,R N Yorks Eng
100 Q9 Ryerson Saskatchewan 49.47N 101.42W
70 J3 Ryes France 49.18N 0.36W
53 U20 Ryfylke *dist* Norway
53 U15 Rygg Norway 61.46N 6.07E
57 L3 Ryhope Tyne and Wear Eng 54.52N 1.21W
95 K3 Rykaartspos S Africa 26.33S 26.39E
62 N4 Ryki Poland 51.38N 21.57E
99 G3 Ryland Ontario 49.43N 83.50W
100 E5 Ryley Alberta 53.17N 112.22W
45 F5 Ryl'sk U.S.S.R. 51.35N 34.39E
12 J5 Rylstone New S Wales 32.51S 149.00E
57 J4 Rylstone N Yorks Eng 54.01N 2.02W
62 N6 Rymanow Poland 49.35N 21.51E
62 K6 Rýmařov Czechoslovakia 49.56N 17.15E
47 L5 Rymovy U.S.S.R. 60.50N 71.28E
62 N2 Ryn Poland 53.57N 21.30E
65 M3 Rynárec Czechoslovakia 49.23N 15.14E
47 D2 Rynda U.S.S.R. 68.53N 36.54E
94 U13 Rynfield Witwatersrand S Africa 26.10S 28.23E
95 L7 Ryno S Africa 31.22S 27.58E
46 P5 Ryn Peski *sandy des* Kazakhstan U.S.S.R.
53 F4 Ryomgard Denmark 56.23N 10.31E
20 P2 Ryōri-zaki *C* Japan 39.02N 141.52E
20 M3 Ryōtsu Japan 38.06N 138.28E
62 L2 Rypin Poland 53.03N 19.23E
Ryrkarpiya *see* Shmidta, Mys
113 A2 Ryrkaypiy U.S.S.R. 68.54N 179.25W
82 L3 Ryshkany U.S.S.R. 47.56N 27.36E
45 G4 Ryshkovo U.S.S.R. 52.10N 35.29E
53 F6 Ryslinge Denmark 55.15N 10.33E
95 L2 Rysmierbult S Africa 26.21S 27.08E
53 U15 Ryssfjøra Norway 61.50N 6.12E
53 X20 Rysstad Norway 59.05N 7.33E
63 F6 Rysum W Germany 53.23N 7.03E
57 L5 Ryther N Yorks Eng 53.51N 1.09W
53 P12 Rytterknægten *mt* Bornholm Denmark 55.07N 14.54E
20 O6 Ryūgasaki Japan 35.51N 140.12E
Ryuko *vol see* Ebeko *vol*
122 D4 Ryukuyu Ridge Pacific Oc
122 D5 Ryukuyu Trench Pacific Oc
17 K7 Ryūkyū Retto *arch* Japan
53 S19 Ryvarden *Lt Ho* Norway 59.32N 5.15E
64 Q2 Rýzmburk Czechoslovakia 50.38N 13.41E
62 H3 Rzepin Poland 52.20N 14.50E
62 N5 Rzeszów Poland 50.04N 22.00E
45 O4 Rzhaksa-Vyselki U.S.S.R. 52.08N 42.01E
45 C2 Rzhavka U.S.S.R. 54.39N 31.38E
45 F1 Rzhev U.S.S.R. 56.15N 34.18E
45 C7 Rzhishchev Ukraine U.S.S.R. 49.58N 31.02E
45 N6 Rzsavskiy U.S.S.R. 50.45N 41.51E
32 G3 Sa'ābād Iran 34.29N 57.20E
69 E6 Saâcy-sur-Marne France 48.57N 3.12E
35 B8 Sa'ad Israel 31.28N 34.32E
34 D9 Sa'ada al Barsa *hills* Saudi Arabia
Saadabad *see* Kārīz
74 K9 Saada,bou *R* Algeria
32 E5 Sa'ādatābād Fārs Iran 30.07N 53.05E
32 F6 Sa'ādatābād Kermān Iran 29.40N 55.50E
95 L4 Saaibult S Africa 28.32S 27.31E
95 N2 Saaiwater S Africa 26.06S 29.08E
64 M6 Saal Bayern W Germany 48.54N 11.57E
63 R4 Saal E Germany 54.19N 12.30E
64 J3 Saal Hessen W Germany 50.19N 10.23E
64 F5 Saal *R* W Germany
88 N7 Saala Algeria 28.39N 0.10W
65 G6 Saalach *R* Austria
65 G7 Saalbach Austria 47.24N 12.39E
64 M2 Saalburg E Germany 50.30N 12.44E
63 P9 Saale *R* E Germany
64 H3 Saale *R* Hessen W Germany
64 M3 Saale *R* Oberfranken, Bayern W Germany
63 Q4 Saaler Bodden *B* E Germany
69 N7 Saales France 48.21N 7.06E
Saale Talsperre *see* Bleilochsperre *res*
64 L2 Saalfeld E Germany 50.39N 11.22E
65 G7 Saalfelden Austria 47.26N 12.52E
87 M9 Saamòggia Somalia 0.20S 42.29E
66 E4 Saane *R* Switzerland
Saane ech Chajara *see* Sā'ān,Es
66 F6 Saanen Switzerland 46.30N 7.16E
66 F5 Saanenmöser Switzerland 46.31N 7.17E
34 E3 Sā'ān,Es Syria 35.18N 37.21E
101 M11 Saanich Vancouver I, Br Col 48.28N 123.22W
35 D1 Sa'ar Israel 33.02N 35.06E
64 B5 Saar *R* W Germany
64 B5 Saarbrücken W Germany 49.15N 6.58E
64 B4 Saarburg W Germany 49.36N 6.33E
46 D1 Sääre Estonia U.S.S.R. 57.55N 22.08E
69 N6 Saarebourg France 48.44N 7.03E
69 N5 Saareguemines France 49.07N 7.04E
46 D1 Saaremaa *isld* Estonia U.S.S.R.
51 M5 Saarenkylä Finland 66.32N 25.50E
Saargemünd *see* Saareguemines
51 O10 Saari Finland 61.38N 29.48E
51 L9 Saarijärvi Finland 62.44N 25.15E
51 N3 Saariselkä *mts* Finland
64 B5 Saarland *land* W Germany
64 B5 Saarlouis W Germany 49.19N 6.45E
63 S8 Saarmund E Germany 52.19N 13.08E
69 M5 Saar-Wellingen W Germany 49.21N 6.49E
66 Q4 Saas Switzerland 46.55N 9.48E
66 H7 Saas-Almagell Switzerland 46.07N 7.58E
69 O7 Saasenheim France 48.15N 7.39E
66 H7 Saaser Visp *R* Switzerland
66 H7 Saas Fee Switzerland 46.07N 7.56E
66 H7 Saas-Grund Switzerland 46.08N 7.57E
66 H7 Saastal *V* Switzerland
60 Q10 Saasveld Netherlands 52.20N 6.48E
87 B4 Sa'ata Sudan 12.39N 29.35E
18 M4 Saätan Kalimantan Indon 3.54N 116.36E
87 G3 Saati Ethiopia 15.35N 39.18E
37 J8 Sā'atlū Iran 37.27N 45.07E
44 J8 Saatly Azerbaydzhan U.S.S.R. 39.55N 48.25E
121 E6 Saavedra Buenos Aires Arg 37.45S 62.26W
121 E3 Saavedra Santa Fé Arg 31.43N 61.20W
39 D2 Saba U.S.S.R. 66.38N 149.30E
116 N6 Saba *isld* Lesser Antilles 17.42N 63.26W
Sabaa-Biâr *see* Sab 'Biyār
116 N6 Saba Bank Leeward Is W I
63 L9 Şababurg W Germany 51.33N 9.32E
82 F6 Šabac Yugoslavia 44.45N 19.41E
75 P4 Sabadell Spain 41.33N 2.07E
20 K6 Sabae Japan 35.58N 136.11E
18 M3 Sabah *state* Malaysia
18 A8 Sabak Pen Malaysia 3.45N 100.59E
113 L9 Sabak,C Aleutian Is 52.21N 173.40E
85 M7 Sabakhâya,El Egypt 24.21N 32.54E
19 C4 Sabal Celebes Indon 0.58S 123.15E
19 A7 Sabalana *isld* Indonesia 6.51S 119.09E
19 A7 Sabalana, Pulau Pulau *islds* Indonesia
18 N9 Sabalan, Kepulauan *islds* Indonesia
32 B1 Sabalān,Kūhhā-ye *mts* Iran
30 A6 Sabalgarh Madhya Prad Indon 26.15N 77.24E
115 P5 Sábalo Panama 8.02N 78.12W
87 D2 Sabaloka Cat Sudan 16.19N 32.40E
119 G3 Saban Venezuela 9.09N 65.54W
117 B2 Sabana Surinam 5.25N 55.55W
116 D3 Sabana,Arch de Cuba
116 K5 Sabana de la Mar Dominican Rep 19.04N 69.24W
115 L3 Sabana Grande Honduras 13.48N 87.15W
119 D2 Sabanalarga Colombia 10.38N 74.55W
33 D3 Sab'ān, Aś Saudi Arabia 27.05N 41.58E
116 J5 Sabaneta Dominican Rep 19.30N 71.21W
119 E2 Sabaneta Venezuela 11.17N 70.00W
19 A3 Sabang Celebes Indon 0.15N 119.53E
18 A3 Sabang Sumatra Indon 5.53N 95.17E
18 K7 Sabangan,Teluk *B* Borneo Indon
119 D8 Sabano Colombia 0.53S 72.37W
36 G2 Şabanözü Turkey 40.28N 33.20E
118 G6 Sabara Brazil 19.54S 43.46W
26 R8 Sabaragamuwa *prov* Sri Lanka
72 G9 Sabarat France 43.06N 1.23E
75 J2 Sabardan *R* Spain
93 H1 Sabarei Kenya 4.19N 36.55E
15 M9 Sabari I Louisiade Arch 11.10S 153.05E
87 K4 Sabar,Jeb Yemen 13.31N 44.01E
29 C6 Sabarkantha *dist* Gujarat India
29 C6 Sabarmati R Gujarat India
19 A7 Sabaru *isld* Indonesia 6.34S 118.53E
93 J6 Saba Saba Kenya 0.50S 37.09E
35 D4 Sabastiya Jordan 32.17N 35.12E
30 A1 Sabathu Himachal Prad India 31.00N 76.59E
93 G6 Sabatia Kenya 0.02S 35.45E
80 F4 Sabatini,Monti Italy
80 H6 Sabaudia Italy 41.18N 13.02E
80 H6 Sabaudia,L.di Italy
30 L7 Sabaur Bihar India 25.15N 87.03E
33 B3 Saba,Wādī *watercourse* Saudi Arabia
120 E8 Sabaya Bolivia 19.02S 68.23W
33 D7 Şabayā *isld* Saudi Arabia 18.35N 41.04E
87 H3 Šabba Ethiopia 14.05N 40.11E
86 M9 Şabbâgh,Gebel *hill* Egypt 28.11N 34.04E
81 D2 Sabbatino,Pta Sardinia 40.48N 9.42E
66 J8 Sabbia Italy 45.52N 8.15E
79 H5 Sabbioneta Italy 45.00N 10.29E
34 E5 Sab'Biyār Syria 33.50N 37.40E
Sabderat *see* Sebderat
32 G3 Sabeh Iran 35.30N 57.58E
93 L5 Sabena Kenya 0.55N 39.31E
15 E5 Saberania Irian Jaya 2.04S 138.19E
109 P2 Sabetha Kansas 39.54N 95.49W
34 D6 Sabhā Jordan 32.19N 36.29E
33 F5 Şabḥā' Saudi Arabia 23.11N 44.41E
86 P3 Şabḥa el Hadītha, Jebel *mt* Jordan 31.22N 35.35E
86 M4 Şabḥa, Gebel el *hill* Egypt 30.45N 34.26E
85 C6 Sabhah *div* Libya
29 A6 Sabhrai Gujarat India 23.01N 69.11E
92 E12 Sabi Zimbabwe 20.22S 30.14E
92 F12 Sabi *R* Zimbabwe
87 F1 Sabidana,Jeb *mt* Sudan 18.04N 36.50E
94 M5 Sabié Mozambique 25.19S 32.16E
94 L5 Sabie S Africa 25.10S 30.48E
94 L5 Sabie *R* S Africa
34 P7 Sābilah,Nahr as *R* Iraq
46 D2 Sabile Latvia U.S.S.R. 57.00N 22.28E
86 O7 Sābil, Wādī *watercourse* Jordan
104 B7 Sabina Ohio 39.30N 83.38W
80 G4 Sabina *reg* Italy
115 F2 Sabinal Mexico 30.58N 107.29W
112 H6 Sabinal Texas 29.19N 99.28W
116 F4 Sabinal,Cayo *isld* Cuba 21.40N 77.20W
77 L7 Sabinal,Pta.del *pt* Spain 36.42N 2.41W
75 K2 Sabiñánigo Spain 42.31N 0.22W
115 J4 Sabinas Mexico 27.50N 101.09W
115 J4 Sabinas Hidalgo Mexico 26.33N 100.10W
50 T14 Sabine Spitsbergen
112 O6 Sabine Texas 29.42N 93.52W
112 O5 Sabine *R* Louisiana/Texas
112 O6 Sabine L Louisiana/Texas
123 K6 Sabine,Mt Antarctica 72.08S 169.10E
48 V8 Sabine Ø *isld* Greenland 74.35N 19.00W
80 G4 Sabini,Monti Italy
96 P12 Sabinosa Hierro Canary Is 27.45N 18.06W
62 N6 Sabinov Czechoslovakia 49.06N 21.05E
93 A7 Sabinyo *mt* Uganda/Rwanda/Zaïre 1.22S 29.36E
77 K4 Sabiote Spain 38.05N 3.18W
29 E4 Sabi R Rajasthan India
44 J8 Sabirabad Azerbaydzhan U.S.S.R. 40.00N 48.28E
33 M9 Şābirīyah,Aş Kuwait 29.54N 47.57E
92 D12 Šabiwa Zimbabwe 20.50S 29.02E
90 H2 Sabka Chad 19.15N 16.35E
34 G3 Sabkha Syria 35.48N 39.17E
88 G8 Sabkhaf Tah *salt L* Morocco
34 E3 Sabkha Marāgha *salt marsh* Syria
33 L6 Sabkhat Abū ar Rūs *salt marsh* Saudi Arabia
85 F4 Sabkhat al Qunayyin *salt marsh* Libya
33 J5 Sabkhat Maṭṭī *salt flats* Saudi Arabia/U.A.E.
34 F4 Sabkhat Mūh *salt marsh* Syria
85 C3 Sabkhat Tāwurghā *salt marsh* Libya
86 K3 Sabkhet el Bardawîl *lagoon* Egypt
19 K5 Sablayan Philippines 12.50N 120.48E
96 E4 Sable I Atlantic Oc 43.57N 60.00W
10 M5 Sable I Coral Sea 19.13S 159.57E
98 N10 Sable I Nova Scotia
122 U13 Sable,I.de Marquesas Is Pacific Oc 7.53S 140.25W
9 A12 Sable,I.de New Caledonia 19.15S 163.48E
98 M10 Sable Island Bank Nova Scotia
106 H5 Sable Pt.,Big Michigan 44.03N 86.31W
106 H6 Sable Pt.,Little Michigan 43.39N 86.33W
98 G10 Sable River Nova Scotia 43.50N 65.05W
72 A2 Sables d'Olonne,Les France 46.30N 1.47W
70 F4 Sables d'Or France 48.39N 2.24W
99 H6 Sables,L.aux Ontario 46.47N 82.20W
99 H6 Sables,R.aux Ontario
70 K6 Sable-sur-Sarthe France 47.50N 0.20W
71 G8 Sablet France 44.12N 5.01E
71 E7 Sablières France 44.33N 4.03E
44 E3 Sablinskoye U.S.S.R. 44.33N 43.14E
71 F10 Sablon,Pte.du France 43.22N 4.33E
71 F6 Sablons France 45.19N 4.47E
117 G8 Saboeiro Brazil 6.30S 39.54W
76 B14 Saboia Portugal 37.30N 8.30W
90 C5 Sabon Birni Nigeria 13.34N 6.20E
76 F5 Sabor *R* Portugal
95 C5 Sabotsy Madagascar 18.51S 47.59E
89 H5 Sabou Upper Volta 12.01N 2.15W
90 G1 Sabozo Niger 21.05N 14.46E
85 B3 Sabrātah Libya 32.50N 12.24E
15 B5 Sabra,Tg *C* Irian Jaya 2.17S 132.18E
104 F7 Sabraton W Virginia 39.36N 79.56W
72 C7 Sabres France 44.09N 0.43W
88 S5 Sabria Tunisia 33.24N 8.46E
123 G3 Sabrina Coast Antarctica
33 M9 Sabriya *oil field* Kuwait 29.50N 47.52E
33 G2 Şabrīyah Kuwait 29.54N 47.57E
53 E4 Sabro Denmark 56.13N 10.02E
76 D6 Sabrosa Portugal 41.15N 7.35W
35 H1 Sabsabah Syria 33.10N 36.02E
33 H3 Sabsab,As Saudi Arabia 26.22N 48.23E
19 K1 Sabtang *isld* Philippines 20.20N 121.52E
25 K9 Sabual Assam India 23.30N 92.33E
15 A5 Sabuda *isld* Irian Jaya 2.40S 131.36E

76 E8 **Sabugal** Portugal 40.20N 7.05W
76 C15 **Sabugo** Portugal 38.49N 9.18W
76 C11 **Sabugueiro** Portugal 38.46N 8.07W
106 D7 **Sabula** Iowa 42.05N 90.11W
93 M5 **Sabuleh** Kenya 0.35N 40.20E
89 H6 **Sabuli** Ghana 10.35N 2.26W
42 C2 **Sabun** U.S.S.R. 61.58N 81.18E
42 C2 **Sabun** *R* U.S.S.R.
44 K7 **Sabunchi** Azerbaydzhan **U.S.S.R.** 40.26N 49.58E
36 E3 **Sabuncu** Turkey 39.35N 30.11E
18 L9 **Sabunting** *isld* Indonesia 7.00S 115.32E
33 E8 **Şabyā** Saudi Arabia 17.07N 42.39E
41 H5 **Sabyda** *R* U.S.S.R.
43 K2 **Sabyndy** Kazakhstan **U.S.S.R.** 50.52N 70.26E
31 B4 **Sabz** Afghanistan 33.03N 62.40E
Sabzawar Afghanistan *see* **Shindand**
Sabzawār Iran *see* **Sabzevār**
Sabzāwārān *see* **Jīroft**
31 F2 **Sabz Bahar** Afghanistan 37.03N 70.15E
32 G2 **Sabzevār** Iran 36.13N 57.38E
29 B1 **Sabzi Mandi** *dist* Delhi **India**
Sabzvārān *see* **Jīroft**
87 F6 **Saca** Ethiopia 8.13N 36.59E
120 E7 **Sacaba** Bolivia 17.21S 66.05W
120 E8 **Sacaca** Bolivia 18.07S 66.25W
77 V14 **Sa Calobra** Balearic Is 39.51N 2.47E
91 G9 **Sacalunga** Angola 11.58S 21.18E
91 H9 **Sacambunge** Angola 10.28S 22.17E
91 D7 **Sacamo** Angola 6.44S 14.55E
121 C9 **Sacanana,Pampa** *plain* Arg
104 L3 **Sacandaga** *R* New York
104 L3 **Sacandaga Res** New York
91 E6 **Sacandica** Angola 5.58S 16.02E
75 J8 **Sacañet** Spain 39.51N 0.44W
121 E3 **Sacanta** Argentina 31.44S 62.50W
111 N8 **Sacaton** Arizona 33.05N 111.42W
76 A11 **Sacavem** Portugal 38.47N 9.06W
115 P8 **Sacbecan** Mexico 18.58N 89.09W
71 M8 **Saccarello,Mt** France 44.03N 7.43E
80 M5 **Saccione,R** Italy
108 P7 **Sac City** Iowa 42.26N 95.00W
80 H5 **Sacco** *R* Italy
79 L4 **Saccolongo** Italy 45.24N 11.45E
75 F6 **Sacecorbo** Spain 40.50N 2.25W
75 E6 **Sacecorbo** *mt* Spain 40.49N 2.33W
75 E7 **Sacedón** Spain 40.29N 2.44W
75 F7 **Sacedoncillo** Spain 40.11N 2.15W
82 J3 **Săcel** Romania 47.39N 24.23E
82 K5 **Săcele** Romania 45.36N 25.40E
77 G3 **Saceruela** Spain 38.56N 4.37W
119 C8 **Sacha** *oil well* Ecuador 0.22S 76.48W
21 D7 **Sachang-ni** N Korea 40.02N 126.57E
103 J4 **Sachem Hd** Connecticut 41.15N 72.42W
97 K7 **Sachigo** *R* Ontario
29 C7 **Sachin** Gujarat **India** 21.03N 72.59E
91 E9 **Sachinemuna** Angola 11.33S 18.00E
29 E1 **Sach Khas** Himachal Prad **India** 33.00N 76.29E
44 E5 **Sachkhere** Georgia **U.S.S.R.** 42.22N 43.24E
93 G5 **Sacho** Kenya 0.22N 35.48E
92 G10 **Sachombe** Mozambique 17.42S 35.15E
21 D10 **Sachŏn** S Korea 35.04N 128.06E
29 E1 **Sach Pass** Himachal Prad **India** 33.01N 76.17E
64 N8 **Sachrang** W Germany 47.42N 12.16E
112 P8 **Sachse** Texas 32.56N 96.37W
66 J4 **Sachseln** Switzerland 46.52N 8.15E
64 F1 **Sachsenberg** W Germany 51.08N 8.48E
65 H8 **Sachsenburg** Austria 46.50N 13.22E
64 L1 **Sachsenburg** E Germany 51.18N 11.09E
64 N3 **Sachsenburg-Georgenthal** E Germany 50.22N 12.28E
63 K8 **Sachsenhagen** W Germany 52.24N 9.16E
64 G1 **Sachsenhausen** W Germany 51.15N 9.00E
97 G3 **Sachs Harbour** N W Terr 72.00N 124.30W
72 G2 **Sacierges-St.Martin** France 46.30N 1.22E
79 M3 **Sacile** Italy 45.58N 12.30E
104 J3 **Sackets Harbor** New York 43.56N 76.07W
64 D8 **Säckingen** W Germany 47.34N 7.56E
98 H8 **Sackville** New Brunswick 45.54N 64.23W
69 C7 **Saclas** France 48.22N 2.07E
117 F8 **Saco** Brazil 7.13S 42.11W
104 P3 **Saco** Maine 43.31N 70.26W
110 S1 **Saco** Montana 48.27N 107.21W
19 L8 **Sacol** *isld* **Philippines** 6.59N 122.15E
66 A7 **Saconnex,Grand** Switzerland 46.15N 6.08E
71 G1 **Sacquenay** France 47.36N 5.20E
58 S11 **Sacquoy Hd** Orkney **Scotland** 59.12N 3.05W
75 C5 **Sacramenia** Spain 41.30N 3.58W
118 F6 **Sacramento** Brazil 19.51S 47.26W
111 C3 **Sacramento** California 38.33N 121.30W
111 C3 **Sacramento** *R* California
109 E8 **Sacramento Mts** New Mexico
120 B2 **Sacramento,Pampa del** *plain* Peru
111 B1 **Sacramento Val** California
111 K7 **Sacramento Wash** *R* Arizona
77 K7 **Sacratif,C** Spain 36.42N 3.28W
98 C5 **Sacré Cœur** Quebec 48.16N 69.52W
98 D5 **Sacré Cœur** Quebec 48.25N 68.39W
118 B3 **Sacre,R** Brazil
80 O5 **Sacro,Monte** Foggia Italy 41.45N 16.03E
81 K3 **Sacro,Monte** Salerno Italy 40.13N 15.25E
76 C3 **Sacro, Pico** *mt* Spain 42.49N 8.27W
82 G3 **Săcueni** Romania 47.20N 22.05E
118 B3 **Sacuriuiná,R** Brazil
76 C2 **Sada** Spain 43.22N 8.15W
35 F2 **Sada** Syria 32.50N 35.45E
75 H3 **Sádaba** Spain 42.17N 1.16W
32 D6 **Sa'dabad** Iran 29.21N 51.00E
30 B5 **Sadabad** Uttar Prad **India** 27.26N 78.02E
Sá da Bandeira *see* **Lubango**
34 D4 **Sadad** Syria 34.21N 36.52E
75 H2 **Sada de Sangüesa** Spain 42.35N 1.25W
Sadah *see* **Sadh**
33 E8 **Şad'ah** Yemen 17.00N 43.45E
33 M9 **Sādah, As** *area* Kuwait
Sadaich *R see* **Sadij** *R*
33 H3 **Sada,Jabal as** *hill* Saudi Arabia 26.34N 48.15E
44 F6 **Sadakhlo** Georgia **U.S.S.R.** 41.14N 44.49E
81 C4 **Sadali** Sardinia 39.49N 9.17E
20 F8 **Sada-misaki** *C* Japan 33.22N 132.01E
21 F10 **Sadamitsu** Japan 34.02N 134.01E
19 A5 **Sadang** *R* Celebes Indon
92 J5 **Sadani** Tanzania 6.05S 38.46E
18 D2 **Sadao** Thailand 6.39N 100.30E
44 F8 **Sadarak** Nakhichevan' **U.S.S.R.** 39.42N 44.50E
29 B2 **Sadar Bazar** *dist* Delhi **India**
28 C2 **Sadaseopet** Andhra Prad **India** 17.38N 77.59E
57 L3 **Sadberge** Durham **Eng** 54.32N 1.28W
31 F4 **Sadda** Pakistan 33.43N 70.25E
87 H8 **Saddei** Ethiopia 4.00N 41.04E
93 N2 **Saddei** Ethiopia 4.00N 41.08E
85 M8 **Sadd el Aali** Egypt 23.54N 32.52E
57 B1 **Saddell** Strathclyde **Scotland** 55.32N 5.31W
35 E1 **Saddîqîne** Lebanon 33.11N 35.19E
57 G3 **Saddleback** *mt* Cumbria **Eng** 54.39N 3.03W
13 G2 **Saddle Hill** Queensland 14.39S 144.47E
14 D4 **Saddle Hill** W Australia 18.30S 121.54E
9 C10 **Saddle I** New Hebrides 13.40S 167.40E
110 A7 **Saddle Mt** Oregon 42.24N 124.08W
110 Q5 **Saddle Mt** Wyoming 44.45N 109.59W
28 G6 **Saddle Pk** Andaman Is 13.10N 93.00E
26 A16 **Saddle Pt** Heard I **Antarctica** 53.01S 73.30E
58 F4 **Saddle,The** *mt* Highland **Scotland** 57.09N 5.26W
25 H7 **Sa Dec** Vietnam 10.19N 105.45E
119 B7 **Sade,L.de** Ecuador 0.32N 79.16W
24 H10 **Sadêng** Xizang Zizhiqu **China** 31.15N 94.46E
82 K2 **Sadgora** U.S.S.R. 48.20N 25.57E
33 L8 **Sadḩ** Oman 17.11N 55.08E
30 A2 **Sadhaura** Haryana **India** 30.22N 77.13E
116 O2 **Sadhoowa** Trinidad & Tobago 10.08N 61.27W
87 E6 **Sadi** Ethiopia 8.50N 35.02E
34 L3 **Sadid** *oil bore* Iraq 35.27N 43.02E
107 M3 **Sadieville** Kentucky 38.22N 84.31W
32 H8 **Sadij** *R* Iran
36 F6 **Sadıklar** Turkey 36.56N 31.50E
89 D5 **Sadiola** Mali 13.51N 11.40W
31 F6 **Sadiqabad** Pakistan 28.16N 70.09E
31 G2 **Sad Istragh** Afghanistan 36.36N 72.13E
28 K2 **Sadiya** Assam **India** 27.49N 95.38E
33 C6 **Sa'diya** Saudi Arabia 20.35N 39.53E
34 N4 **Sa'dīyah,As** Iraq 34.13N 45.07E
34 O6 **Sa'dīyah,Hawr as** *L* Iraq
33 L4 **Sa'dīyyāt** *isld* U.A.E.
95 D2 **Sadjoavato** Madagascar 12.36S 49.20E
Sadjour Souyou *R see* **Sajur Suyi**
32 G2 **Sad-Kharv** Iran 36.20N 57.05E
113 P2 **Sadlerochit** *R* Alaska
76 B12 **Sado** *R* Portugal
43 E5 **Sadoch'ye,Ozero** *L* Uzbekistan **U.S.S.R.**
25 N8 **Sadon** Burma 25.21N 97.54E
44 F5 **Sadon** U.S.S.R. 42.50N 44.03E
18 J5 **Sadong** *R* Sarawak **Malaysia**
20 M3 **Sado-shima** *isld* Japan
86 M3 **Sadot** Egypt 31.13N 34.14E
45 Q9 **Sadovoye** Kalmyk A.S.S.R. **U.S.S.R.** 47.46N 44.31E
44 F2 **Sadovoye** Stavropol' **U.S.S.R.** 45.17N 44.42E
31 B9 **Sadr** *dist* Karachi **Pakistan**
29 C6 **Sadra** Gujarat **India** 23.20N 72.48E
28 E4 **Sadras** Tamil Nadu **India** 12.33N 80.10E
29 C5 **Sadri** Rajasthan **India** 25.12N 73.32E
72 H5 **Sadroc** France 45.17N 1.32E
30 E5 **Sadrpur** Uttar Prad **India** 27.26N 81.08E
86 O10 **Sadr, Wādī** *watercourse* **Saudi Arabia**
30 F5 **Sadullahnagar** Uttar Prad **India** 27.06N 82.24E
Sadulpur *see* **Rajgarh**
33 G4 **Sādūs** Saudi Arabia 25.01N 46.12E
51 E5 **Sädvajaure** *L* Sweden 66.28N 16.30E
41 L8 **Sadyn** U.S.S.R. 64.28N 120.00E
53 S17 **Sæbø** Norway 60.37N 5.07E
53 W18 **Sæbo** Norway 60.25N 7.07E
50 B2 **Sæból** Iceland 66.03N 23.40W
50 B2 **Sæból** Iceland 66.21N 23.07W
53 T19 **Saebøvik** Norway 59.47N 5.42E
53 F2 **Sæby** Nordjylland **Denmark** 57.20N 10.33E
53 H5 **Sæby** Roskilde **Denmark** 55.43N 11.58E
53 G5 **Sæby** Vestjælland **Denmark** 55.33N 11.19E
53 J6 **Sædder** Denmark 55.24N 12.08E
53 B4 **Sædding** Denmark 56.02N 8.33E
53 F5 **Sælvig** Denmark 55.52N 10.33E
15 H4 **Sae Is** Bismarck Arch 0.43S 145.16E
75 E8 **Saelices** Spain 39.55N 2.49W
76 J4 **Saelices del Rio** Spain 42.30N 5.00W
76 J4 **Saelices de Mayorgo** Spain 42.13N 5.12W
50 D4 **Sælingsdalstunga** Iceland 65.15N 21.48W
50 F5 **Sæluhús** Iceland 64.36N 19.45W
63 G8 **Saerbeck** W Germany 52.11N 7.39E
53 E5 **Særslev** Denmark 55.31N 10.11E
53 E2 **Saesing** Denmark 57.22N 10.12E
61 O8 **Saeul** Luxembourg 49.43N 5.59E
53 T18 **Sævareid** Norway 60.11N 5.46E
Safa Saudi Arabia *see* **Lişāfah, Al**
34 D5 **Safa** *lava reg* Syria
90 H7 **Safa** *tribe* Chad
Safad *see* **Zefat**
85 M6 **Safâga I** Egypt 26.45N 33.57E
81 H10 **Safaglione,C.di** Sicily 36.55N 14.24E
47 J8 **Safakulevo** U.S.S.R. 54.58N 62.30E
89 H5 **Safané** Upper Volta 12.09N 3.11W
33 H2 **Safaniya** *oil well* Saudi Arabia 28.00N 48.50E
76 E12 **Safara** Portugal 38.07N 7.13W
44 G7 **Safaraliyev** Azerbaydzhan **U.S.S.R.** 40.46N 46.25E
62 M7 **Šafárikovo** Czechoslovakia 48.25N 20.20E
122 B2 **Safata B** W Samoa, Pacific Oc 14.00S 171.51W
33 G1 **Safay al Maqūf** Iraq 30.07N 46.51E
Safed *see* **Zefat**
31 F1 **Safed Khirs** *mts* Afghanistan
31 F2 **Safed Khirs Pass** Afghanistan 37.42N 70.50E
31 C3 **Safed Koh** *mts* Herat **Afghanistan**
31 F3 **Safed Koh** *mts* Nangarhar **Afghanistan**
Safed Sang *see* **Safid Sagak**
103 B7 **Safe Harbor** Pennsylvania 39.56N 76.23W
34 H2 **Safeh,Es** Syria 36.45N 40.09E
65 O7 **Safen** *R* Austria
66 H2 **Safenwil** Switzerland 47.18N 7.58E
31 C5 **Safer** Afghanistan 30.38N 64.00E
93 M7 **Saferene** Kenya 1.42S 40.44E
14 A4 **Safety Bay** *dist* W Australia 32.18S 115.43E
105 E10 **Safety Harbor** Florida 27.59N 82.43W
35 D6 **Saffa** Jordan 31.54N 35.03E
34 O7 **Şaffāf, Birkat aş** *marsh* Iraq
33 H3 **Şaffānīyah, Ra's as** *C* Saudi Arabia 27.59N 48.51E
86 F6 **Şaff, El** Egypt 29.34N 31.16E
52 G7 **Säffle** Sweden 59.08N 12.55E
107 J9 **Safford** Alabama 32.17N 87.23W
111 P9 **Safford** Arizona 32.50N 109.43W
70 G7 **Saffré** France 47.30N 1.33W
56 M3 **Saffron Walden** Essex **Eng** 52.01N 0.15E
Saffuriya *see* **Zippori**
35 E9 **Safi** Jordan 31.02N 35.28E
84 Y20 **Safi** Malta 35.50N 14.30E
88 J5 **Safi** Morocco 32.18N 9.20W
15 K8 **Safia** Papua New Guinea 9.36S 148.38E
32 G2 **Safiabad** Iran 36.46N 57.56E
Safid Ab *see* **Chashmeh-ye Safid Ab**
32 J5 **Safidabeh** Iran 31.05N 60.30E
32 E6 **Safidār, Kūh-e** *mt* Iran 28.56N 52.51E
32 C4 **Safid Dasht** Lorestān Iran 33.13N 48.50E
34 Q5 **Safid Dasht** Lorestān Iran 33.27N 48.14E
Safid Kūh *mts see* **Paropamisus** *mts*
34 P4 **Safid,Kūh-e-** *mts* Iran
29 E3 **Safidon** Haryana **India** 29.26N 76.42E
32 C2 **Safid Rūd** *R* Iran
32 C2 **Safid Rūd Dam** Iran 36.45N 49.26E
32 J3 **Safid Sagak** Iran 35.39N 60.05E
66 O5 **Safien Platz** Switzerland 46.42N 9.20E
66 O5 **Safiental** *V* Switzerland
30 D6 **Safipur** Uttar Prad **India** 26.45N 80.20E
76 C11 **Safira** Portugal 38.37N 8.49W
118 H6 **Safiras,Serra das** *mts* Brazil
34 D4 **Sāfīta** Syria 34.49N 36.07E
34 G7 **Sāfīyah,Khabrah** *salt L* Saudi Arabia
90 B7 **Safo** Nigeria 9.58N 5.25E
45 K3 **Safonovka** U.S.S.R. 53.18N 38.10E
47 F3 **Safonovo** Arkhangel'sk **U.S.S.R.** 65.43N 47.44E
39 K3 **Safonovo** Magadan **U.S.S.R.** 64.04N 175.55E
45 E1 **Safonovo** Smolensk **U.S.S.R.** 55.08N 33.16E
122 A1 **Safotu** W Samoa, Pacific Oc 13.26S 172.24W
33 E3 **Safrā' al Asyāh** *escarp* Saudi Arabia
33 C4 **Şafrā, Aş** Saudi Arabia 24.04N 38.55E
33 E3 **Şafrā, Aş** Saudi Arabia 26.55N 42.12E
33 F4 **Safrā as Sark** *sand dunes* Saudi Arabia
75 E8 **Safra de Záncara** Spain 39.53N 2.34W
86 N6 **Safra,Gebel,el** *hill* Egypt 29.44N 34.50E
36 F1 **Safranbolu** Turkey 41.16N 32.41E
Safsaf *see* **Sifsufa**
52 H6 **Säfsnäs** Sweden 60.09N 14.29E
86 E4 **Saft el 'Inab** Egypt 30.49N 30.41E
86 E4 **Saft el Mulûk** Egypt 30.56N 30.33E
86 E8 **Saft Rashîn** Egypt 28.58N 30.55E
86 F4 **Saft Turâb** Egypt 30.54N 31.07E
122 A1 **Safune** W Samoa, Pacific Oc 13.26S 172.25W
35 G5 **Safut** Jordan 32.03N 35.49E
33 A7 **Şafwā** Saudi Arabia 26.40N 49.58E
33 H3 **Şafwā** Saudi Arabia 26.39N 49.58E
34 P8 **Şafwān** Iraq 30.06N 47.44E
33 L4 **Safwan** U.A.E. 24.35N 55.47E
Saga *see* **Asu**
43 G3 **Saga** Kazakhstan **U.S.S.R.** 48.48N 63.46E
20 D8 **Saga** Kyūshū Japan 33.16N 130.18E
20 G8 **Saga** Shikoku Japan 33.04N 133.06E
20 C7 **Saga** Tsushima Japan 34.26N 129.22E
24 E11 **Saga** Xizang Zizhiqu **China** 29.30N 85.10E
20 C8 **Saga** *prefect* Japan
91 H9 **Sagaba** Angola 11.16S 23.09E
89 K8 **Sagada** Togo 7.05N 1.34E
20 O3 **Sagae** Japan 38.22N 140.12E
25 C2 **Sagaing** Burma 21.55N 95.56E
25 L9 **Sagaing** *div* Burma
89 F4 **Sagala** Mali 14.09N 6.38W
28 D3 **Sagalair R** Andhra Prad **India**
36 E5 **Sagalassus** *anc site* Turkey 37.38N 30.30E
20 B3 **Sagamihara** Kanagawa Japan
20 N7 **Sagami-nada** *sea* Japan
20 N6 **Sagami-wan** *B* Japan
104 F6 **Sagamore** Pennsylvania 40.46N 79.14W
119 D4 **Sagamoso,R** Colombia
87 F8 **Sagan** *watercourse* Ethiopia
93 J6 **Sagana** Kenya 0.40S 37.13E
100 M2 **Saganaga L** Ontario 48.15N 90.55W
99 H3 **Saganash L** Ontario 49.04N 82.35W
41 N7 **Sagandzha** *R* U.S.S.R.
87 G3 **Saganeiti** Ethiopia 15.02N 39.12E
20 E8 **Saganoseki** Japan 33.16N 131.51E
25 E6 **Saganthit Kyun** *isld* Burma
42 F6 **Sagan-Tolagay** U.S.S.R. 50.00N 95.32E
103 K5 **Sagaponack** Long I, N Y 40.56N 72.16W
28 C2 **Sagar** Gulbarga, Karnataka **India** 16.37N 76.45E
29 F6 **Sagar** Madhya Prad **India** 23.50N 78.44E
28 B3 **Sagar** Shimoga, Karnataka **India** 14.07N 75.00E
29 F6 **Sagar** *dist* Madhya Prad **India**
20 M7 **Sagara** Japan 34.38N 138.11E
92 H5 **Sagara** *tribe* Tanzania
92 E4 **Sagara, L** Tanzania
43 F7 **Sagar-Chaga** Turkmeniya **U.S.S.R.** 37.44N 61.40E
63 T3 **Sagard** E Germany 54.32N 13.35E
44 G6 **Sagaredzho** Georgia **U.S.S.R.** 41.44N 45.16E
29 L7 **Sagar I** W Bengal **India**
31 J10 **Sagaria** Bangladesh 22.11N 91.06E
75 R4 **S'Agaró** Spain 41.47N 3.03E
30 J8 **Sagarpur** Bihar **India** 24.39N 85.02E
41 N4 **Sagastyr** U.S.S.R. 73.27N 126.20E
89 B4 **Sagata** Senegal 15.11N 15.34W
30 H6 **Sagauli** Bihar **India** 26.46N 84.45E
113 N2 **Sagavanirkok** *R* Alaska
63 H7 **Sage** W Germany 52.57N 8.13E
110 P8 **Sage** Wyoming 41.49N 110.59W
110 P1 **Sage Cr** Montana
108 C8 **Sage Cr** Wyoming
52 H6 **Sågen** Sweden 60.17N 14.10E
112 H2 **Sagerton** Texas 33.05N 99.57W
51 E4 **Sagfjord** Norway 68.00N 15.50E
51 F5 **Saggat** *L* Sweden 66.54N 17.50E
86 N5 **Saggi** *watercourse* **Israel**
32 F4 **Saghand** Iran 32.33N 55.12E
103 K5 **Sag Harbor** Long I, N Y 40.59N 72.18W
Saghzi *see* **Sajzi**
75 F5 **Sagides** Spain 41.08N 2.16W
113 S10 **Sagigik I** Aleutian Is 51.59N 173.09W
106 L6 **Saginaw** Michigan 43.25N 83.54W
112 M9 **Saginaw** Texas 32.50N 97.24W
106 L6 **Saginaw B** Michigan
93 E6 **Sagitu I** Uganda 0.01S 33.40E
43 C3 **Sagiz** Kazakhstan **U.S.S.R.** 47.31N 53.16E
43 C3 **Sagiz** *R* Kazakhstan **U.S.S.R.**
97 N6 **Saglek B** Labrador, Nfld
97 M5 **Saglouc** Quebec 62.10N 75.40W
42 E6 **Sagly** U.S.S.R. 50.31N 91.15E
66 D3 **Sagne,la** Switzerland 47.03N 6.48E
106 F3 **Sagola** Michigan 46.05N 88.04W
67 O12 **Sagone** Corsica 42.07N 8.42E
67 O12 **Sagone,G.de** Corsica 42.03N 8.42E
29 D6 **Sagor** Madhya Prad **India** 22.38N 75.40E
77 Q3 **Sagra** Spain 38.49N 0.05W
79 O3 **Sagrado** Italy 45.52N 13.29E
77 L5 **Sagra,La** *mt* Spain 37.57N 2.34W
76 L2 **Sagra,Peña** *mt* Spain 43.10N 4.29W
90 D10 **Sagre, Pta. de** Fernando Póo **Eq Guinea** 3.20N 8.25E
76 B14 **Sagres** Portugal 37.01N 8.56W
76 B14 **Sagres, Pta de** *C* Portugal 37.01N 8.56W
30 G6 **Sagri** Uttar Prad **India** 26.10N 83.16E
79 L2 **Sagron,Pizzo di** *mt* Italy 46.11N 11.56E
15 K6 **Sag Sag** New Britain 5.34S 148.22E
22 D4 **Sagsay** *R* Mongolia
29 D6 **Sagthale** Rajasthan **India** 23.47N 74.48E
25 C2 **Sagu** Burma 20.11N 94.46E
19 C8 **Sagu** Indonesia 8.16S 123.15E
109 D3 **Saguache** Colorado 38.05N 106.10W
116 G4 **Sagua de Tánamo** **Cuba** 20.38N 75.14W
116 D3 **Sagua la Grande** **Cuba** 22.48N 80.06W
111 N8 **Saguaro L** Arizona 33.36N 111.30W
111 O9 **Saguaro Nat. Mon** Arizona 32.12N 110.20W
98 B5 **Saguenay R** Quebec
88 H8 **Saguia el Hamra** *watercourse* **Morocco**
75 K8 **Sagunto** Spain 39.40N 0.17W
53 S19 **Sagvåg** Norway 59.46N 5.25E
29 D6 **Sagwara** Rajasthan **India** 23.42N 74.03E
113 N2 **Sagwon** Alaska 69.22N 148.42W
71 G3 **Sagy** France 46.35N 5.19E
24 F11 **Sa'gya** Xizang Zizhiqu **China** 28.50N 88.10E
44 K3 **Sagyndyk,Mys** *C* Kazakhstan **U.S.S.R.** 44.03N 50.53E
41 H5 **Sagyr** U.S.S.R. 72.29N 103.17E
44 J7 **Sagyrly** Azerbaydzhan **U.S.S.R.** 40.25N 48.26E
30 D7 **Sah** Uttar Prad **India** 25.54N 80.43E
35 H6 **Sahab** Jordan 31.52N 36.00E
Sahabad *see* **Shāhābād**
86 K5 **Saḩâba, Gebel** *hill* Egypt 30.17N 33.08E
30 L6 **Sahabganj** Bihar **India** 26.25N 87.10E
86 O7 **Sahāb,Wādī es** *watercourse* **Saudi Arabia**
33 H3 **Şaḩāf, As** Saudi Arabia 26.55N 48.37E
119 C3 **Sahagun** Colombia 8.58N 75.30W
76 J4 **Sahagún** Spain 42.23N 5.02W
95 B7 **Sahamandrevo** Madagascar 23.15S 45.35E
95 C7 **Sahambano** Madagascar 22.29S 46.15E
32 B2 **Sahand, Kūh-e** *mt* Iran 37.37N 46.29E
30 A5 **Sahar** Uttar Prad **India** 27.38N 77.29E
29 D5 **Sahara** Rajasthan **India** 25.10N 74.15E
73 D3 **Sahara** *des* N Africa
86 M9 **Sahara,Gebel** *hill* Egypt 28.00N 34.08E
30 A3 **Saharanpur** Uttar Prad **India** 29.58N 77.33E
30 A2 **Saharanpur** *dist* Uttar Prad **India**
14 E5 **Sahara Well** W Australia 21.23S 123.30E
88 P4 **Saharien,Atlas** *mts* **Algeria**
30 K7 **Saharsa** Bihar **India** 25.54N 86.36E
30 K7 **Saharsa** *dist* Bihar **India**
95 C6 **Sahasinaka** Madagascar 21.49S 47.51E
30 B4 **Sahaswan** Uttar Prad **India** 28.04N 78.45E
32 F3 **Sahat,Kūh-i** *mt* Iran 35.38N 55.10E
30 H7 **Sahatwar** Uttar Prad **India** 25.50N 84.14E
30 B5 **Sahawar** Uttar Prad **India** 27.48N 78.49E
33 H5 **Sahbā',Wādī as** *watercourse* **Saudi Arabia**
Sahdol *see* **Shahdol**
34 Q4 **Şāhehābād** Iran 34.53N 48.21E
86 K6 **Saheira, Wâdi el** *watercourse* **Egypt**
32 F7 **Sahelī-ye Jazāyer va Banāder-e** *prov* Iran
30 L7 **Sahibganj** Bihar **India** 25.15N 87.40E
30 G6 **Sahibganj** Uttar Prad **India** 26.56N 83.18E
34 K5 **Şāhilīyah** Iraq 33.44N 42.43E
37 C1 **Şahin** Turkey 41.02N 26.51E
37 C3 **Şahinli** Turkey 40.19N 26.45E
87 G5 **Sahint** Ethiopia 10.51N 38.45E
27 L3 **Sahiwal** Pakistan 30.41N 73.11E
31 G5 **Sahiwal** Pakistan 30.14N 73.10E
31 G5 **Sahiwal** Pakistan 31.57N 72.22E
31 G5 **Sahiwal** *dist* **Pakistan**
30 A2 **Sahiya** Uttar Prad **India** 30.36N 77.53E
53 D4 **Sahl** Denmark 56.21N 9.40E
32 H4 **Sahlābād** Iran 32.10N 59.50E
34 M10 **Sahl al Bushuk** *plat* Saudi Arabia
33 C3 **Sahl al Maţrān** Saudi Arabia 26.18N 38.14E
33 M4 **Saḩm** Oman 24.12N 56.51E
33 H6 **Şaḩmā', As** *gravel plain* Saudi Arabia
35 G2 **Sahm el Jawlan** Syria 32.47N 35.56E
34 K8 **Şaḩn, Aş** *plain* Saudi Arabia
32 B3 **Şaḩneh** Iran 34.29N 47.40E
Şahouet el Kameh *see* **Sahwat el Qamh**
82 F7 **Šahovići** Yugoslavia 43.14N 19.39E
86 G9 **Sahra esh Sharqiya** *des* **Egypt**
86 F4 **Şahragt el Kubra** Egypt 30.39N 31.17E
19 E3 **Sahu** Halmahera Indon 1.09N 127.24E
115 E3 **Sahuaripa** Mexico 29.00N 109.13W
111 O10 **Sahuarita** Arizona 41.59N 110.57W
115 H7 **Sahuayo** Mexico 20.05N 102.42W
71 G8 **Sahune** France 44.24N 5.17E
33 D4 **Şāḩūq** *dist* Saudi Arabia
33 D4 **Şāḩūq,Wādī** *watercourse* **Saudi Arabia**
25 K5 **Sa Huynh** Vietnam 14.38N 109.02E
35 J3 **Şahwat el Qamh** Syria 32.35N 36.22E
62 L7 **Šahy** Czechoslovakia 48.04N 18.55E
Sahyadri *mts see* **Western Ghats**
29 D7 **Sahyadriparvat Ra** Maharashtra **India**
34 D3 **Sahyūn** *anc site* Syria 35.36N 36.05E
30 D5 **Sai** *R* Hardoi, Uttar Prad **India**
20 L5 **Sai** *R* Japan
30 F7 **Sai** *R* Jaunpur, Uttar Prad **India**
91 C5 **Saïak** Gabon 2.08S 13.23E
15 G8 **Saibai I** Torres Str, Qnsld 9.23S 142.40E
18 C6 **Saibi** Indonesia 1.22S 98.52E
34 J10 **Sa'ibiyah,As** Saudi Arabia 28.08N 41.48E
25 F9 **Sai Buri** Thailand 6.45N 101.30E
25 F9 **Sai Buri** *R* Thailand
88 O4 **Saïda** Algeria 34.50N 0.10E
34 C5 **Saïda** Lebanon 33.32N 35.22E
35 H3 **Saida** Syria 32.37N 36.14E
32 F6 **Sa'īdābād** Kermān Iran 29.28N 55.44E
32 F2 **Sa'īdābād** Semnān Iran 36.05N 54.18E
30 F7 **Saidabad** Uttar Prad **India** 25.21N 82.07E
74 H9 **Saïda, Mts. de** **Algeria**
25 G6 **Sai Dao Tai,Khao** *mt* Thailand 12.56N 102.12E
28 C8 **Saidapet** *dist* Madras, Tamil Nadu **India**
90 M7 **Said Bundas** Sudan 8.24N 24.48E
88 K10 **Saïd,El** Mauritania 23.32N 6.43W
85 L6 **Sa'id,Es** *reg* Egypt
32 K7 **Sa'īdī** Iran 27.50N 62.20E
74 F9 **Saïdia** Morocco 35.04N 2.15W
15 J6 **Saidor** Papua New Guinea 5.38S 146.28E
31 H8 **Saidpur** Bangladesh 25.48N 89.00E
30 A4 **Saidpur** Bulandshahr, Uttar Prad **India** 28.37N 77.54E
30 G7 **Saidpur** Ghazipur, Uttar Prad **India** 25.33N 83.13E
31 G3 **Saidu** Pakistan 34.43N 72.24E
66 E2 **Saignelégier** Switzerland 47.16N 7.01E
72 J5 **Saignes** France 45.20N 2.28E
20 G5 **Saigō** Japan 36.12N 133.19E
Saigon *see* **Ho Chi Minh**
25 J7 **Saigon** *R* Vietnam
Saih *see* **Sayḩ, As**
Saihan Tal *see* **Sonid Youqi**
22 E6 **Saihan Toroi** Nei Monggol Zizhiqu **China** 41.50N 100.30E
15 K8 **Saiho** Papua New Guinea 8.45S 148.05E
Saihut *see* **Sayḩūt**
85 L9 **Sai I** Sudan 20.40N 30.21E
51 O4 **Saija** Finland 67.07N 28.46E
20 F7 **Saijō** Japan 34.27N 132.43E
20 G8 **Saijō** Japan 33.55N 133.10E
28 K2 **Saikhoa Ghat** Assam **India** 27.46N 95.38E
20 E9 **Saiki** Japan 32.58N 131.51E
20 E8 **Saiki-wan** *B* Japan
Sail *see* **Sayl al Kabīr,As**
29 D6 **Sailana** Madhya Prad **India** 23.28N 74.58E
15 A4 **Saileen** Salawati I, Irian Jaya 1.20S 130.56E
72 J11 **Saillagouse** France 42.28N 2.02E
71 G7 **Saillans** France 44.41N 5.12E
71 D6 **Saillant** France 45.26N 3.55E
71 D4 **Sail-les-Bains** France 46.14N 3.50E
66 E7 **Saillon** Switzerland 46.11N 7.11E
15 A4 **Sailolo** Salawati I, Irian Jaya 1.15S 130.47E
110 K7 **Sailor Cr** Idaho
26 B15 **Sail Rock** Heard I **Antarctica** 52.54S 73.33E
96 R8 **Sail Rock** Madeira Is
71 D5 **Sail-sous-Couzan** France 45.43N 3.58E
21 C7 **Saima** Liaoning **China** 40.59N 124.14E
51 N10 **Saimaa** *L* Finland
51 N10 **Saimaan Canal** Finland/U.S.S.R.
Saimarreh *R see* **Şimareh** *R*
36 J4 **Saimbeyli** Turkey 38.07N 36.08E
32 F5 **Sā'īn** Iran 30.14N 54.18E
115 H6 **Sain Alto** Mexico 23.36N 103.14W
71 F5 **Sain-Bel** France 45.49N 4.35E
71 C3 **Saincaize-Meauce** France 46.55N 3.04E
31 A6 **Saindak** Pakistan 29.16N 61.38E
Sain Diz *see* **Shāhīn Dezh**
69 D2 **Sainghin-en-Weppes** France 50.34N 2.54E
30 A1 **Sainj** Himachal Prad **India** 31.45N 77.18E
Sainkeduk *see* **Selenek**
Saīn Qal'eh *see* **Shāhīn Dezh**
69 G3 **Sains-du-Nord** France 50.06N 4.01E
69 F4 **Sains-Richaumont** France 49.49N 3.43E
58 M7 **St. Abbs** Borders **Scotland** 55.54N 2.08W
Ste Adelaide *see* **Pabos**
99 Q7 **Ste.Adèle** Quebec 45.58N 74.10W
70 L2 **Ste.Adresse** France 49.31N 0.05E
65 N6 **St.Aegyd am Neuwalde** Austria 47.52N 15.35E
72 K8 **St.Affrique** France 43.58N 2.53E
99 T6 **St.Agapit** Quebec 46.34N 71.26W
St. Agatha-Berchem *see* **Berchem**
61 J3 **St.Agatha-Rode** Belgium 50.47N 4.38E
100 U9 **Ste.Agathe** Manitoba 49.35N 97.10W
99 Q6 **Ste.Agathe des Monts** Quebec 46.03N 74.19W
70 M5 **St.Agil** France 48.02N 0.56E
71 D3 **St.Agnan** France 46.30N 3.54E
71 G7 **St.Agnan-en-Vercors** France 44.56N 5.26E
72 B4 **St.Agnant** France 45.53N 0.58W
56 T9 **St.Agnes** Cornwall **Eng** 50.18N 5.13W
99 U3 **Ste. Agnès** Quebec 45.01N 74.25W
56 Q8 **St.Agnes** *isld* Is of Scilly **Eng** 49.54N 6.21W
71 E6 **St.Agrève** France 45.00N 4.24E
72 G1 **St.Aignan** France 47.16N 1.22E
70 H6 **St.Aignan-sur-Roë** France 47.51N 1.08W
72 D5 **St.Aigulin** France 45.10N 0.01W
74 H9 **St.Aime** Algeria 35.54N 0.50E
71 F4 **St.Albain** France 46.25N 4.52E
70 E4 **St.Alban** France 48.34N 2.33W
71 D4 **St.Alban-les-Eaux** France 46.00N 3.56E
56 L4 **St.Albans** Herts **Eng** 51.46N 0.21W
98 R6 **St.Alban's** Newfoundland 47.51N 55.50W
103 L8 **St.Albans** New York 40.42N 73.45W
104 M2 **St.Albans** Vermont 44.49N 73.07W
104 D8 **St.Albans** W Virginia 38.24N 81.53W
11 M9 **St. Albans** *dist* Christchurch **New Zealand**
56 G6 **St.Albans Hd** Dorset **Eng** 50.34N 2.04W
71 C7 **St.Alban-sur-Limagnole** France 44.46N 3.24E
100 D5 **St.Albert** Alberta 53.39N 113.32W
98 C6 **St.Alexandre** Quebec 47.40N 69.40W
99 R6 **St.Alexis des Monts** Quebec 46.27N 73.10W
72 F6 **St.Alvère** France 44.56N 0.48E
71 B6 **St.Alyre-ès-Montagne** France 45.23N 2.59E
61 J4 **St.Amand** Belgium 50.30N 4.33E
71 C1 **St.Amand-en-Puisaye** France 47.32N 3.04E
69 E3 **St.Amand-les-Eaux** France 50.27N 3.26E
70 N6 **St. Amand-Longpré** France 47.41N 1.01E
72 J2 **St. Amand-Mont-Rond** France 46.43N 2.29E
61 G2 **St.Amands** Belgium 51.03N 4.12E
61 F2 **St.Amandsberg** Belgium 51.04N 3.46E
69 H6 **St.Amand-sur-Fion** France 48.49N 4.37E
72 C2 **St.Amand-sur-Sèvre** France 46.52N 0.47W
71 C7 **St.Amans** Lozère France 44.40N 3.26E
71 B9 **St Amans-de-Mounis** Hérault **France** 43.41N 2.58E
72 K6 **St. Amans-des-Cots** France 44.42N 2.40E
72 J9 **St. Amans Soult** France 43.28N 2.28E
71 D5 **St.Amant-Roche-Savine** France 45.34N 3.38E
71 C5 **St.Amant-Tallende** France 45.40N 3.06E
69 N8 **St.Amarin** France 47.53N 7.03E
99 T4 **St.-Ambroise** Quebec 48.33N 71.20W
72 J2 **St.Ambroix** Cher France 46.56N 2.04E
71 E8 **St.Ambroix** Gard France 44.15N 4.12E
71 G4 **St.Amour** France 46.26N 5.20E
98 D5 **St.Anaclet** Quebec 48.29N 68.28W
71 F9 **St.Andiol** France 43.50N 4.56E
65 L8 **St.Andra im Lavanttal** Austria 46.47N 14.49E
61 O4 **St.André** Belgium 50.42N 5.45E
70 F7 **St.André** France 47.20N 2.18W
26 U11 **St Andre** Mauritius, Indian Oc 20.05S 57.34E
26 U14 **St.-André** Réunion Ind Oc 20.57S 55.39E
63 N9 **St.Andreasberg** W Germany 51.43N 10.30E
84 T13 **St.Andreas,C** Cyprus 35.40N 34.36E
84 T13 **St.Andreas Monastery** Cyprus 35.38N 34.35E
95 B4 **St.André,C** Madagascar 16.10S 44.27E
71 F5 **St.André-de-Corcy** France 45.56N 4.57E
71 E8 **St.André-de-Cruzières** France 44.20N 4.12E
72 D6 **St.André-de-Cubzac** France 44.59N 0.27W
70 N4 **St.André-de-l'Eure** France 48.55N 1.17E
71 K7 **St.André-d'Embrun** France 44.35N 6.33E
72 K9 **St.André-de-Roquelongue** France 43.07N 2.50E
71 D9 **St.André-de-Sangonis** France 43.39N 3.30E
71 D8 **St.André-de-Valborgne** France 44.10N 3.40E
71 D2 **St. André-en-Morvan** France 47.23N 3.50E
71 H5 **St.André-le-Gaz** France 45.33N 5.32E
71 K9 **St.André-les-Alpes** France 43.58N 6.30E
70 N4 **St.André,Plaine de** France
105 B7 **St.Andrew** Florida 30.11N 85.44W
116 P1 **St.Andrew** *co* Trinidad & Tobago
116 P6 **St.Andrew** *parish* Barbados
116 L2 **St.Andrew** *parish* Jamaica, W I
105 B7 **St.Andrew B** Florida
58 L6 **St.Andrews** Fife **Scotland** 56.20N 2.48W
98 E8 **St.Andrew's** New Brunswick 45.05N 67.04W
98 N6 **St.Andrew's** Newfoundland 47.45N 59.15W
11 F11 **St.Andrews** New Zealand 44.32S 171.11E
58 T12 **St.Andrews** Orkney **Scotland** 58.57N 2.51W
98 M7 **St.Andrew's Chan** C Breton I, Nova Scotia
105 F7 **St.Andrew Sd** Georgia 30.58N 81.25W
61 C2 **St.Andries** Belgium 51.12N 3.11E
72 E4 **St.Angeau** France 45.50N 0.18E
72 J5 **St.Angel** France 45.30N 2.14E
108 K9 **St.Ann** Nebraska 40.28N 100.42W
116 K1 **St. Ann** *parish* Jamaica, W I
116 B1 **St.Anna-baai** *B* Curaçao **W I** 12.12N 68.57W
60 E13 **St.Annaland** Netherlands 51.37N 4.06E
60 L6 **St.Annaparochie** Netherlands 53.17N 5.40E
60 A3 **St Anna ter Muiden** Netherlands 51.20N 3.27E
70 M4 **Ste.Anne** France 48.35N 0.42E
116 N4 **Ste.Anne** Guadeloupe **W I** 16.13N 61.23W
106 G8 **St.Anne** Illinois 41.02N 87.41W
100 E1 **Ste. Anne** Manitoba 49.40N 96.40W
116 L4 **Ste.Anne** Martinique **W I** 14.26N 60.53W
26 V15 **Ste.-Anne** Réunion Ind Oc 21.04S 55.45E
70 E6 **Ste.Anne-d'Auray** France 47.43N 2.57W
98 B6 **Ste.Anne de Beaupré** Quebec 47.02N 70.58W
99 O10 **Ste. Anne de Bellevue** Quebec 45.24N 73.53W
99 S6 **Ste.Anne de la Pérade** Quebec 46.35N 72.14W
Ste. Anne de la Pocatière *see* **La Pocatière**
98 F4 **Ste.Anne-des-Monts** Quebec 49.07N 66.29W
99 P6 **Ste.Anne du Lac** Quebec 46.52N 75.21W
26 S13 **St.Anne I** Mahé I **Seychelles, Ind Oc** 4.36S 55.30E
98 E3 **Ste.Anne,L** Quebec
100 C5 **Ste. Anne, Lac** Alberta 53.45N 114.51W
98 B6 **Ste.Anne,R** Quebec
70 F2 **St.Annes** Channel Is 49.43N 2.12W
98 M7 **St Anns** C Breton I, Nova Scotia 46.15N 60.40W
13 H5 **St.Anns** Queensland 21.12S 146.55E
98 M7 **St. Anns Bay** C Breton I, Nova Scotia
116 K1 **St.Ann's Bay** Jamaica, **W I** 18.26N 77.12W
57 G2 **St.Ann's Bridge** Dumfries & Galloway **Scotland** 55.13N 3.29W
56 A4 **St.Ann's Hd** Dyfed **Wales** 51.41N 5.10W
108 S6 **St.Ansgar** Iowa 43.25N 92.53W
61 F3 **St.Antelinks** Belgium 50.51N 3.55E
71 D5 **St.Anthême** France 45.32N 3.55E
60 M13 **St.Anthonis** Netherlands 51.38N 5.53E
110 O6 **St.Anthony** Idaho 43.59N 111.40W
98 R2 **St.Anthony** Newfoundland 51.24N 55.37W
St. Antoine *see* **Goodlands**
71 G10 **St.Antoine** Bouches-du-Rhône **France** 43.22N 5.21E
66 D1 **St. Antoine** Haut-Rhin **France** 47.47N 6.46E
66 B4 **St. Antoine** Jura **France** 46.47N 6.20E
67 O12 **St.Antoine,Col** *pass* Corsica 42.10N 8.48E
65 B7 **St.Anton** Tirol **Austria** 47.09N 10.17E
66 Q3 **St. Anton** Vorarlberg **Austria** 47.08N 9.52E
66 Q4 **St.Antönien** Switzerland 46.58N 9.48E
98 C6 **St.Antonin** Quebec 47.45N 69.28W
72 H7 **St. Antonin-Noble-Val** France 44.10N 1.44E
86 H8 **St.Antony,Monastery of** **Egypt**
72 H2 **St.Août** France 46.44N 1.57E
72 F5 **St.Aquilin** France 45.11N 0.30E
70 N3 **St.Aquilin-de-Pacy** France 49.00N 1.21E
71 D6 **St.Arcons-d'Allier** France 45.04N 3.33E
St.Arnaud *see* **Eulma,El**
11 G8 **St.Arnaud** New Zealand 41.49S 172.53E
12 G6 **St.Arnaud** Victoria 36.40S 143.20E
11 G8 **St.Arnaud Ra** **New Zealand**
72 B9 **St. Arnéguy** France 43.06N 1.17W
69 B6 **St Arnoux** France 48.34N 1.58E
98 C6 **St.Arsène** Quebec 47.56N 69.26W
13 B1 **St.Asaph B** N Terr **Australia**
72 F5 **St.Astier** Dordogne **France** 45.09N 0.32E
72 E6 **St.Astier** Lot-et-Garonne **France** 44.43N 0.14E
98 C6 **St.Athanase** Quebec 47.25N 69.26W
71 J8 **St.Auban** Alpes de Haute Provence **France** 44.04N 6.00E
71 K9 **St.Auban** Alpes-Maritimes **France** 43.51N 6.44E
71 G8 **St.Auban-sur-l'Ouvéze** France 44.17N 5.25E
98 B6 **St.Aubert** Quebec 47.10N 70.14W
61 J5 **St.Aubin** Belgium 50.15N 4.35E
70 K3 **St.Aubin** Calvados **France** 49.19N 0.24W
70 F3 **St.Aubin** Channel Is 49.12N 2.10W
71 G2 **St.Aubin** Jura **France** 47.02N 5.20E
66 D4 **St.Aubin** Neuchâtel **Switzerland** 46.54N 6.57E
71 C1 **St. Aubin-Château-Neuf** France 47.50N 3.18E
70 G5 **St.Aubin-d'Aubigné** France 48.16N 1.36W
72 C5 **St.Aubin-de-Blaye** France 45.17N 0.34W
70 L3 **St.Aubin-de-Scellon** France 49.10N 0.29E
70 H4 **St.Aubin-de-Terregatte** France 48.34N 1.19W
70 H5 **St.Aubin-du-Cormier** France 48.16N 1.24W
70 N2 **St.Aubin-le-Cauf** France 49.52N 1.12E
56 W11 **St.Aubin's B** Channel Is
69 J6 **St.Aubin-sur-Aire** France 48.43N 5.27E
72 B4 **St.Augustin** Charente-Maritime **France** 45.42N 1.06W
72 H5 **St.Augustin** Corrèze **France** 45.26N 1.49E
95 A7 **St.Augustin** Madagascar 23.31S 43.46E
64 C2 **St. Augustin** W Germany 50.47N 7.10E
98 O2 **St.Augustin B** Quebec
70 J7 **St.Augustin-des-Bois** France 47.27N 0.46W
105 F8 **St.Augustine** Florida 29.54N 81.19W
98 N2 **St.Augustin R** Quebec
98 O2 **St.Augustin-Saguenay** Quebec 51.15N 58.40W
72 D5 **St.Aulais-la-Chapelle** France 45.26N 0.02W
72 E5 **St.Aulaye** France 45.12N 0.08E
56 B7 **St.Austell** Cornwall **Eng** 50.20N 4.48W
56 B7 **St.Austell B** Cornwall **Eng**
70 M7 **St.Avertin** France 47.22N 0.44E
71 B5 **St.Avit** France 45.52N 2.32E
69 M5 **St.Avold** France 49.06N 6.43E
71 K10 **St.Aygulf** France 43.24N 6.43E
61 D3 **Ste.Baafs-Vijve** Belgium 50.54N 3.24E
71 C5 **St.Babel** France 45.36N 3.17E
99 S6 **St.Barnabé Nord** Quebec 46.24N 72.54W
99 R6 **St. Barthélémi** Quebec 46.12N 73.08W
69 E6 **St.Barthélemy** France 48.49N 3.23E
116 N6 **St Barthélémy** / Lesser Antilles 17.55N 62.50W
72 E6 **St. Barthélemy d'Agenais** France 44.31N 0.22E
72 E5 **St.Barthélemy-de-Bellegarde** France 45.04N 0.13E
72 H10 **St.Barthélemy,Pic de** France 42.49N 1.45E
11 D11 **St.Bathans** New Zealand 44.52S 169.50E
11 D11 **St.Bathan's,Mt** New Zealand 44.44S 169.49E
72 J2 **St.Baudel** France 46.50N 2.11E
71 H10 **Ste.Baume** *hills* France
71 D9 **St.Bauzille-de-Putois** France 43.53N 3.44E
72 E6 **St.Bazeille** France 44.32N 0.06E
72 F10 **St. Béar** France 42.55N 0.42E
72 K7 **St. Beauzély** France 44.10N 2.56E
57 F4 **St.Bees** Cumbria **Eng** 54.29N 3.35W
57 F3 **St.Bees Hd** Cumbria **Eng** 54.31N 3.39W
108 Q6 **St.Benedict** Iowa 43.02N 94.02W
100 M6 **St.Benedict** Saskatchewan 52.34N 105.23W
71 C3 **St.Benin-d'Azy** France 47.00N 3.24E
72 G3 **St. Benoîr-du-Sault** France 46.26N 1.23E
72 J9 **St.Benoit** Aude France 43.01N 2.04E
26 V15 **St.-Benoit** Réunion Ind Oc 21.02S 55.43E
72 E2 **St.Benoit** Vienne France 46.33N 0.20E
98 B7 **St.Benoit Labre** Quebec 46.07N 70.48W
70 P6 **St.Benoît-sur-Loire** France 47.48N 2.18E
71 F3 **St.Bèrain-sur-Dheune** France 46.49N 4.35E
72 A2 **St. Berm-sur-Mer** France 46.36N 1.50W
98 H5 **Ste.Bernadette** Quebec 48.30N 64.49W
99 T6 **St. Bernard** Quebec 46.29N 71.09W
11 H9 **St.Bernard** *mt* New Zealand 42.07S 173.25E
79 B3 **St.Bernard,Col du Grand** *pass* **Italy/Switz** 45.52N 7.11E
79 A3 **St.Bernard,Col du Picco** *pass* **Italy/France** 45.40N 6.53E
99 Q10 **St.Bernard I** Quebec
107 J2 **St.Bernice** Indiana 39.42N 87.30W
71 H5 **St. Béron** France 45.31N 5.43E
70 J5 **St.Berthevin** France 48.04N 0.50W
72 F9 **St.Bertrand-de-Comminges** France 43.02N 0.34E
66 D3 **St.Blaise** Switzerland 47.01N 6.59E
69 N7 **St. Blaise-la-Roche** France 48.24N 7.10E
95 F10 **St.Blaize,C** S Africa 34.12S 22.10E
98 D5 **Ste.Blandine** Quebec 48.23N 68.29W
64 E8 **St.Blasien** W Germany 47.46N 8.08E
61 E3 **St.Blasius-Boekel** Belgium 50.51N 3.43E
56 B7 **St.Blazey** Cornwall **Eng** 50.22N 4.43W
69 J7 **St.Blin** France 48.17N 5.26E
71 F3 **St.Boil** France 46.40N 4.40E
100 U9 **St.Boniface** Manitoba 49.54N 97.07W
72 D5 **St.Bonnet** Charente **France** 45.29N 0.07W
71 J7 **St.Bonnet** Hautes-Alpes **France** 44.40N 6.05E
72 G4 **St.Bonnet-Briance** France 45.42N 1.29E
72 F3 **St. Bonnet de-Bellac** France 46.11N 0.57E
71 E4 **St.Bonnet-de-Joux** France 46.29N 4.26E
72 L3 **St.Bonnet-de-Rochefort** France 46.09N 3.07E
71 E4 **St.Bonnet-des-Bruyères** France 46.17N 4.28E
71 G3 **St.Bonnet-en-Bresse** France 46.51N 5.10E
71 E6 **St.Bonnet-le Château** France 45.25N 4.04E
71 E6 **St.Bonnet-le-Froid** France 45.09N 4.27E
72 C5 **St.Bonnet-sur-Gironde** France 45.22N 0.39W
72 K2 **St. Bonnet Tronçais** Allier France 46.40N 2.41E
71 K6 **St. Bon-Tarentaise** France 45.26N 6.37E
57 H1 **St.Boswells** Borders **Scotland** 55.34N 2.38W
100 L8 **St.Boswells** Saskatchewan 50.04N 106.47W
66 E2 **St.Brais** Switzerland 47.18N 7.07E
71 D2 **St.Brancher** France 47.26N 3.59E
72 F1 **St. Branchs** France 47.15N 0.46E
98 T5 **St.Brendan's** Newfoundland 48.53N 53.40W
70 F7 **St.Brévin-les-Pins** France 47.16N 2.09W
70 F4 **St.Briac** France 48.37N 2.08W
70 H5 **St.Brice-en-Cogles** France 48.25N 1.22W
68 F1 **St.Brice-sous-Forêt** France 49.00N 2.21E
100 B7 **St. Bride, Mt** Alberta 51.34N 115.50W
56 A4 **St.Brides** Dyfed **Wales** 51.46N 5.11W
98 S7 **St Bride's** Newfoundland 46.56N 54.10W
56 A4 **St.Brides B** Dyfed **Wales**
70 E4 **St.Brieuc** France 48.31N 2.45W
70 E4 **St.Brieuc,B.de** France
100 N6 **St.Brieux** Saskatchewan 52.39N 104.54W
69 F8 **St.Bris-le-Vineux** France 47.45N 3.39E
71 E2 **St.Brisson** France 47.16N 4.04E
70 G4 **St.Broladre** France 48.35N 1.38W
56 S9 **St.Buryan** Cornwall **Eng** 50.04N 5.37W
70 M6 **St.Calais** France 47.55N 0.45E
98 B7 **St. Camille** Quebec 46.29N 70.12W
71 G9 **St.Cannat** France 43.37N 5.17E
70 E5 **St.Caradec** France 48.11N 2.51W
70 E5 **St. Carreuc** France 48.24N 2.44W
99 S6 **St.Casimir** Quebec 46.39N 72.09W
70 F4 **St.Cast** France 48.38N 2.15W
107 G11 **St. Catharine, L** Louisiana 30.10N 89.45W
99 L9 **St.Catharines** Ontario 43.10N 79.15W
116 K2 **St.Catherine** *parish* Jamaica, **W I**
99 S10 **St.Catherine Lock** Quebec 45.24N 73.34W
86 L8 **St.Catherine,Monastery of** **Egypt** 28.33N 33.58E
116 P5 **St. Catherine, Mt** Grenada, **W I** 12.10N 61.40W
116 P5 **St Catherine, Mt** Grenada, **W I** 12.10S 61.43W
91 A4 **Ste.Catherine,Pte** Gabon 1.56S 9.20E
58 F6 **St.Catherines** Strathclyde **Scotland** 56.13N 5.02W
105 F6 **St.Catherines I** Georgia 31.35N 81.10W
96 C1 **St. Catherine's Pt** Bermuda 32.24N 64.42W
56 J6 **St.Catherine's Pt** I of Wight **Eng** 50.34N 1.18W
105 F6 **St Catherines Sd** Georgia 31.45N 81.05W
61 L8 **Ste.Cécile** Belgium 49.44N 5.15E
98 B8 **Ste.Cécile** Quebec 45.40N 70.57W
71 D8 **St.Cécile-d'Andorge** France 44.15N 3.58E
71 F8 **St.Cécile-les-Vignes** France 44.15N 4.53E
72 H6 **St.Cére** France 44.52N 1.53E
66 A6 **St.Cergue** Switzerland 46.27N 6.10E
72 J5 **St.Cernin** France 45.03N 2.24E
72 G6 **St.Cernin-de-l'Herm** France 44.38N 1.02E
99 R7 **St.Césaire** Quebec 45.25N 73.01W
71 K9 **St. Cézaire-sur-Siagne** France 43.38N 6.48E
71 K7 **St.Chaffrey** France 44.56N 6.35E
71 G9 **St.Chamas** France 43.32N 5.02E
71 F6 **St.Chamond** France 45.29N 4.32E
71 E9 **St.Chaptes** France 43.58N 4.17E
88 R3 **St.Charles** Algeria 36.47N 6.53E
110 O7 **St.Charles** Idaho 42.06N 111.24W
106 F8 **St.Charles** Illinois 41.56N 88.20W
100 A2 **St.Charles** Manitoba 49.50N 97.15W
106 K6 **St.Charles** Michigan 43.17N 84.09W
108 S6 **St.Charles** Minnesota 43.58N 92.03W
107 F3 **St.Charles** Missouri 38.48N 90.29W
98 B7 **St.Charles** Quebec 46.47N 70.58W
98 P8 **St.Charles R** Quebec
72 H2 **St.Chartier** France 46.40N 1.58E
71 G5 **St.Chef** France 45.37N 5.21E
71 C7 **St. Chély d'apcher** France 44.48N 3.17E
72 K6 **St. Chély d'Aubrac** France 44.36N 2.59E
St. Chély-du-Tarn *see* **Mas-St. Chély**
69 C6 **St.Chéron** France 48.33N 2.06E
71 B10 **St.Chinian** France 43.26N 2.57E
116 B1 **St.Christoffel Berg** *mt* Curaçao **W I** 12.26N 69.07W
71 E8 **St. Christol-lès-Alès** France 44.05N 4.04E
71 H8 **St.Christol,Plat.de** France
72 C5 **St. Christoly Médoc** France 45.20N 0.50W
72 A2 **St.Christophe-du-Ligneron** France 46.50N 1.47W
72 H1 **St. Christophe-en-Bazelle** France 47.12N 1.41E
71 E4 **St.Christophe-en-Brion** France 46.18N 4.18E
71 J7 **St. Christophe-en-Oisans** France 44.52N 6.11E
St.Christopher *isld see* **St.Kitts**
72 C5 **St.Ciers-sur-Gironde** France 45.18N 0.36W
71 E7 **St.Cirgues-en-Montagne** France 44.45N 4.05E
72 H7 **St. Cirq Lapopie** France 44.27N 1.40E
70 H3 **St.Clair** France 49.11N 1.03W
106 M7 **St.Clair** Michigan 42.49N 82.30W
108 R5 **St.Clair** Minnesota 44.03N 93.50W
107 F3 **St.Clair** Missouri 38.21N 90.59W
103 B5 **St.Clair** Pennsylvania 40.43N 76.12W
11 L13 **St.Clair** *bor* Dunedin **New Zealand**
106 M7 **St. Clair, L** Michigan/Ontario
12 H9 **St.Clair,L** Tasmania 42.05S 146.09E
99 H9 **St.Clair R** Ontario/Mich

106 P1 **St.Clair Shores** *dist* Detroit, Michigan
70 O3 **St.Clair-sur-Epte** France 49.12N 1.41E
72 F8 **St.Clar** France 43.54N 0.47E
71 H4 **St.Claude** France 46.23N 5.52E
116 M4 **St.Claude** Guadeloupe W I 16.02N 61.42W
100 T9 **St.Claude** Manitoba 49.40N 98.20W
72 E4 **St. Claud-sur-le-Son** France 45.54N 0.28E
56 C4 **St.Clears** Dyfed Wales 51.50N 4.30W
72 H5 **St.Clément** Corrèze France 45.21N 1.40E
69 M6 **St.Clément** Meurthe-et-Moselle France 48.32N 6.34E
98 C6 **St.Clement** Quebec 47.56N 69.06W
69 E7 **St.Clément** Yonne France 48.13N 3.18E
70 J6 **St. Clement-de-la-Place** France 47.32N 0.43W
99 S7 **Ste.Clothilde** Quebec 45.58N 72.16W
St. Cloud Algeria*see* **Gdyel**
105 F9 **St.Cloud** Florida 28.15N 81.16W
68 D3 **St.Cloud** France 48.51N 2.12E
108 Q4 **St.Cloud** Minnesota 45.34N 94.10W
99 T4 **St.-Cœur-de-Marie** Quebec 48.39N 71.43W
71 F5 **Ste.Colombe** Rhône France 45.31N 4.51E
72 H10 **Ste. Colombe-sur-l'Hers** France 42.57N 1.57E
72 A1 **St. Columban** France 47.01N 1.35W
56 B7 **St.Columb Major** Cornwall Eng 50.26N 4.56W
56 A7 **St.Columb Minor** Cornwall Eng 50.26N 5.03W
58 N3 **St.Combs** Grampian Scotland 57.39N 1.55W
St.Côme Quebec *see* **Linière**
99 R6 **St.Côme** Quebec 46.16N 73.47W
70 H3 **St.Côme-du-Mont** France 49.20N 1.16W
72 J6 **St.Constant** France 44.40N 2.12E
99 S10 **St. Constant** Quebec 45.23N 73.35W
70 L5 **St.Cosme-de-Vair** France 48.16N 0.28E
72 F5 **St. Crépin-de-Richemont** France 45.25N 0.37E
72 C8 **St. Cricq Chalosse** France 43.39N 0.42W
71 G7 **Ste.Croix** Drôme France 44.46N 5.17E
98 E8 **Ste.Croix** New Brunswick 45.33N 67.26W
71 G3 **Ste.Croix** Saône-et-Loire France 46.34N 5.14E
66 C4 **Ste.Croix** Switzerland 46.50N 6.31E
106 B4 **St. Croix** *R* Wisconsin
69 N7 **Ste.Croix-aux-Mines** France 48.16N 7.14E
71 D8 **St. Croix de Vallée Française** France 44.12N 3.44E
69 N7 **Ste.Croix-en-Plaine** France 48.01N 7.23E
95 J9 **St.Croix I** S Africa 33.48S 25.46E
98 E8 **Ste.Croix R** Maine/New Bruns
106 B3 **St.Croix,R** Wisconsin
72 G9 **Ste. Croix-Volvestre** France 43.08N 1.10E
56 J5 **St.Cross** Hants Eng 51.03N 1.19W
72 G6 **St.Cyprien** Dordogne France 44.52N 1.03E
72 G7 **St.Cyprien** Lot France 44.19N 1.16E
98 C6 **St.Cyprien** Quebec 47.53N 69.02W
70 K5 **St.Cyr** Mayenne France 48.26N 0.15W
99 P4 **St. Cyr** Quebec
70 J4 **St.Cyr-du-Bailleul** France 48.34N 0.49W
72 D1 **St.Cyr-en-Bourg** France 47.12N 0.03W
70 O6 **St.Cyr-en-Val** France 47.50N 1.58E
99 S7 **St.Cyrille** Quebec 45.55N 72.25W
100 J4 **St. Cyr Lake** Saskatchewan 54.14N 108.02W
68 B4 **St.Cyr-l'École** France 48.48N 2.04E
71 D1 **St.Cyr-les-Colons** France 47.44N 3.43E
71 H10 **St. Cyr-sur-Mer** France 43.10N 5.43E
69 E6 **St.Cyr-sur-Morin** France 48.55N 3.11E
58 M5 **St.Cyrus** Grampian Scotland 56.47N 2.25W
71 M8 **St. Dalmas-de-Tendée** France 44.03N 7.35E
98 B7 **St.Damien** Quebec 46.38N 70.45W
106 D9 **St.David** Illinois 40.30N 90.02W
116 P1 **St.David** *co* Trinidad & Tobago
98 A5 **St.David de Falardeau** Quebec 48.38N 71.08W
98 R9 **St.David-de-Lévis** Quebec 46.47N 71.12W
St.David Is *see* **Mapia,Pulau Pulau**
56 A4 **St.David's** Dyfed Wales 51.54N 5.16W
98 O5 **St.David's** Newfoundland 48.11N 58.52W
56 A4 **St.David's Hd** Dyfed Wales 51.55N 5.19W
96 C1 **St.David's I** Bermuda 32.23N 64.42W
61 D3 **St.Denijs** Belgium 50.45N 3.22E
61 E3 **St.Denijs-Boekel** Belgium 50.52N 3.43E
61 E2 **St.Denijs-Westrem** Belgium 51.02N 3.40E
72 J9 **St.Denis** Aude France 43.21N 2.14E
61 G5 **St.Denis** Hainaut Belgium 50.29N 4.02E
61 K4 **St.Denis** Namur Belgium 50.32N 4.47E
98 C6 **St.Denis** Quebec 47.30N 69.58W
99 R7 **St. Denis** Quebec 45.46N 73.10W
26 U14 **St.-Denis** Réunion Ind Oc 20.52S 55.27E
68 F2 **St.Denis** Seine-St Denis France 48.57N 2.23E
70 K6 **St.Denis-d'Anjou** France 47.47N 0.27W
70 J5 **St.Denis-de-Gastines** France 48.21N 0.51W
72 H2 **St.Denis-de-Jouhet** France 46.31N 1.52E
72 D6 **St.Denis-de-Pile** France 45.00N 0.12W
72 H4 **St.Denis-des-Murs** France 45.46N 1.34E
72 B3 **St. Denis d'Oléron** Charente-Maritime France 46.02N 1.22W
70 K5 **St.Denis-d'Orques** France 48.02N 0.18W
72 B3 **St. Denis-du-Payré** France 46.25N 1.16W
71 G5 **St.Denis-en-Bugey** France 45.56N 5.19E
72 B2 **St. Denis la Chevasse** France 46.49N 1.22W
72 H6 **St. Denis-lès-Martel** France 44.57N 1.36E
70 K5 **St.Denis-sur-Sarthon** France 48.27N 0.04W
70 F4 **St.Denoual** France 48.32N 2.24W
71 F3 **St. Désert** France 46.45N 4.42E
56 F4 **St.Devereux** Hereford & Worcs Eng 51.59N 2.49W
71 E2 **St.Didier** Côte d'Or France 47.19N 4.10E
71 G8 **St.Didier** Vaucluse France 44.01N 5.07E
71 E6 **St.Didier-en-Velay** France 45.18N 4.16E
71 E3 **St.Didier-sur-Arroux** France 46.50N 4.05E
71 F4 **St. Didier-sur-Chalaronne** France 46.12N 4.49E
71 D5 **St.Didier-sur-Rochefort** France 45.47N 3.51E
69 M7 **St.Dié** France 48.17N 6.57E
71 C5 **St. Dier-d'Auvergne** France 45.41N 3.29E
72 C5 **St.Dizant-du-Bois** France 45.24N 0.34W
72 C5 **St.Dizant-du-Gua** France 45.25N 0.52W
66 D2 **St. Dizier** France 47.28N 6.58E
69 H6 **St.Dizier** Haute-Marne France 48.38N 4.58E
72 F6 **St. Dizier** Lot-et-Garonne France 44.40N 0.38E
72 H3 **St. Dizier Leyrenne** France 46.01N 1.42E
70 F6 **St.Dolay** France 47.33N 2.11W
70 G5 **St Domineuc** France 48.22N 1.51W
99 Q6 **St.Donat** Quebec 46.19N 74.15W
71 F6 **St.Donat-sur-l'Herbasse** France 45.07N 4.59E
99 Q9 **Ste Dorothée** Quebec 45.32N 73.47W
72 J1 **St.Doulchard** France 47.07N 2.20E
108 N8 **St.Edward** Nebraska 41.37N 97.53W
71 H6 **St.Egrève** France 45.15N 5.41E
72 K3 **St. Élay les Mines** France 46.10N 2.49E
113 P7 **St.Elias,C** Alaska 59.50N 144.35W
113 R6 **Saint Elias, Mt** Alaska/Yukon Terr 60.14N 140.50W
101 C5 **St.Elias,Mt** Yukon/Alaska 60.12N 140.57W
101 C5 **St.Elias Mts** Yukon/Alaska
117 C2 **St.Elie** Fr Guiana 4.50N 53.21W
99 S4 **Ste.Elisabeth** Quebec 48.57N 72.10W
72 G9 **St. Elix-le-Château** France 43.17N 1.08E
72 E9 **St.Elix-Theux** France 43.26N 0.29E
116 H2 **St.Elizabeth** *parish* Jamaica, W I
107 H2 **St Elmo** Illinois 39.00N 88.51W
98 C5 **St.Eloi** Quebec 48.03N 69.14W
61 D3 **St.Eloois-Vijve** Belgium 50.54N 3.25E
61 C3 **St.Eloois-Winkel** Belgium 50.52N 3.11E
71 B4 **St.Eloy-les-Mines** France 46.10N 2.50E
99 R8 **St.Elzéar de Laval** Quebec 45.36N 73.42W
99 R6 **Ste. Emélie** Quebec 46.19N 73.39W
71 E3 **St.Emiland** France 46.54N 4.30E
72 D6 **St.Emilion** France 44.54N 0.09W
72 C10 **Ste.Engrâce** France 43.00N 0.48W
71 C8 **Ste.Enimie** France 44.22N 3.25E
71 C3 **St.Ennemond** France 46.40N 3.25E
70 H3 **Sainteny** France 49.14N 1.19W
72 F1 **St.Epain** France 47.09N 0.31E
98 B7 **St.Ephrem** Quebec 46.03N 70.59W
99 L3 **St.Ephrem de Paradis** Quebec 49.09N 79.15W
98 C6 **St Epiphane** Quebec 47.52N 69.22E
70 G5 **St.Erblon** France 48.01N 1.38W
69 F4 **St.Erme-Outre-et-Ramecourt** France 49.31N 3.52E
61 G4 **Saintes** Belgium 50.42N 4.10E
72 C4 **Saintes** France 45.44N 0.38W
116 M4 **Saintes, Îles des** Guadeloupe W I
71 E10 **Stes.Maries-de-la-Mer,les** France 43.27N 4.25E
72 B9 **St.Esteben** France 43.21N 1.12W
72 C5 **St.Estèphe** France 45.17N 0.46W
72 K10 **St.Estève** France 42.43N 2.50E
71 H8 **St. Étienne** Alpes de Haute Provence France 44.02N 5.47E
71 E6 **St.Étienne** Loire France 45.26N 4.23E
69 B2 **St Étienne-au-Mont** France 50.40N 1.39E
72 J4 **St.Étienne-aux-Clos** France 45.35N 2.26E
72 J6 **St. Étienne-Cantalès** France 44.57N 2.13E
72 B9 **St. Étienne-de-Baigorry** France 43.11N 1.20W
71 J6 **St.Étienne-de-Cuines** France 45.20N 6.17E
72 H3 **St.Étienne-de-Fursac** France 46.09N 1.31E
71 D7 **St. Etienne de Lugdarès** France 44.39N 3.57E
72 A1 **St.Étienne-de-Montluc** France 47.19N 1.47W
71 G6 **St.Étienne-de-St.Geoirs** France 45.20N 5.20W
71 K8 **St.Étienne-de-Tinée** France 44.15N 6.57E
71 G4 **St.Étienne-du-Bois** France 46.17N 5.17E
70 N3 **St.Étienne-du-Rouvray** France 49.22N 1.07E
71 H7 **St.Étienne-en-Dévoluy** France 44.41N 5.56E
26 T16 **St. Etienne R** Réunion Ind Oc
71 D8 **St.Étienne-Vallée-Française** France 44.10N 3.51E
99 M4 **St.Eugène** Quebec 48.57N 78.57W
99 S4 **St.-Eugène** Quebec 48.59N 72.19W
72 K7 **St. Eulalie d'Olt** France 44.28N 2.56E
72 B7 **Ste.Eulalie-en-Born** France 44.17N 1.10W
98 D6 **St.Eusèbe** Quebec 47.34N 68.57W
99 R7 **St.Eustache** Quebec 45.34N 73.55W
70 L4 **St.Evroult Notre Dame-du-Bois** France 48.47N 0.28E
98 D5 **St.Fabien** Quebec 48.19N 68.51W
95 O6 **St.Faith's** S Africa 30.31S 30.12E
98 B7 **Ste.Famille** Quebec 46.58N 71.00W
99 P6 **Ste.Famille d'Aumond** Quebec 46.27N 75.52W
71 C1 **St.Fargeau** France 47.38N 3.04E
71 F6 **St.Félicien** France 45.06N 4.37E
99 S4 **St.-Félicien** Quebec 48.38N 72.29W
98 E5 **Ste.Félicité** Quebec 48.54N 67.21W
99 M4 **St. Félix de Dalquier** Quebec 48.45N 78.12W
72 D6 **St.Félix-de-Foncaude** France 44.38N 0.08W
99 R6 **St.Félix de Valois** Quebec 46.10N 73.26W
72 H9 **St. Felix Lauragais** France 43.27N 1.53E
72 H5 **St.Féréole** France 45.14N 1.35E
58 N3 **St.Fergus** Grampian Scotland 57.33N 1.51W
72 E6 **St.Ferme** France 44.43N 0.04E
66 B8 **St. Ferréol** France 45.46N 6.18E
72 H3 **St.Feyre** France 46.08N 1.55E
66 O2 **St.Fiden** Switzerland 47.26N 9.24E
59 L3 **Saintfield** Down N Ireland 54.28N 5.50W
58 H6 **St.Fillans** Tayside Scotland 56.23N 4.07W
59 B8 **St.Finan's B** Kerry Irish Rep 51.50N 10.23W
98 O5 **St.Fintan's** Newfoundland 48.10N 58.50W
71 J7 **St.Firmin** Hautes-Alpes France 44.46N 6.02E
69 L7 **St.Firmin** Meurthe-et-Moselle France 48.25N 6.08E
72 A2 **Ste. Flaive-des-Loups** France 46.36N 1.34W
99 T6 **St.Flavien** Quebec 46.31N 71.35W
69 F7 **St.Flavy** France 48.24N 3.47E
98 E5 **Ste.Florence** Quebec 48.15N 67.13W
67 P11 **St. Florent** Corsica 42.41N 9.18E
72 B2 **St.Florent-des-Bois** France 46.35N 1.19W
67 P11 **St Florent, G. de** Corsica
69 F7 **St.Florentin** France 48.00N 3.44E
70 H7 **St.Florent-le-Vieil** France 47.22N 1.01W
71 E8 **St. Florent-sur-Auzonnet** France 44.14N 4.07E
72 J2 **St.Florent-sur-Cher** France 47.00N 2.14E
71 C5 **St.Floret** France 45.32N 3.05E
72 L5 **St.Flour** France 45.02N 3.05E
72 G2 **St.Flovier** France 46.58N 1.02E
71 F5 **St.Fons** France 45.42N 4.51E
72 C5 **St.Fort-sur-Gironde** France 45.28N 0.43W
72 D4 **St. Fort-sur-le-Né** France 45.35N 0.18W
72 H5 **Ste.Fortunade** France 45.12N 1.46E
99 T7 **St.Fortunat** Quebec 45.58N 71.36W
71 F7 **St. Fortunat-sur-Eyrieux** France 44.49N 4.41E
98 P9 **Ste.-Foy** Quebec 46.47N 71.18W
72 G9 **Ste.Foy-de-Peyrollières** France 43.29N 1.08E
72 E6 **Ste.Foy-la-Grande** France 44.50N 0.15E
71 E5 **Ste.Foy-l'Argentière** France 45.42N 4.28E
71 K5 **Ste.Foy-Tarentaise** France 45.36N 6.53E
72 D4 **St.Fraigne** France 45.57N 0.02W
72 F9 **St.Frajou** France 43.21N 0.51E
109 J2 **St.Francis** Kansas 39.47N 101.47W
104 Q6 **St.Francis** Maine 47.10N 65.54W
104 Q6 **St.Francis** *R* Maine
107 F5 **St. Francis** *R* Missouri/Ark
95 J10 **St.Francis B** S Africa
98 T6 **St.Francis,C** Newfoundland 47.49N 52.49W
95 H10 **St.Francis,C** S Africa 34.13S 24.51E
12 C5 **St.Francis,Is.of** S Australia 32.32S 133.20E
98 A8 **St. Francis, L** Quebec
99 Q7 **St.Francis,L** Quebec
107 J3 **St.Francisville** Illinois 38.36N 87.39W
107 E11 **St.Francisville** Louisiana 30.47N 91.24W
116 N3 **St.François** Guadeloupe W I 16.15N 61.17W
99 S6 **St. François** *R* Quebec
99 T7 **St.François,L** Quebec
71 J6 **St.François-Longchamp** France 45.23N 6.21E
107 F4 **St.Francois Mts** Missouri
99 S7 **St.François Xavier** Quebec 45.32N 72.04W
104 Q7 **St.Froid L** Maine 46.57N 68.38W
71 E7 **St.Front** France 44.59N 4.09E
72 B2 **St.Fulgent** France 46.51N 1.10W
107 E11 **St.Gabriel** Louisiana 30.17N 91.07W
91 J3 **St.Gabriel** Zaïre 0.34N 25.08E
99 R6 **St.Gabriel de Brandon** Quebec 46.17N 73.23W
98 H5 **St.Gabriel de Gaspé** Quebec 48.31N 64.35W
St.Gall *see* **St.Gallen** Switzerland
65 L6 **St.Gallen** Austria 47.42N 14.38E
66 O2 **St.Gallen** Switzerland 47.25N 9.23E
66 N3 **St.Gallen** *canton* Switzerland
65 A7 **St.Gallenkirch** Austria 47.02N 9.59E
71 E5 **St.Galmier** France 45.35N 4.19E
70 L4 **Ste.Gauburge-Ste.Colombe** France 48.42N 0.26E
72 F9 **St.Gaudens** France 43.07N 0.44E
72 H9 **St. Gaudéric** France 43.07N 1.56E
72 G2 **St.Gaultier** France 46.38N 1.26E
98 B8 **St.Gédéon** Quebec 45.52N 70.39W
99 T4 **St.Gédéon** Quebec 48.29N 71.47W
60 T17 **St.Geertruid** Netherlands 50.47N 5.46E
72 D8 **St.Gein** France 43.51N 0.18W
71 D9 **St.Gély-du-Fesc** France 43.41N 3.48E
72 G2 **Ste.Gemme** France 46.52N 1.21E
72 B2 **Ste.Gemme-la-Plaine** France 46.29N 1.07W
71 B6 **St.Genès-Champespe** France 45.25N 2.44E
61 H4 **St.Genesius-Rode** Belgium 50.45N 4.21E
71 E6 **St.Genest-Malifaux** France 45.20N 4.25E
107 F4 **Ste.Genevieve** Missouri 37.58N 90.04W
69 C5 **Ste. Geneviève** Oise France 49.17N 2.13E
99 P10 **Ste Geneviève** Quebec 45.28N 73.49W
98 Q2 **Ste.Geneviève B** Newfoundland
68 E6 **Ste.Geneviève-des-Bois** France 48.39N 2.19E
72 K6 **St.Geneviève-sur-Argence** Aveyron France 44.48N 2.44E
71 F3 **St.Gengoux-le-National** France 46.37N 4.39E
72 G6 **St. Genies** France 44.59N 1.16E
71 E9 **St. Geniès-de-Malgoires** France 43.56N 4.13E
71 J8 **St.Geniez** France 44.15N 6.02E
72 K7 **St. Geniez d'Olt** France 44.28N 2.58E
72 C5 **St. Genis-de-Saintange** France 45.29N 0.34W
71 F5 **St. Genis Laval** France 45.42N 4.47E
71 J4 **St. Génis-Pouilly** France 46.15N 6.02E
71 H5 **St.Genix-sur-Guiers** France 45.36N 5.38E
72 G2 **St.Genou** France 46.55N 1.21E
71 H6 **St.Geoire-en-Valdaine** France 45.28N 5.38E
96 C1 **St.George** Bermuda 32.24N 64.42W
105 E7 **St.George** Georgia 30.32N 82.04W
98 F8 **St.George** New Brunswick 45.08N 66.50W
113 C8 **St. George** Pribilof Is Bering Sea 56.34N 169.31W
13 J8 **St.George** Queensland 28.03S 148.30E
105 G4 **St.George** S Carolina 33.12N 80.34W
103 J8 **St George** Staten I, N Y 40.38N 74.04W
111 L4 **St.George** Utah 37.06N 113.35W
116 O1 **St. George** *co* Trinidad & Tobago
116 P6 **St. George** *parish* Barbados
13 G3 **St. George** *R* Queensland
98 N5 **St.George,C** Newfoundland 48.28N 59.15W
15 M6 **St. George, C** New Ireland 4.52S 152.51E
12 K6 **St.George Hd** New S Wales 35.11S 150.40E
105 C8 **St.George I** Florida 29.40N 84.50W
113 C8 **St. George I** Pribilof Is Bering Sea
64 E7 **St.Georgen** Baden-Württemberg W Germany 48.08N 8.20E
65 L8 **St.Georgen** Kärnten Austria 46.44N 14.55E
65 H6 **St.Georgen** Ober-Österreich Austria 47.57N 13.30E
65 K7 **St.Georgen** Steiermark Austria 47.12N 14.30E
65 N8 **St.Georgen** Steiermark Austria 46.53N 15.35E
65 L6 **St.Georgen am Reith** Austria 47.51N 14.53E
110 A8 **St.George,Pt** California 41.48N 124.15W
14 E4 **St.George Ra** W Australia
103 C7 **St.Georges** Delaware 39.33N 75.39W
117 C3 **St.Georges** Fr Guiana 3.55N 51.49W
116 P5 **St.George's** Grenada, W I 12.04N 61.44W
69 M6 **St.Georges** Moselle France 48.40N 6.55E
98 O5 **St.George's** Newfoundland 48.26N 58.31W
98 B7 **St.Georges** Quebec 46.08N 70.40W
98 H5 **St.Georges** Quebec 48.39N 64.13W
98 N5 **St.George's B** Newfoundland
98 L8 **St. George's B** Nova Scotia
84 Y20 **St George's Bay** Malta
115 P9 **St.George's Cay** *isld* Belize 17.29N 88.10W
15 M6 **St.George's Chan** Bismarck Arch
28 J7 **St.George's Chan** Nicobar Is
54 F11 **St.George's Chan** Wales/Ireland
71 D6 **St.Georges-d'Aurac** France 45.10N 3.32E
72 B4 **St.Georges-de-Didonne** France 45.36N 1.00W
72 K7 **St.Georges-de-Luzençon** France 44.04N 2.59E
72 B2 **St.Georges-de-Montaigu** France 46.56N 1.16W
70 H4 **St.Georges-de-Reintembault** France 48.30N 1.14W
71 F4 **St.Georges-de-Reneins** France 46.04N 4.42E
71 G5 **St.Georges-d'Espéranche** France 45.33N 5.05E
72 B4 **St. Georges d'Oléron** Charente-Maritime France 45.59N 1.18W
72 C3 **St.Georges-du-Bois** France 46.09N 0.44W
70 M3 **St.Georges-du-Mesnil** France 49.12N 0.35E
70 M3 **St. Georges du-Vièvre** France 49.15N 0.33E
71 D5 **St.Georges-en-Couzan** France 45.42N 3.57E
96 C1 **St.George's Harb** Bermuda 32.23N 64.42W
96 C1 **St.Georges I** Bermuda 32.24N 64.42W
56 C7 **St.George's I** Cornwall Eng 50.20N 4.27W
72 E2 **St.Georges-les-Baillargeaux** France 46.41N 0.24E
71 F7 **St.Georges-les-Bains** France 44.51N 4.48E
70 N4 **St.Georges-Motel** Eure France 48.48N 1.22E
70 N5 **St.Georges-sur-Eure** France 48.25N 1.22E
72 H1 **St.Georges-sur-la Prée** France 47.14N 1.55E
70 J7 **St.Georges-sur-Loire** France 47.25N 0.45W
61 M4 **St. Georges-sur-Meuse** Belgium 50.36N 5.22E
69 J8 **St.Geosmes** France 47.50N 5.19E
72 B8 **St.Geours-de-Maremne** France 43.41N 1.14W
71 D4 **St.Gérand-le-Puy** France 46.15N 3.30E
61 J5 **St.Gérard** Belgium 50.21N 4.44E
99 M4 **St.Gérard** Quebec 48.51N 78.14W
99 T7 **St. Gerard-Centre** Quebec 45.45N 71.25W
69 G7 **St.Germain** Aube France 48.16N 4.02E
61 K4 **St.Germain** Belgium 50.35N 4.50E
66 C1 **St. Germain** France 47.43N 6.31E
71 F5 **St.Germain-au-Mont-d'Or** France 45.53N 4.48E
71 C3 **St.Germain-Chassenay** France 46.47N 3.23E
70 J5 **St.Germain-d'Anxure** France 48.12N 0.49W
71 D8 **St.Germain-de-Calberte** France 44.14N 3.49E
72 F3 **St.Germain-de-Confolens** France 46.03N 0.42E
71 H4 **St.Germain-de Joux** France 46.11N 5.44E
70 M5 **St.Germain-de-la-Coudre** France 48.17N 0.36E
71 C4 **St.Germain-des-Fossés** France 46.12N 3.21E
72 G6 **St.Germain-du-Bel-Air** France 44.39N 1.26E
71 G3 **St.Germain-du-Bois** France 46.45N 5.15E
71 F3 **St.Germain-du-Plain** France 46.42N 5.00E
71 C8 **St.Germain-du-Teil** France 44.28N 3.10E
98 B7 **Ste.Germaine** Quebec 46.24N 70.24W
68 B3 **St.Germain-en-Laye** France 48.53N 2.04E
68 C2 **St.Germain,Forêt de** France
70 G3 **St. Germain, Hâvre de** France 49.13N 1.36W
70 L3 **St.Germain-la-Campagne** France 49.03N 0.25E
71 E5 **St.Germain-Laval** France 45.50N 4.01E
71 C6 **St.Germain-Lembron** France 45.27N 3.15E
72 G4 **St.Germain-les-Belles** France 45.37N 1.29E
71 D4 **St.Germain-l'Espinasse** France 46.06N 3.58E
72 H5 **St.Germain-les-Vergnes** France 45.17N 1.36E
71 D6 **St.Germain-l'Herm** France 45.28N 3.32E
71 F1 **St.Germain-Source-Seine** France 47.30N 4.41E
70 G3 **St.Germain-sur-Ay** France 49.14N 1.36W
56 C7 **St.Germans** Cornwall Eng 50.24N 4.18W
72 D8 **St.Germé** France 43.41N 0.08W
69 B5 **St. Germer-de-Fly** France 49.27N 1.48E
71 G6 **St.Gervais** Isère France 45.12N 5.29E
98 B7 **St.Gervais** Quebec 46.43N 70.56W
72 A2 **St.Gervais** Vendée France 46.55N 1.59W
72 K3 **St. Gervais d'Auvergne** France 46.02N 2.49E
71 K5 **St. Gervais-les-Bains** France 45.53N 6.44E
72 E2 **St. Gervais-les-Trois-Clochers** France 46.53N 0.26E
71 C9 **St.Gervais-sur-Mare** France 43.39N 3.02E
72 H7 **St.Géry** France 44.28N 1.34E
61 F5 **St.Ghislain** Belgium 50.27N 3.49E
70 E6 **St.Gildas-de-Rhuis** France 47.30N 2.50W
70 F6 **St.Gildas-des-Bois** France 47.32N 2.02W
70 F7 **St.Gildas,Pte.de** France 47.08N 2.15W
99 T6 **St.Giles** Quebec 46.30N 71.23W
116 M1 **St.Giles Is** Tobago W I 11.21N 60.32W
65 H6 **St.Gilgen** Austria 47.47N 13.22E
71 E9 **St.Gilles** France 43.40N 4.26E
98 A7 **St. Gilles** Quebec 46.29N 71.23W
61 S10 **St.Gilles** *dist* Bruxelles Belgium
72 A2 **St. Gilles-Croix-de-Vie** France 46.42N 1.56W
26 T15 **St.Gilles-les-Bains** Réunion Ind Oc 21.02S 55.14E
70 D5 **St.Gilles-Pligeaux** France 48.22N 3.06W
61 G2 **St.Gillis-bij-Dendermonde** Belgium 51.02N 4.07E
61 G2 **St.Gillis-Waas** Belgium 51.13N 4.08E
71 K4 **St. Gingolph** France 46.23N 6.49E
67 O13 **St Giorgio, Col de** *pass* Corsica 41.53N 8.55E
72 G10 **St.Girons** France 42.59N 1.08E
72 B8 **St.Girons-en-Marensin** France 43.57N 1.18W
52 G7 **St.Gla** *L* Sweden 59.35N 12.30E
64 D3 **St.Goar** W Germany 50.08N 7.43E
St. Goarshausen *see* **Stadt Loreley**
70 C5 **St.Goazec** France 48.09N 3.48W
69 E4 **St.Gobain** France 49.36N 3.23E
98 G5 **St. Godefroy** Quebec 48.05N 65.09W
71 A1 **St.Gondon** France 47.42N 2.29E
66 B3 **St. Gorgon** France 47.01N 6.20E
61 F3 **St.Goriks-Oudenhove** Belgium 50.51N 3.47E
66 L5 **St.Gotthard** *pass* Switzerland 46.34N 8.34E
66 L5 **St. Gotthard Tunnel** Switzerland
56 B4 **St.Govans Hd** Dyfed Wales 51.36N 4.55W
68 E2 **St.Gratien** France 48.58N 2.17E
100 N6 **St.Gregor** Saskatchewan 52.12N 104.50W
98 O4 **St.Gregory,Mt** Newfoundland 49.19N 58.13W
70 B6 **St.Guénolé** France 47.49N 4.22W
99 S7 **St.Guillaume** Quebec 45.53N 72.45W
71 J7 **St.Guillaume,Mt** France 44.36N 6.25E
71 D4 **St.Haon-le-Châtel** France 46.04N 3.55E
106 K5 **St.Helen** Michigan 44.23N 84.24W
111 B3 **St.Helena** California 38.30N 122.28W
96 A13 **St.Helena** *isld* Atlantic Oc 15.58S 5.43W
94 E9 **St.Helena B** S Africa
94 E9 **St.Helena Fontein** S Africa 32.31S 18.20E
96 J10 **St Helena Fracture** Atlantic Oc
106 K4 **St.Helena I** Michigan 45.52N 84.52W
105 G5 **St.Helena Sd** S Carolina
72 C6 **Ste.Hélène** France 44.58N 0.52W
98 C6 **Ste. Hélène** Quebec 47.36N 69.44W
99 S9 **Ste.Hélène,I** Quebec
56 J6 **St.Helen's** I of Wight Eng 50.42N 1.06W
57 H6 **St.Helens** Lancs Eng 53.28N 2.44W
110 C4 **St.Helens** Oregon 45.54N 122.50W
12 J8 **St.Helens** Tasmania 41.16S 148.15E
110 C3 **St.Helens,Mt** Washington 46.12N 122.11W
12 J8 **St.Helens Pt** Tasmania 41.16S 148.20E
70 F3 **St Hélier** Channel Is 49.12N 2.07W
98 H4 **St.Helier** Quebec 49.08N 64.44W
11 D2 **St. Heliers** *dist* Auckland New Zealand
98 B7 **St.Hénédine** Quebec 46.33N 70.59W
98 A7 **St.Henri** Quebec 46.42N 71.04W
99 T7 **St.Herménégilde** Quebec 45.05N 71.40W
72 B2 **Ste.Hermine** France 46.34N 1.03W
29 L1 **Sainthia** W Bengal India 23.55N 87.42E
72 L2 **St.Hilaire** Allier France 46.31N 3.01E
72 J9 **St.Hilaire** Aude France 43.05N 2.18E
72 K3 **St. Hilaire** France 46.07N 2.36E
71 H6 **St.Hilaire** Isère France 45.19N 5.52E
108 O1 **St.Hilaire** Minnesota 48.01N 96.12W
71 B4 **St.Hilaire** Puy-de-Dôme France 46.06N 2.37E
69 G5 **St.Hilaire-au-Temple** France 49.03N 4.23E
72 A1 **St. Hilaire-de-Chaléons** France 47.06N 1.51W
72 B1 **St. Hilaire-de-Loulay** France 47.00N 1.20W
70 G8 **St.Hilaire-de-Riez** France 46.43N 1.56W
72 A2 **St. Hilaire-de-Riez** France 46.44N 1.56W
72 C3 **St.Hilaire-des-Loges** France 46.28N 0.39W
72 C4 **St.Hilaire-de-Villefranche** France 45.51N 0.31W
70 H4 **St. Hilaire-du-Harcouet** France 48.35N 1.05W
71 D3 **St.Hilaire-Fontaine** France 46.46N 3.38E
72 C3 **St.Hilaire-la-Pallud** France 46.16N 0.42W
72 H4 **St.Hilaire-le-Château** France 45.59N 1.54E
69 G5 **St Hilaire-le-Grand** France 49.09N 4.27E
72 D1 **St. Hilaire St. Florent** France 47.17N 0.08W
70 O6 **St.Hilaire-St.Mesmin** France 47.52N 1.50E
84 R14 **St.Hilarion Castle** Cyprus 35.18N 33.16E
13 D6 **Sainthill,Mt** N Terr Australia 22.46S 135.36E
71 K2 **St.Hippolyte** Doubs France 47.19N 6.48E
69 N7 **St.Hippolyte** Haut-Rhin France 48.14N 7.22E
72 G1 **St.Hippolyte** Indre-et-Loire France 47.04N 1.05E
71 D9 **St. Hippolyte-du-Fort** Gard France 43.58N 3.51E
71 K8 **St.Honorat,Mt** France 46.05N 6.45E
71 D3 **St.Honoré** France 46.55N 3.50E
98 A5 **St.Honoré** Quebec 48.33N 71.04W
98 C6 **St.Honoré** Quebec 47.43N 69.10W
70 J3 **Ste.Honorine** France 49.21N 0.47W
70 K3 **Ste.Honorine-du-Fay** France 49.04N 0.30W
71 E6 **St.Hostien** France 45.05N 4.03E
61 M6 **St.Hubert** Belgium 50.02N 5.22E
63 D10 **St.Hubert** W Germany 51.23N 6.26E
61 M3 **St.Huibrechts-Hern** Belgium 50.50N 5.27E
61 M2 **St.Huibrechts-Lille** Belgium 51.13N 5.29E
99 S7 **St.Hyacinthe** Quebec 45.38N 72.57W
53 K5 **St. Ibb** Sweden 55.55N 12.44E
106 K4 **St.Ignace** Michigan 45.53N 84.44W
99 R6 **St.Ignace du Lac** Quebec 46.43N 73.49W
99 B4 **St. Ignace, Isle** Ontario
119 J6 **St.Ignatius** Guyana 3.15N 59.50W
110 L2 **St.Ignatius** Montana 47.19N 114.08W
71 E4 **St.Igny-de-Vers** France 46.15N 4.27E
66 E3 **St. Imier, Val** Switzerland
64 C5 **St.Ingbert** W Germany 49.17N 7.07E
98 B6 **St.Irénée** Quebec 47.35N 70.14W
99 L5 **St.Isidore** Quebec 47.26N 79.17W
99 T7 **St. Isidore** Quebec 45.15N 71.31W
51 G3 **St.Istind** *mt* Norway 68.57N 18.36E
56 C7 **St.Ive** Cornwall Eng 50.29N 4.23W
56 L3 **St.Ives** Cambs Eng 52.20N 0.05W
56 T9 **St.Ives** Cornwall Eng 50.12N 5.29W
56 T9 **St.Ives B** Cornwall Eng
70 C6 **St.Ivy** France 47.58N 3.55W
72 K8 **St.Izaire** France 43.59N 2.43E
60 L6 **St.Jacobiparochie** Netherlands 53.17N 5.37E
98 D6 **St Jacques** New Brunswick 47.25N 68.24W
99 R7 **St.Jacques** Quebec 45.58N 73.35W
70 G5 **St.Jacques-de-la-Lande** France 48.04N 1.44W
72 K5 **St.Jacques-des-Blats** France 45.03N 2.42E
65 F8 **St.Jakob** Austria 46.56N 12.20E
71 G8 **Ste.Jalle** France 44.21N 5.17E
94 P12 **St James** Cape Town S Africa 34.07S 18.28E
70 H4 **St.James** France 48.32N 1.19W
103 H5 **St.James** Long I, N Y 40.54N 73.09W
100 A1 **St.James** Manitoba 49.55N 97.15W
106 J4 **St.James** Michigan 45.45N 85.33W
108 Q5 **St.James** Minnesota 44.00N 94.36W
107 E3 **St James** Missouri 38.00N 91.35W
116 O6 **St.James** *parish* Barbados
116 H1 **St. James** *parish* Jamaica, W I 18.25N 77.56W
101 H9 **St.James,C** Kunghit I, Br Col 51.58N 131.00W
105 E11 **St.James City** Florida 26.30N 82.05W
61 E1 **St.Jan-in-Eremo** Belgium 51.16N 3.35E
60 N9 **St.Jansklooster** Netherlands 52.40N 6.01E
60 E13 **St Jansland** Netherlands 51.40N 4.01E
61 R9 **St.-Jans-Molenbeek** *dist* Bruxelles Belgium
60 D3 **St.Jansteen** Netherlands 51.16N 4.03E
99 L4 **St.Janvier** Quebec 48.54N 79.03W
70 K5 **St.Jean** France 48.02N 0.23W
117 B2 **St.Jean** Fr Guiana 5.25N 54.05W
99 R7 **St.Jean** Quebec 45.18N 73.16W
100 U9 **St.Jean Baptiste** Manitoba 49.15N 97.20W
99 S5 **St.Jean Bosco** Quebec 47.38N 72.38W
70 E6 **St.Jean-Brévelay** France 47.51N 2.43W
72 C4 **St.Jean-d'Angély** France 45.57N 0.31W
72 C4 **St. Jean d'Angle** France 45.49N 0.57W
71 J6 **St.Jean-d'Arves** France 45.13N 6.16E
70 L5 **St.Jean-d'Asse** France 48.08N 0.08E
71 K4 **St. Jean-d'Aulps** France 46.13N 6.40E
71 G5 **St.Jean-de-Bournay** France 45.30N 5.07E
70 H3 **St.Jean-de-Daye** France 49.13N 1.08W
98 C5 **St.Jean de Dieu** Quebec 48.00N 69.05W
99 T8 **St. Jean de Dieu** *dist* Quebec 45.35N 73.31W
71 D9 **St.Jean-de-Fos** France 43.42N 3.33E
71 G2 **St. Jean-de-Losne** France 47.06N 5.16E
72 A9 **St.Jean-de-Luz** France 43.23N 1.39W
72 B8 **St. Jean-de-Marsacq** France 43.38N 1.15W
99 R6 **St.-Jean-de-Matha** Quebec 46.14N 73.33W
71 J6 **St.Jean-de-Maurienne** France 45.17N 6.21E
70 F8 **St.Jean-de-Monts** France 46.47N 2.03W
72 E2 **St.Jean-de-Sauves** France 46.51N 0.06E
71 J5 **St.Jean-de-Sixt** France 45.55N 6.25E
72 H9 **St.Jean-de-Verges** France 43.01N 1.36E
72 C6 **St.Jean-d'Illac** France 44.49N 0.49W
71 D8 **St.Jean-du-Gard** France 44.07N 3.53E
71 G6 **St.Jean-en-Royans** France 45.01N 5.18E
61 K4 **St.Jean-Geest** Belgium 50.44N 4.54E
99 S4 **St.-Jean,L** Quebec
71 F7 **St.Jean-le-Centenier** France 44.35N 4.32E
71 F4 **St.Jean-le-Priche** France 46.23N 4.51E
70 G4 **St.Jean-le-Thomas** France 48.44N 1.31W
72 B9 **St.Jean-Pied-de-Port** France 43.10N 1.14W
98 B6 **St.Jean Port Joli** Quebec 47.13N 70.16W
72 E8 **St.Jean-Poutge** France 43.44N 0.23E
98 H3 **St.Jean,R** Quebec
69 M5 **St.Jean-Rohrbach** France 49.01N 6.53E
71 E8 **St. Jeans-de Maruéjols-et-Avejan** France 44.15N 4.17E
71 E5 **St.Jean-Soleymieux** France 45.30N 4.02E
70 H5 **St.Jean-sur-Couesnon** France 48.17N 1.22W
71 G4 **St.Jean-sur-Reyssouze** France 46.23N 5.03E
71 J4 **St.Jeoire** France 46.08N 6.28E
99 Q7 **St.Jérôme** Quebec 45.47N 74.01W
99 T4 **St.Jérôme** Quebec 48.25N 71.53W
71 F6 **St.Jeure-d'Ay** France 45.09N 4.43E
71 E6 **St.Jeures** France 45.06N 4.13E
112 K2 **St.Jo** Texas 33.42N 97.32W
70 F7 **St.Joachim** France 47.23N 2.10W
98 B6 **St.Joachim** Quebec 47.03N 70.50W
65 E7 **St.Jodok** Austria 47.04N 11.31E
107 D5 **St. Joe** Arkansas 36.01N 92.49W
110 J2 **St.Joe** Idaho 47.19N 116.22W
106 K8 **St.Joe** Indiana 41.19N 84.54W
110 J2 **St. Joe** *R* Idaho
64 E4 **St.Johann** W Germany 49.53N 8.03E
65 K7 **St. Johann am Tauern** Austria 47.21N 14.29E
60 M8 **St.Johannesga** Netherlands 52.56N 5.51E
65 H7 **St.Johann im Pongua** Austria 47.22N 13.13E
65 G8 **St. Johann-im-Walde** Austria 46.55N 12.36E
65 O7 **St.Johann in der Haide** Austria 47.18N 16.02E
65 F6 **St.Johann in Tirol** Austria 47.32N 12.26E
56 W11 **St.John** Channel Is 49.15N 2.08W
St.John Egypt*see* **Zebirget**
109 M4 **St.John** Kansas 37.59N 98.46W
98 F8 **Saint John** New Brunswick 45.16N 66.03W
110 N9 **St.John** Utah 40.22N 112.27W
110 H2 **St.John** Washington 47.04N 117.36W
116 P6 **St.John** *parish* Barbados
89 E8 **St.John** *R* Liberia
104 P3 **St.John** *R* Maine
98 P3 **St John B** Newfoundland
98 R3 **St John, C** Newfoundland 50.01N 55.30W
98 P3 **St John I** Newfoundland 50.49N 57.15W
105 L7 **St John I** Virgin Is 18.21N 64.48W
98 S5 **St.John,L** Newfoundland 48.25N 54.40W
98 E7 **St.John R** Maine/New Bruns
98 G5 **St.John R** Quebec
116 O4 **St. John's** Antigua W I 17.08N 61.50W
111 P7 **St.Johns** Arizona 34.30N 109.24W
106 K6 **St.Johns** Michigan 43.01N 84.31W
98 T6 **St.John's** Newfoundland 47.34N 52.41W
103 C4 **St.Johns** Pennsylvania 41.03N 75.57W
105 G9 **St Johns** *R* Florida
104 N2 **St. Johnsbury** Vermont 44.25N 72.02W
104 N2 **St.Johnsbury** Vermont 44.25N 72.02W
57 J3 **St.John's Chapel** Durham Eng 54.44N 2.11W
56 M2 **St.John's Highway** Norfolk Eng 52.43N 0.17E
59 F2 **St.John's Pt** Donegal Irish Rep 54.34N 8.28W
59 L3 **St.John's Pt** Down N Ireland 54.14N 5.40W
105 F7 **St.Johns R** Florida
59 H2 **St.Johnstown** Donegal Irish Rep 54.56N 7.28W
104 L3 **St.Johnsville** New York 43.00N 74.40W
103 C8 **St Jones** *R* Delaware
70 H3 **St.Jores** France 49.18N 1.25W
66 A8 **St. Jorioz** France 45.50N 6.10E
61 B2 **St.Joris** Belgium 51.09N 2.48E
61 D2 **St.Joris** Belgium 51.07N 3.22E
61 J3 **St.Joris-Weert** Belgium 50.48N 4.40E
61 K3 **St.Joris-Winge** Belgium 50.54N 4.52E
72 G8 **St.Jory** France 43.45N 1.22E
72 F4 **St. Jory-de Chaleix** France 45.30N 0.54E
107 E10 **St Joseph** Louisiana 31.56N 91.15W
116 L3 **St.Joseph** Martinique W I 14.40N 61.03W
106 H7 **St.Joseph** Michigan 42.05N 86.30W
107 B2 **St. Joseph** Missouri 39.46N 94.52W
103 C3 **St.Joseph** Pennsylvania 41.55N 76.00W
98 B7 **St.Joseph** Quebec 46.19N 70.52W
26 U16 **St.-Joseph** Réunion Ind Oc 21.22S 55.37E
116 O1 **St.Joseph** Trinidad & Tobago 10.39N 61.25W
116 P2 **St.Joseph** Trinidad & Tobago 10.19N 61.00W
116 P6 **St.Joseph** *parish* Barbados
105 B8 **St.Joseph B** Florida 29.45N 85.23W
98 S8 **St.Joseph de Lévis** Quebec 46.49N 71.09W
99 G6 **St.Joseph I** Ontario
112 L8 **St.Joseph I** Texas
97 K7 **St.Joseph,L** Ontario 51.00N 91.00W
106 H8 **St.Joseph,R** Michigan
98 T6 **St.Joseph's** Newfoundland 47.06N 53.31W
103 E3 **St.Josephs** New York 41.36N 74.43W
69 B3 **St.Josse** France 50.27N 1.39E
61 S9 **Saint Josse** *dist* Bruxelles Belgium
70 F5 **St. Jouan-de-l'Isle** France 48.16N 2.10W
70 G4 **St Jouan-des-Guerets** France 48.36N 1.58W
70 L2 **St.Jouin** France 49.39N 0.10E
72 D2 **St.Jouin-de-Marnes** France 46.53N 0.03W
99 Q6 **St. Jovite** Quebec 46.07N 74.36W
72 J8 **St.Juéry** France 43.57N 2.12E
84 Y20 **St Julian's** Malta 35.55N 14.30E
84 Y20 **St Julian's Bay** Malta
70 E5 **St.Julien** Côtes-du-Nord France 48.27N 2.49W
72 G9 **St.Julien** Haute-Garonne France 43.14N 1.08E
71 J4 **St.Julien** Haute-Savoie France 46.08N 6.05E
72 J5 **St.Julien-aux-Bois** France 45.08N 2.08E
72 C5 **St. Julien Beychevelle** Gironde France 45.10N 0.44W
71 E7 **St.Julien-Boutières** France 44.58N 4.21E
71 E6 **St.Julien-Chapteuil** France 45.02N 4.03E
71 E8 **St.Julien-de-Cassagnas** France 44.12N 4.11E
71 E4 **St.Julien-de-Civry** France 46.26N 4.14E
72 B1 **St.Julien-de-Concelles** France 47.15N 1.23W
72 A2 **St. Julien-des-Landes** France 46.39N 1.43W
70 H6 **St.Julien-de-Vouvantes** France 47.39N 1.14W
69 E7 **St.Julien-du-Sault** France 48.01N 3.18E
71 K9 **St Julien-du-Verdon** France 43.55N 6.33E
71 H7 **St. Julien-en-Beauchène** France 44.36N 5.42E
72 B7 **St. Julien-en-Born** France 44.03N 1.14W
71 G7 **St.Julien-en-Quint** France 44.50N 5.17E
72 E2 **St.Julien-l'Ars** France 46.33N 0.30E
70 L3 **St.Julien-le-Faucon** France 49.04N 0.05E
71 F6 **St.Julien-Molin-Molette** France 45.20N 4.37E
71 G4 **St.Julien-sur-Reyssouze** France 46.25N 5.05E
71 G4 **St. Julien-sur-Suran** France 46.23N 5.27E
72 F4 **St.Junien** France 45.53N 0.54E
72 H4 **St.Junien-la-Bregère** France 45.53N 1.44E
69 L6 **St.Jure** France 48.57N 6.13E
72 K2 **St.Just** Cher France 46.59N 2.30E
56 S9 **St.Just** Cornwall Eng 50.07N 5.41W
70 G6 **St.Just** Ille-et-Vilaine France 47.46N 1.57W
69 E6 **St. Just-en-Brie** Seine-et-Marne France 48.36N 3.07E
69 C4 **St.Just-en-Chaussée** France 49.31N 2.27E
71 D5 **St.Just-en-Chevalet** France 45.55N 3.50E
72 B9 **St. Just Ibarre** France 43.11N 1.02W
72 D8 **St.Justin** France 43.59N 0.13W
71 E5 **St.Just-la-Pendue** France 45.53N 4.15E
72 B4 **St. Just-Luzac** France 45.48N 1.02W
71 E5 **St. Just-St. Rambert** Loire France 45.30N 4.14E
69 F6 **St.Just-Sauvage** France 48.33N 3.47E
52 K9 **St.Karlsö Lt.Ho** Sweden 57.17N 18.00E
61 J2 **St. Katelijne** Belgium 51.04N 4.32E
61 J2 **St.-Katelijne-Waver** Belgium 51.04N 4.32E
65 M7 **St.Katharein** Austria 47.29N 15.10E
61 G3 **St.Katherina-Lombeek** Belgium 50.52N 4.10E
56 T9 **St.Keverne** Cornwall Eng 50.02N 5.05W
56 B6 **St.Kew Highway** Cornwall Eng 50.33N 4.45W
12 C8 **St.Kilda** *dist* Melbourne, Victoria
58 A1 **St.Kilda** *isld* W Isles Scotland 57.49N 8.34W
116 P3 **St.Kitts** *isld* Leeward Is W I 17.25N 62.45W
61 D2 **St.Kruis** Belgium 51.13N 3.15E
116 B1 **St.Kruis** Curaçao W I 12.23N 69.08W
60 A3 **St.Kruis** Netherlands 51.16N 3.30E
61 F2 **St.Kruis Winkel** Belgium 51.09N 3.49E
61 G3 **St.Kwintens-Lennik** Belgium 50.48N 4.10E
99 R7 **St.Lambert** Quebec 45.29N 73.30W
99 T6 **St.Lambert** Quebec 46.35N 71.12W
14 G2 **St.Lambert,C** W Australia 14.17S 127.43E
72 D1 **St. Lambert des Levées** France 47.17N 0.06E
72 C1 **St.Lambert-du-Lattay** France 47.18N 0.37W
65 K7 **St.Lambrecht** Austria 47.05N 14.18E
61 M3 **St.Lambrechts-Herk** Belgium 50.54N 5.18E
107 D11 **St.Landry** Louisiana 30.50N 92.14W
26 Q15 **St.Lanne Gramont** *isld* Kerguelen Indian Oc
72 F10 **St.Lary** Ariège France 42.56N 0.54E
72 F8 **St.Lary** Gers France 43.43N 0.31E
72 E10 **St. Lary-Soulan** France 42.48N 0.18E
61 E2 **St.Laureins** Belgium 51.14N 3.32E
66 B7 **St. Laurent** France 46.03N 6.21E
117 B2 **St.Laurent** Fr Guiana 5.29N 54.03W
100 U8 **St.Laurent** Manitoba 50.25N 97.58W
99 L4 **St Laurent** Quebec 48.38N 79.18W
99 R9 **St.Laurent** Quebec 45.31N 73.42W
69 L7 **St.Laurent** Vosges France 48.09N 6.27E
St Laurent *R see* **St Lawrence**
72 D9 **St. Laurent-Bretagne** France 43.23N 0.11W
71 E9 **St.Laurent-d'Aigouze** France 43.38N 4.12E
71 F8 **St.Laurent-de-Carnols** France 44.12N 4.32E
72 K11 **St.Laurent-de-Cerdans** France 42.23N 2.37E
72 E4 **St.Laurent-de-Céris** France 45.56N 0.29E
71 E5 **St.Laurent-de-Chamousset** France 45.44N 4.28E
72 K9 **St. Laurent-de-la-Cabrerisse** France 43.05N 2.42E
72 K10 **St.Laurent-de-la-Salanque** France 42.46N 2.59E
71 G5 **St.Laurent-de-Mûre** France 45.41N 5.03E
72 E9 **St. Laurent-de-Neste** France 43.05N 0.28E
70 B1 **St. Laurent-des-Autels** France 47.18N 1.07W
72 E5 **St.Laurent-des-Combes** France 45.21N 0.02E
70 O6 **St.Laurent-des-Eaux** France 47.43N 1.36E
72 L7 **St. Laurent d'Olt** France 44.27N 3.07E
117 C2 **Saint Laurent du Maroni** *dept* Fr Guiana
71 H6 **St.Laurent-du-Pont** France 45.24N 5.44E
70 M2 **St.Laurent-en-Caux** France 49.45N 0.52E
70 M6 **St.Laurent-en-Gâtines** France 47.36N 0.47E
71 H3 **St. Laurent-en-Grandvaux** France 46.34N 5.58E
72 C5 **St.Laurent-et-Benon** France 45.10N 0.50W
71 D7 **St.Laurent-les-Bains** France 44.36N 3.58E
72 H4 **St.Laurent-les-Églises** France 45.57N 1.30E
98 Q9 **St.Laurent R** Quebec
72 F4 **St.Laurent-sur-Gorre** France 45.46N 0.57E
70 J3 **St.Laurent-sur-Mer** France 49.22N 0.51W
69 K5 **St.Laurent-sur-Othain** France 49.24N 5.31E
72 C2 **St. Laurent-sur-Sèvre** France 46.57N 0.53W
72 C2 **St.Laurs** France 46.31N 0.34W
56 J6 **St.Lawrence** I of Wight Eng 50.35N 1.14W
98 R7 **St.Lawrence** Newfoundland 46.54N 55.23W
13 J5 **St.Lawrence** Queensland 22.19S 149.30E
98 M6 **St.Lawrence,C** C Breton I, Nova Scotia 47.03N 60.37W
98 K6 **St.Lawrence,G.of** Canada
113 B5 **St. Lawrence I** Bering Sea
99 O8 **St.Lawrence Islands Nat.Park** Ontario
97 N8 **St.Lawrence R** Canada/U.S.A.
99 P8 **St.Lawrence Seaway** Canada/U.S.A.
100 Q8 **St.Lazare** Manitoba 50.27N 101.19W
61 D4 **St.Léger** Hainaut Belgium 50.42N 3.19E
61 N8 **St.Léger** Luxembourg Belgium 49.37N 5.40E
71 D2 **St.Léger-de-Fougeret** France 47.02N 3.55E
69 B6 **St.Léger-en-Yvelines** France 48.44N 1.46E
72 G3 **St. Léger-Magnazeix** France 46.18N 1.16E
71 E3 **St.Léger-sous-Beuvray** France 46.55N 4.06E
71 F3 **St.Léger-sur-Dheune** France 46.51N 4.38E
66 D6 **St.Legier** Switzerland 46.29N 6.53E
61 J1 **St.Lenaarts** Belgium 51.21N 4.41E
71 D4 **St.Léon** France 46.24N 3.41E
98 A5 **St Leon** Quebec 48.41N 71.29W
98 E5 **St.Léon** Quebec 48.24N 67.28W
98 E6 **St.-Léonard** New Brunswick 47.10N 67.55W
99 R8 **St Léonard** Quebec 45.35N 73.39W
99 S6 **St.Léonard** Quebec 46.06N 72.22W
66 F6 **St.Leonard** Switzerland 46.16N 7.25E
69 M7 **St.Léonard** Vosges France 48.13N 6.56E
72 G4 **St.Léonard-de-Noblat** Haute-Vienne France 45.50N 1.29E
56 N6 **St.Leonards** E Sussex Eng 50.51N 0.34E
11 M12 **St.Leonards** *dist* Dunedin New Zealand
12 M7 **St.Leonards** *dist* Sydney, N S W
99 T4 **St.-Leon-de-Chicoutimi** Quebec 48.40N 71.34W
98 B7 **St.Léon-de-Standon** Quebec 46.29N 70.38W
65 L8 **St.Leonhard** Kärnten Austria 46.58N 14.48E
65 N4 **St.Leonhard** Nieder-Österreich Austria 48.37N 15.33E
65 H6 **St.Leonhard** Salzburg Austria 47.43N 13.03E
65 C7 **St.Leonhard** Tirol Austria 47.04N 10.51E
65 M5 **St.Leonhard am Forst** Austria 48.09N 15.17E
72 L2 **St.Léopardin d'Augy** France 46.42N 3.08E
26 T15 **St.Leu** Réunion Ind Oc 21.09S 55.17E
68 D1 **St.Leu-la-Forêt** France 49.02N 2.15E
98 P1 **St.Lewis R** Labrador, Nfld
99 S7 **St.Liboire** Quebec 45.40N 72.48W
61 F3 **St.Lievens-Esse** Belgium 50.52N 3.53E
61 F3 **St.Lievens-Houtem** Belgium 50.55N 3.52E
72 F7 **Ste.Livrade-sur-Lot** France 44.24N 0.36E
66 B5 **St.Livres** Switzerland 46.31N 6.24E
72 J1 **Ste.Lizaigne** France 47.00N 2.01E
72 G9 **St.Lizier** France 43.01N 1.07E
70 H3 **St.Lô** France 49.07N 1.05W
72 B8 **St. Lon-les-Mains** France 43.37N 1.07W
65 H6 **St.Lorenz** Austria 47.50N 13.22E
65 G8 **St.Lorenzen** Kärnten Austria 46.43N 12.48E
65 L7 **St.Lorenzen** Steiermark Austria 47.15N 14.53E
71 H3 **St. Lothain** France 46.50N 5.38E
71 M1 **St.Louis** France 47.35N 7.34E
116 N4 **St.Louis** Marie Galante, Guadeloupe W I 15.57N 61.19W
106 K6 **St.Louis** Michigan 43.24N 84.35W

107 F3 **St.Louis** Missouri 38.40N 90.15W
98 H7 **St.Louis** Prince Edward I 46.55N 64.10W
26 T16 **St.-Louis** Réunion Ind Oc 21.17S 55.25E
100 M6 **St.Louis** Saskatchewan 52.56N 105.50W
89 A3 **St.Louis** Senegal 16.01N 16.30W
108 S2 **St Louis** *R* Minnesota
98 H7 **St.Louis de Kent** New Brunswick 46.46N 64.59W
98 D6 **St.Louis du Ha Ha** Quebec 47.40N 69.00W
116 H5 **St.Louis du Sud** Haiti 18.19N 73.34W
98 B6 **Ste.Louise** Quebec 47.17N 70.09W
99 R7 **St.Louis,L** Quebec
69 N6 **St.Louis-lès-Bitche** France 49.00N 7.21E
104 C6 **St.Louisville** Ohio 40.10N 82.26W
71 F3 **St.Loup-de-la-Salle** France 46.57N 4.55E
72 D2 **St. Loup-Lamaire** France 46.47N 0.11W
71 D9 **St.Loup,Pic** *mt* France 43.46N 3.46E
69 L8 **St. Loup-sur-Semouse** France 47.53N 6.17E
70 N4 **St.Lubin-des-Joncherets** France 48.45N 1.13E
66 G7 **St.Luc** Switzerland 46.13N 7.37E
116 L4 **Ste.Luce** Martinique W I 14.28N 60.56W
13 K2 **St.Lucia** *dist* Brisbane, Qnsld
116 O8 **St.Lucia** *isld* Windward Is W I
95 P9 **St.Lucia,C** S Africa 28.32S 32.25E
116 O7 **St.Lucia Chan** Windward Is W I
67 P13 **Ste Lucia de Porto Vecchio** Corsica 41.41N 9.20E
95 P9 **St.Lucia Estuary** S Africa 28.23S 32.25E
99 Q6 **Ste. Lucie** Quebec 46.07N 74.13W
105 G10 **St.Lucie Can** Florida
105 G10 **St Lucie Inlet** Florida
105 G10 **St. Lucie R** Florida
116 O6 **St.Lucy** *parish* Barbados
98 B8 **St.Ludger** Quebec 45.45N 70.45W
116 H5 **St.Luis du Nord** Haiti 19.56N 72.44W
St Luke's I Burma*see* **Zadetkale Kyun**
70 F4 **St.Lunaire** France 48.38N 2.06W
98 R2 **St.Lunaire** Newfoundland 51.30N 55.29W
98 R2 **St.Lunaire B** Newfoundland
69 G7 **St.Lye** France 48.21N 4.00E
70 F7 **St.Lyphard** France 47.24N 2.18W
72 G8 **St.Lys** France 43.31N 1.11E
60 G8 **St.Maartensbrug** Netherlands 52.46N 4.44E
60 E13 **St.Maartensdijk** Netherlands 51.33N 4.05E
72 D6 **St.Macaire** Gironde France 44.34N 0.13W
72 C1 **St. Macaire-en-Mauges** France 47.07N 0.59W
59 C5 **St.Macdara's I** Galway Irish Rep 53.18N 9.55W
72 C6 **St.Magne** France 44.32N 0.39W
58 P9 **St.Magnus B** Shetland Scotland
72 D5 **St.Maigrin** France 45.26N 0.16W
72 D3 **St. Maixent l'Ecole** France 46.25N 0.12W
98 B7 **St.Malachie** Quebec 46.32N 70.46W
70 F4 **St.Malo** France 48.39N 2.00W
70 G3 **St.Malo-de-la-Lande** France 49.05N 1.33W
70 F4 **St.Malo,G.de** France
70 F5 **St.Malon-sur-Mel** France 48.05N 2.07W
71 E9 **St. Mamert-du-Gard** France 43.54N 4.11E
72 J6 **St. Mamet-la-Salvetat** France 44.51N 2.20E
68 G3 **St.Mandé** France 48.50N 2.25E
71 H10 **St. Mandrier-sur-Mer** France 43.04N 5.56E
61 K5 **St.Marc** Belgium 50.30N 4.51E
70 B5 **St.Marc** Finistère France 48.24N 4.27W
116 H5 **St.Marc** Haiti 19.08N 72.41W
70 F7 **St.Marc** Loire-Inférieure France 47.15N 2.16W
72 G4 **St.Marc,Barrage de** *res* France 45.55N 1.24E
116 H5 **St.Marc,Can.de** *str* Haiti
99 S6 **St.Marc des Carrières** Quebec 46.40N 72.03W
72 H2 **St.Marcel** Indre France 46.37N 1.30E
79 B3 **St.Marcel** Italy 45.44N 7.27E
98 B7 **St.Marcel** Quebec 46.55N 70.03W
71 G6 **St.Marcellin** Isère France 45.10N 5.20E
71 E5 **St. Marcellin-en-Forez** Loire France 45.30N 4.10E
117 C3 **St.Marcel,Mt** Fr Guiana 2.20N 53.02W
72 K9 **St. Marcel-sur-Aude** Aude France 43.14N 2.55E
72 F9 **St.Marcet** France 43.12N 0.44E
70 H3 **St.Marcouf,Is** France 49.30N 1.09W
70 H5 **St.Marc-sur-Couesnon** France 48.19N 1.22W
71 F1 **St. Marc-sur-Seine** France 47.42N 4.36E
61 N8 **St.Mard** Belgium 49.33N 5.32E
69 F7 **St.Mards-en-Othe** France 48.10N 3.50E
98 P2 **St.Margaret B** Newfoundland
98 J9 **St.Margaret B** Nova Scotia
65 P6 **St.Margarethen** Burgenland Austria 47.49N 16.38E
65 K8 **St.Margarethen** Kärnten Austria 46.34N 14.27E
63 K5 **St.Margarethen** W Germany 53.53N 9.16E
56 O5 **St.Margarets** Kent Eng 51.10N 1.23E
116 L2 **St. Margaret's Bay** Jamaica, W I 18.12N 76.32W
58 T12 **St.Margaret's Hope** Orkney Scotland 58.49N 2.57W
64 E7 **St.Märgen** W Germany 48.00N 8.08E
66 P2 **St.Margrethen** Switzerland 47.28N 9.37E
61 E1 **St.Margriete** Belgium 51.17N 3.33E
70 F7 **Ste.Marguerite** France 47.15N 2.19W
98 B5 **Ste.Marguerite N.E.,R** Quebec
98 B5 **Ste.Marguerite,R** Quebec
98 F3 **Ste. Marguerite, R** Quebec
61 E3 **St.-Maria-Horebeke** Belgium 50.50N 3.41E
61 E3 **St.-Maria-Latem** Belgium 50.53N 3.43E
61 F3 **St.Maria-Lierde** Belgium 50.49N 3.51E
61 F3 **St.Maria-Oudenhove** Belgium 50.50N 3.48E
61 N8 **Ste.Marie** Belgium 49.40N 5.34E
72 K6 **Ste.Marie** France 44.53N 2.54E
107 H3 **Ste.Marie** Illinois 38.55N 88.02W
116 L3 **Ste.Marie** Martinique W I 14.47N 61.00W
98 A7 **Ste. Marie** Quebec 46.26N 71.00W
26 U14 **Ste.-Marie** Réunion Ind Oc 20.53S 55.33E
69 L5 **Ste.Marie-aux-Chênes** France 49.12N 6.02E
69 N7 **Ste.Marie-aux-Mines** France 48.15N 7.11E
95 B8 **Ste.Marie,C** Madagascar 25.34S 45.10E
61 M7 **Ste.Marie-Chevigny** Belgium 49.56N 5.27E
69 N7 **Ste.Marie,Col de** *pass* France 48.15N 7.09E
70 H3 **Ste.Marie-du-Mont** France 49.22N 1.14W
Ste Marie, I *see* **Nosy Boraha, I**
72 D5 **St.Mariens** France 45.08N 0.24W
110 J2 **St.Maries** Idaho 47.19N 116.34W
105 C7 **St.Marks** Florida 30.12N 84.12W
95 L8 **St.Marks** S Africa 32.01S 27.22E
72 K10 **St.Marsal** France 42.33N 2.37E
70 L6 **St. Mars-d'Outille** France 47.52N 0.21E
70 H7 **St.Mars-du-Désert** France 47.22N 1.24W
70 L5 **St.Mars-la-Brière** France 48.02N 0.23E
70 H6 **St.Mars-la-Jaille** France 47.32N 1.10W
70 H5 **St.Mars-sur-la-Futaie** France 48.26N 1.01W
61 G3 **St.Martens-Bodegem** Belgium 50.52N 4.13E
61 E2 **St.Martens-Latem** Belgium 51.01N 3.39E
61 G3 **St.Martens-Lennik** Belgium 50.48N 4.10E
61 F3 **St.Martens-Lierde** Belgium 50.48N 3.50E
61 O4 **St.Martens-Voeren** Belgium 50.45N 5.48E
98 F4 **Ste.Marthe de Gaspé** Quebec 49.11N 66.13W
72 E5 **St.Martial** Charente France 45.23N 0.02E
71 D8 **St.Martial** Gard France 44.03N 3.42E
72 E5 **St. Martial d'Artenset** France 45.01N 0.13E
72 H5 **St.Martial-de-Gimel** France 45.16N 1.52E
72 F4 **St.Martial-de-Valette** France 45.30N 0.39E
72 G6 **St. Martiai-et-St. Aubin-de-Nabirat** France 44.45N 1.16E
61 J4 **St. Martin** Belgium 50.30N 4.38E
65 O6 **St.Martin** Burgenland Austria 47.34N 16.25E
56 V11 **St.Martin** Chan Is 49.27N 2.34W
56 W11 **St.Martin** Channel Is 49.13N 2.03W
66 C8 **St. Martin** France 45.56N 6.39E
100 T7 **St. Martin** Manitoba 51.43N 98.42W
70 F6 **St.Martin** Morbihan France 47.45N 2.15W
65 L4 **St.Martin** Nieder-Österreich Austria 48.41N 14.51E
65 H5 **St.Martin** Ober-Österreich Austria 48.18N 13.26E
65 H7 **St.Martin** Salzburg Austria 47.28N 13.23E
66 F7 **St.Martin** Switzerland 46.11N 7.26E
71 H9 **St.Martin** Var France 43.35N 5.55E
116 N5 **St. Martin** *I* Leeward Is W I 18.05N 63.05W
65 J7 **St.Martin am Grimming** Austria 47.29N 13.59E
106 K4 **St.Martin B** Michigan
69 B2 **St.Martin-Boulogne** France 50.44N 1.39E
116 K3 **St.Martin,C** Martinique W I 14.52N 61.13W
94 D9 **St.Martin,C** S Africa 32.42N 17.59E
69 F5 **St. Martin d'Ablois** France 49.00N 3.52E
71 F8 **St. Martin d'Ardèche** France 44.18N 4.34E
72 B9 **St. Martin d'Arrosa** France 43.13N 1.18W
72 J1 **St. Martin d'Auxigny** France 47.11N 2.24E
69 B6 **St.Martin-de-Bretencourt** France 48.31N 1.56E
71 F9 **St.Martin-de-Crau** France 43.38N 4.47E
71 D7 **St.Martin-de-Fugères** France 44.54N 3.56E
72 B8 **St. Martin de Hinx** France 43.36N 1.16W
70 H4 **St.Martin-de-Landelle** France 48.33N 1.10W
71 D9 **St.Martin-de-Londres** France 43.47N 3.44E
71 K8 **St.Martin d'Entraunes** France 44.09N 6.45E
72 B3 **St.Martin-de-Ré** France 46.12N 1.25W
70 J3 **St.Martin-des-Besaces** France 49.01N 0.51W
72 B8 **St.Martin-de-Seignanx** France 43.33N 1.22W
72 B2 **St.Martin-des-Noyers** France 46.44N 1.11W
71 D4 **St.Martin-d'Estréaux** France 46.13N 3.47E
71 E7 **St.Martin-de-Valamas** France 44.55N 4.22E
72 C8 **St. Martin d'Oney** France 43.56N 0.37W
71 H4 **St. Martin-du-Frêne** France 46.08N 5.33E
71 G4 **St.Martin-du-Mont** France 46.05N 5.20E
71 L9 **St.Martin-du-Var** France 43.49N 7.12E
71 G3 **St.Martin-en-Bresse** France 46.49N 5.03E
70 N2 **St.Martin-en-Campagne** France 49.57N 1.14E
71 G6 **St. Martin-en-Vercors** France 45.01N 5.27E
71 L8 **St. Martin-en-Vésubie** France 44.04N 7.15E
106 H4 **St.Martin I** Michigan 45.31N 86.46W
100 T7 **St. Martin, L** Manitoba
St.Martin-la-Rivière *see* **Valdivienne**
72 F3 **St. Martin-l'Ars** France 46.13N 0.32E
71 D5 **St. Martin-la-Sauveté** France 45.50N 3.55E
70 M7 **St. Martin-le-Beau** France 47.22N 0.55E
66 P7 **St.Martino** Italy 46.15N 9.38E
98 G8 **St.Martins** New Brunswick 45.21N 65.34W
11 M10 **St.Martins** *dist* Christchurch New Zealand
56 R8 **St. Martins** *isld* Is of Scilly Eng 49.58N 6.17W
25 B2 **St.Martin's I** Burma 20.35N 92.22E
70 E3 **St.Martin's Pt** Channel Is 49.25N 2.32W
100 T7 **St. Martin Station** Manitoba 51.44N 98.40W
72 J5 **St. Martin Valmeroux** France 45.07N 2.24E
107 E11 **St.Martinville** Louisiana 30.07N 91.51W
72 F9 **St.Martory** France 43.09N 0.56E
70 F3 **St.Mary** Channel Is 49.14N 2.10W
116 K1 **St. Mary** *parish* Jamaica, W I
110 M1 **St. Mary** *R* Alberta/Montana
89 A5 **St.Mary,C** The Gambia 13.28N 16.47W
55 J5 **St.Mary Cray** London Eng 51.23N 0.07E
98 N3 **St.Mary Is** Quebec 50.12N 59.46W
110 M1 **St. Mary L** Montana 48.45N 113.30W
55 F3 **St.Marylebone** London Eng 51.31N 0.09W
101 P11 **St.Mary,Mt** Br Col 49.55N 116.24W
15 J8 **St Mary, Mt** Papua New Guinea 8.08S 147.02E
12 E4 **St.Mary Pk** S Australia 31.31S 138.34E
98 N3 **St.Mary Reefs** Quebec
100 D9 **St.Mary Res** Alberta
St.Marys Alaska *see* **Andreafsky**
105 F7 **St.Marys** Georgia 30.43N 81.34W
109 O2 **St.Marys** Kansas 39.12N 96.04W
107 G4 **St.Marys** Missouri 37.52N 89.57W
98 T7 **St.Mary's** Newfoundland 46.56N 53.34W
104 A6 **St.Marys** Ohio 40.32N 84.22W
99 J9 **St.Mary's** Ontario 43.15N 81.09W
58 T12 **St.Mary's** Orkney Scotland 58.54N 2.55W
104 G5 **St.Marys** Pennsylvania 41.27N 78.35W
12 J8 **St.Marys** Tasmania 41.33S 148.12E
104 D7 **St.Marys** W Virginia 39.24N 81.13W
56 R8 **St. Marys** *isld* Is of Scilly Eng 49.55N 6.18W
98 T7 **St.Mary's B** Newfoundland
98 F9 **St.Mary's B** Nova Scotia
56 N6 **St. Mary's Bay** Kent Eng 51.00N 0.58E
98 S7 **St Mary's, C** Newfoundland 46.50N 54.12W
104 J8 **St.Marys City** Maryland 38.12N 76.26W
95 P9 **St.Mary's Hill** *mt* S Africa 27.55S 32.35E
57 L2 **St.Mary's I** Northumb Eng 55.04N 1.26W
57 G2 **St.Mary's L** Borders Scotland 55.29N 3.12W
105 F7 **St.Marys R** Florida
106 J9 **St.Marys,R** Indiana
106 K3 **St.Marys,R** Michigan
98 K8 **St.Mary's R** Nova Scotia
105 G4 **St Mathews** S Carolina 33.40N 80.44W
72 F4 **St.Mathieu** France 45.43N 0.46E
98 D5 **St.Mathieu** Quebec 48.12N 68.59W
99 M4 **St.Mathieu** Quebec 48.28N 78.10W
70 A5 **St.Mathieu,Pte de** France 48.20N 4.46W
72 A2 **St.Mathurin** France 46.34N 1.42W
97 B5 **St.Matthew I** Bering Sea 60.30N 172.30W
113 A6 **St. Matthew I** Bering Sea 60.20N 171.00W
St Matthew's I Burma*see* **Zadetkyi Kyun**
15 K4 **St.Matthias Grp** *islds* Bismarck Arch
68 G4 **St. Maur-des-Fossés** France 48.48N 2.27E
72 E7 **Ste.Maure-de-Peyriac** France 44.01N 0.09E
72 F1 **Ste.Maure-de-Touraine** France 47.07N 0.38E
68 G4 **St.Maurice** Paris France 48.49N 2.26E
66 E7 **St.Maurice** Switzerland 46.14N 7.01E
99 R5 **St. Maurice** *R* Quebec
69 F7 **St Maurice-aux-Aiches-Hommes** France 48.18N 3.32E
71 E6 **St.Maurice-de-Lignon** France 45.13N 4.08E
72 F4 **St.Maurice-des-Lions** France 45.58N 0.43E
71 H7 **St. Maurice-en-Trièves** France 44.45N 5.40E
72 D1 **St. Maurice la Fougereuse** Deux Sèvres France 47.02N 0.28W
72 G3 **St.Maurice-la-Souterraine** France 46.13N 1.26E
70 M4 **St. Maurice-les-Charencey** France 48.39N 0.46E
71 D9 **St. Maurice-Navacelles** Hérault France 43.50N 3.30E
71 B4 **St.Maurice-près-Pionsat** France 46.04N 2.36E
69 K5 **St.Maurice-sous-les-Côtes** France 49.01N 5.41E
69 D8 **St.Maurice-sur-Aveyron** France 47.51N 2.55E
71 E5 **St.Maurice-sur-Loire** France 45.58N 4.00E
69 M8 **St.Maurice-sur-Moselle** France 47.52N 6.50E
72 F7 **St.Maurin** France 44.13N 0.55E
56 T9 **St.Mawes** Cornwall Eng 50.09N 5.01W
St Maxime *see* **Scott**
71 K10 **Ste.Maxime** France 43.19N 6.39E
69 C5 **St.Maximin** Oise France 49.13N 2.27E
71 H10 **St. Maximin-la-Sainte Baume** France 43.27N 5.51E
70 D5 **St.Mayeux** France 48.16N 3.00W
72 E5 **St. Méard-de Drône** France 45.14N 0.26E
72 E6 **St.Méard-de-Gurçon** France 44.55N 0.11E
61 M7 **St.Medard** Belgium 49.49N 5.20E
72 D5 **St.Médard-de-Guizières** France 45.01N 0.03W
72 C6 **St.Médard-en-Jalles** France 44.54N 0.42W
70 F5 **St.Meen** France 48.11N 2.12W
107 K3 **St.Meinrad** Indiana 38.11N 86.49W
56 E4 **St.Mellons** S Glam Wales 51.32N 3.07W
70 G4 **St.Méloir-des-Ondes** France 48.39N 1.54W
72 D4 **St. Meme les Carrières** France 45.39N 0.09W
69 H5 **Ste.Menehould** France 49.05N 4.54E
69 H4 **St.Menges** France 49.44N 4.56E
72 L2 **St.Menoux** France 46.36N 3.08E
72 J4 **St.Merd-la-Breuille** France 45.44N 2.26E
70 H3 **Ste.Mère-Église** France 49.24N 1.19W
88 R3 **St.Mérouane** Algeria 36.32N 6.15E
69 F7 **St.Mesmin** Aube France 48.27N 3.56E
72 G5 **St.Mesmin** Dordogne France 45.22N 1.14E
72 C2 **St.Mesmin** Vendée France 46.48N 0.44W
65 M3 **St.Mĕsto** Czechoslovakia 49.01N 15.16E
72 F7 **St.Mézard** France 44.02N 0.33E
113 F5 **St.Michael** Alaska 63.29N 162.10W
65 O7 **St.Michael** Burgenland Austria 47.08N 16.15E
57 H5 **St.Michael** Lancs Eng 53.52N 2.50W
108 M8 **St.Michael** Nebraska 41.01N 98.44W
65 J7 **St. Michael** Salzburg Austria 47.06N 13.38E
65 M7 **St.Michael** Steiermark Austria 47.21N 15.01E
116 O6 **St.Michael** *parish* Barbados
63 K5 **St.Michaelis-donn** W Germany 53.59N 9.07E
111 P6 **St Michaels** Arizona 35.38N 109.08W
104 J8 **St.Michaels** Maryland 38.17N 76.15W
56 T9 **St.Michael's Mount** Cornwall Eng 50.06N 5.29W
69 G4 **St.Michel** Aisne France 49.55N 4.11E
St.Michel Finland*see* **Mikkeli**
72 E9 **St.Michel** Gers France 43.27N 0.25E
70 H6 **St.Michel** Maine-et-Loire France 47.41N 1.08W
70 F7 **St.Michel-Chef-Chef** France 47.11N 2.09W
72 D7 **St. Michel de Castelnau** France 44.17N 0.06W
116 H5 **St.Michel de l'Atalaye** Haiti 19.26N 72.20W
71 J6 **St. Michel-de-Maurienne** France 45.13N 6.29E
99 R6 **St.Michel des Saints** Quebec 46.40N 73.55W
72 B3 **St.Michel-en-l'Herm** France 46.21N 1.15W
72 C2 **St.Michel-Mont Mercure** France 46.50N 0.52W
70 C5 **St.Michel,Mt** Finistère France 48.21N 3.57W
69 K6 **St.Michel,Mt** Meurthe-et-Moselle France 48.42N 5.54E
71 K8 **St. Michel-Peyresq** France 46.03N 6.37E
70 C5 **St.Michel,Res.de** France
69 M7 **St.Michel-sur-Meurthe** France 48.19N 6.52E
116 B1 **St.Michiel** Curaçao W I 12.14N 68.59W
61 C2 **St.Michiels** Belgium 51.12N 3.13E
60 K13 **St.Michielsgestel** Netherlands 51.38N 5.21E
69 K6 **St.Mihiel** France 48.54N 5.33E
69 C2 **St.Momelin** France 50.47N 2.15E
58 L6 **St.Monance** Fife Scotland 56.13N 2.46W
72 D8 **St.Mont** France 43.39N 0.09W
72 H4 **St.Moreil** France 45.51N 1.40E
72 C6 **St.Morillon** France 44.38N 0.33W
66 Q6 **St.Moritz** Switzerland 46.30N 9.51E
66 Q6 **St.Moritzbad** Switzerland 46.29N 9.51E
71 C5 **St.Myon** France 46.00N 3.08E
72 G8 **St.Nauphary** France 43.57N 1.27E
St. Nazaire *see* **Canet-en-Roussillon-St. Nazaire**
70 F7 **St.Nazaire** Loire-Atlantique France 47.17N 2.12W
71 G6 **St.Nazaire-en-Royans** France 45.04N 5.15E
71 G7 **St.Nazaire-le-Désert** France 44.34N 5.17E
71 B5 **St.Nectaire** France 45.35N 2.59E
56 L3 **St.Neots** Cambs Eng 52.14N 0.17W
70 B5 **St.Nic** France 48.12N 4.17W
56 E5 **St.Nicholas** S Glam Wales 51.28N 3.20W
69 L6 **St.Nicholas-de-Port** France 48.38N 6.18E
60 M8 **St.Nicolaasga** Netherlands 52.55N 5.45E
70 N2 **St.Nicolas-d'Aliermont** France 49.53N 1.14E
72 G7 **St. Nicolas-de-la-Grave** France 44.04N 1.02E
70 F6 **St.Nicolas-de-Redon** France 47.39N 2.03W
70 D5 **St.Nicolas-du-Pélem** France 48.18N 3.10W
61 G2 **St.Niklaas** Belgium 51.10N 4.09E
66 H7 **St.Niklaus** Switzerland 46.11N 7.48E
65 L5 **St.Nikola** Austria 48.15N 14.55E
65 K7 **St.Nikolai** Austria 47.19N 14.04E
58 J6 **St.Ninians** Central Scotland 56.06N 3.57W
58 Q10 **St.Ninian's Isle** Shetland Scotland 59.58N 1.21W
71 H6 **St. Nizier-du-Moucherotte** France 45.09N 5.38E
66 C8 **St. Nocolas de Véroce** France 45.52N 6.44E
100 U9 **St.Norbert** Manitoba 49.45N 97.10W
60 U16 **St.Odiliënberg** Netherlands 51.08N 6.00E
60 K13 **St.Oedenrode** Netherlands 51.34N 5.29E
69 C2 **St.-Omer** France 50.45N 2.15E
11 H8 **St.Omer** New Zealand 41.10S 173.56E
98 F5 **St.Omer** Quebec 48.07N 66.16W
108 G5 **St.Onge** S Dakota 44.32N 103.43W
72 C3 **Saintonge** *hist reg* France
72 H8 **St. Orens-de-Gameville** France 43.33N 1.31E
72 G5 **St.Orse** France 45.12N 1.05E
72 E9 **St.Ost** France 43.23N 0.28E
70 H4 **St.Osvin** France 48.41N 1.15W
65 L4 **St.Oswald** Austria 48.31N 14.37E
56 O4 **St.Osyth** Essex Eng 51.49N 1.05E
68 F3 **St.Ouen** France 48.54N 2.21E
70 J5 **St.Ouen-des-Toits** France 48.08N 0.55W
69 G6 **St.Ouen-et-Domprot** Marne France 48.37N 4.25E
69 C5 **St.Ouen-l'Aumône** France 49.02N 2.07E
56 W11 **St.Ouen's B** Channel Is
99 R7 **St.Ours** Quebec 45.53N 73.09W
98 C6 **St.Pacôme** Quebec 47.24N 69.58W
70 G4 **St.Pair** France 48.49N 1.35W
72 B9 **St.Palais** France 43.20N 1.01W
72 B4 **St.Palais-sur-Mer** France 45.39N 1.07W
71 D6 **St.Pal-de-Chalençon** France 45.22N 3.57E
71 E6 **St-Pal-de-Mons** France 45.15N 4.16E
98 C7 **St Pamphile** Quebec 46.58N 69.46W
55 F3 **St.Pancras** London Eng 51.32N 0.08W
65 K6 **St.Pankraz** Austria 47.47N 14.13E
72 G7 **St.Pantaléon** France 44.22N 1.16E
72 J9 **St. Papoul** France 43.20N 2.02E
71 C4 **St. Pardoux** Puy-de-Dôme France 46.03N 3.00E
72 F5 **St. Pardoux-la-Rivière** France 45.30N 0.44E
104 B6 **St. Paris** Ohio 40.06N 83.58W
71 C3 **St. Parize-le-Châtel** France 46.51N 3.10E
69 G7 **St. Parres-les-Vaudes** France 48.10N 4.13E
98 C6 **St. Pascal** Quebec 47.32N 69.48W
70 L6 **St. Paterne** Indre-et-Loire France 47.36N 0.30E
70 L5 **St. Paterne** Sarthe France 48.25N 0.07E
99 N6 **St. Patrice, L** Quebec
116 N2 **St. Patrick** *co* Trinidad & Tobago
100 F4 **St. Paul** Alberta 54.00N 111.18W
71 K7 **St. Paul** Alpes de Haute Provence France 44.31N 6.44E
107 C6 **St. Paul** Arkansas 35.50N 93.48W
65 L8 **St. Paul** Austria 46.43N 14.52E
72 H5 **St. Paul** Corrèze France 45.13N 1.53E
72 G4 **St. Paul** Haute-Vienne France 45.45N 1.26E
107 L2 **St. Paul** Indiana 39.25N 85.39W
109 P4 **St. Paul** Kansas 37.31N 95.11W
108 R4 **St. Paul** Minnesota 45.00N 93.10W
108 M8 **St. Paul** Nebraska 41.13N 98.26W
113 B8 **St. Paul** Pribilof Is Bering Sea 57.05N 170.15W
26 T15 **St. Paul** Réunion Ind Oc 21.00S 55.17E
105 G4 **St. Paul** S Carolina 33.35N 80.24W
104 C10 **St. Paul** Virginia 36.54N 82.18W
89 D8 **St.Paul** *R* Liberia
26 T14 **St. Paul, B. de** Réunion Ind Oc
72 H8 **St. Paul-Cap-de-Joux** France 43.38N 1.58E
72 J10 **St. Paul-de-Fenouillet** France 42.49N 2.29E
72 H10 **St. Paul-de-Jarrat** France 42.55N 1.39E
98 C6 **St. Paul-de-la-Croix** Quebec 47.58N 69.10W
St Paul-de-Montminy *see* **Montminy**
72 F7 **St. Paul d'Espis** France 44.08N 0.58E
98 C5 **St. Paul du Nord** Quebec 48.35N 69.16W
72 B7 **St. Paul-en-Born** France 44.13N 1.08W
71 K9 **St. Paul-en-Forêt** France 43.34N 6.43E
71 D9 **St. Paul-et-Valmalle** France 43.38N 3.42E
98 M6 **St. Paul I** C Breton I, Nova Scotia 47.12N 60.09W
26 G9 **St. Paul Î** Indian Oc 38.44S 77.30E
113 B8 **St. Paul I** Pribilof Is Bering Sea
71 D6 **St. Paulien** France 45.09N 3.49E
99 R6 **St. Paulin** Quebec 46.26N 73.01W
71 E8 **St. Paul-le-Jeune** France 44.20N 4.09E
72 B8 **St. Paul-lès-Dax** France 43.44N 1.03W
71 H9 **St. Paul-lès-Durance** France 43.41N 5.42E
86 J8 **St. Paul, Monastery of** Egypt
98 P2 **St. Paul R** Quebec
96 H8 **St. Paul Rocks** Atlantic Oc 1.00N 29.23W
105 J3 **St. Pauls** N Carolina 34.48N 78.59W
116 O3 **St. Pauls** St Kitts W I 17.25N 62.51W
St. Paul's Bay *see* **San Pawl il Bahar**
55 J5 **St. Paul's Cray** London Eng 51.24N 0.06E
St. Paul's I *see* **Selmunett**
98 P4 **St. Paul's Inlet** Newfoundland
122 V11 **St. Paul's Pt** Pitcairn I Pacific Oc 25.05S 130.05W
71 F8 **St. Paul-Trois-Châteaux** France 44.21N 4.46E
61 G2 **St. Pauwels** Belgium 51.12N 4.06E
72 A1 **St. Pazanne** France 47.06N 1.49W
72 D9 **St. Pé** France 43.06N 0.09W
69 B7 **St. Péravy-la-Colombe** France 48.01N 1.42E
70 O5 **St. Peravy-la-Colombe** France 48.01N 1.40E
71 F7 **St. Péray** France 44.56N 4.50E
71 D2 **St. Père** France 47.27N 3.45E
70 F7 **St. Père-en-Retz** France 47.13N 2.03W
98 C6 **Ste. Perpétue** Quebec 47.02N 69.58W
56 W11 **St. Peter** Channel Is 49.13N 2.11W
107 H3 **St. Peter** Illinois 38.52N 88.51W
108 R5 **St. Peter** Minnesota 44.21N 93.58W
64 E7 **St. Peter** W Germany 48.01N 8.05E
116 O6 **St. Peter** *parish* Barbados
65 K7 **St. Peter am Kammersberg** Austria 47.12N 14.11E
65 N8 **St. Peter am Ottersbach** Austria 46.49N 15.46E
St. Peter and St. Paul Rocks *see* **São Pedro e São Paulo**
98 R1 **St. Peter B** Labrador, Nfld
65 L5 **St. Peter in der Au** Austria 48.03N 14.38E
70 E3 **St. Peter Port** Channel Is 49.27N 2.32W
98 H5 **St. Peter, Pt** Quebec 48.38N 64.12W
98 M8 **St Peters** C Breton I, Nova Scotia 45.40N 60.53W
103 C6 **St. Peters** Pennsylvania 40.11N 75.43W
98 K7 **St Peters** Prince Edward I 46.26N 62.35W
12 B8 **St. Peters** *dist* Adelaide, S Australia
105 E10 **St. Petersburg** Florida 27.45N 82.40W
St Petersburg U.S.S.R.*see* **Leningrad**
66 E3 **St. Peters I** Switzerland
66 N2 **St. Peterzell** Switzerland 47.19N 9.11E
98 T8 **St.-Petronille** Quebec 46.51N 71.08W
56 B4 **St. Petrox** Dyfed Wales 51.39N 4.56W
18 H5 **St. Petrus** *islds* Indonesia 1.55N 108.43E
69 F7 **St. Phal** France 48.07N 3.59E
72 A2 **St. Philbert-de-Bouaine** France 46.59N 1.31W
72 A1 **St. Philbert-de-Grandlieu** France 47.02N 1.38W
98 B7 **St. Philémon** Quebec 46.42N 70.29W
116 P6 **St. Philip** *parish* Barbados
9 C10 **St. Philip and St. James B** New Hebrides
26 V16 **St.-Philippe** Réunion Ind Oc 21.21S 55.46E
60 E13 **St. Philipsland** Netherlands 51.37N 4.10E
99 S7 **St. Pie** Quebec 45.31N 72.55W
61 M7 **St. Pierre** Belgium 49.54N 5.23E
100 E1 **St. Pierre** Manitoba 49.28N 96.58W
116 L3 **St. Pierre** Martinique W I 14.44N 61.11W
26 U12 **St. Pierre** Mauritius, Indian Oc 20.13S 57.32E
70 D6 **St. Pierre** Morbihan France 47.31N 3.08W
99 R10 **St. Pierre** Quebec 45.27N 73.38W
26 U16 **St.-Pierre** Réunion Ind Oc 21.20S 55.29E
98 Q7 **St-Pierre** Saint-Pierre I Atlantic Oc 46.46N 56.12W
116 O1 **St. Pierre** Trinidad & Tobago 10.42N 61.37W
98 Q7 **St. Pierre and Miquelon** *islds* Atlantic Oc
71 J5 **St. Pierre-d'Albigny** France 45.34N 6.10E
70 N3 **St. Pierre-d'Autils** France 49.07N 1.25E
71 H6 **St. Pierre-de C** France 45.21N 5.50E
72 F5 **St. Pierre-de-Chignac** France 45.08N 0.54E
66 E7 **St. Pierre de Clages** Switzerland 46.12N 7.15E
72 F5 **St. Pierre-de-Côle** France 45.22N 0.47E
71 H6 **St. Pierre-de-Grande-Chartreuse** France 45.22N 5.48E
71 C9 **St. Pierre-de-la-Fage** France 43.47N 3.25E
72 F2 **St. Pierre-de-Maillé** France 46.41N 0.51E
71 H6 **St. Pierre-d'Entremont** France 45.25N 5.52E
70 G5 **St. Pierre-de-Plesguen** France 48.27N 1.55W
72 K9 **St. Pierre-des-Champs** France 43.03N 2.35E
72 C2 **St. Pierre-des-Echaubrognes** France 46.59N 0.44W
70 K5 **St. Pierre-des-Nids** France 48.24N 0.06W
72 J8 **St. Pierre-de-Trivisy** France 43.46N 2.26E
72 B4 **St. Pierre-d'Oléron** Charente-Maritime France 45.59N 1.14W
72 C2 **St. Pierre-du-Chemin** France 46.42N 0.42W
70 N3 **St. Pierre-du-Vauvray** France 49.14N 1.13E
70 H2 **St. Pierre-Église** France 49.40N 1.25W
71 J4 **St. Pierre-en-Faucigny** France 46.04N 6.22E
70 L2 **St. Pierre-en-Port** France 49.48N 0.30E
98 Q7 **St. Pierre I** Atlantic Oc
26 D6 **St. Pierre I** Indian Ocean
99 S6 **St. Pierre, L** Quebec
70 H5 **St. Pierre-la-Cour** France 48.07N 1.01W
70 H4 **St. Pierre-Langers** France 48.47N 1.29W
71 C3 **St Pierre-le-Moûtier** France 46.48N 3.06E
70 N3 **St. Pierre-lès-Elbeuf** France 49.16N 1.04E
70 A5 **St. Pierre-Quilbignon** France 48.23N 4.32W
70 K3 **St. Pierre-sur-Dives** France 49.01N 0.02W
70 K5 **St. Pierre-sur-Orthe** France 48.12N 0.13W
71 E7 **St. Pierreville** France 44.48N 4.30E
60 S17 **St. Pieter** Netherlands 50.50N 5.41E
61 F4 **St. Pieters-Kapelle** Hainaut Belgium 50.42N 4.00E
61 B2 **St. Pieters-Kapelle** West Vlaanderen Belgium 51.08N 2.53E
61 G3 **St. Pieters-Leeuw** Belgium 50.47N 4.15E
61 K3 **St. Pieters-Rode** Belgium 50.56N 4.50E
61 O4 **St. Pieters-Voeren** Belgium 50.44N 5.50E
72 F9 **St. Plancard** France 43.11N 0.34E
71 J3 **St. Point** France 46.49N 6.17E
71 J3 **St. Point, L. de** France 46.49N 6.18E
70 H4 **St. Pois** France 48.45N 1.03W
70 H6 **St. Poix** France 47.58N 1.01W
69 C1 **St. Pol** Nord France 51.01N 2.22E
70 C4 **St. Pol-de-Leon** France 48.42N 4.00W
69 C3 **St Pol-sur-Ternoise** Pas de Calais France 50.23N 2.20E
65 N5 **St. Pölten** Austria 48.13N 15.37E
72 G6 **St. Pompont** France 44.44N 1.10E
71 B10 **St. Pons** France 43.29N 2.45E
72 C4 **St. Porchaire** France 45.49N 0.46W
72 G7 **St. Porquier** France 44.00N 1.11E
72 L3 **St. Pourçain-sur-Sioule** France 46.19N 3.16E
66 B6 **St. Prex** Switzerland 46.29N 6.28E
71 F5 **St. Priest** Isère France 45.43N 4.57E
71 D5 **St. Priest** Loire France 45.57N 3.45E
71 B5 **St. Priest-des-Champs** France 45.59N 2.45E
72 G4 **St. Priest-Ligoure** France 45.38N 1.18E
72 G4 **St. Priest-sous-Aixe** France 45.49N 1.06E
72 G4 **St. Priest-Taurion** France 45.53N 1.24E
99 S4 **St.-Prime** Quebec 48.35N 72.22W
72 J5 **St. Privat** France 45.08N 2.06E
71 D7 **St. Privat-d'Allier** France 45.00N 3.41E
69 L5 **St. Privat-la-Montagne** France 49.11N 6.03E
71 D4 **St. Prix** Allier France 46.14N 3.40E
71 F7 **St. Prix** Ardèche France 44.56N 4.30E
72 H7 **St. Projet** France 44.18N 1.46E
72 C2 **St. Prouant** France 46.46N 0.57W
72 E8 **St. Puy** France 43.53N 0.28E
70 E4 **St. Quay-Portrieux** France 48.39N 2.50W
69 E4 **St. Quentin** Aisne France 49.51N 3.17E
70 J6 **St. Quentin** Maine-et-Loire France 47.46N 0.54W
98 E6 **St. Quentin** New Brunswick 47.30N 67.23W
68 A4 **St. Quentin-en-Yvelines** France 48.47N 2.00E
72 J4 **St. Quentin-la-Chabanne** Creuse France 45.52N 2.08E
71 E8 **St. Quentin-la-Poterie** France 44.03N 4.27E
69 B3 **St. Quentin, Pte. de** France 50.17N 1.32E
71 H6 **St. Quentin-sur-Isère** France 45.17N 5.33E
69 N6 **St. Quirin** France 48.37N 7.04E
65 M7 **St. Radegund** Austria 47.11N 15.29E
71 F6 **St. Rambert d'Albon** France 45.17N 4.49E
71 G5 **St. Rambert-en-Bugey** France 45.57N 5.26E
71 K10 **St. Raphael** France 43.26N 6.46E
98 B7 **St. Raphaël** Quebec 46.48N 70.45W
99 T6 **St. Raymond** Quebec 46.54N 71.50W
110 K2 **St. Regis** Montana 47.17N 115.07W
99 T2 **St. Regis** Ontario 44.58N 74.40W
104 L2 **St. Regis** *R* New York
104 L2 **St. Regis Falls** New York 44.40N 74.35W
71 F8 **St. Remèze** France 44.23N 4.30E
99 R7 **St. Rémi** Quebec 45.15N 73.37W
St. Rémi, Quebec *see* **Lac aux Sables**
70 K4 **St. Rémy** Calvados France 48.56N 0.30W
61 H6 **St. Rémy** Hainaut Belgium 50.02N 4.18E
61 N4 **St. Remy** Liège Belgium 50.42N 5.42E
71 F3 **St. Rémy** Saône-et-Loire France 46.45N 4.50E
69 E5 **St. Rémy-Blanzy** France 49.14N 3.20E
71 F9 **St. Rémy-de-Provence** Bouches-du-Rhône France 43.47N 4.49E
70 L5 **St. Rémy-des-Monts** France 48.18N 0.24E
70 G5 **St Remy du Plain** France 48.23N 1.34W
70 L5 **St. Rémy-du-Plain** France 48.21N 0.15E
69 H6 **St. Rémy-en-Bouzemont-St.-Genest-et-I** France 48.38N 4.38E
61 K3 **St. Remy-Geest** Belgium 50.45N 4.51E
68 B5 **St. Rémy-les-Chevreuse** France 48.42N 2.04E
70 N4 **St. Rémy-sur-Avre** France 48.45N 1.16E
71 D5 **St. Rémy-sur-Durolle** France 45.53N 3.35E
70 A5 **St. Renan** France 48.26N 4.37W
71 D2 **St. Révérien** France 47.13N 3.30E
79 B3 **St. Rhémy** Italy 45.50N 7.12E
71 E4 **St. Rigaux, Mt** France 46.13N 4.30E
69 B3 **St. Riquier** France 50.09N 1.58E
99 R7 **St. Robert** Quebec 45.59N 73.01W
98 A8 **St. Romain** Quebec 45.47N 71.08W
72 E3 **St. Romain** Vienne France 46.14N 0.23E
70 L2 **St. Romain-de-Colbosc** France 49.32N 0.21E
71 E5 **St. Romain-le-Puy** France 45.33N 4.07E
71 E3 **St. Romain-sous-Versigny** France 46.39N 4.12E
72 G1 **St. Romain-sur-Cher** France 47.19N 1.24E
71 G6 **St. Romans** France 45.07N 5.20E
72 K7 **St. Rome-de-Cernon** France 44.01N 2.57E
72 K7 **St. Rome-de-Tarn** France 44.03N 2.53E
98 Q10 **St. Romuald d'Etchemin** Quebec 46.46N 71.15W
98 A7 **St Romvald** Quebec 46.45N 71.14W
13 G4 **St. Ronans** Queensland 18.00S 144.42E
116 M3 **Ste. Rose** Guadeloupe W I 16.20N 61.42W
99 R7 **Ste. Rose** Quebec 45.36N 73.47W
26 V15 **Ste-Rose** Réunion Ind Oc 21.07S 55.47E
Ste Rose du Dégelé *see* **Dégelis**
100 S7 **Ste. Rose du Lac** Manitoba 51.04N 99.31W
63 U7 **St. Rudnica** Poland 52.49N 14.14E
65 N7 **St. Ruprecht an der Raab** Austria 47.09N 15.40E
71 F2 **Ste. Sabine** France 47.12N 4.37E
70 N2 **St. Saëns** France 49.40N 1.17E
72 H5 **St. Salvadour** France 45.23N 1.44E
70 E3 **St. Sampson** Channel Is 49.29N 2.31W
70 E5 **St. Samson** France 48.05N 2.46W
72 J6 **St. Santin** France 44.39N 2.12E
72 J2 **St. Saturnin** France 46.31N 2.13E
71 G9 **St. Saturnin-d'Apt** France 43.56N 5.23E
71 F9 **St. Saturnin-lès-Avignon** France 43.57N 4.56E
72 F4 **St. Saud-Lacoussière** France 45.32N 0.48E
69 C4 **St. Sauflieu** France 49.47N 2.15E
71 D2 **St. Saulge** France 47.06N 3.31E
72 E3 **St. Sauvant-d'Aliermont** France 46.22N 0.04E
71 B5 **St. Sauves d'Auvergne** France 45.37N 2.42E
61 E4 **St. Sauveur** Belgium 50.42N 3.36E
70 B5 **St. Sauveur** Finistère France 48.26N 4.00W
69 L8 **St. Sauveur** Haute-Saône France 47.48N 6.23E
72 D10 **St. Sauveur** Hautes-Pyrénées France 42.50N 0.01W
70 K4 **St. Sauveur** Orne France 48.35N 0.07W
99 Q7 **St. Sauveur** Quebec 45.52N 74.11W
71 F7 **St. Sauveur-de-Montagut** France 44.49N 4.35E
71 C1 **St. Sauveur-en-Puisaye** France 47.38N 3.12E
71 G8 **St. Sauveur-Gouvernet** France 44.20N 5.23E
70 H3 **St. Sauveur-Lendelin** France 49.08N 1.25W
70 N4 **St. Sauveur-Levasville** Eure France 48.36N 1.18E
70 G3 **St. Sauveur-le-Vicomte** France 49.23N 1.32W
71 L8 **St. Sauveur-sur-Tinée** France 44.05N 7.07E
72 J3 **St. Sauvier** France 46.24N 2.19E
72 F8 **St. Sauvy** France 43.42N 0.50E
72 D5 **St. Savin** France 45.09N 0.26W
72 F2 **St. Savin** Vienne France 46.34N 0.52E
72 C4 **St. Savinien** France 45.53N 0.40W
72 E3 **St. Saviol** France 46.08N 0.15E
70 L4 **Ste. Scolasse** France 48.35N 0.25E
95 D10 **St. Sebastian B** S Africa
72 H3 **St. Sébastien** France 46.24N 1.32E
72 E3 **St. Secondin** France 46.20N 0.30E
70 B5 **St. Segal** France 48.14N 4.05W
71 F2 **St. Seine-l'Abbaye** France 47.26N 4.48E
72 D6 **St. Selve** France 44.40N 0.30W
71 E7 **St. Sernin** France 44.34N 4.23E
72 K8 **St. Sernin-sur-Rance** France 43.53N 2.36E
69 E7 **St. Sérotin** France 48.15N 3.10E
70 F4 **St. Servan** France 48.38N 2.00W
72 C4 **St. Seurin** France 45.31N 0.50W
72 D5 **St. Seurin-sur-l'Isle** France 45.01N 0.01W
72 C8 **St. Sever** France 43.45N 0.34W
70 H4 **St. Sever-Calvados** France 48.50N 1.03W
72 D4 **Ste. Sévère** Charente France 45.45N 0.14W
72 J3 **Ste. Sévère-sur-Indre** Indre France 46.30N 2.03E
61 M4 **St. Séverin** Belgium 50.32N 5.25E
72 E5 **St. Severin** France 45.18N 0.14E
98 T7 **St. Shott's** Newfoundland 46.39N 53.36W
71 E6 **Ste. Sigolène** France 45.14N 4.15E
98 C6 **St. Siméon** Quebec 47.50N 69.55W
71 G6 **St. Siméon-de-Bressieux** France 45.20N 5.15E
69 E4 **St. Simon** Aisne France 49.45N 3.11E
72 J6 **St. Simon** Cantal France 44.58N 2.30E
98 C5 **St. Simon** Quebec 48.12N 69.02W
105 F6 **St Simons** Georgia 31.08N 81.24W
105 F6 **St Simons I** Georgia 31.10N 81.24W
51 F4 **St. Sjöfallets Nat. Park** Sweden
72 E3 **Ste. Soline** France 46.14N 0.04E
66 A5 **St. Sorlin, Mt** France 46.44N 6.09E
71 J6 **St. Sorlins-d'Arves** France 45.14N 6.16E
72 G3 **St. Sornin-Leulac** France 46.12N 1.18E
69 D5 **St. Soupplets** France 49.03N 2.49E
65 H8 **St. Stefan** Austria 46.38N 13.30E
66 F5 **St. Stephan** Switzerland 46.32N 7.24E
98 E8 **St. Stephen** New Brunswick 45.12N 67.18W
105 H4 **St. Stephen** S Carolina 33.24N 79.56W
108 B7 **St. Stephens** Wyoming 42.59N 108.26W
61 H3 **St. Stevens-Woluwe** Belgium 50.52N 4.27E
66 C4 **St. Sulpice** Neuchâtel Switzerland 46.55N 6.34E
70 M4 **St. Sulpice** Orne France 48.47N 0.40E
72 H8 **St. Sulpice** Tarn France 43.46N 1.40E
66 C5 **St. Sulpice** Vaud Switzerland 46.31N 6.34E
70 G6 **St. Sulpice-des-Landes** France 47.46N 1.35W
72 G3 **St. Sulpice Laurière** France 46.03N 1.28E
72 G3 **St. Sulpice-les-Feuilles** France 46.19N 1.22E
72 G9 **St. Sulpice-sur-Lèze** France 43.20N 1.19E
70 K5 **Ste. Suzanne** France 48.06N 0.21W
26 U14 **Ste.-Suzanne** Réunion Ind Oc 20.54S 55.37E
70 K3 **St. Sylvain** France 49.03N 0.15W
72 G4 **St. Sylvestre** Haute-Vienne France 46.00N 1.22E
98 A7 **St Sylvestre** Quebec 46.23N 71.15W
99 T6 **St. Sylvestre** Quebec 46.21N 71.16W
72 F7 **St. Sylvestre-sur-Lot** Lot-et-Garonne France 44.24N 0.49E
61 G5 **St. Symphorien** Belgium 50.27N 4.00E
72 D7 **St. Symphorien** Gironde France 44.26N 0.29W
71 D7 **St. Symphorien** Lozère France 44.50N 3.37E
71 E5 **St. Symphorien-de-Lay** France 45.57N 4.13E
71 F5 **St. Symphorien-d'Ozon** France 45.38N 4.51E
71 E5 **St. Symphorien-sur-Coise** France 45.38N 4.28E
113 U7 **St. Terese** Alaska 58.31N 134.50W
98 E5 **St. Tharsicius** Quebec 48.33N 67.20W
99 S6 **Ste. Thècle** Quebec 46.48N 72.30W
70 C4 **St. Thégonnec** France 48.32N 3.57W
98 B8 **St. Théophile** Quebec 45.57N 70.30W
99 R7 **Ste. Thérèse** Quebec 45.38N 73.50W
101 N3 **Ste. Thérèse, L** N W Terr 64.38N 121.35W
71 C10 **St. Thibery** France 43.25N 3.25E
69 K7 **St. Thiébault** France 48.12N 5.35E
108 N1 **St. Thomas** N Dakota 48.39N 97.28W
99 J10 **St. Thomas** Ontario 42.46N 81.12W
116 O6 **St. Thomas** *parish* Barbados
116 L2 **St. Thomas** *parish* Jamaica, W I
84 Z20 **St. Thomas B** Malta 35.52N 14.34E
99 S4 **St. Thomas Didyme** Quebec 48.51N 72.41W
28 B8 **St. Thomas Mount** Tamil Nadu India 12.59N 80.11E
72 J1 **Ste. Thorette** France 47.05N 2.12E
70 C6 **St Thurien** France 47.58N 3.37W
99 S6 **St. Tite** Quebec 46.44N 72.34W
98 B6 **St. Tite des Caps** Quebec 47.08N 70.46W
63 D10 **St. Tönis** W Germany 51.19N 6.28E
72 B4 **St. Trajan-les-Bains** France 45.50N 1.12W
71 G4 **St. Trivier-de-Courtes** France 46.26N 5.03E
71 F4 **St Trivier-sur-Moignans** France 46.05N 4.55E
St. Trond *see* **St. Truiden**
71 K10 **St. Tropez** France 43.16N 6.39E
71 K10 **St. Tropez, G. de** France 43.17N 6.40E
91 H6 **St. Trudon** Zaïre 5.03S 23.26E
61 L3 **St. Truiden** Belgium 50.49N 5.11E
56 C2 **St. Tudwal's Is** Gwynedd Wales 52.49N 4.28W
52 J6 **St. Tuna** Sweden 60.28N 15.30E
98 E5 **St Ulric** Quebec 48.46N 67.40W
65 G6 **St. Ulrich** Austria 47.32N 12.34E
61 G3 **St. Ulriks-Kapelle** Belgium 50.53N 4.13E
98 B6 **St. Urbain** Quebec 47.35N 70.33W
66 H3 **St. Urban** Switzerland 47.14N 7.51E
72 H8 **St. Urcisse** France 43.56N 1.37E
72 K6 **St. Urcize** France 44.42N 3.00E
66 E2 **St. Ursanne** Switzerland 47.23N 7.09E
61 G5 **St. Vaast** Belgium 50.27N 4.10E
70 M2 **St. Vaast** France 49.45N 0.44E
70 H2 **St. Vaast-la-Hougue** France 49.35N 1.16W
65 L5 **St. Valentin** Austria 48.11N 14.33E
69 E7 **St. Valérien** France 48.11N 3.07E
70 M2 **St. Valéry-en-Caux** France 49.52N 0.43E
69 B3 **St. Valery-sur-Somme** France 50.11N 1.38E
71 F6 **St. Vallier** Ardèche France 45.11N 4.49E
98 B7 **St. Vallier** Quebec 46.56N 70.46W
71 E3 **St. Vallier** Saône-et-Loire France 46.39N 4.23E
71 K9 **St. Vallier-de-Thiey** Alpes-Maritimes France 43.42N 6.51E
72 D2 **St. Varent** France 46.53N 0.14W
72 H3 **St. Vaury** France 46.12N 1.45E
65 F8 **St. Veit** Öst Tirol Austria 46.56N 12.26E
65 H7 **St. Veit** Salzburg Austria 47.20N 13.10E
65 K8 **St. Veit an der Glan** Austria 46.47N 14.22E
69 D2 **St. Venant** France 50.38N 2.33E
71 C2 **St. Vérain** France 47.30N 3.03E
70 F5 **St. Véran** Côtes-du-Nord France 48.14N 2.27W
71 K7 **St. Véran** Hautes-Alpes France 44.42N 6.52E
99 Q6 **Ste. Véronique** Quebec 46.31N 75.00W
70 O6 **St. Viâtre** France 47.32N 1.55E
70 F7 **St Viaud** France 47.18N 2.01W
72 A1 **St. Viaud** France 47.16N 2.02W
71 H9 **Ste. Victoire, Mtgne** France 43.32N 5.39E
71 F6 **St. Victor** Ardèche France 45.06N 4.40E
98 B7 **St. Victor** Quebec 46.09N 70.55W
71 E4 **St. Victor-sur-Rhins** France 46.01N 4.17E
72 J5 **St. Victour** France 45.27N 2.23E
72 G4 **St. Victurnien** France 45.53N 1.00E
61 M8 **St. Vincent** Belgium 49.41N 5.28E
70 F6 **St. Vincent** France 47.42N 2.09W
79 C3 **St. Vincent** Italy 45.45N 7.38E
116 O8 **St. Vincent** *isld* Windward Is W I 13.15N 61.12W
St. Vincent, C *see* **São Vicente, C. de**
12 H9 **St. Vincent, C** Tasmania 43.15S 145.45E
72 E5 **St. Vincent-de-Connezac** France 45.10N 0.25E
70 L6 **St Vincent-de-Larouer** France 47.49N 0.29E
99 R8 **St. Vincent de Paul** Quebec 45.37N 73.39W
71 E4 **St. Vincent-de-Reins** France 46.04N 4.23E
72 B8 **St. Vincent-de-Tyrosse** France 43.39N 1.18W
12 E5 **St. Vincent, G** S Australia
105 B8 **St. Vincent I** Florida 29.40N 85.08W
72 D3 **St. Vincent-la-Châtre** France 46.13N 0.02W
116 O8 **St. Vincent Passage** Windward Is W I
98 T7 **St. Vincent's** Newfoundland 46.49N 53.40W
72 A3 **St. Vincent-sur-Jard** France 46.25N 1.33W
71 H2 **St. Vit** France 47.11N 5.49E
100 B2 **St. Vital** Manitoba 49.49N 97.10W
106 K4 **St. Vital Pt** Michigan 45.58N 83.58W
72 B5 **St. Vivien-de-Médoc** France 45.26N 1.02W
109 G7 **St. Vrain** New Mexico 34.26N 103.29W
100 H5 **St. Walburg** Saskatchewan 53.38N 109.12W
91 J7 **Ste. Walburge** Zaïre 7.38S 24.30E
70 M2 **St. Wandrille** France 49.32N 0.45E
64 C5 **St. Wendel** W Germany 49.28N 7.10E
56 F4 **St. Weonards** Hereford & Worcs Eng 51.55N 2.44W
60 G13 **St. Willebrord** Netherlands 51.33N 4.35E
116 B1 **St. Willebrordus** Curaçao W I 12.18N 69.04W
99 K10 **St. Williams** Ontario 42.40N 80.26W
65 H6 **St. Wolfgang** Austria 47.45N 13.27E
65 H6 **St. Wolfgangsee** *L* Austria
110 S4 **St. Xavier** Montana 45.27N 107.43W
72 C8 **St. Yaguen** France 43.54N 0.44W
71 E4 **St. Yan** France 46.24N 4.02E
72 G9 **St. Ybars** France 43.15N 1.23E
71 C4 **St. Yorre** France 46.04N 3.27E
72 G4 **St. Yrieix-la-Perche** France 45.31N 1.12E
72 H5 **St. Yrieix-le-Déjalat** France 45.28N 1.57E
98 H4 **St. Yvon** Quebec 49.09N 64.48W
72 D5 **St. Yzan-de-Soudiac** France 45.09N 0.24W
71 H10 **St. Zacharie** France 43.23N 5.42E
70 O5 **Sainville** France 48.25N 1.54E
30 E3 **Saipal** *mt* Nepal 29.53N 81.30E

19 M3 Saipan Palau Is Pacific Oc 6.54N 134.09E
17 P8 Saipan isld Marianas Pacific Oc 15.12N 145.43E
120 F8 Saipurú Bolivia 19.30S 63.18W
Sairam Nor L see Sayram Hu
28 J4 Sairang Mizoram India 23.50N 92.42E
70 H2 Saire R France
70 H2 Saire, Pte. de France 49.36N 1.14W
86 M4 Saisib, Gebel el hill Egypt 30.31N 34.23E
72 C9 Saison R France
72 J9 Saissac France 43.21N 2.10E
20 M6 Saitama prefect Japan
Saiteli see Kadınhanı
25 B1 Saitlai Burma 22.05N 93.35E
20 E9 Saito Japan 32.07N 131.24E
23 B9 Sai Tso Wan Hong Kong 22.18N 114.13E
28 J3 Saitu Manipur India 25.02N 93.54E
Saiun see Saywūn
95 D5 Saivaza Madagascar 19.40S 48.32E
51 K3 Saivomuotka Sweden 68.10N 23.10E
72 D3 Saivres France 46.26N 0.12W
20 E3 Saiwai dist Yokohama Japan
23 B9 Sai Wan Ho Hong Kong 22.16N 114.12E
72 J8 Saix France 43.34N 2.10E
31 E3 Saiydabad Afghanistan 34.01N 68.44E
34 Q3 Saiyid Mazār mt Iran 35.09N 48.19E
31 G5 Saiyidwala Pakistan 31.10N 73.32E
76 L2 Saja R Spain
120 D8 Sajama Bolivia 18.07S 69.00W
120 E8 Sajama Nevado pk Bolivia 18.09S 68.52W
Sajang I see Sayang
30 D6 Sajeti Uttar Prad India 26.03N 80.10E
33 H3 Saji, As Saudi Arabia 27.38N 48.50E
33 D8 Sajid oil well Farasān Is Red Sea 16.52N 41.54E
21 D7 Saji-dong N Korea 41.50N 129.00E
33 F4 Sājir Saudi Arabia 25.09N 44.35E
33 K8 Sājir, Ra's C Oman 16.45N 53.20E
62 M7 Sajó R Hungary
62 M7 Sajószentpéter Hungary 48.12N 20.44E
34 E2 Sajur Suyi R Syria/Turkey
32 E4 Sajzī Iran 32.42N 52.05E
95 F7 Sak R S Africa
94 F8 Sak watercourse S Africa
93 L6 Saka Kenya 0.08S 39.22E
90 B6 Sakaba Nigeria 11.04N 5.35E
91 J9 Sakabinda Zaïre 11.10S 25.20E
Saka Dzong see Saga
20 C3 Sakahama Tōkyō Japan
20 J7 Sakai Japan 34.35N 135.28E
20 G7 Sakaide Japan 34.19N 133.50E
20 G6 Sakaiminato Japan 35.34N 133.12E
34 H9 Sākākah Saudi Arabia 29.59N 40.06E
31 C7 Saka Kalat Pakistan 27.03N 65.06E
44 K3 Sakakuduk Kazakhstan U.S.S.R. 44.18N 50.36E
89 A4 Sakal Senegal 15.47N 16.12W
18 M9 Sakala isld Indonesia 6.56S 116.14E
95 C7 Sakalalina Madagascar 22.21S 46.30E
95 B7 Sakalama-Soaleka Madagascar 23.02S 45.20E
87 F5 Sakalat Ethiopia 11.47N 37.19E
92 E6 Sakalilo Tanzania 8.10S 31.59E
37 F6 Sakaltutan Dağı mt Turkey 39.49N 41.40E
20 N3 Sakamachi Japan 38.10N 139.23E
95 B7 Sakamahily Madagascar 22.48S 45.52E
93 F10 Sakamaliwa Tanzania 4.04S 34.03E
97 M7 Sakami L Quebec 53.10N 77.00W
92 D8 Sakania Zaïre 12.44S 28.34E
31 C8 Sakani, Ras C Pakistan 25.14N 64.29E
20 C1 Sakanoshita Saitama Japan
90 G9 Sakany Cent Afr Rep 5.26N 14.50E
43 G7 Sakar Turkmeniya U.S.S.R. 38.57N 63.45E
Sakar mts see Brannitsa mts
95 B7 Sakaraha Madagascar 22.54S 44.31E
90 L9 Sakarani Cent Afr Rep 5.40N 23.40E
15 K6 Sakar I Bismarck Arch 5.22S 148.10E
Sakarya see Adapazarı
36 E2 Sakarya R Turkey
89 G8 Sakassou Ivory Coast 7.29N 5.19W
20 N3 Sakata Japan 38.55N 139.51E
Sakav see Akçan
Sakavi see Akçan
36 J5 Sakcagözü Turkey 37.12N 36.54E
21 C7 Sakchu N Korea 40.24N 125.01E
25 F6 Sa Keo R Thailand
31 G4 Sakesar Pakistan 32.27N 72.03E
89 L8 Sakété Benin 6.45N 2.45E
25 L8 Sakhala Nagaland India 25.59N 94.32E
40 J6 Sakhalin isld U.S.S.R.
38 O4 Sakhalinskaya Oblast' prov U.S.S.R.
40 H5 Sakhalinskiy Zaliv B U.S.S.R.
33 J4 Sakhāma, As Qatar, The Gulf 25.26N 51.27E
25 K9 Sakhan Assam India 23.50N 92.09E
41 N6 Sakhandzha U.S.S.R. 69.45N 128.12E
41 B4 Sakhanina, Mys C Novaya Zemlya U.S.S.R. 70.34N 55.09E
40 G1 Sakhara R U.S.S.R.
43 K5 Sakharozavodskiy Kazakhstan U.S.S.R. 42.52N 71.28E
29 C3 Sakhi Rajasthan India 28.59N 72.58E
31 F6 Sakhir Sarwar Pakistan 29.59N 70.22E
45 G7 Sakhnovshchina Ukraine U.S.S.R. 49.08N 35.52E
35 G1 Sakhr watercourse Syria
35 G4 Sakhra Jordan 32.22N 35.50E
86 L10 Sakhrat Shag rocks Egypt 27.48N 33.53E
35 H10 Sakhriya watercourse Jordan
35 J9 Sakhriyat, Jebel es mts Jordan
35 H10 Sakhriya Um Marajid watercourse Jordan
44 C9 Şaki Ukraine U.S.S.R. 45.09N 33.36E
46 E3 Šakiai Lithuania U.S.S.R. 55.00N 23.01E
35 G4 Sakib Jordan 32.17N 35.48E
20 H8 Sakihama Japan 33.23N 134.11E
31 D5 Sakir mt Pakistan 31.08N 67.54E
90 L9 Sakiri Cent Afr Rep 5.15N 22.10E
23 K6 Sakishima guntō islds Japan
30 B5 Sakit Uttar Prad India 27.26N 78.46E
28 B4 Sakleshpur Karnataka India 12.59N 75.43E
46 S4 Sakmara U.S.S.R. 52.00N 55.20E
88 P4 Sakni watercourse Algeria
35 E2 Saknīn Israel 32.52N 35.18E
95 D4 Sakoamadinika Madagascar 17.10S 48.02E
25 D3 Sakoi Burma 19.54N 97.02E
29 G7 Sakoli Maharashtra India 21.05N 80.02E
Sakon Nakhon see Muang Sakon Nakhon
103 M4 Sakonnet Pt C Rhode I 41.28N 71.12W
103 M3 Sakonnett R Rhode I
45 P1 Sakony U.S.S.R. 55.22N 43.10E
90 B7 Sakpe Nigeria 9.05N 5.30E
31 E7 Sakrand Pakistan 26.06N 68.20E
18 H4 Sakra, Pulau isld Singapore
30 B7 Sakrar Uttar Prad India 25.21N 78.52E
94 F8 Sakrivier S Africa 30.50S 20.26E
37 D7 Şakşak Dağ mts Turkey
43 F4 Saksaul'skiy Kazakhstan U.S.S.R. 47.06N 61.06E
53 M9 Saksen Faeroes 62.15N 7.10W
53 E5 Saksild Denmark 55.59N 10.15E
53 H7 Sakskøbing Denmark 54.48N 11.39E
29 H6 Sakti Madhya Prad India 22.02N 82.56E
30 F8 Saktisgarh Uttar Prad India 24.58N 82.50E
20 M5 Saku Japan 36.17N 138.29E
20 L6 Sakuma Japan 35.06N 137.49E
20 O6 Sakura Japan 35.43N 140.13E
20 J7 Sakurai Japan 34.31N 135.51E
20 D10 Sakura-jima pen Japan
20 C4 Sakurakabu Kanagawa Japan
29 L3 Sakya Gompa Xizang Zizhiqu 28.55N 88.10E
30 L5 Sakyetang Xizang Zizhiqu 27.58N 87.14E
51 J10 Säkylä Finland 61.04N 22.20E
35 G3 Sal Jordan 32.34N 35.54E
89 P10 Sal isld Cape Verde
45 P9 Sal R U.S.S.R.
93 L9 Şala Coast Kenya 3.06S 39.10E
62 K7 Šala Czechoslovakia 48.10N 17.50E
93 M5 Sala North Eastern Kenya 0.41N 40.09E
87 J10 Sala Somalia 0.46N 42.56E
52 K7 Sala Sweden 59.55N 16.38E
34 P10 Sala hill Saudi Arabia 28.48N 47.08E
25 G7 Sala Andong Tuk Cambodia 11.11N 103.27E
79 H5 Sala Baganza Italy 44.43N 10.13E
19 C5 Salabangka, Pulau Pulau islds Indonesia
46 E1 Salacgriva Latvia U.S.S.R. 57.42N 24.22E
81 L3 Sala Consilina Italy 40.23N 15.35E
75 J8 Salada mt Spain 39.54N 0.49W
75 N3 Salada R Spain
121 B1 Salada, B Chile
75 K5 Salada Grande L Spain 41.02N 0.13W
121 C10 Salada, Gran L Argentina
121 G6 Salada, L Buenos Aires Arg
121 C10 Salada, L Chubut Arg
121 F2 Salada, L Corrientes Arg
115 B1 Salada, L Mexico
75 K5 Salada, L Spain 41.14N 0.11W
121 F2 Saladas Argentina 28.15S 58.40W
86 P7 Salādīkh, Wādī es watercourse Saudi Arabia
121 F5 Saladillo Buenos Aires Arg 35.40S 59.50W
121 E4 Saladillo Córdoba Arg 32.55S 62.23W
121 D4 Saladillo San Luis Arg 33.14S 65.53W
121 E4 Saladillo R Córdoba Argentina
121 E3 Saladillo R Santa Fé Argentina
121 D2 Saladillo, R Santiago del Estero Arg
87 G6 Sala Dingai Ethiopia 9.59N 39.40E
119 C8 Salado Ecuador 0.12S 77.43W
115 J6 Salado Mexico 23.20N 101.59W
112 K5 Salado Texas 30.58N 97.34W
121 B2 Salado R Argentina
116 F4 Salado R Cuba
115 J4 Salado R Mexico
121 D8 Salado R Rio Negro Arg
121 E3 Salado R Santa Fé Argentina
121 F5 Salado, R Buenos Aires Arg
121 C5 Salado, R Mendoza Arg
118 B9 Salado, R Taiwan
109 C7 Salado, Rio New Mexico
89 J7 Salaga Ghana 8.34N 0.28W
87 J10 Salàgle Somalia 1.49N 42.15E
33 D6 'Şalāh Saudi Arabia 21.38N 40.10E
25 G7 Sala Hintoun Cambodia 11.26N 103.10E
34 F5 Salah, Tell mt Jordan 33.03N 38.24E
32 A2 Salahuddin Iraq 36.21N 44.10E
122 A1 Salailua W Samoa, Pacific Oc 13.39S 172.33W
42 D5 Salair U.S.S.R. 54.14N 85.54E
42 C5 Salairskiy Kryazh ridge U.S.S.R.
82 H3 Sălaj div Romania
94 H4 Salajwe Botswana 23.40S 24.46E
18 G9 Salak, Gunung mt Java Indon 6.44S 106.43E
33 M5 Salakh, Jabal mt Oman 22.20N 57.22E
85 O9 Salak, Marsa inlet Sudan 20.27N 37.11E
90 H4 Salal Chad 14.48N 17.12E
85 O9 Salala Kassala Sudan 21.17N 36.16E
85 O9 Salala Kassala Sudan 20.29N 36.34E
33 L8 Salālah Oman 17.00N 54.04E
87 J5 Salala Hills Ethiopia
36 H5 Salam R Turkey
115 O10 Salamá Guatemala 15.06N 90.15W
115 L2 Salamá Honduras 14.52N 86.28W
121 B3 Salamanca Chile 31.46S 70.59W
115 J7 Salamanca Mexico 20.34N 101.12W
104 G4 Salamanca New York 42.11N 78.43W
76 H7 Salamanca Spain 40.58N 5.40W
120 B9 Salamanca dist Lima Peru
75 P8 Salamanca dist Madrid Spain
74 C4 Salamanca prov Spain
26 Q16 Salamanca, Roches rocks Kerguelen Ind Oc 49.48S 69.26E
94 M6 Salamanga Mozambique 26.29S 32.40E
90 K6 Salamat dist Chad
32 B3 Salamatabad Iran 35.40N 47.50E
15 J7 Salamaua Papua New Guinea 7.04S 147.05E
92 G9 Salambidua mt Mozambique 15.52S 34.16E
32 H3 Salāmī Iran 34.43N 59.58E
119 C5 Salamina Colombia 5.24N 75.31W
84 S14 Salamis Cyprus 35.10N 33.55E
84 F6 Salamís isld Greece 37.58N 23.30E
33 G4 Salamiyah, As Saudi Arabia 24.08N 47.24E
76 J3 Salamón Spain 42.57N 5.08W
76 C5 Salamonde Portugal 41.40N 8.05W
106 J9 Salamonie, R Indiana
86 F3 Sâlamûn Egypt 31.05N 31.28E
36 H4 Salanda Turkey 38.52N 34.31E
29 K7 Salandi R Orissa India
81 M2 Salandra Italy 40.32N 16.20E
18 M3 Salang Borneo Indon 4.10N 117.01E
119 B8 Salanga, I Ecuador 1.39S 80.54W
51 F3 Salangen Norway 68.53N 17.50E
31 E3 Salang Tunnel Afghanistan 35.24N 69.08E
122 C2 Salani W Samoa, Pacific Oc 14.00S 171.35W
46 D2 Salantai Lithuania U.S.S.R. 56.03N 21.31E
96 P3 Salao Azores 38.37N 28.40W
81 E8 Salaparuta Sicily 37.47N 13.00E
86 E8 Salaqus Egypt 28.44N 30.50E
77 H6 Salar Spain 37.09N 4.04W
79 K5 Salara Italy 44.59N 11.26E
87 B5 Salara Sudan 11.59N 29.30E
82 G3 Sălard Romania 47.13N 22.02E
75 M2 Salardú Spain 42.42N 0.54E
31 C7 Salari Pakistan 26.46N 64.45E
121 D5 Salas Argentina 34.10S 63.06W
76 G2 Salas Oviedo Spain 43.25N 6.15W
119 B11 Salas Peru 6.18S 79.38W
82 G6 Salas Yugoslavia 44.07N 22.17E
75 D3 Salas de los Infantes Spain 42.02N 3.17W
87 G3 Salassie,E Ethiopia 14.07N 38.16E
19 N5 Salat isld Truk Is Pacific Oc 7.15N 152.01E
72 G9 Salat R France
42 B3 Salat R U.S.S.R.
18 J9 Salatiga Java Indon 7.15S 110.34E
19 N4 Salat Pass Truk Is Pacific Oc 7.15N 152.02E
75 N2 Salau France 42.45N 1.12E
72 C6 Salaunes France 44.57N 0.48W
46 R2 Salaushi U.S.S.R. 56.02N 52.58E
46 S3 Salavat U.S.S.R. 53.22N 55.50E
120 A3 Salaverry Peru 8.14S 78.55W
121 D2 Salavina Argentina 28.46S 63.23W
15 A4 Salawati isld Irian Jaya
19 M7 Salay Mindanao Philippines 8.50N 124.48E
29 A6 Salaya Gujarat India 22.20N 69.40E
19 B7 Salayar Indonesia 6.07S 120.28E
19 B6 Salayar, Selat str Celebes Indon
33 M6 Salayb, Wādī watercourse Oman
122 Q11 Sala y Gómez isld Pacific Oc 26.28S 105.28W
122 Q11 Sala y Gomez Ridge Pacific Oc
121 E6 Salazar Argentina 36.20S 62.11W
119 D4 Salazar Colombia 7.46N 72.46W
75 H2 Salazar R Spain
Salazar Angola see Ndalatando
26 U15 Salazie Réunion Ind Oc 21.02S 55.33E
26 U15 Salazie, Cirque de Réunion Ind Oc
42 E5 Salba U.S.S.R. 53.13N 92.37E
79 A4 Salbertrand Italy 45.04N 6.52E
70 P7 Salbris France 47.26N 2.03E
116 D3 Sal, Cay isld Bahamas 23.41N 80.24W
116 L9 Sal, Cayo de isld Lesser Antilles 11.47N 66.49W
120 C5 Salccantay, Cerro mt Peru 13.06S 72.36W
76 G6 Salce Spain 41.16N 6.13W
76 B4 Salceda de Caselas Spain 42.07N 8.33W
75 C5 Salceda, La Spain 41.04N 3.54W
116 J5 Salcedo Dominican Rep 19.26N 70.25W
75 E2 Salcedo Spain 42.44N 2.58W
120 C4 Sal, Cerros de la hills Peru
113 O4 Salcha R Alaska
113 O4 Salchaket Alaska 64.28N 146.57W
63 P8 Salchau E Germany 52.27N 11.35E
64 O6 Salching W Germany 48.49N 12.35E
82 J7 Salcia Romania 43.56N 24.57E
80 L5 Salcito Italy 41.45N 14.31E
82 H4 Sălciua Romania 46.25N 23.27E
56 D7 Salcombe Devon Eng 50.13N 3.47W
47 N3 Salda U.S.S.R. 58.22N 60.16E
47 J6 Salda R Sverdlovsk U.S.S.R.
47 N4 Salda R Sverdlovsk U.S.S.R.
36 D5 Salda Gölü L Turkey
119 C6 Saldana Colombia 3.57N 75.01W
76 K3 Saldaña Spain 42.31N 4.44W
119 C6 Saldaña, R Colombia
118 G2 Saldanha Brazil 10.27S 42.37W
95 A9 Saldanha S Africa 33.00S 17.56E
95 A9 Saldanhabaai B S Africa
89 C3 Saldé Senegal 16.12N 13.52W
75 H7 Saldón Spain 40.20N 1.26W
75 E4 Salduero Spain 41.54N 2.49W
121 E7 Saldungaray Argentina 38.15S 61.45W
79 J1 Saldura, Pta mt Italy 46.44N 10.44E
46 D2 Saldus Latvia U.S.S.R. 56.38N 22.30E
25 C2 Sale Burma 20.48N 94.43E
57 J6 Sale Greater Manchester Eng 53.26N 2.19W
79 E5 Sale Italy 44.59N 8.48E
88 K4 Salé Morocco 34.04N 6.50W
12 H7 Sale Victoria 38.06S 147.06E
19 E2 Salebabu isld Indonesia 3.55N 126.40E
66 K6 Salecchio Italy 46.19N 8.22E
72 F10 Saléchan France 42.57N 0.38E
105 C6 Sale City Georgia 31.17N 84.02W
107 L6 Sale Creek Tennessee 35.22N 85.08W
116 N3 Salée channel Guadeloupe W I
32 C3 Şālehābād Hamadān Iran 34.55N 48.22E
34 O5 Şālehābād Ilam Iran 33.28N 46.14E
32 F6 Şālehābād Kermān Iran 29.17N 55.50E
32 B4 Şālehābād Kermānshāh Iran 33.27N 46.10E
32 J3 Şālehābād Khorāsān Iran 35.43N 61.03E
18 M10 Saleh, Teluk B Indonesia
47 K3 Salekhard U.S.S.R. 66.33N 66.35E
122 B1 Salelologa W Samoa, Pacific Oc 13.42S 172.10W
15 L6 Salelubu New Britain 5.36S 150.58E
107 L9 Salem Alabama 32.33N 85.15W
107 E5 Salem Arkansas 36.21N 91.51W
103 K4 Salem Connecticut 41.30N 72.16W
105 D8 Salem Florida 29.55N 83.26W
107 H3 Salem Illinois 38.37N 88.58W
107 K3 Salem Indiana 38.38N 86.06W
104 P4 Salem Massachusetts 42.32N 70.53W
107 E4 Salem Missouri 37.38N 91.34W
103 D7 Salem New Jersey 39.35N 75.28W
109 C9 Salem New Mexico 32.42N 107.13W
104 M3 Salem New York 43.11N 73.20W
104 E6 Salem Ohio 40.54N 80.52W
110 B5 Salem Oregon 44.57N 123.01W
95 K9 Salem S Africa 33.28S 26.30E
105 E3 Salem S Carolina 34.53N 82.58W
108 N6 Salem S Dakota 43.45N 97.25W
28 D5 Salem Tamil Nadu India 11.38N 78.08E
104 E9 Salem Virginia 37.17N 80.04W
106 F7 Salem Wisconsin 42.33N 88.04W
104 E7 Salem W Virginia 39.16N 80.34W
103 D7 Salem co New Jersey
28 D5 Salem dist Tamil Nadu India
18 L8 Salembu Besar isld Indonesia 5.35S 114.26E
103 D7 Salem Cr New Jersey
104 O4 Salem Depot New Hampshire 42.46N 71.14W
64 G8 Salemertal W Germany 47.48N 9.18E
81 E8 Salemi Sicily 37.48N 12.48E
28 D5 Salem Junction Tamil Nadu India 11.41N 78.06E
58 E5 Salen Highland Scotland 56.43N 5.48W
58 E5 Salen Mull, Strathclyde Scotland 56.31N 5.56W
52 G5 Sälen Sweden 61.12N 13.19E
81 Q12 Salentina, Pen Italy
29 H6 Salepali Madhya Prad India 22.12N 83.26E
14 E3 Sale, R W Australia
71 J9 Salernes France 43.33N 6.14E
80 L7 Salerno Italy 40.40N 14.46E
81 K3 Salerno prov Italy
80 L8 Salerno, G. di Italy
72 J5 Salers France 45.08N 2.28E
66 D5 Sâles Switzerland 46.38N 6.58E
92 C7 Salesienne Zaïre 11.44S 27.34E
56 N4 Sales Pt Essex Eng 51.45N 0.55E
92 G10 Saleta Mozambique 16.47S 34.27E
29 G7 Saletekri reg Madhya Prad India
71 H7 Salette-Fallavaux, la France 44.50N 5.59E
71 D7 Salettes France 44.51N 3.58E
79 L4 Saletto Italy 45.13N 11.32E
69 C4 Saleux France 49.51N 2.14E
71 J4 Salève, Mt France 46.06N 6.08E
89 H7 Saleye Ivory Coast 8.18N 2.52W
66 P3 Salez Switzerland 47.14N 9.31E
35 D5 Salfit Jordan 32.05N 35.10E
57 J6 Salford Greater Manchester Eng 53.30N 2.16W
119 H9 Salgada Brazil 3.21S 60.07W
118 J2 Salgado Brazil 11.04S 37.27W
117 H8 Salgado R Brazil
121 H2 Salgado Filho airport Brazil 30.00S 51.05W
45 R1 Salgan U.S.S.R. 55.14N 45.30E
66 G6 Salgesch Switzerland 46.19N 7.35E
Salgine see Salqin
44 C9 Salgir R Ukraine U.S.S.R.
44 C10 Salgir R Ukraine U.S.S.R.
62 M7 Salgótarjan Hungary 48.05N 19.47E
117 G9 Salgueiro Brazil 8.04S 39.05W
76 D9 Salgueiro Portugal 39.53N 7.35W
121 D5 Salguero Argentina 34.17S 63.24W
35 E1 Sâlhâni Lebanon 33.08N 35.18E
Sâlhiyé, Es see Qalat es Sālihīya
53 Z18 Salhovd mt Norway 60.10N 8.30E
53 S17 Salhus Hordaland Norway 60.30N 5.15E
53 S20 Salhus Rogaland Norway 59.23N 5.17E
88 N8 Sali Algeria 26.59N 0.01W
31 A5 Salian Afghanistan 31.30N 61.37E
116 P1 Salibea Trinidad & Tobago 10.42N 61.02W
67 O12 Salice Corsica 42.07N 8.54E
81 Q12 Salice Salentino Italy 40.22N 17.58E
79 D6 Saliceto Italy 44.25N 8.10E
81 J8 Sálici Sicily 37.43N 14.38E
81 B2 Salici, Mte Sardinia 40.55N 8.59E
109 D3 Salida Colorado 38.33N 106.01W
72 C9 Salies-de-Béarn France 43.28N 0.55W
72 F9 Salies-du-Salat France 43.06N 0.57E
33 E9 Şalif, As Yemen 15.16N 42.44E
72 G6 Salignac-Eyvignes France 44.58N 1.21E
71 D4 Saligny-sur-Roudon France 46.28N 3.44E
Saliha see Yir'on
Salihabad see Şalehābād
34 O7 Şāliḩ ad Dughaym Iraq 31.10N 46.38E
Şālihīyah, As see Qalat es Sālihīya
36 C4 Salihli Turkey 38.29N 28.08E
33 B10 Salīl, Jazīrat isld S Yemen 12.44N 44.56E
75 H4 Salillas de Jalón Spain 41.34N 1.19W
33 B10 Salīl, Ra's C S Yemen 12.45N 44.56E
31 D4 Salim Afghanistan 32.20N 66.30E
35 F10 Salim watercourse Jordan
92 G8 Salima Malawi 13.45S 34.29E
18 M4 Salimbatu Borneo Indon 2.59N 117.23E
76 F2 Salime, Embalse de res Spain
91 H8 Salimi Zaïre 9.25S 23.35E
33 N9 Sālimīyah, As Kuwait 29.09N 48.05E
25 C2 Salin Burma 20.30N 94.40E
25 C2 Salin R Burma
109 N3 Salina Kansas 38.53N 97.36W
81 J6 Salina Lipari Is Italy 38.34N 14.52E
109 P5 Salina Oklahoma 36.16N 95.10W
111 N3 Salina Utah 38.57N 111.52W
81 J6 Salina isld Lipari Is Italy
84 Y20 Salina B Malta 35.58N 14.26E
115 M9 Salina Cruz Mexico 16.11N 95.12W
116 G3 Salina Pt Acklins I Bahamas 22.13N 74.19W
77 P3 Salinas Alicante Spain 38.31N 0.55W
118 G5 Salinas Brazil 16.10S 42.15W
111 C5 Salinas California 36.39N 121.40W
119 B9 Salinas Ecuador 2.15S 80.58W
75 L2 Salinas Huesca Spain 42.35N 0.14E
105 J8 Salinas Puerto Rico 17.59N 66.18W
115 J6 Salinas San Luis Potosí Mexico 22.40N 101.42W
115 M8 Salinas Veracruz Mexico 18.54N 95.55W
75 Q3 Salinas mt Spain/France 42.26N 2.45E
111 C5 Salinas R California
115 L4 Salinas, B. de Costa Rica
77 W15 Salinas, C. de Balearic Is 39.16N 3.04E
75 E2 Salinas de Añana Spain 42.48N 2.59W
120 E8 Salinas de Garci Mendoza Bolivia 19.42S 67.43W
75 E2 Salinas de Leniz Spain 42.59N 2.35W
75 G7 Salinas del Manzano Spain 40.05N 1.34W
75 G2 Salinas de Oro Spain 42.47N 1.54W
76 L3 Salinas de Pisuerga Spain 42.51N 4.23W
121 D9 Salinas Grande Argentina 42.40S 64.03W
120 B4 Salinas ó Lachay, Pta C Peru 11.20S 77.29W
121 C3 Salinas, Pampa de la plain Arg
109 D8 Salinas Pk New Mexico 33.18N 106.32W
116 J5 Salinas, Pta C Dominican Rep 18.13N 70.35W
122 V11 Salinas Pta C Juan Fernández, Is Pacific Oc 33.37S 78.30W
105 J7 Salinas, Pta pt Puerto Rico 18.28N 66.11W
91 C10 Salinas, Pta. das pt Angola 12.50S 12.54E
115 J4 Salinas Victoria Mexico 26.00N 100.20W
71 F10 Salin-de-Giraud, le France 43.24N 4.44E
71 E8 Salindres France 44.10N 4.09E
58 J6 Saline Fife Scotland 56.07N 3.36W
80 C2 Saline Italy 43.22N 10.48E
106 L7 Saline Michigan 42.12N 83.46W
107 D8 Saline R Arkansas
107 H4 Saline R Illinois
109 L2 Saline R Kansas
116 P1 Saline B Trinidad & Tobago
107 D9 Saline Bayou R Louisiana
107 D10 Saline L Louisiana 31.54N 92.54W
26 T15 Saline, La Réunion Ind Oc 21.04S 55.15E
88 M10 Salines d'Agorgott salt L Mali
111 G5 Saline Val California
104 E6 Salineville Ohio 40.38N 80.39W
25 C2 Salingyi Burma 21.58N 95.07E
120 D11 Salinitas Chile 25.00S 70.00W
117 E5 Salinópolis Brazil 0.35S 47.18W
72 J5 Salins Cantal France 45.12N 2.22E
71 K10 Salins, C. des France 43.16N 6.42E
71 J10 Salins-d'Hyères, les France 43.07N 6.12E
71 H3 Salins-les-Bains France 46.56N 5.53E
71 K6 Salins-les-Thermes France 45.27N 6.32E
19 A5 Salipolo Celebes Indonesia 3.44S 119.29E
120 F12 Sali, R Argentina
76 C14 Salir Portugal 37.14N 8.02W
103 H3 Salisbury Connecticut 41.59N 73.25W
104 K8 Salisbury Maryland 38.22N 75.37W
107 D2 Salisbury Missouri 39.25N 92.47W
105 G2 Salisbury N Carolina 35.20N 80.30W
98 G7 Salisbury New Brunswick 46.02N 65.03W
104 F7 Salisbury Pennsylvania 39.44N 79.05W
12 E5 Salisbury S Australia 34.46S 138.39E
104 M3 Salisbury Vermont 43.54N 73.06W
56 H5 Salisbury Wilts Eng 51.05N 1.48W
92 E10 Salisbury Zimbabwe 17.43S 31.05E
13 K2 Salisbury dist Brisbane, Qnsld
93 D6 Salisbury Channel Uganda
Salisbury I see Solsberi, Ostrov
97 M5 Salisbury I N W Terr 63.30N 77.00W
113 O2 Salisbury, Mt Alaska 69.10N 146.19W
56 G5 Salisbury Plain Wilts Eng
113 T8 Salisbury Sd Alaska
82 H5 Săliste Romania 45.46N 23.53E
81 G8 Salito R Sicily
118 H2 Salitre, R Brazil
120 D12 Salitrosa R Chile
91 F10 Saliveca Angola 12.23S 19.49E
35 G8 Saliya anc site Jordan 31.27N 35.56E
79 K4 Salizzole Italy 45.14N 11.05E
41 L4 Salkay, Ostrov isld U.S.S.R. 73.19N 118.33E
105 F4 Salkehatchie, R S Carolina
34 D6 Salkhad Syria 32.29N 36.42E
29 H1 Salkhia W Bengal India 22.36N 88.20E
29 J7 Salki R Orissa India
53 D4 Sall Denmark 56.17N 9.50E
65 L7 Salla Austria 47.07N 14.58E
51 O5 Salla Finland 66.50N 28.40E
71 K5 Sallanches France 45.56N 6.38E
89 C7 Sallatouk, Pte Guinea 9.05N 13.22W
72 D4 Salle d'Angles France 45.38N 0.20W
72 C1 Salle-de-Vihiers, la France 47.10N 0.37W
79 B3 Salle, La Italy 45.44N 7.04E
75 O4 Sallent Barcelona Spain 41.49N 1.54E
75 K2 Sallent Huesca Spain 42.46N 0.20W
61 H6 Salles Belgium 50.03N 4.15E
72 C6 Salles Gironde France 44.33N 0.52W
72 K7 Salles Curan France 44.11N 2.46E
72 K7 Salles-la-Source France 44.26N 2.30E
71 F8 Salles-sous-Bois Drôme France 44.27N 4.57E
72 H9 Salles-sur-l'Hers France 43.18N 1.46E
105 F4 Salley S Carolina 33.35N 81.17W
63 T9 Sallgast E Germany 51.35N 13.52E
53 C3 Salling pen Denmark 56.12N 9.00E
53 B3 Salling Sund sound Denmark 56.45N 8.50E
59 J5 Sallins Kildare Irish Rep 53.15N 6.40W
121 E6 Salliqueló Argentina 36.45S 62.55W
109 Q6 Sallisaw Oklahoma 35.27N 94.49W
85 O10 Sallom Junction Sudan 19.17N 37.02E
30 F4 Sallyana Nepal 28.21N 82.11E
59 F8 Sallybrook Cork Irish Rep 51.57N 8.24W
98 P4 Sally Cove Newfoundland 49.53N 57.56W
59 K5 Sally Gap Wicklow Irish Rep 53.11N 6.20W
33 M8 Salma Iraq 30.16N 47.41E
85 O6 Salma watercourse Saudi Arabia
32 H4 Salmābād Iran 32.31N 59.50E
33 E3 Salmā, Jabal mts Saudi Arabia
34 M8 Salmān, As Iraq 30.29N 44.34E
36 G3 Salmanlı Turkey 39.54N 34.15E
34 M5 Salmān Pāk Iraq 33.06N 44.37E
30 L7 Salmari Bihar India 25.38N 87.50E
32 A1 Salmas Iran 38.13N 44.50E
Salmean R see Nu Jiang
Salmela see Aapajärvi
75 F6 Salmerón Spain 40.33N 2.29W
47 C5 Salmi U.S.S.R. 61.19N 31.46E
51 N5 Salmivaara Finland 66.48N 28.30E
101 P11 Salmo Br Col 49.11N 117.16W
113 Q3 Salmon Alaska 66.30N 142.40W
110 M4 Salmon Idaho 45.11N 113.55W
101 M8 Salmon R Br Columbia
110 J4 Salmon R Idaho
101 O10 Salmon Arm Br Col 50.41N 119.18W
114 A1 Salmon Bank shoal Hawaiian Is
98 P2 Salmon Bay Quebec 51.25N 57.36W
110 L7 Salmon Creek Res Idaho 42.10N 114.45W
14 F3 Salmond R W Australia
110 L7 Salmon Falls Idaho 42.48N 114.56W
110 L7 Salmon Falls Cr Idaho
101 C2 Salmon Fork Alaska 65.10N 141.50W
113 Q3 Salmon Fork, R Alaska
14 D10 Salmon Gums W Australia 32.59S 121.39E
98 T6 Salmonier Newfoundland 47.11N 53.28W
110 J4 Salmon, Lit R Idaho
110 L5 Salmon Middle Fork R Idaho
110 B8 Salmon Mt California 41.11N 123.25W
98 K4 Salmon R Anticosti I, Que
98 G7 Salmon, R New Brunswick
98 Q5 Salmon Res Newfoundland
104 K3 Salmon Res New York 43.32N 75.52W
110 K5 Salmon River Mts Idaho
110 K5 Salmon S. Fork R Idaho
76 J7 Salmoral Spain 40.48N 5.13W
41 P2 Sal'm, Ostrov isld Franz Josef Land U.S.S.R.
79 C5 Salmour Italy 44.34N 7.47E
66 O1 Salmsach Switzerland 47.33N 9.23E
64 B4 Salmtal W Germany 49.55N 6.51E
64 G3 Salmünster W Germany 50.17N 9.24E
46 S3 Salmysh R U.S.S.R.
47 D3 Sal'nitsa U.S.S.R. 66.24N 35.45E
91 E2 Salo Cent Afr Rep 3.10N 16.08E
51 K11 Salo Finland 60.23N 23.10E
79 J3 Salò Italy 45.37N 10.31E
46 P2 Salobelyak U.S.S.R. 57.09N 48.00E
118 C7 Salobra R Brazil
77 N3 Salobral, El Spain 38.52N 1.55W
77 L3 Salobre Spain 38.36N 2.33W
77 J7 Salobrena Spain 36.45N 3.35W
51 L7 Saloinen Finland 64.39N 24.30E
108 P1 Salol Minnesota 48.52N 95.35W
93 L1 Salole Ethiopia 4.23N 39.33E
87 F2 Saloma Sudan 17.07N 36.31E
45 Q6 Salomatino U.S.S.R. 50.01N 44.50E
111 L8 Salome Arizona 33.49N 113.37W
116 L4 Salomon, C Martinique W I 14.31N 61.07W
27 L11 Salomon Is Chagos Arch Br Indian Oc Terr 5.16S 72.25E
30 E6 Salon Uttar Prad India 26.00N 81.30E
71 H1 Salon R France
71 G9 Salon-de-Provence France 43.38N 5.06E
18 D8 Salong hill Pen Malaysia 3.13N 103.07E
91 G4 Salonga R Zaïre
Salonica see Thessaloníki
93 H9 Salonik Tanzania 3.56S 36.57E
82 G4 Salonta Romania 46.49N 21.40E
56 F2 Salop co England
76 F9 Salor R Spain
76 E10 Salorino Spain 39.29N 7.01W
71 F3 Salornay-sur-Guye France 46.31N 4.33E
79 K2 Salorno Italy 46.14N 11.13E
75 N5 Salou Spain 41.05N 1.08E
75 N5 Salou, C Spain 41.03N 1.10E
89 A4 Saloum R Senegal
51 L10 Salpausselkä reg Finland
37 E5 Şalpazarı Turkey 40.59N 39.11E
115 Q10 Sal, Pta C Honduras 15.55N 87.35W
50 S14 Salpynten pt Spitsbergen 78.12N 12.10E
34 D2 Salqin Syria 36.10N 36.26E
76 B7 Salreu Portugal 40.44N 8.33W
121 D3 Salsacate Argentina 31.20S 65.05W
75 L7 Salsadella Spain 40.25N 0.10E
52 L4 Salsåker Sweden 62.59N 18.20E
76 F5 Salselas Portugal 41.32N 6.51W
72 K10 Salses France 42.50N 2.55E
44 D1 Sal'sk U.S.S.R. 46.30N 41.33E
81 J8 Salso R Enna, Sicily
81 G9 Salso R Sicily
80 N5 Sálsola R Italy
79 G5 Salsomaggiore Italy 44.49N 9.58E
35 F5 Salt Jordan 32.03N 35.44E
75 Q4 Salt Spain 41.59N 2.47E
111 O8 Salt R Arizona
107 L4 Salt R Kentucky
107 E2 Salt R Missouri
95 G8 Salt R S Africa
110 O6 Salt R Wyoming
120 F11 Salta Argentina 24.46S 65.28W
120 F11 Salta prov Argentina
47 L7 Saltaim, Oz L U.S.S.R.
103 H5 Saltaire Long I, N Y 40.38N 73.11W
29 L7 Saltarmukhi R W Bengal India
39 C1 Saltasa-Tas, Gory mts U.S.S.R.
56 C7 Saltash Cornwall Eng 50.24N 4.12W
53 G5 Saltbæk Vig L Denmark 55.44N 11.13E
57 M3 Saltburn Cleveland Eng 54.35N 0.58W
105 L9 Salt Cay isld New Providence I Bahamas 25.06N 77.17W
116 J4 Salt Cay isld Turks Is West Indies 21.21N 71.11W
100 P7 Saltcoats Saskatchewan 51.03N 102.12W
57 D1 Saltcoats Strathclyde Scotland 55.38N 4.47W
106 E9 Salt Cr Illinois
108 D6 Salt Cr Wyoming
104 C7 Salt Cr R Ohio
106 P3 Salt Creek R Chicago, Illinois
51 E4 Saltdal Norway 67.06N 15.25E
112 C4 Salt Draw R Texas
59 J7 Saltee Is Wexford Irish Rep 52.07N 6.36W
51 E5 Saltelv R Norway
51 D4 Salten reg Norway
53 D4 Salten Langsø L Denmark 56.05N 9.35E
57 K5 Saltersbrook S Yorks Eng 53.30N 1.46W
57 M4 Saltersgate N Yorks Eng 54.19N 0.42W
51 D4 Saltfjord inlet Norway 67.15N 14.10E
112 B4 Salt Flat Texas 31.43N 105.06W
57 O6 Saltfleet Lincs Eng 53.26N 0.10E
109 M5 Salt Fork R Oklahoma
112 G1 Salt Fork R Texas
112 J2 Salt Fork R Texas
112 H4 Salt Gap Texas 31.18N 99.37W
59 D5 Salt Hill Galway Irish Rep 53.16N 9.05W
53 K5 Saltholm isld Denmark 55.39N 12.45E
115 J5 Saltillo Mexico 25.30N 101.00W
104 G6 Saltillo Pennsylvania 40.14N 78.01W
107 H6 Saltillo Tennessee 35.22N 88.15W
66 J6 Saltine R Switzerland
112 C4 Salt L Texas 31.24N 104.50W
111 M2 Salt L Utah 39.10N 112.42W
13 E6 Salt Lake Queensland 24.00S 138.25E
95 H5 Salt Lake S Africa 29.17S 24.01E
110 O9 Salt Lake City Utah 40.45N 111.55W
14 C8 Salt Lakes W Australia
14 D6 Salt Lakes W Australia
104 B8 Salt Lick Kentucky 38.06N 83.37W
12 F4 Salt L., The New S Wales 30.09S 142.12E
121 E5 Salto Argentina 34.20S 60.15W
118 F8 Salto Brazil 23.10S 47.16W
76 D5 Salto Portugal 41.38N 7.56W
121 F3 Salto Uruguay 31.27S 57.50W
121 F3 Salto dept Uruguay
78 E6 Salto R Italy
118 H5 Salto da Divisa Brazil 16.04S 39.58W
118 C9 Salto das Sete Quedas falls Paraguay 24.05S 54.17W
115 N9 Salto de Agua Mexico 17.35N 92.20W
119 H5 Salto del Angel waterfall Venez 5.56N 62.30W
81 D4 Salto di Quirra reg Sardinia
118 E8 Salto Grande Brazil 22.53S 49.59W
80 H4 Salto, L. del Italy
51 G4 Saltoluokta Sweden 67.24N 18.30E
111 J8 Salton California 33.29N 115.51W
111 J8 Salton Sea L California
103 G3 Salt Point New York 41.48N 73.47W
89 J9 Saltpond Ghana 5.13N 1.00W
116 L2 Salt Ponds, The Jamaica, W I
53 X19 Saltpyttegga mt Norway 59.53N 7.41E
31 G4 Salt Ra Pakistan
116 K2 Salt River Jamaica, W I 17.50N 77.10W
110 P6 Salt River Ra Wyoming
116 H5 Saltrou Haiti 18.18N 72.05W
52 L7 Saltsjöbaden Sweden 59.15N 18.20E
51 H11 Saltvik Finland 60.16N 20.05E
50 H2 Saltvik Iceland 66.00N 17.21W
104 D10 Saltville Virginia 36.52N 81.48W
111 F2 Salt Wells Nevada 39.23N 118.33W
45 L3 Saltyki U.S.S.R. 53.34N 39.57E
45 Q4 Saltykovka U.S.S.R. 52.07N 44.04E
45 Q4 Saltykovo U.S.S.R. 52.24N 44.20E
122 C2 Saluafata W Samoa, Pacific Oc 13.50S 171.34W
115 F9 Salud hill Panama 9.13N 79.43W
105 F4 Saluda S Carolina 34.00N 81.47W
105 E3 Saluda, R S Carolina
79 N7 Saludecio Italy 43.52N 12.40E
19 C4 Salue Indonesia 1.59S 123.50E
19 C4 Salue Timpaus str Indonesia
79 D4 Saluggia Italy 45.13N 8.01E
29 J2 Salukdih Bihar India 23.06N 85.50E
85 H4 Salûm Egypt 31.31N 25.09E
29 D5 Salumbar Rajasthan India 24.08N 74.05E
85 H4 Salûm, Gulf of Egypt
19 L8 Saluping isld Philippines 6.20N 122.01E
28 F1 Salur Andhra Prad India 18.31N 83.16E
107 C6 Salus Arkansas 35.41N 93.24W
79 D4 Salussola Italy 45.27N 8.07E
117 C2 Salut, Is. du Fr Guiana 5.15N 52.35W
79 B5 Saluzzo Italy 44.39N 7.29E
75 G7 Salvacañete Spain 40.06N 1.30W
76 D13 Salvada Portugal 37.56N 7.46W
75 D1 Salvada, Sierra mts Spain
121 D3 Salvador Argentina 31.47S 65.58W
118 J3 Salvador Brazil 12.58S 38.29W
76 E8 Salvador Portugal 40.05N 7.05W
100 H6 Salvador Saskatchewan 52.12N 109.32W
107 F12 Salvador, L Louisiana 29.49N 90.12W
120 F10 Salvador Mazza Argentina 22.05S 63.45W
98 T5 Salvage Newfoundland 48.41N 53.40W
72 H8 Salvagnac France 43.54N 1.40E
77 C3 Salvaleón Spain 38.30N 6.48W
66 E7 Salvan Switzerland 46.07N 7.02E
117 D5 Salvaterra Brazil 0.45S 48.32W
76 B10 Salvaterra de Magos Portugal 39.01N 8.47W
76 F9 Salvaterra do Extremo Portugal 39.53N 6.54W
115 J7 Salvatierra Mexico 20.14N 100.52W
75 F2 Salvatierra Spain 42.51N 2.23W
77 C4 Salvatierra de los Barros Spain 38.30N 6.40W
76 C4 Salvatierra de Miño Spain 42.05N 8.29W
76 H7 Salvatierra de Tormes Spain 40.35N 5.36W
111 N3 Salvation Cr Utah
13 H6 Salvator, L Queensland 24.42S 147.12E
121 G8 Salvesen Ra S Georgia
72 J7 Salvetat-Peyralès, la France 44.13N 2.12E
71 B9 Salvetat-sur-Agout, la Hérault France 43.36N 2.42E
72 G6 Salviac France 44.41N 1.16E
76 A4 Sálvora, I Spain 42.28N 9.01W
101 J8 Salvus Br Col 54.20N 129.23W
33 J4 Salwah Qatar, The Gulf 24.44N 50.52E
Salween R see Nu Jiang
17 E8 Salween, R Burma/China
44 J8 Sal'yany Azerbaydzhan U.S.S.R. 39.36N 48.59E
104 B9 Salyersville Kentucky 37.43N 83.06W
63 N9 Salza E Germany 51.31N 10.46E
65 J6 Salza R Austria
65 M6 Salza R Austria
65 G7 Salzach R Austria
63 F8 Salzbergen W Germany 52.20N 7.21E
94 D5 Salzbrunn Namibia 24.23S 18.00E
65 H6 Salzburg Austria 47.48N 13.03E
65 G7 Salzburg prov Austria
63 L9 Salzderhelden W Germany 51.48N 9.55E
Salzelmen see Bad Salzelmen
63 M8 Salzgitter W Germany 52.13N 10.20E
63 M8 Salzgitter-Bad W Germany 52.02N 10.21E
63 M8 Salzgitter-Ringelheim W Germany 52.02N 10.19E
65 J6 Salzkammergut reg Austria
63 J9 Salzkotten W Germany 51.40N 8.36E
63 P9 Salzmünde E Germany 51.32N 11.48E
63 O7 Salzwedel E Germany 52.51N 11.10E
110 O6 Sam Idaho 43.44N 111.18W
43 D4 Sam Kazakhstan U.S.S.R. 45.29N 56.02E
29 B4 Sam Rajasthan India 26.50N 70.30E
35 G3 Sama Jordan 32.38N 35.49E
35 H4 Sama Jordan 32.28N 36.14E
35 J2 Sama Syria 32.46N 36.24E
86 G4 Samā'ana, El Egypt 30.48N 31.51E
119 D5 Samacá Colombia 5.28N 73.33W
35 G4 Samad Jordan 32.27N 35.50E
33 N5 Şamad Oman 22.47N 58.12E
19 D4 Samada isld Moluccas Indon 1.35S 124.29E
76 H2 Sama de Langreo Spain 43.18N 5.40W
72 D8 Samadet France 43.38N 0.28W
86 E5 Samâdûn Egypt 30.20N 30.57E
89 F5 Samaflala Mali 13.27N 6.36W
42 F6 Samagaltay U.S.S.R. 50.39N 95.01E
Samah see Ya Xian
34 N10 Samāḩ Arabia/Iraq 28.57N 45.33E
85 E5 Samah Libya 28.14N 19.05E
29 C5 Samai Gujarat India 24.08N 72.53E
89 C7 Samaia Sierra Leone 9.32N 12.26W
32 B4 Samaida Iran 32.06N 47.39E
33 N5 Samā'il Oman 23.18N 58.00E
30 L7 Samaili Bihar India 25.30N 87.16E
120 F8 Samaipata Bolivia 18.08S 63.53W
15 H4 Sama Is Bismarck Arch 1.23S 144.05E
19 C6 Samak Indonesia 4.50S 122.22E
35 F2 Samak watercourse Syria
18 F6 Samak, Tanjung C Indonesia 1.30S 105.55E
19 G1 Samal Luzon Philippines 14.46N 120.33E
19 M8 Samal isld Mindanao Philippines 7.03N 125.44E
122 B1 Samalaeulu W Samoa, Pacific Oc 13.26S 172.16W
18 B3 Samalanga Sumatra Indon 5.11N 96.22E
115 F2 Samalayuca Mexico 31.25N 106.30W
19 K9 Samales Grp islds Philippines
113 C10 Samalga I Aleutian Is 52.47N 169.15W
30 A3 Samalkha Haryana India 29.16N 77.01E
28 F2 Samalkot Andhra Prad India 17.03N 82.15E
86 E9 Samâlût Egypt 28.18N 30.43E
116 K5 Samaná Dominican Republic 19.14N 69.20W
30 A3 Samana Haryana India 29.54N 76.54E
29 E2 Samana Patiala, Punjab India 30.09N 76.15E
116 K5 Samaná, B. de Dominican Republic
116 K5 Samaná, C Dominican Republic 19.20N 69.09W
116 H3 Samana Cay isld Bahamas 23.05N 73.45W
120 A3 Samanco, B. de Peru 9.13S 78.33W
36 H6 Samandağ Turkey 36.07N 35.55E
37 G2 Samandıra Turkey 40.59N 29.13E
31 E2 Samangan Afghanistan 36.15N 68.03E
32 J3 Samangān Iran 35.30N 60.14E
31 D2 Samangan prov Afghanistan
91 J6 Samangwa Zaïre 4.23S 24.10E
20 M2 Samani Japan 42.07N 142.57E
119 C7 Samaniego Colombia 1.22N 77.35W
37 G2 Samanlı Dağ mt Turkey
86 F4 Samannûd Egypt 30.58N 31.14E
91 F9 Samapumba Angola 10.57S 19.32E
99 S3 Samaqua R Quebec
86 O6 Samar Israel 29.47N 35.02E
35 G3 Samar Jordan 32.40N 35.47E
120 D7 Sama, R Peru
19 M6 Samar isld Philippines
35 F9 Samara Jordan 31.12N 35.39E
46 R3 Samara R Kuybyshev U.S.S.R.
45 G8 Samara R Ukraine U.S.S.R.
15 L9 Samarai Papua New Guinea 10.36S 150.39E
40 H8 Samarga U.S.S.R. 47.15N 138.45E
110 N7 Samaria Idaho 42.07N 112.20W
35 D4 Samaria anc site Jordan 32.17N 35.11E
35 C5 Samaria reg Israel/Jordan
119 F5 Samariapo Venezuela 5.16N 67.43W
84 B1 Samarina Greece 40.07N 21.01E
18 M6 Samarinda Borneo Indon 0.30S 117.09E
40 F9 Samarka U.S.S.R. 44.46N 134.12E
43 H7 Samarkand Uzbekistan U.S.S.R. 39.40N 66.57E
34 L4 Sāmarrā Iraq 34.13N 43.52E
34 L4 Sāmarrā oil bore Iraq 34.17N 43.42E
34 L4 Samarra Barrage Iraq 34.13N 43.51E
19 M5 Samar Sea Philippines
43 K3 Samarskoye Karaganda, Kazakhstan U.S.S.R. 49.40N 72.02E
43 P3 Samarskoye Kazakhstan U.S.S.R. 49.03N 83.25E
45 L10 Samarskoye Rostov U.S.S.R. 46.56N 39.40E
31 F6 Samasata Pakistan 29.20N 71.33E
81 B5 Samassi Sardinia 39.29N 8.54E
30 J7 Samastipur Bihar India 25.52N 85.47E
72 F8 Samatan France 43.30N 0.56E
122 B2 Samatau W Samoa, Pacific Oc 13.52S 172.02W
15 A4 Samate Salawati I, Irian Jaya 0.59S 131.03E
81 C5 Samatzai Sardinia 39.29N 9.02E
120 E3 Samaúma Amazonas Brazil 8.40S 67.22W
120 G2 Samaúma Amazonas Brazil 6.20S 61.33W
34 M7 Samawa oil bore Iraq 31.07N 44.58E
34 N7 Samawah, As Iraq 31.18N 45.18E
28 H1 Sam-aye Xizang Zizhiqu 29.17N 91.37E
40 E1 Sama-Yuryakh U.S.S.R. 61.01N 129.10E
91 F10 Samba Angola 12.19S 19.06E
91 G3 Samba Equateur Zaïre 0.13N 21.25E
31 H4 Samba Kashmir 32.32N 75.08E
91 K6 Samba Kivu Zaïre 4.41S 26.23E
18 K6 Samba R Borneo Indon
92 H4 Sambaa tribe Tanzania
91 D8 Samba Caju Angola 8.44S 15.21E
117 E8 Sambaiba Brazil 7.05S 45.20W
89 C5 Sambailo Guinea 12.31N 13.18W
89 C4 Samba Kandji Mauritania 15.01N 12.19W
19 E4 Sambaki, Selat str Moluccas Indon
92 E5 Sambala Tanzania 6.06S 30.33E
18 M5 Sambaliung dist Borneo Indon
29 J7 Sambalpur Orissa India 21.28N 84.04E
29 H7 Sambalpur dist Orissa India
19 B6 Sambapolulu, Gunung mt Indon 5.19S 121.58E
18 J7 Sambar, Tg C Borneo Indon 3.00S 110.18E
18 H5 Sambas Borneo Indon 1.22N 109.15E
89 D4 Sambatara Mali 14.42N 10.41W
95 E3 Sambava Madagascar 14.16S 50.10E
37 D8 Şambayat Turkey 37.41N 38.03E
60 M13 Sambeek Netherlands 51.38N 5.58E
45 L9 Sambek U.S.S.R. 47.47N 39.48E
Sambelong isld see Great Nicobar
20 F6 Sambe-san mt Japan 35.09N 132.38E
30 B4 Sambhal Uttar Prad India 28.35N 78.34E
29 D4 Sambhar Rajasthan India 26.54N 75.16E
29 D4 Sambhar L Rajasthan India
81 M6 Sambiase Italy 38.58N 16.16E
70 N7 Sambin France 47.27N 1.18E
94 F1 Sambio Namibia 17.52S 20.03E
18 N5 Sambit isld Indonesia 1.46N 118.58E
117 G8 Sambito, R Brazil
91 E10 Sambo Huambo Angola 13.03S 16.08E
76 L6 Samboal Spain 41.15N 4.25W
18 M6 Samboja Borneo Indon 1.03S 117.04E
90 E8 Sambolabo Cameroon 7.06N 11.57E
91 F10 Sambongue Angola 12.34S 18.14E
25 J6 Sambor Cambodia 12.46N 106.01E
46 E5 Sambor Ukraine U.S.S.R. 49.31N 23.10E
25 J6 Sambor Dam Cambodia 12.30N 106.01E
121 G6 Samborombón, B Argentina
89 J7 Sambu Ghana 9.26N 0.07W
18 E5 Sambu Indonesia 1.06N 103.54E
93 G8 Sambu mt Tanzania 2.10S 35.56E

18 L6 **Sambuan** Borneo Indon 0.21S 115.32E
81 F8 **Sambuca di Sicilia** Sicily 37.39N 13.06E
79 J6 **Sambuca Pistojese** Italy 44.06N 10.59E
79 B6 **Sambuco** Italy 44.20N 7.04E
81 H8 **Sambughetti, Mte** Sicily 37.50N 14.22E
41 C7 **Samburg** U.S.S.R. 67.02N 78.15E
93 L9 **Samburu** Kenya 3.47S 39.17E
93 H4 **Samburu** *dist* Kenya
93 H4 **Samburu Hills** Kenya
21 E9 **Samchŏk** S Korea 37.30N 129.10E
21 D10 **Samch'ŏnp** S Korea 35.00N 128.05E
29 C5 **Samdari** Rajasthan India 25.47N 72.38E
30 G3 **Samde** Nepal 27.51N 86.41E
37 H8 **Samdi Dağ** *mt* Turkey 37.20N 44.13E
21 D8 **Samd'ŭng** N Korea 38.58N 126.12E
25 E6 **Same** Burma 13.32N 99.31E
19 D8 **Same** Indonesia 9.02S 125.42E
93 J10 **Same** Tanzania 4.04S 37.41E
66 Q5 **Samedan** Switzerland 46.33N 9.53E
88 R8 **Samene** *watercourse* Algeria
69 B2 **Samer** France 50.38N 1.45E
44 E5 **Samertskhle** *mt* Georgia U.S.S.R. 42.43N 43.12E
25 F6 **Samet, Ko** *isld* Thailand 12.33N 101.25E
91 H10 **Sametondo** Angola 12.38S 22.46E
15 B4 **Samfeman** Irian Jaya 0.33S 133.08E
92 D7 **Samfya** Zambia 11.22S 29.34E
87 O4 **Samhah** / S Yemen 12.07N 53.02E
33 J10 **Samḥah** *isld* Socotra Indian Ocean 12.05N 53.00E
33 L8 **Samḥān, Jabal** *escarp* Oman
25 B2 **Sami** Burma 21.21N 93.08E
84 A5 **Sámi** Greece 38.15N 20.39E
31 B7 **Sami** Pakistan 26.03N 63.28E
89 L6 **Samia** Nigeria 11.12N 3.33E
19 C3 **Samia, Tanjung** *C* Celebes Indon 0.58N 123.01E
84 C6 **Samikón** Greece 37.34N 21.35E
66 P3 **Samina Tal** *V* Austria/Liechtenstein
33 E3 **Samīrah** Saudi Arabia 26.30N 42.06E
Samirum Esfahān *see* **Semīrom**
Samirum Fārs *see* **Yazd-e-Khvāst**
89 K3 **Samit** Mali 16.45N 0.52E
33 E8 **Sāmitah** Saudi Arabia 16.37N 42.55E
34 L7 **Samīt, Al** Iraq 31.06N 43.19E
25 D2 **Samka** Burma 20.07N 96.58E
23 B9 **Sam Ka Tsun** Hong Kong 22.17N 114.14E
23 C10 **Sam Kong I** Hong Kong 22.10N 114.17E
88 G9 **Samlat Amgrach** *reg* Morocco
36 C3 **Şamlı** Turkey 39.49N 27.50E
93 K1 **Šamma** Ethiopia 4.37N 38.02E
35 F3 **Samma** Jordan 32.34N 35.41E
26 U7 **Sammanturai** Sri Lanka 7.22N 81.48E
51 K11 **Sammatti** Finland 60.20N 23.50E
81 N2 **Sammichele di Bari** Italy 40.52N 16.57E
35 F3 **Sammu'** Jordan 32.31N 35.44E
Sammu'i *see* **Kefar Shammay**
86 P5 **Samna** Jordan 30.09N 35.40E
33 B4 **Samnah** *well* Saudi Arabia 25.12N 37.20E
25 G5 **Samnak Kado** Thailand 14.09N 102.22E
Samnan *see* **Semnān**
32 E4 **Samnan and Damghan** *reg* Iran
53 T18 **Samnanger** Norway 60.24N 5.42E
53 T18 **Samnangerfjord** *inlet* Norway 60.18N 5.39E
20 B6 **Samnangjin** S Korea 35.21N 128.49E
66 S4 **Samnaun** Switzerland 46.57N 10.22E
66 S4 **Samnaun** *V* Switzerland
65 B7 **Samnaun Gruppe** *mts* Austria
25 H2 **Sam Neua** Laos 20.25N 104.04E
35 E6 **Samniya** *watercourse* Jordan
85 C6 **Samnū** Libya 27.17N 14.53E
76 C2 **Samo** *R* Spain
30 E2 **Samo** *R* Xizang Zizhiqu
89 H5 **Samo** *tribe* Mali/Upper Volta
110 A9 **Samoa** California 40.50N 124.10W
Samoa, East *see* **American Samoa**
Samoa i Sisifo *see* **Western Samoa**
121 B3 **Samo Alto** Chile 30.22S 71.00W
10 S4 **Samoan Is** Pacific Oc
122 A2 **Samoa, Western** *islds* Pacific Oc
29 D4 **Samod** India 27.13N 75.50E
47 E4 **Samoded** U.S.S.R. 63.36N 40.32E
71 K4 **Samoëns** France 46.05N 6.45E
45 Q8 **Samofalovka** U.S.S.R. 48.57N 44.14E
69 D7 **Samois** France 48.27N 2.45E
82 H8 **Samokov** Bulgaria 42.19N 23.34E
79 F2 **Samólaco** Italy 46.14N 9.23E
41 M4 **Samoleta, Ostrov** *isld* U.S.S.R. 73.54N 123.04E
25 D2 **Samon** *R* Burma
76 B11 **Samora Correia** Portugal 38.56N 8.52W
89 G6 **Samorogouan** Upper Volta 11.21N 4.57W
76 E3 **Samos** Spain 42.44N 7.20W
83 H7 **Sámos** *isld* Greece
18 C4 **Samosir** *isld* Sumatra Indon
Samothrace *isld see* **Samothráki**
83 H4 **Samothráki** Thraki Greece 40.27N 25.32E
83 D5 **Samothráki** *isld* Ionian Is Greece 39.46N 19.31E
83 H4 **Samothráki** *isld* Thraki Greece 40.27N 25.32E
42 B2 **Samotlor, Oz** *L* U.S.S.R. 61.07N 76.45E
45 P5 **Samoylovka** U.S.S.R. 51.10N 43.44E
89 H8 **Sampa** Ghana 8.00N 2.36W
121 D4 **Sampacho** Argentina 33.25S 64.45W
19 A5 **Sampaga** Celebes Indon 2.20S 119.10E
19 K4 **Sampaloc Pt** Luzon Philippines 14.45N 120.06E
18 M7 **Sampanahan** Borneo Indon 2.40S 116.14E
18 K9 **Sampang** Indonesia 7.13S 113.15E
31 D5 **Sam Pass** Afghanistan 31.23N 67.22E
75 O4 **Sampedor** Spain 41.47N 1.50E
75 K5 **Samper de Calanda** Spain 41.11N 0.24W
79 B5 **Sampéyre** Italy 44.34N 7.11E
105 L12 **Samphire Cay** *isld* Bahamas 25.12N 76.59W
81 J10 **Sampieri** Sicily 36.44N 14.44E
69 K6 **Sampigny** France 48.49N 5.31E
18 K7 **Sampit** Borneo Indon 2.34S 112.59E
18 K7 **Sampit** *R* Kalimantan Indonesia
18 K7 **Sampit, Teluk** *B* Borneo Indon
19 C6 **Sampolawa** Indonesia 5.36S 122.44E
80 E3 **Samprugnano** Italy 42.43N 11.32E
15 M6 **Sampun** New Britain 5.17S 152.05E
119 C4 **Sampú, R** Panama
45 N4 **Sampur** U.S.S.R. 52.19N 41.36E
91 K8 **Sampwe** Zaïre 9.22S 27.26E
35 G8 **Samra** Jordan 31.22N 35.45E
Şamrah *see* **Mazıdağı**
112 N4 **Sam Rayburn Res** Texas
87 G4 **Samre** Ethiopia 13.17N 39.14E
61 N6 **Samree** Belgium 50.13N 5.38E
86 J9 **Samr el'Abd, Gebel** *hill* Egypt 28.10N 32.40E
86 H9 **Samr el Qa', Gebel** *hill* Egypt 28.13N 32.27E
25 G5 **Samrong** Cambodia 14.12N 103.31E
25 G6 **Samrong** *R* Cambodia
36 F3 **Samsam Göl** *L* Turkey
24 D10 **Samsang** Xizang Zizhiqu China 30.22N 82.57E
37 D8 **Samsat** Turkey 37.30N 38.32E
53 F5 **Samsø** *isld* Denmark
53 F5 **Samsø Bælt** *str* Denmark
107 K10 **Samson** Alabama 31.07N 86.04W
25 H3 **Sam Son** Vietnam 19.44N 105.53E
56 Q8 **Samson** *isld* Is of Scilly Eng 49.56N 6.21W
43 H7 **Samsonono** Turkmeniya U.S.S.R. 38.00N 65.11E
103 F3 **Samsonville** New York 41.53N 74.18W
103 F3 **Sams Pt** *pk* New York 41.41N 74.22W
21 D7 **Samsu** N Korea 41.17N 128.01E
36 J1 **Samsun** Turkey 41.17N 36.22E
36 C5 **Samsun Dağı** *mt* Turkey
43 M5 **Samsy** Kazakhstan U.S.S.R. 43.18N 76.08E
63 S4 **Samtens** E Germany 54.22N 13.18E
35 F3 **Samt, Es** Jordan 32.31N 35.41E
25 H2 **Sam Teu** Laos 20.00N 104.41E
30 B7 **Samthar** Uttar Prad India 25.50N 78.54E
31 E2 **Samti** Afghanistan 37.33N 69.52E
44 E5 **Samtredia** Georgia U.S.S.R. 42.10N 42.22E
18 L7 **Samu** Borneo Indon 2.00S 115.58E
13 C4 **Samuel, Mt** N Terr Australia 19.35S 134.10E
35 D8 **Samu, Es** Jordan 31.24N 35.04E
81 B4 **Samugheo** Sardinia 39.57N 8.57E
25 F8 **Samui, Ko** *isld* Thailand
82 K7 **Samuil** Bulgaria 43.31N 26.45E
41 J3 **Samuila, Ostrov** *isld* U.S.S.R.
20 B5 **Samukawa** Kanagawa Japan
31 G5 **Samundri** Pakistan 31.04N 72.58E
44 H6 **Samur** *R* U.S.S.R.
37 H8 **Samur Dağları** *mts* Turkey
44 H6 **Samurskiy Khrebet** *mts* U.S.S.R.
42 C4 **Samus'** U.S.S.R. 56.49N 84.45E
92 B7 **Samusole** Zaïre 10.02S 24.03E
Samutlu *see* **Temelli**
25 F6 **Samut Sakhon** Thailand 13.31N 100.13E
25 F6 **Samut Songkhram** Thailand 13.25N 100.01E
35 J2 **Samya** Syria 32.47N 36.25E
24 G11 **Samyai** Xizang Zizhiqu China 29.20N 91.29E
31 J1 **Samzumling** Kashmir 34.42N 78.42E
89 G5 **San** Mali 13.21N 4.57W
62 O5 **San** *R* Poland
Sana Iran*see* **Senā**
33 H8 **Sanā** S Yemen 16.02N 49.44E
33 F9 **Şan'ā'** Yemen 15.24N 44.14E
82 D6 **Sana** *R* Yugoslavia
89 H5 **Sanaba** Upper Volta 12.25N 3.47W
35 F1 **Sanabir** Syria 33.00N 35.40E
33 B8 **Sanābis** Bahrain, The Gulf 26.14N 50.34E
33 A7 **Sanābis** Saudi Arabia 26.35N 50.06E
76 F4 **Sanabria, La** *reg* Spain
76 F4 **Sanabria, L. de** Spain 42.08N 6.43W
86 E10 **Şanabu** Egypt 27.30N 30.46E
109 D7 **San Acacia** New Mexico 34.16N 106.55W
75 G3 **San Adrián** Spain 42.20N 1.56W
76 B2 **San Adrián, C** Spain 43.21N 8.50W
75 P5 **San Adrián de Besós** Spain 41.26N 2.13E
121 H1 **Sanaduva** Brazil 27.58S 51.46W
123 B10 **Sanae** *S African Base* Antarctica 70.18S 2.22W
86 F4 **Sanafa** Egypt 30.48N 31.21E
90 F9 **Sanaga** *R* Cameroon
119 C7 **San Agustín** Colombia 1.53N 76.14W
96 V16 **San Agustín** Gran Canaria Canary Is 27.46N 15.32W
75 C6 **San Agustin** Madrid Spain 40.40N 3.37W
109 D10 **San Agustin** Mexico 31.30N 106.16W
75 J7 **San Agustín** Teruel Spain 40.04N 0.42W
120 A9 **San Agustín** *dist* Callao Peru
19 N8 **San Agustin, C** Mindanao Philippines 6.17N 126.12E
75 P3 **San Agustín de Llusanés** Spain 42.05N 2.08E
75 N4 **Sanahuja** Spain 41.53N 1.18E
58 D7 **Sanaigmore** Islay, Strathclyde Scotland 55.51N 6.26W
46 N8 **Sanain** Armenia U.S.S.R. 41.04N 44.39E
90 J1 **Sanaka** *watercourse* Chad
113 F9 **Sanak I** Aleutian Is 54.26N 162.40W
79 M5 **San Alberto** Italy 44.32N 12.09E
30 K5 **Sanam** Nepal 27.27N 86.54E
33 F5 **Sanām** Saudi Arabia 23.38N 44.45E
76 C4 **San Amaro** Spain 42.24N 8.04W
33 J6 **Sanām, As** *des reg* Saudi Arabia
120 A12 **San Ambrosio** *isld* Pacific Oc 26.28S 79.53W
Sanam Chai *see* **Ban Sanam Chai**
35 H1 **Sanamein, Es** Syria 33.04N 36.11E
34 P8 **Sanām, Jabal** *hill* Iraq 30.06N 47.39E
19 D5 **Sanana** Moluccas Indon 2.03S 125.59E
19 E5 **Sanana** *isld* Moluccas Indon
32 B3 **Sanandaj** Iran 35.18N 47.01E
120 F9 **Sanandita** Bolivia 21.40S 63.45W
79 O3 **San Andrea** *isld* Italy
111 D3 **San Andreas** California 38.10N 120.41W
111 B9 **San Andreas L** California
120 F6 **San Andrés** Bolivia 14.57S 64.28W
119 D4 **San Andrés** Colombia 6.52N 72.53W
115 P9 **San Andrés** Guatemala 17.00N 89.52W
96 P9 **San Andrés** La Palma Canary Is 28.47N 17.46W
19 M5 **San Andres** Philippines 13.36N 124.08E
96 S13 **San Andres** Tenerife Canary Is 28.30N 16.11W
121 H6 **San Andrés, B** Chile
75 O5 **San Andrés de la Barca** Spain 41.27N 1.59E
75 P4 **San Andrés de Llevaneras** Spain 41.35N 2.30E
76 H3 **San Andrés del Rabanedo** Spain 42.36N 5.36W
115 O3 **San Andrés, I. de** Caribbean Sea
109 D9 **San Andres Mts** New Mexico
115 M8 **San Andrés Tuxtla** Mexico 18.28N 95.15W
119 D2 **San Angel** Colombia 10.03N 74.15W
112 G4 **San Angelo** Texas 31.28N 100.28W
80 M8 **San Angelo Fasanella** Italy 40.25N 15.19E
112 G4 **San Angelo Res** Texas
96 Q7 **San Antonio da Serra** Madeira Is 32.43N 16.50W
76 F2 **San Antolín de Ibias** Spain 43.03N 6.53W
San Antonia do Zaïre *see* **Sovo**
79 B4 **San Antonino di Susa** Italy 45.06N 7.16E
119 F6 **San Antonio** Amazonas Venez 3.31N 66.47W
121 B1 **San Antonio** Atacamá Chile 27.55S 70.03W
88 B1 **San Antonio** Azores 38.31N 28.24W
115 D6 **San Antonio** Baja Cal Mexico 23.47N 110.06W
115 E6 **San Antonio** Baja Cal Mexico 23.30N 109.40W
115 P9 **San Antonio** Belize 16.18N 89.01W
120 F6 **San Antonio** Bolivia 14.54S 64.37W
121 D2 **San Antonio** Catamarca Arg 28.56S 65.06W
119 D2 **San Antonio** Colombia 11.35N 72.53W
115 M4 **San Antonio** Costa Rica 10.11N 85.26W
105 E9 **San Antonio** Florida 28.22N 82.17W
115 L2 **San Antonio** Honduras 14.21N 87.36W
19 K4 **San Antonio** Luzon Philippines 14.59N 120.04E
109 D8 **San Antonio** New Mexico 33.54N 106.54W
119 D9 **San Antonio** Peru 3.33S 73.53W
120 F11 **San Antonio** Salta Argentina 24.22S 65.18W
121 B4 **San Antonio** Santiago Chile 33.35S 71.39W
121 D1 **San Antonio** Santiago del Estero Arg 27.46S 63.05W
75 H8 **San Antonio** Spain 39.31N 1.11W
119 D4 **San Antonio** Tachira Venez 7.48N 72.28W
112 J6 **San Antonio** Texas 29.25N 98.30W
111 C6 **San Antonio** *R* California
112 K7 **San Antonio** *R* Texas
77 S12 **San Antonio Abad** Balearic Is 38.59N 1.19E
19 H7 **San Antonio B** Philippines
112 L7 **San Antonio B** Texas
116 B4 **San Antonio, C** Cuba 21.50N 84.57W
121 G6 **San Antonio, Cabo** Argentina 36.20S 56.45W
77 S12 **San Antonio, Cala de** *B* Balearic Is
77 R3 **San Antonio, C. de** Spain 38.48N 0.12E
117 C5 **San Antônio da Cachoeira** Brazil 0.52S 52.18W
119 E4 **San Antonio de Caparo** Venez 7.34N 71.28W
120 D7 **San Antonio de Esquilache** Peru 16.08S 70.22W
119 G2 **San Antonio del Golfo** Venez 10.29N 63.57W
120 E9 **San Antonio de Lípez** Bolivia 21.52S 66.58W
115 A2 **San Antonio del Mar** Mexico 31.08N 116.17W
116 C3 **San Antonio de los Baños** Cuba 22.54N 82.31W
120 E11 **San Antonio de los Cobres** Arg 24.10S 66.17W
120 F9 **San Antonio del Parapetí** Bolivia 20.00S 63.14W
119 G2 **San Antonio de M** Venezuela 10.08N 63.47W
119 F3 **San Antonio de Tamanaco** Venez 9.44N 66.06W
91 A2 **San Antonio de Ureca** Fernando Póo Eq Guinea 3.16N 8.39E
79 J2 **San Antonio di Mavignola** Italy 46.11N 10.47E
75 M3 **San Antonio, Embalse de** *res* Spain
121 D8 **San Antonio Este** Argentina 40.46S 64.45W
111 G7 **San Antonio, Mt** California 34.17N 117.36W
112 B4 **San Antonio Mt** Texas 31.59N 105.34W
121 D8 **San Antonio Oeste** Argentina 40.45S 64.58W
102 C5 **San Antonio, Pta** *C* Mexico 29.45N 115.41W
111 C6 **San Antonio Reservoir** California
87 B3 **Sanaqir, Jeb. es** *mt* Sudan 14.10N 28.30E
111 D5 **San Ardo** California 36.02N 120.55W
15 L8 **Sanaroa I** D'Entrecasteaux Is Papua New Guinea 9.45S 151.00E
80 M8 **San Arsenio** Italy 40.26N 15.28E
71 H10 **Sanary-sur-Mer** France 43.07N 5.48E
75 E3 **San Asensio** Spain 42.30N 2.45W
112 G4 **Sanatorium** Texas 31.37N 100.39W
Sanau *see* **Sanāw**
121 F7 **San Augustín** Buenos Aires Arg 38.00S 58.20W
121 C3 **San Augustín** San Juan Arg 30.40S 67.29W
112 N4 **San Augustine** Texas 31.32N 94.09W
33 N5 **Sanāw** Oman 22.32N 58.01E
33 J8 **Sanaw** S Yemen 17.50N 51.01E
29 E2 **Sanawar** Punjab India 30.16N 76.29E
104 O3 **Sanbarnville** New Hampshire 43.34N 71.03W
66 F8 **San Barthelémy** *R* Italy
90 C9 **San Bartholomeo** *R* Nigeria
115 J6 **San Bartolo** Mexico 22.20N 100.05W
96 U8 **San Bartolomé** Lanzarote Canary Is 29.01N 13.38W
76 K9 **San Bartolomé de las Abiertas** Spain 39.50N 4.44W
77 B6 **San Bartolomé de la Torre** Spain 37.26N 7.06W
76 K7 **San Bartolomé de Pinares** Spain 40.32N 4.33W
96 V16 **San Bartolomé de Tirajana** Gran Canaria Canary Is 27.55N 15.34W
66 N7 **San Bartolomeo** Italy 46.05N 9.09E
80 M6 **San Bartolomeo in Galdo** Italy 41.24N 15.01E
79 E2 **San Bartolomeo Valmara** Italy 46.06N 8.41E
81 N3 **San Basilio** Italy 40.19N 16.43E
81 C4 **San Basilio** Sardinia 39.33N 9.12E
75 P5 **San Baudilio de Llobregat** Spain 41.21N 2.02E
79 L7 **San Benedetto, Alpe di** *mts* Italy
80 J3 **San Benedetto del Tronto** Italy 42.57N 13.53E
79 J4 **San Benedetto Po** Italy 45.03N 10.55E
115 D8 **San Benedicto, I** Mexico
79 C4 **San Benigno Canavese** Italy 45.14N 7.47E
77 B3 **San Benito** Badajoz Spain 38.37N 7.10W
77 G3 **San Benito** Ciudad Real Spain 38.34N 4.40W
115 P9 **San Benito** Guatemala 16.56N 89.53W
112 K9 **San Benito** Texas 26.08N 97.39W
111 C5 **San Benito** *R* California
77 O3 **San Benito, Laguna de** *L* Spain 38.55N 1.08W
111 D5 **San Benito Mt** California 36.23N 120.38W
112 M6 **San Bernard** *R* Texas
111 G7 **San Bernardino** California 34.07N 117.18W
118 B9 **San Bernardino** Paraguay 25.16S 57.16W
66 N6 **San Bernardino** Switzerland 46.28N 9.13E
111 H7 **San Bernardino Mts** California
66 N6 **San Bernardino Pass** Switzerland 46.30N 9.11E
19 M5 **San Bernardino Str** Philippines
121 B4 **San Bernardo** Chile 33.37S 70.45W
115 G4 **San Bernardo** Mexico 26.09N 105.31W
119 C3 **San Bernardo, I. de** Colombia 9.45N 75.53W
79 L5 **San Biagio** Italy 44.35N 11.52E
79 M3 **San Biagio di Callalta** Italy 45.41N 12.22E
81 G8 **San Biágio Plátani** Sicily 37.31N 13.32E
121 C2 **San Blas** Argentina 28.25S 67.06W
105 B7 **San Blas** Florida 30.03N 85.37W
115 G7 **San Blas** Nayarit Mexico 21.35N 105.20W
115 E4 **San Blas** Sinaloa Mexico 26.04N 108.46W
115 Q5 **San Blas, Arch. de** Panama
105 B8 **San Blas, C** Florida 29.40N 85.12W
119 B3 **San Blas, G. de** Panama
119 B3 **San Blas, Pta** Panama 9.34N 79.00W
115 P5 **San Blas, Serrania de** *ra* Panama
79 K4 **San Bonifácio** Italy 45.24N 11.16E
120 E6 **San Borja** Bolivia 14.50S 66.52W
115 C3 **San Borja** Mexico 28.48N 113.56W
108 P6 **Sanborn** Iowa 43.10N 95.41W
108 P5 **Sanborn** Minnesota 44.14N 95.08W
108 M3 **Sanborn** N Dakota 46.56N 98.15W
111 A9 **San Bruno** California 37.37N 122.24W
22 E7 **Sanbu** Gansu China 38.35N 100.50E
120 E6 **San Buenaventura** Bolivia 14.30S 67.37W
115 J4 **San Buenaventura** Mexico 27.04N 101.32W
80 L5 **San Buono** Italy 41.58N 14.34E
25 F5 **San Buri** Thailand 15.06N 100.10E
92 G10 **Sanca** Mozambique 17.14S 34.21E
37 E6 **Sancak** Turkey 39.02N 40.23E
77 F5 **San Calixto** Spain 37.57N 5.19W
120 G11 **San Camilo** Argentina 24.35S 61.24W
79 M1 **San Candido** Italy 46.44N 12.17E
79 O3 **San Canzian d'Isonzo** Italy 45.48N 13.28E
75 K4 **San Caprasio** *mt* Spain 41.43N 0.28W
66 R6 **San Carlo** Graubünden Switz 46.21N 10.04E
81 F8 **San Carlo** Sicily 37.37N 13.15E
66 L6 **San Carlo** Ticino Switz 46.25N 8.32E
San Carlos *see* **Luba**
119 F7 **San Carlos** Amazonas Venez 1.54N 67.06W
111 O8 **San Carlos** Arizona 33.22N 110.29W
77 T11 **San Carlos** Balearic Is 39.02N 1.34E
120 F5 **San Carlos** Beni Bolivia 13.13S 65.46W
111 B10 **San Carlos** California 37.30N 122.16W
121 B6 **San Carlos** Chile 36.25S 71.58W
115 J3 **San Carlos** Coahuila Mexico 29.00N 100.54W
119 F3 **San Carlos** Cojedes Venez 9.39N 68.35W
121 D3 **San Carlos** Córdoba Arg 31.10S 65.04W
San Carlos Fernando Póo *see* **Luba**
19 K4 **San Carlos** Luzon Philippines 15.59N 120.22E
121 B4 **San Carlos** Mendoza Arg 33.45S 69.05W
19 L6 **San Carlos** Negros Philippines 10.30N 123.29E
115 M4 **San Carlos** Nicaragua 11.10N 84.45W
115 P5 **San Carlos** Panama 8.29N 79.58W
118 B8 **San Carlos** Paraguay 22.13S 57.19W
120 F11 **San Carlos** Salta Arg 25.52S 65.55W
120 F7 **San Carlos** Santa Cruz Bolivia 17.20S 63.45W
115 K5 **San Carlos** Tamaulipas Mexico 24.36N 98.49W
121 G5 **San Carlos** Uruguay 34.46S 54.58W
90 D10 **San Carlos, B. de** Fernando Póo
121 E3 **San Carlos Centro** Argentina 31.45S 61.05W
121 B8 **San Carlos de Bariloche** Arg 41.11S 71.23W
75 M6 **San Carlos de la Rápita** Spain 40.37N 0.35E
77 K3 **San Carlos del Valle** Spain 38.50N 3.15W
119 E3 **San Carlos del Zulia** Venezuela 9.01N 71.58W
111 O8 **San Carlos L** Arizona 33.13N 110.25W
115 B3 **San Carlos, Mesa de** *tableland* Mexico
118 B8 **San Carlos, R** Paraguay
80 E3 **San Casciano dei Bagni** Italy 42.52N 11.53E
79 K7 **San Casciano in Val di Pesa** Italy 43.39N 11.12E
66 O6 **San Cassiano** Italy 46.17N 9.25E
79 K1 **San Cassiano, Cima** *mt* Italy 46.43N 11.30E
81 R12 **San Cataldo** Italy 40.23N 18.18E
81 G9 **San Cataldo** Sicily 37.29N 14.00E
76 F3 **Sancedo** Spain 42.40N 6.38W
77 V14 **Sancellas** Balearic Is 39.38N 2.53E
75 P4 **San Celoni** Spain 41.42N 2.30E
72 K1 **Sancergues** France 47.09N 2.54E
71 B2 **Sancerre** France 47.20N 2.50E
81 R12 **San Cesarea Terme** Italy 40.02N 18.27E
81 R12 **San Cesário di Lecce** Italy 40.18N 18.10E
79 K5 **San Cesario sul Panaro** Italy 44.33N 11.02E
71 K2 **Sancey-le-Grand** France 47.18N 6.35E
66 C2 **Sancey le Long** France 47.18N 6.37E
23 D5 **Sancha He** *R* Guizhou China
24 C6 **Sanchakou** Xinjiang Uygur Zizhiqu China 39.56N 78.28E
70 O5 **Sancheville** France 48.11N 1.35E
116 K5 **Sánchez** Dominican Republic 19.15N 69.36W
109 E4 **Sanchez Res** Colorado 37.05N 105.24W
29 E6 **Sanchi** Madhya Prad India 23.38N 77.42E
76 K7 **Sanchidrián** Spain 40.54N 4.35W
25 G2 **San Chien Pau** *mt* Laos 21.24N 102.12E
81 M2 **San Chírico Nuovo** Italy 40.41N 16.04E
81 M3 **San Chírico Raparo** Italy 40.11N 16.05E
77 C6 **Sancho, Embalse de** *res* Spain
76 F6 **Sanchón** *R* Spain
76 L6 **Sanchonuño** Spain 41.19N 4.19W
29 B5 **Sanchor** Rajasthan India 24.45N 71.55E
46 O2 **Sanchursk** U.S.S.R. 56.54N 47.11E
81 F8 **San Cipirello** Sicily 37.58N 13.10E
76 D4 **San Ciprián de Viñas** Spain 42.18N 7.52W
89 A1 **San Cipriano, B. de** Mauritania 22.30N 16.45W
80 L7 **San Cipriano Picentino** Italy 40.43N 14.52E
115 K7 **San Ciro de Acosta** Mexico 21.40N 99.50W
77 Y14 **San Clemente** Balearic Is 39.52N 4.11E
111 G8 **San Clemente** California 33.26N 117.36W
121 B5 **San Clemente** Chile 35.32S 71.29W
77 M2 **San Clemente** Spain 39.24N 2.25W
111 F9 **San Clemente I** California 32.55N 118.30W
76 E4 **San Clodio** Spain 42.28N 7.16W
72 K2 **Sancoins** France 46.50N 2.54E
79 F6 **San Colombano Certénoli** Italy 44.22N 9.19E
81 H9 **San Cono** Sicily 37.18N 14.23E
81 M3 **San Constantino Albanese** Italy 40.02N 16.19E
19 N7 **Sanco Pt** Mindanao Philippines 8.15N 126.28E
121 F1 **San Cosme** Argentina 27.20S 58.30W
79 O7 **San Costanzo** Italy 43.46N 13.05E
121 E3 **San Cristóbal** Argentina 30.20S 61.14W
119 D9 **San Cristóbal** Colombia 2.18S 73.02W
116 J5 **San Cristóbal** Dominican Republic 18.27N 70.07W
115 M8 **San Cristóbal** Mexico 18.23N 95.44W
120 E9 **San Cristóbal** Potosí Bolivia 21.05S 67.15W
120 G5 **San Cristóbal** Santa Cruz Bolivia 13.53S 61.51W
119 D4 **San Cristóbal** Venezuela 7.46N 72.15W
77 F5 **San Cristóbal** *mt* Spain 37.45N 5.24W
76 D4 **San Cristóbal de Cea** Spain 42.29N 7.59W
76 H4 **San Cristobal de Entreviñas** Spain 42.03N 5.38W
76 H4 **San Cristóbal de la Polantera** Spain 42.23N 5.55W
115 N9 **San Cristóbal de las Casas** Mexico 16.45N 92.40W
76 K6 **San Cristóbal de la Vega** Spain 41.06N 4.39W
119 B6 **San Cristóbal, I** Galápagos Is 0.52S 89.27W
15 M4 **San Cristobal I** Solomon Is
10 N4 **San Cristóbal Trench** Pacific Oc
115 O10 **San Cristóbal Verapáz** Guatemala 15.21N 90.22W
111 L9 **San Cristobal Wash** *R* Arizona
77 Y14 **San Cristófol** Balearic Is 39.57N 4.03E
26 S14 **Sancta Maria** Mahé I Seychelles, Ind Oc 4.44S 55.29E
77 D8 **Sancti Petri** Spain 36.24N 6.13W
77 F3 **Sancti Spiritus** Badajoz Spain 38.55N 5.09W
116 E4 **Sancti-Spíritus** Cuba 21.55N 79.28W
76 G7 **Sancti-Spiritus** Salamanca Spain 40.42N 6.29W
100 J7 **Sanctuary** Saskatchewan 51.02N 108.07W
75 P5 **San Cugat de Vallés** Spain 41.28N 2.05E
69 K5 **Sancy** France 49.21N 5.56E
53 N10 **Sand** Faeroes 61.50N 6.48W
53 U20 **Sand** Norway 59.28N 6.15E
95 L4 **Sand** *R* Orange Free State S Africa
15 F5 **Sand** *R* Papua New Guinea
94 K4 **Sand** *R* Transvaal S Africa
20 J7 **Sanda** Japan 34.54N 135.12E
91 D6 **Sanda** Zaïre 4.41S 15.26E
57 B2 **Sanda** *isld* Strathclyde Scotland 55.18N 5.34W
50 F6 **Sandá** *R* Árnessýsla Iceland
50 L4 **Sandá** *R* Múlasýsla, Nordhur Iceland
50 K2 **Sandá** *R* Thingeyjarsýsla, Nordhur Iceland
86 E8 **Şandafa el Fâr** Egypt 28.32N 30.40E
53 D6 **Sandager** Denmark 55.19N 9.56E
18 J6 **Sandai** Borneo Indon 1.15S 110.31E
Sandak *see* **Shāndak**
18 N3 **Sandakan** Sabah Malaysia 5.52N 118.04E
19 H9 **Sandakan** *isld* Sabah Malaysia 5.45N 118.00E
29 L4 **Sandakphu Pk** Nepal/India 27.09N 88.05E
35 E3 **Sandala** Israel 32.31N 35.19E
32 D6 **Şandalī, Gardaneh-ye** *pass* Iran 28.54N 51.55E
81 A5 **Sandalo, C** Sardinia 39.09N 8.14E
92 G10 **Sandama** Malawi 16.13S 35.19E
Sandamargatsa *see* **Santmargats**
79 D5 **San Damiano d'Asti** Italy 44.50N 8.04E
79 B6 **San Damiano Macra** Italy 44.29N 7.15E
25 J6 **Sandan** Cambodia 12.42N 106.03E
91 G9 **Sandando** Angola 11.40S 20.48E
53 U15 **Sandane** Norway 61.47N 6.14E
18 M4 **Sandang, Gunung** *mt* Borneo Indon 3.05N 116.56E
79 O2 **San Daniele del Friuli** Italy 46.10N 13.00E
82 H9 **Sandanski** Bulgaria 41.35N 23.16E
22 F7 **Sandaohumiao** Nei Monggol Zizhiqu China 38.16N 104.24E
21 D2 **Sandaoqia** Heilongjiang China 51.09N 126.53E
21 E5 **Sandaotong** Heilongjiang China 45.42N 129.42E
21 D4 **Sandaozhen** Heilongjiang China 47.27N 126.25E
52 K5 **Sandarne** Sweden 61.15N 17.15E
109 H4 **Sand Arroyo** *R* Colorado
50 G7 **Sandasel** Iceland 63.31N 18.13W
44 D1 **Sandata** U.S.S.R. 46.17N 41.46E
63 Q7 **Sandau (Elbe)** E Germany 52.48N 12.03E
92 G4 **Sandawe** *tribe* Tanzania
58 C4 **Sanday** *isld* Highland Scotland 57.03N 6.30W
58 T11 **Sanday** *isld* Orkney Scotland 59.15N 2.30W
58 T11 **Sanday Sd** Orkney Scotland
57 J6 **Sandbach** Cheshire Eng 53.09N 2.22W
64 P6 **Sandbach** W Germany 48.36N 13.18E
52 H10 **Sandbäck** Sweden 56.10N 14.40E
58 G7 **Sandbank** Strathclyde Scotland 55.59N 4.58W
99 H1 **Sandbank L** Ontario 51.08N 82.40W
94 J4 **Sandbult** S Africa 23.42S 27.15E
53 G7 **Sandby** Denmark 54.53N 11.06E
52 G2 **Sanddøla** *R* Norway
53 S14 **Sande** Möre og Romsdal Norway 62.15N 5.27E
52 B5 **Sande** Norway 61.19N 5.48E
53 T20 **Sande** Norway 59.02N 5.36E
76 C6 **Sande** Portugal 41.07N 8.11W
53 T16 **Sande** Sogn og Fjordane Norway 61.20N 5.48E
63 H5 **Sande** W Germany 53.30N 8.01E
52 E7 **Sandefjord** *inlet* Norway
53 T19 **Sandeid** Norway 59.33N 5.52E
53 T19 **Sandeidfjorden** *inlet* Norway 59.31N 5.51E
10 B11 **Sandell B** Macquarie I Pacific Oc 54.40S 158.51E
81 M4 **San Demetrio Corone** Italy 39.34N 16.22E
80 J4 **San Demetrio ne Vestini** Italy 42.18N 13.34E
111 P6 **Sanders** Arizona 35.14N 109.20W
110 J2 **Sanders** Idaho 47.06N 116.45W
108 C3 **Sanders** Montana 46.18N 107.05W
64 M6 **Sandersdorf** W Germany 48.54N 11.38E
63 P9 **Sandersleben** E Germany 51.42N 11.35E
105 E7 **Sanderson** Florida 30.15N 82.18W
112 E5 **Sanderson** Texas 30.08N 102.25W
93 G1 **Sanderson's Gulf** *dry lake* Sudan/Kenya/Ethiopia
55 G5 **Sanderstead** London England 51.20N 0.05W
105 E5 **Sandersville** Georgia 32.59N 82.49W
107 G10 **Sandersville** Mississippi 31.47N 89.02W
30 H7 **Sandes** Bihar India 25.25N 84.44E
63 M5 **Sandesneben** W Germany 53.41N 10.28E
53 B5 **Sandet** Denmark 55.55N 8.52E
53 M9 **Sandevåg** Faeroes 62.03N 7.08W
50 C2 **Sandeyri** Iceland 66.10N 22.51W
50 J7 **Sandfell** Iceland 63.57N 16.48W
Sandfell *mt see* **Balafjöll**
50 E6 **Sandfell** *mt* Árnessýsla Iceland 64.22N 20.19W
50 K4 **Sandfell** *mt* Múlasýsla, Nordhur Iceland 65.25N 15.10W
50 F3 **Sandfell** *mt* Skagafjardharsýsla Iceland 65.42N 19.43E
50 J2 **Sandfell** *mt* Thingeyjarsýsla, Nordhur Iceland 66.07N 16.19W
95 J9 **Sandflats** S Africa 33.26S 25.58E
53 W19 **Sandfloegga** *mt* Norway 59.56N 7.08E
11 N13 **Sandfly B** New Zealand
100 L3 **Sandfly L** Saskatchewan
94 K4 **Sandfontein** S Africa 23.48S 29.01E
104 E8 **Sand Fork** W Virginia 38.55N 80.44W
56 O5 **Sandgate** Kent Eng 51.05N 1.08E
13 L7 **Sandgate** Queensland 27.18S 153.00E
50 C6 **Sandgerdhi** Iceland 64.03N 22.43W
53 Y14 **Sandgrovvatn** *L* Norway 62.24N 8.06E
53 W18 **Sandhaug** Norway 60.11N 7.30E
64 F5 **Sandhausen** W Germany 49.20N 8.39E
57 D3 **Sandhead** Dumfries & Galloway Scotland 54.48N 4.58W
11 B13 **Sand Hill Pt** New Zealand 46.16S 167.21E
105 J2 **Sand Hills** N Carolina
100 H8 **Sand Hills, Great** Saskatchewan
50 K3 **Sandhnúkavatn** *L* Iceland 65.46N 15.36W
58 M3 **Sandhole** Grampian Scotland 57.33N 2.00W
51 D4 **Sandhornøy** *isld* Norway 67.05N 14.10E
56 N5 **Sandhurst** Kent Eng 51.02N 0.34E
57 L4 **Sand Hutton** N Yorks Eng 54.14N 1.25W
Sand I Bismarck Arch *see* **Othlien Reef**
114 E9 **Sand I** Hawaiian Is
122 U2 **Sand I** Midway Is Pacific Oc 28.12N 177.23W
122 U7 **Sand I** Palmyra I Pacific Oc 5.52N 162.06W
19 N4 **Sand I** Truk Is Pacific Oc 7.30N 151.55E
30 C5 **Sandi** Uttar Prad India 27.18N 79.57E
106 D3 **Sand I** Wisconsin 46.59N 90.58W
120 D6 **Sandia** Peru 14.18S 69.25W
112 K7 **Sandia** Texas 28.02N 97.54W
76 D4 **Sandianes** Spain 42.07N 7.45W
109 D6 **Sandia Pk** New Mexico 35.14N 106.26W
120 F9 **San Diego** Bolivia 21.22S 64.15W
111 G9 **San Diego** California 32.45N 117.10W
115 E2 **San Diego** Chihuahua Mexico 30.12N 108.01W
115 G3 **San Diego** Chihuahua Mexico 28.35N 105.36W
115 J7 **San Diego** Guanajuato Mexico 21.30N 100.52W
112 J8 **San Diego** Texas 27.47N 98.15W
121 M10 **San Diego, C** Argentina 54.43S 65.07W
119 G3 **San Diego de Cabrutica** Venez 8.24N 64.55W
36 E4 **Sandıklı** Turkey 38.28N 30.17E
30 D5 **Sandila** Uttar Prad India 27.04N 80.31E
100 F1 **Sandilands** Manitoba 49.20N 96.16W
105 L9 **Sandilands Village** New Providence I Bahamas 25.02N 77.19W
70 P6 **Sandillon** France 47.51N 2.01E
14 B6 **Sandiman, Mt** W Australia 24.24S 115.24E
115 O8 **San Dimas** Campeche Mexico 19.16N 90.28W
115 G5 **San Dimas** Durango Mexico 24.10N 105.59W
18 D7 **Sanding** *isld* Indonesia 3.29S 100.44E
113 D5 **Sand Is** Alaska
103 H2 **Sandisfield** Massachusetts 42.07N 73.09W
122 U1 **Sand Islet** Midway Is Pacific Oc 28.16N 177.24W
47 H3 **Sandivey** *R* U.S.S.R.
95 H9 **Sandkraal** S Africa 33.15S 24.01E
63 H6 **Sandkrug** W Germany 53.03N 8.15E
50 F5 **Sandkúlufell** *mt* Iceland 64.59N 19.38W
65 L4 **Sandl** Austria 48.34N 14.39E
100 H1 **Sand L** Ontario 50.05N 94.35W
99 F5 **Sand Lake** Ontario 47.46N 84.31W
100 S1 **Sand L., Big** Manitoba
Sandli *pass see* **Şandalī, Gardaneh-ye** *pass*
56 O3 **Sandlings** *reg* Suffolk Eng
100 T1 **Sand L., Little** Manitoba
107 L7 **Sand Mt** Alabama
50 H4 **Sandmúladalsa** *R* Iceland
52 D8 **Sandnes** Aust Agder Norway 58.53N 7.45E
50 D3 **Sandnes** Iceland 65.44N 21.36W
52 B8 **Sandnes** Rogaland Norway 58.51N 5.45E
58 P9 **Sandness** Shetland Scotland 60.18N 1.38W
58 P9 **Sandness Hill** Shetland Scotland 60.17N 1.40W
51 C5 **Sandnessjøen** Norway 66.01N 12.40E
76 G7 **Sando** Spain 40.58N 6.07W
53 N10 **Sandø** *isld* Faeroes
91 H8 **Sandoa** Zaïre 9.41S 22.56E
62 N5 **Sandomierz** Poland 50.40N 21.45E
89 A5 **San Domingos** Guinea-Bissau 12.19N 16.13W
80 M4 **San Domino** Italy 42.07N 13.29E
119 C7 **Sandona** Colombia 1.18N 77.28W
79 N3 **San Donà di Piave** Italy 45.38N 12.34E
81 R12 **San Donato di Lecce** Italy 40.16N 18.11E
81 M4 **San Donato di Ninea** Italy 39.42N 16.03E
79 F8 **San Donato Milanese** *dist* Milan Italy
80 J5 **San Donato Val di Comino** Italy 41.42N 13.49E
107 G3 **Sandoval** Illinois 38.38N 89.05W
76 L3 **Sandoval de la Reina** Spain 42.33N 4.06W
13 D5 **Sandover** *R* N Terr Australia
46 K1 **Sandovo** U.S.S.R. 58.28N 36.30E
15 C4 **Sandow** Numfoor I, Irian Jaya 1.03S 134.54E
25 C3 **Sandoway** Burma 18.28N 94.20E
56 J6 **Sandown** I of Wight Eng 50.39N 1.09W
Sandoy *isld see* **Sandø**
53 R17 **Sandøy** *isld* Sogn og Fjordane Norway 60.54N 4.59E
110 J1 **Sandpoint** Idaho 48.17N 116.34W
100 K2 **Sand Point L** Minnesota 48.18N 92.30W
113 G9 **Sand Pt** Alaska 55.20N 160.32W
100 F4 **Sand R** Alberta
95 C6 **Sandrandahy** Madagascar 20.20S 47.18E
36 D5 **Sandras Dağı** *mt* Turkey 37.05N 28.43E
58 A5 **Sandray** *isld* W Isles Scotland 56.53N 7.31W
58 A5 **Sandray, Sound of** W Isles Scotland
79 L3 **Sandrigo** Italy 45.39N 11.37E
13 E6 **Sandringham** Queensland 24.04S 139.02E
11 C2 **Sandringham** *dist* Auckland New Zealand
12 D8 **Sandringham** *dist* Melbourne, Vic
56 N2 **Sandringham House** Norfolk Eng 52.50N 0.31E
94 K5 **Sandriviersspoort** S Africa 24.30S 28.02E
106 G3 **Sands** Michigan 46.25N 87.26W
53 V20 **Sandsavatn** *L* Norway 59.25N 6.35E
85 H6 **Sand Sea, Gt** *reg* Egypt
Sandsele *see* **Lomsele**
57 M3 **Sandsend** N Yorks Eng 54.30N 0.40W
53 U20 **Sandsfjorden** *inlet* Norway 59.22N 6.02E
105 G12 **Sands Key** *isld* Florida 25.30N 80.11W
51 F8 **Sandslån** Sweden 63.02N 17.50E
53 S14 **Sandsøy** *isld* Möre og Romsdal Norway 62.15N 5.26E
101 H9 **Sandspit** Moresby I, Br Col 53.14N 131.50W
65 G8 **Sand Spitze** *mt* Austria 46.47N 12.49E
103 M6 **Sands Point** New York
108 C2 **Sand Springs** Montana 47.06N 107.30W
109 O5 **Sand Springs** Oklahoma 36.08N 96.07W
111 F2 **Sand Springs Salt Flat** *dry lake* Nevada 39.20N 118.30W
95 N3 **Sandspruit** S Africa 27.16S 29.48E
95 K3 **Sandspruit** *R* S Africa
52 E3 **Sandstad** Norway 63.33N 9.06E
63 J6 **Sandstedt** W Germany 53.22N 8.32E
104 H9 **Sandston** Virginia 37.31N 77.18W
108 S3 **Sandstone** Minnesota 46.08N 92.50W
14 C8 **Sandstone** W Australia 27.59S 119.18E
111 M9 **Sand Tank Mts** Arizona
94 T13 **Sandton** S Africa 26.06S 28.04E
98 L4 **Sandtop, C** Anticosti I, Que 49.13N 61.45W
23 D5 **Sandu** Guizhou China 26.04N 106.44E
23 D6 **Sandu** Guizhou China 25.58N 107.57E
23 G4 **Sandu** Jiangxi China 29.10N 114.42E
Sandur *see* **Hellissandur**
50 B3 **Sandur** Isafjardharsýsla, Vestur Iceland 65.52N 23.29W
28 C3 **Sandur** Karnataka India 15.06N 76.31E
106 M6 **Sandusky** Michigan 43.26N 82.50W
104 C5 **Sandusky** Ohio 41.27N 82.42W
104 C5 **Sandusky B** Ohio
104 B5 **Sandusky, R** Ohio
50 E6 **Sandvatn** *L* Árnessýsla Iceland 64.29N 20.28W
50 E6 **Sandvatn** *L* Árnessýsla Iceland 64.25N 20.10W
50 L4 **Sandvatn** *L* Múlasýsla, Nordhur Iceland 65.18N 14.40W
53 U20 **Sandvatn** *L* Rogaland Norway 59.05N 6.23E
50 H3 **Sandvatn** *L* Thingeyjarsýsla, Sudhur Iceland 65.39N 17.06W
50 H4 **Sandvatn** *L* Thingeyjarsýsla, Sudhur Iceland 65.30N 17.11W
53 V21 **Sandvatn** *L* Vest Agder Norway 58.58N 6.38E
53 H6 **Sandved** Denmark 55.16N 11.32E
94 D6 **Sandverhaar** Namibia 26.50S 17.25E
53 P12 **Sandvig** Bornholm Denmark 55.18N 14.48E
50 H4 **Sandvík** Iceland 65.29N 17.28W
53 S14 **Sandvik** Norway 62.04N 5.26E
50 C7 **Sandvik** *inlet* Gullbringusýsla Iceland
50 M4 **Sandvík** *inlet* Múlasýsla, Sudhur Iceland
52 E7 **Sandvika** Norway 59.54N 10.29E
52 K6 **Sandviken** Sweden 60.38N 16.50E
50 L3 **Sandvíkurheidhi** *heath* Iceland
53 V18 **Sandvinvatn** *L* Norway 60.02N 6.33E
95 H9 **Sandvlakte** S Africa 33.35S 24.10E
61 P8 **Sandweiler** Luxembourg 49.37N 6.13E
106 F8 **Sandwich** Illinois 41.38N 88.38W
56 O5 **Sandwich** Kent Eng 51.17N 1.20E
103 O3 **Sandwich** Massachusetts 41.45N 70.29W
97 O7 **Sandwich B** Labrador, Nfld
13 H4 **Sandwich, C** Queensland 18.10S 146.20E
Sandwich Harb *see* **Port d'Ilheo B**
58 Q10 **Sandwick** Shetland Scotland 60.00N 1.14W
31 J10 **Sandwip** Bangladesh 22.29N 91.25E
31 J10 **Sandwip Chan** Bangladesh
100 J5 **Sandwith** Saskatchewan 53.10N 108.00W
56 L3 **Sandy** Beds Eng 52.08N 0.18W
111 J6 **Sandy** Nevada 35.49N 115.36W
110 C4 **Sandy** Oregon 45.24N 122.18W
104 P2 **Sandy** *R* Maine
94 P12 **Sandy B** Cape Town S Africa
10 C10 **Sandy B** Macquarie I Pacific Oc 54.34S 158.58E
11 J2 **Sandy B** North I New Zealand
100 P3 **Sandy B** Saskatchewan 55.32N 102.18W
116 H1 **Sandy Bay** Jamaica, W I 18.26N 78.05W
96 B14 **Sandy Bay** St Helena
11 H8 **Sandy Bay** South I New Zealand
12 F8 **Sandy Bay** *dist* Hobart, Tasmania
100 K1 **Sandybeach L** Ontario 49.55N 92.20W
14 E10 **Sandy Bight** W Australia
13 L6 **Sandy C** Queensland 24.39S 153.14E
12 G8 **Sandy C** Tasmania 41.25S 144.47E
110 O9 **Sandy City** Utah 40.36N 111.53W
13 E4 **Sandy Cr** Queensland
112 L6 **Sandy Cr** Texas
110 Q7 **Sandy Cr** Wyoming
104 J3 **Sandy Creek** New York 43.39N 76.07W
99 O7 **Sandy Creek** Quebec 45.58N 76.33W
99 O7 **Sandy Creek** Quebec 45.58N 76.33W
13 D3 **Sandy Hd** N Terr Australia 16.00S 137.14E
103 H4 **Sandy Hook** Connecticut 41.25N 73.17W
104 B8 **Sandy Hook** Kentucky 38.05N 83.09W
107 G10 **Sandy Hook** Mississippi 31.01N 89.49W
103 F6 **Sandy Hook** *C* New Jersey 40.28N 74.00W
14 D2 **Sandy Is** Indian Oc 14.03S 121.18E
26 A12 **Sandy Is** Rodriguez I Ind Oc 19.42S 63.18E
43 G8 **Sandykachi** Turkmeniya U.S.S.R. 36.36N 62.32E
98 Q4 **Sandy L** Newfoundland
97 K7 **Sandy L** Ontario 53.00N 93.00W
100 R8 **Sandy Lake** Manitoba 50.32N 100.10W
101 U7 **Sandy Lake** Saskatchewan 57.00N 107.15W
59 K4 **Sandymount** Louth Irish Rep 53.58N 6.22W
11 N13 **Sandymount** New Zealand 45.53S 170.37E
11 N13 **Sandymount** *hill* New Zealand 45.54S 170.40E
100 O3 **Sandy Narrows** Saskatchewan 55.04N 103.01W
105 L2 **Sandy Point** N Carolina 35.54N 76.04W
116 P3 **Sandy Point** St Kitts W I 17.22N 62.51W
116 A2 **Sandy Pt** San Salvador I Bahamas 23.57N 74.34W
96 C15 **Sandy Pt** Tristan da Cunha 37.06S 12.18W
103 L4 **Sandy Pt** *C* Rhode I 41.13N 71.34W
103 C4 **Sandy Run** Pennsylvania 41.01N 75.51W
86 G4 **Sân el Hagar** Egypt 30.59N 31.52E
80 J2 **San Elpidio a Mare** Italy 43.13N 13.42E
61 O8 **Sanem** Luxembourg 49.33N 5.56E
76 H3 **San Emiliano** Spain 42.58N 6.00W
25 G3 **Sane, Nam** *R* Laos
121 E5 **San Enrique** Argentina 35.47S 60.23W
118 C9 **San Estanislao** Paraguay 24.36S 56.29W
115 M2 **San Esteban** Honduras 15.19N 85.52W
75 L4 **San Esteban** Huesca Spain 41.54N 0.20E
76 G1 **San Esteban** Oviedo Spain 43.33N 6.05W
75 P3 **San Esteban de Bas** Spain 42.07N 2.28E
75 D4 **San Esteban de Gormaz** Spain 41.34N 3.13W
76 H7 **San Esteban de la Sierra** Spain 40.31N 5.54W
76 K8 **San Esteban del Valle** Spain 40.16N 4.59W
76 F4 **San Esteban de Valdueza** Spain 42.29N 6.35W
76 E4 **San Esteban, Emb de** *res* Spain
121 J6 **San Estéban, G. de** Chile
66 F6 **Sanetsch Pass** Switzerland 46.20N 7.17E
19 K3 **San Fabian** Luzon Philippines 16.15N 120.24E
80 N7 **San Fele** Italy 40.48N 15.33E
80 H6 **San Felice Circeo** Italy 41.14N 13.05E
76 F7 **San Felices de los Gallegos** Spain 40.50N 6.42W
79 K5 **San Felice sul Panaro** Italy 44.51N 11.09E
115 B2 **San Felipe** Baja Cal Mexico 31.03N 114.52W
115 F4 **San Felipe** Chihuahua Mexico 27.20N 106.00W
121 B4 **San Felipe** Chile 32.45S 70.42W
115 J7 **San Felipe** Guanajuato Mexico 21.30N 101.15W
115 O10 **San Felipe** Guatemala 14.40N 91.30W
119 F2 **San Felipe** Venezuela 10.25N 68.40W
75 G7 **San Felipe** *mt* Spain 40.24N 1.52W
121 K9 **San Felipe, B** Chile
116 C4 **San Felipe, Cayos de** *islds* Cuba
111 H8 **San Felipe Cr** California
109 D6 **San Felipe Pueblo** New Mexico 35.26N 106.27W
75 Q4 **San Feliú de Buxalleu** Spain 41.47N 2.35E
75 P4 **San Feliú de Codinas** Spain 41.41N 2.11E
75 R4 **San Feliú de Guixols** Spain 41.47N 3.02E
75 P5 **San Felíu de Llobregat** Spain 41.23N 2.02E
75 Q3 **San Feliú de Pallarols** Spain 42.04N 2.30E
75 P4 **San Feliú Saserra** Spain 41.57N 2.01E
121 B2 **San Félix** Chile 28.58S 70.30W
115 O5 **San Félix** Panama 8.20N 81.50W
120 A12 **San Félix** *isld* Pacific Oc 26.23S 80.05W
80 O6 **San Ferdinando di Puglia** Italy 41.18N 16.05E

121 F5 **San Fernando** Argentina 34.28S 58.30W
115 B3 **San Fernando** Baja Cal Mexico 29.59N 115.10W
111 F7 **San Fernando** California 34.17N 118.27W
121 B5 **San Fernando** Chile 34.40S 71.00W
119 D4 **San Fernando** Colombia 6.15N 74.14W
19 K3 **San Fernando** Luzon Philippines 16.39N 120.19E
19 K4 **San Fernando** Luzon Philippines 15.02N 120.41E
77 D8 **San Fernando** Spain 36.28N 6.12W
115 K5 **San Fernando** Tamaulipas Mexico 24.50N 98.10W
116 O2 **San Fernando** Trinidad & Tobago 10.16N 61.28W
119 F4 **San Fernando de Apure** Venez 7.53N 67.15W
119 F5 **San Fernando de Atabapo** Venez 4.03N 67.45W
118 B5 **San Fernando, R** Bolivia
77 V14 **San Ferriol** Balearic Is 39.34N 2.43E
81 M5 **San Fili** Italy 39.20N 16.08E
81 K7 **San Filippo del Mela** Sicily 38.11N 15.17E
52 H4 **Sånfjället** *mt* Sweden 62.18N 13.30E
109 E4 **Sanford** Colorado 37.16N 105.55W
105 F9 **Sanford** Florida 28.49N 81.17W
104 P3 **Sanford** Maine 43.25N 70.46W
100 U9 **Sanford** Manitoba 49.42N 97.29W
105 H2 **Sanford** N Carolina 35.29N 79.10W
103 D2 **Sanford** New York 42.07N 75.26W
112 C8 **Sanford** Texas 35.43N 101.34W
106 K6 **Sanford L** Michigan 43.44N 84.23W
113 Q5 **Sanford, Mt** Alaska 62.14N 144.08W
14 B7 **Sanford, R** W Australia
116 N2 **San Francique** Trinidad & Tobago 10.05N 61.39W
120 F6 **San Francisco** Bolivia 15.15S 65.31W
111 B4 **San Francisco** California 37.45N 122.27W
121 E3 **San Francisco** Córdoba Argentina 31.29S 62.06W
119 E2 **San Francisco** Lara Venezuela 10.18N 70.22W
115 O5 **San Francisco** Panama 8.19N 80.59W
121 C4 **San Francisco** San Luis Arg 32.38S 66.15W
115 C2 **San Francisco** Sonora Mexico 30.50N 112.40W
119 E2 **San Francisco** Zulia Venez 10.36N 71.39W
109 B8 **San Francisco** *R* New Mexico
111 B4 **San Francisco B** *inlet* California
102 B4 **San Francisco Bay** California
111 B8 **San Francisco Bay Bridge** Cal 37.49N 122.22W
119 B7 **San Francisco, C. de** Ecuador 0.38N 80.05W
112 E6 **San Francisco Cr** Texas
115 G4 **San Francisco de Conchos** Mexico 27.38N 105.18W
115 G10 **San Francisco de la Caleta** Panama 8.59N 79.30W
121 D2 **San Francisco del Chanar** Arg 29.46S 63.50W
115 G4 **San Francisco del Oro** Mexico 26.52N 105.50W
120 F8 **San Francisco del Parapetí** Bolivia 20.00S 63.09W
115 J7 **San Francisco del Rincón** Mexico 21.00N 101.51W
116 J5 **San Francisco de Macoris** Dominican Rep 19.19N 70.15W
121 L7 **San Francisco de Paula, C** Arg 49.44S 67.38W
115 P11 **San Francisco Gotera** El Salvador 13.41N 88.06W
77 S12 **San Francisco Javier** Balearic Is 38.43N 1.26E
120 E12 **San Francisco, Paso de** *pass* Arg/Chile 26.50S 68.20W
120 F10 **San Francisco R** Argentina
119 C4 **San Francisco Solano, Pta** *C* Colombia
81 J7 **San Fratello** Sicily 38.02N 14.36E
81 J7 **San Fratello** *R* Sicily
79 C5 **Sanfrè** Italy 44.45N 7.48E
79 B5 **Sanfront** Italy 44.39N 7.18E
77 P4 **San Fulgencio** Spain 38.07N 0.43W
89 J7 **Sang** Ghana 9.26N 0.15W
91 D9 **Sanga** Angola 11.09S 15.21E
92 G8 **Sanga** Mozambique 12.25S 35.24E
93 B6 **Sanga** Uganda 0.29S 30.56E
91 D6 **Sanga** Zaïre 4.50S 14.59E
93 J5 **Sanga** *mt* Kenya 0.19N 37.22E
119 C7 **San Gabriel** Ecuador 0.35N 77.48W
115 L8 **San Gabriel Chilac** Mexico 18.20N 97.24W
111 F7 **San Gabriel Mts** California
115 C3 **San Gabriel, Pta** *C* Mexico 28.28N 112.50W
111 E9 **San Gabriel R** California
44 J7 **Sangachaly** Azerbaydzhan U.S.S.R. 40.11N 49.27E
Sanga Choling *see* **Sangngagqoiling**
86 G4 **Sangaha** Egypt 30.51N 31.38E
23 A3 **Sa'ngain** Xizang Zizhiqu China 30.47N 98.45E
39 C3 **Sanga-Kyuyel'** U.S.S.R. 62.55N 144.28E
120 B5 **San Gallan, I** Peru 13.52S 76.28W
28 D3 **Sangam** Andhra Prad India 14.36N 79.46E
26 U8 **Sangamankanda Pt** Sri Lanka 7.01N 81.53E
28 A2 **Sangameshwar** Maharashtra India 17.13N 73.35E
29 D8 **Sangamner** Maharashtra India 19.37N 74.18E
106 D9 **Sangamon** *R* Illinois
31 C4 **Sangan** Afghanistan 33.25N 65.01E
32 J6 **Sangān** Balūchestān va Sīstān Iran 28.35N 61.23E
32 H3 **Sangān** Khorāsān Iran 35.08N 59.24E
32 J3 **Sangān** Khorāsān Iran 34.21N 60.10E
31 D6 **Sangan** Pakistan 29.52N 67.42E
33 B7 **Sanganeb** *Lt Ho* Sudan 19.45N 37.25E
29 D4 **Sanganer** Rajasthan India 26.48N 75.48E
31 C4 **Sangan, Koh-i-** *mt* Afghanistan 33.33N 64.56E
34 N4 **Sangar** Iraq 34.39N 45.28E
41 N8 **Sangar** U.S.S.R. 64.02N 127.30E
15 K8 **Sangara** Papua New Guinea 8.48S 148.06E
76 L7 **Sangarcía** Spain 40.56N 4.24W
31 D1 **Sangardak** Uzbekistan U.S.S.R. 38.29N 67.30E
89 C7 **Sangarea B** Guinea 9.50N 13.40W
28 D2 **Sangareddipet** Andhra Prad India 17.37N 78.04E
89 C6 **Sangaredyi** Guinea 11.07N 13.52W
31 F5 **Sangar R** Pakistan
18 M6 **Sangasanga** Borneo Indon 0.36S 117.12E
19 J9 **Sanga Sanga** *isld* Philippines 5.04N 119.46E
89 G5 **Sangasso** Mali 12.04N 5.34W
39 D4 **Sangatolon** U.S.S.R. 61.44N 149.30E
69 B2 **Sangatte** France 50.55N 1.45E
44 J10 **Sangavar** *R* Iran
81 B4 **San Gavino Monreale** Sardinia 39.33N 8.48E
119 B9 **Sangay, Vol** Ecuador 2.03S 78.23W
32 H3 **Sang Bast** Iran 35.59N 59.48E
19 K8 **Sangboy Is** Philippines
31 A4 **Sangbur** Afghanistan 32.51N 61.39E
92 D5 **Sange** Katanga Zaïre 7.01S 28.20E
93 A9 **Sange** Kivu Zaïre 3.04S 29.09E
18 N10 **Sangeang** *isld* Indonesia
22 G6 **Sangejing** Nei Monggol Zizhiqu China 40.10N 105.24E
80 G3 **San Gémini** Italy 42.37N 12.33E
121 E4 **San Genaro** Argentina 32.20S 61.18W
76 B4 **Sangenjo** Spain 42.24N 8.48W
111 E5 **Sanger** California 36.41N 119.35W
108 J2 **Sanger** N Dakota 47.13N 101.00W
112 K2 **Sanger** Texas 33.23N 97.13W
32 H3 **Sangerd** Iran 35.43N 58.04E
63 O10 **Sangerhausen** E Germany 51.29N 11.18E
121 E7 **San German** Argentina 38.22S 62.56W
79 B5 **San Germano Chisone** Italy 44.54N 7.14E
79 D4 **San Germano Vercellese** Italy 45.21N 8.15E
75 M3 **San Gervás, Sierra de** *mts* Spain
32 G6 **Sang-e Safīd** Iran 28.18N 57.55E
32 E3 **Sang-e Sar** Iran 35.42N 53.20E
32 G2 **Sang-e-Sūrakh** Iran 37.03N 56.05E
22 K6 **Sanggan He** *R* Hebei China
18 N10 **Sanggar** Indonesia 8.22S 118.20E
23 C2 **Sanggarmai** Sichuan China 32.06N 102.40E
23 C2 **Sanggarpar** Sichuan China 32.19N 102.31E
18 N10 **Sanggar, Teluk** *B* Indonesia
18 H5 **Sanggau** Borneo Indon 1.04N 109.39E
18 J5 **Sanggau** Borneo Indon 0.08N 110.35E
19 D2 **Sanggeluhang** Indonesia 2.57N 125.30E
19 B5 **Sanggona** Celebes Indonesia 3.40S 121.31E
21 B9 **Sanggou Wan** *B* Shandong China
91 D3 **Sangha** *div* Congo
91 E3 **Sangha** *R* Congo
31 E7 **Sanghar** Pakistan 26.10N 68.59E
31 E8 **Sanghar** *dist* Pakistan
Sanghas *see* **Sankhaș**
29 E3 **Sanghi** Haryana India 29.05N 76.39E
87 F4 **Sangi** Ethiopia 13.00N 36.40E
79 F2 **San Giácomo** Italy 46.21N 9.22E
79 H1 **San Giacomo, L. di** Italy
66 K6 **San Giacomo Pass** Switz/Italy 46.28N 8.27E
66 O6 **San Giacomo, Valle** Italy
19 D2 **Sangihe** *isld* Indonesia
19 D2 **Sangihe, Kep** *islds* Indonesia
119 D4 **San Gil** Colombia 6.35N 73.08W
42 F6 **Sangilen, Nagor'ye** *upland* U.S.S.R.
42 C2 **Sangil'ka** *R* U.S.S.R.
80 D2 **San Gimignano** Italy 43.28N 11.02E
31 C4 **Sangīn** Afghanistan 32.03N 64.50E
75 P4 **San Ginés** Spain 41.31N 2.22E
75 P4 **San Ginés de Vilasar** Spain 41.39N 2.25E
80 H2 **San Ginésio** Italy 43.07N 13.19E
81 L7 **San Giorgio** Sicily 38.16N 15.32E
79 C4 **San Giorgio Canavese** Italy 45.20N 7.48E
79 N2 **San Giorgio della Ricinvelda** Italy 46.03N 12.52E
80 L6 **San Giorgio del Sannio** Italy 41.03N 14.52E
79 E4 **San Giorgio di Lomellina** Italy 45.11N 8.47E
79 O3 **San Giorgio di Nogaro** Italy 45.50N 13.13E
79 K5 **San Giorgio di Piano** Italy 44.39N 11.22E
81 P12 **San Giorgio Iónico** Italy 40.27N 17.23E
80 L6 **San Giorgio la Molara** Italy 41.16N 14.55E
79 G5 **San Giorgio Piacentino** Italy 44.57N 9.44E
79 L1 **San Giovanni** Italy 46.58N 11.57E
81 K3 **San Giovanni a Piro** Italy 40.03N 15.27E
80 K7 **San Giovanni a Tedúcio** Italy 40.49N 14.18E
79 G3 **San Giovanni Bianco** Italy 45.52N 9.39E
80 E2 **San Giovanni d'Asso** Italy 43.09N 11.35E
79 H4 **San Giovanni in Croce** Italy 45.05N 10.22E
81 N5 **San Giovanni in Fiore** Italy 39.15N 16.42E
80 L5 **San Giovanni in Galdo** Italy 41.35N 14.45E
79 K5 **San Giovanni in Persiceto** Italy 44.38N 11.11E
80 N5 **San Giovanni Rotondo** Italy 41.43N 15.44E
81 B5 **San Giovanni Suergiu** Sardinia 39.07N 8.31E
80 K4 **San Giovanni Teatino** Italy 42.24N 14.12E
79 L7 **San Giovanni Valdarno** Italy 43.34N 11.31E
29 D7 **Sangir** Maharashtra India 21.02N 74.51E
79 M4 **San Giuliano** Italy 45.28N 12.17E
81 N2 **San Giuliano, L. di** Italy
79 F4 **San Giuliano Milanese** Italy 45.24N 9.17E
79 H7 **San Giuliano Terme** Italy 43.45N 10.26E
81 F8 **San Giuseppe Iato** Sicily 37.58N 13.11E
80 L7 **San Giuseppe Vesuviano** Italy 40.50N 14.31E
79 M2 **San Giustina** Italy 46.05N 12.02E
79 M7 **San Giustino** Italy 43.33N 12.10E
22 E2 **Sangiyn Dalay Nuur** *L* Mongolia
31 C4 **Sang-i-zard** Afghanistan 33.16N 65.35E
21 D9 **Sangju** S Korea 36.25N 128.08E
18 K8 **Sangkapura** Indonesia 5.53S 112.37E
19 A6 **Sangkarang, Kep** *islds* Indonesia
25 G6 **Sangker** *R* Cambodia
25 E5 **Sangkhla Buri** Thailand 14.57N 98.32E
18 M5 **Sangkulirang** Borneo Indon 1.00N 117.58E
18 N5 **Sangkulirang, Teluk** *B* Indonesia
30 B1 **Sangla** Himachal Prad India 31.24N 78.14E
31 G5 **Sangla** Pakistan 31.42N 73.26E
28 B2 **Sangli** Maharashtra India 16.55N 74.37E
28 B2 **Sangli** *dist* Maharashtra India
31 F2 **Sanglich** Afghanistan 36.20N 71.14E
91 B2 **Sangmelima** Cameroon 2.57N 11.56E
24 E10 **Sangmo Bertik Pass** Xizang Zizhiqu China 30.25N 85.26E
30 B1 **Sangnam** Himachal Prad India 31.46N 78.28E
24 H11 **Sangngagqoiling** Xizang Zizhiqu China 28.35N 93.01E
21 D7 **Sang-ni** N Korea 40.58N 128.10E
91 D8 **Sango** Angola 9.51S 15.44E
29 E5 **Sangod** Rajasthan India 24.58N 76.18E
79 L7 **San Godenzo** Italy 43.55N 11.37E
28 B2 **Sangola** Maharashtra India 17.30N 75.15E
119 B8 **Sangolquí** Ecuador 0.19S 78.30W
47 K3 **Sangompan** U.S.S.R. 66.49N 67.50E
92 K8 **Sangone, B. de** Mozambique
77 O5 **Sangonera** *R* Spain
111 H7 **San Gorgonio Mt** California 34.05N 116.50W
21 D10 **Sango-ri** S Korea 35.25N 126.46E
19 F2 **Sangowo** Moluccas Indonesia 2.09N 128.34E
118 H9 **Sangrador, R** Brazil
30 E7 **Sangramgarh** Uttar Prad India 25.52N 81.30E
75 Q3 **San Grao, Sierra de** *mts* Spain
121 J7 **Sangra, Sa. de** *ra* Arg/Chile
109 E5 **Sangre de Cristo Mts** New Mexico/Colorado
121 E5 **San Gregorio** Argentina 34.18S 62.02W
111 B4 **San Gregorio** California 37.19N 122.25W
121 K9 **San Gregorio** Chile 52.34S 70.10W
121 G4 **San Gregorio** Uruguay 32.35S 55.50W
116 P1 **Sangre Grande** Trinidad & Tobago 10.35N 61.08W
28 J1 **Sangri** Xizang Zizhiqu 29.19N 92.03E
24 G11 **Sangri** Xizang Zizhiqu China 29.16N 92.13E
80 K4 **Sangro** *R* Italy
80 K5 **Sangro, Lago di** Italy
29 D2 **Sangrur** Punjab India 30.16N 75.52E
29 D2 **Sangrur, dist** Punjab India
24 E11 **Sangsang** Xizang Zizhiqu China 29.22N 86.45E
30 H4 **Sangu** Nepal 28.03N 84.38E
92 G6 **Sangu** *tribe* Tanzania
120 C4 **Sanguantiari** *R* Peru
100 C5 **Sangudo** Alberta 53.45N 114.50W
118 B2 **Sangue, R** Brazil
75 H2 **Sangüesa** Spain 42.34N 1.17W
121 E3 **San Guillermo** Argentina 30.23S 61.53W
89 E9 **Sanguin** Liberia 5.14N 9.19W
67 O13 **Sanguinaires, Iles** Corsica 41.53N 8.35E
72 B7 **Sanguinet** France 44.29N 1.04W
79 K4 **Sanguinetto** Italy 45.11N 11.09E
94 M4 **Sangulane** *R* Mozambique
Sangun *see* **Sangān**
31 J10 **Sangu R** Bangladesh
43 K7 **Sangvor** Tadzhikistan U.S.S.R. 38.47N 71.17E
Sangyuan *see* **Wuqiao**
42 L2 **Sangyyakhtakh** U.S.S.R. 60.37N 124.00E
23 E4 **Sangzhi** Hunan China 29.22N 110.10E
89 F6 **Sanhala** Ivory Coast 10.01N 6.48W
Sanhe *see* **Sandu**
22 L7 **Sanhe** Hebei China 40.00N 117.04E
21 B2 **Sanhe** Nei Monggol Zizhiqu China 50.29N 120.10E
23 F2 **Sanhedian** Hubei China 32.18N 113.05E
35 B1 **Sanhedriya** *sub* Jerusalem
21 D1 **Sanhezhan** Heilongjiang China 52.35N 126.01E
118 B10 **San Hilario** Argentina 26.02S 58.42W
115 D5 **San Hilario** Mexico 24.22N 110.58W
75 Q4 **San Hilario Sacalm** Spain 41.53N 2.30E
75 P3 **San Hipólito de Voltrega** Spain 42.01N 2.15E
115 B4 **San Hipólito, Pta** Mexico 26.58N 114.02W
23 F3 **San Hu** *L* Hubei China 30.13N 112.33E
23 D3 **Sanhuizhen** Sichuan China 30.05N 105.38E
86 E7 **Sanhûr** Egypt 29.25N 30.45E
88 H11 **Sani** Mauritania 21.40N 10.33W
77 F9 **Sania Ramel** *airport* Morocco 35.36N 5.20W
105 E11 **Sanibel I** Florida 26.26N 82.10W
121 B8 **Sanico** Argentina 40.15S 70.34W
115 C4 **San Ignacio** Baja Cal Mexico 27.22N 113.00W
115 P9 **San Ignacio** Belize 17.14N 89.03W
120 F6 **San Ignacio** Beni Bolivia 14.54S 65.35W
121 F6 **San Ignacio** Buenos Aires Arg 37.20S 58.25W
121 G1 **San Ignacio** Misiones Arg 27.15S 55.32W
118 B10 **San Ignacio** Paraguay 26.51S 57.00W
119 B10 **San Ignacio** Peru 5.09S 79.00W
118 A5 **San Ignacio** Santa Cruz Bolivia 16.23S 60.59W
120 F7 **San Ignacio** Santa Cruz Bolivia 17.14S 63.33W
115 D2 **San Ignacio** Sonora Mexico 30.42N 110.54W
115 C4 **San Ignacio, L** Mexico
San Ildefonso *see* **La Granja**
109 D6 **San Ildefonso** New Mexico 35.54N 106.06W
19 L3 **San Ildefonso, C** Luzon Philippines 16.02N 122.01E
19 L3 **San Ildefonso Pen** Luzon Philippines
Sanimah, Wādī *watercourse see* **Sanime, Wādī** *water course*
34 E3 **Sanime, Wādī** *watercourse* Syria
20 H6 **San'in Kaigan Nat. Park** Japan
15 E5 **Sanintah** Irian Jaya 2.15S 138.34E
109 E4 **San Isabel** Colorado 37.59N 105.03W
115 N5 **San Isdro** Costa Rica 9.28N 83.42W
121 F5 **San Isidro** Buenos Aires Arg 34.31S 58.30W
121 C3 **San Isidro** La Rioja Arg 31.50S 66.20W
115 F3 **San Isidro** Mexico 28.38N 107.25W
19 M6 **San Isidro** Philippines 11.23N 124.22E
96 R15 **San Isidro** Tenerife Canary Is 28.04N 16.35W
120 B10 **San Isidro** *dist* Lima Peru
121 K9 **San Isidro, C** Chile 53.45S 70.56W
77 H5 **Sanitago de Calatrava** Spain 37.45N 4.10W
103 C2 **Sanitaria Springs** New York 42.09N 75.46W
94 B2 **Sanitatas** Namibia 18.22S 12.48E
63 Q4 **Sanitz** E Germany 54.05N 12.22E
34 K5 **Sanīyah** Iraq 33.48N 42.46E
34 O7 **Sanīyah, Hawr as** *L* Iraq
90 M5 **Saniya Karau** Sudan 13.08N 25.59E
85 D6 **Sāniyet al Fawākhir** Libya 26.05N 17.45E
111 H8 **San Jacinto** California 33.48N 116.58W
119 C3 **San Jacinto** Colombia 9.53N 75.06W
110 L8 **San Jacinto** Nevada 41.52N 114.43W
19 L5 **San Jacinto** Philippines 12.31N 123.45E
111 H8 **San Jacinto Mts** California
112 M5 **San Jacinto, West Fork** *R* Texas
75 O5 **San Jaime dels Domenys** Spain 41.18N 1.34E
29 J3 **Sanjai R** Bihar India
120 F6 **San Javier** Beni Bolivia 14.36S 64.45W
121 B5 **San Javier** Chile 35.40S 71.45W
121 G1 **San Javier** Misiones Arg 27.50S 55.06W
120 G7 **San Javier** Santa Cruz Bolivia 16.22S 62.38W
121 F3 **San Javier** Santa Fé Argentina 30.35S 59.59W
77 P5 **San Javier** Spain 37.49N 0.50W
121 F2 **San Javier R** Argentina
31 E5 **Sanjawi** Pakistan 30.16N 68.25E
32 C2 **Sanjbod** Iran 37.42N 48.24E
93 C6 **Sanje** Uganda 0.47S 31.32E
29 C6 **Sanjeli** Bombay India 23.05N 73.56E
115 J9 **San Jerónimo** Mexico 17.08N 100.28W
120 C2 **San Jerónimo** Peru 7.53S 74.52W
119 C4 **San Jerónimo, Sa. de** *mts* Colombia
Sanjiang *see* **Liannan**
Sanjiang *see* **Jinping**
23 E6 **Sanjiang** Guangxi China 25.46N 109.26E
23 E6 **Sanjiang** Guangxi China 24.21N 110.00E
21 C6 **Sanjiangkou** Liaoning China 43.23N 123.46E
Sanjiaocheng *see* **Haiyan**
21 C6 **Sanjiazi** Liaoning China 42.25N 123.34E
23 B6 **Sanjie** Yunnan China 24.56N 101.07E
20 M4 **Sanjō** Japan 37.38N 138.59E
120 F5 **San Joaquín** Bolivia 13.06S 64.47W
111 D5 **San Joaquin** California 36.35N 120.13W
118 C9 **San Joaquín** Paraguay 24.58S 56.19W
119 G3 **San Joaquín** Venezuela 9.21N 64.30W
111 D4 **San Joaquin** *R* California
120 F5 **San Joaquín, R** Bolivia
111 D4 **San Joaquin Val** California
109 G6 **San Jon** New Mexico 35.07N 103.20W
121 E3 **San Jorge** Argentina 31.50S 61.50W
77 B3 **San Jorge** Badajoz Spain 38.39N 7.04W
75 L6 **San Jorge** Castellón Spain 40.31N 0.20E
115 M4 **San Jorge** Nicaragua 11.28N 85.49W
121 L5 **San Jorge, C** Argentina 45.45S 67.18W
121 L6 **San Jorge, G. de** Argentina
75 M6 **San Jorge, G. de** Spain
15 L3 **San Jorge I** Solomon Is
119 D3 **San Jorge, R** Colombia
77 M7 **San José** Almería Spain 36.46N 2.05W
77 S12 **San José** Balearic Is 38.55N 1.18E
77 D7 **San José** Cádiz Spain 36.30N 6.17W
111 C4 **San Jose** California 37.20N 121.55W
120 E12 **San José** Catamarca Arg 26.46S 66.04W
121 D3 **San José** Córdoba Arg 30.01S 64.35W
115 M5 **San José** Costa Rica 9.59N 84.04W
119 B8 **San José** Ecuador 1.43S 79.01W
119 F6 **San José** Guainia Colombia 2.43N 68.03W
115 O11 **San José** Guatemala 14.00N 90.50W
106 E9 **San Jose** Illinois 40.19N 89.39W
19 K4 **San Jose** Luzon Philippines 15.47N 120.59E
19 K5 **San Jose** Mindoro Philippines 12.25N 121.03E
19 K5 **San Jose** Mindoro Philippines 13.20N 121.20E
115 F10 **San José** Panama 8.56N 79.44W
120 D6 **San José** Peru 14.43S 70.13W
116 H9 **San José** Venezuela 10.02N 72.24W
121 G5 **San José** *dept* Uruguay
119 C6 **San José** *isld* Colombia 3.09N 77.35W
115 D5 **San José** *isld* Mexico
77 C4 **San José** *mt* Spain 38.22N 6.49W
121 D10 **San José, C** Argentina 44.30S 65.17W
76 J6 **San José, Canal de** Spain
115 O8 **San José Carpizo** Mexico 19.25N 90.36W
121 F3 **San José, Cuchilla de** *mt* Uruguay
119 H3 **San José de Amacuro** Venezuela 8.30N 60.30W
19 K6 **San Jose de Buenavista** Philippines 10.45N 121.58E
118 A5 **San José de Chiquitos** Bolivia 17.53S 60.45W
120 E6 **San José de Chupiamonas** Bolivia 14.13S 68.06W
115 D3 **San José de Dimas** Mexico 28.44N 110.21W
121 F3 **San José de Feliciano** Argentina 30.26S 58.46W
115 C4 **San José de Gracia** Baja Cal Mexico 26.29N 112.42W
115 F4 **San José de Gracia** Sinaloa Mexico 26.06N 107.53E
115 D3 **San José de Gracia** Sonora Mexico 29.18N 110.39W
119 G3 **San José de Guanipa** Venezuela 8.54N 64.10W
119 G3 **San José de Guaribe** Venezuela 9.54N 65.50W
121 C3 **San José de Jáchal** Argentina 30.15S 68.46W
121 D3 **San José de la Dormida** Arg 30.20S 63.52W
121 A7 **San José de la Mariquina** Chile 39.30S 73.04W
121 E4 **San José de las Esquinas** Argentina 33.10S 61.40W
116 J5 **San José de las Matas** Dominican Republic 19.23N 70.57W
120 F12 **San José del Boquerón** Argentina 26.05S 63.38W
115 E6 **San José del Cabo** Mexico 23.01N 109.40W
119 D6 **San José del Guaviare** Colombia 2.34N 72.38W
19 J1 **San Jose del Monte** Luzon Philippines 14.47N 121.03E
121 G5 **San José de Mayo** Uruguay 34.27S 56.40W
116 J5 **San José de Ocoa** Dominican Rep 18.49N 70.34W
119 E5 **San José de Ocuné** Colombia 4.16N 70.19W
115 J5 **San José de Raíces** Mexico 24.35N 100.19W
119 F3 **San José de Tiznados** Venezuela 9.26N 67.37W
121 D9 **San José, Golfo** Argentina
115 P5 **San José, I** Panama
115 L2 **San José Mangulile** Honduras 15.04N 86.50W
109 C7 **San Jose, R** New Mexico
118 A6 **San José, Sa. de** *mts* Bolivia
120 G8 **San José, Salinas de** *salt pans* Bolivia
121 B4 **San José, Vol** Chile 33.45S 69.57W
24 C7 **Sanju** Xinjiang Uygur Zizhiqu China 37.10N 78.20E
119 C3 **San Juan** Antioquia Colombia 8.46N 76.33E
77 W14 **San Juan** Balearic Is 39.36N 3.02E
77 Y13 **San Juan** Balearic Is 40.01N 4.09E
112 C6 **San Juan** Chihuahua Mexico 29.34N 104.37W
115 F4 **San Juan** Chihuahua Mexico 26.54N 106.19W
115 J4 **San Juan** Coahuila Mexico 27.00N 101.53W
116 J5 **San Juan** Dominican Rep 18.49N 71.12W
119 D6 **San Juan** Meta Colombia 3.25N 73.50W
19 N7 **San Juan** Mindanao Philippines 8.25N 126.22E
120 B6 **San Juán** Peru 15.22S 75.07W
19 M6 **San Juan** Philippines 10.17N 125.11E
105 K7 **San Juan** Puerto Rico 18.29N 66.08W
121 C3 **San Juan** San Juan Arg 31.33S 68.31W
118 A5 **San Juan** Santa Cruz Bolivia 17.55S 60.01W
120 F7 **San Juan** Santa Cruz Bolivia 17.55S 64.17W
77 D6 **San Juan** Spain 37.23N 6.02W
96 Q14 **San Juan** Tenerife Canary Is 28.11N 16.49W
112 J9 **San Juan** Texas 26.12N 98.10W
116 O1 **San Juan** Trinidad & Tobago 10.40N 61.27W
119 F5 **San Juan** Venezuela 5.10N 66.12W
91 A3 **San Juan** *C* Equat Guinea 1.12N 9.20E
116 D4 **San Juan** *mt* Cuba 21.59N 80.07W
77 K6 **San Juan** *mt* Spain 37.06N 3.07W
121 C3 **San Juan** *prov* Argentina
111 D6 **San Juan** *R* California
115 N4 **San Juan** *R* Costa Rica/Nic
120 B5 **San Juan** *R* Peru
77 D3 **San Juan** *R* Spain
111 P4 **San Juan** *R* Utah etc
77 T11 **San Juan Bautista** Balearic Is 39.05N 1.31E
111 C5 **San Juan Bautista** California 36.50N 121.34W
122 V12 **San Juan Bautista** Juan Fernández, Is Pacific Oc 33.38S 78.30W
118 B10 **San Juan Bautista** Paraguay 26.37S 57.06W
115 K9 **San Juan Bautista lo de Soto** Mexico 16.31N 98.16W
115 L8 **San Juan Bautista Tuxtepec** Mexico 18.05N 96.06W
121 M10 **San Juan, C** Estados I Arg 54.45S 63.46W
111 G8 **San Juan Capistrano** California 33.30N 117.39W
115 L2 **San Juancito** Honduras 14.14N 87.03W
77 Q4 **San Juan de Alicante** Spain 38.25N 0.25W
120 B9 **San Juan de Aurigancho** *dist* Lima Peru
119 D2 **San Juan de César** Colombia 10.49N 73.00W
116 H10 **San Juan de Colon** Venezuela 8.02N 72.17W
115 H5 **San Juan de Guadalupe** Mexico 24.40N 102.49W
119 D2 **San Juan de Guía, C. de** Colombia 11.23N 74.00W
121 A8 **San Juan de la Costa** Chile 40.28S 73.29W
75 J3 **San Juan de la Peña, Monasterio de** *hist ruins* Spain 42.30N 0.40W
96 Q14 **San Juan de la Rambla** Tenerife Canary Is 28.23N 16.39W
75 P3 **San Juan de las Abadesas** Spain 42.13N 2.18E
115 H8 **San Juan de Lima, Pta** *C* Mexico 18.32N 103.41W
115 N4 **San Juan del Norte** Nicaragua 10.58N 83.40W
115 N4 **San Juan del Norte, B. de** Nic
119 F2 **San Juan de los Cayos** Venezuela 11.11N 68.27W
115 H7 **San Juan de los Lagos** Mexico 21.15N 102.20W
119 F3 **San Juan de los Morros** Venez 9.53N 67.23W
77 C6 **San Juan del Puerto** Spain 37.20N 6.50W
115 G5 **San Juan del Río** Durango Mexico 24.48N 104.28W
115 J7 **San Juan del Río** Querétaro Mexico 20.24N 100.00W
115 M4 **San Juan del Sur** Nicaragua 11.16N 85.51W
119 C6 **San Juan de Micay, R** Colombia
76 H1 **San Juan de Nieva** Spain 43.35N 5.55W
119 F4 **San Juan de Payara** Venezuela 7.43N 67.35W
121 M10 **San Juan de Salvamento** Estados I Arg 54.46S 63.50W
76 L8 **San Juan, Embalse de** *res* Spain 40.23N 4.25W
115 M9 **San Juan Evangelista** Mexico 17.55N 95.05W
110 B1 **San Juan I** Washington 48.30N 123.05W
115 C4 **San Juanico, Pta** Mexico 26.02N 112.19W
110 C1 **San Juan Is** Washington
115 F4 **San Juanito** Mexico 27.59N 107.35W
115 F7 **San Juanito, I** Mexico
115 O10 **San Juan Ixcoy** Guatemala 15.38N 91.26W
109 C4 **San Juan Mts** Colo/New Mex
119 C3 **San Juan Nepomucenco** Colombia 9.57N 75.06W
122 U15 **San Juan, Pta** *C* Easter I Pacific Oc 27.03S 109.22W
115 P11 **San Juan, Pta** *C* El Salvador 13.09N 88.26W
96 Q14 **San Juan, Pto. de** Tenerife Canary Is 28.11N 16.49W
121 C3 **San Juan, R** Argentina
119 C5 **San Juan R** Colombia
119 H2 **San Juan, R** Venezuela
77 F6 **San Juan, Sierra de** *mts* Spain
116 C3 **San Juan y Martínez** Cuba 22.18N 83.50W
34 O2 **Sanjūd** Iran 36.31N 46.41E
75 N3 **San Juliá** Andorra 42.28N 1.29E
121 L7 **San Julián** Argentina 49.17S 67.45W
75 D1 **San Julián de Musques** Spain 43.20N 3.08W
75 P3 **San Julián de Vallfogona** Spain 42.11N 2.19E
121 L7 **San Julián, Puerto** *B* Argentina
75 J6 **San Just** *mt* Spain 40.46N 0.49W
121 J4 **San Justo** Buenos Aires Arg 34.40S 58.33W
121 E3 **San Justo** Santa Fé Arg 30.47S 60.32W
76 G4 **San Justo de la Vega** Spain 42.27N 6.01W
76 C3 **San Justo, Pte de** *pass* Pontevedra Spain 42.50N 8.11W
76 J2 **San Justo, Pto. de** *pass* Oviedo/León Spain 43.04N 5.23W
75 J6 **San Just, Sierra de** *mts* Spain
29 E6 **Sankach** Madhya Prad India 23.00N 76.45E
87 F4 **Sankaho** Ethiopia 13.10N 36.24E
28 C6 **Sankaranayinarkovil** Tamil Nadu India 9.11N 77.34E
89 E6 **Sankarani** *R* Guinea/Mali
28 C5 **Sankaridrug** Tamil Nadu India 11.30N 77.52E
30 C5 **Sankasya** Uttar Prad India 27.21N 79.16E
28 B2 **Sankeshwar** Karnataka India 16.20N 74.32E
29 J6 **Sankh** *R* India
32 G2 **Sankhāș** Iran 37.04N 56.52E
29 D3 **Sankhu** Rajasthan India 28.27N 75.22E
94 E2 **Sankora** *watercourse* S Africa
29 H7 **Sankra** Madhya Prad India 20.18N 82.03E
29 B4 **Sankra** Rajasthan India 26.42N 71.42E
53 J5 **Sankt Jørgensbjerg** Denmark 55.39N 12.05E
64 J8 **Sankt Mang** W Germany 47.43N 10.22E
63 J4 **Sankt Peter-Ording** W Germany 54.18N 8.37E
61 P5 **Sankt-Vith** Belgium 50.17N 6.07E
92 G10 **Sankulani** Malawi 16.21S 35.12E
93 L6 **Sankuri** Kenya 0.16S 39.35E
91 H6 **Sankuru** *R* Zaïre
84 X19 **San Lawrenz** Gozo Mediterranean Sea 36.03N 14.12E
118 B8 **San Lázaro** Paraguay 22.08S 57.55W
115 C5 **San Lázaro, C** Mexico 24.49N 112.21W
115 E6 **San Lázaro, Sa. de** *mts* Mexico
79 G4 **San Lazzaro** Piacenza Italy 45.02N 9.44E
79 K6 **San Lázzaro di Savena** Italy 44.28N 11.24E
111 C9 **San Leandro** California 37.43N 122.10W
111 B9 **San Leandro B** California
111 C8 **San Leandro Res** California 37.47N 122.06W
79 M7 **San Leo** Italy 43.54N 12.20E
79 K1 **San Leonardo** Italy 46.49N 11.16E
75 D4 **San Leonardo** Spain 41.49N 3.04W
81 G8 **San Leonardo** *R* Sicily
76 J4 **San Llorente** Spain 42.16N 5.20W
119 E4 **San Lope** Colombia 6.12N 71.56W
San Lorenzo *see* **San Timoteo**
77 Y14 **San Lorenzo** Balearic Is 39.54N 4.04E
120 F6 **San Lorenzo** Beni Bolivia 15.32S 65.46W
111 C9 **San Lorenzo** California 37.41N 122.08W
115 F3 **San Lorenzo** Chihuahua Mexico 29.48N 107.06W
121 F2 **San Lorenzo** Corrientes Arg 28.07S 58.47W
67 P12 **San Lorenzo** Corsica 42.23N 9.17E
119 B7 **San Lorenzo** Ecuador 1.15N 78.51W
115 L3 **San Lorenzo** Honduras 13.24N 87.27W
81 L7 **San Lorenzo** Italy 38.01N 15.50E
109 C9 **San Lorenzo** New Mexico 32.49N 107.56W
115 M3 **San Lorenzo** Nicaragua 12.20N 85.40W
120 E4 **San Lorenzo** Pando Bolivia 11.54S 66.53W
120 D4 **San Lorenzo** Peru 11.29S 69.21W
105 K7 **San Lorenzo** Puerto Rico 18.11N 65.57W
121 E4 **San Lorenzo** Santa Fé Argentina 32.45S 60.45W
120 F9 **San Lorenzo** Tarija Bolivia 21.25S 64.45W
115 C3 **San Lorenzo** *isld* Mexico
79 C7 **San Lorenzo al Mare** Italy 43.52N 7.58E
119 B8 **San Lorenzo, C** Ecuador 1.06S 80.56W
81 D5 **San Lorenzo, C** Sardinia 39.30N 9.39E
76 H1 **San Lorenzo, C** Spain 43.34N 5.36W
121 J6 **San Lorenzo, Cerro** *pk* Arg/Chile 47.40S 72.18W
77 J4 **San Lorenzo de Calatrava** Spain 38.29N 3.49W
77 W14 **San Lorenzo de Descardazar** Balearic Is 39.36N 3.16E
75 F8 **San Lorenzo de la Parrilla** Spain 39.51N 2.22W
76 L7 **San Lorenzo del Escorial** Spain 40.35N 4.09W
75 O3 **San Lorenzo de Morunys** Spain 42.08N 1.35E
76 J8 **San Lorenzo de Tormes** Spain 40.22N 5.30W
79 L1 **San Lorenzo di Sebato** Italy 46.47N 11.55E
75 M4 **San Lorenzo, Embalse de** *res* Spain
120 B5 **San Lorenzo, I** Peru 12.07S 77.15W
79 N7 **San Lorenzo in Campo** Italy 43.36N 12.56E
75 E3 **San Lorenzo, Sierra de** *mts* Spain
81 M7 **San Luca** Italy 38.09N 16.04E
77 D7 **Sanlúcar de Barrameda** Spain 36.46N 6.21W
77 B6 **Sanlúcar de Guadiana** Spain 37.29N 7.28W
77 D6 **Sanlúcar la Mayor** Spain 37.23N 6.13W
115 C4 **San Lucas** Baja Cal Mexico 27.14N 112.15W
115 E6 **San Lucas** Baja Cal Mexico 22.50N 109.52W
120 F9 **San Lucas** Bolivia 20.08S 65.07W
111 C5 **San Lucas** California 36.08N 121.01W
115 E6 **San Lucas, C** Mexico 22.50N 109.55W
119 D4 **San Lucas, Sa. de** *mts* Colombia
81 M5 **San Lucido** Italy 39.18N 16.03E
121 C4 **San Luis** Argentina 33.20S 66.23W
111 K9 **San Luis** Arizona 32.29N 114.45W
111 N9 **San Luis** Arizona 32.05N 111.57W
77 Y14 **San Luis** Balearic Is 39.51N 4.15E
115 F4 **San Luis** Chihuahua Mexico 27.36N 107.45W
109 E4 **San Luis** Colorado 37.03N 105.25W
116 G4 **San Luis** Cuba 20.13N 75.50W
115 P9 **San Luís** Guatemala 16.16N 89.27W
115 J9 **San Luis** Guerrero Mexico 17.16N 100.52W
115 M3 **San Luis** Nicaragua 13.59N 84.10W
119 D9 **San Luis** Peru 2.53S 73.30W
119 E2 **San Luis** Venezuela 11.09N 69.39W
120 B10 **San Luis** *dist* Lima Peru
115 B3 **San Luis** *isld* Mexico 29.58N 114.25W
121 C4 **San Luis** *prov* Argentina
115 K9 **San Luis Acatlán** Mexico 16.48N 98.50W
115 J7 **San Luis de la Paz** Mexico 21.19N 100.32W
121 F1 **San Luis del Palmar** Argentina 27.30S 58.38W
115 D5 **San Luis Gonzaga** Baja Cal Mexico 24.57N 111.14W
115 C2 **San Luisito** Mexico 31.15N 112.26W
115 P10 **San Luis Jilotepeque** Guatemala 14.40N 89.42W
120 F5 **San Luis, L. de** Bolivia 13.45S 64.00W
111 K9 **San Luis, Mesa de** Mexico
111 D6 **San Luis Obispo** California 35.16N 120.40W
111 C6 **San Luis Obispo B** California
115 P10 **San Luis Pajón** Honduras 15.08N 88.25W
112 M6 **San Luis Pass** Texas 29.04N 95.08W
109 D4 **San Luis Pk** Colorado 37.59N 106.56W
115 J6 **San Luis Potosí** Mexico 22.10N 101.00W
115 J6 **San Luis Potosí** *state* Mexico
111 G8 **San Luis Rey** *R* California
115 B1 **San Luis Río Colorado** Mexico 32.26N 114.48W
121 C4 **San Luis, Sa. de** *ra* Argentina
109 E4 **San Luis Valley** Colorado
111 D5 **San Luiz Canal** California
81 B4 **Sanluri** Sardinia 39.34N 8.54E
76 C7 **San Macário** *mt* Portugal 40.53N 8.04W
79 M1 **San Maddalena Vallalta** Italy 46.49N 12.14E
76 D4 **San Mamed, Sierra de** *mts* Spain
76 K4 **San Mamés de Campos** Spain 42.21N 4.34W
121 F6 **San Manuel** Argentina 37.45S 58.58W
19 K4 **San Marcelino** Luzon Philippines 15.00N 120.13E
79 J6 **San Marcello Pistoiese** Italy 44.03N 10.47E
115 D3 **San Marcial** Mexico 28.30N 110.18W
109 C8 **San Marcial** New Mexico 33.42N 107.01W
115 D5 **San Marcial, Pta** *C* Mexico 25.30N 111.03W
81 M4 **San Marco Argentano** Italy 39.33N 16.07E
81 A4 **San Marco, C** Sardinia 39.52N 8.26E
81 F9 **San Marco, C** Sicily 37.30N 13.02E
81 J7 **San Marco d'Alunzio** Sicily 38.09N 14.42E
80 L6 **San Marco dei Cavoti** Italy 41.18N 14.53E
80 N5 **San Marco in Lamis** Italy 41.43N 15.38E
80 M5 **San Marco la Catola** Italy 41.32N 15.01E
121 B3 **San Marcos** Chile 30.55S 71.02W
119 C3 **San Marcos** Colombia 8.38N 75.10W
115 M5 **San Marcos** Costa Rica 9.40N 84.02W
115 K9 **San Marcos** Guerrero Mexico 16.45N 99.22W
115 L3 **San Marcos** Honduras 13.22N 86.50W
115 P10 **San Marcos** Honduras 14.23N 88.55W
115 G7 **San Marcos** Jalisco Mexico 20.48N 104.22W
115 L4 **San Marcos** Nicaragua 11.52N 86.10W
120 A2 **San Marcos** Peru 7.22S 78.09W
96 Q14 **San Marcos** Tenerife Canary Is 28.22N 16.42W
112 K6 **San Marcos** Texas 29.54N 97.57W
115 C4 **San Marcos** *isld* Mexico
66 N7 **San Margherita** Italy 46.01N 9.02E
79 M7 **San Marino** Italy 43.56N 12.26E
79 M7 **San Marino** *rep* Italy
120 G6 **San Martin** Bolivia 14.56S 62.06W
121 D2 **San Martín** Catamarca Arg 29.15S 65.47W
119 D6 **San Martín** Colombia 3.43N 73.42W
121 C4 **San Martín** Mendoza Arg 33.05S 68.28W
115 K8 **San Martín** Mexico 19.46N 98.53W
119 D8 **San Martín** Peru 1.38S 74.37W
121 C3 **San Martín** San Juan Arg 31.28S 68.34W
121 D4 **San Martín** San Luis Argentina 32.27S 65.43W
123 F13 **San Martín** *Arg. Base* Antarctica 68.07S 67.08W
120 B2 **San Martin** *dept* Peru
77 R3 **San Martín, C. de** Spain 38.46N 0.14E
115 K7 **San Martín Chalchicuautla** Mexico 21.20N 98.42W
75 C2 **San Martin de Elines** Spain 42.50N 3.53W
75 C7 **San Martin de la Vega** Spain 40.13N 3.35W
121 B8 **San Martín de los Andes** Arg 40.11S 71.22W
75 G4 **San Martín de Moncayo** Spain 41.51N 1.47W
76 L9 **San Martín de Montalbán** Spain 39.42N 4.23W
76 F2 **San Martín de Oscos** Spain 43.16N 6.57W
76 K9 **San Martín de Pusa** Spain 39.47N 4.38W
75 O4 **San Martín de Tous** Spain 41.33N 1.31E
76 F8 **San Martín de Trevejo** Spain 40.13N 6.46W
75 G2 **San Martín de Unx** Spain 42.32N 1.34W
76 L8 **San Martín de Valdeiglesias** Spain 40.21N 4.24W
115 H7 **San Martín Hidalgo** Mexico 20.28N 103.58W
121 J7 **San Martín, L** Arg/Chile
79 K1 **San Martino** Italy 46.48N 10.14E
79 N2 **San Martino al Tagliamento** Italy 46.02N 12.52E
79 K4 **San Martino Buon Albergo** Italy 45.25N 11.05E
67 O12 **San Martino, Col de** *pass* Corsica 42.12N 8.38E
81 M3 **San Martino d'Agri** Italy 40.14N 16.04E
79 J4 **San Martino dell'Argine** Italy 45.06N 10.31E
79 L2 **San Martino di Castrozza** Italy 46.16N 11.49E
67 P11 **San Martino di Lota** Corsica 42.44N 9.26E
79 L3 **San Martino di Lupari** Italy 45.39N 11.52E
79 L5 **San Martino in Argine** Italy 44.35N 11.37E
79 L1 **San Martino in Badia** Italy 46.41N 11.54E
80 F2 **San Martino in Colle** Italy 43.01N 12.22E
80 M5 **San Martino in Pensilis** Italy 41.52N 15.01E
79 J5 **San Martino in Rio** Italy 44.43N 10.47E
79 K5 **San Martino in Spino** Italy 44.56N 11.14E
66 J7 **San Martino, Pizzo** *mt* Italy 46.02N 8.07E
120 F5 **San Martín, R** Bolivia
115 K8 **San Martín Texmelucan** Mexico 19.20N 98.26W
111 B4 **San Mateo** California 37.33N 122.22W
115 M5 **San Mateo** Costa Rica 9.52N 84.32W
96 V15 **San Mateo** Gran Canaria Canary Is 28.01N 15.32W
19 J1 **San Mateo** Luzon Philippines 14.42N 121.07E
109 C6 **San Mateo** New Mexico 35.20N 107.38W
119 E9 **San Mateo** Peru 3.46S 71.30W
75 L7 **San Mateo** Spain 40.28N 0.10E
119 G3 **San Mateo** Venezuela 9.48N 64.36W
111 C9 **San Mateo Bridge** California 37.35N 122.15W
75 J4 **San Mateo de Gállego** Spain 41.50N 0.45W
115 O10 **San Mateo Ixtatán** Guatemala 15.50N 91.30W
109 C8 **San Mateo Pk** New Mexico 33.36N 107.36W
111 B9 **San Mateo Pt** California 37.34N 122.19W
118 B5 **San Matías** Bolivia 16.23S 58.19W
76 D11 **San Matias** Portugal 38.35N 8.00W
121 D8 **San Matías, Golfo** *gulf* Argentina
99 R5 **Sanmaur** Quebec 47.53N 73.48W
119 F3 **San Mauricio** Venezuela 8.40N 66.22W
81 M3 **San Mauro** Italy 40.29N 16.15E
81 H8 **San Máuro Castelverde** Sicily 37.55N 14.12E
81 N5 **San Mauro Marchesato** Italy 39.06N 16.56E
79 M6 **San Mauro Pascoli** Italy 44.07N 12.25E
23 J4 **Sanmen** Zhejiang China 29.08N 121.22E
25 N1 **San-men Tao** *isld* China 22.26N 114.38E
23 J4 **Sanmen Wan** *B* Zhejiang China
23 F1 **Sanmenxia** Henan China 34.46N 111.17E
98 D6 **San Michel du Squatec** Quebec 47.53N 68.42W
79 K4 **San Michele** Italy 45.26N 11.03E
79 K2 **San Michele all'Adige** Italy 46.12N 11.09E
79 N3 **San Michele al Tagliamento** Italy 45.46N 12.59E
81 H9 **San Michele di Ganzaria** Sicily 37.18N 14.26E
79 B6 **San Michele Prazzo** Italy 44.30N 7.04E
81 B5 **San Michele, Pta** Sardinia 39.21N 8.36E
121 F2 **San Miguel** Argentina 28.01S 57.36W
111 N10 **San Miguel** Arizona 31.38N 111.46W
77 S11 **San Miguel** Balearic Is 39.03N 1.26E
119 B8 **San Miguel** Bolívar Ecuador 1.46S 79.04W
120 G7 **San Miguel** Bolivia 16.43S 61.06W
111 D6 **San Miguel** California 35.45N 120.44W
San Miguel Colombia*see* **Puerto Ospina**
115 P11 **San Miguel** El Salvador 13.28N 88.10W
119 B7 **San Miguel** Esmeraldas Ecuador 0.44N 78.55W
115 P9 **San Miguel** Guatemala 17.09N 89.55W
19 K5 **San Miguel** Luzon Philippines 13.39N 121.22E
109 D9 **San Miguel** New Mexico 32.08N 106.45W
109 E6 **San Miguel** New Mexico 35.23N 105.30W
115 P5 **San Miguel** Panama 8.27N 78.51W
120 C5 **San Miguel** Peru 12.59S 73.54W
75 G2 **San Miguel** Spain 42.57N 2.00W
96 Q15 **San Miguel** Tenerife Canary Is 28.07N 16.38W
119 G3 **San Miguel** Venezuela 9.55N 64.59W
120 B10 **San Miguel** *dist* Lima Peru
121 G10 **San Miguel** *dist* Santiago Chile
109 B3 **San Miguel** *R* Colorado
115 D3 **San Miguel** *R* Mexico
19 L5 **San Miguel B** Luzon Philippines
112 J9 **San Miguel Camargo** Mexico 26.13N 98.37W
112 J7 **San Miguel Cr** Texas
115 J7 **San Miguel de Allende** Mexico 20.56N 100.48W
75 C5 **San Miguel de Bernúy** Spain 41.23N 3.57W
115 G5 **San Miguel de Cruces** Mexico 24.25N 105.50W
76 J3 **San Miguel de Escalada, Monasterio de** Spain 42.33N 5.20W
75 K3 **San Miguel de Foces** *monastery* Spain 42.10N 0.12W
120 E6 **San Miguel de Huachi** Bolivia 15.43S 67.12W
76 H6 **San Miguel de la Ribera** Spain 41.20N 5.35W

76 L6 San Miguel del Arroyo Spain 41.26N 4.29W
121 F5 San Miguel del Monte Arg 35.26S 58.50W
76 J4 San Miguel del Valle Spain 42.02N 5.30W
76 B4 San Miguel de Oya Spain 42.11N 8.49W
120 A2 San Miguel de Pallaques Peru 7.03S 78.54W
77 P5 San Miguel de Salinas Spain 37.59N 0.47W
76 J7 San Miguel de Serrezuela Spain 40.40N 5.17W
120 F12 San Miguel de Tucumán Argentina 26.47S 65.15W
115 H7 San Miguel el Alto Mexico 21.01N 102.24W
115 P5 San Miguel, G. de Panama
111 D7 San Miguel I California 34.02N 120.20W
19 J8 San Miguel Is Philippines
120 E4 San Miguelito Bolivia 11.37S 68.22W
115 M4 San Miguelito Nicaragua 11.22N 84.54W
115 G10 San Miguelito Panama 9.02N 79.30W
120 F6 San Miguel, R Bolivia
118 A6 San Miguel, R Bolivia/Paraguay
119 C7 San Miguel, R Ecuador
115 L9 San Miguel Sola de Vega Mexico 16.31N 96.58W
115 O10 San Miguel Uspantán Guatemala 15.22N 90.50W
75 D3 San Millán *mt* Spain 42.14N 3.12W
75 E3 San Millán de la Cogolla Spain 42.20N 2.52W
75 D2 San Millán de San Zadorni Spain 42.50N 3.09W
23 H5 Sanming Fujian China 26.16N 117.35E
79 J7 San Miniato Italy 43.41N 10.51E
119 B8 San Miquel Cotopaxi Ecuador 1.05S 78.37W
76 G7 San Muñoz Spain 40.47N 6.08W
19 K4 San Narciso Luzon Philippines 15.06N 120.05E
95 K5 Sannaspos S Africa 29.10S 26.34E
72 J3 Sannat France 46.07N 2.23E
84 X19 Sannat Gozo Med Sea 36.01N 14.14E
79 L3 San Nazario Italy 45.50N 11.42E
79 E4 San Nazzaro de Burgondi Italy 45.07N 8.54E
31 D6 Sanni Pakistan 29.11N 67.34E
67 P12 San Nicalao Corsica 42.22N 9.29E
81 N1 Sannicandro di Bari Italy 41.00N 16.49E
80 N5 Sannicandro Garganico Italy 41.50N 15.34E
81 L4 San Nicola Arcella Italy 39.50N 15.48E
81 N5 San Nicola d'Alto Italy 39.17N 16.58E
121 E4 San Nicolas Argentina 33.25S 60.15W
115 G5 San Nicolás Durango Mexico 24.55N 105.25W
96 U15 San Nicolás Gran Canaria Canary Is 27.58N 15.48W
115 K9 San Nicolás Guerrero Mexico 16.26N 98.31W
19 K2 San Nicolas Luzon Philippines 18.10N 120.36E
19 K3 San Nicolas Luzon Philippines 16.06N 120.46E
119 E9 San Nicolás Peru 3.37S 71.36W
115 K5 San Nicolas Tamaulipas Mexico 24.41N 98.48W
120 B6 San Nicolás, B Peru
77 E5 San Nicolás del Puerto Spain 38.00N 5.39W
111 E8 San Nicolas I California 33.15N 119.30W
120 F5 San Nicolas, L Bolivia 12.40S 65.43W
81 B4 San Nicolò d'Arcidano Sardinia 39.41N 8.39E
79 L5 San Nicolò Ferrarese Italy 44.43N 11.43E
81 C5 San Nicolò Gerrei Sardinia 39.30N 9.19E
52 E8 Sannidal Norway 58.55N 9.15E
95 J2 Sannieshof S Africa 26.31S 25.49E
94 H6 Sannieshof Transvaal S Africa 26.31S 25.49E
41 P4 Sannikova, Proliv *str* U.S.S.R.
80 L6 Sannio *reg* Italy
80 L6 Sannio, Monti del Italy
89 E8 Sanniquellie Liberia 7.24N 8.45W
35 D5 Sanniriya Jordan 32.08N 35.03E
Sanniya, Haur *L* see Saniyah, Hawr as *L*
20 P1 Sannohe Japan 40.22N 141.18E
68 D2 Sannois France 48.58N 2.15E
80 M6 Sannoro *R* Italy
58 F7 Sannox Arran, Strathclyde Scotland 55.40N 5.10W
86 F8 Sannûr Egypt 28.59N 31.03E
86 F8 Sannûr, Wâdi *watercourse* Egypt
20 N5 Sano Japan 36.19N 139.32E
121 C2 Sañogasta, Sa. de *ra* Argentina
62 N6 Sanok Poland 49.32N 22.12E
69 M6 Sânon *R* France
111 G8 San Onofre California 33.22N 117.33W
119 C3 San Onofre Colombia 9.45N 75.33W
89 D8 Sanoyie Liberia 6.55N 10.04W
121 L10 San Pablo Argentina 54.17S 66.44W
111 B8 San Pablo California 37.58N 122.21W
121 A8 San Pablo Chile 40.27S 73.02W
119 E5 San Pablo Colombia 5.26N 70.56W
19 J2 San Pablo Luzon Philippines 14.03N 121.19E
115 K7 San Pablo Mexico 20.08N 99.58W
120 C2 San Pablo Peru 7.45S 74.59W
120 E9 San Pablo Potosí Bolivia 21.43S 66.38W
120 F6 San Pablo Santa Cruz Bolivia 15.38S 63.15W
76 L9 San Pablo Spain 39.33N 4.19W
77 E6 San Páblo *airport* Spain 37.24N 5.54W
111 B3 San Pablo B California
115 F4 San Pablo Balleza Mexico 26.58N 106.20W
111 B8 San Pablo Cr California
119 B7 San Pablo, L Ecuador 0.10N 78.14W
111 A8 San Pablo Pt California 37.58N 122.26W
115 B4 San Pablo, Pta *C* Mexico 27.11N 114.30W
120 G7 San Pablo, R Bolivia
111 B8 San Pablo Res California
79 K1 San Pancrázio d'Ultimo Italy 46.36N 11.06E
81 Q12 San Pancrazio Salentino Italy 40.25N 17.50E
80 M5 San Paolo di Civitate Italy 41.44N 15.16E
19 L5 San Pascual Philippines 13.07N 122.59E
84 Y9 San Pawl il Bahar Malta 35.57N 14.24E
115 N5 San Pedrillo, Pta *C* Costa Rica 8.41N 83.43W
120 C6 San Pedro Ayacucho Peru 14.49S 74.05W
115 D6 San Pedro Baja Cal Mexico 23.57N 110.16W
115 Q9 San Pedro Belize 18.00N 87.53W
120 F6 San Pedro Beni Bolivia 14.21S 64.46W
121 F4 San Pedro Buenos Aires Arg 33.43S 59.45W
111 F8 San Pedro California 33.45N 118.19W
120 E9 San Pedro Chile 21.58S 68.30W
120 F8 San Pedro Chuquisaca Bolivia 19.38S 64.26W
119 E5 San Pedro Colombia 4.57N 71.55W
121 D3 San Pedro Córdoba Arg 31.55S 65.19W
89 F9 San Pédro Ivory Coast 4.45N 6.37W
120 F11 San Pedro Jujuy Arg 24.12S 64.55W
120 D4 San Pedro Loreto Peru 10.20S 71.07W
19 K5 San Pedro Mindoro Philippines 12.20N 121.20E
118 C10 San Pedro Misiones Arg 26.38S 54.12W
118 B9 San Pedro Paraguay 24.08S 57.08W
120 F10 San Pedro Salta Arg 22.26S 64.01W
120 G7 San Pedro Santa Cruz Bolivia 16.46S 62.31W
121 D1 San Pedro Santiago del Estero Argentina 27.59S 65.13W
115 E4 San Pedro Sonora Mexico 27.00N 109.53W
77 M3 San Pedro Spain 38.50N 2.11W
118 B9 San Pedro *dept* Paraguay
111 O9 San Pedro *R* Arizona
116 E4 San Pedro *R* Cuba
120 E9 San Pedro *R* Potosí Bolivia
111 E10 San Pedro B California
19 M6 San Pedro B Philippines
121 A8 San Pedro, B.de Chile
115 O10 San Pedro Carchá Guatemala 15.30N 90.12W
111 F8 San Pedro Chan California
77 G8 San Pedro de Alcántara Spain 36.29N 4.58W
119 E5 San Pedro de Arimena Colombia 4.38N 71.37W
120 E10 San Pedro de Atacama Chile 22.55S 68.15W
120 F8 San Pedro de Buena Vista Bolivia 18.11S 66.00W
76 G4 San Pedro de Ceque Spain 42.03N 6.04W
115 E3 San Pedro de la Cueva Mexico 29.20N 109.42W
76 K7 San Pedro del Arroyo Spain 40.48N 4.53W
119 H4 San Pedro de las Bocas Venezuela 6.59N 62.53W
115 H5 San Pedro de las Colonias Mexico 25.50N 102.59W
76 J5 San Pedro de Latarce Spain 41.44N 5.20W
120 A8 San Pedro de Lloc Peru 7.15S 79.28W
118 C10 San Pedro del Paraná Paraguay 26.44S 56.15W
77 P5 San Pedro del Pinatar Spain 37.50N 0.46W
75 C1 San Pedro del Romeral Spain 43.07N 3.49W
116 K5 San Pedro de Macoris Dominican Rep 18.30N 69.18W
77 D3 San Pedro de Mérida Spain 38.57N 6.12W
76 H7 San Pedro de Rozados Spain 40.48N 5.46W
115 B2 San Pedro Mártir, Sa *ra* Mexico
75 F7 San Pedro Palmiches Spain 40.26N 2.24W
75 R3 San Pedro Pescador Spain 42.11N 3.05E
111 A9 San Pedro Pt California 37.34N 122.33W
120 D11 San Pedro, Pta *C* Chile 25.32S 70.43W
120 F8 San Pedro, R Potosí Bolivia
76 F10 San Pedro, Sierra de *mts* Spain
115 P10 San Pedro Sula Honduras 15.26N 88.01W
79 G3 San Pellegrino Italy 45.50N 9.40E
112 K9 San Perlita Texas 26.31N 97.39W
79 E6 San Pier d'Arena Italy 44.24N 8.54E
79 K7 San Piero a Sieve Italy 43.58N 11.19E
79 L7 San Piero in Bagno Italy 43.52N 11.59E
81 J7 San Piero Patti Sicily 38.03N 14.58E
106 H8 San Pierre Indiana 41.11N 86.53W
79 L1 San Pietro Bolzano Italy 46.38N 11.42E
79 M1 San Pietro Bolzano Italy 47.02N 12.04E
81 K6 San Pietro Lipari Is Italy 38.38N 15.05E
81 H9 San Pietro Sicily 37.07N 14.30E
79 O2 San Pietro al Natisone Italy 46.08N 13.29E
79 M3 San Pietro di Feletto Italy 45.56N 12.14E
79 K4 San Pietro di Morúbio Italy 45.15N 11.14E
67 P11 San Pietro di Tenda Corsica 42.37N 9.15E
81 A5 San Pietro, I. di Sardinia
79 J3 San Pietro in Cariano Italy 45.31N 10.53E
79 K5 San Pietro in Casale Italy 44.42N 11.24E
79 L3 San Pietro in Gu Italy 45.37N 11.41E
81 M5 San Pietro in Guarano Italy 39.20N 16.18E
79 M6 San Pietro in Vincoli Italy 44.18N 12.09E
81 Q12 San Pietro Vernótico Italy 40.28N 18.00E
121 L10 San Pio, C Argentina 55.02S 66.25W
110 G1 Sanpoil *R* Washington
79 H5 San Polo d'Enza in Caviano Italy 44.38N 10.26E
79 M3 San Polo di Piave Italy 45.48N 12.23E
75 O4 San Pons, Embalse de *res* Spain 41.57N 1.35E
79 J5 San Possidónio Italy 44.53N 11.00E
25 G3 San, Pou *mt* Laos 19.38N 103.23E
79 F3 San Primo, Monte Italy 45.55N 9.12E
79 K5 San Prospero Italy 44.47N 11.01E
28 B3 Sanquem Goa India 15.13N 74.10E
111 A8 San Quentin California 37.55N 122.29W
57 F2 Sanquhar Dumfries & Galloway Scotland 55.22N 3.56W
115 B2 San Quintín Mexico 30.28N 115.58W
115 A2 San Quintín, C Mexico 30.20N 116.00W
75 P3 San Quirico de Besora Spain 42.06N 2.15E
80 E2 San Quirico d'Orcia Italy 43.04N 11.36E
79 N2 San Quirino Italy 46.02N 12.40E
121 C5 San Rafael Argentina 34.35S 68.24W
118 A5 San Rafael Bolivia 16.44S 60.35W
111 B4 San Rafael California 37.58N 122.30W
119 E5 San Rafael Colombia 6.00N 69.50W
109 C6 San Rafael New Mexico 35.06N 107.53W
76 L7 San Rafael Spain 40.42N 4.12W
119 E2 San Rafael Venezuela 10.58N 71.45W
111 O2 San Rafael *R* Utah
115 L5 San Rafael, Boca *channel* Mexico 25.01N 97.30W
116 K5 San Rafael, C Dominican Rep 19.03N 68.56W
119 F4 San Rafael de Atamaica Venez 7.35N 67.26W
115 L3 San Rafael del Norte Nicaragua 13.12N 86.06W
75 L6 San Rafael del Rio Spain 40.36N 0.20E
116 K5 San Rafael del Yuma Dominican Rep 18.26N 68.40W
111 O3 San Rafael Knob *mt* Utah 38.49N 110.53W
111 E7 San Rafael Mts California
120 F5 San Ramón Beni Bolivia 13.19S 64.41W
115 M4 San Ramón Costa Rica 10.04N 84.31W
115 M3 San Ramón Nicaragua 12.55N 85.50W
120 B4 San Ramón Peru 11.08S 75.18W
120 G7 San Ramón Santa Cruz Bolivia 16.43S 62.39W
121 G5 San Ramon Uruguay 34.18S 55.55W
120 G6 San Ramón, R Bolivia
23 G7 Sanrao Guangdong China 23.55N 116.45E
79 C7 Sanremo Italy 43.48N 7.46E
66 K7 San Rocco Italy 46.01N 8.16E
79 G4 San Rocco al Porto Italy 45.05N 9.41E
112 F7 San Rodrigo *R* Mexico
119 E1 San Román, C Venezuela 12.10N 70.01W
76 G2 San Román de Candamo Spain 43.27N 6.05W
76 K4 San Román de la Cuba Spain 42.15N 4.52W
76 J6 San Román de la Hornija Spain 41.29N 5.17W
121 F2 San Roque Argentina 28.35S 58.45W
77 F8 San Roque Spain 36.13N 5.23W
75 C1 San Roque de Riomiera Spain 43.14N 3.41W
112 J4 San Saba Texas 31.13N 98.44W
112 G5 San Saba *R* Texas
72 C3 Sansais France 46.17N 0.35W
121 F3 San Salvador Argentina 31.38S 58.30W
115 P11 San Salvador El Salvador 13.40N 89.10W
119 E9 San Salvador Peru 2.25S 71.21W
116 A2 San Salvador *isld* Bahamas 24.00N 74.32W
77 W15 San Salvador *mt* Balearic Is 39.27N 3.10E
121 F4 San Salvador *R* Uruguay
75 B2 San Salvador de Cantamuda Spain 42.58N 4.29W
120 F11 San Salvador de Jujuy Argentina 24.10S 65.48W
119 B5 San Salvador, I Galápagos Is 0.16S 90.40W
116 G2 San Salvador, Lit *isld* Bahamas 24.35N 75.58W
66 M8 San Salvatore *mt* Switzerland 45.58N 8.57E
79 E5 San Salvatore Monferrato Italy 44.59N 8.33E
80 O5 San Salvatore, Monte Italy 41.58N 16.10E
81 H8 San Salvatore, Mte Sicily 37.50N 14.04E
80 L4 San Salvo Italy 42.03N 14.44E
89 F5 Sansanding Mali 13.48N 6.01W
15 B4 Sansapor Irian Jaya 0.31S 132.06E
76 C1 San Saturnino Spain 43.32N 8.05W
121 L9 San Sebastián Argentina 53.15S 68.30W
105 J7 San Sebastian Puerto Rico 18.21N 66.59W
75 G1 San Sebastián Spain 43.19N 1.59W
115 C3 San Sebastián *isld* Mexico
121 L9 San Sebastián, B. de Argentina
75 R4 San Sebastián, C.de Spain 41.53N 3.12E
96 P15 San Sebastian de la Gomera Gomera Canary Is 28.06N 17.06W
77 G5 San Sebastián de los Ballesteros Spain 37.39N 4.49W
76 F4 San Sebastián, Embalse de *res* Spain
76 C3 San Sebastían, Mte de Spain 42.41N 8.20W
79 F5 San Sebastiano Curone Italy 44.47N 9.04E
115 L8 San Sebastian Zinacatepec Mexico 18.21N 97.19W
79 B5 San Secondo di Pinerolo Italy 44.52N 7.18E
79 H5 San Secondo Parmense Italy 44.55N 10.13E
79 M7 Sansepolcro Italy 43.34N 12.08E
81 M3 San Severino Lucano Italy 40.02N 16.08E
80 H2 San Severino Marche Italy 43.13N 13.10E
80 M5 San Severo Italy 41.41N 15.23E
23 J5 Sansha Fujian China 26.56N 120.12E
120 E4 San Silvestre Bolivia 11.51S 68.37W
119 E3 San Silvestre Venezuela 8.16N 69.58W
77 B6 San Silvestre de Guzmán Spain 37.23N 7.20W
111 C6 San Simeon California 35.39N 121.11W
111 P9 San Simon Arizona 32.16N 109.14W
103 P9 San Simon Cr Arizona
120 F5 San Simón, R Bolivia
120 F6 San Simón, Serrania *mts* Bolivia
79 E8 San Siro *dist* Milan Italy
82 D6 Sanski Most Yugoslavia 44.46N 16.40E
75 F2 Sansol Spain 42.33N 2.15W
11 K7 Sanson New Zealand 40.12S 175.23E
112 B6 San Sostenes Mexico 29.13N 105.20W
81 M4 San Sosti Italy 39.40N 16.02E
106 M7 Sans Souci Michigan 42.35N 82.35W
79 G4 San Stefano Italy 45.07N 9.44E
79 C7 San Stefano al Mare Italy 43.50N 7.54E
79 N1 San Stéfano di Cadore Italy 46.34N 12.33E
81 H7 San Stefano di Camastra Sicily 38.00N 14.20E
116 M4 Sans Toucher *mt* Guadeloupe W I 16.06N 61.41W
23 E5 Sansui Guizhou China 26.55N 108.34E
22 F3 Sant Mongolia 46.02N 103.42E
110 J2 Santa Idaho 47.10N 116.27W
120 A3 Santa Peru 8.57S 78.37W
120 A3 Santa *isld* Peru 9.01S 78.40W
81 J7 Santa'Agata di Militello Sicily 38.04N 14.08E
79 C5 Santa Albano Stura Italy 44.31N 7.43E
77 D2 Santa Amalia Spain 39.00N 6.01W
79 B4 Santa Ambrogio di Torino Italy 45.06N 7.21E
79 J3 Santa Ambrogio di Valpolicella Italy 45.32N 10.50E
115 P9 Santa Amelia Guatemala 16.18N 90.00W
120 F5 Santa Ana Beni Bolivia 13.46S 65.37W
111 G8 Santa Ana California 33.44N 117.54W
119 B8 Santa Ana Ecuador 1.16S 80.24W
115 P10 Santa Ana El Salvador 14.00N 89.31W
121 F3 Santa Ana Entre Ríos Arg 30.55S 57.55W
120 E6 Santa Ana La Paz Bolivia 15.29S 67.28W
118 A5 Santa Ana Santa Cruz Bolivia 16.38S 60.45W
118 B6 Santa Ana Santa Cruz Bolivia 18.44S 58.45W
115 D2 Santa Ana Sonora Mexico 30.31N 111.08W
77 M3 Santa Ana Spain 38.41N 2.07W
121 D1 Santa Ana Tucumán Arg 27.30S 65.40W
119 G3 Santa Ana Venezuela 9.20N 64.40W
111 G8 Santa Ana *R* California
89 A1 Santa Ana, B.de Mauritania 21.55N 17.00W
76 K9 Santa Ana de Pusa Spain 39.45N 4.43W
76 C11 Santa Ana do Campo Portugal 38.47N 8.02W
75 M4 Santa Ana, Embalse de *res* Spain 41.50N 0.37E
15 M4 Santa Ana I Solomon Is 10.53S 162.28E
77 C5 Santa Ana la Real Spain 37.52N 6.44W
111 G8 Santa Ana Mts California
119 D3 Santa Ana, Playones de *L* Colombia 9.23N 74.37W
119 D3 Santa Ana, R Venezuela
75 F4 Santa Ana, Sierra de *mts* Spain
79 E4 Santa Angelo di Lomellina Italy 45.14N 8.39E
79 M7 Santa Angelo in Vado Italy 43.40N 12.24E
79 F4 Santa Angelo Lodigiano Italy 45.14N 9.25E
115 E6 Santa Anita Mexico 23.10N 109.40W
112 H4 Santa Anna Texas 31.43N 99.21W
119 F6 Santa Bárbara Amazonas Venez 3.59N 67.09W
119 C5 Santa Bárbara Antioquia Colombia 5.53N 75.37W
120 F11 Santa Bárbara Argentina 24.10S 64.20W
96 Q4 Santa Barbara Azores 38.23N 28.13W
96 T3 Santa Bárbara Azores 38.42N 27.21W
96 V5 Santa Bárbara Azores 36.59N 25.06W
119 E4 Santa Bárbara Barinas Venez 7.48N 71.10W
119 H4 Santa Bárbara Bolívar Venez 7.10N 62.05W
111 E7 Santa Barbara California 34.25N 119.41W
121 B6 Santa Bárbara Chile 37.40S 72.00W
115 P10 Santa Bárbara Honduras 14.56N 88.11W
118 B4 Santa Bárbara Mato Grosso Brazil 15.37S 59.05W
115 G4 Santa Bárbara Mexico 26.48N 105.50W
118 G6 Santa Bárbara Minas Gerais Brazil 19.57S 43.20W
119 G3 Santa Bárbara Monagas Venez 9.36N 63.38W
119 B6 Santa Bárbara Nariño Colombia 2.32N 78.00W
116 C4 Santa Bárbara Pinos, I de Cuba 21.49N 82.58W
75 L6 Santa Bárbara Spain 40.43N 0.29E
77 L6 Santa Bárbara *mt* Spain 37.23N 2.50W
111 D7 Santa Barbara Chan California
77 B5 Santa Bárbara de Casas Spain 37.48N 7.11W
76 D14 Santa Barbara de Nexe Portugal 37.06N 7.58W
118 F8 Santa Barbara d'Oeste Brazil 22.45S 47.20W
76 D13 Santa Bárbara dos Padrões Portugal 37.38N 7.59W
121 H2 Santa Bárbara do Sul Brazil 28.24S 53.17W
118 J5 Santa Bárbara, I Brazil 17.59S 38.38W
111 E8 Santa Barbara I California 33.29N 119.01W
120 G7 Santa Bárbara R Santa Cruz Bolivia
111 E7 Santa Barbara Res California 34.31N 119.40W
118 B4 Santa Bárbara, Sa.de *mts* Mato Grosso do Sul Brazil
118 D7 Santa Bárbara, Sa.de *mts* Mato Grosso do Sul Brazil
96 T3 Santa Bárbara, Serra de *mt* Azores 38.44N 27.20W
96 V15 Santa Brigida Gran Canaria Canary Is 28.02N 15.30W
75 G3 Santacara Spain 42.23N 1.33W
120 E10 Santa Catalina Argentina 22.00S 66.02W
120 D11 Santa Catalina Chile 25.13S 69.44W
119 C2 Santa Catalina Colombia 10.36N 75.17W
119 A3 Santa Catalina Panama 8.45N 81.19W
119 H3 Santa Catalina Venezuela 8.31N 61.54W
115 D5 Santa Catalina *isld* Mexico
75 F1 Santa Catalina, C Spain 43.22N 2.30W
111 F8 Santa Catalina, G.of California
111 F8 Santa Catalina I California 33.25N 118.25W
15 M4 Santa Catalina I Solomon Is 10.55S 162.30E
115 B3 Santa Catarina Baja Cal Mexico 29.32N 115.18W
115 J5 Santa Catarina Nuevo León Mexico 25.44N 100.30W
76 D14 Santa Catarina Portugal 37.09N 7.47W
118 E10 Santa Catarina *state* Brazil
76 C12 Santa Catarina de Sitimos Portugal 38.23N 8.26W
115 L9 Santa Catarina Juquíla Mexico 16.15N 97.20W
118 E10 Santa Catarina, I. de Brazil
81 A3 Santa Caterina Sardinia 40.07N 8.29E
81 N6 Santa Caterina dello Iónio Italy 38.32N 16.31E
79 H2 Santa Caterina Valfurva Italy 46.26N 10.29E
81 H8 Santa Caterina Villarmosa Sicily 37.35N 14.03E
116 B1 Santa Catharina Curaçao W I 12.14N 68.50W
121 J1 Santa Cecilia Brazil 27.00S 50.18W
118 F10 Santa Cecilia *dist* São Paulo Brazil
75 J2 Santa Cilia de Jaca Spain 42.34N 0.43W
111 C4 Santa Clara California 37.21N 121.58W
115 F3 Santa Clara Chihuahua Mexico 29.20N 107.02W
119 E9 Santa Clara Colombia 2.43S 69.56W
116 E3 Santa Clara Cuba 22.25N 79.58W
104 L2 Santa Clara New York 44.37N 74.30W
76 C8 Santa Clara Portugal 40.12N 8.26W
111 K10 Santa Clara Sonora Mexico 31.41N 114.30W
111 L4 Santa Clara Utah 37.08N 113.40W
122 U12 Santa Clara *I* Juan Fernández, Is Pacific Oc
111 E7 Santa Clara *R* California
76 C14 Santa Clara-a-Nova Portugal 37.29N 8.09W
76 C13 Santa Clara a Velha Portugal 37.31N 8.28W
76 C13 Santa Clara, Barragem de *res* Portugal 37.32N 8.26W
91 A3 Santa Clara, C Gabon 0.33N 9.17E
76 D13 Santa Clara de Louredo Portugal 37.58N 7.52W
121 G4 Santa Clara de Olimar Uruguay 32.50S 54.54W
119 B9 Santa Clara, I Ecuador 3.15S 80.23W
109 D5 Santa Clara Pk New Mexico 36.02N 106.24W
107 K3 Santa Claus Indiana 38.08N 86.56W
119 D9 Santa Clotilde Peru 2.33S 73.44W
75 Q4 Santa Coloma de Farnés Spain 41.52N 2.39E
75 P5 Santa Coloma de Grammanet Spain 41.28N 2.14E
75 N4 Santa Coloma de Queralt Spain 41.32N 1.23E
76 G4 Santa Colomba de Somoza Spain 42.26N 6.15W
76 J3 Santa Columba de Curueño Spain 42.45N 5.25W
91 D9 Santa Comba Angola 11.23S 15.08E
76 E7 Santa Comba Portugal 40.57N 7.08W
76 B2 Santa Comba Spain 43.02N 8.49W
76 C8 Santa Comba Dão Portugal 40.23N 8.07W
76 F5 Santa Comba de Rossas Portugal 41.40N 6.49W
79 L1 Santa Cristina Italy 46.34N 11.44E
81 K9 Santa Croce, C Sicily 37.15N 15.16E
81 J10 Santa Croce Camerina Sicily 36.50N 14.32E
80 L6 Santa Croce del Sánnio Italy 41.23N 14.44E
80 L5 Santa Croce di Magliano Italy 41.43N 14.59E
79 M2 Santa Croce, L.di Italy 46.07N 12.21E
80 N7 Santa Croce, Monte Italy 40.47N 15.35E
79 J7 Santa Croce sull'Arno Italy 43.43N 10.46E
119 E9 Santa Cruz Amazonas Brazil 3.53S 69.30W
91 E7 Santa Cruz Angola 6.56S 16.23E
116 A1 Santa Cruz Aruba W I 12.31N 69.59W
88 A1 Santa Cruz Azores 39.28N 31.08W
88 B1 Santa Cruz Azores 39.05N 28.00W
76 B12 Santa Cruz Baixo Alentejo Portugal 38.02N 8.42W
76 D14 Santa Cruz Baixo Alentejo Portugal 37.26N 7.55W
119 B11 Santa Cruz Cajamarca Peru 6.40S 79.00W
111 B5 Santa Cruz California 36.58N 122.03W
121 B5 Santa Cruz Chile 34.38S 71.27W
77 G5 Santa Cruz Cordoba Spain 37.45N 4.39W
115 M4 Santa Cruz Costa Rica 10.15N 85.35W
76 A10 Santa Cruz Estremadura Portugal 39.07N 9.23W
75 J2 Santa Cruz Huesca Spain 42.31N 0.40W
116 J2 Santa Cruz Jamaica, W I 18.03N 77.43W
120 B1 Santa Cruz Loreto Peru 5.14S 75.51W
19 G1 Santa Cruz Luzon Philippines 14.55N 120.34E
19 J4 Santa Cruz Luzon Philippines 15.47N 119.53E
19 K3 Santa Cruz Luzon Philippines 17.08N 120.27E
19 K4 Santa Cruz Luzon Philippines 14.16N 121.24E
96 Q7 Santa Cruz Madeira Is 32.41N 16.48W
28 A1 Santa Cruz Maharashtra India 19.07N 72.53E
115 D2 Santa Cruz Mexico 31.18N 110.40W
109 D6 Santa Cruz New Mexico 35.59N 106.02W
117 C6 Santa Cruz Pará Brazil 2.35S 53.38W
117 D5 Santa Cruz Pará Brazil 0.35S 49.10W
19 L7 Santa Cruz Philippines 9.31N 123.08E
117 J8 Santa Cruz Rio Grande do Norte Brazil 6.09S 35.58W
120 F7 Santa Cruz Santa Cruz Bolivia 17.45S 63.14W
119 E3 Santa Cruz Venezuela 8.25N 71.38W
120 F7 Santa Cruz *dept* Bolivia
115 D5 Santa Cruz *isld* Mexico 25.19N 110.42W
75 G5 Santa Cruz *mt* Spain 41.07N 1.35W
121 K7 Santa Cruz *prov* Argentina
121 K8 Santa Cruz *R* Argentina
115 O10 Santa Cruz Barillas Guatemala 15.50N 91.20W
10 N4 Santa Cruz Basin Pacific Oc
118 H5 Santa Cruz Cabrália Brazil 16.17S 39.03W
111 E7 Santa Cruz Chan California
96 R1 Santa Cruz da Graciosa Azores 39.06N 28.01W
96 P2 Santa Cruz das Flores Azores 39.28N 31.08W
76 C7 Santa Cruz da Trapa Portugal 40.46N 8.09W
75 C1 Santa Cruz de Bezana Spain 43.27N 3.54W
75 F2 Santa Cruz de Campezo Spain 42.40N 2.20W
118 E5 Santa Cruz de Goiás Brazil 17.19S 48.33W
75 D3 Santa Cruz de Juarros Spain 42.15N 3.28W
96 P10 Santa Cruz de la Palma La Palma Canary Is 28.41N 17.46W
76 H10 Santa Cruz de la Sierra Spain 39.20N 5.50W
75 D8 Santa Cruz de la Zarza Spain 39.59N 3.11W
77 J6 Santa Cruz del Comercio Spain 37.04N 3.58W
77 L3 Santa Cruz de los Cáñamos Spain 38.39N 2.51W
115 O10 Santa Cruz del Quiché Guatemala 15.02N 91.06W
76 L8 Santa Cruz del Retamar Spain 40.08N 4.14W
116 F4 Santa Cruz del Sur Cuba 20.44N 78.00W
75 C2 Santa Cruz del Tozo Spain 42.40N 3.54W
75 H8 Santa Cruz de Moya Spain 39.57N 1.16W
77 K3 Santa Cruz de Mudela Spain 38.39N 3.28W
96 S13 Santa Cruz de Tenerife Tenerife Canary Is 28.28N 16.15W
115 Q10 Santa Cruz de Yojoa Honduras 14.54N 87.55W
119 E3 Santa Cruz de Zulia Venezuela 8.56N 71.59W
91 G12 Santa Cruz do Cuando Rivungo Angola 16.13S 21.57E
118 E8 Santa Cruz do Rio Pardo Brazil 22.54S 49.37W
121 H2 Santa Cruz do Sul Brazil 29.42S 52.25W
111 E8 Santa Cruz I California 34.00N 119.40W
119 B5 Santa Cruz, I Galápagos Is 0.38S 90.23W
118 K8 Santa Cruz, I. de Brazil 22.52S 43.08W
10 O4 Santa Cruz Is Solomon Is
111 B4 Santa Cruz Mts California
116 J2 Santa Cruz Mts Jamaica, W I
117 B6 Santa Cruz, R Brazil
75 G5 Santa Cruz, Sierra de *mts* Spain
81 B5 Santadi Sardinia 39.06N 8.42E
81 J8 Santa Doménica Vittoria Sicily 37.55N 14.53E
86 F4 Santa, El Egypt 30.46N 31.08E
120 F9 Santa Elena Bolivia 20.31S 64.46W
121 E6 Santa Elena Buenos Aires Arg 37.25S 60.39W
119 B9 Santa Elena Ecuador 2.16S 80.52W
121 F3 Santa Elena Entre Ríos Arg 30.58S 59.47W
79 L4 Santa Elena Italy 45.11N 11.43E
120 C2 Santa Elena Loreto Peru 6.02S 74.04W
77 J4 Santa Elena Spain 38.21N 3.32W
112 J9 Santa Elena Texas 26.46N 98.30W
119 H5 Santa Elena Venezuela 4.37N 61.07W
119 B9 Santa Elena, B.de Ecuador
115 M4 Santa Elena, C Costa Rica 10.54N 85.56W
76 H4 Santa Elena de Jamuz Spain 42.15N 5.54W
77 L7 Santa Elena, Pta Spain 36.43N 2.38W
120 E7 Santa Elena, R Bolivia
121 E5 Santa Eleonora Argentina 34.43S 62.40W
77 G5 Santaella Spain 37.34N 4.51W
75 E2 Santa Engracia, Embalse del *res* Spain
118 F7 Santa Eudóxia Brazil 21.45S 47.47W
77 G3 Santa Eufemia Spain 38.36N 4.54W
77 V14 Santa Eugenia Balearic Is 39.38N 2.50E
76 B3 Santa Eugenia de Ribeira Spain 42.33N 8.59W
76 E10 Santa Eulália Alto Alentejo Portugal 39.01N 7.15W
76 C7 Santa Eulalia Beira Alta Portugal 40.33N 8.08W
75 H6 Santa Eulalia Spain 40.34N 1.20W
77 T12 Santa Eulalia del Río Balearic Is 38.59N 1.33E
76 E2 Santa Eulalia de Oscos Spain 43.17N 7.02W
75 P4 Santa Eulalia de Riuprimer Spain 41.55N 2.11E
120 D9 Santa Fé Chile 21.53S 69.32W
115 L2 Santa Fé Honduras 15.54N 86.05W
109 E6 Santa Fe New Mexico 35.41N 105.57W
115 O5 Santa Fé Panama 8.29N 80.50W
19 L5 Santa Fe Philippines 12.10N 122.01E
116 C4 Santa Fé Pinos, I de Cuba 21.45N 82.45W
75 P4 Santa Fe Spain 41.47N 2.27E
77 J6 Santafé Spain 37.11N 3.43W
121 E3 Santa Fé *prov* Argentina
77 L7 Santa Fé de Mondújar Spain 36.58N 2.31W
119 B6 Santa Fé, I Galápagos Is 0.57S 90.07W
105 E8 Santa Fe L Florida 29.44N 82.14W
105 E8 Santa Fe R Florida
117 E9 Santa Filomena Brazil 9.06S 45.52W
80 E3 Santa Fiora Italy 42.50N 11.55E
75 D2 Santa Gadea Spain 42.43N 3.04W
77 X14 Santa Galdana, Cala de *B* Balearic Is
79 K5 Sant'Agata Bolognese Italy 44.39N 11.08E
80 L6 Sant 'Agata de' Goti Italy 41.05N 14.30E
81 L4 Sant'Agata di Esaro Italy 39.37N 15.59E
80 M6 Sant'Agata di Puglia Italy 41.09N 15.24E
79 M7 Sant'Agata Feltria Italy 43.52N 12.12E
115 E6 Santa Genovéva *pk* Mexico 23.16N 109.50W
79 J2 Santa Gertrude d'Ultimo Italy 46.29N 10.52E
115 G4 Santa Gertrudis Mexico 27.48N 105.52W
79 F4 Santa Giuletta Italy 45.02N 9.11E
81 B4 Santa Giusta Sardinia 39.53N 8.37E
81 A2 Santa Giusta, Mte Sardinia 40.49N 8.15E
79 K5 Sant'Agostino Italy 44.47N 11.23E
31 H8 Santahar Bangladesh 24.45N 89.03E
117 E6 Santa Helena Maranhão Brazil 2.15S 45.15W
117 B7 Santa Helena Pará Brazil 5.00S 56.20W
118 E5 Santa Helena de Goiás Brazil 17.53S 50.36W
23 D3 Santai Sichuan China 31.05N 105.02E
24 D3 Santai Xinjiang Uygur Zizhiqu China 44.40N 81.29E
24 F3 Santai Xinjiang Uygur Zizhiqu China 44.08N 88.53E
23 B5 Santai Yunnan China 26.00N 101.07E
118 G10 Santa Ifigènia *dist* São Paulo Brazil
118 H3 Santa Inês Brazil 13.21S 39.48W
77 E3 Santa Inés *mt* Spain 38.32N 5.37W
121 J9 Santa Inés, I Chile
121 L10 Santa Inéz, C Argentina 54.12S 67.05W
76 D13 Santa Iria Baixo Alentejo Portugal 37.53N 7.34W
76 E15 Santa Iria Estremadura Portugal 38.51N 9.05W
120 E9 Santa Isabel Bolivia 21.35S 66.31W
118 A3 Santa Isabel Brazil 13.35S 60.45W
121 E4 Santa Isabel Buenos Aires Arg 33.56S 61.40W
119 B9 Santa Isabel Ecuador 3.22S 79.22W
Santa Isabel Fernando Póo *see* Malabo
121 C6 Santa Isabel La Pampa Argentina 36.15S 66.54W
120 C1 Santa Isabel Loreto Peru 5.47S 74.30W
105 J8 Santa Isabel Puerto Rico 17.58N 66.24W
120 C7 Santa Isabel de Sihuas Peru 16.20S 72.09W
117 D8 Santa Isabel do Araguaia Brazil 6.05S 48.22W
118 E2 Santa Isabel do Morro Brazil 11.36S 50.37W
15 L2 Santa Isabel I Solomon Is
117 G6 Santa Isabel, I. Grande de Brazil
90 D10 Santa Isabel, Pico de *mt* Fernando Póo Eq Guinea 3.36N 8.45E
115 B2 Santa Isabel,Sa *ra* Mexico
119 D8 Santa Julia Colombia 1.44S 72.25W
121 G10 Santa Julia *dist* Santiago Chile
118 F6 Santa Juliana Brazil 19.18S 47.32W
76 D11 Santa Justa Alto Alentejo Portugal 38.45N 7.52W
76 C10 Santa Justa Ribatejo Portugal 39.01N 8.17W
121 E1 Santa Justina Argentina 27.40S 62.40W
75 F3 Santa, La Spain 42.13N 2.21W
81 K8 Sant.Aléssio, C Sicily 37.55N 15.22E
75 M4 Santa Liña Spain 41.56N 0.47E
29 K5 Santal Parganas *dist* Bihar India
29 B6 Santalpur Gujarat India 23.46N 71.12E
80 C2 Santa Luce Italy 43.28N 10.33E
121 F2 Santa Lucia Argentina 28.58S 59.05W
119 B8 Santa Lucía Ecuador 1.45S 79.58W
96 V16 Santa Lucía Gran Canaria Canary Is 27.55N 15.33W
115 M3 Santa Lucía Nicaragua 12.28N 85.50W
116 F4 Santa Lucía Oriente Cuba 21.01N 76.01W
116 C3 Santa Lucía Pinar del Rio Cuba 22.39N 83.59W
81 D2 Santa Lucia Sardinia 40.35N 9.47E
77 P5 Santa Lucía Spain 37.35N 0.58W
121 G5 Santa Lucía Uruguay 34.26S 56.25W
115 O10 Santa Lucía Cotz Guatemala 14.20N 91.00W
81 K7 Santa Lucia del Mela Sicily 38.08N 15.17E
67 P13 Santa Lucia di Tallano Corsica 41.41N 9.04E
121 F2 Santa Lucía R Argentina
121 G5 Santa Lucía R Uruguay
111 C5 Santa Lucia Ra California
120 D9 Santa Lucía Victoria Chile 20.44S 69.43W
118 C6 Santa Luísa, Sa.de *mts* Brazil
118 E3 Santa Luiza, Sa.de *mts* Brazil
118 H2 Santaluz Brazil 11.15S 39.23W
96 Q4 Santa Luzia Azores 38.33N 28.24W
117 H8 Santa Luzia Paraíba Brazil 6.48S 36.52W
76 C13 Santa Luzia Portugal 37.44N 8.24W
89 O10 Santa Luzia *isld* Cape Verde 16.30N 24.35W
76 D8 Santa Luzia, Barragem de *res* Portugal 40.05N 7.52W
121 D10 Santa Magdalena de Gali Arg 44.05S 65.30W
75 L7 Santa Magdalena de Pulpis Spain 40.21N 0.18E
67 P14 Santa Manza, G.de Corsica 41.25N 9.15E
76 B12 Santa Margarida da Serra Portugal 38.07N 8.36W
76 C12 Santa Margarida do Sado Portugal 38.07N 8.21W
121 E2 Santa Margarita Argentina 28.18S 61.35W
77 W14 Santa Margarita Balearic Is 39.42N 3.05E
111 D6 Santa Margarita California 35.22N 120.36W
115 D5 Santa Margarita *isld* Mexico
111 G8 Santa Margarita *R* California
81 F8 Santa Margherita di Belice Sicily 37.42N 13.02E
79 F6 Santa Margherita Ligure Italy 44.19N 9.12E
117 A5 Santa Maria Amazonas Brazil 1.45S 58.32W
117 A6 Santa Maria Amazonas Brazil 2.30S 58.10W
119 H9 Santa María Amazonas Brazil 2.55S 60.25W
119 J9 Santa María Amazonas Brazil 2.32S 58.10W
120 F2 Santa Maria Amazonas Brazil 6.52S 64.40W
77 V14 Santa Maria Balearic Is 39.39N 2.46E
111 D7 Santa Maria California 34.56N 120.25W
89 P10 Santa Maria Cape Verde 16.38N 22.57W
115 N5 Santa María Costa Rica 9.40N 83.58W
115 G5 Santa María Mexico 25.58N 105.20N
120 E4 Santa Maria Pando Bolivia 10.45S 67.39W
117 B6 Santa Maria Pará Brazil 2.37S 54.55W
119 D8 Santa Maria Peru 1.24S 74.40W
120 F6 Santa María Santa Cruz Bolivia 15.28S 63.22W
66 S5 Santa Maria Switzerland 46.37N 10.27E
119 F4 Santa María Venezuela 6.36N 67.10W
92 D7 Santa Maria Zambia 11.09S 29.59E
96 U4 Santa Maria *isld* Azores 36.58N 25.07W
121 A6 Santa María *isld* Chile
9 C10 Santa Maria *isld* New Hebrides
111 L7 Santa Maria *R* Arizona
115 F2 Santa María *R* Mexico
121 G3 Santa Maria *R* Rio Grande do Sul Brazil
121 G5 Santa Maria, C Uruguay 34.38S 54.07W
80 K6 Santa Maria Capua Vetere Italy 41.05N 14.15E
116 E3 Santa María, Cayo Cuba 22.40N 79.00W
91 C10 Santa Maria, C.de Angola 13.25S 12.32E
94 M6 Santa Maria, C.de Mozambique 26.07S 32.56E
76 D15 Santa Maria, C.de Portugal 36.58N 7.55W
118 F4 Santa Maria, Chapadão de *hills* Brazil
117 D9 Santa Maria das Barreiras Brazil 8.50S 49.40W
118 G3 Santa Maria da Vitória Brazil 13.26S 44.09W
75 K3 Santa Maria de Belsué, Embalse de *res* Spain 42.19N 0.21W
75 C1 Santa Maria de Cayón Spain 43.18N 3.51W
75 P3 Santa María de Corcó Spain 42.02N 2.23E
115 F4 Santa María de Cuevas Mexico 27.55N 106.23W
119 G3 Santa María de Ipire Venezuela 8.51N 65.21W
75 F5 Santa María de la Huerta Spain 41.15N 2.10W
75 D4 Santa Maria de las Hoyas Spain 41.46N 3.09W
76 J7 Santa María del Berrocal Spain 40.31N 5.23W
75 C3 Santa María del Campo Spain 42.08N 3.59W
75 F8 Santa María del Campo Rus Spain 39.34N 2.26W
79 F5 Santa Maria della Versa Italy 44.59N 9.17E
96 S13 Santa Maria del Mar Tenerife Canary Is 28.26N 16.18W
76 H4 Santa María del Páramo Spain 42.21N 5.45W
115 J7 Santa María del Río Mexico 21.50N 100.45W
79 F6 Santa Maria del Taro Italy 44.26N 9.29E
75 F7 Santa María del Val Spain 40.30N 2.03W
119 D9 Santa María de Nanay Peru 3.51S 73.51W
77 N6 Santa María de Nieva Spain 37.28N 2.00W
75 P4 Santa María de Palautordera Spain 41.42N 2.37E
77 G5 Santa María de Trassierra Spain 37.56N 4.53W
76 H5 Santa Maria de Valverde Spain 41.56N 5.56W
81 R13 Santa Maria di Léuca, C Italy 39.48N 18.23E
81 J8 Santa Maria di Licodia Sicily 37.32N 14.54E
120 G2 Santa Maria dos Marmelos Amazonas Brazil 5.06S 61.42W
120 G2 Santa Maria dos Marmelos Brazil 7.04S 62.52W
118 G6 Santa Maria do Suaçuí Brazil 18.09S 42.21W
119 B6 Santa María, I Galápagos Is 1.20S 90.28W
81 C1 Santa Maria I Sardinia 41.18N 9.23E
76 L6 Santa Maria la Real de Nieva Spain 41.04N 4.25W
115 F2 Santa María, L.de Mexico
118 G7 Santa Maria Madalena Brazil 21.58S 42.02W
79 D2 Santa Maria Maggiore Italy 46.08N 8.28E
111 M7 Santa Maria Mts Arizona
80 H2 Santa Maria Nuova Italy 43.29N 13.18E
120 B6 Santa María, Pta *C* Peru 14.43S 75.54W
118 C7 Santa Maria, R Mato Grosso do Sul Brazil
119 B3 Santa María, R Panama
118 F4 Santa Maria, Sa. de *mts* Brazil
67 O13 Santa Maria Siché Corsica 41.53N 8.59E
121 B6 Santa Mariá, V *vol* Argentina 36.15S 69.22W
76 H2 Santa Marina Spain 43.09N 5.57W
76 H3 Santa Marina del Rey Spain 42.30N 5.51W
81 J6 Santa Marina Salina Lipari Is Italy 38.34N 14.52E
80 E4 Santa Marinella Italy 42.02N 11.52E
77 M2 Santa Marta Albacete Spain 39.09N 2.18W
77 C3 Santa Marta Badajoz Spain 38.37N 6.39W
119 D2 Santa Marta Colombia 11.18N 74.10W
91 C10 Santa Marta, C Angola 13.52S 12.24E
76 G9 Santa Marta de Magasca Spain 39.30N 6.06W
76 D6 Santa Marta de Penguião Portugal 41.12N 7.46W
121 J2 Santa Marta Grande, C Brazil 28.43S 48.50W
76 D1 Santa Marta, R.de *B* Spain
119 D2 Santa Marta, Sa.Nev.de *mts* Colombia
118 D6 Santa Martha, Serra de *mts* Brazil
Santa Maura *isld see* Levkás
66 M8 Sant Ambrogio Italy 45.51N 8.48E
111 F7 Santa Monica California 34.00N 118.25W
112 G7 Santa Mónica Coahuila Mexico 28.13N 100.39W
112 K9 Santa Monica Texas 26.22N 97.38W
111 F8 Santa Monica B California
111 C8 Santa Monica Mts California
18 M6 Santan Borneo Indon 0.01S 117.30E
119 F7 Santana Amazonas Brazil 0.16N 67.15W
118 G3 Santana Bahia Brazil 12.58S 44.03W
117 A6 Santana Brazil 2.36S 58.00W
96 P7 Santana Madeira Is 32.48N 16.54W
76 A12 Sant'Ana Portugal 38.28N 9.06W
118 G9 Santana *dist* São Paulo Brazil
118 D6 Santana *R* Mato Grosso do Sul Brazil
121 G3 Santana, Coxilha de *mts* Brazil/Uruguay
121 H3 Santana da Boa Vista Brazil 30.58S 53.10W
76 C14 Sant Ana da Serra Portugal 37.30N 8.18W
76 D13 Sant'Ana de Cambas Portugal 37.37N 7.32W
117 G6 Santana do Acarau Brazil 3.27S 40.10W
117 G8 Santana do Cariri Brazil 7.14S 39.45W
117 H9 Santana do Ipanema Brazil 9.19S 37.15W
121 G3 Santana do Livramento Brazil 30.52S 55.30W
76 C11 Santana do Mato Portugal 38.53N 8.24W
117 H7 Santana do Matos Brazil 5.59S 36.31W
117 F6 Santana, I Brazil 2.20S 43.40W
119 C6 Santander Colombia 3.00N 76.25W
75 C1 Santander Spain 43.28N 3.48W

119 D4 Santander div Colombia
74 E1 Santander prov Spain
75 C1 Santander, B.de Spain
81 D5 Sant' Andrea Sardinia 39.22N 9.34E
81 Q12 Sant 'Andrea isld Italy 40.03N 17.59E
81 N6 Sant'Andrea Apostolo dello Iónio Italy 38.37N 16.32E
81 K8 Sant'Andrea, C Sicily 37.52N 15.19E
81 C5 Sant'Andrea Frius Sardinia 39.28N 9.10E
77 X14 Santandria, Cala de B Balearic Is
81 K3 Sant'Angelo a Fasanella Italy 40.27N 15.20E
81 G9 Sant'Angelo, C Sicily 37.06N 13.54E
80 M7 Sant'Angelo de Lombardi Italy 40.55N 15.11E
81 J7 Sant' Angelo di Brolo Sicily 38.07N 14.53E
79 N7 Sant'Angelo in Lizzola Italy 43.49N 12.48E
24 H3 Santanghu Xinjiang Uygur Zizhiqu China 44.16N 93.22E
81 E8 Santa Ninfa Sicily 37.47N 12.53E
111 N8 Santan Mt Arizona 33.12N 111.41W
79 B6 Sant'Anna, Colle pass Italy/France 44.13N 7.07E
118 H8 Sant'Anna, I. de Brazil
81 A5 Sant'Antioco Sardinia 39.04N 8.27E
81 A5 Sant'Antioco, I.di Sardinia
81 A4 Sant'Antonio di Santadi Sardinia 39.43N 8.28E
81 B3 Sant'Antonio Mte Sardinia 40.14N 8.41E
77 W15 Santañy Balearic Is 39.22N 3.07E
San-tao-kou see Helong
76 L8 Santa Olalla Spain 40.02N 4.25W
77 D5 Santa Olalla de Cala Spain 37.54N 6.14W
Santa Ona I see Santa Ana I.
81 K9 Santa Panagia, C Sicily 37.07N 15.18E
75 Q3 Santa Pau Spain 42.08N 2.34E
111 E7 Santa Paula California 34.20N 119.05W
28 F1 Santapilly Andhra Prad India 18.05N 83.47E
77 P4 Santa Pola Spain 38.12N 0.32W
77 P4 Santa Pola, B.de Spain
77 O4 Santa Pola C.de Spain 38.13N 0.29W
111 N2 Santaquin Utah 39.58N 111.48W
117 G7 Santa Quitéria Brazil 4.20S 40.10W
117 F6 Santa Quitéria do Maranhão Brazil 3.33S 42.35W
120 A3 Santa, R Peru
76 D7 Santar Portugal 40.34N 7.54W
81 M3 Sant'Arcangelo Italy 40.15N 16.17E
79 M6 Sant'Arcangelo di Romagna Italy 44.04N 12.26E
81 M3 Sant'Arcangelo, Mte Italy 40.13N 16.23E
121 D5 Santa Regina Argentina 34.33S 63.12W
117 B6 Santarém Brazil 2.26S 54.41W
76 B10 Santarém Portugal 39.14N 8.40W
76 B10 Santarém dist Portugal
116 E3 Santaren Chan Bahamas
119 G4 Santa Rita Bolívar Venez 7.06N 63.23W
119 D7 Santa Rita Colombia 0.48N 73.36W
19 L1 Santa Rita Guam Pacific Oc 13.23N 144.40E
119 F3 Santa Rita Guarico Venez 8.08N 66.18W
117 A8 Santa Rita Mato Grosso Brazil 7.37S 58.15W
110 N1 Santa Rita Montana 48.41N 112.22W
109 B9 Santa Rita New Mexico 32.48N 108.04W
115 G10 Santa Rita Panama 9.04N 79.31W
117 J8 Santa Rita Paraíba Brazil 7.08S 35.00W
76 D14 Santa Rita Portugal 37.11N 7.34W
119 E2 Santa Rita Zulia Venez 10.35N 71.30W
118 D5 Santa Rita do Araguaia Brazil 17.21S 53.07W
118 F8 Santa Rita do Sapucaí Brazil 22.15S 45.43W
119 E9 Santa Rita do Weil Brazil 3.33S 69.20W
120 D3 Santa Rosa Acre Brazil 9.30S 70.30W
119 F7 Santa Rosa Amazonas Venez 1.30N 66.55W
91 C11 Santa Rosa Angola 15.45S 11.56E
119 G3 Santa Rosa Anzoátegui Venez 9.37N 64.20W
119 F4 Santa Rosa Apure Venezuela 6.36N 67.58W
120 E6 Santa Rosa Beni Bolivia 14.10S 66.54W
120 F4 Santa Rosa Beni Bolivia 11.41S 65.17W
111 B3 Santa Rosa California 38.26N 122.43W
119 E6 Santa Rosa Colombia 3.33N 69.47W
121 D3 Santa Rosa Córdoba Arg 31.08S 63.20W
115 M4 Santa Rosa Costa Rica 10.51N 85.38W
119 B9 Santa Rosa Ecuador 3.29S 79.57W
121 D6 Santa Rosa La Pampa Argentina 36.37S 64.17W
119 D9 Santa Rosa Loreto Peru 3.02S 73.07W
19 J2 Santa Rosa Luzon Philippines 14.19N 121.07E
121 C4 Santa Rosa Mendoza Arg 33.15S 68.10W
109 F7 Santa Rosa New Mexico 34.56N 104.42W
115 J5 Santa Rosa Nuevo León Mexico 24.12N 100.19W
115 F10 Santa Rosa Panama Canal Zone 9.11N 79.40W
118 C10 Santa Rosa Paraguay 26.51S 56.50W
120 D6 Santa Rosa Puno Peru 14.38S 70.45W
121 G1 Santa Rosa Rio Grande do Sul Brazil 27.50S 54.29W
121 C8 Santa Rosa Rio Negro Arg 40.03S 66.40W
120 E11 Santa Rosa Salta Arg 24.27S 66.39W
121 D4 Santa Rosa San Luis Argentina 32.21S 65.15W
115 P8 Santa Rosa Yucatán Mexico 19.58N 88.51W
120 B9 Santa Rosa dist Lima Peru
19 M1 Santa Rosa mt Guam Pacific Oc 13.32N 144.55E
115 M2 Santa Rosa de Aguán Honduras 15.55N 85.40W
119 C5 Santa Rosa de Cabal Colombia 4.52N 75.37W
115 P10 Santa Rosa de Copán Honduras 14.48N 88.43W
120 G7 Santa Rosa de la Mina Bolivia 16.36S 62.39W
120 G7 Santa Rosa de la Roca Bolivia 16.03S 61.35W
115 Q11 Santa Rosa de Lima El Salvador 13.38N 87.52W
121 G9 Santa Rosa de Locobe dist Santiago Chile
120 G7 Santa Rosa del Palmar Bolivia 16.52S 26.24W
119 C4 Santa Rosa de Osas Colombia 6.40N 75.27W
119 C8 Santa Rosa de Otas Ecuador 0.58S 77.29W
119 C7 Santa Rosa de Sucumbio Ecuador 0.21N 77.08W
119 D5 Santa Rosa de Viterbo Colombia 5.55N 72.59W
111 D8 Santa Rosa I California 34.00N 120.05W
107 J11 Santa Rosa I Florida
118 B6 Santa Rosa, L Bolivia 18.58S 58.44W
112 H2 Santa Rosa L Texas 33.55N 99.17W
115 C4 Santa Rosalía Mexico 27.20N 112.20W
119 G4 Santa Rosalía Venezuela 7.30N 65.40W
111 H8 Santa Rosa Mts California
110 H8 Santa Rosa Pk Nevada 41.35N 117.40W
121 G1 Santa Rosa R Brazil
110 H8 Santa Rosa Ra Nevada
111 N9 Santa Rosa Wash R Arizona
81 K3 Sant'Arsenio Italy 40.28N 15.29E
80 E4 Santa Severa Italy 42.01N 11.59E
81 N5 Santa Severina Italy 39.08N 16.55E
76 J4 Santas Martas Spain 42.25N 5.22W
79 L7 Santa Sofia Italy 43.57N 11.54E
76 C11 Santa Sofia Portugal 38.37N 8.05W
76 D11 Santa Susana Alto Alentejo Portugal 38.34N 7.40W
76 C12 Santa Susana Baixo Alentejo Portugal 38.27N 8.24W
121 E1 Santa Sylvina Argentina 27.55S 61.15W
94 G2 Santatadibe R Botswana
Santa Tecla see Nueva San Salvador
76 B5 Santa Tecla, Pta de pt Spain 41.52N 8.53W
121 E4 Santa Teresa Argentina 33.30S 60.45W
119 H5 Santa Teresa Bolívar Venez 4.44N 61.05W
118 H6 Santa Teresa Espírito Santo Brazil 19.55S 40.36W
119 F2 Santa Teresa Miranda Venez 10.15N 66.39W
115 G6 Santa Teresa Nayarit Mexico 22.28N 104.42W
115 L5 Santa Teresa Tamaulipas Mexico 25.19N 97.50W
118 J9 Santa Teresa dist Rio de Janeiro Brazil 22.56S 43.12W
81 K8 Santa Teresa di Riva Sicily 37.57N 15.23E
76 H7 Santa Teresa, Embalse de res Spain
81 C1 Santa Teresa Gallura Sardinia 41.14N 9.12E
118 E3 Santa Teresa, R Brazil
13 C6 Santa Theresa Mission N Terr Australia 24.10S 134.28E
96 R13 Santa Úrsula Tenerife Canary Is 28.25N 16.30W
81 K8 Santa Venerina Sicily 37.42N 15.09E
76 C13 Santa Victoria Portugal 37.58N 8.01W
120 F10 Santa Victoria Salta Arg 22.15S 65.00W
120 G10 Santa Victoria Salta Arg 22.17S 62.44W
120 F10 Santa Victoria, Sa mts Argentina
118 E6 Santa Vitória Brazil 18.51S 50.06W
121 H4 Santa Vitória do Palmar Brazil 33.32S 53.25W
80 H2 Santa Vittoria in Matenano Italy 43.04N 13.30E
81 C4 Santa Vittoria, Mte Sardinia 39.46N 9.19E
111 D7 Santa Ynez California 34.37N 120.05W
111 D7 Santa Ynez R California
111 D7 Santa Ynez Mts California
111 H8 Santa Ysabel California 33.08N 116.40W
Santa Ysabel isld see Santa Isabel /
75 N4 Sant Climens Spain 41.58N 1.25E
99 L4 Sante Agnes Quebec 48.07N 79.04W
108 N7 Santee Nebraska 42.50N 97.51W
105 G4 Santee Dam S Carolina 33.27N 80.09W
105 H4 Santee Pt S Carolina 33.07N 79.15W
105 H4 Santee, R S Carolina
76 E5 Sante Estêvão Trás os Montes e Alto Douro Portugal 41.45N 7.25W
105 D2 Santeetlah, L N Carolina
121 E3 Sante Fé Argentina 31.38S 60.43W
80 L5 Sant' Elia a Pianisi Italy 41.37N 14.53E
81 C5 Sant' Elia, C Sardinia 39.11N 9.10E
81 G9 Sant' Elisabetta Sicily 37.27N 13.33E
77 U14 San Telmo Balearic Is 39.35N 2.21E
115 A2 San Telmo Mexico 31.00N 116.06W
115 H8 San Telmo, Pta C Mexico 18.20N 103.30W
80 H4 Sante Marie Italy 42.07N 13.12E
79 C5 Sántena Italy 44.57N 7.46E
71 F3 Santenay Côte d'Or France 46.55N 4.42E
70 N6 Santenay France 47.32N 1.05E
81 N2 Santeramo in Colle Italy 40.47N 16.45E
79 L6 Santerno R Italy
76 K3 Santervás de la Vega Spain 42.30N 4.48W
75 G1 Santesteban Spain 43.07N 1.40W
81 L7 Sant' Eufémia d'Aspromonte Italy 38.16N 15.51E
81 L6 Sant' Eufémia, G. di Italy
81 M6 Sant' Eufémia Lamézia Italy 38.56N 16.15E
70 O5 Santeuil France 48.23N 1.44E
79 D4 Santhià Italy 45.22N 8.11E
115 E6 Santiago Baja Cal Mexico 23.32N 109.47W
118 B6 Santiago Bolivia 18.25S 59.37W
121 G2 Santiago Brazil 29.11S 54.52W
121 B4 Santiago Chile 33.30S 70.40W
115 G8 Santiago Colima Mexico 19.08N 104.20W
116 J5 Santiago Dominican Rep 19.30N 70.42W
19 K3 Santiago Luzon Philippines 16.45N 121.34E
115 J5 Santiago Nuevo León Mexico 25.28N 100.09W
115 O5 Santiago Panama 8.08N 80.59W
118 C10 Santiago Paraguay 27.08S 56.45W
120 B6 Santiago Peru 14.14S 75.44W
76 E9 Santiago mt Spain 39.36N 7.13W
121 B4 Santiago prov Chile
115 M10 Santiago Astata Mexico 16.00N 95.42W
115 O10 Santiago Atitlán Guatemala 14.39N 91.12W
121 H8 Santiago, C Chile 50.46S 75.26W
115 O5 Santiago, Cerro pk Panama 8.34N 81.42W
120 A8 Santiago de Cao Peru 7.58S 79.13W
77 B1 Santiago de Carbajo Spain 39.36N 7.15W
120 B5 Santiago de Chocorvos Peru 13.50S 75.12W
120 A3 Santiago de Chuco Peru 8.07S 78.10W
76 J8 Santiago de Collado Spain 40.25N 5.21W
76 B3 Santiago de Compostela Spain 42.52N 8.33W
116 G4 Santiago de Cuba Cuba 20.00N 75.49W
120 E7 Santiago de Huata Bolivia 16.06S 68.53W
77 L4 Santiago de la Espada Spain 38.06N 2.33W
76 J7 Santiago de la Puebla Spain 40.48N 5.17W
76 G9 Santiago del Campo Spain 39.38N 6.22W
121 D1 Santiago del Estero Argentina 27.47S 64.15W
121 D1 Santiago del Estero prov Arg 27.48S 64.15W
96 Q14 Santiago del Teide Tenerife Canary Is 28.18N 16.49W
120 D7 Santiago de Machaca Bolivia 17.02S 69.10W
115 P11 Santiago de María El Salvador 13.28N 88.28W
120 E5 Santiago de Pacaguaras Bolivia 13.05S 68.00W
120 B10 Santiago de Sucro dist Lima Peru
76 B12 Santiago do Cacém Portugal 38.01N 8.42W
76 C11 Santiago do Escoural Portugal 38.32N 8.10W
115 G7 Santiago Ixcuintla Mexico 21.50N 105.11W
76 E11 Santiago Maior Portugal 38.33N 7.29W
76 G4 Santiago Millas Spain 42.23N 6.06W
112 D6 Santiago Mts Texas
115 G5 Santiago Papasquiaro Mexico 25.00N 105.27W
112 D6 Santiago Pk Texas 29.50N 103.26W
111 G8 Santiago Pk mt California 33.42N 117.34W
90 D10 Santiago, Pta. de Fernando Póo Eq Guinea 3.12N 8.43E
96 Q14 Santiago, Pto. de Tenerife Canary Is 28.14N 16.50W
119 B7 Santiago, R Ecuador
119 C10 Santiago, R Peru
115 G7 Santiago, R.Grande de Mexico
118 B6 Santiago, Sa.de mts Bolivia
121 D3 Santiago Temple Argentina 31.28S 63.20W
115 G5 Santiaguillo, L.de Mexico
110 C5 Santiam, N R Oregon
110 C5 Santiam, S R Oregon
76 H2 Santibañez Spain 43.06N 5.40W
75 D5 Santibáñez de Ayllón Spain 41.20N 3.18W
76 H8 Santibáñez de Béjar Spain 40.30N 5.35W
76 K3 Santibañez de la Peña Spain 42.48N 4.45W
76 G4 Santibañez de Vidriales Spain 42.05N 6.00W
76 G8 Santibañez el Bajo Spain 40.10N 6.14W
75 C3 Santibáñez-Zarzaguda Spain 42.29N 3.46W
19 B3 Santigi Celebes Indon 1.22N 120.55E
89 J6 Santijan Ghana 10.28N 1.22W
79 H5 Sant'Ilario d'Enza Italy 44.46N 10.27E
76 L2 Santillana Spain 43.24N 4.06W
76 L4 Santillana de Campos Spain 42.22N 4.23W
76 M7 Santillana, Embalse de res Spain 40.43N 3.50W
119 E3 San Timoteo Venezuela 9.50N 71.05W
76 D8 Santinho mt Portugal 40.28N 7.32W
77 G7 Santi Petri mt Spain 36.50N 4.35W
77 D6 Santiponce Spain 37.26N 6.03W
Santipui see Santipur
29 L6 Santipur W Bengal India 23.14N 88.29E
76 E2 San Tirso de Aores Spain 43.24N 7.08W
66 O2 Säntis mt Switzerland 47.15N 9.21E
76 C3 Santiso Spain 42.52N 8.03W
77 K4 Santisteban del Puerto Spain 38.15N 3.11W
76 L2 Santiurde de Reinosa Spain 43.04N 4.05W
76 K6 Santiuste Spain 41.10N 4.35W
76 H6 Santiz Spain 41.12N 5.54W
22 C2 Santmargrats Mongolia 48.35N 95.25E
112 J3 Santo Texas 32.34N 98.14W
76 E11 Santo Aleixo Alto Alentejo Portugal 38.55N 7.25W
76 E12 Santo Aleixo Baixo Alentejo Portugal 38.04N 7.09W
76 E12 Santo Amador Portugal 38.08N 7.18W
96 R4 Santo Amaro Azores 38.27N 28.10W
118 J3 Santo Amaro Bahia Brazil 12.35S 38.41W
117 F6 Santo Amaro Maranhão Brazil 2.31S 43.10W
76 D11 Santo Amaro Portugal 38.59N 7.35W
118 H7 Santo Amaro de Campos Brazil 21.59S 41.05W
118 F8 Santo Amaro, I.de Brazil 23.55S 46.14W
118 D7 Santo Anastácio Brazil 21.57S 51.43W
118 F8 Santo André Brazil 23.39S 46.29W
76 B12 Santo André Portugal 38.02N 8.45W
76 B12 Santo André, Lagoa de Portugal
121 G2 Santo Angelo Brazil 28.17S 54.15W
96 S4 Santo Antão Azores 38.33N 27.48W
89 O10 Santo Antão isld Cape Verde
119 G9 Santo Antonio Amazonas Brazil 3.25S 63.38W
119 H9 Santo Antônio Amazonas Brazil 2.22S 60.58W
96 Q4 Santo Antonio Azores 38.33N 28.21W
117 E8 Santo Antônio Maranhão Brazil 6.40S 46.10W
91 B12 Santo Antonio Príncipe São Tomé & Principe, Gulf of Guinea 1.37N 7.27E
117 J8 Santo Antônio Rio Grande do Norte Brazil 6.15S 35.27W
118 G6 Santo Antônio R Brazil
118 J3 Santo Antônio, C Brazil 13.01S 38.27W
118 E8 Santo Antônio da Platina Brazil 23.16S 50.04W
118 H3 Santo Antônio de Jesus Brazil 12.59S 39.16W
119 F9 Santo Antônio do Içá Brazil 3.05S 67.56W
118 C4 Santo Antônio do Leverger Brazil 15.45S 56.02W
118 F7 Santo Antônio do Monte Brazil 20.06S 45.17W
91 C7 Santo Antonio do Zaire Angola 6.12S 12.23E
96 T1 Santo Antônio Fenaes de Luz Azores 37.37N 25.43W
118 J5 Santo Antônio, Pta Brazil 16.10S 38.55W
119 H8 Santo Antônio, R Brazil
118 B5 Santo Corazón Bolivia 17.57S 58.46W
76 E8 Santo Cornélio mt Portugal 40.21N 7.10W
121 G1 Santo Cristo R Brazil
121 F6 Santo Domingo Argentina 36.44S 57.35W
115 B3 Santo Domingo Baja Cal Mexico 28.10N 114.08W
115 C5 Santo Domingo Baja California Mexico 25.34N 112.00W
116 D3 Santo Domingo Cuba 22.35N 80.27W
116 K5 Santo Domingo Dominican Rep 18.30N 69.57W
115 P10 Santo Domingo Guatemala 15.56N 89.45W
115 M3 Santo Domingo Nicaragua 12.15N 84.59W
120 D5 Santo Domingo Peru 13.49S 69.38W
115 J6 Santo Domingo San Luis Potosí Mexico 23.20N 101.45W
119 D4 Santo Domingo Venezuela 7.34N 72.06W
116 G4 Santo Domingo, Cay isld Cuba 21.41N 75.46W
96 P9 Santo Domingo de Garafia La Palma Canary Is 28.49N 16.56W
75 E3 Santo Domingo de la Calzada Spain 42.26N 2.57W
119 B8 Santo Domingo de los Colorados Ecuador 0.13S 79.09W
75 D4 Santo Domingo de Silos Spain 41.58N 3.25W
119 E3 Santo Domingo, R Venezuela
115 M9 Santo Domingo Tehuantepec Mexico 16.21N 95.16W
118 H7 Santo Eduardo Brazil 21.15S 41.28W
96 V5 Santo Espírito Azores 36.58N 25.03W
76 D14 Santo Estêvão Algarve Portugal 37.07N 7.43W
76 C5 Santo Estêvão Minho Portugal 41.31N 8.20W
76 B11 Santo Estevão Ribatejo Portugal 38.52N 8.44W
76 B11 Santo Estevão R Portugal
118 G6 Santo Hipólito Brazil 18.16S 44.10W
118 G2 Santo Inácio Brazil 11.09S 42.45W
76 C7 Santo João do Monte Portugal 40.36N 8.14W
Santokhe see Santanghu
75 K6 Santolea Spain 40.45N 0.22W
75 K6 Santolea, Embalse de L Spain 40.45N 0.20W
76 C8 Santo Martinho Portugal 40.17N 8.09W
76 G5 Santo Martinho de Angueira Portugal 41.38N 6.21W
119 G3 San Tomé Venezuela 9.00N 64.09W
77 O4 Santomera Spain 38.03N 1.03W
76 E8 Santo Miguel de Acha Portugal 40.01N 7.19W
81 B5 Santo, Mte Sardinia 39.02N 8.55E
57 D4 Santon Isle of Man U.K. 54.06N 4.35W
75 D1 Santoña Spain 43.27N 3.26W
21 D6 Santong He R Jilin China
19 M6 Santo Niño isld Philippines 11.56N 124.25E
81 M6 Sant' Onofrio Italy 38.41N 16.09E
118 G3 Santo Onofre, R Brazil
76 C7 Santo Pedro Velho mt Portugal 40.53N 8.17W
80 G4 Sant'Oreste Italy 42.14N 12.31E
Santoríni isld see Thíra
118 F8 Santos Brazil 23.56S 46.22W
119 F11 Santos Dumont Amazonas Brazil 6.27S 68.18W
118 G7 Santos Dumont Minas Gerais Brazil 21.30S 43.34W
118 J9 Santos Dumont, Aeroporto Brazil 22.55S 43.10W
81 N1 Santo Spirito Italy 41.09N 16.45E
77 F4 Santos, Sierra de los mts Spain
81 L7 Santo Stefano Italy 38.10N 15.48E
79 D5 Santo Stefano Belbo Italy 44.43N 8.14E
79 F5 Santo Stefano d'Aveto Italy 44.33N 9.27E
81 K7 Santo Stefano di Briga Sicily 38.06N 15.28E
81 F8 Santo Stéfano Quisquina Sicily 38.37N 13.29E
79 N3 Santo Stino di Livenza Italy 45.44N 12.40E
76 C6 Santo Tirso Portugal 41.20N 8.29W
115 A2 Santo Tomás Baja Cal Mexico 31.32N 116.26W
115 F3 Santo Tomás Chihuahua Mexico 28.40N 107.32W
115 L3 Santo Tomás Nicaragua 12.46N 87.25W
115 M3 Santo Tomás Nicaragua 12.04N 85.02W
120 C6 Santo Tomás Peru 14.27S 72.07W
120 C6 Santo Tomás R Peru
111 H10 Santo Tomás, Pta C Mexico 31.34N 116.40W
121 G2 Santo Tomé Argentina 28.31S 56.03W
77 K4 Santo Tomé Spain 38.02N 3.06W
75 C5 Santo Tomé del Puerto Spain 41.11N 3.35W
76 H5 Santovenia Spain 41.52N 5.42W
76 D8 Santo Vicente de Beira Portugal 40.02N 7.34W
60 G10 Santpoort Netherlands 52.26N 4.38E
59 K5 Santry Dublin Irish Rep 53.24N 6.15W
75 O5 Sant Sadurní de Noya Spain 41.25N 1.47E
23 G4 Santu Jiangxi China 29.10N 114.42E
75 P3 Santuario de Nuria Spain 42.23N 2.09E
81 H8 Santuario di Gibilmanna Sicily 37.59N 14.01E
77 W15 Santucri ruin Balearic Is 39.26N 3.10E
81 B3 Santu Lussurgiu Sardinia 40.08N 8.39E
22 L6 Santunying Hebei China 40.15N 118.11E
75 D1 Santurce Spain 43.20N 3.03W
75 E3 Santurde Spain 42.23N 2.59W
20 D4 Sanuki Japan 35.16N 139.53E
35 D4 Sanur Jordan 32.21N 35.15E
121 E4 San Urbano Argentina 33.40S 61.28W
121 J6 San Valentín, Cerro pk Chile 46.33S 73.20W
79 J1 San Valentino alla Muta Italy 46.47N 10.32E
80 J4 San Valentino in Abruzzo Citeriore Italy 42.13N 13.39E
121 G5 San Vazquez Uruguay 34.46S 56.20W
80 F3 San Venanzo Italy 42.52N 12.16E
79 M3 San Vendemiano Italy 45.53N 12.21E
81 B3 San Vero Milis Sardinia 40.02N 8.36E
70 L2 Sanvic France 49.31N 0.07E
121 F5 San Vicente Argentina 35.00S 58.27W
120 E9 San Vicente Bolivia 21.11S 66.25W
121 B5 San Vicente Chile 34.27S 71.05W
115 P11 San Vicente El Salvador 13.38N 88.42W
19 L2 San Vicente Luzon Philippines 18.30N 122.09E
115 A2 San Vicente Mexico 31.20N 116.15W
75 E2 San Vicente Spain 42.33N 2.44W
76 C12 San Vicente mt Portugal 38.19N 8.01W
121 M10 San Vicente, C Argentina 54.43S 65.16W
76 E10 San Vicente de Alcántara Spain 39.22N 7.08W
120 B5 San Vicente de Cañete Peru 13.06S 76.23W
75 O4 San Vicente de Castellet Spain 41.40N 1.52E
76 L2 San Vicente de la Barquera Spain 43.23N 4.24W
76 G5 San Vicente de la Cabeza Spain 41.47N 6.14W
119 D6 San Vicente del Caguán Colombia 2.07N 74.47W
76 K6 San Vicente del Palacio Spain 41.13N 4.51W
77 P4 San Vicente del Raspeig Spain 38.25N 0.31W
76 K8 San Vicente, Sierra de mts Spain
81 K6 San Vicenzo Lipari Is Italy 38.48N 15.15E
80 H2 San Vicino, Monte Italy 43.19N 13.04E
79 L1 San Vigilio Italy 46.42N 11.56E
80 C2 San Vincenzo Italy 43.06N 10.32E
80 J5 San Vincenzo Valle Roveto Italy 41.51N 13.33E
79 K3 San Vito Italy 45.41N 11.23E
81 D5 San Vito Sardinia 39.27N 9.33E
79 N3 San Vito al Tagliamento Italy 45.55N 12.51E
81 P12 San Vito, C Italy 40.25N 17.13E
81 E7 San Vito, C Sicily 38.12N 12.43E
80 K4 San Vito Chietino Italy 42.18N 14.26E
81 Q11 San Vito de Normanni Italy 40.40N 17.42E
79 M2 San Vito di Cadore Italy 46.28N 12.13E
81 E7 San Vito lo Capo Sicily 38.11N 12.43E
80 G5 San Vito Romano Italy 41.53N 12.59E
81 M6 San Vito sullo Iónio Italy 38.43N 16.25E
66 N7 San Vittore Switzerland 46.14N 9.08E
22 C6 Sanwei Shan mt Gansu China 40.05N 95.02E
72 D2 Sanxay France 46.30N 0.01W
21 C4 Sanxing Heilongjiang China 47.37N 125.01E
Sanya see Ya Xian
93 J9 Sanya Tanzania 3.24S 37.06E
119 E6 San Yanaro Colombia 2.46N 69.41W
Sanyati R see Umniati R
112 H8 San Ygnacio Texas 27.04N 99.26W
23 B5 Sanying Yunnan China 26.17N 100.04E
111 G9 San Ysidro California 32.33N 117.02W
109 D6 San Ysidro New Mexico 35.34N 106.46W
20 A2 Sanyū Tōkyō Japan
23 E1 Sanyuan Shaanxi China 34.40N 108.56E
21 C6 Sanyuanpu Jilin China 42.04N 125.05E
81 L3 Sanza Italy 40.14N 15.33E
91 E7 Sanza Pombo Angola 7.20S 16.00E
79 H4 San Zeno Naviglio Italy 45.29N 10.13E
21 C3 Sanzhan Heilongjiang China 49.38N 125.18E
21 C5 Sanzhan Heilongjiang China 45.32N 125.40E
76 H6 Sanzoles Spain 41.26N 5.34W
Sao see Ban Sao
117 F8 São Aleixo Brazil 6.32S 42.42W
121 J2 São Antônio Rio Grande do Sul Brazil 29.43S 50.30W
120 F3 São Antônio Rondônia Brazil 8.49S 63.58W
117 J8 São Antonio, Pta.de C Brazil 6.58S 34.50W
76 C14 São Barnabé Portugal 37.22N 8.10W
96 U3 São Bartolomeu Azores 38.41N 27.18W
76 B12 São Bartolomeu Portugal 38.01N 8.37W
76 C14 São Bartolomeu de Messines Portugal 37.15N 8.17W
76 D12 São Bartolomeu do Outeiro Portugal 38.21N 7.54W
117 G7 São Benedito Ceará Brazil 4.03S 40.52W
117 F6 São Benedito do Rio Préto Brazil 3.21S 43.35W
117 B9 São Benedito, R Brazil
120 F2 São Bento Amazonas Brazil 7.37S 65.22W
117 F6 São Bento Maranhão Brazil 2.45S 44.48W
119 H6 São Bento Roraima Brazil 3.00N 60.35W
76 D11 São Bento do Cortiço Portugal 38.56N 7.34W
76 D11 São Bento do Mato Portugal 38.44N 7.46W
117 J7 São Bento do Norte Brazil 5.02S 36.00W
117 F6 São Bernardo Brazil 3.25S 42.28W
118 F8 São Bernardo do Campo Brazil 23.45S 46.34W
121 G2 São Borja Brazil 28.35S 56.01W
76 D14 São Bras de Alportel Portugal 37.08N 7.54W
76 C12 São Brás de Regedouro Portugal 38.26N 8.04W
76 D13 São Braz Portugal 37.54N 7.37W
91 C9 São Braz, C de Angola 10.02S 13.22E
96 Q4 São Caetano Azores 38.26N 28.26W
117 D5 São Caetano de Odivelas Brazil 0.44S 48.04W
118 G10 São Caetano do Sul Brazil 23.37S 46.34W
120 F3 São Carlos Rondônia Brazil 9.46S 63.08W
120 F3 São Carlos Rondônia Brazil 9.05S 64.06W
118 D10 São Carlos Santa Catarina Brazil 27.10S 53.06W
118 F8 São Carlos São Paulo Brazil 22.02S 47.53W
Sao Chi R see Hsiao Ch'i R
Saochow see Suzhou
76 D6 São Cipriano Portugal 41.03N 8.00W
89 A1 São Cipriano, B.de Morocco
118 J10 São Conrado Brazil 23.00S 43.15W
76 C12 São Cristovão Portugal 38.27N 8.18W
118 J2 São Cristóvão Sergipe Brazil 10.59S 37.10W
118 J9 São Cristóvão sub Rio de Janeiro Brazil 22.54S 43.14W
118 G3 São Desidério Bahia Brazil 12.19S 44.59W
118 G3 São Desidério, R Brazil
90 H3 Saodinga Chad 16.31N 16.49E
118 F3 São Domingos Brazil 13.25S 46.19W
76 B13 São Domingos Portugal 37.55N 8.32W
76 C16 São Domingos de Ranna Portugal 38.42N 9.20W
118 D6 São Domingos, R Mato Grosso do Sul Brazil
120 F4 São Domingos, R Rondônia Brazil
118 F3 São Domingos, Sa.de mts Brazil
76 C10 São Facundo Portugal 39.22N 8.05W
118 G4 São Felipe, Sa.de mts Brazil
118 H3 São Félix Bahia Brazil 12.44S 39.01W
118 E2 São Félix Mato Grosso Brazil 11.36S 50.40W
117 C8 São Félix Pará Brazil 6.43S 51.56W
117 F8 São Félix de Balsas Brazil 6.59S 45.00W
118 H7 São Fidélis Brazil 21.37S 41.40W
89 O11 São Filipe Cape Verde 14.52N 24.29W
120 D4 São Francisco Acre Brazil 10.58S 69.33W
120 G1 São Francisco Amazonas Brazil 5.39S 60.14W
118 G4 São Francisco Minas Gerais Brazil 15.51S 44.52W
76 B12 São Francisco da Serra Portugal 38.06N 8.40W
121 G2 São Francisco de Assis Brazil 29.32S 55.07W
121 J2 São Francisco de Paula Brazil 29.23S 50.30W
118 E6 São Francisco de Sales Brazil 19.54S 49.48W
117 F8 São Francisco do Maranhão Brazil 6.15S 42.55W
118 E10 São Francisco do Sul Brazil 26.17S 48.39W
118 E10 São Francisco, I.de Brazil 26.19S 48.38W
120 E4 São Francisco, R Acre Brazil
117 J2 São Francisco, R Bahia Brazil
118 D9 São Francisco, R Paraná Brazil
118 K9 São Francisco, Saco de gulf Brazil
121 G3 São Gabriel Brazil 30.24S 54.20W
76 C11 São Geraldo Portugal 38.46N 8.12W
118 G8 São Gonçalo Brazil 22.48S 43.05W
76 D6 São Gonçalo Portugal 41.15N 7.56W
118 F6 São Gonçalo do Abaeté Brazil 18.19S 45.51W
117 H6 São Goncalo do Amirante Brazil 3.36S 38.59W
118 G6 São Gonçalo do Pará Brazil 19.59S 44.53W
118 F7 São Gonçalo do Sapucaí Brazil 21.54S 45.35W
118 F6 São Gotardo Brazil 19.21S 46.01W
76 C4 São Gregório Portugal 42.08N 8.12W
76 D11 São Gregório Portugal 34.48N 7.55W
92 G6 Sao Hill Tanzania 8.19S 35.11E
76 B7 São Jacinto Portugal 40.40N 8.44W
121 H2 São Jerônimo Brazil 29.59S 51.43W
118 C5 São Jerônimo, Sa.de mts Brazil
119 F8 São João Amazonas Brazil 0.30S 66.26W
96 Q4 São João Azores 38.26N 28.20W
118 G2 Sao João Piauí Brazil 10.24S 44.09W
118 D8 São João R Paraná Brazil
118 F4 São João da Aliança Brazil 14.46S 47.30W
118 H7 São João da Barra Brazil 21.39S 41.04W
117 A9 São João da Barra R Brazil
118 F7 São João da Boa Vista Brazil 21.59S 46.45W
76 C7 São João da Madeira Portugal 40.54N 8.30W
76 E6 São João da Pesqueira Portugal 41.08N 7.24W
118 G4 São João da Ponte Brazil 15.58S 43.59W
76 B10 São João da Ribeira Portugal 39.17N 8.50W
76 E15 São João da Talha Portugal 38.49N 9.06W
76 D14 São João da Venda Portugal 37.03N 7.58W
118 G7 São João del Rei Brazil 21.08S 44.15W
118 H8 São João de Meriti sub Rio de Janeiro. Brazil 22.48S 43.22W
118 H8 São João de Meriti, R Brazil
76 C13 São João de Negrilhos Portugal 37.57N 8.10W
76 D7 São João de Tarouca Portugal 40.59N 7.45W
117 D7 São João do Araguaia Brazil 5.24S 48.41W
118 D8 São João do Caiuá Brazil 22.50S 52.30W
117 H8 São João do Cariri Brazil 7.22S 36.30W
118 G4 São João do Paraíso Brazil 15.22S 42.06W
117 F9 São João do Piauí Brazil 8.21S 42.14W
76 D13 São João dos Caldeireiros Portugal 37.37N 7.47W
117 F8 São João dos Patos Brazil 6.29S 43.44W
91 C11 São João do Sul Angola 15.46S 12.06E
118 E9 São João do Triunfo Brazil 25.42S 50.22W
118 G6 São João Evangelista Brazil 18.31S 42.45W
117 F5 São João, Is.de Brazil 1.20S 45.00W
118 G7 São João Nepomuceno Brazil 21.33S 43.04W
118 D3 São João, R Mato Grosso Brazil
120 G3 São João, Sa.de mts Brazil
76 C12 São João, Sa.de mts Portugal
119 F7 São Joaquim Amazonas Brazil 0.01N 67.15W
117 E6 São Joaquim Pará Brazil 2.06S 47.46W
121 J2 São Joaquim Santa Catarina Brazil 28.08S 49.58W
118 F7 São Joaquim da Barra Brazil 20.36S 47.51W
117 F7 São Joaquim dos Melos Brazil 5.46S 44.45W
96 R3 São Jorge isld Azores 38.40N 28.03W
94 M4 São Jorge do Limpopo Mozambique 22.44S 32.03E
96 P7 São Jorge, Pta.de pt Madeira Is 32.50N 16.55W
119 F8 São José Amazonas Brazil 0.23S 66.20W
120 E3 São José Amazonas Brazil 9.38S 67.07W
121 J1 São José Santa Catarina Brazil 27.35S 48.40W
117 F6 São José, B.de Brazil
117 H9 São José da Laje Brazil 8.59S 36.02W
118 C4 São José da Serra Brazil 15.40S 55.10W
117 J8 São José de Mipibu Brazil 6.02S 35.12W
117 H8 São José de Piranhas Brazil 7.04S 38.24W
119 H7 São José do Anauá Brazil 0.59N 61.27W
117 H8 São José do Belmonte Brazil 7.48S 38.45W
118 H7 São José do Calçado Brazil 21.01S 41.37W
117 H8 São José do Egito Brazil 7.26S 37.16W
117 E5 São José do Gurupi Brazil 1.34S 46.10W
121 H4 São José do Norte Brazil 32.00S 52.01W
117 F8 São José do Peixe Brazil 7.25S 42.38W
118 F7 São José do Rio Pardo Brazil 21.35S 46.49W
118 E7 São José do Rio Prêto Brazil 20.50S 49.20W
118 F8 São José dos Campos Brazil 23.07S 45.52W
118 E7 São José dos Dourados R Brazil
118 E9 São José dos Pinhais Brazil 25.34S 49.13W
91 C10 São José, Pta.de pt Angola 12.35S 13.13E
118 E2 São José, R Brazil
76 E10 São Julião Portugal 39.18N 7.18W
76 C16 São Julião da Barra Lt Ho Portugal 38.40N 9.20W
19 E3 Saolat, Bukit mt Halmahera Indonesia 0.43N 127.58E
76 E12 São Leonardo Portugal 38.22N 7.16W
121 H2 São Leopoldo Brazil 29.45S 51.11W
118 C5 São Lourenço Mato Grosso Brazil 16.37S 55.02W
118 F8 São Lourenço São Paulo Brazil 22.08S 45.05W
117 F7 São Lourenço do Ipixuna Brazil 4.25S 44.55W
121 H3 São Lourenço do Sul Brazil 31.25S 52.00W
118 C5 São Lourenço, Pantanal de swamp Brazil
96 Q7 São Lourenço, Pta. de Madeira Is 32.43N 16.39W
118 C5 São Lourenço, R Brazil
91 E9 São Lucas Angola 10.59S 16.08E
120 E4 São Luis Acre Brazil 10.17S 67.08W
117 F6 São Luís Maranhão Brazil 2.34S 44.16W
117 B7 São Luís Pará Brazil 4.22S 56.02W
120 F2 São Luís de Cassianã Brazil 7.15S 64.54W
121 G2 São Luís Gonzaga Brazil 28.25S 55.00W
117 F6 São Luís, I.de Brazil
76 B13 São Luiz Portugal 37.43N 8.40W
76 C12 São Mamede do Sádão Portugal 38.09N 8.20W
76 E10 São Mamede, Sa.de mts Portugal
76 D12 São Manços Portugal 38.28N 7.45W
118 E8 São Manuel Brazil 22.40S 48.35W
São Manuel, R see Teles Pires, R
119 F7 São Marcelino Brazil 0.54N 67.15W
76 E13 São Marcos Portugal 37.47N 7.26W
117 F6 São Marcos, B.de Brazil
76 D12 São Marcos da Abóbada Portugal 38.27N 7.54W
76 D13 São Marcos da Ataboeira Portugal 37.42N 7.57W
76 C14 São Marcos da Serra Portugal 37.21N 8.22W
118 F5 São Marcos, R Brazil
117 G9 São Maria da Boa Vista Brazil 8.47S 39.51W
117 A7 São Martinho Brazil 5.45S 57.21W
94 M5 São Martinho Mozambique 25.17S 33.15E
76 C11 São Martinho Portugal 38.31N 8.29W
76 B11 São Martinho R Portugal
76 C13 São Martinho das Amoreiras Portugal 37.39N 8.24W
76 A9 São Martinho do Porto Portugal 39.31N 9.08W
96 Q4 São Mateus Azores 38.27N 28.27W
118 H6 São Mateus Brazil 18.44S 39.53W
118 E9 São Mateus do Sul Brazil 25.58S 50.29W
118 H6 São Mateus, R Brazil
76 D12 São Matias Portugal 38.07N 7.51W
96 T1 São Miguel isld Azores 37.33N 25.27W
76 D14 São Miguel mt Portugal 37.06N 7.49W
118 F4 São Miguel R Minas Gerais Brazil
76 D11 São Miguel de Machede Portugal 38.38N 7.44W
118 E3 São Miguel do Araguaia Brazil 13.15S 50.15W
76 D13 São Miguel do Pinheiro Portugal 37.32N 7.50W
117 H9 São Miguel dos Campos Brazil 9.48S 36.04W
117 D5 São Miguel dos Macacos Brazil 1.07S 50.28W
117 G7 São Miguel do Tapuio Brazil 5.30S 41.16W
120 F5 São Miguel, R Rondônia Brazil
116 K5 Saona, I Dominican Rep 18.09N 68.42W
66 A3 Saône France 47.14N 6.06E
Saône castle see Sahyūn anc.site
71 F4 Saône R France
67 H6 Saône-et-Loire dept France
29 F7 Saoner Maharashtra India 21.25N 79.02E
91 C11 São Nicolau Angola 14.19S 12.23E
121 G2 São Nicolãu Brazil 28.12S 55.15W
89 O10 São Nicolau isld Cape Verde
117 G7 São Nicolau, R Brazil
118 F8 São Paulo Brazil 23.33S 46.39W
118 D8 São Paulo state Brazil
119 F9 São Paulo de Olivença Brazil 3.34S 68.55W
119 H10 São Pedro Amazonas Brazil 5.51S 61.25W
119 J10 São Pedro Amazonas Brazil 4.39S 59.53W
120 G1 São Pedro Amazonas Brazil 5.50S 61.20W
96 U4 São Pedro Azores 36.59N 25.08W
76 B15 São Pedro Portugal 38.47N 9.23W
120 F3 São Pedro Rondônia Brazil 9.04S 63.16W
118 F8 São Pedro São Paulo Brazil 22.33S 47.57W
118 G8 São Pedro da Aldeia Brazil 22.46S 42.06W
76 A10 São Pedro da Cadeira Portugal 39.04N 9.22W
76 B5 São Pedro da Torre Portugal 41.59N 8.40W
76 A9 São Pedro de Muel Portugal 39.45N 9.01W
76 D14 São Pedro de Solis Portugal 37.29N 7.54W
120 E3 São Pedro do Destêrro Brazil 8.35S 67.25W
117 F7 São Pedro do Piauí Brazil 5.55S 42.45W
121 G2 São Pedro do Sul Brazil 29.35S 54.10W
76 C7 São Pedro do Sul Portugal 40.46N 8.04W
117 F1 São Pedro e São Paulo rocks Atlantic Oc 0.56N 29.22W
117 G9 São Pedro, R Brazil
25 G3 Sao Pou mt Laos 19.10N 103.30E
117 E8 São Raimundo das Mangabeiras Brazil 7.00S 45.30W
117 F9 São Raimundo Nonato Brazil 9.00S 42.39W
89 D4 Saorane Mali 14.21N 10.51W
71 M9 Saorge France 43.59N 7.34E
118 G2 São Rita de Cassia Brazil 11.00S 44.30W
76 C11 São Romão Alto Alentejo Portugal 38.34N 8.18W
76 E11 São Romão Alto Alentejo Portugal 38.46N 7.19W
120 E1 São Romão Amazonas Brazil 5.53S 67.50W
118 F5 São Romão Minas Gerais Brazil 16.21S 45.08W
76 C12 São Romão do Sado Portugal 38.14N 8.21W
96 T1 São Roque Azores 37.30N 25.38W
118 F8 São Roque Brazil 23.31S 47.09W
117 J7 São Roque, C.de Brazil 5.28S 35.17W
118 J3 São Roque do Paraguaçu Brazil 12.53S 38.53W
96 Q4 São Roque do Pico Azores 38.32N 28.19W
120 C2 São Salvador Acre Brazil 7.28S 73.18W
São Salvador Angola see M 'Banza Congo
96 U3 São Sebastião Azores 38.41N 27.06W
117 C7 São Sebastião Pará Brazil 5.50S 52.36W
120 G3 São Sebastião Rondônia Brazil 9.52S 61.57W
118 F8 São Sebastião São Paulo Brazil 23.48S 45.26W
117 D5 São Sebastião da Boa Vista Brazil 1.41S 49.30W
120 G2 São Sebastião de Tapuru Brazil 6.31S 62.15W
118 F7 São Sebastião do Paraíso Brazil 20.54S 46.59W
76 D13 São Sebastião dos Carros Portugal 37.33N 7.46W
118 G4 São Sebastião dos Poções Brazil 14.33S 44.22W
118 F8 São Sebastião, I.de Brazil 23.53S 45.17W
92 G13 São Sebastião, Pta Mozambique 22.05S 35.32E
121 H3 São Sepé Brazil 30.10S 53.31W
120 G5 São Simão, R Brazil
118 E6 São Simão Goiás Brazil 18.58S 50.32W
118 F7 São Simão São Paulo Brazil 21.27S 47.35W
76 B13 São Teotonio Portugal 37.30N 8.42W
76 B13 São Teotonio mt Portugal 37.30N 8.42W
89 P11 São Tiago isld Cape Verde
91 A12 São Tomé São Tomé São Tomé & Principe, Gulf of Guinea 0.19N 6.43E
73 E5 São Tomé isld Gulf of Guinea 0.25N 6.35E
118 H7 São Tomé, C.de Brazil 21.54S 40.59W
73 E5 São Tomé & Principe Gulf of Guinea
76 B11 São Torcato Portugal 38.52N 8.31W
71 G7 Saou France 44.39N 5.04E
88 T3 Saouaf Tunisia 36.12N 10.12E
35 E1 Saouane Lebanon 33.14N 35.26E
89 J4 Saouga Upper Volta 14.25N 0.04W
25 G7 Sa Oui Cambodia 10.55N 103.23E
88 N7 Saoura watercourse Algeria
76 E11 São Vicente Alto Alentejo Portugal 38.57N 7.13W
118 F8 São Vicente Brazil 23.57S 46.23W
96 P7 São Vicente Madeira Is 32.48N 17.03W
76 E5 São Vicente Trás os Montes e Alto Douro Portugal 41.51N 7.15W
89 O10 São Vicente isld Cape Verde
76 B14 São Vicente, C. de Lt Ho Portugal 37.01N 8.59W
117 F6 São Vicente Ferrer Brazil 2.55S 44.54W
120 E7 Sapahaqui Bolivia 16.40S 67.58W
83 H3 Sápai Greece 41.02N 25.44E
120 B5 Sapallanga Peru 12.07S 75.07W
36 E2 Sapanca Turkey 40.41N 30.15E
36 E2 Sapanca Gölü L Turkey
15 J7 Sapanda Papua New Guinea 7.20S 146.31E
Sapangbato see Mabalacat
118 F2 Sapão R Brazil
Sapar Shāhābād see Separ Shāhābād
19 F5 Saparua Moluccas Indon 3.35S 128.37E
19 F5 Saparua isld Moluccas Indon
76 A11 Sapataria Portugal 38.57N 9.11W
90 B9 Sapele Nigeria 5.55N 5.46E
109 E6 Sapello New Mexico 35.46N 105.15W
105 F6 Sapelo I Georgia 31.26N 81.15W
105 F6 Sapelo Sd Georgia 31.31N 81.12W
19 A8 Sape Selat str Indonesia
18 N10 Sape, Teluk B Indonesia
91 H8 Sapeza Zaïre 9.31S 23.56E
36 D3 Şaphane Turkey 39.02N 29.14E
25 H2 Sa Phin, Pou mt Vietnam 21.26N 104.19E
84 C8 Sapiéntza isld Greece 36.45N 21.42E
109 C3 Sapinero Colorado 38.28N 107.19W
95 J9 Sapkamma S Africa 33.22S 25.03E
70 L4 Sap, le France 48.53N 0.20E

19 K3 **Sapocoy, Mt** Luzon Philippines 17.29N 121.00E
89 J5 **Saponé** Upper Volta 12.03N 1.43W
115 Q6 **Sapo, Serranía del** *mts* Panama
120 B2 **Saposoa** Peru 6.53S 76.45W
89 J6 **Sapoui** Upper Volta 11.34N 1.44W
89 G7 **Sapoutan** Ivory Coast 9.38N 4.05W
45 M3 **Sapozhok** U.S.S.R. 53.56N 40.44E
109 K2 **Sappa Cr** Kansas
79 N1 **Sappada** Italy 46.34N 12.40E
60 Q7 **Sappemeer** Netherlands 53.10N 6.47E
33 B10 **Sapper B** S Yemen
110 M3 **Sapphire Mts** Montana
51 J4 **Sappisaasi** Sweden 67.52N 21.35E
20 L1 **Sapporo** Japan 43.05N 141.21E
41 L4 **Sappyya, Ozero** *L* U.S.S.R. 72.43N 118.16E
81 L3 **Sapri** Italy 40.04N 15.38E
89 D2 **Sapti** Mauritania 18.20N 10.25W
91 F10 **Sapu** Angola 12.28S 19.26E
117 B6 **Sapucaia** Brazil 3.22S 56.58W
117 B5 **Sapucuá, L** Brazil
18 L9 **Sapudi** *isld* Indonesia
109 O5 **Sapulpa** Oklahoma 36.01N 96.06W
18 M3 **Sapulut** Sabah Malaysia 4.41N 116.30E
92 D7 **Sapwe** Zaïre 10.55S 28.14E
32 H4 **Sāqī** Iran 33.08N 59.15E
33 G6 **Saqiyat an Nāth** Saudi Arabia 21.58N 46.40E
33 E3 **Sāq, Jabal** *mt* Saudi Arabia 26.20N 43.09E
86 F6 **Şaqqâra** Egypt 29.51N 31.14E
32 B2 **Saqqez** Iran 36.14N 46.15E
Saqqiz *see* **Saqqez**
33 E8 **Saqr** Saudi Arabia 17.46N 43.10E
35 H5 **Saqra, Es** *mt* Jordan 32.10N 36.03E
119 B8 **Saquisilí** Ecuador 0.51S 78.53W
33 B8 **Sar** Bahrain, The Gulf 26.12N 50.29E
31 H9 **Sara** Bangladesh 24.04N 89.06E
90 F1 **Sara** Niger 20.46N 12.35E
89 M9 **Sara** Nigeria 5.36N 5.16E
89 H6 **Sara** Upper Volta 11.45N 3.50W
32 B2 **Sarāb** Āzārbāījān-e Khāvarī Iran 37.56N 47.35E
32 H4 **Sarāb** Khorāsān Iran 33.10N 59.56E
33 H9 **Sarab** S Yemen 14.55N 48.38E
34 M5 **Sarabādī** Iraq 33.01N 44.50E
32 B4 **Sarāb-e Meymeh** Iran 33.12N 46.59E
86 K7 **Sarabît el Khâdim** *ruins* Egypt 29.02N 33.27E
25 F5 **Sara Buri** Thailand 14.32N 100.53E
117 A6 **Saracá, L** Amazonas Brazil
81 M4 **Saracena** Italy 39.46N 16.10E
81 E7 **Saraceno, Pta.di** Sicily 38.07N 12.39E
120 D6 **Saracocha, L** Peru 15.49S 70.38W
29 B7 **Saradiya** Gujarat India 21.38N 70.03E
Sarafand *see* **Zerifin**
89 H4 **Sarafere** Mali 15.49N 3.39W
Sarafina *see* **Bernal**
31 E4 **Sarafsar** Afghanistan 33.05N 68.55E
112 D4 **Saragosa** Texas 31.03N 103.39W
Saragossa *see* **Zaragoza**
119 B9 **Saraguro** Ecuador 3.42S 79.18W
30 A1 **Sarahan** Himachal Prad India 31.33N 77.32E
30 A2 **Sarahan** Himachal Prad India 30.42N 77.11E
12 D2 **Sarah, Mt** S Australia 26.59S 135.14E
31 D4 **Sarai** Afghanistan 32.45N 67.37E
30 J7 **Sarai** Bihar India 25.47N 85.15E
30 A8 **Sarai** Madhya Prad India 24.32N 77.12E
45 N3 **Sarai** U.S.S.R. 53.44N 41.00E
Sarai Aghat *see* **Sankasya**
30 C6 **Sarai Ajitmal** Uttar Prad India 26.35N 79.18E
30 E7 **Sarai Akil** Uttar Prad India 25.23N 81.31E
30 C6 **Sarai Ekdil** Uttar Prad India 26.44N 79.07E
29 J2 **Saraikela** Bihar India 22.42N 85.56E
30 F7 **Sarai Khwaja** Uttar Prad India 25.52N 82.40E
31 J9 **Sarail** Bangladesh 24.05N 91.07E
30 F6 **Sarai Mir** Uttar Prad India 26.02N 82.55E
31 G5 **Sarai Sidhu** Pakistan 30.35N 72.02E
51 M7 **Säräisniemi** Finland 64.27N 26.50E
82 E7 **Sarajevo** Yugoslavia 43.52N 18.26E
30 F7 **Sara Kheta** Uttar Prad India 25.58N 82.40E
32 J2 **Sarakhs** Iran 36.32N 61.07E
84 C1 **Sarakina** Kozáni Greece 40.02N 21.39E
84 C2 **Sarakina** Tríkkala Greece 39.40N 21.38E
83 F4 **Saraklí** Greece 40.44N 23.03E
43 D2 **Saraktash** U.S.S.R. 51.48N 56.24E
42 D5 **Sarala** U.S.S.R. 54.53N 89.14E
43 C3 **Saralzhin** Kazakhstan U.S.S.R. 49.30N 54.58E
84 Q15 **Sarama** Cyprus 34.57N 32.32E
117 B2 **Saramacca** *dist* Surinam
117 B2 **Saramacca** *R* Surinam
25 L8 **Sarameti** *mt* Burma/India 25.45N 95.02E
72 F8 **Saramon** France 43.32N 0.46E
30 K8 **Saran** Bihar India 24.29N 86.19E
43 L3 **Saran'** Kazakhstan U.S.S.R. 49.47N 73.02E
30 H6 **Saran** *dist* Bihar India
47 H7 **Sarana** U.S.S.R. 56.28N 57.45E
113 L9 **Sarana B** Aleutian Is
106 J7 **Saranac** Michigan 42.55N 85.13W
104 M2 **Saranac** *R* New York
104 L2 **Saranac Lake** New York 44.20N 74.10W
92 G4 **Saranda** Tanzania 5.42S 34.59E
83 D5 **Sarandë** Albania 39.53N 20.00E
121 H1 **Sarandi** Brazil 27.57S 52.51W
121 K4 **Sarandi** Buenos Aires Arg 34.41S 58.21W
121 G4 **Sarandí del Yí** Uruguay 33.18S 55.38W
121 G4 **Sarandi Grande** Uruguay 33.43S 56.19W
15 H6 **Sarang** Papua New Guinea 4.48S 145.40E
19 M9 **Sarangani** *isld* Philippines 5.28N 125.28E
19 M9 **Sarangani B** Mindanao Philippines
19 M9 **Sarangani Is** Philippines
19 M9 **Sarangani Str** Mindanao Philippines
29 H7 **Sarangarh** Madhya Prad India 21.38N 83.09E
29 E6 **Sarangpur** Madhya Prad India 23.35N 76.32E
18 J6 **Saran, Gunung** *mt* Borneo Indon 0.25S 111.18E
39 H7 **Sarannoye Ozero** *L* Komandorskiye O-va U.S.S.R. 55.17N 166.13E
47 J4 **Saranpaul'** U.S.S.R. 64.15N 60.58E
45 R2 **Saransk** U.S.S.R. 54.12N 45.10E
47 M3 **Sarany** U.S.S.R. 58.32N 58.48E
Sara Ostrov *see* **Narimanabad**
Saraphi *see* **Ban Saraphi**
46 R2 **Sarapul** U.S.S.R. 56.30N 53.49E
40 G7 **Sarapul'skoye** U.S.S.R. 48.50N 136.00E
87 L6 **Sarar** *reg* Somalia
118 B4 **Sararé, R** Brazil
119 E4 **Sarare, R** Venezuela
30 J7 **Sarari** Bihar India 25.09N 85.57E
32 G7 **Sārās** Iran 27.32N 57.33E
105 E10 **Sarasota** Florida 27.20N 82.32W
105 E10 **Sarasota B** Florida
105 E10 **Sarasota Key** *isld* Florida 27.20N 82.34W
29 B6 **Saraswati R** Gujarat India
46 G6 **Sarata** Ukraine U.S.S.R. 46.00N 29.40E
30 K8 **Sarath** Bihar India 24.16N 86.51E
112 N5 **Saratoga** Texas 30.17N 94.31W
108 D8 **Saratoga** Wyoming 41.28N 106.48W
104 M3 **Saratoga L** New York 43.02N 73.44W
104 M3 **Saratoga Springs** New York 43.04N 73.47W
18 J5 **Saratok** Sarawak Malaysia 1.45N 111.16E
45 R5 **Saratov** U.S.S.R. 51.30N 45.55E
44 C3 **Saratovskaya** U.S.S.R. 44.44N 39.14E
46 N4 **Saratovskaya Oblast'** *prov* U.S.S.R.
45 U4 **Saratovskoye Vdkhr** *res* U.S.S.R.
84 E3 **Saratzí** *mt* Greece 39.19N 22.40E
30 C5 **Sarauth Pawayan** Uttar Prad India 27.28N 79.05E
32 K7 **Saravan** Iran 27.25N 62.17E
25 J5 **Saravane** Laos 15.43N 106.24E
118 J8 **Saravatá, Ilha do** Brazil 22.49S 43.17W
19 L6 **Saravia** Philippines 10.54N 122.59E
25 E6 **Sarawa** *R* Burma
18 J5 **Sarawak** *state* Malaysia
37 H7 **Saray** Hakkâri Turkey 38.38N 44.10E
44 H9 **Sarāy** Iran 38.14N 46.55E
36 C1 **Saray** İstanbul Turkey 41.27N 27.56E
89 D5 **Saraya** Senegal 12.45N 11.45W
30 G6 **Saraya** Uttar Prad India 26.06N 83.48E
119 C8 **Sarayacu** Ecuador 1.45S 77.30W
30 D5 **Sarayan** *R* Uttar Prad India
37 J2 **Saray Burun** *C* İstanbul Turkey 41.01N 28.58E
43 B4 **Saraychik** Kazakhstan U.S.S.R. 47.29N 51.42E
36 H1 **Saraycik** Amasya Turkey 41.00N 35.10E
37 G2 **Saraycık** Kocaeli Turkey 40.42N 29.32E
36 D5 **Sarayköy** Turkey 37.54N 28.56E
36 F4 **Sarayönü** Turkey 38.16N 32.27E
32 J7 **Sarbāz** Iran 26.40N 61.20E
32 J7 **Sarbāz** *R* Iran
32 J7 **Sarbāz** *reg* Iran
28 H2 **Sarbhang** Bhutan 26.52N 90.16E
32 H4 **Sarbīsheh** Iran 32.35N 59.50E
62 L9 **Sárbogárd** Hungary 46.54N 18.38E
24 F2 **Sarbulak** Xinjiang Uygur Zizhiqu China 46.55N 89.12E
79 J2 **Sarca** *R* Italy
68 F2 **Sarcelles** France 49.00N 2.24E
79 J2 **Sarche** Italy 46.03N 10.57E
63 T9 **Särchen** E Germany 51.34N 13.54E
81 C4 **Sarcidano** *reg* Sardinia
121 B2 **Sarco** Chile 28.50S 71.27W
107 B4 **Sarcoxie** Missouri 37.04N 94.09W
30 F4 **Sarda** *R* Nepal
30 D4 **Sarda** *R* Uttar Prad India
32 J7 **Sardāb** Iran 26.43N 61.34E
31 F2 **Sardab Pass** Afghanistan 36.43N 71.31E
85 A7 **Sardalas** Libya 25.50N 10.35E
76 B13 **Sardão, C** *Lt Ho* Portugal 37.36N 8.49W
Sardap *see* **Sardāb**
81 B4 **Sardara** Sardinia 39.37N 8.49E
32 B1 **Sardari** Iran 38.01N 46.12E
43 J7 **Sardarova Karakhana, im** Tadzhikistan U.S.S.R. 38.36N 68.48E
29 D6 **Sardarpur** Madhya Prad India 22.41N 75.02E
29 D3 **Sardarshahr** Rajasthan India 28.30N 74.30E
32 A2 **Sar Dasht** Iran 36.09N 45.29E
32 C4 **Sardasht** Iran 32.33N 48.52E
81 B3 **Sardegna** *isld* Italy
72 H3 **Sardent** France 46.03N 1.52E
30 A3 **Sardhana** Uttar Prad India 29.09N 77.36E
84 B4 **Sardhínina** Greece 38.53N 21.12E
96 U14 **Sardina** Gran Canaria Canary Is 28.09N 15.42W
96 V16 **Sardina** Gran Canaria Canary Is 27.52N 15.26W
77 F8 **Sardina, C** Spain 36.20N 5.14W
115 M4 **Sardinal** Costa Rica 10.29N 85.40W
96 U14 **Sardina, Pta** *pt* Gran Canaria Canary Is 28.10N 15.44W
119 D3 **Sardinata** Colombia 8.07N 72.47W
93 L3 **Sardindina Plain** Kenya
Sardinia *see* **Sardegna**
104 B7 **Sardinia** Ohio 39.01N 83.50W
77 H4 **Sardinilla** *R* Spain
105 F5 **Sardis** Georgia 32.58N 82.47W
107 G7 **Sardis** Mississippi 34.25N 89.56W
104 E7 **Sardis** Ohio 39.37N 80.56W
107 H6 **Sardis** Tennessee 35.28N 88.19W
36 C4 **Sardis** *anc site* Turkey 38.28N 28.02E
107 G7 **Sardis L** Mississippi 34.24N 89.48W
48 U16 **Sârdloq** Greenland 60.35N 46.00W
76 C9 **Sardoal** Portugal 39.32N 8.10W
66 O4 **Sardona, Piz** *mt* Switzerland 46.56N 9.16E
Sarduiyeh *see* **Dar Mazār**
91 F10 **Sare** Angola 12.15S 19.59E
72 A9 **Sare** France 43.19N 1.34W
93 F6 **Sare** Kenya 0.55S 34.33E
33 J4 **Sareb Rās as** *C* U.A.E. 24.18N 51.45E
31 C3 **Sarecha** Afghanistan 34.51N 64.45E
19 A7 **Sarege** *isld* Indonesia 7.04S 118.41E
79 K4 **Sarego** Italy 45.24N 11.25E
51 F4 **Sareks Nat.Park** Sweden
51 F4 **Sarektjåkkå** *mt* Sweden 67.29N 17.40E
18 L6 **Sarempaka, Gunung** *mt* Borneo Indon 1.45S 115.44E
87 G4 **Sarenga** *mt* Ethiopia 12.40N 39.31E
30 D6 **Sareni** Uttar Prad India 26.08N 80.51E
79 K1 **Sarentini, Monti** *mts* Italy
79 K1 **Sarentino** Italy 46.39N 11.22E
34 N4 **Sar-e-Pol-e-āzahāb** Iran 34.28N 45.52E
107 C9 **Sarepta** Louisiana 32.52N 93.27W
Sar Eskandar *see* **Hashtrūd**
88 P7 **Saret** *watercourse* Algeria
30 L8 **Sareya** Bihar India 24.35N 87.02E
89 H3 **Sareyamou** Mali 16.07N 3.06W
32 F5 **Sar-e Yazd** Iran 31.36N 54.34E
43 K7 **Sarezskoye Oz** *L* Tadzhikistan U.S.S.R.
79 H3 **Sarezzo** Italy 45.39N 10.12E
48 S10 **Sarfánguaq** Greenland 66.55N 53.00W
66 O3 **Sargans** Switzerland 47.03N 9.27E
88 F10 **Sarga, Punta** *C* Mauritania 23.37N 16.00W
77 M5 **Sarga, Sierra** *mts* Spain
96 D6 **Sargasso Sea** Atlantic Oc
47 L7 **Sargatskoye** U.S.S.R. 55.35N 73.30E
70 L5 **Sarge** France 48.07N 0.15E
111 C5 **Sargent** California 36.55N 121.34W
108 L8 **Sargent** Nebraska 41.39N 99.22W
75 C2 **Sargentes de la Lora** Spain 42.46N 3.52W
113 N6 **Sargent Icefield** Alaska
111 K10 **Sargent, Pta** *C* Mexico 31.38N 114.47W
109 D3 **Sargents** Colorado 38.23N 106.26W
119 D9 **Sargentu Loros** Peru 3.47S 74.37W
70 M6 **Sargé-sur-Braye** France 47.56N 0.52E
31 G4 **Sargodha** Pakistan 32.01N 72.40E
31 G4 **Sargodha** *div* Pakistan
31 G4 **Sargodha** *dist* Pakistan
90 J7 **Sarh** Chad 9.08N 18.22E
30 D6 **Sarh** Uttar Prad India 26.14N 80.20E
32 J6 **Sarhad** *reg* Iran
31 G2 **Sarhad-i-Wakhan** Afghanistan 36.59N 73.31E
89 F7 **Sarhala** Ivory Coast 8.22N 6.08W
88 L6 **Sarhro, Jbel** *mts* Morocco
32 E2 **Sārī** Iran 36.33N 53.06E
36 E3 **Sarı** *R* Turkey
83 J9 **Sária** *isld* Greece 35.53N 27.14E
81 M4 **Saria, Mte** Italy 39.58N 16.08E
Sar-i-Asiab *see* **Hūtak**
15 L9 **Sariba I** Papua New Guinea 10.40S 150.40E
31 D3 **Sar-i-Bum** Afghanistan 35.31N 67.10E
115 D2 **Sáric** Mexico 31.08N 111.22W
37 C2 **Sariçêali** Turkey 40.59N 26.23E
113 E9 **Sarichef, C** Aleutian Is 54.38N 164.59W
35 D3 **Sarid** Israel 32.40N 35.13E
35 C5 **Sarida** *watercourse* Israel/Jordan
44 F10 **Sārī Dāsh** *mt* Iran 37.54N 44.27E
67 O12 **Sari d'Orcino** Corsica 42.03N 8.49E
119 F6 **Saridu, L** Colombia 3.54N 68.05W
76 H2 **Sariego** Spain 43.24N 5.32W
33 F3 **Sarīf, As** Saudi Arabia 26.35N 44.13E
17 P8 **Sarigan** *isld* Marianas Pacific Oc 16.43N 145.47E
31 J1 **Sarigh Jilganang** *L* Kashmir 34.43N 79.39E
37 F5 **Sarigöl** Çoruh Turkey 41.00N 40.59E
36 D4 **Sarigöl** Manisa Turkey 38.16N 28.41E
37 F5 **Sarigöl** Turkey 40.59N 41.30E
35 G3 **Sarih, Es** Jordan 32.30N 35.53E
37 G5 **Sarıkamış** Turkey 40.19N 42.35E
36 G6 **Sarıkavak** Turkey 36.33N 33.39E
36 H3 **Sarıkaya** Turkey 39.27N 35.09E
18 J4 **Sarikei** Sarawak Malaysia 2.07N 111.30E
43 J8 **Sar-i-Kia** Afghanistan 36.28N 67.54E
Sarikol Range *see* **Sarykol'skiy Khrebet** *mts*
37 D3 **Sarıköy** Balikesir Turkey 40.13N 27.36E
36 E3 **Sarıköy** Eskişehir Turkey 39.42N 31.28E
30 C7 **Sarila** Uttar Prad India 25.47N 79.40E
37 D1 **Sarılanköy** Turkey 41.08N 27.40E
76 B11 **Sarilhos Grandes** Portugal 38.41N 8.58W
13 J5 **Sarina** Queensland 21.25S 149.15E
43 K7 **Sarinay** Tadzhikistan U.S.S.R. 39.25N 71.42E
75 K4 **Sariñena** Spain 41.47N 0.10W
36 F3 **Sarıoba** Turkey 39.54N 32.05E
36 H3 **Sarıoğlan** Kayseri Turkey 39.05N 35.57E
32 A2 **Sar-i-Pirān** *mt* Iraq 36.50N 44.19E
31 D3 **Sar-i-Pul** Bamiyan Afghanistan 35.30N 66.40E
31 C2 **Sar-i-Pul** Jozjan Afghanistan 36.13N 65.55E
32 F2 **Sārī Qamīsh** Iran 37.52N 55.30E
44 H8 **Sārī Qamīsh** *R* Iran
85 F6 **Sarir** Libya 27.40N 22.15E
30 E7 **Sarira** Uttar Prad India 25.26N 81.19E
120 C1 **Sariria, R** Peru
31 H9 **Sarishabari** Bangladesh 24.35N 89.50E
44 F8 **Sārī Sū** Iran 39.23N 44.54E
37 G7 **Sarısu** Turkey 38.59N 42.52E
112 K8 **Sarita** Texas 27.14N 97.48W
21 C8 **Sariwŏn** N Korea 38.30N 125.45E
36 E2 **Sarıyar Barajı** *dam* Turkey 40.03N 31.25E
37 F1 **Sarıyer** Turkey 41.11N 29.03E
Sariz Iran*see* **Sīrīz**
36 J4 **Sarız** Turkey 38.29N 36.30E
51 L7 **Sarjakylä** Finland 64.04N 25.10E
30 E5 **Sarju** *R* Bahraich, Uttar Prad India
30 D4 **Sarju** *R* Kheri, Uttar Prad India
70 F3 **Sark** *isld* Channel Is Eng 49.26N 2.22W
62 N9 **Sarkad** Hungary 46.44N 21.25E
43 N4 **Sarkand** Kazakhstan U.S.S.R. 45.24N 79.55E
Sarkaor *R see* **Sarkör** *watercourse*
29 B4 **Sarkari Tara** Rajasthan India 27.39N 70.52E
57 G3 **Sark Bay** Eng/Scot 54.58N 3.04W
44 H8 **Sarkhāneh Beyg** Iran 39.25N 47.20E
36 E4 **Şarkîkaraağaş** Turkey 38.04N 31.22E
36 J3 **Şarkışla** Turkey 39.21N 36.27E
Sar Koh *see* **Sar Kūh**
32 J7 **Sarkör** *watercourse* Iran
37 D2 **Şarköy** Turkey 40.37N 27.07E
32 K7 **Sar Kūh** Iran 27.34N 62.40E
31 D6 **Sarlath Range** Pakistan/Afghanistan
72 G6 **Sarlat-la-Canéda** France 44.54N 1.12E
65 J4 **Sarleinsbach** Austria 48.33N 13.55E
108 M1 **Sarles** N Dakota 48.58N 99.00W
72 F5 **Sarliac-sur-l'Isle** France 45.14N 0.52E
44 E4 **Sarmakovo** U.S.S.R. 43.44N 43.14E
31 C4 **Sarmalan** Afghanistan 33.53N 64.03E
87 J5 **Sarman Didinte** Ethiopia 10.32N 42.20E
46 R2 **Sarmanovo** U.S.S.R. 55.15N 52.32E
82 J4 **Sărmaşu** Romania 46.46N 24.10E
30 J8 **Sarmatanr** Bihar India 24.21N 85.39E
79 F4 **Sarmato** Italy 45.04N 9.29E
30 J7 **Sarmera** Bihar India 25.16N 85.47E
15 E4 **Sarmi** Irian Jaya 1.51S 138.45E
121 K5 **Sarmiento** Chubut Argentina 45.38S 69.08W
121 D5 **Sarmiento** Cordoba Arg 34.08S 64.44W
121 J8 **Sarmiento, Canal** *str* Chile
121 J8 **Sarmiento, L** Chile
121 K10 **Sarmiento, Mte** Chile 54.27S 70.48W
24 E4 **Sarmin Ula** *mt ra* Xinjiang Uygur Zizhiqu China
82 H5 **Sarmizegetusa** Romania 45.32N 22.45E
42 C1 **Sarmsabun** *R* U.S.S.R.
56 E2 **Sarn** Powys Wales 52.31N 3.11W
52 G5 **Särna** Sweden 61.40N 13.10E
76 D9 **Sarnadas** Portugal 39.44N 7.38W
76 D9 **Sarnadas de São Simão** Portugal 39.57N 7.46W
80 H2 **Sarnano** Italy 43.02N 13.18E
30 G7 **Sarnath** Uttar Prad India 25.23N 83.02E
56 C3 **Sarnau** Dyfed Wales 52.08N 4.28W
Sarneh Iran*see* **Sar Ney**
32 B4 **Sarneh** Iran 33.38N 47.06E
66 J4 **Sarnen** Switzerland 46.54N 8.15E
66 J4 **Sarner See** *L* Switzerland
56 F3 **Sarnesfield** Hereford & Worcs Eng 52.10N 2.55W
32 G7 **Sar Ney** Iran 27.03N 57.22E
99 H10 **Sarnia** Ontario 42.57N 82.24W
79 G3 **Sarnico** Italy 45.40N 9.58E
80 L7 **Sarno** Italy 40.48N 14.37E
46 F4 **Sarny** Ukraine U.S.S.R. 51.21N 26.31E
52 F9 **Särö** Sweden 57.31N 11.55E
19 B5 **Saroako** Celebes Indonesia 2.33S 121.22E
31 E3 **Sarobi** Afghanistan 34.40N 69.46E
18 E7 **Sarolangum** Sumatra Indon 2.14S 102.44E
95 C9 **Saron** S Africa 33.11S 19.01E
84 F6 **Saronikós Kólpos** *gulf* Greece
79 F3 **Saronno** Italy 45.38N 9.02E
37 C2 **Saros** *isld* Turkey 40.37N 26.43E
37 C2 **Saros Körfezi** *gulf* Turkey
62 N7 **Sárospatak** Hungary 48.19N 21.30E
47 K3 **Saroto** U.S.S.R. 65.43N 68.58E
29 C5 **Sarotra** Gujarat India 24.24N 72.36E
95 B8 **Sarotsetatsy** Madagascar 24.24S 45.02E
Saroute *R see* **Sarūt** *R*
45 P2 **Sarova** U.S.S.R. 54.55N 43.19E
45 R9 **Sarpa** U.S.S.R. 47.06N 45.31E
45 R9 **Sarpa, Oz** *L* Kalmyk A.S.S.R. U.S.S.R.
19 N3 **Sar Pass** Palau Is Pacific Oc
30 F6 **Sarpataha** Uttar Prad India 26.06N 82.31E
45 R9 **Sarpinskaya Nizmennost'** *plain* U.S.S.R.
45 Q8 **Şarpinskiye Ozera** *L* Volgograd U.S.S.R.
82 F8 **Šar Planina** *mts* Yugoslavia
52 F7 **Sarpsborg** Norway 59.17N 11.06E
108 D4 **Sarpy** Montana 45.48N 106.56W
81 C5 **Sarrabus** *reg* Sardinia
69 N5 **Sarralbe** France 49.00N 7.01E
69 N6 **Sarraltroff** France 48.46N 7.04E
72 C9 **Sarrance** France 43.02N 0.36W
72 E10 **Sarrancolin** France 42.58N 0.22E
72 K6 **Sarrans, Barrage de** *res* France 44.50N 2.44E
76 D5 **Sarraquinhos** Portugal 41.47N 7.40W
71 F6 **Sarras** France 45.11N 4.48E
75 L7 **Sarratella** Spain 40.19N 0.01E
55 B1 **Sarratt** Herts England 51.41N 0.30W
66 C5 **Sarraz, la** Switzerland 46.40N 6.31E
79 B3 **Sarre** Italy 45.43N 7.15E
56 O5 **Sarre** Kent Eng 51.21N 1.14E
69 N6 **Sarre** *R* France
75 N5 **Sarreal** Spain 41.27N 1.15E
76 D4 **Sarreaus** Spain 42.06N 7.36W
69 N6 **Sarre-Union** France 48.56N 7.05E
76 E3 **Sarria** Spain 42.47N 7.25W
75 Q3 **Sarriá de Ter** Spain 42.01N 2.49E
71 F8 **Sarrians** France 44.05N 4.59E
75 J7 **Sarrión** Spain 40.09N 0.49W
89 G5 **Sarro** Mali 13.45N 5.13W
75 M5 **Sarroca** Spain 41.27N 0.34E
81 C5 **Sarroch** Sardinia 39.03N 9.01E
67 O12 **Sarrola Carcopino** Corsica 42.01N 8.50E
72 D8 **Sarron** France 43.36N 0.16W
35 G5 **Sarrut** Jordan 32.09N 35.57E
47 H7 **Sars** U.S.S.R. 56.30N 57.08E
31 F3 **Sarsashi** Afghanistan 34.15N 70.31E
30 A2 **Sarsawa** Uttar Prad India 30.01N 77.24E
34 O3 **Sarshiv** Iran 35.45N 46.30E
32 B3 **Sarshive** Iran 35.42N 46.28E
30 L7 **Sarsi Istamrar** Bihar India 25.51N 87.18E
79 M7 **Sarsina** Italy 43.55N 12.08E
61 F5 **Sars-la-Bruyère** Belgium 50.23N 3.52E
61 G5 **Sars-la-Buissière** Belgium 50.20N 4.13E
69 D3 **Sars, le** France 50.05N 2.48E
69 G3 **Sars-Poteries** France 50.10N 4.02E
26 E16 **Sars Seamount** S Pacific Oc 59.40S 68.45W
63 L8 **Sarstedt** W Germany 52.14N 9.51E
61 O4 **Sart** Belgium 50.31N 5.56E
35 D5 **Sarta** Jordan 32.06N 35.05E
34 N2 **Sārtakeh** Iran 36.18N 45.34E
24 F2 **Sartal** Xinjiang Uygur Zizhiqu China 46.42N 87.44E
43 N8 **Sartala** Kirgiziya U.S.S.R. 40.00N 71.27E
31 F7 **Sartanahu** Pakistan 26.22N 70.02E
39 A2 **Sartang** *R* U.S.S.R.
61 K5 **Sart-Bernard** Belgium 50.24N 4.57E
61 K6 **Sart-Custinne** Belgium 50.00N 4.55E
61 H4 **Sart-Dames-Avelines** Belgium 50.34N 4.30E
80 E3 **Sarteano** Italy 42.59N 11.52E
67 O13 **Sartène** Corsica 41.37N 8.58E
61 J6 **Sart-en-Fagne** Belgium 50.09N 4.37E
61 J5 **Sart-Eustache** Belgium 50.22N 4.36E
67 F5 **Sarthe** *dept* France
70 K5 **Sarthe** *R* France
44 G6 **Sartichala** Georgia U.S.S.R. 41.43N 45.11E
70 H4 **Sartilly** France 48.45N 1.26W
79 E4 **Sartirana Lomellina** Italy 45.07N 8.40E
42 B5 **Sartlan, Ozero** *L* U.S.S.R.
45 T8 **Sartol'gen** Kazakhstan U.S.S.R. 48.55N 47.02E
68 D2 **Sartrouville** France 48.57N 2.11E
61 K5 **Sart-st.-Laurent** Belgium 50.24N 4.45E
Sartu *see* **Anda**
47 J4 **Sartyn'ya** U.S.S.R. 63.22N 63.11E
20 N2 **Sarubetsu-gawa** *R* Japan
32 D3 **Sarud** *R* Iran
20 L2 **Sarufuto** Japan 42.31N 142.03E
21 J5 **Sarufutsu** Japan 45.17N 142.17E
36 C4 **Saruhanlı** Turkey 38.43N 27.35E
15 F8 **Saru, L** Papua New Guinea
81 C3 **Sarule** Sardinia 40.13N 9.10E
29 J3 **Sarum** Xizang Zizhiqu 29.10N 85.52E
20 F6 **Sarumasa-yama** *mt* Japan 35.05N 132.57E
31 D7 **Saruna** Pakistan 26.28N 66.58E
31 D7 **Saruna R** Pakistan
29 J6 **Saru Pk** Bihar India 23.33N 84.33E
29 C3 **Sarupsar** Rajasthan India 29.25N 73.50E
32 C3 **Saruq** Iran 34.22N 49.35E
32 B2 **Sārūq** *R* Iran
30 A3 **Sarurpur** Uttar Prad India 29.02N 77.14E
34 D3 **Sarūt** *R* Syria
31 B5 **Saru Tara** *ruins* Afghanistan 30.41N 62.11E
15 J7 **Saruwaged Ra** Papua New Guinea
32 E4 **Sarv** Iran 32.21N 53.20E
32 J7 **Sarvāb** Iran 26.04N 61.05E
32 B3 **Sarvabad** Iran 35.10N 46.28E
65 P7 **Sárvár** Hungary 47.15N 16.59E
32 E6 **Sarvestān** Iran 29.16N 53.13E
75 K2 **Sarvisé** Spain 42.35N 0.07W
Sarvistan *see* **Sarvestān**
62 L9 **Sárviz** *R* Hungary
34 P4 **Sarv Now** Iran 34.10N 47.07E
52 G4 **Särvsjö** Sweden 62.38N 13.10E
30 D7 **Sarwai** Madhya Prad India 25.11N 80.17E
31 E4 **Sarwand Pass** Afghanistan 32.41N 68.41E
30 H8 **Sarwan Khas** Bihar India 24.33N 84.59E
29 D4 **Sarwar** Rajasthan India 26.02N 75.04E
29 C8 **Sarya** *R* Maharashtra India
43 J6 **Saryagach** Kazakhstan U.S.S.R. 41.29N 69.10E
43 J7 **Saryassiya** Uzbekistan U.S.S.R. 38.27N 67.58E
43 F4 **Sarybasat** Kazakhstan U.S.S.R. 46.37N 60.25E
43 L6 **Sarybulak** Kirgiziya U.S.S.R. 40.52N 73.54E
43 F4 **Sarychaganak, Zaliv** *gulf* Kazakhstan U.S.S.R.
43 J7 **Sary-Chashma** Tadzhikistan U.S.S.R. 37.45N 69.52E
40 N7 **Sarycheva, Pik** *vol* Kuril Is U.S.S.R. 48.06N 153.12E
40 N7 **Sarychevo** Kuril Is U.S.S.R. 48.05N 153.10E
44 C10 **Sarych, Mys** *C* Ukraine U.S.S.R. 44.23N 33.43E
43 M7 **Sarydala** Uzbekistan U.S.S.R. 41.10N 70.28E
44 M7 **Sarydepe** Turkmeniya U.S.S.R. 40.58N 52.59E
43 N5 **Sarydzhas** Kazakhstan U.S.S.R. 42.54N 79.34E
43 N6 **Sarydzhaz** *R* Kirgiziya U.S.S.R.
37 E7 **Saryekşan Dağı** *mt* Turkey 38.40N 40.14E
42 E6 **Saryg Bel'** U.S.S.R. 51.04N 90.50E
42 F6 **Saryg-Sep** U.S.S.R. 51.33N 95.36E
43 M4 **Sary-Ishikotrau, Peski** *sand des* Kazakhstan U.S.S.R.
43 C4 **Sarykamys** Kazakhstan U.S.S.R. 46.15N 53.33E
43 D6 **Sarykamysh, Ozera** *lakes* Turkmeniya U.S.S.R.
43 D6 **Sarykamyshskaya, Kotlovina** *depression* Turkmeniya U.S.S.R.
31 H1 **Sarykol'skiy Khrebet** *mts* U.S.S.R./China
43 L4 **Sarykomey** Kazakhstan U.S.S.R. 45.15N 74.10E
43 G2 **Sarykopa, Ozero** *L* Kazakhstan U.S.S.R.
43 N8 **Sarykurgan** Uzbekistan U.S.S.R. 40.21N 71.03E
43 G2 **Sarymoin, Ozero** *L* Kazakhstan U.S.S.R.
43 F3 **Saryoba** Kazakhstan U.S.S.R. 49.15N 60.25E
43 P4 **Saryolen** Kazakhstan U.S.S.R. 47.16N 84.05E
43 N5 **Sary-Ozek** Kazakhstan U.S.S.R. 44.22N 78.00E
43 L4 **Sary-Shagan** Kazakhstan U.S.S.R. 46.08N 73.32E
43 H4 **Sarysu** *R* Kazakhstan U.S.S.R.
44 L3 **Sarytash** Kazakhstan U.S.S.R. 44.29N 51.10E
43 L7 **Sary-Tash** Kirgiziya U.S.S.R. 39.45N 73.10E
47 H4 **Sar'yudin** U.S.S.R. 62.41N 57.41E
43 G8 **Sary-Yazikskoye, Vdkhr** *res* Turkmeniya U.S.S.R.
79 G6 **Sarzana** Italy 44.07N 9.57E
70 E6 **Sarzeau** France 47.32N 2.46W
76 D9 **Sarzedas** Portugal 39.50N 7.41W
76 D6 **Sarzedo** Beira Alta Portugal 41.01N 7.39W
76 E8 **Sarzedo** Beira Baixa Portugal 40.22N 7.25W
44 L4 **Sarzha** Kazakhstan U.S.S.R. 43.11N 51.30E
35 E1 **Sasa** Israel 33.02N 35.23E
87 J7 **Sasa Baneh** Ethiopia 7.52N 43.39E
111 N10 **Sasabe** Arizona 31.31N 111.31W
115 D2 **Sásabe** Mexico 31.30N 111.32W
18 C5 **Sasak** Sumatra Indonesia 0.000 99.45E
101 H10 **Sasamat, L** Br Col 49.20N 122.54W
76 L4 **Sasamón** Spain 42.25N 4.02W
15 K2 **Sasamungga** Choiseul I Solomon Is 7.05S 156.45E
34 K2 **Sāsān** *oil well* Iraq 36.27N 42.22E
30 H8 **Sasaram** Bihar India 24.58N 84.01E
15 L3 **Sasari, Mt** Santa Isabel I Solomon Is 8.13S 159.33E
19 A8 **Sasar, Tanjung** *C* Indonesia 9.23S 119.58E
44 E5 **Sasashi** Georgia U.S.S.R. 42.48N 43.00E
20 J6 **Sasayama** Japan 35.03N 135.12E
64 D7 **Sasbach** W Germany 48.08N 7.38E
62 L9 **Sásd** Hungary 46.15N 18.06E
76 E2 **Sasdonigas** Spain 43.24N 7.25W
20 C8 **Sasebo** Japan 33.10N 129.42E
30 D6 **Sashendi** Uttar Prad India 26.25N 80.09E
97 J7 **Saskatchewan** *prov* Canada
100 O5 **Saskatchewan R** Saskatchewan
100 K6 **Saskatchewan R., N** Alberta/Sask
100 J8 **Saskatchewan R., S** Saskatchewan
100 L6 **Saskatoon** Saskatchewan 52.10N 106.40W
100 Q5 **Saskeram L** Manitoba 53.50N 101.32W
41 K5 **Saskylakh** U.S.S.R. 71.56N 114.06E
115 M3 **Saslaya** *pk* Nicaragua 13.26N 84.56W
113 Q10 **Sasmik, C** Aleutian Is 51.39N 177.58W
30 B5 **Sasni** Uttar Prad India 27.43N 78.05E
29 B6 **Sasoi** *R* Bombay India
95 L2 **Sasolburg** S Africa 26.50S 27.51E
37 F7 **Sason** Turkey 38.22N 41.25E
37 F7 **Sason** *R* Turkey
45 N2 **Sasovo** U.S.S.R. 54.21N 41.58E
112 J6 **Saspamco** Texas 29.14N 98.19W
60 B3 **Sasput** Netherlands 51.22N 3.36E
65 N8 **Sass** *R* Austria
101 R5 **Sass** *R* N W Terr
103 C8 **Sassafras** Maryland 39.23N 75.48W
105 E2 **Sassafras Mt** S Carolina 35.04N 82.48W
103 B8 **Sassafras R** Maryland
66 R6 **Sassalbo** *mt* Switzerland 46.21N 10.06E
33 K4 **Sassan** *oil well* The Gulf 25.33N 53.10E
89 F9 **Sassandra** Ivory Coast 4.58N 6.08W
89 F9 **Sassandra** *R* Ivory Coast
64 K4 **Sassanfahr** W Germany 49.49N 10.59E
81 L3 **Sassano** Italy 40.20N 15.34E
81 B2 **Sassari** Sardinia 40.43N 8.34E
81 A2 **Sassari** *prov* Sardinia
79 D6 **Sassello** Italy 44.29N 8.29E
63 S4 **Sassen** E Germany 54.02N 13.11E
71 H6 **Sassenage** France 45.13N 5.39E
63 H9 **Sassenberg** W Germany 51.59N 8.02E
63 N7 **Sassenburg** W Germany 52.33N 10.43E
66 G7 **Sasseneire** *mt* Switzerland 46.08N 7.32E
60 G11 **Sassenheim** Netherlands 52.14N 4.31E
70 M2 **Sassetot** France 49.48N 0.32E
80 C2 **Sassetta** Italy 43.08N 10.38E
63 T3 **Sassnitz** E Germany 54.32N 13.40E
79 M7 **Sassocorvaro** Italy 43.47N 12.30E
80 G2 **Sassoferrato** Italy 43.26N 12.51E
79 K6 **Sasso Marconi** Italy 44.23N 11.14E
66 Q6 **Sasso Moro, Monte** Italy 46.20N 9.55E
89 E9 **Sasstown** Liberia 4.44N 8.25W
81 B2 **Sassu, Mte** Sardinia 40.43N 8.55E
79 J5 **Sassuolo** Italy 44.32N 10.47E
75 K5 **Sástago** Spain 41.19N 0.21W
43 K5 **Sas-Tobe** Kazakhstan U.S.S.R. 42.33N 70.01E
121 E3 **Sastre** Argentina 31.46S 61.47W
93 J7 **Sasumia Dam** Kenya 1.02S 37.21E
20 C7 **Sasuna** Japan 34.38N 129.23E
30 E7 **Sasur** *R* Uttar Prad India
28 B1 **Sasvad** Maharashtra India 18.20N 74.01E
60 C4 **Sas-Van-Gent** Netherlands 51.14N 3.48E
43 O4 **Sasykkol', Ozero** *L* Kazakhstan U.S.S.R.
45 S9 **Sasykoli** U.S.S.R. 47.35N 46.59E
46 J6 **Sasyk Oz** *L* Crimea U.S.S.R.
46 G6 **Sasyk, Oz** *L* Izmail, Ukraine U.S.S.R.
39 A1 **Sasyl Uyalakh** U.S.S.R. 68.39N 134.35E
53 Z17 **Såta** *mt* Buskerud Norway 60.48N 8.33E
50 D5 **Såta** *mt* Iceland 64.50N 21.35W
53 T18 **Såta** *mt* Norway 60.26N 5.59E
53 U15 **Såta** *mt* Sogn og Fjordane Norway 61.57N 6.02E
53 W16 **Såta** *mt* Sogn og Fjordane Norway 61.28N 7.07E
89 D5 **Satadougou** Mali 12.39N 11.25W
37 G7 **Şatak Dağları** *mts* Turkey
89 G8 **Satama Sokoura** Ivory Coast 7.55N 4.27W
20 D10 **Sata-misaki** *C* Japan 31.00N 130.39E
29 D7 **Satana** Maharashtra India 20.38N 74.12E
109 B6 **Satan Pass** New Mexico 35.38N 108.07W
109 K4 **Satanta** Kansas 37.26N 100.59W
76 D7 **Satão** Portugal 40.45N 7.45W
76 D7 **Satão** *R* Portugal
122 B1 **Satapuala** W Samoa, Pacific Oc 13.49S 172.00W
28 B2 **Satara** Maharashtra India 17.43N 74.05E
94 L5 **Satara** Transvaal S Africa 24.25S 31.46E
41 O7 **Satara** U.S.S.R. 67.19N 130.29E
28 B2 **Satara** *dist* Maharashtra India
47 L5 **Satarino** U.S.S.R. 60.59N 71.40E
122 A1 **Sataua** W Samoa, Pacific Oc 13.26S 172.40W
30 B2 **Satdog** Uttar Prad India 30.14N 78.21E
97 H2 **Satellite B** N W Terr
90 K9 **Satéma** Cent Afr Rep 4.15N 21.46E
18 M9 **Satengar** *isld* Indonesia 7.32S 117.20E
52 J6 **Säter** Sweden 60.21N 15.45E
63 G6 **Saterland** *reg* W Germany
115 F4 **Satevó** Mexico 27.58N 106.08W
30 J8 **Satgawan** Bihar India 24.42N 85.52E
30 A3 **Satheri** Uttar Prad India 29.14N 77.40E
71 F5 **Sathonay-Village** France 45.50N 4.53E
53 W14 **Såthorn** *mt* Norway 62.06N 7.20E
30 F6 **Sathri** Uttar Prad India 26.43N 82.04E
66 A7 **Satigny** Switzerland 46.13N 6.02E
105 F7 **Satilla** *R* Georgia
71 F6 **Satillieu** France 45.10N 4.37E
95 P8 **Satine, L** Mozambique 26.45S 32.51E
45 N4 **Satinka** U.S.S.R. 52.24N 41.41E
120 C4 **Satipo** Peru 11.19S 74.37W
120 C4 **Satipo, R** Peru
89 G6 **Satiri** Upper Volta 11.28N 4.01W
Satırlar *see* **Yeşilova** Burdur Turkey
45 P1 **Satis** U.S.S.R. 55.01N 43.48E
51 G4 **Satishaure** *L* Sweden 67.30N 18.40E
47 L5 **Satka** U.S.S.R. 55.06N 58.59E
31 J10 **Satkania** Bangladesh 22.00N 92.02E
31 H9 **Satkhira** Bangladesh 22.43N 89.06E
57 K3 **Satley** Durham Eng 54.47N 1.49W
29 F8 **Satmala Ra** Andhra Prad/Maharashtra India
30 D8 **Satna** Madhya Prad India 24.33N 80.50E
30 D8 **Satna** *dist* Madhya Prad India
30 D8 **Satna** *R* Madhya Prad India
18 M10 **Satonda** *isld* Indonesia 8.06S 117.45E
30 C2 **Satopanth** *mt* Uttar Prad India 30.49N 79.14E
82 D6 **Šator** *mt* Yugoslavia 44.09N 16.37E
62 N7 **Şátoraljaújhely** Hungary 48.22N 21.39E
65 O4 **Šatov** Czechoslovakia 48.49N 16.01E
63 P5 **Satow** E Germany 53.59N 11.54E
29 D7 **Satpura Range** Madhya Prad India
80 N7 **Satriano di Lucania** Italy 40.32N 15.38E
30 E6 **Satrikh** Uttar Prad India 26.51N 81.12E
95 B7 **Satrokala** Madagascar 22.20S 45.41E
63 L3 **Satrup** W Germany 54.42N 9.37E
20 D10 **Satsuma-hantō** *pen* Japan
Sattahip *see* **Ban Sattahipp**
51 K4 **Sattajärvi** Sweden 67.04N 23.20E
51 M4 **Sattanen** Finland 67.31N 26.40E
66 P3 **Satteins** Austria 47.13N 9.40E
66 L3 **Sattel** Switzerland 47.04N 8.38E
15 J7 **Sattelburg** Papua New Guinea 6.29S 147.46E
28 E2 **Sattenapalle** Andhra Prad India 16.27N 80.10E
25 C3 **Satthwa** Burma 19.52N 95.34E
31 J3 **Satti** Kashmir 34.26N 77.47E
52 K4 **Sättna** Sweden 62.28N 17.10E
65 K8 **Sattnitz** *reg* Austria
28 C6 **Sattur** Tamil Nadu India 9.23N 77.56E
18 L7 **Satui** Borneo Indon 3.49S 115.29E
82 H3 **Satu Mare** Romania 47.48N 22.52E
25 F9 **Satun** Thailand 6.40N 100.01E
122 B1 **Satupaitea** W Samoa, Pacific Oc 13.44S 172.18W
110 B1 **Saturna I** Br Col 48.47N 123.07W
80 E3 **Saturnia** Italy 42.37N 11.32E
110 E3 **Satus** Washington 46.15N 120.10W
48 T7 **Såtut** Greenland 70.50N 51.30W
29 E6 **Satwas** Madhya Prad India 22.32N 76.42E
28 C5 **Satyamangalam** Tamil Nadu India 11.31N 77.15E
47 J6 **Satyga** U.S.S.R. 59.56N 64.41E
65 L8 **Saualpe** *mts* Austria
53 U19 **Sauanuten** *mt* Norway 59.58N 6.28E
53 W19 **Sauarflått** *plat* Norway
18 L9 **Saubi** *isld* Indonesia 7.00S 115.28E
98 H2 **Saubosq, L** Quebec
66 B5 **Saubraz** Switzerland 46.32N 6.21E
72 B8 **Saubusse** France 43.40N 1.10W
75 E5 **Sauca** Spain 41.01N 2.32W
72 C6 **Saucats** France 44.38N 0.42W
121 F3 **Sauce** Argentina 30.05S 58.46W
120 B2 **Sauce** Peru 6.44S 76.11W
115 J5 **Sauceda** Mexico 25.55N 101.18W
111 M9 **Sauceda Mts** Arizona
121 F3 **Sauce de Luna** Argentina 31.15S 59.09W
76 H9 **Saucedilla** Spain 39.51N 5.40W
77 F6 **Saucejo, El** Spain 37.05N 5.06W
76 F6 **Saucelle** Spain 41.03N 6.46W
76 F6 **Saucelle, Embalse de** *res* Spain
121 E7 **Sauce, R** Argentina
121 D4 **Sauces** Argentina 32.38S 64.35W
107 G11 **Saucier** Mississippi 30.37N 89.10W
71 C9 **Sauclières** France 43.59N 3.22E
53 U19 **Sauda** Norway 59.38N 6.23E
120 F1 **Saudade** Brazil 5.55S 64.15W
53 U19 **Saudafjorden** *inlet* Norway 59.35N 6.18E
53 U19 **Saudasjøen** Norway 59.38N 6.19E
118 H2 **Saúde** Brazil 10.54S 40.25W
118 G10 **Saúde** *dist* São Paulo Brazil
53 U14 **Saudehorn** *mt* Norway 62.14N 6.09E
50 D4 **Saudhafell** Iceland 65.01N 21.37W
50 F4 **Saudhafell** *mt* Húnavatnssýsla, Austur Iceland 65.06N 19.36W
50 F6 **Saudhafell** *mt* Rangárvallasýsla Iceland 64.05N 19.41W
50 G6 **Saudhafell** *mt* Rangárvallasýsla Iceland 64.23N 18.39W
50 K2 **Saudhanes** Iceland 66.15N 15.13W
50 G2 **Saudhanes** *Lt Ho* Iceland 66.11N 18.58W
50 F3 **Saudhárkrókur** Iceland 65.45N 19.39W
50 B3 **Saudhlauksdalur** Iceland 65.33N 23.58W
27 E4 **Saudi Arabia** *kingdom* Saudi Arabia
69 J7 **Saudron** France 48.29N 5.20E
75 P4 **Sau, Embalse de** *res* Spain 41.57N 2.20E
64 B4 **Sauer** *R* W Germany etc
64 M8 **Sauerlach** W Germany 47.58N 11.40E
64 D1 **Sauerland** *reg* W Germany
118 B3 **Sauêruiná, R** Brazil
19 M8 **Saug** *R* Mindanao Philippines
106 H7 **Saugatuck** Michigan 42.40N 86.11W
103 H4 **Saugatuck Res** Connecticut 41.17N 73.22W
99 J8 **Saugeen** *R* Ontario
103 G2 **Saugerties** New York 42.05N 73.56W
72 C7 **Saugnacq-et-Muret** France 44.24N 0.46W
76 F8 **Saúgo, El** Spain 40.25N 6.32W
Saugor *see* **Sagar**
101 K9 **Saugstad, Mt** Br Col 52.16N 126.29W
71 D7 **Saugues** France 44.56N 3.34E
104 Q8 **Saugus** *dist* Boston, Mass
18 A8 **Sauh, Tanjong** *C* Pen Malaysia 3.46N 100.47E
Sāūībolāgh *see* **Mahābād**
121 C1 **Saujil** Argentina 27.32S 67.37W
18 A7 **Sauk** Pen Malaysia 4.55N 100.55E
108 Q4 **Sauk** *R* Minnesota
110 D1 **Sauk** *R* Washington
108 Q4 **Sauk Center** Minnesota 45.43N 94.58W
106 E6 **Sauk City** Wisconsin 43.16N 89.44W
46 E2 **Saukenai** Lithuania U.S.S.R. 55.49N 22.50E
15 B4 **Saukorem** Irian Jaya 0.36S 133.12E
108 Q4 **Sauk Rapids** Minnesota 45.35N 94.10W
117 C3 **Saül** Fr Guiana 3.32N 53.15W
71 J8 **Saulce, la** France 44.25N 6.00E
69 H4 **Saulces-Monclin** France 49.34N 4.30E
71 F7 **Saulce-sur-Rhône** France 44.41N 4.48E
66 E2 **Saulcy** Switzerland 47.18N 7.10E
71 A1 **Sauldre, Grande** *R* France 47.34N 2.15E
71 A2 **Sauldre, Petite** *R* France 47.27N 2.21E
70 K5 **Saule, Mt.du** France 48.21N 0.23W
64 H7 **Saulgau** W Germany 48.01N 9.31E
72 F3 **Saulgé** France 46.22N 0.53E
72 D1 **Saulgé l'Hôpital** France 47.18N 0.27W
64 L8 **Saulgrub** W Germany 47.40N 11.02E
71 E2 **Saulieu** France 47.17N 4.14E
46 E2 **Saulkrasti** Latvia U.S.S.R. 57.20N 24.28E
98 F9 **Saulnierville** Nova Scotia 44.16N 66.08W
66 C1 **Saulnot** France 47.34N 6.38E
71 G2 **Saulon-la-Rue** France 47.13N 5.05E
71 G8 **Sault** France 44.05N 5.25E
98 C5 **Sault au Mouton** Quebec 48.32N 69.18W
98 C5 **Sault-aux-Cochons, R** Quebec
72 C8 **Sault-de-Navailles** France 43.33N 0.40W
106 K3 **Sault Ste.Marie** Michigan 46.29N 84.22W
99 F6 **Sault Ste.Marie** Ontario 46.32N 84.20W
71 J1 **Saulx** France 47.42N 6.17E
69 H6 **Saulx** *R* France
69 N7 **Saulxures** France 48.24N 7.08E
69 M8 **Saulxures-sur-Moselotte** France 47.57N 6.47E
72 J2 **Saulzais-le-Potier** France 46.36N 2.29E
35 G3 **Saum** Jordan 32.34N 35.48E
13 L5 **Saumarez Reef** Gt Barrier Reef Australia
116 J5 **Saumâtre, Étang** *L* Haiti 18.35N 72.00W
70 N5 **Saumeray** France 48.15N 1.21E
15 A7 **Saumlaki** Moluccas Indon 7.59S 131.22E
72 B6 **Saumos** France 44.56N 1.00W
72 D1 **Saumur** France 47.16N 0.05W
98 K2 **Saumur, L** Quebec
51 N4 **Saunavaara** Finland 67.03N 27.30E
28 B3 **Saundatti** Karnataka India 15.47N 75.10E
100 B6 **Saunders** Alberta 52.28N 115.40W
11 E12 **Saunders, C** New Zealand 45.54S 170.45E
56 B4 **Saundersfoot** Dyfed Wales 51.43N 4.43W
121 E9 **Saunders I** Falkland Is 51.20S 60.10W
123 A14 **Saunders I** S Sandwich Is Atlantic Oc 57.48S 26.28W
13 B2 **Saunders, Mt** N Terr Australia 13.35S 131.51E
14 F8 **Saunders Ra** W Australia
103 M3 **Saunderstown** Rhode I 41.31N 71.25W
25 E8 **Saung** Thailand 8.37N 99.24E
25 N8 **Saungka** Burma 25.32N 97.30E
56 C5 **Saunton** Devon Eng 51.07N 4.12W
Sauqira, Ras *see* **Şawqirah, Ra's** *cape*
44 K3 **Saura** Kazakhstan U.S.S.R. 44.13N 50.51E
30 L7 **Saura** *R* Bihar India
72 H10 **Saurat** France 42.52N 1.31E
50 D6 **Saurbær** Borgarfjardharsýsla Iceland 64.25N 21.38W
50 G4 **Saurbær** Eyjafjardharsýsla Iceland 65.28N 18.10W
50 D6 **Saurbær** Kjósarsýsla Iceland 64.17N 21.51W
50 K2 **Saurbær** Múlasýsla, Nordhur Iceland 66.05N 15.08W
50 K2 **Saurbœjarvatn** *L* Iceland 66.03N 15.15W
15 K6 **Sauren** New Britain 5.58S 148.53E
90 C6 **Sauri** Nigeria 11.42N 6.45E
79 N2 **Sauris** Italy 46.28N 12.42E
24 E2 **Saur, Khrebet** *mts* Kazakhstan/Xinjiang Uygur Zizhiqu
81 M3 **Sauro** *R* Italy
65 M8 **Sausal** *reg* Austria
111 B4 **Sausalito** California 37.51N 122.30W
89 K6 **Sausanné Mango** Togo 10.23N 0.35E
29 F7 **Sausar** Madhya Prad India 21.42N 78.52E
70 H2 **Saussemesnil** France 49.34N 1.28W
71 G10 **Sausset-les-Pins** France 43.20N 5.05E
71 F2 **Saussy** France 47.28N 5.00E
19 B4 **Sausu** Celebes Indon 1.01S 120.30E
91 F9 **Sautar** Angola 11.09S 18.26E
66 C3 **Saut du Doubs** *falls* France/Switz 47.04N 6.42E
65 C7 **Sautens** Austria 47.13N 10.52E
98 J2 **Sauterelles, L.aux** Quebec
72 D6 **Sauternes** France 44.32N 0.21W
116 P5 **Sauteurs** Grenada, W I 12.14N 61.38W
61 G6 **Sautin** Belgium 50.10N 4.14E
61 J6 **Sautour** Belgium 50.10N 4.34E
72 A1 **Sautron** France 47.17N 1.40W
72 G3 **Sauvagnac, Puy de** *pk* France 46.01N 1.27E
71 B5 **Sauvagnat** France 45.46N 2.36E
72 D9 **Sauvagnon** France 43.24N 0.23W
71 D9 **Sauve** France 43.56N 3.56E
72 D6 **Sauve, la** France 44.46N 0.18W
72 E6 **Sauvetat-du-Dropt, la** France 44.39N 0.20E
72 F8 **Sauvetat, la** France 43.51N 0.32E
71 C8 **Sauveterre, Causse de** *plat* France
72 C9 **Sauveterre-de-Béarn** France 43.24N 0.56W
72 D6 **Sauveterre-de-Guyenne** France 44.42N 0.04W
72 J7 **Sauveterre-de-Rouergue** France 44.13N 2.18E
72 G6 **Sauveterre-la-Lémance** France 44.35N 1.01E
72 H4 **Sauviat-sur-Vige** France 45.54N 1.36E
51 K11 **Sauvo** Finland 60.22N 22.44E
60 P6 **Sauwerd** Netherlands 53.18N 6.32E
71 C5 **Sauxillanges** France 45.33N 3.22E
121 A5 **Sauzal** Maule Chile 35.46S 72.05W
121 B5 **Sauzal** O'Higgins Chile 34.15S 70.42W
96 R13 **Sauzal** Tenerife Canary Is 28.29N 16.27W
71 K8 **Sauze, le** France 44.22N 6.41E
72 G7 **Sauzet** France 44.25N 1.16E
72 E3 **Sauzé Vaussais** France 46.08N 0.07E
70 D7 **Sauzon** France 47.22N 3.13W
45 B2 **Sava** Belorussiya U.S.S.R. 54.23N 30.47E
115 L2 **Savá** Honduras 15.30N 86.16W
81 Q12 **Sava** Italy 40.24N 17.33E
82 F6 **Sava** *R* Yugoslavia
103 A8 **Savage** Maryland 39.09N 76.50W
107 F7 **Savage** Mississippi 34.37N 90.12W
108 F2 **Savage** Montana 47.28N 104.10W
108 E6 **Savageton** Wyoming 43.53N 105.46W
10 S4 **Savaii** Western Samoa 13.40S 172.16W
122 B1 **Savaii** *isld* W Samoa, Pacific Oc 13.44S 172.18W
37 E7 **Şavak** Turkey 38.56N 39.10E
46 M4 **Savala** *R* U.S.S.R.
Savalan, Kuh-i- *see* **Sabalan, Kūhha-ye** *mts*
89 L8 **Savalou** Benin 7.59N 2.03E
Savanat *see* **Eştahbānāt**
98 A2 **Savane, R** Quebec
116 A1 **Savaneta** Aruba W I 12.27N 69.57W
106 D7 **Savanna** Illinois 42.06N 90.07W
109 P7 **Savanna** Oklahoma 34.51N 95.52W
105 F5 **Savannah** Georgia 32.04N 81.07W
26 U13 **Savannah** Mauritius, Indian Oc 20.29S 57.37E
107 B2 **Savannah** Missouri 39.57N 94.49W
104 C6 **Savannah** Ohio 40.58N 82.23W
107 H6 **Savannah** Tennessee 35.12N 88.15W
105 G6 **Savannah Beach** Georgia 32.00N 80.50W
13 F4 **Savannah Downs** Queensland 19.29S 141.44E
105 D3 **Savannah R** S Carolina/Georgia
25 H4 **Savannakhet** Laos 16.34N 104.45E
116 H1 **Savanna la Mar** Jamaica, W I 18.13N 78.08W
100 M1 **Savant Lake** Ontario 50.16N 90.44W
28 A3 **Savantvadi** Maharashtra India 15.55N 73.52E
28 B3 **Savanur** Karnataka India 14.58N 75.27E
52 M3 **Sävar** Sweden 63.55N 20.30E
52 M2 **Sävaran** *R* Sweden
79 B3 **Savaranche, Val** Italy
87 J10 **Savarò** Somalia 0.59N 43.44E
36 C3 **Savaştepe** Turkey 39.20N 27.38E
91 E12 **Savate** Angola 16.45S 17.59E
51 J6 **Sävatnäs** Sweden 65.46N 21.50E
36 G3 **Savcılı** Turkey 39.13N 33.43E
89 L7 **Savé** Benin 8.04N 2.37E

72 G8 **Save** R France
94 N3 **Save** R Mozambique
32 D3 **Sāveh** Iran 35.00N 50.22E
81 N5 **Savelli** Italy 39.18N 16.47E
89 J7 **Savelugu** Ghana 9.35N 0.48W
42 G4 **Savel'yevskaya** U.S.S.R. 56.10N 100.02E
79 K6 **Sàvena** R Italy
70 G7 **Savenay** France 47.22N 1.57W
82 K3 **Săveni** Romania 47.58N 26.57E
69 O6 **Saver** R France
72 H9 **Saverdun** France 43.14N 1.33E
119 J5 **Saveretik** Guyana 4.56N 59.58W
56 H5 **Savernake Forest** Wilts Eng
69 N6 **Saverne** France 48.45N 7.22E
108 C8 **Savery** Wyoming 41.02N 107.27W
108 C8 **Savery Cr** Wyoming
69 F7 **Savières** France 48.24N 3.57E
66 F6 **Saviese** Switzerland 46.17N 7.22E
79 C5 **Savigliano** Italy 44.39N 7.39E
72 F5 **Savignac-les-Eglises** France 45.17N 0.56E
80 M6 **Savignano Irpino** Italy 41.14N 15.11E
70 L6 **Savigne** France 47.37N 0.04E
70 L5 **Savigné-l'Evêque** France 48.04N 0.18E
70 L7 **Savigné-sur-Lathan** France 47.27N 0.19E
79 K6 **Savigno** Italy 44.23N 11.05E
79 E5 **Savignone** Italy 44.33N 8.59E
66 C5 **Savigny** Switzerland 46.33N 6.45E
71 G3 **Savigny-en-Revermont** France 46.38N 5.25E
71 B2 **Savigny-en Sancerre** France 47.27N 2.48E
72 E1 **Savigny-en-Véron** Indre-et-Loire France 47.13N 0.09E
71 F2 **Savigny-lès-Beaune** France 47.04N 4.48E
70 M6 **Savigny-sur-Braye** France 47.53N 0.49E
68 F5 **Savigny-sur-Orge** France 48.41N 2.22E
48 S4 **Savigsivik** Greenland 76.03N 64.58W
103 J3 **Saville Dam** Connecticut 41.55N 72.58W
41 A4 **Savina** R Novaya Zemlya U.S.S.R.
41 B4 **Savina, Bukhta** B Novaya Zemlya U.S.S.R.
75 G5 **Saviñán** Spain 41.26N 1.34W
Saviñao see **Escairón**
71 J7 **Savines-le-lac** France 44.31N 6.24E
82 B4 **Savinja** R Yugoslavia
45 T6 **Savinka** U.S.S.R. 50.05N 47.06E
46 M2 **Savino** Ivanovo U.S.S.R. 56.30N 41.20E
47 G3 **Savino** Komi U.S.S.R. 65.08N 50.31E
47 H4 **Savinobor** U.S.S.R. 63.39N 56.30E
40 H5 **Savinsk** U.S.S.R. 52.10N 140.22E
47 E4 **Savinskiy** U.S.S.R. 62.57N 40.12E
45 J7 **Savintsy** Ukraine U.S.S.R. 49.23N 37.05E
79 M6 **Sávio** Italy 44.20N 12.20E
79 M7 **Sávio** R Italy
82 G4 **Săvîrşin** Romania 46.00N 22.15E
51 N10 **Savitaipale** Finland 61.14N 27.45E
28 A2 **Savitri R** Maharashtra India
29 C6 **Şavli** Gujarat India 22.33N 73.16E
82 E8 **Šavnik** Yugoslavia 42.58N 19.06E
99 F3 **Savoff** Ontario 49.56N 84.58W
66 P5 **Savognin** Switzerland 46.36N 9.37E
15 L3 **Savo I** Solomon Is 9.10S 159.50E
67 K7 **Savoie** dept France
67 K7 **Savoie** prov France
71 E1 **Savoisy** France 47.42N 4.23E
37 J8 **Sāvojbolāgh** R Iran
101 N10 **Savona** Br Col 50.43N 120.51W
79 D6 **Savona** Italy 44.18N 8.28E
104 H4 **Savona** New York 42.17N 77.14W
79 D6 **Savona** prov Italy
51 O10 **Savonlinna** Finland 61.54N 28.55E
51 O9 **Savonranta** Finland 62.10N 29.11E
113 B5 **Savoonga** St Lawrence I Bering Sea 63.40N 170.31W
44 E1 **Savos'kin** U.S.S.R. 46.44N 42.49E
45 C1 **Savost'ye** U.S.S.R. 55.23N 31.00E
66 D1 **Savoureuse** R France
107 H9 **Savoy** Mississippi 32.17N 88.48W
110 R1 **Savoy** Montana 48.29N 108.33W
82 N2 **Savran** U.S.S.R. 48.09N 30.04E
36 J5 **Savron** R Turkey
37 G4 **Savşat** Turkey 41.15N 42.30E
52 H9 **Sävsjö** Sweden 57.25N 14.40E
52 J10 **Sävsjöstrom** Sweden 57.00N 15.25E
79 P4 **Savudrija** Yugoslavia 45.29N 13.30E
82 A5 **Savudrija Rtič** pt Yugoslavia 45.30N 13.30E
51 N4 **Savukoski** Finland 67.19N 28.10E
37 F8 **Savur** Turkey 37.34N 40.53E
9 S5 **Savusavu** Vanua Levu Fiji 16.48S 179.20E
9 S5 **Savusavu B** Vanua Levu Fiji
19 B8 **Savu Sea** Indonesia
40 O6 **Savushkino** Kuril Is U.S.S.R. 50.44N 156.19E
94 H2 **Savuti** Botswana 18.38S 24.05E
81 M5 **Savuto** R Italy
84 B6 **Savvália** Greece 37.49N 21.18E
42 K6 **Savvo-Borzya** U.S.S.R. 50.44N 118.25E
25 C2 **Saw** Burma 21.12N 94.08E
34 G5 **Şawab, Wādī aş** watercourse Iraq
33 F5 **Şawādah, As** reg Saudi Arabia
18 L4 **Sawah** Borneo Indon 2.28N 115.14E
18 D6 **Sawahlunto** Sumatra Indon 0.41S 100.52E
15 D4 **Sawai** Irian Jaya 1.50S 137.10E
19 F5 **Sawai** Moluccas Indon 2.58S 129.05E
9 U8 **Sawaieke** Ngau Fiji 18.00S 179.15E
29 E5 **Sawai Madhopur** Rajasthan India 26.00N 76.28E
29 E4 **Sawai Madhopur** dist Rajasthan India
19 F5 **Sawai, Teluk** B Moluccas Indon
18 H9 **Sawall, Gunung** mt Java Indon 7.12S 108.15E
25 N8 **Sawan** Burma 26.02N 97.31E
18 E5 **Sawang** Indonesia 0.45N 103.21E
25 E4 **Sawankhalok** Thailand 17.19N 99.50E
29 D5 **Sawar** Rajasthan India 25.46N 75.15E
20 K2 **Sawara** Hokkaido Japan 42.08N 140.41E
20 O6 **Sawara** Honshu Japan 35.52N 140.31E
20 M4 **Sawasaki-bana** C Japan 37.48N 138.12E
109 D2 **Sawatch Ra** Colorado
99 L1 **Sawayan Pt** Quebec 51.39N 79.19W
33 F9 **Sawbah** Yemen 14.02N 44.34E
100 Q1 **Sawbill** Manitoba 57.38N 101.44W
56 M4 **Sawbridgeworth** Herts Eng 51.50N 0.09E
33 L8 **Sawdā** isld Arabian Sea 17.30N 55.51E
85 C5 **Sawdā', Jabal as** mts Libya
100 D4 **Sawdy** Alberta 54.52N 113.24W
15 B4 **Saweba, Tg** C Irian Jaya 0.44S 133.57E
15 C4 **Sawek** Biak I, Irian Jaya 0.50S 135.30E
59 H2 **Sawel** mt Londonderry N Ireland 54.49N 7.03W
87 H7 **Sawena** Ethiopia 7.22N 41.16E
85 B4 **Sawfajjin** watercourse Libya
Sawi see **Ban Sawi**
25 E7 **Sawi, Ao** B Thailand
28 H6 **Sawi B** Nicobar Is
35 E5 **Sawiya** Jordan 32.05N 35.16E
85 C5 **Sawknah** Libya 29.04N 15.47E
122 U7 **Sawle Pt** Palmyra I Pacific Oc 5.53N 162.06W
57 J5 **Sawley** Lancs Eng 53.55N 2.20W
57 K4 **Sawley** N Yorks Eng 54.06N 1.37W
87 M6 **Sawl Haud** reg Somalia
109 L4 **Sawlog Cr** Kansas
33 H8 **Sawm, As** S Yemen 16.11N 49.17E
101 O3 **Sawmill Bay** N W Terr 65.48N 119.25W
92 D11 **Sawmills** Zimbabwe 19.31S 28.02E
15 H7 **Saw Mts** Papua New Guinea
33 M7 **Şawqirah B** Oman
33 M7 **Şawqirah, Ra's** C Oman 18.08N 56.37E
86 O6 **Şawr** mt Jordan 29.51N 35.16E
33 A3 **Şawrah,Aş** Saudi Arabia 27.49N 35.24E
33 C3 **Şawrah, Aş** Saudi Arabia 26.03N 38.30E
56 M3 **Sawston** Cambs Eng 52.07N 0.10E
113 N4 **Sawtooth Mt** Alaska 65.25N 149.30W
110 K5 **Sawtooth Ra** Idaho
110 E1 **Sawtooth Ra** Washington
19 B9 **Sawu** isld Indonesia
109 M4 **Sawyer** Kansas 37.31N 98.41W
108 J1 **Sawyer** N Dakota 48.06N 101.05W
106 G5 **Sawyer** Wisconsin 44.49N 87.23W
110 B8 **Sawyers Bar** California 41.18N 123.09W
11 M12 **Sawyers Bay** New Zealand 45.49S 170.37E
99 T7 **Sawyerville** Quebec 45.20N 71.34W
77 P3 **Sax** Spain 38.33N 0.49W
66 O3 **Sax** Switzerland 47.14N 9.27E
13 F4 **Saxby** R Queensland
13 G5 **Saxby Downs** Queensland 20.05S 142.30E
66 D8 **Saxe, la** Italy 45.48N 6.58E
90 G8 **Saxe, Pic** mt Cameroon 7.58N 14.26E
66 H5 **Saxeten** Switzerland 46.38N 7.50E
71 C2 **Saxi-Bourdon** France 47.03N 3.28E
57 M6 **Saxilby** Lincs Eng 53.17N 0.40W
104 K9 **Saxis** Virginia 37.55N 75.44W
113 W9 **Saxman** Alaska 55.21N 131.35W
56 O3 **Saxmundham** Suffolk Eng 52.13N 1.29E
52 J2 **Saxnäs** Sweden 64.57N 15.20E
66 E7 **Saxon** Switzerland 46.09N 7.11E
106 D3 **Saxon** Wisconsin 46.30N 90.25W
56 O2 **Saxthorpe** Norfolk Eng 52.50N 1.09E
104 G6 **Saxton** Pennsylvania 40.13N 78.15W
11 H9 **Saxton Pass** New Zealand 42.03S 173.16E
53 K5 **Saxtorp** Sweden 55.49N 12.58E
89 G5 **Say** Mali 13.50N 4.57W
89 L5 **Say** Niger 13.08N 2.20E
34 C3 **Saya** Syria 35.04N 35.58E
98 E5 **Sayabec** Quebec 48.35N 67.41W
25 F3 **Sayaboury** Laos 19.18N 101.46E
26 E6 **Saya de Malha Bank** Indian Oc
19 F3 **Sayafi** isld Moluccas Indon 0.30N 128.50E
43 M4 **Sayak** Kazakhstan U.S.S.R. 47.02N 77.28E
43 N4 **Sayakskaya Pristan'** Kazakhstan U.S.S.R. 46.38N 77.31E
28 D6 **Sayalkudi** Tamil Nadu India 9.09N 78.26E
120 B4 **Sayán** Peru 11.10S 77.08W
15 A3 **Sayang** isld Irian Jaya 0.20N 129.55E
42 G5 **Sayansk** U.S.S.R. 54.00N 102.06E
42 E6 **Sayanskiy Khrebet** mts U.S.S.R.
33 G8 **Şay'ar** tribe Saudi Arabia 16.45N 46.19E
33 H8 **Şayar** tribe S Yemen
43 G7 **Sayat** Turkmeniya U.S.S.R. 38.48N 63.54E
75 E7 **Sayatón** Spain 40.22N 2.51W
115 O9 **Sayaxché** Guatemala 16.34N 90.14W
Sayda see **Saïda**
64 P2 **Sayda** E Germany 50.43N 13.25E
41 O6 **Saydy** U.S.S.R. 68.43N 134.12E
84 B5 **Sayéika** Greece 38.06N 21.28E
25 D8 **Sayer I** Thailand
12 G5 **Sayers Lake** New S Wales 32.46S 143.20E
90 E7 **Sayfo** Nigeria 8.04N 11.10E
45 S10 **Saygachiy** U.S.S.R. 46.52N 46.18E
Saygatka see **Chaykovskiy**
33 F8 **Şayḩ** Yemen 17.03N 44.54E
33 M6 **Şayḩ al Aḩmar** area Oman
22 H4 **Sayhandulaan** Mongolia 44.41N 108.57E
22 F4 **Sayhan-Ovoo** Mongolia 45.30N 103.57E
85 C5 **Sayḩ ar Rashādah** Libya 29.59N 14.51E
33 G5 **Sayḩ, As** Saudi Arabia 22.14N 46.50E
33 J3 **Sayhāt** Saudi Arabia 26.28N 50.04E
33 J9 **Sayhūt** S Yemen 15.12N 51.12E
35 D10 **Sayif** watercourse Israel
35 H5 **Sayih** watercourse Jordan
45 S8 **Saykhin** Kazakhstan U.S.S.R. 48.49N 46.46E
29 B6 **Sayla** dist Gujarat India
33 D6 **Sayl al Kabīr, As** Saudi Arabia 21.38N 40.30E
103 D5 **Saylorsburg** Pennsylvania 40.54N 75.19W
108 R8 **Saylorville Reservoir** Iowa
42 D7 **Saylyugem, Khrebet** mts U.S.S.R.
51 M9 **Säynätsalo** Finland 62.09N 25.42E
22 H4 **Saynshand** Mongolia 44.58N 110.10E
Sayn Shanda see **Saynshand**
40 G9 **Sayon** U.S.S.R. 45.52N 137.44E
24 D3 **Sayram Hu** L Xinjiang Uygur Zizhiqu China
109 L6 **Sayre** Oklahoma 35.18N 99.38W
103 A3 **Sayre** Pennsylvania 41.58N 76.31W
103 F6 **Sayreville** New Jersey 40.28N 74.21W
34 N2 **Saysārim** Iran 36.04N 45.46E
115 H8 **Sayula** Jalisco Mexico 19.52N 103.36W
115 M9 **Sayula** Veracruz Mexico 17.50N 95.01W
115 H8 **Sayula, L.de** Mexico
43 C5 **Say-Utes** Kazakhstan U.S.S.R. 44.06N 53.12E
103 H5 **Sayville** Long I, N Y 40.44N 73.05W
101 L10 **Sayward** Br Col 50.19N 125.58W
33 H9 **Saywūn** S Yemen 15.59N 48.44E
33 M7 **Sayy** Oman 19.40N 57.36E
41 O9 **Sayylyk** U.S.S.R. 62.29N 134.50E
39 B1 **Sayylyk** Yakutsk U.S.S.R. 67.48N 135.42E
41 L8 **Sayylyk** Yakutsk U.S.S.R. 64.03N 118.20E
76 G5 **Sazadón, Portillo de** pass Spain 41.53N 6.01W
83 C4 **Sazan** isld Albania 40.30N 19.15E
65 N2 **Sázava** Jihlava Czech 49.34N 15.52E
65 L2 **Sázava** Praha Czech 49.53N 14.54E
65 N2 **Sázava** R Czechoslovakia
46 P6 **Sazdy** Kazakhstan U.S.S.R. 46.58N 49.15E
47 H7 **Sazhino** U.S.S.R. 56.21N 58.15E
31 G3 **Sazin** Pakistan 35.32N 73.31E
37 F1 **Sazlı** R Turkey
37 F1 **Sazlibosna Çitlihan** Turkey 41.12N 28.41E
46 L2 **Sazonovo** U.S.S.R. 55.14N 39.40E
88 N7 **Sbaa** Algeria 28.13N 0.10W
Sbadeh-i-Tashk see **Tashk**
89 C2 **Sbaya** Mauritania 19.00N 13.45W
88 S4 **Sbeitla** Tunisia 35.13N 9.03E
35 G2 **Sbitah, Es** Syria 32.58N 35.46E
58 B3 **Scadavay, L** N Uist, W Isles Scotland 57.37N 7.16W
14 D10 **Scaddan** W Australia 33.27S 121.43E
70 C5 **Scaër** France 48.02N 3.43W
80 L7 **Scafati** Italy 40.44N 14.32E
57 G4 **Sca Fell** mt Cumbria Eng 54.27N 3.14W
57 G4 **Scafell Pike** mt Cumbria Eng 54.28N 3.12W
71 K9 **Scaffarels, les** France 43.58N 6.42E
57 M6 **Scaftworth** Notts Eng 53.25N 1.00W
81 N5 **Scala Coeli** Italy 39.27N 16.54E
58 D6 **Scalasaig** Strathclyde Scotland 56.04N 6.12W
57 N4 **Scalby** N Yorks Eng 54.18N 0.27W
81 L4 **Scalea** Italy 39.49N 15.47E
79 J6 **Scale, Corno alle** mt Italy 44.07N 10.49E
106 D7 **Scales Mound** Illinois 42.28N 90.15W
66 Q5 **Scaletta Pass** Switzerland 46.42N 9.56E
81 K7 **Scaletta Zanclea** Sicily 38.03N 15.28E
79 G2 **Scalino, Pizzo** mt Italy 46.17N 9.58E
58 Q9 **Scalloway** Shetland Scotland 60.08N 1.17W
59 F6 **Scalp** mt Galway Irish Rep 53.00N 8.29W
58 C3 **Scalpay** isld Harris, W Isles Scotland 57.52N 6.40W
58 E4 **Scalpay** isld Highland Scotland
59 H1 **Scalp Mt** Donegal Irish Rep 55.05N 7.22W
59 K5 **Scalp, The** pass Dublin Irish Rep 53.14N 6.12W
71 E9 **Scamandre, Etang de** L France 43.37N 4.22E
57 N6 **Scamblesby** Lincs Eng 53.18N 0.05W
113 E6 **Scammon Bay** Alaska 61.50N 165.35W
57 M6 **Scampton** Lincs Eng 53.18N 0.35W
81 N5 **Scandale** Italy 39.07N 16.58E
100 E8 **Scandia** Alberta 50.18N 112.02W
109 N2 **Scandia** Kansas 39.48N 97.47W
79 J5 **Scandiano** Italy 44.36N 10.41E
80 G4 **Scandriglia** Italy 42.10N 12.51E
80 J5 **Scanno** Italy 41.54N 13.53E
80 J5 **Scanno, Lago di** Italy 41.56N 13.52E
81 B3 **Scano di Montiferro** Sardinia 40.13N 8.35E
80 D3 **Scansano** Italy 42.41N 11.20E
100 V8 **Scanterbury** Manitoba 50.24N 96.36W
103 J3 **Scantic** Connecticut 41.54N 72.33W
81 N3 **Scanzano** Italy 40.15N 16.42E
100 F7 **Scapa** Alberta 51.52N 112.00W
58 S12 **Scapa Flow** firth Orkney Scotland
58 T12 **Scapa Pier** Orkney Scotland 58.57N 2.58W
110 C4 **Scappoose** Oregon 45.46N 122.54W
58 J2 **Scaraben** mt Highland Scotland 58.13N 3.36W
81 H10 **Scaramia, C** Sicily 36.48N 14.30E
58 E6 **Scarba** isld Strathclyde Scotland 56.11N 5.42W
94 P12 **Scarborough** Cape Town S Africa 34.12S 18.22E
57 N4 **Scarborough** N Yorks Eng 54.17N 0.24W
99 E10 **Scarborough** Ontario 43.44N 79.16W
116 M1 **Scarborough** Tobago W I 11.11N 60.45W
14 A1 **Scarborough** dist Perth, W Australia
99 E10 **Scarborough Bluffs** Ontario
19 H4 **Scarborough Shoal** S China Sea 15.05N 117.45E
89 C7 **Scarcies, Gt** R Guinea/Sierra Leone
89 C7 **Scarcies, Lit** R Sierra Leone
58 G3 **Scardroy Lodge** Highland Scotland 57.31N 4.58W
58 K1 **Scarfskerry** Highland Scotland 58.39N 3.16W
11 G9 **Scargill** New Zealand 42.57S 172.57E
59 B8 **Scariff, I** Kerry Irish Rep 51.44N 10.15W
58 C6 **Scarinish** Tiree, Strathclyde Scotland 56.30N 6.49W
66 S5 **Scarl** Switzerland 46.43N 10.20E
103 C6 **Scarlets Mill** Pennsylvania 40.13N 75.51W
66 S5 **Scarl Tal** V Switzerland
79 C5 **Scarnafigi** Italy 44.41N 7.34E
58 B2 **Scarp** isld Harris, W Isles Scotland 58.02N 7.07W
Scarpanto isld see **Kárpathos**
69 D3 **Scarpe** R France
79 K7 **Scarperia** Italy 44.00N 11.21E
111 B10 **Scarper Pk** mt California 37.32N 122.26W
59 E6 **Scarriff** Clare Irish Rep 52.55N 8.37W
100 R9 **Scarth** Manitoba 49.44N 100.56W
59 K3 **Scarva** Down N Ireland 54.20N 6.22W
98 N7 **Scatarie I** C Breton I, Nova Scotia 46.02N 59.43W
58 Q9 **Scatsta** Shetland Scotland 60.26N 1.18W
59 C6 **Scattery I** Clare Irish Rep 52.37N 9.31W
57 F2 **Scaur Water** R Dumfries & Galloway Scotland
58 D4 **Scavaig, L** Skye, Highland Scotland
25 J9 **Scawfell Shoal** S China Sea
57 L4 **Scawton** N Yorks Eng 54.15N 1.09W
12 C5 **Sceale Bay** S Australia 33.00S 134.15E
68 E4 **Sceaux** Hauts-de-Seine France 48.47N 2.18E
70 M5 **Çeaux** Sarthe France 48.06N 0.35E
82 D7 **Šćedro** isld Yugoslavia 43.05N 16.40E
108 H6 **Scenic** S Dakota 43.46N 102.32W
100 H8 **Sceptre** Saskatchewan 50.53N 109.14W
80 L4 **Scerni** Italy 42.07N 14.35E
66 P3 **Scesaplana** mt Austria/Switz 47.04N 9.43E
71 H1 **Scey-sur-Saône-et-St. Albin** France 47.40N 5.58E
63 N6 **Schaale** R E Germany
63 N5 **Schaalsee** L Germany
66 P3 **Schaan** Liechtenstein 47.10N 9.31E
60 M11 **Schaarsbergen** Netherlands 52.02N 5.52E
Schachen see **Bad Schachen**
66 M4 **Schächen Tal** V Switzerland
66 M4 **Schächentaler Windgälle** mt Switzerland 46.53N 8.48E
Schadow see **Alt-Schadow**
103 B6 **Schaefferstown** Pennsylvania 40.18N 76.18W
61 S9 **Schaerbeek** dist Bruxelles Belgium
60 U17 **Schaesberg** Netherlands 50.54N 6.00E
65 H6 **Schafberg** mt Austria 47.47N 13.26E
66 S5 **Schaf Berg** mt Italy/Switz 46.35N 10.30E
66 P3 **Schafboden** mt Liechtenstein 47.05N 9.34E
61 L3 **Schaffen** Belgium 51.00N 5.05E
106 G4 **Schaffer** Michigan 45.46N 87.17W
66 L1 **Schaffhausen** Switz 47.42N 8.38E
66 L1 **Schaffhausen** canton Switzerland
53 C7 **Schafflund** W Germany 54.45N 9.11E
63 P10 **Schafstädt** E Germany 51.23N 11.47E
60 K14 **Schaft** Netherlands 51.18N 5.28E
64 M8 **Schaftlach** W Germany 47.46N 11.42E
60 H8 **Schagen** Netherlands 52.47N 4.47E
60 L13 **Schaijk** Netherlands 51.45N 5.38E
69 N6 **Schalbach** France 48.50N 7.10E
64 P6 **Schalding** W Germany 48.37N 13.23E
63 G8 **Schale** W Germany 52.27N 7.38E
64 L3 **Schalkau** E Germany 50.23N 11.01E
60 N10 **Schalkhaar** Netherlands 52.16N 6.11E
64 D1 **Schalksmühle** W Germany 51.15N 7.32E
60 J12 **Schalkwijk** Netherlands 51.59N 5.11E
108 P7 **Schaller** Iowa 42.30N 95.19W
64 D8 **Schallstadt-Wolfenweiler** W Germany 47.58N 7.45E
61 L5 **Schaltin** Belgium 50.22N 5.07E
66 O5 **Schams** V Switzerland
60 N14 **Schandelo** Netherlands 51.25N 6.11E
66 Q5 **S-chanf** Switzerland 46.37N 9.59E
66 P4 **Schanfigg** V Switzerland
66 H4 **Schangnau** Switzerland 46.50N 7.53E
66 Q4 **Schanielen** R Switzerland
66 N3 **Schänis** Switzerland 47.10N 9.03E
32 J4 **Schao** R Iran/Afghanistan
63 G8 **Schapen** W Germany 52.25N 7.32E
66 O5 **Scharans** Switzerland 46.44N 9.28E
65 H5 **Schärding** Austria 48.28N 13.27E
60 C2 **Scharendijke** Netherlands 51.44N 3.50E
63 H5 **Scharhörn** isld W Germany
S-charl see **Scarl**
63 U8 **Scharmützelsee** L E Germany
63 N6 **Scharnebeck** W Germany 53.18N 10.30E
60 L7 **Scharnegoutum** Netherlands 53.03N 5.41E
65 D7 **Scharnitz** Austria 47.23N 11.17E
65 J6 **Scharnstein** Austria 47.54N 13.58E
63 G6 **Scharrel** W Germany 53.04N 7.42E
60 L8 **Scharsterbrug** Netherlands 52.57N 5.46E
60 J9 **Scharwoude** Netherlands 52.37N 5.00E
45 L8 **Schast'ye** Ukraine U.S.S.R. 48.45N 39.06E
65 B6 **Schattwald** Austria 47.32N 10.28E
66 Q4 **Schatzalp** Switzerland 46.48N 9.49E
66 M2 **Schauen Berg** mt Switzerland 47.28N 8.52E
64 G1 **Schauenburg** W Germany 51.14N 9.10E
64 M3 **Schauenstein** W Germany 50.16N 11.46E
64 D8 **Schauinsland** mt W Germany 47.55N 7.55E
63 K8 **Schaumburg** W Germany 52.12N 9.13E
64 N8 **Schechen** W Germany 47.56N 12.08E
64 H6 **Schechingen** W Germany 48.52N 9.56E
60 Q7 **Scheemda** Netherlands 53.10N 6.59E
95 O3 **Scheepersnek** S Africa 27.50S 30.42E
95 D9 **Scheepersrus** S Africa 33.53S 20.22E
64 G7 **Scheer** W Germany 48.04N 9.18E
66 M4 **Scheerhorn** mt Switzerland 46.49N 8.50E
63 L3 **Scheersberg** mt W Germany 54.44N 9.46E
60 N9 **Scheerwolde** Netherlands 52.45N 6.01E
63 K6 **Scheessel** W Germany 53.11N 9.29E
66 Q1 **Scheffau** W Germany 47.32N 9.53E
97 N7 **Schefferville** Quebec 54.50N 67.00W
80 G2 **Schéggia** Italy 43.24N 12.40E
80 G3 **Scheggino** Italy 42.43N 12.51E
65 M5 **Scheibbs** Austria 48.01N 15.11E
19 N4 **Scheiben** isld Truk Is Pacific Oc 7.29N 151.50E
65 N5 **Scheibmühl** Austria 48.04N 15.37E
66 L3 **Scheidegg** Switzerland 47.02N 8.31E
65 A6 **Scheidegg** W Germany 47.35N 9.52E
66 J5 **Scheidegg, Grosse** mt Switz 46.39N 8.07E
66 H5 **Scheidegg, Klein** Switzerland 46.36N 7.58E
65 K7 **Scheifling** Austria 47.09N 14.26E
64 K4 **Scheinfeld** W Germany 49.40N 10.30E
61 E3 **Schelde** R Belgium
61 H2 **Schelde** R Belgium
61 E3 **Schelderode** Belgium 50.58N 3.43E
61 F3 **Scheldewindeke** Belgium 50.56N 3.47E
64 H7 **Schelklingen** W Germany 48.24N 9.45E
111 K3 **Schell Creek Ra** Nevada
61 H2 **Schelle** Belgium 51.08N 4.20E
61 F2 **Schellebelle** Belgium 51.01N 3.55E
Schellenberg see **Marktschellenberg**
60 H10 **Schellingwoude** Netherlands 52.23N 4.58E
60 H12 **Schelluinen** Netherlands 51.51N 4.55E
61 F3 **Schendelbeke** Belgium 50.47N 3.54E
104 M4 **Schenectady** New York 42.48N 73.57W
63 K4 **Schenefeld** W Germany 54.04N 9.29E
63 L5 **Schenefeld** W Germany 53.35N 9.48E
103 E1 **Schenevus** New York 42.33N 74.49W
103 E1 **Schenevus Cr** New York
65 K4 **Schenkenfelden** Austria 48.31N 14.22E
64 H2 **Schenklengsfeld** W Germany 50.49N 9.53E
61 G3 **Schepdaal** Belgium 50.50N 4.12E
63 F8 **Schepsdorf-Lohne** Niedersachsen W Ger 52.29N 7.13E
63 K9 **Scherfede** W Germany 51.32N 9.01E
63 E9 **Schermbeck** W Germany 51.41N 6.51E
60 H9 **Schermer** dist Netherlands
60 H9 **Schermerhorn** Netherlands 52.36N 4.54E
64 K1 **Schernberg** E Germany 51.20N 10.47E
61 K3 **Scherpenheuvel** Belgium 50.59N 4.59E
60 E13 **Scherpenisse** Netherlands 51.33N 4.06E
60 M8 **Scherpenzeel** Friesland Netherlands 52.50N 5.53E
60 K11 **Scherpenzeel** Gelderland Netherlands 52.05N 5.30E
112 J6 **Schertz** Texas 29.35N 98.17W
66 N1 **Scherzingen** Switzerland 47.38N 9.14E
66 G4 **Scherzligen** Switzerland 46.46N 7.38E
65 A7 **Schesaplana** mt Austria 47.05N 9.43E
64 L4 **Schesslitz** W Germany 49.58N 11.03E
60 F11 **Scheveningen** Netherlands 52.05N 4.16E
80 K5 **Schiavi di Abruzzo** Italy 41.48N 14.30E
60 F12 **Schie** canal Netherlands
65 O6 **Schieblingkirchen** Austria 47.40N 16.09E
60 F12 **Schiedam** Netherlands 51.55N 4.25E
63 K9 **Schieder** W Germany 51.54N 9.09E
58 H5 **Schiehallion** mt Tayside Scotland 56.40N 4.08W
66 M1 **Schiener Berg** mts W Germany 47.42N 8.55E
66 H6 **Schienhorn** mt Switzerland 46.28N 7.57E
61 P7 **Schieren** Luxembourg 49.50N 6.06E
64 N6 **Schierling** W Germany 48.48N 12.04E
60 N5 **Schiermonnikoog** Netherlands 53.28N 6.10E
60 N5 **Schiermonnikoog** isld Netherlands
66 P4 **Schiers** Switzerland 46.58N 9.42E
63 S8 **Schiessplatz** E Germany 52.06N 13.23E
64 F2 **Schiffenberg** W Germany 50.34N 8.44E
66 E4 **Schiffenen-see** L Switzerland
64 E5 **Schifferstadt** W Germany 49.24N 8.23E
61 P8 **Schifflange** Luxembourg 49.30N 6.01E
64 C5 **Schiffweiler** W Germany 49.22N 7.07E
60 G14 **Schijf** Netherlands 51.30N 4.33E
60 K13 **Schijndel** Netherlands 51.37N 5.27E
66 N3 **Schild** mt Switzerland 47.03N 9.08E
63 R10 **Schildau** E Germany 51.28N 12.57E
61 J2 **Schilde** Belgium 51.14N 4.35E
63 N6 **Schilde** R E Germany
60 Q6 **Schildmeer** L Netherlands 53.16N 6.50E
60 Q7 **Schildwolde** Netherlands 53.14N 6.50E
63 R6 **Schillersdorf** E Germany 53.21N 12.50E
63 L8 **Schillerslage** W Germany 52.28N 9.58E
63 H5 **Schillighörn** pt W Germany
64 J5 **Schillingsfürst** W Germany 49.18N 10.18E
79 H2 **Schilpario** Italy 46.01N 10.09E
66 O3 **Schils** R Switzerland
64 E7 **Schiltach** W Germany 48.17N 8.21E
65 N4 **Schiltern** Austria 48.32N 15.38E
66 H5 **Schilthorn** mt Switzerland 46.33N 7.50E
66 H6 **Schilthorn** mt Switzerland 46.26N 7.45E
66 J4 **Schimberg** Switzerland 46.57N 8.06E
60 T17 **Schimmert** Netherlands 50.55N 5.50E
60 T17 **Schinnen** Netherlands 50.57N 5.53E
60 T17 **Schin op Geul** Netherlands 50.51N 5.52E
60 T17 **Schinveld** Netherlands 50.57N 5.59E
66 J2 **Schinznach** Switzerland 47.28N 8.08E
79 K3 **Schio** Italy 45.43N 11.21E
63 D8 **Schipbeek** R Netherlands
60 H10 **Schiphol** Netherlands 52.18N 4.48E
60 F12 **Schipluiden** Netherlands 51.59N 4.19E
69 N7 **Schirmeck** France 48.29N 7.12E
81 K8 **Schisò, C** Sicily 37.49N 15.17E
82 L3 **Schitu Duca** Romania 47.00N 27.50E
63 Q10 **Schkeuditz** E Germany 51.24N 12.13E
64 M1 **Schkölen** E Germany 51.03N 11.50E
63 T9 **Schlabendorf** E Germany 51.49N 13.50E
65 J7 **Schladming** Austria 47.24N 13.42E
65 J7 **Schladminger Tauern** mts Austria
64 E3 **Schlangenbad** W Germany 50.06N 8.07E
66 N4 **Schlans** Switzerland 46.46N 9.01E
66 Q4 **Schlappintal** R Switzerland
Schlarigna see **Celerina**
64 C1 **Schlebusch** Nordrhein-Westfalen W Germany 51.02N 7.04E
63 L3 **Schlei** inlet W Germany
64 B2 **Schleiden (Eifel)** W Germany 50.32N 6.29E
15 L5 **Schleinitz Ra** New Ireland
69 P6 **Schleithal** France 48.59N 8.04E
66 K1 **Schleitheim** Switzerland 47.45N 8.30E
64 M2 **Schleiz** E Germany 50.34N 11.49E
63 P5 **Schlemmin** E Germany 53.54N 11.51E
65 C7 **Schlenker-Spitze** mt Austria 47.15N 10.35E
108 P7 **Schleswig** Iowa 42.10N 95.25W
63 L3 **Schleswig** W Germany 54.32N 9.34E
62 E1 **Schleswig-Holstein** land W Germany
64 O2 **Schlettau** E Germany 50.33N 12.58E
64 K2 **Schleusingen** E Germany 50.30N 10.46E
64 K2 **Schleusinger-Neundorf** E Germany 50.32N 10.50E
48 U1 **Schley Fd., G.B** Greenland
64 M4 **Schlicht** W Germany 49.36N 11.48E
63 S9 **Schlieben** E Germany 51.44N 13.24E
64 D8 **Schliengen** W Germany 47.45N 7.35E
66 P1 **Schlier** W Germany 47.45N 9.40E
66 K2 **Schlieren** Switzerland 47.23N 8.27E
64 M8 **Schliersee** W Germany 47.44N 11.53E
64 H3 **Schlüchtern** W Germany 50.21N 9.32E
66 P3 **Schlins** Austria 47.13N 9.43E
64 H2 **Schlitz** W Germany 50.41N 9.34E
64 N8 **Schloss** isld W Germany 47.52N 12.25E
63 J9 **Schloss-Holte** W Germany 51.55N 8.35E
63 J9 **Schloss Neuhaus** W Germany 51.44N 8.43E
64 L1 **Schlossvippach** E Germany 51.07N 11.08E
64 K1 **Schlotheim** E Germany 51.15N 10.40E
64 E8 **Schluchsee** W Germany 47.49N 8.11E
69 N7 **Schlucht, Col de la** pass France 48.03N 7.01E
63 K8 **Schlüsselburg** W Germany 52.29N 9.05E
64 K4 **Schlüsselfeld** W Germany 49.45N 10.38E
63 N5 **Schlutup** Lübeck W Germany 53.53N 10.48E
66 H5 **Schmadribach Falls** Switzerland 46.31N 7.55E
64 J2 **Schmalkalden** E Germany 50.43N 10.28E
64 E1 **Schmallenberg** W Germany 51.09N 8.16E
63 A2 **Schmargendorf** dist W Berlin W Germany
63 O7 **Schmarsau** W Germany 52.54N 11.22E
64 B5 **Schmelz** W Germany 49.28N 6.50E
66 M3 **Schmerikon** Switzerland 47.14N 8.57E
64 M5 **Schmidmühlen** W Germany 49.16N 11.56E
Schmidt isld see **Shmidta, Ostrov**
64 B3 **Schmidthein** W Germany 50.25N 6.34E
95 H4 **Schmidtsdrif** S Africa 28.41S 24.03E
64 K2 **Schmiedefeld** E Germany 50.36N 10.49E
64 Q2 **Schmiedelberg** E Germany 50.51N 13.41E
65 G7 **Schmittenhöhe** mt Austria 47.20N 12.45E
64 F1 **Schmittlotheim** W Germany 51.09N 8.55E
26 C10 **Schmitt-Ott Seamount** S Atlantic Oc
64 N2 **Schmölln** Leipzig E Germany 50.53N 12.22E
63 U6 **Schmölln** Neubrandenburg E Germany 53.18N 14.06E
64 K7 **Schmutter** R W Germany
64 M4 **Schnabelwaid** W Germany 49.48N 11.35E
63 P6 **Schnackenburg** W Germany 53.03N 11.34E
64 N7 **Schnaitsee** W Germany 48.05N 12.23E
64 L4 **Schnaittach** W Germany 49.34N 11.20E
64 N4 **Schnaittenbach** W Germany 49.33N 12.01E
66 M2 **Schnebelhorn** mt Switzerland 47.19N 8.59E
103 C5 **Schnecksville** Pennsylvania 40.40N 75.37W
65 N6 **Schneealpe** mt Austria 47.43N 15.36E
64 O2 **Schneeberg** E Germany 50.35N 12.38E
65 K6 **Schnee Berg** mt Austria 47.53N 14.25E
65 N6 **Schneeberg** mt Austria 47.47N 15.48E
69 N6 **Schnee Berg** mt France 48.36N 7.16E
64 M3 **Schneeberg** mt W Germany 50.03N 11.53E
65 H5 **Schneegattem** Austria 48.02N 13.18E
63 K7 **Schneeren** W Germany 52.31N 9.20E
Schneidemühl see **Piła**
63 O9 **Schneidlingen** E Germany 51.54N 11.27E
64 O8 **Schneizlreuth** W Germany 47.41N 12.48E
64 J5 **Schnelldorf** W Germany 49.11N 10.14E
66 Q2 **Schnepfau** Austria 47.22N 9.57E
63 L6 **Schneverdingen** W Germany 53.07N 9.48E
65 L7 **Schober Pass** Austria 47.28N 14.40E
63 K3 **Schobüll** W Germany 54.31N 9.01E
65 M7 **Schöckl** mt Austria 47.13N 15.29E
65 K7 **Schöder** Austria 47.12N 14.05E
116 L3 **Schœlcher** Martinique W I 14.37N 61.07W
95 F9 **Schoemanshoek** S Africa 33.29S 22.15E
69 O7 **Schöenau** France 48.14N 7.40E
61 Q5 **Schoenberg** Belgium 50.17N 6.16E
106 E5 **Schofield** Wisconsin 44.54N 89.36W
114 A4 **Schofield Barracks** Hawaiian Is 21.29N 158.04W
66 J2 **Schöftland** Switzerland 47.18N 8.04E
104 L4 **Schoharie** New York 42.40N 74.20W
103 F2 **Schoharie Cr** New York
103 F2 **Schoharie Res** New York
60 M9 **Schokkerhaven** Netherlands
60 L9 **Schokland** dist Netherlands
65 E7 **Scholastika** Austria 47.30N 11.44E
63 Q7 **Schollene** E Germany 52.41N 12.13E
66 L5 **Schollenen** pass Switzerland 46.39N 8.36E
64 G3 **Schöllkrippen** W Germany 50.05N 9.14E
64 F6 **Schömberg** W Germany 48.48N 8.38E
64 F7 **Schömberg** W Germany 48.13N 8.46E
65 J6 **Schön** mt Austria 47.43N 13.48E
64 E7 **Schonach** W Germany 48.09N 8.12E
64 G6 **Schönaich** W Germany 48.40N 9.05E
64 D8 **Schönau** Baden-Württemberg W Germany 47.47N 7.54E
64 F5 **Schönau** Baden-Württemberg W Germany 49.27N 8.49E
64 J2 **Schönau** E Germany 50.56N 10.26E
69 M3 **Schönau** Nordrhein-Westfalen W Germany 50.30N 6.47E
64 P6 **Schönberg** Bayern W Germany 48.51N 13.21E
65 N4 **Schönberg** Neider Österreich Austria 48.32N 15.43E
63 R7 **Schönberg** Potsdam E Germany 52.59N 12.31E
63 N5 **Schönberg** Rostock E Germany 53.51N 10.57E
64 M2 **Schönberg** Sachsen E Germany 50.31N 12.58E
64 N3 **Schönberg** Sachsen E Germany 50.11N 12.19E
63 M4 **Schönberg** Schleswig Holstein W Germany 54.24N 10.23E
65 D7 **Schönberg** Tirol Austria 47.12N 11.24E
66 L3 **Schönbrunn** Switzerland 47.11N 8.34E
66 G3 **Schönbühl** Switzerland 47.01N 7.31E
64 L7 **Schondorf** W Germany 48.03N 11.05E
64 H3 **Schondra** W Germany 50.16N 9.52E
63 P8 **Schönebeck (Elbe)** E Germany 52.01N 11.45E
63 B2 **Schöneberg** dist W Berlin
64 N3 **Schöneck** Berlin W Germany 50.24N 12.20E
64 A3 **Schönecken-Wetteldorf** W Germany 50.10N 6.28E
64 E6 **Schönegründ** W Germany 48.34N 8.24E
63 T8 **Schöneiche** E Germany 52.28N 13.43E
64 C5 **Schönenberg-Kubelberg** W Germany 49.25N 7.22E
66 N2 **Schönengrund** Switzerland 47.20N 9.14E
66 J2 **Schönenwerd** Switzerland 47.23N 8.01E
63 U6 **Schönermark** E Germany 53.06N 14.05E
63 S9 **Schönewalde** E Germany 51.49N 13.14E
64 B3 **Schönfeld** W Germany 50.19N 6.33E
64 K8 **Schongau** W Germany 47.49N 10.54E
65 O4 **Schöngrabern** Austria 48.37N 16.03E
63 L9 **Schönhagen** W Germany 51.42N 9.32E
63 Q7 **Schönhausen** E Germany 52.36N 12.02E
64 O3 **Schönheide** E Germany 50.30N 12.33E
63 N8 **Schöningen** W Germany 52.08N 10.58E
64 O4 **Schönsee** W Germany 49.31N 12.34E
64 H5 **Schöntal** W Germany 49.20N 9.33E
64 O5 **Schönthal** W Germany 49.21N 12.37E
64 J3 **Schonungen** W Germany 50.03N 10.20E
64 E7 **Schönwald** W Germany 48.06N 8.13E
63 S7 **Schönwalde** E Germany 52.41N 13.27E
63 N4 **Schönwalde am Bungsberg** W Germany 54.12N 10.45E
104 R1 **Schoodic L** Maine
104 R2 **Schoodic Pt** Maine 44.21N 68.04W
106 J7 **Schoolcraft** Michigan 42.07N 85.39W
95 J7 **Schoombee** S Africa 31.27S 25.30E
61 G2 **Schoonaarde** Belgium 51.00N 4.00E
60 B3 **Schoondijke** Netherlands 51.21N 3.33E
60 H12 **Schoonhoven** Netherlands 51.57N 4.51E
60 P8 **Schoonloo** Netherlands 52.54N 6.41E
60 Q8 **Schoonoord** Netherlands 52.50N 6.45E
117 A1 **Schoon Ord** Guyana 6.45N 58.15W
60 J12 **Schoonrewoerd** Netherlands 51.55N 5.07E
60 G9 **Schoorl** Netherlands 52.42N 4.41E
64 D8 **Schopfheim** W Germany 47.38N 7.50E
63 T7 **Schopfurth** E Germany 52.51N 13.42E
63 N8 **Schöppenstedt** W Germany 52.08N 10.47E
63 F8 **Schöppingen** W Germany 52.06N 7.14E
69 N5 **Schorbach** France 49.04N 7.25E
61 B2 **Schore** Belgium 51.07N 2.51E
60 C3 **Schore** Netherlands 51.28N 4.00E
61 E3 **Schorisse** Belgium 50.48N 3.41E
64 H6 **Schorndorf** W Germany 48.48N 9.33E
63 G5 **Schortens** W Germany 53.33N 7.47E
61 H1 **Schoten** Belgium 51.15N 4.30E
60 M8 **Schoterzijl** Netherlands 52.48N 5.49E
64 G3 **Schotten** W Germany 50.30N 9.08E
65 N6 **Schottwien** Austria 47.40N 15.52E
66 H3 **Schötz** Switzerland 47.08N 7.59E
12 J8 **Schouten I** Tasmania 42.20S 148.15E
15 H5 **Schouten Is** Papua New Guinea
60 C2 **Schouwen** isld Netherlands
60 O6 **Schouwerzijl** Netherlands 53.20N 6.27E
60 K7 **Schraard** Netherlands 53.05N 5.27E
103 A3 **Schrader** R Pennsylvania
15 H6 **Schrader Mt** Papua New Guinea 4.59S 144.05E
75 L2 **Schrader, Pico** mt Spain 42.42N 0.25E
110 G2 **Schrag** Washington 47.05N 118.50W
64 E7 **Schramberg** W Germany 48.14N 8.24E
65 D7 **Schrankogl** mt Austria 47.03N 11.07E
63 P10 **Schraplau** E Germany 51.26N 11.40E
66 H4 **Schrattenfluh** mt Switzerland 46.51N 7.59E
65 N4 **Schrattental** Austria 48.44N 15.55E
66 P4 **Schrau** R Switzerland
66 J5 **Schreckhorn, Grosser** mt Switz 46.36N 8.07E
66 J5 **Schreckhorn, Kleiner** Switzerland 46.37N 8.07E
64 G2 **Schrecksbach** W Germany 50.50N 9.18E
99 C4 **Schreiber** Ontario 48.48N 87.17W
65 M4 **Schrems** Austria 48.48N 15.05E
63 Q6 **Schrepkow** E Germany 53.00N 12.06E
63 N5 **Schretstaken** W Germany 53.35N 10.33E
61 J2 **Schriek** Belgium 51.02N 4.42E
64 F5 **Schriesheim** W Germany 49.29N 8.40E
64 L6 **Schrobenhausen** W Germany 48.33N 11.16E
65 B7 **Schröcken** Austria 47.17N 10.05E
104 M3 **Schroon L** New York
104 M3 **Schroon Lake** New York 43.51N 73.47W
64 H5 **Schrozberg** W Germany 49.21N 9.58E
65 A7 **Schruns** Austria 47.06N 9.56E
111 M9 **Schuchuli** Arizona 32.14N 112.39W
94 H1 **Schuckmannsburg** Namibia 17.34S 24.48E
61 D2 **Schuiferskapelle** Belgium 51.02N 3.20E
61 L3 **Schulen** Belgium 50.57N 5.10E
112 L6 **Schulenburg** Texas 29.41N 96.57W
63 L8 **Schulenburg** W Germany 52.12N 9.46E
100 G8 **Schuler** Alberta 50.22N 110.05W
59 C8 **Schull** Cork Irish Rep 51.32N 9.33W
64 M1 **Schulpforta** E Germany 51.08N 11.45E
Schuls see **Scuol**
109 P6 **Schulter** Oklahoma 35.32N 95.58W
13 K1 **Schultz Can** Brisbane, Qnsld
101 Z3 **Schultz L** N W Terr 64.55N 97.32W
63 U7 **Schulzendf** E Germany 52.41N 14.07E
63 T8 **Schulzendorf** E Germany 52.22N 13.32E
99 J4 **Schumacher** Ontario 48.30N 81.16W
63 N8 **Schunter** R W Germany
66 F3 **Schüpfen** Switzerland 47.02N 7.24E
66 J4 **Schüpfheim** Switzerland 46.57N 8.02E
111 F3 **Schurz** Nevada 38.57N 118.48W
64 H8 **Schussen** R W Germany
64 D7 **Schutterwald** W Germany 48.28N 7.55E
95 K3 **Schuttesdraai** S Africa 27.30S 26.40E
63 F8 **Schüttorf** W Germany 52.19N 7.13E
61 Q8 **Schuttrange** Luxembourg 49.37N 6.16E
65 P6 **Schutzen** Austria 47.52N 16.38E
108 N8 **Schuyler** Nebraska 41.28N 97.02W
104 G9 **Schuyler** Virginia 37.48N 78.44W
104 M3 **Schuylerville** New York 43.06N 73.37W
103 B5 **Schuylkill** co Pennsylvania
103 C6 **Schuylkill** R Pennsylvania
103 B5 **Schuylkill Haven** Pennsylvania 40.38N 76.12W
63 Q5 **Schwaan** E Germany 53.57N 12.07E
64 K5 **Schwabach** W Germany 49.20N 11.02E
64 J7 **Schwaben** dist Bayern W Germany
64 L7 **Schwabhausen** W Germany 48.18N 11.22E
64 F7 **Schwäbische Alb** mts W Germany
64 H6 **Schwäbisch Gmünd** W Germany 48.49N 9.48E
64 H5 **Schwäbisch Hall** W Germany 49.07N 9.45E
64 K7 **Schwabmünchen** W Germany 48.10N 10.45E
63 K4 **Schwabstedt** W Germany 54.23N 9.12E
64 G8 **Schwackenreute** W Germany 47.56N 9.04E
66 O2 **Schwägalp** Switzerland 47.16N 9.20E
64 M7 **Schwaig** W Germany 48.19N 11.50E
64 G5 **Schwaigern** W Germany 49.09N 9.03E
63 K9 **Schwalenberg** W Germany 51.53N 9.10E
65 M5 **Schwallenbach** Austria 48.21N 15.25E
64 G2 **Schwalm** R W Germany
64 G2 **Schwalmtal** Hessen W Germany 50.41N 9.18E
64 A1 **Schwalmtal** Nordrhein-Westfalen W Germany 51.13N 6.13E
69 L1 **Schwalmtal** W Germany 51.14N 6.16E
66 L2 **Schwamendingen** Switzerland 47.23N 8.36E
65 M8 **Schwanberg** Austria 46.46N 15.13E
64 L5 **Schwand** W Germany 49.18N 11.08E
66 N3 **Schwanden** Switzerland 47.01N 9.05E
64 N5 **Schwandorf in Bayern** W Germany 49.20N 12.07E
63 O9 **Schwanebeck** E Germany 51.58N 11.08E
65 J5 **Schwanenstadt** Austria 48.03N 13.47E
18 K6 **Schwaner Pegunungan** mts Borneo Indonesia
63 J6 **Schwanewede** W Germany 53.14N 8.34E
65 C6 **Schwangau** W Germany 47.36N 10.47E
63 N6 **Schwanheide** E Germany 53.26N 10.41E
63 L3 **Schwansen** reg W Germany
66 G6 **Schwarenbach** Switzerland 46.27N 7.38E
63 L7 **Schwarmstedt** W Germany 52.41N 9.37E
123 A5 **Schwartz Ra** Antarctica
63 R6 **Schwarz** E Germany 53.14N 12.47E
64 L2 **Schwarza** Gera E Germany 50.41N 11.19E
64 K2 **Schwarza** Suhl E Germany 50.37N 10.32E
64 L2 **Schwarza** R E Germany etc
66 J1 **Schwarza** R W Germany
Schwarzach see **Rheinmünster**
65 H7 **Schwarzach** Austria 47.19N 13.09E
64 O6 **Schwarzach** Bayern W Germany 48.55N 12.49E
66 Q2 **Schwarzach** Vorarlberg Austria 47.27N 9.46E
64 L5 **Schwarzach** R W Germany
64 N5 **Schwarzach** R W Germany
65 N6 **Schwarzau im Gebirge** Austria 47.49N 15.43E
64 L2 **Schwarzburg** E Germany 50.38N 11.11E
63 S9 **Schwarze Elster** R E Germany
66 H5 **Schwarze Lütschine** R Switz
65 M4 **Schwarzenau** Austria 48.45N 15.16E
64 M3 **Schwarzenbach** W Germany 50.17N 11.36E
64 M3 **Schwarzenbach an der Saale** W Germany 50.13N 11.56E
63 M6 **Schwarzenbek** W Germany 53.29N 10.28E
66 Q2 **Schwarzenberg** Austria 47.26N 9.52E
64 O2 **Schwarzenberg** E Germany 50.31N 12.48E
66 J3 **Schwarzenberg** Luzern Switz 47.01N 8.12E
64 K4 **Schwarzenberg** W Germany 49.41N 10.32E
64 G2 **Schwarzenborn** Hessen W Germany 50.56N 9.28E
64 B3 **Schwarzenborn** Rheinland Pfalz W Germany 50.02N 6.43E
66 F4 **Schwarzenburg** Bern Switz 46.49N 7.21E
66 G4 **Schwarzenegg** Switzerland 46.48N 7.48E
64 N5 **Schwarzenfeld** W Germany 49.23N 12.09E
64 H3 **Schwarzenfels** W Germany 50.18N 9.38E
64 A3 **Schwarzer Mann** mt W Germany 50.15N 6.23E
64 O5 **Schwarzer Regen** R W Germany
64 N5 **Schwarzhofen** W Germany 49.23N 12.21E
66 H7 **Schwarzhorn** mt Switzerland 46.13N 7.46E
66 J5 **Schwarzhorn** mt Switzerland 46.42N 8.03E
66 Q5 **Schwarz Horn** mt Switzerland 46.45N 9.56E
94 D5 **Schwarzrand** mts Namibia
66 G8 **Schwarzsee** Switzerland 45.59N 7.43E
66 F5 **Schwarz See** L Switzerland 46.40N 7.17E
64 E8 **Schwarzwald** mts W Germany
66 J5 **Schwarzwaldalp** Switzerland 46.41N 8.08E
64 B4 **Schwarzwälder Hochwald** mts W Germany
113 J3 **Schwatka Mts** Alaska
65 E7 **Schwaz** Austria 47.21N 11.44E
65 O5 **Schwechat** Austria 48.09N 16.29E
63 U6 **Schwedt an der Oder** E Germany 53.04N 14.17E
66 F5 **Schwefelbergbad** Switzerland 46.43N 7.26E
64 B4 **Schweich** W Germany 49.49N 6.46E
65 M4 **Schweiggers** Austria 48.41N 15.04E
64 D7 **Schweighausen** W Germany 48.13N 7.59E
64 J2 **Schweina** E Germany 50.49N 10.21E
63 M7 **Schweinau** W Germany 53.00N 10.25E
64 J3 **Schweinfurt** W Germany 50.03N 10.16E
63 S9 **Schweinitz** E Germany 51.48N 13.03E
66 G1 **Schweizerhalle** Switzerland 47.32N 7.41E
48 U13 **Schweizerland** Greenland
95 J3 **Schweizer-Reneke** S Africa 27.11S 25.20E
95 J3 **Schweizer-Renekedam** res S Africa 27.09S 25.21E
66 Q3 **Schweizer Tor** pass Austria/Switz 47.03N 9.48E
66 O2 **Schwellbrunn** Switzerland 47.22N 9.15E
64 C1 **Schwelm** W Germany 51.17N 7.18E
66 O2 **Schwende** Switzerland 47.18N 9.26E
64 J7 **Schwendi** W Germany 48.10N 10.00E
66 J4 **Schwendi Kaltbad** Switzerland 46.54N 8.08E
Schwenningen see **Villingen-Schwenningen**
64 F7 **Schwenningen** W Germany 48.03N 8.32E
63 T10 **Schwepnitz** E Germany 51.20N 13.58E
63 O5 **Schwerin** E Germany 53.38N 11.25E
63 O6 **Schwerin** reg E Germany
63 O5 **Schweriner See** L E Germany
65 L5 **Schwertberg** Austria 48.17N 14.37E
63 G10 **Schwerte** W Germany 51.26N 7.34E
66 L2 **Schwerzenbach** Switzerland 47.22N 8.39E
64 F5 **Schwetzingen** W Germany 49.22N 8.35E
63 T5 **Schwichtenberg** E Germany 53.42N 13.43E
62 H3 **Schwieloch-see** L E Germany
63 R8 **Schwielowsee** L E Germany
63 K5 **Schwinge** W Germany 53.33N 9.24E
63 K5 **Schwinge** R W Germany
63 R5 **Schwinkendorf** E Germany 53.38N 12.42E
63 P9 **Schwittersdorf** E Germany 51.34N 11.42E
66 L3 **Schwyz** Switzerland 47.02N 8.39E
66 L3 **Schwyz** canton Switzerland
66 H5 **Schynige Platte** mt Switzerland 46.39N 7.54E
81 F8 **Sciacca** Sicily 37.31N 13.05E
93 N3 **Sciama, El** Somalia 2.47N 41.01E
87 K9 **Sciao** Somalia 3.25N 45.19E
81 G8 **Sciara** Sicily 37.55N 13.47E
81 J10 **Scicli** Sicily 36.48N 14.43E
70 N2 **Scie** R France
98 R10 **Scie, R. á la** Quebec
71 J4 **Sciez** France 46.20N 6.22E
81 M5 **Scigliano** Italy 39.07N 16.18E
81 L7 **Scilla** Italy 38.15N 15.43E
87 H10 **Şcimbirale** Somalia 1.35N 41.15E
62 J4 **Scinawa** Poland 51.26N 16.25E
104 H4 **Scio** New York 42.10N 77.59W
104 D6 **Scio** Ohio 40.24N 81.06W
79 C4 **Sciolze** Italy 45.05N 7.53E
66 C7 **Scionzier** France 46.04N 6.33E
103 D5 **Sciota** Pennsylvania 40.56N 75.20W
104 C8 **Scioto** R Ohio
104 C8 **Sciotoville** Ohio 38.46N 82.53W
111 M2 **Scipio** Utah 39.15N 112.09W
103 N2 **Scituate** Massachusetts 42.12N 70.43W
103 L3 **Scituate Res** Rhode I
81 G8 **Sclafani** Sicily 37.48N 13.52E
100 R7 **Sclater** Manitoba 51.56N 100.36W
61 L5 **Sclayn** Belgium 50.29N 5.02E
56 B4 **Scleddau** Dyfed Wales 51.58N 5.00W

82 H5 Scoarţa Romania 45.02N 23.29E
108 E1 Scobey Montana 48.48N 105.28W
79 F6 Scoffera, Passo della pass Italy 44.29N 9.08E
111 N2 Scofield Utah 39.44N 111.10W
111 N2 Scofield Res Utah 39.47N 111.09W
81 A2 Scoglietti, Pta Sardinia 40.56N 8.11E
80 B4 Scóglio d'Africa Lt Ho Italy 42.21N 10.04E
81 H10 Scoglitti Sicily 36.54N 14.26E
56 O3 Scole Norfolk Eng 52.22N 1.10E
100 E7 Scollard Alberta 51.57N 112.46W
12 K4 Scone New S Wales 32.01S 150.53E
107 H9 Scooba Mississippi 32.51N 88.29W
79 D3 Scopa Italy 45.48N 8.07E
79 D3 Scopello Italy 45.46N 8.06E
66 M5 Scopi mt Switzerland 46.34N 8.50E
81 E8 Scorace, Mte Sicily 37.59N 12.47E
72 E2 Scorbé-Clairvaux France 46.48N 0.26E
81 L7 Scorda, Mte Italy 38.12N 16.00E
81 J9 Scordia Sicily 37.18N 14.51E
58 D3 Score B Skye, Highland Scotland
58 Q9 Score Hd Shetland Scotland 60.11N 1.05W
48 U11 Scoresby Land Greenland
48 V12 Scoresbysund Greenland 70.30N 22.00W
48 V12 Scoresby Sund sound Greenland
70 D6 Scorff, R France
14 F9 Scorpion Bight W Australia
81 R12 Scorrano Italy 40.05N 18.18E
110 G9 Scossa Nevada 40.45N 118.35W
57 K4 Scotch Corner N Yorks Eng 54.26N 1.40W
57 H4 Scotforth Lancs Eng 54.02N 2.48W
108 M8 Scotia Nebraska 41.28N 98.39W
99 L7 Scotia Ontario 45.31N 79.18W
110 H1 Scotia Washington 48.06N 117.10W
101 G6 Scotia Bay Br Col 59.36N 133.51W
123 A13 Scotia Ridge Antarctica
123 A14 Scotia Sea Antarctica
54 G5 Scotland British Isles
108 N6 Scotland S Dakota 43.09N 97.43W
112 J2 Scotland Texas 33.40N 98.29W
12 M5 Scotland I New S Wales 33.39S 151.18E
103 G6 Scotland Lt. Ship New Jersey 40.28N 73.49W
105 K1 Scotland Neck N Carolina 36.08N 77.27W
107 E11 Scotlandville Louisiana 30.31N 91.12W
98 H8 Scots Bay Nova Scotia 45.19N 64.25W
98 K8 Scotsburn Nova Scotia 45.40N 62.51W
100 J9 Scotsguard Saskatchewan 49.44N 108.09W
99 T7 Scotstown Quebec 45.32N 71.17W
105 E5 Scott Georgia 32.33N 82.43W
107 E8 Scott Mississippi 33.35N 91.02W
104 A6 Scott Ohio 40.58N 84.35W
98 A7 Scott Quebec 46.30N 71.04W
100 J6 Scott Saskatchewan 52.23N 108.49W
110 C8 Scott R California
12 E4 Scott R S Australia
110 B8 Scott Bar California 41.45N 123.01W
123 H6 Scott Base N Z Base Antarctica 77.51S 166.45E
95 O6 Scottburgh S Africa 30.17S 30.45E
13 A2 Scott, Cape N Terr Australia 13.30S 129.48E
101 J10 Scott, Cape Vancouver I, Br Col 50.47N 128.24W
109 K3 Scott City Kansas 38.28N 100.55W
123 H6 Scott Coast Antarctica
104 F6 Scottdale Pennsylvania 40.05N 79.36W
57 M5 Scotter Lincs Eng 53.30N 0.40W
123 E2 Scott Glacier Antarctica 66.30S 100.30E
14 E4 Scott Headland mt W Australia 18.59S 124.21E
97 M3 Scott Inlet N W Terr
101 J10 Scott Is Br Columbia 50.48N 128.38W
101 U6 Scott L Sask/N W Terr
110 C7 Scott, Mt Oregon 42.55N 122.02W
123 A5 Scott Mts Antarctica
11 G1 Scott Pt New Zealand 34.32S 172.44E
14 D2 Scott Reef Indian Oc 14.05S 121.50E
106 J7 Scotts Michigan 42.12N 85.27W
108 G8 Scottsbluff Nebraska 41.52N 103.40W
108 G8 Scotts Bluff Nat. Mon Nebraska 41.51N 103.45W
107 L7 Scottsboro Alabama 34.40N 86.00W
107 L3 Scottsburg Indiana 38.42N 85.47W
110 B6 Scottsburg Oregon 43.40N 123.50W
104 G10 Scottsburg Virginia 36.46N 78.49W
111 N8 Scottsdale Arizona 33.27N 111.59W
12 J8 Scottsdale Tasmania 41.09S 147.31E
105 B7 Scotts Ferry Florida 30.19N 85.09W
116 O7 Scotts Head Dominica, W I 15.12N 61.22W
96 A2 Scott's Hill Bermuda 32.18N 64.53W
98 L7 Scottsville C Breton I, Nova Scotia 46.11N 61.10W
109 N2 Scottsville Kansas 39.33N 97.56W
107 K5 Scottsville Kentucky 36.43N 86.12W
104 G9 Scottsville Virginia 37.49N 78.31W
106 H6 Scottville Michigan 43.57N 86.18W
13 J5 Scottville Queensland 20.31S 147.45E
111 G4 Scotty's Castle California 37.01N 117.21W
111 G4 Scottys Junction Nevada 37.21N 117.08W
56 N2 Scoulton Norfolk Eng 52.34N 0.55E
58 F2 Scourie Highland Scotland 58.20N 5.08W
58 Q10 Scousburgh Shetland Scotland 59.57N 1.20W
100 M9 Scout Lake Saskatchewan 49.25N 106.00W
59 G4 Scrabby Cavan Irish Rep 53.53N 7.32W
58 J1 Scrabster Highland Scotland 58.37N 3.34W
107 C6 Scranton Arkansas 35.21N 93.32W
109 P3 Scranton Kansas 38.47N 95.46W
108 G3 Scranton N Dakota 46.08N 103.05W
103 C4 Scranton Pennsylvania 41.25N 75.40W
59 C5 Screeb Galway Irish Rep 53.23N 9.33W
15 G5 Screw R Papua New Guinea
104 J3 Scriba New York 43.27N 76.26W
108 O8 Scribner Nebraska 41.39N 96.40W
58 D6 Scridain, L Strathclyde Scotland
80 G2 Scritto Italy 43.14N 12.33E
12 A6 Scrivener Dam Canberra Australia 35.18S 149.05E
79 E5 Scrivia R Italy
57 L6 Scrooby Notts Eng 53.25N 1.01W
99 H10 Scudder Ontario 41.47N 82.39W
99 M8 Scugog, L Ontario
12 A5 Scullin dist Canberra Australia
57 M5 Scunthorpe Humberside Eng 53.35N 0.39W
66 S4 Scuol Switzerland 46.48N 10.18E
80 H4 Scurcola Marsicana Italy 42.04N 13.20E
81 M5 Scuro, Mte Italy 39.20N 16.24E
58 B4 Scurrival Pt Barra, W Isles Scotland 57.04N 7.28W
87 N5 Scusciuban Somalia 10.18N 50.12E
Scutari see Üsküdar
Scutari Albaniasee Shkodër
Scutari L see Skadarsko Jezero L
58 U11 Scuthvie B Orkney Scotland 59.18N 2.25W
61 L5 Scy Belgium 50.18N 5.13E
118 G10 Sé dist São Paulo Brazil
105 K1 Seaboard N Carolina 36.30N 77.27W
14 C9 Seabrook, L W Australia
14 C7 Seabrook, Mt W Australia 25.30S 117.41E
103 G5 Sea Cliff Long I, N Y 40.52N 73.39W
11 E12 Seacliff New Zealand 45.41S 170.39E
12 A9 Seacliff dist Adelaide, S Australia
112 L7 Seadrift Texas 28.25N 96.44W
12 G7 Sea Elephant B King I, Tasmania
104 K8 Seaford Delaware 38.39N 75.35W
56 M6 Seaford E Sussex Eng 50.46N 0.06E
99 J9 Seaforth Ontario 43.33N 81.24W
14 C3 Seaforth W Australia 32.06S 116.00E
58 C3 Seaforth, L Lewis, W Isles Scotland
100 O4 Seager Wheeler L Saskatchewan
112 E3 Seagraves Texas 32.56N 102.35W
105 H2 Seagrove N Carolina 35.32N 79.46W
57 L3 Seaham Durham Eng 54.50N 1.20W
98 G1 Seahorse Newfoundland/Labrador 52.11N 65.44W
19 H6 Seahorse Bank Philippines 10.48N 117.50E
97 L5 Seahorse Pt N W Terr 63.45N 80.10W
57 K1 Seahouses Northumb Eng 55.35N 1.38W
101 G11 Sea I Br Col 49.12N 123.11W
105 F6 Sea I Georgia 31.11N 81.21W
103 E8 Sea Isle City New Jersey 39.09N 74.47W
56 M5 Seal Kent Eng 51.17N 0.14E
12 G6 Sea L Victoria 35.31S 142.54E
97 K6 Seal R Manitoba
96 B15 Seal B Tristan da Cunha 37.09S 12.18W
111 E10 Seal Beach California 33.45N 118.05W
98 R1 Seal Bight Labrador, Nfld 52.27N 55.40W
113 H9 Seal C Alaska 56.00N 158.30W
95 G10 Seal, C S Africa 34.07S 23.24E
116 J4 Seal Cays islds Caicos Is W I 21.10N 71.40W
98 F9 Seal Cove New Brunswick 44.38N 66.52W
98 Q4 Seal Cove Newfoundland 49.57N 56.22W
107 L9 Seale Alabama 32.17N 85.11W
114 A1 Seal I Hawaiian Is 27.55N 176.15W
104 R3 Seal I Maine 43.53N 68.46W
11 F9 Seal I New Zealand 42.02S 171.22E
95 B10 Seal I S Africa 34.08S 18.35E
121 E10 Sea Lion Is Falkland Is
12 H7 Seal Is Victoria 38.52S 146.40E
101 T3 Seal L N W Terr
11 N13 Seal Pt Dunedin New Zealand 45.54S 170.37E
95 H10 Seal Pt S Africa 34.14S 24.50E
11 B13 Seal Pt Stewart I New Zealand 47.13S 167.52E
110 A5 Seal Rock Oregon 44.30N 124.04W
111 A9 Seal Rocks islds California 37.46N 122.31W
112 L6 Sealy Texas 29.48N 96.09W
11 E10 Sealy, Mt New Zealand 43.48S 170.01E
11 E10 Sealy Pass New Zealand 43.25S 170.33E
111 J4 Seaman Ra Nevada
57 N4 Seamer N Yorks Eng 54.14N 0.27W
58 G7 Sea Mill Strathclyde Scotland 55.41N 4.52W
94 P11 Sea Point dist Cape Town S Africa
76 B5 Seara Portugal 41.44N 8.37W
111 K6 Searchlight Nevada 35.28N 114.55W
99 F6 Searchmont Ontario 46.47N 84.05W
107 E6 Searcy Arkansas 35.14N 91.43W
111 G6 Searles California 35.30N 117.36W
111 G6 Searles L California 35.45N 117.20W
102 G6 Searles Lake California
104 R2 Searsport Maine 44.27N 68.56W
98 N6 Searston Newfoundland 47.50N 59.20W
57 G4 Seascale Cumbria Eng 54.24N 3.29W
111 C5 Seaside California 36.36N 121.50W
110 B4 Seaside Oregon 45.59N 123.54W
103 F7 Seaside Heights New Jersey 39.56N 74.05W
103 F7 Seaside Park New Jersey 39.55N 74.05W
57 G3 Seatoller Cumbria Eng 54.31N 3.10W
56 E6 Seaton Devon Eng 50.43N 3.05W
57 K2 Seaton Burn Tyne and Wear Eng 55.03N 1.37W
57 K2 Seaton Delaval Northumb Eng 55.04N 1.31W
57 L2 Seaton Sluice Northumb Eng 55.05N 1.28W
11 D6 Seatoun dist Wellington New Zealand
103 A9 Seat Pleasant Maryland 38.54N 76.54W
110 C2 Seattle Washington 47.35N 122.20W
101 D5 Seattle, Mt Yukon/Alaska 60.03N 139.12W
13 H4 Seaview Ra Queensland
11 H9 Seaward Kaikoura Ra New Zealand
122 U1 Seaward Roads channel Midway Is Pacific Oc 28.13N 177.25W
116 P6 Seawell airport Barbados 13.05N 59.30W
19 B9 Seba Indonesia 10.29S 121.54E
74 K9 Sebaa Rous hills Algeria
100 C5 Seba Beach Alberta 53.34N 114.43W
115 L3 Sebaco Nicaragua 12.51N 86.08W
104 P3 Sebago L Maine
18 J6 Sebajan, Bukit hill Borneo Indon 1.09S 110.58E
18 M6 Sebakung Borneo Indon 1.36S 116.30E
92 E11 Sebakwe R Zimbabwe
60 O7 Sebaldeburen Netherlands 53.13N 6.18E
18 D5 Sebanga Sumatra Indon 1.15N 101.20E
25 H4 Se Bang Fai R Laos
25 K4 Se Bang Hieng R Laos
18 F5 Sebangka isld Indonesia
Sebastea anc site see Sivas
105 G10 Sebastian Florida 27.50N 80.29W
112 K9 Sebastian Texas 26.21N 97.49W
121 D3 Sebastián Elcano Argentina 30.09S 63.35W
115 B3 Sebastián Vizcaíno, B Mexico
104 Q2 Sebasticook R Maine
104 Q2 Sebasticook L Maine 44.52N 69.15W
111 B3 Sebastopol California 38.23N 122.50W
107 G9 Sebastopol Mississippi 32.33N 89.20W
18 M3 Sebatik isld Kalimantan/Sabah
18 K4 Sebauh Sarawak Malaysia 3.10N 113.16E
89 K5 Sebba Upper Volta 13.35N 0.32E
53 D3 Sebbersund Denmark 56.58N 9.35E
87 F3 Sebderat Ethiopia 15.25N 36.40E
88 N4 Sebdou Algeria 34.37N 1.21W
91 C4 Sébé R Gabon
18 J5 Sebedau Borneo Indon 0.02N 111.06E
108 P3 Sebeka Minnesota 46.38N 95.03W
89 E5 Sébékoro Mali 12.58N 9.00W
36 F2 Seben Turkey 40.25N 31.36E
Sebenico see Šibenik
Seberey see Sevrey
115 D4 Seberi, Cerro pk Mexico 27.48N 110.13W
65 N7 Sebersdorf Austria 47.13N 16.00E
82 H5 Sebeş Romania 45.58N 23.34E
18 F8 Sebesi isld Indonesia 5.58S 105.30E
82 H5 Sebeşul R Romania
82 H5 Sebesului, Munţii mts Romania
39 B2 Sebetka Chibagalakhskiy Khrebet ra U.S.S.R.
106 L6 Sebewaing Michigan 43.44N 83.26W
46 G2 Sebezh U.S.S.R. 56.16N 28.25E
Sebha see Sabhah
37 D5 Şebinkarahisar Turkey 40.19N 38.25E
82 G4 Şebiş Romania 46.22N 22.06E
88 F9 Sebjet Aarred salt L Morocco 26.00N 14.12W
88 F11 Sebjet Afuidich salt L Mauritania
88 F10 Sebjet Agreich salt L Mauritania
88 G9 Sebjet Agsumal salt L Morocco
88 G8 Sebjet Agueneiguin salt L Morocco
88 G8 Sebjet Aridal salt L Morocco
88 F10 Sebjet Doloo Esder salt L Mauritania
88 G10 Sebjet Dumus salt L Mauritania
88 F10 Sebjet El Cursiat salt L Mauritania
89 A1 Sebjet el Mahariat salt L Mauritania 22.15N 16.32W
89 A1 Sebjet Fares salt L Mauritania 22.30N 16.20W
88 G10 Sebjet Galb Um Dueial salt L Mauritania
89 A1 Sebjet Lemheiris salt L Mauritania 22.09N 16.49W
89 C1 Sebjet Lemmuilha salt L Mauritania 22.00N 13.15W
88 G10 Sebjet Saasaiat salt L Morocco
89 A1 Sebjet Tenmud salt L Mauritania 21.50N 16.36W
88 F10 Sebjet Tennuaca salt L Mauritania
88 E10 Sebjet Tentuatalet salt L Mauritania
88 F10 Sebjet Tidsit salt L Mauritania
88 G8 Sebjet Um Deboaa salt L Morocco
74 F9 Sebkha bou Areq L Morocco
88 M4 Sebkha bou Areq Saïdia salt L Morocco
78 C13 Sebkhat Kelbia salt L Tunisia 35.50N 10.17E
88 G10 Sebkhet Idjil Mauritania
88 Q5 Sebkhet Safioune salt L Algeria
88 K8 Sebkra salt L Algeria
88 H9 Sebkra salt L Mauritania
88 L8 Sebkra Aïne Belbela salt L Algeria
88 O8 Sebkra Azz el Matti salt L Algeria
89 C1 Sebkra de Chinchane salt flats Mauritania
89 D1 Sebkra d'El Iteha salt lakes Mauritania 22.13N 11.18W
89 B2 Sebkra de Ndaghamcha salt L Mauritania 18.30N 15.55W
88 O7 Sebkra de Timimoun salt L Algeria
88 G10 Sebkra de Timjati Mauritania
88 K8 Sebkra de Tindouf salt L Algeria
88 N4 Sebkra d'Oran Algeria
88 N7 Sebkra el Mellah salt L Algeria
88 S4 Sebkra en Noual salt L Algeria
88 O8 Sebkra Mekerrhane salt L Algeria
88 H9 Sebkra Oum el Drouss Guebli Mauritania
88 H9 Sebkra Oum el Drouss Telli salt L Mauritania
88 T4 Sebkra Sidi el Hani salt L Algeria 35.20N 10.20E
18 D7 Seblat Sumatra Indonesia 3.13S 101.39E
18 D7 Seblat R Sumatra Indonesia
18 E7 Seblat, Gunung mt Sumatra Indonesia 2.52S 102.08E
62 H5 Sebnitz E Germany 50.59N 14.18E
104 P8 Sebodmook Maine 45.55N 69.45W
104 R1 Seboeis L Maine 45.28N 68.54W
69 F4 Seboncourt France 49.57N 3.31E
104 P8 Seboomook L Maine
88 L5 Sebou R Morocco
107 J4 Sebree Kentucky 37.36N 87.31W
104 H10 Sebrell Virginia 36.47N 77.08W
105 F10 Sebring Florida 27.30N 81.28W
104 D6 Sebring Ohio 40.56N 81.01W
46 N4 Sebryakovo U.S.S.R. 50.02N 43.18E
88 Q6 Sebseb watercourse Algeria
18 M3 Sebuku Borneo Indon 4.01N 117.01E
18 M7 Sebuku isld Borneo Indon
18 M4 Sebuku R Borneo Indon
18 M4 Sebuku, Teluk B Borneo Indon
18 J5 Sebuyau Sarawak Malaysia 1.30N 110.54E
41 G6 Sebyaki, Ozero L U.S.S.R.
65 N2 Seč Pardubice Czech 49.52N 15.40E
64 P4 Seč Plzeň Czech 49.35N 13.30E
75 M5 Secá, Embalse de res Spain 41.30N 0.31E
121 B10 Seca, L Argentina
76 K6 Seca, La Spain 41.25N 4.55W
76 E4 Seca, Sierra mts Spain
119 A4 Secas, Is Panama 7.59N 82.06W
103 J7 Secaucus New Jersey 40.48N 74.04W
118 J8 Secca, I Brazil 22.51S 43.11W
78 C4 Secchia R La Spezia Italy
79 J5 Secchia R Modena Italy
105 E3 Secession L S Carolina 34.19N 82.37E
25 H4 Se Cham, R Laos
31 A4 Sechchah Post Afghanistan 32.39N 61.03E
98 C1 Séchelles, L Quebec
101 M11 Sechelt Pen Br Columbia
45 R1 Sechenovo U.S.S.R. 55.14N 45.55E
Secher see Sesher
119 B10 Sechura Peru 5.39S 80.50W
119 A10 Sechura, B. de Peru
119 B11 Sechura, Des. de Peru
80 K5 Secine, Monte Italy 41.43N 14.10E
65 L7 Seckau Austria 47.17N 14.48E
65 L7 Seckauer Alpen mts Austria
69 E2 Séclin France 50.33N 3.02E
121 L7 Seco R Argentina
76 F7 Seco R Portugal
75 L6 Seco R Spain
121 K7 Seco, L Argentina
72 D2 Secondigny France 46.37N 0.24W
104 O1 Second L New Hampshire
89 O11 Secos, Is Cape Verde 15.10N 24.40W
62 N7 Sečovce Czechoslovakia 48.42N 21.40E
79 P4 Sečovlje Yugoslavia 45.28N 13.37E
100 L8 Secretan Saskatchewan 50.30N 106.28W
11 A12 Secretary I New Zealand
28 D2 Secunderabad Andhra Prad India 17.27N 78.27E
120 F6 Sécure, R Bolivia
62 L8 Séd R Hungary
75 M5 Sed R Spain
46 D2 Seda Lithuania U.S.S.R. 56.10N 22.02E
76 D10 Seda Portugal 39.11N 7.46W
76 D10 Seda R Portugal
19 C9 Sedah Indonesia 10.46S 123.16E
100 G7 Sedalia Alberta 51.40N 110.39W
109 F2 Sedalia Colorado 39.25N 104.57W
107 H5 Sedalia Kentucky 36.39N 88.37W
107 C3 Sedalia Missouri 38.42N 93.15W
104 B7 Sedalia Ohio 39.44N 83.28W
69 H4 Sedan France 49.42N 4.57E
109 O4 Sedan Kansas 37.07N 96.11W
109 G5 Sedan New Mexico 36.08N 103.07W
12 E5 Sedan S Australia 34.34S 139.19E
39 F5 Sedanka U.S.S.R. 57.39N 159.00E
113 D10 Sedanka I Aleutian Is 53.50N 166.10W
42 G4 Sedannovskaya, Shiv falls U.S.S.R. 56.50N 101.25E
75 C2 Sedano Spain 42.42N 3.44W
57 H4 Sedbergh Cumbria Eng 54.20N 2.31W
87 G6 Seddisto Ethiopia 9.13N 39.40E
11 J8 Seddon New Zealand 41.42S 174.06E
97 O2 Seddon, Kap C Greenland 75.20N 58.20W
11 G8 Seddonville New Zealand 41.33S 172.00E
37 B3 Seddülbahir Turkey 40.03N 26.12E
35 C10 Sede Boqer Israel 30.53N 34.47E
35 B7 Sede Dawid Israel 31.36N 34.41E
39 E2 Sededema R U.S.S.R.
35 F1 Sede Eli'ezer Israel 33.03N 35.34E
35 F4 Sede Eliyyahu Israel 32.27N 35.31E
37 G2 Sedef isld Turkey 40.52N 29.09E
79 N2 Sedegliano Italy 46.02N 12.59E
32 E5 Sedeh Fārs Iran 30.47N 52.10E
32 H4 Sedeh Khorāsān Iran 33.18N 59.12E
35 E2 Sede Ilan Israel 32.45N 35.25E
77 H7 Sedella Spain 36.51N 4.02W
47 M7 Sedel'nikovo U.S.S.R. 56.58N 75.15E
35 C7 Sede Moshe Israel 31.37N 34.48E
35 E3 Sede Nahum Israel 32.32N 35.29E
35 F1 Sede Nehemya Israel 33.11N 35.37E
71 H8 Séderon France 44.12N 5.32E
35 B7 Sederot Israel 31.31N 34.35E
35 E4 Sede Terumot Israel 32.26N 35.29E
35 B8 Sede Zevi Israel 31.27N 34.43E
56 H3 Sedgeberrow Hereford & Worcs Eng 52.02N 1.58W
57 L3 Sedgefield Durham Eng 54.39N 1.26W
56 G2 Sedgeley W Midlands Eng 52.33N 2.08W
56 F5 Sedgemoor moorland Somerset Eng
100 F6 Sedgewick Alberta 52.48N 111.41W
109 H1 Sedgwick Colorado 40.56N 102.33W
109 N4 Sedgwick Kansas 37.56N 97.26W
104 R2 Sedgwick Maine 44.19N 68.39W
30 H7 Sedha Bihar India 25.18N 84.25E
89 B5 Sedhiou Senegal 12.44N 15.30W
79 M2 Sédico Italy 46.07N 12.06E
18 E10 Sedili Kechil, Tg C Pen Malaysia 1.51N 104.10E
81 B3 Sedilo Sardinia 40.11N 8.55E
81 B2 Sedini Sardinia 40.52N 8.48E
65 K2 Sedlčany Czechoslovakia 49.40N 14.26E
64 Q3 Sedlec Severočeský Czech 50.29N 13.43E
65 M2 Sedlec Stredočeský Czech 49.58N 15.18E
65 L2 Sedlec Prčice Czechoslovakia 49.34N 14.32E
56 N6 Sedlescombe E Sussex Eng 50.56N 0.32E
100 O8 Sedley Saskatchewan 50.10N 104.00W
65 J3 Sedlice Czechoslovakia 49.23N 13.57E
45 C5 Sednev Ukraine U.S.S.R. 51.38N 31.35E
35 E9 Sedom Israel 31.04N 35.23E
35 E9 Sedom, Har hills Israel
111 N7 Sedona Arizona 34.53N 111.45W
25 H5 Se Done R Laos
35 C7 Sedot Mikha Israel 31.44N 34.55E
35 C4 Sedot Yam Israel 32.30N 34.54E
41 F2 Sedova, Arkhipelag islds U.S.S.R.
41 A3 Sedova, Pik pk Novaya Zemlya U.S.S.R. 73.29N 55.00E
41 B2 Sedova, Zaliv gulf Novaya Zemlya U.S.S.R. 74.13N 59.41E
88 R3 Sédrata Algeria 36.06N 7.31E
79 E4 Sedriano Italy 45.29N 8.58E
110 C1 Sedro Woolley Washington 48.30N 122.15W
66 M5 Sedrun Switzerland 46.41N 8.47E
46 E2 Seduva Lithuania U.S.S.R. 55.42N 23.46E
65 H6 See Austria 47.49N 13.27E
70 H4 See R France
66 O2 Seealpsee L Switzerland 47.16N 9.24E
65 K7 Seebach Austria 47.11N 14.03E
66 L2 Seebach Switzerland 47.25N 8.33E
63 U5 Seebad Ahlbeck Rostock E Germany 53.56N 14.12E
63 U5 Seebad Heringsdorf E Germany 53.58N 14.10E
63 M4 Seebad Laboe W Germany 54.24N 10.13E
63 N4 Seebad Neustadt Schleswig Holstein W Germany 54.06N 10.48E
63 N4 Seebad Neustadt W Germany 54.06N 10.48E
100 C7 Seebe Alberta 51.10N 114.59W
66 G3 Seeberg Switzerland 47.10N 7.41E
64 K2 Seebergen E Germany 50.55N 10.48E
65 L9 Seeberg-sattel pass Austria 46.26N 14.31E
64 N8 Seebruck W Germany 47.56N 12.29E
64 E8 Seebrugg W Germany 47.47N 8.12E
63 P10 Seeburg E Germany 51.30N 11.42E
66 L4 Seedorf Switzerland 46.53N 8.37E
63 T7 Seefeld E Germany 52.38N 13.42E
65 O4 Seefeld Nieder-Österreich Austria 48.44N 16.11E
65 D7 Seefeld Tirol Austria 47.21N 11.12E
64 D8 Seefelden W Germany 47.52N 7.39E
59 E7 Seefin mt Cork Irish Rep 52.02N 8.56W
59 C7 Seefin mt Kerry Irish Rep 52.03N 9.55W
59 G7 Seefin mt Waterford Irish Rep 52.13N 7.36W
64 K8 Seeg W Germany 47.39N 10.36E
65 J6 Seehaus Austria 47.45N 13.58E
63 O8 Seehausen Magdeburg E Germany 52.07N 11.18E
63 T6 Seehausen Neubrandenburg E Germany 53.13N 13.53E
63 P7 Seehausen (Altmark) Magdeburg E Germany 52.54N 11.45E
94 D6 Seeheim Namibia 26.50S 17.45E
64 F4 Seeheim W Germany 49.46N 8.40E
66 F5 Seehorn mt Switzerland 46.34N 7.28E
94 D4 Seeis Namibia 22.29S 17.39E
65 H6 Seekirchen Austria 47.54N 13.08E
95 F9 Seekoegat S Africa 33.05S 22.30E
95 H6 Seekoei R S Africa
94 Q12 Seekoeivlei pond Cape Town S Africa 34.03S 18.31E
103 M3 Seekonk Massachusetts 41.48N 71.20W
66 E3 Seeland reg Switzerland
64 D7 Seelbach W Germany 48.20N 7.56E
110 M2 Seeley Lake Montana 47.12N 113.30W
99 O8 Seeleys Bay Ontario 44.28N 76.16W
123 G10 Seelig, Mt Antarctica 82.30S 103.00W
64 N2 Seelingstädt Gera E Germany 50.46N 12.14E
64 O1 Seelingstädt Leipzig E Germany 51.16N 12.43E
66 L4 Seelisberg Switzerland 46.58N 8.36E
64 C2 Seelscheid W Germany 50.51N 7.18E
103 D3 Seelyville Pennsylvania 41.35N 75.18W
53 B6 Seem Denmark 55.19N 8.50E
66 M2 Seen Switzerland 47.28N 8.46E
56 G5 Seend Wilts Eng 51.21N 2.05W
66 J2 Seengen Switzerland 47.20N 8.12E
64 P1 Seerhausen E Germany 51.16N 13.15E
70 L4 Sées France 48.36N 0.10E
63 H3 Seesand sandbank W Germany
63 M9 Seesen W Germany 51.54N 10.11E
64 L8 Seeshaupt W Germany 47.49N 11.18E
65 L7 Seetaler Alpen Austria
65 J7 Seethal Austria 47.10N 13.56E
66 L3 Seewen Schwyz Switz 47.02N 8.38E
66 G2 Seewen Solothurn Switz 47.27N 7.39E
65 M6 Seewiesen Austria 47.38N 15.17E
65 P6 Seewinkel reg Austria
66 P4 Seewis Switzerland 46.58N 9.39E
71 K5 Séez France 45.37N 6.49E
66 O3 Seez R Switzerland
66 O3 Seez Tal V Switzerland
Şefaatli see Kızılkoca
89 C7 Sefadu Sierra Leone 8.39N 10.58W
36 B4 Seferihisar Turkey 38.11N 26.50E
88 N8 Sefiat Djedid Algeria 27.22N 0.41W
32 D4 Sēfīd Dasht Iran 32.13N 51.14E
32 D5 Sefīd,Kūh-e mts Khuzestān Iran
32 C4 Sefīd, Kūh-e mt Lorestān Iran 33.38N 48.04E
74 G10 Sefioun R Algeria
80 G2 Sefro Italy 43.09N 12.57E
88 L5 Sefrou Morocco 33.50N 4.50W
11 G10 Sefton New Zealand 43.14S 172.42E
11 E10 Sefton, Mt New Zealand 43.44S 170.03E
87 J7 Segag Ethiopia 7.40N 42.49E
72 H9 Ségala, le France 43.20N 1.50E
72 J7 Ségalas reg France
52 E5 Segalstad Norway 61.14N 10.14E
18 N3 Segama R Sabah Malaysia
18 C9 Segamat Pen Malaysia 2.30N 102.48E
18 H9 Segara Andkan lagoon Java Indon
82 H6 Segarcea Romania 44.06N 23.43E
89 L6 Segbana Benin 10.56N 3.42E
89 D8 Segbwema Sierra Leone 7.59N 10.50W
15 B5 Sege Irian Jaya 2.11S 132.16E
44 L4 Segendy Kazakhstan U.S.S.R. 43.50N 51.02E
19 A6 Segeri Celebes Indon 4.41S 119.35E
81 E8 Segesta ruins Sicily 37.57N 12.51E
15 A4 Seget Irian Jaya 1.25S 130.59E
35 D2 Segev Israel 32.52N 35.15E
47 C4 Segezha U.S.S.R. 63.42N 34.19E
39 B4 Seginel-yy U.S.S.R. 61.20N 137.07E
43 H4 Segiz, Ozera L Kazakhstan U.S.S.R.
Segl see Sils-Baselgia
Segl see Sils-Maria
70 D5 Seglien France 48.06N 3.10W
66 N4 Segnes Pass Switzerland 46.54N 9.13E
80 H5 Segni Italy 41.42N 13.02E
111 P2 Sego Utah 39.03N 109.42W
72 D4 Segonzac France 45.37N 0.13W
75 K8 Segorbe Spain 39.51N 0.30W
89 F5 Ségou Mali 13.28N 6.18W
119 D4 Segovia Colombia 7.08N 74.39W
76 L7 Segovia Spain 40.57N 4.07W
112 H5 Segovia Texas 30.25N 99.41W
74 E3 Segovia prov Spain
Segovia R see Coco R
47 C4 Segozero, Ozero L U.S.S.R.
70 J6 Segré France 47.41N 0.51W
75 M4 Segre R Spain
70 L5 Segrie France 48.11N 0.01E
113 S9 Seguam I Aleutian Is 52.20N 172.30W
113 S9 Seguam Pass Aleutian Is
90 F1 Seguedine Niger 20.09N 12.55E
89 F8 Séguéla Ivory Coast 7.58N 6.44W
89 C1 Seguelil watercourse Mauritania
109 K2 Seguin Kansas 39.20N 100.35W
115 J5 Seguín Mexico 25.29N 101.46W
112 K6 Seguin Texas 29.34N 97.58W
35 C7 Segula Israel 31.40N 34.47E
113 O9 Segula I Aleutian Is 52.00N 178.08E
76 F4 Segundera, Sierra mts Spain
109 F4 Segundo Colorado 37.08N 104.44W
121 E3 Segundo R Argentina
18 M5 Seguntur Borneo Indon 1.56N 117.50E
72 K7 Ségur France 44.18N 2.50E
76 F9 Segura Portugal 39.50N 6.59W
77 L4 Segura R Spain
77 N4 Segura R Spain
77 L4 Segura de la Sierra Spain 38.18N 2.39W
77 C4 Segura de León Spain 38.07N 6.32W
75 J6 Segura de los Baños Spain 40.56N 0.57W
77 L4 Segura, Sierra de mts Spain
76 K8 Segurilla Spain 40.02N 4.53W
72 G5 Ségur le Château France 45.26N 1.18E
29 L2 Sehara W Bengal India 23.05N 87.49E
Seh Deh see Sedeh
63 L4 Sehestedt W Germany 54.22N 9.49E
Sehhamza see Bahemdan
94 G3 Sehithwa Botswana 20.28S 22.43E
Sehkuheh see Sekūheh
Sehlabad see Sahlābād
95 N5 Sehlabathebe Lesotho 29.52S 29.05E
63 L8 Sehnde W Germany 52.19N 9.59E
19 D4 Seho isld Moluccas Indon 2.00S 124.20E
29 E6 Sehore Madhya Prad India 23.12N 77.08E
29 E6 Sehore dist Madhya Prad India
89 B3 Sehout el Ma Mauritania 16.52N 15.19W
32 H4 Seh Qal'eh Iran 33.40N 58.25E
31 D7 Sehwan Pakistan 26.26N 67.52E
76 D8 Seia Portugal 40.25N 7.42W
76 D8 Seia R Portugal
110 B8 Seiad Valley California 41.51N 123.11W
64 L3 Seibelsdorf W Germany 50.13N 11.25E
109 H2 Seibert Colorado 39.17N 102.52W
82 J4 Seica Mare Romania 46.01N 24.07E
70 H6 Seiche R France
70 K6 Seiches France 47.35N 0.21W
35 D4 Seidā Jordan 32.23N 35.07E
51 N1 Seida Norway 70.13N 28.07E
35 F3 Seidur Jordan 32.37N 35.42E
64 P2 Seiffen E Germany 50.39N 13.28E
90 K6 Seifou Chad 11.15N 21.36E
85 N8 Seiga, Gebel mt Egypt 22.38N 34.20E
13 E4 Seigals Creek N Terr Australia 17.35S 137.33E
71 K5 Seigne, Col. de la pass France/Italy 45.46N 6.49E
69 F8 Seignelay France 47.55N 3.36E
98 C1 Seignelay, R Quebec
72 K7 Seigné, Mt France 44.13N 2.55E
34 H2 Seigneur Tahtâni Syria 36.50N 40.34E
72 B8 Seignosse France 43.42N 1.22W
71 K8 Seignus, le France 44.14N 6.37E
66 L8 Seih, Wâdi watercourse Egypt
20 D3 Seijō dist Tōkyō Japan
25 C2 Seikpyu Burma 20.51N 94.48E
25 C2 Seiktein Burma 21.02N 95.13E
58 E6 Seil isld Strathclyde Scotland 56.17N 5.37W
86 E7 Seila Egypt 29.21N 30.58E
50 F3 Seila Iceland 65.33N 19.30W
51 K1 Seiland isld Norway 70.25N 23.10E
72 H5 Seilhac France 45.22N 1.42E
109 M5 Seiling Oklahoma 36.09N 98.56W
69 L6 Seille R Moselle France
71 F3 Seille R Saône-et-Loire France
61 L4 Seilles Belgium 50.30N 5.05E
53 S17 Seim Hordaland Norway 60.37N 5.16E
53 V17 Seim Hordaland Norway 60.35N 6.42E
53 X16 Seimsdal Norway 61.15N 7.38E
51 K9 Seinäjoki Finland 62.45N 22.55E
69 E7 Seine R France
70 K2 Seine, B. de la France
67 G4 Seine-et-Marne dept France
67 F3 Seine-Maritime dept France
69 G7 'Seine', Rés France
69 C6 Seine-St. Denis dept France
90 M5 Seingo Sudan 12.30N 24.34E
82 H3 Seini Romania 47.45N 23.18E
70 A5 Sein, I. de France 48.02N 4.51W
18 H5 Seipenyu Borneo Indonesia 0.15N 109.07E
34 E5 Seiqal, Khabrat es salt marsh Syria
72 F9 Seissan France 43.29N 0.36E
65 L5 Seitenstetten Austria 48.03N 14.40E
90 H6 Seitla Chad 11.25N 16.30E
47 M6 Seitova U.S.S.R. 55.14N 60.24E
44 J1 Seitovka U.S.S.R. 46.43N 48.05E
121 H3 Seival Brazil 31.27S 53.45W
72 G10 Seix France 42.51N 1.10E
96 P7 Seixal Madeira Is 32.48N 17.08W
76 A11 Seixal Portugal 38.38N 9.06W
76 B14 Seixe R Portugal
76 D8 Seixo da Beira Portugal 40.27N 7.52W
18 M7 Sejaka Borneo Indon 3.32S 116.15E
53 G5 Sejerø Denmark 55.53N 11.10E
53 G5 Sejerø isld Denmark 55.53N 11.10E
53 G5 Sejerø Bugt B Denmark
53 B3 Sejerslev Denmark 56.56N 8.53E
53 E3 Sejlflod Denmark 56.59N 10.07E
62 O1 Sejny Poland 54.07N 23.22E
53 D4 Sejs Denmark 56.08N 9.37E
53 B6 Sejstrup Denmark 55.27N 8.44E
45 P6 Sekachi U.S.S.R. 50.30N 43.37E
18 J5 Sekadau Kalimantan Indonesia 0.01N 110.51E
18 D9 Sekakap, Tg C Pen Malaysia 2.20N 103.56E
95 M6 Sekakes Lesotho 30.02S 28.21E
25 J5 Se Kamane R Laos
18 F6 Sekanak, Teluk B Sumatra Indon
93 D5 Sekanyonyi Uganda 0.30N 32.08E
93 G6 Sekauani mt Kenya 0.23S 35.04E
18 E7 Sekayu Sumatra Indon 2.50S 103.54E
93 E9 Seke Tanzania 3.20S 33.30E
91 J6 Seke Zaïre 5.08S 25.47E
91 C6 Seke Bama Zaïre 5.21S 13.17E
93 F10 Sekenke Tanzania 4.16S 34.09E
37 E8 Sekerli Turkey 37.34N 39.23E
87 G4 Seket Ethiopia 13.23N 39.53E
35 C9 Sekher watercourse Israel
20 K6 Seki Japan 35.30N 136.54E
18 J6 Sekima Borneo Indon 1.42S 111.35E
20 D2 Sekimachi dist Tōkyō Japan
18 F8 Sekincau mt Sumatra Indon 5.10S 104.25E
18 F8 Sekincau R Sumatra
37 G6 Sekir Dağ mt Turkey 39.40N 42.44E
82 L2 Sekiryany U.S.S.R. 48.25N 27.27E
53 X15 Sekkebreen glacier Norway 61.50N 7.36E
53 W13 Sekken Norway 62.39N 7.21E
94 G5 Sekoma Pan Botswana 24.41S 23.50E
89 J9 Sekondi Ghana 4.59N 1.43W
41 M7 Sekondya U.S.S.R. 66.40N 124.01E
25 J6 Se Kong R Cambodia
25 J5 Se Kong R Laos
65 O3 Sekoř mt Czechoslovakia 49.27N 16.25E
84 C6 Sékoula Greece 37.35N 21.53E
88 Q10 Seksen Ahni Algeria 23.32N 5.21E
42 C4 Sektinskoye U.S.S.R. 55.11N 81.22E
32 J5 Sekūheh Iran 30.44N 61.30E
52 E5 Sel Norway 61.49N 9.35E
84 C7 Séla Greece 37.12N 21.47E
89 G5 Sela Mali 13.37N 4.59W
24 F10 Se La pass Xizang Zizhiqu 30.18N 87.59E
50 L3 Selá R Iceland
18 D7 Selagan R Sumatra Indon
110 E3 Selah Washington 46.40N 120.31W
87 G5 Selakulla Ethiopia 10.10N 38.29E
18 J5 Selalang Sarawak Malaysia 2.00N 111.19E
18 A6 Selama Pen Malaysia 5.12N 100.40E
61 O8 Selange Belgium 49.37N 5.51E
18 B8 Selangor R Pen Malaysia
18 B8 Selangor state Pen Malaysia
25 J4 Se La Nong R Laos
51 M10 Selänpää Finland 61.04N 26.50E
15 L5 Selapiu I Bismarck Arch 2.40S 150.35E
18 E7 Selara Ladangpait Sumatra Indon 2.25S 103.40E
50 B3 Selárdalur Iceland 65.46N 23.49W
50 K3 Selárdalur V Múlasýsla, Nordhur Iceland
50 D3 Selárdalur V Strandasýsla Iceland
81 C5 Selargius Sardinia 39.16N 9.10E
15 A8 Selaru isld Moluccas Indon
15 B5 Selassi Irian Jaya 3.11S 132.42E
18 D7 Selatan isld Indonesia
18 L8 Selatan, Tg C Borneo Indon 4.09S 114.36E
88 Q4 Selat Djebel mt Algeria 35.25N 4.04E
18 B9 Selat Kering, Pulau isld Pen Malaysia
18 H6 Selatpampang Borneo Indon 0.15S 109.11E
18 E5 Selatpanjang Sumatra Indon 0.58N 102.40E
69 D14 Selat Sipora str Indonesia
113 H3 Selawik Alaska 66.35N 160.10W
113 H3 Selawik R Alaska
113 G3 Selawik L Alaska 66.30N 160.40W
75 C1 Selaya Spain 43.13N 3.48W
19 B7 Selayar isld Indonesia
64 N3 Selb W Germany 50.11N 12.08E
93 K4 Selberawawa Kenya 1.12N 38.04E
64 M3 Selbitz W Germany 50.18N 11.46E
53 S19 Selbjørn isld Norway 59.59N 5.12E
53 S19 Selbjørnfjord inlet Norway 59.57N 5.12E
56 K5 Selborne Hants Eng 51.06N 0.56W
66 M4 Selbsanft mt Switzerland 46.50N 8.59E
52 F3 Selbu Norway 63.14N 11.03E
52 F3 Selbusjøen L Norway
57 L5 Selby N Yorks Eng 53.48N 1.04W
108 K4 Selby S Dakota 45.30N 100.02W
113 K3 Selby, L Alaska 66.55N 155.40W
104 K8 Selbyville Delaware 38.28N 75.15W
Selçuk see Akıncılar
53 C3 Selde Denmark 56.48N 9.03E
109 K2 Selden Kansas 39.33N 100.34W
103 H5 Selden Long I, N Y 40.52N 73.03W
98 S4 Seldom Newfoundland 49.36N 54.10W
113 M7 Seldovia Alaska 59.29N 151.45W
15 A4 Sele Irian Jaya 1.22S 131.06E
80 M7 Sele R Italy
92 C13 Selebi-Pikwe Botswana 22.01S 27.50E
41 O6 Selebir U.S.S.R. 68.32N 132.38E
45 F4 Selechnya U.S.S.R. 52.23N 34.23E
94 U14 Selection Park S Africa 26.17S 28.26E
87 K5 Selei Somalia 10.12N 44.18E
92 J11 Selem Zanzibar 6.03S 39.14E
40 E5 Selemdzha R U.S.S.R.
40 E5 Selemdzhinsk U.S.S.R. 52.34N 131.05E
34 E3 Selemīya Syria 35.01N 37.02E
Sélémiyé see Selemīya
36 D4 Selendi Turkey 38.45N 28.52E
42 H6 Selenduma U.S.S.R. 50.55N 106.15E
15 B4 Selenek Irian Jaya 0.45S 132.09E
42 H6 Selenga R U.S.S.R.
93 J8 Selengai Kenya 2.11S 37.15E
22 F2 Selenge Mongolia 49.34N 104.15E
91 F4 Selenge Zaïre 1.58S 18.11E
22 G2 Selenge prov Mongolia
22 G2 Selenge Mörön R Mongolia
42 H6 Selenginsk U.S.S.R. 52.03N 106.43E
83 D4 Selenicë Albania 40.33N 19.39E
39 B1 Selennyakh R U.S.S.R.
63 M4 Selent W Germany 54.17N 10.26E
63 M4 Selenter See L W Germany
37 E6 Selepur Turkey 39.36N 39.50E
15 A4 Sele, Selat str Irian Jaya
69 N7 Sélestat France 48.16N 7.28E
51 H6 Selet Sweden 65.04N 21.00E
18 J2 Seletar Singapore 1.25N 103.52E
18 J2 Seletar R Singapore
18 J2 Seletar, Pulau isld Singapore
18 J2 Seletar Res Singapore
82 J3 Seletin U.S.S.R. 47.50N 25.12E
45 B3 Selets Belorussiya U.S.S.R. 53.51N 30.15E
43 L2 Selety R Kazakhstan U.S.S.R.
43 L1 Seletyteniz, Ozero L Kazakhstan U.S.S.R.
34 M5 Seleucia anc site Iraq 33.05N 44.35E
Seleucia anc site Turkeysee Silifke
Seleucia Pieria see Samandağ
36 E4 Selevir Barajı res Turkey 38.33N 30.45E
50 M5 Seley isld Iceland 64.59N 13.35W
45 C1 Selezni U.S.S.R. 55.39N 31.30E
45 U4 Seleznikha U.S.S.R. 52.15N 48.39E
50 G4 Selfjall mt Iceland 65.29N 18.49W
50 K2 Selfjöll mt Iceland 66.20N 15.44W
69 K1 Selfkant W Germany 51.01N 5.55E
50 L3 Selfljót R Iceland
50 E7 Selfoss Iceland 63.56N 20.59W
108 K3 Selfridge N Dakota 46.02N 100.57W
40 G7 Selgon U.S.S.R. 49.35N 135.26E
75 L4 Selgua Spain 41.56N 0.07E
55 F5 Selhurst London Eng 51.24N 0.06W
84 D5 Selianítika Greece 38.16N 22.01E
47 F4 Selib U.S.S.R. 63.42N 48.30E
89 C4 Sélibabi Mauritania 15.14N 12.11W
45 J8 Selidovo Ukraine U.S.S.R. 48.06N 37.16E
64 F3 Seligenstadt W Germany 50.02N 8.58E
46 J2 Seliger, Oz L U.S.S.R.
111 M6 Seligman Arizona 35.19N 112.52W
107 C5 Seligman Missouri 36.32N 93.58W
45 R3 Seliksa U.S.S.R. 53.14N 45.15E
74 K10 Selim Algeria 34.55N 3.44E
90 L9 Selim Cent Afr Rep 4.56N 23.41E
18 B8 Selim Pen Malaysia 3.50N 101.27E
37 G5 Selim Turkey 40.27N 42.46E
87 D4 Selima Sudan 13.01N 32.01E
85 K9 Selîma Oasis Sudan 21.22N 29.19E
18 K5 Selimbau Borneo Indon 0.36N 112.09E
36 E6 Selimiye Antalya Turkey 36.45N 31.23E
37 K2 Selimiye İstanbul Turkey 41.01N 29.02E
36 C5 Selimiye Muğla Turkey 37.22N 27.42E
18 B8 Selim River Pen Malaysia 3.48N 101.24E
44 H8 Selin R Iran
92 F12 Selinda, Mt Zimbabwe 20.24S 32.43E
94 G2 Selinda Spillway watercourse Botswana
84 D8 Selínitsa Greece 36.49N 22.18E
84 C6 Selinoús Greece 37.35N 21.37E
104 J6 Selinsgrove Pennsylvania 40.51N 76.51W
81 E8 Selinunte ruins Sicily 37.35N 12.50E
45 A1 Selishche Belorussiya U.S.S.R. 55.36N 29.44E
45 P2 Selishchi U.S.S.R. 54.29N 43.30E
45 T9 Selitrennoye U.S.S.R. 47.11N 47.28E
43 B1 Selit'va-Russkaya U.S.S.R. 53.48N 50.45E
45 N8 Selivanovskaya U.S.S.R. 48.50N 41.42E
47 L5 Seliyarovo U.S.S.R. 61.18N 70.10E
46 J2 Selizharovo U.S.S.R. 56.50N 33.31E
50 H7 Seljaland Skaftafellssýsla, Vestur Iceland 63.55N 17.50W
53 S14 Selje Norway 62.03N 5.22E
53 S14 Selje isld Norway 62.03N 5.18E
53 V19 Seljestad Norway 59.53N 6.40E
53 V19 Seljestadjuvet gorge Norway 59.51N 6.43E
52 D7 Seljord Norway 59.30N 8.40E
52 D7 Seljordsvatnet L Norway
63 O9 Selke R E Germany
57 H1 Selkirk Borders Scotland 55.33N 2.50W
109 J3 Selkirk Kansas 38.27N 101.34W
100 V8 Selkirk Manitoba 50.10N 96.52W
106 K5 Selkirk Michigan 44.19N 84.05W
99 L10 Selkirk Ontario 42.51N 79.54W
Selkirk co see Borders reg
100 S5 Selkirk I Manitoba
101 O10 Selkirk Mts Br Col
77 Q3 Sella Spain 38.37N 0.17W
76 J2 Sella R Spain
120 F9 Sella Cercado Bolivia 21.25S 64.45W
58 Q8 Sellafirth Shetland Scotland 60.40N 1.02W
79 L1 Sella Gruppo di mts Italy 46.31N 11.51E
88 Q3 Sellam R Algeria
87 B4 Sellama Sudan 12.51N 29.46E
50 H4 Sellandafjall mt Iceland 65.25N 17.03W
76 J2 Sellano Spain 43.15N 5.13W
84 D7 Sellasía Greece 37.10N 22.25E
70 G6 Sel, le France 47.55N 1.36W
69 C4 Selle R France
110 D2 Selleck Washington 47.22N 121.53W
116 J5 Selle, La mt Haiti 18.12N 71.59W
75 Q4 Sellera, La Spain 41.58N 2.37E
107 L3 Sellersburg Indiana 38.25N 85.46W
103 D6 Sellersville Pennsylvania 40.21N 75.19W
75 M3 Selles, Embalse de res Spain
70 O7 Selles-St. Denis France 47.23N 1.55E
72 H1 Selles-sur-Cher France 47.16N 1.33E
69 D7 Selle-sur-le-Bied, la France 48.04N 2.52E
Sellheim see Marlow
13 H5 Sellheim R Queensland
84 K11 Selliá Crete 35.12N 24.23E
71 H3 Sellières France 46.50N 5.34E
63 T4 Sellin E Germany 54.23N 13.41E
56 N5 Sellindge Kent Eng 51.07N 1.00E
60 R8 Sellingen Netherlands 52.57N 7.09E
50 J4 Sellönd reg Iceland
Sellore I Burmasee Saganthit Kyun
65 D7 Sellrain Austria 47.13N 11.14E
111 N10 Sells Arizona 31.55N 111.53W
40 E1 Sellyakait-Sellya, Vozvyshennost mts U.S.S.R.
41 Q5 Sellyakh R U.S.S.R.
41 P5 Sellyakhskaya Guba gulf U.S.S.R.
62 K10 Sellye Hungary 45.52N 17.51E
63 F9 Selm W Germany 51.42N 7.27E
107 J9 Selma Alabama 32.24N 87.01W
111 E5 Selma California 36.34N 119.38W
105 J2 Selma N Carolina 35.32N 78.18W
110 B7 Selma Oregon 42.18N 123.36W
107 H6 Selmer Tennessee 35.10N 88.34W
76 D12 Selmes Portugal 38.08N 7.45W
Selmi see Meşkinan
76 F3 Selmo R Spain
63 N5 Selmsdorf E Germany 53.53N 10.52E
84 Y20 Selmunett isld Malta 35.58N 14.25E
50 F3 Selnes Iceland 65.58N 19.56W
65 M8 Selnica Yugoslavia 46.33N 15.29E
61 H6 Seloignes Belgium 50.01N 4.15E
70 N6 Selommes France 47.46N 1.12E
66 D2 Seloncourt France 47.28N 6.53E
18 M10 Selong Indonesia 8.38S 116.30E
71 G1 Selongey France 47.36N 5.11E
71 J8 Sélonnet France 44.23N 6.18E
95 N1 Selonsrivier S Africa 25.37S 29.38E
74 F9 Selouane Morocco 35.04N 2.56W
88 M4 Selouáne Morocco 35.05N 3.00W
92 H6 Selous Game Reserve Tanzania
101 G4 Selous, Mt Yukon Terr 62.57N 132.29W
53 R17 Seløy I Norway
53 R17 Seløy isld Norway
26 S14 Sel Pt Mahé I Seychelles, Ind Oc 4.43S 55.32E
53 V16 Selseng Norway 61.20N 6.55E
56 K6 Selsey W Sussex Eng 50.44N 0.48W
56 K6 Selsey Bill prom W Sussex Eng 50.43N 0.48W
63 K6 Selsingen W Germany 53.23N 9.13E
53 J5 Selsø Denmark 55.45N 12.02E
56 O5 Selstead Kent Eng 51.09N 1.10E
50 D3 Selströnd coast Iceland
50 F7 Selsundsfjall mt Iceland 63.57N 19.50W
52 J3 Selsviken Sweden 63.10N 16.00E
64 D2 Selters W Germany 50.31N 7.45E
52 K3 Seltjärn Sweden 63.34N 18.00E
50 C6 Seltjarnarnes Iceland 64.09N 22.01W
45 F3 Sel'tso U.S.S.R. 53.22N 34.08E
53 M9 Selttenæs Faeroes 62.09N 7.15W
46 Q2 Selty U.S.S.R. 57.19N 52.12E
63 S5 Seltz E Germany 53.46N 13.14E
69 P6 Seltz France 48.54N 8.06E
15 A7 Selu isld Moluccas Indon
18 G7 Selui isld Indonesia 3.14S 107.30E
92 D11 Selukwe Zimbabwe 19.40S 30.00E
92 D11 Selukwe dist Zimbabwe
18 E8 Seluma Sumatra Indon 4.07S 102.30E

66 O3 **Selun** *mt* Switzerland 47.09N 9.16E
70 H4 **Selune** *R* France
121 E2 **Selva** Argentina 29.46S 62.02W
77 V14 **Selva** Balearic Is 39.45N 2.53E
79 L1 **Selva** Italy 46.33N 11.47E
79 M2 **Selva di Cadore** Italy 46.27N 12.03E
79 K3 **Selva di Progno** Italy 45.37N 11.09E
88 F6 **Selvagens, Ilhas** Atlantic Oc
75 N5 **Selva, La** Spain 41.13N 1.08E
32 A2 **Selvānā** Iran 37.24N 44.54E
72 K7 **Selve, la** France 44.06N 2.32E
50 F3 **Selvik** *inlet* Iceland
50 D7 **Selvogur** *reg* Iceland
110 K3 **Selway** *R* Idaho
13 F5 **Selwyn** Queensland 21.31S 140.30E
101 V5 **Selwyn L** N W Terr
101 H3 **Selwyn Mts** Yukon Terr
13 F5 **Selwyn Ra** Queensland
108 L2 **Selz** N Dakota 47.52N 99.52W
64 E4 **Selz** *R* W Germany
66 F3 **Selzach** Switzerland 47.13N 7.27E
65 K6 **Selzthal** Austria 47.33N 14.19E
92 G11 **Semacueza** Mozambique 19.12S 34.45E
15 B5 **Semai** *isld* Irian Jaya 3.09S 132.30E
70 L5 **Semallé** France 48.29N 0.10E
83 D4 **Seman** *R* Albania
18 A7 **Semanggol** Pen Malaysia 4.57N 100.36E
18 F8 **Semangka, Teluk** *B* Sumatra Indonesia
34 D2 **Semān, Jebel** *mts* Syria
100 N7 **Semans** Saskatchewan 51.22N 104.45W
18 J10 **Semanu** Java Indon 8.01S 110.39E
12 A7 **Semaphore Bay** S Australia 34.51S 138.29E
30 L7 **Semapur** Bihar India 25.32N 87.28E
18 J9 **Semarang** Java Indon 6.58S 110.29E
18 J6 **Semarangkai** Kalimantan Indonesia 0.000 110.22E
30 E8 **Semaria** Madhya Prad India 24.47N 81.08E
18 H5 **Sematan** Sarawak Malaysia 1.50N 109.44E
19 C9 **Semau** *isld* Indonesia 10.15S 123.25E
18 M6 **Semayang, Danau** *L* Borneo Indon
93 C6 **Sembabule** Uganda 0.04S 31.31E
71 D6 **Sembadel** France 45.17N 3.41E
18 M4 **Sembakung** *R* Borneo Indon
18 G2 **Sembawang** Singapore 1.27N 103.50E
18 J2 **Sembawang** *dist* Singapore
18 H2 **Sembawang** *R* Singapore
91 D3 **Sembé** Congo 1.38N 14.35E
89 C8 **Sembehun** Sierra Leone 7.54N 12.32W
28 E4 **Sembiem** Tamil Nadu India 13.07N 80.15E
18 C7 **Sembilan, Bukit** *hill* Pen Malaysia 4.24N 102.01E
18 H3 **Sembilan Str** Singapore
70 M6 **Semblançay** France 47.30N 0.35E
91 C7 **Sembo** *R* Angola
66 E7 **Sembrancher** Switzerland 46.05N 7.09E
18 D9 **Sembrong** *R* Pen Malaysia
37 H8 **Şemdinli** Turkey 37.18N 44.32E
87 C4 **Šemeih** Sudan 12.43N 30.53E
71 D3 **Semelay** France 46.52N 3.51E
36 F2 **Semen Dağ** *mt* Turkey
91 F5 **Semendua** Zaïre 3.10S 18.06E
36 J1 **Semenlik Göl** *L* Turkey
46 N2 **Semenov** U.S.S.R. 56.42N 44.30E
39 G5 **Semenova, Mys** *C* U.S.S.R. 58.59N 163.41E
45 D4 **Semenovka** Chernigov, Ukraine U.S.S.R. 52.08N 32.36E
45 E7 **Semenovka** Poltava, Ukraine U.S.S.R. 49.36N 33.10E
45 R6 **Semenovka** U.S.S.R. 50.29N 45.20E
44 E7 **Semenovka** Zaporozh'ye, Ukraine U.S.S.R. 47.20N 36.19E
46 O2 **Semenovo** U.S.S.R. 57.19N 45.41E
41 O4 **Semenovskiy, Ostrov** *isld* U.S.S.R. 74.15N 132.45E
46 M1 **Semenovskoye** Kostroma U.S.S.R. 57.42N 42.12E
66 M7 **Sementina** Switzerland 46.12N 8.59E
46 M1 **Sementsovo** U.S.S.R. 58.38N 40.20E
18 B9 **Semenyih** Pen Malaysia 2.56N 101.50E
89 K7 **Sémére** Benin 9.35N 1.28E
40 F5 **Semertak** U.S.S.R. 52.57N 132.32E
18 K10 **Semeru** *mts* Java Indon
81 B3 **Semestene** Sardinia 40.24N 8.44E
45 L9 **Semibalki** U.S.S.R. 47.01N 39.03E
113 L9 **Semichi Is** Aleutian Is
113 J8 **Semidi Is** Alaska
89 F8 **Sémien** Ivory Coast 7.41N 7.10W
47 E6 **Semigorodnyaya** U.S.S.R. 59.46N 40.10E
45 M9 **Semikarakorskiy** U.S.S.R. 47.31N 40.49E
45 O1 **Semilovo** U.S.S.R. 55.04N 42.12E
45 L5 **Semiluki** U.S.S.R. 51.44N 39.01E
62 J5 **Semily** Czechoslovakia 50.38N 15.20E
81 L7 **Seminara** Italy 38.20N 15.52E
107 G10 **Seminary** Mississippi 31.32N 89.30W
56 G5 **Semington** Wilts Eng 51.21N 2.10W
108 D7 **Seminoe Dam** Wyoming 42.09N 106.56W
108 D7 **Seminoe Res** Wyoming
109 O6 **Seminole** Oklahoma 35.15N 96.40W
112 E3 **Seminole** Texas 32.43N 102.39W
105 C7 **Seminole, L** Florida
42 D6 **Seminskiy Khrebet** *mts* U.S.S.R.
45 M2 **Semion** U.S.S.R. 54.04N 40.10E
66 M6 **Semione** Switzerland 46.25N 8.58E
43 G2 **Semiozernoye** Kazakhstan U.S.S.R. 52.22N 64.06E
42 L5 **Semiozernyy** U.S.S.R. 53.45N 120.28E
42 J7 **Semiozer'ye** U.S.S.R. 49.52N 110.25E
43 O2 **Semipalatinsk** Kazakhstan U.S.S.R. 50.26N 80.16E
43 H1 **Semipolka** Kazakhstan U.S.S.R. 54.08N 67.15E
45 B6 **Semipolki** Ukraine U.S.S.R. 50.43N 30.55E
19 K5 **Semirara** *isld* Philippines 12.05N 121.23E
19 K6 **Semirara Is** Philippines
32 D5 **Semirom** Iran 31.20N 51.50E
113 O10 **Semisopochnoi I** Aleutian Is 52.00N 179.40E
18 J5 **Semitau** Borneo Indon 0.30N 111.59E
43 N2 **Semiyarka** Kazakhstan U.S.S.R. 50.52N 78.23E
43 L2 **Semiz-Bugu** Kazakhstan U.S.S.R. 50.14N 74.50E
45 E1 **Semlevo** U.S.S.R. 55.04N 33.59E
93 B5 **Semliki** *R* Zaïre/Uganda
63 R4 **Semlow** E Germany 54.12N 12.41E
Semlyachik Tsentral'nyy *vol see* **Bol'shoy Semlyachik** *vol*
87 M7 **Sèmmade** Somalia 7.12N 48.32E
39 B4 **Semmedaban, Khrebet** *mts* U.S.S.R.
63 T7 **Semmelberg** *mt* E Germany 52.44N 13.56E
53 Y15 **Semmeltind** *mt* Norway 61.32N 8.26E
65 N6 **Semmering** Austria 47.38N 15.50E
65 N6 **Semmering** *pass* Austria
57 J4 **Semmer Water** *L* N Yorks Eng 54.17N 2.07W
61 E3 **Semmerzake** Belgium 50.57N 3.40E
85 L9 **Semna E** Sudan 21.31N 30.59E
32 E3 **Semnān** Iran 35.30N 53.25E
32 E3 **Semnān** *prov* Iran
85 L9 **Semna W** Sudan 21.29N 30.56E
33 A3 **Semna, Wâdi** *watercourse* Egypt
70 G6 **Semnon** *R* France
19 E4 **Semo** Halmahera Indon 0.07S 127.43E
61 L7 **Semois** *R* Belgium
61 N8 **Semois** *R* Belgium
91 F5 **Semondane** Zaïre 3.31S 18.24E
66 J3 **Sempach** Switzerland 47.08N 8.12E
66 J3 **Sempacher See** *L* Switzerland
79 P3 **Sempas** Yugoslavia 45.56N 13.44E
18 N3 **Semporna** Sabah Malaysia 4.27N 118.36E
80 H5 **Semprevisa, Monte** Italy 41.34N 13.06E
18 K10 **Sempu I** Indonesia 8.27S 112.44E
65 M7 **Semriach** Austria 47.14N 15.24E
66 D5 **Semsales** Switzerland 46.35N 6.56E
51 E5 **Semskfjell** *mt* Norway 66.41N 15.20E
117 B7 **Sem Tripa** Brazil 4.38S 54.04W
45 E4 **Semtsy** U.S.S.R. 52.50N 33.29E
93 F9 **Semu** *watercourse* Tanzania
18 K7 **Semuda** Borneo Indon 2.49S 112.54E
88 F10 **Semul** *reg* Mauritania
71 E2 **Semur-en Auxios** France 47.30N 4.20W
71 E4 **Semur-en-Brionnais** France 46.16N 4.05E
72 C4 **Semussac** France 45.36N 0.55W
92 D11 **Semwe** *R* Zimbabwe
47 E3 **Semzha** U.S.S.R. 66.09N 44.15E
41 J7 **Sen** *R* U.S.S.R.
120 E4 **Sena** Bolivia 11.35S 67.13W
32 D6 **Senā** Iran 28.26N 51.38E
92 G10 **Sena** Mozambique 17.26S 35.01E
75 K4 **Sena** Spain 41.43N 0.03W
117 G7 **Senador Pompeu** Brazil 5.30S 39.25W
87 G3 **Senafe** Ethiopia 14.43N 39.26E
18 D10 **Senai** Pen Malaysia 1.36N 103.38E
18 M2 **Senaja** Sabah Malaysia 6.46N 117.04E
15 F8 **Senajo** Irian Jaya 8.15S 140.44E
74 K10 **Senalba, Djebel** *mts* Algeria
79 J1 **Senales, Val di** *V* Italy
81 C2 **Senalonga, Pta** Sardinia 40.42N 9.19E
120 E3 **Sena Madureira** Brazil 9.05S 68.41W
26 U7 **Senanayake Samudra** *L* Sri Lanka
18 D10 **Senang** *isld* Singapore 1.10N 103.44E
92 A10 **Senanga** Zambia 16.09S 23.16E
69 B4 **Sénarpont** France 49.53N 1.44E
68 G5 **Sénart, Forêt de** France
71 G9 **Sénas** France 43.45N 5.05E
100 H9 **Senate** Saskatchewan 49.15N 109.45W
107 F5 **Senath** Missouri 36.08N 90.10W
107 G7 **Senatobia** Mississippi 34.35N 89.58W
20 J7 **Senboku** Japan 34.31N 135.29E
41 N6 **Sencha** U.S.S.R. 67.52N 126.25E
89 K8 **Senchi** Ghana 6.15N 0.09E
120 F10 **Senda Hachada** Argentina 23.05S 63.57W
20 O3 **Sendai** Honshu Japan 38.16N 140.52E
20 D10 **Sendai** Kyūshū Japan 31.50N 130.17E
20 D10 **Sendai** *R* Japan
76 F5 **Sendas** Portugal 41.36N 6.50W
94 D7 **Sendeling's Drift** Namibia 28.12S 16.53E
89 K2 **Sendemane** Mali 18.48N 1.28E
63 F9 **Senden** Nordrhein-Westfalen W Germany 51.50N 7.28E
64 J7 **Senden** W Germany 48.20N 10.04E
63 G9 **Sendenhorst** W Germany 51.50N 7.50E
76 D6 **Sendim** Trás os Montes e Alto Douro Portugal 41.03N 7.32W
76 G6 **Sendim** Trás os Montes e Alto Douro Portugal 41.23N 6.25W
24 H10 **Sêndo** Xizang Zizhiqu China 31.43N 95.16E
89 C6 **Sendomoli, Mt** Guinea 11.40N 12.11W
90 E7 **Sendridi** Nigeria 8.33N 10.24E
29 F7 **Sendurjana** Maharashtra India 21.06N 78.04E
18 J6 **Senduruhan** Borneo Indon 0.55S 110.47E
89 J8 **Sene** *R* Ghana
18 B9 **Senebui, Tg** *C* Sumatra Indon 2.19N 101.06E
62 K7 **Senec** Czechoslovakia 48.13N 17.25E
106 F8 **Seneca** Illinois 41.19N 88.35W
109 O2 **Seneca** Kansas 39.50N 96.04W
107 B5 **Seneca** Missouri 36.50N 94.36W
108 K7 **Seneca** Nebraska 42.03N 100.52W
110 G5 **Seneca** Oregon 44.09N 118.58W
105 E3 **Seneca** S Carolina 34.41N 82.59W
108 L4 **Seneca** S Dakota 45.04N 99.31W
104 J4 **Seneca Falls** New York 42.57N 76.47W
104 J4 **Seneca L** New York
104 D7 **Senecaville** Ohio 39.58N 81.28W
104 D7 **Senecaville Res** Ohio
88 S4 **Sened** Tunisia 34.30N 9.19E
61 H4 **Seneffe** Belgium 50.32N 4.15E
89 C4 **Sénégal** *R* W Africa
89 B4 **Senegal** *rep* W Africa
81 B3 **Seneghe** Sardinia 40.05N 8.37E
95 L4 **Senekal** S Africa 28.19S 27.38E
40 G4 **Seneka, Mys** *C* U.S.S.R. 54.16N 137.44E
77 M6 **Senés** Spain 37.12N 2.20W
81 D3 **Senes, Mte** Sardinia 40.29N 9.40E
67 O13 **Senetosa, Pta di** Corsica 41.33N 8.46E
106 J3 **Seney** Michigan 46.21N 85.56W
71 J9 **Senez** France 43.55N 6.24E
63 U9 **Senftenberg** E Germany 51.31N 14.01E
92 E6 **Senga Hill** Zambia 9.24S 31.13E
93 E8 **Senga Pt** Tanzania 2.24S 33.06E
91 H2 **Senge** Zaïre 3.45N 22.40E
30 E1 **Senge Khambal** Xizang Zizhiqu 31.23N 81.37E
53 J5 **Sengeløse** Denmark 55.41N 12.16E
60 K14 **Sengelsbroek** Netherlands 51.17N 5.20E
30 E1 **Sengephu** Xizang Zizhiqu 31.21N 81.31E
47 G2 **Sengeyskiy, Ostrov** *isld* U.S.S.R. 68.28N 51.00E
18 D10 **Senggarang** Pen Malaysia 1.45N 103.02E
45 U3 **Sengiley** U.S.S.R. 53.57N 48.46E
44 D2 **Sengileyevka, Ozero** *L* U.S.S.R.
44 D2 **Sengileyevskaya** U.S.S.R. 45.02N 41.40E
44 L5 **Sengirli, Mys** *C* Kazakhstan U.S.S.R. 42.06N 52.24E
19 B6 **Sengkang** Celebes Indonesia 4.09S 120.02E
84 Z20 **Senglea** Malta 35.54N 14.31E
72 F10 **Sengouagnet** France 42.59N 0.47E
65 K6 **Sengsengebirge** *mts* Austria
91 D7 **Senguele** Angola 7.15S 14.48E
121 K5 **Senguerr, R** Argentina
92 D1 **Senguli** Zaïre 1.17N 28.59E
92 J7 **Sengwa** Tanzania 11.11S 38.25E
92 D10 **Sengwa** *R* Zimbabwe
63 H5 **Sengwärden** W Germany 53.36N 8.04E
76 D13 **Senhora da Graca de Padrões** Portugal 37.33N 7.58W
76 D11 **Senhora da Graça do Divor** Portugal 38.39N 7.59W
96 T3 **Senhora do Pilar** Azores 38.41N 27.20W
Senhora do Porto Barragem *res see* **Guilhofrei, Barragem de**
118 H2 **Senhor do Bonfim** Brazil 10.28S 40.11W
88 N4 **Senia, Es** *aer* Algeria 35.48N 0.35W
82 D2 **Senica** Czechoslovakia 48.40N 17.20E
62 K6 **Senice** Czechoslovakia 49.38N 17.05E
65 Q2 **Senice nad Hané** Czechoslovakia 49.37N 17.06E
79 O7 **Senigallia** Italy 43.43N 13.13E
Şenik *see* **Geliguzan**
79 L6 **Šenio** *R* Italy
36 E4 **Senirkent** Turkey 38.07N 30.34E
81 B4 **Senis** Sardinia 39.49N 8.57E
81 M3 **Senise** Italy 40.08N 16.18E
82 B5 **Senj** Yugoslavia 45.00N 14.55E
51 F2 **Senja** *isld* Norway 69.15N 17.20E
23 K6 **Senkaku gunto** *islds* Japan 25.46N 123.32E
37 G5 **Senkaya** Turkey 40.33N 42.17E
47 G3 **Sen'kina** U.S.S.R. 65.52N 51.00E
92 B10 **Senkobo** Zambia 17.38S 25.58E
45 J7 **Sen'kovo** Ukraine U.S.S.R. 49.31N 37.40E
36 J6 **Şenköy** Turkey 36.02N 36.08E
41 K6 **Şenkyabasa** U.S.S.R. 68.45N 112.32E
41 L6 **Sënkyu** *R* U.S.S.R.
95 G1 **Senlac** S Africa 25.49S 23.44E
100 H6 **Senlac** Saskatchewan 52.29N 109.46W
72 D7 **Sen, le** France 44.08N 0.29W
40 F8 **Senlin Shan** *mt pk* Jilin China 43.12N 130.35E
21 E6 **Senlin Shan** *mt pk* Jilin China 43.12N 130.35E
69 D5 **Senlis** France 49.12N 2.35E
75 P4 **Senmanat** Spain 41.36N 2.09E
87 D4 **Sennar** Sudan 13.31N 33.38E
81 B3 **Sennariolo** Sardinia 40.13N 8.33E
44 A2 **Sennaya** U.S.S.R. 45.17N 37.00E
61 G4 **Senne** *R* Belgium
61 S9 **Senne** *R* Belgium
63 J9 **Senne** *reg* W Germany
71 F3 **Sennecey-le-Grand** France 46.35N 4.48E
63 J9 **Sennelager** W Germany 51.46N 8.44E
53 B3 **Sennels** Denmark 56.58N 8.48E
56 S9 **Sennen** Cornwall Eng 50.03N 5.42W
53 T16 **Senneset** Norway 61.17N 5.49E
63 J9 **Sennestadt** W Germany 51.57N 8.35E
99 N4 **Senneterre** Quebec 48.24N 77.16W
70 L2 **Senneville** France 49.47N 0.25E
99 O10 **Senneville** Quebec 45.26N 73.54W
45 A2 **Senno** Belorussiya U.S.S.R. 54.50N 29.43E
81 B2 **Sennori** Sardinia 40.48N 8.36E
45 S4 **Sennoy** U.S.S.R. 52.12N 46.58E
66 P2 **Sennwald** Switzerland 47.16N 9.31E
56 D4 **Sennybridge** Powys Wales 51.57N 3.34W
25 H4 **Se Noi** *R* Laos
105 C4 **Senoia** Georgia 33.17N 84.34W
70 N4 **Senonches** France 48.34N 1.03W
69 M7 **Senones** France 48.24N 6.59E
76 B11 **Señora da Atalaia** Portugal 38.42N 8.55W
81 C4 **Senorbi** Sardinia 39.33N 9.08E
121 A8 **Seno Reloncavi** *gulf* Chile
89 C4 **Sénoudébou** Senegal 14.27N 12.12W
72 H8 **Senouillac** France 43.57N 1.56E
71 D6 **Senouire** *R* France
76 D1 **Senra** Spain 43.39N 7.50W
20 J7 **Senri** Japan 34.49N 135.30E
69 E7 **Sens** France 48.12N 3.18E
70 G5 **Sens-de-Bretagne** France 48.20N 1.32W
66 F4 **Sense** *R* Switzerland
61 L7 **Sensenruth** Belgium 49.49N 5.04E
25 H6 **Sen, Stung** *R* Cambodia
115 P11 **Sensuntepeque** El Salvador 13.54N 88.35W
66 S4 **Sent** Switzerland 46.49N 10.21E
82 F5 **Senta** Yugoslavia 45.55N 20.06E
15 F5 **Sentani, Danau** *L* Irian Jaya
18 J5 **Sentarum Danau** *L* Borneo Indon
43 O3 **Sentas** Kazakhstan U.S.S.R. 49.20N 82.30E
72 F10 **Sentein** France 42.53N 0.58E
72 G10 **Sentenac-d'Oust** France 42.53N 1.09E
92 B4 **Sentery** Zaïre 5.19S 25.43E
30 C4 **Senthal** Uttar Prad India 28.31N 79.32E
66 E1 **Sentheim** France 47.45N 7.04E
66 A5 **Sentier, le** Switzerland 46.37N 6.15E
111 L9 **Sentinel** Arizona 32.53N 113.12W
109 L6 **Sentinel** Oklahoma 35.10N 99.12W
108 G3 **Sentinel Butte** N Dakota 46.56N 103.50W
101 N8 **Sentinel Peak** Br Columbia 54.56N 121.59W
123 G11 **Sentinel Ra** Antarctica
115 G7 **Sentispac** Mexico 21.50N 105.20W
117 G9 **Sento Sé** Brazil 9.41S 41.16W
15 F5 **Senu** *R* Papua New Guinea
69 H5 **Senuc** France 49.18N 4.50E
61 M5 **Seny** Belgium 50.28N 5.24E
39 M3 **Senyavina, Proliv** *str* U.S.S.R.
91 A3 **Senye** Equat Guinea 1.38N 9.50E
37 F8 **Şenyurt** Turkey 37.06N 40.39E
20 E7 **Senzaki** Japan 34.24N 131.11E
20 E9 **Sen-zaki** *C* Honshu Japan 32.50N 132.00E
61 H6 **Senzeille** Belgium 50.11N 4.28E
63 R7 **Senzke** E Germany 52.40N 12.38E
20 B4 **Senzu** Kanagawa Japan
75 N3 **Seo de Urgel** Spain 42.22N 1.27E
30 B3 **Seohara** Uttar Prad India 29.13N 78.36E
66 J2 **Seon** Switzerland 47.21N 8.10E
29 G7 **Seonath R** *R* Madhya Prad India
30 B6 **Seondha** Madhya Prad India 26.09N 78.47E
30 A1 **Seoni** Himachal Prad India 31.14N 77.06E
29 F6 **Seoni** Madhya Prad India 22.06N 79.36E
29 F8 **Seoni** Maharashtra India 19.38N 79.50E
29 F6 **Seoni** *dist* Madhya Prad India
29 E6 **Seoni-Malwa** Madhya Prad India 22.29N 77.31E
29 H7 **Seorinarayan** Madhya Prad India 21.46N 82.40E
21 D9 **Seoul** S Korea 37.30N 127.00E
72 G7 **Séoune** *R* France
19 F5 **Sepa** Moluccas Indon 3.19S 129.04E
18 K6 **Sepandan** Borneo Indon 1.17S 112.21E
18 K6 **Sepang** Borneo Indon 1.24S 113.54E
18 B9 **Sepang** Pen Malaysia 2.41N 101.44E
18 E10 **Sepang, Tanjong** *C* Pen Malaysia 1.22N 104.17E
18 L9 **Sepanjang** *isld* Indonesia
109 B9 **Separ** New Mexico 32.12N 108.26W
11 H7 **Separation Pt** New Zealand 40.47S 173.00E
14 E6 **Separation Well** W Australia 22.57S 123.56E
32 B3 **Separ Shāhābād** Iran 35.15N 47.51E
18 M5 **Sepasu** Borneo Indon 0.42N 117.40E
120 F3 **Sepatini, R** Brazil
30 A6 **Şepau** Rajasthan India 26.49N 77.45E
65 K3 **Šepekov** Czechoslovakia 49.26N 14.25E
118 G8 **Sepetiba, B. de** Brazil
66 E6 **Sépey, le** Switzerland 46.22N 7.04E
15 F6 **Sepik** *R* Papua New Guinea
18 L4 **Seping** *R* Sarawak Malaysia
80 L6 **Sepino** Italy 41.24N 14.37E
72 F1 **Sepmes** France 47.04N 0.40E
62 K2 **Sępolno** Poland 53.26N 17.30E
28 K2 **Sepon** Assam India 27.08N 94.51E
25 J4 **Sepone** Laos 16.41N 106.14E
25 J4 **Se Pone** *R* Laos
62 N1 **Sępopol** Poland 54.15N 21.00E
21 D8 **Sep'o-ri** N Korea 38.35N 127.23E
120 G2 **Sepoti, R** Brazil
118 B4 **Sepotuba** *R* Brazil
63 F9 **Seppenrade** W Germany 51.46N 7.23E
71 L1 **Seppois** France 47.32N 7.10E
71 F5 **Septême** France 45.34N 5.00E
71 G10 **Septêmes-les-Vallons** France 43.24N 5.22E
82 J8 **Septemvri** Bulgaria 42.11N 24.09E
69 B6 **Septeuil** France 48.54N 1.40E
72 H7 **Septfonds** France 44.11N 1.37E
61 O8 **Septfontaines** Luxembourg 49.42N 5.58E
70 J5 **Sept-Forges** France 48.29N 0.32W
98 F3 **Sept Iles** Quebec 50.13N 66.22W
66 P6 **Septimer Pass** Switzerland 46.26N 9.38E
13 J5 **Septimus** Queensland 21.14S 148.46E
70 D4 **Sept Isles, les** France 48.54N 3.27W
98 B2 **Sept-Milles, L** Quebec
71 H4 **Septmoncel** France 46.22N 5.54E
61 M5 **Septon** Belgium 50.22N 5.25E
76 G7 **Sepulcro Hilario** Spain 40.42N 6.11W
18 K9 **Sepulu** Indonesia 6.54S 112.56E
75 C5 **Sepúlveda** Spain 41.18N 3.45W
75 C5 **Sepúlveda, Tierra de** *reg* Spain
18 F8 **Seputih** *R* Sumatra Indon
72 D3 **Sepvret** France 46.16N 0.08W
95 M6 **Seqhobong** S Africa 30.26S 28.26E
79 N2 **Sequals** Italy 46.10N 12.50E
107 L6 **Sequatchie** *R* Tennessee
88 H8 **Sequen** *reg* Morocco
76 G7 **Sequeros** Spain 40.31N 6.02W
76 J5 **Sequillo** *R* Spain
110 B1 **Sequim** Washington 48.05N 123.06W
111 F5 **Sequoia National Park** California 36.35N 118.45W
32 B2 **Serā** Iran 36.22N 46.09E
15 A7 **Sera** *isld* Moluccas Indon
37 F6 **Şerafeddin Dağları** *mts* Turkey
45 O7 **Serafimovich** U.S.S.R. 49.33N 42.42E
44 F2 **Serafimovskoye** U.S.S.R. 45.14N 43.58E
30 B8 **Serai** Madhya Prad India 24.33N 78.06E
34 C3 **Serai** Syria 35.46N 35.57E
69 G4 **Seraincourt** France 49.37N 4.12E
61 N4 **Seraing** Belgium 50.37N 5.31E
61 M4 **Seraing-le-Château** Belgium 50.37N 5.18E
84 R14 **Serakhis** *R* Cyprus
43 F8 **Serakhs** Turkmeniya U.S.S.R. 36.34N 61.14E
28 C2 **Seram** Karnataka India 17.13N 77.14E
19 F5 **Seram** *isld* Moluccas Indon
29 M2 **Serampore** W Bengal India 22.44N 88.21E
26 M6 **Seram Sea** Indonesia
95 D5 **Seranantsara** Madagascar 18.30S 49.05E
72 J5 **Sérandon** France 45.22N 2.18E
18 G9 **Serang** Java Indon 6.07S 106.09E
18 J2 **Serangoon** Singapore 1.23N 103.55E
18 K2 **Serangoon Harb** Singapore
18 K2 **Serangoon, Pulau** *isld* Singapore
71 D9 **Séranne, Mtgne, de la** France
80 G3 **Serano, Monte** Italy 42.52N 12.48E
71 K9 **Séranon** France 43.46N 6.42E
76 C1 **Serantes** Spain 43.30N 8.15W
86 H5 **Serapeum** Egypt 30.29N 32.22E
76 E5 **Serapicos** Portugal 41.36N 7.26W
18 H4 **Serasan** *isld* Indonesia
18 H4 **Serasan, Selat** *str* Indonesia
87 K3 **Serat** *reg* Yemen
87 J2 **Serat, Jebel** *mts* Yemen
79 H7 **Seravezza** Italy 43.59N 10.13E
87 L7 **Seraweina** Ethiopia 7.58N 46.18E
Seraya *see* **Serai**
18 H4 **Seraya** *isld* Indonesia 2.40N 108.33E
19 A8 **Seraya** *isld* Indonesia 8.22S 119.53E
18 L10 **Seraya, Gunung** *mt* Bali Indon 8.24S 115.36E
18 H3 **Seraya, Pulau** *isld* Singapore
18 H9 **Serayu** *R* Java Indonesia
86 L8 **Serbâl, Gebel** *hill* Egypt 28.39N 33.38E
81 B5 **Serbariu** Sardinia 39.10N 8.32E
82 F7 **Serbia** *reg* Yugoslavia
44 A7 **Serbka** Ukraine U.S.S.R. 47.02N 30.48E
24 H10 **Sêrca** Xizang Zizhiqu China 31.43N 95.20E
82 J5 **Şercaia** Romania 45.49N 25.09E
78 C4 **Serchio** *R* Italy
75 O3 **Serchs** Spain 42.09N 1.51E
18 A6 **Serdang** Pen Malaysia 5.16N 100.34E
18 F8 **Serdang, Tg** *C* Sumatra Indon 4.26S 105.50E
Serdar *see* **Kaypak**
46 N4 **Serdoba** *R* U.S.S.R.
45 Q4 **Serdobsk** U.S.S.R. 52.29N 44.13E
39 M2 **Serdtse-Kamen', Mys** *C* U.S.S.R. 67.00N 171.43W
87 H4 **Sereba** Ethiopia 13.12N 40.31E
42 F4 **Serebrovo** U.S.S.R. 55.26N 97.50E
47 M3 **Serebryanka** U.S.S.R. 57.58N 58.59E
47 M3 **Serebryanka** *R* U.S.S.R.
47 L7 **Serebryanoye** U.S.S.R. 55.42N 74.21E
43 P3 **Serebryansk** Kazakhstan U.S.S.R. 49.44N 83.16E
47 D2 **Serebryanskiy** U.S.S.R. 68.54N 35.40E
45 K2 **Serebryanye Prudy** U.S.S.R. 54.28N 38.45E
92 H5 **Serebu** *mt* Tanzania 7.30S 36.09E
62 K7 **Sered** Czechoslovakia 48.19N 17.45E
45 G1 **Sereda** Moscow U.S.S.R. 55.53N 35.30E
46 M1 **Sereda** Yaroslavl' U.S.S.R. 58.01N 40.30E
45 F4 **Seredina-Buda** Ukraine U.S.S.R. 52.10N 34.03E
46 G1 **Seredka** U.S.S.R. 58.11N 28.10E
42 K6 **Seredyanka** U.S.S.R. 51.45N 120.10E
37 D5 **Şerefiye** Turkey 40.09N 37.46E
36 G4 **Şereflikoçhisar** Turkey 38.56N 33.31E
79 F3 **Seregno** Italy 45.39N 9.12E
47 G5 **Seregovo** U.S.S.R. 62.20N 50.40E
72 G4 **Séreilhac** France 45.46N 1.05E
69 F8 **Serein** *R* France
18 B9 **Seremban** Pen Malaysia 2.42N 101.54E
77 E3 **Serena, La** *reg* Spain
92 G3 **Serengeti Nat.Park** Tanzania
93 F8 **Serengeti Plain** Tanzania
18 J6 **Serengka** Borneo Indon 1.50S 110.41E
92 E8 **Serenje** Zambia 13.12S 30.15E
87 J9 **Serenli** Somalia 2.19N 42.15E
117 E8 **Sereno** *R* Brazil
70 F6 **Serent** France 47.50N 2.29W
93 E4 **Serere** Uganda 1.31N 33.27E
93 G9 **Sereri, L** Tanzania 3.53S 35.53E
46 F5 **Seret** *R* Ukraine U.S.S.R.
46 N2 **Serezha** *R* Gor'kiy U.S.S.R.
42 E4 **Serezha** *R* Krasnoyarsk U.S.S.R.
95 L3 **Serfontein** S Africa 27.23S 27.28E
84 H7 **Serfopoúla** *isld* Greece 37.15N 24.35E
46 S1 **Serga** U.S.S.R. 57.45N 57.05E
47 H6 **Ser'ga** U.S.S.R. 57.49N 56.55E
45 R1 **Sergach** U.S.S.R. 55.32N 45.27E
108 O7 **Sergeant Bluff** Iowa 42.24N 96.20W
103 E6 **Sergeantsville** New Jersey 40.27N 74.57W
22 G3 **Sergelen** Mongolia 47.44N 106.56E
36 C1 **Sergen** Turkey 41.42N 27.42E
41 E3 **Sergeya Kirova, Ostrova** *islds* U.S.S.R.
45 V6 **Sergey Aula** Kazakhstan U.S.S.R. 50.20N 49.30E
43 J2 **Sergeyevka** Akmolinsk, Kazakhstan U.S.S.R. 51.38N 68.11E
40 D6 **Sergeyevka** Amur U.S.S.R. 50.45N 127.14E
43 H1 **Sergeyevka** Kazakhstan U.S.S.R. 53.53N 67.23E
47 M7 **Sergeyevka** Novosibirsk U.S.S.R. 56.28N 76.10E
40 F10 **Sergeyevka** Primor'ye U.S.S.R. 43.20N 133.23E
45 L6 **Sergeyevka** Voronezh U.S.S.R. 50.25N 39.47E
42 D4 **Sergeyevo** U.S.S.R. 57.19N 86.05E
69 E7 **Sergines** France 48.20N 3.17E
47 K5 **Sergino** U.S.S.R. 62.30N 65.40E
118 J2 **Sergipe** *R* Brazil
118 J2 **Sergipe** *state* Brazil
44 E3 **Sergiyevka** U.S.S.R. 44.56N 42.45E
Sergiyevo *see* **Zagorsk**
46 Q3 **Sergiyevsk** U.S.S.R. 53.56N 51.00E
45 P6 **Sergiyevskaya** U.S.S.R. 50.15N 43.48E
45 K4 **Sergiyevskoye** U.S.S.R. 52.59N 38.51E
93 G5 **Sergo** Kenya 0.39N 35.24E
44 H5 **Sergokala** U.S.S.R. 42.27N 47.42E
84 D5 **Sergoúla** Greece 38.24N 22.04E
47 D3 **Sergozero, Ozero** *L* U.S.S.R. 66.44N 36.45E
22 D8 **Serh** Qinghai China 36.58N 98.25E
18 L3 **Seria** Brunei 4.39N 114.23E
18 J5 **Serian** Sarawak Malaysia 1.10N 110.35E
79 G3 **Seriana, Val** *V* Italy
79 G3 **Seriate** Italy 45.41N 9.44E
18 C4 **Seribudolok** Sumatra Indon 2.56N 98.36E
93 L4 **Sericho** Kenya 1.08N 39.07E
81 M2 **Serico, Monte** Italy 40.52N 16.09E
117 H8 **Seridó** *R* Brazil
69 B5 **Sérifontaine** France 49.21N 1.47E
84 H7 **Sérifos** Greece 37.09N 24.30E
84 H7 **Sérifos** *isld* Greece
84 H7 **Sérifou, Stenón** *str* Greece
70 C5 **Sérignac** France 48.26N 3.41W
71 C10 **Sérignan** Hérault France 43.17N 3.17E
71 F8 **Sérignan-du-Comtat** Vaucluse France 44.11N 4.51E
36 E6 **Serik** Turkey 36.55N 31.06E
24 B6 **Serikbuya** Xinjiang Uygur Zizhiqu China 39.11N 77.56E
37 H2 **Serin** *R* Turkey
75 Q3 **Seriñá** Spain 42.10N 2.45E
95 B5 **Serinam** Madagascar 19.40S 44.40E
61 L6 **Serinchamps** Belgium 50.14N 5.14E
120 G4 **Seringal Setenta** Brazil 10.21S 62.35W
14 D2 **Seringapatam Reef** Indian Oc 13.41S 122.05E
117 D8 **Seringa, Sa da** *mts* Brazil
80 L7 **Serino** Italy 40.51N 14.52E
79 G3 **Sério** *R* Italy
15 F8 **Serki** Papua New Guinea 8.10S 141.56E
41 M7 **Serki** *R* U.S.S.R.
88 R10 **Serkout** *mt* Algeria 23.35N 6.46E
88 R10 **Serkout** *reg* Algeria
41 E7 **Serkovo** U.S.S.R. 66.36N 88.05E
12 E4 **Serle, Mt** S Australia 30.34S 138.55E
69 C7 **Sermaises** France 48.17N 2.12E
69 H6 **Sermaize-les-Bains** France 48.47N 4.55E
66 D1 **Sermamagny** France 47.42N 6.50E
67 P12 **Sermano** Corsica 42.19N 9.15E
19 F8 **Sermata** *isld* Indon 8.13S 128.55E
19 F8 **Sermata, Kep** *islds* Indon
66 J8 **Sermenza** *R* Italy
79 K4 **Sermide** Italy 45.01N 11.18E
48 V13 **Sermiligâq** Greenland 65.55N 36.30W
48 S15 **Sermiligârssuk** *fjord* Greenland
48 U16 **Sermilik** Greenland 60.25N 44.55W
48 S13 **Sermilik** *fjord* Greenland
48 U13 **Sermilik** *fjord* Greenland
15 F5 **Sermo** *R* Irian Jaya
80 G5 **Sermoneta** Italy 41.33N 12.59E
71 F4 **Sermoyer** France 46.29N 4.58E
76 C9 **Sernache do Bom Jardim** Portugal 39.49N 8.11W
76 C7 **Sernada** Portugal 40.41N 8.27W
76 K4 **Serna, La** Spain 42.25N 4.40W
76 E7 **Sernancelhe** Portugal 40.54N 7.30W
66 Q4 **Serneus** Switzerland 46.53N 9.51E
66 N4 **Sernf Tal** *V* Switzerland
79 O2 **Sernio, Monte** Italy 46.29N 13.08E
63 U6 **Sernitz** *R* E Germany
63 Q8 **Serno** E Germany 52.01N 12.26E
40 K10 **Sernovodsk** Kuril Is U.S.S.R. 43.55N 145.37E
46 Q3 **Sernovodsk** Kuybyshev U.S.S.R. 53.57N 51.20E
46 O7 **Sernovodskoye** U.S.S.R. 43.20N 45.09E
46 P2 **Sernur** U.S.S.R. 56.52N 49.02E
43 E7 **Sernyy-Zavod** Turkmeniya U.S.S.R. 40.00N 58.18E
89 D4 **Séro** Mali 14.44N 11.00W
76 C6 **Seroa** Portugal 41.15N 8.27W
62 N3 **Serock** Poland 52.31N 21.01E
121 E4 **Serodino** Argentina 32.33S 60.52W
116 A1 **Seroe Colorado** Aruba W I 12.26N 69.53W
46 O6 **Seroglazovka** U.S.S.R. 47.00N 47.28E
121 B3 **Serón** Chile 30.21S 70.47W
77 M6 **Serón** Spain 37.20N 2.29W
75 F5 **Serón de Nágima** Spain 41.30N 2.12W
93 F8 **Seronera** Tanzania 2.23S 34.49E
60 C2 **Serooskerke** Schouwen Netherlands 51.42N 3.49E
60 B2 **Serooskerke** Walcheren Netherlands 51.33N 3.36E
75 L5 **Serós** Spain 41.27N 0.24E
88 R9 **Serouenout** Algeria 24.18N 7.25E
89 D3 **Séroumeli** Mauritania 16.03N 11.27W
47 J6 **Serov** U.S.S.R. 59.42N 60.32E
43 N8 **Serovo** Uzbekistan U.S.S.R. 40.28N 71.12E
94 J4 **Serowe** Botswana 22.25S 26.44E
76 D13 **Serpa** Portugal 38.00N 7.37W
76 D13 **Serpa** Portugal 37.56N 7.36W
117 A6 **Serpa, I. de** Brazil
Serpa Pinto *see* **Menongue**
81 C5 **Serpeddi, Pta** Sardinia 39.22N 9.18E
81 D5 **Serpentara, I** Sardinia 39.08N 9.38E
113 E4 **Serpentine Hot Springs** Alaska 65.50N 164.49W
12 A3 **Serpentine Lakes** S Australia
101 J12 **Serpentine R** Br Columbia
14 B9 **Serpentine, R** W Australia
98 A4 **Serpent, R. au** Quebec
119 H2 **Serpent's Mouth** *str* Venezuela
76 C8 **Serpins** Portugal 40.09N 8.11W
74 G6 **Serpis** *R* Spain
29 L3 **Serpo La** *pass* India/Xizang Zizhiqu 28.05N 88.44E
45 J2 **Serpukhov** U.S.S.R. 54.53N 37.25E
69 K8 **Serqueux** Haute-Marne France 48.00N 5.45E
70 O2 **Serqueux** Seine-Inférieure France 49.38N 1.32E
70 M3 **Serquigny** France 49.07N 0.42E
118 H7 **Serra** Brazil 20.06S 40.16W
76 C9 **Serra** Portugal 39.35N 8.18W
75 K8 **Serra** Spain 39.42N 0.26W
79 L7 **Serra, Alpe di** *mts* Italy
118 E10 **Serra Alta** Brazil 26.15S 49.24W
118 F4 **Serra Bonita** Brazil 15.10S 46.50W
80 M5 **Serracapriola** Italy 41.48N 15.10E
76 K6 **Serrada** Spain 41.27N 4.52W
118 F4 **Serra das Araras** Brazil 15.37S 45.24W
76 A10 **Serra de El Rei** Portugal 39.20N 9.20W
75 E3 **Serradero** *mt* Spain 42.20N 2.36W
81 M2 **Serra di Corvo, L. di** Italy
81 G9 **Serradifalco** Sicily 37.28N 13.53E
67 O13 **Serra di Ferro** Corsica 41.45N 8.47E
76 G9 **Serradilla** Spain 39.50N 6.09W
76 G7 **Serradilla del Arroyo** Spain 40.31N 6.22W
67 P13 **Serra di Scopamene** Corsica 41.46N 9.06E
117 C4 **Serra do Navio** Brazil 1.00N 52.05W
76 E10 **Serra do Rosário** Portugal 39.06N 7.19W
63 Q5 **Serrahn** E Germany 53.41N 12.22E
83 F3 **Sérrai** Greece 41.03N 23.33E
79 C4 **Serra, La** *mts* Italy
81 B5 **Serramanna** Sardinia 39.26N 8.56E
79 J6 **Serramazzoni** Italy 44.25N 10.47E
81 B5 **Serra Miai, Mte** Sardinia 39.14N 8.35E
79 J7 **Serra, Monte** *mt* Italy 43.46N 10.33E
116 D7 **Serrana Bank** Caribbean Sea
116 D7 **Serranilla Bank** Caribbean Sea
76 K8 **Serranillos** Spain 40.20N 4.55W
121 J7 **Serrano** *isld* Chile 48.30S 74.40W
118 D6 **Serranópolis** Brazil 18.15S 51.55W
81 A2 **Serra, R** Sardinia
Serraria *isld see* **Queimada ou Serraria**
81 M6 **Serra San Bruno** Italy 38.35N 16.20E
80 G2 **Serra San Quirico** Italy 43.27N 13.01E
80 G2 **Serra Sant' Abbondio** Italy 43.29N 12.46E
81 M5 **Serrastretta** Italy 39.01N 16.25E
117 H9 **Serra Talhada** Brazil 8.01S 38.17W
88 S3 **Serrat, C** *C* Tunisia 37.17N 9.15E
66 B8 **Serraval** France 45.48N 6.20E
79 K3 **Serravalle all' Adige** Italy 45.49N 11.01E
80 G2 **Serravalle di Chienti** Italy 43.04N 12.57E
79 J7 **Serravalle Pistojese** Italy 43.54N 10.49E
79 E5 **Serravalle Scrivia** Italy 44.44N 8.51E
79 D3 **Serravalle Sesia** Italy 45.41N 8.18E
80 M7 **Serre** Salerno Italy 40.34N 15.11E
69 F4 **Serre** *R* France
71 K7 **Serre Chevalier** France 44.55N 6.30E
76 H9 **Serrejón** Spain 39.50N 5.48W
81 B5 **Serrenti** Sardinia 39.30N 8.58E
71 J8 **Serre Ponçon, Barrage de** France 44.27N 6.16E
72 H10 **Serrère Pic de** *mt* France 42.37N 1.35E
71 H8 **Serres** Hautes-Alpes France 44.25N 5.42E
72 E7 **Serres** *reg* France
72 H10 **Serres-sur-Arget** France 42.57N 1.31E
121 D3 **Serrezuela** Argentina 30.38S 65.26W
81 C4 **Serri** Sardinia 39.43N 9.09E
53 D2 **Serridslev** Denmark 57.19N 10.00E
71 F6 **Serrières** France 45.19N 4.45E
71 G5 **Serrières-de-Briord** France 45.48N 5.27E
71 H5 **Serrières-en-Chantagne** France 45.53N 5.52E
118 J2 **Serrinha** Bahia Brazil 11.38S 38.56W
79 M7 **Serriola, Bocca** *pass* Italy 43.31N 12.21E
117 G8 **Serrita** Brazil 7.52S 39.18W
118 G6 **Sêrro** Brazil 18.38S 43.22W
76 J8 **Serrota, La** *mt* Spain 40.30N 5.05W
121 B8 **Serrucho** *pk* Argentina 41.36N 71.03W
88 S3 **Sers** Tunisia 36.04N 8.57E
81 N5 **Sersale** Italy 39.01N 16.44E
61 F3 **Serskamp** Belgium 50.59N 3.56E
88 Q9 **Sersouf** *watercourse* Algeria
88 O4 **Sersou, Plateaux du** Algeria
76 C9 **Sertã** Portugal 39.48N 8.05W
76 C9 **Serta** *R* Portugal
36 E5 **Sertaç** Turkey 37.22N 30.06E
117 H9 **Sertânia** Brazil 8.04S 37.15W
118 D8 **Sertanópolis** Brazil 23.03S 51.04W
118 F7 **Sertãozinho** Brazil 21.08S 47.59W
23 B2 **Sêrtar** Sichuan China 32.13N 100.10E
66 Q5 **Sertig Dörfli** Switzerland 46.44N 9.52E
66 Q4 **Sertig-Tal** *V* Switzerland
66 Q5 **Sertig-Tal** *V* Switzerland
18 F9 **Sertung** *isld* Indonesia 6.06S 105.23E
15 A7 **Serua** *isld* Moluccas Indon 6.20S 130.02E
18 C8 **Serudom** *mt* Pen Malaysia 3.48N 102.58E
15 D4 **Serui** Yapen I, Irian Jaya 1.53S 136.15E
94 J3 **Serule** Botswana 21.58S 27.20E
29 C3 **Seruna** Rajasthan India 28.06N 73.46E
18 H6 **Serutu** *isld* Indonesia
18 C3 **Seruwai** Sumatra Indonesia 4.20N 98.10E
18 K7 **Seruyan** *R* Borneo Indon
69 M8 **Servance** France 47.49N 6.40E
72 K3 **Servant** France 46.08N 2.55E
71 C7 **Serverette** France 44.43N 3.23E
83 E4 **Sérvia** Greece 40.11N 22.01E
71 C10 **Servian** France 43.25N 3.18E
84 A2 **Servianá** Greece 39.33N 20.55E
110 E5 **Service Creek** Oregon 44.49N 120.01W
12 F6 **Serviceton** Victoria 36.22S 141.02E
80 H2 **Servigliano** Italy 43.04N 13.30E
61 K5 **Serville** Belgium 50.15N 4.47E
109 E5 **Servilleta** New Mexico 36.31N 105.56W
66 B2 **Servin** France 47.18N 6.28E
71 K5 **Servoz** France 45.55N 6.46E
19 E8 **Serwaru** Indon 8.10S 127.41E
23 A2 **Sêrxü** Sichuan China 33.02N 97.50E
69 G4 **Séry** Ardennes France 49.34N 4.20E
39 M2 **Serykh Gusey, Ostrova** *islds* U.S.S.R.
69 E4 **Séry-les-Mezières** France 49.46N 3.26E
40 D6 **Seryshevo** U.S.S.R. 51.12N 128.16E
75 K4 **Sesa** Spain 42.00N 0.15W
30 A7 **Sesai Buzurg** Madhya Prad India 25.19N 77.37E
30 A7 **Sesaipura** Madhya Prad India 25.33N 77.11E
25 J6 **Se San** *R* Cambodia
25 H4 **Se Sang Soi** *R* Laos
89 M3 **Sesao** Mali 16.59N 4.03E
18 M4 **Sesayap** Borneo Indon 3.34N 117.01E
18 M4 **Sesayap** *R* Borneo Indon
85 L9 **Sese** Sudan 20.05N 30.31E
100 N1 **Seseganaga L** Ontario
93 D6 **Sese Is** Uganda
99 K4 **Sesekinika** Ontario 48.13N 80.14W
9 R5 **Seseleka** *mt* Vanua Levu Fiji 16.47S 178.31E
75 C7 **Seseña** Spain 40.06N 3.42W
19 E4 **Sesepe** Moluccas Indon 1.29S 127.57E
94 B2 **Sesfontein** Namibia 19.07S 13.39E
28 D3 **Seshachalam Hills** Andhra Prad India
45 E3 **Seshcha** U.S.S.R. 53.45N 32.22E
92 B10 **Sesheko** Zambia 17.28S 24.20E
34 H3 **Sesher** Syria 35.18N 40.34E
87 F7 **Seshia Mts** Ethiopia
79 D3 **Sésia** *R* Italy
66 J8 **Sesia, Valle della** Italy
18 M3 **Sesibu** Borneo Indon 4.01N 116.30E
76 A12 **Sesimbra** Portugal 38.26N 9.06W
51 K6 **Seskarön** *isld* Sweden 65.43N 23.45E
59 K5 **Seskin, Mt** Dublin Irish Rep 53.15N 6.25W
84 U16 **Seskli** *isld* Greece 36.30N 27.53E
75 F3 **Sesma** Spain 42.29N 2.05W
19 B8 **Sesok** Indonesia 8.47S 120.02E
20 P8 **Sesoko** Okinawa Japan 26.40N 127.55E
20 P8 **Sesoko-jima** *isld* Okinawa Japan
91 G10 **Sessa** Angola 13.56S 20.40E
66 M7 **Sessa** Switzerland 46.01N 8.48E
80 J6 **Sessa Aurunca** Italy 41.14N 13.56E
80 K5 **Sessano** Italy 41.38N 14.20E
91 G8 **Sesse** Angola 8.09S 20.57E
89 K7 **Sessé** Benin 9.28N 1.51E
53 U15 **Sesseggja** *mt* Norway 61.44N 6.01E
69 O6 **Sessenheim** France 48.48N 7.59E
107 G3 **Sesser** Illinois 38.05N 89.01W
64 K3 **Sesslach** W Germany 50.12N 10.52E
53 W19 **Sessnut** *mt* Norway 59.42N 7.23E
79 G6 **Sesta Godano** Italy 44.18N 9.40E
75 D1 **Sestao** Spain 43.18N 3.00W
79 M7 **Sestino** Italy 43.43N 12.18E
79 M1 **Sesto** Italy 46.42N 12.22E
66 L9 **Sesto Calende** Italy 45.43N 8.38E
79 K7 **Şesto Fiorentino** Italy 43.50N 11.12E
62 O1 **Šeštokai** U.S.S.R. 54.20N 23.30E
79 J6 **Sestola** Italy 44.14N 10.46E
79 F7 **Sesto San Giovanni** *dist* Milan Italy
46 K2 **Sestra** *R* U.S.S.R.
75 G5 **Sestrica** Spain 41.29N 1.36W
79 A5 **Sestriere** Italy 44.58N 6.54E
79 A5 **Sestriere, Col** *pass* Italy 44.57N 6.53E
79 F6 **Sestri Levante** Italy 44.16N 9.23E
79 E6 **Sestri Ponente** Italy 44.25N 8.51E
47 B5 **Sestroretsk** U.S.S.R. 60.09N 29.58E
81 C5 **Sestu** Sardinia 39.18N 9.06E
37 C3 **Sestus** *anc site* Turkey 40.14N 26.24E
66 S5 **Sesvenna, Piz** *mt* Italy/Switz 46.43N 10.24E
20 J7 **Seta** Japan 34.59N 135.53E
93 D5 **Seta** Uganda 0.20N 32.52E
95 M6 **Setabataba** S Africa 30.35S 28.20E
31 G8 **Setabganj** Bangladesh 25.38N 88.36E
20 D3 **Setagaya** *dist* Tōkyō Japan
20 D8 **Setaka** Japan 33.09N 130.28E
20 J2 **Setana** Japan 42.27N 139.52E
18 B8 **Setapak** Pen Malaysia 3.11N 101.42E
103 H5 **Setauket** Long I, N Y 40.57N 73.07W
50 B5 **Setberg** Iceland 64.58N 23.14W
75 P3 **Setcases** Spain 42.23N 2.18E
56 M2 **Setchey** Norfolk Eng 52.42N 0.25E
71 D10 **Sète** France 43.25N 3.43E
96 T1 **Sete Cidades, L** Azores 37.37N 25.47W
37 F7 **Setek** Turkey 38.14N 41.57E
118 G6 **Sete Lagoas** Brazil 19.29S 44.15W
77 F7 **Setenil** Spain 36.52N 5.10W
117 B9 **Sete Quedas, Cachoeira das** *falls* Brazil 9.21S 56.46W
118 D8 **Sete Quedas, Ilha Grande ou** *isld* Brazil
118 C9 **Sete Quedas, Salto das** *falls* Paraguay 24.05S 54.17W
53 W20 **Setesdal** *V* Norway
93 L3 **Setetio** Kenya 2.58N 39.08E
104 D8 **Seth** W Virginia 38.06N 81.40W
30 E3 **Seti** *R* Nepal
30 H4 **Seti** *R* Nepal
88 Q3 **Sétif** Algeria 36.11N 5.24E
76 B10 **Setil** Portugal 39.07N 8.46W
75 G6 **Setiles** Spain 40.44N 1.37W
87 F3 **Setit,R** Sudan/Ethiopia
95 J2 **Setlagodi** S Africa 26.16S 25.07E
95 H2 **Setlagodi** *watercourse* S Africa
30 F5 **Set Mahet** Uttar Prad India 27.32N 82.05E
20 L6 **Seto** Honshu Japan 35.14N 137.06E
20 C9 **Seto** Kyūshū Japan 33.00N 129.39E
20 F8 **Seto Naikai** *sea* Japan
25 J5 **Set, Pou** *mt* Laos 15.34N 106.19E
45 M7 **Setraki** U.S.S.R. 49.22N 40.49E
25 C4 **Setsan** Burma 16.02N 95.21E
88 K5 **Settat** Morocco 33.04N 7.37W
91 A5 **Setté Cama** Gabon 2.32S 9.46E
40 G1 **Sette Daban, Khrebet** *ra* U.S.S.R.
100 U1 **Settee L** Manitoba
81 C5 **Sette Fratelli, Mte** Sardinia 39.18N 9.27E
79 C4 **Séttimo Torinese** Italy 45.09N 7.46E
79 C3 **Séttimo Vittone** Italy 45.33N 7.50E
100 T3 **Setting L** Manitoba
57 J4 **Settle** N Yorks Eng 54.04N 2.16W
96 B11 **Settlement** Ascension I 7.58S 14.22W
9 B7 **Settlement** Wake I Pacific Oc 19.17N 166.38E
13 E3 **Settlement Cr** Queensland
105 H11 **Settlement Pt** Bahamas 26.42N 79.01W
94 K5 **Settlers** S Africa 25.02S 28.30E
71 E2 **Settons, Res. des** France 47.11N 4.04E
89 E9 **Settra Kru** Liberia 4.58N 8.52W
76 B11 **Setúbal** Portugal 38.31N 8.54W
76 B11 **Setúbal** *dist* Portugal
76 B12 **Setúbal, B. de** Portugal
64 M5 **Seubersdorf** W Germany 49.10N 11.30E
72 C4 **Seudre** *R* France
72 C4 **Seugne** *R* France
81 C4 **Seui** Sardinia 39.50N 9.19E
64 K4 **Seukendorf** W Germany 49.31N 10.54E
47 K5 **Seul'** *R* U.S.S.R.
106 J4 **Seul Choix Pt** Michigan 45.57N 85.55W
18 A3 **Seulimeum** Sumatra Indon 5.21N 95.29E
97 K7 **Seul, Lac** *L* Manitoba
70 J3 **Seulles** *R* France
81 C4 **Seulo** Sardinia 39.52N 9.15E
18 B4 **Seumanyam** Sumatra Indon 3.45N 96.39E
71 G2 **Seurre** France 47.00N 5.10E
66 L1 **Seuzach** Switzerland 47.32N 8.44E
75 P4 **Seva** Spain 41.50N 2.17E
44 F7 **Sevan** Armenia U.S.S.R. 40.33N 44.56E
44 G7 **Sevan,Ozero** *L* Armenia U.S.S.R.
120 E8 **Sevaruyo** Bolivia 19.25S 66.52W
44 C10 **Sevastopol'** Ukraine U.S.S.R. 44.36N 33.31E
53 B4 **Sevel** Denmark 56.28N 8.53E
66 O3 **Sevelen** Switzerland 47.07N 9.30E
110 J4 **Seven Devils** *mts* Idaho
13 D3 **Seven Emu** N Terr Australia 16.20S 137.09E
95 K9 **Seven Fountains** S Africa 33.26S 26.20E
59 E8 **Seven Hd** Cork Irish Rep 51.34N 8.42W
59 B7 **Seven Hogs, The** *islds* Kerry Irish Rep 52.20N 10.03W
Seven Hunters *see* **Flannan Is.**
Seven Is *see* **Sept Iles**
98 F3 **Seven Islands B** Quebec
109 C6 **Seven Lakes** New Mexico 35.45N 107.56W
14 B6 **Seven Mile Cr** W Australia
56 M5 **Sevenoaks** Kent Eng 51.16N 0.12E
95 O5 **Sevenoaks** S Africa 29.13S 30.36E
Seven Pagodas *see* **Mahabalipuram**
100 G9 **Seven Persons** Alberta 49.53N 110.54W
112 J7 **Seven Sisters** Texas 28.01N 98.34W
Seven Sisters Falls *waterfall see* **Syv Söstrefosser** *falls*
56 G4 **Seven Springs** Glos Eng 51.52N 2.02W
105 K2 **Seven Springs** N Carolina 35.12N 77.50W
110 G9 **Seven Troughs** Nevada 40.27N 118.47W
101 N10 **Seventy Mile House** Br Columbia 51.21N 121.25W
60 N14 **Sevenum** Netherlands 51.25N 6.02E
103 A7 **Seven Valleys** Pennsylvania 39.51N 76.45W
39 H3 **Sever** U.S.S.R. 62.59N 166.09E
76 E9 **Sever** *R* Spain
70 F6 **Sévérac** France 47.34N 2.05W
72 L7 **Sévérac, Causse de** *plat* France
72 L7 **Sévérac-le-Château** France 44.20N 3.04E
109 P2 **Severance** Kansas 39.45N 95.16W
76 C7 **Sever do Vouga** Portugal 40.44N 8.22W
40 N7 **Severgina** *vol* Kuril Is U.S.S.R. 49.07N 154.31E
40 N7 **Severgina, Proliv** *str* Kuril Is U.S.S.R.
121 G3 **Severino Ribeiro** Brazil 30.07S 56.02W
103 A8 **Severn** Maryland 39.08N 76.41W
95 F2 **Severn** S Africa 26.35S 22.52E
12 K3 **Severn** *R* New S Wales
97 L6 **Severn** *R* Ontario
99 L8 **Severn** *R* Ontario
103 A8 **Severna Park** Maryland 39.04N 76.37W
41 F7 **Severnaya** *R* U.S.S.R.
40 D3 **Severnaya Bruingra** *mt* U.S.S.R. 56.16N 126.29E
41 C4 **Severnaya Karga, Mys** *C* U.S.S.R. 72.46N 75.25E
47 H5 **Severnaya Mylva** *R* U.S.S.R.
45 D4 **Severnaya Rassukha** U.S.S.R. 52.53N 33.00E
41 B2 **Severnaya Sul'meneva, Guba** *gulf* Novaya Zemlya U.S.S.R.

38 K1 Severnaya Zemlya arch Arctic Oc
47 F2 Severnayy Kolguyev, O U.S.S.R. 69.28N 49.01E
56 F2 Severn Gorge Shropshire Eng
39 H6 Severnoye Komandorskiye O-va U.S.S.R. 55.49N 166.01E
42 B4 Severnoye Novosibirsk U.S.S.R. 56.20N 78.10E
43 C1 Severnoye Orenburg U.S.S.R. 54.07N 52.31E
41 F7 Severnoye, Ozero L U.S.S.R.
103 A8 Severn R Maryland
56 F4 Severn, R Wales/England
56 G3 Severn Stoke Hereford & Worcs Eng 52.06N 2.12W
56 F4 Severn Tunnel Junc Gwent Wales 51.35N 2.46W
44 M6 Severnykh Promyslov Ozero No. 6 Turkmeniya U.S.S.R. 41.37N 52.44E
47 M5 Severnyy Chelyabinsk U.S.S.R. 55.51N 60.30E
47 L8 Severnyy Kazakhstan U.S.S.R. 53.44N 74.55E
42 D5 Severnyy Kemerovo U.S.S.R. 54.45N 88.09E
47 J2 Severnyy Komi U.S.S.R. 67.32N 64.02E
45 O4 Severnyy Tambov U.S.S.R. 52.40N 42.24E
47 J5 Severnyy U.S.S.R. 60.58N 60.23E
44 L3 Severnyy Aktau, Khrebet mts Kazakhstan U.S.S.R.
39 G1 Severnyy Anyuyskiy Khrebet ra U.S.S.R.
43 D4 Severnyy Chink Ustyurta escarp Kazakhstan U.S.S.R.
47 E4 Severnyy Dvina R U.S.S.R.
41 A3 Severnyy Gusinyy Nos, Mys C Novaya Zemlya U.S.S.R. 72.08N 51.47E
43 N7 Severnyy Kanal Uzbekistan U.S.S.R.
40 G4 Severnyy, Mys C U.S.S.R. 55.10N 137.32E
41 F3 Severnyy, Ostrov isld U.S.S.R. 77.15N 90.45E
47 H5 Severnyy Ural mts U.S.S.R.
40 J4 Severnyy Zaliv B Sakhalin U.S.S.R.
42 J4 Severo Baykal'skoye Nagor'ye highland U.S.S.R.
64 P3 Severočeský Kraj div Czechoslovakia
42 D6 Severo Chuyskiy, Khrebet mts U.S.S.R.
45 K8 Severodonetsk U.S.S.R. 48.58N 38.29E
47 D4 Severodvinsk U.S.S.R. 64.35N 39.50E
47 K8 Severo-Kazakhstan terr U.S.S.R.
40 O6 Severo-Kuril'sk Kuril Is U.S.S.R. 50.40N 156.01E
65 P2 Severomoravský reg Czechoslovakia
47 C2 Severomorsk U.S.S.R. 69.05N 33.30E
42 J4 Severo-Muyskiy Khrebet mts U.S.S.R.
47 D4 Severoonezhsk U.S.S.R. 62.35N 39.46E
44 F4 Severo-Osetinskaya A.S.S.R U.S.S.R.
41 E5 Severo-Sibirskaya Nizmennost' lowland U.S.S.R.
47 H5 Severoural'sk U.S.S.R. 60.10N 59.56E
41 H3 Severo-Vostochnyy Khrebet mts U.S.S.R.
39 H6 Severo-Vostochnyy Mys C Komandorskiye O-va U.S.S.R. 55.18N 116.18E
41 D4 Severo-Vostochnyy, Mys C U.S.S.R. 73.32N 80.33E
42 E2 Severo-Yeniseyskiy U.S.S.R. 60.22N 93.08E
45 K2 Severo Zadonsk U.S.S.R. 54.01N 38.25E
39 H6 Severo-Zapadnyy, Mys C Komandorskiye O-va U.S.S.R. 55.18N 165.48E
45 K8 Seversk Ukraine U.S.S.R. 48.52N 38.07E
44 B3 Severskaya U.S.S.R. 44.51N 38.42E
45 M8 Severskiy Donets R U.S.S.R.
109 O4 Severy Kansas 37.38N 96.14W
70 H3 Sèves R France
79 F3 Seveso Italy 45.38N 9.08E
65 L3 Sevětín Czechoslovakia 49.07N 14.35E
51 O2 Sevettijärvi Finland 69.32N 28.40E
67 O12 Sevi, Col de pass Corsica 42.13N 8.50E
111 M3 Sevier Utah 38.37N 112.14W
111 M2 Sevier R Utah
111 N2 Sevier Bridge Res Utah 39.20N 111.55W
111 M2 Sevier Des Utah
111 L2 Sevier L Utah 39.00N 113.10W
105 D2 Sevierville Tennessee 35.53N 83.34W
70 F5 Sévignac France 48.21N 2.21W
72 D9 Sévignacq France 43.27N 0.14W
72 D9 Sévignacq Meyracq France 43.07N 0.25W
69 G4 Sévigny-Waleppe France 49.36N 4.05E
119 C5 Sevilla Colombia 4.16N 75.58W
77 E6 Sevilla Spain 37.24N 5.59W
74 D7 Sevilla prov Spain
116 F4 Sevilla R Cuba
76 L8 Sevilla la Nueva Spain 40.20N 4.02W
Seville see Sevilla
76 K9 Sevilleja de la Jara Spain 39.35N 4.58W
121 F6 Sevinge Argentina 36.14S 57.44W
37 E3 Şevketiye Balikesir Turkey 40.06N 27.51E
37 C2 Şevketiye Çanakkale Turkey 40.24N 26.52E
53 S20 Sevlandsvik Norway 59.16N 5.12E
82 J7 Sevlievo Bulgaria 43.00N 27.07E
82 J2 Sevola mt U.S.S.R. 48.32N 24.05E
80 H3 Sevo, Pizzo di pk Italy 42.40N 13.21E
68 H2 Sevran France 48.57N 2.32E
72 C2 Sèvre R France
72 C3 Sèvre-Niortaise R France
68 D4 Sèvres France 48.49N 2.13E
22 F5 Sevrey Mongolia 43.33N 102.13E
71 J5 Sévrier France 45.51N 6.08E
71 G4 Sevron R France
45 F4 Sevsk U.S.S.R. 52.08N 34.31E
47 J4 Sev Sos'va R U.S.S.R.
89 D8 Sewa R Sierra Leone
29 D7 Sewand R Maharashtra India
107 L6 Sewanee Tennessee 35.11N 85.54W
113 N6 Seward Alaska 60.05N 149.34W
109 M3 Seward Kansas 38.10N 98.49W
108 N9 Seward Nebraska 40.54N 97.08W
109 N6 Seward Oklahoma 35.47N 97.30W
104 F6 Seward Pennsylvania 40.25N 79.02W
101 C5 Seward Glacier Yukon/Alaska
123 F12 Seward Mts Antarctica
113 D4 Seward Pen Alaska
121 B5 Sewell Chile 34.05S 70.25W
69 M8 Sewen France 47.49N 6.55E
15 C6 Sewer Moluccas Indon 5.53S 134.44E
15 G8 Sewerimabu Papua New Guinea 8.36S 143.17E
95 E9 Seweweekspoort S Africa 33.21S 21.25E
104 E6 Sewickley Pennsylvania 40.34N 80.13W
28 B7 Sewri dist Bombay India
60 K7 Sexbierum Netherlands 53.13N 5.29E
72 J5 Sexcles France 45.02N 2.00E
101 O8 Sexsmith Alberta 55.21N 118.50W
115 G4 Sextín Mexico 26.12N 105.32W
20 C4 Seya Kanagawa Japan
93 J4 Seya watercourse Kenya
44 J10 Seyādūn Iran 37.48N 48.54E
31 B4 Seyah Band Koh mts Afghanistan
47 L1 Sëyakha U.S.S.R. 70.11N 72.30E
47 K1 Seyakha R U.S.S.R.
42 E5 Seyba U.S.S.R. 52.32N 94.56E
115 O8 Seybaplaya Mexico 19.45N 90.42W
88 R3 Seybouse R Algeria
27 H10 Seychelles islds Indian Oc
26 Q13 Seychelles Bank Indian Oc
Seychelles Mauritius Ridge see Mascarene Ridge
72 E6 Seyches France 44.34N 0.18E
63 R9 Seyda E Germany 51.53N 12.55E
47 J3 Seyda U.S.S.R. 67.03N 63.00E
50 L4 Seydhisfjördhur Iceland 65.16N 14.02W
50 C2 Seydhisfjördhur B Ísafjardharsýsla, Nordhur Iceland
50 M4 Seydhisfjördhur B Múlasýsla, Nordhur Iceland
53 N9 Seydhtorva C Faeroes 62.24N 6.35W
36 H2 Seydim Turkey 40.32N 34.48E
36 F5 Seydişehir Turkey 37.25N 31.51E
32 A1 Seydvān Iran 38.32N 45.03E
31 G2 Seydzh Tadzhikistan U.S.S.R. 37.14N 72.03E
70 G3 Seye R France
Seyhan see Adana
37 E7 Seyhan R Diyarbakır Turkey
36 H6 Seyhan R Turkey
36 H5 Seyhan Barajı dam Turkey 37.02N 35.18E
36 E1 Seyhler Turkey 41.01N 30.17E
37 H6 Seyhli Gülü marsh Turkey
44 G7 Seyidlyar Azerbaydzhan U.S.S.R. 40.14N 46.05E
36 E3 Seyit R Turkey
36 E3 Seyitgazi Turkey 39.27N 30.42E
37 C3 Seyitli Turkey 40.20N 26.24E
45 D5 Seym R Ukraine U.S.S.R.
46 J4 Seym R Ukraine/Kursk U.S.S.R.
40 D3 Seym R Yakutsk U.S.S.R.
39 E3 Seymchan U.S.S.R. 62.54N 152.26E
41 N6 Seymchan R U.S.S.R.
37 E1 Seymen Turkey 41.07N 27.58E
39 D4 Seymkan R U.S.S.R.
103 H4 Seymour Connecticut 41.24N 73.05W
107 L3 Seymour Indiana 38.57N 85.55W
108 R9 Seymour Iowa 40.40N 93.08W
107 D4 Seymour Missouri 37.07N 92.46W
95 K8 Seymour S Africa 32.33S 26.46E
112 H2 Seymour Texas 33.36N 99.16W
12 H6 Seymour Victoria 37.01S 145.10E
106 F5 Seymour Wisconsin 44.32N 88.21W
13 E4 Seymour R Queensland
101 H10 Seymour Cr. Br Columbia
119 B5 Seymour, I Galápagos Is 0.23S 90.17W
101 H10 Seymour, Mt Br Columbia 49.25N 122.57W
13 C6 Seymour Ra N Terr Australia
71 J8 Seyne France 44.21N 6.20E
71 E8 Seynes France 44.08N 4.18E
71 H10 Seyne-sur-Mer, la France 43.05N 5.53E
51 N11 Seyskari, Ostrov isld U.S.S.R. 60.01N 28.22E
71 H5 Seyssel France 45.57N 5.50E
72 G8 Seysses France 43.30N 1.18E
36 F5 Seytan Dağı mt Turkey 37.18N 31.32E
37 E6 Şeytan Dağları mts Turkey
41 N7 Seytchan R U.S.S.R.
66 B9 Seythenex France 45.44N 6.17E
66 C7 Seytroux France 46.15N 6.37E
82 B5 Sežana Yugoslavia 45.42N 13.51E
69 F6 Sézanne France 48.44N 3.44E
95 O6 Sezela S Africa 30.25S 30.40E
65 N1 Sezemice Czechoslovakia 50.04N 15.51E
46 J2 Sezha R U.S.S.R.
93 D4 Sezibwa R Uganda
76 D7 Sezures Portugal 40.42N 7.38W
80 H6 Sezze Italy 41.29N 13.04E
84 C8 Sfaktiría isld Greece 36.56N 21.40E
88 T4 Sfax Tunisia 34.45N 10.43E
81 D4 Sferracavallo, C Sardinia 39.43N 9.42E
82 K5 Sfîntu Gheorghe Brasov Romania 45.51N 25.48E
82 M6 Sfîntu Gheorghe Constanţa Romania 44.52N 29.37E
82 M6 Sfîntu Gheorghe R Romania
34 E2 Sfira Syria 36.05N 37.21E
Sfiré see Sfira
74 G9 Sfisef Algeria 35.13N 0.17W
60 J11 's Graveland Netherlands 52.15N 5.07E
60 G12 's Gravendeel Netherlands 51.47N 4.37E
60 F11 's Gravenhage Netherlands 52.05N 4.16E
60 H13 's Gravenmoer Netherlands 51.39N 4.56E
60 C3 's Gravenpolder Netherlands 51.28N 3.54E
61 J1 's Gravenwezel Belgium 51.15N 4.34E
60 E11 's Gravenzande Netherlands 52.00N 4.10E
58 G4 Sgurr a'Choire Ghlais mt Highland Scotland 57.27N 4.55W
58 D4 Sgurr Alasdair mt Skye, Highland Scotland 57.12N 6.14W
58 F3 Sgurr Mór mt Highland Scotland 57.41N 5.01W
58 F4 Sgurr na Lapaich mt Highland Scotland 57.22N 5.04W
84 R15 Sha Cyprus 34.57N 33.23E
35 D2 Sha'ab Israel 32.53N 35.14E
35 C6 Sha'alvim Israel 31.53N 34.59E
33 M4 Sha'am U.A.E. 26.00N 56.04E
22 H9 Shaanxi prov China
33 E7 Sha'ar, Ash Saudi Arabia 18.24N 42.27E
35 F3 Sha'ar HaGolan Israel 32.41N 35.36E
34 E4 Sha'ar, Jebel mts Syria
43 J8 Shaartuz Tadzhikistan U.S.S.R. 37.15N 68.07E
86 E3 Shâba Egypt 31.12N 30.46E
Shabachah, Ash see Shabakah, Ash
34 L8 Shabakah, Ash Iraq 30.48N 43.42E
31 D6 Shaban Pakistan 28.07N 66.52E
92 E12 Shabani Zimbabwe 20.20S 30.05E
100 N2 Shabaqua Ontario 48.35N 89.54W
86 E3 Shabâs el Malh Egypt 31.12N 30.39E
86 E3 Shabâs el Shuhada Egypt 31.05N 30.44E
87 D3 Shabasha Sudan 14.10N 32.18E
86 E3 Shabâs 'Imeir Egypt 31.06N 30.47E
85 C6 Shabb Ash Libya 27.35N 14.46E
106 F8 Shabbona Illinois 41.47N 88.53W
85 K8 Shab, El Egypt 22.20N 29.45E
44 B1 Shabel'sk U.S.S.R. 46.50N 38.50E
32 A1 Shabestar Iran 38.10N 45.38E
Shabgudar see Ḩasanābād
34 C9 Shabibi, Jebel esh mt Jordan 29.58N 35.17E
Shabicha, Ash see Shabakah, Ash
31 A4 Shabik Afghanistan 32.54N 61.01E
33 H4 Sha'b, Jabal ash mts Saudi Arabia
82 M7 Shabla Bulgaria 43.31N 28.32E
47 N5 Shablish U.S.S.R. 56.17N 61.42E
47 N5 Shablish, Oz L U.S.S.R. 56.15N 61.38E
45 G4 Shablykino U.S.S.R. 52.51N 35.12E
86 F6 Shabramant Egypt 29.56N 31.11E
47 M4 Shabrovskiy U.S.S.R. 56.38N 60.38E
34 L8 Shabrūm, Ash Iraq 30.10N 43.58E
91 K5 Shabunda Zaïre 2.42S 27.20E
47 J6 Shaburovo U.S.S.R. 59.42N 67.08E
Shabwa anc site see Shabwah
33 G9 Shabwah S Yemen 15.22N 47.00E
23 D5 Shachang Guizhou China 27.20N 106.03E
24 B6 Shache Xinjiang Uygur Zizhiqu China 38.27N 77.16E
100 J8 Shackleton Saskatchewan 50.42N 108.36W
123 G7 Shackleton Coast Antarctica
123 G8 Shackleton Glacier Antarctica
123 D2 Shackleton Ice Shelf Antarctica
123 H7 Shackleton Inlet Antarctica
123 D10 Shackleton Ra Antarctica
33 D6 Shadād Saudi Arabia 21.20N 40.02E
31 D7 Shadadkot Pakistan 27.48N 67.56E
Shaddadi see Shedadi
32 C5 Shādegān Iran 30.40N 48.40E
108 H4 Shadehill Res S Dakota
Shadgan see Shādegān
34 J1 Shadhka Syria 37.06N 41.45E
23 G5 Shadi Jiangxi China 26.05N 114.47E
30 G7 Shadiabad Uttar Prad India 25.41N 83.22E
31 D6 Shadihar Pakistan 28.03N 67.34E
31 D5 Shadikhak Pass Afghanistan 31.18N 67.30E
32 E5 Shādkām R Iran
45 W1 Shadki U.S.S.R. 55.44N 50.13E
35 E3 Shadmot Devora Israel 32.42N 35.26E
Shadpur see Shāhpūr
32 J7 Shadrad Iran 27.37N 60.53E
34 C8 Shadra, Esh mts Jordan
42 E4 Shadrino U.S.S.R. 55.55N 91.08E
47 J7 Shadrinsk U.S.S.R. 56.08N 63.32E
33 A3 Shadwân isld Egypt 27.29N 34.00E
103 F2 Shady New York 42.04N 74.10W
107 K10 Shady Grove Alabama 31.55N 86.11W
105 D7 Shady Grove Florida 30.18N 83.38W
103 A9 Shady Side Maryland 38.51N 76.32W
104 E7 Shadyside Ohio 39.57N 80.46W
43 K7 Shadzud Tadzhikistan U.S.S.R. 37.45N 72.24E
Shafā 'Amr see Shefar'am
30 C3 Shafakhana Uttar Prad India 29.10N 79.09E
87 G5 Shafartak Ethiopia 10.03N 38.14E
44 J10 Shafā Rūd Iran 37.36N 49.11E
86 O6 Sha'fat Ibn Jad ra Jordan
32 G2 Shafī'abad Iran 36.44N 56.34E
35 B7 Shafir Israel 31.41N 34.42E
46 R3 Shafranovo U.S.S.R. 54.00N 54.46E
43 G6 Shafrikan Uzbekistan U.S.S.R. 40.08N 64.30E
40 D4 Shafrova U.S.S.R. 54.01N 127.24E
111 E6 Shafter California 35.30N 119.16W
110 L9 Shafter Nevada 40.52N 114.27W
112 C6 Shafter Texas 29.50N 104.19W
56 G5 Shaftesbury Dorset Eng 51.01N 2.12W
33 M10 Shaga, As area Saudi Arabia/Kuwait
90 A8 Shagamu Nigeria 6.50N 3.43E
43 E4 Shagan R Kazakhstan U.S.S.R.
43 N2 Shagan R Kazakhstan U.S.S.R.
21 B7 Shagang Liaoning China 40.19N 122.12E
46 G6 Shagany, Oz L Ukraine U.S.S.R.
Shagedu see Jungar Qi
113 H5 Shageluk Alaska 62.35N 159.35W
33 B3 Shaghab Saudi Arabia 27.11N 36.29E
33 K8 Shaghawāt, Wādī watercourse S Yemen
35 F6 Shaghur Jordan 31.50N 35.39E
26 B15 Shag I Heard I Antarctica 52.55S 73.34E
Shaglāwa see Shaqlāwa
43 K1 Shaglyteniz, Ozero L Kazakhstan U.S.S.R.
42 E6 Shagonar U.S.S.R. 51.34N 92.55E
11 E12 Shag Pt New Zealand 45.28S 170.48E
11 E12 Shag R New Zealand
123 B16 Shag Rocks S Georgia S Atlantic Oc
Shagwut Wādī see Shaghawāt, Wādī watercourse
31 B4 Shagzak Afghanistan 33.57N 63.08E
87 G4 Shaha watercourse Ethiopia
30 C5 Shahabad Hardoi, Uttar Prad India 27.39N 79.56E
32 B3 Shāhābād Iran 34.08N 46.35E
28 C2 Shahabad Karnataka India 17.07N 76.54E
30 A2 Shahabad Punjab India 30.09N 76.52E
30 A7 Shahabad Rajasthan India 25.15N 77.09E
30 B4 Shahabad Rampur, Uttar Prad India 28.34N 79.00E
30 G7 Shahabad dist Bihar India
29 D7 Shahada Maharashtra India 21.32N 74.30E
18 B9 Shah Alam Pen Malaysia 3.02N 101.31E
31 B7 Shahana Pakistan 27.31N 63.47E
34 O4 Shāhān, Kūh-i- mt Iran 34.34N 46.05E
28 B3 Shahapur Karnataka India 15.51N 74.38E
29 C8 Shahapur Maharashtra India 19.25N 73.20E
35 B7 Shahar Israel 31.37N 34.43E
34 D6 Shahba Syria 32.50N 36.38E
31 D5 Shahbad Pass Afghanistan 31.41N 66.26E
31 D8 Shahbandar Pakistan 24.08N 67.56E
31 C7 Shahbaz Kalat Pakistan 26.40N 64.01E
31 H10 Shahbazpur R Bangladesh
31 D8 Shahbeg Pakistan 25.26N 67.29E
31 D8 Shah Bilawal Pakistan 25.50N 67.10E
32 G5 Shahdāb Iran 30.27N 57.44E
31 E8 Shahdadpur Pakistan 25.56N 68.40E
30 A4 Shahdara Delhi India 28.40N 77.18E
31 H5 Shahdara Pakistan 31.39N 74.23E
31 G4 Shahdheri Pakistan 33.43N 73.00E
29 G6 Shahdol Madhya Prad India 23.19N 81.26E
29 G6 Shahdol dist Madhya Prad India
22 K8 Shahe Hebei China 36.50N 114.29E
22 L8 Shahe Shandong China 37.04N 119.48E
Shahezhen see Linze
Shahezhen see Jiujiang
Shahezi see Wan Xian
31 D3 Shah Fuladi mt Pakistan 34.39N 67.39E
30 F6 Shahganj Juanpur, Uttar Prad India 26.03N 82.41E
30 F8 Shahganj Mirzapur, Uttar Prad India 24.42N 82.57E
30 C8 Shahgarh Madhya Prad India 24.18N 79.08E
29 A4 Shahgarh Rajasthan India 27.08N 69.56E
85 F3 Shahhat Libya 32.48N 21.54E
31 G5 Shah Husain Pakistan 31.36N 72.01E
Shāhī see Ghaem Shahr
34 N2 Shahīdān Iraq 36.19N 45.00E
31 D3 Shahidan Kabul Afghanistan 34.50N 67.37E
31 C4 Shahidan Kandahar Afghanistan 32.31N 64.48E
Shāhī, Daryācheh i L see Rezā'īyeh, Daryācheh-ye
31 B8 Shahid, Ras C Pakistan 25.12N 63.01E
Shahidulla see Xaidulla
32 B2 Shāhīn Dezh Iran 36.43N 46.35E
31 D2 Shah Injir Afghanistan 36.20N 67.09E
32 A2 Shahi Pen Iran
31 C6 Shah Ismail Afghanistan 29.43N 64.22E
30 C5 Shahjahanpur Uttar Prad India 27.53N 79.55E
30 C4 Shahjahanpur dist Uttar Prad India
32 G2 Shāh Jehān, Kūh-e mts Iran
31 D4 Shahjui Afghanistan 32.31N 67.24E
32 F2 Shāh Kūh mts Iran
32 H5 Shāh Kūh mt Iran 31.46N 59.40E
32 F2 Shah Kūh Bālā Iran 36.35N 54.32E
32 E3 Shahmīrzād Iran 35.49N 53.28E
22 M6 Shahousuo Liaoning China 40.29N 120.31E
32 F2 Shāh Pasand Iran 37.02N 55.18E
Shāhpūr see Salmas
29 E6 Shahpur Betul, Madhya Prad Ind 22.12N 77.58E
31 E7 Shahpur Hyderabad Pakistan 26.11N 68.44E
31 E6 Shahpur Kalat Pakistan 28.43N 68.29E
28 C2 Shahpur Karnataka India 16.42N 76.47E
29 G6 Shahpur Mandla, Madhya Prad India 23.00N 81.03E
29 E7 Shahpur Nimar, Madhya Prad India 21.13N 76.15E
31 G4 Shahpur Rawalpindi Pakistan 32.15N 72.32E
29 F6 Shahpur Sagar, Madhya Prad India 23.52N 79.02E
29 F6 Shahpura Madhya Prad India 23.28N 79.58E
29 G6 Shahpura Madhya Prad India 23.10N 80.45E
29 D5 Shahpura Rajasthan India 25.38N 75.01E
33 J7 Shahr Saudi Arabia 19.16N 51.42E
Shahrābād see Shahrabad Kord
32 G2 Shahrabad Kord Iran 37.28N 56.45E
Shahrāban see Miqdādīyah, Al
31 C3 Shahrak Afghanistan 34.06N 64.18E
34 P2 Shahrak Gīlān Iran 36.25N 47.32E
32 D2 Shahrak Tehrān Iran 36.14N 50.55E
32 J4 Shāhrakht Iran 33.38N 60.14E
33 E7 Shahran tribe Saudi Arabia
32 F5 Shahr-e Bābak Iran 30.08N 55.04E
32 J3 Shahr-e-Now Iran 35.00N 60.15E
32 D4 Shahrezā Iran 32.01N 51.55E
31 F2 Shahr-i-Buzurg Afghanistan 37.17N 70.10E
31 D5 Shahrig Pakistan 30.11N 67.45E
31 F2 Shahr-i-Munjan Afghanistan 36.01N 70.52E
Shahr-i-Nau see Shahr-e-Now
44 H10 Shahrī, R Iran
31 D5 Shahr-i-Safa Afghanistan 31.49N 66.23E
Shahr-i-Tajan see Sārī
Shahriza see Shahrezā
32 D4 Shahr Kord Iran 32.20N 50.52E
Shahr Kurd see Shahr Kord
Shahr Rai see Shahr Rey
32 D3 Shahr Rey Iran 35.35N 51.27E
31 F6 Shahr Sultan Pakistan 29.38N 71.08E
Shahrūd see Emāmrūd
32 C2 Shāh Rūd R Iran
32 F3 Shahrud Bustam reg Iran
Shahrukh see Shāhrakht
32 D2 Shahsavār Iran 36.49N 50.54E
32 H6 Shāh Savārān, Kūh-e mts Iran
Shahsawar see Shahsavār
43 E8 Shāh Taqī Iran 36.00N 59.22E
34 O4 Shahu, Kuh-e- mt Iran 34.59N 46.29E
31 C6 Shah Umar Pakistan 29.14N 64.19E
44 H9 Shāhverdī Iran 38.24N 47.17E
30 B8 Shahzad R Uttar Prad India
30 A2 Shahzadpur Haryana India 30.26N 77.01E
Shaibara isld see Shaybārā
33 M8 Sha'ib ash Shich watercourse Iraq
35 D5 Sha'if watercourse Jordan
31 E5 Shaighalu Pakistan 31.10N 68.59E
Shaikhan see Shaykhān
32 A2 Shaikh Bāzit Dāgh mt Iran 37.47N 44.50E
31 C6 Shaikh Husain mt Pakistan 29.08N 65.48E
Shaikh, Shaib ash see Shaykh, Sha'īb Ash watercourse
Shaikh Shu'aib isld see Sheykh Sho'eyb
Shaik Sa'ad see Shaykh Sa'd
47 J5 Shaim U.S.S.R. 60.18N 64.08E
86 M5 Sha'īra, Gebel hill Egypt 30.06N 34.17E
86 M6 Sha'īra, Gebel hill Egypt 29.34N 34.29E
85 L5 Sha'Ira, Gebel mt Egypt 28.45N 31.49E
31 J9 Shaistagang Bangladesh 24.25N 91.40E
21 J9 Shaistaganj Bangladesh 24.16N 91.25E
Shaitur see Shayṭūr
33 K7 Shai'yt S Yemen 18.15N 52.06E
33 H4 Shaj'ah, Jabal mt Saudi Arabia 24.58N 49.34E
29 E6 Shajapur Madhya Prad India 23.27N 76.21E
29 D6 Shajapur dist Madhya Prad India
35 G3 Shajara Jordan 32.39N 35.56E
34 F2 Shajara, Esh Syria 36.16N 38.10E
21 C7 Shajianzi Liaoning China 41.03N 125.30E
93 L9 Shakajila Kenya 3.05S 39.30E
92 C9 Shakalama mt Zambia 15.20S 27.31E
93 M8 Shaka, Ras pt Kenya 2.34S 40.36E
32 B2 Shakar Bolāghī Iran 37.02N 47.41E
95 P5 Shakaskraal S Africa 29.27S 31.14E
91 F7 Shakenge Zaïre 6.14S 18.41E
99 B3 Shakespeare I Ontario 49.38N 88.25W
43 J8 Shakh Tadzhikistan U.S.S.R. 37.03N 68.05E
44 J9 Shakhagach Azerbaydzhan U.S.S.R. 38.36N 48.52E
43 N7 Shakhand Uzbekistan U.S.S.R. 40.54N 71.29E
44 G8 Shakhbuz Nakhichevan' U.S.S.R. 39.24N 45.31E
44 G7 Shakhdagskiy Khrebet mts U.S.S.R.
31 F2 Shakhdara R Tadzhikistan U.S.S.R.
32 H4 Shākhen Iran 33.19N 59.33E
Shakhin see Shākhen
45 H6 Shakhovo U.S.S.R. 50.52N 36.45E
45 G1 Shakhovskaya U.S.S.R. 56.03N 35.32E
43 K6 Shakhrikhan Uzbekistan U.S.S.R. 40.46N 72.01E
43 J7 Shakhristan Tadzhikistan U.S.S.R. 39.47N 68.49E
43 H7 Shakhrisyabz Uzbekistan U.S.S.R. 39.05N 66.49E
40 J7 Shakhtersk Sakhalin U.S.S.R. 49.11N 142.11E
46 L5 Shakhtersk Ukraine U.S.S.R. 48.08N 38.25E
39 K3 Shakhterskiy U.S.S.R. 64.47N 177.38E
43 L3 Shakhtinsk Kazakhstan U.S.S.R. 49.46N 72.45E
43 E3 Shakhty Kazakhstan U.S.S.R. 48.27N 58.30E
45 M9 Shakhty Rostov U.S.S.R. 47.43N 40.16E
46 O1 Shakhun'ya U.S.S.R. 57.41N 46.46E
90 A7 Shaki Nigeria 8.39N 3.25E
31 E4 Shakin Afghanistan 32.30N 69.15E
33 D7 Shākir isld Saudi Arabia 18.52N 40.25E
108 R5 Shakopee Minnesota 44.49N 93.30W
20 F3 Shakotan-dake mt Japan 43.15N 140.25E
20 K1 Shakotan-misaki C Japan 43.24N 140.19E
31 J2 Shaksgam Kashmir 36.08N 76.31E
43 D1 Shaksha Bashkir U.S.S.R. 54.45N 56.16E
86 E7 Shakshūk Egypt 29.29N 30.40E
113 G4 Shaktoolik Alaska 64.20N 161.10W
90 C7 Shaku Nigeria 9.20N 6.45E
29 A1 Shakūrpūr Delhi India 28.41N 77.08E
24 H8 Shalakuei pass Qinghai China 35.48N 93.39E
47 E5 Shalakusha U.S.S.R. 62.15N 40.17E
87 G7 Shala,L Ethiopia
101 M10 Shalalth Br Columbia 50.43N 122.12W
32 D4 Shālamzār Iran 32.02N 50.45E
21 D5 Shalan Heilongjiang China 44.13N 128.52E
23 F8 Shalang Guangdong China 21.40N 111.16E
Shalar R see Shilēr R
87 L5 Shalau Somalia 10.46N 46.45E
41 Q4 Shalaurova, Mys C U.S.S.R. 73.10N 143.30E
Shalav see Shelār
56 H5 Shalbourne Wilts Eng 51.23N 1.33W
43 J6 Shaldarai, Step' Kazakhstan U.S.S.R.
43 N2 Shalday Kazakhstan U.S.S.R. 51.55N 78.45E
46 N2 Shaldezh U.S.S.R. 56.50N 44.59E
33 H6 Shalfā, Ash Saudi Arabia 21.50N 49.39E
56 K5 Shalford Surrey Eng 51.13N 0.35W
47 D5 Shalgachëva U.S.S.R. 62.18N 39.38E
43 K3 Shalgiya Kazakhstan U.S.S.R. 47.34N 70.40E
28 H2 Shali Bhutan 27.30N 91.35E
44 G4 Shali Checheno Ingush A.S.S.R. U.S.S.R. 43.10N 45.55E
45 V1 Shali Tatar A.S.S.R. U.S.S.R. 55.42N 49.38E
29 G2 Shalimar Pt Calcutta, W Bengal
Shalinhe see Gangca
42 E4 Shalinskoye U.S.S.R. 55.42N 93.45E
29 F2 Shalkar Himachal Prad India 32.00N 78.33E
43 B2 Shalkar Ural'sk, Kazakhstan U.S.S.R. 50.34N 51.46E
43 F2 Shalkar Karashatau salt L Kazakhstan U.S.S.R. 50.26N 61.07E
43 B2 Shalkar, Ozero L Kazakhstan U.S.S.R.
43 F2 Shalkar Yega Kara salt L U.S.S.R. 50.15N 60.53E
35 G3 Shallala watercourse Jordan
34 M10 Shallālah, Ash Saudi Arabia 28.08N 44.40E
59 F6 Shallee mt Tipperary Irish Rep 52.47N 8.16W
105 J4 Shallotte N Carolina 33.58N 78.25W
112 E2 Shallowater Texas 33.41N 102.00W
101 F1 Shallow B N W Terr
99 J8 Shallow Lake Ontario 44.38N 81.06W
86 J5 Shallûfa, El Egypt 30.07N 32.33E
86 E3 Shâlma Egypt 31.15N 30.52E
58 K1 Shalmstry Highland Scotland 58.33N 3.30W
93 M8 Shalu, L Kenya 2.08S 40.28E
23 B3 Shaluli Shan mt ra Sichuan China
28 L1 Shalunli mt Assam India 28.58N 96.02E
31 H3 Shalurah Kashmir 34.30N 74.08E
35 C7 Shalwa Israel 31.34N 34.46E
47 M4 Shalya U.S.S.R. 57.17N 58.48E
45 F5 Shalygino Ukraine U.S.S.R. 51.35N 34.07E
42 D5 Shalym U.S.S.R. 52.48N 87.50E
Sha'm see Sha'am
32 G7 Shām Iran 26.40N 57.23E
89 J9 Shama Ghana 5.03N 1.35W
92 F5 Shama R Tanzania
45 T8 Shamak Kazakhstan U.S.S.R. 48.26N 47.52E
86 P5 Shamākh Jordan 30.30N 35.31E
43 K6 Shamaldy Say Kirgiziya U.S.S.R. 41.17N 72.11E
Shamālīya, Al Bādiya ash see Badiet esh Shām desert
39 G5 Shamanka R U.S.S.R.
42 D6 Shaman, Khrebet mts U.S.S.R.
39 E2 Shamankina R U.S.S.R.
33 G9 Shamarīyah S Yemen 15.12N 47.40E
47 H7 Shamary U.S.S.R. 57.24N 58.19E
33 E2 Shāmat al Akbād sand dune area Saudi Arabia
33 M6 Shamāţīţ,Ash sandy reg Oman
32 C4 Shambār Iran 32.35N 49.36E
87 C7 Shambe Sudan 7.08N 30.48E
87 F6 Shambo Ethiopia 9.32N 37.03E
91 F7 Shambungu Zaïre 7.23S 18.38E
91 G7 Shambwania Zaïre 6.35S 20.01E
35 D2 Shamerat Israel 32.57N 35.06E
Sham, Esh see Damascus Syria
28 H2 Shamgong Dzong Bhutan 27.13N 90.40E
30 K7 Shamhu Bihar India 25.19N 86.13E
32 G7 Shamīl Iran 27.32N 56.51E
35 F1 Shamir Israel 33.10N 35.39E
33 K5 Shāmis oil field U.A.E. 23.55N 53.43E
34 F4 Shāmīyah des Syria/Iraq
Shāmīyah, Ash see Bādiyah al Janūbīyah, Al
34 M7 Shāmīyah, Ash Iraq 31.56N 44.37E
44 H4 Shamkhal U.S.S.R. 43.05N 47.20E
44 G7 Shamkhor Azerbaydzhan U.S.S.R. 40.50N 46.00E
44 G7 Shamkhor-chay R Azerbaydzhan U.S.S.R.
32 G3 Shāmkūh Iran 35.46N 57.51E
30 A3 Shamli Uttar Prad India 29.27N 77.18E
33 D3 Shammar tribe Saudi Arabia
103 A5 Shamokin Pennsylvania 40.46N 76.35W
103 A5 Shamokin R Pennsylvania
40 K7 Shamovo Sakhalin U.S.S.R. 49.02N 144.21E
105 D8 Shamrock Florida 29.38N 83.08W
109 O6 Shamrock Oklahoma 35.55N 96.36W
100 L8 Shamrock Saskatchewan 50.11N 106.41W
112 D8 Shamrock Texas 35.13N 100.15W
32 F5 Shams anc site Iran 31.04N 55.03E
30 B5 Shamsabad Agra, Uttar Prad India 27.01N 78.07E
30 C5 Shamsabad Farukhabad, Uttar Prad India 27.31N 79.26E
33 C10 Shamsān, Jebel S Yemen 12.47N 45.01E
34 F2 Shams ed Dīn Gharbi Syria 36.14N 38.10E
Shamsh see Shams
23 B9 Sham Shui Po Hong Kong 22.19N 114.08E
91 F7 Shamuhombo Zaïre 7.50S 18.59E
91 F7 Sha Musenge Zaïre 7.17S 18.59E
92 E10 Shamva Zimbabwe 17.20S 31.38E
92 E10 Shamva dist Zimbabwe
25 E2 Shan aut area Burma
35 G6 Sha'nab anc site Jordan 31.51N 35.46E
28 D2 Shanabad Andhra Prad India 17.09N 78.05E
Shanafiyah see Shinafīyah, Ash
59 D6 Shanagolden Limerick Irish Rep 52.35N 9.05W
86 F4 Shanawân Egypt 30.30N 31.00E
86 F7 Shanawīya, El Egypt 29.09N 31.08E
Shanchengzhen see Nanjing
42 E6 Shanchi U.S.S.R. 51.43N 91.58E
31 A5 Shand Chakhansur Afghanistan 31.26N 61.50E
31 B5 Shand Chakhansur Afghanistan 31.11N 62.47E
32 J6 Shāndak Iran 28.28N 60.27E
103 F2 Shandaken New York 42.07N 74.25W
22 E7 Shandan Gansu China 38.50N 101.08E
32 C2 Shāndarman Iran 37.24N 49.05E
22 K5 Shandian He R Nei Monggol Zizhiqu China
32 H2 Shāndīz Iran 36.18N 59.10E
111 D6 Shandon California 35.38N 120.22W
58 G6 Shandon Strathclyde Scotland 56.03N 4.49W
22 K8 Shandong prov China
34 N5 Shandrūkh Iraq 33.20N 45.22E
31 G2 Shandur Pass Kashmir/Pakistan 36.05N 72.40E
91 K9 Shangalowe Zaïre 10.48S 26.35E
47 E5 Shangaly U.S.S.R. 61.09N 43.22E
92 D11 Shangani Zimbabwe 19.41S 29.20E
92 C11 Shangani R Zimbabwe
22 L6 Shangbancheng Hebei China 40.50N 118.02E
23 G2 Shangcai Henan China 33.15N 114.20E
23 G3 Shangcheng Henan China 31.51N 115.27E
21 C6 Shangchengzhen Jilin China 42.28N 125.31E
Shang-ch'iu see Shangqiu
28 G1 Shang Chu R Xizang Zizhiqu
23 F8 Shangchuan Dao isld Guangdong China 21.42N 112.47E
22 J6 Shangdu Nei Monggol Zizhiqu China 41.34N 113.42E
Shangdundu see Linchuan
23 G4 Shangfu Jiangxi China 28.40N 115.00E
23 G4 Shanggao Jiangxi China 28.16N 114.55E
23 B2 Shang Gongma Qinghai China 33.44N 99.40E
21 B12 Shanghai Shanghai China 31.06N 121.22E
23 J3 Shanghai Shanghai China 31.06N 121.22E
23 G6 Shanghang Fujian China 25.03N 116.25E
22 L8 Shanghe Shandong China 37.20N 117.11E
22 K6 Shanghuanggi Hebei China 41.30N 116.30E
Shangji see Xichuan
23 E2 Shangjin Hubei China 33.10N 109.55E
23 E3 Shangkan Hubei China 31.47N 110.20E
23 E7 Shanglin Guangxi China 23.26N 108.32E
23 E2 Shangnan Shaanxi China 33.31N 110.50E
91 H12 Shangombo Zambia 16.28S 22.10E
Shangpaihe see Feixi
23 G1 Shangqui Henan China 34.27N 115.07E
23 H4 Shangrao Jiangxi China 28.28N 117.54E
23 H4 Shangrao Jiangxi China 28.28N 117.54E
23 G2 Shangshui Henan China 33.36N 114.38E
24 G10 Shangshung pass Xizang Zizhiqu 30.57N 91.40E
23 E7 Shangsi Guangxi China 22.13N 108.03E
23 H2 Shangtang Jiangsu China 33.23N 118.03E
23 E2 Shang Xian Shaanxi China 33.53N 109.56E
22 J7 Shangyangwu Shanxi China 38.50N 112.30E
22 J6 Shangyi Hebei China 41.05N 113.57E
23 G6 Shangyou Jiangxi China 25.56N 114.40E
24 C5 Shangyou Sk L Xinjiang Uygur Zizhiqu China
24 C5 Shangyou Yichang Xinjiang Uygur Zizhiqu China 40.27N 81.00E
23 J3 Shangyu Zhejiang China 30.03N 120.52E
23 B7 Shangyun Yunnan China 23.04N 99.50E
21 D5 Shangzhi Heilongjiang China 45.13N 127.59E
22 F3 Shanh Mongolia 47.07N 102.56E
22 L7 Shanhaiguan Hebei China 39.59N 119.45E
Shanhe see Zhengning
21 D5 Shanhetun Heilongjiang China 44.33N 127.14E
90 F6 Shani Nigeria 10.11N 12.05E
110 E4 Shaniko Oregon 45.02N 120.45W
30 J3 Shanjo Nepal 27.54N 86.52E
92 A10 Shanjo tribe Zambia
30 E7 Shankargarh Uttar Prad India 25.11N 81.37E
56 J6 Shanklin I of Wight Eng 50.38N 1.10W
23 G4 Shankou Jiangxi China 28.50N 114.32E
24 H4 Shankou Xinjiang Uygur Zizhiqu China 42.02N 94.08E
104 G6 Shanksville Pennsylvania 40.02N 78.56W
24 G11 Shannan reg Xizang Zizhiqu China
103 L4 Shannock Rhode I 41.27N 71.38W
105 B3 Shannon Georgia 34.21N 85.03W
106 E7 Shannon Illinois 42.09N 89.46W
107 H7 Shannon Mississippi 34.07N 88.45W
11 K7 Shannon New Zealand 40.32S 175.24E
95 K5 Shannon S Africa 29.09S 26.19E
48 V8 Shannon isld Greenland
59 E6 Shannon Airport Clare Irish Rep 52.42N 8.57W
59 F5 Shannonbridge Offaly Irish Rep 53.17N 8.03W
108 Q9 Shannon City Iowa 40.56N 94.16W
59 C6 Shannon, Mth of the Irish Rep
59 F3 Shannon,R Leitrim etc Irish Rep
87 G6 Shano Ethiopia 9.20N 39.21E
90 C5 Shanomo Nigeria 12.06N 7.57E
24 G4 Shanshan Xinjiang Uygur Zizhiqu China 42.51N 90.14E
22 G8 Shanshui He R Ningxia China
86 E5 Shanshûr Egypt 30.22N 31.00E
Shansi prov Chinasee Shanxi
39 D1 Shanskoye U.S.S.R. 70.08N 147.22E
21 D6 Shansonggang Jilin China 42.34N 126.17E
40 G4 Shantarskiye Ostrova islds U.S.S.R.
29 L1 Shanti Niketan W Bengal India 23.42N 87.41E
59 J3 Shantonagh Monaghan Irish Rep 54.03N 6.52W
23 G7 Shantou Guangdong China 23.23N 116.39E
41 B2 Shantsa, Mys C Novaya Zemlya U.S.S.R. 74.45N 55.30E
23 A8 Shan Tseng Hong Kong 22.22N 114.03E
Shantung prov Chinasee Shandong
Shantung Pen. see Liaodong Bandao
92 F3 Shanwa Tanzania 2.22S 33.45E
23 G7 Shanwei Guangdong China 22.48N 115.22E
22 J7 Shanxi prov China
23 G1 Shan Xian Shandong China 34.51N 116.09E
23 E2 Shanyang Shaanxi China 33.33N 109.53E
23 H6 Shanyao Fujian China 25.07N 118.44E
22 J7 Shanyin Shanxi China 39.25N 112.56E
23 H2 Shaobo Jiangsu China 32.29N 119.30E
23 F5 Shaodong Hunan China 27.15N 111.43E
22 G7 Shaogangpu Ningxia China 38.09N 106.04E
23 F6 Shaoguan Guangdong China 24.54N 113.33E
23 F5 Shaoshan Hunan China 27.55N 112.33E
23 H5 Shaowu Fujian China 27.21N 117.27E
23 J3 Shaoxing Zhejiang China 30.02N 120.35E
23 F5 Shaoyang Hunan China 26.59N111.16E
23 F5 Shaoyang Hunan China 27.10N 111.25E
57 H3 Shap Cumbria Eng 54.32N 2.41W
91 G6 Shapembe Zaïre 4.50S 20.42E
39 F6 Shapina R U.S.S.R.
58 T11 Shapinsay isld Orkney Scotland 59.03N 2.51W
58 T11 Shapinsay Sd Orkney Scotland
45 O5 Shapkino U.S.S.R. 51.44N 42.21E
47 G3 Shapkino R U.S.S.R.
45 E1 Shapkovo U.S.S.R. 55.46N 33.22E
42 D6 Shapshal'skiy Khrebet mts U.S.S.R.
44 H3 Shapshur U.S.S.R. 44.57N 46.56E
32 D6 Shapur anc site Iran 29.45N 51.38E
87 E3 Shaqarab Sudan 14.50N 35.51E
35 H1 Shaqhab Syria 33.15N 36.10E
33 D2 Shaqīq, Ash Saudi Arabia 29.27N 40.08E
24 F3 Shaqiuhe Xinjiang Uygur Zizhiqu China 45.00N 88.52E
34 M2 Shaqlāwa Iraq 36.25N 44.22E
33 M9 Shaqq, Ash area Kuwait
33 G8 Shaqqat al Kharītah sand ridge Saudi Arabia
90 M4 Shaqq el Giefer, Wadi watercourse Sudan
87 A4 Shaqq el Khadir Sudan 12.02N 26.25E
33 F4 Shaqra' Saudi Arabia 25.18N 45.15E
35 H2 Shaqra Syria 32.54N 36.15E
24 D3 Shaquanzi Xinjiang Uygur Zizhiqu China 44.40N 83.03E
33 F4 Sha'rā', Ash Saudi Arabia 24.18N 44.13E
40 G1 Sharabarma U.S.S.R. 60.32N 135.03E
87 A4 Sharafa Sudan 12.02N 27.07E
32 A1 Sharaf-khāneh Iran 38.11N 45.29E
Shara Gol see Dang He
Sharakpur see Sharqpur
42 H6 Sharalday U.S.S.R. 51.01N 107.40E
31 D4 Sharan Afghanistan 33.28N 66.19E
46 R3 Sharan U.S.S.R. 54.50N 54.00E
46 O2 Sharanga U.S.S.R. 57.09N 46.30E
31 E5 Sharan Jogizai Pakistan 31.02N 68.33E
45 Q1 Sharapovo U.S.S.R. 55.16N 44.41E
47 K1 Sharapov Shar, Zaliv B U.S.S.R.
Sharasume see Altay
42 H5 Shara-Togot U.S.S.R. 53.02N 106.52E
33 G8 Sharawrah Saudi Arabia 17.28N 47.06E
34 D10 Sharawrā, Jabal mts Saudi Arabia
Sharbatāt, Ra's see Sharbithāt, Ra's cape
33 M8 Sharbithāt, Ra's C Oman 17.55N 56.24E
32 G6 Shārb Māh Iran 28.01N 57.10E
99 O8 Sharbot Lake Ontario 44.45N 76.42W
42 C5 Sharchino U.S.S.R. 53.11N 81.49E
31 H3 Shardi Kashmir 34.47N 74.14E
Shardin see Māmātīn
90 B7 Share Nigeria 8.50N 4.55E
93 C9 Shareka mt Tanzania 3.48S 31.59E
32 H4 Sharfa'ī Iran 32.02N 59.04E
30 J6 Sharfuddinpur Bihar India 26.07N 85.33E
Shargain Tsagān Nur L see Tsagaan Nuur
42 J6 Shargal'dzhin U.S.S.R. 52.25N 114.48E
Shargol see Kargil
43 J7 Shargun Uzbekistan U.S.S.R. 38.31N 67.56E
24 H10 Shargung La pass Xizang Zizhiqu China 30.52N 94.42E
21 K6 Shari Japan 43.56N 144.41E
34 M4 Shārī, Buḩayrat L Iraq
Sharifa see Sherifa oil well
Sharifabad see Shafi'abad
32 H2 Sharīfābad Khorāsān Iran 36.01N 59.24E
34 P2 Sharīfābād Kordestān Iran 36.01N 47.40E
Sharif-khaneh see Sharaf-khāneh
47 L6 Sharipova U.S.S.R. 54.43N 59.38E
46 S3 Sharipovo U.S.S.R. 54.58N 55.30E
22 G2 Shariyn gol Mongolia 49.15N 106.30E
Sharja see Sharjah
33 A3 Shār, Jabal mt Saudi Arabia 27.39N 35.45E
33 L4 Sharjah U.A.E. 25.20N 55.26E
86 P10 Shar, Jebel mt Saudi Arabia 27.39N 35.44E
46 R2 Sharkan U.S.S.R. 57.19N 53.51E
13 B1 Shark B N Terr Australia
Shark Bay see Denham W Australia
19 J6 Shark Fin B Philippines
28 H1 Sharkha-leb La pass Xizang Zizhiqu 28.34N 91.32E
33 J9 Sharkhāt S Yemen 15.10N 51.00E
46 G2 Sharkovshchina Belorussiya U.S.S.R. 55.19N 27.30E
13 H2 Shark Reef Gt Barrier Reef Australia 14.06S 146.50E
43 D7 Sharlauk Turkmeniya U.S.S.R. 38.14N 55.39E
46 R3 Sharlyk U.S.S.R. 52.58N 54.46E
35 G9 Sharma watercourse Jordan
34 C10 Sharmah, Ash Saudi Arabia 28.01N 35.18E
86 N9 Sharm Dabba inlet Saudi Arabia
86 N9 Sharm el Kusara inlet Saudi Arabia
86 M10 Sharm el Sheikh Egypt 27.51N 34.16E
86 M10 Sharm el Sheikh inlet Egypt 27.52N 34.18E
86 N9 Sharm Mujawwa inlet Saudi Arabia
33 B4 Sharm Yanbu gulf Saudi Arabia 24.12N 37.55E
56 J2 Sharnford Leics Eng 52.31N 1.16W
86 E3 Sharnûb Egypt 31.01N 30.34E
103 H3 Sharon Connecticut 41.53N 73.28W
105 E4 Sharon Georgia 33.32N 82.49W
109 M4 Sharon Kansas 37.15N 98.25W
103 M2 Sharon Massachusetts 42.08N 71.11W
106 J5 Sharon Michigan 44.35N 85.04W
108 N2 Sharon N Dakota 47.36N 97.53W
109 L5 Sharon Oklahoma 36.17N 99.21W
104 E5 Sharon Pennsylvania 41.16N 80.30W
107 H5 Sharon Tennessee 36.15N 88.49W
104 N3 Sharon Vermont 43.47N 72.27W
106 F7 Sharon Wisconsin 42.30N 88.43W
35 E3 Sharona Israel 32.43N 35.28E
35 C5 Sharon, Plain of Israel
109 J3 Sharon Springs Kansas 38.54N 101.46W
45 G6 Sharovka Ukraine U.S.S.R. 50.01N 35.28E
108 K5 Sharpe, L S Dakota
23 C8 Sharp I Hong Kong
15 M8 Sharp I Papua New Guinea 9.17S 152.35E
56 G4 Sharpness Glos Eng 51.44N 2.29W
56 B6 Sharpnose headland Cornwall Eng 50.55N 4.34W
111 A9 Sharp Park California 37.38N 122.29W
104 J9 Sharps Virginia 37.50N 76.42W
108 Q9 Sharpsburg Iowa 40.48N 94.38W
104 H7 Sharpsburg Maryland 39.27N 77.46W
112 F9 Sharpstown dist Houston, Texas 29.42N 95.30W
106 H9 Sharpsville Indiana 40.24N 86.05W
104 K8 Sharptown Maryland 38.31N 75.45W
103 D7 Sharptown New Jersey 39.39N 75.22W
34 L3 Sharqāţ Iraq 35.30N 43.14E
34 C5 Sharqi, Jebel esh mts Lebanon
86 G4 Sharqîya div Egypt
33 M5 Sharqiyah, Ash reg Oman
31 H5 Sharqpur Pakistan 31.29N 74.08E
35 B8 Sharsheret Israel 31.24N 34.36E
44 G2 Sharshuk U.S.S.R. 45.36N 45.41E
103 B5 Shartlesville Pennsylvania 40.32N 76.07W
86 E8 Shârûna Egypt 28.37N 30.50E
86 E8 Shârûna, Wâdî watercourse Egypt
22 D3 Shar Us Gol R Mongolia
33 J9 Sharwayn, Ra's C S Yemen 15.20N 51.40E
33 E3 Shary Saudi Arabia 27.14N 43.29E
46 O1 Shar'ya U.S.S.R. 58.22N 45.20E
42 D4 Sharypovo U.S.S.R. 55.32N 89.10E
87 E7 Shasha Ethiopia 6.29N 35.59E
Shashamanna see Shashemenē
92 D12 Shashani R Zimbabwe
94 J3 Shashe Botswana 21.25S 27.28E
94 K3 Shashe R Botswana

92 E11 Shashe R Zimbabwe
87 G7 Shashemenē Ethiopia 7.13N 38.33E
23 F3 Shashi Hubei China 30.16N 112.20E
29 A1 Shashtrinagar dist Delhi India
Shaspeh R see Shūl R
110 C9 Shasta California 40.36N 122.30W
110 C8 Shasta R California
110 C9 Shasta L California 40.45N 122.20W
110 C8 Shasta, Mt California 41.25N 122.12W
45 K5 Shatalovka U.S.S.R. 51.08N 38.16E
35 G4 Shatana Jordan 32.26N 35.52E
86 F5 Shatânûf Egypt 30.15N 31.04E
34 N2 Shataveh R Iran
85 B6 Shāţi watercourse Libya
23 F6 Shatian Hunan China 25.52N 113.47E
23 B8 Sha Tin Hong Kong 22.22N 114.10E
45 Q1 Shatki U.S.S.R. 55.10N 44.07E
43 F8 Shatlyk Turkmeniya U.S.S.R. 37.30N 61.30E
Shatnat as Salmas, Wadi see Shetnet es Salmas, Wādī watercourse
45 P1 Shatovka U.S.S.R. 55.16N 43.44E
Shatra see Shaţrah, Ash
34 O7 Shaţrah, Ash Iraq 31.26N 46.10E
47 J7 Shatrovo U.S.S.R. 56.32N 64.40E
30 L4 Shatsal Xizang Zizhiqu 28.11N 87.22E
45 N2 Shatsk U.S.S.R. 54.02N 41.45E
34 P8 Shatt al 'Arab R Iran/Iraq
32 A4 Shatt al Hillah R Iraq
34 M6 Shatt al Hindīyah R Iraq
86 J6 Shatt, El Egypt 29.57N 32.36E
32 D6 Shaţţ, Ra's ash C Iran 29.10N 50.40E
109 L5 Shattuck Oklahoma 36.16N 99.55W
45 L1 Shatura U.S.S.R. 55.32N 39.30E
45 L1 Shaturtorf U.S.S.R. 55.34N 39.25E
86 P4 Shaubak Jordan 30.33N 35.35E
43 N4 Shaukar, Poluostrov pen Kazakhstan U.S.S.R. 46.30N 78.15E
23 B9 Shau Kei Wan Hong Kong 22.16N 114.13E
43 J5 Shaul'der Kazakhstan U.S.S.R. 42.45N 68.18E
35 G4 Shaumar watercourse Jordan
44 C3 Shaumyan U.S.S.R. 44.18N 39.17E
44 F6 Shaumyani Georgia U.S.S.R. 41.22N 44.46E
44 H7 Shaumyanovsk Azerbaydzhan U.S.S.R. 40.24N 46.33E
100 J9 Shaunavon Saskatchewan 49.40N 108.25W
28 B3 Shavarati R Karnataka India
47 C4 Shaverki U.S.S.R. 63.11N 31.27E
111 E4 Shaver L California 37.07N 119.19W
104 F8 Shavers Fork R W Virginia
35 D2 Shave Ziyyon Israel 32.59N 35.05E
44 G5 Shaviklde mt U.S.S.R. 42.14N 45.35E
121 F6 Shaw Argentina 36.38S 59.45W
107 F8 Shaw Mississippi 33.36N 90.49W
Shawak see Shawāq
87 D4 Shawal, Esh Sudan 13.32N 32.39E
31 F3 Shawal Pass Pakistan/Afghan 35.36N 71.35E
24 E3 Shawan Xinjiang Uygur Zizhiqu China 44.20N 85.45E
24 E3 Shawan ruins Xinjiang Uygur Zizhiqu China 45.05N 85.08E
99 K7 Shawanaga Ontario 45.32N 80.18W
103 F3 Shawangunk Kill R New York
103 E4 Shawangunk Mts New York
106 F5 Shawano Wisconsin 44.46N 88.38W
106 F5 Shawano L Wisconsin
33 B3 Shawāq Saudi Arabia 27.19N 36.26E
86 E7 Shawâshna, El Egypt 29.23N 30.36E
58 C2 Shawbost Lewis, W Isles Scotland 58.18N 6.41W
99 Q7 Shawbridge Quebec 45.52N 74.06W
56 F2 Shawbury Shropshire Eng 52.47N 2.39W
57 F2 Shawhead Dumfries & Galloway Scotland 55.04N 3.47W
13 J5 Shaw I Queensland 20.29S 149.05E
99 S6 Shawinigan Quebec 46.33N 72.45W
110 Q3 Shawmut Montana 46.20N 109.31W
104 C7 Shawnee Ohio 39.36N 82.14W
109 O6 Shawnee Oklahoma 35.20N 96.55W
108 F7 Shawnee Wyoming 42.46N 105.00W
107 H4 Shawneetown Illinois 37.42N 88.21W
14 C5 Shaw, R W Australia
35 H1 Shawrah Syria 33.16N 36.02E
34 H5 Shawr, Ash hill Iraq 33.01N 40.22E
103 A7 Shawsville Maryland 39.38N 76.34W
99 O7 Shawville Quebec 45.36N 76.30W
23 H5 Sha Xi R Fujian China
23 H5 Sha Xian Fujian China 26.27N 117.42E
Shayar see Xayar
33 L5 Shaybah oil field Saudi Arabia 22.35N 54.05E
34 K10 Shaybāni, Ash Saudi Arabia 28.30N 42.05E
33 B4 Shaybārā isld Saudi Arabia 25.30N 36.50E
39 G3 Shayboveem R U.S.S.R.
43 M7 Shaydan Tadzhikistan U.S.S.R. 40.42N 70.22E
86 E6 Shâyib, El Egypt 29.50N 30.56E
85 M6 Shâyib El Banât, Gebel mt Egypt 26.59N 33.29E
34 M7 Shaykh' Abbūd Shinīn Iraq 31.54N 44.59E
34 L2 Shaykhān Iraq 36.47N 43.27E
34 P6 Shaykh Fāris Iraq 32.03N 47.37E
Shaykh Ibrāhīm see Sheikh Ibrāhīm
Shaykh, Jabal Ash mt see Hermōn, Mt
34 O6 Shaykh Jūwī Iraq 32.24N 46.45E
Shaykh Miskin see Sheikh Miskīn
34 O6 Shaykh Sa'd Iraq 32.32N 46.18E
34 J7 Shaykh, Sha'īb ash watercourse Iraq
34 M4 Shaykh Shunayf, Ash Iraq 34.02N 44.37E
33 B9 Shaykh 'Uthmān S Yemen 12.53N 44.58E
33 B9 Shaykh 'Uthmān Airport S Yemen 12.53N 44.58E
47 H5 Shaytanovka U.S.S.R. 62.03N 58.01E
32 F5 Shayţūr Iran 31.32N 55.49E
34 P10 Shazaf, Ash Saudi Arabia/Kuwait 28.25N 48.05E
32 C4 Shāzand Iran 33.54N 49.28E
22 C7 Shazaoyuan Gansu China 39.58N 94.20E
33 D3 Shaẓāẓ, Jabal mts Saudi Arabia
23 J3 Shazhou Jiangsu China 31.52N 120.33E
Shchapinskaya Sopka vol see Kizimen, Sopka vol
46 F3 Shchara R Belorussiya U.S.S.R.
40 M8 Shchekal Kuril Is U.S.S.R. 46.10N 150.16E
45 J3 Shchekino U.S.S.R. 54.00N 37.34E
45 G2 Shchelkanovo U.S.S.R. 54.36N 35.28E
45 K1 Shchelkovo U.S.S.R. 55.56N 38.05E
47 M5 Shchelkun U.S.S.R. 56.19N 60.58E
45 G2 Shcheloki U.S.S.R. 54.53N 35.07E
42 E5 Shchelovatka U.S.S.R. 54.56N 92.35E
47 G3 Shchel'yayur U.S.S.R. 65.16N 53.17E
Shcherbakov see Rybinsk
39 G2 Shcherbakovo U.S.S.R. 65.12N 160.36E
43 N1 Shcherbakty Kazakhstan U.S.S.R. 52.31N 78.11E
44 B7 Shcherbani Ukraine U.S.S.R. 47.31N 31.44E
41 J3 Shcherberina, Mys C U.S.S.R. 77.03N 106.58E
45 J1 Shcherbinka U.S.S.R. 55.30N 37.36E
45 F3 Shchigry Kaluga U.S.S.R. 53.40N 35.00E
45 H5 Shchigry Kursk U.S.S.R. 51.52N 36.54E
82 H1 Shchirets U.S.S.R. 49.40N 23.51E
45 C5 Shchors Ukraine U.S.S.R. 51.50N 31.59E
45 F8 Shchorsk Ukraine U.S.S.R. 48.20N 34.07E
43 K1 Shchuchinsk Kazakhstan U.S.S.R. 52.59N 70.14E
47 K3 Shchuch'ya R U.S.S.R.
47 J7 Shchuch'ye Kurgan U.S.S.R. 55.20N 62.42E
47 K3 Shchuch'ye Tyumen U.S.S.R. 67.12N 68.38E
45 M5 Shchuch'ye Voronezh U.S.S.R. 51.46N 40.30E
47 K7 Shchuch'ye, Oz L U.S.S.R. 55.35N 67.30E
47 H7 Shchuch'ye Ozero U.S.S.R. 56.28N 56.39E
47 H4 Shchugor R U.S.S.R.
45 K1 Shchurovo U.S.S.R. 55.04N 38.47E
119 J6 Shea Guyana 2.48N 59.04W
87 E7 Shea Ghimirra Ethiopia 7.01N 35.50E
58 F3 Sheallag, L. na Highland Scotland 57.47N 5.20W
110 H6 Sheaville Oregon 43.06N 117.03W
45 P9 Shebalin U.S.S.R. 47.23N 43.37E
42 D6 Shebalino U.S.S.R. 51.14N 85.45E
100 M2 Shebandowan L Ontario
45 H6 Shebekino U.S.S.R. 50.25N 36.54E
45 H7 Shebelinka Ukraine U.S.S.R. 49.27N 36.31E
42 F5 Sheberta U.S.S.R. 54.36N 99.59E
44 L3 Shebir Kazakhstan U.S.S.R. 44.49N 52.04E
44 H10 Sheblī Iran 37.58N 46.39E
106 G6 Sheboygan Wisconsin 43.46N 87.44W
90 E7 Shebshi Mts Nigeria
40 J8 Shebunino Sakhalin U.S.S.R. 46.24N 141.50E
Shechem see Nablus
34 H2 Shedadi Syria 36.02N 40.44E
110 B5 Shedd Oregon 44.28N 123.07W
99 J10 Shedden Ontario 42.44N 81.20W
59 K2 Sheddings, The Antrim N Ireland 54.55N 6.05W
35 B6 Shedema Israel 31.50N 34.44E
33 H4 Shedgum oil field Saudi Arabia 25.46N 49.20E
98 H7 Shediac New Brunswick 46.13N 64.35W
44 D3 Shedok U.S.S.R. 44.13N 40.50E
59 H4 Sheelin, L Cavan etc Irish Rep 53.48N 7.20W
99 N7 Sheenboro Quebec 45.58N 77.15W
113 Q2 Sheenjek R Alaska
101 O9 Sheep Cr Alberta
108 E7 Sheep Cr Wyoming
59 G1 Sheep Haven B Donegal Irish Rep 55.12N 7.52W
56 K4 Sheep Lane Beds Eng 51.58N 0.39W
95 O2 Sheepmoor S Africa 26.43S 30.18E
109 C2 Sheep Mt Colorado 39.56N 107.10W
111 J5 Sheep Pk mt Nevada 36.35N 115.18W
103 J5 Sheep Ra Nevada
111 J5 Sheep Ra Nevada
Sheeps Hd see Muntervary Hd
103 M8 Sheepshead Bay New York 40.36N 73.57W
60 C3 's Heer-Abtskerke Netherlands 51.28N 3.53E
60 C3 's Heer-Arendskerke Netherlands 51.30N 3.50E
60 O12 's Heerenberg Netherlands 51.52N 6.15E
60 C3 's Heerenhoek Netherlands 51.27N 3.46E
60 C2 's Heer-Hendrikskinderen Netherlands 51.30N 3.52E
100 F7 Sheerness Alberta 51.30N 111.40W
56 N5 Sheerness Kent Eng 51.27N 0.45E
98 K9 Sheet Harbour Nova Scotia 44.56N 62.31W
58 K5 Shee Water R Tayside Scotland
35 D2 Shefar'am Israel 32.48N 35.10W
35 C5 Shefayyim Israel 32.13N 34.49E
35 C8 Shefela reg Israel
35 E2 Shefer Israel 32.56N 35.27E
107 J7 Sheffield Alabama 34.45N 87.40W
106 E8 Sheffield Illinois 41.22N 89.43W
108 R7 Sheffield Iowa 42.53N 93.11W
103 H2 Sheffield Massachusetts 42.06N 73.22W
11 G10 Sheffield New Zealand 43.23S 172.02E
104 F5 Sheffield Pennsylvania 41.43N 79.03W
57 K6 Sheffield S Yorks Eng 53.23N 1.30W
12 H8 Sheffield Tasmania 41.24S 146.19E
112 F5 Sheffield Texas 30.42N 101.52W
104 C5 Sheffield Lake Ohio 41.31N 82.04W
56 L3 Shefford Beds Eng 52.02N 0.20W
29 E7 Shegaon Maharashtra India 20.48N 76.47E
42 C4 Shegarka R U.S.S.R.
47 F4 Shegmas U.S.S.R. 64.40N 49.18E
99 J7 Sheguiandah Ontario 45.53N 81.57W
100 O7 Sheho Saskatchewan 51.37N 103.17W
23 D3 Shehong Sichuan China 30.53N 105.19E
23 D3 Shehong Sichuan China 30.53N 105.19E
Shehuén R see Chalía R
31 F4 Sheik Budin Pakistan 32.16N 70.48E
87 K6 Sheikh Somalia 9.56N 45.13E
87 K5 Sheikh, El Somalia 10.28N 44.18E
86 M9 Sheikh el 'Arab, Gebel hill Egypt 28.24N 34.01E
35 F4 Sheikh Husein Bridge Israel/Jordan 32.30N 35.34E
34 F3 Sheikh Ibrāhīm Syria 35.07N 38.52E
87 D5 Sheikh Idris Sudan 11.47N 33.33E
35 B1 Sheikh Jarrah sub Jerusalem
34 C5 Sheikh, Jebel esh mt Lebanon/Syria 33.24N 35.50E
34 D6 Sheikh Miskīn Syria 32.49N 36.10E
30 J7 Sheikhpura Bihar India 25.09N 85.50E
86 L9 Sheikh Riyâh inlet Egypt
35 H2 Sheikh Sa'd Syria 32.50N 36.02E
86 E10 Sheikh Timai, El Egypt 27.52N 30.51E
86 F8 Sheikh, Wâdî el watercourse Egypt
86 L8 Sheikh, Wâdi el watercourse Egypt
35 G2 Shejara, Esh Syria 32.46N 35.53E
99 F3 Shekak R Ontario
32 F4 Shekār Āb Iran 33.39N 55.34E
29 D4 Shekhawati reg Rajasthan India
45 M4 Shekhman' U.S.S.R. 52.32N 40.27E
31 H5 Shekhupura Pakistan 31.42N 74.08E
31 G5 Shekhupura dist Pakistan
44 H6 Sheki Azerbaydzhan U.S.S.R. 41.12N 47.10E
46 O8 Sheki Azerbaydzhan U.S.S.R. 41.12N 47.10E
103 G3 Shekomeko New York 41.55N 73.35W
47 D6 Sheksna R U.S.S.R.
23 B9 Shek Tong Tsui Hong Kong 22.16N 114.07E
42 C5 Shelabolikha U.S.S.R. 53.25N 82.35E
32 J5 Shelag R Iran/Afghanistan
39 J1 Shelagskiy U.S.S.R. 70.04N 170.30E
39 J1 Shelagskiy, Mys C U.S.S.R. 70.08N 170.20E
32 G2 Shelami, Reshteh-ye mts Iran
45 U1 Shelanga U.S.S.R. 55.31N 49.00E
32 C4 Shelār Iran 32.19N 49.41E
42 F4 Shelayevo U.S.S.R. 56.56N 97.44E
104 C9 Shelbiana Kentucky 37.26N 82.29W
107 D2 Shelbina Missouri 39.40N 92.01W
107 J2 Shelburn Indiana 39.11N 87.24W
98 G10 Shelburne Nova Scotia 43.47N 65.20W
99 K8 Shelburne Ontario 44.05N 80.13W
104 M2 Shelburne Vermont 44.22N 73.15W
13 G1 Shelburne B Queensland 11.50S 142.50E
104 N4 Shelburne Falls Massachusetts 42.35N 72.45W
106 G8 Shelby Indiana 41.12N 87.21W
108 P8 Shelby Iowa 41.31N 95.26W
106 H6 Shelby Michigan 43.36N 86.22W
107 F8 Shelby Mississippi 33.58N 90.47W
110 O1 Shelby Montana 48.30N 111.52W
105 F2 Shelby N Carolina 35.16N 81.34W
108 N8 Shelby Nebraska 41.13N 97.24W
104 C6 Shelby Ohio 40.52N 82.40W
107 H2 Shelbyville Illinois 39.24N 88.48W
107 L2 Shelbyville Indiana 39.31N 85.46W
107 L3 Shelbyville Kentucky 38.13N 85.12W
107 D2 Shelbyville Missouri 39.48N 92.01W
107 K6 Shelbyville Tennessee 35.29N 86.30W
112 N4 Shelbyville Texas 31.46N 94.05W
107 H2 Shelbyville, Lake res Illinois
106 G9 Sheldon Illinois 40.46N 87.33W
108 P6 Sheldon Iowa 43.10N 95.40W
107 B4 Sheldon Missouri 37.40N 94.19W
108 N3 Sheldon N Dakota 46.35N 97.30W
95 J9 Sheldon S Africa 33.03S 25.52E
106 D4 Sheldon Wisconsin 45.20N 90.57W
101 H4 Sheldon Mt Yukon Terr 62.44N 131.21W
113 E5 Sheldons Point Alaska 62.30N 165.00W
104 N2 Sheldon Springs Vermont 44.53N 73.00W
103 M2 Sheldonville Massachusetts 42.02N 71.23W
98 H3 Sheldrake Quebec 50.18N 64.54W
Sheldrake I see Luodou Sha
42 G6 Shelekhov U.S.S.R. 52.12N 104.01E
40 N6 Shelekhova Kuril Is U.S.S.R. 50.20N 155.22E
42 F4 Shelekhova U.S.S.R. 55.42N 97.40E
113 K8 Shelikof Str Alaska
44 G4 Shelkovskaya U.S.S.R. 43.32N 46.20E
108 C5 Shell Wyoming 44.33N 107.45W
108 P3 Shell R Minnesota
107 G12 Shell Beach Louisiana 29.51N 89.41W
100 L5 Shellbrook Saskatchewan 53.14N 106.24W
108 B8 Shell Cr Wyoming
108 C5 Shell Cr Wyoming
90 F7 Shellen Nigeria 9.51N 12.03E
110 N6 Shelley Idaho 43.25N 112.07W
12 K5 Shellharbour New S Wales 34.35S 150.52E
58 C3 Shell L Lewis, W Isles Scotland 58.00N 6.30W
100 K5 Shell Lake Saskatchewan 53.19N 107.06W
106 C4 Shell Lake Wisconsin 45.44N 91.56W
14 F8 Shell Lakes W Australia
105 C6 Shellman Georgia 31.45N 84.38W
100 Q8 Shellmouth Manitoba 50.57N 101.30W
110 B9 Shell Mt California 40.08N 123.05W
108 S7 Shell Rock Iowa 42.42N 92.33W
108 S7 Shellrock R Iowa
106 C7 Shellsburg Iowa 42.04N 91.50W
35 D1 Shelomi Israel 33.04N 35.08E
46 G1 Shelon' R U.S.S.R.
42 K6 Shelopugino U.S.S.R. 51.42N 117.32E
110 A9 Shelter Cove California 40.03N 124.04W
23 C9 Shelter I Hong Kong
103 K4 Shelter I Long I, N Y 41.05N 72.17W
103 K4 Shelter Island Long I, N Y 41.04N 72.20W
11 C13 Shelter Pt Stewart I New Zealand 47.07S 168.14E
39 D5 Shel'tinga Zaliv B U.S.S.R.
103 H4 Shelton Connecticut 41.19N 73.06W
108 M9 Shelton Nebraska 40.48N 98.40W
110 B2 Shelton Washington 47.13N 123.05W
59 K6 Shelton Abbey Wicklow Irish Rep 52.51N 6.10W
47 D5 Sheltozero U.S.S.R. 61.22N 35.21E
35 A10 Sheluhat Qeren hill Israel 30.58N 34.26E
35 E4 Sheluhot Israel 32.28N 35.29E
93 F10 Shelui Tanzania 4.19S 34.15E
Shelyakino see Sovetskoye Belgorod U.S.S.R.
32 D2 Shem Iran 36.02N 51.48E
44 J7 Shemakha Azerbaydzhan U.S.S.R. 40.38N 48.37E
47 L5 Shemakhao U.S.S.R. 56.14N 58.50E
34 J4 Shemlān, Sabkhat salt marsh Syria
43 O2 Shemonaikha Kazakhstan U.S.S.R. 50.38N 81.55E
46 Q2 Shemordan U.S.S.R. 56.12N 50.28E
85 K10 Shemsi Sudan 19.02N 29.57E
45 T2 Shemursha U.S.S.R. 54.54N 47.30E
113 M9 Shemya I Aleutian Is 52.45N 174.05E
45 R4 Shemysheyka U.S.S.R. 52.54N 45.22E
108 P9 Shenandoah Iowa 40.48N 95.22W
103 B5 Shenandoah Pennsylvania 40.49N 76.11W
104 G8 Shenandoah Virginia 38.30N 78.38W
104 G8 Shenandoah R Virginia
104 H7 Shenandoah Junc W Virginia 39.22N 77.52W
104 F8 Shenandoah Mts W Virginia
104 G8 Shenandoah Nat. Park Virginia
104 E5 Shenango R Pennsylvania
104 E5 Shenango Res Penn/Ohio 41.17N 80.24W
43 H3 Shenber Kazakhstan U.S.S.R. 49.46N 66.08E
22 J7 Shenchi Shanxi China 39.05N 112.10E
28 C6 Shencottah Tamil Nadu India 8.59N 77.15E
90 D7 Shendam Nigeria 8.49N 9.31E
87 D2 Shendi Sudan 16.41N 33.22E
21 F4 Shending Shan mts Heilongjiang China
21 F4 Shending Shan mt pk Heilongjiang China 46.37N 133.36E
87 J7 Sheneli Ethiopia 6.40N 43.31E
89 C8 Shenge Sierra Leone 7.54N 12.54W
83 D3 Shëngjin Albania 41.48N 19.34E
24 E4 Shengli Daban pass Xinjiang Uygur Zizhiqu China
Sheng-li Feng see Pobedy, Pik mt
24 C5 Shengli Qichang Xinjiang Uygur Zizhiqu China 40.20N 80.05E
24 D5 Shengli Shibachang Xinjiang Uygur Zizhiqu China 40.38N 81.35E
24 D5 Shengli Shijiuchang Xinjiang Uygur Zizhiqu China 40.33N 81.29E
24 D5 Shengli Shiliuchang Xinjiang Uygur Zizhiqu China 40.40N 81.28E
24 C5 Shengli Shisanchang Xinjiang Uygur Zizhiqu China 40.45N 80.46E
21 C4 Shengping Heilongjiang China 46.12N 125.20E
21 B12 Shengsi Zhejiang China 30.43N 122.27E
21 B12 Shengsi Liedao islds Zhejiang China
23 J4 Sheng Xian Zhejiang China 29.36N 120.42E
83 D3 Shenjt Mal i mts Albania
31 E2 Shen Khan Bandar Afghanistan 37.08N 68.38E
47 E5 Shenkursk U.S.S.R. 62.05N 42.58E
22 K5 Shenlang (Xulun Ho) Qi Nei Monggol Zizhiqu China 42.15N 116.10E
22 H7 Shenmu Shaanxi China 38.54N 110.19E
82 F9 Shën Ndue-Madh mt Albania 41.22N 20.10E
23 E3 Shennongjia Hubei China 31.44N 110.43E
23 G2 Shenqiu Henan China 33.25N 115.06E
Shensi prov Chinasee Shaanxi
46 Q3 Shentala U.S.S.R. 54.28N 51.30E
14 E8 Shenton, Mt W Australia 27.59S 123.20E
Shentza Dzong see Xainza
22 K7 Shen Xian Hebei China 38.00N 115.30E
22 K8 Shen Xian Shandong China 36.15N 115.44E
21 C7 Shenyang Liaoning China 41.50N 123.26E
22 K7 Shenze Hebei China 38.12N 115.14E
Shenzhen see Bao'an
30 J6 Sheohar Bihar India 26.31N 85.18E
29 E5 Sheopur Madhya Prad India 25.41N 76.42E
100 D7 Shepard Alberta 51.00N 113.56W
123 J10 Shepard I Antarctica 74.25S 132.00W
45 A2 Shepelevichi Belorussiya U.S.S.R. 54.08N 29.32E
46 F4 Shepetovka Ukraine U.S.S.R. 50.12N 27.01E
Shephela reg see Shefela region
106 K6 Shepherd Michigan 43.33N 84.42W
110 R4 Shepherd Montana 35.58N 108.20W
112 M5 Shepherd Texas 30.29N 95.01W
55 E3 Shepherds Bush London England 51.30N 0.14W
104 H7 Shepherdstown W Virginia 39.24N 77.49W
107 L4 Shepherdsville Kentucky 38.00N 85.42W
101 G7 Sheppard, Mt Br Columbia 57.41N 132.35W
12 H6 Shepparton Victoria 36.25S 145.26E
14 E8 Shepperd, L W Australia
55 B5 Shepperton Surrey Eng 51.23N 0.28W
56 N5 Sheppey isld Kent Eng 51.25N 0.50E
103 B5 Sheppton Pennsylvania 40.53N 76.08W
43 B5 Shepte Kazakhstan U.S.S.R. 44.08N 52.07E
56 F5 Shepton Mallet Somerset Eng 51.12N 2.33W
45 G5 Sheptukhovka U.S.S.R. 51.26N 35.10E
23 F2 Sheqi Henan China 33.07N 112.55E
90 M6 Sherab Sudan 10.44N 24.41E
43 H7 Sherabad Uzbekistan U.S.S.R. 37.45N 67.01E
87 F7 Sherada Ethiopia 7.18N 36.25E
42 G5 Sheragul U.S.S.R. 54.28N 101.00E
97 L3 Sherard, C N W Terr 74.40N 80.25W
31 A4 Sher Bakhsh Afghanistan 33.32N 1.58E
47 L8 Sherbakul' U.S.S.R. 54.38N 72.22E
45 N2 Sherbatovka U.S.S.R. 54.48N 41.45E
103 M2 Sherborn Massachusetts 42.15N 71.22W
56 F6 Sherborne Dorset Eng 50.57N 2.31W
95 J7 Sherborne S Africa 31.21S 25.01E
89 C8 Sherbro channel Sierra Leone
89 C8 Sherbro I Sierra Leone
98 L8 Sherbrooke Nova Scotia 45.10N 61.58W
99 T7 Sherbrooke Quebec 45.24N 71.54W
98 H9 Sherbrooke L Nova Scotia
108 Q6 Sherburn Minnesota 43.38N 94.42W
57 M4 Sherburn N Yorks Eng 54.10N 0.32W
104 K4 Sherburne New York 42.41N 75.30W
15 K5 Sherburne Reef Bismarck Arch 3.20S 148.00E
57 L5 Sherburn in Elmet N Yorks Eng 53.48N 1.15W
59 J4 Shercock Cavan Irish Rep 54.00N 6.54W
90 H1 Sherda Chad 20.06N 16.44E
31 E4 Sher-Dahan Pass Afghanistan 33.40N 68.33E
56 L5 Shere Surrey Eng 51.13N 0.28W
85 M10 Shereik Sudan 18.44N 33.37E
56 J5 Sherfield Hants Eng 51.19N 1.01W
28 J2 Shergaon Assam India 27.06N 92.16E
29 C4 Shergarh Jodhpur, Rajasthan India 26.19N 72.24E
29 E5 Shergarh Kota, Rajasthan India 24.41N 76.32E
30 A5 Shergarh Uttar Prad India 27.48N 77.39E
30 H8 Sherghati Bihar India 24.34N 84.48E
107 D7 Sheridan Arkansas 34.18N 92.22W
106 H9 Sheridan Indiana 40.08N 86.13W
106 J6 Sheridan Michigan 43.13N 85.06W
110 N4 Sheridan Montana 45.27N 112.12W
110 B4 Sheridan Oregon 45.07N 123.24W
108 D5 Sheridan Wyoming 44.48N 106.57W
97 N1 Sheridan, C N W Terr 82.30N 60.30W
109 H3 Sheridan Lake Colorado 38.28N 102.17W
110 P5 Sheridan, Mt Wyoming 44.16N 110.34W
34 E4 Sherifa oil bore Syria 34.30N 37.22E
57 L4 Sheriff Hutton N Yorks Eng 54.05N 1.00W
12 D5 Sheringa S Australia 33.48S 135.12E
56 O2 Sheringham Norfolk Eng 52.57N 1.12E
87 F2 Sherit Ethiopia 16.40N 37.49E
47 K4 Sherkaly U.S.S.R. 62.49N 65.28E
43 J8 Sher Khan Bandar Afghanistan 37.16N 68.49E
31 D6 Sher Khan Qala Afghanistan 29.55N 66.20E
59 D9 Sherkin I Cork Irish Rep 51.28N 9.25W
14 C5 Sherlock, R W Australia
42 K6 Sherlovaya Gora U.S.S.R. 50.32N 116.15E
103 H3 Sherman Connecticut 41.34N 73.30W
107 H7 Sherman Mississippi 34.20N 88.50W
104 F4 Sherman New York 42.10N 79.37W
103 D3 Sherman Pennsylvania 41.59N 75.26W
112 L2 Sherman Texas 33.39N 96.35W
101 Z2 Sherman Basin N W Terr
104 Q8 Sherman Mills Maine 45.53N 68.23W
110 K9 Sherman Mt Nevada 40.08N 115.35W
110 O7 Sherman Pk Idaho 42.29N 111.31W
108 M8 Sherman Res Nebraska 41.18N 98.52W
85 N6 Sherm, El Egypt 27.52N 34.18E
45 J1 Shermet'yevo airport U.S.S.R. 56.00N 37.25E
30 K3 Sherpani Col pass Nepal 27.52N 87.02E
31 E3 Sherpur Afghanistan 34.33N 69.09E
31 H9 Sherpur Bogra Bangladesh 24.40N 89.29E
31 H8 Sherpur Mymensingh Bangladesh 25.00N 90.01E
30 G7 Sherpur Uttar Prad India 25.36N 83.49E
31 H2 Sher Qila Kashmir 36.05N 74.03E
100 Q3 Sherridon Manitoba 55.07N 101.05W
104 K3 Sherrill New York 43.05N 75.36W
30 L4 Sherson Nepal 27.49N 87.05E
56 G4 Sherston Wilts Eng 51.35N 2.13W
28 C6 Shertally Kerala India 9.40N 76.21E
60 K13 's Hertogenbosch Netherlands 51.41N 5.19E
Sherwan see Shīrvān
108 J1 Sherwood N Dakota 48.58N 101.38W
112 G4 Sherwood Texas 31.17N 100.47W
92 D11 Sherwood Zimbabwe 18.44S 29.50E
13 K2 Sherwood dist Brisbane, Qnsld
11 E10 Sherwood Downs New Zealand 43.57S 170.52E
101 W5 Sherwood L N W Terr 60.57N 103.21W
120 C3 Sheshea, R Peru
103 B3 Sheshequn Pennsylvania 41.52N 76.30W
46 Q2 Sheshma R U.S.S.R.
32 G2 Sheshtamad Iran 36.03N 57.45E
23 G3 She Shui R Hubei China
101 H6 Sheslay Br Col 58.18N 131.52W
101 H6 Sheslay R Br Columbia
39 D1 Shestakova U.S.S.R. 68.10N 147.13E
46 Q1 Shestakovo Kirov U.S.S.R. 58.58N 50.10E
39 G3 Shestakovo Magadan U.S.S.R. 62.43N 164.43E
108 P5 Shetek, L Minnesota
54 K2 Shetland islds Scotland
58 Q9 Shetland isld area Scotland
34 F3 Shetnet es Salmas, Wādī watercourse Syria
44 L3 Shetpe Kazakhstan U.S.S.R. 44.09N 52.06E
35 E1 Shetula Israel 33.05N 35.18E
35 B6 Shetulim Israel 31.47N 34.40E
28 D5 Shevaroy Hills Tamil Nadu India
43 B5 Shevchenko Kazakhstan U.S.S.R. 43.37N 51.11E
45 J8 Shevchenko Ukraine U.S.S.R. 48.14N 37.11E
45 J7 Shevchenkova Ukraine U.S.S.R. 49.40N 37.11E
Sheveluch vol see Shiveluch, Sopka vol
29 D8 Shevgaon Maharashtra India 19.21N 75.14E
40 F4 Shevli U.S.S.R. 54.06N 133.14E
40 F5 Shevli R U.S.S.R.
108 P2 Shevlin Minnesota 47.32N 95.15W
42 H5 Shevykan U.S.S.R. 54.25N 106.48E
87 G6 Shewa prov Ethiopia
23 H4 She Xian Anhui China 29.53N 118.27E
22 J8 She Xian Hebei China 38.00N 115.30E
42 K1 Sheya U.S.S.R. 62.52N 117.32E
23 J2 Sheyang Jiangsu China 33.46N 120.15E
108 L2 Sheyenne N Dakota 47.49N 99.08W
108 N3 Sheyenne R N Dakota
34 O3 Sheykh 'Aţţār Iran 35.29N 46.28E
34 O4 Sheykh Hasan Iran 34.26N 46.12E
32 E7 Sheykh Sho'eyb isld Iran
32 D5 Sheykkī Iran 30.14N 51.25E
35 E2 Shezor Israel 32.56N 35.20E
58 D3 Shiant Is Lewis, W Isles Scotland
58 D3 Shiant, Sound of Lewis, W Isles Scotland
40 N7 Shiashkotan, O isld Kuril Is U.S.S.R. 48.45N 154.00E
106 K6 Shiawassee, R Michigan
34 M7 Sh'īb Abū Ma'ris watercourse Iraq
33 H9 Shibām S Yemen 15.58N 48.34E
22 D6 Shiban Jing well Nei Monggol Zizhiqu China 41.45N 98.25E
22 D7 Shibaocheng Gansu China 39.54N 96.30E
31 C2 Shibarghan Afghanistan 36.40N 65.42E
31 E3 Shibar Pass Afghanistan 34.55N 68.18E
20 N4 Shibata Japan 37.57N 139.20E
22 J6 Shibatai Nei Monggol Zizhiqu China 40.56N 112.55E
21 C1 Shibazhan Heilongjiang China 52.27N 125.23E
86 F9 Shibb, El hill Egypt 28.22N 31.03E
21 K6 Shibecha Japan 43.17N 144.34E
20 H2 Shibetsu Kamikawa Japan 44.10N 142.21E
20 L2 Shibetsu Nemuro Japan 43.40N 145.10E
31 C6 Shibian Pass Afghan/Pakistan 29.36N 64.38E
86 E4 Shibîn el Kôm Egypt 30.33N 31.00E
86 F5 Shibîn El Qanâtir Egypt 30.19N 31.19E
23 E5 Shibing Guizhou China 27.02N 108.06E
24 F10 Shib La pass Xizang Zizhiqu China 30.01N 88.03E
86 F5 Shiblanga Egypt 30.29N 31.16E
40 K10 Shibotsu-jima isld Kuril Is U.S.S.R. 43.30N 146.09E
Shibrum, Ash see Shabrūm, Ash
20 M5 Shibukawa Japan 36.30N 138.59E
20 E10 Shibushi Japan 31.30N 131.07E
20 E10 Shibushi-wan B Japan
33 J8 Shibut mt S Yemen 17.02N 51.51E
20 D2 Shibuya dist Tōkyō Japan
22 L8 Shibuzi Shandong China 36.07N 119.06E
23 D5 Shichang Guizhou China 27.33N 105.58E
23 G5 Shicheng Jiangxi China 26.22N 116.14E
20 P1 Shichinohe Japan 40.42N 141.08E
19 M4 Shichiyo Is Truk Is Pacific Oc
108 N9 Shickley Nebraska 40.25N 97.35W
103 B4 Shickshinny Pennsylvania 41.39N 76.09W
98 F5 Shickshock Mts Quebec
23 H2 Shicun Anhui China 33.46N 117.19E
34 F8 Shidād al Mismā salt L Saudi Arabia
20 A4 Shidahara Kanagawa Japan
21 B9 Shidao Shandong China 36.54N 122.23E
21 B9 Shidao Wan B Shandong China
43 L2 Shiderty R Kazakhstan U.S.S.R.
23 B6 Shidian Yunnan China 24.42N 99.12E
86 P6 Shīdīya, Wādī esh watercourse Jordan
109 O5 Shidler Oklahoma 36.46N 96.40W
20 H7 Shido Japan 34.19N 134.10E
Shidongsi see Gaolan
31 F2 Shidud Afghanistan 37.40N 71.29E
58 F4 Shiel Bridge Highland Scotland 57.12N 5.26W
58 E3 Shieldaig Highland Scotland 57.31N 5.40W
13 D2 Shield, C N Terr Australia 13.16S 136.20E
109 K3 Shields Kansas 38.36N 100.28W
108 J3 Shields N Dakota 46.14N 101.09W
58 E5 Shiel, L Highland Scotland
Shif see Jazireh-ye Shif
23 C3 Shifang Sichuan China 31.08N 104.10E
56 G2 Shifnal Shropshire Eng 52.41N 2.22W
20 K6 Shiga prefect Japan
90 L4 Shigaib Sudan 15.00N 23.35E
23 B7 Shigaojing Yunnan China 22.47N 101.24E
31 H3 Shigar Kashmir 35.27N 75.43E
Shigatse see Xigazê
98 G5 Shigawake Quebec 48.07N 65.06W
28 B3 Shiggaon Karnataka India 15.00N 75.28E
Shighala see Shaighalu
35 C8 Shigma watercourse Israel
22 C6 Shigong Gansu China 40.25N 95.45E
45 U3 Shigony U.S.S.R. 53.25N 48.40E
85 N9 Shigrib, Jebel mt Sudan 20.25N 34.10E
85 M9 Shigrib, Wadi watercourse Sudan
23 B5 Shigu Yunnan China 26.50N 99.58E
22 H6 Shiguaigou Nei Monggol Zizhiqu China 40.52N 110.14E
34 C7 Shihān mt Jordan 31.22N 35.42E
33 K8 Shihan, Wādī watercourse S Yemen/Oman
Shih-ch'üan Ho see Shiquan He
24 E3 Shihezi Xinjiang Uygur Zizhiqu China 44.19N 86.10E
34 M8 Shīhiyāt, Ash hills Iraq
30 B1 Shih-pu-ch'i Shan-k'ou pass Xizang Zizhiqu/India 31.50N 78.50E
33 H9 Shiḥr, Ash S Yemen 14.46N 49.40E
Shiḥr & Mukalla sultanate see Qu'ayţī sultanate
Shih-tai see Guangyang
20 M4 Shiiya Japan 37.28N 138.38E
83 D3 Shijak Albania 41.21N 19.33E
23 C3 Shijiaba Sichuan China 30.19N 104.48E
Shijiao see Fogang
22 K7 Shijiazhuang Hebei China 38.04N 114.28E
22 J7 Shijiazhuang Shanxi China 38.36N 112.02E
22 K7 Shijingshan Beijing China 39.55N 116.12E
23 H3 Shijiu Hu L Jiangsu China
23 H1 Shijiusuo Shandong China 35.25N 119.25E
23 K6 Shika Ishigakishima Japan 24.21N 124.10E
20 K2 Shikabe Japan 42.03N 140.49E
100 M1 Shikag L Ontario 49.45N 90.40W
20 H7 Shikama Japan 34.48N 134.39E
23 E8 Shikang Guangxi China 21.46N 109.20E
Shikarab see Shekār Āb
35 F5 Shikara, Esh Jordan 32.14N 35.44E
30 H5 Shikarpur Bihar India 27.07N 84.28E
28 B3 Shikarpur Karnataka India 14.16N 75.18E
31 E7 Shikarpur Pakistan 27.58N 68.42E
30 B4 Shikarpur Uttar Prad India 28.17N 78.00E
31 B6 Shikar R Pakistan
43 E6 Shikh Turkmeniya U.S.S.R. 40.02N 58.26E
45 T4 Shikhany U.S.S.R. 52.06N 47.12E
45 T1 Shikhazany U.S.S.R. 55.34N 47.24E
20 C1 Shiki Saitama Japan 35.50N 139.35E
19 N4 Shiki Is Truk Is Pacific Oc
20 N7 Shikine-jima isld Japan 34.19N 139.11E
30 B5 Shikohabad Uttar Prad India 27.06N 78.35E
20 F8 Shikoku isld Japan
20 F8 Shikoku-sanchi mts Japan
22 G8 Shikong Ningxia China 37.32N 105.42E
40 K10 Shikotan Kuril Is U.S.S.R. 43.51N 146.47E
40 K10 Shikotan isld Kuril Is U.S.S.R.
21 K6 Shikotan tō isld Japan 43.47N 148.45E
20 L2 Shikotsu-ko L Japan
20 K2 Shikotsu Toya Nat. Park Japan
45 T4 Shikovka U.S.S.R. 52.37N 47.24E
42 E4 Shila U.S.S.R. 56.34N 93.00E
47 F5 Shilador U.S.S.R. 61.47N 49.53E
43 E2 Shil'da U.S.S.R. 51.49N 59.46E
57 K3 Shildon Durham Eng 54.38N 1.39W
47 E4 Shilega U.S.S.R. 63.48N 44.04E
34 N3 Shilēr R Iraq
43 P3 Shilikarym Kazakhstan U.S.S.R. 48.08N 83.59E
Shiliu see Changjiang
42 K6 Shilka U.S.S.R. 51.55N 116.01E
40 A5 Shilka R U.S.S.R.
39 D5 Shilkan U.S.S.R. 59.24N 145.38E
58 B3 Shillay isld W Isles Scotland 57.48N 7.15W
59 J6 Shillelagh Wicklow Irish Rep 52.45N 6.32W
89 C7 Shilling, C Sierra Leone 8.11N 13.10W
56 J4 Shillingford Oxon Eng 51.39N 1.09W
99 K4 Shillington Ontario 48.33N 80.40W
104 K6 Shillington Pennsylvania 40.17N 75.59W
28 H3 Shillong Meghalaya India 25.34N 91.53E
87 C6 Shilluk tribe Sudan
43 A2 Shil'naya Balka Kazakhstan U.S.S.R. 50.36N 48.58E
45 V6 Shil'naya Balka Kazakhstan U.S.S.R. 50.34N 49.02E
103 D8 Shiloh New Jersey 39.28N 75.18W
35 E5 Shiloh anc site Jordan 32.03N 35.18E
107 H6 Shiloh Nat. Mil. Park Tennessee 35.08N 88.20W
23 F7 Shilong Guangdong China 23.05N 113.50E
23 E7 Shilong Guangxi China 23.54N 109.33E
22 H8 Shilou Shanxi China 36.58N 110.52E
45 U2 Shilovka U.S.S.R. 54.06N 48.31E
45 M2 Shilovo Ryazan' U.S.S.R. 54.20N 40.56E
45 K3 Shilovo Tula U.S.S.R. 53.10N 38.34E
56 J3 Shilton Warwicks Eng 52.28N 1.23W
22 D3 Shilüüstey Mongolia 46.55N 97.14E
Shima see Longhai
23 G5 Shima Jiangxi China 27.00N 115.42E
20 D9 Shimabara Japan 32.48N 130.20E
20 M7 Shimada Japan 34.50N 138.10E
20 H2 Shimadadai Chiba Japan
20 F3 Shimamaki Japan 42.42N 140.01E
20 E7 Shimane prefect Japan
40 D5 Shimanovsk U.S.S.R. 52.02N 127.35E
23 F2 Shimantan Sk res Henan China 33.23N 113.23E
20 G9 Shimanto-gawa R Japan
23 E8 Shimao Ling volcano Guangdong China 20.35N 110.10E
93 L10 Shimba Hills Kenya
Shimbar see Shambār
93 M5 Shimbirre Kenya 0.31N 40.36E
93 M4 Shimbirri Kenya 1.05N 40.34E
23 F4 Shimen Hunan China 29.35N 111.15E
22 L6 Shimenzhai Hebei China 40.10N 119.36E
Shimenzhen see Yunlong
23 C4 Shimian Sichuan China 29.08N 102.28E
20 M1 Shimizu Hokkaido Japan 43.01N 142.51E
20 M6 Shimizu Honshu Japan 35.01N 138.29E
20 A3 Shimizu Kanagawa Japan
Shimmanato see Shimminato
20 L5 Shimminato Japan 36.48N 137.05E
87 H7 Shimo Ethiopia 7.15N 40.05E
20 P1 Shimoburo Japan 41.26N 141.05E
20 M7 Shimoda Japan 34.40N 138.55E
20 O5 Shimodate Japan 36.20N 140.00E
20 B1 Shimo-Fujisawa Saitama Japan
20 B4 Shimo-Furusawa Kanagawa Japan
28 B4 Shimoga Karnataka India 13.56N 75.31E
28 B3 Shimoga dist Karnataka India
20 B3 Shimo-gawara Tōkyō Japan
20 E7 Shimogō Japan 34.05N 131.22E
20 C2 Shimo-Hōya dist Tōkyō Japan
20 H5 Shimo-Izumi Chiba Japan
20 D9 Shimo-jima isld Japan
20 P4 Shimo-Kitaba Japan 37.12N 141.00E
20 C10 Shimo-Koshiki-jima isld Japan
20 A3 Shimo-Kuzawa Kanagawa Japan
20 B4 Shimo-Mizo Kanagawa Japan
93 L10 Shimoni Kenya 4.37S 39.22E
20 M5 Shimonita Japan 36.12N 138.47E
20 D8 Shimonoseki Japan 33.59N 130.58E
20 C7 Shimono-shima isld Japan
20 B4 Shimo-Ogino Kanagawa Japan
20 B4 Shimoppara Kanagawa Japan
45 O1 Shimorskoye U.S.S.R. 55.19N 42.02E
20 B1 Shimo-Shinden Saitama Japan
20 D10 Shimo-Taniguchi Japan 31.38N 130.22E
20 E9 Shimo-Tashima Japan 32.03N 131.26E
20 N5 Shimotsuma Japan 36.10N 139.58E
20 C4 Shimotsuruma Kanagawa Japan
20 A1 Shimo-Yaganuki Saitama Japan
20 B3 Shimo-Yugi Tōkyō Japan
35 D3 Shimron Israel 32.42N 35.12E
28 C4 Shimsha R Karnataka India
46 H1 Shimsk U.S.S.R. 58.12N 30.45E
20 D2 Shimura dist Tōkyō Japan
34 M7 Shinafiyāh, Ash Iraq 31.34N 44.38E
20 E3 Shinagawa dist Tōkyō Japan
34 N2 Shinak Pass Iraq/Iran 36.42N 45.04E
23 E7 Shinan Guangxi China 22.54N 109.55E
20 M4 Shinano-gawa R Japan
33 M4 Shināş Oman 24.45N 56.30E
31 B4 Shindand Afghanistan 33.16N 62.05E
20 B4 Shindenjuku Kanagawa Japan
20 K7 Shindō Japan 34.50N 136.13E
86 E3 Shîn, El Egypt 31.01N 30.53E
112 K6 Shiner Texas 29.26N 97.11W
58 H2 Shiness Highland Scotland 58.05N 4.30W
58 H3 Shin Falls Highland Scotland 57.56N 4.25W
92 D8 Shingana Zaïre 12.50S 29.00E
25 M7 Shingbwiyang Burma 26.41N 96.10E
25 N7 Shing-Gai Burma 27.20N 97.55E
31 E5 Shinghar Pakistan 31.45N 69.50E
28 K1 Shingke Gompa Xizang Zizhiqu 29.34N 95.49E
104 G5 Shinglehouse Pennsylvania 41.58N 78.11W
11 H8 Shingle Pk mt New Zealand 41.57S 173.21E
106 H3 Shingleton Michigan 46.21N 86.28W
110 D9 Shingletown California 40.30N 121.55W
30 D2 Shing-lhap cha Xizang Zizhiqu 30.32N 80.58E
29 E1 Shingo Pass Kashmir 33.00N 77.08E
43 O3 Shingozha Kazakhstan U.S.S.R. 47.43N 80.40E
31 H2 Shingshal Kashmir 36.29N 75.19E
31 H2 Shingshal Pass Kashmir 36.26N 75.38E
23 C10 Shing Shi Mun channel Hong Kong
20 J8 Shingū Japan 33.42N 136.00E
94 L4 Shingwidzi, Gr R S Africa/Moz
103 D2 Shinhopple New York 42.02N 75.04W
23 C4 Shinian Sichuan China 29.17N 102.22E
99 J5 Shining Tree Ontario 47.35N 81.15W
20 F6 Shinji-ko L Japan
20 O3 Shinjō Japan 38.45N 140.18E
20 E2 Shinjuku dist Tōkyō Japan
31 E4 Shinkai Hills Afghanistan
91 K9 Shinkolobwe Zaïre 11.10S 26.40E
58 G2 Shin, L Highland Scotland
20 E7 Shin-Nanyō Japan 34.05N 131.41E
31 D5 Shin Narai Thana Afghanistan 31.19N 66.43E
103 J5 Shinnecock B Long I, N Y
104 E7 Shinnston W Virginia 39.23N 80.18W
20 M5 Shinonoi Japan 36.35N 138.08E
31 F3 Shinpokh Pakistan 34.18N 71.13E
58 H3 Shin, R Highland Scotland
59 G6 Shinrone Offaly Irish Rep 52.59N 7.55W
34 D4 Shinshār Syria 34.36N 36.45E
20 L7 Shinshiro Japan 34.53N 137.29E
20 M1 Shintoku Japan 43.04N 142.50E
120 D5 Shintuya Peru 12.41S 71.12W
93 E9 Shinyanga Tanzania 3.40S 33.25E
93 C9 Shinyanga reg Tanzania
20 P3 Shiogama Japan 38.19N 141.00E
20 L5 Shiojiri Japan 36.08N 137.58E
20 J8 Shiono-misaki C Japan 33.28N 135.47E
20 O5 Shioya-zaki C Japan 36.59N 140.58E
Shipai see Huaining
56 M5 Shipborne Kent Eng 51.15N 0.17E
103 F7 Ship Bottom New Jersey 39.39N 74.11W
116 F2 Ship Channel Cay isld Bahamas 24.50N 76.49W
98 S6 Ship Cove Newfoundland 47.06N 54.03W
56 N2 Shipdham Norfolk Eng 52.37N 0.53E
107 H11 Ship I Mississippi 30.14N 88.56W
23 C7 Shiping Yunnan China 23.43N 102.27E
42 K5 Shipishka U.S.S.R. 54.15N 115.20E
47 F5 Shipitsino U.S.S.R. 61.20N 46.26E
82 K8 Shipka Pass Bulgaria 42.46N 25.33E
56 G2 Shipley Shropshire Eng 52.34N 2.17W
57 K5 Shipley W Yorks Eng 53.50N 1.47W
100 N5 Shipman Saskatchewan 53.29N 104.59W
45 J7 Shipovatoye Ukraine U.S.S.R. 49.55N 37.26E
98 H6 Shippegan New Brunswick 47.45N 64.44W
104 H6 Shippensburg Pennsylvania 40.03N 77.32W
109 B5 Shiprock New Mexico 36.46N 108.42W
109 B5 Ship Rock Pk New Mexico 36.41N 108.50W
99 T4 Shipshaw R Quebec
99 T4 Shipshaw Dam Quebec 48.28N 71.17W
107 E13 Ship Shoal Lt. Ho Gulf of Mexico 28.55N 91.06W
56 H3 Shipston-on-Stour Warwicks Eng 52.04N 1.37W
57 L4 Shipton N Yorks Eng 54.01N 1.09W
56 F2 Shipton Shropshire Eng 52.31N 2.39W
56 H4 Shipton-under-Wychwood Oxon Eng 51.52N 1.35W
Shipu see Huanglong
23 J4 Shipu Zhejiang China 29.13N 121.57E
42 C6 Shipunovo U.S.S.R. 52.15N 82.14E
39 G7 Shipunskiy, Mys C U.S.S.R. 53.07N 160.05E
39 G7 Shipunskiy, Poluostrov pen U.S.S.R.
24 C9 Shiqanthe Xizang Zizhiqu China 32.30N 79.45E
33 H8 Shiqāq al Ma'ātīf sand dunes S Yemen
23 E5 Shiqian Guizhou China 27.24N 108.11E
Shiqiao see Panyu
23 F7 Shiqiao Guangxi China 23.50N 111.28E
35 B7 Shiqma watercourse Israel
33 L9 Shiqqat al Qalib V Kuwait
33 L9 Shiqqat Ibn Şuqayh V Kuwait
23 E2 Shiquan Shaanxi China 33.03N 108.25E
24 C9 Shiquan He R Xizang Zizhiqu China
90 E6 Shira Nigeria 11.30N 10.03E
42 D5 Shira U.S.S.R. 54.32N 89.55E
33 K4 Shirā'awh isld The Gulf 25.03N 52.18E
32 C1 Shīrābād Iran 38.10N 48.57E
31 D5 Shirah Afghanistan 31.53N 66.55E
20 J8 Shirahama Japan 33.39N 135.22E
20 J3 Shirakami-misaki C Japan 41.25N 140.13E
20 O4 Shirakawa Fukushima Japan 37.07N 140.11E
20 K5 Shirakawa Toyama Japan 36.14N 136.56E
44 G6 Shirakskaya Step Georgia U.S.S.R.
20 N5 Shirane-san mt Tochigi Japan 36.49N 139.23E
20 M6 Shirane san mt Yamanashi Japan 35.42N 138.12E
20 L2 Shiraoi Japan 42.34N 141.19E
123 B6 Shirasebreen Antarctica
123 H8 Shirase Coast Antarctica
34 K8 Shīr, Ash ridge Saudi Arabia
93 F7 Shirati Tanzania 1.08S 34.01E
32 E6 Shīrāz Iran 29.38N 52.34E
86 G3 Shirbîn Egypt 31.13N 31.31E
43 K7 Shirden Afghanistan 37.49N 70.15E
92 G9 Shire R Malawi
92 G9 Shire Highlands Malawi
32 B1 Shīreh Jīn Iran 38.00N 47.31E
21 D7 Shiren Jilin China 41.55N 126.33E
21 K5 Shiretoko-misaki C Japan 44.24N 145.20E
31 C7 Shireza Pakistan 27.49N 65.40E
20 K1 Shiribeshi sub-prefect Hokkaido Japan
Shiribeshi-yama see Yōtei-an mt
43 G5 Shirikrabat Kazakhstan U.S.S.R. 44.08N 62.23E
Shirin see Khosrow Shīrīn
43 J6 Shirin U.S.S.R. 40.22N 69.04E
31 D6 Shirinab R Pakistan
30 B1 Shiring La pass Xizang Zizhiqu 31.49N 78.58E
45 O3 Shiringushi U.S.S.R. 53.50N 42.45E
Shirinkotan O isld see Chirinkotan O
34 Q3 Shīrīn Su Iran 35.28N 48.30E
31 C2 Shīrīn Tagāb Afghanistan 36.49N 65.01E
20 P1 Shiriya-zaki C Japan 41.24N 141.30E
33 E4 Shi'r, Jabal mts Saudi Arabia
43 D4 Shirkala dist Kazakhstan U.S.S.R.
45 G5 Shirkovo U.S.S.R. 51.24N 35.33E

32 F5 **Shir Kūh** *mt* Iran 31.39N 54.03E
107 D6 **Shirley** Arkansas 35.39N 92.20W
107 L2 **Shirley** Indiana 39.54N 85.34W
103 D7 **Shirley** New Jersey 39.34N 75.14W
56 H3 **Shirley** W Midlands Eng 52.24N 1.48W
11 M9 **Shirley** *dist* Christchurch New Zealand
20 H1 **Shiroi** Chiba Japan 35.49N 140.06E
20 O4 **Shiroishi** Japan 38.00N 140.38E
45 D10 **Shirokaya Balka** Ukraine U.S.S.R. 46.56N 32.03E
47 M4 **Shirokaya, Gora** *mt* U.S.S.R. 57.36N 59.43E
40 J6 **Shirokaya Pad** Sakhalin U.S.S.R. 50.14N 142.14E
47 M4 **Shirokaya Rechka** U.S.S.R. 56.48N 60.30E
40 E7 **Shirokiy** Amur U.S.S.R. 49.44N 129.30E
39 D3 **Shirokiy** Magadan U.S.S.R. 63.02N 147.58E
45 T4 **Shirokiy Buyerak** U.S.S.R. 52.07N 47.44E
45 R5 **Shirokiy Karamysh** U.S.S.R. 51.21N 45.02E
45 C9 **Shirokolanovka** Ukraine U.S.S.R. 47.10N 31.25E
41 P5 **Shirokostan, Poluostrov** *pen* U.S.S.R.
42 F4 **Shirokovo** U.S.S.R. 55.25N 99.24E
45 E9 **Shirokoye** Ukraine U.S.S.R. 47.41N 33.16E
28 H1 **Shirong** Xizang Zizhiqu 29.25N 91.09E
20 K6 **Shirotori** Japan 35.50N 136.50E
20 L5 **Shirouma-dake** *pk* Japan 36.43N 137.43E
29 D7 **Shirpur** Maharashtra India 21.21N 74.56E
33 N6 **Shirq, Ra's as** *C* Oman 21.39N 59.29E
85 L8 **Shirshir, Gebel** *mt* Egypt 23.54N 30.16E
22 D5 **Shirten Höloy Gobi** *des* Mongolia/China
32 B4 **Shīrvān** Kermānshāh Iran 33.34N 46.52E
32 G2 **Shīrvān** Khorāsān Iran 37.25N 57.55E
44 H7 **Shirvanskaya Step'** Azerbaydzhan U.S.S.R.
34 M2 **Shirwan Mazīn** Iraq 36.59N 44.12E
24 G4 **Shisanjianfang** Xinjiang Uygur Zizhiqu China 43.10N 91.15E
21 C2 **Shisanzhan** Heilongjiang China 51.20N 125.40E
47 L7 **Shish** *R* U.S.S.R.
45 F7 **Shishaki** Ukraine U.S.S.R. 49.55N 34.00E
113 F9 **Shishaldin** *vol* Aleutian Is 54.45N 163.58W
39 G6 **Shishel** *mt* U.S.S.R. 57.22N 160.15E
39 G6 **Shish Gora** *mt* U.S.S.R. 55.45N 161.09E
22 D1 **Shishhid Gol** *R* Mongolia
45 Q7 **Shishikin** U.S.S.R. 49.12N 44.07E
20 H8 **Shishikui** Japan 33.34N 134.18E
20 C7 **Shishimi** Japan 34.30N 129.19E
44 G7 **Shishkaya** Armenia U.S.S.R. 40.18N 45.41E
113 D3 **Shishmaref** Alaska 66.15N 166.11W
113 E3 **Shishmaref Inlet** Alaska
23 F4 **Shishou** Hubei China 29.40N 111.20E
86 E4 **Shisht el'An'âm** Egypt 30.52N 30.44E
21 C2 **Shisizhan** Heilongjiang China 51.35N 125.44E
88 P4 **Shisseb** *R* Algeria
33 K7 **Shişur,Ash** Oman 18.14N 53.36E
23 H3 **Shitai** Anhui China 30.12N 117.26E
22 G7 **Shitaning** Ningxia China 39.16N 106.11E
20 L6 **Shitara** Japan 35.08N 137.31E
34 L6 **Shithāthah** Iraq 32.34N 43.30E
42 F4 **Shitkino** U.S.S.R. 56.25N 98.21E
21 C2 **Shitou Shan** *mt pk* Nei Monggol Zizhiqu China 51.02N 125.18E
30 E6 **Shiugarh** Uttar Prad India 26.32N 81.15E
29 B4 **Shiv** Rajasthan India 26.11N 71.14E
30 D6 **Shivarajpur** Uttar Prad India 26.41N 80.09E
39 G6 **Shiveluch, Sopka** *vol* Kamchatka U.S.S.R. 56.38N 161.19E
42 E4 **Shivera** U.S.S.R. 56.21N 93.29E
30 A7 **Shivpuri** Madhya Prad India 25.26N 77.39E
30 A7 **Shivpuri** *dist* Madhya Prad India
35 B10 **Shivta** *anc site* Israel 30.53N 34.38E
Shivuh *see* **Bandar-e Shiū**
111 L5 **Shivwits Plat** Arizona
31 F2 **Shiwa L** Afghanistan 37.23N 71.08E
23 D7 **Shiwan Dashan** *mts* Guangxi China
21 A2 **Shiwei** Nei Monggol Zizhiqu China 51.22N 119.54E
23 G6 **Shixing** Guangdong China 25.03N 114.05E
23 E2 **Shiyan** Hubei China 32.31N 110.45E
23 D4 **Shiyangchang** Sichuan China 29.52N 105.30E
22 F7 **Shiyang He** *R* Ningxia China
23 E4 **Shiye** Sichuan China 28.22N 109.02E
21 C2 **Shiyizhan** Heilongjiang China 51.09N 125.58E
Shizhaihe *see* **Zhenping**
23 E4 **Shizhu** Sichuan China 30.02N 108.07E
Shizilu *see* **Junan**
23 C6 **Shizong** Yunnan China 24.53N 104.00E
20 P3 **Shizugawa** Japan 38.41N 141.30E
22 G7 **Shizuishan** Ningxia China 39.04N 106.22E
22 H8 **Shizuiyi** Shaanxi China 37.18N 110.10E
20 O2 **Shizukuishi** Japan 39.44N 140.52E
20 M2 **Shizunai** Japan 42.20N 142.23E
20 M7 **Shizuoka** Japan 34.59N 138.24E
20 L7 **Shizuoka** *prefect* Japan
44 E5 **Shkhara** *mt* U.S.S.R. 43.00N 43.10E
45 K1 **Shkin'** U.S.S.R. 55.10N 38.30E
45 B2 **Shklov** Belorussiya U.S.S.R. 54.16N 30.16E
83 D2 **Shkodër** Albania 42.03N 19.01E
40 F10 **Shkotovo** U.S.S.R. 43.22N 132.14E
82 F9 **Shkumbin** *R* Albania
44 C1 **Shkurinskaya** U.S.S.R. 46.36N 39.22E
46 J1 **Shlino** *R* U.S.S.R.
87 K7 **Shllave** Ethiopia 6.07N 44.45E
45 H6 **Shlyakhovo** U.S.S.R. 50.42N 36.51E
47 M7 **Shmakovka** Novosibirsk U.S.S.R. 56.34N 76.55E
42 B3 **Shmakovka** Tomsk U.S.S.R. 57.41N 77.25E
38 J1 **Shmidta, Ostrov** *isld* U.S.S.R.
40 J4 **Shmidta Poluostrov** *pen* Sakhalin U.S.S.R.
44 E2 **Shnakovskoye** Stavropol' U.S.S.R. 45.09N 42.01E
46 M6 **Shnakovskoye** U.S.S.R. 45.09N 42.01E
20 L5 **Shō** *R* Japan
Shoa *prov see* **Shewa**
107 K11 **Shoal** *R* Florida
11 C1 **Shoal B** New Zealand
13 B1 **Shoal B** N Terr Australia
14 D10 **Shoal C** W Australia 33.51S 121.10E
98 T5 **Shoal Harbour** Newfoundland 48.12N 54.00W
12 K5 **Shoalhaven R** New S Wales
100 G1 **Shoal L** Ontario 49.30N 95.00W
100 R8 **Shoal Lake** Manitoba 50.28N 100.35W
100 U8 **Shoal Lakes** Manitoba
107 K3 **Shoals** Indiana 38.40N 86.47W
13 K5 **Shoalwater B** Queensland
20 F7 **Shōbara** Japan 34.52N 133.00E
20 H7 **Shōdo-shima** *isld* Japan
56 N4 **Shoeburyness** Essex Eng 51.32N 0.48E
56 N4 **Shoebury Ness** *pt* Essex Eng 51.31N 0.47E
98 R4 **Shoe Cove** Newfoundland 49.56N 55.35W
11 K3 **Shoe I** New Zealand 36.59S 175.57E
103 C6 **Shoemakersville** Pennsylvania 40.29N 75.58W
87 E5 **Shogali** Ethiopia 10.40N 35.11E
32 H2 **Shoghlābād** Iran 36.50N 58.40E
Shohi Pass *see* **Tal Pass**
103 D4 **Shohola Cr** Pennsylvania
20 M6 **Shōji** Japan 35.32N 138.37E
41 B4 **Shokal'skogo, Ostrov** *isld* U.S.S.R.
41 H2 **Shokal'skogo, Proliv** *str* U.S.S.R.
20 L1 **Shokambetsu-dake** *mt* Japan 43.42N 141.33E
Sho-kha Dzong *see* **Xoka**
28 J1 **Sho Kha Dzong** Xizang Zizhiqu 29.56N 93.50E
47 L5 **Shokurovo** U.S.S.R. 56.20N 59.08E
47 D5 **Shola** *R* U.S.S.R.
43 G2 **Sholaksay** Kazakhstan U.S.S.R. 51.45N 64.45E
43 K2 **Sholakshalkar, Ozero** *L* Kazakhstan U.S.S.R.
28 B2 **Sholapur** Maharashtra India 17.43N 75.56E
28 B2 **Sholapur** *dist* Maharashtra India
44 J6 **Shollar** Azerbaydzhan U.S.S.R. 41.37N 48.39E
14 B5 **Sholl I** W Australia 20.57S 115.52E
41 K7 **Shologontsy** U.S.S.R. 66.16N 114.00E
51 Q6 **Sholopovo** Karelia U.S.S.R. 65.22N 32.40E
30 H3 **Shomare** Nepal 27.52N 86.48E
34 E4 **Shōmarīye, Jebel** *mts* Syria
47 C3 **Shomba** U.S.S.R. 65.07N 33.02E
35 E1 **Shomera** Israel 33.05N 35.17E
Shomron *reg see* **Samaria** *region*
47 G4 **Shomvukva** U.S.S.R. 63.40N 51.49E
43 E4 **Shomyshkol'** Kazakhstan U.S.S.R. 46.30N 59.20E
92 D9 **Shona** *tribe* Zambia
24 G4 **Shona Nor** *L* Xinjiang Uygur Zizhiqu China 42.40N 92.10E
90 B7 **Shonga** Nigeria 9.02N 5.08E
28 H2 **Shongar** Bhutan 27.15N 90.05E
95 P8 **Shongwe** S Africa 27.26S 32.23E
86 E4 **Shôni** Egypt 30.45N 30.55E
19 N3 **Shonian Harb** Palau Is Pacific Oc
55 H4 **Shooters Hill** London Eng 51.28N 0.04E
Shopando *see* **Xobando**
43 M2 **Shoptykul'** Kazakhstan U.S.S.R. 51.16N 75.45E
35 B8 **Shoqeda** Israel 31.26N 34.31E
29 E1 **Shor** Himachal Prad India 32.50N 76.30E
31 D6 **Shoran** Pakistan 28.51N 67.30E
28 C5 **Shoranur** Kerala India 10.46N 76.15E
31 C8 **Shorap** Pakistan 25.45N 65.34E
44 E5 **Shorapani** Georgia U.S.S.R. 42.03N 43.09E
28 C2 **Shorapur** Karnataka India 16.31N 76.44E
31 C5 **Shorawak** Afghanistan 31.48N 64.16E
31 C6 **Shorawak** *reg* Afghanistan
44 J7 **Shorbachi** Azerbaydzhan U.S.S.R. 40.14N 48.57E
44 G8 **Shorbulag** Azerbaydzhan U.S.S.R. 40.02N 46.03E
55 F3 **Shoreditch** London Eng 51.32N 0.05W
55 K5 **Shoreham** Kent England 51.20N 0.11E
103 J5 **Shoreham** Long I, N Y 40.58N 72.53W
56 L6 **Shoreham-by-Sea** W Sussex Eng 50.49N 0.16W
106 G6 **Shorewood** Wisconsin 43.05N 87.52W
32 A2 **Shor Gol** *L* Iran
93 B8 **Shori** Rwanda 2.09S 30.17E
43 D6 **Shorkazakhly, Solonchak** *salt marsh* Turkmeniya U.S.S.R.
31 G5 **Shorkot** Pakistan 30.49N 72.08E
31 H1 **Shorkul', Oz** *L* Tadzhikistan U.S.S.R.
56 M5 **Shorne** Kent Eng 51.25N 0.26E
Shoro *see* **Shūrū**
24 D10 **Shoro Tso** *L* Xizang Zizhiqu China 31.20N 83.15E
43 N8 **Shorsu** Uzbekistan U.S.S.R. 40.17N 70.50E
44 J8 **Shorsulu** Azerbaydzhan U.S.S.R. 39.27N 48.51E
43 K2 **Shortandy** Kazakhstan U.S.S.R. 51.45N 71.01E
111 M5 **Short Creek** Arizona 36.59N 112.59W
100 R7 **Shortdale** Manitoba 51.14N 101.00W
31 D2 **Shor Tepe** Afghanistan 37.22N 66.49E
107 L9 **Shorter** Alabama 32.23N 85.58W
12 E2 **Short, L** S Australia
15 J2 **Shortland I** Solomon Is 7.05S 155.45E
14 C10 **Short, Mt** W Australia 33.28S 119.53E
104 H4 **Shortsville** New York 42.56N 77.14W
56 J6 **Shorwell** I of Wight Eng 50.39N 1.21W
111 H6 **Shoshone** California 35.58N 116.17W
110 L7 **Shoshone** Idaho 42.57N 114.25W
108 B5 **Shoshone** *R* Wyoming
110 Q5 **Shoshone Cavern Nat. Mon** Wyoming 44.30N 109.06W
110 L7 **Shoshone Falls** Idaho 42.38N 114.30W
110 P5 **Shoshone L** Wyoming 44.22N 110.45W
111 G3 **Shoshone Mts** Nevada
110 Q5 **Shoshone N. Fork** *R* Wyoming
111 H5 **Shoshone Pk** *mt* Nevada 36.58N 116.20W
110 Q5 **Shoshone S. Fork** *R* Wyoming
94 J4 **Shoshong** Botswana 22.59S 26.30E
108 B6 **Shoshoni** Wyoming 43.15N 108.04W
45 E5 **Shostka** Ukraine U.S.S.R. 51.53N 33.30E
56 O4 **Shotley** Suffolk Eng 51.58N 1.15E
57 K3 **Shotley Bridge** Durham Eng 54.52N 1.51W
11 C11 **Shotover R** New Zealand
57 G6 **Shotton** Clwyd Wales 53.12N 3.02W
23 H4 **Shouchang** Zhejiang China 29.22N 119.12E
23 E6 **Shoucheng** Guangxi China 25.11N 109.46E
22 L8 **Shouguang** Shandong China 36.53N 118.45E
113 Q3 **Shoulder Mt** Alaska 67.50N 143.43W
100 E8 **Shouldice** Alberta 50.44N 112.53W
23 H5 **Shouning** Fujian China 27.30N 119.29E
110 L4 **Shoup** Idaho 45.24N 114.19W
23 G2 **Shou Xian** Anhui China 32.40N 116.42E
Shouyang *see* **Shou Xian**
22 J8 **Shouyang** Shanxi China 37.54N 113.08E
23 E2 **Shouyang Shan** *mt pk* Shaanxi China 33.56N 108.24E
35 B8 **Shoval** Israel 31.25N 34.45E
108 R3 **Shovel Lake** Minnesota 46.56N 93.42W
44 C2 **Shovgenovskiy** U.S.S.R. 45.01N 40.14E
Showa *Antarctic Base see* **Syowa**
87 E3 **Showak** Sudan 14.21N 35.50E
20 K2 **Shōwa-Shin-zan** *vol* Japan 42.34N 140.54E
111 O7 **Show Low** Arizona 34.16N 110.03W
47 E2 **Shoyna** U.S.S.R. 67.47N 44.13E
47 E5 **Shozhma** U.S.S.R. 61.58N 40.14E
Shozu *see* **Shūzū**
83 D3 **Shpatit, Mal i** *mts* Albania
82 M2 **Shpikov** U.S.S.R. 48.47N 28.31E
45 N5 **Shpikulovo** U.S.S.R. 51.45N 41.54E
39 B4 **Shpil'-Tarbagannakh, Gora** *mt* U.S.S.R. 61.10N 138.25E
45 C7 **Shpola** Ukraine U.S.S.R. 49.00N 31.25E
53 X18 **Shrekken** *mt* Norway 60.13N 7.47E
41 G4 **Shrenk** *R* U.S.S.R.
104 C6 **Shreve** Ohio 40.42N 82.02W
107 C9 **Shreveport** Louisiana 32.30N 93.46W
103 L2 **Shrewsbury** Massachusetts 42.18N 71.43W
103 A7 **Shrewsbury** Pennsylvania 39.46N 76.41W
56 F2 **Shrewsbury** Shropshire Eng 52.43N 2.45W
107 H12 **Shrewsbury** *dist* New Orleans, Louisiana 29.57N 90.09W
56 H5 **Shrewton** Wilts Eng 51.12N 1.55W
28 B1 **Shrigonda** Maharashtra India 18.39N 74.44E
56 H4 **Shrivenham** Oxon Eng 51.36N 1.39W
44 G6 **Shroma** Georgia U.S.S.R. 41.51N 45.42E
Shropshire *co see* **Salop**
103 G4 **Shrub Oak** New York 41.20N 73.50W
59 D4 **Shrule** Mayo Irish Rep 53.32N 9.05W
45 F6 **Shtepovka** Ukraine U.S.S.R. 50.49N 34.20E
45 K8 **Shterovka** Ukraine U.S.S.R. 48.19N 38.59E
41 G3 **Shturmanov, Poluostrov** *pen* U.S.S.R.
39 D3 **Shturmovoy** U.S.S.R. 62.50N 149.45E
39 E7 **Shtyubelya, Sopka** *vol* Kamchatka U.S.S.R. 51.50N 157.32E
34 P8 **Shu'aiba** Iraq 30.24N 47.41E
23 C3 **Shuajingsi** Sichuan China 31.50N 102.51E
23 F5 **Shuanfeng** Hunan China 27.32N 112.06E
23 B6 **Shuangbai** Yunnan China 24.50N 101.35E
21 D5 **Shuangcheng** Heilongjiang China 45.24N 126.14E
21 C5 **Shuangchengpu** Jilin China 44.08N 124.42E
21 B5 **Shuanggang** Jilin China 45.07N 122.58E
21 B5 **Shuanggang** Jilin China 45.03N 122.58E
23 F2 **Shuanggou** Hubei China 32.12N 112.23E
21 E3 **Shuanghedagang** Heilongjiang China 48.58N 129.59E
21 D6 **Shuanghezhen** Jilin China 43.29N 126.08E
Shuanghuyu *see* **Zizhou**
Shuangjiang *see* **Tongdao**
23 B7 **Shuangjiang** Yunnan China 23.25N 99.49E
23 G1 **Shuangji He** *R* Henan China
Shuang-liao *see* **Shuangliao**
21 C6 **Shuangliao** Jilin China 43.30N 123.29E
23 C3 **Shuangliu** Sichuan China 30.34N 103.58E
21 C6 **Shuangshan** Jilin China 43.43N 123.51E
Shuangshipu *see* **Feng Xian**
22 D6 **Shuangtapu** Gansu China 40.31N 96.30E
24 H5 **Shuangtapu** Gansu China 40.31N 96.30E
21 C6 **Shuangyang** Jilin China 43.35N 125.37E
21 E4 **Shuangyashan** Heilongjiang China 46.42N 131.20E
33 N10 **Shu'aybah** Kuwait 29.02N 48.10E
Shuaybah, Ash *see* **Shu'aiba**
33 E3 **Shu'āybah, Ash** Saudi Arabia 27.51N 42.48E
33 J8 **Shu'ayt, Wādī** *watercourse* S Yemen
34 M10 **Shu'bah, Ash** Saudi Arabia 28.56N 44.42E
43 D3 **Shubar-Kuduk** Kazakhstan U.S.S.R. 49.08N 56.30E
43 D3 **Shubarshi** Kazakhstan U.S.S.R. 57.11N 48.35E
Shubash *R see* **Bezeq** *R*
33 E4 **Shubaykīyah, Ash** Saudi Arabia 25.12N 43.23E
33 E4 **Shubayrimah** Saudi Arabia 24.36N 43.35E
Shubayt, Jabal *see* **Shubeit, Jebel**
34 E3 **Shubeit, Jebel** *mts* Syria
98 J8 **Shubenacadie** Nova Scotia 45.05N 63.25W
98 J9 **Shubenacadie L** Nova Scotia
108 P9 **Shubert** Nebraska 40.14N 95.42W
41 B4 **Shuberta, Mys** *C* Belyy, Ostrov U.S.S.R. 73.11N 71.35E
41 B3 **Shuberta, Zaliv** *gulf* Novaya Zemlya U.S.S.R.
39 G6 **Shubertovo** U.S.S.R. 55.59N 162.00E
113 P2 **Shublik Mts** Alaska
45 B7 **Shubovka** Ukraine U.S.S.R. 49.45N 30.46E
86 Q12 **Shubrâ** *dist* Cairo Egypt
86 Q11 **Shubrâ El Kheima** Cairo Egypt 30.06N 31.15E
86 E3 **Shubra Khît** Egypt 31.02N 30.42E
33 E5 **Shubramīyah** Saudi Arabia 23.58N 42.48E
33 F4 **Shubrāmīyah** Saudi Arabia 24.12N 44.10E
33 K10 **Shu'b, Ra's** *C* Socotra Ind Oc 12.30N 53.18E
107 H10 **Shubuta** Mississippi 31.51N 88.41W
23 G3 **Shucheng** Anhui China 31.31N 117.00E
120 B1 **Shucushuyacu** Peru 6.02S 75.53W
42 C3 **Shudel'ka** U.S.S.R. 58.04N 81.20E
35 F6 **Shu'eib** *R* Jordan
35 F6 **Shu'eib Bridge** Jordan 31.58N 35.43E
35 D4 **Shufa** Jordan 32.16N 35.05E
24 B6 **Shufu** Xinjiang Uygur Zizhiqu China 39.20N 75.33E
43 M2 **Shuga** Kazakhstan U.S.S.R. 52.28N 75.01E
47 L3 **Shuga** U.S.S.R. 66.20N 71.30E
47 L3 **Shuga** *R* U.S.S.R.
28 J3 **Shuganu** Manipur India 24.19N 93.50E
43 K8 **Shugnan** Tadzhikistan U.S.S.R. 37.33N 71.35E
43 K8 **Shugnansk Khrebet** *mts* Tadzhikistan U.S.S.R.
43 K7 **Shugnou** Tadzhikistan U.S.S.R. 38.38N 70.24E
47 C6 **Shugozero** U.S.S.R. 59.54N 34.10E
47 K5 **Shugur** U.S.S.R. 60.13N 66.31E
92 H6 **Shuguri Falls** Tanzania 8.30S 37.25E
46 Q3 **Shugurovo** U.S.S.R. 54.31N 52.10E
33 H9 **Shuḩayr** S Yemen 14.41N 49.26E
23 H1 **Shu He** *R* Shandong China
23 E2 **Shuhekou** Shaanxi China 32.55N 109.41E
45 E2 **Shui** U.S.S.R. 54.13N 33.35E
23 D4 **Shuibatang** Guizhou China 28.43N 107.05E
23 C5 **Shuicheng** Guizhou China 26.42N 104.49E
Shuiding *see* **Huocheng**
21 C7 **Shuifeng Sk** *res* Liaoning China
Shuiji *see* **Laixi**
23 H5 **Shuiji** Fujian China 27.13N 118.20E
Shuijiahu *see* **Changfeng**
23 H5 **Shuikou** Fujian China 26.18N 118.47E
23 F7 **Shuikou** Guangdong China 22.27N 112.28E
23 E6 **Shuikou** Guizhou China 25.55N 109.18E
Shuiluocheng *see* **Zhuanglang**
23 B4 **Shuiluo He** *R* Sichuan China
21 D5 **Shuiquliu** Jilin China 44.34N 127.04E
22 M7 **Shuishiying** Liaoning China 38.52N 121.21E
Shuizhai *see* **Wuhua**
Shuizhai *see* **Xiangcheng**
22 B7 **Shuizhan** Qinghai China 38.00N 91.46E
31 F6 **Shujaabad** Pakistan 29.53N 71.23E
Shujabad *see* **Shujaabad**
29 E6 **Shujalpur** Madhya Prad India 23.21N 76.46E
23 B6 **Shujie** Yunnan China 24.42N 100.47E
47 J5 **Shukhtungort** U.S.S.R. 62.25N 64.00E
87 E3 **Shukriya** *tribe* Sudan
110 D1 **Shuksan** Washington 48.55N 121.43W
110 D1 **Shuksan, Mt** Washington 48.50N 121.36W
32 D5 **Shūl** *R* Iran
21 D5 **Shulan** Jilin China 44.23N 126.55E
24 B6 **Shule** Xinjiang Uygur Zizhiqu China 39.25N 76.03E
22 D6 **Shulehe** Gansu China 40.26N 96.51E
22 C6 **Shule He** *R* Gansu China
22 D7 **Shule He** *R* Gansu China
22 D7 **Shule Nanshan** *mts* Qinghai China
45 M4 **Shul'gino** U.S.S.R. 52.14N 40.50E
Shulgistan *see* **Shūrjestān**
Shulinzhao *see* **Dalad Qi**
106 D7 **Shullsburg** Wisconsin 42.34N 90.14W
22 K8 **Shulu** Hebei China 37.52N 115.19E
Shülüsete *see* **Shilüüstey**
113 G9 **Shumagin Is** Alaska
45 H5 **Shumakovo** Kursk U.S.S.R. 51.30N 36.38E
43 E5 **Shumanay** Uzbekistan U.S.S.R. 42.36N 59.04E
Shumariyah, Jabal ash *see* **Shōmariye, Jebel**
85 C4 **Shumaykh** *watercourse* Libya
93 M5 **Shumbura** Kenya 0.45N 40.06E
93 K10 **Shume** Tanzania 4.42S 38.12E
43 G2 **Shumekty** Kazakhstan U.S.S.R. 50.15N 64.13E
82 K7 **Shumen** Bulgaria 43.17N 26.55E
45 S1 **Shumerlya** U.S.S.R. 55.30N 46.25E
47 J7 **Shumikha** U.S.S.R. 55.15N 63.14E
45 A1 **Shumilino** Belorussiya U.S.S.R. 55.18N 29.37E
45 N7 **Shumilinskaya** U.S.S.R. 49.59N 41.29E
47 G5 **Shumina** U.S.S.R. 60.18N 53.47E
Shumkai *see* **Cenxi**
112 F6 **Shumla** Texas 29.46N 101.26W
33 G3 **Shumlūl, Ash** Saudi Arabia 26.29N 47.19E
40 O6 **Shumshu, O** *isld* Kuril Is U.S.S.R.
42 F5 **Shumskiy** U.S.S.R. 54.48N 99.11E
46 F4 **Shumskoye** Ukraine U.S.S.R. 50.10N 26.08E
21 B4 **Shumugou** Nei Monggol Zizhiqu China 46.09N 120.48E
111 O7 **Shumway** Arizona 34.24N 110.05W
45 D3 **Shumyachi** U.S.S.R. 53.52N 32.25E
35 F6 **Shuna** Jordan 31.54N 35.34E
35 F6 **Shunat Nimrin** Jordan 31.54N 35.37E
86 G6 **Shûna, Wâdi el** *watercourse* Egypt
23 H5 **Shunchang** Fujian China 26.54N 117.45E
23 F7 **Shunde** Guangdong China 22.50N 113.16E
47 C4 **Shunga** U.S.S.R. 62.34N 34.58E
45 S8 **Shungay** Kazakhstan U.S.S.R. 48.32N 46.45E
113 J3 **Shungnak** Alaska 66.53N 157.10W
Shungrutruga *see* **Xungru**
43 N8 **Shunk** Kirgiziya U.S.S.R. 40.10N 71.20E
103 A3 **Shunk** Pennsylvania 41.33N 76.44W
Shun-ning *see* **Fengqing**
47 M4 **Shunut, Gora** *mt* U.S.S.R. 56.32N 59.44E
22 K6 **Shunyi** Beijing China 40.09N 116.36E
23 D7 **Shuolong** Guangxi China 22.48N 107.05E
22 J7 **Shuo Xian** Shanxi China 39.20N 112.25E
43 O7 **Shupan** Uzbekistan U.S.S.R. 41.03N 72.05E
31 H4 **Shupiyan** Kashmir 33.43N 74.50E
33 E8 **Shuqayq, Ash** Saudi Arabia 17.43N 42.03E
35 D6 **Shuqba** Jordan 31.59N 35.03E
35 F7 **Shuqeiq** Jordan 31.30N 35.43E
35 F8 **Shuqeiq** *watercourse* Jordan
33 G7 **Shuqqān al Araţī** *sand ridge* Saudi Arabia
33 H6 **Shuqqān, Ash** *des area* Saudi Arabia
33 F8 **Shuqqat Najrān** *des area* Saudi Arabia
33 F10 **Shuqrā** S Yemen 13.23N 45.44E
107 H9 **Shuqualak** Mississippi 32.59N 88.35W
32 E6 **Shūr** *R* Fārs Iran
32 F5 **Shūr** *R* Iran
32 J5 **Shūr** *R* Iran
32 H3 **Shūr** *R* Khorāsān Iran
32 H4 **Shur** *R* Khorāsān Iran
34 K2 **Shūra** Iraq 36.17N 42.18E
44 J7 **Shuraabad** Azerbaydzhan U.S.S.R. 40.47N 49.30E
34 L3 **Shūra, Ash** Iraq 35.59N 43.12E
32 D4 **Shurâb** Bakhtāri va Chahār Mahāll Iran 32.19N 50.03E
32 F4 **Shūrāb** Esfahān Iran 33.06N 55.20E
32 G4 **Shūrāb** Khorāsān Iran 33.43N 56.30E
43 K6 **Shurab** Tadzhikistan U.S.S.R. 40.06N 70.33E
32 D3 **Shūr Āb** Tehrān Iran 34.24N 51.17E
32 G5 **Shūr Āb** *R* Iran
34 P3 **Shūrāb-e-Hezāreh** Iran 35.27N 47.50E
45 V1 **Shuran** U.S.S.R. 55.23N 49.54E
Shurayf, Ash *see* **Khaybar**
43 J7 **Shurchi** Uzbekistan U.S.S.R. 38.01N 67.49E
32 E4 **Shureghestan** Iran 33.17N 52.03E
32 H6 **Shūr Gaz** Iran 29.10N 59.16E
Shurgistan *see* **Shureghestan**
37 J8 **Shūr Gol** *L* Iran
20 P9 **Shuri** Okinawa Japan 26.11N 127.43E
42 J4 **Shurinda** U.S.S.R. 55.18N 113.25E
32 E5 **Shūrjestān** Iran 31.25N 52.27E
46 Q2 **Shurma** U.S.S.R. 57.00N 50.20E
32 J6 **Shūrū** Iran 29.10N 60.15E
34 N7 **Shuruppak** *anc site* Iraq 31.45N 45.34E
24 E10 **Shuru Tso** *L* Xizang Zizhiqu China 30.10N 86.15E
Shurwayn, Ras *see* **Sharwayn Ra's** *cape*
Shurwein, Ras *see* **Sharwayn Ra's** *cape*
42 C5 **Shurygino** U.S.S.R. 54.06N 82.59E
47 J3 **Shuryshkarskiy Sor, Oz** *L* U.S.S.R.
47 K3 **Shuryshkary** U.S.S.R. 65.56N 65.20E
32 J5 **Shusf** Iran 31.49N 60.01E
32 C4 **Shūsh** Iran 32.12N 48.20E
44 H8 **Shusha** Azerbaydzhan U.S.S.R. 39.44N 46.45E
42 E5 **Shushenskoye** U.S.S.R. 53.16N 92.00E
86 K4 **Shûshet el Maghâra** *hill* Egypt 30.39N 33.23E
83 D4 **Shushicë** *R* Albania
31 J3 **Shushot** Kashmir 34.03N 77.40E
32 C4 **Shushtar** Iran 32.03N 48.51E
119 C8 **Shushufindi** *oil well* Ecuador 0.10S 76.41W
45 G5 **Shustovo** U.S.S.R. 51.47N 35.05E
101 O10 **Shuswap L** Br Columbia
31 C4 **Shutar Gardaneh** Afghanistan 32.01N 65.30E
31 E4 **Shutargardan Pass** Afghanistan 33.57N 69.22E
31 C3 **Shutar Khun Pass** Afghanistan 34.20N 64.53E
103 K2 **Shutesbury** Massachusetts 42.27N 72.25W
23 B9 **Shu Tsai** Hong Kong 22.19N 114.13E
12 H4 **Shuttleton** New S Wales 32.08S 146.08E
35 A9 **Shu'uth, Esh** Egypt 31.15N 34.14E
35 B8 **Shuva** Israel 31.27N 34.32E
45 Q2 **Shuvary** U.S.S.R. 54.11N 44.28E
34 H8 **Shuwayhiţīyah** Saudi Arabia 20.23N 40.09E
33 M9 **Shuwaykh** Kuwait 29.20N 47.58E
33 L8 **Shuwaymīyah, Ra's ash** *C* Oman 17.52N 55.53E
35 D4 **Shuweika** Jordan 32.20N 35.02E
46 M2 **Shuya** Ivanovo U.S.S.R. 56.49N 41.23E
47 C5 **Shuya** Karelia U.S.S.R. 62.00N 34.12E
113 L7 **Shuyak I** Alaska 58.33N 152.30W
113 L7 **Shuyak Str** Alaska
23 H1 **Shuyang** Jiangsu China 34.08N 118.53E
47 C4 **Shuyeretskoye** U.S.S.R. 64.44N 34.43E
43 M2 **Shuyreksor, Oz** *L* Kazakhstan U.S.S.R.
46 M1 **Shuyskoye** U.S.S.R. 59.19N 41.02E
35 D7 **Shuyukh** Jordan 31.34N 35.09E
Shuzch *see* **Sūzā**
20 M7 **Shuzenji** Japan 35.00N 138.55E
32 F6 **Shūzū** Iran 29.53N 54.29E
Shwangcheng *see* **Shuangcheng**
Shwangliao *see* **Shuangliao**
Shwang-shan *see* **Shuangshan**
25 C3 **Shwebandaw** Burma 19.13N 95.33E
25 C1 **Shwebo** Burma 22.35N 95.42E
25 N9 **Shwebo** Burma 24.26N 97.05E
25 C3 **Shwedaung** Burma 18.44N 95.12E
25 M8 **Shwedwin** Burma 25.20N 95.59E
25 D4 **Shwegun** Burma 17.09N 97.39E
25 D4 **Shwegyin** Burma 17.56N 96.59E
25 M9 **Shweli** *R* Burma
25 D2 **Shwenyaung** Burma 20.48N 96.58E
31 J2 **Shyok** Kashmir 34.13N 78.12E
31 K3 **Shyok** Kashmir 34.15N 80.10E
31 J3 **Shyok R** Kashmir
15 C7 **Sia** Moluccas Indon 6.48S 134.20E
18 C5 **Siabu** Sumatra Indon 1.00N 99.28E
31 J3 **Siachen Glacier** Kashmir
32 C2 **Siādūn** Iran 37.45N 48.58E
71 K9 **Siagne** *R* France
31 B7 **Siahan Ra** Pakistan
32 B2 **Sīāh Chaman** Iran 37.37N 47.09E
32 A1 **Sīāh Chashmeh** Iran 39.02N 44.22E
31 D2 **Siahgird** Afghanistan 36.57N 67.03E
32 G2 **Siah Khaneh Pass** Iran 37.16N 57.21E
31 C4 **Siah Koh** *mts* Afghanistan
32 E3 **Sīāh Kūh** *mts* Iran
32 J5 **Sīāh Kūh** *mt* Iran 31.30N 60.52E
31 C5 **Siah Sang Pass** Afghanistan 31.48N 65.33E
Siahsien *see* **Hsia-hsien**
Siahwayuan *see* **Hsia-hua-yüan**
18 D5 **Siak** *R* Sumatra Indon
Siakiang *see* **Hsia-chiang**
18 E5 **Siak Sri Inderapura** Sumatra Indon 0.50N 102.05E
Siakwan *see* **Hsia-kuan**
Sialk *anc site see* **Kāshān**
32 D4 **Sialk** *anc mon* Iran 34.00N 51.29E
31 H4 **Sialkot** Pakistan 32.29N 74.35E
31 H4 **Sialkot** *dist* Pakistan
15 J7 **Sialum** Papua New Guinea 6.02S 147.37E
Siam *see* **Thailand**
94 G2 **Siambissa** Botswana 18.01S 23.18E
30 C8 **Siamri** *R* Madhya Prad India
Sian *see* **Xi'an**
Sian *see* **Xi'an**
40 D5 **Sian** U.S.S.R. 53.20N 126.54E
Siang-cheng *see* **Hsiang-ch'eng**
28 K1 **Siang Frontier Div** Assam India
Siangho *see* **Xianghe**
Sianghsien *see* **Xiangzhou**
Siangning *see* **Xiangning**
Siang Shuikow *see* **Xiangshui**
Siangsiang *see* **Xiangxing**
Siangtan *see* **Xiangtan**
Siangtu *see* **Xiangdu**
Siangtung *see* **Xiangdong**
Siangyin *see* **Xiangyin**
Siangyuan *see* **Xiangyuan**
92 C10 **Siankondobo** Zambia 17.16S 27.05E
84 U17 **Siánna** *mt* Rhodes 36.10N 27.50E
62 J1 **Sianów** Poland 54.15N 16.20E
Siaochengtze *see* **Xiaocheng**
Siaohingkai Hu *L see* **Xingkai Hu**
Siaohoki *see* **Xiaohexi**
Siaohsien *see* **Xiao Xian**
Siaokan *see* **Xiaogan**
Siaokin *see* **Xiaojin**
Siaoshan *see* **Xiaoshan**
Siaowutai Shan *mt see* **Xiaowutai Shan**
119 G7 **Siapa, R** Venezuela
75 C1 **Sia, Portillo de la** *pass* Spain 43.09N 3.34W
Siapu *see* **Xiapu**
32 J6 **Siāreh** Iran 28.04N 60.14E
19 N7 **Siargao** *isld* Philippines
103 O4 **Siasconset** Massachusetts 41.15N 69.58W
19 K9 **Siasi** Philippines 5.33N 120.50E
19 K9 **Siasi** *isld* Philippines 5.33N 120.52E
15 J6 **Siassi** Papua New Guinea
15 J6 **Siassi Is** Bismarck Arch
30 G6 **Siat** Uttar Prad India 26.07N 83.51E
83 E4 **Siátista** Greece 40.16N 21.34E
19 L7 **Siaton** Philippines 9.05N 123.05E
19 D2 **Şiau** *isld* Indonesia 2.45N 125.25E
46 E2 **Šiauliai** Lithuania U.S.S.R. 55.51N 23.20E
93 E5 **Siavona** *mt* Uganda 0.16N 33.51E
92 D10 **Siavonga** Zambia 16.33S 28.42E
19 K1 **Siayan** *isld* Philippines 20.54N 121.53E
44 J6 **Siazan'** Azerbaydzhan U.S.S.R. 41.06N 49.10E
32 K7 **Sīb** Iran 27.15N 62.04E
33 N5 **Sīb** Oman 23.40N 58.11E
33 A4 **Sibā'i, Gebel** *mt* Egypt 25.43N 34.08E
85 M7 **Sibâîya, El** Egypt 25.10N 32.39E
32 D4 **Sībak** Iran 32.51N 50.02E
116 F4 **Sibanicú** Cuba 21.14N 77.32W
81 M4 **Sibari** *sta* Italy 39.45N 16.28E
24 F2 **Sibati** Xinjiang Uygur Zizhiqu China 47.15N 88.20E
43 E1 **Sibay** Bashkir U.S.S.R. 52.43N 58.39E
19 K6 **Sibay** *isld* Philippines 11.51N 121.30E
95 P8 **Sibayi** S Africa 27.20S 32.45E
95 P8 **Sibayi, L** S Africa 27.22S 32.40E
100 G7 **Sibbald** Alberta 51.24N 110.10W
60 T17 **Sibbe** Netherlands 50.52N 5.49E
51 L11 **Sibbo** Finland 60.22N 25.20E
32 H4 **Sīb Chah** Iran 32.15N 59.05E
60 P10 **Sibculo** Netherlands 52.28N 6.38E
87 A5 **Şibdu** Sudan 10.57N 26.17E
82 C7 **Šibenik** Yugoslavia 43.45N 15.55E
16 J2 **Siberia** *reg* U.S.S.R.
18 C7 **Siberimanua** Indonesia 2.08S 99.34E
18 C7 **Siberu, Selat** Indonesia
18 C6 **Siberut** *isld* Indonesia
18 C6 **Siberut, Selat** *str* Indonesia
31 D6 **Sibi** Pakistan 29.31N 67.54E
31 E6 **Sibi** *dist* Pakistan
15 G8 **Sibidiri** Papua New Guinea 8.58S 142.16E
18 A4 **Sibigo** Indonesia 2.50N 95.58E
39 D2 **Sibik** *R* U.S.S.R.
80 H3 **Sibillini, Monti** Italy
39 F1 **Sibir'** U.S.S.R. 68.29N 158.30E
86 F4 **Sibirbâi** Egypt 30.50N 31.01E
47 K4 **Sibirskiye Uvaly** *marsh* U.S.S.R.
41 K4 **Sibirskiy, Mys** *C* U.S.S.R. 74.43N 112.00E
40 F9 **Sibirtsevo** U.S.S.R. 44.12N 132.25E
41 C4 **Sibiryakova, Ostrov** *isld* U.S.S.R.
91 C5 **Sibiti** Congo 3.40S 13.24E
93 F9 **Sibiti** *R* Tanzania
82 J5 **Sibiu** Romania 45.46N 24.09E
15 K8 **Sibium Mts** Papua New Guinea
56 N4 **Sible Hedingham** Essex Eng 51.58N 0.35E
106 F9 **Sibley** Illinois 40.35N 88.23W
108 P6 **Sibley** Iowa 43.25N 95.43W
107 C9 **Sibley** Louisiana 32.32N 93.17W
99 B4 **Sibley Prov. Park** Ontario
66 L1 **Siblingen** Switzerland 47.43N 8.31E
19 B3 **Siboa** Celebes Indon 0.31N 120.02E
118 G2 **Sibó, I. do** Brazil 12.00S 43.28W
18 C5 **Sibolga** Sumatra Indon 1.42N 98.48E
18 C5 **Sibolga, Teluk** *B* Sumatra Indonesia
19 K5 **Sibolon** *isld* Philippines 12.07N 121.35E
19 B3 **Siboluton** Celebes Indonesia 0.45N 120.36E
116 G5 **Siboney** Cuba 19.57N 75.42W
25 L9 **Sibong** Manipur India 24.21N 94.18E
18 C4 **Siborongborong** Sumatra Indon 2.13N 98.58E
65 B7 **Sibratsgfall** Austria 47.26N 10.03E
64 J8 **Sibratshofen** W Germany 47.38N 10.05E
61 N7 **Sibret** Belgium 49.58N 5.38E
28 K2 **Sibsagar** Assam India 26.58N 94.39E
28 J2 **Sibsagar** *dist* Assam India
57 O6 **Sibsey** Lincs Eng 53.02N 0.01E
18 J4 **Sibu** Sarawak Malaysia 2.18N 111.49E
18 E9 **Sibu** *isld* Pen Malaysia
120 B3 **Sibuas** Peru 8.33S 77.36W
19 L8 **Sibuco** Mindanao Philippines 7.18N 122.05E
19 L8 **Sibuco B** Mindanao Philippines 7.18N 122.04E
85 M8 **Sibû, El** Egypt 22.44N 32.32E
19 L8 **Sibuguey** *R* Mindanao Philippines
19 L8 **Sibuguey B** Mindanao Philippines
90 J9 **Sibut** Cent Afr Rep 5.46N 19.06E
18 K3 **Sibuti** Sarawak Malaysia 4.05N 113.47E
19 J9 **Sibutu** *isld* Philippines 4.46N 119.28E
19 J9 **Sibutu Pass** Philippines
19 L5 **Sibuyan** *isld* Philippines
19 L5 **Sibuyan Sea** Philippines
92 E5 **Sibwesa** Tanzania 6.27S 30.42E
82 H4 **Sic** Romania 46.58N 23.54E
37 H2 **Sicak** *R* Turkey
19 K2 **Sicapoo** *mt* Luzon Philippines 18.01N 120.58E
120 E7 **Sicasica** Bolivia 17.23S 67.44W
119 E8 **Sicayari, Mesa de** *plat* Colombia
12 E4 **Siccus** *R* S Australia
32 E4 **Si Chah** Iran 33.50N 52.40E
Sichang *see* **Xichang**
25 F6 **Si Chang, Ko** *isld* Thailand 13.10N 100.48E
75 K7 **Sichar, Embalse de** *res* Spain 40.00N 0.17W
Siche *see* **Xiche**
Sichon *see* **Ban Sichon**
Sichow *see* **Xinzhou**
23 C3 **Sichuan** *prov* China
23 C3 **Sichuan Pendi** *basin* Sichuan China
Sichung *see* **Xichong**
71 H10 **Sicié, C** France 43.03N 5.49E
80 M7 **Sicignano** Italy 40.34N 15.18E
81 G8 **Sicilia** *I* Italy
78 D11 **Sicilian Chan** Mediterranean Sea
Sicily *see* **Sicilia**
107 E10 **Sicily Island** Louisiana 31.51N 91.40E
100 R2 **Sickle L** Manitoba
115 M2 **Sico** Honduras 15.52N 85.13W
19 L6 **Sicogon** *isld* Philippines 11.26N 123.16E
76 B9 **Sicó, Sa.de** *mts* Portugal
120 D6 **Sicuani** Peru 14.21S 71.13W
81 F9 **Siculiana** Sicily 37.20N 13.26E
81 F9 **Şiculiana Marina** Sicily 37.21N 13.23E
82 E5 **Šid*** Yugoslavia 45.06N 19.16E
41 H7 **Sida** *R* U.S.S.R.
85 C4 **Sidādah** Libya 31.29N 14.45E
Sidair, Sha'ib *see* **Sudayr, Sha'īb** *watercourse*
87 G8 **Sidamo** *prov* Ethiopia
19 E3 **Sidangoli** Halmahera Indon 0.55N 127.29E
90 D2 **Sidaouet** Niger 18.34N 8.03E
33 H9 **Sidarah** S Yemen 14.31N 48.04E
85 E4 **Sidar, As** Libya 30.38N 18.20E
18 H5 **Sidas** Borneo Indon 0.16N 109.43E
19 D3 **Sidate** Celebes Indon 1.12N 124.25E
40 G9 **Sidatun** U.S.S.R. 45.20N 135.28E
95 K9 **Sidbury** S Africa 33.25S 26.10E
56 F5 **Sidcot** Avon Eng 51.19N 2.50W
55 J4 **Sidcup** London England 51.26N 0.06E
60 Q7 **Siddeburen** Netherlands 53.15N 6.52E
13 B6 **Siddeley Ra** N Terr Australia
86 P9 **Sidd, Es** Saudi Arabia 28.01N 35.44E
57 J6 **Siddington** Cheshire Eng 53.14N 2.14W
28 D1 **Siddipett** Andhra Prad India 18.07N 78.51E
Side *anc site see* **Selimiye**
51 J9 **Sideby** Finland 62.03N 21.20E
15 L9 **Sideia I** Papua New Guinea 10.38S 150.45E
107 J2 **Sidell** Illinois 39.55N 87.50W
86 G6 **Sid el Na'âm, Gebel** *hill* Egypt 29.48N 31.44E
19 A5 **Sidenreng, Danau** *L* Celebes Indon 4.00S 119.54E
52 L3 **Sidensjö** Sweden 63.18N 18.38E
81 M7 **Siderno Marina** Italy 38.16N 16.17E
56 O2 **Sidestrand** Norfolk Eng 52.55N 1.22E
100 H8 **Sidewood** Saskatchewan 50.03N 109.00W
85 L6 **Sidfa** Egypt 27.01N 31.22E
56 E6 **Sidford** Devon Eng 50.42N 3.15W
30 D5 **Sidhauli** Uttar Prad India 27.18N 80.50E
83 G4 **Sidherítis** *isld* Greece 40.02N 25.06E
30 E8 **Sidhi** Madhya Prad India 24.24N 81.54E
29 H5 **Sidhi** *dist* Madhya Prad India
83 F3 **Sidhirókastron** Makedhonia Greece 41.14N 23.23E
84 C7 **Sidhirókastron** Messinía Greece 37.20N 21.46E
31 G5 **Sidhnai** Pakistan 30.35N 72.10E
28 D3 **Sidhout** Andhra Prad India 14.30N 78.58E
29 C6 **Sidhpur** Gujarat India 23.57N 72.28E
30 B5 **Sidhpura** Uttar Prad India 27.38N 78.51E
50 H6 **Sídhujökull** *ice cap* Iceland 64.08N 17.55W
50 D5 **Sídhumúli** Iceland 64.42N 21.21W
88 O7 **Sidi Abdallah** Algeria 28.38N 0.20E
88 M4 **Sidi Ahmed** Morocco 34.04N 3.00W
88 P4 **Sidi Aïssa** Algeria 35.53N 3.45E
74 H8 **Sidi Ali** Algeria 36.07N 0.25E
88 N4 **Sidi Ali Ben Youb** Algeria 34.59N 0.45W
88 K4 **Sidi Allal Bahraou** Morocco 34.02N 6.32W
85 H4 **Sidi Barrani** Egypt 31.38N 25.58E
88 N4 **Sidi-bel-Abbès** Algeria 35.15N 0.39W
88 J5 **Sidi Bennour** Morocco 32.40N 8.25W
78 C13 **Sidi bou Ali** Tunisia 35.57N 10.28E
88 K6 **Sidi Bou Othmane** Morocco 31.59N 7.54W
88 S4 **Sidi bou Zid** Tunisia 35.01N 9.30E
88 J5 **Sidi Brahim** Morocco 33.02N 8.32W
88 J6 **Sidi Chiker** Morocco 31.45N 8.38W
74 E9 **Sidi Dris** Morocco 35.11N 3.33W
88 M9 **Sidi el Habib** Algeria 24.31N 3.43E
85 H4 **Sidi et Tehami** Libya 31.50N 24.14E
88 H7 **Sidi Ifni** Morocco 29.24N 10.12W
88 L4 **Sidi Kacem** Morocco 34.15N 5.49W
18 C4 **Sidikalang** Sumatra Indon 2.43N 98.25E
88 Q4 **Sidi Khaled** Algeria 34.23N 4.55E
88 Q5 **Sidi Krelil** Algeria 33.50N 5.55E
88 K5 **Sidi Lamine** Morocco 32.57N 6.07W
88 S6 **Sidi Maabet** Algeria 30.11N 9.08E
88 O7 **Sidi Mannsour** Algeria 29.44N 0.20E
88 J5 **Sidi Moussa** Morocco 33.00N 8.50W
88 Q8 **Sidi Moussa** *watercourse* Algeria
88 S4 **Sidi Nasr Allah** Tunisia 35.15N 9.50E
88 Q4 **Sidi Okba** Algeria 34.48N 5.54E
85 H4 **Sidi Omar** Egypt 31.24N 24.57E
88 K6 **Sidi Rahhal** Morocco 31.40N 7.30W
88 S4 **Sidi Saad** Tunisia 35.22N 9.50E
88 S4 **Sidi Saad Dam** Tunisia
85 A3 **Sidi Sa'īd** Libya 33.05N 11.50E
86 E3 **Sidi Sâlim** Egypt 31.16N 30.47E
88 L4 **Sidi Slimane** Morocco 34.17N 5.57W
88 J5 **Sidi Smail** Morocco 32.51N 8.32W
88 T5 **Sidi Toui** Tunisia 32.48N 11.22E
85 H4 **Sidi 'Umar** Libya 30.51N 24.51E
88 O4 **Sidi Youssef** Algeria 34.49N 0.39E
101 V4 **Sid L** N W Terr
28 C4 **Sidlaghatta** Karnataka India 13.25N 77.53E
58 K6 **Sidlaw Hills** Tayside Scotland
56 K6 **Sidlesham** W Sussex Eng 50.47N 0.48W
123 H10 **Sidley, Mt** Antarctica 77.12S 129.00W
28 H2 **Sidli** Assam India 26.31N 90.30E
88 O3 **Sid M'Hamed Benali** Algeria 36.13N 0.51E
56 E6 **Sidmouth** Devon Eng 50.41N 3.15W
13 G2 **Sidmouth, C** Queensland 13.20S 143.35E
106 F3 **Sidnaw** Michigan 46.31N 88.43W
106 F9 **Sidney** Illinois 40.01N 88.04W
108 P9 **Sidney** Iowa 40.46N 95.40W
100 S9 **Sidney** Manitoba 49.54N 99.02W
108 F2 **Sidney** Montana 47.42N 104.10W
108 H8 **Sidney** Nebraska 41.09N 103.00W
103 D2 **Sidney** New York 42.19N 75.24W
104 A6 **Sidney** Ohio 40.16N 84.10W
101 M11 **Sidney** Vancouver I, Br Col 48.39N 123.25W
103 D2 **Sidney Center** New York 42.18N 75.16W
105 C3 **Sidney Lanier, L** Georgia
89 F6 **Sido** Mali 11.37N 7.29W
19 B3 **Sidoan** Celebes Indon 0.19N 120.12E
18 K9 **Sidoarjo** Java Indon 7.27S 112.42E
72 J8 **Sidobre** *reg* France
25 C2 **Sidoktaya** Burma 20.26N 94.14E
19 A4 **Sidole, Bukit** *mt* Celebes Indon 0.30S 119.54E
Sidon *see* **Saida**
41 D7 **Sidorovsk** U.S.S.R. 66.35N 82.18E
Sidra, Golfo di *see* **Sirte, Gulf of**
86 K8 **Sidri, Wâdi** *watercourse* Egypt
118 C7 **Sidrolândia** Brazil 20.53S 54.58W
86 E5 **Sidûd** Egypt 30.25N 30.54E
64 C2 **Siebengebirge** *mts* W Germany
60 N13 **Siebengewald** Netherlands 51.39N 6.07E
64 P1 **Siebenlehn** E Germany 51.02N 13.19E
66 P1 **Sieberatsweiler** W Germany 47.37N 9.42E
66 M3 **Siebnen** Switzerland 47.11N 8.54E
72 D4 **Siecq** France 45.48N 0.12W
66 K5 **Siedelhorn** *mt* Switzerland 46.32N 8.16E
63 J7 **Siedenburg** W Germany 52.43N 8.56E
62 N3 **Siedlce** Poland 52.10N 22.18E
64 D2 **Sieg** *R* W Germany
64 E2 **Siegbach** W Germany 50.45N 8.17E
64 C2 **Siegburg** W Germany 50.48N 7.13E
Siegelsdorf *see* **Seukendorf**
64 E2 **Siegen** W Germany 50.52N 8.02E
64 M6 **Siegenburg** W Germany 48.45N 11.53E
41 O8 **Siegen-Kyuel'** U.S.S.R. 64.06N 130.16E
103 C5 **Siegersville** Pennsylvania 40.38N 75.35W
69 F7 **Sièges, les** France 48.10N 3.32E
65 O5 **Sieghartskirchen** Austria 48.16N 16.02E
64 O8 **Siegsdorf** W Germany 47.50N 12.40E
Siehcheng *see* **Pei Xian**
Siehmaho *see* **Xiemahe**
Siehyang Tao *see* **Xieyang Dao**
15 K4 **Siemens, C** Bismarck Arch 1.18S 149.35E
62 O3 **Siemiatycze** Poland 52.25N 22.50E
25 J5 **Siem Pang** Cambodia 14.09N 106.23E
25 G6 **Siem Reap** Cambodia 13.21N 103.50E
80 D2 **Siena** Italy 43.19N 11.19E
80 D2 **Siena** *prov* Italy
Sienfeng *see* **Xianfeng**
Sienhsien *see* **Xian Xian**
62 O5 **Sieniawa** Poland 50.11N 22.38E
Sienku *see* **Xianju**
70 H4 **Sienne** *R* France
Sienning *see* **Xianning**
Sienyang *see* **Xianyang**
51 K4 **Sieppijärvi** Finland 67.09N 23.59E
62 L4 **Sieradz** Poland 51.35N 18.41E
62 J3 **Sieraków** Poland 52.39N 16.04E
69 L5 **Sierck-les-Bains** France 49.26N 6.22E
71 L1 **Sierentz** France 47.40N 7.27E
65 O5 **Sierndorf** Austria 48.27N 16.10E
65 K5 **Sierning** Austria 48.04N 14.18E
62 M3 **Sierpc** Poland 52.52N 19.40E
76 H7 **Sierpe, La** Spain 40.40N 5.50W
121 E6 **Sierra Bayas** Argentina 36.59S 60.10W
112 B4 **Sierra Blanca** Texas 31.10N 105.22W
111 D2 **Sierra Buttes** *mt* California 39.37N 120.39W
121 E6 **Sierra Chica** Argentina 36.50S 60.10W
121 C8 **Sierra Colorada** Argentina 40.34S 67.48W
76 G10 **Sierra de Fuentes** Spain 39.26N 6.17W
75 J3 **Sierra de Luna** Spain 42.03N 0.55W
77 G6 **Sierra de Yeguas** Spain 37.07N 4.52W
75 K7 **Sierra Engarcerán** Spain 40.16N 0.01W
120 D10 **Sierra Gorda** Chile 22.50S 69.18W
121 D8 **Sierra Grande** Argentina 41.34S 65.21W
89 C7 **Sierra Leone** *rep* W Africa
96 J8 **Sierra Leone Basin** Atlantic Oc
89 C7 **Sierra Leone C** Sierra Leone 8.31N 13.20W
96 H8 **Sierra Leone Rise** Atlantic Oc
111 D6 **Sierra Madre Mts** California
115 H4 **Sierra Mojada** Mexico 27.19N 103.42W
121 D8 **Sierra, Pta** *C* Argentina 41.30S 65.00W
121 C9 **Sierra Rosada** Argentina 42.47S 68.08W
111 D2 **Sierraville** California 39.37N 120.21W
111 O10 **Sierra Vista** Arizona 31.34N 110.21W
66 G6 **Sierre** Switzerland 46.18N 7.33E
77 M6 **Sierro** Spain 37.19N 2.23W
64 D3 **Siershahn** W Germany 50.28N 7.46E
77 P2 **Siete Aguas** Spain 39.28N 0.55W
76 J6 **Siete Iglesias de Trabancos** Spain 41.21N 5.10W
118 B8 **Siete Puntas** *R* Paraguay
63 R6 **Sietow** E Germany 53.27N 12.35E
82 J3 **Sieu** Romania 47.00N 24.31E
79 K7 **Sieve** *R* Italy
63 Q7 **Sieversdorf** E Germany 52.49N 12.24E
63 M8 **Sievershausen** W Germany 52.22N 10.08E
51 L8 **Sievi** Finland 63.55N 24.30E
18 B5 **Sifahandra** Indonesia 1.30N 97.20E
33 N5 **Sifah, As** Oman 23.30N 58.45E
33 C2 **Şifān** Saudi Arabia 29.36N 39.45E
23 D7 **Şifang Ling** *mts* Guangxi China
21 D4 **Sifangtai** Heilongjiang China 46.52N 126.53E
87 H4 **Sifani** Ethiopia 12.18N 40.19E
90 B5 **Sifawa** Nigeria 12.49N 5.10E
36 G3 **Sife Gölü** *L* Turkey
Sifeng *see* **Xifeng**
89 F7 **Sifié** Ivory Coast 8.00W 7.04W
83 G8 **Sífnos** *isld* Greece
35 E1 **Sifsufa** Israel 33.01N 35.26E
100 R7 **Sifton** Manitoba 51.21N 100.09W

101 K7 Sifton Pass Br Columbia 57.57N 126.17W
88 N4 Sig Algeria 35.31N 0.11W
53 B5 Sig Denmark 55.40N 8.34E
47 C3 Sig U.S.S.R. 65.31N 34.16E
36 B4 Siğacik Turkey 38.12N 26.47E
93 D9 Siga Hills Tanzania
33 K7 Sigani Saudi Arabia 19.24N 52.20E
52 E6 Sigdal Norway 60.04N 9.38E
72 K9 Sigean France 43.02N 2.58E
72 K9 Sigean, Etang de L France 43.05N 3.00E
107 H2 Sigel Illinois 39.14N 88.30W
104 F5 Sigel Pennsylvania 41.17N 79.08W
75 K4 Sigena mt Spain 41.39N 0.03W
18 C6 Sigep Indonesia 0.59S 98.50E
18 C6 Sigep, Tanjung C Indonesia 0.56S 98.52E
51 E3 Sigerfjord Norway 68.40N 15.33E
66 Q1 Siggen W Germany 47.42N 9.57E
87 J8 Siggia Somalia 3.59N 43.24E
84 Y20 Siġġiewi Malta 35.51N 14.26E
82 H3 Sighet Romania 47.56N 23.53E
82 J4 Sighişoara Romania 46.12N 24.48E
57 H2 Sighty Crag mt Cumbria Eng 55.07N 2.38W
80 G2 Sigillo Italy 43.20N 12.44E
33 K10 Sigirah Socotra Ind Oc 12.38N 54.18E
37 E3 Sığırcı Turkey 40.14N 28.04E
66 M7 Sigirino Switzerland 46.05N 8.55E
26 S6 Sigiriya Sri Lanka 7.57N 80.46E
18 J3 Siglap dist Singapore
18 A3 Sigli Sumatra Indon 5.21N 95.56E
50 G2 Siglufjördhur Iceland 66.09N 18.55W
50 B4 Siglunes Iceland 65.27N 23.40W
50 B4 Sigluneshlídhar coast 65.18N 23.55W
19 L6 Sigma Philippines 11.25N 122.39E
64 G7 Sigmaringen W Germany 48.05N 9.13E
65 N4 Sigmundsherberg Austria 48.42N 15.46E
79 K7 Signa Italy 43.47N 11.06E
44 G6 Signakhi Georgia U.S.S.R. 41.34N 46.00E
111 L7 Signal Arizona 34.29N 113.37W
111 E10 Signal Hill California 33.47N 118.10W
94 P11 Signal Hill Cape Town S Africa 33.55S 18.24E
11 M12 Signal Hill Dunedin New Zealand 45.51S 170.33E
107 L6 Signal Mountain Tennessee 35.07N 85.21W
111 K8 Signal Pk mt Arizona 33.23N 114.04W
66 G4 Signau Switzerland 46.56N 7.45E
71 H10 Signes France 43.17N 5.50E
81 P11 Signora Pulita, Mte Italy 40.47N 17.23E
81 H9 Signore, Poggio di mt Sicily 37.14N 14.09E
123 C14 Signy U.K. Base S Orkney Is S Atlantic Oc 60.54S 45.56W
69 G4 Signy-l'Abbaye France 49.42N 4.25E
69 G4 Signy-le-Petit France 49.54N 4.17E
72 D4 Sigogne France 45.44N 0.10W
18 C7 Sigoisoinan Indonesia 2.05S 99.35E
93 G4 Sigor Kenya 1.29N 35.26E
72 E6 Sigoulès France 44.45N 0.25E
106 B8 Sigourney Iowa 41.19N 92.12W
42 D1 Sigovo U.S.S.R. 62.46N 87.01E
50 H3 Sigridharstadhaskógur wood Iceland
66 G5 Sigriswil Switzerland 46.43N 7.43E
119 B9 Sigsig Ecuador 3.04S 78.50W
52 K7 Sigtuna Sweden 59.36N 17.44E
115 L2 Siguatepeque Honduras 14.39N 87.48W
75 E5 Sigüenza Spain 41.04N 2.38W
75 H2 Sigues Spain 42.37N 1.00W
89 E6 Siguiri Guinea 11.28N 9.07W
93 E5 Sigulu I Uganda 0.07N 33.48E
111 N3 Sigurd Utah 38.49N 111.56W
50 J1 Sigurdharstadhavík inlet Iceland
70 N2 Sigy-en-Bray France 49.33N 1.29E
35 G5 Sihan Jordan 32.09N 35.45E
95 P8 Sihangwana S Africa 27.04S 32.25E
25 C1 Sihaung Myauk Burma 22.53N 94.08E
29 G7 Sihawa Madhya Prad India 20.25N 81.98E
30 F8 Sihawal Madhya Prad India 24.35N 82.14E
22 L6 Siheyong Hebei China 41.46N 117.48E
66 M3 Sihl R Switzerland
95 N7 Sihlitho S Africa 31.25S 29.28E
66 M3 Sihlsee L Switzerland 47.08N 8.46E
Siho see Hsi-ho
23 H2 Sihong Jiangsu China 33.26N 118.12E
30 B7 Sihor Madhya Prad India 25.44N 78.06E
29 G6 Sihora Madhya Prad India 23.30N 80.09E
29 F7 Sihora Maharashtra India 21.28N 79.58E
95 L8 Sihotu S Africa 32.30S 27.59E
Sihsien Anhui see She Xian
23 F7 Sihui Guangdong China 23.25N 112.27E
Sihwa see Xihua
51 J10 Siikainen Finland 61.52N 21.50E
47 B4 Siikajoki R Finland
51 N8 Siilinjärvi Finland 63.05N 27.40E
40 G8 Siin U.S.S.R. 46.35N 135.25E
Siipyy see Sideby
35 D7 Si'ir Jordan 31.35N 35.09E
37 F8 Siirt Turkey 37.56N 41.56E
31 E7 Sijawal Pakistan 27.49N 68.11E
60 H9 Sijbekarspel Netherlands 52.43N 4.59E
61 D2 Sijsele Belgium 51.12N 3.19E
29 A6 Sika Gujarat India 22.26N 69.47E
33 J4 Sikak, As Qatar, The Gulf 24.39N 50.54E
84 G5 Sikáminos Greece 38.17N 23.44E
30 A4 Sikandarabad Bulandshahr, Uttar Prad India 28.28N 77.42E
30 D5 Sikandarabad Kheri, Uttar Prad India 27.57N 80.30E
30 H6 Sikandarpur Uttar Prad India 26.02N 84.03E
30 A5 Sikandra Agra, Uttar Prad India 27.14N 77.56E
30 E7 Sikandra Allahabad, Uttar Prad Ind 25.36N 81.59E
30 K8 Sikandra Bihar India 24.57N 86.02E
30 C6 Sikandra Kanpur, Uttar Prad Ind 26.22N 79.38E
30 B5 Sikandra Rao Uttar Prad India 27.42N 78.21E
101 M7 Sikanni Chief Br Columbia 57.11N 122.43W
101 M7 Sikanni Chief R Br Columbia
29 D4 Sikar Rajasthan India 27.33N 75.12E
29 D4 Sikar dist Rajasthan India
31 E3 Sikaram mt Afghanistan 34.04N 69.58E
30 H7 Sikarhata Bihar India 25.17N 84.29E
18 C7 Sikariman Indonesia 2.35S 99.59E
30 L8 Sikaripara Bihar India 24.14N 87.29E
89 G6 Sikasso Mali 11.18N 5.38W
25 M9 Sikaw Burma 23.49N 97.06E
84 E8 Sikéa Greece 36.46N 22.56E
52 M2 Sikeå Sweden 64.09N 20.55E
37 H7 Şikefti Turkey 38.10N 44.11E
19 B6 Sikeli Indonesia 5.16S 121.51E
39 C2 Sikerin U.S.S.R. 67.30N 142.59E
107 D9 Sikes Louisiana 32.04N 92.30W
107 G5 Sikeston Missouri 36.52N 89.33W
38 N4 Sikhote Alin Gory mts U.S.S.R.
84 D2 Sikiá Greece 39.49N 22.03E
42 H2 Sikili, Porog falls U.S.S.R. 61.32N 109.10E
83 G8 Síkinos Greece
84 E6 Sikión Greece 37.58N 22.43E
Sikionía see Kiáton
53 X15 Sikkelbreen glacier Norway 61.51N 7.34E
29 L4 Sikkim state India
62 L10 Siklós Hungary 45.51N 18.18E
113 B5 Siknik C St Lawrence I Bering Sea 63.10N 170.19W
19 E3 Siko isld Moluccas Indon 0.09N 127.06E
92 F4 Sikonge Tanzania 5.38S 32.46E
84 E2 Sikoúrion Greece 39.46N 22.35E
30 A5 Sikri Patti Rajasthan India 27.34N 77.05E
51 F5 Sikselet Sweden 66.15N 17.55E
39 E2 Siktemey U.S.S.R. 67.12N 153.05E
30 L6 Sikti Bihar India 26.24N 87.33E
41 M6 Siktyakh U.S.S.R. 69.56N 125.00E
41 N6 Siktyakh R U.S.S.R.
18 M2 Sikuati Sabah Malaysia 6.54N 116.39E
19 B3 Sikutu Celebes Indonesia 0.51N 120.38E
76 F3 Sil R Spain
29 K2 Silabati R W Bengal India
47 M5 Silach, Oz L U.S.S.R. 56.00N 60.45E
25 E8 Si, Laem C Thailand 9.24N 99.18E
53 U14 Silafjorden inlet Norway 62.25N 6.05E
19 M6 Silago Philippines 10.31N 125.08E
81 M5 Sila, Grande mts Italy
81 M5 Sila, Greca mts Italy
18 C6 Silagui Indonesia 1.14S 98.57E
31 F3 Silala Afghanistan 34.30N 70.53E
81 M5 Şila, La mts Italy
46 D2 Silale Lithuania U.S.S.R. 55.31N 22.08E
90 B5 Silame Nigeria 13.00N 4.53E
79 J1 Silandro Italy 46.38N 10.47E
19 H2 Silang Luzon Philippines 14.13N 120.59E
18 J5 Silantek, Gunung mt Kalimantan/Sarawak 1.02N 111.02E
81 B3 Silanus Sardinia 40.18N 8.54E
30 J7 Silao Bihar India 25.05N 85.25E
115 J7 Silao Mexico 20.56N 101.28W
81 M5 Sila Piccola mts Italy
19 M5 Sila Pt Philippines 12.25N 125.20E
107 H10 Silas Alabama 31.47N 88.21W
18 J5 Silat Borneo Indon 0.24N 111.48E
35 D3 Silat el Harithiya Jordan 32.31N 35.14E
88 Q9 Silaten, Mt Algeria 25.38N 5.55E
26 Q4 Silavattura Sri Lanka 8.43N 79.58E
18 A3 Silawaih Agam vol Sumatra Indon 5.29N 95.35E
19 L6 Silay Philippines 10.45N 122.59E
63 U8 Silberberg E Germany 52.15N 14.03E
66 Q3 Silber Tal V Austria
66 Q3 Silberthal Austria 47.06N 9.59E
28 J3 Silchar Assam India 24.49N 92.47E
29 K2 Silda W Bengal India 22.37N 86.50E
51 J1 Silda isld Norway 70.17N 21.42E
53 S14 Sildegapet B Norway 62.05N 5.12E
37 G1 Şile Turkey 41.11N 29.38E
79 M3 Sile R Italy
79 M3 Silea Italy 45.39N 12.18E
57 G4 Silecroft Cumbria Eng 54.14N 3.20W
112 G7 Silencio Mexico 28.03N 101.00W
66 L4 Silenen Switzerland 46.48N 8.41E
61 H6 Silenrieux Belgium 50.13N 4.25E
59 K3 Silent Valley Res Down N Ireland 54.08N 6.00W
105 H2 Siler City N Carolina 35.43N 79.29W
28 E2 Sileru R Andhra Prad etc India
77 L4 Siles Spain 38.23N 2.34W
110 R4 Silesia Montana 45.33N 108.50W
62 K5 Silesia reg Poland/Czech
88 Q10 Silet Algeria 22.40N 4.34E
70 D5 Silfiac France 48.09N 3.09W
50 F4 Silfrastadhir Iceland 65.26N 19.12W
30 D3 Silgarhi-Doti Nepal 29.14N 80.58E
28 J2 Silghat Assam India 26.36N 92.56E
26 Q12 Silhouette I Seychelles, Ind Oc 4.29S 55.12E
89 H6 Sili Upper Volta 11.37N 2.29W
23 E6 Silian Guangxi China 24.02N 108.52E
78 C12 Siliana Tunisia 36.05N 9.23E
78 C12 Siliana R Tunisia
18 B9 Siliau Pen Malaysia 2.36N 101.52E
108 S2 Silica Minnesota 47.16N 93.00W
36 G6 Silifke Turkey 36.22N 33.57E
41 K6 Siligir R U.S.S.R.
81 B2 Siligo Sardinia 40.35N 8.44E
29 L4 Siliguri W Bengal India 26.42N 88.30E
87 J5 Silil Somalia 10.58N 43.30E
84 D6 Silímna Greece 37.30N 22.19E
24 F10 Siling Co L Xizang Zizhiqu China 31.45N 88.50E
30 A6 Silipur Madhya Prad India 26.05N 77.02E
81 B5 Siliqua Sardinia 39.18N 8.48E
81 B2 Silis R Sardinia
122 A1 Silisili pk W Samoa, Pacific Oc 13.34S 172.27W
Silistat see Bozkır
82 L6 Silistra Bulgaria 44.06N 27.17E
37 E1 Silivri Turkey 41.05N 28.15E
52 E7 Siljan Norway 59.17N 9.42E
52 H6 Siljan L Sweden 60.55N 14.50E
53 D4 Silkeborg Denmark 56.10N 9.34E
57 K5 Silkstone S Yorks Eng 53.33N 1.33W
77 Q2 Silla Spain 39.22N 0.25W
120 E8 Sillajhuay cord Bolivia/Chile 19.46S 68.42W
59 J3 Sillan L Cavan Irish Rep 54.00N 6.55W
79 H6 Sillano Italy 44.13N 10.18E
71 J9 Sillans-la-Cascade France 43.34N 6.10E
79 L6 Sillaro R Italy
36 F5 Sille Turkey 37.56N 32.26E
76 C3 Silleda Spain 42.42N 8.15W
69 L6 Sillegny France 49.00N 6.10E
76 B4 Silleiro, C Spain 42.07N 8.54W
70 K5 Sillé-le-Guillaume France 48.10N 0.08W
69 G5 Sillery France 49.12N 4.09E
98 Q9 Sillery dist Quebec 46.46N 71.15W
29 J2 Silli Bihar India 23.24N 85.52E
65 F8 Sillian Austria 46.46N 12.26E
70 L4 Silli-en-Gouffern France 48.45N 0.04E
77 C4 Sillo, Arroyo de R Spain
29 D7 Sillod Maharashtra India 20.20N 75.42E
70 D4 Sillon-de-Talbert France 48.53N 3.05W
57 G3 Silloth Cumbria Eng 54.52N 3.23W
61 F4 Silly Belgium 50.38N 3.55E
83 H3 Sílo mt Greece 41.08N 25.52E
35 B1 Siloam, Pool of Jerusalem
107 B5 Siloam Springs Arkansas 36.10N 94.31W
15 L5 Silom New Ireland 3.13S 151.58E
30 C8 Silon Madhya Prad India 24.40N 79.49E
37 G8 Silopi Turkey 37.15N 42.27E
47 J2 Silovayakha R U.S.S.R.
66 P6 Sils-Baselgia Switzerland 46.28N 9.45E
112 N5 Silsbee Texas 30.20N 94.10W
100 W3 Silsby L Manitoba
66 P6 Silser See L Switzerland
85 M7 Silsila, Gebel es mts Egypt
66 Q6 Sils-Maria Switzerland 46.27N 9.46E
Silsoe see Bessie's Castle
109 C2 Silt Colorado 39.32N 107.40W
100 N8 Silton Saskatchewan 50.49N 104.54W
90 G3 Siltoü Chad 16.46N 15.33E
18 H5 Siluas Borneo Indon 1.15N 109.50E
90 B8 Siluko Nigeria 6.35N 5.10E
18 M10 Silungblanak Indonesia 8.52S 116.10E
32 J8 Silūp R Iran
107 K8 Şiluria Alabama 33.14N 86.51W
46 D2 Šilutė Lithuania U.S.S.R. 55.18N 21.30E
119 G8 Silva, I. da Brazil 0.23S 64.25W
37 F7 Silvan Turkey 38.08N 41.00E
118 E5 Silvânia Brazil 16.39S 48.37W
79 E5 Silvano d'Orba Italy 44.42N 8.40E
66 Q6 Silvaplana Switzerland 46.28N 9.48E
66 Q6 Silvaplaner See L Switzerland
Silva Porto see Bié
103 B3 Silvara Pennsylvania 41.42N 76.08W
76 D8 Silvares Portugal 40.08N 7.40W
29 C7 Silvassa Dadra & Nagar Haveli India 20.13N 73.03E
116 K4 Silver Bank West Indies
116 J4 Silver Bank Passage West Indies
106 C2 Silver Bay Minnesota 47.15N 91.17W
103 N3 Silver Beach Massachusetts 41.38N 70.39W
111 N9 Silverbell Arizona 32.26N 111.31W
110 N3 Silver Bow Montana 46.00N 112.40W
99 L5 Silver Centre Ontario 47.12N 79.30W
110 J6 Silver City Idaho 43.02N 116.44W
107 F8 Silver City Mississippi 33.05N 90.30W
109 B9 Silver City New Mexico 32.47N 108.16W
111 M2 Silver City Utah 39.55N 112.09W
107 F10 Silver Creek Mississippi 31.38N 90.01W
108 N8 Silver Creek Nebraska 41.20N 97.40W
104 F4 Silver Creek New York 42.32N 79.12W
110 F6 Silver Creek Oregon
108 E8 Silver Crown Wyoming 41.11N 105.02W
109 O4 Silverdale Kansas 37.03N 96.54W
57 H4 Silverdale Lancs Eng 54.10N 2.49W
11 J3 Silverdale New Zealand 36.39S 174.42E
65 B8 Silverettahorn mt Austria 46.52N 10.06E
100 F6 Silver Heights Alberta 52.19N 111.14W
99 B4 Silver Islet Ontario 48.22N 88.50W
110 E6 Silver L Oregon 43.06N 120.54W
110 F6 Silver L Oregon 43.21N 119.24W
111 H6 Silver Lake California 35.23N 116.05W
103 N2 Silver Lake Massachusetts 42.02N 70.48W
106 G3 Silver Lake Michigan 46.39N 87.50W
59 F6 Silvermines Tipperary Irish Rep 52.48N 8.14W
98 P4 Silver Mt pk Newfoundland 49.38N 57.17W
103 G2 Silvernails New York 42.01N 73.40W
102 G4 Silverpeak Nevada
111 G4 Silverpeak Nevada 37.46N 117.39W
11 L11 Silverpeak mt New Zealand 45.44S 170.27E
111 G4 Silver Peak Ra Nevada
54 L9 Silver Pit North Sea
13 G2 Silver Plains Queensland 14.00S 143.38E
103 A8 Silver Spring Maryland 39.00N 77.01W
104 M9 Silver Spring dist Washington D C
104 G4 Silver Springs New York 42.41N 78.06W
110 N4 Silver Star Montana 45.41N 112.17W
101 O10 Silver Star Prov. Park Br Columbia
56 J3 Silverstone Northants Eng 52.06N 1.02W
11 L12 Silver Stream New Zealand
95 G4 Silver Streams S Africa 28.20S 23.34E
101 K10 Silverthrone Mt Br Columbia 51.30N 126.03W
109 C4 Silverton Colorado 37.48N 107.40W
103 F6 Silverton New Jersey 40.01N 74.08W
12 F4 Silverton New S Wales 31.55S 141.14E
110 C4 Silverton Oregon 45.01N 122.47W
95 M1 Silverton S Africa 25.45S 28.18E
112 F1 Silverton Texas 34.28N 101.18W
110 D1 Silverton Washington 48.04N 121.35W
55 H3 Silvertown London Eng 51.30N 0.02E
12 K7 Silverwater dist Sydney, N S W
117 A6 Silves Brazil 2.48S 58.08W
76 C14 Silves Portugal 37.11N 8.26W
Silves, Barragem res see Arade, Barragem de
121 C4 Silveyra, L Argentina
80 K3 Silvi Italy 43.33N 14.06E
119 C6 Silvia Colombia 2.42N 76.22W
19 E8 Silvícola Indonesia 8.38S 127.01E
110 F6 Silvies R Oregon
106 D8 Silvis Illinois 41.32N 90.25W
115 O8 Silvituc Mexico 18.44N 90.15W
60 O12 Silvolde Netherlands 51.54N 6.24E
85 M7 Silwa Bahari Egypt 24.40N 32.59E
35 B1 Silwān sub Jerusalem Israel
94 P12 Silwermyn R Cape Town S Africa
64 B5 Silwingen W Germany 49.26N 6.34E
41 O7 Silyan-Kyuyel' U.S.S.R. 65.20N 130.01E
39 D2 Silyap R U.S.S.R.
51 R3 Silyavr, Ozero L U.S.S.R. 68.33N 34.29E
41 Q5 Sil'yeyaki U.S.S.R. 71.29N 144.17E
65 C7 Silz Austria 47.16N 10.56E
47 H8 Sim U.S.S.R. 55.00N 57.40E
47 H8 Sim R U.S.S.R.
25 N8 Sima Burma 25.02N 97.42E
95 B2 Sima Comoros, Indian Oc 12.11S 44.18E
91 C5 Sima Congo 2.23S 13.40E
34 L4 Simād Iraq 34.16N 43.20E
53 W17 Simadalen V Norway 60.30N 7.10E
35 G8 Simakiya Jordan 31.19N 35.48E
18 C6 Simaleke Hilir Indonesia 1.12S 98.38E
18 C6 Simalubek Indonesia 1.30S 98.49E
30 M6 Simana Basti W Bengal India 26.59N 88.09E
76 K5 Simancas Spain 41.35N 4.50W
71 F3 Simandre France 46.37N 4.59E
18 J5 Simanggang Sarawak Malaysia 1.10N 111.32E
66 M6 Simano mt Switzerland 46.28N 9.00E
18 C6 Simansih Indonesia 1.34S 98.49E
23 B7 Simao Yunnan China 22.42N 101.23E
118 J2 Simão Dias Brazil 10.48S 37.47W
19 L5 Simara isld Philippines 12.48N 122.02E
119 G5 Simaraña Venezuela 4.35N 63.56W
99 M5 Simàrd, L Quebec
32 B4 Şimareh R Iran
29 J5 Šimaria Bihar India 24.05N 84.58E
30 J7 Simaria Ghat Bihar India 25.25N 86.00E
19 B3 Simatang Celebes Indonesia 1.02N 120.24E
77 Q2 Simat de Valldigna Spain 39.03N 0.19W
36 D3 Simav Turkey 39.05N 28.59E
36 C2 Simav R Turkey
37 E3 Simav Çayı R Turkey
36 D3 Simav Gölü L Turkey
37 E3 Sımavlı Turkey 40.12N 27.52E
81 B4 Simaxis Sardinia 39.56N 8.42E
33 D8 Simayr isld Saudi Arabia 17.50N 41.24E
93 J8 Simba Kenya 2.10S 37.36E
91 H3 Simba Zaïre 0.38N 22.59E
64 O6 Simbach W Germany 48.34N 12.45E
64 P7 Simbach am Inn W Germany 48.16N 13.02E
120 A2 Simbal Peru 8.00S 78.51W
81 M6 Simbario Italy 38.37N 16.20E
15 L5 Simberi I Bismarck Arch 2.40S 151.56E
86 F4 Simbillâwein, El Egypt 30.53N 31.27E
93 E10 Simbo Tabora Tanzania 4.39S 33.28E
15 J3 Simbo I Solomon Is 8.08S 156.32E
29 B7 Simbor isld Gujarat India 20.46N 71.21E
80 H5 Simbruini, Monti Italy
45 H1 Simbukhovo U.S.S.R. 55.23N 36.19E
88 J6 Sim, C Morocco 31.23N 9.53W
99 K10 Simcoe Ontario 42.50N 80.19W
99 L8 Simcoe, L Ontario 44.23N 79.18W
29 J6 Simdega Bihar India 22.35N 84.31E
44 C10 Simeiz Ukraine U.S.S.R. 44.26N 33.59E
37 G7 Simek Turkey 38.19N 42.07E
87 F4 Simēn reg Ethiopia
42 H1 Simenga U.S.S.R. 62.42N 108.25E
108 K7 Simeon Nebraska 42.38N 100.42W
113 H9 Simeonof I Alaska 54.55N 159.15W
53 D3 Simested Denmark 56.42N 9.34E
53 C3 Simested Å R Denmark
81 J8 Simeto R Sicily
18 B4 Simeuluë isld Indonesia
44 C10 Simferopol' Ukraine U.S.S.R. 44.57N 34.05E
84 U16 Sími Greece 36.36N 27.51E
84 U16 Simi isld Greece
84 D6 Simiádhes Greece 37.39N 22.20E
71 H9 Simiane-la-Rotonde France 43.59N 5.33E
Simien reg see Simēn reg
30 E3 Simikot Nepal 29.58N 81.49E
79 J1 Similaun mt Italy 46.47N 10.52E
32 J7 Simish watercourse Iran
119 D4 Simití Colombia 7.57N 73.57W
82 H9 Simitli Bulgaria 41.51N 23.09E
48 R11 Simiutak Greenland 66.02N 53.45W
92 F3 Simiyu R Tanzania
93 F8 Simiyu watercourse Tanzania
93 M8 Simkara Kenya 2.31S 40.18E
45 S2 Simkino U.S.S.R. 54.15N 46.08E
109 F2 Simla Colorado 39.09N 104.06W
30 A1 Simla Himachal Prad India 31.07N 77.09E
29 H1 Simla dist Calcutta, W Bengal
82 H3 Simlăul 'Silvaniei Romania 47.12N 22.49E
35 H1 Simlin Syria 33.02N 36.06E
66 F5 Simme R Switzerland
53 C4 Simmelkær Denmark 56.17N 9.01E
64 L4 Simmelsdorf W Germany 49.36N 11.20E
64 D4 Simmer R W Germany
64 A2 Simmerath W Germany 50.36N 6.19E
64 D4 Simmern W Germany 49.59N 7.32E
107 E11 Simmesport Louisiana 30.59N 91.49W
66 O3 Simmi R Switzerland
100 J9 Simmie Saskatchewan 49.56N 108.06W
111 E6 Simmler California 35.20N 119.58W
79 B8 Simmons Quebec 45.28N 75.50W
112 J7 Simmons Texas 28.24N 98.18W
116 G3 Simms Long I Bahamas 23.31N 75.14W
110 O2 Simms Montana 47.30N 111.55W
112 N2 Simms Texas 33.21N 94.31W
105 K9 Simms Pt New Providence I Bahamas 25.02N 77.33W
62 O1 Simnas Lithuania U.S.S.R. 54.24N 23.38E
51 L6 Simo Finland 65.39N 25.01E
52 E7 Simoa R Norway
51 M6 Simojoki R Finland
115 N9 Simojovel Mexico 17.14N 92.40W
51 N11 Simola Finland 60.55N 28.15E
111 G3 Simon Nevada 38.35N 117.51W
14 E9 Simon W Australia 31.50S 123.05E
119 B9 Simón Bolívar airport Ecuador 2.13S 79.55W
116 J10 Simon Bolivar Nat Park Venezuela
57 J2 Simonburn Northumb Eng 55.03N 2.12W
101 O8 Simonette R Alberta
28 K1 Simong Moling Assam India 28.36N 95.03E
100 Q4 Şimonhouse Manitoba 54.28N 101.22W
62 N7 Šimonka mt Czechoslovakia 48.57N 21.30E
99 P7 Simon, L Quebec
94 P12 Simonsbaai B Cape Town S Africa
56 D5 Simonsbath Somerset Eng 51.09N 3.45W
60 F12 Simonshaven Netherlands 51.49N 4.17E
Simonstad see Simonstown
52 J8 Simonstorp Sweden 58.45N 16.10E
95 B10 Simonstown S Africa 34.12S 18.26E
60 O5 Simonszand isld Netherlands 53.31N 6.24E
101 K10 Simoom Sound Br Columbia 50.44N 126.28W
84 C6 Simópoulon Greece 37.50N 21.34E
72 F9 Simorre France 43.27N 0.44E
Simoş see Uçum Bitlis
18 J6 Simpang Borneo Indon 1.04S 110.05E
18 E5 Simpang Sumatra Indon 0.07N 103.15E
18 F6 Simpang Sumatra Indon 1.15S 104.05E
18 A8 Simpang Ampat Pen Malaysia 3.54N 100.56E
18 B4 Simpang-kiri R Sumatra Indonesia
18 M2 Simpang Mangayau, Tanjong C Sabah Malaysia 7.00N 116.44E
18 D10 Simpang Rengam Pen Malaysia 1.49N 103.18E
51 O10 Simpele Finland 61.26N 29.20E
Simpeln see Simplon
60 T17 Simpelveld Netherlands 50.50N 5.59E
52 K9 Simpevarp Sweden 57.25N 16.40E
117 G8 Simplício Mendes Brazil 7.47S 41.51W
66 J7 Simplon Switzerland 46.12N 8.04E
66 J7 Simplon Pass Switzerland 46.15N 8.03E
66 J6 Simplon Tunnel Italy/Switz
109 N2 Simpson Kansas 39.23N 97.56W
108 S6 Simpson Minnesota 43.58N 92.24W
110 P1 Simpson Montana 48.55N 110.13W
103 C3 Simpson Pennsylvania 41.36N 75.30W
100 M7 Simpson Saskatchewan 51.28N 105.28W
101 Q1 Simpson B N W Terr
13 D6 Simpson Des N Terr Australia
14 F7 Simpson Hill W Australia 26.30S 126.34E
121 J5 Simpson, I Chile 45.50S 73.45W
99 C4 Simpson I Ontario 48.47N 87.40W
101 R5 Simpson Is N W Terr
101 K1 Simpson L N W Terr 68.08N 126.39W
15 K9 Simpson, Mt Papua New Guinea 10.05S 149.36E
111 H2 Simpson Park Mts Nevada
97 L4 Simpson Pen N W Terr
121 J5 Simpson, R Chile
101 Y1 Simpson Str N W Terr
105 E3 Simpsonville S Carolina 34.43N 82.16W
29 J4 Simra Nepal 27.10N 85.00E
30 K6 Simrahi Bihar India 26.19N 86.51E
30 E6 Simrauta Uttar Prad India 26.28N 81.24E
30 K7 Simri Bakhtiarpur Bihar India 25.44N 86.36E
52 H11 Simrishamn Sweden 55.35N 14.20E
110 C8 Sims California 41.05N 122.23W
112 G9 Sims Bayou R Texas
103 J3 Simsbury Connecticut 41.53N 72.48W
15 L8 Simsim I Trobriand Is Papua New Guinea 8.24S 150.29E
64 N8 Simssee L W Germany 47.51N 12.15E
110 D5 Simtustus, L Oregon
92 K8 Simuco Mozambique 14.00S 40.35E
18 B6 Simuk isld Indonesia 0.05S 97.50E
92 D12 Simukwe R Zimbabwe
18 J5 Simunjan Sarawak Malaysia 1.22N 110.45E
19 J9 Simunul isld Philippines 4.54N 119.50E
40 M8 Simushir O isld Kuril Is U.S.S.R.
Simusiru-fuji vol see Prevo vol
37 E6 Sin Turkey 39.11N 39.24E
61 G2 Sinaai Belgium 51.09N 4.03E
18 B4 Sinabang Indonesia 2.27N 96.24E
18 C4 Sinabung mt Sumatra Indon 3.13N 98.20E
82 C6 Sinac Yugoslavia 44.49N 15.22E
87 L8 Sinadogo Somalia 5.21N 46.13E
33 A3 Sināfir isld Saudi Arabia 27.55N 34.40E
86 N10 Sināfir isld Saudi Arabia
31 C4 Sinai Afghanistan 33.17N 64.56E
108 N5 Sinai S Dakota 44.16N 97.02W
86 K7 Sinai pen Egypt
82 K5 Sinaia Romania 45.20N 25.33E
Sinai, Mt see Mûsa, Gebel
115 F5 Sinaloa state Mexico
80 E2 Sinalunga Italy 43.13N 11.43E
119 E2 Sinamaica Venezuela 11.06N 71.52W
23 E5 Sinan Guizhou China 27.56N 108.22E
37 F8 Sinan Turkey 37.53N 40.59E
83 D4 Sinanaj Albania 40.22N 19.52E
82 G5 Sînandrei Romania 45.50N 21.11E
21 C8 Sinanju N Korea 39.33N 125.36E
36 F3 Sinanlı Turkey 39.10N 32.27E
84 S14 Sina Oros mt Cyprus 35.22N 33.52E
28 B1 Sina R Maharashtra India
47 N5 Sinara R U.S.S.R.
84 W22 Sinarádhes Corfu 39.34N 19.51E
47 M5 Sinara, Oz L U.S.S.R. 56.08N 60.45E
40 N7 Sinarka vol Kuril Is U.S.S.R. 48.53N 154.11E
113 J1 Sinaru Alaska 70.57N 157.30W
85 A4 Sināwan Libya 31.03N 10.37E
31 F3 Sinawi Afghanistan 35.40N 70.45E
92 C10 Sinazongwe Zambia 17.14S 27.27E
25 C3 Sinbaungwe Burma 19.44N 95.10E
25 M9 Sinbo Burma 24.44N 97.03E
25 E6 Sinbyubyin Burma 13.47N 98.18E
25 E5 Sinbyudaing Burma 14.01N 98.56E
25 C2 Sinbyugyun Burma 20.38N 94.40E
36 E4 Sincalı Turkey 38.45N 30.14E
37 D6 Sincan Turkey 39.26N 37.54E
119 C3 Sincé Colombia 9.14N 75.08W
119 C3 Sincelejo Colombia 9.17N 75.23W
69 E4 Sinceny France 49.36N 3.17E
71 E2 Sincey-lès-Rouvray France 47.26N 4.08E
Sinchan see Hsin-chan
Sinchang see Xinzhan
21 D9 Sinch'ang S Korea 36.50N 126.55E
Sinchar see Xinzhai
Sincheng see Xincheng
Sinchengtze see Xinchengzi
Sinchiehchi see Xinjieji
Sinchow see Xinzhou
37 D7 Sincik Turkey 38.05N 38.32E
108 C8 Sinclair Wyoming 41.45N 107.06W
11 B6 Sinclair Hd New Zealand 41.22S 174.43E
105 D4 Sinclair L Georgia
101 N9 Sinclair Mills Br Col 54.00N 121.40W
12 C4 Sinclair, Pt S Australia 32.05S 132.59E
58 K2 Sinclairs B Highland Scotland 58.30N 3.07W
104 F4 Sinclairville New York 42.18N 79.16W
118 H3 Sincora, Serra do mts Brazil
Sind see Thul Pakistan
31 E8 Sind reg Pakistan
91 C6 Sinda Congo 4.51S 12.03E
40 G7 Sinda U.S.S.R. 48.58N 136.16E
53 E2 Sindal Denmark 57.29N 10.13E
19 L7 Sindañgan Mindanao Philippines 8.13N 123.01E
19 L7 Sindañgan B Mindanao Philippines
18 G9 Sindangbarang Java Indon 7.26S 107.01E
91 B4 Sindara Gabon 1.07S 10.41E
Sindari see Sindri
19 B8 Sindeh, Teluk B Indonesia
82 L7 Sindel Bulgaria 43.07N 27.38E
64 G6 Sindelfingen W Germany 48.43N 9.01E
89 K4 Sinder Niger 14.29N 1.22E
60 O12 Sinderen Netherlands 51.54N 6.29E
47 J5 Sindeya U.S.S.R. 60.04N 61.30E
28 C2 Sindgi Karnataka India 16.57N 76.15E
30 B6 Sindh R Madhya Prad India
29 E6 Sindhara Madhya Prad India 23.50N 77.12E
30 C5 Sindhauli Uttar Prad India 27.58N 79.58E
30 J5 Sindhuli Garhi Nepal 27.17N 85.58E
90 K6 Sindi Chad 11.34N 20.31E
46 E1 Sindi Estonia U.S.S.R. 58.28N 24.41E
29 F7 Sindi Maharashtra India 20.48N 78.59E
81 B3 Sindia Sardinia 40.18N 8.40E
53 B4 Sinding Ringkøbing Denmark 56.13N 8.52E
53 C4 Sinding Viborg Denmark 56.12N 9.29E
Sındıran see Yenice Ankara Turkey
36 C3 Sındırgı Turkey 39.13N 28.10E
Sindiskom see Yalnızçam
86 F5 Sindiyûn Egypt 30.15N 31.12E
29 E8 Sindkhed Maharashtra India 19.58N 76.10E
29 D7 Sindkheda Maharashtra India 21.17N 74.47E
28 C3 Sindnur Karnataka India 15.46N 76.44E
47 G4 Sindor U.S.S.R. 62.48N 51.57E
69 M2 Sindorf W Germany 50.54N 6.40E
89 G6 Sindou Upper Volta 10.35N 5.04W
28 B1 Sindphana R Maharashtra India
29 K1 Sindri Bihar India 23.45N 86.42E
29 B5 Sindri Rajasthan India 25.32N 71.58E
64 G5 Sindringen W Germany 49.17N 9.30E
31 F5 Sind Sagar Doab interfluve Pakistan
89 C7 Sindugu Sierra Leone 9.13N 12.17W
89 C5 Sine Senegal 13.37N 12.52W
71 K9 Sine, Col de la pass France 43.45N 6.52E
40 J8 Sinegorsk Sakhalin U.S.S.R. 47.08N 142.40E
45 M9 Sinegorskiy U.S.S.R. 48.00N 40.52E
47 G6 Sinegor'ye U.S.S.R. 59.45N 50.50E
37 D3 Sinekçi Turkey 40.17N 27.24E
37 E1 Sinekli Turkey 41.14N 28.13E
45 G8 Sinel'nikovo Ukraine U.S.S.R. 48.19N 35.32E
89 L6 Sinendé Benin 10.19N 2.22E
76 B13 Sines Portugal 37.58N 8.52W
76 B13 Sines, C.de Lt Ho Portugal 37.58N 8.53W
66 S4 Sinestra, Val Switzerland
51 L5 Sinettä Finland 66.39N 25.26E
77 W14 Sineu Balearic Is 39.39N 3.00E
45 F6 Sinevka Ukraine U.S.S.R. 50.35N 34.07E
15 L6 Sinewit, Mt New Britain 4.43S 151.58E
45 F3 Sinezerki U.S.S.R. 53.01N 34.30E
Sinfeng see Xinfeng
89 G8 Sinfra Ivory Coast 6.35N 5.56W
Sinfu see Jianping (Sinfu)
25 E2 Sing Burma 21.22N 98.06E
87 D4 Singa Sudan 13.11N 33.55E
103 F5 Singac New Jersey 40.53N 74.14W
30 D4 Singahi Uttar Prad India 28.18N 80.54E
25 D2 Singaingmyo Burma 21.43N 96.04E
90 J7 Singako Chad 9.50N 19.24E
21 D7 Singalpa N Korea 41.20N 127.50E
28 C5 Singanallur Tamil Nadu India 11.01N 77.02E
31 J4 Singa Pass Kashmir 33.59N 76.54E
18 E5 Singapore rep S E Asia
18 F5 Singapore, Str.of Singapore etc
28 F1 Singapuru Orissa India 19.02N 82.46E
18 L10 Singaraja Bali Indon 8.06S 115.07E
28 E2 Singareni Andhra Prad India 17.33N 80.19E
9 S8 Singatoka Viti Levu Fiji 18.10S 177.30E
9 S8 Singatoka R Viti Levu Fiji
25 F5 Sing Buri Thailand 14.56N 100.21E
87 F7 Singe Ethiopia 6.22N 36.19E
64 F8 Singen W Germany 47.45N 8.50E
Singer see Qinggir
107 C11 Singer Louisiana 30.39N 93.25W
29 D3 Singhana Rajasthan India 28.05N 75.52E
29 J6 Singhbum dist Orissa India
30 K7 Singheswar Bihar India 26.00N 86.49E
92 G5 Singida reg Tanzania
93 F10 Singida reg Tanzania
24 F4 Singim Xinjiang Uygur Zizhiqu China 42.57N 89.45E
82 J4 Sîngiorgiu de Padure Romania 46.27N 24.50E
93 H7 Singiraini Kenya 1.54S 36.29E
93 B6 Singiro mt Uganda 0.15S 30.31E
83 F4 Singitikós, Kólpos G Greece
30 K7 Singja Bihar India 25.51N 86.10E
25 M8 Singkaling Hkamti Burma 26.01N 95.39E
30 F3 Singkar mt Nepal 27.57N 86.35E
18 D6 Singkarak Sumatra Indon 0.41S 100.38E
18 H5 Singkawang Borneo Indon 0.57N 108.57E
18 F6 Singkep isld Indonesia
18 B4 Singkilbaru Sumatra Indon 2.16N 97.47E
18 C5 Singkuang Sumatra Indon 1.03N 98.55E
57 H5 Singleton Lancs Eng 53.51N 2.56W
12 K4 Singleton New S Wales 32.38S 151.00E
13 C5 Singleton N Terr Australia 20.50S 134.20E
112 M5 Singleton Texas 30.40N 95.59W
56 K6 Singleton W Sussex Eng 50.55N 0.46W
13 B5 Singleton, Mt N Terr Australia 22.03S 130.39E
14 B8 Singleton, Mt W Australia 29.28S 117.19E
41 N7 Singnei R U.S.S.R.
24 B9 Singo La pass Kashmir/India 32.55N 77.07E
29 D5 Singoli Madhya Prad India 24.59N 75.22E
25 M9 Singon Burma 23.45N 95.56E
18 B6 Singor R Pen Malaysia
Singora see Songkhla
15 J6 Singorkai Papua New Guinea 5.54S 146.54E
21 D8 Singosan N Korea 38.50N 127.27E
28 H3 Singra Assam India 25.55N 91.10E
30 F7 Singramau Uttar Prad India 25.55N 80.22E
28 J2 Singri Assam India 26.35N 92.30E
28 G3 Singrimari Assam India 25.45N 89.57E
Singsingsia see Xingxingxia
Sing-tai see Xingtai
Singtang see Xingtang
Singtze see Xingzi
25 C1 Singu Burma 22.32N 95.59E
29 G6 Singwara Madhya Prad India 23.26N 80.59E
21 D8 Sin'gye N Korea 38.32N 126.37E
33 F7 Sinh, Jabal mt Saudi Arabia 18.42N 44.41E
25 N8 Sinhkung Burma 25.41N 98.20E
21 D7 Sinhŭng N Korea 40.10N 127.36E
Sinhwa see Xinhua
21 D11 Sinhyo-ri S Korea 33.16N 126.35E
84 W22 Siniais Corfu 39.45N 19.53E
83 E4 Siniátsikon mt Greece 40.25N 21.35E
35 F10 Sinifha Jordan 30.51N 35.33E
19 K4 Siniloan Luzon Philippines 14.25N 121.25E
Sining see Xining
Sining Ho see Huang Shui
81 D2 Siniscola Sardinia 40.34N 9.42E
Siniya see Saniyah
45 K5 Siniye Lipyagi U.S.S.R. 51.22N 38.30E
43 F2 Siniy Shikhan U.S.S.R. 52.02N 60.01E
82 D7 Sinj Yugoslavia 43.43N 16.39E
19 B6 Sinjai Celebes Indon 5.07S 120.15E
82 E7 Sinjajevina mts Yugoslavia
34 J2 Sinjār Iraq 36.20N 41.51E
34 J2 Sinjār, Jabal mts Syria
32 A2 Sinji Iran 37.54N 44.45E
35 E5 Sinjil Jordan 32.02N 35.16E
31 C5 Sinjiri Afghanistan 31.35N 65.31E
31 E3 Sinjitak Pass Afghanistan 35.41N 68.31E
Sinkai Ho R Liaoning see Xinkai He R
Sinkan see Xingan
25 M9 Sinkan Burma 24.07N 97.03E
85 O10 Sinkat Sudan 18.55N 36.48E
22 J9 Sinkiang Shanxi China 35.37N 111.13E
Sinkiang aut reg Chinasee Xinjiang Uygur Zizhiqu aut reg China
Sin Kiang R see Xin Jiang
Sinkiang Uighur aut reg Chinasee Xinjiang Uygur Zizhiqu
Sinkiang-Uighur Aut. Reg. Chinasee Xinjiang Uygur Zizhiqu aut reg China
104 B7 Sinking Spring Ohio 39.04N 83.24W
89 E7 Sinko Guinea 8.53N 8.16W
76 K6 Sinlabajos Spain 4.05N 4.50W
Sinlitun see Xinlitun
21 D8 Sinmak N Korea 38.25N 126.17E
Sinmakiao see Xinmaqiao
21 C8 Sinmi isld N Korea
Sinmin see Xinmin
Sinminchen see Xincheng
64 E2 Sinn W Germany 50.39N 8.20E
64 H3 Sinn R W Germany
81 C5 Sinnai Sardinia 39.18N 9.13E
117 C2 Sinnamary Fr Guiana 5.28N 53.00W
117 C2 Sinnamary R Fr Guiana
26 U7 Sinnamuhattuvaram Sri Lanka 7.11N 81.56E
29 D8 Sinnar Maharashtra India 19.52N 74.02E
86 J6 Sinn Bishr, Gebel hill Egypt 29.40N 32.58E
Sinneh see Sanandaj
85 L8 Sinn el Kaddâb rock escarp Egypt
104 G5 Sinnemahoning Pennsylvania 41.50N 78.06W
81 M3 Sinni R Italy
82 F4 Sînnicolau Mare Romania 46.05N 20.38E
Sinning see Xining
57 M4 Sinnington N Yorks Eng 54.15N 0.51W
64 H3 Sinntal W Germany 50.16N 9.39E
86 E7 Sinnûris Egypt 29.25N 30.52E
89 B3 Sinoboval Senegal 16.22N 15.03W
Sinoe see Greenville Liberia
82 M6 Sinoe, L Romania
92 E10 Sinoia Zimbabwe 17.21S 30.13E
36 H1 Sinop Turkey 42.02N 35.09E
36 H1 Sinop Burun C Turkey 42.02N 35.14E
Sinope see Sinop
81 L7 Sinopoli Italy 38.16N 15.53E
115 D2 Sinoquipe Mexico 30.09N 110.14W
44 D10 Sinor, Pereval pass Ukraine U.S.S.R. 44.54N 35.04E
121 J2 Sinos R Brazil
21 D7 Sinp'o N Korea 40.00N 128.13E
21 E7 Sinpung-dong N Korea 41.05N 129.10E
21 D8 Sinp'yŏng N Korea 38.54N 126.45E
95 M5 Sinqu R Lesotho
95 M5 Sinqunyane R Lesotho
66 K3 Sins Switzerland 47.12N 8.24E
64 F5 Sinsheim W Germany 49.16N 8.52E
61 M5 Sinsin Belgium 50.17N 5.15E
40 D1 Sinskoye U.S.S.R. 61.09N 126.50E
64 A4 Sinspelt W Germany 49.58N 6.20E
Sintai see Xintai
100 O8 Sintaluta Saskatchewan 50.29N 103.29W
82 G4 Sintana Romania 46.20N 21.30E
18 J5 Sintang Borneo Indon 0.03N 111.31E
116 N6 Sint Eustatius isld Leeward Is W I 17.33N 63.00W
Sintien see Xintian
61 B3 Sint-Jan Belgium 50.52N 2.54E
116 N5 Sint Maarten isld Leeward Is W I 18.05N 63.05W
116 A1 Sint Nicolaas Aruba W I 12.27N 69.54W
112 K7 Sinton Texas 28.02N 97.33W
60 H9 Sint Pancras Netherlands 52.40N 4.47E
76 A11 Sintra Portugal 38.48N 9.22W
76 A11 Sintra, Sa.de ra Portugal
Sintsun see Xincun
Sintu see Xindu
26 S9 Sinuggala Sri Lanka 6.31N 80.52E
87 M6 Sinugif Somalia 8.30N 49.00E
21 C7 Sinŭiju N Korea 40.04N 124.25E
113 D4 Sinuk Alaska 64.34N 166.15W
119 C3 Sinú, R Colombia
87 B4 Sinut Sudan 12.10N 29.05E
93 J8 Sinya Tanzania 2.45S 37.03E
46 F3 Sinyavka Belorussiya U.S.S.R. 52.58N 26.30E
46 G2 Sinyaya R Pskov U.S.S.R.
41 N9 Sinyaya R Yakutsk U.S.S.R.
Sinyeh see Xinye
Sinyu see Xinyu
42 K3 Sinyuga U.S.S.R. 57.44N 115.15E
45 B8 Sinyukha R Ukraine U.S.S.R.
46 H5 Sinyukha R Ukraine U.S.S.R.
64 E6 Sinzheim W Germany 48.45N 8.10E
69 P6 Sinzheim W Germany 48.46N 8.10E
64 C2 Sinzig W Germany 50.32N 7.15E
93 F5 Sio Kenya 0.13N 34.01E
15 J6 Sio Papua New Guinea 5.58S 147.22E
53 F7 Siø isld Denmark 54.58N 10.42E
62 L9 Sió R Hungary
75 M4 Sio R Spain
19 L8 Siocon Mindanao Philippines 7.40N 122.10E
62 L9 Siófok Hungary 46.54N 18.03E
92 A10 Sioma Zambia 16.39S 23.36E
92 A10 Sioma Ngwezi Nat. Park Zambia
70 G6 Sion France 47.44N 1.35W
66 F7 Sion Switzerland 46.14N 7.22E
58 F2 Sionascaig, L Highland Scotland 58.04N 5.11W
28 B7 Sion Causeway Bombay India 19.04N 72.53E
28 B7 Sion R Bombay India
44 G6 Sionstroy Georgia U.S.S.R. 41.59N 45.02E
72 F6 Siorac-en-Perigord France 44.50N 0.59E
48 R3 Siorapaluk Greenland 77.48N 70.58W
79 F2 S. Iorio, Passo di pass Italy/Switz 46.10N 9.09E
15 L3 Siota Solomon Is 8.08S 160.18E
71 B4 Sioule R France
71 B5 Sioulet R France
108 O6 Sioux Center Iowa 43.05N 96.10W
108 O7 Sioux City Iowa 42.30N 96.28W
108 O6 Sioux Falls S Dakota 43.34N 96.42W
100 L1 Sioux Lookout Ontario 50.05N 91.55W
100 H1 Sioux Narrows Ontario 49.27N 94.06W
108 P7 Sioux Rapids Iowa 42.53N 95.08W
115 O11 Sipacate Guatemala 13.56N 91.10W
19 L7 Sipalay Philippines 9.45N 122.25E
117 B3 Sipaliwini R Surinam
18 J5 Sipang, Tanjong C Sarawak Malaysia 1.49N 110.22E
Sipapo mt see Paraque, Cerro
119 F5 Sipapo, R Venezuela
116 O2 Siparia Trinidad & Tobago 10.08N 61.31W
25 M9 Sipein Burma 23.34N 96.48E
Siping see Huangpin
21 C6 Siping Jilin China 43.15N 124.25E
37 H8 Sipirez Dağ mt Turkey
18 L3 Sipitang Sabah Malaysia 5.02N 115.32E
100 U3 Sipiwesk Manitoba 55.27N 97.24W
100 U3 Sipiwesk L Manitoba
123 G11 Siple U.S.A. Base Antarctica 76.00S 84.00W
123 H8 Siple Coast Antarctica
123 J10 Siple, Mt Antarctica 73.25S 122.50W
92 E10 Sipolilo Zimbabwe 16.43S 30.43E
92 E10 Sipolilo dist Zimbabwe
18 C7 Sipora isld Indonesia
18 C7 Sipora, Selat str Indonesia
51 N11 Sippola Finland 60.46N 27.00E
29 D6 Sipra R Madhya Prad India
Sipri see Shivpuri
107 J8 Sipsey Alabama 33.49N 87.06W
107 J8 Sipsey R Alabama
15 K6 Sipul New Britain 5.51S 148.44E
72 H10 Siquer, Pic de mt France 42.39N 1.30E
19 L7 Siquijor Philippines 9.12N 123.32E
19 L7 Siquijor isld Philippines 9.13N 123.35E
92 H9 Siquirire Mozambique 15.08S 37.43E
115 N4 Siquirres Costa Rica 10.05N 83.30W
119 E2 Siquisique Venezuela 10.36N 69.45W
86 K7 Sîq, Wâdi el watercourse Egypt
35 E4 Sir Jordan 32.22N 35.19E
35 G6 Sir R Jordan
28 C4 Sira Karnataka India 13.45N 76.53E
52 C8 Sira R Norway
71 J7 Sirac mt France 44.48N 6.19E
Si Racha see Ban Si Racha
81 K9 Siracusa Sicily 37.04N 15.18E
81 J9 Siracusa prov Sicily
83 J6 Sira Dağları mts Turkey
33 C10 Sīrah isld S Yemen 12.47N 45.04E
31 H9 Sirajganj Bangladesh 24.27N 89.42E
89 E5 Sirakoro Mali 12.40N 9.10W
101 N9 Sir Alexander, Mt Br Col 53.56N 120.27W
33 M6 Sirāl, Ra's C Oman 20.10N 57.49E
37 E5 Siran Turkey 40.12N 39.07E
31 D8 Siranda L Pakistan
35 G9 Sirat el Heiran anc site Jordan 31.04N 35.50E
30 E7 Sirathu Uttar Prad India 25.39N 81.18E
61 F4 Sirault Belgium 50.30N 3.47E
89 K5 Sirba R Niger/Upper Volta
33 K4 Şir Banī Yās isld U.A.E.
Şir Bū Nu'air isld see Şir Bū Nu'air
33 L4 Şir Bū Nu'air isld The Gulf 25.15N 54.14E
98 S4 Sir Charles Hamilton Sd Newfoundland
13 G1 Sir Charles Hardy Is Gt Barrier Reef Australia
30 J8 Sirdala Bihar India 24.40N 85.24E
52 C8 Sirdalsvatn L Norway
32 C2 Sirdān Iran 36.39N 49.23E
100 B8 Sir Douglas, Mt Alberta/Br Col 50.44N 115.15W
87 E7 Sire Kefa Ethiopia 6.55N 35.36E

87 F6 **Sire** Walaga Ethiopia 9.02N 36.52E
15 H7 **Sirebi** R Papua New Guinea
13 D3 **Sir Edward Pellew Group** islds N Terr Australia
89 D7 **Sirekude** Sierra Leone 9.59N 11.51W
106 B4 **Siren** Wisconsin 45.48N 92.22W
39 M3 **Sireniki** U.S.S.R. 64.28N 173.56W
80 J4 **Sirente, Monte** Italy 42.09N 13.37E
82 K3 **Siret** Romania 47.55N 26.05E
82 K3 **Siretul** R Romania
35 F8 **Sirfa** Jordan 31.20N 35.39E
32 J8 **Sirgān** Iran 25.25N 60.25E
13 B1 **Sir George Hope Is** N Terr Australia
14 F2 **Sir Graham Moore Is** W Australia
30 K6 **Sirha** Nepal 26.39N 86.13E
34 E7 **Sirhān, Wādi** depression Saudi Arabia/Jordan
29 E2 **Sirhind** Punjab India 30.39N 76.28E
87 G6 **Siri** Ethiopia 8.19N 39.29E
29 B3 **Siri** anc site Delhi India 28.32N 77.13E
82 G4 **Siria** Romania 46.16N 21.38E
15 M9 **Siri, C** Louisiade Arch 11.40S 153.45E
25 F4 **Siri Kit Dam** Thailand 17.40N 100.32E
18 J4 **Sirik, Tanjong** C Sarawak Malaysia 2.50N 111.20E
86 E9 **Sirîrîya, El** Egypt 28.19N 30.45E
Şiris see **Hakif**
30 H8 **Siris** Bihar India 24.50N 84.15E
35 E4 **Siris** Jordan 32.19N 35.17E
12 D5 **Sir Isaac Pt** S Australia 34.24S 135.11E
31 E5 **Siritoi R** Pakistan
32 F5 **Sirīz** Iran 30.59N 55.56E
32 J8 **Sirjā** Iran 25.32N 61.23E
101 J4 **Sir James McBrien, Mt** N W Terr 62.15N 128.01W
14 D7 **Sir James, Mt** W Australia 25.26S 121.58E
Sirjan see **Sa'īdābād**
32 F6 **Sirjān** salt waste Iran
32 G7 **Sirk** Iran 26.28N 57.07E
28 D5 **Sirkazhi** Tamil Nadu India 11.15N 79.45E
36 F2 **Sirkeli** Turkey 40.08N 32.51E
53 B4 **Sir Kirke** Denmark 56.25N 8.37E
51 L4 **Sirkka** Finland 67.52N 24.50E
51 L5 **Sirkkakoski** Finland 66.41N 24.24E
3 E8 **Sirmaur** Madhya Prad India 24.49N 87.23E
79 J4 **Sirmione** Italy 45.29N 10.36E
30 A2 **Sirmur** Himachal Prad India 30.30W 77.40E
30 A2 **Sirmur** dist Himachal Prad India
30 A6 **Sir Muttra** Rajasthan India 26.31N 77.22E
84 D6 **Sírna** Greece 37.31N 22.06E
83 H8 **Sírna** isld Greece 36.22N 26.42E
66 M2 **Sirnach** Switzerland 47.28N 8.59E
37 G8 **Şirnak** Turkey 37.33N 42.27E
51 N6 **Sirniö** Finland 65.50N 28.11E
37 D7 **Siro** R Turkey
71 J3 **Sirod** France 46.44N 6.00E
29 C5 **Sirohi** Rajasthan India 25.53N 72.58E
29 C5 **Şirohi** dist Rajasthan India
82 D7 **Široki Brijeg** Yugoslavia 43.21N 17.36E
93 F4 **Siroko** Uganda 1.16N 34.16E
79 P7 **Sirolo** Italy 43.32N 13.37E
18 B5 **Sirombu** Indonesia 0.58N 97.25E
28 E1 **Sironcha** Maharashtra India 18.52N 80.01E
29 E5 **Sironj** Madhya Prad India 24.05N 77.39E
79 L2 **Siror** Italy 46.11N 11.51E
30 D3 **Siror** Nepal 29.21N 80.45E
83 G7 **Síros** Greece 37.26N 24.55E
83 G7 **Síros** isld Greece
45 A1 **Sirotino** Belorussiya U.S.S.R. 55.23N 29.37E
45 P7 **Sirotinskaya** U.S.S.R. 49.15N 43.40E
45 P9 **Sirotskiy** U.S.S.R. 47.17N 43.22E
88 K6 **Siroua Jbel** mt Morocco 30.44N 7.35W
36 B1 **Sırpsındığı** Turkey 41.45N 26.31E
28 D1 **Sirpur** Andhra Prad India 19.28N 79.36E
29 E7 **Sirpur** Maharashtra India 20.12N 77.04E
31 E8 **Sir R** Pakistan
Sirrain isld see **Sirrayn I**
33 D7 **Sirrayn I** Saudi Arabia 19.37N 40.40E
87 J7 **Sirrei** Ethiopia 6.42N 42.05E
86 L4 **Sirr, El** reg Egypt
90 D2 **Sirret, Mt** Niger 19.20N 9.09E
111 F6 **Sirretta Pk** mt California 35.56N 118.20W
33 L4 **Sirri** isld The Gulf 25.55N 54.32E
29 D3 **Sirsa** Haryana India 29.32N 75.04E
30 F7 **Sirsa** Uttar Prad India 25.16N 82.06E
30 B5 **Sirsa** R Uttar Prad India
30 B5 **Sirsaganj** Uttar Prad India 27.02N 78.42E
101 P10 **Sir Sandford, Mt** Br Columbia 51.40N 117.55W
30 G6 **Sirsi** Basti, Uttar Prad India 26.32N 83.06E
28 B3 **Sirsi** Karnataka India 14.40N 74.51E
30 A7 **Sirsi** Madhya Prad India 25.02N 77.17E
30 B4 **Sirsi** Moradabad, Uttar Prad India 28.38N 78.37E
28 D1 **Sirsilla** Andhra Prad India 18.24N 78.48E
86 E4 **Sirsina** Egypt 30.36N 30.54E
30 A7 **Sirsod** Madhya Prad India 25.29N 77.30E
29 G7 **Sirsundi** Maharashtra India 20.28N 80.28E
Sirte see **Surt**
85 C4 **Sirte Des** Libya
Sirte, Gulf Of see **Khalīj Surt**
12 A2 **Sir Thomas, Mt** S Australia 27.09S 129.45E
77 F3 **Siruela** Spain 38.58N 5.03W
28 C3 **Siruguppa** Karnataka India 15.41N 76.53E
19 D8 **Sirung** vol Indonesia 8.30S 124.08E
28 B2 **Sirur** Karnataka India 16.08N 75.51E
28 B1 **Sirur** Maharashtra India 18.50N 74.23E
Sirv see **Sarv**
37 G7 **Sirvan** Turkey 38.03N 42.01E
34 O3 **Sirvān** R Iran
28 D3 **Sirvel** Andhra Prad India 15.20N 78.32E
33 F9 **Şirwāḩ** Yemen 15.29N 45.02E
Sirwān R see **Diyālā** R
101 O9 **Sir Wilfrid Laurier, Mt** Br Col 52.48N 119.49W
13 G2 **Sir William Thompson Ra** Queensland
100 F4 **Sir Winston Churchill Prov. Park** Alberta
37 F4 **Sirya** Turkey 41.08N 41.52E
32 H4 **Siryan** Iran 33.50N 58.32E
Sis see **Kozan**
120 B2 **Sisa** Peru 6.39S 76.41W
31 D8 **Sisa Creek** Pakistan
30 H4 **Sisaghat Bazar** Nepal 28.06N 84.16E
30 E5 **Sisaiya Thana** Uttar Prad India 27.34N 81.20E
82 C5 **Sisak** Yugoslavia 45.30N 16.22E
25 H5 **Sisaket** Thailand 15.08N 104.18E
32 D5 **Sisakht** Iran 30.50N 51.30E
115 O7 **Sisal** Mexico 21.10N 90.02W
77 M2 **Sisante** Spain 39.25N 2.12W
76 B2 **Sisargas Is** Spain 43.22N 8.50W
66 E3 **Siselen** Switzerland 47.02N 7.12E
95 F3 **Sishen** S Africa 27.47S 22.59E
95 F3 **Sisheu Valley** S Africa
Sishui see **Xishui**
23 F1 **Sishui** Henan China 34.51N 113.12E
23 H1 **Sishui** Shandong China 35.45N 117.19E
44 G8 **Sisian** Armenia U.S.S.R. 39.35N 45.58E
Sisiang see **Xixiang**
100 S6 **Sisib L** Manitoba
66 L4 **Sisikon** Switzerland 46.57N 8.38E
89 J6 **Sisili** R Upper Volta/Ghana
42 E5 **Sisim** R U.S.S.R.
Sisimiut see **Holsteinsborg**
100 Q3 **Sisipuk L** Man/Sask
106 F2 **Siskiwit B** Michigan
110 C7 **Siskiyou** Oregon 42.04N 122.37W
110 B8 **Siskiyou Mts** California
37 K1 **Şişli** Turkey 41.03N 29.01E
80 F3 **Sismano** Italy 42.41N 12.26E
115 F4 **Sisoguichic** Mexico 27.48N 107.30W
30 D7 **Sisolar** Uttar Prad India 25.40N 80.15E
25 G6 **Sisophon** Cambodia 13.37N 102.58E
37 D5 **Sisorta** Turkey 40.26N 38.03E
111 D7 **Sisquoc** California 34.53N 120.15W
111 E7 **Sisquoc** R California
66 H2 **Sissach** Switzerland 47.28N 7.48E
15 G5 **Sissano** Papua New Guinea 3.02S 142.01E
108 N4 **Sisseton** S Dakota 45.39N 97.03W
56 N5 **Sissinghurst** Kent Eng 51.07N 0.35E
98 E6 **Sisson Branch Res** New Brunswick
66 P6 **Sissone, Madone** mt Italy/Switz 46.18N 9.43E
69 F4 **Sissonne** France 49.35N 3.54E
69 F4 **Sissonne, Camp de** France
32 J5 **Sistan** reg Iran
32 J5 **Sīstan, Daryācheh-ye** salt marsh Iran
112 J6 **Sisterdale** Texas 30.00N 98.45W
71 H8 **Sisteron** France 44.16N 5.56E
110 D5 **Sisters** Oregon 44.17N 121.32W
96 B11 **Sisters Pk** Ascension I 7.56S 14.23W
11 J10 **Sisters, The** islds Chatham Is Pacific Oc 43.34S 176.48W
26 R12 **Sisters, The** islds Seychelles, Ind Oc 4.16S 55.52E
113 G5 **Sisters, The** mt Alaska 63.19N 161.50W
14 F7 **Sisters, The** mt W Australia 26.15S 126.42E
104 D7 **Sistersville** W Virginia 39.33N 81.01W
64 B3 **Sistig** W Germany 50.29N 6.31E
42 F5 **Sistig-Khem** U.S.S.R. 52.43N 95.32E
80 H6 **Sisto** R Italy
30 G5 **Siswa Bazar** Uttar Prad India 27.09N 83.45E
30 K6 **Siswar** Bihar India 26.26N 86.28E
30 G5 **Siswa Tal** Uttar Prad India 27.27N 83.08E
46 L1 **Sit** R U.S.S.R.
92 E5 **Sitalike** Tanzania 6.35S 31.07E
30 J6 **Sitamarhi** Bihar India 26.36N 85.30E
29 D6 **Sitamau** Madhya Prad India 24.00N 75.26E
95 C4 **Sitampiky** Madagascar 16.40S 46.06E
19 J9 **Sitankai** Philippines 4.43N 119.25E
30 D5 **Sitapur** Uttar Prad India 27.33N 80.40E
30 D7 **Sitapur** Uttar Prad India 25.11N 80.52E
30 D5 **Sitapur** dist Uttar Prad India
51 F3 **Sitasjaure** L Sweden 68.00N 17.20E
75 O5 **Sitges** Spain 41.14N 1.49E
83 F4 **Sithoniá** pen Greece
84 O11 **Sitía** Crete 35.13N 26.06E
24 H4 **Sitian** Xinjiang Uygur Zizhiqu China 42.03N 94.35E
18 A7 **Sitiawan** Pen Malaysia 4.11N 100.42E
101 G1 **Sitidgi L** N W Terr 68.29N 133.37W
118 F4 **Sítio da Abadia** Brazil 14.52S 46.11W
76 C14 **Sítio das Éguas** Portugal 37.19N 8.04W
118 G3 **Sítio do Mato** Brazil 13.04S 43.29W
118 F3 **Sítio Grande** Brazil 12.27S 45.05W
113 U8 **Sitka** Alaska 57.05N 135.20W
109 L4 **Sitka** Kansas 37.11N 99.39W
113 L8 **Sitkalidak I** Alaska 57.05N 153.20W
113 L8 **Sitkinak I** Alaska 56.35N 154.10W
113 L8 **Sitkinak Str** Alaska
41 E6 **Sitkovo** U.S.S.R. 69.13N 85.59E
110 B6 **Sitkum** Oregon 43.10N 123.51W
30 E8 **Sitlaha** Madhya Prad India 24.57N 81.30E
82 F8 **Sitnica** R Yugoslavia
47 K7 **Sitnikovo** U.S.S.R. 56.25N 67.53E
80 O1 **Sitno** Yugoslavia 43.41N 16.09E
51 G4 **Sitojaure** L Sweden 67.15N 18.25E
84 C4 **Sitoména** Greece 38.43N 21.32E
31 F6 **Sitpur** Pakistan 29.13N 70.50E
85 J5 **Sitra** oasis Egypt
33 B8 **Sitrah** Bahrain, The Gulf 26.08N 50.38E
33 J3 **Sitrah** isld Bahrain, The Gulf 26.06N 50.40E
76 H4 **Sitrama de Tera** Spain 42.00N 5.55W
25 D4 **Sittang** R Burma
60 T17 **Sittard** Netherlands 51.00N 5.52E
25 L9 **Sittaung** Burma 24.09N 94.36E
41 N8 **Sitte** R U.S.S.R.
63 L6 **Sittensen** W Germany 53.17N 9.30E
66 O2 **Sitter** R Switzerland
66 N1 **Sitterdorf** Switzerland 47.31N 9.14E
65 L8 **Sittersdorf** Austria 46.33N 14.37E
56 N5 **Sittingbourne** Kent Eng 51.21N 0.44E
87 F3 **Sittona** Ethiopia 14.25N 37.23E
47 M5 **Sittseva** U.S.S.R. 55.47N 59.43E
28 J5 **Sittwe** Burma 20.09N 92.55E
18 L9 **Situbondo** Java Indon 7.40S 114.01E
65 N4 **Sitzendorf** Austria 48.35N 15.57E
63 R10 **Sitzenroda** E Germany 51.28N 12.59E
23 B8 **Siu Lek Yuen** Hong Kong 22.22N 114.12E
19 C5 **Siumbatu** Celebes Indon 2.46S 122.04E
19 C6 **Siumpu** isld Indonesia 5.41S 122.32E
122 C2 **Siumu** W Samoa, Pacific Oc 14.00S 171.46W
Siuni see **Siyunī**
Siuning see **Xiuning**
51 M6 **Siuruanjoki** R Finland
Siushan see **Xiushan**
Siu-shui see **Xiushui**
84 M11 **Síva** Crete 35.13N 25.02E
28 D6 **Sivaganga** Tamil Nadu India 9.50N 78.30E
28 C6 **Sivakasi** Tamil Nadu India 9.26N 77.50E
40 D5 **Sivaki** U.S.S.R. 52.38N 126.44E
37 E7 **Sivan** Turkey 38.34N 40.18E
32 E5 **Sivand** Iran 30.06N 52.56E
36 J3 **Sivas** Turkey 39.44N 37.01E
28 C4 **Sivasamudram I** Karnataka India 12.16N 77.08E
44 C8 **Sivash** lagoon Crimea, Ukraine U.S.S.R.
44 D8 **Sivash, Oz** lagoon Ukraine U.S.S.R.
44 D8 **Sivashskoye** Ukraine U.S.S.R. 46.24N 34.34E
36 D4 **Sivaslı** Turkey 38.30N 29.40E
47 J3 **Sivaya Maska** U.S.S.R. 66.38N 62.30E
37 H8 **Şivelân** Turkey 37.54N 44.02E
39 F2 **Sïver** R U.S.S.R.
37 E8 **Siverek** Turkey 37.46N 39.19E
47 K7 **Siverga, Oz** L U.S.S.R. 55.25N 68.50E
46 H1 **Siverskiy** U.S.S.R. 59.20N 30.00E
45 B1 **Siverst** U.S.S.R. 56.01N 30.50E
79 H3 **Siviano** Italy 45.43N 10.05E
75 K3 **Sivil** mt Spain 42.14N 0.01W
45 Q2 **Sivin'** U.S.S.R. 54.21N 44.15E
66 D5 **Siviriez** Switzerland 46.40N 6.53E
47 J3 **Sivomaskinskiy** U.S.S.R. 66.45N 62.44E
47 F2 **Sivri** isld Turkey 40.53N 28.58E
37 E7 **Sivrice** Turkey 38.26N 39.18E
36 F3 **Sivrihisar** Turkey 39.29N 31.32E
36 H3 **Sivri Tepe** mt Turkey 39.30N 35.51E
61 G6 **Sivry** Belgium 50.10N 4.11E
69 J5 **Sivry-sur-Meuse** France 49.20N 5.16E
39 E5 **Sivuch** U.S.S.R. 59.04N 152.28E
39 G6 **Sivuchy, Mys** C U.S.S.R. 56.45N 163.14E
40 H5 **Sivuk** U.S.S.R. 53.45N 140.14E
19 B5 **Siwa** Celebes Indon 3.44S 120.24E
85 H5 **Siwa** Egypt 29.11N 25.31E
30 E7 **Siwaith** Uttar Prad India 25.35N 81.53E
29 E2 **Siwalik Ra** India/Nepal
30 H6 **Siwan** Bihar India 26.14N 84.21E
29 C5 **Siwana** Rajasthan India 25.37N 72.28E
29 D3 **Siwani** Haryana India 28.58N 75.39E
85 H5 **Siwa Oasis** Egypt
110 A7 **Sixes** Oregon 42.50N 124.29W
71 H10 **Six-Fours-la-Plage** France 43.05N 5.50E
23 H2 **Si Xian** Anhui China 33.30N 117.58E
22 E8 **Sixin** Qinghai China 37.10N 99.44E
66 L5 **Six Madun** mt Switzerland 46.38N 8.40E
59 E6 **Sixmilebridge** Clare Irish Rep 52.45N 8.46W
59 H2 **Six Mile Cross** Tyrone N Ireland 54.33N 7.07W
107 E12 **Six Mile L** Louisiana
71 K4 **Sixt** Haute-Savoie France 46.04N 6.48E
70 F6 **Sixt** Ille-et-Vilaine France 47.47N 2.03W
101 C3 **Sixtymile** Yukon Terr 64.01N 140.42W
47 E4 **Siya** U.S.S.R. 63.38N 41.40E
85 O8 **Siyâl Is** Egypt 22.49N 36.06E
26 U8 **Siyambalanduwa** Sri Lanka 6.54N 81.32E
30 B4 **Siyana** Uttar Prad India 28.37N 78.04E
Siyang see **Hsi-yang**
23 H2 **Siyang** Jiangsu China 33.46N 118.49E
23 H2 **Siyang** Jiangsu China 33.46N 118.49E
110 M1 **Siyeh, Mt** Montana 48.46N 113.39W
87 E1 **Siyeteb** Sudan 18.00N 35.01E
44 G1 **Siygachiy** U.S.S.R. 46.50N 46.26E
22 H6 **Siyitang** Nei Monggol Zizhiqu China 41.18N 108.32E
28 K1 **Siyom** R Assam India
37 C2 **Sıyullu** Turkey 40.49N 26.35E
32 E4 **Sīyunī** Iran 32.20N 52.12E
76 A10 **Sizandro** R Portugal
95 N5 **Sizanenjana** S Africa 29.51S 29.54E
92 C10 **Sizarira Hills** Zimbabwe
36 G1 **Sizerli** Turkey 41.11N 34.06E
56 P3 **Sizewell** Suffolk Eng 52.13N 1.36E
22 J6 **Sizhiwang (Dorbod) Qi** Nei Monggol Zizhiqu China 41.35N 111.42E
40 H6 **Siziman** U.S.S.R. 50.45N 140.25E
42 F6 **Sizin** U.S.S.R. 51.22N 95.58E
22 J6 **Siziwang (Dorbod) Qi** Nei Monggol Zizhiqu China 41.35N 111.42E
70 B5 **Sizun** France 48.25N 4.05W
47 G3 **Sizyabsk** U.S.S.R. 65.05N 53.38E
53 G5 **Sjælland** isld Denmark
53 G5 **Sjællands Odde** pen Denmark 56.00N 11.18E
50 F3 **Sjafarborg** Iceland 65.44N 19.36W
52 L3 **Själevad** Sweden 63.19N 18.40E
53 D4 **Sjelle** Denmark 56.12N 9.57E
82 F7 **Sjenica** Yugoslavia 43.16N 20.00E
53 T20 **Sjernarøy** Norway 59.15N 5.50E
53 T20 **Sjernarøy** isld Norway 59.15N 5.50E
52 E5 **Sjoa** R Norway
52 H11 **Sjöbo** Sweden 55.37N 13.45E
53 Y13 **Sjødøla** mt Norway 62.35N 8.06E
53 V14 **Sjøholt** Norway 62.29N 6.50E
50 B3 **Sjónfridh** mt Iceland 65.49N 23.02W
53 B3 **Sjørring** Denmark 56.58N 8.36E
53 C4 **Sjørslev** Denmark 56.19N 9.28E
53 C4 **Sjørup** Denmark 56.26N 9.06E
50 B4 **Sjöundá Skor** C Iceland 65.25N 23.56W
52 H2 **Sjoutnäs** Sweden 64.37N 14.55E
51 F3 **Sjøvegan** Norway 68.54N 17.50E
52 G9 **Sjövik** Sweden 57.55N 12.20E
52 H2 **Sjulsåsen** Sweden 64.21N 14.45E
51 J6 **Sjulsmark** Sweden 65.32N 21.30E
50 U12 **Sjuøyane** Spitsbergen
52 G3 **Skäckerfjällen** mt Sweden 63.50N 12.45E
82 E8 **Skadarsko Jezero** L Yugoslavia/Albania
53 E4 **Skåde** Denmark 56.06N 10.13E
44 B8 **Skadovsk** Ukraine U.S.S.R. 46.07N 32.56E
53 B6 **Skæbæk** Denmark 55.10N 8.47E
53 N9 **Skælingsfjall** mt Faeroes 62.06N 6.59W
53 G6 **Skælskør** Denmark 55.16N 11.18E
48 V6 **Skærfjorden** fjord Greenland
53 D5 **Skærup** Denmark 55.39N 9.37E
53 J5 **Skævinge** Denmark 55.55N 12.10E
84 E6 **Skafidháki** Greece 37.34N 22.41E
53 X20 **Skafså** Norway 59.25N 8.00E
50 G6 **Skaftá** R Iceland
50 J6 **Skaftáfell** Iceland 64.02N 16.59W
50 H7 **Skaftafellsfjara** sand spit Iceland
50 H6 **Skaftafellsfjöll** mt Iceland 64.05N 17.05W
50 J6 **Skaftafellsjökull** ice cap Iceland 64.03N 16.55W
50 J6 **Skaftafellssýsla, Austur** co Iceland
50 G7 **Skaftafellssýsla, Vestur** co Iceland
50 G7 **Skaftárdalur** Iceland 63.48N 18.28W
50 G6 **Skaftárjökull** ice cap Iceland 64.15N 18.00W
50 H7 **Skaftárós** str Iceland 63.40N 17.48W
50 G7 **Skaftártunga** delta Iceland
52 K9 **Skaftet** Sweden 57.39N 16.35E
52 L6 **Skäfthammar** Sweden 60.09N 18.15E
50 F3 **Skagafjardharsýsla** co Iceland
50 F3 **Skagafjördhur** B Iceland
50 C6 **Skagaflös** C Iceland 64.05N 22.44W
50 E2 **Skagaheidhi** heath Iceland
53 X16 **Skagastølstindane** mt Norway 61.28N 7.53E
Skagaströnd see **Höfdhakaupstadhur**
50 E2 **Skagatá** C Iceland 66.07N 20.06W
53 F1 **Skagen** Denmark 57.44N 10.37E
53 E1 **Skagen, Gl** Denmark 57.44N 10.34E
52 H8 **Skagern** L 58.59N 14.15E
52 D9 **Skagerrak** channel Den/Norway
52 E5 **Skaget** mt Norway 61.17N 9.13E
110 D1 **Skagit** R Washington
113 U7 **Skagway** Alaska 59.23N 135.20W
50 G7 **Skál** Iceland 63.45N 18.16W
34 A4 **Skala** Cyprus 34.54N 33.38E
84 E6 **Skála** Greece 37.42N 22.39E
84 E8 **Skála** Lakonía Greece 36.51N 22.40E
84 C7 **Skála** Messinía Greece 37.11N 22.00E
53 W15 **Skåla** mt Norway 61.52N 7.00E
50 D6 **Skálafell** mt Iceland 64.15N 21.28W
82 K2 **Skala Podolskaya** U.S.S.R. 48.51N 26.11E
50 L2 **Skálar** Iceland 66.20N 14.43W
46 F5 **Skalat** Ukraine U.S.S.R. 49.20N 25.59E
50 B2 **Skálavík** inlet Iceland
53 K4 **Skälderviken** B Sweden
53 N9 **Skálebotn** Faeroes 62.12N 6.51W
53 N10 **Skálevig** Faeroes 61.50N 6.40W
50 C4 **Skáleyjar** isld Iceland 65.27N 22.40W
50 E6 **Skalholt** Iceland 64.08N 20.31W
50 D4 **Skálholtsvík** Iceland 65.27N 21.15W
50 E4 **Skali** Iceland 65.10N 20.02W
65 P3 **Skalice** Czechoslovakia 49.30N 16.37E
65 K3 **Skalice** R Czechoslovakia
41 D4 **Skalistaya, Gora** mt U.S.S.R. 72.51N 82.33E
51 G5 **Skalka** L Sweden 66.53N 18.50E
51 P1 **Skallelv** Norway 70.11N 30.20E
53 A5 **Skallingen** pen Denmark 55.30N 8.15E
52 K8 **Skällvik** Sweden 58.25N 16.40E
50 G7 **Skálm** R Iceland
50 C3 **Skálmarfjördhur** B Iceland
50 C3 **Skálmarnesmúli** Iceland 65.31N 22.43W
62 K4 **Skalmierzyce** Poland 51.42N 17.58E
64 N3 **Skalná** Czechoslovakia 50.10N 12.23E
53 G7 **Skalø** isld Denmark 54.58N 11.22E
53 C3 **Skals** Denmark 56.34N 9.25E
53 C3 **Skals Å** R Denmark
110 C4 **Skamania** Washington 45.38N 122.03W
53 E5 **Skamby** Denmark 55.31N 10.17E
53 D6 **Skamlingsbanke** mt Denmark 55.25N 9.34E
84 A2 **Skamnéli** Greece 39.54N 20.52E
53 D4 **Skanderborg** Denmark 56.02N 9.57E
Skanderborg co see **Vejle**
106 G3 **Skandia** Michigan 46.23N 87.14W
52 G11 **Skåne** reg Sweden
104 J4 **Skaneateles** New York 42.57N 76.27W
104 J4 **Skaneateles L** New York
106 F3 **Skanee** Michigan 46.52N 88.11W
53 T19 **Skånevik** Norway 59.43N 5.58E
53 T19 **Skånevikfjord** inlet Norway 59.42N 5.46E
51 F3 **Skånland** Norway 68.35N 16.36E
53 D4 **Skannerup** Denmark 56.13N 9.45E
52 J8 **Skänninge** Sweden 58.24N 15.05E
53 K6 **Skanör** Sweden 55.24N 12.48E
48 S8 **Skansen** Greenland 69.28N 52.30W
52 J2 **Skansholm** Sweden 64.41N 16.20E
51 F6 **Skansnäs** Sweden 65.45N 17.04E
84 H3 **Skantzoúra** isld Greece 39.05N 24.06E
50 B3 **Skapadalur** Iceland 65.31N 23.49W
52 G8 **Skara** Sweden 58.23N 13.25E
52 G8 **Skaraborg** dist Sweden
58 S11 **Skara Brae** Orkney Scotland 59.03N 3.20W
53 X18 **Skarbu** Norway 60.05N 7.41E
53 U16 **Skardfjell** mt Sogn og Fjordane Norway 61.17N 6.15E
50 C4 **Skardh** Dalasýsla Iceland 65.17N 22.20W
50 E6 **Skardh** Rangárvallasýsla Iceland 64.01N 20.07W
50 K6 **Skardhsfjördhur** B Iceland
50 D6 **Skardhsheidhi** heath Iceland
13 F1 **Skardon** R Queensland
52 G4 **Skardørsfjell** mt Norway 62.54N 12.05E
31 H3 **Skardu** Kashmir 35.18N 75.44E
31 H3 **Skardu** dist Kashmir
53 S20 **Skåre** Norway 59.26N 5.16E
53 V19 **Skare** Norway 59.57N 6.35E
53 Y18 **Skarfjell** mt Telemark Norway 60.01N 8.13E
52 F6 **Skarnes** Norway 60.14N 11.41E
53 X17 **Skåro** Norway 60.40N 8.00E
53 E6 **Skarø** isld Denmark 55.01N 10.29E
53 B5 **Skarrild** Denmark 55.59N 8.54E
52 G4 **Skarsfjället** mt Sweden 62.47N 12.15E
53 Y17 **Skarsgård** Norway 60.41N 8.17E
53 Z14 **Skarstind** mt Norway 62.01N 8.35E
62 L1 **Skarszewy** Poland 54.04N 18.25E
53 F6 **Skårup** Denmark 55.06N 10.42E
53 N10 **Skarvanaes** Faeroes 61.48N 6.45W
53 Y14 **Skarvdalsegga** mt Norway 62.03N 8.04E
53 R17 **Skarvøy** Lt Ho Norway 60.31N 4.50E
52 K2 **Skarvsjö** Sweden 64.58N 17.10E
62 N4 **Skaryszew** Poland 51.20N 21.16E
62 M4 **Skarżysko-Kamienna** Poland 51.07N 20.52E
53 B5 **Skast** Denmark 55.31N 8.34E
53 B6 **Skast** Denmark 55.04N 8.43E
52 J5 **Skästra** Sweden 61.42N 16.00E
52 H10 **Skatelöv** Sweden 56.46N 14.35E
58 M4 **Skateraw** Grampian Scotland 57.02N 2.09W
52 H7 **Skattkärr** Sweden 59.25N 13.42E
52 J5 **Skattungen** L Sweden 61.10N 15.05E
46 E2 **Skaudvilė** Lithuania U.S.S.R. 55.28N 22.38E
53 V19 **Skaulen** mt Norway 59.38N 6.35E
53 B4 **Skave** Denmark 56.23N 8.49E
62 M6 **Skawina** Poland 49.59N 19.49E
58 R9 **Skaw Taing** Shetland Scotland 60.23N 0.54W
Skaw, The C see **Skagen**
99 K6 **Skead** Ontario 46.40N 80.45W
59 H4 **Skeagh L** Cavan Irish Rep 53.57N 7.00W
101 J8 **Skeena** R Br Col
101 K8 **Skeena Crossing** Br Col 55.06N 127.48W
101 J7 **Skeena Mts** Br Col
57 G2 **Skeen, L** Dumfries & Galloway Scotland 55.26N 3.19W
50 F3 **Skefilsstadhir** Iceland 65.55N 19.54W
50 L2 **Skeggjastadhir** Iceland 66.01N 14.52W
50 D4 **Skeggöxl** mt Iceland 65.15N 22.00W
57 O6 **Skegness** Lincs Eng 53.10N 0.21E
53 U15 **Skei** Norway 61.34N 6.29E
50 E6 **Skeidh** dist Iceland
50 J7 **Skeidhará** R Iceland
50 H6 **Skeidharárjökull** ice cap Iceland 64.02N 17.15W
50 H7 **Skeidharársandur** sand reg Iceland
50 F8 **Skeidhflötur** Iceland 63.26N 19.08W
53 H6 **Skelby** Storstrøm Denmark 55.19N 11.42E
53 H7 **Skelby** Storstrøm Denmark 54.38N 11.55E
58 Q9 **Skelda Ness** prom Shetland Scotland 60.09N 1.28W
53 D7 **Skelde** Denmark 54.52N 9.44E
13 D3 **Skeleton** R N Terr Australia
53 C4 **Skelhøje** Denmark 56.22N 9.18E
50 D3 **Skeljavík** Iceland 65.42N 21.40W
45 G9 **Skel'ki** Ukraine U.S.S.R. 47.25N 35.08E
52 M2 **Skellefteå** Sweden 64.47N 20.59E
51 H6 **Skellefte älv** R Sweden
52 N2 **Skelleftehamn** Sweden 64.40N 21.12E
59 A8 **Skelligs Lt.Ho.,The** Kerry Irish Rep 51.47N 10.30W
58 Q9 **Skellister** Shetland Scotland 60.17N 1.10W
112 C8 **Skellytown** Texas 35.34N 101.11W
57 H5 **Skelmersdale** Lancs Eng 53.33N 2.48W
58 G7 **Skelmorlie** Strathclyde Scotland 55.51N 4.53W
57 M3 **Skelton** Cleveland Eng 54.33N 0.59W
57 H3 **Skelton** Cumbria Eng 54.43N 2.51W
53 E3 **Skelund** Denmark 56.46N 10.13E
52 G9 **Skene** Sweden 57.30N 12.35E
58 M4 **Skene, L.of** Grampian Scotland 57.09N 2.22W
56 F4 **Skenfrith** Gwent Wales 51.53N 2.47W
84 F4 **Skepastí** Greece 38.50N 23.20E
84 D5 **Skepastón** Greece 38.02N 22.04E
37 B2 **Skepastón, Ákra** C Samothráki Greece 40.27N 25.43E
50 C6 **Skerjafjördhur** B Iceland
94 G7 **Skerpioenpunt** S Africa 28.53S 22.05E
59 K4 **Skerries** Dublin Irish Rep 53.35N 6.07W
57 D6 **Skerries Lt.Ho** Gwynedd Wales 53.25N 4.36W
58 B6 **Skerryvore L.H** Strathclyde Scotland 56.20N 7.05W
15 F5 **S Keten** mts Irian Jaya
95 N4 **Skeurklip** mt S Africa 28.10S 29.32E
56 D4 **Skewen** W Glam Wales 51.40N 3.51W
84 G5 **Skhimatárion** Greece 38.20N 23.35E
84 C8 **Skhíza** isld Greece 36.43N 21.46E
84 M11 **Skhoiniá** Crete 35.03N 25.18E
83 H8 **Skhoinoúsa** isld Greece 36.53N 25.31E
52 F7 **Ski** Norway 59.43N 10.52E
84 F3 **Skíathos** Greece 39.10N 23.30E
84 F3 **Skíathos** isld Greece
84 F3 **Skíathou, Dhíavlos** str Greece
109 O5 **Skiatook** Oklahoma 36.24N 96.03W
59 D8 **Skibbereen** Cork Irish Rep 51.33N 9.15W
53 B4 **Skibbild** Denmark 56.10N 8.51E
53 H5 **Skibby** Denmark 55.46N 11.58E
53 C5 **Skibet** Denmark 55.43N 9.27E
53 J6 **Skibinge** Denmark 55.07N 12.03E
51 H2 **Skibotn** Norway 69.25N 20.15E
53 A3 **Skibsted Fjord** inlet Denmark 56.40N 8.28E
105 F6 **Skidaway I** Georgia 31.55N 81.02W
57 N5 **Skidby** Humberside Eng 53.48N 0.27W
57 G3 **Skiddaw** mt Cumbria Eng 54.40N 3.08W
101 G9 **Skidegate** Graham I, Br Col 53.19N 132.02W
46 E3 **Skidel'** Belorussiya U.S.S.R. 53.37N 24.19E
104 J7 **Skidmore** Maryland 39.01N 76.27W
112 K7 **Skidmore** Texas 28.16N 97.42W
52 E7 **Skien** Norway 59.14N 9.37E
62 M4 **Skierniewice** Poland 51.58N 20.10E
100 F9 **Skiff** Alberta 49.32N 111.48W
51 J11 **Skiftet Kihti** Finland
88 R3 **Skikda** Algeria 36.53N 6.54E
113 M6 **Skilak L** Alaska 60.25N 150.20W
107 H3 **Skillet** R Illinois
52 H9 **Skillingaryd** Sweden 57.27N 14.05E
84 R14 **Skilloura** Cyprus 35.13N 33.10E
57 G3 **Skinburness** Cumbria Eng 54.53N 3.22W
53 Y16 **Skinegga** mt Norway 61.20N 8.20E
50 J2 **Skinnastadhur** Iceland 66.04N 16.25W
103 B3 **Skinners Eddy** Pennsylvania 41.37N 76.08W
53 B3 **Skinnerup** Denmark 56.59N 8.41E
52 J7 **Skinnskatteberg** Sweden 59.51N 15.44E
58 F7 **Skipness** Strathclyde Scotland 55.46N 5.22W
58 B4 **Skiport, L** S Uist, W Isles Scotland 57.19N 7.15W
11 C11 **Skippers** New Zealand 44.52S 168.41E
11 C11 **Skippers Ra** New Zealand
57 N5 **Skipsea** Humberside Eng 53.59N 0.13W
95 D10 **Skipskop** S Africa 34.33S 20.24E
57 J5 **Skipton** N Yorks Eng 53.58N 2.01W
12 G6 **Skipton** Victoria 37.40S 143.40E
58 K7 **Skirling** Borders Scotland 55.39N 3.30W
84 H4 **Skiropoúla** isld Greece 38.50N 24.21E
84 H4 **Skíros** Greece 38.55N 24.34E
84 H4 **Skíros** isld Greece
57 H3 **Skirwith** Cumbria Eng 54.41N 2.35W
84 E2 **Skiti** Greece 39.41N 22.49E
53 C3 **Skive** Denmark 56.34N 9.02E
Skive Å see **Karup Å**
53 C3 **Skive Fjord** inlet Denmark 56.36N 9.05E
53 Y15 **Skjåk** Norway 61.53N 8.21E
50 E6 **Skjaldbreidharhraun** lava field Iceland
50 E6 **Skjaldbreidhur, mt** Iceland 64.24N 20.45W
50 H3 **Skjalfandafljot** R Iceland
50 H2 **Skjálfandi** B Iceland
53 V18 **Skjeggedalsfoss** waterfall Norway 60.06N 6.47E
51 D5 **Skjelåtind** mt Norway 66.44N 14.30E
53 T15 **Skjelbreivatn** L Norway 61.42N 5.47E
53 D3 **Skjellerup** Denmark 56.38N 9.52E
53 U18 **Skjelnes** Norway 60.05N 6.00E
53 W17 **Skjerdal** Norway 60.57N 7.12E
53 R17 **Skjerjehamn** Norway 60.56N 4.58E
53 A5 **Skjern** Denmark 55.57N 8.30E
53 D4 **Skjern** Denmark 56.27N 9.47E
53 B5 **Skjern Å** R Denmark
51 E4 **Skjerstad** Norway 67.15N 15.05E
53 V17 **Skjervefossen** waterfall Norway 60.35N 6.37E
51 H1 **Skjervøy** Norway 70.03N 20.56E
53 D4 **Skjød** Denmark 56.18N 9.55E
53 T19 **Skjold** Norway 59.30N 5.36E
53 T20 **Skjoldafjord** inlet Norway 59.26N 5.37E
53 T20 **Skjoldastraumen** Norway 59.25N 5.39E
53 B3 **Skjoldborg** Denmark 56.55N 8.37E
53 X16 **Skjolden** Norway 61.29N 7.36E
53 E7 **Skjoldnæs** C Denmark 54.59N 10.13E
97 P5 **Skjoldungen Ø** / Greenland 63.15N 41.30W
53 Y15 **Skjøli** R Norway
51 F3 **Skjomen** Norway 68.15N 17.25E
51 E4 **Skjønsta** Norway 67.12N 15.45E
53 Y13 **Skjorta** mt Möre og Romsdal Norway 62.39N 8.14E
53 U15 **Skjørta** mt Sogn og Fjordane Norway 61.37N 6.23E
41 M5 **Sklad** U.S.S.R. 71.57N 123.28E
84 D7 **Sklavokhóri** Greece 37.01N 22.26E
84 C7 **Sklirón** Greece 37.27N 21.55E
84 E2 **Sklíthron** Greece 39.37N 22.53E
84 B2 **Sklíva, mt** Greece 39.36N 21.14E
62 L6 **Skoczów** Poland 49.49N 18.45E
53 C6 **Skodborg** Denmark 55.25N 9.10E
53 V13 **Skodje** Norway 62.30N 6.43E
53 B5 **Skodsbøl** Denmark 55.53N 8.34E
53 K5 **Skodsborg** Denmark 55.50N 12.36E
53 E4 **Skødstrup** Denmark 56.16N 10.19E
95 J10 **Skoenmakerskop** S Africa 34.02S 25.34E
97 S2 **Skœrfjorden** B Greenland
53 V13 **Şkœringen** mt Norway 62.35N 6.45E
82 B4 **Škofja Loka** Yugoslavia 46.09N 14.19E
52 K5 **Skog** Gävleborg Sweden 61.10N 16.50E
52 L4 **Skog** Norrland Sweden 62.56N 18.05E
53 Y16 **Skogadalsbøen** Norway 61.28N 8.01E
50 F7 **Skógafoss** waterfall Iceland 63.32N 19.30W
51 L2 **Skoganvarre** Norway 69.49N 25.05E
50 L3 **Skógar** Múlasýsla, Nordhur Iceland 65.46N 14.55W
50 F7 **Skógar** Rangárvallasýsla Iceland 63.32N 19.28W
50 J2 **Skogar** Thingeyjarsýsla, Nordhur Iceland 69.09N 16.32W
51 O2 **Skogerøy** Norway 69.53N 29.55E
52 G7 **Skoghall** Sweden 59.20N 13.30E
50 F7 **Skógshraun** lava field Iceland
53 Y16 **Skogstad** Norway 61.12N 8.22E
56 A4 **Skokholm I** Dyfed Wales 51.42N 5.16W
106 R1 **Skokie** dist Chicago, Illinois
43 F3 **Skol'** Kazakhstan U.S.S.R. 49.38N 60.40E
46 E5 **Skole** Ukraine U.S.S.R. 49.00N 23.30E
52 J7 **Sköllersta** Sweden 59.08N 15.23E
84 C6 **Skóllis** mt Greece 37.57N 21.35E
56 A4 **Skomer I** Dyfed Wales 51.45N 5.18W
51 C4 **Skomvœr** isld Norway 67.29N 12.00E
51 F9 **Skön** Sweden 62.27N 17.28E
53 S14 **Skongsnes** Lt Ho Norway 62.02N 5.07E
101 Q11 **Skookumchuk** Br Col 49.54N 115.46W
95 K3 **Skoonspruit** S Africa 27.37S 26.36E
95 K2 **Skoonspruit** R S Africa
84 G3 **Skópelos** Greece 39.07N 23.43E
84 G3 **Skópelos** isld Greece
83 G6 **Skópelos Kaloyeroi** isld Greece 38.08N 25.16E
84 G3 **Skópelou, Dhíavlos** str Greece
53 N10 **Skopen** Faeroes 61.54N 6.52W
53 N10 **Skopen Fjord** channel Faeroes 61.55N 6.52W
84 O11 **Skopí** Crete 35.10N 26.02E
84 D6 **Skopí** Greece 37.33N 22.23E
84 D3 **Skopiá** Greece 39.09N 22.28E
45 L3 **Skopin** U.S.S.R. 53.50N 39.34E
82 G8 **Skopje** Yugoslavia 42.00N 21.28E
53 U14 **Skopshorn** mt Norway 62.21N 6.30E
50 B4 **Skorarhlídhar** cliff Iceland
62 L2 **Skórcz** Poland 53.48N 18.31E
53 W13 **Skorgenes** Norway 62.34N 7.06E
45 J5 **Skorodnoye** U.S.S.R. 51.05N 37.15E
47 L6 **Skorodum** U.S.S.R. 57.50N 70.54E
52 G2 **Skorovatn** Norway 64.39N 13.05E
53 S14 **Skorpa** isld Möre og Romsdal Norway 62.20N 5.30E
53 R15 **Skorpa** isld Sogn og Fjordane Norway 61.36N 4.51E
52 K3 **Skorped** Sweden 63.23N 17.55E
53 D3 **Skørping** Denmark 56.50N 9.55E
53 T19 **Skorpo** isld Hordaland Norway 59.54N 5.37E
53 T19 **Skorpo** isld Hordaland Norway 59.57N 5.50E
50 D5 **Skorradalsvatn** L Iceland 64.30N 21.21W
50 M4 **Skorrastadhur** Iceland 65.08N 13.49W
53 G7 **Skørringe** Denmark 54.45N 11.23E
50 L2 **Skoruvík** Iceland 66.21N 14.43W
31 F2 **Skorzar** Afghanistan 36.13N 70.50E
45 N8 **Skosyrskaya** U.S.S.R. 48.24N 41.19E
84 D6 **Skotiní** Greece 37.47N 22.25E
52 E7 **Skotselv** Norway 59.53N 9.54E
50 C3 **Skötufjördhur** B Iceland
84 B3 **Skoulikariá** Greece 39.11N 21.16E
84 D7 **Skoúra** Greece 37.01N 22.29E
84 Q14 **Skouriotissa** Cyprus 35.05N 32.53E
84 B6 **Skourokhóri** Greece 37.41N 21.21E
84 E8 **Skoútari** Greece 36.40N 22.30E
15 D4 **Skouten, Kepulauan** arch Irian Jaya
53 F7 **Skovballe** Denmark 54.59N 10.33E
53 D4 **Skovby** Århus Denmark 56.09N 9.57E
53 E5 **Skovby** Fyn Denmark 55.32N 10.05E
53 D7 **Skovby** Sønderjylland Denmark 54.53N 10.00E
52 H8 **Skövde** Sweden 58.24N 13.52E
53 B5 **Skovlund** Denmark 55.45N 8.42E
40 C5 **Skovorodino** U.S.S.R. 54.00N 123.53E
104 Q2 **Skowhegan** Maine 44.46N 69.44W
100 S7 **Skownan** Manitoba 51.58N 99.35W
53 C2 **Skræm** Denmark 57.04N 9.20E
50 E3 **Skrapatunga** Iceland 65.43N 20.10W
52 F6 **Skreia** Norway 60.38N 10.57E
53 V20 **Skreinuten** mt Norway 59.25N 6.55E
53 X18 **Skrekjen** mt Norway 60.13N 7.48E
53 Y20 **Skrevatn** L Norway 59.20N 8.07E
50 G3 **Skridha** Iceland 65.43N 18.20W
50 E6 **Skridhan** mt Iceland 64.22N 20.40W
50 L5 **Skridhdalur** V Iceland
50 F5 **Skridhufell** mt Iceland 64.37N 19.55W
53 X15 **Skridulaupbre** glacier Norway 61.57N 7.37E
84 E5 **Skripoú** Greece 38.29N 22.58E
53 F7 **Skrøbelev** Denmark 54.56N 10.46E
51 J5 **Skröven** Sweden 66.46N 21.55E
53 T20 **Skrubburdnut** mt Norway 59.22N 5.50E
50 M5 **Skrúdhur** isld Iceland 64.55N 13.40W
53 V14 **Skruven** mt Norway 62.10N 6.47E
53 C6 **Skrydstrup** Denmark 55.14N 9.15E
53 Y18 **Skrykken** L Norway 60.16N 8.05E
39 D3 **Skrytyy** U.S.S.R. 63.04N 148.13E
18 D10 **Skudai** Pen Malaysia 1.32N 103.39E
18 H2 **Skudai** R Pen Malaysia
53 S20 **Skudeneshavn** Norway 59.10N 5.16E
50 J4 **Skuggadyngja** mt Iceland 65.27N 16.27W
94 L5 **Skukuza** S Africa 25.01S 31.35E
53 J5 **Skuldelev** Denmark 55.48N 12.02E
52 F7 **Skulerud** Norway 59.41N 11.32E
53 U17 **Skulestadmo** Norway 60.40N 6.28E
111 H5 **Skull Pk** mt Nevada 36.45N 116.13W
111 M7 **Skull Valley** Arizona 34.31N 112.40W
82 L3 **Skulyany** U.S.S.R. 47.19N 27.39E
50 L4 **Skúmhöttur** mt Iceland 65.02N 14.29W
53 K4 **Skummeslöv** Sweden 56.28N 12.59E
107 G8 **Skuna** R Mississippi
106 C9 **Skunk, R** Iowa
53 N10 **Skuø** Faeroes 61.47N 6.48W
53 N10 **Skuø** isld Faeroes 61.47N 6.48W
46 D2 **Skuodas** Lithuania U.S.S.R. 56.12N 21.32E
41 B4 **Skuratova, Mys** C U.S.S.R. 73.01N 69.24E
45 J2 **Skuratovskiy** U.S.S.R. 54.05N 37.36E
53 Y18 **Skurdalen** V Norway 60.27N 8.20E
52 G11 **Skurup** Sweden 55.28N 13.30E
Skutari see **Üsküdar**
65 N2 **Skuteč** Czechoslovakia 49.51N 15.59E
52 K6 **Skutskär** Sweden 60.39N 17.25E
50 B2 **Skutulsfjördhur** B Iceland
50 H3 **Skútustadhir** Iceland 65.34N 17.02W
Skúvoy see **Skuø**
Skúvoyar Bjørg mt see **Knúkur**
46 G5 **Škvira** Ukraine U.S.S.R. 49.42N 29.40E
65 L1 **Škvorec** Czechoslovakia 50.03N 14.44E
44 C9 **Skvortsovo** Ukraine U.S.S.R. 45.05N 33.50E
113 M6 **Skwentna** Alaska 61.56N 151.15W
113 L6 **Skwentna** R Alaska
62 J3 **Skwierzyna** Poland 52.35N 15.30E
53 E6 **Skydebjerg** Denmark 55.22N 10.03E
58 D4 **Skye** isld Highland Scotland
50 L4 **Skýhnukur** mt Iceland 65.21N 14.10W
53 W18 **Skykkjedalsfossen** waterfall Norway 60.29N 7.15E
110 D2 **Skykomish** Washington 47.42N 121.21W
121 J5 **Skyring, Pen** Chile
121 J9 **Skyring, Seno** gulf Chile
103 D4 **Skytop** Pennsylvania 41.14N 75.14W
53 W19 **Skyvatn** L Norway 59.37N 7.10E
95 O1 **Slaaihoek** S Africa 25.44S 30.34E
95 M4 **Slabberts** S Africa 28.26S 28.12E
65 J1 **Slabce** Czechoslovakia 50.00N 13.42E
15 L9 **Slade I** Louisiade Arch 10.38S 151.15E
14 G6 **Sladen Water** W Australia 24.45S 128.18E
44 B1 **Sladkiy, Liman** lagoon U.S.S.R.
47 L7 **Sladkovo** U.S.S.R. 55.31N 70.20E
47 J6 **Sladkovskoye** U.S.S.R. 57.46N 64.10E
53 N9 **Slættaratindur** mt Faeroes 62.18N 7.00W
53 G6 **Slagelse** Denmark 55.24N 11.23E
57 J3 **Slaggyford** Northumb Eng 54.52N 2.30W
60 P9 **Slagharen** Netherlands 52.37N 6.34E
107 C10 **Slagle** Louisiana 31.12N 93.09W
53 H6 **Slaglille** Denmark 55.27N 11.38E
51 G6 **Slagnäs** Sweden 65.36N 18.10E
57 H5 **Slaidburn** Lancs Eng 54.00N 2.26W
35 D1 **Slaiyeb, Bahr Es** B Lebanon
57 J3 **Slaley** Northumb Eng 54.55N 2.03W
58 J7 **Slamannan** Central Scotland 55.57N 3.51W
18 H9 **Slamet, Gunung** mt Java Indon 7.14S 109.10E
113 P5 **Slana** Alaska 62.42N 144.02W
62 M7 **Slana** R Czechoslovakia
59 J4 **Slane** Meath Irish Rep 54.43N 6.33W
59 J7 **Slaney, R** Wexford etc Irish Rep
94 F8 **Slang Berg** S Africa 31.32S 20.48E
53 J5 **Slangerup** Denmark 55.51N 12.11E
94 P12 **Slangkop** Cape Town S Africa 34.09S 18.21E
95 B10 **Slangkoppunt** pt S Africa 34.09S 18.20E
82 K5 **Slănic** Romania 45.14N 25.58E
82 D8 **Slano** Yugoslavia 42.48N 17.53E
46 G1 **Slantsy** U.S.S.R. 59.09N 28.09E
62 H5 **Šlaný** Czechoslovakia 50.14N 14.05E
65 P3 **Šlapanice** Czechoslovakia 49.11N 16.43E
64 N3 **Slapany** Czechoslovakia 50.03N 12.25E
58 D4 **Slapin, L** Skye, Highland Scotland 57.10N 6.01W
65 K2 **Slapská nádrž** res Czechoslovakia
56 D7 **Slapton** Devon Eng 50.17N 3.39W
45 O7 **Slashchevskaya** U.S.S.R. 49.52N 42.22E
13 H4 **Slashers Reefs** Gt Barrier Reef Australia
103 C5 **Slatedale** Pennsylvania 40.44N 75.40W
103 D5 **Slateford** Pennsylvania 40.57N 75.08W
99 D4 **Slate Is** Ontario
109 C1 **Slater** Colorado 40.59N 107.22W
107 C2 **Slater** Missouri 39.13N 93.03W
108 F8 **Slater** Wyoming 41.55N 104.50W
111 G6 **Slate Ra** California
103 L2 **Slatersville** Rhode I 42.00N 71.35W
103 B2 **Slaterville Springs** New York 42.23N 76.21W
107 G8 **Slate Springs** Mississippi 33.45N 89.23W
14 G4 **Slatey, R** W Australia
82 J6 **Slatina** Romania 44.26N 24.22E
103 C5 **Slatington** Pennsylvania 40.45N 75.37W
112 F2 **Slaton** Texas 33.26N 101.40W
52 J6 **Slättberg** Sweden 60.48N 15.15E
53 S19 **Slåtterøy** Lt Ho Norway 59.54N 5.05E
53 S20 **Slåttevik** Norway 59.18N 5.29E
104 E8 **Slatyfork** W Virginia 38.25N 80.07W
107 E11 **Slaughter** Louisiana 30.42N 91.10W
103 D9 **Slaughter Beach** Delaware 38.54N 75.18W
18 J10 **Slaung** Java Indon 8.01S 111.24E
39 H3 **Slautnoye** U.S.S.R. 63.12N 168.00E
40 E5 **Slava** U.S.S.R. 52.08N 129.18E
89 L8 **Slave Coast** W Africa
33 C10 **Slave I** S Yemen 12.48N 45.02E
100 C3 **Slave L** Alberta 55.17N 114.43W
100 B3 **Slave L., Lesser** Alberta
101 Q5 **Slave Pt** Great Slave L, N W Terr 61.11N 115.59W
101 R5 **Slave R** N W Terr/Alberta
100 C3 **Slave R.,Lesser** Alberta
43 N1 **Slavgorod** Altay U.S.S.R. 53.01N 78.37E
45 B3 **Slavgorod** Belorussiya U.S.S.R. 53.25N 31.00E
45 G6 **Slavgorod** Sumy, Ukraine U.S.S.R. 50.36N 35.22E
45 G8 **Slavgorod** Ukraine U.S.S.R. 48.05N 35.30E
62 N1 **Slavinek** U.S.S.R. 54.48N 21.01E
46 G1 **Slavkovichi** U.S.S.R. 57.31N 29.01E
65 P3 **Slavkov n Brna** Czech 49.10N 16.53E
40 L9 **Slavnoye** Kuril Is U.S.S.R. 45.27N 148.44E
40 J6 **Slavo** Sakhalin U.S.S.R. 51.01N 142.41E
82 D5 **Slavonia** reg Yugoslavia
65 M3 **Slavonice** Czechoslovakia 49.01N 15.22E
82 D5 **Slavonska Požega** Yugoslavia 45.20N 17.40E
82 H8 **Slavovvrŭkh** mt Bulgaria 42.07N 23.50E
82 H2 **Slavsko** U.S.S.R. 48.51N 23.26E
46 F4 **Slavuta** Ukraine U.S.S.R. 50.20N 26.58E
43 J6 **Slavyanka** Kazakhstan U.S.S.R. 40.39N 68.31E
40 E10 **Slavyanka** Primorsk U.S.S.R. 42.52N 131.20E
45 J8 **Slavyansk** Ukraine U.S.S.R. 48.51N 37.36E
Slavyanskaya see **Slavyansk-na-Kubani**
44 B2 **Slavyansk-na-Kubani** U.S.S.R. 45.14N 38.08E
62 J4 **Sława** Poland 51.52N 16.04E
62 O4 **Sławatycze** Poland 51.43N 23.30E
62 K1 **Sławno** Poland 54.21N 16.40E
62 J2 **Sławoborze** Koszalin Poland 53.53N 15.42E
63 U5 **Sławoborze** Szczecin Poland 53.36N 14.20E
108 P6 **Slayton** Minnesota 43.59N 95.42W
57 N7 **Sleaford** Lincs Eng 53.00N 0.24W
12 D5 **Sleaford B** S Australia
59 B7 **Slea Hd** Kerry Irish Rep 52.06N 10.27W
58 E4 **Sleat, Aird of** Skye, Highland Scotland 57.02N 5.58W
58 D4 **Sleat, Pt.of** Skye, Highland Scotland 57.01N 6.01W
58 E4 **Sleat, Sd.of** Highland Scotland
53 W18 **Sledalsrusta** mt Norway 60.08N 7.06E
113 D4 **Sledge I** Alaska 64.30N 166.14W
50 L3 **Sledhbrjótur** Iceland 65.35N 14.30W
100 K4 **Sled L** Saskatchewan
57 M4 **Sledmere** Humberside Eng 54.04N 0.35W
29 G6 **Sleemanabad** Madhya Prad India 23.38N 80.18E
60 Q8 **Sleen** Netherlands 52.47N 6.48E
97 M6 **Sleeper Is** Hudson B, N W Terr
106 H5 **Sleeping Bear Pt** Michigan 44.55N 86.04W
108 Q5 **Sleepy Eye** Minnesota 44.19N 94.45W
113 J6 **Sleetmute** Alaska 61.40N 157.11W
61 E2 **Sleidinge** Belgium 51.08N 3.41E
57 M4 **Sleights** N Yorks Eng 54.26N 0.40W
Slēmānī see **Sulaymānīyah**
60 T17 **Slenaken** Netherlands 50.46N 5.51E
60 N6 **Şlenk** Netherlands
62 L3 **Slesiń** Poland 52.22N 18.14E
123 D10 **Slessor Glacier** Antarctica
50 C2 **Slétta** Ísafjardharsýsla, Nordhur Iceland 66.19N 22.57W
50 L4 **Slétta** Múlasýsla, Sudhur Iceland 65.01N 14.15W
53 S20 **Sletta** Norway 59.28N 5.08E
53 V19 **Slettadalen** V Norway 59.42N 6.30E
53 U19 **Slettadalshytta** Norway 59.45N 6.30E
50 E4 **Sléttafell** mt Iceland 65.00N 20.51W
53 K5 **Sletten** Denmark 55.57N 12.33E
48 U16 **Sletten** Greenland 60.41N 45.17W
53 F4 **Sletterhage** C Denmark 56.06N 10.32E
53 X16 **Sletterust** Norway 61.16N 8.01E
53 C2 **Slettestrand** Denmark 57.09N 9.23E
51 N1 **Slettnes** Lt Ho Norway 71.05N 28.10E
53 Y16 **Slettningen** L Norway 61.13N 8.07E
53 Y18 **Slettnut** mt Norway 60.07N 8.08E
50 J2 **Sléttuheidhi** heath Iceland
65 K6 **Sleyrling** Austria 47.49N 14.08E
107 G11 **Slidell** Louisiana 30.17N 89.49W
112 K2 **Slidell** Texas 33.22N 97.25W
103 F2 **Slide Mt** New York 42.00N 74.25W
52 E5 **Slidre** Norway 61.06N 9.00E
84 Z20 **Sliema** Malta 35.55N 14.31E
59 B7 **Slievanea** mt Kerry Irish Rep 52.10N 10.10W
59 G3 **Slieve Anierin** mt Leitrim Irish Rep 54.06N 7.58W
59 G6 **Slieveardagh Hills** Tipperary etc Irish Rep
59 E5 **Slieve Aughty Mts** Galway Irish Rep
59 H3 **Slieve Beagh** mt Tyrone N Ireland 54.21N 7.12W
59 E6 **Slieve Bernagh** ra Clare Irish Rep
59 G5 **Slieve Bloom Mts** Leix Irish Rep
59 D6 **Slieve Callan** hill Clare Irish Rep 52.51N 9.16W
59 C3 **Slieve Car** mt Mayo Irish Rep 54.04N 9.39W
59 L3 **Slieve Donard** mt Down N Ireland 54.11N 5.55W
59 D5 **Slieve Elva** mt Clare Irish Rep 53.05N 9.16W
59 F6 **Slievefelim Mts** Limerick Irish Rep
59 J2 **Slieve Gallion** hill Londonderry N Ireland 54.45N 6.45W
59 D3 **Slieve Gamph** mts Mayo etc Irish Rep
59 H2 **Slieve Kirk** hill Tyrone N Ireland 54.55N 7.18W
59 E2 **Slieve League** mt Donegal Irish Rep 54.39N 8.42W

59 C7 Slieve Mish Mts Kerry Irish Rep
59 C8 Slieve Miskish Mts Cork Irish Rep
59 B3 Slievemore *hill* Mayo Irish Rep 54.01N 10.03W
59 H4 Slieve-na-Calliagh *hill* Meath Irish Rep 53.45N 7.06W
59 G3 Slievenakilla *hill* Cavan Irish Rep 54.11N 7.57W
59 G7 Slievenaman *mt* Tipperary Irish Rep 52.25N 7.34W
59 F7 Slievenamuck *hills* Tipperary Irish Rep 52.26N 8.14W
59 G3 Slieve Rushen *mt* Fermanagh N Ireland 54.09N 7.37W
59 F2 Slieve Snaght *mt* Donegal Irish Rep 54.59N 8.07W
59 H1 Slieve Snaght *mt* Donegal Irish Rep 55.12N 7.20W
59 E2 Slieve Tooey *mt* Donegal Irish Rep 54.45N 8.37W
58 D4 Sligachan Skye, Highland Scotland 57.17N 6.10W
104 F5 Sligo Pennsylvania 41.06N 79.30W
59 F3 Sligo Sligo Irish Rep 54.17N 8.28W
59 E3 Sligo *co* Irish Rep
59 E3 Sligo B Sligo Irish Rep 54.18N 8.40W
60 M12 Slijk-Ewijk Netherlands 51.53N 5.47E
61 B2 Slijpe Belgium 51.09N 2.51E
53 H6 Slimminge Denmark 55.27N 11.58E
53 V16 Slinde Norway 61.09N 6.55E
56 K6 Slindon W Sussex Eng 50.52N 0.39W
60 P11 Slinge *R* Netherlands
106 F6 Slinger Wisconsin 43.20N 88.18W
57 M4 Slingsby N Yorks Eng 54.09N 0.56W
46 G4 Slipchitsy Ukraine U.S.S.R. 50.30N 28.50E
56 L3 Slip End Herts Eng 52.01N 0.08W
11 K4 Slipper I New Zealand 37.02S 175.57E
104 E5 Slippery Rock Pennsylvania 41.04N 80.03W
52 L9 Slite Sweden 57.43N 18.50E
82 K8 Sliven Bulgaria 42.40N 26.19E
65 N9 Slivnica Yugoslavia 46.27N 15.38E
82 H8 Slivnitsa Bulgaria 42.50N 23.00E
108 O7 Sloan Iowa 42.14N 96.14W
110 L2 Sloan Montana 47.29N 114.21W
111 J6 Sloan Nevada 35.58N 115.14W
111 D2 Sloat California 39.53N 120.44W
103 F4 Sloatsburg New York 41.09N 74.12W
45 C1 Sloboda Smolensk U.S.S.R. 55.31N 31.51E
47 M4 Sloboda Sverdlovsk U.S.S.R. 57.01N 59.35E
45 M5 Sloboda Voronezh U.S.S.R. 51.09N 40.17E
47 F5 Slobodchikovo U.S.S.R. 61.46N 48.16E
46 G5 Slobodka Ukraine U.S.S.R. 47.56N 29.18E
46 Q1 Slobodskoy U.S.S.R. 58.42N 50.10E
46 G6 Slobodzeya Moldavia U.S.S.R. 46.42N 29.40E
82 J6 Slobozia Romania 44.30N 25.14E
82 L6 Slobozia Romania 44.34N 27.23E
101 P11 Slocan Br Col 49.46N 117.28W
101 P11 Slocan L Br Col
60 Q7 Slochteren Netherlands 53.14N 6.48E
107 L10 Slocomb Alabama 31.06N 85.36W
60 B3 Sloe *inlet* Netherlands
52 G10 Slöinge Sweden 56.54N 12.40E
101 G6 Sloko *R* Br Col
46 F3 Slonim Belorussiya U.S.S.R. 53.05N 25.21E
45 J6 Slonovka U.S.S.R. 50.39N 37.46E
62 H3 Słońsk Poland 52.32N 14.48E
Slonta *see* Suluntah
60 H8 Slootdorp Netherlands 52.50N 4.58E
60 L8 Sloten Friesland Netherlands 52.53N 5.39E
60 H10 Sloten Noord-Holland Netherlands 52.20N 4.48E
60 H10 Sloterdijk Netherlands 52.24N 4.50E
60 L8 Sloter Meer *L* Netherlands 52.55N 5.38E
53 G6 Slots Bjergby Denmark 55.23N 11.21E
51 L1 Slotten Norway 70.44N 24.30E
15 K2 Slot, The *str* Solomon Is
26 D9 Slot van Capelle *seamount* Indian Oc 36.50S 41.20E
56 K4 Slough Berks Eng 51.31N 0.36W
65 P3 Sloup Czechoslovakia 49.26N 16.45E
Sloûq *see* Slug
62 L7 Slovakia *old prov* Czechoslovakia
46 G4 Slovechna *R* Belorussiya U.S.S.R.
46 G4 Slovechno Ukraine U.S.S.R. 51.23N 28.20E
Slovenia *rep see* Slovenija *rep*
82 B5 Slovenija *rep* Yugoslavia
65 M9 Slovenjgradec Yugoslavia 46.30N 15.04E
82 C4 Slovenska Bistrica Yugoslavia 46.24N 15.35E
62 L7 Slovenské Pravno Czechoslovakia 48.52N 18.39E
62 L7 Slovenské Rudohorie Czechoslovakia
62 L7 Slovensko *aut reg* Czechoslovakia
113 L5 Slow Fork *R* Alaska
58 G6 Sloy, L Strathclyde Scotland 56.16N 4.47W
41 E3 Slozhnyy, Ostrov *isld* U.S.S.R.
62 H3 Słubice Poland 52.20N 14.35E
46 F4 Sluch' *R* Ukraine U.S.S.R.
79 J1 Sluderno Italy 46.40N 10.35E
47 G5 Sludka U.S.S.R. 62.00N 50.09E
92 A9 S.Lueti *R* Zambia
34 G2 Slug Syria 36.36N 39.07E
58 M4 Slug Road Grampian Scotland
60 A3 Sluis Netherlands 51.18N 3.23E
60 E13 Sluis Netherlands 51.38N 4.07E
60 C3 Sluiskil Netherlands 51.17N 3.50E
61 N3 Sluizen Belgium 50.46N 5.32E
62 H5 Sluknov Czechoslovakia 51.00N 14.25E
82 C5 Slunj Yugoslavia 45.06N 15.33E
62 K3 Słupca Poland 52.17N 17.52E
62 K1 Słupia *R* Poland
62 K1 Słupsk Poland 54.28N 17.00E
95 J1 Slurry S Africa 25.49S 25.52E
46 G3 Slutsk Belorussiya U.S.S.R. 53.02N 27.31E
50 J3 Slúttnes *C* Iceland 65.39N 16.58W
57 H4 Slyne Lancs Eng 54.06N 2.48W
59 B5 Slyne Hd Galway Irish Rep 53.24N 10.13W
53 V13 Slyngstad Norway 62.33N 6.31E
42 G6 Slyudyanka U.S.S.R. 51.40N 103.40E
Smaâne, Jebel es *see* Semân, Jebel
107 D8 Smackover Arkansas 33.21N 92.43W
58 J6 Sma' Glen *V* Tayside Scotland 56.27N 3.48W
57 H1 Smailholm Borders Scotland 55.37N 2.34W
52 H9 Småland *reg* Sweden
53 G6 Smålandsfarvandet *sea* Denmark
110 N5 Small Idaho 44.13N 112.24W
57 L7 Smalley Derbys Eng 53.00N 1.23W
19 N4 Small I Truk Is Pacific Oc 7.28N 151.57E
100 U1 Small L Manitoba 57.40N 97.20W
14 F7 Small, L W Australia 26.38S 125.37E
15 L3 Small Nggela *isld* Solomon Is 9.10S 160.20E
104 Q3 Small Pt Maine 43.42N 69.51W
54 G11 Smalls Rock Lt.Ho Wales 51.43N 5.45W
97 N7 Smallwood Res Labrador, Nfld 54.00N 64.00W
88 H8 Smara Morocco 26.44N 11.41W
56 N5 Smarden Kent Eng 51.09N 0.41E
101 U4 Smart L N W Terr
100 N5 Smeaton Saskatchewan 53.30N 104.50W
53 X16 Smeddalsvatn *L* Norway 61.10N 8.00E
65 K4 Smědeč Czechoslovakia 48.58N 14.10E
82 F6 Smederevo Yugoslavia 44.40N 20.56E
82 F6 Smederevska Palanka Yugoslavia 44.23N 21.00E
52 J6 Smedjebacken Sweden 60.08N 15.25E
61 F3 Smeerebbe-Vloerzegem Belgium 50.49N 3.56E
45 C7 Smela Ukraine U.S.S.R. 49.15N 31.54E
53 Y21 Smeland Norway 58.56N 8.13E
45 E6 Smeloye Ukraine U.S.S.R. 50.55N 33.37E
51 P1 Smelror Norway 70.24N 31.00E
59 B7 Smerwick Harb Kerry Irish Rep 52.12N 10.23W
104 G5 Smethport Pennsylvania 41.48N 78.26W
56 H3 Smethwick W Midlands Eng 52.30N 1.58W
61 F3 Smetlede Belgium 50.58N 3.55E
50 C2 Smidhjuvík *inlet* Iceland
41 B2 Smidovich Novaya Zemlya U.S.S.R. 74.58N 56.02E
40 F7 Smidovich U.S.S.R. 48.35N 133.45E
53 J4 Smidstrup Denmark 56.06N 12.13E
62 K3 Śmigiel Poland 52.01N 16.31E
74 K10 S'Mila Algeria 34.46N 3.10E
60 O8 Smilde Netherlands 52.57N 6.28E
100 H7 Smiley Saskatchewan 51.38N 109.27W
112 K6 Smiley Texas 29.16N 97.40W
46 G3 Smilovichi Belorussiya U.S.S.R. 53.45N 28.00E
46 F2 Smiltene Latvia U.S.S.R. 57.28N 26.00E
82 J9 Smilyan Bulgaria 41.29N 24.46E
82 J7 Smîrdiosa Romania 43.50N 25.27E
62 J5 Smiřice Czechoslovakia 50.19N 15.50E
45 Q1 Smirnovo Gor'kiy U.S.S.R. 55.19N 44.22E
43 J1 Smirnovo Kazakhstan U.S.S.R. 54.31N 69.27E
40 J7 Smirnykh Sakhalin U.S.S.R. 49.44N 142.56E
84 A3 Smirtoúla Greece 39.02N 20.44E
100 C3 Smith Alberta 55.11N 114.02W
121 E5 Smith Argentina 35.30S 61.35W
111 E3 Smith Nevada 38.48N 119.20W
87 F7 Smith *mt* Ethiopia 6.10N 36.16E
110 A7 Smith *R* California
104 F10 Smith *R* Virginia
101 M2 Smith Arm *inlet* N W Terr
113 K1 Smith B Alaska
97 M2 Smith B N W Terr
107 G3 Smithboro Illinois 38.55N 89.20W
103 B2 Smithboro New York 42.02N 76.25W
103 F6 Smithburg New Jersey 40.12N 74.21W
13 F3 Smithburne R Queensland
Smith, C *see* Nord, Pte
109 M2 Smith Center Kansas 39.46N 98.46W
101 K8 Smithers Br Col 54.45N 127.10W
57 H3 Smithfield Cumbria Eng 54.59N 2.52W
105 J2 Smithfield N Carolina 35.30N 78.21W
108 L9 Smithfield Nebraska 40.35N 99.42W
104 F7 Smithfield Pennsylvania 39.47N 79.48W
103 L3 Smithfield Rhode I 41.55N 71.34W
95 K6 Smithfield S Africa 30.13S 26.32E
112 M9 Smithfield Texas 32.49N 97.12W
110 O8 Smithfield Utah 41.50N 111.50W
104 J9 Smithfield Virginia 36.59N 76.40W
104 E7 Smithfield W Virginia 39.30N 80.35W
28 G6 Smith I Andaman Is
97 M5 Smith I Hudson B, N W Terr 60.40N 78.45W
104 J8 Smith I Maryland 38.01N 76.01W
105 K4 Smith I N Carolina 33.52N 77.59W
123 E14 Smith I S Shetland Is Antarctica 63.00S 62.30W
104 K9 Smith I Virginia 37.07N 75.56W
110 C1 Smith I Washington 48.21N 122.51W
123 K6 Smith Inlet Antarctica
107 J8 Smith, L.M.,Res Alabama
104 F9 Smith Mountain Lake *res* Virginia
110 J1 Smith Pk Idaho 48.50N 116.37W
98 J8 Smith Pt Nova Scotia 45.52N 63.25W
110 O2 Smith R Montana
101 K6 Smith River Br Col 59.56N 126.28W
110 A8 Smith River California 41.56N 124.09W
12 L5 Smiths Cr New S Wales
97 M2 Smiths Sd N W Terr
99 O8 Smiths Falls Ontario 44.54N 76.01W
110 J5 Smiths Ferry Idaho 44.18N 116.04W
107 K4 Smiths Grove Kentucky 37.02N 86.14W
54 M10 Smiths Knoll North Sea
107 C3 Smithton Missouri 38.40N 93.09W
12 H8 Smithton Tasmania 40.52S 145.07E
103 H5 Smithtown Long I, N Y 40.52N 73.13W
103 H5 Smithtown B Long I, N Y
12 L4 Smithtown-Gladstone New S Wales 31.04S 152.53E
105 C6 Smithville Georgia 31.56N 84.14W
107 B2 Smithville Missouri 39.23N 94.33W
103 F7 Smithville New Jersey 39.30N 74.28W
109 Q7 Smithville Oklahoma 34.29N 94.38W
107 L6 Smithville Tennessee 35.59N 85.49W
112 K6 Smithville Texas 30.01N 97.10W
104 D7 Smithville W Virginia 39.04N 81.06W
103 C2 Smithville Flats New York 42.23N 75.48W
108 G6 Smithwick S Dakota 43.18N 103.14W
94 P12 Smitswinkelbaai *B* Cape Town S Africa
50 L3 Smjörfjöll *mt* Iceland 65.35N 14.49W
50 K3 Smjörvatnsheidhi *heath* Iceland
45 D1 Smogiri U.S.S.R. 55.05N 32.21E
110 F9 Smoke Creek Des Nevada
104 F8 Smoke Hole W Virginia 38.52N 79.18W
101 K1 Smoking Mts N W Terr
101 O8 Smoky *R* Alberta
12 C4 Smoky Bay S Australia 32.24S 134.13E
98 M7 Smoky C C Breton I, Nova Scotia 46.38N 60.20W
12 L4 Smoky C New S Wales 30.55S 153.05E
13 E5 Smoky Cr Queensland
99 H2 Smoky Falls Ontario 50.03N 82.11W
109 L3 Smoky Hill *R* Colorado/Kansas
109 K2 Smoky Hills Kansas
100 E4 Smoky Lake Alberta 54.08N 112.26W
52 D3 Smøla *isld* Norway 63.25N 8.00E
46 Q4 Smolenka U.S.S.R. 52.00N 50.00E
45 D2 Smolensk U.S.S.R. 54.49N 32.04E
46 H3 Smolenskaya Oblast' *prov* U.S.S.R.
45 C2 Smolensko-Moskovskaya Vozvyshennost *heights* U.S.S.R.
42 D6 Smolenskoye U.S.S.R. 52.18N 85.04E
46 G3 Smolevichi Belorussiya U.S.S.R. 54.00N 28.01E
84 A1 Smólikas *mt* Greece 40.05N 20.56E
82 J9 Smolyan Bulgaria 41.34N 24.42E
40 F10 Smolyanninovo U.S.S.R. 43.15N 132.24E
45 B2 Smolyany Belorussiya U.S.S.R. 54.36N 30.14E
58 G1 Smoo Highland Scotland 58.33N 4.44W
110 P7 Smoot Wyoming 42.37N 110.55W
99 J3 Smooth Rock Falls Ontario 49.17N 81.37W
99 A2 Smoothrock L Ontario
100 L4 Smoothstone L Saskatchewan
100 L3 Smoothstone R Saskatchewan
53 X13 Smørbottind *mt* Norway 62.37N 7.41E
53 T15 Smørdal Norway 61.57N 5.56E
46 F3 Smorgon' Belorussiya U.S.S.R. 54.20N 26.20E
53 R15 Smørhamn Norway 61.46N 4.57E
53 V14 Smørskredtindane *mt* Norway 62.12N 6.46E
53 Y15 Smorstabbre *glacier* Norway 61.33N 8.04E
46 F5 Smotrich Ukraine U.S.S.R. 48.59N 26.32E
82 K2 Smotrich *R* U.S.S.R.
45 D6 Smotriki Ukraine U.S.S.R. 50.20N 32.24E
65 N3 Smrček *mt* Czechoslovakia 49.19N 15.49E
61 M6 Smuid Belgium 50.02N 5.16E
82 L7 Smyadovo Bulgaria 43.02N 27.01E
45 G1 Smychka U.S.S.R. 56.04N 35.58E
112 E2 Smyer Texas 33.35N 102.10W
52 G11 Smygehamn Sweden 55.20N 13.25E
123 G12 Smyley *isld* Antarctica 72.26S 78.20W
Smyrna *see* İzmir
103 C8 Smyrna Delaware 39.18N 75.37W
105 C4 Smyrna Georgia 33.53N 84.31W
104 K4 Smyrna New York 42.42N 75.34W
107 K6 Smyrna Tennessee 35.59N 86.32W
103 C8 Smyrna *R* Delaware
104 Q7 Smyrna Mills Maine 46.07N 68.09W
121 J9 Smyth, Canal *str* Chile
61 B2 Snaaskerke Belgium 51.10N 2.57E
50 K5 Snæfell *mt* Iceland 64.48N 15.34W
57 E4 Snaefell *mt* Isle of Man U.K. 54.16N 4.28W
50 B5 Snæfellsjökull *ice cap* Iceland 64.40N 23.46W
50 B5 Snæfellsnessýsla *co* Iceland
25 H7 Snaipol Cambodia 11.39N 105.15E
57 L5 Snaith Humberside Eng 53.41N 1.01W
108 J7 Snake *R* Nebraska
101 G3 Snake *R* Yukon Terr
13 B1 Snake Bay N Terr Australia 11.22S 130.38E
13 A3 Snake Cr N Terr Australia
111 K2 Snake Ra Nevada
110 J4 Snake R. Canyon Idaho
110 G3 Snake River Washington 46.25N 118.40W
110 P5 Snake River Wyoming 44.10N 110.40W
110 M7 Snake R. Plain Idaho
12 A7 Snapper Pt S Australia 34.47S 138.31E
116 F3 Snap Pt Andros Bahamas 23.44N 77.34W
53 E5 Snaptun Denmark 55.49N 10.03E
101 Q3 Snare L N W Terr 64.09N 114.40W
101 U6 Snare L Saskatchewan 58.29N 107.43W
101 P4 Snare River N W Terr 63.27N 116.18W
11 B9 Snares Is Pacific Oc
50 J2 Snartarstadhanúpur *mt* Iceland 66.21N 16.26W
50 J2 Snartarstadhir Iceland 66.17N 16.24W
53 E6 Snarup Denmark 55.10N 10.27E
52 G2 Snåsa Norway 64.15N 12.23E
52 G3 Snasahögarna *mt* Sweden 63.10N 12.15E
52 F2 Snåsavatn *L* Norway
105 C7 Sneads Florida 30.42N 84.58W
53 B3 Snedsted Denmark 56.54N 8.32E
60 L7 Sneek Netherlands 53.02N 5.40E
60 L7 Sneeker Meer *L* Netherlands 53.03N 5.45E
60 L7 Sneek Trek *canal* Netherlands
59 C8 Sneem Kerry Irish Rep 51.50N 9.45W
94 E9 Sneeuberg *mt* S Africa 32.30S 19.10E
95 H7 Sneeuberg *mts* S Africa
95 C8 Sneeukop S Africa 32.49S 19.24E
53 M9 Sneis *mt* Faeroes 62.10N 7.03W
53 B4 Snejbjerg Denmark 56.08N 8.55E
53 K4 Snekkersten Denmark 56.01N 12.37E
61 C2 Snellegem Belgium 51.10N 3.08E
111 D4 Snelling California 37.31N 120.25W
56 N2 Snettisham Norfolk Eng 52.53N 0.30E
53 B5 Sneum Å *R* Denmark
41 E6 Snezhnogorsk U.S.S.R. 67.60N 87.58E
45 K8 Snezhnoye Donetsk, Ukraine U.S.S.R. 48.01N 38.46E
39 J2 Snezhnoye Magadan U.S.S.R. 65.27N 173.01E
62 J5 Sněžka *mt* Czechoslovakia 50.45N 15.37E
82 B5 Snežnik *mt* Yugoslavia 45.36N 14.35E
62 N2 Śniadowo Poland 53.03N 22.00E
62 N2 Śniardwy, Jezioro *L* Poland
45 D9 Snigirevka Ukraine U.S.S.R. 47.04N 32.49E
53 T19 Snilstveitøy *isld* Norway 59.58N 5.55E
Snîmê, Ouâdi *see* Sanime, Wādi *watercourse*
62 N6 Snina Czechoslovakia 49.00N 22.10E
103 N3 Snipatuit Pond *L* Massachusetts
100 A3 Snipe L Alberta 55.09N 116.40W
53 T14 Snipsøyrvatn Norway 62.20N 6.00E
58 D3 Snizort, Loch Skye, Highland Scotland
50 G6 Snjóalda *R* Iceland
50 L5 Snjótindur *pk* Iceland 64.31N 14.35W
53 F6 Snøde Denmark 55.05N 10.55E
60 M12 Snodenhoek Netherlands 51.56N 5.51E
56 M5 Snodland Kent Eng 51.20N 0.27E
50 C2 Snæfjall *mt* Iceland 66.11N 22.46W
50 C2 Snæfjallaströnd: *coast* Iceland
53 Q12 Snogebæk Bornholm Denmark 55.02N 15.08E
53 D5 Snoghøj Denmark 55.31N 9.43E
52 E4 Snøhetta *mt* Norway 62.19N 9.16E
110 C2 Snohomish Washington 47.55N 122.05W
53 U14 Snøhorn *mt* Norway 62.07N 6.17E
50 D4 Snoksdalur Iceland 65.01N 21.45W
53 J5 Snoldelev Denmark 55.34N 12.09E
53 V15 Snønipa *mt* Norway 61.40N 6.43E
53 V19 Snønuten *mt* Norway 59.31N 6.50E
116 M2 Snook Pt Jamaica, W I 17.53N 76.12W
45 E3 Snopot' U.S.S.R. 53.53N 33.40E
110 D2 Snoqualmie Washington 47.31N 121.50W
110 D2 Snoqualmie Pass Washington 47.25N 121.24W
52 G5 Snössvallen Sweden 61.55N 13.30E
25 J6 Snoul Cambodia 12.05N 106.25E
45 D4 Snov *R* U.S.S.R.
106 M6 Snover Michigan 43.27N 82.57W
101 W5 Snowbird L N W Terr
113 L6 Snowcap Mt Alaska 61.29N 154.00W
110 B8 Snowden California 41.21N 123.01W
100 N5 Snowden Saskatchewan 53.30N 104.45W
57 E6 Snowdon *mt* Gwynedd Wales 53.04N 4.05W
101 S4 Snowdrift N W Terr 62.24N 110.42W
101 S4 Snowdrift, R N W Terr
111 O7 Snowflake Arizona 34.32N 110.05W
100 T9 Snowflake Manitoba 49.03N 98.37W
104 K8 Snow Hill Maryland 38.11N 75.23W
105 K2 Snow Hill N Carolina 35.26N 77.39W
123 E14 Snow Hill I Antarctica 63.57S 57.10W
123 E15 Snow I S Shetland Is Antarctica 62.55S 61.30W
107 E7 Snow Lake Arkansas 34.03N 91.01W
100 R4 Snow Lake Manitoba 54.56N 100.02W
109 C2 Snowmass Mt Colorado 39.07N 107.05W
99 O8 Snow Road Ontario 44.56N 76.42W
104 H5 Snow Shoe Pennsylvania 41.02N 77.58W
110 K1 Snowshoe Pk Montana 48.16N 115.43W
12 E5 Snowtown S Australia 33.47S 138.14E
110 N8 Snowville Utah 41.58N 112.45W
110 K9 Snow Water L Nevada 40.48N 115.00W
12 J6 Snowy *R* Victoria
12 J6 Snowy Mts New S Wales/Victoria
Snubbin *mt see* Høvdin
12 H9 Snug Tasmania 43.04S 147.16E
116 H3 Snug Corner Acklins I Bahamas 22.33N 73.52W
Snuyen *see* Hsiu-jen
46 F5 Snyatyn Ukraine U.S.S.R. 48.30N 25.50E
108 O8 Snyder Nebraska 41.42N 96.47W
109 M7 Snyder Oklahoma 34.40N 98.58W
112 G3 Snyder Texas 32.43N 100.54W
103 C5 Snyders Pennsylvania 40.44N 75.52W
103 D5 Snydersville Pennsylvania 40.57N 75.18W
103 A5 Snydertown Pennsylvania 40.52N 76.40W
45 H3 Snykhovo U.S.S.R. 53.54N 36.12E
52 J7 Snyten Sweden 59.59N 16.01E
95 B5 Soahany Madagascar 18.40S 44.12E
95 B5 Soahazo Madagascar 19.19S 44.24E
14 E6 Soakage Well W Australia 24.12S 123.54E
11 B12 Soaker, Mt New Zealand 45.23S 167.14E
95 B4 Soalala Madagascar 16.05S 45.21E
95 B7 Soalanivo Madagascar 23.30S 44.40E
95 A7 Soalara Madagascar 23.36S 43.44E
76 E8 Soalheira Portugal 40.01N 7.29W
95 B5 Soaloka Madagascar 18.30S 45.15E
95 B7 Soamanonga Madagascar 23.50S 44.46E
90 G8 Soang Cameroon 7.45N 14.04E
95 D4 Soanierana-Ivongo Madagascar 16.53S 49.35E
95 C5 Soanindrariny Madagascar 19.52S 47.14E
21 D10 Soan-kundo *islds* S Korea
51 P9 Soanlakhti Karelia U.S.S.R. 62.02N 31.04E
94 H3 Soa Pan *salt pan* Botswana
110 F2 Soap Lake Washington 47.23N 119.29W
15 G7 Soari *R* Papua New Guinea
56 J2 Soar, R Leics Eng
82 J5 Soarș Romania 45.55N 24.56E
19 E3 Soasiu Moluccas Indon 0.40N 127.25E
119 D4 Soatá Colombia 6.23N 72.40W
95 B5 Soatanana Madagascar 18.44S 44.25E
79 K4 Soave Italy 45.26N 11.15E
95 C6 Soavina Madagascar 20.21S 46.52E
95 D6 Soavina Madagascar 20.21S 48.18E
95 C5 Soavinandriana Madagascar 19.09S 46.43E
58 D4 Soay *isld* Highland Scotland 57.08N 6.14W
58 A1 Soay *isld* W Isles Scotland 57.50N 8.38W
66 N6 Soazza Switzerland 46.22N 9.14E
46 G5 Sob *R* Ukraine U.S.S.R.
87 F3 Soba Ethiopia 14.50N 37.00E
90 D6 Soba Nigeria 10.58N 8.04E
87 D3 Soba Sudan 15.27N 32.40E
42 G2 Soba *R* U.S.S.R.
41 F6 Sobachye, Ozero *L* U.S.S.R.
30 D2 Sobala Uttar Prad India 30.03N 80.36E
91 E11 Soba Matias Angola 14.16S 17.53E
87 D6 Sobat,R Sudan
76 D4 Sober Spain 42.29N 7.35W
64 D4 Sobernheim W Germany 49.47N 7.40E
65 L3 Soběslav Czechoslovakia 49.16N 14.44E
15 F5 Sobger *R* Irian Jaya
29 F6 Sobhapur Madhya Prad India 22.47N 78.17E
45 M1 Sobinka U.S.S.R. 55.59N 40.01E
46 Q4 Sobolev U.S.S.R. 51.59N 51.49E
45 F2 Sobolevka U.S.S.R. 54.14N 34.56E
39 F7 Sobolevo U.S.S.R. 54.14N 155.59E
39 D1 Sobonoydokh U.S.S.R. 70.02N 145.10E
41 N7 Sobopol U.S.S.R. 67.06N 126.30E
41 M7 Sobopol Mayan *R* U.S.S.R.
90 H1 Soborom Chad 21.03N 17.09E
65 M8 Soboth Austria 46.41N 15.03E
65 Q1 Sobotin Czechoslovakia 50.02N 17.08E
62 K5 Sobótka Poland 50.55N 16.45E
20 E9 Sobo zan *mt* Japan 32.48N 131.22E
76 F7 Sobradillo Spain 40.55N 6.48W
117 C7 Sobrado Pará Brazil 5.30S 52.45W
117 G9 Sobrado Piauí Brazil 9.22S 40.48W
76 C2 Sobrado Spain 43.02N 8.02W
76 C6 Sobrado de Paiva Portugal 41.02N 8.16W
120 D3 Sobral Brazil 9.10S 70.26W
117 G6 Sobral Ceará Brazil 3.45S 40.20W
76 E12 Sobral da Adiça Portugal 38.02N 7.16W
76 D8 Sobral de Cazegas Portugal 40.12N 7.45W
76 A10 Sobral de Monte Agraço Portugal 39.01N 9.09W
76 D9 Sobral do Campo Portugal 40.00N 7.34W
62 N7 Sobrance Czechoslovakia 48.44N 22.10E
111 B8 Sobrante Ridge California
29 D2 Sobraon Punjab India 31.08N 74.59E
75 K2 Sobrarbe *reg* Spain
76 D9 Sobreira Formosa Portugal 39.46N 7.51W
76 L2 Sobrelapeña Spain 43.15N 4.29W
76 J2 Sobrescobio Spain 43.14N 5.28W
47 K3 Sobtyegan *R* U.S.S.R.
53 E7 Søby Svendborg Denmark 54.57N 10.16E
53 C3 Søby Viborg Denmark 56.32N 9.08E
53 C4 Søby Sø *L* Denmark 56.03N 9.04E
79 P2 Soča Yugoslavia 46.20N 13.40E
79 P2 Soča *R* Italy
67 O12 Soccia Corsica 42.11N 8.54E
25 J1 Soc Giang Vietnam 22.55N 106.02E
62 M3 Sochaczew Poland 52.15N 20.13E
44 C4 Sochi U.S.S.R. 43.35N 39.46E
21 D9 Söch'ön S Korea 36.06N 126.42E
42 E3 Sochur *R* U.S.S.R.
105 D4 Social Circle Georgia 33.40N 83.44W
Société, Is.de la *see* Society Is
105 H3 Society Hill S Carolina 34.30N 79.51W
122 M10 Society Is Pacific Oc
11 L10 Sockburn New Zealand 43.33S 172.33E
Socna *see* Sawnah
121 B3 Soco Chile 30.42S 71.28W
72 A9 Socoa France 43.24N 1.41W
77 N4 Socobos Spain 38.20N 1.59W
120 F9 Sococha Bolivia 22.00S 65.29W
120 E11 Socompa Chile 24.28S 68.18W
120 E11 Socompa *vol* Arg/Chile 24.25S 68.15W
118 F8 Socorro Brazil 22.34S 46.32W
119 D4 Socorro Colombia 6.30N 73.16W
109 D7 Socorro New Mexico 34.04N 106.55W
Socorro *isld see* Guamblin I
115 D8 Socorro, I Mexico
120 D7 Socosani Peru 16.15S 71.44W
120 A2 Socota Peru 6.18S 78.40W
87 P4 Socotra / S Yemen
Socotra-Chagos *see* Carlsberg Ridge
77 L2 Socuéllamos Spain 39.18N 2.48W
87 D5 Soda Sudan 11.20N 33.53E
101 M9 Soda Creek Br Col 52.22N 122.15W
21 J1 Sŏdaemun-gu *dist* Seoul S Korea
111 E6 Soda L California 35.15N 119.55W
111 H6 Soda L California 35.10N 116.05W
51 M4 Sodankylä Finland 67.26N 26.35E
31 J1 Soda Plains Kashmir
110 O7 Soda Springs Idaho 42.40N 111.35W
111 F3 Sodaville Nevada 38.20N 118.06W
87 E6 Soddo Ethiopia 8.38N 35.50E
Soddu *see* Sodo
107 L6 Soddy Tennessee 35.17N 85.10W
64 F3 Södel W Germany 50.23N 8.49E
90 D9 Soden I Cameroon 4.30N 8.51E
52 K5 Söderala Sweden 61.17N 17.00E
52 L7 Söderby-Karl Sweden 59.53N 18.43E
52 K6 Söderfors Sweden 60.23N 17.20E
52 K5 Söderhamn Sweden 61.19N 17.10E
52 J8 Söderköping Sweden 58.28N 16.20E
52 J7 Södermanland *dist* Sweden
52 K7 Södertälje Sweden 59.11N 17.39E
31 H4 Sodhra Pakistan 32.26N 74.12E
50 G5 Sodhulfell *mt* Iceland 64.39N 18.54W
87 B3 Sodiri Sudan 14.23N 29.06E
95 G6 Sodium S Africa 30.11S 23.09E
87 F7 Sodo Ethiopia 6.49N 37.41E
52 F8 Södra Bullaren Sweden 58.45N 11.35E
52 G6 Södra Finnskoga Sweden 60.41N 12.35E
52 J10 Södra Möckleby Sweden 56.20N 16.25E
52 G7 Södra Ny Sweden 59.09N 13.07E
51 D6 Södra Storfjället *mt* Sweden 65.38N 14.45E
52 J9 Södra Vi Sweden 57.45N 15.45E
53 E3 Sødring Denmark 56.38N 10.20E
75 D1 Sodupe Spain 43.11N 3.04W
29 F6 Sodurpur Madhya Prad India 23.24N 78.29E
104 H3 Sodus New York 43.14N 77.04W
104 J3 Sodus Pt New York 43.16N 76.59W
19 D8 Soë Timor Indon 9.51S 124.16E
53 U14 Søbo Norway 62.12N 6.28E
20 D8 Soeda Japan 33.35N 130.51E
99 S10 Sœurs, I.des Quebec
90 K2 Soéka Chad 18.49N 20.08E
46 D1 Soela väin *str* Estonia U.S.S.R.
76 C5 Soengas Portugal 41.38N 8.12W
60 L14 Soerendonk Netherlands 51.18N 5.35E
60 K11 Soest Netherlands 52.10N 5.20E
63 H9 Soest W Germany 51.34N 8.06E
60 K11 Soestdijk Netherlands 52.11N 5.19E
63 G7 Soeste *R* W Germany
60 K11 Soesterberg Netherlands 52.07N 5.17E
84 D3 Sofadhítikos *R* Greece
Sofala *see* Beira
12 J5 Sofala New S Wales 33.00S 149.45E
34 C5 Sofar Lebanon 33.48N 35.39E
81 D1 Soffi, I Sardinia 41.04N 9.35E
Sofia *see* Sofiya
109 G5 Sofia New Mexico 36.29N 103.51W
95 D3 Sofia *R* Madagascar
84 D3 Sofiádhes Greece 39.12N 22.15E
84 F6 Sofikón Greece 37.47N 23.03E
45 P4 Sof'ino Saratov U.S.S.R. 52.11N 43.56E
45 P5 Sofino Saratov U.S.S.R. 51.42N 43.55E
82 H8 Sofiya Bulgaria 42.40N 23.18E
45 E8 Sofiyevka Dnepropetrovsk, Ukraine U.S.S.R. 48.04N 33.55E
44 C8 Sofiyevka Kherson, Ukraine U.S.S.R. 46.34N 34.04E
44 E2 Sofiyevka Stavropol' U.S.S.R. 45.42N 42.27E
40 F5 Sofiysk Khabarovsk U.S.S.R. 52.19N 133.55E
40 H6 Sofiysk Khabarovsk U.S.S.R. 51.32N 139.46E
64 H7 Söflingen W Germany 48.23N 9.57E
51 F10 Söforsa Sweden 61.45N 17.00E
47 C3 Sofporog U.S.S.R. 65.47N 31.30E
37 F8 Softek Dağları *mts* Turkey
53 E4 Søften Denmark 56.14N 10.06E
21 H13 Sōfu gan *rock* Japan 29.50N 140.22E
91 K9 Sofumwango Zaïre 11.19S 27.16E
50 D6 Sog *R* Iceland
92 J5 Soga Tanzania 6.52S 38.57E
89 K8 Sogakofe Ghana 6.01N 0.35E
119 D5 Sogamoso Colombia 5.43N 72.56W
36 F1 Soğanli *R* Turkey
37 E5 Soğanlı Dağları *mts* Turkey
32 H8 Sogār Iran 25.52N 58.06E
40 F6 Sogda U.S.S.R. 50.24N 132.14E
42 J3 Sogdiondon U.S.S.R. 57.42N 112.09E
63 G7 Sögel W Germany 52.51N 7.31E
15 H6 Sogeram *R* Papua New Guinea
15 J8 Sogeri Papua New Guinea 9.30S 147.33E
93 K1 Soghidda Ethiopia 4.15N 38.42E
93 L2 Sogile Guda Kenya/Ethiopia 3.35N 39.41E
43 L8 Soglasiya, Pik *mt* Tadzhikistan U.S.S.R. 37.16N 73.45E
79 M6 Sogliano al Rubicone Italy 44.01N 12.18E
53 T16 Sogn *reg* Norway
52 C8 Sogndal Norway 58.40N 6.45E
Sogndal Rogaland Norway*see* Hauge
53 W16 Sogndal Sogn og Fjordane Norway 61.13N 7.05E
53 W16 Sogndalen *V* Norway 61.16N 7.00E
53 W16 Sogndalsfjord *inlet* Norway 61.12N 7.02E
52 D8 Søgne Norway 58.05N 7.49E
53 S16 Sognefjorden *inlet* Norway
69 E7 Sognes France 48.21N 3.29E
53 U15 Sogn og Fjordane *co* Norway
41 N5 Sogo U.S.S.R. 71.33N 129.05E
19 M6 Sogod Philippines 10.22N 124.59E
19 M6 Sogod B Philippines
93 H2 Sogo Hills Kenya
47 K5 Sogom U.S.S.R. 60.32N 68.00E
22 E5 Sogo Nur *L* Nei Monggol Zizhiqu China
23 B2 Sogruma Qinghai China 32.32N 100.52E
37 F3 Soğukpinar Turkey 40.04N 29.07E
36 E2 Söğüt Turkey 40.02N 30.10E
37 F3 Söğütalan Turkey 40.04N 28.34E
36 D5 Söğüt Gölü *L* Turkey
36 E2 Söğütlü Turkey 40.54N 30.27E
37 C7 Söğütlü *R* Turkey
24 H10 Sog Xian Xizang Zizhiqu China 31.50N 93.44E
32 D4 Soh Iran 33.25N 51.29E
85 L6 Sohâg Egypt 26.33N 31.42E
30 E8 Sohagi Madhya Prad India 24.59N 81.41E
29 F6 Sohagpur Madhya Prad India 22.43N 78.14E
56 M3 Soham Cambs Eng 52.20N 0.20E
15 J1 Sohano Bougainville I Papua New Guinea 5.26S 154.39E
31 G4 Sohan R Pakistan
33 M4 Șohār Oman 24.23N 56.45E
31 G4 Sohawa Pakistan 33.12N 73.29E
30 D8 Sohawal Madhya Prad India 24.35N 80.46E
61 M5 Soheit-Tinlot Belgium 50.29N 5.23E
29 H7 Sohela Orissa India 21.20N 83.24E
61 L6 Sohier Belgium 50.04N 5.04E
30 A4 Sohna Haryana India 28.15N 77.04E
25 E5 Sohng Gwe, Khao *mt* Burma/Thailand 14.22N 98.33E
21 D7 Sŏho-ri N Korea 40.05N 128.22E
31 B7 Sohrag Pakistan 26.31N 62.50E
64 H1 Söhrewald W Germany 51.13N 9.35E
So-hsien *see* Sog Xian
21 C10 Sohŭksan *isld* S Korea 34.05N 125.07E
30 E6 Sohwal Uttar Prad India 26.44N 81.58E
61 H3 Soignes, Forêt de Belgium
61 G4 Soignies Belgium 50.35N 4.04E
23 A3 Soila Xizang Zizhiqu China 30.40N 97.07E
71 H1 Soing-Cubry-Charentenay France 47.35N 5.53E
70 O7 Soings-en-Sologne France 47.26N 1.31E
51 L9 Soini Finland 62.53N 24.10E
69 E5 Soissons France 49.23N 3.20E
69 C6 Soisy Essonne France 48.39N 2.27E
68 E2 Soisy Val d'Oise France 49.00N 2.18E
68 G6 Soisy-sur-Seine France 48.39N 2.28E
121 C5 Soitue Argentina 36.02S 67.55W
69 F6 Soizy-aux-Bois France 48.49N 3.44E
20 G7 Sōja Japan 34.40N 133.42E
29 C5 Sojat Rajasthan India 25.53N 73.45E
29 C5 Sojat Road Rajasthan India 25.48N 73.49E
30 B8 Sojna Uttar Prad India 24.32N 78.54E
19 L7 Sojoton Pt Philippines 9.59N 122.28E
65 P8 Sojtör Hungary 46.42N 16.55E
46 Q3 Sok *R* U.S.S.R.
20 E1 Sōka Japan 35.50N 139.49E
46 E4 Sokal' Ukraine U.S.S.R. 50.30N 24.10E
91 C4 Soke Gabon 1.23N 12.12E
36 C5 Söke Turkey 37.45N 27.26E
91 J8 Sokele Zaïre 9.54S 24.40E
Sok Gompa *see* Sog Xian
43 K7 Sokh Uzbekistan U.S.S.R. 39.59N 71.09E
43 N8 Sokh *R* Kirgiziya U.S.S.R.
40 E1 Sokholokh U.S.S.R. 60.20N 130.14E
42 J6 Sokhondo U.S.S.R. 51.52N 112.29E
42 J7 Sokhondo, Gora *mt* U.S.S.R. 49.45N 111.10E
47 L2 Sokhonto, Oz *L* U.S.S.R.
42 H6 Sokhor, Gora *mt* U.S.S.R. 51.18N 105.10E
83 F4 Sokhós Greece 40.49N 23.23E
41 K7 Sokhsolokh *R* U.S.S.R.
31 D2 Sokhta-Qala Afghanistan 36.02N 66.05E
19 B5 Sokita Celebes Indon 2.27S 121.55E
Sok Kwu Wan *see* Picnic B Hong Kong
86 E6 Soknopaios *ruins* Egypt 29.32N 30.40E
82 G7 Soko Banja Yugoslavia 43.40N 21.51E
89 K7 Sokodé Togo 8.59N 1.11E
40 M2 Sokol Magadan U.S.S.R. 59.50N 150.57E
40 J8 Sokol Sakhalin U.S.S.R. 47.14N 142.48E
46 M1 Sokol Vologda U.S.S.R. 59.28N 40.04E
62 O2 Sokółka Poland 53.26N 23.30E
46 Q2 Sokolka U.S.S.R. 55.38N 51.28E
65 P3 Sokolnice Czechoslovakia 49.07N 16.43E
62 L4 Sokolniki Poland 51.19N 18.19E
46 E6 Sokolniki *dist* Moscow U.S.S.R.
89 F4 Sokolo Mali 14.53N 6.11W
89 F6 Sokolo Mali 10.52N 6.59W
64 O3 Sokolov Czechoslovakia 50.11N 12.38E
43 J1 Sokolovka Kazakhstan U.S.S.R. 55.08N 69.10E
42 F4 Sokolovka Krasnoyarsk U.S.S.R. 56.22N 96.46E
40 F10 Sokolovka Primor'ye U.S.S.R. 42.56N 133.57E
42 C4 Sokolovka Tomsk U.S.S.R. 57.30N 83.45E
42 C5 Sokolovo Altay U.S.S.R. 52.32N 84.47E
47 H3 Sokolovo Komi U.S.S.R. 65.25N 57.00E
45 O4 Sokolovo Tambov U.S.S.R. 52.55N 42.16E
45 L9 Sokolovo-Kundryuchenskiy U.S.S.R. 47.47N 39.57E
62 N5 Sokołów Małopolski Poland 50.12N 22.07E
62 N3 Sokołów Podlaski Poland 52.25N 22.15E
47 C3 Sokolozero U.S.S.R. 66.21N 30.57E
47 C3 Sokolozero, Oz *L* U.S.S.R.
46 N2 Sokol'skoye U.S.S.R. 57.05N 43.10E
62 O3 Sokoły Poland 53.00N 22.42E
97 R4 Søkongens Ø *isld* Greenland 68.15N 29.59W
20 Q8 Sokoniya Okinawa Japan 26.34N 128.08E
87 G4 Sokota Ethiopia 12.40N 39.02E
90 B5 Sokoto Nigeria 13.02N 5.15E
90 B5 Sokoto *R* Nigeria
42 K6 Soktuy-Milozan U.S.S.R. 50.03N 117.55E
23 B8 So Kun Tan Hong Kong 22.21N 114.06E
45 R5 Sokur U.S.S.R. 51.59N 45.45E
90 E5 Sokwa Nigeria 12.09N 10.20E
90 B5 Sokwoi Nigeria 13.30N 4.55E
43 D4 Sokyrbulak Kazakhstan U.S.S.R. 46.57N 57.07E
85 L5 Sôl Egypt 29.22N 31.15E
116 F4 Sola Cuba 21.40N 77.40W
52 B8 Sola Norway 58.53N 5.36E
91 K6 Sola Zaïre 5.08S 27.06E
115 L9 Sola de Vega, San Miguel Mexico 16.31N 96.58W
79 L3 Solagna Italy 45.49N 11.44E
93 H5 Solai Kenya 0.03N 36.09E
77 C3 Solana de los Barros Spain 38.44N 6.33W
77 H4 Solana del Pino Spain 38.28N 4.04W
77 K3 Solana, La Spain 38.56N 3.14W
11 A13 Solander I New Zealand 46.37S 166.53E
81 M3 Solandrella *R* Italy
121 F6 Solanet Argentina 36.52S 58.31W
19 K3 Solano Luzon Philippines 16.31N 121.10E
109 F6 Solano New Mexico 35.51N 104.04W
119 F7 Solano Venezuela 2.00N 66.58W
121 L5 Solano, B Argentina
81 E7 Solanto, Pta.di *pt* Sicily 38.11N 12.46E
75 C1 Solares Spain 43.23N 3.43W
121 F2 Solari Argentina 29.23S 58.13W
81 K9 Solarino Sicily 37.07N 15.08E
67 P13 Solaro Corsica 41.54N 9.20E
80 K7 Solaro, Monte Italy 40.33N 14.13E
81 B4 Solarussa Sardinia 39.53N 8.40E
65 E7 Solbad Hall Austria 47.17N 11.31E
52 K3 Solberg Sweden 63.48N 17.40E
51 F2 Solbergfjord *inlet* Norway 69.05N 17.20E
52 F7 Solbergfoss Norway 59.37N 11.10E
53 E3 Solbjerg Nordjylland Denmark 56.49N 10.10E
53 B3 Solbjerg Viborg Denmark 56.52N 8.43E
53 E4 Solbjerg Sø *L* Denmark 56.03N 10.03E
88 G9 Solb Taiaret *reg* Morocco
82 K3 Solca Romania 47.40N 25.50E
119 C9 Soldado Bartra Peru 2.34S 75.47W
119 B9 Soldados, Cerro *mt* Ecuador 2.56S 79.13W
44 F3 Soldato Aleksandrovskoye U.S.S.R. 44.16N 43.45E
39 H3 Soldatovo U.S.S.R. 64.41N 169.49E
44 F4 Soldatskaya U.S.S.R. 43.51N 43.50E
45 U2 Soldatskaya Tashla U.S.S.R. 54.00N 48.13E
45 R7 Soldatsko-Stepnoye U.S.S.R. 49.31N 45.31E
65 C8 Sölden Austria 46.58N 11.00E
75 O2 Soldeu Andorra 42.34N 1.39E
108 P8 Soldier Iowa 41.59N 95.46W
109 P2 Soldier Kansas 39.30N 95.59W
104 B8 Soldier Kentucky 38.16N 83.19W
108 P8 Soldier *R* Iowa
105 B11 Soldier Key *isld* Florida 25.36N 80.07W
111 N2 Soldier Summit Utah 39.55N 111.07W
113 M6 Soldotna Alaska 60.29N 151.04W
62 L2 Solec Kujawski Poland 53.04N 18.10E
121 E3 Soledad Argentina 30.38S 60.52W
111 C5 Soledad California 36.25N 121.20W
119 D2 Soledad Colombia 10.54N 74.48W
119 G3 Soledad Venezuela 8.10N 63.36W
115 L8 Soledad de Doblado Mexico 19.02N 96.25W
120 D2 Soledade Amazonas Brazil 6.36S 69.07W
117 H8 Soledade Paraíba Brazil 7.01S 36.17W
121 H2 Soledade Rio Grande do Sul Brazil 29.03S 52.35W
110 A1 Soleduck *R* Washington
66 D3 Soleil, Mt Switzerland 47.10N 6.59E
81 C5 Soleminis Sardinia 39.21N 9.12E
52 F5 Sølen *mt* Norway 61.53N 11.33E
41 D6 Solenaya *R* U.S.S.R.
41 D6 Solenayo *R* U.S.S.R.
44 E1 Solenoye Kalmyk A.S.S.R. U.S.S.R. 46.20N 42.32E
45 F8 Solenoye Ukraine U.S.S.R. 48.12N 34.53E
47 M8 Solenoye, Oz *L* Novosibirsk U.S.S.R.
44 D2 Solenoye, Oz *L* Stavropol' U.S.S.R.
44 C9 Solenoye Oz *L* Ukraine U.S.S.R.
45 S9 Solenoye Zaymishche U.S.S.R. 47.55N 46.07E
115 M4 Solentiname, Is.de Nicaragua
56 J6 Solent, The *channel* Hants Eng
45 M9 Solenyy U.S.S.R. 47.15N 40.48E
67 P13 Solenzara Corsica 41.51N 9.24E
54 L9 Sole Pit North Sea
77 K5 Solera Spain 37.41N 3.22W
79 E5 Solero Italy 44.55N 8.30E
79 L4 Solesino Italy 45.10N 11.45E
69 F3 Solesmes Nord France 50.11N 3.30E
70 K6 Solesmes Sarthe France 47.51N 0.18W
79 J2 Sole, Val di *V* Italy
50 G5 Sóleyjarhöfdhi *mt* Iceland 64.31N 18.47W
51 J8 Solf Finland 63.01N 21.40E
72 C7 Solférino France 44.09N 0.54W
79 J4 Solferino Italy 45.22N 10.34E
53 V18 Solfonn *glacier* Norway 60.02N 6.57E
47 E5 Solginskiy U.S.S.R. 61.07N 41.30E
42 E4 Solgonskiy Kryazh *ridge* U.S.S.R.
37 F7 Solhan Turkey 38.58N 40.03E
53 S17 Solheim Norway 60.53N 5.28E
50 F7 Sólheimajökull *ice cap* Iceland 63.35N 19.18W
50 F8 Sólheimar Iceland 63.30N 19.19W
50 F8 Sólheimasandur Jökulsá-a *R* Iceland
53 Y18 Solheimsstul Norway 60.18N 8.20E
53 V19 Solheimsvik Norway 59.32N 6.37E
84 Q14 Soli *ruins* Cyprus 35.08N 32.48E
46 M1 Soligalich U.S.S.R. 59.02N 42.15E
72 G4 Solignac Haute-Vienne France 45.45N 1.16E
71 D7 Solignac-sur-Loire Haute-Loire France 44.58N 3.53E
79 G5 Solignano Italy 44.38N 9.59E
70 M4 Soligny-la-Trappe France 48.37N 0.32E
46 G3 Soligorsk Belorussiya U.S.S.R. 52.50N 27.32E
56 H3 Solihull W Midlands Eng 52.25N 1.45W
47 H6 Solikamsk U.S.S.R. 59.40N 56.45E
95 C6 Solila Madagascar 21.24S 46.36E
43 C2 Sol'-Iletsk U.S.S.R. 51.09N 55.00E
78 C12 Soliman Tunisia 36.41N 10.30E
115 Q8 Solimán, Pta Mexico 19.50N 87.27W
119 F9 Solimões, R Brazil
80 P1 Solin Yugoslavia 43.33N 16.30E
64 C1 Solingen W Germany 51.10N 7.05E
115 J8 Solis Mexico 19.58N 100.01W
119 E3 Solita Venezuela 9.12N 71.46W
26 P16 Solitaire, Î Kerguelen Ind Oc 50.00S 68.35E
75 N5 Solivella Spain 41.27N 1.10E
79 P3 Solkan Yugoslavia 45.58N 13.39E
65 K7 Sölker Tauern *mts* Austria
65 F6 Söll Austria 47.31N 12.12E
67 O13 Sollacaro Corsica 41.44N 8.54E
77 Q2 Sollana Spain 39.17N 0.23W
77 W14 s'Olla, Pta, de Balearic Is 39.43N 3.28E
58 B3 Sollas N Uist, W Isles Scotland 57.39N 7.22W
52 K3 Sollefteå Sweden 63.09N 17.15E
65 O6 Sollenau Austria 47.54N 16.16E
52 K7 Sollentuna Sweden 59.26N 17.56E
77 V14 Sóller Balearic Is 39.46N 2.42E
53 K5 Søllerød Denmark 55.48N 12.30E
53 G7 Søllested Denmark 54.49N 11.17E
52 E5 Sollia Norway 61.47N 10.24E
63 R9 Söllichau E Germany 51.38N 12.38E
71 J10 Solliès-Pont France 43.11N 6.02E
63 K9 Solling *mts* W Germany
63 N8 Söllingen W Germany 52.06N 10.55E
64 E3 Solms W Germany 50.32N 8.25E
52 K7 Solna Sweden 59.22N 17.59E
45 H1 Solnechnogorsk U.S.S.R. 56.10N 37.00E
40 G6 Solnechnyy U.S.S.R. 50.35N 136.36E
64 L6 Solnhofen W Germany 48.54N 11.00E
52 E5 Sølnkletten *mt* Norway 61.55N 10.18E
44 B3 Solntsedar U.S.S.R. 44.34N 38.02E
Solo *see* Surakarta
18 J9 Solo *R* Java Indon
18 K9 Solo *R* Kalimantan Indonesia
82 K1 Solobkovtsy U.S.S.R. 49.04N 26.57E
45 Q7 Solodcha U.S.S.R. 49.40N 44.18E
45 R8 Solodniki U.S.S.R. 48.24N 45.17E
80 L7 Solofra Italy 40.49N 14.51E
70 N7 Sologne *reg* France
19 D3 Solok Celebes Indon 0.48N 124.05E
18 D6 Solok Sumatra Indon 0.45S 100.42E
115 O10 Sololá Guatemala 14.46N 91.09W
93 K2 Sololo Kenya 3.34N 38.39E
47 C5 Solomennoye U.S.S.R. 61.55N 34.19E
44 F3 Solomenskoye U.S.S.R. 44.13N 44.19E
72 F8 Solomiac France 43.49N 0.54E
113 E4 Solomon Alaska 64.33N 164.29W
111 P9 Solomon Arizona 32.49N 109.37W
109 N3 Solomon Kansas 38.55N 97.24W
109 M2 Solomon *R* Kansas
9 N9 Solomon Is Pacific Oc
122 F9 Solomon Is.Ridge Pacific Oc
10 L3 Solomons Basin Solomon Sea
15 K7 Solomon Sea Pacific Oc
35 D7 Solomon's Pools *anc site* Jordan 31.41N 35.10E
30 A2 Solon Himachal Prad India 30.54N 77.06E
106 C8 Solon Iowa 41.48N 91.30W
21 B4 Solon Nei Monggol Zizhiqu China 46.36N 121.17E
104 D5 Solon Ohio 41.24N 81.27W
42 C6 Soloneshnoye U.S.S.R. 51.46N 84.12E
43 L2 Solonichki Kazakhstan U.S.S.R. 50.04N 73.15E
117 H7 Solonópole Brazil 5.43S 39.00W
106 C3 Solon Springs Wisconsin 46.22N 91.48W
42 K5 Solontsovo U.S.S.R. 54.28N 115.35E
80 L6 Solopaca Italy 41.12N 14.33E
19 C8 Solor *isld* Indonesia 8.30S 123.01E
52 F6 Sølor *reg* Norway
75 F5 Solorio, Sierra del *mts* Spain
19 C8 Solor, Kep *islds* Indonesia
75 C1 Solórzano Spain 43.23N 3.35W
76 K7 Solosancho Spain 40.33N 4.55W
45 L2 Solotcha U.S.S.R. 54.49N 39.51E
66 G3 Solothurn Switzerland 47.13N 7.32E
66 G2 Solothurn *canton* Switzerland
43 H5 Solotobe Kazakhstan U.S.S.R. 44.36N 66.00E
47 D3 Solovetskiye Ostrova *islds* U.S.S.R.
40 C4 Solov'yevsk Amur U.S.S.R. 54.15N 124.28E
42 K7 Solov'yevsk Chita U.S.S.R. 49.55N 115.45E
45 M3 Solovyye U.S.S.R. 53.21N 40.06E
66 O4 Sol, Piz *mt* Switzerland 46.58N 9.23E
96 R12 Sol, Pta del *pt* Fuerteventura Canary Is 28.04N 14.35W
69 G3 Solre-le-Château France 50.11N 4.05E
53 U16 Solrenningshutte Norway 61.00N 6.08E
61 G6 Solre-St.Géry Belgium 50.13N 4.15E
61 G5 Solre-sur-Sambre Belgium 50.18N 4.10E
53 J5 Solrød Strand Denmark 55.33N 12.12E
41 O2 Solsberi, Ostrov *isld* Franz Josef Land U.S.S.R.
75 O4 Solsona Spain 42.00N 1.31E
Solstad *see* Holm
53 B6 Sølsted Denmark 55.01N 8.52E
65 D7 Solstein *mt* Austria 47.18N 11.20E
53 T18 Solstrand Norway 60.11N 5.31E
53 R18 Șolsvik Norway 60.27N 4.58E
82 C7 Șolta *isld* Yugoslavia
32 G6 Sōlṭānābād Kermān Iran 28.22N 56.15E
32 H2 Soltānābād Khorāsān Iran 36.25N 58.02E
32 H3 Solṭānābād Khorāsān Iran 34.13N 59.58E

32 H3 Solţānābād Khorāsān Iran 35.54N 59.17E
32 C5 Solţānābād Khuzestān Iran 30.57N 49.48E
32 D3 Solţānābād Tehrān Iran 35.30N 51.08E
44 G10 Soltān Dāgh mt Iran 37.46N 46.20E
31 B4 Soltān-e Bakvā Afghanistan 32.14N 62.56E
32 D6 Soltāni, Khowr-e B Iran
32 C2 Solţāniyeh Iran 36.24N 48.50E
44 G9 Solţān Jahangir, Kūh-e mt Iran 38.37N 46.04E
32 H2 Solţān Meydān Iran 36.46N 58.24E
32 B4 Solţanqoli Iran 33.51N 46.26E
63 L7 Soltau W Germany 52.59N 9.50E
42 D5 Solton U.S.S.R. 52.52N 86.31E
46 H1 Sol'tsy U.S.S.R. 58.12N 30.30E
Soluch see Sulūq
53 R16 Solund Norway 61.05N 4.50E
82 G9 Solunska mt Yugoslavia 41.44N 21.31E
81 G7 Solunto ruin Sicily 38.06N 13.32E
56 A4 Solva Dyfed Wales 51.54N 5.12W
50 G4 Sölvadalur V Iceland
111 D7 Solvang California 34.36N 120.09W
104 J3 Solvay New York 43.03N 76.15W
76 D5 Solveira Portugal 41.50N 7.40W
52 H10 Sölvesborg Sweden 56.04N 14.35E
53 W16 Solvorn Norway 61.18N 7.15E
82 J2 Solvotvin U.S.S.R. 48.42N 24.24E
47 F5 Sol'vychegodsk U.S.S.R. 61.21N 46.49E
57 F3 Solway Firth Scot/Eng
92 C8 Solwezi Zambia 12.11S 26.23E
42 F4 Solyanka Krasnoyarsk U.S.S.R. 56.01N 95.15E
42 L2 Solyanka Yakutsk U.S.S.R. 60.28N 120.42E
96 T9 Solyplayas Fuerteventura Canary Is 28.42N 13.51W
Som see Sawm, As
20 O4 Sōma Japan 37.48N 140.56E
36 C3 Soma Turkey 39.10N 27.36E
92 D11 Somabula Zimbabwe 19.41S 29.41E
21 D12 Somachi Japan 28.20N 130.00E
66 O6 Somággia Italy 46.16N 9.26E
69 E3 Somain France 50.21N 3.18E
73 J5 Somalia rep East Africa
26 D5 Somali Basin Indian Oc
Somaliland see Somalia
Somali Republic see Somalia
93 F8 Somanda Tanzania 2.46S 34.01E
86 K6 Somâr, Gebel ra Egypt
86 J6 Somâr, Wâdi watercourse Egypt
66 B4 Sombacourt France 46.57N 6.16E
71 F2 Sombernon France 47.18N 4.42E
91 G8 Sombo Angola 8.42S 20.59E
87 F7 Sombo Ethiopia 7.31N 36.37E
82 E5 Sombor Yugoslavia 45.46N 19.09E
99 H10 Sombra Ontario 42.42N 82.28W
61 J4 Sombreffe Belgium 50.32N 4.36E
90 C9 Sombreiro R Nigeria
115 H6 Sombrerete Mexico 23.38N 103.40W
121 K9 Sombrero Chile 52.50S 69.23W
116 N5 Sombrero I Leeward Is W I 18.37N 63.26W
28 H7 Sombrero Chan Nicobar Is
105 F13 Sombrero Key isld Florida 24.38N 81.07W
121 J2 Sombrio, L.do Brazil
82 H3 Şomcuţa Mare Romania 47.29N 23.30E
91 K6 Somene Zaïre 5.50S 26.52E
66 L6 Someo Switzerland 46.18N 8.40E
103 D7 Somerdale New Jersey 39.52N 75.02W
60 L14 Someren Netherlands 51.23N 5.42E
60 L14 Someren-Eind Netherlands 51.22N 5.45E
51 K11 Somero Finland 60.37N 23.30E
103 K3 Somers Connecticut 41.58N 72.26W
108 Q7 Somers Iowa 42.22N 94.22W
110 L1 Somers Montana 48.07N 114.15W
103 G4 Somers New York 41.20N 73.41W
106 G7 Somers Wisconsin 42.40N 87.55W
96 A2 Somerset Bermuda 32.18N 64.53W
109 C3 Somerset Colorado 38.55N 107.28W
107 M4 Somerset Kentucky 37.05N 84.38W
100 T9 Somerset Manitoba 49.26N 98.39W
103 M3 Somerset Massachusetts 41.47N 71.08W
104 F6 Somerset Pennsylvania 40.02N 79.05W
13 G1 Somerset Queensland 10.45S 142.35E
12 H8 Somerset Tasmania 41.00S 145.48E
112 J6 Somerset Texas 29.13N 98.40W
56 E5 Somerset co England
103 E5 Somerset co New Jersey
95 J8 Somerset East S Africa 32.44S 25.35E
96 A2 Somerset I Bermuda
97 K3 Somerset I N W Terr 73.30N 93.00W
13 L7 Somerset Res Queensland
104 N3 Somerset Res Vermont
95 B10 Somerset West S Africa 34.05S 18.51E
56 M3 Somersham Cambs Eng 52.23N 0.01E
103 E8 Somers Point New Jersey 39.18N 74.36W
104 P3 Somersworth New Hampshire 43.15N 70.52W
111 K9 Somerton Arizona 32.35N 114.44W
56 F5 Somerton Somerset Eng 51.03N 2.44W
103 M2 Somerville Massachusetts 42.24N 71.07W
103 E5 Somerville New Jersey 40.34N 74.36W
107 G6 Somerville Tennessee 35.14N 89.24W
112 L5 Somerville Texas 30.22N 96.33W
104 P9 Somerville dist Boston, Mass
112 L5 Somerville Res Texas
110 B8 Somesbar California 41.23N 123.30W
11 D5 Somes I New Zealand 41.15S 174.50E
11 J11 Somes Pt Chatham Is Pacific Oc 43.49S 176.51W
82 H3 Someşul R Romania
82 H4 Someşul Cald R Romania
82 J3 Someşul Mare R Romania
28 H3 Someswari R India/Bangladesh
76 H1 Somió Spain 43.32N 5.36W
80 G3 Somma Italy 42.40N 12.44E
79 J4 Sommacampagna Italy 45.24N 10.51E
79 E3 Somma Lombardo Italy 45.41N 8.42E
13 H7 Sommariva Queensland 26.25S 146.35E
79 C5 Sommariva del Bosco Italy 44.46N 7.47E
81 G9 Sommatino Sicily 37.20N 14.00E
69 H5 Sommauthe France 49.29N 4.58E
80 K7 Somma Vesuviana Italy 40.52N 14.26E
67 G3 Somme dept France
69 B3 Somme R France
69 G6 Somme R Marne France
69 J5 Sommedieue France 49.05N 5.27E
61 M5 Somme-Leuze Belgium 50.20N 5.22E
60 E12 Sommelsdijk Netherlands 51.45N 4.09E
52 H8 Sommen Sweden 58.08N 14.59E
52 J8 Sommen L Sweden 58.05N 15.15E
69 H5 Sommepy-Tahure France 49.15N 4.33E
64 L1 Sömmerda E Germany 51.10N 11.07E
53 C6 Sommersted Denmark 55.18N 9.19E
69 G6 Sommesous France 48.45N 4.12E
69 H5 Somme-Suippe France 49.07N 4.37E
61 M8 Sommethonne Belgium 49.35N 5.27E
69 H5 Somme-Tourbe France 49.06N 4.40E
69 H7 Sommevoire France 48.25N 4.51E
61 K5 Sommière Belgium 50.17N 4.51E
71 E9 Sommières France 43.47N 4.05E
72 E3 Sommieres du-Clain France 46.17N 0.22E
25 H2 Som Mong Vietnam 21.12N 104.20E
30 A4 Somna Uttar Prad India 28.02N 77.56E
29 B7 Somnath Gujarat India 20.50N 70.31E
39 H4 Somneniya, Bukhta B U.S.S.R.
41 C2 Somneniy, Poluostrov pen Novaya Zemlya U.S.S.R. 75.35N 63.40E
40 H5 Somnitel'nyy U.S.S.R. 52.13N 139.07E
82 D4 Somogy co Hungary
62 K9 Somogyszob Hungary 46.19N 17.20E
62 K9 Somogyvár Hungary 46.34N 17.40E
106 F8 Somonauk Illinois 41.37N 88.42W
75 J3 Somontano reg Spain
77 M6 Somontin Spain 37.24N 2.23W
75 C5 Somosierra Spain 41.08N 3.35W
75 C5 Somosierra, Sierra de mts Spain
9 T5 Somosomo Taveuni Fiji 16.48S 179.59W
9 T5 Somosomo Str Vanua Levu Fiji
115 L3 Somotillo Nicaragua 13.01N 86.53W
115 L3 Somoto Nicaragua 13.29N 86.36W
45 F4 Somovo Orël U.S.S.R. 52.51N 35.00E
45 H3 Somovo Tula U.S.S.R. 53.53N 36.30E
76 D1 Somozas Spain 43.32N 7.56W
29 J8 Sompeta Andhra Prad India 18.58N 84.39E
62 L3 Sompolno Poland 52.22N 18.30E
72 C10 Somport pass France/Spain 42.48N 0.31W
56 L6 Sompting W Sussex Eng 50.50N 0.21W
69 G6 Sompuis France 48.42N 4.23E
121 C8 Somuncurá, Mesa Volcánica de mts Argentina
41 R5 Somuttakh-Uolbut, Oz L U.S.S.R. 71.13N 146.00E
25 N7 Somutu Burma 27.20N 98.41E
28 B4 Somvarpet Karnataka India 12.38N 75.46E
66 M5 Somvix Switzerland 46.43N 8.55E
66 M5 Somvixer Tal V Switzerland
61 H5 Somzée Belgium 50.18N 4.29E
60 K13 Son Netherlands 51.30N 5.30E
52 F7 Son Norway 59.32N 10.42E
76 B3 Son Spain 42.43N 9.00W
30 H8 Son R Bihar etc India
115 O5 Soná Panama 8.00N 81.20W
91 D6 Sona Bata Zaïre 4.53S 15.13E
30 B7 Sonagir Madhya Prad India 25.44N 78.25E
115 L2 Sonaguera Honduras 15.38N 86.18W
29 J6 Sonahatu Bihar India 23.11N 85.48E
30 L7 Sonahula Bihar India 25.05N 87.10E
30 L7 Sonaili Bazar Bihar India 25.37N 87.43E
28 J2 Sonai R Assam India
30 A7 Sonaj Madhya Prad India 25.15N 77.49E
40 G6 Sonakh U.S.S.R. 51.28N 135.07E
29 H7 Sonakhan Madhya Prad India 21.34N 82.35E
29 E7 Sonala Maharashtra India 20.52N 77.01E
43 K3 Sonaly Kazakhstan U.S.S.R. 49.39N 70.29E
29 L2 Sonamukhi W Bengal India 23.18N 87.25E
28 H4 Sonamura Tripura India 23.29N 91.14E
28 K2 Sonari Assam India 27.00N 95.04E
30 D4 Sonaripur Uttar Prad India 28.26N 80.43E
29 F5 Sonar R Madhya Prad India
30 K7 Sonbarsa Raj Bihar India 25.42N 86.43E
77 V14 Son Bonet Balearic Is 39.36N 2.42E
66 E3 Sonceboz Switzerland 47.12N 7.12E
69 B6 Sonchamp France 48.35N 1.53E
21 C8 Sŏnch'ŏn N Korea 39.43N 124.57E
21 D10 Sŏnch'ŏn-ni S Korea 35.42N 127.14E
75 C2 Soncillo Spain 42.58N 3.48W
79 G4 Soncino Italy 45.24N 9.52E
95 J9 Sondags R S Africa
79 H2 Sondalo Italy 46.20N 10.19E
47 C4 Sondaly U.S.S.R. 63.20N 33.00E
53 B3 Søndbjerg Denmark 56.38N 8.35E
60 L8 Sondel Netherlands 52.52N 5.36E
95 N3 Sonder S Africa 27.18S 29.05E
53 C7 Sønderå R Denmark
53 D4 Sønderbæk Denmark 56.30N 9.52E
53 G6 Sønder Bjerge Vestjælland Denmark 55.17N 11.26E
53 D5 Sønder Bjerre Vejle Denmark 55.47N 9.52E
53 D6 Sønder Bjert Denmark 55.27N 9.34E
53 D7 Sønderborg Denmark 54.55N 9.48E
53 A5 Sønder Bork Denmark 55.49N 8.18E
53 E6 Sønder Broby Denmark 55.14N 10.17E
53 J6 Sønder Dalby Denmark 55.19N 12.05E
53 B3 Sønder Dråby Denmark 56.53N 8.51E
53 B5 Sønder Felding Denmark 55.57N 8.47E
53 D7 Sønderhav Denmark 54.52N 9.30E
53 A5 Sønder Havrvig Denmark 55.56N 8.10E
53 A6 Sønderho Denmark 55.21N 8.28E
53 E6 Sønder Højrup Denmark 55.17N 10.28E
53 D2 Sønderholm Denmark 57.01N 9.45E
53 C7 Sønder Hostrup Denmark 54.59N 9.28E
53 B6 Sønder Hygum Denmark 55.22N 8.59E
53 B6 Sønderjylland co Denmark
53 E3 Sønder Kongerslev Denmark 56.53N 10.08E
53 A4 Sønder Lem Denmark 56.04N 8.25E
53 A4 Sønder Nissum Denmark 56.19N 8.12E
53 B5 Sønder Omme Denmark 55.51N 8.54E
53 D3 Sønder Onsild Denmark 56.35N 9.47E
53 C4 Sønder Rind Denmark 56.24N 9.29E
63 N10 Sondershausen E Germany 51.23N 10.52E
53 E6 Søndersø Denmark 55.29N 10.16E
53 D6 Sønder Stenderup Denmark 55.28N 9.38E
53 D2 Sønder Tranders Denmark 57.01N 9.59E
53 D3 Sønderup Denmark 56.49N 9.40E
53 A4 Søndervig Denmark 56.08N 8.07E
53 D6 Sønder Vilstrup Denmark 55.12N 9.32E
53 A5 Sønder Vium Denmark 55.50N 8.26E
107 E9 Sondheimer Louisiana 32.32N 91.10W
75 E1 Sondica airport Spain 43.17N 2.52W
53 Y14 Söndre Grøna R Norway 62.07N 8.15E
53 U18 Söndre Hamlagrø Norway 60.30N 6.07E
48 R11 Söndre Isortoq fjord Greenland
53 Y18 Söndre Skarvevatn L Norway 60.18N 8.11E
Sondrestrom Air Base see Søndre Strømfjord
48 S10 Søndre Strømfjord Greenland 67.05N 50.30W
48 S6 Søndre Upernavik Greenland 72.05N 55.30W
79 G2 Sondrio Italy 46.11N 9.52E
79 G2 Sondrio prov Italy
92 G10 Sone Mozambique 17.20S 34.55E
75 K8 Soneja Spain 39.49N 0.26W
71 G6 Sône, la France 45.07N 5.17E
28 C1 Sonepet Maharashtra India 19.03N 76.31E
29 H7 Sonepur Orissa India 20.50N 83.58E
Soneri see Sonari
103 A4 Sonestown Pennsylvania 41.22N 76.34W
90 F7 Song Nigeria 9.49N 12.39E
18 K4 Song Sarawak Malaysia 2.01N 112.32E
30 B2 Song R Uttar Prad India
91 D6 Songa Zaïre 5.49S 14.22E
53 W19 Songa R Norway
21 F5 Song'acha He R Heilongjiang China
29 B7 Songad Gujarat India 21.42N 71.58E
92 J6 Songa Manara I Tanzania 9.05S 39.34E
53 X19 Songavatn L Norway 59.51N 7.34E
25 K6 Song Ba R Vietnam
23 F5 Songbai Hunan China 26.38N 112.33E
25 J1 Song Bang Giang R Vietnam
25 J7 Song Be R Vietnam
Song Bo R see Noire R N Vietnam
25 H2 Song Boi R Vietnam
23 G3 Songbu Hubei China 31.07N 114.51E
21 K1 Sŏngbuk-ku dist Seoul S Korea
25 H3 Song Ca R Vietnam
25 K6 Song Cai R Vietnam
25 K6 Song Cau Vietnam 13.26N 109.12E
25 H2 Song Chay R Vietnam
21 D8 Sŏngchŏn N Korea 39.12N 126.15E
25 J8 Song Co Chien R Vietnam
25 H3 Song Con R Vietnam
25 H8 Song Cua Lon R Vietnam
21 K1 Songdong-gu dist Seoul S Korea
52 E8 Songe Norway 58.41N 9.02E
92 G7 Songea Tanzania 10.42S 35.39E
69 B4 Songeons France 49.33N 1.51E
53 U20 Songesand Norway 59.01N 6.20E
25 H1 Song Gam R Vietnam
25 J4 Song Giang R Vietnam
23 B5 Songgui Yunnan China 26.22N 100.17E
25 K5 Song Ha Giao R Vietnam
25 H7 Song Hau Giang R Vietnam
21 D6 Songhua Hu res Jilin China
21 D5 Songhua Jiang R Heilongjiang China
21 E4 Songhua Jiang R Heilongjiang China
Songjiachuan see Wubu
Songjiang see Antu
23 J3 Songjiang Shanghai China 13.00N 121.13E
23 D4 Songkan Guizhou China 28.33N 106.50E
25 F9 Songkhla Thailand 7.12N 100.35E
25 G4 Song Khram, Mae Nam R Thailand
23 C7 Song koi R Vietnam
23 G6 Songkou Guangdong China 24.28N 116.24E
25 J2 Song Ky Cung R Vietnam
21 B3 Songling Nei Monggol Zizhiqu China 48.00N 121.05E
22 M6 Song Ling mts Liaoning China
25 E1 Songlong Burma 22.41N 98.53E
25 K7 Song Luy R Vietnam
25 F2 Song Ma R Vietnam
25 H2 Song Ma R Vietnam
23 C6 Songming Yunnan China 25.23N 102.59E
25 H7 Song Moy R Vietnam
25 J7 Song Nha Be R Vietnam
91 D7 Songo Angola 7.30S 14.56E
92 F9 Songo Mozambique 15.36S 32.45E
89 C7 Songo Sierra Leone 8.27N 12.53W
89 K5 Songoï tribe Niger
91 D6 Songololo Zaïre 5.40S 14.05E
25 H8 Song Ong Doc R Vietnam
90 M9 Songopai Cent Afr Rep 5.54N 24.15E
92 J6 Songo Songo I Tanzania 8.31S 39.30E
93 F2 Songot mt Kenya 3.59N 34.30E
23 C2 Songpan Sichuan China 32.40N 103.30E
28 H3 Songsak Meghalaya India 25.40N 90.40E
23 E4 Songtao Miaozu Zizhixian Guizhou China 28.09N 109.10E
25 K5 Song Tra Khuc R Vietnam
21 D11 Sŏngŭm-ni S Korea 83.25N 127.00E
37 G3 Songurpaşa Turkey 40.12N 29.29E
25 H7 Song Vam Co Dong R Vietnam
25 H7 Song Vam Co Tay R Vietnam
25 K5 Song Ve R Vietnam
92 F6 Songwe Malawi 9.43S 33.55E
92 F6 Songwe R Tanzania
23 H5 Songxi Fujian China 27.37N 118.42E
23 H5 Song Xi R Fujian China
23 F1 Song Xian Henan China 34.01N 112.02E
21 C4 Song Zhan Heilongjiang China 46.13N 125.40E
23 F3 Songzi Hubei China 30.08N 111.50E
25 K5 Son Ha Vietnam 15.03N 108.33E
25 K7 Son Hai Vietnam 11.25N 109.01E
29 H6 Sonhat Madhya Prad India 23.28N 82.35E
25 K6 Son Hoa Vietnam 13.03N 108.59E
92 J4 Soni Tanzania 4.54S 38.20E
79 H2 Sónico Italy 46.10N 10.22E
22 J5 Sonid Youqi Nei Monggol Zizhiqu China 43.58N 113.59E
22 J5 Sonid Zuoqi Nei Monggol Zizhiqu China 42.30N 113.00E
30 A4 Sonipat Haryana India 29.00N 77.01E
93 G8 Sonja Tanzania 2.15S 35.54E
21 E7 Sŏnjin N Korea 40.50N 129.05E
29 E6 Sonkach Madhya Prad India 23.00N 76.24E
51 N8 Sonkajärvi Finland 63.40N 27.30E
43 L6 Sonkel, Oz L Kirgiziya U.S.S.R.
30 A5 Sonkh Uttar Prad India 27.24N 77.30E
25 G2 Son La Vietnam 21.20N 103.55E
66 L6 Sonlerto Switzerland 46.23N 8.33E
31 D8 Sonmiani Pakistan 25.25N 66.40E
31 D8 Sonmiani B Pakistan
72 D4 Sonnac France 45.51N 0.17W
53 V14 Sønnavinds Nipa mt Norway 62.19N 6.31E
65 G7 Sonnblick mt Austria 47.03N 12.57E
65 H7 Sonnblick, Gross mt Austria 47.04N 13.26E
64 L3 Sonneberg E Germany 50.22N 11.10E
64 L3 Sonnefeld W Germany 50.13N 11.08E
66 K3 Sonnenberg Switzerland 47.03N 8.18E
79 D2 Sonnenhorn mt Italy/Switz 46.18N 8.25E
64 P6 Sonnen-Wald mts W Germany
108 E4 Sonnette Montana 45.22N 105.51W
63 T9 Sonnewalde E Germany 51.42N 13.39E
56 K5 Sonning Berks Eng 51.29N 0.55W
100 K6 Sonningdale Saskatchewan 52.23N 107.40W
80 B2 Sonninno Italy 43.26N 10.21E
80 H6 Sonnino Italy 41.25N 13.15E
66 Q3 Sonntag Austria 47.14N 9.54E
65 E7 Sonnwend Gebrige mts Austria
89 H5 Sono Upper Volta 12.53N 3.30W
20 J6 Sonobe Japan 35.09N 135.25E
66 M6 Sonogno Switzerland 46.22N 8.47E
115 C2 Sonoita Ariz/Mexico 31.53N 112.52W
111 O10 Sonoita Arizona 31.40N 110.40W
111 L10 Sonoita R Mexico
111 B3 Sonoma California 38.17N 122.28W
110 H9 Sonoma Pk Nevada 40.53N 117.36W
110 H9 Sonoma Ra Nevada
95 L1 Sonop S Africa 25.40S 27.42E
118 F2 Sono, R Goiás Brazil
118 F5 Sono, R Minas Gerais Brazil
111 N8 Sonora Arizona 33.10N 111.00W
111 D4 Sonora California 38.00N 120.21W
98 L8 Sonora Nova Scotia 45.03N 61.52W
112 G5 Sonora Texas 30.34N 100.39W
115 D3 Sonora R Mexico
115 D3 Sonora state Mexico
102 D4 Sonoran Desert Calif/Arizona
111 E3 Sonora Pk mt California 38.20N 119.39W
30 J7 Sonpur Bihar India 25.42N 85.11E
30 E5 Sonpur Uttar Prad India 27.55N 81.43E
32 B3 Sonqor Iran 34.45N 47.39E
77 V14 Son San Juan airport Balearic Is 39.33N 2.43E
63 D9 Sonsbeck W Germany 51.36N 6.22E
75 C8 Sonseca con Casalgordo Spain 39.40N 3.59W
77 W14 Son Serra Balearic Is 39.43N 3.13E
77 W14 Son Servera Balearic Is 39.37N 3.20E
42 E5 Sonskiy U.S.S.R. 54.13N 90.11E
95 K6 Sonskyn S Africa 30.47S 26.28E
119 C5 Sonsón Colombia 5.45N 75.18W
115 P11 Sonsonate El Salvador 13.43N 89.44W
17 M10 Sonsorol islds Caroline Is Pacific Oc 5.20N 132.13E
95 F3 Sonstraal S Africa 27.07S 22.29E
25 H2 Son Tay Vietnam 21.06N 105.32E
30 L6 Sonthe Bihar India 26.10N 87.46E
64 J6 Sontheim Baden-Württemberg W Germany 48.32N 10.18E
64 J7 Sontheim Bayern W Germany 48.00N 10.21E
65 B6 Sonthofen W Germany 47.31N 10.18E
64 H1 Sontra W Germany 51.05N 9.56E
66 D3 Sonvilier Switzerland 47.08N 6.58E
30 E5 Sonwan Uttar Prad India 27.39N 81.45E
39 E2 Sonyakina R U.S.S.R.
104 H4 Sonyea New York 42.41N 77.50W
70 L6 Sonzay France 47.32N 0.28E
106 K3 Soo Canals Canada/U.S.A.
113 C5 Sooghmeghat St Lawrence I, Bering Sea 63.20N 167.12W
101 M11 Sooke Vancouver I, Br Col 48.20N 123.42W
66 N3 Sool Switzerland 47.01N 9.06E
64 D4 Soonwald mts W Germany
72 B8 Soorts-Hossegor France 43.41N 1.24W
90 L2 Soounga Chad 19.00N 22.08E
120 F8 Sopachuy Bolivia 19.30S 64.30W
121 G3 Sopas R Uruguay
105 C7 Sopchoppy Florida 30.34N 84.30W
75 M3 Sopeira Spain 42.19N 0.44E
75 M3 Sopeira, Embalse de res Spain
109 P7 Soper Oklahoma 34.03N 95.43W
105 E5 Soperton Georgia 32.23N 82.37W
Sop Huai Hai see Ban Sop Huai Hai
19 F2 Sopi Moluccas Indon 2.34N 128.26E
19 F2 Sopi, Tanjung C Moluccas Indon 2.39N 128.34E
25 G3 Sop Khao Laos 19.55N 103.16E
56 H6 Sopley Dorset Eng 50.47N 1.47W
87 A6 Sopo watercourse Sudan
45 J3 Sopochinka U.S.S.R. 53.38N 37.30E
39 F6 Sopochnaya R U.S.S.R.
41 D5 Sopochnaya Karga U.S.S.R. 71.55N 82.39E
39 F6 Sopochnoye U.S.S.R. 55.55N 156.10E
Sopot see Vazovgrad
62 L1 Sopot Poland 54.27N 18.31E
46 E3 Sopotskin Belorussiya U.S.S.R. 53.49N 23.42E
71 L1 Soppe-le-Bas France 47.43N 7.06E
66 E1 Sopper-le-Haut France 47.44N 7.04E
Sop Prap see Ban Sop Prap
81 G9 Soprano, C Sicily 37.09N 13.44E
65 P6 Sopron Hungary 47.40N 16.35E
98 Q4 Sop's Arm Newfoundland 49.46N 56.56W
31 H3 Sopur Kashmir 34.19N 74.30E
19 D3 Soputan, Gunung mt Celebes Indon 1.11N 124.48E
111 C5 Soquel California 37.00N 121.58W
76 D10 Sor R Portugal
76 D1 Sor R Spain
80 J5 Sora Italy 41.43N 13.37E
28 B3 Sorab Karnataka India 14.28N 75.09E
52 H9 Söraby Sweden 57.01N 14.55E
20 L1 Sorachi sub-prefect Hokkaido Japan
20 L1 Sorachi-gawa R Japan
29 J8 Sorada Orissa India 19.46N 84.29E
79 H5 Soragna Italy 44.56N 10.07E
80 E3 Sorano Italy 42.41N 11.43E
30 E7 Soraon Uttar Prad India 25.37N 81.51E
120 D7 Sorapa Peru 16.33S 69.40W
79 M1 Sorapis mt Italy 46.31N 12.13E
120 C5 Soras, R Peru
120 E6 Sorata Bolivia 15.47S 68.38W
37 H8 Soratap Dağları mts Turkey
80 G4 Soratte, Monte Italy 42.15N 12.30E
90 F7 Sorau Nigeria 9.44N 13.12E
50 P9 Søraustkapp C Jan Mayen I 71.00N 7.59W
67 P12 Sorba, Col de pass Corsica 42.09N 9.11E
77 M6 Sorbas Spain 37.06N 2.07W
74 E3 Sorbe R Spain
52 G5 Sörberget Sweden 61.39N 13.10E
69 L5 Sorbey France 49.03N 6.19E
57 E3 Sorbie Dumfries & Galloway Scotland 54.48N 4.26W
53 T20 Sørbø Norway 59.08N 5.40E
79 H5 Sorbolo Italy 44.51N 10.27E
53 T14 Sør-Brandal Norway 62.10N 5.35E
50 O9 Sørbreen glacier Jan Mayen I 71.01N 8.10W
52 J4 Sörbygden Sweden 62.48N 16.15E
53 G6 Sørbymagle Denmark 55.22N 11.28E
69 K6 Sorcy-St.-Martin France 48.43N 5.38E
72 B8 Sorde l'Abbaye France 43.32N 1.03W
41 O8 Sordoginskiy Khrebet mts U.S.S.R.
40 G2 Sordongnokh Khabarovsk U.S.S.R. 59.25N 136.12E
39 C3 Sordongnokh Yakutsk U.S.S.R. 63.10N 144.03E
39 D1 Sordongnookh U.S.S.R. 70.13N 146.00E
39 D4 Sordonnakh U.S.S.R. 62.09N 148.09E
95 P8 Sordwana B S Africa 33.02S 32.40E
72 C7 Sore France 44.20N 0.35W
18 G9 Soreang Java Indon 7.02S 107.28E
61 L5 Sorée Belgium 50.24N 5.08E
53 T16 Søreide Norway 61.06N 5.53E
99 R6 Sorel Quebec 46.03N 73.06W
12 H9 Sorell Tasmania 42.15S 147.33E
12 H8 Sorell, C Tasmania 42.12S 145.12E
12 H8 Sorell L Tasmania 42.05S 147.09E
15 C4 Sorenarwa, Selat str Irian Jaya
66 J4 Sörenberg Switzerland 46.50N 8.02E
30 M5 Soreng India 27.10N 88.12E
35 B6 Soreq R Israel
86 N2 Soreq watercourse Israel
79 G4 Soresina Italy 45.17N 9.51E
72 J9 Sorèze France 43.27N 2.04E
52 K4 Sörfjärden Sweden 62.02N 17.25E
51 C5 Sørfjorden Norway 66.29N 13.20E
53 V18 Sørfjorden inlet Hordaland Norway
53 T18 Sørfjorden inlet Norway 60.27N 5.30E
52 F2 Sør Flatanger Norway 64.27N 10.46E
51 E4 Sørfold Norway 67.30N 15.30E
50 U13 Sørfonna glacier Spitsbergen 79.35N 22.00E
52 J2 Sörfors Sweden 64.37N 15.30E
79 J4 Sorgà Italy 45.13N 10.59E
63 K4 Sorge R W Germany
72 F5 Sorges France 45.19N 0.52E
81 C3 Sorgono Sardinia 40.02N 9.07E
71 F8 Sorgues France 44.00N 4.52E
72 K8 Sorgues R France
53 S15 Sørgulen Norway 61.43N 5.06E
36 H3 Sorgun Turkey 39.49N 35.10E
37 H3 Sorgun R Turkey
50 R11 Sørhamna B Spitsbergen 74.21N 19.11E
53 X16 Sørheim Norway 61.25N 7.30E
79 F6 Sori Italy 44.22N 9.06E
75 F4 Soria Spain 41.46N 2.28W
74 F3 Soria prov Spain
121 F4 Soriano Uruguay 33.25S 58.21W
121 F4 Soriano dept Uruguay
81 M6 Soriano Cálabro Italy 38.35N 16.14E
80 F4 Soriano nel Cimino Italy 42.25N 12.14E
72 F1 Sorigny France 47.15N 0.41E
76 H8 Sorihuela Spain 40.27N 5.41W
77 K4 Sorihuela de Guadalimar Spain 38.15N 3.03W
18 C5 Sorikmerapi mt Sumatra Indon 0.38N 99.15E
61 L5 Sorinne-la-Longue Belgium 50.23N 5.02E
61 K5 Sorinnes Belgium 50.16N 4.59E
66 K9 Soriso Italy 45.44N 8.25E
50 O10 Sør-jan Jan Mayen I
47 D6 Sorka U.S.S.R. 59.40N 36.01E
38 A1 Sørkapp isld Svalbard Arctic Ocean 76.28N 16.40E
50 T16 Sørkapp Land Spitsbergen
50 T16 Sørkappøya isld Spitsbergen 76.28N 16.40E
32 D3 Sorkh Āb anc site Iran 34.18N 50.10E
32 E3 Sorkheh Iran 35.25N 53.10E
32 F4 Sorkh, Kūh-e mts Iran
51 H2 Sørkjosen Norway 69.47N 20.51E
53 S17 Sor Kvingo Norway 60.44N 5.24E
75 F2 Sorlada Spain 42.37N 2.13W
50 O10 Sørlaguna L Jan Mayen I 70.58N 8.33W
52 H2 Sørli Norway 64.15N 13.50E
Sorlings see Isles of Scilly
52 M3 Sörmjöle Sweden 63.40N 20.00E
57 E1 Sorn Strathclyde Scotland 55.30N 4.18W
72 J4 Sornac-St. Germain-Lavolps France 45.40N 2.11E
66 F2 Sorne R Switzerland
53 H6 Sorø Denmark 55.26N 11.34E
29 K7 Soro Orissa India 21.18N 86.49E
Sorø co see Vestjælland
118 F8 Sorocaba Brazil 23.30S 47.32W
45 V1 Soroch'i Gory U.S.S.R. 55.24N 49.59E
46 R4 Sorochinsk U.S.S.R. 52.29N 53.15E
42 G6 Sorok U.S.S.R. 52.20N 100.09E
46 G5 Soroki Moldavia U.S.S.R. 48.08N 28.12E
42 C5 Sorokino Altay U.S.S.R. 53.47N 84.58E
42 E5 Sorokino Krasnoyarsk U.S.S.R. 54.11N 91.35E
42 D6 Sorokino U.S.S.R. 52.27N 85.03E
40 C3 Sorokinskiy U.S.S.R. 56.27N 125.15E
62 L8 Soroksár Hungary 47.24N 19.10E
17 O10 Sorol isld Caroline Is Pacific Oc 8.09N 140.25E
43 M4 Sorolen Kazakhstan U.S.S.R. 47.26N 75.34E
81 J8 Soro, Mte Sicily 37.56N 14.42E
30 B5 Soron Uttar Prad India 27.54N 78.45E
15 A4 Sorong Irian Jaya 0.50S 131.17E
119 H7 Sororoca Brazil 0.44N 61.30W
117 D7 Sororó, R Brazil
46 G2 Sorot R U.S.S.R.
93 E4 Soroti Uganda 1.42N 33.37E
93 E4 Soroti sta Uganda 1.46N 33.40E
51 K1 Sørøya isld Norway 70.35N 22.30E
51 K1 Sørøysund channel Norway
Sorp see Reşadiye Bitlis Turkey
75 N2 Sorpe Spain 42.39N 1.05E
63 G10 Sorpetalsperre L W Germany 52.20N 7.56E
76 B11 Sorraia R Portugal
51 G2 Sørreisa Norway 69.08N 18.08E
101 O10 Sorrento Br Col 50.51N 119.29W
80 K7 Sorrento Italy 40.37N 14.23E
107 F11 Sorrento Louisiana 30.11N 90.53W
104 R2 Sorrento Maine 44.30N 68.11W
12 G7 Sorrento Victoria 38.22N 144.19E
94 C3 Sorris Sorris Namibia 20.57S 14.50E
123 B8 Sør-Rondane mts Antarctica 72.00S 25.00E
51 O4 Sorsatunturi mt Finland 67.25N 29.40E
51 F6 Sorsele Sweden 65.32N 17.34E
52 G5 Sörsjön Sweden 61.24N 13.10E
42 D5 Sorsk U.S.S.R. 53.51N 87.30E
53 U20 Sør Skår Norway 59.08N 6.05E
81 B2 Sorso Sardinia 40.48N 8.35E
19 M5 Sorsogon Luzon Philippines 12.59N 124.01E
75 N3 Sort Spain 42.25N 1.07E
47 C5 Sortavala U.S.S.R. 61.40N 30.40E
81 K9 Sortino Sicily 37.10N 15.02E
51 E3 Sortland Norway 68.44N 15.25E
47 G5 Sortopolovskaya U.S.S.R. 60.57N 50.09E
85 L10 Sortot Sudan 19.01N 30.28E
52 E4 Sør-Trøndelag co Norway
53 H7 Sortsø Denmark 54.55N 11.59E
37 G1 Sortullu Turkey 41.03N 29.45E
108 H4 Sorum S Dakota 45.28N 102.55W
47 K4 Sorum R U.S.S.R.
53 G7 Sørup Denmark 54.49N 11.25E
63 L3 Sörup W Germany 54.43N 9.40E
53 B4 Sørvad Denmark 56.16N 8.40E
51 J1 Sørvær Norway 70.38N 21.59E
53 M9 Sørvåg Faeroes 62.04N 7.17W
53 M9 Sørvågs Vatn L Faeroes 62.04N 7.19W
52 G4 Sörvattnet Sweden 64.10N 13.00E
46 D1 Sörve pen Estonia U.S.S.R.
50 N10 Sørvestkapp C Jan Mayen I 70.49N 9.04W
46 P1 Sorvizhi U.S.S.R. 57.58N 48.28E
75 E3 Sorzano Spain 42.20N 2.32W
72 E7 Sos France 44.03N 0.09E
21 D9 Sŏsan S Korea 36.49N 126.26E
75 H3 Sos del Rey Católico Spain 42.30N 1.13W
63 M9 Söse R W Germany
45 O3 Sosedka U.S.S.R. 53.14N 42.39E
20 D3 Soshigaya dist Tōkyō Japan
81 F8 Sósio R Sicily
45 G4 Soskovo U.S.S.R. 52.43N 35.24E
42 H2 Sosna Irkutsk U.S.S.R. 61.00N 106.30E
47 J8 Sosna Kazakhstan U.S.S.R. 53.51N 64.33E
46 L4 Sosna R U.S.S.R.
121 B5 Sosneado pk Argentina 34.45S 70.00W
45 D5 Sosnitsa Ukraine U.S.S.R. 51.31N 32.31E
47 G4 Sosnogorsk U.S.S.R. 63.32N 53.55E
47 C4 Sosnovets U.S.S.R. 64.27N 34.30E
45 B1 Sosnovka Belorussiya U.S.S.R. 55.06N 30.10E
42 H5 Sosnovka Buryat U.S.S.R. 54.10N 109.32E
45 T1 Sosnovka Cheboksary U.S.S.R. 56.10N 47.12E
45 R1 Sosnovka Gor'kiy U.S.S.R. 55.42N 45.30E
43 L5 Sosnovka Kirgiziya U.S.S.R. 42.38N 73.55E
47 E3 Sosnovka Murmansk U.S.S.R. 66.31N 40.39E
45 P4 Sosnovka Penza U.S.S.R. 52.24N 43.30E
45 S4 Sosnovka Saratov U.S.S.R. 52.23N 46.56E
45 N3 Sosnovka Tambov U.S.S.R. 53.13N 41.24E
47 C5 Sosnovo U.S.S.R. 60.33N 30.11E
45 S3 Sosnovoborsk U.S.S.R. 53.17N 46.15E
42 J5 Sosnovo-Ozerskoye U.S.S.R. 52.32N 111.30E
45 P1 Sosnovskoye U.S.S.R. 55.47N 43.10E
47 C3 Sosnovyy U.S.S.R. 66.01N 32.40E
42 C2 Sosnovyy Bor U.S.S.R. 61.34N 80.55E
47 K5 Sosnovyy Mys U.S.S.R. 62.00N 66.19E
45 V3 Sosnovyy Solonets U.S.S.R. 53.17N 49.30E
62 L5 Sosnowiec Poland 50.16N 19.07E
51 M7 Soso Finland 64.50N 25.54E
107 G10 Soso Mississippi 31.46N 89.17W
93 K6 Sosoma Kenya 0.56S 38.43E
61 K5 Sosoye Belgium 50.18N 4.47E
71 L9 Sospel France 43.52N 7.27E
79 H4 Sospiro Italy 45.06N 10.10E
79 M2 Sospirolo Italy 46.09N 12.04E
90 G10 Sosso Cent Afr Rep 3.55N 15.28E
72 F10 Şost France 42.56N 0.32E
82 C4 Šoštanj Yugoslavia 46.23N 15.04E
20 Q8 Sosu Okinawa Japan 26.50N 128.18E
47 J6 Sos'va U.S.S.R. 59.10N 61.50E
47 J6 Sos'va R U.S.S.R.
47 J4 Sos'vinskaya Kul'tbaza U.S.S.R. 63.36N 62.01E
46 L6 Sosyka U.S.S.R. 46.11N 38.49E
44 C1 Sosyka R U.S.S.R.
30 C5 Sot R Uttar Prad India
121 B3 Sotaquí Chile 30.36S 71.10W
119 C6 Sotará, Vol Colombia 2.14N 76.35W
53 X15 Sotaseter Norway 61.49N 7.41E
75 J8 Sot de Chera Spain 39.37N 0.55W
120 F4 Sotério R Brazil
75 E3 Sotés Spain 42.24N 2.36W
76 H1 Sotiello Spain 43.30N 5.42W
93 G6 Sotik Kenya 0.40S 35.08E
37 D6 Şotik Turkey 39.03N 38.15E
77 E4 Sotillo R Spain
76 K8 Sotillo de la Adrada Spain 40.17N 4.35W
75 E4 Sotillo del Rincón Spain 41.55N 2.35W
75 E6 Sotillo, El Spain 40.52N 2.38W
84 S14 Sotira Cyprus 35.01N 33.57E
51 N7 Sotkamo Finland 64.11N 28.28E
44 F2 Sotnikovskoye U.S.S.R. 45.01N 43.47E
121 D3 Soto Argentina 30.50S 65.00W
76 G2 Soto de la Barca, Embalse de res Spain
76 H4 Soto de la Vega Spain 42.20N 5.53W
76 G1 Soto del Barco Spain 43.31N 6.05W
75 C6 Soto del Real Spain 40.45N 3.46W
76 H2 Soto de Rey Spain 43.18N 5.53W
115 K6 Soto la Marina Mexico 23.44N 98.10W
76 B4 Sotomayor Spain 42.19N 8.34W
75 J3 Sotonera, Embalse de la res Spain 42.07N 0.40W
75 C3 Sotopalacios Spain 42.27N 3.40W
75 F7 Sotos Spain 40.11N 2.10W
76 G8 Sotoserrano Spain 40.26N 6.03W
89 K7 Sotouboua Togo 8.33N 0.58E
76 H3 Soto y Amío Spain 42.46N 5.53W
53 S18 Sotra isld Norway 60.20N 5.03E
76 L3 Sotresgudo Spain 42.35N 4.11W
47 M6 Sotsgorod U.S.S.R. 55.15N 61.20E
45 K6 Sotsgorodok U.S.S.R. 50.10N 38.08E
43 N3 Sotsial Kazakhstan U.S.S.R. 48.37N 78.02E
67 P13 Sotta Corsica 41.33N 9.11E
66 C5 Sottens Switzerland 46.40N 6.45E
70 G2 Sottevast France 49.32N 1.36W
70 N3 Sotteville France 49.25N 1.05E
81 E10 Sottile, Pta Lampedusa, I di Italy 35.29N 12.38E
51 H11 Sottunga Finland 60.06N 20.40E
77 L2 Sotuélamos Spain 39.02N 2.34W
72 G7 Soturac France 44.30N 1.01E
115 P7 Sotuta Mexico 20.36N 89.00W
90 L9 Soua Cent Afr Rep 5.30N 22.16E
Souâb, Ouâdi es see Suāb, Wādī Es watercourse
69 H5 Souain-Perthus-lès-Hurlus France 49.11N 4.33E
72 J8 Soual France 43.33N 2.07E
70 M5 Souance France 48.15N 0.51E
91 D2 Souanké Congo 2.03N 14.02E
Souar see Tell es Suwar
88 T4 Souassi tribe Tunisia
71 C9 Soubès France 43.46N 3.21E
72 C5 Soubran France 45.22N 0.31W
89 F9 Soubré Ivory Coast 5.50N 6.35W
69 D3 Souchez France 50.24N 2.45E
11 H8 Soucis, C New Zealand 41.03S 173.35E
72 D3 Soudan Deux Sèvres France 46.25N 0.08W
70 H6 Soudan Loire-Inférieure France 47.44N 1.18W
13 D5 Soudan N Terr Australia 20.02S 137.00E
103 D6 Souderton Pennsylvania 40.17N 75.19W
84 K11 Soúdhas, Kólpos gulf Crete
90 J1 Soudou Chad 21.30N 18.18E
72 F9 Soueich France 43.02N 0.47E
Soueïda see Suweidiya, Es
72 G10 Soueix France 42.53N 1.11E
90 D10 Souelaba, C Cameroon 3.50N 9.30E
70 P7 Souesmes France 47.27N 2.10E
88 P8 Souf watercourse Algeria
88 R5 Souf El Oued Algeria 33.21N 6.54E
69 O6 Soufflenheim France 48.50N 7.57E
83 H3 Souflíon Greece 41.12N 26.18E
116 O8 Soufrière St Lucia, W I 13.53N 61.04W
116 M4 Soufrière mt Guadeloupe W I 16.03N 61.40W
116 O8 Soufrière mt St Vincent St Vincent, W I 13.21N 61.11W
70 K5 Sougé-le Ganelon France 48.18N 0.03W
61 N5 Sougné Belgium 50.29N 5.42E
89 C6 Sougueta Guinea 10.10N 12.32W
88 O4 Sougueur Algeria 35.12N 1.30E
69 B7 Sougy France 48.03N 1.47E
70 O5 Sougy France 48.05N 1.42E
72 G6 Souillac France 44.53N 1.29E
26 U13 Souillac Mauritius, Indian Oc 20.31S 57.31E
69 J5 Souilly France 49.01N 5.18E
90 H2 Souinga Chad 19.33N 16.36E
88 R3 Souk Ahras Algeria 36.14N 8.00E
Soukaïk see Suqeiq
77 F10 Souk-el-Arba des-Beni Hassan Morocco 35.21N 5.23W
74 D10 Souk-el-Arba-du-Rharb Morocco 34.43N 5.58W
89 K2 Souk, Es Mali 18.48N 1.12E
77 E9 Souk-et-Had des Rharbia Morocco 35.32N 5.57W
Soukhne see Sukhne, Es
88 K5 Souk-Jemaâ-Oulad-Abbou Morocco 33.11N 7.52W
77 D10 Souk-Khemis-du-Sahel Morocco 35.16N 6.06W
88 L4 Souk Larbat Gharb Morocco 34.42N 5.59W
89 E7 Soukouralla Guinea 9.10N 8.01W
77 E10 Souk-Sebt des Beni-Zarfet Morocco 35.16N 5.51W
77 F9 Souk-Tieta-Taghremt Morocco 35.48N 5.29W
77 E10 Souk-Tnine-de-Sidi-el-Yamani Morocco 35.22N 5.59W
21 D9 Sŏul S Korea 37.32N 127.00E
72 B4 Soulac-sur-Mer France 45.31N 1.06W
69 H7 Soulaines-Dhuys France 48.23N 4.45E
72 G10 Soulan France 42.55N 1.14E
99 O7 Soulanges Can Quebec
72 J10 Soulatge France 42.53N 2.29E
57 J4 Soulby Westmor Eng 54.30N 2.23W
70 J5 Soulgé-sur-Quette France 48.04N 0.34W
70 L5 Souligné France 48.08N 0.14E
70 L6 Souligné France 47.58N 0.01E
72 A2 Soullans France 46.48N 1.54W
61 J6 Soulme Belgium 50.12N 4.44E
72 D10 Soulom France 42.57N 0.05W
69 N7 Soultzerem France 48.04N 7.07E
69 N8 Soultz-Haut-Rhin France 47.53N 7.14E
69 N8 Soultzmatt France 47.58N 7.15E
69 O6 Soultz-sous-Forêts France 48.56N 7.53E
61 O4 Soumagne Belgium 50.37N 5.45E
72 J3 Soumans France 46.18N 2.19E
72 D10 Soum-du-Moun-Né mt France 42.53N 0.12W
88 Q3 Soummam R Algeria
72 D9 Soumoulou France 43.17N 0.12W
61 H6 Soumoy Belgium 50.12N 4.26E
90 H1 Sounadom Chad 20.57N 17.05E
89 E7 Soundédou Guinea 8.20N 9.30W
28 G6 Sound I Andaman Is
100 G6 Sounding L Alberta 52.10N 110.30W
89 J3 Sounfal,Mt Mali 16.20N 1.10W
88 O11 Sounfat Mali 20.53N 0.38E
84 Q15 Souni Cyprus 34.43N 32.54E
90 E3 Sountellane Niger 16.48N 11.40E
69 D7 Souppes-sur-Loing France 48.11N 2.45E
72 C8 Souprosse France 43.47N 0.42W
72 B8 Souquet France 43.58N 1.03W
Sour see Tyr Lebanon
Soûrâne see Sūrān
59 G3 Source of the Shannon L Cavan Irish Rep 54.14N 7.55W
95 M4 Sources, Mt-aux- Lesotho 28.46S 28.54E
70 J4 Sourdeval France 48.43N 0.55W
113 P5 Sourdough Alaska 62.32N 145.30W
117 D5 Soure Brazil 0.40S 48.30W
76 B8 Soure Portugal 40.04N 8.38W
88 P3 Sour el Ghozlane Algeria 36.10N 3.41E
100 R9 Souris Manitoba 49.38N 100.17W
108 K1 Souris N Dakota 48.56N 100.41W
98 K7 Souris Prince Edward I 46.22N 62.16W
97 J8 Souris R Man/N Dakota
112 N5 Sour Lake Texas 30.08N 94.25W
103 E6 Sourland Mts New Jersey
90 M8 Sourmane Cent Afr Rep 6.39N 24.52E
72 J10 Sournia France 42.43N 2.25E
89 H5 Sourou Upper Volta 12.56N 3.15W
Sourou R see Bagué R
89 H5 Sourou R Mali/Upper Volta
84 E3 Soúrpi Greece 39.06N 22.54E
70 O5 Sours France 48.25N 1.35E
72 J5 Soursac France 45.17N 2.11E
56 C6 Sourton Devon Eng 50.42N 4.04W
88 J6 Sous tribe Morocco
117 H8 Sousa Brazil 6.41S 38.14W
76 C6 Sousa R Portugal
91 D10 Sousa Lara Angola 12.28S 14.10E
72 J6 Sousceyrac France 44.53N 2.02E
66 B7 Sous Dine, Montagne de mt France 46.01N 6.19E
117 C6 Sousel Brazil 2.38S 51.55W
76 D11 Sousel Portugal 38.57N 7.40W
72 D5 Sousmoulins France 45.20N 0.20W
88 J6 Souss R Morocco
88 T4 Sousse Tunisia 35.50N 10.38E
89 A4 Soussoum Senegal 14.34N 16.48W
72 B8 Soustons France 43.45N 1.19W
72 B8 Soustons,Etang de L France 43.47N 1.20W
95 G8 Sout R S Africa
95 G2 Soutbos S Africa 26.09S 23.58E
76 F6 Soutelo Portugal 41.24N 6.44W
57 L3 Souter Lt.Ho Tyne and Wear Eng 54.58N 1.21W
72 G3 Souterraine,la France 46.14N 1.29E
73 G8 South Africa,Rep.of Africa
55 C3 Southall London England 51.31N 0.23W
108 M1 Southam N Dakota 48.10N 98.32W
56 J3 Southam Warwicks Eng 52.15N 1.23W
103 J9 South Amboy New Jersey 40.29N 74.17W
56 J6 Southampton Hants Eng 50.55N 1.25W
103 K5 Southampton Long I, N Y 40.54N 72.24W
103 J2 Southampton Massachusetts 42.14N 72.44W
98 H8 Southampton Nova Scotia 45.32N 64.21W
99 J8 Southampton Ontario 44.29N 81.22W
97 L5 Southampton, C N W Terr 62.05N 83.45W
97 L5 Southampton I N W Terr 65.00N 85.00W
56 J6 Southampton Water inlet Hants Eng
28 G7 South Andaman isld Andaman Is
104 H9 South Anna R Virginia
South Arabia see Southern Yemen
103 F6 Southard New Jersey 40.08N 74.14W
123 G2 Southard,C Antarctica 66.38S 122.50E
103 M3 South Attleboro Massachusetts 41.56N 71.20W
11 L4 South Auckland-Bay of Plenty stat area New Zealand
97 N6 South Aulatsivik I Labrador, Nfld 56.45N 61.30W
10 G7 South Australia state Australia
26 K9 South Australian Basin Indian Oc
South B Nicobar Is see Galathea B
99 J7 South B Ontario
109 C8 South Baldy mt New Mexico 33.59N 107.10W
57 L3 South Bank Cleveland Eng 54.35N 1.10W
104 C5 South Bass I Ohio 41.39N 82.49W
105 G11 South Bay Florida 26.40N 80.44W
99 H7 South Baymouth Ontario 45.34N 82.02W
14 A2 South Beach dist Perth, W Australia
14 B2 South Belmont dist Perth, W Australia
106 E7 South Beloit Illinois 42.29N 89.02W
106 H8 South Bend Indiana 41.40N 86.15W
112 J3 South Bend Texas 33.00N 98.41W
110 B3 South Bend Washington 46.39N 123.48W
104 P3 South Berwick Maine 43.14N 70.49W
103 G1 South Bethlehem New York 42.32N 73.51W
116 F2 South Bight B Andros Bahamas 24.00N 77.58W
56 A4 South Bishop Lt.Ho Dyfed Wales 51.52N 5.25W
13 J6 South Blackwater Queensland 23.52S 148.31E
116 G3 South Bluff C Acklins I Bahamas 22.13N 74.13W
106 J5 South Boardman Michigan 44.39N 85.17W
56 M5 Southborough Kent Eng 51.10N 0.15E
103 L2 Southborough Massachusetts 42.18N 71.31W
104 G10 South Boston Virginia 36.42N 78.58W
106 L5 South Branch Michigan 44.29N 83.56W
56 D7 South Brent Devon Eng 50.25N 3.50W
103 K2 Southbridge Massachusetts 42.05N 72.02W
11 G10 Southbridge New Zealand 43.48S 172.16E
13 K1 South Brisbane dist Brisbane, Qnsld
98 Q4 South Brook Newfoundland 49.25N 56.04W
11 G10 Southbrook New Zealand 43.20S 172.38E
98 H9 South Brookfield Nova Scotia 44.23N 64.58W
93 C6 South Buganda dist Uganda
11 F11 Southburn New Zealand 44.27S 171.06E
103 H4 Southbury Connecticut 41.28N 73.13W
26 B13 South C Prince Edward I Ind Oc 46.41S 37.57E
11 B13 South C Stewart I New Zealand 47.16S 167.38E
116 J4 South Caicos isld Caicos Is W I 21.31N 71.30W
103 D3 South Canaan Pennsylvania 41.30N 75.26W
109 E3 South Canon Colorado 38.25N 105.14W
South Cape see Ka Lae
9 T5 South Cape Taveuni Fiji 17.00S 179.57E
102 K4 South Carolina state U.S.A.
103 N3 South Carver Massachusetts 41.51N 70.44W
57 M5 South Cave Humberside Eng 53.46N 0.35W
19 G2 South Chan Luzon Philippines
106 K4 South Chan Michigan
104 B7 South Charleston Ohio 39.48N 83.37W

104 D8 **South Charleston** W Virginia 38.22N 81.44W
104 Q2 **South China** Maine 44.24N 69.36W
17 H8 **South China Sea** S E Asia
14 A1 **South City Beach** *dist* Perth, W Australia
30 K2 **South Col** *pass* Xizang Zizhiqu/Nepal 27.59N 86.57E
104 L2 **South Colton** New York 44.31N 74.54W
28 G7 **South Coral Bank** Andaman Is
103 K3 **South Coventry** Connecticut 41.46N 72.18W
102 F2 **South Dakota** *state* U.S.A.
103 N3 **South Dartmouth** Massachusetts 41.36N 70.56W
104 F4 **South Dayton** New York 42.21N 79.03W
57 H2 **Southdean** Borders Scotland 55.22N 2.35W
103 J2 **South Deerfield** Massachusetts 42.29N 72.37W
56 K6 **South Downs** *chalk hills* W Sussex Eng
94 H5 **South East** *dist* Botswana
96 B11 **South East B** Ascension I 7.58S 14.18W
113 C5 **Southeast C** St Lawrence I Bering Sea 62.56N 169.41W
12 H9 **South East C** Tasmania 43.38S 146.48E
12 H7 **South East C** Victoria 39.08S 146.25E
90 D9 **South Eastern** *state* Nigeria
96 C11 **South East Hd** Ascension I 7.58S 14.18W
114 A1 **Southeast I** Hawaiian Is 27.56N 176.10W
26 S14 **South-East I** Mahé I Seychelles, Ind Oc 4.40S 55.32E
14 E10 **South East Is** W Australia 34.20S 123.30E
122 N15 **Southeast Pacific Basin** Pacific Oc
116 H4 **Southeast Pt** Great Inagua Bahamas 20.58N 73.09W
103 L4 **Southeast Pt** Rhode I 41.10N 71.05W
10 A12 **South East Reef** Macquarie I Pacific Oc 54.47S 158.52E
10 F12 **South East Rock** Lord Howe I Pacific Oc 31.48S 159.18E
103 H2 **South Egremont** Massachusetts 42.10N 73.25W
101 W7 **Southend** Saskatchewan 56.16N 103.22W
57 B2 **Southend** Strathclyde Scotland 55.20N 5.38W
56 N4 **Southend Airport** Essex Eng 51.35N 0.42E
56 N4 **Southend-on-Sea** Essex Eng 51.33N 0.43E
106 B8 **South English** Iowa 41.27N 92.03W
26 V13 **South Entrance** Mauritius, Indian Oc
15 G8 **South Entrance** *str* Papua New Guinea
93 B6 **Southern** *dist* Uganda
92 G9 **Southern** *prov* Malawi
26 S9 **Southern** *prov* Sri Lanka
92 B10 **Southern** *prov* Zambia
11 E10 **Southern Alps** *mts* New Zealand
110 M3 **Southern Cross** Montana 46.11N 113.16W
13 H5 **Southern Cross** Queensland 20.06S 146.10E
14 C9 **Southern Cross** W Australia 31.14S 119.16E
90 L6 **Southern Darfur** *prov* Sudan
56 D5 **Southerndown** Mid Glam Wales 51.28N 3.36W
98 T6 **Southern Harbour** Newfoundland 47.44N 53.58W
92 G6 **Southern Highlands** Tanzania
87 B5 **Southern Kordofan** *prov* Sudan
34 M2 **Southern Kurdistan** *reg* Iraq
26 E11 **Southern Ocean**
107 G10 **Southern Pine Hills** Mississippi
105 H2 **Southern Pines** N Carolina 35.12N 79.23W
89 C8 **Southern Prov** Sierra Leone
14 B2 **Southern R** Perth, W Australia
Southern Rhodesia *see* **Zimbabwe**
31 E4 **Southern Waziristan** *reg* Pakistan
56 M2 **Southery** Norfolk Eng 52.32N 0.23E
58 L5 **South Esk, R** Tayside Scotland
14 F5 **South Esk Tableland** W Australia
100 N8 **Southey** Saskatchewan 50.57N 104.33W
95 L7 **Southeyville** S Africa 31.48S 27.28E
107 E2 **South Fabius** *R* Missouri
103 E3 **South Fallsburg** New York 41.42N 74.07W
57 M5 **South Ferriby** Humberside Eng 53.41N 0.30W
103 H2 **Southfield** Massachusetts 42.06N 73.14W
103 F4 **Southfields** New York 41.14N 74.11W
10 R7 **South Fiji Ridge** Pacific Oc
11 B12 **South Fiord** New Zealand
103 H4 **Southford** Connecticut 41.27N 73.10W
56 O5 **South Foreland** *headland* Kent Eng 51.09N 1.23E
110 B9 **South Fork** California 40.21N 123.55W
109 D4 **South Fork** Colorado 37.39N 106.39W
104 G6 **South Fork** Pennsylvania 40.22N 78.47W
100 J9 **South Fork** Saskatchewan 49.35N 108.46W
111 D3 **South Fork American** *R* California
111 A2 **South Fork Eel** *R* California
108 M7 **South Fork Elkhorn** *R* Nebraska
111 F6 **South Fork Kern** *R* California
104 F8 **South Fork, South Branch** *R* W Virginia
103 L3 **South Foster** Rhode I 41.50N 71.43W
116 P3 **South Friar's B** St Kitts W I
107 H5 **South Fulton** Tennessee 36.30N 88.53W
35 E2 **South Galilee** *reg* Israel
55 F2 **Southgate** London Eng 51.38N 0.07W
111 E9 **South Gate** *dist* Los Angeles, California
123 F5 **South Geomagnetic Pole (1975)** Antarctica 78.40S 109.33E
121 G8 **South Georgia** *islds* Atl Oc
117 H6 **South Georgia** *isld* S Atlantic Oc
103 C3 **South Gibson** Pennsylvania 41.44N 75.38W
107 D1 **South Gifford** Missouri 40.02N 92.40W
103 E2 **South Gilboa** New York 42.24N 74.34W
56 E5 **South Glamorgan** *co* Wales
103 J3 **South Glastonbury** Connecticut 41.40N 72.36W
107 B3 **South Grand R** Missouri
103 J2 **South Hadley** Massachusetts 42.15N 72.35W
103 J2 **South Hadley Falls** Massachusetts 42.13N 72.36W
98 M7 **South Harbour** C Breton I, Nova Scotia 46.51N 60.28W
58 P10 **South Harbour** Shetland Scotland 59.31N 1.39W
56 K6 **South Harting** W Sussex Eng 50.58N 0.54W
31 J10 **South Hatia I** Bangladesh
109 N4 **South Haven** Kansas 37.02N 97.25W
106 H7 **South Haven** Michigan 42.25N 86.16W
58 Q9 **South Havra** *isld* Shetland Scotland 60.02N 1.22W
56 K6 **South Hayling** Hants Eng 50.47N 0.59W
12 M7 **South Hd** New S Wales 33.51S 151.17E
11 J3 **South Hd** New Zealand 36.27S 174.11E
95 A9 **South Hd** S Africa 33.06S 17.58E
97 K5 **South Henik L** N W Terr 61.30N 98.00W
96 A16 **South Hill** Tristan da Cunha 37.20S 12.44W
104 G10 **South Hill** Virginia 36.44N 78.10W
114 C7 **South Hilo** *dist* Hawaiian Is
12 F8 **South Hobart** *dist* Hobart, Tasmania
105 F1 **South Holston L** Tennessee
122 E5 **South Honshu Ridge** Pacific Oc
93 H3 **South Horr** Kenya 2.07N 36.55E
112 G9 **South Houston** Texas 29.37N 95.13W
103 H5 **South Huntington** Long I, N Y 40.50N 73.25W
13 C1 **South I** Australia 11.36S 133.28E
26 V2 **South I** Cocos Is Ind Oc 12.12S 96.55E
93 H3 **South I** Kenya 2.35N 36.38E
11 C10 **South I** New Zealand
100 T2 **South Indian Lake** Manitoba 56.48N 98.56W
103 J3 **Southington** Connecticut 41.36N 72.53W
11 J13 **South Islet** Antipodes Is Pacific Oc 49.45S 178.50E
19 J7 **South Islet** Philippines 8.44N 119.48E
100 F1 **South Junction** Manitoba 49.03N 95.44W
28 B4 **South Kanara** *dist* Karnataka India
57 N6 **South Kelsey** Lincs Eng 53.28N 0.26W
106 G7 **South Kenosha** Wisconsin 42.32N 87.50W
57 L4 **South Kilvington** N Yorks Eng 54.15N 1.21W
93 H6 **South Kinangop** Kenya 0.42S 36.37E
29 J6 **South Koel R** Bihar India
114 B7 **South Kohala** *dist* Hawaiian Is
114 B8 **South Kona** *dist* Hawaiian Is
9 K6 **South Korea** *rep* Asia
103 E2 **South Kortright** New York 42.20N 74.45W
112 M8 **Southlake** Texas 32.56N 97.09W
112 F2 **Southland** Texas 33.21N 101.33W
11 B12 **Southland** *stat area* New Zealand
98 K8 **South Lochaber** Nova Scotia 45.22N 62.03W
108 L8 **South Loup** *R* Nebraska
92 E8 **South Luangwa Nat. Park** Zambia
106 L7 **South Lyon** Michigan 42.28N 83.39W
26 D9 **South Madagascar Ridge** Indian Oc
123 J3 **South Magnetic Pole (1975)** Antarctica 65.46S 139.34W
103 J3 **South Manchester** Connecticut 41.46N 72.31W
12 C7 **South Melbourne** *dist* Melbourne, Vic
105 G12 **South Miami** Florida 25.41N 80.19W
103 G3 **South Milbrook** New York 41.46N 73.42W
105 L1 **South Mills** N Carolina 36.29N 76.20W
106 G7 **South Milwaukee** Wisconsin 42.58N 87.52W
56 L4 **South Mimms** Herts Eng 51.43N 0.15W
56 N4 **Southminster** Essex Eng 51.40N 0.50E
13 J5 **South Molle I** Queensland 20.17S 148.52E
56 D5 **South Molton** Devon Eng 51.01N 3.50W
103 C3 **South Montrose** Pennsylvania 41.47N 75.55W
112 K10 **Southmost** Texas 25.51N 97.24W
104 H7 **South Mt** Pennsylvania
101 K5 **South Nahanni** *R* N W Terr
113 J7 **South Naknek** Alaska 58.42N 157.00W
South Nelson *see* **Chatham Head**
58 O9 **South Ness** *prom* Shetland Scotland 60.06N 2.05W
103 D1 **South New Berlin** New York 42.32N 75.23W
11 N9 **South New Brighton** New Zealand 43.32S 172.44E
105 F6 **South Newport** Georgia 31.37N 81.25W
105 B10 **South New River Canal** Florida
103 H4 **South Norwalk** Connecticut 41.06N 73.25W
56 M4 **South Ockendon** Essex Eng 51.32N 0.18E
103 K4 **Southold** Long I, N Y 41.04N 72.25W
103 G7 **South Orange** New Jersey 40.45N 74.16W
123 C14 **South Orkney Is** S Atlantic Oc
103 O3 **South Orleans** Massachusetts 41.46N 69.59W
104 K4 **South Otselic** New York 42.49N 75.47W
57 L4 **South Otterington** N Yorks Eng 54.16N 1.25W
103 C2 **South Oxford** New York 42.23N 75.38W
93 J10 **South Pare Mts** Tanzania
104 P2 **South Paris** Maine 44.14N 70.33W
104 D7 **South Parkersburg** W Virginia 39.15N 81.33W
19 N5 **South Pass** Truk Is Pacific Oc 7.14N 151.48E
110 R7 **South Pass** Wyoming 42.20N 108.55W
14 A7 **South Passage** W Australia
110 R7 **South Pass City** Wyoming 42.27N 108.48W
106 E9 **South Pekin** Illinois 40.30N 89.40W
56 F6 **South Perrott** Dorset Eng 50.52N 2.46W
14 B2 **South Perth** *dist* Perth, W Australia
56 F6 **South Petherton** Somerset Eng 50.58N 2.49W
56 C6 **South Petherwin** Cornwall Eng 50.37N 4.24W
107 L6 **South Pittsburg** Tennessee 35.01N 85.41W
109 E2 **South Platte** Colorado 39.25N 105.10W
109 E2 **South Platte** *R* Colorado
103 C1 **South Plymouth** New York 42.34N 75.35W
123 F8 **South Polar Plat** Antarctica
123 F8 **South Pole** Antarctica
99 J4 **South Porcupine** Ontario 48.30N 81.02W
103 H4 **Southport** Connecticut 41.08N 73.17W
107 K2 **Southport** Indiana 39.40N 86.08W
57 G5 **Southport** Merseyside Eng 53.39N 3.01W
105 J4 **Southport** N Carolina 33.55N 78.00W
98 T5 **Southport** Newfoundland 48.03N 53.38W
95 O6 **Southport** S Africa 30.40S 30.30E
104 P3 **South Portland** Maine 43.37N 70.14W
98 K4 **South Pt** Anticosti I, Que 49.04N 62.17W
96 A12 **South Pt** Ascension I 7.59S 14.24W
116 P6 **South Pt** Barbados 13.02N 59.32W
26 V4 **South Pt** Christmas I Ind Oc 10.32S 105.43E
116 G3 **South Pt** Long I Bahamas 22.51N 74.53W
11 A12 **South Pt** South I New Zealand 45.49S 166.25E
58 K7 **South Queensferry** Lothian Scotland 55.59N 3.25W
105 J3 **South R** N Carolina
106 F2 **South Range** Michigan 47.04N 88.38W
59 G7 **South Riding** *div* Tipperary Irish Rep
105 H12 **South Riding Rock** Bahamas 25.14N 79.10W
103 F6 **South River** New Jersey 40.26N 74.23W
99 L7 **South River** Ontario 45.50N 79.23W
58 T12 **South Ronaldsay** *isld* Orkney Scotland 58.47N 2.56W
92 F7 **South Rukuru** *R* Malawi
56 M2 **South Runcton** Norfolk Eng 52.39N 0.25E
95 O7 **South Sand** *hd* S Africa 31.19S 30.00E
123 A14 **South Sandwich Is** S Atlantic Oc
96 H14 **South Sandwich Trench** Atlantic Oc
111 B4 **South San Francisco** California 37.39N 122.25W
103 G1 **South Schodack** New York 42.31N 73.43W
59 D5 **South Sd** Galway Irish Rep
56 J6 **Southsea** Hants Eng 50.46N 1.05W
100 S1 **South Seal R** Manitoba
103 E8 **South Seaville** New Jersey 39.11N 74.46W
18 J2 **South Seletar** *dist* Singapore
28 G7 **South Sentinel** *isld* Andaman Is 11.00N 92.12E
123 E15 **South Shetland Is** S Atlantic Oc
57 L2 **South Shields** Tyne and Wear Eng 55.00N 1.25W
11 N9 **Southshore** New Zealand 43.32S 172.45E
122 A5 **Southside** Canton I Pacific Oc 2.50S 171.41W
108 O7 **South Sioux City** Nebraska 42.28N 96.24W
108 O6 **South Sioux Falls** S Dakota 43.30N 96.43W
101 P11 **South Slocan** Br Col 49.28N 117.32W
South Son *mt see* **Bamus Mt**
57 D6 **South Stack Lt. Ho** Gwynedd Wales 53.19N 4.42W
103 D4 **South Sterling** Pennsylvania 41.17N 75.21W
110 R8 **South Superior** Wyoming 41.44N 108.56W
111 N2 **South Tent** *mt* Utah 39.24N 111.24W
56 H5 **South Tidworth** Hants Eng 51.14N 1.40W
108 F7 **South Torrington** Wyoming 42.03N 104.12W
109 E6 **South Truchas Pk** New Mexico 35.58N 105.38W
103 O3 **South Truro** Massachusetts 41.58N 70.04W
58 B4 **South Uist** *isld* W Isles Scotland
103 D8 **South Vineland** New Jersey 39.28N 75.02W
56 O2 **South Walsham** Norfolk Eng 52.40N 1.29E
55 F3 **Southwark** London England 51.30N 0.06W
55 F4 **Southwark** *borough* London England
103 A3 **South Waverly** Pennsylvania 42.00N 76.34W
57 M6 **Southwell** Notts Eng 53.05N 0.58W
South West Africa *see* **Namibia**
26 A16 **South West B** Heard I Antarctica
105 K9 **South West B** New Providence I Bahamas
96 A12 **South West Bay** Ascension I
11 B7 **South West C** Auckland Is Pacific Oc 50.50S 165.53E
98 L6 **Southwest C** Madeleine Is, Que 47.15N 62.00W
113 B5 **Southwest C** St Lawrence I Bering Sea 63.19N 171.30W
11 B13 **Southwest C** Stewart I New Zealand 47.17S 167.29E
12 H9 **South West C** Tasmania 43.32S 145.59E
13 L5 **South-West Cay** *isld* Gt Barrier Reef Australia 21.50S 153.22E
15 L9 **South West Ent** Louisiade Arch 11.10S 151.50E
103 F2 **South Westerlo** New York 42.27N 74.02W
13 J3 **South-West I** Gt Barrier Reef Australia 16.59S 149.55E
12 H7 **South West I** Tasmania 39.31S 147.07E
26 E9 **South-West Indian Ridge** Indian Oc
101 J11 **South Westminster** Br Col 49.12N 122.53W
122 L12 **Southwest Pacific Basin** Pacific Oc
South West Peru Ridge *see* **Nasca Ridge**
15 J5 **Southwest Pt** Admiralty Is 2.13S 146.30E
98 J4 **Southwest Pt** Anticosti I, Que 49.24N 63.36W
105 J11 **Southwest Pt** Bahamas 26.31N 78.48W
105 K12 **Southwest Pt** Bahamas 25.51N 77.12W
116 G1 **South West Pt** Jamaica, W I 18.11N 78.14W
10 A11 **South West Pt** Macquarie I Pacific Oc 54.46S 158.48E
105 L8 **South West Pt** Virgin Is 17.42N 64.54W
96 A14 **South West Pt** *C* St Helena 16.00S 5.48W
106 J8 **South Whitley** Indiana 41.05N 85.39W
103 J2 **Southwick** Massachusetts 42.03N 72.46W
103 C4 **South Wilkes Barre** Pennsylvania 41.13N 75.55W
104 H5 **South Williamsport** Pennsylvania 41.14N 77.02W
104 P3 **South Windham** Maine 43.44N 70.26W
103 J3 **South Windsor** Connecticut 41.49N 72.37W
56 P3 **Southwold** Suffolk Eng 52.20N 1.40E
56 M2 **South Wootton** Norfolk Eng 52.47N 0.26E
103 E1 **South Worcester** New York 42.31N 74.46W
27 G6 **South Yemen (People's Dem Rep)** S W Asia
57 L6 **South Yorkshire** *co* Eng
56 D6 **South Zeal** Devon Eng 50.44N 3.54W
76 F8 **Souto** Beira Alta Portugal 40.21N 6.58W
76 C9 **Souto** Ribatejo Portugal 39.34N 8.14W
76 B9 **Souto da Carpolhosa** Portugal 39.50N 8.50W
95 K4 **Soutpan** S Africa 28.42S 26.05E
95 H2 **Soutpan** *salt pan* S Africa 26.34S 24.53E
94 K4 **Soutpansberg** *mts* S Africa
58 L7 **Soutra Hill** Lothian Scotland 55.49N 2.53W
11 D12 **Soutra Hill** *mt* New Zealand 45.33S 169.50E
95 F8 **Soutriviervlei** *salt L* S Africa
95 G5 **Soutvleipan** *salt pan* S Africa 29.42S 23.12E
72 D3 **Souvigne** France 46.22N 0.12W
72 L2 **Souvigny** France 46.33N 3.10E
61 H5 **Souvret** Belgium 50.27N 4.21E
76 C8 **Souzelas** Portugal 40.17N 8.25W
76 C6 **Souzelo** Portugal 41.04N 8.14W
80 E3 **Sovana** Italy 42.31N 11.38E
82 J4 **Sovata** Romania 46.35N 25.03E
82 K5 **Soveja** Romania 45.59N 26.41E
81 N6 **Soverato** Italy 38.42N 16.33E
100 K7 **Sovereign** Saskatchewan 51.30N 107.40W
67 P12 **Soveria** Corsica 42.20N 9.10E
81 M5 **Soveria Mannelli** Italy 39.05N 16.22E
81 N6 **Soveria Simeri** Italy 38.57N 16.42E
79 M2 **Sovérzene** Italy 46.13N 12.18E
61 L5 **Sovet** Belgium 50.18N 5.02E
46 D2 **Sovetsk** Kaliningrad U.S.S.R. 55.02N 21.50E
46 P1 **Sovetsk** Kirov U.S.S.R. 57.39N 48.59E
44 D3 **Sovetskaya** Krasnodar U.S.S.R. 44.46N 41.13E
45 O7 **Sovetskaya** Rostov U.S.S.R. 49.01N 42.07E
44 F3 **Sovetskaya** Stavropol' U.S.S.R. 44.03N 44.04E
40 H7 **Sovetskaya Gavan'** U.S.S.R. 48.57N 140.16E
39 M1 **Sovetskaya, Gora** *mt* Vrangelya, Ostrov U.S.S.R. 71.02N 179.05W
42 E5 **Sovetskaya Khakassiya** U.S.S.R. 54.06N 91.30E
41 D7 **Sovetskaya Rechka** U.S.S.R. 66.45N 83.45E
40 E5 **Sovetskiy** Amur U.S.S.R. 53.57N 129.55E
43 K6 **Sovetskiy** Kirgiziya U.S.S.R. 40.12N 71.18E
47 B5 **Sovetskiy** Leningrad U.S.S.R. 60.32N 28.40E
43 J7 **Sovetskiy** Tadzhikistan U.S.S.R. 38.04N 69.35E
47 J5 **Sovetskiy** Tyumen U.S.S.R. 61.24N 63.31E
44 D9 **Sovetskiy** Ukraine U.S.S.R. 45.20N 34.56E
45 L6 **Sovetskoye** Belgorod U.S.S.R. 50.22N 39.03E
45 S1 **Sovetskoye** Cheboksary U.S.S.R. 55.52N 46.32E
44 G5 **Sovetskoye** Checheno Ingush A.S.S.R. U.S.S.R. 42.52N 45.44E
44 F4 **Sovetskoye** Kabardino-Balkar A.S.S.R. U.S.S.R. 43.17N 43.34E
45 Q9 **Sovetskoye** Kalmyk A.S.S.R. U.S.S.R. 47.19N 44.32E
43 N5 **Sovetskoye** Kirgiziya U.S.S.R. 42.39N 78.23E
45 S5 **Sovetskoye** Saratov U.S.S.R. 51.26N 46.45E
41 D7 **Sovetskoye, Ozero** *L* U.S.S.R.
9 S8 **Sovi Bay** Viti Levu Fiji 18.15S 177.32E
80 D2 **Sovicille** Italy 43.17N 11.14E
53 U13 **Søvik** Norway 62.32N 6.17E
53 V14 **Søvik** Norway 62.26N 6.45E
53 E5 **Søvind** Denmark 55.54N 10.00E
91 C7 **Sovo** Angola 7.11S 12.24E
47 E3 **Sovpol'ye** U.S.S.R. 65.21N 44.00E
Sowa *see* **Dagxoi**
15 F8 **Sowau** Irian Jaya 8.01S 140.59E
57 K5 **Sowerby Bridge** W Yorks Eng 53.43N 1.54W
94 S14 **Soweto** Witwatersrand S Africa 26.17S 27.50E
37 J8 **Sowfi** Iran
32 G6 **Sowghān** Iran 28.20N 56.56E
61 N5 **Soy** Belgium 50.17N 5.30E
115 N9 **Soyaló** Mexico 16.55N 92.55W
21 J5 **Sōya-misaki** *C* Japan 45.33N 141.58E
47 E3 **Soyana** *R* U.S.S.R.
61 J5 **Soye** Belgium 50.27N 4.44E
71 J2 **Soye** France 47.26N 6.27E
64 N7 **Soyen** W Germany 48.06N 12.13E
66 F2 **Soyhieres** Switzerland 47.24N 7.22E
37 F6 **Söylemez** Turkey 39.47N 41.47E
39 D1 **Soylyk** U.S.S.R. 69.14N 146.00E
71 F7 **Soyons** France 44.53N 4.51E
115 E3 **Soyopa** Mexico 28.47N 109.39W
93 G5 **Soy Road** Kenya 0.40N 35.11E
45 B4 **Sozh** *R* Belorussiya U.S.S.R.
47 G6 **Sozimskiy** U.S.S.R. 59.43N 52.10E
82 L8 **Sozopol** Bulgaria 42.23N 27.42E
79 E4 **Sozzago** Italy 45.24N 8.43E
61 O5 **Spa** Belgium 50.29N 5.52E
116 B2 **Spaanse Baai** *B* Curaçao W I
60 G10 **Spaarndam** Netherlands 52.25N 4.40E
81 K7 **Spadafora** Sicily 38.13N 15.23E
81 C3 **Spada, Mte** Sardinia 40.04N 9.23E
81 E9 **Spadillo,Pta** Pantelleria I Italy 36.50N 12.00E
39 D5 **Spafar'yeva,O** *isld* U.S.S.R. 59.09N 149.00E
64 F7 **Spaichingen** W Germany 48.05N 8.44E
74 **Spain** *rep* Europe
60 K10 **Spakenburg** Netherlands 52.15N 5.23E
50 E3 **Spákonufell** Iceland 65.50N 20.11W
62 M4 **Spała** Poland 51.32N 20.10E
Spalato *see* **Split**
66 L7 **Spalavera, Mt** Italy 46.03N 8.38E
110 J3 **Spalding** Idaho 46.27N 116.48W
56 L2 **Spalding** Lincs Eng 52.47N 0.10W
108 M8 **Spalding** Nebraska 41.41N 98.21W
100 N6 **Spalding** Saskatchewan 52.22N 104.30W
12 E5 **Spalding** S Australia 33.29S 138.40E
56 L3 **Spaldwick** Cambs Eng 52.20N 0.21W
65 J2 **Spálené Poříčí** Czechoslovakia 49.38N 13.38E
81 A5 **Spalmatore, Pta** Sardinia 39.06N 8.15E
64 K5 **Spalt** W Germany 49.11N 10.56E
122 A5 **Spam I** Canton I Pacific Oc 2.47S 171.43W
60 H9 **Spanbroek** Netherlands 52.42N 4.56E
63 S7 **Spandau** W Berlin W Germany 52.32N 13.13E
53 B6 **Spandet** Denmark 55.16N 8.54E
52 J9 **Spångenäs** Sweden 57.36N 16.07E
64 H1 **Spangenberg** W Germany 51.08N 9.40E
31 K4 **Spanggur** Kashmir 33.30N 78.40E
31 K4 **Spanggur Tso** *L* Kashmir/Xizang Zizhiqu
110 H2 **Spangle** Washington 47.26N 117.22W
104 G6 **Spangler** Pennsylvania 40.38N 78.46W
98 T6 **Spaniard's Bay** Newfoundland 47.38N 53.20W
99 H6 **Spanish** Ontario 46.12N 82.21W
110 O9 **Spanish Fork City** Utah 40.07N 111.39W
57 D4 **Spanish Hd** Isle of Man U.K. 54.03N 4.46W
109 F4 **Spanish Pks** Colorado 37.23N 104.58W
96 B2 **Spanish Pt** Bermuda 32.18N 64.49W
59 D6 **Spanish Pt** Clare Irish Rep 52.51N 9.27W
99 J6 **Spanish R** Ontario
116 K2 **Spanish Town** Jamaica, W I 17.59N 76.58W
81 E7 **Sparagio,Mte** Sicily 38.04N 12.47E
80 K6 **Sparanise** Italy 41.12N 14.06E
52 F3 **Sparbu** Norway 63.55N 11.23E
81 C1 **Spargi, I** Sardinia 41.15N 9.22E
53 C4 **Sparkær** Denmark 56.29N 9.14E
56 F5 **Sparkford** Somerset Eng 51.02N 2.34W
103 G4 **Sparkill** New York 41.02N 73.56W
107 D8 **Sparkman** Arkansas 33.55N 92.51W
105 D6 **Sparks** Georgia 31.15N 83.28W
108 K7 **Sparks** Nebraska 42.58N 100.20W
111 E2 **Sparks** Nevada 39.34N 119.46W
109 O6 **Sparks** Oklahoma 35.36N 96.50W
106 E8 **Sparland** Illinois 41.02N 89.26W
64 M3 **Sparnberg** E Germany 50.25N 11.47E
106 K4 **Sparr** Michigan 45.03N 84.34W
66 H6 **Sparrhorn** *mt* Switzerland 46.25N 8.00E
103 E4 **Sparrow Bush** New York 41.24N 74.42W
103 B8 **Sparrows Point** Maryland 39.14N 76.28W
Sparta *see* **Spárti**
105 E4 **Sparta** Georgia 33.17N 82.58W
107 G3 **Sparta** Illinois 38.06N 89.41W
106 J6 **Sparta** Michigan 43.10N 85.44W
107 C5 **Sparta** Missouri 37.00N 93.06W
105 F1 **Sparta** N Carolina 36.30N 81.07W
103 E4 **Sparta** New Jersey 41.03N 74.36W
110 H5 **Sparta** Oregon 44.52N 117.20W
81 L7 **Spartà** Sicily 38.17N 15.33E
107 L6 **Sparta** Tennessee 35.55N 85.30W
106 D6 **Sparta** Wisconsin 43.57N 90.50W
50 F5 **Spartakvisl** *R* Iceland
105 F3 **Spartanburg** S Carolina 34.56N 81.57W
104 F5 **Spartansburg** Pennsylvania 41.50N 78.43W
77 E9 **Spartel,C** Morocco 35.47N 5.56W
84 D7 **Spárti** Greece 37.05N 22.25E
84 W22 **Spartilla** Corfu 39.43N 19.50E
81 M8 **Spartivento,C** Italy 37.56N 16.04E
81 B6 **Spartivento,C** Sardinia 38.53N 8.52E
84 B4 **Spártos** Greece 38.54N 21.06E
81 M4 **Sparviere,Mte** Italy 39.55N 16.22E
80 C3 **Sparviero** *isld* Italy 42.48N 10.43E
101 Q11 **Sparwood** Br Col 49.45N 114.45W
45 F2 **Spas-Demensk** U.S.S.R. 54.24N 34.01E
45 M1 **Spas-Klepiki** U.S.S.R. 55.08N 40.13E
42 D5 **Spassk** U.S.S.R. 52.47N 87.46E
47 C5 **Spasskaya Guba** U.S.S.R. 62.11N 33.45E
40 F9 **Spassk Dal'niy** U.S.S.R. 44.37N 132.37E
45 R1 **Spasskoye** Gor'kiy U.S.S.R. 55.50N 45.42E
43 J2 **Spasskoye** Kazakhstan U.S.S.R. 52.07N 68.32E
44 F2 **Spasskoye** Stavropol' U.S.S.R. 45.05N 43.42E
45 M2 **Spassk-Ryazanskiy** U.S.S.R. 54.24N 40.25E
66 L7 **Spasu** Italy 46.06N 8.42E
84 G6 **Spáta** Greece 37.58N 23.55E
84 F4 **Spathári** Greece 38.46N 23.26E
101 J7 **Spatsizi Plateau Wilderness Prov. Park** Br Col
64 D3 **Spay** W Germany 50.15N 7.38E
112 L6 **Speaks** Texas 29.16N 96.43W
58 G5 **Spean Bridge** Highland Scotland 56.53N 4.54W
108 G5 **Spearfish** S Dakota 44.28N 103.51W
100 T7 **Spearhill** Manitoba 51.20N 98.22W
14 D6 **Spear Hill** W Australia 24.30S 121.27E
112 C7 **Spearman** Texas 36.12N 101.13W
109 L4 **Spearville** Kansas 37.51N 99.51W
14 A3 **Spearwood** *dist* Perth, W Australia
81 R13 **Spécchia** Italy 39.56N 18.19E
63 R6 **Specker-see** *L* E Germany
104 R9 **Spectacle I** Massachusetts
12 L4 **Spectacle I** New S Wales 33.32S 151.13E
104 L3 **Speculator** New York 43.30N 74.23W
100 F4 **Spedden** Alberta 54.09N 111.41W
121 E10 **Speedwell I** Falkland Is 52.20S 59.45W
109 P7 **Speer** Oklahoma 34.07N 95.35W
108 F8 **Speer** Wyoming 41.03N 104.53W
66 N3 **Speer** *mt* Switzerland 47.12N 9.08E
100 K6 **Speers** Saskatchewan 52.43N 107.32W
96 A14 **Speery I** St Helena 16.02S 5.46W
66 O2 **Speicher** Switzerland 47.25N 9.27E
64 B4 **Speicher** W Germany 49.56N 6.39E
64 M4 **Speichersdorf** W Germany 49.52N 11.46E
64 M7 **Speichersee** *L* W Germany 48.13N 11.45E
116 O6 **Speightstown** Barbados 13.15N 59.39W
65 M7 **Speik Kopf** *mt* Austria 47.14N 15.03E
57 H6 **Speke** Merseyside Eng 53.20N 2.51W
93 E8 **Speke Gulf** Tanzania
60 U17 **Spekholzerheide** Netherlands 50.52N 6.01E
80 G3 **Spello** Italy 42.59N 12.41E
67 O11 **Speloneato** Corsica 42.34N 8.59E
58 E6 **Spelve,L** Mull, Strathclyde Scotland 56.23N 5.43W
113 N6 **Spenard** Alaska 61.05N 150.00W
97 K4 **Spence Bay** N W Terr 69.30N 93.20W
101 Z1 **Spence Bay** N W Terr 69.19N 93.30W
112 G4 **Spence, E.V., Res** Texas
110 N5 **Spencer** Idaho 44.21N 112.11W
107 K2 **Spencer** Indiana 39.18N 86.46W
108 P6 **Spencer** Iowa 43.08N 95.08W
103 L2 **Spencer** Massachusetts 42.15N 71.59W
108 M7 **Spencer** Nebraska 42.52N 98.42W
103 B2 **Spencer** New York 42.12N 76.30W
108 N6 **Spencer** S Dakota 43.45N 97.35W
106 D5 **Spencer** Wisconsin 44.43N 90.18W
104 D8 **Spencer** W Virginia 38.48N 81.22W
94 C5 **Spencer B** Namibia 25.40S 14.50E
113 T7 **Spencer,C** Alaska 58.13N 136.40W
12 D6 **Spencer,C** S Australia 35.19S 136.54E
98 Q9 **Spencer Crique** *B* Quebec 46.47N 71.14W
12 D5 **Spencer G** S Australia
104 P1 **Spencer L** Maine 45.25N 70.17W
104 H3 **Spencerport** New York 43.12N 77.46W
113 D4 **Spencer,Pt** Alaska 65.10N 167.00W
13 A3 **Spencer Ra** N Terr Australia
13 C1 **Spencer Ra** N Terr Australia
103 G2 **Spencertown** New York 42.19N 73.32W
104 A6 **Spencerville** Ohio 40.43N 84.22W
99 O1 **Spencerville** Ontario 44.51N 75.33W
11 N8 **Spencerville Park** New Zealand 43.26S 172.42E
101 N10 **Spences Bridge** Br Col 50.23N 121.21W
63 H8 **Spenge** W Germany 52.08N 8.29E
57 K3 **Spennymoor** Durham Eng 54.42N 1.35W
11 G9 **Spenser Mts** New Zealand
86 E10 **Speos Artemidos** *ruins* Egypt 27.55N 30.52E
63 S8 **Sperenberg** E Germany 52.08N 13.22E
52 E6 **Sperillen** *L* Norway 60.30N 10.05E
84 D4 **Sperkhiás** Greece 38.54N 22.07E
84 D4 **Sperkhós** *R* Greece
53 W15 **Sperle** Norway 61.33N 7.18E
100 U9 **Sperling** Manitoba 49.32N 97.43W
81 H8 **Sperlinga** Sicily 37.46N 14.22E
80 H6 **Sperlonga** Italy 41.16N 13.22E
61 B2 **Spermalie** Belgium 51.03N 2.52E
81 A6 **Sperone,C** Sardinia 38.57N 8.23E
59 H2 **Sperrin Mts** Tyrone N Ireland
104 G8 **Sperryville** Virginia 38.41N 78.13W
95 L3 **Spes Bona** S Africa 27.07S 27.07E
64 G4 **Spessart** *mts* W Germany
103 B8 **Spesutie I** Maryland 39.28N 76.05W
56 G3 **Spetchley** Hereford & Worcs Eng 52.11N 2.09W
84 F7 **Spétsai** Greece 37.16N 23.09E
84 F7 **Spétsai** *isld* Greece
84 F7 **Spetsopoúla** *isld* Greece 37.14N 23.10E
60 L10 **Speulde** Netherlands 52.16N 5.43E
58 K3 **Spey Bay** Grampian Scotland 57.40N 3.06W
58 J4 **Spey Bridge** Grampian Scotland 57.19N 3.38W
64 E5 **Speyer** W Germany 49.18N 8.26E
64 E5 **Speyer** *R* W Germany
58 K3 **Spey R** Scotland
116 M1 **Speyside** Tobago W I 11.17N 60.32W
31 D6 **Spezand** Pakistan 29.59N 67.01E
70 C5 **Spézet** France 48.12N 3.43W
79 G6 **Spezia** *prov* Italy
79 G6 **Spezia,G.di** *B* Italy
79 G6 **Spezia,La** Italy 44.07N 9.48E
81 E7 **Speziale,Mte** Sicily 38.07N 12.46E
81 M4 **Spezzano Albanese** Italy 39.40N 16.19E
81 M5 **Spezzano della Sila** Italy 39.17N 16.20E
97 M4 **Spicer Is** N W Terr 68.00N 77.30W
59 D5 **Spiddle** Galway Irish Rep 53.15N 9.18W
41 B2 **Spidvel', Mys** *C* Novaya Zemlya U.S.S.R. 74.59N 55.40E
63 G5 **Spiekeroog** W Germany 53.47N 7.43E
65 N8 **Spielfeld** Austria 46.43N 15.38E
61 F5 **Spiennes** Belgium 50.27N 3.59E
60 O8 **Spier** Netherlands 52.48N 6.27E
60 H9 **Spierdijk** Netherlands 52.39N 4.56E
61 D4 **Spiere** Belgium 50.43N 3.21E
69 N5 **Spiesen** W Germany 49.19N 7.09E
64 C5 **Spiesen-Elversberg** W Germany 49.18N 7.09E
66 G5 **Spiez** Switzerland 46.42N 7.41E
79 D5 **Spigno Monferrato** Italy 44.33N 8.20E
80 N5 **Spigno,Monte** Italy 41.46N 15.55E
60 Q6 **Spijk** Groningen Netherlands 53.23N 6.50E
60 J12 **Spijk** Zuid Holland Netherlands 51.52N 5.03E
60 F12 **Spijkenisse** Netherlands 51.52N 4.19E
107 C1 **Spikard** Missouri 40.13N 93.37W
113 R3 **Spike Mt** Alaska 67.40N 141.37W
84 B2 **Spilaion** Greece 40.00N 21.18E
79 K5 **Spilamberto** Italy 44.32N 11.01E
84 J10 **Spiliá** Crete 35.31N 23.46E
84 Q15 **Spilia** Cyprus 34.57N 32.58E
84 E2 **Spiliá** Greece 39.48N 22.38E
79 N2 **Spilimbergo** Italy 46.07N 12.54E
81 L6 **Spilinga** Italy 38.37N 15.55E
52 F2 **Spillum** Norway 64.27N 11.32E
57 O6 **Spilsby** Lincs Eng 53.11N 0.05E
66 Q5 **Spina** Switzerland 46.45N 9.47E
81 L3 **Spina,Monte La** Italy 40.02N 15.55E
53 N11 **Spinarnir** *mt* Faeroes 61.26N 6.43W
81 M2 **Spinazzola** Italy 40.58N 16.06E
31 D5 **Spin Bāldak** Afghanistan 31.01N 66.23E
69 K5 **Spincourt** France 49.20N 5.40E
105 F2 **Spindale** N Carolina 35.21N 81.21W
65 L6 **Spindeleben** *mt* Austria 47.56N 14.41E
79 M4 **Spinea** Italy 45.29N 12.09E
80 J3 **Spinetoli** Italy 42.53N 13.46E
79 E5 **Spinetta** Italy 44.53N 8.41E
14 F7 **Spinifex Ra** W Australia
58 H3 **Spinningdale** Highland Scotland 57.52N 4.15W
79 F4 **Spino** Italy 45.24N 9.29E
81 L3 **Spinoso** Italy 40.16N 15.58E
31 D4 **Spintak** Afghanistan 32.32N 67.47E
31 E6 **Spintangi** Pakistan 29.53N 68.10E
31 F4 **Spinwam** Pakistan 33.13N 70.25E
94 F8 **Spioenberg I** *mt* S Africa 31.18S 21.38E
94 E8 **Spioenberg II** *mt* S Africa 31.00S 19.47E
94 S14 **Spioenkop** *mt* S Africa 26.26S 27.55E
95 N4 **Spioenkopdam** *res* S Africa 28.40S 29.29E
11 B12 **Spire Pk** *mt* New Zealand 45.24S 167.29E
110 J2 **Spirit L** Idaho 47.58N 116.54W
108 P6 **Spirit L** Iowa 43.29N 95.08W
110 C3 **Spirit L** Washington 46.17N 122.08W
108 P6 **Spirit Lake** Iowa 42.55N 95.07W
110 C3 **Spirit Lake** Washington 46.16N 122.10W
101 O8 **Spirit River** Alberta 55.46N 118.51W
11 G1 **Spirits B** New Zealand
108 M3 **Spiritwood** N Dakota 46.56N 98.30W
100 K5 **Spiritwood** Saskatchewan 53.24N 107.33W
44 K1 **Spirkin Oseredok.Ostrov** *isld* Kazakhstan U.S.S.R. 46.33N 49.54E
109 Q6 **Spiro** Oklahoma 35.16N 94.36W
46 J2 **Spirovo** U.S.S.R. 57.28N 35.00E
31 D4 **Spirsang Pass** Afghanistan 32.06N 67.19E
66 S4 **Spiss** Austria 46.58N 10.27E
62 M6 **Spišská Belá** Czechoslovakia 49.12N 20.25E
62 M7 **Spišská Nová Ves** Czechoslovakia 48.58N 20.35E
62 M6 **Spišské Podhradie** Czechoslovakia 49.00N 20.47E
44 F7 **Spitak** Armenia U.S.S.R. 40.51N 44.19E
57 M6 **Spital** Lincs Eng 53.24N 0.33W
65 K6 **Spital am Pyhrn** Austria 47.41N 14.22E
65 N6 **Spital am Semmering** Austria 47.36N 15.45E
58 K5 **Spital of Glenshee** Tayside Scotland 56.48N 3.29W
26 B16 **Spit B** Heard I Antarctica
53 Y15 **Spiterstulen** Norway 61.38N 8.24E
56 J6 **Spithead** *channel* Hants Eng
29 E1 **Spiti R** Himachal Prad India
26 B16 **Spit Pt** Heard I Antarctica 53.07S 73.51E
14 C5 **Spit Pt** W Australia 20.04S 119.00E
Spitsbergen *arch see* **Svalbard** *archipelago*
50 T14 **Spitsbergen** *isld* Svalbard
44 E2 **Spitsevka** U.S.S.R. 45.08N 42.31E
95 F9 **Spitskop** *mt* Cape Province S Africa 33.22S 22.23E
95 J5 **Spitskop** *mt* S Africa 29.57S 25.19E
58 N7 **Spittal** Northumb England 55.45N 2.00W
65 H8 **Spittal an der Drau** Austria 46.48N 13.30E
96 C1 **Spittal Pond** Bermuda 32.19N 64.43W
11 N10 **Spit,The** *pt* New Zealand 43.34S 172.45E
65 M5 **Spitz** Austria 48.53N 15.27E
66 L5 **Spitzberge** *mts* Switzerland
94 C3 **Spitzkopje** *mt* Namibia 21.50S 15.08E
66 N3 **Spitzmeilen** *mt* Switzerland 47.02N 9.15E
53 B4 **Spjald** Denmark 56.08N 8.32E
53 U14 **Spjelkavik** Norway 62.28N 6.22E
53 Y20 **Spjotsodd** Norway 59.22N 8.30E
39 E5 **Splavnaya** U.S.S.R. 59.53N 150.35E
112 M5 **Splendora** Texas 30.13N 95.11W
82 C7 **Split** Yugoslavia 43.31N 16.28E
98 H8 **Split,C** Nova Scotia 45.20N 64.30W
100 V2 **Split L** Manitoba
100 V2 **Split Lake** Manitoba 56.16N 96.08W
100 W2 **Split Lake** Manitoba 56.01N 95.49W
110 G8 **Split Pk** Nevada 41.49N 118.27W
79 G2 **Spluga,Monte** Italy 46.12N 9.34E
66 O5 **Splügen** Switzerland 46.34N 9.21E
66 O5 **Splügen Pass** Italy/Switz 46.31N 9.21E
65 N8 **Spodnje Hoče** Yugoslavia 46.30N 15.38E
53 F7 **Spodsbjerg** Denmark 54.56N 10.50E
112 G6 **Spofford** Texas 29.10N 100.26W
57 L5 **Spofforth** N Yorks Eng 53.57N 1.26W
110 H2 **Spokane** Washington 47.40N 117.25W
110 H2 **Spokane** *R* Washington
44 D3 **Spokoynaya** Krasnodar U.S.S.R. 44.15N 41.24E
39 D3 **Spokoynaya** Yakutsk U.S.S.R. 63.58N 145.30E
40 D3 **Spokoynyy** U.S.S.R. 57.42N 128.04E
79 H1 **Spol** *R* Italy
66 R5 **Spöl** *R* Switzerland
84 B4 **Spoláïta** Greece 38.42N 21.21E
80 G3 **Spoleto** Italy 42.44N 12.44E
80 K4 **Spoltore** Italy 42.27N 14.08E
100 F7 **Spondin** Alberta 51.50N 111.38W
25 H6 **Spong** Cambodia 13.27N 105.33E
63 S5 **Sponholz** E Germany 53.33N 13.23E
61 L5 **Spontin** Belgium 50.19N 5.01E
106 C4 **Spooner** Wisconsin 45.50N 91.53W
110 E8 **Spooner Res** California 41.01N 120.36W
106 D9 **Spoon,R** Illinois
83 H7 **Sporádhes** *islds* Greece
63 P6 **Spornitz** E Germany 53.24N 11.44E
39 E4 **Spornoye** U.S.S.R. 62.22N 151.05E
53 E4 **Spørring** Denmark 56.18N 10.09E
53 W15 **Spørteggbre** *glacier* Norway 61.37N 7.28E
41 D2 **Spory Navolok,Mys** *C* Novaya Zemlya U.S.S.R. 76.07N 68.26E
79 D6 **Spotorno** Italy 44.13N 8.25E
103 F6 **Spotswood** New Jersey 40.23N 74.23W
12 C7 **Spotswood** *dist* Melbourne, Vic
108 E5 **Spotted Horse** Wyoming 44.42N 105.50W
111 J5 **Spotted Ra** Nevada
Spoûfiyé *see* **Giv'at Yo'ay**
99 H6 **Spragge** Ontario 46.13N 82.40W
107 K9 **Sprague** Alabama 32.08N 86.18W
100 F1 **Sprague** Manitoba 49.02N 95.36W
110 H2 **Sprague** Washington 47.17N 117.58W
106 D5 **Sprague** Wisconsin 44.09N 90.08W
110 G2 **Sprague L** Washington 47.15N 118.04W
110 D7 **Sprague River** Oregon 42.28N 121.30W
64 H6 **Spraitbach** W Germany 48.52N 9.46E
63 M7 **Sprakensehl** W Germany 52.46N 10.29E
60 J13 **Sprangsevaart** Netherlands 51.40N 5.03E
17 H10 **Spratly Is.** S China Sea 8.45N 111.54E
110 F5 **Spray** Oregon 44.50N 119.46W
82 E6 **Spreča** *R* Yugoslavia
114 E6 **Spreckelsville** Hawaiian Is 20.48N 156.24W
62 H4 **Spree** *R* E Germany
95 D9 **Spreeufontein** S Africa 33.23S 20.45E
63 T9 **Spreewald** *mts* E Germany
62 H4 **Spremberg** E Germany 51.35N 14.22E
64 F3 **Sprendlingen** Hessen W Germany 50.01N 8.41E
64 E4 **Sprendlingen** Rheinland-Pfalz W Germany 49.52N 8.01E
50 G5 **Sprengisandur** *reg* Iceland
79 M3 **Spresiano** Italy 45.47N 12.16E
11 M10 **Spreydon** *dist* Christchurch New Zealand
61 N4 **Sprimont** Belgium 50.30N 5.40E
112 M5 **Spring** Texas 30.05N 95.30W
107 E5 **Spring** *R* Arkansas
109 Q5 **Spring** *R* Oklahoma
110 N8 **Spring B** Utah 41.36N 112.55W
94 D7 **Springbok** S Africa 29.44S 17.56E
104 E5 **Springboro** Pennsylvania 41.48N 80.21W
112 J6 **Spring Branch** Texas 29.56N 98.27W
108 G1 **Spring Brook** N Dakota 48.16N 103.30W
101 P8 **Springburn** Alberta 55.56N 116.55W
11 F10 **Springburn** New Zealand 43.41S 171.28E
103 C6 **Spring City** Pennsylvania 40.11N 75.33W
107 M6 **Spring City** Tennessee 35.41N 84.52W
111 N2 **Spring City** Utah 39.29N 111.30W
100 D9 **Spring Coulee** Alberta 49.24N 113.02W
108 J9 **Spring Cr** Nebraska
13 E4 **Spring Cr** N Terr Australia
13 F6 **Spring Cr** Queensland
11 H8 **Spring Creek** New Zealand 41.28S 173.59E
107 B5 **Springdale** Arkansas 36.11N 94.10W
110 P4 **Springdale** Montana 45.44N 110.14W
111 H4 **Springdale** Nevada 37.02N 116.46W
98 Q4 **Springdale** Newfoundland 49.30N 56.06W
111 M4 **Springdale** Utah 37.10N 113.00W
110 H1 **Springdale** Washington 48.05N 117.45W
63 L8 **Springe** W Germany 52.13N 9.33E
66 Q1 **Springen** Austria 47.31N 9.58E
109 F5 **Springer** New Mexico 36.22N 104.36W
109 N7 **Springer** Oklahoma 34.20N 97.09W
99 Q3 **Springer,Mt** Quebec 49.49N 74.51W
111 P7 **Springerville** Arizona 34.09N 109.18W
109 H4 **Springfield** Colorado 37.26N 102.36W
105 F5 **Springfield** Georgia 32.22N 81.20W
110 N6 **Springfield** Idaho 43.05N 112.42W
107 G2 **Springfield** Illinois 39.49N 89.39W
107 L4 **Springfield** Kentucky 37.42N 85.18W
93 G5 **Springfield** Kenya 0.47N 35.09E
103 J2 **Springfield** Massachusetts 42.07N 72.35W
108 Q5 **Springfield** Minnesota 44.15N 94.58W
107 C4 **Springfield** Missouri 37.11N 93.19W
98 G8 **Springfield** New Brunswick 45.41N 65.51W
11 F10 **Springfield** New Zealand 43.20S 171.56E
98 H9 **Springfield** Nova Scotia 44.37N 64.52W
99 K10 **Springfield** Ontario 42.49N 80.57W
110 B5 **Springfield** Oregon 44.03N 123.01W
13 G7 **Springfield** Queensland 25.52S 143.06E
105 F4 **Springfield** S Carolina 33.31N 81.16W
108 N7 **Springfield** S Dakota 42.52N 97.53W
107 K5 **Springfield** Tennessee 36.30N 86.54W
104 N3 **Springfield** Vermont 43.18N 72.29W
107 G2 **Springfield, L** Illinois 39.43N 89.37W
57 H5 **Springfields** Lancs Eng 53.38N 2.40W
95 J6 **Springfontein** S Africa 30.16S 25.42E
117 A1 **Spring Garden** Guyana 7.00N 58.33W
103 F3 **Spring Glen** New York 41.40N 74.25W
103 A5 **Spring Glen** Pennsylvania 40.38N 76.38W
106 D6 **Spring Green** Wisconsin 43.11N 90.04W
106 C6 **Spring Grove** Minnesota 43.34N 91.37W
104 J7 **Spring Grove** Pennsylvania 39.53N 76.54W
121 K9 **Springhill** Chile 52.40S 69.22W
107 C9 **Springhill** Louisiana 33.00N 93.29W
98 H8 **Springhill** Nova Scotia 45.40N 64.04W
107 K6 **Spring Hill** Tennessee 35.43N 86.58W
57 F2 **Springholm** Dumfries & Galloway Scotland 55.01N 3.52W
105 J2 **Spring Hope** N Carolina 35.57N 78.08W
106 H6 **Spring Lake** Michigan 43.04N 86.10W
103 F6 **Spring Lake** New Jersey 40.09N 74.02W
112 E1 **Springlake** Texas 34.14N 102.19W
95 K9 **Springmount** S Africa 33.40S 26.02E
111 J5 **Spring Mts** Nevada
103 K4 **Springs** Long I, N Y 41.02N 72.20W
94 U14 **Springs** S Africa 26.16S 28.26E
100 P7 **Springside** Saskatchewan 51.21N 102.46W
11 G9 **Springs Junction** New Zealand 42.20S 172.09E
11 G10 **Springston** New Zealand 43.40S 172.26E
13 J6 **Springsure** Queensland 24.09S 148.04E
103 D7 **Springton Res** Pennsylvania 39.58N 75.23W
103 D5 **Springtown** Pennsylvania 40.32N 75.17W
112 K3 **Springtown** Texas 32.58N 97.41W
104 P3 **Springvale** Maine 43.28N 70.48W
13 F6 **Springvale** Queensland 23.34S 140.43E
13 G3 **Springvale** Queensland 15.50S 144.59E
14 G4 **Springvale** W Australia 17.52S 127.35E
12 E8 **Springvale** *dist* Melbourne, Victoria
108 S6 **Spring Valley** Minnesota 43.41N 92.24W
103 F4 **Spring Valley** New York 41.07N 74.02W
95 K8 **Spring Valley** S Africa 32.16S 26.17E
100 M9 **Spring Valley** Saskatchewan 49.55N 105.31W
112 F8 **Spring Valley** *dist* Houston, Texas 29.48N 95.30W
108 L7 **Springview** Nebraska 42.49N 99.45W
107 K8 **Springville** Alabama 33.46N 86.28W
104 G4 **Springville** New York 42.31N 78.41W
103 C3 **Springville** Pennsylvania 41.42N 75.55W
110 O9 **Springville** Utah 40.10N 111.36W
104 H4 **Springwater** New York 42.38N 77.34W
100 J7 **Springwater** Saskatchewan 51.58N 108.23W
57 N5 **Sproatley** Humberside Eng 53.48N 0.11W
63 F10 **Sprockhövel** W Germany 51.20N 7.14E
53 Y18 **Sprogen** *L* Norway 60.63N 8.13E
53 F6 **Sprogø** *isld* Denmark 55.20N 10.58E
63 L6 **Sprötze** W Germany 53.18N 9.47E
57 J1 **Sprouston** Borders Scotland 55.37N 2.23W
106 L5 **Spruce** Michigan 44.52N 83.29W
98 O5 **Spruce Brook** Newfoundland 48.43N 58.12W
99 L7 **Sprucedale** Ontario 45.29N 79.28W
104 F8 **Spruce Knob** *mt* W Virginia 38.43N 79.33W
100 H5 **Spruce Lake** Saskatchewan 53.34N 109.05W
110 L9 **Spruce Mt** Nevada 40.35N 114.49W
105 E2 **Spruce Pine** N Carolina 35.56N 82.04W
103 E5 **Spruce Run Res** New Jersey
103 F2 **Spruceton** New York 42.12N 74.19W
95 M2 **Sprucewell** S Africa 26.42S 28.40E
100 S9 **Spruce Woods Prov. Park** Manitoba
60 G13 **Sprundel** Netherlands 51.32N 4.35E
111 M4 **Spry** Utah 37.55N 112.28W
60 C3 **Spui** Netherlands 51.18N 3.53E
60 E12 **Spui** *R* Netherlands
78 H9 **Spulico,C** Italy 39.57N 16.38E
112 G2 **Spur** Texas 33.28N 100.54W
100 C3 **Spurfield** Alberta 55.15N 114.15W
112 N5 **Spurger** Texas 30.42N 94.12W
109 B8 **Spur L** New Mexico 33.59N 108.54W
58 T11 **Spur Ness** *prom* Orkney Scotland 59.11N 2.42W
57 O5 **Spurn Hd** Humberside Eng 53.36N 0.07E
113 L6 **Spurr,Mt** Alaska 61.19N 152.18W
82 E8 **Spuž** Yugoslavia 42.32N 19.10E
61 J5 **Spy** Belgium 50.29N 4.43E
63 D9 **Spyck** W Germany 51.49N 6.12E
100 Q8 **Spy Hill** Saskatchewan 50.37N 101.42W
95 H4 **Spytfontein** S Africa 28.53S 24.41E
101 M11 **Squamish** Br Col 49.41N 123.11W
104 O3 **Squam L** New Hampshire
104 Q10 **Squantum** Massachusetts 42.17N 71.00W
104 Q7 **Squapan L** Maine
110 P2 **Square Butte** Montana 47.30N 110.11W
33 B10 **Square I** S Yemen 12.46N 44.56E
104 Q6 **Square L** Maine
Squattack *see* **San Michel du Squatec**
98 L3 **Squaw L** Quebec

108 Q2 Squaw Lake Minnesota 47.48N 94.10W
100 O5 Squaw Rapids Dam Saskatchewan 53.39N 103.24W
103 N4 Squibnocket Pt C Massachusetts 41.18N 70.47W
81 N6 Squillace Italy 38.46N 16.31E
81 N6 Squillace,G.di Italy
81 R12 Squinzano Italy 40.26N 18.03E
57 G5 Squires Gate airport Lancs England 53.46N 3.03W
14 G7 Squires,Mt W Australia 26.18S 127.33E
113 G3 Squirrel R Alaska
99 F2 Squirrel R Ontario
18 J9 Sragen Java Indon 7.24S 111.00E
88 K5 Srarhna tribe Morocco
82 F8 Srbica Kosovo i Metohija Yugoslavia 42.45N 20.48E
82 G9 Srbica Makedonija Yugoslavia 41.35N 21.02E
82 F6 Srbija rep Yugoslavia
82 F5 Srbobran Yugoslavia 45.32N 19.48E
45 D6 Srebnoye Ukraine U.S.S.R. 50.39N 32.57E
82 E6 Srebrnica Yugoslavia 44.06N 19.20E
82 L8 Sredetska R Bulgaria
40 C3 Sredina Aldana U.S.S.R. 56.39N 123.05E
39 F7 Sredinnyy Khrebet ra U.S.S.R.
65 O9 Središče Yugoslavia 46.23N 16.17E
82 H8 Sredna Gora mts Bulgaria
40 B3 Srednaya Olëkma U.S.S.R. 57.57N 121.44E
40 D6 Sredne-belaya U.S.S.R. 50.40N 128.00E
40 M8 Srednego O-va islds Kuril Is U.S.S.R. 47.30N 152.50E
39 F6 Sredne-Kamchatsk U.S.S.R. 55.39N 159.45E
39 E2 Srednekolymsk U.S.S.R. 67.27N 153.35E
45 H2 Sredne Russkaya Vozvyshennost' uplands U.S.S.R.
38 J2 Sredne-Sibirskoye Ploskogor'ye tableland U.S.S.R.
47 M4 Sredneural'sk U.S.S.R. 57.00N 60.29E
47 C3 Sredneye Kuyto,Oz L U.S.S.R.
39 E4 Srednikan U.S.S.R. 62.04N 152.31E
82 J9 Sredni Rodopi mts Bulgaria
39 E5 Sredniy U.S.S.R. 59.11N 153.20E
45 L5 Sredniy Ikorets U.S.S.R. 51.04N 39.45E
42 K4 Sredniy Kalar U.S.S.R. 55.55N 117.28E
39 E5 Sredniy,Mys C U.S.S.R. 59.20N 154.48E
41 F3 Sredniy,Ostrov isld U.S.S.R. 77.06N 90.02E
47 M5 Sredniy Ural mts U.S.S.R.
40 F6 Sredniy Urgal U.S.S.R. 51.15N 133.03E
42 B3 Sredniy Vasyugan U.S.S.R. 59.18N 78.11E
44 D1 Sredniy Yegorlyk U.S.S.R. 46.22N 40.47E
44 D1 Sredniy Yegorlyk R U.S.S.R.
45 Q8 Srednyaya Akhtuba U.S.S.R. 48.44N 44.50E
39 G4 Srednyaya Itkana U.S.S.R. 61.39N 162.20E
40 C4 Srednyaya Larba R U.S.S.R.
47 M1 Srednyaya Nevka R Leningrad U.S.S.R.
40 C4 Srednyaya Nyukzha U.S.S.R. 55.13N 123.31E
40 B4 Srednyaya Olekma U.S.S.R. 55.25N 120.30E
39 H4 Srednyaya Pakhacha U.S.S.R. 60.44N 169.14E
43 B2 Srednyaya Pokrovka U.S.S.R. 51.39N 50.07E
25 J6 Sre Khtum Cambodia 12.11N 106.56E
62 K3 Śrem Poland 52.07N 17.00E
82 E6 Srem Raca Yugoslavia 44.55N 19.19E
82 F6 Sremska Mitrovica Yugoslavia 44.59N 19.39E
82 F5 Sremski Karlovci Yugoslavia 45.11N 19.56E
25 J6 Srepok R Cambodia
42 K6 Sretensk U.S.S.R. 52.15N 117.52E
42 F4 Sretenskoye U.S.S.R. 56.28N 96.30E
25 G7 Sre Umbell Cambodia 11.08N 103.46E
18 D9 Sri Buat isld Pen Malaysia
29 D2 Sri Govindpur Punjab India 31.42N 75.33E
28 E4 Sriharikota I Andhra Prad
29 J8 Srikakulam Andhra Prad India 18.19N 84.00E
29 H8 Srikakulam dist Andhra Prad India
30 B2 Sri Kanta mt Uttar Prad India 30.55N 78.51E
27 N8 Sri Lanka rep S Asia
29 D4 Sri Madhopur Rajasthan India 27.26N 75.38E
31 J9 Srimangal Bangladesh 24.20N 91.40E
29 B4 Sri Mohangarh Rajasthan India 27.17N 71.18E
30 L7 Srinagar Bihar India 25.57N 87.22E
30 B2 Srinagar Garhwal, Uttar Prad India 30.12N 78.47E
30 C7 Srinagar Hamirpur, Uttar Prad India 25.11N 79.46E
31 H3 Srinagar Kashmir 34.08N 74.50E
28 B4 Sringeri Karnataka India 13.26N 75.13E
31 H9 Sripur Bangladesh 24.14N 90.26E
28 D5 Srirangam Tamil Nadu India 10.51N 78.44E
28 C4 Srīrangapatam Karnataka India 12.25N 76.41E
28 D2 Srisailam Andhra Prad India 16.06N 78.54E
25 F4 Sri Thep ruins Thailand 16.20N 101.05E
28 C6 Srivaikuntam Tamil Nadu India 8.40N 77.56E
28 A1 Srivardhan Maharashtra India 18.04N 73.03E
28 C6 Srivilliputtur Tamil Nadu India 9.31N 77.41E
82 D6 Srnetica Yugoslavia 44.26N 16.40E
62 K3 Środa Poland 52.15N 17.15E
62 K4 Środa Śląska Poland 51.10N 16.39E
42 D6 Srostki U.S.S.R. 52.25N 85.46E
28 F1 Srungavarapukota Andhra Prad India 18.05N 83.15E
120 D2 S. Sebastião Brazil 7.30S 70.30W
Ssu-ch'uan prov see Sichuan
Ssu-tzu-wang Ch'i see Sizhiwang (Dorbod) Qi
13 F3 Staaten R Queensland
103 G3 Staatsburg New York 41.51N 73.56W
65 O4 Staatz Austria 48.41N 16.30E
51 L1 Stabburselv R Norway
63 Q4 Stäbelow E Germany 54.02N 12.02E
63 O4 Staberhuk pt W Germany 54.24N 11.19E
66 M8 Stabio Switzerland 45.52N 8.57E
110 D4 Stabler Washington 45.48N 122.00W
61 H1 Stabroek Belgium 51.20N 4.22E
53 A4 Staby Denmark 56.16N 8.15E
58 A1 Stac an Armin rock Boreray, W Isles Scotland 57.53N 8.30W
58 C2 Stacashal mt Lewis, W Isles Scotland 58.14N 6.36W
66 M4 Stachelberg Switzerland 46.56N 9.00E
66 P3 Stachler Kops mt Liechtenstein 47.08N 9.37E
58 G2 Stack,L Highland Scotland 58.20N 4.55W
99 J5 Stackpool Ontario 47.53N 81.54W
54 H3 Stack Skerry isld Scotland
59 C7 Stack's Mts Kerry Irish Rep
58 A1 Stac Lee rock Boreray, W Isles Scotland 57.52N 8.30W
58 F2 Stac Polly mt Highland Scotland 58.02N 5.12W
110 E9 Stacy California 40.15N 120.03W
105 L3 Stacy N Carolina 34.52N 76.26W
63 K5 Stade W Germany 53.36N 9.28E
66 K1 Stadel Switzerland 47.32N 8.28E
61 C3 Staden Belgium 50.58N 3.01E
64 F3 Staden W Germany 50.19N 8.55E
56 J4 Stadhampton Oxon Eng 51.42N 1.08W
50 C4 Stadharfell Iceland 65.07N 22.11W
50 L3 Stadharheidhi heath Iceland
50 D4 Stadharhólskirkja Iceland 65.23N 21.58W
50 C5 Stadharhraun Iceland 64.45N 22.06W
50 B5 Stadharsveit dist Iceland
50 B5 Stadhastadhur Iceland 64.49N 23.00W
84 D7 Stádhion Greece 37.27N 22.25E
50 C4 Stadhur Bardhastrandarsýsla, Austur Iceland 65.29N 22.22W
50 C7 Stadhur Gullbringusýsla Iceland 63.49N 22.32W
50 D4 Stadhur Húnavatnssýsla, Vestur Iceland 65.08N 21.03W
50 C2 Stadhur Ísafjardharsýsla, Nordhur Iceland 66.15N 22.49W
50 B2 Stadhur Ísafjardharsýsla, Vestur Iceland 66.20N 23.02W
50 B2 Stadhur Ísafjardharsýsla, Vestur Iceland 66.07N 23.32W
50 D3 Stadhur Strandasýsla Iceland 65.47N 21.50W
53 A4 Stadil Denmark 56.12N 8.13E
53 A4 Stadil Fjord inlet Denmark 56.09N 8.13E
65 J7 Stadl Austria 47.06N 13.59E
53 S14 Stadlandet headland Norway 62.08N 5.13E
65 O5 Stadlau Austria 48.14N 16.27E
65 J5 Stadl Paura Austria 48.05N 13.52E
60 Q7 Stadskanaal Netherlands 53.00N 6.55E
60 Q7 Stads Kanaal canal Netherlands
64 F2 Stadt Allendorf W Germany 50.50N 8.58E
64 N5 Stadtamhof W Germany 49.02N 12.07E
64 K7 Stadtbergen W Germany 48.20N 10.50E
61 Q8 Stadtbredimus Luxembourg 49.33N 6.22E
63 K8 Stadthagen W Germany 52.19N 9.13E
64 L2 Stadtilm E Germany 50.46N 11.04E
64 B3 Stadtkyll W Germany 50.21N 6.32E
63 H6 Stadtland W Germany 53.24N 8.24E
64 J3 Stadtlauringen W Germany 50.11N 10.24E
64 J2 Stadtlengsfeld E Germany 50.47N 10.07E
63 E8 Stadtlohn W Germany 52.00N 6.56E
64 D3 Stadt Loreley W Germany 50.10N 7.44E
63 L9 Stadtoldendorf W Germany 51.53N 9.37E
64 G4 Stadtprozelten W Germany 49.47N 9.25E
Stadtremda see Remda
64 M2 Stadtroda E Germany 50.51N 11.44E
69 Q3 Stadt Schwalbach W Germany 50.09N 8.32E
64 J4 Stadt Schwarzach W Germany 49.48N 10.11E
64 M3 Stadtsteinach W Germany 50.10N 11.32E
66 L3 Stäfa Switzerland 47.14N 8.45E
50 L6 Stafafell Iceland 64.26N 14.52W
58 D6 Staffa isld Strathclyde Scotland 56.26N 6.21W
66 J2 Staffelbach Switzerland 47.17N 8.03E
63 R7 Staffelde E Germany 52.44N 12.58E
64 L8 Staffelsee L W Germany 47.41N 11.10E
64 L3 Staffelstein W Germany 50.06N 11.00E
58 D3 Staffin Skye, Highland Scotland 57.38N 6.12W
58 D3 Staffin isld Highland Scotland
80 H2 Staffolo Italy 43.26N 13.11E
79 F5 Staffora R Italy
103 K3 Stafford Connecticut 41.59N 72.17W
109 M4 Stafford Kansas 37.57N 98.36W
108 M7 Stafford Nebraska 42.20N 98.28W
56 G2 Stafford Staffs Eng 52.48N 2.07W
112 F9 Stafford Texas 29.37N 95.33W
104 H8 Stafford Virginia 38.26N 77.27W
13 K1 Stafford dist Brisbane, Qnsld
56 G2 Staffordshire co England
103 K3 Stafford Springs Connecticut 41.57N 72.17W
50 D5 Stafholt Iceland 64.40N 21.36W
101 Q4 Stagg L N W Terr 62.55N 115.30W
79 H7 Stagno Italy 43.36N 10.21E
81 D5 Stagno dei Colostrai L Sardinia 39.22N 9.37E
81 A4 Stagno di Cabras L Sardinia
81 C5 Stagno di Cagliari Sardinia
81 A2 Stagno di Casaraccio L Sardinia 40.56N 8.13E
87 J10 Stagno di Gumbi flood plain Somalia
81 A2 Stagno di Pilo L Sardinia 40.52N 8.17E
81 B4 Stagno di Santa Guista L Sardinia 39.53N 8.35E
81 D2 Stagno di San Teodoro Sardinia 40.48N 9.40E
81 E8 Stagnone, Is. dello Sicily 37.53N 12.28E
81 A3 Stagno Sale Porcus L Sardinia 40.03N 8.27E
56 K3 Stagsden Beds Eng 52.08N 0.34W
57 J2 Stagshaw Bank Northumb Eng 55.01N 2.01W
59 C3 Stags of Broadhaven rocks Mayo Irish Rep 54.22N 9.47W
63 S4 Stahlbrode E Germany 54.14N 13.16E
63 S8 Stahnsdorf E Germany 52.23N 13.13E
66 M1 Stahringen W Germany 47.46N 8.58E
46 E1 Staicele Latvia U.S.S.R. 57.45N 24.48E
59 B8 Staigue Fort Kerry Irish Rep 51.51N 10.02W
65 K6 Stainach Austria 47.33N 14.07E
57 L5 Staincross W Yorks Eng 53.36N 1.29W
57 K3 Staindrop Durham Eng 54.35N 1.48W
55 A4 Staines Surrey England 51.26N 0.30W
121 J8 Staines Pen Chile
55 B4 Staines Reservoirs Surrey England
57 J4 Stainforth N Yorks Eng 54.06N 2.16W
68 F2 Stains France 48.57N 2.22E
69 J6 Stainville France 48.39N 5.11E
65 M8 Stainz Austria 46.54N 15.17E
57 E2 Stair Strathclyde Scotland 55.29N 4.28W
57 M3 Staithes Cleveland Eng 54.33N 0.48W
81 M8 Staiti Italy 38.00N 16.02E
62 N7 Stakčín Czechoslovakia 49.00N 22.13E
56 G3 Stakenbridge Hereford & Worcs Eng 52.25N 2.09W
45 K8 Stakhanov Ukraine U.S.S.R. 48.34N 38.40E
41 H5 Stakhanova,Im U.S.S.R. 71.46N 101.40E
53 S20 Stakkastadvatn L Norway 59.28N 5.23E
50 C6 Stakksfjördhur B Iceland
53 B5 Stakroge Denmark 55.54N 8.52E
82 G7 Stalać Yugoslavia 43.40N 21.26E
52 K7 Stålboga Sweden 59.13N 16.50E
56 G6 Stalbridge Dorset Eng 50.58N 2.23W
66 H7 Stalden Switzerland 46.14N 7.53E
81 N6 Staletti, Pta. di Italy 38.46N 16.35E
56 P2 Stalham Norfolk Eng 52.47N 1.31E
53 V17 Stalheim Norway 60.50N 6.41E
61 C2 Stalhille Belgium 51.13N 3.04E
47 C4 Stalina Kanal U.S.S.R.
Stalina,Khr mts see Khan Tengri,Pik
41 F2 Stalina, Zaliv B U.S.S.R.
Stalingrad see Volgograd
101 L6 Stalin,Mt Br Col 58.16N 124.48W
Stalino Ukraine see Donetsk
Stalinsk see Novokuznetsk
103 D3 Stalker Pennsylvania 41.50N 75.07W
65 H8 Stall Austria 46.53N 13.02E
66 P6 Stallerberg pass Switzerland 46.28N 9.37E
57 J4 Stalling Busk N Yorks Eng 54.16N 2.07W
64 O5 Stallwang W Germany 49.03N 12.40E
82 J5 Stàlpeni Romania 45.06N 25.00E
106 K3 Stalwart Michigan 46.06N 84.14W
100 M7 Stalwart Saskatchewan 51.15N 105.28W
95 L9 Stalwart Pt S Africa 33.27S 27.13E
57 J6 Stalybridge Greater Manchester Eng 53.29N 2.04W
116 G3 Sta. Marie, C Long I Bahamas 23.42N 75.21W
82 J7 Stamboliyski Dam Bulgaria 43.05N 25.10E
61 E4 Stambruges-Grandglise Belgium 50.31N 3.43E
37 J2 Stambul İstanbul Turkey 41.01N 28.55E
103 G4 Stamford Connecticut 41.03N 73.32W
56 L2 Stamford Lincs Eng 52.39N 0.29W
103 E2 Stamford New York 42.24N 74.38W
13 G5 Stamford Queensland 21.16S 143.48E
108 J6 Stamford S Dakota 43.54N 101.06W
112 H3 Stamford Texas 32.57N 99.48W
57 M5 Stamford Bridge Humberside Eng 53.59N 0.55W
112 H2 Stamford,L Texas
65 O5 Stammersdorf Austria 48.18N 16.24E
64 L6 Stammham W Germany 48.52N 11.29E
66 M1 Stammheim Switzerland 47.38N 8.47E
84 B4 Stamná Greece 38.31N 21.17E
53 T17 Stamnes Norway 60.40N 5.45E
66 P6 Stampa Switzerland 46.21N 9.37E
Stampalia isld see Astipálaia
110 D2 Stampede Washington 47.16N 121.22W
60 F13 Stampersgat Netherlands 51.37N 4.27E
107 M3 Stamping Ground Kentucky 38.20N 84.39W
94 E5 Stampriet Namibia 24.20S 18.28E
107 C8 Stamps Arkansas 33.21N 93.30W
64 O5 Stamsried W Germany 49.16N 12.35E
51 D3 Stamsund Norway 68.07N 13.50E
59 K4 Stamullin Meath Irish Rep 53.37N 6.16W
104 G8 Stanadsville Virginia 38.18N 78.25W
107 B1 Stanberry Missouri 40.15N 94.40W
39 E1 Stanchik U.S.S.R. 70.50N 150.09E
53 U14 Standal Norway 62.16N 6.25E
100 E7 Standard Alberta 51.07N 112.56W
111 O7 Standard Arizona 34.17N 110.15W
60 G13 Standdaarbuiten Netherlands 51.37N 4.31E
95 N2 Standerton S Africa 26.57S 29.14E
57 H5 Standish Greater Manchester Eng 53.36N 2.41W
106 L6 Standish Michigan 43.59N 83.58W
56 M4 Standon Herts Eng 51.53N 0.02E
110 M8 Standrod Utah 42.00N 113.25W
110 F4 Stanfield Oregon 45.46N 119.12W
107 K2 Stanford Indiana 39.06N 86.41W
107 M4 Stanford Kentucky 37.30N 84.40W
110 P2 Stanford Montana 47.09N 110.13W
95 C10 Stanford S Africa 34.26S 19.26E
56 G3 Stanford Bridge Hereford & Worcs Eng 52.17N 2.25W
56 M4 Stanford-le-Hope Essex Eng 51.31N 0.26E
55 K1 Stanford Rivers Essex Eng 51.41N 0.12E
103 G3 Stanfordville New York 41.53N 73.43W
52 L9 Stånga Sweden 57.17N 18.30E
52 F6 Stange Norway 60.40N 11.05E
95 P5 Stanger S Africa 29.20S 31.18E
58 T11 Stanger Hd Orkney Scotland 59.16N 2.53W
79 L4 Stanghella Italy 45.08N 11.46E
53 T17 Stanghelle Norway 60.33N 5.44E
52 D4 Stangvik Norway 62.55N 8.30E
57 J3 Stanhope Durham Eng 54.45N 2.01W
103 E5 Stanhope New Jersey 40.55N 74.43W
116 F2 Staniard Creek Andros Bahamas 24.50N 77.55W
45 L8 Stanichno Luganskoye Ukraine U.S.S.R. 48.38N 39.30E
111 D4 Stanislaus R California
45 D10 Stanislav Kherson, Ukraine U.S.S.R. 46.31N 32.20E
Stanislav Ukraine see Ivano-Frankovsk
82 H8 Stanke Dimitrov Bulgaria 42.15N 23.18E
64 P4 Staňkov Czechoslovakia 49.33N 13.04E
121 E10 Stanley Falkland Is 51.45S 57.56W
23 B10 Stanley Hong Kong 22.12N 114.12E
110 L5 Stanley Idaho 44.13N 114.55W
105 F2 Stanley N Carolina 35.23N 81.06W
108 H1 Stanley N Dakota 48.21N 102.25W
98 F7 Stanley New Brunswick 46.17N 66.45W
109 E6 Stanley New Mexico 35.08N 105.57W
109 P7 Stanley Oklahoma 34.33N 95.30W
12 H8 Stanley Tasmania 40.46S 145.20E
58 K6 Stanley Tayside Scotland 56.29N 3.28W
104 G8 Stanley Virginia 38.35N 78.30W
106 D5 Stanley Wisconsin 44.58N 90.56W
115 P9 Stanley airport Belize 17.28N 88.12W
92 D1 Stanley mt Zaïre 0.25N 29.52E
23 B10 Stanley B Hong Kong
Stanley Falls see Boyoma Falls
100 N3 Stanley Mission Saskatchewan 55.27N 104.33W
23 B10 Stanley Mound Hong Kong 22.13N 114.12E
12 G7 Stanley,Mt King I, Tasmania 40.02S 144.03E
11 G9 Stanley,Mt New Zealand 42.16S 172.41E
13 B6 Stanley,Mt N Terr Australia 22.48S 130.32E
93 A5 Stanley,Mt Uganda/Zaïre 0.23N 29.54E
Stanley Pool see Pool Malebo
28 C5 Stanley Res Tamil Nadu India
Stanleyville see Kisangani
57 H6 Stanlow Cheshire Eng 53.17N 2.52W
100 F7 Stanmore Alberta 51.35N 111.31W
55 D2 Stanmore London England 51.37N 0.19W
92 D12 Stanmore Zimbabwe 20.41S 29.01E
41 M4 Stannakh Khocho U.S.S.R. 73.00N 121.39E
106 G2 Stannard Rock Lt.Ho Michigan 47.09N 87.13W
115 P9 Stann Creek Belize 16.59N 88.13W
57 J2 Stannersburn Northumb Eng 55.10N 2.26W
57 K2 Stannington Northumb Eng 55.06N 1.40W
84 B4 Stános Greece 38.48N 21.10E
39 F1 Stanovaya U.S.S.R. 69.36N 159.30E
47 L7 Stanovka U.S.S.R. 56.49N 72.18E
47 J6 Stanovoy U.S.S.R. 58.47N 63.11E
42 J4 Stanovoye Nagor'ye highland U.S.S.R.
40 B3 Stanovoy Khrebet mts U.S.S.R.
45 H4 Stanovoy Kolodez' U.S.S.R. 52.50N 36.16E
65 E7 Stans Austria 47.23N 11.43E
66 K4 Stans Switzerland 46.57N 8.23E
12 E5 Stansbury S Australia 34.55S 137.48E
66 K4 Stanserhorn mt Switzerland 46.56N 8.21E
14 G5 Stansmore Ra W Australia
66 K4 Stansstad Switzerland 46.59N 8.21E
56 M4 Stanstead Abbots Herts Eng 51.47N 0.01E
Stansted see London Airport (Stansted)
56 M4 Stansted Essex Eng 51.54N 0.12E
13 K8 Stanthorpe Queensland 28.37S 151.52E
108 P9 Stanton Iowa 40.59N 95.06W
107 N4 Stanton Kentucky 37.51N 83.51W
106 J6 Stanton Michigan 43.19N 85.04W
108 J2 Stanton N Dakota 47.20N 101.23W
108 N8 Stanton Nebraska 41.57N 97.13W
56 N3 Stanton Suffolk Eng 52.19N 0.53E
107 G6 Stanton Tennessee 35.28N 89.24W
112 F3 Stanton Texas 32.07N 101.47W
54 E6 Stanton Banks N Atlantic Oc
43 H7 Stantsiya Yakkabag Uzbekistan U.S.S.R. 39.01N 66.41E
56 H4 Stanway Glos Eng 51.59N 1.55W
55 B4 Stanwell Surrey Eng 51.27N 0.29W
57 H3 Stanwix Cumbria Eng 54.54N 2.55W
106 J6 Stanwood Michigan 43.35N 85.30W
110 C1 Stanwood Washington 48.16N 122.22W
65 C7 Stanzach Austria 47.24N 10.35E
50 L5 Stapaey isld Iceland 64.38N 14.19W
50 G3 Stapar mt Iceland 65.43N 18.42W
63 N9 Stapelburg E Germany 51.55N 10.40E
60 N9 Staphorst Netherlands 52.38N 6.12E
57 L7 Stapleford Notts Eng 52.56N 1.15W
56 H5 Stapleford Wilts Eng 51.08N 1.55W
55 K2 Stapleford Abbots Essex Eng 51.39N 0.11E
55 K1 Stapleford Tawney Essex Eng 51.40N 0.11E
56 N5 Staplehurst Kent Eng 51.10N 0.33E
108 Q3 Staples Minnesota 46.20N 94.48W
107 J11 Stapleton Alabama 30.45N 87.48W
105 E4 Stapleton Georgia 33.12N 82.29W
108 K8 Stapleton Nebraska 41.29N 100.40W
103 J8 Stapleton Staten I, N Y 40.37N 74.05W
57 K3 Stapleton Yorks Eng 54.30N 1.35W
50 R11 Stappen C Spitsbergen 74.20N 19.05E
101 P1 Stapylton B N W Terr
107 F9 Star Mississippi 32.03N 90.03W
105 H2 Star N Carolina 35.24N 79.48W
112 J4 Star Texas 31.28N 98.20W
45 F3 Star' U.S.S.R. 53.37N 34.09E
13 H4 Star R Queensland
46 D4 Starachowice Poland 51.03N 21.00E
46 G3 Stara Dorogi Belorussiya U.S.S.R. 53.02N 28.18E
62 M6 Stará L'ubovňa Czechoslovakia 49.16N 20.40E
82 E5 Stara Moravica Yugoslavia 45.50N 19.26E
82 F6 Stara Pazova Yugoslavia 45.00N 20.10E
82 H7 Stara Planina mts Bulgaria
65 N3 Stará Říše Czechoslovakia 49.10N 15.35E
64 O3 Stará-Role Czechoslovakia 50.15N 12.50E
47 M3 Staratel' U.S.S.R. 57.53N 60.02E
45 M5 Staraya Chigla U.S.S.R. 51.19N 40.20E
41 E7 Staraya Igarka U.S.S.R. 67.27N 86.32E
45 N6 Staraya Kriusha U.S.S.R. 50.12N 41.11E
45 T4 Staraya Kulatka U.S.S.R. 52.44N 47.38E
47 L5 Staraya Maskara U.S.S.R. 55.59N 59.13E
45 U2 Staraya Mayna U.S.S.R. 54.36N 48.57E
45 M6 Staraya Melovaya U.S.S.R. 50.17N 40.50E
45 S6 Staraya Poltavka U.S.S.R. 50.29N 46.29E
45 V4 Staraya Porubezhka U.S.S.R. 52.03N 49.10E
45 U3 Staraya Racheyka U.S.S.R. 53.25N 48.02E
45 B4 Staraya Rudnya Belorussiya U.S.S.R. 52.52N 30.16E
46 H1 Staraya Russa U.S.S.R. 58.00N 31.22E
46 G5 Staraya Sinyava Ukraine U.S.S.R. 49.38N 27.39E
45 T4 Staraya Terevka U.S.S.R. 52.53N 47.30E
45 B2 Staraya Vodva Belorussiya U.S.S.R. 52.05N 30.10E
47 K5 Staraya Vorpavla U.S.S.R. 61.08N 65.10E
82 K8 Stara Zagora Bulgaria 42.25N 25.37E
100 U9 Starbuck Manitoba 49.47N 97.38W
108 P4 Starbuck Minnesota 45.35N 95.35W
110 G3 Starbuck Washington 46.32N 118.07W
122 L9 Starbuck I Line Is Pacific Oc 5.37S 155.55W
107 E8 Star City Arkansas 33.56N 91.52W
106 H9 Star City Indiana 40.58N 86.34W
100 N6 Star City Saskatchewan 52.52N 104.20W
104 F7 Star City W Virginia 39.41N 79.58W
13 G2 Starcke Queensland 14.50S 144.58E
56 E6 Starcross Devon Eng 50.38N 3.27W
65 N3 Stařeč Czechoslovakia 49.13N 15.48E
65 M3 Staré Hobzí Czechoslovakia 49.01N 15.27E
64 O4 Staré Sedliště Czechoslovakia 49.45N 12.42E
65 K2 Staré Sedlo Czechoslovakia 49.31N 14.10E
Stargard see Burg Stargard
62 J2 Stargard Poland 53.21N 15.01E
15 M4 Star Harb San Cristobal I Solomon Is 10.53S 162.18E
53 T15 Stårheim Norway 61.55N 5.46E
39 H2 Starichkova U.S.S.R. 65.14N 168.58E
39 D1 Starikovo U.S.S.R. 71.07N 149.15E
46 O3 Stari Kulatka U.S.S.R. 52.48N 47.30E
82 D6 Stari Majdan Yugoslavia 44.50N 16.35E
62 N6 Starina Czechoslovakia 49.04N 22.15E
45 R8 Staritsa Astrakhan' U.S.S.R. 48.14N 45.55E
46 J2 Staritsa Kalinin U.S.S.R. 56.29N 34.59E
40 J7 Staritsa Sakhalin U.S.S.R. 48.36N 141.59E
42 C3 Staritsa Tomsk U.S.S.R. 58.10N 80.32E
111 O10 Stark Arizona 31.22N 110.03W
110 L2 Stark Montana 47.06N 114.29W
104 O2 Stark New Hampshire 44.36N 71.25W
105 E8 Starke Florida 29.55N 82.06W
66 O3 Starkenbach Switzerland 47.12N 9.16E
110 J5 Starkey Idaho 44.51N 116.27W
110 G4 Starkey Oregon 45.14N 118.25W
11 K11 Star Keys islds Chatham Is Pacific Oc 44.12S 175.58W
107 C11 Starks Louisiana 30.19N 93.40W
109 F4 Starkville Colorado 37.06N 104.33W
107 H8 Starkville Mississippi 33.27N 88.50W
108 M1 Starkweather N Dakota 48.29N 98.52W
106 E3 Starlake Wisconsin 46.02N 89.28W
66 S5 Starlex,Piz mt Italy/Switz 46.40N 10.24E
50 L5 Starmýrarfjörur sand spit Iceland
50 L5 Starmyri Iceland 64.33N 14.35W
64 L7 Starnberg W Germany 48.00N 11.20E
64 L8 Starnberger See L W Germany
42 C6 Staroaleyskoye U.S.S.R. 51.01N 82.01E
45 K7 Star'obel'sk Ukraine U.S.S.R. 49.16N 38.56E
45 K9 Starobeshevo Ukraine U.S.S.R. 47.45N 38.03E
46 F3 Starobin Belorussiya U.S.S.R. 52.40N 27.29E
42 D5 Starobochaty U.S.S.R. 54.12N 86.13E
45 D4 Starodub U.S.S.R. 52.35N 32.46E
40 J8 Starodubskoye Sakhalin U.S.S.R. 47.24N 142.47E
62 L2 Starogard Poland 53.58N 18.30E
44 G4 Starogladkovskaya U.S.S.R. 43.39N 46.26E
45 J9 Staroignat'yevka Ukraine U.S.S.R. 47.33N 37.49E
41 J2 Starokadomskogo,O isld U.S.S.R.
82 M4 Starokazache U.S.S.R. 46.20N 30.00E
46 F5 Starokonstantinov Ukraine U.S.S.R. 49.48N 27.10E
45 L2 Staroletovo U.S.S.R. 54.51N 39.30E
44 E2 Staromar'yevka U.S.S.R. 45.05N 42.15E
44 C1 Starominskaya U.S.S.R. 46.33N 39.04E
45 H9 Staromlinovka Ukraine U.S.S.R. 47.42N 36.51E
44 B2 Staronizhestebliyevskaya U.S.S.R. 45.24N 38.24E
82 L8 Staro Oryakhovo Bulgaria 42.59N 27.49E
43 M5 Staropokrovka Kirgiziya U.S.S.R. 44.47N 75.16E
44 B1 Staroshcherbinovskaya U.S.S.R. 46.38N 38.40E
62 O2 Starosielce Poland 53.08N 23.03E
82 L1 Staro Sinyava U.S.S.R. 49.35N 27.39E
47 L7 Starosoldatskoye U.S.S.R. 56.12N 72.38E
43 D1 Starosubkhangulovo Bashkir U.S.S.R. 53.07N 57.29E
45 T3 Starotimoshkino U.S.S.R. 53.39N 47.31E
44 A2 Starotitarovskaya U.S.S.R. 45.13N 37.38E
42 K6 Starotsurukhaytuy U.S.S.R. 50.12N 119.22E
47 M4 Staroutkinsk U.S.S.R. 57.15N 59.20E
47 F6 Starovercheskaya U.S.S.R. 59.35N 48.33E
45 G7 Staroverovka Ukraine U.S.S.R. 49.33N 35.43E
46 R2 Staroye Baysarovo U.S.S.R. 55.29N 53.50E
41 M7 Staroye Linde U.S.S.R. 65.55N 121.02E
45 Q2 Staroye Shaygovo U.S.S.R. 54.20N 44.28E
45 T2 Staroye Shaymurzino U.S.S.R. 54.45N 47.59E
45 Q2 Staroye Sindrovo U.S.S.R. 54.25N 44.07E
45 R4 Staroye Slavkino U.S.S.R. 52.34N 45.07E
45 M3 Staroyur'yevo U.S.S.R. 53.19N 40.42E
45 L2 Starozhilovo U.S.S.R. 54.14N 39.54E
110 G9 Star Pk Nevada 40.32N 118.10W
103 B9 Starr Maryland 38.59N 76.01W
103 D3 Starrucca Pennsylvania 41.54N 75.29W
45 A1 Star Selo Belorussiya U.S.S.R. 55.14N 29.53E
56 D7 Start Pt Devon Eng 50.13N 3.38W
58 U11 Start Pt Orkney Scotland 59.17N 2.24W
53 B5 Starup Denmark 55.39N 8.49E
64 P4 Starý Plzenec Czechoslovakia 49.42N 13.29E
62 M6 Stary Sącz Poland 49.33N 20.36E
82 H1 Stary Sambor U.S.S.R. 49.25N 22.59E
47 L5 Staryy Belokatay U.S.S.R. 55.48N 59.02E
44 H3 Staryy Biryuzyak U.S.S.R. 44.49N 46.54E
42 K6 Staryy Chindant U.S.S.R. 50.34N 115.30E
41 P5 Staryy Dom U.S.S.R. 71.48N 139.50E
45 T2 Staryye Aybesi U.S.S.R. 54.57N 47.01E
45 S4 Staryye Burasy U.S.S.R. 52.18N 46.06E
46 R2 Staryye Zyattsy U.S.S.R. 57.20N 52.40E
43 E3 Staryy Karabutak Kazakhstan U.S.S.R. 49.47N 59.55E
41 H5 Staryy Kayak U.S.S.R. 71.30N 103.20E
39 C5 Staryy Kheydzhan U.S.S.R. 59.55N 144.45E
45 O5 Staryy Khopër U.S.S.R. 51.31N 42.58E
44 D9 Staryy Krym Crimea, Ukraine U.S.S.R. 45.03N 35.06E
45 J9 Staryy Krym Donetsk, Ukraine U.S.S.R. 47.10N 37.30E
44 F4 Staryy Lesken U.S.S.R. 43.24N 43.56E
39 J3 Staryy Mayn U.S.S.R. 64.31N 171.13E
46 R2 Staryy Menzelyabash U.S.S.R. 55.12N 52.41E
47 L3 Staryy Nadym U.S.S.R. 65.33N 72.45E
44 H2 Staryy Olenichevo U.S.S.R. 45.34N 47.06E
42 K5 Staryy Olov U.S.S.R. 52.30N 116.40E
45 J5 Staryy Oskol U.S.S.R. 51.20N 37.50E
46 J1 Staryy Ryad U.S.S.R. 58.01N 34.59E
45 H6 Staryy Saltov Ukraine U.S.S.R. 50.06N 36.47E
44 H4 Staryy Terek R U.S.S.R.
63 P9 Stassfurt E Germany 51.51N 11.35E
62 N5 Staszów Poland 50.33N 21.07E
108 R7 State Center Iowa 42.01N 93.10W
104 H6 State College Pennsylvania 40.48N 77.52W
107 H10 State Line Mississippi 31.25N 88.29W
Staten I see Estados, I. de los
103 K8 Staten Island New York
26 A14 State President Swart Pk Marion I Ind Oc 46.54S 37.44E
105 F5 Statesboro Georgia 32.28N 81.47W
105 G2 Statesville N Carolina 35.46N 80.54W
52 E7 Stathelle Norway 59.03N 9.42E
66 P4 Stätzerhorn Switzerland 46.46N 9.31E
66 H5 Staubbach Falls Switzerland
64 P1 Stauchitz E Germany 51.15N 13.14E
64 O8 Staudach-Egerdach W Germany 47.46N 12.30E
64 D8 Staufen Baden-Württemberg W Germany 47.54N 7.45E
65 B6 Staufen W Germany 47.33N 10.02E
64 F2 Staufenberg W Germany 50.40N 8.45E
110 E6 Stauffer Oregon 43.29N 120.07W
56 G4 Staunton Glos Eng 51.58N 2.19W
107 G2 Staunton Illinois 39.01N 89.49W
104 F8 Staunton Virginia 38.10N 79.05W
53 R16 Stauren Norway 61.21N 4.50E
53 S15 Stavang Sogn og Fjordane Norway 61.32N 5.12E
53 T21 Stavanger Norway 58.58N 5.45E
53 W19 Ståvatn L Norway 59.49N 7.11E
61 J5 Stave Belgium 50.17N 4.40E
101 M11 Stave L Br Col 49.21N 122.19W
61 A3 Stavele Belgium 50.56N 2.40E
57 H4 Staveley Cumbria Eng 54.23N 2.49W
57 L6 Staveley Derbys Eng 53.16N 1.20W
61 O5 Stavelot Belgium 50.24N 5.56E
100 D8 Stavely Alberta 50.10N 113.35W
63 S5 Staven E Germany 53.37N 13.24E
Stavenhagen see Reuterstadt Stavenhagen
60 E13 Stavenisse Netherlands 51.35N 4.00E
60 K8 Staveren Netherlands 52.53N 5.21E
56 J3 Staverton Northants Eng 52.15N 1.12W
53 R16 Stavfjorden inlet Norway
53 S16 Stavnes Norway 61.25N 5.08E
53 A5 Stavning Denmark 55.58N 8.23E
53 F3 Stavnshoved C Denmark 56.32N 10.47E
53 S15 Stavøy isld Norway 61.34N 5.06E
53 J6 Stavreby Denmark 55.06N 12.09E
53 F6 Stavreshoved C Denmark 55.29N 10.45E
84 C6 Stavrodhrómi Greece 37.42N 21.57E
41 E3 Stavrolitovaya, Gora mt U.S.S.R. 75.20N 89.50E
44 D2 Stavropol' Stavropol' U.S.S.R. 45.03N 41.59E
43 H1 Stavropolka Kazakhstan U.S.S.R. 52.51N 66.31E
44 D2 Stavropol'skaya Vozvyshennost' highlands U.S.S.R.
46 M7 Stavropol'skiy Kray terr U.S.S.R.
84 Q14 Stavros Cyprus 35.02N 32.28E
84 A5 Stavrós Itháki Greece 38.27N 20.39E
84 D3 Stavrós Lárisa Greece 39.18N 22.15E
83 G3 Stavroúpolis Greece 41.12N 24.45E
45 M1 Stavrovo U.S.S.R. 56.08N 40.00E
84 R15 Stavrovouni Monastery Cyprus 34.53N 33.28E
12 G6 Stawell Victoria 37.06S 142.52E
13 G5 Stawell R Queensland
62 N2 Stawiski Poland 53.23N 22.10E
62 L4 Stawiszyn Poland 51.56N 18.04E
57 N4 Staxton N Yorks Eng 54.11N 0.26W
45 B6 Stayki Ukraine U.S.S.R. 50.05N 30.54E
99 K8 Stayner Ontario 44.25N 80.06W
110 C5 Stayton Oregon 44.48N 122.27W
79 H7 Stazzema Italy 43.59N 10.18E
111 E2 Steamboat Nevada 39.24N 119.45W
109 D1 Steamboat Springs Colorado 40.28N 106.51W
33 B10 Steamer Pt S Yemen 12.48N 44.59E
107 M5 Stearns Kentucky 36.41N 84.29W
62 M2 Stębark Poland 53.30N 20.09E
113 F5 Stebbins Alaska 63.32N 162.20W
66 H5 Stechelberg Switzerland 46.33N 7.55E
63 Q7 Stechow E Germany 52.39N 12.28E
66 M1 Steckborn Switzerland 47.38N 8.59E
60 P6 Stedum Netherlands 53.19N 6.42E
65 J6 Steeg Österreich Austria 47.37N 13.38E
65 B7 Steeg Tirol Austria 47.15N 10.18E
60 N11 Steeg, De Netherlands 52.02N 6.04E
74 J8 Steeg Ou De L'o. Flodda barrage Algeria
107 K8 Steele Alabama 33.56N 86.11W
107 G5 Steele Missouri 36.07N 89.50W
108 O9 Steele City Nebraska 40.02N 97.00W
113 R4 Steele Creek Alaska 64.15N 141.24W
123 E13 Steele I Antarctica
101 C5 Steele, Mt Yukon Terr 61.03N 140.21W
107 G3 Steeleville Illinois 38.00N 89.40W
99 D3 Steel L Ontario
94 L5 Steelpoort S Africa 24.48S 30.11E
99 D4 Steel R Ontario
95 N3 Steel's Drift S Africa 27.21S 29.29E
10 V10 Steel's Pt Norfolk I Pacific Oc 29.02S 167.59E
103 A6 Steelton Pennsylvania 40.13N 76.51W
107 E4 Steelville Missouri 37.57N 91.21W
101 P6 Steen R Alberta
60 F13 Steenbergen Noord-Brabant Netherlands 51.35N 4.19E
60 F13 Steenbergsche Vliet R Netherlands
15 D6 Steenboom, Tandjung C Irian Jaya 4.55S 136.50E
60 N11 Steenderen Netherlands 52.04N 6.14E
61 H2 Steendorp Belgium 51.07N 4.17E
61 H3 Steenhuffel Belgium 51.00N 4.17E
61 F3 Steenhuize-Wijnhuize Belgium 50.50N 3.54E
94 L5 Steenkamps Berg mts S Africa
95 E8 Steenkampsvlakte S Africa 32.09S 21.37E
61 A2 Steenkerke Belgium 51.03N 2.41E
61 G4 Steenkerque Belgium 50.38N 4.04E
15 B5 Steenkool Irian Jaya 2.07S 133.37E
61 J3 Steenokkerzeel Belgium 50.55N 4.31E
101 P6 Steen River Alberta 59.37N 117.17W
60 K14 Steensel Netherlands 51.23N 5.21E
110 G7 Steens Mt Oregon 42.45N 118.33W
97 O2 Steenstrups Gletscher glacier Greenland 75.00N 56.00W
69 D2 Steenvoorde France 50.49N 2.35E
69 D2 Steenwerck France 50.41N 2.45E
60 N8 Steenwijk Netherlands 52.47N 6.07E
60 N8 Steenwijkerdiep canal Netherlands
60 P9 Steenwijksmoer Netherlands 52.40N 6.41E
100 M5 Steep Creek Saskatchewan 53.18N 105.18W
100 O3 Steephill L Saskatchewan
56 E5 Steepholm isld Somerset Eng 51.21N 3.07W
23 C9 Steep I Hong Kong 22.16N 114.18E
56 N4 Steeple Essex Eng 51.42N 0.47E
121 D9 Steeple I Falkland Is 51.00S 61.15W
19 J7 Steep Pt Philippines 9.30N 118.12E
14 A7 Steep Pt W Australia 26.09S 113.11E
100 T7 Steep Rock Manitoba 41.26N 98.48W
100 L2 Steep Rock Lake Ontario 48.50N 91.38W
14 B6 Steere, Mt W Australia 24.57S 116.20E
57 K5 Steeton W Yorks Eng 53.54N 1.57W
81 M6 Stefanaconi Italy 38.40N 16.08E
84 E3 Stefanavíkion Greece 39.28N 22.45E
82 L3 Stefaneşti Romania 47.44N 27.15E
84 G5 Stefáni Greece 38.10N 23.33E
84 E8 Stefaniá Greece 36.51N 22.36E
Stefanie L see Chew Bahir L
123 B4 Stefansson B Antarctica
97 J3 Stefansson I N W Terr 73.30N 105.30W
64 F2 Steffenberg W Germany 50.50N 8.33E
121 B10 Steffen, Cerro pk Arg/Chile 44.25S 71.40W
15 L5 Steffen Str Bismarck Arch
66 G4 Steffisburg Switzerland 46.47N 7.38E
66 M2 Steg Switzerland 47.21N 8.56E
108 G8 Stegall Nebraska 41.52N 103.56W
53 Y18 Stegaros Norway 60.05N 8.17E
53 J7 Stege Denmark 54.59N 12.18E
53 J6 Stege Bugt B Denmark 55.02N 12.15E
63 P8 Stegelitz E Germany 52.12N 11.55E
53 J7 Stege Nor L Denmark 54.59N 12.20E
106 G8 Steger Illinois 41.28N 87.39W
65 O7 Stegersbach Austria 47.10N 16.10E
94 L6 Stegi Swaziland 26.30S 32.00E
63 A2 Steglitz dist W Berlin
110 E1 Stehekin Washington 48.20N 120.40W
65 K7 Steiermark prov Austria
51 D4 Steigen Norway 67.57N 15.00E
64 J4 Steigerwald hills W Germany
60 N14 Steijl Netherlands 51.20N 6.08E
95 P3 Steilrand S Africa 27.47S 31.15E
66 H1 Stein Aargau Switz 47.33N 7.57E
65 N5 Stein Austria 48.25N 15.35E
60 T17 Stein Netherlands 50.58N 5.45E
66 N3 Stein St Gallen Switz 47.13N 9.15E
58 C3 Stein Skye, Highland Scotland 57.31N 6.35W
66 M1 Stein Thurgau Switz 47.40N 8.52E
64 L5 Stein W Germany 49.25N 11.01E
65 D7 Steinach Austria 47.06N 11.28E
64 L3 Steinach E Germany 50.25N 11.10E
66 O1 Steinach Switzerland 47.30N 9.27E
64 J5 Steinach W Germany 49.27N 10.17E
65 M5 Steinakirchen Austria 48.05N 15.03E
50 F7 Steinar Iceland 63.33N 19.43W
64 G3 Steinau W Germany 50.18N 9.29E
108 O9 Steinauer Nebraska 40.12N 96.15W
64 J2 Steinbach E Germany 50.50N 10.21E
69 N8 Steinbach France 47.49N 7.09E
100 V9 Steinbach Manitoba 49.32N 96.40W
64 E6 Steinbach W Germany 48.43N 8.10E
64 K2 Steinbach Hallenberg E Germany 50.42N 10.34E
65 E6 Steinberg Austria 47.32N 11.49E
53 X17 Steinbergdalshytta Norway 60.47N 7.35E
69 N6 Steinbourg France 48.47N 7.25E
53 Y13 Steinbruhøgda mt Norway 62.36N 8.29E
66 F1 Steinbrunn-le-Bas France 47.41N 7.22E
66 F1 Steinbrunn-le-Haut France 47.40N 7.21E
53 Y16 Steinbusjøen L Norway 61.16N 8.21E
65 H6 Steindorf Austria 47.57N 13.15E
53 W17 Steine Norway 60.52N 7.20E
66 L3 Steinen Switzerland 47.03N 8.37E
64 D8 Steinen W Germany 47.39N 7.45E
65 G7 Steinernes Meer mts Austria
53 S17 Steinesto Norway 60.31N 5.20E
63 H7 Steinfeld W Germany 52.35N 8.13E
61 O8 Steinfort Luxembourg 49.39N 5.55E
64 K8 Steingaden W Germany 47.41N 10.51E
50 C3 Steingrimsfjardharheidhi heath Iceland
50 D3 Steingrímsfjördhur B Iceland
63 H8 Steinhagen W Germany 52.00N 8.25E
105 D8 Steinhatchee Florida 29.40N 83.23W
94 E3 Steinhausen Namibia 21.49S 18.20E
53 U21 Steinheia moor Norway 58.57N 6.20E
64 L3 Steinheid E Germany 50.27N 11.03E
64 J7 Steinheim Bayern W Germany 48.01N 10.10E
64 F3 Steinheim Hessen W Germany 50.06N 8.56E
63 K9 Steinheim Nordrhein-Westfalen W Germany 51.51N 9.05E
63 M5 Steinhorst W Germany 53.43N 10.28E
63 K8 Steinhuder Meer L W Germany
63 L5 Steinkirchen W Germany 53.34N 9.37E
52 F3 Steinkjer Norway 64.00N 11.30E
94 D7 Steinkopf S Africa 29.18S 17.43E
53 T20 Steinnesvåg Norway 59.10N 5.50E
65 G6 Steinpass Austria/W Germany 47.41N 12.46E
65 L7 Steinplan mt Austria 47.10N 14.54E
109 B9 Steins New Mexico 32.13N 108.59W
61 P8 Steinsel Luxembourg 49.41N 6.08E
64 F5 Steinsfurt W Germany 49.15N 8.55E
53 T17 Steinsland Norway 60.55N 5.58E
53 T17 Steinslandsvatn L Norway 60.53N 5.58E
50 H7 Steinsmýri Iceland 63.39N 18.00W
53 R16 Steinsund Norway 61.04N 4.49E
53 T15 Steinsvik Norway 62.00N 5.52E
50 L2 Steintún Iceland 66.04N 14.42W
64 L3 Steinwiesen W Germany 50.18N 11.28E
65 K3 Štěken Czechoslovakia 49.15N 14.01E
61 G2 Stekene Belgium 51.12N 4.03E
39 E4 Stekol'nyy U.S.S.R. 60.00N 150.57E
79 D6 Stella Italy 44.23N 8.30E
105 K3 Stella N Carolina 34.57N 77.09W
108 P9 Stella Nebraska 40.15N 95.48W
95 H2 Stella S Africa 26.33S 24.52E
79 G2 Stella, Corno mt Italy 46.03N 9.48E
26 T15 Stella Matutina Réunion Ind Oc 21.11S 55.18E
81 K3 Stella, Monte della Italy 40.13N 15.04E
79 D6 Stellanello Italy 44.01N 8.03E
66 O6 Stella, Pizzo mt Italy 46.23N 9.25E
98 K8 Stellarton Nova Scotia 45.34N 62.30W
79 K5 Stellata Italy 44.57N 11.25E
63 M6 Stelle W Germany 53.22N 10.07E
95 B9 Stellenbosch S Africa 33.56S 18.51E
60 E12 Stellendam Netherlands 51.48N 4.01E
113 Q6 Steller, Mt Alaska 60.31N 143.10W
67 P11 Stello mt Corsica 42.47N 9.25E
79 J1 Stelvio Italy 46.37N 10.32E
79 H1 Stelvio, Passo di pass Italy 46.32N 10.27E
105 J1 Stem N Carolina 36.13N 78.44W
61 O4 Stembert Belgium 50.36N 5.54E
103 C5 Stemlersville Pennsylvania 40.51N 75.36W
63 K7 Stemmen W Germany 52.52N 9.21E
52 D3 Stemshang Norway 63.19N 8.44E
63 H8 Stemwede W Germany 52.26N 8.25E
84 D1 Sténa Sarandapórou pass Greece 40.08N 22.03E
69 J5 Stenay France 49.29N 5.12E
53 A3 Stenbjerg Denmark 56.56N 8.23E
53 S18 Stend Norway 60.15N 5.21E
63 P7 Stendal E Germany 52.36N 11.52E
46 E2 Stende Latvia U.S.S.R. 57.06N 22.31E
53 D5 Stenderup Denmark 55.47N 9.50E
61 B2 Stene Belgium 51.12N 2.55E
100 P7 Stenen Saskatchewan 51.53N 102.22W
53 E2 Stenhøj Denmark 57.23N 10.21E
12 D6 Stenhouse Bay S Australia 35.17S 126.56E
23 B10 Stenhouse, Mt Hong Kong 22.11N 114.07E
79 J2 Sténico Italy 46.03N 10.51E
84 G4 Stení Dhírfios Greece 38.35N 23.50E
53 D3 Stenild Denmark 56.41N 9.42E
53 H5 Stenlille Denmark 55.32N 11.37E
53 J5 Stenløse Denmark 55.47N 12.13E
58 P9 Stenness Shetland Scotland 60.29N 1.37W
58 S11 Stenness, L of Orkney Scotland 59.00N 3.15W
84 D7 Stenón Greece 37.30N 22.27E
58 D3 Stenscholl Skye, Highland Scotland 57.38N 6.14W
51 F6 Stensele Sweden 65.05N 17.10E
52 H9 Stensjön Sweden 57.36N 14.42E
52 H8 Stenstorp Sweden 58.15N 13.45E
51 H6 Stenstrask Sweden 65.13N 19.50E
53 F6 Stenstrup Denmark 55.08N 10.31E
51 H5 Stenträsk Sweden 66.20N 19.50E
52 F8 Stenungsund Sweden 58.05N 11.55E
53 F4 Stenvad Denmark 56.28N 10.39E
46 F4 Stepan Ukraine U.S.S.R. 51.09N 26.18E
44 H8 Stepanakert Azerbaydzhan U.S.S.R. 39.48N 46.45E
44 K7 Stepana Razina Azerbaydzhan U.S.S.R. 40.25N 50.01E
45 Q2 Stepana Razina, imeni U.S.S.R. 54.53N 44.15E
44 F6 Stepanavan Armenia U.S.S.R. 41.01N 44.24E
65 O2 Stěpánov Czechoslovakia 49.32N 16.22E
45 J8 Stepanovka Donetsk, Ukraine U.S.S.R. 48.38N 37.02E
43 D2 Stepanovka Kazakhstan U.S.S.R. 50.29N 56.30E
44 D8 Stepanovka Zaporozh'ye, Ukraine U.S.S.R. 46.29N 35.33E
45 N1 Stepantsevo U.S.S.R. 56.07N 41.40E
63 O5 Stepenitz R E Germany
63 P6 Stepenitz R E Germany
64 N8 Stephanskirchen W Germany 47.51N 12.10E
64 O6 Stephansposching W Germany 48.50N 12.50E
15 H6 Stephan Str Papua New Guinea
108 O1 Stephen Minnesota 48.28N 96.52W
107 C8 Stephens Arkansas 33.26N 93.04W
12 F3 Stephens R New S Wales
11 H7 Stephens, C New Zealand 41.43S 173.57E
104 G7 Stephens City Virginia 39.05N 78.14W
12 F5 Stephen's Creek New S Wales 31.50S 141.30E
101 H8 Stephens I Br Col 54.09N 130.40W
11 H7 Stephens I New Zealand 41.42S 174.00E
106 G4 Stephenson Michigan 45.25N 87.38W
11 H1 Stephenson I New Zealand 34.59S 173.48E
113 V8 Stephens Pass Alaska
98 O5 Stephenville Newfoundland 48.33N 58.34W
112 J3 Stephenville Texas 32.12N 98.13W
98 O5 Stephenville Crossing Newfoundland 48.31N 58.28W
44 B2 Stepnaya U.S.S.R. 45.47N 38.28E
55 G3 Stepney London Eng 51.31N 0.04W
Stepnoy see Elista
45 R8 Stepnoy U.S.S.R. 48.57N 45.36E
47 J8 Stepnoye Chelyabinsk U.S.S.R. 54.06N 60.21E

Stepnoye Kalmyk A.S.S.R. U.S.S.R. see Yashalta
43 L5 Stepnoye Kirgiziya U.S.S.R. 43.14N 73.58E
45 S5 Stepnoye Saratov U.S.S.R. 51.22N 46.48E
44 F3 Stepnoye Stavropol' U.S.S.R. 44.15N 44.36E
43 K1 Stepnyak Kazakhstan U.S.S.R. 52.52N 70.49E
113 H9 Stepovak B Alaska
53 C6 Stepping Denmark 55.21N 9.23E
122 D1 Steps Pt C Amer Samoa Pacific Oc 14.23S 170.46W
111 K2 Steptoe Nevada 39.32N 114.55W
64 H3 Sterbfritz W Germany 50.18N 9.41E
83 E6 Stereá Ellás div Greece
84 C3 Sterea Ellas reg Greece
95 G7 Sterkaar S Africa 31.05S 23.42E
94 R13 Sterkfontein S Africa 26.04S 27.42E
95 N4 Sterkfonteindam res Orange Free State S Africa 28.26S 29.03E
95 N1 Sterkloop S Africa 25.31S 29.51E
60 L14 Sterksel Netherlands 51.21N 5.37E
95 L6 Sterkspruit S Africa 30.31S 27.22E
95 K7 Sterkstroom S Africa 31.34S 26.33E
66 O6 Sterla, Pizzo mt Italy 46.28N 9.24E
101 T3 Sterlet L N W Terr 64.45N 109.36W
112 F1 Sterley Texas 34.12N 101.23W
43 D1 Sterlibashevo Bashkir U.S.S.R. 53.27N 55.15E
113 M6 Sterling Alaska 60.31N 150.48W
109 G1 Sterling Colorado 40.37N 103.13W
103 L3 Sterling Connecticut 41.43N 71.50W
106 E8 Sterling Illinois 41.48N 89.43W
109 M3 Sterling Kansas 38.13N 98.13W
103 L2 Sterling Massachusetts 42.27N 71.46W
106 K5 Sterling Michigan 44.02N 84.02W
108 K3 Sterling N Dakota 46.49N 100.16W
108 O9 Sterling Nebraska 40.28N 96.22W
109 M7 Sterling Oklahoma 34.45N 98.12W
103 D4 Sterling Pennsylvania 41.21N 75.24W
111 N2 Sterling Utah 39.10N 111.44W
112 G4 Sterling City Texas 31.50N 101.00W
113 K5 Sterling Landing Alaska 62.51N 155.49W
109 G1 Sterling Res Colorado 40.48N 103.18W
46 S3 Sterlitamak U.S.S.R. 53.40N 55.59E
84 E6 Stérna Greece 37.43N 22.36E
63 P5 Şternberg E Germany 54.43N 11.50E
62 K6 Šternberk Czechoslovakia 49.45N 17.20E
66 M2 Sternenberg Switzerland 47.23N 8.55E
84 K10 Stérnes Crete 35.31N 24.09E
65 K4 Sternstein mt Austria 48.34N 14.18E
61 J3 Sterrebeek Belgium 50.52N 4.31E
15 F6 Sterren, Pegunungan mts Irian Jaya
47 D5 Steshevskaya U.S.S.R. 61.57N 37.45E
62 K3 Stęszew Poland 52.16N 16.39E
65 O5 Stetteldorf Austria 48.25N 16.01E
64 G7 Stetten W Germany 48.07N 9.05E
66 G1 Stetten W Germany 47.36N 7.40E
Stettin see Szczecin
15 L6 Stettin B New Britain
63 U5 Stettiner Haff L E Ger/Poland
100 E6 Stettler Alberta 52.21N 112.40W
95 C9 Stettyn S Africa 33.52S 19.21E
106 H3 Steuben Michigan 46.12N 86.27W
106 D6 Steuben Wisconsin 43.11N 90.52W
104 E6 Steubenville Ohio 40.22N 80.39W
63 Q9 Steutz E Germany 51.53N 12.05E
56 L4 Stevenage Herts Eng 51.55N 0.14W
84 E5 Steveníkoi Greece 38.21N 22.54E
99 E3 Stevens Ontario 49.33N 85.50W
11 G7 Stevens, Mt New Zealand 40.49S 172.26E
107 L7 Stevenson Alabama 34.51N 85.49W
110 D4 Stevenson Washington 45.42N 121.55W
100 U9 Stevenson airfield Manitoba 49.58N 97.13W
12 C2 Stevenson R S Australia
100 W5 Stevenson L Manitoba
14 D10 Stevenson's L W Australia 33.05S 121.00E
106 E5 Stevens Point Wisconsin 44.32N 89.33W
103 C3 Stevens Pt Pennsylvania 41.57N 75.32W
58 G7 Stevenston Strathclyde Scotland 55.39N 4.45W
113 N4 Stevens Village Alaska 66.01N 149.10W
103 B9 Stevensville Maryland 39.00N 76.19W
106 H7 Stevensville Michigan 42.01N 86.31W
110 L3 Stevensville Montana 46.32N 114.05W
103 B3 Stevensville Pennsylvania 41.45N 76.11W
60 T16 Stevensweert Netherlands 51.07N 5.51E
56 J4 Steventon Oxon Eng 51.38N 1.20W
63 F9 Stever R W Germany
101 G12 Steveston Lulu I, Br Col 49.08N 123.12W
53 J6 Stevns reg Denmark 55.18N 12.20E
53 J6 Stevns Klint cliff Denmark 55.19N 12.28E
61 M3 Stevoort Belgium 50.55N 5.15E
106 E8 Steward Illinois 41.52N 89.01W
48 V12 Steward Ø isld Greenland 69.50N 22.55W
107 H2 Stewardson Illinois 39.16N 88.39W
101 H8 Stewart Br Col 55.56N 130.01W
108 Q5 Stewart Minnesota 44.43N 94.30W
111 E2 Stewart Nevada 39.07N 119.45W
101 D4 Stewart Yukon Terr 63.19N 139.26W
13 G2 Stewart R Queensland
101 D4 Stewart R Yukon Terr
13 C1 Stewart, C N Terr Australia 11.58S 134.46E
100 N5 Stewart Cr Saskatchewan
101 E4 Stewart Crossing Yukon Terr 63.22N 136.41W
121 K10 Stewart, I Chile 54.55S 71.15W
11 B13 Stewart I New Zealand
10 N3 Stewart Is Pacific Oc 8.28S 162.34E
14 C10 Stewart, Mt W Australia 32.36S 119.36E
58 G7 Stewarton Strathclyde Scotland 55.41N 4.31W
103 A7 Stewartstown Pennsylvania 39.45N 76.36W
59 J2 Stewartstown Tyrone N Ireland 54.35N 6.41W
107 B2 Stewartsville Missouri 39.45N 94.30W
103 D5 Stewartsville New Jersey 40.42N 75.07W
116 J1 Stewart Town Jamaica, W I 18.23N 77.27W
100 K8 Stewart Valley Saskatchewan 50.38N 107.50W
108 S6 Stewartville Minnesota 43.51N 92.29W
98 J8 Stewiacke Nova Scotia 45.09N 63.22W
63 K7 Steyerberg W Germany 52.34N 9.02E
56 L6 Steyning W Sussex Eng 50.53N 0.20W
95 J7 Steynsburg S Africa 31.20S 25.50E
95 K5 Steynspruit S Africa 29.01S 26.42E
95 L3 Steynsrus S Africa 27.57S 27.34E
56 A4 Steynton Dyfed Wales 51.44N 5.01W
65 K5 Steyr Austria 48.04N 14.25E
65 K6 Steyr R Austria
65 K5 Steyregg Austria 48.18N 14.23E
95 H9 Steytlerville S Africa 33.20S 24.20E
98 N6 Sth Branch Newfoundland 47.56N 59.02W
53 C3 S. Thise Denmark 56.43N 9.08E
79 L7 Stia Italy 43.48N 11.43E
56 C6 Stibb Cross Devon Eng 50.55N 4.14W
110 K5 Stibnite Idaho 44.54N 115.20W
57 O6 Stickford Lincs Eng 53.08N 0.02E
63 G6 Stickhausen W Germany 53.13N 7.38E
57 O6 Stickney Lincs England 53.06N 0.01E
108 M6 Stickney S Dakota 43.35N 98.26W
63 N9 Stiege E Germany 51.41N 10.54E
60 M6 Stiens Netherlands 53.15N 5.45E
56 N2 Stiffkey Norfolk Eng 52.57N 0.56E
65 N5 Stift Göttweig Austria 48.23N 15.38E
50 B2 Stigahlídh coast Iceland
53 W17 Stiganosa mt Norway 60.55N 7.02E
109 P6 Stigler Oklahoma 35.16N 95.08W
81 M3 Stigliano Italy 40.24N 16.14E
81 M7 Stignano Italy 38.25N 16.28E
52 K4 Stigsjö Sweden 62.38N 17.40E
53 G6 Stigsnæs pen Denmark 55.13N 11.15E
101 H7 Stikine R Alaska/Br Col
101 H6 Stikine Ranges Br Col
113 V8 Stikine Str Alaska
95 E10 Stilbaai S Africa 34.23S 21.24E
95 E10 Stilbaai B S Africa
95 E10 Stilbaaistrand S Africa 34.21S 21.25E
112 F4 Stiles Texas 31.25N 101.35W
107 K2 Stilesville Indiana 39.37N 86.38W
84 E4 Stilís Greece 38.55N 22.37E
53 D4 Stilling Denmark 56.04N 10.00E
57 L4 Stillington N Yorks Eng 54.06N 1.06W
106 E7 Stillman Valley Illinois 42.06N 89.11W
103 B8 Still Pond Maryland 39.20N 76.03W
108 S4 Stillwater Minnesota 45.03N 92.45W
111 F2 Stillwater Nevada 39.31N 118.33W
103 E4 Stillwater New Jersey 41.02N 74.53W
109 N5 Stillwater Oklahoma 36.07N 97.03W
103 B4 Stillwater Pennsylvania 41.09N 76.23W
110 L1 Stillwater R Montana
102 F2 Stillwater Ra Nevada
111 F2 Stillwater Ra Nevada
103 D3 Stillwater Res Pennsylvania 41.41N 75.30W
81 M7 Stilo Italy 38.29N 16.28E
81 N7 Stilo, Punta Italy 38.27N 16.24E
56 L3 Stilton Cambs Eng 52.29N 0.17W
79 K1 Stilves Italy 46.53N 11.29E
95 O3 Stilwater S Africa 27.47S 30.45E
109 Q6 Stilwell Oklahoma 35.50N 94.37W
84 E6 Stimánga Greece 37.55N 22.42E
84 D6 Stimfalías L Greece 37.51N 22.27E
110 M1 Stimson, Mt Montana 48.30N 113.37W
57 D2 Stinchar, R Strathclyde Scotland
108 J9 Stinking Water Cr Nebraska
112 C8 Stinnett Texas 35.49N 101.27W
81 A2 Stintino Sardinia 40.57N 8.14E
81 K3 Ştio Italy 40.18N 15.15E
82 G9 Ştip Yugoslavia 41.44N 22.12E
60 L14 Stiphout Netherlands 51.29N 5.37E
84 H5 Stíra isld Greece 38.09N 24.14E
100 E9 Stirling Alberta 49.34N 112.30W
58 J6 Stirling Central Scotland 56.07N 3.57W
58 N4 Stirling Grampian Scotland 57.28N 1.48W
11 D13 Stirling New Zealand 46.17S 169.50E
13 C5 Stirling N Terr Australia 21.44S 133.44E
99 N8 Stirling Ontario 44.18N 77.33W
12 E5 Stirling S Australia 35.00S 139.01E
Stirling co see Strathclyde and Central regions
12 A6 Stirling dist Canberra Australia
111 C2 Stirling City California 39.55N 121.31W
13 A3 Stirling Cr N Terr Australia
14 C9 Stirling, Mt W Australia 31.50S 117.49E
14 D8 Stirling, Mt W Australia 28.32S 121.03E
12 D4 Stirling North S Australia 32.30S 137.27E
14 C10 Stirling Ra W Australia
79 H5 Stirone R Italy
108 N3 Stirum N Dakota 46.14N 97.48W
103 G3 Stissing New York 41.54N 73.41W
110 K3 Stites Idaho 46.06N 116.00W
56 T9 Stithians Cornwall Eng 50.11N 5.10W
100 V3 Ştitt Manitoba 55.50N 96.40W
65 P2 Štíty Czechoslovakia 49.59N 16.47E
106 D7 Stitzer Wisconsin 42.56N 90.38W
65 M7 Stiwoll Austria 47.07N 15.13E
52 L9 Stjärnarve Sweden 57.17N 18.14E
52 J6 Stjärnsund Sweden 60.26N 16.10E
51 K1 Stjernøya isld Norway 70.17N 22.40E
52 F3 Stjørdal Norway 63.27N 10.57E
52 F3 Stjørdalselva R Norway
58 K7 Stobo Borders Scotland 55.38N 3.20W
57 H2 Stobs Borders Scotland 55.23N 2.47W
56 M4 Stock Essex Eng 51.40N 0.26E
64 G8 Stockach W Germany 47.51N 9.01E
66 K4 Stöckalp Switzerland 46.48N 8.17E
52 H9 Stockaryd Sweden 57.18N 14.35E
56 J5 Stockbridge Hants Eng 51.07N 1.29W
103 H2 Stockbridge Massachusetts 42.17N 73.20W
106 K7 Stockbridge Michigan 42.27N 85.11W
104 C8 Stockdale Ohio 38.57N 82.52W
112 K6 Stockdale Texas 29.13N 97.58W
63 N5 Stockelsdorf W Germany 53.54N 10.38E
65 O5 Stockerau Austria 48.24N 16.13E
103 D5 Stockertown Pennsylvania 40.45N 75.15W
69 M6 Stock, Étang du L France 48.45N 6.56E
110 O2 Stockett Montana 47.22N 111.10W
108 N9 Stockham Nebraska 40.43N 97.58W
64 L3 Stockheim Bayern W Germany 50.18N 11.17E
64 G3 Stockheim Hessen W Germany 50.18N 9.02E
104 Q6 Stockholm Maine 47.03N 68.10W
103 F4 Stockholm New Jersey 41.05N 74.30W
100 P8 Stockholm Saskatchewan 50.40N 102.18W
52 L7 Stockholm Sweden 59.20N 18.05E
52 K7 Stockholm dist Sweden
66 G5 Stockhorn mt Switzerland 46.42N 7.33E
12 J5 Stockinbingal New S Wales 34.39S 148.05E
103 G2 Stockport Columbia, New York 42.19N 73.44W
57 J6 Stockport Greater Manchester Eng 53.25N 2.10W
104 D7 Stockport Ohio 39.33N 81.48W
57 J4 Stocks Res Lancs Eng 54.00N 2.25W
107 J10 Stockton Alabama 31.00N 87.52W
111 C4 Stockton California 37.58N 121.20W
56 F3 Stockton Hereford & Worcs Eng 52.15N 2.41W
106 D7 Stockton Illinois 42.21N 90.02W
109 L2 Stockton Kansas 39.27N 99.17W
100 S9 Stockton Manitoba 49.37N 99.28W
104 K8 Stockton Maryland 38.03N 75.26W
107 C4 Stockton Missouri 37.43N 93.49W
103 E6 Stockton New Jersey 40.24N 74.58W
12 K5 Stockton New S Wales 32.54S 151.48E
11 F8 Stockton New Zealand 41.37S 171.57E
110 N9 Stockton Utah 40.28N 112.21W
106 D3 Stockton I Wisconsin 46.56N 90.35W
113 O1 Stockton Is Alaska
57 L3 Stockton on Tees Cleveland Eng 54.34N 1.19W
107 C4 Stockton Reservoir Missouri
104 R2 Stockton Springs Maine 44.30N 68.52W
108 K9 Stockville Nebraska 40.33N 100.20W
62 N4 Stoczek Łukowski Poland 51.59N 21.58E
64 P4 Stod Czechoslovakia 49.39N 13.11E
52 F2 Stod Norway 64.04N 11.40E
106 C6 Stoddart Wisconsin 43.37N 91.11W
52 K4 Stöde Sweden 62.27N 16.35E
50 M5 Stodh Iceland 64.51N 13.59W
50 M5 Stödhvarfjördhur B Iceland
53 T19 Stødle Norway 59.41N 6.00E
45 D2 Stodolische U.S.S.R. 54.10N 32.38E
113 W8 Stoeckl, Mt Alaska/Br Col 56.21N 130.50W
58 F2 Stoer Highland Scotland 58.12N 5.20W
58 F2 Stoer, Pt. of Highland Scotland 58.16N 5.23W
94 K5 Stoffberg S Africa 25.29S 29.49E
95 G1 Stoffelshoek S Africa 25.57S 23.15E
53 C4 Stoholm Denmark 56.29N 9.09E
11 H8 Stoke New Zealand 41.20S 173.17E
55 C6 Stoke d'Abernon Surrey Eng 51.19N 0.22W
56 N2 Stoke Ferry Norfolk Eng 52.34N 0.31E
56 D7 Stoke Fleming Devon Eng 50.19N 3.36W
56 K4 Stoke Mandeville Bucks Eng 51.47N 0.49W
56 K4 Stokenchurch Bucks Eng 51.40N 0.55W
55 G3 Stoke Newington London Eng 51.34N 0.04W
56 D7 Stokenham Devon Eng 50.16N 3.40W
57 J6 Stoke on Trent Staffs Eng 53.00N 2.10W
56 C7 Stoke Pt Devon Eng 50.17N 4.03W
56 F3 Stokesay Shropshire Eng 52.25N 2.49W
99 J7 Stokes Bay Ontario 45.00N 81.23W
121 J8 Stokes, Cerro pk Arg/Chile 50.48S 73.16W
105 H1 Stokesdale N Carolina 36.15N 79.59W
121 A10 Stokes, I Chile 44.42S 74.32W
14 D10 Stokes Inlet W Australia 33.47S 121.09E
57 L4 Stokesley N Yorks Eng 54.28N 1.11W
11 J8 Stokes, Mt New Zealand 41.06S 174.07E
12 G7 Stokes Pt King I, Tasmania 40.11S 143.58E
11 C2 Stokes Pt New Zealand 36.49S 174.46E
13 B3 Stokes Ra N Terr Australia
46 F4 Stokhod R Ukraine U.S.S.R.
61 T9 Stokkel Bruxelles Belgium
61 N2 Stokkem Belgium 51.01N 5.45E
53 G7 Stokkemarke Denmark 54.51N 11.23E
50 D7 Stokkseyri Iceland 63.50N 21.04W
50 L6 Stokksnes C Iceland 64.15N 14.58W
52 E2 Stokksund Norway 64.03N 10.05E
53 S19 Stokksund sound Norway 59.48N 5.17E
60 P11 Stokkum Netherlands 52.14N 6.30E
51 D3 Stokmarknes Norway 68.34N 14.55E
61 M3 Ştokrooie Belgium 50.58N 5.16E
65 N3 Štoky Czechoslovakia 49.30N 15.35E
Stol mt see Hochstuhl
82 D7 Stolac Yugoslavia 43.04N 17.56E
63 N9 Stolberg (Harz) E Germany 51.34N 10.57E
64 A2 Stolberg (Rheinland) W Germany 50.45N 6.15E
45 V1 Stolbishchi U.S.S.R. 55.40N 49.15E
43 P3 Stolboukha Kazakhstan U.S.S.R. 50.00N 84.30E
39 E3 Stolbovaya Magadan U.S.S.R. 64.46N 153.51E
45 J1 Stolbovaya Moscow U.S.S.R. 55.14N 37.30E
41 A3 Stolbovoy Novaya Zemlya U.S.S.R. 73.15N 53.55E
39 G6 Stolbovoye, Ozero L U.S.S.R. 56.39N 162.38E
39 G6 Stolbovoy, Mys C U.S.S.R. 56.42N 163.19E
41 P4 Stolbovoy, Ostrov isld U.S.S.R.
46 F3 Stolbtsy Belorussiya U.S.S.R. 53.30N 26.44E
39 M3 Stoletiya, Mys C U.S.S.R. 64.21N 173.45W
62 M7 Stolica mt Czechoslovakia 48.46N 20.15E
46 F4 Stolin Belorussiya U.S.S.R. 51.52N 26.51E
64 O2 Stollberg E Germany 50.42N 12.47E
63 H5 Stollhamm W Germany 53.32N 8.22E
53 S19 Stolmen isld Norway 60.00N 5.06E
82 J6 Stolnici Romania 44.31N 24.48E
Stolp see Słupsk
63 U7 Stolpe E Germany 52.59N 14.08E
53 T16 Stølsvatn L Norway 61.02N 5.45E
96 B16 Stoltenhoff I Tristan da Cunha 37.26S 12.32W
60 H12 Stolwijk Netherlands 51.58N 4.46E
63 K7 Stolzenau W Germany 52.31N 9.05E
94 E7 Stolzenfels Namibia 28.31S 19.38E
64 D3 Stolzenfels W Germany 50.18N 7.36E
84 D5 Stómion Korinthía Greece 38.08N 22.29E
84 E2 Stómion Lárisa Greece 39.52N 22.44E
64 B1 Stommeln W Germany 51.02N 6.45E
60 H9 Stompetoren Netherlands 52.37N 4.49E
60 F11 Stompwijk Netherlands 52.06N 4.28E
65 N3 Stonařov Czechoslovakia 49.18N 15.35E
80 O2 Stončica, Rtic pt Yugoslavia 43.04N 16.15E
56 K4 Stone Bucks Eng 51.49N 0.53W
56 G4 Stone Glos Eng 51.40N 2.27W
110 N7 Stone Idaho 42.00N 112.41W
57 J7 Stone Staffs Eng 52.54N 2.10W
56 F5 Ston Easton Somerset Eng 51.17N 2.33W
104 E5 Stoneboro Pennsylvania 41.21N 80.07W
50 U15 Stonebreen glacier Spitsbergen 77.45N 24.30E
56 H3 Stonebridge W Midlands Eng 52.27N 1.40W
109 F3 Stone City Colorado 38.26N 104.53W
99 N6 Stonecliffe Ontario 46.12N 77.54W
111 F7 Stone Corral L Oregon 42.37N 119.41W
23 B9 Stonecutters I Hong Kong 22.18N 114.08E
109 G1 Stoneham Colorado 40.37N 103.41W
98 A7 Stoneham Quebec 47.00N 71.22W
103 E8 Stone Harbor New Jersey 39.03N 74.46W
58 M5 Stonehaven Grampian Scotland 56.58N 2.13W
13 G6 Stonehenge Queensland 24.20S 143.15E
56 H5 Stonehenge mon Wilts Eng 51.11N 1.51W
103 O3 Stone Horse Lightship Massachusetts 41.33N 69.59W
56 G4 Stonehouse Glos Eng 51.45N 2.17W
58 J7 Stonehouse Strathclyde Scotland 55.43N 4.00W
106 C4 Stone Lake Wisconsin 45.51N 91.32W
101 L6 Stone Mountain Prov. Park Br Col
105 C4 Stone Mt Georgia 33.48N 84.10W
109 B4 Stoner Colorado 37.36N 108.19W
103 F3 Stone Ridge New York 41.52N 74.09W
103 C6 Stonersville Pennsylvania 40.18N 75.48W
107 K6 Stones River Nat. Mil. Park Tennessee
96 B14 Stone Top Bay St Helena 15.58S 5.38W
103 L2 Stoneville Massachusetts 42.14N 71.50W
109 E4 Stonewall Colorado 37.10N 105.01W
100 U8 Stonewall Manitoba 50.08N 97.20W
107 H9 Stonewall Mississippi 32.09N 88.49W
109 O7 Stonewall Oklahoma 34.40N 96.33W
112 J5 Stonewall Texas 30.14N 98.41W
58 B4 Stoneybridge S Uist, W Isles Scotland 57.17N 7.24W
99 L9 Stoney Creek Ontario 43.13N 79.46W
57 D3 Stoneykirk Dumfries & Galloway Scotland 54.50N 4.59W
53 S16 Stongfjorden Norway 61.26N 5.10E
53 S16 Stongfjorden inlet Norway 61.25N 5.08E
51 F2 Stonglandet Norway 69.05N 17.10E
109 H4 Stonington Colorado 37.17N 102.12W
103 L4 Stonington Connecticut 41.20N 71.54W
107 G2 Stonington Illinois 39.38N 89.11W
104 R2 Stonington Maine 44.11N 68.41W
103 A5 Stonington Pennsylvania 40.52N 76.40W
53 W17 Stonndalen Norway 60.50N 7.21E
56 K4 Stonor Oxon Eng 51.36N 0.57W
113 K6 Stony R Alaska
93 J7 Stony Athi Kenya 1.36S 37.01E
100 M8 Stony Beach Saskatchewan 50.28N 105.08W
103 H5 Stony Brook Long I, N Y 40.56N 73.08W
103 J4 Stony Creek Connecticut 41.16N 72.45W
104 H10 Stony Creek Virginia 36.57N 77.25W
111 B2 Stonyford California 39.22N 122.34W
116 L2 Stony Hill Jamaica, W I 18.05N 76.48W
96 B15 Stonyhill Pt C Tristan da Cunha 37.09S 12.17W
100 U8 Stony Mountain Manitoba 50.05N 97.17W
100 D5 Stony Plain Alberta 53.33N 114.00W
105 F2 Stony Point N Carolina 35.53N 81.04W
103 G4 Stony Point New York 41.15N 73.59W
104 J3 Stony Pt New York 43.51N 76.16W
11 E11 Stony R New Zealand
101 V6 Stony Rapids Saskatchewan 59.14N 105.48W
113 J6 Stony River Alaska 61.48N 156.45W
56 K3 Stony Stratford Bucks Eng 52.04N 0.52W
65 O6 Stoober, R Austria
99 H1 Stooping R Ontario
63 L5 Stör R W Germany
52 J7 Storå Sweden 59.44N 15.10E
53 C4 Storå R Denmark
52 H3 Storåbränna Sweden 63.54N 14.55E
Stóra Dímun isld see Store Dimon
50 B3 Stora Eyarvatn L Iceland 65.42N 23.04W
53 N9 Stórafjall mt Faeroes 62.09N 6.43W
53 N10 Stórafjall mt Faeroes 61.48N 6.41W
53 S16 Storaker Norway 61.11N 5.05E
50 F6 Stóra Laxá R Iceland
52 F7 Stora Le L Sweden
51 H5 Stora Lule älv R Sweden
51 G4 Stora Lulevatten L Sweden 67.20N 19.00E
52 G4 Storån R Sweden
51 G4 Stora Sjöfallet L Sweden 67.30N 18.10E
51 G6 Storavan L Sweden 65.45N 18.10E
53 T20 Storavatn L Rogaland Norway 59.23N 5.34E
50 D4 Stórá Vatnshorn Iceland 65.04N 21.33W
50 J3 Stora Viti mt Iceland 65.52N 16.52W
51 G6 Storberg Sweden 65.32N 19.00E
51 H11 Storby Finland 60.13N 19.31E
53 T19 Stord Norway 59.47N 5.31E
53 W14 Stordal Möre og Romsdal Norway 62.23N 7.00E
52 F3 Stordal Nord-Tröndelag Norway 63.18N 11.48E
53 U19 Stordalsvatn L Norway 59.42N 6.05E
53 D3 Store Ajstrup Denmark 56.57N 9.32E
53 D3 Store Arden Denmark 56.46N 9.54E
53 F5 Store Bælt str Denmark
53 D3 Store Binderup Denmark 56.47N 9.35E
51 D6 Store Børgefjeld mts Norway
53 S15 Storebotnvatn L Norway 61.43N 5.27E
53 Y16 Storebottegga mt Norway 61.02N 8.25E
52 J9 Storebro Sweden 57.36N 15.30E
53 B6 Store Darum Denmark 55.26N 8.39E
53 N10 Store Dimon isld Faeroes 61.43N 6.45W
62 H6 Stóredoóceskóy reg Czechoslovakia
53 V18 Storeflåtten mt Norway 60.25N 6.50E
53 G5 Store Fuglede Denmark 55.36N 11.15E
53 W16 Storehaug mt Norway 61.10N 7.07E
53 J6 Store Heddinge Denmark 55.19N 12.24E
48 R9 Store Hellefiskebanke Greenland
53 C7 Store Jyndevad Denmark 54.54N 9.09E
53 S18 Store Kalsøy isld Norway 60.08N 5.05E
53 K7 Storeklint cliffs Denmark 54.57N 12.03E
48 V6 Store Koldewey isld Greenland
51 M1 Storelv R Norway
52 F5 Stor-Elvdal Norway 61.32N 11.02E
53 K5 Store Magleby Denmark 55.36N 12.39E
53 H5 Store Meløse Denmark 55.33N 11.44E
51 O1 Store Molvik Norway 70.45N 28.38E
Store Momhøj hill see Mombjerge
52 E3 Støren Norway 63.03N 10.16E
53 E7 Store Rise Denmark 54.51N 10.25E
53 W17 Storeskavjen mt Norway 60.44N 7.17E
53 X17 Store Skuta mt Norway 60.37N 7.52E
53 J6 Store Spjellerup Denmark 55.17N 12.15E
53 J6 Store Tårnby Denmark 55.23N 12.16E
53 T15 Store Toren mt Norway 62.00N 5.56E
53 T17 Storevatn L Hordaland Norway 60.33N 5.35E
53 U15 Storevatn L Norway 61.40N 6.05E
53 X15 Storevatn L Opland Norway 61.37N 7.56E
53 D2 Store Vildmose moor Denmark 57.10N 9.45E
53 X18 Storfjell mt Telemark Norway 60.04N 7.55E
53 W14 Storfjellet mt Möre og Romsdal Norway 62.10N 7.30E
53 U17 Storfjellet mt Norway 60.55N 6.03E
53 V14 Storfjord inlet Norway 62.10N 6.34E
53 T15 Storfjord L Norway 61.38N 5.45E
53 U14 Storfjorden inlet Norway
50 T15 Storfjorden inlet Spitsbergen
51 H6 Storfors Norrbotten Sweden 65.52N 20.30E
52 H7 Storfors Värmland Sweden 59.33N 14.16E
51 D5 Storforshei Norway 66.24N 14.35E
53 Y14 Storhø mt Norway 62.18N 8.25E
53 Y14 Storhø mt Norway 62.11N 8.00E
53 Y15 Storhø mt Norway 61.46N 8.18E
50 E8 Stórhöfdhi prom Iceland 63.24N 20.17W
52 J3 Storhögen Sweden 63.22N 15.10E
52 B4 Storholmen isld Norway 62.37N 5.55E
53 U14 Storhorn mt Norway 62.10N 6.27E
97 L2 Stor I N W Terr 79.00N 86.00W
50 D5 Stóri As Iceland 64.42N 21.05W
50 D5 Stórias Iceland 64.38N 21.04W
50 F7 Stóri Dalur Iceland 63.38N 19.58W
50 K3 Stórifoss waterfall Iceland 65.57N 15.35W
50 F7 Stórihver Iceland 63.57N 19.08W
50 B3 Stóri Laugardalur Iceland 65.40N 23.54W
50 E6 Stórinupur Iceland 64.04N 20.10W
50 E4 Stórisandur reg Iceland
52 H2 Storjorm L Sweden 64.40N 14.10E
63 P5 Störkanal E Germany
97 G3 Storkerson B N W Terr
50 F7 Stórkonufell mt Iceland 63.47N 19.19W
63 T8 Storkow E Germany 52.16N 13.56E
52 G3 Storlien Sweden 63.20N 12.05E
52 L2 Storlögda Sweden 64.08N 18.20E
63 L5 Stormarn reg W Germany
12 J9 Storm B Tasmania
95 K7 Stormberg S Africa 31.17S 26.18E
95 K6 Stormberg mt S Africa 30.57S 26.41E
95 K7 Stormberge mts S Africa
108 P7 Storm L Iowa
108 P7 Storm Lake Iowa 42.39N 95.11W
45 K7 Stormovo Ukraine U.S.S.R. 49.05N 38.55E
95 G9 Stormrivier S Africa 33.59S 23.52E
95 D10 Stormsvlei S Africa 34.05S 20.05E
103 G3 Stormville New York 41.34N 73.44W
100 K1 Stormy L Ontario 49.23N 92.20W
80 N6 Stornara Italy 41.17N 15.46E
80 N6 Stornarella Italy 41.17N 15.44E
53 W15 Stornosa mt Norway 61.49N 7.20E
58 D2 Stornoway Lewis, W Isles Scotland 58.13N 6.22W
100 P7 Stornoway Saskatchewan 51.18N 102.01W
58 D2 Stornoway Harbour Lewis, W Isles Scotland
79 J3 Storo Italy 45.51N 10.35E
53 R16 Storøy isld Norway 61.06N 4.42E
50 V12 Storøya isld Spitsbergen 80.07N 28.00E
39 G6 Storozh R U.S.S.R.
39 F4 Storozhevoy, Mys C U.S.S.R. 61.50N 158.47E
47 G5 Storozhevsk U.S.S.R. 62.00N 52.20E
46 F5 Storozhinets Ukraine U.S.S.R. 48.11N 25.40E
52 G3 Storrensjön L Sweden 63.47N 12.35E
56 L6 Storrington W Sussex Eng 50.55N 0.28W
53 Y20 Storroan mt Norway 59.17N 8.12E
103 K3 Storrs Connecticut 41.48N 72.15W
58 D3 Storr, The mt Skye, Highland Scotland 57.30N 6.11W
52 M2 Storsavarträsk Sweden 64.25N 19.55E
53 U19 Storsjæker Norway 59.35N 6.18E
52 G4 Storsjö Sweden 62.49N 13.05E
52 F5 Storsjøen L Norway
52 F6 Stør-sjøen L Norway 60.25N 11.40E
52 K6 Storsjön L Gävleborg Sweden 60.35N 16.45E
52 G4 Storsjön L Jämtland Sweden 62.50N 13.10E
52 H3 Storsjön L Jämtland Sweden
51 F3 Storsteinsfjellet mt Norway 68.14N 17.54E
53 G7 Storstrøm co Denmark
48 U6 Storstrømmen glacier Greenland
53 H7 Storstrømmen str Denmark 54.57N 11.57E
51 H6 Storsund Sweden 65.36N 20.40E
60 J6 Stortemelk channel Netherlands
100 Q9 Storthoaks Saskatchewan 49.23N 101.38W
51 F6 Storuman Sweden 65.05N 17.10E
51 F6 Storuman L Sweden 65.14N 16.50E
50 H4 Stóruvellir Iceland 65.29N 17.40W
52 H5 Storvarden mt Sweden 61.36N 13.55E
52 G4 Storvigelen mt Norway 62.34N 12.04E
52 K6 Storvik Sweden 60.37N 16.30E
51 F6 Stor-vindeln L Sweden 65.45N 17.05E
53 E2 Storvorde Denmark 57.01N 10.07E
108 D5 Story Wyoming 44.35N 106.55W
108 R7 Story City Iowa 42.10N 93.34W
121 H7 Stosch I Chile 49.10S 75.30W
66 P2 Stoss Switzerland 47.22N 9.31E
64 M1 Stössen E Germany 51.07N 11.57E
64 K8 Stotten W Germany 47.44N 10.42E
64 L1 Stotternheim E Germany 51.04N 11.02E
51 C5 Støttvaer Norway 66.56N 13.30E
103 G2 Stottville New York 42.17N 73.45W
53 D5 Stouby Denmark 55.42N 9.48E
103 B6 Stouchsburg Pennsylvania 40.23N 76.15W
99 L9 Stouffville Ontario 43.59N 79.15W
103 M2 Stoughton Massachusetts 42.08N 71.05W
100 O9 Stoughton Saskatchewan 49.40N 103.01W
106 E7 Stoughton Wisconsin 42.55N 89.14W
56 K6 Stoughton W Sussex Eng 50.54N 0.53W
61 O5 Stoumont Belgium 50.25N 5.48E
83 E4 Stoupí Greece 40.14N 22.30E
56 G3 Stourbridge W Midlands Eng 52.27N 2.09W
56 G6 Stourpaine Dorset Eng 50.54N 2.12W
56 G3 Stourport Hereford & Worcs Eng 52.21N 2.16W
56 H6 Stour, R Dorset Eng
56 O4 Stour, R Essex etc Eng
56 O5 Stour, R Kent Eng
56 G3 Stour, R Staffs etc Eng
56 G3 Stourton Staffs Eng 52.27N 2.13W
104 C7 Stoutsville Ohio 39.36N 82.48W
107 D3 Stover Missouri 38.25N 93.00W
53 E4 Støvring Århus Denmark 56.30N 10.12E
53 D3 Støvring Nordjylland Denmark 56.53N 9.52E
58 L7 Stow Borders Scotland 55.42N 2.51W
103 C6 Stowe Pennsylvania 40.15N 75.40W
104 N2 Stowe Vermont 44.28N 72.44W
112 N6 Stowell Texas 29.47N 94.22W
56 N3 Stowmarket Suffolk Eng 52.11N 1.00E
56 H4 Stow-on-the-Wold Glos Eng 51.56N 1.44W
40 E5 Stoyba U.S.S.R. 52.49N 131.47E
82 E8 Stožac mt Yugoslavia 42.49N 19.14E
79 M4 Stra Italy 45.24N 12.00E
63 R9 Straach E Germany 51.56N 12.36E
59 H2 Strabane Tyrone N Ireland 54.49N 7.27W
59 H2 Strabane Bridge Tyrone N Ireland 54.49N 7.28W
58 L4 Strachan Grampian Scotland 57.01N 2.32W
15 G8 Strachan I Papua New Guinea
101 G10 Strachan, Mt Br Col 49.25N 123.12W
58 F6 Strachur Strathclyde Scotland 56.10N 5.04W
66 S4 Strada Switzerland 46.53N 10.27E
59 B7 Stradbally Kerry Irish Rep 52.14N 10.04W
59 H5 Stradbally Leix Irish Rep 53.01N 7.09W
59 H7 Stradbally Waterford Irish Rep 52.07N 7.27W
56 O3 Stradbroke Suffolk Eng 52.19N 1.16E
79 F4 Stradella Italy 45.04N 9.18E
65 N8 Straden Austria 46.49N 15.53E
59 H4 Stradone Cavan Irish Rep 53.59N 7.14W
56 M2 Stradsett Norfolk Eng 52.37N 0.28E
63 D10 Straelen W Germany 51.27N 6.15E
107 C4 Strafford Missouri 37.15N 93.10W
12 H8 Strahan Tasmania 42.08S 145.21E
66 H7 Strahlhorn mt Switzerland 46.01N 7.55E
111 N4 Straight Cliffs ra Utah
61 M7 Straimont Belgium 49.48N 5.23E
57 D2 Straiton Strathclyde Scotland 55.19N 4.33W
57 H5 Straits Lancs Eng 53.42N 2.43W
105 H12 Straits of Florida Florida
65 J3 Strakonice Czechoslovakia 49.16N 13.54E
82 K8 Straldzha Bulgaria 42.35N 26.40E
58 J5 Straloch Tayside Scotland 56.45N 3.35W
63 S4 Stralsund E Germany 54.18N 13.06E
79 C4 Strambino Italy 45.23N 7.53E
60 L15 Stramproij Netherlands 51.12N 5.44E
59 G7 Strancally Castle Waterford Irish Rep 52.05N 7.53W
65 L2 Strančice Czechoslovakia 49.57N 14.40E
52 F5 Strand Hedmark Norway 61.18N 11.15E
95 B10 Strand S Africa 34.06S 18.50E
53 V14 Stranda Möre og Romsdal Norway 62.18N 6.56E
50 D7 Strandarkirkja Iceland 63.50N 21.42W
50 D2 Strandasýsla co Iceland
53 C3 Strandby Nordjylland Denmark 56.48N 9.13E
53 F2 Strandby Nordjylland Denmark 57.30N 10.31E
53 V20 Stranddalshytta Norway 59.27N 6.42E
63 M4 Strande W Germany 54.27N 10.10E
53 U18 Strandebarm Norway 60.15N 6.02E
53 W20 Strandefjell mt Norway 59.22N 7.10E
53 Z17 Strandefjord L Norway 60.36N 8.30E
53 X17 Strandevatn L Norway 60.42N 7.48E
50 L3 Strandhöfn Iceland 65.55N 14.37W
53 T18 Strandvik Norway 60.09N 5.41E
108 N9 Strang Nebraska 40.25N 97.35W
50 F4 Strangakvísl R Iceland
105 J10 Strangers Cay isld Bahamas 27.05N 78.10W
59 L3 Strangford Down N Ireland 54.22N 5.34W
59 L2 Strangford L Down N Ireland 54.30N 5.35W
52 K7 Strängnäs Sweden 59.22N 17.02E
52 J8 Strångsjö Sweden 58.54N 16.12E
13 C3 Strangways R N Terr Australia
13 C6 Strangways Ra N Terr Australia
12 D3 Strangways Springs S Australia 29.08S 136.35E
59 G2 Stranorlar Donegal Irish Rep 54.48N 7.46W
57 C3 Stranraer Dumfries & Galloway Scotland 54.54N 5.02W
100 J7 Stranraer Saskatchewan 51.43N 108.30W
69 O6 Strasbourg France 48.35N 7.45E
100 N7 Strasbourg Saskatchewan 51.05N 104.58W
109 F2 Strasburg Colorado 39.44N 104.19W
63 T5 Strasburg E Germany 53.31N 13.46E
107 H2 Strasburg Illinois 39.22N 88.39W
108 K3 Strasburg N Dakota 46.09N 100.10W
104 D6 Strasburg Ohio 40.36N 81.34W
103 B7 Strasburg Pennsylvania 39.59N 76.11W
104 G7 Strasburg Virginia 39.00N 78.22W
82 M3 Strasheny U.S.S.R. 47.09N 28.39E
65 J2 Strašice Czechoslovakia 43.44N 13.46E
65 N8 Strass Steiermark Austria 46.44N 15.38E
65 E7 Strass Tirol Austria 47.24N 11.50E
52 J7 Stråssa Sweden 59.45N 15.13E
Strassbessenbach see Bessenbach
65 K8 Strassburg Austria 46.54N 14.20E
66 P3 Strassburger Hütte Austria 47.04N 9.42E
61 P8 Strassen Luxembourg 49.37N 6.05E
64 C2 Strassenhaus W Germany 50.33N 7.25E
65 M7 Strassgang Austria 47.02N 15.24E
63 U10 Strassgräbchen E Germany 51.22N 14.06E
64 O6 Strasskirchen W Germany 48.50N 12.45E
65 H6 Strasswalchen Austria 47.59N 13.15E
111 E5 Stratford California 36.11N 119.50W
103 H4 Stratford Connecticut 41.12N 73.08W
108 R7 Stratford Iowa 42.15N 93.56W
55 G3 Stratford London England 51.33N 00.000
104 O2 Stratford New Hampshire 44.40N 71.34W
11 J6 Stratford New Zealand 39.20S 174.18E
109 O7 Stratford Oklahoma 34.50N 96.57W
99 K9 Stratford Ontario 43.22N 81.00W
98 A8 Stratford Quebec 45.47N 71.19W
108 M4 Stratford S Dakota 45.19N 98.19W
112 B7 Stratford Texas 36.21N 102.05W
12 H7 Stratford Victoria 37.57S 147.05E
106 D5 Stratford Wisconsin 44.48N 90.05W
56 H3 Stratford-on-Avon Warwicks Eng 52.12N 1.41W
59 J6 Stratford-on-Slaney Wicklow Irish Rep 52.59N 6.40W
103 H4 Stratford Pt C Connecticut 41.09N 73.07W
56 N4 Stratford St. Mary Suffolk Eng 51.59N 1.00E
103 H4 Stratford Shoal New York 41.04N 73.03W
58 E3 Strath Highland Scotland 57.44N 5.42W
12 E6 Strathalbyn S Australia 35.13S 138.54E
58 H7 Strathaven Strathclyde Scotland 55.41N 4.05W
58 K4 Strath Avon V Grampian Scotland
58 H2 Strath Bagastie V Highland Scotland
58 H7 Strathblane Central Scotland 55.59N 4.18W
58 L4 Strathbogie dist Grampian Scotland
58 G3 Strath Bran V Highland Scotland
58 J5 Strath Bran V Tayside Scotland
58 H2 Strath Brora V Highland Scotland
58 G3 Strath Carron V Highland Scotland
100 R8 Strathclair Manitoba 50.25N 100.26W
58 F7 Strathclyde reg Scotland
101 L11 Strathcona Prov. Park Vancouver I, Br Col
58 G3 Strath Conon V Highland Scotland
58 J4 Strath Dearn V Highland Scotland
58 K4 Strathdon Grampian Scotland 57.12N 3.05W
58 L4 Strathdon V Grampian Scotland
58 J6 Strath Earn V Tayside Scotland
58 H4 Strath Errick V Highland Scotland
12 L7 Strathfield dist Sydney, N S W
58 G6 Strath Fillan V Central Scotland
58 J2 Strath Halladale V Highland Scotland
58 F3 Strathkanaird Highland Scotland 57.57N 5.08W
13 G3 Strathleven Queensland 15.52S 143.22E
98 L7 Strathlorne C Breton I, Nova Scotia 46.11N 61.18W
103 E8 Strathmere New Jersey 39.12N 74.39W
58 K6 Strathmiglo Fife Scotland 56.17N 3.16W
100 D7 Strathmore Alberta 51.05N 113.18W
13 G4 Strathmore Queensland 17.48S 142.32E
58 K5 Strathmore V Tayside Scotland
58 H4 Strath Nairn V Highland Scotland
101 M9 Strathnaver Br Col 53.21N 122.32W
58 H2 Strath Naver V Highland Scotland
58 J2 Strath of Kildonan V Highland Scotland
15 L9 Strathord I Louisiade Arch 10.10S 151.50E
58 G3 Strath Oykel V Highland Scotland
58 G3 Strathpeffer Highland Scotland 57.34N 4.33W
58 H3 Strathrory, R Highland Scotland
99 J10 Strathroy Ontario 42.57N 81.40W
58 J4 Strath Spey V Highland/Grampian Scotland
58 J1 Strathy Highland Scotland 58.33N 3.59W
58 H1 Strathy, Pt Highland Scotland 58.35N 4.01W
58 H1 Strathy, R Highland Scotland
58 H6 Strathyre Central Scotland 56.19N 4.19W
84 B4 Strátos Greece 38.41N 21.19E
109 H2 Stratton Colorado 39.18N 102.36W
56 B6 Stratton Cornwall Eng 50.50N 4.31W
104 P1 Stratton Maine 45.07N 70.27W
108 J9 Stratton Nebraska 40.09N 101.12W
64 O6 Straubing W Germany 48.53N 12.35E
53 T17 Straume Norway 60.52N 5.58E
52 D3 Straumen Möre og Romsdal Norway 63.20N 8.06E
51 D4 Straumen Nordland Norway 67.15N 14.46E
53 V14 Straumgjerde Norway 62.20N 6.35E
Straumnes C see Blakknes cape
50 B2 Straumnes C Ísafjardharsýsla, Nordhur Iceland 66.26N 23.08W
50 F2 Straumnes C Skagafjardharsýsla Iceland 66.05N 19.22W
53 X20 Straumsfjord L Norway 59.05N 7.45E
53 U14 Straumshamn Norway 62.04N 6.04E
50 C6 Straumsvik Iceland 64.03N 22.04W
63 U9 Straupitz E Germany 51.55N 14.09E
63 T7 Strausberg E Germany 52.34N 13.53E
109 D10 Strauss New Mexico 31.52N 106.43W
64 K1 Straussfurt E Germany 51.10N 11.00E
103 B6 Strausstown Pennsylvania 40.30N 76.11W
53 T15 Stravme Norway 61.45N 5.55E
110 Q3 Straw Montana 46.51N 109.48W
111 J2 Strawberry Nevada 39.38N 115.46W
107 E5 Strawberry R Arkansas
110 P9 Strawberry R Utah
101 H11 Strawberry Hill Br Col 49.09N 122.55W
110 G5 Strawberry Mt Oregon 44.19N 118.42W
106 C7 Strawberry Point Iowa 42.41N 91.32W
110 O9 Strawberry Res Utah 40.10N 111.07W
99 R5 Strawhat Depot Quebec 47.12N 73.33W
106 F9 Strawn Illinois 40.39N 88.24W
112 J3 Strawn Texas 32.34N 98.31W
122 U7 Strawn I Palmyra I Pacific Oc 5.53N 162.05W
64 O4 Stráž Czechoslovakia 49.40N 12.46E
65 M9 Straze Yugoslavia 46.25N 15.11E
65 M2 Strážiště mt Czechoslovakia 49.32N 15.01E
65 L3 Stráž nad Nežárkou Czech 49.04N 14.54E
62 K7 Strážnice Czechoslovakia 48.54N 17.20E
64 P5 Ştrážov Czechoslovakia 49.19N 13.15E
62 M6 Štrba Czechoslovakia 49.04N 20.05E
12 C5 Streaky Bay S Australia 32.50S 134.15E
12 C5 Streaky Bay B S Australia
100 G5 Streamstown Alberta 53.28N 110.14W
55 F4 Streatham London Eng 51.26N 0.07W
56 J4 Streatley Berks Eng 51.32N 1.10W
106 F8 Streator Illinois 41.07N 88.53W
65 K2 Středočeský reg Czechoslovakia
62 L7 Středoslovenský reg Czechoslovakia
61 H5 Strée Hainaut Belgium 50.17N 4.18E
61 M5 Strée Liège Belgium 50.29N 5.20E
60 G12 Streefkerk Netherlands 51.54N 4.45E
108 L3 Streeter N Dakota 46.40N 99.20W
112 H5 Streeter Texas 30.47N 99.24W
112 L4 Streetman Texas 31.53N 96.22W
84 C6 Stréfi Ilía Greece 37.40N 21.33E
84 C7 Stréfi Messinía Greece 37.03N 21.53E
79 P2 Stregna Italy 46.08N 13.35E
82 H6 Strehaia Romania 44.37N 23.10E
63 S10 Strehla E Germany 51.22N 13.14E
14 E9 Streich Mound W Australia 30.28S 123.44E
64 L4 Streitberg W Germany 49.48N 11.13E
50 M5 Streitishvarf hill Iceland 64.45N 14.00W
82 H5 Streiul R Romania
82 J6 Strejeştii de Jos Romania 44.32N 24.16E
64 P4 Střela R Czechoslovakia
66 Q4 Strela Pass Switzerland 46.49N 9.47E
45 H5 Streletskoye U.S.S.R. 51.45N 36.16E
65 O3 Střelice Czechoslovakia 49.09N 16.30E
45 K5 Strelitsa U.S.S.R. 51.36N 38.55E
63 S6 Ştrelitz-Alt E Germany 53.20N 13.06E
42 E3 Ştrelka Krasnoyarsk U.S.S.R. 58.04N 93.03E
39 E3 Strelka Magadan U.S.S.R. 63.15N 152.50E
39 E4 Strelka Magadan U.S.S.R. 61.54N 152.13E
42 G2 Strelka-Chunya U.S.S.R. 61.45N 102.48E
44 D9 Strelkovoye Ukraine U.S.S.R. 45.54N 34.54E
53 B5 Strellev Denmark 55.48N 8.33E
14 C5 Strelley W Australia 20.35S 119.02E
14 C5 Strelley R W Australia
47 D3 Strel'na U.S.S.R. 66.04N 38.43E
47 D3 Strel'na R U.S.S.R.
45 L7 Strel'tsovka U.S.S.R. 49.18N 39.52E
65 O7 Strem Austria 47.03N 16.25E
65 O7 Strem R Austria
63 Q8 Stremme R E Germany
46 F1 Strenči Latvia U.S.S.R. 57.39N 25.42E
65 L5 Strengberg Austria 48.09N 14.40E
65 B7 Strengen Austria 47.08N 10.29E
52 D7 Strengen Norway 59.17N 8.58E
57 L4 Strensall N Yorks Eng 54.02N 1.03W
61 G5 Strepy Belgium 50.27N 4.07E
79 E3 Stresa Italy 45.53N 8.32E
82 G8 Strešer mt Yugoslavia 42.38N 22.11E
45 B4 Streshin Belorussiya U.S.S.R. 52.44N 30.06E
57 J6 Stretford Greater Manchester Eng 53.27N 2.19W
56 M3 Stretham Cambs Eng 52.21N 0.14E
66 R6 Stretta, Piz mt Italy/Switz 46.29N 10.03E
57 H6 Stretton Cheshire Eng 53.21N 2.35W
57 L6 Stretton Derbys Eng 53.09N 1.24W
14 C10 Stretton W Australia 32.30S 117.42E
64 J3 Streu R W Germany
64 K3 Streufdorf E Germany 50.21N 10.41E
Streymoy isld see Strømø
42 B2 Strezhevoy U.S.S.R. 60.42N 77.34E
53 D5 Strib Denmark 55.33N 9.47E
65 P3 Stříbrná mt Czechoslovakia 49.22N 16.58E
65 L2 Stříbrná Skalice Czechoslovakia 49.54N 14.52E
64 P4 Stříbro Czechoslovakia 49.45N 13.01E
58 M3 Strichen Grampian Scotland 57.35N 2.05W
99 J3 Strickland Ontario 49.17N 81.50W
15 G7 Strickland R Papua New Guinea
79 L2 Strigno Italy 46.04N 11.32E
60 H13 Strijbeek Netherlands 51.30N 4.47E
95 O8 Strijdom Dam, J.G res S Africa 27.21S 31.58E
60 G13 Strijen Netherlands 51.45N 4.34E
60 G13 Strijensas Netherlands 51.43N 4.35E
61 F3 Strijpen Belgium 50.52N 3.48E
112 N4 Striker Creek Res Texas 31.57N 94.58W
51 D5 Strimasund Sweden 66.04N 14.55E
83 F3 Strimón R Greece
83 F4 Strimonikós, Kólpos G Greece
103 A6 Strinestown Pennsylvania 40.05N 76.46W
107 G10 Stringer Mississippi 31.53N 89.18W
109 O7 Stringtown Oklahoma 34.28N 96.04W
58 F7 Striven, L Strathclyde Scotland
15 C5 Striwo R Irian Jaya
44 E3 Strizhament mt U.S.S.R. 44.47N 42.03E
47 L7 Strizhovo U.S.S.R. 55.50N 74.35E
82 E5 Striživojna Yugoslavia 45.14N 18.22E
65 M3 Strmilov Czechoslovakia 49.10N 15.12E
121 K7 Strobel, L Argentina
65 H6 Strobl Austria 47.43N 13.30E
53 J6 Strøby Denmark 55.24N 12.18E
60 L11 Stroe Netherlands 52.11N 5.41E
121 E8 Stroeder Argentina 40.11S 62.35W
84 B7 Strofádhes isld Greece 37.15N 21.00E
84 F4 Strofiliá Greece 38.49N 23.25E
63 J7 Ströhen W Germany 52.32N 8.42E
59 F4 Strokestown Roscommon Irish Rep 53.47N 8.06W
52 K5 Ström Sweden 61.54N 17.28E
63 T6 Strom R E Germany
58 K1 Stroma isld Highland Scotland 58.41N 3.09W
61 H3 Strombeek-Bever Belgium 50.54N 4.21E
63 H9 Stromberg Nordrhein-Westfalen W Germany 51.48N 8.12E
64 D4 Stromberg Rheinland-Pfalz W Germany 49.57N 7.48E
81 K6 Stromboli isld Lipari Is Italy 38.48N 15.15E
81 K6 Strombolicchio isld Lipari Is Italy 38.49N 15.16E
100 E6 Strome Alberta 52.49N 112.04W
58 E4 Stromeferry Highland Scotland 57.21N 5.34W
52 M2 Strömfors Sweden 64.52N 20.25E
45 K1 Stromin U.S.S.R. 56.05N 38.30E
52 F3 Strømmen Norway 63.53N 11.16E
58 S12 Stromness Orkney Scotland 58.57N 3.18W
121 G8 Stromness S Georgia 54.11S 36.43W
84 D4 Strómni Greece 38.42N 22.15E
53 M9 Strømø isld Faeroes
51 F10 Strömsbruk Sweden 61.52N 17.20E
108 N8 Stromsburg Nebraska 41.09N 97.36W
52 G10 Strömsnäsbruk Sweden 56.35N 13.45E
52 F8 Strömstad Sweden 58.56N 11.11E
52 J3 Strömsund Sweden 63.51N 15.35E

52 H2 **Ströms vattudal** *L* Sweden 63.55N 15.30E
66 K8 **Strona** *R* Italy
58 G6 **Stronachlachar** Central **Scotland** 56.16N 4.35W
108 E5 **Stroner** Wyoming 44.55N 105.02W
107 D8 **Strong** Arkansas 33.08N 92.21W
104 P2 **Strong** Maine 44.48N 70.15W
107 H8 **Strong** Mississippi 33.41N 88.37W
50 T15 **Strongbreen** *glacier* Spitsbergen 77.30N 17.00E
109 O3 **Strong City** Kansas 38.24N 96.34W
109 L6 **Strong City** Oklahoma 35.41N 99.37W
100 L7 **Strongfield** Saskatchewan 51.20N 106.36W
106 D9 **Stronghurst** Illinois 40.44N 90.54W
84 W22 **Strongilí** Corfu 39.31N 19.55E
15 J7 **Strong, Mt** Papua **New Guinea** 7.59S 147.00E
81 O5 **Strongoli** Italy 39.16N 17.03E
106 K3 **Strongs** Michigan 46.22N 84.57W
104 D5 **Strongsville** Ohio 41.18N 81.50W
58 G6 **Stronmilchan** Strathclyde **Scotland** 56.25N 5.00W
53 S18 **Strøno** *isld* **Norway** 60.09N 5.22E
58 T11 **Stronsay** *isld* Orkney **Scotland** 59.07N 2.37W
58 T11 **Stronsay Firth** Orkney **Scotland**
65 O4 **Stronsdorf** **Austria** 48.39N 16.18E
58 E5 **Strontian** Highland **Scotland** 56.42N 5.34W
60 N7 **Stroobos** **Netherlands** 53.14N 6.13E
56 M5 **Strood** Kent **Eng** 51.24N 0.28E
61 D2 **Strooibrug** **Belgium** 51.14N 3.27E
62 N6 **Stropkov** **Czechoslovakia** 49.12N 21.40E
65 L4 **Stropnice** **Czechoslovakia** 48.45N 14.45E
79 D4 **Stroppiana** Italy 45.14N 8.27E
79 B5 **Stroppo** Italy 44.30N 7.07E
105 F3 **Strother** S Carolina 34.24N 81.24W
56 G4 **Stroud** Glos **Eng** 51.45N 2.12W
109 O6 **Stroud** Oklahoma 35.45N 96.41W
12 K4 **Stroud Road** New S Wales 32.18S 151.58E
103 D5 **Stroudsburg** Pennsylvania 41.00N 75.11W
84 P15 **Stroumbi** **Cyprus** 34.54N 32.29E
53 K4 **Strövelstorp** **Sweden** 56.11N 12.52E
84 R14 **Strovolos** **Cyprus** 35.08N 33.21E
12 F6 **Struan** S Australia 37.08S 140.49E
58 J5 **Struan** Tayside **Scotland** 56.46N 3.58W
65 G6 **Strub Pass** **Austria** 47.35N 12.40E
63 G6 **Strücklingen** **W Germany** 53.07N 7.40E
65 L5 **Strudengau** *V* **Austria**
53 B4 **Struer** **Denmark** 56.29N 8.37E
82 F9 **Struga** **Yugoslavia** 41.10N 20.41E
46 G1 **Strugi Krasnye** **U.S.S.R.** 58.18N 29.01E
95 D10 **Struisbaai** **S Africa** 34.48S 20.03E
95 D10 **Struispunt** *pt* **S Africa** 34.41S 20.14E
106 C5 **Strum** Wisconsin 44.33N 91.23W
82 H8 **Struma** *R* **Bulgaria**
56 A3 **Strumble Hd** Dyfed **Wales** 52.02N 5.04W
82 H9 **Strumica** **Yugoslavia** 41.26N 22.39E
82 H9 **Strumitsa** *R* **Yugoslavia** etc
45 K1 **Strunino** **U.S.S.R.** 56.22N 38.37E
53 S18 **Strusshamn** **Norway** 60.24N 5.10E
104 E5 **Struthers** Ohio 41.03N 80.35W
99 E4 **Struthers** Ontario 48.43N 85.51W
50 E5 **Strútur** *mt* **Iceland** 64.46N 20.40W
58 G4 **Struy** Highland **Scotland** 57.25N 4.40W
64 P3 **Stružná** **Czechoslovakia** 50.15N 13.00E
82 H1 **Stry** *R* **U.S.S.R.**
82 J8 **Stryama** *R* **Bulgaria**
95 G5 **Strydenburg** **S Africa** 29.56S 23.40E
95 G9 **Strydomsvlei** **S Africa** 33.13S 23.04E
95 J2 **Strydpoort** **S Africa** 26.59S 25.58E
110 L1 **Stryker** Montana 48.40N 114.44W
104 A5 **Stryker** Ohio 41.31N 84.24W
62 M4 **Stryków** **Poland** 51.55N 19.33E
53 V15 **Stryn** **Norway** 61.55N 6.44E
53 F7 **Strynø** **Denmark** 54.54N 10.35E
53 F7 **Strynø** *isld* **Denmark** 54.54N 10.35E
53 W15 **Strynsvatn** *L* **Norway** 61.55N 7.03E
46 F5 **Strypa** *R* Ukraine **U.S.S.R.**
50 L5 **Strýta** **Iceland** 64.40N 14.22W
50 F5 **Strýtur** *mt* **Iceland** 64.48N 19.35W
82 H1 **Stryy** Ukraine **U.S.S.R.** 49.16N 23.51E
82 H1 **Stryy** *R* Ukraine **U.S.S.R.**
62 J5 **Strzegom** **Poland** 50.59N 16.20E
62 J3 **Strzelce** **Poland** 52.53N 15.31E
12 F3 **Strzelecki Cr** S Australia
13 C5 **Strzelecki, Mt** N Terr **Australia** 21.08S 133.52E
12 J8 **Strzelecki, Pk** Tasmania 40.20S 148.05E
62 K5 **Strzelin** **Poland** 50.48N 17.03E
62 L3 **Strzelno** **Poland** 52.38N 18.10E
62 N6 **Strzyżów** **Poland** 49.52N 21.47E
105 G10 **Stuart** Florida 27.12N 80.16W
108 Q8 **Stuart** Iowa 41.30N 94.20W
108 L7 **Stuart** Nebraska 42.36N 99.09W
109 O7 **Stuart** Oklahoma 34.55N 96.06W
104 E10 **Stuart** Virginia 36.38N 80.19W
13 K7 **Stuart** *R* Queensland
13 B6 **Stuart Bluff Ra** N Terr **Australia**
12 D3 **Stuart Creek** S Australia 29.43S 137.01E
113 F5 **Stuart I** Alaska 63.36N 162.30W
101 L8 **Stuart L** Br Columbia
110 E2 **Stuart, Mt** Washington 47.29N 120.47W
11 B11 **Stuart Mts** **New Zealand**
13 B1 **Stuart Pt** N Terr **Australia** 12.09S 131.12E
101 L8 **Stuart R** Br Col
12 C3 **Stuart Ra** S Australia
12 J5 **Stuart Town** New S Wales 32.51S 149.08E
65 G7 **Stubachtal** *V* **Austria**
65 D7 **Stubaier Alpen** *mts* **Austria**
65 D7 **Stubai tal** *V* **Austria**
65 L7 **Stub Alpe** *mts* **Austria**
53 J7 **Stubbekøbing** **Denmark** 54.53N 12.04E
63 J6 **Stubben** **W Germany** 53.25N 8.47E
63 T3 **Stubbenkammer** **E Germany** 54.34N 13.40E
53 B4 **Stubbergd Sø** *L* **Denmark** 56.25N 8.56E
53 F4 **Stubbe Sø** *L* **Denmark** 56.16N 10.43E
26 V4 **Stubbings Pt** Christmas I **Ind Oc** 10.33S 105.42E
Stubel *vol see* **Shtyubelya, Sopka** *vol*
65 C8 **Stuben** Tirol **Austria** 46.58N 10.33E
65 B7 **Stuben** Vorarlberg **Austria** 47.09N 10.10E
65 N7 **Stubenberg** **Austria** 47.15N 15.48E
65 M6 **Stübming** *R* **Austria**
46 F2 **Stuchka** Latvia **U.S.S.R.** 56.39N 25.24E
65 M3 **Studená** **Czechoslovakia** 49.12N 15.18E
65 O3 **Studenec** **Czechoslovakia** 49.13N 16.03E
45 D3 **Studenets** **U.S.S.R.** 53.54N 32.05E
82 K9 **Studen Kladenets Dam** **Bulgaria**
45 J4 **Studenoye** **U.S.S.R.** 52.09N 37.38E
45 V4 **Studentsy** **U.S.S.R.** 52.47N 49.13E
65 N7 **Studenzen** **Austria** 47.02N 15.46E
13 B5 **Studholme Hills** N Terr **Australia**
11 F11 **Studholme Junction** **New Zealand** 44.44S 171.08E
11 E11 **Studholme, Mt** **New Zealand** 44.40S 170.56E
82 J7 **Studina** **Romania** 43.59N 24.22E
111 D8 **Studio City** California 34.09N 118.24W
56 H6 **Studland** Dorset **Eng** 50.39N 1.58W
56 H3 **Studley** Warwicks **Eng** 52.16N 1.52W
56 G5 **Studley** Wilts **Eng** 51.27N 2.04W
53 B4 **Studsgård** **Denmark** 56.06N 8.55E
52 K8 **Studsvik** **Sweden** 58.45N 17.17E
95 G9 **Studtis** **S Africa** 33.32S 23.58E
Stuer *see* **Bad Stuer**
53 Y14 **Stugufláten** **Norway** 62.17N 8.10E
52 J3 **Stugun** **Sweden** 63.10N 15.40E
64 E8 **Stühlingen** **W Germany** 47.45N 8.27E
65 N6 **Stuhteck** *mt* **Austria** 47.35N 15.48E
58 Q8 **Stuis, Nev of** Shetland **Scotland** 60.39N 1.10W
61 B2 **Stuivekenskerke** **Belgium** 51.05N 2.50E
63 J9 **Stukenbrock** **W Germany** 51.54N 8.40E
42 C5 **Stukovo** **U.S.S.R.** 53.13N 83.23E
58 C2 **Stulaval** *mt* Harris, W Isles **Scotland** 58.01N 6.52W
58 B4 **Stulaval** *mt* S Uist, W Isles **Scotland** 57.12N 7.18W
58 B4 **Stuley** *isld* S Uist, W Isles **Scotland** 57.12N 7.15W
56 M3 **Stump Cross** Cambs **Eng** 52.05N 0.11E
105 M2 **Stumpy Point** N Carolina 35.43N 75.44W
63 Q9 **Stumsdorf** **E Germany** 51.37N 12.04E
25 H6 **Stung Chinle** *R* **Cambodia**
25 H7 **Stung Kos Sla** *R* **Cambodia**
25 G6 **Stung Mong Borey** *R* **Cambodia**
25 H6 **Stung Porong** *R* **Cambodia**
25 H6 **Stung Stong** *R* **Cambodia**
25 G6 **Stung Tamyong** *R* **Cambodia**
25 G7 **Stung Tasal** *R* **Cambodia**
25 H6 **Stung Treng** **Cambodia** 13.31N 105.59E
51 K2 **Stuorajavrre** *L* **Norway** 69.06N 22.48E
101 K9 **Stupendous Mt** Br Col 52.20N 126.14W
45 K2 **Stupino** **U.S.S.R.** 54.53N 38.07E
79 O2 **Stupizza** Italy 46.13N 13.28E
79 D4 **Stura** *R* **Italy**
79 B4 **Stura di Ala** *R* **Italy**
79 B6 **Stura di Delmonte** *R* **Italy**
79 B4 **Stura di Val Grande** *R* **Italy**
79 B4 **Stura di Viù** **Italy**
103 K2 **Sturbridge** Massachusetts 42.06N 72.05W
12 B4 **Sturdee** S Australia 31.46S 132.24E
123 K5 **Sturge I** **Antarctica** 67.30S 164.20E
107 D2 **Sturgeon** Missouri 39.13N 92.15W
99 K6 **Sturgeon** *R* Ontario
100 U6 **Sturgeon B** Manitoba
106 J4 **Sturgeon B** Michigan
106 G5 **Sturgeon Bay** Wisconsin 44.51N 87.21W
106 G5 **Sturgeon Bay Can** Wisconsin
99 L6 **Sturgeon Falls** Ontario 46.22N 79.57W
101 P8 **Sturgeon L** Alberta 55.06N 117.31W
99 M8 **Sturgeon L** Ontario
100 L2 **Sturgeon L** Ontario 48.25N 91.35W
100 M1 **Sturgeon L** Ontario
100 Q4 **Sturgeon Landing** Saskatchewan 54.18N 101.49W
100 C5 **Sturgeon R** Alberta
106 H3 **Sturgeon, R** Michigan
106 K4 **Sturgeon, R** Michigan
100 L5 **Sturgeon R** Saskatchewan
107 J4 **Sturgis** Kentucky 37.32N 88.00W
106 J8 **Sturgis** Michigan 41.48N 85.25W
107 G8 **Sturgis** Mississippi 33.20N 89.05W
109 H5 **Sturgis** Oklahoma 36.54N 102.05W
100 P7 **Sturgis** Saskatchewan 51.58N 102.32W
108 G5 **Sturgis** S Dakota 44.27N 103.31W
79 E6 **Sturla** Italy 44.23N 8.59E
56 M3 **Sturmer** Essex **Eng** 52.04N 0.28E
56 G6 **Sturminster Newton** Dorset **Eng** 50.56N 2.19W
62 L8 **Štúrovo** **Czechoslovakia** 47.49N 18.40E
81 A4 **Sturraggia, C** Sardinia 39.58N 8.23E
56 O5 **Sturry** Kent **Eng** 51.18N 1.07E
12 D6 **Sturt B** S Australia
13 A4 **Sturt Cr** N Terr **Australia**
14 G4 **Sturt Cr** W Australia
14 G4 **Sturt Creek** W Australia 19.12S 128.08E
14 G4 **Sturt Creek** W Australia 19.08S 128.12E
13 F8 **Sturt Des** Qnsld/S Aust
106 G7 **Sturtevant** Wisconsin 42.42N 87.55W
12 F3 **Sturt, Mt** New S Wales 29.35S 141.42E
57 M6 **Sturton** Lincs **Eng** 53.19N 0.41W
13 C3 **Sturt Plain** N Terr **Australia**
12 A8 **Sturt, R** S Australia
69 O5 **Stürzelbronn** **France** 49.04N 7.35E
64 E5 **Stutensee** **W Germany** 49.04N 8.29E
95 L8 **Stutterheim** **S Africa** 32.35S 27.26E
107 E7 **Stuttgart** Arkansas 34.30N 91.32W
109 L2 **Stuttgart** Kansas 39.47N 99.27W
64 G6 **Stuttgart** **W Germany** 48.47N 9.12E
64 K2 **Stützerbach** **E Germany** 50.38N 10.52E
94 F8 **Stuurman** **S Africa** 31.21S 20.09E
103 G2 **Stuyvesant** New York 42.23N 73.47W
103 G2 **Stuyvesant Falls** New York 42.22N 73.44W
46 G4 **Stviga** *R* Ukraine/Belorussiya **U.S.S.R.**
52 J4 **Styggberget** **Sweden** 62.14N 16.20E
53 M9 **Stykket** **Faeroes** 62.07N 7.01W
50 C4 **Stykkishólmur** **Iceland** 65.05N 22.44W
46 F4 **Styr** *R* Ukraine **U.S.S.R.**
53 V17 **Styvi** **Norway** 60.56N 6.55E
11 M9 **Styx** *sub* Christchurch **New Zealand**
11 M8 **Styx R** **New Zealand**
75 O4 **Sú** **Spain** 41.54N 1.34E
94 J3 **Sua** **Botswana** 20.24S 26.08E
34 H4 **Suàb, Wādi es** *watercourse* **Syria**
118 G6 **Suaçuí Grande, R** **Brazil**
85 L5 **Suâdi** **Egypt** 28.04N 30.51E
18 K4 **Suai** Sarawak **Malaysia** 3.40N 113.37E
15 G5 **Suain** Papua **New Guinea** 3.20S 142.50E
58 C2 **Suainval** *mt* Lewis, W Isles **Scotland** 58.10N 6.57W
58 C2 **Suainval, L** Lewis, W Isles **Scotland**
119 D4 **Suaita** **Colombia** 6.07N 73.30W
85 O10 **Suakin** **Sudan** 19.08N 37.17E
93 G4 **Suam** *R* **Kenya**
60 N7 **Suameer** **Netherlands** 53.11N 6.00E
106 F5 **Suamico** Wisconsin 44.38N 88.03W
21 D8 **Suan** **N Korea** 38.40N 126.24E
76 L2 **Suances** **Spain** 43.25N 4.03W
Suancheng *see* **Xuancheng**
Suanhan *see*
Suanhwa *see*
15 L9 **Suao** Papua **New Guinea** 10.39S 150.03E
23 J6 **Su-ao** **Taiwan** 24.33N 121.48E
119 F4 **Suapure, R** **Venezuela**
115 E3 **Suaqui** **Mexico** 29.10N 109.40W
115 E3 **Suaqui Grande** **Mexico** 28.22N 109.52W
30 C3 **Suar** Uttar Prad **India** 29.01N 79.03E
50 B4 **Suarbær** Bardhastrandarsýsla, Vestur Iceland 65.29N 23.58W
71 L1 **Suarce** **France** 47.35N 7.05E
121 E3 **Suardi** **Argentina** 30.32S 61.58W
119 C6 **Suárez** **Colombia** 2.55N 76.41W
119 D4 **Suaréz, R** **Colombia**
91 G8 **Suarimo** **Angola** 9.38S 20.24E
61 K5 **Suarlée** **Belgium** 50.29N 4.47E
76 E2 **Suarna** *R* **Spain**
116 M10 **Suarta** **Venezuela** 8.22N 65.12W
44 K3 **Suat** Kazakhstan **U.S.S.R.** 44.34N 50.55E
15 L2 **Suavanao** Santa Isabel I **Solomon Is** 7.36S 158.42E
60 M7 **Suawoude** **Netherlands** 53.11N 5.55E
34 P6 **Sub'a 'Abar** **Iran** 32.34N 47.16E
33 M10 **Subaith** **Kuwait** 28.55N 47.55E
18 E7 **Suban Jerigi** Sumatra **Indonesia** 3.40S 103.59E
28 H2 **Subankhata** Assam **India** 26.46N 91.24E
19 L5 **Suban Pt** **Philippines** 13.10N 122.00E
28 J2 **Subansiri Frontier Division** Assam **India**
29 K6 **Subarnarekhal R** Bihar/W Bengal **India**
32 C3 **Sūbāshī** **Iran** 35.11N 48.12E
46 E2 **Subate** Latvia **U.S.S.R.** 55.59N 26.00E
33 G3 **Subay** *dist* **Saudi Arabia**
33 C2 **Subayhah** **Saudi Arabia** 29.59N 38.41E
33 E10 **Şubayhī** *tribe* **S Yemen**
33 H9 **Şubaykh** **S Yemen** 15.13N 48.21E
33 E7 **Subaykhah, As** **Saudi Arabia** 19.08N 43.20E
79 L7 **Subbiano** **Italy** 43.34N 11.52E
42 E5 **Subbotino** **U.S.S.R.** 53.04N 91.58E
35 H8 **Subeiban, Jebel** *mts* **Jordan**
23 H2 **Subei Guangai Zongqu** *canal* Jiangsu **China**
Subeihi *see* **Şubayhī** *tribe*
35 F5 **Subeihi** **Jordan** 32.09N 35.42E
22 C7 **Subei Monggolzu Zizhixian** Gansu **China** 39.30N 94.59E
Subeita *anc site see* **Shivta**
66 Q2 **Subers Ach** *R* **Austria**
33 C5 **Şubh,Jabal** *mts* **Saudi Arabia**
18 H4 **Subi** *isld* **Indonesia**
92 E3 **Subi** *tribe* **Tanzania**
80 H5 **Subiaco** **Italy** 41.56N 13.06E
14 A1 **Subiaco** *dist* Perth, W Australia
19 F1 **Subic B** Luzon **Philippines**
75 E2 **Subijana** **Spain** 42.50N 2.53W
18 H4 **Subi Kecil** *isld* **Indonesia** 3.01N 108.50E
88 G11 **Subjet Lemmuilha** *salt L* **Morocco**
86 F5 **Subk el Ahad** **Egypt** 30.19N 31.01E
110 M7 **Sublett** Idaho 42.21N 113.10W
106 E8 **Sublette** Illinois 41.38N 89.16W
109 K4 **Sublette** Kansas 37.28N 100.52W
112 L6 **Sublime** Texas 29.29N 96.48W
82 F4 **Subotica** **Yugoslavia** 46.04N 19.41E
22 L4 **Subrag** Nei Monggol Zizhiqu **China** 44.13N 118.26E
93 G7 **Subugu** *mt* **Kenya** 1.38S 35.50E
117 H7 **Sucatinga** **Brazil** 4.17S 38.00W
76 E6 **Sucçães** **Portugal** 41.30N 7.15W
107 D4 **Success** Missouri 37.25N 92.06W
100 J8 **Success** Saskatchewan 50.28N 108.06W
79 H6 **Succiso, Alpe di** *mts* **Italy** 44.20N 10.12E
70 G7 **Sucé** **France** 47.21N 1.31W
82 K3 **Suceava** **Romania** 47.37N 26.18E
82 K3 **Suceava** *R* **Romania**
117 G7 **Sucesso** **Brazil** 4.54S 40.35W
62 M6 **Sucha** **Poland** 49.44N 19.35E
62 J2 **Suchan** **Poland** 53.18N 15.15E
40 F10 **Suchan** *R* **U.S.S.R.**
65 L4 **Suchdol** **Czechoslovakia** 48.53N 14.53E
62 M4 **Suchedniów** **Poland** 51.03N 20.50E
120 D6 **Suches, L** **Peru**
66 B4 **Suchet** *mt* **Switzerland** 46.47N 6.28E
115 N9 **Suchiapa** **Mexico** 16.39N 93.06W
115 N10 **Suchiate, Mariscal** **Mexico** 14.40N 92.11W
115 L9 **Suchixtepec** **Mexico** 16.08N 96.29W
Suchow *see* **Yibin**
62 O2 **Suchowola** **Poland** 53.34N 23.05E
63 D10 **Süchteln** **W Germany** 51.17N 6.22E
66 C5 **Suchy** **Switzerland** 46.44N 6.36E
110 C1 **Sucia I** Washington 48.46N 122.54W
77 P5 **Sucina** **Spain** 37.54N 0.57W
119 C4 **Sucio, R** **Colombia**
110 H6 **Sucker Cr** Oregon/Idaho
113 Q7 **Suckling C** Alaska 60.00N 143.50W
15 K8 **Suckling, Mt** Papua **New Guinea** 9.49S 148.53E
63 P6 **Suckow** **E Germany** 53.19N 11.58E
59 F4 **Suck, R** Roscommon etc **Irish Rep**
120 F8 **Sucre** **Bolivia** 19.05S 65.15W
119 D3 **Sucre** **Colombia** 8.50N 74.45W
119 B8 **Sucre** **Ecuador** 1.21S 80.27W
119 C3 **Sucre** *div* **Colombia**
119 G2 **Sucre** *state* **Venezuela**
119 F5 **Sucuaro** **Colombia** 4.36N 68.50W
117 A8 **Sucunduri, R** **Brazil**
118 D7 **Sucuriu, R** **Brazil**
68 H4 **Sucy-en-Brie** **France** 48.46N 2.32E
69 D6 **Sucy-en-Brie** **France** 48.47N 2.31E
89 L8 **Sud** *dept* **Benin**
89 G9 **Sud** *dept* **Ivory Coast**
46 K1 **Suda** **U.S.S.R.** 59.10N 37.28E
46 K1 **Suda** *R* **U.S.S.R.**
44 D10 **Sudak** Ukraine **U.S.S.R.** 44.52N 34.57E
112 E1 **Sudan** Texas 34.04N 102.32W
73 G4 **Sudan** *rep* **Africa**
75 M4 **Sudanell** **Spain** 41.32N 0.34E
46 N1 **Suday** **U.S.S.R.** 58.59N 43.00E
33 F4 **Sudayr** *dist* **Saudi Arabia**
34 N8 **Sudayr, Sha'ib** *watercourse* **Iraq**
45 J4 **Sudbishchi** **U.S.S.R.** 52.56N 37.38E
43 C2 **Sud'bodarovka** **U.S.S.R.** 52.23N 53.54E
56 H2 **Sudbury** Derbys **Eng** 52.53N 1.44W
55 D3 **Sudbury** London **Eng** 51.34N 0.19W
103 M2 **Sudbury** Massachusetts 42.23N 71.25W
99 J6 **Sudbury** Ontario 46.30N 81.01W
13 J5 **Sudbury** Queensland 22.15S 148.35E
56 N3 **Sudbury** Suffolk **Eng** 52.02N 0.44E
103 M2 **Sudbury Res** Massachusetts 42.20N 71.30W
87 C6 **Sudd** *swamp* **Sudan**
117 A1 **Suddie** **Guyana** 7.07N 58.31W
63 O6 **Sude** *R* **E Germany**
63 J3 **Süderau** *R* **W Germany/Denmark**
63 H3 **Süderaue** *inlet* **W Germany**
63 L3 **Süderbrarup** **W Germany** 54.38N 9.47E
63 M7 **Süderburg** **W Germany** 52.54N 10.28E
63 K4 **Süderhastedt** **W Germany** 54.03N 9.13E
63 J4 **Süderhöft** **W Germany** 54.17N 8.41E
63 J3 **Süderlügum** **W Germany** 54.52N 8.55E
63 J4 **Süderoog** *isld* **W Germany**
89 L8 **Sud-Est** *dept* **Benin**
Sudest, C *see* **Siri, C.**
62 J5 **Sudety** *mts* **Poland/Czech**
63 J4 **Südfall** *isld* **W Germany**
50 C2 **Súdhavik** **Iceland** 66.02N 22.59W
50 H4 **Sudhurárhraun** *lava field* **Iceland**
50 L5 **Sudhurdalur** *V* **Iceland**
50 E8 **Sudhurey** *isld* **Iceland** 63.23N 20.19W
50 B2 **Sudhureyri** **Iceland** 66.08N 23.30W
50 B3 **Sudhurfirdhir** *B* **Iceland**
50 E5 **Sudhurjökull** *ice cap* **Iceland** 64.35N 20.00W
Sudhuroy *see* **Syderø**
46 L2 **Sudilova** **U.S.S.R.** 57.20N 38.48E
15 D6 **Sudirman, Pegunungan** *mts* Irian Jaya
46 M1 **Sudislavl'** **U.S.S.R.** 57.50N 41.39E
Sudkhar *see* **Sad-Kharv**
103 C8 **Sudlersville** Maryland 39.11N 75.51W
63 E9 **Südlohn** **W Germany** 51.56N 6.51E
45 M1 **Sudogda** **U.S.S.R.** 55.58N 40.50E
65 L2 **Sudoměřice** **Czechoslovakia** 49.31N 14.39E
65 L3 **Sudoměřice** **Czechoslovakia** 49.18N 14.33E
21 D9 **Sudong-ni** **S Korea** 36.01N 126.42E
41 D3 **Sudorova, Os** *isld* **U.S.S.R.** 75.06N 82.00E
45 C3 **Sudorovichi** Belorussiya **U.S.S.R.** 53.04N 31.09E
45 E4 **Sudost'** *R* **U.S.S.R.**
89 K8 **Sud-Ouest** *dept* **Benin**
26 T13 **Sud Ouest, Pte** Mauritius, **Indian Oc** 20.27S 57.18E
26 N15 **Sud, Pte** St Paul I **Ind Oc** 38.44S 77.31E
86 J6 **Sudr** **Egypt** 29.40N 32.42E
39 C1 **Sudrolakh** **U.S.S.R.** 68.15N 143.00E
86 J6 **Sudr, Wâdi** *watercourse* **Egypt**
Suduroy *isld see* **Syderø**
45 G5 **Sudzha** **U.S.S.R.** 51.11N 35.17E
87 A7 **Sue** *watercourse* **Sudan**
77 Q2 **Sueca** **Spain** 39.13N 0.19W
103 B5 **Suedburg** Pennsylvania 40.32N 76.58W
89 D8 **Suehn** **Liberia** 6.37N 10.43W
35 G8 **Su'eida** *watercourse* **Jordan**
35 F8 **Su'eidat** **Jordan** 31.17N 35.38E
81 C4 **Suelli** Sardinia 39.34N 9.08E
113 V9 **Suemez I** Alaska 55.15N 133.20W
112 E6 **Sue Pk** Texas 29.25N 102.58W
47 K7 **Suer'** *R* **U.S.S.R.**
48 U10 **Suess Land** **Greenland**
70 N6 **Suèvres** **France** 47.40N 1.28E
96 C2 **Sue Wood Bay** **Bermuda**
86 J6 **Suez** **Egypt** 29.59N 32.33E
86 H3 **Suez Canal** **Egypt**
86 K9 **Suez, G.of** **Egypt**
35 G4 **Suf** **Jordan** 32.19N 35.50E
86 M3 **Sufa** **Egypt** 31.13N 34.10E
33 H9 **Sufāl, As** **S Yemen** 14.09N 48.43E
33 D5 **Şufaynah** **Saudi Arabia** 23.09N 40.33E
33 F2 **Şufayri, Aş** **Saudi Arabia** 28.31N 45.46E
34 N10 **Şufayri Aş** **Saudi Arabia** 28.32N 45.49E
Şufeina *see* **Şufaynah**
66 O5 **Sufers** **Switzerland** 46.35N 9.23E
103 F4 **Suffern** New York 41.07N 74.09W
100 F8 **Suffield** Alberta 50.13N 111.11W
103 J3 **Suffield** Connecticut 41.58N 72.38W
110 Q2 **Suffolk** Montana 47.29N 109.21W
104 J10 **Suffolk** Virginia 36.44N 76.37W
56 N3 **Suffolk** *co* **England**
103 H5 **Suffolk** *co* Long I, N Y
103 M2 **Suffolk** *co* Massachusetts
15 H4 **Suf I** Bismarck Arch 0.53S 145.31E
32 A1 **Sūfiān** **Iran** 38.15N 45.59E
43 O8 **Sufi-Kishlak** Uzbekistan **U.S.S.R.** 40.44N 72.40E
43 L6 **Sufi-Kurgan** Kirgiziya **U.S.S.R.** 40.01N 73.30E
86 G4 **Sufîya, El** **Egypt** 30.56N 31.46E
Sufu *see* **K'a-shih**
42 E6 **Sug-Aksy** **U.S.S.R.** 51.28N 91.15E
79 K2 **Sugana, Val** *V* **Italy**
50 B2 **Súgandafjördhur** *B* **Iceland**
20 H6 **Sugano yama** *mt* **Japan** 35.23N 134.27E
110 O6 **Sugar** Idaho 43.55N 111.44W
109 G3 **Sugar City** Colorado 38.14N 103.40W
103 A3 **Sugar Creek** Pennsylvania
104 F5 **Sugar Grove** Pennsylvania 41.59N 79.21W
104 D10 **Sugar Grove** Virginia 36.46N 81.26W
106 K3 **Sugar, L** Michigan
112 M6 **Sugar Land** Texas 29.37N 95.40W
103 F4 **Sugar Loaf** New York 41.20N 74.18W
Sugar Loaf *mt* Rio de Janeiro *see* **Pão de Açúcar**
14 C6 **Sugarloaf Hill** W Australia 24.00S 119.45E
105 F13 **Sugarloaf Key** *isld* Florida 24.38N 81.32W
59 C8 **Sugarloaf Mt** Cork **Irish Rep** 51.43N 9.38W
98 B8 **Sugarloaf Mt** Maine 45.02N 70.18W
10 E11 **Sugarloaf Passage** Lord Howe I **Pacific Oc**
23 B8 **Sugar Loaf Peak** Hong Kong 22.22N 114.11E
12 L4 **Sugarloaf Pt** New S Wales 32.25S 152.30E
96 B13 **Sugar Loaf Pt** St Helena 15.54S 5.43W
15 G6 **Sugarloaf, The** *mt* Papua **New Guinea** 5.47S 143.45E
106 E7 **Sugar, R** Wisconsin
103 B3 **Sugar Run** Pennsylvania 41.38N 76.14W
Sugaru *see* **Sogār**
20 K7 **Suga-shima** *isld* **Japan**
24 G3 **Sugaytu Bulak** *spring* Xinjiang Uygur Zizhiqu **China** 45.00N 93.20E
19 N6 **Sugbuhan Pt** **Philippines** 10.04N 126.04E
42 H5 **Sugdzha** **U.S.S.R.** 54.56N 106.59E
41 P9 **Sugdzha** *R* **U.S.S.R.**
64 J4 **Sugenheim** **W Germany** 49.36N 10.27E
71 C5 **Sugères** **France** 45.36N 3.25E
66 Q3 **Suggadin** *R* **Austria**
100 P4 **Suggi L** Saskatchewan
Sughun *see* **Sowghān**
20 H6 **Sugi** **Japan** 35.06N 134.55E
18 E5 **Sugi** *isld* **Indonesia**
20 D2 **Suginami** *dist* Tōkyō **Japan**
20 D5 **Sugita** Kanagawa **Japan**
41 O8 **Suglan** **U.S.S.R.** 64.12N 134.00E
36 F5 **Suğla Sölü** *L* **Turkey**
61 K7 **Sugny** **Belgium** 49.48N 4.54E
42 C3 **Sugot** **U.S.S.R.** 58.00N 82.52E
39 F3 **Sugoy** *R* **U.S.S.R.**
Sugsundong Gompa *see* **Ya-la**
41 P5 **Sugulan** **U.S.S.R.** 70.38N 138.30E
24 B6 **Sugun** Xinjiang Uygur Zizhiqu **China** 39.46N 76.45E
18 M2 **Sugut** *R* Sabah **Malaysia**
93 H4 **Suguta** *watercourse* **Kenya**
93 E7 **Suguti** **Tanzania** 1.47S 33.41E
18 M2 **Sugut, Tg** *C* Sabah **Malaysia** 6.25N 117.45E
82 J7 **Suhaia, L** **Romania** 43.41N 25.19E
18 J5 **Suhaid** Borneo **Indon** 0.35N 111.59E
22 C7 **Suhai Hu** *L* Qinghai **China** 38.50N 93.50E
34 P6 **Suhain** **Iraq** 32.13N 47.28E
22 G6 **Suhai Obo** Nei Monggol Zizhiqu **China** 40.18N 106.23E
22 G7 **Suhait** Nei Monggol Zizhiqu **China** 39.37N 105.06E
Şuhār *see* **uhār**
33 M4 **Şuhār** **Oman** 24.25N 56.45E
22 G1 **Sühbaatar** **Mongolia** 50.10N 106.14E
22 J3 **Sühbaatar** *prov* **Mongolia**
Suhe Bator *see* **Sühbaatar**
64 K2 **Suhl** **E Germany** 50.37N 10.43E
64 K2 **Suhl** *reg* **E Germany**
Suhmātā *see* **Zur'iel**
82 D5 **Suhopolje** **Yugoslavia** 45.48N 17.29E
66 J2 **Suhr** **Switzerland** 47.23N 8.05E
66 J3 **Suhr** *R* **Switzerland**
33 F5 **Suhul** *tribe* **Saudi Arabia**
33 K5 **Suhūl al Kidan** *des area* **Saudi Arabia**
36 E4 **Şuhut** **Turkey** 38.33N 30.32E
31 E6 **Sui** **Pakistan** 28.39N 69.21E
30 K8 **Suiabathan** Bihar **India** 24.51N 86.41E
118 D2 **Suiá Missu, R** **Brazil**
110 E1 **Suiattle Pass** Washington 48.12N 120.57W
21 E4 **Suibin** Heilongjiang **China** 47.19N 121.52E
23 H4 **Suichang** Zhejiang **China** 28.35N 119.15E
23 G5 **Suichuan** Jiangxi **China** 26.26N 114.34E
22 H8 **Suide** Shaanxi **China** 37.35N 110.05E
21 F4 **Suidong** Heilongjiang **China** 47.24N 132.05E
76 C4 **Suido, Sierra del** *mts* **Spain**
21 E5 **Suifenhe** Heilongjiang **China** 44.25N 131.06E
21 E6 **Suifen He** *R* Heilongjiang **China**
29 B5 **Suigam** Gujarat **India** 24.10N 71.23E
21 D4 **Sui-hua** Heilongjiang **China** 46.40N 127.00E
23 C4 **Suijang** Sichuan **China** 28.29N 103.55E
23 F7 **Sui Jiang** *R* Guangdong **China**
Sui-lai *see* **Manas**
21 D4 **Suileng** Heilongjiang **China** 47.14N 127.07E
71 C2 **Suilly-la-Tour** **France** 47.19N 3.04E
58 F2 **Suilven, mt** Highland **Scotland** 58.07N 5.08W
23 E5 **Suining** Hunan **China** 26.34N 109.50E
23 H2 **Suining** Jiangsu **China** 33.54N 117.58E
23 D3 **Suining** Sichuan **China** 30.31N 105.33E
121 F5 **Suipacha** **Argentina** 34.46S 59.44W
120 F9 **Suipacha** **Bolivia** 21.35S 65.41W
23 G2 **Suiping** Henan **China** 33.08N 114.04E
69 G5 **Suippe** *R* **France**
69 H5 **Suippes** **France** 49.08N 4.32E
69 H5 **Suippes, Camp de** **France**
59 H7 **Suir, R** Waterford etc **Irish Rep**
30 J7 **Suitha** Bihar **India** 25.32N 85.07E
103 A9 **Suitland** Maryland 38.51N 76.55W
31 F6 **Sui Vehar** **Pakistan** 29.17N 71.35E
23 E8 **Suixi** Guangdong **China** 21.23N 110.14E
23 G1 **Sui Xian** Henan **China** 34.26N 115.08E
23 F3 **Sui Xian** Hubei **China** 31.46N 113.22E
23 D5 **Suiyang** Guizhou **China** 27.56N 107.10E
23 D4 **Suiyangchang** Guizhou **China** 28.06N 107.45E
69 J8 **Suize** *R* **France**
22 M6 **Suizhong** Liaoning **China** 40.19N 120.22E
22 G5 **Suj** Nei Monggol Zizhiqu **China** 42.07N 107.59E
30 F7 **Sujanganj** Uttar Prad **India** 25.47N 82.17E
29 D4 **Sujangarh** Rajasthan **India** 27.43N 74.35E
29 D1 **Sujanpur** Gurdaspur, Punjab **India** 32.19N 75.38E
29 E2 **Sujanpur** Himachal Prad **India** 31.49N 76.32E
31 E8 **Sujawal** **Pakistan** 24.36N 68.06E
Suji *see* **Haixing**
87 G7 **Suka** **Ethiopia** 6.35N 39.11E
18 G9 **Sukabumi** Java **Indon** 6.55S 106.50E
18 H6 **Sukadana** Borneo **Indon** 1.15S 109.57E
18 F8 **Sukadana** Sumatra **Indon** 5.02S 105.34E
18 H6 **Sukadana, Teluk** *B* Borneo **Indon**
20 O4 **Sukagawa** **Japan** 37.15N 140.21E
18 J7 **Sukamara** Borneo **Indon** 2.45S 111.10E
18 G9 **Sukanegara** Java **Indon** 7.08S 107.01E
18 J7 **Sukaraja** Borneo **Indon** 2.23S 110.35E
Sukarnapura *see* **Jayapura**
Sukarno, Geb *mt see* **Jaya, Puntjak**
18 N3 **Sukau** Sabah **Malaysia** 5.30N 118.16E
21 C8 **Sukch'ŏn** **N Korea** 39.24N 125.40E
93 M4 **Sukela** **Kenya** 1.17N 40.11E
29 E5 **Suket** Jhalawar, Rajasthan **Ind** 24.21N 76.00E
29 E5 **Suket** Kota, Rajasthan **India** 24.40N 76.06E
51 N8 **Sukeva** **Finland** 63.50N 27.30E
41 L6 **Sukhana** **U.S.S.R.** 68.45N 118.32E
40 F8 **Sukhanovka** **U.S.S.R.** 46.06N 133.54E
45 B3 **Sukhari** Belorussiya **U.S.S.R.** 53.58N 30.44E
30 C5 **Sukhata** *R* Uttar Prad **India**
42 H5 **Sukhaya** **U.S.S.R.** 52.31N 107.05E
42 D1 **Sukhaya** *R* **U.S.S.R.**
41 E7 **Sukhaya Tunguska** **U.S.S.R.** 65.06N 88.01E
41 E8 **Sukhaya Tunguska** *R* **U.S.S.R.**
30 K5 **Sukhchauri** **Nepal** 27.05N 86.22E
82 J7 **Sukhindol** **Bulgaria** 43.11N 25.10E
45 G2 **Sukhinichi** **U.S.S.R.** 54.07N 35.21E
35 H5 **Sukhna, Es** **Jordan** 32.08N 36.04E
Sukhnah *see* **Sukhne, Es**
34 F4 **Sukhne, Es** **Syria** 34.56N 38.52E
86 N8 **Sukhn, Gebel** *hill* **Egypt** 28.46N 34.35E
42 E4 **Sukhobuzimskoye** **U.S.S.R.** 56.30N 93.16E
45 K3 **Sukhodolskiy** **U.S.S.R.** 53.43N 38.16E
47 E6 **Sukhona** *R* **U.S.S.R.**
25 E4 **Sukhothai** **Thailand** 17.00N 99.51E
40 D6 **Sukhotino** **U.S.S.R.** 51.00N 127.01E
45 P6 **Sukhov 2-oy** **U.S.S.R.** 50.00N 43.29E
45 N9 **Sukhoy** **U.S.S.R.** 47.07N 41.24E
47 N4 **Sukhoy Log** **U.S.S.R.** 56.54N 62.01E
41 A3 **Sukhoy Nos, Mys** *C* Novaya Zemlya **U.S.S.R.** 73.45N 53.39E
47 K3 **Sukhoy Paloy** *R* **U.S.S.R.**
42 E3 **Sukhoy-Pit** **U.S.S.R.** 58.50N 92.49E
30 K6 **Sukhpur** Bihar **India** 26.04N 86.33E
47 J8 **Sukhtelinskiy** Kazakhstan **U.S.S.R.** 53.59N 60.05E
44 D4 **Sukhumi** Georgia **U.S.S.R.** 43.01N 41.01E
87 D4 **Suki, Es** **Sudan** 13.22N 33.52E
95 N2 **Sukkelaar** **S Africa** 26.35S 29.32E
48 R11 **Sukkertoppen** **Greenland** 65.25N 52.40W
47 O4 **Sukkertoppen Isflade** *ice field* **Greenland**
20 J2 **Sukki** **Japan** 42.35N 139.50E
47 C4 **Sukkozero** **U.S.S.R.** 32.18N 63.11E
31 E7 **Sukkur** **Pakistan** 27.42N 68.54E
31 E7 **Sukkur** *dist* **Pakistan**
31 E7 **Sukkur Barrage** **Pakistan** 27.40N 68.52E
29 K2 **Suklara** W Bengal **India** 23.11N 86.20E
30 F5 **Sukli** *R* Uttar Prad **India**
28 E1 **Sukma** Madhya Prad **India** 18.22N 81.45E
93 G4 **Suk Mts** **Kenya**
18 J9 **Sukoharjo** Java **Indon** 7.40S 110.50E
91 K4 **Sukomakanga** **Zaïre** 1.10S 27.02E
63 P5 **Sukow** **E Germany** 53.34N 11.34E
40 G8 **Sukpay** *R* **U.S.S.R.**
40 G8 **Sukpay Datani** **U.S.S.R.** 47.56N 136.43E
Sukre *R see* **Lakhish** *R*
29 C5 **Sukri R** Rajasthan **India**
94 D3 **Sukses** **Namibia** 21.01S 16.52E
39 E3 **Suksukan** **U.S.S.R.** 63.14N 153.32E
47 H7 **Suksun** **U.S.S.R.** 57.10N 57.22E
29 H7 **Suktel R** Orissa **India**
Sukulum *see* **Yuwil**
92 F3 **Sukuma** *tribe* **Tanzania**
20 F9 **Sukumo** **Japan** 32.59N 132.42E
20 F9 **Sukumo-wan** *B* **Japan**
19 C8 **Sukun** *isld* **Indonesia** 8.05S 122.09E
101 N8 **Sukunka** *R* Br Col
93 H5 **Sukuta lol Marmar** **Kenya** 0.42N 36.42E
93 H5 **Sukuta Mugie** **Kenya** 0.43N 36.37E
35 F9 **Sul** **Jordan** 31.04N 35.44E
76 C7 **Sul** **Portugal** 40.50N 8.03W
110 M4 **Sula** Montana 45.50N 113.59W
53 R16 **Sula** *isld* **Norway** 61.08N 4.55E
53 U14 **Sula** *isld* **Norway** 62.25N 6.10E
47 G3 **Sula** *R* Arkhangel'sk **U.S.S.R.**
45 D7 **Sula** *R* Ukraine **U.S.S.R.**
115 L2 **Sulaco** **Honduras** 14.57N 87.15W
Sulaiman Beg *see* **Sulaymān Beg**
Sulaimānīya *see* **Sulaymānīyah**
31 E6 **Sulaiman Ra** **Pakistan**
Sulaiyil *see* **Sulayyil, As**
44 H4 **Sulak** Dagestan **U.S.S.R.** 43.19N 47.33E
45 U5 **Sulak** Saratov **U.S.S.R.** 51.50N 48.22E
44 H4 **Sulak** *R* **U.S.S.R.**
19 D5 **Sula, Kep** *islds* Moluccas **Indon**
Sulakyurt *see* **Konur**
52 D3 **Sula Lt.House** **Norway** 63.50N 8.30E
47 E5 **Sulanda** *R* **U.S.S.R.**
32 D5 **Sūlār** **Iran** 31.56N 51.55E
54 F3 **Sula Sgeir** *isld* **Scotland**
18 D6 **Sulasih, Gunung** *mt* Sumatra **Indon** 1.00S 100.39E
19 M6 **Sulat** **Philippines** 11.48N 125.26E
18 M10 **Sulat** *isld* **Indonesia** 8.19S 116.43E
113 K4 **Sulatna** *R* Alaska
113 K4 **Sulatna Crossing** Alaska 64.06N 155.38W
19 B4 **Sulawesi** *isld* **Indonesia**
19 B5 **Sulawesi Selatan** *prov* **Indonesia**
19 B4 **Sulawesi Tengah** *prov* **Indonesia**
19 B3 **Sulawesi Utara** *prov* **Indonesia**
34 M4 **Sulaymān Beg** **Iraq** 34.50N 44.40E
34 N3 **Sulaymānīyah** **Iraq** 35.32N 45.27E
33 D3 **Sulaymī, As** **Saudi Arabia** 26.18N 41.22E
33 F6 **Sulayyil, As** **Saudi Arabia** 20.28N 45.35E
33 F6 **Sulayyimah** **Saudi Arabia** 21.43N 45.35E
Sulayyul, As *see* **Sulayyil, As**
85 L9 **Sulb** *ruin* **Sudan** 20.26N 30.22E
33 H4 **Şulb, Aş** *plain* **Saudi Arabia**
57 E4 **Sulby** Isle of Man **U.K.** 54.19N 4.29W
117 D5 **Sul, Canal do** *channel* **Brazil**
81 B5 **Sulcis** *reg* Sardinia
53 U20 **Suldal** **Norway** 59.29N 6.30E
53 U20 **Suldalslågen** *V* **Norway** 59.28N 6.20E
53 V20 **Suldalsosen** **Norway** 59.30N 6.31E
53 V19 **Suldalsvatn** *L* **Norway**
39 D2 **Suldkkan** *R* **U.S.S.R.**
53 D3 **Suldrup** **Denmark** 56.51N 9.43E
62 J3 **Sulechów** **Poland** 52.05N 15.37E
62 J3 **Sulęcin** **Poland** 52.24N 15.08E
32 E2 **Suledeh** **Iran** 36.34N 52.02E
66 H5 **Sulegg** *mt* **Switzerland** 46.38N 7.52E
Sulehdeh *see* **Suledeh**
31 G5 **Suleimanki** **Pakistan** 30.19N 73.53E
47 M4 **Sulem** **U.S.S.R.** 57.32N 59.09E
Sulemanke *see* **Suleimanki**
50 K3 **Sulendur** *mt* **Iceland** 65.33N 15.31W
95 M7 **Sulenkama** **S Africa** 31.01S 28.41E
15 G5 **Sulen, Mt** Papua **New Guinea** 3.25S 142.12E
81 D2 **Su Lernu** *R* Sardinia
53 V20 **Suleskar** **Norway** 59.01N 6.56E
54 H3 **Sule Skerry** Orkney **Scotland** 59.05N 4.20W
53 U14 **Sulesund** **Norway** 62.24N 6.08E
53 Y16 **Suletind** *mt* **Norway** 61.07N 8.07E
47 L5 **Suleya** **U.S.S.R.** 55.11N 58.50E
36 J5 **Süleymanlı** **Turkey** 37.53N 36.50E
63 M5 **Sülfeld** **W Germany** 53.48N 10.12E
41 O9 **Sulgachi** **U.S.S.R.** 61.35N 132.55E
66 N1 **Sulgen** **Switzerland** 47.33N 9.12E
53 Y15 **Sulheim** **Norway** 61.47N 8.24E
93 L2 **Suli** **Ethiopia** 4.00N 39.58E
91 K4 **Sulia** **Zaïre** 1.37S 26.37E
117 F2 **Sul, I. do** Martin Vaz **Atlantic Oc**
71 F4 **Sulignat** **France** 46.11N 4.58E
22 C8 **Suli Hu** *L* Qinghai **China**
18 D6 **Suliki** Sumatra **Indon** 0.08S 100.24E
89 D8 **Sulima** **Sierra Leone** 6.59N 11.34W
82 M5 **Sulina** **Romania** 45.07N 29.40E
82 M5 **Sulina** *R* **Romania**
63 J7 **Sulingen** **W Germany** 52.41N 8.47E
22 D8 **Sulin Gol He** *R* Qinghai **China**
82 K3 **Sulița** **Romania** 47.39N 26.59E
51 E4 **Sulitjelma** **Norway** 67.10N 16.05E
51 E4 **Sulitjelma** *mt* **Norway** 67.10N 16.24E
51 N10 **Sulkava** **Finland** 61.50N 28.25E
39 H7 **Sulkovskogo, Mys** *C* Komandorskiye O-va **U.S.S.R.** 54.52N 167.31E
35 D1 **Sullamah Shel Zor** *anc site* **Israel** 33.05N 35.06E
119 B10 **Sullana** **Peru** 4.52S 80.39W
59 D8 **Sullane R** Cork **Irish Rep**
107 H8 **Sulligent** Alabama 33.53N 88.10W
107 H2 **Sullivan** Illinois 39.35N 88.37W
107 J2 **Sullivan** Indiana 39.05N 87.24W
107 E3 **Sullivan** Missouri 38.13N 91.10W
103 E3 **Sullivan** *co* New York
103 A4 **Sullivan** *co* Pennsylvania
101 K10 **Sullivan Bay** Br Col 50.55N 126.52W
Sullivan I Burma*see* **Lanbi Kyun**
100 F6 **Sullivan L** Alberta
12 A5 **Sullivans Cr** Canberra **Australia**
103 A2 **Sullivanville** New York 42.13N 76.46W
87 G4 **Sullo** *watercourse* **Ethiopia**
58 Q9 **Sullom** Shetland **Scotland** 60.27N 1.20W
58 Q9 **Sullom Voe** *B* Shetland **Scotland** 60.27N 1.20W
108 S8 **Sully** Iowa 41.34N 92.50W
70 P6 **Sully-la Chapelle** **France** 47.59N 2.11E
70 P6 **Sully-sur-Loire** **France** 47.46N 2.22E
65 M8 **Sulm** *R* **Austria**
80 J4 **Sulmona** **Italy** 42.03N 13.56E
51 P8 **Sulo, Ozero** *L* Karelia **U.S.S.R.** 63.39N 31.00E
107 C11 **Sulphur** Louisiana 30.13N 93.24W
110 G9 **Sulphur** Nevada 40.55N 118.44W
109 O7 **Sulphur** Oklahoma 34.31N 96.58W
112 O2 **Sulphur** *R* Texas/Arkansas
111 M3 **Sulphurdale** Utah 38.34N 112.35W
95 P3 **Sulphur Springs** **S Africa** 27.11S 31.05E
112 M2 **Sulphur Springs** Texas 33.09N 95.36W
112 E3 **Sulphur Springs Cr** Texas
66 Q5 **Sulsanna, Val** **Switzerland**
53 D2 **Sulsted** **Denmark** 57.10N 9.59E
52 G3 **Sulstua** **Norway** 63.41N 12.02E
35 H9 **Sulsul, Jeb. es** *mts* **Jordan**
99 H5 **Sultan** Ontario 47.36N 82.47W
110 D2 **Sultan** Washington 47.53N 121.48W
37 D7 **Sultan** *R* **Turkey**
35 G9 **Sultan** *watercourse* **Jordan**
Sultanabad *see* **Arāk**
Sultanabad *see* **Solţānābād**
28 D1 **Sultanabad** Andhra Prad **India** 18.35N 79.19E
34 N7 **Sultān al Wal'ah** **Iraq** 31.26N 45.07E
85 D4 **Sulţān, As** **Libya** 31.07N 17.10E
32 K2 **Sultanbent** Turkmeniya **U.S.S.R.** 37.09N 62.21E
36 E4 **Sultan Dağları** *mts* **Turkey**
93 J8 **Sultan Hamud** **Kenya** 2.02S 37.23E
36 G4 **Sultanhanı** **Turkey** 38.15N 33.35E
36 C5 **Sultanhisar** **Turkey** 37.52N 28.10E
Sultani, Khor *see* **Soltānī, Khowr-e** *Bay*
Sultanıye *see* **Karapınar**
37 G2 **Sultaniye** **Turkey** 40.35N 29.45E
Sultaniyeh *see* **Solţānīyeh**
31 B6 **Sultan, Koh-i-** *ra* **Iran/Pakistan**
44 H8 **Sultanly** Azerbaydzhan **U.S.S.R.** 39.17N 47.03E
Sultan Maidan *see* **Soltān Meydān**
37 G6 **Sultanmut** **Turkey** 30.07N 42.44E
29 D2 **Sultanpur** Kapurthala, Punjab **India** 31.13N 75.12E
30 B3 **Sultanpur** Saharanpur, Uttar Prad **India** 29.45N 78.07E
30 F6 **Sultanpur** Sultanpur, Uttar Prad **India** 26.15N 82.04E
30 E6 **Sultanpur** *dist* Uttar Prad **India**
36 H4 **Sultansazlığı** *marsh* **Turkey**
44 E3 **Sultanskoye** **U.S.S.R.** 44.36N 42.41E
47 M5 **Sultayeva** **U.S.S.R.** 55.29N 61.21E
63 R5 **Sülten** **E Germany** 53.38N 12.56E
15 L6 **Sulu** New Britain 5.27S 150.59E
19 M6 **Suluan** *isld* **Philippines** 10.45N 125.58E
19 J9 **Sulu Arch** **Philippines**
93 K3 **Sulugona** *locality* **Kenya**
36 F4 **Sülüklü** **Turkey** 38.54N 32.20E
113 K5 **Sulukna** *R* Alaska
87 G6 **Sululta** **Ethiopia** 9.10N 38.43E
28 J2 **Sulung** Assam **India** 27.11N 93.20E
85 F3 **Suluntah** **Libya** 32.34N 21.39E
85 F4 **Sulūq** **Libya** 31.39N 20.18E
35 F2 **Suluqiye** **Syria** 32.59N 35.44E
28 E4 **Suluru** Andhra Prad **India** 13.44N 80.03E
36 J3 **Sulusaray** **Turkey** 40.00N 36.05E
17 J10 **Sulu Sea** **Philippines**
44 J7 **Sulut** Azerbaydzhan **U.S.S.R.** 40.44N 48.28E
43 H1 **Suly** Kazakhstan **U.S.S.R.** 53.46N 66.30E
43 J7 **Sulyukta** Kirgiziya **U.S.S.R.** 39.59N 69.31E
66 P2 **Sulz** **Austria** 47.18N 9.39E
64 F7 **Sulz** **W Germany** 48.21N 8.38E
65 H7 **Sulzau** **Austria** 47.30N 13.10E
64 H5 **Sulzbach** Baden-Württemberg **W Germany** 49.00N 9.30E
64 C5 **Sulzbach** Saarland **W Germany** 49.18N 7.04E
64 M4 **Sulzbach-Rosenberg** **W Germany** 49.30N 11.46E
65 A6 **Sulzberg** **Austria** 47.32N 9.55E
64 J8 **Sulzberg** **W Germany** 47.41N 10.21E
123 J9 **Sulzberger B** **Antarctica**
64 D8 **Sulzburg** Baden-Württemberg **W Germany** 47.50N 7.45E
64 L5 **Sulzbürg** Bayern **W Germany** 49.11N 11.25E
64 H5 **Sulzdorf** Baden-Württemberg **W Germany** 49.05N 9.52E
64 K3 **Sulzdorf** Bayern **W Germany** 50.14N 10.35E
Sülze *see* **Bad Sülze**
63 M7 **Sülze** **W Germany** 52.45N 10.02E
113 R6 **Sulzer, Mt** Alaska 61.35N 141.35W
64 F5 **Sulzfeld** **W Germany** 49.06N 8.51E
66 Q3 **Sulzfluh** *mt* **Austria/Switz** 47.02N 9.51E
64 J4 **Sulzheim** **W Germany** 49.57N 10.22E
64 J3 **Sulzthal** **W Germany** 50.07N 10.02E
119 C8 **Sumaco, Vol** **Ecuador** 0.36S 77.39W
82 F6 **Sumadija** *reg* **Yugoslavia**
Sumaichah *see* **Dujayl, Ad**
Sumair al Muhammad *see* **Sumayr al Muḩammad**
31 C3 **Sumak** **Afghanistan** 34.43N 65.49E
19 C3 **Sumalata** Celebes **Indon** 0.59N 122.31E
121 D2 **Sumampa** **Argentina** 29.25S 63.29W
32 A4 **Sūmar** **Iran** 33.52N 45.36E
42 D2 **Sumarokovo** **U.S.S.R.** 61.45N 89.40E
110 C1 **Sumas** Washington 49.00N 122.16W
15 H4 **Sumasuma I** Bismarck Arch 1.29S 144.05E
Sumatera *see* **Sumatra**
18 C4 **Sumatera** *isld* **Indonesia**
18 D6 **Sumatera Barat** *prov* Sumatra **Indonesia**
18 E7 **Sumatera Selatan** *prov* Sumatra **Indon**
18 C4 **Sumatera Utara** *prov* Sumatra **Indonesia**
105 C7 **Sumatra** Florida 30.02N 84.59W
108 C3 **Sumatra** Montana 46.38N 107.31W
17 E11 **Sumatra** *isld* **Indonesia**
120 G2 **Sumaúma** **Brazil** 7.49S 60.02W
19 L1 **Sumay** Guam **Pacific Oc** 13.27N 144.39E
34 N5 **Sumayr al Muḩammad** **Iraq** 33.38N 45.05E
91 C7 **Sumba** **Angola** 6.15S 12.38E
19 A8 **Sumba** *isld* **Indonesia**
91 F3 **Sumba, I** **Zaïre** 1.42N 19.30E
18 N5 **Sumbang, Teluk** *B* Borneo **Indon**
43 D7 **Sumbar** *R* Turkmeniya **U.S.S.R.**
19 A8 **Sumba, Selat** *str* **Indonesia**
86 F4 **Sumbât** **Egypt** 30.49N 31.12E
18 M10 **Sumbawa** *isld* **Indonesia**
18 M10 **Sumbawa Besar** **Indonesia** 8.30S 117.25E
92 E5 **Sumbawanga** **Tanzania** 7.58S 31.36E
120 D6 **Sumbay** **Peru** 15.59S 71.24W
22 H3 **Sümber** **Mongolia** 46.31N 108.42E
53 N11 **Sumbiarfles** *isld* **Faeroes** 61.22N 6.40W
75 G1 **Sumbilla** **Spain** 43.10N 1.40W
18 J9 **Sumbing, Gunung** *mt* Java **Indon** 7.23S 110.02E
18 D7 **Sumbing, Gunung** *mt* Sumatra **Indon** 2.25S 101.47E
53 N11 **Sumbø** **Faeroes** 61.25N 6.43W
92 E6 **Sumbu** **Zambia** 8.35S 30.30E
92 E6 **Sumbu Nat. Park** **Zambia**
58 Q10 **Sumburgh** *aer* Shetland **Scotland** 59.53N 1.17W
58 Q10 **Sumburgh Hd** Shetland **Scotland** 59.51N 1.16W
58 Q10 **Sumburgh Roost** *current* Shetland Scotland
89 D8 **Sumbuya** **Sierre Leone** 7.39N 11.58W
30 B1 **Sumdeo** Himachal Prad **India** 31.26N 78.44E
31 J1 **Sumdo** Kashmir 35.03N 78.45E
23 B4 **Sumdo** Sichuan **China** 29.12N 100.10E
101 G7 **Sumdum** Alaska 57.40N 133.30W
28 L1 **Sum Dzong** Xizang Zizhiqu 29.44N 96.10E
117 H8 **Sumé** **Brazil** 7.37S 36.53W
18 G9 **Sumedang** Java **Indon** 6.54S 107.55E
32 C2 **Sūme 'eh Sarā** **Iran** 37.17N 49.18E
62 K9 **Sümeg** **Hungary** 47.00N 17.20E
87 A6 **Sumeih** **Sudan** 9.50N 27.39E
71 D9 **Sumène** **France** 43.59N 3.43E
18 K9 **Sumenep** **Indonesia** 7.01S 113.51E
30 H5 **Sumesar Range** **Nepal**
44 K7 **Sumgait** Azerbaydzhan **U.S.S.R.** 40.35N 49.38E
44 J7 **Sumgait** *R* Azerbaydzhan **U.S.S.R.**
51 M9 **Sumiainen** **Finland** 62.39N 26.05E
20 E2 **Sumida** *dist* Tōkyō **Japan**
33 N5 **Sum'il** **Oman** 22.19N 58.01E
21 H12 **Sumisu jima** *isld* **Japan** 31.27N 140.05E
66 G3 **Sumiswald** **Switzerland** 47.02N 7.45E
107 J8 **Sumiton** Alabama 33.45N 87.02W
35 G5 **Sumiya** **Jordan** 32.10N 35.47E
43 H1 **Sumki** Kurgan **U.S.S.R.** 55.04N 65.45E
45 S1 **Sumki** Mariy A.S.S.R. **U.S.S.R.** 56.15N 46.15E
33 G3 **Şummān, Aş** *reg* **Saudi Arabia**
33 H5 **Şummān,Aş** *rocky plat* **Saudi Arabia**
34 K2 **Summēl** **Iraq** 36.52N 42.50E
65 K4 **Summerau** **Austria** 48.33N 14.28E
57 K4 **Summer Bridge** N Yorks **Eng** 54.03N 1.41W
109 O2 **Summerfield** Kansas 39.59N 96.26W
104 D7 **Summerfield** Ohio 39.48N 81.21W
112 E1 **Summerfield** Texas 34.43N 102.30W
98 S4 **Summerford** Newfoundland 49.29N 54.50W
106 H4 **Summer I** Michigan 45.34N 86.38W
58 F2 **Summer Is** Highland **Scotland** 58.01N 5.26W
110 E7 **Summer L** Oregon 42.50N 120.45W
110 E7 **Summer Lake** Oregon 42.54N 120.50W
101 O11 **Summerland** Br Col 49.35N 119.41W
107 L5 **Summer Shade** Kentucky 36.52N 85.43W
98 P4 **Summerside** Newfoundland 49.00N 57.59W
98 J7 **Summerside** Prince Edward I 46.24N 63.46W
123 B5 **Summers Pk** **Antarctica** 69.30S 60.25E
99 U2 **Summerstown** Ontario 45.04N 74.34W
107 E4 **Summersville** Missouri 37.10N 91.40W
104 E8 **Summersville** W Virginia 38.17N 80.52W

104 E8 **Summersville Lake** res West Virginia 38.15N 80.54W
105 G4 **Summerton** S Carolina 33.38N 80.23W
105 E5 **Summertown** Georgia 32.45N 82.17W
98 T5 **Summerville** Newfoundland 48.27N 53.33W
104 F5 **Summerville** Pennsylvania 41.09N 79.11W
105 G4 **Summerville** S Carolina 33.02N 80.11W
113 N5 **Summit** Alaska 63.19N 149.19W
111 G7 **Summit** California 34.20N 117.26W
107 F10 **Summit** Mississippi 31.18N 90.29W
110 M1 **Summit** Montana 48.20N 113.21W
103 F5 **Summit** New Jersey 40.43N 74.23W
109 B9 **Summit** New Mexico 32.28N 108.59W
99 F5 **Summit** Ontario 47.09N 84.12W
110 B5 **Summit** Oregon 44.39N 123.35W
115 F10 **Summit** Panama Canal Zone 9.04N 79.39W
108 N4 **Summit** S Dakota 45.18N 97.02W
111 M4 **Summit** Utah 37.47N 112.56W
106 Q3 **Summit** dist Chicago, Illinois
11 L7 **Summit** mt New Zealand 40.28S 176.09E
106 J5 **Summit City** Michigan 44.33N 85.30W
103 C5 **Summit Hill** Pennsylvania 40.49N 75.52W
113 P5 **Summit L** Alaska 63.08N 145.30W
101 L6 **Summit L** Br Col 58.35N 124.40W
110 F8 **Summit L** Nevada 41.30N 119.04W
101 M8 **Summit Lake** Br Col 54.17N 122.38W
111 H2 **Summit Mt** Nevada 39.25N 116.27W
109 D4 **Summit Pk** Colorado 37.29N 106.43W
103 B5 **Summit Station** Pennsylvania 40.34N 76.13W
109 D4 **Summitville** Colorado 37.27N 106.36W
106 J9 **Summitville** Indiana 40.21N 85.39W
103 F3 **Summitville** New York 41.37N 74.27W
107 L6 **Summitville** Tennessee 35.22N 85.59W
65 N4 **Šumná** Czechoslovakia 48.56N 15.52E
30 G2 **Sumna Glacier** Nepal
31 J1 **Sumnal** Kashmir 35.44N 78.41E
31 K3 **Sumnal** Kashmir 35.45N 80.45E
107 J3 **Sumner** Illinois 38.43N 87.52W
106 B7 **Sumner** Iowa 42.52N 92.06W
107 C2 **Sumner** Missouri 39.38N 93.13W
11 G10 **Sumner** New Zealand 43.35S 172.47E
11 G9 **Sumner, L** New Zealand 42.41S 172.15E
115 V8 **Sumner Str** Alaska
20 N4 **Sumon-dake** mt Japan 37.23N 139.10E
62 K10 **Sumony** Hungary 45.59N 17.55E
20 H7 **Sumoto** Japan 34.20N 134.53E
19 A6 **Sumpangbinangae** Celebes Indon 4.25S 119.39E
25 N8 **Sumpawng Mata** Burma 26.04N 97.53E
65 P2 **Šumperk** Czechoslovakia 49.57N 16.59E
25 N8 **Sumprabum** Burma 26.38N 97.36E
110 G5 **Sumpter** Oregon 44.45N 118.10W
31 F7 **Sumrahu** Pakistan 26.31N 70.01E
107 G10 **Sumrall** Mississippi 31.25N 89.33W
45 F6 **Sumskaya Oblast'** prov Ukraine U.S.S.R.
47 D4 **Sumskiy Posad** U.S.S.R. 64.12N 35.29E
105 G4 **Sumter** S Carolina 33.54N 80.22W
47 D4 **Sumuta** U.S.S.R. 60.39N 86.15E
86 E8 **Sumusta el Waqf** Egypt 28.56N 30.51E
45 F6 **Sumy** Ukraine U.S.S.R. 50.55N 34.49E
24 J11 **Sumzom** Xizang Zizhiqu China 29.45N 96.14E
66 L8 **Suna** Italy 45.56N 8.33E
93 F7 **Suna** Kenya 1.06S 34.29E
92 G4 **Suna** Tanzania 5.24S 34.47E
46 G1 **Suna** U.S.S.R. 57.52N 50.01E
20 L1 **Sunagawa** Japan 43.30N 141.55E
Sunaisila see **Sunaysilah** L
29 D2 **Sunam** Punjab India 30.06N 75.51E
31 J8 **Sunamganj** Bangladesh 25.04N 91.24E
21 C8 **Sunan** N Korea 39.12N 125.40E
22 E7 **Sunan Yugurzu Zizhixian** Gansu China 38.51N 99.34E
58 E5 **Sunart** dist Highland Scotland
58 E5 **Sunart, L** Highland Scotland
33 L5 **Sunaynah** Oman 23.39N 55.58E
34 J3 **Sunaysilah** L Iraq
109 B1 **Sunbeam** Colorado 40.34N 108.12W
110 L5 **Sunbeam** Idaho 44.16N 114.45W
107 M5 **Sunbright** Tennessee 36.14N 84.40W
32 A3 **Sunbula Kūh** mts Iran
101 O1 **Sunburst** Montana 48.54N 111.55W
105 L1 **Sunbury** N Carolina 36.27N 76.37W
104 C6 **Sunbury** Ohio 40.14N 82.52W
103 A5 **Sunbury** Pennsylvania 40.52N 76.47W
55 B5 **Sunbury** Surrey Eng 51.24N 0.25W
12 G7 **Sunbury** Victoria 37.36S 144.45E
121 E3 **Sunchales** Argentina 30.58S 61.35W
64 N6 **Sünching** W Germany 48.53N 12.22E
121 D1 **Suncho Corral** Argentina 27.55S 63.27W
21 C8 **Sunch'ŏn** N Korea 39.23N 125.59E
21 D10 **Sunch'ŏn** S Korea 34.56N 127.28E
109 M4 **Sun City** Kansas 37.23N 98.54W
103 Q4 **Suncook** New Hampshire 43.07N 71.27W
Suncun see **Xinwen**
53 N9 **Sund** Faeroes 62.03N 6.51W
53 S18 **Sund** Norway 60.13N 5.10E
122 C9 **Sunda** I Indonesia
122 B8 **Sunda Is., Greater** Indonesia
108 F5 **Sundance** Wyoming 44.23N 104.22W
18 L3 **Sundar** Sarawak Malaysia 4.55N 115.15E
28 G5 **Sundarbans** tidal forest India/Bangladesh
30 J6 **Sundargarh** Orissa India 22.04N 84.08E
29 J6 **Sundargarh** dist Orissa India
30 A1 **Sundarnagar** Himachal Prad India 31.32N 76.54E
30 L8 **Sundarpahar** Bihar India 24.46N 87.22E
29 E6 **Sundarsi** Madhya Prad India 23.12N 76.30E
18 F9 **Sunda, Selat** str Java/Sumatra S E Asia
26 K6 **Sunda Trench** Indian Oc
13 C3 **Sunday Cr** N Terr Australia
14 F7 **Sunday Hill** W Australia 25.20S 127.05E
Sunday I see **Raoul I**
95 H8 **Sundays** R S Africa
14 E3 **Sunday Str** W Australia
121 D5 **Sundblad** Argentina 35.46S 63.10W
53 B3 **Sundby** Denmark 56.53N 8.41E
53 B3 **Sundby** Norway 60.14N 11.49E
52 K7 **Sundbyberg** Sweden 59.22N 17.58E
53 T19 **Sunde** Hordaland Norway 59.50N 5.43E
52 E3 **Sunde** Nord-Trøndelag Norway 63.30N 9.12E
53 U15 **Sunde** Sogn og Fjordane Norway 61.32N 6.27E
53 M9 **Sundene** inlet Faeroes 62.19N 7.08W
103 P4 **Sunderland** Massachusetts 42.28N 72.35W
99 L8 **Sunderland** Ontario 44.16N 79.04W
57 L3 **Sunderland** Tyne and Wear Eng 54.55N 1.23W
59 G4 **Sunderlin, L** W Meath Irish Rep 53.30N 7.40W
63 H10 **Sundern** W Germany 51.20N 8.00E
53 D7 **Sundeved** reg Denmark
53 T18 **Sundfjord** Norway 60.03N 5.50E
71 L2 **Sundgau** reg France 47.41N 7.01E
36 E3 **Sündiken Dağı** mt Turkey 39.57N 31.14E
18 H9 **Sundoro, Gunung** mt Java Indon 7.18S 109.58E
100 F1 **Sundown** Manitoba 49.08N 96.12W
103 F1 **Sundown** New York 41.53N 74.27W
12 C2 **Sundown** S Australia 26.11S 133.09E
112 E2 **Sundown** Texas 33.27N 102.28W
100 C7 **Sundre** Alberta 51.49N 114.46W
52 L9 **Sundre** Gotland Sweden 56.56N 18.15E
52 L9 **Sundridge** Ontario 45.46N 79.25W
53 C4 **Sunds** Denmark 56.13N 9.03E
53 Y19 **Sundsbørnvatn** L Norway 59.33N 8.25E
52 J4 **Sundsjö** Sweden 63.00N 15.10E
53 Y20 **Sundsli** Norway 59.01N 8.17E
53 C3 **Sundstrup** Denmark 56.37N 9.19E
52 K4 **Sundsvall** Sweden 62.22N 17.20E
43 G7 **Sunduki, Peski** sand des Turkmeniya U.S.S.R.
42 J7 **Sunduyka** U.S.S.R. 49.40N 110.12E
53 T18 **Sundvor** Norway 60.05N 5.46E
53 R9 **Sundwana** S Africa 31.28S 28.05E
106 K7 **Sunfield** Michigan 42.45N 85.00W
107 F8 **Sunflower** Mississippi 33.32N 90.32W
107 F8 **Sunflower** R Mississippi
93 B5 **Sunge** Uganda 0.55N 30.53E
21 F5 **Sungacha** R China/U.S.S.R.
18 M7 **Sungaianyar** Borneo Indon 2.56S 116.20E
18 E5 **Sungaiapit** Sumatra Indonesia 1.05N 102.10E
18 J5 **Sungaibatu** Borneo Indon 0.56N 110.44E
18 A6 **Sungai Bayor** Pen Malaysia 5.15N 100.48E
18 D6 **Sungaidareh** Sumatra Indon 0.58S 101.31E
18 D6 **Sungaigerong** Sumatra Indon 2.59S 104.54E
18 E5 **Sungaiguntung** Sumatra Indonesia 0.17N 103.32E
18 H6 **Sungaikakap** Borneo Indon 0.11S 109.12E
18 G6 **Sungailiat** Indonesia 1.49S 106.07E
18 D6 **Sungailimau** Sumatra Indon 0.33S 100.08E
18 D6 **Sungaipenuh** Sumatra Indon 2.00S 101.28E
18 L6 **Sungaipinang** Borneo Indon 0.50S 114.13E
18 D6 **Sungaisalak** Sumatra Indon 0.29S 103.00E
18 G7 **Sungaiselan** Indonesia 2.21S 106.00E
18 M6 **Sungaitiram** Borneo Indon 0.50S 117.10E
Sungari R see **Songhua Jiang**
Sungari Res see **Songhua Hu**
18 B8 **Sungei Besi** Pen Malaysia 3.02N 101.42E
18 B8 **Sungei Buloh** Pen Malaysia 3.14N 101.19E
18 D8 **Sungei Lembing** Pen Malaysia 3.54N 103.02E
18 C9 **Sungei Mati** Pen Malaysia 2.08N 102.33E
18 A6 **Sungei Petani** Pen Malaysia 5.36N 100.29E
18 C9 **Sungei Rambai** Pen Malaysia 2.06N 102.18E
18 B7 **Sungei Siput** Pen Malaysia 4.49N 101.03E
19 A6 **Sungguminasa** Celebes Indon 5.14S 119.28E
87 B4 **Sungikai** Sudan 12.18N 29.54E
18 B8 **Sungkai** Pen Malaysia 3.57N 101.19E
111 P10 **Sunglow** Arizona 31.51N 109.26W
92 F10 **Sungo** Mozambique 16.36S 33.58E
Sungqu see **Songpan**
18 F7 **Sungsang** Sumatra Indonesia 2.22S 104.50E
91 E4 **Sungu** Zaïre 1.05S 17.21E
36 G2 **Sungurlu** Turkey 40.10N 34.23E
64 M7 **Sünhausen** W Germany 48.30N 11.39E
99 C2 **Suni** Ontario 50.14N 87.23W
81 B3 **Suni** Sardinia 40.17N 8.33E
18 M3 **Suniston Besar, Gunong** mt Sabah Malaysia 5.31N 116.04E
22 K7 **Suning** Hebei China 38.26N 115.49E
120 D6 **Sunipani, Nev.de** pk Peru 14.38S 70.07W
64 P3 **Sunipek** Czechoslovakia 50.28N 13.15E
82 D5 **Sunja** Yugoslavia 45.21N 16.35E
26 T5 **Sunkankuli** Sri Lanka 8.17N 81.20E
15 M9 **Sunken Barrier, The** Louisiade Arch
30 K5 **Sun Kosi** R Nepal
107 L2 **Sunman** Indiana 39.14N 85.05W
53 U18 **Sunndal** Norway 60.06N 6.17E
52 D4 **Sunndal** R Norway
52 D4 **Sunndalsøra** Norway 62.39N 8.37E
53 W15 **Sunndalssæter** Norway 61.53N 7.17E
52 H3 **Sunne** Jämtland Sweden 63.07N 14.30E
52 G7 **Sunne** Värmland Sweden 59.52N 13.05E
53 S16 **Sunnfjord** reg Norway
52 F11 **Sunniland** Florida 26.14N 81.22W
87 B7 **Sunni, water course** Sudan
53 U14 **Sunnmøre** reg Norway
50 K3 **Sunnudalsa** R Iceland
50 L3 **Sunnudalur** Iceland 65.37N 14.58W
13 J7 **Sunnybank** Queensland 27.00S 149.10E
13 K2 **Sunnybank** dist Brisbane, Qnsld
98 K8 **Sunnybrae** Nova Scotia 45.24N 62.30W
100 C5 **Sunnybrook** Alberta 53.15N 114.12W
53 V14 **Sunnylven** Norway 62.05N 6.52E
53 V14 **Sunnylvsfjorden** inlet Norway 62.10N 7.00E
100 F7 **Sunnynook** Alberta 51.19N 111.40W
94 G3 **Sunnyside** Botswana 21.39S 22.01E
111 J3 **Sunnyside** Nevada 38.26N 115.03W
98 T6 **Sunnyside** Newfoundland 47.52N 53.58W
110 Q2 **Sunnyside** Utah 39.34N 110.24W
110 E3 **Sunnyside** Washington 46.20N 120.01W
112 F9 **Sunnyside** dist Houston, Texas 29.38N 95.22W
100 D7 **Sunnyslope** Alberta 51.43N 113.32W
79 E3 **Suno** Italy 45.38N 8.32E
106 E6 **Sun Prairie** Wisconsin 43.11N 89.15W
Sunqur see **Sonqor**
110 N2 **Sun R** Montana
112 C8 **Sunray** Texas 36.01N 101.50W
113 N6 **Sunrise** Alaska 60.51N 149.29W
111 Q6 **Sunrise** Arizona 35.18N 111.10W
108 F7 **Sunrise** Wyoming 42.20N 104.42W
110 Q2 **Sun River** Montana 47.32N 111.43W
30 Q3 **Sunsagra** Xizang Zizhiqu 31.31N 80.25E
18 B6 **Sunsas, Sa.de** mts Bolivia
107 D11 **Sunset** Louisiana 30.24N 92.05W
110 G2 **Sunset** Utah 41.08N 112.02W
112 K2 **Sunset** Texas 33.28N 97.46W
111 E10 **Sunset Beach** California 33.43N 118.04W
114 A4 **Sunset Beach** Hawaiian Is 21.39N 158.05W
111 N6 **Sunset Crater Nat.Mon** Arizona 35.21N 111.30W
101 P8 **Sunset House** Alberta 55.05N 116.54W
111 N6 **Sunshine** Arizona 35.08N 111.02W
110 G5 **Sunshine** Wyoming 44.01N 109.01W
12 B7 **Sunshine** dist Melbourne, Vic
Sunshine I see **Chau Kung**
100 K1 **Sunstrum** Ontario 50.04N 92.33W
90 E8 **Suntar** Nigeria 7.55N 10.22E
42 K2 **Suntar** U.S.S.R. 62.10N 117.35E
39 B3 **Suntar Khayata, Khrebet** mts U.S.S.R.
63 K8 **Süntel** hills W Germany
18 G2 **Sunter** Jakarta Indonesia 6.09S 106.54E
18 G2 **Sunter, Kali** R Indonesia
18 B7 **Sunting** mt Pen Malaysia 4.50N 101.53E
113 N5 **Suntrana** Alaska 63.52N 148.50W
31 B8 **Sunstar** Pakistan 25.31N 62.02E
95 O6 **Sunwich Port** S Africa 30.40S 30.32E
21 D3 **Sunwu** Heilongjiang China 49.29N 127.15E
Sunwui see **Xinhui**
Sunyang see **Xunyang**
89 H8 **Sunyani** Ghana 7.22N 2.18W
Sunyi see **Xunyi**
44 G4 **Suoja** Finland 61.43N 33.22E
51 M9 **Suolahti** Finland 62.35N 25.50E
41 K4 **Suolama** R U.S.S.R.
51 K2 **Suolovuobme** Norway 69.37N 23.30E
51 M4 **Suomussalmi** Finland 61.21N 27.30E
100 M2 **Suomi** Ontario 48.15N 90.00W
51 O7 **Suomussalmi** Finland 64.52N 29.10E
Suŏ-nada see **Japan**
51 O7 **Suonenjoki** Finland 62.40N 27.06E
51 N9 **Suonenjoki** Finland 62.40N 27.06E
40 C2 **Suon-Tit** U.S.S.R. 58.10N 123.42E
51 S1 **Suordakh** U.S.S.R. 67.45N 139.30E
51 N3 **Suosjarvi** Finland 61.45N 26.20E
51 M10 **Suonne L** Finland 61.45N 26.20E
47 L2 **Suoyarvi** Karelia U.S.S.R. 62.02N 32.20E
51 G4 **Suorva** Sweden 67.35N 18.14E
47 C5 **Suozhen** see **Huantai**
79 E6 **Sup** Italy 44.19N 8.31E
28 B3 **Supa** Karnataka India 15.18N 74.35E
111 M5 **Supai** Arizona 36.15N 112.43W
120 D3 **Supamo, R** Venezuela
30 K7 **Supaul** Darbhanga, Bihar India 25.57N 86.15E
30 K6 **Supaul** Saharsa, Bihar India 26.07N 86.36E
120 B4 **Supe** Lima Peru 10.49S 77.40W
100 H7 **Superb** Saskatchewan 51.55N 109.23W
72 F10 **Superbagnères** France 42.46N 0.35E
43 H7 **Superfosfatnyy** Uzbekistan U.S.S.R. 39.38N 66.50E
111 N8 **Superior** Arizona 33.18N 111.06W
109 E2 **Superior** Colorado 39.56N 105.11W
110 L2 **Superior** Montana 47.12N 114.52W
108 N3 **Superior** Nebraska 40.02N 98.02W
106 D3 **Superior** Wisconsin 46.42N 92.05W
108 D7 **Superior** Wyoming 41.46N 108.58W
79 J4 **Superiore, L** Italy 45.10N 10.45E
115 M9 **Superior, L** Mexico
106 C2 **Superior, L** U.S.A./Canada
25 F5 **Suphan Buri** Thailand 14.14N 100.07E
37 G3 **Süphan Dağı** mt Turkey 38.59N 42.49E
53 V16 **Suphella** Norway 61.27N 6.49E
53 V15 **Suphellenipa** mt Norway 61.31N 6.50E
80 H5 **Supino** Italy 41.37N 13.13E
15 D2 **Supiori** isld Biak I, Irian Jaya 0.35S 135.30E
111 F9 **Supplee** Oregon 44.03N 119.41W
103 C6 **Suplee** Pennsylvania 40.06N 75.52W
42 F8 **Supoy** R Ukraine U.S.S.R.
45 C7 **Süpplingen** W Germany 52.13N 10.55E
47 K6 **Supra** U.S.S.R. 58.01N 69.30E
62 O2 **Supraśl** Poland 53.13N 23.19E
46 D6 **Supsa** Georgia U.S.S.R. 42.02N 41.50E
44 D6 **Supsa** R Georgia U.S.S.R.
Supu see **Hsü-p'u**
19 E2 **Supu** Halmahera Indon 2.11N 127.57E
18 F4 **Su, Pulau Pulau** islds Irian Jaya 0.20S 132.09E
29 K2 **Supur** W Bengal India 23.00N 86.53E
82 H3 **Supurunu** Turkey 40.19N 89.11E
82 H3 **Supurunu** Kirgiziya U.S.S.R. 42.28N 73.59E
33 F8 **Suq al Gamal** Sudan 12.50N 27.40E
33 F8 **Sūq al Khamīs** Libya
34 G8 **Sūq al Inān** Yemen 16.50N 44.05E
33 G8 **Sūq al Jum'ah** Yemen 16.08N 44.10E
33 G8 **Sūq ar Rubū'** Saudi Arabia 20.44N 40.51E
34 G8 **Sūq ash Shuyūkh** Iraq 30.53N 46.28E
35 F1 **Suq Sū** Turkey 43.11N 35.41E
Suqfiye see **Giv'at Yo'ay**
23 H2 **Suqian** Jiangsu China 33.57N 118.18E
21 A2 **Suqin Nei** Monggol Zizhiqu China 50.26N 119.40E
Şuqrah Bay see **Şawqirah Bay**
Şuqrah, Ra's C see **Şawqirah, Ra's**
33 C4 **Sūq Suwayq** Saudi Arabia 24.19N 38.30E
Suquţrá isld see **Socotra**
43 N8 **Sur** Kirgiziya U.S.S.R. 39.57N 71.15E
33 N5 **Şūr** Oman 22.34N 59.32E
47 F4 **Sura** Arkhangel'sk U.S.S.R. 63.38N 45.28E
107 F5 **Sura** Nigeria 8.05N 8.11E
45 R3 **Sura** Penza U.S.S.R. 53.52N 45.45E
52 J7 **Sura** Sweden 59.42N 16.10E
45 F3 **Sura** R U.S.S.R.
31 B8 **Surab** Pakistan 28.29N 66.19E
18 K7 **Surabaya** Java Indon 7.14S 112.45E
86 E4 **Surad** Egypt 30.59N 30.54E
29 J8 **Surada** Orissa India 19.46N 84.29E
45 Q1 **Surad'yevo** U.S.S.R. 55.25N 44.44E
Surag see **Surak**
29 C6 **Surai** Pakistan 29.08N 66.00E
29 D3 **Surajgarh** Rajasthan India 28.18N 75.48E
32 H8 **Surak** Iran 25.40N 58.50E
18 J9 **Surakarta** Java Indon 7.32S 110.50E
19 A4 **Surampai** Celebes Indon 0.51S 119.37E
46 B5 **Surami** Georgia U.S.S.R. 42.02N 43.44E
44 F5 **Surami** Georgia U.S.S.R.
37 G5 **Sūran** Iran 27.18N 61.58E
34 E3 **Sūran** Syria 35.18N 36.44E
72 B1 **Surani** R France
62 L7 **Surany** Czechoslovakia 48.04N 18.10E
87 H7 **Surar** Ethiopia 7.27N 40.55E
11 D3 **Suraru** Pakistan 27.22N 68.13E
29 D4 **Surat** Gujarat India 21.10N 72.54E
13 J7 **Surat** Queensland 27.10S 149.05E
29 C7 **Surat** dist Gujarat India
30 B3 **Suratgarh** Uttar Prad India 27.12N 81.20E
29 C3 **Suratgarh** Rajasthan India 29.20N 73.59E
25 E8 **Surat Thani** Thailand 9.09N 99.20E
62 O3 **Suraż** Poland 52.55N 22.59E
45 B1 **Surazh** Belorussiya U.S.S.R. 55.24N 30.44E
45 D4 **Surazh** U.S.S.R. 53.00N 32.22E
35 B2 **Sür Bāhir** Jordan 31.44N 35.14E
13 K2 **Surbiton** Queensland 23.05S 146.40E
55 B6 **Surbiton** London England 51.23N 0.18W
95 L8 **Surbiton** S Africa 32.23S 27.15E
92 B5 **Surbo** Italy 40.23N 18.08E
81 R12 **Surbo** Italy 40.23N 18.08E
122 U16 **Sur, C** Easter I Pacific Oc 27.11S 109.26W
82 F6 **Surčin** Yugoslavia 44.48N 20.19E
76 F3 **Surcio, Pico** mt Spain 42.55N 6.50W
34 N3 **Sürdāsh** Iraq 35.52N 45.04E
70 L4 **Surdon** France 48.40N 0.10E
82 H3 **Surduc** Romania 47.13N 23.20E
82 G8 **Surdulica** Yugoslavia 42.41N 22.11E
61 Q7 **Sûre** R Luxembourg
86 O7 **Sureibit, Jebel** mt Saudi Arabia 29.22N 35.28E
35 J2 **Sur el Leja** Syria 32.58N 36.18E
29 B6 **Surendranagar** Gujarat India 22.44N 71.43E
29 B6 **Surendranagar** dist Gujarat India
66 L4 **Surenen Pass** Switzerland 46.50N 8.33E
68 D3 **Suresnes** France 48.52N 2.13E
115 N5 **Suretka** Costa Rica 9.36N 82.58W
66 O5 **Suretta Horn** mt Switzerland 46.32N 9.23E
111 D7 **Surf** California 34.40N 120.35W
103 F7 **Surf City** New Jersey 39.40N 74.10W
101 J9 **Surf Inlet** Br Col 53.02N 128.54W
103 O4 **Surfside** Massachusetts 41.15N 70.05W
29 C7 **Surgana** Maharashtra India 20.32N 73.40E
72 F3 **Surgères** France 46.07N 0.44W
116 C3 **Surgidero de Batabanó** Cuba 22.41N 82.19W
37 F8 **Sürgücü** Turkey 37.37N 40.43E
29 H6 **Surguja** dist Madhya Prad India
42 A2 **Surgut** Tyumen U.S.S.R. 61.13N 73.20E
41 E8 **Surgutikha** U.S.S.R. 63.52N 87.25E
71 D1 **Surgy** France 47.31N 3.30E
60 N7 **Surhuisterveen** Netherlands 53.11N 6.10E
60 N7 **Surhuizum** Netherlands 53.12N 6.10E
29 L1 **Suri** W Bengal India 23.54N 87.32E
72 F8 **Sūri** isld Iran 25.54N 54.30E
75 O4 **Suria** Spain 41.50N 1.45E
82 H5 **Surianu** mt Romania 45.32N 23.34E
30 E5 **Surianwan** Uttar Prad India 25.28N 82.22E
28 D2 **Suriapet** Andhra Prad India 17.10N 79.37E
28 N2 **Suribachi-yama** hill Iwo Jima Pacific Oc 24.45N 141.17E
61 J6 **Surice** Belgium 50.11N 4.42E
35 D7 **Surif** Jordan 31.39N 35.04E
19 M7 **Surigao** Mindanao Philippines 9.47N 125.29E
19 M6 **Surigao Str** Philippines
119 D6 **Surimena** Colombia 3.54N 73.25W
72 E3 **Surin** France 46.04N 0.23E
25 G5 **Surin** Thailand 14.53N 103.29E
117 H1 **Surinam** terr S America
106 F4 **Suring** Wisconsin 45.01N 88.24W
45 P1 **Surinskoye** U.S.S.R. 53.31N 48.29E
15 J8 **Surinumu Res** Papua New Guinea 9.31S 147.30E
119 E4 **Suripá** Venezuela 7.47N 69.57W
119 E4 **Suripá, R** Venezuela
120 D8 **Surire, Salar de** salt pan Chile 18.50S 69.00W
29 G8 **Surjagarh** Maharashtra India 19.36N 80.28E
31 C2 **Surkhab** R Afghanistan
32 E3 **Surkhab** Iran 35.58N 52.58E
Surkhab see **Sorkh Ab**
43 H6 **Surkhan** Uzbekistan U.S.S.R. 37.44N 67.30E
43 J7 **Surkhandar'inskaya Obl** U.S.S.R.
43 H7 **Surkhandar'ya** R U.S.S.R.
31 D4 **Surkhbed Pass** Afghanistan 32.24N 66.08E
31 C5 **Surkhduz** Afghanistan 31.14N 64.10E
Surkheh see **Sorkheh**
30 E4 **Surkhet** Nepal 28.36N 81.36E
Surkh, Kuh-e see **Sorkh, Kuh-e** mts
43 K7 **Surkhob** R Tadzhikistan U.S.S.R.
85 B3 **Surman** Libya 32.49N 12.35E
35 G1 **Surman** Syria 33.06N 35.50E
33 F8 **Surmaq** Iran 31.03N 52.50E
69 F6 **Surmelin** R France
37 F5 **Sürmene** Turkey 40.56N 40.03E
52 D4 **Surnadalsøra** Norway 62.58N 8.43E
82 H8 **Sûrnena Gora** mts Bulgaria
24 D10 **Surng Ru** R Xizang Zizhiqu
31 E1 **Surnge La** pass Xizang Zizhiqu 31.01N 81.58E
45 F1 **Surovatikha** U.S.S.R. 55.45N 43.55E
45 O8 **Surovikino** U.S.S.R. 48.37N 42.51E
66 D5 **Surpierre** Switzerland 46.45N 6.52E
101 O6 **Surprise** Br Col 59.37N 133.25W
108 N8 **Surprise** Nebraska 41.08N 97.18W
103 G2 **Surprise** New York 42.24N 73.56W
9 A12 **Surprise I** New Caledonia 18.29S 163.07E
101 G6 **Surprise L** Br Col 59.40N 133.11W
99 Q3 **Surprise, L.de la** Quebec
111 C5 **Sur, Pt** California 36.18N 121.55W
29 C4 **Surpura** Rajasthan India 27.41N 73.25E
35 H4 **Surra** Jordan 32.24N 36.09E
105 E6 **Surrency** Georgia 31.43N 82.12W
100 H2 **Surrey** N Dakota 48.16N 101.10W
101 J11 **Surrey** co Br Col
56 L5 **Surrey** co England
100 M7 **Surrey Centre** Br Col 49.07N 122.46W
95 P4 **Surreyvale** S Africa 28.05S 31.02E
66 M5 **Surrhein** Switzerland 46.43N 8.57E
86 P10 **Surr, Wādi es** watercourse Saudi Arabia
104 J10 **Surry** Virginia 37.08N 76.50W
30 J6 **Sursand** Bihar India 26.38N 85.43E
51 M11 **Sur Sari, Ostrov** isld U.S.S.R. 60.05N 27.00E
66 J3 **Sursee** Switzerland 47.11N 8.07E
26 D2 **Sur Singh** Punjab India 31.22N 74.45E
45 R3 **Sursk** U.S.S.R. 53.04N 45.42E
45 G2 **Surskoye** U.S.S.R. 54.30N 46.44E
86 D3 **Surt** Libya 31.10N 16.39E
70 G3 **Surtainville** France 49.27N 1.49W
50 E6 **Surtsey** isld Iceland 63.18N 20.38W
53 Z15 **Surtsøyi** mt Norway 61.32N 8.35E
50 E8 **Surtseyjan** isld Iceland 63.18N 20.37W
50 E5 **Surtshellir** rift Iceland
56 K8 **Surtuanan** Kenya 2.09N 37.16E
117 D6 **Surubiú, R** Brazil
37 D9 **Sürüc** Turkey 36.59N 38.24E
87 L5 **Suruc** mt Somalia 10.44N 47.15E
20 M6 **Suruga-wan** B Japan
Suruk see **Sārūq** R
Suruk see **Saruq**
41 O7 **Surutkakh** Yakutsk U.S.S.R. 65.18N 132.53E
18 F7 **Surulangun** Sumatra Indon 2.35S 102.47E
18 E5 **Surumu, R** Brazil
19 N8 **Surup** Mindanao Philippines 6.22N 126.10E
32 Q7 **Surup Spit** Iran 27.11N 56.12E
113 L8 **Survey Pass** Alaska 67.52N 154.10W
11 H1 **Surville Cliffs** hd New Zealand 34.25S 173.03E
30 A7 **Surwaya** Madhya Prad India 25.26N 77.55E
71 E5 **Sury-le-Comtal** France 45.32N 4.11E
87 K7 **Suryu** Ethiopia 7.05N 45.01E
70 E6 **Surzur** France 47.35N 2.37W
Süs see **Susch**
79 B4 **Susa** Italy 45.08N 7.02E
20 E7 **Susa** Japan 34.39N 131.36E
Susa Tunisia see **Sousse**
Susa anc site see **Shūsh**
53 H6 **Suså** R Denmark 58.24N 11.36E
82 C8 **Sušac** isld Yugoslavia 42.46N 16.30E
82 B5 **Sušak** Yugoslavia 45.19N 14.28E
20 F6 **Susaki** Japan 33.22N 133.16E
20 E8 **Susami** Japan 33.32N 135.29E
43 L6 **Susamyr** Kirgiziya U.S.S.R. 42.08N 73.59E
111 D2 **Susan** R California
10 C2 **Susangerd** Iran 31.40N 48.06E
32 C5 **Susangerd** Iran 31.40N 48.06E
42 G5 **Susanino** N Korea 40.33N 127.46E
40 H5 **Susanino** Khabarovsk U.S.S.R. 52.46N 140.09E
46 O1 **Susanino** Kostroma U.S.S.R. 58.08N 41.30E
20 M1 **Susanoo** see Japan 35.11N 138.50E
110 E9 **Susanville** California 40.26N 120.40W
110 G5 **Susanville** Oregon 44.33N 118.46W
66 O3 **Susch** Switzerland 46.45N 10.05E
115 Q4 **Susegana** Italy 45.51N 12.15E
37 D5 **Suşehri** Turkey 40.12N 38.06E
63 M7 **Süsel** W Germany 54.04N 10.43E
Susemangmati see **Hsü-shui**
34 P3 **Su Sīāh** mt Iran 35.24N 47.09E
65 O2 **Sušice** Czechoslovakia 49.14N 13.32E
35 F2 **Susita** anc site Israel 32.46N 35.39E
113 M6 **Susitna** Alaska 61.30N 150.34W
113 O5 **Susitna** R Alaska
113 N6 **Susitna L** Alaska 62.26N 146.40W
29 G2 **Susner** Madhya Prad India 23.57N 76.08E
29 E9 **Susong** Anhui China 30.08N 116.08E
23 G3 **Susong** N Korea 41.52N 129.19E
22 J6 **Susong** Anhui China 30.08N 116.08E
12 G3 **Susoong** Thailand 7.15N 99.38E
76 G3 **Suspiron, El** mt Spain 42.46N 6.11W
62 O3 **Suspiro, Pto.del** pass Spain 37.03N 3.39W
77 J6 **Suspiro, Pto.del** pass Spain 37.03N 3.39W
103 B2 **Susquehanna** Pennsylvania 41.56N 75.38W
103 C5 **Susquehanna** co Pennsylvania
103 E2 **Susquehanna** R N Y/Penn
103 D3 **Susquehanna, West Branch** R Penn
114 E6 **Susques** Argentina 23.33S 66.29W
72 F4 **Sussac** France 45.39N 1.38E
63 P10 **Susser See** L E Germany 51.30N 11.40E
98 G8 **Sussex** New Brunswick 45.43N 65.32W
103 E4 **Sussex** New Jersey 41.12N 74.36W
108 D8 **Sussex** Wyoming 43.42N 106.19W
Sussex co see **W. Sussex** and **E. Sussex**
103 D9 **Sussex** co Delaware
103 E4 **Sussex** co New Jersey
104 L10 **Sussex** co Virginia
105 K5 **Sustenhorn** mt Switzerland 46.42N 8.27E
66 K5 **Susten Pass** Switzerland 46.44N 8.27E
60 O13 **Süsteren** Netherlands 51.04N 5.51E
63 T16 **Süsteren** W Germany 50.59N 5.57E
71 J9 **Sustut Pk** Br Col 56.31N 126.38W
15 L3 **Susubona** Santa Isabel I Solomon Is 8.17S 159.29E
18 M3 **Susul** Sabah Malaysia 4.55N 116.44E
113 K8 **Susulatna** R Alaska
39 D3 **Susuman** U.S.S.R. 62.46N 148.08E
29 K2 **Susunia Hill** W Bengal India 23.23N 87.00E
19 G3 **Susunu** Irian Jaya 2.54S 133.40E
36 C3 **Susurluk** Turkey 39.55N 28.10E
37 G5 **Susuz** Turkey 40.47N 43.10E
37 E8 **Susuz Dağları** mts Turkey
37 D1 **Susuzmüsellim** Turkey 41.07N 27.04E
93 H7 **Suswa** mt Kenya 1.10S 36.21E
18 C5 **Sut** mt Sumatra Indon 1.46N 99.18E
31 J4 **Sutak** Kashmir 23.05N 77.32E
40 D4 **Sutam** U.S.S.R. 56.56N 127.32E
40 D3 **Sutam** R U.S.S.R.
40 D3 **Sutamo-Gonamskiy Khr** mts U.S.S.R.
111 E2 **Sutcliffe** Nevada 39.55N 119.35W
36 E5 **Sütçüler** Turkey 37.31N 31.00E
81 G8 **Sutera** Sicily 37.32N 13.44E
82 L5 **Suteşti** Romania 45.13N 27.27E
39 E1 **Sutgun** U.S.S.R. 67.52N 153.58E
108 P7 **Sutherland** Iowa 42.58N 95.30W
108 J8 **Sutherland** Nebraska 41.10N 101.08W
12 L8 **Sutherland** N S Wales 34.02S 151.06E
95 D8 **Sutherland** S Africa 32.24S 20.40E
Sutherland co see **Highland** reg
11 B11 **Sutherland Falls** waterfall New Zealand 44.48S 167.46E
14 F7 **Sutherland Ra** W Australia
108 J7 **Sutherland Res** Nebraska
11 B11 **Sutherland Sd** New Zealand
110 B6 **Sutherlin** Oregon 43.23N 123.20W
80 O2 **Sutivan** Yugoslavia 43.23N 16.30E
36 D4 **Sutlej** Turkey 38.08N 29.59E
27 L4 **Sutlej** R Pakistan/India
24 C10 **Sutlej** R Xizang Zizhiqu
31 G5 **Sutlej** R Pakistan
37 J2 **Sütlüce** Turkey 41.03N 28.53E
80 G7 **Sutri** Italy 42.14N 12.14E
Sut Ta see **Ban Sut Ta**
111 D3 **Sutter Creek** California 38.24N 120.50W
97 N7 **Sutterton** Lincs Eng 52.54N 0.08W
56 D9 **Sutton** Cambs Eng 52.23N 0.07E
55 E5 **Sutton** London England 51.22N 0.12W
103 Q3 **Sutton** Massachusetts 42.09N 71.46W
108 K2 **Sutton** N Dakota 47.24N 98.26W
108 N9 **Sutton** Nebraska 40.37N 97.52W
11 E12 **Sutton** New Zealand 45.35S 170.08E
57 L4 **Sutton** N Yorks Eng 54.14N 1.15W
99 L8 **Sutton** Ontario 44.18N 79.22W
99 S7 **Sutton** Quebec 45.05N 72.36W
95 F3 **Sutton** S Africa 27.26S 22.50E
104 E8 **Sutton** W Virginia 38.41N 80.43W
55 E5 **Sutton** bor London England
55 K5 **Sutton at Hone** Kent Eng 51.25N 0.14E
99 L5 **Sutton Bay** Ontario 47.35N 79.41W
55 H7 **Sutton Benger** Wilts Eng 51.31N 2.05W
56 M2 **Sutton Bridge** Lincs Eng 52.46N 0.12E
56 H2 **Sutton Coldfield** W Midlands Eng 52.34N 1.48W
57 L6 **Sutton in Ashfield** Notts Eng 53.08N 1.15W
104 E8 **Sutton Lake** res W Virginia
57 O6 **Sutton on Sea** Lincs Eng 53.19N 0.17E
56 M2 **Sutton St.James** Lincs Eng 52.45N 0.05E
56 J5 **Sutton Scotney** Hants Eng 51.10N 1.21W
13 H5 **Suttor** R Queensland
20 J2 **Suttsu** Japan 42.49N 140.04E
40 G8 **Sutungu** U.S.S.R. 46.38N 136.00E
51 N5 **Sutun'ya** U.S.S.R. 69.00N 131.01E
40 F6 **Sutur** R U.S.S.R.
39 D1 **Suturuokha-Térdé** U.S.S.R. 68.33N 146.07E
113 J8 **Sutwik I** Alaska 56.35N 157.10W
46 D7 **Suuk** dist Moscow U.S.S.R.
15 M3 **Su'u** Malaita I Solomon Is 9.12S 161.03E
15 N4 **Su'u Holo** Ulawa I Solomon Is 9.45S 161.58E
94 R14 **Suurbekom** S Africa 26.18S 27.45E
95 J9 **Suurberg** Cape Province S Africa 33.21S 25.45E
95 J7 **Suurberg** mt Cape Province S Africa 31.13S 25.38E
95 J9 **Suurberge** mts S Africa
95 D10 **Suurbraak** S Africa 34.00S 20.39E
46 F1 **Suure-Jaani** Estonia U.S.S.R. 58.34N 25.24E
95 J8 **Suurfontein** S Africa 32.09S 25.03E
9 T8 **Suva** Viti Levu Fiji 18.08S 178.25E
82 G7 **Suva Planina** mts Yugoslavia
82 F8 **Suva Reka** Yugoslavia 42.21N 20.50E
66 H3 **Suva** Switzerland 47.34N 37.37E
28 E3 **Suvarnamukhi** R Andhra Prad India
51 N9 **Suvasvesi** L Finland 62.40N 28.10E
80 C2 **Suvereto** Italy 43.05N 10.40E
81 M6 **Suvero, C** Italy 38.57N 16.10E
Suvla, C see **Anafarta Liman** bay
Suvla, C see **Büyük Kemikli Burun**
42 J5 **Suvo** U.S.S.R. 53.42N 110.59E
42 G4 **Suvorka** U.S.S.R. 56.28N 103.52E
45 H2 **Suvorov** U.S.S.R. 54.08N 36.30E
122 L9 **Suvorov I** Cook Is Pacific Oc 13.15S 163.05W
82 L7 **Suvorovo** Bulgaria 43.20N 27.36E
40 G9 **Suvorovo** Primorsk U.S.S.R. 44.14N 133.53E
82 M5 **Suvorovo** Ukraine U.S.S.R. 45.35N 29.00E
82 E5 **Suvo Rudište** mt Yugoslavia 43.15N 20.49E
20 M5 **Suwa** Japan 36.02N 138.09E
33 F9 **Suwādi, As** Yemen 14.16N 45.20E
Suwaiqiya, Hawr as L see
Suwayqiyah, Hawr as L
Suwair see **Suwayr**
Suwairqiya see **Suwayriqiyah, As**
20 M5 **Suwa ko** L Japan
62 O1 **Suwałki** Poland 54.06N 22.56E
Suwan see **Hu-wan**
25 F5 **Suwannaphum** Thailand 15.36N 103.46E
105 D8 **Suwannee** Florida 29.20N 83.09W
105 D8 **Suwannee** R Florida
100 R2 **Suwannee, L** Manitoba
105 F7 **Suwannee, R** Georgia
105 E7 **Suwannee Sound** Florida
105 E7 **Suwannoochee Cr** Georgia
21 D11 **Suwanose jima** isld Japan 29.37N 129.44E
18 M5 **Suwarrow** see Suvorov I
Suwaran, Gunung mt Borneo Indon 1.52N 117.41E
Suwayda, As see **Suweidiya, Es**
33 M5 **Suwayh, As** Oman 22.06N 59.40E
33 M5 **Suwayq, As** Oman 23.49N 57.30E
33 C5 **Suwayqiyah, Hawr as** L Iraq
33 M6 **Suwayr** Saudi Arabia 30.05N 40.17E
33 M6 **Suwayrah, As** Iraq 32.57N 44.47E
33 M6 **Suwayrqiyah, As** Saudi Arabia 23.14N 40.20E
35 J4 **Suwaysah** Syria 33.00N 35.56E
34 D6 **Suwayś, As** Egypt 29.58N 32.33E
34 B10 **Suweilih** C Saudi Arabia 28.41N 34.37E
35 H5 **Suweilih** Jordan 32.02N 35.50E
15 E6 **Suweima** Jordan 31.45N 35.35E
Suweimi watercourse Jordan
86 N6 **Suweiqa, Gebel** hill Egypt 29.50N 34.45E
Suweiri see **Şuwayrah, As**
Suweis, El see **Suez**
21 D9 **Suwŏn** S Korea 37.16N 126.59E
23 H2 **Su Xian** Anhui China 33.38N 117.02E
22 M7 **Suxik** Qinghai China 38.23N 94.08E
92 M9 **Suye, L** Zambia 14.27S 27.30E
Suyetikha see **Biryusinsk**
47 J5 **Suyevatpaul** U.S.S.R. 61.38N 60.22E
52 G6 **Suy'ga** U.S.S.R. 57.31N 38.50E
43 O3 **Suykbulak** Kazakhstan U.S.S.R. 49.51N 80.25E
119 B10 **Suyo** Peru 4.33S 80.01W
Suyung see **Hsü-yung**
44 H3 **Suyutkina Kosa** U.S.S.R. 44.11N 47.13E
44 H3 **Suyutkina Kosa, Mys** C U.S.S.R. 44.15N 47.42E
32 G7 **Sūza** Iran 26.50N 56.05E
43 G5 **Suzak** Kazakhstan U.S.S.R. 44.07N 68.27E
20 M5 **Suzaka** Japan 36.38N 138.20E
26 R15 **Suzanne, Pte** Kerguelen Ind Oc 49.28S 70.25E
42 G4 **Suzdal'** U.S.S.R. 56.26N 40.29E
66 E3 **Suze** R Switzerland
71 F8 **Suze-la-Rousse** France 44.17N 4.50E
45 F4 **Suzemka** U.S.S.R. 52.20N 34.06E
70 L6 **Suze-sur-Sarthe, la** France 47.54N 0.02E
Suzhou see **Jiuquan**
23 J3 **Suzhou** Jiangsu China 31.21N 120.40E
44 L6 **Suz, Mys** C Kazakhstan U.S.S.R. 41.46N 52.26E
71 G2 **Suzon** R France
99 T4 **Suzor Côté, L** Quebec 48.02N 71.26W
20 K4 **Suzu** Japan 37.25N 137.10E
18 K9 **Suzuka** Japan 34.51N 136.35E
20 J4 **Suzu-misaki** C Japan 37.30N 137.21E
42 C5 **Suzun** U.S.S.R. 53.46N 82.12E
79 G5 **Suzzara** Italy 45.00N 10.45E
53 J5 **Svabensverk** Sweden 61.04N 15.45E
53 H6 **Sværdborg** Denmark 55.06N 11.53E
53 U16 **Sværeford** Norway 61.17N 6.29E
57 J2 **Svågan** R Sweden
51 H5 **Svågstra** mt Sweden 66.19N 16.15E
34 B2 **Svalbard** arch Arctic Oc
50 K2 **Svalbard** Thingeyjarsýsla, Nordhur Iceland 66.12N 15.43W
50 G3 **Svalbardhseyri** Thingeyjarsýsla, Sudhur Iceland 65.45N 18.02W
50 K2 **Svalbardshnúpur** mt Iceland 66.04N 15.52W
53 G5 **Svallerup** Denmark 55.37N 11.11E
53 B5 **Svalvogar** Iceland 65.54N 23.50W
34 B2 **Svalyava** U.S.S.R. 48.33N 23.00E
80 T14 **Svanbergfjellet** mt Spitsbergen 78.40N 18.20E
53 U19 **Svandal** Norway 59.37N 6.16E
53 Q12 **Svaneke** Bornholm Denmark 55.08N 15.10E
44 E5 **Svanetskiy Khrebet** mts Georgia U.S.S.R.
53 E6 **Svanninge** Denmark 55.08N 10.15E
53 G9 **Svanøy** isld Norway 61.30N 5.05E
52 S16 **Svanskog** Sweden 59.11N 12.35E
52 G7 **Svanstein** Sweden 66.39N 23.50E
51 K4 **Svanvik** Norway 69.25N 30.00E
41 F5 **Svapa** R U.S.S.R.
51 J4 **Svappavaara** Sweden 67.41N 21.05E
50 G3 **Svarfadhardalur** V Iceland
52 E7 **Svarstad** Norway 59.25N 9.56E
Svartå see **Mustio**
52 H7 **Svartå** Ørebro Sweden 59.13N 14.08E
52 K8 **Svärta** Sødermanland Sweden 58.50N 17.10E
50 F4 **Svartá** R Húnavatnssýsla, Austur Iceland
50 F5 **Svartá** R Iceland
50 G6 **Svartá** R Rangárvallasýsla Iceland
50 H4 **Svartá** R Thingeyjarsýsla, Sudhur Iceland
50 G7 **Svartahnuksfjöll** mt Iceland 63.52N 18.48W
52 H7 **Svartälven** R Sweden
50 H4 **Svartárkot** Iceland 65.20N 17.16W
50 H4 **Svartárvatn** L Iceland 65.21N 17.15W
50 B5 **Svartbakafell** mt Iceland 64.54N 23.24W
53 N9 **Svartbakstindur** mt Faeroes 62.16N 6.59W
51 K5 **Svartbyn** Sweden 66.14N 22.50E
53 V13 **Svartebøkvatn** L Norway 62.32N 6.52E
48 S6 **Svartenhuk Halvø** pen Greenland
53 S15 **Svartevatn** L Norway 61.42N 5.19E
50 B2 **Svarthamar** mt Iceland 66.05N 23.17W
51 D5 **Svartisen** mt Norway 66.40N 13.56E
51 F5 **Svartlå** Sweden 66.00N 21.15E
52 J6 **Svartnäs** Sweden 60.54N 16.10E
51 J6 **Svartöstaden** Sweden 65.34N 22.14E
53 W20 **Svarvarnutén** mt Norway 59.12N 7.24E
39 E1 **Svatay** U.S.S.R. 67.56N 151.52E
45 K7 **Svatovo** Ukraine U.S.S.R. 49.24N 38.11E
51 N6 **Svatsum** Norway 61.19N 9.51E
25 H7 **Svay Rieng** Cambodia 11.05N 105.48E
52 F5 **Sveagruva** Spitsbergen 77.55N 16.45E
46 P1 **Svecha** U.S.S.R. 58.20N 47.31E
52 G11 **Svedala** Sweden 55.30N 13.15E
41 B3 **Svedomskogo, Mys** C Novaya Zemlya U.S.S.R. 71.50N 55.35E
52 M2 **Svedun** Sweden 64.39N 20.55E
50 C4 **Svefneyjar** isld Iceland 65.22N 22.50W
52 H4 **Sveg** Sweden 62.02N 14.20E
53 X15 **Sveigdalsbre** glacier Norway 61.37N 7.43E
50 J4 **Sveinagjá** rift Iceland
Sveinseyri see **Tunga** Bardhastrandarsýsla Iceland
50 G6 **Sveinstindur** pk Iceland 64.06N 18.25W
53 S19 **Sveio** Norway 59.33N 5.21E
53 S15 **Svelgen** Norway 61.47N 5.18E
52 E7 **Svelvik** Norway 59.37N 10.24E
46 F2 **Švenčionėliai** Lithuania U.S.S.R. 55.10N 26.00E
46 F2 **Švenčionys** Lithuania U.S.S.R. 55.09N 26.10E
53 F6 **Svendborg** Denmark 55.04N 10.38E
Svendborg co see **Fyn**
48 R2 **Svendborg Sund** str Denmark 55.03N 10.38E
52 G9 **Svenljunga** Sweden 57.30N 13.05E
123 C4 **Svenner Is** Antarctica 69.00S 76.50E
52 J7 **Svennevad** Sweden 59.02N 15.23E
51 C6 **Svenningdal** V Norway
110 B3 **Svensen** Oregon 46.10N 123.39W
51 F2 **Svensgrunnen** shoal Norway
50 V14 **Svenskøya** isld Spitsbergen 78.45N 26.45E
53 F5 **Svenstrup** Nordjylland Denmark 56.58N 9.52E
53 D6 **Svenstrup** Sønderjylland Denmark 55.02N 9.50E
53 D6 **Sverbeyevo** U.S.S.R. 53.35N 123.15E
46 D7 **Sverdlov** dist Moscow U.S.S.R.
45 Q5 **Sverdlovo** Saratov U.S.S.R. 51.15N 44.35E
44 A8 **Sverdlovo** Ukraine U.S.S.R. 46.41N 30.55E
47 M4 **Sverdlovsk** Sverdlovsk U.S.S.R. 56.52N 60.35E
45 L8 **Sverdlovsk** Ukraine U.S.S.R. 48.05N 39.37E
43 G7 **Sverdlovsk** Uzbekistan U.S.S.R. 39.46N 64.15E
38 F3 **Sverdlovskaya Oblast'** prov U.S.S.R.
97 K1 **Sverdrup Chan** N W Terr
97 J2 **Sverdrup Is** N W Terr
41 C4 **Sverdrup, Ostrov** isld U.S.S.R. 74.30N 74.22E
45 E5 **Svessa** Ukraine U.S.S.R. 51.57N 33.58E
82 C7 **Sveti Andrija** isld Yugoslavia 43.02N 15.45E
82 C5 **Sveti Ivan Zelina** Yugoslavia 45.57N 16.16E
45 C4 **Svetilovichi** Belorussiya U.S.S.R. 52.47N 31.18E
82 G9 **Sveti Nikole** Yugoslavia 41.51N 21.56E
65 M2 **Světlá nad Sázavou** Czech 49.40N 15.25E
40 H8 **Svetlaya** Primor'ye U.S.S.R. 46.30N 138.14E
39 D3 **Svetlaya** Yakutsk U.S.S.R. 64.04N 145.28E
46 C3 **Svetlogorsk** U.S.S.R. 54.57N 20.06E
44 E2 **Svetlograd** Stavropol' U.S.S.R. 45.21N 42.50E
40 G8 **Svetlovodnaya** U.S.S.R. 46.30N 136.38E
45 J5 **Svetlovodsk** Ukraine U.S.S.R. 49.05N 33.15E
46 R2 **Svetloye** Udmurt A.S.S.R. U.S.S.R. 57.02N 53.40E
62 M1 **Svetloye** U.S.S.R. 54.35N 20.22E
44 G2 **Svetloye, Oz** L U.S.S.R.
42 K3 **Svetlyy** Irkutsk U.S.S.R. 58.28N 116.02E
47 L6 **Svetlyy** Orenburg U.S.S.R. 50.47N 60.50E
47 J1 **Svetlyy** Yakutsk U.S.S.R. 57.47N 127.55E
40 G1 **Svetlyy** Yakutsk U.S.S.R. 61.15N 137.12E
45 Q8 **Svetlyy Yar** U.S.S.R. 48.29N 44.47E
47 B5 **Svetogorsk** U.S.S.R. 61.07N 28.50E
51 O10 **Svetogorsk** U.S.S.R. 61.04N 28.56E
47 D2 **Svetozarevo** Yugoslavia 44.00N 21.15E
45 O2 **Svezhen'kaya** U.S.S.R. 54.00N 42.28E
50 H6 **Sviandkur** mt Iceland 64.45N 16.15E
45 C4 **Svidhnur** isld Iceland 65.24N 22.39W
65 L3 **Svidník** mt Czechoslovakia 49.24N 14.58E
62 N6 **Švidovok** Ukraine U.S.S.R. 49.30N 31.56E
84 P5 **Švihov** Czechoslovakia 49.29N 13.17E
45 K8 **Svilaja** mt Yugoslavia 43.49N 16.31E
82 G6 **Svilajnac** Yugoslavia 44.15N 21.11E
82 K9 **Svilengrad** Bulgaria 41.45N 26.14E
50 D6 **Svínadalsá** R Iceland
50 G8 **Svínadalur** Iceland 63.43N 18.22W
50 J7 **Svínafell** Iceland 63.59N 16.51W
50 H7 **Svínafellsfjara** sand spit Iceland
50 H7 **Svínafellsjökull** ice cap Iceland 64.01N 16.50W
50 F3 **Svínavatn** Iceland 65.32N 19.58W
50 E5 **Svínavatn** L Iceland 65.32N 20.05W
53 F6 **Svindinge** Denmark 55.13N 10.42E
52 E6 **Svinesund** mt Norway 61.48N 6.20E
53 G5 **Svinninge** Denmark 55.43N 11.28E
53 O9 **Svinø** Faeroes 62.17N 6.18W
53 O9 **Svinø** isld Faeroes 62.17N 6.18W
Svinoy see **Svinø**
44 J8 **Svinoy** isld Azerbaydzhan U.S.S.R. 39.46N 49.36E
53 S14 **Svinøy** Lt Ho Norway 62.20N 5.15E
43 H7 **Svintsovyy Rudnik** Turkmeniya U.S.S.R. 37.57N 66.30E
39 C6 **Sv. Iony, O** U.S.S.R.
46 F3 **Svir'** Belorussiya U.S.S.R. 54.48N 26.28E
47 C5 **Svir'** R U.S.S.R.
47 C5 **Sviritsa** U.S.S.R. 60.28N 32.51E
47 C5 **Svirsk** U.S.S.R. 53.03N 103.20E
47 C5 **Svir'stroy** U.S.S.R. 60.48N 32.48E
45 P4 **Svishchevka** U.S.S.R. 52.50N 43.44E
82 J7 **Svishtov** Bulgaria 43.36N 25.22E
47 C5 **Svisloch'** Belorussiya U.S.S.R. 53.28N 29.00E
46 G3 **Svisloch'** R Belorussiya U.S.S.R.
45 C1 **Svistovichi** U.S.S.R. 55.15N 31.54E
65 P3 **Svitava** R Czechoslovakia
65 P3 **Svitávka** Czechoslovakia 49.31N 16.36E
65 P3 **Svitavy** Czechoslovakia 49.46N 16.28E
45 C1 **Svityaga** R U.S.S.R.
45 H5 **Svoboda** U.S.S.R. 51.58N 36.19E
40 D6 **Svobodnyy** Amur U.S.S.R. 51.24N 128.02E
45 R4 **Svobodnyy** Saratov U.S.S.R. 52.20N 46.20E
44 B8 **Svobodnyy Port** Ukraine U.S.S.R. 46.20N 31.52E
51 M1 **Svœrholtklubben** C Norway 70.57N 26.40E
65 P3 **Svogerslev** Denmark 55.38N 12.02E
64 Q3 **Svojetín** Czechoslovakia 50.12N 13.38E
65 M1 **Svojšice** Czechoslovakia 50.01N 15.02E
64 O4 **Svojšín** Czechoslovakia 49.46N 12.55E
51 D2 **Svolvær** Norway 68.15N 14.40E
41 M3 **Svóni** mt Greece 39.09N 21.42E
52 C5 **Svorkmo** Norway 63.12N 9.45E
65 O3 **Svratka** Czechoslovakia 49.43N 16.02E
65 O2 **Svratka** R Czechoslovakia
82 G7 **Svrljig** Yugoslavia 43.25N 22.06E
82 C7 **Svrljiške Planina** mts Yugoslavia
46 M2 **Svyatogor'ye** U.S.S.R. 57.08N 29.49E
47 F2 **Svyatoy Nos, Mys** C Arkhangel'sk U.S.S.R. 67.45N 48.32E
47 D2 **Svyatoy Nos, Mys** C Murmansk U.S.S.R. 68.11N 39.50E
41 Q4 **Svyatoy Nos, Mys** C Yakutsk U.S.S.R. 72.50N 140.46E
42 H5 **Svyatoy Nos, Poluostrov** pen U.S.S.R.
47 C5 **Svyatozero** U.S.S.R. 61.32N 33.39E
25 D3 **Swa** R Burma
31 G3 **Swabi** Pakistan 34.06N 72.34E
Swabue see **Shanwei**
95 J8 **Swaershoek** S Africa 32.30S 25.25E
56 N2 **Swaffham** Norfolk Eng 52.39N 0.41E
13 K5 **Swain Reefs** Gt Barrier Reef Australia
105 E5 **Swainsboro** Georgia 32.36N 82.21W
122 B4 **Swains I** Samoa Pacific Oc 11.04S 171.06W
26 G16 **Swain's I** S Pacific Oc 59.30S 100.00W
57 N6 **Swainsthorpe** Norfolk Eng 52.34N 1.17E
56 G5 **Swainswick** Avon Eng 51.26N 2.21W
94 C4 **Swakop** watercourse Namibia
94 C4 **Swakopmund** Namibia 22.40S 14.34E
57 J4 **Swaledale** V N Yorks Eng
57 J4 **Swale, R** N Yorks Eng
56 N5 **Swale, The** channel Kent Eng
10 O4 **Swallow Is** Santa Cruz Is Pacific Oc 10.21S 166.17E
17 H10 **Swallow Reef** S China Sea 7.25N 113.45E
109 F3 **Swallows** Colorado 38.18N 104.35W
60 N15 **Swalmen** Netherlands 51.13N 6.02E
100 D7 **Swalwell** Alberta 51.33N 113.15W

11 L12 Swampy Summit mt New Zealand 45.47S 170.28E
28 C3 Swamthalli Karnataka India 14.52N 76.38E
56 H6 Swanage Dorset Eng 50.37N 1.58W
14 A2 Swanbourne Beach dist Perth, W Australia
12 G6 Swan Hill Victoria 35.23S 143.37E
100 B4 Swan Hills Alberta 54.41N 115.20W
116 C6 Swan Is Caribbean Sea 17.25N 83.56W
12 J8 Swan Is Tasmania 40.42S 148.08E
101 J8 Swan L Br Columbia 55.49N 128.38W
100 R6 Swan L Manitoba
110 M2 Swan L Montana 47.57N 113.52W
108 L4 Swan L S Dakota 45.18N 99.50W
111 M2 Swan L Utah 39.10N 112.45W
100 T9 Swan Lake Manitoba 49.25N 98.48W
110 M2 Swan Lake Montana 47.55N 113.50W
103 E3 Swan Lake New York 41.45N 74.47W
55 K5 Swanley Kent Eng 51.24N 0.12E
59 G3 Swanlinbar Cavan Irish Rep 54.12N 7.42W
105 E2 Swannanoa N Carolina 35.36N 82.25W
58 S11 Swannay, L Orkney Scotland 59.08N 3.12W
100 P6 Swan Plain Saskatchewan 52.08N 102.01W
14 E3 Swan Pt W Australia 16.23S 122.58E
105 L2 Swanquarter N Carolina 35.24N 76.20W
100 B3 Swan R Alberta
100 Q6 Swan R Man/Sask
110 M2 Swan R Montana
14 B9 Swan R W Australia
12 E5 Swan Reach S Australia 34.34S 139.10E
100 Q6 Swan River Manitoba 52.06N 101.17W
108 R2 Swan River Minnesota 47.04N 93.11W
105 K3 Swansboro N Carolina 34.43N 77.08W
111 L7 Swansea Arizona 34.11N 113.50W
103 M3 Swansea Massachusetts 41.45N 71.11W
12 K5 Swansea New S Wales 33.05S 150.40E
105 F4 Swansea S Carolina 33.45N 81.06W
12 J8 Swansea Tasmania 42.08S 148.00E
56 D4 Swansea W Glam Wales 51.38N 3.57W
56 D4 Swansea B W Glam Wales
104 R2 Swans I Maine
100 K7 Swanson Saskatchewan 51.42N 107.10W
101 J9 Swanson Bay Br Columbia 53.00N 128.27W
108 J9 Swanson Res Nebraska 40.10N 101.07W
56 N4 Swan Street Essex Eng 51.58N 0.36E
108 N9 Swanton Nebraska 40.23N 97.05W
104 B5 Swanton Ohio 41.36N 83.54W
104 M2 Swanton Vermont 44.56N 73.08W
63 S4 Swantow E Germany 54.18N 13.20E
12 K3 Swan Vale New S Wales 29.43S 151.25E
110 O6 Swan Valley Idaho 43.27N 111.20W
108 Q4 Swanville Minnesota 45.50N 94.20W
56 O2 Swardeston Norfolk Eng 52.35N 1.15E
95 N6 Swartberg S Africa 30.15S 29.20E
95 C10 Swartberg mt Cape Province S Africa 34.11S 19.29E
95 E9 Swartberg mt Cape Province S Africa 33.22S 21.55E
103 D7 Swarthmore Pennsylvania 39.54N 75.21W
95 K8 Swart-kei R S Africa
94 P12 Swartkopberge mts Cape Town S Africa
95 J9 Swartkops S Africa 33.52S 25.36E
95 J9 Swartkops R S Africa
26 B14 Swart Pk hill Marion I Indian Oc 46.53S 37.46E
95 K2 Swartplaas S Africa 26.09S 26.56E
95 K1 Swartruggens S Africa 25.40S 26.42E
95 K1 Swartruggens mts S Africa
103 E4 Swartswood New Jersey 41.05N 74.50W
111 L2 Swasey Pk mt Utah 39.24N 113.19W
99 K4 Swastika Ontario 48.07N 80.06W
103 A6 Swatara Cr Pennsylvania
91 E7 Swa Tende Zaïre 7.13S 17.07E
31 G3 Swat Kohistan reg Pakistan
57 N7 Swaton Lincs Eng 52.56N 0.19W
Swatow see Shantou
31 G3 Swat R Pakistan
59 J2 Swatragh Londonderry N Ireland 54.54N 6.40W
31 G3 Swat, reg Pakistan
94 L6 Swaziland kingdom Africa
108 Q6 Swea City Iowa 43.25N 94.19W
49 H4 Sweden kingdom N Europe
103 D7 Swedesboro New Jersey 39.45N 75.18W
58 E7 Sween, L Strathclyde Scotland 55.59N 5.39W
112 M6 Sweeny Texas 29.02N 95.45W
59 H7 Sweep, The Waterford Irish Rep 52.14N 7.15W
13 E3 Sweers I Queensland 17.05S 139.35E
110 J6 Sweet Idaho 43.58N 116.19W
110 O1 Sweetgrass Montana 48.59N 111.58W
107 D7 Sweet Home Arkansas 34.39N 92.13W
110 C5 Sweet Home Oregon 44.24N 122.25W
112 K6 Sweet Home Texas 29.20N 97.06W
107 C3 Sweet Springs Missouri 38.57N 93.25W
103 B4 Sweet Valley Pennsylvania 41.17N 76.09W
109 L6 Sweetwater Oklahoma 35.27N 99.56W
107 M6 Sweetwater Tennessee 35.36N 84.29W
112 G3 Sweetwater Texas 32.27N 100.25W
108 B7 Sweetwater R Wyoming
95 D10 Swellendam S Africa 34.01S 20.26E
112 G2 Swenson Texas 33.14N 100.19W
18 B7 Swettenham, Gunong mt Pen Malaysia 4.37N 101.30E
121 J7 Swett, Pen Chile
62 J5 Świdnica Poland 50.51N 16.29E
62 J2 Świdwin Poland 53.46N 15.44E
62 J5 Świebodzice Poland 50.51N 16.20E
62 J3 Świebodzin Poland 52.15N 15.31E
62 L2 Świecie Poland 53.25N 18.25E
113 K6 Swift R Alaska
101 H6 Swift R Br Col/Yukon Terr
104 P2 Swift R Maine
98 S6 Swift Current Newfoundland 47.53N 54.15W
100 K8 Swift Current Saskatchewan 50.17N 107.49W
100 J8 Swiftcurrent Cr Saskatchewan
60 L9 Swifterbant Netherlands 52.34N 5.38E
113 L5 Swift Fork, R Alaska
107 E6 Swifton Arkansas 35.49N 91.09W
110 C3 Swift Res Washington 46.04N 122.05W
101 H5 Swift River Yukon Terr 60.02N 133.10W
110 A1 Swiftsure Bank Lightship Vancouver I, Br Col 48.34N 124.59W
103 D4 Swiftwater Pennsylvania 41.06N 75.20W
59 G1 Swilly, L Donegal Irish Rep 55.10N 7.32W
59 G2 Swilly, R Donegal Irish Rep
56 D5 Swimbridge Devon Eng 51.03N 3.58W
63 U5 Swina channel Poland 53.52N 14.20E
95 N4 Swinburne S Africa 28.20S 29.16E
103 J9 Swinburne I New York 40.34N 74.33W
56 H4 Swindon Wilts Eng 51.34N 1.47W
Swinemünde see Swinoujście
57 N7 Swineshead Lincs Eng 52.57N 0.10W
59 E4 Swinford Mayo Irish Rep 53.57N 8.57W
103 E3 Swinging Bridge Res New York
109 G3 Swink Colorado 38.01N 103.37W
95 J4 Swinkpan salt pan S Africa 28.29S 25.36E
62 H2 Swinoujście Poland 53.55N 14.18E
58 M7 Swinton Borders Scotland 55.43N 2.15W
57 J5 Swinton Greater Manchester Eng 53.31N 2.21W
64 B2 Swisttal W Germany 50.41N 6.54E
49 F7 Switzerland rep Cent Europe
60 N14 Swolgen Netherlands 51.29N 6.07E
58 S12 Swona isld Orkney Scotland 58.44N 3.03W
59 K5 Swords Dublin Irish Rep 53.28N 6.13W
13 F5 Swords Ra Queensland
56 F6 Swyre Dorset Eng 50.42N 2.41W
47 L3 Syadaykharvuta U.S.S.R. 67.10N 73.58E
45 D5 Syadrino Ukraine U.S.S.R. 51.50N 32.29E
39 D1 Syagan Akh U.S.S.R. 68.54N 148.56E
41 Q6 Syagannakh U.S.S.R. 68.55N 143.23E
41 M7 Syalakh U.S.S.R. 66.12N 124.10E
29 K6 Syambazar W Bengal India 22.52N 87.40E
47 C5 Syamozero, Ozero L U.S.S.R.
47 E5 Syamzha U.S.S.R. 60.01N 41.04E
29 H3 Syang Nepal 28.49N 83.42E
39 D1 Syangannakh U.S.S.R. 68.33N 149.28E
47 C6 Syas' R U.S.S.R.
47 F6 Syava U.S.S.R. 58.00N 46.14E
47 L2 Syavtato L U.S.S.R.
108 E8 Sybille Cr Wyoming
59 B7 Sybil Pt Kerry Irish Rep 52.10N 10.27W
107 K8 Sycamore Alabama 33.15N 86.12W
106 F8 Sycamore Illinois 41.59N 88.41W
104 B6 Sycamore Ohio 40.56N 83.11W
105 F4 Sycamore S Carolina 33.03N 81.14W
45 C10 Sychavka Ukraine U.S.S.R. 46.40N 31.09E
45 F1 Sychevka U.S.S.R. 55.51N 34.16E
62 K4 Sycow Poland 51.19N 17.40E
42 E5 Syda R U.S.S.R.
55 G4 Sydenham London Eng 51.25N 0.03W
99 O8 Sydenham Ontario 44.24N 76.36W
11 M10 Sydenham dist Christchurch New Zealand
53 N10 Syderø isld Faeroes
53 N10 Syderø Fjord channel Faeroes
56 N2 Syderstone Norfolk Eng 52.52N 0.43E
50 K3 Sydhri Hágangur mt Iceland 65.49N 15.12W
50 G7 Sydhri Ófœra R Iceland
53 O9 Sydhritangi C Faeroes 62.11N 6.25W
Sydhstibær see Hrisey
48 U11 Sydkap Greenland 71.19N 25.00W
98 M7 Sydney C Breton I, Nova Scotia 46.10N 60.10W
12 K5 Sydney New S Wales 33.55S 151.10E
10 V11 Sydney B Norfolk I Pacific Oc 29.05S 167.57E
10 S2 Sydney I Phoenix Is Pacific Oc 4.30S 171.30W
13 E3 Sydney I Queensland 16.40S 139.30E
98 M7 Sydney Mines C Breton I, Nova Scotia 46.16N 60.15W
95 H4 Sydney-on-Vaal S Africa 28.27S 24.18E
9 D5 Sydney Pt Ocean I Pacific Oc 0.53S 169.36E
48 U16 Sydprøven Greenland 60.30N 45.35W
95 L2 Syferbult S Africa 26.00S 27.20E
95 K7 Syfergat S Africa 31.27S 26.26E
53 S18 Syfteland Norway 60.13N 5.29E
53 X15 Sygnefjell mts Norway
63 J7 Syke W Germany 52.55N 8.49E
108 L2 Sykeston N Dakota 47.28N 99.23W
104 J7 Sykesville Maryland 39.21N 76.58W
104 G5 Sykesville Pennsylvania 41.03N 78.50W
53 V14 Sykkylven Norway 62.23N 6.35E
39 E1 Syklanya U.S.S.R. 69.42N 151.15E
47 G5 Syktyvkar U.S.S.R. 61.42N 50.45E
39 E2 Sykynakh R U.S.S.R.
107 K8 Sylacauga Alabama 33.10N 86.15W
107 D6 Sylamore Arkansas 35.57N 92.05W
52 G3 Sylarna mt Norway 63.01N 12.13E
39 E1 Sylgy-Ytar Yakutsk U.S.S.R. 67.50N 154.57E
39 E2 Sylgy-Ytar Yakutsk U.S.S.R. 66.10N 151.11E
31 J8 Sylhet Bangladesh 24.53N 91.51E
31 J9 Sylhet dist Bangladesh
63 H3 Sylt isld W Germany
53 T14 Sylte Möre og Romsdal Norway 62.03N 5.38E
53 W14 Sylte Möre og Romsdal Norway 62.18N 7.17E
51 P1 Syltefjord inlet Norway 70.32N 30.10E
53 A7 Sylt-Ost W Germany 54.51N 8.27E
105 D2 Sylva N Carolina 35.23N 83.13W
47 H6 Sylva Perm U.S.S.R. 58.04N 56.42E
47 M4 Sylva Sverdlovsk U.S.S.R. 57.19N 58.47E
47 H7 Sylva R U.S.S.R.
104 G7 Sylvan Pennsylvania 39.44N 78.02W
72 K8 Sylvanès France 43.50N 2.57E
109 M2 Sylvan Grove Kansas 39.02N 98.23W
105 F5 Sylvania Georgia 32.45N 81.40W
12 L8 Sylvania New S Wales 34.01S 151.06E
104 B5 Sylvania Ohio 41.42N 84.42W
100 N6 Sylvania Saskatchewan 52.41N 104.00W
14 D6 Sylvania W Australia 23.39S 120.00E
100 C6 Sylvan L Alberta 52.20N 114.03W
110 P5 Sylvan Pass Wyoming 44.29N 110.05W
53 U16 Sylvarnes Norway 61.05N 6.18E
65 E6 Sylvensteinstausee L W Germany 47.35N 11.31E
105 D6 Sylvester Georgia 31.32N 83.52W
112 G3 Sylvester Texas 32.44N 100.16W
13 D4 Sylvester, L N Terr Australia
98 R5 Sylvester, Mt Newfoundland 48.10N 55.04W
109 M4 Sylvia Kansas 37.58N 98.24W
94 C5 Sylvia Hill Namibia 25.10S 14.56E
101 L6 Sylvia, Mt Br Columbia 58.02N 124.28W
47 M3 Sylvitsa R U.S.S.R.
42 D2 Sym U.S.S.R. 60.23N 88.18E
42 D2 Sym R U.S.S.R.
58 Q9 Symbister Shetland Scotland 60.21N 1.02W
115 H5 Symon Mexico 24.44N 102.40W
56 F4 Symond's Yat Glos Eng 51.51N 2.38W
19 L5 Syndicate Philippines 12.28N 123.25E
41 O6 Synegey U.S.S.R. 69.24N 134.35E
53 Y18 Synhøvd mt Norway 60.15N 8.25E
14 F3 Synnott, Mt W Australia 16.41S 125.20E
14 F3 Synnott Ra W Australia
42 J4 Synnyr, Khrebet mts U.S.S.R.
Synod Inn see Post-Mawr
45 N1 Syntul U.S.S.R. 55.00N 41.19E
47 J3 Synya R U.S.S.R.
47 K5 Syn'yakha R U.S.S.R.
42 D5 Synzas U.S.S.R. 53.00N 88.50E
82 L3 Synzhereya U.S.S.R. 47.37N 28.10E
103 G5 Syosset Long I, N Y 40.49N 73.31W
123 A6 Syowa Jap Base Antarctica 69.00S 39.35E
106 J8 Syracuse Indiana 41.24N 85.45W
Syracuse Italy see Siracusa
109 J4 Syracuse Kansas 37.59N 101.46W
108 O9 Syracuse Nebraska 40.40N 96.12W
104 J3 Syracuse New York 43.03N 76.10W
110 N8 Syracuse Utah 41.05N 112.07W
43 J6 Syrdar'ya Uzbekistan U.S.S.R. 40.51N 60.40E
43 H5 Syr-Dar'ya R U.S.S.R.
43 H6 Syr Dar'ya, Oblast prov Uzbekistan U.S.S.R.
84 R15 Syrgatis R Cyprus
34 E3 Syria rep S W Asia
25 D4 Syriam Burma 16.45N 96.17E
Syrian Desert see Badiet es Sham des
47 K5 Syrkovoye, Oz L U.S.S.R.
53 G2 Syr Odde, cape Denmark 57.19N 11.13E
45 C1 Syrokorenskiye U.S.S.R. 55.03N 31.57E
47 L6 Syrostan U.S.S.R. 55.04N 59.55E
45 L4 Syrskiy U.S.S.R. 52.34N 39.29E
41 E4 Syruta, Oz L U.S.S.R. 72.59N 88.45E
41 H4 Syrutaturku, Oz L U.S.S.R. 74.23N 103.40E
53 W18 Sysenvatn L Norway 60.25N 7.25E
47 M5 Sysert' U.S.S.R. 56.30N 60.50E
104 R1 Sysladobsis L Maine
51 M10 Sysmä Finland 61.33N 25.40E
47 G5 Sysola R U.S.S.R.
41 P5 Systengnakh U.S.S.R. 71.15N 136.13E
56 J2 Syston Leics Eng 52.42N 1.04W
46 J2 Syt'kovo U.S.S.R. 56.32N 34.00E
47 L5 Sytomino U.S.S.R. 61.13N 71.18E
41 O6 Sytygan-Lebi U.S.S.R. 69.17N 134.27E
41 O5 Sytygan-Tala, Bukhta B U.S.S.R.
40 A3 Sytykanskiy Porog falls U.S.S.R. 57.45N 118.35E
39 B1 Syuge-Khaya, Gora mt U.S.S.R. 68.18N 136.51E
41 K8 Syul'dzhyukyar U.S.S.R. 63.14N 113.32E
47 E5 Syuma R U.S.S.R.
46 Q2 Syumsi U.S.S.R. 57.08N 51.12E
46 R2 Syun' R U.S.S.R.
47 L5 Syuribayevo U.S.S.R. 55.26N 59.04E
40 H6 Syurkum U.S.S.R. 50.05N 140.30E
40 H6 Syurkum, Mys C U.S.S.R. 50.04N 140.41E
41 M5 Syuryakh-Dzhangy, Vozvyshennost' heights U.S.S.R.
41 K5 Syuryakh-Dzhangy, Vozvyshennost' mts U.S.S.R.
39 C2 Syuryuktyakh R U.S.S.R.
41 O7 Syuryun-Kyuyel' U.S.S.R. 65.09N 130.43E
82 J9 Syutkya mt Bulgaria 41.50N 23.59E
45 P5 Syvatoslavka U.S.S.R. 51.20N 43.25E
53 T14 Syvde Norway 62.06N 5.46E
53 T14 Syvdefjord inlet Norway 62.08N 5.42E
53 W14 Syv Søstrefosser falls Norway 62.08N 7.05E
45 U3 Syzran' U.S.S.R. 53.10N 48.29E
45 T3 Syzran' R U.S.S.R.
62 L9 Szabadszállás Hungary 46.54N 19.15E
82 G2 Szabolcs-Szatmár co Hungary
62 L4 Szadek Poland 51.40N 18.56E
15 F7 Szaga, L Papua New Guinea
62 K2 Szamocin Poland 53.01N 17.05E
62 N7 Szamosszeg Hungary 48.02N 22.22E
62 K3 Szamotuły Poland 52.36N 16.34E
62 K8 Szany Hungary 47.28N 17.20E
62 M9 Szarvas Hungary 46.51N 20.35E
62 O5 Szczebrzeszyn Poland 50.42N 22.59E
62 H2 Szczecin Poland 53.25N 14.32E
62 K2 Szczecinek Poland 53.42N 16.41E
62 H2 Szczecinski, Zalew inlet Poland/E Ger
62 M5 Szczekociny Poland 50.38N 19.49E
62 L4 Szczerców Poland 51.18N 19.09E
62 N5 Szczucin Poland 50.18N 21.04E
62 N2 Szczuczyn Poland 53.36N 22.19E
62 M2 Szczytno Poland 53.33N 20.59E
Szechwan prov China see Sichuan
62 M7 Szécsény Hungary 48.07N 19.30E
62 M9 Szeged Hungary 46.15N 20.09E
62 N8 Szeghalom Hungary 47.01N 21.09E
Szehsien see Si Xian
Szehung see Sihong
62 L8 Székesfehérvár Hungary 47.11N 18.22E
62 L9 Szekszárd Hungary 46.21N 18.41E
Szelu see Haiyuan Guangxi
Szemao see Simao
62 M7 Szendrő Hungary 48.24N 20.40E
Szengen see Huanjian
62 L8 Szentendre Hungary 47.40N 19.02E
62 M9 Szentes Hungary 46.40N 20.17E
65 O8 Szentgotthárd Hungary 46.57N 16.18E
62 K9 Szentlőrinc Hungary 46.02N 17.58E
62 N7 Szerencs Hungary 48.10N 21.11E
62 K8 Szigetköz dist Hungary
62 K9 Szigetvár Hungary 46.01N 17.50E
62 M7 Szikszó Hungary 48.12N 20.58E
62 N2 Szkwa R Poland
62 J4 Szlichtyngowa Poland 51.43N 16.16E
62 L8 Szob Hungary 47.49N 18.52E
62 M8 Szolnok Hungary 47.10N 20.10E
82 F3 Szolnok co Hungary
65 P7 Szombathely Hungary 47.14N 16.38E
62 J4 Szprotawa Poland 51.35N 15.32E
62 M2 Szreńsk Poland 53.02N 20.10E
62 L2 Sztum Poland 53.55N 19.00E
62 K3 Szubin Poland 53.00N 17.43E
62 M4 Szydłowiec Poland 51.14N 20.50E
40 D4 Taaga, Khrebet mts U.S.S.R.
95 F7 Taaibosberg mts S Africa
Taalintehdas see Dalsbruk
19 K4 Taal, L Luzon Philippines 14.00N 121.00E
33 F8 Ta'ām Yemen 16.14N 44.44E
15 B6 Taām isld Moluccas Indonesia 5.45S 132.12E
93 E2 Taan Uganda 3.48N 33.48E
35 D3 Taanach anc site Jordan 32.32N 35.13E
35 E3 Taanach dist Israel
122 B12 Taapuna Tahiti Pacific Oc 17.35S 149.36W
60 P7 Taarlo Netherlands 53.02N 6.38E
51 H3 Taavätno R Sweden
62 L9 Tab Hungary 46.45N 18.01E
91 F10 Taba Angola 13.05S 18.58E
19 L5 Tabaco Luzon Philippines 13.21N 123.44E
119 B7 Tabacundo Ecuador 0.03N 78.13W
89 C5 Tabadian Senegal 13.15N 13.29W
32 H2 Tabadkān Iran 36.27N 59.55E
41 O9 Tabaga Yakutsk U.S.S.R. 61.45N 130.50E
41 N9 Tabago Yakutsk U.S.S.R. 61.52N 129.42E
33 E3 Tābah Saudi Arabia 27.01N 42.08E
96 S13 Tabaiba Tenerife Canary Is 28.25N 16.20W
120 G3 Tabajara Brazil 8.57S 62.07W
31 B5 Tabaksar Afghanistan 31.55N 63.15E
15 K4 Tabalo Bismarck Arch 1.25S 149.37E
120 B2 Tabalosos Peru 6.26S 76.37W
18 L10 Tabanan Bali Indon 8.31S 115.05E
76 L4 Tabanera de Cerrato Spain 42.01N 4.08W
89 K4 Tabango Mali 15.47N 0.25E
88 O12 Tabankort Mali 19.44N 1.00E
89 K3 Tabankort Mali 17.44N 0.20E
37 D3 Tabanköy Turkey 40.03N 27.25E
95 N6 Tabankulu S Africa 30.58S 29.19E
87 C5 Tabanya Sudan 10.32N 30.01E
116 O2 Tabaquite Trinidad & Tobago 10.23N 61.18W
76 H5 Tábara Spain 41.49N 5.57W
35 G5 Tabarbaur Jordan 32.00N 35.57E
15 M5 Tabar I Bismarck Arch 2.58S 152.07E
15 M5 Tabar Is Bismarck Arch
78 B12 Tabarka Tunisia 36.55N 8.45E
89 N5 Tabaroua Niger 13.32N 6.57E
32 G4 Ţabas Khorāsān Iran 33.37N 56.54E
32 J4 Ţabas Khorāsān Iran 32.48N 60.14E
115 O5 Tabasará, Sa. de mts Panama
115 H7 Tabasco Mexico 21.54N 102.43W
115 N8 Tabasco state Mexico
32 G5 Tabāsin Iran 31.14N 57.51E
32 D6 Tābask, Kūh-e mt Iran 29.53N 51.54E
98 O3 Tabatière, La Quebec 50.51N 58.59W
118 E7 Tabatinga Brazil 21.41S 48.40W
119 E10 Tabatinga Brazil 4.14S 69.44W
117 F10 Tabatinga, Sa. da mts Brazil
119 H7 Tabatinga, Serra mts Brazil
44 F6 Tabatskuri, Oz L Georgia U.S.S.R.
25 M7 Tabawng Ga Burma 26.35N 96.32E
25 C1 Tabayin Burma 22.39N 95.20E
19 K3 Tabayoo, Mt Luzon Philippines 16.40N 120.54E
Tabbaghaj see Tūp Āghāj
14 F7 Tabba Pan W Australia
86 F6 Tabbîn, El Egypt 29.47N 31.18E
88 M7 Tabelbala Algeria 29.23N 3.15W
88 R8 Tabelbalet Algeria 27.21N 6.54E
88 O7 Tabelkoza Algeria 29.47N 0.50E
25 H6 Tabeng Cambodia 13.31N 104.52E
100 E9 Taber Alberta 49.48N 112.09W
88 R4 Taberdga Algeria 35.02N 7.03E
52 H9 Taberg Sweden 57.42N 14.05E
103 E7 Tabernacle New Jersey 39.51N 74.43W
77 M6 Tabernas Spain 37.03N 2.22W
77 M6 Tabernas, R. de Spain
77 Q2 Tabernes de Valldigna Spain 39.05N 0.15W
77 M6 Taberno Spain 37.29N 2.04W
100 E9 Taber Prov. Park Alberta
91 C8 Tabi Angola 8.10S 13.22E
88 N4 Tabia Algeria 35.02N 0.45W
9 D4 Tabiang Ocean I Pacific Oc 0.52S 169.35E
24 E10 Tabia Tsaka L Xizang Zizhiqu China
9 A3 Tabik islet Marshall Is Pacific Oc 9.17N 166.58E
9 A3 Tabik Channel Marshall Is Pacific Oc
92 D1 Tabili Zaïre 0.04N 28.01E
110 P9 Tabiona Utah 40.21N 110.43W
18 E6 Tabir R Sumatra Indon
9 B6 Tabiteuea atoll Kiribati, Pacific Oc 1.25S 174.50E
96 P9 Tablado, El La Palma Canary Is 28.50N 17.54W
121 A9 Tablaruca, Pta C Chile 42.56S 74.16W
19 L5 Tablas isld Philippines
121 B3 Tablas, C Chile 31.53S 71.38W
19 K5 Tablas Str Philippines
119 E2 Tablazo, B. de Venezuela
15 K9 Table Bay Papua New Guinea
95 B9 Table Bay S Africa
12 H8 Table C Tasmania 40.56S 145.45E
11 N6 Table Cape New Zealand 39.06S 178.02E
19 J7 Table Hd Philippines 9.36N 118.43E
11 B13 Table Hill Stewart I New Zealand 47.02S 167.51E
23 C9 Table I Hong Kong 22.18N 114.18E
25 J2 Table, I. de la Vietnam 20.57N 107.30E
28 G6 Table Is Andaman Is 14.11N 93.21E
89 D8 Table, La mt Liberia 6.13N 10.02W
14 F3 Tableland W Australia 17.15S 126.48E
113 Q2 Table Mt Alaska 68.24N 143.43W
98 N6 Table Mt Newfoundland 47.43N 59.12W
95 B9 Table Mt S Africa 33.58S 18.25E
19 J6 Table Pt Philippines 10.02N 118.38E
26 V16 Table, Pte de la Réunion Ind Oc 21.19S 55.49E
108 B8 Table Rock Wyoming 41.38N 108.16W
107 C5 Table Rock Lake res Missouri 36.38N 93.17W
13 G4 Tabletop, Mt Queensland 18.28S 144.40E
94 P11 Table View Cape Town S Africa 33.49S 18.28E
89 K8 Tabligbo Togo 6.35N 1.30E
77 H3 Tablillas R Spain
76 D3 Taboada Spain 42.42N 7.46W
76 D4 Taboadela Spain 42.15N 7.49W
119 H9 Taboca Brazil 2.27S 61.52W
117 A6 Tabocal Brazil 3.05S 58.06W
120 F2 Tabocal R Brazil
118 C6 Taboco, R Brazil
115 G11 Taboga Panama 8.47N 79.33W
115 G11 Taboga, I Panama
115 G11 Taboguilla, I Panama
117 G10 Taboleiro reg Brazil
65 L3 Tábor Czechoslovakia 49.25N 14.39E
108 P9 Tabor Iowa 40.54N 95.40W
108 N7 Tabor S Dakota 42.58N 97.40W
39 E1 Tábor U.S.S.R. 71.20N 150.20E
92 E5 Tabora reg Tanzania
105 J3 Tabor City N Carolina 34.09N 79.53W
35 E3 Tabor, Mt Israel 32.41N 35.24E
47 J6 Tabory U.S.S.R. 58.35N 64.30E
43 J6 Taboshar Tadzhikistan U.S.S.R. 40.36N 69.40E
89 F9 Tabou Ivory Coast 4.28N 7.20W
32 B1 Tabrīz Iran 38.05N 46.18E
25 H2 Ta Bu Vietnam 21.26N 104.02E
76 C8 Tábua Portugal 40.22N 8.01W
76 D6 Tabuaço Portugal 41.07N 7.34W
75 G4 Tabuenca Spain 41.42N 1.32W
33 B2 Tabūk Saudi Arabia 28.22N 36.32E
20 E8 Tabuka Japan 33.35N 131.42E
12 L3 Tabulam New S Wales 28.50S 152.35E
117 A7 Tabuleiro Brazil 5.03S 58.25W
43 N1 Tabuny U.S.S.R. 52.45N 78.45E
40 E6 Taburachka U.S.S.R. 51.58N 129.31E
96 P9 Taburiente, Caldera de mt La Palma Canary Is 28.45N 17.45W
80 L6 Taburno, Monte Italy 41.05N 14.36E
98 G6 Tabusintac R New Brunswick
33 K9 Tabut S Yemen 15.59N 52.12E
18 C5 Tabuyung Sumatra Indon 0.51N 98.59E
92 D6 Tabwe tribe Zambia
9 C10 Tabwemasana Pk New Hebrides 15.20S 166.40E
52 L7 Täby Sweden 59.29N 18.04E
47 H8 Tabynsk U.S.S.R. 54.00N 56.28E
117 H9 Tacaimbó Brazil 8.17S 36.15W
117 C5 Tacaipu, Sa mts Brazil
117 B4 Tacalé Brazil 1.45N 54.56W
115 J8 Tacámbaro Mexico 19.15N 101.30W
115 N10 Tacaná, Vol. de Mexico/Guatemala 15.08N 92.06W
121 E2 Tacanitas Argentina 28.40S 62.33W
117 H9 Tacaratu Brazil 9.05S 38.07W
119 G2 Tacarigua, L. de Venezuela 10.16N 65.58W
119 C3 Tacarouna, Cerro mt Panama 8.07N 77.19W
115 P7 Tacchibichén Mexico 20.28N 88.52W
66 O7 Taceno Italy 46.02N 9.23E
24 E3 Tachakou Xinjiang Uygur Zizhiqu China 45.26N 84.50E
24 D2 Tacheng Xinjiang Uygur Zizhiqu China 46.42N 82.00E
64 O7 Tacherting W Germany 48.04N 12.35E
23 J6 Ta-chia Taiwan 24.20N 120.34E
20 C9 Tachibana-wan B Japan
20 B2 Tachikawa Tōky Japan 35.42N 139.28E
113 D6 Tachikuga Alaska 60.02N 167.10W
Ta-ch'ing Shan mts see Daqing Shan
Ta-ch'in-t'a-la see Naiman Qi
119 D3 Táchira Venezuela 8.09N 72.15W
119 D4 Táchira state Venezuela
85 A6 Tachiumet Libya 26.19N 10.05E
25 L3 Tachou Dao isld Guangdong China
64 O4 Tachov Czechoslovakia 49.48N 12.38E
81 N5 Tacina R Italy
120 G1 Taciuã, L Brazil
12 L4 Tacking Pt New S Wales 31.33S 152.50E
19 M6 Tacloban Philippines 11.15N 125.01E
111 K9 Tacna Arizona 32.40N 114.00W
119 E9 Tacna Colombia 2.21S 70.37W
120 D8 Tacna Peru 18.00S 70.15W
120 D7 Tacna dept Peru
69 B6 Tacoignières France 48.51N 1.40E
110 C2 Tacoma Washington 47.16N 122.30W
104 C1 Tacony dist Philadelphia, Penn
120 E7 Tacopaya Bolivia 17.47S 66.30W
120 F11 Taco Pozo Argentina 25.34S 63.15W
120 D7 Tacora, Vol Chile 17.40S 69.45W
96 R13 Tacoronte Tenerife Canary Is 28.28N 16.25W
92 H10 Tacuane Mozambique 16.22S 36.31E
118 B6 Tacuaral Bolivia 18.59S 58.02W
118 B10 Tacuaras Paraguay 26.52S 57.59W
121 G3 Tacuarembó Uruguay 31.42S 56.00W
121 G4 Tacuarembó dept Uruguay
121 G3 Tacuarembó R Uruguay
121 H4 Tacuarí, R Uruguay
118 C8 Tacuatí Paraguay 23.25S 56.46W
115 C10 Tacubaya dist Mexico
59 K7 Tacumshin L Wexford Irish Rep 52.12N 6.28W
115 E3 Tacupeto Mexico 28.50N 109.10W
119 H6 Tacutu, R Brazil
20 N4 Tadami-gawa R Japan
57 L5 Tadcaster N Yorks Eng 53.53N 1.16W
95 H3 Tadcaster S Africa 27.52S 24.49E
88 R10 Tadeinte Algeria 23.00N 7.43E
88 O7 Tademaït, Plateau du Algeria
101 L1 Tadenet L N W Terr
9 C13 Tadine Loyalty Is Pacific Oc 21.31S 167.53E
88 L6 Tadirhoust Morocco 31.50N 5.00W
89 B2 Tadjakant Mauritania 18.39N 14.32W
88 P5 Tadjemout Algeria 33.55N 2.33E
88 S8 Tadjentourt Algeria 27.40N 8.28E
88 R10 Tadjetaret Algeria 22.41N 7.52E
88 R10 Tadjettaret watercourse Algeria
88 L7 Tadjine, Djebel ben mts Algeria
88 P9 Tadjmout Algeria 25.32N 3.42E
87 J5 Tadjoura Djibouti 11.49N 42.56E
87 J5 Tadjoura, G. de Djibouti
88 P5 Tadjrouna Algeria 33.30N 2.05E
56 J5 Tadley Hants Eng 51.21N 1.08W
56 L3 Tadlow Cambs Eng 52.07N 0.09W
74 K8 Tadmaït Algeria 36.45N 3.55E
56 J3 Tadmarton Oxon Eng 52.02N 1.25W
Tadmor see Palmyra
11 G8 Tadmor New Zealand 41.26S 172.47E
119 C5 Tadó Colombia 5.16N 76.32W
20 L1 Tadoshi Japan 43.49N 142.04E
20 G7 Tadotsu Japan 34.15N 133.43E
98 C5 Tadoussac Quebec 48.09N 69.43W
28 C3 Tadpatri Andhra Prad India 14.55N 77.59E
28 C1 Tadwale Maharashtra India 18.26N 76.10E
43 N8 Tadzhik Uzbekistan U.S.S.R. 40.27N 71.02E
43 K7 Tadzhikabad Tadzhikistan U.S.S.R. 39.06N 70.53E
38 F5 Tadzhikskaya S.S.R U.S.S.R.
Tadzhik S.S.R see Tadzhikskaya S.S.R
96 U7 Tae Lanzarote Canary Is 29.02N 13.38W
53 B3 Tæbring Denmark 56.48N 8.38E
21 C8 Taechŏn N Korea 39.54N 125.31E
21 C9 Taech'ŏngdo isld S Korea
21 D9 Taech'ŏn-ni S Korea 36.25N 126.35E
21 C8 Taedasa-do N Korea 39.49N 124.26E
21 D8 Taedong R N Korea
21 C8 Taedong-man B N Korea
21 D10 Taegu S Korea 35.52N 128.36E
21 E9 Taeha-Dong S Korea 37.40N 130.50E
21 C10 Taehŭksan isld S Korea 34.40N 125.25E
21 D9 Taejŏn S Korea 36.20N 127.26E
122 D14 Taenga atoll Tuamotu Is Pacific Oc 16.18S 143.05W
21 D8 Taep'o-ri S Korea 38.05N 128.35E
53 J7 Tærø isld Denmark 54.58N 12.07E
21 C7 Taeyu-dong N Korea 40.16N 125.36E
10 S5 Tafahi isld Pacific Oc 15.52S 173.55W
75 G2 Tafalla Spain 52.32N 1.41W
35 H3 Tafas Syria 32.44N 36.05E
88 R9 Tafasaset watercourse Algeria
Tafelbaai see Table Bay
95 J7 Tafelberg S Africa 31.37S 25.14E
Tafelberg mt Cape Province see Table Mt
116 B1 Tafelberg mt Curaçao W I 12.23N 69.09W
95 E8 Tafelberg mt S Africa 32.16S 21.35E
117 B3 Tafelberg pk Surinam 3.55N 56.09W
88 J6 Tafelney, C Morocco 31.08N 9.53W
Ta-feng see Ta-chung-chi
15 C7 Tafermaär Moluccas Indon 6.49S 134.12E
66 E4 Tafers Switzerland 46.49N 7.13E
88 M4 Tafersit Morocco 35.03N 3.32W
56 E4 Taf-fechan Res Powys Wales 51.50N 3.23W
56 E4 Taff, R Mid Glam/S Glam Wales
56 E4 Taff's-well S Glam Wales 51.33N 3.16W
35 D7 Taffuh Jordan 31.32N 35.03E
32 E6 Tafihān Iran 29.30N 52.38E
34 C8 Tafila Jordan 30.52N 35.36E
35 F10 Tafila, Jeb. el mt Jordan 30.58N 35.30E
88 L6 Tafilalt reg Morocco
96 V15 Tafira Alta Gran Canaria Canary Is 28.04N 15.28W
89 G7 Tafiré Ivory Coast 9.03N 5.04W
120 F12 Tafi Viejo Argentina 26.43S 65.17W
53 W14 Tafjord Norway 62.14N 7.25E
88 N4 Tafna R Algeria
89 J8 Tafo Ghana 6.15N 0.20W
109 F5 Tafoya New Mexico 36.27N 104.06W
56 B4 Taf, R Dyfed Wales
88 O4 Tafraoua Algeria 34.33N 0.10E
88 J7 Tafraoute Morocco 29.40N 8.58W
Tafrash see Tafresh
88 G8 Tafraut Morocco 27.23N 13.18W
32 D3 Tafresh Iran 34.40N 50.00E
111 E6 Taft California 35.08N 119.28W
32 F5 Taft Iran 31.45N 54.14E
109 P6 Taft Oklahoma 35.45N 95.34W
112 K8 Taft Texas 27.59N 97.25W
32 J6 Taftān, Kūh-e mt Iran 28.37N 61.08E
103 D4 Tafton Pennsylvania 41.25N 75.10W
103 K3 Taftville Connecticut 41.35N 72.03W
28 J7 Tafwap Nicobar Is 7.14N 93.40E
122 A1 Taga W Samoa, Pacific Oc 13.44S 172.27W
113 H4 Tagagawik R Alaska
113 R10 Tagalak I Aleutian Is 51.59N 175.41W
15 G6 Tagan Papua New Guinea 5.39S 143.40E
96 S13 Taganana Tenerife Canary Is 28.33N 16.12W
14 E10 Tagan Harb W Australia
39 D4 Taganka U.S.S.R. 61.20N 148.50E
45 K9 Taganrog U.S.S.R. 47.14N 38.55E
45 K9 Taganrogskiy Zaliv gulf U.S.S.R.
19 M5 Tagapula isld Philippines 12.05N 124.10E
31 G2 Tagarkaty Pass Tadzhikistan U.S.S.R. 37.37N 72.59E
25 M9 Tagaung Burma 23.33N 96.06E
53 W17 Tågavatn L Norway 60.37N 7.23E
20 D8 Tagawa Japan 33.40N 130.48E
45 T2 Tagay U.S.S.R. 54.20N 47.35E
19 H2 Tagaytay Luzon Philippines 14.05N 120.55E
19 H2 Tagaytay Ridge Luzon Philippines
19 L7 Tagbilaran Philippines 9.38N 123.53E
88 O4 Tagdempt Algeria 35.20N 1.15E
87 A2 Tageru, Jeb mt Sudan 16.30N 27.05E
66 N1 Tägerwilen Switzerland 47.38N 9.13E
30 E2 Tage Tsangpo R Xizang Zizhiqu
90 D2 Taggafadi Niger 18.36N 9.13E
121 H7 Taggart, I Chile 49.30S 75.32W
79 C7 Taggia Italy 43.52N 7.50E
Taghistan see Chāh-e Tāqestān
88 M6 Taghit Algeria 30.57N 2.03W
103 G2 Taghkanic Cr New York
88 S12 Taghmeurt Niger 18.49N 8.50E
59 J7 Taghmon Wexford Irish Rep 52.19N 6.39W
85 D5 Taghrīfat Libya 29.12N 17.22E
47 J6 Tagil R U.S.S.R.
44 D5 Tagiloni Georgia U.S.S.R. 42.32N 41.44E
101 F5 Tagish Yukon Terr 60.18N 134.16W
101 F6 Tagish L Br Columbia
80 H4 Tagliacozzo Italy 42.05N 13.15E
79 N2 Tagliamento R Italy
79 M4 Táglio di Po Italy 45.01N 12.12E
42 G5 Tagna U.S.S.R. 53.35N 101.52E
24 C8 Tagnek Xizang Zizhiqu China 34.10N 81.25E
71 E3 Tagnière, la France 46.47N 4.12E
69 G5 Tagnon France 49.27N 4.17E
59 K7 Tagoat Wexford Irish Rep 52.15N 6.23W
19 M7 Tagoloan R Mindanao Philippines
19 L7 Tagolo Pt Mindanao Philippines 8.42N 123.23E
77 T11 Tagomago isld Balearic Is 39.02N 1.39E
88 L7 Tagounite Morocco 29.58N 5.36W
24 F10 Tagra R Xizang Zizhiqu
88 R11 Tagrina watercourse Algeria
52 K3 Tågsjöberg Sweden 63.40N 16.45E
82 J4 Tagu Romania 46.55N 24.03E
118 G2 Taguá Brazil 11.45S 44.30W
118 F3 Taguatinga Brazil 12.16S 46.25W
118 F3 Taguatinga, Serra mts Brazil
19 L6 Tagubanhan isld Philippines 11.07N 123.07E
19 K3 Tagudin Luzon Philippines 16.59N 120.28E
88 N11 Taguenout Hagguerét Mali 21.14N 0.48W
89 J1 Taguenout Hagguerét Mali 21.14N 0.48W
88 F9 Taguersimet Morocco 24.09N 15.10W
88 P4 Taguine Algeria 34.52N 2.20E
42 F4 Tagul R U.S.S.R.
15 M9 Tagula Louisiade Arch 11.21S 153.11E
15 M9 Tagula I Louisiade Arch
42 F5 Tagul'skiy Khrebet mts U.S.S.R.
19 M8 Tagum Mindanao Philippines 7.25N 125.54E
108 J1 Tagus N Dakota 48.22N 101.57W
Tagus R Portugal see Tejo R
Tagus R Spain see Tajo R
41 N7 Tagyndzhinskiy Krebet mts U.S.S.R.
88 G8 Tah Morocco 27.45N 13.02W
122 A15 Tahaa isld Society Is Pacific Oc 16.40S 151.30W
88 R10 Tahabert Algeria 23.05N 7.52E
11 D13 Tahakopa New Zealand 46.32S 169.25E
77 M6 Tahal Spain 37.14N 2.16W
88 L4 Tahala Morocco 34.04N 4.25W
18 C7 Tahan R Pen Malaysia
122 D15 Tahanéa atoll Tuamotu Is Pacific Oc 16.45S 144.40W
18 C7 Tahan, Gunong mt Pen Malaysia 4.34N 102.17E
20 L7 Tahara Japan 34.40N 137.18E
122 C12 Taharuu, R Tahiti Pacific Oc
88 Q10 Tahat, Mt Algeria 23.18N 5.33E
122 C11 Tahaute, R Tahiti Pacific Oc
25 N7 Tahawndam Burma 28.10N 97.44E
21 C1 Tahe Heilongjiang China 52.21N 124.48E
21 C2 Ta He R Heilongjiang China
11 H2 Taheke New Zealand 35.27S 173.43E
44 J10 Tāher Gurāb Iran 37.24N 49.16E
32 E7 Tāherī Iran 27.43N 52.20E
32 G7 Taherū'ī Iran 26.35N 57.07E
101 G6 Tahi R Br Columbia
96 V8 Tahiche Lanzarote Canary Is 29.00N 13.33W
88 Q10 Tahifet Algeria 22.58N 5.55E
Tahir see Arguvan
Tahiri see Tāherī
101 R1 Tahiryuak L Victoria I, N W Terr 70.56N 112.20W
101 H6 Tahitan Br Col 58.02N 131.02W
122 C12 Tahiti isld Society Is Pacific Oc
122 B15 Tahiti, Archipel de Pacific Oc
31 B6 Tahlab R Iran/Pakistan
109 Q6 Tahlequah Oklahoma 35.57N 94.58W
111 D2 Tahoe City California 39.10N 120.09W
111 D2 Tahoe, L Calif/Nevada 39.05N 120.00W
101 T1 Tahoe L Victoria I, N W Terr
111 D3 Tahoe Valley California 38.55N 120.00W
112 F2 Tahoka Texas 33.11N 101.48W
11 J6 Tahora New Zealand 39.02S 174.48E
11 L7 Tahoraiti New Zealand 40.14S 176.04E
89 M4 Tahoua Niger 14.57N 5.19E
89 M4 Tahoua reg Niger
89 K8 Tahoun Togo 7.06N 1.40E
106 J3 Tahquamenon Falls Michigan 46.34N 85.17W
106 J3 Tahquamenon, R Michigan
34 N7 Tahrir Iraq 31.58N 45.24E
32 G6 Tahrūd Iran 29.27N 57.48E
32 G6 Tahrūd R Iran
25 E2 Ta Hsai Burma 20.55N 98.28E
101 K11 Tahsis Br Col 49.56N 126.40W
74 H9 Taht R Algeria
85 L6 Tahta Egypt 26.47N 31.31E
36 D3 Tahtaköprü Turkey 39.56N 29.37E
36 E6 Tahtali Dağ mt Turkey 36.32N 30.26E
36 J4 Tahtalı Dağı mt Turkey 38.46N 36.45E
101 K9 Tahtsa R Br Columbia
120 E8 Tahua Bolivia 19.55S 67.45W
120 D4 Tahuamanú Peru 11.23S 69.27W
120 D4 Tahuamanú, R Peru
122 V14 Tahuata isld Marquesas Is Pacific Oc 9.58S 139.05W
19 D2 Tahulandang isld Indonesia 2.22N 125.26E
19 D2 Tahuna Indonesia 3.38N 125.30E
11 K4 Tahuna New Zealand 37.29S 175.32E
75 N3 Tahús Spain 42.18N 1.11E
86 E5 Tahwâi Egypt 30.22N 30.52E
89 F9 Tai Ivory Coast 5.52N 7.28W
87 F5 Taia mt Ethiopia 10.50N 36.38E
Taiabad see Tayyebāt
89 C7 Taiama Sierra Leone 8.15N 12.01W
T'ai-an see Yi'an
21 B7 Tai'an Liaoning China 41.29N 122.25E
22 L8 Tai'an Shandong China 36.15N 117.10E
122 D12 Taiarapu pen Tahiti Pacific Oc
122 D14 Taiaro atoll Tuamotu Is Pacific Oc 15.42S 144.34W
11 O11 Taiaroa Hd New Zealand 45.46S 170.43E
23 C9 Tai Au Mun Hong Kong 22.17N 114.17E
23 H4 Taibai Jiangxi China 29.06N 117.38E
23 D1 Taibai Shaanxi China 34.02N 107.18E
23 D2 Taibai Shan mt pk Shaanxi China 33.58N 107.42E
109 F7 Taiban New Mexico 34.26N 104.01W
Taïbé see Taiyibah, At
35 F1 Taïbé, Ett Lebanon 33.17N 35.31E
Taïbé Ett Syria see Taiyibah, Et
77 M4 Taibilla R Spain
77 N4 Taibilla, Canal de Spain
77 M4 Taibilla, Sierra de mts Spain
96 P12 Taibique Hierro Canary Is 27.42N 17.59W
29 L4 Taibpur Bihar India 26.22N 88.13E
23 J3 Taicang Jiangsu China 31.30N 121.05E
23 J6 T'ai-chung Taiwan 24.09N 120.40E
23 J6 T'ai-chung-hsien Taiwan 24.15N 120.43E
88 J7 Taïdalt Morocco 28.40N 9.48W
23 H1 Tai'erzhuang Shandong China 34.36N 117.46E
33 D6 Ţā'if, Aţ Saudi Arabia 21.15N 40.21E
Taigong see Taijiang
22 J8 Taigu Shanxi China 37.24N 112.31E
23 B9 Tai Hang Hong Kong 22.16N 114.11E
22 K7 Taihang Shan mts Hebei China
23 F1 Taihang Shan mts Shanxi China
22 J8 Taihang Shan mts Shanxi/Hebei China
11 K6 Taihape New Zealand 39.40S 175.48E
23 G2 Taihe Anhui China 33.10N 115.40E
23 G5 Taihe Jiangxi China 26.47N 114.52E
Taihezhen see Shehong
20 Q8 Taiho Okinawa Japan 26.39N 128.07E
23 G3 Taihu Anhui China 30.22N 116.20E
23 J3 Tai Hu L Jiangsu China
23 E5 Taijiang Guizhou China 26.37N 108.20E
22 B8 Taijnar He R Qinghai China
Taikang see Dorbod Monggolzu Zizhixian
23 G1 Taikang Henan China 34.01N 114.59E
31 D4 Taikhak Afghanistan 33.32N 67.47E
20 N2 Taiki Japan 42.27N 143.17E
25 C4 Taikkyi Burma 17.16N 95.55E
93 H10 Taikus Tanzania 4.04S 36.40E
21 C4 Tailai Heilongjiang China 46.25N 123.25E
18 C6 Taileleo Indonesia 1.45S 99.08E
12 E6 Tailem Bend S Australia 35.17S 139.27E
Tailfingen see Neckartailfingen
64 G7 Tailfingen W Germany 48.15N 9.01E
70 K4 Taillebois France 48.48N 0.26W
72 C4 Taillebourg France 45.51N 0.38W
71 H6 Taillefer mt France 45.02N 5.55E
61 O6 Tailles Belgium 50.14N 5.45E
70 H5 Taillis France 48.12N 1.14W
Tai Long Head see D'Aguilar, C
59 K5 Tailor's Rock Dublin Irish Rep 53.29N 6.02W
121 H4 Taim Brazil 32.29S 52.32W
Taima see Taymā'
20 B4 Taima Kanagawa Japan
31 B4 Taimani reg Afghanistan
42 F2 Taimba U.S.S.R. 60.21N 98.59E
58 H3 Tain Highland Scotland 57.48N 4.04W
89 H8 Tain R Ghana
23 J7 T'ai-nan Taiwan 23.01N 120.14E
87 E7 Taine Ethiopia 7.52N 34.50E
71 C1 Taingy France 47.37N 3.25E
121 J2 Tainhas R Brazil
23 H5 Taining Fujian China 26.54N 117.10E
71 F6 Tain-l'Hermitage France 45.05N 4.50E
23 B8 Tai No Hong Kong 22.23N 114.13E
61 D4 Taintignes Belgium 50.33N 3.21E
69 M7 Taintrux France 48.15N 6.53E
79 K2 Táio Italy 46.18N 11.05E
118 G4 Taiobeiras Brazil 15.47S 42.13W
15 J1 Taiof I Papua New Guinea 5.30S 154.40E
122 U13 Tai-o-haé Marquesas Is Pacific Oc 8.55S 140.04W
Taion see Ta-an
51 O9 Taipale Finland 62.37N 29.20E
51 N10 Taipalsaari Finland 61.10N 28.05E
118 F3 Taipas Brazil 12.15S 47.08W
23 J6 T'ai-pei Taiwan 25.05N 121.32E
23 H3 Taiping Anhui China 30.19N 118.11E
23 D7 Taiping Guangxi China 22.35N 106.59E
23 E7 Taiping Guangxi China 23.40N 110.39E
18 A7 Taiping Pen Malaysia 4.54N 100.42E
22 E7 Taipingbao Gansu China 38.55N 100.40E
21 C5 Taipingchuan Jilin China 44.25N 123.07E
21 D6 Taipingchuan Jilin China 42.35N 127.18E
21 E3 Taipinggou Heilongjiang China 48.08N 130.40E
21 B4 Taiping Ling mt pk Nei Monggol Zizhiqu China 47.33N 120.24E
21 C7 Taipingshao Liaoning China 40.52N 125.10E
117 J7 Taipu Brazil 5.36S 35.35W
28 K2 Taipudia Assam India 27.41N 94.25E
20 O4 Taira Japan 37.04N 140.54E
20 Q8 Taira Okinawa Japan 26.38N 128.09E
20 O1 Tairadate-kaikyō str Japan
21 D11 Taira shima isld Japan 29.42N 129.32E
11 K4 Tairua New Zealand 37.01S 175.52E
32 A3 Tairuq Iraq 34.33N 45.39E
35 E1 Taïr Zebna Lebanon 33.14N 35.23E
18 E8 Tais Sumatra Indon 4.05S 102.29E
20 J2 Taisei Japan 42.14N 139.48E
20 H2 Taisetsuzan Nat.Park Japan
119 C9 Taisha Ecuador 2.24S 77.31W
20 F6 Taisha Japan 35.26N 132.40E
23 F7 Taishan Guangdong China 22.15N 112.45E
23 F7 Taishan Guangdong China 22.17N 112.46E
23 H5 Taishun Zhejiang China 27.35N 119.45E
65 J5 Taiskirchen Austria 48.16N 13.34E
88 H7 Taissa, Jbel mts Morocco
11 E4 Taita New Zealand 41.11S 174.57E
93 K9 Taita dist Kenya
93 K9 Taita Hills Kenya
23 B10 Tai Tam B Hong Kong
23 B9 Tai Tam Harbour Hong Kong
23 B10 Tai Tam Pen Hong Kong
23 B9 Tai Tam Res Hong Kong 22.15N 114.12E
121 J6 Taitao, Pen. de Chile
121 J5 Taitao, Pta Chile 45.50S 75.10W
121 H5 Taitao, Pta C Chile 45.50S 75.06W
11 L11 Taitapu New Zealand 43.40S 172.34E
24 F6 Taitema Hu L Xinjiang Uygur Zizhiqu China
20 E2 Taitō dist Tōkyō Japan
22 L6 Taitouying Hebei China 40.01N 119.11E
23 J7 T'ai-tung Taiwan 22.43N 121.10E
22 L6 Taituying Hebei China 40.01N 119.11E

51 N6 Taivalkoski Finland 65.35N 28.20E
51 J11 Taivassalo Finland 60.30N 21.30E
23 B8 Tai Wai Hong Kong 22.23N 114.10E
23 B10 Tai Wan Hong Kong 22.10N 114.13E
23 J7 Taiwan *nat rep* E Asia
23 H6 T'ai-wan Hai-hsia *str* China/Taiwan
23 H6 T'aiwan Haixia *str* Guangdong China
23 C9 Tai Wan Tau Hong Kong 22.17N 114.17E
23 H2 Tai Xian Jiangsu China 32.31N 120.08E
23 J2 Taixing Jiangsu China 32.08N 120.00E
84 D7 Taïyetos Óros *mts* Greece
35 D4 Taiyiba Israel 32.16N 35.01E
35 E3 Taiyiba Israel 32.36N 35.27E
34 C8 Taiyiba Jordan 30.15N 35.27E
35 E6 Taiyiba Jordan 31.57N 35.18E
35 F3 Taiyiba Jordan 32.33N 35.43E
35 F3 Taiyiba *R* Jordan
35 H3 Taiyibah, At Syria 32.33N 36.15E
35 F2 Taiyibah, Et Syria 32.57N 35.43E
86 M6 Taiyiba, Wâdî *watercourse* Egypt
86 N8 Taiyib el Ism, Jebel *mt* Saudi Arabia 28.36N 34.54E
22 J8 Taiyuan Shanxi China 37.50N 112.30E
22 J8 Taiyue Shan *mts* Shanxi China
21 G10 Taiza Japan 35.46N 135.08E
21 C7 Taize He *R* Liaoning China
24 H10 Taizhao Xizang Zizhiqu China 30.00N 93.01E
Taizhou *see* Linhai
23 H2 Taizhou Jiangsu China 32.27N 119.56E
23 J4 Taizhou Wan *B* Zhejiang China
21 C7 Taizi He *R* Liaoning China

33 F10 Ta'izz Yemen 13.35N 44.02E
32 F5 Tājābād Iran 30.02N 54.22E
31 E7 Tajal Pakistan 26.53N 69.04E
18 G7 Tajam, Gunung *hill* Indonesia 2.49S 107.50E
Tajandu *see* Tayandu
85 C7 Tajarḥī Libya 24.21N 14.28E
85 G7 Tāj, At Libya 24.13N 23.19E
78 B13 Tajerouine Tunisia 35.53N 8.32E
88 S4 Tajerouine Tunisia 35.51N 8.34E
120 E6 Tajibo Bolivia 14.07S 66.33W
Tajik S.S.R *see* Tadzhikskaya S.S.R
20 N4 Tajima Japan 37.11N 139.46E
20 L6 Tajimi Japan 35.22N 137.10E
21 E7 Tajin-dong N Korea 41.14N 129.45E
109 D7 Tajique New Mexico 34.45N 106.18W
87 N5 Tajis *mt* Somalia 11.41N 51.05E
115 C2 Tajito Mexico 31.00N 112.23W
76 G9 Tajo *R* Spain
28 L1 Tajobum Assam India 28.22N 96.34E
30 J7 Tajpur Bihar India 25.51N 85.41E
32 D3 Tajrīsh Iran 35.48N 51.20E
120 F9 Tajsara, Cord de *mts* Bolivia
88 R10 Tajuienout Algeria 23.18N 6.38E
115 O10 Tajumulco, Vol. de Guatemala 15.03N 91.54W
75 E6 Tajuña, R Spain
96 P10 Tajuya La Palma Canary Is 28.37N 17.52W
25 E4 Tak Thailand 16.51N 99.08E
9 D1 Taka *atoll* Marshall Is Pacific Oc 11.07N 169.40E
84 D7 Táka *L* Greece 37.26N 22.22E
32 B2 Takāb Iran 36.24N 47.06E
93 M2 Takabba Kenya 3.27N 40.14E
20 M4 Takada Japan 37.06N 138.16E
20 P3 Takagi Japan 38.22N 141.08E
20 O5 Takahagi Japan 36.42N 140.42E
20 J6 Takahama Japan 35.30N 135.32E
20 E10 Takaharu Kyūshū Japan 31.52N 131.03E
20 G7 Takahashi Japan 34.48N 133.38E
20 G7 Takahashi-gawa *R* Japan
20 O3 Takahata Japan 38.00N 140.10E
34 Q2 Takah Qayasī, Kūh-e- *mt* Iran 36.42N 48.02E
20 D2 Takaido *dist* Tōkyō Japan
20 C3 Takaishi Kanagawa Japan
20 E9 Takaj Japan 32.10N 131.26E
11 G7 Takaka New Zealand 40.52S 172.49E
29 E7 Takal Madhya Prad India 21.43N 76.32E
88 R10 Takalous *watercourse* Algeria
89 K2 Takalout Mali 18.09N 1.23E
43 N7 Takalyk 2-oy Uzbekistan U.S.S.R. 40.43N 71.55E
117 A2 Takama Guyana 5.30N 58.00W
89 J3 Takamadasset, Mts. du Mali
26 S14 Takamaka Mahé I Seychelles, Ind Oc 4.46S 55.30E
20 H7 Takamatsu Japan 34.20N 134.01E
20 E9 Takamori Japan 32.49N 131.08E
20 A2 Takane Saitama Japan
20 O1 Takanosu Japan 40.16N 140.21E
46 Q2 Takanysh U.S.S.R. 55.52N 51.02E
20 K5 Takaoka Honshu Japan 36.47N 137.00E
20 E10 Takaoka Kyūshū Japan 31.58N 131.20E
11 L7 Takapau New Zealand 40.02S 176.22E
122 C14 Takapoto *atoll* Tuamotu Is Pacific Oc 14.35S 145.13W
11 J3 Takapuna New Zealand 36.48S 174.47E
11 C5 Takapu Road New Zealand 41.11S 174.49E
21 D11 Takara jima *isld* Japan 29.06N 129.14E
122 D14 Takaroa *atoll* Tuamotu Is Pacific Oc 14.30S 144.58W
28 G2 Takarpo Xizang Zizhiqu 27.35N 89.08E
20 H7 Takasago Japan 34.45N 134.46E
20 M5 Takasaki Honshu Japan 36.20N 139.00E
20 E7 Taka-shima *isld* Honshu Japan 34.51N 131.50E
20 C8 Taka-shima *isld* Kyūshū Japan 33.28N 129.44E
28 H7 Takashin Nicobar Is 8.10N 93.30E
21 H10 Takato Japan 35.55N 138.06E
94 F4 Takatshwana Botswana 22.36S 21.55E
20 A2 Takatsuki Tōkyō Japan
20 F8 Takatsuki yama *mt* Japan 33.11N 132.39E
119 J6 Takatu *R* Guyana
11 J3 Takatu Pt New Zealand 36.22S 174.53E
93 L9 Takaungu Kenya 3.42S 39.51E
25 E2 Ta-Kaw Burma 21.13N 98.40E
20 L5 Takayama Japan 36.09N 137.16E
Takazze *watercourse see* Tekezē *watercourse*
25 F9 Tak Bai Thailand 6.25N 101.59E
20 H6 Takeda Honshu Japan 35.20N 134.49E
Takedatsu *see* Taketazu
20 K6 Takefu Japan 35.54N 136.10E
20 F7 Takehara Japan 34.20N 132.52E
56 M4 Takeley Essex Eng 51.52N 0.15E
43 J6 Takeli Tadzhikistan U.S.S.R. 40.34N 69.26E
20 F7 Takemori Japan 34.05N 132.02E
20 E1 Takenozuka *dist* Tōkyō Japan
25 H7 Takeo Cambodia 11.00N 104.46E
20 D8 Takeo Japan 33.13N 130.00E
25 H7 Takeo *R* Cambodia
20 C7 Takeshiki Japan 34.18N 129.18E
21 E12 Take-shima *isld* Japan 30.51N 130.28E
21 E9 Take-shima *rocks* Japan
20 C3 Takeshita Kanagawa Japan
32 C2 Takestān Iran 36.02N 49.40E
53 T16 Taket *mt* Norway 61.17N 5.32E
20 E8 Taketa Kyūshū Japan 33.00N 131.23E
91 F5 Taketa Zaïre 3.13S 19.08E
21 E11 Taketazu Japan 33.40N 131.33E
Takeum *see* Rawas
43 J7 Takfan Tadzhikistan U.S.S.R. 39.14N 68.36E
34 M9 Takhādīd Iraq 29.58N 44.32E
31 E2 Takhar *prov* Afghanistan
29 G6 Takhatpur Madhya Prad India 22.09N 81.55E
88 O4 Takhemaret Algeria 35.10N 0.39E
43 E6 Takhiatash Uzbekistan U.S.S.R. 42.21N 59.36E

101 F5 Takhini *R* N W Terr
Ta Khli *see* Ban Ta Khli
40 H5 Takhta Khabarovsk U.S.S.R. 53.10N 139.51E
44 E2 Takhta Stavropol' U.S.S.R. 45.54N 42.08E
43 E6 Takhta Turkmeniya U.S.S.R. 41.36N 59.55E
43 G8 Takhta-Bazar Turkmeniya U.S.S.R. 35.38N 62.54E
43 J1 Takhtabrod Kazakhstan U.S.S.R. 52.36N 67.33E
43 F5 Takhtakupyr Uzbekistan U.S.S.R. 43.01N 60.15E
44 B3 Takhtamukay U.S.S.R. 44.57N 38.59E
40 C4 Takhtamygda U.S.S.R. 54.14N 123.38E
32 C4 Takht Apān, Kūh-e *mt* Iran 33.01N 49.25E
31 C5 Takhta Pul Post Afghanistan 31.17N 65.58E
39 E4 Takhtayamsk U.S.S.R. 60.12N 154.40E
32 E6 Takht-e Jamshid *anc site* Iran 29.57N 52.52E
31 F5 Takht-i-Sulaiman *mt* Pakistan 31.36N 70.01E
32 D2 Takht-i-Suleiman *mt* Iran 36.23N 50.59E
39 E4 Takhtoyama *R* U.S.S.R.
15 J2 Taki Bougainville I Papua New Guinea 6.31S 155.53E
101 R2 Takijuq L N W Terr
20 L1 Takikawa Japan 43.35N 141.55E
110 B7 Takilma Oregon 42.04N 123.37W
18 B3 Takingeun Sumatra Indon 4.37N 96.48E
21 J5 Takinoue Japan 44.12N 143.07E
100 R3 Takipy Manitoba 55.25N 100.56W
37 E8 Takırtukur Dağı *mt* Turkey
Takistan *see* Takestān
11 B12 Takitimo Mts New Zealand
Takket *see* Ain el Hadjadj
Taklakot *see* Burang
101 L8 Takla L Br Col
101 L8 Takla Landing Br Col 55.28N 125.58W

Takla Makan *see* Taklimakan Shamo
53 S16 Takle Norway 61.02N 5.20E
24 D6 Taklimakan Shamo *basin* Xinjiang Uygur Zizhiqu China
39 C3 Takloun, Gora *mt* U.S.S.R. 64.03N 143.48E
85 F3 Taknis Libya 32.26N 21.08E

43 J7 Takob Tadzhikistan U.S.S.R. 38.52N 68.56E
20 G6 Tako-bana *C* Japan 35.37N 133.06E
103 A9 Takoma Park Maryland 38.59N 77.00W
104 N8 Takoma Park *dist* Washington D C/Md
89 J9 Takoradi Ghana 4.55N 1.45W
113 J5 Takotna Alaska 63.00N 156.10W
11 H2 Takou B New Zealand
23 B9 Tak Pak Uk Hong Kong 22.19N 114.12E
28 K1 Takpa Shili *mt* Xizang Zizhiqu 30.10N 94.40E
28 J1 Takpa Shiri *mt* Assam India 28.10N 92.52E
28 H1 Takra Xizang Zizhiqu 28.17N 91.16E
37 J2 Taksim *dist* Istanbul Turkey 41.02N 28.58E
113 F6 Takslesluk L Alaska 61.04N 163.00W
Taktak *see* Ţaqţaq

101 G6 Taku Br Col 59.38N 133.50W
122 S15 Taku Mangaréva Pacific Oc 23.05S 134.56W
101 G6 Taku *R* Br Columbia
15 J2 Takuan, Mt Bougainville I Papua New Guinea 6.29S 155.37E
Takua Pa *see* Ban Takua Pa
101 F5 Taku Arm *L* Yukon/Br Col
25 E8 Takua Thung Thailand 8.22N 98.27E
113 V7 Taku Harbor Alaska 58.03N 134.00W
90 D8 Takum Nigeria 7.18N 9.59E
122 E14 Takumé *atoll* Tuamotu Is Pacific Oc 15.53S 142.10W
91 E6 Takundi Zaïre 4.45S 16.39E
23 A7 Ta Kut Burma 22.15N 98.58E
15 M3 Takwa Malaita I Solomon Is 8.21S 160.47E
Tal *see* Tut
31 G3 Tal Pakistan 35.31N 72.20E
76 B3 Tal Spain 42.47N 9.00W
90 L7 Tala Cent Afr Rep 9.30N 22.40E
86 E4 Tala Egypt 30.41N 30.56E
121 G5 Tala Uruguay 34.24S 55.45W
19 D5 Talaga Moluccas Indon 2.13S 125.56E
31 G4 Talagang Pakistan 32.55N 72.29E
121 B4 Talagante Chile 33.40S 70.50W
32 J8 Talagh Ramazan Iran 25.59N 60.15E
88 O9 Talahouait Algeria 24.52N 1.05E
25 J7 Ta Lai Vietnam 11.22N 107.24E
26 Q3 Talaimannar Sri Lanka 9.05N 79.43E
72 K9 Talairan France 43.02N 2.39E
72 B5 Talais France 45.29N 1.04W
29 C7 Talaja Gujarat India 21.20N 72.08E
89 M2 Talak *reg* Niger
42 K6 Talakan Chita U.S.S.R. 51.59N 120.12E
40 F7 Talakan Khabarovsk U.S.S.R. 49.39N 133.19E
18 D5 Talakmau, Gunung *mt* Sumatra Indon 0.10N 100.00E
39 D2 Tala-Kyuyel' Yakutsk U.S.S.R. 66.25N 150.00E
39 F1 Tala-Kyuyel' Yakutsk U.S.S.R. 68.34N 155.35E
29 B7 Talala Gujarat India 21.00N 70.39E
109 P5 Talala Oklahoma 36.33N 95.40W
45 C6 Talalayevka Chernigov, Ukraine U.S.S.R. 50.57N 31.55E
45 E6 Talalayevka Sumy, Ukraine U.S.S.R. 50.50N 33.09E
74 E10 Talamagait Morocco 34.53N 3.45W
75 C6 Talamanca de Jarama Spain 40.44N 3.31W
75 G4 Talamantes Spain 41.44N 1.40W
31 G5 Talamba Pakistan 30.30N 72.18E
80 D3 Talamone Italy 42.33N 11.08E
80 D4 Talamone, Golfo di Italy
91 E8 Tala Mugongo Angola 9.42S 17.14E
95 O4 Talana S Africa 28.10S 30.17E
81 C3 Talana Sardinia 40.03N 9.30E
40 E7 Talandzha U.S.S.R. 49.30N 131.32E
Talang *see* Teleng
115 L2 Talanga Honduras 14.25N 87.06W
18 E7 Talang Akar Sumatra Indon 3.15S 103.45E
18 F7 Talangbatu Sumatra Indon 3.59S 105.29E
18 F7 Talangbetutu Sumatra Indon 2.48S 104.42E
18 D7 Talang, Gunung *mt* Sumatra Indon 2.03S 101.21E
18 F7 Talang Jimar Sumatra Indon 3.29S 104.16E
21 B2 Talangkong Nei Monggol Zizhiqu China 51.45N 122.03E
18 F7 Talangrimbo Sumatra Indon 3.26S 105.25E
26 U6 Talankuda Sri Lanka 7.39N 81.45E
28 K2 Talap Assam India 27.43N 95.34E
119 A10 Talara Peru 4.38S 81.18W
77 J7 Talará Spain 36.57N 3.32W
31 B8 Talar-i-Band *mts* Pakistan
77 F2 Talarrubias Spain 39.03N 5.14W
43 K6 Talas Kirgiziya U.S.S.R. 42.30N 72.13E
36 H4 Talas Turkey 38.42N 35.35E
43 K5 Talas *R* Kazakhstan U.S.S.R.
15 L6 Talasea New Britain 5.20S 150.01E
43 K6 Talasskiy Alatau, Khrebet *mts* U.S.S.R.
Talat *see* Maha Sarakham
95 C6 Talata-Ampano Madagascar 21.32S 47.03E
19 C4 Talatakoh *isld* Indonesia 0.20S 122.08E
34 D4 Talat Mūsa *mt* Lebanon 34.02N 36.29E
56 E6 Talaton Devon Eng 50.47N 3.20W
41 O6 Tala-Tumsa U.S.S.R. 67.42N 130.39E
71 E6 Talaudière, la France 45.29N 4.25E
19 E2 Talaud, Kep *islds* Indonesia
88 J6 Talaut n 'Yakoub Morocco 31.00N 8.09W
76 G9 Talaván Spain 39.43N 6.18W
77 N3 Talave, Embalse de *res* Spain 38.30N 1.53W
76 K9 Talavera de la Reina Spain 39.58N 4.50W
118 C10 Talavera, I Paraguay 27.30N 56.25W
77 C3 Talavera la Real Spain 38.53N 6.46W
26 R5 Talawa Sri Lanka 8.14N 80.21E
26 S8 Talawakele Sri Lanka 6.57N 80.40E
13 F4 Talawanta Queensland 18.38S 140.15E
26 U7 Talawayaya Sri Lanka 7.16N 81.30E
15 K6 Talawe, Mt New Britain 5.34S 148.24E
25 N8 Talawgyi Burma 25.04N 97.24E
26 Q5 Talawila Sri Lanka 8.08N 79.42E
42 F4 Talaya Irkutsk U.S.S.R. 55.37N 97.44E
39 E4 Talaya Magadan U.S.S.R. 61.22N 152.45E
19 M8 Talayan Mindanao Philippines 6.56N 124.24E
77 N5 Talayón *mt* Spain 37.34N 1.33W
76 H9 Talayuela Spain 39.59N 5.36W
75 H8 Talayuelas Spain 39.50N 1.18W
75 F8 Talayuelo *mt* Spain 39.57N 2.04W
21 D6 Talazhan Jilin China 43.45N 128.35E
34 P6 Talazī *R* Iran
30 B7 Talbahat Uttar Prad India 25.02N 78.26E
14 E9 Talbot W Australia 30.43S 123.30E
103 B9 Talbot *co* Maryland
14 F2 Talbot, C W Australia 13.49S 126.42E
105 F7 Talbot I Florida 30.28N 81.27W
97 M2 Talbot Inlet N W Terr
100 S4 Talbot L Manitoba
14 F7 Talbot, Mt W Australia 26.08S 126.40E
105 C5 Talbotton Georgia 32.41N 84.31W
12 J4 Talbragar *R* New S Wales
121 B5 Talca Chile 35.28S 71.40W
121 B5 Talca *prov* Chile
121 A6 Talcahuano Chile 36.40S 73.10W
121 B4 Talca, Pta *C* Chile 33.28S 71.45W
29 J7 Talcher Orissa India 21.00N 85.18E
89 L4 Talcho Niger 14.44N 3.28E
112 M2 Talco Texas 33.22N 95.06W
104 E9 Talcott W Virginia 37.40N 80.46W
40 C5 Taldan U.S.S.R. 53.41N 124.48E
46 L2 Taldom U.S.S.R. 56.49N 37.30E
13 F4 Taldora Queensland 19.34S 141.17E
66 P1 Taldorf W Germany 47.44N 9.31E
43 E5 Taldyk Kara-Kalpak, Uzbekistan U.S.S.R. 43.44N 59.13E
43 F6 Taldyk Kara-Kalpak, Uzbekistan U.S.S.R. 41.59N 60.24E
31 G1 Taldyk *pass* Tadzhikistan U.S.S.R. 39.47N 73.14E
45 V6 Taldykuduk Kazakhstan U.S.S.R. 50.07N 49.30E
43 N4 Taldy-Kurgan Kazakhstan U.S.S.R. 45.02N 78.23E
43 N5 Taldysu Kirgiziya U.S.S.R. 42.49N 78.30E
66 E8 Talefre, Aiguille de *mt* France/Italy 45.54N 7.00E
28 B1 Talegaon Poona, Maharashtra India 18.41N 74.14E
29 F7 Talegaon Wardha, Maharashtra India 20.20N 78.10E
87 M6 Taleh Somalia 9.09N 48.22E
32 C4 Taleh Zang Iran 32.50N 48.45E
32 D5 Tal-e Khosravī Iran 30.50N 51.29E
9 T13 Taleki Tonga *atoll* Tonga, Pacific Oc 20.24S 174.32W
9 T13 Taleki Vavu'u *atoll* Tonga, Pacific Oc 20.20S 174.32W
77 F10 Talembote Morocco 35.16N 5.08W
29 E6 Talen Madhya Prad India 23.32N 76.48E
72 C6 Talence France 44.50N 0.35W
110 C7 Talent Oregon 42.16N 122.48W
66 C5 Talent *R* Switzerland
56 D2 Talerddig Powys Wales 52.35N 3.34W
44 J10 Ţālesh, Kūhhā-ye *mts* Iran
86 M5 Tal'et el Badan *hill* Egypt 30.27N 34.03E
43 M5 Talgar Kazakhstan U.S.S.R. 43.17N 77.15E
14 C5 Talga R W Australia
56 E4 Talgarth Powys Wales 52.00N 3.15W
53 T20 Talgje Norway 59.07N 5.51E
53 T20 Talgje *isld* Norway 59.07N 5.51E
30 C5 Talgram Uttar Prad India 27.03N 79.40E
87 E1 Talguharai Sudan 18.19N 35.56E
28 B3 Talgupka Karnataka India 14.09N 74.50E
85 H7 Talh *wadi* Egypt
76 C7 Talhadas Portugal 40.40N 8.19W
33 E8 Talḥah Saudi Arabia 17.48N 43.30E
32 F6 Tal Halāl Iran 28.50N 55.02E
76 F6 Talhas Portugal 41.29N 6.41W
33 G9 Talḥ, Aţ S Yemen 15.02N 47.22E
12 C5 Talia S Australia 33.16S 134.53E
19 D4 Taliabu *isld* Moluccas Indon
19 M6 Talibon Philippines 10.09N 124.20E
Ta-lien *see* Luda

77 B3 Táliga Spain 38.32N 7.01W
30 L7 Talihari Bihar India 25.05N 87.44E
109 P7 Talihina Oklahoma 34.46N 95.04W
Tal-i-Khusrovi *see* Tal-e Khosravī
28 C2 Talikota Karnataka India 16.31N 76.20E
19 M8 Talikud *isld* Mindanao Philippines 6.56N 125.41E
19 J2 Talim *isld* Luzon Philippines
117 B4 Talimã Brazil 1.59N 55.05W
43 H7 Talimardzhan Turkmeniya U.S.S.R. 38.10N 65.27E
31 E3 Tal-i-Mir Ghazi Afghanistan 35.44N 69.20E
120 F9 Talina Bolivia 21.47S 65.47W
Taling *see* Teleng
88 K6 Taliouine Morocco 30.30N 7.48W
28 B4 Taliparamba Kerala India 12.02N 75.20E
87 C8 Tali Post Sudan 5.55N 30.44E
31 E2 Taliq-an Afghanistan 36.46N 69.29E
19 L6 Talisay Philippines 10.15N 123.46E
19 M7 Talisayan Mindanao Philippines 8.58N 124.57E
19 D3 Talisei *isld* Indonesia 1.50N 125.06E
Talish Mts *see* Talyshskiye Gory *mts*
42 C6 Talitsa Altay U.S.S.R. 51.06N 84.22E
45 K4 Talitsa Lipetsk U.S.S.R. 52.44N 38.44E
47 J5 Talitsa Sverdlovsk U.S.S.R. 61.11N 60.22E
47 J7 Talitsa Sverdlovsk U.S.S.R. 57.04N 63.44E
47 L4 Talitsa Sverdlovsk U.S.S.R. 56.50N 58.48E
45 M4 Talitskiy Chamlyk U.S.S.R. 52.03N 40.34E
18 M10 Taliwang Indonesia 8.45S 116.55E
Tal-i-Zangu *see* Taleh Zang
80 N3 Taljola, Rtic *pt* Yugoslavia 42.58N 16.00E
87 J7 Talkalk Ethiopia 6.25N 43.50E
63 N5 Talkau W Germany 53.34N 10.34E
57 J6 Talke Staffs Eng 53.04N 2.16W
113 M5 Talkeetna Alaska 62.20N 150.09W
113 N5 Talkeetna *R* Alaska
113 N6 Talkeetna Mts Alaska
32 B1 Talkeh *R* Iran
86 F3 Talkha Egypt 31.04N 31.22E
32 G4 Talkhi Āb Iran 33.14N 57.50E
24 D3 Talki Davan *pass* Xinjiang Uygur Zizhiqu China 44.28N 81.05E
51 O3 Talkkunapää *mt* Finland 68.11N 28.45E
50 A3 Tálknafjördhur *B* Iceland
50 A3 Tálkni *C* Iceland 65.39N 24.05W
30 E3 Talkot Nepal 29.37N 81.19E
86 E9 Talla Egypt 28.05N 30.43E
79 L7 Talla Italy 43.36N 11.47E
90 H8 Talla *tribe* Cent Afr Rep
85 G8 Tallāb, Aţ Libya 24.01N 23.12E
37 G9 Tall Abū Zāhir Iraq 36.52N 42.29E
107 K8 Talladega Alabama 33.25N 86.07W
34 K2 Tall 'Āfar Iraq 36.22N 42.27E
59 K5 Tallaght Dublin Irish Rep 53.17N 6.22W
107 G10 Tallahala *R* Mississippi
105 C7 Tallahassee Florida 30.26N 84.19W
107 F7 Tallahatchie *R* Mississippi
34 O8 Tall al Laḥm Iraq 30.47N 46.24E
Tall al Muqayyar *see* Ur of the Chaldees
Tall al Warkā *see* Erech
56 C7 Talland Cornwall Eng 50.20N 4.29W
12 H6 Tallangatta Victoria 36.14S 147.19E
77 O5 Tallante Spain 37.38N 1.10W
105 B4 Tallapoosa Georgia 33.43N 85.19W
107 L8 Tallapoosa *R* Ala/Georgia
71 J8 Tallard France 44.28N 6.03E
57 G2 Talla Res Borders Scotland 55.29N 3.25W
52 J5 Tallåsen Sweden 61.52N 16.00E
107 L9 Tallassee Alabama 32.31N 85.54W
86 D4 Tallât el Gabâbîn *hill* Egypt 30.32N 30.05E
86 D4 Tallât el Garw *hill* Egypt 30.37N 30.13E
Tall Bisah *see* Tell Bīsa
72 B8 Taller France 43.52N 1.04W
14 B8 Tallering Pk W Australia 28.03S 115.38E
56 D4 Talley Dyfed Wales 51.58N 3.59W
56 L2 Tallington Lincs Eng 52.40N 0.24W
46 E1 Tallinn Estonia U.S.S.R. 59.22N 24.48E
51 J5 Talljärv Sweden 66.17N 22.20E
34 L2 Tall Kayf Iraq 36.30N 43.08E
Tall Köchak *see* Tel Kotchek
71 J5 Talloires France 45.50N 6.14E
67 P12 Tallone Corsica 42.09N 9.29E
35 E1 Talloûssa Lebanon 33.14N 35.29E
59 F7 Tallow Waterford Irish Rep 52.05N 8.00W
100 P6 Tall Pines Saskatchewan 52.20N 102.38W
107 G2 Tallula Illinois 39.58N 89.58W
107 E9 Tallulah Louisiana 32.22N 91.12W
34 K2 Tall 'Uwaynāt Iraq 36.43N 42.19E
35 E4 Talluza Jordan 32.16N 35.14E
111 A2 Talmage California 39.07N 123.10W
109 N2 Talmage Kansas 39.02N 97.16W
108 P9 Talmage Nebraska 40.32N 96.00W
100 O9 Talmage Saskatchewan 49.46N 103.40W
79 O3 Talmassons Italy 45.56N 13.07E
71 G2 Talmay France 47.22N 5.27E
35 B8 Talme Bilu Israel 31.27N 34.38E
42 C5 Tal'menka U.S.S.R. 53.50N 83.36E
88 H12 Talmeust Mauritania 19.01N 11.35W
35 C6 Talme Yehi'el Israel 31.45N 34.46E
35 B7 Talmey Yafe Israel 31.37N 34.36E
88 N7 Talmine Algeria 29.22N 0.30W
72 A3 Talmont-St. Hilaire France 46.28N 1.36W
41 E6 Talnakh U.S.S.R. 69.30N 88.52E
39 F6 Tal'niki U.S.S.R. 55.40N 155.44E
42 G5 Tal'niki U.S.S.R. 52.50N 102.18E
45 B8 Tal'noye Ukraine U.S.S.R. 48.55N 30.40E
22 B2 Tal Nuur *L* Mongolia
29 D7 Taloda Maharashtra India 21.32N 74.11E
87 C5 Talodi Sudan 10.40N 30.25E
19 L1 Talofofo B Guam Pacific Oc
19 L1 Talofolo Guam Pacific Oc 13.20N 144.46E
109 M5 Taloga Oklahoma 36.02N 98.58W
88 P9 Talohak Algeria 24.46N 2.20E
31 C8 Taloi Ra Pakistan
18 N5 Talok Borneo Indon 1.00N 118.53E
28 J2 Talong Assam India 27.31N 92.56E
25 E2 Ta-long Burma 21.26N 98.37E
81 C3 Taloro *R* Sardinia
88 G12 Talorza Mauritania 18.57N 12.22W
25 G2 Ta Loung San *mt* Laos 21.54N 102.08E
88 J7 Taloust Morocco 29.31N 9.40W
45 M5 Talovaya U.S.S.R. 51.06N 40.45E
44 H3 Talovka Dagestan U.S.S.R. 44.16N 46.37E
39 H4 Talovka Kamchatka U.S.S.R. 62.27N 165.19E
42 E4 Talovka Krasnoyarsk U.S.S.R. 57.12N 93.09E
45 R7 Talovka Volgograd U.S.S.R. 49.59N 45.02E
39 H4 Talovka *R* U.S.S.R.
46 Q4 Talovoye Kazakhstan U.S.S.R. 51.35N 50.35E
39 G4 Talovskoye, Oz *L* U.S.S.R. 61.15N 164.57E
40 E4 Taloye Amur U.S.S.R. 54.06N 129.25E
42 F4 Taloye Krasnoyarsk U.S.S.R. 55.23N 95.45E
40 D1 Taloye Yakutsk U.S.S.R. 60.28N 127.36E
109 E5 Talpa New Mexico 36.19N 105.36W
112 H4 Talpa Texas 31.46N 99.44W
115 G7 Talpa *pk* Mexico 20.22N 104.58W
29 H7 Talpada Orissa India 21.10N 83.22E
116 O2 Talparo R Trinidad & Tobago
31 G3 Tal Pass Pakistan 35.46N 72.15E
26 R10 Talpe Sri Lanka 6.01N 80.18E
26 S7 Talpitigala Sri Lanka 7.04N 80.59E
35 B2 Talpiyot *sub* Jerusalem
105 C7 Talquin, L Florida 30.25N 84.32W
95 J4 Talsen S Africa 28.01S 25.22E
35 C6 Tal Shaḥar Israel 31.48N 34.54E
46 E2 Talsi Latvia U.S.S.R. 57.18N 22.39E
88 M5 Talsinnt Morocco 32.33N 3.30W
52 M2 Tålsmark Sweden 64.02N 20.30E
120 D11 Taltal Chile 25.26S 70.33W
120 D11 Taltal *R* Chile
59 E3 Talt, L Sligo Irish Rep 54.05N 8.55W
101 S5 Taltson R N W Terr
18 C5 Talu Sumatra Indon 0.20N 99.59E
19 C3 Taludaä Celebes Indon 0.23N 123.28E
19 K9 Talue *isld* Philippines 5.45N 121.01E
18 D6 Taluk Sumatra Indon 0.33S 101.34E
40 B3 Taluma U.S.S.R. 56.34N 122.00E
25 H3 Ta Lus, C Vietnam 19.14N 105.47E
32 B3 Talvar *R* Iran
79 K1 Tálvera *R* Italy
51 K1 Talvik Norway 70.05N 22.52E
13 J8 Talwood Queensland 28.29S 149.25E
86 E5 Talya Egypt 30.16N 31.00E
42 G6 Tal'yan U.S.S.R. 52.12N 103.15E
12 G4 Talyawalka *R* New S Wales
56 D3 Talybont Dyfed Wales 52.29N 3.59W
57 F6 Tal-y-cafn Gwynedd Wales 53.13N 3.47W
32 C1 Talyshskiye Gory *mts* Iran/U.S.S.R.
47 H4 Talyy U.S.S.R. 64.41N 55.50E
45 R1 Talyzino U.S.S.R. 55.06N 45.50E
88 M6 Talzaza Algeria 31.57N 2.23W
44 H5 Talzi U.S.S.R. 42.53N 47.27E
108 S8 Tama Iowa 41.58N 92.42W
20 B3 Tama Tōkyō Japan
20 N6 Tama *R* Japan
18 L4 Tamabo Ra Sarawak Malaysia
88 P11 Tamada Algeria 21.34N 3.20E
90 C2 Tamadalt Niger 18.20N 7.55E
88 S7 Tamadanet Algeria 28.46N 9.14E
25 C1 Tamadaw Burma 22.53N 95.14E
96 P11 Tamaduste Hierro Canary Is 27.49N 17.53W
20 D3 Tamagawa *dist* Tōkyō Japan
20 C3 Tama-gawa *R* Japan
89 M3 Tamaia Niger 17.52N 5.28E
75 D5 Tamajón Spain 41.00N 3.15W
39 J4 Tamak U.S.S.R. 60.45N 171.30E
11 D2 Tamaki New Zealand 36.53S 174.52E
11 D2 Tamaki R New Zealand
45 P4 Tamala U.S.S.R. 52.34N 43.14E
14 A7 Tamala W Australia 26.42S 113.47E
86 E4 Tamalâi Egypt 30.30N 30.51E
119 D3 Tamalameque Colombia 8.52N 73.51W
89 J7 Tamale Ghana 9.26N 0.49W
19 A5 Tamalea Celebes Indonesia 2.29S 119.21E
23 J7 Ta-ma-li Taiwan 22.37N 121.00E
Tamaliyeh *see* Temileh
42 D5 Tamalyk U.S.S.R. 53.40N 89.40E
34 N8 Tamāma, At *ridge* Iraq
76 H6 Tamame Spain 41.19N 5.53W
76 G7 Tamames Spain 40.40N 6.06W

91 C10 Tama,Mt Angola 13.50S 13.32E
44 A2 Taman' U.S.S.R. 45.12N 36.43E
20 D9 Tamana Japan 32.52N 130.35E
9 C6 Tamana *I* Kiribati, Pacific Oc 2.30S 176.00E
119 C5 Tamana *mt* Colombia 5.07N 76.11W
88 J6 Tamanar Morocco 31.03N 9.42W
119 D10 Tamanco Peru 5.49S 74.18W
117 J9 Tamandare Brazil 9.45S 35.05W
88 N12 Tamandouririt Mali 19.50N 1.58W
87 J7 Tamangale Ethiopia 7.28N 43.22E
121 F7 Tamangueyu Argentina 38.15S 58.45W
18 C7 Taman Negara Nat.Park Pen Malaysia
20 G7 Tamano Japan 34.29N 133.56E
88 Q10 Tamanrasset Algeria 22.50N 5.28E
88 P10 Tamanrasset *watercourse* Algeria
44 E9 Tamanskiy Zaliv *B* U.S.S.R.
25 L8 Tamanthi Burma 25.20N 95.18E
19 B4 Tamanusi Celebes Indonesia 1.48S 121.18E
103 C5 Tamaqua Pennsylvania 40.47N 75.58W
119 G8 Tamaquari, I Brazil 0.28S 64.51W
29 J2 Tamar Bihar India 23.02N 85.40E
119 D5 Támara Colombia 5.51N 72.09W
79 L5 Tamara Italy 44.52N 11.47E
108 R3 Tamarack Minnesota 46.38N 93.06W
20 E9 Tamarai Japan 32.56N 131.20E
119 D4 Tamar,Alto de *mt* Colombia 7.31N 74.21W
86 N6 Tamarâni,Wâdi el *watercourse* Egypt
Tamarīdah *see* Ḥadībū
Tamarike *see* Mariu
26 T13 Tamarin Mauritius, Indian Oc 20.20S 57.22E
119 G3 Tamarindo Venezuela 9.38N 63.06W
75 L4 Tamarite de Litera Spain 41.52N 0.25E
75 R4 Tamariu Spain 41.55N 3.12E
107 G3 Tamaroa Illinois 38.09N 89.11W
66 M7 Tamaro, Mt Switzerland 46.06N 8.51E
45 C6 Tamarovka Ukraine U.S.S.R. 50.22N 31.51E
56 C6 Tamar,R Cornwall/Devon Eng
12 H8 Tamar R Tasmania
120 D9 Tamarugal, Pampa del *plain* Chile
62 L9 Tamási Hungary 46.39N 18.17E
89 M4 Tamaské Niger 14.49N 5.43E
Tamatave *see* Toamasina
89 N3 Tamat Edderit Niger 17.52N 6.39E
20 O5 Tamatsukuri Japan 36.08N 140.23E
115 K6 Tamaulipas *state* Mexico
115 K6 Tamaulipas,Sa.de *ra* Mexico
121 B3 Tamaya Chile 30.33S 71.25W
120 C3 Tamaya,R Peru
115 F5 Tamazula Durango Mexico 24.55N 106.58W
115 H8 Tamazula Jalisco Mexico 19.41N 103.19W
115 L9 Tamazulápam Mexico 17.41N 97.33W
115 K7 Tamazunchale Mexico 21.18N 98.46W
89 D6 Tamba Guinea 11.52N 10.39W
93 G5 Tambach Kenya 0.36N 35.34E
64 K2 Tambach Dietharz E Germany 50.46N 10.36E
89 C5 Tambacounda Senegal 13.45N 13.40W
89 C5 Tambala Senegal 13.45N 12.52W
18 L4 Tambalan Kalimantan Indonesia 3.12N 115.40E
Tambao *see* Tambāv
89 K4 Tambao Upper Volta 14.48N 0.05E
119 H10 Tambaqui Brazil 5.14S 62.45W
92 G10 Tambara Mozambique 16.42S 34.14E
32 J8 Tambāv Iran 25.28N 61.21E
90 B5 Tambawel Nigeria 12.24N 4.40E
117 J8 També Brazil 7.22S 35.05W
19 B6 Tambea Celebes Indon 4.14S 121.37E
28 G7 Tambeibui Andaman Is 10.32N 92.30E
18 G5 Tambelan *isld* Indonesia 0.59N 107.35E
18 G5 Tambelan,Kep *islds* Indonesia
14 C10 Tambellup W Australia 34.03S 117.36E
92 C10 Tambero Zambia 16.10S 27.30E
47 L1 Tambey U.S.S.R. 71.31N 71.55E
47 L1 Tambey *R* U.S.S.R.
32 C5 Tambiān Iran 31.48N 49.32E
86 E8 Tambidi Egypt 28.37N 30.46E
121 B2 Tambillos,Nevado de los *pk* Chile 28.58S 70.46W
18 N3 Tambisan Sabah Malaysia 5.29N 119.08E
120 C5 Tambo Ayacucho Peru 12.51S 74.00W
120 A2 Tambo Cajamarca Peru 7.35S 78.42W
13 H6 Tambo Queensland 24.52S 146.15E
91 K8 Tambo Zaïre 8.21S 27.14E
12 J6 Tambo *R* Victoria
19 N7 Tamboa Point Mindanao Philippines 8.05N 126.27E
120 C5 Tambobamba Peru 13.51S 72.09W
120 B5 Tambo de Mora Peru 13.30S 76.08W
119 B10 Tambo Grande Peru 4.58S 80.22W
95 A4 Tambohorano Madagascar 17.30S 43.59E
19 B7 Tambolongang *isld* Indonesia 6.43S 120.25E
120 D5 Tambopata,R Peru
79 F2 Tambo, Pizzo *pk* Italy 46.29N 9.16E
115 G5 Tambor Mexico 25.08N 105.27W
120 D7 Tambo,R Peru
18 M10 Tambora,Gunung *mt* Indonesia 8.16S 117.59E
121 G3 Tambores Uruguay 31.50S 56.17W
117 G7 Tamboril Brazil 4.50S 40.18W
12 H6 Tamboritha,Mt Victoria 37.29S 146.40E
119 D9 Tamboryacu,R Peru
45 N4 Tambov U.S.S.R. 52.44N 41.28E
46 M3 Tambovskaya Oblast' *prov* U.S.S.R.
76 B3 Tambre *R* Spain
14 C5 Tambrey W Australia 21.51S 117.45E
19 A4 Tambu Celebes Indonesia 0.01S 119.53E
15 G6 Tambul Papua New Guinea 5.58S 144.00E
18 M3 Tambunan Sabah Malaysia 5.52N 116.22E
18 M3 Tambunan Bukit *hill* Sabah Malaysia 4.44N 116.38E
87 A8 Tambura Sudan 5.38N 27.30E
118 H3 Tamburi Brazil 13.04S 40.30W
19 A3 Tambu,Teluk *B* Celebes Indon
26 R5 Tambutta Sri Lanka 8.05N 80.13E
18 M2 Tambuyukon,Gunong *mt* Sabah Malaysia 6.15N 116.36E
22 C4 Tamch Mongolia 45.41N 93.58E
89 D3 Tamchaket Mauritania 17.23N 10.37W
43 D3 Tamdy Kazakhstan U.S.S.R. 49.45N 57.16E
43 G6 Tamdybulak Uzbekistan U.S.S.R. 41.46N 64.36E
43 G6 Tamdytau,Gory *mts* Uzbekistan U.S.S.R.
119 E4 Tame Colombia 6.27N 71.42W
76 C6 Tamega *R* Portugal
88 Q12 Tamegaout *reg* Algeria
Tamehi *see* Tamch
121 K7 Tamel Aike Argentina 48.13S 71.00W
88 R8 Tamelrik *reg* Algeria
88 S3 Tamera Tunisia 37.01N 9.09E
43 J5 Tamerlanovka Kazakhstan U.S.S.R. 42.34N 69.13E
89 B2 Tamersguid Mauritania 18.16N 14.26W
88 R4 Tamerza Tunisia 34.23N 7.54E
88 P8 Tamesguidat Algeria 27.25N 3.50E
90 D2 Tamgak,Mts Niger
43 J4 Tamgaly Oz *L* Kazakhstan U.S.S.R.
115 L7 Tamiahua Mexico 21.18N 97.28W
115 L7 Tamiahua, L. de Mexico
105 F12 Tamiami Canal Florida
18 B3 Tamiang *R* Sumatra Indon
18 C3 Tamiang,Udjung *C* Sumatra Indon 4.26N 98.17E
28 C5 Tamil Nadu *state* India
103 D4 Tamiment Pennsylvania 41.08N 75.01W
85 G3 Tamīmī, at Libya 32.20N 23.02E
66 O4 Tamina *R* Switzerland
61 J5 Tamines Belgium 50.27N 4.37E
66 O4 Tamins Switzerland 46.50N 9.25E
22 E3 Tamirïn Gol *R* Mongolia
33 H8 Tamis S Yemen 16.55N 48.59E
82 F5 Tamiš *R* Yugoslavia
118 D3 Tamitatoala,R Brazil
47 D4 Tamitsa U.S.S.R. 64.10N 38.05E
86 E7 Tâmîya Egypt 29.29N 30.57E
33 E4 Tamīyah,Jabal *mt* Saudi Arabia 25.35N 42.01E
Tamizhagam *state see* Tamil Nadu *state*
93 G4 Tamkal Camp Kenya 1.22N 35.29E
43 G3 Tamkamys Kazakhstan U.S.S.R. 49.33N 63.32E
30 H6 Tamkuhi Uttar Prad India 26.42N 84.11E
25 K5 Tam Ky Vietnam 15.32N 108.30E
88 M5 Tamlelt, Plaine de Morocco
29 K6 Tamluk W Bengal India 22.17N 87.58E
30 F2 Tamlung La *pass* Xizang Zizhiqu 30.27N 82.01E
30 F2 Tamlung Tso *L* Xizang Zizhiqu 30.28N 82.04E
80 L6 Tammaro *R* Italy
Tammerfors *see* Tampere
Tammisaari *see* Ekenäs
107 G4 Tamms Illinois 37.13N 89.16W
35 E4 Tammun Jordan 32.17N 35.23E
52 K6 Tämnaren *L* Sweden 60.10N 17.25E
71 D2 Tamnay-en-Bazois France 47.03N 3.44E
76 D3 Tamoga *R* Spain
18 D9 Tamok *R* Pen Malaysia
115 K6 Tamos Mexico 22.15N 98.00W
95 C7 Tamotamo Madagascar 24.00S 46.11E
105 E10 Tampa Florida 27.58N 82.38W
109 N3 Tampa Kansas 38.31N 97.11W
105 E10 Tampa B Florida
26 T4 Tampalakamam Sri Lanka 8.30N 81.05E
18 F8 Tampang Sumatra Indon 5.54S 104.43E
32 H7 Tamp-e Gīrān Iran 27.23N 58.07E
51 K10 Tampere Finland 61.32N 23.45E
106 E8 Tampico Illinois 41.36N 89.48W
115 L6 Tampico Mexico 22.18N 97.52W
108 D1 Tampico Montana 48.19N 106.50W
18 C9 Tampin Pen Malaysia 2.26N 102.14E
18 K3 Tampine *dist* Singapore
117 C3 Tampoc *R* Fr Guiana
26 U16 Tampon,Le Réunion Ind Oc 21.16S 55.32E
25 K5 Tam Quam Vietnam 14.34N 109.03E
35 D2 Tamra Israel 32.51N 35.12E
35 E3 Tamra Israel 32.38N 35.24E
33 F6 Tamrah Saudi Arabia 20.27N 45.26E

15 B4 Tamrau, Peg *mts* Irian Jaya
88 H9 Tamreïkat *hills* Mauritania
88 J6 Tamri Morocco 30.46N 9.50W
Tamridah *see* Ḥadībū
88 S9 Tamrit *ruins* Algeria 24.42N 9.32E
22 L3 Tamsagbulag Mongolia 47.10N 117.21E
22 F6 Tamsag Bulag Nei Monggol Zizhiqu China 40.45N 103.33E
88 K9 Tamsagout Mali 24.09N 6.23W
120 C1 Tamshiyacu Peru 4.00S 72.59W
28 H1 Tam-shul Xizang Zizhiqu 28.25N 91.25E
65 J7 Tamsweg Austria 47.08N 13.49E
25 L9 Tamu Burma 24.56N 94.20E
34 O2 Tamūgheh Iran 36.13N 46.08E
115 K6 Tamuín Mexico 22.00N 98.44W
19 K8 Tamuk *isld* Philippines 6.26N 121.50E
19 L1 Tamuning Guam Pacific Oc 13.29N 144.47E
30 L6 Tamur *R* Nepal
77 G3 Tamurejo Spain 38.59N 4.56W
104 O3 Tamworth New Hampshire 43.52N 71.16W
12 K4 Tamworth New S Wales 31.07S 150.57E
99 O8 Tamworth Ontario 44.28N 76.59W
56 H2 Tamworth Staffs Eng 52.39N 1.40W
Tan *see* Ban Tan
43 M3 Tan Kazakhstan U.S.S.R. 48.02N 75.57E
120 D8 Tana Chile 19.28S 69.56W
51 N1 Tana Norway 70.26N 28.14E
9 D12 Tana *isld* New Hebrides
113 Q6 Tana *R* Alaska
93 K6 Tana *R* Kenya
20 J8 Tanabe Japan 33.43N 135.22E
20 J8 Tanabe-wan *B* Japan
118 E7 Tanabi Brazil 20.36S 49.35W
113 Q5 Tanacross Alaska 63.21N 143.30W
113 S9 Tanadak I Aleutian Is 52.05N 172.57W
113 Q5 Tanada L Alaska 62.25N 143.25W
89 N2 Ta-n-Adar Niger 18.40N 7.11E
51 N1 Tanafjord *inlet* Norway
113 P10 Tanaga I Aleutian Is 51.50N 178.00W
113 P10 Tanaga Pass Aleutian Is
84 G5 Tanágra Greece 38.20N 23.32E
81 L3 Tánagro *R* Italy
20 O4 Tanagura Japan 37.02N 140.22E
18 C6 Tanahbala *isld* Indonesia
18 C5 Tanahbatu Sumatra Indon 0.45N 99.30E
19 B7 Tanahjampea *isld* Indonesia 7.04S 120.39E
18 C6 Tanahmasa *isld* Indonesia
15 F7 Tanahmerah Irian Jaya 6.08S 140.18E
18 M4 Tanahmerah Kalimantan Indonesia 3.45N 117.31E
18 B9 Tanah Merah Pen Malaysia 2.36N 101.48E
18 E3 Tanah Merah Pen Malaysia 5.50N 102.08E
51 O1 Tanahorn *mt* Norway 70.50N 28.50E
18 B10 Tanahputih Sumatra Indon 1.41N 101.04E
18 H9 Tanah, Tanjung *C* Java Indon 6.30S 108.32E
Tanajib,Ras *see* Tanāqīb,Ra's *cape*
113 C10 Tanak,C Aleutian Is 53.35N 168.00W
19 A6 Tanakeke *isld* Celebes Indon 5.30S 119.18E
30 D3 Tanakpur Uttar Prad India 29.04N 80.06E
87 F4 Tana,L Ethiopia
89 H4 Tanal Mali 15.21N 2.59W
113 K6 Tanalian Pt Alaska 60.10N 154.20W
41 C5 Tanama *R* U.S.S.R.
26 T9 Tanamalwila Sri Lanka 6.26N 81.07E
13 A4 Tanami N Terr Australia 19.58S 129.43E
86 F5 Tanân Egypt 30.15N 31.14E
25 J7 Tan An Vietnam 10.32N 106.24E
113 L4 Tanana Alaska 65.11N 152.10W
113 N4 Tanana *R* Alaska
Tananarive *see* Antananarive
95 C7 Tanandava Madagascar 22.40S 46.53E
53 T21 Tananger Norway 58.56N 5.36E
18 M6 Tanangrogot Kalimantan Indonesia 1.55S 116.11E
88 K6 Tanannt Morocco 31.50N 6.52W
88 N11 Tanaok Mali 20.33N 0.08W
33 H3 Tanāqīb,Ra's *C* Saudi Arabia 27.50N 48.52E
51 N1 Tana,R Finland/Norway
71 E7 Tanargue *mt* France 44.37N 4.06E
93 L7 Tana River *dist* Kenya
79 E5 Tanaro *R* Italy
85 A5 Tānārūt *watercourse* Libya
20 C2 Tanashi *dist* Tōkyō Japan
19 J2 Tanauan Luzon Philippines 14.04N 121.08E
19 M6 Tanauan Philippines 11.05N 125.01E
81 D2 Tanaunella Sardinia 40.42N 9.45E
9 T7 Tanavuso Pt Viti Levu Fiji 17.35S 178.30E
19 J2 Tanay Luzon Philippines 14.30N 121.17E
30 K5 Tanba Kosi *R* Nepal
13 F7 Tanbar Queensland 25.41S 142.00E
32 F7 Tanb-e bozorg *isld* Iran 26.15N 55.17E
14 C5 Tanberry,R W Australia
75 M6 Tancada,L.de la Spain 40.39N 0.44E
70 L3 Tancarville France 49.29N 0.28E
20 P9 Tancha Okinawa Japan 26.27N 127.48E
23 H1 Tancheng Shandong China 34.39N 118.21E
21 D7 Tanch'ŏn N Korea 40.32N 128.58E
115 H8 Tancitario,Cerro de *pk* Mexico 19.26N 102.18W
115 K7 Tancuayalab Mexico 21.42N 98.36W
30 F6 Tanda Faizabad, Uttar Prad India 26.33N 82.39E
30 A1 Tanda Himachal Prad India 31.35N 76.54E
89 H8 Tanda Ivory Coast 7.45N 3.03W
30 B4 Tanda Rampur, Uttar Prad India 28.58N 78.57E
41 O8 Tanda *R* U.S.S.R.
19 N7 Tandag Mindanao Philippines 9.04N 126.12E
37 F2 Tan Dağı *mt* Turkey 40.32N 28.54E
Tandaho *see* Tendaho
82 L6 Tăndărei Romania 45.39N 27.43E
91 F12 Tandaué Angola 17.00S 18.05E
29 D2 Tanda Urmar Punjab India 31.38N 75.44E
29 G8 Tandawara Madhya Prad India 19.20N 81.12E
53 D6 Tanderup Denmark 55.22N 9.51E
29 E1 Tandi Himachal Prad India 32.32N 77.00E
29 D2 Tandiala Punjab India 31.32N 75.06E
28 C7 Tandiarpet *dist* Madras, Tamil Nadu India
121 F6 Tandil Argentina 37.18S 59.10W
121 F6 Tandil, Sa. del *ra* Argentina
95 J8 Tandjiesberg *mts* S Africa
90 H7 Tandjilé Chad
18 N4 Tandjungbatu Borneo Indon 2.15N 118.06E
31 E8 Tando Adam Pakistan 25.44N 68.41E
31 E8 Tando Alahyar Pakistan 25.28N 68.44E
31 E8 Tando Bago Pakistan 24.48N 68.59E
31 E8 Tando Muhammad Khan Pakistan 25.07N 68.35E
12 F5 Tandou L New S Wales
42 B4 Tandovo,Ozero *L* U.S.S.R.
59 K3 Tandragee Armagh N Ireland 54.22N 6.25W
95 B7 Tandrano Madagascar 22.05S 44.38E
52 H5 Tandsjöborg Sweden 61.40N 14.40E
53 D7 Tandslet Denmark 54.56N 9.58E
19 K9 Tandu Batu Philippines 5.59N 121.17E
19 K9 Tandubatu *isld* Philippines 5.14N 120.16E
29 G7 Tandula *R* Madhya Prad India
28 C2 Tandur Hyderabad India 17.17N 77.33E
28 D1 Tandur Karimnagar, Andhra Prad India 19.10N 79.29E
31 E6 Tanduri Pakistan 29.42N 68.00E
11 M5 Taneatua New Zealand 38.03S 177.01E
21 E12 Tanega shima *isld* Japan
20 P1 Taneichi Japan 40.23N 141.44E
88 S8 Tan Emellel Algeria 27.36N 9.40E
25 E3 Tanen Taunggyi *mts* Burma/Thailand
58 F3 Tanera More *isld* Highland Scotland 57.58N 5.30W
19 E4 Taneti *isld* Moluccas Indon 0.06S 127.14E
19 A6 Tanette Celebes Indon 4.35S 119.38E
62 O5 Tanew *R* Poland
104 H7 Taneytown Maryland 39.40N 77.11W
88 N10 Tanezrouft *reg* Algeria
88 O9 Tanezrouft,Route du Algeria
88 O10 Tanezrouft Tan-Ahenet *reg* Algeria
85 A7 Tanezzuft *watercourse* Libya
57 K4 Tanfield N Yorks Eng 54.12N 1.35W
34 F5 Tanf,Jebel *mt* Syria 33.32N 38.43E
Tang *see* Tangmai
32 H8 Tang Iran 25.25N 59.53E
59 G4 Tang W Meath Irish Rep 53.32N 7.47W
91 E3 Tanga Congo 1.29N 17.41E
15 H6 Tanga Papua New Guinea 4.25S 144.58E
92 J4 Tanga Tanzania 5.07S 39.05E
42 J6 Tanga U.S.S.R. 51.02N 111.32E
93 K10 Tanga *reg* Tanzania
31 H9 Tangail Bangladesh 24.15N 89.55E
31 H9 Tangail *dist* Bangladesh
15 M5 Tanga Is Bismarck Arch
92 H11 Tangalane,Ponta *pt* Mozambique 18.01S 37.00E
90 H3 Tangaléa Chad 16.29N 17.56E
26 S10 Tangalla Sri Lanka 6.02N 80.47E
Tanganyika *see* Tanzania
93 A9 Tanganyika, L E Africa
92 D4 Tanganyika, Lake Kigoma Tanzania 4.51S 29.41E
32 F2 Tangar Iran 37.25N 55.46E
121 H1 Tangará Brazil 27.11S 51.14W
15 L3 Tangarare Guadalcanal I Solomon Is 9.29S 159.35E
90 H2 Tangashinga Chad 18.38N 17.55E
50 L3 Tangaspordhur *C* Iceland 65.48N 14.46W
28 C6 Tangasseri Kerala India 8.54N 76.35E
90 B5 Tangaza Nigeria 13.19N 4.55E
Tangdan *see* Dongchuan
Tangdukou *see* Shaoyang

60 R7 Tange-Alteveer Netherlands 53.03N 7.00E
32 E6 Tang-e Karam Iran 29.03N 53.38E
32 F2 Tangeli Iran 37.27N 54.45E
53 X18 Tangen Norway 60.02N 7.33E
77 E9 Tanger Morocco 35.48N 5.50W

18 G9 Tangerang Java Indon 6.14S 106.36E
63 P8 Tangerhütte E Germany 52.26N 11.49E
63 P7 Tangermünde E Germany 52.34N 11.58E
53 D4 Tange Sø L Denmark 56.20N 9.37E
24 H10 Tanggo Xizang Zizhiqu China 31.40N 93.17E
23 C2 Tanggor Sichuan China 33.27N 102.30E
22 L7 Tanggu Tianjin China 39.00N 117.42E
24 G9 Tanggula (Dangla) Shan mt ra Xizang Zizhiqu China
24 G9 Tanggula Shankou pass Xizang Zizhiqu China 32.45N 92.24E
24 G8 Tanggulashanqu Qinghai China 34.10N 92.23E
23 F2 Tanghe Henan China 32.45N 112.48E
22 K7 Tang He R Hebei China
23 F2 Tang He R Hubei China
Tangi see Tungi
31 F3 Tangi Pakistan 34.18N 71.42E
40 J6 Tangi Sakhalin U.S.S.R. 51.14N 142.10E
Tangier see Tanger
98 K9 Tangier Nova Scotia 44.48N 62.43W
98 K9 Tangier Grand L Nova Scotia
104 K9 Tangier I Virginia 37.48N 76.00W
11 K7 Tangimoana New Zealand 40.18S 175.15E
107 F11 Tangipahoa R Miss/Louisiana
Tang-i-Panj see Tang Panj
21 D9 Tangjin S Korea 36.55N 126.34E
18 K6 Tangkahan Borneo Indonesia 1.36S 113.55E
18 C9 Tangkak Pen Malaysia 2.14N 102.33E
19 B5 Tangkeleboke,Gunung mt Celebes Indonesia 3.06S 121.23E
18 G9 Tangkuban Perahu,Gunung mt Java Indon 6.48S 107.32E
28 H2 Tangla Assam India 26.40N 91.57E
23 B1 Tanglag Qinghai China 34.01N 99.30E
112 L5 Tanglewood Texas 30.30N 96.59W
Tanglha Ra see Tanggula (Dangla) Shan
23 A9 Tang Lung Chau isld Hong Kong 22.20N 114.03E
24 H10 Tangmai Xizang Zizhiqu China 30.10N 95.09E
30 L4 Tangmoche Xizang Zizhiqu 28.11N 87.15E
41 M8 Tangnary R U.S.S.R.
91 D8 Tango Angola 8.07S 15.41E
89 D4 Tango Mali 15.04N 10.19W
13 G5 Tangorin Queensland 21.48S 144.16E
11 H2 Tangowahine New Zealand 35.52S 173.57E
51 D3 Tangøya isld Norway
32 C4 Tang Panj Iran 32.58N 48.41E
Tang Pass see Tanggula Shankou
23 E8 Tangpeng Guangdong China 21.48N 110.07E
Tang-Rah see Tangar
32 H8 Tang,Ra's-e C Iran 25.21N 59.52E
24 E10 Tangra Yumco L Xizang Zizhiqu China 31.00N 86.15E
18 A3 Tangse Sumatra Indon 5.01N 95.54E
22 L7 Tangshan Hebei China 39.37N 118.05E
23 C5 Tangtang Yunnan China 26.30N 104.09E
23 E5 Tangtou Guizhou China 27.44N 108.15E
23 G7 Tangtouxia Guangdong China 22.45N 114.05E
19 L7 Tangub Mindanao Philippines 8.04N 123.44E
19 L6 Tangub Philippines 10.35N 122.57E
89 K6 Tanguiéta Benin 10.35N 1.19E
28 K1 Tangu La pass India/Xizang Zizhiqu 28.55N 94.09E
21 E3 Tangwanghe Heilongjiang China 48.26N 129.32E
21 E4 Tangwang He R Heilongjiang China
23 H4 Tangxi Zhejiang China 29.04N 119.21E
22 K7 Tang Xian Hebei China 38.48N 114.54E
23 F3 Tangxianzhen Hubei China 32.00N 113.08E
25 E1 Tang-yan Burma 22.29N 98.22E
23 E4 Tangyan He R Sichuan China
22 K8 Tangyi Shandong China 36.27N 115.42E
21 E4 Tangyuan Heilongjiang China 46.45N 129.56E
24 E10 Tangyung Tso L Xizang Zizhiqu China 31.30N 86.30E
118 H4 Tanhaçu Brazil 14.03S 41.15W
51 N4 Tanhua Finland 67.32N 27.30E
25 H7 Tani Cambodia 10.46N 104.39E
23 A3 Taniantaweng Shan mts Xizang Zizhiqu China
20 K6 Tanigumi Japan 35.36N 136.32E
15 A7 Tanimbar,Kep islds Indonesia
71 K4 Taninges France 46.07N 6.35E
15 B5 Tanisepata Irian Jaya 2.46S 132.04E
89 A2 Tanit,Baie de Mauritania
20 D10 Taniyama Japan 31.30N 130.30E
34 N3 Tānjarō R Iraq
19 L7 Tanjay Philippines 9.31N 123.10E
18 B8 Tanjong Malim Pen Malaysia 3.43N 101.27E
18 B7 Tanjong Rambutan Pen Malaysia 4.41N 101.08E
Tanjore see Thanjavur
18 L7 Tanjung Borneo Indon 2.08S 115.23E
18 E5 Tanjungbalai Indonesia 1.00N 103.19E
18 C4 Tanjungbalai Sumatra Indonesia 2.59N 99.46E
19 E5 Tanjungbaliha Moluccas Indon 2.25S 126.03E
18 M5 Tanjungbatu Borneo Indon 0.45N 117.29E
18 N5 Tanjungbuayabuaya isld Borneo Indon
18 E7 Tanjungenim Sumatra Indonesia 3.45S 103.46E
18 F8 Tanjungkarang Sumatra Indon 5.22S 105.18E
18 E7 Tanjung Luntar Sumatra Indon 3.35S 103.44E
18 D4 Tanjungmengidan Sumatra Indon 2.42N 100.03E
18 G7 Tanjungpandan Indonesia 2.44S 107.36E
18 F5 Tanjungpinang Indonesia 0.55N 104.28E
18 G9 Tanjung Priok Java Indon 6.08S 106.46E
18 C4 Tanjungpura Sumatra Indon 3.57N 98.16E
18 K6 Tanjungpusu Borneo Indon 0.02S 113.32E
18 F7 Tanjungraja Sumatra Indon 3.14S 104.49E
18 M4 Tanjungredeb Borneo Indon 2.09N 117.29E
18 G7 Tanjungrusa Indonesia 3.12S 107.45E
18 H6 Tanjungsaleh isld Borneo Indon
18 M4 Tanjungselor Borneo Indon 2.52N 117.21E
18 J6 Tanjungwaringin Borneo Indon 1.48S 111.05E
31 F4 Tank Pakistan 32.14N 70.29E
12 E3 Tankamarinna,L S Australia
51 N3 Tankapirtti Finland 68.16N 27.20E
88 S8 Tan Kena Bordj Algeria 26.35N 9.32E
112 G4 Tankersly Texas 31.22N 100.40W
29 C7 Tankhala Gujarat India 21.58N 72.50E
42 H6 Tankhoy U.S.S.R. 51.32N 105.05E
39 A1 Tanki R U.S.S.R.
47 J6 Tankovichi U.S.S.R. 59.45N 60.45E
42 D2 Tankovo U.S.S.R. 60.42N 89.49E
Tank,Ras see Tang,Ra's-e cape
31 J2 Tankse Kashmir 34.03N 78.13E
31 K3 Tankse Kashmir 34.01N 80.08E
69 G8 Tanlay France 47.51N 4.05E
47 L3 Tanlovo U.S.S.R. 65.12N 73.29E
47 L3 Tanlovo R U.S.S.R.
25 C3 Tanlwe R Burma
25 K7 Tan My Vietnam 11.42N 108.50E
64 O7 Tann Bayern W Germany 48.19N 12.55E
64 J2 Tann Thüringen W Germany 50.38N 10.02E
Tanna see Tana
64 M3 Tanna E Germany 50.29N 11.52E
Tanna isld see Tana
58 L5 Tannadice Tayside Scotland 56.43N 2.52W
52 G4 Tännäs Sweden 62.27N 12.40E
66 P1 Tannau W Germany 47.39N 9.39E
69 H4 Tannay France 49.31N 4.50E
71 D2 Tannay France 47.22N 3.36E
63 N9 Tanne E Germany 51.43N 10.43E
103 D3 Tanners Falls Pennsylvania 41.40N 75.18W
103 F2 Tannersville New York 42.12N 74.09W
103 D4 Tannersville Pennsylvania 41.03N 75.17W
64 N4 Tännesberg W Germany 49.31N 12.20E
64 J6 Tannhausen Baden-Württemberg Germany 48.59N 10.23E
65 C7 Tannheim Austria 47.30N 10.32E
64 J8 Tannheim W Germany 48.00N 10.05E
66 H4 Tann Horn mt Switzerland 46.47N 7.59E
51 M6 Tannila Finland 65.30N 26.00E
100 M1 Tannin Ontario 49.40N 91.00W
35 C3 Tanninim R Israel
53 E1 Tannis Bugt B Denmark
53 E1 Tannisby Denmark 57.36N 10.12E
64 L2 Tannroda E Germany 50.51N 11.15E
50 D4 Tannstadhabakki Iceland 65.16N 21.05W
42 E6 Tannu Ola ra U.S.S.R.
33 A7 Tannurah,Ra's at C Saudi Arabia 26.38N 50.11E
89 H8 Tano R Ghana
9 T13 Tano'a atoll Tonga, Pacific Oc 20.20S 174.35W
88 Q9 Tanombella Algeria 25.30N 5.49E
19 L7 Tañon Str Philippines
89 H9 Tanoso Ghana 5.22N 2.39W
29 B4 Tanot Rajasthan India 27.44N 70.17E
88 H11 Tanoucherte Mauritania 20.38N 11.50W
90 D4 Tanout Niger 15.05N 8.50E
111 P9 Tanque Arizona 32.36N 109.33W
115 H4 Tanque Alvarez Mexico 27.56N 102.32W
115 K7 Tanquián Mexico 21.38N 98.40W
88 P12 Tan Ramir Mali 19.48N 2.50E
23 J6 Tan-shui Taiwan 25.13N 121.29E
30 G5 Tansing Nepal 27.51N 83.33E
43 N4 Tansyk Kazakhstan U.S.S.R. 47.17N 79.54E
86 F4 Tanta Egypt 30.48N 31.00E
25 C1 Tantabin Burma 22.54N 95.34E
25 D3 Tantabin Burma 19.50N 96.22E
100 Q8 Tantallon Saskatchewan 50.32N 101.50W
58 L6 Tantallon Castle Lothian Scotland 56.04N 2.39W
89 H7 Tantama Ivory Coast 9.31N 2.39W
12 F7 Tantanoola S Australia 37.44S 140.30E
88 H7 Tan-Tan-Tarfaya Morocco 28.30N 11.02W
91 K9 Tantara Zaïre 11.04S 26.31E
69 L7 Tantonville France 48.29N 6.08E
63 U6 Tantow E Germany 53.16N 14.22E
115 K7 Tantoyuca Mexico 21.21N 98.12W
30 A6 Tantpur Uttar Prad India 26.51N 77.29E
Tanţūra see Dor
28 E2 Tanuku Andhra Prad India 16.48N 81.45E
13 C3 Tanumbirini N Terr Australia 16.05S 134.49E
113 E6 Tanunak Alaska 60.34N 165.15W
12 E5 Tanunda S Australia 34.34S 138.56E
28 B5 Tanur Kerala India 10.59N 75.52E
72 J7 Tanus France 44.07N 2.18E
21 D9 Tanyang S Korea 36.55N 128.20E
46 S2 Tanyn R U.S.S.R.
47 H7 Tanyp R U.S.S.R.
18 G2 Tanyung Priok Jakarta Indonesia 6.06S 106.53E
39 J3 Tanyurer R U.S.S.R.
19 H2 Tanza Luzon Philippines 14.24N 120.51E
73 H6 Tanzania fed rep E Africa
101 H6 Tanzilla R Br Col
21 B5 Tao'an Jilin China 45.25N 122.46E
94 G2 Taoghe R Botswana
23 C1 Tao He R Gansu China
23 J4 Taohua Dao isld Zhejiang China
Taohuaping see Longhui
23 F4 Taojiang Hunan China 28.35N 112.05E
25 E7 Tao,Ko isld Thailand 10.03N 99.51E
95 C8 Taolañaro Madagascar 25.01S 47.00E
22 G7 Taole Ningxia China 38.45N 106.45E
23 H1 Taoluo Shandong China 35.15N 119.25E
108 S6 Taopi Minnesota 43.34N 92.36W
81 K8 Taormina Sicily 37.51N 15.17E
109 E5 Taos New Mexico 36.24N 105.35W
88 M10 Taoudenni Mali 22.38N 3.58E
88 H12 Taoujafet Mauritania 18.55N 11.50W
89 B2 Taoumi Mauritania 18.49N 14.41W
88 L4 Taounate Morocco 34.25N 4.39W
88 S7 Taouratine Algeria 28.22N 9.20E
88 O8 Taourirt Algeria 26.40N 0.20E
88 M4 Taourirt Morocco 34.25N 2.53W
88 L6 Taouz Morocco 30.53N 4.01W
23 F4 Taoyuan Hunan China 28.55N 111.16E
23 J6 T'ao-yüan Taiwan 25.00N 121.15E
Tap see Huyut
47 K7 Tap R U.S.S.R.
46 F1 Tapa Estonia U.S.S.R. 59.16N 25.50E
19 K9 Tapaan Pass Philippines
120 E7 Tapacari Bolivia 17.31S 66.32W
115 N10 Tapachula Mexico 14.54N 92.15W
122 C2 Tapaga Pt C W Samoa, Pacific Oc 14.01S 171.25W
18 B7 Tapah Pen Malaysia 4.07N 101.16E
18 C8 Tapah hill Pen Malaysia 3.36N 102.10E
18 B7 Tapah Road Pen Malaysia 4.08N 101.11E
118 C2 Tapaiuna R Brazil
117 B6 Tapajós,R Brazil
18 C4 Tapakkuda Sumatra Indon 3.58N 98.30E
18 B4 Tapaktuan Sumatra Indon 3.15N 97.12E
29 D7 Tapal Maharashtra India 21.29N 75.05E
19 A5 Tapalang Celebes Indon 2.49S 118.53E
121 E6 Tapalque Argentina 36.21S 60.01W
Tapan see Mansurlu
18 D7 Tapan Sumatra Indon 2.14S 101.02E
9 R12 Tapana / Tonga, Pacific Oc 18.43S 174.00W
117 B3 Tapanahoni R Surinam
115 M9 Tapanatepec Mexico 16.23N 94.11W
11 D12 Tapanui New Zealand 45.57S 169.17E
117 B6 Tapará,I.Grande do Brazil
117 C6 Tapara, Sa. do mts Brazil
46 N8 Taparavani,Oz L Georgia U.S.S.R.
19 E4 Tapat isld Moluccas Indon 1.09S 127.25E
120 F1 Tapauá Amazonas Brazil 5.42S 64.15W
120 E2 Tapauá,R Brazil
11 G8 Tapawera New Zealand 41.23S 172.48E
119 H8 Tapera Brazil 0.36S 61.44W
121 H2 Tapera Rio Grande do Sul Brazil 28.32S 52.55W
119 H8 Tapera,R Brazil
118 H3 Taperoá Bahia Brazil 13.35S 39.07W
117 H8 Taperoá Paraíba Brazil 7.12S 37.46W
121 H3 Tapes Brazil 30.42S 51.24W
121 H3 Tapes,Pta.de C Brazil 30.50S 51.20W
89 E8 Tapeta Liberia 6.36N 8.52W
64 K6 Tapfheim W Germany 48.39N 10.41E
76 F1 Tapia de Casariego Spain 43.34N 6.56W
19 L8 Tapiantana isld Philippines 6.17N 122.00E
118 B6 Tapia,Sa.de mts Bolivia
120 C2 Tapiche,R Peru
115 N9 Tapijulapa Mexico 17.29N 92.44W
91 K2 Tapili Zaïre 3.23N 27.34E
45 N9 Tapilinsky U.S.S.R. 47.24N 41.09E
15 J8 Tapini Papua New Guinea 8.16S 146.55E
51 L11 Tapiola Finland 60.09N 24.43E
76 J5 Tapioles Spain 41.52N 5.30W
118 G3 Tapiracanga Brazil 12.15S 44.30W
119 G7 Tapirapecó,Sa mts Venez/Brazil
118 D2 Tapirapé,R Brazil
118 B4 Tapirapuã Brazil 14.51S 57.33W
18 C8 Tapis mt Pen Malaysia 4.02N 102.54E
9 D4 Tapiwa Ocean I Pacific Oc 0.52S 169.34E
115 E4 Tapizuelas Mexico 26.40N 108.50W
30 L5 Taplejung Nepal 27.21N 87.41E
89 K5 Tapoa R Upper Volta/Niger
62 K9 Tapolca Hungary 46.54N 17.29E
25 E2 Ta-pom Burma 21.34N 99.32E
86 C4 Taposiris ruins Egypt 30.57N 29.31E
104 J9 Tappahannock Virginia 37.55N 76.54W
Tappah Zārdik see Tepe Zārdik
30 A4 Tappal Uttar Prad India 28.02N 77.34E
103 G4 Tappan New York 41.01N 73.57W
104 D6 Tappan Res Ohio 40.19N 81.07W
32 D3 Tappeh,Kūh-e hills Iran
108 L3 Tappen N Dakota 46.54N 99.38W
53 H6 Tappernøje Denmark 55.10N 12.00E
20 O1 Tappi-zaki C Japan 41.14N 140.21E
53 C6 Taps Denmark 55.24N 9.30E
47 J5 Tapsuy R U.S.S.R.
29 C7 Tapti R Maharashtra/Madhya Prad India
40 B5 Taptugary U.S.S.R. 53.44N 120.04E
11 K3 Tapu New Zealand 36.59S 175.33E
11 H8 Tapuaenuku mt New Zealand 42.00S 173.39E
19 K9 Tapul Philippines 5.44N 120.55E
19 K9 Tapul Grp islds Philippines
25 C3 Tapun Burma 18.24N 95.29E
18 D5 Tapung R Sumatra Indon
120 G1 Tapurú Brazil 4.15S 61.50W
119 G8 Tapurucuara Brazil 0.23S 65.01W
122 D1 Taputapu,C Amer Samoa Pacific Oc 14.20S 170.51W
11 C6 Taputerenga I Wellington New Zealand 41.21S 174.46E
33 L8 Ţāqah Oman 17.02N 54.23E
33 F10 Taqar mt Yemen 13.53N 44.07E
32 B3 Tāq-e Bostan Iran 34.22N 47.08E
32 H3 Taqīābād Iran 35.35N 59.10E
Taq-i-Bustan mts see Tāq-e Bostan
34 M3 Taqtaq Iraq 35.53N 44.36E
34 L6 Taqţaqanah, Aţ Iraq 32.02N 43.55E
118 H9 Taquara Rio de Janeiro Brazil 22.55S 43.24W
121 J2 Taquara Rio Grande do Sul Brazil 29.36S 50.46W
118 D4 Taquara,Serra da mts Brazil
121 H2 Taquarembo Brazil 29.26S 53.44W
118 D5 Taquarí Mato Grosso do Sul Brazil 17.51S 53.14W
121 H2 Taquarí Rio Grande do Sul Brazil 29.45S 51.47W
121 H2 Taquarí R Rio Grande do Sul Brazil
118 C6 Taquari, Pantanal do swamp Brazil
118 C6 Taquari,R Mato Grosso do Sul Brazil
118 E7 Taquaritinga Brazil 21.23S 48.33W
118 D7 Taquaruçu R Brazil
Tara Iran see Tarz
59 J4 Tara Meath Irish Rep 53.34N 6.35W
99 J8 Tara Ontario 44.28N 81.09W
13 K7 Tara Queensland 27.16N 150.26E
47 L7 Tara U.S.S.R. 56.55N 74.24E
92 C10 Tara Zambia 16.56S 26.50E
19 K5 Tara isld Philippines 12.20N 120.16E
82 E7 Tara mt Yugoslavia 43.54N 19.21E
47 M7 Tara R U.S.S.R.
82 E7 Tara R Yugoslavia
90 E7 Taraba R Nigeria
30 E6 Tarabganj Uttar Prad India 26.57N 81.59E
86 H7 Tarabîl,El hill Egypt 29.12N 32.12E
120 F8 Tarabuco Bolivia 19.13S 65.02W
Tarābulus al Gharb see Tripoli Libya
Tarābulus esh Shām see Tripoli Lebanon
75 D6 Taracena Spain 40.39N 3.08W
93 F2 Tarach watercourse Kenya
120 D6 Taraco Peru 15.19S 69.58W
119 F7 Taracua Brazil 0.06N 68.23W
11 L6 Taradale New Zealand 39.33S 176.52E
34 N7 Tarād al Kahf Iraq 31.58N 45.58E
71 J10 Taradeau France 43.27N 6.25E
29 F6 Taradehi Madhya Prad India 23.18N 79.22E
75 P4 Taradell Spain 41.53N 2.18E
89 P11 Tarafo, Punta Cape Verde 15.58N 22.50W
87 D2 Taragma Sudan 16.50N 33.35E
12 J6 Tarago New S Wales 35.05S 149.10E
59 J4 Tara Hill Meath Irish Rep 53.35N 6.37W
31 F8 Tar Ahmad Rind Pakistan 25.12N 70.42E
30 D7 Tarahuwan Uttar Prad India 25.12N 80.54E
30 A8 Tarai Madhya Prad India 24.38N 77.56E
29 L4 Tarai jungle Nepal/India
Taraíra R see Traíra
120 F9 Tarairí Bolivia 21.02S 53.28W
33 J6 Tarā'īz, Aţ sand dunes Saudi Arabia
96 S11 Tarajalejo-Playa Fuerteventura Canary Is 28.10N 14.13W
18 M4 Tarakan Borneo Indon 3.20N 117.38E
18 M4 Tarakan isld Borneo Indon
20 D9 Taraki Japan 32.16N 130.57E
31 D4 Tarakki reg Afghanistan
36 E2 Taraklı Turkey 40.24N 30.29E
82 M4 Tarakliya Moldavia U.S.S.R. 46.33N 29.08E
82 M5 Tarakliya Moldavia U.S.S.R. 45.51N 28.42E
11 G7 Tarakohe New Zealand 40.51S 172.54E
37 E7 Taraksu Turkey 38.03N 39.02E
31 A5 Tarakun,Ruins of Afghanistan 30.21N 61.34E
40 K10 Taraku-shima isld Kuril Is U.S.S.R. 43.37N 146.15W
120 E10 Tara, L Chile
12 J5 Taralga New S Wales 34.12S 149.50E
11 F9 Taramakau R New Zealand
19 D8 Taramana Indonesia 8.13S 124.54E
76 E2 Taramundi Spain 43.21N 7.06W
41 B5 Taran U.S.S.R. 71.21N 73.00E
12 J5 Tarana New S Wales 33.31S 149.55E
29 D3 Tārānagar Rajasthan India 28.40N 75.06E
11 J6 Taranaki stat area New Zealand
11 J5 Taranaki Bight, N New Zealand
11 J6 Taranaki Bight,S New Zealand
118 B5 Taranaquis Bolivia 17.45S 59.15W
75 D7 Tarancón Spain 40.01N 3.01W
29 C5 Taranga Hill Gujarat India 24.00N 72.43E
11 J2 Taranga I New Zealand 35.58S 174.45E
30 G3 Tarangan Nepal 27.53N 86.39E
93 G10 Tarangire Nat. Park Tanzania
47 K8 Tarangul,Oz L Kazakhstan U.S.S.R. 54.02N 68.25E
39 E5 Taran Mys C U.S.S.R. 59.09N 151.08E
58 B3 Taransay isld W Isles Scotland 57.53N 7.03W
81 P12 Táranto Italy 40.28N 17.15E
81 P11 Táranto prov Italy
81 N4 Táranto, Golfo di Italy
120 D8 Tarapacá Chile 19.58S 69.31W
119 E9 Tarapaca Colombia 2.56S 69.46W
120 D8 Tarapacá prov Chile
15 M3 Tarapaina Malaita I Solomon Is 9.24S 161.21E
120 F8 Tarapaya Bolivia 19.30S 65.47W
31 B4 Tarapkan, P-i- pass Afghanistan 33.15N 63.50E
11 L6 Taraponui mt New Zealand 39.09S 176.45E
120 B2 Tarapoto Peru 6.31S 76.23W
84 D8 Tárapsa Greece 36.54N 22.29E
30 K7 Tarapur Bihar India 25.05N 86.39E
29 C8 Tarapur Chinchani Maharashtra India 19.52N 72.42E
Taraq el Aalab see Tarq el'Alab
Taraq el Hbâri see Tarq el Hbâri
Taraq Naaje see Tarq Nâje
Taraq Sidâoui see Tarq Sidâui
71 E5 Tarare France 45.54N 4.26E
11 K7 Tararua Ra New Zealand
41 O6 Taras U.S.S.R. 69.10N 134.11E
71 F9 Tarascon Bouches-du-Rhône France 43.48N 4.39E
72 H10 Tarascon-sur-Ariège France 42.51N 1.35E
45 B7 Tarashcha Ukraine U.S.S.R. 49.35N 30.20E
32 G4 Tarasht Iran 33.57N 57.14E
45 K7 Tarasovka Ukraine U.S.S.R. 49.37N 38.25E
47 F3 Tarasovo U.S.S.R. 66.14N 46.43E
42 G5 Tarasovskiy U.S.S.R. 54.20N 102.58E
45 M8 Tarasovskiy U.S.S.R. 48.44N 40.22E
88 S8 Tarat Algeria 26.09N 9.10E
120 E7 Tarata Bolivia 17.35S 66.04W
18 D5 Taratalbuluh Sumatra Indon 0.25N 101.29E
120 D3 Tarauacá Brazil 8.06S 70.45W
120 D2 Tarauacá,R Brazil
122 T15 Tarauru-roa isld Gambier Is Pacific Oc 23.06S 134.50W
122 R15 Tara-Vai isld Gambier Is Pacific Oc 23.08S 135.02W
122 D12 Taravao B Tahiti Pacific Oc
122 C12 Taravao,Isthmus of Tahiti Pacific Oc
75 G6 Taravilla Spain 40.42N 1.59W
67 O13 Taravo R Corsica
9 B5 Tarawa atoll Kiribati, Pacific Oc 1.30N 173.00E
15 G5 Tarawai I Papua New Guinea 3.14S 143.15E
Tarawasi see Armopa
11 L6 Tarawera New Zealand 39.01S 176.35E
11 L5 Tarawera L New Zealand
11 L5 Tarawera, Mt New Zealand 38.14S 176.32E
88 S11 Tarazit Niger 20.04N 8.13E
88 S11 Tarazit,Massif de mts Niger
76 J6 Tarazona Salamanca Spain 41.10N 5.15W
75 G4 Tarazona Zaragoza Spain 41.54N 1.44W
77 N2 Tarazona de la Mancha Spain 39.16N 1.55W
53 K5 Tårbæk Denmark 55.48N 12.37E
Tarbagatai see Tacheng
42 H6 Tarbagatay Buryat U.S.S.R. 51.30N 107.20E
42 H6 Tarbagatay Chita U.S.S.R. 51.15N 109.05E
43 P4 Tarbagatay,Khrebet mts Kazakhstan U.S.S.R.
93 M3 Tarbaj Hill Kenya 2.12N 40.10E
58 J3 Tarbat Ness prom Highland Scotland 57.52N 3.46W
31 G3 Tarbela Dam Pakistan 34.06N 72.50E
77 Q3 Tárbena Spain 38.42N 0.07W
58 C3 Tarbert Harris, W Isles Scotland 57.54N 6.49W
59 D6 Tarbert Kerry Irish Rep 52.34N 9.22W
58 F7 Tarbert Strathclyde Scotland 55.52N 5.26W
58 C3 Tarbert, E.L Harris, W Isles Scotland
58 E7 Tarbert,L Jura, Strathclyde Scotland 55.58N 5.55W
58 C3 Tarbert, W.L Harris, W Isles Scotland
58 F7 Tarbert, W.L Strathclyde Scotland
72 E9 Tarbes France 43.14N 0.05E
58 G6 Tarbet Strathclyde Scotland 56.12N 4.43W
57 E1 Tarbolton Strathclyde Scotland 55.31N 4.29W
105 K2 Tarboro N Carolina 35.54N 77.34W
13 F5 Tarbrax Queensland 21.05S 142.25E
85 C7 Tarbū Libya 26.00N 15.09E
86 F7 Tarbûl Abu Khashirât, Gebel hill Egypt 29.13N 31.21E
86 L8 Tarbûsh,Gebel hill Egypt 28.36N 33.50E
82 K4 Tarcaului, Munţii mts Romania
66 A3 Tarcenay France 47.09N 6.06E
79 O2 Tarcento Italy 46.13N 13.13E
30 E2 Tarchan Xizang Zizhiqu 30.58N 81.20E
61 H5 Tarcienne Belgium 50.18N 4.30E
13 F7 Tarco Queensland 26.30S 141.46E
12 G5 Tarcoola New S Wales 33.27S 142.38E
12 C4 Tarcoola S Australia 30.43S 134.34E
12 H4 Tarcoon New S Wales 30.19S 146.43E
12 C2 Tarcoonyinna,R S Australia
12 J6 Tarcutta New S Wales 35.17S 147.50E
75 C3 Tardajos Spain 42.21N 3.49W
75 E4 Tardelcuende Spain 41.36N 2.39W
28 A8 Tardeo dist Bombay India
72 J3 Tardes R France
72 C9 Tardets Sorholus France 43.07N 0.51W
75 J4 Tardienta Spain 41.59N 0.33W
72 C2 Tardière,la France 46.40N 0.43W
72 F4 Tardoire R France
40 H7 Tardoki Yani,Gory mt U.S.S.R. 48.50N 138.04E
14 B8 Tardun W Australia 28.47S 115.44E
88 P9 Taredjerdja Algeria 25.12N 2.32E
12 K4 Taree New S Wales 31.54S 152.26E
87 H5 Tareina Ethiopia 10.48N 40.36E
12 G4 Tarella New S Wales 30.55S 143.06E
51 K4 Tärendö Sweden 67.10N 22.40E
71 K5 Tarentaise reg France
104 F6 Tarentum Pennsylvania 40.37N 79.46W
41 F4 Tareya U.S.S.R. 73.19N 90.37E
41 F4 Tareya R U.S.S.R.
33 L7 Ţarfā, Aţ Oman 19.00N 55.30E
33 E8 Ţarfā, Ra's Aţ C Saudi Arabia 17.03N 42.21E
34 H5 Tarfat,At Iraq 33.27N 40.02E
86 F9 Tarfa,Wâdi el watercourse Egypt
33 A4 Tarfawi,Gebel mt Egypt 24.19N 34.54E
88 G8 Tarfaya Morocco 27.58N 12.55W
58 L5 Tarfside Tayside Scotland 56.54N 2.50W
57 D3 Tarf Water R Dumfries & Galloway Scotland
74 K9 Targa R Algeria
21 C4 Targan Heilongjiang China 46.11N 124.08E
89 M3 Targan Niger 16.30N 5.47E
Targhan see Tarqān
42 J5 Targinskiy U.S.S.R. 54.25N 110.32E
24 E10 Targo R Xizang Zizhiqu
72 D6 Targon France 44.44N 0.14W
82 H6 Târgu Carbuneşti Romania 44.57N 23.32E
74 E10 Targuist Morocco 34.57N 4.18W
82 H3 Târgu Lăpuş Romania 47.28N 23.51E
43 P3 Targyn Kazakhstan U.S.S.R. 49.32N 82.47E
32 B4 Tarhān Iran 33.23N 47.19E
36 H3 Tarhana Turkey 39.55N 35.45E
88 Q10 Tarhaouhaout Algeria 22.41N 5.56E
88 L6 Tarhbalt Morocco 30.39N 5.20W
105 J3 Tarheel N Carolina 34.42N 78.49W
88 J7 Tarhjijt Morocco 28.59N 9.26W
88 L9 Tarhmanant Algeria 24.43N 4.15W
85 B3 Tarhunāh Libya 32.27N 13.36E
85 B3 Tarhunāh, Jabal mts Libya
85 G8 Tarhūnī, Jabal at mt Libya 22.10N 22.12E
15 G6 Tari Papua New Guinea 5.52S 142.58E
15 G6 Tari R Papua New Guinea
22 H6 Tarian Gol Nei Monggol Zizhiqu China 40.05N 109.11E
22 E2 Tariat Mongolia 48.07N 99.32E
119 D4 Tariba Venezuela 7.48N 72.10W
33 E7 Tarib, Wādī watercourse Saudi Arabia
33 K4 Tarif U.A.E. 24.03N 53.45E
33 K4 Tarif U.A.E. 24.03N 53.46E
77 E8 Tarifa Spain 36.01N 5.36W
33 E9 Tarifah Yemen 14.22N 43.46E
103 J3 Tariffville Connecticut 41.55N 72.46W
19 L3 Tarigtig Pt Luzon Philippines 16.24N 122.13E
120 F9 Tarija Bolivia 21.33S 64.45W
120 F9 Tarija dept Bolivia
120 F9 Tarija R Bolivia
19 N4 Tarik isld Truk Is Pacific Oc 7.21N 151.47E
28 B4 Tarikere Karnataka India 13.43N 75.46E
11 J6 Tariki New Zealand 39.14S 174.16E
94 F2 Tarikora Namibia 18.50S 20.55E
15 D5 Tariku R Irian Jaya
33 H8 Tarim S Yemen 16.08N 48.58E
Tarim Basin see Tarim Pendi
Tarim Darya R see Yarkant He
93 F7 Tarime Tanzania 1.20S 34.24E
24 F5 Tarim Erchang Xinjiang Uygur Zizhiqu China 40.43N 87.07E
24 E5 Tarim He R Xinjiang Uygur Zizhiqu China
24 D6 Tarim Pendi basin Xinjiang Uygur Zizhiqu China
Tarim & Saywūn sultanate see Kathīri state
18 B4 Taring Sumatra Indon 3.51N 97.30E
120 F9 Taringuiti Bolivia 21.25S 63.09W
31 C4 Tarīn Kowt Afghanistan 32.52N 65.53E
Tari Nor see Dalai Nur
15 E5 Taritatu R Irian Jaya
18 M2 Taritipan Sabah Malaysia 6.39N 116.55E
34 M3 Tarjil Iraq 35.22N 44.29E
95 J8 Tarka R S Africa
47 L2 Tarkasale U.S.S.R. 68.23N 71.52E
95 K8 Tarkastad S Africa 32.01S 26.16E
Tarkh see Tarq
44 B9 Tarkhankut, Mys C U.S.S.R. 45.28N 32.30E
44 B9 Tarkhankutskaya Vozvyshennost' heights Ukraine U.S.S.R.
107 A1 Tarkio Missouri 40.27N 95.24W
110 L2 Tarkio Montana 47.01N 114.44W
24 F10 Tarko La pass Xizang Zizhiqu China 31.34N 89.57E
38 G2 Tarko-Sale U.S.S.R. 64.55N 77.50E
31 D3 Tarkuch Afghanistan 35.22N 66.32E
89 J9 Tarkwa Ghana 5.16N 1.59W
121 K7 Tar,L Argentina
19 K4 Tarlac Luzon Philippines 15.29N 120.35E
19 K4 Tarlac R Luzon Philippines
24 E5 Tarlak Xinjiang Uygur Zizhiqu China 41.52N 84.15E
58 L4 Tarland Grampian Scotland 57.08N 2.52W
37 G2 Tarla Tepe mt Turkey 40.22N 29.29E
57 H5 Tarleton Lancs Eng 53.41N 2.50W
94 R13 Tarlton S Africa 26.05S 27.38E
53 B5 Tarm Denmark 55.55N 8.32E
120 B4 Tarma Junín Peru 11.28S 75.41W
119 E9 Tarma Loreto Peru 3.15S 71.42W
34 M5 Tarmiyah, Aţ Iraq 33.40N 44.25E
63 K6 Tarmstedt W Germany 53.14N 9.04E
67 G9 Tarn dept France
72 H8 Tarn R France
30 A2 Tarna Himachal Prad India 30.48N 77.27E
76 J2 Tarna Spain 43.06N 5.13W
62 M8 Tarna R Hungary
51 E6 Tärnaby Sweden 65.44N 15.20E
31 D5 Tarnak R Afghanistan
76 J2 Tarna,Pto de pass Spain 43.05N 5.12W
53 K5 Tårnby Denmark 55.37N 12.36E
67 F8 Tarn-et-Garonne dept France
72 L7 Tarn,Gorges du France
Tarnguk see Dongco
62 N5 Tarnobrzeg Poland 50.35N 21.40E
47 E5 Tarnogskiy Gorodok U.S.S.R. 60.32N 43.33E
100 M6 Tarnopol Saskatchewan 52.43N 105.23W
72 B8 Tarnos France 43.33N 1.27W
63 Q5 Tarnow E Germany 53.47N 12.02E
62 N6 Tarnów Poland 50.01N 20.59E
62 L5 Tarnowskie Gory Poland 50.28N 18.40E
24 J12 Taro Burma 26.22N 96.10E
20 P2 Tarō Japan 39.44N 141.59E
79 H5 Taro R Italy
15 L3 Taroaniara Solomon Is 9.09S 160.13E
15 L6 Tarobi New Britain 5.30S 150.46E
15 B5 Tarof Irian Jaya 2.14S 132.27E
24 E10 Tarok Tso L Xizang Zizhiqu China 31.10N 84.00E
32 F6 Ţārom Iran 28.10N 55.44E
45 F8 Taromskoy Ukraine U.S.S.R. 48.26N 34.49E
15 M6 Taron New Ireland 4.24S 153.03E
13 K7 Tarong Queensland 26.50S 151.50E
12 F9 Taronga Tasmania 42.58S 147.20E
72 D8 Taron-Sadirac Viellenave France 43.30N 0.14W
13 J7 Taroom Queensland 25.39S 149.50E
12 F9 Taroona Tasmania 42.58S 147.22E
90 J1 Tarou Chad 20.39N 19.15E
90 D3 Tarouadji,Mts Niger
76 D6 Tarouca Portugal 41.01N 7.36W
88 J6 Taroudannt Morocco 30.31N 8.55W
63 K3 Tarp W Germany 54.40N 9.25E
31 H9 Tarpasa Bangladesh 23.38N 90.16E
13 D4 Tarpaulin Swamp N Terr Australia
112 H6 Tarpley Texas 29.38N 99.18W
105 E9 Tarpon Springs Florida 28.08N 82.45W
57 H6 Tarporley Cheshire Eng 53.10N 2.40W
32 D4 Tarq Esfahān Iran 33.20N 51.50E
32 H5 Ţārq Khorāsān Iran 31.50N 59.55E
32 D5 Ţarqān Iran 31.49N 51.42E
34 F5 Tarq el'Alab watercourses Syria
34 G4 Tarq el Hbâri watercourses Syria
34 G4 Tarq Nâje watercourses Syria
34 G4 Tarq Sidâui watercourses Syria
80 E4 Tarquinia Italy 42.23N 11.45E
35 D7 Tarqumiya Jordan 31.34N 35.01E
105 J1 Tar,R N Carolina
59 G7 Tar,R Tipperary Irish Rep
75 N5 Tarragona Spain 41.07N 1.15E
74 H3 Tarragona prov Spain
51 H5 Tårrajaur Sweden 66.27N 19.40E
12 H8 Tarraleah Tasmania 42.20S 146.21E
12 H4 Tarran Hills New S Wales
107 K8 Tarrant City Alabama 33.38N 86.46W
56 G6 Tarrant Hinton Dorset Eng 50.54N 2.05W
13 E3 Tarrant,Pt Queensland 17.20S 139.30E
11 D11 Tarras New Zealand 44.52S 169.26E
75 P4 Tarrasa Spain 41.34N 2.00E
75 N4 Tárrega Spain 41.39N 1.09E
51 F4 Tarrekaise mt Sweden 67.02N 17.20E
65 C7 Tarrenz Austria 47.17N 10.47E
13 K8 Tarrewinna Queensland 28.12S 150.10E
76 B13 Tarro Portugal 37.53N 8.42W
75 N4 Tarroja Spain 41.44N 1.17E
109 E2 Tarryall Colorado 39.07N 105.28W
109 E2 Tarryall Cr Colorado
105 E5 Tarrytown Georgia 32.19N 82.33W
103 F4 Tarrytown New York 41.05N 73.51W
53 E2 Tårs Nordjylland Denmark 57.23N 10.08E
53 G7 Tårs Storstrøm Denmark 54.53N 11.02E
53 H7 Tårs Storstrøm Denmark 54.50N 11.38E
74 F9 Tarsa,C Algeria 34.28N 1.50W
86 L3 Tarsag Egypt 31.09N 33.57E
90 J1 Tarsaou Chad 20.09N 18.22E
65 G5 Tarsdorf Austria 48.05N 12.50E
33 B10 Tarshayn, Ra's C S Yemen 12.47N 44.59E
Tarshīha see Me'ona
81 M4 Tarsia Italy 39.37N 16.16E
79 P4 Tarski Zaliv gulf Yugoslavia
44 F5 Tarskoye U.S.S.R. 42.57N 44.48E
90 J1 Tarso Emisou mts Chad
90 H1 Tarso Kobour mts Chad
90 J1 Tarso Kozen mts Chad
90 J1 Tarso Mohi mts Chad
90 H1 Tarso Ourari mts Chad
90 J1 Tarso Taro mt Chad 20.21N 18.23E
90 H1 Tarso Tieroko mts Chad
90 H1 Tarso Tiri mts Chad
90 H1 Tarso Toon mts Chad
90 H1 Tarso Voon mts Chad
36 H6 Tarsus Turkey 36.52N 34.52E
53 H7 Tårs Vig B Denmark 54.53N 11.39E
22 B8 Tart Qinghai China 37.05N 92.58E
43 C6 Tarta Turkmeniya U.S.S.R. 40.01N 52.48E
120 F10 Tartagal Argentina 22.32S 63.50W
121 F2 Tartagal Argentina 28.35S 59.52W
79 G2 Tartano Italy 46.07N 9.42E
88 F9 Tartar Morocco 25.25N 14.45W
79 K4 Tartaro R Italy
Tartary,Gulf of see Tatarskiy Proliv
72 C8 Tartas France 43.50N 0.48W
42 B4 Tartas R U.S.S.R.
Tartoûs see Tartūs
46 F1 Tartu Estonia U.S.S.R. 58.20N 26.44E
89 F9 Tartuke Libya 5.13N 7.59W
34 C4 Tartūs Syria 34.55N 35.52E
93 L9 Taru Kenya 3.45S 39.10E
93 A3 Taru Zaïre 2.54N 29.25E
Ta Ruang see Ban Ta Ruang
Tarum Iran see Ţārom
35 C6 Tarum Israel 31.46N 34.58E
24 D5 Tarum Xinjiang Uygur Zizhiqu China 41.02N 83.15E
20 L2 Tarumae-yama mt Japan 42.44N 141.24E
20 K6 Tarumi Japan 35.41N 136.33E
118 H6 Tarumirim Brazil 19.17S 41.59W
20 D10 Tarumizu Japan 31.30N 130.40E
44 H3 Tarumovka U.S.S.R. 44.06N 46.33E
25 M7 Tarung Hka R Burma
45 J2 Tarusa U.S.S.R. 54.44N 37.14E
86 F4 Tārût Egypt 30.32N 31.28E
33 J3 Tārūt isld Saudi Arabia 26.35N 50.05E
33 A7 Tārūt B Saudi Arabia
46 G6 Tarutino Ukraine U.S.S.R. 46.09N 29.04E
33 A7 Tārūt,Jazīrat / Saudi Arabia
18 C4 Tarutung Sumatra Indon 2.01N 98.54E
15 K2 Taruvana Choiseul I Solomon Is 6.52S 156.58E
52 E3 Tarva isld Norway 63.48N 9.26E
53 W17 Tarven mt Norway 60.46N 7.11E
58 M4 Tarves Grampian Scotland 57.23N 2.14W
57 H6 Tarvin Cheshire Eng 53.12N 2.46W
79 P1 Tarvisio Italy 46.30N 13.35E
120 G6 Tarvo Bolivia 15.05S 60.38W
120 G6 Tarvo,R Bolivia
84 Z20 Tarxien Malta 35.52N 14.32E
32 G5 Tarz Iran 31.25N 56.34E
74 H8 Tarzout Algeria 36.29N 1.04E
85 A7 Tarz Ulli Libya 25.32N 10.08E
99 K4 Tarzwell Ontario 48.01N 80.01W
86 J4 Ţâsa, El reg Egypt
36 E6 Taşağil Turkey 36.55N 31.16E
112 B6 Tasajera,Sierra mts Mexico
Tasak,Kuh see Tābask,Kūh-e mt
30 K4 Tasam Xizang Zizhiqu 28.10N 86.26E
43 L4 Tasaral Kazakhstan U.S.S.R. 46.17N 74.00E
43 L4 Tasaral,Ostrov isld Kazakhstan U.S.S.R. 46.15N 74.01E
96 U15 Tasarte Gran Canaria Canary Is 27.56N 15.46W
85 B7 Tasawah Libya 25.58N 13.30E
43 H5 Tas-Buget Kazakhstan U.S.S.R. 44.46N 65.31E
66 H7 Täsch Switzerland 46.06N 7.47E
99 M4 Taschereau Quebec 48.40N 78.42W
Taşcı see Bakırdağı
109 K2 Tasco Kansas 39.21N 100.19W
112 B8 Tascosa Texas 35.31N 102.16W
88 R9 Tasedjibest mts Algeria
88 R11 Taseggafit,Mt Algeria 21.10N 7.08E
101 M10 Taseko R Br Col
101 M10 Taseko,Mt Br Col 51.12N 123.07W
88 O12 Tasendjit Mali 19.37N 1.25E
48 S12 Taserssuaq fjord Greenland
90 D3 Tasessat Niger 17.44N 8.45E
42 E3 Taseyeva R U.S.S.R.
42 E4 Taseyevo U.S.S.R. 57.13N 94.50E
28 B2 Tasgaon Maharashtra India 17.04N 74.41E
32 F2 Tāsh Iran 36.34N 54.46E
42 D7 Tashakta U.S.S.R. 49.44N 89.14E
32 D5 Tashān Iran 30.52N 50.10E
43 E6 Tashauz Turkmeniya U.S.S.R. 41.49N 59.58E
24 G6 Tash Davan pass Xinjiang Uygur Zizhiqu China 39.02N 91.16E
45 V3 Tashelka U.S.S.R. 53.46N 49.28E
22 D6 Tashi Gansu China 40.15N 95.58E
43 N8 Tashiak Uzbekistan U.S.S.R. 40.30N 71.47E
Tashi Bhup Tso L see Zhaxi Co
Tashi Chho Dzong see Thimbu
28 H2 Tashigang Bhutan 27.19N 91.33E
Tashigong see Zhaxigang
30 L5 Tashirakha Xizang Zizhiqu 27.58N 87.40E
32 E6 Tashk Iran 29.46N 53.42E
43 J6 Tashkent Uzbekistan U.S.S.R. 41.16N 69.13E
43 G8 Tashkepri Turkmeniya U.S.S.R. 36.16N 62.08E
43 G8 Tashkeprinskoye Vdkhr res Turkmeniya U.S.S.R.
43 K6 Tash-Kumyr Kirgiziya U.S.S.R. 41.21N 72.14E
Tash Kurghan see Taxkorgan
Tash Kurghan R see Taxkorgan
46 R4 Tashla U.S.S.R. 51.43N 52.41E
Tashmalik see Akto
99 C2 Tashota Ontario 50.13N 87.40W
42 D5 Tashtagol U.S.S.R. 52.49N 87.57E
42 D6 Tashtyp U.S.S.R. 52.52N 89.54E
18 H9 Tasikmalaya Java Indon 7.20S 108.16E
35 G2 Tasil Syria 32.50N 35.58E
33 H9 Taşilah S Yemen 15.12N 48.08E
53 F7 Tåsinge isld Denmark 55.00N 10.35E
97 O3 Tasiussaq Greenland 73.20N 56.00W
52 J2 Tåsjö Sweden 64.13N 16.00E
52 J2 Tåsjön L Sweden 64.15N 15.50E
90 E4 Task Niger 14.56N 10.46E
39 E3 Taskan U.S.S.R. 62.57N 150.20E
53 W14 Taskedalstind mt Norway 62.23N 7.22E
36 F6 Taşkent Turkey 36.54N 32.28E
90 E4 Tasker Niger 15.08N 10.41E
43 O4 Taskesken Kazakhstan U.S.S.R. 47.15N 80.45E
42 E4 Taskino U.S.S.R. 56.20N 92.50E
37 G2 Taşkopru İzmir Turkey 40.54N 29.45E
36 G1 Taşköprü Kastamonu Turkey 41.30N 34.12E
15 L5 Taskul Bismarck Arch 2.34S 150.25E
39 A1 Tas-Kumsa U.S.S.R. 68.40N 133.16E
42 F6 Taskyl,Khrebet mts U.S.S.R.
39 C3 Tas-Kystabys,Khrebet ra U.S.S.R.
37 G6 Taşlıçay Turkey 39.37N 43.23E
11 H7 Tasman B New Zealand
11 E10 Tasman Glacier New Zealand 43.35S 170.12E
12 H9 Tasman Hd Tasmania 43.30S 147.15E
12 G9 Tasmania state Australia
11 E10 Tasman,Mt New Zealand 43.33S 170.10E
11 G7 Tasman Mts New Zealand
12 J9 Tasman Pen Tasmania
10 K10 Tasman Plateau Southern Oc
11 E10 Tasman R New Zealand
10 L9 Tasman Sea Pacific Oc
82 H3 Tăşnad Romania 47.30N 22.33E
65 O3 Tasov Czechoslovakia 49.18N 16.06E
36 J2 Taşova Turkey 40.45N 36.20E
56 O2 Tas,R Norfolk Eng
37 H7 Taşrumi Turkey 38.49N 44.04E
59 J3 Tassagh Armagh N Ireland 54.16N 6.39W
77 F10 Tassaot,Jebel mt Morocco 35.15N 5.06W
89 M3 Tassara Niger 16.52N 5.40E
71 F2 Tasselot,Mt France 47.24N 4.47E
97 M6 Tassialouc, L Quebec
89 A1 Tassiast reg Mauritania
88 P12 Tassili du Hoggar mts Algeria
88 Q8 Tassili N' Ajjer mts Algeria
88 R10 Tassili Tin Eggolé mts Algeria
89 C7 Tasso I Sierra Leone 8.35N 13.00W
53 J5 Tåstrup Denmark 55.39N 12.19E
41 N8 Tas-Tumus Yakutsk U.S.S.R. 64.14N 126.46E
41 O5 Tas-Tumus Yakutsk U.S.S.R. 70.42N 131.00E
43 J5 Tasty Kazakhstan U.S.S.R. 44.42N 69.06E
36 G6 Taşucu Turkey 36.18N 33.52E
32 A1 Tasūj Iran 38.18N 45.18E
42 J2 Tas-Yuryakh U.S.S.R. 61.45N 113.05E
88 K7 Tata Morocco 29.44N 7.56W
122 B11 Tataa,Pt Tahiti Pacific Oc 17.33S 149.36W
82 E3 Tatabanya Hungary 47.31N 18.25E
15 H4 Tatak I Bismarck Arch 0.54S 145.30E
122 F15 Tatakoto atoll Tuamotu Is Pacific Oc 17.17S 138.20W
Tatāl see Dadal
19 K8 Tatalan isld Philippines 6.15N 121.51E
22 C8 Tatalin Gol R Qinghai China
19 F3 Tatam Halmahera Indon 1.30N 128.23E
98 J8 Tatamagouche Nova Scotia 45.43N 63.19W
15 L3 Tatamba Santa Isabel I Solomon Is 8.23S 159.48E
103 D5 Tatamy Pennsylvania 40.44N 75.14W
29 J2 Tatanagar Bihar India 22.47N 86.14E
88 T5 Tataouine Tunisia 33.00N 10.28E
11 K5 Tatara mt New Zealand 38.37S 175.00E
82 M5 Tatarbunary U.S.S.R. 45.50N 29.39E
47 M8 Tatarka U.S.S.R. 54.00N 75.09E
36 B1 Tatarlar Turkey 41.46N 26.54E
45 C2 Tatarsk Smolensk U.S.S.R. 54.15N 31.34E
38 E3 Tatarskaya A.S.S.R U.S.S.R.
47 M5 Tatarskaya-Karabolka U.S.S.R. 55.56N 61.12E
40 J6 Tatarskiy Proliv str U.S.S.R.
45 T3 Tatarskiy Sayman U.S.S.R. 53.18N 47.07E
41 E8 Tatarskoye U.S.S.R. 64.46N 87.56E
Tatars Pass see Yablonitse,Pereval pass
18 K4 Tatau Sarawak Malaysia 2.55N 112.50E
37 J8 Tātā'u R Iran
15 L5 Tatau I Bismarck Arch 2.50S 151.51E
42 H6 Tataurovo Buryat U.S.S.R. 52.10N 107.29E
42 J6 Tataurovo Chita U.S.S.R. 51.38N 112.56E
32 A2 Tatavi R Iran
105 C3 Tate Georgia 34.25N 84.24W
89 F9 Taté Ivory Coast 4.48N 7.32W
100 N7 Tate Saskatchewan 51.27N 104.52W
13 G3 Tate R Queensland
20 O2 Tateai Japan 39.18N 140.18E
20 N5 Tatebayashi Japan 36.14N 139.30E
13 C2 Tate Bluff hill N Terr Australia 14.09S 134.23E
20 J6 Tateishi-misaki C Japan 35.45N 135.57E
20 H4 Tateno-shimbata Chiba Japan
94 J3 Tate, R Botswana
20 J3 Tateura Japan 41.58N 140.08E
20 N7 Tateyama Japan 34.59N 139.50E
20 L5 Tate yama mt Japan 36.39N 137.32E
101 P5 Tathlina L N W Terr
33 E7 Tathlith Saudi Arabia 19.35N 43.31E
33 E7 Tathlith, Wādī watercourse Saudi Arabia
23 C9 Tathong Chan Hong Kong
23 C9 Tathong Pt Hong Kong 22.14N 114.16E
12 J6 Tathra New S Wales 36.44S 149.58E
Ta-ting see Dafang
28 J1 Tatingka Xizang Zizhiqu 29.32N 93.25E
45 R5 Tatishchevo U.S.S.R. 51.42N 45.36E
113 O6 Tatitlek Alaska 60.51N 146.39W
25 D2 Tatkon Burma 20.07N 96.11E
101 L10 Tatla L Br Col 51.59N 124.25W
101 L10 Tatla Lake Br Col 51.54N 124.39W
101 K7 Tatlatui Prov. Park Br Col
113 K6 Tatlawiksuk,R Alaska
101 L10 Tatlayoko Lake Br Columbia 51.39N 124.23W
101 M10 Tatlow,Mt Br Col 51.22N 123.52W
108 B5 Tatman Mt Wyoming 44.18N 108.26W
97 K6 Tatnam,C Manitoba 57.25N 90.55W
113 R4 Tatonduk R Alaska/Yukon Terr
12 H6 Tatong Victoria 36.46S 146.03E
Tatra mts see Tatry mts
Tatran see Tatrang
24 E6 Tatrang Xinjiang Uygur Zizhiqu China 38.29N 85.38E
62 M6 Tatry mts Czech/Poland
22 E4 Tatsain Tsagaan Nuur L Mongolia 45.05N 101.25E

Tatsaitan see Ta-ch'ai-tan
24 G11 Ta-tse Xizang Zizhiqu 29.51N 91.33E
101 E6 Tatshenshini R Br Col
Tatsienlu see Kangding
45 N8 Tatsinskiy U.S.S.R. 48.11N 41.17E
20 H7 Tatsuno Japan 34.54N 134.30E
20 K4 Tatsuruhama Japan 37.03N 136.52E
31 D8 Tatta Pakistan 24.44N 67.58E
31 D8 Tatta dist Pakistan
41 O8 Tatta R U.S.S.R.
57 N6 Tattershall Lincs Eng 53.07N 0.11W
43 L5 Tatty Kazakhstan U.S.S.R. 43.11N 73.22E
118 G10 Tatuapé dist São Paulo Brazil
118 F8 Tatuí Brazil 23.22S 47.53W
121 B2 Tatul,Sa.de mts Chile
109 G8 Tatum New Mexico 33.16N 103.18W
112 N3 Tatum Texas 32.20N 94.32W
109 N7 Tatums Oklahoma 34.29N 97.28W
Ta-t'ung see Datong
Ta-tun-kou see Antung Liaoning
12 H6 Tatura Victoria 36.26S 145.14E
37 F5 Tatus Dağları mts Turkey
37 G7 Tatvan Turkey 38.31N 42.15E
42 C4 Tat'yanovka U.S.S.R. 56.53N 83.36E
Ta-tzu see Ta-tse
45 T7 Tau Kazakhstan U.S.S.R. 49.41N 47.16E
53 T20 Tau Norway 59.04N 5.55E
122 F1 Tau isld Amer Samoa Pacific Oc 14.15S 169.27W
9 S10 Tau islet Tonga, Pacific Oc 21.00S 175.00W
117 G8 Tauá Brazil 6.04S 40.26W
19 M4 Taualap Pass Truk Is Pacific Oc 7.29N 151.35E
119 H9 Tauapeçaçu Brazil 2.39S 60.57W
117 B6 Tauari Brazil 3.05S 55.05W
120 F1 Tauaria Brazil 5.38S 63.52W
120 D1 Tauaru,I Brazil 4.07S 69.24W
64 L2 Taubach E Germany 50.56N 11.24E
118 F8 Taubaté Brazil 23.00S 45.36W
64 H5 Tauber R W Germany
64 H4 Tauberbischofsheim W Germany 49.38N 9.41E
64 J5 Tauberzell W Germany 49.27N 10.09E
63 R10 Taucha E Germany 51.24N 12.31E
63 U8 Tauche E Germany 52.09N 14.10E
44 L3 Tauchik Kazakhstan U.S.S.R. 44.22N 51.21E
122 E15 Tauére atoll Tuamotu Is Pacific Oc 17.18S 141.30W
65 F7 Tauern-kopf mt Austria 47.09N 12.29E
66 E3 Täuffelen Switzerland 47.04N 7.13E
87 C6 Taufikia Sudan 9.23N 31.38E
65 J5 Taufkirchen Austria 48.25N 13.32E
64 N7 Taufkirchen W Germany 48.20N 12.08E
64 G2 Taufstein mt W Germany 50.31N 9.16E
11 J3 Tauhoa New Zealand 36.23S 174.29E
117 A4 Tauini,R Brazil
43 M5 Taukum,Peski sand des Kazakhstan U.S.S.R.
91 F10 Taula Angola 12.32S 19.12E
9 R13 Taula islet Tonga, Pacific Oc 18.50S 174.01W
122 B4 Taulaga Swains I Pacific Oc 11.03S 171.05W
71 J9 Taulanne France 43.52N 6.27E
70 C4 Taulé France 48.36N 3.55W
71 F8 Taulignan France 44.26N 4.58E
30 G5 Taulihawa Nepal 27.33N 83.03E
53 D5 Taulov Denmark 55.33N 9.38E
43 D7 Taumakindzhi Turkmeniya U.S.S.R. 39.29N 55.40E
11 K5 Taumarunui New Zealand 38.53S 175.16E
11 B3 Taumatarea Pt New Zealand 36.59S 174.38E
120 C3 Taumaturgo Brazil 8.54S 72.51W
107 F4 Taum Sauk Mt Missouri 37.34N 90.44W
118 C7 Taunay Brazil 20.18S 56.00W
95 H3 Taung S Africa 27.32S 24.48E
9 R12 Taunga isld Tonga, Pacific Oc 18.44S 174.01W
25 D5 Taungbon Burma 15.24N 97.50E
25 C2 Taungdwingyi Burma 20.01N 95.20E
25 M9 Taunggon Burma 23.43N 96.32E
25 D2 Taung-gyi Burma 20.55N 96.53E
25 D2 Taunglau Burma 21.59N 97.26E
25 D4 Taungnyo Ra Burma
25 C2 Taungtha Burma 21.16N 95.25E
25 C3 Taungup Burma 18.50N 94.14E
122 B11 Taunoa Tahiti Pacific Oc 17.30S 149.33W
30 J8 Taunsa Bihar India 24.57N 85.09E
31 F5 Taunsa Pakistan 30.43N 70.41E
31 F5 Taunsa Barrage Pakistan 30.42N 70.50E
103 M3 Taunton Massachusetts 41.54N 71.05W
56 E5 Taunton Somerset Eng 51.01N 3.06W
64 E3 Taunus mts W Germany
69 P3 Taunusstein W Germany 50.09N 8.06E
11 J10 Taupeka Pt Chatham Is Pacific Oc 43.43S 176.28W
51 L11 Taupila Finland 60.08N 24.45E
11 K4 Taupiri New Zealand 37.38S 175.12E
11 L5 Taupo New Zealand 38.42S 176.06E
11 K5 Taupo,L New Zealand
Tāūq see Dāqūq
34 M4 Tāūq Chāy R Iraq
59 D7 Taur mt Cork Irish Rep 52.14N 9.07W
46 D2 Tauragė Lithuania U.S.S.R. 55.12N 22.16E
11 J6 Taurakawa mt New Zealand 39.20S 174.42E
119 D5 Tauramena Colombia 5.02N 72.43W
11 L4 Tauranga New Zealand 37.42S 176.11E
11 L4 Tauranga Harb inlet New Zealand
99 R6 Taureau, L Quebec
15 H7 Tauri R Papua New Guinea
81 M7 Taurianova Italy 38.22N 16.01E
72 G4 Taurion R France
81 R13 Taurisano Italy 39.57N 18.13E
Tauriuiná,R see Verde,R Mato Grosso Brazil
11 H2 Tauroa Pt New Zealand 35.11S 173.06E
42 A3 Taurovy U.S.S.R. 59.38N 73.17E
Taurus Mts see Toros Dağları
Taushkan Darya R see Toxkan He
72 B6 Taussat France 44.43N 1.04W
75 H4 Tauste Spain 41.55N 1.15W
75 H4 Tauste,Can.de Spain
122 V11 Tautama isld Pitcairn I Pacific Oc 25.05S 130.06W
122 D12 Tautira Tahiti Pacific Oc 17.45S 149.10W
122 D12 Tautira B Tahiti Pacific Oc 17.45S 149.08W
122 D12 Tautira, Pt Tahiti Pacific Oc 17.44S 149.09W
24 F9 Tau Tso L Xizang Zizhiqu China 32.50N 88.40E
11 D13 Tautuku Pen New Zealand 46.38S 169.29E
15 K1 Tauu I Papua New Guinea 4.51S 157.04E
15 K1 Tauu Is Papua New Guinea
71 B5 Tauves France 45.34N 2.37E
39 D5 Tauy R U.S.S.R.
39 D5 Tauysk U.S.S.R. 59.45N 149.16E
39 D5 Tauyskaya Guba gulf U.S.S.R.
44 G7 Tauz Azerbaydzhan U.S.S.R. 41.00N 45.36E
Tavālesh,Kūhhá-ye mts see Talyshskiye Gory mts
66 N5 Tavanasa Switzerland 46.45N 9.04E
97 K5 Tavani N W Terr 62.00N 93.20W
66 E3 Tavannes Switzerland 47.13N 7.13E
105 F9 Tavares Florida 28.49N 81.45W
118 K8 Tavares,I.do Brazil 22.49S 43.06W
79 K7 Tavarnelle Val di Pesa Italy 43.33N 11.11E
75 K7 Tavaruela mt Spain 40.30N 0.25W
36 D5 Tavas Turkey 37.33N 29.04E
36 D5 Tavas Ovasi plat Turkey
Tavastehus see Hämeenlinna
39 F4 Tavatuma U.S.S.R. 61.48N 157.52E
47 M4 Tavatuy U.S.S.R. 57.04N 60.09E
47 M4 Tavatuy,Ozero L U.S.S.R. 57.10N 60.35E
69 F4 Tavaux-et Pontséricourt France 49.44N 3.55E
39 K2 Tavayvaam R U.S.S.R.
47 K6 Tavda U.S.S.R. 58.04N 65.12E
47 J6 Tavda R U.S.S.R.
71 F8 Tavel France 44.01N 4.42E
52 M2 Tavelsjö Sweden 64.03N 20.05E
81 N5 Taverna Italy 39.02N 16.35E
71 E2 Tavernay France 47.01N 4.12E
66 M7 Taverne Switzerland 46.04N 8.56E
79 K3 Tavernelle Italy 45.32N 11.28E
80 F2 Tavernelle Italy 43.02N 12.08E
97 M4 Taverner Bay N W Terr
71 J9 Tavernes France 43.35N 6.01E
105 G12 Tavernier Florida 25.02N 80.30W
79 H3 Tavernola Bergamo Italy 45.42N 10.03E
56 B4 Tavernspite Dyfed Wales 51.48N 4.38W
68 D1 Taverny Paris France 49.01N 2.04E
69 C5 Taverny Val d'Oise France 49.02N 2.13E
75 P4 Tavertet Spain 42.00N 2.25E
93 J9 Taveta Kenya 3.23S 37.40E
66 L5 Tavetsch, Val V Switzerland
9 T5 Taveuni isld Fiji
81 R13 Taviano Italy 39.59N 18.05E
61 M5 Tavier Belgium 50.30N 5.28E
67 P12 Tavignano R Corsica
61 O6 Tavigny Belgium 50.07N 5.50E
43 K7 Tavil'dara Tadzhikistan U.S.S.R. 38.44N 70.31E
76 D14 Tavira Portugal 37.07N 7.39W
76 D14 Tavira,Ilha de Portugal 37.04N 7.37W
56 C6 Tavistock Devon Eng 50.33N 4.08W
99 K9 Tavistock Ontario 43.19N 80.50W
37 G6 Tavo Turkey 39.46N 42.40E
80 K4 Tavo R Italy
81 D2 Tavolara, I Sardinia 40.55N 9.43E
80 M5 Tavoliere della Puglia reg Italy
81 Q11 Tavoliere di Lecce reg Italy
43 M1 Tavolzhan Kazakhstan U.S.S.R. 52.44N 77.25E
35 E3 Tavor R Israel
76 D6 Távora R Portugal
Tavor, Har mt see Tabor,Mt
25 E5 Tavoy Burma 14.02N 98.12E
25 E6 Tavoy R Burma
Tavoy I Burma see Mali Kyun
25 E6 Tavoy Pt Burma 13.32N 98.09E
40 E10 Tavrichanka U.S.S.R. 43.22N 131.54E
66 S5 Tavrii,Piz mt Switzerland 46.42N 10.18E
84 C3 Tavropoú, Tekhnití Limni res Greece
37 E2 Tavşan isld Turkey 40.28N 28.07E
37 E2 Tavşan isld Turkey 40.22N 27.47E
37 G2 Tavşancıl Turkey 40.47N 29.35E
37 G2 Tavşanlı Kocaeli Turkey 40.50N 29.33E
36 D3 Tavşanlı Kütahya Turkey 39.34N 29.28E
9 S7 Tavua Viti Levu Fiji 17.27S 177.51E
9 R7 Tavua isld Fiji 17.37S 177.09E
56 C6 Tavy,R Devon Eng
11 J8 Tawa New Zealand 41.10S 174.50E
33 C10 Tawāhī S Yemen 12.48N 45.00E
Tawakhal see Tōwakal
112 M3 Tawakoni,L Texas
34 N9 Tawal,At neutral terr Arabia/Iraq
15 M9 Tawal Reef Louisiade Arch
28 H2 Tawang Assam India 27.34N 91.54E
18 B3 Tawar,Danau L Sumatra Indon
90 C7 Tawari Nigeria 8.17N 6.54E
106 L5 Tawas B Michigan
106 L5 Tawas City Michigan 44.16N 83.33W
100 D4 Tawatinaw Alberta 54.19N 113.30W
100 D4 Tawatinaw R Alberta
18 M3 Tawau Sabah Malaysia 4.16N 117.54E
30 H3 Taweche mt Nepal 27.54N 86.47E
87 A4 Taweisha Sudan 12.19N 26.40E
11 J2 Tawhiti Rahi isld New Zealand 35.29S 174.45E
92 J6 Tawi Tanzania 8.20S 38.50E
90 M5 Tawila Sudan 13.30N 24.54E
33 C2 Ţawīl, At area Saudi Arabia
87 E3 Tawil,Jeb mt Sudan 14.42N 34.42E
59 D5 Tawin I Galway Irish Rep 53.13N 9.02W
31 H4 Tawi R Kashmir
19 K9 Tawitawi isld Philippines
19 K9 Tawitawi Grp islds Philippines
33 F6 Ţaw, Jabal at mts Saudi Arabia
33 D6 Ţawlah, At Saudi Arabia 20.11N 41.23E
87 J8 Tawlei,El Ethiopia 5.44N 42.17E
25 M8 Tawmaw Burma 25.42N 96.19E
59 C4 Tawnyard L Mayo Irish Rep 53.39N 9.39W
56 C5 Taw,R Devon Eng
23 J7 Ta-wu Taiwan 22.17N 120.54E
85 C3 Tāwurghā Libya 32.02N 15.08E
115 K8 Taxco Mexico 18.32N 99.36W
65 G7 Taxenbach Austria 47.18N 12.58E
52 K7 Taxinge Sweden 59.13N 17.21E
24 B7 Taxkorgan Tajik Zizhixian Xinjiang Uygur Zizhiqu China 37.47N 75.14E
120 B3 Tayabamba Peru 8.16S 77.16W
19 K5 Tayabas B Philippines
40 D2 Tayakhtakh U.S.S.R. 59.20N 126.45E
18 J6 Tayan Borneo Indon 0.02S 110.01E
15 B6 Tayandu Moluccas Indon 5.32S 132.20E
15 B6 Tayandu, Pulau Pulau islds Moluccas Indon
47 M6 Tayandy U.S.S.R. 54.47N 61.04E
35 E4 Tayasir Jordan 32.20N 35.24E
47 C2 Taybola U.S.S.R. 68.32N 33.10E
58 L6 Tay Bridge Fife/Tayside Scotland 56.27N 2.59W
40 G9 Tayezhnaya U.S.S.R. 45.19N 136.38E
42 E4 Tayëzhnyy U.S.S.R. 56.15N 94.59E
58 K6 Tay,Firth of Scotland
37 C2 Tayfur Turkey 40.24N 26.29E
42 D4 Tayga U.S.S.R. 56.05N 85.30E
32 D3 Tāygān Iran 34.30N 50.41E
39 G4 Taygonos,Mys C U.S.S.R. 60.36N 160.10E
39 G4 Taygonos Poluostrov pen U.S.S.R.
35 G1 Tayhah Syria 33.09N 36.00E
58 E7 Tayinloan Strathclyde Scotland 55.40N 5.39W
40 F4 Taykanskiy,Khrebet mts U.S.S.R.
58 H6 Tay,L Tayside Scotland
14 D10 Tay,L W Australia
59 K5 Tay,L Wicklow Irish Rep 53.07N 6.15W
111 O7 Taylor Arizona 34.29N 110.05W
107 C8 Taylor Arkansas 33.03N 93.30W
101 N7 Taylor Br Col 56.09N 120.40W
107 G7 Taylor Mississippi 34.16N 89.35W
107 E2 Taylor Missouri 39.57N 91.31W
108 L8 Taylor Nebraska 41.47N 99.23W
103 C1 Taylor New York 42.33N 75.54W
103 C4 Taylor Pennsylvania 41.23N 75.43W
112 K5 Taylor Texas 30.35N 97.26W
110 D2 Taylor Washington 47.27N 121.54W
106 C5 Taylor Wisconsin 44.21N 91.07W
12 A6 Taylor mt A.C.Terr Australia 35.23S 149.05E
13 C5 Taylor R N Terr Australia
101 X1 Taylor I N W Terr 69.12N 101.40W
109 C6 Taylor,Mt New Mexico 35.14N 107.36W
11 F10 Taylor,Mt New Zealand 43.31S 171.19E
113 J6 Taylor Mts Alaska
109 D3 Taylor Park Res Colorado 38.42N 106.49W
105 B3 Taylor Ridge Georgia
105 E3 Taylors S Carolina 34.54N 82.10W
103 C8 Taylors Bridge Delaware 39.25N 75.36W
14 B3 Taylors Crossing W Australia 32.08S 115.55E
11 N10 Taylors Mistake New Zealand 43.35S 172.46E
95 F1 Taylor's Pan salt pan S Africa 25.59S 22.49E
109 F5 Taylor Springs New Mexico 36.19N 104.30W
107 L3 Taylorsville Kentucky 38.01N 85.21W
107 G10 Taylorsville Mississippi 31.50N 89.25W
105 F2 Taylorsville N Carolina 35.56N 81.10W
104 D7 Taylorsville Ohio 39.52N 81.56W
107 G2 Taylorville Illinois 39.32N 89.18W
33 C3 Taymā' Saudi Arabia 27.37N 38.30E
98 F7 Taymouth New Brunswick 46.13N 66.39W
58 J5 Taymouth Castle Tayside Scotland 56.36N 3.59W
41 G8 Taymura R U.S.S.R.
41 M4 Taymylyr U.S.S.R. 72.34N 121.48E
41 F6 Taymyr U.S.S.R. 68.16N 90.07E
41 H2 Taymyra,Mys C U.S.S.R. 78.10N 102.45E
41 G3 Taymyr,Ostrov isld U.S.S.R.
41 H4 Taymyr,Ozero L U.S.S.R.
41 G3 Taymyrskaya Guba U.S.S.R.
41 D4 Taymyrskiy Nats Okrug dist U.S.S.R.
41 G3 Taymyrskyy Zaliv U.S.S.R.
43 J1 Tayncha Kazakhstan U.S.S.R. 53.30N 69.50E
25 J7 Tay Ninh Vietnam 11.21N 106.07E
58 F6 Taynuilt Strathclyde Scotland 56.26N 5.15W
58 L6 Tayport Fife Scotland 56.27N 2.53W
58 J5 Tay,R Tayside Scotland
42 F4 Tayshet U.S.S.R. 55.56N 98.01E
22 D3 Tayshir Mongolia 46.41N 96.26E
95 O4 Tayside S Africa 28.04S 30.24E
58 J5 Tayside reg Scotland
33 E2 Taysīyah,At plat Saudi Arabia
43 C3 Taysoygan, Peski sand des Kazakhstan U.S.S.R.
19 J1 Taytay Luzon Philippines 14.35N 121.08E
19 J6 Taytay Philippines 10.47N 119.32E
19 J6 Taytay B Philippines
19 M6 Taytay Pt Philippines 10.42N 125.08E
18 J9 Tayu Java Indon 6.32S 111.02E
21 C2 Tayuan Heilongjiang China 51.28N 124.22E
42 H4 Tayura U.S.S.R. 57.00N 106.35E
32 J3 Tayyebāt Iran 34.44N 60.45E
34 B10 Ţayyib al Ism Saudi Arabia 28.35N 34.49E
41 D7 Taz U.S.S.R. 66.02N 82.07E
41 C7 Taz R U.S.S.R.
88 L4 Taza Morocco 34.16N 4.01W
Taza Khurmatli see Tāza Khurmātū
34 M3 Tāza Khurmātū Iraq 35.29N 44.21E
20 O2 Tazawa ko L Japan
25 M9 Taze Burma 24.01N 95.22E
44 J10 Tāzehābād Iran 37.34N 49.14E
32 B1 Tāzeh Kand Āzārbāījān-e Khāvarī Iran 39.31N 48.00E
44 H9 Tāzeh Kand Āzārbāījān-e Khāvarī Iran 38.21N 46.51E
37 J9 Tazeh Qāl'eh Iran 36.38N 46.03E
88 K6 Tazenakht Morocco 30.35N 7.12W
85 F7 Tazerbo oasis Libya
104 D9 Tazewell Virginia 37.07N 81.34W
21 C4 Tazicheng Nei Monggol Zizhiqu China 46.37N 123.04E
113 K7 Tazimina Lakes Alaska
101 T6 Tazin R N W Terr/Sask
101 T6 Tazin L Saskatchewan
82 K4 Tazlăul R Romania
113 O6 Tazlina R Alaska
113 O6 Tazlina L Alaska 61.50N 146.30W
76 J1 Tazones Spain 43.32N 5.23W
88 R4 Tazoult-Lambèse Algeria 35.31N 6.15E
41 C6 Tazovskaya Guba gulf U.S.S.R.
41 C7 Tazovskiy U.S.S.R. 67.28N 78.43E
41 C6 Tazovskiy Poluostrov pen U.S.S.R.
25 N7 Tazungdam Burma 28.02N 97.39E
88 L6 Tazzarine Morocco 30.48N 5.37W
88 M5 Tazzouguert Morocco 32.03N 3.48W
Tbal,Wadi watercourse see Tubal,Wādī at watercourse
44 F6 Tbilisi Georgia U.S.S.R. 41.43N 44.48E
44 C2 Tbilisskaya U.S.S.R. 45.23N 40.13E
Tchad,Lac see Chad,L
90 H6 Tchagen Chad 10.01N 16.17E
89 K7 Tchamba Togo 9.04N 1.32E
92 A6 Tchamba Zaïre 9.57S 22.22E
89 L7 Tchaourou Benin 8.58N 2.40E
Tchârher Bâzâr see Kagher Bazār
91 A4 Tchengue Gabon 0.44S 8.50E
91 B5 Tchibanga Gabon 2.49S 11.00E
91 B5 Tchibenda, L Congo
90 J3 Tchié Chad 17.08N 18.55E
89 E8 Tchien Liberia 6.01N 8.12W
90 G1 Tchigai, Plat. du Chad/Niger
91 D11 Tchihepepe Angola 15.50S 14.09E
91 B5 Tchimba L Congo
25 J2 Tching Lan Xan, I Vietnam 21.00N 107.50E
89 M4 Tchin-Tabaradene Niger 15.58N 5.56E
91 C11 Tchivara mt Angola 14.16S 13.52E
Tchobâne Bey see Choban Bey
90 G7 Tchollíré Cameroon 8.26N 14.09E
107 F8 Tchula Mississippi 33.11N 90.12W
62 L1 Tczew Poland 54.05N 18.46E
108 O6 Tea S Dakota 43.27N 96.49W
76 C4 Tea R Spain
82 J4 Teaca Romania 46.55N 24.30E
115 G6 Teacapán Mexico 22.31N 105.43W
109 G9 Teague New Mexico 32.16N 103.12W
112 L4 Teague Texas 31.38N 96.18W
14 D7 Teague,L W Australia
122 D13 Téahupo Tahiti Pacific Oc 17.51S 149.15W
122 A9 Te Aiti Pt C Rarotonga Pacific Oc 21.11S 59.47W
122 R15 Téakaréraga,Pte C Gambier Is Pacific Oc 23.09S 135.03W
95 M2 Teakworth S Africa 26.46S 28.50E
57 K3 Team Valley Tyne and Wear Eng 54.57N 1.37W
11 B12 Te Anau New Zealand 45.24S 167.44E
11 B12 Te Anau, L New Zealand
103 J6 Teaneck New Jersey 40.53N 74.01W
11 J5 Te Anga New Zealand 38.15S 174.51E
58 E4 Teangue Skye, Highland Scotland 57.07N 5.51W
80 K6 Teano Italy 41.15N 14.05E
14 C6 Teano Ra W Australia
115 N9 Teapa Mexico 17.35N 92.56W
108 D6 Teapot Dome mt Wyoming 43.16N 106.12W
119 F8 Tea,R Brazil
59 B7 Tearaght Lt.Ho Cork Irish Rep 52.04N 10.39W
11 N4 Te Araroa New Zealand 37.38S 178.25E
11 K4 Te Aroha New Zealand 37.32S 175.43E
35 B8 Te'ashur Israel 31.22N 34.39E
11 B2 Te Atatu Auckland New Zealand 36.50S 174.38E
13 C5 Tea Tree N Terr Australia 22.05S 133.22E
122 S15 Téauorongo,Pte C Mangaréva Pacific Oc 23.06S 134.57W
122 S15 Te-Ava-nui-o-Tupa channel Gambier Is Pacific Oc 23.11S 134.52W
122 B11 Teavaro Society Is Pacific Oc 17.29S 149.46W
11 K8 Te Awaiti New Zealand 41.29S 175.34E
11 K5 Te Awamutu New Zealand 38.00S 175.20E
15 D4 Teba Irian Jaya 1.32S 137.53E
77 G7 Teba Spain 36.59N 4.55W
89 K2 Tebahalet Mali 18.50N 0.08E
18 F8 Tebak,Gunung mt Sumatra Indonesia 5.01S 104.35E
75 F8 Tébar Spain 39.30N 2.11W
57 H4 Tebay Cumbria Eng 54.26N 2.35W
18 J5 Tebedu Sarawak Malaysia 1.05N 110.22E
90 L5 Tebella Plat Sudan
40 L9 Teben'kova vol Kuril Is U.S.S.R. 45.02N 147.57E
15 H7 Tebera, L Papua New Guinea 6.42S 144.39E
44 D4 Teberda U.S.S.R. 43.28N 41.46E
44 D4 Teberda R U.S.S.R.
101 Y4 Tebesjuak L N W Terr
88 S4 Tébessa Algeria 35.21N 8.06E
88 S4 Tébessa, Mts. de Algeria
118 B10 Tebicuary Paraguay 26.30S 58.10W
118 B10 Tebicuary, R Paraguay
18 C4 Tebingtinggi Sumatra Indon 3.20N 99.08E
18 E7 Tebingtinggi Sumatra Indon 3.37S 103.09E
18 E5 Tebingtinggi isld Sumatra Indon
92 H10 Tebo Mozambique 16.17S 37.19E
94 N4 Tebo Mozambique 22.25S 34.13E
18 D6 Tebo R Sumatra Indonesia
88 S3 Tebourba Tunisia 36.54N 9.50E
88 S3 Teboursouk Tunisia 36.24N 9.15E
18 D10 Tebrau Pen Malaysia 1.32N 103.47E
86 E7 Tebtunis ruins Egypt 29.06N 30.45E
Tebuk see Tabūk
44 G5 Tebulos Mta mt Georgia U.S.S.R. 42.34N 45.17E
41 Q5 Tebyulekh U.S.S.R. 70.40N 143.33E
115 H8 Tecalitlán Mexico 19.20N 103.01W
115 L8 Tecamachalco Mexico 18.52N 97.44W
115 A1 Tecate Mexico 32.33N 116.38W
36 J3 Tecer R Turkey
72 K11 Tech R France
47 J7 Techa R U.S.S.R.
65 H8 Techendorf Austria 46.44N 13.18E
89 J8 Techiman Ghana 7.38N 1.53W
91 D12 Techipa watercourse Angola
82 M6 Techirghiol Romania 44.03N 28.37E
11 G9 Technical,Mt New Zealand 42.25S 172.22E
119 D5 Techo airport Colombia 4.35N 74.10W
63 Q6 Techow E Germany 53.09N 12.23E
36 J5 Tecirli Turkey 37.10N 36.04E
64 G6 Teck W Germany 48.36N 9.29E
121 B9 Tecka Argentina 43.28S 70.53W
121 B9 Tecka, R Argentina
63 G8 Tecklenburg W Germany 52.13N 7.49E
52 G11 Teckomatorp Sweden 55.52N 13.05E
115 P7 Tecoh Mexico 20.42N 89.30W
109 E6 Tecolote New Mexico 35.27N 105.17W
109 E7 Tecolote New Mexico 34.01N 105.41W
115 G7 Tecolotlán Mexico 20.10N 104.07W
115 L7 Tecolutla Mexico 20.30N 97.00W
110 L8 Tecoma Nevada 41.20N 114.06W
115 H8 Tecomán Mexico 18.52N 103.50W
111 H6 Tecopa California 35.51N 116.12W
115 F4 Tecorichic Mexico 26.45N 106.46W
115 E3 Tecoripa Mexico 28.38N 109.58W
115 O10 Tecpán Guatemala 14.48N 90.56W
115 J9 Técpan Mexico 17.13N 100.41W
115 G6 Tecuala Mexico 22.24N 105.30W
82 L5 Tecuci Romania 45.50N 27.27E
106 L7 Tecumseh Michigan 42.01N 83.56W
107 D5 Tecumseh Missouri 36.34N 92.15W
108 O9 Tecumseh Nebraska 40.22N 96.12W
109 O6 Tecumseh Oklahoma 35.15N 96.56W
99 H10 Tecumseh Ontario 42.18N 82.53W
87 J8 Ted Somalia 4.26N 43.51E
85 E9 Teda Chad/Libya
56 D6 Tedburn St.Mary Devon Eng 50.44N 3.41W
88 K5 Tedders Morocco 33.38N 6.17W
55 C4 Teddington London Eng 51.25N 0.20W
11 M11 Teddington New Zealand 43.40S 172.40E
42 C2 Tedel'kynak U.S.S.R. 60.22N 83.44E
89 E4 Tédeneib Mauritania 15.50N 9.00W
88 R10 Tedjeret Algeria 23.58N 6.13E
88 R11 Tedjert Algeria 21.23N 6.25E
89 N3 Tedjidda n-Adrar Niger 17.08N 7.24E
88 O11 Tedjoudjemet Mali 20.11N 1.33E
88 Q3 Tedlès,C Algeria 36.55N 4.09E
20 K5 Tedori-gawa R Japan
43 F8 Tedzhen Turkmeniya U.S.S.R. 37.26N 60.30E
43 F8 Tedzhen R Turkmeniya/Iran
43 F8 Tedzhenstroy Turkmeniya U.S.S.R. 36.57N 60.50E
95 J7 Teebus S Africa 31.22S 25.40E
20 Q9 Teema Okinawa Japan 26.33N 128.03E
100 D6 Tees Alberta 52.30N 113.25W
57 J3 Teesdale V Durham Eng
95 O2 Teespruit R S Africa
57 L4 Tees,R N Yorks etc Eng
57 L3 Teesside dist Cleveland Eng
99 J9 Teeswater Ontario 43.59N 81.18W
19 J7 Teeth,The mt Philippines 9.20N 118.17E
119 G9 Tefé Brazil 3.24S 64.45W
120 F1 Tefé R Amazonas Brazil
36 D5 Tefenni Turkey 37.19N 29.45E
119 G9 Tefé,R Brazil
96 T10 Tefia Fuerteventura Canary Is 28.31N 14.01W
52 M3 Teg Sweden 63.48N 20.10E
18 H9 Tegal Java Indon 6.52S 109.07E
87 F3 Tegalhusi Sudan 15.51N 36.19E
84 D7 Tegea ruins Greece 37.28N 22.25E
60 N14 Tegelen Netherlands 51.21N 6.08E
66 K1 Tegerfelden Switzerland 47.33N 8.17E
43 N5 Tegermen' Kazakhstan U.S.S.R. 43.23N 79.36E
64 M8 Tegernsee W Germany 47.42N 11.46E
41 O2 Tegetkhof,Mys C Franz Josef Land U.S.S.R. 80.06N 58.01E
88 Q12 Teggert Algeria 19.45N 5.59E
81 L3 Teggiano Italy 40.22N 15.33E
88 M5 Teggour Morocco 33.10N 3.50W
88 M9 Teggueur Algeria 25.48N 3.40W
89 N3 Tegguidda In Tessoum Niger 17.26N 6.37E
67 P11 Teghime,Col de pass Corsica 42.41N 9.23E
30 J7 Teghra Bihar India 25.31N 85.57E
90 C6 Tegina Nigeria 10.02N 6.10E
18 F8 Teginenéng Sumatra Indonesia 5.16S 105.12E
79 H2 Teglio Italy 46.11N 10.05E
Tegre prov see Tigrē prov
121 D4 Tegua Argentina 32.43S 64.20W
9 C9 Tegua isld New Hebrides 13.15S 166.36E
115 L2 Tegucigalpa Honduras 14.05N 87.14W
96 S13 Tegueste Tenerife Canary Is 28.31N 16.20W
96 U7 Teguise Lanzarote Canary Is 29.04N 13.38W
42 D4 Tegul'det U.S.S.R. 57.20N 88.13E
92 C12 Tegwani R Zimbabwe
40 E1 Tegyul'te-Tërde U.S.S.R. 60.10N 130.08E
111 F6 Tehachapi California 35.08N 118.27W
111 F7 Tehachapi Mts California
33 J9 Tehair S Yemen 15.45N 50.42E
110 C9 Tehama California 40.01N 122.10W
11 J3 Te Hana New Zealand 36.14S 174.32E
11 G1 Te Hapua New Zealand 34.32S 172.57E
30 B7 Teharka Madhya Prad India 25.18N 78.54E
11 L6 Te Haroto New Zealand 39.08S 176.36E
11 L6 Te Hauke New Zealand 39.47S 176.41E
Tehchow see Te-chou
97 K4 Tehek L N W Terr 65.10N 96.00W
18 B5 Tehemberau Indonesia 1.30N 97.26E
Teheran see Tehrān
87 F2 Tehilla Sudan 17.42N 36.06E
85 A7 Tehi n Abahoha pass Libya
89 H7 Téhini Ivory Coast 9.39N 3.32W
19 F5 Tehoru Moluccas Indonesia 3.20S 129.28E
32 D3 Tehrān Iran 35.40N 51.26E
32 D3 Tehrān prov Iran
Tehri Madhya Prad see Tikamgarh
30 B2 Tehri Uttar Prad India 30.21N 78.29E
30 B2 Tehri Garhwal dist Uttar Prad India
30 H7 Tehtu Bihar India 25.07N 85.00E
115 L8 Tehuacán Mexico 18.30N 97.26W
115 M10 Tehuantepec, G.de Mexico
115 M9 Tehuantepec,Istmo de isthmus Mexico
122 R6 Tehuantepec Ridge Pacific Oc
115 M9 Tehuantepec,Sto.Domingo Mexico 16.21N 95.13W
115 K8 Tehuitzingo Mexico 18.20N 98.16W
80 A2 Teia,Pta.della Italy 43.04N 9.52E
64 L2 Teichel E Germany 50.47N 11.18E
96 Q14 Teide Pico de mt Tenerife Canary Is 28.17N 16.39W
56 C3 Teifi,R Dyfed Wales
90 M4 Teiga Plat Sudan
56 E6 Teignmouth Devon Eng 50.33N 3.30W
56 D6 Teign,R Devon Eng
87 D4 Teigo Sudan 13.09N 33.40E
50 D5 Teigsfjall mt Iceland 64.53N 21.34W
Teiha,Et see Tayhah
76 E4 Teijeira,La Spain 42.24N 7.29W
37 E8 Teilharbecircibi watercourse Turkey
71 B4 Teilhet France 46.06N 2.49E
72 K3 Teilhet France 46.06N 2.49E
70 G6 Teillay France 47.48N 1.31W
70 H7 Teille France 47.28N 1.16W
71 F7 Teil,le France 44.33N 4.40E
72 J8 Teillet France 43.50N 2.20E
70 J4 Teilleul,le France 48.32N 0.53W
71 K9 Teillon mt France 43.50N 6.36E
Teinach see Bad Teinach-Zavelstein
11 L5 Te Iringa mt New Zealand 38.59S 176.12E
86 E4 Teirîya, El Egypt 30.39N 30.45E
64 N6 Teisbach W Germany 48.37N 12.28E
64 O8 Teisenberg mt W Germany 47.48N 12.46E
64 O8 Teisendorf W Germany 47.50N 12.50E
51 K10 Teisko Finland 61.43N 23.50E
72 K6 Teissières-les-Boulies France 44.50N 2.32E
58 H6 Teith,R Central Scotland
82 H4 Teius Romania 46.12N 23.40E
117 H8 Teixeira Brazil 7.08S 37.11W
76 D8 Teixeira Portugal 40.15N 7.45W
91 D10 Teixeira da Silva Angola 12.11S 15.52E
Teixeira de Sousa see Luan
89 A5 Teixeira Pinto Guinea-Bissau 12.03N 16.00W
118 G7 Teixeiras Brazil 20.40S 42.50W
118 E9 Teixeira Soares Brazil 25.20S 50.24W
76 E8 Teixoso Portugal 40.19N 7.27W
76 E7 Teja R Portugal
75 G7 Tejadillos Spain 40.08N 1.38W
76 H8 Tejado,El Spain 40.27N 5.32W
18 L10 Tejakula Bali Indon 8.09S 115.19E
32 E2 Tejan,Rūd-e R Iran
76 H7 Tejares Spain 40.58N 5.41W
96 U15 Tejeda Gran Canaria Canary Is 27.59N 15.35W
76 H8 Tejeda de Tiétar Spain 40.01N 5.52W
77 J7 Tejeda,Sierra mts Spain
76 E2 Tejeiro Spain 43.06N 7.30W
76 G2 Tejera Spain 43.21N 6.23W
31 H9 Tejgaon Bangladesh 23.46N 90.22E
96 R13 Tejina Tenerife Canary Is 28.32N 16.22W
53 P12 Tejn Bornholm Denmark 55.15N 14.51E
111 F7 Tejon Pass California 34.49N 118.54W
120 C3 Tejo,R Brazil
28 L2 Teju Assam India 27.54N 96.10E
118 E6 Tejuco,R Brazil
115 J8 Tejupilco Mexico 18.55N 100.10W
11 M4 Te Kaha New Zealand 37.44S 177.52E
15 B4 Tekai mt Irian Jaya 1.01S 132.53E
18 C7 Tekai R Pen Malaysia
18 C8 Tekam R Pen Malaysia
108 O8 Tekamah Nebraska 41.48N 96.12W
11 E10 Tekapo,L New Zealand
11 E11 Tekapo R New Zealand
11 M5 Te Karaka New Zealand 38.28S 177.53E
30 H8 Tekari Bihar India 24.57N 84.50E
11 K4 Te Kauwhata New Zealand 37.24S 175.08E
11 K5 Te Kawa New Zealand 38.06S 175.18E
115 P7 Tekax Mexico 20.11N 89.18W
36 D1 Teke Turkey 41.06N 29.40E
37 B3 Teke Burun C Turkey 40.03N 26.11E
43 F3 Tekeli Aktyubinsk, Kazakhstan U.S.S.R. 48.08N 60.10E
43 N5 Tekeli Taldy-Kurgan, Kazakhstan U.S.S.R. 44.47N 79.00E
37 C5 Tekeli Dağ mts Turkey
43 L1 Teke,Ozero L Kazakhstan U.S.S.R.
43 O5 Tekes Kazakhstan U.S.S.R. 42.40N 80.01E
24 D4 Tekes Xinjiang Uygur Zizhiqu China 43.10N 81.44E
24 C4 Tekes He R Xinjiang Uygur Zizhiqu China
90 J8 Tekévére Cent Afr Rep 7.46N 19.54E
87 G4 Tekezē watercourse Ethiopia
24 G11 Tekhar La pass Xizang Zizhiqu China 29.31N 91.55E
45 A3 Tekhtin Belorussiya U.S.S.R. 53.51N 29.42E
24 C7 Tekiliktag mt pk Xinjiang Uygur Zizhiqu China 36.30N 80.26E
40 F7 Tekin U.S.S.R. 48.52N 133.50E
11 F9 Te Kinga New Zealand 42.37S 171.30E
37 D2 Tekirdağ Turkey 40.59N 27.31E
37 D2 Tekir Dağlari mts Turkey
11 H6 Te Kiri New Zealand 39.25S 173.59E
29 J8 Tekkali Andhra Prad India 18.37N 84.15E
37 G3 Tekke Turkey 40.08N 29.41E
28 D2 Tekmal Andhra Prad India 17.59N 78.02E
37 F6 Tekman Turkey 39.39N 41.31E
44 H10 Tekmeh Dāsh Iran 37.42N 46.57E
28 J5 Teknaf Bangladesh 20.52N 92.18E
110 H2 Tekoa Washington 47.14N 117.04E
11 G9 Tekoa,Mt New Zealand 42.40S 172.38E
122 E15 Tekokota atoll Tuamotu Is Pacific Oc 17.18S 142.27W
115 P7 Tekom Mexico 20.34N 88.14W
18 E10 Tekong Besar isld Singapore
18 K2 Tekong Kechil,Pulau isld Singapore
106 K7 Tekonsha Michigan 42.05N 85.00W
11 B6 Te Kopahou mt New Zealand 41.21S 174.43E
11 H3 Te Kopuru New Zealand 36.02S 173.56E
122 A10 Te Kou pk Rarotonga Pacific Oc 21.14S 159.46W
88 P10 Tekouyat, Irh. watercourse Algeria
90 K2 Tekro Chad 19.32N 20.56E
37 E8 Tektek Dağları mts Turkey
41 O9 Tektyur U.S.S.R. 62.10N 130.00E
19 C4 Teku Celebes Indon 0.44S 123.27E
11 K5 Te Kuiti New Zealand 38.20S 175.10E
115 L2 Tela Honduras 15.46N 87.25W
92 D8 Tela Zaïre 12.06S 28.35E
35 E3 Tel 'Adashim Israel 32.39N 35.18E
74 G10 Télagh Algeria 34.48N 0.36W
88 N4 Télagh Algeria 34.51N 0.38W
35 D1 Tel Akhziv anc site Israel 33.03N 35.06E
35 D2 Tel Akko anc site Israel 32.55N 33.06E
34 L3 Tel' Ali Iraq 35.20N 43.39E
Tel al Lahm see Tall al Lahm
Tel al Shaur see Tel' ash Shawr
35 B7 Telamim Israel 31.35N 34.40E
18 F5 Telan isld Indonesia 0.42N 104.37E
113 L6 Telaquana,L Alaska 61.00N 153.50W
35 D8 Tel 'Arad anc site Israel 31.17N 35.08E
121 D2 Telaritos Argentina 29.29S 65.42W
35 C5 Tel Arshaf anc site Israel 32.12N 34.48E
89 K2 Tela-Sabet Mali 19.10N 0.28E
35 B6 Tel Ashdod anc site Israel 31.45N 34.39E
35 B7 Tel Ashqelon anc site Israel 31.40N 34.33E
34 K2 Tel' ash Shawr Iraq 36.31N 42.09E
53 R18 Telavåg Norway 60.15N 5.00E
35 F1 Tel Avel Bet Ma'akha anc site Israel 33.15N 35.34E
44 G6 Telavi Georgia U.S.S.R. 41.56N 45.30E
35 C5 Tel Aviv-Yafo Israel 32.05N 34.46E
35 C7 Tel Azeqa anc site Israel 31.42N 34.57E
42 D5 Tel'bes U.S.S.R. 53.15N 87.27E
35 F3 Tel Bet She'an Israel 32.30N 35.30E
35 C7 Tel Bet Shemesh anc site Israel 31.45N 34.58E
35 F3 Tel Bet Yerah anc site Israel 32.42N 35.34E
65 M3 Telč Czechoslovakia 49.12N 15.28E
115 P7 Telchac Puerto Mexico 21.21N 89.20W
45 H3 Tel'ch'ye U.S.S.R. 53.22N 36.21E
82 J3 Telciu Romania 47.25N 24.24E
35 F1 Tel Dan anc site Israel 33.15N 35.39E
96 V15 Telde Gran Canaria Canary Is 28.01N 15.25W
26 S7 Teldeniya Sri Lanka 7.18N 80.47E
35 C8 Tel Devir Israel 31.27N 34.54E
91 J2 Tele R Zaïre
89 E7 Telebadou Guinea 9.09N 9.42W
15 F6 Telefomin Papua New Guinea 5.08S 141.31E
18 K7 Telegapulang Borneo Indonesia 2.54S 112.23E
45 Q4 Telegino U.S.S.R. 52.55N 44.31E
81 F8 Telegrafo,Pizzo mt Sicily 37.37N 13.10E
23 B9 Telegraph Bay Hong Kong
101 H7 Telegraph Creek Br Col 57.56N 131.10W
90 F1 Telei watercourse Niger
90 M6 Teleihun Sudan 10.57N 25.18E
35 F6 Teleilet el Ghassul anc site Jordan 31.48N 35.36E
93 H3 Telekis Volcano Kenya 2.21N 36.38E
45 L4 Telelyuy' U.S.S.R. 52.24N 39.55E
118 E9 Têlemaco Borba Brazil 24.20S 50.44W
53 X19 Telemark co Norway
42 J5 Telemba U.S.S.R. 52.45N 113.15E
119 C7 Telembi,R Colombia
18 C8 Telemong R Pen Malaysia
121 D6 Telén Argentina 36.20S 65.31W
18 M5 Telen R Borneo Indon
46 G5 Teleneshty Moldavia U.S.S.R. 47.35N 28.17E
32 J8 Teleng Balūchestān va Sīstān Iran 25.48N 61.04E
32 G7 Teleng Banāder va Jazāyer-e Baḩr-e Oman Iran 26.44N 57.15E
76 G4 Teleno, El mt Spain 42.20N 6.24W
82 J6 Teleorman div Romania
82 J6 Teleormanul R Romania
112 L2 Telephone Texas 33.47N 96.02W
88 R9 Telertheba, Djebel mt Algeria 24.10N 6.50E
111 G5 Telescope Pk mt California 36.11N 117.05W
116 P5 Telescope Pt Grenada, W I 12.07N 61.36W
80 L6 Telese Italy 41.13N 14.31E
117 A9 Teles Pires, R Brazil
42 D6 Teletskoye, Oz L U.S.S.R.
35 C8 Tel Eyton anc mound Israel 31.29N 34.56E
89 H2 Telfel Mali 19.05N 3.35W
56 G2 Telford Salop 52.42N 2.28W
65 D7 Telfs Austria 47.19N 11.05E
Tel Gat see Jatt
70 B5 Telgruc France 48.14N 4.21W
63 G9 Telgte W Germany 51.59N 7.46E
76 C6 Telhado Portugal 41.27N 8.28W
35 D2 Tel Hannaton anc site Israel 32.47N 35.15E
35 B7 Tel Hasi anc site Israel 31.33N 34.44E
35 F1 Tel Hazor anc site Israel 33.01N 35.34E
76 D15 Telheiras Portugal 38.46N 9.10W
76 B14 Telheiro Algarve Portugal 37.11N 8.45W
76 E12 Telheiro Alto Alentejo Portugal 38.27N 7.22W
76 B13 Telheiro Baixo Alentejo Portugal 37.36N 8.37W
42 E6 Teli U.S.S.R. 51.05N 90.12E
115 L3 Telica Nicaragua 12.30N 86.52W
88 M10 Telig Mali 22.38N 3.40W
89 C6 Teliméle Guinea 10.54N 13.02W
82 J7 Telish Bulgaria 43.20N 24.15E
Tel Kaif see Tall Kayf
34 D4 Telkalakh Syria 34.40N 36.18E
35 F2 Tel Kinnerot anc site Israel 32.52N 35.32E
34 K2 Tel Kotchek Syria 36.48N 42.04E
101 K8 Telkwa Br Col 54.44N 127.05W
Tell see Ben 'Ammi
112 G1 Tell Texas 34.23N 100.24W
Tell Abiad see Tell el Abyad,Et
Tell Afar see Tall 'Āfar
35 C7 Tel Lakhish anc site Israel 31.34N 34.51E
69 K4 Tellancourt France 49.31N 5.38E
28 D4 Tellar Tamil Nadu India 12.25N 79.33E
81 J10 Tellaro R Sicily
34 D5 Tell Asfar mt Syria 33.07N 36.42E
34 H2 Tell Beidar Syria 36.43N 40.34E
34 D4 Tell Bīsa Syria 34.51N 36.44E
Tell Bisseh see Tell Bīsa
86 P4 Tell Burmā hill Jordan 30.37N 35.50E
Tell Chehâb see Tell esh Shehāb
107 K4 Tell City Indiana 37.56N 86.46W
35 F5 Tell Deir 'Alla anc site Jordan 32.12N 35.37E
Tell ech Chaar mt see Tell esh Sha'r
36 J7 Tell Ejine Syria 35.50N 37.03E
51 H5 Tellejokk Sweden 66.06N 19.50E
34 F2 Tell el Abyad,Et Syria 36.41N 38.59E
86 H4 Tell el Ahmar, El Egypt 30.54N 32.24E
34 F2 Tell el Ahmar,Et Syria 36.42N 38.08E
86 E10 Tell el Amarna Egypt 27.38N 30.52E
86 J3 Tell el Farama hill Egypt 31.03N 32.32E
86 G4 Tell el Kebîr,El Egypt 30.33N 31.46E
86 H3 Tell el Lûli hill Egypt 31.02N 32.24E
35 F9 Tell el Meisa mt Jordan 31.08N 35.40E
Tell el Milh see Tel Malhata
34 O8 Tell el Obeid anc site Iraq 30.58N 46.05E
Tell el Quadi see Tel Dan anc site
113 D4 Teller Alaska 65.12N 166.23W
35 G1 Tell esh Sha'r mt Syria 33.11N 35.57E
35 G3 Tell esh Shehāb Syria 32.41N 35.58E
34 H3 Tell es Suwar Syria 35.31N 40.38E
34 H3 Tell Fajāmi Syria 35.54N 40.52E
35 J5 Tell Hamra Hamad tomb Jordan 32.03N 36.18E
28 B5 Tellicherry Kerala India 11.44N 75.29E
107 M6 Tellico Plains Tennessee 35.22N 84.18W
98 F3 Tellier Quebec 50.21N 66.12W
61 L6 Tellin Belgium 50.05N 5.13E
63 K4 Tellingstedt W Germany 54.13N 9.17E
34 G2 Tell Khanzīr Syria 36.44N 39.51E
35 F6 Tell Nimrin anc site Jordan 31.54N 35.37E
119 C6 Tello Colombia 3.06N 75.08W
34 O7 Telloh Iraq 31.37N 46.09E
86 G4 Tell Râk Egypt 30.54N 31.43E
74 J8 Tell,Reg.du Algeria
Tell Sa'wa see Tel Yeshua
66 L4 Tells Platte Switzerland 46.56N 8.38E
34 H2 Tell Tamer Syria 36.40N 40.22E
Tell 'Urād see Tel 'Arad
109 C4 Telluride Colorado 37.57N 107.48W
42 G5 Tel'ma U.S.S.R. 52.42N 103.45E
35 D9 Tel Malhata anc site Israel 31.13N 35.02E
Tel'mana, im see Zharlykamys
45 K9 Tel'manovo Ukraine U.S.S.R. 47.24N 38.02E
43 E6 Tel'mansk Turkmeniya U.S.S.R. 42.04N 60.00E
35 C7 Tel Maresha anc site Israel 31.36N 34.54E
35 D3 Tel Megiddo anc site Israel 32.35N 35.11E
22 D2 Telmen Nuur L Mongolia
88 J6 Telmest Morocco 31.51N 9.23W
35 B8 Tel Mifsah anc site Israel 31.28N 34.39E
35 C8 Tel Milha hill Israel 31.28N 34.46E
35 C4 Tel Mond Israel 32.16N 34.54E
35 C7 Tel Nagila anc site Israel 31.31N 34.45E
40 J7 Tel'novskiy Sakhalin U.S.S.R. 49.20N 142.10E
110 H4 Telocaset Oregon 45.07N 117.49W
76 D6 Telões Portugal 41.27N 7.41W
30 L5 Telok Nepal 27.22N 87.50E
18 B7 Telok Anson Pen Malaysia 4.00N 101.02E
18 J3 Telok Blanga dist Singapore
18 B9 Telok Datok Pen Malaysia 2.49N 101.31E
115 K8 Teloloapán Mexico 18.21N 99.52W
18 B7 Telom R Pen Malaysia
88 K6 Telouet Morocco 31.17N 7.15W
47 H4 Telpos-Iz,Gora mt U.S.S.R. 63.56N 59.02E
35 F3 Tel Qazir Israel 36.42N 35.37E
35 F1 Tel Qedesh anc site Israel 33.07N 35.31E
29 H7 Tel R Madhya Prad/Orissa India
35 A8 Tel Re'im anc site Israel 31.24N 34.26E
121 C9 Telsen Argentina 42.29S 66.53W
35 B8 Tel Ser'a anc site Israel 31.24N 34.40E
35 A8 Tel Sharuhen anc site Israel 31.17N 34.29E
35 C2 Tel Shiqmona anc site Israel 32.50N 34.57E
35 C8 Tel Shoqet anc site Israel 31.18N 34.54E
46 D2 Telšiai Lithuania U.S.S.R. 55.58N 22.16E
99 E3 Teltaka Ontario 49.59N 85.08W
63 S8 Teltow E Germany 52.25N 13.14E
18 H6 Telukbatang Borneo Indonesia 0.53S 109.46E
18 M4 Telukbayur Borneo Indon 2.10N 117.24E
18 D6 Telukbayur Sumatra Indonesia 1.02S 100.22E
18 F8 Telukbetung Sumatra Indon 5.28S 105.16E
18 B5 Telukdalam Indonesia 0.33N 97.48E
18 E5 Teluklanjut Sumatra Indon 0.05N 103.32E
26 T8 Telulla Sri Lanka 6.36N 81.07E
19 F5 Teluti,Teluk B Moluccas Indon
Tel Uwainat see Tall 'Uwaynāt
30 K8 Telwabazar Bihar India 24.42N 86.33E
35 C8 Tel Yeshua anc site Israel 31.16N 34.59E
Tel Yits-haq see Tel Yizhaq
35 C4 Tel Yizhaq Israel 32.16N 34.52E
35 E3 Tel Yosef Israel 32.33N 35.24E
35 C8 Tel Ziqlag anc site Israel 31.24N 34.52E
42 G4 Tem' U.S.S.R. 55.20N 100.45E
89 J9 Tema Ghana 5.40N 0.01W
89 J5 Tema Upper Volta 13.00N 1.49W
88 R5 Témacine Algeria 32.53N 6.03E
122 A11 Temae,L Society Is Pacific Oc 17.29S 149.48W
18 H5 Temaju isld Borneo Indon 0.30N 108.50E
104 H9 Teman Virginia 37.56N 77.38W
18 J5 Temangga Borneo Indon 0.30N 111.26E
18 J9 Temanggung Java Indon 7.22S 110.12E
122 A10 Te Mansa pk Rarotonga Pacific Oc 21.14S 159.45W
115 L7 Temapache Mexico 21.00N 97.39W
88 R10 Temasint Algeria 23.18N 7.40E
Temassinin see Fort Flatters
115 P7 Temax Mexico 21.10N 88.53W
115 L8 Temaxcal Mexico 18.20N 96.21W
18 C7 Tembeling Pen Malaysia 4.04N 102.19E
41 G8 Tembenchi U.S.S.R. 64.58N 58.55E
41 G7 Tembenchi R U.S.S.R.
41 G7 Tembenchi, Ozero L U.S.S.R.
18 E7 Tembesi R Sumatra Indon
92 G10 Tembe-Tembe Mozambique 17.28S 35.19E
84 E2 Témbi V Greece
18 E6 Tembilahan Sumatra Indonesia 0.16S 103.14E
Tembiun see Tambiān
75 D8 Tembleque Spain 39.41N 3.30W
111 D6 Temblor Ra California
91 E7 Tembo Aluma Angola 7.42S 17.15E
91 B3 Temboni R Gabon/Equat Guinea
92 F9 Tembué Mozambique 14.54S 32.53E
95 M7 Tembuland reg S Africa
15 B4 Tembuni R Irian Jaya
92 D5 Tembwe Pt Zaïre 6.30S 29.29E
111 G8 Temecula California 33.30N 117.09W
65 K3 Temelín Czechoslovakia 49.12N 14.22E
36 F3 Temelli Turkey 39.42N 32.20E
42 F6 Temenchulu, Gora mt U.S.S.R. 50.00N 96.44E

18 B6 Temengor Pen Malaysia 5.20N 101.21E
56 F3 Teme, R Hereford & Worcs etc Eng
82 F5 Temerin Yugoslavia 45.23N 19.54E
18 C8 Temerloh Pen Malaysia 3.28N 102.25E
45 N2 Temgenevo U.S.S.R. 54.22N 41.58E
18 F5 Temiang isld Indonesia
18 E3 Temiang, Bukit hill Pen Malaysia 5.30N 102.25E
32 C4 Temileh Iran 33.54N 48.06E
15 A4 Teminabuan Irian Jaya 1.30S 131.59E
43 D3 Temir Kazakhstan U.S.S.R. 49.09N 57.06E
44 C2 Temirgoyevskaya U.S.S.R. 45.07N 40.21E
43 L2 Temirtau Kazakhstan U.S.S.R. 50.05N 72.55E
42 D5 Temirtau U.S.S.R. 53.11N 87.30E
98 A2 Temiscamie L Quebec
98 A2 Temiscamie R Quebec
98 D6 Temiscouata, L Quebec
99 L6 Témiskaming Quebec 46.44N 79.05W
90 J6 Temki Chad 11.33N 18.17E
45 F1 Temkino U.S.S.R. 55.05N 35.00E
36 H3 Temlik Turkey 39.25N 34.47E
12 G8 Temma Tasmania 41.14S 144.48E
51 M7 Temmes Finland 64.41N 25.35E
42 G6 Temnik R U.S.S.R.
45 P2 Temnikov U.S.S.R. 54.39N 43.14E
44 E3 Temnolesskaya U.S.S.R. 44.52N 42.06E
42 K5 Temnyy U.S.S.R. 53.26N 118.40E
24 H11 Têmo Xizang Zizhiqu China 29.30N 94.44E
81 B3 Temo R Sardinia
28 K1 Temo Gomba Xizang Zizhiqu 29.31N 94.28E
12 H5 Temora New S Wales 34.22S 147.30E
115 F3 Temósachic Mexico 28.58N 107.50W
45 R3 Temovka Penza U.S.S.R. 53.09N 45.00E
39 D5 Temp U.S.S.R. 59.48N 149.45E
115 M4 Tempate Costa Rica 10.22N 85.42W
30 J4 Tempathang Nepal 28.01N 85.48E
41 P3 Temp, Bukhta gulf U.S.S.R.
111 N8 Tempe Arizona 33.25N 111.55W
Tempe V see Témbi
19 A6 Tempe, Danau L Celebes Indon 4.06S 119.57E
63 B2 Tempelhof dist W Berlin
106 L8 Temperance Michigan 41.47N 83.32W
119 D8 Tempestad Peru 1.19S 74.55W
18 E6 Tempino Sumatra Indon 1.42S 103.30E
81 C2 Tempio Pausania Sardinia 40.54N 9.07E
57 G2 Templand Dumfries & Galloway Scotland 55.09N 3.26W
58 K7 Temple Lothian Scotland 55.49N 3.05W
104 P2 Temple Maine 44.41N 70.16W
106 J5 Temple Michigan 44.02N 85.01W
109 M7 Temple Oklahoma 34.17N 98.15W
103 C6 Temple Pennsylvania 40.25N 75.55W
112 K4 Temple Texas 31.06N 97.22W
13 G1 Temple B Queensland
56 C3 Temple Bar Dyfed Wales 52.10N 4.09W
56 G5 Temple Combe Somerset Eng 51.00N 2.25W
70 G7 Temple-de-Bretagne, le France 47.20N 1.47W
13 B6 Temple Downs N Terr Australia 24.15S 132.06E
56 O5 Temple Ewell Kent Eng 51.09N 1.16E
59 E3 Templehouse L Sligo Irish Rep 54.06N 8.35W
72 C6 Temple, le France 44.53N 0.59W
59 G6 Templemore Tipperary Irish Rep 52.48N 7.50W
59 K2 Templepatrick Antrim N Ireland 54.42N 6.06W
19 H6 Templer Bank Philippines 11.05N 117.14E
55 F3 Temples London Eng 51.31N 0.07W
57 H3 Temple Sowerby Cumbria Eng 54.39N 2.35W
12 E7 Templestowe dist Melbourne, Vic
59 L3 Temple, The Down N Ireland 54.29N 5.55W
111 D6 Templeton California 35.34N 120.42W
104 F6 Templeton Pennsylvania 40.56N 79.27W
Templeton Queensland see Mittagong
13 E5 Templeton R Queensland
59 G6 Templetouhy Tipperary Irish Rep 52.47N 7.43W
61 D4 Templeuve Belgium 50.38N 3.17E
103 C8 Templeville Maryland 39.08N 75.46W
63 T6 Templin E Germany 53.07N 13.30E
61 K5 Temploux Belgium 50.28N 4.46E
59 H3 Tempo Fermanagh N Ireland 54.23N 7.27W
115 K7 Tempoal Mexico 21.32N 98.23W
91 F10 Tempué Angola 13.27S 18.53E
77 E7 Tempul, Can.de Spain
63 P5 Tempzin E Germany 53.46N 11.40E
47 K6 Temryak, Oz L U.S.S.R. 59.20N 67.00E
44 A2 Temryuk U.S.S.R. 45.16N 37.24E
44 A2 Temryukskiy Zaliv B U.S.S.R.
61 G2 Temse Belgium 51.08N 4.13E
121 A7 Temuco Chile 38.45S 72.40W
11 F11 Temuka New Zealand 44.12S 171.16E
108 K3 Temvik N Dakota 46.24N 100.15W
91 C6 Temvo Zaïre 5.28S 13.13E
43 E1 Temyasovo Bashkir U.S.S.R. 53.01N 58.08E
119 C8 Tena Ecuador 1.00S 77.48W
115 O7 Tenabo Mexico 20.02N 90.12W
110 J9 Tenabo Nevada 40.19N 116.41W
110 J9 Tenabo, Mt Nevada 40.10N 116.36W
115 G8 Tenacatita Mexico 19.18N 104.46W
103 K6 Tenafly New Jersey 40.56N 73.57W
112 N4 Tenaha Texas 31.56N 94.25W
113 U8 Tenakee Springs Alaska 57.48N 135.15W
51 K11 Tenala Finland 60.05N 23.20E
28 E2 Tenali Andhra Prad India 16.13N 80.36E
39 E1 Tenalr U.S.S.R. 69.00N 150.05E
115 G7 Tenamaxtlán Mexico 20.13N 104.11W
11 G8 Te Namu New Zealand 41.24S 172.04E
115 K8 Tenancingo Mexico 19.00N 98.35W
115 K8 Tenango Mexico 19.10N 99.34W
90 F8 Tenangour Cameroon 7.51N 12.59E
25 E6 Tenasserim Burma 12.05N 99.00E
25 D4 Tenasserim div Burma
25 E6 Tenasserim R Burma
25 D6 Tenasserim I Burma
71 H5 Tenay France 45.55N 5.31E
60 P6 Ten Boer Netherlands 53.17N 6.42E
89 A1 Tenbrourt watercourse Mauritania
56 F3 Tenbury Shropshire Eng 52.19N 2.35W
56 B4 Tenby Dyfed Wales 51.41N 4.43W
99 G6 Tenby Bay Ontario 46.07N 83.55W
71 E6 Tence France 45.07N 4.18E
91 F3 Tenda tribe Zaïre
79 C6 Tenda, Colle di pass Italy/France 44.09N 7.34E
87 H5 Tendaho Ethiopia 11.41N 40.58E
Tendanye I see Tarawai I
71 M8 Tende France 44.05N 7.35E
28 H6 Ten Degree Chan Andaman/Nicobar Is Indian Ocean
89 C3 Tendel Mauritania 16.59N 12.51W
87 C4 Tendelti Sudan 13.01N 31.55E
75 K2 Tendeñera, Pico de mt Spain 42.40N 0.12W
20 O3 Tendō Japan 38.22N 140.22E
78 B12 Tendouba Tunisia 36.30N 8.45E
110 M5 Tendoy Idaho 44.59N 113.37W
88 N5 Tendrara Morocco 33.04N 1.59W
88 M5 Tendrara, Jbel mt Morocco 33.02N 2.01W
66 B5 Tendre, Mt Switzerland 46.36N 6.19E
56 O4 Tendring Essex Eng 51.53N 1.08E
44 B8 Tendrovskaya Kosa sand spit Ukraine U.S.S.R.
44 B8 Tendrovskiy Zaliv B Ukraine U.S.S.R.
72 H2 Tendu France 46.39N 1.33E
29 F6 Tendukheda Madhya Prad India 23.08N 78.55E
37 H6 Tendürük Dağı mt Turkey 39.23N 43.53E
76 G7 Tenebrón Spain 40.38N 6.21W
75 C6 Tenebroso, Embalse del res Spain 40.59N 3.39W
89 L3 Tenekert Mali 17.45N 3.09E
89 G4 Tenenkou Mali 14.28N 4.55W
118 B2 Tenente Marques, R Brazil
90 D1 Ténéré reg Niger
90 E1 Ténéré du Tafassasset reg Niger
96 Q14 Tenerife isld Canary Is 28.15N 16.35W
77 N6 Teñerife mt Spain 37.17N 1.45W
88 O3 Ténès Algeria 36.35N 1.18E
74 H8 Ténès, C Algeria 36.34N 1.03E
82 K8 Tenevo Bulgaria 42.21N 26.32E
30 L4 Teng Xizang Zizhiqu 28.05N 87.21E
18 H2 Tengah dist Singapore 1.23N 103.43E
23 A6 Tengchong Yunnan China 25.02N 98.28E
Tengchow see Penglai
Tengchow see Qingdao
18 G3 Tengeh R Singapore
15 L4 Te Nggano L Solomon Is 11.50S 160.28E
18 D9 Tenggaroh, Tanjong C Pen Malaysia 2.15N 103.58E
18 M6 Tenggarong Borneo Indon 0.23S 117.00E
18 K9 Tengger mts Java Indon
22 F7 Tengger Shamo sand dunes Nei Monggol Zizhiqu China
23 E9 Tenggiao Guangdong China 18.30N 109.46E
18 E3 Tenggol isld Pen Malaysia 4.52N 103.44E
18 M2 Tenghilan Sabah Malaysia 6.15N 116.17E
40 J5 Ten'gi Sakhalin U.S.S.R. 52.44N 141.59E
18 B8 Tengi R Pen Malaysia
43 J2 Tengiz, Ozero L Akmolinsk, Kazakhstan U.S.S.R.
30 G4 Teng Kangpoche mt Nepal 27.48N 86.35E
92 D4 Tengo Zaïre 5.26S 28.12E
19 K8 Tengolan isld Philippines 6.32N 121.47E
Tengpoche Gonda see Thyangboche
23 E9 Tengqiao Hainan Dao, Guangdong China 18.30N 109.46E
92 G10 Tengua Mozambique 16.15S 35.46E
45 O2 Ten'gushevo U.S.S.R. 54.45N 42.44E
23 E7 Teng Xian Guangxi China 23.18N 110.52E
23 H1 Teng Xian Shandong China 35.10N 117.14E

13 G7 Tenham Queensland 25.40S 142.58E
104 D2 Ten Hills dist Baltimore, Md
52 H9 Tenhult Sweden 57.45N 14.20E
88 F10 Tenialig Mauritania 23.10N 14.02W
90 L3 Ténibé Chad 17.31N 23.14E
79 A6 Ténibres Italy/France 44.17N 6.58E
88 G8 Teniegrad Morocco 26.10N 12.06W
121 B5 Teniente Chile 34.05S 70.22W
120 E7 Teniente Bullain Bolivia 17.59S 67.00W
88 P6 Teniet el Anz pass Algeria 31.50N 3.09E
66 M5 Tenigerbad Switzerland 46.42N 8.57E
64 D7 Teningen W Germany 48.06N 7.47E
110 C3 Tenino Washington 46.52N 122.50W
66 P3 Tenins Switzerland 47.01N 9.33E
89 F6 Ténintou Mali 11.18N 7.40W
74 G9 Ténira Algeria 35.03N 0.34W
47 L7 Tenis, Oz L Omsk U.S.S.R.
47 J8 Teniz, Ozero L Kazakhstan U.S.S.R.
28 C6 Tenkasi Tamil Nadu India 8.58N 77.22E
91 K9 Tenke Katanga Zaïre 10.34S 26.12E
91 K9 Tenke Katanga Zaïre 11.24S 26.48E
42 K2 Tenke U.S.S.R. 62.00N 116.35E
39 L1 Tenkergynpilgyn, Laguna lagoon U.S.S.R.
45 U1 Ten'ki U.S.S.R. 55.26N 48.59E
109 Q6 Tenkiller Ferry Res Oklahoma
89 J6 Tenkodogo Upper Volta 11.54N 0.19W
28 J8 Tenlaa Nicobar Is 7.00N 93.53E
103 G3 Tenmile R New York
98 Q2 Ten Mile L Newfoundland
103 E3 Ten Mile River New York 41.34N 75.00W
66 O4 Tenna Switzerland 46.45N 9.21E
80 J2 Tenna R Italy
103 E3 Tennanah Lake New York 41.54N 74.57W
110 D8 Tennant California 41.36N 121.54W
13 C4 Tennant Creek N Terr Australia 19.31S 134.15E
65 H6 Tennen Gebirge mts Austria
103 F6 Tennent New Jersey 40.17N 74.20W
102 J3 Tennessee state U.S.A.
107 M6 Tennessee, Little R Tennessee
109 D2 Tennessee Pass Colorado 39.22N 106.20W
107 J6 Tennessee R Tennessee etc
66 D7 Tenneverge, Col de pass France/Switz 46.05N 6.53E
61 N6 Tenneville Belgium 50.06N 5.32E
53 V13 Tennfjord Norway 62.32N 6.36E
51 C4 Tennholmen Lt Ho Norway 67.19N 13.30E
105 E5 Tennille Georgia 32.55N 83.50W
51 O4 Tenniöjoki R Finland
112 G4 Tennyson Texas 31.43N 100.20W
11 G9 Tennyson, L New Zealand 42.11S 172.45E
121 B5 Teno Chile 34.51S 71.13W
121 B5 Teno R Chile
51 M2 Tenojoki R Finland
122 R15 Ténoko isld Mangaréva Pacific Oc 23.05S 135.00W
18 L3 Tenom Sabah Malaysia 5.07N 115.57E
96 P14 Teno, Pta.de pt Tenerife Canary Is 28.21N 16.55W
115 O9 Tenosique Mexico 17.30N 91.24W
88 G7 Tenouchad Morocco 28.01N 12.08W
60 P6 Ten Post Netherlands 53.18N 6.44E
121 J5 Tenquehuén I Chile 45.43S 74.47W
20 J7 Tenri Japan 34.36N 135.49E
20 L7 Tenryū Japan 34.50N 137.48E
20 L6 Tenryū-gawa R Japan
107 E9 Tensas R Louisiana
107 J11 Tensaw R Alabama
110 J2 Tensed Idaho 47.10N 116.57W
88 J6 Tensift R Morocco
108 C5 Ten Sleep Wyoming 44.02N 107.26W
108 Q2 Tenstrike Minnesota 47.35N 94.40W
19 B4 Tentena Celebes Indonesia 1.46S 120.40E
56 N5 Tenterden Kent Eng 51.05N 0.41E
14 B10 Tenterden W Australia 34.26S 117.32E
12 K3 Tenterfield New S Wales 29.01S 152.04E
105 F12 Ten Thousand Is Florida
113 K7 Ten Thousand Smokes, V. of Alaska
101 T4 Tent L N W Terr 62.25N 108.00W
19 B3 Tentolomatinan, Gunung mt Celebes Indon 0.59N 121.50E
30 A6 Tentra Madhya Prad India 26.12N 77.18E
58 L6 Tents Muir dist Fife Scotland
77 D4 Tentudia mt Spain 38.04N 6.20W
76 B8 Tentugal Portugal 40.14N 8.35W
76 B3 Teo Spain 42.45N 8.31W
Teoao see Yoboki
115 H7 Teocalitche Mexico 21.28N 102.35W
115 L8 Teocello Mexico 19.24N 97.00W
79 M6 Teodorano Italy 44.05N 12.06E
118 D8 Teodoro Sampaio Brazil 22.27S 52.31W
118 H5 Teófilo Otôni Brazil 17.52S 41.31W
82 K1 Teofipol U.S.S.R. 49.51N 26.25E
19 K8 Teomabal isld Philippines 6.18N 120.53E
122 S15 Téoné-Kura, Pte Mangaréva Pacific Oc 23.08S 134.57W
30 E7 Teonthar Madhya Prad India 25.00N 81.38E
115 N9 Teopisca Mexico 16.31N 92.31W
80 M7 Teora Italy 40.51N 15.16E
115 K8 Teotihuacan ruins Mexico 19.42N 98.51W
115 L8 Teotitán Mexico 18.10N 97.08W
88 R8 Teouit Algeria 27.53N 6.33E
89 H8 Tepa Ghana 7.00N 2.05W
19 F7 Tepa Indon 7.52S 129.35E
115 E3 Tepachi Mexico 29.32N 109.30W
122 S15 Tépaeturu, Pte C Mangaréva Pacific Oc 23.04S 134.56W
115 H8 Tepalcatepec Mexico 19.11N 102.50W
115 K8 Tepalcingo Mexico 18.38N 98.51W
51 L3 Tepasto Finland 68.01N 24.40E
115 H7 Tepatitlán Mexico 20.50N 102.46W
Tepe see Behramki
82 G8 Tepe mt Yugoslavia 42.43N 21.31E
34 L2 Tepe Gawra anc site Iraq 36.31N 43.14E
37 D7 Tepehan Turkey 38.06N 38.45E
115 G5 Tepehuanes Mexico 25.22N 105.42W
115 K8 Tepeji Mexico 19.55N 99.21W
Tepeköy see Karakoçan
43 F5 Tepekul' Uzbekistan U.S.S.R. 43.09N 60.25E
83 D4 Tepelenë Albania 40.19N 20.01E
115 L9 Tepelmemec Mexico 17.54N 97.25W
64 O4 Tepelska Plošina tableland Czechoslovakia
37 G2 Tepeören Turkey 40.57N 29.22E
119 H6 Tepequem, Sa hills Brazil
92 J8 Tepere Mozambique 13.56S 38.50E
115 L7 Tepetzintla Mexico 21.11N 97.51W
115 L8 Tepexi de Rodriguez Mexico 18.36N 97.58W
34 M3 Tepe Zārdik Iraq 35.40N 44.21E
115 G7 Tepic Mexico 21.30N 104.51W
64 O4 Teplá Czechoslovakia 49.59N 12.52E
64 O3 Teplá R Czechoslovakia
47 M3 Teplaya Gora U.S.S.R. 58.32N 59.06E
64 Q2 Teplice Czechoslovakia 50.40N 13.49E
64 O3 Teplička Czechoslovakia 50.07N 12.51E
82 M2 Teplik U.S.S.R. 48.40N 29.45E
41 O1 Teplits, Bukhta B Franz Josef Land U.S.S.R.
47 G5 Teplogorka U.S.S.R. 61.21N 52.29E
45 K8 Teplogorsk Ukraine U.S.S.R. 48.36N 38.36E
46 Q4 Teplovka U.S.S.R. 51.30N 51.30E
45 J3 Teploye U.S.S.R. 53.36N 37.43E
115 C2 Tepoca, C Mexico 30.16N 112.50W
115 C3 Tepoca, C Mexico 29.21N 112.30W
11 L6 Te Pohue New Zealand 39.14S 176.42E
115 L9 Teposcolula Mexico 17.32N 97.30W
122 D15 Tepoto I Tuamotu Is Pacific Oc 16.45S 144.15W
122 E14 Tepoto I Tuamotu Is Pacific Oc 14.00S 141.20W
11 N5 Te Puia New Zealand 38.05S 178.20E
11 L4 Te Puke New Zealand 37.47S 176.22E
119 D5 Tequendama, Salto de cat Colombia 4.36N 74.19W
115 H7 Tequila Mexico 20.52N 103.48W
115 M9 Tequisistlán Mexico 16.26N 95.39W
115 K7 Tequisquiapán Mexico 20.32N 99.54W
115 L8 Tequixtepec Mexico 18.06N 97.55W
35 B8 Tequma Israel 31.27N 34.34E
75 R3 Ter R Spain
89 K4 Téra Niger 14.01N 0.45E
76 D11 Tera R Portugal
76 G5 Tera R Spain
60 G11 Ter Aar Netherlands 52.11N 4.42E
20 M4 Teradomari Japan 37.38N 138.46E
Terai see Tarai jungle
20 P3 Teraike Japan 38.39N 141.17E
28 C5 Terakanambi Karnataka India 11.50N 76.44E
87 C8 Terakeka Sudan 5.32N 31.43E
61 G3 Teralfene Belgium 50.53N 4.06E
31 J3 Teram Kangri mt Kashmir 35.42N 77.03E
80 J3 Teramo Italy 42.40N 13.43E
80 J3 Teramo prov Italy
115 N9 Terán Mexico 16.45N 93.10W
76 E11 Terana Portugal 38.36N 7.25W
12 G7 Terang Victoria 38.14S 143.00E
60 R8 Ter-Apel Netherlands 52.52N 7.05E
18 J6 Teratak Borneo Indon 0.45S 110.33E
31 E6 Teratani R Pakistan
18 M10 Terawangan isld Indonesia 8.20S 116.02E
11 J8 Terawhiti, C New Zealand 41.17S 174.35E
60 M8 Terband Netherlands 52.59N 5.55E
19 F7 Terbang Selatan isld Indon 7.22S 128.34E
19 F7 Terbang Utara isld Indonesia 7.16S 128.34E
60 O12 Terborg Netherlands 51.55N 6.22E
45 K4 Terbun'y U.S.S.R. 52.08N 38.16E
37 E6 Tercan Turkey 39.47N 40.23E
72 F2 Tercé France 46.31N 0.34E
96 T3 Terceira isld Azores 38.43N 27.13W
121 D4 Tercero R Argentina
109 E4 Tercio Colorado 37.04N 105.02W
89 E7 Tere Guinea 9.55N 8.45W
46 F5 Terebovlya Ukraine U.S.S.R. 49.18N 25.44E
15 G5 Terebu Papua New Guinea 3.46S 143.50E
45 K2 Terebush U.S.S.R. 54.21N 38.10E
93 C2 Terego Uganda 3.08N 31.03E
82 G5 Teregova Romania 45.10N 22.16E

11 K7 Te Rehunga New Zealand 40.12S 176.02E
44 F4 Terek U.S.S.R. 43.28N 44.11E
44 G4 Terek R U.S.S.R.
42 E6 Tere-Khol' U.S.S.R. 50.05N 94.59E
42 F6 Tere-Khol', Oz L U.S.S.R. 50.40N 97.29E
45 C4 Terekhovka Belorussiya U.S.S.R. 52.13N 31.28E
44 G3 Terekli Mekteb U.S.S.R. 44.11N 45.53E
43 K6 Terek-Say Kirgiziya U.S.S.R. 41.28N 71.11E
24 A6 Terek Tau mts Kirgiziya/Xinjiang Uygur Zizhiqu
24 A5 Terek Tau R Xinjiang Uygur Zizhiqu China
42 D6 Terektinskiy Khrebet mts U.S.S.R.
45 V8 Terekty Kazakhstan U.S.S.R. 48.32N 49.02E
100 R9 Terence Manitoba 49.44N 100.20W
98 J9 Terence Bay Nova Scotia 44.27N 63.44W
45 U3 Teren'ga U.S.S.R. 53.20N 48.25E
18 E3 Terengganu R Pen Malaysia
18 E3 Terengganu state Pen Malaysia
45 E2 Terenino U.S.S.R. 54.30N 33.35E
118 C7 Terenos Brazil 20.22S 54.49W
43 E2 Terensay U.S.S.R. 51.33N 59.28E
18 M6 Terentang, Pulau isld Borneo Indon
59 K5 Terenure Dublin Irish Rep 53.19N 6.17W
43 G4 Teren-Uzyak Kazakhstan U.S.S.R. 45.05N 64.57E
118 D9 Teresa Cristina Brazil 24.46S 51.07W
45 S4 Tereshka R U.S.S.R.
82 H2 Tereshva R U.S.S.R.
117 F7 Teresina Brazil 5.09S 42.46W
119 E7 Teresita Colombia 0.45N 69.26W
118 G8 Teresópolis Brazil 22.27S 42.59W
62 O3 Terespol Poland 52.04N 23.35E
28 H7 Teressa isld Nicobar Is
122 U15 Terevaka pk Easter I Pacific Oc 27.05S 109.23W
120 F7 Terevinto Bolivia 17.44S 63.22W
Terewah L see Narran L
12 H3 Terewah, L New S Wales
117 C4 Terezinha Brazil 0.59N 52.02W
41 J3 Terezy Klavenes, Zaliv gulf U.S.S.R.
76 D13 Terges R Portugal
69 E4 Tergnier France 49.39N 3.18E
90 D3 Tergoulaouène Niger 16.29N 8.48E
22 C7 Tergun Daba Shan mts Qinghai China
61 H2 Terhagen Belgium 51.05N 4.24E
30 L5 Terhathum Nepal 27.08N 87.33E
88 L10 Terhazza Mali 23.38N 5.22W
60 H13 Terheijden Netherlands 51.38N 4.45E
88 Q10 Terhenanet Algeria 23.10N 5.28E
88 Q6 Terhir watercourse Algeria
22 E2 Terhiyn Tsagaan Nuur L Mongolia
60 D3 Ter Hole Netherlands 51.18N 4.02E
60 M7 Terhorne Netherlands 53.03N 5.46E
18 C8 Teriang Pen Malaysia 3.14N 102.24E
47 D2 Teriberka U.S.S.R. 69.10N 35.11E
47 C2 Teriberka R U.S.S.R.
47 D2 Teriberskiy, Mys C U.S.S.R. 69.15N 35.14E
15 F7 Terik Irian Jaya 6.54S 140.15E
Terinam Tso L see Zhari Namco
18 B4 Teripa R Sumatra Indon
18 G3 Teritip C Singapore 1.18N 103.39E
90 K6 Terkama Chad 11.08N 21.16E
90 K3 Terkei Chad 16.46N 21.35E
90 K2 Terkezi Chad 18.20N 21.29E
36 D1 Terkos Gölü L Turkey
79 K1 Terlano Italy 46.32N 11.15E
112 D6 Terlingua Texas 29.20N 103.39W
112 D6 Terlingua Cr Texas
81 N1 Terlizzi Italy 41.08N 16.33E
121 B6 Termas de Chillan Chile 74.52S 71.31W
36 J1 Terme Turkey 41.12N 37.00E
36 G2 Terme R Turkey
79 B6 Terme di Valdieri Italy 44.12N 7.16E
79 B6 Terme di Vinádio Italy 44.17N 7.04E
79 K2 Termeno Italy 46.21N 11.15E
75 M4 Termens Spain 41.43N 0.46E
61 M8 Termes Belgium 49.42N 5.28E
72 K10 Termes France 43.00N 2.32E
43 H8 Termez Uzbekistan U.S.S.R. 37.15N 67.15E
71 K6 Termignon France 45.17N 6.49E
111 D10 Terminal I California
14 D10 Termination I W Australia 34.31S 122.00E
90 D5 Termini Niger 13.45N 8.48E
70 O5 Terminiers France 48.05N 1.44E
81 G8 Termini Imerese Sicily 37.59N 13.42E
81 G7 Termini Imerese, Golfo di Sicily
80 G4 Terminillo, Monte Italy 42.29N 13.00E
80 L7 Terminio, Monte Italy 40.50N 14.56E
75 M6 Término, C Spain 40.56N 0.51E
75 D2 Terminón Spain 42.43N 3.27W
115 O8 Términos, L.de Mexico
44 G2 Termita U.S.S.R. 45.07N 45.17E
90 E3 Termit, N Niger 16.02N 11.05E
110 E9 Termo California 40.53N 120.27W
80 L4 Termoli Italy 42.00N 15.00E
59 H2 Termon Tyrone N Ireland 54.36N 7.02W
59 K4 Termonfeckin Louth Irish Rep 53.46N 6.16W
45 O8 Termosin U.S.S.R. 48.11N 42.39E
60 R6 Termunten Netherlands 53.18N 7.03E
60 M6 Ternaard Netherlands 53.23N 5.58E
61 G3 Ternat Belgium 50.52N 4.11E
19 G2 Ternate Luzon Philippines 14.17N 120.44E
19 E3 Ternate Moluccas Indonesia 0.48N 127.23E
19 E3 Ternate isld Moluccas Indonesia 0.50N 127.19E
26 Q12 Ternay, C Seychelles, Ind Oc 4.29S 55.23E
26 R14 Ternay Pass Mahé I Seychelles, Ind Oc
65 K6 Ternberg Austria 47.57N 14.23E
53 E3 Terndrup Denmark 56.49N 10.05E
72 L6 Ternes, les France 45.00N 3.00E
60 C3 Terneuzen Netherlands 51.20N 3.50E
40 G9 Terney U.S.S.R. 45.05N 136.36E
56 F2 Ternhill Shropshire Eng 52.53N 2.33W
114 C2 Tern I Hawaiian Is 23.56N 166.32W
80 G3 Terni Italy 42.34N 12.39E
80 F3 Terni prov Italy
46 F5 Ternopol' Ukraine U.S.S.R. 49.35N 25.39E
46 F5 Ternopol'skaya Oblast' prov Ukraine U.S.S.R.
45 H9 Ternovatoye Ukraine U.S.S.R. 47.52N 36.12E
45 D9 Ternovka Ukraine U.S.S.R. 47.03N 32.02E
45 G8 Ternovka Ukraine U.S.S.R. 48.31N 35.57E
46 N4 Ternovka U.S.S.R. 51.19N 42.58E
45 N5 Ternovka Voronezh U.S.S.R. 51.41N 41.38E
45 P5 Ternovoye U.S.S.R. 51.02N 43.43E
44 C2 Ternovskaya U.S.S.R. 45.53N 40.26E
45 E6 Terny Ukraine U.S.S.R. 51.00N 33.59E
45 E8 Terny Ukraine U.S.S.R. 48.05N 33.35E
18 B8 Terolak Pen Malaysia 3.52N 101.21E
18 A7 Terong Pen Malaysia 4.43N 100.42E
18 A7 Teronoh Pen Malaysia 4.23N 100.58E
80 F2 Terontola Italy 43.12N 12.01E
96 V15 Teror Gran Canaria Canary Is 27.03N 15.32W
11 J6 Te Roti New Zealand 39.30S 174.17E
74 D10 Teroual Morocco 34.40N 5.14W
12 E5 Terowie S Australia 33.11S 138.55E
40 K7 Terpeniya, Mys C Sakhalin U.S.S.R. 48.38N 144.43E
40 J7 Terpeniya Zaliv B Sakhalin U.S.S.R.
47 K7 Terpugovo U.S.S.R. 55.59N 66.15E
39 H2 Terpukhoy, Gora mt U.S.S.R. 65.17N 168.45E
84 P15 Terra Cyprus 34.57N 32.25E
104 F7 Terra Alta W Virginia 39.25N 79.35W
111 E6 Terra Bella California 35.58N 119.03W
115 M3 Terrabona Nicaragua 12.41N 85.59W
101 J8 Terrace Br Col 54.31N 128.32W
99 C4 Terrace Bay Ontario 48.47N 87.06W
14 D8 Terraces, The hills W Australia
96 U3 Terra-Chã Azores 38.41N 27.15W
80 H6 Terracina Italy 41.17N 13.15E
80 H6 Terracina, Golfo di Italy
75 Q3 Terradas Spain 42.19N 2.50E
51 C6 Terråk Norway 65.05N 12.22E
109 N8 Terral Oklahoma 34.54N 97.56W
81 B4 Terralba Sardinia 39.43N 8.38E
98 S5 Terra Nova Newfoundland 48.30N 54.14W
123 J6 Terra Nova B Antarctica
81 M4 Terranova di Pollino Italy 39.59N 16.18E
81 M4 Terranova di Sibari Italy 39.39N 16.20E
98 S5 Terra Nova Nat.Park Newfoundland
98 S5 Terra Nova R Newfoundland
79 L7 Terranuova Bracciolini Italy 43.33N 11.35E
119 J10 Terra Preta Brazil 5.09S 59.22W
117 B6 Terra Santa Brazil 2.07S 56.26W
76 C5 Terras do Bouro Portugal 41.43N 8.18W
81 F7 Terrasini Favarotta Sicily 38.09N 13.05E
99 O10 Terrasse Vaudreuil Quebec 45.23N 73.55W
72 G5 Terrasson-la-Villedieu France 45.07N 1.18E
80 J5 Terratta, La mt Italy 41.53N 13.50E
72 F8 Terraube France 43.55N 0.33E
115 F3 Terrazas Mexico 28.56N 106.14W
123 J3 Terre Adélie Antarctica
110 D5 Terrebonne Oregon 44.22N 121.11W
99 R7 Terrebonne Quebec 45.42N 73.37W
107 F12 Terrebonne B Louisiana
116 M4 Terre de Bas I Guadeloupe W I 15.43N 61.38W
116 N4 Terre de Haut isld Guadeloupe W I 15.52N 61.35W
107 J2 Terre Haute Indiana 39.27N 87.24W
103 B6 Terre Hill Pennsylvania 40.10N 76.04W
112 L3 Terrell Texas 32.43N 96.17W
98 S6 Terrenceville Newfoundland 47.41N 54.44W
71 E6 Terrenoire France 45.27N 4.21E
26 U16 Terre Sainte Réunion Ind Oc 21.20S 55.30E
9 F13 Terres Australes Françaises islands terr Southern Oc
110 N6 Terreton Idaho 43.51N 112.25W
70 H3 Terrette R France
12 M5 Terrey Hills New S Wales 33.41S 151.15E
75 G7 Terriente Spain 40.18N 1.30W

77 F7 Terril mt Spain 37.00N 5.11W
66 E2 Terri, le Mont Switzerland 47.23N 7.10E
77 L3 Terrinches Spain 38.37N 2.50W
56 M2 Terrington Norfolk Eng 52.46N 0.18E
57 M4 Terrington N Yorks Eng 54.07N 0.58W
66 N5 Terri, Piz mt Switzerland 46.36N 9.02E
66 D6 Territet Switzerland 46.26N 6.56E
Territoire Français des Afars et des Issas see French Territory of the Afars and Issas
75 F3 Terroba Spain 42.16N 2.26W
121 K9 Terromontes, Pampa de los plain Chile
72 H6 Terrou France 44.46N 1.59E
76 E11 Terrugem Alto Alentejo Portugal 38.50N 7.20W
76 A11 Terrugem Estremadura Portugal 38.50N 9.22W
107 F9 Terry Mississippi 32.05N 90.19W
108 E3 Terry Montana 46.50N 105.20W
103 H3 Terryville Connecticut 41.40N 73.01W
45 Q6 Tersa R U.S.S.R.
43 J2 Tersakkan R Kazakhstan U.S.S.R.
60 J6 Terschelling isld Netherlands
60 K6 Terschellinger Wad flats Netherlands
60 L11 Terschuur Netherlands 52.10N 5.31E
79 B3 Tersiva mt Italy 45.37N 7.28E
36 G4 Tersizhan Gölü L Turkey
43 M6 Terskey Alatau, Khrebet mts Kirgiziya U.S.S.R.
47 D3 Terskiy Bereg coast U.S.S.R.
53 G5 Tersløse Denmark 55.31N 11.30E
81 D4 Tertenia Sardinia 39.42N 9.35E
87 C5 Terter Sudan 11.57N 31.43E
44 G7 Terter R Azerbaydzhan U.S.S.R.
39 E1 Tertik U.S.S.R. 67.56N 153.39E
61 F5 Tertre Belgium 50.28N 3.49E
75 H7 Teruel Spain 40.21N 1.06W
74 G4 Teruel prov Spain
18 B4 Terumon Sumatra Indonesia 2.52N 97.36E
25 E9 Terutao isld Thailand
82 L7 Tervel Bulgaria 43.45N 27.28E
51 M9 Tervo Finland 62.57N 26.48E
51 L5 Tervola Finland 66.05N 24.50E
61 M5 Terwagne Belgium 50.27N 5.21E
29 B5 Terwara Gujarat India 24.02N 71.43E
60 N7 Terwispel Netherlands 53.02N 6.03E
60 N10 Terwolde Netherlands 52.17N 6.06E
45 H1 Teryayevo U.S.S.R. 56.10N 36.09E
45 J4 Teryazh'ye U.S.S.R. 52.38N 37.17E
44 E5 Terzhola Georgia U.S.S.R. 42.11N 43.00E
82 D6 Tešanj Yugoslavia 44.37N 18.00E
88 P9 Tesaret watercourse Algeria
109 N2 Tescott Kansas 39.02N 97.53W
72 H8 Tescou R France
89 M2 Tesellamane watercourse Niger
79 L2 Tésero Italy 46.18N 11.31E
96 S11 Teseyeraque Fuerteventura Canary Is 28.15N 14.07W
45 O1 Tesha U.S.S.R. 55.31N 42.50E
46 N2 Tesha R U.S.S.R.
113 L1 Teshekpuk L Alaska 70.20N 154.00W
89 J9 Teshi Ghana 5.34N 0.11W
22 F2 Teshig Mongolia 49.58N 102.31E
20 H7 Te-shima I Japan 34.29N 134.05E
21 J5 Teshio Japan 44.53N 141.46E
20 M1 Teshio dake mt Japan 43.59N 142.54E
82 G7 Tešica Yugoslavia 43.27N 21.45E
30 H3 Tesinga Nepal 27.50N 86.45E
22 D2 Tesiyn Gol R Mongolia
75 C2 Tesla, Sierra de mts Spain
101 G5 Teslin Yukon Terr 60.10N 132.42W
101 F5 Teslin R Yukon/Br Col
101 G5 Teslin L Yukon/Br Col
112 E5 Tesnus Texas 30.07N 102.55W
24 D10 Te-so-erh-mi-t'ang Hu L Xizang Zizhiqu 30.35N 83.15E
79 N3 Tésolo Italy 45.32N 12.38E
93 M4 Tesore Kenya 1.02N 40.02E
76 H6 Teso Santo mt Spain 41.14N 5.54W
118 E4 Tesouras, R Brazil
118 D5 Tesouro Brazil 16.04S 53.30W
46 H1 Tesovo-Netyl'skiy U.S.S.R. 59.00N 31.10E
74 G9 Tessala, Mts.du Algeria
89 K1 Tessalit Mali 20.11N 1.02E
90 C5 Tessaoua Niger 13.46N 7.55E
88 K5 Tessaout R Morocco
87 F3 Tessenai Ethiopia 15.33N 36.41E
61 L2 Tessenderlo Belgium 51.04N 5.05E
87 F3 Tessenei Ethiopia 14.58N 37.47E
80 E4 Tessennano Italy 42.28N 11.47E
66 M7 Tesserete Switzerland 46.04N 8.58E
100 K7 Tessier Saskatchewan 51.48N 107.26W
63 Q4 Tessin E Germany 54.02N 12.29E
94 N3 Tessolo Mozambique 21.52S 34.02E
72 C4 Tesson France 45.39N 0.40W
53 Z18 Tessungtind mt Norway 60.07N 8.36E
70 H4 Tessy France 48.58N 1.04W
81 C1 Testa, C Sardinia 41.15N 9.09E
63 L6 Testedt W Germany 53.18N 9.43E
72 B6 Teste, la France 44.39N 1.09W
61 K2 Testelt Belgium 51.01N 4.57E
Teştik see Mindeval
78 C12 Testour Tunisia 36.33N 9.28E
56 H5 Test, R Hants Eng
109 E6 Tesuque New Mexico 35.45N 105.57W
37 G3 Teşvikiye Turkey 40.08N 29.17E
62 K8 Tét Hungary 47.30N 17.31E
72 K10 Tet R France
101 L9 Tetachuck L Br Col
98 F6 Tetagouche R New Brunswick
30 J6 Tetaria Bihar India 26.24N 85.12E
120 D10 Tetas, Pta C Chile 23.32S 70.39W
56 G4 Tetbury Glos Eng 51.39N 2.10W
90 K7 Tete Cent Afr Rep 8.43N 20.04E
92 F10 Tete Mozambique 16.10S 33.35E
92 F9 Tete dist Mozambique
98 N3 Tête à la Baleine Quebec 50.43N 59.20W
66 G8 Tête Blanche mt Italy/Switz 45.59N 7.35E
66 B8 Tête de Parmelan mt France 45.57N 6.15E
66 D3 Tête de Rang mt Switzerland 47.04N 6.51E
122 S15 Tétégégié isld Gambier Is Pacific Oc 23.05S 134.53W
101 O9 Tête Jaune Cache Br Col 52.57N 119.25W
11 L5 Te Teko New Zealand 38.03S 176.48E
115 J9 Tetela Mexico 17.58N 100.06W
15 K3 Tetepare I Solomon Is 8.45S 157.30E
103 J6 Teterboro Airport New Jersey 40.51N 74.04W
69 M5 Téterchen France 49.14N 6.34E
42 G2 Tetere U.S.S.R. 60.10N 102.12E
42 G2 Tetere R U.S.S.R.
46 G4 Teterev R Ukraine U.S.S.R.
60 H13 Teteringen Netherlands 51.37N 4.49E
63 R5 Teterow E Germany 53.47N 12.35E
82 J8 Teteven Bulgaria 42.54N 24.18E
42 H2 Teteya R U.S.S.R.
57 N6 Tetford Lincs Eng 53.16N 0.01W
122 B15 Tetiaroa atoll Society Is Pacific Oc 17.05S 149.30W
40 E2 Tetinnyakh U.S.S.R. 58.56N 130.45E
96 T10 Tetir Fuerteventura Canary Is 28.31N 13.57W
46 G5 Tetiyev Ukraine U.S.S.R. 49.22N 29.40E
45 F5 Tetkino U.S.S.R. 51.16N 34.16E
113 Q5 Tetlin Alaska 63.05N 142.32W
113 Q5 Tetlin Junction Alaska 63.20N 142.40W
113 Q5 Tetlin L Alaska 63.05N 142.50W
110 O2 Teton R Montana
110 O6 Tetonia Idaho 43.49N 111.10W
110 P6 Teton Ra Wyoming
77 F9 Tetouan Morocco 35.34N 5.22W
82 F8 Tetovo Yugoslavia 42.00N 20.59E
84 C7 Tetrávi, Óros mt Greece 37.22N 21.57E
30 J7 Tetrawan Bihar India 25.08N 85.34E
99 S8 Tetreauville Quebec 45.37N 73.32W
47 D3 Tetrino U.S.S.R. 66.03N 38.16E
44 F6 Tetri Tskaro Georgia U.S.S.R. 41.33N 44.30E
56 J4 Tetsworth Oxon Eng 51.43N 1.01W
64 L3 Tettau W Germany 50.28N 11.16E
63 G5 Tettens W Germany 53.38N 7.54E
64 H8 Tettnang W Germany 47.40N 9.36E
Te-tu see Dedu
Tetuán Morocco see Tetouan
75 O6 Tetuan dist Madrid Spain
31 H10 Tetulia R Bangladesh
45 U2 Tetyushi U.S.S.R. 54.55N 48.49E
64 N1 Teuchern E Germany 51.08N 12.02E
20 C10 Teuchi Japan 31.38N 129.40E
120 G11 Teuco R Argentina
94 D4 Teufelsbach Namibia 22.10S 17.01E
65 N7 Teufelstein mt Austria 47.28N 15.38E
66 O2 Teufen Switzerland 47.23N 9.23E
65 K7 Teufenbach Austria 47.08N 14.23E
64 P7 Teufenberg Austria 48.24N 13.29E
60 N11 Teuge Netherlands 52.14N 6.02E
120 E2 Teuini Brazil 7.57N 67.15W
81 B6 Teulada Sardinia 38.58N 8.46E
77 R3 Teulada Spain 38.44N 0.06E
81 B6 Teulada, C Sardinia 38.52N 8.38E
81 B6 Teulada, G. di Sardinia
115 H7 Teul de Gonzales Ortega Mexico 21.30N 103.28W
100 U8 Teulon Manitoba 50.26N 97.18W
19 F7 Teun isld Indon 6.58S 129.08E
18 A3 Teunom R Sumatra Indon
63 T8 Teupitz E Germany 52.08N 13.38E
21 J5 Teuri isld Japan 44.27N 141.20E
64 L3 Teuschnitz W Germany 50.23N 11.23E
115 M3 Teustepe Nicaragua 12.21N 85.51W
65 H5 Teutenburg Austria 48.24N 13.28E
63 H8 Teutoburger Wald hills W Germany
51 J9 Teuva Finland 62.29N 21.45E
52 J4 Tevansjö Sweden 62.05N 15.30E
28 C6 Tevaram Tamil Nadu India 9.55N 77.18E
37 E9 Tevem Turkey 36.44N 39.37E
70 B4 Téven-Kerbrat France 48.41N 4.09W
80 F5 Tevere R Italy
Teverga see Plaza, La
11 D12 Teviot New Zealand 45.38S 169.24E
95 J7 Teviot S Africa 31.41S 25.36E
57 H2 Teviotdale V Borders Scotland
57 H2 Teviot, R Borders Scotland

47 L6 Tevriz U.S.S.R. 57.31N 72.20E
11 B13 Te Waewae B New Zealand
18 K6 Tewah Borneo Indon 1.05S 113.43E
94 J4 Tewane Botswana 22.50S 27.02E
18 L6 Teweh R Borneo Indon
11 J6 Te Wera New Zealand 39.14S 174.35E
11 L5 Te Whaiti New Zealand 38.34S 176.46E
11 J11 Te Whanga lagoon Chatham Is Pacific Oc
11 K8 Te Wharau New Zealand 41.11S 175.50E
56 G4 Tewkesbury Glos Eng 51.59N 2.09W
23 C1 Tewo Gansu China 34.07N 103.15E
101 L11 Texada I Br Col
112 N2 Texarkana Texas/Arkansas 33.28N 94.02W
112 N2 Texarkana. L Texas 33.19N 94.10W
103 A8 Texas Maryland 39.28N 76.38W
13 K8 Texas Queensland 28.50S 151.09E
102 F4 Texas state U.S.A.
112 N6 Texas City Texas 29.23N 94.55W
115 K8 Texcoco Mexico 19.32N 98.52W
60 H7 Texel isld Netherlands
60 H8 Texel Stroom channel Netherlands
109 J5 Texhoma Texas/Oklahoma 36.30N 101.47W
109 G7 Texico New Mexico 34.14N 103.05W
112 B7 Texline Texas 36.23N 103.02W
109 L6 Texola Oklahoma 35.13N 99.59W
109 O8 Texoma, L Oklahoma
112 F4 Texon Texas 31.13N 101.43W
42 E2 Teya U.S.S.R. 60.18N 92.43E
42 E2 Teya R U.S.S.R.
95 L5 Teyateyaneng Lesotho 29.09S 27.45E
46 M2 Teykovo U.S.S.R. 56.50N 40.35E
72 H6 Teyssieu France 44.55N 1.58E
31 C4 Teyvareh Afghanistan 33.21N 64.25E
95 O9 Teza S Africa 28.31S 32.08E
46 M2 Teza R U.S.S.R.
Tezaf see Tīgh Āb
43 F6 Tezebazar Uzbekistan U.S.S.R. 42.10N 60.05E
44 F7 Tezhler mt Armenia U.S.S.R. 40.42N 44.31E
115 L8 Teziutlán Mexico 19.49N 97.22W
115 K8 Tezontepec Mexico 19.53N 98.50W
28 J2 Tezpur Assam India 26.38N 92.49E
79 L3 Tezze Trento Italy 45.59N 11.41E
79 L3 Tezze Vicenza Italy 45.41N 11.43E
85 A4 Tghuttah Libya 30.15N 10.28E
Thabana Ntlenyana mt see Thadentsonyane
95 N5 Thabana-Ntlenyana mt Lesotho 29.28S 29.16E
95 K5 Thaba Nchu S Africa 29.13S 26.50E
95 K5 Thaba Nchu mt S Africa 29.15S 26.54E
95 O3 Thabankulu mt S Africa 27.30S 30.21E
95 L5 Thaba Putsoa mt Lesotho 29.44S 27.55E
95 L6 Thaba Putsoa mts Lesotho
25 C4 Thabaung Burma 17.03N 94.48E
94 J5 Thabazimbi S Africa 24.41S 27.21E
25 D1 Thabeikkyin Burma 22.51N 96.03E
25 G4 Tha Bo Thailand 17.52N 102.34E
71 K6 Thabor, Mt France 45.07N 6.38E
86 M9 Thabt, Gebel el mt Egypt 28.16N 34.01E
25 D2 Thabyedaung Burma 21.16N 96.05E
24 D9 Thachap Kangri mt pk Xizang Zizhiqu China 33.29N 82.14E
109 N8 Thackerville Oklahoma 33.48N 97.08W
33 F4 Thādiq Saudi Arabia 25.20N 45.54E
24 C10 Thaga La pass Xizang Zizhiqu 31.27N 79.09E
29 H6 Thagaon Madhya Prad India 23.05N 82.20E
25 E6 Thagyettaw Burma 13.45N 98.08E
Tha Hin see Lop Buri
25 J2 Thai Binh Vietnam 20.30N 106.12E
25 K5 Thai Binh Vietnam 14.59N 108.52E
25 J4 Thai Duong Thuong Vietnam 16.36N 107.36E
17 F8 Thailand kingdom S E Asia
17 F9 Thailand, G. of Cambodia/Thailand
Thai Muang see Ban Thai Muang
25 H2 Thai Nguyen Vietnam 21.31N 105.55E
28 C1 Thair Maharashtra India 18.22N 76.14E
72 B3 Thairé France 46.05N 1.01W
33 H3 Thaj Saudi Arabia 26.50N 48.45E
Thak see Namco
9 U4 Thakau Matathuthu reef Fiji 16.09S 179.43W
9 T5 Thakaundrove Pen Vanua Levu Fiji
9 U4 Thakau Vuthovutho reef Fiji 16.08S 179.35W
Tha Kham see Ban Tha Kham
25 E8 Tha Khanon Thailand 9.02N 98.57E
25 H4 Thakhek Laos 17.22N 104.50E
30 B3 Thakurdwara Uttar Prad India 29.12N 78.52E
31 G8 Thakurgaon Bangladesh 26.05N 88.34E
29 G7 Thakurtola Madhya Prad India 21.40N 81.01E
65 G8 Thal Austria 46.48N 12.39E
64 J2 Thal E Germany 50.54N 10.23E
31 F4 Thal Pakistan 33.24N 70.32E
66 P2 Thal Switzerland 47.28N 9.35E
88 S4 Thala Tunisia 35.35N 8.40E
25 H6 Thalabarivat Cambodia 13.35N 105.57E
25 E8 Thalang Thailand 8.00N 98.21E
23 A4 Thala Pass China/Burma 28.10N 98.10E
30 D3 Thalara Nepal 29.40N 80.59E
Tha Lat see Ban Tha Lat'
31 J1 Thaldat Kashmir 35.15N 79.30E
31 F5 Thal Desert Pakistan
63 O9 Thale E Germany 51.46N 11.03E
25 F9 Thale Luang L Thailand
95 M8 Thaleni S Africa 32.12S 28.25E
25 F9 Thale Noi L Thailand
65 M8 Thalerhof airport Austria 46.59N 15.27E
64 B4 Thalfang W Germany 49.45N 7.00E
65 H6 Thalgau Austria 47.52N 13.15E
64 O2 Thalheim E Germany 50.42N 12.51E
66 L1 Thalheim Switzerland 47.34N 8.45E
Tha Li see Ban Tha Li
66 O5 Thalkirch Switzerland 46.39N 9.17E
13 J8 Thallon Queensland 28.39S 148.49E
105 F6 Thalmann Georgia 31.18N 81.42W
64 L5 Thalmässing W Germany 49.05N 11.14E
31 C6 Thalo Pakistan 28.10N 64.29E
33 G6 Thalthānah, Jabal ath mt Saudi Arabia 21.51N 46.56E
66 L2 Thalwil Switzerland 47.17N 8.35E
85 E6 Thamad Bū Hashishah Libya 26.28N 18.45E
86 M6 Thamad, El Egypt 29.40N 34.18E
94 H5 Thamaga Botswana 24.46S 25.21E
94 G2 Thamalakane R Botswana
Thamami, Ath see Thumāmī, Ath
33 K8 Thamarīt Oman 17.44N 53.59E
33 L8 Thamarīt Oman 17.47N 54.00E
33 F10 Thamar, Jabal mt S Yemen 13.53N 45.15E
56 K4 Thame Oxon Eng 51.45N 0.59W
56 K4 Thame, R Bucks etc Eng
11 K4 Thames New Zealand 37.08S 175.35E
103 K4 Thames R Connecticut
99 H10 Thames R Ontario
55 C5 Thames Ditton Surrey Eng 51.24N 0.20W
11 K4 Thames, Firth of New Zealand
99 J9 Thamesford Ontario 43.03N 81.01W
56 N4 Thames Haven Essex Eng 51.31N 0.31E
55 J4 Thamesmead London England 51.30N 0.07E
56 N4 Thames, R England
99 J10 Thamesville Ontario 42.33N 81.59W
30 G3 Thami Nepal 27.50N 86.39E
30 G3 Thami Khola R Nepal
25 E6 Thamikla Kyun isld Burma
85 D4 Thāmit wadi Libya
Tham Khae see Ban Tham Khae
30 G3 Thammu Nepal 27.49N 86.42E
86 P8 Thamri, Wādī eth watercourse Saudi Arabia
64 K1 Thamsbrück E Germany 51.09N 10.38E
30 H4 Thamserku Nepal 27.48N 86.48E
52 E3 Thamshamn Norway 63.18N 9.53E
33 H8 Thamūd S Yemen 17.22N 49.58E
28 A1 Thana Maharashtra India 19.14N 73.02E
29 C8 Thana dist Maharashtra India
30 A3 Thana Bhawan Uttar Prad India 29.35N 77.25E
30 E5 Thanagaon Uttar Prad India 27.28N 81.15E
29 E4 Thana Gazi Rajasthan India 27.23N 76.18E
30 A7 Thana Kasba Rajasthan India 25.14N 77.19E
25 D4 Thanatpin Burma 17.16N 96.34E
25 D5 Thanbyuzayat Burma 15.58N 97.44E
29 D6 Thandla Madhya Prad India 23.00N 74.38E
113 U7 Thane Alaska 58.14N 134.14W
13 K8 Thane Queensland 28.08S 151.39E
Thanesar see Kurukshetra
30 A3 Thanesar Haryana India 29.58N 76.48E
56 O5 Thanet, I.of reg Kent Eng 51.22N 1.15E
25 K5 Thang Binh Vietnam 15.43N 108.20E
30 G3 Thangmoche Nepal 27.51N 86.39E
14 D4 Thangoo W Australia 18.10S 122.26E
13 K6 Thangool Queensland 24.38S 150.42E
31 K4 Thangra Kashmir 33.14N 78.55E
25 H3 Thanh Hoa Vietnam 19.49N 105.48E
25 J2 Thanh Moi Vietnam 21.33N 107.06E
25 H1 Thanh Thuy Vietnam 22.55N 104.53E
25 H8 Thanh Tri Vietnam 9.25N 105.47E
35 F9 Thaniya Jordan 31.10N 35.43E
33 G9 Thaniyah, Jabal mt Yemen 15.50N 46.22E
28 D5 Thanjavur Tamil Nadu India 10.46N 79.09E
28 D5 Thanjavur dist Tamil Nadu India
57 F1 Thankerton Strathclyde Scotland 55.38N 3.39W
25 E8 Than Kyun isld Burma
25 L9 Thanlon Manipur India 24.18N 93.17E
69 N8 Thann France 47.49N 7.05E
64 N7 Thann W Germany 48.15N 12.04E
64 J7 Thannhausen W Germany 48.17N 10.28E
31 D8 Thano Bula Khan Pakistan 25.23N 67.51E
25 G2 Than Uyen Vietnam 21.58N 103.54E
69 N7 Thanvillé France 48.20N 7.20E
30 J5 Thapagaon Nepal 27.51N 85.19E

25 F4 Tha Pla Thailand 17.40N 100.30E
Thap Phung see Ban Thap Phung
25 E8 Thap Put Thailand 8.32N 98.40E
Thapsacus anc site see Dibse
25 E7 Thap Sakae Thailand 11.30N 99.35E
29 B6 Thara Gujarat India 24.00N 71.51E
25 E6 Tharabwin Burma 12.19N 99.03E
29 B5 Tharad Gujarat India 24.26N 71.44E
64 Q2 Tharandt E Germany 50.59N 13.35E
93 H10 Tharangire watercourse Tanzania
31 E8 Thar Des Pakistan/India
30 B6 Tharet Madhya Prad India 26.01N 78.39E
13 G8 Thargomindah Queensland 27.59S 143.45E
29 K3 Thargram W Bengal India 22.26N 87.00E
30 K8 Thari Sonarai Bihar India 24.24N 86.54E
30 A2 Tharoch Himachal Prad India 30.59N 77.42E
25 F5 Tha Rong Thailand 15.37N 101.06E
Tharparkar dist see Mirpur Khas
31 E8 Thar Parkar div Pakistan
25 C4 Tharrawaddy Burma 17.37N 95.48E
25 C4 Tharrawaw Burma 17.40N 95.29E
81 A4 Tharros anc site Sardinia 39.53N 8.25E
77 B5 Tharsis Spain 37.36N 7.07W
34 K4 Tharthar oil well Iraq 34.07N 42.44E
34 L5 Tharthār Canal Iraq
34 K3 Tharthār, Wādī ath watercourse Iraq
33 L5 Tharwāniyyah U.A.E. 23.07N 54.02E
Tha Sala see Ban Tha Sala
Tha Song Yang see Ban Tha Song Yang
83 G4 Thásos Greece 40.46N 24.42E
56 J5 Thatcham Berks Eng 51.25N 1.15W
111 P9 Thatcher Arizona 32.50N 109.46W
109 F4 Thatcher Colorado 37.33N 104.07W
110 O7 Thatcher Idaho 42.26N 111.44W
93 J7 Thatha mt Kenya 1.04S 37.45E
30 B2 Thati Kathur Uttar Prad India 30.36N 78.40E
25 J1 That Khe Vietnam 22.15N 106.26E
25 D4 Thaton Burma 16.56N 97.20E
Tha Tum see Ban Tha Tum
71 D10 Thau, Etang de L France 43.25N 3.38E
72 K2 Thaumiers France 46.49N 2.39E
25 L9 Thaungdut Burma 24.26N 94.45E
25 E4 Thaungyin R Burma/Thailand
Tha Uthen see Ban Tha Uthen
33 E10 Thawbānī Yemen 13.20N 43.24E
56 M4 Thaxted Essex Eng 51.57N 0.20E
65 M4 Thaya Austria 48.52N 15.18E
65 N4 Thaya R Austria
34 G8 Thāyāt, Ath hill Saudi Arabia 30.23N 39.20E
25 D6 Thayawthadangyi Kyun isld Burma
107 E5 Thayer Missouri 36.32N 91.33W
25 E6 Thayetchaung Burma 13.52N 98.17E
25 C3 Thayetmyo Burma 19.20N 95.10E
25 M9 Thayetta Burma 24.33N 96.39E
110 P7 Thayne Wyoming 42.56N 111.00W
66 L1 Thayngen Switzerland 47.49N 8.43E
25 B3 Thazi Burma 19.40N 93.51E
25 C3 Thazi Burma 20.00N 95.04E
25 D2 Thazi Burma 20.50N 96.04E
56 J5 Theale Berks Eng 51.27N 1.04W
111 M9 Theba Arizona 32.54N 112.54W
12 A8 Thebarton dist Adelaide, S Aust
100 J5 The Battlefords Prov.Park Saskatchewan
Thebes see Thívai
107 G4 Thebes Illinois 37.12N 89.26W
85 M7 Thebes ruins Egypt 25.41N 32.40E
87 O4 The Brothers islds S Yemen
108 K8 Thedford Nebraska 41.59N 100.32W
99 J9 Thedford Ontario 43.09N 81.51W
63 K7 Thedinghausen W Germany 52.57N 9.01E
13 L7 Theebine Queensland 25.57S 152.30E
25 C3 Thegon Burma 18.39N 95.26E
69 O5 Theileischweiler-Fröschen W Germany 49.16N 7.35E
72 J1 Theillay France 47.18N 2.02E
70 H6 Theil, le Ille-et-Vilaine France 47.56N 1.26W
70 M5 Theil, le Orne France 48.15N 0.41E
25 E7 Theinkun Burma 11.52N 99.08E
25 D4 Theinzeik Burma 17.00N 97.12E
64 N1 Theissen E Germany 51.05N 12.07E
50 J3 Theistareykjabunga mt Iceland 65.51N 16.53W
70 E6 Theix France 47.38N 2.38W
30 F7 Thekman Uttar Prad India 25.53N 82.57E
101 T5 Thekulthili L N W Terr 61.03N 110.00W
56 D6 Thelbridge Devon Eng 50.54N 3.43W
88 S4 Thélepte Tunisia 35.04N 8.38E
105 E7 Thelma Georgia 30.49N 82.49W
101 W3 Thelon R N W Terr
53 D4 Them Denmark 56.06N 9.33E
93 B7 Thema, L Rwanda
64 K2 Themar E Germany 50.30N 10.37E
93 H9 Themi R Tanzania
72 H6 Thémines France 44.45N 1.48E
72 C4 Thénac France 45.40N 0.39W
72 G2 Thenay Indre France 46.37N 1.25E
70 N7 Thenay Loir-et-Cher France 47.24N 1.18E
66 B9 Thenésol France 45.43N 6.23E
72 K2 Theneuille France 46.35N 2.52E
72 D2 Thénezay France 46.43N 0.02W
94 L4 Thengwe S Africa 22.48S 30.30E
88 P3 Thénia Algeria 36.43N 3.34E
88 P4 Theniet el Had Algeria 35.47N 2.01E
72 G5 Thenon France 45.08N 1.05E
107 H11 Theodore Alabama 30.32N 88.11W
13 K7 Theodore Queensland 25.00S 150.06E
100 P7 Theodore Saskatchewan 51.26N 102.58W
111 O8 Theodore Roosevelt L Arizona
108 G2 Theodore Roosevelt Nat.Mem.Park N Dakota
66 G8 Theodul Pass Italy/Switz 45.58N 7.43E
30 A1 Theog Himachal Prad India 31.07N 77.21E
84 D6 Theóktiston Greece 37.48N 22.07E
84 G5 Theológos Évvoia Greece 38.29N 23.48E
84 D7 Theológos Lakonía Greece 37.08N 22.27E
13 B5 Theo, Mt N Terr Australia 21.20S 131.10E
71 K9 Théoule-sur-Mer France 43.30N 6.56E
Thepha see Ban Thepha
104 K2 Theresa New York 44.14N 75.49W
106 F6 Theresa Wisconsin 43.32N 88.26W
13 J6 Theresa R Queensland
26 R14 Thérèse I Mahé I Seychelles, Ind Oc 4.40S 55.23E
100 F4 Therien Alberta 54.15N 111.15W
107 F12 Theriot Louisiana 29.25N 90.48W
83 F4 Thermaïkós Kólpos G Greece
66 J6 Thermen Switzerland 46.20N 8.02E
Thermia isld see Kíthnos
84 H7 Thérmion, Stenón str Greece
111 L3 Thermo Utah 38.12N 113.11W
84 C4 Thérmon Greece 38.35N 21.40E
84 E4 Thermopílai pass Greece 38.50N 22.35E
108 B6 Thermopolis Wyoming 43.39N 108.12W
50 K2 Thernuvatn L Iceland 66.19N 15.47W
95 K4 Theron S Africa 28.19S 26.46E
123 D10 Theron Mts Antarctica
69 C2 Thérouanne France 50.38N 2.15E
66 G1 Therwil Switzerland 47.30N 7.33E
99 G5 The Shoals Prov. Park Ontario
97 G3 Thesiger B N W Terr
84 F5 Thespiaí Greece 38.17N 23.10E
84 D3 Thessalía prov Greece
99 G6 Thessalon Ontario 46.15N 83.34W
83 F4 Thessaloníki Greece 40.38N 22.58E
Thessaly prov see Thessalía
56 N3 Thetford Norfolk Eng 52.25N 0.45E
98 A7 Thetford Mines Quebec 46.07N 71.16W
25 C5 Thetkethaung R Burma
56 N3 Thet, R Norfolk Eng
95 K4 Theunissen S Africa 28.25S 26.44E
70 O5 Theuville France 48.20N 1.36E
61 O4 Theux Belgium 50.32N 5.49E
12 C4 Thevenard S Australia 32.10S 133.40E
14 A5 Thevenard I W Australia 21.25S 115.00E
98 H2 Thévet, L Quebec 51.50N 64.15W
72 J2 Thevet St. Julien France 46.38N 2.04E
55 J1 Theydon Bois Essex Eng 51.40N 0.05E
55 J1 Theydon Garnon Essex Eng 51.40N 0.07E
55 J1 Theydon Mount Essex Eng 51.40N 0.09E
71 H6 Theys France 45.19N 6.00E
71 C10 Thézan-lès-Béziers France 43.25N 3.10E
71 H8 Thèze Alpes de Haute Provence France 44.18N 5.56E
72 D9 Thèze Pyrénées Atlantiques France 43.29N 0.20W
72 G1 Thézée France 47.20N 1.18E
68 F4 Thiais France 48.46N 2.23E
83 D5 Thiamis R Greece
72 F3 Thiat France 46.16N 0.58E
69 K6 Thiaucourt France 48.57N 5.52E
61 N8 Thiaumont Belgium 49.43N 5.44E
93 J6 Thiba R Kenya
70 L3 Thiberville France 49.08N 0.27E
69 G6 Thibie France 48.56N 4.13E
107 F12 Thibodaux Louisiana 29.47N 90.50W
70 M3 Thibouville France 49.09N 0.44E
100 U3 Thicket Portage Manitoba 55.20N 97.42W
100 E2 Thickwood Hills Alberta
69 H6 Thiéblemont-Farémont France 48.42N 4.44E
108 O1 Thief R Minnesota
108 P1 Thief L Minnesota
108 O1 Thief River Falls Minnesota 48.08N 96.12W
110 H4 Thief Valley Res Oregon 45.00N 117.44W
66 C4 Thièle R Switzerland
123 F9 Thiel Mts Antarctica
110 C6 Thielsen, Mt Oregon 43.09N 122.05W
71 D3 Thiel-sur-Acolin France 46.30N 3.35E
79 K3 Thiene Italy 45.43N 11.29E
106 G6 Thiensville Wisconsin 43.14N 88.00W
69 E4 Thiérache hills France
66 G4 Thierachern Switzerland 46.46N 7.35E
66 K5 Thierberg Hinter mt Switzerland 46.42N 8.24E
66 D5 Thierrens Switzerland 46.43N 6.46E
71 D5 Thiers France 45.51N 3.33E
64 N3 Thiersheim W Germany 50.04N 12.08E
74 H9 Thiersville Algeria 35.14N 0.09E
69 J5 Thierville-sur-Meuse France 49.10N 5.20E
89 A4 Thiès Senegal 14.49N 16.52W
89 A4 Thiès reg Senegal
81 B2 Thiesi Sardinia 40.32N 8.43E
63 T4 Thiessow E Germany 54.17N 13.43E
87 B7 Thiet Sudan 7.37N 28.49E
61 G5 Thieu Belgium 50.28N 4.06E
61 E4 Thieulain Belgium 50.37N 3.36E
61 G4 Thieusies Belgium 50.31N 4.03E
72 K5 Thiézac France 45.00N 2.38E
93 J7 Thika Kenya 1.03S 37.05E
93 H6 Thika R Kenya
9 T1 Thikombia isld Fiji 15.45S 179.58W
27 L8 Thiladunmathi Atoll Maldives, Ind Oc 6.30N 72.50E
15 K4 Thilenius, C Bismarck Arch 1.35S 149.50E
89 B3 Thillé-Boubacar Senegal 16.30N 15.05W
70 O3 Thilliers-en-Vexin, les France 49.14N 1.37E
69 M8 Thillot, le France 47.53N 6.47E
86 J7 Thilmet, Gebel hill Egypt 29.00N 32.32E
86 L9 Thimân, Wâdi watercourse Egypt
28 G2 Thimbu Bhutan 27.32N 89.43E
28 G2 Thimbu R Bhutan
61 H5 Thiméon Belgium 50.29N 4.26E
70 N4 Thimert-Gâtelles France 48.34N 1.18E
30 J5 Thimi Nepal 27.41N 85.24E
61 O4 Thimister Belgium 50.39N 5.52E
61 E4 Thimougies Belgium 50.38N 3.31E
61 H4 Thines Belgium 50.36N 4.22E
50 K6 Thinganes Iceland 64.17N 15.06W
50 J2 Thingeyjarsýsla, Nordhur co Iceland
50 J2 Thingeyjarsýsla, Nordhur co Iceland
50 H3 Thingeyjarsýsla, Sudhur co Iceland
50 E3 Thingeyrasandur sand reg Iceland
50 B3 Thingeyri Iceland 65.53N 23.27W
50 B3 Thingmannaheidhi heath Iceland
50 L4 Thingmúli Iceland 65.02N 14.38W
50 D6 Thingvallavatn L Iceland 64.10N 21.10W
50 D6 Thingvellir Iceland 64.15N 21.06W
69 H4 Thin-le-Moutier France 49.43N 4.30E
87 H3 Thio Ethiopia 14.41N 40.57E
9 B13 Thio New Caledonia 21.36S 166.12E
69 L5 Thionville France 49.22N 6.11E
89 H5 Thiou Upper Volta 13.51N 2.34W
83 G8 Thíra Greece 36.24N 25.27E
83 G8 Thíra isld Greece
83 G8 Thirasía isld Greece 36.26N 25.21E
85 L10 Third Cataract Sudan 19.42N 30.20E
72 C2 Thiré France 46.33N 1.00W
61 G5 Thirimont Belgium 50.16N 4.14E
57 G3 Thirlmere L Cumbria Eng 54.32N 3.04W
57 G3 Thirlspot Cumbria Eng 54.33N 3.03W
70 N5 Thiron-Gardais France 48.18N 1.01E
57 L4 Thirsk N Yorks Eng 54.14N 1.20W
57 K2 Thirston Northumb Eng 55.17N 1.42W
14 D9 Thirsty, Mt W Australia 32.05S 121.38E
Thirthar, Wadi see Tharthār, Wādī ath watercourse
91 D7 'Thirty One' de Janeiro Angola 6.57S 15.35E
99 K7 Thirty Thousand Is Ontario
61 L4 Thisnes Belgium 50.40N 5.03E
53 B3 Thisted Viborg Denmark 56.58N 8.42E
Thisted co see Viborg
50 K2 Thistilfjördhur B Iceland
111 N2 Thistle Utah 39.59N 111.31W
54 L1 Thistle oil field North Sea 61.22N 1.27E
12 D5 Thistle I S Australia 35.00S 136.08E
101 T3 Thistle L N W Terr 64.58N 108.41W
84 E5 Thísvi Greece 38.15N 22.58E
9 T2 Thithia isld Fiji 17.45S 179.20W
25 C1 Thitseingyi Burma 22.23N 95.56E
17 H9 Thitu islds S China Sea
25 M9 Thityabin Burma 23.25N 95.35E
84 F5 Thívai Greece 38.19N 23.19E
70 N5 Thivars France 48.23N 1.27E
72 F5 Thiviers France 45.24N 0.56E
71 E4 Thizy France 46.02N 4.18E
50 K4 Thjódhfell mt Iceland 65.28N 15.37W
50 F6 Thjófafoss waterfall Iceland 64.03N 19.53W
50 K5 Thjófahnukar mt Iceland 64.45N 15.39W
50 E7 Thjorsá inlet Iceland
50 F6 Thjórsá R Iceland
50 E7 Thjórsárbru Iceland 63.56N 20.39W
50 F6 Thjórsárdalur V Iceland
101 T5 Thoa R N W Terr
71 J8 Thoard France 44.10N 6.08E
Thoen see Muang Thoen
25 F3 Thoeng Thailand 19.43N 100.10E
108 D1 Thoeny Montana 48.55N 106.57W
71 H4 Thoirette France 46.16N 5.33E
69 B6 Thoiry France 48.52N 1.48E
71 F4 Thoissey France 46.10N 4.48E
71 E2 Thoisy-la-Berchère France 47.15N 4.21E
Thok Amar see Gêrzê
84 D7 Thoknía Greece 37.25N 22.05E
60 E13 Tholen Netherlands 51.32N 4.13E
60 E13 Tholen isld Netherlands
64 C5 Tholey W Germany 49.29N 7.03E
66 C6 Thollon France 46.23N 6.42E
71 H9 Tholonet France 43.31N 5.32E
69 M7 Tholy, Le France 48.05N 6.44E
109 M6 Thomas Oklahoma 35.46N 98.46W
104 F7 Thomas W Virginia 39.08N 79.32W
111 E4 Thomas A.Edison, L California 37.20N 119.00W
105 K11 Thomas B Bahamas
107 D2 Thomas Hill Reservoir Missouri
97 K1 Thomas Hubbard, C N W Terr 81.30N 94.40W
112 F3 Thomas, J.B., L Texas
12 E2 Thomas, L S Australia
111 H8 Thomas Mt California 33.37N 116.41W
11 G10 Thomas, Mt New Zealand 43.11S 172.20E
14 B6 Thomas, R W Australia
13 B6 Thomas Res N Terr Australia 23.40S 130.48E
65 J5 Thomasroith Austria 48.05N 13.37E
122 V15 Thomasset, Rocher Marquesas Is Pacific Oc 10.22S 138.40W
107 J9 Thomaston Alabama 32.15N 87.39W
103 H3 Thomaston Connecticut 41.40N 73.05W
105 C5 Thomaston Georgia 32.55N 84.20W
104 Q2 Thomaston Maine 44.04N 69.14W
112 K6 Thomaston Texas 29.00N 97.10W
103 H3 Thomaston Res Connecticut
59 H6 Thomastown Kilkenny Irish Rep 52.31N 7.08W
107 G9 Thomastown Mississippi 32.52N 89.40W
107 J10 Thomasville Alabama 31.56N 87.43W
105 D7 Thomasville Georgia 30.50N 83.59W
107 E5 Thomasville Missouri 36.48N 91.31W
105 G2 Thomasville N Carolina 35.54N 80.04W
9 U5 Thombia islet Fiji 16.28S 179.40W
25 E8 Thom Chob, Lem C Thailand 8.35N 98.13E
70 N4 Thomer-la-Sogne France 48.56N 1.10E
69 D7 Thomery France 48.24N 2.47E
61 P6 Thommen Belgium 50.13N 6.05E
116 J5 Thomonde Haiti 19.00N 71.59W
103 L3 Thompson Connecticut 41.58N 71.52W
108 R6 Thompson Iowa 43.22N 93.45W
100 U3 Thompson Manitoba 55.45N 97.54W
106 H4 Thompson Michigan 45.54N 86.20W
108 N2 Thompson N Dakota 47.47N 97.09W
103 C3 Thompson Pennsylvania 41.51N 75.32W
111 P3 Thompson Utah 38.58N 109.42W
101 N10 Thompson R Br Col
107 C1 Thompson R Missouri
110 K2 Thompson Falls Montana 47.36N 115.20W
104 Q10 Thompson I Massachusetts 42.20N 71.01W
14 B3 Thompson L W Australia 32.09S 115.50E
101 R4 Thompson Lake N W Terr 62.40N 113.22W
101 S4 Thompson Landing N W Terr 62.58N 110.40W
13 B6 Thompson, Mt N Terr Australia 25.00S 131.40E
113 P6 Thompson Pass Alaska 61.09N 145.45W
112 M6 Thompsons Texas 29.30N 95.36W
11 A12 Thompson Sd New Zealand
18 J3 Thompson Village Singapore 1.21N 103.51E
103 J2 Thompsonville Connecticut 42.00N 72.36W
106 J5 Thompsonville Michigan 44.32N 85.57W
105 E4 Thomson Georgia 33.28N 82.31W
106 D8 Thomson Illinois 41.58N 90.05W
13 G6 Thomson R Queensland
10 L8 Thomson Deep Tasman Sea
14 B6 Thomson, Mt W Australia 23.58S 115.50E
11 C12 Thomson Mts New Zealand
61 L5 Thon Belgium 50.28N 5.01E
25 F6 Thonburi Thailand 13.43N 100.27E
31 J4 Thondhe Kashmir 33.32N 77.00E
71 J5 Thônes France 45.53N 6.20E
18 H2 Thong Hoe Singapore 1.25N 103.43E
29 K3 Thong La pass Xizang Zizhiqu 28.27N 86.18E
50 G2 Thönglabakki Iceland 66.09N 18.05W
25 D4 Thongwa Burma 16.45N 96.34E
69 J7 Thonnance-les-Joinville France 48.27N 5.10E
101 T3 Thonokied L N W Terr
71 J4 Thonon-les-Bains France 46.22N 6.30E
71 K8 Thorame-Haute France 44.06N 6.34E
87 B6 Thorangop Sudan 9.10N 29.42E
71 D7 Thoras France 44.52N 3.33E
66 G3 Thorberg Switzerland 47.01N 7.34E
50 L5 Thórdalsheidhi heath Iceland
50 H3 Thordarstadaskógur wood Iceland
50 F3 Thórdharhöfdhi prom Iceland 65.58N 19.31W
50 H6 Thórdharhyrna mt Iceland 64.17N 17.32W
70 M6 Thore France 47.47N 0.58E
72 J8 Thoré R France
109 B6 Thoreau New Mexico 35.24N 108.13W
70 L6 Thorée France 47.41N 0.03E
61 K4 Thorembais-les-Bëguines Belgium 50.40N 4.49E
61 K4 Thorembais-St-Trond Belgium 50.38N 4.48E
71 K9 Thorenc France 43.49N 6.48E
71 J4 Thorens-Glières France 46.00N 6.15E
42 G4 Thorez Irkutsk U.S.S.R. 55.10N 100.35E
Thorez Ukraine see Torez
50 B5 Thorgeirsfell mt Iceland 64.51N 23.10W
50 G2 Thorgeirsfjördhur B Iceland
100 D4 Thorhild Alberta 54.12N 113.07W
61 F4 Thoricourt Belgium 50.37N 3.57E
72 B2 Thorigny Vendée France 46.37N 1.15W
69 E7 Thorigny Yonne France 48.18N 3.25E
68 K3 Thorigny-sur-Marne France 48.53N 2.42E
50 L6 Thórisdalur Iceland 64.26N 14.55W
50 E5 Thorisdalur V Iceland
50 K5 Thóriseyjar islds Iceland
66 F4 Thörishaus Switzerland 46.54N 7.22E
50 E5 Thorisjökull ice cap Iceland 64.33N 20.43W
50 G6 Thóristindur pk Iceland 64.11N 18.53W
50 F5 Thórisvatn L Iceland 64.50N 19.27W
50 G6 Thórisvatn L Iceland 64.15N 18.53W
50 C7 Thorkötlustadhir Iceland 63.51N 22.24W
65 M6 Thörl Austria 47.32N 15.13E
50 D7 Thorlákshöfn Iceland 63.51N 21.23W
71 F9 Thor, le France 43.55N 5.00E
13 G8 Thorlindah, L Queensland 28.55S 144.50E
50 C6 Thormödhssker rock Iceland 64.25N 22.19W
60 T16 Thorn Netherlands 51.10N 5.51E
57 L3 Thornaby Cleveland Eng 54.34N 1.18W
56 O2 Thornage Norfolk Eng 52.54N 1.04E
106 J7 Thornapple, R Michigan
104 H8 Thornburg Virginia 38.09N 77.31W
56 F4 Thornbury Avon Eng 51.37N 2.32W
11 C13 Thornbury New Zealand 46.19S 168.06E
99 K8 Thornbury Ontario 44.34N 80.27W
56 J3 Thornby Northants Eng 52.22N 1.00W
112 K5 Thorndale Texas 30.36N 97.14W
103 K2 Thorndike Massachusetts 42.12N 72.20W
11 C5 Thorndon dist Wellington New Zealand
111 F3 Thorne Nevada 38.36N 118.35W
57 M5 Thorne S Yorks Eng 53.37N 0.58W
57 L5 Thorner W Yorks Eng 53.52N 1.25W
56 L2 Thorney Hunts Eng 52.37N 0.07W
95 J8 Thorngrove S Africa 32.40S 25.48E
58 H6 Thornhill Central Scotland 56.10N 4.09W
57 F2 Thornhill Dumfries & Galloway Scotland 55.15N 3.46W
99 L9 Thornhill Ontario 43.49N 79.26W
95 J9 Thornhill S Africa 33.54S 25.08E
103 C4 Thornhurst Pennsylvania 41.10N 75.35W
12 K6 Thornleigh dist Sydney, N S W
60 H7 t'Horntje Netherlands 53.01N 4.47E
107 D8 Thornton Arkansas 33.46N 92.30W
58 K6 Thornton Fife Scotland 56.10N 3.09W
108 R7 Thornton Iowa 42.57N 93.22W
112 L4 Thornton Texas 31.25N 96.35W
110 H2 Thornton Washington 47.07N 117.25W
13 E4 Thornton R Queensland
57 M4 Thornton Dale N Yorks Eng 54.14N 0.43W
55 F5 Thornton Heath London Eng 51.24N 0.06W
13 F4 Thorntonia Queensland 18.58S 140.31E
57 L4 Thornton le Street N Yorks Eng 54.16N 1.22W
106 H9 Thorntown Indiana 40.06N 86.37W
95 O5 Thornville S Africa 29.45S 30.24E
50 D4 Thóroddsstadhir Iceland 65.13N 21.02W
50 H3 Thóroddsstadhur Iceland 65.52N 17.32W
99 L9 Thorold Ontario 43.08N 79.14W
50 F7 Thórólfsfell mt Iceland 63.43N 19.40W
110 E2 Thorp Washington 47.04N 120.40W
106 D5 Thorp Wisconsin 44.58N 90.48W
11 G8 Thorpe New Zealand 41.17S 172.54E
56 O2 Thorpe Norfolk Eng 52.38N 1.20E
56 O4 Thorpe-le-Soken Essex Eng 51.52N 1.10E
56 O2 Thorpe Market Norfolk Eng 52.53N 1.20E
56 P3 Thorpeness Suffolk Eng 52.11N 1.36E
53 E4 Thorsager Denmark 56.21N 10.28E
100 C5 Thorsby Alberta 53.16N 114.02W
53 N9 Thorshavn Faeroes 62.02N 6.47W
123 A7 Thorshavnfjella mts Antarctica
50 K2 Thórshöfn Iceland 66.12N 15.17W
50 C3 Thorskafjardharheidhi heath Iceland
50 C3 Thorskafjördhur B Iceland
50 F7 Thorsmörk forest Iceland
53 D4 Thorsø Denmark 56.18N 9.48E
100 U1 Thorsteinson L Manitoba
50 G3 Thorvalasdalur V Iceland
123 G8 Thorvald Nilsen Mts Antarctica
30 K5 Those Nepal 27.36N 86.16E
25 H7 Thot Not Vietnam 10.17N 105.31E
72 D1 Thouarcé France 47.16N 0.30W
72 D2 Thouaret R France
72 D2 Thouars France 46.59N 0.13W
72 C2 Thouarsais-Bouildroux France 46.37N 0.53W
28 K3 Thoubal Manipur India 24.40N 94.00E
72 D2 Thouet R France
14 C5 Thouin Pt W Australia 20.27S 118.05E
72 C3 Thou, le France 46.05N 0.55W
84 D7 Thouría Greece 37.05N 22.03E
70 H6 Thourie France 47.52N 1.28W
69 D5 Thourotte France 49.29N 2.52E
Thourout see Torhout
104 J2 Thousand Islands Ontario/N Y
111 N3 Thousand Lake Mt Utah 38.26N 111.29W
110 L8 Thousand Spring Cr Nevada
110 L7 Thousand Springs Idaho 42.45N 114.50W
93 K7 Thowa watercourse Kenya
82 K9 Thrace hist reg Bulgaria/Turkey
83 Thraki div Greece
112 K5 Thrall Texas 30.36N 97.20W
110 E3 Thrall Washington 46.56N 120.31W
50 L5 Thrandarjökull ice cap Iceland 64.42N 14.55W
84 M11 Thrapsanós Crete 35.11N 25.16E
56 K3 Thrapston Northants Eng 52.24N 0.32W
50 E6 Thrastaskogur wood Iceland
12 J6 Thredbo New S Wales 36.30S 148.19E
103 E5 Three Bridges New Jersey 40.32N 74.47W
27 L11 Three Brothers islds Chagos Arch Br Indian Oc Terr
110 K7 Three Creek Idaho 42.06N 115.10W
110 O4 Three Forks Montana 45.54N 111.32W
100 D7 Three Hills Alberta 51.43N 113.15W
12 G8 Three Hummock I Tasmania 40.27S 144.56E
57 N7 Threekingham Lincs Eng 52.55N 0.23W
11 C2 Three Kings New Zealand 36.54S 174.45E
10 O8 Three Kings Basin Pacific Oc
11 G1 Three Kings Is New Zealand
13 D3 Three Knobs mt N Terr Australia 16.30S 135.27E
106 E4 Three Lakes Wisconsin 45.48N 89.10W
13 G2 Three Mile Opening, First & Second straits Gt Barrier Reef Australia
106 H8 Three Oaks Michigan 41.49N 86.37W
25 E5 Three Pagodas Pass Burma/Thailand 15.17N 98.24E
100 T3 Threepoint L Manitoba
89 H9 Three Points, C Ghana 4.43N 2.06W
111 F5 Three Rivers California 36.25N 118.55W
103 K2 Three Rivers Massachusetts 42.11N 72.22W
106 J8 Three Rivers Michigan 41.58N 85.39W
109 D8 Three Rivers New Mexico 33.17N 106.06W
Three Rivers Quebec see Trois Rivières
112 J7 Three Rivers Texas 28.29N 98.12W
98 N5 Three Rock Cove Newfoundland 48.38N 59.05W
95 G7 Three Sisters S Africa 31.54S 23.06E
Three Sisters Solomon Is see Olu Malau Is
13 G1 Three Sisters islds Queensland
110 D5 Three Sisters mts Oregon
14 B8 Three Springs W Australia 29.34S 115.45E
57 G3 Threlkeld Cumbria Eng 54.38N 3.03W
57 J4 Threshfield N Yorks Eng 54.04N 2.01W
50 K4 Thríhyrningsvatn L Iceland 65.11N 15.46W
50 H5 Thrihyrningur ice cap Iceland 64.40N 17.25W
50 H5 Thríhyrningur mt Iceland 64.58N 17.17W
50 F7 Thrihyrningur mt Rangárvallasýsla Iceland 63.47N 19.59W
50 E5 Thrístapafell mt Iceland 64.48N 20.15W
50 F4 Thrístikla L Iceland 65.15N 19.45W
50 J3 Thrístikluvatn L Iceland 65.59N 16.11W
112 H2 Throckmorton Texas 33.11N 99.12W
25 G5 Throm Cambodia 14.19N 103.25E
103 C4 Throop Pennsylvania 41.27N 75.36W
57 K2 Thropton Northumb Eng 55.19N 1.57W
14 E8 Throssell, L W Australia 27.33S 124.10E
14 E7 Throssell, Mt W Australia 25.58S 122.39E
14 D5 Throssel Ra W Australia
58 K2 Thrumster Highland Scotland 58.23N 3.09W
57 L6 Thrybergh S Yorks Eng 53.28N 1.17W
28 G1 Thubden Xizang Zizhiqu 29.24N 88.30E
25 J5 Thu Bon R Vietnam
101 S5 Thubun Ls N W Terr
12 J5 Thuddungra New S Wales 34.10S 148.09E
72 J10 Thués-entre-Valls France 41.31N 2.14E
71 E7 Thueyts France 44.40N 4.14E
50 G3 Thúfnavellir Iceland 65.40N 18.34W
50 G5 Thúfovötn lakes Iceland
79 A3 Thuile, la Italy 45.43N 6.57E
71 K8 Thuiles, les France 44.24N 6.34E
28 J7 Thuillier, Mt Nicobar Is 7.08N 93.45E
61 H5 Thuillies Belgium 50.18N 4.20E
61 H5 Thuin Belgium 50.21N 4.18E
72 K10 Thuir France 42.38N 2.45E
30 H3 Thukla Nepal 27.56N 86.49E
31 E6 Thul Pakistan 28.14N 68.50E
87 D6 Thul Sudan 8.31N 32.06E
87 D6 Thul watercourse Sudan
48 S3 Thule Greenland 77.30N 69.29W
Thule Air Base see Dundas
123 A13 Thule, Southern isld S Sandwich Is Atl Oc
61 E5 Thulin Belgium 50.26N 3.44E
Thuling see T'olin
64 O2 Thum E Germany 50.40N 12.58E
61 E4 Thumaide Belgium 50.33N 3.38E
Thumail, Wadi watercourse see Thumayl, Wādī watercourse
33 F3 Thumāmī, Ath Saudi Arabia 27.36N 44.59E
34 K5 Thumayl, Wādī watercourse Iraq
110 P5 Thumb Wyoming 44.27N 110.35W
11 E10 Thumbs, The mt New Zealand 43.35S 170.42E
Thumrayt see Thamarīt
66 G4 Thun Switzerland 46.46N 7.38E
13 G7 Thunda Queensland 25.28S 143.05E
14 B8 Thundelarra W Australia 28.54S 117.07E
106 L4 Thunder B Michigan
100 O2 Thunder B Ontario
100 O2 Thunder Bay Ontario 48.27N 89.12W
109 N6 Thunderbird, Lake Oklahoma
108 H4 Thunder Butte Cr S Dakota
99 G2 Thunderhouse Falls Ontario 50.03N 83.12W
100 C4 Thunder Lake Prov.Park Alberta
113 G2 Thunder Mt Alaska 68.40N 160.20W
66 M1 Thundorf Switzerland 47.33N 8.57E
66 G5 Thuner See L Switzerland
64 H4 Thüngen W Germany 49.56N 9.52E
25 E8 Thung Maphrao Thailand 8.33N 98.19E
25 E8 Thung Song Thailand 8.10N 99.41E
25 E9 Thung Wa Thailand 7.01N 99.43E
69 N8 Thur R France
66 L1 Thur R Switzerland
71 K6 Thures, Col de pass France 45.02N 6.39E
71 C5 Thuret France 45.58N 3.15E
71 G3 Thurey France 46.45N 5.05E
66 M1 Thurgau canton Switzerland
50 K3 Thuridharvatn L Iceland 65.35N 15.11W
65 A7 Thüringen Austria 47.13N 9.47E
71 F5 Thurins France 45.41N 4.38E
63 R5 Thürkow E Germany 53.50N 12.34E
59 G6 Thurles Tipperary Irish Rep 52.41N 7.49W
56 D7 Thurlestone Devon Eng 50.16N 3.51W
12 G3 Thurloo Downs New S Wales 29.18S 143.30E
108 D3 Thurlow Montana 46.16N 106.20W
107 L9 Thurlow Dam Alabama 32.32N 85.52W
104 H7 Thurmont Maryland 39.37N 77.26W
64 L3 Thurnau W Germany 50.01N 11.24E
56 J2 Thurnby Leics Eng 52.38N 1.02W
65 F7 Thurn Pass Austria 47.20N 12.25E
53 F6 Thurø Denmark 55.03N 10.43E
53 F6 Thurø isld Denmark 55.03N 10.43E
57 G3 Thursby Cumbria Eng 54.51N 3.03W
13 F1 Thursday I Queensland 10.37S 142.10E
58 J1 Thurso Highland Scotland 58.35N 3.32W
99 P7 Thurso Quebec 45.36N 75.15W
58 J1 Thurso Bay Highland Scotland
58 J2 Thurso, R Highland Scotland
123 H12 Thurston I Antarctica
71 C1 Thury France 47.35N 3.17E
70 K4 Thury-Harcourt France 48.59N 0.28W
66 O5 Thusis Switzerland 46.42N 9.27E
71 H5 Thusy France 45.56N 5.58E
101 K7 Thutade L Br Col
30 G5 Thuthibari Uttar Prad India 27.26N 83.42E
50 K6 Thveit L Iceland
50 J2 Thverá Thingeyjarsýsla, Nordhur Iceland 66.08N 16.25W
50 H3 Thvera Thingeyjarsýsla, Sudhur Iceland 65.44N 17.10W
50 D5 Thverá R Mýrasýsla Iceland
50 E7 Thverá R Rangárvallasýsla Iceland
50 J6 Thverartindur pk Iceland 64.14N 16.11W
50 D6 Thverfell mt Iceland 64.28N 21.04W
50 G3 Thverfjall mt Iceland 65.59N 18.53W
56 O3 Thwaite Suffolk Eng 52.17N 1.06E
53 B3 Thy reg Denmark
30 H3 Thyangboche Nepal 27.51N 86.46E
Thyatera anc site see Akhisar
53 A3 Thyborøn Denmark 56.43N 8.13E
50 G7 Thykkvabæjarklaustur Iceland 63.31N 18.20W
50 E7 Thykkvibær Iceland 63.44N 20.35W
61 J5 Thy-le-Bauduin Belgium 50.18N 4.31E
61 H5 Thy-le-Château Belgium 50.17N 4.25E
13 G7 Thylungra Queensland 26.05S 143.25E
61 K5 Thynes Belgium 50.17N 4.59E
66 F7 Thyon Switzerland 46.11N 7.23E
53 C5 Thyregod Denmark 55.54N 9.16E
50 D6 Thyrill Iceland 64.24N 21.26W
91 D6 Thysville Zaïre 5.16S 14.53E
16 K4 Tia New S Wales 31.11S 150.34E
32 G7 Tiāb Iran 27.03N 56.55E
120 D7 Tiabaya Peru 16.28S 71.36W
120 E7 Tiahuanaco Bolivia 16.38S 68.40W
119 E2 Tía Juana Venezuela 10.18N 71.24W
81 C3 Tiana Sardinia 40.04N 9.09E
21 D6 Tianbaoshan Jilin China 42.55N 128.55E
22 E6 Tiancang Gansu China 40.36N 99.39E
23 H2 Tianchang Anhui China 32.37N 118.57E
22 E7 Tiancheng Gansu China 39.48N 99.28E
23 D7 Tiandeng Guangxi China 23.06N 107.07E
23 D7 Tiandong Guangxi China 23.37N 107.06E
23 D6 Tian'e Guangxi China 25.06N 107.19E
44 F5 Tianeti Georgia U.S.S.R. 42.07N 44.08E
117 G6 Tianguá Brazil 3.45S 41.00W
115 K7 Tianguistengo Mexico 20.46N 98.39W
23 E6 Tianhe Guangxi China 24.55N 108.40E
22 L7 Tianjin Tianjin China 39.08N 117.12E
22 E8 Tianjun Qinghai China 37.18N 99.04E
23 D6 Tianlin Guangxi China 24.20N 106.11E
23 F3 Tianmen Hubei China 30.38N 113.20E
21 E6 Tianqiaoling Jilin China 43.36N 129.35E
23 C3 Tianquan Sichuan China 30.05N 102.53E
Tianshan see Ar Horqin Qi
24 D4 Tian Shan mt ra Xinjiang Uygur Zizhiqu China
21 D4 Tiansheng Heilongjiang China 46.53N 127.30E
23 D1 Tianshui Gansu China 34.25N 105.58E
24 C8 Tianshuihai Xinjiang Uygur Zizhiqu China 35.17N 79.30E
22 C6 Tianshuijing Gansu China 40.15N 95.23E
24 H5 Tianshuijing Gansu China 40.15N 95.23E
23 J4 Tiantai Zhejiang China 29.11N 121.03E
25 L1 Tiantang Guangdong China 22.35N 112.00E
23 D7 Tianyang Guangxi China 23.50N 106.52E
Tianyi see Ningcheng
Tianzhen see Gaoqing
22 K6 Tianzhen Shanxi China 40.29N 114.04E
23 E5 Tianzhu Guizhou China 26.56N 109.08E
22 F8 Tianzhu Zangzu Zizhixian Gansu China 37.17N 102.54E
121 G3 Tiaraju Brazil 30.14S 54.24W
122 C11 Tiarel Tahiti Pacific Oc 17.32S 149.20W
88 O4 Tiaret Algeria 35.20N 1.20E
88 T6 Tiaret Tunisia 30.52N 10.05E
9 A13 Tiari New Caledonia 20.16S 164.20E
79 J3 Tiarno Italy 45.54N 10.41E
13 L7 Tiaro Queensland 25.43S 152.34E
Tiâs see Tiyās
96 U8 Tias Lanzarote Canary Is 28.57N 13.38W
89 G9 Tiassalé Ivory Coast 5.53N 4.57W
93 G4 Tiati mt Kenya 1.16N 35.55E
122 C2 Tiavea W Samoa, Pacific Oc 13.57S 171.25W
118 E9 Tibagi Brazil 24.29S 50.29W
118 E9 Tibagi, R Brazil
90 E7 Tibak Nigeria 8.40N 11.52E
119 D5 Tibaná Colombia 5.19N 73.25W
90 F8 Tibati Cameroon 6.25N 12.33E
117 H7 Tibau Brazil 4.50S 37.15W
31 F6 Tibba Pakistan 29.59N 71.54E
87 F6 Tibbe Ethiopia 9.02N 37.12E
88 Q10 Tibeghim Algeria 22.39N 4.30E
Tiber R see Tevere R
88 M6 Tiberbatine Algeria 31.21N 3.08W
35 F2 Tiberias Israel 32.48N 35.32E
35 F2 Tiberias, L Israel
80 D7 Tiberina, I Roma Italy
79 M7 Tiberina, Val Italy
110 O1 Tiber Res Montana 48.20N 111.04W
85 D8 Tibesti Libya 25.31N 18.11E
90 G1 Tibesti mt reg Chad
85 D8 Tibesti, Sarīr gravel des Libya
Tibet aut reg China see Xizang Zizhiqu
41 C7 Tibeysalya U.S.S.R. 67.13N 79.28E
29 D3 Tibi Rajasthan India 29.23N 74.16E
77 P3 Tibi Spain 38.32N 0.35W
75 P5 Tibidabo mt Spain 41.26N 2.07E
89 L5 Tibiri Niger 13.08N 3.59E
89 N5 Tibiri Niger 13.35N 7.05E
117 B2 Tibiti R Surinam
99 N4 Tiblemont Quebec 48.19N 77.20W
82 J3 Tibleşului, Munţii mts Romania
35 H2 Tibnah Syria 32.59N 36.13E
34 P6 Ţib, Nahr aţ R Iraq
34 G3 Tibne Syria 35.38N 39.49E
Tibni see Tibne
35 E1 Tibnine Lebanon 33.11N 35.25E
119 J5 Tiboku Falls Guyana 5.44N 59.36W
12 F3 Tibooburra New S Wales 29.28S 142.04E
30 A3 Tibri Haryana India 29.06N 77.03E
29 H3 Tibrikot Nepal 29.00N 82.44E
52 H8 Tibro Sweden 58.25N 14.11E
116 H10 Tibu Colombia 8.40N 72.43W
119 C5 Tibugá, Esenada G Colombia
111 A8 Tiburon California 37.53N 122.27W
115 C3 Tiburón I Mexico
115 Q5 Tiburón, C Colombia/Panama 8.41N 77.18W
19 L5 Ticao isld Philippines
56 M5 Ticehurst E Sussex Eng 51.02N 0.24E
65 O2 Tichá Orlice R Czechoslovakia
99 O8 Tichborne Ontario 44.40N 76.41W
88 L5 Tichchoukt, Jbel mt Morocco 33.27N 4.42W
100 K7 Tichfield Saskatchewan 51.16N 107.02W
Tichidi mt see Tousside, Pic mt
89 E2 Tichitt Mauritania 18.21N 9.29W
88 F11 Tichla Mauritania 21.35N 14.58W
66 L6 Ticino canton Switzerland
79 E4 Ticino R Italy/Switz
57 L6 Tickhill S Yorks Eng 53.26N 1.06W
56 J2 Ticknall Derbys Eng 52.49N 1.28W
104 M3 Ticonderoga New York 43.51N 73.26W
121 A9 Tictoc, B.de Chile
121 A9 Tictoc, Cerro pk Chile 43.43S 72.35W
115 P7 Ticul Mexico 20.22N 89.31W
86 E3 Tida Egypt 31.14N 30.48E
52 H8 Tidaholm Sweden 58.12N 13.55E
95 K8 Tidbury's Toll S Africa 32.39S 26.40E
25 L9 Tiddim Burma 23.28N 93.42E
23 B8 Tide Cove Hong Kong 22.24N 114.11E
90 J1 Tidedi watercourse Chad
98 F6 Tide Head New Brunswick 47.58N 66.49W
100 F8 Tide L Alberta
28 J7 Tiden Nicobar Is 7.03N 93.35E
57 K6 Tideswell Derbys Eng 53.17N 1.46W
110 B5 Tidewater Oregon 44.26N 123.54W
35 B8 Tid-har Israel 31.23N 34.38E
33 D7 Tidhkār isld Saudi Arabia 18.56N 40.38E
88 O8 Tidikelt reg Algeria
104 F5 Tidioute Pennsylvania 41.42N 79.26W
74 D10 Tidiquin mt Morocco 34.51N 4.33W
89 D2 Tidjikdja Mauritania 18.29N 11.31W
12 E2 Tidna Hill S Australia 26.29S 137.58E
98 H8 Tidnish Nova Scotia 45.59N 64.02W
79 F5 Tidone R Italy
Tidore see Soasiu
89 A2 Tidra,I Mauritania 19.40N 16.20W
75 G2 Tiebas Spain 42.41N 1.39W
89 J6 Tiébélé Upper Volta 11.04N 0.57W
89 G8 Tiebissou Ivory Coast 7.10N 5.10W
90 H1 Tiéboro Chad 21.20N 17.06E
88 R8 Tiedou, Djebel mt Algeria 26.26N 7.09E
76 J5 Tiedra Spain 41.39N 5.16W
66 P5 Tiefencastel Switzerland 46.40N 9.35E
23 E3 Tiefeng Shan mt ra Sichuan China
63 T7 Tiefensee E Germany 52.41N 13.51E
69 N6 Tieffenbach France 48.54N 7.15E
61 D3 Tiegem Belgium 50.48N 3.29E
89 F7 Tieio Ivory Coast 8.30N 6.34W
113 P6 Tiekel Alaska 61.20N 145.21W
89 F6 Tiekongoba Mali 11.25N 6.35W
60 K12 Tiel Netherlands 51.53N 5.26E
89 B4 Tiel Senegal 14.58N 15.05W
61 K2 Tielen Belgium 51.14N 4.54E
21 D4 Tieli Heilongjiang China 46.57N 128.02E
21 C6 Tieling Liaoning China 42.19N 123.52E
24 C8 Tielongtan Xinjiang Uygur Zizhiqu China 35.10N 79.32E
61 G2 Tielrode Belgium 51.07N 4.11E
61 K3 Tielt Brabant Belgium 50.57N 4.54E
61 D3 Tielt West Vlaanderen Belgium 51.00N 3.20E
76 K2 Tielve Spain 43.16N 4.47W
76 L8 Tiemblo, El Spain 40.25N 4.29W
89 F5 Tiembougou Mali 12.40N 6.22W
89 F7 Tiéme Ivory Coast 9.39N 7.18W
Tien-ch'eng see Dianbai
T'ien-chiu-an see Fengyang
T'ien-chou see Tianyang
61 K3 Tienen Belgium 50.48N 4.56E
60 F13 Tiengemeten Netherlands 51.44N 4.19E
64 E8 Tiengen W Germany 47.38N 8.18E
60 J11 Tienhoven Netherlands 52.10N 5.05E
Tien-hsi see Lucheng
T'ien-pao see Debao
60 N14 Tienraij Netherlands 51.30N 6.06E
27 M1 Tien Shan mts Xinjiang Uygur Zizhiqu/U.S.S.R.
Tientsin see Tianjin
T'ien-yang see Napo
25 J2 Tien Yen Vietnam 21.19N 107.25E
95 H6 Tierberg mt S Africa 30.20S 24.17E
70 K6 Tiercé France 47.37N 0.28W
95 K4 Tierfontein S Africa 28.01S 26.18E
75 G4 Tierga Spain 41.37N 1.36W
63 B1 Tiergarten dist W Berlin W Germany
95 H3 Tierkloof S Africa 27.04S 24.46E
75 H2 Tiermas Spain 42.37N 1.07W
52 K6 Tierp Sweden 60.20N 17.30E
95 K5 Tierpoortdam res S Africa 29.25S 26.10E
119 C3 Tierra Alta Colombia 8.08N 76.06W
121 B1 Tierra Amarilla Chile 27.28S 70.17W
109 D5 Tierra Amarilla New Mexico 36.42N 106.34W
115 L8 Tierra Blanca Mexico 18.28N 96.21W
120 B2 Tierra Blanca Peru 6.34S 75.10W
115 K9 Tierra Colorada Mexico 17.10N 99.30W
76 K6 Tierra de Arévalo reg Spain
77 C3 Tierra de Barros reg Spain
76 K4 Tierra de Campos reg Spain
121 L10 Tierra del Fuego terr Argentina
121 K10 Tierra del Fuego, Isla Grande de Arg/Chile
76 H5 Tierra del Pan reg Spain
76 H6 Tierra del Vino reg Spain
76 G6 Tierras de Sayago reg Spain
94 Q11 Tiervlei Cape Town S Africa 33.55S 18.36E
75 G6 Tierzo Spain 40.45N 1.55W
77 F5 Tiesa mt Spain 37.58N 5.23W
108 E8 Tie Siding Wyoming 41.06N 105.31W
76 H8 Tiétar, R Spain
118 F8 Tietê Brazil 23.04S 47.41W
118 E7 Tietê R Brazil
12 B2 Tietkens, Mt S Australia 26.44S 130.10E
110 E3 Tieton Washington 46.43N 120.46W
12 C2 Tieyon S Australia 26.10S 133.49E
85 N10 Tifaieb watercourse Sudan
88 H8 Tifariti Morocco 26.04N 10.32W
80 K6 Tifata, Monte Italy 41.07N 14.17E
89 B1 Tiferchai Mauritania 21.10N 15.43W
88 J6 Tiferhal Morocco 30.04N 9.34W
89 B1 Tiferzas Mauritania 20.03N 14.29W
110 F1 Tiffany Mt Washington 48.41N 119.56W
87 F7 Tiffi Ethiopia 6.12N 36.55E
106 C8 Tiffin Iowa 41.42N 91.40W
104 B5 Tiffin Ohio 41.07N 83.11W
74 H10 Tiffrit Algeria 34.55N 0.24E
88 K5 Tiflet Morocco 33.54N 6.18W
Tiflis see Tbilisi
19 E3 Tifore isld Moluccas Indonesia 0.58N 126.10E
35 B8 Tifraḥ Israel 31.19N 34.40E
74 E9 Tifriste Morocco 35.01N 3.33W
105 D6 Tifton Georgia 31.27N 83.31W
105 D6 Tifton Upland reg Georgia
19 E5 Tifu Moluccas Indon 3.41S 126.24E
9 C13 Tiga isld Loyalty Is Pacific Oc 21.10S 167.52E
18 L3 Tiga isld Sabah Malaysia 5.44N 115.40E
113 E9 Tigalda I Aleutian Is 54.09N 165.00W
96 P10 Tigalete La Palma Canary Is 28.32N 17.46W
18 E6 Tigapuluh, Pegunungan mts Sumatra Indonesia
Tigara see Point Hope
110 C4 Tigard Oregon 45.26N 122.47W
89 K5 Tigba Upper Volta 12.10N 0.02E
44 L3 Tigen Kazakhstan U.S.S.R. 44.29N 52.05E
110 H1 Tiger Washington 48.42N 117.24W
105 F3 Tiger, R S Carolina
106 E5 Tigerton Wisconsin 44.44N 89.03W
32 J7 Tigh Āb Iran 27.40N 60.46E
58 B3 Tighary N Uist, W Isles Scotland 57.37N 7.30W
58 F7 Tighnabruaich Strathclyde Scotland 55.56N 5.14W
87 K8 Tigieglò Somalia 4.02N 44.30E
39 F5 Tigil' U.S.S.R. 57.49N 158.40E
39 F6 Tigil' R U.S.S.R.
42 C6 Tigiretskiy Khrebet mts U.S.S.R.
29 J7 Tigiria Orissa India 20.28N 85.34E
88 H7 Tiglid Morocco 28.28N 10.16W
79 D5 Tigliole Italy 44.53N 8.04E
66 J8 Tignaga, Pizzo mt Italy 45.57N 8.04E
79 J3 Tignale Italy 45.45N 10.43E
105 E4 Tignall Georgia 33.53N 82.48W
120 D8 Tignamar Chile 18.35S 69.30W
71 K5 Tignes France 45.29N 6.54E
71 K5 Tignes, Barrage de France 45.30N 6.55E
98 H7 Tignish Prince Edward I 46.58N 64.03W
88 J7 Tigouraine Morocco 28.43N 9.03W
87 G4 Tigrē prov Ethiopia
120 C1 Tigre R Peru
115 K6 Tigre, Cerro del pk Mexico 23.04N 99.18W
119 C9 Tigre, R Peru
119 G3 Tigre, R Venezuela
121 B3 Tigre, Sa ra Argentina
120 C1 Tigrillo R Peru
34 L4 Tigris R Iraq/Turkey
43 E5 Tigrovyy Khvost, Mys C Kazakhstan U.S.S.R. 43.55N 58.44E
88 J7 Tigsert, Oued wadi Morocco
88 P8 Tiguelguemine Algeria 26.15N 3.34E
88 S8 Tiguentourine Algeria 27.52N 9.08E
90 J2 Tigui Mali 18.35N 18.46E
57 D2 Tig, Water of R Strathclyde Scotland
70 P6 Tigy France 47.48N 2.12E
25 M9 Tigyaing Burma 23.49N 96.09E
74 K8 Tigzirt Algeria 36.54N 3.54E
33 E8 Tihāmah reg Saudi Arabia
61 M4 Tihange Belgium 50.32N 5.15E
86 M6 Tîh, Gebel el plat Egypt
11 K5 Tihoi New Zealand 38.37S 175.43E
53 B4 Tihøje mt Denmark 56.13N 8.41E
Tihran see Ţīrān
Ti-hua see Ürümqi
115 L7 Tihuatlán Mexico 20.46N 97.33W
19 B5 Tiinampuu Celebes Indon 2.38S 121.25E
45 V2 Tiinsk U.S.S.R. 54.24N 49.39E
120 F6 Tijamuchi, R Bolivia
29 E4 Tijara Rajasthan India 27.56N 76.55E
96 P10 Tijarafe La Palma Canary Is 28.43N 17.57W
109 D6 Tijeras New Mexico 35.04N 106.23W
85 A3 Tiji Libya 32.01N 11.20E
89 B2 Tijirit watercourse Mauritania
60 M7 Tijnje Netherlands 53.02N 6.00E
117 E5 Tijoca Brazil 1.07S 46.30W
77 M6 Tíjola Spain 37.21N 2.26W
115 A1 Tijuana Mexico 32.29N 117.10W
118 H10 Tijuca, L.da Brazil
118 H10 Tijucamar Brazil 23.01S 43.19W

118 J9 Tijúca, Pico da *mt* Brazil 22.57S 43.18W
118 E10 Tijucas Brazil 27.15S 48.40W
118 E10 Tijucas, B. de Brazil 27.15S 48.30W
98 G3 Tika Quebec 50.54N 65.57W
122 B14 Tikahau *atoll* Tuamotu Is Pacific Oc 15.00S 148.10W
30 E6 Tikaitnagar Uttar Prad India 26.57N 81.31E
115 P9 Tikal *ruins* Guatemala 17.13N 89.24W
30 B8 Tikamgarh Madhya Prad India 24.44N 78.50E
30 B8 Tikamgarh *dist* Madhya Prad India
24 F5 Tikanlik Xinjiang Uygur Zizhiqu China 40.36N 87.40E
89 J5 Tikaré Upper Volta 13.15N 1.43W
29 J7 Tikarpara Dam Orissa India 20.32N 84.56E
113 H6 Tikchik L Alaska 59.58N 158.20W
122 D14 Tikéi *isld* Tuamotu Is Pacific Oc 14.52S 144.32W
Tikelik Tagh *mt see* Tekiliktag
39 F6 Tikhaya *R* U.S.S.R.
42 G5 Tikhonovka U.S.S.R. 53.10N 104.10E
44 C2 Tikhoretsk U.S.S.R. 45.52N 40.07E
47 C3 Tikhtozero U.S.S.R. 65.34N 30.22E
47 C6 Tikhvin U.S.S.R. 59.35N 33.29E
113 J1 Tikikluk Alaska 70.50N 156.20W
88 K6 Tikirt Morocco 30.56N 7.08W
11 N4 Tikitiki New Zealand 37.48S 178.26E
9 S8 Tikituru *mt* Viti Levu Fiji 17.59S 177.59E
30 A1 Tiklik Himachal Prad India 31.22N 77.43E
44 F8 Tikmeh-ye Bāīā Iran 39.22N 44.32E
90 D9 Tiko Cameroon 4.02N 9.19E
11 L6 Tikokino New Zealand 39.49S 176.27E
10 O4 Tikopia Santa Cruz Is Pacific Oc 12.10S 168.50E
34 L4 Tikrīt Iraq 34.36N 43.42E
31 J3 Tikse Kashmir 34.01N 77.44E
47 C4 Tiksha U.S.S.R. 64.04N 32.35E
47 C3 Tikshozero, Oz *L* U.S.S.R.
41 N5 Tiksi U.S.S.R. 71.40N 128.45E
30 H6 Tikulia Bihar India 26.57N 84.33E
Til *see* Azakpur
30 E3 Tila *R* Nepal
35 G6 Tila el Ali Jordan 31.59N 35.51E
29 J5 Tilaiya Bihar India 24.20N 85.38E
29 J5 Tilaiya Res Bihar India
19 C3 Tilamuta Celebes Indon 0.32N 122.23E
115 M8 Tilapán Mexico 18.22N 95.21W
86 G10 Tilat Hassan *hill* Egypt 27.32N 31.46E
29 D4 Tilaunia Rajasthan India 26.38N 74.58E
32 F2 Tilavar Iran 36.52N 55.43E
37 C9 Tılbeşar Ovası *plat* Turkey
13 H8 Tilbooroo Queensland 27.49S 145.08E
60 J13 Tilburg Netherlands 51.34N 5.05E
56 M5 Tilbury Essex Eng 51.28N 0.23E
99 H10 Tilbury Ontario 42.15N 82.26W
101 H11 Tilbury I Br Col 49.09N 123.02W
120 F10 Tilcara Argentina 23.36S 65.23W
12 F3 Tilcha S Australia 29.38S 140.54E
107 G3 Tilden Illinois 38.12N 89.40W
108 N7 Tilden Nebraska 42.05N 97.50W
112 J7 Tilden Texas 28.27N 98.34W
61 J3 Tildonk Belgium 50.57N 4.38E
87 K9 Tile Somalia 3.08N 45.48E
82 G3 Tileagd Romania 47.03N 22.11E
90 J5 Tilégey Chad 12.24N 19.56E
86 H7 Tileimât, El *hill* Egypt 29.05N 32.20E
88 L8 Tilemsï el Fasi Algeria 27.01N 4.21W
88 M9 Tilemsi Ould Haïda Algeria 25.32N 3.16W
105 G2 Tilery, L N Carolina
61 N4 Tilff Belgium 50.34N 5.35E
108 G5 Tilford S Dakota 44.18N 103.28W
72 C8 Tilh France 43.35N 0.50W
30 C5 Tilhar Uttar Prad India 27.57N 79.45E
88 O8 Tilia *watercourse* Algeria
39 H4 Tilichiki U.S.S.R. 60.27N 166.06E
46 H6 Tiligul *R* Ukraine U.S.S.R.
45 C10 Tiligulo-Berezanka Ukraine U.S.S.R. 46.55N 31.25E
45 C10 Tiligul'skiy Liman *lagoon* Ukraine U.S.S.R.
25 C2 Tilin Burma 21.41N 94.06E
84 M11 Tílissos Crete 35.18N 25.00E
89 K4 Tillabéri Niger 14.28N 1.27E
72 E9 Tillac France 43.28N 0.17E
110 B4 Tillamook Oregon 45.28N 123.50W
110 A4 Tillamook Rock Oregon 45.56N 124.01W
28 J7 Tillanchong I Nicobar Is
70 O5 Tillay le Peneux France 48.09N 1.46E
52 K7 Tillberga Sweden 59.52N 16.39E
100 F8 Tillebrook Prov. Park Alberta
71 G2 Tille, R France
61 N6 Tillet Belgium 50.01N 5.32E
61 N4 Tilleur Belgium 50.37N 5.32E
100 F8 Tilley Alberta 50.28N 111.38W
89 M3 Tillia Niger 16.07N 4.50E
65 G8 Tilliach Austria 46.43N 12.38E
58 J6 Tillicoultry Central Scotland 56.09N 3.45W
61 K4 Tillier Belgium 50.32N 4.57E
72 B1 Tillières France 47.08N 1.10W
70 N4 Tillières-sur-Avre France 48.46N 1.03E
60 Q10 Tilligte Netherlands 52.24N 6.58E
53 G7 Tillitse Denmark 54.46N 11.10E
105 F5 Tillman S Carolina 32.28N 81.07W
105 L11 Tilloo Cay Bahamas 26.26N 76.59W
72 D3 Tillou France 46.09N 0.08W
69 H5 Tilloy-et-Bellay France 49.01N 4.36E
58 M7 Till, R Northumberland England
99 K10 Tillsonburg Ontario 42.53N 80.44W
61 J4 Tilly Belgium 50.33N 4.33E
72 G3 Tilly Indre France 46.24N 1.13E
69 J6 Tilly-sur-Meuse Meuse France 49.00N 5.27E
70 J3 Tilly-sur-Seulles France 49.10N 0.37W
88 Q8 Tilmas el Mra Algeria 27.44N 5.09E
88 P7 Tilmas Ferkla Algeria 28.40N 3.00E
39 G5 Til'myg, Gora *mt* U.S.S.R. 58.22N 160.37E
89 C3 Tilogne Senegal 16.00N 13.40W
19 D8 Tilomar Indonesia 9.22S 125.09E
120 E10 Tilomonte Chile 23.49S 68.13W
83 J8 Tílos *isld* Greece
12 G4 Tilpa New S Wales 30.58S 144.27E
88 P5 Tilrhemt Algeria 33.10N 3.21E
56 H5 Tilshead Wilts Eng 51.14N 1.58W
Tilsit *see* Sovetsk Kaliningrad
57 H7 Tilstock Shropshire Eng 52.56N 2.42W
100 Q9 Tilston Manitoba 49.23N 101.20W
47 J3 Til'tim U.S.S.R. 65.15N 63.28E
59 G3 Tiltinbane *mt* Cavan Irish Rep 54.13N 7.52W
98 S4 Tilting Newfoundland 49.42N 54.05W
105 C3 Tilton Georgia 34.39N 84.57W
106 G9 Tilton Illinois 40.06N 87.39W
56 K2 Tilton Leics Eng 52.38N 0.54W
104 O3 Tilton New Hampshire 43.27N 71.37W
58 J5 Tilt, R Tayside Scotland
19 A4 Tilu, Bukit *mt* Celebes Indon 1.30S 119.48E
53 A4 Tim Denmark 56.12N 8.19E
45 J5 Tim U.S.S.R. 51.36N 37.07E
85 L6 Tima Egypt 26.58N 31.28E
93 E10 Tima Tanzania 4.27S 33.57E
33 E9 Timā Yemen 15.36N 42.50E
53 A4 Tim Å *R* Denmark
99 L5 Timagami Ontario 47.04N 79.47W
99 K6 Timagami, L Ontario
18 H3 Timah *hill* Singapore 1.21N 103.47E
59 H6 Timahoe Leix Irish Rep 52.58N 7.12W
119 C7 Timaná Colombia 1.58N 75.55W
118 B7 Timane, R Paraguay
96 U8 Timanfaya Lanzarote Canary Is 28.59N 13.42W
47 F3 Timanskiy Kryazh *ridge* U.S.S.R.
37 G7 Timar Turkey 38.49N 43.23E
15 D6 Timare Irian Jaya 4.18S 136.38E
29 E6 Timarni Madhya Prad India 22.22N 77.13E
11 F11 Timaru New Zealand 44.23S 171.14E
35 H1 Timarus Syria 33.09N 36.10E
46 Q3 Timashevo U.S.S.R. 53.26N 51.10E
44 B2 Timashevsk U.S.S.R. 45.38N 38.56E
79 N1 Timau Italy 46.35N 13.00E
93 J5 Timau Kenya 0.05N 37.15E
79 O1 Timau, Pizzo di *mt* Italy 46.36N 13.01E
57 G2 Tima Water *R* Borders Scotland
89 A1 Timazine Mauritania 21.09N 16.36W
84 L11 Timbákion Crete 35.04N 24.45E
107 F12 Timbalier B Louisiana
107 F12 Timbalier I Louisiana
117 J8 Timbaúba Brazil 7.29S 35.17W
45 T2 Timbayevo U.S.S.R. 54.55N 47.55E
89 E3 Timbédra Mauritania 16.17N 8.16W
110 B4 Timber Oregon 45.44N 123.18W
13 B3 Timber Creek N Terr Australia 15.34S 130.24E
105 J1 Timberlake N Carolina 36.16N 78.58W
108 J4 Timber Lake S Dakota 45.25N 101.06W
111 H4 Timber Mt Nevada 37.06N 116.28W
56 E5 Timberscombe Somerset Eng 51.10N 3.29W
89 C6 Timbi Madina Guinea 11.11N 12.31W
119 C6 Timbío Colombia 2.20N 76.40W
119 C6 Timbiquí Colombia 2.43N 77.45W
117 F7 Timbiras Brazil 4.15S 43.54W
89 D6 Timbo Guinea 10.36N 11.51W
89 E9 Timbo Liberia 5.37N 9.43W
26 S9 Timbolketiya Sri Lanka 6.25N 80.48E
12 G7 Timboon Victoria 38.32S 143.02E
118 E10 Timbo, R Brazil
93 G5 Timboroa Kenya 0.04N 35.33E
94 O2 Timbue, I Mozambique 18.50S 36.20E
Timbuktu *see* Tombouctou
18 N3 Timbun Mata *isld* Sabah Malaysia
117 A1 Timehri *airfield* Guyana 6.30N 58.12W
88 O11 Timeiaouine Algeria 20.27N 1.50E
65 J6 Timelkam Austria 47.59N 13.37E
88 K6 Timelloughit Morocco 31.10N 7.20W
88 G9 Timel-lusa Morocco 25.15N 12.03W
88 J6 Timezgadiouine Morocco 30.54N 9.04W
84 A2 Tímfi Óros *mts* Greece
84 C4 Timfristós Greece 38.55N 21.51E
84 C4 Timfristós *mt* Greece 38.57N 21.50E
88 R4 Timgad *ruins* Algeria 35.29N 6.28E
88 Q11 Timg'aouine Algeria 21.37N 4.30E
88 L5 Timhadite Morocco 33.15N 5.09W
84 Q15 Timi Cyprus 34.43N 32.30E
90 D2 Timia Niger 18.09N 8.46E
15 G6 Timibunke Papua New Guinea 4.11S 153.40E
88 K6 Timidert Morocco 30.40N 6.18W
88 O7 Timimoun Algeria 29.15N 0.14E
39 E2 Timir-Atakh-Tas U.S.S.R. 66.24N 151.45E
89 A2 Timiris, C Mauritania 19.21N 16.28W
42 C4 Timiryazevskiy U.S.S.R. 56.29N 84.48E
82 G5 Timiş *div* Romania
99 L5 Timiskaming, L Quebec/Ontario
82 G5 Timişoara Romania 45.45N 21.15E
82 G5 Timişul *R* Romania
87 F2 Timitatei Sudan 16.01N 36.10E
47 J5 Timkapaul' U.S.S.R. 61.29N 62.22E
30 A2 Timli Uttar Prad India 30.22N 77.43E
63 N5 Timmendorfer Strand W Germany 54.00N 10.47E
52 H8 Timmersdala Sweden 58.31N 13.45E
88 R11 Ti-m-mersoi *watercourse* Niger
99 J4 Timmins Ontario 48.30N 81.20W
88 P11 Ti-m Misaou Algeria 21.55N 3.08E
105 H3 Timmonsville S Carolina 34.08N 79.56W
82 G7 Timok *R* Yugoslavia
59 E8 Timoleague Cork Irish Rep 51.38N 8.46W
59 J6 Timolin Kildare Irish Rep 52.59N 6.48W
117 F7 Timon Brazil 5.08S 42.52W
103 A8 Timonium Maryland 39.27N 76.37W
17 L13 Timor *isld* East Indies
Timorlaut *see* Tanimbar, Kep *Is*
17 K14 Timor Sea Aust/Indon
26 M7 Timor Trough Timor Sea
Timoshenko *see* Omchak
46 N1 Timoshino Kostroma U.S.S.R. 57.50N 44.31E
47 D5 Timoshino Vologda U.S.S.R. 60.08N 36.14E
121 E5 Timote Argentina 35.22S 62.13W
119 E3 Timotes Venezuela 9.00N 70.47W
88 N7 Timoudi Algeria 29.21N 1.12W
18 L6 Timpah Borneo Indon 1.39S 114.26E
111 J4 Timpahute Ra Nevada
110 O9 Timpanogos Cave Nat.Mon Utah 40.33N 111.34W
109 G4 Timpas Colorado 37.48N 103.47W
19 D4 Timpaus Indonesia 1.53S 124.01E
14 E7 Timperley Ra W Australia
110 N9 Timpie Utah 40.45N 112.39W
112 N4 Timpson Texas 31.55N 94.25W
40 D2 Timpton *R* U.S.S.R.
52 K4 Timrå Sweden 62.29N 17.20E
53 B4 Timring Denmark 56.10N 8.45E
105 A2 Tims Ford L Tennessee
47 G5 Timsher U.S.S.R. 60.43N 54.45E
47 G5 Timsher *R* U.S.S.R.
15 D6 Timuka Irian Jaya 4.46S 136.33E
66 O6 Timun *mt* Italy/Switz 46.28N 9.25E
43 J5 Timur Kazakhstan U.S.S.R. 42.48N 68.25E
30 J4 Timure Nepal 28.15N 85.24E
11 G10 Timutimu Hd New Zealand 43.55S 172.58E
35 D4 Tin *watercourse* Jordan
90 L4 Tina Sudan 15.00N 22.50E
34 F2 Tinā Syria 36.28N 38.50E
95 M6 Tina *R* S Africa
19 M9 Tinaca Pt Mindanao Philippines 5.34N 125.20E
119 F3 Tinaco Venezuela 9.44N 68.28W
86 H3 Tîna, El Egypt 31.03N 32.22E
95 N7 Tina Falls S Africa 31.13S 29.01E
19 L4 Tinaga *isld* Philippines 14.29N 122.55E
59 K6 Tinahely Wicklow Irish Rep 52.48N 6.28W
28 L1 Tinai Assam India 28.05N 97.00E
75 E7 Tinajas Spain 40.19N 2.35W
96 U7 Tinajo Lanzarote Canary Is 29.03N 13.41W
11 C5 Tinakori Hills New Zealand
10 O4 Tinakula *isld* Santa Cruz Is Pacific Oc 10.28S 165.40E
76 D9 Tinalhas Portugal 39.57N 7.32W
88 T9 Tin Alkoum Libya 24.42N 10.13E
76 L2 Tinamayor. Ría de *B* Spain
19 A5 Tinambung Celebes Indon 3.32S 119.01E
88 Q11 Tin Amzi *watercourse* Algeria etc
119 F3 Tinaquillo Venezuela 9.57N 68.20W
89 L3 Tin Asaguid Mali 17.09N 2.01E
88 O9 Tin-atanai Algeria 25.52N 1.37E
88 J10 Tin Bessaïs Mauritania 23.11N 8.21W
82 G4 Tinca Romania 46.46N 21.58E
70 J4 Tinchebray France 48.46N 0.44W
69 C3 Tincques France 50.21N 2.29E
88 Q10 Tin Dahar Algeria 22.58N 4.32E
88 N11 Ti-n Daksen el Haoua Mali 21.19N 0.27W
88 N11 Ti-n Daksen el Melah Mali 21.16N 0.30W
110 K7 Tindall Idaho 42.17N 115.53W
87 C8 Tindalo Sudan 5.40N 31.06E
89 K6 Tindangou Upper Volta 11.10N 0.53E
50 E3 Tindar Iceland 65.34N 20.06W
81 K7 Tindari, C Sicily 38.08N 15.03E
50 E6 Tindaskagi *ridge* Iceland
50 F3 Tindastóll *mt* Iceland 65.51N 19.48W
96 T9 Tindaya Fuerteventura Canary Is 28.35N 13.59W
53 U21 Tindefjell *mt* Norway 58.56N 6.14E
53 V19 Tinden *mts* Norway 59.45N 6.37E
89 L3 Ti-n Dermine Mali 16.37N 2.23E
50 F7 Tindfjallajökull *ice cap* Iceland 63.48N 19.35W
89 J1 Ti-n Didin Mali 21.39N 0.11W
28 D4 Tindivanam Tamil Nadu India 12.15N 79.41E
88 J8 Tindouf Algeria 27.42N 8.10W
53 N10 Tindur *mt* Faeroes 61.51N 6.45W
30 D7 Tindwari Uttar Prad India 25.37N 80.32E
Tiné *see* Tinā
88 R11 Tinedin *watercourse* Niger
71 L8 Tinée *R* France
88 Q10 Tinef Algeria 22.03N 4.50E
89 H3 Tin Eguethar Mali 17.11N 2.49W
89 L3 Ti-n Ekkart Mali 16.28N 3.20E
88 P7 Tineldjame Algeria 28.26N 2.29E
111 F4 Tinemaha Res California 37.04N 118.14W
76 G2 Tineo Spain 43.20N 6.24W
88 L6 Tinerhir Morocco 31.28N 5.30W
88 O7 Tinerkouk *reg* Algeria
85 A8 Tin Er Rada *mt* Algeria 23.48N 11.00E
89 L3 Tin Essako *watercourse* Mali
89 L2 Ti-n-Essalak Mali 18.52N 2.25E
88 N12 Tin Ethisane Mali 19.03N 0.52W
88 O11 Tin Etiki Algeria 21.59N 0.04E
88 L7 Tinfouchy Algeria 28.52N 5.49W
88 R7 Tin Fouye Algeria 28.28N 7.42E
13 L1 Tingalpa *dist* Brisbane, Qnsld
93 H8 Tingatinga Tanzania 2.52S 36.55E
18 E9 Tinggi *isld* Pen Malaysia
12 K3 Tingha New S Wales 29.58S 151.16E
23 A8 Ting Kau Hong Kong 22.22N 114.04E
25 M8 Tingkawk Sakan Burma 26.05N 96.43E
24 E10 Ting La *pass* Xizang Zizhiqu China 30.25N 86.45E
53 C7 Tinglev Denmark 54.57N 9.15E
108 Q9 Tingley Iowa 40.50N 94.11W
113 F2 Tingmerkpuk Mt Alaska 68.32N 162.30W
97 P5 Tingmiarmiut Ø / Greenland 62.35N 42.20W
120 B3 Tingo María Peru 9.08S 75.54W
23 E5 Tingping Hunan China 26.08N 110.18E
89 F6 Tingrela Ivory Coast 10.26N 6.20W
24 E11 Tingri Xizang Zizhiqu China 28.33N 86.40E
24 F11 Tingri Xizang Zizhiqu China 28.43N 87.08E
23 G4 Tingsiqiao Hubei China 29.52N 114.11E
52 J10 Tingsryd Sweden 56.31N 15.00E
52 L9 Tingstäde Sweden 57.45N 18.36E
96 U7 Tinguatón Lanzarote Canary Is 29.02N 13.42W
90 F8 Tinguéré Cameroon 7.24N 12.35E
121 B5 Tinguiririca *vol* Chile 34.47S 70.22W
52 D4 Tingvoll Norway 62.56N 8.13E
99 T7 Tingwick Quebec 45.54N 71.57W
15 K5 Tingwon Grp *islds* Bismarck Arch
15 K5 Tingwon I Bismarck Arch 2.37S 149.40E
Ting-yüan-ying *see* Alxa Zuoqi
Tingzhou *see* Changting
118 J3 Tinharé, I.de Brazil 13.28S 38.58W
76 E5 Tinhela Portugal 41.43N 7.18W
25 H3 Tinh Gia Vietnam 18.30N 105.38E
17 P9 Tinian *isld* Marianas Pacific Oc 14.58N 145.38E
88 K10 Tinioulig Mauritania 22.39N 7.12W
11 M5 Tiniroto New Zealand 38.47S 177.34E
48 U13 Tiniteqilaq Greenland 65.55N 37.50W
66 P5 Tinizong Switzerland 46.37N 9.37E
33 E3 Tin,Jabal *mts* Saudi Arabia
18 L4 Tinjar *R* Sarawak Malaysia
87 E6 Tinji Ethiopia 8.41N 35.28E
18 F9 Tinjil *islds* Java Indon 6.58S 105.45E
88 S11 Tin Keradet *reg* Niger
89 D6 Tinkisso *R* Guinea
88 S8 Tin Kret *mt* Algeria 26.08N 8.31E
11 H9 Tinline, Mt New Zealand 42.27S 173.07E
85 A8 Tin Merzouga *mts* Algeria
52 D6 Tinn Norway 60.01N 8.45E
13 H8 Tinnenburra Queensland 28.40S 145.30E
Tinnevelley *see* Tirunelveli
53 X18 Tinnholen *L* Norway 60.16N 7.36E
52 D7 Tinnoset Norway 59.55N 9.03E
52 D7 Tinnsjø *L* Norway
121 C2 Tinogasta Argentina 28.05S 67.32W
79 G6 Tino, I.del *isld* Italy 44.02N 9.51E
19 B3 Tinombo Celebes Indon 0.25N 120.16E
18 D7 Tinopo *isld* Indonesia
96 P11 Tiñor Hierro Canary Is 27.47N 17.57W
83 G7 Tinos Greece 37.33N 25.08E
83 G7 Tínos *isld* Greece 37.33N 25.08E
77 O5 Tiñoso, C Spain 37.32N 1.06W
89 D2 Tin Ouadine Mauritania 18.04N 11.52W
30 L8 Tinpahar Bihar India 25.00N 87.43E
15 J1 Tinputz Papua New Guinea 5.36S 156.02E
89 L3 Tin Raidane *watercourse* Mali
88 P11 Tin Rerhoh Algeria 20.43N 3.58E
88 R11 Tin Seririne *watercourse* Algeria
42 F4 Tinskaya U.S.S.R. 55.27N 95.07E
107 D8 Tinsman Arkansas 33.39N 92.21W
89 E8 Tinsou Liberia 7.27N 9.25W
14 C5 Tinstane, Mt W Australia 21.16S 118.40E
28 K2 Tinsukia Assam India 27.28N 95.20E
88 O11 Ti-n-Tadjant Algeria 21.13N 1.35E
56 B6 Tintagel Cornwall Eng 50.40N 4.45W
56 B6 Tintagel Hd Cornwall Eng 50.41N 4.46W
108 O3 Tintah Minnesota 46.00N 96.20W
61 N7 Tintange Belgium 49.53N 5.45E
88 S10 Tin Taourdi Algeria 22.50N 8.02E
88 R10 Tin Tarabine Algeria 23.13N 6.49E
88 R10 Tin Tarabine *watercourse* Algeria
88 Q8 Tin Tarha *mt* Algeria 26.10N 5.55E
88 Q8 Tin Te Iremt *mt* Algeria 26.51N 5.26E
70 G5 Tinténiac France 48.20N 1.50W
56 F4 Tintern Gwent Wales 51.43N 2.41W
61 N8 Tintigny Belgium 49.41N 5.31E
120 F8 Tin Tin Bolivia 18.02S 65.23W
121 E1 Tintina Argentina 27.00S 62.45W
12 F5 Tintinara S Australia 35.52S 140.04E
88 Q9 Tin Tires Algeria 25.04N 5.53E
90 D9 Tinto Cameroon 5.32N 9.36E
57 F1 Tinto *hill* Strathclyde Scotland 55.36N 3.39W
77 C6 Tinto *R* Spain
88 N11 Tin Tounannt Mali 20.16N 0.26W
11 L7 Tinui New Zealand 40.52S 176.06E
11 F10 Tinwald New Zealand 43.56S 171.43E
88 R7 Tin Yagguin Algeria 28.55N 7.13E
39 A1 Tinyay U.S.S.R. 67.56N 131.34E
89 J4 Tinye Upper Volta 14.26N 1.28W
30 C1 Tinzam Sampa Xizang Zizhiqu 31.45N 79.05E
88 P12 Tin Zaouatene Algeria 19.58N 2.58E
66 P5 Tinzen Horn *mt* Switzerland 46.37N 9.41E
107 D10 Tioga Louisiana 31.23N 92.27W
108 H1 Tioga N Dakota 48.26N 102.57W
104 H5 Tioga Pennsylvania 41.54N 77.08W
112 L2 Tioga Texas 33.31N 96.56W
104 E8 Tioga W Virginia 38.26N 80.40W
103 B2 Tioga *co* New York
104 H5 Tioga *R* Pennsylvania
103 B2 Tioga Center New York 42.04N 76.21W
111 E4 Tioga Pass California 37.55N 119.18W
89 F6 Tiola Mali 11.10N 6.10W
90 J6 Tiole Chad 10.24N 19.40E
18 E9 Tioman I Pen Malaysia
99 H4 Tionaga Ontario 48.05N 82.06W
79 J2 Tione di Trento Italy 46.02N 10.43E
110 D8 Tionesta California 41.39N 121.20W
104 F5 Tionesta Pennsylvania 41.31N 79.30W
104 F5 Tionesta Creek Res Pennsylvania
18 D9 Tiong,Gunong *mt* Pen Malaysia 2.25N 103.20E
89 F6 Tiongui Mali 10.34N 6.17W
19 G6 Tioor *isld* Moluccas Indon 4.45S 131.44E
90 J1 Tioro Chad 20.30N 18.31E
19 C6 Tioro Indonesia 4.41S 122.37E
19 C6 Tioro,Selat *str* Indonesia
88 R11 Tiouardiouine Aguelman Algeria 21.59N 6.48E
104 K4 Tioughnioga *R* New York
89 A2 Tiouilit Anagoum Mauritania 18.51N 16.02W
89 B3 Tiourourt Mauritania 17.45N 15.56W
88 N5 Tiout Algeria 32.48N 0.25W
15 A4 Tipin Salawati I, Irian Jaya 0.58S 130.48E
115 L3 Tipitapa Nicaragua 12.08N 86.04W
104 A7 Tipp City Ohio 39.57N 84.12W
106 H8 Tippecanoe Indiana 41.12N 86.06W
106 H9 Tippecanoe,R Indiana
59 F7 Tipperary Tipperary Irish Rep 52.29N 8.10W
59 F6 Tipperary *co* Irish Rep
107 F8 Tippo Mississippi 33.55N 90.10W
111 E5 Tipton California 36.03N 119.20W
106 H9 Tipton Indiana 40.18N 86.03W
106 C8 Tipton Iowa 41.46N 91.08W
109 M2 Tipton Kansas 39.21N 98.28W
107 D3 Tipton Missouri 38.41N 92.49W
109 L7 Tipton Oklahoma 34.31N 99.08W
56 G2 Tipton W Midlands Eng 52.32N 2.05W
111 K6 Tipton, Mt Arizona 35.33N 114.11W
107 G5 Tiptonville Tennessee 36.21N 89.30W
104 D9 Tiptop Virginia 37.13N 81.28W
99 D4 Tip Top Hill Ontario 48.16N 86.02W
56 N4 Tiptree Essex Eng 51.49N 0.45E
95 H9 Tiptree S Africa 33.40S 24.59E
120 E6 Tipuani Bolivia 15.33S 68.03W
119 C8 Tiputini,R Ecuador
119 E7 Tiquié,R Brazil
115 O10 Tiquisate Guatemala 14.16N 91.21W
86 F3 Tîra Egypt 31.06N 31.14E
35 C5 Tira Israel 32.14N 34.57E
35 D6 Tira Jordan 31.52N 35.08E
93 E4 Tira Uganda 1.36N 33.32E
117 E6 Tiracambu,Sa.do *mts* Brazil
31 F4 Tirah *reg* Pakistan
32 D4 Tīrān Iran 32.41N 51.08E
Tir'an Israel *see* Tur'an
33 A3 Tīrān *isld* Saudi Arabia 27.58N 34.35N
Tirana *see* Tiranë
83 D3 Tiranë Albania 41.20N 19.49E
71 D6 Tiranges France 45.19N 3.59E
87 D8 Tirangolé Sudan 4.33N 32.50E
35 E2 Tir'an Har *hill* Israel 32.48N 35.23E
79 H2 Tirano Italy 46.13N 10.11E
28 K2 Tirap Frontier Div Assam India
26 R5 Tirappane Sri Lanka 8.13N 80.31E
33 E3 Tirāq,Jabal al *escarp* Saudi Arabia
120 F7 Tiraque Bolivia 17.23S 65.41W
46 G6 Tiraspol' Moldavia U.S.S.R. 46.50N 29.38E
86 H4 Tir'at el 'Abbâsîya *canal* Egypt
86 F4 Tir'at el Bûhîya *canal* Egypt
86 G5 Tir'at el Ismâ'ilîya *canal* Egypt
86 F4 Tir'at el Mansûrîya *canal* Egypt
35 C2 Tirat Karmel Israel 32.46N 34.58E
Tirat Tsevi *see* Tirat Zevi
35 C5 Tirat Yehuda Israel 32.00N 34.56E
35 F4 Tirat Zevi Israel 32.25N 35.32E
11 K4 Tirau New Zealand 37.58S 175.46E
11 L7 Tiraumea New Zealand 40.37S 176.09E
94 D5 Tiraz Mts Namibia
36 C4 Tire Turkey 38.04N 27.45E
37 D4 Tirebolu Turkey 41.01N 38.49E
58 C5 Tiree *isld* Strathclyde Scotland
41 N7 Tirekh U.S.S.R. 66.50N 129.33E
39 B1 Tirekhtyakh Yakutsk U.S.S.R. 68.55N 136.49E
39 C3 Tirekhtyakh Yakutsk U.S.S.R. 64.50N 143.30E
39 D1 Tirekhtyakh Yakutsk U.S.S.R. 68.39N 147.07E
41 O8 Tirekh-Yuryuya U.S.S.R. 64.46N 133.07E
90 H1 Tirenno Chad 21.36N 17.25E
79 L2 Tires Italy 46.28N 11.31E
88 O11 Tirest Mali 20.18N 1.05E
75 D8 Tirez,L.de Spain 39.33N 3.22W
39 C3 Tirgelir U.S.S.R. 64.11N 142.45E
75 E2 Tirgo Spain 42.32N 2.57W
82 J6 Tîrgovişte Romania 44.56N 25.27E
82 L3 Tîrgu Frumos Romania 47.12N 27.00E
82 H5 Tîrgu Jiu Romania 45.03N 23.18E
82 J6 Tîrgului *R* Romania
82 J4 Tîrgu Mureş Romania 46.33N 24.34E
82 K3 Tîrgu Neamţ Romania 47.12N 26.25E
82 K4 Tîrgu Ocna Romania 46.17N 26.37E
82 K4 Tîrgu Secuesc Romania 46.00N 26.08E
88 P9 Tirhatimine Algeria 25.45N 3.15E
30 J6 Tirhut *div* Bihar India
31 K4 Tiri Kashmir 33.40N 80.02E
31 D6 Tiri Pakistan 29.52N 66.52E
31 F2 Tirich Mir *mt* Pakistan 36.18N 71.55E
75 L7 Tirig Spain 40.25N 0.05E
37 F2 Tirilye Turkey 40.24N 28.47E
86 O10 Tirīm,Wādī *watercourse* Saudi Arabia
84 E6 Tirins Greece 37.36N 22.48E
81 N6 Tiriolo Italy 38.57N 16.30E
93 E4 Tiriri Uganda 1.54N 33.28E
88 S10 Tiririne Algeria 23.38N 8.29E
88 G10 Tiris *reg* Mauritania/Morocco
11 J3 Tiritiri Matangi I New Zealand 36.36S 174.54E
Tirlemont *see* Tienen
47 H8 Tirlyanskiy U.S.S.R. 54.12N 58.30E
84 C2 Tirna Greece 39.30N 21.33E
28 C1 Tirna R Maharashtra India
82 J4 Tîrnava Mare *R* Romania
82 J4 Tîrnava Mică *R* Romania
82 J4 Tîrnăveni Diciosânmărtin Romania 46.20N 24.17E
84 D2 Tírnavos Greece 39.45N 22.18E
19 B6 Tiro Celebes Indon 5.29S 120.26E
89 D7 Tiro Guinea 9.47N 10.43W
104 C6 Tiro Ohio 40.53N 82.46W
29 F7 Tirodi Madhya Prad India 21.40N 79.44E
65 C7 Tirol *prov* Austria
79 K1 Tirolo Italy 46.42N 11.09E
75 D3 Tirón *R* Spain
118 F6 Tiros Brazil 18.58S 45.55W
77 F3 Tiros *mt* Spain 38.42N 5.20W
35 C6 Tirosh Israel 31.45N 34.54E
90 L7 Tiroun Goulou Cent Afr Rep 9.43N 22.12E
31 A3 Tirpul Afghanistan 34.34N 61.20E
79 H7 Tirrenia Italy 43.37N 10.17E
26 U7 Tirrukkovil Sri Lanka 7.07N 81.51E
58 H2 Tirry,R Highland Scotland
64 N4 Tirschenreuth W Germany 49.53N 12.20E
81 C3 Tirso *R* Sardinia
53 F4 Tirstrup Denmark 56.18N 10.42E
77 H3 Tirteafuera Spain 38.46N 4.15W
28 B4 Tirthahalli Karnataka India 13.41N 75.10E
29 K7 Tirtol Orissa India 20.17N 86.22E
11 J5 Tirua Pt New Zealand 38.24S 174.37E
121 A7 Tirua,Pta *C* Chile 38.21S 73.32W
28 D6 Tiruchendur Tamil Nadu India 8.29N 78.07E
28 C5 Tiruchengodu Tamil Nadu India 11.25N 77.54E
28 D5 Tiruchirapalli Tamil Nadu India 10.50N 78.43E
28 D5 Tiruchirapalli *dist* Tamil Nadu India
28 D5 Tirukkoyilur Tamil Nadu India 11.59N 79.13E
28 D6 Tirumangalam Tamil Nadu India 9.50N 78.01E
28 D5 Tirumayam Tamil Nadu India 10.15N 78.46E
28 C6 Tirunelveli Tamil Nadu India 8.45N 77.43E
28 C6 Tirunelveli *dist* Tamil Nadu India
120 C2 Tiruntán Peru 7.54S 74.59W
28 K2 Tirup Assam India 27.16N 95.46E
28 D4 Tirupati Andhra Prad India 13.39N 79.25E
28 D4 Tiruppattur Tamil Nadu India 12.29N 78.34E
28 D5 Tiruppattur Tamil Nadu India 10.07N 78.39E
28 C5 Tiruppur Tamil Nadu India 11.05N 77.20E
28 D4 Tiruttani Andhra Prad India 13.12N 79.35E
28 D5 Tirutturaippundi Tamil Nadu India 10.31N 79.39E
28 D4 Tiruvallur Tamil Nadu India 13.07N 79.54E
28 D5 Tiruvalur Tamil Nadu India 10.45N 79.48E
28 D4 Tiruvannamalai Tamil Nadu India 12.15N 79.05E
28 D4 Tiruvettipuram Tamil Nadu India 12.41N 79.32E
14 F5 Tiru Well W Australia 21.33S 125.55E
30 C6 Tirwa Uttar Prad India 26.58N 79.49E
28 C6 Tisaiyanvilai Tamil Nadu India 8.26N 77.49E
100 N6 Tisdale Saskatchewan 52.51N 104.01W
88 R9 Tisemt Algeria 24.59N 6.10E
87 M5 Tisgieh Somalia 10.49N 49.27E
45 B8 Tishkovka Ukraine U.S.S.R. 48.30N 30.57E
44 J1 Tishkovo U.S.S.R. 46.01N 48.38E
107 H7 Tishomingo Mississippi 34.37N 88.15W
109 O7 Tishomingo Oklahoma 34.15N 96.41W
87 F5 Tisisat Falls *waterfall* Ethiopia 11.32N 37.30E
34 D6 Tisiya Syria 32.23N 36.26E
Tisïyah *see* Tisiya
88 S10 Tiska *mt* Algeria 22.20N 8.16E
106 E8 Tiskilwa Illinois 41.17N 89.32W
42 C3 Tiskino U.S.S.R. 58.05N 83.08E
53 C6 Tislund Denmark 55.13N 9.08E
88 O5 Tismouline Algeria 33.41N 0.20E
52 J8 Tisnaren *L* Sweden 58.57N 16.00E
65 O3 Tišnov Czechoslovakia 49.22N 16.24E
62 M7 Tisovec Czechoslovakia 48.42N 19.55E
88 L4 Tissa Morocco 34.22N 4.38W
82 H2 Tissa *R* U.S.S.R.
26 T9 Tissamaharama Sri Lanka 6.17N 81.18E
61 H2 Tisselt Belgium 51.02N 4.22E
88 O4 Tissemsilt Algeria 35.37N 1.48E
88 R10 Tissertassine Algeria 22.48N 6.37E
81 B2 Tissi Sardinia 40.41N 8.34E
Tissia *see* Tisiya
57 K6 Tissington Derbys Eng 53.04N 1.44W
88 K7 Tissinnt Morocco 29.55N 7.20W
53 G5 Tissø *L* Denmark 55.35N 11.18E
29 L4 Tista *R* W Bengal/Sikkim India
52 F7 Tistedal Norway 59.08N 11.25E
88 M4 Tistutin Morocco 35.01N 3.10W
77 F10 Tisuka *mt* Morocco 35.10N 5.14W
42 D4 Tisul' U.S.S.R. 55.45N 88.16E
53 J4 Tisvildeleje Denmark 56.04N 12.05E
62 N7 Tisza *R* Hungary
62 N8 Tiszacsege Hungary 47.43N 21.00E
62 M8 Tiszafüred Hungary 47.38N 20.45E
62 M9 Tiszakécske Hungary 46.56N 20.04E
62 N7 Tiszalök Hungary 48.01N 21.20E
62 N8 Tiszavasvari Hungary 47.56N 21.20E
82 G3 Tiszavasvári Hungary 47.56N 21.21E
88 O8 Tit Oasis Algeria 26.58N 1.29E
88 Q10 Tit Oasis Algeria 22.59N 5.11E
28 K2 Titabar Assam India 26.36N 94.12E
88 N8 Titaf Algeria 27.26N 0.13W
29 M2 Titagarh W Bengal India 22.44N 88.24E
75 H8 Titaguas Spain 39.53N 1.06W
11 D4 Titahi Bay New Zealand 41.06S 174.50E
113 K2 Titaluk *R* Alaska
31 G8 Titalyah Bangladesh 26.30N 88.28E
84 D2 Titarísios *R* Greece
41 N5 Tit-Ary U.S.S.R. 71.55N 127.02E
56 J6 Titchfield Hants Eng 50.51N 1.13W
89 B6 Tite Guinea-Bissau 11.45N 15.25W
74 K9 Titeri,Mts.du Algeria
84 E4 Tithoréa Greece 38.35N 22.40E
31 G3 Tithwal Kashmir 34.26N 73.52E
120 D7 Titicaca,I Bolivia 16.01S 69.14W
120 D6 Titicaca, Lago Peru/Bolivia
80 F3 Titignano Italy 42.46N 12.17E
18 A6 Titi Karangan Pen Malaysia 5.32N 100.37E
122 B10 Titikaveka Rarotonga Pacific Oc 21.16S 159.45W
11 B3 Titirangi New Zealand 36.56S 174.40E
119 C4 Titiribi Colombia 6.03N 75.48W
64 E8 Titisee-Neustadt W Germany 47.55N 8.10E
29 H7 Titlagarh Orissa India 20.18N 83.11E
66 K4 Titlis *mt* Switzerland 46.46N 8.27E
113 L4 Titna *R* Alaska
88 R10 Tit-n-Afara Algeria 23.46N 7.00E
80 N7 Tito Italy 40.34N 15.40E
82 E8 Titograd Yugoslavia 42.28N 19.17E
108 Q6 Titonka Iowa 43.14N 94.03W
47 C2 Titovka *R* U.S.S.R.
45 P3 Titovo U.S.S.R. 53.17N 43.41E
82 F7 Titovo Užice Yugoslavia 43.52N 19.50E
82 G9 Titov Veles Yugoslavia 41.43N 21.49E
52 D3 Titran Norway 63.42N 8.22E
30 A3 Titron Uttar Prad India 29.40N 77.20E
56 M5 Titsey Surrey Eng 51.17N 0.01E
106 K6 Tittabawassee,R Michigan
53 T19 Tittelsnes Norway 59.43N 5.33E
64 L6 Titting W Germany 48.59N 11.15E
64 P6 Tittling W Germany 48.45N 13.24E
64 O7 Tittmoning W Germany 48.03N 12.46E
93 K3 Titu Kenya 2.49N 38.55E
82 K6 Titu Romania 44.40N 25.32E
91 J2 Titule Zaïre 3.14N 25.32E
119 C3 Titumate Colombia 8.17N 77.05W
28 H6 Titup Nicobar Is 9.10N 92.44E
105 G9 Titusville Florida 28.37N 80.50W
104 F5 Titusville Pennsylvania 41.37N 79.42W
69 L1 Titz W Germany 51.01N 6.26E
23 B9 Tiu Keng Wan Hong Kong 22.18N 114.13E
58 D2 Tiumpan Hd Lewis, W Isles Scotland 58.15N 6.10W
30 A2 Tiuni Uttar Prad India 30.56N 77.51E
75 N4 Tiurana Spain 41.59N 1.15E
47 K1 Tiuteyyakha *R* U.S.S.R.
93 J7 Tiva Kenya 1.26S 37.54E
93 L8 Tiva *watercourse* Kenya
89 A4 Tivaouane Senegal 14.57N 16.45W
67 P14 Tivarello Corsica 41.29N 9.08E
29 C4 Tivari Rajasthan India 26.34N 72.56E
52 H8 Tived Sweden 58.47N 14.32E
75 M6 Tivenys Spain 40.54N 0.31E
56 E6 Tiverton Devon Eng 50.55N 3.29W
98 F9 Tiverton Nova Scotia 44.24N 66.14W
99 J8 Tiverton Ontario 44.15N 81.33W
103 M3 Tiverton Rhode Island 41.08N 71.12W
75 M5 Tivisa Spain 41.02N 0.44E
80 G5 Tivoli Italy 41.58N 12.48E
103 G2 Tivoli New York 42.04N 73.55W
112 L7 Tivoli Texas 28.26N 96.54W
11 C13 Tiwai Point New Zealand 46.36S 168.22E
90 L6 Tiwal,Wâdi *watercourse* Sudan
93 L10 Tiwi Kenya 4.15S 39.34E
33 N5 Tīwī Oman 22.49N 59.13E
115 P7 Tixkokob Mexico 21.00N 89.25W
115 K9 Tixtla Mexico 17.35N 99.22W
34 E4 Tiyās Syria 34.36N 37.41E
25 E6 Ti-ywa Burma 12.43N 98.58E
115 H7 Tizapán el Alto Mexico 20.11N 103.02W
115 K8 Tizayuca Mexico 19.51N 99.00W
88 G12 Tizegui Mauritania 19.45N 13.45W
89 C2 Tizegui Mauritania 18.15N 12.35W
74 H9 Tizi Algeria 35.17N 0.07E
74 E10 Tizi Ifri Morocco 34.53N 4.13W
115 P7 Tizimín Mexico 21.10N 88.09W
88 J7 Tizi Mlil *pass* Morocco 29.48N 8.50W
88 K6 Tizi n' Aït Imguer *pass* Morocco 31.25N 7.30W
88 L5 Tizi-n-Talrhemt Morocco 32.35N 4.29W
88 J6 Tizi n'Test *pass* Morocco 30.51N 8.18W
88 K6 Tizi n'Tichka *pass* Morocco 31.10N 7.30W
88 Q3 Tizi Ouzou Algeria 36.44N 4.05E
90 D3 Tizizilet Niger 17.43N 9.20E
119 F3 Tiznados,R Venezuela
24 B7 Tiznap He *R* Xinjiang Uygur Zizhiqu China
88 J7 Tiznit Morocco 29.43N 9.44W
115 J5 Tizoc Mexico 25.45N 101.59W
89 M4 Tizouari Niger 15.09N 4.57E
74 E10 Tiztoutine Morocco 34.58N 3.10W
79 K7 Tizzana Italy 43.50N 11.00E
67 O13 Tizzano Corsica 41.32N 8.50E
79 H5 Tizzano val Parma Italy 44.31N 10.12E
90 N9 Tizzio Cent Afr Rep 5.54N 26.01E
53 B6 Tjæreborg Denmark 55.28N 8.35E
53 G6 Tjæreby Denmark 55.15N 11.22E
Tjalang *see* Calang
60 M7 Tjalleberd Netherlands 53.00N 5.56E
52 J8 Tjällmo Sweden 58.44N 15.20E
Tjamara *see* Camara
51 G5 Tjåmotis Sweden 66.56N 18.30E
Tjamplong *see* Camplong
Tjangkuang, Tandjung *see* Cangkuang, Tanjung
Tjapalulu, Selat *str see* Capalulu, Selat
Tjarat, Tandjung *C see* Carat, Tanjung
50 G4 Tjarnir Iceland 65.17N 18.15W
51 E7 Tjärnmytberget Sweden 64.28N 15.28E
51 H4 Tjårrokiehle *mt* Sweden 67.23N 20.20E
51 F5 Tjeggelvas *L* Sweden 66.35N 17.40E
51 E3 Tjeldøya *isld* Norway 68.30N 16.20E
53 R17 Tjeldstø Norway 60.35N 4.51E
53 R17 Tjeldstø Norway 60.35N 4.51E
53 D3 Tjele Denmark 56.32N 9.38E
53 D3 Tjele Langsø *L* Denmark 56.32N 9.38E
15 D6 Tjemara *R* Irian Jaya
Tjemaru, Gunung *mt see* Cemaru, Gunung *mt*
Tjempi, Teluk *B see* Cempi, Teluk
Tjendrawasih *pen see* Cendrawasih *pen.*
Tjenrana *see* Cenrana
Tjepu *see* Cepu
Tjereme, Gunung *mt see* Cereme, Gunung *mt*
60 L8 Tjerkgaast Netherlands 52.54N 5.41E
60 L7 Tjerkwerd Netherlands 52.03N 5.30E
53 S19 Tjernagel Norway 59.38N 5.20E
60 M8 Tjeuke Meer *L* Netherlands
Tjiamis *see* Ciamis
Tjiandjur *see* Cianjur
Tjibadak *see* Cibadak
Tjibatu *see* Cibatu
Tjibuni *R see* Cibuni *R*
Tjidjulang *see* Cijulang
Tjidua *see* Cidua
Tjihara *see* Cihara
Tjikadjang *see* Cikajang
Tjikampek *see* Cikampek
Tjilatjap *see* Cilacap
Tjiledug *see* Ciledug
Tjimahi *see* Cimahi
Tjimanuk *R see* Cimanuk *R*
Tjimpu *see* Cimpu
Tjina, Tg *C see* Cina, Tanjung *C*
Tjipatudja *see* Cipatuja
Tjirebon *see* Cirebon
Tjitarum *R see* Citarum *R*
53 V20 Tjodanvatn *L* Norway 59.02N 6.43E
Tjomal *R see* Comal *R*
52 E7 Tjøme *isld* Norway 59.10N 10.30E
50 G3 Tjörn Eyjafjardharsýsla Iceland 65.56N 18.32W
50 E3 Tjörn Húnavatnssýsla, Vestur Iceland 65.39N 20.46W
52 F8 Tjörn *isld* Sweden 58.05N 11.40E
50 H2 Tjörnes *C* Iceland 66.13N 17.07W
50 H2 Tjörnes *pen* Iceland
53 M9 Tjørnevig Faeroes 62.17N 7.09W
53 B4 Tjørring Denmark 56.10N 8.56E
51 C6 Tjøtta Norway 65.50N 12.25E
53 V16 Tjugum Norway 61.13N 6.33E
60 L7 Tjum Netherlands 53.09N 5.34E
18 E7 Tjurup Sumatra Indonesia 3.31S 102.32E
50 U15 Tjuvfjorden *inlet* Spitsbergen
15 E6 T Keten *mts* Irian Jaya
44 B3 Tkhab *mt* U.S.S.R. 44.34N 38.23E
44 C3 Tkhach *mt* U.S.S.R. 44.04N 40.25E
44 E5 Tkibuli Georgia U.S.S.R. 42.21N 43.00E
44 D5 Tkvaroheli Georgia U.S.S.R. 42.51N 41.42E
115 L9 Tlacolula Mexico 16.58N 96.23W
115 M8 Tlacotalpán Mexico 18.38N 95.40W
115 H4 Tlahualilo Mexico 26.06N 103.25W
115 K8 Tlalnepantla Mexico 19.34N 99.12W
115 K8 Tlálpan Mexico 19.19N 99.10W
115 J8 Tlalpujahua de Rayon Mexico 19.50N 100.10W
115 K8 Tlaltizapan Mexico 18.42N 99.06W
115 K8 Tlancualpican Mexico 18.26N 98.40W
115 K9 Tlapa Mexico 17.34N 98.32W
115 L8 Tlapacoyan Mexico 19.58N 97.13W
115 H7 Tlaquepaque Mexico 20.39N 103.15W
115 K8 Tlaxcala Mexico 19.20N 98.12W
115 K8 Tlaxcala *state* Mexico
115 K8 Tlaxco Mexico 19.38N 98.06W
115 K7 Tlaxcoapán Mexico 20.08N 99.12W
115 L9 Tlaxiaco Mexico 17.18N 97.42W
101 H9 Tlell Graham I, Br Col 53.35N 131.56W
88 N4 Tlemcen Algeria 34.53N 1.21W
88 N4 Tlemcen,Monts de Algeria
89 M4 Tlemcès Niger 15.32N 4.57E
77 E10 Tleta-des-Beni Yder-Cherki Morocco 35.24N 5.30W
88 L4 Tleta Ketama Morocco 34.55N 4.34W
77 E10 Tleta Rissana Morocco 35.14N 6.00W
88 J5 Tleta Sidi Bouguedra Morocco 32.16N 9.00W
Tlété Ouâte Rharbi,Jebel *mt see* Gharbi Jebel *mt*
95 H2 Tlhakgamengspruit *watercourse* S Africa
95 H2 Tlhakmeng S Africa 26.28S 24.22E
85 D5 Tlisan Libya 28.24N 17.32E
82 J2 Tlumach U.S.S.R. 48.51N 25.00E
62 N3 Tłuszcz Poland 52.25N 21.25E
44 G5 Tlyadal' U.S.S.R. 42.07N 46.13E
44 G5 Tlyarata U.S.S.R. 42.05N 46.24E
46 O8 Tlyarata U.S.S.R. 42.08N 46.20E
46 K2 T'ma *R* U.S.S.R.
85 C6 Tmassah Libya 26.22N 15.47E
39 K2 Tnekveem *R* U.S.S.R.
88 M9 Tni Haïa Algeria 24.17N 3.15E
25 D4 To *R* Burma
116 G4 Toa *R* Cuba
115 O5 Toabré Panama 8.41N 80.19W
101 L6 Toad R Br Col
19 N2 Toagel Mlungui Palau Is Pacific Oc 7.33N 134.29E
95 D5 Toamasina Madagascar 18.10S 49.23E
79 J6 Toano Italy 44.23N 10.33E
122 D13 Toanoano Tahiti Pacific Oc 17.52S 149.12W
110 L9 Toano Mts Nevada
18 J3 Toa Payoh *dist* Singapore
11 M5 Toatoa New Zealand 38.05S 177.30E
122 C14 Toau *atoll* Tuamotu Is Pacific Oc 15.50S 146.00W
121 D6 Toay Argentina 36.43S 64.22W
88 G8 Tob Morocco 26.50N 12.51W
20 K7 Toba Japan 34.29N 136.51E
23 A3 Toba Xizang Zizhiqu China 31.17N 97.37E
31 D5 Toba and Kakar Ras Pakistan
18 C4 Toba, Danau *L* Sumatra Indon
75 G7 Toba, Embalse de la *res* Spain 40.13N 1.55W
31 G6 Toba Gargaji Pakistan 29.22N 72.50E
116 M1 Tobago *isld* West Indies 11.15N 60.40W
105 L7 Tobago Is Virgin Is 18.28N 64.51W
116 M1 Tobago, Little / Tobago W I 11.17N 60.31W
101 L10 Toba Inlet Br Col
89 D9 Tobakoni Pt Liberia 5.49N 10.00W
75 E5 Toba,La Spain 41.00N 2.59W
75 D2 Tobalina,Valle de Spain
47 K2 Tobanto,Ozero *L* U.S.S.R. 69.20N 69.20E
110 L9 Tobar Nevada 40.53N 114.54W
77 N3 Tobarra Spain 38.36N 1.41W
121 E2 Tobas Argentina 28.08S 62.44W
20 D8 Tobata Japan 33.53N 130.50E
31 G5 Toba Tek Singh Pakistan 30.54N 72.30E
19 C6 Tobea *isld* Indonesia 4.36S 122.45E
66 N1 Tobel Switzerland 47.31N 9.02E
19 E3 Tobelo Halmahera Indon 1.45N 127.59E
19 F3 Tobelo *isld* Halmahera Indon 1.46N 128.00E
59 J2 Tobermore Londonderry N Ireland 54.48N 6.42W
13 E5 Tobermorey N Terr Australia 22.15S 137.51E
58 D5 Tobermory Mull, Strathclyde Scotland 56.37N 6.05W
99 J7 Tobermory Ontario 45.15N 81.39W
13 G7 Tobermory Queensland 27.16S 143.40E
20 L1 Tōbetsu Japan 43.14N 141.31E
17 M11 Tobi *isld* Caroline Is Pacific Oc 3.01N 131.10E
75 E3 Tobía Spain 42.18N 2.50W
75 E3 Tobía *R* Spain
91 C8 Tobias Angola 9.40S 13.15E
108 N9 Tobias Nebraska 40.25N 97.20W
118 J2 Tobias Barreto Brazil 11.07S 38.01W
20 N10 Tobiishi-hana *C* Iwo Jima Pacific Oc 24.45N 141.17E
48 V12 Tobin, Kap *C* Greenland 70.20N 22.00W
100 O5 Tobin L Saskatchewan
14 F5 Tobin,L W Australia
110 H9 Tobin,Mt Nevada 40.24N 117.31W
98 E6 Tobique R New Brunswick
20 N2 Tobi-shima *isld* Japan 39.12N 139.32E
19 G5 Tobo Moluccas Indon 3.33S 130.10E
18 G7 Toboali Indonesia 3.00S 106.30E
43 G1 Tobol Kazakhstan U.S.S.R. 52.45N 62.34E
47 K7 Tobol *R* U.S.S.R.
19 B4 Toboli Celebes Indon 0.41S 120.05E
47 K6 Tobol'sk U.S.S.R. 58.15N 68.12E
116 J1 Tobolski Jamaica, W I 18.22N 77.23W
15 L3 Tobona I Solomon Is 8.03S 158.56E
25 K6 To Bong Vietnam 12.46N 109.19E
21 K1 Tobong-gu *dist* Seoul S Korea
19 L6 Toboso Philippines 10.42N 123.30E
75 D8 Toboso,El Spain 39.30N 3.00W
89 K6 Tobré Benin 10.08N 2.00E
Tobruch *see* Tubruq
47 G2 Tobseda U.S.S.R. 68.34N 52.16E
13 E5 Toby *R* Queensland
103 D4 Tobyhanna Pennsylvania 41.11N 75.25W
103 D4 Tobyhanna State Park Pennsylvania
47 G4 Tobysh U.S.S.R. 63.15N 53.06E
47 G3 Tobysh *R* U.S.S.R.
120 B3 Tocache Nuevo Peru 8.09S 76.26W
119 D5 Tocaima Colombia 4.30N 74.38W
13 G6 Tocal Queensland 23.51S 143.20E
72 F5 Tocane-St.Apre France 45.15N 0.30E
117 D9 Tocantínia Brazil 9.31S 48.18W
117 E8 Tocantinópolis Brazil 6.20S 47.29W
117 D6 Tocantins, R Brazil
118 E4 Tocantinzinha *R* Brazil
105 D3 Toccoa Georgia 34.34N 83.21W
80 J4 Tocco da Casauria Italy 42.13N 13.55E
79 D2 Toce *R* Italy
66 K7 Toceno Italy 46.09N 8.28E
76 B8 Tocha Portugal 40.19N 8.45W
93 D3 Tochi *R* Uganda
20 N5 Tochigi Japan 36.23N 139.46E
20 N5 Tochigi *prefect* Japan
20 N4 Tochio Japan 37.27N 139.00E
31 F4 Tochi R Pakistan
65 J2 Tochovice Czechoslovakia 49.36N 13.59E
77 E5 Tocina Spain 37.37N 5.44W
52 F7 Töcksfors Sweden 59.30N 11.50E
120 D10 Toco Chile 22.05S 69.35W
116 P1 Toco Trinidad & Tobago 10.49N 60.57W
119 G3 Toco Venezuela 9.09N 64.51W
115 L2 Tocoa Honduras 15.40N 86.01W
120 E10 Toconao Chile 23.11S 68.00W
77 J6 Tocón, El Spain 37.14N 3.58W
120 D10 Tocopilla Chile 22.05S 70.10W

120 E10 Tocorpuri,Cerro de pk Bolivia/Chile 22.26S 67.53W
Tocra see Tūkrah
115 G10 Tocumen airport Panama
119 B3 Tocumen,Aeródromo Nacional Panama 9.05N 79.22W
12 H6 Tocumwal New S Wales 35.51S 145.34E
119 F2 Tocuyo de la Costa Venezuela 11.04N 68.23W
119 F2 Tocuyo,R Venezuela
85 M7 Tōd Egypt 25.34N 32.32E
20 D1 Toda Saitama Japan
29 E4 Toda Bhim Rajasthan India 26.52N 76.49E
52 D4 Todal Norway 62.48N 8.45E
29 D4 Toda Rai Singh Rajasthan India 26.02N 75.35E
113 L3 Todatonten L Alaska 66.10N 152.59W
56 K4 Toddington Beds Eng 51.57N 0.32W
98 F7 Todd,Mt New Brunswick 46.33N 66.42W
13 B2 Todd,Mt N Terr Australia 14.04S 132.07E
53 Y18 Toddøla R Norway 60.20N 8.22E
13 C6 Todd R N Terr Australia
14 F7 Todd Ra W Australia
86 E4 Tōd,El Egypt 30.48N 30.36E
19 D4 Todeli Moluccas Indon 1.40S 124.30E
75 G6 Todelisgo Spain 40.43N 1.40W
93 G1 Todenyang Kenya 4.32N 35.55E
82 L7 Toder Ikonomovo Bulgaria 43.39N 27.10E
63 M5 Todesfelde W Germany 53.54N 10.11E
29 C5 Todgarh Rajasthan India 25.38N 73.58E
58 L5 Todhills Tayside Scotland 56.33N 2.56W
80 F3 Todi Italy 42.47N 12.24E
66 M4 Tödi mt Switzerland 46.48N 8.56E
12 C2 Todmorden S Australia 27.04S 134.49E
57 J5 Todmorden W Yorks Eng 53.43N 2.05W
20 Q2 Todoga-saki C Japan 39.31N 142.03E
21 K3 Todohokke Japan 41.44N 141.09E
75 K6 Todolella Spain 40.38N 0.15W
121 A8 Todos los Santos,L Chile
118 J3 Todos os Santos,B de Brazil
120 F7 Todos Santos Bolivia 16.36S 65.08W
115 D6 Todos Santos Mexico 23.28N 110.14W
111 H10 Todos Santos, B. de Mexico
111 H10 Todos Santos, I de Mexico 31.46N 116.45W
88 L6 Todra R Morocco
93 B2 Todro Zaïre 3.21N 30.14E
32 F7 Todrūyeh Iran 27.18N 54.46E
64 D8 Todtmoos W Germany 47.45N 8.00E
64 D8 Todtnau W Germany 47.50N 7.56E
42 F6 Todzha,Oz L U.S.S.R. 52.27N 96.30E
59 D9 Toe Hd Cork Irish Rep 51.30N 9.12W
58 B3 Toe Hd Harris, W Isles Scotland 57.50N 7.07W
25 E5 Toe Jaga,Khao mt Burma/Thailand 15.10N 98.14E
61 O8 Toernich Belgium 49.39N 5.47E
94 F7 Toeslaan S Africa 28.20S 20.30E
11 C13 Toetoes B New Zealand
79 M1 Tofane,Le mt Italy 46.33N 12.04E
66 H4 Toffen Switzerland 46.52N 7.30E
100 E5 Tofield Alberta 53.22N 112.39W
101 L11 Tofino Vancouver I, Br Col 49.05N 125.51W
52 G9 Tofta Sweden 57.11N 12.20E
53 N9 Tofte Faeroes 62.06N 6.44W
106 D2 Tofte Minnesota 47.34N 90.51W
53 B6 Tofterup Denmark 55.40N 8.50E
53 C6 Toftlund Denmark 55.12N 9.04E
53 R18 Toftøy isld Norway 60.29N 4.56E
53 T20 Toftøy isld Norway 59.16N 5.41E
113 M4 Tofty Alaska 65.10N 151.00W
9 T12 Tofua isld Tonga, Pacific Oc 19.45S 175.05W
9 C9 Toga isld New Hebrides 13.26S 166.41E
20 G6 Togane Japan 35.34N 140.22E
29 D2 Togano,Monte Italy 46.05N 8.23E
20 F1 Togasaki Saitama Japan
88 D3 Togba Mauritania 17.29N 10.12W
66 N2 Toggenburg V Switzerland
59 K4 Togher Louth Irish Rep 53.51N 6.18W
20 K4 Togi Japan 37.08N 136.44E
113 G7 Togiak Alaska 59.05N 160.30W
113 G7 Togiak R Alaska
113 G7 Togiak B Alaska
113 H7 Togiak L Alaska 59.40N 159.38W
19 B3 Togian isld Indonesia 0.23S 121.55E
19 B4 Togian,Kep islds Indonesia
64 O7 Töging W Germany 48.14N 12.36E
Togliatti see Tol'yatti
87 E1 Togni Sudan 18.02N 35.05E
87 F2 Tognuf Ethiopia 16.12N 37.28E
15 G8 Togo Papua New Guinea 9.11S 142.44E
100 Q7 Togo Saskatchewan 51.25N 101.38W
89 K8 Togo rep W Africa
89 K8 Togo,L Togo 6.18N 1.32E
Tögrög see Tögrög
Togoy see Taras
22 C4 Tögrög Mongolia 45.47N 94.59E
22 F4 Tögrög Mongolia 45.31N 103.00E
Togrog Ul see Qahar Youyi Qianqi
22 J6 Togtoh Nei Monggol Zizhiqu China 40.20N 111.10E
20 P8 Toguchi Okinawa Japan 26.40N 127.53E
21 C13 Toguchi Okinawa Japan 29.40N 128.10E
42 C4 Toguchin U.S.S.R. 55.14N 84.23E
42 D5 Togul U.S.S.R. 53.29N 85.59E
42 C3 Togur U.S.S.R. 58.23N 82.48E
47 J8 Toguzak R Kazakhstan U.S.S.R.
43 F3 Toguz Kazakhstan U.S.S.R. 47.32N 60.32E
110 F9 Tohakum Pk Nevada 40.11N 119.26W
87 F1 Tohamiyam Sudan 18.20N 36.15E
29 D3 Tohana Haryana India 29.41N 75.58E
106 B6 Tohatchi New Mexico 35.53N 108.46W
87 N5 Tohēn Somalia 11.46N 51.14E
18 F5 Tohenbatu mt Sarawak Malaysia 1.22N 113.22E
122 A11 Tohiea pk Society Is Pacific Oc 17.33S 149.48W
37 D7 Tohma R Turkey
51 P9 Tohmajärvi Finland 62.15N 30.21E
20 M5 Tohogne Belgium 50.23N 5.29E
51 L8 Toholampi Finland 63.46N 24.15E
22 G6 Tohom Nei Monggol Zizhiqu China 40.43N 105.46E
105 F9 Tohopekaliga L Florida 28.15N 81.24W
18 C10 Tohor,Tanjong C Pen Malaysia 1.51N 102.42E
24 D8 To Huping Tso L Xizang Zizhiqu China 34.10N 83.05E
20 K3 Toi Japan 41.44N 141.03E
20 M7 Toi Japan 34.50N 138.45E
122 B1 Toiavea pk W Samoa, Pacific Oc 13.35S 172.19W
28 G8 Toibalewe Andaman Is 10.26N 92.34E
28 G8 Toibuebe Andaman Is 10.40N 92.21E
51 L10 Toijala Finland 61.11N 23.50E
19 C4 Toili Celebes Indonesia 1.25S 122.23E
108 T2 Toimi Minnesota 47.22N 91.50W
20 E10 Toi-misaki C Japan 31.22N 131.21E
79 E4 Toirano Italy 44.07N 8.12E
95 L8 Toise River S Africa 32.28S 27.23E
51 K9 Toisvesi L Finland
51 M9 Toivakka Finland 62.06N 26.10E
109 L5 Toivola Michigan 47.00N 88.48W
111 G3 Toiyabe Ra Nevada
76 C12 Tojal Portugal 38.28N 8.02W
75 B4 Toja,La Spain 42.29N 8.50W
19 B4 Tojo Celebes Indon 1.19S 121.13E
29 G7 Tōjō Japan 34.51N 133.12E
65 J2 Tok mt Czechoslovakia 49.42N 13.53E
43 C1 Tok R Orenburg U.S.S.R.
92 B10 Toka tribe Zambia
11 K5 Tokaanu New Zealand 38.57S 175.47E
20 C3 Tokachi R Japan
20 M1 Tokachi sub-prefect Hokkaido Japan
20 M1 Tokachi-dake mt Japan 43.27N 142.41E
20 C3 Tokagi Chiba Japan
22 G2 Tokaj Hungary 48.08N 21.24E
62 N7 Tokaj Hungary 48.08N 21.23E
37 C5 Tokal R Turkey
19 B4 Tokala, Gunung mt Celebes Indon 1.36S 121.41E
20 M4 Tōkamachi Japan 37.08N 138.44E
33 B7 Tokan Sudan 18.26N 37.45E
11 C13 Tokanui New Zealand 46.35S 168.58E
87 F1 Tokar Sudan 18.27N 37.41E
21 D11 Tokara rettō arch Japan
43 J4 Tokarevka Kazakhstan U.S.S.R. 50.07N 73.10E
45 N4 Tokarevka U.S.S.R. 52.00N 41.10E
42 J5 Tokarevo U.S.S.R. 54.50N 41.16E
45 H6 Tokari U.S.S.R. 61.11N 34.23E
45 O1 Tokarikha U.S.S.R. 57.50N 45.21E
37 D8 Tokaris Turkey 37.45N 38.49E
35 J8 Tokat Turkey 40.19N 36.35E
36 J2 Tokat Turkey 40.20N 36.35E
11 H3 Tokatoka New Zealand 36.03S 173.59E
21 C4 Tŏkchŏk-kundo islds S Korea
19 B5 Toke Celebes Indon 2.48S 120.27E
122 K9 Tokelau is Pacific Oc
109 P9 Tokewanna Pk Utah 40.48N 110.38W
84 R15 Tokhni Cyprus 34.45N 33.20E
42 F2 Tokhoma R U.S.S.R.
43 L7 Tokhtamysh Tadzhikistan U.S.S.R. 37.51N 74.41E
20 L6 Toki Japan 35.25N 137.12E
108 M2 Tokio N Dakota 47.56N 98.49W
112 E2 Tokio Texas 33.12N 102.34W
9 A6 Toki Pt Peale I Pacific Oc 19.19N 166.35E
20 G6 Tokitsu Japan 32.50N 129.50E
21 J5 Tokiwa Japan 44.44N 142.18E
42 H2 Tokiya U.S.S.R. 65.10N 107.15E
113 Q5 Tok Junction Alaska 63.20N 143.10W
52 D7 Tokke R Norway
52 E7 Tokke-vatn L Norway 59.05N 9.20E
45 K3 Toko U.S.S.R. 59.58N 119.55E
42 K3 Tokko R U.S.S.R.
Tokkuztara see Gongliu
36 J4 Toklar Turkey 38.25N 36.02E
113 M2 Toklat Alaska 64.30N 150.25W
113 M5 Toklat R Alaska
36 J5 Toklu Dağı mt Turkey 37.43N 36.08E
42 H3 Tokma U.S.S.R. 58.18N 105.45E
Tokmak see Eşme
43 M5 Tokmak Kirgiziya U.S.S.R. 42.49N 75.15E
45 G9 Tokmak Ukraine U.S.S.R. 47.13N 35.43E
44 L5 Tokmak,Mys C Kazakhstan U.S.S.R. 42.47N 52.17E
11 J6 Toko New Zealand 39.19S 174.25E
19 B5 Tokolimbu Celebes Indonesia 2.48S 121.36E
11 K7 Tokomaru New Zealand 40.27S 175.31E
11 N5 Tokomaru Bay New Zealand 38.10S 178.20E
20 K7 Tokoname Japan 34.50N 136.50E
21 K5 Tokoro Japan 44.07N 144.04E
11 K5 Tokoroa New Zealand 38.13S 175.53E
20 B5 Tokorozawa Saitama Japan 35.48N 139.28E
122 R16 Tokorua isld Gambier Is Pacific Oc 23.11S 135.04W
43 M4 Tokrau R Kazakhstan U.S.S.R.
43 D4 Toksha-Kuznetsova U.S.S.R. 62.37N 38.03E
113 E6 Toksook Bay Alaska 60.30N 165.07W
51 P11 Toksovo U.S.S.R. 60.10N 30.30E
Toksu see Xihe
24 F4 Toksun Xinjiang Uygur Zizhiqu China 42.45N 87.38E
43 L6 Toktogul Kirgiziya U.S.S.R. 41.48N 72.48E
45 E4 Tokty Kazakhstan U.S.S.R. 45.23N 82.12E
9 U9 Toku isld Tonga, Pacific Oc 18.10S 174.10W
9 T12 Tokulu atoll Tonga, Pacific Oc 20.07S 174.48W
39 A2 Tokuma U.S.S.R. 67.05N 134.15E
18 L6 Tokung Borneo Indon 0.21S 114.25E
21 D12 Tokuno shima isld Japan
39 F2 Tokur-Yurakh R U.S.S.R.
20 H7 Tokushima Japan 34.03N 134.34E
20 G8 Tokushima prefect Japan
20 E7 Tokuyama Japan 34.04N 131.48E
92 E12 Tokwe R Zimbabwe
20 C2 Tōkyō Japan 35.40N 139.45E
Tōkyō Bay see Tōkyō-wan
20 E3 Tōkyō-kō harb Tōkyō Japan
20 D2 Tōkyō-To capital dist Tōkyō Japan
20 C3 Tōkyō-wan B Japan
19 M4 Tol isld Truk Is Pacific Oc
115 M4 Tola Nicaragua 11.28N 85.57W
11 N5 Tolaga B New Zealand
11 N5 Tolaga Bay New Zealand 38.24S 178.20E
30 F3 Tolambau Glacier Nepal
109 G7 Tolar New Mexico 34.27N 103.57W
112 K3 Tolar Texas 32.25N 97.56W
121 C1 Tolar,Cerro pk Catamarca Arg 27.20S 67.16W
121 C2 Tolar,Cerro pk La Rioja Arg 28.05S 68.20W
39 G6 Tolbachik mt Kamchatka U.S.S.R. 55.49N 160.22E
46 S3 Tolbazy U.S.S.R. 54.00N 55.50E
60 O7 Tolbert Netherlands 53.10N 6.21E
22 D2 Tolbonur Mongolia 49.25N 90.15E
22 A2 Tolbo Nuur L Mongolia
82 L7 Tolbukhin Bulgaria 43.34N 27.51E
42 O5 Tolbuzine U.S.S.R. 53.10N 125.24E
103 B8 Tolchester Beach Maryland 39.13N 76.14W
115 O5 Tolé Panama 8.16N 81.40W
76 L10 Toledana,La Spain 39.16N 4.15W
118 D9 Toledo Brazil 24.46S 53.40W
120 C1 Toledo Brazil 5.54S 73.10W
121 B1 Toledo Chile 27.18S 70.27W
119 D4 Toledo Colombia 7.20N 72.27W
107 H2 Toledo Illinois 39.16N 88.15W
108 S7 Toledo Iowa 42.00N 92.32W
104 D5 Toledo Ohio 41.40N 83.35W
110 B5 Toledo Oregon 44.37N 123.57W
76 L9 Toledo Spain 39.52N 4.02W
110 C3 Toledo Washington 46.26N 122.51W
76 L9 Toledo prov Spain
112 O4 Toledo Bend Res Texas/Louisiana
76 L9 Toledo,Mtes.de Spain
Toledo see Tulmaythah
80 H2 Tolentino Italy 43.12N 13.17E
80 E4 Tolfa Italy 42.09N 11.56E
80 E4 Tolfa,Monti della Italy
53 Q6 Tolga Norway 62.26N 11.01E
54 ... Tolga Algeria 34.40N 5.21E
52 F4 Tolga Norway 62.26N 11.01E
Tolgon Hayrhan see Dölgöön
19 M4 Tol Harb Truk Is Pacific Oc 7.22N 151.38E
24 D3 Toli Xinjiang Uygur Zizhiqu China 45.57N 83.40E
15 E5 Tol R Irian Jaya
95 A7 Toliara Madagascar 23.20S 43.41E
119 C6 Tolima div Colombia
115 K7 Tolimán Mexico 20.56N 99.56W
119 C5 Tolima,Nevado del vol Colombia 4.39N 75.22W
Toling see Zanda
Töling see Zanda
19 B3 Tolitoli Celebes Indon 1.05N 120.50E
19 B3 Tolitoli,Teluk B Celebes Indon
63 L3 Tolk W Germany 54.35N 9.39E
42 D8 Tol'ka U.S.S.R. 64.01N 81.55E
67 O13 Tolla Corsica 41.58N 8.59E
115 K7 Tollan ruins Mexico 20.02N 99.18W
103 K3 Tolland Connecticut 41.52N 72.22W
103 H2 Tolland Massachusetts 42.05N 73.01W
103 K3 Tolland co Connecticut
52 H11 Tollarp Sweden 55.56N 14.00E
60 L9 Tollebeek Netherlands 52.40N 5.40E
61 G4 Tollembeek Belgium 50.44N 4.00E
62 D5 Tollense R E Germany
63 S6 Tollense-see L E Germany
56 M7 Tolleshunt D'Arcy Essex Eng 51.46N 0.48E
111 M8 Tolleson Arizona 33.29N 112.15W
108 J1 Tolley N Dakota 48.45N 101.50W
112 E4 Tollhouse California 37.01N 119.25W
80 K4 Tollo Italy 42.21N 14.19E
55 B3 Tollose Denmark 55.37N 11.47E
75 H5 Tollos,L.de los Spain 36.51N 6.01W
41 C2 Tollya, Gory mts Novaya Zemlya U.S.S.R.
41 P3 Tollya,Plato U.S.S.R.
41 P4 Tollya,Zaliv B U.S.S.R.
29 H2 Tollygunge dist Calcutta, W Bengal
58 C3 Tolmachan Harris, W Isles Scotland 57.57N 6.54W
43 F5 Tolmacheva,Ostrov isld Uzbekistan U.S.S.R. 44.13N 60.35E
46 G1 Tolmachevo U.S.S.R. 58.57N 29.51E
79 Q2 Tolmezzo Italy 46.24N 13.01E
79 R2 Tolmin Yugoslavia 46.11N 13.45E
62 L9 Tolna Hungary 46.26N 18.47E
82 E4 Tolna co Hungary
53 E6 Tolne Denmark 57.29N 10.20E
91 F5 Tolo Zaïre 2.55S 18.34E
115 M4 Toloa Honduras 15.43N 87.45W
45 A2 Tolochin Belorussiya U.S.S.R. 54.25N 29.42E
15 J6 Tolokiwa I Bismarck Arch 5.23S 147.37E
39 D5 Tolon Magadan U.S.S.R. 59.49N 148.48E
42 Q3 Tolon Yakutsk U.S.S.R. 59.30N 111.32E
112 H2 Tolono Illinois 39.58N 88.16W
75 E2 Tolono mt Spain 42.38N 2.46W
76 D2 Tolos Greece 37.31N 22.51E
75 F1 Tolosa Spain 43.09N 2.04W
76 D8 Tolosa Portugal 39.25N 7.43W
75 B5 Tolo,Teluk B Celebes Indon
113 M4 Tolovana R Alaska
77 G7 Tolox Spain 36.41N 4.54W
77 G7 Tolox,Sierra de mts Spain
21 D10 Tolsan isld S Korea
58 D2 Tolsta Hd Lewis, W Isles Scotland 58.20N 6.10W
82 K2 Tolstoe U.S.S.R. 48.52N 25.43E
77 F6 Tolstoy,Mys C U.S.S.R.
42 N2 Tolstyy Byk,Porog falls U.S.S.R. 57.58N 102.40E
42 G4 Tol'sty-Les Ukraine U.S.S.R. 51.24N 29.48E
111 N9 Toltec Arizona 32.48N 111.37W
121 A7 Toltén Chile 39.13S 73.15W
121 A7 Toltén,R Chile
119 C3 Tolú Colombia 9.16N 75.35W
107 H3 Toluca Illinois 41.01N 89.08W
115 K8 Toluca Mexico 19.20N 99.40W
89 J7 Tolundipe Ghana 9.01N 1.32W
75 K5 Tolva Spain 42.07N 0.34E
51 P5 Tolvant,Ozero L U.S.S.R. 66.55N 31.00E
47 E5 Tolvayarvi Karelia U.S.S.R. 62.14N 31.45E
82 M2 Tolve Italy 40.42N 16.02E
47 D5 Tolvuya U.S.S.R. 62.29N 35.17E
56 F5 Tolworth London Eng 51.23N 0.17E
41 K2 Tolyatti U.S.S.R. 53.32N 49.24E
45 V2 Tolybay Kazakhstan U.S.S.R. 50.33N 62.15E
42 D8 Tolzat R France
42 D3 Tom' R Amur U.S.S.R.
42 C4 Tom' R Tomsk/Kemerovo U.S.S.R.
98 J2 Toma Mozambique 12.58S 38.49E
89 J4 Toma Upper Volta 12.46N 2.51W
106 D6 Tomah Wisconsin 43.59N 90.30W
105 D6 Tomahawk Wisconsin 45.27N 89.42W
11 M13 Tomahawk Lagoon New Zealand 45.54S 170.33E
20 L2 Tomakomai Japan 42.39N 141.33E
45 F9 Tomakovka Ukraine U.S.S.R. 47.48N 34.45E
Toman Agha see Tūmān Āqā
18 L3 Tomani Sabah Malaysia 4.51N 115.52E
9 T11 Tomanivi mt Viti Levu Fiji 17.37S 178.01E
119 G8 Tomar Brazil 0.26S 63.57W
43 L4 Tomar Kazakhstan U.S.S.R. 46.23N 75.06E
76 C9 Tomar Portugal 39.36N 8.25W
20 J2 Tomari Japan 42.39N 140.35E
21 K5 Tomari Sakhalin U.S.S.R. 47.45N 142.04E
84 A3 Tómaros mt Greece 39.29N 20.48E
45 H6 Tomarovka U.S.S.R. 50.41N 36.15E
35 F3 Tomarza Turkey 38.27N 35.47E
120 F7 Tomas Barrón Bolivia 17.35S 67.30W
121 F3 Tomas Gomensoro Uruguay 30.28S 57.28W
62 O4 Tomashevka U.S.S.R. 51.34N 23.36E
82 L2 Tomashpol U.S.S.R. 48.33N 28.31E
121 K10 Tomas, I Chile 55.25S 69.40W
118 E8 Tomasina Brazil 23.44S 49.57W
62 O5 Tomaszów Lubelski Poland 50.29N 23.23E
62 M4 Tomaszów Mazowiecka Poland 51.33N 20.00E
58 J4 Tomatin Highland Scotland 57.20N 3.59W
115 G8 Tomatlán Mexico 19.54N 105.18W
120 E8 Tomave Bolivia 20.06S 66.31W
65 O9 Tomaž Yugoslavia 46.29N 16.05E
118 H2 Tombador,Sa do mts Bahia Brazil
118 B3 Tombador,Sa.do mts Mato Grosso Brazil
90 J8 Tombaggo tribe Cent Afr Rep
112 M5 Tomball Texas 30.04N 95.38W
20 F6 Tombara Japan 35.05N 132.45E
89 D5 Tombé Mali 12.46N 10.54W
87 C8 Tombe Sudan 5.52N 31.40E
26 U11 Tombeau B Mauritius, Indian Oc
72 E7 Tombebœuf France 44.30N 0.29E
107 H8 Tombigbee R Alabama/Miss
19 C4 Tombila,Gunung mt Indonesia 1.28S 122.59E
95 N7 Tombo S Africa 31.38S 29.23E
91 C7 Tomboco Angola 6.50S 13.20E
19 B5 Tomboli Celebes Indonesia 3.56S 121.22E
121 D10 Tombo,Pta C Argentina 44.05S 65.12W
120 C4 Tombo,R Peru
118 G7 Tombos Brazil 20.53S 42.03W
89 H3 Tombouctou Mali 16.49N 2.59W
11 G1 Tom Bowling B New Zealand
111 O10 Tombstone Arizona 31.44N 110.04W
94 J4 Tomburke S Africa 23.05S 28.00E
58 F4 Tomdoun Highland Scotland 57.04N 5.02W
121 A6 Tomé Chile 36.38S 72.57W
19 C6 Tomea isld Indonesia 5.47S 123.55E
36 F4 Tömek Turkey 38.02N 32.36E
52 H11 Tomelilla Sweden 55.33N 14.00E
77 K2 Tomelloso Spain 39.09N 3.01W
91 A12 Tomé,Pico de mt São Tomé
São Tomé & Principe, Gulf of Guinea 0.13N 6.33E
59 E6 Tomgraney Clare Irish Rep 52.54N 8.38W
90 G4 Tomi R Cent Afr Rep
58 H3 Tomich Highland Scotland 57.18N 4.49W
58 G4 Tomich Highland Scotland 57.30N 4.27W
21 D11 Tomie Japan 32.31N 128.46E
99 L6 Tomiko Ontario 46.34N 79.25W
120 F8 Tomina Bolivia 19.15S 64.30W
89 C6 Tomine R Guinea
12 J5 Tomingley New S Wales 32.06S 148.15E
19 C2 Tomini Celebes Indon 0.31N 120.30E
89 G5 Tominian Mali 13.17N 4.36W
19 B3 Tomini,Teluk B Celebes Indon
76 B5 Tomiño Spain 41.59N 8.46W
58 K4 Tomintoul Grampian Scotland 57.15N 3.24W
20 P4 Tomioka Honshu Japan 37.20N 141.00E
20 M5 Tomioka Japan 36.14N 138.45E
20 E9 Tomioka Japan 32.25N 131.37E
Tomitaka see Hyūga
20 M2 Tomiuchi Japan 42.54N 142.16E
103 G4 Tom Jones Cove New York 41.16N 73.59W
14 G7 Tomkinson Ras S Aust/W Aust
51 C5 Tømmerås isld Norway 66.15N 12.50E
53 E5 Tømmerby Denmark 57.04N 9.01E
52 E3 Tommerby Fjord L Denmark 57.03N 8.58E
53 E5 Tømmerup Denmark 55.19N 10.13E
53 E6 Tømmerup Stationsby Denmark 55.21N 10.12E
40 D2 Tommot U.S.S.R. 59.04N 126.20E
58 K4 Tomnavoulin Grampian Scotland 57.19N 3.20W
119 F6 Tomo Colombia 2.37N 67.31W
20 G7 Tomo Japan 34.22N 133.21E
115 F3 Tomochic Mexico 28.20N 107.50W
20 Q3 Tomogashima-suidō str Japan
19 H7 Tomohon Celebes Indon 1.28N 124.55E
19 B5 Tomori Albania
119 F5 Tomo, R Colombia
19 B5 Tomori,Teluk B Celebes Indon
84 B4 Tomorrit,Mal i e mts Albania
42 H4 Tompa U.S.S.R. 55.08N 109.45E
100 J8 Tompkins Saskatchewan 50.04N 108.49W
103 G1 Tompkins co New York
108 K7 Tompkins Center Michigan 42.22N 84.32W
107 L5 Tompkinsville Kentucky 36.43N 85.41W
19 C2 Tompo Celebes Indon 0.59N 120.20E
39 B3 Tompo U.S.S.R. 63.56N 135.51E
39 B3 Tompo R U.S.S.R.
14 C6 Tom Price W Australia 22.45S 117.50E
14 C6 Tom Price,Mt W Australia 22.49S 117.51E
53 V13 Tomra Norway 62.34N 6.55E
24 F10 Tomra Xizang Zizhiqu China 30.52N 87.30E
52 E7 Tomrefjord inlet Norway 62.38N 6.41E
118 F6 Toms R New Jersey
87 E6 Tomsa Ethiopia 8.38N 43.03E
42 D4 Tomsk U.S.S.R. 56.30N 85.05E
42 C3 Tomsk obl U.S.S.R.
26 V3 Tom's Ridge Christmas I Ind Oc 10.27S 105.36E
103 F7 Toms River New Jersey 39.57N 74.12W
39 D1 Tomsyu U.S.S.R. 67.49N 146.07E
39 A2 Tomtor U.S.S.R. 67.05N 132.40E
39 A2 Tomtor U.S.S.R. 67.10N 134.36E
42 P3 Tomtor U.S.S.R. 63.18N 143.14E
42 O2 Tomtor U.S.S.R. 62.52N 132.48E
41 O8 Tomtor U.S.S.R. 62.48N 131.06E
15 G7 Tomu R Papua New Guinea
Tomük see Elvanlı
20 M1 Tomuraushi-yama mt Japan 43.33N 142.49E
20 H4 Tomuro Kanagawa Japan
44 F3 Tomuzlovka R U.S.S.R.
113 Q6 Tom White,Mt Alaska 60.40N 143.40W
76 K4 Tona Spain 41.52N 2.14E
115 F4 Tonachic Mexico 26.58N 107.11W
115 N5 Tonalá Chiapas Mexico 16.08N 93.41W
115 M8 Tonalá Veracruz Mexico 18.14N 94.10W
111 K8 Tonalea Arizona 36.20N 110.58W
115 G7 Tonalá Jalisco Mexico
79 J2 Tonale,Passo del pass Italy 46.16N 10.35E
22 P3 Tonami Japan 36.40N 136.55E
119 F8 Tonantins Brazil 2.46S 67.45W
119 E7 Tonantins, R Brazil
119 F9 Tonara Sardinia 40.02N 9.11E
110 F1 Tonasket Washington 48.42N 119.28W
112 F3 Tonate Fr Guiana 5.00N 52.28W
104 H1 Tonawanda New York 43.01N 78.54W
56 M8 Tonbridge Kent Eng 51.12N 0.16E
20 H8 Tonda Japan 33.38N 135.23E
15 G8 Tonda Papua New Guinea 8.55S 141.33E
19 C3 Tondano Celebes Indon 1.19N 124.56E
76 C7 Tondela Portugal 40.31N 8.05W
53 C7 Tønder Denmark 54.57N 8.53E
Tønder co see Sønderjylland
99 E3 Tondern Ontario 49.19N 85.03W
28 D6 Tondi Tamil Nadu India 9.44N 79.00E
88 F10 Tondibi Mali
91 E10 Tondo Zaïre 0.53S 18.09E
92 E9 Tondongwe mt Zimbabwe 16.20S 30.15E
53 E5 Tondorf W Germany 50.28N 6.44E
115 H10 Tondu Mid Glam Wales 51.33N 3.36W
66 D8 Tondu,Mt France 45.46N 6.45E
50 T15 Tonefjellet mt Spitsbergen 77.06N 15.30E
61 P6 Tone-gawa R Japan
56 D13 Tonelagee mt Wicklow Irish Rep 53.03N 6.23W
19 N3 Tonelik isld Truk Is Pacific Oc 7.41N 151.48E
56 E6 Tone,R Somerset Eng
79 K3 Tonezza Italy 45.52N 11.21E
56 G3 Tong Shropshire Eng 52.41N 2.18W
96 H2 Tonga New S Wales 30.30S 143.47E
87 C6 Tonga Sudan 9.22N 31.00E
9 U14 Tonga island grp Pacific Oc
92 C10 Tonga tribe Zambia
95 P5 Tongaat S Africa 29.35S 31.07E
11 H7 Tonga I New Zealand 40.57S 173.05E
12 H1 Tonga I Papua New Guinea
12 G6 Tongala Victoria 36.15S 144.57E
23 H8 Tong 'An Fujian China 24.43N 118.07E
24 S5 Tong'an Xizang Zizhiqu China
82 H3 Tonganoxie Kansas 39.06N 95.06W
109 P2 Tongaporutu New Zealand 38.48S 174.36E
23 C1 Tong'anyi Gansu China 25.18N 104.39E
15 J3 Tongaporutu New Zealand 38.48S
122 L9 Tongareva atoll Cook Is Pacific Oc 9.00S 158.00W
10 R6 Tonga Ridge sea feature Pacific Oc
11 K6 Tongariro Nat.Park New Zealand
11 K6 Tongariro vol New Zealand 39.08S 175.42E
9 S10 Tongatapu / Tonga, Pacific Oc
9 R11 Tongatapu Group island grp
Tonga, Pacific Oc
10 S6 Tonga Trench Pacific Oc
23 F2 Tongbai Henan China 32.25N 113.25E
23 F2 Tongbai Shan mts Hubei China
21 D4 Tongbei Heilongjiang China 47.46N 126.43E
Tongcheng see Dong'e
23 G3 Tongcheng Anhui China 31.07N 116.56E
23 F4 Tongcheng Hubei China 29.16N 113.51E
22 K5 Tongchuan Shaanxi China 35.05N 109.02E
21 K1 Tongdaemun-gu dist Seoul S Korea
23 C4 Tongdao Dongzu Zizhixian Hunan China 26.20N 109.36E
22 C3 Tongde Qinghai China 35.18N 100.40E
23 B1 Tongeren Belgium 50.47N 5.28E
60 M10 Tongeren Netherlands 52.21N 5.55E
61 N2 Tongerlo Antwerp Belgium 51.07N 4.55E
61 L4 Tongerlo Limburg Belgium 51.08N 5.40E
23 E3 Tonggu Jiangxi China 28.35N 114.16E
22 B4 Tongguan Shaanxi China 34.35N 110.21E
23 E4 Tongguan Yunnan China 23.17N 101.29E
22 D6 Tonggu Jiao pt Hainan China
25 L3 Tonghai Yunnan China 24.07N 102.45E
23 C6 Tonghe Heilongjiang China 45.58N 128.44E
21 B7 Tonghua Jilin China 41.42N 125.45E
21 C7 Tonghua Jilin China 41.45N 125.50E
21 D10 Tongjiang Heilongjiang China 47.39N 132.26E
21 F4 Tongjiang Heilongjiang China 47.39N 132.26E
23 D3 Tongjiang Sichuan China 31.57N 107.15E
24 E9 Tongka Tso L Xizang Zizhiqu China 32.09N 84.43E
21 D4 Tongken He R Heilongjiang China
23 D8 Tongking, Gulf of Vietnam/China
57 E3 Tongland Dumfries & Galloway Scotland 54.52N 4.02W
23 D4 Tongliang Sichuan China 29.53N 106.02E
21 B6 Tongliao Nei Monggol Zizhiqu China 43.37N 122.15E
23 H3 Tongling Anhui China 30.57N 117.40E
23 H3 Tongling Anhui China 30.58N 117.48E
23 H4 Tonglu Zhejiang China 29.50N 119.38E
21 E10 Tongnae S Korea 35.11N 129.05E
21 C3 Tongnan Heilongjiang China 48.13N 125.00E
23 D3 Tongnan Sichuan China 30.13N 105.50E
25 J6 Tong Noy Cambodia 13.44N 106.59E
42 K1 Tongo R U.S.S.R.
9 C11 Tongoa isld New Hebrides
95 B7 Tongobory Madagascar 23.30S 44.20E
121 B3 Tongoi, B Chile
121 B3 Tongoy Chile 30.16S 71.31W
Tong Po Chau see Middle I Hong Kong
Tongquan see Malong
19 K8 Tongquil isld Philippines 6.01N 121.50E
23 E5 Tongren Guizhou China 27.44N 109.10E
23 B1 Tongren Qinghai China 35.30N 101.55E
Tongres Belgium see Tongeren
61 F4 Tongres-Notre-Dame Belgium 50.35N 3.47E
61 F4 Tongres-St.Martin Belgium 50.35N 3.48E
28 H2 Tongsa Bhutan 27.33N 90.30E
28 H2 Tongsa R Bhutan
Tongshan see Xuzhou
23 G4 Tongshan Hubei China 29.39N 114.30E
25 E2 Tongta Burma 20.21N 99.18E
24 H8 Tongtian He R Qinghai China
24 G9 Tongtianheyan Qinghai China 33.50N 92.19E
58 H2 Tongue Highland Scotland 58.28N 4.25W
108 E3 Tongue R Montana
58 H2 Tongue,Kyle of sea loch Highland Scotland 58.27N 4.26W
116 F2 Tongue of the Ocean Bahamas
11 B6 Tongue Pt New Zealand 41.21S 174.39E
108 D4 Tongue River Res Montana
42 L2 Tongulakh U.S.S.R. 61.58N 124.42E
Tongustarau see Gongliu
23 D1 Tongwei Gansu China 35.06N 105.26E
22 K7 Tong Xian Beijing China 39.55N 116.40E
23 D1 Tongxiang Zhejiang China 30.39N 120.34E
22 G8 Tongxin Ningxia China 37.01N 106.08E
22 L5 Tongxing Nei Monggol Zizhiqu China 43.40N 117.37E
23 G1 Tongxu Henan China 34.30N 114.30E
21 D8 Tongyang N Korea 39.05N 126.51E
21 C5 Tongyu Jilin China 44.48N 123.01E
21 C7 Tongyuanpu Liaoning China 40.45N 123.58E
Tongyuk see Dongjug
23 D6 Tongzhou Guizhou China 25.40N 107.05E
23 D4 Tongzi Guizhou China 28.08N 106.49E
23 E2 Tonhil Mongolia 46.19N 93.54E
106 E8 Tonica Illinois 41.12N 89.03W
115 M3 Tonila Mexico 28.37N 109.34W
115 H8 Tonila Mexico 19.24N 103.31W
87 B7 Tonj Sudan 7.18N 28.41E
Tonj R see Ibba R
87 B7 Tonj watercourse Sudan
53 W16 Tønjum Norway 61.03N 7.30E
53 X16 Tønjumdal V Norway 61.01N 7.31E
29 D4 Tonk Rajasthan India 26.10N 75.50E
29 D4 Tonk dist Rajasthan India
109 N5 Tonkawa Oklahoma 36.40N 97.18W
113 M7 Tonki C Alaska 58.20N 152.00W
25 H5 Tonkin reg Vietnam
46 O2 Tonkino U.S.S.R. 57.24N 46.38E
Tonkon Point see Tonggu Jiao
25 H5 Tonle Repou R Laos/Cambodia
25 G7 Tonle Sap L Cambodia
25 H7 Tonle Sap R Cambodia
72 C4 Tonnay Boutonne France 45.58N 0.42W
72 D4 Tonnay Charente France 45.57N 0.53W
72 E7 Tonneins France 44.24N 0.19E
72 H2 Tonnerre France 47.51N 3.59E
69 F8 Tønning Denmark 55.59N 9.40E
63 G3 Tønning W Germany 54.19N 8.57E
20 P2 Tōno Japan 39.20N 141.31E
111 G3 Tonopah Nevada 38.05N 117.15W
119 G3 Tonoro,R Venezuela
20 G3 Tonoshō Japan 34.28N 134.11E
111 H7 Tonosí Panama 7.25N 80.22W
115 O6 Tonosi Panama 7.25N 80.22W
70 D4 Tonquédec France 48.41N 3.24W
66 H8 Tonriggia Italy 45.54N 9.09E
30 F6 Tons R Faizabad, Uttar Prad India
30 D8 Tons R Madhya Prad etc India
30 E1 Tons R Tehri Garhwal, Uttar Prad India
52 E7 Tønsberg Norway 59.16N 10.25E
60 L10 Tonsel Netherlands 52.20N 5.37E
112 G8 Tonsina Alaska 61.35N 145.14W
121 E8 Tonsoi,Sa ra Argentina
61 O8 Tontelange Belgium 49.43N 5.49E
111 N8 Tonto Basin Arizona 33.55N 111.18W
111 N8 Tonto Nat.Mon Arizona 33.40N 111.04W
19 N4 Tonuamu isld Truk Is Pacific Oc 7.18N 151.42E
9 T13 Tonumea atoll Tonga, Pacific Oc 20.25S 174.54W
14 H3 Tonvarjeh Iran 35.23N 58.37E
37 H5 Tonya Turkey 40.52N 39.17E
93 C4 Tonya Uganda 1.35N 21.05E
56 C4 Tonyrefail Mid Glam Wales 51.36N 3.25W
74 G8 Tonzang Burma 23.39N 93.46E
25 B1 Tonzi Burma 24.39N 94.56E
15 L9 Tonzona R Alaska
13 J8 Toobeah Queensland 28.22S 149.50E
18 B9 Toodyay W Australia 31.35S 116.26E
110 N9 Tooele Utah 40.32N 112.18W
12 B7 Toogoolawah Queensland 27.05S 152.19E
12 G6 Toolebuc New S Wales 35.01S 143.20E
14 G9 Toolgana W Australia 31.33S 128.34E
12 D5 Toolige S Australia 33.51S 135.41E
113 B6 Toolik R Alaska
12 F6 Toolondo Victoria 36.55S 142.00E
12 J6 Tooma R New S Wales
13 G7 Toompine Queensland 27.12S 144.15E
59 F6 Toomyvara Tipperary Irish Rep 52.51N 8.02W
13 F5 Toorak Queensland 21.05S 141.46E
12 D7 Toorak dist Melbourne, Vic
13 G4 Tooraweenah New S Wales 31.31S 148.55E
95 H8 Toorberg mt S Africa 32.08S 24.05E
55 F4 Tooting Graveney London Eng 51.25N 0.10W
119 G7 Tootobi, R Brazil
13 G6 Toowong dist Brisbane, Qnsld
13 K8 Toowoomba Queensland 27.35S 151.54E
12 D7 Top Afghanistan 34.15N 68.50E
113 J1 Topagoruk R Alaska
82 L8 Topalu Romania 44.31N 28.03E
120 B1 Topa,R Peru
77 H5 Topares Spain 37.51N 2.13W
77 M5 Topares,Sierra de mts Spain
111 N10 Topawa Arizona 31.50N 111.48W
26 A12 Topaze B Rodriguez I Ind Oc
111 E3 Topaz L Calif/Nevada 38.40N 119.31W
112 K2 Topaz Mt Utah 39.42N 112.50W
42 C5 Topchikha U.S.S.R. 52.49N 83.13E
67 H4 Tope de Coroa mt Madeira
57 K6 Topcliffe N Yorks Eng 54.10N 1.23W
107 L2 Topeka Indiana 41.33N 85.33W
107 H4 Topeka Kansas 39.02N 95.41W
37 J8 Tophane dist İstanbul Turkey 41.01N 28.58E
115 F5 Topia Mexico 25.12N 106.32W
80 G3 Topino R Italy
42 K5 Topkanovo U.S.S.R. 54.41N 38.30E
30 L5 Topke Gola Nepal 27.39N 87.35E
52 G6 Topki U.S.S.R. 55.20N 85.40E
42 C4 Topki U.S.S.R. 62.58N 147.31E
39 D3 Topko,Gora mt U.S.S.R. 57.06N 137.18E
82 E8 Topľa R Czechoslovakia
62 M7 Topľa reg Madhya Prad India
100 B4 Topland Alberta 54.22N 114.56W
84 C2 Topland Albania 42.13N 19.52E
101 G7 Topley Lodge Br Col 54.46N 126.10W
82 F8 Toplice R Yugoslavia
82 B2 Toplica Yugoslavia 45.46N 15.04E
82 J4 Toplița Romania 46.56N 25.20E
121 A5 Topocalma Pta C Chile 34.10S 72.02W
111 K7 Topock Arizona 34.44N 114.27W
96 S4 Topo, Ilhéu do isld Azores 38.33N 27.46W
82 B6 Topola Yugoslavia 44.15N 20.41E
82 G9 Topolčani Yugoslavia 41.13N 21.28E
62 L7 Topol'čany Czechoslovakia 48.33N 18.10E
86 G6 Topoli Kazakhstan U.S.S.R. 47.58N 51.38E
52 K6 Topólia Greece 35.25N 23.41E
83 F9 Topólia Greece 38.29N 23.10E
19 G7 Topolinyy U.S.S.R. 64.05N 136.10E
82 H8 Topolnitsa R Bulgaria
115 G4 Topolobampo Mexico 25.36N 109.04W
82 K6 Topoloveni Romania 44.49N 25.05E
82 K8 Topolovgrad Bulgaria 42.05N 26.20E
85 M9 Topolšica Yugoslavia 46.24N 15.02E
109 D1 Toponas Colorado 40.04N 106.47W
67 D6 Topornya U.S.S.R. 59.51N 38.20E
42 C4 Topozero,Oz L U.S.S.R.
101 E7 Toppenish Washington 46.23N 120.18W
28 D3 Toppur Sri Lanka 8.23N 81.18E
14 C2 Topraisar Romania 44.01N 28.29E
43 F7 Toprak-Kala anc site Uzbekistan U.S.S.R. 41.55N 60.45E
36 J5 Toprakkale Turkey 37.05N 36.07E
47 E4 Topsa U.S.S.R. 62.38N 43.40E
104 S1 Topsfield Maine 45.25N 67.44W
56 F6 Topsham Devon Eng 50.42N 3.27W
104 Q3 Topsham Maine 43.57N 69.59W
102 B5 Topton Pennsylvania 40.30N 75.42W
83 C3 Topusko Yugoslavia 45.18N 15.59E
120 D7 Toquepala Peru 17.24S 70.25W
111 L4 Toquerville Utah 37.16N 113.16W
76 D3 Toques Spain 42.58N 7.59W
111 G3 Toquima Ra Nevada
54 N6 Tor oil field North Sea 56.41N 3.18E
15 E5 Tor R Irian Jaya
89 F5 Tora Ivory Coast 9.26N 6.53W
75 N4 Torá Spain 41.49N 1.25E
87 B9 Tora Zaïre 3.20N 29.10E
19 N4 Tora isld Truk Is Pacific Oc 7.39N 151.53E
42 F5 Tora-Khem U.S.S.R. 52.31N 96.13E
87 C5 Tora Kit Sudan 11.00N 32.36E
76 H4 Toral de los Guzmanes Spain 42.15N 5.34W
76 F3 Toral de los Vados Spain 42.32N 6.47W
Toraman see Halilçavuş
81 M4 Torano Castello Italy 39.31N 16.09E
75 J8 Torás Spain 39.55N 0.33W
47 K2 Torasovey,Ostrov isld U.S.S.R.
120 D7 Torata Peru 17.28S 70.02W
19 D3 Torawitan, Tanjung C Celebes Indon 1.45N 125.00E
98 L8 Tor B Nova Scotia
14 C11 Tor B W Australia
83 J6 Torbah Turkey 38.10N 27.22E
31 D5 Tor Baldak mt Afghanistan 30.55N 66.19E
36 C4 Torbalı Turkey 38.07N 27.08E
32 H7 Torbat-e Heydariyeh Iran 35.15N 59.08E
32 J3 Torbat-e Jām Iran 35.16N 60.36E
Torbat-i-Shaikh Jam see Torbat-e Jām
56 D7 Torbay Devon Eng 50.27N 3.32W
98 T6 Torbay Newfoundland 47.40N 52.42W
98 L8 Tor B Nova Scotia 45.11N 61.20W
66 H7 Torbel Switzerland 46.15N 7.52E
52 G5 Tørberget Norway 61.08N 12.06E
113 L6 Torbert,Mt Alaska 61.28N 152.20W
45 P2 Torbeyevo Mordovian A.S.S.R. U.S.S.R. 54.05N 43.14E
45 F1 Torbeyevo Smolensk U.S.S.R. 55.29N 34.15E
46 J1 Torbino U.S.S.R. 58.37N 32.50E
79 H3 Torbole Italy 45.31N 10.07E
79 J3 Tórbole Italy 45.52N 10.52E
53 Z14 Torbua Norway 62.26N 8.33E
77 G7 Torcal,El reg Spain
81 K3 Torchiara Italy 40.19N 15.03E
81 R12 Torchiarolo Italy 40.28N 18.03E
106 J4 Torch L Michigan
71 G5 Torcieu France 45.55N 5.24E
59 C8 Torc Mt Kerry Irish Rep 51.59N 9.31W
56 D7 Tor Cross Devon Eng 50.16N 3.39W
70 N2 Torcy-le-Grand France 49.48N 1.10E
87 J10 Torda Somalia 0.05S 42.44E
76 J5 Tordehumos Spain 41.49N 5.10W
75 Q4 Tordera Spain 41.42N 2.43E
75 Q4 Tordera R Spain
76 K6 Tordesillas Spain 41.30N 5.00W
75 G6 Tordesilos Spain 40.40N 1.35W
80 J3 Tordino R Italy
75 C3 Tordomar Spain 42.03N 3.53W
12 F5 Tor Downs New S Wales 32.54S 142.03E
76 B2 Tordoya Spain 43.06N 8.36W
51 K6 Töre Sweden 65.55N 22.40E
52 H8 Töreboda Sweden 58.41N 14.07E
53 H7 Toreby Denmark 54.46N 11.47E
53 K4 Torekov Sweden 56.26N 12.39E
50 S15 Torellbreen glacier Spitsbergen 77.10N 15.00E
50 T15 Torell Land reg Spitsbergen
75 P3 Torelló Spain 42.02N 2.16E
60 M11 Torenberg mt Netherlands 52.14N 5.52E
76 F3 Toreno Spain 42.42N 6.31W
19 C5 Toreo Celebes Indon 3.43S 122.17E
11 M4 Tore New Zealand 37.56S 177.29E
52 K7 Toresund Sweden 59.20N 17.15E
75 E5 Torete R Spain
42 G6 Torey U.S.S.R. 50.31N 104.48E
45 K9 Torez Ukraine U.S.S.R. 48.00N 38.38E
50 G7 Torfajökull ice cap Iceland 63.53N 18.58W
50 K6 Torfastadhir Iceland 64.11N 20.30W
52 K7 Torfinnsbu Norway 61.22N 8.35E
53 U17 Torfinnsvatn L Norway 60.33N 6.16E
50 K6 Torfnahnúkur mt Iceland 65.11N 18.18W
72 B1 Torfou France 47.03N 1.07W
50 G4 Torfufell mt Iceland 65.16N 18.21W
51 M8 Torfuhorn C Iceland 66.04N 14.39W
42 E6 Torgalyg U.S.S.R. 51.23N 92.56E
63 S9 Torgau E Germany 51.34N 13.01E
63 U5 Torgelow E Germany 53.37N 14.00E
51 C8 Torget isld Norway 65.23N 12.09E
79 F2 Torgiano Italy 43.02N 12.26E
66 G8 Torgnon Italy 45.47N 7.34E
61 M8 Torgny Belgium 49.31N 5.29E
79 K3 Torgo U.S.S.R. 58.30N 119.50E
41 P5 Torgo,Ozero L U.S.S.R. 70.50N 138.30E
42 H4 Torgovoye U.S.S.R. 47.01N 43.51E
46 Q2 Torgun R U.S.S.R.
74 Q4 Torgun R U.S.S.R.
58 G4 Torgyle Highland Scotland 57.11N 4.49W
52 J10 Torhamn Sweden 56.05N 15.50E
61 D7 Torhout Belgium 51.04N 3.06E
59 F3 Tori Bihar India 23.44N 84.48E
87 D7 Tori Ethiopia 7.53N 33.35E
19 B4 Toribulu Celebes Indon 0.23S 120.01E
20 O6 Toride Japan 35.54N 140.07E
30 F7 Tori Fatehpur Madhya Prad India 25.27N 79.06E
70 J3 Torigny-sur-Vire France 49.02N 0.59W
76 J5 Torija Spain 40.44N 3.02W
76 H9 Toril Cáceres Spain 39.55N 5.46W
71 F4 Toril Teruel Spain 40.15N 1.29W
115 D7 Torin Mexico 27.36N 110.15W
79 C4 Torino Italy 45.04N 7.40E
79 B4 Torino prov Italy
80 C4 Torino di Sangro Italy 42.12N 14.33E
87 C8 Torit Sudan
79 C3 Tori,R Sudan
21 C12 Tori-shima isld Amami Guntō Japan 27.54N 128.15E
21 D11 Tori shima isld Honshu Japan 32.14N 128.06E
21 H12 Tori shima isld Ogasawara-Guntō Japan 30.28N 140.18E
87 D8 Torit Sudan 4.27N 32.31E
81 N2 Toritto Italy 41.00N 16.40E
118 D5 Torixoreu Brazil 16.09S 52.24W
32 B2 Torkamān Iran 37.35N 47.24E
32 F7 Tor Khama Pakistan 34.08N 71.10E
31 F4 Torkhan Pakistan 33.08N 70.06E
46 H1 Torkovichi U.S.S.R. 58.52N 30.21E
57 M6 Torksey Lincs Eng 53.18N 0.45W
75 K2 Torla Spain 42.37N 0.06W
43 K3 Torlun Kazakhstan U.S.S.R. 44.42N 51.28E
51 N3 Tornänen Finland 68.36N 27.30E
42 B2 Tornemtor,Oz L U.S.S.R.
14 E2 Torment, Pt W Australia 17.03S 123.38E
78 H6 Tormes R Spain
75 F4 Tormillo,El Spain 41.52N 0.02W
75 H7 Tormón Spain 40.13N 1.22W
28 H2 Tormoshangsa Bhutan 27.30N 91.04E
76 A10 Tormos Portugal 38.42N 7.59W
100 C9 Tornado Mt Alberta 49.57N 114.35W
66 Q6 Tornadri Italy 46.17N 9.58E
77 L5 Tornajuelos mt Spain 37.56N 2.42W
58 J3 Tornapress Highland Scotland 57.25N 5.36W
81 J8 Tornatore Poggio mt Sicily 37.53N 14.37E
76 H8 Tornavacas Spain 40.15N 5.41W
53 D1 Tornby Denmark 57.32N 9.58E
Torneå see Tornio
51 J4 Torne älv R Sweden
76 L10 Torneros,Sierra de los mts Spain
65 L5 Tornesch W Germany 53.43N 9.44E
58 H4 Tornesss Highland Scotland 57.18N 4.21W
58 S12 Tor Ness pt Orkney Scotland 58.46N 3.17W
51 H3 Torneträsk Sweden 68.14N 19.40E
51 J3 Torne-träsk L Sweden
66 E6 Tornettaz mt Switzerland 46.23N 7.10E
98 N6 Torngat Mts Newfoundland/Labrador
28 F6 Torniella Italy 43.08N 11.10E
82 F7 Tornik mt Yugoslavia 43.40N 19.40E
80 H4 Tornimparte Italy 42.18N 13.18E
52 E7 Torning Denmark 56.17N 9.20E
53 E6 Torning Denmark 56.17N 9.26E
51 L6 Tornio Finland 65.52N 24.12E
51 L6 Tornionjoki R Sweden/Finland
51 L6 Tornio Italy 45.51N 9.07E
79 H6 Tornol,El Spain 40.08N 5.57W
80 E3 Tornola Italy 44.28N 9.38E
100 K4 Tornow E Germany 53.04N 13.21E
121 E7 Tornquist Argentina 38.08S 62.15W
89 D9 Tor Nigeria 10.05N 9.05E
75 C4 Toro Spain 41.31N 5.24W
52 L7 Torö Sweden 58.50N 17.50E
55 D4 Torø isld Denmark 55.15N 9.53E
15 A4 Torobi I Irian Jaya
19 C6 Torobuku Celebes Indonesia 4.26S 122.27E
76 J6 Toro,Canal de Spain
121 C3 Toro,Cerro de pk Arg/Chile 29.10S 69.48W
89 K5 Torodi Niger 13.18N 1.45E
79 F1 Toro,El Spain 39.59N 0.46W
77 Y14 Toro,El mt Balearic Is 39.59N 4.06E
82 J3 Torom mt Romania 47.44N 24.43E
77 U15 Toro,I.del Balearic Is 39.27N 2.29E
81 A6 Toro,I.il Sardinia 38.52N 8.24E
88 C7 Torok Cameroon 10.03N 14.36E
122 K15 Torokina Bougainville I Papua New Guinea 6.15S 155.02E
62 M8 Törökszentmiklós Hungary 47.11N 20.26E
121 J8 Toro,L.del Chile
53 Y16 Torolmen L Norway 61.16N 8.05E
40 G4 Torom U.S.S.R. 54.35N 135.44E
40 G5 Torom R U.S.S.R.
84 G5 Toronaios Kólpos gulf Greece
109 P4 Toronto Kansas 37.49N 95.57W
12 K5 Toronto New S Wales 33.01S 151.36E
104 E6 Toronto Ohio 40.29N 80.38W
99 L9 Toronto Ontario 43.42N 79.25W
99 D10 Toronto Harb Ontario
99 D10 Toronto I.Airport Ontario 43.37N 79.24W
109 P4 Toronto Res Kansas
103 E5 Toronto Res New York 41.37N 74.50W
120 F9 Toropalca Bolivia 20.35S 65.22W
46 H2 Toropets U.S.S.R. 56.30N 31.40E
115 J5 Toro,Pico del pk Mexico 24.32N 101.50W
111 H8 Toro Pk mt California 33.32N 116.27W
121 B4 Toro,Pta C Chile 33.47S 71.45W

93 F3 Toror mt Uganda 2.49N 34.11E
90 H5 Tororo Chad 13.22N 16.43E
93 F5 Tororo Uganda 0.42N 34.12E
36 G5 Toros Dağı mt Turkey
36 F6 Toros Dağları ra Turkey
75 J8 Toro,Sierra del mts Spain
76 K5 Torozos,Mtes Spain
52 J4 Torp Sweden 62.32N 16.10E
81 D2 Torpè Sardinia 40.38N 9.41E
58 L4 Torphins Grampian Scotland 57.06N 2.38W
46 M2 Torpino U.S.S.R. 56.31N 40.39E
56 C7 Torpoint Cornwall Eng 50.22N 4.11W
52 J4 Torpshammar Sweden 62.29N 16.25E
121 G3 Torquato Severo Brazil 31.04S 54.10W
56 D7 Torquay Devon Eng 50.28N 3.30W
100 O9 Torquay Saskatchewan 49.09N 103.31W
95 G5 Torquay Dam res Cape Province S Africa 29.39S 23.52E
76 L4 Torquemada Spain 42.02N 4.19W
81 B2 Torralba Sardinia 40.31N 8.46E
75 F5 Torralba Spain 41.09N 2.29W
75 F7 Torralba Spain 40.18N 2.18W
75 K4 Torralba de Aragón Spain 41.56N 0.30W
77 J2 Torralba de Calatrava Spain 39.01N 3.44W
75 E4 Torralba del Burgo Spain 41.38N 2.55W
75 H6 Torralba de los Sisones Spain 50.53N 1.28W
76 J9 Torralba de Oropesa Spain 39.56N 5.09W
111 D9 Torrance California 33.50N 118.20W
99 L8 Torrance Ontario 44.59N 79.35W
58 G3 Torrandhu Bridge Highland Scotland 57.42N 4.52W
76 C12 Torrão Baixo Alentejo Portugal 38.18N 8.13W
76 C6 Torrão Douro Litoral Portugal 41.05N 8.18W
79 F5 Torrazza Coste Italy 44.58N 9.05E
77 F7 Torre Alháquime Spain 36.55N 5.14W
80 K7 Torre Annunziata Italy 40.45N 14.27E
75 H7 Torre Baja Spain 40.06N 1.15W
79 K3 Torrebelvicino Italy 45.43N 11.19E
79 E4 Torre Beretti Italy 45.04N 8.40E
75 E4 Torreblacos Spain 41.40N 2.52W
75 L7 Torreblanca Spain 40.14N 0.12E
77 J5 Torreblascopedro Spain 37.59N 3.39W
77 D6 Torre, Brazo de la R Spain
76 L7 Torrecaballeros Spain 40.59N 4.01W
77 G4 Torrecampo Spain 38.29N 4.41W
77 K5 Torre Cardela Spain 37.30N 3.21W
81 R11 Torre Cavallo tower Italy 40.38N 18.01E
80 D4 Torre Ciana,Pta.di Italy 42.22N 11.09E
75 K6 Torrecilla de Alcañiz Spain 40.58N 0.06W
76 K9 Torrecilla de la Jara Spain 39.42N 4.46W
76 J6 Torrecilla de la Orden Spain 41.13N 5.13W
76 G8 Torrecilla de los Angeles Spain 40.15N 6.25W
75 E3 Torrecilla en Cameros Spain 42.15N 2.38W
76 H9 Torrecillas de la Tiesa Spain 39.35N 5.44W
76 C11 Torre da Gadanha Portugal 38.34N 8.18W
76 D10 Torre das Vargens Portugal 39.17N 7.57W
75 B9 Torre de Abraham, Embalse de res Spain
76 D12 Torre de Coelheiras Portugal 38.25N 7.50W
76 E5 Torre de Dona Chama Portugal 41.38N 7.07W
76 F8 Torre de Don Miguel Spain 40.14N 6.34W
75 K7 Torre de Embesora Spain 40.20N 0.05W
76 L8 Torre de Esteban Hambrán,La Spain 40.10N 4.14W
76 C7 Torredeita Portugal 40.39N 8.01W
77 K3 Torre de Juan Abad Spain 38.35N 3.04W
77 E6 Torre del Aguila,Embalse res Spain 37.03N 5.45W
75 D6 Torre del Burgo Spain 40.47N 3.05W
77 J5 Torre del Campo Spain 37.46N 3.53W
81 H2 Torre del Greco Italy 40.46N 14.22E
79 F4 Torre del Mangano Italy 45.15N 9.07E
77 H7 Torre del Mar Spain 36.44N 4.06W
75 N5 Torredembarra Spain 41.09N 1.24E
77 C3 Torre de Miguel Sesmero Spain 38.36N 6.48W
76 E6 Tôrre de Moncorvo Portugal 41.10N 7.03W
80 J4 Torre de' Passeri Italy 42.14N 13.56E
79 N3 Torre di Mosto Italy 45.42N 12.43E
81 R12 Torre di Rocca Vecchia ruins Italy 40.17N 18.26E
79 H7 Torre d. Lago Puccini Italy 43.49N 10.17E
77 J5 Torredonjimeno Spain 37.45N 3.58W
76 E7 Torre do Terranho Portugal 40.53N 7.23W
87 K10 Torre,El Somalia 1.23N 44.21E
79 L4 Torréglia Italy 45.20N 11.44E
75 M4 Torregrosa Spain 41.35N 0.50E
81 K7 Torregrotta Sicily 38.12N 15.22E
76 L6 Torreiglesias Spain 41.06N 4.02W
76 G9 Torrejoncillo Spain 39.54N 6.28W
75 D7 Torrejón de Ardoz Spain 40.27N 3.29W
75 C7 Torrejón de la Calzada Spain 40.12N 3.48W
75 D6 Torrejón del Rey Spain 40.38N 3.20W
76 G9 Torrejón el Rubio Spain 39.46N 6.01W
77 E1 Torrejón, Embalse de res Spain
76 K7 Torre,La Spain 40.35N 4.58W
75 H6 Torre la Cárcel Spain 40.36N 1.19W
75 C6 Torrelaguna Spain 40.50N 3.33W
75 G4 Torrelapaja Spain 41.35N 1.57W
76 L2 Torrelavega Spain 43.21N 4.03W
77 P4 Torrellano Spain 38.18N 0.35W
75 G4 Torrellas Spain 41.53N 1.46W
76 J5 Torrelobatón Spain 41.39N 5.02W
75 C6 Torrelodones Spain 40.35N 3.56W
80 M5 Torremaggiore Italy 41.41N 15.17E
80 G3 Torre Maggiore,Monte Italy 42.38N 12.37E
77 Q3 Torremanzanas Spain 38.37N 0.26W
77 C3 Torremayor Spain 38.54N 6.33W
77 D3 Torremegia Spain 38.47N 6.24W
76 G10 Torremocha Spain 39.20N 6.11W
77 H7 Torremolinos Spain 36.38N 4.30W
77 H7 Torremolinos,Pta.de Spain 36.36N 4.30W
75 E2 Torremontalbo Spain 42.30N 2.40W
80 E2 Torrenieri Italy 43.05N 11.33E
12 A6 Torrens dist Canberra Australia
13 H5 Torrens R Queensland
13 H5 Torrens Cr Queensland 20.50S 145.00E
12 A7 Torrens I S Australia
12 E4 Torrens, Lake S Australia
12 B8 Torrens Park dist Adelaide, S Aust
12 B8 Torrens,R S Australia
121 G2 Torrent Argentina 28.46S 56.29W
66 G7 Torrent, Col de pass Switz 46.08N 7.33E
77 Q2 Torrente Spain 39.27N 0.28W
75 L5 Torrente de Cinca Spain 41.28N 0.19E
66 G6 Torrenthorn mt Switzerland 46.23N 7.41E
77 K3 Torrenueva Spain 38.39N 3.22W
115 H5 Torreón Mexico 25.34N 103.25W
76 G10 Torreorgaz Spain 39.23N 6.16W
81 K3 Torre Orsaja Italy 40.07N 15.28E
77 P5 Torre Pacheco Spain 37.45N 0.56W
79 B5 Torre Pellice Italy 44.49N 7.13E
77 K4 Torreperogil Spain 38.02N 3.17W
77 J5 Torrequebradilla Spain 37.55N 3.40W
76 G10 Torrequemada Spain 39.22N 6.14W
121 J2 Torres Brazil 29.20S 49.43W
115 D3 Torres Mexico 28.47N 110.48W
77 J5 Torres Spain 37.47N 3.30W
19 M4 Torres isld Truk Is Pacific Oc 7.20N 151.27E
77 J5 Torres R Spain
75 C4 Torresandino Spain 41.49N 3.55W
79 G2 Torre Santa Maria Italy 46.14N 9.51E
81 Q12 Torre Santa Susanna Italy 40.28N 17.44E
75 E6 Torresaviñán,La Spain 40.59N 2.35W
76 H1 Torres, C Spain 43.34N 5.41W
77 L4 Torres de Albánchez Spain 38.25N 2.40W
88 L4 Torres de Alcala Morocco 35.10N 4.17W
74 E9 Torres de Alealá Morocco 35.07N 4.18W
75 H4 Torres de Berrellén Spain 41.45N 1.04W
76 H5 Torres de Carrizal Spain 41.36N 5.40W
75 M4 Torres de Segre Spain 41.32N 0.31E
9 C9 Torres Is New Hebrides
76 B10 Torres Novas Portugal 39.28N 8.32W
121 J2 Torres Pta,dos C Brazil 29.20S 49.43W
13 F1 Torres Strait Queensland
10 N4 Torres Trench Pacific Oc
76 A10 Torres Vedras Portugal 39.05N 9.15W
80 N7 Torretta,Monte Italy 40.47N 15.50E
76 C13 Torre Va Portugal 37.49N 8.52W
77 P5 Torrevieja Spain 37.59N 0.40W
77 P4 Torrevieja, Salinas de salt pan Spain 38.00N 0.44W
111 N3 Torrey Utah 38.18N 111.25W
80 G4 Torricella in Sabina Italy 42.16N 12.52E
80 K4 Torricella Peligna Italy 42.02N 14.16E
76 F10 Torrico de San Pedro mt Spain 39.25N 6.58W
79 J3 Torri del Benaco Italy 45.37N 10.41E
56 C6 Torridge, R Devon Eng
58 E3 Torridon Highland Scotland 57.33N 5.31W
58 E3 Torridon,L Highland Scotland
58 E3 Torridon, Upper L Highland Scotland
79 F5 Torriglia Italy 44.31N 9.09E
75 J7 Torrijas Spain 40.02N 0.58W
75 G5 Torrijo Spain 41.28N 1.53W
76 L9 Torrijos Spain 39.59N 4.18W
53 E5 Torrild Denmark 55.59N 10.03E
53 A3 Tørring Ringkøbing Denmark 56.35N 8.16E
53 C5 Tørring Vejle Denmark 55.51N 9.29E
100 D7 Torrington Alberta 51.50N 113.32W
103 H3 Torrington Connecticut 41.48N 73.08W
56 C6 Torrington Devon Eng 51.57N 4.09W
12 K3 Torrington New S Wales 29.20S 151.40E
108 F7 Torrington Wyoming 42.05N 104.11W
76 B14 Torrinha Portugal 37.15N 8.32W
57 C1 Torrisdale Strathclyde Scotland 55.34N 5.30W
58 J2 Torrish Lodge Highland Scotland 58.08N 3.45W
80 E2 Torrita di Siena Italy 43.09N 11.46E
76 B12 Torroal Portugal 38.19N 8.44W
13 C1 Tor Rock mt N Terr Australia 11.58S 133.04E
80 K7 Torro del Greco Italy 40.47N 14.23E
75 R3 Torroella de Montgri Spain 42.02N 3.08E
52 G3 Torröjen L Sweden 63.55N 13.10E
66 N6 Torrone d'Orza mt Switzerland 46.21N 9.05E
75 E6 Torronteras Spain 40.34N 2.35W
90 J1 Torros Source Chad 20.56N 18.26E
Torrowangee see Podamacca
77 J7 Torrox Spain 36.46N 3.57W
77 J7 Torrox Pta pt Spain 36.44N 3.57W
75 E8 Torrubia del Campo Spain 39.53N 2.58W
75 F4 Torrubia de Soria Spain 41.39N 2.05W
58 J6 Torryburn Fife Scotland 56.03N 3.38W
52 J6 Torsåker Sweden 60.31N 16.30E
52 K3 Torsåker Sweden 63.07N 17.44E
28 G2 Torsa R Bhutan
52 J10 Torsås Sweden 56.24N 16.00E
53 D7 Tørsbøl Denmark 54.55N 9.31E
52 G4 Torsborg Sweden 62.50N 13.30E
52 G6 Torsby Sweden 60.07N 13.00E
53 X14 Torsdalen V Norway 62.05N 7.45E
52 J7 Torshälla Sweden 59.25N 16.28E
53 W19 Torsheller Norway 59.45N 7.05E
53 E2 Torshøj Denmark 57.21N 10.20E
53 W17 Torskarnuten mt Norway 60.53N 7.25E
51 F2 Torsken Norway 69.20N 17.06E
53 C2 Torslev Denmark 57.05N 9.30E
53 A4 Torsminde Denmark 56.23N 8.08E
53 U18 Torsnes Norway 60.14N 6.13E
53 U16 Torsnesstøl Norway 61.20N 6.26E
53 V18 Torsnut mt Norway 60.16N 6.31E
53 V16 Torstadnakken mt Norway 61.22N 6.56E
53 A4 Torsted Ringkøbing Denmark 56.12N 8.26E
53 D5 Torsted Vejle Denmark 55.50N 9.49E
53 B5 Torstrup Kirke Denmark 55.41N 8.34E
51 H1 Torsvåg Norway 70.15N 19.30E
53 X14 Torsvatn L Norway 62.09N 7.49E
75 H7 Tortajada Spain 40.24N 1.05W
75 Q3 Tortellá Spain 42.14N 2.39E
56 V11 Torteval Channel Is 49.26N 2.38W
57 F2 Torthorwald Dumfries & Galloway Scotland 55.05N 3.32W
43 J5 Tortkol' Kazakhstan U.S.S.R. 42.53N 68.55E
43 L2 Tortkuduk Kazakhstan U.S.S.R. 51.44N 74.14E
98 M2 Tort L.Le Quebec
75 F8 Tórtola Cuenca Spain 39.55N 2.09W
75 D6 Tórtola Guadalajara Spain 40.42N 3.07W
119 H3 Tortola, I Venezuela
105 L7 Tortola I Virgin Is 18.28N 64.40W
121 B2 Tortolas,Cerro las pk Arg/Chile 29.55S 69.55W
76 L5 Tõrtoles de Esgueva Spain 41.49N 4.02W
81 D4 Tortoli Sardinia 39.56N 9.40E
79 E5 Tortona Italy 44.54N 8.52E
81 G8 Torto,R Sicily
81 L4 Tortora Italy 39.57N 15.49E
80 J3 Tortoreto Italy 42.48N 13.56E
81 J7 Tortorici Sicily 38.02N 14.49E
75 M6 Tortosa Spain 40.49N 0.31E
Tortosa castle see Tartūs
75 M6 Tortosa,C.de Spain 40.44N 0.54E
76 D8 Tortosendo Portugal 40.15N 7.31W
116 H4 Tortue, Île de la Haiti 20.05N 72.57W
75 G6 Tortuera Spain 40.58N 1.48W
75 D6 Tortuero Spain 40.56N 3.21W
119 A6 Tortuga, I Galápagos Is 1.00S 90.55W
115 K6 Tortuga, L Mexico
119 C3 Tortuguilla isld Colombia 9.03N 76.28W
37 F5 Tortum Turkey 40.20N 41.36E
37 F5 Tortum Gölü L Turkey
43 M6 Toruaygr Kirgiziya U.S.S.R. 42.29N 76.20E
32 F3 Torūd Iran 35.25N 55.06E
19 B4 Torue Celebes Indonesia 0.58S 120.18E
Torugart Pass see Turugart Shankou
43 M6 Torugart,Pereval pass Kirgiziya/Xinjiang Uygur Zizhiqu 40.30N 75.23E
53 C3 Torum Denmark 56.45N 9.04E
62 L2 Toruń Poland 53.01N 18.35E
52 G10 Torup Sweden 56.57N 13.05E
37 E5 Torut Turkey 40.35N 39.18E
46 F1 Tõrva Estonia U.S.S.R. 58.00N 26.00E
53 S20 Torvastad Norway 59.23N 5.15E
52 H8 Torved Sweden 58.50N 14.05E
57 G4 Torver Cumbria Eng 54.21N 3.06W
53 X13 Torvik Norway 62.33N 7.37E
53 U18 Tørvikbygd Norway 60.19N 6.10E
77 K7 Torviscon Spain 36.52N 3.17W
76 J9 Torviscoso Spain 39.56N 5.27W
53 W14 Torvløysa mt Norway 62.12N 7.17E
52 K2 Torvsjö Sweden 64.22N 17.20E
53 T16 Torvund Norway 61.09N 5.40E
99 M8 Tory Hill Ontario 44.58N 78.18W
59 F1 Tory I Donegal Irish Rep 55.16N 8.13W
59 F1 Tory I.Lt.Ho Donegal Irish Rep 55.16N 8.13W
62 N7 Torysa R Czechoslovakia
59 F1 Tory Sd Donegal Irish Rep 55.14N 8.15W
46 J2 Torzhok U.S.S.R. 57.02N 34.51E
62 J3 Torzym Poland 52.18N 15.05E
20 G8 Tosa Japan 33.29N 133.25E
Tosa Fall see Caso di Frua
92 G5 Tosamaganga Tanzania 7.51S 35.33E
20 F9 Tosa-Shimizu Japan 32.47N 132.58E
20 G8 Tosa-wan B Japan
20 G8 Tosa-Yamada Japan 33.40N 133.40E
89 J3 Tosaye Mali 16.51N 0.33W
95 G1 Tosca S Africa 25.53S 23.58E
58 E4 Toscaig Highland Scotland 57.23N 5.49W
79 J7 Toscana reg Italy
78 C6 Toscano, Arcipelago Italy
115 D5 Tosca,Pta C Mexico 24.20N 111.40W
79 J3 Toscolano Italy 45.38N 10.36E
51 C6 Tosen Norway 65.16N 12.50E
51 C6 Tosenfjord inlet Norway 65.15N 12.40E
65 C7 Tösens Austria 47.02N 10.37E
29 D3 Tosham Haryana India 28.56N 75.58E
20 K7 Tōshi-jima isld Japan
20 E2 Toshima dist Tōkyō Japan
20 N7 To-shima isld Japan 34.32N 139.16E
20 P1 Tōshima-yama mt Japan 40.02N 141.40E
93 N4 Tosilei Somalia 1.26N 41.24E
39 D3 Toskan R U.S.S.R.
36 H1 Tosköy Turkey 41.24N 35.56E
51 P12 Tosna R U.S.S.R.
46 H1 Tosno U.S.S.R. 59.25N 30.40E
22 D8 Toson Hu L Qinghai China
66 L2 Töss Switzerland 47.30N 8.43E
66 M2 Töss R Switzerland
75 O3 Tossa mt Spain 42.20N 1.54E
75 Q4 Tossa, C Spain 41.44N 2.56E
75 Q4 Tossa de Mar Spain 41.43N 2.56E
52 G5 Tossåsen Sweden 62.57N 13.15E
72 B8 Tosse France 43.41N 1.20W
40 J5 Tossi Sakhalin U.S.S.R. 53.16N 143.13E
80 J3 Tossicia Italy 42.33N 13.34E
79 L6 Tossignano Italy 44.17N 11.37E
90 E8 Tosso Cameroon 6.57N 10.14E
121 E2 Tostado Argentina 29.15S 61.45W
76 A2 Tosto,C Spain 43.11N 9.11W
110 O3 Toston Montana 46.10N 111.26W
41 K4 Tostuya U.S.S.R. 73.14N 113.35E
20 D8 Tosu Japan 33.24N 130.29E
36 G1 Tosya Turkey 41.02N 34.02E
62 L5 Toszek Poland 50.27N 18.32E
93 G4 Tot Kenya 1.12N 35.39E
53 X19 Totak L Norway
119 D5 Tota, L Colombia 5.35N 72.56W
19 B5 Totala Celebes Indonesia 2.56S 121.09E
77 O5 Totana Spain 37.46N 1.30W
76 L9 Totanés Spain 39.43N 4.14W
Totapella mt see Totupola
11 F9 Totara Flat New Zealand 42.18S 171.36E
11 H2 Totara North New Zealand 35.03S 173.45E
11 H7 Totaranui New Zealand 40.49S 173.00E
92 B10 Totela,tribe Zambia
52 F6 Toten reg Norway
94 G3 Toteng Botswana 20.25S 23.00E
63 L6 Tötensen W Germany 53.24N 9.55E
70 N2 Tôtes France 49.40N 1.03E
65 J6 Totes Gebirge mts Austria
87 J9 Totias Somalia 3.56N 43.57E
62 M9 Tótkomlós Hungary 46.25N 20.44E
56 H6 Totland I of Wight Eng 50.40N 1.32W
53 S15 Totland Norway 61.56N 5.24E
53 U20 Tøtlandsvik Norway 59.16N 6.20E
57 K6 Totley S Yorks Eng 53.19N 1.32W
47 E6 Tot'ma U.S.S.R. 59.59N 42.44E
56 D7 Totnes Devon Eng 50.25N 3.41W
117 B2 Totness Surinam 5.50N 56.14W
96 S10 Toto Fuerteventura Canary Is 28.17N 14.06W
90 C7 Toto Nigeria 8.26N 7.05E
95 F3 Toto mt S Africa 27.47S 22.40E
115 L9 Totolápan Mexico 16.40N 96.18W
115 O10 Totonicapán Guatemala 14.58N 91.12W
120 F7 Totora Bolivia 17.40S 65.10W
121 B1 Totoral Chile 27.51S 71.05W
121 D2 Totoralejos Argentina 29.35S 64.50W
121 B2 Totoralillo Chile 29.31S 71.19W
89 E8 Totota Liberia 6.50N 10.00W
9 T3 Totoya isld Fiji 18.56S 179.50W
15 B6 Totrean Moluccas Indon 5.51S 132.54E
91 F6 Totshi Zaïre 5.30S 19.18E
46 R3 Totskoye U.S.S.R. 52.32N 52.48E
20 C5 Totsuka Japan 35.24N 139.32E
123 C10 Tottan-fjella ra Antarctica
123 G2 Totten Glacier Antarctica
55 F2 Tottenham London England 51.35N 0.05W
12 H4 Tottenham New S Wales 32.14S 147.24E
99 L8 Tottenham Ontario 44.02N 79.48W
103 J9 Tottenville Staten I, N Y 40.30N 74.15W
55 E2 Totteridge London Eng 51.38N 0.12W
57 J5 Tottington Greater Manchester Eng 53.37N 2.20W
56 N2 Tottington Norfolk Eng 52.31N 0.47E
56 J6 Totton Hants Eng 50.56N 1.29W
20 H6 Tottori Japan 35.32N 134.12E
20 G6 Tottori prefect Japan
26 S8 Totupola mt Sri Lanka 6.51N 80.47E
90 H2 Touaoul watercourse Chad
89 N1 Touaret Niger 20.17N 7.08E
89 C6 Touba Guinea 11.36N 13.00W
89 F7 Touba Ivory Coast 8.22N 7.42W
89 D4 Touba Mali 14.00N 10.40W
89 B4 Touba Senegal 14.51N 15.54W
88 K6 Toubkal mt Morocco 31.03N 7.57W
90 F4 Toubou tribe Chad/Niger
72 G9 Touch R France
123 D10 Touchdown Hills Antarctica
70 H7 Touches,les France 47.27N 1.26W
110 G3 Touchet Washington 46.03N 118.40W
110 G3 Touchet R Washington
100 N7 Touchwood Hills Saskatchewan
71 C1 Toucy France 47.44N 3.18E
21 D6 Toudao Jiang R Jilin China
22 G6 Toudaoqiao Nei Monggol Zizhiqu China 40.36N 107.06E
22 L5 Toufendi Nei Monggol Zizhiqu China 43.05N 118.41E
72 G7 Touffailles France 44.17N 1.03E
88 L9 Toufourine Mali 24.34N 4.45W
89 H5 Tougan Upper Volta 13.06N 3.03W
72 F8 Touget France 43.42N 0.55E
88 R5 Touggourt Algeria 33.08N 6.04E
103 C7 Toughkenamon Pennsylvania 39.50N 75.45W
89 B6 Tougnifili Guinea 10.20N 14.25W
22 C6 Tougong Gansu China 40.28N 95.41E
90 H2 Tougoumma Chad 19.42N 17.46E
89 D6 Tougue Guinea 11.29N 11.48W
89 E2 Touijinet Mauritania 18.19N 9.00W
88 K9 Touila Mauritania 25.55N 6.15W
88 O5 Touilet Makna mt Algeria 33.40N 1.30E
88 R9 Toukmatine mt Algeria 24.48N 7.08E
89 E5 Toukoto Mali 13.27N 9.52W
89 D5 Toukoundia Guinea 12.23N 11.29W
69 K6 Toul France 48.41N 5.54E
89 E8 Toulépleu Ivory Coast 6.37N 8.27W
23 J7 Tou-lin Taiwan 23.42N 120.32E
70 A5 Toulinguet,Pte,du France 48.17N 4.38W
98 E3 Toulnustouc R Quebec
76 E9 Toulões Portugal 39.56N 7.02W
106 E8 Toulon Illinois 41.05N 89.54W
110 G9 Toulon Nevada 40.04N 118.38W
71 H10 Toulon Var France 43.07N 5.55E
72 L2 Toulon-sur-Allier France 46.32N 3.22E
71 E3 Toulon-sur-Arroux France 46.41N 4.08E
71 G9 Touloubre R France
72 K10 Toulouges France 42.40N 2.50E
72 G8 Toulouse France 43.37N 1.27E
89 D4 Toumba Oumou Mauritania 15.35N 11.05W
89 F7 Toumbougou Ivory Coast 9.37N 6.34W
85 C8 Toummo Libya/Niger 22.35N 14.10E
85 C8 Toummo,Mts.of Libya
89 G8 Toumodi Ivory Coast 6.34N 5.01W
89 G6 Toumou Mali 11.49N 5.23W
90 K5 Toumtouna Chad 13.41N 22.00E
89 G5 Touna Mali 13.04N 5.51W
23 J7 Tou-nan Taiwan 23.39N 120.28E
88 L7 Tounassine Algeria 28.20N 4.45W
90 F7 Toungo Nigeria 8.20N 12.03E
25 D3 Toungoo Burma 18.57N 96.26E
89 C6 Tountourou Guinea 11.28N 12.12W
89 G9 Toupah Ivory Coast 5.17N 4.34W
70 L3 Touques France 49.21N 0.08E
70 L3 Touques R France
69 E6 Touquin France 48.44N 3.01E
67 F5 Touraine prov France
25 G3 Tourakom Laos 18.25N 102.31E
Tourane see Da Nang
26 N13 Tourbières marsh Amsterdam I Ind Oc
72 E5 Tour Blanche, la France 45.22N 0.28E
70 C5 Tourch France 48.02N 3.50W
69 E2 Tourcoing France 50.44N 3.10E
66 E6 Tour d'Ai mt Switzerland 46.23N 7.01E
71 H9 Tour-d'Aigues France 43.43N 5.33E
66 D6 Tour de Peilz,la Switzerland 46.28N 6.52E
66 E5 Tour de Trême,la Switzerland 46.37N 7.04E
71 G5 Tour-du-Pin,la France 45.34N 5.26E
89 H4 Touré Mali 14.55N 3.09W
76 D5 Tourem Portugal 41.54N 7.54W
71 J10 Tour-Fondue,la France 43.01N 6.10E
101 U3 Tourgis L N W Terr
66 D8 Tour, Glacier du France
76 A2 Touriñán, C Spain 43.04N 9.19W
88 H10 Tourine Mauritania 22.23N 11.50W
61 K3 Tourinnes-la-Grosse Belgium 50.47N 4.45E
61 J4 Tourinnes-St.-Lambert Belgium 50.38N 4.43E
70 G2 Tourlaville France 49.38N 1.34W
72 E10 Tourmalet,Col du pass France 42.54N 0.09E
61 D4 Tournai Belgium 50.36N 3.24E
66 G8 Tournanche,Valle Italy
69 D6 Tournan-en-Brie France 48.44N 2.46E
120 C3 Tournavista Peru 8.53S 74.44W
61 M7 Tournay Belgium 49.52N 5.24E
72 E9 Tournay France 43.10N 0.16E
72 F8 Tournecoupe France 43.52N 0.49E
72 L8 Tournemire France 43.58N 3.01E
66 B8 Tournette, la mt France 45.50N 6.16E
71 F6 Tournon Ardèche France 45.05N 4.49E
72 G7 Tournon d'Agenais France 44.24N 1.00E
72 F2 Tournon-St.Martin Indre-et-Loire France 46.45N 0.57E
71 F3 Tournus France 46.33N 4.55E
70 O3 Tourny France 49.12N 1.33E
76 D7 Touro Portugal 40.53N 7.46W
76 C3 Touro Spain 42.52N 8.18W
76 F7 Tourões R Spain/Portugal
121 G2 Touro Passo Brazil 29.40S 56.50W
117 J7 Touros Brazil 5.10S 35.29W
90 F7 Touroua Cameroon 9.05N 12.59E
70 M4 Tourouvre France 48.36N 0.40E
61 E4 Tourpes Belgium 50.34N 3.39E
71 L9 Tourrette-sur-Loup France 43.43N 7.03E
70 M7 Tours France 47.23N 0.42E
72 E1 Tour-St. Gélin, la France 47.03N 0.25E
66 D7 Tour Sallière mt Switzerland 46.08N 6.55E
71 D5 Tours-sur-Meymont France 45.40N 3.34E
71 C9 Tour-sur-Orb,la France 43.39N 3.09E
69 H4 Tourteron France 49.32N 4.39E
72 G5 Tourtoirac France 45.16N 1.04E
71 H10 Tourves France 43.25N 5.55E
98 B6 Tourville Quebec 47.05N 70.00W
70 N3 Tourville-la-Rivière France 49.20N 1.07E
70 L2 Tourville-les-Ifs France 49.42N 0.24E
70 O5 Toury France 48.11N 1.56E
77 P2 Tous Spain 39.10N 0.40W
75 J9 Tous,Embalse de res Spain
90 H1 Toussidé,Pic mt Chad 21.04N 16.29E
69 C7 Tousson France 48.21N 2.27E
71 J6 Toussuire, la France 45.16N 6.17E
10 B11 Toutcher, C Macquarie I Pacific Oc 54.41S 158.50E
91 H1 Touté Cent Afr Rep 4.11N 22.01E
69 C3 Toutencourt France 50.02N 2.27E
100 S7 Toutes Aides Manitoba 51.32N 99.31W
110 C3 Toutle Washington 46.20N 122.40W
71 H6 Touvet,le France 45.22N 5.58E
72 A2 Touvois France 46.55N 1.40W
95 E9 Touws R S Africa
95 D9 Touwsrivier S Africa 33.20S 20.02E
88 G11 Touyerma Mauritania 20.36N 13.25W
85 E8 Touzaugou Libya 22.24N 19.28E
64 O3 Toužím Czechoslovakia 50.03N 12.59E
22 G2 Töv prov Mongolia
119 E3 Tovar Venezuela 8.22N 71.50W
45 K3 Tovarkovskiy U.S.S.R. 53.41N 38.14E
52 D8 Tovdal Norway 58.47N 8.15E
52 D8 Tovdalselv R Norway
48 S12 Tovqussaq Greenland 64.55N 52.15W
20 O1 Towada-Hachimantai Nat. Park Japan
20 O1 Towada ko L Japan
Towa Dzong see Lhozhag
11 J2 Towai New Zealand 35.29S 174.10E
11 D5 Towai hill New Zealand 41.14S 174.56E
119 J4 Towakaima Guyana 7.16N 59.59W
34 M3 Towakal Iraq 35.43N 44.53E
12 J6 Towamba New S Wales 37.09S 149.43E
106 F9 Towanda Illinois 40.34N 88.54W
109 N4 Towanda Kansas 37.48N 97.02W
103 B3 Towanda Pennsylvania 41.46N 76.27W
103 A3 Towanda R Pennsylvania
19 B6 Towari Celebes Indon 4.38S 121.31E
56 K3 Towcester Northants Eng 52.08N 1.00W
108 S2 Tower Minnesota 47.47N 92.19W
108 N3 Tower City N Dakota 46.57N 97.40W
103 A5 Tower City Pennsylvania 40.36N 76.34W
55 G3 Tower Hamlets bor London Eng 51.32N 0.02W
107 H2 Tower Hill Illinois 39.23N 88.58W
13 G5 Tower Hill Queensland 22.00S 144.01E
13 G5 Towerhill R Queensland
Tower I see Genovesa, I.
110 P5 Tower Junction Wyoming 44.55N 110.24W
11 A12 Towing Hd New Zealand 45.24S 166.46E
57 K3 Towlaw Durham Eng 54.45N 1.49W
11 L13 Town Belt dist Dunedin New Zealand
109 H3 Towner Colorado 38.27N 102.06W
108 K1 Towner N Dakota 48.20N 100.24W
103 G4 Towners New York 41.28N 73.36W
111 G5 Townes Pass California 36.25N 117.16W
107 J8 Townley Alabama 33.48N 87.25W
103 C8 Town Point Maryland 39.29N 75.55W
103 C8 Townsend Delaware 39.24N 75.42W
105 F6 Townsend Georgia 31.32N 81.32W
110 O3 Townsend Montana 46.20N 111.30W
105 D2 Townsend Tennessee 35.41N 83.47W
106 F4 Townsend Wisconsin 45.21N 88.35W
12 J6 Townsend,Mt New S Wales 36.24S 148.15E
13 K5 Townshend,C Queensland 22.10S 150.30E
13 K5 Townshend I Queensland 22.15S 150.32E
13 D3 Towns R N Terr Australia
13 H4 Townsville Queensland 19.13S 146.48E
104 F5 Townville Pennsylvania 41.42N 79.54W
87 E7 Towot Sudan 6.10N 34.25E
31 B3 Towraghondi Afghanistan 35.14N 62.16E
12 M8 Towra Pt New S Wales 34.00S 151.10E
103 A8 Towson Maryland 39.25N 76.36W
19 B5 Towuti,Danau L Celebes Indon
Towyn see Tywyn
56 C4 Towy,R Dyfed Wales
34 Q3 Towzlū Iran 35.38N 48.36E
105 D2 Toxaway,L N Carolina
24 C5 Toxkan He R Xinjiang Uygur Zizhiqu China
59 L3 Toy Down N Ireland 54.26N 5.40W
112 D4 Toyah Texas 31.19N 103.48W
112 D4 Toyah L Texas
20 K2 Tōya-ko L Japan
20 L5 Toyama Japan 36.42N 137.14E
20 L5 Toyama prefect Japan
20 L5 Toyama wan B Japan
39 M2 Toygunen U.S.S.R. 67.04N 173.50W
20 L7 Toyo R Japan
20 B3 Toyoda Tōkyō Japan
20 G7 Toyohama Japan 34.04N 133.38E
20 L7 Toyohashi Japan 34.46N 137.22E
20 L7 Toyokawa Japan 34.47N 137.24E
20 J7 Toyonaka Japan 34.48N 135.35E
41 O8 Toyon-Tirekh U.S.S.R. 65.00N 130.33E
20 H6 Toyooka Japan 35.35N 134.48E
20 N4 Toyosaka Japan 37.55N 139.13E
20 L6 Toyota Japan 35.05N 137.09E
51 K9 Töysä Finland 62.38N 23.50E
75 K3 Tozal de Guara mt Spain 42.18N 0.14W
75 N3 Tozal del Orri mt Spain 42.25N 1.12E
Tozanlı see Almus
88 S5 Tozeur Tunisia 33.55N 8.07E
113 L4 Tozitna R Alaska
76 H9 Tozo R Spain
44 H6 Tpig U.S.S.R. 41.47N 47.36E
76 E2 Trabada Spain 43.25N 7.11W
76 F3 Trabadelo Spain 42.39N 6.53W
76 G6 Trabanca Spain 41.14N 6.23W
76 J7 Trabancos R Spain
79 M7 Trabaria,Bocca pass Italy 43.36N 12.13E
76 G5 Trabazos Spain 41.45N 6.29W
64 C4 Traben-Trarbach W Germany 49.57N 7.07E
81 G8 Trabia Sicily 37.59N 13.39E
81 A1 Trabucato,Pta Sardinia 41.03N 8.20E
37 E4 Trabzon Turkey 41.00N 39.43E
98 H6 Tracadie New Brunswick 47.32N 64.57W
98 L8 Tracadie Nova Scotia 45.38N 61.40W
98 F8 Tracey New Brunswick 45.41N 66.42W
66 H5 Trachsellauenen Switzerland 46.32N 7.55E
66 G3 Trachselwald Switzerland 47.01N 7.45E
81 E9 Tracino, Pta Pantelleria I Italy 36.48N 12.03E
25 J8 Tra Cu Vietnam 9.42N 106.18E
111 C4 Tracy California 37.43N 121.27W
71 B2 Tracy France 47.19N 2.53E
108 S8 Tracy Iowa 41.16N 92.52W
108 P5 Tracy Minnesota 44.15N 95.38W
107 L6 Tracy City Tennessee 35.15N 85.45W
69 E5 Tracy-le-Mont France 49.28N 3.01E
79 E3 Tradate Italy 45.43N 8.54E
100 O3 Trade L Saskatchewan
52 H9 Trädet Sweden 57.59N 13.33E
89 E9 Trade Town Liberia 5.42N 9.50W
107 J4 Tradewater R Kentucky
Tradom see Zhongba
108 S7 Traer Iowa 42.10N 92.28W
109 K2 Traer Kansas 39.56N 100.41W
77 D8 Trafalgar,C Spain 36.11N 6.02W
76 A11 Trafaria Portugal 38.40N 9.14W
66 L7 Traffiume Italy 46.03N 8.41E
107 K8 Trafford Alabama 33.47N 86.45W
105 F11 Trafford, L Florida 26.25N 81.30W
79 J1 Trafoi Italy 46.33N 10.31E
121 B8 Traful R Argentina
121 B8 Traful, L Argentina
75 G7 Tragacete Spain 40.21N 1.51W
84 B6 Traganon Greece 37.52N 21.20E
85 C7 Trāghan Libya 25.59N 14.26E
65 M6 Tragöss Oberort Austria 47.33N 15.05E
65 L5 Tragwein Austria 48.20N 14.38E
11 C2 Traherne I Auckland New Zealand
82 L4 Traian Romania 46.36N 27.07E
82 L5 Traian Romania 45.10N 27.46E
75 G6 Traid Spain 40.40N 1.50W
Traighli see Tralee
121 A7 Traiguén Chile 38.15S 72.45W
121 J5 Traiguén, L Chile 45.40S 73.45W
75 L6 Traiguera Spain 40.32N 0.17E
101 P11 Trail Br Col 49.04N 117.39W
110 C7 Trail Oregon 42.40N 122.50W
108 K4 Trail City S Dakota 45.27N 100.43W
50 O10 Traill,Kapp Jan Mayen I Arctic Oc 70.54N 8.45W
48 U10 Traill Ø isld Greenland
69 E7 Trainel France 48.25N 3.26E
14 D6 Trainor Hills W Australia
101 N5 Trainor L N W Terr 60.23N 120.18W
69 C8 Trainou France 47.58N 2.05E
70 P6 Traînou France 47.59N 2.06E
117 H9 Traipu Brazil 9.56S 37.00W
119 E8 Traíra, R Colombia/Brazil
117 G6 Trairi Brazil 3.18S 39.18W
117 J8 Trairí R Brazil
65 N5 Traisen Austria 48.03N 15.37E
65 N5 Traisen R Austria
65 M6 Traisenberg mt Austria 47.52N 15.29E
65 O5 Traiskirchen Austria 48.01N 16.18E
65 N5 Traismauer Austria 48.22N 15.46E
70 M3 Trait,le France 49.29N 0.47E
64 O5 Traitsching W Germany 49.10N 12.40E
95 F9 Traka R S Africa
46 E3 Trakai Lithuania U.S.S.R. 54.38N 24.52E
84 D6 Trakhi Óros mts Greece
47 G4 Trakt U.S.S.R. 62.40N 51.26E
107 F8 Tralake Mississippi 33.16N 90.40W
59 C7 Tralee Kerry Irish Rep 52.16N 9.42W
59 C7 Tralee B Kerry Irish Rep 52.15N 9.55W
75 G7 Tramacastilla Spain 40.25N 1.35W
76 C10 Tramagal Portugal 39.26N 8.13W
121 J2 Tramandai Brazil 29.58S 50.06W
119 H5 Tramán Tepuí mt Venezuela 5.39N 62.36W
71 F4 Tramayes France 46.18N 4.35E
25 K7 Tram Bo Vietnam 11.59N 108.34E
66 E3 Tramelan Switzerland 47.13N 7.07E
72 E10 Tramezaygues France 42.47N 0.17E
25 H7 Tram Kak Cambodia 10.54N 104.40E
25 H7 Tram Khnar Cambodia 11.15N 104.50E
81 B2 Tramontana Pta Sardinia 40.53N 8.38E
79 N2 Tramonti di Sopra Italy 46.19N 12.47E
79 N2 Tramonti di Sotto Italy 46.17N 12.48E
59 H7 Tramore Waterford Irish Rep 52.10N 7.10W
59 H7 Tramore B Waterford Irish Rep 52.08N 7.08W
100 J6 Tramping Lake Saskatchewan 52.10N 108.57W
81 L3 Tramutola Italy 40.18N 15.48E
79 B4 Trana Italy 45.02N 7.25E
25 N6 Trana Xizang Zizhiqu 28.30N 98.30E
52 J8 Tranås Sweden 58.03N 15.00E
53 E4 Tranbjerg Denmark 56.06N 10.09E
76 E15 Trancão,R Portugal
120 F12 Trancas Argentina 26.11S 65.20W
69 F7 Trancault France 48.22N 3.33E
72 B3 Tranche-sur-Mer,la France 46.21N 1.26W
77 L4 Tranco de Beas,Embalse de el L Spain 38.07N 2.46W
77 L4 Tranco,El reg Spain
118 H5 Trancoso Brazil 16.36S 39.08W
76 E7 Trancoso Portugal 40.46N 7.21W
53 V14 Trandal Norway 62.16N 6.30E
53 E7 Tranderup Denmark 54.53N 10.23E
35 G1 Trâne L Syria 33.14N 35.46E
53 F5 Tranebjerg Denmark 55.50N 10.36E
53 F7 Tranekær Denmark 55.00N 10.51E
52 G9 Tranemo Sweden 57.30N 13.20E
58 L7 Tranent Lothian Scotland 55.57N 2.57W
25 E9 Trang Thailand 7.30N 99.18E
95 B5 Trangahy Madagascar 19.05S 44.31E
15 C7 Trangan isld Moluccas Indon
12 J4 Trangie New S Wales 32.03S 148.01E
53 N10 Trangisvåg Faeroes 61.34N 6.50W
53 N10 Trangisvåg Fjord Faeroes 61.32N 6.45W
80 O6 Trani Italy 41.17N 16.25E
69 H7 Trannes France 48.18N 4.35E
95 C8 Tranomaro Madagascar 24.35S 46.28E
95 B8 Tranoroa Madagascar 24.42S 45.05E
95 B8 Tranovaho Madagascar 25.18S 44.58E
51 F2 Tranøy Norway 69.08N 17.25E
28 D5 Tranquebar Tamil Nadu India 11.04N 79.50E
75 G5 Tranquera,Embalse de la res Spain 41.14N 1.47W
121 G3 Tranqueras Uruguay 31.13S 55.45W
111 D5 Tranquillity California 36.39N 120.17W
120 F10 Tranquitos Argentina 22.40S 63.52W
70 G4 Trans France 48.30N 1.35W
70 G5 Trans Ille-et-Vilaine France 48.30N 1.35W
123 F9 Transantarctic Mts Antarctica
100 V9 Transcona Manitoba 49.55N 97.00W
71 J9 Trans-en-Provence Var France 43.30N 6.30E
61 L7 Transinne Belgium 50.00N 5.12E
95 M7 Transkei Bantu Homeland S Africa
93 F5 Trans-Nzoia dist Kenya
52 G5 Transtrand Kopparberg Sweden 61.06N 13.20E
52 G6 Transtrand Värmland Sweden 60.34N 13.05E
94 J5 Transvaal prov S Africa
26 B14 Transvaal Cove Marion I Ind Oc
82 J4 Transylvania old prov Romania
Transylvanian Alps see Carpaţii Meridionali Munţii mts
58 J2 Trantlebeg Highland Scotland 58.27N 3.53W
53 C2 Tranum Denmark 57.08N 9.29E
18 B8 Tranum Pen Malaysia 3.44N 101.51E
53 C2 Tranum Strand coast Denmark
25 H8 Tra On Vietnam 9.58N 105.58E
79 G2 Traona Italy 46.09N 9.32E
81 E7 Trápani Sicily 38.02N 12.32E
81 E8 Trápani prov Sicily
30 C1 Trape R Xizang Zizhiqu
Trapezus anc site see Trabzon
79 C6 Trappa Italy 44.11N 7.59E
104 J8 Trappe Maryland 38.40N 76.04W
103 D6 Trappe Pennsylvania 40.13N 75.30W
110 L4 Trapper Pk Montana 45.55N 114.19W
68 A4 Trappes France 48.47N 2.00E
95 K9 Trappes Valley S Africa 33.27S 26.53E
121 H3 Trapua R Brazil
57 G1 Traquair Borders Scotland 55.36N 3.05W
12 H7 Traralgon Victoria 38.12S 146.32E
74 F9 Traras,Mts.des Algeria
52 H10 Traryd Sweden 56.35N 13.45E
89 B3 Trarza reg Mauritania
18 B8 Tras Pen Malaysia 3.45N 101.47E
80 J5 Trasacco Italy 41.57N 13.33E
79 O2 Trasaghis Italy 46.18N 13.04E
28 G1 Trashigang Xizang Zizhiqu 29.18N 88.09E
30 F3 Trashi Labtsa pass Nepal 27.52N 86.35E
77 E4 Trasierra Spain 38.11N 5.59W
80 F2 Trasimeno, Lago L Italy
51 H6 Träskholm Sweden 65.14N 20.05E
107 D7 Traskwood Arkansas 34.24N 92.41W
76 H8 Tras la Sierra mts Spain
75 D1 Traslavina Spain 43.14N 3.13W
76 D4 Trasmiras Spain 42.02N 7.37W
75 G4 Trasobares Spain 41.39N 1.39W
76 D5 Trás-os-Montes hist reg Portugal
74 C3 Trás os Montes e Alto Douro prov Portugal
76 D2 Trasparga Spain 43.11N 7.50W
66 J7 Trasquera Italy 46.13N 8.14E
64 B4 Trassem W Germany 49.35N 6.32E
79 H6 Trassilico Italy 44.02N 10.24E
25 G6 Trat Thailand 12.16N 102.30E
81 B5 Tratalias Sardinia 39.06N 8.34E
81 D3 Trattasu,Mte Sardinia 40.04N 9.43E
66 E1 Traubach-le-Bas France 47.39N 7.05E
66 E1 Traubach-le-Haut France 47.41N 7.05E
65 K5 Traun Austria 48.14N 14.15E
65 J6 Traun R Austria
106 H3 Traunik Michigan 46.16N 86.59W
65 J6 Traunkirchen Austria 47.48N 13.48E
65 G6 Traunreut W Germany 47.58N 12.33E
65 J6 Traunsee L Austria
65 M5 Traunstein Austria 48.27N 15.08E
64 O8 Traunstein W Germany 47.52N 12.39E
65 J6 Traunstein mt Austria 47.53N 13.51E
41 H3 Trautfetter R U.S.S.R.
79 H3 Travagliato Italy 45.31N 10.05E
101 H2 Travaillant L N W Terr 67.40N 131.48W
76 C8 Travanca Portugal 40.19N 8.11W
63 N5 Trave R W Germany
96 B11 Traveller's Hill Ascension I 7.57S 14.23W
12 F5 Travellers L New S Wales
105 E3 Travellers Rest S Carolina 34.58N 82.27W
63 N5 Travemünde W Germany 53.57N 10.53E
63 M5 Travenberg W Germany 53.52N 10.25E
100 E8 Travers Alberta 50.18N 112.30W
66 C4 Travers Switzerland 46.56N 6.40E
123 A14 Traversay Is S Sandwich Is Atlantic Oc
106 J4 Traverse B,Grand Michigan
106 J4 Traverse B.,Little Michigan
106 J5 Traverse City Michigan 44.46N 85.38W
121 G9 Traverse Is S Sandwich Is Atl Oc
108 O4 Traverse,L S Dakota
113 H4 Traverse Pk Alaska 65.10N 159.19W
79 H5 Traversetolo Italy 44.38N 10.23E
71 L7 Traversette,Col de la pass France/Italy 44.43N 7.03E
98 B5 Travers,L Quebec 48.45N 70.35W
11 G9 Travers, Mt New Zealand 42.01S 172.47E
66 C4 Travers, Val de Switzerland
66 N5 Travesasch Switzerland 46.40N 9.13E
121 C5 Travesia Puntana reg Argentina
121 C4 Travesia Tunuyán reg Argentina
103 K8 Travis Staten I, N Y 40.35N 74.12W
112 J5 Travis,L Texas
39 G4 Travka U.S.S.R. 61.56N 160.30E
82 D6 Travnik Yugoslavia 44.13N 17.40E
42 B5 Travnoye U.S.S.R. 54.14N 79.39E
79 G5 Travo Italy 44.52N 9.33E
67 P13 Travo R Corsica
57 J5 Trawden Lancs Eng 53.51N 2.08W
112 N4 Trawick Texas 31.47N 94.44W
57 F7 Trawsfynydd Gwynedd Wales 52.54N 3.55W
71 K10 Trayas,Le France 43.28N 6.55E
121 C8 Trayén Niyeu Argentina 41.10S 68.26W
14 C9 Trayning W Australia 31.09S 117.16E
61 H5 Trazegnies Belgium 50.28N 4.20E
76 B3 Trazo Spain 43.00N 8.30W
81 P11 Trazzonara,Mte Italy 40.37N 17.24E
82 C4 Trbovlje Yugoslavia 46.10N 15.02E
103 D2 Treadwell New York 42.20N 75.03W
57 D6 Tre-Arddur B Gwynedd Wales 53.16N 4.40W
116 J2 Treasure Beach Jamaica, W I 17.53N 77.45W
111 B8 Treasure I California 37.50N 122.22W
15 J2 Treasury Is Solomon Is
113 J4 Treat I Alaska 66.00N 156.00W
63 U8 Trebatsch E Germany 52.05N 14.10E
79 F5 Trebbia R Italy
63 S8 Trebbin E Germany 52.13N 13.13E
63 O7 Trebel W Germany 52.59N 11.20E
63 R5 Trebel R E Germany
65 N3 Třebelovice Czechoslovakia 49.02N 15.41E
72 J9 Trèbes France 43.12N 2.26E
70 C4 Trébeurden France 48.46N 3.34W
65 N3 Třebíč Czechoslovakia 49.14N 15.53E
82 E8 Trebinje Yugoslavia 42.44N 18.20E
81 N4 Trebisacce Italy 39.52N 16.32E
82 E8 Trebišnica R Yugoslavia
62 N7 Trebišov Czechoslovakia 48.39N 21.40E
82 D7 Trebižat R Yugoslavia
Trebizond see Trabzon
65 K3 Třebkov Czechoslovakia 49.21N 14.03E
11 A13 Treble Mt New Zealand 46.01S 166.42E
63 U7 Trebnitz E Germany 52.32N 14.14E
82 C5 Trebnje Yugoslavia 45.55N 15.01E
65 L3 Třeboň Czechoslovakia 49.01N 14.45E
70 B5 Tréboul France 48.06N 4.22W
65 O2 Třebovice Czechoslovakia 49.53N 16.29E
70 D5 Trébrivan France 48.18N 3.28W
64 O1 Trebsen E Germany 51.18N 12.45E
77 D7 Trebujena Spain 36.52N 6.11W
65 P2 Třebůrka R Czechoslovakia
81 K8 Trecastagni Sicily 37.37N 15.05E
56 D4 Trecastle Powys Wales 51.58N 3.38W
79 E4 Trecate Italy 45.26N 8.44E
79 K4 Trecenta Italy 45.02N 11.28E
109 B7 Trechado New Mexico 34.35N 108.25W
56 E4 Tredegar Gwent Wales 51.47N 3.16W
79 J3 Tredici Comuni reg Italy
56 H3 Tredington Warwicks Eng 52.06N 1.37W
70 E6 Trédion France 47.47N 2.35W
79 L6 Tredozio Italy 44.04N 11.45E
70 C4 Trédrez France 48.42N 3.34W
60 T17 Treebeek Netherlands 50.56N 5.56E
27 L7 Tree I Laccadive Is Ind Oc 11.28N 72.15E
25 M4 Tree I Paracel Islands S China Sea
56 S9 Treen Cornwall Eng 50.02N 5.39W
63 K4 Treene R W Germany
101 R2 Tree R N W Terr
65 J8 Treffen Austria 46.42N 13.52E
70 G6 Treffieux France 47.37N 1.32W
71 G4 Treffort France 46.16N 5.22E
64 J1 Treffurt E Germany 51.08N 10.15E
81 H8 Trefinaite, Serra delle mt Sicily 37.57N 14.24E
57 G6 Trefnant Clwyd Wales 53.13N 3.25W
57 F6 Trefriw Gwynedd Wales 53.09N 3.49W
56 D3 Tregaron Dyfed Wales 52.13N 3.55W
100 N8 Tregarva Saskatchewan 50.38N 104.46W
70 C4 Trégastel France 48.49N 3.30W
70 C4 Trégastel-Primel France 48.43N 3.49W
79 K3 Tregnago Italy 45.31N 11.10E
110 L1 Trego Montana 48.43N 114.53W
110 F9 Trego Nevada 40.47N 119.10W
106 C4 Trego Wisconsin 45.54N 91.49W
56 B7 Tregony Cornwall Eng 50.16N 4.55W
70 D4 Trégorrois reg France
13 K4 Tregosse Islets & Reefs Gt Barrier Reef Australia
70 D4 Treguier France 48.47N 3.14W
70 C6 Trégunc France 47.51N 3.52W
100 T9 Treherne Manitoba 49.39N 98.41W
25 H8 Tre, Hon isld Vietnam 9.59N 104.50E
25 K6 Tre, Hon islds Vietnam 12.14N 109.18E
52 L3 Trehönningsjö Sweden 63.42N 18.50E
70 B5 Tréhou, le France 48.23N 4.09W
80 H2 Tréia Italy 43.18N 13.19E
63 K3 Treia W Germany 54.32N 9.19E
66 L4 Treib Switzerland 46.59N 8.36E
65 K8 Treibach Austria 46.53N 14.28E
58 G5 Treig, L Highland Scotland 56.48N 4.44W
72 H4 Treignac France 45.32N 1.47E
72 J3 Treignat France 46.21N 2.20E
61 J6 Treignes Belgium 50.06N 4.40E
71 C1 Treigny France 47.33N 3.11E
70 G7 Treillières France 47.20N 1.37W
121 G4 Treinta-y-Tres Uruguay 33.16S 54.17W
121 G4 Treinta-y-Tres dept Uruguay
28 J8 Treis I Nicobar Is Ind Oc 7.28N 93.33E
64 C3 Treis-Karden W Germany 50.11N 7.18E
47 M4 Treka U.S.S.R. 57.09N 59.30E
13 E5 Trekelano Queensland 21.32S 139.50E
50 S14 Tre Kroner mt Spitsbergen 78.52N 13.15E
50 D3 Trékyllisheidhi heath Iceland
50 D2 Trékyllisvík inlet Iceland
66 D8 Tre la Tête mt France/Italy 45.48N 6.48E
92 E10 Trelawney Zimbabwe 17.30S 30.30E
116 J1 Trelawney parish Jamaica, W I
70 K7 Trélazé France 47.27N 0.28W
63 L6 Trelde W Germany 53.19N 9.48E
53 D5 Trelde Næs C Denmark 55.38N 9.53E
121 D9 Trelew Argentina 43.13S 65.15W
66 A6 Trélex Switzerland 46.26N 6.13E
52 G11 Trelleborg Sweden 55.22N 13.10E
56 F4 Trellech Gwent Wales 51.46N 2.43W
69 G3 Trélon France 50.04N 4.06E

69 F5 **Tréloup** France 49.05N 3.37E
57 E7 **Tremadoc** Gwynedd **Wales** 52.56N 4.09W
56 C2 **Tremadog B** Gwynedd **Wales**
72 B4 **Tremblade, la** France 45.46N 1.08W
70 H5 **Tremblay** France 48.26N 1.28W
68 H2 **Tremblay-les-Gonesse** France 48.58N 2.34E
70 N4 **Tremblay-les-Villages** France 48.37N 1.24E
26 V16 **Tremblet** Réunion **Ind Oc** 21.18S 55.48E
101 L8 **Trembleur L** Br Col
61 J3 **Tremelo** Belgium 50.59N 4.42E
109 F6 **Trementina** New Mexico 35.28N 104.27W
72 C1 **Trémentines** France 47.09N 0.46W
64 K3 **Tremersdorf** W Germany 50.21N 10.57E
76 B10 **Tremês** Portugal 39.21N 8.45W
66 N8 **Tremezzo** Italy 45.59N 9.14E
80 N4 **Tremiti** Italy 42.07N 13.32E
80 M4 **Tremiti, I, di** Italy 42.07N 15.30E
66 Q6 **Tremoggia, Piz** *mt* Switzerland 46.22N 9.49E
106 E9 **Tremont** Illinois 40.33N 89.30W
107 H7 **Tremont** Mississippi 34.13N 88.15W
103 B5 **Tremont** Pennsylvania 40.38N 76.22W
110 N8 **Tremonton** Utah 41.43N 112.10W
70 F5 **Trémorel** France 48.12N 2.17W
79 J3 **Tremósine Pieve** Italy 45.48N 10.45E
64 P4 **Třemošná** Czechoslovakia 49.50N 13.25E
72 K7 **Trémouilles** France 44.15N 2.37E
75 M3 **Tremp** Spain 42.10N 0.54E
106 C5 **Trempealeau** Wisconsin 44.01N 91.27W
106 C5 **Trempealeau** *R* Wisconsin
63 M5 **Tremsbüttel** W Germany 53.44N 10.19E
65 J2 **Třemšín** *mt* Czechoslovakia 49.34N 13.46E
25 H8 **Trem Trem** *R* Vietnam
106 H3 **Trenary** Michigan 46.13N 86.59W
99 S5 **Trenche** *R* Quebec
62 L7 **Trenčín** Czechoslovakia 48.53N 18.00E
53 C3 **Trend Å** *R* Denmark
63 K9 **Trendelburg** W Germany 51.34N 9.23E
121 D5 **Trenel** Argentina 35.42S 64.08W
53 T18 **Trengereid** Norway 60.26N 5.37E
18 J10 **Trenggalek** Java Indon 8.01S 111.38E
Trengganu *R see* **Terengganu** *R*
Trengganu *state see* **Terengganu** *state*
79 E7 **Trenno** *dist* Milan Italy
121 E5 **Trenque Lauquén** Argentina 35.56S 62.43W
72 C7 **Trensacq** France 44.13N 0.44W
Trent *see* **Trento**
63 S3 **Trent** E Germany 54.32N 13.16E
112 G3 **Trent** Texas 32.30N 100.07W
66 D7 **Trent** *R* France/Switz
99 L8 **Trent Can** Ontario
72 F7 **Trentels** France 44.27N 0.52E
57 J7 **Trentham** Staffs Eng 52.58N 2.12W
79 J2 **Trentino** *reg* Italy
56 J2 **Trent Junction** Derbys Eng 52.53N 1.16W
79 K2 **Trento** Italy 46.04N 11.08E
79 J2 **Trento** *prov* Italy
80 K7 **Tréntola** Italy 40.58N 14.10E
105 E8 **Trenton** Florida 29.37N 82.50W
106 L7 **Trenton** Michigan 42.05N 83.06W
107 C1 **Trenton** Missouri 40.04N 93.37W
108 G1 **Trenton** N Dakota 48.06N 103.50W
108 J9 **Trenton** Nebraska 40.11N 101.01W
103 E6 **Trenton** New Jersey 40.15N 74.43W
104 K3 **Trenton** New York 43.17N 75.13W
98 K8 **Trenton** Nova Scotia 45.37N 62.38W
104 A7 **Trenton** Ohio 39.29N 84.27W
99 N8 **Trenton** Ontario 44.07N 77.34W
105 F4 **Trenton** S Carolina 33.44N 81.51W
107 H6 **Trenton** Tennessee 35.59N 88.59W
105 K2 **Trent, R** N Carolina
57 M6 **Trent, R** Notts etc Eng
79 H4 **Trenzano** Italy 45.29N 10.00E
70 N4 **Tréon** France 48.41N 1.20E
13 B1 **Trepang B** N Terr Australia
98 T7 **Trepassey** Newfoundland 46.45N 53.20W
98 T7 **Trepassey B** Newfoundland
82 F8 **Trepča** Yugoslavia 42.56N 20.55E
70 N1 **Tréport, le** France 50.04N 1.22E
79 J6 **Tre Potenze, Alpe** *mt* Italy 44.07N 10.38E
79 O1 **Treppo Carnico** Italy 46.33N 13.02E
71 G5 **Trept** France 45.41N 5.19E
99 C3 **Treptow L** Ontario 49.53N 87.11W
81 R12 **Trepuzzi** Italy 40.24N 18.04E
80 E2 **Trequanda** Italy 43.11N 11.40E
66 M8 **Tresa** *R* Italy/Switz
121 E5 **Tres Algarrobas** Argentina 35.14S 62.46W
79 G6 **Tresana** Italy 44.15N 9.54E
121 G4 **Tres Arboles** Uruguay 32.25S 56.45W
121 E7 **Tres Arroyos** Argentina 38.26S 60.17W
70 G6 **Tresboeuf** France 47.53N 1.32W
120 G2 **Três Casas** Brazil 6.58S 62.38W
121 L7 **Tres Cerros** Argentina 48.12S 67.32W
71 H8 **Trescléoux** France 44.21N 5.41E
56 R8 **Tresco** *isld* Is of Scilly Eng 49.57N 6.20W
118 F7 **Três Corações** Brazil 21.44S 45.15W
79 G3 **Trescore Balneario** Italy 45.42N 9.50E
120 F10 **Tres Cruces** Argentina 22.54S 65.32W
121 B2 **Tres Cruces** Chile 29.24S 70.56W
121 C1 **Tres Cruces, Nevados** *mt* Chile 27.05S 68.46W
63 N9 **Treseburg** E Germany 51.44N 10.58E
79 B4 **Tresenta** *mt* Italy 45.30N 7.15E
119 C7 **Tres Esquinas** Colombia 0.43N 75.14W
53 W13 **Tresfjord** Norway 62.31N 7.08E
53 W13 **Tresfjord** *inlet* Norway 62.35N 7.07E
53 V18 **Tresfonn** *mt* Norway 60.13N 6.50E
74 F9 **Tres Forcas, C** Morocco 35.26N 2.57W
58 D6 **Treshnish Isles** Strathclyde **Scotland** 56.30N 6.25W
79 J2 **Tre Signori, Corno dei** *mt* Italy 46.20N 10.31E
79 M1 **Tre Signori, Picco dei** *mt* Italy/Austria 47.04N 12.14E
79 G2 **Tre Signori, Pizzo dei** *mt* Italy 46.01N 9.32E
118 A10 **Tres Isletas** Argentina 26.17S 60.27W
75 E8 **Tresjuncos** Spain 39.41N 2.46W
82 G9 **Treska** *R* Yugoslavia
82 E7 **Treskavica** *mt* Yugoslavia 43.35N 18.20E
118 D7 **Três Lagoas** Brazil 20.46S 51.43W
121 K7 **Tres Lagos** Argentina 49.35S 71.32W
109 B7 **Tres Lagunas** New Mexico 34.23N 108.06W
121 E6 **Tres Lomas** Argentina 36.30S 62.50W
120 F4 **Tres Mapejos** Bolivia 11.35S 65.39W
118 F6 **Três Marias Dam** Brazil 18.15S 45.15W
119 G3 **Tres Matas** Venezuela 8.27N 65.15W
121 H6 **Tres Montes, G** Chile
121 H6 **Tres Montes, Pen** Chile
58 T11 **Tres Ness** *prom* Orkney **Scotland** 59.14N 2.30W
81 B3 **Tresnuraghes** Sardinia 40.16N 8.31E
75 D2 **Trespaderne** Spain 42.47N 3.24W
121 H1 **Trés Passos** Brazil 27.33S 53.55W
115 N10 **Tres Picos** Mexico 15.53N 93.29W
121 B9 **Tres Picos** *pk* Argentina 42.25S 71.46W
121 E7 **Tres Picos, Cerro** *pk* Argentina 38.13S 61.50W
109 E5 **Tres Piedras** New Mexico 36.38N 105.58W
111 C5 **Tres Pinos** California 36.45N 121.19W
118 F7 **Três Pontas** Brazil 21.23S 45.29W
91 C9 **Tres Pontas, C.das** Angola 10.28S 13.32E
121 C4 **Tres Porteñas** Argentina 32.50S 68.20W
121 B1 **Tres Puentes** Chile 27.49S 70.05W
121 M6 **Tres Puntas, C** Argentina 47.05S 65.55W
118 G8 **Três Rios** Brazil 22.06S 43.15W
118 J9 **Três Rios, Serra dos** *mts* Brazil
70 M6 **Tresson** France 47.55N 0.35E
65 M3 **Třešt** Czechoslovakia 49.17N 15.29E
58 Q9 **Tresta** Shetland **Scotland** 60.15N 1.21W
120 D2 **Três Unidos** Brazil 6.37S 69.30W
120 B1 **Tres Unidos** Peru 5.05S 75.36W
115 L8 **Tres Valles** Mexico 18.18N 96.09W
115 M8 **Tres Zapotes** *ruins* Mexico 18.30N 95.30W
71 D4 **Treteau** France 46.23N 3.31E
66 E7 **Trétien, Le** Switzerland 46.07N 7.01E
39 G4 **Tretiy, Ostrov** *isld* U.S.S.R. 61.45N 162.30E
75 D1 **Treto** Spain 43.22N 3.28W
56 E4 **Tretower** Powys **Wales** 51.54N 3.11W
71 H10 **Trets** France 43.26N 5.40E
52 E5 **Tretten** Norway 61.16N 10.21E
Treuburg *see* **Olecko**
64 K6 **Treuchtlingen** W Germany 48.57N 10.55E
64 N2 **Treuen** W Germany 50.32N 12.18E
63 R8 **Treuenbrietzen** E Germany 52.06N 12.52E
53 Z20 **Treungen** Norway 59.01N 8.32E
70 E5 **Trévé** France 48.13N 2.47W
77 K6 **Trevélez** Spain 37.00N 3.15W
69 J6 **Tréveray** France 48.36N 5.24E
71 C8 **Trèves** France 44.05N 3.23E
Treves W Germany *see* **Trier**
70 C5 **Trévézal, Roc** *mt* France 48.24N 3.56W
80 G3 **Trevi** Italy 42.53N 12.45E
75 D2 **Treviana** Spain 42.34N 3.04W
76 G2 **Trevias** Spain 43.30N 6.26W
80 M6 **Trevico** Italy 41.03N 15.14E
70 J3 **Trévières** France 49.18N 0.55W
79 G3 **Treviglio** Italy 45.32N 9.35E
80 F4 **Trevignano** Roma Italy 42.09N 12.15E
79 M3 **Trevignano** Treviso Italy 45.44N 12.04E
71 K2 **Trévillers** France 47.16N 6.50E
75 E2 **Treviño** Spain 42.44N 2.45W
79 M3 **Treviso** Italy 45.40N 12.15E
79 L3 **Treviso** *prov* Italy
76 E6 **Trevões** Portugal 41.05N 7.26W
72 L2 **Trévol** France 46.39N 3.18E
26 Q12 **Trevor Pt** Silhouette I **Seychelles, Ind Oc** 4.30S 55.12E
103 A5 **Trevorton** Pennsylvania 40.47N 76.41W
56 A6 **Trevose Hd** Cornwall Eng 50.33N 5.01W
71 F5 **Trévoux** France 45.57N 4.46E
103 C5 **Trexler** Pennsylvania 40.38N 75.51W
103 C5 **Trexlertown** Pennsylvania 40.33N 75.36W
66 D4 **Trey** Switzerland 46.47N 6.56E
64 G2 **Treysa** W Germany 50.55N 9.11E
66 E5 **Treyvaux** Switzerland 46.44N 7.08E
71 C5 **Trézioux** France 45.43N 3.29E
79 E8 **Trezzano San Naviglio** *dist* Milan Italy
79 G3 **Trezzo-sull 'Adda** Italy 45.37N 9.31E
65 N2 **Trhová Kamenice** Czechoslovakia 49.48N 15.48E
65 L4 **Trhove Sviny** Czechoslovakia 48.51N 14.39E
65 M2 **Trhovy Štěpánov** Czechoslovakia 49.43N 15.01E
52 J9 **Triabo** Sweden 57.15N 15.30E
12 J8 **Triabunna** Tasmania 42.27S 147.56E
76 E3 **Triacastela** Spain 42.45N 7.14W
70 C4 **Triagoz, les** France 48.53N 3.40W
72 B3 **Triaize** France 46.24N 1.12W
13 D2 **Trial B** N Terr Australia
44 F6 **Trialetskiy Khrebet** *mts* Georgia U.S.S.R.
84 V17 **Triánda** Rhodes Greece 36.25N 28.10E
101 P8 **Triangle** Alberta 55.25N 116.40W
110 J7 **Triangle** Idaho 42.47N 116.36W
103 C2 **Triangle** New York 42.20N 75.53W
25 N8 **Triangle, The** *reg* Burma
83 H8 **Tría Nisiá** *isld* Greece 36.16N 26.45E
69 J6 **Triaucourt-en-Argonne** France 48.58N 5.04E
31 G3 **Tribal Territory** Kashmir
62 L7 **Tribeč** *mts* Czechoslovakia
70 H3 **Tribehou** France 49.13N 1.15W
30 K6 **Tribeniganj** Bihar India 26.09N 86.53E
30 G5 **Tribeni Ghat** Nepal 27.28N 83.56E
64 E7 **Triberg** W Germany 48.07N 8.14E
63 R4 **Tribsees** E Germany 54.06N 12.45E
13 H3 **Tribulation, C** Queensland 16.03S 145.30E
109 J3 **Tribune** Kansas 38.27N 101.46W
100 O9 **Tribune** Saskatchewan 49.15N 103.51W
81 M2 **Tricarico** Italy 40.37N 16.09E
81 R13 **Tricase** Italy 39.55N 18.22E
79 D4 **Tricerro** Italy 45.14N 8.19E
79 O2 **Tricesimo** Italy 46.10N 13.13E
95 N2 **Trichardt** S Africa 26.30S 29.13E
Trichinopoly *see* **Tiruchirapalli**
28 C5 **Trichur** Kerala India 10.32N 76.14E
28 C5 **Trichur** *dist* Kerala India
117 G7 **Trici** Brazil 5.59S 40.32W
56 H6 **Trickett's Cross** Dorset Eng 50.48N 1.54W
69 D4 **Tricot** France 49.34N 2.36E
12 H5 **Trida** New S Wales 33.00S 145.01E
110 G8 **Trident Pk** Nevada 41.55N 118.26W
65 K7 **Trieben** Austria 47.29N 14.30E
64 N2 **Triebes** E Germany 50.41N 12.01E
69 B5 **Trie-Château** France 49.18N 1.50E
64 P6 **Triefenried** W Germany 48.58N 13.05E
81 D3 **Triei** Sardinia 40.02N 9.39E
68 B2 **Triel-sur-Seine** France 48.59N 2.01E
66 J3 **Triengen** Switzerland 47.14N 8.05E
Trient *see* **Trento**
66 D7 **Trient** Switzerland 46.03N 7.00E
66 E7 **Trient, Glacier du** Switzerland
64 B4 **Trier** W Germany 49.45N 6.39E
64 K5 **Triesdorf** W Germany 49.13N 10.41E
66 P3 **Triesen** Liechtenstein 47.07N 9.32E
79 P3 **Trieste** Italy 45.39N 13.47E
79 P3 **Trieste** *prov* Italy
79 O3 **Trieste, G.di** *B* Italy
72 E9 **Trie-sur-Baïse** France 43.19N 0.23E
69 K5 **Trieux** France 49.19N 5.57E
70 D4 **Trieux** *R* France
64 P7 **Triftern** W Germany 48.23N 13.01E
120 F8 **Trigal** Bolivia 18.16S 64.07W
71 J9 **Trigance** France 43.45N 6.27E
81 N1 **Triggiano** Italy 41.04N 16.55E
82 B4 **Triglav** *mt* Yugoslavia 46.21N 13.59E
84 H5 **Tríglia** Greece 38.01N 24.00E
70 F7 **Trignac** France 47.20N 2.11W
81 G8 **Trigna, Pizzo** *mt* Sicily 37.57N 13.34E
80 L5 **Trigno, R** Italy
79 G4 **Trigolo** Italy 45.19N 9.48E
96 Q3 **Trigo, Mte** Azores 38.44N 28.17W
76 H2 **Trigueiro** *mt* Spain 43.17N 5.30W
69 D8 **Triguères** France 47.57N 2.59E
77 C6 **Trigueros** Spain 37.24N 6.50W
76 K5 **Trigueros del Valle** Spain 41.50N 4.40W
Trigu Tso *L see* **Chigu Co** *L*
84 F3 **Tríkeri** Greece 39.06N 23.05E
84 F7 **Tríkeri** *isld* Greece 37.16N 23.17E
84 F3 **Tríkeri, Dhíavlos** *str* Greece
45 C9 **Trikhaty** Ukraine U.S.S.R. 47.07N 31.49E
84 B4 **Trikhonís, Límni** *L* Greece
84 C2 **Tríkkala** Greece 39.33N 21.46E
84 C2 **Tríkkala** *prov* Greece
84 B4 **Tríklinos** Greece 38.58N 21.27E
84 S14 **Trikomo** Cyprus 35.16N 33.54E
15 E6 **Trikora, Pk** Irian Jaya 4.15S 138.41E
84 C5 **Tríkorfon** Greece 38.26N 21.54E
84 D5 **Tríkorfon** *mt* Greece 38.27N 22.04E
45 C9 **Trikraty** Ukraine U.S.S.R. 47.42N 31.24E
105 E9 **Trilby** Florida 28.29N 82.13W
9 S10 **Trilithon** *anc mon* Tonga, Pacific Oc 21.08S 175.03W
59 H3 **Trillick** Tyrone **N Ireland** 54.27N 7.30W
75 E6 **Trillo** Spain 40.42N 2.35W
29 E1 **Triloknath** Himachal Prad India 32.42N 76.41E
69 D6 **Trilport** France 48.57N 2.57E
99 F2 **Trilsbeck L** Ontario 50.49N 84.05W
59 J4 **Trim** Meath Irish Rep 53.34N 6.47W
66 H2 **Trimbach** Switzerland 47.22N 7.53E
57 L3 **Trimdon** Durham Eng 54.42N 1.25W
56 O2 **Trimingham** Norfolk Eng 52.54N 1.24E
56 O4 **Trimley** Suffolk Eng 51.59N 1.19E
65 G5 **Trimmelkam** Austria 48.02N 12.52E
66 P4 **Trimmis** Switzerland 46.54N 9.34E
Trimmu Barrage *see* **Emerson Barrage**
108 Q6 **Trimont** Minnesota 43.43N 94.41W
14 B5 **Trimouille I** W Australia 20.23S 115.33E
72 G3 **Trimouille, la** France 46.28N 1.02E
58 H5 **Trinafour** Tayside **Scotland** 56.45N 4.05W
115 D2 **Trincheras** Mexico 30.22N 111.32W
109 F4 **Trinchere** Colorado 37.03N 104.04W
26 T4 **Trincomalee** Sri Lanka 8.34N 81.13E
118 E5 **Trindade** Brazil 16.40S 49.27W
76 D13 **Trindade** Portugal 37.53N 7.54W
117 E2 **Trindade, I da** Atlantic Oc
53 M9 **Trindholm** *isld* Faeroes 62.04N 7.29W
88 L4 **Trine, El** Morocco 35.23N 5.56W
56 K4 **Tring** Herts Eng 51.48N 0.40W
84 B2 **Tringía** *mt* Greece 39.38N 21.24E
98 B7 **Tring Jonction** Quebec 46.17N 71.00W
120 F6 **Trinidad** Bolivia 14.46S 64.50W
110 A8 **Trinidad** California 41.04N 124.08W
119 E5 **Trinidad** Colombia 5.25N 71.39W
109 F4 **Trinidad** Colorado 37.11N 104.31W
116 D4 **Trinidad** Cuba 21.48N 80.00W
115 P10 **Trinidad** Honduras 15.07N 88.11W
118 C10 **Trinidad** Paraguay 27.09S 55.43W
120 A1 **Trinidad** Peru 4.29S 78.33W
19 M5 **Trinidad** Philippines 12.05N 124.32E
121 G4 **Trinidad** Uruguay 33.30S 56.51W
110 E2 **Trinidad** Washington 47.14N 120.01W
121 E7 **Trinidad** *isld* Argentina
Trinidad *isld* Brazil *see* **Trindade, I. da**
116 O1 **Trinidad** *isld* West Indies
116 O9 **Trinidad and Tobago** *nation* W I
115 E10 **Trinidad B** Panama
121 H7 **Trinidad, G** Chile
77 E6 **Trinidad, La** Spain 37.10N 5.38W
79 C5 **Trinità** Italy 44.30N 7.45E
81 E8 **Trinitá, L** Sicily 37.43N 12.45E
80 O6 **Trinitapoli** Italy 41.22N 16.06E
116 L3 **Trinite** Martinique W I 14.44N 60.58W
70 M4 **Trinité-de-Réville, la** France 48.58N 0.32E
70 E5 **Trinité-Porhoët, la** France 48.05N 2.33W
70 D6 **Trinité-sur-Mer, la** France 47.36N 3.02W
56 W11 **Trinity** Channel Is 49.14N 2.05W
98 T5 **Trinity** Newfoundland 48.22N 53.24W
98 T5 **Trinity** Newfoundland 48.58N 53.55W
112 M5 **Trinity** Texas 30.58N 95.25W
110 B9 **Trinity** *R* California
112 L3 **Trinity** *R* Texas
98 T5 **Trinity B** Newfoundland
13 H3 **Trinity B** Queensland
110 C8 **Trinity Center** California 41.01N 122.43W
116 P2 **Trinity Hills** Trinidad & Tobago 10.07N 61.07W
113 K8 **Trinity Is** Alaska
13 H3 **Trinity Opening** *str* Gt Barrier Reef Australia
110 G9 **Trinity Ra** Nevada
110 B9 **Trinity S. Fork** *R* California
28 J7 **Trinkat** *isld* Nicobar Is
87 F1 **Trinkitat** *B* Sudan
79 D4 **Trino** Italy 45.12N 8.18E
76 E7 **Trinta** Portugal 40.30N 7.21W
84 C7 **Tríodhos** Greece 37.05N 21.59E
23 C9 **Trio Is** Hong Kong 22.17N 114.18E
26 U11 **Triolet** Mauritius, Indian Oc 20.04S 57.32E
76 K3 **Triollo** Spain 42.56N 4.40W
80 N5 **Triolo** *R* Italy
105 B3 **Trion** Georgia 34.34N 85.19W
81 N5 **Trionto** *R* Italy
81 N4 **Trionto, C** Italy 39.38N 16.47E
79 C7 **Triora** Italy 44.00N 7.46E
84 D7 **Trípi** Greece 37.06N 22.21E
81 K7 **Tripi** Sicily 38.03N 15.06E
84 C6 **Tripití** Greece 37.34N 21.47E
28 C8 **Triplicane** *dist* Madras, Tamil Nadu India
108 S7 **Tripoli** Iowa 42.49N 92.15W
34 C4 **Tripoli** Lebanon 34.27N 35.50E
85 B3 **Tripoli** Libya 32.58N 13.12E
84 D6 **Trípolis** Greece 37.31N 22.22E
Tripolis Lebanon *see* **Tripoli**
85 B4 **Tripolitania** *reg* Libya
45 B6 **Tripol'ye** Ukraine U.S.S.R. 50.07N 30.43E
84 C6 **Tripótama** Greece 37.52N 21.54E
84 D7 **Tripótamos** Greece 37.22N 22.05E
108 N6 **Tripp** S Dakota 43.13N 97.59W
64 D5 **Trippstadt** W Germany 49.22N 7.47E
64 M2 **Triptis** E Germany 50.44N 11.51E
28 C6 **Tripunittura** Kerala India 9.56N 76.21E
28 H4 **Tripura** *state* India
84 Q15 **Tripylos** *mt* Cyprus 34.59N 32.40E
98 N3 **Triquet, L** Quebec
63 J4 **Trischen** *isld* W Germany
64 O4 **Tři Sekery** Czechoslovakia 49.57N 12.38E
65 G8 **Tristach** Austria 46.49N 12.48E
96 B15 **Tristan da Cunha** *I* Tristan da Cunha
96 B15 **Tristan da Cunha** *islds* Atlantic Oc
89 B6 **Tristao, I** Guinea 10.55N 14.55W
96 O6 **Tristão, Pta.do** *pt* Madeira Is 32.52N 17.13W
84 D4 **Tristenon** Greece 38.37N 22.03E
30 C2 **Trisul** *mt* Uttar Prad India 30.19N 79.48E
30 J5 **Trisuli Dam** Nepal 27.54N 85.08E
69 E3 **Trith-St.-Léger** France 50.19N 3.30E
25 H7 **Tri Ton** Vietnam 10.26N 105.01E
25 L5 **Triton I** Paracel Islands **S China Sea**
15 C5 **Triton, Teluk** *B* Irian Jaya 3.45S 134.10E
63 M5 **Trittau** W Germany 53.37N 10.24E
115 L3 **Triunfo** Honduras 13.06N 87.01W
117 H8 **Triunfo** Pernambuco **Brazil** 7.48S 38.05W
121 H2 **Triunfo** Rio Grande do Sul **Brazil** 29.58S 51.43W
120 F4 **Triunfo** Rondônia **Brazil** 11.56S 64.17W
117 C8 **Triunfo, R** Brazil
28 C6 **Trivandrum** Kerala India 8.30N 76.57E
28 C6 **Trivandrum** *dist* Kerala India
84 H8 **Trivássalon** Greece 36.45N 24.26E
80 L5 **Trivento** Italy 41.47N 14.33E
61 G5 **Trivieres** Belgium 50.27N 4.09E
80 N7 **Trivigno** Italy 40.34N 15.59E
72 K5 **Trizac** France 45.15N 2.32E
84 D5 **Trizónia** *isld* Greece 38.22N 22.04E
62 K7 **Trnava** Czechoslovakia 48.23N 17.35E
65 L2 **Trnavka** *R* Czechoslovakia
79 P2 **Trnovo** Yugoslavia 46.17N 13.33E
70 K3 **Troarn** France 49.11N 0.10W
15 L8 **Trobriand I** Papua New Guinea 8.30S 151.05E
15 L8 **Trobriand Is** Papua New Guinea
58 J5 **Trochry** Tayside **Scotland** 56.33N 3.40W
64 G7 **Trochtelfingen** W Germany 48.18N 9.15E
100 D7 **Trochu** Alberta 51.50N 113.10W
53 T15 **Trodalsvatn** *L* Norway 61.33N 5.59E
79 K2 **Tródena** Italy 46.19N 11.22E
51 C6 **Trœna** *isld* Norway 66.30N 12.05E
53 V16 **Troegga** *mt* Norway 61.15N 6.43E
53 F6 **Troense** Denmark 55.02N 10.39E
65 M7 **Trofaiach** Austria 47.25N 15.01E
79 C5 **Trofarello** Italy 44.59N 7.44E
45 N9 **Trofimov** U.S.S.R. 47.52N 41.17E
41 N4 **Trofimovsk** U.S.S.R. 72.50N 127.52E
41 N4 **Trofimovskaya Protoka** *canal* U.S.S.R.
66 O2 **Trogen** Switzerland 47.25N 9.28E
82 C7 **Trogir** Yugoslavia 43.32N 16.15E
82 D7 **Troglav** *mt* Yugoslavia 43.57N 16.36E
61 L4 **Trognée** Belgium 50.41N 5.08E
80 M6 **Troia** Italy 41.22N 15.19E
81 J8 **Troina** Sicily 37.47N 14.37E
81 J8 **Troina** *R* Sicily
26 T15 **Trois-Bassins** Réunion Ind Oc 21.05S 55.18E
72 H3 **Trois Cornes** *hill* France 46.13N 1.45E
64 C2 **Troisdorf** W Germany 50.49N 7.09E
71 J8 **Trois-Evêchés, les** *mt* France 44.17N 6.30E
69 N6 **Troisfontaines-la-Ville** France 48.40N 7.08E
72 E1 **Trois Moutiers, les** France 47.04N 0.01E
98 C5 **Trois Pistoles** Quebec 48.08N 69.10W
61 O5 **Trois-Ponts** Belgium 50.23N 5.53E
116 M4 **Trois Rivières** Guadeloupe W I 15.57N 61.38W
99 S6 **Trois Rivières** Quebec 46.21N 72.34W
72 G10 **Trois Seigneurs, Pic des** *mt* France 42.50N 1.26E
26 R16 **Trois Swains, les** *islds* Kerguelen **Ind Oc** 49.44S 69.55E
66 D7 **Troistorrents** Switzerland 46.14N 6.55E
71 C3 **Trois-Vèvres** France 46.55N 3.24E
61 P6 **Troisvierges** Luxembourg 50.07N 6.00E
45 M2 **Troitsa** U.S.S.R. 54.24N 40.14E
47 J8 **Troitsk** Chelyabinsk **U.S.S.R.** 54.08N 61.33E
42 E4 **Troitsk** Krasnoyarsk **U.S.S.R.** 57.22N 94.50E
45 P2 **Troitsk** Mordovian A.S.S.R. **U.S.S.R.** 54.06N 43.50E
42 J5 **Troitskiy** Buryat **U.S.S.R.** 54.38N 113.10E
45 J1 **Troitskiy** Moscow **U.S.S.R.** 55.27N 37.19E
43 L1 **Troitskiy** Omsk **U.S.S.R.** 54.53N 73.16E
46 R4 **Troitskiy** Orenburg **U.S.S.R.** 50.43N 54.42E
47 J7 **Troitskiy** Sverdlovsk **U.S.S.R.** 57.08N 63.44E
45 P6 **Troitskiy** Volgograd **U.S.S.R.** 50.14N 43.03E
42 G5 **Troitskiy Zavod** U.S.S.R. 53.28N 102.10E
47 H4 **Troitsko-Pechorsk** U.S.S.R. 62.40N 56.08E
45 D9 **Troitsko-Safonovo** Ukraine **U.S.S.R.** 47.46N 32.52E
42 C5 **Troitskoye** Altay **U.S.S.R.** 53.01N 84.43E
44 F6 **Troitskoye** Georgia **U.S.S.R.** 41.10N 43.49E
44 F1 **Troitskoye** Kalmyk A.S.S.R. **U.S.S.R.** 46.24N 44.14E
40 G7 **Troitskoye** Khabarovsk **U.S.S.R.** 49.25N 136.32E
45 K7 **Troitskoye** Lugansk, Ukraine **U.S.S.R.** 49.54N 38.16E
43 C1 **Troitskoye** Orenburg **U.S.S.R.** 53.20N 52.50E
43 D2 **Troitskoye** Orenburg **U.S.S.R.** 52.18N 56.26E
47 K5 **Troitskoye** Tyumen **U.S.S.R.** 61.09N 68.10E
45 N5 **Troitskoye** Voronezh **U.S.S.R.** 51.18N 41.29E
84 F7 **Troizín** Greece 37.30N 23.21E
116 K1 **Troja** Jamaica, W I 18.12N 76.56W
53 N9 **Troldenæs** Faeroes 62.23N 6.48W
53 B5 **Troldhede** Denmark 55.59N 8.45E
53 N10 **Troldhoved** *isld* Faeroes 61.56N 6.58W
50 H5 **Trölladyngja** *vol* Iceland 64.54N 17.16W
50 G6 **Tröllahraun** *lava field* Iceland
50 F3 **Trollakirkja** *mt* Skagafjardharsýsla **Iceland** 65.41N 19.55W
50 D4 **Tröllakirkja Snjöfjöll** *mt* Iceland 65.01N 21.11W
50 D3 **Tröllatunga** Iceland 65.38N 21.40W
51 D3 **Trollfjord** *inlet* Norway 68.22N 15.00E
52 G8 **Trollhättan** Sweden 58.17N 12.20E
52 E4 **Trollheimen** *mts* Norway
Trølhøvdi *isld see* **Troldhoved**
53 X14 **Trollstigheim** *pass* Norway 62.25N 7.40E
53 W13 **Trolltind** *mt* Norway 62.35N 7.00E
53 X14 **Trolltindane** *mt* Norway 62.29N 7.43E
53 W14 **Trollvatn** *L* Norway 62.28N 7.20E
118 J4 **Tromba Grande, Pta** Brazil 14.16S 38.58W
28 A1 **Trombay** Maharashtra India 19.01N 72.58E
117 B5 **Trombetas, R** Brazil
26 E7 **Tromelin I** Indian Oc 15.51S 54.25E
79 E4 **Tromello** Italy 45.13N 8.52E
121 B6 **Tromen, V** *vol* Argentina 36.50S 70.05W
58 H4 **Tromie, R** Highland **Scotland**
63 S3 **Tromper Wiek** *B* E Germany
79 H3 **Trompia, Val** *V* Italy
95 J6 **Trompsburg** S Africa 30.02S 25.47E
51 G3 **Troms** *co* Norway
51 G2 **Tromsdalen** Norway 69.40N 19.00E
51 G2 **Tromsø** Norway 69.42N 19.00E
42 A2 **Trom'yegan** *R* U.S.S.R.
111 G6 **Trona** California 35.46N 117.24W
121 B8 **Tronador** *pk* Arg/Chile 41.10S 71.50W
71 H6 **Tronche, la** France 45.13N 5.45E
70 G4 **Tronchet, le** France 48.30N 1.52W
75 K6 **Tronchón** Spain 40.37N 0.25W
76 E5 **Tronco** Portugal 41.46N 7.17W
51 F3 **Trondenes** Norway 68.50N 16.35E
52 E3 **Trondheim** Norway 63.36N 10.23E
52 E3 **Trondheimsfjord** *inlet* Norway
52 F4 **Tronfjell** *mt* Norway 62.09N 10.45E
53 K3 **Trönninge** Sweden 56.38N 12.59E
52 K5 **Trönö** Sweden 61.24N 17.00E
Tronoh *see* **Teronoh**
66 K7 **Trontano** Italy 46.08N 8.20E
80 H3 **Tronto** *R* Italy
53 Y20 **Trontveit** Norway 59.05N 8.28E
69 J6 **Tronville-en-Barrois** France 48.43N 5.16E
66 L7 **Tronzano** Italy 46.05N 8.44E
79 D4 **Tronzano Vercellese** Italy 45.20N 8.11E
70 M6 **Trôo** France 47.47N 0.48E
84 Q15 **Troödos** Cyprus 34.55N 32.53E
84 Q15 **Troödos** *mts* Cyprus
94 F7 **Trooilapspan** S Africa 28.40S 21.25E
57 E2 **Trool, L** Dumfries & Galloway **Scotland** 55.05N 4.30W
57 D1 **Troon** Strathclyde **Scotland** 55.32N 4.40W
61 N4 **Trooz** Belgium 50.34N 5.42E
84 C6 **Trópaia** Greece 37.43N 21.57E
117 A7 **Tropas, R** Brazil
81 L6 **Tropea** Italy 38.40N 15.54E
118 G4 **Tropeiros, Serra dos** *mts* Brazil
111 M4 **Tropic** Utah 37.36N 112.05W
83 D2 **Tropojë** Albania 42.23N 20.10E
52 K8 **Trosa** Sweden 58.54N 17.35E
47 H3 **Trosh** U.S.S.R. 66.24N 56.08E
108 O6 **Trosky** Minnesota 43.54N 96.14W
45 G4 **Trosna** U.S.S.R. 52.25N 35.45E
100 N9 **Trossachs** Saskatchewan 49.38N 104.13W
58 H6 **Trossachs, The** *defile* Central **Scotland**
64 F7 **Trossingen** W Germany 48.05N 8.38E
59 K1 **Trostan** *mt* Antrim **N Ireland** 55.03N 6.10W
64 O7 **Trostberg** W Germany 48.01N 12.34E
53 E6 **Trøstrup Korup** Denmark 55.26N 10.17E
45 F6 **Trostyanets** Ukraine **U.S.S.R.** 50.30N 34.59E
82 M2 **Trostyanets** Ukraine **U.S.S.R.** 48.35N 29.10E
63 P9 **Trotha** E Germany 51.31N 11.58E
108 G2 **Trotters** N Dakota 47.20N 103.57W
82 K4 **Trotuşul** *R* Romania
109 D1 **Troublesome** Colorado 40.04N 106.17W
14 F2 **Troughton I** W Australia 13.44S 126.05E
72 K10 **Trouillas** France 42.37N 2.48E
84 S14 **Troulli** Cyprus 35.01N 33.37E
75 L2 **Troumous, Cirque de** France 42.45N 0.09E
25 H6 **Troun** Cambodia 13.47N 105.21E
112 M3 **Troup** Texas 32.08N 95.07W
109 L4 **Trousdale** Kansas 37.50N 99.05W
98 F6 **Trousers L** New Brunswick
107 D10 **Trout** Louisiana 31.41N 92.09W
101 N5 **Trout** *R* N W Terr
57 H4 **Troutbeck** Cumbria **Eng** 54.25N 2.55W
111 L6 **Trout Cr** Arizona
110 E5 **Trout Cr** Oregon
106 E3 **Trout Creek** Michigan 46.29N 89.01W
110 K2 **Trout Creek** Montana 47.53N 115.43W
103 D2 **Trout Creek** New York 42.12N 75.17W
99 L7 **Trout Creek** Ontario 45.59N 79.22W
111 L2 **Trout Creek** Utah 39.40N 113.49W
101 P10 **Trout L** Br Col 50.35N 117.29W
106 J3 **Trout L** Michigan 46.12N 85.01W
101 N5 **Trout L** N W Terr
97 K7 **Trout L** Ontario 51.10N 93.20W
106 E3 **Trout L** Wisconsin 46.04N 89.40W
110 Q5 **Trout Pk** Wyoming 44.37N 109.30W
100 C2 **Trout R** Alberta
101 L6 **Trout R** Br Col
98 O4 **Trout River** Newfoundland 49.29N 58.08W
104 H5 **Trout Run** Pennsylvania 41.23N 77.03W
104 G5 **Troutville** Pennsylvania 41.02N 78.47W
104 F9 **Troutville** Virginia 37.25N 79.55W
70 L3 **Trouville** France 49.22N 0.05E
76 C9 **Troviscal** Portugal 39.52N 8.01W
56 G5 **Trowbridge** Wilts Eng 51.20N 2.13W
57 L7 **Trowell** Notts Eng 52.57N 1.16W
56 O2 **Trowse Newton** Norfolk Eng 52.37N 1.19E
12 H8 **Trowutta** Tasmania 41.02S 145.05E
107 L10 **Troy** Alabama 31.49N 86.00W
110 J3 **Troy** Idaho 46.44N 116.47W
107 K3 **Troy** Indiana 38.00N 86.50W
116 J1 **Troy** Jamaica, W I 18.15N 77.37W
109 P2 **Troy** Kansas 39.45N 95.06W
107 F3 **Troy** Missouri 38.59N 90.59W
110 K1 **Troy** Montana 48.28N 115.55W
105 H2 **Troy** N Carolina 35.23N 79.54W
104 N4 **Troy** New Hampshire 42.50N 72.12W
104 M4 **Troy** New York 42.43N 73.43W
104 A6 **Troy** Ohio 40.02N 84.12W
110 H4 **Troy** Oregon 45.58N 117.26W
103 A3 **Troy** Pennsylvania 41.48N 76.47W
112 K4 **Troy** Texas 31.12N 97.20W
104 E7 **Troy** W Virginia 39.02N 80.48W
36 B3 **Troy** *anc site* Turkey 39.55N 26.17E
121 C1 **Troya** *R* Argentina
82 J8 **Troyan** Bulgaria 42.52N 24.42E
45 L3 **Troyekurovo** Lipetsk **U.S.S.R.** 53.25N 39.45E
45 J3 **Troyekurovo** Tula **U.S.S.R.** 53.28N 37.28E
69 G7 **Troyes** France 48.18N 4.05E
41 D3 **Troynoy, Ostrov** *isld* U.S.S.R. 76.00N 83.00E
69 J5 **Troyon** France 49.00N 5.29E
111 J3 **Troy Pk** *mt* Nevada 38.18N 115.31W
88 S4 **Trozza, Jebel** *mt* Tunisia 35.34N 9.35E
64 N3 **Tršnice** Czechoslovakia 50.07N 12.24E
62 M6 **Trstená** Czechoslovakia 49.22N 19.35E
82 F7 **Trstenik** Yugoslavia 43.36N 21.00E
119 C4 **Truandó, R** Colombia
13 D1 **Truant I** N Terr **Australia** 11.36S 136.49E
100 N9 **Truax** Saskatchewan 49.55N 104.58W
66 H4 **Trub** Switzerland 46.57N 7.54E
66 O3 **Trübbach** Switzerland 47.05N 9.29E
45 E4 **Trubchevsk** U.S.S.R. 52.36N 33.46E
45 L4 **Trubetchino** U.S.S.R. 52.53N 39.32E
45 C6 **Trubezh** *R* Ukraine U.S.S.R.
76 H2 **Trubia** Spain 43.20N 5.59W
76 H2 **Trubia** *R* Spain
66 H4 **Trubschachen** Switzerland 46.55N 7.52E
66 K4 **Trübsee** *L* Switzerland 46.47N 8.24E
79 B3 **Truc Blanc** *mt* Italy 45.32N 7.08E
25 J7 **Truc Giang** Vietnam 10.03N 106.36E
109 E5 **Truchas** New Mexico 36.02N 105.50W
76 G4 **Truchas** Spain 42.15N 6.25W
76 G4 **Truchillas** Spain 42.14N 6.28W
69 O6 **Truchtersheim** France 48.40N 7.36E
33 K4 **Trucial Coast** The Gulf
Trucial States S *see* **United Arab Emirates**
Trucial 'Umān *see* **United Arab Emirates**
111 D2 **Truckee** California 39.20N 120.10W
111 E2 **Truckee** *R* Nevada
44 H2 **Trudfront** U.S.S.R. 45.55N 47.41E
42 E4 **Trudnovo** U.S.S.R. 56.41N 91.28E
40 F10 **Trudovoye** U.S.S.R. 43.17N 132.07E
45 A1 **Trudy** Belorussiya **U.S.S.R.** 55.38N 29.21E
47 N1 **Trudyashchikhsya, Ostrov** *isld* Leningrad U.S.S.R.
72 K7 **Truel, le** France 44.03N 2.44E
13 B5 **Truer Ra** N Terr **Australia**
14 E7 **Truer Tableland** W Australia
Trufawi *see* **Bi'r Ţarūfawī**
99 M5 **Truite, la** *L* Quebec
77 D3 **Trujillanos** Spain 38.57N 6.16W
119 C5 **Trujillo** Colombia 4.08N 76.21W
115 L2 **Trujillo** Honduras 15.55N 86.00W
109 F6 **Trujillo** New Mexico 35.32N 104.43W
120 A3 **Trujillo** Peru 8.06S 79.00W
76 H10 **Trujillo** Spain 39.28N 5.53W
119 E3 **Trujillo** Venezuela 9.20N 70.38W
119 E3 **Trujillo** *state* Venezuela
77 J6 **Trujillos** Spain 37.28N 3.48W
17 Q10 **Truk Is** Caroline Is **Pacific Oc**
19 M4 **Truk Is** *island grp* **Pacific Oc**
26 D12 **Truls I** *rock* Southern Oc 56.07S 23.39E
108 Q6 **Truman** Minnesota 43.49N 94.26W
107 F6 **Trumann** Arkansas 35.40N 90.30W
103 A1 **Trumansburg** New York 42.34N 76.40W
76 D2 **Trumao** *R* Spain
103 H4 **Trumbull** Connecticut 41.15N 73.12W
108 M9 **Trumbull** Nebraska 40.42N 98.15W
111 L5 **Trumbull, Mt** Arizona 36.25N 113.08W
66 H5 **Trümmelbach Falls** Switzerland 46.34N 7.55E
56 M3 **Trumpington** Cambs Eng 52.11N 0.07E
82 H8 **Trŭn** Bulgaria 42.50N 22.37E
70 L4 **Trun** France 48.50N 0.02E
66 M5 **Trun** Switzerland 46.45N 8.59E
12 J5 **Trundle** New S Wales 32.54S 147.35E
25 J1 **Trung Khanh Phu** Vietnam 22.50N 106.32E
44 E2 **Trunovskoye** U.S.S.R. 45.28N 42.09E
56 A7 **Truro** Cornwall **Eng** 50.16N 5.03W
108 R8 **Truro** Iowa 41.12N 93.51W
103 O3 **Truro** Massachusetts 42.00N 70.02W
98 J8 **Truro** Nova Scotia 45.24N 63.18W
12 E5 **Truro** S Australia 34.23S 139.09E
18 L3 **Trusan** Sarawak **Malaysia** 4.47N 115.19E
18 L3 **Trusan** *R* Sarawak **Malaysia**
112 H2 **Truscott** Texas 33.45N 99.48W
82 L3 **Truşeşti** Romania 47.45N 27.01E
64 J2 **Trusetal** E Germany 50.46N 10.23E
46 E5 **Truskavets** Ukraine **U.S.S.R.** 49.16N 23.31E
59 F3 **Truskmore** *mt* Sligo **Irish Rep** 54.23N 8.22W
14 D10 **Truslove** W Australia 33.19S 121.40E
18 M3 **Trus Madi, Gunung** *mt* Sabah **Malaysia** 5.34N 116.29E
47 G3 **Trusovo** U.S.S.R. 65.26N 51.18E
107 K8 **Trussville** Alabama 33.37N 86.37W
53 F4 **Trustrup** Denmark 56.21N 10.47E
101 M7 **Trutch** Br Col 57.42N 123.00W
101 M7 **Trutch Creek** Br Col
109 C8 **Truth or Consequences** New Mexico 33.08N 107.16W
62 J5 **Trutnov** Czechoslovakia 50.34N 15.55E
70 J4 **Truttemer-le-Petit** France 48.47N 0.50W
104 J4 **Truxton** New York 42.43N 76.03W
71 C7 **Truyère** *R* France
82 J8 **Tryavna** Bulgaria 42.50N 25.29E
108 K8 **Tryon** Nebraska 41.33N 100.57W
11 K3 **Tryphena** New Zealand 36.18S 175.27E
84 S14 **Trypimeni** Cyprus 35.18N 33.38E
52 G5 **Trysil** Norway 61.22N 12.16E
52 F5 **Trysilelva** *R* Norway
46 E2 **Tryškiai** Lithuania **U.S.S.R.** 56.02N 22.33E
62 J2 **Trzcianka** Poland 53.01N 16.25E
62 J1 **Trzebiatow** Poland 54.03N 15.15E
62 H2 **Trzebiez** Poland 53.38N 14.31E
62 K4 **Trzebnica** Poland 51.20N 17.01E
62 K3 **Trzemeszno** Poland 52.33N 17.48E
82 B4 **Tržič** Yugoslavia 46.22N 14.18E
84 P15 **Tsadha** Cyprus 34.50N 32.28E
22 G3 **Tsagaandelger** Mongolia 46.22N 107.39E
22 D3 **Tsagaanhayrhan** Mongolia 47.28N 96.45E
22 C3 **Tsagaan Nuur** *L* Mongolia
22 G4 **Tsagaan-Ovoo** Mongolia 45.49N 105.19E
22 D2 **Tsagaan-Uul** Mongolia 49.56N 98.52E
22 E1 **Tsagaan Üür** Mongolia 50.30N 101.30E
44 F1 **Tsagan Khak, Oz** *L* U.S.S.R.
42 J6 **Tsagan-Khurtey, Khrebet** *mts* U.S.S.R.
45 R9 **Tsagan-Nur** Kalmyk A.S.S.R. **U.S.S.R.** 47.23N 45.16E
Tsagān Obōni *see* **Tsagaan-Ovoo**
Tsagān Olom *see* **Tayshir**
44 E5 **Tsageri** Georgia **U.S.S.R.** 42.39N 42.46E
24 C8 **Tsaggar Tso** *L* Xizang Zizhiqu **China**
44 E6 **Tsagveri** Georgia **U.S.S.R.** 41.48N 43.26E
24 C9 **Tsaka La** *L* Xizang Zizhiqu **China**
24 C9 **Tsaka La** *pass* Kashmir 33.23N 78.55E
84 A5 **Tsakarisiánon** Greece 38.10N 20.40E
44 H6 **Tsakhur** U.S.S.R. 41.41N 47.05E
42 G6 **Tsakir** U.S.S.R. 50.28N 103.35E
105 E9 **Tsala Apopka L** Florida
44 E5 **Tsalendzhikha** Georgia **U.S.S.R.** 42.37N 42.06E
44 F6 **Tsalka** Georgia **U.S.S.R.** 41.34N 44.04E
44 F6 **Tsalkinskoye, Vdkhr** *res* Georgia **U.S.S.R.**
91 D4 **Tsama** Congo 0.33S 14.38E
83 D5 **Tsamandás** Greece 39.46N 20.21E
30 J3 **Tsambur** Nepal 27.55N 86.49E
30 L5 **Tsanga** Xizang Zizhiqu 27.53N 87.25E
84 F3 **Tsangarádha** Greece 39.23N 23.10E
Ts'ang-hsien *see* **Cangzhou**
Tsangpo *R see* **Yarlung Zangbo Jiang**
30 C1 **Tsang Tsangpo** *R* Xizang Zizhiqu
84 A5 **Tsannáta** Greece 38.08N 20.45E
Tsaparang *see* **Tse-pu-lung**
95 D3 **Tsarahonenana** Madagascar 15.28S 48.28E
95 C4 **Tsaramandroso** Madagascar 16.20S 47.03E
95 C4 **Tsaratanana** Madagascar 16.46S 47.40E
95 D2 **Tsaratanana, Massif du** *mts* Madagascar
45 F1 **Tsarevo-Zaymishche** U.S.S.R. 55.24N 34.48E
45 Q3 **Tsarevshchina** U.S.S.R. 53.37N 44.45E
45 F8 **Tsarichanka** Ukraine **U.S.S.R.** 48.55N 34.30E
94 D5 **Tsaris Mts** Namibia
84 D2 **Tsaritsáni** Greece 39.53N 22.14E
82 K7 **Tsar Kaloyan** Bulgaria 43.36N 26.14E
Tsarsko Selo *see* **Pushkin**
45 Q8 **Tsatsa** U.S.S.R. 48.13N 44.40E
95 M6 **Tsatsana** *mt* Lesotho 30.29S 28.10E
45 Q8 **Tsatsa, Oz** *L* U.S.S.R.
94 G3 **Tsau** Botswana 20.12S 22.22E
94 H2 **Tsaugara Pan** Botswana 19.55S 25.18E
93 K8 **Tsavo** Kenya 2.59S 38.28E
93 K9 **Tsavo** *R* Kenya
93 K9 **Tsavo Nat.Park** Kenya
101 G12 **Tsawwassen** Br Col 49.03N 123.06W
66 Q3 **Tschagguns** Austria 47.05N 9.54E
94 C6 **Tschaukaib** Namibia 26.34S 15.40E
66 P6 **Tscheisch Horn** *mt* Switzerland 46.27N 9.31E
66 O3 **Tscherlach** Switzerland 47.08N 9.21E
108 J3 **Tschida, L** N Dakota
88 N7 **Tseibat** *watercourse* Algeria
93 K6 **Tseikuru** Kenya 0.19S 38.14E
88 O6 **Tseldja** Algeria 31.32N 1.30E
44 D1 **Tselina** U.S.S.R. 46.33N 41.02E
43 Q1 **Tselinnoye** U.S.S.R. 53.05N 85.43E
44 F1 **Tselinnyy** Kalmyk A.S.S.R. **U.S.S.R.** 46.38N 44.36E
43 F2 **Tselinnyy** Orenburg **U.S.S.R.** 50.47N 60.47E
43 K2 **Tselinograd** Kazakhstan **U.S.S.R.** 51.10N 71.28E
45 F3 **Tsementnyy** Bryansk **U.S.S.R.** 53.25N 34.25E
47 M4 **Tsementnyy** Sverdlovsk **U.S.S.R.** 57.30N 60.09E
23 B9 **Tseng Lan** Hong Kong 22.19N 114.15E
22 E3 **Tsenher** Mongolia 47.14N 101.46E
22 H3 **Tsenhermandal** Mongolia 47.44N 109.00E
47 F4 **Tsenogora** U.S.S.R. 64.54N 46.44E
41 M8 **Tsental'no-Yakutskaya' Ravnina** *lowland* U.S.S.R.
42 D4 **Tsentral'nyy** U.S.S.R. 55.14N 87.35E
47 H6 **Tsentral'nyy Kospashskiy** U.S.S.R. 59.01N 57.52E
94 E5 **Tses** Namibia 25.58N 18.08E
30 E1 **Tseti La** *pass* Xizang Zizhiqu 31.13N 81.24E
22 C3 **Tsetseg** Mongolia 46.37N 93.06E
22 D2 **Tsetserleg** Mongolia 49.33N 97.39E
22 E3 **Tsetserleg** Mongolia 47.26N 101.22E
23 C9 **Tseung Kwan O** Hong Kong 22.19N 144.14E
66 F6 **Tseuzier, Lac de** Switzerland
89 K8 **Tsévié** Togo 6.26N 1.18E
94 G6 **Tshabong** Botswana 26.03S 22.27E
91 H7 **Tshabuta** Zaïre 7.42N 23.07E
94 F5 **Tshane** Botswana 24.05S 21.54E
91 K9 **Tshangalele** Zaïre 10.50S 27.03E
43 E4 **Tshchebas, Zaliv** *gulf* Kazakhstan **U.S.S.R.**
44 C2 **Tshchikskoye Vdkhr** *res* **U.S.S.R.**
91 C6 **Tshela** Zaïre 4.57S 12.57E
91 J6 **Tshele** Zaïre 4.54S 25.23E
94 J3 **Tshesebe** Botswana 20.48S 27.37E
92 A6 **Tshibamba** Zaïre 9.08S 22.35E
92 D7 **Tshibambo** Zaïre 10.12S 28.46E
92 D3 **Tshibinda** Zaïre 2.20S 28.43E
91 B5 **Tshibobo, Pte** Gabon 3.50S 11.04E
91 H6 **Tshibumbuba** Zaïre 5.15S 22.10E
92 A4 **Tshibumbula** Zaïre 5.15S 22.10E
95 H1 **Tshidilamolomo** S Africa 25.50S 24.41E
91 G7 **Tshikapa** Zaïre 6.28S 20.48E
91 F7 **Tshikuku** Zaïre 6.25S 19.58E
91 H7 **Tshikula** Zaïre 6.10S 22.49E
91 G7 **Tshikulela** Zaïre 6.17S 21.34E
91 H7 **Tshilenge** Zaïre 6.17S 23.48E
91 K9 **Tshilongo** Zaïre 10.30S 26.01E
91 H7 **Tshilunde** Zaïre 6.27S 23.40E
91 H8 **Tshimbalanga** Zaïre 9.40S 23.06E
91 J7 **Tshimboko** Zaïre 7.01S 24.30E
91 H7 **Tshimbulu** Zaïre 6.27S 22.54E
91 H9 **Tshindjamba** Zaïre 10.52S 22.43E
91 G7 **Tshinota** Zaïre 7.02S 20.58E
92 C8 **Tshinsenda** Zaïre 12.20S 27.56E
91 G7 **Tshisuku** Zaïre 6.23S 21.20E
91 G7 **Tshitadi** Zaïre 6.46S 21.43E
91 J6 **Tshofa** Zaïre 5.13S 25.16E
93 B8 **Tshohoha Nord, L** Rwanda
93 B8 **Tshohoha, Sud, L** Rwanda/Burundi
94 L5 **Tshokwane** Transvaal **S Africa** 24.48S 31.52E
92 C11 **Tshontanda** Zimbabwe 18.33S 26.31E
91 J3 **Tshopo** *R* Zaïre
91 G4 **Tshuapa** *R* Zaïre
94 G4 **Tshukudu** Botswana 22.32S 23.27E
91 J6 **Tshumbe Ste.Marie** Zaïre 4.10S 24.21E
91 E5 **Tshumbiri** Zaïre 2.38S 16.18E
94 G4 **Tshwaane** Botswana 22.26S 22.02E
93 A8 **Tshyanika** Rwanda 2.25S 29.39E
95 C5 **Tsiafajavona** *mt* Madagascar 19.20S 47.15E
Tsian *see* **Chi-an**
95 B5 **Tsianaloka** Madagascar 18.08S 44.50E
95 B5 **Tsiandro** Madagascar 18.42S 44.53E
Tsianglo *see* **Ch'ang-lo**
95 B6 **Tsianiny** Madagascar 21.20S 44.01E
Tsiaotso *see* **Chiao-tso**
95 D6 **Tsiatosika** Madagascar 21.10S 48.14E
95 C4 **Tsiazonano** *mt* Madagascar 17.55S 46.44E
82 M1 **Tsibulev** U.S.S.R. 49.06N 29.50E
Tsienkian *see* **Ch'ien-chiang**
Tsienshan *see* **Ch'ien-shan**
Tsienwei *see* **Ch'ien-wei**
94 H3 **Tsigara** Botswana 20.18S 25.50E
41 B2 **Tsigol'ko, Ova** *islds* Novaya Zemlya U.S.S.R.
Tsiho *see* **Ch'i-ho**
95 B8 **Tsihombe** Madagascar 25.19S 45.30E
Tsikiotsing *see* **Ch'i-chiao-ching**
37 D2 **Tşıklı** Turkey 40.52N 27.19E
Tsikura *vol see* **Chikurachki** *vol*
Tsîl *see* **Tasil**
47 F3 **Tsil'ma** *R* U.S.S.R.
95 A8 **Tsimanampetsotsa, L** Madagascar 24.08S 43.45E
95 B6 **Tsimazava** Madagascar 20.40S 45.41E
95 B8 **Tsimilofo** Madagascar 24.56S 45.10E
45 O9 **Tsimlyansk** U.S.S.R. 47.36N 42.06E
45 O9 **Tsimlyanskoye Vdkhr** *res* U.S.S.R.
40 H6 **Tsimmermanovka** U.S.S.R. 51.22N 139.15E
Tsimo *see* **Chi-mo**
Tsim Tsa Tsui *see* **Kowloon Pt**
Tsin *see* **Zin** *water course*
Tsinan *see* **Jinan**
Tsincheng *see* **Jincheng**
95 G3 **Tsineng** S Africa 27.05S 23.05E
83 G3 **Tsínga** *mt* Greece 41.23N 24.44E
Tsingan *see* **Jing'an**
Tsingfeng *see* **Qingfeng**
Tsinghai *prov* China *see* **Qinghai**
Tsingho *see* **Jinghe**
Tsinghocheng *see* **Qinghecheng**
Tsinghuachen *see* **Bo'ai**
Tsinghuiho *see* **Qingshuihe**
Tsingkang *see* **Qinggang**
Tsingkiang *see* **Jingjiang**
Tsingkien *see* **Qingjian**
Tsingkien Ho *R see* **Qingjian He**
Tsingkow *see* **Ganyu**
Tsinglo *see* **Jingle**
Tsingmai *see* **Chengmai**
Tsingning *see* **Jingning**
Tsingping *see* **Qingping**
Tsingpu *see* **Qingpu**
Tsingshen *see* **Qingshen**
Tsingshui *see* **Qingshui**
Tsingsi *see* **Jingxi**
Tsingsu *see* **Qingxu**
Tsingtao *see* **Qingdao**
Tsingteh *see* **Jingde**
Tsingtien *see* **Qingtian**
Tsingtung *res see* **Qingtongxia Sk**
23 B8 **Tsing Yi I** Hong Kong
Tsingyuan Sichuan *see* **Qingshen**
Tsingyun *see* **Qingyuan**
25 G1 **Tsinh Ho** Vietnam 22.25N 103.19E
Tsinhsien *see* **Jinxian**
Tsining *see* **Jining**
95 C3 **Tsinjomitondraka** Madagascar 15.39S 47.10E
Tsinkiang *see* **Jinjiang**
Tsinkong *see* **Qianjiang**
Tsinshui *see* **Qinshui**
23 B9 **Tsin Shui Wan** Hong Kong 22.14N 114.11E
Tsinsien *see* **Jinxian**
94 D2 **Tsintsabis** Namibia 18.45S 17.51E
Tsinyang *see* **Qinyang**
Tsinyun *see* **Jinyun**
84 D2 **Tsiótion** Greece 39.36N 22.04E
42 K4 **Tsipa** *R* U.S.S.R.
40 G2 **Tsipanda** U.S.S.R. 58.11N 135.04E
42 J5 **Tsipikan** U.S.S.R. 54.58N 113.15E
95 C5 **Tsiroanomandidy** Madagascar 18.44S 46.02E
19 N4 **Tsis** *isld* Truk Is **Pacific Oc** 7.18N 151.49E
84 E7 **Tsitália** Greece 37.08N 22.51E
44 G6 **Tsiteli Tskaro** Georgia **U.S.S.R.** 41.27N 46.05E
94 H4 **Tsitle** Botswana 23.12S 25.39E
95 B6 **Tsitondroina** Madagascar 21.19S 45.59E

95 M7 Tsitsa R S Africa
Tsitsihar see Qiqihar
95 G9 Tsitsikamaberge mts S Africa
95 H10 Tsitsikama Pt S Africa 34.11S 24.29E
101 L9 Tsitsutl Peak Br Col 52.44N 125.50W
95 D5 Tsivangiana Madagascar 19.39S 48.48E
84 K11 Tsivarás Crete 35.26N 24.10E
45 T1 Tsivil'sk U.S.S.R. 55.50N 47.28E
41 B3 Tsivol'ki, Zaliv gulf Novaya Zemlya U.S.S.R.
95 C8 Tsivory Madagascar 24.03S 46.05E
Tsiyang see Jiyang
44 E5 Tskhaltubo Georgia U.S.S.R. 42.20N 42.40E
44 E5 Tskhenis Tskali R Georgia U.S.S.R.
44 F5 Tskhinvali Georgia U.S.S.R. 42.14N 43.58E
46 F3 Tsna R Belorussiya U.S.S.R.
46 J2 Tsna R Kalinin U.S.S.R.
45 N2 Tsna R Ryazan' U.S.S.R.
44 G6 Tsnori Georgia U.S.S.R. 41.34N 46.03E
31 J2 Tso R Kashmir/Xizang Zizhiqu
35 E9 Tsoar anc site Jordan 31.01N 35.28E
23 B9 Tso Chui Wan Hong Kong 22.14N 114.14E
94 F2 Tsodilo Hills Botswana 18.47S 21.48E
Tsofit see Zofit
22 D4 Tsogt Mongolia 45.24N 96.42E
22 G5 Tsogttsetsiy Mongolia 43.45N 105.40E
Tso-hsien see Zuozhou
31 K4 Tsokr L Kashmir 33.20N 78.00E
95 M7 Tsolo S Africa 31.19S 28.45E
95 L8 Tsomo S Africa 32.02S 27.50E
95 L7 Tsomo R S Africa
Tsomonang R see Bangong Co
28 J1 Tsomora Xizang Zizhiqu 29.44N 92.24E
31 K4 Tso Morari L Kashmir
Ts'o-na see Cona
Tsona Dzong see Cona
Tso-shui see Zhashui
84 C5 Tsoukaléïka Akhaïa Greece 38.09N 21.39E
84 D7 Tsoukaléïka Messinía Greece 37.12N 22.00E
84 F3 Tsoungriá isld Greece 39.07N 23.30E
44 F7 Tsovagyukh Armenia U.S.S.R. 40.38N 44.59E
20 K7 Tsu Japan 34.41N 136.30E
20 M4 Tsubame Japan 37.40N 138.56E
20 K5 Tsubata Japan 36.42N 136.44E
44 G2 Tsubu U.S.S.R. 45.30N 46.15E
20 O5 Tsuchiura Japan 36.05N 140.11E
44 H5 Tsudakhar U.S.S.R. 42.20N 47.11E
20 D2 Tsudanuma Japan 35.42N 140.02E
23 B8 Tsuen Wan Hong Kong 22.22N 114.06E
20 E9 Tsugao Japan 32.24N 131.14E
20 F5 Tsugaru-kaikyō str Japan
20 N4 Tsugawa Japan 37.42N 139.28E
20 P9 Tsuha Okinawa Japan 26.10N 127.48E
20 L6 Tsukechi Japan 35.41N 137.25E
20 P9 Tsuken-jima isld Okinawa Japan
20 G3 Tsukigata Japan 43.30N 141.40E
20 E9 Tsukumi Japan 33.00N 131.51E
44 E5 Tsulukidze Georgia U.S.S.R. 42.20N 42.28E
94 D2 Tsumeb Namibia 19.13S 17.42E
94 D4 Tsumis Namibia 23.43S 17.28E
94 F2 Tsumkwe Namibia 19.37S 20.30E
Tsungjen see Chongren
Tsungkow see Songkou
Tsungsin see Chongxin
Tsungteh see Chongde
Tsungtso see Chongzuo
92 F11 Tsungwisi Zimbabwe 18.41S 32.20E
Tsungyang see Chongyang
29 L4 Tsunthang Sikkim India 27.38N 88.35E
Tsunyi see Zunyi
44 H5 Tsurib U.S.S.R. 42.15N 46.51E
Tsur Moshe see Zur Moshe
30 H3 Tsuro Og Nepal 27.53N 86.49E
20 M6 Tsuru Japan 35.36N 138.54E
20 K6 Tsuruga Japan 35.40N 136.05E
20 K6 Tsuruga-wan B Japan
20 K5 Tsurugi Japan 36.29N 136.38E
20 H8 Tsurugi-san mt Japan 33.50N 134.04E
20 B3 Tsurumi Ku dist Japan 35.28N 139.33E
20 N3 Tsuruoka Japan 38.42N 139.50E
20 E8 Tsurusaki Japan 33.17N 131.45E
20 K6 Tsushima Japan 35.11N 136.45E
20 C7 Tsushima isld Japan
20 C8 Tsushima kaikyō str Japan
20 C7 Tsutsu Japan 34.08N 129.10E
20 E7 Tsuwano Japan 34.29N 131.45E
20 H6 Tsuyama Japan 35.04N 134.01E
20 D8 Tsuyazaki Japan 33.49N 130.27E
45 C7 Tsvetkovo Ukraine U.S.S.R. 49.08N 31.32E
47 K5 Tsyngaly U.S.S.R. 60.13N 69.42E
47 C2 Tsyp Navolok U.S.S.R. 69.45N 33.01E
45 K1 Tsyurupi, im U.S.S.R. 55.29N 38.29E
45 D10 Tsyurupinsk Ukraine U.S.S.R. 46.35N 32.43E
24 H10 Tu Xizang Zizhiqu 31.00N 94.53E
76 E6 Tua Portugal 41.12N 7.25W
91 E5 Tua Zaïre 3.38S 16.38E
15 H7 Tua R Papua New Guinea
76 E6 Tua R Portugal
11 N5 Tuahine Pt New Zealand 38.43S 178.06E
11 M5 Tuai New Zealand 38.50S 177.10E
11 J4 Tuakau New Zealand 37.15S 174.58E
15 B6 Tual Moluccas Indonesia 5.38S 132.40E
59 E4 Tuam Galway Irish Rep 53.31N 8.50W
11 H8 Tuamarina New Zealand 41.26S 173.59E
15 K6 Tuam I Bismarck Arch 5.56S 148.04E
122 C14 Tuamotu, Arch. des Pacific Oc
122 E15 Tuamotu Is Pacific Oc
122 M10 Tuamotu Ridge Pacific Oc
122 D15 Tuanaké atoll Tuamotu Is Pacific Oc 16.40S 144.12W
18 L7 Tuanan Borneo Indon 2.07S 114.22E
25 G2 Tuan Giao Vietnam 21.35N 103.25E
18 B4 Tuangku isld Indonesia
9 R12 Tu'anuku Tonga, Pacific Oc 18.40S 174.02W
23 D5 Tuanxi Guizhou China 27.30N 107.17E
11 D13 Tuapeka Mouth New Zealand 46.02S 169.32E
115 N2 Tuapi Nicaragua 14.10N 83.20W
51 P9 Tuapovaara Finland 62.29N 30.39E
44 C3 Tuapse U.S.S.R. 44.06N 39.05E
18 M2 Tuaran Sabah Malaysia 6.12N 116.12E
89 H3 Tuareg tribe Mali
18 F3 Tuas Singapore 1.19N 103.40E
18 F3 Tuas dist Singapore
122 B1 Tuasivi W Samoa, Pacific Oc 13.38S 172.08W
18 F8 Tua, Tanjung C Sumatra Indonesia 5.55S 105.44E
11 B13 Tuatapere New Zealand 46.09S 167.42E
58 D5 Tuath, L Mull, Strathclyde Scotland 56.30N 6.15W
42 G4 Tuba U.S.S.R. 57.25N 102.58E
42 E5 Tuba R U.S.S.R.
111 N10 Tubac Arizona 31.37N 111.03W
111 N5 Tuba City Arizona 36.09N 111.18W
34 P8 Ţūbah, Aţ Iraq 30.27N 47.30E
19 F4 Tubalai Moluccas Indon 1.37S 128.20E
34 J6 Tubal, Wādī at watercourse Iraq
18 K9 Tuban Java Indon 6.55S 112.01E
94 H5 Tubane Botswana 24.46S 24.18E
121 J2 Tubarão Brazil 28.29S 49.00W
121 J2 Tubarão, R Brazil
35 E4 Tubas Jordan 32.19N 35.22E
94 C4 Tubas watercourse Namibia
18 K4 Tubau Sarawak Malaysia 3.10N 113.41E
33 B2 Tubayq, Aţ Saudi Arabia
34 E9 Tubayq, At mts Saudi Arabia
19 J7 Tubbataha Reefs Philippines
59 E3 Tubbercurry Sligo Irish Rep 54.03N 8.43W
60 Q10 Tubbergen Netherlands 52.25N 6.46E
100 J8 Tuberose Saskatchewan 50.57N 108.06W
86 E7 Tubhâr Egypt 29.19N 30.42E
118 J8 Tubiacanga, Pta. de Brazil 22.48S 43.14W
19 K8 Tubigan isld Philippines 6.25N 120.47E
19 K5 Tubili Pt Philippines 13.10N 120.30E
75 C2 Tubilla del Agua Spain 42.43N 3.48W
64 G6 Tübingen W Germany 48.32N 9.04E
43 E1 Tubinskiy Bashkir U.S.S.R. 52.52N 58.13E
61 G4 Tubize Belgium 50.42N 4.12E
90 C6 Tubo R Nigeria
15 L8 Tuboa I D'Entrecasteaux Is Papua New Guinea 9.10S 150.52E
19 L7 Tubod Mindanao Philippines 8.04N 123.48E
79 H1 Tubre Italy 46.38N 10.28E
14 A5 Tubridgi Pt W Australia 21.53S 114.37E
85 G3 Tubruq Libya 32.06N 23.56E
122 M10 Tubuai I Tubuai Is Pacific Oc 23.23S 149.27W
122 M10 Tubuai Is Pacific Oc
Tubuai Manu see Maïao
18 M4 Tubu, R Borneo Indon
115 D2 Tubutama Mexico 30.52N 111.29W
119 F2 Tucacas Venezuela 10.50N 68.22W
119 H8 Tucandera Brazil 1.07S 62.49W
110 H3 Tucannon R Washington
118 J2 Tucano Brazil 10.57S 38.46W
121 A6 Tucapel, Pta C Chile 37.36S 73.40W
118 B6 Tucavaca Bolivia 18.36S 58.47W
118 B6 Tucavaca, R Bolivia
72 K10 Tuchan France 42.53N 2.43E
63 Q8 Tucheim E Germany 52.18N 12.11E
23 C5 Tucheng Guizhou China 26.05N 104.35E
Tuchengtze see Xiabancheng
101 J5 Tuchitua Yukon Terr 60.58N 129.03W
101 L6 Tuchodi R Br Col
62 K2 Tuchola Poland 53.36N 17.50E
62 N6 Tuchów Poland 49.54N 21.01E
103 E8 Tuckahoe New Jersey 39.17N 74.45W
103 G5 Tuckahoe New York 40.57N 73.49W
103 C9 Tuckahoe R Maryland
14 C7 Tuckanarra W Australia 27.10S 118.05E
103 O4 Tuckernuck I Massachusetts
96 C1 Tucker's Town Bermuda 32.20N 64.42W
103 F7 Tuckerton New Jersey 39.36N 74.20W
14 E4 Tuckfield, Mt W Australia 18.47S 124.57E
111 O9 Tucson Arizona 32.15N 110.57W
111 N9 Tucson Mts Arizona
119 D3 Tucuco, R Venezuela
87 G3 Tucul Ethiopia 14.48N 38.15E
120 F12 Tucumán prov Argentina
109 G6 Tucumcari New Mexico 35.11N 103.44W
117 D7 Tucunduba, Cachoeira rapids Brazil 4.02S 49.38W
121 C3 Tucunuco Argentina 30.34S 68.38W
Tucunupucú see Hernandarias
117 B7 Tucuparé Brazil 5.05S 55.52W
119 G3 Tucupido Venezuela 9.18N 65.48W
119 H3 Tucupita Venezuela 9.02N 62.04W
119 D2 Tucuracas Colombia 11.47N 72.30W
117 D6 Tucuruí Brazil 3.42S 49.44W
118 G9 Tucuruvi dist São Paulo Brazil
115 Q5 Tucutí Panama 8.02N 77.50W
62 J2 Tuczno Poland 53.12N 16.08E
19 C9 Tudameda Indonesia 10.53S 122.58E
76 L2 Tudanca Spain 43.10N 4.22W
32 C4 Tū Dār Iran 33.49N 48.02E
28 D1 Tudaram Andhra Prad India 18.51N 79.30E
53 G6 Tude Å R Denmark
72 H5 Tudeils France 45.03N 1.47E
75 G3 Tudela Spain 42.04N 1.37W
76 K5 Tudela de Duero Spain 41.35N 4.35W
33 K8 Tudho Oman 17.46N 53.04E
99 J3 Tudhope Ontario 49.15N 81.40W
77 D4 Tudia, Sierra de mts Spain
Tudīran see Todrūyeh
87 F3 Tudluk Ethiopia 15.05N 37.08E
111 C2 Tudor California 39.00N 121.37W
75 H8 Tuéjar Spain 39.46N 1.04W
76 E5 Tuela R Portugal
53 H6 Tuelsø L Denmark 55.27N 11.36E
13 H8 Tuen Queensland 28.33S 145.38E
79 K3 Tuénho Italy 46.20N 11.02E
28 K2 Tuensang Nagaland India 26.16N 94.45E
28 K2 Tuensang dist Nagaland India
117 D6 Tueré, R Brazil
76 H4 Tuerto R Spain
36 J4 Tufanbeyli Seyhan Turkey 38.15N 36.13E
33 H3 Ţufayḩ Saudi Arabia 26.55N 49.46E
33 N10 Tuffat al Ad'amī area Saudi Arabia
70 M5 Tuffe France 48.07N 0.31E
15 K8 Tufi Papua New Guinea 9.08S 149.20E
58 U11 Tuft Ness prom Orkney Scotland 59.19N 2.26W
56 B4 Tufton Dyfed Wales 51.56N 4.51W
37 G7 Tug Turkey 38.27N 42.16E
105 D3 Tugaloo L S Carolina 34.43N 83.20W
22 G8 Tugao Gansu China 36.19N 105.11E
100 L8 Tugaske Saskatchewan 50.54N 106.15W
56 K2 Tugby Leics Eng 52.36N 0.52W
87 L6 Tug Der wadi Somalia
95 P5 Tugela S Africa 29.11S 31.25E
95 O4 Tugela R S Africa
95 O4 Tugela Ferry S Africa 28.45S 30.28E
104 C9 Tug Fork R Kentucky
12 K5 Tuggerah Bay New S Wales
113 K8 Tugidak I Alaska 56.30N 154.40W
19 M6 Tugnug Pt Philippines 11.22N 125.38E
45 N5 Tugolukovo U.S.S.R. 51.57N 41.40E
47 J5 Tugrovskiy U.S.S.R. 61.40N 64.49E
97 O3 Tugssâq Greenland 73.00N 56.00W
48 V13 Tugtiliq fjord Greenland
19 A3 Tuguan isld Celebes Indonesia 0.40N 119.50E
19 N8 Tugubun Pt Mindanao Philippines 7.00N 126.28E
19 K3 Tuguegarao Luzon Philippines 17.36N 121.44E
47 J7 Tugulym U.S.S.R. 57.02N 64.40E
40 G5 Tugur U.S.S.R. 53.44N 136.45E
40 G5 Tugur R U.S.S.R.
40 G5 Tugurskiy Zaliv B U.S.S.R.
42 G5 Tugutuy U.S.S.R. 52.40N 104.50E
93 L5 Tug Wein Kenya 0.48N 39.18E
Tuht see Yapraklı
25 N7 Tuhtong Burma 27.39N 98.14E
11 G8 Tui New Zealand 41.34S 172.45E
18 C9 Tui R Pen Malaysia
120 E6 Tuichi, R Bolivia
Tui-la-ma-miao see Tui Lamin Sum
22 H6 Tui Lamin Sum Nei Monggol Zizhiqu China 41.56N 110.42E
42 D5 Tuim U.S.S.R. 54.21N 89.55E
Tuimazy oil field see Tuymazy
96 T11 Tuineje Fuerteventura Canary Is 28.18N 14.03W
94 K5 Tuinplaas S Africa 25.00S 28.36E
119 C3 Tuira, R Panama
Tuisarkan see Tūysarkān
32 G7 Tujak Iran 26.01N 57.14E
Tujiabu see Yongxiu
18 C7 Tujoh, Bukit hill Pen Malaysia 4.22N 102.01E
60 N8 Tuk Netherlands 52.48N 6.05E
18 C4 Tuka Sumatra Indon 2.10N 98.24E
41 H6 Tukalan R U.S.S.R.
43 D1 Tukan Bashkir U.S.S.R. 53.51N 57.28E
19 C6 Tukangbesi, Kep islds Indonesia
87 F6 Tuka Ra Ethiopia
34 N9 Tukayyid Iraq 29.46N 45.38E
93 M7 Tukeli Kenya 1.04S 40.53E
86 E10 Tukh Egypt 27.41N 30.48E
86 F5 Tûkh Egypt 30.21N 31.11E
86 E4 Tûkh Dalaka Egypt 30.39N 30.54E
86 F4 Tûkh el Aqlâm Egypt 30.53N 31.25E
11 L6 Tukituki R New Zealand
113 H7 Tuklung Alaska 58.49N 159.30W
25 G6 Tuk Luy Cambodia 12.04N 103.29E
42 H4 Tukolon' U.S.S.R. 55.25N 107.40E
91 G6 Tukope Zaïre 4.37S 20.25E
85 F3 Tūkrah Libya 32.32N 20.35E
87 B5 Tukswana Sudan 11.07N 29.48E
101 G1 Tuktoyaktuk N W Terr 69.27N 133.00W
29 H3 Tukucha Nepal 28.41N 83.39E
41 O8 Tukulan R U.S.S.R.
87 F4 Tukul Duma Ethiopia 13.33N 37.00E
46 E2 Tukums Latvia U.S.S.R. 56.58N 23.10E
18 J6 Tukung, Bukit mt Borneo Indon 0.58S 111.54E
40 D5 Tukuringra, Khrebet mts U.S.S.R.
44 G3 Túkuy Mekteb U.S.S.R. 44.20N 45.04E
92 F6 Tukuyu Tanzania 9.14S 33.39E
31 D3 Tukzar Afghanistan 35.57N 66.21E
43 N8 Tul' Uzbekistan U.S.S.R. 40.08N 71.05E
122 E1 Tula Amer Samoa Pacific Oc 14.15S 170.35W
115 K7 Tula Hidalgo Mexico 20.01N 99.21W
81 B2 Tula Sardinia 40.44N 8.59E
115 K6 Tula Tamaulipas Mexico 23.00N 99.41W
45 J2 Tula U.S.S.R. 54.11N 37.38E
93 L6 Tula watercourse Kenya
100 P4 Tulabi Lake Saskatchewan 54.44N 102.58W
Tula Gol R see Tuul Gol
22 B8 Tulagt Ar Gol R Qinghai China
41 N9 Tulagy-Kil'dem U.S.S.R. 62.18N 129.50E
22 D7 Tulai Nanshan mt ra Qinghai China
22 D7 Tulai Shan mt ra Qinghai China
31 B4 Tulak Afghanistan 33.58N 63.44E
101 N11 Tulameen Br Col 49.33N 120.45W
115 K7 Tulancingo Mexico 20.06N 98.20W
91 F11 Tülandangombe Angola 14.56S 18.20E
18 F8 Tulangbawang R Sumatra Indon
111 E5 Tulare California 36.13N 119.22W
108 M5 Tulare S Dakota 44.45N 98.31W
111 E5 Tulare L lake bed California
109 D8 Tularosa New Mexico 33.04N 106.02W
109 B8 Tularosa Mts New Mexico
109 D9 Tularosa Valley New Mexico
28 F1 Tulasi mt Madhya Prad/Orissa India 18.42N 82.04E
33 F3 Ţulayḩī, Aţ Saudi Arabia 27.30N 44.10E
41 J4 Tulay-Kiryaka-Tas, Vozvyshennost' mts U.S.S.R.
95 C9 Tulbagh S Africa 33.17S 19.09E
94 F8 Tulbagh mt S Africa 30.56S 20.43E
119 C7 Tulcan Ecuador 0.50N 77.48W
82 M5 Tulcea Romania 45.10N 28.50E
46 G5 Tul'chin Ukraine U.S.S.R. 48.40N 28.49E
89 F8 Tule Ivory Coast 7.55N 6.03W
119 D2 Tulé Venezuela 10.56N 72.06W
111 E5 Tule R California
75 G4 Tulebras Spain 41.59N 1.41W
112 F1 Tule Cr Texas
32 E3 Tuleh Semnān Iran 34.38N 52.45E
Tūleh Tehrān Iran see Tūreh
110 D8 Tule L California 41.54N 121.31W
29 L4 Tule-la pass India 27.10N 88.50E
110 D8 Tulelake California 41.58N 121.29W
110 E8 Tule Lake Res California 41.05N 120.25W
101 Y4 Tulemalu L N W Terr
51 Q10 Tulema-yoku R Karelia U.S.S.R.
71 F8 Tulette France 44.17N 4.56E
43 O8 Tuleyken Kirgiziya U.S.S.R. 40.29N 72.51E
Tulha see Tuleh
92 D12 Tuli Zimbabwe 21.59S 29.15E
92 D12 Tuli R Zimbabwe
112 F1 Tulia Texas 34.32N 101.46W
25 M7 Tulieng Assam India 27.39N 96.18E
21 B2 Tulihe Nei Monggol Zizhiqu China 50.26N 121.43E
113 C10 Tulik Vol Aleutian Is 53.25N 168.04W
29 L3 Tuling Pass Xizang Zizhiqu 28.16N 88.59E
62 L3 Tuliszków Poland 52.05N 18.19E
28 C1 Tuljapur Maharashtra India 18.03N 76.10E
35 D4 Tulkarm Jordan 32.19N 35.02E
59 E6 Tulla Clare Irish Rep 52.52N 8.45W
59 J2 Tullaghoge Tyrone N Ireland 54.37N 6.43W
107 K6 Tullahoma Tennessee 35.21N 86.12W
58 G5 Tulla, L Strathclyde Scotland 56.33N 4.47W
12 C6 Tullamarine dist Melbourne, Vic
12 J5 Tullamore New S Wales 32.39S 147.39E
59 H5 Tullamore Offaly Irish Rep 53.16N 7.30W
72 H5 Tulle France 45.16N 1.46E
Tullear see Tolia
53 F7 Tullebølle Denmark 54.58N 10.50E
12 H5 Tullibigeal New S Wales 33.30S 146.48E
64 N7 Tulling W Germany 48.05N 12.04E
71 G6 Tullins France 45.18N 5.29E
65 O5 Tulln Austria 48.20N 16.03E
65 N5 Tullner Feld reg Austria
58 G5 Tulloch Station Highland Scotland 56.53N 4.42W
107 D10 Tullos Louisiana 31.50N 92.20W
59 J6 Tullow Carlow Irish Rep 52.48N 6.44W
87 G6 Tullu Milki Ethiopia 9.59N 38.20E
90 M6 Tullus Sudan 11.07N 24.31E
104 J4 Tully New York 42.47N 76.06W
13 H4 Tully Queensland 17.55S 145.59E
13 H4 Tully R Queensland
59 K3 Tullydonnel Armagh N Ireland 54.04N 6.30W
13 H4 Tully Falls Queensland 17.48S 145.42E
59 G2 Tullyhomman Bridge Fermanagh N Ireland 54.33N 7.49W
13 E3 Tully Inlet Queensland
59 J3 Tullynagrow Monaghan Irish Rep 54.11N 6.44W
103 E6 Tullytown Pennsylvania 40.08N 74.49W
85 F3 Tulmaythah Libya 32.42N 20.55E
47 C2 Tuloma R U.S.S.R.
21 E4 Tulongshan Heilongjiang China 46.23N 130.10E
47 C4 Tulos, Ozero L U.S.S.R.
82 K8 Tulovo Bulgaria 42.33N 25.32E
47 H5 Tulpan U.S.S.R. 61.25N 57.18E
109 P5 Tulsa Oklahoma 36.07N 95.58W
101 G6 Tulsequah Br Col 58.39N 133.35W
30 L7 Tulsihata W Bengal India 25.27N 87.54E
30 L7 Tulsipur Bihar India 25.22N 87.03E
30 F5 Tulsipur Uttar Prad India 27.32N 82.24E
59 F4 Tulsk Roscommon Irish Rep 53.47N 8.15W
44 C3 Tul'skaya U.S.S.R. 44.31N 40.14E
46 K3 Tul'skaya Oblast' prov U.S.S.R.
53 D4 Tulstrup Denmark 56.07N 9.48E
87 A4 Tulu Sudan 12.54N 26.17E
119 C5 Tuluá Colombia 4.05N 76.12W
24 B5 T'u-lu-ka-erh-t'e Shan-k'ou see Turagart Shankou
113 G6 Tuluksak Alaska 61.04N 160.58W
115 Q7 Tulum ruins Mexico 20.10N 87.29W
121 C4 Tulumaya R Argentina
120 B4 Tulumayo, R Peru
47 H7 Tulumbasy U.S.S.R. 57.27N 57.40E
121 C3 Tulum, Valle de Argentina
42 G5 Tulun U.S.S.R. 54.32N 100.35E
18 J10 Tulungagung Java Indon 8.03S 111.54E
28 H1 Tulung Churbu Gomba Xizang Zizhiqu 29.40N 90.21E
28 J2 Tulung La pass India/Xizang Zizhiqu 27.49N 92.16E
19 J6 Tuluran isld Philippines 11.00N 119.17E
119 G7 Tulu-Tuloi, Serra mts Brazil
47 H7 Tulva R U.S.S.R.
19 G5 Tum Moluccas Indon 3.36S 130.20E
45 M1 Tuma U.S.S.R. 55.08N 40.35E
102 K8 Tuma R Nicaragua
111 N10 Tumacacori Nat.Mon Arizona 31.34N 111.04W
119 B7 Tumaco Colombia 1.51N 78.46W
93 L8 Tumade Kenya 2.34S 39.53E
19 N8 Tumadgo Pt Mindanao Philippines 6.48N 126.15E
15 L8 Tuma I Trobriand Is Papua New Guinea 8.23S 150.52E
30 A8 Tumain Madhya Prad India 24.29N 77.43W
110 D5 Tumalo Oregon 44.09N 121.20W
32 J3 Tūmān Āqā Iran 34.54N 61.02E
31 H1 Tumanchi R Xinjiang Uygur Zizhiqu China
45 F1 Tumanovo U.S.S.R. 55.24N 34.33E
47 K6 Tuman, Oz L U.S.S.R. 59.37N 66.15E
42 F4 Tumanshet U.S.S.R. 55.50N 97.17E
39 K3 Tumanskiy U.S.S.R. 64.03N 178.10E
39 F4 Tumany U.S.S.R. 60.55N 155.57E
44 F7 Tumanyan Armenia U.S.S.R. 40.59N 44.38E
41 N8 Tumara R U.S.S.R.
41 P5 Tumat U.S.S.R. 70.50N 139.30E
87 E5 Tumat watercourse Sudan
41 N4 Tumatskaya Protoka canal U.S.S.R.
42 F6 Tumat-Tayga, Khrebet mts U.S.S.R.
119 J5 Tumatumari Guyana 5.17N 58.59W
91 D9 Tumba Angola 11.07S 14.58E
91 D6 Tumba Bas-Zaïre Zaïre 5.27S 14.54E
91 G4 Tumba Equateur Zaïre 1.50S 20.09E
91 H5 Tumba Kasai-Oriental Zaïre 3.10S 23.36E
91 F5 Tumba tribe Zaïre
91 F4 Tumba, L Zaïre 0.45S 18.00E
19 M8 Tumbao Mindanao Philippines 7.08N 124.22E
81 A1 Tumbarino, Pta Sardinia 41.03N 8.13E
12 J6 Tumbarumba New S Wales 35.49S 148.01E
92 J11 Tumbatu I Zanzibar 5.50S 39.13E
120 F10 Tumbaya Argentina 23.50S 65.26W
119 B9 Tumbes Peru 3.37S 80.27W
119 B9 Tumbes dept Peru
119 B9 Tumbes, R Ecuador/Peru
115 H8 Tumbiscatio Mexico 18.31N 102.21W
56 C4 Tumble Dyfed Wales 51.48N 4.07W
104 P1 Tumbledown Mt Maine 45.28N 70.30W
13 B2 Tumbling Waters N Terr Australia 12.50S 130.56E
93 K6 Tumboni Kenya 0.47S 38.26E
45 P1 Tumbotino U.S.S.R. 56.00N 43.00E
84 Z21 Tumbrell Pt Malta 35.50N 14.34E
91 D6 Tumbumami Zaïre 5.58S 15.19E
118 B9 Tumburús Argentina 25.50S 58.15W
91 K9 Tumbwe Zaïre 11.26S 27.19E
57 N6 Tumby Lincs Eng 53.08N 0.09W
12 D5 Tumby Bay S Australia 34.20S 136.05E
22 H6 Tumd Youqi Nei Monggol Zizhiqu China 40.35N 110.32E
22 J6 Tumd Zuoqi Nei Monggol Zizhiqu China 40.46N 111.12E
35 G4 Tumeira Jordan 32.24N 35.59E
21 E6 Tumen Jilin China 42.56N 129.47E
22 D3 Tümen Mongolia 46.11N 96.02E
21 E6 Tumen Jiang R Jilin China
21 E6 Tumen R China/U.S.S.R.
22 F8 Tumenzi Gansu China 37.37N 103.05E
119 H4 Tumeremo Venezuela 7.17N 61.30W
119 H4 Tumereng Guyana 6.13N 60.03W
Tumgiran see Tamp-e Gīrān
19 J9 Tumindao isld Philippines 4.44N 119.25E
118 H6 Tumiritinga Brazil 18.59S 41.37W
28 C4 Tumkur Karnataka India 13.20N 77.06E
28 C4 Tumkur dist Karnataka India
28 H1 Tum La pass Xizang Zizhiqu 28.16N 90.44E
58 H5 Tummel Bridge Tayside Scotland 56.43N 4.01W
58 J5 Tummel, L Tayside Scotland 56.43N 3.55W
58 H5 Tummel, R Tayside Scotland
40 H7 Tumnin U.S.S.R. 49.42N 140.04E
40 H7 Tumnin R U.S.S.R.
19 L1 Tumon B Guam Pacific Oc
31 B7 Tump Pakistan 26.06N 62.24E
18 E2 Tumpat Pen Malaysia 6.13N 102.10E
25 G6 Tumpor, Phnom mt Cambodia 12.24N 103.01E
29 F7 Tumsar Maharashtra India 21.24N 79.48E
43 H7 Tumshuk Uzbekistan U.S.S.R. 39.53N 67.24E
89 J6 Tumu Ghana 10.55N 1.59W
117 B3 Tumucumaque, Sa mts Brazil/Surinam
29 H8 Tumudibandh Orissa India 19.59N 83.46E
41 N8 Tumul U.S.S.R. 62.58N 129.40E
120 E6 Tumupasa Bolivia 14.08S 67.55W
120 F9 Tumusla Bolivia 20.30S 65.35W
12 J6 Tumut New S Wales 35.20S 148.14E
12 J6 Tumut R New S Wales
46 R2 Tumutuk U.S.S.R. 55.00N 53.20E
24 C5 Tumxuk Xinjiang Uygur Zizhiqu China 41.27N 79.57E
52 G8 Tun Sweden 58.26N 12.45E
29 B6 Tuna Gujarat India 22.59N 70.04E
52 K4 Tuna Sweden 62.20N 17.10E
19 M8 Tuna B Mindanao Philippines 6.20N 124.03E
119 D7 Tunaima, L Colombia 0.45N 73.15W
116 O1 Tunapuna Trinidad & Tobago 10.38N 61.23W
120 E7 Tunari pk Bolivia 17.17S 66.23W
121 H2 Tunas Brazil 29.14S 52.47W
116 E4 Tunas de Zaza Cuba 21.39N 79.34W
121 E5 Tunas, L Argentina
Tunb see Tanb-e bozorg
12 H8 Tunbridge Tasmania 42.08S 147.26E
Tunbridge Wells, Royal see Royal Tunbridge Wells
36 B1 Tunca R Bulgaria/Turkey
36 D3 Tunçbilek Turkey 39.39N 29.28E
37 E6 Tunceli Turkey 39.07N 39.34E
23 E9 Tunchang Guangdong China 19.29N 110.10E
12 K4 Tuncurry New S Wales 32.17S 152.29E
30 B5 Tundla Uttar Prad India 27.13N 78.14E
47 E4 Tundra U.S.S.R. 64.14N 40.44E
53 X15 Tundradalen V Norway 61.48N 7.51E
85 K10 Tundubai Sudan 18.36N 28.35E
92 F6 Tunduma Tanzania 9.19S 32.48E
92 H7 Tunduru Tanzania 11.08S 37.21E
82 K8 Tundzha R Bulgaria
53 J5 Tune Denmark 55.36N 12.12E
35 G6 Tuneib, Et Jordan 31.48N 35.57E
121 B4 Tunel la Cumbre Arg/Chile
76 C14 Tunes Portugal 37.10N 8.11W
50 B3 Tunga Bardhastrandarsýsla Iceland 65.38N 23.49W
50 C2 Tunga Isafjardharsýsla Nordhur Iceland 66.26N 22.56W
28 B4 Tunga R Karnataka India
28 B3 Tungabhadra Dam Karnataka India 15.00N 75.50E
28 C3 Tungabhadra R Andrha Prad/Mysore India
28 C3 Tungabhadra Res Karnataka India
Tung-an see Mishan
87 C5 Tungaru Sudan 10.12N 30.41E
53 X14 Tungaseter Norway 62.14N 7.55E
53 V15 Tungastølen Norway 61.32N 6.59E
Tungchangtai see Xinbin
T'ung-cheng see Zhongdong
23 J7 Tung-chiang Taiwan 22.26N 120.30E
Tungchow see Tongzhou
60 L15 Tungelroij Netherlands 51.13N 5.44E
22 G7 Tunggalag Nur Nei Monggol Zizhiqu China 38.43N 105.07E
92 K7 Tunghi, B.de Mozambique
Tung-hsing-chen see Chunhua Jilin
31 H9 Tungi Bangladesh 23.55N 90.24E
89 D7 Tungie Sierra Leone 8.30N 11.34W
40 B4 Tungir R U.S.S.R.
40 A4 Tungirskiy Khrebet mts U.S.S.R.
Tungki Chiang R see Sung Ch'i
18 N3 Tungku Sabah Malaysia 5.05N 119.00E
18 C8 Tungku hill Pen Malaysia 3.50N 102.15E
Tung-liao see Liaoyuan
Tung Lung isld see Lam Tong
50 F6 Tungnaá R Iceland
50 G6 Tungnaá reg Iceland
50 G6 Tungnaárfjöll mt Iceland 64.15N 18.15W
50 G6 Tungnaárjökull ice cap Iceland 64.20N 18.05W
50 H5 Tungnafell, mt Iceland 64.46N 17.51W
50 H5 Tungnafellsjökull ice cap Iceland 64.45N 17.55W
50 G3 Tungnahryggsjökull ice cap Iceland 65.43N 18.47W
42 L1 Tungnary R U.S.S.R.
42 K5 Tungokochen U.S.S.R. 53.35N 115.35E
24 H9 Tung-pu-le-t'u Shan-k'ou pass Qinghai China 33.57N 94.50E
23 J7 Tung Shan mt Taiwan 23.27N 120.56E
23 J6 Tung-shih Taiwan 24.13N 120.54E
110 G9 Tungsten Nevada 40.48N 118.08W
101 J5 Tungsten N W Terr 61.59N 128.09W
90 L6 Tungsunga, Jebel mt Sudan 11.30N 23.21E
9 T12 Tungua atoll Tonga, Pacific Oc 20.00S 174.45W
50 E6 Túngufell Iceland 64.17N 20.10W
50 F3 Tungufjall mt Skagafjardharsýsla Iceland 65.34N 19.03W
50 H4 Tungufjall mt Thingeyjarsýsla, Sudhur Iceland 65.28N 17.45W
50 E6 Tungufljót R Iceland
50 H2 Tunguheidhi heath Iceland
93 A1 Tungu, Jeb Sudan 4.21N 29.59E
18 K5 Tungun, Bukit mt Borneo Indon 0.30N 113.12E
119 B8 Tungurahua prov Ecuador
119 B8 Tungurahua, Vol Ecuador 1.30S 78.26W
39 E4 Tunguska U.S.S.R. 61.20N 151.42E
41 N8 Tungus-Khaya U.S.S.R. 64.58N 125.16E
41 F5 Tungusy U.S.S.R. 70.41N 94.15E
41 F5 Tungusy I-ye U.S.S.R. 70.36N 92.25E
92 J12 Tunguu Zanzibar 6.12S 39.20E
50 R11 Tunheim Spitsbergen 73.29N 19.13E
52 D6 Tunhovdfjord L Norway 60.25N 8.55E
28 F2 Tuni Andhra Prad India 17.23N 82.36E
119 C6 Tunía Colombia 2.44N 76.31W
107 F7 Tunica Mississippi 34.41N 90.23W
88 T3 Tunis Tunisia 36.50N 10.13E
88 T3 Tunis, G. de gulf Tunisia
73 E2 Tunisia rep N Africa
103 B9 Tunis Mills Maryland 38.49N 76.10W
119 D5 Tunja Colombia 5.33N 73.23W
42 G6 Tunka U.S.S.R. 51.46N 102.31E
30 E2 Tun-kang Xizang Zizhiqu 30.36N 81.19E
115 P7 Tunkás Mexico 20.54N 88.42W
103 C3 Tunkhannock Pennsylvania 41.32N 75.46W
103 C3 Tunkhannock Cr Pennsylvania
42 G6 Tunkinskiye Gol'tsy mts U.S.S.R.
22 J8 Tunliu Shanxi China 36.13N 112.50E
52 F4 Tunna R Norway
12 J8 Tunnack Tasmania 42.27S 147.27E
93 G6 Tunnel Kenya 0.13S 35.23E
14 C6 Tunnel Cr W Australia
99 G6 Tunnel Dam Ontario 46.26N 83.24W
104 F7 Tunnelton W Virginia 39.23N 79.45W
52 G2 Tunnsjø L Norway 64.45N 13.25E
53 E5 Tunø Denmark 55.57N 10.27E
53 E5 Tunø isld Denmark 55.57N 10.27E
42 H1 Tunor U.S.S.R. 62.35N 105.58E
53 W15 Tunsbergdalsbre glacier Norway
57 J6 Tunstall Staffs Eng 53.05N 2.13W
56 O3 Tunstall Suffolk Eng 52.09N 1.27E
61 P8 Tuntange Luxembourg 49.43N 6.00E
113 F6 Tuntutuliak Alaska 60.22N 162.38W
97 N6 Tunungayualok I Labrador, Nfld 56.00N 61.00W
121 B4 Tunuyán Argentina 33.35S 69.00W
121 B4 Tunuyán R Argentina
121 C4 Tunuyán, Sa.de ra Argentina
23 H4 Tunxi Anhui China 29.43N 118.20E
30 J3 Tuo Nepal 27.54N 86.50E
42 L2 Tuobuya U.S.S.R. 62.13N 116.01E
23 F6 Tuojiang Hunan China 25.12N 111.35E
23 C3 Tuo Jiang R Sichuan China
22 M7 Tuoji Dao isld Liaoning China
40 C1 Tuolba R U.S.S.R.
22 D7 Tuole Qinghai China 38.54N 98.26E
25 H6 Tuol Khpos Cambodia 12.01N 104.25E
111 D4 Tuolumne California 37.59N 120.15W
111 D4 Tuolumne R California
111 E4 Tuolumne Meadows California 37.51N 119.25W
51 L7 Tuomioja Finland 64.38N 25.04E
23 C5 Tuomogou Sichuan China 27.40N 102.24E
40 C2 Tuora U.S.S.R. 59.28N 125.16E
41 N5 Tuora-Sis, Khrebet mts U.S.S.R.
39 C3 Tuora-Yuryakh R U.S.S.R.
80 F2 Tuoro sul Trasimeno Italy 43.12N 12.04E
66 Q5 Tuors, Val Switzerland
39 B2 Tuostakh U.S.S.R. 67.25N 137.06E
39 B1 Tuostakh R U.S.S.R.
Tuotuohe see Tanggulashanqu
24 G8 Tuotuo He R Qinghai China
42 J1 Tuoy-Khaya U.S.S.R. 62.33N 111.25E
21 C2 Tuozaminnutuke Nei Monggol Zizhiqu China 50.11N 123.02E
118 E7 Tupā Brazil 21.57S 50.28W
118 E6 Tupaciguara Brazil 18.34S 48.45W
32 B2 Tūp Āghāj Iran 36.05N 47.52E
Tupai see Motu Iti
119 H8 Tupanaóca Brazil 1.11S 61.50W
120 G1 Tupana, R Brazil
121 H2 Tupanciretа Brazil 29.05S 53.50W
121 G2 Tuparai Brazil 29.11S 56.15W
11 N4 Tuparoa New Zealand 37.56S 178.25E
119 F5 Tuparro, R Colombia
107 H7 Tupelo Mississippi 34.15N 88.43W
109 O7 Tupelo Oklahoma 34.36N 96.26W
45 C5 Tupichev Ukraine U.S.S.R. 51.45N 31.28E
40 A4 Tupik Chita U.S.S.R. 54.29N 120.00E
46 J2 Tupik U.S.S.R. 55.40N 33.32E
117 A6 Tupinambarama, I Brazil
118 E4 Tupiraçaba Brazil 14.39S 48.31W
117 D9 Tupirama Brazil 8.58S 48.10W
117 D9 Tupiratins Brazil 8.27S 48.07W
120 F9 Tupiza Bolivia 21.27S 65.45W
111 E6 Tupman California 35.18N 119.21W
51 L7 Tupos Finland 64.53N 25.30E
101 N8 Tupper Br Col 55.30N 120.01W
104 L2 Tupper L New York
104 L2 Tupper Lake New York 44.14N 74.29W
104 L2 Tupper L, Lit New York 44.03N 74.38W
121 B4 Tupungato Argentina 33.24S 69.07W
121 B4 Tupungato pk Arg/Chile 33.20S 69.50W
Tuqaiyid see Tukayyid
35 G3 Tuqbul Jordan 32.36N 35.48E
Tuqtaqana see Ţaqţaqanah, Aţ
21 B5 Tuquan Nei Monggol Zizhiqu China 45.26N 121.42E
119 C7 Túquerres Colombia 1.06N 77.37W
72 G4 Tuquet-de-la-Garde mt France 45.40N 1.05E
23 F8 Tuqu Wan B Guangdong China
86 F6 Tura Egypt 29.56N 31.16E
28 H3 Tura Meghalaya India 25.32N 90.14E
92 F4 Tura Tanzania 5.30S 33.50E
41 H8 Tura U.S.S.R. 64.20N 100.17E
24 E7 Tura Xinjiang Uygur Zizhiqu China 37.34N 86.27E
47 J6 Tura R U.S.S.R.
33 D6 Turabah Saudi Arabia 21.15N 41.34E
33 E2 Turabah Saudi Arabia 28.18N 42.56E
33 D6 Turabah, Wādī watercourse Saudi Arabia
31 C5 Turabaz Afghanistan 31.07N 65.49E
119 G4 Turagua, Serrania mts Venezuela
28 D5 Turaiyur Tamil Nadu India 11.13N 78.35E
41 M4 Turakh U.S.S.R. 73.00N 124.00E
11 K7 Turakina New Zealand 40.02S 175.12E
11 K7 Turakina R New Zealand
11 J8 Turakirae Hd New Zealand 41.27S 174.56E
13 K8 Turallin Queensland 27.50S 151.10E
42 F2 Turama U.S.S.R. 61.19N 96.45E
15 G7 Turama R., Delta of Papua New Guinea
42 G6 Turan Buryat U.S.S.R. 51.40N 101.38E
32 G3 Turan Iran 35.39N 56.42E
35 E2 Tur'an Israel 32.46N 35.22E
42 E6 Turan Tuvinsk U.S.S.R. 52.11N 93.58E
40 E6 Turana, Khrebet mts U.S.S.R.
11 K6 Turangi New Zealand 39.00S 175.49E
36 C3 Turanlı Turkey 39.10N 27.20E
78 E6 Turano R Italy
80 G4 Turano, L.di Italy
43 D7 Turanskaya Nizmennost' lowland U.S.S.R.
66 S4 Turasp Switzerland 46.47N 10.16E
33 H3 Turayf Saudi Arabia 27.31N 48.38E
34 F7 Turayf Saudi Arabia 31.43N 38.35E
33 J6 Turayqā', Aţ Saudi Arabia 21.22N 51.00E
119 C2 Turbaco Colombia 10.20N 75.25W
33 E9 Turbah Yemen 15.06N 43.02E
33 E10 Turbah, At Yemen 12.42N 43.29E
70 E7 Turballe, la France 47.21N 2.30W
47 G5 Turbanovo U.S.S.R. 60.05N 50.46E
31 B8 Turbat Pakistan 26.00N 63.06E
Turbat-i-Haidari see Torbat-e-Heydarīyeh
66 M2 Turbenthal Switzerland 47.27N 8.51E
93 K2 Turbi Kenya 2.20N 38.24E
71 L9 Turbie, la France 43.45N 7.24E
79 E3 Turbigo Italy 45.32N 8.44E
119 C3 Turbo Colombia 8.06N 76.44W
93 G5 Turbo Kenya 0.37N 35.05E
75 M3 Turbón mt Spain 42.25N 0.30E
59 B5 Turbot I Galway Irish Rep 53.30N 10.09W
103 A4 Turbotville Pennsylvania 41.07N 76.46W
82 M1 Turbov U.S.S.R. 49.20N 28.47E
82 H6 Turburea Romania 44.42N 23.29E
47 D4 Turchasovo U.S.S.R. 63.05N 39.12E
81 E9 Turchi, B.d Pantelleria I Italy 36.45N 12.02E
76 H3 Turcia Spain 42.31N 5.52W
76 A10 Turcifal Portugal 39.02N 9.16W
69 N7 Turckheim France 48.06N 7.17E
120 E8 Turco Bolivia 18.12S 68.12W
82 H4 Turda Romania 46.35N 23.50E
45 J3 Turdey U.S.S.R. 53.21N 38.00E
14 C6 Turee Cr W Australia
76 L6 Turégano Spain 41.09N 4.01W
32 C3 Tūreh Tehrān Iran 34.04N 49.19E
122 F16 Turéia atoll Tuamotu Is Pacific Oc 20.49S 138.30W
62 L3 Turek Poland 52.01N 18.30E
86 L9 Tûr, El Egypt 28.14N 33.36E
72 H5 Turenne France 45.04N 1.34E
79 L1 Tures, Val di V Italy
90 B5 Tureta Nigeria 12.40N 5.37E
66 S5 Turettas mt Switzerland 46.36N 10.21E
Turfan see Turpan
24 F4 Turfan Depression Xinjiang Uygur Zizhiqu China
94 T13 Turffontein S Africa 26.15S 28.02E
22 E1 Türga Nuur L Mongolia
43 L2 Turgay Akmolinsk, Kazakhstan U.S.S.R. 51.46N 72.45E
43 G3 Turgay Kustanay, Kazakhstan U.S.S.R. 49.38N 63.25E
43 G3 Turgay R Kazakhstan U.S.S.R.
43 G3 Turgayskaya Dolina V Kazakhstan U.S.S.R.
43 G2 Turgayskaya Oblast' Kazakhstan U.S.S.R.
43 F2 Turgayskaya Stolovaya Strana tableland Kazakhstan U.S.S.R.
22 B2 Turgen Uul pk Mongolia 49.40N 91.20E
99 L3 Turgeon R Quebec
31 F2 Turghan Pass Afghanistan 37.26N 70.41E
66 K2 Turgi Switzerland 47.30N 8.16E
82 K7 Tŭrgovishte Bulgaria 43.14N 26.37E
47 M6 Turgoyak U.S.S.R. 55.10N 60.10E
47 M6 Turgoyak, Oz L U.S.S.R. 55.08N 60.04E
72 G10 Turgulla, Pic de mt France 42.44N 1.19E
36 C5 Turgut Muğla Turkey 37.22N 28.02E
36 F4 Turğut Turkey 38.38N 31.49E
36 C4 Turgutlu Turkey 38.30N 27.43E
92 E12 Turgwe R Zimbabwe
36 J2 Turhal Turkey 40.23N 36.05E
120 E10 Turi Chile 22.13S 68.15W
46 F1 Türi Estonia U.S.S.R. 58.48N 25.28E
81 O2 Turi Italy 40.55N 17.02E
93 G6 Turi Kenya 0.17S 35.47E
75 J8 Turia R Spain
117 E5 Turiaçu Brazil 1.40S 45.22W
117 E1 Turiaçu, B. de Brazil
117 E6 Turiaçu, R Brazil
119 F2 Turiamo Venezuela 10.30N 67.50W
44 H7 Turianchay R Azerbaydzhan U.S.S.R.
92 H5 Turiani Tanzania 6.10S 37.38E
120 E6 Turiapo R Bolivia
62 L7 Turiec R Czechoslovakia
116 E3 Turiguano, Isla Cuba 22.17N 78.36W
12 M6 Turimetta Hd New S Wales 33.42S 151.19E
100 E9 Turin Alberta 49.59N 112.35W
Turin Italy see Torino
104 K3 Turin New York 43.38N 75.25W
47 J6 Turinsk U.S.S.R. 58.03N 63.42E
47 J6 Turinskaya-Sloboda U.S.S.R. 57.38N 64.20E
77 P2 Turís Spain 39.23N 0.43W
40 E9 Turiy Rog U.S.S.R. 45.13N 131.59E
62 K8 Türje Hungary 47.00N 17.07E
Tur, Jebel et mt see Olives, Mt.of
46 E5 Turka Ukraine U.S.S.R. 49.10N 23.02E
42 H5 Turka U.S.S.R. 52.56N 108.15E
42 H5 Turka R U.S.S.R.
93 G2 Turkana dist Kenya
41 M4 Turkannakh U.S.S.R. 73.22N 123.30E
30 H6 Turkauliya Bihar India 26.36N 84.49E
58 H6 Turk, Bridge of Central Scotland 56.13N 4.25W
36 G1 Türkeli Turkey 41.57N 34.26E
37 D2 Türkeli isld Turkey 40.31N 27.28E
64 L7 Türkenfeld W Germany 48.06N 11.05E
43 J5 Turkestan Kazakhstan U.S.S.R. 43.17N 68.16E
38 F4 Turkestan reg U.S.S.R.
43 J7 Turkestanskiy Khrebet mts U.S.S.R.
62 M8 Túrkeve Hungary 47.06N 20.42E
112 G1 Turkey Texas 34.24N 100.54W
16 C5 Turkey rep W Asia
14 G3 Turkey Cr W Australia
14 G3 Turkey Creek W Australia 17.04S 128.15E
107 E10 Turkey Lake res Louisiana
109 F6 Turkey Mts New Mexico
103 B8 Turkey Pt Maryland 39.27N 76.00W
106 C7 Turkey, R Iowa
64 K7 Türkheim W Germany 48.03N 10.39E
45 P4 Turki U.S.S.R. 52.00N 43.16E
116 J4 Turk I., Grand Turks Is W I 21.30N 71.07W
30 J6 Turki Kharar Bihar India 26.19N 85.21E
64 C4 Türkismühle W Germany 49.35N 7.07E
Turkmanchai see Torkamān
36 E3 Turkmen Dağı mt Turkey
43 F8 Turkmen-Kala Turkmeniya U.S.S.R. 37.27N 62.20E
43 G8 Turkmenkarakul' Turkmeniya U.S.S.R. 35.45N 62.37E
38 E4 Turkmenskaya S.S.R U.S.S.R.
43 C7 Turkmenskiy Zaliv B Turkmeniya U.S.S.R.
Turkmen S.S.R see Turkmenskaya S.S.R
36 J5 Türkoğlu Turkey 37.24N 36.49E
96 B13 Turk's Cap mt St Helena 15.56S 5.39W
116 J4 Turks Is West Indies
116 J4 Turks Island Passage West Indies
51 J11 Turku Finland 60.27N 22.15E
51 J10 Turku Pori dist Finland
93 G2 Turkwel watercourse Kenya
75 C8 Turleque Spain 39.36N 3.37W
111 D4 Turlock California 37.29N 120.50W
111 D4 Turlock L California 37.35N 120.35W
66 H8 Turlo Pass Italy 45.54N 7.58E
118 G5 Turmalina Brazil 17.17S 42.45W
35 E5 Turmus 'Aiya Jordan 32.02N 35.20E
33 E3 Turmus, Wādī at watercourse Saudi Arabia
101 J6 Turnagain R Br Col
11 L7 Turnagain, C New Zealand 40.28S 176.38E
15 G8 Turnagain I Torres Str, Qnsld 9.35S 142.16E
65 M6 Turnau Austria 47.34N 15.22E
100 Q5 Turnberry Manitoba 53.27N 101.42W
57 D2 Turnberry Strathclyde Scotland 55.19N 4.50W
100 S4 Turnbull Manitoba 54.34N 99.29W
13 B5 Turnbull, Mt N Terr Australia 21.00S 131.48E
102 J7 Turneffe I Belize
104 P2 Turner Maine 44.16N 70.16W
106 L5 Turner Michigan 44.07N 83.49W
110 R1 Turner Montana 48.50N 108.26W
110 C5 Turner Oregon 44.50N 122.57W
110 H3 Turner Washington 46.25N 117.52W
104 F2 Turner dist Baltimore, Md
12 A6 Turner dist Canberra Australia
108 E6 Turnercrest Wyoming 43.34N 105.42W
14 B6 Turner, Mt W Australia 22.49S 117.30E
14 C5 Turner R W Australia
14 G4 Turner River W Australia 17.46S 128.13E
104 N4 Turners Falls Massachusetts 42.37N 72.34W
89 C8 Turner's Pen Sierra Leone
103 D7 Turnersville New Jersey 39.46N 75.03W
100 C8 Turner Valley Alberta 50.43N 114.19W
110 P7 Turnerville Wyoming 42.51N 110.53W
58 K7 Turnhouse aer Lothian Scotland 55.58N 3.22W
61 K1 Turnhout Belgium 51.19N 4.57E
69 M2 Türnich W Germany 50.52N 6.45E
65 M6 Türnitz Austria 47.57N 15.30E
101 T7 Turnor L Saskatchewan
62 J5 Turnov Czechoslovakia 50.36N 15.10E
36 H2 Türnük Turkey 40.44N 35.25E
82 J7 Turnu Măgurele Romania 43.44N 24.53E
82 J5 Turnu Roşu Romania 45.33N 24.17E
82 H6 Turnu Severin Romania 44.36N 22.39E
103 E2 Turnwood New York 42.02N 74.42W
93 M7 Turo Kenya 1.37S 40.06E
43 M3 Turobay Kazakhstan U.S.S.R. 48.55N 77.12E
62 O5 Turobin Poland 50.50N 22.45E
42 D6 Turochak U.S.S.R. 52.15N 87.10E
109 M4 Turon Kansas 37.48N 98.26W
77 K7 Turón Spain 36.52N 3.04W
12 J5 Turon R New S Wales
77 G7 Turón R Spain
12 K6 Tuross R New S Wales
46 G4 Turov Belorussiya U.S.S.R. 52.04N 27.40E
46 L4 Turoyo U.S.S.R. 51.34N 38.32E
24 F4 Turpan Xinjiang Uygur Zizhiqu China 42.55N 89.06E
24 F4 Turpan Zhan Xinjiang Uygur Zizhiqu China 43.10N 89.06E
120 B5 Turpicotay, Cord. de Peru
109 K5 Turpin Oklahoma 36.51N 100.54W

76 B10 Turquel Portugal 39.27N 8.58W
116 F4 Turquino *mt* Cuba 20.00N 76.50W
109 D9 Turquoise New Mexico 32.27N 106.04W
113 K6 Turquoise L Alaska 60.50N 154.00W
65 J8 Turrach Austria 46.58N 13.53E
35 G3 Turra, Et Jordan 32.38N 35.59E
12 L6 Turramurra *dist* Sydney, N S W
77 N6 Turre Spain 37.10N 1.53W
107 F6 Turrell Arkansas 35.20N 90.15W
12 D3 Turret Ra S Australia
115 N5 Turrialba Costa Rica 9.56N 83.40W
115 N4 Turrialba, Vol Costa Rica 10.02N 83.48W
71 J8 Turriers France 44.24N 6.10E
58 M3 Turriff Grampian Scotland 57.32N 2.28W
77 M6 Turrillas Spain 37.02N 2.15W
81 A2 Turritano *reg* Sardinia
81 D1 Turritta, Monte Sardinia 41.06N 9.31E
75 F3 Turruncún Spain 42.09N 2.06W
34 N5 Tursāq Iraq 33.26N 45.47E
46 P2 Tursha U.S.S.R. 56.55N 47.36E
Turshiz *see* Kāshmar
81 M3 Tursi Italy 40.14N 16.29E
47 J5 Tursuntskiy Tuman, Oz *L* U.S.S.R. 60.32N 64.00E
43 J7 Tursunzade Tadzhikistan U.S.S.R. 38.32N 68.15E
22 E1 Turta Mongolia 51.31N 100.42E
53 X16 Turtagrø Norway 61.30N 7.48E
47 K6 Turtas *R* U.S.S.R.
43 F6 Turtkul' Uzbekistan U.S.S.R. 41.30N 61.00E
108 S1 Turtle *R* Ontario
98 H8 Turtle Creek New Brunswick 45.58N 64.56W
100 J5 Turtleford Saskatchewan 53.25N 108.58W
13 G1 Turtlehead I Queensland 10.56S 142.40E
13 K3 Turtle I Gt Barrier Reef Australia 17.12S 152.00E
14 C5 Turtle I W Australia 19.54S 118.54E
19 J8 Turtle Is Philippines
89 C8 Turtle Is Sierra Leone
100 J5 Turtle L Saskatchewan
108 K2 Turtle Lake N Dakota 47.32N 100.54W
106 B4 Turtle Lake Wisconsin 45.23N 92.09W
100 R9 Turtle Mountain Provincial Park Manitoba
108 K1 Turtle Mts Manitoba/N Dakota
13 A2 Turtle Pt N Terr Australia 14.55S 129.10E
66 G6 Turtmann Switzerland 46.18N 7.43E
66 G7 Turtmann Tal *V* Switzerland
51 K5 Turtola Finland 66.39N 23.55E
108 M4 Turton S Dakota 45.03N 98.06W
41 H7 Turu *R* U.S.S.R.
11 K4 Turua New Zealand 37.14S 175.35E
24 B5 Turugart Shankou *pass* China/U.S.S.R. 40.33N 74.04E
41 E7 Turukhan *R* U.S.S.R.
41 E7 Turukhansk U.S.S.R. 65.49N 88.00E
42 K2 Turukta U.S.S.R. 60.32N 116.35E
47 K5 Turumeyevo U.S.S.R. 60.35N 68.29E
87 C5 Turum,Jeb *mt* Sudan 11.38N 31.06E
Turun *see* Turan
117 A4 Turuna, R Brazil
42 H6 Turuntayevo U.S.S.R. 52.15N 107.40E
53 D6 Turup Denmark 55.18N 9.59E
37 E6 Türüsmek Turkey 39.03N 39.26E
Turut *see* Ţorūd
28 C3 Turuvanur Karnataka India 14.27N 76.26E
56 K3 Turvey Beds Eng 52.10N 0.38W
121 J2 Turvo Brazil 28.50S 49.42W
121 H1 Turvo *R* Rio Grande do Sul Brazil
118 E7 Turvo *R* São Paulo Brazil
118 E8 Turvo *R* São Paulo Brazil
118 E5 Turvo, R Goiás Brazil
45 B1 Tury U.S.S.R. 55.39N 30.59E
47 G4 Tur'ya U.S.S.R. 62.49N 50.40E
46 E4 Tur'ya *R* Ukraine U.S.S.R.
62 L6 Turzovka Czechoslovakia 49.24N 18.35E
32 H2 Ţūs Iran 36.30N 59.31E
77 M4 Tus *R* Spain
81 H8 Tusa Sicily 37.59N 14.14E
111 M6 Tusayan Arizona 35.58N 112.08W
107 J8 Tuscaloosa Alabama 33.12N 87.33W
80 E4 Tuscania Italy 42.25N 11.53E
104 D6 Tuscarawas *R* Ohio
110 J8 Tuscarora Nevada 41.19N 116.14W
103 B5 Tuscarora Pennsylvania 40.47N 76.02W
104 H6 Tuscarora Mt Pennsylvania
66 E3 Tüscherz Switzerland 47.07N 7.12E
107 H2 Tuscola Illinois 39.49N 88.18W
112 H3 Tuscola Texas 32.13N 99.47W
110 K2 Tuscor Montana 47.58N 115.43W
107 J7 Tuscumbia Alabama 34.42N 87.41W
107 D3 Tuscumbia Missouri 38.14N 92.29W
53 H5 Tuse Denmark 55.43N 11.38E
53 H5 Tuse Næs *C* Denmark 55.47N 11.47E
32 G3 Tusharīk Iran 34.44N 57.10E
44 L3 Tushchibek Kazakhstan U.S.S.R. 44.09N 51.56E
44 L3 Tushchikuduk Kazakhstan U.S.S.R. 44.44N 51.57E
35 B8 Tushiyya Israel 31.27N 34.32E
107 L9 Tuskegee Alabama 32.25N 85.41W
59 K7 Tusker Rock Lt.Ho Wexford Irish Rep 52.12N 6.12W
98 G10 Tusket Nova Scotia 43.53N 65.58W
45 H5 Tuskor' *R* U.S.S.R.
82 K4 Tuşnad Romania 46.11N 25.56E
53 V14 Tussavatn *L* Norway 62.05N 6.38E
64 K7 Tussenhausen W Germany 48.06N 10.35E
40 G6 Tusser U.S.S.R. 50.06N 136.57E
64 O7 Tüssling W Germany 48.12N 12.37E
72 E4 Tusson France 45.56N 0.04E
103 D3 Tusten New York 41.34N 75.02W
111 G8 Tustin California 33.43N 117.49W
106 J5 Tustin Michigan 44.06N 85.29W
52 D3 Tustna *isld* Norway 63.10N 8.10E
113 M6 Tustumena L Alaska 60.10N 150.50W
53 U14 Tusvik Norway 62.23N 6.28E
62 M4 Tuszyn Poland 51.36N 19.33E
32 F4 Tūt Iran 32.34N 54.27E
37 D8 Tut Turkey 37.50N 37.59E
91 K7 Tuta Zaïre 6.40S 26.55E
32 G6 Tūtak Iran 29.20N 57.30E
37 G6 Tutak Turkey 39.34N 42.48E
76 E12 Tutalga *R* Portugal
11 H2 Tutamoe Ra New Zealand
32 H7 Tūtān Iran 26.23N 59.01E
46 L1 Tutayev U.S.S.R. 57.52N 39.31E
56 H2 Tutbury Staffs Eng 52.52N 1.40W
43 N8 Tutek Kirgiziya U.S.S.R. 40.17N 71.17E
108 J6 Tuthill S Dakota 43.09N 101.29W
31 F4 Tutia Khel Pakistan 32.39N 70.09E
28 D6 Tuticorin Tamil Nadu India 8.48N 78.10E
82 F7 Tutin Yugoslavia 43.00N 20.20E
11 L6 Tutira L New Zealand 39.14S 176.53E
51 O5 Tutiyarvi Karelia U.S.S.R. 66.33N 29.54E
36 H1 Tütmen Tepesi *mt* Turkey 41.26N 35.28E
113 K6 Tutna L Alaska 60.22N 155.20W
18 L4 Tutoh *R* Sarawak Malaysia
117 F6 Tutóia Brazil 2.46S 42.20W
11 C11 Tutoko Pk *mt* New Zealand 44.34S 168.01E
41 F7 Tutonchana *R* U.S.S.R.
41 F7 Tutonchana, Vozvyshennost' *heights* U.S.S.R.
41 F8 Tutonchany U.S.S.R. 64.14N 93.48E
18 L3 Tutong Brunei 4.51N 114.40E
82 L4 Tutova *R* Romania
63 S5 Tutow E Germany 53.55N 13.13E
82 K6 Tutrakan Bulgaria 44.02N 26.40E
101 F5 Tutshi L Yukon Terr 60.08N 134.50W
110 L7 Tuttle Idaho 42.52N 114.50W
108 K2 Tuttle N Dakota 47.09N 100.00W
109 N6 Tuttle Oklahoma 35.18N 97.48W
64 K2 Tüttleben E Germany 50.56N 10.48E
109 O2 Tuttle Creek Res Kansas
108 Q6 Tuttle L Minnesota
64 F8 Tuttlingen W Germany 47.59N 8.49E
40 H7 Tutto U.S.S.R. 48.54N 139.59E
9 T4 Tutu *isld* Fiji 16.13S 179.35E
15 L8 Tutubea Papua New Guinea 9.34S 150.40E
92 F4 Tutubu Tanzania 5.28S 32.43E
122 D1 Tutuila / Amer Samoa Pacific Oc
94 J3 Tutume Botswana 20.26S 27.02E
94 J3 Tutumi *watercourse* Botswana
86 E7 Tuţûn Egypt 29.09N 30.46E
37 E3 Tütüncü Turkey 40.05N 27.42E
119 C5 Tutunendo Colombia 5.46N 76.35W
37 G4 Tütünlü Turkey 41.09N 42.04E
120 D7 Tutupaca *vol* Peru 17.00S 70.22W
42 H5 Tutura U.S.S.R. 54.45N 105.10E
115 L9 Tututepec Mexico 16.10N 97.40W
19 F7 Tutuwawang Indon 8.00S 129.47E
107 F7 Tutwiler Mississippi 34.01N 90.27W
64 L8 Tutzing W Germany 47.54N 11.17E
22 F2 Tuul Gol *R* Mongolia
51 L10 Tuulos Finland 61.07N 24.50E
51 P9 Tuupovarra Finland 62.30N 30.40E
51 O9 Tuusniemi Finland 62.50N 28.32E
122 U16 Tuutapu *crater* Easter I Pacific Oc 27.08S 109.24W
53 Y17 Tuv Norway 60.53N 8.29E
Tuva A.O *see* Tuvinskaya Aut. Oblast'
122 J9 Tuvalu Pacific Ocean
9 C8 Tuvalu *state, islds* Pacific Oc
10 R6 Tuvana-i-Ra *isld* Pacific Oc 21.00S 178.42W
10 R6 Tuvana-i-Tholo *isld* Pacific Oc 21.03S 178.57W
53 X18 Tuvaseter Norway 60.27N 8.00E
38 J3 Tuvinskaya Aut.Oblast' *aut prov* U.S.S.R.
22 J3 Tüvshinshiree Mongolia 46.05N 111.54E
9 S8 Tuvutau *mt* Viti Levu Fiji 18.05S 177.46E
9 U2 Tuvutha *isld* Fiji 17.40S 178.50W
86 E9 Ţuwa Beni Ibrâhîm Egypt 28.05N 30.41E
35 H8 Tuwai *watercourse* Jordan
34 H5 Tuwaila Iraq 33.27N 40.16E
Tuwairifa *see* Ţuwayrifah, Aţ
34 C9 Tuwayīlel Hāj *mt* Jordan 29.49N 35.55E
33 F4 Tuwayq, Jabal *escarp* Saudi Arabia
33 G5 Tuwayq, Jabal *reg* Saudi Arabia
33 C4 Ţuwayrah Saudi Arabia 25.52N 38.32E
33 H6 Ţuwayrifah, Aţ Saudi Arabia 21.28N 49.37E
Tuwayrij *see* Hindīyah, Al
33 D3 Ţuwayyah, Aţ Saudi Arabia 27.39N 40.59E
111 L5 Tuweep Arizona 36.23N 113.03W
22 H7 Tuwei He *R* Shaanxi China
34 D8 Tuweiyil esh Shiqāq *mt* Jordan 30.35N 36.07E
33 C5 Tuwwal Saudi Arabia 22.19N 39.08E
113 L6 Tuxedni B Alaska
100 A1 Tuxedo Manitoba 49.52N 97.13W
105 E2 Tuxedo N Carolina 35.13N 82.28W
103 F4 Tuxedo Park New York 41.12N 74.12W
65 E7 Tuxer Gebirge *mts* Austria
57 M6 Tuxford Notts Eng 53.14N 0.54W
100 M8 Tuxford Saskatchewan 50.34N 105.35W
23 E3 Tuxiang Sichuan China 30.45N 109.11E
115 H8 Tuxpan Jalisco Mexico 19.31N 103.20W
115 G7 Tuxpan Nayarit Mexico 21.58N 105.20W
115 L7 Tuxpan Veracruz Mexico 20.58N 97.23W
115 N10 Tuxtla Chico Mexico 14.58N 92.11W
115 N9 Tuxtla Gutiérrez Mexico 16.45N 93.09W
76 B4 Túy Spain 42.03N 8.39W
47 L6 Tuy *R* U.S.S.R.
101 H6 Tuya L Br Col 59.05N 130.38W
25 K6 Tuy An Vietnam 13.20N 109.15E
25 H2 Tuyen Quang Vietnam 21.48N 105.18E
25 K6 Tuy Hoa Vietnam 13.02N 109.15E
46 R3 Tuymazy U.S.S.R. 54.38N 53.40E
119 F2 Tuy, R Venezuela
32 C3 Tūysarkān Iran 34.31N 48.30E
43 N5 Tuyuk Kazakhstan U.S.S.R. 43.05N 79.30E
24 B5 Tuyuk-boto Hoynak Pass *mt pass* Xinjiang Uygur Zizhiqu China
24 B5 Tuyuk-boto Moynak Pass Kirgiziya/Xinjiang Uygur Zizhiqu 40.34N 76.45E
72 E9 Tuzaguet France 43.05N 0.26E
72 C7 Tuzan, le France 44.27N 0.35W
44 M3 Tuzbair, Sor *mud flat* Kazakhstan U.S.S.R.
36 G4 Tuz Gölü *L* Turkey
111 N7 Tuzigoot Nat. Mon Arizona 34.48N 112.00W
43 H6 Tuzkan, Oz *L* Kazakhstan U.S.S.R. 40.37N 67.30E
Tuz Khurmatli *see* Tuz Khurmātū
34 M4 Tuz Khurmātū Iraq 34.56N 44.38E
36 H6 Tuzla Turkey 36.42N 35.06E
82 E6 Tuzla Yugoslavia 44.33N 18.41E
37 F6 Tuzla *R* Turkey
37 F2 Tuzla Burun *C* Turkey 40.25N 29.05E
37 F2 Tuzlaçiftliği Turkey 40.25N 29.05E
37 C2 Tuzla Gölü *L* Edirne Turkey 40.37N 26.17E
36 H3 Tuzla Gölü *L* Kayseri Turkey
46 L5 Tuzlov *R* U.S.S.R.
37 H5 Tuzluca Turkey 40.02N 43.39E
Tuzlu Göl *see* Namak-e Mīqhān, Kavīr-e *salt lake*
37 C3 Tuzlu Gölü Turkey 40.17N 26.16E
36 F4 Tuzlukçu Turkey 38.29N 31.38E
82 N5 Tuzly U.S.S.R. 45.50N 30.05E
28 K3 Tuzu R India/Burma
52 G9 Tvååker Sweden 57.04N 12.25E
52 M2 Tvärålund Sweden 64.05N 19.35E
51 J6 Tvärån Sweden 65.34N 21.05E
39 F6 Tvayan U.S.S.R. 55.22N 156.15E
53 E4 Tved Århus Denmark 56.12N 10.27E
53 F6 Tved Fyn Denmark 55.06N 10.38E
53 E3 Tvede Denmark 56.33N 10.12E
52 D8 Tvedestrand Norway 58.36N 8.55E
53 T20 Tveit Norway 59.21N 5.48E
53 W18 Tveit Norway 60.30N 7.11E
53 T18 Tveita Norway 60.16N 5.57E
53 T18 Tveitakvitingen *mt* Norway 60.19N 5.55E
53 Z20 Tveitsund Norway 59.02N 8.31E
Tver *see* Kalinin
53 N10 Tverå Faeroes 61.34N 6.48W
Tvereya *see* Tiberias
53 U14 Tverfjell *mt* Norway 62.25N 6.11E
53 X15 Tverrådalskyrkja *mt* Norway 61.45N 7.40E
53 V17 Tverrbotnanut *mt* Norway 60.58N 6.47E
53 Y15 Tverrfjellet *mt* Norway 61.51N 8.05E
53 W14 Tverrfjord *mt* Norway 62.08N 7.15E
44 C3 Tverskaya U.S.S.R. 44.35N 39.38E
53 E1 Tversted Denmark 57.36N 10.12E
46 K2 Tvertsa *R* U.S.S.R.
53 V17 Tvinde Norway 60.43N 6.29E
52 J10 Tving Sweden 56.18N 15.30E
53 D5 Tvingstrup Denmark 55.55N 9.55E
53 B4 Tvis Denmark 56.20N 8.44E
50 J7 Tvísker *isld* Iceland 63.56N 16.12W
82 K8 Tvŭrditsa Bulgaria 42.41N 25.52E
60 J11 't Waal Netherlands 52.00N 5.08E
33 L9 Twai al Hashāsh *mt* Iraq 29.52N 46.55E
94 F2 Twaka Namibia 18.59S 20.08E
66 E3 Twann Switzerland 47.06N 7.10E
25 C4 Twante Burma 16.44N 95.58E
62 K4 Twardogóra Poland 51.22N 17.28E
58 S11 Twatt Orkney Scotland 59.06N 3.17W
99 N8 Tweed Ontario 44.29N 77.19W
60 Q8 Tweede Exloërmond Netherlands 52.55N 6.56E
100 F4 Tweedie Alberta 54.54N 111.46W
58 M7 Tweed, R Borders/Northumberland Scot/Eng
57 G1 Tweedsmuir Borders Scotland 55.30N 3.27W
57 G2 Tweedsmuir Hills Scotland
101 K9 Tweedsmuir Provincial Park Br Col
95 M3 Tweeling S Africa 27.33S 28.31E
95 L5 Tweespruit S Africa 29.11S 27.02E
60 N11 Twello Netherlands 52.14N 6.07E
100 L9 Twelve Mile L Saskatchewan
113 P4 Twelvemile Summit *pass* Alaska 65.25N 146.00W
59 C4 Twelve Pins, The *mts* Galway Irish Rep 53.32N 9.50W
65 J7 Tweng Austria 47.12N 13.37E
60 P11 Twente Kanaal *canal* Netherlands
29 L6 Twenty-four Parganas *dist* W Bengal India
111 H7 Twentynine Palms California 34.09N 116.03W
Twenty-six Baku Commissars *see* Bakinskikh Komissarov, im 26
91 F4 Tweya Zaïre 0.54S 18.58E
55 C4 Twickenham London England 51.27N 0.21W
60 N7 Twijzel Netherlands 53.14N 6.06E
14 F9 Twilight Cove W Australia
98 S4 Twillingate Newfoundland 49.38N 54.45W
65 L8 Twimberg Austria 46.55N 14.51E
110 B1 Twin Washington 48.10N 123.58W
110 N4 Twin Bridges Montana 45.33N 112.20W
108 O4 Twin Brooks S Dakota 45.11N 96.48W
112 G4 Twin Buttes Res Texas
100 O2 Twin City Ontario 48.23N 89.28W
110 L7 Twin Falls Idaho 42.34N 114.30W
97 N7 Twin Falls Labrador, Nfld 53.22N 64.26W
14 F5 Twin Heads *mt* W Australia 20.16S 126.35E
13 G2 Twin Humps *pk* Queensland 13.52S 143.05E
106 K5 Twin L Michigan 44.52N 84.20W
106 H6 Twin Lake Michigan 43.21N 86.12W
113 K6 Twin Lakes Alaska 60.40N 154.00W
101 P7 Twin Lakes Alberta 57.47N 117.30W
109 D2 Twin Lakes Colorado 39.04N 106.23W
103 E4 Twin Lakes Pennsylvania 41.23N 74.52W
98 R4 Twin L, N Newfoundland
98 R4 Twin L, S Newfoundland
110 L6 Twin Ls. Res Idaho 43.16N 114.49W
104 O2 Twin Mt New Hampshire 44.16N 71.32W
25 M9 Twinnge Burma 23.10N 96.02E
111 D2 Twin Pk *mt* California 39.06N 120.14W
110 L5 Twin Pks Idaho 44.37N 114.28W
111 A9 Twin Pks San Francisco, Cal 37.45N 122.27W
14 C10 Twin Pks W Australia 34.38S 117.55E
33 C10 Twin Rocks S Yemen 12.49N 45.01E
14 D10 Twin Rocks W Australia 34.25S 122.24E
12 E3 Twins Cr S Australia
12 D4 Twins, The S Australia 30.00S 135.17E
11 G8 Twins, The *mt* New Zealand 41.15S 172.40E
108 O2 Twin Valley Minnesota 47.16N 96.16W
60 J9 Twisk Netherlands 52.45N 5.04E
110 E1 Twisp Washington 48.22N 120.08W
63 J7 Twistringen W Germany 52.48N 8.38E
112 D8 Twitty Texas 35.21N 100.14W
11 E11 Twizel New Zealand 44.14S 170.06E
56 D6 Two Bridges Devon Eng 50.34N 3.58W
109 H4 Two Butte Cr Colorado
109 H4 Two Buttes Colorado 37.33N 102.25W
100 R8 Two Creeks Manitoba 50.00N 101.00W
106 G5 Two Creeks Wisconsin 44.19N 87.33W
110 P3 Twodot Montana 46.25N 110.04W
12 K6 Twofold B New S Wales
106 C2 Two Harbors Minnesota 47.02N 91.40W
113 L8 Two Headed I Alaska 56.55N 153.39W
100 F5 Two Hills Alberta 53.43N 111.42W
59 G6 Twomileborris Tipperary Irish Rep 52.40N 7.43W
110 P5 Two Ocean Pass Wyoming 44.03N 110.10W
106 G5 Two Rivers Wisconsin 44.10N 87.33W
112 C2 Two Rivers Res New Mexico
100 O3 Two Rivers, The Saskatchewan 55.47N 103.10W
11 E10 Two Thumbs Ra New Zealand
56 J2 Twycross Leics Eng 52.39N 1.30W
95 K1 Twyfelspoort S Africa 25.39S 26.31E
56 K5 Twyford Berks Eng 51.29N 0.53W
56 J5 Twyford Hants Eng 51.01N 1.19W
57 E3 Twynholm Dumfries & Galloway Scotland 54.52N 4.05W
56 D4 Twyn-Llanan Dyfed Wales 51.54N 3.49W
53 X16 Tya *R* Norway
82 H2 Tyachevo U.S.S.R. 48.00N 23.42E
28 C8 Tyagaraya Nagar *dist* Madras, Tamil Nadu India
36 H5 Tyana *anc site* Turkey 37.48N 34.36E
43 L6 Tyan-Shan' *mts* U.S.S.R./China
43 L6 Tyan'-Shanskaya Oblast' *prov* Kirgiziya U.S.S.R.
42 K3 Tyanya U.S.S.R. 59.05N 119.53E
40 B2 Tyanya *R* U.S.S.R.
46 H5 Tyasmin *R* Ukraine U.S.S.R.
40 K9 Tyatino Kuril Is U.S.S.R. 44.15N 146.16E
40 K9 Tyatya *vol* Kuril Is U.S.S.R. 44.21N 146.15E
42 D4 Tyazhinskiy U.S.S.R. 56.11N 88.30E
105 G5 Tybee Roads S Carolina
53 H6 Tybjerg Denmark 55.21N 11.50E
111 H3 Tybo Nevada 38.22N 116.25W
53 D6 Tybrind Vig *B* Denmark 55.24N 9.48E
42 F2 Tychany U.S.S.R. 61.43N 97.15E
42 F2 Tychany *R* U.S.S.R.
42 B4 Tychkino U.S.S.R. 56.13N 77.35E
62 J2 Tychowo Poland 53.56N 16.15E
62 L5 Tychy Poland 50.08N 18.56E
52 F3 Tydal Norway 63.04N 11.33E
56 M2 Tydd St. Mary Lincs Eng 52.45N 0.09E
101 F7 Tyee Alaska 57.02N 134.35N
110 A1 Tyee Washington 48.04N 124.23W
39 D4 Tyellakh U.S.S.R. 62.07N 148.31E
104 G9 Tye River Virginia 37.41N 78.58W
104 F7 Tygart L Virginia
104 F8 Tygart Valley Virginia
40 D5 Tygda U.S.S.R. 53.09N 126.16E
40 D5 Tygda *R* U.S.S.R.
39 H2 Tygyin-Kail'rpyn *R* U.S.S.R.
47 L6 Tygys *R* U.S.S.R.
110 N7 Tyhee Idaho 42.57N 112.27W
59 J3 Tyholland Monaghan Irish Rep 54.16N 6.54W
53 Y16 Tyin Norway 61.13N 8.15E
53 Y16 Tyin *L* Norway
53 Y16 Tyinholmen Norway 61.22N 8.15E
40 J6 Tyk Sakhalin U.S.S.R. 51.44N 141.45E
39 A1 Tykakh *R* U.S.S.R.
62 O2 Tykocin Poland 53.13N 22.46E
95 L8 Tylden S Africa 32.07S 27.05E
108 O5 Tyler Minnesota 44.16N 96.08W
104 G5 Tyler Pennsylvania 41.14N 78.34W
112 M3 Tyler Texas 32.22N 95.18W
110 H2 Tyler Washington 47.26N 117.46W
103 D3 Tyler Hill Pennsylvania 41.42N 75.07W
112 M3 Tyler, L Texas 32.12N 95.08W
107 F10 Tylertown Mississippi 31.06N 90.09W
39 G3 Tylkhoy U.S.S.R. 62.35N 163.30E
39 G3 Tylkhoy *R* U.S.S.R.
40 G4 Tyl'skiy Khrebet *mts* U.S.S.R.
53 D2 Tylstrup Denmark 57.12N 9.58E
42 C3 Tym *R* U.S.S.R.
62 M6 Tymbark Poland 49.44N 20.20E
39 G5 Tymlat U.S.S.R. 59.28N 163.08E
40 D4 Tymna *R* U.S.S.R.
39 K3 Tymna, Laguna *lagoon* U.S.S.R.
40 J6 Tymovskoye Sakhalin U.S.S.R. 50.50N 142.43E
39 B2 Tympy U.S.S.R. 67.26N 135.39E
39 D3 Tymtey *R* U.S.S.R.
60 P7 Tynaarlo Netherlands 53.05N 6.37E
59 F5 Tynagh Galway Irish Rep 53.09N 8.22W
47 L6 Tynay U.S.S.R. 58.28N 70.14E
40 C4 Tynda *R* U.S.S.R.
100 V8 Tyndall Manitoba 50.05N 96.40W
108 N7 Tyndall S Dakota 42.59N 97.51W
11 E10 Tyndall, Mt New Zealand 43.20S 170.41E
81 K7 Tyndaris *ruins* Sicily 38.08N 15.02E
52 K4 Tynderö Sweden 62.28N 17.40E
40 C4 Tyndinskiy U.S.S.R. 55.11N 124.34E
58 G6 Tyndrum Central Scotland 56.27N 4.43W
57 K3 Tyne and Wear *co* Eng
65 M1 Týnec Nad Labem Czechoslovakia 50.03N 15.21E
57 L2 Tynemouth Tyne and Wear Eng 55.01N 1.24W
42 D1 Tynep U.S.S.R. 62.49N 88.52E
58 L6 Tyne, R Lothian Scotland 56.01N 2.35W
57 K3 Tyne, R Northumb Eng
100 J7 Tyner Saskatchewan 51.00N 108.29W
98 J7 Tyne Valley Prince Edward I 46.36N 63.57W
52 H6 Tyngsjö Sweden 60.22N 13.50E
65 K3 Týn nad Vltavou Czechoslovakia 49.14N 14.25E
57 F2 Tynron Dumfries & Galloway Scotland 55.13N 3.53W
52 F4 Tynset Norway 62.17N 10.47E
56 D2 Tyn-y-groes Gwynedd Wales 52.48N 3.54W
113 O5 Tyone *R* Alaska
113 M6 Tyonek Alaska 61.01N 151.20W
42 G5 Typta U.S.S.R. 54.33N 104.30E
34 C5 Tyr Lebanon 33.16N 35.12E
40 H5 Tyr U.S.S.R. 52.58N 139.50E
Tyre *see* Tyr
59 L3 Tyrella Down N Ireland 54.16N 5.45W
42 G5 Tyret' U.S.S.R. 53.40N 102.20E
52 E6 Tyrifjorden *L* Norway
52 H10 Tyringe Sweden 56.09N 13.35E
103 H2 Tyringham Massachusetts 42.15N 73.12W
42 H5 Tyrka U.S.S.R. 54.30N 107.10E
40 F3 Tyrkan *R* U.S.S.R.
40 F6 Tyrma U.S.S.R. 50.06N 132.15E
40 E6 Tyrma *R* U.S.S.R.
82 L2 Tyrnovo Moldavia U.S.S.R. 48.20N 27.45E
45 N2 Tyrnovo U.S.S.R. 54.29N 41.04E
44 E4 Tyrnyauz U.S.S.R. 43.22N 42.54E
105 E2 Tyron N Carolina 35.13N 82.14W
109 B9 Tyrone New Mexico 32.41N 108.18W
104 G6 Tyrone Pennsylvania 40.41N 78.15W
59 H2 Tyrone *co* N Ireland
12 G6 Tyrrell *R* Victoria
101 V4 Tyrrell L N W Terr 63.10N 105.20W
12 G6 Tyrrell, L Victoria
59 H5 Tyrrellspass W Meath Irish Rep 53.23N 7.22W
78 D8 Tyrrhenian Sea S Europe
53 D5 Tyrsted Denmark 55.50N 9.52E
39 B4 Tyry *R* U.S.S.R.
53 T20 Tysbær Norway 59.20N 5.30E
53 U20 Tysdal Norway 59.07N 6.10E
53 U20 Tysdalsvatn *L* Norway 59.05N 6.06E
51 E3 Tysfjord Norway 68.07N 16.25E
53 T18 Tysnes Norway 60.02N 5.33E
53 S19 Tysnesøy *isld* Norway 59.59N 5.30E
53 V14 Tyssa Norway 62.28N 6.44E
53 T18 Tysse Norway 60.22N 5.45E
53 T17 Tyssebotn Norway 60.37N 5.35E
53 V18 Tyssedal Norway 60.07N 6.35E
52 K8 Tystberga Sweden 58.51N 17.15E
53 H6 Tystrup Denmark 55.22N 11.35E
53 H6 Tystrup Sø *L* Denmark 55.21N 11.37E
62 O5 Tyszowce Poland 50.36N 23.41E
39 H1 Tytyl', Ozero *L* U.S.S.R. 67.19N 169.27E
39 C2 Tyubelyakh U.S.S.R. 65.20N 143.11E
44 K3 Tyub-Karagan, Mys *C* Kazakhstan U.S.S.R. 44.40N 50.19E
44 K3 Tyub-Karagan Poluostrov *pen* Kazakhstan U.S.S.R.
47 M5 Tyubuk U.S.S.R. 56.04N 60.58E
41 N8 Tyugene U.S.S.R. 62.36N 126.08E
41 N8 Tyugene *R* U.S.S.R.
39 C2 Tyugyuren U.S.S.R. 67.12N 142.40E
47 L7 Tyukalinsk U.S.S.R. 55.55N 72.10E
42 D4 Tyukhtet U.S.S.R. 56.34N 89.16E
41 L8 Tyukyan *R* U.S.S.R.
43 M6 Tyulek Kirgiziya U.S.S.R. 41.54N 75.41E
44 K3 Tyulen'i, Ostrova *islds* Kazakhstan U.S.S.R.
44 K7 Tyuleniy *isld* Azerbaydzhan U.S.S.R. 40.13N 50.22E
44 H3 Tyuleniy, Ostrova *isld* U.S.S.R. 44.28N 47.30E
39 J4 Tyulen'ye Ozero, Bukhta *B* U.S.S.R.
43 D2 Tyul'gan U.S.S.R. 52.23N 56.09E
47 K5 Tyuli U.S.S.R. 60.45N 69.41E
47 H6 Tyul'kino U.S.S.R. 59.51N 56.29E
43 K6 Tyul'kubas Kazakhstan U.S.S.R. 42.30N 70.14E
45 W1 Tyulyachi U.S.S.R. 55.54N 50.13E
42 D4 Tyulyapsy U.S.S.R. 57.30N 89.37E
47 K7 Tyumen' U.S.S.R. 57.11N 65.29E
43 H5 Tyumen'-Aryk Kazakhstan U.S.S.R. 44.00N 66.56E
38 F2 Tyumenskaya Oblast' *prov* U.S.S.R.
42 C5 Tyumentsevo U.S.S.R. 53.18N 81.30E
39 C3 Tyumsyu U.S.S.R. 63.43N 142.15E
41 L7 Tyung *R* U.S.S.R.
41 O9 Tyungulyu U.S.S.R. 62.18N 130.45E
43 H2 Tyuntyugur Kazakhstan U.S.S.R. 52.20N 65.50E
43 H1 Tyuntyugur, Ozero *L* Kazakhstan U.S.S.R. 52.43N 65.53E
43 N5 Tyup Kirgiziya U.S.S.R. 42.45N 78.20E
Tyuratam *see* Leninsk
43 N7 Tyurya-Kurgan Uzbekistan U.S.S.R. 41.00N 71.30E
47 C2 Tyuva Guba U.S.S.R. 69.13N 33.40W
100 O8 Tyvan Saskatchewan 50.02N 103.47W
82 M1 Tyvrov U.S.S.R. 49.01N 28.30E
56 C2 Tywyn Gwynedd Wales 52.35N 4.05W
87 G3 Tzado Medri Ethiopia 14.28N 38.05E
60 M12 't Zand Gelderland Netherlands 51.55N 5.56E
60 H8 't Zand Noord-Holland Netherlands 52.50N 4.45E
60 Q6 't Zandt Netherlands 53.22N 6.46E
94 L4 Tzaneen S Africa 23.50S 30.09E
Tzekam *see* Zijin
84 M11 Tzermiádhes Crete 35.11N 25.29E
Tzeyang *see* Hancheng
84 B3 Tzoumerka *mts* Greece
115 P7 Tzucacab Mexico 20.04N 89.03W
23 J6 Tz'u-kao Shan *pk* Taiwan
60 L7 Tzummarum Netherlands 53.14N 5.33E
91 D10 Uaba Angola 13.49S 14.54E
117 C3 Uaca *R* Brazil
87 J10 Uacalla Iero Somalia 1.45N 42.39E
119 H5 Uacauyén Venezuela 4.59N 61.44W
87 H9 Uach, El *reg* Somalia
120 G5 Uacurizal Brazil 13.30S 61.40W
88 G9 Uad Aarred *watercourse* Morocco
89 A1 Uad Archan *watercourse* Mauritania
88 F9 Uad Assag *watercourse* Morocco
89 B1 Uad Atui *watercourse* Mauritania
88 G9 Uad Auleitis *watercourse* Morocco
88 G8 Uad Bu Craa *watercourse* Morocco
Uaddan *see* Waddān
88 H8 Uad Echdari *watercourse* Morocco
88 G9 Uad el Feida *watercourse* Morocco
88 G8 Uad el Jat *watercourse* Morocco
88 G8 Uad el Marmuza *watercourse* Morocco
88 H8 Uad Erni *watercourse* Morocco
88 H8 Uad Gaddar *watercourse* Morocco
88 E11 Uad Legraitifa *watercourse* Mauritania
88 H8 Uad Lejcheibi *watercourse* Morocco
88 G8 Uad Lemhairiz *watercourse* Morocco
88 H8 Uad Mesuar *watercourse* Morocco
88 H8 Uad Quesat *watercourse* Morocco
88 G9 Uad Seleyina *watercourse* Morocco
88 J8 Uad Sen Amera *watercourse* Morocco
88 J8 Uad Sluguiat *watercourse* Morocco
88 H8 Uad Tasua *watercourse* Morocco
88 F10 Uad Tēbel-Lit *watercourse* Morocco
88 F10 Uad Tennuaca *watercourse* Morocco
88 F11 Uad Tenuaiur *watercourse* Mauritania
88 J8 Uad Tenuchchad *watercourse* Morocco
88 F11 Uad Teralal *watercourse* Mauritania
88 H8 Uad Ternit *watercourse* Morocco
88 H8 Uad Timel-lusa *watercourse* Morocco
88 H8 Uad Uein Terguet *watercourse* Morocco
88 J8 Uad Um Chamel Hamra *watercourse* Morocco
88 F11 Uad Yelua *watercourse* Mauritania
88 F10 Uad Yenna *watercourse* Mauritania
122 C2 Uafato W Samoa, Pacific Oc 13.56S 171.27W
122 U13 Ua Huka *isld* Marquesas Is Pacific Oc 8.55S 139.32W
119 E7 Uainambi Colombia 1.45N 69.49W
87 J9 Ualac, El Somalia 3.30N 43.04E
39 G5 Uala, Zaliv *B* U.S.S.R.
113 H7 Ualik, L Alaska 59.07N 159.30W
15 L8 Uama I D'Entrecasteaux Is Papua New Guinea 9.25S 151.00E
87 M10 Uama Idu Somalia 1.04S 41.21E
91 H12 Uamanda Angola 16.30S 22.06E
91 E7 Uamba Angola 7.21S 16.10E
91 E8 Uamba *R* Angola
58 E4 Uamh, L.nam Skye, Highland Scotland 57.06N 5.55W
58 E5 Uamh, L. nan Highland Scotland 56.53N 5.49W
13 G5 Uanda Queensland 21.34S 144.54E
91 D7 Uando Angola 7.06S 15.26E
87 K9 Uanle Uen Somalia 2.40N 44.50E
114 E6 Uaoa B Hawaiian Is
122 U14 Ua Pu / Marquesas Is Pacific Oc 9.25S 140.00W
15 G8 Uapumba I Papua New Guinea 8.05S 143.40E
119 G9 Uara Brazil 2.39S 65.39W
87 K7 Uardere Ethiopia 7.00N 45.20E
93 N4 Uar Dud Scimbirale Somalia 1.39N 41.21E
87 K9 Uar Dugullè Somalia 2.18N 44.30E
93 N4 Uar Gallo Somalia 1.08N 41.08E
87 L7 Uargalò Somalia 6.15N 47.24E
117 A8 Uari Brazil 6.24S 57.11W
119 G9 Uarini Brazil 2.57S 65.09W
87 K8 Uariomo Somalia 4.31N 45.32E
14 B6 Uaroo W Australia 22.47S 115.30E
87 L8 Uarot, El Somalia 4.02N 47.35E
87 K9 Uarre, El Somalia 3.45N 45.11E
87 K9 Uarsciek Somalia 2.17N 45.44E
87 H9 Uarti Hadded Somalia 3.24N 41.35E
119 F7 Uaruma Brazil 0.23N 68.52W
119 G5 Uasadi-Jidi, Sierra *mts* Venez
93 G5 Uasin Gishu *dist* Kenya
93 J5 Uaso *R* Kenya
119 G6 Uatatás, R Brazil
119 J9 Uatumã, R Brazil
117 G9 Uauá Brazil 9.46S 39.28W
119 G6 Uauaris, R Brazil
119 F8 Uaupés Brazil 0.07S 67.05W
119 F8 Uaupés, R Brazil
115 P9 Uaxactún Guatemala 17.25N 89.39W
33 F6 U'ayfirah Saudi Arabia 20.06N 44.57E
33 F2 U'aywij Saudi Arabia 28.54N 44.08E
33 E2 U'aywij, Wādī *watercourse* Saudi Arabia
85 A4 Uazzen Libya 31.58N 10.38E
118 G7 Ubá Brazil 21.08S 42.59W
90 F6 Uba Nigeria 10.29N 13.13E
43 O2 Uba *R* Kazakhstan U.S.S.R.
64 A2 Übach-Palenberg W Germany 50.55N 6.06E
60 T17 Ubachsberg Netherlands 50.51N 5.57E
92 F4 Ubada Tanzania 5.11S 33.24E
43 H1 Ubagan *R* Kazakhstan U.S.S.R.
118 G5 Ubaí Brazil 16.15S 44.45W
15 L6 Ubai New Britain 5.40S 150.42E
'Ubaidat, Safawiyat *watercourse see* Ubaydāt, Sha'īb al *water course*
34 H5 Ubaila Iraq 33.07N 40.14E
118 H4 Ubaitaba Brazil 14.17S 39.19W
Ubaiyidh, Wadi al *see* Ubayyiḑ, Wādī al *water course*
117 G6 Ubajara Brazil 3.52S 40.54W
33 E9 'Ubāl Yemen 14.55N 43.29E
43 D5 Ubal Karabaur *ridge* Uzbekistan U.S.S.R.
43 D5 Ubal Muzbel' *ridge* Kazakhstan U.S.S.R.
91 F1 Ubangi *R* Zaïre
Ubangi Shari *see* Central African Rep
91 G12 Ubango *reg* Angola
Ubari Libya *see* Awbārī
119 D5 Ubate Colombia 5.20N 73.50W
31 E6 Ubauro Pakistan 28.08N 69.43E
34 J7 Ubaydāt, Sha'īb al *watercourse* Iraq
33 E10 'Ubaydīyah Yemen 13.09N 43.18E
71 J8 Ubaye France 44.28N 6.22E
71 K8 Ubaye *R* France
33 J6 'Ubaylah, Al Saudi Arabia 21.59N 51.00E
33 G6 'Ubaylah, Al *area* Saudi Arabia
33 J6 'Ubaylah, Al *well* Saudi Arabia 21.51N 50.39E
34 J6 Ubayyiḑ, Wādī al *watercourse* Arabia/Iraq
53 G5 Ubby Denmark 55.38N 11.13E
20 E8 Ube Japan 33.57N 131.16E
77 K4 Ubeda Spain 38.01N 3.22W
77 K4 Ubeda, Loma de *hills* Spain
'Ubeid, Jabal *see* 'Udayd, Jabal al *mt*
Ubeid, Khor-al- *see* Udayd, Khawr al *Bay*
97 O3 Ubekendt Ejland *isld* Greenland 71.10N 53.30W
65 M7 Übelbach Austria 47.14N 15.14E
118 F6 Uberaba Brazil 19.47S 47.57W
118 B5 Uberaba, L Bolivia/Brazil
64 B5 Überherrn W Germany 49.15N 6.42E
118 E6 Uberlândia Brazil 18.57S 48.17W
64 G8 Überlingen W Germany 47.46N 9.10E
64 G8 Überlinger See *L* W Germany
64 N8 Übersee W Germany 47.49N 12.29E
90 C8 Ubiaja Nigeria 6.39N 6.23E
93 L5 Ubibule Kenya 0.17N 39.41E
75 E1 Ubidea Spain 43.02N 2.41W
75 C3 Ubierna Spain 42.30N 3.41W
63 S9 Ubigau E Germany 51.35N 13.17E
18 D10 Ubin *isld* Singapore
120 D7 Ubinas Peru 16.22S 70.50W
44 B3 Ubinka *R* U.S.S.R.
18 J2 Ubin, Pulau *isld* Singapore
42 B4 Ubinskoye U.S.S.R. 55.20N 79.42E
42 C4 Ubinskoye Oz *L* U.S.S.R.
39 J2 Ubiyenka U.S.S.R. 65.15N 171.06E
106 M6 Ubly Michigan 43.44N 82.58W
25 G4 Ubolratna Res Thailand
95 O9 Ubombo S Africa 27.35S 32.05E
95 O9 Ubombo *mts* S Africa
Ubon *see* Muang Ubon
91 J4 Ubondo Zaïre 0.57S 25.40E
25 H5 Ubon Ratchathani Thailand 15.15N 104.50E
46 G4 Ubort' *R* Ukraine/Belorussiya U.S.S.R.
41 D4 Uboynaya U.S.S.R. 73.36N 82.18E
71 K9 Ubraye France 43.54N 6.43E
77 F7 Ubrique Spain 36.41N 5.27W
77 F7 Ubrique, Sierra de *mts* Spain
Ubsa Nūr *L see* Uvs Nuur
64 F5 Ubstadt-Weiher W Germany 49.10N 8.38E
18 L10 Ubud Bali Indon 8.30S 115.18E
91 J4 Ubundu Zaïre 0.24S 25.30E
121 D4 Ucacha Argentina 33.03S 64.30W
120 C1 Ucayali, R Peru
37 G2 Uçburun Yarımada *pen* Turkey 40.49N 29.17E
67 O12 Ucciani Corsica 42.02N 8.58E
61 R10 Uccle *dist* Bruxelles Belgium
75 D6 Uceda Spain 40.50N 3.28W
75 D4 Ucero Spain 41.42N 3.04W
75 D4 Ucero *R* Spain
37 H2 Uçgaziler Turkey 40.51N 29.57E
31 F6 Uch Bahawalpur Pakistan 27.18N 71.12E
31 E6 Uch Jacobabad Pakistan 28.30N 69.12E
43 G7 Uch-Adzhi Turkmeniya U.S.S.R. 38.07N 62.53E
47 H8 Uchaly U.S.S.R. 54.22N 59.30E
41 G8 Uchami U.S.S.R. 63.52N 96.33E
41 G8 Uchami *R* U.S.S.R.
32 D2 Ūchān Iran 36.18N 50.34E
43 O4 Uch-Aral Kazakhstan U.S.S.R. 46.08N 80.55E
71 E9 Uchaud France 43.45N 4.17E
20 O4 Uchigō Japan 37.03N 140.49E
20 F8 Uchiko Japan 33.32N 132.40E
97 K7 Uchi Lake Ontario 51.04N 92.34W
36 H4 Üçhisar Turkey 38.40N 34.46E
20 K2 Uchiura-wan *B* Japan
20 H2 Uchiyama Chiba Japan
120 B3 Uchiza Peru 8.24S 76.27W
71 F3 Uchizy France 46.31N 4.53E
44 E4 Uchkeken U.S.S.R. 43.58N 42.34E
43 O8 Uch-Korgon Kirgiziya U.S.S.R. 40.14N 72.06E
43 G6 Uch Kuduk Uzbekistan U.S.S.R. 41.27N 64.30E
44 E4 Uchkulan U.S.S.R. 43.26N 42.08E
43 N8 Uchkupryuk Uzbekistan U.S.S.R. 40.33N 71.04E
63 J7 Uchte W Germany 52.31N 8.54E
63 P7 Uchte *R* E Germany
43 L6 Uchterek Kirgiziya U.S.S.R. 41.46N 73.11E
31 D8 Uchto *R* Pakistan
Uch Turfan *see* Wushi
40 E2 Uchur *R* U.S.S.R.
43 N8 Uch'yar Uzbekistan U.S.S.R. 40.55N 71.05E
76 K4 Ucieza *R* Spain
61 L7 Ucimont Belgium 49.50N 5.03E
69 L5 Uckange France 49.18N 6.10E
64 C2 Uckerath W Germany 50.44N 7.22E
63 U4 Ückeritz E Germany 54.01N 14.04E
56 M6 Uckfield E Sussex Eng 50.58N 0.06E
Üçköşe *see* Ovacık Erzurum Turkey
63 T9 Uckro E Germany 51.52N 13.37E
75 E8 Uclés Spain 39.58N 2.52W
101 L11 Ucluelet Vancouver I, Br Col 48.55N 125.34W
110 O6 Ucon Idaho 43.36N 111.58W
36 F5 Üçpınar Turkey 37.07N 32.17E
108 D5 Ucross Wyoming 44.34N 106.32W
66 G4 Uctendorf Switzerland 46.47N 7.34E
91 D8 Ucua Angola 8.43S 14.08E
37 G7 Uçum Bitlis Turkey 38.02N 42.39E
37 G7 Uçum Turkey 38.28N 43.20E
42 H6 Uda *R* Buryat U.S.S.R.
40 F4 Uda *R* Khabarovsk U.S.S.R.
41 K7 Udachnyy U.S.S.R. 66.20N 112.58E
Udain, Al *see* Udayn, Al
29 D4 Udaipur Jhunjhunu, Rajasthan Ind 27.40N 75.32E
29 J7 Udaipur Orissa India 21.41N 85.58E
29 C5 Udaipur Udaipur, Rajasthan India 24.36N 73.47E
29 C5 Udaipur *dist* Rajasthan India
30 K6 Udaipur Garhi Nepal 26.57N 86.30E
28 D5 Udaiyarpalaiyam Tamil Nadu India 11.15N 79.20E
28 J2 Udalguri Assam India 26.46N 92.08E
28 C5 Udamalpet Tamil Nadu India 10.37N 77.16E
93 L8 Udan Kenya 2.51S 39.35E
39 C2 Udanna U.S.S.R. 65.55N 143.31E
29 H7 Udanti R Orissa India
121 F6 Udaquilla Argentina 36.31S 58.30W
39 D3 Udarnik U.S.S.R. 63.08N 147.58E
44 E3 Udarnyy U.S.S.R. 44.16N 42.24E
26 S9 Uda Walawe *res* Sri Lanka 6.27N 80.50E
45 D6 Uday *R* Ukraine U.S.S.R.
28 D3 Udayagiri Andhra Prad India 14.54N 79.18E
29 E6 Udayagiri Madhya Prad India 23.31N 77.47E
29 J7 Udayagiri Hill Orissa India 20.18N 85.51E
29 F6 Udayapur Madhya Prad India 23.55N 78.03E
33 J4 'Udayd, Jabal al *mt* U.A.E. 24.30N 51.30E
33 J4 Udayd, Khawr al *B* U.A.E 24.33N 51.30E
33 H4 'Udayliyah, Al Saudi Arabia 25.07N 49.18E
33 E10 Udayn, Al Yemen 13.58N 43.59E
33 H5 'Udaynān Saudi Arabia 23.31N 48.36E
35 F2 Udaysah Syria 32.49N 35.43E
82 C6 Udbina Yugoslavia 44.31N 15.47E
53 E3 Udby Århus Denmark 56.35N 10.18E
53 H5 Udby Denmark 55.46N 11.43E
53 D6 Udby Fyn Denmark 55.26N 9.52E
53 E3 Udbyhøj Denmark 56.38N 10.19E
53 E3 Udbyneder Denmark 56.40N 10.16E
60 M10 Uddel Netherlands 42.15N 5.47E
52 F8 Uddevalla Sweden 58.20N 11.56E
58 H7 Uddingston Strathclyde Scotland 55.50N 4.06W
51 F6 Uddjaur *L* Sweden 65.55N 17.50E
33 J4 'Udeid, Khōr al *gulf* Qatar/U.A.E.
92 H5 Udekwa Tanzania 7.39S 36.25E
60 L13 Uden Netherlands 51.40N 5.37E
60 J13 Udenhout Netherlands 51.37N 5.09E
63 M10 Uder E Germany 51.22N 10.04E
65 E7 Uderns Austria 47.19N 11.52E
31 E8 Udero Lal Pakistan 25.40N 68.36E
28 C1 Udgir Maharashtra India 18.26N 77.11E
31 H4 Udhampur Kashmir 32.55N 75.07E
31 H4 Udhampur *dist* Kashmir
86 P5 Udhruḩ Jordan 30.20N 35.36E
90 C8 Udi Nigeria 6.15N 7.24E
30 B6 Udi Uttar Prad India 26.43N 78.56E
14 E4 Udialla W Australia 18.01S 123.45E
76 L2 Udias Spain 43.21N 4.15W
19 N5 Udidan *isld* Truk Is Pacific Oc 7.11N 151.57E
35 C4 Udim Israel 32.16N 34.51E
79 O2 Udine Italy 46.04N 13.14E
42 F5 Udinskiy Khrebet *mts* U.S.S.R.
28 B4 Udipi Karnataka India 13.23N 74.45E
29 C4 Udit Rajasthan India 27.32N 72.45E
Udjir *isld see* Ujir
64 P3 Udlice Czechoslovakia 50.27N 13.28E
38 E3 Udmurtskaya A.S.S.R U.S.S.R.
20 E10 Udo Japan 31.41N 131.26E
44 D3 Udobnaya U.S.S.R. 44.18N 41.31E
40 A3 Udokan Khrebet *mts* U.S.S.R.
46 J1 Udomlya U.S.S.R. 57.54N 35.00E
20 N7 Udone-jima *isld* Japan 34.28N 139.18E
25 G4 Udon Thani Thailand 17.25N 102.45E
13 B6 Udor, Mt N Terr Australia 23.30S 130.52E
19 N4 Udot *isld* Truk Is Pacific Oc 7.24N 151.44E
39 F7 Udova *R* Kamchatka U.S.S.R.
40 G4 Udskaya Guba *B* U.S.S.R.
40 F4 Udskoye U.S.S.R. 54.33N 134.25E
90 E6 Udubo Nigeria 11.52N 10.35E
26 R9 Udugama Sri Lanka 6.13N 80.20E
82 K8 Udvoy *mts* Bulgaria
45 H6 Udy Ukraine U.S.S.R. 50.24N 36.04E
40 E4 Udykhin *R* U.S.S.R.
40 H5 Udyl', Oz *L* U.S.S.R.
41 L5 Udzha U.S.S.R. 71.19N 116.50E
41 L5 Udzha *R* U.S.S.R.
44 H7 Udzhary Azerbaydzhan U.S.S.R. 40.29N 47.37E
66 F4 Ueberstorf Switzerland 46.52N 7.19E
87 J10 Uebi Gofca,R Somalia
87 K9 Uebi Scebeli,R Somalia
19 B4 Uëbonti Celebes Indon 0.55S 121.39E
63 U5 Uecker *R* E Germany
63 S6 Ueckermark *reg* E Germany
63 U5 Ueckermünde E Germany 53.45N 14.03E
20 M5 Ueda Japan 36.27N 138.13E
63 D9 Uedem W Germany 51.39N 6.16E
63 G8 Ueffeln W Germany 52.27N 7.54E
87 J9 Uegit Somalia 3.48N 43.15E
108 O8 Uehling Nebraska 41.42N 96.30W
20 D9 Ueki Japan 32.54N 130.42E
41 L4 Uele *R* U.S.S.R.
91 H2 Uele *R* Zaïre
39 N2 Uelen U.S.S.R. 66.13N 169.48W
39 L2 Uel'kal' U.S.S.R. 65.32N 179.19W
93 N6 Uel Mur Somalia 0.02S 41.18E
63 E7 Uelsen W Germany 52.30N 6.54E
63 J4 Uelvesbüll W Germany 54.25N 8.55E
63 N7 Uelzen W Germany 52.58N 10.34E
47 K1 Uengan, Mys *C* U.S.S.R. 70.42N 66.43E
20 K7 Ueno Japan 34.45N 136.08E
20 N6 Uenohara Japan 35.40N 139.07E
63 E10 Uerdingen W Germany 51.22N 6.37E
91 K1 Uere *R* Zaïre
64 B3 Uess *R* W Germany
66 M1 Uesslingen Switzerland 47.35N 8.50E
63 L5 Uetersen W Germany 53.42N 9.40E
66 L2 Uetli Berg Switzerland 47.21N 8.31E
39 A1 Uettyakh U.S.S.R. 67.37N 134.27E
63 M8 Uetze W Germany 52.27N 10.12E
47 H8 Ufa Bashkir U.S.S.R. 54.45N 55.58E
47 M5 Ufa Chelyabinsk U.S.S.R. 55.46N 60.08E
47 M5 Ufa *R* U.S.S.R.
47 M4 Ufaleyskiy Khrebet *mts* U.S.S.R.
87 E5 Uffat *watercourse* Sudan
60 O8 Uffelte Netherlands 52.47N 6.17E
64 J4 Uffenheim W Germany 49.32N 10.15E
56 O3 Ufford Suffolk Eng 52.07N 1.20E
47 H7 Ufimka U.S.S.R. 56.44N 58.09E
47 H7 Ufimskiy U.S.S.R. 56.45N 58.15E
43 C7 Ufra Turkmeniya U.S.S.R. 40.00N 53.05E
56 J3 Ufton Warwicks Eng 52.16N 1.26W
47 F5 Uftyuga *R* Arkhangel'sk U.S.S.R.
47 E5 Uftyuga *R* Vologda U.S.S.R.
96 U8 Uga Lanzarote Canary Is 28.54N 13.45W
94 D2 Ugab *watercourse* Namibia
40 D4 Ugagli U.S.S.R. 54.50N 127.00E
113 J8 Ugaiushak I Alaska 56.48N 156.55W
113 L8 Ugak B Alaska
113 L8 Ugak I Alaska 57.24N 152.19W
92 E4 Ugalla Tanzania 5.47S 31.10E
92 E4 Ugalla *R* Tanzania
113 E9 Ugamak I Aleutian Is 54.14N 164.50W
73 H5 Uganda *rep* E Africa
113 L8 Uganik I Alaska 57.55N 153.25W
113 J8 Ugashik Alaska 57.32N 157.25W
113 J8 Ugashik B Alaska
113 J8 Ugashik Lakes Alaska
60 M11 Ugchelen Netherlands 52.11N 5.55E
42 J6 Ugdan U.S.S.R. 52.10N 113.31E
53 C7 Uge Denmark 54.58N 9.19E
81 R13 Ugento Italy 39.55N 18.10E
53 H5 Ugerløse Denmark 55.35N 11.40E
26 S8 Uggalkaltota Sri Lanka 6.39N 80.53E
53 T19 Uggdal Norway 60.00N 5.31E
53 E4 Uggelhüse Denmark 56.28N 10.13E
53 E1 Uggerby Denmark 57.34N 10.07E
53 E1 Uggerby Å *R* Denmark
53 E5 Uggerslev Denmark 55.32N 10.19E
81 R12 Uggiano la Chiesa Italy 40.06N 18.28E
66 M8 Uggiate Italy 45.49N 8.58E
90 B9 Ughelli Nigeria 5.33N 6.00E
32 J7 Ughin Iran 26.36N 60.06E
95 M7 Ugie S Africa 31.11S 28.13E

58 N3 Ugie, R Grampian Scotland
Ugi I see Uki I
77 K7 Ugíjar Spain 36.58N 3.03W
53 E2 Ugilt Denmark 57.26N 10.10E
71 J5 Ugine France 45.45N 6.25E
40 J7 Uglegorsk Sakhalin U.S.S.R. 49.01N 142.04E
45 K8 Uglegorsk Ukraine U.S.S.R. 48.18N 38.18E
40 F10 Uglekamensk U.S.S.R. 43.15N 133.11E
47 H6 Ugleural'sk U.S.S.R. 59.08N 57.35E
46 L1 Uglich U.S.S.R. 57.30N 38.20E
82 D7 Ugljane Yugoslavia 43.35N 16.46E
82 E6 Ugljevik Yugoslavia 44.38N 19.01E
46 J1 Uglovka U.S.S.R. 58.13N 33.30E
40 E6 Uglovoya U.S.S.R. 52.00N 129.17E
42 C6 Uglovskoye U.S.S.R. 51.17N 80.11E
45 D4 Ugly-Zavod Ukraine U.S.S.R. 52.09N 32.53E
90 C8 Ugo Nigeria 6.09N 6.03E
45 H1 Ugodskiy Zavod U.S.S.R. 55.02N 36.44E
Ugoi see Ujiji
39 K3 Ugol'naya U.S.S.R. 64.41N 175.17E
41 G4 Ugol'naya R U.S.S.R.
39 K3 Ugol'naya, Bukhta gulf U.S.S.R.
39 D2 Ugol'naya Zyryanka U.S.S.R. 65.45N 150.00E
Ugol'nyy Magadan U.S.S.R. see Beringovskiy
39 K3 Ugol'nyye Kopi U.S.S.R. 64.45N 177.49E
39 G4 Ugol'nyy, Mys C U.S.S.R. 61.00N 163.29E
39 F7 Ugon, Sopka vol U.S.S.R. 54.34N 159.45E
40 C2 Ugoyan U.S.S.R. 59.20N 125.20E
45 F2 Ugra U.S.S.R. 54.46N 34.20E
45 G2 Ugra R U.S.S.R.
88 G8 Ugranat reg Morocco
Ugtal see Govĭ-Ugtaal
30 D6 Ugu Uttar Prad India 26.48N 80.19E
39 F4 Ugulan U.S.S.R. 60.27N 155.08E
40 C3 Ugumru R U.S.S.R.
41 L6 Ugumun U.S.S.R. 69.38N 115.17E
40 D2 Ugun U.S.S.R. 58.45N 128.30E
36 G2 Uğurludağ Turkey 40.27N 34.28E
42 A2 Ugut U.S.S.R. 60.31N 74.07E
43 L6 Ugyut Kirgiziya U.S.S.R. 41.23N 74.53E
26 U7 Uhana Sri Lanka 7.22N 81.38E
92 G6 Uhanyana Tanzania 8.55S 34.50E
87 C2 Uheimir, El watercourse Sudan
62 K6 Uherské Hradiště Czechoslovakia 49.05N 17.30E
62 K6 Uherský Brod Czechoslovakia 49.01N 17.40E
64 H6 Uhingen W Germany 48.43N 9.35E
64 P4 Úhlava R Czechoslovakia
103 D5 Uhlerstown Pennsylvania 40.31N 75.05W
64 K4 Uhlfeld W Germany 49.40N 10.44E
66 K1 Ühlingen W Germany 47.43N 8.18E
65 M2 Uhlirké Czechoslovakia 49.53N 15.04E
100 T2 Uhlman L Manitoba
64 L2 Uhlstädt E Germany 50.44N 11.28E
53 C5 Uhre Denmark 55.56N 9.03E
104 D6 Uhrichsville Ohio 40.25N 81.23W
62 O4 Uhrusk Poland 51.20N 23.38E
30 D5 Ui R Uttar Prad India
118 G2 Uibaí Brazil 11.07S 42.16W
75 C9 Uicario, Embalse de res Spain
58 D3 Uig Skye, Highland Scotland 57.35N 6.22W
91 D7 Uige Angola 7.45S 15.09E
91 D7 Uige dist Angola
9 U12 Uiha isld Tonga, Pacific Oc 19.54S 174.24W
19 N5 Uijec isld Truk Is Pacific Oc 7.11N 151.57E
21 D9 Ŭijŏngbu S Korea 37.48N 127.00E
21 C7 Uiju N Korea 40.09N 124.36E
61 N3 Uikhoven Belgium 50.55N 5.43E
43 C3 Uil Kazakhstan U.S.S.R. 49.08N 54.43E
43 D3 Uil R Kazakhstan U.S.S.R.
44 F5 Uilpata U.S.S.R. 42.47N 43.49E
33 M10 Uinā' al Ahmadī Kuwait 29.05N 48.09E
66 S4 Uina, Val d' Switzerland
111 L5 Uinkaret Plat Arizona
87 H9 Uinle, El Somalia 3.00N 41.40E
47 H7 Uinskoye U.S.S.R. 56.51N 56.30E
110 P9 Uinta R Utah
110 P9 Uinta Mts Utah
21 D10 Uiryŏng S Korea 35.20N 128.00E
94 C3 Uis Namibia 21.08S 14.49E
21 D9 Uisŏng S Korea 36.21N 128.45E
61 F2 Uitbergen Belgium 51.01N 3.58E
60 J10 Uitdam Netherlands 52.25N 5.05E
95 J9 Uitenhage S Africa 33.46S 25.25E
60 G9 Uitgeest Netherlands 52.32N 4.43E
60 H11 Uithoorn Netherlands 52.14N 4.50E
60 P6 Uithuizen Netherlands 53.24N 6.41E
60 P6 Uithuizermeeden Netherlands 53.25N 6.44E
61 C1 Uitkerke Belgium 51.18N 3.09E
95 H8 Uitkoms Cape Province S Africa 32.45S 24.39E
95 N2 Uitkoms Transvaal S Africa 26.50S 29.35E
95 K5 Uitsig S Africa 29.20S 26.36E
95 N2 Uitspanning S Africa 26.45S 29.55E
95 H3 Uitvalskop S Africa 27.19S 24.56E
117 A1 Uitvlugt Guyana 6.52N 58.18W
60 Q6 Uitwierde Netherlands 53.22N 6.54E
9 B2 Ujae atoll Marshall Is Pacific Oc 9.00N 165.40E
44 H10 Ujān R Iran
48 S8 Ujarasugssuk Greenland 69.50N 52.30W
62 L5 Ujazd Poland 50.23N 18.20E
30 C5 Ujhani Uttar Prad India 28.00N 79.00E
20 J7 Uji Japan 34.54N 135.48E
21 E12 Uji-guntō islds Japan
20 N5 Ujiie Japan 36.42N 139.57E
92 D4 Ujiji Tanzania 4.55S 29.39E
15 C6 Ujir I Moluccas Indon 5.38S 134.18E
29 D6 Ujjain Madhya Prad India 23.11N 75.50E
29 D6 Ujjain dist Madhya Prad India
76 H2 Ujo Spain 43.12N 5.47W
62 L8 Újpest Hungary 47.33N 19.05E
62 K2 Ujście Poland 53.03N 16.44E
75 H2 Ujué Spain 42.30N 1.30W
19 B7 Ujung Indonesia 7.06S 120.46E
19 B6 Ujunglamuru Celebes Indonesia 4.42S 120.02E
19 A6 Ujung Pandang Celebes Indon 5.09S 119.28E
42 F4 Uk U.S.S.R. 55.06N 98.51E
20 Q8 Uka Okinawa Japan 26.51N 128.14E
39 G5 Uka U.S.S.R. 57.50N 162.02E
39 G5 Uka R U.S.S.R.
94 E7 Ukamas Namibia 28.01S 19.44E
92 J12 Ukanga I Zanzibar 6.15S 39.18E
42 F4 Ukar U.S.S.R. 55.05N 99.15E
93 E7 Ukara I Tanzania 1.50S 33.03E
20 L4 Ukawa Japan 37.15N 137.04E
33 F3 'Ukayrishah Saudi Arabia 27.23N 44.22E
43 N8 Ukchi Uzbekistan U.S.S.R. 40.21N 71.00E
90 C8 Ukehe Nigeria 6.40N 7.24E
39 J4 Ukelayat U.S.S.R. 61.46N 173.23E
39 J4 Ukelayat R U.S.S.R.
92 F3 Ukerewe I Tanzania 2.09S 32.52E
Ukhaidhir see Ukhaydir
34 L6 Ukhaydir anc site Iraq 32.27N 43.36E
33 F8 Ukhdūd Saudi Arabia 17.34N 44.20E
30 C2 Ukhimath Uttar Prad India 30.31N 79.06E
45 M3 Ukholovo U.S.S.R. 53.48N 40.30E
28 K3 Ukhrul Manipur India 25.08N 94.24E
47 G4 Ukhta Komi U.S.S.R. 63.33N 53.44E
47 D5 Ukhtoma U.S.S.R. 60.09N 38.03E
41 M7 Ukhunku U.S.S.R. 67.05N 123.50E
111 A2 Ukiah California 39.09N 123.12W
110 G4 Ukiah Oregon 45.08N 118.55W
20 P9 Ukibaru-jima isld Okinawa Japan 26.16N 128.00E
15 M4 Uki I Solomon Is 10.17S 161.45E
39 G5 Ukinskaya Guba gulf U.S.S.R.
20 F2 Ukita dist Tōkyō Japan
Ukitsu see Muroto
48 U13 Ukîverajik Greenland 65.45N 38.00W
113 C4 Ukivok Alaska 65.00N 168.00W
30 E8 Ukme R Madhya Prad India
46 E2 Ukmerge Lithuania U.S.S.R. 55.14N 24.49E
52 J8 Ukna Sweden 58.04N 16.20E
42 D7 Ukok, Ploskogor'ye tableland U.S.S.R.
39 G6 Ukolka R U.S.S.R.
40 G4 Ukoy, Mys C U.S.S.R. 55.38N 136.46E
Ukraine see Ukrainskaya S.S.R
Ukrainian S.S.R see Ukrainskaya S.S.R.
42 B4 Ukrainka Novosibirsk U.S.S.R. 56.52N 78.18E
47 L8 Ukrainka Omsk U.S.S.R. 54.40N 71.20E
38 B4 Ukrainskaya S.S.R U.S.S.R.
82 D6 Ukrina R Yugoslavia
51 Q10 Uksun R Karelia U.S.S.R.
47 J7 Uksyanskoye U.S.S.R. 56.00N 63.00E
62 N2 Ukta Poland 53.41N 21.29E
41 R5 Ukta U.S.S.R. 70.44N 145.15E
47 F4 Uktym U.S.S.R. 62.43N 49.00E
20 C8 Uku-jima isld Japan
41 L6 Ukukit R U.S.S.R.
40 D2 Ukulan U.S.S.R. 59.03N 126.15E
93 L10 Ukunda Kenya 4.18S 39.33E
40 G5 Ukurunry, Mys C U.S.S.R. 53.55N 137.45E
93 E2 Ukuti Uganda 3.40N 33.31E
39 K3 Ukvushvuynen, Gory mts U.S.S.R.
87 E7 Ukwaa Sudan 6.41N 34.35E
93 F5 Ukwala Kenya 0.12N 34.12E
93 D9 Ukwene mt Tanzania 3.41S 32.21E
94 F4 Ukwi Pan salt pan Botswana 23.33S 20.34E
36 C5 Ula Turkey 37.08N 28.25E
33 B3 'Ulā, Al Saudi Arabia 26.38N 37.57E
22 G3 Ulaanbaatar Mongolia 47.54N 106.52E
22 H5 Ulaanbadrah Mongolia 43.41N 109.59E
24 F1 Ulaan Davaa pass Mongolia/U.S.S.R. 49.15N 88.05E
22 B2 Ulaangom Mongolia 49.59N 92.00E
Ula bayan Mönhö see Uulbayan
85 J4 Ulâd Ali dist Egypt
85 B4 Ulad Mshiahia tribe Libya
41 O7 Ulaga U.S.S.R. 66.11N 131.39E
Ulagqat see Wuqia
37 F2 Ulagu Burun C Turkey 40.22N 28.41E
33 F9 'Ulah tribe Yemen/S Yemen
Ulai see Ulāy, Kūh-e mt
41 N9 Ulakhan U.S.S.R. 61.40N 129.15E
40 G2 Ulakhan-Bam, Khrebet ra U.S.S.R.
42 J2 Ulakhan Botuobuya R U.S.S.R.
39 D2 Ulakhan-Chistay, Khrebet ra U.S.S.R.
41 L8 Ulakhan-Kyuyel' U.S.S.R. 63.50N 116.40E
42 J2 Ulakhan, Porog falls U.S.S.R. 61.58N 110.30E
39 D1 Ulakhan-Sis, Kryazh ridge U.S.S.R.
39 E1 Ulakh-Ebe, Oz L U.S.S.R. 68.45N 155.00E
113 P10 Ulak I Aleutian Is 51.24N 178.59W
19 N4 Ulalu isld Truk Is Pacific Oc 7.25N 151.41E
91 H8 Ulamba Zaïre 9.09S 23.41E
15 L6 Ulamona New Britain 5.01S 151.15E
Ulan see Otog Qi
12 J4 Ulan New S Wales 32.14S 149.48E
22 D8 Ulan Qinghai China 36.55N 98.30E
Ulān Badaraha see Ulaanbadrah
Ulan Bator see Ulaanbaatar
22 G7 Ulan Buh Shamo desert Nei Monggol Zizhiqu China
22 G6 Ulan Buh Shamo mt ra Nei Monggol Zizhiqu China
42 H5 Ulan-Burgasy, Khrebet mts U.S.S.R.
44 F1 Ulan Erge Kalmyk A.S.S.R. U.S.S.R. 46.17N 44.52E
Ulān Gōm see Ulaangom
Ulanhad see Chifeng
22 K4 Ulan Hobor Nei Monggol Zizhiqu China 44.22N 114.54E
Ulan Hot see Horqin Youyi Qianqi
Ulan Hua see Sizhiwang (Dorbod) Qi
21 B5 Ulan Hua Jilin China 44.45N 122.40E
46 O6 Ulan Khol U.S.S.R. 45.24N 46.50E
24 F4 Ulanlinggi Xinjiang Uygur Zizhiqu China 42.47N 87.15E
42 G5 Ulan-Obusa U.S.S.R. 53.40N 103.50E
82 L1 Ulanov U.S.S.R. 49.42N 28.10E
22 F6 Ulan Suhai Nei Monggol Zizhiqu China 41.12N 104.14E
22 H6 Ulansuhai Nur L Nei Monggol Zizhiqu China
22 E6 Ulan Tohoi Nei Monggol Zizhiqu China 40.55N 101.26E
42 H6 Ulan-Ude U.S.S.R. 51.55N 107.40E
24 G8 Ulan Ula mt ra Qinghai China
24 G8 Ulan Ul Hu L Qinghai China
Ulap see Kabwum
26 S7 Ulapane Sri Lanka 7.07N 80.34E
121 C3 Ulapes Argentina 31.31S 66.16W
121 C3 Ulapes, Sa ra Argentina
15 M5 Ulaputur New Ireland 3.47S 152.30E
39 E1 Ularovskaya Guba gulf U.S.S.R.
13 H7 Ularunda Queensland 26.48S 147.04E
37 C6 Ulaş Turkey 39.27N 37.04E
81 D4 Ulassai Sardinia 39.48N 9.31E
24 E4 Ulasutai Shankou pass Xinjiang Uygur Zizhiqu China 43.03N 85.49E
15 M3 Ulawa I Solomon Is 9.45S 161.55E
15 L6 Ulawun, Mt New Britain 5.06S 151.20E
92 H5 Ulaya Tanzania 7.02S 36.55E
32 H6 Ulāy, Kūh-e mt Iran 29.02N 59.34E
33 G4 Ulayyah plat Saudi Arabia
43 P2 Ul'ba Kazakhstan U.S.S.R. 50.16N 83.22E
40 G5 Ul'banskiy Zaliv B U.S.S.R.
61 M3 Ulbeek Belgium 50.51N 5.19E
39 C5 Ul'beya U.S.S.R. 59.22N 144.20E
39 C4 Ul'beya R U.S.S.R.
39 C5 Ul'beya R U.S.S.R.
53 C3 Ulbjerg Denmark 56.38N 9.22E
57 O6 Ulceby Cross Lincs Eng 53.15N 0.07E
21 E9 Ulchin S Korea 37.00N 129.26E
82 E9 Ulcinj Yugoslavia 41.56N 19.12E
95 H4 Ulco S Africa 28.21S 24.15E
57 G3 Uldale Cumbria Eng 54.43N 3.10W
53 D5 Uldum Denmark 55.51N 9.36E
Uldza see Bayan Uul
77 O4 Ulea Spain 38.09N 1.19W
Uleåborg see Oulu
Uled Saidan see Fuqahā', Al
52 E7 Ulefoss Norway 59.17N 9.15E
92 F6 Uleia Tanzania 8.06S 32.38E
77 M6 Uleila del Campo Spain 37.11N 2.11W
108 O2 Ulen Minnesota 47.04N 96.16W
42 D5 Ulen' U.S.S.R. 54.07N 89.45E
12 F3 Ulenia L New S Wales 29.57S 142.24E
60 T17 Ulestraten Netherlands 50.54N 5.47E
92 G6 Ulete Tanzania 8.09S 35.25E
42 J6 Ulety U.S.S.R. 51.24N 112.29E
53 A4 Ulfborg Denmark 56.17N 8.20E
53 A4 Ulfborg Kirkeby Denmark 56.18N 8.22E
64 J1 Ulfen W Germany 51.03N 10.01E
50 D6 Úlfljótsvatn Iceland 64.06N 21.04W
50 D6 Úlfljótsvatn L Iceland 64.06N 21.03W
50 E5 Úlfsvatn L Iceland 64.54N 20.35W
60 O12 Ulft Netherlands 51.53N 6.23E
22 L4 Ulgai Nei Monggol Zizhiqu China 45.43N 118.22E
22 L4 Ulgain Gol R Nei Monggol Zizhiqu China
37 G4 Ulgar Dağ mt Turkey 41.26N 42.43E
37 C3 Ulgardere Turkey 40.18N 26.29E
57 K2 Ulgham Northumb Eng 55.13N 1.38W
41 L8 Ulgumdzha U.S.S.R. 63.43N 118.24E
29 C8 Ulhasnagar Maharashtra India 19.15N 73.08E
113 C10 Uliaga I Aleutian Is 53.05N 169.45W
Uliassutai see Uliastay
Uliastai see Dong Ujimqin Qi
22 D3 Uliastay Mongolia 47.42N 96.52E
Uliástay Davan pass see Ulasutai Shankou
64 P4 Ulice Czechoslovakia 49.46N 13.10E
60 H14 Ulicoten Netherlands 51.27N 4.51E
19 N5 Ulifauro Pass Truk Is Pacific Oc 7.14N 151.42E
19 N5 Uligar Pass Truk Is Pacific Oc 7.12N 151.58E
91 K5 Ulindi R Zaïre
15 H6 Ulingan Papua New Guinea 4.32S 145.23E
39 C5 Ul'inskiy Khrebet ra U.S.S.R.
19 M4 Uliperu isld Truk Is Pacific Oc 7.17N 151.33E
17 N9 Ulithi atoll Caroline Is Pacific Oc 10.00N 139.40E
82 C6 Uljan isld Yugoslavia 44.04N 15.10E
82 G5 Uljma Yugoslavia 45.02N 21.10E
42 H4 Ul'kan U.S.S.R. 57.15N 107.20E
42 H4 Ul'kan R Irkutsk U.S.S.R.
40 F3 Ulkan R Khabarovsk U.S.S.R.
43 G3 Ul'kayak R Kazakhstan U.S.S.R.
53 D7 Ulkebøl Denmark 54.56N 9.51E
43 K1 Ul'kenkaroy, Oz L Kazakhstan U.S.S.R.
42 J7 Ulkhun-Partiya U.S.S.R. 49.53N 112.48E
53 C5 Ulkind Denmark 55.49N 9.08E
46 G2 Ulla Belorussiya U.S.S.R. 55.10N 29.14E
46 G3 Ulla R Belorussiya U.S.S.R.
53 U20 Ulla R Norway 59.21N 6.29E
76 C3 Ulla R Spain
12 K6 Ulladulla New S Wales 35.21S 150.25E
52 L4 Ullånger Sweden 63.00N 18.10E
31 H9 Ullapara Bangladesh 24.20N 89.34E
58 F3 Ullapool Highland Scotland 57.54N 5.10W
52 G9 Ullared Sweden 57.07N 12.45E
51 J4 Ullatti Sweden 67.02N 21.50E
53 V20 Ullatun Norway 59.23N 6.32E
51 K8 Ullava Finland 63.43N 23.56E
53 T16 Ulldalsvatn L Norway 61.12N 5.57E
75 L6 Ulldecona Spain 40.36N 0.20E
75 M5 Ulldemolins Spain 41.19N 0.53E
53 V18 Ullensvang Norway 60.19N 6.40E
53 F6 Ullerslev Denmark 55.21N 10.40E
53 D7 Ullerup Denmark 54.58N 9.40E
107 G4 Ullin Illinois 37.17N 89.10W
53 C3 Ullits Denmark 56.43N 9.18E
120 E7 Ulloma Bolivia 17.29S 68.31W
51 H2 Ullsfjord Norway 69.32N 19.34E
51 H2 Ullsfjord inlet Norway 69.40N 19.45E
57 H3 Ullswater L Cumbria Eng 54.35N 2.55W
44 H6 Ulluchay R U.S.S.R.
21 E9 Ullung do isld S Korea
21 C8 Ŭllyul N Korea 38.29N 125.10E
107 E7 Ulm Arkansas 34.35N 91.29W
110 O2 Ulm Montana 47.25N 111.30W
64 H7 Ulm W Germany 48.24N 10.00E
108 D5 Ulm Wyoming 44.39N 106.36W
12 L3 Ulmarra New S Wales 29.37S 153.03E
76 C10 Ulme Portugal 39.18N 8.25W
64 B3 Ulmen W Germany 50.13N 6.59E
82 K5 Ulmeni Romania 45.04N 26.40E
65 L5 Ulmerfeld Austria 48.04N 14.50E
69 P2 Ulmtal W Germany 50.35N 8.18E
115 M2 Ulmukhuas Nicaragua 14.20N 84.30W
82 E7 Ulog Yugoslavia 43.24N 18.19E
92 G9 Ulongue Mozambique 14.34S 34.21E
12 E2 Uloowaranie, L S Australia
39 E1 Ulovo U.S.S.R. 70.33N 154.01E
57 G4 Ulpha Cumbria Eng 54.20N 3.15W
29 E1 Ul R Punjab India
52 G9 Ulricehamn Sweden 57.57N 13.25E
66 K5 Ulrichen Switzerland 46.31N 8.18E
14 E7 Ulrich Ra W Australia
65 J4 Ulrichsberg Austria 48.41N 13.55E
65 O5 Ulrichskirchen Austria 48.24N 16.29E
64 G2 Ulrichstein W Germany 50.35N 9.11E
53 S18 Ulriken mt Norway 60.23N 5.22E
52 J3 Ulriksfors Sweden 63.50N 15.40E
60 O6 Ulrum Netherlands 53.22N 6.20E
21 E10 Ulsan S Korea 35.32N 129.21E
63 L3 Ülsby W Germany 54.38N 9.36E
53 E2 Ulsted Denmark 57.05N 10.16E
53 T14 Ulsteinvik Norway 62.21N 5.53E
103 A3 Ulster Pennsylvania 41.50N 76.30W
103 F3 Ulster co New York
59 G2 Ulster prov Irish Rep
64 H2 Ulster R E & W Germany
59 H3 Ulster Canal Monaghan Irish Rep
103 G3 Ulster Park New York 41.51N 73.59W
116 J1 Ulster Spring Jamaica, W I 18.19N 77.32W
53 F5 Ulstrup Denmark 55.44N 10.58E
53 D4 Ulstrup Viborg Denmark 56.23N 9.48E
81 C2 Ultana, Monti Sardinia
51 G4 Ultevis mts Sweden
12 G6 Ultima Victoria 35.30S 143.20E
121 J8 Ultima Esperanza, Seno inlet Chile
13 D6 Ultim, Mt N Terr Australia 22.30S 135.15E
79 J1 Ultimo, Val di V Italy
19 D2 Ulu Indonesia 2.44N 125.25E
93 J7 Ulu Kenya 1.49S 37.09E
36 F2 Ulu R Bolu Turkey
37 C3 Ulu R Çanakkale Turkey
36 G2 Ulu R Çankırı Turkey
37 G1 Ulu R İstanbul Turkey
40 D1 Ulu R U.S.S.R.
115 P10 Ulua R Honduras
37 D8 Ulubaba Dağı mt Turkey 37.58N 38.10E
18 C7 Ulu Bakar, Gunong mt Pen Malaysia 4.16N 102.54E
18 J3 Ulu Bedok dist Singapore
37 D5 Ulubey Ordu Turkey 40.54N 37.44E
36 D4 Ulubey Uşak Turkey 38.27N 29.18E
36 E4 Uluborlu Turkey 38.06N 30.28E
37 G3 Ulu Dağları mts Turkey
37 G8 Uludere Turkey 37.25N 42.51E
19 J6 Ulugan B Philippines 10.04N 118.47E
37 H8 Ulugh Dāgh mt Iran 37.10N 44.48E
Ulugh Muztagh mt see Muztag
Ulug-Khem R see Verkhniy Yenisey R
24 A6 Ulugqat Xinjiang Uygur Zizhiqu China 39.45N 74.10E
41 N8 Ulugur U.S.S.R. 63.36N 126.15E
92 H5 Uluguru Mts Tanzania
9 T5 Uluinggalau mt Taveuni Fiji 16.52S 18.000
87 D5 Ulu,Jeb mt Sudan 10.45N 33.31E
18 D4 Ulu Kali, Gunong mt Pen Malaysia 3.23N 101.50E
18 D9 Ulu Kemapan hill Pen Malaysia 2.37N 103.12E
36 G5 Ulukışla Turkey 37.33N 34.29E
40 F2 Ulukuut U.S.S.R. 59.36N 134.57E
17 P10 Ulul isld Caroline Is Pacific Oc 8.36N 149.39E
18 B6 Ulu Laho, Bukit hill Pen Malaysia 5.42N 101.27E
18 K5 Ululselua, Bukit mt Borneo Indon 1.09N 113.12E
95 O9 Ulundi Natal S Africa 28.18S 31.26E
24 F2 Ulungur He R Xinjiang Uygur Zizhiqu China
24 F2 Ulungur Hu L Xinjiang Uygur Zizhiqu China 47.10N 87.10E
42 J5 Ulunkhan U.S.S.R. 54.50N 110.58E
114 E6 Ulupalakua Hawaiian Is 20.38N 156.23W
18 H3 Ulu Pandan dist Singapore
36 F1 Ulus Turkey 41.35N 32.38E
83 J5 Ulus Dağ mt Turkey 39.19N 28.23E
18 B6 Ulu Soh, Gunong mt Pen Malaysia 5.04N 101.05E
43 H3 Ulutau Kazakhstan U.S.S.R. 48.37N 67.00E
43 H4 Ulutau, Gory mts Kazakhstan U.S.S.R.
18 D10 Ulu Tiram Pen Malaysia 1.36N 103.48E
43 J1 Ulu-Togo U.S.S.R. 63.00N 113.12E
18 B8 Ulu Yam Pen Malaysia 3.26N 101.38E
42 D3 Ulu-Yul R U.S.S.R.
58 D6 Ulva isld Strathclyde Scotland 56.28N 6.12W
53 Y14 Ulvåa R Norway
53 X14 Ulvådalsvatn L Norway 62.15N 7.51E
50 T14 Ulvebreen glacier Spitsbergen 78.10N 19.00E
60 H13 Ulvenhout Netherlands 51.33N 4.48E
57 G4 Ulverston Cumbria Eng 54.12N 3.06W
12 H8 Ulverstone Tasmania 41.09S 146.10E
53 S15 Ulvesundet sound Norway 61.57N 5.08E
53 V17 Ulvik Norway 60.34N 6.54E
51 J10 Ulvila Finland 61.26N 21.55E
52 L3 Ulvön isld Sweden 63.04N 18.40E
53 J6 Ulvshale pen Denmark 55.03N 12.16E
53 J7 Ulv Sund sound Denmark 54.59N 12.12E
39 C5 Ulya U.S.S.R. 58.51N 141.51E
39 C5 Ulya R U.S.S.R.
29 G2 Ulyagan R U.S.S.R.
46 P2 Ul'yankovo U.S.S.R. 55.24N 47.50E
45 F6 Ul'yanovka Ukraine U.S.S.R. 50.58N 34.18E
45 G3 Ul'yanovo U.S.S.R. 53.42N 35.31E
45 U2 Ul'yanovsk U.S.S.R. 54.19N 48.22E
46 O3 Ul'yanovskaya Oblast' prov U.S.S.R.
43 L2 Ul'yanovskoye Kazakhstan U.S.S.R. 50.05N 73.44E
42 K6 Ulyatuy U.S.S.R. 51.12N 116.15E
110 L4 Ulysses Idaho 45.28N 114.09W
109 J4 Ulysses Kansas 37.36N 101.23W
108 N8 Ulysses Nebraska 41.05N 97.12W
43 G3 Ulyzhilanshik R Kazakhstan U.S.S.R.
75 G2 Ulzama R Spain
Ulzburg see Henstedt-Ulzburg
83 D3 Ulzë,L i Albania 41.40N 20.00E
21 B1 Uma Nei Monggol Zizhiqu China 52.33N 120.41E
87 F2 Umadam Sudan 16.30N 36.10E
79 P4 Umag Yugoslavia 45.26N 13.31E
90 C7 Umaisha Nigeria 8.01N 7.12E
113 R10 Umak I Aleutian Is 51.52N 176.00W
120 E7 Umala Bolivia 17.21S 68.00W
40 F6 Umaltinskiy U.S.S.R. 51.58N 133.37E
115 P7 Umán Mexico 20.51N 89.43W
46 H5 Uman' Ukraine U.S.S.R. 48.45N 30.10E
19 N4 Uman isld Truk Is Pacific Oc
48 T7 Umánaq Greenland 70.40N 52.00W
Ûmánarssuaq see Farvel, Kap
91 G2 Umangi Zaïre 2.05N 21.27E
121 C2 Umango, Cerro pk Argentina 29.00S 68.40W
31 C6 Umarao Pakistan 28.05N 65.22E
15 C6 Umari Irian Jaya 4.25S 135.19E
29 G6 Umaria Madhya Prad India 23.30N 80.52E
34 D7 'Umarī, Qa'el salt L Jordan
29 E8 Umarkhed Maharashtra India 19.36N 77.46E
29 H8 Umarkot Orissa India 19.39N 82.18E
31 E8 Umarkot Pakistan 25.22N 69.48E
12 E2 Umaroona, L S Australia
15 H7 Umasia Papua New Guinea 7.03S 145.00E
19 L1 Umatac Guam Pacific Oc 13.18N 144.40E
20 J4 Umatate Chiba Japan
105 F9 Umatilla Florida 28.57N 81.42W
110 F4 Umatilla Oregon 45.54N 119.20W
110 F4 Umatilla R Oregon
110 A1 Umatilla Reef Lightship Washington 48.11N 124.52W
19 M7 Umayan R Mindanao Philippines
120 D6 Umayo, L Peru 15.46S 70.13W
33 M5 'Umayrī, Wādī watercourse Oman
47 C3 Umba U.S.S.R. 66.40N 34.17E
93 K10 Umba R Tanzania
51 R4 Umba R U.S.S.R.
104 O2 Umbagog L New Hampshire
18 C9 Umbai Pen Malaysia 2.06N 102.24E
13 D2 Umbakumba Groote Eylandt, N Terr Australia 13.47S 136.50E
112 B9 Umbarger Texas 34.58N 102.06W
29 C7 Umbarpada Gujarat India 21.26N 73.33E
13 C7 Umbeara N Terr Australia 25.50S 133.40E
90 L7 Umbelasha watercourse Sudan
56 D5 Umberleigh Bridge Devon Eng 51.00N 3.59W
80 F2 Umbertide Italy 43.18N 12.20E
95 O6 Umbogintwini S Africa 30.01S 30.55E
15 J6 Umboi I Bismarck Arch
47 C2 Umbozero L U.S.S.R.
66 S5 Umbrail, Piz mt Italy/Switz 46.33N 10.25E
87 F3 Umbrega Ethiopia 14.18N 36.33E
11 D12 Umbrella Mts New Zealand
116 H1 Umbrella Pt Jamaica, W I 18.31N 77.54W
77 D6 Umbrete Spain 37.22N 6.10W
80 F3 Umbria prov Italy
77 C6 Umbria, Pta pt Spain 37.10N 6.58W
76 D14 Umbrias de Camacho Portugal 37.15N 7.38W
75 D4 Umbria, Sierra de la mts Spain
81 N5 Umbriatico Italy 39.21N 16.55E
80 G2 Umbro-Marchigiano, Appno mts Italy
51 D5 Umbukta Norway 66.10N 14.35E
15 K5 Umbukul Bismarck Arch 2.28S 149.59E
95 N4 Umbulwana S Africa 28.36S 29.50E
95 O5 Umbumbulu S Africa 29.58S 30.43E
117 J8 Umbuzeiro Brazil 7.40S 35.36W
95 P5 Umdloti Beach S Africa 29.40S 31.07E
52 M3 Umeå Sweden 63.50N 20.15E
52 M3 Ume älv R Sweden
35 G5 Um ed Dananir Jordan 32.05N 35.49E
35 G5 Um ed Dananir R Jordan
34 C6 Um ed Daraj, Jebel mt Jordan 32.18N 35.48E
35 F5 Um el 'Amad Jordan 32.06N 35.45E
35 G6 Um el 'Amad Jordan 31.47N 35.54E
35 G6 Um el Hanafish Jordan 31.49N 35.52E
34 C9 Um el Hashim, Jebel mt Jordan 29.28N 35.17E
35 F9 Um el Khanazir Jordan 31.01N 35.40E
35 G6 Um el Kundum Jordan 31.50N 35.53E
35 G7 Um el Malid anc site Jordan 31.39N 35.54E
35 G4 Um el Manabi anc site Jordan 32.22N 35.45E
35 G6 Um el Qanafid Jordan 31.50N 35.49E
34 H2 Um el Quseir Syria 36.34N 40.32E
19 F4 Umera Moluccas Indon 0.09S 129.37E
35 G7 Um er Risas anc site Jordan 31.30N 35.55E
45 O2 Umet U.S.S.R. 54.08N 42.55E
95 O9 Umfolozi R S Africa
51 E6 Umfors Sweden 65.58N 15.05E
100 L1 Umfreville Ontario 49.54N 91.30W
92 D10 Umfuli R Zimbabwe
52 L2 Umgransele Sweden 64.42N 18.20E
92 C11 Umguza Zimbabwe 19.25S 27.51E
35 G9 Um Hamat Jordan 31.02N 35.46E
65 C7 Umhausen Austria 47.09N 10.55E
95 P5 Umhlali S Africa 29.29S 31.13E
95 P5 Umhlanga Rocks S Africa 29.44S 31.05E
92 D10 Umi R Zimbabwe
76 C3 Umia R Spain
113 L2 Umiat Alaska 69.25N 152.20W
114 C7 Umikoa Hawaiian Is 19.58N 155.23W
87 C3 Um Inderaba Sudan 15.12N 31.50E
101 U2 Umingmaktok N W Terr 67.48N 108.00W
34 C9 Um Ishrīn, Jebel mt Jordan 29.35N 35.27E
35 F5 Um Jauza Jordan 32.06N 35.44E
95 O6 Umkomaas S Africa 30.13S 30.48E
95 O6 Umkomaas R S Africa
95 O5 Umlaasweg S Africa 29.44S 30.31E
28 J3 Umlaiteng Assam India 25.48N 92.03E
34 N7 Umma anc site Iraq 31.38N 45.52E
86 M9 Umm Adawi, Wâdi watercourse Egypt
86 J4 Umm 'Agârim hill Egypt 30.50N 32.50E
85 N8 Umm Akpa, Gebel mt Sudan 23.42N 35.10E
85 C6 Umm al 'Abīd Libya 27.29N 15.01E
Umm al Amzd see Umm el 'Amad
85 C6 Umm al Arānib Libya 26.08N 14.43E
33 K5 'Umm al Ashtān U.A.E. 23.42N 53.32E
34 O7 Umm al Baqar, Hawr L Iraq
33 C5 Umm al Birak Saudi Arabia 23.28N 39.16E
Umm-al-Guwein see 'Umm al Qaiwain
Umm al Ḩayt see Ramlat Amilḩayt sand dunes
87 D2 Umm Ali Sudan 17.02N 33.43E
86 L6 Umm 'Ali, Gebel hill Egypt 29.56N 33.56E
85 C6 Umm al Izām Libya 26.03N 15.20E
33 F3 Umm al Jamājim Saudi Arabia 26.56N 45.19E
33 M9 Umm al Madāfi' mt Kuwait 29.46N 47.20E
33 L4 'Umm al Qaiwain U.A.E. 25.32N 55.35E
33 D3 Umm al Qalbān Saudi Arabia 27.50N 41.29E
Umm al Quwain see 'Umm al Qaiwain
33 K4 'Umm al Sheif oil field The Gulf 25.08N 52.08E
34 K4 Umm al Tūz Iraq 34.47N 42.42E
63 S4 Ummanz isld E Germany
34 K4 Umm ar Rughība Iraq 34.32N 42.50E
86 J8 Umm Arta, Wâdi watercourse Egypt
86 L4 Umm Asâgîl, Gebel hill Egypt 30.45N 33.32E
33 L6 Umm as Samīm salt flat Saudi Arabia/Oman
33 L5 Umm az Zumūl U.A.E. 22.42N 55.12E
33 J4 Umm Bâb Qatar, The Gulf 25.09N 50.50E
87 A3 Umm Badr Sudan 14.13N 27.58E
86 J10 Umm Balad, Wâdi watercourse Egypt
87 D5 Umm Barbit Sudan 10.56N 32.32E
87 A3 Umm Bayada depression Sudan 14.56N 27.00E
87 B4 Umm Bel Sudan 13.31N 28.03E
86 K8 Umm Bugma Egypt 28.59N 33.21E
90 L6 Umm Dafag Sudan 10.28N 23.20E
87 B4 Umm Defeis Sudan 12.42N 29.15E
87 E4 Umm Doga,Jeb mt Sudan/Ethiopia 12.12N 35.29E
87 B3 Umm Dubban Sudan 14.11N 29.43E
87 C3 Umm Durag, Jeb mt Sudan 14.45N 30.10E
35 G2 Umm ed Dananir Syria 32.57N 35.49E
34 E4 Umm el 'Amad Syria 34.47N 37.01E
35 H1 Umm el 'Awsaj Syria 33.05N 36.04E
86 G4 Umm el Diyâb Egypt 30.57N 31.35E
35 D3 Umm el Fahm Israel 32.31N 35.09E
86 F8 Umm el Ḩawâya, Gebel hill Egypt 28.43N 31.07E
35 H3 Umm el Mayadin Syria 32.35N 36.12E
35 J1 Umm el Qusur Syria 33.11N 36.20E
86 K4 Umm el Ruweisât hill Egypt 30.52N 33.04E
64 K3 Ummerstadt E Germany 50.15N 10.50E
85 E5 Umm Farud Libya 29.11N 18.14E
86 N7 Umm Garfein, Wâdi watercourse Saudi Arabia
87 D4 Umm Garr Sudan 13.49N 32.23E
85 C5 Umm Ghayr Libya 28.21N 14.18E
87 E3 Umm Gidad Sudan 14.16N 35.40E
33 M10 Umm Gudair oil field Kuwait 28.55N 47.40E
32 B6 Umm Gudair oil well Saudi Arabia 28.45N 47.35E
85 N7 Umm Gurâf, Gebel mt Egypt 24.25N 34.17E
Umm Hagar see Om Hajer
86 N5 Umm Hallûf, Gebel hill Egypt 30.14N 34.35E
90 L6 Umm Haraz Sudan 11.58N 23.14E
33 B3 Umm Ḩarb Saudi Arabia 26.35N 36.40E
86 O7 Umm Ḩashīm, Jebel mt Jordan 29.26N 35.16E
87 A3 Umm Heglig Sudan 14.11N 26.38E
87 C5 Umm Heitan Sudan 11.30N 30.06E
86 M5 Umm Ḩuşaira hill Egypt 30.21N 34.15E
87 C3 Umm Inderab Sudan 15.58N 30.41E
86 M9 Umm 'Isheirât, Gebel hill Egypt 28.20N 34.22E
86 H6 Umm Itla, Wâdi watercourse Egypt
86 O7 Umm Jasir Saudi Arabia 29.06N 35.14E
34 K10 Umm Junayyih Saudi Arabia 28.44N 42.12E
87 A4 Umm Keddada Sudan 13.33N 26.35E
87 B4 Umm Kereidim Sudan 13.42N 29.50E
86 J5 Umm Khisheib, Gebel hill Egypt 30.12N 32.58E
86 J5 Umm Khisheib, Wâdi watercourse Egypt
87 D4 Umm Koweika Sudan 13.10N 32.16E
90 M4 Umm Lahai Sudan 15.41N 25.54E
33 B4 Umm Lajj Saudi Arabia 25.03N 37.17E
87 A5 Umm Leilaya Sudan 11.55N 27.20E
86 M7 Umm Mafrûd, Gebel hill Egypt 29.10N 34.13E
86 J5 Umm Makhassa, Gebel hill Egypt 30.20N 32.59E
90 M5 Umm Marahik Sudan 13.55N 25.27E
86 L4 Umm Mitmam, Gebel hill Egypt 30.48N 33.33E
33 C5 Umm Mukhbār, Jabal mts Saudi Arabia
85 N7 Umm Naqqât, Gebel mt Egypt 25.31N 34.13E
33 B8 Umm Na'sān isld Bahrain, The Gulf
33 M8 Umm Niqqā area Kuwait
34 C10 Umm Nukhaylah Saudi Arabia 28.49N 35.30E
34 F9 Umm Nukhaylah hill Saudi Arabia 29.28N 38.36E
86 J10 Umm 'Omeiyid, Wâdi watercourse Egypt
33 N10 Umm Qaşbā C Saudi Arabia 28.26N 48.32E
34 P8 Umm Qaşr Iraq 30.02N 47.55E
87 A3 Umm Qozein Sudan 14.11N 27.16E
33 A3 Umm Quşur isld Saudi Arabia 27.56N 35.15E
86 O10 Umm Qusūr isld Saudi Arabia
86 J9 Umm Rabul, Gebel hill Egypt 28.20N 32.40E
34 M10 Umm Radmah Saudi Arabia 28.42N 44.42E
85 L10 Umm Rahau Sudan 18.53N 32.00E
86 G5 Umm Raqm, Gebel hill Egypt 30.15N 31.52E
86 M8 Umm Ri', Gebel hill Egypt 38.42N 34.13E
86 G6 Umm Rihiyât, Gebel hill Egypt 29.53N 31.52E
86 O9 Umm Rijm Saudi Arabia 28.22N 35.05E
87 D3 Umm Rimta Sudan 14.51N 32.06E
86 P8 Umm Rizim, Wādī watercourse Saudi Arabia
87 C4 Umm Ruwaba Sudan 12.50N 31.20E
90 L4 Umm Saggat, Wadi watercourse Sudan
33 J4 Umm Sa'id Qatar, The Gulf 24.59N 51.37E
87 C3 Umm Saiyala Sudan 14.24N 31.08E
33 C5 Umm Samā Saudi Arabia 22.30N 39.34E
85 L8 Umm Shâghir, Jebel mt Egypt 23.15N 31.38E
34 D9 Umm Shaitiya Saudi Arabia 29.14N 36.10E
86 P7 Umm Shallāl, Wādī watercourse Saudi Arabia
86 L9 Umm Shomar, Gebel hill Egypt 28.22N 33.56E
86 J10 Umm Sidar, Wâdi watercourse Egypt
90 M4 Umm Sidr Darfur Sudan 14.29N 25.10E
87 D3 Umm Sidr Kordofan Sudan 15.09N 32.03E
34 K6 Umm Sijla, Sha'īb watercourse Iraq
86 G8 Umm Sirrâb, Wâdi watercourse Egypt
87 B3 Umm Suneita Sudan 15.11N 28.54E
87 B3 Umm Sunta Sudan 15.10N 28.03E
86 J8 Umm Tinâssib, Gebel hill Egypt 28.30N 32.34E
86 J8 Umm Tinâssib, Wâdi watercourse Egypt
87 C2 Umm Tub Sudan 17.44N 31.42E
33 B4 Umm Urūmah isld Saudi Arabia 25.43N 36.35E
33 F5 Umm Wazir Saudi Arabia 22.21N 44.55E
113 C10 Umnak I Aleutian Is 53.20N 168.20W
113 C10 Umnak Pass Aleutian Is
51 E6 Umnäs Sweden 65.27N 16.05E
95 N7 Umngazana S Africa 31.42S 29.23E
92 D11 Umniati Zimbabwe 18.39S 29.49E
92 D10 Umniati R Zimbabwe
41 G7 Umnyn Syverma, Khrebet mts U.S.S.R.
64 L2 Umpferstedt E Germany 50.58N 11.25E
92 J9 Umpilua Mozambique 14.10S 38.36E
110 B6 Umpqua R Oregon
91 E10 Umpulo Angola 12.40S 17.40E
35 G4 Um Qantara Jordan 32.15N 35.56E
35 F3 Um Qeis Jordan 32.39N 35.41E
35 G8 Um Quleib anc site Jordan 31.24N 35.48E
35 G6 Um Quseir Jordan 31.53N 35.55E
36 E3 Umraniye Turkey 39.10N 31.12E
29 F7 Umrer Maharashtra India 20.50N 79.24E
30 A8 Umri Madhya Prad India 24.48N 77.18E
35 G7 Um Rummana Jordan 31.45N 35.52E
35 G7 Um Shujeira el Gharbiya Jordan 31.31N 35.51E
92 D11 Umsweswe Zimbabwe 18.23S 29.52E
92 E11 Umsweswe R Zimbabwe
92 F11 Umtali Zimbabwe 19.00S 32.40E
92 F11 Umtali dist Zimbabwe
95 M7 Umtata S Africa 31.35S 28.47E
95 O6 Umtentweni S Africa 30.42S 30.29E
90 C9 Umuahia Nigeria 5.31N 7.26E
118 D8 Umuarama Brazil 23.43S 52.57W
15 G8 Umuda I Papua New Guinea 8.25S 143.45E
9 S12 Umuna isld Tonga, Pacific Oc 18.41S 173.56W
37 C3 Umurbey Bursa Turkey 40.15N 26.37E
37 G2 Umurbey Çanakkale Turkey 40.25N 29.11E
37 C3 Umurbey R Turkey
95 O5 Umvoti R S Africa
92 E10 Umvukwe Ra Zimbabwe
92 E10 Umvukwes Zimbabwe 16.59S 30.59E
92 E11 Umvuma Zimbabwe 19.19S 30.35E
35 F9 Umyan Jordan 31.10N 35.38E
95 N6 Umzimhlava R S Africa
95 N6 Umzimkulu S Africa 30.16S 29.56E
95 O6 Umzimkulu R S Africa
95 N6 Umzimvubu R S Africa
92 D12 Umzingwani R Zimbabwe
95 O6 Umzinto S Africa 30.19S 30.40E
95 O6 Umzumbe S Africa 30.37S 30.33E
35 G5 Um Zuweitina Jordan 32.02N 35.53E
118 H4 Una Brazil 15.18S 39.06W
29 E2 Una Himachal Prad India 31.28N 76.19E
75 G7 Uña Spain 40.14N 1.59W
47 D4 Una U.S.S.R. 64.31N 38.15E
117 J9 Una R Brazil
82 C5 Una R Yugoslavia
20 K2 Unabetsu-dake mt Japan 43.55N 144.53E
76 G4 Uña de Quintana Spain 42.06N 6.09W
50 C2 Unadhsdalur Iceland 66.06N 22.35W
105 D5 Unadilla Georgia 32.16N 83.46W
103 D2 Unadilla New York 42.20N 75.18W
104 K4 Unadilla R New York
118 F5 Unaí Brazil 16.24S 46.49W
31 E3 Unai Pass Afghanistan 34.27N 68.25E
40 D4 Unakho R U.S.S.R.
113 G5 Unalakleet Alaska 63.52N 160.50W
113 G5 Unalakleet R Alaska
113 D10 Unalaska Aleutian Is 53.51N 166.35W
113 D10 Unalaska I Aleutian Is 53.40N 166.40W
75 G7 Uña, L. de Spain 40.14N 2.00W
113 D10 Unalga I Aleutian Is 54.00N 166.10W
113 P10 Unalga I Aleutian Is 51.36N 179.05W
11 G9 Una, Mt New Zealand 42.13S 172.36E
92 G8 Unango Mozambique 12.51S 35.23E
30 B7 Unao Madhya Prad India 25.36N 78.36E
Unao Uttar Prad see Unnao
50 L3 Unaós Iceland 65.35N 14.01W
58 G2 Unapool Highland Scotland 58.14N 5.00W
119 G2 Unare, L. de Venezuela 10.05N 65.23W
119 G3 Unare, R Venezuela
51 M4 Unari Finland 67.07N 25.38E
30 A8 Unarsi Madhya Prad India 24.18N 77.21E
48 V12 Unarteq Greenland 70.20N 21.59W
30 G6 Unaul Uttar Prad India 26.38N 83.17E
19 B4 Unauna isld Indonesia 0.10S 121.35E
33 E3 'Unayzah Saudi Arabia 26.06N 43.58E
34 G6 'Unayzah, Jabal mt Iraq/Jordan/Saudi Arabia 32.09N 39.11E
75 H3 Uncastillo Spain 42.21N 1.08W
103 K4 Uncasville Connecticut 41.26N 72.06W
30 D8 Unchahra Madhya Prad India 24.22N 80.46E
30 D5 Unchaulia Uttar Prad India 27.48N 80.05E
120 E8 Uncía Bolivia 18.28S 66.35W
109 C3 Uncompahgre Pk Colorado 38.04N 107.28W
109 B3 Uncompahgre Plateau Colorado
42 K6 Unda U.S.S.R. 51.46N 117.00E
42 K6 Unda R U.S.S.R.
52 H8 Unden L Sweden 58.50N 14.30E
52 H8 Undenäs Sweden 58.38N 14.25E
95 N5 Underberg S Africa 29.47S 29.30E
12 F6 Underbool Victoria 35.10S 141.50E
51 C8 Undersåker Norway 63.20N 13.18E
53 E2 Understed Denmark 57.23N 10.28E
52 L6 Understen Lt Ho Sweden 60.18N 18.56E
52 J5 Undersvik Sweden 61.36N 16.20E
53 D5 Underup Denmark 55.57N 9.42E
66 E2 Undervelier Switzerland 47.18N 7.13E
108 P8 Underwood Iowa 41.24N 95.41W
108 P3 Underwood Minnesota 46.17N 95.52W
108 J2 Underwood N Dakota 47.28N 101.10W
42 K6 Undino-Posel'ye U.S.S.R. 51.27N 116.18E
50 E4 Undirfell Iceland 65.24N 20.15W
53 H5 Undløse Denmark 55.37N 11.36E
45 U2 Undory U.S.S.R. 54.36N 48.24E
53 W17 Undredal Norway 60.57N 7.06E
9 T4 Undu Pt Vanua Levu Fiji 16.07S 179.55W
19 B9 Undu, Tanjung C Sumba Indonesia 10.03S 120.53E
41 M7 Undylyung R U.S.S.R.
15 K6 Unea I Bismarck Arch 4.54S 149.10E
45 D4 Unecha U.S.S.R. 52.52N 32.42E
119 F8 Uneiuxi, R Brazil
86 P5 'Uneiza Jordan 30.29N 35.51E
64 P4 Úněšov Czechoslovakia 49.51N 13.10E
47 D4 Unezhma U.S.S.R. 63.54N 36.50E
113 G9 Unga Alaska 55.10N 160.35W
113 G9 Unga I Alaska 55.15N 160.40W
113 G4 Ungalik Alaska 64.34N 161.00W
113 G4 Ungalik R Alaska
12 H5 Ungarie New S Wales 33.38S 147.00E
12 D5 Ungarra S Australia 34.09S 136.00E
97 N6 Ungava B Quebec
46 G6 Ungeny Moldavia U.S.S.R. 47.10N 27.43E
15 F7 Ungerem Papua New Guinea 6.30S 141.12E
64 J8 Ungerhausen W Germany 48.00N 10.16E
21 E6 Unggi N Korea 42.19N 130.24E
94 N4 Unguana Mozambique 23.04S 35.17E
40 E2 Unguële R U.S.S.R.
92 K12 Unguja Ukuu Zanzibar 6.19S 39.23E
91 H5 Ungundu Zaïre 3.44S 23.50E
87 F2 Ungwatiri Sudan 16.52N 36.10E
76 D8 Unhais da Serra Portugal 40.16N 7.39W
76 E15 Unhos Portugal 38.49N 9.07W
65 K1 Unhošt Czechoslovakia 50.06N 14.08E
31 C4 Uni Afghanistan 32.44N 65.10E
117 F7 União Brazil 4.34S 42.51W
120 D3 União Brazil 9.15S 70.55W
118 D10 União da Vitória Brazil 26.13S 51.05W
119 H8 União do Mararà Brazil 0.58S 61.51W
117 J9 União dos Palmares Brazil 9.08S 36.02W
29 D4 Uniara Tonk, Rajasthan India 26.08N 75.16E
29 E5 Uniara Tonk, Rajasthan India 25.54N 76.03E
105 E1 Unicoi Tennessee 36.13N 82.21W
96 B12 Unicorn Pt Ascension I 7.59S 14.19W
62 K6 Uničov Czechoslovakia 49.48N 17.05E
62 L4 Uniejów Poland 51.59N 18.48E
82 B6 Unije, I Yugoslavia 44.40N 14.15E
119 D6 Unilla, R Colombia
113 E9 Unimak Aleutian Is 54.25N 164.50W
113 E9 Unimak B Aleutian Is
113 E9 Unimak I Aleutian Is 55.00N 164.00W
113 E9 Unimak Pass Aleutian Is
89 F9 Uni, Mt Liberia 4.53N 7.46W
120 C4 Unini Peru 10.41S 73.59W
119 H8 Unini, R Brazil
121 D5 Unión Argentina 35.09S 65.55W
109 G1 Union Colorado 40.23N 103.30W
103 K3 Union Connecticut 42.00N 72.09W
108 R7 Union Iowa 42.15N 93.03W
107 F11 Union Louisiana 30.06N 90.54W
104 Q2 Union Maine 44.12N 69.18W
107 G9 Union Mississippi 32.34N 89.09W
107 E3 Union Missouri 38.27N 91.01W
108 P9 Union Nebraska 40.49N 95.56W
103 F5 Union New Jersey 40.42N 74.17W
109 N6 Union Oklahoma 35.25N 97.56W
110 H4 Union Oregon 45.14N 117.50W
118 C9 Unión Paraguay 24.45S 56.33W
105 F3 Union S Carolina 34.42N 81.37W
104 E9 Union W Virginia 37.36N 80.34W
103 F5 Union co New Jersey
116 O8 Union I Grenadines W I 12.36N 61.26W
121 E7 Unión, Bahía Argentina
103 F6 Union Beach New Jersey 40.27N 74.11W
104 H7 Union Bridge Maryland 39.34N 77.12W
103 B2 Union Center New York 42.08N 76.04W
106 D6 Union Center Wisconsin 43.40N 90.19W
107 F10 Union Church Mississippi 31.42N 90.46W
106 J7 Union City Michigan 42.03N 85.08W
103 L7 Union City New Jersey 40.46N 74.02W
104 A6 Union City Ohio 40.13N 84.48W
104 F5 Union City Pennsylvania 41.56N 79.51W
107 G5 Union City Tennessee 36.26N 89.03W
110 C7 Union Creek Oregon 42.55N 122.26W
98 P9 Union Crique B Quebec 46.46N 71.16W
103 C3 Uniondale Pennsylvania 41.42N 75.30W
95 G9 Uniondale S Africa 33.40S 23.07E
95 G9 Uniondale Road S Africa 33.29S 23.01E
116 D3 Unión de Reyes Cuba 22.49N 81.31W
110 H3 Union Flat Cr Washington
110 E3 Union Gap Washington 46.35N 120.30W
59 D8 Unionhall Cork Irish Rep 51.33N 9.08W
Union Is see Tokelau Is
103 D8 Union L New Jersey
77 P5 Unión, La Spain 37.37N 0.53W
105 F2 Union Mills N Carolina 35.30N 81.59W
111 M7 Union, Mt Arizona 34.27N 112.24W
16 E3 Union of Soviet Socialist Republics (U.S.S.R.) Europe/Asia
110 Q6 Union Pass Wyoming 43.29N 109.50W
105 D4 Union Pt Georgia 33.37N 83.05W
100 U9 Union Pt Manitoba 49.30N 97.03W
107 L9 Union Springs Alabama 32.08N 85.44W
104 J4 Union Springs New York 42.51N 76.42W
107 B2 Union Star Missouri 39.59N 94.36W
107 J9 Uniontown Alabama 32.27N 87.30W
107 J4 Uniontown Kentucky 37.43N 87.56W
104 F7 Uniontown Pennsylvania 39.54N 79.44W
26 U13 Union Vale Mauritius, Indian Oc 20.27S 57.39E
103 J3 Unionville Connecticut 41.45N 72.53W
108 S9 Unionville Iowa 40.49N 92.40W
106 L6 Unionville Michigan 43.41N 83.29W
107 C1 Unionville Missouri 40.28N 93.01W
110 G9 Unionville Nevada 40.26N 118.07W
103 E4 Unionville New York 41.18N 74.34W

103 C7 Unionville Pennsylvania 39.54N 75.45W
104 H8 Unionville Virginia 38.16N 77.59W
82 H4 Unirea Romania 46.24N 23.50E
62 L2 Unisław Poland 53.12N 18.20E
33 K5 United Arab Emirates The Gulf
United Arab Republic see Egypt, Arab Rep. of
49 B5 United Kingdom of Gt. Britain & N. Ireland (U.K.) W Europe
102 United States of America (U.S.A.) N America
97 L1 United States Ra N W Terr
79 M6 Uniti, Fiume R Italy
47 C4 Unitsa U.S.S.R. 62.38N 34.29E
104 Q2 Unity Maine 44.37N 69.21W
110 G5 Unity Oregon 44.26N 118.11W
100 H6 Unity Saskatchewan 52.27N 109.10W
107 G7 University Mississippi 34.22N 89.35W
107 F3 University City Missouri 38.42N 90.20W
29 C6 Unjha Gujarat India 23.48N 72.29E
64 C2 Unkel W Germany 50.35N 7.14E
65 G6 Unken Austria 47.39N 12.43E
47 L5 Unkurda U.S.S.R. 55.48N 59.23E
41 O7 Unkyur U.S.S.R. 66.35N 132.45E
39 E2 Unkyur Yakutsk U.S.S.R. 65.23N 151.00E
41 O9 Unkyur Yakutsk U.S.S.R. 62.28N 131.48E
12 A8 Unley dist Adelaide, S Aust 34.57S 138.35E
40 E6 Un'ma R U.S.S.R.
63 G9 Unna W Germany 51.32N 7.41E
30 D6 Unnao Uttar Prad India 26.32N 80.30E
30 D6 Unnao dist Uttar Prad India
52 H9 Unnaryd Sweden 57.37N 13.45E
89 A6 Uno,I Guinea-Bissau 11.15N 16.20W
39 H4 Unomachi U.S.S.R. 60.41N 166.05E
76 K2 Unquera Spain 43.23N 4.31W
121 D3 Unquillo Argentina 31.15S 64.17W
64 L6 Unsernherrn W Germany 48.44N 11.28E
47 D4 Unskaya Guba gulf U.S.S.R.
58 R8 Unst isld Shetland Scotland 60.45N 0.55W
64 K1 Unstrut R E Germany
21 D7 Unt'aek N Korea 40.35N 128.13E
30 G8 Untari Bihar India 24.17N 83.30E
20 P8 Unten Okinawa Japan 26.42N 128.00E
66 J5 Unteraar Glacier Switzerland
65 H6 Unter Ach Austria 47.49N 13.29E
66 L3 Unter-Ägeri Switzerland 47.08N 8.36E
66 Q1 Unter Argen R W Germany
65 N6 Unterberg mt Austria 47.57N 15.50E
Unter Deufstetten see Fichtenau
65 H8 Unter-drau-tal V Austria
66 O2 Untereggen Switzerland 47.27N 9.28E
66 K1 Unter Eggingen W Germany 47.42N 8.24E
66 L2 Unter Embrach Switzerland 47.30N 8.36E
66 R4 Unter Engadin V Switzerland
64 H3 Unterfranken dist Bayern W Ger
65 H8 Untergailtal V Austria
64 Q6 Untergriesbach Bayern W Germany 48.35N 13.41E
64 F5 Unter Grombach W Germany 49.06N 8.34E
64 H6 Untergröningen W Germany 48.55N 9.54E
64 M7 Unterhaching W Germany 48.03N 11.37E
66 M3 Unter Iberg Switzerland 47.03N 8.47E
66 L2 Unter Illnau Switzerland 47.25N 8.44E
65 E7 Unter-inn-tal V Austria
64 J6 Unterkochen W Germany 48.48N 10.14E
63 M7 Unterlüss W Germany 52.49N 10.18E
64 K3 Untermerzbach W Germany 50.08N 10.53E
64 H5 Untermünkheim W Germany 49.09N 9.44E
64 K5 Untern-Bibert W Germany 49.25N 10.38E
69 Q5 Unter-Owisheim W Germany 49.09N 8.40E
65 O6 Unter Piesting Austria 47.53N 16.09E
66 P1 Unter-Reitnau W Germany 47.35N 9.40E
64 O8 Untersberg mt W Germany 47.42N 13.59E
66 M4 Unter Schächen Switzerland 46.52N 8.47E
64 F5 Unter Schwarzach W Germany 49.22N 8.59E
64 G8 Untersee L W Germany
66 H5 Unterseen Switzerland 46.41N 7.46E
64 M3 Unter Steinach W Germany 50.08N 11.32E
Untersteinbach see Rauhenebrach
65 J7 Unter-tal V Austria
65 J7 Unter Tauern Austria 47.18N 13.31E
64 J8 Unter-Thingau W Germany 47.47N 10.30E
63 T6 Unteruecker-see L E Germany
64 G8 Unteruhldingen W Germany 47.44N 9.15E
66 P4 Untervaz Switzerland 46.56N 9.32E
66 J4 Unterwalden canton Switzerland
66 K5 Unterwasser Switzerland 46.32N 8.21E
65 L5 Unter Weissenbach Austria 48.27N 14.48E
66 N1 Unter-Zell W Germany 47.43N 9.02E
64 M7 Unter Zolling W Germany 48.26N 11.46E
47 K4 Untor, Oz L U.S.S.R. 62.30N 65.20E
44 H5 Untsukul' U.S.S.R. 42.42N 46.49E
119 G7 Unturán, Sa.de mts Venezuela
113 W8 Unuk R Alaska
24 G8 Unuli Horog Qinghai China 35.10N 91.50E
70 N5 Unverre France 48.11N 1.05E
100 H6 Unwin Saskatchewan 52.57N 109.52W
40 E4 Un'ya R Amur U.S.S.R.
47 H5 Un'ya R Komi U.S.S.R.
93 D2 Unyama R Uganda
37 C4 Ünye Turkey 41.09N 37.15E
20 D9 Unzen-Amakusa Nat. Park Japan
20 D9 Unzen-dake pk Japan 32.46N 130.16E
46 N1 Unzha U.S.S.R. 58.01N 44.00E
46 N1 Unzha R U.S.S.R.
65 K7 Unzmarkt Austria 47.12N 14.28E
121 E6 Unzue Argentina 36.10S 61.00W
75 G2 Unzue Spain 42.39N 1.38W
87 G2 Uodgan Ethiopia 17.20N 38.40E
39 E1 Uolbut U.S.S.R. 68.07N 154.05E
39 C3 Uol'chan U.S.S.R. 64.44N 142.39E
39 C3 Uol'chan R U.S.S.R.
87 F6 Uolchitte Ethiopia 8.15N 37.42E
9 U12 Uoleva isld Tonga, Pacific Oc 19.53S 174.24W
80 D4 Uomo, Capo d' Italy 42.24N 11.06E
9 U12 Uonuku Hahake atoll Tonga, Pacific Oc 19.58S 174.30W
42 J4 Uoyan U.S.S.R. 56.08N 111.40E
20 L5 Uozu Japan 36.50N 137.25E
45 H3 Upa R U.S.S.R.
110 P9 Upalco Utah 40.17N 110.13W
91 D10 Upanda, Sa mts Angola
119 B9 Upano, R Ecuador
39 K3 Upanu U.S.S.R. 62.49N 179.35E
30 H5 Upardang Garhi Nepal 27.46N 84.35E
29 H6 Upar Ghat reg Madhya Prad India
119 H3 Upata Venezuela 8.02N 62.25W
56 H5 Upavon Wilts Eng 51.18N 1.49W
21 C9 Upchŏ-ri N Korea 37.53N 125.09E
91 K8 Upemba, L Zaïre
91 K8 Upemba, Parc Nat. de l' Zaïre
29 K6 Uperbada Orissa India 22.10N 86.07E
48 S5 Upernavik Greenland 72.40N 56.05W
12 C6 Upfield dist Melbourne, Vic
58 J7 Uphali Lothian Scotland 55.56N 3.31W
108 K1 Upham N Dakota 48.36N 100.44W
56 F5 Uphill Avon Eng 51.20N 2.59W
57 H5 Upholland Lancs Eng 53.33N 2.44W
19 M1 Upi Guam Pacific Oc 13.35N 144.56E
19 M8 Upi Mindanao Philippines 6.57N 124.10E
119 D5 Upía, R Colombia
94 F7 Upington S Africa 28.28S 21.14E
111 G7 Upland California 34.06N 117.38W
106 J9 Upland Indiana 40.28N 85.30W
108 M9 Upland Nebraska 40.20N 98.53W
95 G9 Uplands S Africa 33.58S 23.19E
99 P7 Uplands airport Ontario 45.18N 75.43W
29 B7 Upleta Gujarat India 21.47N 70.21E
55 K3 Upminster London England 51.33N 0.15E
113 H6 Upnuk L Alaska 60.22N 159.00W
47 C2 Upolaksha U.S.S.R. 67.30N 31.58E
122 B2 Upolu isld W Samoa, Pacific Oc
114 B6 Upolu Pt Hawaiian Is Pacific Oc 20.16N 155.52W
44 D3 Upornaya U.S.S.R. 44.22N 41.02E
56 E6 Upottery Devon Eng 50.52N 3.10W
89 H6 Upper reg Ghana
101 P10 Upper Arrow L Br Col
103 D5 Upper Black Eddy Pennsylvania 40.33N 75.07W
98 G7 Upper Blackville New Brunswick 46.39N 65.50W
56 K2 Upper Broughton Notts Eng 52.50N 0.59W
99 R2 Upper Canada Village Ontario 44.57N 75.05W
56 E3 Upper Chapel Powys Wales 52.04N 3.28W
Upper Chindwin see Mawlaik
59 F6 Upperchurch Tipperary Irish Rep 52.43N 8.01W
57 H3 Upper Denton Cumbria Eng 54.59N 2.36W
99 E8 Upper Duck I Ontario 45.30N 75.37W
59 K3 Upper Fathom Armagh N Ireland 54.08N 6.19W
98 D6 Upper Frenchville Maine 47.18N 68.22W
30 A3 Upper Ganga Canal Uttar Prad India
57 K6 Upper Hulme Staffs Eng 53.09N 1.58W
98 P4 Upper Humber R Newfoundland
11 K8 Upper Hutt New Zealand 41.06S 175.06E
98 E7 Upper Kent New Brunswick 46.34N 67.45W
56 C4 Upper Killay W Glam Wales 51.37N 4.02W
110 D7 Upper Klamath L Oregon 42.25N 122.00W
110 E8 Upper L California 41.45N 120.10W
59 C8 Upper L Kerry Irish Rep 51.58N 9.35W
101 F5 Upper Laberge Yukon Terr 60.54N 135.12W
111 B2 Upper Lake California 39.10N 122.55W
103 C4 Upper Lehigh Pennsylvania 41.02N 75.54W
101 J5 Upper Liard Yukon Terr 60.01N 129.02W
103 C2 Upper Lisle New York 42.22N 75.57W
116 P2 Upper Manzanilla Trinidad & Tobago 10.32N 61.03W
104 J8 Upper Marlboro Maryland 38.46N 76.45W
11 G8 Upper Moutere New Zealand 41.18S 173.00E
98 K8 Upper Musquodoboit Nova Scotia 45.10N 62.58W
87 D6 Upper Nile prov Sudan
55 F4 Upper Norwood London Eng 51.25N 0.05W
95 O10 Upper Nseleni S Africa 28.34S 31.40E
103 G2 Upper Red Hook New York 42.02N 73.51W
110 O5 Upper Red Rock L Montana 44.37N 111.44W
104 B6 Upper Sandusky Ohio 40.48N 83.17W
56 G3 Upper Sapey Hereford & Worcs Eng 52.16N 2.28W
104 L2 Upper Saranac L New York
97 M6 Upper Seal L Quebec
109 Q5 Upper Spavinaw L Oklahoma
98 J8 Upper Stewiacke Nova Scotia 45.14N 63.02W
104 F8 Upper Tract W Virginia 38.46N 79.18W
98 H9 Upper Vaughan Nova Scotia 44.50N 64.14W
104 H8 Upperville Virginia 39.00N 77.54W
89 H5 Upper Volta rep W Africa
56 K6 Upper Waltham W Sussex Eng 50.55N 0.40W
12 H7 Upper Yarra Dam Victoria 37.43S 145.56E
Upper Zaïre prov see Zaïre Supérieure prov
28 B4 Uppinangadi Karnataka India 12.50N 75.13E
56 K2 Uppingham Leics Eng 52.35N 0.43W
52 K7 Upplands Väsby Sweden 59.29N 17.50E
52 K7 Uppsala Sweden 59.55N 17.38E
52 K7 Uppsala dist Sweden
50 J4 Upptyppingar mt Iceland 65.02N 16.15W
26 T4 Uppuveli Sri Lanka 8.36N 81.12E
29 H6 Uprara Madhya Prad India 22.39N 82.48E
113 A6 Upright, C St Matthew I Bering Sea 60.20N 172.12W
108 Q4 Upsala Minnesota 45.48N 94.35W
100 M1 Upsala Ontario 49.03N 90.30W
98 F6 Upsalquitch New Brunswick 47.49N 66.55W
98 F6 Upsalquitch R New Brunswick
50 G3 Upsaströnd coast Iceland
53 V17 Upsete Norway 60.43N 7.01E
31 J4 Upshi Kashmir 33.48N 72.26E
50 G3 Upsir Iceland 65.59N 18.29W
106 D3 Upson Wisconsin 46.23N 90.24W
13 J4 Upstart B Queensland
13 J4 Upstart, C Queensland 19.45S 147.47E
56 O5 Upstreet Kent Eng 51.20N 1.12E
56 C6 Upton Cornwall Eng 50.31N 4.25W
56 G3 Upton Hereford & Worcs Eng 52.04N 2.13W
107 L4 Upton Kentucky 37.24N 85.57W
104 O2 Upton Maine 44.42N 71.02W
103 L2 Upton Massachusetts 42.10N 71.35W
103 E7 Upton New Jersey 39.57N 74.31W
108 F5 Upton Wyoming 44.05N 104.36W
56 G3 Upton Warren Hereford & Worcs Eng 52.19N 2.06W
19 N5 Uput isld Truk Is Pacific Oc 7.14N 152.00E
85 D5 'Uqayb watercourse Libya
85 E4 'Uqaylah, Al Libya 30.15N 19.12E
33 H9 'Uqaymah, Al S Yemen 14.30N 48.15E
33 J4 'Uqayr, Al Saudi Arabia 25.37N 50.14E
33 E9 'Uqbān, Al isld Yemen 15.30N 42.24E
87 D3 Uqda, El Sudan 14.02N 33.33E
34 C8 'Uqeiqa, Wādī watercourse Jordan
33 F9 Uqīyah, Al Yemen 14.06N 45.46E
34 H5 Uqla Sawāb Iraq 33.56N 40.06E
34 O9 'Uqlat al 'Udhaybah Iraq 29.47N 47.00E
33 E4 'Uqlat aş Şuqūr Saudi Arabia 25.47N 42.15E
Uqturpan see Wushi
Ur see Ur of the Chaldees anc site
119 C3 Urabá, G. de Colombia
115 H11 Urabá, I Panama
Uracas islds see Farallon de Pajaros islds
64 G6 Urach W Germany 48.30N 9.25E
119 H3 Uracoa Venezuela 9.03N 62.27W
22 H6 Urad Qianqi Nei Monggol Zizhiqu China 40.41N 108.34E
22 H6 Urad Zhongu Liaheqi Nei Monggol Zizhiqu China 41.39N 108.30E
32 G5 Ūrāf Iran 30.12N 56.00E
58 Q9 Ura Firth Shetland Scotland 60.27N 1.29W
20 C5 Uraga Japan 35.15N 139.42E
26 R9 Uragaha Sri Lanka 6.20N 80.05E
20 C5 Uraga-suidō str Japan
20 M4 Uragawara Japan 37.10N 138.27E
47 M5 Uraim R U.S.S.R.
39 C5 Urak Khabarovsk U.S.S.R. 59.15N 142.45E
39 C5 Urak Khabarovsk U.S.S.R. 59.33N 141.13E
39 C5 Urak R U.S.S.R.
28 C5 Urakam Kerala India 10.26N 76.15E
42 H3 Urakan U.S.S.R. 58.40N 106.00E
20 M2 Urakawa Hokkaido Japan 42.10N 142.46E
20 L6 Urakawa Honshu Japan 35.03N 137.42E
110 K1 Ural Montana 48.38N 115.15W
12 H5 Ural mt New S Wales 33.23S 146.13E
43 B2 Ural R U.S.S.R.
47 M4 Uralets U.S.S.R. 57.40N 59.39E
47 H6 Uralka R U.S.S.R.
12 K4 Uralla New S Wales 30.40S 151.31E
Ural Mts see Uralskiy Khrebet mts
40 D5 Uralovka U.S.S.R. 52.28N 128.04E
46 Q4 Ural'sk Kazakhstan U.S.S.R. 51.19N 51.20E
38 E3 Uralskiy Khrebet mts U.S.S.R.
14 F5 Ural Well W Australia 22.08S 125.17E
15 C5 Urama R Irian Jaya
92 E4 Urambo Tanzania 5.02S 32.00E
15 H7 Uramu I Papua New Guinea 7.37S 144.37E
28 A1 Uran Maharashtra India 18.51N 72.59E
12 H6 Urana New S Wales 35.21S 146.19E
12 H6 Urana, L New S Wales
13 E5 Urandangie Queensland 21.35S 138.20E
118 G4 Urandi Brazil 14.49S 42.38W
13 L7 Urangan Queensland 25.19S 152.46E
107 D10 Urania Louisiana 31.52N 92.18W
101 T6 Uranium City Saskatchewan 59.32N 108.43W
26 T7 Uraniya Sri Lanka 7.13N 81.07E
53 Y16 Uranostind mt Norway 61.26N 8.10E
26 R7 Urapola Sri Lanka 7.06N 80.09E
13 C2 Urapunga N Terr Australia 14.41S 134.32E
119 H6 Uraricaá, R Brazil
119 H6 Uraricoera Brazil 3.28N 61.05W
119 G6 Uraricuera, R Brazil
14 E9 Uraryie W Australia 31.14S 123.27E
81 B4 Uras Sardinia 39.42N 8.42E
39 D1 Urasalakh U.S.S.R. 69.09N 145.20E
43 J7 Ura-Tyube Tadzhikistan U.S.S.R. 39.58N 68.59E
119 H5 Uraucaima, Sa hills Brazil
20 L1 Urausunai Japan 43.26N 141.48E
28 C3 Uravakonda Andhra Prad India 14.57N 77.15E
109 B3 Uravan Colorado 38.24N 108.46W
20 B1 Urawa Japan 35.52N 139.40E
47 J6 Uray U.S.S.R. 60.07N 64.49E
20 F2 Urayasu Japan 35.40N 139.54E
33 N10 'Urayfijān Kuwait 28.54N 48.12E
33 H4 Uray'irah Saudi Arabia 25.59N 48.50E
33 F3 'Urayq ad Duḩūl des area Saudi Arabia
33 C2 Urayq, Al des Saudi Arabia
33 G3 'Urayq Sāqān sand ridge Saudi Arabia
33 G10 'Urays, Jabal al mts S Yemen
43 D1 Urazmetovo Bashkir U.S.S.R. 53.51N 55.28E
45 R1 Urazovka U.S.S.R. 55.25N 45.37E
45 K6 Urazovo U.S.S.R. 50.05N 38.05E
106 F9 Urbana Illinois 40.07N 88.12W
106 J9 Urbana Indiana 40.53N 85.47W
106 C7 Urbana Iowa 42.13N 91.53W
107 C4 Urbana Missouri 37.52N 93.10W
104 B6 Urbana Ohio 40.06N 83.45W
79 N7 Urbania Italy 43.40N 12.31E
104 J9 Urbanna Virginia 37.38N 76.36W
117 F6 Urbano Santos Brazil 3.14S 43.25W
75 F2 Urbasa, Sierra de mts Spain
79 E6 Urbe Italy 44.29N 8.35E
75 C3 Urbel R Spain
75 C2 Urbel del Castillo Spain 42.37N 3.50W
69 M8 Urbès France 47.53N 6.58E
76 H2 Urbies Spain 43.13N 5.41W
79 N7 Urbino Italy 43.43N 12.38E
67 P12 Urbino, Etang d' L Corsica 42.02N 9.28E
75 E3 Urbión, L. de Spain 42.01N 2.53W
75 E3 Urbión Sierra de mts Spain
80 H2 Urbisaglia Italy 43.12N 13.22E
72 K2 Urçay France 46.37N 2.35E
69 F5 Urcel France 49.30N 3.35E
56 H5 Urchfont Wilts Eng 51.19N 1.56W
120 D5 Urcos Peru 13.40S 71.38W
46 P5 Urda Kazakhstan U.S.S.R. 48.44N 47.30E
77 J2 Urda Spain 39.25N 3.43W
39 E1 Urdakh U.S.S.R. 68.13N 150.29E
53 W20 Urdalsnuten mt Norway 59.10N 7.10E
75 G1 Urdax Spain 43.15N 1.31W
50 L3 Urdharhjalli mt Iceland 65.39N 14.38W
50 G4 Urdharvötn lakes Iceland
50 G3 Urdhir Iceland 65.52N 18.40W
76 B3 Urdilde Spain 42.49N 8.45W
72 C10 Urdos France 42.53N 0.33W
22 E3 Urd Tamir Gol R Mongolia
44 K3 Urduk, Mys C Kazakhstan U.S.S.R. 44.23N 50.52E
47 G3 Urdyuzhskoye Oz L U.S.S.R.
43 O4 Urdzhar Kazakhstan U.S.S.R. 47.06N 81.33E
46 G3 Urech'ye Belorussiya U.S.S.R. 52.59N 27.50E
87 J9 Ure, El Somalia 3.50N 43.05E
Ureg Nūr L see Örög Nuur L
86 E4 Urein Egypt 30.58N 30.42E
47 L7 Urekhovo Omsk U.S.S.R. 57.30N 70.50E
44 D6 Ureki Georgia U.S.S.R. 41.57N 41.46E
39 M3 Ureliki U.S.S.R. 64.25N 173.14W
46 O1 Uren' U.S.S.R. 57.30N 45.50E
41 C7 Urengoy U.S.S.R. 65.59N 78.30E
11 J5 Urenui New Zealand 38.58S 174.24E
9 C10 Ureparapara isld New Hebrides 13.32S 167.17E
72 B9 Urepel France 43.04N 1.25W
57 J4 Ure, R N Yorks Eng
115 D3 Ures Mexico 29.26N 110.24W
60 N7 Ureterp Netherlands 53.06N 6.10E
11 M5 Urewera Country dist New Zealand
11 M5 Urewera Nat. Pk New Zealand
42 B4 Urez U.S.S.R. 55.55N 77.05E
37 D8 Urfa Turkey 37.08N 38.45E
64 L8 Urfeld W Germany 47.37N 11.21E
86 J10 'Urf, Gebel el hill Egypt 27.49N 32.55E
85 C4 Urfilla tribe Libya
64 A2 Urft-Stausee res W Germany 50.35N 6.27E
90 F6 Urga Nigeria 11.29N 13.25E
43 E5 Urga Uzbekistan U.S.S.R. 43.36N 58.29E
46 O2 Urga R U.S.S.R.
40 F6 Urgal R U.S.S.R.
22 C2 Urgamal Mongolia 48.26N 94.20E
75 N4 Urgel, Can. de Spain
75 M4 Urgel, Llanos de plain Spain
43 F6 Urgench Uzbekistan U.S.S.R. 41.35N 60.41E
87 G7 Urgoma Mts Ethiopia
31 E4 Urgun Afghanistan 32.52N 69.10E
36 H4 Ürgüp Turkey 38.39N 34.55E
43 H7 Urgut Uzbekistan U.S.S.R. 39.29N 67.15E
24 E2 Urho Xinjiang Uygur Zizhiqu China 46.05N 84.51E
31 H3 Uri Kashmir 34.05N 74.03E
81 A2 Uri Sardinia 40.38N 8.30E
66 L4 Uri canton Switzerland
71 H6 Uriage-les-Bains France 45.06N 5.50E
107 J10 Uriah Alabama 31.20N 87.30W
11 F9 Uriah, Mt New Zealand 42.02S 171.43E
119 E4 Uribante, R Venezuela
119 D6 Uribe Colombia 3.16N 74.22W
121 J8 Uribe, Canal str Chile
119 D2 Uribia Colombia 11.45N 72.19W
120 G6 Uribicha Bolivia 15.23S 62.55W
121 D6 Uriburu Argentina 36.32S 63.50W
107 B3 Urich Missouri 38.28N 94.01W
110 P8 Urie Wyoming 41.20N 110.20W
94 C5 Uri-hauchab Mts Namibia
40 E7 Uril U.S.S.R. 49.14N 130.31E
35 B8 Urim Israel 31.18N 34.31E
20 M1 Urimaku Japan 43.08N 143.03E
13 G8 Urimbin Queensland 28.15S 143.46E
66 N8 Urio Italy 45.53N 9.08E
120 F9 Uriondo Bolivia 21.43S 64.40W
115 F4 Urique Mexico 27.14N 107.50W
102 E5 Urique R Mexico
66 L4 Uri Rotstock mt Switzerland 46.52N 8.32E
12 G3 Urisino New S Wales 29.44S 143.49E
11 L8 Uriti Pt New Zealand 41.06S 176.05E
51 P12 Uritsk U.S.S.R. 59.49N 30.10E
43 H1 Uritskoye Kazakhstan U.S.S.R. 53.21N 65.30E
45 K4 Uritskoye Lipetsk U.S.S.R. 52.02N 38.10E
45 Q5 Uritskoye Saratov U.S.S.R. 51.27N 44.58E
42 L2 Uritskoye U.S.S.R. 60.35N 122.25E
120 B1 Urituyacu, R Peru
33 E9 'Urj, Al Yemen 15.11N 42.52E
51 K10 Urjala Finland 61.06N 23.35E
60 L9 Urk Netherlands 52.40N 5.35E
40 C5 Urkan R U.S.S.R.
40 D4 Urkan R U.S.S.R.
44 H5 Urkarakh U.S.S.R. 42.09N 47.36E
43 P4 Urkashar, Khrebet mts Xinjiang Uygur Zizhiqu China
53 V14 Urke Norway 62.13N 6.35E
60 L9 Urkervaart canal Netherlands
36 B4 Urla Turkey 38.19N 26.47E
82 K6 Urlaţi Romania 44.59N 26.15E
59 E4 Urlaur L Mayo Irish Rep 53.51N 8.45W
53 D5 Urlev Denmark 55.46N 9.48E
59 G6 Urlingford Kilkenny Irish Rep 52.43N 7.35W
42 H6 Urluk U.S.S.R. 50.03N 107.55E
30 C7 Urmal R Madhya Prad India
'Urman see 'Ormān
47 H8 Urman U.S.S.R. 54.55N 56.55E
47 K5 Urmannyy U.S.S.R. 61.36N 67.52E
45 T1 Urmary U.S.S.R. 55.42N 47.58E
43 J7 Urmetan Tadzhikistan U.S.S.R. 39.28N 68.15E
40 F7 Urmi R U.S.S.R.
Urmia see Reẕā'īyeh
Urmia L see Reẕā'īyeh, Daryācheh-ye L
32 A2 Urmia, L Iran
60 T17 Urmond Netherlands 50.59N 5.46E
47 L6 Urna R U.S.S.R.
66 O2 Urnäsch Switzerland 47.19N 9.17E
66 O2 Urnäsch R Switzerland
66 N3 Urnen, Nieder Switzerland 47.08N 9.04E
66 N3 Urnen, Ober Switzerland 47.07N 9.04E
66 M4 Urner Boden V Switzerland
66 L4 Urner See L Switzerland
53 W16 Urnes Norway 61.17N 7.20E
23 C8 Urn I Hong Kong
47 L6 Urninskoye Boloto marsh U.S.S.R.
53 X20 Urnosa mt Norway 59.25N 7.39E
92 K12 Uroa Zanzibar 6.06S 39.25E
34 O8 Ur of the Chaldees anc site Iraq 30.56N 46.08E
75 F1 Urola R Spain
82 G8 Uroševac Yugoslavia 42.21N 21.09E
40 A6 Urov R U.S.S.R.
101 G1 Urquhart L N W Terr 69.05N 132.01W
76 E10 Urra Portugal 39.14N 7.24W
77 M6 Urracal Spain 37.24N 2.21W
119 C4 Urrao Colombia 6.16N 76.10W
75 K5 Urrea de Gaén Spain 41.09N 0.29W
75 H4 Urrea de Jalón Spain 41.40N 1.14W
121 D7 Urre Lauquen, L Argentina
50 D3 Urridhavötn lakes Iceland
75 H2 Urries Spain 42.31N 1.07W
57 F2 Urr, L Dumfries & Galloway Scotland 55.09N 3.56W
76 E6 Urros Trás os Montes e Alto Douro Portugal 41.05N 7.01W
76 G6 Urrós Trás os Montes e Alto Douro Portugal 41.20N 6.28W
75 H2 Urroz Spain 42.46N 1.28W
57 F2 Urr Water R Dumfries & Galloway Scotland
87 F6 Ursa Ethiopia 8.36N 36.52E
106 C9 Ursa Illinois 40.04N 91.20W
43 J6 Ursat'yevskaya Uzbekistan U.S.S.R. 40.14N 68.46E
64 J7 Ursberg W Germany 48.15N 10.28E
61 D2 Ursel Belgium 51.08N 3.30E
60 H9 Ursem Netherlands 52.37N 4.54E
66 H3 Ursenbach Switzerland 47.08N 7.46E
64 M5 Ursensollen W Germany 49.24N 11.47E
66 L5 Urseren-Tal V Switzerland
45 M1 Urshel'skiy U.S.S.R. 55.41N 40.15E
111 K4 Ursine Nevada 37.59N 114.15W
42 D5 Ursk U.S.S.R. 54.31N 85.27E
64 H6 Urspring W Germany 48.31N 9.55E
52 N2 Ursviken Sweden 64.42N 21.10E
72 B9 Urt France 43.30N 1.17W
31 H2 Urtabal Pass Afghan/U.S.S.R. 37.26N 74.32E
42 C4 Urtam U.S.S.R. 56.10N 83.59E
34 J10 Urţayyan Saudi Arabia 28.36N 41.39E
43 E2 Urtazym U.S.S.R. 52.13N 58.46E
81 B3 Urtigu, Mte Sardinia 40.08N 8.37E
66 S5 Urtiota Spitze mt Italy/Switz 46.39N 10.24E
22 C8 Urt Moron Qinghai China 36.53N 93.00E
22 C8 Urt Moron He R Qinghai China
115 E4 Uruáchic Mexico 27.51N 108.14W
118 E4 Uruaçu Brazil 14.38S 49.06W
118 E4 Uruana Brazil 15.32S 49.40W
115 H8 Uruapan Mexico 19.26N 102.04W
Urūbah see Aruba
120 C5 Urubamba Peru 13.20S 72.07W
120 C4 Urubamba, R Peru
119 G8 Urubaxi, R Brazil
26 S9 Urubokka Sri Lanka 6.18N 80.38E
118 D7 Urubupungá, Salto do falls Brazil 20.35S 51.30W
119 J9 Urubu, R Brazil
117 G6 Uruburetama Brazil 3.40S 39.28W
117 A6 Urucará Brazil 2.30S 57.45W
117 A8 Urucu R Amazonas Brazil
118 H4 Uruçuca Brazil 14.36S 39.19W
117 F8 Uruçuí Brazil 7.14S 44.30W
118 F5 Urucuia Brazil 16.05S 45.45W
118 F5 Urucuia, R Brazil
117 F9 Uruçuí Prêto, R Brazil
117 F9 Uruçuí, Sa.do mts Brazil
118 B6 Urucum Brazil 19.08S 57.33W
120 F1 Urucu, R Amazonas Brazil
117 C5 Urucuricaia, I Brazil
117 A6 Urucurituba Brazil 2.38S 57.36W
76 J5 Urueña Spain 41.42N 5.11W
93 F10 Urugu Tanzania 4.39S 34.12E
121 F2 Uruguaiana Brazil 29.45S 57.05W
118 D10 Uruguai, R Brazil
117 A9 Uruguatos, R Brazil
117 H4 Uruguay R Uruguay
117 H4 Uruguay rep S America
121 G1 Uruguay, R Brazil
Uruk anc site see Erech
44 F5 Urukh R U.S.S.R.
20 H2 Urū ko L Japan
19 N2 Urukthapel isld Palau Is Pacific Oc
47 M5 Urukul' U.S.S.R. 55.50N 61.20E
42 J6 Urul'ga U.S.S.R. 51.50N 114.50E
39 D3 Urul'tun, Oz L U.S.S.R. 63.46N 148.15E
Urumchi see Ürümqi
75 G1 Urumea R Spain
34 D2 Urum es Sughra Syria 36.09N 36.55E
39 J2 Urumkuveem R U.S.S.R.
24 F4 Ürümqi Xinjiang Uygur Zizhiqu China 43.43N 87.38E
53 Y17 Urunda R Norway
18 B4 Urung Indon 2.37N 96.08E
12 L4 Urunga New S Wales 30.30S 152.28E
Urungu R see Ulungur He
Urungu Nor L see Ulungur Hu
92 D10 Urungwe dist Zimbabwe
19 L1 Uruno Pt Guam Pacific Oc 13.37N 144.50E
117 G6 Uruoca Brazil 3.17S 40.34W
44 D4 Urup U.S.S.R. 43.52N 41.10E
44 D3 Urup R U.S.S.R.
120 G4 Urupá, R Brazil
40 M9 Urup, Ostrov isld Kuril Is U.S.S.R.
40 M8 Urup, Proliv str Kuril Is U.S.S.R.
33 G6 'Urūq al Akdān sand dunes Saudi Arabia
33 G7 'Urūq al Awārik des area Saudi Arabia
33 G8 'Urūq al Kuthayyib sand ridge Saudi Arabia
33 K6 'Urūq al Mahlakah sand dunes Saudi Arabia
33 K6 'Urūq al Mūsá sand dunes Saudi Arabia
33 K6 'Urūq al Mu'tariḑah, Al sand dunes Saudi Arabia
33 G6 'Urūq ar Rumaylah sand dunes Saudi Arabia
33 L6 'Urūq ash Shaybah sand dunes Saudi Arabia
33 L6 'Urūq as Sārit sand dunes Saudi Arabia
33 G8 'Urūq az Zayzá sand dunes Saudi Arabia
33 J7 'Urūq Ḑahyah sandy des S Yemen
80 M5 Ururi Italy 41.48N 15.01E
40 B4 Urusha U.S.S.R. 54.04N 122.51E
40 B5 Urusha R U.S.S.R.
44 G4 Urus-Martan U.S.S.R. 43.09N 45.35E
45 L3 Urusovo U.S.S.R. 53.31N 39.36E
121 J2 Urussanga Brazil 28.34S 49.16W
46 R3 Urussu U.S.S.R. 54.38N 53.29E
118 F4 Urutágua Brazil 14.43S 47.05W
118 E5 Urutaí Brazil 17.28S 48.15W
117 C5 Urutai, I Brazil
11 J5 Uruti New Zealand 38.57S 174.31E
120 E8 Uru Uru L Bolivia
92 E5 Uruwira Tanzania 6.25S 31.20E
119 H5 Uruyén Venezuela 5.40N 62.26W
31 D4 Uruzgan Afghanistan 32.58N 66.39E
31 C4 Uruzgan prov Afghanistan
72 F6 Urval France 44.48N 0.57E
123 D14 Urville, I. d' Antarctica 63.13S 56.25W
70 G2 Urville-Nacqueville France 49.41N 1.45W
15 D4 Urville, Tanjung d' C Irian Jaya 1.29S 137.55E
94 F4 Urwi Botswana 23.24S 20.26E
42 D7 Uryl' Berel' Kazakhstan U.S.S.R. 49.16N 86.20E
20 L1 Uryu-gawa R Japan
21 J5 Uryū-ko L Japan
42 K5 Uryum R U.S.S.R.
42 K6 Uryumkan R U.S.S.R.
41 K4 Uryung-Kyaya U.S.S.R. 72.52N 113.31E
41 Q5 Uryung-Ulakh, Oz L U.S.S.R.
42 D4 Uryup R U.S.S.R.
40 A5 Uryupino U.S.S.R. 52.16N 120.00E
45 O6 Uryupinsk U.S.S.R. 50.49N 42.01E
76 C13 Urza mt Portugal 37.37N 8.04W
46 P2 Urzhum U.S.S.R. 57.08N 50.00E
45 T2 Urzhumskoye U.S.S.R. 54.19N 47.50E
82 K6 Urziceni Romania 44.43N 26.39E
64 B4 Ürzig W Germany 49.58N 7.00E
81 D3 Urzulei Sardinia 40.06N 9.31E
69 B5 Us France 49.05N 2.00E
42 E6 Us R U.S.S.R.
20 E8 Usa Japan 33.31N 131.22E
93 H9 Usa Tanzania 3.24S 36.51E
42 D5 Usa U.S.S.R. 54.05N 88.37E
47 J3 Usa R Komi U.S.S.R.
46 P3 Usa R Kuybyshev U.S.S.R.
19 K8 Usada isld Philippines 6.07N 120.33E
93 E8 Usagara Tanzania 2.46S 33.01E
77 D4 Usagre Spain 38.21N 6.10W
36 D4 Uşak Turkey 38.42N 29.25E
94 C4 Usakos Namibia 22.01S 15.32E
40 H5 Usal'gin U.S.S.R. 53.37N 138.15E
93 K10 Usambara Mts Tanzania
35 E5 Usarīn Jordan 32.07N 35.19E
30 H7 Usas Bihar India 25.03N 84.45E
110 F3 U.S. Atomic Energy Comm Res Washington
110 N6 U.S. Atomic Energy Comm Reserve Idaho
33 F9 'Usaylān S Yemen
121 E10 Usborne, Mt Falkland Is 51.35S 58.57W
Usburjan see Esfarjan
79 F6 Uscio Italy 44.24N 9.10E
75 G5 Used Spain 41.04N 1.34W
63 T5 Usedom E Germany 53.53N 13.55E
63 U5 Usedom isld E Germany
30 C5 Usehat Uttar Prad India 27.48N 79.14E
28 J1 Usekyang Xizang Zizhiqu 29.44N 92.12E
61 O7 Useldange Luxembourg 49.47N 5.59E
81 B4 Usellus Sardinia 39.48N 8.51E
93 E6 Usengi Kenya 0.04S 34.04E
75 K7 Useras Spain 40.09N 0.10W
92 E5 Usevia Tanzania 7.05S 31.14E
33 C6 Usfān Saudi Arabia 21.55N 39.25E
35 D2 Usha Israel 32.48N 35.06E
46 G2 Ushachi Belorussiya U.S.S.R. 55.11N 28.31E
113 L7 Ushagat I Alaska 58.56N 152.20W
39 D5 Ushakova, Mys C Khabarovsk U.S.S.R. 59.11N 145.50E
39 M1 Ushakova, Mys C Vrangelya, Ostrov U.S.S.R. 71.29N 179.43E
38 G1 Ushakova, Ostrov isld Kara Sea Arctic Oc 81.30N 79.00E
47 K6 Ushakovo U.S.S.R. 57.31N 68.28E
39 M1 Ushakovskiy Vrangelya, Ostrov U.S.S.R. 71.05N 178.30W
Ushaktal see Uxxaktal
Ushan see Üchān
Ushant see Ouessant, I.d'
43 K5 Usharal Kazakhstan U.S.S.R. 43.48N 70.30E
93 E7 Ushashi Tanzania 1.59S 33.59E
33 F4 Ushayqir Saudi Arabia 25.21N 45.13E
33 D6 'Ushayrah Saudi Arabia 21.46N 40.42E
33 F4 'Ushayrah Saudi Arabia 25.36N 45.49E
44 E4 Ushba mt Georgia U.S.S.R. 43.09N 42.43E
93 D10 Ushetu Tanzania 4.09S 32.16E
19 N3 Ushi isld Truk Is Pacific Oc 7.41N 151.50E
20 C9 Ushibuka Japan 32.12N 130.00E
93 L8 Ushingo Kenya 2.47S 39.40E
45 O3 Ushinka U.S.S.R. 53.29N 42.50E
93 C9 Ushirombo Tanzania 3.30S 31.57E
40 M8 Ushishir caldera Kuril Is U.S.S.R. 47.31N 152.49E
20 L4 Ushitsu Japan 37.16N 137.09E
20 D8 Ushizu Japan 33.15N 130.10E
39 K2 Ushkan'iy, Gory mts U.S.S.R.
39 F6 Ushkh R U.S.S.R.
39 G6 Ushki U.S.S.R. 56.11N 160.00E
39 D5 Ushki Zaliv B U.S.S.R.
45 N1 Ushna R U.S.S.R.
Ushnuiyeh see Oshnovīyeh
43 E5 Ushsay Uzbekistan U.S.S.R. 43.49N 58.48E
Ushtaran, Kuh-i- see Oshtorān Kūh mt
Ushtarinan see Oshtorīnān
43 N4 Ush-Tobe Kazakhstan U.S.S.R. 45.15N 77.59E
121 L10 Ushuaia Argentina 54.48S 68.19W
40 D5 Ushumun U.S.S.R. 52.48N 126.27E
39 G2 Ushurakchan, Gory mts U.S.S.R.
93 E7 Usimbiti Tanzania 1.21S 33.51E
117 B8 Usina Brazil 7.42S 54.40W
92 E4 Usinge Tanzania 5.10S 31.19E
64 F3 Usingen W Germany 50.20N 8.33E
81 B2 Usini Sardinia 40.40N 8.33E
15 H6 Usino Papua New Guinea 5.40S 145.31E
47 H3 Usinsk U.S.S.R. 65.57N 57.27E
45 U3 Usinskoye U.S.S.R. 53.20N 48.42E
56 F4 Usk Gwent Wales 51.43N 2.54W
110 H1 Usk Washington 48.20N 117.17W
30 G5 Uska Uttar Prad India 27.12N 83.07E
58 B4 Uskavagh, L W Isles Scotland 57.27N 7.15W
53 T19 Uskedal Norway 59.56N 5.53E
56 E4 Usk, R Powys/Gwent Wales
Üskub see Skopje
37 K2 Üsküdar Turkey 41.01N 29.03E
36 C1 Üsküp Turkey 41.44N 27.23E
63 L9 Uslar W Germany 51.39N 9.38E
64 Q4 Uslava R Czechoslovakia
32 G3 Usmaj Iran 35.59N 57.39E
45 L4 Usman' U.S.S.R. 52.02N 39.43E
79 F3 Usmate Italy 45.39N 9.21E
40 C2 Usmun U.S.S.R. 58.19N 125.12E
45 C1 Usmyn' U.S.S.R. 55.51N 31.08E
121 C3 Usno Argentina 30.33S 67.33W
47 F4 Usogorsk U.S.S.R. 63.25N 48.38E
92 F4 Usoke Tanzania 5.05S 32.21E
42 E3 Usolka R U.S.S.R.
47 H6 Usol'ye U.S.S.R. 59.28N 56.31E
42 G5 Usol'ye-Sibirskoye U.S.S.R. 52.48N 103.40E
90 C8 Usonigbe Nigeria 6.01N 6.10E
65 Q2 Usov Czechoslovakia 49.47N 17.01E
46 G4 Usovo Ukraine U.S.S.R. 51.20N 28.01E
75 H2 Usoz, Embalse de res Spain 42.52N 1.21W
121 B4 Uspallata Argentina 32.43S 69.24W
43 M1 Uspenka Kazakhstan U.S.S.R. 52.56N 77.24E
45 E8 Uspenka Kirovograd, Ukraine U.S.S.R. 48.55N 33.38E
45 L8 Uspenka Lugansk, Ukraine U.S.S.R. 48.21N 39.11E
45 H9 Uspenovka Ukraine U.S.S.R. 47.47N 36.24E
40 D5 Uspenovka U.S.S.R. 53.25N 126.50E
44 D2 Uspenskaya U.S.S.R. 45.45N 41.03E
43 L3 Uspenskiy Kazakhstan U.S.S.R. 48.41N 72.43E
44 D3 Uspenskoye U.S.S.R. 44.50N 41.23E
60 P6 Usquert Netherlands 53.24N 6.37E
30 C6 Usrahar Uttar Prad India 26.57N 79.18E
81 C4 Ussassai Sardinia 39.49N 9.24E
72 H10 Ussat France 42.49N 1.37E
72 C3 Usseau France 46.11N 0.35W
79 B4 Usseglio Italy 45.14N 7.13E
72 K5 Ussel Cantal France 45.05N 2.56E
72 J4 Ussel Corrèze France 45.32N 2.18E
57 N6 Usselby Lincs Eng 53.26N 0.21W
64 F1 Usseln W Germany 51.16N 8.41E
53 J5 Usserød Denmark 55.54N 12.30E
72 F3 Usson-du-Poitou France 46.17N 0.32E
71 D6 Usson-en-Forez France 45.24N 3.56E
72 J10 Usson-les-Bains France 42.44N 2.06E
21 F4 Ussuri R China/U.S.S.R.
40 E10 Ussuriysk U.S.S.R. 43.48N 131.59E
70 K4 Ussy France 48.56N 0.16W
53 Y17 Usta R Norway
46 O2 Usta R U.S.S.R.
42 E5 Ust'-Abakan U.S.S.R. 53.50N 91.25E
40 J6 Ust'-Agnevo Sakhalin U.S.S.R. 50.35N 142.09E
47 F5 Ust' Alekseyevo U.S.S.R. 60.25N 46.22E
40 F1 Ust'Allakh U.S.S.R. 60.40N 134.50E
41 O8 Ust'-Amginskoye U.S.S.R. 62.42N 135.00E
31 D6 Usta Muhammad Pakistan 28.07N 68.00E
53 Y18 Ustaoset Norway 60.30N 8.02E
72 B9 Ustaritz France 43.24N 1.27W
41 F5 Ust'-Avam U.S.S.R. 71.10N 92.50E
47 N5 Ust'bagaryak U.S.S.R. 56.07N 61.54E
42 H5 Ust'-Barguzin U.S.S.R. 53.26N 109.00E
39 J2 Ust'-Belaya U.S.S.R. 65.30N 173.15E
39 F6 Ust'-Belogolovoye U.S.S.R. 57.03N 156.35E
39 E4 Ust'-Bokhapcha U.S.S.R. 62.08N 150.33E
42 G6 Ust' Bokson U.S.S.R. 52.10N 100.18E
39 F7 Ust'-Bol'sheretsk U.S.S.R. 52.50N 156.15E
45 O6 Ust'-Buzulukskaya U.S.S.R. 50.10N 42.10E
45 N9 Ust'-Bystryanskaya U.S.S.R. 47.48N 41.02E
42 E5 Ust'-Byur' U.S.S.R. 53.50N 90.16E
42 L2 Ust'-Chara U.S.S.R. 60.15N 120.58E
39 B2 Ust' Charky U.S.S.R. 66.45N 136.33E
42 C6 Ust'-Charyshskaya Pristan' U.S.S.R. 52.24N 83.41E
39 J1 Ust'-Chaun U.S.S.R. 68.45N 171.31E
42 C3 Ust'-Chaya U.S.S.R. 58.18N 82.30E
42 H2 Ust'-Chayka U.S.S.R. 60.10N 107.02E
47 G5 Ust' Chernaya Perm U.S.S.R. 60.27N 52.36E
42 K5 Ust'-Chernaya U.S.S.R. 52.59N 119.00E
42 B3 Ust'-Chizhapka U.S.S.R. 59.03N 79.35E
82 H2 Ustchorna U.S.S.R. 48.21N 23.56E
42 B3 Ust'-Churul'ka U.S.S.R. 58.37N 79.27E
47 H6 Ust' Dolgaya U.S.S.R. 59.56N 57.20E
45 M9 Ust' Donetskiy U.S.S.R. 47.40N 40.57E
40 D5 Ust' Dymo U.S.S.R. 52.07N 128.12E
44 D3 Ust'-Dzhegutinskaya U.S.S.R. 44.03N 41.59E
53 Y17 Ustedal Norway 60.32N 8.11E
53 X17 Ustekveikja R Norway
42 E6 Ust'-Elegest U.S.S.R. 51.35N 94.06E
66 L2 Uster Switzerland 47.21N 8.49E
53 X18 Ustevatnet L Norway 60.30N 7.57E
45 O8 Ust'-Gryaznovskiy U.S.S.R. 48.49N 42.09E
81 F6 Ustica Italy 38.43N 13.12E
81 F6 Ustica isld Italy
42 G4 Ust'-Ilga U.S.S.R. 54.59N 105.00E
41 J8 Ust'-Ilimpeya U.S.S.R. 63.16N 105.38E
42 G3 Ust' Ilimsk U.S.S.R. 58.03N 102.39E
42 J6 Ust'-Ilya U.S.S.R. 50.24N 113.50E
47 H4 Ust' Ilych U.S.S.R. 62.31N 56.49E
62 H5 Ústí nad Labem Czech 50.41N 14.00E
65 O2 Ústí nad Orlicí Czechoslovakia 49.58N 16.24E
45 D9 Ustinovka Ukraine U.S.S.R. 47.58N 32.32E
47 L6 Ustinovo U.S.S.R. 54.49N 60.00E
47 L6 Ust' Ishim U.S.S.R. 57.45N 71.05E
62 K1 Ustka Poland 54.35N 16.50E
42 G5 Ust'-Kada U.S.S.R. 54.29N 103.00E
42 C6 Ust'-Kalmanka U.S.S.R. 52.09N 83.18E
39 G6 Ust'-Kamchatsk U.S.S.R. 56.14N 162.28E
43 P3 Ust'-Kamenogorsk Kazakhstan U.S.S.R. 49.58N 82.36E
42 F2 Ust'-Kamo U.S.S.R. 60.44N 97.31E
42 C6 Ust'-Kan Gorno-Altay U.S.S.R. 50.58N 84.53E
42 E4 Ust'-Kan Krasnoyarsk U.S.S.R. 56.32N 93.47E
47 K2 Ust'-Kara U.S.S.R. 69.12N 65.00E
42 F3 Ust' Karabula U.S.S.R. 58.24N 97.11E
42 K5 Ust'-Karenga U.S.S.R. 54.26N 116.28E
42 K5 Ust'-Karsk U.S.S.R. 52.45N 118.48E
47 H8 Ust' Katav U.S.S.R. 54.51N 58.10E
42 F4 Ust'-Kaytym U.S.S.R. 57.23N 95.30E
42 E4 Ust'-Kemchug U.S.S.R. 57.16N 90.27E
39 F6 Ust'-Khayryuzovo U.S.S.R. 57.11N 156.45E
45 O7 Ust'-Khoperskiy U.S.S.R. 49.34N 42.25E
47 H7 Ust' Kishert U.S.S.R. 57.25N 57.11E
47 G4 Ust' Koin U.S.S.R. 63.10N 51.14E
42 D6 Ust'-Koksa U.S.S.R. 50.16N 85.39E
42 B2 Ust'Kolik'yegan U.S.S.R. 61.08N 78.10E
47 G5 Ust' Kulom U.S.S.R. 61.43N 53.40E
45 S5 Ust'-Kurdyum U.S.S.R. 51.40N 46.12E
41 E7 Ust'-Kureyka U.S.S.R. 66.30N 87.17E
42 H4 Ust'-Kut U.S.S.R. 56.48N 105.42E
41 P5 Ust'-Kuyga U.S.S.R. 70.01N 135.43E
42 H6 Ust'-Kyakhta U.S.S.R. 50.32N 106.20E
44 C2 Ust'-Labinsk U.S.S.R. 45.14N 39.41E
47 J6 Ust' Loz'va U.S.S.R. 59.34N 62.20E
40 B5 Ust' Lubiya U.S.S.R. 52.35N 120.12E
47 H3 Ust' Lyzha U.S.S.R. 65.45N 56.38E
47 J5 Ust'-Man'ya U.S.S.R. 62.15N 60.15E
40 F1 Ust' Maya U.S.S.R. 60.25N 134.28E
39 J2 Ust'-Mayn U.S.S.R. 65.05N 172.26E
40 F2 Ust'-Mil' U.S.S.R. 59.40N 133.00E
40 A2 Ust' Molvo U.S.S.R. 59.50N 119.28E
41 E7 Ust'-Mukduyka U.S.S.R. 66.44N 88.28E
40 A5 Ust' Nachin U.S.S.R. 52.22N 119.11E
47 G5 Ust' Nem U.S.S.R. 61.38N 54.50E
39 C3 Ust'-Nera U.S.S.R. 64.35N 143.14E
39 E4 Ust'-Nerega U.S.S.R. 61.50N 151.31E
40 F6 Ust' Niman U.S.S.R. 51.24N 132.41E
40 B3 Ust' Nyukzha U.S.S.R. 56.31N 121.39E
41 L4 Ust'-Olenek U.S.S.R. 72.59N 119.57E
39 D4 Ust' Omchug U.S.S.R. 61.08N 149.38E
42 G5 Ust'-Ordynskiy U.S.S.R. 52.50N 104.42E
42 G5 Ust'-Ordynskiy Buryat Nats.Okrug dist U.S.S.R.
72 G10 Ustou France 42.50N 1.16E
82 J9 Ustovo Bulgaria 41.33N 24.50E
42 K6 Ust'-Ozernaya U.S.S.R. 50.45N 117.05E
42 D3 Ust'-Ozernoye U.S.S.R. 58.54N 87.47E
42 E5 Ust' Paden'ga U.S.S.R. 61.55N 42.31E
39 H3 Ust' Penzhino U.S.S.R. 62.32N 165.11E
47 E4 Ust' Pinega U.S.S.R. 64.10N 41.59E
42 E3 Ust'-Pit U.S.S.R. 58.59N 91.45E
45 Q7 Ust'-Pogozh'ye U.S.S.R. 49.29N 44.37E
41 D6 Ust'-Port U.S.S.R. 69.44N 84.23E
42 C6 Ust'-Pustynka U.S.S.R. 51.30N 83.07E
47 E5 Ust' Puya U.S.S.R. 61.45N 42.30E
47 F5 Ust' Reka U.S.S.R. 62.19N 46.52E
47 K4 Ustrem U.S.S.R. 64.21N 65.28E
62 O6 Ustrzyki Dolne Poland 49.24N 22.38E
47 C5 Ust' Sara U.S.S.R. 60.14N 34.06E
40 C2 Ust'-Seligdar U.S.S.R. 59.08N 125.29E
45 O5 Ust'-Shcherbedino U.S.S.R. 51.53N 42.54E
47 H4 Ust'-Shchugor U.S.S.R. 64.16N 57.30E
39 F6 Ust'-Sopochnoye U.S.S.R. 56.08N 155.45E
39 E4 Ust'-Srednikan U.S.S.R. 62.25N 152.19E
39 E3 Ust'-Sugoy U.S.S.R. 64.15N 154.35E
47 J5 Ust'-Tapsuy U.S.S.R. 62.25N 61.42E
47 L7 Ust' Tara U.S.S.R. 56.42N 74.41E
47 M7 Ust' Tarka U.S.S.R. 55.35N 75.42E
40 E6 Ust'-Tashino U.S.S.R. 51.05N 129.36E
41 O8 Ust'-Tatta U.S.S.R. 63.02N 133.17E
47 L7 Ust' Tava U.S.S.R. 57.16N 71.51E
39 F5 Ust'-Tigil' U.S.S.R. 58.00N 158.10E
40 D2 Ust'-Timpton U.S.S.R. 58.49N 127.11E
47 G3 Ust' Tsil'ma U.S.S.R. 65.28N 52.09E
42 C3 Ust'-Tym U.S.S.R. 59.29N 80.06E
40 E6 Ust'Tyrma U.S.S.R. 50.31N 131.17E
37 F6 Üstükran Turkey 39.18N 41.17E
42 D6 Ust'-Ulagan U.S.S.R. 50.39N 88.00E
47 H5 Ust' Uls U.S.S.R. 60.35N 58.29E
40 F6 Ust' Umalta U.S.S.R. 51.39N 133.15E
42 K5 Ust'-Undurga U.S.S.R. 53.10N 118.10E
40 E4 Ust'-Un'ya Amur U.S.S.R. 54.24N 129.50E
47 H5 Ust' Un'ya Komi U.S.S.R. 61.52N 56.55E
47 E4 Ust' Ura U.S.S.R. 63.06N 44.41E
40 F6 Ust'-Urgal U.S.S.R. 51.12N 132.31E
40 C4 Ust' Urkima U.S.S.R. 55.16N 123.16E
42 H6 Ust'-Urluk U.S.S.R. 50.00N 107.45E
40 B5 Ust' Urov U.S.S.R. 52.14N 120.41E
47 H3 Ust' Usa Komi U.S.S.R. 66.00N 57.00E
42 E6 Ust'-Usa Krasnoyarsk U.S.S.R. 52.09N 92.21E
39 E3 Ust'-Utinaya U.S.S.R. 62.34N 151.27E
47 J8 Ust' Uyskoye U.S.S.R. 54.16N 63.52E
46 O3 Ust'-Uza U.S.S.R. 52.59N 45.20E
47 F4 Ust' Vacherga U.S.S.R. 63.20N 48.30E
47 E4 Ust' Vaga U.S.S.R. 62.42N 42.45E
42 G4 Ust'-Vikhoreva U.S.S.R. 56.48N 101.25E
47 H4 Ust'-Voya U.S.S.R. 64.28N 57.40E
39 F5 Ust'-Voyampolka U.S.S.R. 58.32N 159.13E
39 G5 Ust' Vym' U.S.S.R. 62.15N 50.25E
47 F4 Ust' Vyyskaya U.S.S.R. 63.02N 46.44E
42 E5 Ust'ya R U.S.S.R.
42 F5 Ust'-Yaga U.S.S.R. 54.45N 98.15E
41 P5 Ust'-Yansk U.S.S.R. 70.56N 136.30E
42 E3 Ustye Krasnoyarsk U.S.S.R. 57.46N 94.40E
47 D6 Ust'ye Vologda U.S.S.R. 59.38N 39.40E
46 L2 Ust'ye R U.S.S.R.
47 K2 Ust' Yuribey U.S.S.R. 68.58N 69.30E
43 D5 Ustyurt, Plato Kazakhstan U.S.S.R.
46 K1 Ustyuzhna U.S.S.R. 58.49N 36.28E
47 L8 Ust' Zaostrovka U.S.S.R. 54.49N 73.35E
42 J5 Ust' Zaza U.S.S.R. 53.15N 111.30E
19 C9 Usu Indonesia 10.32S 123.25E
24 E3 Usu Xinjiang Uygur Zizhiqu China 44.21N 84.41E
20 M5 Usuda Japan 36.07N 138.29E
20 K2 Usu-dake mt Japan 42.34N 140.47E
42 K5 Usugli U.S.S.R. 52.40N 115.20E
92 F5 Usuhilo Tanzania 6.23S 33.59E
44 H6 Usukh Chay U.S.S.R. 41.30N 47.48E
20 E8 Usuki Japan 33.07N 131.48E
93 E9 Usule Tanzania 3.43S 33.18E
115 P11 Usulután El Salvador 13.20N 88.25W
115 O9 Usumacinta R Mex/Guatemala
39 E1 Usum-Kyuyel' U.S.S.R. 67.39N 154.30E
18 L4 Usun Apau Plat Sarawak Malaysia
42 J2 Usun, Porog falls U.S.S.R. 62.22N 111.25E

75 F1 Usúrbil Spain 43.16N 2.02W
93 F10 Usure Tanzania 4.39S 34.22E
94 L6 Usutu R Swaziland
47 H6 Us'va U.S.S.R. 58.44N 57.42E
47 H6 Us'va R U.S.S.R.
45 B1 Usvyaty U.S.S.R. 55.45N 30.45E
46 H4 Ut Belorussiya U.S.S.R. 52.18N 31.10E
15 D6 Uta Irian Jaya 4.33S 136.03E
19 F3 Uta isld Moluccas Indon 0.02N 129.38E
90 C9 Utagba Uno Nigeria 5.56N 6.19E
102 D3 Utah state U.S.A.
31 D4 Utahal Afghanistan 32.44N 67.21E
110 O9 Utah L Utah 40.10N 111.50W
51 M7 Utajärvi Finland 64.45N 26.26E
53 T19 Utåker Norway 59.47N 5.55E
122 C12 Utaofai Tahiti Pacific Oc 17.39S 149.18W
15 D6 Uta R Irian Jaya
18 D7 Utara isld Indonesia
20 L1 Utashinai Japan 43.32N 142.03E
42 G6 Utata U.S.S.R. 50.50N 102.45E
9 R12 'Uta Vava'u isld Tonga, Pacific Oc 18.35S 174.00W
33 D5 'Utaybah tribe Saudi Arabia
'Utaybah, Buḩarai al L see Ateibe,Bahret el L
33 H3 Utayyiq Saudi Arabia 27.10N 48.36E
53 T19 Utbjoa Norway 59.41N 5.36E
120 A1 Utcubamba,R Peru
108 P7 Ute Iowa 42.04N 95.42W
75 J4 Utebo Spain 41.42N 1.00W
109 G6 Ute Cr New Mexico
93 F7 Utegi Tanzania 1.19S 34.15E
71 L9 Utelle France 43.55N 7.15E
91 G12 Utembo R Angola
46 F2 Utena Lithuania U.S.S.R. 55.30N 25.35E
92 J6 Utenge, L Tanzania 8.00S 38.25E
92 F6 Utengule Mbeya Tanzania 8.55S 33.20E
92 G6 Utengule Morogoro Tanzania 8.56S 35.41E
109 E5 Ute Park New Mexico 36.34N 105.06W
29 B5 Uterlai Rajasthan India 25.50N 71.30E
64 P4 Uterý Czechoslovakia 49.56N 13.01E
43 M1 Utës Kazakhstan U.S.S.R. 52.39N 76.31E
39 J2 Utesiki U.S.S.R. 65.04N 173.41E
92 J6 Utete Tanzania 8.00S 38.49E
46 Q3 Utevka U.S.S.R. 52.58N 51.00E
29 E4 Utgir Rajasthan India 26.08N 76.57E
Uthai Thani see Muang Uthai Thani
33 B2 Uthayli. Al Saudi Arabia 28.14N 36.48E
33 F4 Uthaythiyah Saudi Arabia 25.10N 45.23E
53 R17 Uthella Norway 60.40N 4.58E
63 J6 Uthlede W Germany 53.18N 8.34E
50 E6 Úthlidh Iceland 64.17N 20.28W
Uthmāniyah see Osmāniya
33 H4 Uthmaniyah, Al Saudi Arabia 24.16N 49.23E
35 G1 Uthmaniye Syria 33.13N 35.59E
25 E5 U Thong Thailand 14.16N 99.52E
25 H5 Uthumphon Phisai Thailand 15.03N 104.10E
118 B3 Utiariti Brazil 13.00S 58.20W
109 K3 Utica Kansas 38.38N 100.11W
107 J4 Utica Kentucky 37.36N 87.07W
106 L7 Utica Michigan 42.37N 83.03W
106 C6 Utica Minnesota 43.58N 91.56W
107 F9 Utica Mississippi 32.08N 90.40W
107 C2 Utica Missouri 39.44N 93.38W
110 P3 Utica Montana 46.58N 110.06W
108 N9 Utica Nebraska 40.55N 97.20W
104 K3 Utica New York 43.06N 75.15W
104 C6 Utica Ohio 40.14N 82.27W
75 H8 Utiel Spain 39.33N 1.13W
52 L2 Utifällan Sweden 64.05N 19.00E
100 V3 Utik L Manitoba
11 K6 Utiku New Zealand 39.43S 175.50E
100 B3 Utikuma L Alberta
115 L1 Utila Honduras 16.05N 86.51W
118 H3 Utinga Brazil 12.01S 41.03W
118 H3 Utinga R Brazil
44 D9 Utinoye Ukraine U.S.S.R. 45.38N 34.59E
92 E5 Utinta Tanzania 7.10S 30.30E
9 D1 Utirik atoll Marshall Is Pacific Oc 11.19N 169.49E
39 F5 Utkholok U.S.S.R. 57.34N 157.11E
39 F5 Utkholokskiy,Mys C U.S.S.R. 57.55N 157.00E
52 J11 Utklippan isld Sweden 55.58N 15.45E
52 J10 Utlängan isld Sweden 56.02N 15.50E
112 K5 Utley Texas 30.13N 97.27W
109 G4 Utleyville Colorado 37.17N 103.04W
44 D8 Utlyukskiy Liman gulf U.S.S.R.
53 V18 Utne Norway 60.25N 6.37E
20 D9 Uto Japan 32.42N 130.40E
52 L8 Utö Sweden 58.56N 18.20E
51 J12 Utö Lt Ho Finland 59.47N 21.20E
113 L4 Utopia Alaska 65.59N 153.54W
13 C5 Utopia N Terr Australia 22.14S 134.37E
112 H6 Utopia Texas 29.36N 99.33W
48 S13 Utorqarmiut Greenland 63.45N 51.30W
121 D6 Utracán Argentina 37.13S 64.31W
30 F5 Utraula Uttar Prad India 27.20N 82.25E
60 J11 Utrecht Netherlands 52.06N 5.07E
95 O3 Utrecht S Africa 27.40S 30.20E
60 J11 Utrecht prov Netherlands
77 E6 Utrera Spain 37.10N 5.47W
75 J6 Utrillas Spain 40.49N 0.51W
53 Y16 Utrovatn L Norway 61.11N 8.11E
44 F2 Ut Sala U.S.S.R. 45.54N 44.46E
103 E2 Utsayantha Mt New York 42.23N 74.36W
44 F5 Utsera Georgia U.S.S.R. 42.39N 43.32E
53 R20 Utsira Norway 59.19N 4.54E
51 N2 Utsjoki Finland 69.54N 27.01E
50 C6 Útskálar Iceland 64.05N 22.40W
53 T20 Utstein Kloster Norway 59.06N 5.36E
20 N5 Utsunomiya Japan 36.33N 139.52E
44 G1 Utta U.S.S.R. 46.24N 46.01E
28 C6 Uttamapalaiyam Tamil Nadu India 9.47N 77.20E
28 D4 Uttangarai Tamil Nadu India 12.17N 78.31E
25 F4 Uttaradit Thailand 17.38N 100.05E
30 B2 Uttarkashi Uttar Prad India 30.45N 78.19E
30 B2 Uttarkashi dist Uttar Prad India
29 F3 Uttar Pradesh state India
65 H5 Uttendorf Austria 48.09N 13.07E
52 J7 Uttersberg Sweden 59.45N 15.39E
53 G7 Uttersley Denmark 54.55N 11.12E
99 L7 Utterson Ontario 45.13N 79.20W
64 L7 Utting W Germany 48.01N 11.05E
64 H4 Üttingen W Germany 49.48N 9.43E
57 K7 Uttoxeter Staffs Eng 52.54N 1.52W
66 O1 Uttwil Switzerland 47.36N 9.20E
41 O7 Uttyakh U.S.S.R. 65.38N 132.45E
Utu see Miao'ergou
92 C2 Utu Zaïre 1.45S 27.58E
93 A2 Utua R Zaïre
105 J7 Utuado Puerto Rico 18.17N 66.41W
24 E2 Utubulak Xinjiang Uygur Zizhiqu China 46.50N 86.15E
40 D4 Utugey R U.S.S.R.
113 G2 Utukok R Alaska
42 G6 Utulik U.S.S.R. 51.32N 104.01E
91 K4 Utumba Zaïre 1.08S 26.51E
9 R12 Utungake isld Tonga, Pacific Oc 18.41S 174.02W
10 O4 Utupua isld Santa Cruz Is Pacific Oc 11.20S 166.30E
122 A15 Uturoa Society Is Pacific Oc 16.44S 151.25W
46 R4 Utva R Kazakhstan U.S.S.R.
52 B6 Utvar Lt Ho Norway 60.55N 4.33E
53 V15 Utvik Norway 61.48N 6.32E
64 O3 Útvina Czechoslovakia 50.05N 12.57E
42 B5 Utyanka U.S.S.R. 54.42N 79.48E
43 H1 Utyatskoye U.S.S.R. 55.10N 65.07E
39 C2 Utychan R U.S.S.R.
63 S5 Utzedel E Germany 53.52N 13.09E
66 G3 Utzensdorf Switzerland 47.07N 7.33E
51 O10 Uukuniem Finland 61.46N 29.59E
22 J3 Uulbayan Mongolia 46.28N 112.05E
22 J2 Uuldza Mongolia 49.03N 112.35E
22 J2 Uuldza Gol R Mongolia
51 L9 Uurainen Finland 62.30N 25.28E
22 E1 Üür Gol R Mongolia
Uusikaarlepyy see Nykarleby
51 L11 Uusimaa dist Finland
51 P9 Uusi Värtsilä Finland 62.12N 30.30E
26 T7 Uva Sri Lanka 7.08N 81.07E
46 Q2 Uva U.S.S.R. 57.00N 52.10E
108 F7 Uva Wyoming 42.09N 104.56W
26 T8 Uva prov Sri Lanka
82 F7 Uvac R Yugoslavia
111 K2 Uvada Nevada 39.40N 114.05W
119 E6 Uva,Laguna L Colombia 3.30N 71.39W
105 E5 Uvalda Georgia 32.02N 82.30W
112 H6 Uvalde Texas 29.14N 99.49W
65 L1 Uvaly Czechoslovakia 50.05N 14.45E
119 E6 Uva,R Colombia
39 K1 Uvargin U.S.S.R. 69.46N 176.27E
45 B4 Uvarovichi Belorussiya U.S.S.R. 52.35N 30.44E
45 G1 Uvarovka U.S.S.R. 55.33N 35.43E
45 O5 Uvarovo U.S.S.R. 51.59N 42.15E
47 K6 Uvat U.S.S.R. 59.10N 68.49E
39 J1 Uvatkyn R U.S.S.R.
10 R4 Uvea isld Îles Wallis Pacific Oc 13.22S 176.12W
122 J9 Uvéa isld Wallis Is Pacific Oc 13.22S 176.12W
46 O4 Uvek U.S.S.R. 51.27N 45.58E
47 J8 Uvel'ka R U.S.S.R.
47 J8 Uvel'skiy U.S.S.R. 54.28N 61.20E
71 K8 Uvernet-Fours France 44.21N 6.38E
47 M5 Uvil'dy, Oz L U.S.S.R. 55.31N 60.30E
92 E4 Uvinza Tanzania 5.08S 30.23E
93 A9 Uvira Zaïre 3.24S 29.05E
48 T7 Uvkusigssat Greenland 71.00N 52.05W
48 S6 Uvkusigssat Fd Greenland
95 O6 Uvongo Beach S Africa 30.50S 30.25E
22 B2 Uvs prov Mongolia
22 B1 Uvs Nuur L Mongolia
20 F8 Uwa Japan 33.22N 132.32E
20 E9 Uwae Japan 32.08N 131.30E
30 F4 Uwagaon Nepal 28.25N 82.50E
'Uwaina see 'Uwaynah, Al
34 D10 Uwainid,Wādī al watercourse Saudi Arabia
20 F8 Uwajima Japan 33.13N 132.32E
33 F5 'Uwayjā', Al Saudi Arabia 22.21N 45.24E
33 J5 'Uwayjā', Al Saudi Arabia 22.24N 50.36E
33 H3 'Uwaynah,Al Saudi Arabia 26.46N 48.24E
33 B3 'Uwaynidhiyah, Al isld Saudi Arabia 26.37N 36.04E
33 E1 'Uwayqīlah, Al Saudi Arabia 30.20N 42.15E
33 B3 'Uwayrid, Harrat al lava flow Saudi Arabia
34 F8 Uwaysiţ Saudi Arabia 30.32N 38.09E
85 H9 'Uweinat,Jebel mt Sudan 21.56N 25.04E
114 C8 Uwekahuna pk Hawaiian Is 19.25N 155.17W
90 D9 Uwet Nigeria 5.15N 8.11E
18 G5 Uwi isld Indonesia 1.05N 107.25E
92 G5 Uwimbi Tanzania 6.58S 35.23E
15 F7 Uwimmerah R Irian Jaya
50 H3 Uxahver hot springs Iceland 65.51N 17.05W
55 B3 Uxbridge London England 51.33N 0.29W
103 L2 Uxbridge Massachusetts 42.05N 71.38W
99 L8 Uxbridge Ontario 44.07N 79.09W
71 E3 Uxeau France 46.40N 4.00E
22 H7 Uxin Ju Nei Monggol Zizhiqu China 39.07N 109.03E
22 H7 Uxin Qi Nei Monggol Zizhiqu China 38.25N 108.59E
117 B7 Uxituba Brazil 4.15S 55.46W
115 P7 Uxmal ruins Mexico 20.21N 89.46W
24 F4 Uxxaktal Xinjiang Uygur Zizhiqu China 42.15N 87.16E
47 J8 Uy R Chelyabinsk U.S.S.R.
47 L7 Uy R Omsk U.S.S.R.
113 K8 Uyak B Alaska
43 F5 Uyaly Kazakhstan U.S.S.R. 44.36N 60.52E
43 F5 Uyaly,Ostrov isld Kazakhstan U.S.S.R. 44.36N 61.00E
43 O4 Uyaly,Ozero L Kazakhstan U.S.S.R.
40 F3 Uyan R U.S.S.R.
41 O8 Uyana R U.S.S.R.
39 C1 Uyandi U.S.S.R. 69.25N 140.52E
39 C1 Uyandina R U.S.S.R.
22 F3 Uyanga Mongolia 46.29N 102.20E
42 E4 Uyar U.S.S.R. 55.50N 94.18E
43 M8 Uyas Tadzhikistan U.S.S.R. 40.23N 69.55E
34 D10 'Uyaynah,Al Saudi Arabia 28.55N 36.03E
58 R8 Uyea isld Unst, Shetland Scotland 60.40N 0.54W
58 Q8 Uyea I Shetland Scotland 60.37N 1.25W
58 R8 Uyeasound Shetland Scotland 60.41N 0.55W
41 P5 Uyëdey U.S.S.R. 71.30N 136.38E
41 D3 Uyedineniya, Ostrov isld U.S.S.R. 77.30N 82.30E
47 G3 Uyeg U.S.S.R. 65.45N 51.59E
39 C4 Uyega U.S.S.R. 60.45N 142.45E
47 M5 Uyelgi,Oz L U.S.S.R. 55.47N 61.35E
47 E4 Uyemskiy U.S.S.R. 64.39N 40.50E
43 K6 Uygursay Uzbekistan U.S.S.R. 40.51N 71.02E
90 C9 Uyo Nigeria 5.01N 7.56E
22 B3 Üyönch Mongolia 46.05N 92.07E
22 B3 Üyönch Gol R Mongolia
93 D10 Uyowa Tanzania 4.33S 32.01E
36 D4 Uysal Dağ mt Turkey 38.15N 28.51E
25 M8 'Uyu Chaung R Burma
43 K5 Uyuk Kazakhstan U.S.S.R. 43.46N 70.54E
42 E6 Uyuk U.S.S.R. 52.06N 94.06E
35 D8 'Uyun Abu Kheit Jordan 31.30N 35.03E
33 C4 'Uyūn,Al Saudi Arabia 24.35N 39.35E
33 E3 'Uyūn, Al Saudi Arabia 26.31N 43.43E
86 D7 'Uyûn el Ruwayân Egypt 29.05N 30.17E
35 G2 'Uyun Hadid Syria 32.52N 35.49E
120 E9 Uyuni Bolivia 20.28S 66.47W
120 E9 Uyuni,Salar de salt pan Bolivia
86 J6 'Uyûn Mûsa Egypt 29.53N 32.39E
62 N7 Už R U.S.S.R./Czech
72 B7 Uza France 44.02N 1.12W
35 C7 'Uza Israel 31.35N 34.46E
45 R4 Uza R U.S.S.R.
'Uzair,Al see 'Uzayr Al
72 J2 Uzay-le-Venon France 46.49N 2.26E
33 E3 'Uzaym, Al Saudi Arabia 26.34N 42.30E
34 M4 'Uzaym, Nahr al R Iraq
34 P7 'Uzayr,Al Iraq 31.20N 47.26E
38 F4 Uzbekskaya S.S.R U.S.S.R.
Uzbek S.S.R see Uzbekskaya S.S.R
24 A6 Uzbel Shankou pass Xinjiang Uygur Zizhiqu China 38.34N 73.34E
43 D7 Uzboy R Turkmeniya U.S.S.R.
46 F3 Uzda Belorussiya U.S.S.R. 53.28N 27.11E
82 F5 Uzdin Yugoslavia 45.11N 20.36E
70 E5 Uzel France 48.17N 2.51W
66 B2 Uzelle France 47.28N 6.27E
44 M4 Uzen' Kazakhstan U.S.S.R. 43.30N 53.00E
71 E7 Uzer France 44.32N 4.21E
72 H5 Uzerche France 45.25N 1.34E
71 E8 Uzès France 44.01N 4.25E
43 L6 Uzgen Kirgiziya U.S.S.R. 40.48N 73.14E
46 G4 Uzh R Ukraine U.S.S.R.
42 C5 Uzhanikha U.S.S.R. 54.41N 81.07E
46 D5 Uzhgorod Ukraine U.S.S.R. 48.38N 22.15E
82 H2 Uzhok U.S.S.R. 48.59N 22.52E
42 D4 Uzhur U.S.S.R. 55.19N 89.50E
82 F7 Užicka Pozega Yugoslavia 43.51N 20.03E
92 K12 Uzi I Zanzibar 6.21S 39.24E
Uzinki see Ouzinkie
42 H6 Uzkiy Lug U.S.S.R. 50.46N 108.00E
45 B1 Uzkoye U.S.S.R. 55.46N 30.33E
45 K3 Uzlovaya U.S.S.R. 53.55N 38.11E
45 R5 Uzmor'ye U.S.S.R. 51.15N 45.55E
66 M3 Uznach Switzerland 47.13N 8.59E
46 N2 Uzola R U.S.S.R.
36 B4 Uzon isld Turkey
75 J2 Uztárroz Spain 42.54N 0.56W
37 G1 Üzümce Turkey 41.10N 29.15E
36 F5 Üzümlo Turkey 37.33N 31.37E
36 D6 Üzümlü Turkey 36.44N 29.14E
83 H6 Uzun isld Turkey
43 M5 Uzun-Agach Kazakhstan U.S.S.R. 43.36N 76.19E
43 M5 Uzun-Agach Kazakhstan U.S.S.R. 42.40N 76.20E
24 E3 Uzunbulak Xinjiang Uygur Zizhiqu China 45.18N 84.10E
37 J9 Üzün Darreh Iran 36.44N 45.46E
32 B2 Üzün Darreh R Iran
92 G6 Uzungwa reg Tanzania
37 D5 Uzunisa Turkey 40.56N 37.52E
37 C1 Uzunköprü Turkey 41.18N 26.40E
44 E9 Uzunlarskoye Ozero L Ukraine U.S.S.R.
45 K2 Uzunovo U.S.S.R. 54.34N 38.38E
Uzun Qizil R see Qezel Owzan R
32 F1 Uzun Su Turkmeniya U.S.S.R. 39.11N 55.46E
66 N2 Uzwil, Nieder Switzerland 47.27N 9.09E
66 N2 Uzwil,Ober Switzerland 47.26N 9.08E
43 F5 Uzynkair Kazakhstan U.S.S.R. 44.39N 61.16E
90 L7 Va watercourse Cent Afr Rep
122 C2 Vaaifetu pk W Samoa, Pacific Oc 13.55S 171.39W
51 M9 Vaajakoski Finland 62.16N 25.56E
95 G4 Vaal R S Africa
51 M7 Vaala Finland 64.35N 26.50E
61 J3 Vaalbeek Belgium 50.50N 4.41E
95 M2 Vaaldam res S Africa 27.00S 28.15E
94 E8 Vaalfontein S Africa 31.46S 19.55E
95 H4 Vaal Hartz Weir L S Africa 28.07S 24.57E
51 N11 Vaalimaa Finland 60.38N 27.52E
95 K7 Vaalkop mt S Africa 31.21S 26.32E
95 M1 Vaalplaas S Africa 25.40S 28.53E
60 U17 Vaals Netherlands 50.46N 6.01E
95 K2 Vaalsig S Africa 26.59S 26.37E
94 K5 Vaalwater S Africa 24.20S 28.03E
39 K3 Vaamochkino,Ozero L U.S.S.R.
51 M8 Vaaraslahti Finland 63.22N 26.45E
60 L14 Vaarsel Netherlands 51.23N 5.41E
70 L6 Vaas France 47.40N 0.19E
51 J8 Vaasa Finland 63.06N 21.36E
51 J9 Vaasa dist Finland
60 M10 Vaassen Netherlands 52.18N 5.59E
60 N10 Vaassen Netherlands 52.23N 6.05E
51 L4 Vaattojärvi Finland 67.15N 24.10E
53 H7 Våbensted Denmark 54.48N 11.36E
43 G6 Vabkent Uzbekistan U.S.S.R. 40.02N 64.31E
45 G5 Vablya U.S.S.R. 51.55N 35.27E
72 J8 Vabre France 43.41N 2.25E
72 K8 Vabres-l'Abbaye France 43.57N 2.50E
62 L8 Vác Hungary 47.46N 19.08E
120 F8 Vaca Guzman Bolivia 19.54S 63.45W
121 J2 Vacaria Brazil 28.31S 50.52W
118 G5 Vacaría R Minas Gerais Brazil
121 J2 Vacaria,Campo da plain Brazil
118 C7 Vacaria,R Mato Grosso do Sul Brazil
118 C7 Vacaria,Serra mts Brazil
121 C9 Vacas,L Argentina
111 C3 Vacaville California 38.21N 122.00W
95 E10 Vacca,C S Africa 34.20S 21.53E
81 A6 Vacca,I.la Sardinia 38.56N 8.26E
67 P13 Vacca Morta, Punta della mt Corsica 41.39N 9.10E
71 F9 Vaccarès, Etang de L France 43.32N 4.35E
67 P13 Vaccia,Col de la pass Corsica 41.50N 9.05E
64 J2 Vacha E Germany 50.45N 10.03E
47 C4 Vacha Karelia U.S.S.R. 63.59N 33.30E
45 O1 Vacha U.S.S.R. 55.46N 42.45E
26 R14 Vache I Mahé I Seychelles, Ind Oc 4.41S 55.27E
116 H5 Vache, Île-à- Haiti 18.04N 73.40W
71 K4 Vacheresse France 46.20N 6.40E
71 K7 Vachette,la France 44.55N 6.41E
44 H5 Vachi Dagestan U.S.S.R. 42.04N 47.12E
26 U12 Vacoas Mauritius, Indian Oc 20.18S 57.29E
71 F8 Vacqueyras France 44.08N 4.59E
45 Q1 Vad U.S.S.R. 55.30N 44.14E
46 N3 Vad R U.S.S.R.
80 B2 Vada Italy 43.21N 10.27E
29 C8 Vada Maharashtra India 19.40N 73.11E
80 B2 Vada,Secche di shoal Italy
76 C5 Vade Portugal 41.46N 8.25W
110 C3 Vader Washington 46.25N 122.58W
50 J5 Vadhalda mt Iceland 64.59N 16.29W
53 T16 Vadheim Norway 61.12N 5.50E
50 H3 Vadhlaheidhi heath Iceland
50 M4 Vadhlavík inlet Iceland
Vadi see Savantvadi
76 J7 Vadillo de la Sierra Spain 40.37N 5.06W
45 E1 Vadino U.S.S.R. 55.16N 33.18E
45 P3 Vadinsk U.S.S.R. 53.42N 43.02E
109 E5 Vadito New Mexico 36.12N 105.41W
53 U20 Vadla Norway 59.19N 6.26E
29 C6 Vadnagar Gujarat India 23.48N 72.40E
79 D6 Vado, Capo C Italy 44.15N 8.27E
75 C4 Vadocondes Spain 41.38N 3.34W
29 C6 Vadodara Gujarat India
29 C6 Vadodara Gujarat India 22.19N 73.14E
75 D5 Vado,Embalse de El res Spain 41.03N 3.20W
79 D6 Vado Ligure Italy 44.16N 8.26E
77 J4 Vadollano Spain 38.07N 3.34W
47 C3 Vadozero,Oz L U.S.S.R.
66 Q5 Vadret,Piz mt Switzerland 46.42N 9.58E
51 O1 Vadsø Norway 70.05N 29.47E
52 H8 Vadstena Sweden 58.26N 14.55E
82 M6 Vadu Romania 44.27N 28.45E
53 D2 Vadum Denmark 57.07N 9.54E
66 P3 Vaduz Liechtenstein 47.08N 9.32E
51 C4 Værøy Norway 67.40N 12.40E
53 H7 Væggerløse Denmark 54.43N 11.56E
53 R16 Værlandet isld Norway 61.18N 4.44E
53 J5 Værløse Denmark 55.47N 12.23E
53 G5 Værslev Denmark 55.39N 11.13E
84 K11 Váfes Crete 35.21N 24.10E
53 N11 Våg Faeroes 61.29N 6.49W
53 S20 Våg Norway 59.28N 5.29E
47 E5 Vaga R U.S.S.R.
52 E5 Vågåmo Norway 61.52N 9.10E
51 D3 Vagan Norway 68.14N 14.30E
82 C6 Vaganski mt Yugoslavia 44.20N 15.34E
Vágar isld see Vågø
47 K6 Vagay Tyumen U.S.S.R. 57.58N 69.00E
47 K7 Vagay Tyumen U.S.S.R. 56.30N 67.16E
47 K7 Vagay R U.S.S.R.
53 T18 Våge Hordaland Norway 60.03N 5.33E
53 V19 Våge Rogaland Norway 59.34N 6.40E
53 N11 Våg Fjord Faeroes 61.29N 6.43W
51 O2 Vaggatem L Norway 69.15N 29.20E
52 H9 Vaggeryd Sweden 57.30N 14.10E
15 K2 Vaghena I Solomon Is 7.25S 157.44E
42 D4 Vagino U.S.S.R. 56.23N 89.50E
50 H3 Vaglaskógur wood Iceland
79 K7 Vaglia Italy 43.54N 11.17E
80 N7 Vaglio Basilicata Italy 40.40N 15.55E
69 M7 Vagney France 48.00N 6.43E
52 K8 Vagnhärad Sweden 58.57N 17.32E
53 M9 Vågø isld Faeroes
76 B7 Vagos Portugal 40.33N 8.42W
89 D8 Vagra Liberia 7.12N 10.59W
52 G6 Vägsjöfors Sweden 60.17N 13.04E
53 W19 Vågslid Norway 59.46N 7.25E
53 S15 Vågsøy isld Norway 61.57N 5.05E
53 W13 Vagstranda Norway 62.36N 7.20E
71 E7 Vagué France 44.33N 4.25E
62 L8 Váh R Czechoslovakia
51 J8 Vähäkyrö Finland 63.04N 22.05E
86 O5 Vahel Israel 30.02N 35.04E
122 F15 Vahitahi atoll Tuamotu Is Pacific Oc 18.35S 138.50W
123 D10 Vahsel Bay Antarctica 77.49S 35.00W
121 G8 Vahsel, C S Georgia 54.45S 35.45W
76 D10 Vaiamonte Portugal 39.06N 7.30W
122 D13 Vaiau,Pt Tahiti Pacific Oc 17.53S 149.10W
107 G8 Vaiden Mississippi 33.21N 89.44W
28 D6 Vaigai R Tamil Nadu India
48 S7 Vaigat channel Greenland
70 K5 Vaiges France 48.03N 0.28W
64 F6 Vaihingen W Germany 48.56N 8.58E
122 C12 Vaihiria,L Tahiti Pacific Oc 17.40S 149.25W
122 U16 Vaihu Easter I Pacific Oc 27.10S 109.22W
29 D8 Vaijapur Maharashtra India 19.58N 74.46E
28 C6 Vaikam Kerala India 9.45N 76.24E
46 F1 Väike-Maarja Estonia U.S.S.R. 59.10N 26.20E
111 O9 Vail Arizona 32.02N 110.44W
58 P9 Vaila isld Shetland Scotland 60.12N 1.35W
15 H7 Vailala R Papua New Guinea
79 G4 Vailate Italy 45.28N 9.36E
9 S7 Vaileka Viti Levu Fiji 17.22S 178.10E
122 C2 Vailima W Samoa, Pacific Oc 13.51S 171.45W
71 G1 Vaillant France 47.43N 5.10E
66 C6 Vailly France 46.18N 6.32E
69 F5 Vailly-sur-Aisne France 49.24N 3.32E
71 B2 Vailly-sur-Sauldre France 47.28N 2.38E
122 B1 Vailoa W Samoa, Pacific Oc 13.42S 172.16W
122 C2 Vailoa W Samoa, Pacific Oc 14.00S 171.24W
103 F4 Vails Gate New York 41.27N 74.04W
9 S10 Vaina Tonga, Pacific Oc 21.12S 175.10W
51 N11 Vainikkala Finland 60.51N 28.28E
28 C6 Vaippar R Tamil Nadu India
69 K7 Vair R France
122 F16 Vairaatéa isld Tuamotu Is Pacific Oc 19.14S 139.19W
80 K6 Vairano Patenora Italy 41.20N 14.08E
122 C12 Vairao Tahiti Pacific Oc 17.48S 149.17W
66 J7 Vaira,Valle Switzerland
72 A2 Vairé France 46.36N 1.46W
66 A2 Vaire-le-Grand France 47.17N 6.10E
68 J3 Vaires-sur-Marne France 48.52N 2.38E
29 D2 Vairowal Punjab India 31.22N 75.10E
30 B6 Vaisali R Madhya Prad India
71 G8 Vaison-la-Romaine France 44.14N 5.04E
72 H7 Vaissac France 44.02N 1.33E
122 V14 Vaitahu Marquesas Is Pacific Oc 9.56S 139.05W
122 A15 Vaitape Society Is Pacific Oc 16.30S 151.45W
122 B14 Vaitepaoa Tuamotu Is Pacific Oc 16.10S 148.14W
122 A15 Vaitoare Society Is Pacific Oc 16.41S 151.26W
122 D1 Vaitogi Amer Samoa Pacific Oc 14.22S 170.44W
122 D12 Vaitoto Tahiti Pacific Oc 17.47S 149.07W
9 D8 Vaitupu isld Tuvalu, Pacific Ocean 7.28S 178.41E
122 B1 Vaiusu W Samoa, Pacific Oc 13.47S 171.47W
71 J1 Vaivre France 47.38N 6.06E
51 F9 Väja Sweden 62.59N 17.40E
51 H5 Vajkijaur Sweden 66.42N 19.50E
9 R12 Vaka'eitu isld Tonga, Pacific Oc 18.43S 174.06W
90 L7 Vakaga dist Cent Afr Rep
26 T5 Vakarai Sri Lanka 8.08N 81.26E
82 H8 Vakarel Bulgaria 42.35N 23.40E
39 J3 Vakarevo U.S.S.R. 64.53N 171.53E
52 H6 Vakern Sweden 60.23N 14.10E
37 E4 Vakfıkebir Turkey 41.03N 39.19E
42 B2 Vakh R U.S.S.R.
43 K8 Vakhanskiy Khrebet mts Tadzhikistan/Afghan
84 C6 Vákhlia Greece 37.47N 21.57E
84 D8 Vakhón Greece 36.41N 22.25E
40 J7 Vakhrushev Sakhalin U.S.S.R. 48.57N 142.58E
43 J7 Vakhsh R Tadzhikistan U.S.S.R.
43 J7 Vakhshstroy Tadzhikistan U.S.S.R. 37.45N 68.51E
46 O1 Vakhtan U.S.S.R. 57.53N 46.47E
32 H6 Vakīlābād Iran 29.00N 58.34E
53 X14 Vakkerstøylen Norway 62.16N 7.49E
47 C4 Vaknavolok U.S.S.R. 64.55N 30.39E
53 T18 Vaksdal Norway 60.29N 5.45E
91 C6 Vaku Zaïre 5.15S 13.13E
50 K3 Vakursstadhir Iceland 65.43N 15.00W
15 L8 Vakuta I Trobriand Is Papua New Guinea 8.52S 151.09E
95 M2 Val S Africa 26.48S 28.56E
40 J5 Val Sakhalin U.S.S.R. 52.30N 143.07E
51 P10 Valaam, Ostrov isld Karelia U.S.S.R. 61.21N 31.00E
75 H7 Valacloche Spain 40.11N 1.05W
52 G3 Vålådalen Sweden 63.09N 13.00E
76 B6 Valadares Douro Litoral Portugal 41.05N 8.38W
76 C4 Valadares Minho Portugal 42.04N 8.22W
76 A9 Valado Portugal 39.35N 9.01W
50 F6 Valafell mt Iceland 64.06N 19.35W
39 A1 Valagannakh U.S.S.R. 67.58N 133.40E
39 F7 Valaginskiy Khrebet ra U.S.S.R.
26 U6 Valaichchenai Sri Lanka 7.54N 81.32E
66 F7 Valais canton Switzerland
46 Q1 Valamaz U.S.S.R. 57.32N 52.01E
82 H9 Valandovo Yugoslavia 41.19N 22.34E
70 E4 Val André, le France 48.36N 2.33W
66 D3 Valangin Switzerland 47.01N 6.55E
84 D2 Valanídha Greece 39.53N 22.05E
72 C1 Valanjou France 47.12N 0.34W
52 H7 Valåsen Sweden 59.17N 14.35E
62 K6 Valasske Klobouky Czech 49.10N 18.00E
62 K6 Valasske Meziříčí Czechoslovakia 49.29N 17.57E
103 G2 Valatie New York 42.25N 73.40W
103 G2 Valatie Kill R New York
46 G4 Valavsk Belorussiya U.S.S.R. 51.40N 28.38E
84 H4 Valáxa isld Greece 38.50N 24.29E
99 P6 Val Barrette Quebec 46.31N 75.22W
66 N6 Valbella Switzerland 46.25N 9.09E
66 P4 Valbella Switzerland 46.46N 9.34E
71 K8 Valberg France 46.06N 6.56E
51 D3 Valberg Norway 68.12N 14.00E
79 H2 Valbondione Italy 46.02N 10.01E
71 H7 Valbonnais France 44.53N 5.53E
98 E5 Val Brilliant Quebec 48.32N 67.34W
76 L5 Valbuena de Duero Spain 41.38N 4.17W
60 M12 Valburg Netherlands 51.54N 5.47E
76 F3 Valcarce R Spain
75 H1 Valcarlos Spain 43.05N 1.18W
76 K3 Valcavadillo mt Spain 42.34N 4.45W
82 J5 Valcea div Romania
121 C8 Valcheta Argentina 40.42S 66.08W
79 C3 Valchiusella Italy 45.32N 7.42E
41 R5 Valch'ya R U.S.S.R.
99 S7 Valcourt Quebec 45.30N 72.20W
75 L5 Valcuerna R Spain
79 K3 Valdagno Italy 45.39N 11.18E
71 J2 Valdahom France 47.08N 6.20E
Valdai Hills see Valdayskaya Vozvyshennost' heights
69 M8 Val d'Ajol, le France 47.55N 6.31E
76 K4 Valdavia R Spain
28 D4 Valdavur Tamil Nadu India 12.01N 79.44E
47 D4 Valday Karelia U.S.S.R. 63.28N 35.36E
46 J1 Valday Novgorod U.S.S.R. 57.59N 33.10E
46 J2 Valdayskaya Vozvyshennost' heights U.S.S.R.
76 M3 Valdeajos Spain 42.46N 3.55W
75 K6 Valdealgorfa Spain 40.59N 0.02W
77 G3 Valdeazogues R Spain
71 L8 Valdeblore France 44.05N 7.12E
76 J10 Valdecaballeros Spain 39.15N 5.11W
75 F7 Valdecabras Spain 40.09N 2.02W
117 D5 Val de Caes airport Brazil 1.23S 48.30W
76 L5 Valdecañas de Cerrato Spain 42.00N 4.10W
76 H9 Valdecañas de Tajo Spain 39.46N 5.37W
76 J9 Valdecañas, Embalse de res Spain
76 L3 Valdecebollas mt Spain 42.58N 4.21W
75 H7 Valdecebro Spain 40.22N 1.03W
75 E7 Valdeconcha Spain 40.27N 2.52W
75 J6 Valdeconejos Spain 40.47N 0.53W
75 H7 Valdecuenca Spain 40.18N 1.24W
76 H2 Valdediós Spain 43.26N 5.32W
76 J3 Valdefresno Spain 42.34N 5.29W
76 G10 Valdefuentes Spain 39.16N 6.08W
76 H4 Valdefuentes del Páramo Spain 42.19N 5.50W
76 G9 Valdegamas mt Spain 39.35N 6.05W
77 N2 Valdeganga Spain 39.09N 1.41W
75 D2 Valdegovia Spain 42.50N 3.06W
76 H8 Valdehijaderos Spain 40.25N 5.53W
77 N5 Valdeinfierno,Embalse de L Spain 37.49N 1.58W
76 J9 Valdelacasa de Tajo Spain 39.44N 5.17W
75 E6 Valdelagua Spain 40.40N 2.45W
75 D7 Valdelaguna Spain 40.10N 3.23W
77 C5 Valdelarco Spain 37.57N 6.40W
75 J7 Valdelinares Spain 40.24N 0.37W
75 H6 Valdellosa mt Spain 40.53N 1.22W
76 J3 Valdeluqueros Spain 42.58N 5.25W
75 D4 Valdemaluque Spain 41.40N 3.03W
69 C6 Val-de-Marne dept France
46 E2 Valdemarpils Latvia U.S.S.R. 57.20N 22.32E
52 K8 Valdemarsvik Sweden 58.13N 16.35E
75 G7 Valdemeca,Sierra de mts Spain
75 G7 Valdeminguete,Sierra de mts Spain
75 G7 Valdemorillo de la Sierra Spain 40.02N 1.48W
75 C7 Valdemoro Spain 40.12N 3.40W
75 E7 Valdemoro del Rey Spain 40.15N 2.38W
75 G7 Valdemoro Sierra Spain 40.06N 1.46W
75 C2 Valdenoceda Spain 42.51N 3.35W
75 D6 Valdenoches Spain 40.41N 3.05W
76 G8 Valdeobispo Spain 40.05N 6.15W
75 F6 Valdeolivas Spain 40.30N 2.26W
76 F4 Valdeorras reg Spain
77 K3 Valdepeñas Spain 38.46N 3.24W
77 J5 Valdepeñas de Jaén Spain 37.36N 3.50W
76 J3 Valdepiélago Spain 42.51N 5.24W
76 J3 Valdepolo Spain 42.34N 5.14W
76 L3 Valdeprado del Río Spain 42.52N 4.05W
76 L7 Valdeprados Spain 40.49N 4.15W
76 J4 Valderaduey R Spain
76 J4 Valderas Spain 42.05N 5.27W
72 J7 Valderiès France 44.01N 2.13E
53 U13 Valderøya isld Norway 62.30N 6.08E
76 G4 Valderrey Spain 42.23N 6.02W
75 L6 Valderrobres Spain 40.53N 0.09E
106 G5 Valders Wisconsin 44.04N 87.51W
76 H3 Valdesamario Spain 42.43N 5.56W
75 H5 Val de San Martín Spain 41.03N 1.27W
76 L8 Val de Santo Domingo Spain 40.01N 4.19W
75 E6 Valdesaz Spain 40.44N 2.58W
99 P7 Val des Bois Quebec 45.54N 75.36W
105 F2 Valdese N Carolina 35.43N 81.35W
121 D9 Valdés,Pen Argentina
75 F4 Valdespina Spain 41.35N 2.26W
98 H5 Val-d'Espoir Quebec 48.31N 64.23W
76 K6 Valdestillas Spain 41.28N 4.47W
76 J3 Valdeteja Spain 42.55N 5.26W
77 D3 Valdetorres Spain 38.55N 6.05W
76 J9 Valdeverdeja Spain 39.48N 5.15W
76 H4 Valdevimbre Spain 42.25N 5.37W
113 O6 Valdez Alaska 61.07N 146.17W
109 F4 Valdez Colorado 37.07N 104.41W
119 B7 Valdez Ecuador 1.13N 79.00W
75 N6 Valdezarza dist Madrid Spain
79 H2 Valdidentro Italy 46.29N 10.17E
79 B6 Valdieri Italy 44.16N 7.23E
76 K7 Valdihuelo mt Spain 40.38N 4.31W
75 D7 Valdilecha Spain 40.18N 3.19W
66 D7 Val d'Illiez Switzerland 46.13N 6.54E
71 K6 Val-d'Isère France 45.27N 7.00E
121 A7 Valdivia Chile 39.46S 73.15W
119 C4 Valdivia Colombia 7.10N 75.25W
121 A8 Valdivia prov Chile
Valdivia Basin see Atlantic-Indian-Antarctic Basin
72 F2 Valdivienne France 46.32N 0.39E
70 H5 Val-d'Izé France 48.11N 1.18W
77 G3 Valdmanco del Esteras Spain 38.56N 4.50W
79 L3 Valdobbiádene Italy 45.54N 11.59E
71 K1 Valdoie France 47.40N 6.51E
69 B5 Val-d'Oise dept France
71 H10 Valdonne France 43.25N 5.35E
99 N4 Val-d 'Or Quebec 48.07N 77.47W
105 D7 Valdosta Georgia 30.51N 83.51W
76 C1 Valdoviño Spain 43.36N 8.08W
52 D5 Valdres reg Norway
79 J3 Valdritta,Cima mt Italy 45.43N 10.50E
71 H7 Valdrôme France 44.30N 5.35E
76 J4 Valdunquillo Spain 42.03N 5.18W
75 K5 Valdurrios,Sierra de mts Spain
70 E3 Vale Channel Is 49.29N 2.33W
44 E6 Vale Georgia U.S.S.R. 41.35N 42.54E
110 H6 Vale Oregon 43.59N 117.15W
108 G5 Vale S Dakota 44.36N 103.25W
82 G3 Valea-lui-Mihai Romania 47.30N 22.08E
82 J3 Valea Vişeului Romania 47.51N 24.11E
64 P3 Valeč Czechoslovakia 50.10N 13.16E
76 D13 Vale de Açor Portugal 37.47N 7.51W
76 E7 Vale de Azares Portugal 40.37N 7.23W
76 C7 Vale de Cambra Portugal 40.51N 8.24W
76 B10 Vale de Cavalos Portugal 39.17N 8.31W
76 F8 Vale de Espinho Portugal 40.18N 6.48W
76 E6 Vale de Figueira Portugal 41.08N 7.20W
76 C12 Vale de Gaio, Barragem de res Portugal 38.16N 8.15W
76 C12 Vale de Guizo Portugal 38.18N 8.29W
76 D10 Vale de Junça Portugal 39.24N 7.53W
76 E8 Vale de Prazeres Portugal 40.07N 7.26W
76 B10 Vale de Santarém Portugal 39.12N 8.45W
76 C13 Vale de Santiago Portugal 37.45N 8.25W
76 E13 Vale de Vargo Portugal 37.59N 7.24W
76 D10 Vale do Pezo Portugal 39.21N 7.39W
91 D10 Vale do Queve Angola 12.27S 15.49E
76 B12 Vale dos Reis Portugal 38.25N 8.30W
76 B7 Valega Portugal 40.50N 8.35W
79 J4 Valéggio sul Mincio Italy 45.22N 10.44E
53 T19 Valen Norway 59.50N 5.48E
118 H3 Valença Brazil 13.22S 39.06W
76 D6 Valença do Douro Portugal 41.09N 7.33W
76 B4 Valença do Minho Portugal 42.02N 8.38W
117 G8 Valença do Piauí Brazil 6.26S 41.46W
72 H1 Valençay France 47.10N 1.33E
72 E4 Valence Charente France 45.53N 0.18E
71 F7 Valence Drôme France 44.56N 4.54E
72 F7 Valence d'Agen France 44.07N 0.54E
72 J7 Valence d'Albigeois France 44.02N 2.24E
69 D7 Valence-en-Brie France 48.27N 2.54E
72 E8 Valence-sur-Baïse France 43.53N 0.24E
77 Q2 Valencia Spain 39.29N 0.24W
116 P1 Valencia Trinidad & Tobago 10.40N 61.11W
119 F2 Valencia Venezuela 10.14N 67.59W
74 G5 Valencia prov Spain
74 G6 Valencia reg Spain
76 E10 Valencia de Alcántara Spain 39.25N 7.14W
76 H4 Valencia de Don Juan Spain 42.17N 5.31W
77 E4 Valencia de las Torres Spain 38.25N 6.00W
77 B4 Valencia del Mombuey Spain 38.15N 7.06W
77 D4 Valencia del Ventoso Spain 38.15N 6.29W
77 Q2 Valencia,G.de Spain
59 B8 Valencia I Kerry Irish Rep 51.55N 10.20W
119 F2 Valencia, Lac de Venezuela 10.13N 67.30W
69 F3 Valenciennes France 50.22N 3.32E
66 O4 Valendas Switzerland 46.47N 9.17E
82 K5 Vălenii de Munte Romania 45.10N 26.02E
66 O4 Valens Switzerland 46.58N 9.29E
71 H9 Valensole France 43.50N 5.59E
80 E3 Valentano Italy 42.34N 11.49E
71 K2 Valentigney France 47.27N 6.50E
15 E6 Valentijn Keten mts Irian Jaya
117 F7 Valentim,Sa.do mts Brazil
40 F10 Valentin U.S.S.R. 43.09N 134.15E
111 L6 Valentine Arizona 35.23N 113.40W
72 F9 Valentine France 43.06N 0.42E
107 F12 Valentine Louisiana 29.38N 90.28W
110 R2 Valentine Montana 47.19N 108.26W
108 K7 Valentine Nebraska 42.53N 100.31W
79 E4 Valenza Italy 45.01N 8.38E
19 H1 Valenzuela Luzon Philippines 14.44N 120.57E
77 H5 Valenzuela Spain 37.47N 4.14W
77 J3 Valenzuela de Calatrava Spain 38.51N 3.46W
121 H8 Valenzuela, I Chile 51.10S 74.50W
52 F6 Våler Norway 60.48N 11.38E
112 H4 Valera Texas 31.46N 99.34W
119 E3 Valera Venezuela 9.21N 70.38W
75 F8 Valera de Abajo Spain 39.46N 2.09W
75 F8 Valeria Spain 39.49N 2.09W
53 S17 Valestrand Norway 60.30N 5.25E
53 S19 Valestrand Norway 59.40N 5.28E
Valetta see Valletta
71 H10 Valette-du-Var, la France 43.08N 6.00E
53 T19 Valevåg Norway 59.42N 5.30E
53 V21 Valevatn Norway 58.55N 6.44E
53 V21 Valevatn L Vest Agder Norway 58.56N 6.48E
118 H5 Vale Verde Brazil 16.30S 39.22W
76 D8 Valezim Portugal 40.21N 7.43W
80 G2 Valfábbrica Italy 43.09N 12.36E
75 K4 Valfarta Spain 41.34N 0.08W
46 F1 Valga Estonia U.S.S.R. 57.44N 26.00E
76 B3 Valga Spain 42.42N 8.38W
99 K4 Val Gagné Ontario 48.37N 80.37W
66 M8 Valganna Italy 45.54N 8.50E
71 E7 Valgorge France 44.35N 4.08E
77 V15 Valgornera Balearic Is 39.22N 2.51E
79 B6 Valgrana Italy 44.24N 7.22E
81 H9 Valguarnera Caropepe Sicily 37.30N 14.23E
28 B1 Valha Maharashtra India 18.12N 74.13E
103 G4 Valhalla New York 41.04N 73.35W
95 M1 Valhalla S Africa 25.50S 28.09E
50 T13 Valhallfonna glacier Spitsbergen 79.46N 17.00E
76 E8 Valhelhas Portugal 40.24N 7.25W
75 G6 Valhermoso Spain 40.47N 1.58W
115 O5 Valiente,Pen Panama 9.10N 81.45W
110 N1 Valier Montana 48.19N 112.14W
Valif I see Walis I.
9 S5 Valili Pk Vanua Levu Fiji 16.39S 179.09E
84 D5 Valimí Greece 38.05N 22.16E
67 O13 Valinco,G.de Corsica 41.40N 8.50E
53 K4 Välinge Sweden 56.12N 12.50E
84 C7 Valíra Greece 37.10N 21.59E
72 G11 Valira R Andorra etc
82 F6 Valjevo Yugoslavia 44.16N 19.56E
51 M2 Valjok Norway 69.41N 25.50E
71 J7 Valjouffrey-la-Chapelle France 44.53N 6.01E
75 L6 Valjunquera Spain 40.57N 0.01E
39 K1 Val'karay U.S.S.R. 69.54N 175.53E
51 L10 Valkeakoski Finland 61.17N 24.05E
51 M11 Valkeala Finland 60.56N 26.50E
51 L5 Valkeavaara mt Finland 66.15N 24.40E
39 K3 Valkelvaam U.S.S.R. 62.44N 177.50E
60 T17 Valkenburg Limburg Netherlands 50.52N 5.50E
60 F11 Valkenburg Zuid Holland Netherlands 52.11N 4.26E
60 K14 Valkenswaard Netherlands 51.21N 5.27E
65 P4 Valké Pavlovice Czechoslovakia 48.54N 16.48E
45 G7 Valki Ukraine U.S.S.R. 49.51N 35.38E
51 M11 Valko Finland 60.25N 26.15E
Valkom see Valko
39 J1 Val'kumey U.S.S.R. 69.35N 170.12E
29 B7 Vallabhipur Gujarat India 20.52N 71.58E
71 F9 Vallabregues France 43.51N 4.37E
77 P3 Vallada Spain 38.54N 0.41W
115 P7 Valladolid Mexico 20.40N 88.11W
76 K5 Valladolid Spain 41.39N 4.45W
74 D3 Valladolid prov Spain
91 B3 Valladolid de los Bimbiles Equat Guinea 1.48N 10.40E
77 O5 Valladolises Spain 37.47N 1.07W
99 N4 Val-Laflamme Quebec 48.32N 77.38W
75 H7 Vallanca Spain 40.04N 1.21W
50 L4 Vallanes Iceland 65.12N 14.34W
79 L1 Vallarga Italy 46.51N 11.44E
79 K3 Vallarsa R Italy
79 K3 Vallarsa Raossi Italy 45.47N 11.08E
80 M6 Vallata Italy 41.03N 15.16E
87 M5 Vallata del Darror V Somalia
71 L9 Vallauris France 43.35N 7.03E
58 B3 Vallay isld W Isles Scotland 57.40N 7.25W
75 O4 Vallbona Spain 41.31N 1.43E
75 M5 Vallclara Spain 41.23N 0.59E
53 W14 Valldal Norway 62.19N 7.17E
53 V19 Valldalen V Norway 59.53N 6.52E
53 W14 Valldalen V Norway 62.20N 7.25E
53 V19 Valldalsseter Norway 59.57N 6.57E
77 Q3 Vall de Alcalá Spain 38.48N 0.15W
77 Q3 Vall de Ebo Spain 38.49N 0.10W
77 V14 Valldemosa Balearic Is 39.43N 2.36E
75 K8 Vall de Uxó Spain 39.49N 0.15W
111 M6 Valle Arizona 35.39N 112.11W
71 J10 Val,le France 43.26N 6.04E
53 X20 Valle Norway 59.12N 7.32E
76 D1 Valle Spain 43.43N 7.38W
96 Q15 Valle Tenerife Canary Is 28.06N 16.39W
119 C6 Valle div Colombia
80 J3 Valle Castellana Italy 42.44N 13.30E
115 K4 Vallecillo Mexico 26.40N 99.58W
75 G7 Vallecillo,El Spain 40.14N 1.34W
121 C3 Vallecito Argentina 31.47S 67.55W
119 F3 Vallecito Venezuela 9.54N 68.29W
109 C4 Vallecito Res Colorado 37.24N 107.34W
109 D5 Vallecitos New Mexico 36.29N 106.08W
80 H6 Vallecorsa Italy 41.27N 13.25E
121 B2 Valle Cura,R.del Argentina
67 P12 Valle d'Alesani Corsica 42.19N 9.24E
78 A3 Valle d'Aosta aut reg Italy
77 G7 Valle de Abdalagis Spain 36.56N 4.41W
115 G7 Valle de Banderas Mexico 20.50N 105.18W
115 J8 Valle de Bravo Mexico 19.12N 100.10W
76 L2 Valle de Cabuérniga Spain 43.14N 4.18W
76 F3 Valle de Finolledo Spain 42.43N 6.41W
119 F3 Valle de la Pascua Venezuela 9.15N 66.00W
77 E3 Valle de la Serena Spain 38.42N 5.48W
77 C4 Valle de Matamoros Spain 38.24N 6.48W
115 F4 Valle de Olivos Mexico 27.14N 106.18W
Valle de Oro see Ferreira Spain
115 F4 Valle de Rosario Mexico 27.20N 106.19W
77 C4 Valle de Santa Ana Spain 38.22N 6.47W
115 J7 Valle de Santiago Mexico 20.25N 101.15W
115 G4 Valle de Zaragoza Mexico 27.29N 105.48W
79 H2 Valle di Sotto Italy 46.26N 10.21E
81 G8 Valledolmo Sicily 37.45N 13.50E
76 F2 Valledor,Sierra de mts Spain
119 D2 Valledupar Colombia 10.31N 73.16W
98 B7 Vallée Junction Quebec 46.22N 70.58W
121 C3 Valle Fértil,Sa.de mts Argentina
120 F10 Valle Grande Argentina 23.28S 64.57W
120 F8 Valle Grande Bolivia 18.30S 64.06W
Valle Gran Rey see Calera Mexico
96 O15 Valle Gran Rey Gomera Canary Is 28.07N 17.19W
96 R13 Valle Guerra Tenerife Canary Is 28.30N 16.23W
121 L5 Valle Hermosa Argentina 45.45S 68.30W
121 B4 Valle Hermosa,Paso de Arg/Chile 32.21S 70.16W
96 O14 Vallehermoso Gomera Canary Is 28.12N 17.15W
115 L5 Valle Hermoso Mexico 25.47N 97.49W
71 H4 Valleiry France 46.06N 5.57E
111 B3 Vallejo California 38.05N 122.14W
79 M2 Valle,La Italy 46.17N 12.04E
76 L6 Vallelado Spain 41.24N 4.26W
81 M6 Vallelonga Italy 38.39N 16.17E
81 G8 Vallelunga Pratameno Sicily 37.41N 13.50E
80 J6 Vallemaio Italy 41.22N 13.49E
52 N2 Vallen Västerbotten Sweden 64.28N 21.00E
52 K3 Vallen Västernorrland Sweden 63.47N 16.45E
115 L9 Valle Nacional Mexico 17.47N 96.18W
121 B2 Vallenar Chile 28.36S 70.45W
64 D3 Vallendar W Germany 50.24N 7.37E
53 H6 Vallensved Denmark 55.17N 11.40E
69 H7 Vallentigny France 48.27N 4.33E
80 H5 Vallepietra Italy 41.56N 13.14E
71 D8 Valleraugue France 44.05N 3.38E
81 B5 Vallermosa Sardinia 39.22N 8.48E
66 B1 Vallerois le Bois France 47.33N 6.18E
80 J5 Vallerotonda Italy 41.33N 13.55E
115 K7 Valles, Ciudad de Mexico 22.00N 99.00W
75 P4 Vallés,El reg Spain
121 C9 Valle Superior V Argentina
72 H8 Vallesvilles France 43.35N 1.38E
72 B1 Vallet France 47.10N 1.16W
95 D9 Valletjies S Africa 33.32S 20.28E
84 Z20 Valletta Malta 35.54N 14.32E
57 D6 Valley Gwynedd Wales 53.17N 4.34W
107 F9 Valley Mississippi 32.46N 90.29W
108 O8 Valley Nebraska 41.19N 96.22W
98 J8 Valley Nova Scotia 45.22N 63.10W
110 H1 Valley Washington 48.12N 117.44W
64 M8 Valley W Germany 47.53N 11.47E
110 Q5 Valley Wyoming 44.09N 109.37W
109 N4 Valley Center Kansas 37.51N 97.23W
100 K7 Valley Centre Saskatchewan 51.48N 107.51W

108 N3 Valley City N Dakota 46.57N 97.58W
109 P2 Valley Falls Kansas 39.21N 95.27W
110 E7 Valley Falls Oregon 42.29N 120.16W
99 Q7 Valleyfield Quebec 45.15N 74.08W
103 D6 Valley Forge Pennsylvania 40.06N 75.27W
107 L7 Valley Head Alabama 34.32N 85.38W
19 L3 Valley Head Luzon Philippines 17.54N 122.14E
104 E8 Valley Head W Virginia 38.33N 80.03W
112 K4 Valley Mills Texas 31.40N 97.29W
107 F3 Valley Park Missouri 38.35N 90.30W
110 L8 Valley Pass Nevada 41.09N 114.28W
107 L3 Valley Station Kentucky 38.06N 85.52W
103 M8 Valley Stream Long I, N Y 40.40N 73.42W
101 P8 Valleyview Alberta 55.02N 117.17W
103 A5 Valley View Pennsylvania 40.40N 76.32W
112 K2 Valley View Texas 33.30N 97.11W
12 B7 Valley View *dist* Adelaide, S Aust
75 N4 Vallfogona de Riucorp Spain 41.34N 1.15E
51 J8 Vallgrund Finland 63.11N 21.18E
Vallgrund *isld see* Rappaluoto
50 F3 Vallholt Iceland 65.30N 19.24W
109 P7 Valliant Oklahoma 34.01N 95.06W
75 L6 Vallibona Spain 40.36N 0.02E
79 K3 Valli del Pasúbio Italy 45.44N 11.16E
72 J4 Vallières France 45.54N 2.01E
72 G10 Vallier, Mont *mt* France 42.48N 1.04E
28 C6 Vallikodu Kerala India 9.13N 76.50E
99 P6 Val Limoges Quebec 46.43N 75.53W
71 G1 Vallinot, le Haute-Marne France 47.47N 5.19E
70 M2 Valliquerville France 49.36N 0.41E
53 J6 Valløby Denmark 55.24N 12.15E
81 K3 Vallo della Lucania Italy 40.14N 15.16E
80 G3 Vallo di Nero Italy 42.46N 12.52E
81 K3 Vallo,G.di Italy
71 J6 Valloire France 45.09N 6.28E
79 L7 Vallombrosa Italy 43.44N 11.34E
72 K2 Vallon-en-Sully France 46.32N 2.36E
71 K6 Vallonet,Pointe du *mt* France 45.20N 6.53E
107 K3 Vallonia Indiana 38.50N 86.06W
71 E8 Vallon-Pont-d'Arc France 44.24N 4.24E
70 K6 Vallon-sur-Gée France 47.58N 0.04W
66 B5 Vallorbe Switzerland 46.43N 6.23E
71 K4 Vallorcine France 46.01N 6.56E
71 J7 Vallouise France 44.49N 6.30E
52 E7 Valløy Norway 59.15N 10.29E
75 N5 Valls Spain 41.18N 1.15E
52 J5 Vallsta Sweden 61.30N 16.25E
65 B7 Valluga *mt* Austria 47.10N 10.13E
66 R4 Vallüla *mt* Austria 46.57N 10.07E
52 K5 Vallvik Sweden 61.11N 17.15E
75 J5 Valmadrid Spain 41.26N 0.53W
75 D3 Valmala Spain 42.19N 3.16W
100 K9 Val Marie Saskatchewan 49.15N 107.44W
75 D1 Valmaseda Spain 43.11N 3.11W
77 H4 Valmayor *R* Spain
61 N3 Val-Meer Belgium 50.47N 5.36E
46 F1 Valmiera Latvia U.S.S.R. 57.32N 25.29E
76 L8 Valmojado Spain 40.12N 4.05W
75 N5 Valmoll Spain 41.14N 1.15E
69 C5 Valmondois France 49.06N 2.12E
70 M2 Valmont France 49.44N 0.31E
109 E9 Valmont New Mexico 32.44N 105.59W
80 G5 Valmontone Italy 41.47N 12.55E
79 G5 Valmozzola Italy 44.35N 9.52E
69 H5 Valmy France 49.05N 4.47E
110 H9 Valmy Nevada 40.48N 117.07W
75 C1 Valnera *mt* Spain 43.09N 3.40W
79 F5 Val.Noci,L.di *L* Italy 44.30N 9.03E
52 L6 Valö Sweden 60.18N 18.10E
70 H2 Valognes France 49.31N 1.28W
69 D5 Valois *plain* France
44 D9 Valok Ukraine U.S.S.R. 45.46N 34.57E
Valona *see* Vlorë
76 C7 Valonga Portugal 40.37N 8.27W
76 D10 Valongo Alto Alentejo Portugal 39.10N 7.52W
76 C6 Valongo Douro Litoral Portugal 41.11N 8.30W
77 K6 Válor Spain 37.00N 3.05W
76 K5 Valoria la Buena Spain 41.48N 4.32W
76 E5 Valpaços Portugal 41.36N 7.17W
99 L3 Val-Paradis Quebec 49.10N 79.17W
28 C5 Valparai Tamil Nadu India 10.19N 76.58E
118 E7 Valparaíso Brazil 21.16S 50.54W
121 B4 Valparaíso Chile 33.05S 71.40W
107 K11 Valparaiso Florida 30.30N 86.31W
106 G8 Valparaiso Indiana 41.28N 87.04W
115 H6 Valparaíso Mexico 22.44N 103.32W
108 O8 Valparaiso Nebraska 41.06N 96.50W
100 N6 Valparaiso Saskatchewan 52.51N 104.12W
121 B4 Valparaíso *prov* Chile
79 B3 Valpelline Italy 45.50N 7.20E
66 F8 Valpelline *R* Italy
80 C2 Valpiana Italy 43.00N 10.50E
82 E5 Valpovo Yugoslavia 45.39N 18.25E
98 A8 Val-Racine Quebec 45.30N 71.06W
71 C10 Valras-Plage France 43.16N 3.18E
71 F8 Valréas France 44.22N 4.59E
77 H2 Valronquillo *mt* Spain 39.01N 4.20W
71 C10 Valros France 43.26N 3.22E
66 N5 Vals Switzerland 46.37N 9.12E
95 L3 Vals *R* S Africa
66 E5 Valsainte Switzerland 46.40N 7.13E
84 A5 Valsamáta Greece 38.10N 20.36E
79 B3 Valsavaranche Italy 45.36N 7.13E
95 B10 Valsbaai *B* S Africa
53 H7 Vålse Denmark 54.56N 11.48E
76 L6 Valseca Spain 41.00N 4.10W
96 V15 Valsequillo Gran Canaria Canary Is 27.59N 15.29W
77 F4 Valsequillo Spain 38.24N 5.20W
66 N5 Valserrhein *R* Switzerland
66 N5 Valser Tal *V* Switzerland
110 B5 Valsetz Oregon 44.50N 123.39W
53 D3 Valsgård Denmark 56.41N 9.52E
66 S4 Val Sinestra Switzerland 46.52N 10.21E
81 M3 Valsinni Italy 40.10N 16.26E
52 H2 Valsjöbyn Sweden 64.04N 14.15E
52 J7 Valskog Sweden 59.27N 15.58E
71 E7 Vals-les-Bains France 44.40N 4.23E
71 E5 Valsonne France 45.56N 4.27E
51 J8 Valsörarna *isld* Finland 63.25N 21.05E
95 M4 Valsrivier S Africa 28.09S 28.07E
52 H8 Valstad Sweden 58.08N 13.55E
79 L3 Valstagna Italy 45.52N 11.40E
15 D8 Vals, Tanjung *C* Irian Jaya 8.26S 137.35E
79 K1 Valsura *R* Italy
71 F2 Val Suzon France 47.25N 4.53E
84 F1 Válta Khalkidhikí Greece 40.03N 23.25E
84 E5 Válta Korinthía Greece 38.00N 22.39E
84 C7 Válta Messinía Greece 37.06N 21.37E
75 F6 Valtablado del Rio Spain 40.43N 2.24W
75 F4 Valtajeros Spain 41.56N 2.13W
79 G2 Valtellina *physical reg* Italy
41 P3 Val'tera, Mys *C* U.S.S.R. 75.21N 137.10E
84 D6 Valtesiníkon Greece 37.42N 22.05E
99 C8 Val Tetreau Quebec 45.26N 75.45W
84 D7 Valtétsi Greece 37.28N 22.16E
60 Q8 Valthe Netherlands 52.50N 6.54E
60 Q8 Valthermond Netherlands 52.53N 6.59E
50 L4 Valthjófsstadhur Iceland 65.01N 15.00W
65 P4 Valtice Czechoslovakia 48.45N 16.45E
51 O8 Valtimo Finland 63.39N 28.50E
80 G2 Valtopina Italy 43.03N 12.45E
84 C3 Váltou, Óri *mts* Greece
79 C3 Valtournanche Italy 45.52N 7.37E
72 K5 Valuéjols France 45.03N 2.56E
76 D5 Valugas Portugal 41.31N 7.33W
46 N6 Valuyevka U.S.S.R. 46.43N 43.40E
45 K6 Valuyki U.S.S.R. 50.13N 38.06E
96 P11 Valverde Hierro Canary Is 27.48N 17.55W
81 A2 Valverde Sardinia 40.33N 8.24E
75 D7 Valverde de Alcalá Spain 40.24N 3.18W
77 C4 Valverde de Burguillos Spain 38.19N 6.32W
75 F8 Valverde de Júcar Spain 39.43N 2.13W
76 J8 Valverde de la Vera Spain 40.07N 5.29W
76 H3 Valverde de la Virgen Spain 42.33N 5.41W
77 C5 Valverde del Camino Spain 37.35N 6.45W
77 C3 Valverde de Leganés Spain 38.40N 6.58W
76 F8 Valverde del Fresno Spain 40.14N 6.52W
77 E4 Valverde de Llerena Spain 38.13N 5.49W
76 L7 Valverde del Majano Spain 40.57N 4.14W
75 D5 Valverde de los Arroyos Spain 41.07N 3.14W
77 D3 Valverde de Mérida Spain 38.55N 6.14W
76 J4 Valverde-Enrique Spain 42.18N 5.18W
75 F8 Valverdejo Spain 39.37N 2.02W
51 J5 Valvträsk Sweden 66.08N 21.50E
82 K3 Vama Romania 47.34N 25.42E
15 K6 Vambu I Bismarck Arch 4.39S 149.17E
53 C6 Vamdrup Denmark 55.26N 9.18E
52 H5 Våmhus Sweden 61.07N 14.30E
92 K7 Vamizi, I Mozambique 11.01S 40.40E
52 F7 Vamma Norway 59.33N 11.10E
51 K10 Vammala Finland 61.20N 22.55E
53 D3 Vammen Denmark 56.32N 9.35E
84 K11 Vámos Crete 35.25N 24.11E
62 N8 Vámospércs Hungary 47.30N 21.51E
29 J8 Vamsadhara R Andhra Prad India
84 D8 Vámvaka Greece 36.35N 22.25E
112 M3 Van Texas 32.32N 95.38W
51 L10 Vanajanselkä *L* Finland
112 L2 Van Alstyne Texas 33.26N 96.34W
108 C3 Vananda Montana 46.25N 107.00W
15 J8 Vanapa *R* Papua New Guinea
84 D2 Vánari Greece 39.32N 22.00E
69 H6 Vanault-les-Dames France 48.51N 4.46E
122 F16 Vanavana *isld* Tuamotu Is Pacific Oc 20.43S 139.49W
42 G2 Vanavarva U.S.S.R. 60.25N 102.15E
99 S5 Van Bruyssel Quebec 47.58N 72.10W
107 B6 Van Buren Arkansas 35.28N 94.25W
106 J9 Van Buren Indiana 40.38N 85.31W
104 R6 Van Buren Maine 47.10N 67.59W
107 E5 Van Buren Missouri 36.59N 91.01W
72 E3 Vançais France 46.18N 0.03E
25 K6 Van Canh Vietnam 13.39N 108.58E
61 N8 Vance Belgium 49.40N 5.40E
70 M6 Vancé France 47.50N 0.39E
104 R8 Vanceboro Maine 45.35N 67.27W
105 K2 Vanceboro N Carolina 35.20N 77.08W
104 B8 Vanceburg Kentucky 38.36N 83.21W
43 K7 Vanch Tadzhikistan U.S.S.R. 38.25N 71.25E
25 H2 Van Chan Vietnam 21.36N 104.29E
43 K7 Vanchskiy,Khrebet *mts* Tadzhikistan U.S.S.R.
101 M11 Vancouver Br Col 49.13N 123.06W
110 C4 Vancouver Washington 45.38N 122.40W
113 E6 Vancouver,C Alaska 60.32N 165.28W
14 C10 Vancouver,C W Australia 34.55S 118.11E
101 H11 Vancouver Height Br Col 49.17N 123.00W
101 K10 Vancouver I Br Col
121 J8 Vancouver,I Chile 51.20S 74.10W
101 G11 Vancouver Inter.Airport Br Col 49.11N 123.12W
101 D5 Vancouver,Mt Yukon/Alaska 60.19N 139.44W
Vanda *see* Vantaa
15 D5 Van Dalen *R* Irian Jaya
107 G3 Vandalia Illinois 38.58N 89.05W
107 E2 Vandalia Missouri 39.19N 91.29W
65 A7 Vandans Austria 47.07N 9.52E
53 A3 Vandborg Denmark 56.33N 8.11E
100 Q1 Vandekerckhove L Manitoba
53 C5 Vandel Denmark 55.43N 9.13E
69 K7 Vandeléville France 48.25N 6.00E
75 M5 Vandellós Spain 41.01N 0.49E
26 U6 Vandeloos B Sri Lanka
105 L2 Vandemere N Carolina 35.12N 76.40W
71 D3 Vandenesse Nièvre France 46.55N 3.45E
71 F2 Vandenesse-en-Auxois France 47.13N 4.37E
95 L2 Vanderbijlpark S Africa 26.41S 27.50E
106 K4 Vanderbilt Michigan 45.09N 84.39W
112 L7 Vanderbilt Texas 28.49N 96.38W
104 F6 Vandergrift Pennsylvania 40.36N 79.34W
101 M8 Vanderhoof Br Col 54.00N 124.00W
40 L9 Van-der-Lind,Mys *C* Kuril Is U.S.S.R. 45.30N 149.21E
13 D3 Vanderlin I N Terr Australia
107 B7 Vandervoort Arkansas 34.22N 94.22W
53 B2 Vandet Sø *L* Denmark 57.01N 8.33E
60 M14 Van Deurne Kanaal *canal* Netherlands
13 B1 Van Diemen,C N Terr Australia 11.10S 130.25E
13 E3 Van Diemen,C Queensland 16.31S 139.45E
13 B1 Van Diemen G N Terr Australia
13 F3 Van Diemen R Queensland
120 F7 Vandiola Bolivia 17.03S 65.11W
103 D3 Vandling Pennsylvania 41.38N 75.29W
47 K5 Vandmtor,Oz *L* U.S.S.R.
79 L1 Vandóies Italy 46.49N 11.44E
72 C3 Vandré France 46.03N 0.45W
99 R5 Vandry Quebec 47.52N 73.35W
107 G5 Vanduser Missouri 37.00N 89.41W
110 A9 Van Duzen *R* California
95 N2 Van Dyksdrif S Africa 26.06S 29.19E
52 G8 Vänern *L* Sweden
52 F8 Vänersborg Sweden 58.23N 12.19E
76 L3 Vañes Spain 42.55N 4.30W
32 D4 Vāneshan Iran 33.19N 50.19E
103 A2 Van Etten New York 42.10N 76.33W
60 H8 Van Ewijcksluis Netherlands 52.53N 4.52E
53 P12 Vang Bornholm Denmark 55.16N 14.45E
52 D5 Vang Norway 61.09N 8.20E
79 K1 Vanga Italy 46.34N 11.23E
93 L10 Vanga Kenya 4.40S 39.13E
91 F6 Vanga Zaïre 4.30S 18.26E
95 C7 Vangaindrano Madagascar 23.21S 47.35E
42 E3 Vangash U.S.S.R. 59.58N 93.35E
56 M4 Vange Essex Eng 51.34N 0.28E
37 G7 Van Gölü *L* Turkey 38.33N 42.46E
Vangou *see* Lazo
53 Y16 Vangsmjøsa *L* Norway 61.10N 8.30E
53 V16 Vangsnes Norway 61.10N 6.40E
53 U17 Vangsvatn *L* Hordaland Norway 60.37N 6.20E
53 Z14 Vangsvatn *L* Opland Norway 62.19N 8.32E
100 K9 Vanguard Saskatchewan 49.54N 107.15W
15 K3 Vangunu I Solomon Is 8.40S 158.00E
25 G3 Vang Vieng Laos 18.55N 102.28E
103 F6 Van Hiseville New Jersey 40.07N 74.21W
108 H2 Van Hook N Dakota 47.58N 102.21W
112 C4 Van Horn Texas 31.03N 104.51W
109 F5 Van Houten New Mexico 36.47N 104.34W
44 E5 Vani Georgia U.S.S.R. 42.04N 42.31E
99 D8 Vanier Ontario 45.27N 75.40W
98 P8 Vanier Quebec 46.49N 71.16W
10 O4 Vanikoro Is Santa Cruz Is Pacific Oc 11.42S 166.50E
66 E5 Vanil Noir *mt* Switzerland 46.32N 7.09E
15 F5 Vanimo Papua New Guinea 2.40S 141.17E
40 H7 Vanino U.S.S.R. 49.05N 140.14E
Vanishan *see* Vāneshan
28 C4 Vanivilasa Sagara *L* Karnataka India
28 D4 Vaniyambadi Tamil Nadu India 12.43N 78.37E
52 L2 Vänjaurbäck Sweden 64.22N 18.35E
26 Q4 Vankala Sri Lanka 8.52N 79.56E
39 L1 Vankarem U.S.S.R. 67.50N 175.51W
39 L2 Vankarem *R* U.S.S.R.
39 L1 Vankarem Laguna U.S.S.R.
41 P5 Van'kina,Guba *gulf* U.S.S.R.
99 Q7 Vankleek Hill Ontario 45.31N 74.40W
69 G7 Vanlay France 48.02N 4.01E
108 K5 Van Metre S Dakota 44.10N 100.49W
50 T15 Van Mijenfjorden *inlet* Spitsbergen
51 H1 Vanna *isld* Norway 70.10N 19.40E
52 M3 Vännäs Sweden 63.56N 19.50E
26 Q5 Vannativillu Sri Lanka 8.10N 79.52E
69 F7 Vanne *R* France
70 E6 Vannes France 47.40N 2.44W
70 P6 Vannes-sur-Cosson France 47.43N 2.13E
25 K6 Van Ninh Vietnam 12.37N 109.13E
52 G9 Vannum Sweden 57.50N 13.10E
79 L2 Vanoi *R* Italy
71 K6 Vanoise,Col de la *pass* France 45.23N 6.48E
109 O7 Vanoss Oklahoma 34.46N 96.52W
95 N4 Van Reenen S Africa 28.22S 29.23E
15 D5 Van Rees, Pegunungan *mts* Irian Jaya
94 E8 Vanrhynsdorp S Africa 31.36S 18.45E
13 F3 Vanrook Queensland 16.59S 141.54E
13 F3 Vanrook *R* Queensland
95 O4 Van Rooyen S Africa 28.07S 30.22E
95 H8 Van Ryneveldspasdam *res* S Africa 32.12S 24.31E
75 N3 Vansa *R* Spain
104 C9 Vansant Virginia 37.15N 82.06W
52 H6 Vansbro Sweden 60.32N 14.15E
100 L6 Vanscoy Saskatchewan 52.01N 106.59W
14 F2 Vansittart B W Australia
97 L4 Vansittart I N W Terr 66.00N 84.00W
71 E8 Vans,les France 44.25N 4.08E
95 L5 Van Stadensrus S Africa 29.59S 27.01E
60 O7 Van Starkenborgh Kanaal *canal* Netherlands
51 L11 Vantaa Finland 60.18N 24.57E
51 L11 Vantaa *R* Finland
100 L9 Vantage Saskatchewan 49.52N 106.01W
110 F3 Vantage Washington 46.57N 120.00W
108 F7 Van Tassell Nebraska 42.40N 104.02W
9 C10 Vanua Lava *isld* New Hebrides
9 S1 Vanua Levu *isld* Fiji
9 S2 Vanua Levu Barrier Reef Fiji
9 U2 Vanua Mbalavu *isld* Fiji 17.15S 178.55W
47 K3 Vanuyto U.S.S.R. 66.30N 69.30E
68 E4 Vanves France 48.50N 2.17E
69 H8 Vanvey France 47.50N 4.43E
53 U19 Vanvik Norway 59.33N 6.23E
108 R9 Van Wert Iowa 40.51N 93.48W
104 A6 Van Wert Ohio 40.53N 84.36W
95 E9 Vanwyksdorp S Africa 33.45S 21.28E
94 S14 Van Wyksrust S Africa 26.20S 27.55E
94 F8 Van Wyks Vlei S Africa 30.22S 21.50E
25 H2 Van Yen Vietnam 21.03N 104.41E
53 T14 Vanylven Norway 62.05N 5.33E
53 S14 Vanylvsfjord *inlet* Norway 62.07N 5.13E
53 S14 Vanylvsgapet *B* Norway 62.12N 5.20E
107 D5 Vanzant Missouri 36.57N 92.18W
47 K4 Vanzevat U.S.S.R. 64.15N 66.00E
42 C2 Vanzhil'kynak U.S.S.R. 60.29N 84.02E
26 B13 Van Zinderen Baaker Pk *hill* Prince Edward I Indian Oc 46.38S 37.56E
26 B13 Van Zinderen Bakker Pk Prince Edward I Ind Oc 46.38S 37.56E
79 D3 Vanzone Italy 45.59N 8.07E
9 C14 Vao New Caledonia 22.39S 167.30E
72 H7 Vaour France 44.05N 1.47E
65 N2 Vápenný Podol Czechoslovakia 49.54N 15.40E
46 G5 Vapnyarka Ukraine U.S.S.R. 48.31N 28.44E
79 G3 Vaprio d'Adda Italy 45.35N 9.32E
76 D14 Vaqueiros Portugal 37.22N 7.44W
67 K9 Var *dept* France
71 L9 Var *R* France
52 G8 Vara Sweden 58.16N 12.55E
79 G6 Vara *R* Italy
28 B3 Varada R Karnataka India
77 M2 Vara de Rey Spain 39.26N 2.17W
116 D3 Varadero Cuba 23.10N 81.16W
70 H7 Varades France 47.24N 1.02W
71 H9 Varages France 43.36N 5.58E
29 B6 Varahi Gujarat India 23.48N 71.29E
72 H7 Varaire France 44.22N 1.42E
79 B5 Varaita *R* Italy
72 D4 Varaize France 45.55N 0.24W
32 J6 Varaj Iran 28.34N 60.57E
53 T18 Varaldsøy Norway 60.06N 5.59E
53 T18 Varaldsøy *isld* Norway 60.07N 6.00E
79 E3 Varallo Pombia Italy 45.41N 8.37E
79 D3 Varallo Sésia Italy 45.49N 8.15E
Varamerik *see* Yayla
32 D3 Varāmīn Iran 35.19N 51.40E
30 G7 Varanasi Uttar Prad India 25.20N 83.00E
30 F7 Varanasi *dist* Uttar Prad India
47 H2 Varandey U.S.S.R. 68.49N 58.00E
51 O1 Varanger fjorden *inlet* Norway
51 O1 Varangerhalvøya *pen* Norway 70.22N 29.40E
69 L6 Varangéville France 48.39N 6.18E
66 L8 Varano Italy 45.46N 8.42E
79 H5 Varano de Melegari Italy 44.41N 10.02E
80 N5 Varano,Lago di Italy
96 V1 Vara,Pico da *mt* Azores 37.33N 25.13W
77 G4 Varas *R* Spain
32 E7 Varāvī Iran 27.26N 53.07E
70 K3 Varaville France 49.15N 0.10W
36 H2 Varay Turkey 40.28N 35.38E
82 C4 Varaždin Yugoslavia 46.18N 16.21E
79 E6 Varazze Italy 44.22N 8.34E
52 G9 Varberg Sweden 57.06N 12.15E
32 C4 Varcheh Iran 33.45N 49.54E
Varchin *see* Varcheh
107 G8 Vardaman Mississippi 33.53N 89.11W
28 D2 Vardannapet Andhra Prad India 17.47N 79.34E
82 G9 Vardar *R* Yugoslavia
53 A5 Varde Denmark 55.38N 8.30E
53 B5 Varde Å *R* Denmark
37 J5 Vardenik Armenia U.S.S.R. 40.08N 45.26E
44 G7 Vardenis Armenia U.S.S.R. 40.11N 45.43E
84 C4 Vardhoúsia Óri *mts* Greece
44 G7 Vardinek Armenia U.S.S.R. 40.10N 45.30E
51 H11 Vårdö Finland 60.16N 20.20E
51 P1 Vardø Norway 70.22N 31.06E
46 L1 Varegovo U.S.S.R. 57.42N 39.25E
63 H6 Varel W Germany 53.24N 8.08E
25 K6 Varella, Mui *C* Vietnam 12.53N 109.28E
66 G6 Varen Switzerland 46.19N 7.37E
46 E3 Varėna Lithuania U.S.S.R. 54.10N 24.40E
61 K2 Varendonk Belgium 51.05N 4.57E
70 M2 Varengeville France 49.54N 0.58E
70 G3 Varenguebec France 49.20N 1.31W
44 B2 Varenikovskaya U.S.S.R. 45.07N 37.39E
44 F3 Varenikovskiy U.S.S.R. 44.29N 44.23E
79 F2 Varenna Italy 46.01N 9.17E
70 J4 Varenne *R* France
68 H4 Varenne-St.Hilaire,la France 48.47N 2.30E
69 J5 Varennes-en-Argonne France 49.13N 5.03E
69 D8 Varennes-en-Gâtinais Loiret France 47.53N 2.39E
71 F3 Varennes-le-Grand France 46.42N 4.53E
71 G4 Varennes-St.Sauveur France 46.29N 5.15E
72 L3 Varennes-sur-Allier France 46.19N 3.24E
69 K8 Varennes-sur-Amance France 47.54N 5.38E
72 H1 Varennes-sur-Fouzon France 47.12N 1.36E
82 E6 Vareš Yugoslavia 44.10N 18.20E
79 E3 Varese Italy 45.49N 8.49E
79 E3 Varese *prov* Italy
79 E3 Varese, L. di *L* Italy
79 G6 Varese Ligure Italy 44.22N 9.36E
72 G5 Varetz France 45.12N 1.26E
71 F6 Vareze *R* France
40 F9 Varfolomeyevka Primor'ye U.S.S.R. 44.19N 133.27E
45 U6 Varfolomeyevka Saratov U.S.S.R. 50.02N 48.11E
52 G8 Vårgårda Sweden 58.05N 12.47E
121 B5 Vargas Argentina 34.43S 69.22W
119 C9 Vargas Guerra Peru 2.58S 77.42W
47 K7 Vargashi U.S.S.R. 55.19N 65.51E
53 X17 Vargebre *mt* Norway 60.41N 7.30E
117 F6 Vargem Grande Brazil 3.35S 43.57W
117 G9 Vargem,R Brazil
118 F7 Varginha Brazil 21.33S 45.25W
84 G6 Vári Greece 37.50N 23.48E
60 K12 Varik Netherlands 51.49N 5.22E
72 H9 Varilhes France 43.02N 1.37E
120 D11 Varillas Chile 24.00S 70.10W
105 J2 Varina N Carolina 35.36N 78.49W
52 H8 Våring Sweden 58.30N 13.58E
37 G7 Varis Burun *C* Turkey 38.23N 42.53E
76 F6 Variz Portugal 41.21N 6.36W
70 O5 Varize France 48.06N 1.30E
51 G5 Varjisträsk Sweden 66.02N 19.30E
41 D7 Varka-Syl'-Ky *R* U.S.S.R.
51 N9 Varkaus Finland 62.20N 27.50E
39 F4 Varkhalam U.S.S.R. 61.48N 159.30E
39 F4 Varkhalamskiy, Mys *C* U.S.S.R. 61.38N 159.30E
84 A3 Varlaám Greece 39.25N 20.54E
47 J8 Varlamovo U.S.S.R. 54.40N 60.35E
14 C10 Varley,L W Australia 32.42S 119.21E
50 F3 Varmahlidh Iceland 65.33N 19.29W
52 G7 Värmland *dist* Sweden
79 N3 Varmo Italy 45.53N 12.59E
82 L7 Varna Bulgaria 43.12N 27.57E
79 L1 Varna Italy 46.45N 11.38E
103 B2 Varna New York 42.27N 76.27W
43 F1 Varna U.S.S.R. 53.25N 60.51E
107 G11 Varnado Louisiana 30.52N 89.50W
53 D6 Varnæs Denmark 55.01N 9.35E
52 H9 Värnamo Sweden 57.11N 14.03E
28 A2 Varna R Maharashtra India
52 G6 Värnäs Sweden 60.26N 13.15E
46 O2 Varnavino U.S.S.R. 57.28N 45.02E
47 J2 Varnek U.S.S.R. 69.45N 60.01E
109 E7 Varney New Mexico 34.19N 105.33W
62 H5 Varnsdorf Czechoslovakia 50.57N 14.35E
105 F5 Varnville S Carolina 32.50N 81.04W
47 L3 Varnya U.S.S.R. 66.45N 71.30E
84 S14 Varosha Cyprus 35.06N 33.58E
62 K8 Városlőd Hungary 47.10N 17.40E
84 D8 Varoúsia Greece 36.56N 22.11E
72 E4 Vars Charente France 45.46N 0.08E
71 K7 Vars Hautes-Alpes France 44.37N 6.41E
31 F2 Varsaj Afghanistan 36.12N 70.02E
71 K7 Vars,Col du *pass* France 44.33N 6.43E
61 C2 Varsenare Belgium 51.12N 3.09E
47 F3 Varsh,Ozero *L* U.S.S.R. 66.08N 47.58E
79 G5 Varsi Italy 44.39N 9.50E
84 D7 Vársova Greece 37.06N 22.22E
60 O12 Varsseveld Netherlands 51.56N 6.28E
53 E3 Vårst Denmark 56.52N 10.04E
44 H6 Vartashen Azerbaydzhan U.S.S.R. 41.05N 47.25E
53 U14 Vartdal,Nordre Norway 62.19N 6.10E
53 U14 Vartdalsfjord *inlet* Norway 62.18N 6.02E
53 U14 Vartdal,Sør Norway 62.18N 6.05E
84 B6 Vartholomíon Greece 37.52N 21.12E
37 F6 Varto Turkey 39.10N 41.28E
52 H8 Vartofta Sweden 58.06N 13.40E
59 K5 Vartry Res Wicklow Irish Rep 53.04N 6.12W
28 C6 Varttirayiruppu Tamil Nadu India 9.38N 77.37E
30 F7 Varuna *R* Uttar Prad India
66 Q6 Varuna,Piz di *mt* Italy/Switz 46.22N 9.59E
45 D6 Varva Ukraine U.S.S.R. 50.30N 32.45E
83 E7 Varvára *mt* Greece 37.11N 21.41E
82 G7 Varvarin Yugoslavia 43.43N 21.20E
45 C9 Varvarovka Nikolayev, Ukraine U.S.S.R. 47.00N 31.55E
45 G7 Varvarovka Poltava, Ukraine U.S.S.R. 49.33N 35.13E
84 B6 Varvásaina Greece 37.40N 21.30E
42 B2 Var'yegan U.S.S.R. 62.00N 76.46E
32 E4 Varzaneh Iran 32.26N 52.43E
32 B1 Varzaqān Iran 38.33N 46.40E
34 P5 Varzarīn,Kūh-e- *mt* Iran 33.12N 47.07E
121 H1 Varzea *R* Rio Grande do Sul Brazil
117 G8 Várzea Alegre Brazil 6.51S 39.18W
118 G5 Várzea da Palma Brazil 17.30S 44.45W
117 F8 Várzea Grande Brazil 6.32S 42.05W
118 E9 Varzea, R Paraná Brazil
118 G3 Várzeas Brazil 12.22S 44.38W
79 F5 Varzi Italy 44.49N 9.12E
47 D2 Varzino U.S.S.R. 68.20N 38.30E
79 D2 Varzo Italy 46.13N 8.15E
43 J7 Varzob Tadzhikistan U.S.S.R. 38.49N 68.54E
43 J7 Varzobskaya G.E.S *H E Station* Tadzhikistan U.S.S.R. 38.43N 68.50E
47 D3 Varzuga U.S.S.R. 66.25N 36.39E
47 D3 Varzuga *R* U.S.S.R.
71 C2 Varzy France 47.21N 3.23E
43 N7 Varzyk Uzbekistan U.S.S.R. 41.09N 71.29E
82 D3 Vas *co* Hungary
Vasa *see* Vaasa
118 J2 Vasa Barris,R Brazil
46 E1 Vasalemma Estonia U.S.S.R. 59.15N 24.18E
84 E7 Vasarás Greece 37.10N 22.30E
62 N7 Vásárosnémény Hungary 48.10N 22.18E
53 K4 Väsby Sweden 56.13N 12.37E
76 D14 Vascão *R* Portugal
82 H4 Vaşcau Romania 46.28N 22.30E
70 N3 Vascœuil France 49.27N 1.23E
121 H3 Vasconcelos Brazil 30.37S 51.32W
75 E2 Vascongadas *hist reg* Spain
74 F2 Vascongadas *reg* Spain
47 F4 Vashka *R* U.S.S.R.
82 J2 Vashkovtsy U.S.S.R. 48.24N 25.30E
47 K4 Vashnel U.S.S.R. 64.40N 67.19E
110 C2 Vashon I Washington 47.25N 122.30W
Vasht *see* Khāsh
108 L2 Vashti N Dakota 47.13N 99.06W
112 J2 Vashti Texas 33.34N 98.03W
84 C6 Vasiláki Greece 37.39N 21.45E
46 G4 Vasilevichi Belorussiya U.S.S.R. 52.19N 29.48E
84 D3 Vasilí Greece 39.20N 22.23E
50 T16 Vasilievbreen *glacier* Spitsbergen 76.50N 17.00E
84 A4 Vasilikí Levkás Greece 38.38N 20.37E
84 C2 Vasilikí Tríkkala Greece 39.38N 21.43E
84 C5 Vasilikón Akhaïa Greece 38.07N 21.44E
84 G5 Vasilikón Évvoia Greece 38.25N 23.40E
84 C7 Vasilikón Messinía Greece 37.16N 21.53E
84 R15 Vasilikos Cyprus 34.42N 33.20E
46 H4 Vasil'kov Ukraine U.S.S.R. 50.12N 30.15E
45 H8 Vasil'kovka Ukraine U.S.S.R. 48.13N 36.02E
84 B4 Vasilópoulon Greece 38.35N 21.04E
45 S1 Vasil'sursk U.S.S.R. 56.07N 46.00E
43 P3 Vasil'yevka Kazakhstan U.S.S.R. 49.48N 82.32E
45 G9 Vasil'yevka Ukraine U.S.S.R. 47.26N 35.16E
45 N6 Vasil'yevka U.S.S.R. 50.56N 41.00E
40 N6 Vasil'yevo Kuril Is U.S.S.R. 50.02N 155.16E
45 U1 Vasil'yevo U.S.S.R. 55.50N 48.45E
47 F4 Vasil'yevo U.S.S.R. 63.00N 45.40E
47 M2 Vasil'yevskiy Ostrov *isld* Leningrad U.S.S.R.
47 L7 Vasiss U.S.S.R. 57.20N 74.45E
122 U10 Vaskess B Christmas I Pacific Oc 1.50N 157.30W
47 L4 Vask'ino U.S.S.R. 56.46N 58.50E
46 G1 Vasknarva Estonia U.S.S.R. 59.00N 27.42E
51 M3 Vaskojoki *R* Finland
37 D7 Vaskovan Turkey 38.57N 38.58E
45 D2 Vas'kovo U.S.S.R. 54.18N 32.34E
62 L9 Vaskút Hungary 46.07N 19.00E
72 D2 Vasles France 46.35N 0.02W
82 L4 Vaslui Romania 46.37N 27.46E
105 H2 Vass N Carolina 35.14N 79.14W
29 A3 Vassant Vihar Delhi India 28.33N 77.10E
100 F1 Vassar Manitoba 49.08N 95.50W
106 L6 Vassar Michigan 43.23N 83.33W
53 W19 Vassdalsegga *mt* Norway 59.46N 7.09E
60 Q10 Vasse Netherlands 52.26N 6.50E
66 O8 Vassena Italy 45.56N 9.18E
53 U15 Vassenden Norway 61.45N 6.20E
53 U16 Vassenden Norway 61.29N 6.06E
53 S15 Vasset Norway 61.34N 5.29E
53 T15 Vassetvatn *L* Norway 61.33N 5.30E
53 W17 Vassfjøra *mt* Norway 60.37N 7.01E
51 G3 Vassijaure Sweden 68.25N 18.16E
72 H4 Vassivière,Barrage de France 45.49N 1.54E
53 Y18 Vasstulan Norway 60.21N 8.29E
53 W15 Vassvendegga *mts* Norway 62.00N 7.25E
70 J4 Vassy Calvados France 48.51N 0.40W
71 E1 Vassy Yonne France 47.34N 4.10E
46 O6 Vasta U.S.S.R. 47.12N 47.30E
Vastan *see* Gevaş
51 F4 Vastenjaure *L* Sweden 67.30N 16.35E
52 J7 Västerås Sweden 59.36N 16.32E
52 J2 Västerbotten *dist* Sweden
52 G6 Västerdalälven *R* Sweden
51 F5 Västerfjäll Sweden 66.44N 17.25E
52 L7 Västerhaminge Sweden 59.07N 18.06E
52 J7 Västermo Sweden 59.06N 16.05E
52 K2 Västermyrriset Sweden 64.24N 18.00E
52 K3 Västernorrland *dist* Sweden
52 K9 Västervik Sweden 57.45N 16.40E
53 K5 Väst Klagstorp Sweden 55.31N 13.00E
52 K6 Västland Sweden 60.28N 17.35E
52 J7 Västmanland *dist* Sweden
80 L4 Vasto Italy 42.07N 14.43E
80 K5 Vastogirardi Italy 41.47N 14.15E
63 N6 Vastorf W Germany 53.12N 10.33E
52 G7 Västra Amtervik Sweden 59.44N 13.06E
52 K9 Västra Ed Sweden 58.00N 16.30E
52 M3 Västra Kvarken *channel* Sweden
52 J9 Västra Ryd Sweden 57.47N 15.10E
52 H10 Västra Torsås Sweden 56.39N 14.30E
52 J7 Västra Vingåker Sweden 59.07N 16.05E
52 G7 Väst Silen *L* Sweden
42 B3 Vasyugan *R* U.S.S.R.
65 P7 Vat Hungary 47.16N 16.47E
42 B2 Vata U.S.S.R. 61.08N 75.48E
72 H1 Vatan France 47.05N 1.48E
Vaté *isld see* Efate
53 V15 Våtedalen *V* Norway 61.39N 6.31E
58 C3 Vaternish Pt Skye, Highland Scotland 57.37N 6.39W
58 A5 Vatersay *isld* W Isles Scotland 56.56N 7.32W
9 C9 Vatganai *islet* New Hebrides 13.20S 167.20E
28 B2 Vathar Maharashtra India 17.56N 74.14E
63 P8 Väthen E Germany 52.26N 11.47E
84 A4 Vathí Meganísi I Greece 38.40N 20.46E
83 H7 Vathí Sámos Greece 37.44N 26.59E
84 G5 Vathí Voiotía Greece 38.24N 23.36E
83 E8 Váthia Greece 36.29N 22.29E
9 S7 Vatia Pt Viti Levu Fiji 17.24S 177.50E
81 L6 Vaticano, C Italy 38.37N 15.50E
80 F5 Vaticano,Citta del Italy 41.54N 12.27E
15 L3 Vatilau I Solomon Is 8.53S 160.02E
84 S14 Vatili Cyprus 35.07N 33.40E
92 H9 Vatiua Mozambique 14.15S 37.22E
50 F7 Vatnafjöll *mt* Iceland 63.56N 19.38W
50 H6 Vatnajökull *ice cap* Iceland 64.30N 17.00W
53 W20 Vatndalsvatn *L* Aust Agder Norway 59.28N 7.15E
53 U14 Vatne Norway 62.08N 6.16E
53 V13 Vatne Norway 62.33N 6.38E
53 V14 Vatnedalsvatn *L* Möre og Romsdal Norway 62.00N 6.54E
53 V13 Vatnefjord *inlet* Norway 62.37N 6.37E
50 B3 Vatneyri Iceland 65.36N 23.59W
50 E4 Vatnsdalsá *R* Iceland
50 E4 Vatnsdalsfjall *mt* Iceland 65.28N 20.15W
50 J5 Vatnsfell *mt* Iceland 64.59N 16.47W
50 C3 Vatnsfjördhur Iceland 65.57N 22.28W
50 B3 Vatnsfjördhur *B* Iceland
50 E3 Vatnsnes *pen* Iceland
39 J4 Vatnya U.S.S.R. 61.17N 172.23E
52 L7 Vätö Sweden 59.48N 18.55E
9 U3 Vatoa *isld* Fiji 19.50S 178.15W
95 D5 Vatomandry Madagascar 19.20S 48.58E
82 J3 Vatra Dornei Romania 47.20N 25.21E
69 G6 Vatry France 48.49N 4.15E
53 T20 Vats Norway 59.29N 5.45E
53 T19 Vatsvatn *L* Norway 59.31N 5.44E
50 C3 Vattarfjördhur *B* Iceland
50 C3 Vattarnes Iceland 65.38N 22.41W
50 M5 Vattarnes *C* Iceland 64.57N 13.43W
52 H8 Vättern *L* Sweden
66 O4 Vättis Switzerland 46.55N 9.27E
52 K5 Vattrång Sweden 61.54N 17.15E
9 T7 Vatu-I-Ra Channel Fiji
9 T7 Vatu-i-Thake *islet* Fiji 17.19S 178.46E
9 S7 Vatukoula Viti Levu Fiji 17.30S 177.53E
9 S9 Vatulele *isld* Fiji 18.30S 177.38E
45 C7 Vatutino Ukraine U.S.S.R. 49.01N 31.01E
9 U6 Vatu Vara *isld* Fiji 17.25S 179.34W
42 B2 Vat' Yegan *R* U.S.S.R.
42 C1 Vatyl'ka *R* U.S.S.R.
69 J6 Vaubécourt France 48.56N 5.07E
61 J6 Vaucelles Belgium 50.07N 4.45E
69 F6 Vauchamps France 48.53N 3.38E
69 F7 Vauchassis France 48.14N 3.55E
71 D2 Vauclaix France 47.14N 3.50E
105 F4 Vaucluse S Carolina 33.39N 81.51W
67 J8 Vaucluse *dept* France
12 M7 Vaucluse *dist* Sydney, N S W
71 G9 Vaucluse,Mts.de France
71 H1 Vauconcourt-Nervezain France 47.39N 5.49E
70 L2 Vaucottes France 49.44N 0.17E
69 K6 Vaucouleurs France 48.36N 5.40E
69 M6 Vaucourt France 48.40N 6.41E
68 C3 Vaucresson France 48.50N 2.09E
66 B5 Vaud *canton* Switzerland
69 L7 Vaudémont France 48.24N 6.02E
66 D5 Vauderens Switzerland 46.38N 6.52E
69 F7 Vaudeurs France 48.08N 3.34E
72 H4 Vaud-Gelade,Barrage de la France 45.50N 1.56E
69 E6 Vaudoy-en-Brie France 48.41N 3.06E
70 N3 Vaudreuil, le France 49.15N 1.13E
71 K2 Vaufrey France 47.21N 6.54E
13 B5 Vaughan Springs N Terr Australia 22.15S 130.50E
110 O2 Vaughn Montana 47.35N 111.34W
109 E7 Vaughn New Mexico 34.35N 105.14W
68 E3 Vaugirard Paris France 48.50N 2.18E
71 F5 Vaugneray France 45.44N 4.39E
68 H2 Vaujours France 48.56N 2.34E
66 B5 Vaulion Switzerland 46.42N 6.24E
66 D5 Vaulruz Switzerland 46.38N 7.00E
71 D1 Vault-de-Lugny France 47.31N 3.51E
61 D4 Vaulx Belgium 50.35N 3.26E
61 H6 Vaulx Belgium 50.03N 4.22E
71 D4 Vaumas France 46.26N 3.37E
119 D7 Vaupés *div* Colombia
119 E7 Vaupés,R Colombia
71 H9 Vauvenargues France 43.33N 5.35E
71 E9 Vauvert France 43.41N 4.16E
70 G2 Vauville France 49.38N 1.50W
69 L8 Vauvillers France 47.55N 6.06E
72 K1 Vauvise *R* France
66 B4 Vaux France 46.48N 6.15E
69 J5 Vaux France 49.13N 5.30E
61 N5 Vaux-Chavanne Belgium 50.18N 5.42E
71 D2 Vaux, Etang de *L* France 47.11N 3.35E
61 L4 Vaux-et Borset Belgium 50.37N 5.14E
100 E8 Vauxhall Alberta 50.05N 112.09W
61 N7 Vaux-lez-Rosières Belgium 49.55N 5.34E
61 N4 Vaux-sous-Chèvremont Belgium 50.36N 5.38E
71 G1 Vaux-sur-Aubigny France 47.40N 5.18E
61 N7 Vaux-sur-Sûre Belgium 49.55N 5.34E
29 B5 Vav Gujarat India 24.22N 71.32E
95 D4 Vavatenina Madagascar 17.25S 49.11E
53 Y17 Vavatn *L* Norway 60.58N 8.25E
9 R13 Vava'u Group *islds* Tonga, Pacific Oc
39 E1 Vavilon, Ozero *L* U.S.S.R. 68.30N 151.16E
69 J6 Vavincourt France 48.49N 5.12E
89 F8 Vavoua Ivory Coast 7.22N 6.36W
46 Q2 Vavozh U.S.S.R. 56.48N 52.00E
26 R4 Vavuniya Sri Lanka 8.45N 80.30E
100 J5 Vawn Saskatchewan 53.08N 108.39W
52 L7 Vaxholm Sweden 59.25N 18.21E
52 H10 Växjö Sweden 56.52N 14.50E
70 G6 Vay France 47.34N 1.42W
28 D4 Vayalpad Andhra Prad India 13.38N 78.37E
39 J3 Vayegi U.S.S.R. 63.56N 170.46E
47 H1 Vaygach U.S.S.R. 70.28N 58.59E
47 J1 Vaygach, Ostrov *isld* U.S.S.R.
84 F5 Váyia Greece 38.18N 23.10E
28 C5 Vayittiri Kerala India 11.31N 76.02E
47 E4 Vaymuga *R* U.S.S.R.
72 H6 Vayrac France 44.57N 1.42E
72 F4 Vayrs France 45.46N 0.50E
42 E2 Vayvida U.S.S.R. 60.53N 94.15E
118 F5 Vazante Brazil 17.53S 46.56W
72 G7 Vazerac France 44.12N 1.19E
47 F4 Vazhgort U.S.S.R. 63.55N 47.15E
37 D6 Vazıldan Turkey 39.10N 38.01E
95 C5 Vazobe *mt* Madagascar 18.24S 47.17E
82 J8 Vazovgrad Bulgaria 42.39N 24.43E
121 E7 Vázquez Argentina 38.11S 60.10W
79 M3 Vazzola Italy 45.51N 12.23E
115 J4 V. Carranza, Presa *res* Mexico
42 C4 Vdovino U.S.S.R. 56.04N 82.08E
118 F4 Veadeiros Brazil 14.05S 47.26W
25 G7 Veal Renh Cambodia 10.42N 103.48E
71 E5 Veauche France 45.34N 4.17E
72 K1 Veaugues France 47.15N 2.44E
53 D3 Vebbestrup Denmark 56.44N 9.50E
108 N4 Veblen S Dakota 45.53N 97.18W
53 X13 Veblungsnes Norway 62.33N 7.41E
52 N2 Vebomark Sweden 64.24N 21.00E
71 D8 Vébron France 44.15N 3.34E
79 H7 Vecchiano Italy 43.47N 10.23E
63 M8 Vechelde W Germany 52.17N 10.22E
60 O9 Vecht *R* Neth/W Germany
63 H7 Vechta W Germany 52.44N 8.17E
63 H7 Vechta *R* W Germany
63 F8 Vechte *R* W Germany
76 J3 Vecilla,La Spain 42.50N 5.24W
76 H7 Vecinos Spain 40.47N 5.52W
63 L10 Veckerhagen W Germany 51.29N 9.35E
52 K7 Veckholm Sweden 59.32N 17.21E
69 M8 Vecoux France 47.58N 6.39E
76 B8 Veda, L. da Portugal 40.16N 8.49W
28 D5 Vedaranniyam Tamil Nadu India 10.20N 79.50E
28 C5 Vedasandur Tamil Nadu India 10.33N 77.58E
66 M7 Vedasca, Val Italy/Switz
53 S20 Vedavågen Norway 59.18N 5.13E
53 K5 Vedbæk Denmark 55.52N 12.35E
53 H5 Vedde Denmark 55.32N 11.33E
52 G9 Veddige Sweden 57.17N 12.20E
53 E3 Veddum Denmark 56.47N 10.12E
82 J6 Vedea Romania 44.45N 24.39E
79 M3 Vedelago Italy 45.41N 12.02E
44 G5 Vedeno U.S.S.R. 42.58N 46.06E
53 A4 Vedersø Denmark 56.14N 8.11E
52 J7 Vedevåg Sweden 59.32N 15.15E
44 F8 Vedi Armenia U.S.S.R. 39.55N 44.44E
121 E5 Vedia Argentina 34.30S 61.31W
76 C3 Vedra Spain 42.46N 8.28W
77 S12 Vedrá *isld* Balearic Is 38.52N 1.12E
72 L5 Vedrines St. Loup France 45.05N 3.16E
53 E5 Vedslet Denmark 55.58N 10.01E
53 C6 Vedsted Sønderjylland Denmark 55.12N 9.22E
52 G8 Vedum Sweden 58.11N 13.00E
106 G9 Veedersburg Indiana 40.06N 87.15W
60 R7 Veelerveen Netherlands 53.04N 7.08E
60 Q7 Veendam Netherlands 53.07N 6.53E
60 L11 Veenendaal Netherlands 52.03N 5.33E
60 O7 Veenhuizen Netherlands 53.02N 6.24E
60 M7 Veenwouden Netherlands 53.14N 5.59E
60 B2 Veere Netherlands 51.33N 3.40E
61 K2 Veerle Belgium 51.04N 4.59E
60 B2 Veerse Meer *L* Netherlands
63 N7 Veerssen W Germany 52.57N 10.33E
53 C5 Veerst Denmark 55.34N 9.15E
53 E6 Veflinge Denmark 55.29N 10.11E
Vefsn *see* Halsöy
51 C6 Vefsna *R* Norway
103 E2 Vega New York 42.16N 74.32W
112 B8 Vega Texas 35.14N 102.26W
51 B6 Vega *isld* Norway 65.38N 11.52E
105 J7 Vega Baja Puerto Rico 18.27N 66.23W
76 H3 Vegacervera Spain 42.53N 5.34W
115 L7 Vega de Alatorre Mexico 20.02N 96.40W
76 K3 Vega de Almanza,La Spain 42.44N 5.00W
76 K2 Vega de Liébana,La Spain 43.06N 4.39W
76 G3 Vega de Los Viejos,La Spain 42.58N 6.13W
76 H2 Vega del Rey Spain 43.07N 5.49W
76 E2 Vegadeo Spain 43.27N 7.04W
75 C1 Vega de Pas Spain 43.10N 3.46W
76 G5 Vega de Tera Spain 42.00N 6.08W
76 F3 Vega de Valcarce Spain 42.40N 6.57W
76 E4 Vega,La Spain 42.15N 7.01W
77 J6 Vega,La *reg* Spain
76 J3 Vegamian Spain 42.56N 5.17W
41 H2 Vega,Mys *C* U.S.S.R. 77.10N 103.00E
75 C5 Veganzones Spain 41.12N 4.00W
76 L4 Vegapagar *mt* Spain 42.08N 4.19W
113 N10 Vega Pt Aleutian Is 51.50N 177.19E
76 J3 Vegaquemada Spain 42.49N 5.20W
76 G3 Vegarienza Spain 42.48N 6.03W
52 D8 Vegårs Vatn *L* Norway 58.50N 8.50E
76 J3 Vegas *mt* Spain 42.41N 5.21W
76 J3 Vegas del Condado Spain 42.41N 5.22W
76 L7 Vegas de Matute Spain 40.47N 4.16W
53 K4 Vegeån *R* Sweden
63 J6 Vegesack Bremen W Germany 53.11N 8.37E
53 D3 Veggerby Denmark 56.54N 9.39E
52 E6 Veggli Norway 60.02N 9.11E
60 L13 Veghel Netherlands 51.37N 5.33E
81 Q12 Veglie Italy 40.20N 17.58E
67 O12 Vegno, Capo di *mt* Corsica 42.26N 8.47E
83 E4 Vegorrítis,L Greece
100 E5 Vegreville Alberta 53.30N 112.02W
53 U14 Vegsund Norway 62.26N 6.23E
120 B4 Végueta Peru 11.04S 77.37W
109 D7 Veguita New Mexico 34.30N 106.46W
63 Q6 Vehlow E Germany 53.02N 12.20E
51 J11 Vehmaa Finland 60.41N 21.40E
31 F5 Vehoa Pakistan 31.11N 70.45E
31 F5 Vehoa R Pakistan
53 Y19 Vehuskjerringa *mt* Norway 59.38N 8.04E
80 F4 Veiano Italy 42.13N 12.06E
50 C2 Veidhileysufjördhur *B* Iceland
50 H7 Veidhiós *B* Iceland 63.43N 17.44W
50 G6 Veidhivötn *lakes* Iceland
53 W18 Veig *R* Norway 60.24N 7.06E
66 B6 Veigy France 46.16N 6.15E
47 D5 Veilikaya Guba U.S.S.R. 62.13N 35.11E
51 M1 Veines Norway 70.38N 26.33E
52 G10 Veinge Sweden 56.33N 13.05E
99 D3 Vein L Ontario 49.08N 86.20W
121 E5 Veinticinco de Mayo Buenos Aires Arg 35.27S 60.10W
121 C6 Veinticinco de Mayo La Pampa Arg 38.00S 67.48W
121 C5 Veinticinco de Mayo Mendoza Arg 34.32S 68.35W
80 F4 Veio *ruins* Italy 42.02N 12.24E
117 C6 Veiros Brazil 2.05S 52.07W
76 D11 Veiros Portugal 38.57N 7.30W
31 E8 Veirwaro Pakistan 24.06N 68.30E
53 W16 Veitastrondsvatn *L* Norway 61.25N 7.04E
65 E6 Veitsberg *mt* Austria 47.34N 11.58E
65 M6 Veitsch Austria 47.05N 15.30E
65 M6 Veitschalpe *mt* Austria 47.39N 15.25E
64 H4 Veitshöchheim W Germany 49.51N 9.53E
53 V18 Veivatn *L* Norway 60.14N 6.55E
53 J4 Vejby Denmark 56.04N 12.09E
53 C6 Vejen Denmark 55.29N 9.13E
77 E8 Vejer de la Frontera Spain 36.15N 5.58W
53 A5 Vejers Denmark 55.37N 8.09E
53 D4 Vejerslev Denmark 56.19N 9.44E
53 D2 Vejgård Denmark 57.03N 9.52E
53 E4 Vejlby Århus Denmark 56.12N 10.13E
53 D5 Vejlby Vejle Denmark 55.37N 9.44E
53 D5 Vejle Denmark 55.43N 9.33E
53 C5 Vejle *co* Denmark
53 D5 Vejle Fjord *inlet* Denmark 55.43N 9.40E
53 H6 Vejlø Denmark 55.11N 11.47E
62 G5 Vejprty Czechoslovakia 50.30N 13.03E
53 G5 Vejrhøj *mt* Denmark 55.48N 11.24E
53 G6 Vejrø *isld* Storstrøm Denmark 55.03N 11.22E
53 F5 Vejrø *isld* Vestjælland Denmark 55.58N 10.46E
53 B4 Vejrum Ringkøbing Denmark 56.27N 8.36E
53 D4 Vejrum Viborg Denmark 56.27N 9.35E
53 B5 Vejrup Denmark 55.31N 8.48E
53 E7 Vejsnæs Nokke *C* Denmark 54.59N 10.26E
53 F6 Vejstrup Fyn Denmark 55.07N 10.43E
53 D6 Vejstrup Vejle Denmark 55.24N 9.33E
43 F7 Vekil'-Bazar Turkmeniya U.S.S.R. 37.43N 61.59E
53 J5 Veksø Denmark 55.46N 12.15E
47 E5 Vel *R* U.S.S.R.
121 F6 Vela Argentina 37.25S 59.30W
119 D1 Vela,C.de la Colombia 12.14N 72.13W
29 C7 Velachha Gujarat India 21.26N 73.06E
76 K9 Velada Spain 39.58N 4.59W
76 D9 Velada *dam* Portugal 39.34N 7.38W
61 J5 Velaine Belgium 50.28N 4.37E
61 D4 Velaines Belgium 50.40N 3.30E
26 Q2 Velanai *isld* Sri Lanka 9.40N 79.54E
84 F9 Velanidhia Greece 36.28N 23.10E
66 F8 Velan,Monte Italy 45.53N 7.16E
66 F8 Velan, Mt Italy/Switz 45.53N 7.15E
84 B3 Velaóra Greece 39.02N 21.27E
109 E5 Velarde New Mexico 36.10N 105.58W
115 H5 Velardeña Mexico 25.04N 103.44W
96 Q3 Velas Azores 38.42N 28.13W
116 B9 Velas,C Costa Rica 10.22N 85.53W
112 M7 Velasco Texas 28.57N 95.24W
119 B6 Velasco Ibarra Galápagos Is 1.15S 90.27W
72 A9 Velate, Pto de Spain 43.04N 1.37W
71 D7 Velay,Mts.du France
121 G5 Velázquez Uruguay 34.05S 54.16W
63 F10 Velbert W Germany 51.22N 7.03E
64 M5 Velburg W Germany 49.15N 11.40E
95 B8 Velddrif S Africa 32.47S 18.10E
61 C2 Veldegem Belgium 51.06N 3.10E
65 K8 Velden Austria 46.38N 14.03E
60 N14 Velden Netherlands 51.25N 6.10E
64 M4 Velden W Germany 49.36N 11.31E
64 N7 Velden W Germany 48.21N 12.16E
60 K14 Veldhoven Netherlands 51.24N 5.24E
28 C3 Veldurti Andhra Prad India 15.35N 77.55E
61 N3 Veldwezelt Belgium 50.52N 5.38E
82 B6 Velebit *mts* Yugoslavia
77 M6 Velefique Spain 37.12N 2.24W
82 L8 Veleka *R* Bulgaria
63 E9 Velen W Germany 51.53N 6.59E
62 L8 Velencei Tó *L* Hungary 47.11N 18.32E
82 C4 Velenje Yugoslavia 46.23N 15.08E
65 K4 Velešin Czechoslovakia 48.50N 14.28E

84 E3 Velestínon Greece 39.23N 22.45E
45 O1 Velet'ma U.S.S.R. 55.20N 42.25E
119 D4 Vélez Colombia 6.02N 73.43W
77 M5 Vélez Blanco Spain 37.41N 2.05W
77 J7 Vélez de Benaudalla Spain 36.50N 3.30W
77 H7 Vélez Málaga Spain 36.47N 4.06W
77 N5 Velez,R.,de Spain
77 M5 Vélez Rubio Spain 37.39N 2.04W
51 C6 Velfjord Norway 65.23N 12.31E
63 R4 Velgast E Germany 54.17N 12.49E
118 G6 Velhas,R Brazil
40 G6 Veli U.S.S.R. 51.40N 135.31E
28 D5 Veliar R Tamil Nadu India
Velibaba see Aras Turkey
84 E8 Veliés Greece 36.43N 22.56E
82 D5 Velika Yugoslavia 45.27N 17.40E
82 C5 Velika Gorica Yugoslavia 45.44N 16.05E
82 G6 Velika Gradište Yugoslavia 44.46N 21.30E
82 B5 Velika Kapela mts Yugoslavia
82 G6 Velika Plana Yugoslavia 44.20N 21.01E
47 F3 Velikaya U.S.S.R. 67.21N 47.52E
47 F6 Velikaya R Kirov U.S.S.R.
39 K3 Velikaya R Magadan U.S.S.R.
46 G2 Velikaya R Pskov U.S.S.R.
45 E7 Velikaya Bagachka Ukraine U.S.S.R. 49.47N 33.45E
40 G9 Velikaya Kema U.S.S.R. 45.31N 137.12E
45 J6 Velikaya Mikhaylovka U.S.S.R. 50.46N 37.36E
45 F7 Velikaya Rublevka Ukraine U.S.S.R. 49.54N 34.52E
80 O2 Veliki Drvenik Yugoslavia 43.27N 16.08E
82 K1 Velikie Borki U.S.S.R. 49.32N 25.45E
45 C7 Velikiy Bukrin Ukraine U.S.S.R. 49.57N 31.19E
45 J6 Velikiy Burluk Ukraine U.S.S.R. 50.05N 37.25E
46 H2 Velikiye-Luki U.S.S.R. 56.19N 30.31E
45 E6 Velikiye-Sorochintsy Ukraine U.S.S.R. 50.02N 33.56E
47 F5 Velikiy Ustyug U.S.S.R. 60.48N 46.15E
43 J6 Velikoalekseyevskiy Uzbekistan U.S.S.R. 40.40N 68.45E
45 M1 Velikodvorskiy U.S.S.R. 55.14N 40.40E
28 D3 Velikonda Ra mts Andhra Prad India
82 K7 Veliko Tŭrnovo Bulgaria 43.04N 25.39E
47 G3 Velikovisochnoye U.S.S.R. 67.12N 52.03E
46 M1 Velikovo U.S.S.R. 59.15N 42.05E
Veliköy see Merya
45 M1 Velikoye,Oz U.S.S.R.
76 J5 Velilla Spain 41.33N 5.01W
75 L4 Velilla de Cinca Spain 41.35N 0.15E
75 K5 Velilla de Ebro Spain 41.22N 0.26W
75 F5 Velilla de Medinaceli Spain 41.10N 2.20W
120 D6 Velille R Peru
72 E6 Vélines France 44.51N 0.06E
89 B5 Vélingara Senegal 13.12N 14.05W
82 H8 Velingrad Bulgaria 42.01N 23.59E
80 G4 Velino R Italy
80 H4 Velino,Monte Italy 42.09N 13.24E
45 C1 Velizh U.S.S.R. 55.36N 31.13E
68 D4 Vélizy-Villacoublay France 48.47N 2.12E
65 O3 Velká Biteš Czechoslovakia 49.18N 16.14E
62 L7 Velká Fatra mts Czechoslovakia
62 N7 Vel'ké Kapušány Czechoslovakia 48.34N 22.05E
62 L6 Velké Karlovice Czechoslovakia 49.20N 18.15E
65 O3 Velké Meziříčí Czechoslovakia 49.22N 16.02E
65 P2 Velké Opatovice Czechoslovakia 49.37N 16.40E
62 L6 Vel'ke Raca mt Czechoslovakia 49.24N 18.55E
82 G2 Velki Bereznyy U.S.S.R. 48.54N 22.27E
50 S13 Velkomstpynten C Spitsbergen 79.50N 12.27E
65 L2 Velký Blaník mt Czechoslovakia 49.38N 14.53E
65 M1 Velký Osek Czechoslovakia 50.07N 15.11E
62 K8 Vel'ký Žitný Ostrov reg Czechoslovakia
65 L9 Vellach Austria 46.27N 14.32E
65 L9 Vellach R Austria
15 K2 Vella G Solomon Is
63 N6 Vellahn E Germany 53.24N 10.58E
15 K2 Vella Lavella I Solomon Is 7.45S 156.35E
26 R3 Vellankulam Sri Lanka 9.11N 80.07E
79 J7 Vellano Italy 43.57N 10.43E
64 H5 Vellberg W Germany 49.05N 9.59E
53 V14 Velle Norway 62.18N 6.40E
61 G5 Vellereille-les-Brayeux Belgium 50.23N 4.09E
61 G5 Vellèreille-le-Sec Belgium 50.24N 4.04E
72 H2 Velles France 46.41N 1.38E
76 H6 Vellés,La Spain 41.05N 5.35W
80 G5 Velletri Italy 41.41N 12.47E
53 D4 Vellev Denmark 56.23N 9.50E
71 K2 Vellevans France 47.19N 6.30E
71 H1 Vellexon-Queutrey-et-Vaudey France 47.34N 5.47E
53 A4 Velling Denmark 56.03N 8.19E
52 G11 Vellinge Sweden 55.29N 13.00E
50 G3 Vellir Iceland 65.56N 18.30W
75 E7 Vellisca Spain 40.08N 2.49W
84 E6 Véllon Greece 37.58N 22.45E
28 D4 Vellore Tamil Nadu India 12.56N 79.09E
75 L2 Vellos R Spain
72 C3 Velluire France 46.25N 0.55W
61 L3 Velm Belgium 50.47N 5.08E
42 E2 Vel'mo R U.S.S.R.
42 E2 Vel'mo 1-oye U.S.S.R. 61.03N 93.03E
42 E2 Vel'mo 2-oye U.S.S.R. 61.00N 93.25E
69 J4 Velosnes France 49.30N 5.27E
84 H5 Veloúsia Greece 38.23N 24.05E
79 K3 Velo Veronese Italy 45.37N 11.06E
60 M12 Velp Gelderland Netherlands 52.00N 5.59E
61 L3 Velpe R Belgium
63 N8 Velpke W Germany 52.24N 10.56E
60 G10 Velsen Netherlands 52.28N 4.39E
47 E5 Vel'sk U.S.S.R. 61.05N 42.06E
53 T14 Velsvik Norway 62.12N 5.53E
53 T14 Velsvikskåla mt Norway 62.10N 5.52E
47 G2 Vel't U.S.S.R. 68.02N 50.00E
61 J3 Veltem-Beisem Belgium 50.54N 4.38E
63 S7 Velten E Germany 52.42N 13.12E
66 L1 Veltheim Switzerland 47.31N 8.43E
60 M13 Veltum Netherlands 51.31N 5.58E
69 D3 Vélu France 50.07N 2.57E
60 L11 Veluwe physical reg Netherlands
60 L10 Veluwemeer L Netherlands
108 K1 Velva N Dakota 48.04N 100.55W
44 J6 Vel'velichay R Azerbaydzhan U.S.S.R.
51 P12 Vel'ye,Ozero L U.S.S.R. 59.00N 30.12E
61 F3 Velzeke-Ruddershove Belgium 50.53N 3.47E
96 F7 Vema Fracture Atlantic Oc
28 D1 Vemalwada Andhra Prad India 18.30N 78.53E
26 F6 Vema Trough Indian Ocean
53 A4 Vemb Denmark 56.21N 8.22E
28 C6 Vembanād L Kerala India
52 H4 Vemdalen Sweden 62.29N 13.55E
58 Q9 Vementry I Shetland Scotland 60.20N 1.28W
51 D9 Vemhan Sweden 62.21E 14.14E
53 G6 Vemmelev Denmark 55.22N 11.16E
53 F7 Vemmenæs Denmark 54.59N 10.40E
53 Y19 Vemork Norway 59.52N 8.28E
40 J8 Vemor'ye Sakhalin U.S.S.R. 47.50N 142.30E
28 D3 Vempalle Andhra Prad India 14.20N 78.26E
65 O3 Vémyslice Czechoslovakia 49.02N 16.16E
53 K5 Ven isld Sweden 55.55N 12.45E
52 J9 Vena Sweden 57.31N 16.00E
52 E5 Venabygd Norway 61.35N 10.05E
67 P12 Venaco Corsica 42.13N 9.08E
119 D5 Venadillo Colombia 4.45N 74.55W
115 N4 Venado,I.de Nicaragua
121 E4 Venado Tuerto Argentina 33.45S 61.56W
80 K6 Venafro Italy 41.28N 14.03E
79 B4 Venálzio Italy 45.09N 7.01E
119 H5 Venamo,Cerro mt Venezuela 5.59N 61.28W
119 H4 Venamo,R Venezuela
121 H2 Venâncio Aires Brazil 29.37S 52.08W
108 H9 Venango Nebraska 40.46N 102.01W
13 F4 Vena Park Queensland 18.33S 141.14E
71 E1 Venarey France 47.32N 4.25E
71 E2 Venarey-les-Laumes France 47.32N 4.26E
79 C4 Venaria Italy 45.08N 7.38E
80 H3 Venarotta Italy 42.53N 13.30E
79 B5 Venasca Italy 44.33N 7.23E
110 G6 Venator Oregon 43.21N 118.17W
71 L9 Vence France 43.43N 7.06E
120 G1 Vencedor Brazil 5.17S 60.46W
118 E8 Venceslau Bráz Brazil 23.50S 49.46W
61 K6 Vencimont Belgium 50.02N 4.55E
94 L4 Venda Bantu Homeland S Africa
79 L4 Venda hill Italy 45.20N 11.42E
76 D5 Venda Nova Portugal 41.40N 7.58W
71 D9 Vendargues France 43.39N 3.58E
76 C15 Venda Seca Portugal 38.47N 9.17W
76 C11 Vendas Novas Portugal 38.41N 8.27W
72 B5 Vendays-Montalivet France 45.21N 1.04W
67 E6 Vendée dept France
72 C2 Vendée R France 46.30N 0.42W
Vendelus B see Vandeloos B
71 E4 Vendenesse-les-Charolles France 46.27N 4.20E
69 O6 Vendenheim France 48.40N 7.43E
69 E4 Vendeuil France 49.42N 3.22E
69 G7 Vendeuvre-sur-Barse France 48.14N 4.29E
53 V18 Vendevatn L Norway 60.13N 6.44E
81 K10 Vendicari isld Sicily 36.48N 15.07E
69 D3 Vendin-le-Vieil France 50.29N 2.53E
66 E2 Vendlincourt Switzerland 47.28N 7.09E
72 G2 Vendœuvres France 46.48N 1.20E
70 N6 Vendôme France 47.48N 1.04E
75 O5 Vendrell Spain 41.13N 1.33E
69 H4 Vendresse France 49.36N 4.47E
53 D2 Vendsyssel reg Denmark
60 P9 Venebrügge Netherlands 52.33N 6.40E
119 C7 Venecia Colombia 1.32N 75.30W
120 D4 Venecia Peru 11.52S 69.27W
65 F7 Venediger,Gruppe mt Austria 47.07N 12.20E
115 J6 Venegas Mexico 23.51N 100.56W
66 M9 Venegono Italy 45.44N 8.54E
71 G9 Venelles France 43.35N 5.28E
80 F4 Venere,Monte Italy 42.21N 12.11E
72 G9 Venerque France 43.26N 1.27E
72 J8 Venès France 43.44N 2.11E
79 M4 Veneta, Laguna lagoon Italy
65 C7 Venet-Berg mt Austria 47.09N 10.40E
113 O3 Venetie Alaska 67.00N 146.30W
113 O3 Venetie Landing Alaska 66.38N 146.00W
84 C8 Venétiko isld Greece 36.40N 21.50E
45 K2 Venev U.S.S.R. 54.22N 38.15E
120 E2 Veneza, L Brazil 6.26S 68.55W
79 M4 Venezia Italy 45.26N 12.20E
79 M4 Venezia prov Italy
79 N2 Venezia reg Italy
79 N4 Venezia,G.di B Italy
117 G1 Venezuela rep S America
119 E2 Venezuela,G.de Venezuela
96 D7 Venezuelan Basin Caribbean Sea
53 D4 Veng Denmark 56.07N 9.54E
42 B4 Vengerovo U.S.S.R. 55.41N 76.44E
53 X13 Vengetindane mt Norway 62.30N 7.50E
28 A3 Vengurla Maharashtra India 15.53N 73.41E
60 J9 Venhuizen Netherlands 52.40N 5.13E
76 H6 Venialbo Spain 41.23N 5.32W
113 H8 Veniaminof Vol Alaska 56.13N 159.20W
100 E4 Venice Alberta 54.43N 112.03W
111 C9 Venice California 33.59N 118.28W
105 E10 Venice Florida 27.05N 82.26W
Venice Italy see Venezia
107 G12 Venice Louisiana 29.16N 89.23W
107 L12 Venice dist St Louis, Ill 38.40N 90.10W
119 F8 Veni,R Brazil
71 F5 Vénissieux France 45.42N 4.46E
66 D8 Veni,Valle Italy
52 H6 Venjan Sweden 60.58N 13.55E
28 D4 Venkatagiri Andhra Prad India 13.59N 79.35E
28 E1 Venkatapalem Orissa India 18.05N 81.48E
28 E1 Venkatapuram Andhra Prad Ind 18.19N 80.34E
108 N3 Venlo N Dakota 46.30N 97.25W
60 N14 Venlo Netherlands 51.22N 6.10E
95 F4 Venn S Africa 28.02S 22.54E
100 M7 Venn Saskatchewan 51.37N 105.11W
58 H6 Vennachar,L Central Scotland 56.13N 4.20W
53 D2 Vennebjerg Denmark 57.28N 9.51E
63 E7 Vennebrügge W Germany 52.33N 6.43E
56 C6 Venngreen Devon Eng 50.53N 4.19W
53 B3 Venø Denmark 56.33N 8.38E
53 B3 Venø isld Denmark 56.33N 8.38E
53 B3 Venø Bugt B Denmark 56.30N 8.40E
66 C5 Venoge R Switzerland
80 N7 Venosa Italy 40.57N 15.49E
71 J7 Venosc France 44.59N 6.07E
99 O7 Venosta Quebec 45.51N 76.01W
79 J1 Venosta,Val V Italy
53 B3 Venø Sund sound Denmark 56.33N 8.35E
69 F8 Venoy France 47.48N 3.37E
60 M13 Venray Netherlands 51.32N 5.59E
72 B5 Vensac France 45.24N 1.02W
Vensmoen see Rökland
65 C8 Vent Austria 46.53N 10.56E
46 D2 Venta R Latvia U.S.S.R.
77 H4 Venta de Azuel Spain 38.20N 4.20W
76 K5 Venta de Baños Spain 41.55N 4.30W
77 H4 Venta de Cardeña Spain 38.16N 4.20W
77 H4 Venta del Charco Spain 38.12N 4.16W
77 O2 Venta del Moro Spain 39.29N 1.22W
77 K4 Venta de los Santos Spain 38.22N 3.04W
77 G4 Venta del Puerto mt Spain 38.11N 4.31W
109 D6 Ventana, La New Mexico 35.47N 107.57W
115 E5 Ventana,Pta.de la Mexico 24.04N 109.48W
121 E7 Ventana,Sa ra Argentina
76 F2 Venta Nueva Spain 43.04N 6.38W
75 Q8 Ventas dist Madrid Spain 40.25N 3.40W
77 J6 Ventas de Huelma Spain 37.04N 3.49W
76 D3 Ventas de Narón Spain 42.50N 7.44W
77 H7 Ventas de Zafarraya Spain 36.57N 4.06W
71 H8 Ventavon France 44.22N 5.54E
53 H5 Vented Denmark 55.40N 11.34E
95 L4 Ventersburg S Africa 28.05S 27.08E
95 K2 Ventersdorp S Africa 26.19S 26.50E
95 L2 Venterskroon S Africa 26.53S 27.15E
94 R14 Venterspost S Africa 26.18S 27.39E
94 R14 Venterspost West S Africa 26.17S 27.38E
95 J6 Venterstad S Africa 30.47S 25.48E
71 D7 Venteuges France 44.59N 3.31E
67 P14 Ventilegne, Golfo di Corsica 41.26N 9.05E
77 H3 Ventillas Spain 38.30N 4.17W
79 C7 Ventimiglia Italy 43.47N 7.37E
122 B15 Vent,Is.du Society Is Pacific Oc
67 P13 Ventiseri Corsica 41.57N 9.18E
115 M4 Ventisiete de Abril Costa Rica 10.13N 85.44W
121 B8 Ventisquero pk Arg/Chile 41.47S 71.42W
122 A15 Vent,Is.sous le Society Is Pacific Oc
56 J6 Ventnor I of Wight Eng 50.36N 1.11W
103 F8 Ventnor New Jersey 39.21N 74.29W
81 O2 Vento,Mte.,del Italy 40.50N 17.14E
77 V15 Ventosa,C Balearic Is 39.10N 2.59E
76 J7 Ventosa del Rio Almar Spain 40.55N 5.20W
76 L3 Ventosa de Pisuerga Spain 42.32N 4.18W
75 F7 Ventosa,La Spain 40.12N 2.26W
80 H7 Ventotene Italy 40.48N 13.25E
80 H7 Ventotène, I. di Italy 40.48N 13.25E
71 G8 Ventoux,Mt France 44.09N 5.16E
69 M8 Ventron France 47.56N 6.52E
59 B7 Ventry Kerry Irish Rep 52.08N 10.22W
63 P5 Ventschow E Germany 53.47N 11.35E
40 E8 Ventselevo U.S.S.R. 47.48N 131.59E
46 D2 Ventspils Latvia U.S.S.R. 57.22N 21.31E
119 F5 Ventuari,R Venezuela
111 E7 Ventura California 34.15N 119.18W
75 C6 Venturada Spain 40.47N 3.40W
108 L4 Venturia N Dakota 45.59N 99.31W
80 C2 Venturina Italy 43.02N 10.35E
105 F10 Venus Florida 27.05N 81.25W
112 K3 Venus Texas 32.26N 97.07W
12 C5 Venus Bay S Australia
12 H7 Venus Bay Victoria
122 C11 Vénus,Pt Tahiti Pacific Oc 17.28S 149.29W
115 H8 Venustiano Carranza Mexico 19.43N 103.41W
47 L1 Venuyyeuo R U.S.S.R.
79 O2 Venzone Italy 46.20N 13.08E
65 P7 Vép Hungary 47.14N 16.44E
28 C7 Vepery dist Madras, Tamil Nadu India
47 C5 Vepsovskaya,Vozvyshennost' heights U.S.S.R.
121 E2 Vera Argentina 29.30S 60.08W
77 N6 Vera Spain 37.15N 1.51W
112 H2 Vera Texas 33.39N 99.32W
121 D10 Vera Bahía Argentina
120 E3 Vera Cruz Amazonas Brazil 8.07S 67.09W
115 L8 Veracruz Mexico 19.11N 96.10W
76 D12 Vera Cruz Portugal 38.13N 7.40W
118 E8 Vera Cruz São Paulo Brazil 22.15S 49.46W
115 L7 Veracruz state Mexico
75 G1 Vera de Bidasoa Spain 43.16N 1.41W
118 B10 Vera,L Paraguay 26.00S 57.36W
75 J2 Veral R Spain
76 H8 Vera,La V Spain
Veramin see Varāmīn
121 H2 Veranópolis Brazil 28.57S 51.37W
9 C11 Verao isld New Hebrides 17.34S 168.13E
96 T9 Vera,Pta.de la Fuerteventura Canary Is 28.45N 13.55W
29 B7 Veraval Gujarat India 20.53N 70.28E
79 E3 Verbania Italy 45.56N 8.34E
103 G3 Verbank New York 41.44N 73.43W
Verbano,Lago see Maggiore,Lago
107 K9 Verbena Alabama 32.45N 86.32W
69 D5 Verberie France 49.18N 2.45E
81 L4 Verbicaro Italy 40.46N 15.55E
66 E7 Verbier Switzerland 46.06N 7.13E
46 L2 Verbilki U.S.S.R. 56.30N 37.36E
45 D8 Verblyuzhka Ukraine U.S.S.R. 48.21N 32.54E
45 N1 Verbovskiy U.S.S.R. 55.30N 42.00E
46 P5 Verbovsky Kazakhstan U.S.S.R. 49.30N 49.00E
66 O7 Verceja Italy 46.12N 9.28E
79 D4 Vercelli Italy 45.19N 8.26E
79 D3 Vercelli prov Italy
71 J2 Vercel-Villedieu-le-Camp France 47.11N 6.23E
37 F5 Verçenik Tepe mt Turkey 40.43N 40.55E
66 C7 Verchaix France 46.06N 6.40E
63 R5 Verchen E Germany 53.52N 12.55E
99 R7 Verchères Quebec 45.45N 73.21W
72 D1 Verchers,les France 47.09N 0.17W
71 G7 Vercors dist France
71 J8 Verdaches France 44.16N 6.20E
52 F3 Verdal R Norway
52 F3 Verdalsøra Norway 63.47N 11.23E
19 K5 Verde isld Philippines 13.31N 121.05E
111 N7 Verde R Arizona
118 A4 Verde R Bolivia/Brazil
118 E4 Verde R Brazil
118 E6 Verde R Minas Gerais Brazil
Verde, C see Vert,C
116 G3 Verde,Cay isld Bahamas 22.02N 75.11W
118 G4 Verde Grande R Brazil
111 N7 Verde Hot Springs Arizona 32.24N 111.41W
119 C2 Verde,I Colombia 11.05N 75.00W
19 K5 Verde Island Pass Philippines
121 A10 Verde,L Aisén Chile 44.15S 72.00W
121 C9 Verde,L Argentina
120 E12 Verde,L Atacamá Chile 26.53S 68.28W
120 E10 Verde,L Bolivia 22.47S 67.50W
108 M7 Verdel Nebraska 42.49N 98.10W
81 M7 Verde,la R Italy
72 D6 Verdelais France 44.36N 0.15W
79 G3 Verdello Italy 45.37N 9.37E
109 M6 Verden Oklahoma 35.04N 98.06W
63 K7 Verden W Germany 52.56N 9.14E
121 E7 Verde,Pen Argentina
118 G4 Verde Pequeno,R Brazil
121 D8 Verde R Argentina
118 G2 Verde,R Bahia Brazil
118 D6 Verde, R Brazil
118 E5 Verde,R Goiás Brazil
118 D7 Verde,R Mato Grosso do Sul Brazil
118 F5 Verde, R Minas Gerais/Goiás Brazil
118 B8 Verde,R Paraguay
70 N6 Verdes France 47.58N 1.26E
84 C2 Verdhikoúsa Greece 39.47N 21.59E
111 D2 Verdi California 39.32N 120.00W
71 H9 Verdière,la France 43.39N 5.55E
108 M7 Verdigre Nebraska 42.37N 98.03W
109 P5 Verdigris R Okla/Kansas
100 F9 Verdigris L Alberta 49.17N 112.00W
72 D4 Verdille France 45.53N 0.06W
118 D5 Verdinho,Serra do mts Brazil
45 D1 Verdino U.S.S.R. 55.27N 32.20E
108 P9 Verdon Nebraska 40.09N 95.42W
71 J9 Verdon R France
71 J9 Verdon, Grand Cañon du France
72 B4 Verdon-sur-Mer,le France 45.33N 1.04W
99 S10 Verdun Quebec 45.28N 73.35W
72 G8 Verdun-sur-Garonne France 43.49N 1.13E
71 G3 Verdun-sur-le-Doubs France 46.53N 5.01E
69 J5 Verdun-sur-Meuse Meuse France 49.10N 5.24E
81 F9 Verdura R Sicily
76 D4 Verea Spain 42.05N 7.58W
46 H2 Vereche Belorussiya U.S.S.R. 55.36N 30.22E
77 H3 Veredas Spain 38.40N 4.22W
60 R7 Vereenigd Kanaal Netherlands
95 L2 Vereeniging S Africa 26.41S 27.56E
100 P7 Veregin Saskatchewan 51.35N 102.01W
53 U15 Vereide Norway 61.48N 6.08E
45 C3 Veremeyki Belorussiya U.S.S.R. 53.46N 31.16E
90 F7 Vere Mts Nigeria
108 H2 Verendrye Nat.Mon N Dakota 47.58N 102.32W
99 N5 Vérendrye, Parc Prov. de la Quebec
41 E8 Vereshchagino Krasnoyarsk U.S.S.R. 64.15N 87.37E
47 G6 Vereshchagino Perm U.S.S.R. 58.07N 54.45E
45 C4 Vereshchaki U.S.S.R. 52.43N 31.40E
45 C5 Veresoch' Ukraine U.S.S.R. 51.18N 31.47E
46 K1 Verestovo,Oz L U.S.S.R.
46 M3 Veret'ye U.S.S.R. 54.38N 40.34E
43 M8 Verevkino Tadzhikistan U.S.S.R. 40.16N 70.04E
45 H1 Vereya U.S.S.R. 55.20N 36.12E
72 H8 Verfeil Haute-Garonne France 43.39N 1.39E
72 H7 Verfeil Tarn-et-Garonne France 44.11N 1.52E
89 B6 Verga,C Guinea 10.11N 14.29W
121 F5 Vergara Argentina 35.25S 57.47W
120 D10 Vergara Chile 22.27S 69.37W
75 F1 Vergara Spain 43.07N 2.25W
121 H4 Vergara Uruguay 32.58S 53.54W
108 P3 Vergas Minnesota 46.39N 95.50W
79 K6 Vergato Italy 44.17N 11.07E
69 M6 Vergaville France 48.50N 6.44E
77 R3 Vergel Spain 38.51N 0.01E
95 H1 Vergeleë S Africa 25.46S 24.10E
66 L7 Vergeletto Switzerland 46.14N 8.36E
13 G6 Vergemont Queensland 23.32S 143.00E
13 G6 Vergemont R Queensland
104 M2 Vergennes Vermont 44.11N 73.16W
75 R3 Verges Spain 42.04N 3.03E
79 M7 Verghereto Italy 43.47N 12.00E
79 E3 Vergiate Italy 45.44N 8.41E
80 L7 Vergine,Monte Italy 40.56N 14.44E
67 O12 Vergio,Col de pass Corsica 42.18N 8.53E
61 H6 Vergnies Belgium 50.12N 4.18E
72 F5 Vergt France 45.02N 0.44E
76 E5 Verín Spain 41.55N 7.26W
64 G7 Veringenstadt W Germany 48.10N 9.14E
Verin Gukasyan see Gukasyan
44 F7 Verin Talin Armenia U.S.S.R. 40.23N 43.53E
118 E6 Veríssimo Brazil 19.44S 48.19W
91 G8 Verissimo Sarmento Angola 8.08S 20.38E
95 K4 Verkeerdevlei S Africa 28.50S 26.46E
45 S8 Verkh. Baskunchak U.S.S.R. 48.12N 46.44E
39 H4 Verkhnaya Pakhacha U.S.S.R. 61.00N 169.14E
42 J4 Verkhneangarskiy Khrebet mts U.S.S.R.
47 H8 Verkhnearshinskiy U.S.S.R. 54.23N 58.34E
43 E1 Verkhne-Avzyan Bashkir U.S.S.R. 53.00N 57.40E
44 B3 Verkhnebakanskiy U.S.S.R. 44.50N 37.40E
43 O2 Verkhneberezovskiy Kazakhstan U.S.S.R. 50.17N 82.10E
45 P7 Verkhne Buzinovka U.S.S.R. 49.05N 43.15E
45 F8 Verkhne-dneprovsk Ukraine U.S.S.R. 48.36N 34.36E
45 E2 Verkhnedneprovskiy U.S.S.R. 55.35N 32.26E
46 G2 Verkhnedvinsk Belorussiya U.S.S.R. 55.48N 28.00E
45 O8 Verkhne Gnutoye U.S.S.R. 48.15N 42.14E
40 G9 Verkhne Imanskiy U.S.S.R. 45.00N 135.25E
41 E8 Verkhneimbatskoye U.S.S.R. 63.12N 88.01E
39 F7 Verkhne-Kamchatsk U.S.S.R. 54.37N 158.22E
39 F7 Verkhne-Kolpakovo U.S.S.R. 54.37N 155.53E
39 E2 Verkhne-Kolymsk U.S.S.R. 65.38N 150.40E
39 D3 Verkhne-Kolymskoye Nagor'ye uplands U.S.S.R.
45 P8 Verkhne Kumskiy U.S.S.R. 48.05N 43.27E
39 G6 Verkhne-Ozernaya U.S.S.R. 57.21N 161.45E
43 F1 Verkhnesanarskiy U.S.S.R. 54.12N 60.31E
45 N4 Verkhne Spasskoe U.S.S.R. 52.35N 41.54E
45 N8 Verkhne-Svechnikov U.S.S.R. 48.59N 41.34E
47 D5 Verkhne Svirskoye Vdkhr res U.S.S.R. 61.05N 35.20E
45 L8 Verkhne Teploye Ukraine U.S.S.R. 48.50N 39.25E
47 C2 Verkhnetulomskiy U.S.S.R. 68.37N 32.00E
43 E1 Verkhneural'sk U.S.S.R. 53.52N 59.14E
42 E6 Verkhneusinskoye U.S.S.R. 52.14N 93.02E
42 B2 Verkhne-Vartovskoye U.S.S.R. 60.05N 79.05E
42 B2 Verkhne-Vartovskoye U.S.S.R. 60.05N 79.05E
41 M8 Verkhnevilyuysk U.S.S.R. 63.28N 120.15E
46 R2 Verkhne Yarkeyevo U.S.S.R. 55.28N 54.29E
45 K8 Verkhneye Ukraine U.S.S.R. 48.52N 38.30E
47 M4 Verkhneye Dubrovo U.S.S.R. 56.46N 61.02E
42 B4 Verkhneye Krasnoyarka U.S.S.R. 56.20N 77.58E
47 J4 Verkhneye Nil'dino U.S.S.R. 63.16N 61.30E
39 F6 Verkhneye Oblukovino U.S.S.R. 55.13N 156.01E
42 B3 Verkhneye Panino U.S.S.R. 59.40N 79.09E
42 D3 Verkhneye Skoblino U.S.S.R. 57.31N 88.44E
39 E3 Verkhniy At-Uryakh' U.S.S.R. 62.40N 150.16E
39 D3 Verkhniy Debin U.S.S.R. 62.51N 148.50E
47 H7 Verkhniye Kigi U.S.S.R. 55.23N 58.38E
40 C3 Verkhniye Kolbochi U.S.S.R. 56.04N 125.01E
47 H7 Verkhniye Tatyshly U.S.S.R. 56.12N 55.57E
44 F5 Verkhniy Fiagdon U.S.S.R. 42.47N 44.15E
45 N5 Verkhniy Karachan U.S.S.R. 51.28N 41.46E
47 H8 Verkhniy Katav U.S.S.R. 54.38N 58.15E
45 M9 Verkhniy Khomutets U.S.S.R. 47.00N 40.45E
47 J4 Verkhniy Khurumpaul' U.S.S.R. 63.58N 61.00E
42 E5 Verkhniy Kuzhebar U.S.S.R. 53.23N 93.16E
45 P3 Verkhniy Lomov U.S.S.R. 53.29N 43.31E
45 K4 Verkhniy Lomovets U.S.S.R. 52.15N 38.37E
45 G4 Verkhniy Lyubazh U.S.S.R. 52.14N 35.51E
47 J4 Verkhniy Lyulyukary U.S.S.R. 63.19N 64.28E
45 M6 Verkhniy Mamon U.S.S.R. 50.10N 40.24E
42 D6 Verkhniy Matur U.S.S.R. 52.44N 89.28E
47 M7 Verkhniy Mayzass U.S.S.R. 56.42N 76.50E
47 M4 Verkhniy Neyvinskiy U.S.S.R. 57.20N 60.05E
45 F9 Verkhniy Rogachik Ukraine U.S.S.R. 47.15N 34.22E
39 E3 Verkhniy Seymchan U.S.S.R. 62.45N 152.30E
47 G2 Verkhniy Shar U.S.S.R. 68.21N 50.45E
42 H6 Verkhniy Shergol'dzhin U.S.S.R. 50.12N 108.20E
47 M5 Verkhniy Sysert' U.S.S.R. 56.26N 60.45E
47 M4 Verkhniy Tagil U.S.S.R. 57.22N 59.58E
42 F4 Verkhniy Tugusha U.S.S.R. 55.56N 96.30E
47 M5 Verkhniy Ufaley U.S.S.R. 56.05N 60.14E
42 E6 Verkhniy Yenisey R U.S.S.R.
42 D5 Verkhniy Zub,Gora mt U.S.S.R. 53.50N 89.14E
40 D2 Verkhnyaya Amga U.S.S.R. 59.41N 126.59E
42 J4 Verkhnyaya Angara R U.S.S.R.
41 D7 Verkhnyaya Baikha U.S.S.R. 65.33N 84.56E
42 F2 Verkhnyaya Chunku U.S.S.R. 61.59N 97.45E
47 J3 Verkhnyaya Inta U.S.S.R. 66.00N 60.11E
42 C5 Verkhnyaya Irmen' U.S.S.R. 54.35N 82.15E
45 L5 Verkhnyaya Khava U.S.S.R. 51.51N 40.00E
42 K6 Verkhnyaya Khila U.S.S.R. 52.05N 115.55E
45 F9 Verkhnyaya Khortitsa Ukraine U.S.S.R. 47.53N 35.00E
40 C4 Verkhnyaya Larba R U.S.S.R.
45 N7 Verkhnyaya Makayevka U.S.S.R. 49.09N 41.05E
45 T4 Verkhnyaya Maza U.S.S.R. 52.58N 47.56E
47 M4 Verkhnyaya Oslyanka U.S.S.R. 57.57N 58.50E
47 M4 Verkhnyaya Pyshma U.S.S.R. 56.59N 60.30E
47 N3 Verkhnyaya Salda U.S.S.R. 58.05N 60.30E
45 O9 Verkhnyaya Serebryakovka U.S.S.R. 47.22N 42.15E
47 N4 Verkhnyaya Sinyachikha U.S.S.R. 58.02N 61.40E
45 F6 Verkhnyaya Syrovatka Ukraine U.S.S.R. 50.50N 34.58E
42 B4 Verkhnyaya Tarka U.S.S.R. 56.37N 77.30E
41 F4 Verkhnyaya Taymyra R U.S.S.R.
45 M5 Verkhnyaya Tishanka U.S.S.R. 51.21N 40.35E
47 F5 Verkhnyaya Toyma U.S.S.R. 62.10N 45.12E
47 F5 Verkhnyaya Toyma R U.S.S.R.
47 F5 Verkhnyaya Toz'ma U.S.S.R. 60.34N 45.11E
47 M3 Verkhnyaya Tura U.S.S.R. 58.22N 59.50E
42 B3 Verkhnyaya Vol'dzha U.S.S.R. 58.17N 79.18E
47 H6 Verkhnyaya Yarva U.S.S.R. 59.30N 57.35E
43 Q3 Verkhnyaya Yelovka Kazakhstan U.S.S.R. 48.51N 85.46E
42 J4 Verkhnyaya Zaimka U.S.S.R. 55.52N 110.05E
42 G5 Verkhnyaya Zima U.S.S.R. 53.48N 101.45E
42 H5 Verkholensk U.S.S.R. 54.08N 105.40E
46 P1 Verkhoshizhem'ye U.S.S.R. 58.00N 49.09E
42 F3 Verkhoturovo U.S.S.R. 58.24N 95.18E
47 J6 Verkhotur'ye U.S.S.R. 58.54N 60.50E
44 G5 Verkhovani Georgia U.S.S.R. 42.24N 45.30E
47 E5 Verkhovazh'e U.S.S.R. 60.45N 41.57E
45 F8 Verkhovtsevo Ukraine U.S.S.R. 48.29N 34.15E
45 J4 Verkhov'ye U.S.S.R. 52.49N 37.14E
39 A1 Verkhoyansk U.S.S.R. 67.35N 133.25E
45 S4 Verkhozim U.S.S.R. 52.55N 46.20E
45 O4 Verkh. Shibryay U.S.S.R. 52.02N 42.33E
43 O2 Verkhubinka Kazakhstan U.S.S.R. 50.30N 82.25E
47 C3 Verkneye Kuyto, Oz L U.S.S.R.
47 M4 Verkniye Sergi U.S.S.R. 56.39N 59.31E
46 P4 Verkniy Kushum U.S.S.R. 51.32N 48.18E
42 J7 Verkniy Ul'khun U.S.S.R. 49.35N 112.32E
45 U1 Verkniy Uslon U.S.S.R. 55.45N 48.58E
47 F4 Verkola U.S.S.R. 63.51N 45.12E
95 N3 Verkykerskop S Africa 27.54S 29.15E
61 M4 Verlaine Belgium 50.37N 5.19E
61 M5 Verlée Belgium 50.22N 5.17E
50 T12 Verlegenhuken C Spitsbergen 80.03N 16.30E
100 J8 Verlo Saskatchewan 50.19N 108.37W
53 Y14 Verma Norway 62.21N 8.03E
53 X14 Verma R Norway 62.53N 7.58E
95 E10 Vermaaklikheid S Africa 34.18S 21.01E
95 K2 Vermaas S Africa 26.31S 26.00E
66 F6 Vermala Switzerland 46.19N 7.29E
69 E4 Vermand France 49.52N 3.09E
87 H8 Verme Falls Ethiopia 5.22N 40.19E
76 A10 Vermelha Portugal 39.16N 9.06W
117 E9 Vermelho,R Goiás Brazil
118 E4 Vermelho,R Goiás Brazil
117 D7 Vermelho,R Pará Brazil
71 D1 Vermenton France 47.40N 3.43E
53 X14 Vermevatn L Norway 62.21N 7.50E
79 J2 Vermiglio Italy 46.18N 10.41E
100 G5 Vermilion Alberta 53.21N 110.52W
107 J2 Vermilion Illinois 39.34N 87.34W
104 C5 Vermilion Ohio 41.24N 82.21W
107 D11 Vermilion R Louisiana
107 D12 Vermilion Bay Louisiana
100 J1 Vermilion Bay Ontario 49.51N 93.21W
101 Q6 Vermilion Chutes Alberta 58.22N 114.51W
111 M4 Vermilion Cliffs ra Utah
100 K1 Vermilion L Ontario 50.02N 92.10W
100 G5 Vermilion Prov.Park Alberta 53.25N 110.59W
100 G5 Vermilion R Alberta
109 O2 Vermillion Kansas 39.43N 96.18W
108 O7 Vermillion S Dakota 42.48N 96.55W
108 O7 Vermillion R S Dakota
108 S2 Vermillion L Minnesota
106 F8 Vermillion,R Illinois
99 R5 Vermillion,R Quebec
108 S2 Vermillion Range mts Minnesota
83 E4 Vermion mts Greece
76 F7 Vermiosa Portugal 40.50N 6.53W
76 B9 Vermoil Portugal 39.50N 8.40W
76 C6 Vermoim Portugal 41.25N 8.28W
106 D9 Vermont Illinois 40.18N 90.26W
102 M2 Vermont state U.S.A.
70 J6 Vern France 47.36N 0.49W
45 O3 Vernadovka U.S.S.R. 53.19N 42.25E
40 N6 Vernadskogo mt Kuril Is U.S.S.R. 50.32N 155.49E
110 Q9 Vernal Utah 40.26N 109.32W
111 C4 Vernalis California 37.36N 121.18W
79 C6 Vernante Italy 44.14N 7.32E
70 L7 Vernantes France 47.23N 0.03E
71 D8 Vernarède,la France 44.18N 4.00E
79 G5 Vernasca Italy 44.48N 9.50E
66 E7 Vernayaz Switzerland 46.08N 7.03E
66 D6 Vernaz,Col de pass France/Switz 46.19N 6.49E
79 G6 Vernazza Italy 44.08N 9.42E
110 P8 Verne Wyoming 41.35N 110.05W
99 K6 Verner Ontario 46.26N 80.07W
71 C6 Vernet-la-Varenne France 45.28N 3.27E
72 J10 Vernet-les-Bains France 42.32N 2.23E
71 B5 Verneugheol France 45.46N 2.37E
70 M4 Verneuil Eure France 48.44N 0.55E
69 F5 Verneuil Marne France 49.06N 3.40E
69 D6 Verneuil-l'Etang France 48.39N 2.50E
72 G1 Verneuil sur-Indre France 47.04N 1.03E
94 F8 Verneukpan S Africa 30.04S 21.01E
94 F7 Verneuk Pan salt L S Africa 29.57S 21.05E
64 B2 Vernich W Germany 50.44N 6.50E
66 A7 Vernier Switzerland 46.13N 6.05E
66 B3 Vernierfontaine France 47.07N 6.20E
53 E6 Verninge Denmark 55.18N 10.13E
79 K6 Vérnio Italy 44.03N 11.10E
72 H9 Verniolle France 43.05N 1.38E
70 L7 Vernoil France 47.22N 0.04E
81 R12 Vernole Italy 40.17N 18.19E
107 H8 Vernon Alabama 33.43N 88.08W
111 P7 Vernon Arizona 34.16N 109.41W
101 O10 Vernon Br Col 50.17N 119.19W
109 H2 Vernon Colorado 39.57N 102.18W
103 K3 Vernon Connecticut 41.49N 72.29W
70 N3 Vernon Eure France 49.05N 1.29E
105 B7 Vernon Florida 30.36N 85.43W
107 L3 Vernon Indiana 38.59N 85.39W
103 F4 Vernon New Jersey 41.12N 74.29W
104 K3 Vernon New York 43.05N 75.31W
98 K7 Vernon Prince Edward I 46.11N 62.54W
112 H1 Vernon Texas 34.11N 99.17W
110 N9 Vernon Utah 40.06N 112.27W
104 N4 Vernon Vermont 42.46N 72.34W
72 E3 Vernon Vienne France 46.26N 0.27E
83 E4 Vérnon mt Greece 40.40N 21.25E
110 B4 Vernonia Oregon 45.52N 123.13W
13 B1 Vernon Is N Terr Australia
107 C10 Vernon, Lake Louisiana
14 C6 Vernon,Mt W Australia 24.09S 118.00E
70 M7 Vernou France 47.27N 0.57E
116 M4 Vernou Guadeloupe W I 16.10N 61.39W
70 O7 Vernou-en-Sologne France 47.30N 1.41E
71 F7 Vernoux-en-Vivarais France 44.53N 4.39E
40 D6 Vernoye U.S.S.R. 51.14N 128.40E
70 G5 Vern-sur-Seiche France 48.03N 1.36W
69 L5 Verny France 49.00N 6.12E
75 L3 Vero R Spain
105 G10 Vero Beach Florida 27.39N 80.24W
83 E4 Véroia Greece 40.32N 22.11E
79 H4 Verolanuova Italy 45.19N 10.05E
79 C4 Verolengo Italy 45.11N 7.58E
80 H5 Veroli Italy 41.41N 13.26E
79 K4 Verona Italy 45.26N 11.00E
107 C5 Verona Missouri 36.58N 93.49W
108 M3 Verona N Dakota 46.22N 98.06W
103 H7 Verona New Jersey 40.50N 74.15W
99 O8 Verona Ontario 44.30N 76.41W
106 E7 Verona Wisconsin 42.59N 89.34W
108 D5 Verona Wyoming 44.43N 106.40W
79 J4 Verona prov Italy
121 F5 Veronica Argentina 35.25S 57.16W
71 E4 Vérosvres France 46.25N 4.26E
71 G5 Verpillière France 45.38N 5.09E
95 J2 Verplig S Africa 26.58S 25.03E
12 D5 Verran S Australia 33.50S 136.16E
61 G2 Verrebroek Belgium 51.15N 4.12E
60 L13 Verreheide Netherlands 51.35N 5.42E
79 C3 Verrès Italy 45.41N 7.42E
107 E12 Verret, L Louisiana
116 H5 Verrettes Haiti 19.03N 72.38W
71 F2 Verrey-sous-Salmaise France 47.26N 4.40E
76 B8 Verride Portugal 40.08N 8.43W
72 C2 Verrie,la France 46.58N 1.00W
72 F3 Verrières France 46.25N 0.36E
68 E5 Verrièrres-le-Buisson France 48.45N 2.17E
15 M6 Verron Ra New Ireland
72 D2 Verruyes France 46.31N 0.16W
68 C4 Versailles France 48.48N 2.08E
107 L2 Versailles Indiana 39.04N 85.16W
107 M3 Versailles Kentucky 38.02N 84.45W
107 D3 Versailles Missouri 38.25N 92.51W
104 A6 Versailles Ohio 40.14N 84.27W
120 F5 Versalles Bolivia 12.42S 63.23W
66 O4 Versam Switzerland 46.48N 9.22E
66 L7 Vérscio Switzerland 46.12N 8.44E
71 H3 Vers-en-Montagne France 46.48N 5.55E
47 J5 Vershina Sverdlovsk U.S.S.R. 60.55N 62.12E
47 K5 Vershina Tyumen U.S.S.R. 61.50N 68.30E
42 K6 Vershino-Darasunskiy U.S.S.R. 52.22N 115.32E
42 E4 Vershino Rybnoye U.S.S.R. 55.16N 94.17E
42 K6 Vershino-Shakhtaminskiy U.S.S.R. 51.20N 117.15E
53 Y17 Versjøen L Norway 60.48N 8.30E
63 H8 Versmold W Germany 52.03N 8.09E
66 A6 Versoix Switzerland 46.17N 6.10E
66 A6 Versoix R France/Switz
72 K8 Versols-et-Lapeyre France 43.54N 2.56E
70 K3 Verson France 49.09N 0.28W
71 F9 Vers-Pont-du-Gard France 43.58N 4.32E
95 G7 Verster S Africa 31.37S 23.10E
70 K3 Ver-sur-Mer France 49.20N 0.30W
72 C7 Vert France 44.05N 0.34W
71 C5 Vertaizon France 45.46N 3.17E
79 J1 Vertana,Cima mt Italy 46.33N 10.38E
89 A4 Vert,C Senegal 14.43N 17.33W
98 J7 Verte,Baie Nova Scotia/New Brunswick 46.00N 64.00W
70 C6 Verte,I France 47.46N 3.48W
98 C5 Verte,I Quebec 48.05N 69.25W
72 E5 Verteillac France 45.20N 0.22E
117 J8 Vertentes Brazil 7.50S 35.54W
118 D2 Vertentes,R Brazil
62 L8 Verteshegység mts Hungary
72 E7 Verteuil-d'Agenais France 44.28N 0.26E
72 E4 Verteuil-sur-Charente France 45.59N 0.14E
72 C5 Vertheuil France 45.16N 0.49W
116 E4 Vertientes Cuba 21.18N 78.11W
121 D5 Vertiz Argentina 35.26S 63.55W
69 B3 Verton France 50.23N 1.40E
98 N2 Verton,L Quebec
72 B1 Vertou France 47.10N 1.28W
84 G4 Vertoúra Greece 38.38N 23.37E
79 G3 Vértova Italy 45.49N 9.51E
45 P4 Vertunovskaya U.S.S.R. 52.26N 43.35E
69 G6 Vertus France 48.54N 4.00E
45 P8 Vertyachiy U.S.S.R. 48.56N 43.55E
79 M7 Verucchio Italy 43.59N 12.26E
95 P5 Verulam S Africa 29.39S 31.03E
84 D7 Vérvaina Greece 37.22N 22.27E
61 O4 Verviers Belgium 50.36N 5.52E
69 F4 Vervins France 49.50N 3.55E
65 B7 Verwall Gruppe mts Austria
56 H6 Verwood Dorset Eng 50.53N 1.52W
100 M9 Verwood Saskatchewan 49.32N 105.40W
66 M6 Verzasca,Valle Switzerland
79 N2 Verzegnis,Monte Italy 46.23N 12.54E
65 O8 Veržej Yugoslavia 46.35N 16.10E
69 G5 Verzenay France 49.10N 4.09E
79 B5 Verzuolo Italy 44.36N 7.28E
69 G5 Verzy France 49.09N 4.10E
51 M9 Vesanto Finland 62.56N 26.24E
67 P12 Vescovato Corsica 42.30N 9.26E
61 N4 Vesdre R Belgium
72 J2 Vesdun France 46.33N 2.27E
70 O4 Vesegre R France
47 H8 Veselaya,Gora mt U.S.S.R. 54.35N 58.00E
62 K7 Veselí Jihomoravský Czech 48.58N 17.25E
65 L3 Veselí nad Lužnice Czechoslovakia 49.12N 14.43E
44 A7 Veselinovo Ukraine U.S.S.R. 47.22N 31.14E
47 L6 Veselovka Chelyabinsk U.S.S.R. 54.59N 59.32E
47 H6 Vesëlovka Sverdlovsk U.S.S.R. 59.41N 59.56E
45 K9 Veselo-Voznesenka U.S.S.R. 47.07N 38.21E
43 N1 Veselovskoye U.S.S.R. 54.02N 78.45E
45 N9 Veselovskoye Vdkhr res U.S.S.R.
45 F9 Veseloye Ukraine U.S.S.R. 47.01N 34.56E
45 E8 Veselye Terny Ukraine U.S.S.R. 48.04N 33.35E
45 M9 Veselyy Rostov U.S.S.R. 47.06N 40.45E
45 P9 Veselyy Volgograd U.S.S.R. 47.50N 43.01E
43 H1 Veselyy Podol Kazakhstan U.S.S.R. 53.34N 65.58E
40 G10 Veselyy Yar U.S.S.R. 43.56N 135.24E
66 A7 Vésenaz Switzerland 46.15N 6.13E
66 A6 Vesenex France 46.22N 6.10E
70 K6 Vesgre R France
45 N7 Veshenskaya U.S.S.R. 49.39N 41.45E
45 S2 Veshkayma U.S.S.R. 54.05N 47.00E
47 E4 Veshkoma U.S.S.R. 64.22N 43.09E
68 C3 Vésinet,le France 48.54N 2.09E
120 A3 Vesique Peru 9.14S 78.28W
69 G5 Vesle R France
53 B2 Vesløs Denmark 57.02N 8.58E
70 H3 Vesly France 49.16N 1.30W
47 G4 Veslyana U.S.S.R. 62.58N 51.00E
47 G5 Veslyana R U.S.S.R.
71 J1 Vesoul France 47.38N 6.09E
109 M2 Vesper Kansas 39.03N 98.19W
106 E5 Vesper Wisconsin 44.29N 89.58W
79 E4 Vespolate Italy 45.21N 8.40E
Vespucio see Ciro Echesortu
60 K14 Vessem Netherlands 51.25N 5.17E
42 J3 Vesseniy U.S.S.R. 58.20N 114.50E
52 G10 Vessige Sweden 56.59N 12.40E
108 P5 Vesta Minnesota 44.30N 95.26W
53 V21 Vest Agder co Norway
103 B2 Vestal New York 42.05N 76.03W
103 B2 Vestal Center New York 42.02N 76.01W
50 F4 Vestari Jökulsá R Iceland
51 E3 Vestbygd Norway 68.20N 15.34E
50 L4 Vestdalseyri Iceland 65.17N 14.01W
65 N2 Vestecká hora mt Czechoslovakia 49.45N 15.45E
79 K3 Vestenanuova Italy 45.34N 11.13E
53 G7 Vestenskov Denmark 54.47N 11.07E
121 C9 Vester Argentina 43.45S 67.38W
53 E6 Vester Åby Denmark 55.06N 10.23E
51 D3 Vesterålen islds Norway
53 B3 Vester Assels Denmark 56.43N 8.40E
53 D3 Vester Bjerregrav Denmark 56.35N 9.31E
53 G7 Vesterborg Denmark 54.52N 11.17E
48 S12 Vesterbygd hist reg Greenland
53 H6 Vester Egede Denmark 55.17N 11.59E
53 H6 Vester Egesborg Denmark 55.09N 11.50E
53 E6 Vester Hæsinge Denmark 55.12N 10.15E
53 E2 Vester Hassing Denmark 57.04N 10.08E
53 D2 Vester Hjermitslev Denmark 57.17N 9.46E
53 C3 Vester Hornum Denmark 56.50N 9.22E
53 K4 Vester Karup Sweden 56.25N 12.47E
53 C5 Vesterlund Denmark 55.55N 9.20E
53 P12 Vestermarie Bornholm Denmark 55.07N 14.50E
53 C5 Vester Nebel Denmark 55.34N 9.25E
53 B5 Vester Nykirke Denmark 55.31N 8.42E
53 F2 Vesterøhavn Denmark 57.18N 10.57E
53 E6 Vester Skerninge Denmark 55.05N 10.28E
53 D7 Vester Sottrup Denmark 54.58N 9.43E
53 G7 Vester Tirsted Denmark 54.44N 11.21E
53 D3 Vester Tørslev Denmark 56.36N 9.55E
53 C2 Vester Torup Denmark 57.07N 9.08E
53 B2 Vester Vandet Denmark 57.01N 8.36E
53 B6 Vester Vedsted Denmark 55.18N 8.42E
53 D4 Vester Velling Denmark 56.26N 9.52E
53 A3 Vestervig Denmark 56.46N 8.20E
Vestfj-dal see Vest-fjordalen
53 Y19 Vest-fjordalen V Norway
51 C4 Vestfjorden inlet Norway
52 E7 Vestfold co Norway
123 C4 Vestfold Hills Antarctica
50 T13 Vestfonna glacier Spitsbergen 79.55N 20.00E
48 T13 Vest Grønland reg Greenland
118 D7 Véstia Brazil 20.19S 51.22W
53 G6 Vestjælland co Denmark
53 M9 Vestmanhavn Faeroes 62.09N 7.11W
50 E8 Vestmannaeyjar Iceland 63.25N 20.15W
50 E8 Vestmannaeyjar islds Iceland
53 W13 Vestnes Norway 62.38N 7.04E
39 E7 Vestnik,Bukhta gulf U.S.S.R.
79 H3 Vestone Italy 45.43N 10.24E
53 S20 Vestre Bokn isld Norway
53 S20 Vestrebokn isld Norway
50 E4 Vesturá R Húnavatnssýsla, Vestur Iceland
50 K3 Vestura R Múlasýsla, Nordhur Iceland
50 K3 Vesturárdalur V Iceland
50 E3 Vesturhópsholar Iceland 65.32N 20.40W
50 E4 Vesturhópsvatn L Iceland 65.28N 20.40W
50 L6 Vesturhorn C Iceland 64.17N 14.54W
50 E7 Vestur Landeyjar interfluve Iceland 63.43N 20.20W
50 K5 Vesturöræfi des Iceland
51 D3 Vestvågøy isld Norway 68.10N 13.50E
71 L9 Vésubie R France
80 K7 Vesuvio vol Italy 40.49N 14.26E
46 K1 Ves'yegonsk U.S.S.R. 58.38N 37.19E
62 K8 Veszprém Hungary 47.06N 17.54E
82 D3 Veszprém co Hungary
62 K8 Veszprémvarsány Hungary 47.25N 17.52E
62 N9 Vésztő Hungary 46.55N 21.15E
95 J3 Vet R S Africa
108 J6 Vetal S Dakota 43.12N 101.23W
28 E3 Vetapalem Andhra Prad India 15.50N 80.23E
9 U4 Vetauua isld Fiji 15.57S 179.25W
42 K4 Vetekhtina U.S.S.R. 55.20N 120.00E
100 F6 Veteran Alberta 52.01N 111.10W
103 F2 Veteran New York 42.05N 74.01W
108 F8 Veteran Wyoming 41.57N 104.23W
69 B5 Vétheuil France 49.04N 1.42E
45 C4 Vetka Belorussiya U.S.S.R. 52.35N 31.13E
52 J9 Vetlanda Sweden 57.26N 15.05E
53 V16 Vetlefjord Norway 61.18N 6.34E
46 O1 Vetluga U.S.S.R. 57.50N 45.42E
46 O1 Vetluga R U.S.S.R.
46 O1 Vetluzhskiy U.S.S.R. 58.26N 45.28E

46 O2 **Vetluzhskiy** U.S.S.R. 57.04N 45.01E
82 K7 **Vetovo** Bulgaria 43.42N 26.16E
80 F4 **Vetralla** Italy 42.19N 12.03E
71 J4 **Vétraz-Monthoux** France 46.10N 6.15E
82 J8 **Vetren** Bulgaria 42.15N 24.03E
39 D4 **Vetrenyy** U.S.S.R. 61.49N 149.50E
46 G2 **Vetrino** Belorussiya U.S.S.R. 55.24N 28.30E
95 K4 **Vetrivier** S Africa 28.29S 26.42E
66 F7 **Vétroz** Switzerland 46.14N 7.17E
65 M3 **Větrý Jenikov** Czechoslovakia 49.29N 15.29E
63 U9 **Vetschau** E Germany 51.47N 14.05E
79 M1 **Vetta d'Italia** *mt* Italy/Austria 47.05N 12.11E
51 J4 **Vettäsjärvi** Sweden 67.24N 21.40E
53 H6 **Vetterslev** Denmark 55.23N 11.48E
53 X16 **Vetti** Norway 61.22N 7.55E
53 X16 **Vettisfossen** *waterfall* Norway 61.23N 7.57E
79 H6 **Vetto** Italy 44.29N 10.20E
80 H3 **Vettore,Monte** Italy 42.49N 13.17E
64 B2 **Vettweiss** W Germany 50.44N 6.35E
39 H4 **Vetvey** U.S.S.R. 60.48N 166.05E
72 E2 **Veude** *R* France
70 M2 **Veules** France 49.53N 0.54E
70 M2 **Veulettes** France 49.51N 0.36E
53 Y20 **Veum** Norway 59.17N 8.05E
25 J6 **Veun Kham** Cambodia 13.54N 106.01E
72 L2 **Veurdre,la** France 46.46N 3.02E
71 H6 **Veurey-Voroize** France 45.16N 5.36E
61 A2 **Veurne** Belgium 51.04N 2.40E
69 G5 **Veuve,La** France 49.02N 4.19E
107 L3 **Vevay** Indiana 38.45N 85.08W
51 C6 **Vevelstad** Norway 65.43N 12.30E
87 D7 **Veveno,R** Sudan
65 O3 **Veverská Bitýška** Czechoslovakia 49.17N 16.26E
66 D6 **Vevey** Switzerland 46.28N 6.51E
83 E4 **Vévi** Greece 40.47N 21.38E
53 S16 **Vevring** Norway 61.30N 5.24E
66 F7 **Vex** Switzerland 46.13N 7.24E
58 F2 **Veyatie, L** Highland Scotland 58.08N 5.03W
45 K6 **Veydelevka** U.S.S.R. 50.09N 38.29E
39 J1 **Veyeman** U.S.S.R. 69.51N 174.46E
71 G4 **Veyle** *R* France
71 H7 **Veynes** France 44.31N 5.49E
111 L4 **Veyo** Utah 37.21N 113.41W
71 C5 **Veyre-Monton** France 45.40N 3.09E
66 A8 **Veyrier** France 45.53N 6.10E
66 A7 **Veyrier** Switzerland 46.11N 6.12E
32 C5 **Veys** Iran 31.30N 48.54E
64 B2 **Veytal** W Germany 50.37N 6.43E
66 D6 **Veytaux** Switzerland 46.26N 6.56E
41 J3 **Vezdekhodnaya** *R* U.S.S.R.
76 J5 **Vezdemarbán** Spain 41.38N 5.23W
71 D2 **Vézelay** France 47.28N 3.43E
69 L7 **Vézelise** France 48.29N 6.06E
71 E8 **Vézénobres** France 44.03N 4.08E
72 H5 **Vézère** *R* France
47 G4 **Vezhayu** U.S.S.R. 62.34N 54.50E
82 J8 **Vezhen** *mt* Bulgaria 42.45N 24.22E
45 E5 **Vezhevka** Ukraine U.S.S.R. 51.00N 33.46E
47 G4 **Vezh'yudor** U.S.S.R. 63.04N 51.01E
66 M7 **Vezia** Switzerland 46.02N 8.56E
69 K5 **Vezin** France 49.29N 5.31E
72 C1 **Vezins** Maine-et-Loire France 47.07N 0.42W
72 K7 **Vézins-de-Lévézou** France 44.16N 2.56E
36 H1 **Vezirköprü** Turkey 41.09N 35.27E
61 E4 **Vezon** Belgium 50.34N 3.30E
69 M6 **Vezouse** *R* France
79 H2 **Vezza di Oglio** Italy 46.14N 10.24E
79 L2 **Vezzana,Cima di** *mt* Italy 46.18N 11.50E
67 P12 **Vezzani** Corsica 42.10N 9.15E
79 K2 **Vezzano** Italy 46.05N 11.00E
79 G6 **Vezzano Ligure** Italy 44.08N 9.53E
70 O5 **Viabon** France 48.13N 1.42E
75 M3 **Viacamp** Spain 42.08N 0.37E
120 E7 **Viacha** Bolivia 16.40S 68.17W
79 J5 **Viadana** Italy 44.56N 10.31E
76 D5 **Viade** Portugal 41.45N 7.51W
56 L3 **Via Devana** *hist route* Eng
15 H5 **Viai I** Papua New Guinea 3.23S 144.25E
Vialar *see* **Tissemsilt**
71 D8 **Vialas** France 44.20N 3.52E
66 O5 **Via Mala** *gorge* Switzerland
121 J3 **Viamão** Brazil 30.05S 51.00W
121 D4 **Viamonte** Argentina 33.46S 63.03W
121 L9 **Viamonte** Argentina 53.55S 67.28W
109 Q6 **Vian** Oklahoma 35.30N 94.59W
91 C8 **Viana** Angola 8.54S 13.23E
117 F6 **Viana** Brazil 3.15S 44.59W
118 H7 **Viana** Brazil 20.21S 40.30W
75 F2 **Viana** Spain 42.31N 2.22W
76 K5 **Viana de Cega** Spain 41.31N 4.45W
76 D12 **Viana do Alentejo** Portugal 38.20N 8.00W
76 B5 **Viana do Castelo** Portugal 41.41N 8.50W
61 P7 **Vianden** Luxembourg 49.56N 6.12E
61 F4 **Viane** Belgium 50.44N 3.56E
72 K8 **Viane** France 43.44N 2.35E
60 M13 **Vianen** Noord-Brabant Netherlands 51.43N 5.51E
60 J12 **Vianen** Zuid Holland Netherlands 52.00N 5.05E
79 J5 **Viano** Italy 44.32N 10.38E
76 E4 **Viano del Bollo** Spain 42.11N 7.07W
118 E5 **Vianópolis** Brazil 16.44S 48.33W
77 M3 **Vianos** Spain 38.38N 2.30W
51 L6 **Viantie** Finland 65.41N 24.57E
77 E5 **Viar** *R* Spain
79 H7 **Viareggio** Italy 43.52N 10.15E
79 D5 **Viarigi** Italy 44.58N 8.22E
72 K7 **Viarouges** France 44.15N 2.50E
71 C10 **Vias** France 43.19N 3.25E
76 B4 **Viascon** Spain 42.29N 8.32W
77 M7 **Viátor** Spain 36.54N 2.25W
72 J7 **Viaur** *R* France
53 W14 **Viavatn** *L* Norway 62.06N 7.25E
72 J6 **Viazac** France 44.38N 2.04E
100 O8 **Vibank** Saskatchewan 50.20N 103.59W
81 L3 **Vibonati** Italy 40.06N 15.35E
77 H5 **Viboras** *R* Spain
53 C4 **Viborg** Denmark 56.28N 9.25E
108 N6 **Viborg** S Dakota 43.10N 97.04W
53 B3 **Viborg** *co* Denmark
115 N2 **Viborillas, Cayos** *islds* Caribbean Sea
81 M6 **Vibo Valentia** Italy 38.40N 16.06E
70 M5 **Vibraye** France 48.03N 0.44E
53 E4 **Viby** Århus Denmark 56.08N 10.11E
53 J5 **Viby** Roskilde Denmark 55.33N 12.03E
52 L3 **Vibyggerå** Sweden 63.04N 18.20E
75 C7 **Vicálvaro** Spain 40.24N 3.35W
77 L7 **Vicar** Spain 36.50N 2.38W
81 G8 **Vicari** Sicily 37.50N 13.34E
75 B10 **Vicario, Embalse de** *res* Spain
79 K7 **Vicchio** Italy 43.56N 11.28E
72 G10 **Vicdessos** France 42.46N 1.28E
Viçe *see* **Fındıklı** Çoruh
123 D14 **Vicecomodoro Marambio** *Arg Base* Antarctica 64.14S 56.43W
72 E9 **Vic-en-Bigorre** France 43.23N 0.04E
115 A2 **Vicente Guerrero** Mexico 30.48N 116.00W
121 J3 **Vicente López** Buenos Aires Arg 34.31S 58.30W
111 F8 **Vicente,Pt** California 33.44N 118.26W
79 L3 **Vicenza** Italy 45.33N 11.32E
79 K3 **Vicenza** *prov* Italy
100 M9 **Viceroy** Saskatchewan 49.29N 105.26W
71 D10 **Vic, Etang de** *L* France 43.30N 3.50E
72 E8 **Vic-Fézensac** France 43.46N 0.19E
75 P4 **Vich** Spain 41.56N 2.16E
119 E5 **Vichada** *div* Colombia
119 E5 **Vichada, R** Colombia
121 G3 **Vichadero** Uruguay 31.45S 54.41W
120 F9 **Vichoca** Bolivia 20.42S 65.30W
61 D3 **Vichte** Belgium 50.50N 3.25E
61 P7 **Vichten** Luxembourg 49.48N 6.00E
46 M2 **Vichuga** U.S.S.R. 57.12N 41.50E
121 A5 **Vichuquén** Chile 34.50S 72.05W
71 C4 **Vichy** France 46.08N 3.25E
109 L5 **Vici** Oklahoma 36.09N 99.20W
75 K3 **Vicien** Spain 42.04N 0.26W
57 G4 **Vickerstown** Cumbria Eng 54.06N 3.15W
111 L8 **Vicksburg** Arizona 33.47N 113.45W
106 J7 **Vicksburg** Michigan 42.07N 85.33W
107 F9 **Vicksburg** Mississippi 32.21N 90.51W
107 F9 **Vicksburg Nat. Mil. Park** Miss
71 C5 **Vic-le-Comte** France 45.39N 3.16E
71 E9 **Vic-les-Fesq** France 43.52N 4.05E
67 O12 **Vico** Corsica 42.10N 8.48E
80 N5 **Vico del Gargano** Italy 41.53N 15.58E
80 K7 **Vico Equense** Italy 40.39N 14.26E
79 C6 **Vicoforte** Italy 44.22N 7.53E
80 F4 **Vico,Lago di** Italy
79 J7 **Vicopisano** Italy 43.42N 10.35E
75 H5 **Vicor,Sierra de** *mts* Spain
117 H9 **Viçosa** Alagoas Brazil 9.22S 36.10W
118 G7 **Viçosa** Minas Gerais Brazil 20.45S 42.53W
117 G6 **Viçosa do Ceará** Brazil 3.34S 41.05W
117 D4 **Vicosa, I** Brazil
66 P6 **Vicosoprano** Switzerland 46.22N 9.38E
80 G4 **Vicovaro** Italy 42.01N 12.54E
82 K3 **Vicovu de Sus** Romania 47.55N 25.39E
72 J2 **Vicq Exemplet** France 46.38N 2.09E
72 G4 **Vicq-sur-Breuilh** France 45.38N 1.23E
72 F2 **Vicq-sur-Gartempe** France 46.44N 0.51E
69 E5 **Vic-sur-Aisne** France 49.24N 3.07E
72 K6 **Vic-sur-Cère** France 44.59N 2.36E
69 M6 **Vic-sur-Seille** France 48.47N 6.31E
109 E3 **Victor** Colorado 38.43N 105.08W
110 O6 **Victor** Idaho 43.37N 111.09W
106 B8 **Victor** Iowa 41.43N 92.19W
110 L3 **Victor** Montana 46.25N 114.10W
104 H4 **Victor** New York 42.59N 77.26W
15 F6 **Victor Emanuel Ra** Papua New Guinea
12 E6 **Victor Harbour** S Australia 35.36S 138.35E
74 J9 **Victor Hugo** Algeria 35.25N 1.50E
121 E4 **Victoria** Argentina 32.40S 60.10W
90 D9 **Victoria** Cameroon 4.01N 9.12E
84 X19 **Victoria** Gozo Medit Sea 36.03N 14.14E
116 P5 **Victoria** Grenada, W I 12.12N 61.42W
89 B6 **Victoria** Guinea 10.50N 14.32W
115 L2 **Victoria** Honduras 14.57N 87.24W
23 G7 **Victoria** Hong Kong 22.16N 114.13E
109 L3 **Victoria** Kansas 38.51N 99.09W
18 L3 **Victoria** Labuan, Sabah Malaysia 5.20N 115.14E
19 K4 **Victoria** Luzon Philippines 15.35N 120.40E
26 R13 **Victoria** Mahé I Ind Oc 4.37S 55.27E
121 A7 **Victoria** Malleco Chile 38.15S 72.27W
98 T6 **Victoria** Newfoundland 47.48N 53.13W
82 J5 **Victoria** Romania 45.44N 24.41E
26 Q12 **Victoria** Seychelles, Ind Oc 4.38S 55.28E
112 K7 **Victoria** Texas 28.49N 97.01W
121 K9 **Victoria** Tierra del Fuego Chile 52.52S 69.24W
110 B1 **Victoria** Vancouver I, Br Col 48.25N 123.22w
104 G10 **Victoria** Virginia 36.59N 78.16W
116 O2 **Victoria** *co* Trinidad & Tobago
92 E12 **Victoria** *dist* Zimbabwe
92 E12 **Victoria** *prov* Zimbabwe
121 E4 **Victoria** *R* Argentina
10 J9 **Victoria** *state* Australia
95 F10 **Victoria Bay** S Africa
100 V8 **Victoria Beach** Manitoba 50.43N 96.32W
115 K6 **Victoria,Ciudad** Mexico 23.43N 99.10W
96 R13 **Victoria de Acentejo,La** Tenerife Canary Is 28.26N 16.28W
116 F4 **Victoria de las Tunas** Cuba 20.58N 76.59W
13 H5 **Victoria Downs** Queensland 20.44S 146.21E
92 B10 **Victoria Falls** Zambia/Zimbabwe 17.55S 25.52E
91 J12 **Victoria Falls** Zimbabwe 17.55S 25.51E
92 B10 **Victoria Falls** Zimbabwe 18.00S 25.48E
92 B10 **Victoria Falls Nat. Park** Zimbabwe
48 R1 **Victoria Fjord** Greenland
26 S14 **Victoria Harb** Mahé I Ind Oc
23 B9 **Victoria Harbour** Hong Kong
99 L8 **Victoria Harbour** Ontario 44.45N 79.46W
116 A2 **Victoria Hill** San Salvador I Bahamas 24.02N 74.28W
121 J5 **Victoria,I** Chile 45.20S 74.00W
Victoria I Franz Josef Land U.S.S.R. *see* **Viktoriya,Ostrov**
97 H3 **Victoria I** N W Terr
Victoria,L *see* **Zorkul', Ozero**
12 F5 **Victoria,L** New S Wales 34.00S 141.15E
12 G5 **Victoria L** New S Wales 32.30S 143.25E
99 N5 **Victoria,L** Quebec
12 J6 **Victoria,L** Victoria
77 G5 **Victoria,La** Spain 37.41N 4.51W
93 D6 **Victoria, Lake** Tanzania/Uganda/Kenya
123 H6 **Victoria Land** Antarctica
Victoria,Mt *see* **Tomaniivi** Fiji
25 B2 **Victoria Mt** Burma 21.12N 93.55E
11 G9 **Victoria, Mt** New Zealand 42.02S 172.08E
15 J8 **Victoria,Mt** Papua New Guinea 8.52S 147.32E
11 C5 **Victoria, Mt** *hill* Wellington New Zealand 41.18S 174.48E
93 C3 **Victoria Nile** *R* Uganda
14 B2 **Victoria Park** *dist* Perth, W Aust
12 K5 **Victoria Pass** New S Wales 33.30S 150.15E
23 B9 **Victoria Pk** Hong Kong 22.18N 114.08E
10 B11 **Victoria Pt** Macquarie I Pacific Oc 54.40S 158.55E
98 P5 **Victoria R** Newfoundland
13 B3 **Victoria R** N Terr Australia
11 G9 **Victoria Ra** New Zealand
14 A8 **Victoria Ra** W Australia
98 P5 **Victoria Res** Newfoundland
13 B3 **Victoria River Downs** N Terr Australia 16.20S 131.00E
118 C9 **Victoria,Sa.de la** *ra* Argentina
101 X1 **Victoria Str** N W Terr
11 H2 **Victoria Valley** New Zealand 35.09S 173.26E
99 T6 **Victoriaville** Quebec 46.04N 71.57W
95 G7 **Victoria West** S Africa 31.25S 23.08E
121 D6 **Victorica** Argentina 36.15S 65.25W
119 F6 **Victorino** Venezuela 2.51N 67.51W
98 L3 **Victor L** Quebec
111 G7 **Victorville** California 34.31N 117.18W
89 F9 **Victory** Ivory Coast 4.50N 6.22W
11 O12 **Victory Beach** New Zealand
13 C7 **Victory Downs** N Terr Australia 25.59S 132.55E
15 K8 **Victory,Mt** Papua New Guinea 9.13S 149.05E
123 J6 **Victory Mts** Antarctica
121 B3 **Vicuña** Chile 30.00S 70.44W
121 D4 **Vicuña Mackenna** Argentina 33.53S 64.25W
108 E2 **Vida** Montana 47.50N 105.27W
110 C5 **Vida** Oregon 44.10N 122.36W
53 B7 **Vidå** *R* Denmark
76 D5 **Vidago** Portugal 42.38N 7.33W
111 K7 **Vidal** California 34.07N 114.30W
121 J9 **Vidal, I** Chile 52.00S 74.40W
105 E5 **Vidalia** Georgia 32.14N 82.24W
107 E10 **Vidalia** Louisiana 31.33N 91.26W
95 P9 **Vidal,Kaap** *C* S Africa 28.08S 32.33E
75 H2 **Vidángoz** Spain 42.48N 1.01W
76 A10 **Vidas** Portugal 39.22N 9.02W
26 R3 **Vidattaltivu** Sri Lanka 9.01N 80.03E
71 J10 **Vidauban** France 43.26N 6.26E
112 K7 **Vidauri** Texas 28.26N 97.10W
76 D8 **Vide** Portugal 40.17N 7.46W
53 B4 **Videbæk** Denmark 56.08N 8.38E
118 D10 **Videira** Brazil 26.58S 51.06W
82 K6 **Videle** Romania 44.15N 25.34E
53 N9 **Viderejde** Faeroes 62.23N 6.31W
53 O9 **Viderø** *isld* Faeroes 62.20N 6.30W
53 W15 **Videseter** Norway 61.56N 7.15E
50 K2 **Vídharfjall** *mt* Iceland 66.15N 15.45W
50 K2 **Vidharvötn** *lakes* Iceland
50 D6 **Vidhey** Iceland 64.10N 21.51W
50 M4 **Vidhfjördhur** *B* Iceland
50 D3 **Vidhidalsa** Iceland 65.40N 21.36W
50 E4 **Vidhidalsá** *R* Iceland
50 E4 **Vídhidalsfjall** *mt* Iceland 65.24N 20.28W
50 E4 **Vídhidalstunga** Iceland 65.22N 20.37W
50 K4 **Vidhidalur** Iceland 65.30N 15.58W
50 F3 **Vidhimyri** Iceland 65.32N 19.30W
50 J3 **Vidhirhóll** Iceland 65.43N 16.02W
50 L5 **Vidhivellir** Iceland 64.59N 14.59W
Vidhoy *isld see* **Viderø**
50 F3 **Vidhvík** Iceland 65.46N 19.17W
50 L2 **Vidhvík** *inlet* Iceland
76 K2 **Vidiago** Spain 43.24N 4.42W
76 D11 **Vidigão** Portugal 38.48N 7.44W
76 D12 **Vidigueira** Portugal 38.12N 7.48W
82 H7 **Vidin** Bulgaria 44.00N 22.50E
76 G1 **Vidio,C** Spain 43.35N 6.14W
29 E6 **Vidisha** Madhya Prad India 23.30N 77.50E
72 F4 **Vidix** France 45.47N 0.45E
75 D4 **Vid,La** Spain 41.37N 3.29W
47 C5 **Vidlitsa** U.S.S.R. 61.12N 32.21E
82 G7 **Vidojevica** *mt* Yugoslavia 43.08N 21.33E
76 G6 **Vidola,La** Spain 41.09N 6.28W
79 M3 **Vidor** Italy 45.52N 12.03E
100 H9 **Vidora** Saskatchewan 49.21N 109.25W
71 E9 **Vidourie** *R* France
82 K5 **Vidra** Bârlad Romania 45.56N 26.55E
82 K6 **Vidra** Bucureşti Romania 44.16N 26.11E
75 Q4 **Vidreras** Spain 41.48N 2.47E
77 L4 **Vidriera,La** Spain 38.04N 2.32W
53 D1 **Vidstrup** Denmark 57.31N 9.58E
76 D8 **Vidual** Portugal 40.07N 7.52W
82 E8 **Viduša** *mts* Yugoslavia
46 F2 **Vidzy** Belorussiya U.S.S.R. 55.23N 26.32E
47 G5 **Vidz'yuyar** U.S.S.R. 60.53N 51.20E
70 L3 **Vie** *R* Calvados France
72 A2 **Vie** *R* Vendée France
64 O5 **Viechtach** W Germany 49.05N 12.54E
95 M7 **Viedgesville** S Africa 31.43S 28.42E
121 D8 **Viedma** Argentina 40.45S 63.00W
121 J7 **Viedma,L** Argentina
65 L4 **Viehberg** *mt* Austria 48.34N 14.38E
71 C6 **Vieille-Brioude** France 45.16N 3.23E
72 B2 **Vieillevigne** France 46.58N 1.20W
76 B9 **Vieira** Estremadura Portugal 39.52N 8.56W
76 C5 **Vieira** Minho Portugal 41.38N 8.08W
76 K2 **Vieja,Peña** *mt* Spain 43.10N 4.50W
120 B6 **Viejas,I.de las** Peru 14.16S 76.14W
77 C4 **Vieja,Sierra** *mt* Spain 38.30N 6.33W
112 C5 **Vieja,Sierra** *mts* Texas
115 C2 **Viejo, Cerro** *pk* Mexico 30.18N 112.20W
96 Q14 **Viejo,Pico** *mt* Tenerife Canary Is 28.16N 16.41W
72 D8 **Viella** France 43.36N 0.08W
75 M2 **Viella** Spain 42.41N 0.47E
75 M2 **Viella, Túnel de** *pass* Spain 42.39N 0.46E
72 E10 **Vielle-Aure** France 42.49N 0.18E
70 M4 **Vielle-Lyre, la** France 48.55N 0.45E
70 B8 **Vielle-St. Girons** France 43.56N 1.18W
72 J8 **Vielmur-sur-Agout** France 43.37N 2.06E
61 O5 **Vielsalm** Belgium 50.17N 5.55E
69 E6 **Viels-Maisons** France 48.54N 3.23E
71 G2 **Vielverge** France 47.17N 5.26E
61 M4 **Viemme** Belgium 50.38N 5.16E
53 J6 **Viemose** Denmark 55.02N 12.08E
63 N9 **Vienenburg** W Germany 51.57N 10.35E
25 F2 **Vieng Pou Kha** Laos 20.39N 101.05E
Vienna Austria *see* **Wien**
105 D5 **Vienna** Georgia 32.05N 83.49W
107 H4 **Vienna** Illinois 37.24N 88.55W
104 K8 **Vienna** Maryland 39.29N 75.50W
107 E3 **Vienna** Missouri 38.12N 91.59W
103 E5 **Vienna** New Jersey 40.53N 74.54W
108 N5 **Vienna** S Dakota 44.42N 97.30W
104 H8 **Vienna** Virginia 38.56N 77.17W
104 D7 **Vienna** W Virginia 39.20N 81.33W
71 F5 **Vienne** France 45.32N 4.54E
67 F6 **Vienne** *dept* France
72 F3 **Vienne** *R* France
69 H5 **Vienne-la-Ville** France 49.10N 4.52E
69 H5 **Vienne-le-Château** France 49.11N 4.54E
121 B3 **Vientes,Paso del** *pass* Arg/Chile 30.44S 70.17W
25 G4 **Vientiane** Laos 17.59N 102.38E
121 B6 **Viento, C. del** *ra* Argentina
96 O14 **Viento, Pta. del** *pt* Gomera Canary Is 28.09N 17.21W
77 N5 **Viento,Sierra del** *mts* Spain
105 K7 **Vieques,I.de** Puerto Rico
63 U5 **Viereck** E Germany 53.33N 14.03E
51 M8 **Vieremä** Finland 63.48N 27.00E
95 K3 **Vierfontein** S Africa 27.05S 26.45E
60 M10 **Vierhouten** Netherlands 52.20N 5.50E
63 M6 **Vierlande** *reg* W Germany
60 N13 **Vierlingsbeek** Netherlands 51.36N 6.01E
64 F4 **Viernheim** W Germany 49.32N 8.35E
60 E12 **Vierpolders** Netherlands 51.53N 4.10E
63 U6 **Vierraden** E Germany 53.06N 14.18E
61 J2 **Viersel** Belgium 51.12N 4.39E
64 A1 **Viersen** W Germany 51.16N 6.24E
61 M5 **Vierset-Barse** Belgium 50.29N 5.18E
Vier Töre *see* **Packsattel**
70 J3 **Vierville-sur-Mer** France 49.23N 0.55W
66 K3 **Vierwaldstätter See** *L* Switz
72 J1 **Vierzon** France 47.14N 2.03E
115 H5 **Viesca** Mexico 25.21N 102.50W
63 Q6 **Viesecke** E Germany 53.02N 12.02E
64 L1 **Vieselbach** E Germany 51.00N 11.08E
46 F2 **Viesite** Latvia U.S.S.R. 56.20N 25.31E
70 J4 **Viessoix** France 48.50N 0.48W
80 O5 **Vieste** Italy 41.52N 16.11E
61 H5 **Viesville** Belgium 50.29N 4.25E
17 G8 **Vietnam** *people's rep* Indo-China
25 H2 **Vietri** Vietnam 21.20N 105.26E
80 N7 **Vietri di Potenza** Italy 40.36N 15.31E
80 L7 **Vietri sul Mare** Italy 40.40N 14.44E
63 R7 **Vietznitz** E Germany 52.44N 12.38E
72 B8 **Vieux-Boucau-les-Bains** France 43.47N 1.24W
116 N3 **Vieux-Bourg** Guadeloupe W I 16.21N 61.31W
116 M4 **Vieux Fort** Guadeloupe W I 15.57N 61.42W
116 O8 **Vieux Fort** St Lucia, W I 13.46N 60.58W
116 M4 **Vieux Fort,Pte.du** Guadeloupe W I 15.57N 61.43W
61 H4 **Vieux-Genappe** Belgium 50.37N 4.26E
116 M4 **Vieux-Habitants** Guadeloupe W I 16.04N 61.45W
66 B4 **Vieux les Hôpitaux** France 46.47N 6.22E
61 N5 **Vieuxville** Belgium 50.24N 5.33E
61 L4 **Vieux-Waleffe** Belgium 50.37N 5.12E
71 M8 **Vievola** France 44.06N 7.34E
112 H3 **View** Texas 32.20N 99.55W
71 H6 **Vif** France 45.03N 5.40E
50 D6 **Vifilsfell** *mt* Iceland 64.02N 21.34W
50 L4 **Vifilsstadhaflói** *R* Iceland
53 H5 **Vig** Denmark 55.51N 11.36E
46 N1 **Viga** *R* U.S.S.R.
19 K3 **Vigan** Luzon Philippines 17.35N 120.23E
71 D9 **Vigan,le** France 43.59N 3.36E
79 L5 **Vigarano Mainarda** Italy 44.51N 11.30E
118 H8 **Vigário Geral** Brazil 22.49S 43.19W
79 J4 **Vigásio** Italy 45.19N 10.56E
53 W15 **Vigdal** Norway 61.30N 7.18E
53 S19 **Vigdarvatn** *L* Norway 59.32N 5.22E
79 F8 **Vigentino** *dist* Milan Italy
72 G5 **Vigeois** France 45.22N 1.30E
79 E4 **Vigevano** Italy 45.19N 8.51E
66 K7 **Vigezzo,Valle** Italy
81 M4 **Viggianello** Italy 39.58N 16.05E
81 L3 **Viggiano** Italy 40.20N 15.54E
66 M8 **Viggiu** Italy 45.52N 8.54E
117 D5 **Vigia** Brazil 0.50S 48.07W
76 C13 **Vigia** *mt* Portugal 37.37N 8.23W
121 L7 **Vigiá,C** Argentina 48.35S 66.52W
115 Q8 **Vigía Chico** Mexico 19.49N 87.32W
70 P6 **Viglain** France 47.44N 2.17E
53 U20 **Viglesdalshytta** Norway 59.09N 6.26E
80 H5 **Viglio,Monte** Italy 41.53N 13.23E
69 C3 **Vignacourt** France 50.01N 2.13E
79 D4 **Vignale** Italy 45.01N 8.23E
80 F4 **Vignanello** Italy 42.23N 12.17E
79 F4 **Vignate** Italy 45.30N 9.22E
72 D10 **Vignemale,Pic de** France 42.46N 0.08W
71 C8 **Vignes,les** France 44.17N 3.13E
69 K6 **Vigneulles-les-Hattonchâtel** France 48.59N 5.43E
69 G4 **Vigneux-Hocquet** France 49.45N 4.00E
68 F5 **Vigneux-sur-Seine** France 48.42N 2.25E
79 K6 **Vignola** Italy 44.29N 11.01E
81 C1 **Vignola** *R* Sardinia
69 J7 **Vignory** France 48.17N 5.06E
79 M1 **Vigo** Italy 46.30N 12.29E
76 B4 **Vigo** Spain 42.15N 8.44W
79 K2 **Vigo d'Anaunia** Italy 46.16N 11.06E
79 L2 **Vigo di Fassa** Italy 46.26N 11.41E
79 K2 **Vigolo Vattaro** Italy 46.01N 11.12E
79 B5 **Vigone** Italy 44.50N 7.29E
79 L4 **Vigonza** Italy 45.26N 12.00E
76 B4 **Vigo, Ría de** *B* Spain
14 C5 **Vigors,Mt** W Australia 22.32S 118.14E
53 U13 **Vigra** Norway 62.33N 6.05E
52 B4 **Vigra Giske** Norway
52 B8 **Vigrestad** Norway 58.34N 5.43E
53 H7 **Vigsnæs** Denmark 54.54N 11.40E
53 B2 **Vigsø** Denmark 57.06N 8.44E
53 B2 **Vigsø Bugt** *B* Denmark 57.08N 8.45E
75 E3 **Viguera** Spain 42.19N 2.32W
50 C2 **Vigur** *isld* Iceland 66.04N 22.48W
79 E5 **Viguzzolo** Italy 44.54N 8.55E
69 L5 **Vigy** France 49.12N 6.18E
51 L7 **Vihanti** Finland 64.29N 25.00E
31 G5 **Vihari** Pakistan 30.03N 72.32E
72 C1 **Vihiers** France 47.09N 0.31W
62 N7 **Vihorlát** *mts* Czechoslovakia
51 L11 **Vihti** Finland 60.25N 24.16E
51 K10 **Viiala** Finland 61.16N 23.45E
51 O9 **Viinijärvi** *L* Finland 62.45N 29.15E
51 M5 **Viiri** Finland 66.24N 26.30E
51 M8 **Viitasaari** Finland 63.06N 25.47E
29 C6 **Vijapur** Gujarat India 23.34N 72.47E
28 A2 **Vijayadurg** Maharashtra India 16.34N 73.22E
Vijayanagar *see* **Hampi**
28 C6 **Vijayāpati** Tamil Nadu India 8.12N 77.45E
28 E2 **Vijayawada** Andhra Prad India 16.34N 80.40E
60 T17 **Vijlen** Netherlands 50.47N 5.58E
72 J3 **Vijon** France 46.25N 2.06E
83 D4 **Vijosë** *R* Albania
50 F8 **Vík** Iceland 63.25N 19.00W
51 C6 **Vik** Nordland Norway 65.19N 12.10E
53 U20 **Vik** Rogaland Norway 59.21N 6.13E
52 H6 **Vika** Sweden 60.56N 14.30E
52 J6 **Vika** Sweden 60.31N 15.45E
51 M5 **Vikajärvi** Finland 66.37N 26.10E
53 M9 **Víkar** Faeroes 62.08N 7.23W
28 C2 **Vikarabad** Andhra Prad India 17.20N 77.54E
52 J6 **Vikarbyn** Sweden 60.57N 15.00E
53 X14 **Vikdalsvatn** *L* Sogn og Fjordane Norway 62.05N 7.35E
53 T17 **Vike** Hordaland Norway 60.42N 5.35E
53 Y13 **Vike** Möre og Romsdal Norway 62.33N 8.10E
53 T20 **Vikedal** Norway 59.30N 5.55E
53 K4 **Viken** Sweden 56.09N 12.36E
52 E7 **Vikersund** Norway 59.58N 9.59E
52 H7 **Vikersvik** Sweden 59.27N 14.50E
53 Y13 **Vikesaksa** *mt* Norway 62.35N 8.14E
53 T20 **Vikevåg** Norway 59.06N 5.41E
53 T19 **Vikevik** Norway 59.36N 5.36E
53 K5 **Vikhog** Sweden 55.44N 12.59E
42 G4 **Vikhorevka** U.S.S.R. 56.10N 101.02E
82 H9 **Vikhren** *mt* Bulgaria 41.47N 23.22E
100 F5 **Viking** Alberta 53.07N 111.50W
54 M9 **Viking** *oil field* North Sea 53.28N 2.19E
50 J2 **Vikingavatn** *L* Iceland 66.06N 16.49W
54 M2 **Viking Bank** North Sea
52 J6 **Vikmanshyttan** Sweden 60.19N 15.55E
52 F2 **Vikna** Norway 64.54N 10.58E
52 F2 **Vikna** *isld* Norway 64.55N 10.55E
50 H2 **Víknafjöll** *mt* Iceland 66.03N 17.49W
53 U18 **Vikøy** Norway 60.20N 6.11E
53 U16 **Viksdalen** Sogn og Fjordane Norway 61.21N 6.07E
53 V16 **Viksdalen** Sogn og Fjordane Norway 61.04N 6.35E
53 T16 **Viksdalsvatn** *L* Sogn og Fjordane Norway 61.19N 6.00E
52 K4 **Viksjo** Sweden 62.45N 17.30E
53 V16 **Viksøyri** Norway 61.05N 6.35E
53 Y18 **Vikstøl** Norway 60.13N 8.23E
48 K11 **Viktoriya,Ostrov** *isld* Franz Josef Land U.S.S.R. 80.10N 37.00E
43 G1 **Viktorovka** Kazakhstan U.S.S.R. 52.50N 62.31E
42 E2 **Viktorovskiy** U.S.S.R. 60.01N 93.07E
41 B2 **Vikulova,Mys** *C* Novaya Zemlya U.S.S.R. 74.36N 60.00E
47 L7 **Vikulovo** U.S.S.R. 56.51N 70.30E
50 J4 **Vikursandur** *sand reg* Iceland
9 C11 **Vila** New Hebrides 17.45S 168.18E
117 D5 **Vila Aramá** Brazil 0.58S 50.15W
19 D8 **Vila Armindo Monteiro** Timor 9.01S 125.24E
91 C11 **Vila Arriaga** Angola 14.44S 13.24E
96 S6 **Vila-Baleira** Madeira Is 33.04N 16.20W
118 J10 **Vila Balneária** Brazil 23.01S 43.18W
75 N5 **Vilabella** Spain 41.15N 1.20E
76 B4 **Vilaboa** Spain 42.21N 8.39W
76 E11 **Vila Boim** Portugal 38.52N 7.17W
117 B7 **Vila Braga** Brazil 4.20S 56.07W
120 F8 **Vilacaya** Bolivia 19.58S 65.31W
76 C6 **Vilacova da Lixa** Portugal 41.18N 8.09W
75 O3 **Vilada** Spain 42.08N 1.55E
92 H10 **Vila da Maganja** Mozambique 17.20S 37.31E
76 D7 **Vila da Ponte** Portugal 40.56N 7.30W
89 O10 **Vila da Ribeira Brava** Cape Verde 16.38N 24.17W
89 O10 **Vila das Pombas** Cape Verde 17.10N 25.00W
88 B1 **Vila Das Velas** Azores 38.34N 28.15W
Vila de Cangamba *see* **Cangamba**
76 B7 **Vila de Feira** Portugal 40.55N 8.32W
76 D12 **Vila de Frades** Portugal 38.13N 7.49W
94 M5 **Vila de João Belo** Mozambique 25.04S 33.38E
19 D8 **Vila de Liquiçá** Indonesia 8.36S 125.20E
19 E8 **Vila de Manatuto** Indonesia 8.33S 126.03E
75 R3 **Vilademat** Spain 42.08N 3.05E
75 Q3 **Vilademuls** Spain 42.08N 2.52E
76 C9 **Vila de Rei** Portugal 39.41N 8.09W
19 E8 **Vila de Salazar** Indonesia 8.30S 126.28E
89 P10 **Vila de Sal-Rei** Cape Verde 16.12N 22.58W
37 G5 **Vilâdikars** Turkey 40.31N 42.59E
76 B14 **Vila do Bispo** Portugal 37.05N 8.53W
76 B6 **Vila do Conde** Portugal 41.21N 8.45W
89 P11 **Vila do Maio** Cape Verde 15.12N 23.15W
96 U5 **Vila do Porto** Azores 36.57N 25.10W
117 E1 **Vila dos Remédios** Fernando de Noronha Atl Oc 3.50S 32.25W
89 P11 **Vila do Tarrafal** Cape Verde 15.17N 23.45W
75 P4 **Viladrau** Spain 41.51N 2.23E
89 J3 **Vila du Tilemsi** *watercourse* Mali
76 E11 **Vila Fernando** Alto Alentejo Portugal 38.55N 7.19W
76 E8 **Vila Fernando** Beira Alta Portugal 40.29N 7.08W
76 D9 **Vila Flôr** Alto Alentejo Portugal 39.31N 7.48W
96 Q14 **Vilaflor** Tenerife Canary Is 28.09N 16.38W
76 E6 **Vila Flôr** Trás os Montes e Alto Douro Portugal 41.18N 7.09W
118 G10 **Vila Formosa** *dist* São Paulo Brazil
76 B11 **Vila Franca de Xira** Portugal 38.57N 8.59W
96 U2 **Vila Franca do Campo** Azores 37.28N 25.27W
76 E7 **Vila France das Naves** Portugal 40.44N 7.16W
76 B11 **Vila Fresca de Azeitão** Portugal 38.31N 8.59W
92 F9 **Vila Gamito** Mozambique 14.11S 32.59E
19 D8 **Vila General Carmona** Indonesia 8.43S 125.37E
Vila General Machado *see* **General Machado**
94 M5 **Vila Gomes da Costa** Mozambique 24.19S 33.38E
118 G9 **Vila Guilherme** *dist* São Paulo Brazil
Vila Henrique de Carvalho *see* **Henrique de Carvalho**
70 H5 **Vilaine** *R* Ille-et-Vilaine France
70 F6 **Vilaine** *R* Morbihan France
118 J9 **Vila Isabel** Brazil 22.56S 43.15W
118 F9 **Vila Jaguara** *dist* São Paulo Brazil
75 R3 **Vilajuiga** Spain 42.20N 3.05E
75 M3 **Vilaller** Spain 42.29N 0.43E
75 P3 **Vilallonga de Ter** Spain 42.20N 2.19E
94 M5 **Vila Luisa** Mozambique 25.44S 32.41E
Vila Luso *see* **Luso**
92 G11 **Vila Machado** Mozambique 19.18S 34.11E
118 F10 **Vila Madalena** *dist* São Paulo Brazil
120 E10 **Vilama, L** Argentina
118 G9 **Vila Maria** *dist* São Paulo Brazil
118 G10 **Vila Mariana** *dist* São Paulo Brazil
Vila Mariano Machado *see* **Mariano Machado**
89 O10 **Vila Maria Pia** Cape Verde 17.13N 25.04W
118 G10 **Vila Matilde** *dist* São Paulo Brazil
120 F4 **Vila Murtinho** Brazil 10.21S 65.19W
66 P3 **Vilan** *mt* Switzerland 47.02N 9.37E
94 N4 **Vilanculos** Mozambique 22.01S 35.19E
46 F2 **Vilāni** Latvia U.S.S.R. 56.32N 26.58E
76 A11 **Vila Nogueira de Azeitão** Portugal 38.31N 9.01W
91 E10 **Vila Nova** Angola 12.38S 16.03E
96 U3 **Vila Nova** Azores 38.47N 27.10W
117 B7 **Vila Nova** Pará Brazil 4.23S 56.07W
76 D12 **Vila Nova** Portugal 38.15N 7.54W
118 H9 **Vila Nova** Rio de Janeiro Brazil 22.52S 43.26W
76 D4 **Vilanova** Spain 42.10N 7.58W
91 F12 **Vila Nova da Armada** Angola 16.18S 19.05E
76 B5 **Vila Nova da Cerveira** Portugal 41.57N 8.44W
76 B10 **Vila Nova da Rainha** Portugal 39.02N 8.56W
76 C12 **Vila Nova de Baronia** Portugal 38.17N 8.03W
76 B6 **Vila Nova de Famalicão** Portugal 41.24N 8.31W
76 E6 **Vila Nova de Fozcôa** Portugal 41.05N 7.09W
76 B13 **Vila Nova de Milfontes** Portugal 37.43N 8.47W
76 B9 **Vila Nova de Ourém** Portugal 39.40N 8.35W
76 D7 **Vila Nova de Paiva** Portugal 40.51N 7.44W
75 P4 **Vilanova de Sau** Spain 41.57N 2.23E
91 D9 **Vila Nova do Seles** Angola 11.24S 14.19E
89 O11 **Vila Nova Sintra** Cape Verde 14.49N 24.41W
Vila Paiva d'Andrade *see* **Andrada**
94 N2 **Vila Paiva de Andrada** Mozambique 18.44S 34.03E
118 H8 **Vila Pedro II** Brazil 22.49S 43.21W
Vila Pereira d'Eca *see* **Pereira d'Eca**
76 C3 **Vilapouca** Spain 42.32N 8.19W
76 D6 **Vila Pouca de Aguiar** Portugal 41.30N 7.38W
76 B5 **Vila Praia de Âncora** Portugal 41.48N 8.52W
118 G10 **Vila Prudente** *dist* São Paulo Brazil
76 A10 **Vilar** Portugal 39.11N 9.07W
76 E5 **Vilarandelo** Portugal 41.39N 7.19W
76 C5 **Vilar da Veiga** Portugal 41.41N 8.11W
76 D6 **Vila Real** Portugal 41.17N 7.45W
76 D6 **Vila Real** *dist* Portugal
76 E14 **Vila Real de Santo Antonio** Portugal 37.12N 7.25W
76 E5 **Vilarelho da Raia** Portugal 41.50N 7.27W
76 F7 **Vilar Formoso** Portugal 40.37N 6.50W
76 E6 **Vilarica** *R* Portugal
76 E6 **Vilarinho das Azenhas** Portugal 41.22N 7.13W
76 D6 **Vilarinho de Samardã** Portugal 41.22N 7.43W
117 C5 **Vilarinho do Monte** Brazil 1.36S 52.00W
76 F6 **Vilarinho dos Gallegos** Portugal 41.16N 6.38W
76 F8 **Vilar Maior** Portugal 40.23N 6.56W
Vila Robert Williams *see* **Robert Williams**
76 E5 **Vilar Seco** Portugal 41.53N 7.10W
76 F7 **Vilar Torpim** Portugal 40.50N 6.56W
76 D12 **Vila Ruiva** Portugal 38.15N 7.56W
109 H4 **Vilas** Colorado 37.23N 102.26W
108 N5 **Vilas** S Dakota 44.02N 97.36W
91 D8 **Vila Salazar** Angola 9.18S 14.54E
76 C2 **Vilasantar** Spain 43.05N 8.08W
75 P4 **Vilasar de Mar** Spain 41.30N 2.24E
76 B6 **Vila Seca** Portugal 41.30N 8.41W
75 N5 **Vilaseca** Spain 41.06N 1.09E
Vila Serpa Pinto *see* **Serpa Pinto**
Vila Teixeira da Silva *see* **Teixeira da Silva**
75 P4 **Vilatorta** Spain 41.55N 2.20E
28 D6 **Vilattikulam** Tamil Nadu India 9.10N 78.11E
92 F9 **Vila Vasco da Gama** Mozambique 14.55S 32.17E
117 C3 **Vila Velha** Brazil 3.16N 51.14W
118 H7 **Vila Velha** Brazil 20.23S 40.18W
76 D9 **Vila Velha de Rodão** Portugal 39.39N 7.40W
76 C5 **Vila Verde** Minho Portugal 41.39N 8.27W
76 C15 **Vila Verde** Portugal 38.50N 9.22W
76 E13 **Vila Verde de Ficalho** Portugal 37.57N 7.18W
76 E5 **Vila Verde de Raia** Portugal 41.47N 7.25W
Vila Verissimo Sarmento *see* **Verissimo Sarmento**
76 E11 **Vila Viçosa** Portugal 38.46N 7.25W
28 C6 **Vilayankod** Tamil Nadu India 8.17N 77.13E
120 C5 **Vilcabamba,Cord** *mts* Peru
120 D5 **Vilcanota** *R* Peru
120 D5 **Vilcanota,Cord.de** *mts* Peru
82 H5 **Vîlcanului,Munţii** *mts* Romania
41 O2 **Vil'cheka,Ostrov** *isld* Franz Josef Land U.S.S.R. 79.52N 58.30E
41 P2 **Vil'cheka,Zemlya** *isld* Franz Josef Land U.S.S.R.
77 J4 **Vilches** Spain 38.13N 3.30W
53 B4 **Vildbjerg** Denmark 56.12N 8.47E
53 B3 **Vile** Denmark 56.44N 8.52E
47 F5 **Viled'** *R* U.S.S.R.
121 E1 **Vilelas** Argentina 27.59S 62.40W
39 J3 **Vilel'khem** *R* U.S.S.R.
64 P3 **Vilémov** Karlovy Vary Czech 50.19N 13.19E
65 N2 **Vilémov** Pardubice Czech 49.49N 15.32E
72 F7 **Vileneuve-sur-Lot** France 44.25N 0.43E
46 F3 **Vileyka** Belorussiya U.S.S.R. 54.30N 26.50E
47 G5 **Vil'gort** Komi U.S.S.R. 61.39N 50.41E
47 H5 **Vil'gort** Perm U.S.S.R. 60.36N 56.25E
52 K2 **Vilhelmina** Sweden 64.38N 16.40E
118 A3 **Vilhena** Brazil 12.40S 60.08W
39 F4 **Viliga-Kushka** U.S.S.R. 61.35N 156.55E
39 F4 **Viliginskiy,Mys** *C* U.S.S.R.
46 F1 **Viljandi** Estonia U.S.S.R. 58.22N 25.30E
95 L2 **Viljoensdrif** S Africa 26.44S 27.55E
95 C10 **Viljoenshof** S Africa 34.40S 19.40E
95 K3 **Viljoenskroon** S Africa 27.13S 26.57E
95 O3 **Viljoenspos** S Africa 27.35S 30.30E
62 O1 **Vilkavišhkis** Lithuania U.S.S.R. 54.39N 23.02E
41 S3 **Vil'kitskogo,Ostrov** *isld* Novosibirskiye O-va U.S.S.R. 75.44N 152.15E
41 C4 **Vil'kitskogo,Ostrov** *isld* U.S.S.R.
41 H2 **Vil'kitskogo,Proliv** *str* U.S.S.R.
46 G6 **Vilkovo** Ukraine U.S.S.R. 45.28N 29.32E
120 F9 **Villa Abecia** Bolivia 21.00S 65.18W
80 G5 **Villa Adriana** *ruins* Italy 41.57N 12.47E
115 F2 **Villa Ahumada** Mexico 30.38N 106.30W
121 D7 **Villa Alba** Argentina 38.02S 63.31W
121 B4 **Villa Alemana** Chile 33.02S 71.25W
115 L9 **Villa Alta** Mexico 17.21N 96.09W
116 J5 **Villa Altagracia** Dominican Rep 18.43N 70.13W
115 B10 **Villa Alvaro** *dist* Mexico City Mexico
121 F2 **Villa Ana** Argentina 28.28S 59.40W
121 E1 **Villa Ángela** Argentina 27.34S 60.45W
Villa Aroma *see* **Sicasica**
121 C5 **Villa Atuel** Argentina 34.50S 67.58W
79 K4 **Villa Bartolomea** Italy 45.09N 11.22E
79 M1 **Villabassa** Italy 46.44N 12.10E
81 F7 **Villabate** Sicily 38.05N 13.27E
120 F4 **Villa Bella** Bolivia 10.22S 65.22W
Villa Bens *see* **Tarfaya**
121 E1 **Villa Berthet** Argentina 27.17S 60.26W
77 B6 **Villablanca** Spain 37.18N 7.20W
76 G3 **Villablino** Spain 42.57N 6.19W
76 H2 **Villabona** Spain 43.27N 5.49W
76 J5 **Villabrágima** Spain 41.49N 5.07W
121 E1 **Villa Brana** Argentina 27.18S 62.55W
Villa Bruzual *see* **Turén**
76 J6 **Villabuena del Puente** Spain 41.23N 5.24W
72 G5 **Villac** France 45.11N 1.16E
121 E5 **Villa Cañás** Argentina 34.00S 61.35W
75 D8 **Villacañas** Spain 39.38N 3.20W
77 Y14 **Villa Carlos** Balearic Is 39.53N 4.17E
75 C1 **Villacarriedo** Spain 43.14N 3.48W
77 K4 **Villacarrillo** Spain 38.07N 3.05W
121 C2 **Villa Castelli** Argentina 28.58S 68.14W
76 L7 **Villacastín** Spain 40.46N 4.25W
65 J8 **Villach** Austria 46.37N 13.51E
76 F4 **Villachica o de Sanabria, Lago de** Spain 42.08N 6.43W
81 B5 **Villacidro** Sardinia 39.28N 8.44E
75 E4 **Villaciervos** Spain 41.46N 2.38W
Villa Cisneros *see* **Dakhla**
121 C3 **Villa Colón** Argentina 31.40S 68.20W
121 E3 **Villa Concepción del Tío** Arg 31.23N 62.46W
75 D7 **Villaconejos** Spain 40.06N 3.29W
121 E4 **Villa Constitución** Argentina 33.15S 60.20W
115 D5 **Villa Constitución** Mexico 24.59N 111.40W
115 G4 **Villa Coronado** Mexico 26.45N 105.10W
115 N9 **Villa Corzo** Mexico 16.12N 93.15W
76 K4 **Villada** Spain 42.15N 4.59W
79 G3 **Villa d'Almè** Italy 45.45N 9.37E
115 H8 **Villa de Alvarez** Mexico 19.18N 103.41W
89 P11 **Villa de Assomada** Cape Verde 15.07N 23.34W
79 D4 **Villadeati** Italy 45.04N 8.10E
76 F3 **Villadecanes** Spain 42.35N 6.46W
115 N10 **Villa de Comaltitlán** Mexico 15.14N 92.34W
115 H6 **Villa de Cos** Mexico 23.20N 102.20W
119 F2 **Villa de Cura** Venezuela 10.00N 67.30W
75 D8 **Villa de Don Fadrique, La** Spain 39.37N 3.14W
115 C9 **Villa de Guadalupe** Mexico
120 B1 **Villa de Jumbilla** Peru 5.53S 77.51W
76 G8 **Villa del Campo** Spain 40.09N 6.26W
76 L8 **Villa del Prado** Spain 40.16N 4.18W
76 F9 **Villa del Rey** Spain 39.40N 6.49W
77 H5 **Villa del Río** Spain 37.59N 4.17W
121 D3 **Villa del Rosario** Argentina 31.38S 63.34W
76 G5 **Villadepera** Spain 41.33N 6.08W
77 O2 **Villa de Ves** Spain 39.13N 1.15W
76 L3 **Villadiego** Spain 42.31N 4.01W
79 H2 **Villa di Tir** Italy 46.12N 10.07E
121 D3 **Villa Dolores** Argentina 31.58S 65.15W
81 H8 **Villadoro** Sicily 37.41N 14.16E
79 D2 **Villa d'Ossola** Italy 46.04N 8.16E
76 K3 **Villaeles de Valdavia** Spain 42.34N 4.35W
76 J6 **Villaescusa** Spain 41.12N 5.28W
75 E8 **Villaescusa de Haro** Spain 39.37N 2.40W
79 L4 **Villa Estense** Italy 45.10N 11.41E
79 C5 **Villafalletto** Italy 44.33N 7.32E
75 K7 **Villafamés** Spain 40.07N 0.04W
121 F3 **Villa Federal** Argentina 30.58S 58.46W
115 N9 **Villa Flores** Mexico 16.16N 93.15W
118 B10 **Villa Florida** Paraguay 26.25S 57.08W
76 K4 **Villafrades de Campos** Spain 42.05N 4.59W
118 B10 **Villa Franca** Paraguay 26.14S 58.20W
75 G3 **Villafranca** Spain 42.18N 1.45W
79 D5 **Villafranca d'Asti** Italy 44.54N 8.02E
77 W14 **Villafranca de Bonany** Balearic Is 39.34N 3.05E
77 G5 **Villafranca de Córdoba** Spain 37.58N 4.34W
76 F3 **Villafranca del Bierzo** Spain 42.36N 6.49W
75 H6 **Villafranca del Campo** Spain 40.41N 1.21W
75 K7 **Villafranca del Cid** Spain 40.26N 0.16W
77 D3 **Villafranca de los Barros** Spain 38.34N 6.20W
77 K2 **Villafranca de los Caballeros** Spain 39.26N 3.21W
75 O5 **Villafranca del Penedès** Spain 41.20N 1.42E
75 F1 **Villafranca de Oria** Spain 43.04N 2.10W
79 J4 **Villafranca di Verona** Italy 45.22N 10.51E
79 G6 **Villafranca in Lunigiana** Italy 44.17N 9.57E
75 D3 **Villafranca-Montes de Oca** Spain 42.23N 3.18W
79 L3 **Villafranca Padovana** Italy 45.30N 11.48E
79 C5 **Villafranca Piemonte** Italy 44.47N 7.30E
77 D6 **Villafranco del Guadalquivir** Spain 37.08N 6.10W
77 Q4 **Villafranqueza** Spain 38.24N 0.29W
81 F8 **Villafrati** Sicily 37.54N 13.29E
76 J5 **Villafrechós** Spain 41.54N 5.14W
75 C3 **Villafría de Burgos** Spain 42.22N 3.35W
75 C4 **Villafruela** Spain 41.55N 3.55W
76 L5 **Villafuerte** Spain 41.44N 4.19W
79 L4 **Villaga** Italy 45.23N 11.32E
76 B3 **Villagarcía de Arosa** Spain 42.35N 8.45W
76 J5 **Villagarcia de Campos** Spain 41.46N 5.12W
77 D4 **Villagarcia de la Torre** Spain 38.18N 6.05W
77 N2 **Villagarcía del Llano** Spain 39.20N 1.51W
76 G3 **Villagatón** Spain 42.38N 6.11W
112 N5 **Village Cr** Texas
112 N5 **Village Mills** Texas 30.30N 94.24W
121 D3 **Villa General Mitre** Argentina 30.43S 64.02W
121 C4 **Villa General Roca** Argentina 32.34S 66.30W
66 G1 **Village Neuf** France 47.36N 7.34E
76 G3 **Villager** Spain 42.57N 6.20W
77 D3 **Villagonzalo** Spain 38.52N 6.13W
115 K5 **Villagrán** Mexico 24.29N 99.30W
81 D4 **Villagrande Strisaili** Sardinia 39.58N 9.31E
107 H2 **Villa Grove** Illinois 39.54N 88.10W
121 F3 **Villaguay** Argentina 31.55S 59.01W
121 F2 **Villa Guillermina** Argentina 28.15S 59.29W
77 G4 **Villaharta** Spain 38.09N 4.54W
118 B9 **Villa Hayes** Paraguay 25.05S 57.25W
115 N8 **Villahermosa** Mexico 18.00N 92.53W
77 L3 **Villahermosa** Spain 38.46N 2.52W
75 K7 **Villahermosa del Río** Spain 40.12N 0.25W
121 F3 **Villa Hernandarias** Argentina 31.15S 59.59W
76 L4 **Villahizán de Treviño** Spain 42.29N 4.06W
75 C3 **Villahoz** Spain 42.05N 3.55W
121 D5 **Villa Huidobro** Argentina 34.50S 64.34W
120 D7 **Villa Industrial** Chile 17.47S 69.42W
71 F1 **Villaines-en-Duesmois** France 47.42N 4.31E
70 K5 **Villaines-la-Jubel** France 48.20N 0.17W
72 F1 **Villaines-les-Rochers** France 47.13N 0.30E
70 K6 **Villaines-sous-Malicorne** France 47.46N 0.05W
120 F9 **Villa Ingavi** Bolivia 21.40S 63.34W
121 D7 **Villa Iris** Argentina 38.12S 63.12W
77 Q3 **Villajoyosa** Spain 38.31N 0.14W
115 L7 **Villa Juárez** Mexico 20.19N 97.58W
121 C3 **Villa Krause** Argentina 31.35S 68.33W
80 B4 **Villa,La** Montecristo I Italy 42.20N 10.18E
79 K3 **Villa Lagarina** Italy 45.55N 11.02E
76 D2 **Villalba** Lugo Spain 43.17N 7.41W
76 L7 **Villalba** Madrid Spain 40.38N 4.00W
81 G8 **Villalba** Sicily 37.39N 13.51E
75 J6 **Villalba Alta** Spain 40.37N 0.58W
75 H7 **Villalba Baja** Spain 40.26N 1.05W
76 K3 **Villalba de Guardo** Spain 42.42N 4.49W
77 D6 **Villalba del Alcor** Spain 37.24N 6.29W
75 F7 **Villalba de la Sierra** Spain 40.14N 2.06W
76 K5 **Villalba de los Alcores** Spain 41.51N 4.52W
75 L5 **Villalba de los Arcos** Spain 41.07N 0.24E
77 C3 **Villalba de los Barros** Spain 38.36N 6.31W
75 E7 **Villalba del Rey** Spain 40.21N 2.39W
75 E2 **Villalba de Rioja** Spain 42.37N 2.53W
76 G6 **Villalcampo, Embalse de** *res* Spain
115 J4 **Villaldama** Mexico 26.30N 100.29W
75 G5 **Villalengua** Spain 41.27N 1.50W
75 E8 **Villalgordo del Marquesado** Spain 39.41N 2.31W
80 K6 **Villa Literno** Italy 41.01N 14.05E
75 C3 **Villalmanzo** Spain 42.03N 3.44W
79 E7 **Villa Lonati** *dist* Milan Italy
76 J4 **Villalón de Campos** Spain 42.05N 5.03W
121 E7 **Villalonga** Argentina 39.55S 62.35W
77 Q3 **Villalonga** Spain 38.53N 0.12W
76 J5 **Villalpando** Spain 41.51N 5.25W
77 N2 **Villalpardo** Spain 39.28N 1.38W
76 H5 **Villalube** Spain 41.36N 5.32W
75 C7 **Villaluenga** Spain 40.02N 3.54W
77 F7 **Villaluenga del Rosario** Spain 36.42N 5.24W
121 K5 **Villa Lugano** *dist* Buenos Aires Argentina
76 K4 **Villalumbroso** Spain 42.12N 4.45W

79 E5 Villalvernia Italy 44.49N 8.51E
115 K5 Villa Mainero Mexico 24.35N 99.36W
77 N2 Villamalea Spain 39.22N 1.36W
75 K8 Villamalur Spain 39.57N 0.25W
76 H4 Villamañán Spain 42.19N 5.35W
76 H4 Villamandos Spain 42.11N 5.35W
77 L3 Villamanrique Spain 38.34N 3.00W
77 D6 Villamanrique de la Condesa Spain 37.15N 6.18W
75 D7 Villamanrique de Tajo Spain 40.04N 3.15W
76 L8 Villamanta Spain 40.18N 4.06W
81 B4 Villamar Sardinia 39.37N 8.58E
75 J8 Villamarchante Spain 39.34N 0.39W
121 D4 Villa María Argentina 32.25S 63.15W
76 D4 Villamarín Spain 42.28N 7.53W
120 E9 Villa Martín Bolivia 20.46S 67.45W
77 E7 Villamartín Spain 36.52N 5.38W
76 E4 Villamartín de Valdeorras Spain 42.25N 7.04W
81 B5 Villamassargia Sardinia 39.17N 8.38E
115 G4 Villa Matamoros Mexico 26.48N 105.35W
120 F11 Villa Matoque Argentina 25.50S 63.45W
75 J4 Villamayor Spain 41.42N 0.43W
77 H3 Villamayor de Calatrava Spain 38.47N 4.08W
76 J5 Villamayor de Campos Spain 41.54N 5.22W
75 E8 Villamayor de Santiago Spain 39.44N 2.56W
69 B7 Villamblain France 48.01N 1.33E
72 F5 Villamblard France 45.02N 0.33E
76 E2 Villamea Spain 43.20N 7.14W
76 G3 Villameca, Embalse de *res* Spain 42.40N 6.07W
76 L4 Villamediana Spain 42.03N 4.21W
76 G3 Villamejil Spain 42.34N 6.02W
76 H10 Villamesías Spain 39.15N 5.52W
76 F8 Villamiel Spain 40.12N 6.46W
119 A6 Villamil Galápagos Is 0.56S 90.59W
79 H6 Villaminozzo Italy 44.22N 10.28E
76 J3 Villamizar Spain 42.32N 5.08W
76 J4 Villamol Spain 42.25N 5.03W
120 F9 Villa Montes Bolivia 21.15S 63.30W
76 H6 Villamor de los Escuderos Spain 41.15N 5.34W
75 C8 Villamuelas Spain 39.49N 3.44W
76 K5 Villamuriel de Cerrato Spain 41.57N 4.30W
61 L7 Villance Belgium 49.58N 5.13E
72 D7 Villandraut France 44.28N 0.22W
119 C8 Villano Ecuador 1.30S 77.28W
76 A2 Villano, C Coruña Spain 43.10N 9.13W
75 E1 Villano, C Viscaya Spain 43.26N 2.56W
119 C8 Villano, R Ecuador
94 K4 Villa Nora S Africa 23.34S 28.01E
79 D6 Villanova d'Albenga Italy 44.03N 8.08E
79 C5 Villanova d'Asti Italy 44.57N 7.56E
81 C4 Villanovafranca Sardinia 39.39N 9.01E
79 L5 Villanova Marchesana Italy 44.59N 11.58E
79 C6 Villanova Mondovi Italy 44.21N 7.46E
79 D4 Villanova Monferrato Italy 45.11N 8.28E
81 A2 Villanova Monteleone Sardinia 40.31N 8.29E
79 C5 Villanova Solaro Italy 44.44N 7.35E
81 C4 Villanova Tulo Sardinia 39.47N 9.14E
79 F4 Villanterio Italy 45.13N 9.21E
75 J2 Villanúa Spain 42.40N 0.32W
76 K5 Villanubla Spain 41.42N 4.50W
121 D4 Villa Nueva Argentina 32.30S 63.15W
119 D2 Villanueva Colombia 10.37N 72.58W
115 P10 Villa Nueva Honduras 15.14N 88.00W
115 H6 Villanueva Mexico 22.24N 102.53W
109 E6 Villanueva New Mexico 35.15N 105.23W
76 E2 Villanueva Spain 43.28N 7.18W
75 D8 Villanueva de Alcardete Spain 39.40N 3.00W
75 L7 Villanueva de Alcolea Spain 40.14N 0.04E
75 F6 Villanueva de Alcorón Spain 40.40N 2.15W
77 H6 Villanueva de Algaidas Spain 37.11N 4.27W
75 C3 Villanueva de Argaño Spain 42.23N 3.55W
76 B3 Villanueva de Arosa Spain 42.34N 8.49W
75 C8 Villanueva de Bogas Spain 39.43N 3.39W
75 E3 Villanueva de Cameros Spain 42.10N 2.39W
77 P2 Villanueva de Castellón Spain 39.05N 0.31W
77 G4 Villanueva de Córdoba Spain 38.20N 4.38W
75 J4 Villanueva de Gállego Spain 41.47N 0.49W
76 K7 Villanueva de Gomez Spain 40.53N 4.43W
75 M4 Villanueva de la Barca Spain 41.41N 0.44E
76 K6 Villanueva del Aceral Spain 41.02N 4.53W
77 G7 Villanueva de La Concepción Spain 36.55N 4.31W
77 L3 Villanueva de la Fuente Spain 38.42N 2.42W
77 N2 Villanueva de la Jara Spain 39.26N 1.58W
77 J4 Villanueva de la Reina Spain 38.00N 3.54W
77 K4 Villanueva del Arzobispo Spain 38.10N 3.00W
77 B5 Villanueva de las Cruces Spain 37.38N 7.00W
77 E3 Villanueva de la Serena Spain 38.58N 5.48W
76 G8 Villanueva de la Sierra Spain 40.12N 6.24W
76 J4 Villanueva de las Manzanas Spain 42.28N 5.29W
77 K5 Villanueva de las Torres Spain 37.34N 3.05W
76 J8 Villanueva de la Vera Spain 40.08N 5.28W
76 J5 Villanueva del Campo Spain 41.59N 5.25W
77 G4 Villanueva del Duque Spain 38.24N 4.59W
77 B4 Villanueva del Fresno Spain 38.23N 7.10W
75 H5 Villanueva del Huerva Spain 41.21N 1.02W
77 B6 Villanueva de los Castillejos Spain 37.30N 7.15W
77 F4 Villanueva del Rey Spain 38.12N 5.09W
77 E5 Villanueva del Río Spain 37.38N 5.41W
77 H6 Villanueva del Rosario Spain 37.00N 4.21W
77 H6 Villanueva de Mesía Spain 37.13N 4.00W
77 J3 Villanueva de San Carlos Spain 38.37N 3.54W
77 F6 Villanueva de San Juan Spain 37.04N 5.11W
77 H6 Villanueva de Tapia Spain 37.10N 4.20W
77 H6 Villanueva de Trabuco Spain 37.02N 4.20W
75 O5 Villanueva y Geltrú Spain 41.13N 1.43E
76 K3 Villanuño de Valdavia Spain 42.31N 4.30W
79 H3 Villanuova sul Clisi Italy 45.37N 10.27E
62 L10 Villány Hungary 45.51N 18.26E
76 G4 Villaobispo Spain 42.29N 6.04W
121 F2 Villa Ocampo Argentina 28.28S 59.20W
115 G4 Villa Ocampo Mexico 26.29N 105.30W
76 E2 Villaodrid Spain 43.20N 7.11W
118 B10 Villa Oliva Paraguay 26.00S 57.57W
115 G4 Villa O. Pereyra Durango Mexico 26.30N 105.40W
79 P3 Villa Opicina Italy 45.41N 13.47E
120 F8 Villa Oropeza Bolivia 19.12S 65.16W
79 L1 Villa Ottone Italy 46.52N 11.57E
77 L3 Villapalacios Spain 38.35N 2.38W
115 E3 Villa Pesqueira Mexico 29.08N 109.58W
81 M4 Villapiana Italy 39.50N 16.28E
79 E7 Villa Pizzone *dist* Milan Italy
71 D3 Villapourçon France 46.57N 3.57E
81 D5 Villaputzu Sardinia 39.27N 9.35E
76 H4 Villaquejida Spain 42.08N 5.36W
115 M4 Villa Quesada Costa Rica 10.16N 84.26W
76 H3 Villaquilambre Spain 42.39N 5.34W
120 F8 Villar Bolivia 19.40S 64.20W
77 G4 Villaralto Spain 38.28N 4.59W
75 C2 Villarcayo Spain 42.56N 3.34W
66 B7 Villard France 46.13N 6.26E
71 J6 Villar-d'Arène France 45.02N 6.20E
71 H6 Villard-Bonnot France 45.15N 5.53E
71 H6 Villard-de-Lans France 45.05N 5.33E
71 K6 Villard-du-Planay France 45.27N 6.42E
76 D4 Villar de Barrio Spain 42.10N 7.36W
76 E5 Villardebos Spain 41.54N 7.19W
75 E8 Villar de Cañas Spain 39.47N 2.35W
77 N3 Villar de Chinchilla Spain 38.55N 1.31W
76 F7 Villar de Ciervo Spain 40.45N 6.45W
76 G5 Villardeciervos Spain 41.56N 6.16W
75 F7 Villar de Domingo Garcia Spain 40.14N 2.18W
76 J5 Villardefrades Spain 41.43N 5.15W
75 J8 Villar del Arzobispo Spain 39.44N 0.50W
76 G6 Villar del Buey Spain 41.19N 6.13W
75 G8 Villar del Humo Spain 39.51N 1.39W
76 J9 Villar del Pedroso Spain 39.43N 5.11W
77 J3 Villar del Pozo Spain 38.51N 3.58W
77 C2 Villar del Rey Spain 39.07N 6.50W
75 H6 Villar del Salz Spain 40.41N 1.30W
75 F8 Villar del Saz de Arcas Spain 39.56N 2.05W
75 F7 Villar de Olalla Spain 40.01N 2.12W
76 G6 Villar de Peralonso Spain 41.02N 6.14W
76 G8 Villar de Plasencia Spain 40.08N 6.01W
77 E2 Villar de Rena Spain 39.05N 5.49W
76 J5 Villárdiga Spain 41.49N 5.28W
77 J5 Villardompardo Spain 37.50N 4.00W
66 B8 Villards, les France 45.55N 6.22E
71 H4 Villard-sur-Bienne France 46.30N 5.54E
121 C7 Villa Regina Argentina 39.06S 67.06W
75 D7 Villarego de Salvanés Spain 40.10N 3.18W
75 E3 Villarejo Spain 42.22N 2.53W
75 E8 Villarejo de Fuentes Spain 39.47N 2.42W
75 F6 Villarejo de Medina Spain 40.57N 2.20W
76 K9 Villarejo de Montalbán Spain 39.46N 4.35W
75 F3 Villar, El Spain 42.19N 2.05W
76 E6 Villarelho, Sa. de Portugal
75 C6 Villar, Embalse del *res* Spain 40.58N 3.34W
76 J3 Villarente Spain 42.32N 5.28W
76 H6 Villares de la Reina Spain 41.01N 5.39W
75 E8 Villares del Saz Spain 39.50N 2.31W
14 D4 Villaret, C W Australia 18.21S 122.04E
118 B9 Villa Rey Paraguay 24.42S 57.20W
77 J5 Villargordo Spain 37.56N 3.43W
75 H8 Villargordo del Cabriel Spain 39.32N 1.27W
105 C4 Villa Rica Georgia 33.43N 84.46W
76 H5 Villarín de Campos Spain 41.47N 5.38W
76 G6 Villarino Spain 41.16N 6.28W
76 E4 Villarino de Conso Spain 42.10N 7.10W
121 D8 Villarino, Pta *C* Argentina 40.47S 64.54W
75 J6 Villarluengo Spain 40.39N 0.32W
81 H8 Villarosa Sicily 37.36N 14.11E
75 H6 Villarquemado Spain 40.31N 1.17W
76 K4 Villarrabé Spain 42.25N 4.48W
76 K4 Villarramiel Spain 42.02N 4.55W
77 C6 Villarrasa Spain 37.23N 6.36W
75 F1 Villarreal Guipuzcoa Spain 43.06N 2.18W
75 E2 Villarreal de Alava Spain 42.59N 2.38W
75 K8 Villarreal de los Infantes Castellón Spain 39.56N 0.08W
121 A7 Villarrica* Chile 39.15S 72.15W
118 C9 Villarrica Paraguay 25.45S 56.28W
121 A6 Villarrica, L Chile
121 B7 Villarrica, Vol Chile 39.25S 71.55W
77 L2 Villarrobledo Spain 39.16N 2.36W
77 L4 Villarrodrigo Spain 38.29N 2.37W
75 F3 Villarroya Spain 42.08N 2.04W
75 G5 Villarroya de la Sierra Spain 41.28N 1.48W
75 J6 Villarroya de los Pinares Spain 40.31N 0.40W
77 G5 Villarrubia Spain 37.51N 4.55W
77 J2 Villarrubia de los Ojos Spain 39.14N 3.36W
75 D8 Villarrubia de Santiago Spain 39.58N 3.22W
75 E8 Villarrubio Spain 39.56N 2.54W
72 F5 Villars Dordogne France 45.26N 0.44E
71 E6 Villars Loire France 45.28N 4.21E
66 E6 Villars Switzerland 46.18N 7.03E
71 K8 Villars-Colmars France 44.10N 6.37E
72 C4 Villars-en-Pons France 45.37N 0.37W
71 K2 Villars-les-Blamont France 47.22N 6.52E
71 G4 Villars-les-Dombes France 46.00N 5.02E
71 L9 Villars-sur-Var France 43.56N 7.06E
77 N2 Villarta Spain 39.26N 1.39W
76 K10 Villarta de los Montes Spain 39.13N 4.48W
77 K2 Villarta de San Juan Spain 39.15N 3.25W
103 E8 Villas New Jersey 39.02N 74.55W
76 J3 Villasabariego Spain 42.31N 5.25W
81 C5 Villasalto Sardinia 39.29N 9.24E
75 D1 Villasana de Mena Spain 43.05N 3.16W
121 C2 Villa Sanagasta Argentina 29.16S 67.00W
76 L4 Villasandino Spain 42.22N 4.06W
81 L7 Villa San Giovanni Italy 38.13N 15.38E
121 F4 Villa San José Argentina 32.01S 58.20W
121 D2 Villa San Martin Argentina 28.15S 64.12W
81 B5 Villa San Pietro Sardinia 39.03N 9.00E
80 K5 Villa Santa Maria Italy 41.57N 14.21E
75 D1 Villasante Spain 43.04N 3.29W
79 N2 Villa Santina Italy 46.25N 12.55E
76 K4 Villasarracino Spain 42.24N 4.31W
121 D5 Villa Saúce Argentina 35.18S 63.18W
75 E5 Villasayas Spain 41.20N 2.36W
121 G4 Villasboas Uruguay 33.09S 56.30W
75 C8 Villaseca Spain 39.57N 3.53W
76 G6 Villaseco de los Gamitos Spain 41.02N 6.07W
76 G6 Villaseco de los Reyes Spain 41.10N 6.12W
76 J3 Villaselán Spain 42.33N 5.03W
75 C8 Villasequilla de Yepes Spain 39.53N 3.44W
120 F8 Villa Serrano Bolivia 19.06S 64.23W
76 L4 Villasilos Spain 42.20N 4.09W
81 D5 Villasimius Sardinia 39.08N 9.32E
81 K9 Villasmundo Sicily 37.15N 15.07E
81 B5 Villasor Sardinia 39.23N 8.57E
76 F8 Villasrubias Spain 40.20N 6.38W
75 H7 Villastar Spain 40.17N 1.09W
79 C5 Villastellone Italy 44.55N 7.45E
75 D3 Villasur de Herreros Spain 42.19N 3.23W
120 F8 Villa Talavera Bolivia 19.45S 65.28W
75 D8 Villatobas Spain 39.54N 3.20W
76 J7 Villatoro Spain 40.34N 5.07W
76 J7 Villatoro, Pto. de *pass* Spain 40.33N 5.07W
77 O2 Villatoya Spain 39.20N 1.20W
75 G2 Villatuerta Spain 42.39N 2.00W
76 J3 Villaturiel Spain 42.30N 5.29W
121 C2 Villa Unión Argentina 29.17S 68.12W
115 J3 Villa Unión Coahuila Mexico 28.14N 100.44W
115 G6 Villa Unión Durango Mexico 23.59N 104.01W
121 E2 Villa Unión Santiago del Estero Arg 29.27S 62.46W
115 F6 Villa Unión Sinaloa Mexico 23.10N 106.12W
81 B4 Villa Urbana Sardinia 39.53N 8.47E
121 E3 Villa Urquiza Argentina 31.38S 60.22W
75 G2 Villava Spain 42.50N 1.37W
121 D5 Villa Valeria Argentina 34.21S 64.56W
116 J5 Villa Vásquez Dominican Rep 19.46N 71.29W
96 T9 Villaverde Fuerteventura Canary Is 28.37N 13.54W
75 C7 Villaverde Spain 40.21N 3.43W
76 J3 Villaverde de Arcayos Spain 42.36N 5.02W
77 L4 Villaverde de Guadalimar Spain 38.28N 2.30W
77 E5 Villaverde del Río Spain 37.35N 5.52W
75 D1 Villaverde de Trucios Spain 43.14N 3.15W
77 M3 Villaverde, L. de Spain 38.49N 2.23W
79 K3 Villaverla Italy 45.39N 11.30E
119 D5 Villavicencio Colombia 4.09N 73.38W
76 J2 Villaviciosa Spain 43.29N 5.26W
77 F4 Villaviciosa de Córdoba Spain 38.05N 5.02W
75 C7 Villaviciosa de Odón Spain 40.21N 3.54W
75 E6 Villaviciosa de Tajuña Spain 40.47N 2.50W
76 J1 Villaviciosa, Ría de *B* Spain
76 G7 Villavieja de Yeltes Spain 40.53N 6.28W
120 F7 Villa Viscarra Bolivia 18.00S 65.32W
76 L5 Villaviudas Spain 41.58N 4.20W
76 F2 Villayón Spain 43.27N 6.41W
66 A8 Villaz France 45.57N 6.11E
76 E5 Villaza Spain 41.55N 7.30W
76 K3 Villazanzo de Valderaduey Spain 42.32N 4.58W
120 F10 Villazon Bolivia 22.05S 65.35W
66 D5 Villaz-St. Pierre Switzerland 46.44N 6.58E
69 N7 Villé France 48.21N 7.18E
70 N6 Ville-aux-Clèrcs, la France 47.56N 1.06E
70 H4 Villebaudon France 48.58N 1.10W
71 G5 Villebois France 45.51N 5.26E
72 E5 Villebois-Lavalette France 45.29N 0.18E
72 G8 Villebrumier France 43.54N 1.27E
69 D7 Villecerf France 48.19N 2.51E
72 E9 Villecomtal-sur-Arros France 43.24N 0.13E
72 K6 Villecomtal Aveyron France 44.32N 2.32E
71 G1 Villecomte France 47.31N 5.02E
71 J9 Villecroze France 43.35N 6.16E
72 K9 Villedaigne France 43.13N 2.51E
68 D4 Ville d'Avray France 48.49N 2.10E
121 D2 Ville de María Argentina 29.55S 63.44W
69 G8 Villedieu Côte d'Or France 47.55N 4.22E
72 E3 Villedieu du Clain, la Vienne France 46.28N 0.22E
69 L8 Villedieu-en-Fontenette, la France 47.47N 6.12E
72 D3 Villedieu, la Charente France 46.04N 0.19W
72 H4 Villedieu, la Creuse France 45.44N 1.54E
71 D7 Villedieu, la Lozère France 44.43N 3.32E
72 B1 Villedieu-la-Blouère Maine-et-Loire France 47.09N 1.03W
70 H4 Villedieu-les-Poêtes France 48.50N 1.13W
72 H2 Villedieu-sur-Indre France 46.51N 1.33E
70 M2 Villedomer France 47.33N 0.53E
70 M6 Villedomer France 47.31N 0.57E
68 E6 Ville-du-Bois, la France 48.40N 2.16E
66 B3 Ville du Pont France 47.01N 6.28E
61 L4 Ville-en-Hesbaye Belgium 50.37N 5.07E
69 F5 Ville-en-Tardenois France 49.11N 3.48E
72 E3 Villefagnan France 46.01N 0.05E
71 D8 Villefort France 44.27N 3.56E
72 K3 Villefranche France 46.24N 2.52E
72 F9 Villefranche Gers France 43.25N 0.43E
69 E8 Villefranche Yonne France 47.57N 3.09E
72 J8 Villefranche d'Albigeois France 43.54N 2.19E
72 J10 Villefranche-de-Conflent France 42.35N 2.22E
72 H9 Villefranche-de-Lauragais France 43.24N 1.42E
72 E6 Villefranche-de-Lonchat France 44.52N 0.04E
72 K7 Villefranche-de-Panat France 44.05N 2.41E
72 J7 Villefranche-de-Rouergue France 44.21N 2.02E
72 G6 Villefranche-du-Périgord France 44.37N 1.05E
72 H1 Villefranche-sur-Cher France 47.17N 1.46E
71 L9 Villefranche-sur-Mer France 43.42N 7.18E
71 F5 Villefranche-sur-Saône France 46.00N 4.43E
76 L4 Villegas Spain 42.28N 4.01W
120 A9 Villegas *dist* Callao Peru
71 B2 Villegenon France 47.26N 2.34E
68 F4 Villejuif France 48.47N 2.23E
75 H7 Villel Spain 40.14N 1.12W
121 F5 Villela Argentina 35.55S 59.03W
115 J7 Villela Mexico 21.42N 100.44W
71 G9 Villelaure France 43.43N 5.25E
72 D10 Villelongue France 42.57N 0.02W
69 D7 Villemaréchal France 48.15N 2.53E
99 L5 Ville Marie Quebec 47.21N 79.26W
69 F7 Villemaur-sur-Vanne France 48.16N 3.45E
98 R9 Villemay Quebec 46.48N 71.11W
70 N4 Villemeux-sur-Eure France 48.41N 1.27E
68 G3 Villemomble France 48.53N 2.30E
99 M4 Villemontel Quebec 48.38N 78.22W
69 G7 Villemorien France 48.05N 4.18E
72 G8 Villemur-sur-Tarn France 43.52N 1.30E
77 P3 Villena Spain 38.39N 0.52W
69 F6 Villenauxe-la-Grande France 48.35N 3.34E
72 C6 Villenave-d'Ornon France 44.47N 0.32W
71 F4 Villeneuve Ain France 46.01N 4.50E
72 J7 Villeneuve France 44.26N 2.01E
66 D6 Villeneuve Switzerland 46.24N 6.56E
69 F7 Villeneuve-au-Chemin France 48.05N 3.52E
71 C6 Villeneuve-d'Allier Haute-Loire France 45.12N 3.23E
69 E2 Villeneuve d'Ascq France 50.37N 3.10E
71 F7 Villeneuve-de-Berg France 44.33N 4.30E
71 G6 Villeneuve-de-Marc France 45.27N 5.06E
72 D8 Villeneuve de-Marsan France 43.54N 0.18W
72 F9 Villeneuve-de-Rivière France 43.08N 0.39E
72 D3 Villeneuve-la-Comtesse France 46.06N 0.30W
68 E2 Villeneuve-la-Garonne France 48.56N 2.19E
69 E7 Villeneuve-la-Guyard France 48.20N 3.04E
69 F7 Villeneuve-l'Archevêque France 48.14N 3.35E
69 D6 Villeneuve-le-Comte France 48.48N 2.50E
68 G5 Villeneuve-le-Roi France 48.44N 2.25E
71 F9 Villeneuve-les-Avignon France 43.57N 4.48E
71 C10 Villeneuve-les-Béziers France 43.19N 3.16E
69 E7 Villeneuve-les-Bordes France 48.29N 3.04E
71 D9 Villeneuve-les-Maguelonne France 43.32N 3.52E
69 C5 Villeneuve-les-Sablons France 49.15N 2.05E
71 L9 Villeneuve-Loubet France 43.40N 7.07E
69 C6 Villeneuve-St. Georges France 48.44N 2.27E
71 E2 Villeneuve-sous-Charigny France 47.26N 4.24W
72 L2 Villeneuve-sur-Allier France 46.40N 3.14E
69 E7 Villeneuve-sur-Yonne France 48.05N 3.18E
72 H9 Villenouvelle France 43.26N 1.39E
72 G1 Villentrois France 47.11N 1.28E
68 J2 Villeparisis France 48.57N 2.37E
68 H2 Villepinte France 48.58N 2.31E
107 D11 Ville Platte Louisiana 30.40N 92.19W
70 M2 Villequier France 49.31N 0.40E
72 F6 Villeréal France 44.38N 0.45E
76 K5 Villerías Spain 41.56N 4.52W
70 N6 Villeromain France 47.44N 1.09E
61 F5 Villerot Belgium 50.29N 3.48E
72 K10 Villerouge Termenès France 42.59N 2.36E
99 T6 Villeroy Quebec 46.23N 71.53W
69 K5 Villers France 49.28N 5.49E
61 N4 Villers-aux-Tours Belgium 50.30N 5.31E
70 J3 Villers-Bocage Calvados France 49.05N 0.39W
69 C4 Villers-Bocage Somme France 50.00N 2.20E
69 D4 Villers-Carbonnel France 49.53N 2.55E
69 E5 Villers-Cotterêts France 49.15N 3.06E
61 H6 Villers-deux-Eglises Belgium 50.12N 4.29E
61 M8 Villers-devant-Orval Belgium 49.37N 5.20E
69 H5 Villers-en-Argonne France 49.01N 4.56E
69 E3 Villers-en-Cauchies France 50.14N 3.24E
61 J6 Villers-en-Fagne Belgium 50.08N 4.35E
70 L4 Villers-en-Ouche France 48.51N 0.27E
71 J1 Villersexel France 47.33N 6.26E
71 H3 Villers-Farlay France 47.00N 5.45E
61 M8 Villers-la-Loue Belgium 49.34N 5.29E
61 H6 Villers-la-Tour Belgium 50.02N 4.16E
61 J4 Villers-la-Ville Belgium 50.35N 4.32E
61 M4 Villers-le-Bouillet Belgium 50.35N 5.15E
71 K2 Villers-le-Lac France 47.04N 6.40E
61 L4 Villers-le-Peuplier Belgium 50.39N 5.05E
61 M4 Villers-le-Temple Belgium 50.31N 5.22E
61 M4 Villers-l'Evêque Belgium 50.42N 5.26E
61 K4 Villers-lez-Heest Belgium 50.32N 4.50E
61 E4 Villers-Notre-Dame Belgium 50.37N 3.44E
69 E3 Villers-Outreaux France 50.02N 3.18E
69 H8 Villers-Patras France 47.56N 4.32E
61 H4 Villers-Perwin Belgium 50.32N 4.29E
61 J5 Villers-Poterie Belgium 50.21N 4.33E
61 E4 Villers-St.Amand Belgium 50.37N 3.44E
61 N5 Villers-Ste. Gertrude Belgium 50.22N 5.35E
61 G5 Villers-St. Ghislain Belgium 50.26N 4.03E
61 L6 Villers-sur-Lesse Belgium 50.09N 5.06E
69 J5 Villers-sur-Meuse France 49.01N 5.25E
69 G3 Villers-sur-Nicole France 50.20N 4.01E
61 N8 Villers-sur-Semois Belgium 49.42N 5.34E
69 K5 Villerupt-la-Montagne France 49.28N 5.55E
70 L3 Villerville France 49.23N 0.07E
69 G7 Villery France 48.11N 4.01E
69 G6 Villeseneux France 48.50N 4.09E
69 H7 Ville-sous-Laferté France 48.07N 4.48E
61 G5 Ville-sur-Haine Belgium 50.28N 4.04E
69 H5 Ville-sur-Tourbe France 49.11N 4.48E
119 D5 Villeta Colombia 5.01N 74.28W
118 B9 Villeta Paraguay 25.29S 57.34W
66 E7 Villette Switzerland 46.05N 7.13E
66 E5 Villette, la Switzerland 46.36N 7.15E
71 F5 Villeurbanne France 45.46N 4.54E
71 D9 Villeveyrac France 43.30N 3.38E
84 F5 Villia Greece 38.10N 23.20E
121 C3 Villicun, Sa *ra* Argentina
71 F4 Villié-Morgon France 46.10N 4.40E
72 G2 Villiers France 46.53N 1.11E
95 M3 Villiers S Africa 27.02S 28.37E
66 D3 Villiers Switzerland 47.05N 6.59E
70 J6 Villiers-Charlemagne France 47.56N 0.40W
95 C9 Villiersdorp S Africa 33.59S 19.17E
72 C3 Villiers-en-Plaine France 46.25N 0.32W
68 F1 Villiers-le-Bel France 49.01N 2.23E
69 J7 Villiers-le-Sec France 48.06N 5.03E
69 E8 Villiers-St. Benoît France 47.48N 3.13E
69 E6 Villiers-St. Georges France 48.39N 3.25E
68 H4 Villiers-sur-Marne France 48.50N 2.34E
66 J1 Villigen Switzerland 47.32N 8.12E
53 N9 Villingadalsfjall *mt* Faeroes 62.24N 6.32W
50 E7 Villingaholt Iceland 63.53N 20.45W
64 E7 Villingen-Schwenningen W Germany 48.03N 8.28E
108 Q9 Villisca Iowa 40.57N 94.59W
64 E3 Villmar W Germany 50.23N 8.13E
66 J2 Villmergen Switzerland 47.21N 8.15E
66 J2 Villnachern Switzerland 47.29N 8.10E
76 L4 Villodrigo Spain 42.09N 4.06W
76 K4 Villoldo Spain 42.15N 4.36W
75 G8 Villora Spain 39.45N 1.36W
77 O5 Villora, Sierra de *mts* Spain
75 K6 Villores Spain 40.40N 0.13W
76 J7 Villoria Spain 41.00N 5.22W
69 J6 Villotte-sur-Aire France 48.52N 5.20E
76 J9 Villuercas, Sierra, de las *mts* Spain
28 D5 Villupuram Tamil Nadu India 11.58N 79.28E
63 T4 Vilm *isld* E Germany 54.19N 13.32E
79 H3 Vilminore de Scalve Italy 45.59N 10.05E
100 F4 Vilna Alberta 54.06N 111.59W
53 R16 Vilnes Norway 61.19N 4.58E
53 R16 Vilnesfjord *inlet* Norway 61.18N 4.59E
46 F3 Vilnius Lithuania U.S.S.R. 54.40N 25.19E
46 E3 Vilnya *R* Lithuania U.S.S.R.
Vilnyus *see* Vilnius
75 Q4 Vilovi de Oñar Spain 41.54N 2.44E
79 K1 Vilpiano Italy 46.34N 11.14E
51 L9 Vilppula Finland 62.02N 24.30E
65 C6 Vils Austria 47.34N 10.37E
53 B3 Vils Denmark 56.47N 8.44E
64 O6 Vils *R* Nieder-Bayern W Germany
64 M5 Vils *R* Oberpfalz, Bayern W Germany
64 N7 Vilsbiburg W Germany 48.26N 12.22E
64 M4 Vilseck W Germany 49.36N 11.50E
64 P6 Vilshofen W Germany 48.38N 13.12E
52 H10 Vilshult Sweden 56.21N 14.30E
53 B6 Vilslev Denmark 55.25N 8.42E
53 C3 Vilsted Denmark 56.54N 9.18E
60 O9 Vilsteren Netherlands 52.30N 6.21E
53 B3 Vilsund Denmark 56.53N 8.38E
53 B3 Vilsund *inlet* Denmark 56.50N 8.37E
60 T17 Vilt Netherlands 50.52N 5.48E
66 O3 Vilters Switzerland 47.02N 9.27E
82 E8 Vilusi Yugoslavia 42.44N 18.34E
76 F6 Vilvestre Spain 41.06N 6.44W
61 H3 Vilvoorde Belgium 50.56N 4.25E
45 O1 Vilya U.S.S.R. 55.14N 42.14E
44 J9 Vilyashchay *R* Azerbaydzhan U.S.S.R.
39 F7 Vilyuchinskaya Bukhta *gulf* U.S.S.R.
39 K4 Vilyuneyskaya U.S.S.R. 62.14N 175.15E
39 F7 Vilyuy U.S.S.R. 52.48N 158.33E
38 L2 Vilyuy *R* U.S.S.R.
41 M8 Vilyuysk U.S.S.R. 63.46N 121.35E
42 J2 Vilyuyskoye Vdkhr *res* U.S.S.R.
75 N5 Vimbodi Spain 41.24N 1.03E
76 A10 Vimeiro Portugal 39.11N 9.19W
79 F3 Vimercate Italy 45.37N 9.22E
76 A2 Vimianzo Spain 43.06N 9.03W
76 D11 Vimieiro Portugal 38.50N 7.50W
80 E6 Viminale, Monte *hill* Roma Italy
76 F5 Vimioso Portugal 41.35N 6.31W
52 J9 Vimmerby Sweden 57.40N 15.50E
52 H6 Vimo Sweden 60.50N 14.20E
69 D8 Vimory France 47.57N 2.41E
70 L4 Vimoutiers France 48.55N 0.12E
51 K8 Vimpeli Finland 63.10N 23.50E
65 J3 Vimperk Czechoslovakia 49.04N 13.46E
69 D3 Vimy France 50.22N 2.49E
107 H7 Vina Alabama 34.21N 88.03W
111 B2 Vina California 39.56N 122.01W
75 J5 Vinaceite Spain 41.15N 0.35W
121 B4 Viña del Mar Chile 33.02S 71.35W
79 B6 Vinádio Italy 44.18N 7.10E
46 E5 Vinagradov Ukraine U.S.S.R. 48.08N 23.00E
75 M5 Vinaixa Spain 41.25N 0.59E
77 P4 Vinalapó *R* Spain
104 R2 Vinalhaven Maine 44.03N 68.50W
61 L4 Vinalmont Belgium 50.34N 5.14E
75 L7 Vinaroz Spain 40.29N 0.28E
71 G6 Vinay France 45.12N 5.24E
72 J10 Vinça France 42.39N 2.29E
26 V16 Vincendo Réunion Ind Oc 21.22S 55.41E
68 G3 Vincennes France 48.51N 2.27E
107 J3 Vincennes Indiana 38.42N 87.30W
123 F2 Vincennes Bay Antarctica
68 G4 Vincennes, Bois de *wood* Paris France
107 K8 Vincent Alabama 33.22N 86.26W
104 D7 Vincent Ohio 39.22N 81.41W
112 F3 Vincent Texas 32.29N 101.14W
12 F9 Vincent Cr Tasmania
103 E7 Vincentown New Jersey 39.57N 74.45W
10 U10 Vincent, Pt Norfolk I Pacific Oc 29.01S 167.55E
119 B8 Vinces Ecuador 1.37S 79.45W
119 B8 Vinces, R Ecuador
69 L7 Vincey France 48.20N 6.19E
80 L6 Vinchiaturo Italy 41.24N 14.35E
121 C2 Vinchina Argentina 28.45S 68.15W
120 C5 Vinchos Peru 13.16S 74.21W
79 J7 Vinci Italy 43.47N 10.56E
53 B4 Vind Denmark 56.16N 8.33E
53 T20 Vindafjorden *inlet* Norway 59.27N 5.52E
50 H3 Vindbelgjarfjall *mt* Iceland 65.37N 17.05W
53 C3 Vindblæs Denmark 56.56N 9.20E
53 G7 Vindeby Denmark 54.56N 11.09E
53 Y19 Vindegga *mt* Norway 59.47N 8.27E
75 F6 Vindel Spain 40.35N 2.23W
52 L2 Vindelälven *R* Sweden
51 G6 Vindelgransele Sweden 65.06N 18.14E
52 M2 Vindeln Sweden 64.11N 19.45E
14 B7 Vinden, Mt W Australia 27.00S 115.35E
61 E2 Vinderhoute Belgium 51.05N 3.39E
53 C4 Vinderslev Denmark 56.15N 9.27E
53 B4 Vinderup Denmark 56.29N 8.48E
91 D6 Vindevoghel Zaïre 4.39S 15.11E
50 L3 Vindfell Iceland 65.45N 14.38W
29 D6 Vindhya Ra Madhya Prad India
53 D4 Vinding Vejle Denmark 56.02N 9.35E
53 D5 Vinding Vejle Denmark 55.40N 9.35E
53 F6 Vindinge Denmark 55.19N 10.44E
53 B4 Vinding Kirke Denmark 56.17N 8.40E
45 O2 Vindrey U.S.S.R. 54.15N 43.00E
53 Z19 Vindsjå *L* Norway 59.57N 8.30E
75 M5 Vinebre Spain 41.11N 0.35E
103 D8 Vineland New Jersey 39.29N 75.02W
41 O2 Viner-Neyshtadt, Ostrov *isld* Franz Josef Land U.S.S.R.
72 H2 Vineuil Indre France 46.55N 1.38E
70 N6 Vineuil Loir-et-Cher France 47.35N 1.22E
103 N4 Vineyard Haven Massachusetts 41.28N 70.36W
103 N4 Vineyard Sound Massachusetts
103 N4 Vineyard Sound Lt Ship Massachusetts 41.23N 71.00W
82 G4 Vinga Romania 46.00N 21.14E
53 D4 Vinge Denmark 56.24N 9.48E
71 G1 Vingeanne *R* France 47.38N 5.22E
53 S15 Vingen Norway 61.50N 5.20E
72 K10 Vingrau France 42.51N 2.48E
98 J3 Vingt-deuxième Mille, L. du Que
70 L4 Vingt Hanaps France 48.31N 0.07E
25 H3 Vinh Vietnam 18.42N 105.41E
76 E5 Vinhais Portugal 41.50N 7.00W
25 K7 Vinh Cam Ranh *B* Vietnam
25 K6 Vinh Giat Vietnam 12.41N 109.20E
25 J4 Vinh Linh Vietnam 17.04N 106.59E
25 H8 Vinh Loi Vietnam 9.17N 105.44E
25 H7 Vinh Long Vietnam 10.15N 105.59E
25 H8 Vinh Rach Gia *B* Vietnam
25 H2 Vinh Yen Vietnam 21.18N 105.36E
71 G4 Viniat France 46.15N 5.13E
82 H9 Vinica Yugoslavia 41.53N 22.30E
75 E3 Viniegra de Abajo Spain 42.09N 2.53W
75 E3 Viniegra de Arriba Spain 42.06N 2.50W
108 P3 Vining Minnesota 46.16N 95.30W
109 P5 Vinita Oklahoma 36.39N 95.11W
53 U19 Vinjanuten *mt* Norway 59.31N 6.30E
53 U17 Vinje Hordaland Norway 60.47N 6.30E
53 X19 Vinje Telemark Norway 59.37N 7.51E
52 E3 Vinjeora Norway 63.12N 9.00E
53 X19 Vinjevatn *L* Norway 59.37N 7.51E
29 A6 Vinjhan Gujarat India 23.04N 69.02E
82 H6 Vînju Mare Romania 44.25N 22.52E
95 D8 Vinkekuil S Africa 32.42S 20.28E
53 D4 Vinkel Denmark 56.25N 9.33E
60 K13 Vinkel Netherlands 51.42N 5.28E
60 H11 Vinkeveen Netherlands 52.14N 4.56E
82 E5 Vinkovci Yugoslavia 45.16N 18.49E
61 D2 Vinkt Belgium 51.01N 3.29E
51 J2 Vinnelys Norway 69.38N 21.15E
46 G5 Vinnitsa Ukraine U.S.S.R. 49.11N 28.30E
46 G5 Vinnitskaya Oblast' *prov* Ukraine U.S.S.R.
45 V3 Vinnovka U.S.S.R. 53.12N 49.40E
44 F4 Vinogradnoye U.S.S.R. 43.43N 44.30E
82 H2 Vinogradov Ukraine U.S.S.R. 48.09N 23.01E
44 B8 Vinogradovo Ukraine U.S.S.R. 46.22N 32.56E
71 H9 Vinon-sur-Verdon France 43.43N 5.48E
79 C5 Vinovo Italy 44.57N 7.38E
71 G8 Vinsobres France 44.19N 5.03E
109 L7 Vinson Oklahoma 34.55N 99.52W
123 G11 Vinson Massif *mts* Antarctica 78.02S 22.00W
52 E5 Vinstra Norway 61.36N 9.45E
52 E5 Vinstra *R* Norway
19 K2 Vintar Luzon Philippines 18.16N 120.40E
106 B7 Vinton Iowa 42.10N 92.01W
107 C11 Vinton Louisiana 30.10N 93.36W
104 F9 Vinton Virginia 37.17N 79.54W
52 H7 Vintrosa Sweden 59.15N 14.55E
82 H4 Vinţul de Jos Romania 46.00N 23.30E
77 H7 Viñuela Spain 36.52N 4.08W
75 D6 Viñuelas Spain 40.47N 3.20W
75 E4 Vinuesa Spain 41.55N 2.46W
28 D2 Vinukonda Andhra Prad India 16.04N 79.45E
91 D5 Vinza Congo 3.25S 14.32E
92 E4 Vinza *tribe* Tanzania
63 P7 Vinzelberg E Germany 52.34N 11.40E
47 K7 Vinzili U.S.S.R. 57.00N 65.48E
72 C9 Viodos France 43.15N 0.52W
63 K3 Viöl W Germany 54.34N 9.12E
110 D9 Viola California 40.32N 121.40W
103 C8 Viola Delaware 39.02N 75.35W
110 H3 Viola Idaho 46.51N 117.01W
106 D8 Viola Illinois 41.12N 90.34W
109 N4 Viola Kansas 37.31N 97.40W
106 D6 Viola Wisconsin 43.31N 90.42W
110 P7 Viola Wyoming 42.16N 110.21W
123 E12 Violante Inlet Antarctica
79 H2 Viola, Val *V* Italy
71 E5 Violay France 45.52N 4.22E
116 E4 Violeta Cuba 21.57N 78.26W
100 B5 Violet Grove Alberta 53.10N 115.10W
71 D9 Viols-le-Fort France 43.45N 3.42E
66 D6 Vionnaz Switzerland 46.19N 6.54E
69 K5 Vionville France 49.06N 5.57E
94 D7 Viooldrif S Africa 28.50S 17.39E
70 H9 Vioreau, Grand Res. de France 47.32N 1.25W
14 G3 Viotti Pk W Australia 15.00S 127.37E
79 J2 Vioz, Monte *mt* Italy 46.24N 10.38E
79 P3 Vipacco *R* Italy/Yugoslavia
79 K1 Vipiteno Italy 46.54N 11.27E
72 J3 Viplaix France 46.28N 2.22E
120 F12 Vipos Argentina 26.28S 65.21W
63 R6 Vipperow E Germany 53.20N 12.42E
19 E8 Viqueque Indonesia 8.52S 126.23E
82 C6 Vir *isld* Yugoslavia 44.17N 15.03E
52 J8 Virå Sweden 58.46N 16.25E
66 M7 Vira Switzerland 46.06N 8.56E
19 M5 Virac Philippines 13.35N 124.14E
19 M5 Virac Pt Philippines 13.33N 124.13E
66 M7 Vira Gambarogno Switzerland 46.09N 8.51E
29 C6 Viramgam Gujarat India 23.08N 72.04E
36 D3 Virancık Turkey 39.26N 29.32E
47 D4 Virandozero U.S.S.R. 64.04N 35.57E
36 J3 Viranşehir Kayseri Turkey 39.01N 36.39E
37 E8 Viranşehir Urfa Turkey 37.13N 39.45E
28 B4 Virarajendrapet Karnataka India 12.12N 75.46E
31 F8 Virawah Pakistan 24.31N 70.46E
82 G6 Vîrciorova Romania 44.43N 22.29E
29 D7 Virdel Maharashtra India 21.20N 74.44E
107 G2 Virden Illinois 39.30N 89.46W
100 R9 Virden Manitoba 49.50N 100.57W
51 J3 Virdni *mt* Finland 68.58N 21.25E
70 J4 Vire France 48.50N 0.53W
70 H3 Vire *R* France
52 H9 Vireda Sweden 57.55N 14.40E
14 B5 Virehow, Mt W Australia 21.13S 116.23E
91 C11 Virei Angola 15.43S 12.52E
61 H6 Virelles Belgium 50.04N 4.20E
69 H3 Vireux France 50.06N 4.44E
69 G7 Virey-sous-Bar France 48.08N 4.18E
82 H4 Vîrfurile Romania 46.19N 22.32E
110 P1 Virgelle Montana 48.01N 110.15W
118 G5 Virgem da Lapa Brazil 16.47S 42.21W
65 F7 Virgen Austria 47.01N 12.28E
77 H4 Virgen de la Cabeza Spain 38.10N 4.05W
77 B5 Virgen de la Peña *mt* Huelva Spain 37.36N 7.12W
75 J2 Virgen de la Peña *mt* Zaragoza Spain 42.41N 1.00W
75 G4 Virgen, Sierra de la *mts* Spain
65 F7 Virgental *V* Austria
109 O4 Virgil Kansas 37.59N 96.01W
103 B1 Virgil New York 42.30N 76.14W
108 M5 Virgil S Dakota 44.18N 98.25W
110 D9 Virgilia California 40.02N 121.07W
104 G10 Virgillina Virginia 36.33N 78.47W
111 L5 Virgin *R* Ariz/Utah/Nev
61 G4 Virginal-Samme Belgium 50.38N 4.13E
105 M7 Virgin Gorda *isld* Virgin Is 18.30N 64.26W
59 H4 Virginia Cavan Irish Rep 53.50N 7.05W
110 N7 Virginia Idaho 42.30N 112.10W
107 F2 Virginia Illinois 39.57N 90.12W
108 S2 Virginia Minnesota 47.30N 92.28W
108 O9 Virginia Nebraska 40.14N 96.30W
11 G9 Virginia New Zealand 42.56S 172.21E
95 K4 Virginia S Africa 28.06S 26.53E
102 L3 Virginia *state* U.S.A.
104 K10 Virginia Beach Virginia 36.51N 75.59W
110 O4 Virginia City Montana 45.18N 111.56W
111 E2 Virginia City Nevada 39.19N 119.39W
105 B11 Virginia Key *isld* Florida 25.44N 80.07W
14 E8 Virginia Ra W Australia
99 L4 Virginiatown Ontario 48.09N 79.36W
116 M5 Virgin Is (UK) W Indies
116 M5 Virgin Is (U.S.A) W Indies
111 K5 Virgin Mts Nevada/Arizona
118 G6 Virginópolis Brazil 18.49S 42.39W
105 L7 Virgin Passage *str* Virgin Is
71 G6 Virieu France 45.29N 5.29E
71 H5 Virieu-le-Grand France 45.51N 5.39E
71 E5 Virigneux France 45.42N 4.22E
71 H5 Virignin France 45.43N 5.42E
51 F4 Virihaure *L* Sweden 67.25N 16.30E
71 G6 Viriville France 45.18N 5.12E
82 D4 Virje Yugoslavia 46.04N 16.59E
58 Q10 Virkie Shetland Scotland 59.53N 1.18W
53 D4 Virklund Denmark 56.08N 9.34E
51 M9 Virmasvesi *L* Finland
64 C3 Virneburg W Germany 50.20N 7.05E
68 D4 Viroflay France 48.47N 2.11E
51 N11 Virolahti Finland 60.30N 27.40E
106 D6 Viroqua Wisconsin 43.33N 90.54W
82 D5 Virovitica Yugoslavia 45.50N 17.25E
82 E8 Virpazar Yugoslavia 42.14N 19.06E
29 B7 Virpur Gujarat India 21.51N 70.46E
84 H5 Vírra Greece 38.18N 24.09E
51 K9 Virrat Finland 62.14N 23.50E
52 J9 Virserum Sweden 57.20N 15.30E
51 N9 Virtasalmi Finland 62.09N 27.30E
82 J6 Vîrtoapele Romania 44.10N 25.14E
61 N8 Virton Belgium 49.34N 5.32E
120 A3 Virú Peru 8.24S 78.40W
28 C6 Virudunagar Tamil Nadu India 9.35N 77.57E
46 F1 Viru-Jaagupi-Lisaku Estonia U.S.S.R. 59.10N 26.25E
93 A7 Virunga *mts* Zaïre
93 A7 Virunga, Parc *nat park* Zaïre
71 J4 Viry Haute-Savoie France 46.07N 6.03E
71 H4 Viry Jura France 46.18N 5.45E
45 F5 Viry Ukraine U.S.S.R. 51.02N 34.25E
68 F5 Viry-Châtillon France 48.40N 2.23E
80 O2 Vis Yugoslavia 43.03N 16.11E
82 C7 Vis *isld* Yugoslavia
111 E5 Visalia California 36.20N 119.18W
71 F8 Visan France 44.19N 4.57E
79 H4 Visano Italy 45.19N 10.23E
28 B1 Visapur Maharashtra India 18.53N 74.42E
75 J2 Visaurin *mt* Spain 42.47N 0.38W
29 B7 Visavadar Gujarat India 21.22N 70.52E
19 L6 Visayan Sea Philippines
95 E10 Visbaai *B* S Africa 34.15S 21.55E
53 E3 Visborg Denmark 56.45N 10.10E
53 B6 Visby Sønderjylland Denmark 55.01N 8.48E
52 L9 Visby Sweden 57.37N 18.20E
53 A3 Visby Viborg Denmark 56.48N 8.29E
79 O3 Visco Italy 45.53N 13.21E
118 G7 Visconde do Rio Branco Brazil 21.00S 42.51W
100 M7 Viscount Saskatchewan 51.57N 105.37W
97 J3 Viscount Melville Sd N W Terr
53 Y15 Visdalen *V* Norway 61.39N 8.55E
61 N4 Visé Belgium 50.44N 5.42E
82 E7 Višegrad Yugoslavia 43.47N 19.20E
79 M2 Visentin, Col *mt* Italy 46.03N 12.17E
79 N6 Viserba Italy 44.05N 12.32E
117 E5 Viseu Brazil 1.10S 46.09W
76 D7 Viseu Portugal 40.40N 7.55W
76 D7 Viseu *dist* Portugal
82 J3 Vişeu de Sus Romania 47.43N 23.24E
82 J3 Vişeul *R* Romania
28 F2 Vishakhapatnam Andhra Prad India 17.42N 83.24E
28 F2 Vishakhapatnam *dist* Andhra Prad India
28 A2 Vishalgarh Maharashtra India 16.55N 73.46E
47 G5 Vishera *R* Komi U.S.S.R.
46 H1 Vishera *R* Novgorod U.S.S.R.
46 P1 Vishkil' U.S.S.R. 58.05N 48.19E
82 K1 Vishnevets U.S.S.R. 49.54N 25.44E
43 K2 Vishnevka Kazakhstan U.S.S.R. 50.51N 72.13E
45 S7 Vishnevka U.S.S.R. 49.26N 46.45E
47 M5 Vishnevogorsk U.S.S.R. 55.59N 60.33E
45 P4 Vishnevoye U.S.S.R. 52.40N 43.28E
94 P12 Vishoek Cape Town S Africa 34.08S 18.25E
94 P12 Vishoekbaai *B* Cape Town S Africa
75 H6 Visiedo Spain 40.41N 1.06W
47 H6 Visim Perm U.S.S.R. 58.40N 56.10E
47 M4 Visim Sverdlovsk U.S.S.R. 57.42N 59.29E
47 J4 Visim *R* U.S.S.R.
47 M4 Visimo Utkinsk U.S.S.R. 57.45N 59.19E
82 J7 Vişina Veche Romania 43.53N 24.26E
52 H8 Visingsö Sweden 58.02N 14.20E
52 G9 Viskafors Sweden 57.37N 12.50E
52 G9 Viskan *R* Sweden
46 F2 Viški Latvia U.S.S.R. 56.10N 26.55E
80 O2 Viški Kanal *str* Yugoslavia
53 G5 Viskinge Denmark 55.40N 11.17E
52 H10 Vislanda Sweden 56.46N 14.30E
66 L6 Visletto Switzerland 46.18N 8.38E
115 D3 Visnaga Mexico 28.50N 111.15W
29 C6 Visnagar Gujarat India 23.41N 72.36E
53 S20 Visnes Rogaland Norway 59.21N 5.14E
53 V15 Visnes Sogn og Fjordane Norway 61.54N 6.44E
79 P4 Višnjan Yugoslavia 45.16N 13.43E
77 E6 Viso del Alcor, El Spain 37.24N 5.43W
77 J3 Viso del Marqués Spain 38.32N 3.34W
77 G4 Viso, El Spain 38.29N 4.57W
82 E7 Visoko Yugoslavia 44.00N 18.10E
82 G9 Visoko *mt* Yugoslavia 41.11N 21.37E
123 A14 Visokoi I S Sandwich Is Atl Oc 56.43S 27.15W
79 B5 Viso, Monte Italy 44.40N 7.05E
66 H6 Visp Switzerland 46.18N 7.53E
66 H6 Visperterminen Switzerland 46.16N 7.54E
95 J7 Visrivier S Africa 31.55S 25.25E
71 D6 Vissac-Auteyrac France 45.06N 3.37E
28 E2 Vissannapeta Andhra Prad India 16.58N 80.50E
52 J10 Vissefjärda Sweden 56.31N 15.35E
63 L7 Visselhövede W Germany 52.59N 9.34E
61 K3 Vissenaken Belgium 50.50N 4.54E
53 E6 Vissenbjerg Denmark 55.23N 10.08E
80 H3 Visso Italy 42.56N 13.05E
66 G7 Vissoye Switzerland 46.13N 7.36E
111 G8 Vista California 33.12N 117.15W
100 R8 Vista Manitoba 50.36N 100.47W
119 F7 Vista Alegre Amazonas Brazil 1.29N 68.10W
119 F11 Vista Alegre Amazonas Brazil 6.15S 68.13W
119 H10 Vista Alegre Amazonas Brazil 4.55S 60.01W
118 C6 Vista Alegre Mato Grosso do Sul Brazil 19.33S 56.11W
119 H7 Vista Alegre Roraima Brazil 1.42N 61.09W
75 K7 Vistabella del Maestrazgo Spain 40.18N 0.18W
110 K8 Vista Res Nevada 49.18N 115.15W
53 F4 Vistoft Denmark 56.12N 10.32E
83 G3 Vistonís,L Greece
Vistula *R* *see* Wisła *R*
60 O6 Visvliet Netherlands 53.16N 6.15E
28 K3 Viswema Nagaland India 25.34N 94.10E
82 J7 Vit *R* Bulgaria
100 V9 Vita Manitoba 49.08N 96.39W
81 E8 Vita Sicily 37.52N 12.49E
80 B3 Vita, C. delle Italy 42.53N 10.25E
31 E6 Vitakri Pakistan 29.39N 69.22E
19 L8 Vitali *isld* Mindanao Philippines 7.21N 122.21E
119 F5 Vita, R Colombia
120 B5 Vitarte Peru 12.03S 76.51W
65 K3 Vitava *R* Czechoslovakia
45 B1 Vitebsk Belorussiya U.S.S.R. 55.10N 30.14E
45 B1 Vitebskaya Oblast' *prov* Belorussiya U.S.S.R.
66 H8 Vitello, Corno *mt* Italy 45.48N 7.48E
45 E4 Vitemlya U.S.S.R. 52.23N 33.23E
80 F4 Viterbo Italy 42.24N 12.06E
80 E4 Viterbo *prov* Italy
69 L6 Viterne France 48.35N 6.01E
82 D6 Viterog Planina *mts* Yugoslavia
15 J6 Vitiaz Str Papua New Guinea
120 F9 Vitichi Bolivia 20.14S 65.22W
76 G6 Vitigudino Spain 41.00N 6.26W
9 R2 Viti Levu *isld* Fiji
9 T7 Viti Levu B Viti Levu Fiji
42 J3 Vitim U.S.S.R. 59.28N 112.35E
42 J3 Vitim *R* U.S.S.R.
42 J3 Vitimskiy U.S.S.R. 58.18N 113.15E
42 J5 Vitimskoye Ploskogor'ye *tableland* U.S.S.R.
84 D6 Vitína Greece 37.40N 22.10E

82 D7 Vitina Yugoslavia 43.17N 17.29E
65 M4 Vitis Austria 48.46N 15.12E
15 J2 Vito Bougainville I Papua New Guinea 6.10S 155.25E
120 D8 Vitor Chile 18.45S 70.21W
120 D7 Vitor Peru 16.29S 71.50W
80 F4 Vitorchiano Italy 42.28N 12.10E
96 R1 Vitória Azores 39.05N 28.04W
117 C6 Vitória Brazil 2.52S 52.00W
118 H7 Vitória Espírito Santo Brazil 20.19S 40.21W
75 E2 Vitoria Spain 42.51N 2.40W
118 H4 Vitória da Conquista Brazil 14.53S 40.52W
117 J9 Vitoria de Santa Antão Brazil 8.10S 35.14W
117 F6 Vitória do Mearim Brazil 3.30S 44.54W
120 C7 Vitor, R Peru
81 J8 Vito, Serra di *mt* Sicily 37.47N 14.44E
70 N5 Vitray-en-Beauce France 48.17N 1.26E
70 H5 Vitré France 48.07N 1.12W
98 N2 Vitré, L Quebec
69 K8 Vitrey-sur-Mance France 47.49N 5.46E
61 J5 Vitrival Belgium 50.23N 4.39E
69 C8 Vitry-aux-Loges France 47.57N 2.20E
69 D3 Vitry-en-Artois France 50.20N 2.58E
69 G6 Vitry-la-Ville France 48.51N 4.28E
69 H6 Vitry-le-François France 48.44N 4.36E
71 D3 Vitry-sur-Loire France 46.40N 3.43E
68 F4 Vitry-sur-Seine France 48.47N 2.24E
52 G6 Vitsand Sweden 60.20N 12.57E
93 A6 Vitshumbi Zaïre 0.41S 29.21E
Vitsi *mt see* Vérnon
51 J4 Vittangi Sweden 67.41N 21.40E
51 J4 Vittangi älv *R* Sweden
53 A5 Vittarp Denmark 55.42N 8.23E
71 F2 Vitteaux France 47.24N 4.32E
69 K7 Vittel France 48.12N 5.58E
53 E4 Vitten Denmark 56.18N 10.01E
52 K7 Vittinge Sweden 59.53N 17.04E
99 K10 Vittoria Ontario 42.46N 80.20W
81 J10 Vittoria Sicily 36.58N 14.32E
87 K10 Vittorio d'Africa Somalia 1.39N 44.40E
84 Z20 Vittoriosa Malta 35.54N 14.32E
79 M3 Vittorio Veneto Italy 45.59N 12.18E
52 H10 Vittsjö Sweden 56.20N 13.40E
Vitu Is Bismarck Arch *see* Witu Is.
80 L6 Vitulano Italy 41.10N 14.39E
51 K5 Vitvattnet Sweden 66.03N 23.14E
17 Q3 Vityaz Depth *trough* Pacific Oc 44.18N 150.30E
10 R6 Vityaz Depth III Pacific Oc 31.43S 177.12W
45 C8 Vityazevka Ukraine U.S.S.R. 48.01N 31.52E
44 A2 Vityazevskiy Liman *lagoon* U.S.S.R.
66 K3 Vitznau Switzerland 47.01N 8.30E
79 B4 Viù Italy 45.14N 7.22E
53 C5 Viuf Denmark 55.36N 9.30E
53 Y18 Viuvatn *L* Norway 60.08N 8.00E
71 J4 Viuz-en-Sallaz France 46.09N 6.26E
71 E6 Vivarais, Mts. du France
67 P12 Vivario Corsica 42.10N 9.10E
79 N2 Vivaro Italy 46.05N 12.47E
53 E3 Vive Denmark 56.43N 10.03E
61 N4 Vivegnis Belgium 50.42N 5.39E
75 J6 Vivel del Río Martín Spain 40.53N 0.57W
53 W18 Viveli Norway 60.20N 7.08E
75 J8 Viver Spain 39.55N 0.36W
76 D1 Vivero Spain 43.39N 7.35W
71 D6 Viverols France 45.26N 3.54E
79 D4 Viverone, L. di Italy 45.25N 8.02E
76 D1 Vivero, Ría de *B* Spain
77 L3 Viveros Spain 38.47N 2.35W
42 F1 Vivi U.S.S.R. 63.59N 97.46E
42 F1 Vivi *R* U.S.S.R.
107 C9 Vivian Louisiana 32.51N 94.00W
108 K6 Vivian S Dakota 43.56N 100.18W
71 F8 Viviers France 44.28N 4.41E
71 H5 Viviers-du-Lac, le France 45.39N 5.55E
70 G4 Vivier-sur-Mer, Le France 48.36N 1.46W
72 J6 Viviez France 44.34N 2.12E
15 L8 Vivigani Papua New Guinea 9.19S 150.22E
53 E4 Vivild Denmark 56.29N 10.27E
41 F7 Vivi, Ozero *L* U.S.S.R.
80 E3 Vivo d'Orcia Italy 42.56N 11.38E
70 L5 Vivoin France 48.14N 0.10E
72 E3 Vivonne France 46.26N 0.16E
12 D6 Vivonne S Australia 35.58S 137.10E
12 D6 Vivonne B S Australia
121 F6 Vivorata Argentina 37.43S 57.40W
51 J4 Vivungi Sweden 67.46N 22.10E
61 L7 Vivy Belgium 49.52N 5.02E
9 R7 Viwa *isld* Fiji 17.10S 176.45E
72 C3 Vix France 46.22N 0.51W
Vizagapatnam *see* Vishakhapatnam
115 C4 Vizcaíno, Des. de Mexico
75 D3 Vizcaínos Spain 42.06N 3.17W
115 B4 Vizcaíno, Sa *ra* Mexico
74 F1 Vizcaya *prov* Spain
75 K5 Vizcuerno, Sierra del *mts* Spain
36 C1 Vize Turkey 41.34N 27.45E
76 C6 Vizela *R* Portugal
41 C2 Vize, Mys *C* Novaya Zemlya U.S.S.R. 76.30N 64.47E
38 G1 Vize, O *isld* Kara Sea Arctic Oc 79.00N 77.00E
48 M11 Vize, Ostrov *isld* U.S.S.R. 79.35N 77.00E
47 F3 Vizhas U.S.S.R. 66.35N 46.01E
47 F3 Vizhas *R* U.S.S.R.
47 F3 Vizhas, Ozero *L* U.S.S.R. 66.20N 46.20E
47 H5 Vizhay Perm U.S.S.R. 60.57N 57.58E
47 J5 Vizhay Tyumen U.S.S.R. 61.16N 60.05E
28 F1 Vizianagaram Andhra Prad India 18.07N 83.30E
84 C6 Vizíkion Greece 37.43N 21.58E
71 H6 Vizille France 45.05N 5.45E
79 P4 Vižinada Yugoslavia 45.20N 13.46E
47 G5 Vizinga U.S.S.R. 61.06N 50.05E
82 L6 Viziru Romania 45.00N 27.43E
75 F3 Vizmanos Spain 42.02N 2.24W
82 D1 Vizovice Czechoslovakia 49.15N 17.55E
67 P12 Vizzavona Corsica 42.08N 9.08E
67 P12 Vizzavona, Col de *pass* Corsica 42.07N 9.07E
79 L1 Vizze *R* Italy
81 J9 Vizzini Sicily 37.10N 14.45E
120 D6 V.J. Jose Perez Bolivia 15.12S 69.03W
41 A3 Vkhodnoy, Mys *C* Novaya Zemlya U.S.S.R. 73.15N 53.28E
41 A4 Vkhodnoy, Mys *C* Novaya Zemlya U.S.S.R. 70.40N 54.47E
60 F12 Vlaardingen Netherlands 51.55N 4.20E
65 J3 Vlachovo Březí Czechoslovakia 49.05N 13.57E
82 L3 Vlădeni Romania 47.24N 27.21E
82 G8 Vladičin Han Yugoslavia 42.42N 22.01E
Vladikavkaz *see* Ordzhonikidze
45 M1 Vladimir U.S.S.R. 56.08N 40.25E
82 F6 Vladimirci Yugoslavia 44.36N 19.45E
46 F4 Vladimirets Ukraine U.S.S.R. 51.28N 26.03E
45 J9 Vladimirovka Donetsk, Ukraine U.S.S.R. 47.44N 37.23E
45 U4 Vladimirovka Kuybyshev U.S.S.R. 52.42N 48.58E
44 B7 Vladimirovka Nikolayev U.S.S.R. 47.31N 32.55E
42 C5 Vladimirovka Novosibirsk U.S.S.R. 55.00N 84.07E
44 F3 Vladimirovka Stavropol' U.S.S.R. 44.45N 44.44E
46 Q4 Vladimirovka Ural'sk, Kazakhstan U.S.S.R. 50.50N 51.10E
40 J7 Vladimirovo Sakhalin U.S.S.R. 49.16N 143.59E
43 G1 Vladimirovskiy Kustanay, Kazakhstan U.S.S.R. 53.30N 64.02E
46 L2 Vladimirskaya Oblast' *prov* U.S.S.R.
45 E1 Vladimirskiy Tupik Smolensk U.S.S.R. 55.42N 33.22E
46 E4 Vladimir-Volynskiy Ukraine U.S.S.R. 50.51N 24.19E
44 D9 Vladislavovka Ukraine U.S.S.R. 45.11N 35.21E
40 E10 Vladivostok U.S.S.R. 43.09N 131.53E
61 B2 Vladslo Belgium 51.03N 2.55E
47 D6 Vladychnoye U.S.S.R. 58.52N 39.35E
60 R7 Vlagtwedde Netherlands 53.02N 7.07E
82 G8 Vlajna *mt* Yugoslavia 42.47N 21.56E
95 H3 Vlakfontein S Africa 27.40S 24.03E
84 A5 Vlakháta Greece 38.15N 20.36E
84 D6 Vlakhérna Greece 37.43N 22.15E
84 E8 Vlakhióti Greece 36.52N 22.42E
84 C6 Vlákhoi Greece 37.39N 21.51E
84 D7 Vlakhokerasiá Greece 37.22N 22.22E
84 C5 Vlakhomándra Greece 38.26N 21.43E
84 C7 Vlakhópoulon Greece 37.02N 21.47E
84 D6 Vlakhorráfti Greece 37.31N 22.01E
84 D2 Vlakhoviánni Greece 39.44N 22.05E
95 N3 Vlakpoort S Africa 27.08S 29.58E
94 K5 Vlakte S Africa 24.38S 29.03E
95 F9 Vlakteplaas S Africa 33.30S 22.42E
61 B3 Vlamertinge Belgium 50.51N 2.49E
14 A5 Vlaming Hd W Australia 21.55S 114.00E
26 N14 Vlaming, Pte *C* Amsterdam I Indian Ocean 37.54S 77.32E
65 O4 Vlasatice Czechoslovakia 48.57N 16.29E
82 E6 Vlasenica Yugoslavia 44.11N 18.59E
82 F6 Vlasić *mts* Yugoslavia
82 D6 Vlašić Planina *mts* Yugoslavia
65 L2 Vlašim Czechoslovakia 49.42N 14.54E
82 G8 Vlasotince Yugoslavia 42.59N 22.07E
41 O5 Vlasovo U.S.S.R. 70.49N 134.37E
84 C7 Vlássi Greece 37.03N 21.49E
65 J2 Vlastec *mt* Czechoslovakia 49.56N 13.48E
62 K7 Vlčany Czechoslovakia 48.00N 17.55E
60 N8 Vledder Netherlands 52.51N 6.11E
95 E9 Vleifontein S Africa 33.10S 21.03E
95 E9 Vleiland S Africa 33.22S 21.11E
60 J11 Vleuten Netherlands 52.07N 5.01E
61 G3 Vlezenbeek Belgium 50.48N 4.14E
60 H6 Vlieland *isld* Netherlands
60 L14 Vlierden Netherlands 51.27N 5.45E
61 M3 Vliermaalroot Belgium 50.52N 5.25E
61 F3 Vlierzele Belgium 50.56N 3.54E
60 J6 Vliestroom *channel* Netherlands
60 F11 Vliet *canal* Netherlands
60 J13 Vlijmen Netherlands 51.42N 5.14E
61 K1 Vlimmeren Belgium 51.18N 4.47E
61 C1 Vlissegem Belgium 51.15N 3.04E
60 B3 Vlissingen Netherlands 51.27N 3.35E
60 U16 Vlodrop Netherlands 51.08N 6.05E
84 D2 Vlokhós Greece 39.32N 22.06E
83 C4 Vlorë Albania 40.29N 19.29E
83 C4 Vlorës, Gji i *B* Albania
63 J8 Vlotho W Germany 52.11N 8.51E
65 J4 Vltava *R* Czechoslovakia
45 J1 Vnukovo U.S.S.R. 55.36N 37.22E
39 G4 Vnutrennyaya Guba *gulf* U.S.S.R.
79 L4 Vo Italy 45.19N 11.38E
79 H3 Vobarno Italy 45.38N 10.30E
79 F5 Vobbia Italy 44.36N 9.02E
112 H5 Voca Texas 31.01N 99.12W
65 J5 Vöckla *R* Austria
65 J5 Vöcklabruck Austria 48.01N 13.40E
65 H5 Vöcklamarkt Austria 48.01N 13.29E
109 K2 Voda Kansas 39.04N 100.02W
25 J7 Vo Dat Vietnam 11.08N 107.33E
53 B6 Vodder Denmark 55.14N 8.52E
61 J6 Vodecée Belgium 50.12N 4.35E
61 J6 Vodelée Belgium 50.10N 4.44E
82 C7 Vodice Yugoslavia 43.47N 15.47E
95 C7 Voditanjona Madagascar 22.04S 47.40E
82 K7 Voditsa Bulgaria 43.21N 26.02E
47 D5 Vodla *R* U.S.S.R.
47 D5 Vodlozero, Ozero *L* U.S.S.R.
65 K3 Vodňany Czechoslovakia 49.09N 14.12E
82 B6 Vodnjan Yugoslavia 44.59N 13.52E
47 G4 Vodnyy U.S.S.R. 63.30N 53.21E
79 M2 Vodo Italy 46.25N 12.15E
Vodop'yanovo *see* Donskoye
53 E2 Vodskov Denmark 57.07N 10.02E
58 Q9 Voe Shetland Scotland 60.21N 1.15W
53 D4 Voel Denmark 56.12N 9.42E
95 J8 Voël *R* S Africa
95 C9 Voëlvlei S Africa 33.22S 19.00E
53 E3 Voer Denmark 56.31N 10.17E
63 E9 Voerde W Germany 51.33N 6.40E
63 F10 Voerde W Germany 51.19N 7.24E
60 T17 Voerendaal Netherlands 50.53N 5.55E
53 D4 Voerladegård Denmark 56.02N 9.45E
53 F2 Voerså Denmark 57.13N 10.30E
25 J6 Voeune Sai Cambodia 13.59N 106.48E
89 K8 Vogan Togo 6.20N 1.33E
50 C7 Vogar Iceland 63.59N 22.24W
15 L8 Vogel, C Papua New Guinea 9.54S 150.00E
65 D7 Vogelkar-Spitze *mt* Austria 47.27N 11.27E
64 G2 Vogelsberg *mts* W Germany
61 H6 Vogenée Belgium 50.15N 4.27E
79 F5 Voghera Italy 44.59N 9.01E
79 L5 Voghiera Italy 44.46N 11.45E
66 H8 Vogna, Valle Italy
53 C3 Vognsild Denmark 56.46N 9.26E
79 D2 Vogogna Italy 46.01N 8.18E
66 M7 Vogorno Switzerland 46.13N 8.52E
66 M7 Vogorno, L. di Switzerland
66 M7 Vogorno, Pizzo di *mt* Switzerland 46.14N 8.53E
64 M2 Vogtland *reg* E Germany
47 J4 Vogulka *R* U.S.S.R.
9 B13 Voh New Caledonia 20.57S 164.44E
64 M6 Vohburg W Germany 48.46N 11.38E
64 N4 Vohenstrauss W Germany 49.37N 12.20E
95 D5 Vohibanany Madagascar 18.49S 49.04E
95 D6 Vohilava Madagascar 21.04S 48.00E
95 E2 Vohimarina Madagascar 13.22S 50.00E
95 D6 Vohimasina Madagascar 21.49S 48.06E
95 D4 Vohimena Madagascar 17.20S 48.39E
95 C7 Vohipana Madagascar 23.31S 47.30E
95 C7 Vohipeno Madagascar 22.21S 47.51E
95 C6 Vohipisaka Madagascar 20.10S 47.00E
64 F1 Vöhl W Germany 51.13N 8.58E
Vohlemar *see* Vohimarina
46 F1 Võhma Estonia U.S.S.R. 58.39N 25.29E
64 E7 Vöhrenbach W Germany 48.03N 8.18E
64 J7 Vöhringen W Germany 48.16N 10.05E
64 C1 Vohwinkel Nordrhein-Westfalen W Germany 51.13N 7.05E
93 K9 Voi Kenya 3.23S 38.35E
93 L9 Voi *watercourse* Kenya
69 K6 Void-Vacon France 48.41N 5.38E
63 S4 Voigdehagen E Germany 54.17N 13.07E
58 H6 Voil, L Central Scotland 56.20N 4.26W
69 H6 Voillecomte France 48.30N 4.52E
46 J4 Voina U.S.S.R. 52.20N 34.19E
82 L3 Voineşti Romania 47.05N 27.27E
89 E7 Voinjama Liberia 8.25N 9.42W
44 C9 Voinka Ukraine U.S.S.R. 45.51N 33.59E
82 J1 Voinolov U.S.S.R. 49.08N 24.29E
84 E5 Voiotía *prov* Greece
69 H7 Voire *R* France
71 H6 Voiron France 45.22N 5.35E
71 J4 Voirons *mt* France 46.13N 6.22E
82 G5 Voislova Romania 45.30N 22.28E
71 H3 Voiteur France 46.45N 5.36E
65 M7 Voitsberg Austria 47.04N 15.09E
65 K5 Voitsdorf Austria 48.02N 14.03E
53 C6 Vojens Denmark 55.15N 9.19E
52 J2 Vojmsjön *L* Sweden 64.45N 16.30E
82 C5 Vojnić* Yugoslavia 45.19N 15.41E
64 N3 Vojtanov Czechoslovakia 50.10N 12.19E
82 E5 Vojvodina *aut reg* Yugoslavia
15 H5 Vokeo *isld* Papua New Guinea 3.13S 144.06E
47 F6 Vokhma *R* U.S.S.R.
47 G5 Vol' *R* U.S.S.R.
65 J4 Volary Czechoslovakia 48.55N 13.53E
53 X17 Volavatn *L* Buskerud Norway 60.47N 7.45E
108 E4 Volborg Montana 45.50N 105.40W
120 F10 Volcán Argentina 23.57S 65.41W
120 E10 Volcán, Cerro *pk* Arg/Bolivia 22.15S 66.40W
121 B3 Volcán, Cerro del *pk* Chile 30.30S 70.18W
109 D2 Volcano Colorado 39.59N 106.43W
Volcano B *see* Uchiura-wan
114 C8 Volcano House Hawaiian Is 19.25N 155.15W
19 H2 Volcano I Luzon Philippines
Volcano Is *see* Kazan-retto
121 F6 Volcán, Sa. del *ra* Argentina
45 V4 Volchanka U.S.S.R. 52.34N 49.59E
45 H6 Volchansk Ukraine U.S.S.R. 50.19N 36.55E
47 H6 Volchansk U.S.S.R. 59.58N 6.00E
42 C5 Volchikha U.S.S.R. 52.02N 80.20E
46 K1 Volchina *R* U.S.S.R.
45 M4 Volchki U.S.S.R. 52.30N 40.44E
45 H8 Volchya *R* Ukraine U.S.S.R.
53 U14 Volda Norway 62.09N 6.05E
53 T14 Voldafjord *inlet* Norway 62.10N 5.58E
53 F4 Voldby Århus Denmark 56.28N 10.53E
53 D4 Voldby Vejle Denmark 56.14N 9.54E
47 G5 Vol'dino U.S.S.R. 62.18N 54.07E
53 E4 Voldum Denmark 56.22N 10.11E
60 J10 Volendam Netherlands 52.30N 5.04E
106 C7 Volga Iowa 42.47N 91.31W
108 O5 Volga S Dakota 44.19N 96.56W
46 L1 Volga U.S.S.R. 57.58N 38.22E
106 C7 Volga *R* Iowa
46 O4 Volga *R* U.S.S.R.
45 P8 Volga-Donskoy Kanal U.S.S.R.
46 J2 Volga, Oz *L* U.S.S.R.
47 D5 Volgo-Balt (I.V. Lenin) Kanal *canal* U.S.S.R.
45 O9 Volgodonsk U.S.S.R. 47.35N 42.08E
46 N5 Volgograd U.S.S.R. 48.45N 44.30E
46 N5 Volgogradskaya Oblast' *prov* U.S.S.R.
46 O5 Volgogradskoye Vodokhranilishche *res* U.S.S.R.
47 E7 Volgorechensk U.S.S.R. 57.28N 41.21E
69 E8 Volgré France 47.56N 3.20E
52 K2 Volgsele Sweden 64.06N 16.45E
52 K2 Volgsjöfors Sweden 64.34N 16.40E
84 A6 Volimais Greece 37.52N 20.40E
108 N7 Volin S Dakota 42.58N 97.11W
83 H6 Volissós Greece 38.29N 25.54E
9 T7 Voli Voli Pt Viti Levu Fiji 17.21S 178.10E
64 J4 Volkach W Germany 49.52N 10.15E
60 L13 Volkel Netherlands 51.39N 5.40E
64 J1 Volkenroda E Germany 51.16N 10.35E
60 F13 Volkerak *estuary* Netherlands
65 L8 Völkermarkt Austria 46.40N 14.38E
64 J3 Völkershausen W Germany 50.29N 10.18E
47 C6 Volkhov U.S.S.R. 59.54N 32.15E
46 H1 Volkhov *R* U.S.S.R.
64 B5 Völklingen W Germany 49.15N 6.51E
63 K10 Volkmarsen W Germany 51.24N 9.06E
45 G3 Volkonskoye U.S.S.R. 53.55N 35.40E
82 L1 Volkovintsy U.S.S.R. 49.12N 27.40E
46 E3 Volkovysk Belorussiya U.S.S.R. 53.10N 24.28E
63 L8 Völksen W Germany 52.13N 9.38E
95 N3 Volksrust S Africa 27.22S 29.54E
53 W13 Voll Norway 62.32N 7.27E
60 M9 Vollenhove Netherlands 52.41N 5.58E
61 G3 Vollezele Belgium 50.46N 4.01E
71 D5 Vollore-Ville France 45.48N 3.35E
53 W14 Vollseter Norway 62.02N 7.02E
63 J9 Völmerstod *mt* W Germany 51.49N 8.57E
69 N5 Volmunster France 49.08N 7.22E
39 F3 Volna, Gora *mt* U.S.S.R. 63.31N 155.10E
71 F2 Volnay Côte d'Or France 47.00N 4.47E
70 L6 Volnay Sarthe France 47.57N 0.28E
106 H6 Volney Michigan 43.42N 86.02W
45 F8 Vol'nogorsk Ukraine U.S.S.R. 48.30N 34.01E
45 J9 Volnovakha Ukraine U.S.S.R. 47.36N 37.32E
45 T9 Vol'noye Astrakhan' U.S.S.R. 47.10N 47.43E
47 L8 Vol'noye Omsk U.S.S.R. 54.24N 71.16E
45 G9 Vol'nyansk Ukraine U.S.S.R. 47.55N 35.29E
47 M1 Vol'nyy, Ostrov *isld* Leningrad U.S.S.R.
45 H5 Volobuyevo U.S.S.R. 51.52N 36.18E
41 F5 Volochanka U.S.S.R. 70.59N 94.48E
40 F7 Volochayevka U.S.S.R. 48.35N 134.25E
46 F5 Volochisk Ukraine U.S.S.R. 49.34N 26.10E
39 G1 Volochsk U.S.S.R. 68.28N 160.19E
45 P1 Volodarsk U.S.S.R. 56.14N 43.10E
44 J1 Volodarskiy U.S.S.R. 46.25N 48.32E
43 J1 Volodarskoye Kazakhstan U.S.S.R. 53.19N 68.05E
47 E5 Volodskaya U.S.S.R. 62.21N 42.00E
46 L1 Vologda U.S.S.R. 59.10N 39.55E
69 M7 Vologne *R* France
41 E6 Vologochan U.S.S.R. 69.30N 87.15E
47 D5 Vologodskaya Oblast' *prov* U.S.S.R.
46 H2 Volok U.S.S.R. 56.58N 31.15E
45 G1 Volokolamsk U.S.S.R. 56.02N 35.56E
42 H3 Volokon U.S.S.R. 58.28N 106.40E
45 J6 Volokonovka U.S.S.R. 50.28N 37.52E
47 F3 Volokovaya U.S.S.R. 66.29N 48.13E
51 Q8 Volom *R* Karelia U.S.S.R.
47 F3 Volonga U.S.S.R. 67.05N 47.44E
71 J8 Volonne France 44.07N 6.01E
84 E3 Vólos Greece 39.22N 22.57E
45 L8 Voloshino U.S.S.R. 48.55N 39.57E
47 D5 Voloshka U.S.S.R. 61.24N 40.00E
46 G1 Volosovo U.S.S.R. 59.30N 29.32E
46 H1 Volot U.S.S.R. 57.59N 30.42E
82 H2 Volovets U.S.S.R. 48.44N 23.14E
45 J4 Volovo Lipetsk U.S.S.R. 52.02N 37.54E
45 K3 Volovo Tula U.S.S.R. 53.32N 38.02E
82 H2 Volovo U.S.S.R. 48.31N 23.31E
45 F2 Voloye U.S.S.R. 54.12N 34.34E
79 C4 Volpiano Italy 45.12N 7.47E
63 O8 Völpke E Germany 52.08N 11.07E
48 U12 Volquart Boons Kyst *coast* Greenland
63 S5 Völschow E Germany 53.54N 13.20E
80 E3 Volsini, Monti Italy
45 T4 Vol'sk U.S.S.R. 52.04N 47.22E
94 R13 Volstruisfontein S Africa 26.12S 27.33E
95 G9 Volstruisleegte S Africa 33.06S 23.26E
53 E2 Volstrup Denmark 57.19N 10.27E
117 H9 Volta Brazil 9.13S 38.14W
111 D4 Volta California 37.06N 120.57W
89 K8 Volta *R* Ghana/Togo
89 K8 Volta *reg* Ghana
89 J6 Volta Blanche *R* Upper Volta
89 H5 Volta Blanche *watercourse* Upper Volta
79 E5 Voltággio Italy 44.37N 8.51E
108 K1 Voltaire N Dakota 48.02N 100.50W
14 F2 Voltaire, C W Australia 14.15S 125.36E
89 J7 Volta,L Ghana
79 J4 Volta Mantovana Italy 45.20N 10.39E
89 G6 Volta Noire *R* Upper Volta
118 G8 Volta Redonda Brazil 22.31S 44.05W
89 J6 Volta Rouge *R* Upper Volta/Ghana
80 C2 Volterra Italy 43.24N 10.52E
47 E4 Volteva U.S.S.R. 64.31N 44.14E
76 L7 Voltoya *R* Spain
79 E6 Voltri Italy 44.26N 8.45E
80 M6 Volturara Appula Italy 41.30N 15.04E
80 L7 Volturara Irpina Italy 40.53N 14.55E
80 M6 Volturino Italy 41.29N 15.08E
81 L3 Volturino, Monte Italy 40.24N 15.49E
80 K6 Volturno *R* Italy
121 E9 Volunteer Pt Falkland Is 51.32S 57.44W
103 L3 Voluntown Connecticut 41.35N 71.51W
15 K6 Volupai New Britain 5.17S 149.58E
45 H7 Volvenkovo Ukraine U.S.S.R. 49.15N 36.49E
71 C5 Volvic France 45.53N 3.02E
83 F4 Vólvi,L Greece
71 H9 Volx France 43.53N 5.50E
47 J4 Vol'ya *R* U.S.S.R.
65 J3 Volyně Czechoslovakia 49.11N 13.53E
65 J3 Volynka *R* Czechoslovakia
45 U1 Volzhsk U.S.S.R. 55.51N 48.22E
Volzhskiy *see* Nizhnevolzhsk
44 H1 Volzhskiy Astrakhan' U.S.S.R. 46.39N 47.51E
45 Q8 Volzhskiy Volgograd U.S.S.R. 48.48N 44.45E
90 G6 Voma Cameroon 11.23N 14.30E
80 J3 Vomano *R* Italy
9 R7 Vomo *isld* Fiji 17.30S 177.15E
50 E7 Vomúlastadhir Iceland 63.40N 20.10W
84 C5 Vomvokioí Greece 38.25N 21.49E
109 H2 Vona Colorado 39.17N 102.45W
50 H5 Vonarskardh *pass* Iceland 64.40N 17.52W
53 U15 Vonavatn *L* Norway 61.37N 6.01E
15 K3 Vona Vona I Solomon Is 8.15S 157.05E
100 L6 Vonda Saskatchewan 52.20N 106.06W
95 G9 Vondeling S Africa 33.21S 23.08E
95 B6 Vondrove Madagascar 21.47S 44.09E
95 C7 Vondrozo Madagascar 22.50S 47.20E
61 K6 Vonêche Belgium 50.03N 4.59E
113 K5 Von Frank Mt Alaska 63.31N 154.20W
47 E4 Vonga U.S.S.R. 64.42N 43.15E
53 C5 Vonge Denmark 55.52N 9.26E
71 G2 Vonges France 47.17N 5.24E
53 W15 Vongsen *mt* Norway 61.34N 7.21E
84 A4 Vónitsa Greece 38.55N 20.53E
118 D2 Von Martius, Cachoeira *waterfall* Brazil 10.08S 52.54W
71 G4 Vonnas France 46.13N 5.00E
72 E3 Vonne *R* France
50 T14 Von Postbreen *glacier* Spitsbergen 78.25N 18.30E
53 D6 Vonsbæk Denmark 55.17N 9.37E
53 C6 Vonsild Vejle Denmark 55.28N 9.29E
28 D3 Vontimitta Andhra Prad India 14.24N 79.00E
93 K7 Voo Kenya 1.40S 38.19E
95 F10 Voorbaai S Africa 34.09S 22.06E
60 F11 Voorburg Netherlands 52.04N 4.22E
61 F3 Voorde Belgium 50.49N 3.57E
60 M14 Voordeldonk Netherlands 51.24N 5.46E
61 B3 Voormezele Belgium 50.49N 2.52E
60 E12 Voorne *isld* Netherlands
60 E12 Voornse Kan *canal* Netherlands
60 F11 Voorschoten Netherlands 52.08N 4.26E
60 N11 Voorst Netherlands 52.10N 6.10E
60 L11 Voorthuizen Netherlands 52.12N 5.36E
45 D2 Vop' *R* U.S.S.R.
50 L3 Vopnafjördhur Iceland 65.46N 14.50W
50 L3 Vopnafjördhur *B* Iceland
51 J8 Vörå Finland 63.10N 22.15E
66 N4 Vorab *mt* Switzerland 46.53N 9.05E
65 A7 Vorarlberg *prov* Austria
65 N7 Vorau Austria 47.25N 15.53E
66 M3 Vorauen Switzerland 47.02N 8.58E
53 C5 Vorbasse Denmark 55.38N 9.09E
60 O11 Vorden Netherlands 52.07N 6.18E
63 H8 Vörden W Germany 52.30N 8.06E
65 L7 Vordernberg Austria 47.30N 14.59E
66 M5 Vorderrhein *R* Switzerland
66 M3 Vorderthal Switzerland 47.07N 8.54E
84 D7 Vordhónia Greece 37.08N 22.19E
50 E6 Vórdhufell *mt* Iceland 64.05N 20.31W
53 H6 Vordingborg Denmark 55.01N 11.55E
71 H6 Voreppe France 45.18N 5.38E
71 D6 Vorey France 45.11N 3.55E
45 D3 Vorga U.S.S.R. 53.45N 32.45E
53 B4 Vorgod Denmark 56.05N 8.42E
53 B4 Vorgod Å *R* Denmark
84 F3 Voríai Sporádhes *islds* Greece
53 W18 Vøringsfossen *waterfall* Norway 60.25N 7.15E
84 D8 Vórion Greece 36.58N 22.15E
84 F4 Vórios Evvoïkos Kólpos *gulf* Greece
28 K1 Vorjing *mt* Assam India 28.19N 94.20E
47 J3 Vorkuta U.S.S.R. 67.27N 64.00E
52 F6 Vorma *R* Norway
51 K12 Vormsi *isld* Estonia 59.00N 23.15E
53 D3 Vorning Denmark 56.32N 9.45E
47 M4 Vorob'i U.S.S.R. 57.15N 59.49E
45 M6 Vorob'yevka U.S.S.R. 50.40N 40.55E
42 G4 Vorob'yevo Irkutsk U.S.S.R. 57.22N 102.15E
47 M7 Vorob'yevo Novosibirsk U.S.S.R. 56.09N 76.30E
45 F1 Vorob'yevo Smolensk U.S.S.R. 55.14N 34.45E
42 D2 Vorogovo U.S.S.R. 61.04N 89.30E
45 O4 Vorona *R* U.S.S.R.
45 C3 Voronevo Belorussiya U.S.S.R. 53.43N 31.44E
45 E5 Voronezh Ukraine U.S.S.R. 51.46N 33.30E
45 L5 Voronezh U.S.S.R. 51.40N 39.13E
45 L4 Voronezh *R* U.S.S.R.
46 L4 Voronezhskaya Oblast' *prov* U.S.S.R.
41 F2 Voronina, Ostrov *isld* U.S.S.R. 78.10N 93.46E
45 B6 Voronkov Ukraine U.S.S.R. 50.14N 30.55E
45 D4 Voronok U.S.S.R. 52.21N 32.40E
82 M1 Voronovitsa U.S.S.R. 49.06N 28.49E
47 E3 Voronov, Mys *C* U.S.S.R. 66.33N 42.20E
46 F3 Voronovo Belorussiya U.S.S.R. 54.09N 25.19E
42 C4 Voronovo U.S.S.R. 56.03N 83.49E
42 J3 Vorontsovka Irkutsk U.S.S.R. 58.55N 113.00E
43 O3 Vorontsovka Kazakhstan U.S.S.R. 49.00N 81.30E
47 J6 Vorontsovka Sverdlovsk U.S.S.R. 59.39N 60.10E
44 C9 Vorontsovka Ukraine U.S.S.R. 45.51N 33.49E
45 M6 Vorontsovka Voronezh U.S.S.R. 50.38N 40.22E
46 G2 Vorontsovo U.S.S.R. 57.18N 28.43E
47 D2 Voronya *R* U.S.S.R.
46 M1 Voron'ye U.S.S.R. 58.00N 42.01E
Voroshilov *see* Ussuriysk
43 F7 Voroshilova, im Turkmeniya U.S.S.R. 37.51N 60.08E
45 L8 Voroshilovgrad Ukraine U.S.S.R. 48.35N 39.20E
45 H9 Voroshilovka Ukraine U.S.S.R. 47.39N 36.43E
45 R4 Voroshilovo Penza U.S.S.R. 52.27N 45.16E
45 S5 Voroshilovo Saratov U.S.S.R. 51.08N 46.39E
47 F6 Voroshno U.S.S.R. 59.56N 45.35E
44 G8 Vorotan *R* U.S.S.R.
45 R1 Vorotynets U.S.S.R. 56.04N 45.50E
45 H2 Vorotynsk U.S.S.R. 54.28N 36.03E
39 F7 Vorovskaya *R* U.S.S.R.
45 N1 Vorovskogo, im U.S.S.R. 55.43N 41.09E
45 F5 Vorozhba Sumy, Ukraine U.S.S.R. 51.10N 34.15E
45 F6 Vorozhba Sumy, Ukraine U.S.S.R. 50.42N 34.40E
42 E3 Vorozheyka U.S.S.R. 58.14N 90.03E
63 S5 Vorpommern *reg* E Germany
84 L11 Vórroi Crete 35.04N 24.48E
Vors *see* Baraqueville
61 K2 Vorselaar Belgium 51.12N 4.46E
63 N8 Vorsfelde W Germany 52.27N 10.52E
45 G6 Vorskla *R* U.S.S.R.
45 P1 Vorsma U.S.S.R. 56.00N 43.15E
61 L2 Vorst Belgium 51.05N 5.01E
63 D10 Vorst W Germany 51.18N 6.25E
60 L13 Vorstenbosch Netherlands 51.40N 5.34E
95 G1 Vorstershoop S Africa 25.50S 23.02E
46 F1 Võrtsjärv *L* Estonia U.S.S.R.
46 F1 Võru Estonia U.S.S.R. 57.48N 26.54E
43 K7 Vorukh Tadzhikistan U.S.S.R. 39.51N 70.35E
53 E4 Vorup Denmark 56.26N 10.03E
47 J5 Vor'ya *R* U.S.S.R.
47 J5 Vor'yapaul' U.S.S.R. 62.07N 61.59E
47 G4 Vorykva *R* U.S.S.R.
95 F6 Vosburg S Africa 30.35S 22.52E
67 K4 Vosges *dept* France
69 M8 Vosges *mts* France
45 N9 Voskhod U.S.S.R. 47.27N 41.51E
45 K1 Voskresensk U.S.S.R. 55.19N 38.43E
42 K5 Voskresenskaya U.S.S.R. 53.15N 119.30E
43 D1 Voskresenskoye Bashkir U.S.S.R. 52.07N 56.09E
47 M5 Voskresenskoye Chelyabinsk U.S.S.R. 56.04N 60.51E
46 O2 Voskresenskoye Gor'kiy U.S.S.R. 56.49N 45.28E
45 K3 Voskresenskoye Lipetsk U.S.S.R. 53.11N 38.45E
45 S5 Voskresenskoye Saratov U.S.S.R. 51.49N 46.55E
47 D6 Voskresenskoye Vologda U.S.S.R. 59.27N 37.58E
94 T14 Vosloorus Witwatersrand S Africa 26.22S 28.14E
45 T5 Vosnesenka U.S.S.R. 51.30N 47.15E
44 E2 Vosnesenskoye U.S.S.R. 45.49N 43.26E
53 U17 Voss Norway 60.38N 6.25E
53 U17 Voss *reg* Norway
53 U17 Vossa *R* Norway 60.38N 6.13E
53 W17 Vossaskavl *mt* Norway 60.40N 7.06E
61 K1 Vosselaar Belgium 51.19N 4.53E
61 E2 Vosselare Belgium 51.02N 3.34E
61 J3 Vossem Belgium 50.50N 4.34E
Vossestrand *see* Framnes
Vossevangen *see* Voss
95 O2 Vossman's Beacon S Africa 26.15S 30.30E
47 D2 Vostochnaya Litsa U.S.S.R. 68.40N 37.45E
43 P3 Vostochno Kazakhstanskaya Oblast' *prov* Kazakhstan U.S.S.R.
43 M4 Vostochno-Kounradskiy Kazakhstan U.S.S.R. 47.00N 75.09E
40 J6 Vostochno Sakhalinskiy Khrebet *mts* Sakhalin U.S.S.R.
41 R4 Vostochno Sibirskoye More *sea* U.S.S.R.
40 J5 Vostochnyy Sakhalin U.S.S.R. 53.30N 143.08E
40 J7 Vostochnyy Sakhalin U.S.S.R. 48.15N 142.36E
47 J6 Vostochnyy U.S.S.R. 58.45N 61.45E
43 E5 Vostochnyy Chink Ustyurta *ridge* Uzbekistan U.S.S.R.
41 D4 Vostochnyy Kammennyy, Ostrov *isld* U.S.S.R.
44 B2 Vostochnyy, Liman *lagoon* U.S.S.R.
42 E5 Vostochnyy Sayan *mts* U.S.S.R.
123 F5 Vostok *U.S.S.R. Base* Antarctica 78.28S 106.48E
123 F13 Vostok, C Antarctica 69.00S 72.00W
122 M9 Vostok I Line Is Pacific Oc 10.05S 152.23W
44 F2 Vostok Manych *R* U.S.S.R.
43 E4 Vostrozhdeniya, Ostrov *isld* Uzbekistan U.S.S.R. 45.06N 59.13E
47 K5 Vostykhoy U.S.S.R. 61.12N 67.48E
112 N5 Votaw Texas 30.25N 94.40W
112 N5 Voth Texas 30.10N 94.11W
65 L2 Votice Czechoslovakia 49.38N 14.38E
46 R2 Votkinsk U.S.S.R. 57.00N 54.00E
46 R2 Votkinskoye Vdkhr *res* U.S.S.R.
53 Z17 Votna *R* Norway
61 N4 Vottem Belgium 50.40N 5.35E
118 E7 Votuporanga Brazil 20.26S 49.53W
Votyak *see* Udmurtskaya A.S.S.R.
91 E10 Vouga Angola 12.14S 16.49E
76 D7 Vouga *R* Portugal
71 F2 Vougeot France 47.10N 4.58E
66 B7 Vougy France 46.04N 6.30E
71 E4 Vougy France 46.06N 4.07E
72 C3 Vouhé France 46.10N 0.48W
72 E2 Vouillé Vienne France 46.38N 0.10E
71 K2 Voujeaucourt France 47.29N 6.46E
84 J11 Voukoliés Crete 35.28N 23.47E
84 G6 Voúla Greece 37.50N 23.45E
84 C3 Voulgára *mt* Greece 39.06N 21.54E
84 B3 Voulgarélion Greece 39.22N 21.11E
84 E2 Voulgariní Greece 39.35N 22.47E
72 E3 Voulon France 46.22N 0.14E
90 L7 Voulou Cent Afr Rep 8.36N 22.28E
71 F7 Voulte-sur-Rhône, la France 44.47N 4.47E
69 D7 Voulx France 48.16N 2.59E
90 F10 Voumo *watercourse* Cameroon
84 B6 Voúnargon Greece 37.44N 21.25E
72 F2 Vouneuil-sur-Vienne France 46.44N 0.32E
84 Q14 Vouni *ruins* Cyprus 35.09N 32.47E
84 D5 Vouraïkós *R* Greece
90 D9 Vouri *R* Cameroon
83 E4 Voúrinos *mt* Greece 40.11N 21.40E
72 L3 Voussac France 46.20N 3.03E
90 E9 Vouté *tribe* Cameroon
71 D1 Voutenay-sur-Cure France 47.34N 3.46E
72 G5 Voutezac France 45.18N 1.27E
84 B2 Voutonási Greece 39.47N 21.07E
70 K5 Voutré France 48.08N 0.18W
84 C3 Voutsikáki *mt* Greece 39.17N 21.38E
84 D2 Vouvála Greece 40.00N 22.05E
72 C2 Vouvant France 46.35N 0.46W
70 M7 Vouvray France 47.25N 0.48E
66 D6 Vouvry Switzerland 46.21N 6.53E
72 E4 Vouzan France 45.35N 0.22E
71 D4 Vouzance *R* France
76 C7 Vouzela Portugal 40.43N 8.07W
72 J1 Vouzeron France 47.16N 2.12E
69 H5 Vouziers France 49.25N 4.41E
70 P6 Vouzon France 47.39N 2.02E
70 O5 Voves France 48.16N 1.37E
90 M8 Vovodo *R* Cent Afr Rep
84 B2 Vovoúsa Greece 39.57N 21.04E
66 A7 Vovray France 46.05N 6.10E
52 J5 Voxnan Sweden 61.20N 15.30E
52 J5 Voxnan *R* Sweden
52 H9 Voxtorp Sweden 57.07N 14.05E
46 Q1 Voya *R* U.S.S.R.
39 F5 Voyampolka U.S.S.R. 58.25N 159.15E
39 F5 Voyampolka *R* U.S.S.R.
39 J3 Voyegi *R* U.S.S.R.
45 L5 Voyevo U.S.S.R. 51.25N 39.20E
45 F1 Voyevodino U.S.S.R. 55.44N 34.51E
42 D5 Voyevodskoye U.S.S.R. 52.49N 85.41E
41 H7 Voyevolikhan *R* U.S.S.R.
123 G2 Voyeykov Ice Shelf Antarctica
47 J3 Voykar *R* U.S.S.R.
44 C9 Voykovo Ukraine U.S.S.R. 45.31N 33.54E
47 C3 Voynitsa U.S.S.R. 65.10N 30.15E
37 F3 Voyvoda Turkey 40.08N 28.27E
47 G4 Voy Vozh U.S.S.R. 62.56N 54.55E
47 H4 Voyvozh U.S.S.R. 64.19N 55.12E
15 K2 Voza Choiseul I Solomon Is 6.55S 156.40E
44 F2 Vozdvizhenskoye U.S.S.R. 45.50N 43.40E
47 F4 Vozhayel' U.S.S.R. 63.15N 49.30E
47 G4 Vozhayel' U.S.S.R. 62.49N 51.21E
47 E5 Vozhega U.S.S.R. 60.25N 40.11E
47 D5 Vozhe, Ozero *L* U.S.S.R.
46 Q1 Vozhgaly U.S.S.R. 58.12N 50.10E
47 F4 Vozhgora U.S.S.R. 64.32N 48.20E
41 R3 Vozneseniya, Guba *gulf* U.S.S.R.
43 K2 Voznesenka Kazakhstan U.S.S.R. 52.25N 70.14E
44 F1 Voznesenovka U.S.S.R. 46.15N 44.24E
45 C9 Voznesensk Ukraine U.S.S.R. 47.34N 31.21E
47 M6 Voznesenskiy U.S.S.R. 54.59N 61.22E
45 D7 Voznesenskoye Ukraine U.S.S.R. 49.45N 32.10E
45 O2 Voznesenskoye U.S.S.R. 54.53N 42.45E
47 D5 Voznesenye U.S.S.R. 61.03N 35.30E
45 U4 Vozrozhdeniye U.S.S.R. 52.42N 48.07E
40 J7 Vozvrashcheniye Sakhalin U.S.S.R. 49.59N 142.12E
43 K1 Vozvyshenskiy Kazakhstan U.S.S.R. 54.26N 70.59E
40 D6 Vozzhayevka U.S.S.R. 50.46N 128.38E
43 E7 Vpadiny Unguz, Solonchakovyye *salt marshes* Turkmeniya U.S.S.R.
53 D2 Vrå Denmark 57.21N 9.57E
62 L7 Vráble Czechoslovakia 48.15N 18.15E
53 Z20 Vrådal Norway 59.20N 8.32E
53 C4 Vrads Denmark 56.03N 9.28E
84 N11 Vrakhási Crete 35.16N 25.33E
84 E6 Vrakháti Greece 37.57N 22.47E
84 A6 Vrakhiónas *mt* Greece 37.49N 20.42E
84 C5 Vrakhnéïka Greece 38.10N 21.40E
53 Y20 Vråliosen Norway 59.22N 8.10E
82 D7 Vran *mt* Yugoslavia 43.40N 17.30E
82 K5 Vrancea *div* Romania
82 K5 Vrancei, Munţii *mts* Vrancea Romania
65 K2 Vrané Czechoslovakia 49.57N 14.24E
84 W23 Vranganiótika Corfu 39.28N 19.55E
40 H4 Vrangelya Mys *C* U.S.S.R. 54.19N 138.45E
39 M1 Vrangelya, Ostrov *isld* U.S.S.R.
82 D7 Vranica *mts* Yugoslavia
82 G8 Vranje Yugoslavia 42.33N 21.54E
65 N4 Vranov Brno Czech 48.54N 15.48E
62 N7 Vranov Prešov Czech 48.54N 21.40E
65 N4 Vranovská nádrž *res* Czechoslovakia
61 G2 Vrasene Belgium 51.13N 4.12E
82 H7 Vratsa Bulgaria 43.12N 23.32E
65 N4 Vratěnín Czechoslovakia 48.54N 15.37E
53 Y20 Vråvatn *L* Norway 59.21N 8.15E
65 K3 Vráž Czechoslovakia 49.23N 14.08E
82 D6 Vrbas *R* Yugoslavia
62 K5 Vrbno Czechoslovakia 50.08N 17.20E
82 C5 Vrbovsko Yugoslavia 45.24N 15.05E
62 J5 Vrchlabí Czechoslovakia 50.38N 15.35E
65 L2 Vrchotovy Janovice Czech 49.40N 14.35E
65 M3 Vrchy Jihlavské *mts* Czech
65 N2 Vrch Žďárská *mts* Czech
82 F5 Vrdnik Yugoslavia 45.06N 19.49E
65 M2 Vrdy Bučice Czechoslovakia 49.56N 15.28E
69 K7 Vrécourt France 48.10N 5.43E
95 N3 Vrede S Africa 27.25S 29.10E
95 L3 Vredefort S Africa 27.00S 27.22E
63 E8 Vreden W Germany 52.03N 6.50E
95 A8 Vredenburg S Africa 32.55S 18.00E
119 J4 Vreed en Hoop Guyana 6.50N 58.12W
60 J11 Vreeland Netherlands 52.13N 5.02E
63 G7 Vrees W Germany 52.54N 7.45E
60 J11 Vreeswijk Netherlands 52.01N 5.05E
61 J2 Vremde Belgium 51.11N 4.33E
53 D2 Vrensted Denmark 57.21N 9.48E
61 M4 Vreren Belgium 50.45N 5.30E
53 F6 Vresen *isld* Denmark 55.13N 10.55E
61 K7 Vresse Belgium 49.52N 4.56E
84 D7 Vrésthena Greece 37.14N 22.30E
70 G3 Vrétot, le France 49.27N 1.43W
52 H7 Vretstorp Sweden 59.03N 14.51E
43 J6 Vrevskiy Uzbekistan U.S.S.R. 40.56N 68.54E
82 D7 Vrgorac Yugoslavia 43.12N 17.20E
82 B5 Vrhnika Yugoslavia 45.58N 14.15E
28 D5 Vriddhachalam Tamil Nadu India 11.33N 79.20E
53 C4 Vridsted Denmark 56.27N 9.02E
60 P7 Vries Netherlands 53.05N 6.35E
60 P10 Vriezenveen Netherlands 52.25N 9.37E
69 H4 Vrigne-aux-Bois France 49.43N 4.51E
52 H9 Vrigstad Sweden 57.20N 14.30E
60 H13 Vrijhoeve-Capelle Netherlands 51.40N 5.00E
13 F1 Vrilya Pt Queensland 11.20S 142.02E
66 N5 Vrin Switzerland 46.39N 9.07E
30 A5 Vrindavan Uttar Prad India 27.36N 77.41E
94 D3 Vrindskap Namibia 20.10S 16.15E
71 J3 Vrine, La France 46.59N 6.20E
84 D3 Vrísais Greece 39.15N 22.20E
84 C7 Vrises Greece 37.15N 21.43E
84 H4 Vrísis Greece 38.33N 24.03E
31 F2 Vrist Afghanistan 37.21N 71.28E
53 A3 Vrist Denmark 56.36N 8.09E
69 H5 Vrizy France 49.26N 4.40E
82 C7 Vrlika Yugoslavia 43.55N 16.26E
82 F7 Vrnjačka Banja Yugoslavia 43.36N 20.52E
82 C5 Vrnograč Yugoslavia 45.10N 15.56E
61 N3 Vroenhoven Belgium 50.50N 5.39E
53 A5 Vrøgum Denmark 55.39N 8.18E
84 Q14 Vroisha Cyprus 35.04N 32.40E
69 B3 Vron France 50.19N 1.46E
36 B4 Vrondádhes Khíos Greece 38.25N 26.08E
84 E8 Vrondamás Greece 36.58N 22.29E
60 P10 Vroomshoop Netherlands 52.28N 6.35E
53 C4 Vroue Denmark 56.27N 9.03E
64 P3 Vroutek Czechoslovakia 50.11N 13.23E
60 L6 Vrouwenparochie Netherlands 53.17N 5.42E
60 B2 Vrouwenpolder Netherlands 51.35N 3.37E
60 K8 Vrouwenzand Netherlands
80 O1 Vrpolje Yugoslavia 43.42N 16.01E
82 G5 Vršac Yugoslavia 45.07N 21.19E
79 P4 Vrsar Yugoslavia 45.08N 13.37E
62 L6 Vrútky Czechoslovakia 49.07N 18.50E
95 H2 Vryburg S Africa 26.57S 24.44E
95 O3 Vryheid S Africa 27.45S 30.48E
64 O5 Všeruby Czechoslovakia 49.21N 12.59E
64 P4 Všeruby Czechoslovakia 49.50N 13.15E
62 K6 Vsetín Czechoslovakia 49.20N 18.00E
113 C10 Vsevidof I Aleutian Is 53.00N 168.30W
113 C10 Vsevidof, Mt *vol* Aleutian Is 53.10N 168.40W
47 H5 Vsevolodo Blagodatskiy U.S.S.R. 60.30N 59.57E
51 P11 Vsevolozhskiy U.S.S.R. 60.03N 30.41E
45 F2 Vskhody U.S.S.R. 54.40N 34.08E
39 H1 Vstrechnyy U.S.S.R. 68.03N 165.32E
62 L7 Vtáčnik *mts* Czechoslovakia
45 N3 Vtoryye Levyye Lamki U.S.S.R. 53.16N 41.06E
92 G7 Vua Malawi 10.15S 34.09E
71 H4 Vuache, Mtgne.de France 46.04N 5.56E
66 E5 Vuadens Switzerland 46.37N 7.02E
43 N8 Vuadil' Uzbekistan U.S.S.R. 40.10N 71.44E
9 U3 Vuanggava *isld* Fiji 18.50S 178.55W
66 C5 Vuarrens Switzerland 46.42N 6.38E
25 H2 Vu Ban Vietnam 20.27N 105.27E
82 J9 Vŭcha *R* Bulgaria
61 N3 Vucht Belgium 50.58N 5.43E
82 F8 Vučitrn Yugoslavia 42.49N 20.59E
91 F6 Vudi Zaïre 5.55S 18.56E
72 A1 Vue France 47.13N 1.52W
66 B5 Vufflens Switzerland 46.32N 6.29E
60 K13 Vught Netherlands 51.39N 5.19E
66 A3 Vuillafans France 47.04N 6.14E
66 D5 Vuissens Switzerland 46.45N 6.46E
66 D5 Vuisternens Switzerland 46.40N 6.56E
66 C4 Vuitebœuf Switzerland 46.48N 6.33E
82 E5 Vuka *R* Yugoslavia
82 E5 Vukovar Yugoslavia 45.19N 19.01E
47 H4 Vuktyl U.S.S.R. 63.52N 57.20E
93 E5 Vukula Uganda 0.57N 33.37E
25 M4 Vuladdore Reef Paracel Islands S China Sea
100 D8 Vulcan Alberta 50.27N 113.12W
82 H5 Vulcan Romania 45.22N 23.16E
81 J7 Vulcanello, Mte Lipari Is Italy 38.26N 14.58E
81 J7 Vulcano *isld* Lipari Is Italy
81 E10 Vulcano Mte Linosa, I di Italy 35.53N 12.53E
80 M6 Vulgano *R* Italy
25 H3 Vu Liet Vietnam 18.43N 105.22E
66 E4 Vully, Mt Switzerland 46.58N 7.06E
66 S4 Vulpera Switzerland 46.47N 10.17E
80 N7 Vulture, Monte Italy 40.56N 15.38E
111 M8 Vulture Mts Arizona
15 L3 Vuluva Solomon Is 8.30S 159.51E
39 K1 Vul'vuveem *R* U.S.S.R.
15 M6 Vunadadir New Britain 4.22S 152.15E
15 M6 Vunapope New Britain 4.22S 152.15E
9 T5 Vuna Pt Taveuni Fiji 16.55S 179.53E
25 K4 Vung da Nang *B* Vietnam
25 K5 Vung Dunq Quat *B* Vietnam
25 K7 Vung Phan Thiet *B* Vietnam
25 J7 Vung Tou Vietnam 10.21N 107.04E
92 D11 Vungu *R* Zimbabwe
9 T8 Vunindawa Viti Levu Fiji 17.49S 178.21E
9 S3 Vunisea Kandavu Fiji 19.04S 178.10E
51 N7 Vuokatti Finland 64.07N 28.15E
51 O11 Vuoksa *R* U.S.S.R.
51 O10 Vuoksenniska Finland 61.13N 28.50E
51 M7 Vuolijoki Finland 64.09N 27.00E
51 H5 Vuollerim Sweden 66.26N 20.40E
51 N5 Vuostimo Finland 66.55N 27.24E
51 N3 Vuotso Finland 68.05N 27.10E
51 J5 Vuottas Sweden 66.25N 21.45E
82 K8 Vŭrbitsa Bulgaria 42.59N 26.40E
45 S1 Vurnary U.S.S.R. 55.29N 46.58E
93 B3 Vurra Uganda 2.54N 30.43E
61 E3 Vurste Belgium 50.57N 3.41E
53 C2 Vust Denmark 57.07N 9.05E
45 T1 Vutabosi U.S.S.R. 55.27N 47.27E
82 L4 Vutcani Romania 46.26N 27.59E
28 E2 Vuyyuru Andhra Prad India 16.23N 80.51E
65 M8 Vuzenica Yugoslavia 46.36N 15.11E
43 G1 Vvedenka Kazakhstan U.S.S.R. 54.01N 63.44E
40 D6 Vvedenovka U.S.S.R. 51.24N 128.10E
47 J7 Vvedenskoye U.S.S.R. 55.20N 64.01E
92 F6 Vwawa Tanzania 9.07S 32.55E
110 F8 Vya Nevada 41.35N 119.51W
Vyake Marya *see* Väike Maarja
47 D3 Vyalozero, Oz *L* U.S.S.R.
46 N1 Vyaltsevo U.S.S.R. 59.05N 43.51E
29 C7 Vyara Gujarat India 21.09N 73.28E
47 C5 Vyartsilya U.S.S.R. 62.08N 30.45E
46 Q2 Vyatka *R* U.S.S.R.
46 Q2 Vyatskiye Polyany U.S.S.R. 56.14N 51.08E
45 O3 Vyazemka U.S.S.R. 53.38N 42.41E
40 F8 Vyazemskiy U.S.S.R. 47.31N 134.45E
45 F1 Vyaz'ma U.S.S.R. 55.12N 34.17E
45 E1 Vyaz'ma *R* U.S.S.R.
45 R4 Vyazmino U.S.S.R. 52.18N 45.40E
45 O1 Vyazniki U.S.S.R. 56.14N 42.08E
46 O5 Vyazovka Astrakhan' U.S.S.R. 48.18N 45.39E
45 R5 Vyazovka Saratov U.S.S.R. 51.49N 45.46E
45 S4 Vyazovka Saratov U.S.S.R. 52.10N 46.44E
45 U4 Vyazovka Ul'yanovsk U.S.S.R. 52.51N 48.20E
45 P6 Vyazovka Volgograd U.S.S.R. 50.52N 43.58E
45 G8 Vyazovok Ukraine U.S.S.R. 48.38N 35.46E
45 H5 Vyazovoye U.S.S.R. 51.07N 37.00E
46 G2 Vybor U.S.S.R. 57.10N 29.15E
47 B5 Vyborg U.S.S.R. 60.45N 28.41E
51 N11 Vyborgskiy Zaliv *gulf* U.S.S.R.
47 F5 Vychegda *R* U.S.S.R.
62 J5 Východočeský *reg* Czechoslovakia
62 M7 Východoslovenský *reg* Czechoslovakia
64 O5 Vydra *R* Czechoslovakia
42 H6 Vydrino Buryat U.S.S.R. 51.35N 105.38E
42 F4 Vydrino Irkutsk U.S.S.R. 56.51N 99.00E
45 P1 Vyezdnoye U.S.S.R. 55.23N 43.45E
47 D4 Vyg *R* U.S.S.R.
46 N3 Vyglyadovka U.S.S.R. 53.18N 43.30E
82 N4 Vygoda U.S.S.R. 46.34N 30.27E
45 F3 Vygonichi U.S.S.R. 53.07N 34.06E
47 C4 Vygozero, Ozero *L* U.S.S.R.

41 B3 **Vykhodnoy, Mys** *C* Novaya Zemlya U.S.S.R. 73.14N 56.17E
45 O1 **Vyksa** U.S.S.R. 55.19N 42.11E
61 M5 **Vyle-et-Tharoul** Belgium 50.27N 5.16E
71 J1 **Vy-lès-Lure** France 47.38N 6.27E
47 G4 **Vym'** *R* U.S.S.R.
47 F5 **Vymsk** U.S.S.R. 60.21N 48.10E
42 B1 **Vyngapur** U.S.S.R. 64.12N 76.40E
28 C5 **Vypin** *isld* Kerala India
65 P2 **Výprachtice** Czechoslovakia 49.59N 16.40E
46 G1 **Vyra** U.S.S.R. 59.21N 29.50E
46 H1 **Vyritsa** U.S.S.R. 59.28N 30.20E
56 E2 **Vyrnwy, L** Powys Wales 52.47N 3.30W
56 E2 **Vyrnwy, R** Powys Wales
Vyrts'yarv, Oz *L see* **Võrtsjärv** *L*
45 T2 **Vyry** U.S.S.R. 54.10N 47.54E
44 C2 **Vyselki** U.S.S.R. 45.35N 39.39E
45 O3 **Vysha** U.S.S.R. 53.52N 42.25E
42 C6 **Vyshe-Ivanovskiy Belok, Gora** *mt* Kazakhstan U.S.S.R. 50.19N 83.55E
45 R3 **Vysheley** U.S.S.R. 53.26N 45.27E
Vyshka *see* **Bakinskikh Komissarov, im.26** Turkmeniya
45 C4 **Vyshkov** U.S.S.R. 52.28N 31.40E
46 J1 **Vyshniy-Volochek** U.S.S.R. 57.34N 34.23E
65 Q3 **Vyškov** Czechoslovakia 49.17N 17.01E
65 M3 **Vyskytná** Czechoslovakia 49.26N 15.22E
65 N2 **Vysočina** *reg* Czechoslovakia
65 L4 **Vysoka** *mt* Czech 48.43N 14.46E
62 L6 **Vysoká** *mt* Severomoravský Czech 49.24N 18.20E
45 V1 **Vysokaya Gora** U.S.S.R. 55.55N 49.18E
39 G5 **Vysokaya Gora** *mt* U.S.S.R. 58.52N 164.10E
47 H5 **Vysokaya Parma** *plat* U.S.S.R.
65 O2 **Vysoké Mýto** Czechoslovakia 49.57N 16.10E
45 H2 **Vysokinichi** U.S.S.R. 54.54N 36.55E
41 C2 **Vysokiy, Mys** *C* Novaya Zemlya U.S.S.R. 74.45N 60.35E
41 R3 **Vysokiy, Mys** *C* U.S.S.R. 75.38N 146.30E
42 C4 **Vysokiy Yar** U.S.S.R. 57.18N 82.00E
40 H6 **Vysokogornyy** U.S.S.R. 50.05N 139.11E
44 C7 **Vysokopolye** Ukraine U.S.S.R. 47.29N 33.31E
45 H1 **Vysokovsk** U.S.S.R. 56.20N 36.33E
62 O3 **Vysokoye** Belorussiya U.S.S.R. 52.23N 23.23E
46 J2 **Vysokoye** Kalinin U.S.S.R. 56.41N 35.00E
45 R5 **Vysokoye** Saratov U.S.S.R. 51.01N 45.29E
47 B5 **Vysotsk** U.S.S.R. 60.37N 28.31E
45 B6 **Vysshaya-Dubechnya** Ukraine U.S.S.R. 50.44N 30.39E
65 K4 **Vyšší Brod** Czechoslovakia 48.37N 14.18E
47 D5 **Vytegra** U.S.S.R. 61.04N 36.27E
42 C4 **V'yuny** U.S.S.R. 55.31N 82.58E
39 H4 **Vyvenka** U.S.S.R. 60.11N 165.32E
39 H4 **Vyvenka** *R* U.S.S.R.
47 N3 **Vyya** Sverdlovsk U.S.S.R. 58.20N 60.36E
47 N3 **Vyya** Sverdlovsk U.S.S.R. 58.35N 59.58E
47 F4 **Vyya** *R* U.S.S.R.

89 H6 **Wa** Ghana 10.07N 2.28W
28 L1 **Wa** Xizang Zizhiqu 29.32N 96.30E
63 L3 **Waabs** W Germany 54.32N 10.00E
Waadt *canton see* **Vaud** *canton*
64 K8 **Waal** W Germany 48.00N 10.46E
60 K12 **Waal** *R* Netherlands
60 H7 **Waal, De** Texel Netherlands 53.04N 4.49E
60 K14 **Waalre** Netherlands 51.23N 5.27E
60 J13 **Waalwijk** Netherlands 51.42N 5.04E
61 L3 **Waanrode** Belgium 50.55N 5.00E
61 F3 **Waarbeke** Belgium 50.47N 3.58E
61 C2 **Waardamme** Belgium 51.07N 3.13E
60 E14 **Waarde** Netherlands 51.25N 4.05E
60 K12 **Waardenburg** Netherlands 51.50N 5.15E
60 H11 **Waarder** Netherlands 52.04N 4.49E
60 J7 **Waard gronden** *sandbank* Netherlands
61 H2 **Waarloos** Belgium 51.06N 4.27E
61 D3 **Waarmaarde** Belgium 50.47N 3.30E
61 E2 **Waarschoot** Belgium 51.09N 3.36E
63 S4 **Waase** E Germany 54.28N 13.11E
61 G2 **Waasmunster** Belgium 51.07N 4.05E
87 D6 **Waat** Sudan 8.11N 32.10E
99 D2 **Wababimiga L** Ontario 50.21N 86.24W
15 G6 **Wabag** Papua New Guinea 5.28S 143.40E
33 M5 **Wabāl** Oman 23.12N 57.52E
100 C5 **Wabamun** Alberta 53.35N 114.28W
100 C5 **Wabamun L** Alberta 53.35N 114.30W
98 T6 **Wabana** Newfoundland 47.40N 52.57W
87 H7 **Wabara** Ethiopia 6.21N 40.33E
87 K6 **Wab Arorih** Ethiopia 8.07N 45.15E
100 D3 **Wabasca** Alberta 55.58N 113.56W
101 Q7 **Wabasca** *R* Alberta
100 D2 **Wabasca L, North** Alberta
100 D3 **Wabasca L, South** Alberta
107 F7 **Wabash** Arkansas 34.25N 90.49W
106 J9 **Wabash** Indiana 40.47N 85.48W
107 J3 **Wabash** *R* Ill/Indiana
106 J9 **Wabash** *R* Indiana
108 S5 **Wabasha** Minnesota 44.23N 92.02W
107 H3 **Wabash, Little** *R* Illinois
105 G10 **Wabasso** Florida 27.45N 80.27W
108 P5 **Wabasso** Minnesota 44.27N 95.16W
99 F4 **Wabatongushi L** Ontario
86 K6 **Wabeira, El** Egypt 29.32N 33.06E
106 F4 **Wabeno** Wisconsin 45.27N 88.38W
Wabern *see* **Egling**
64 G1 **Wabern** Hessen W Germany 51.06N 9.21E
100 K1 **Wabigoon** Ontario 49.43N 92.32W
100 K1 **Wabigoon L** Ontario 49.45N 92.40W
99 R4 **Wabino** *R* Quebec
100 O1 **Wabinosh L** Ontario
85 E6 **Wābirī** Libya 27.19N 18.05E
99 C2 **Waboose Dam** Ontario 50.45N 88.00W
99 F6 **Wabos** Ontario 46.50N 84.10W
100 T4 **Wabowden** Manitoba 54.57N 98.38W
33 G3 **Wabrah** Saudi Arabia 27.24N 47.24E
62 L2 **Wąbrzezno** Poland 53.18N 18.55E
15 G8 **Wabuda I** Papua New Guinea 8.20S 143.40E
23 G2 **Wabu Hu** *L* Anhui China
97 N7 **Wabush** Nfld/Labrador 52.53N 66.50W
111 E2 **Wabuska** Nevada 39.09N 119.13W
105 J3 **Waccamaw, L** N Carolina 34.28N 78.31W
105 J3 **Waccamaw, R** N & S Carolina
105 E8 **Waccasassa B** Florida
90 D5 **Wacha** Niger 13.21N 9.15E
93 L3 **Wachadima Plain** Kenya
104 K9 **Wachapreague** Virginia 37.36N 75.43W
64 H5 **Wachbach** W Germany 49.26N 9.46E
64 E5 **Wachenheim** W Germany 49.26N 8.11E
64 K4 **Wachenroth** W Germany 49.46N 10.44E
20 J6 **Wachi** *R* Japan
87 G5 **Wachit,R** Ethiopia
63 R7 **Wachow** E Germany 52.32N 12.45E
64 C2 **Wachtberg** W Germany 50.38N 7.12E
61 F2 **Wachtebeke** Belgium 51.10N 3.52E
63 D10 **Wachtendonk** W Germany 51.24N 6.18E
64 G3 **Wächtersbach** W Germany 50.15N 9.18E
60 P9 **Wachtum** Netherlands 52.43N 6.45E
63 G7 **Wachtum** W Germany 52.48N 7.42E
103 L2 **Wachusett Res** Massachusetts 42.23N 71.45W
122 M11 **Wachusett Shoal** Pacific Oc 32.10S 150.40W
63 K4 **Wacken** W Germany 54.01N 9.24E
113 W9 **Wacker** Alaska 55.27N 131.46W
108 N9 **Waco** Nebraska 40.55N 97.28W
98 G2 **Waco** Quebec 51.27N 65.35W
112 K4 **Waco** Texas 31.33N 97.10W
108 R5 **Waconia** Minnesota 44.51N 93.48W
98 G2 **Wacouno R** Quebec
31 D7 **Wad** Pakistan 27.21N 66.30E
20 O6 **Wada** Honshu Japan 35.02N 140.01E
90 M5 **Wada'a** Sudan 12.52N 25.48E
87 L6 **Wadamago** Somalia 8.52N 46.15E
14 D6 **Wadara Hills** W Australia
87 C4 **Wad'Ashana** Sudan 13.00N 31.44E
20 H6 **Wadayama** Japan 35.22N 134.49E
87 A4 **Wad Banda** Sudan 13.08N 27.56E
87 D2 **Wad Ban Naqa** Sudan 16.32N 33.09E
12 H8 **Waddamana** Tasmania 42.08S 146.43E
85 D5 **Waddān** Libya 29.10N 16.10E
60 J7 **Waddenzee** *shallow sea* Netherlands
14 C9 **Wadderin** W Australia 31.57S 118.27E
56 K4 **Waddesdon** Bucks Eng 51.51N 0.56W
57 J5 **Waddington** Lancs Eng 53.54N 2.24W
57 M6 **Waddington** Lincs Eng 53.10N 0.32W
104 K2 **Waddington** New York 44.52N 75.12W
101 L10 **Waddington, Mt** Br Col 51.22N 125.14W
60 G11 **Waddinxveen** Netherlands 52.03N 4.38E
26 Q8 **Wadduwa** Sri Lanka 6.39N 79.56E
107 L3 **Waddy** Kentucky 38.08N 85.06W
105 J2 **Wade** N Carolina 35.10N 78.44W
56 B6 **Wadebridge** Cornwall Eng 50.32N 4.50W
87 D5 **Wadega** Sudan 10.30N 33.54E
87 D4 **Wad el Haddad** Sudan 13.50N 33.30E
87 E4 **Wad el Huri** Sudan 13.54N 35.14E
108 P3 **Wadena** Minnesota 46.26N 95.08W
100 O7 **Wadena** Saskatchewan 51.57N 103.48W
87 D4 **Wad en Nail** Sudan 12.32N 34.08E
87 D3 **Wad en Nau** Sudan 14.10N 33.34E
60 K12 **Wadenoijen** Netherlands 51.52N 5.22E
66 L3 **Wädenswil** Switzerland 47.14N 8.41E
64 B4 **Wadern** W Germany 49.32N 6.54E
63 H9 **Wadersloh** W Germany 51.44N 8.15E
105 G3 **Wadesboro** N Carolina 34.59N 80.03W
11 C5 **Wadestown** *dist* Wellington New Zealand
29 E7 **Wadgaon** Akola, Maharashtra India 20.32N 77.00E
28 A1 **Wadgaon** Poona, Maharashtra India 18.46N 73.41E
90 N5 **Wad Gellab** Sudan 12.35N 26.50E
87 D2 **Wad Hamid** Sudan 16.31N 32.51E
98 T4 **Wadham Is** Newfoundland 49.32N 53.50W
101 K10 **Wadhams** Br Col 51.31N 127.31W
87 A5 **Wad Hassib** Sudan 11.42N 26.50E
87 D3 **Wad Hassuna** Sudan 15.49N 33.23E
87 K7 **Wadhel** Ethiopia 7.53N 44.29E
56 M5 **Wadhurst** E Sussex Eng 51.04N 0.21E
Wadhwan *see* **Surendranagar**
28 C2 **Wadi** Karnataka India 17.00N 76.58E
90 F7 **Wadi** Nigeria 9.44N 13.05E
35 B1 **Wadi el Joz** *sub* Jerusalem
85 K10 **Wadi el Qa'ab** *reg* Sudan
35 G6 **Wadi es Sir** Jordan 31.57N 35.49E
86 K8 **Wadi Feirân** *oil well* Egypt 28.40N 33.13E
35 D7 **Wadi Fukin** Jordan 31.42N 35.06E
33 A4 **Wâdi Gimâl** *isld* Egypt 24.40N 35.11E
85 L9 **Wadi Halfa** Sudan 21.46N 31.17E
33 D5 **Wādī Ḩammah** Saudi Arabia 22.03N 40.16E
12 D5 **Wadikee** S Australia 33.18S 136.12E
35 F3 **Wādī Khālid Sta** Syria 32.44N 35.45E
86 O5 **Wādī Mūsā** Jordan 30.19N 35.29E
26 U7 **Wadinagala** Sri Lanka 7.07N 81.31E
103 E7 **Wading** *R* New Jersey
103 J5 **Wading River** Long I, N Y 40.57N 72.50W
87 D3 **Wadi Seidna** Sudan 15.47N 32.32E
87 D3 **Wad Lemeid** Sudan 15.12N 33.00E
107 L8 **Wadley** Alabama 33.07N 85.36W
105 E5 **Wadley** Georgia 32.51N 82.22W
87 D3 **Wad Medani** Sudan 14.24N 33.30E
87 D3 **Wad Nimr** Sudan 14.32N 32.10E
21 C12 **Wadomari** Japan 27.25N 128.40E
62 L6 **Wadowice** Poland 49.54N 19.29E
87 D3 **Wad Ra'iya** Sudan 14.21N 33.10E
87 D3 **Wad Rawa** Sudan 15.10N 33.11E
101 G10 **Wadsley** Br Col 49.21N 123.14W
111 E2 **Wadsworth** Nevada 39.38N 119.18W
104 D5 **Wadsworth** Ohio 41.02N 81.43W
57 L6 **Wadworth** S Yorks Eng 53.28N 1.08W
21 D10 **Waegwan** S Korea 35.59N 128.20E
112 K6 **Waelder** Texas 29.42N 97.19W
25 G4 **Waeng** Thailand 16.17N 103.59E
Waeng Noi *see* **Ban Waeng Noi**
95 D10 **Waenhuiskrans** S Africa 34.40S 20.14E
21 B5 **Wafang** Nei Monggol Zizhiqu China 43.25N 121.42E
Wafangdian *see* **Fu Xian**
91 G4 **Wafania** Zaïre 1.23S 20.22E
87 K7 **Wafdoog** Ethiopia 6.31N 44.57E
33 N5 **Wāfī, Al** Oman 22.10N 59.12E
33 M10 **Wafra** *oil field* Saudi Arabia/Kuwait 28.37N 47.56E
15 G7 **Waga** *R* Papua New Guinea
20 O2 **Waga-gawa** *R* Japan
31 G5 **Wagah** Pakistan 31.32N 74.36E
99 B2 **Wagaming** Ontario 50.16N 88.54W
23 C5 **Wagang** Sichuan China 27.59N 103.21E
107 H10 **Wagarville** Alabama 31.27N 88.03W
15 G5 **Wagasu** *R* Papua New Guinea
60 H13 **Wagenberg** Netherlands 51.40N 44.45E
60 Q6 **Wagenborgen** Netherlands 53.15N 6.56E
63 J7 **Wagenfeld** W Germany 52.33N 8.37E
60 L12 **Wageningen** Netherlands 51.58N 5.40E
117 B2 **Wageningen** Surinam 5.44N 56.45W
60 J8 **Wagenpad** Netherlands
97 K4 **Wager Bay** N W Terr 65.55N 90.40W
13 E4 **Waggabundi** Queensland 19.29S 139.24E
12 H6 **Wagga Wagga** New S Wales 35.07S 147.24E
66 M3 **Wäggi Tal** *V* Switzerland
29 C7 **Waghai** Gujarat India 20.44N 73.36E
14 B10 **Wagin** W Australia 33.20S 117.15E
Wagina I *see* **Vaghena I.**
64 O8 **Waging am See** W Germany 47.56N 12.45E
64 O8 **Waginger See** *L* W Germany
66 M3 **Wägitaler See** *L* Switzerland 47.05N 8.56E
95 O3 **Wag-'n-bietjie** S Africa 27.06S 30.15E
61 J4 **Wagneléey** Belgium 50.32N 4.32E
118 H3 **Wagner** Brazil 12.15S 41.12W
110 R1 **Wagner** Montana 48.23N 108.06W
108 M6 **Wagner** S Dakota 43.05N 98.18W
103 C4 **Wagners** Pennsylvania 41.07N 75.32W
109 P6 **Wagoner** Oklahoma 35.58N 95.23W
109 F5 **Wagon Mound** New Mexico 36.01N 104.44W
110 F6 **Wagontire** Oregon 43.15N 119.53W
109 D4 **Wagon Wheel Gap** Colorado 37.47N 106.50W
65 H7 **Wagrain** Austria 47.20N 13.18E
105 H3 **Wagram** N Carolina 34.54N 79.24W
63 M4 **Wagrien** *reg* W Germany
62 K3 **Wągrowiec** Poland 52.49N 17.11E
Wagsa *see* **Wāqişah**
15 B5 **Wagura** *mt* Irian Jaya 2.47S 133.53E
31 G4 **Wah** Pakistan 33.50N 72.44E
61 M6 **Waha** Belgium 50.12N 5.21E
110 J3 **Waha** Idaho 46.12N 116.50W
85 E5 **Waha** Libya 28.08N 19.51E
19 F5 **Wahai** Moluccas Indon 2.48S 129.29E
26 S4 **Wahalkada Tank** Sri Lanka
11 K4 **Waharoa** New Zealand 37.45S 175.45E
85 L7 **Wâhât el-Khârga, el** *oasis* Egypt
85 F5 **Waḩat Jālū** *oasis* Libya
114 A5 **Wahiawa** Hawaiian Is 21.30N 158.00W
33 N6 **Wahībah Sands** Oman
33 G9 **Waḩidī** *sultanate* S Yemen
11 K4 **Wahi L** New Zealand 37.34S 175.08E
93 E7 **Wahi Pt** Tanzania 1.40S 33.34E
89 F6 **Wahiré** Ivory Coast 10.06N 6.56W
61 O7 **Wahl** Luxembourg 49.50N 5.55E
64 F4 **Wahlen** W Germany 49.37N 8.52E
50 T13 **Wahlenbergfjorden** *inlet* Spitsbergen
64 C2 **Wahn** W Germany 50.51N 7.06E
63 K7 **Wahnebergen** W Germany 52.53N 9.15E
87 F4 **Wahni** Ethiopia 12.43N 36.43E
93 H9 **Wahoga Chini** Tanzania 3.32S 36.59E
108 O8 **Wahoo** Nebraska 41.14N 96.40W
108 O3 **Wahpeton** N Dakota 46.16N 96.36W
63 S9 **Wahrenbrück** E Germany 51.33N 13.22E
63 N7 **Wahrenholz** W Germany 52.37N 10.38E
12 L6 **Wahroonga** *dist* Sydney, N S W
111 L3 **Wah Wah Mts** Utah
28 A2 **Wai** Maharashtra India 17.57N 73.57E
114 B5 **Waiahole** Hawaiian Is 21.29N 157.51W
114 B9 **Waiahukini** Hawaiian Is 18.56N 155.42W
114 B6 **Waiaka** Hawaiian Is 20.02N 155.41W
114 E6 **Waiakoa** Hawaiian Is 20.46N 156.20W
114 E3 **Waialeale** *pk* Hawaiian Is 22.03N 159.30W
114 A4 **Waialee** Hawaiian Is 21.41N 158.03W
114 A4 **Waialua** Hawaiian Is 21.35N 158.08W
114 D5 **Waialua** Hawaiian Is 21.07N 156.46E
114 A4 **Waialua** *dist* Hawaiian Is
114 A4 **Waialua Bay** Hawaiian Is
114 A5 **Waianae** Hawaiian Is 21.26N 158.11W
114 A5 **Waianae** *dist* Hawaiian Is
114 A5 **Waianae Range** Hawaiian Is
11 E12 **Waianakarua** New Zealand 45.17S 170.49E
11 C13 **Waianiwa** New Zealand 46.29S 168.15E
11 B6 **Waiariki R** New Zealand
11 C11 **Waiatoto R** New Zealand
11 H9 **Waiau** New Zealand 42.39S 173.02E
11 M5 **Waiau R** North I New Zealand
11 B12 **Waiau R** South I New Zealand
11 H9 **Waiau R** South I New Zealand
15 B4 **Waibeem** Irian Jaya 0.29S 132.59E
64 G6 **Waiblingen** W Germany 48.50N 9.20E
64 N4 **Waidhaus** W Germany 49.39N 12.30E
65 M4 **Waidhofen** Austria 48.50N 15.18E
65 L6 **Waidhofen an der Ybbs** Austria 47.58N 14.47E
65 G6 **Waidring** Austria 47.36N 12.34E
15 A4 **Waigama** Misoöl I, Irian Jaya 1.52S 129.49E
14 G8 **Waigen Lakes** W Australia
15 A4 **Waigeo** *isld* Irian Jaya
64 J4 **Waigolshausen** W Germany 49.58N 10.07E
15 C6 **Waigua** Moluccas Indon 5.58S 134.29E
11 E11 **Waihao Downs** New Zealand 44.47S 170.55E
11 E11 **Waihao Forks** New Zealand 44.46S 170.57E
11 F11 **Waihao R** New Zealand
11 H1 **Waiharara** New Zealand 34.57S 173.14E
114 D6 **Waihee** Hawaiian Is 20.55N 156.31W
114 D6 **Waihee** *R* Hawaiian Is
114 D6 **Waihee Pt** Hawaiian Is 20.56N 156.31W
11 K3 **Waiheke I** New Zealand 36.48S 175.07E
11 K4 **Waihi** New Zealand 37.22S 175.51E
11 K4 **Waihi Beach** New Zealand 37.22S 175.57E
11 B13 **Waihoaka** New Zealand 46.16S 167.43E
11 E13 **Waihola** New Zealand 46.03S 170.02E
11 E13 **Waihola, L** New Zealand 46.01S 170.04E
11 H8 **Waihopai R** New Zealand
11 H1 **Waihopo** New Zealand 34.45S 173.06E
11 E10 **Waiho R** New Zealand
11 K4 **Waihou** New Zealand 37.34S 175.41E
11 K4 **Waihou R** New Zealand
11 H2 **Waihu** New Zealand 35.46S 173.43E
11 M6 **Waihua** New Zealand 39.07S 177.08E
91 J5 **Waika** Zaïre 2.27S 25.42E
19 A8 **Waikabubak** Indonesia 9.40S 119.25E
114 D6 **Waikahalulu B** Hawaiian Is
11 C12 **Waikaia** New Zealand 45.44S 168.54E
11 C12 **Waikaia Plain** New Zealand
11 D12 **Waikaia R** New Zealand
11 D12 **Waikaka** New Zealand 45.56S 169.02E
11 K7 **Waikanae** New Zealand 40.52S 175.03E
114 B4 **Waikane** Hawaiian Is 21.30N 157.52W
114 D6 **Waikapu** Hawaiian Is 21.50N 156.30W
114 B8 **Waikapuna B** Hawaiian Is
11 M5 **Waikareiti, L** New Zealand
11 K4 **Waikare L** New Zealand 37.26S 175.13E
11 M5 **Waikaremoana, L** New Zealand
11 G9 **Waikari** New Zealand 42.58S 172.42E
11 M6 **Waikari R** New Zealand
11 J4 **Waikato R** New Zealand
11 D13 **Waikawa** New Zealand 46.39S 169.09E
11 J8 **Waikawa** New Zealand 41.15S 174.04E
19 A8 **Waikelo, Teluk** *B* Indonesia 9.25S 119.05E
12 E5 **Waikerie** S Australia 34.11S 139.59E
114 B7 **Waikii** Hawaiian Is 19.51N 150.40W
14 A4 **Waikiki** W Aust
114 B5 **Waikiki Beach** Hawaiian Is 21.17N 157.52W
11 M5 **Waikohu** New Zealand 38.27S 177.49E
11 D13 **Waikoikoi** New Zealand 46.01S 169.10E
11 M6 **Waikokopu** New Zealand 39.05S 177.50E
11 E12 **Waikouaiti** New Zealand 45.38S 170.41E
11 L11 **Waikouaiti R** New Zealand
11 B13 **Waikouro** New Zealand 46.07S 167.59E
11 C3 **Waikowhai** *dist* Auckland New Zealand
9 U5 **Wailangi Lala** *islet* Fiji 16.45S 179.11W
114 D5 **Wailau** Hawaiian Is 21.10N 156.49E
114 C7 **Wailea** Hawaiian Is 19.52N 155.08W
9 S5 **Wailevu** Vanua Levu Fiji 16.25S 179.21E
114 D6 **Wailkuku** *dist* Hawaiian Is
61 M5 **Waillet** Belgium 50.16N 5.18E
9 T8 **Wailotua** Viti Levu Fiji 17.46S 178.24E
114 F3 **Wailua** Hawaiian Is 22.04N 159.20W
114 F3 **Wailua** *R* Hawaiian Is
114 E6 **Wailua Bay** Hawaiian Is
114 D6 **Wailuku** Hawaiian Is 20.54N 156.30W
114 C7 **Wailuku** *R* Hawaiian Is
11 B3 **Waima** New Zealand 36.57S 174.38E
11 C13 **Waimahaka** New Zealand 46.32S 168.50E
11 G10 **Waimakariri R** New Zealand
11 H2 **Waimamaku** New Zealand 35.32S 173.30E
11 M5 **Waimana** New Zealand 38.08S 177.04E
114 B5 **Waimanalo** Hawaiian Is 21.20N 157.43W
114 B5 **Waimanalo Beach** Hawaiian Is 21.20N 157.42W
11 F8 **Waimangaroa** New Zealand 41.42S 171.48E
114 B6 **Waimanu B** Hawaiian Is
114 B7 **Waima Pt** Hawaiian Is 19.57N 155.51W
11 M6 **Waimarama** New Zealand 39.46S 177.02E
11 F8 **Waimarie** New Zealand 41.33S 171.58E
11 F11 **Waimate** New Zealand 44.45S 171.03E
11 J3 **Waimauku** New Zealand 36.47S 174.30E
114 A4 **Waimea** Hawaiian Is 21.39N 158.04W
114 B6 **Waimea** Hawaiian Is 20.02N 155.20W
114 E4 **Waimea** Hawaiian Is 21.57N 159.40W
114 D4 **Waimea** *dist* Hawaiian Is
114 E3 **Waimea** *dist* Hawaiian Is
114 A4 **Waimea Bay** Hawaiian Is 21.38N 158.04W
114 E4 **Waimea Canyon** Hawaiian Is
61 P5 **Waimes** Belgium 50.25N 6.07E
11 K5 **Waimiha** New Zealand 38.37S 175.19E
23 D2 **Wainapu** Gansu China 33.10N 105.08E
57 O6 **Wainfleet** Lincs Eng 53.07N 0.14E
29 G6 **Wainganga** Madhya Prad India 22.30N 80.06E
29 F7 **Wainganga R** Maharashtra etc India
19 B8 **Waingapu** Indonesia 9.40S 120.16E
11 K7 **Waingawa** New Zealand 40.58S 175.36E
119 J3 **Waini** *R* Guyana
114 E3 **Wainiha** Hawaiian Is 22.12N 159.32W
114 E3 **Wainiha** *R* Hawaiian Is
11 F9 **Wainihinihi** New Zealand 42.46S 171.20E
119 J3 **Waini Pt** Guyana 8.24N 59.48W
106 E3 **Wainola** Michigan 46.43N 89.00W
11 D6 **Wainuiomata** New Zealand 41.17S 174.56E
11 D6 **Wainuiomata R** New Zealand
9 R5 **Wainunu B** Vanua Levu Fiji
113 G1 **Wainwright** Alaska 70.39N 160.10W
100 G6 **Wainwright** Alberta 52.50N 110.51W
113 O4 **Wainwright Air Force Base** Alaska 64.49N 147.40W
11 M5 **Waioeka R** New Zealand
114 B8 **Waiohinu** Hawaiian Is 19.05N 155.36W
11 L5 **Waiotapu** New Zealand 38.18S 176.24E
11 J2 **Waiotira** New Zealand 35.56S 174.12E
11 K6 **Waiouru** New Zealand 39.29S 175.40E
11 D13 **Waipahi** New Zealand 46.08S 169.16E
114 A5 **Waipahu** Hawaiian Is 21.24N 158.01W
11 M5 **Waipaoa** New Zealand 38.32S 177.58E
11 H2 **Waipapakauri** New Zealand 35.02S 173.16E
11 C13 **Waipapa Pt** New Zealand 46.41S 168.51E
11 K4 **Waipa R** New Zealand
11 G10 **Waipara** New Zealand 43.03S 172.47E
11 G10 **Waipara R** New Zealand
11 L6 **Waipawa** New Zealand 39.48S 176.36E
11 E12 **Waipiata** New Zealand 45.12S 170.09E
114 B6 **Waipio** Hawaiian Is 20.08N 155.36W
114 B6 **Waipio B** Hawaiian Is
114 E6 **Waipio Bay** Hawaiian Is
114 E8 **Waipio Pen** Hawaiian Is 21.22N 157.58W
11 J4 **Waipipi** New Zealand 37.14S 174.42E
11 N5 **Waipiro B** New Zealand
11 N5 **Waipiro Bay** New Zealand 38.02S 178.21E
11 E12 **Waipori, L** New Zealand 45.59S 170.08E
11 J2 **Waipu** New Zealand 35.59S 174.29E
11 L6 **Waipukurau** New Zealand 39.59S 176.33E
11 N4 **Waipu R** New Zealand
29 G7 **Wairagarh** Maharashtra India 20.28N 80.09E
11 L5 **Wairakei** New Zealand 38.37S 176.07E
11 K8 **Wairarapa, L** New Zealand
11 H8 **Wairau R** New Zealand
11 H8 **Wairau Valley** New Zealand 41.33S 173.32E
86 M10 **Wâ'ir, Gebel** *hill* Egypt 27.58N 34.16E
11 C13 **Wairio** New Zealand 46.01S 168.02E
11 M6 **Wairoa** New Zealand 39.03S 177.25E
11 L5 **Wairoa** *L* New Zealand
11 J2 **Wairoa Falls** *waterfall* New Zealand 35.46S 174.05E
11 M5 **Wairoa R** New Zealand
11 J2 **Wairua R** New Zealand
11 D13 **Wairuna** New Zealand 46.11S 169.19E
Wais *see* **Veys**
15 A4 **Waisai** Waigeo, Irian Jaya 0.14S 130.30E
64 L4 **Waischenfeld** W Germany 49.50N 11.20E
11 L5 **Waitahanui** New Zealand 38.48S 176.07E
11 E9 **Waitaha R** New Zealand
11 D12 **Waitahuna** New Zealand 46.00S 169.48E
11 K4 **Waitakaruru** New Zealand 37.14S 175.24E
11 E11 **Waitaki L** New Zealand 44.40S 170.22E
11 E11 **Waitaki R** New Zealand
11 J11 **Waitangi** Chatham Is Pacific Oc 43.58S 176.32W
11 J2 **Waitangi** New Zealand 35.18S 174.06E
31 G3 **Waitar** Pakistan 34.58N 73.58E
11 J5 **Waitara** New Zealand 38.59S 174.13E
12 L6 **Waitara** *dist* Sydney, N S W
11 K7 **Waitarere** New Zealand 40.33S 175.12E
11 J4 **Waitaretu** New Zealand 37.31S 174.51E
11 E12 **Waitati** New Zealand 45.45S 170.35E
13 B5 **Waite** *R* N Terr Australia
11 C2 **Waitemata Harb** *inlet* Auckland New Zealand
10 B11 **Waite, Mt** Macquarie I Pacific Oc 54.38S 158.52E
14 D8 **Waite, Mt** W Australia 27.33S 121.59E
58 S12 **Waith Bridge** Orkney Scotland 58.59N 3.15W
11 K4 **Waitoa** New Zealand 37.37S 175.39E
11 K5 **Waitomo** *caves* New Zealand 38.14S 175.08E
11 J6 **Waitotara** New Zealand 39.48S 174.42E
11 J6 **Waitotara R** New Zealand
Waitsap *see* **Huaiji**
110 G3 **Waitsburg** Washington 46.17N 118.09W
100 M6 **Waitville** Saskatchewan 52.53N 105.26W
11 J4 **Waiuku** New Zealand 37.15S 174.44E
11 F9 **Waiuta** New Zealand 42.17S 171.50E
11 J3 **Waiwera** New Zealand 36.35S 174.42E
11 D13 **Waiwera South** New Zealand 46.15S 169.30E
19 F5 **Waiya** Moluccas Indon 3.11S 128.55E
9 T5 **Waiyevo** Taveuni Fiji 16.50S 179.59E
65 J5 **Waizenkirchen** Austria 48.20N 13.52E
87 J6 **Wajale** Ethiopia 9.37N 43.30E
33 B3 **Wajh, Al** Saudi Arabia 26.16N 36.28E
33 F7 **Wajīd, Jabal al** *mts* Saudi Arabia
20 H8 **Wajiki** Japan 33.51N 134.30E
20 K4 **Wajima** Japan 37.23N 136.53E
93 M4 **Wajir** Kenya 1.46N 40.05E
93 L4 **Wajir** *dist* Kenya
93 M4 **Wajir Bor** Kenya 1.46N 40.36E
28 C3 **Wajrakarur** Andhra Prad India 15.03N 77.22E
18 B3 **Wak** Sumatra Indonesia 4.22N 96.59E
91 G3 **Waka** Equateur Zaïre 0.59N 20.16E
91 G4 **Waka** Equateur Zaïre 0.52S 20.05E
87 F7 **Waka** Ethiopia 7.02N 37.20E
20 D8 **Wakamatsu** Kyūshū Japan 33.56N 130.48E
20 B9 **Wakamatsu-jima** *isld* Japan 32.58N 129.00E
99 H5 **Wakami L** Ontario 47.29N 82.50W
11 F10 **Wakanui** New Zealand 43.59S 171.51E
11 B13 **Wakaputa Pt** New Zealand 46.24S 167.48E
11 L6 **Wakarara Ra** New Zealand
11 L12 **Wakari** *dist* Dunedin New Zealand
106 H8 **Wakarusa** Indiana 41.32N 86.02W
20 H6 **Wakasa** Japan 35.21N 134.22E
20 J6 **Wakasa-wan** *B* Japan
19 E5 **Waka, Tanjung** *C* Moluccas Indon 2.29S 126.03E
11 C12 **Wakatipu, L** New Zealand
100 M6 **Wakaw** Saskatchewan 52.40N 105.45W
9 U7 **Wakaya** *isld* Fiji 17.39S 179.01E
20 J7 **Wakayama** Japan 34.12N 135.10E
20 J8 **Wakayama** *prefect* Japan
20 P3 **Wakayanagi** Japan 38.46N 141.08E
15 E4 **Wakde** *isld* Irian Jaya 1.56S 138.59E
21 F10 **Wake** Japan 34.50N 134.10E
109 L2 **Wa Keeney** Kansas 39.02N 99.53W
116 J1 **Wakefield** Jamaica, W I 18.24N 77.44W
109 N2 **Wakefield** Kansas 39.14N 97.01W
106 E3 **Wakefield** Michigan 46.29N 89.55W
108 O7 **Wakefield** Nebraska 42.18N 96.51W
11 H8 **Wakefield** New Zealand 41.24S 173.02E
103 B7 **Wakefield** Pennsylvania 39.47N 76.11W
99 P7 **Wakefield** Quebec 45.38N 75.56W
103 L4 **Wakefield** Rhode I 41.26N 71.30W
104 H10 **Wakefield** Virginia 36.57N 77.02W
57 L5 **Wakefield** W Yorks Eng 53.42N 1.29W
105 J2 **Wake Forest** N Carolina 35.59N 78.30W
98 H5 **Wakeham** Quebec 48.50N 64.33W
9 A7 **Wake I** Pacific Oc
93 M3 **Wak, El** Kenya 2.48N 40.55E
25 C4 **Wakema** Burma 16.36N 95.11E
117 A1 **Wakenaam I** Guyana 7.05N 58.29W
106 H8 **Wakerton** Indiana 41.28N 86.29W
56 N4 **Wakes Colne** Essex Eng 51.55N 0.44E
31 G2 **Wakhan** *reg* Afghanistan
31 H2 **Wakhjir** Afghanistan 37.03N 74.11E
31 H2 **Wakhjir Pass** Afghanistan etc 37.06N 74.43E
20 H7 **Waki** Japan 34.03N 134.10E
20 O1 **Wakinosawa** Japan 41.08N 140.49E
87 G3 **Wakiro,R** Ethiopia
109 N5 **Wakita** Oklahoma 36.54N 97.55W
21 J5 **Wakkanai** Japan 45.26N 141.43E
61 D3 **Wakken** Belgium 50.56N 3.24E
95 O3 **Wakkerstroom** S Africa 27.21S 30.10E
Wako *see* **Watcomb**
99 G6 **Wakomata L** Ontario 46.35N 83.20W
12 G6 **Wakool** New S Wales 35.30S 144.25E
12 G6 **Wakool** *R* New S Wales
100 S9 **Wakopa** Manitoba 49.04N 99.50W
108 K4 **Wakpala** S Dakota 45.40N 100.31W
33 J4 **Wakrah, Al** Qatar, The Gulf 25.09N 51.36E
15 A4 **Wakre** Waigeo, Irian Jaya 0.19S 131.08E
15 K7 **Waku** New Britain 6.09S 149.05E
105 C7 **Wakulla** Florida 30.14N 84.47W
15 J1 **Wakunai** Bougainville I Papua New Guinea 5.52S 155.10E
20 P3 **Wakuya** Japan 38.30N 141.09E
99 K2 **Wakwayowkastic** *R* Ontario
92 F4 **Wala** *R* Tanzania
82 H6 **Walachia** *old prov* Romania
15 M3 **Walade** Malaita I Solomon Is 9.38S 161.30E
87 J8 **Waladeh** Ethiopia 4.20N 42.03E
87 E5 **Waladura,Jeb** Ethiopia 10.20N 35.50E
Walaga *prov see* **Welega** *prov*
21 C1 **Walagan** Heilongjiang China 52.37N 124.31E
28 D4 **Walajapet** Tamil Nadu India 12.56N 79.23E
92 D8 **Walamba** Zambia 13.30S 28.45E
111 L6 **Walapai** Arizona 35.18N 113.55W
92 F4 **Wala, R** Tanzania
26 S9 **Walasmulla** Sri Lanka 6.10N 80.42E
26 S9 **Walawe Ganga** *R* Sri Lanka
63 O8 **Walbeck** E Germany 52.18N 11.05E
56 P3 **Walberswick** Suffolk Eng 52.19N 1.39E
69 O6 **Walbourg** France 48.53N 7.47E
104 B5 **Walbridge** Ohio 41.35N 83.32W
62 J5 **Wałbrzych** Poland 50.48N 16.19E
64 H1 **Walburg** W Germany 51.12N 9.46E
12 K4 **Walcha** New S Wales 31.00S 151.36E
65 G7 **Walchen** Austria 47.18N 12.41E
65 D6 **Walchensee** *L* W Germany 47.36N 11.23E
60 B2 **Walcheren** *isld* Netherlands
65 F6 **Walchsee** Austria 47.40N 12.19E
66 L3 **Walchwil** Switzerland 47.06N 8.31E
101 K8 **Walcott** Br Columbia 54.31N 126.53W
106 D8 **Walcott** Iowa 41.35N 90.44W
108 O3 **Walcott** N Dakota 46.32N 96.58W
108 D8 **Walcott** Wyoming 41.46N 106.50W
56 O2 **Walcott Gap** Norfolk Eng 52.51N 1.30E
14 E3 **Walcott Inlet** W Australia
123 F9 **Walcott, Mt** Antarctica 85.20S 86.00W
61 H5 **Walcourt** Belgium 50.15N 4.26E
62 J2 **Wałcz** Poland 53.17N 16.29E
66 O2 **Wald** Appenzell Switzerland 47.25N 9.29E
64 G8 **Wald** Baden-Württemberg W Germany 47.56N 9.11E
65 F7 **Wald** Salzburg Austria 47.16N 12.14E
65 L7 **Wald** Steiermark Austria 47.27N 14.41E
66 M2 **Wald** Zürich Switz 47.17N 8.56E
65 L5 **Wald Aist** *R* Austria
64 F5 **Waldangeloch** W Germany 49.13N 8.50E
94 D3 **Waldau** Namibia 21.54S 16.45E
65 N7 **Waldbach** Austria 47.28N 15.50E
61 Q7 **Waldbillig** Luxembourg 49.48N 6.17E
64 D4 **Waldböckelheim** W Germany 49.49N 7.44E
61 Q8 **Waldbredimus** Luxembourg 49.33N 6.17E
64 C2 **Waldbreitbach** W Germany 50.33N 7.25E
64 D2 **Waldbröl** W Germany 50.52N 7.37E
64 G5 **Waldbrunn** Baden-Württemberg W Germany 49.27N 9.05E
64 G5 **Waldbrunn** Hessen W Germany 49.27N 9.05E
66 P1 **Waldburg** W Germany 47.45N 9.43E
14 B6 **Waldburg Ra** W Australia
63 T9 **Walddrehna** E Germany 51.46N 13.38E
64 M4 **Waldeck** Bayern W Germany 49.51N 11.58E
64 G1 **Waldeck** Hessen W Germany 51.12N 9.05E
100 K8 **Waldeck** Saskatchewan 50.22N 107.32W
109 D1 **Walden** Colorado 40.43N 106.19W
103 F3 **Walden** New York 41.40N 74.10W
64 G6 **Waldenbuch** W Germany 48.38N 9.09E
Waldenburg *see* **Wałbrzych**
107 F6 **Waldenburg** Arkansas 35.32N 90.57W
64 O2 **Waldenburg** E Germany 50.52N 12.36E
66 G2 **Waldenburg** Switzerland 47.23N 7.45E
64 H5 **Waldenburg** W Germany 49.11N 9.40E
64 N4 **Waldershof** W Germany 49.59N 12.05E
64 D5 **Waldfischbach-Burgalben** W Germany 49.17N 7.39E
65 L5 **Waldhausen** Austria 48.17N 14.58E
64 P1 **Waldheim** E Germany 51.04N 13.03E
100 L6 **Waldheim** Saskatchewan 52.39N 106.40W
87 G5 **Waldia** Ethiopia 11.50N 39.36E
71 L1 **Waldighofen** France 47.33N 7.20E
64 H1 **Waldkappel** W Germany 51.09N 9.52E
66 O2 **Waldkirch** Switzerland 47.27N 9.17E
64 D7 **Waldkirch** W Germany 48.05N 7.58E
66 J1 **Waldkirch** W Germany 47.39N 8.11E
64 Q6 **Waldkirchen** W Germany 48.45N 13.38E
64 N7 **Waldkraiburg** W Germany 48.13N 12.24E
64 F4 **Wald-Michelbach** W Germany 49.35N 8.50E
64 O5 **Waldmünchen** W Germany 49.23N 12.43E
64 N4 **Wald Naab** *R* W Germany
61 Q2 **Waldniel** W Germany 51.13N 6.15E
107 C8 **Waldo** Arkansas 33.22N 93.18W
100 B9 **Waldo** Br Columbia 49.14N 115.10W
105 E8 **Waldo** Florida 29.46N 82.11W
109 M2 **Waldo** Kansas 39.09N 98.48W
104 B6 **Waldo** Ohio 40.25N 83.11W
106 G6 **Waldo** Wisconsin 43.39N 87.58W
104 Q2 **Waldoboro** Maine 44.06N 69.25W
110 C6 **Waldo L** Oregon 43.44N 122.04W
104 J8 **Waldorf** Maryland 38.38N 76.56E
108 R6 **Waldorf** Minnesota 43.58N 93.42W
110 A5 **Waldport** Oregon 44.25N 124.05W
107 B7 **Waldron** Arkansas 34.54N 94.09W
100 P8 **Waldron** Saskatchewan 50.53N 102.35W
123 G2 **Waldron, C** Antarctica 66.08S 116.00E
11 L13 **Waldronville** New Zealand 45.55S 170.25E
64 N4 **Waldsassen** W Germany 50.00N 12.19E
Waldsee *see* **Bad Waldsee**
64 E8 **Waldshut** W Germany 47.37N 8.14E
66 O2 **Waldstatt** Switzerland 47.22N 9.17E
64 J7 **Waldstetten** W Germany 48.20N 10.18E
64 N4 **Waldthurn** W Germany 49.40N 12.20E
69 M5 **Waldwisse** France 49.25N 6.32E
19 C4 **Waleabahi** *isld* Indonesia 0.15S 122.20E
19 C4 **Waleakodi** *isld* Indonesia 0.15S 122.13E
19 C4 **Walea, Selat** *str* Indonesia
34 G5 **Walej, Sha'īb al** *watercourse* Iraq
61 H2 **Walem** Belgium 51.04N 4.27E
93 L1 **Walena** Ethiopia 4.36N 39.23E
30 L5 **Waleng** Nepal 27.31N 87.11E
66 N3 **Walensee** *L* Switzerland
66 O3 **Walenstadt** Switzerland 47.08N 9.19E
93 N1 **Walenzu** Ethiopia 4.25N 41.19E
113 C4 **Wales** Alaska 65.38N 168.09W
103 K2 **Wales** Massachusetts 42.04N 72.13W
108 T2 **Wales** Minnesota 47.13N 91.41W
108 M1 **Wales** N Dakota 48.55N 98.35W
111 N2 **Wales** Utah 39.29N 111.39W
54 H10 **Wales** *principality* British Isles
87 B10 **Walese** *tribe* Zaïre
97 L4 **Wales I** N W Terr 68.00N 86.50W
93 M7 **Walesidu** Kenya 1.07S 40.09E
89 J6 **Walewale** Ghana 10.25N 0.41W
61 P8 **Walferdange** Luxembourg 49.39N 6.08E
63 O5 **Walfisch** *isld* E Germany 53.57N 11.26E
29 E7 **Walgaon** Maharashtra India 21.06N 77.45E
87 F6 **Walga, R** Ethiopia
12 J4 **Walgett** New S Wales 30.03S 148.10E
123 H11 **Walgreen Coast** Antarctica
61 J4 **Walhain-St.-Paul** Belgium 50.37N 4.42E
108 N1 **Walhalla** N Dakota 48.57N 97.54W
105 D3 **Walhalla** S Carolina 34.46N 83.05W
64 N5 **Walhalla** *mt* W Germany 49.02N 12.14E
31 E6 **Walhar** Pakistan 28.08N 70.00E
66 F1 **Walheim** France 47.38N 7.16E
69 L2 **Walheim** W Germany 50.42N 6.10E
61 P4 **Walhorn** Belgium 50.41N 6.03E
33 F10 **Walī 'Abd ar Raḩim** S Yemen 13.05N 44.21E
89 B5 **Waliba** The Gambia 13.26N 14.02W
93 M6 **Waligiro** Kenya 0.01S 40.16E
92 D2 **Walikale** Zaïre 1.29S 28.05E
15 J7 **Walinga** Papua New Guinea 6.17S 147.43E
15 B6 **Walir** *isld* Moluccas Indonesia 5.42S 132.18E
15 G5 **Walis I** Papua New Guinea 3.15S 143.15E
Waliso *see* **Welso**
14 A8 **Walkaway** W Australia 28.58S 114.45E
63 R5 **Walkendorf** E Germany 53.58N 12.31E
63 N9 **Walkenried** W Germany 51.36N 10.38E
110 C8 **Walker** California 41.50N 122.50W
106 C7 **Walker** Iowa 42.17N 91.48W
109 L3 **Walker** Kansas 38.53N 99.05W
107 F11 **Walker** Louisiana 30.30N 90.51W
108 Q2 **Walker** Minnesota 47.06N 94.34W
107 B4 **Walker** Missouri 37.54N 94.14W
108 J4 **Walker** S Dakota 45.56N 101.07W
111 E2 **Walker** *R* Nevada
13 B6 **Walker** *R* N Terr Australia
13 F3 **Walker** *R* Queensland
95 C10 **Walker B** S Africa
101 O1 **Walker B** Victoria I, N W Terr
58 K7 **Walkerburn** Borders Scotland 55.38N 3.02W
105 J10 **Walker Cay** *isld* Bahamas 27.17N 78.25W
113 K3 **Walker L** Alaska 67.10N 154.30W
100 V4 **Walker L** Manitoba
111 F3 **Walker L** Nevada 38.40N 118.43W
98 E3 **Walker L** Quebec
123 H12 **Walker Mts** Antarctica
56 L4 **Walkern** Herts Eng 51.55N 0.07W
111 F6 **Walker Pass** California 35.41N 118.04W
95 F10 **Walker Pt** S Africa 34.05S 22.58E
13 D2 **Walker R** N Terr Australia
18 L3 **Walker Ra** Sabah Malaysia
104 E8 **Walkersville** W Virginia 38.52N 80.27W
99 J8 **Walkerton** Ontario 44.08N 81.10W
105 G1 **Walkertown** N Carolina 36.11N 80.10W
103 F3 **Walker Valley** New York 41.37N 74.22W
106 H6 **Walkerville** Michigan 43.43N 86.09W
110 N3 **Walkerville** Montana 46.02N 112.32W
95 L2 **Walkerville** S Africa 26.25S 27.58E
12 A8 **Walkerville** *dist* Adelaide, S Aust
Walkite *see* **Uolchitte**
66 G4 **Walkringen** Switzerland 46.57N 7.38E
108 H5 **Wall** S Dakota 44.00N 102.14W
56 H2 **Wall** Staffs Eng 52.40N 1.50W
14 A8 **Wallabi Group** *islds* W Australia
13 E3 **Wallaby I** Queensland 16.25S 139.48E
13 F3 **Wallaby I** Queensland 15.10S 142.00E
12 C4 **Wallaby, Mt** S Australia 31.59S 134.43E
110 K2 **Wallace** Idaho 47.28N 115.55W
109 J3 **Wallace** Kansas 38.55N 101.55W
106 G4 **Wallace** Michigan 45.18N 87.34W
105 K3 **Wallace** N Carolina 34.42N 78.00W
108 J9 **Wallace** Nebraska 40.51N 101.10W
98 J8 **Wallace** Nova Scotia 45.48N 63.26W
99 M7 **Wallace** Ontario 45.23N 78.05W
108 N4 **Wallace** S Dakota 45.05N 97.27W
104 E7 **Wallace** W Virginia 39.24N 80.32W
99 H10 **Wallaceburg** Ontario 42.34N 82.22W
107 C9 **Wallace L** Louisiana 32.20N 93.45W
100 B4 **Wallace Mt** Alberta 54.58N 115.47W
99 J10 **Wallacetown** Ontario 42.37N 81.28W
13 H7 **Wallal** Queensland 26.37S 146.10E
14 D4 **Wallal Downs** W Australia 19.50S 120.45E
14 C9 **Wallambin, L** W Australia
13 K8 **Wallangarra** Queensland 28.51S 151.52E
14 D5 **Wallani Well** W Australia 20.01S 120.05E
13 H8 **Wallan, R** Queensland
12 E5 **Wallaroo** S Australia 33.57S 137.36E
57 G6 **Wallasey** Merseyside Eng 53.26N 3.03W
13 B3 **Wallaston, Mt** N Terr Australia 17.00S 131.28E
64 E2 **Wallau** W Germany 50.55N 8.29E
12 H6 **Walla Walla** New S Wales 35.48S 146.52E
110 G3 **Walla Walla** Washington 46.05N 118.18W
110 G4 **Walla Walla** *R* Oregon
13 C7 **Wall Creek** N Terr Australia 25.57S 134.45E
64 J2 **Walldorf** E Germany 50.36N 10.23E
64 F5 **Walldorf** W Germany 49.18N 8.39E
64 G4 **Walldürn** W Germany 49.35N 9.23E
94 D8 **Wallekraal** S Africa 30.21S 17.27E
87 E6 **Wallel, Tulu** *mt* Ethiopia 8.53N 34.52E
63 Q10 **Wallendorf** E Germany 51.22N 12.05E
64 L3 **Wallendorf** E Germany 50.29N 11.12E
64 L3 **Wallenfels** W Germany 50.15N 11.28E
63 H8 **Wallenhorst** W Germany 52.22N 8.00E
103 D4 **Wallenpaupack L** Pennsylvania
63 L8 **Wallensen** W Germany 52.02N 9.37E
65 P6 **Wallern** Austria 47.44N 16.57E
64 O6 **Wallersdorf** W Germany 48.45N 12.45E
65 H6 **Wallersee** *L* Austria 47.55N 13.10E
64 F1 **Wallershöhe** *mt* W Germany 51.07N 8.32E
64 J6 **Wallerstein** W Germany 48.54N 10.30E
63 O10 **Wallhausen** E Germany 51.28N 11.15E
14 B3 **Walliabup** W Australia 32.05S 115.51E
103 J4 **Wallingford** Connecticut 41.28N 72.49W
11 L7 **Wallingford** New Zealand 40.14S 176.38E
56 J4 **Wallingford** Oxon Eng 51.37N 1.08W
104 N3 **Wallingford** Vermont 43.28N 72.59W
55 F5 **Wallington** London Eng 51.22N 0.09W
103 J6 **Wallington** New Jersey
112 L6 **Wallis** Texas 29.38N 96.05W
Wallis *canton see* **Valais** *canton*
66 L2 **Wallisellen** Switzerland 47.25N 8.36E
10 R4 **Wallis, Iles** Pacific Oc 13.16S 176.15W
12 K4 **Wallis L** New S Wales
103 F3 **Wallkill** New York 41.36N 74.11W
103 F3 **Wallkill** *R* New York
108 P7 **Wall Lake** Iowa 42.18N 95.02W
64 D3 **Wallmerod** W Germany 50.29N 7.57E
14 B6 **Wall, Mt** W Australia 22.50S 116.50E
13 K6 **Walloon** Queensland 24.55S 150.15E
106 K4 **Walloon L** Michigan 45.15N 85.00W
104 K9 **Wallops I** Virginia
110 H4 **Wallowa** Oregon 45.35N 117.31W
110 H4 **Wallowa** *R* Oregon
110 H4 **Wallowa L** Oregon 45.20N 117.14W
110 H4 **Wallowa Mts** Oregon
58 P9 **Walls** Shetland Scotland 60.14N 1.34W
63 K3 **Wallsbüll** W Germany 54.46N 9.15E
65 L5 **Wallsee** Austria 48.10N 14.44E
12 K5 **Wallsend** New S Wales 32.53S 151.39E
57 K3 **Wallsend** Tyne and Wear Eng 55.00N 1.31W
63 O7 **Wallstawe** E Germany 52.48N 11.03E
63 J8 **Wallucke** W Germany 52.16N 8.44E
110 G3 **Wallula** Washington 46.05N 118.55W
110 F3 **Wallula, L** Washington
13 J7 **Wallumbilla** Queensland 26.35S 149.10E
63 Q9 **Wallwitzhafen** E Germany 51.53N 12.14E
31 B4 **Walma** Afghanistan 33.25N 63.51E
56 O5 **Walmer** Kent Eng 51.13N 1.24E
95 J9 **Walmer** S Africa 33.57S 25.35E
101 T4 **Walmsley L** N W Terr
57 G4 **Walney I** Cumbria Eng 54.05N 3.15W
106 E8 **Walnut** Illinois 41.33N 89.36W
109 P4 **Walnut** Kansas 37.37N 95.04W
107 H7 **Walnut** Mississippi 34.57N 88.55W
109 K3 **Walnut** *R* Kansas
111 N6 **Walnut Canyon Nat. Mon** Arizona 35.10N 111.29W
105 G1 **Walnut Cove** N Carolina 36.28N 80.09W
107 G9 **Walnut Grove** Mississippi 32.35N 89.27W
107 C4 **Walnut Grove** Missouri 37.24N 93.32W
112 N8 **Walnut Hills** Dallas, Texas 32.52N 96.52W
103 C5 **Walnutport** Pennsylvania 40.46N 75.36W
107 F5 **Walnut Ridge** Arkansas 36.03N 90.58W
112 K3 **Walnut Springs** Texas 32.03N 97.45W
28 L1 **Walong** Assam India 28.08N 96.58E
12 F6 **Walpeup** Victoria 35.09S 141.59E
103 M2 **Walpole** Massachusetts 42.09N 71.15W
104 N3 **Walpole** New Hampshire 43.04N 72.26W
56 O3 **Walpole** Suffolk Eng 52.19N 1.29E
9 D14 **Walpole, I** Pacific Oc 22.39S 168.57E
113 C8 **Walrus I** Pribilof Is Bering Sea 57.10N 169.55W
113 G7 **Walrus, Is** Alaska
56 H2 **Walsall** W Midlands Eng 52.35N 1.58W
69 N5 **Walschbronn** France 49.09N 7.29E
64 K1 **Walschleben** E Germany 51.04N 10.57E
64 E3 **Walsdorf** W Germany 50.16N 8.17E
109 F4 **Walsenburg** Colorado 37.36N 104.48W
100 G9 **Walsh** Alberta 49.57N 110.03W
109 H4 **Walsh** Colorado 37.24N 102.17W
13 G3 **Walsh** Queensland 16.38S 143.54E
13 G3 **Walsh** *R* Queensland
101 D5 **Walsh, Mt** Yukon Terr 61.03N 139.58W
61 L4 **Walshoutem** Belgium 50.43N 5.05E
56 N2 **Walsingham** Norfolk Eng 52.54N 0.52E
60 D3 **Walsoorden** Netherlands 51.22N 4.02E
63 L7 **Walsrode** W Germany 52.52N 9.35E
63 E9 **Walsum** W Germany 51.32N 6.41E
87 E7 **Walta** Ethiopia 7.05N 35.52E
28 F2 **Waltair** Andhra Prad India 17.45N 83.25E
64 J8 **Waltenhofen** W Germany 47.39N 10.20E
105 G5 **Walterboro** S Carolina 32.54N 80.21W
30 F6 **Walterganj** Uttar Prad India 26.51N 82.44E
109 M7 **Walters** Oklahoma 34.22N 98.18W
64 K2 **Waltershausen** E Germany 50.54N 10.34E
66 Q1 **Waltershofen** W Germany 47.45N 9.55E
13 G8 **Walter's Ra** Queensland
107 G8 **Walthall** Mississippi 33.37N 89.19W
57 N5 **Waltham** Humberside Eng 53.31N 0.06W
103 M2 **Waltham** Massachusetts 42.23N 71.14W
108 S6 **Waltham** Minnesota 43.49N 92.51W
110 P2 **Waltham** Montana 47.34N 110.54W
99 O7 **Waltham** Quebec 45.55N 76.57W
104 O9 **Waltham** *dist* Boston, Mass
55 G1 **Waltham Abbey** Essex Eng 51.41N 00.000
56 L4 **Waltham Cross** Herts Eng 51.42N 0.02W
55 G2 **Waltham Forest** *bor* London England
56 K2 **Waltham-on-the-Wolds** Leics Eng 52.49N 0.49W
55 G3 **Walthamstow** London Eng 51.34N 0.01W
108 O7 **Walthill** Nebraska 42.08N 96.30W
108 C6 **Waltman** Wyoming 43.05N 107.12W
106 H9 **Walton** Indiana 40.40N 86.16W
107 M3 **Walton** Kentucky 38.51N 84.38W
103 D2 **Walton** New York 42.11N 75.09W
11 K4 **Walton** New Zealand 37.44S 175.43E
98 J8 **Walton** Nova Scotia 45.14N 64.00W
99 J9 **Walton** Ontario 43.40N 81.19W
104 D8 **Walton** W Virginia 38.40N 81.26W
116 E6 **Walton Bank** Caribbean Sea
106 J5 **Walton Junction** Michigan 44.32N 85.23W
55 B5 **Walton-on-Thames** Surrey England 51.23N 0.25W
56 O4 **Walton-on-the-Naze** Essex Eng 51.51N 1.16E
55 C5 **Walton Reservoirs** Surrey England
107 G3 **Waltonville** Illinois 38.14N 89.01W
63 F9 **Waltrop** W Germany 51.37N 7.25E
94 C4 **Walvis B** Namibia
96 L12 **Walvis Basin** Atlantic Oc
94 C4 **Walvis Bay** Namibia 22.59S 14.31E

96 K12 Walvis Ridge Atlantic Oc
87 K7 Wal Wal Ethiopia 7.05N 45.25E
106 F7 Walworth Wisconsin 42.31N 88.36W
14 C9 Walyahmoing hill W Australia 30.37S 118.51E
64 F5 Walzbuchtal W Germany 49.01N 8.40E
66 P2 Walzenhausen Switzerland 47.27N 9.38E
31 F3 Wama Afghanistan 35.12N 70.50E
92 D2 Wama Zaïre 0.57N 28.18E
93 C5 Wamala, L Uganda
91 K6 Wamaza Zaïre 4.14S 27.02E
91 H4 Wamba Equateur Zaïre 1.37S 22.30E
87 A9 Wamba Haut-Zaïre Zaïre 2.10N 27.59E
93 J5 Wamba Kenya 0.58N 37.19E
90 D7 Wamba Nigeria 8.57N 8.42E
76 K5 Wamba Spain 41.40N 4.54W
91 E6 Wamba R Zaïre
61 G3 Wambeek Belgium 50.51N 4.10E
12 H5 Wamboyne New S Wales 33.36S 147.19E
109 O2 Wamego Kansas 39.12N 96.17W
60 K12 Wamel Netherlands 51.53N 5.27E
15 E5 Wamena Irian Jaya 3.50S 138.38E
15 L8 Wamera I Papua New Guinea 9.16S 150.57E
15 B5 Wami Irian Jaya 2.45S 133.18E
92 J5 Wami R Tanzania
110 D4 Wamic Oregon 45.16N 121.14W
30 G4 Wamitaksar Nepal 28.11N 83.17E
19 E5 Wamlana Moluccas Indon 3.05S 126.31E
Wampo see Ombu
104 E6 Wampum Pennsylvania 40.54N 80.23W
19 E5 Wamsasi Moluccas Indon 3.31S 126.10E
19 E5 Wamsisi Moluccas Indon 3.45S 126.59E
108 B8 Wamsutter Wyoming 41.40N 108.00W
93 J7 Wamunyu Kenya 1.25S 37.33E
93 J7 Wamunyu Kenya 1.24S 37.35E
15 D8 Wan Irian Jaya 8.23S 137.55E
31 E4 Wana Pakistan 32.15N 69.34E
12 G3 Wanaaring New S Wales 29.42S 144.14E
90 M5 Wana Hills Sudan
11 D11 Wanaka New Zealand 44.43S 169.10E
11 D11 Wanaka, L New Zealand
103 C5 Wanamakers Pennsylvania 40.40N 75.50W
23 G5 Wan'an Jiangxi China 26.25N 114.44E
15 C6 Wanapiri Irian Jaya 4.31S 135.59E
99 K6 Wanapitei L Ontario
103 F4 Wanaque New Jersey 41.02N 74.17W
103 F4 Wanaque Res New Jersey
106 H8 Wanatah Indiana 41.25N 86.53W
87 E5 Wanbera Ethiopia 10.40N 35.39E
12 F5 Wanbi S Australia 34.46S 140.19E
108 J6 Wanblee S Dakota 43.35N 101.39W
11 F12 Wanbrow, C New Zealand 45.07S 171.00E
61 K6 Wancennes Belgium 50.06N 4.58E
23 B9 Wan Chai Hong Kong 22.16N 114.09E
23 B10 Wan Chai Hong Kong 22.09N 114.14E
105 M2 Wanchese N Carolina 35.51N 75.39W
12 F3 Wancoocha, L S Australia
118 C10 Wanda Argentina 26.05S 54.30W
95 H5 Wanda S Africa 29.36S 24.26E
15 C5 Wandammen, Teluk B Irian Jaya
12 C4 Wandana S Australia 32.04S 133.45E
21 F4 Wanda Shan mts Heilongjiang China
48 U1 Wandels Hav sea Greenland
48 H9 Wandels Sea Arctic Oc
89 G7 Wanderama Ivory Coast 8.37N 4.25W
100 E3 Wandering River Alberta 55.10N 112.25W
64 K2 Wandersleben E Germany 50.54N 10.50E
63 K3 Wanderup W Germany 54.42N 9.20E
23 A6 Wandingzhen Yunnan China 24.01N 98.00E
28 D4 Wandiwash Tamil Nadu India 12.33N 79.35E
55 E4 Wandle, R London England
63 S7 Wandlitz E Germany 52.46N 13.28E
21 D10 Wando S Korea 34.22N 126.40E
13 J7 Wandoan Queensland 26.09S 149.51E
13 G4 Wando Vale Queensland 19.38S 144.52E
61 N4 Wandre Belgium 50.40N 5.40E
Wandsbeck see Hamburg
55 E4 Wandsworth London England 51.27N 0.11W
12 G2 Wandsworth Queensland 25.03S 143.38E
13 G7 Wandsworth Queensland 25.03S 143.38E
55 E4 Wandsworth bor London Eng
92 G4 Waneti Tanzania 5.32S 36.00E
109 N7 Wanette Oklahoma 34.57N 97.02W
61 J5 Wanfercée-Baulet Belgium 50.28N 4.35E
Wanfow see Yunfu
64 J1 Wanfried W Germany 51.11N 10.11E
21 B7 Wanfu Liaoning China 40.05N 122.34E
23 G1 Wanfu He R Shandong China
87 B9 Wanga Zaïre 2.59N 29.14E
13 G8 Wangamurra R Queensland
12 G6 Wanganella New S Wales 35.13S 144.53E
11 J6 Wanganui New Zealand 39.56S 175.02E
11 J6 Wanganui R North I New Zealand
11 E10 Wanganui R South I New Zealand
12 H6 Wangaratta Victoria 36.22S 146.20E
12 D5 Wangary S Australia 34.30S 135.26E
89 J7 Wangasi-Turu Ghana 8.56N 0.39W
23 D2 Wangcang Sichuan China 32.17N 106.20E
23 D4 Wangcaoba Guizhou China 28.11N 107.28E
23 E4 Wangcun Hunan China 28.45N 109.57E
22 J7 Wangcun Shanxi China 39.54N 112.47E
Wangda see Zogang
24 F11 Wangdain Xizang Zizhiqu China 28.55N 89.11E
23 D6 Wangdian Guangxi China 24.08N 106.17E
87 D6 Wangding Sudan 8.07N 33.03E
22 K7 Wangdu Hebei China 38.45N 115.08E
28 G2 Wangdu Phodrang Bhutan 27.26N 89.55E
53 F8 Wangels W Germany 54.16N 10.45E
63 N4 Wangels W Germany 54.16N 10.45E
66 G3 Wangen Bern Switzerland 47.14N 7.40E
66 M3 Wangen Schwyz Switzerland 47.12N 8.54E
66 H2 Wangen Solothurn Switzerland 47.21N 7.52E
66 L2 Wangen Zürich Switzerland 47.25N 8.39E
61 J5 Wangenies Belgium 50.28N 4.31E
64 H8 Wangen im Allgäu W Germany 47.42N 9.50E
66 F4 Wangen, Nieder Switzerland 46.55N 7.22E
63 G5 Wangerland reg W Germany
63 G5 Wangerooge W Germany 53.47N 7.54E
56 P3 Wangford Suffolk Eng 52.22N 1.37E
19 B9 Wanggameti mt Indonesia 10.05S 120.15E
23 F6 Wanggao Guangxi China 24.34N 111.18E
15 C5 Wanggar R Irian Jaya
22 D8 Wang Gaxun Qinghai China 36.40N 98.50E
Wanggezhuang see Jiaonan
93 M7 Wangi Kenya 1.59S 40.56E
66 M2 Wängi Switzerland 47.30N 8.57E
12 E3 Wangianna S Australia 29.39S 138.00E
19 C6 Wangiwangi isld Indonesia 5.23S 123.36E
23 F4 Wangjiachang Hunan China 29.52N 111.37E
21 E4 Wangjiadian Heilongjiang China 47.49N 130.18E
23 G3 Wangjiadian Hubei China 31.28N 114.02E
23 G3 Wangjiang Anhui China 30.10N 116.44E
22 H8 Wangjiaping Shaanxi China 36.25N 109.11E
25 E5 Wangka Thailand 15.07N 98.29E
87 B6 Wang Kai Sudan 9.03N 29.23E
Wang-K'uei see Wangkui
21 D4 Wangkui Heilongjiang China 46.50N 126.29E
23 C10 Wanglan I Hong Kong 22.10N 114.18E
87 C6 Wang Lei Sudan 9.11N 30.55E
23 E7 Wangmao Guangxi China 22.08N 109.53E
23 D6 Wangmo Guizhou China 25.08N 106.08E
89 G7 Wangolodougou Ivory Coast 9.56N 5.11W
23 G1 Wangqiao Henan China 34.44N 115.15E
21 E6 Wangqing Jilin China 43.17N 129.45E
66 O3 Wangs Switzerland 47.02N 9.26E
Wang Saphung see Ban Wang Saphung
Wang Ta Mua see Ban Wang Ta Mua
30 B1 Wangtu Himachal Prad India 31.32N 78.02E
23 F1 Wangwu Shan mts Shanxi China
Wang-yeh-miao see Horqin Youyi Qianqi
Wangying see Huaiyin
25 E2 Wan Hsa-la Burma 20.26N 98.40E
92 C2 Wanianga tribe Zaïre
91 J3 Wanie Rukula Zaïre 0.13N 25.34E
15 K8 Wanigela Papua New Guinea 9.22S 149.10E
19 C6 Wani, Gunung mt Indonesia 4.30S 123.05E
107 F10 Wanilla Mississippi 31.39N 90.09W
20 K2 Wanishi Japan 42.23N 141.00E
21 B8 Wanjialing Liaoning China 39.54N 122.10E
29 B6 Wankaner Gujarat India 22.35N 71.00E
63 M4 Wankendorf W Germany 54.07N 10.12E
Wan Kiang R see Huan Chiang
92 C11 Wankie Zimbabwe 18.20S 26.25E
92 C11 Wankie dist Zimbabwe
92 C11 Wankie Game Reserve Zimbabwe
Wanks R see Coco R
23 A8 Wan-lai-kam Burma 21.20N 98.25E
100 Q4 Wanless Manitoba 54.11N 101.21W
61 L6 Wanlin Belgium 50.09N 5.04E
57 F2 Wanlockhead Dumfries & Galloway Scotland 55.24N 3.47W
14 G8 Wanna Lakes W Australia
33 H3 Wannān, Al Saudi Arabia 26.56N 48.27E
108 P1 Wannaska Minnesota 48.38N 95.41W
61 O5 Wanne Belgium 50.22N 5.55E
63 F9 Wanne-Eickel W Germany 51.31N 7.09E
61 E3 Wannegem-Lede Belgium 50.53N 3.33E
66 J6 Wannehorn, Gt mt Switzerland 46.30N 8.06E
14 B9 Wanneroo W Australia 31.40S 115.35E
23 H4 Wannian Jiangxi China 28.36N 116.51E
23 E9 Wanning Guangdong China 18.55N 110.27E
63 S8 Wannsee W Berlin W Germany 52.26N 13.11E
15 L6 Wanopo New Britain 5.59S 150.47E
90 E8 Wanor, mt Nigeria 7.41N 11.18E
22 K6 Wanquan Hebei China 40.53N 114.49E
60 M13 Wanroij Netherlands 51.40N 5.50E
23 E1 Wanrong Shanxi China 35.25N 110.49E
57 K2 Wansbeck, R Northumb Eng
93 C3 Wanseko Uganda 2.11N 31.25E
56 L2 Wansford Cambs Eng 52.35N 0.25W
23 E5 Wanshan Guizhou China 27.33N 109.11E
23 F8 Wanshan Qundao isld Guangdong China
60 N13 Wanssum Netherlands 51.32N 6.05E
55 H3 Wanstead London Eng 51.34N 0.02E
11 L7 Wanstead New Zealand 40.08S 176.33E
56 G5 Wanstrow Somerset Eng 51.11N 2.25W
56 J4 Wantage Oxon Eng 51.36N 1.25W
103 G5 Wantagh Long I, N Y 40.40N 73.30W
15 F5 Wantipi Papua New Guinea 3.20S 141.58E
69 O6 Wantzenau, la France 48.40N 7.50E
99 K6 Wanup Ontario 46.24N 80.49W
22 K7 Wan Xian Hebei China 38.51N 115.08E
23 E3 Wanxian Sichuan China 30.54N 108.20E
23 E3 Wan Xian Sichuan China 30.48N 108.17E
23 E2 Wanyuan Sichuan China 32.05N 108.08E
23 G4 Wanzai Jiangxi China 28.06N 114.27E
85 B6 Wanzarīk Libya 27.31N 13.29E
61 L4 Wanze Belgium 50.32N 5.13E
61 F3 Wanzele Belgium 50.58N 3.57E
Wanzhi see Wuhu
63 O8 Wanzleben E Germany 52.04N 11.27E
11 K5 Waotu New Zealand 38.09S 175.42E
104 A6 Wapakoneta Ohio 40.34N 84.13W
15 L9 Wapamoiwa Papua New Guinea 9.38S 150.32E
109 O7 Wapanucka Oklahoma 34.23N 96.26W
110 E3 Wapato Washington 46.28N 120.25W
100 N4 Wapawekka Hills Saskatchewan
100 N4 Wapawekka L Saskatchewan
100 Q8 Wapella Saskatchewan 50.16N 101.59W
110 N6 Wapello Idaho 43.17N 112.13W
106 C8 Wapello Iowa 41.10N 91.13W
15 G6 Wapenamanda Papua New Guinea 5.39S 143.54E
60 N10 Wapenveld Netherlands 52.26N 6.05E
19 E5 Waperan Moluccas Indon 3.08S 126.53E
100 N1 Wapikaimaski L Ontario
100 S3 Wapisu L Manitoba
101 O8 Wapiti R Alberta/Br Col
110 Q5 Wapiti Ra Wyoming
91 K5 Wapono Zaïre 3.08S 27.10E
19 E5 Wapotin Moluccas Indon 3.05S 126.41E
107 F4 Wappapello Lake res Missouri 37.00N 90.20W
103 J3 Wapping Connecticut 41.50N 72.33W
103 G3 Wappinger Cr New York
103 G3 Wappingers Falls New York 41.36N 73.55W
65 N4 Wappoltenreith Austria 48.46N 15.35E
60 N8 Wapserveen Netherlands 52.49N 6.15E
108 S7 Wapsipinicon R Iowa
89 K7 Wapuli Ghana 9.43N 0.10E
100 P2 Wapus L Saskatchewan
98 O2 Wapustagamau L Quebec
103 B4 Wapwallopen Cr Pennsylvania
34 N10 Waqba, Al Arabia/Iraq 28.46N 45.31E
23 C2 Waqên Sichuan China 33.05N 102.34E
34 D7 Waqf es Suwwān, Jebel mts Jordan
86 E4 Wâqid Egypt 30.42N 30.45E
34 L8 Wāqişah Iraq 30.34N 43.48E
35 F3 Waqqas Jordan 32.32N 35.36E
33 H5 Waqr Saudi Arabia 23.49N 49.00E
33 F8 Waqr Maryamah Yemen 16.30N 45.07E
95 L8 Waqu S Africa 32.12S 27.06E
103 N3 Waquoit Village Massachusetts 41.37N 70.31W
93 B3 War Uganda 2.36N 30.53E
104 D9 War W Virginia 37.19N 81.42W
20 D1 Warabi Japan 35.50N 139.41E
87 J6 Wara Eban tribe Ethiopia
33 M10 Warah Kuwait 29.00N 47.58E
31 D7 Warah Pakistan 27.28N 67.49E
31 G3 Warai Post Pakistan 35.00N 72.06E
Waraj see Varaj
31 C4 Waraja Afghanistan 33.34N 64.02E
15 A5 Warakaget I Irian Jaya 2.15S 130.37E
26 R7 Warakapola Sri Lanka 7.13N 80.14E
12 A6 Waramanga dist Canberra Australia
103 H3 Waramaug L Connecticut 41.42N 73.23W
87 K7 Warandab Ethiopia 7.09N 44.10E
28 D2 Warangal Andhra Prad India 18.00N 79.35E
28 D1 Warangal dist Andhra Prad India
12 H6 Waranga Res Victoria 36.35S 145.05E
29 G7 Wara Seoni Madhya Prad India 21.46N 80.08E
31 D3 Waras Pass Afghanistan 34.08N 66.45E
12 H8 Waratah Tasmania 41.27S 145.32E
12 H7 Waratah B Victoria
Waravi see Varāvī
108 R2 Warba Minnesota 47.09N 93.16W
33 N9 Warbah, Jazīrat isld Kuwait 30.00N 48.05E
56 L3 Warboys Cambs Eng 52.24N 0.06W
13 G6 Warbreccan Queensland 24.18S 142.50E
15 C4 Warbumi Irian Jaya 1.13S 134.10E
100 C5 Warburg Alberta 53.12N 114.22W
63 K10 Warburg W Germany 51.28N 9.10E
12 H7 Warburton Victoria 37.49S 145.44E
12 D3 Warburton R S Australia
14 F7 Warburton Mission W Australia 26.05S 126.34E
12 C4 Warburton Ra S Australia
14 F7 Warburton Ra W Australia
31 G4 Warcha Pakistan 32.24N 72.04E
61 P5 Warche R Belgium
61 D4 Warchin Belgium 50.37N 3.26E
61 D4 Warcoing Belgium 50.42N 3.21E
57 J3 Warcop Cumbria Eng 54.32N 2.23W
69 K5 Warcq France 49.11N 5.39E
107 H9 Ward Alabama 32.21N 88.19W
11 J8 Ward New Zealand 41.51S 174.10E
13 H7 Ward R Queensland
31 E3 Wardak prov Afghanistan
12 D5 Wardang I S Australia 34.30S 137.20E
86 J6 Wardân, Wâdi watercourse Egypt
93 M5 Wardeglo Kenya 0.14N 40.44E
95 M3 Warden S Africa 27.50S 28.58E
110 F3 Warden Washington 46.58N 119.02W
63 H6 Wardenburg W Germany 53.03N 8.12E
100 E6 Warden Junction Alberta 52.16N 112.44W
104 G7 Wardensville W Virginia 39.04N 78.36W
95 J3 Warden's Vlei L S Africa 27.43S 25.40E
Warder see Uardere
60 J9 Warder Netherlands 52.34N 5.01E
29 F7 Wardha Maharashtra India 20.41N 78.40E
29 F7 Wardha dist Maharashtra India
29 F7 Wardha R Maharashtra India
58 S12 Ward Hill Hoy, Orkney Scotland 58.54N 3.20W
58 S12 Ward Hill Orkney Scotland 58.57N 3.10W
15 K8 Ward Hunt, C Papua New Guinea 8.04S 148.08E
97 M1 Ward Hunt I N W Terr 83.10N 74.30W
15 K8 Ward Hunt Str Papua New Guinea
11 D6 Ward I New Zealand 41.18S 174.52E
84 Y20 Wardija Ridge Malta
61 O7 Wardin Belgium 49.59N 5.48E
56 J3 Wardington Oxon Eng 52.07N 1.17W
34 J2 Wardiya Iraq 36.18N 41.42E
100 F8 Wardlow Alberta 50.56N 111.31W
11 B12 Ward, Mt New Zealand 45.38S 167.14E
11 D10 Ward, Mt New Zealand 43.53S 169.51E
101 Q11 Wardner Br Columbia 49.28N 115.22W
103 K7 Wards I New York 40.48N 73.56W
101 L7 Ware Br Col 57.26N 125.41W
56 L4 Ware Herts Eng 51.49N 0.02W
103 K2 Ware Massachusetts 42.15N 72.15W
103 K2 Ware R Massachusetts
11 H6 Warea New Zealand 39.14S 173.49E
92 C3 Warega tribe Zaïre
61 D3 Waregem Belgium 50.53N 3.26E
56 G6 Wareham Dorset Eng 50.41N 2.07W
103 N3 Wareham Massachusetts 41.46N 70.43W
103 J3 Warehouse Pt Connecticut 41.56N 72.37W
61 M4 Waremme Belgium 50.41N 5.15E
63 R5 Waren E Germany 53.32N 12.42E
15 D5 Waren Irian Jaya 2.19S 136.19E
13 F6 Warenda Queensland 22.35S 140.30E
63 G9 Warendorf W Germany 51.57N 8.00E
57 K1 Warenford Northumb Eng 55.33N 1.46W
11 D13 Warepa New Zealand 46.16S 169.36E
13 B4 Ware Ra N Terr Australia
105 E6 Waresboro Georgia 31.14N 82.29W
105 E3 Ware Shoals S Carolina 34.24N 82.13W
61 L4 Waret-l'Evêque Belgium 50.33N 5.04E
103 F7 Waretown New Jersey 39.47N 74.12W
60 P6 Warffum Netherlands 53.23N 6.34E
60 M7 Warga Netherlands 53.09N 5.50E
93 M2 War Gedud Kenya 3.10N 40.56E
93 J5 Warges mt Kenya 0.58N 37.24E
Wargi see Weriji
56 K4 Wargrave Berks Eng 51.31N 0.53W
87 C6 Wargur Sudan 8.58N 31.06E
59 K5 War Hill Wicklow Irish Rep 53.08N 6.15W
Wari see Savantvadi
33 G3 Warī'ah, Al Saudi Arabia 27.52N 47.30E
33 G3 Warī'ah, Al ridge Saudi Arabia
12 K3 Warialda New S Wales 29.33S 150.36E
15 C4 Wariap Irian Jaya 1.33S 134.10E
15 J7 Waria, R Papua New Guinea
31 D9 Wari Creek Pakistan
87 L6 Waridad Somalia 9.17N 46.11E
15 L9 Wari I Louisiade Arch 10.55S 151.05E
15 C6 Warilau isld Moluccas Indon 5.22S 134.31E
63 P5 Warin E Germany 53.48N 11.43E
25 H5 Warin Chamrap Thailand 15.11N 104.51E
112 J6 Waring Texas 29.57N 98.49W
113 H3 Waring Mts Alaska
59 K3 Waringstown Down N Ireland 54.26N 6.18W
15 F5 Waris Irian Jaya 3.09S 140.57E
30 J7 Waris Aliganj Bihar India 25.02N 85.39E
30 J7 Warisnagar Bihar India 25.57N 85.52E
61 K4 Warisoulx Belgium 50.32N 4.52E
26 R6 Wariyapola Sri Lanka 7.37N 80.15E
23 B4 Warizhên Sichuan China 28.30N 100.53E
90 D6 Warji Nigeria 11.12N 9.47E
57 J2 Wark Northumb Eng 55.05N 2.13W
58 M7 Wark Northumb Eng 55.38N 2.16W
62 N4 Warka Poland 51.46N 21.10E
30 H8 War Khas Bihar India 24.44N 84.32E
11 J3 Warkworth New Zealand 36.23S 174.42E
57 K2 Warkworth Northumb Eng 55.21N 1.36W
99 N8 Warkworth Ontario 44.12N 77.53W
110 K1 Warland Montana 48.30N 115.16W
23 B4 Warli Sichuan China 28.00N 101.30E
56 L5 Warlingham Surrey Eng 51.19N 0.04W
69 D3 Warloy-Baillon France 50.00N 2.30E
15 C6 Warmar isld Moluccas Indon 5.49S 134.12E
94 E7 Warmbad Namibia 28.29S 18.41E
94 K5 Warmbad S Africa 24.55S 28.15E
Warmbaths see Warmbad S.Africa
101 G6 Warm Bay Hotsprings Br Col 59.24N 133.35W
63 L8 Warmbüchen W Germany 52.28N 9.45E
60 G9 Warmenhuizen Netherlands 52.43N 4.45E
64 M4 Warmensteinach W Germany 49.59N 11.47E
69 G5 Warmeriville France 49.20N 4.03E
56 J3 Warmington Warwicks Eng 52.08N 1.24W
56 G5 Warminster Wilts Eng 51.13N 2.12W
60 G11 Warmond Netherlands 52.12N 4.30E
94 B2 Warmquelle Namibia 19.10S 13.50E
63 J8 Warmsen W Germany 52.28N 8.52E
105 C5 Warm Springs Georgia 32.53N 84.42W
110 N3 Warmsprings Montana 46.11N 112.48W
111 H3 Warm Springs Nevada 38.12N 116.24W
111 K2 Warm Springs Nevada 39.39N 114.49W
110 D5 Warm Springs Oregon 44.47N 121.18W
104 F8 Warm Springs Virginia 38.03N 79.48W
110 G6 Warm Springs Res Oregon 43.40N 118.15W
56 G6 Warmwell Dorset Eng 50.41N 2.22W
61 K5 Warnant Belgium 50.19N 4.50E
61 L4 Warnant-Dreye Belgium 50.36N 5.13E
99 B3 Warneford Ontario 49.34N 88.04W
63 Q4 Warnemünde E Germany 54.12N 12.05E
100 E9 Warner Alberta 49.20N 112.14W
104 O3 Warner New Hampshire 43.18N 71.51W
109 P6 Warner Oklahoma 35.31N 95.21W
108 M4 Warner S Dakota 45.19N 98.30W
110 F7 Warner Lakes Oregon
110 E8 Warner Mts Calif/Oregon
105 D5 Warner Robins Georgia 32.35N 83.37W
111 H8 Warner Springs California 33.19N 116.38W
103 D4 Warnertown Pennsylvania 41.10N 75.28W
120 F7 Warnes Bolivia 17.30S 63.11W
61 B3 Warneton Belgium 50.45N 2.57E
56 J5 Warnford Hants Eng 51.00N 1.06W
56 L5 Warnham W Sussex Eng 51.06N 0.22W
88 O3 Warnier Algeria 36.15N 1.15E
12 L3 Warning, Mt New S Wales 28.26S 153.12E
63 P5 Warnow Schwerin E Germany 53.47N 11.53E
63 Q5 Warnow R E Germany
60 K8 Warns Netherlands 52.53N 5.24E
60 N11 Warnsveld Netherlands 52.08N 6.14E
28 C1 Waronda Maharashtra India 19.27N 77.59E
14 B10 Waroona W Australia 32.51S 115.50E
29 F7 Warora Maharashtra India 20.15N 79.05E
61 F5 Warquignies Belgium 50.24N 3.50E
13 K7 Warra Queensland 26.56S 150.50E
14 F5 Warrabuda Well W Australia 21.24S 126.02E
12 F6 Warracknabeal Victoria 36.15S 142.28E
12 K5 Warragamba Res New S Wales
12 H7 Warragul Victoria 38.11S 145.55E
87 G5 Warra Hailu Ethiopia 10.40N 39.32E
12 E3 Warrakalanna, L S Australia
12 D5 Warramboo S Australia 33.14S 135.36E
14 C8 Warramboo mt W Australia 28.02S 117.49E
12 J3 Warrambool R New S Wales
35 G4 Warran watercourse Jordan
12 E2 Warrandirinna, L S Australia
12 G8 Warrane Tasmania 42.52S 147.22E
86 Q11 Warrâq el 'Arab Cairo Egypt
86 Q11 Warrâq el Hadr Cairo Egypt
14 D5 Warrawagine W Australia 20.52S 120.43E
12 H3 Warrego R New S Wales/Queensland
13 H6 Warrego Ra Queensland
111 P10 Warren Arizona 31.25N 109.54W
107 D8 Warren Arkansas 33.38N 92.05W
103 H3 Warren Connecticut 41.45N 73.20W
110 K4 Warren Idaho 45.16N 115.40W
106 E7 Warren Illinois 42.29N 89.59W
106 J9 Warren Indiana 40.42N 85.25W
103 K2 Warren Massachusetts 42.13N 72.11W
108 O1 Warren Minnesota 48.12N 96.48W
110 R4 Warren Montana 45.04N 108.39W
104 O3 Warren New Hampshire 43.56N 71.54W
12 H4 Warren New S Wales 31.44S 147.53E
104 E5 Warren Ohio 41.15N 80.49W
99 K6 Warren Ontario 46.27N 80.20W
104 F5 Warren Pennsylvania 41.52N 79.09W
103 M3 Warren Rhode I 41.44N 71.17W
112 N5 Warren Texas 30.35N 94.26W
104 G9 Warren Virginia 37.47N 78.35W
103 D5 Warren co New Jersey
106 N1 Warren dist Detroit, Michigan
103 B3 Warren Center Pennsylvania 41.57N 76.11W
97 L3 Warrender, C N W Terr 74.30N 82.00W
103 F7 Warren Grove New Jersey 39.45N 74.24W
113 V9 Warren I Alaska 55.53N 133.55W
100 U5 Warren Landing Manitoba 53.42N 97.54W
14 E8 Warren, Mt W Australia 27.44S 123.22E
59 K3 Warrenpoint Down N Ireland 54.06N 6.15W
101 G1 Warren Pt N W Terr 69.43N 132.31W
14 B10 Warren, R W Australia
106 D5 Warrens Wisconsin 44.07N 90.31W
107 G2 Warrensburg Illinois 39.56N 89.02W
107 C3 Warrensburg Missouri 38.46N 93.44W
104 M3 Warrensburg New York 43.28N 73.47W
105 E4 Warrenton Georgia 33.23N 82.40W
107 E3 Warrenton Missouri 38.50N 91.08W
105 J1 Warrenton N Carolina 36.24N 78.11W
110 B3 Warrenton Oregon 46.10N 123.56W
95 H4 Warrenton S Africa 28.07S 24.51E
104 H8 Warrenton Virginia 38.43N 77.48W
90 B9 Warri Nigeria 5.36N 5.46E
110 Q1 Warrick Montana 48.04N 109.36W
14 B8 Warriedar mt W Australia 29.04S 117.09E
13 H5 Warrigal Queensland 20.40S 145.17E
12 F3 Warri House New S Wales 29.00S 141.56E
12 D3 Warrina S Australia 28.10S 135.49E
12 D3 Warriners Cr S Australia
57 H6 Warrington Cheshire Eng 53.24N 2.37W
107 J11 Warrington Florida 30.23N 87.19W
11 E12 Warrington New Zealand 45.43S 170.37E
107 K8 Warrior Alabama 33.49N 86.50W
107 J8 Warrior R Alabama
15 G8 Warrior Reefs Torres Str, Qnsld
12 E4 Warriota R S Australia
12 G7 Warrnambool Victoria 38.23S 142.03E
108 P1 Warroad Minnesota 48.54N 95.20W
12 D5 Warrow S Australia 34.22S 135.25E
12 J4 Warrumbungle Ra New S Wales
13 F8 Warry Warry R Queensland
61 O4 Warsage Belgium 50.44N 5.46E
31 F3 Warsak Dam Pakistan 34.12N 71.20E
106 C9 Warsaw Illinois 40.21N 91.25W
106 J8 Warsaw Indiana 41.13N 85.52W
107 M3 Warsaw Kentucky 38.47N 84.55W
107 C3 Warsaw Missouri 38.14N 93.23W
105 J2 Warsaw N Carolina 35.01N 78.07W
104 G4 Warsaw New York 42.45N 78.07W
Warsaw Poland see Warszawa
104 J9 Warsaw Virginia 37.57N 76.46W
65 K6 Warscheneck mt Austria 47.40N 14.15E
87 M6 Warsengeli tribe Somalia
57 K6 Warslow Staffs Eng 53.07N 1.53W
100 E4 Warspite Alberta 54.06N 112.31W
63 H10 Warstein W Germany 51.26N 8.20E
62 M3 Warszawa Poland 52.15N 21.00E
62 H2 Warszów Poland 53.54N 14.20E
62 J3 Warta R Poland
65 N6 Wartberg Austria 47.32N 15.30E
64 J2 Wartburg E Germany 50.58N 10.17E
95 O5 Wartburg S Africa 29.26S 30.35E
105 C1 Wartburg Tennessee 36.08N 84.37W
60 M7 Wartena Netherlands 53.09N 5.54E
64 N7 Wartenberg W Germany 48.24N 12.00E
66 P3 Wartenstein Switzerland 47.01N 9.31E
57 M5 Warter Humberside Eng 53.57N 0.40W
65 B7 Warth Austria 47.16N 10.11E
64 H7 Warthausen W Germany 48.08N 9.48E
100 J7 Wartime Saskatchewan 51.13N 108.10W
63 U6 Wartin E Germany 53.15N 14.10E
56 M6 Wartling E Sussex Eng 50.51N 0.21E
57 H5 Warton Lancs Eng 53.46N 2.54W
14 F3 Warton Ra W Australia
107 K6 Wartrace Tennessee 35.31N 86.21W
95 L6 War Trail S Africa 30.42S 27.45E
19 G5 Waru Moluccas Indon 3.26S 130.37E
29 F7 Warud Maharashtra India 21.29N 78.22E
91 K7 Waruwa tribe Zaïre
34 H4 Wa'r, Wādī watercourse Syria
57 H3 Warwick Cumbria Eng 54.54N 2.50W
105 D6 Warwick Georgia 31.49N 83.56W
103 C8 Warwick Maryland 39.25N 75.47W
108 M2 Warwick N Dakota 47.51N 98.51W
103 F4 Warwick New York 41.15N 74.21W
103 C6 Warwick Pennsylvania 40.10N 75.47W
99 T7 Warwick Quebec 45.57N 71.59W
13 K8 Warwick Queensland 28.12S 152.00E
103 M3 Warwick Rhode I 41.42N 71.23W
56 H3 Warwick Warwicks Eng 52.17N 1.34W
13 D2 Warwick Chan N Terr Australia
56 H3 Warwickshire co England
15 B4 Waryori R Irian Jaya
61 M5 Warzée Belgium 50.27N 5.26E
23 B4 Warzhong Sichuan China 28.10N 100.50E
101 Q11 Wasa Br Col 49.46N 115.43W
15 C5 Wasado, Gunung mt Irian Jaya 3.20S 134.42E
99 K8 Wasaga Beach Ontario 44.31N 80.02W
90 B6 Wasagu Nigeria 11.20N 5.50E
33 J6 Was'ah, Al des area Saudi Arabia
111 N2 Wasatch Ra Utah
95 O4 Wasbank S Africa 28.19S 30.07E
58 S11 Wasbister Orkney Scotland 59.10N 3.04W
111 E6 Wasco California 35.35N 119.21W
110 E4 Wasco Oregon 45.36N 120.41W
106 C3 Wascott Wisconsin 46.09N 91.48W
57 G4 Wasdale Cumbria Eng 54.26N 3.20W
90 D7 Wase Nigeria 9.04N 9.54E
90 D7 Wase R Nigeria
108 R5 Waseca Minnesota 44.05N 93.29W
100 H5 Waseca Saskatchewan 53.06N 109.27W
101 T7 Wasekamio L Saskatchewan 56.47N 108.48W
66 H3 Wasen Switzerland 47.03N 7.48E
26 S6 Wasgomuwa game reserve Sri Lanka
117 A2 Washabo Surinam 5.17N 57.17W
99 L8 Washago Ontario 44.45N 79.20W
87 J8 Washago watercourse Ethiopia
110 Q6 Washakie Needles mt Wyoming 43.47N 109.18W
31 B7 Washap Pakistan 27.09N 63.28E
106 E9 Washburn Illinois 40.55N 89.18W
104 Q7 Washburn Maine 46.47N 68.10W
108 J2 Washburn N Dakota 47.18N 101.01W
112 C8 Washburn Texas 35.10N 101.35W
106 D3 Washburn Wisconsin 46.41N 90.53W
101 U1 Washburn L Victoria I, N W Terr
110 P5 Washburn, Mt Wyoming 44.49N 110.26W
11 F11 Washdyke New Zealand 44.20S 171.14E
56 E5 Washford Somerset Eng 51.11N 3.22W
98 M3 Washikuti Quebec 50.16N 60.47W
29 E7 Washim Maharashtra India 20.10N 77.11E
99 S3 Washimeska R Quebec
107 C8 Washington Arkansas 33.47N 93.41W
103 H3 Washington Connecticut 41.38N 73.18W
104 J8 Washington Dist of Columbia U.S.A. 38.55N 77.00W
105 E4 Washington Georgia 33.43N 82.46W
106 E9 Washington Illinois 40.43N 89.24W
107 J3 Washington Indiana 38.40N 87.10W
106 C8 Washington Iowa 41.18N 91.43W
109 N2 Washington Kansas 39.49N 97.03W
107 D11 Washington Louisiana 30.37N 92.03W
103 H2 Washington Massachusetts 42.22N 73.07W
107 E3 Washington Missouri 38.33N 91.01W
105 K2 Washington N Carolina 35.33N 77.04W
104 N3 Washington New Hampshire 43.12N 72.06W
103 E5 Washington New Jersey 40.45N 74.59W
104 E6 Washington Pennsylvania 40.11N 80.16W
112 L5 Washington Texas 30.19N 96.11W
57 K3 Washington Tyne and Wear Eng 54.54N 1.31W
111 L4 Washington Utah 37.08N 113.30W
104 G8 Washington Virginia 38.43N 78.11W
106 H4 Washington Wisconsin 45.24N 86.56W
56 L6 Washington W Sussex Eng 50.54N 0.25W
103 L3 Washington co Rhode I
102 B1 Washington state U.S.A.
103 B7 Washington Boro Pennsylvania 40.00N 76.28W
104 B7 Washington Court House Ohio 39.32N 83.27W
104 N10 Washington Highlands Washington D C U.S.A. 38.51N 77.00W
122 L7 Washington I Line Is Pacific Oc 5.00N 161.00W
106 H4 Washington I Wisconsin 45.23N 86.54W
105 G9 Washington, L Florida 28.08N 80.46W
97 N1 Washington Land Greenland
104 O2 Washington, Mt New Hampshire 44.17N 71.19W
103 F4 Washingtonville New York 41.25N 74.10W
103 A4 Washingtonville Pennsylvania 41.04N 76.40W
31 B4 Washir Afghanistan 32.14N 63.52E
109 M6 Washita R Oklahoma
110 Q4 Washoe Montana 45.09N 109.12W
110 C4 Washougal Washington 45.35N 122.21W
100 V7 Washow B Manitoba
31 F3 Washpe Pass Afghanistan 35.20N 71.24E
56 M2 Wash, The G England
110 G3 Washtucna Washington 46.45N 118.19W
31 C7 Washuk Pakistan 27.43N 64.50E
28 B1 Wasi Maharashtra India 18.33N 75.50E
33 G4 Wasi' Saudi Arabia 24.24N 47.47E
33 J5 Wasi' Saudi Arabia 23.50N 50.47E
15 B4 Wasian Irian Jaya 1.51S 133.21E
86 H4 Wasifîya, El Egypt 30.35N 32.13E
69 G4 Wasigny France 49.38N 4.23E
113 N6 Wasilla Alaska 61.35N 149.30W
15 C5 Wasior Irian Jaya 2.38S 134.27E
15 C6 Wasir isld Moluccas Indon 5.32S 134.15E
35 F1 Wāsit Syria 33.08N 35.44E
34 O6 Wasit anc site Iraq 32.12N 46.20E
33 C5 Wāsiţah Saudi Arabia 23.54N 38.57E
33 M5 Wāsiţ, Al Oman 22.26N 57.59E
33 N5 Wāsiţ, Al Oman 22.19N 58.14E
100 R9 Waskada Manitoba 49.05N 100.49W
100 V2 Waskaiowaka L Manitoba
100 E4 Waskatenau Alberta 54.06N 112.46W
100 L5 Waskesiu L Saskatchewan 53.58N 106.45W
100 L5 Waskesiu Lake Saskatchewan 53.56N 106.05W
108 Q1 Waskish Minnesota 48.11N 94.30W
112 N3 Waskom Texas 32.28N 94.05W
61 E4 Wasmes Belgium 50.33N 3.32E
61 F5 Wasmes Belgium 50.25N 3.51E
61 F5 Wasmuel Belgium 50.27N 3.51E
93 K5 Waso Kenya 0.52N 38.23E
91 J5 Wasongola tribe Zaïre
62 K4 Wąsosz Poland 51.31N 16.40E
115 M2 Waspan Nicaragua 14.42N 84.01W
60 H13 Waspik Netherlands 51.42N 4.57E
89 B5 Wassadou Senegal 12.44N 14.11W
103 G3 Wassaic New York 41.48N 73.32W
20 M1 Wassamu Japan 44.01N 142.25E
105 G6 Wassaw Sd Georgia 31.56N 80.58W
61 L4 Wasseiges Belgium 50.37N 5.00E
69 N6 Wasselonne France 48.39N 7.28E
66 L5 Wassen Switzerland 46.43N 8.37E
60 F11 Wassenaar Netherlands 52.09N 4.23E
64 A1 Wassenberg W Germany 51.06N 6.10E
94 E6 Wasser Namibia 26.08S 18.08E
64 J6 Wasseralfingen W Germany 48.53N 10.08E
66 O2 Wasserauen Switzerland 47.17N 9.26E
61 Q8 Wasserbillig Luxembourg 49.43N 6.30E
66 P1 Wasserburg W Germany 47.34N 9.39E
64 N7 Wasserburg am Inn W Germany 48.03N 12.15E
66 H2 Wasserfluh mt Switzerland 47.26N 8.01E
64 H2 Wasserkuppe mt W Germany 50.30N 9.58E
63 N9 Wasserleben E Germany 51.56N 10.45E
64 K5 Wassermungenau W Germany 49.13N 10.54E
64 K5 Wassertrüdingen W Germany 49.02N 10.37E
69 F3 Wassigny France 50.00N 3.36E
111 F3 Wassuk Ra Nevada
69 H7 Wassy France 48.30N 4.59E
33 C5 Wasta Saudi Arabia 23.54N 38.50E
108 H5 Wasta S Dakota 44.04N 102.26W
86 F7 Wasta, El Egypt 29.20N 31.12E
57 G4 Wast Water L Cumbria Eng 54.26N 3.18W
15 J6 Wasu Papua New Guinea 5.59S 147.12E
15 G8 Wasua Papua New Guinea 8.18S 142.57E
15 K7 Wasum New Britain 6.03S 149.20E
64 J2 Wasungen E Germany 50.40N 10.22E
99 O3 Waswanipi Quebec 49.30N 76.20W
99 O3 Waswanipi R Quebec
33 N6 Waţā, Al sandy reg Oman
99 K4 Watabeag L Ontario
106 D8 Wataga Illinois 41.02N 90.17W
26 U8 Watagoda mt Sri Lanka 6.42N 81.28E
19 B6 Watampone Celebes Indon 4.33S 120.20E
93 L9 Watamu Kenya 3.23S 40.00E
15 H5 Watan Papua New Guinea 3.56S 144.35E
19 A6 Watansoppeng Celebes Indon 4.22S 119.57E
86 G5 Waţan, Wâdi watercourse Egypt
20 O3 Watari Honshu Japan 38.02N 140.52E
108 J4 Watauga S Dakota 45.56N 101.32W
112 M9 Watauga Texas 32.51N 97.16W
105 E1 Watauga L Tennessee
105 E1 Watauga R Tennessee
26 S8 Watawala Sri Lanka 6.57N 80.32E
64 L8 Watchensee L W Germany
56 E5 Watchet Somerset Eng 51.12N 3.20W
103 L4 Watch Hill Rhode I 41.18N 71.52W
100 L1 Watcomb Ontario 49.50N 91.20W
56 M3 Waterbeach Cambs Eng 52.16N 0.11E
94 D3 Waterberg Namibia 20.28S 17.13E
94 D3 Waterberg mts Namibia
104 P3 Waterboro Maine 43.33N 70.44W
103 H3 Waterbury Connecticut 41.33N 73.03W
104 N2 Waterbury Vermont 44.21N 72.46W
116 F3 Water Cays islds Andros Bahamas 23.40N 77.50W
99 L9 Waterdown Ontario 43.20N 79.54W
105 G3 Wateree Pond S Carolina
105 G3 Wateree, R S Carolina
56 K4 Waterend Herts Eng 51.48N 0.31W
10 B11 Waterfall B Macquarie I Pacific Oc 54.40S 158.55E
10 A11 Waterfall L Macquarie I Pacific Oc 54.45S 158.51E
59 K1 Waterfoot Antrim N Ireland 55.04N 6.04W
111 D4 Waterford California 37.37N 120.46W
103 K4 Waterford Connecticut 41.20N 72.08W
99 K10 Waterford Ontario 42.55N 80.19W
104 F5 Waterford Pennsylvania 41.57N 80.00W
95 J9 Waterford S Africa 33.05S 25.01E
59 H7 Waterford Waterford Irish Rep 52.15N 7.06W
59 G7 Waterford co Irish Rep
59 J7 Waterford Harb Waterford Irish Rep 52.10N 6.57W
103 E7 Waterford Works New Jersey 39.44N 74.52W
56 T9 Watergate B Cornwall Eng
59 F7 Watergrasshill Cork Irish Rep 52.00N 8.20W
100 S6 Waterhen L Manitoba
100 J4 Waterhen L Saskatchewan
101 T8 Waterhen Lake Saskatchewan 54.30N 108.17W
13 C2 Waterhouse R N Terr Australia
13 C6 Waterhouse Ra N Terr Australia
105 L7 Water I Virgin Is 18.21N 64.57W
60 F11 Wateringen Netherlands 52.02N 4.16E
94 E8 Waterklip S Africa 31.16S 18.10E
95 J6 Waterkloof S Africa 30.19S 25.18E
60 B3 Waterlandkerkje Netherlands 51.19N 3.33E
61 E1 Waterland-Oudeman Belgium 51.18N 3.36E
107 H7 Waterloo Alabama 34.54N 88.05W
107 C8 Waterloo Arkansas 33.32N 93.15W
61 H4 Waterloo Belgium 50.43N 4.24E
107 F3 Waterloo Illinois 38.20N 90.10W
106 J8 Waterloo Indiana 41.22N 85.02W
108 S7 Waterloo Iowa 42.30N 92.20W
110 N4 Waterloo Montana 45.44N 112.10W
103 E5 Waterloo New Jersey 40.55N 74.46W
104 J4 Waterloo New York 42.55N 76.53W
11 D5 Waterloo New Zealand
13 A3 Waterloo N Terr Australia 17.00S 129.14E
99 K9 Waterloo Ontario 43.28N 80.32W
99 S7 Waterloo Quebec 45.21N 72.31W
89 C7 Waterloo Sierra Leone 8.24N 13.05W
117 B2 Waterloo Surinam 5.45N 56.51W
58 J5 Waterloo Tayside Scotland 56.31N 3.34W
116 O2 Waterloo Trinidad & Tobago 10.28N 61.28W
106 F6 Waterloo Wisconsin 43.11N 89.00W
56 E6 Waterloo Cross Devon Eng 50.55N 3.21W
Waterloo I see King George I
56 J6 Waterlooville Hants Eng 50.53N 1.02W
61 S10 Watermael dist Bruxelles Belgium
106 F8 Waterman Illinois 41.47N 88.47W
121 K10 Waterman, I Chile 55.23S 70.00W
103 K5 Water Mill Long I, N Y 40.55N 72.21W
94 K4 Waterpoort S Africa 22.53S 29.32E
107 E10 Waterproof Louisiana 31.49N 91.25W
106 K5 Waters Michigan 44.53N 84.42W
57 E2 Waterside Strathclyde Scotland 55.21N 4.28W
106 E3 Watersmeet Michigan 48.18N 89.10W
110 M1 Waterton Lakes Nat. Park Alberta
100 D9 Waterton Park Alberta 49.06N 113.54W
103 H3 Watertown Connecticut 41.32N 73.08W
108 R5 Watertown Minnesota 44.58N 93.51W
104 K3 Watertown New York 43.57N 75.56W
108 N5 Watertown S Dakota 44.54N 97.08W
107 K5 Watertown Tennessee 36.05N 86.10W
106 F6 Watertown Wisconsin 43.12N 88.46W
104 P9 Watertown dist Boston, Mass 42.21N 71.10W
95 M2 Waterval R S Africa
95 O1 Waterval-Boven S Africa 25.40S 30.20E
12 E5 Watervale S Australia 33.58S 138.39E
107 G7 Water Valley Mississippi 34.09N 89.39W
112 G4 Water Valley Texas 31.40N 100.44W
95 O1 Waterval-Onder S Africa 25.40S 30.23E
103 H3 Waterville Connecticut 41.36N 73.03W
109 O2 Waterville Kansas 39.42N 96.45W
59 B8 Waterville Kerry Irish Rep 51.50N 10.10W
104 Q2 Waterville Maine 44.34N 69.41W
108 R5 Waterville Minnesota 44.12N 93.30W
104 K4 Waterville New York 42.55N 95.24W
98 H8 Waterville Nova Scotia 45.03N 64.41W
99 T7 Waterville Quebec 45.16N 71.52W
110 E2 Waterville Washington 47.38N 120.04W
61 E1 Watervliet Belgium 51.17N 3.38E
104 M4 Watervliet New York 42.43N 73.42W
100 F2 Waterways Alberta 56.41N 111.19W
18 J9 Wates Java Indonesia 7.48S 110.07E
55 C2 Watford Herts England 51.39N 0.24W
99 J10 Watford Ontario 42.57N 81.52W
108 G2 Watford City N Dakota 47.49N 103.19W
Wathar see Vathar
109 Q2 Wathena Kansas 39.44N 94.58W
14 B9 Watheroo W Australia 30.19S 116.03E
87 C6 Wath Kel Sudan 9.25N 30.50E
101 P8 Watino Alberta 55.41N 117.40W
86 N7 Watîr, Wâdi watercourse Egypt
109 F2 Watkins Colorado 39.45N 104.36W
108 Q4 Watkins Minnesota 45.19N 94.25W
104 J4 Watkins Glen New York 42.23N 76.53W
105 D4 Watkinsville Georgia 33.51N 83.26W
15 B6 Watlaär Moluccas Indon 5.27S 133.07E
Watlam see Yulin Guangxi
58 R8 Watlee, L. of Shetland Scotland 60.43N 0.55W
Watling, I see San Salvador
56 J3 Watling Street hist route England
56 J4 Watlington Oxon Eng 51.39N 1.01W
15 A7 Watmuri Moluccas Indon 7.31S 131.32E
15 M6 Watom I Bismarck Arch 4.08S 152.05E
109 M6 Watonga Oklahoma 35.52N 98.26W
18 F9 Waton, Tanjung C Indonesia 6.36S 105.08E
61 A3 Watou Belgium 50.51N 2.37E
19 F3 Watowato, Bukit mt Halmahera Indonesia 1.00N 128.07E
109 F6 Watrous New Mexico 35.46N 104.59W
100 M7 Watrous Saskatchewan 51.40N 105.29W
93 A2 Watsa Zaïre 3.02N 29.33E
106 G9 Watseka Illinois 40.46N 87.45W
91 G4 Watsi Kengo Zaïre 0.49S 20.34E
58 P9 Wats Ness prom Shetland Scotland 60.14N 1.41W
107 E8 Watson Arkansas 33.52N 91.17W
108 P4 Watson Minnesota 45.00N 95.48W
107 A1 Watson Missouri 40.29N 95.37W
100 N6 Watson Saskatchewan 52.09N 104.31W
12 B4 Watson S Australia 30.30S 131.33E
12 B5 Watson dist Canberra Australia
13 F2 Watson R Queensland
101 J5 Watson Lake Yukon Terr 60.02N 128.47W
12 M7 Watson's Bay dist Sydney, N S W
104 J5 Watsontown Pennsylvania 41.04N 76.52W
111 C5 Watsonville California 36.53N 121.49W
26 Q8 Wattala Sri Lanka 7.01N 79.54E
26 S7 Wattegama Sri Lanka 7.20N 80.41E
26 U8 Wattegama Uva Sri Lanka 6.48N 81.30E
69 C2 Watten France 50.50N 2.13E
58 K2 Watten Highland Scotland 58.28N 3.19W
13 G5 Watten Queensland 21.02S 144.00E
58 K2 Watten, L Highland Scotland 58.29N 3.20W
65 E7 Wattens Austria 47.18N 11.37E
63 F10 Wattenscheid W Germany 51.27N 7.07E
66 G4 Wattenwil Switzerland 46.46N 7.31E
12 D3 Wattiwarriganna R S Australia
94 T14 Wattles S Africa 26.16S 28.10E
12 G3 Wattle Vale New S Wales 30.00S 143.30E
101 P6 Watt Mt Alberta 58.39N 117.36W
14 F7 Watt, Mt W Australia 26.51S 126.18E
56 N2 Watton Norfolk Eng 52.34N 0.50E
56 L4 Watton-at-Stone Herts Eng 51.52N 0.07W
61 C4 Wattrelos Belgium 51.41N 3.12E
109 Q5 Watts Oklahoma 36.05N 94.35W
107 M6 Watts Bar Dam Tennessee 35.36N 84.47W
107 M6 Watts Bar L Tennessee
104 F4 Wattsburg Pennsylvania 42.01N 79.52W
15 L9 Watts I Papua New Guinea 10.39S 151.20E
66 N2 Wattwil Switzerland 47.18N 9.06E
93 K7 Watu Kenya 1.59S 38.10E
91 G5 Watu Zaïre 3.18S 20.03E
19 G6 Watubela, Kep islds Moluccas Indon
19 B4 Watukama Celebes Indon 1.41S 120.03E
19 B4 Watukancoa Celebes Indonesia 1.31S 121.51E
103 M3 Watuppa Pond L Massachusetts
19 B5 Watuwila, Bukit mt Celebes Indon 3.48S 121.35E
85 J5 Watya, El oasis Egypt
65 C8 Watze-Spitze mt Austria 46.59N 10.48E
64 O8 Watzmann mt W Germany 47.33N 12.55E
15 J7 Wau Papua New Guinea 7.22S 146.40E
87 B7 Wau Sudan 7.40N 28.04E
87 A7 Wau watercourse Sudan
60 U17 Waubach Netherlands 50.55N 6.03E
99 K7 Waubamick Ontario 45.29N 80.01W
99 L8 Waubaushene Ontario 44.45N 79.42W
108 N4 Waubay S Dakota 45.20N 97.20W
108 N4 Waubay L S Dakota
12 L4 Wauchope New S Wales 31.27S 152.43E
13 C5 Wauchope N Terr Australia 20.48S 134.15E
100 Q9 Wauchope Saskatchewan 49.35N 101.51W
105 F10 Wauchula Florida 27.33N 81.49W
106 B6 Waucoma Iowa 43.03N 92.01W
110 G1 Wauconda Washington 48.45N 118.59W
61 G5 Waudrez Belgium 50.26N 4.09E
100 G1 Waugh Manitoba 49.39N 95.10W
19 A4 Waukara, Gunung mt Celebes Indon 1.15S 119.45E
12 E4 Waukaringa S Australia 32.18S 139.27E
14 D5 Waukarlycarly, L W Australia 21.21S 121.53E
108 R8 Waukee Iowa 41.37N 93.52W
106 G7 Waukegan Illinois 42.21N 87.52W
106 F6 Waukesha Wisconsin 43.01N 88.14W
109 N5 Waukomis Oklahoma 36.16N 97.55W
106 C6 Waukon Iowa 43.15N 91.29W
61 K6 Waulsort Belgium 50.12N 4.52E
108 J9 Wauneta Nebraska 40.27N 101.22W
106 E5 Waupaca Wisconsin 44.23N 89.04W
106 F6 Waupun Wisconsin 43.37N 88.44W
103 L3 Wauregan Connecticut 41.45N 71.55W
109 N7 Waurika Oklahoma 34.12N 98.00W
108 N7 Wausa Nebraska 42.30N 97.33W
106 E5 Wausau Wisconsin 44.58N 89.40W
106 G4 Wausaukee Wisconsin 45.23N 87.57W

104 A5 Wauseon Ohio 41.33N 84.09W
106 E5 Wautoma Wisconsin 44.05N 89.17W
106 F6 Wauwatosa Wisconsin 43.04N 88.02W
66 J3 Wauwil Switzerland 47.11N 8.02E
103 O4 Wauwinet Massachusetts 41.20N 69.59W
106 D6 Wauzeka Wisconsin 43.05N 90.55W
13 B3 Wave Hill N Terr Australia 17.30S 130.56E
107 J2 Waveland Indiana 39.54N 87.02W
107 G11 Waveland Mississippi 30.16N 89.25W
13 K1 Wavell Heights dist Brisbane, Qnsld
56 P3 Waveney, R Suffolk Eng
11 J6 Waverley New Zealand 39.46S 174.35E
98 J9 Waverley Nova Scotia 44.48N 63.38W
95 K7 Waverley S Africa 31.55S 26.27E
11 M13 Waverley dist Dunedin New Zealand
12 M7 Waverley dist Sydney, N S W
105 F6 Waverly Georgia 31.05N 81.44W
107 G2 Waverly Illinois 39.36N 89.57W
108 S7 Waverly Iowa 42.43N 92.29W
109 P3 Waverly Kansas 38.23N 95.36W
107 C2 Waverly Missouri 39.11N 93.32W
108 O9 Waverly Nebraska 40.57N 96.31W
103 A2 Waverly New York 42.01N 76.33W
104 C7 Waverly Ohio 39.07N 82.59W
103 C3 Waverly Pennsylvania 41.32N 75.42W
108 O4 Waverly S Dakota 45.00N 96.59W
107 J5 Waverly Tennessee 36.04N 87.49W
104 H9 Waverly Virginia 37.02N 77.10W
110 H2 Waverly Washington 47.20N 117.14W
104 E1 Waverly dist Baltimore, Md
105 C5 Waverly Hall Georgia 32.41N 84.34W
13 F7 Waverney Queensland 25.18S 141.56E
60 H11 Waverveen Netherlands 52.13N 4.54E
69 C2 Wavrans-sur-l'Aa France 50.41N 2.08E
61 J4 Wavre Belgium 50.43N 4.37E
61 L6 Wavreille Belgium 50.07N 5.15E
69 D2 Wavrin France 50.34N 2.57E
100 E6 Wavy L Alberta
25 D4 Waw Burma 17.26N 96.40E
19 G2 Wawa Luzon Philippines 14.05N 120.37E
90 B7 Wawa Nigeria 9.55N 4.26E
99 F4 Wawa Ontario 48.04N 84.49W
89 K8 Wawa R Ghana/Togo
99 M3 Wawagosic R Quebec
99 J4 Wawaitin Falls Ontario 48.22N 81.30W
85 D7 Wāw al Kabīr Libya 25.21N 16.41E
100 S9 Wawanesa Manitoba 49.36N 99.40W
85 D7 Wāw an Nāmūs Libya 24.53N 17.49E
103 F3 Wawarsing New York 41.45N 74.22W
106 J8 Wawasee, L Indiana 41.23N 85.42W
15 L8 Wawiwa I D'Entrecasteaux Is Papua New Guinea 9.15S 150.45E
57 N5 Wawne Humberside England 53.48N 0.20W
19 B5 Wawo Celebes Indon 3.41S 121.04E
15 G7 Wawoi R Papua New Guinea
111 E4 Wawona California 37.32N 119.39W
100 Q9 Wawota Saskatchewan 49.56N 101.59W
19 C5 Wawotobi Celebes Indon 3.51S 122.06E
112 L3 Waxahachie Texas 32.23N 96.52W
56 P2 Waxham Norfolk Eng 52.47N 1.38E
105 G3 Waxhaw N Carolina 34.56N 80.46W
23 C1 Waxü Gansu China 34.25N 102.15E
64 A3 Waxweiler W Germany 50.06N 6.23E
24 F6 Waxxari Xinjiang Uygur Zizhiqu China 38.43N 87.10E
107 F9 Way Mississippi 32.45N 90.02W
9 R7 Waya isld Fiji 17.19S 177.09E
19 F2 Wayabula Moluccas Indon 2.19N 128.13E
15 A3 Wayag isld Irian Jaya 0.11N 130.03E
9 R7 Waya Lailai isld Fiji 17.22S 177.20E
19 F3 Wayamli Halmahera Indon 0.59N 128.30E
110 O7 Wayan Idaho 42.59N 111.23W
23 B6 Wayao Yunnan China 25.34N 99.12E
Wayaobu see Zichang
19 E4 Wayaua Moluccas Indon 0.44S 127.38E
61 H5 Wayaux Belgium 50.29N 4.29E
105 E6 Waycross Georgia 31.12N 82.22W
25 G8 Way, Ko isld Gulf of Thailand 9.55N 102.55E
14 D7 Way, L W Australia
106 C8 Wayland Iowa 41.07N 91.40W
104 C9 Wayland Kentucky 37.26N 82.48W
103 M2 Wayland Massachusetts 42.22N 71.22W
106 J7 Wayland Michigan 42.40N 85.40W
107 E1 Wayland Missouri 40.23N 91.34W
104 H4 Wayland New York 42.33N 77.36W
86 R11 Wâyli el Kubra, El Cairo Egypt
103 D3 Waymart Pennsylvania 41.35N 75.26W
100 E7 Wayne Alberta 51.23N 112.40W
104 P2 Wayne Maine 44.22N 70.04W
106 L7 Wayne Michigan 42.18N 83.23W
107 C5 Wayne Missouri 36.40N 93.59W
108 N7 Wayne Nebraska 42.13N 97.03W
104 H4 Wayne New York 42.28N 77.08W
109 N7 Wayne Oklahoma 34.55N 97.19W
103 D6 Wayne Pennsylvania 40.03N 75.23W
104 C8 Wayne W Virginia 38.14N 82.27W
103 D3 Wayne co Pennsylvania
107 H3 Wayne City Illinois 38.20N 88.38W
105 E4 Waynesboro Georgia 33.04N 82.01W
107 H10 Waynesboro Mississippi 31.40N 88.40W
104 H7 Waynesboro Pennsylvania 39.45N 77.36W
107 J6 Waynesboro Tennessee 35.20N 87.49W
104 G8 Waynesboro Virginia 38.04N 78.54W
104 D6 Waynesburg Ohio 40.41N 81.16W
104 E7 Waynesburg Pennsylvania 39.54N 80.14W
106 E9 Waynesville Illinois 40.14N 89.09W
107 D4 Waynesville Missouri 37.48N 92.11W
105 E2 Waynesville N Carolina 35.30N 82.58W
104 A7 Waynesville Ohio 39.32N 84.05W
109 M5 Waynoka Oklahoma 36.35N 98.53W
61 H4 Ways Belgium 50.37N 4.28E
108 G7 Wayside Nebraska 42.59N 103.15W
112 F1 Wayside Texas 34.48N 101.33W
93 L7 Wayu Kenya 1.31S 39.39E
25 N8 Waza Burma 25.56N 97.31E
90 G6 Waza Cameroon 11.25N 14.35E
31 E4 Wazi Khwa Afghanistan 32.09N 68.16E
92 C3 Wazimba tribe Zaïre
29 B1 Wazīrabad Delhi India 28.43N 77.14E
31 H4 Wazirabad Pakistan 32.23N 74.10E
30 J8 Wazirganj Bihar India 24.47N 85.15E
29 A1 Wazīrpūr Delhi India 28.41N 77.10E
43 K7 Waznud Afghanistan 38.00N 71.16E
62 L2 Wda R Poland
55 D2 Wealdstone London Eng 51.36N 0.20W
56 M5 Weald, The reg W & E Sussex and Kent Eng
57 K3 Weardale V Durham Eng
57 J3 Wear Head Durham Eng 54.45N 2.13W
57 K3 Wear, R Durham/Tyne and Wear Eng
13 D3 Wearyan R N Terr Australia
13 H3 Weary B Queensland
107 B2 Weatherby Missouri 39.54N 94.16W
57 J4 Weathercote N Yorks Eng 54.12N 2.24W
109 M6 Weatherford Oklahoma 35.32N 98.44W
112 K3 Weatherford Texas 32.47N 97.48W
103 C5 Weatherly Pennsylvania 40.57N 75.50W
107 C4 Weaubleau Missouri 37.54N 93.32W
107 L8 Weaver Alabama 33.42N 85.49W
106 C5 Weaver Minnesota 44.13N 91.56W
57 H6 Weaverham Cheshire Eng 53.16N 2.35W
100 V6 Weaver L Manitoba
57 H6 Weaver, R Cheshire Eng
57 M4 Weaverthorpe N Yorks Eng 54.07N 0.32W
110 C9 Weaverville California 40.44N 122.57W
93 K1 Web Ethiopia 4.30N 38.38E
107 L10 Webb Alabama 31.14N 85.20W
107 F8 Webb Mississippi 33.56N 90.22W
100 J8 Webb Saskatchewan 50.10N 108.15W
112 H8 Webb Texas 27.48N 99.27W
107 B4 Webb City Missouri 37.08N 94.29W
87 H8 Webbe Gestro,R Ethiopia
61 L3 Webbekom Belgium 50.58N 5.04E
109 P6 Webbers Falls Res Oklahoma
87 H7 Webbe Shibeli,R Ethiopia
14 G6 Webb, Mt W Australia 22.59S 128.25E
99 J6 Webbwood Ontario 46.16N 81.53W
11 L7 Weber New Zealand 40.22S 176.20E
109 G7 Weber City New Mexico 34.38N 103.38W
89 F9 Webo Liberia 4.52N 7.37W
109 E2 Webster Colorado 39.26N 105.45W
105 E9 Webster Florida 28.37N 82.03W
106 B8 Webster Iowa 41.26N 92.10W
103 B7 Webster Maryland 39.36N 76.10W
103 L2 Webster Massachusetts 42.04N 71.53W
108 M1 Webster N Dakota 48.19N 98.50W
104 H3 Webster New York 43.13N 77.27W
108 N4 Webster S Dakota 45.19N 97.31W
106 B4 Webster Wisconsin 45.54N 92.22W
108 R7 Webster City Iowa 42.30N 93.50W
107 F3 Webster Groves Missouri 38.35N 90.23W
109 L2 Webster Res Kansas 39.24N 99.27W
93 F5 Webuye Kenya 0.36N 34.47E
61 K1 Wechelderzande Belgium 51.16N 4.48E
112 M4 Weches Texas 31.32N 95.17W
64 O2 Wechselburg E Germany 51.00N 12.47E
19 E3 Weda Halmahera Indon 0.20N 127.52E
26 U8 Wedagama Sri Lanka 6.46N 81.45E
19 F3 Weda, Teluk B Halmahera Indon
15 L9 Wedau Papua New Guinea 10.07S 150.06E
95 H4 Wedberg S Africa 28.19S 24.45E
60 R7 Wedde Netherlands 53.04N 7.04E
121 D10 Weddell I Falkland Is
123 D11 Weddell Sea Antarctica
63 L7 Weddemark W Germany 52.33N 9.35E
11 E12 Wedderburn New Zealand 45.03S 170.03E
110 A7 Wedderburn Oregon 42.27N 124.26W
12 G6 Wedderburn Victoria 36.26S 143.39E
63 B1 Wedding dist W Berlin W Germany
63 K4 Weddinghusen W Germany 54.13N 9.06E
63 K4 Weddingstedt W Germany 54.14N 9.06E
63 L5 Wedel W Germany 53.35N 9.42E
50 S15 Wedel Jarlsberg Land Spitsbergen
13 B6 Wedge, Central Mt N Terr Australia 22.55S 131.50E
105 G4 Wedgefield S Carolina 33.53N 80.32W
14 B9 Wedge I W Australia 30.53S 115.10E
101 M10 Wedge Mt Br Col 50.07N 122.49W
13 B6 Wedge, Mt N Terr Australia 23.50S 131.50E
98 G10 Wedgeport Nova Scotia 43.44N 65.58W
56 F5 Wedmore Somerset Eng 51.14N 2.49W
56 G2 Wednesbury W Midlands Eng 52.34N 2.00W
15 G9 Wednesday I Torres Str, Qnsld 10.31S 142.16E
107 L8 Wedowee Alabama 33.20N 85.29W
15 B6 Weduar, Tg C Moluccas Indon 5.59S 132.50E
92 D12 Wedza Zimbabwe 20.14S 29.51E
92 E11 Wedza Zimbabwe 18.35S 31.35E
92 E11 Wedza dist Zimbabwe
60 K14 Weebosch Netherlands 51.18N 5.17E
110 C8 Weed California 41.26N 122.23W
99 T7 Weedon Quebec 45.43N 71.28W
56 J3 Weedon Beck Northants Eng 52.14N 1.05W
104 J3 Weedsport New York 43.04N 76.34W
104 G5 Weedville Pennsylvania 41.17N 78.30W
56 H2 Weeford Staffs Eng 52.39N 1.46W
103 J7 Weehawken New Jersey 40.47N 74.02W
15 A4 Weeim isld Irian Jaya 1.30S 130.14E
100 P6 Weekes Saskatchewan 52.34N 102.54W
121 J9 Week, Is Chile 53.10S 74.18W
107 E12 Weeks Louisiana 29.50N 91.49W
104 C9 Weeksbury Kentucky 37.19N 82.44W
Weeks I see Puketutu I
103 E7 Weekstown New Jersey 39.36N 74.36W
105 L1 Weeksville N Carolina 36.13N 76.10W
61 K1 Weelde Belgium 51.24N 5.00E
56 O4 Weeley Essex Eng 51.52N 1.07E
58 J5 Weem Tayside Scotland 56.38N 3.55W
12 J3 Weemelah New S Wales 29.02S 149.15E
95 O4 Weenen S Africa 28.50S 30.06E
63 F6 Weener W Germany 53.11N 7.21E
108 O9 Weeping Water Nebraska 40.52N 96.09W
61 H3 Weerde Belgium 50.58N 4.29E
60 Q8 Weerdinge Netherlands 52.49N 6.55E
60 Q10 Weerselo Netherlands 52.22N 6.50E
61 G2 Weert Belgium 51.06N 4.12E
60 L14 Weert Netherlands 51.15N 5.42E
112 K7 Weesatche Texas 28.52N 97.28W
66 N3 Weesen Switzerland 47.08N 9.06E
60 J10 Weesp Netherlands 52.18N 5.03E
12 A5 Weetangera dist Canberra Australia
12 H5 Weethalle New S Wales 33.54S 146.34E
56 N3 Weeting Norfolk Eng 52.28N 0.37E
63 L8 Weetzen W Germany 52.17N 9.39E
12 J4 Wee Waa New S Wales 30.34S 149.27E
63 D9 Weeze W Germany 51.37N 6.13E
63 O8 Wefensleben E Germany 52.11N 11.10E
63 O8 Weferlingen E Germany 52.19N 11.03E
64 A1 Wegberg W Germany 51.08N 6.16E
69 L1 Wegberg W Germany 51.09N 6.14E
Wegdam see Hengevelde
63 O9 Wegeleben E Germany 51.53N 11.11E
63 O8 Wegenstedt E Germany 52.24N 11.12E
66 K3 Weggis Switzerland 47.02N 8.26E
63 J8 Wegholm W Germany 52.23N 8.50E
62 J4 Węgliniec Poland 51.19N 15.12E
62 N1 Wegorapa R Poland/U.S.S.R.
62 N1 Węgorzewo Poland 54.13N 21.45E
62 J2 Węgorzyno Poland 53.31N 15.31E
62 N3 Węgrów Poland 52.22N 22.00E
65 M6 Wegscheid Austria 47.42N 15.20E
64 Q6 Wegscheid W Germany 48.37N 13.50E
87 J8 Wegwet, El Ethiopia 5.28N 42.17E
18 A3 Weh isld Sumatra Indonesia
60 O6 Wehe Netherlands 53.22N 6.25E
64 F7 Wehingen W Germany 48.08N 8.49E
60 N12 Wehl Netherlands 51.58N 6.13E
64 D8 Wehr W Germany 47.37N 7.55E
66 H1 Wehra R W Germany
63 K9 Wehrden W Germany 51.42N 9.22E
64 F3 Wehrheim W Germany 50.18N 8.33E
66 O4 Weiber Sattel mt Switzerland 46.54N 9.28E
22 L6 Weichang Hebei China 41.59N 117.30E
64 L6 Weichering W Germany 48.43N 11.20E
65 M6 Weichselboden Austria 47.41N 15.11E
23 G1 Weichuan Henan China 34.19N 114.01E
64 N2 Weida E Germany 50.47N 12.04E
64 N2 Weida R E Germany
64 M4 Weidenberg W Germany 49.56N 11.43E
64 N4 Weiden in der Oberpfalz W Germany 49.40N 12.10E
64 H6 Weidenstetten W Germany 48.33N 10.00E
64 L3 Weidhausen W Germany 50.12N 11.09E
106 K6 Weidman Michigan 43.41N 84.59W
60 L7 Weidum Netherlands 53.09N 5.45E
22 L8 Weifang Shandong China 36.44N 119.10E
21 B9 Weihai Shandong China 37.30N 122.04E
21 D5 Weihe Heilongjiang China 44.56N 128.20E
23 D1 Wei He R Gansu China
23 G1 Wei He R Henan China
64 N6 Weihmichl W Germany 48.35N 12.05E
Wei-hsin see Weixin
64 H5 Weikersheim W Germany 49.29N 9.54E
64 D8 Weil W Germany 47.35N 7.40E
66 G1 Weil W Germany 47.36N 7.39E
64 E3 Weilburg W Germany 50.29N 8.15E
64 F6 Weil-der-Stadt W Germany 48.45N 8.53E
66 Q1 Weiler W Germany 47.36N 9.56E
61 P8 Weiler-la-Tour Luxembourg 49.32N 6.12E
65 A6 Weiler-Simmerberg W Germany 47.35N 9.55E
64 B2 Weilerswist W Germany 50.45N 6.50E
64 H6 Weilheim Baden-Württemberg W Germany 48.37N 9.33E
64 L8 Weilheim Bayern W Ger 47.50N 11.10E
66 J1 Weilheim W Germany 47.39N 8.14E
61 K5 Weillen Belgium 50.16N 4.49E
12 H3 Weilmoringle New S Wales 29.16S 146.55E
64 E3 Weilmünster W Germany 50.26N 8.23E
64 E3 Weilnau W Germany 50.18N 8.26E
64 J5 Weiltingen W Germany 49.02N 10.29E
22 J6 Weilu Shanxi China 40.08N 112.46E
87 J4 Weima watercourse Ethiopia/Djibouti
64 L2 Weimar E Germany 50.59N 11.20E
112 L6 Weimar Texas 29.42N 96.49W
23 E1 Weinan Shaanxi China 34.30N 109.30E
66 S4 Weinberg Switzerland 46.57N 10.30E
64 Q1 Weinböhla E Germany 51.12N 13.35E
107 F6 Weiner Arkansas 35.38N 90.55W
112 H2 Weinert Texas 33.28N 99.43W
66 N1 Weinfelden Switzerland 47.33N 9.07E
64 F5 Weingarten Baden-Württemberg W Ger 49.02N 8.32E
64 H8 Weingarten Baden-Württemberg W Ger 47.49N 9.40E
64 E5 Weingarten Rheinland-Pfalz W Ger 49.15N 8.18E
64 F4 Weinheim W Germany 49.31N 8.41E
66 K2 Weiningen Switzerland 47.25N 8.26E
23 C5 Weining Yizu Huizu Miaozu Zizhixian Guizhou China 26.51N 104.12E
64 G5 Weinsberg W Germany 49.09N 9.18E
65 M5 Weinsberg mt Austria 48.23N 15.03E
64 G6 Weinstadt W Germany 48.45N 9.25E
64 E5 Weinstrasse dist W Germany
13 F2 Weipa Queensland 12.35S 141.56E
110 K3 Weippe Idaho 46.25N 115.56W
56 N4 Weir Essex Eng 51.35N 0.36E
107 G8 Weir Mississippi 33.15N 89.19W
99 Q7 Weir Quebec 45.56N 74.34W
112 K5 Weir Texas 30.43N 97.35W
13 J8 Weir R Queensland
14 B7 Weiragoo Ra W Australia
109 Q4 Weir City Kansas 37.18N 94.45W
100 M5 Weirdale Saskatchewan 53.27N 105.13W
23 D1 Weirong Gansu China 35.22N 105.47E
105 F9 Weirsdale Florida 28.59N 81.57W
104 E6 Weirton W Virginia 40.24N 80.37W
64 N3 Weischlitz E Germany 50.27N 12.03E
58 Q9 Weisdale Voe B Shetland Scotland 60.12N 1.20W
110 J5 Weiser Idaho 44.15N 116.59W
110 J5 Weiser R Idaho
23 B6 Weishan Yunnan China 25.15N 100.20E
23 G1 Weishan Hu L Shandong China
23 G1 Weishi Henan China 34.28N 114.10E
Weishui see Jingxing
64 B4 Weiskirchen W Germany 49.34N 6.49E
64 L3 Weismain W Germany 50.06N 11.15E
64 F6 Weissach W Germany 48.51N 8.54E
66 Q1 Weissach R Austria/W Germany
65 C6 Weissbach W Germany 47.36N 10.34E
66 O2 Weissbad Switzerland 47.18N 9.26E
65 H8 Weissbriach Austria 46.43N 13.15E
65 H7 Weisseck mt Austria 47.10N 13.24E
65 J6 Weissenbach Ober-Österreich Austria 47.48N 13.33E
65 C7 Weissenbach Tirol Austria 47.28N 10.39E
65 H8 Weissenbach R Austria
66 F5 Weissenburg Switzerland 46.40N 7.29E
64 L5 Weissenburg in Bayern W Germany 49.02N 11.00E
64 M1 Weissenfels E Germany 51.12N 11.58E
64 J7 Weissenhorn W Germany 48.18N 10.10E
65 M5 Weissenkirchen Austria 48.25N 15.29E
64 L1 Weissensee Erfurt E Germany 51.12N 11.05E
65 H8 Weissensee L Austria
64 M3 Weissenstadt W Germany 50.06N 11.53E
64 H6 Weissenstein W Germany 48.42N 9.54E
66 N5 Weissenstein mt Graubünden Switz 46.38N 9.14E
66 G3 Weissenstein mt Solothurn Switz 47.15N 7.31E
69 N3 Weissenthurm W Germany 50.25N 7.27E
64 M3 Weisser Main R W Germany
64 O5 Weisser Regen R W Germany
66 Q4 Weissfluh mt Switzerland 46.51N 9.48E
66 G7 Weisshorn mt Switzerland 46.07N 7.43E
66 P4 Weiss Horn mt Switzerland 46.46N 9.37E
66 Q4 Weiss Horn mt Switzerland 46.46N 9.58E
65 L7 Weisskirchen Austria 47.09N 14.44E
66 M2 Weisslingen Switzerland 47.26N 8.46E
66 J7 Weissmies Switzerland 46.08N 8.01E
94 E5 Weissrand Mts Namibia
107 L7 Weiss Res Alabama
66 O3 Weisstannen Switzerland 47.00N 9.21E
66 O4 Weisstannen-Tal V Switzerland
61 P6 Weiswampach Luxembourg 50.08N 6.05E
66 O3 Weite Switzerland 47.06N 9.30E
69 O2 Weitefeld W Germany 50.44N 7.55E
63 S4 Weitenhagen E Germany 54.03N 13.25E
65 K8 Weitensfeld Austria 46.52N 14.13E
65 N4 Weitersfeld Austria 48.48N 15.49E
65 L5 Weitersfelden Austria 48.29N 14.45E
64 J8 Weitnau W Germany 47.39N 10.10E
23 H6 Weitou Fujian China 24.33N 118.32E
65 L4 Weitra Austria 48.43N 14.55E
110 B8 Weitschpec California 41.11N 123.43W
101 U7 Weitzel L Saskatchewan 57.44N 106.42W
95 L2 Weiveld S Africa 26.58S 27.37E
65 N8 Weixelbaum Austria 46.45N 15.53E
23 B5 Weixi Yunnan China 27.12N 99.16E
22 K8 Wei Xian Hebei China 36.59N 115.15E
22 L8 Wei Xian Shandong China 36.46N 119.14E
23 C5 Weixin Yunnan China 27.55N 104.51E
24 H5 Weiya Xinjiang Uygur Zizhiqu China 41.46N 94.30E
23 C1 Weiyuan Gansu China 35.06N 104.20E
23 C4 Weiyuan Sichuan China 29.35N 104.40E
23 B7 Weiyuan Jiang R Yunnan China
65 N7 Weiz Austria 47.13N 15.38E
65 K8 Weizelsdorf Austria 46.33N 14.13E
64 E8 Weizen W Germany 47.46N 8.28E
Weizhou see Wenchuan
23 E8 Weizhou Dao isld Guangdong China 21.03N 109.08E
Wejh see Wajh, Al
62 L1 Wejherowo Poland 54.36N 18.12E
100 S4 Wekusko Manitoba 54.31N 99.45W
100 S4 Wekusko L Manitoba
105 F8 Welaka Florida 29.29N 81.41W
25 N8 Welatam Burma 26.35N 98.24E
57 L6 Welbeck Abbey Notts Eng 53.16N 1.09W
12 C2 Welbourn Hill S Australia 27.24S 134.05E
112 E3 Welch Texas 32.56N 102.07W
104 D9 Welch W Virginia 37.26N 81.36W
108 Q6 Welcome Minnesota 43.40N 94.39W
13 G3 Welcome Queensland 15.20S 144.40E
94 E8 Welcome Kop mt S Africa 30.27S 18.10E
123 J5 Welcome Mt Antarctica 72.00S 160.02E
61 E3 Welden Belgium 50.53N 3.40E
64 K6 Welden W Germany 48.27N 10.40E
14 D8 Weld, Mt W Australia 28.48S 122.30E
111 F6 Weldon California 35.40N 118.20W
106 F9 Weldon Illinois 40.07N 88.46W
108 R9 Weldon Iowa 40.55N 93.42W
105 K1 Weldon N Carolina 36.28N 77.40W
100 M6 Weldon Saskatchewan 53.00N 105.30W
112 M4 Weldon Texas 31.02N 95.36W
107 C1 Weldon R Missouri
109 G1 Weldona Colorado 40.21N 103.57W
14 B7 Weld Ra W Australia
14 D6 Weld Spring W Australia 24.57S 121.44E
109 O6 Weleetka Oklahoma 35.21N 96.08W
87 E6 Welega prov Ethiopia
18 J9 Weleri Java Indon 7.00S 110.02E
56 J5 Welford Berks Eng 51.28N 1.25W
56 J3 Welford Northants Eng 52.25N 1.03W
13 G7 Welford Downs Queensland 25.10S 143.18E
93 M4 Wel Garas Kenya 1.37N 40.59E
94 U13 Welgedag S Africa 26.12S 28.29E
95 K4 Welgelee S Africa 28.13S 26.50E
26 R10 Weligama Sri Lanka 5.59N 80.26E
26 T9 Weligatta Sri Lanka 6.12N 81.10E
26 T6 Welikanda Sri Lanka 7.56N 81.15E
26 S8 Welimada Sri Lanka 6.54N 80.55E
26 T9 Weliwewa Sri Lanka 6.20N 81.01E
61 O4 Welkenraedt Belgium 50.39N 5.58E
95 K3 Welkom S Africa 27.59S 26.44E
60 N13 Well Netherlands 51.33N 6.05E
57 K4 Well N Yorks Eng 54.14N 1.36W
99 L10 Welland Ontario 45.59N 79.14W
99 L10 Welland Can Ontario
56 K2 Welland, R Northants etc Eng
14 A4 Wellard dist Perth, W Aust
26 R6 Wellawa Sri Lanka 7.34N 80.22E
26 T8 Wellawaya Sri Lanka 6.44N 81.07E
105 E7 Wellborn Florida 30.13N 82.50W
61 G3 Welle Belgium 50.54N 4.03E
63 L6 Welle W Germany 53.14N 9.47E
Welle I see Sanaroa I
61 M3 Wellen Belgium 50.50N 5.21E
61 Q8 Wellenstein Luxembourg 49.31N 6.21E
60 N13 Wellerlooi Netherlands 51.33N 6.07E
64 H1 Wellerode Wald W Germany 51.15N 9.35E
56 H3 Wellesbourne Hastings Warwicks Eng 52.12N 1.35W
122 U2 Welles Harbor Midway Is Pacific Oc 28.12N 177.24W
103 M2 Wellesley Massachusetts 42.18N 71.18W
92 E10 Wellesley Zimbabwe 17.40S 30.40E
13 E3 Wellesley Is Queensland
13 E3 Wellesley Is.,S Queensland
101 D4 Wellesley L Yukon Terr 62.18N 139.50W
103 O3 Wellfleet Massachusetts 41.56N 70.01W
108 K9 Wellfleet Nebraska 40.46N 100.44W
103 O3 Wellfleet Harbor Massachusetts
64 L6 Wellheim W Germany 48.49N 11.06E
61 L6 Wellin Belgium 50.05N 5.07E
56 K3 Wellingborough Northants Eng 52.19N 0.42W
57 M6 Wellingore Lincs Eng 53.06N 0.32W
107 L8 Wellington Alabama 33.49N 85.55W
109 E1 Wellington Colorado 40.42N 105.01W
106 G9 Wellington Illinois 40.33N 87.41W
109 N4 Wellington Kansas 37.17N 97.25W
111 E3 Wellington Nevada 38.45N 119.23W
98 S5 Wellington Newfoundland 48.54N 54.00W
12 J5 Wellington New S Wales 32.33S 148.59E
11 J8 Wellington New Zealand 41.17S 174.47E
98 J9 Wellington Nova Scotia 44.51N 63.35W
104 C5 Wellington Ohio 41.11N 82.13W
99 N9 Wellington Ontario 43.59N 77.21W
98 H7 Wellington Prince Edward I 46.28N 64.00W
95 C9 Wellington S Africa 33.39S 19.00E
12 E6 Wellington S Australia 35.21S 139.23E
56 F2 Wellington Shropshire Eng 52.43N 2.31W
56 E6 Wellington Somerset Eng 50.59N 3.15W
112 G1 Wellington Texas 34.52N 100.13W
111 O2 Wellington Utah 39.33N 110.45W
11 K6 Wellington stat area New Zealand
101 U1 Wellington B N W Terr
99 N9 Wellington B Ontario
97 K2 Wellington Chan N W Terr
121 J7 Wellington, I Chile
11 C6 Wellington International Airport New Zealand 41.20S 174.49E
12 H7 Wellington, L Victoria
12 F8 Wellington, Mt Tasmania 42.55S 147.14E
14 D7 Wellington Ra W Australia
112 E2 Wellman Texas 33.03N 102.25W
109 N2 Wells Kansas 39.10N 97.34W
104 P3 Wells Maine 43.20N 70.35W
108 R6 Wells Minnesota 43.44N 93.48W
110 L8 Wells Nevada 41.08N 114.58W
104 L3 Wells New York 43.24N 74.17W
56 N2 Wells Norfolk Eng 52.58N 0.51E
56 F5 Wells Somerset Eng 51.13N 2.39W
112 N4 Wells Texas 31.29N 94.58W
104 H5 Wellsboro Pennsylvania 41.45N 77.18W
103 D2 Wells Bridge New York 42.22N 75.14W
108 S7 Wellsburg Iowa 42.28N 92.52W
103 A2 Wellsburg New York 42.02N 76.45W
104 E6 Wellsburg W Virginia 40.15N 80.37W
11 J3 Wellsford New Zealand 36.16S 174.32E
101 N9 Wells Gray Provincial Park Br Col
13 G6 Wellshot Queensland 23.48S 144.30E
100 R1 Wells L Manitoba
14 E7 Wells, L W Australia
14 F3 Wells, Mt W Australia 17.30S 127.05E
14 D6 Wells Ra W Australia
104 N2 Wells River Vermont 44.09N 72.06W
104 C7 Wellston Ohio 39.06N 82.33W
107 E2 Wellsville Missouri 39.04N 91.33W
104 H4 Wellsville New York 42.07N 77.56W
110 O8 Wellsville Utah 41.39N 111.56W
111 K9 Wellton Arizona 32.39N 114.09W
100 S8 Wellwood Manitoba 50.02N 99.20W
87 H8 Welmal,R Ethiopia
87 M6 Welo Somalia 9.25N 48.55E
87 G5 Welo prov Ethiopia
114 C7 Weloka Hawaiian Is 19.57N 155.13W
65 K5 Wels Austria 48.10N 14.02E
64 B4 Welschbillig W Germany 49.51N 6.35E
69 O1 Welschen-Enest W Germany 51.02N 8.00E
66 G2 Welschenrohr Switzerland 47.16N 7.32E
63 U6 Welse R E Germany
98 F8 Welsford New Brunswick 45.28N 66.21W
107 D11 Welsh Louisiana 30.12N 92.50W
56 F2 Welshampton Shropshire Eng 52.55N 2.51W
98 F9 Welshpool New Brunswick 44.53N 66.58W
56 E2 Welshpool Powys Wales 52.40N 3.09W
14 B2 Welshpool dist Perth, W Aust
87 F6 Welso Ethiopia 8.33N 38.00E
57 G3 Welton Cumbria Eng 54.47N 3.00W
63 G9 Welver W Germany 51.37N 7.57E
95 L2 Welverdiend S Africa 26.23S 27.17E
56 L4 Welwyn Herts Eng 51.50N 0.13W
100 Q8 Welwyn Saskatchewan 50.20N 101.35W
56 L4 Welwyn Garden City Herts Eng 51.48N 0.13W
64 H6 Welzheim W Germany 48.53N 9.38E
56 F2 Wem Shropshire Eng 52.51N 2.44W
91 G4 Wema Zaïre 0.32S 21.50E
93 F10 Wembere R Tanzania
101 O8 Wembley Alberta 55.09N 119.09W
55 D3 Wembley London England 51.33N 0.18W
14 A1 Wembley dist Perth, W Aust
14 A1 Wembley Downs dist Perth, W Aust
91 J6 Wembo Nyama Zaïre 4.14S 24.27E
56 C7 Wembury Devon Eng 50.19N 4.05W
64 K6 Wemding W Germany 48.53N 10.45E
60 C2 Wemeldinge Netherlands 51.31N 4.00E
61 H3 Wemmel Belgium 50.54N 4.18E
58 G7 Wemyss Bay Strathclyde Scotland 55.52N 4.53W
116 F2 Wemyss Bight Eleuthera I Bahamas 24.49N 76.14W
119 H4 Wenamu R Guyana
22 K7 Wen'an Hebei China 38.52N 116.29E
110 E2 Wenatchee Washington 47.26N 120.20W
110 E2 Wenatchee R Washington
110 E2 Wenatchee L Washington 47.50N 120.48W
110 D2 Wenatchee Mts Washington
23 E9 Wenchang Guangdong China 19.41N 110.46E
23 J5 Wencheng Zhejiang China 27.44N 120.10E
89 H8 Wenchi Ghana 7.45N 2.02W
23 C3 Wenchuan Sichuan China 31.20N 103.48E
110 E9 Wendel California 40.22N 120.14W
110 L7 Wendell Idaho 42.47N 114.42W
108 O3 Wendell Minnesota 46.01N 96.05W
105 J2 Wendell N Carolina 35.47N 78.24W
64 D4 Wendelsheim W Germany 49.46N 8.00E
64 L5 Wendelstein W Germany 49.21N 11.10E
64 N8 Wendel Stein mt W Germany 47.42N 12.01E
111 L8 Wenden Arizona 33.52N 113.30W
64 D2 Wenden W Germany 50.57N 7.55E
69 O2 Wenden W Germany 50.49N 7.52E
21 B9 Wendeng Shandong China 37.10N 122.00E
56 M3 Wendens Ambo Essex Eng 52.00N 0.12E
15 C5 Wendesi Irian Jaya 2.33S 134.17E
63 Q6 Wendisch Priborn E Germany 53.21N 12.16E
63 O7 Wendland reg W Germany
56 J4 Wendlebury Oxon Eng 51.53N 1.10W
56 N2 Wendling Norfolk Eng 52.41N 0.51E
110 C5 Wendling Oregon 44.12N 122.48W
87 G7 Wendo Ethiopia 6.39N 38.21E
63 O5 Wendorf E Germany 53.55N 11.26E
56 K4 Wendover Bucks Eng 51.46N 0.46W
110 L9 Wendover Utah 40.45N 114.02W
108 F7 Wendover Wyoming 42.20N 104.54W
108 K5 Wendte S Dakota 44.15N 100.40W
61 C1 Wenduine Belgium 51.18N 3.05E
99 G5 Wenebegon L Ontario
23 C1 Wenfengzhen Gansu China 34.55N 104.38E
65 L6 Weng Austria 47.37N 14.31E
91 F3 Wenga Zaïre 1.03N 19.21E
23 D5 Weng'an Guizhou China 27.01N 107.28E
91 H3 Wenge Zaïre 0.03N 23.59E
66 H5 Wengen Switzerland 46.37N 7.56E
64 J8 Wengen W Germany 47.41N 10.09E
66 H5 Wengern Alp mt Switzerland 46.34N 7.58E
64 B4 Wengerohr W Germany 49.58N 6.56E
66 F3 Wengi Switzerland 47.05N 7.25E
23 F4 Wengjiang Hunan China 28.44N 113.26E
23 B4 Wengshui Yunnan China 28.30N 99.50E
23 G6 Wengyuan Guangdong China 24.22N 114.08E
23 H1 Wen He R Shandong China
64 H2 Wenigentaft E Germany 50.47N 9.57E
64 G3 Wenings W Germany 50.22N 9.11E
87 G6 Wenji Ethiopia 8.30N 39.30E
23 C3 Wenjiang Sichuan China 30.45N 103.40E
23 J4 Wenling Zhejiang China 28.23N 121.22E
13 G2 Wenlock Queensland 13.05S 142.57E
13 F1 Wenlock R Queensland
56 F2 Wenlock Edge limestone ridge Shropshire Eng
119 A4 Wenman, I Galápagos Is 1.23N 91.49W
63 L8 Wennigsen W Germany 52.17N 9.34E
55 K3 Wennington London Eng 51.30N 0.13E
65 C7 Wenns Austria 47.09N 10.44E
106 E8 Wenona Illinois 41.04N 89.03W
103 D7 Wenonah New Jersey 39.47N 75.09W
Wenpingzhen see Ludian
24 G9 Wenquan Qinghai China 33.28N 91.40E
23 E3 Wenquan Sichuan China 31.20N 108.30E
24 C3 Wenquan Xinjiang Uygur Zizhiqu China 44.59N 81.04E
23 C7 Wenshan Yunnan China 23.25N 104.15E
23 G1 Wenshang Shandong China 35.47N 116.31E
23 D4 Wenshui Guizhou China 28.25N 106.35E
22 J8 Wenshui Shanxi China 37.26N 112.03E
57 K4 Wensley N Yorks Eng 54.18N 1.52W
12 G7 Wensleydale Victoria 38.24S 144.01E
57 K4 Wensleydale V N Yorks Eng
24 C5 Wensu Xinjiang Uygur Zizhiqu China 41.15N 80.11E
56 O2 Wensum, R Norfolk Eng
57 L5 Wentbridge W Yorks Eng 53.39N 1.15W
104 O3 Wentworth New Hampshire 43.52N 71.54W
12 F5 Wentworth New S Wales 34.06S 141.55E
108 O6 Wentworth S Dakota 43.59N 96.58W
98 J8 Wentworth Centre Nova Scotia 45.39N 63.35W
107 F3 Wentzville Missouri 38.49N 90.50W
15 B5 Wenut Irian Jaya 3.15S 133.21E
56 E5 Wenvoe S Glam Wales 51.27N 3.16W
23 F1 Wenxi Shanxi China 35.24N 111.05E
23 C2 Wen Xian Gansu China 32.55N 104.40E
23 F1 Wen Xian Henan China 34.56N 113.05E
64 N5 Wenzenbach W Germany 49.06N 12.14E
23 J4 Wenzhou Zhejiang China 28.02N 120.40E
105 F10 Weohyakapka L Florida 27.49N 81.24W
110 B9 Weott California 40.19N 123.54W
95 L5 Wepener S Africa 29.44S 27.03E
61 K5 Wépion Belgium 50.26N 4.52E
30 A5 Wer Rajasthan India 27.00N 77.11E
93 E4 Wera Uganda 1.52N 33.46E
26 S7 Weragamtota Sri Lanka 7.20N 80.59E
26 U8 Weragoda Sri Lanka 7.02N 81.36E
31 F3 Weran Pass Afghanistan 35.33N 70.31E
63 T7 Werbellin E Germany 52.54N 13.43E
63 T7 Werbellinsee L E Germany
63 P7 Werben (Elbe) E Germany 52.52N 11.58E
63 S9 Werbig E Germany 51.56N 13.12E
61 N5 Werbomont Belgium 50.23N 5.41E
61 J3 Werchter Belgium 50.58N 4.42E
94 G5 Werda Botswana 25.17S 23.18E
95 K2 Werda S Africa 26.45S 26.15E
64 N2 Werdau E Germany 50.44N 12.23E
66 O3 Werdenberg Switzerland 47.11N 9.28E
63 R8 Werder (Havel) E Germany 52.23N 12.56E
64 D1 Werdohl W Germany 51.15N 7.48E
65 H7 Werfen Austria 47.29N 13.12E
15 B5 Weri Irian Jaya 3.14S 132.39E
87 G4 Weri watercourse Ethiopia
61 N5 Weris Belgium 50.20N 5.32E
Werken see Zarren-Werken
60 H12 Werkendam Netherlands 51.48N 4.54E
60 K11 Werkhoven Netherlands 52.01N 5.15E
63 G9 Werl W Germany 51.33N 7.53E
63 G7 Werlte W Germany 52.52N 7.42E
61 M3 Werm Belgium 50.50N 5.28E
64 C1 Wermelskirchen W Germany 51.08N 7.14E
64 O1 Wermsdorf E Germany 51.17N 12.57E
64 H4 Wern R W Germany
64 N4 Wernberg W Germany 49.32N 12.10E
63 G9 Werne an der Lippe W Germany 51.39N 7.38E
64 J4 Werneck W Germany 49.59N 10.06E
101 F3 Wernecke Mts Yukon Terr
108 H2 Werner N Dakota 47.22N 102.26W
103 B6 Wernersville Pennsylvania 40.19N 76.06W
63 T7 Werneuchen E Germany 52.38N 13.44E
64 H3 Wernfeld W Germany 50.01N 9.44E
100 U2 Wernham L Manitoba
60 G14 Wernhout Netherlands 51.27N 4.39E
63 N9 Wernigerode E Germany 51.51N 10.48E
65 H4 Wernstein Austria 48.31N 13.28E
64 J1 Werra R E Ger/W Ger
63 J8 Werre R W Germany
12 G7 Werribee Victoria 37.55S 144.44E
12 F5 Werrimull Victoria 34.24S 141.39E
12 K4 Werris Creek New S Wales 31.20S 150.41E
63 G9 Werse R W Germany
64 J8 Wertach W Germany 47.37N 10.25E
64 K7 Wertach R W Germany
63 E9 Werth W Germany 51.48N 6.30E
64 H4 Wertheim W Germany 49.45N 9.32E
66 J3 Werthenstein Switzerland 47.04N 8.07E
63 H8 Werther W Germany 52.05N 8.25E
64 K6 Wertingen W Germany 48.33N 10.41E
60 J9 Wervershoof Netherlands 52.44N 5.09E
61 C3 Wervik Belgium 50.47N 3.03E
19 F8 Werwaru Moluccas Indon 8.15S 128.09E
103 C5 Wescosville Pennsylvania 40.34N 75.33W
63 E9 Wesel W Germany 51.39N 6.37E
64 D5 Weselberg W Germany 49.21N 7.36E
63 R6 Wesenberg E Germany 53.17N 12.58E
65 J5 Wesenufer Austria 48.28N 13.50E
63 H5 Weser estuary W Germany
63 J6 Weser R W Germany
63 J8 Wesergebirge hills W Germany
19 E7 Wesiri Indon 7.36S 126.38E
109 J3 Weskan Kansas 38.54N 101.57W
87 E8 Weska Weka Ethiopia 5.51N 35.37E
112 K9 Weslaco Texas 26.10N 97.59W
99 N8 Weslemkoon, L Ontario
108 R6 Wesley Iowa 43.06N 93.59W
104 S2 Wesley Maine 44.57N 67.40W
98 T4 Wesleyville Newfoundland 49.08N 53.36W
104 E4 Wesleyville Pennsylvania 42.08N 80.01W
61 J3 Wespelaar Belgium 50.58N 4.38E
63 J4 Wesselburen W Germany 54.13N 8.56E
13 D1 Wessel C N Terr Australia 11.03S 136.45E
64 B2 Wesseling W Germany 50.50N 6.58E
13 D1 Wessel Is N Terr Australia
95 K3 Wessels S Africa 27.48S 26.41E
95 K3 Wesselsbron S Africa 27.51S 26.21E
95 O4 Wesselsnek S Africa 28.22S 30.05E
60 T16 Wessem Netherlands 51.09N 5.53E
60 M15 Wessem-Nederweert Kanaal canal Netherlands
108 M5 Wessington S Dakota 44.28N 98.42W
108 M5 Wessington Springs S Dakota 44.06N 98.35W
64 L8 Wessobrunn W Germany 47.53N 11.01E
107 D8 Wesson Arkansas 33.07N 92.49W
107 F10 Wesson Mississippi 31.42N 90.26W
107 G8 West Mississippi 33.12N 89.47W
112 K4 West Texas 31.47N 97.08W
92 D12 Westacre Zimbabwe 0.21S 28.25E
104 A7 West Alexandria Ohio 39.44N 84.33W
13 B1 West Alligator R N Terr Australia
106 G6 West Allis Wisconsin 43.01N 88.00W
12 C5 Westall, Pt S Australia 32.52S 134.05E
13 K6 West Arm Pt Queensland 23.30S 150.40E
103 G2 West Athens New York 42.18N 73.50W
103 B3 West Auburn Pennsylvania 41.43N 76.07W
57 K3 West Auckland Durham Eng 54.38N 1.43W
26 J6 West Australian Basin Indian Oc
26 H8 West Australian Ridge Indian Oc
57 N4 West Ayton N Yorks Eng 54.14N 0.29W
105 B7 West B Florida
13 A3 West Baines R N Terr Australia
104 P3 West Baldwin Maine 43.51N 70.47W
29 C5 West Banas R Gujarat/Rajasthan India
103 O3 West Barnstable Massachusetts 41.43N 70.22W
56 F6 West Bay Dorset Eng 50.43N 2.46W
105 B7 Westbay Florida 30.17N 85.53W
116 D5 West Bay Grand Cayman I W I 19.25N 81.21W
26 A16 West Bay Heard I Antarctica
107 G12 West Bay Louisiana 29.04N 89.20W
112 M6 West Bay Texas
12 A8 West Beach S Australia 34.58S 138.31E
60 H9 West Beemster Netherlands 52.34N 4.53E
108 Q7 West Bend Iowa 42.58N 94.25W
100 O7 West Bend Saskatchewan 51.28N 103.41W
106 F6 West Bend Wisconsin 43.26N 88.13W
29 K6 West Bengal state India
West Berlin see Berlin
63 G8 West-Bevern W Germany 52.02N 7.48E
107 J8 West Blocton Alabama 33.07N 87.08W
103 L2 Westboro Massachusetts 42.17N 71.37W
107 A1 Westboro Missouri 40.33N 95.20W
99 C9 Westboro Ontario 45.24N 75.46W
106 D4 Westboro Wisconsin 45.22N 90.17W
100 T8 Westbourne Manitoba 50.08N 98.33W
103 L2 West Boylston Massachusetts 42.22N 71.47W
106 C8 West Branch Iowa 41.40N 91.21W
106 K5 West Branch Michigan 44.16N 84.14W
103 H2 West Branch Res Connecticut
103 G4 West Branch Res New York 41.25N 73.42W
57 K5 West Bretton W Yorks Eng 53.38N 1.34W
101 O11 Westbridge Br Columbia 49.11N 119.00W
103 M2 West Bridgewater Massachusetts 42.02N 71.02W
57 L7 West Bridgford Notts Eng 52.56N 1.08W
60 J11 Westbroek Netherlands 52.09N 5.08E
56 H2 West Bromwich W Midlands Eng 52.31N 1.59W
103 K4 Westbrook Connecticut 41.17N 72.27W
104 P3 Westbrook Maine 43.41N 70.22W
108 P5 Westbrook Minnesota 44.03N 95.23W
112 F3 Westbrook Texas 32.22N 101.02W
103 K2 West Brookfield Massachusetts 42.14N 72.09W
103 E3 Westbrookville New York 41.31N 74.33W
104 O2 West Burke Vermont 44.38N 71.59W
103 A3 West Burlington Pennsylvania 41.46N 76.41W
58 Q9 West Burra isld Shetland Scotland 60.05N 1.21W
57 K4 West Burton N Yorks Eng 54.16N 1.58W
56 G4 Westbury Glos Eng 51.50N 2.24W
103 G5 Westbury Long I, N Y 40.46N 73.34W
56 F2 Westbury Shropshire Eng 52.41N 2.57W
12 H8 Westbury Tasmania 41.30S 146.47E
56 G5 Westbury Wilts Eng 51.16N 2.11W
110 O1 West Butte mt Montana 48.58N 111.31W
110 R1 West Butte mt Montana 48.54N 108.58W
108 F1 Westby N Dakota 48.53N 104.02W
12 H6 Westby New S Wales 35.29S 147.27E
106 D6 Westby Wisconsin 43.38N 90.53W
26 A16 West C Heard I Antarctica 53.02S 73.17E
11 A12 West C New Zealand 45.55S 166.25E
113 A5 West C St Lawrence I Bering Sea 63.22N 171.50W
58 J7 West Calder Lothian Scotland 55.51N 3.35W
103 G2 West Camp New York 42.08N 73.55W
14 C11 West Cape Howe W Australia 35.06S 117.31E
104 A7 West Carrollton Ohio 39.40N 84.14W
30 H2 West Changri Glacier Nepal
101 F1 West Channel N W Terr
111 C9 Westchester California 33.58N 118.24W
103 K3 Westchester Connecticut 41.33N 72.24W
103 C7 West Chester Pennsylvania 39.58N 75.37W
103 G4 Westchester co New York
106 F8 West Chicago Illinois 41.54N 88.13W
112 L9 Westcliff Texas 32.42N 97.23W
109 E3 Westcliffe Colorado 38.08N 105.28W
56 F6 West Coker Somerset Eng 50.56N 2.43W
30 K3 West Col pass Nepal 27.52N 86.59E
103 D3 Westcolang Pennsylvania 41.30N 75.00W
112 M6 West Columbia Texas 29.09N 95.41W
108 S5 West Concord Minnesota 44.08N 92.54W
103 D6 West Conshohocken Pennsylvania 40.04N 75.18W
103 G2 West Copake New York 42.05N 73.35W
28 G6 West Coral Bank Andaman Is
103 H3 West Cornwall Connecticut 41.52N 73.22W
111 G7 West Covina California 34.04N 117.56W
103 G2 West Coxsackie New York 42.21N 73.49W
103 F7 West Creek New Jersey 39.38N 74.18W
103 A2 West Danby New York 42.19N 76.35W
106 F5 West De Pere Wisconsin 44.26N 88.05W
108 R8 West Des Moines Iowa 41.34N 93.42W
29 L5 West Dinajpur dist W Bengal India
60 C4 Westdorpe Netherlands 51.14N 3.50E
98 J9 West Dover Nova Scotia 44.28N 63.45W
55 B3 West Drayton London Eng 51.30N 0.28W
99 G7 West Duck I Ontario 45.45N 83.00W
60 G10 Westeinder Plassen L Netherlands
105 J11 West End Bahamas 26.41N 79.00W
111 G6 Westend California 35.41N 117.25W
105 H2 West End N Carolina 35.14N 79.34W
13 K2 West End dist Brisbane, Qnsld
63 A1 Westend dist W Berlin W Germany
61 B2 Westende Belgium 51.10N 2.46E
60 N9 Westenhotte Netherlands 52.32N 6.03E
60 B2 Westenschouwen Netherlands 51.40N 3.43E
63 L4 Westensee L W Germany
60 P8 Westerbork Netherlands 52.50N 6.36E
64 D2 Westerburg W Germany 50.34N 7.59E
11 F10 Westerfield New Zealand 43.50S 171.38E
56 M5 Westerham Kent Eng 51.16N 0.05E
100 H8 Westerham Saskatchewan 50.57N 109.40W
60 K14 Westerhoven Netherlands 51.20N 5.24E
63 G8 Westerkappeln W Germany 52.19N 7.54E
57 G2 Westerkirk Dumfries & Galloway Scotland 55.11N 3.03W
60 H8 Westerland Netherlands 52.54N 4.55E
63 H3 Westerland W Germany 54.54N 8.19E
60 Q7 Westerlee Netherlands 53.08N 6.59E
61 K2 Westerlo Belgium 51.05N 4.55E
103 F1 Westerlo New York 42.32N 74.03W
103 L4 Westerly Rhode I 41.22N 71.50W
60 M8 Westermeer Netherlands 52.58N 5.48E
108 N9 Western Nebraska 40.24N 97.12W
93 B5 Western dist Uganda
93 F5 Western prov Kenya
26 Q8 Western prov Sri Lanka
92 A9 Western prov Zambia
89 H9 Western reg Ghana
90 A8 Western state Nigeria
89 C7 Western Area prov Sierra Leone
10 D6 Western Australia state Australia
11 A9 Western Chain islds Snares Is Pacific Oc
13 C3 Western Cr N Terr Australia
30 J2 Western Cwm cirque Nepal
87 A8 Western Equatoria prov Sudan
27 L6 Western Ghats mts India
11 J12 Western Group islds Bounty Is Pacific Oc
98 H10 Western Head Nova Scotia 44.00N 64.40W
15 H5 Western I Admiralty Is 2.13S 146.00E
99 K7 Western Is Ontario
58 B3 Western Isles reg Scotland
104 F7 Westernport Maryland 39.29N 79.03W
12 H7 Western Port B Victoria
101 U2 Western R N W Terr
13 G5 Western R Queensland
11 J11 Western Reef islds Chatham Is Pacific Oc 43.52S 176.58W
56 Q8 Western Rocks Is of Scilly Eng 49.52N 6.24W
88 F10 Western Sahara reg N Africa
122 A2 Western Samoa islds Pacific Oc
63 M9 Westerode W Germany 51.32N 10.13E
60 C3 Westerschelde channel Netherlands
63 G6 Westerstede W Germany 53.15N 7.56E
60 M12 Westervoort Netherlands 51.58N 5.58E
64 D2 Westerwald reg W Germany
60 R7 Westerwoldsche A R Netherlands
109 M3 Westfall Kansas 38.57N 98.02W
110 H6 Westfall Oregon 43.59N 117.43W
103 N3 West Falmouth Massachusetts 41.36N 70.38W
56 F2 West Felton Shropshire Eng 52.49N 2.58W
56 N6 Westfield E Sussex Eng 50.55N 0.35E
107 J2 Westfield Illinois 39.28N 88.00W
103 J2 Westfield Massachusetts 42.07N 72.45W
103 F5 Westfield New Jersey 40.39N 74.21W
104 F4 Westfield New York 42.20N 79.34W
11 D3 Westfield New Zealand 36.55S 174.51E
104 H5 Westfield Pennsylvania 41.56N 77.33W
106 E6 Westfield Wisconsin 43.54N 89.31W
14 B3 Westfield dist Perth, W Aust
103 J2 Westfield R Massachusetts

98 F8 Westfield Beach New Brunswick 45.22N 66.17W
103 K3 Westford Connecticut 41.55N 72.11W
103 B6 West Fork Arkansas 35.55N 94.11W
94 P12 Westfort Cape Town S Africa 34.03S 18.21E
107 H4 West Frankfort Illinois 37.55N 88.57W
60 B2 Westgat channel Netherlands
60 G8 Westgat channel Netherlands
57 J3 Westgate Durham Eng 54.45N 2.08W
13 H7 Westgate Queensland 26.33S 146.10E
56 O5 Westgate-on-Sea Kent Eng 51.23N 1.21E
110 M1 West Glacier Montana 48.30N 113.59W
56 D4 West Glamorgan co Wales
58 L7 West Gordon Borders Scotland 55.41N 2.34W
103 J2 West Granville Massachusetts 42.05N 72.56W
105 E6 West Green Georgia 31.38N 82.44W
103 L3 West Greenwich Center Rhode I 41.39N 71.45W
103 C7 West Grove Pennsylvania 39.50N 75.50W
13 J7 Westgrove Queensland 25.36S 148.26E
56 J3 West Haddon Northants Eng 52.20N 1.04W
55 H3 West Ham London Eng 51.32N 0.01E
101 G12 Westham I Br Columbia 49.06N 123.12W
104 C8 West Hamlin W Virginia 38.17N 82.12W
103 J5 Westhampton Long I, N Y 40.49N 72.39W
11 M12 West Harbour bor Dunedin New Zealand
103 J2 West Hartford Connecticut 41.46N 72.45W
103 J2 West Hartland Connecticut 42.00N 72.58W
103 J4 West Haven Connecticut 41.16N 72.56W
103 G4 West Haverstraw New York 41.14N 73.59W
103 D4 West Hawley Pennsylvania 41.29N 75.12W
64 K4 Westheim Bayern W Germany 49.59N 10.31E
64 K7 Westheim Bayern W Germany 48.22N 10.49E
63 J10 Westheim Nordrhein-Westfalen W Ger 51.29N 8.54E
107 F7 West Helena Arkansas 34.32N 90.40W
57 M4 West Heslerton N Yorks Eng 54.10N 0.37W
12 F8 West Hobart dist Hobart, Tasmania
64 E4 West-Hofen W Germany 49.55N 8.25E
69 P4 Westhofen W Germany 49.24N 8.15E
112 K6 Westhoff Texas 29.11N 97.30W
69 N6 Westhoffen France 48.36N 7.26E
110 B1 Westholme Vancouver I, Br Col 48.52N 123.43W
108 J1 Westhope N Dakota 48.56N 101.02W
110 G9 West Humboldt Ra Nevada
103 F3 West Hurley New York 41.59N 74.06W
95 J3 Westhuyzen S Africa 27.31S 25.28E
28 G6 West I Andaman Is 13.35N 92.51E
26 V2 West I Cocos Is Ind Oc 12.10S 96.49E
13 D3 West I N Terr Australia
123 C3 West Ice Shelf Antarctica
63 G10 Westig W Germany 51.22N 7.45E
60 G12 Westkapelle Netherlands 51.53N 4.31E
102 M6 West Indies arch Caribbean Sea
West Irian Indonesia see Irian Jaya
105 F1 West Jefferson N Carolina 36.25N 81.29W
104 B7 West Jefferson Ohio 39.56N 83.17W
61 D1 Westkapelle Belgium 51.19N 3.18E
60 A2 Westkapelle Netherlands 51.32N 3.27E
61 C2 Westkerke Belgium 51.10N 3.01E
58 G7 West Kilbride Strathclyde Scotland 55.42N 4.51W
103 F2 West Kill New York 42.13N 74.25W
103 L4 West Kingston Rhode I 41.30N 71.32W
57 G6 West Kirby Merseyside Eng 53.22N 3.10W
110 F8 West L Nevada 41.36N 119.39W
104 B6 West Lafayette Indiana 40.26N 86.56W
104 D6 West Lafayette Ohio 40.17N 81.46W
122 U7 West Lagoon Palmyra I Pacific Oc
110 A6 Westlake Oregon 43.53N 124.08W
99 G4 West Lake reg Tanzania
23 A10 West Lamma Channel Hong Kong
13 G6 Westland Queensland 23.59S 143.49E
11 D10 Westland stat area New Zealand
11 D10 Westland Nat. Park New Zealand
103 D1 West Laurens New York 42.32N 75.20W
56 H5 West Lavington Wilts Eng 51.17N 2.00W
13 E5 West Leichhardt Queensland 20.35S 139.40E
95 L3 Westleigh S Africa 27.35S 27.19E
56 P3 Westleton Suffolk Eng 52.16N 1.35E
104 K3 West Leyden New York 43.27N 75.28W
30 J2 West Lhotse Glacier Nepal
106 C8 West Liberty Iowa 41.33N 91.16W
109 B3 West Liberty Kentucky 37.56N 83.16W
104 B6 West Liberty Ohio 40.14N 83.46W
58 K7 West Linton Borders Scotland 55.46N 3.22W
114 D8 West Loch Hawaiian Is
100 D4 Westlock Alberta 54.12N 113.50W
103 F6 West Long Branch New Jersey 40.17N 74.02W
56 C7 West Looe Cornwall Eng 50.21N 4.28W
99 J10 West Lorne Ontario 42.36N 81.35W
West Lothian co see Lothian and Central regions
56 G6 West Lulworth Dorset Eng 50.38N 2.15W
92 B8 West Lunga R Zambia
93 B8 West Lunga Nat. Park Zambia
57 M4 West Lutton N Yorks Eng 54.06N 0.34W
60 F12 Westmaas Netherlands 51.47N 4.29E
West Malaysia div see Peninsular Malaysia
61 J1 Westmalle Belgium 51.18N 4.42E
56 M5 West Malling Kent Eng 51.18N 0.25E
104 A7 West Manchester Ohio 39.54N 84.37W
99 O7 Westmeath Ontario 45.49N 76.54W
59 G4 Westmeath co Irish Rep
61 K2 Westmeerbeek Belgium 51.04N 4.50E
107 F6 West Memphis Arkansas 35.09N 90.11W
56 J5 West Meon Hants Eng 51.01N 1.05W
56 N4 West Mersea Essex Eng 51.47N 0.55E
56 L6 Westmeston E Sussex Eng 50.54N 0.05W
104 E5 West Middlesex Pennsylvania 41.10N 80.27W
56 G3 West Midlands co England
103 J4 West Milford New York 41.08N 74.22W
104 A7 West Milton Ohio 39.57N 84.19W
55 F3 Westminster London England 51.30N 0.09W
104 J7 Westminster Maryland 39.35N 77.00W
95 L5 Westminster S Africa 29.10S 27.09E
105 D3 Westminster South Carolina 34.40N 83.10W
104 N3 Westminster Vermont 43.03N 72.29W
55 E3 Westminster, City of bor London England
55 C5 West Molesey Surrey Eng 51.24N 0.22W
107 D9 West Monroe Louisiana 32.30N 92.08W
56 H6 West Moors Dorset Eng 50.49N 1.55W
109 O2 Westmoreland Kansas 39.24N 96.27W
104 M2 Westmoreland New Hampshire 42.59N 72.25W
13 E3 Westmoreland Queensland 17.18S 138.12E
107 K5 Westmoreland Tennessee 36.34N 86.18W
111 J8 Westmorland California 33.00N 115.37W
Westmorland co see Cumbria co
116 G1 Westmorland parish Jamaica, W I
99 S9 Westmount Quebec 45.30N 73.36W
103 B4 West Nanticoke Pennsylvania 41.43N 76.01W
103 J7 West New York New Jersey 40.48N 74.01W
92 D12 West Nicholson Zimbabwe 21.06S 29.25E
29 D7 West Nimar dist Madhya Prad India
108 P8 West Nishnabotna R Iowa
112 G6 West Nueces R Texas
94 L6 Westoe Dam Transvaal S Africa 26.26S 30.35E
95 O2 Westoe Dam res S Africa 26.28S 30.30E
106 H7 West Olive Michigan 42.56N 86.10W
104 G4 Weston Connecticut 41.13N 73.23W
110 H5 Weston Idaho 42.03N 111.59W
103 M2 Weston Massachusetts 42.22N 71.17W
106 K8 Weston Michigan 41.46N 84.04W
107 C2 Weston Missouri 39.26N 94.56W
108 P8 Weston Nebraska 41.12N 96.47W
11 E12 Weston New Zealand 45.05S 170.55E
104 B5 Weston Ohio 41.19N 83.49W
99 C10 Weston Ontario 43.43N 79.29W
110 G4 Weston Oregon 45.50N 118.24W
18 L3 Weston Sabah Malaysia 5.14N 115.35E
57 H7 Weston Shropshire Eng 52.51N 2.40W
56 G2 Weston Staffs Eng 52.50N 2.02W
104 F7 Weston W Virginia 39.03N 80.28W
109 K5 Weston Wyoming 44.38N 105.20W
12 A6 Weston dist Canberra Australia
95 L2 Westonaria S Africa 26.20S 27.40E
12 A6 Weston Creek dist Canberra Australia
104 J2 West Oneonta New York 42.29N 75.07W
103 E3 West Oneonta Res New York
56 J4 Weston-on-the-Green Oxon Eng 51.52N 1.14W
56 F5 Weston-super-Mare Avon Eng 51.21N 2.59W
103 H7 West Orange New Jersey 40.48N 74.14W
61 A3 Westouter Belgium 50.48N 2.45E
112 H2 Westover Texas 33.30N 99.01W
63 F6 Westoverledingen W Germany 53.08N 7.33E
West Pakistan see Pakistan
105 G11 West Palm Beach Florida 26.42N 80.05W
111 B8 West Palm Beach Canal Florida
West Passage see Toogel Mlungui
56 F5 West Pennard Somerset Eng 51.09N 2.39W
113 V8 West Petersburg Alaska 56.51N 133.00W
113 V4 Westphalia Indiana 38.51N 87.13W
109 P3 Westphalia Kansas 38.11N 95.28W
103 B3 West Pike Pennsylvania 41.46N 77.43W
103 C4 West Pittston Pennsylvania 41.20N 75.48W
107 E5 West Plains Missouri 36.44N 91.51W
111 D3 West Point California 38.23N 120.32W
105 B5 West Point Georgia 32.54N 85.10W
106 G9 Westpoint Indiana 40.21N 87.01W
106 C9 West Point Iowa 40.42N 91.27W
107 L4 West Point Kentucky 38.00N 85.59W
107 H8 West Point Mississippi 33.35N 88.40W
108 O8 West Point Nebraska 41.50N 96.40W
103 G4 West Point New York 41.23N 73.58W
104 J9 West Point Virginia 37.33N 76.49W
113 P4 West Point mt Alaska 64.59N 144.40W
93 G4 West Pokot dist Kenya
111 A2 Westport California 39.39N 123.45W
103 H4 Westport Connecticut 41.09N 73.22W
107 L2 Westport Indiana 39.11N 85.35W
103 M3 Westport Massachusetts 41.37N 71.04W
59 C4 Westport Mayo Irish Rep 53.48N 9.32W
98 Q4 Westport Newfoundland 49.48N 56.39W
104 M2 West Port New York 44.13N 73.39W
11 F8 Westport New Zealand 41.46S 171.38E
99 O8 Westport Ontario 44.40N 76.26W
110 B3 Westport Oregon 46.08N 123.25W
108 M4 Westport S Dakota 45.39N 98.31W
107 H6 Westport Tennessee 35.55N 88.20W
110 A3 Westport Washington 46.52N 124.07W
103 D5 West Portal New Jersey 40.39N 75.02W
100 A3 West Prairie R Alberta
98 H4 West Pt Anticosti I, Que 49.55N 64.32W
98 H7 West Pt Prince Edward I 46.38N 64.26W
26 B13 West Pt Prince Edward I Ind Oc 46.38S 37.52E
98 M10 West Pt Sable I, Nova Scotia 43.57N 60.08W
12 D6 West Pt S Australia 35.00S 135.54E
12 G8 West Pt Tasmania 40.57S 144.43E
96 A16 West Pt Tristan da Cunha 37.19S 12.44W
98 G10 West Pubnico Nova Scotia 43.39N 65.49W
116 A1 Westpunt Curaçao W I 12.22N 69.09W
West R see Hsi Chiang R
94 R13 West Rand S Africa 26.07S 27.45E
57 N6 West Rasen Lincs Eng 53.24N 0.24W
100 Q5 Westray Manitoba 53.35N 101.24W
58 T11 Westray isld Orkney Scotland 59.18N 2.59W
58 T11 Westray Firth Orkney Scotland
103 C6 West Reading Pennsylvania 40.19N 75.57W
99 J5 Westree Ontario 47.26N 81.34W
61 F3 Westrem Belgium 50.58N 3.52E
63 G6 West Rhauderfehn W Germany 53.08N 7.35E
64 C5 Westrich reg W Germany
103 A9 West River Maryland 38.51N 76.36W
101 L9 West Road R Br Col
104 P9 West Roxbury dist Boston, Mass 42.16N 71.11W
61 C3 Westrozebeke Belgium 50.56N 3.01E
58 L7 Westruther Borders Scotland 55.45N 2.35W
104 M3 West Rutland Vermont 43.36N 73.04W
98 Q2 West St Modeste Labrador, Nfld 51.38N 56.42W
107 H3 West Salem Illinois 38.31N 88.01W
104 D6 West Salem Ohio 40.58N 82.06W
106 C6 West Salem Wisconsin 43.54N 91.04W
25 M4 West Sand I Paracel Islands S China Sea
58 Q8 West Sandwick Shetland Scotland 60.35N 1.10W
103 F2 West Saugerties New York 42.07N 74.04W
103 H5 West Sayville Long I, N Y 40.43N 73.06W
56 J5 West Shefford Berks Eng 51.29N 1.27W
103 F3 West Shokan New York 41.58N 74.18W
11 L6 Westshore New Zealand 39.28S 176.53E
108 P7 Westside Iowa 42.05N 95.08W
110 E7 West Side Oregon 42.07N 120.30W
12 F7 West Sister I Tasmania 39.42S 147.55E
54 L9 West Sole oil field North Sea 53.43N 1.10E
60 B3 West-Souburg Netherlands 51.28N 3.35E
103 J2 West Springfield Massachusetts 42.06N 72.38W
104 O2 West Stewartstown New Hampshire 44.59N 71.30W
103 H2 West Stockbridge Massachusetts 42.20N 73.23W
103 J3 West Suffield Connecticut 41.59N 72.42W
56 K6 West Sussex co England
56 B7 West Taphouse Cornwall Eng 50.26N 4.36W
58 F7 West Tarbert Strathclyde Scotland 55.51N 5.27W
60 J6 West Terschelling Netherlands 53.22N 5.13E
103 N4 West Tisbury Massachusetts 41.22N 70.51W
12 A8 West Torrens dist Adelaide, S Aust
103 E4 Westtown N Y 41.20N 74.32W
103 D6 West Trenton New Jersey 40.16N 74.48W
103 E6 West Union Illinois 39.12N 87.39W
106 C7 West Union Iowa 42.57N 91.49W
104 B8 West Union Ohio 38.48N 83.33W
104 E7 West Union W Virginia 39.18N 80.47W
104 A5 West Unity Ohio 41.35N 84.26W
101 G10 West Vancouver co Br Col
105 D7 Westville Florida 30.47N 85.52W
106 G8 Westville Illinois 40.02N 87.38W
106 H8 Westville Indiana 41.33N 86.54W
103 D7 Westville New Jersey 39.52N 75.08W
98 K8 Westville Nova Scotia 45.34N 62.44W
109 Q6 Westville Oklahoma 35.59N 94.36W
102 K3 West Virginia state U.S.A.
61 B2 West Vlaanderen prov Belgium
61 A4 Westvleteren Belgium 50.56N 2.43E
111 E3 West Walker R Nevada
56 C6 Westward Ho Devon Eng 51.02N 4.15W
103 K2 West Warren Massachusetts 42.13N 72.14W
103 B3 West Warren Pennsylvania 41.57N 76.16W
103 L3 West Warwick Rhode I 41.42N 71.33W
110 G8 Westwater Utah 39.05N 109.08W
58 L5 West Water R Tayside Scotland
107 H13 Westwego Louisiana 29.57N 90.09W
55 G4 West Wickham London Eng 51.22N 0.02W
104 E5 West Winfield New York 42.53N 75.16W
57 K4 West Witton N Yorks Eng 54.17N 1.54W
111 C1 Westwood California 40.20N 121.00W
103 M2 Westwood Massachusetts 42.14N 71.14W
103 F5 Westwood New Jersey 41.00N 74.02W
13 K6 Westwood Queensland 23.37S 150.12E
12 F7 Westwood Lakes Florida 25.44N 80.25W
112 L9 Westworth Fort Worth, Texas 32.45N 97.24W
12 H5 West Wyalong New S Wales 33.54S 147.12E
56 K4 West Wycombe Bucks Eng 51.39N 0.49W
29 A1 West Yamuna Can Delhi India
110 O5 West Yellowstone Montana 44.40N 111.07W
103 A7 West York Pennsylvania 39.57N 76.45W
57 K5 West Yorkshire co Eng
60 G10 Westzaan Netherlands 52.28N 4.44E
19 F7 Wetan isld Indon 7.52S 129.32E
19 E8 Wetar isld Indon
19 E7 Wetar,Selat str Indon
100 D6 Wetaskiwin Alberta 52.57N 113.20W
95 O6 Wet,De S Africa 33.35S 19.30E
94 A6 Wete Pemba I 5.03S 39.41E
95 J2 Wete Zaire 4.35S 24.30E
91 J6 Wetetnagami R Quebec
99 O3 Wethau E Germany 51.08N 11.51E
64 M1 Wetheral Cumbria Eng 54.53N 2.50W
57 J2 Wetherby W Yorks Eng 53.56N 1.23W
57 L5 Wethersfield Connecticut 41.43N 72.40W
103 J3 Wetlet Burma 22.43N 95.22E
25 C1 Wetmore Colorado 38.14N 105.06W
108 O9 Wetmore Texas 29.34N 98.26W
112 J6 Wet Mts Colorado
109 E3 Wetonka S Dakota 45.36N 98.46W
108 M4 Wetter W Germany 50.54N 8.45E
64 F3 Wetter R W Germany
64 F3 Wetterau reg W Germany
64 F3 Wetteren Belgium 51.00N 3.53E
61 G2 Wetterhorn mt Switzerland 46.39N 8.08E
65 J5 Wetter-Spitze mt Austria 47.13N 10.22E
66 K2 Wetterstein Gebirge mts Austria
65 B7 Wettin E Germany 51.35N 11.49E
65 B7 Wettingen Switzerland 47.28N 8.20E
63 K5 Wettringen W Germany 52.13N 7.20E
62 K5 Wetumka Oklahoma 35.13N 96.17W
109 M6 Wetumpka Alabama 32.33N 86.13W
107 K9 Wetwang Humberside Eng 54.01N 0.34W
57 M4 Wetwun Burma 22.20N 96.38E
25 D1 Wetzikon Switzerland 47.19N 8.48E
66 M2 Wetzlar W Germany 50.33N 8.30E
64 F3 Wetzstein mt E Germany 50.26N 11.27E
64 H3 Weurt Netherlands 51.51N 5.49E
61 C3 Wevelgem Belgium 50.48N 3.12E
65 E5 Wevelinghoven W Germany 51.07N 6.38E
64 B1 Wever Iowa 40.42N 91.14W
106 C9 Wevertown New York 43.38N 73.57W
104 M3 Wevok see Cape Lisburne
105 B7 Wewahitchka Florida 30.06N 85.12W
107 H7 Wewak Papua New Guinea 3.35S 143.35E
15 G5 Wewoka Oklahoma 35.09N 96.30W
109 O6 Wexford Wexford Irish Rep 52.20N 6.27W
59 K7 Wexford co Irish Rep
59 J7 Wexford B Wexford Irish Rep 52.23N 6.20W
59 J7 Wexford Harb Wexford Irish Rep 52.20N 6.25W
59 K7 Weyakwin L Saskatchewan
100 L4 Weyauwega Wisconsin 44.20N 88.55W
106 F5 Weybourne Norfolk Eng 52.57N 1.09E
56 O2 Weybridge Surrey England 51.22N 0.28W
55 B6 Weyburn Saskatchewan 49.39N 103.51W
100 O9 Weyer Austria 47.52N 14.39E
65 L6 Weyerbusch W Germany 50.43N 7.34E
64 D2 Weyerhauser Wisconsin 45.25N 91.25W
106 D5 Weyersheim France 48.43N 7.48E
69 O6 Weyer W Germany 50.27N 10.23E
64 F3 Weyhill Hants Eng 51.13N 1.32W
56 H5 Weyland,Pegunungan mts Irian Jaya
15 C5 Weymouth Dorset Eng 50.36N 2.28W
56 G6 Weymouth Massachusetts 42.14N 70.58W
103 N2 Weymouth Nova Scotia 44.26N 66.00W
98 G9 Weymouth B Queensland
13 G1 Weymouth Bay Dorset Eng 50.37N 2.25W
56 G6 Weymouth,C Queensland 12.35S 143.27E
13 G2 Weyprecht-breen glacier Jan Mayen I 71.07N 8.19W
50 O9 Weyprecht, Kapp C see Payer, Kapp
55 B5 Wey, R Surrey England
61 O3 Weyregg Austria 47.54N 13.35E
61 P5 Weywertz Belgium 50.26N 6.10E
95 N6 Weza S Africa 30.37S 29.43E
61 K3 Wezemaal Belgium 50.57N 4.46E
61 H3 Wezembeek-Oppem Belgium 50.51N 4.29E
60 M10 Wezep Netherlands 52.28N 6.00E
60 N10 Wezepe Netherlands 52.20N 6.12E
60 P8 Wezup Netherlands 52.48N 6.44E
61 D4 Wez-Velvain Belgium 50.32N 3.24E
11 K5 Whakamaru New Zealand 38.26S 175.50E
11 J2 Whakapara New Zealand 35.32S 174.18E
11 M5 Whakapunaki mt New Zealand 38.50S 177.34E
11 L7 Whakataki New Zealand 40.52S 176.17E
11 M4 Whakatane New Zealand 37.56S 177.00E
11 L5 Whakatane R New Zealand
113 U8 Whale B Alaska
25 E7 Whale B Burma
14 C6 Whaleback,Mt W Australia 23.25S 119.42E
12 M5 Whale Beach dist Sydney, N S W 33.37S 151.20E
113 D10 Whalebone C Aleutian Is 53.30N 166.45W
116 K12 Whale Cay isld Bahamas 25.24N 77.45W
58 Q8 Whale Firth Shetland Scotland 60.37N 1.07W
Whale I New Zealand see Motuhora
98 P2 Whale I Quebec 51.22N 57.43W
122 U8 Whaler Anchorage Fanning I Pacific Oc 3.52N 159.23W
57 J7 Whale Rock pt S Africa 31.55S 29.13E
95 N7 Whales,B.of Antarctica
123 J8 Whaley Bridge Derbys Eng 53.20N 1.59W
57 K6 Whaleyville Virginia 36.34N 76.43W
104 J10 Whallan R New S Wales
12 J3 Whalley Lancs Eng 53.50N 2.24W
57 J5 Whalsay isld Shetland Scotland 60.22N 0.59W
58 R9 Whalton Northumb Eng 55.08N 1.47W
57 K2 Whangaehu New Zealand 40.01S 175.08E
11 K6 Whangaehu R New Zealand
11 K6 Whangamata New Zealand 37.13S 175.54E
11 K4 Whangamomona New Zealand 39.08S 174.42E
11 J6 Whanganui Inlet New Zealand
11 G7 Whangaparaoa New Zealand 37.32S 178.00E
11 M4 Whangaparaoa Pen New Zealand
11 J3 Whangape New Zealand 35.22S 173.14E
11 H2 Whangape Harb inlet New Zealand
11 H2 Whangape L New Zealand 37.28S 175.04E
11 K4 Whangarei New Zealand 35.43S 174.20E
11 J2 Whangarei Harb inlet New Zealand
11 J2 Whangaroa New Zealand 35.03S 173.48E
11 H2 Whangaroa Harb inlet New Zealand
11 J2 Wharanui New Zealand 41.58S 174.06E
11 J7 Whareama New Zealand 40.58S 176.02E
11 L7 Whareama R New Zealand
11 L8 Wharekauhu New Zealand 45.53S 170.43E
11 O13 Wharerata New Zealand 38.53S 177.54E
11 M5 Wharfe R N Yorks/W Yorks Eng
57 K4 Wharfe,R N Yorks Eng
57 J4 Wharram le Street N Yorks Eng 54.05N 0.40W
57 M4 Wharton New Jersey 40.54N 74.35W
103 E5 Wharton Pennsylvania 41.32N 78.02W
104 G5 Wharton Texas 29.19N 96.06W
112 L6 Wharton L N W Terr
101 Y1 Whataroa New Zealand 43.18S 170.22E
11 E10 Whataroa R New Zealand
11 E10 Whatatutu New Zealand 38.23S 177.51E
11 M5 Whatawhata New Zealand 37.48S 175.10E
11 K4 What Cheer Iowa 41.23N 92.21W
106 B8 Whatcom,L Washington
110 C1 Whately Massachusetts 42.27N 72.39W
103 J2 Whatley Alabama 31.39N 87.42W
107 J10 Whaup Hill Dumfries & Galloway Scotland 54.49N 4.29W
57 E3 Whau R New Zealand
11 B2 Wheatfield Indiana 41.11N 87.02W
106 G8 Wheatland California 39.01N 121.24W
111 C2 Wheatland Iowa 41.49N 90.50W
106 D8 Wheatland Wyoming 42.03N 104.57W
108 F7 Wheatland Res Wyoming 41.50N 105.37W
108 E8 Wheatley Arkansas 34.55N 91.08W
107 F7 Wheatley Notts Eng 53.22N 0.52W
57 M6 Wheatley Ontario 42.05N 82.27W
99 H10 Wheatley Bridge Oxon Eng 51.45N 1.10W
56 J4 Wheaton Illinois 41.54N 88.06W
106 F8 Wheaton Kansas 39.30N 96.19W
109 O2 Wheaton Minnesota 45.49N 96.30W
108 O4 Wheaton Missouri 36.45N 94.05W
107 B5 Wheatsheaf I New Zealand Pacific Oc
10 F12 Wheddon Cross Somerset Eng 51.08N 3.32W
56 D5 Wheeler Kansas 39.46N 101.44W
109 J2 Wheeler Oregon 45.41N 123.53W
110 B4 Wheeler Texas 35.26N 100.17W
112 D8 Wheeler Wisconsin 45.03N 91.54W
106 C5 Wheeler R Saskatchewan
101 V7 Wheeler Dam Alabama 34.47N 87.24W
107 J7 Wheeler L N W Terr 63.21N 114.59W
101 O4 Wheeler Lake Alabama 34.45N 87.15W
107 J8 Wheeler Pk New Mexico 36.34N 105.25W
109 E5 Wheeler Pk mt Nevada 38.59N 114.19W
111 K3 Wheeler Ridge California 35.00N 118.58W
111 F6 Wheelersburg Ohio 38.44N 82.51W
104 C8 Wheeler Springs California 34.30N 119.18W
111 E7 Wheelerville Pennsylvania 41.35N 76.47W
103 A3 Wheeling W Virginia 40.05N 80.43W
104 E6 Wheelock Cheshire Eng 53.07N 2.23W
57 J6 Wheelock N Dakota 48.20N 103.25W
108 D1 Wheelwright Argentina 33.46S 61.14W
121 E4 Wheelwright Kentucky 37.21N 82.45W
104 C9 Whelan,Mt Queensland 23.25S 138.50E
13 E6 Whenuapai Auckland New Zealand 36.47S 174.38E
11 B1 Whernside mt N Yorks Eng 54.14N 2.23W
57 J4 Wherwell Hants Eng 51.11N 1.26W
56 J5 Whetstone London England 51.38N 0.10W
55 E2 Whicham Cumbria Eng 54.14N 3.20W
57 G4 Whickham Tyne and Wear Eng 54.57N 1.40W
57 K3 Whidbey I Washington 48.20N 122.40W
110 C1 Whidbey Is S Australia
12 C4 Whidbey Pt S Australia 34.30S 135.10E
12 D6 Whiddon Down Devon Eng 50.43N 3.51W
56 E6 Whiddy I Cork Irish Rep 51.41N 9.30W
59 B8 Whigham Georgia 30.53N 84.20W
105 C8 Whim Creek W Australia 20.52S 117.51E
14 C5 Whimple Devon Eng 50.46N 3.22W
56 E6 Whinham Mt S Australia 26.08S 130.10E
12 B2 Whiphill Minnesota 47.03N 94.22W
108 L3 Whippany New Jersey 40.49N 74.25W
103 F6 Whipple Pt Nevada 39.51N 94.45W
57 F3 Whipple,Mt Alaska/Br Col 56.40N 131.40W
113 W8 Whipsnade Beds Eng 51.52N 0.33W
98 F9 Whiskey Gap Alberta 49.03N 113.03W
56 K4 Whiskey Jack Landing Manitoba 54.27N 98.00W
100 D9 Whistleduck Creek N Terr Australia
100 S2 Whistlefield Strathclyde Scotland 56.06N 4.49W
13 D5 Whitaker Alabama 30.46N 88.08W
58 G6 Whitakers N Carolina 36.04N 77.43W
107 H11 Whitbourne Newfoundland 47.26N 53.33W
105 K1 Whitburn Lothian Scotland 55.52N 3.42W
98 T6 Whitburn Tyne and Wear Eng 54.57N 1.21W
58 J7 Whitby Cheshire Eng 53.16N 2.55W
57 L3 Whitby New Zealand 41.06S 174.52E
57 H6 Whitby N Yorks Eng 54.29N 0.37W
11 D4 Whitby Ontario 43.52N 78.56W
57 M4 Whitchurch Avon Eng 51.25N 2.34W
99 M9 Whitchurch Bucks Eng 51.53N 0.51W
56 F5 Whitchurch Hants Eng 51.14N 1.20W
56 K4 Whitchurch Hereford & Worcs Eng 51.52N 2.39W
56 J5 Whitchurch S Glam Wales 51.32N 3.14W
56 F4 Whitchurch Shropshire Eng 52.58N 2.41W
56 E5 Whitcombe Dorset Eng 50.41N 2.24W
57 H7 Whitcombe Pass New Zealand 43.14S 170.58E
56 G6 White S Dakota 44.25N 96.39W
11 E10 White R Alaska/Yukon Terr
108 O5 White R Arizona
113 R6 White R Arkansas
111 O8 White R Nevada
107 E6 White R S Dakota
111 J3 White R Texas
111 F3 White R Utah/Colorado
108 J6 White R Vermont
112 E3 White R Washington
111 P2 White R Yukon Terr
104 N3 Whiteabbey Antrim N Ireland 54.42N 5.53W
110 C4 Whiteadder Water R Borders Scotland
101 C6 White Bear Newfoundland
59 K2 White Bear Saskatchewan 50.55N 108.12W
58 M7 White Bear L Minnesota
98 Q3 Whitebear Pt N W Terr 68.09N 103.18W
100 J8 White Bear R Newfoundland
98 P6 White Bear Res Newfoundland
98 P5 White Bird Idaho 45.48N 116.17W
110 J4 White Bluff Tennessee 36.04N 87.14W
107 J5 White Bluffs Washington 46.40N 119.28W
110 F3 White Bridge Highland Scotland 57.13N 4.30W
58 H4 Whiteburn Borders Scotland 55.53N 2.23W
58 M7 White Butte S Dakota 45.56N 102.20W
108 H4 Whitecap L Manitoba
100 W2 White Castle Louisiana 30.10N 91.11W
107 E11 Whitechapel London Eng 51.31N 0.03W
55 G3 White City Florida 29.54N 85.13W
105 B8 White City Florida 27.26N 80.19W
105 G10 White City Kansas 38.47N 96.45W
109 O3 White Cliffs New S Wales 30.50S 143.08E
12 G4 White Cloud Kansas 39.58N 95.20W
109 P2 White Cloud Michigan 43.34N 85.47W
106 J6 White Coomb mt Dumfries & Galloway/Borders Scotland 55.26N 3.20W
57 G2 Whitecourt Alberta 54.10N 115.38W
100 B4 White Deer Texas 35.27N 101.11W
112 C8 White Earth N Dakota 48.24N 102.45W
108 H1 White Esk R Dumfries & Galloway Scotland
57 G2 Whiteface Texas 33.35N 102.36W
112 E2 Whiteface Mt New York 44.23N 73.54W
104 M2 Whitefield Greater Manchester Eng 53.34N 2.18W
57 J5 Whitefield New Hampshire 44.23N 71.37W
104 O2 Whitefish Montana 48.25N 114.21W
110 L1 Whitefish Ontario 46.23N 81.20W
99 J6 Whitefish B Michigan
106 K3 Whitefish Bay Wisconsin 43.07N 87.54W
106 G6 Whitefish Falls Ontario 46.07N 81.44W
99 J6 Whitefish L Alaska 61.20N 160.00W
113 H6 Whitefish L Alaska 60.59N 154.50W
113 K6 Whitefish L Alberta 54.25N 111.58W
100 F4 Whitefish L Michigan 46.10N 85.45W
106 J3 Whitefish L Minnesota
108 O3 Whitefish L Montana 48.27N 114.23W
110 L1 Whitefish L N W Terr
101 U4 Whitefish L Ontario 48.14N 90.00W
100 N2 Whitefish Point Michigan 46.47N 84.57W
106 K3 Whitefish Pt Michigan 46.46N 84.58W
106 K3 Whitefish R Michigan
106 H4 Whitefish Ra Montana
110 L1 Whiteflat Texas 34.08N 100.51W
112 G1 Whiteford Maryland 39.44N 76.21W
103 B7 White Fox Saskatchewan 53.28N 104.06W
100 N5 White Fox R Saskatchewan
100 N5 Whitegate Clare Irish Rep 52.56N 8.23W
59 F6 Whitegate Cork Irish Rep 51.50N 8.14W
59 F8 Whitegull L Quebec 55.20N 64.30W
97 N6 White Hall Illinois 39.27N 90.22W
107 F2 Whitehall Kilkenny Irish Rep 52.41N 7.01W
59 H8 Whitehall Maryland 39.37N 76.37W
103 A7 Whitehall Michigan 43.24N 86.20W
106 H6 Whitehall Montana 45.53N 112.06W
110 N4 Whitehall New York 43.32N 73.26W
104 M3 Whitehall Wisconsin 44.22N 91.20W
106 C5 Whitehall Res Massachusetts 42.14N 71.35W
103 L2 Whitehaven Cumbria Eng 54.33N 3.35W
57 F3 White Haven Pennsylvania 41.04N 75.47W
103 C4 Whitehead Antrim N Ireland 54.45N 5.43W
59 L2 White Hill Ascension I 7.57S 14.19W
96 B11 White Hill Dumfries & Galloway Scotland 54.51N 4.55W
57 D3 White Hill Lancs Eng 54.02N 2.30W
57 J5 White Hills Alaska
113 N2 White Hills Arizona 35.45N 114.22W
111 K6 Whitehills Grampian Scotland 57.40N 2.35W
58 L3 White Hope see Woolibar
110 D8 White Horse California 41.18N 121.25W
101 F5 Whitehorse Yukon Terr 60.41N 135.08W
103 N3 White Horse Beach Massachusetts 41.56N 70.34W
56 H4 White Horse Hills Wilts etc Eng
110 L9 White Horse Pass Nevada 40.18N 114.21W
116 L2 White Horses Jamaica, W I 17.52N 76.29W
59 L2 Whitehouse Antrim N Ireland 54.39N 5.55W
58 F7 Whitehouse Strathclyde Scotland 55.48N 5.29W
103 E5 White House Sta New Jersey 40.37N 74.46W
123 A5 White I Antarctica
123 H7 White I Antarctica 78.10S 167.30E
11 M4 White I New Zealand 37.30S 177.12E
11 M13 White I New Zealand 45.57S 170.30E
97 L4 White I N W Terr 65.50N 85.00W
White I Spitsbergen see Kvitöya
58 L6 Whitekirk Lothian Scotland 56.02N 2.39W
107 D12 White L Louisiana
106 H6 White L Michigan
13 A5 White L N Terr/W Aust
106 H8 White L Ontario
99 O7 White L Ontario
14 G5 White,L W Australia 21.15S 129.00E
106 F4 White L Wisconsin 45.10N 88.46W
103 E3 White Lake New York 41.41N 74.50W
99 O7 White Lake Ontario 45.22N 76.29W
108 M6 White Lake S Dakota 43.43N 98.41W
White Land see Belaya Zemlya,O-va is
15 K6 Whiteman Ra New Britain
12 J8 Whitemark Tasmania 40.07S 148.00E
103 C5 White Mills Pennsylvania 41.32N 75.12W
113 F4 White Mountain Alaska 64.40N 163.30W
113 O4 White Mountains Alaska
100 F1 Whitemouth Manitoba 49.58N 95.59W
101 F1 Whitemouth R Manitoba
100 F1 Whitemouth L Manitoba
59 J7 White Mt Wexford Irish Rep 52.29N 6.50W
111 F4 White Mts California
101 P7 Whitemud R Alberta
58 G1 Whiten Head Highland Scotland 58.34N 4.35W
87 D4 White Nile prov Sudan
White Nile R see Bahr el Abiad
White Nile R Sudan see Bahr el Jebel
87 D3 White Nile Dam Sudan 15.18N 32.30E
112 M2 White Oak Creek Texas
107 C8 White Oak L Arkansas 33.40N 93.05W
105 K3 White Oak Swamp N Carolina
White Oil Springs see Naft-e Safid oil field
100 L1 White Otter L Ontario 49.10N 91.50W
108 H5 White Owl S Dakota 44.36N 102.22W
106 M5 Whiteparish Wilts Eng 51.01N 1.39W
59 K1 White Park B Antrim N Ireland 55.15N 6.27W
101 F6 White Pass Br Col 59.36N 135.08W
110 C3 White Pass Washington 46.38N 121.25W
106 J8 White Pigeon Michigan 41.48N 85.39W
110 E2 White Pine Michigan 46.45N 89.35W
110 K2 Whitepine Montana 47.49N 115.34W
105 D1 White Pine Tennessee 36.07N 83.17W
111 J2 White Pine Ra Nevada
105 G1 White Plains N Carolina 36.27N 80.41W
103 G4 White Plains New York 41.02N 73.46W
115 N8 Whiteport New York 41.54N 74.03W
98 R2 White Pt Belle Isle, Nfld 51.53N 55.25W
96 A14 White Pt mt St Helena 16.00S 5.46W
13 D6 White Quartz Hill mt N Terr Australia 23.04S 135.32E
100 B8 White,R Br Col
109 C2 White,R Colorado
116 K1 White R,Jamaica, W I
108 D2 White,R Ontario
99 E4 White,R Ontario
106 D3 White,R Wisconsin
110 G6 Whiteriver Arizona 33.51N 109.58W
99 E4 White River Ontario 48.35N 85.16W
94 E5 White River S Africa 25.20S 31.00E
108 K6 White River S Dakota 43.34N 100.45W
104 N3 White River Junction Vermont 43.41N 72.21W
110 C2 White River Valley Nevada
96 B12 White Rock Ascension I 7.59S 14.21W
101 J12 White Rock Br Col 49.02N 122.50W
112 O9 White Rock Dallas, Texas 32.50N 96.43W
110 D3 White Rock Nevada 41.44N 116.10W
109 M2 White Rock Cr Kansas
11 B5 White Rock Hill New Zealand 41.16S 174.41E
112 O9 White Rock L Dallas, Texas
111 K3 White Rock Pk mt Nevada 38.11N 114.08W
White Russia see Belorussiya S.S.R.
95 L4 Whites S Africa 28.01S 27.00E
101 K9 Whitesail L Br Col
110 D3 White Salmon Washington 45.45N 121.28W
101 P6 Whitesand R Alberta
100 P7 Whitesand R Saskatchewan
95 D10 Whitesands S Africa 34.23S 20.50E
56 A4 Whitesand's B Dyfed Wales 51.55N 5.18W
109 D9 White Sands Missile Range New Mexico 32.22N 106.23W
109 D9 White Sands Nat.Mon New Mexico
104 K3 Whitesboro New York 43.11N 75.21W
98 F8 Whites Brook New Brunswick 47.46N 67.18W
105 C4 Whitesburg Georgia 33.30N 84.56W
104 C9 Whitesburg Kentucky 37.07N 82.52W
109 F9 Whites City New Mexico 32.09N 104.23W
White Sea see Beloye More
101 T8 White Settlement Texas 32.46N 97.26W
112 L9 Whiteshell Prov. Park Manitoba
100 F1 Whiteside,Canal channel Chile
121 K9 White Spruce Alberta 45.10N 123.12W
110 B3 Whitestone Florida 30.21N 82.47W
105 E8 White Springs Florida 30.21N 82.47W
103 G5 Whitestone New York 40.48N 73.48W
100 U2 Whitestone L Manitoba
110 P3 White Sulphur Springs Montana 46.32N 110.55W
103 E3 White Sulphur Springs New York 41.48N 74.48W
104 E9 White Sulphur Springs W Virginia 37.48N 80.20W
103 D3 Whites Valley Pennsylvania 41.42N 75.22W
107 K4 Whitesville Kentucky 37.40N 86.51W
103 F6 Whitesville New Jersey 40.04N 74.16W
104 H4 Whitesville New York 42.02N 77.46W
104 D9 Whitesville W Virginia 37.58N 81.33W
110 E3 White Swan Washington 46.23N 120.44W
100 M4 Whiteswan Lakes Saskatchewan
108 E1 Whitetail Montana 48.56N 105.10W
95 O9 White Umfolozi R S Africa
105 J3 Whiteville N Carolina 34.20N 78.42W
107 G6 Whiteville Tennessee 35.20N 89.10W
89 J7 White Volta R Ghana
110 S1 Whitewater Montana 48.46N 107.38W
109 B9 Whitewater New Mexico 32.34N 108.07W
106 F7 Whitewater Wisconsin 42.50N 88.44W
107 L2 Whitewater R Indiana
105 F12 Whitewater B Florida
99 A2 Whitewater L Ontario
12 B4 White Well S Australia 31.26S 131.00E
13 G5 Whitewood Queensland 21.30S 143.35E
100 P8 Whitewood Saskatchewan 50.19N 102.16W
108 G5 Whitewood S Dakota 44.29N 103.41W
108 N5 Whitewood,L S Dakota 44.20N 97.20W
112 L2 Whitewright Texas 33.32N 96.24W
12 H6 Whitfield Victoria 36.49S 146.22E
57 E3 Whithorn Dumfries & Galloway Scotland 54.44N 4.25W
116 H1 Whithorn Jamaica, W I 18.16N 78.02W
11 K3 Whitianga New Zealand 36.50S 175.43E
108 O7 Whiting Iowa 42.08N 96.10W
109 P2 Whiting Kansas 39.35N 95.37W
104 S2 Whiting Maine 44.47N 67.10W
103 F7 Whiting New Jersey 39.58N 74.23W
101 G6 Whiting R Alaska/Br Col
57 C2 Whiting Bay Arran, Strathclyde Scotland 55.29N 5.06W
104 N2 Whitingham Res Vermont 42.50N 72.55W
103 J2 Whitinsville Massachusetts 42.08N 71.40W
100 K6 Whitkow Saskatchewan 52.57N 107.51W
100 F9 Whitla Alberta 49.57N 111.08W
Whitland see Hendy-gwyn
110 O1 Whitlash Montana 48.55N 111.16W
57 D2 Whitletts Strathclyde Scotland 55.29N 4.35W
57 L5 Whitley N Yorks Eng 53.41N 1.09W
57 L2 Whitley Bay Tyne and Wear Eng 55.03N 1.25W
107 M5 Whitley City Kentucky 36.45N 84.29W
108 K4 Whitlocks Crossing S Dakota 45.03N 100.18W
103 N2 Whitman Massachusetts 42.05N 70.55W
108 M1 Whitman N Dakota 48.10N 98.08W
108 J7 Whitman Nebraska 42.04N 101.32W
110 G3 Whitman Mission National Mon Washington 46.05N 118.24W
105 F3 Whitmire S Carolina 34.30N 81.39W
56 E3 Whitney Hereford & Worcs Eng 52.07N 3.04W
108 G7 Whitney Nebraska 42.48N 103.15W
111 J5 Whitney Nevada 36.06N 115.05W
99 M7 Whitney Ontario 45.29N 78.15W
110 G5 Whitney Oregon 44.40N 118.17W
112 K4 Whitney Texas 31.58N 97.20W
112 K4 Whitney, L Texas
111 F5 Whitney, Mt California 36.35N 118.17W
103 C2 Whitney Point New York 42.20N 75.58W
103 C2 Whitney Pt.Res New York
56 C7 Whitsand B Cornwall Eng
112 J7 Whitsett Texas 28.38N 98.17W
56 O5 Whitstable Kent Eng 51.22N 1.02E
56 C6 Whitstone Cornwall Eng 50.45N 4.27W
13 J5 Whitsunday I Queensland
13 J5 Whitsunday Pass Queensland
112 J3 Whitt Texas 32.57N 98.03W
104 E7 Whittaker W Virginia 39.49N 80.48W
108 Q6 Whittemore Iowa 43.03N 94.25W
106 L5 Whittemore Michigan 44.13N 83.50W
113 N6 Whittier Alaska 60.45N 148.48W
111 F8 Whittier California 33.58N 118.02W
57 K2 Whittingham Northumb Eng 55.24N 1.54W
57 H4 Whittington Lancs Eng 54.11N 2.36W
56 E2 Whittington Shropshire Eng 52.52N 3.00W
56 M3 Whittlebury Northants Eng 52.05N 0.59W
95 K8 Whittlesea S Africa 32.10S 26.50E
12 H7 Whittlesea Victoria 37.31S 145.08E
56 L3 Whittlesey Cambs Eng 52.34N 0.08W
55 C4 Whitton London Eng 51.27N 0.21W
12 H5 Whitton New S Wales 34.31S 146.11E
56 E3 Whitton Powys Wales 52.19N 3.05W
57 K3 Whittonstall Northumb Eng 54.55N 1.53W
13 G5 Whitula R Queensland
57 K5 Whitwell Derbys Eng 53.18N 1.12W
107 L6 Whitwell Tennessee 35.11N 85.31W
57 J5 Whitworth Lancs Eng 53.40N 2.10W
101 V5 Wholdaia L N W Terr
12 B5 Whyalla S Australia 33.04S 137.34E
98 L8 Whycocomagh C Breton I, N S 45.58N 61.08W
12 G3 Whyjonta New S Wales 29.42S 142.30E
25 E3 Wiang Pa Pao Thailand 19.21N 99.29E
25 E2 Wiang Phran Thailand 20.25N 99.55E
99 J8 Wiarton Ontario 44.44N 81.10W
93 E3 Wiawer Uganda 2.43N 33.40E
89 H8 Wiawso Ghana 6.15N 2.30W
58 B4 Wiay isld W Isles Scotland 57.24N 7.13W
62 K5 Wiązów Poland 50.50N 17.10E
110 K2 Wibaux Montana 47.00N 104.14W
61 N6 Wibrin Belgium 50.10N 5.43E
61 L2 Wichelen Belgium 51.01N 3.58E
64 G4 Wichtelhahn W Germany 50.05N 9.08E
109 N4 Wichita Kansas 37.43N 97.20W
112 J2 Wichita R Texas
112 J2 Wichita Falls Texas 33.55N 98.30W
109 M7 Wichita Mts Oklahoma
60 O11 Wichmond Netherlands 52.05N 6.15E
66 C2 Wichtrach Switzerland 46.52N 7.35E
58 K2 Wick Highland Scotland 58.26N 3.06W
56 D5 Wick Mid Glam Wales 51.27N 3.33W
106 E5 Wickatunk New Jersey 40.22N 74.15W
63 G10 Wickede W Germany 51.30N 7.52E
111 M8 Wickenburg Arizona 33.59N 112.44W
98 K4 Wickenden L Anticosti I, Que
110 C1 Wickepin W Australia 32.45S 117.31E
101 L10 Wickersham Washington 48.40N 122.13W
112 D4 Wickett Texas 33.31N 103.01W
56 N4 Wickford Essex Eng 51.38N 0.31E
103 M3 Wickford Rhode I 41.34N 71.27W
56 J6 Wickham Hants Eng 50.54N 1.10W
13 B5 Wickham R N Terr Australia
56 P3 Wickhambrook Suffolk Eng 52.11N 0.33E
12 G7 Wickham, C King I, Tasmania 39.35S 143.59E
56 O3 Wickham Market Suffolk Eng 52.09N 1.22E
13 A3 Wickham Mt N Terr Aust 16.50S 129.30E
99 S7 Wickham West Quebec 45.45N 72.31W
110 D6 Wickiup Res Oregon 43.41N 121.44W
107 G5 Wickliffe Kentucky 36.58N 89.04W
11 O12 Wickliffe B New Zealand
59 J6 Wicklow Wicklow Irish Rep 52.59N 6.03W
59 J6 Wicklow co Irish Rep
59 K6 Wicklow Hd Wicklow Irish Rep 52.58N 6.00W
59 K6 Wicklow Mts Wicklow Irish Rep
64 A1 Wickrath W Germany 51.08N 6.25E
56 G4 Wickwar Avon Eng 51.36N 2.24W
56 F5 Wick Water R Highland Scotland
105 A5 Wiconisco Pennsylvania 40.35N 76.42W
62 L4 Widawa Poland 51.27N 18.51E
62 L4 Widawka R Poland
99 L4 Widdifield Ontario 46.25N 79.20W
113 J8 Wide B Alaska
13 J8 Wide B New Britain
13 L7 Wide B Queensland
56 D6 Widecombe Devon Eng 50.35N 3.48W
58 T10 Wide Firth Orkney Scotland 59.02N 2.58W
12 B2 Wide Gum,R S Australia
56 B6 Widemouth B Cornwall Eng
56 M4 Widford Herts Eng 51.50N 0.04E
14 D9 Widgiemooltha W Australia 31.35S 121.40E
19 F4 Widi,Kep islds Moluccas Indon
56 J2 Widmerpool Cross Road Notts Eng 52.51N 1.02W
66 P2 Widnau Switzerland 47.24N 9.38E
57 H6 Widnes Merseyside Eng 53.22N 2.44W
18 J9 Widodaren Java Indonesia 7.21S 111.17E
61 M4 Widooie Belgium 50.44N 5.25E
34 H6 Widyan,Al des Arabia/Iraq
86 F6 Widy,El Egypt 29.31N 31.16E
64 F4 Wiebelsbach W Germany 49.50N 8.58E
64 C5 Wiebelskirchen W Germany 49.22N 7.12E
62 L4 Więcbork Poland 53.21N 17.29E
63 R4 Wieck E Germany 54.26N 12.35E
64 F4 Wied R W Germany
Wiedenbrück see Rheda-Wiedenbrück
66 G2 Wiedlisbach Switzerland 47.15N 7.39E
65 J8 Wiedweg Austria 46.50N 13.23E
63 H6 Wiefelstede W Germany 53.15N 8.08E
95 G8 Wiegnaarspoort S Africa 32.38S 23.12E
64 L1 Wiehe E Germany 51.16N 11.25E
63 J8 Wiehengebirge hills W Germany
64 D2 Wiehl W Germany 50.58N 7.34E
63 S3 Wiek E Germany 54.37N 13.17E
61 K2 Wiekevorst Belgium 51.07N 4.48E
62 M2 Wielbark Poland 53.24N 20.55E
62 K3 Wieleń Poland 52.53N 16.10E
62 M6 Wieliczka Poland 50.00N 20.02E
61 C2 Wielsbeke Belgium 50.54N 3.23E
62 L4 Wieluń Poland 51.12N 18.31E
65 O5 Wien Austria 48.13N 16.22E
65 O5 Wien R Austria
65 O6 Wiener Neustadt Austria 47.49N 16.15E

65 N5 Wiener Wald mts Austria
63 M7 Wienhausen W Germany 52.34N 10.11E
65 M4 Wieningerberg mt Austria 48.49N 15.23E
50 O10 Wien,Kapp Jan Mayen I 70.51N 8.49W
113 M4 Wien L Alaska 64.21N 151.20W
63 O7 Wiepke E Germany 52.37N 11.20E
62 N4 Wieprz R Poland
61 K5 Wierde Belgium 50.26N 4.57E
60 P10 Wierden Netherlands 52.21N 6.35E
63 N7 Wieren W Germany 52.53N 10.41E
112 O4 Wiergate Texas 31.01N 93.42W
60 H8 Wieringermeer reg Netherlands
60 H8 Wieringerwaard Netherlands 52.50N 4.52E
60 J8 Wieringerwerf Netherlands 52.51N 5.01E
61 E4 Wiers Belgium 50.31N 3.32E
60 N6 Wierum Netherlands 53.24N 6.01E
62 L4 Wieruszów Poland 51.19N 18.09E
62 N4 Wierzbnik Poland 51.02N 21.03E
62 L2 Wierzchucin Poland 53.33N 18.07E
62 L2 Wierzyca R Poland
65 M8 Wies Austria 46.44N 15.17E
64 D8 Wies W Germany 47.45N 7.46E
64 N4 Wiesau W Germany 49.54N 12.10E
64 E3 Wiesbaden W Germany 50.05N 8.15E
64 D8 Wiese R W Germany
65 M5 Wieselburg Austria 48.08N 15.09E
66 P5 Wiesen Switzerland 46.42N 9.43E
64 P2 Wiesenbad E Germany 50.37N 13.03E
63 Q8 Wiesenburg E Germany 52.08N 12.27E
66 M1 Wiesendangen Switzerland 47.32N 8.48E
64 H6 Wiesensteig W Germany 48.34N 9.38E
64 L4 Wiesent R W Germany
64 J4 Wiesentheid W Germany 49.48N 10.23E
64 L4 Wiesenttal W Germany 49.49N 11.15E
64 D5 Wieslautern W Germany 49.07N 7.49E
64 F5 Wiesloch W Germany 49.17N 8.42E
61 K6 Wiesme Belgium 50.09N 4.59E
63 G6 Wiesmoor W Germany 53.25N 7.43E
63 F7 Wietmarschen W Germany 52.31N 7.07E
63 L7 Wietze W Germany 52.40N 9.48E
63 L7 Wietze R W Germany
63 K7 Wietzen W Germany 52.43N 9.04E
63 L7 Wietzendorf W Germany 52.55N 9.59E
61 G3 Wieze Belgium 50.58N 4.05E
57 H5 Wigan Greater Manchester Eng 53.33N 2.38W
66 H4 Wiggen Switzerland 46.54N 7.55E
66 H3 Wigger R Switzerland
109 F1 Wiggins Colorado 40.04N 104.04W
107 G11 Wiggins Mississippi 30.52N 89.10W
56 J6 Wight, Isle of England
56 F3 Wigmore Hereford & Worcs Eng 52.19N 2.51W
101 V5 Wignes L N W Terr
66 N1 Wigoltingen Switzerland 47.36N 9.02E
62 O1 Wigry,Jezioro L Poland
56 J2 Wigston Leics Eng 52.36N 1.05W
57 G3 Wigton Cumbria Eng 54.49N 3.09W
57 E3 Wigtown Dumfries & Galloway Scotland 54.52N 4.26W
Wigtown co see Dumfries & Galloway reg
57 E3 Wigtown B Dumfries & Galloway Scotland
61 E5 Wihéries Belgium 50.23N 3.45E
61 N4 Wihogne Belgium 50.43N 5.30E
60 L12 Wijchen Netherlands 51.48N 5.44E
61 M2 Wijchmaal Belgium 51.08N 5.25E
60 L8 Wijckel Netherlands 52.53N 5.37E
60 M7 Wijde Ee L Netherlands
50 T13 Wijdefjorden inlet Spitsbergen
60 J9 Wijdenes Netherlands 52.38N 5.10E
60 H10 Wijde Wormer dist Netherlands
61 L3 Wijer Belgium 50.54N 5.13E
60 N10 Wijhe Netherlands 52.23N 6.08E
60 S17 Wijk Limburg Netherlands 50.51N 5.42E
60 J12 Wijk Noord-Brabant Netherlands 51.46N 5.08E
60 G10 Wijk-aan-Zee Netherlands 52.30N 4.35E
60 K12 Wijk-bij-Duurstede Netherlands 51.58N 5.21E
60 O9 Wijk,De Netherlands 52.40N 6.17E
60 T17 Wijlre Netherlands 50.50N 5.54E
60 T17 Wijnandsrade Netherlands 50.54N 5.53E
61 J2 Wijnegem Belgium 51.13N 4.32E
60 H12 Wijngaarden Netherlands 51.51N 4.45E
60 N7 Wijnjeterp Netherlands 53.02N 6.12E
60 M6 Wijns Netherlands 53.15N 5.50E
61 N2 Wijshagen Belgium 51.06N 5.34E
60 P8 Wijster Netherlands 52.49N 6.30E
61 B3 Wijtschate Belgium 50.47N 2.53E
111 L7 Wikieup Arizona 34.42N 113.36W
99 J7 Wikwemikong Ontario 45.48N 81.44W
66 J1 Wil Aargau Switzerland 47.34N 8.09E
66 N2 Wil Switzerland 47.28N 9.03E
66 L1 Wil Zürich Switzerland 47.37N 8.31E
66 M2 Wila Switzerland 47.26N 8.51E
93 E3 Wila mt Uganda 2.07N 33.41E
26 U8 Wila Oya R Sri Lanka
108 O9 Wilber Nebraska 40.30N 96.56W
99 M7 Wilberforce Ontario 45.03N 78.15W
13 D1 Wilberforce,C N Terr Australia 11.52S 136.34E
90 C9 Wilberforce I Nigeria 5.00N 6.10E
11 F10 Wilberforce R New Zealand
110 N3 Wilborn Montana 46.54N 112.24W
103 K2 Wilbraham Massachusetts 42.08N 72.26W
110 B6 Wilbur Oregon 43.19N 123.21W
110 G2 Wilbur Washington 47.45N 118.42W
105 E1 Wilbur Dam Tennessee 36.22N 82.10W
56 M3 Wilburton Cambs Eng 52.21N 0.11E
109 P7 Wilburton Oklahoma 34.57N 95.20W
56 K3 Wilby Northants Eng 52.17N 0.45W
56 O3 Wilby Suffolk Eng 52.18N 1.17E
12 G4 Wilcannia New S Wales 31.05S 143.33E
66 L1 Wilchingen Switzerland 47.39N 8.29E
107 B1 Wilcox Missouri 40.23N 94.58W
108 L9 Wilcox Nebraska 40.22N 99.11W
104 G5 Wilcox Pennsylvania 41.36N 79.40W
100 N8 Wilcox Saskatchewan 50.09N 104.44W
Wilczek I see Vil'cheka,O
Wilczek Land see Vil'cheka,Zemlya
65 L6 Wildalpen Austria 47.40N 14.59E
63 T8 Wildau E Germany 52.19N 13.35E
64 F6 Wildbad W Germany 48.45N 8.33E
64 M8 Wildbad Kreuth W Germany 47.37N 11.45E
63 R7 Wildberg E Germany 52.53N 12.38E
64 F6 Wildberg W Germany 48.37N 8.45E
98 R4 Wild Bight Newfoundland 49.38N 55.56W
111 H2 Wildcat Pk mt Nevada 39.01N 116.53W
100 V3 Wilde Manitoba 55.40N 96.50W
64 J2 Wildeck W Germany 50.57N 10.02E
66 J2 Wildegg Switzerland 47.25N 8.10E
15 E6 Wildeman R Irian Jaya
69 P2 Wilden W Germany 50.48N 8.05E
65 P4 Wilden-Dürnbach Austria 48.47N 16.31E
64 O2 Wildenfels E Germany 50.40N 12.36E
64 L7 Wildenroth W Germany 48.08N 11.10E
69 M8 Wildenstein France 47.58N 6.59E
64 O3 Wildenthal E Germany 50.27N 12.38E
107 L5 Wilder Tennessee 36.16N 85.06W
61 L3 Wilderen Belgium 50.49N 5.09E
101 O9 Wilderness Prov.Park Alberta
107 H6 Wildersville Tennessee 35.47N 88.22W
66 H5 Wilderswil Switzerland 46.41N 7.53E
60 Q7 Wildervank Netherlands 53.04N 6.52E
63 H7 Wildeshausen W Germany 52.54N 8.26E
94 P12 Wildevoëlvlei pond Cape Town S Africa 34.07S 18.21E
64 H3 Wildflecken W Germany 50.22N 9.56E
95 H7 Wildfontein S Africa 31.05S 24.50E
100 O2 Wild Goose Ontario 48.33N 89.01W
66 O3 Wildhaus Switzerland 47.13N 9.22E
66 F6 Wildhorn mt Switzerland 46.22N 7.22E
110 P1 Wild Horse Alberta 49.00N 110.13W
110 K8 Wildhorse Res Nevada 41.40N 115.49W
66 O2 Wildkirchli Switzerland 47.17N 9.25E
113 M3 Wild L Alaska 67.30N 151.40W
100 P4 Wildnest L Saskatchewan 54.59N 102.20W
65 N8 Wildon Austria 46.53N 15.31E
112 B8 Wildorado Texas 35.13N 102.14W
63 S8 Wildpark E Germany 52.24N 13.02E
64 J8 Wildpoldsried W Germany 47.46N 10.24E
108 O2 Wild Rice R Minnesota
108 O3 Wild Rice R N Dakota
108 G1 Wildrose N Dakota 48.39N 103.11W
106 E5 Wild Rose Wisconsin 44.12N 89.16W
64 O7 Wildshut Austria 48.02N 12.50E
65 C8 Wild-Spitze mt Austria 46.53N 10.53E
66 G6 Wildstrubel mts Switzerland
95 L1 Wildt,De S Africa 25.39S 27.57E
100 B5 Wildwood Alberta 53.38N 115.14W
105 E9 Wildwood Florida 28.53N 82.03W
103 E9 Wildwood New Jersey 38.59N 74.49W
26 T6 Wilegama Sri Lanka 7.30N 81.09E
109 H3 Wiley Colorado 38.09N 102.43W
64 F6 Wilferdingen W Germany 48.57N 8.35E
66 J1 Wilfingen W Germany 47.40N 8.06E
64 F7 Wilflingen W Germany 48.09N 8.44E
99 E2 Wilgar Ontario 50.02N 85.22W
95 M3 Wilge R S Africa
95 N1 Wilge R S Africa
12 C4 Wilgena S Australia 30.48S 134.46E
123 D3 Wilhelm II Land Antarctica
60 C2 Wilhelminadorp Netherlands 51.32N 3.54E
60 H13 Wilhelmina Kanaal canal Netherlands
60 N8 Wilhelminaoord Netherlands 52.52N 6.10E
15 H6 Wilhelm,Mt Papua New Guinea 5.46S 144.59E
50 U13 Wilhelmøya isld Spitsbergen 79.05N 20.30E
62 H4 Wilhelm-Pieck-Stadt E Germany 51.59N 14.42E
65 N5 Wilhelmsburg Austria 48.07N 15.37E
63 L5 Wilhelmsburg Hamburg W Germany 53.32N 9.57E
63 H5 Wilhelmshaven W Germany 53.32N 8.07E
63 S8 Wilhelmshorst E Germany 52.20N 13.04E
94 D3 Wilhelmstal Namibia 21.54S 16.19E
63 O5 Wiligrad E Germany 53.45N 11.26E
18 J9 Wilis mt Java Indon 7.49S 111.50E
64 N2 Wilkau-Hasslau E Germany 50.40N 12.30E
Wilkes U.S.A. Base see Casey Australian Base
103 C4 Wilkes Barre Pennsylvania 41.15N 75.50W
105 F1 Wilkesboro N Carolina 36.08N 81.09W
123 H3 Wilkes Coast Antarctica
9 A7 Wilkes I Pacific Oc 19.18N 166.34E
123 E3 Wilkes Land Antarctica
100 J6 Wilkie Saskatchewan 52.27N 108.42W
123 E13 Wilkins Coast Antarctica
123 F13 Wilkins Ice Shelf Antarctica
12 C3 Wilkinson Lakes S Australia
59 J4 Wilkinstown Meath Irish Rep 53.45N 6.43W
105 D6 Willacoochee Georgia 31.20N 83.03W
111 M6 Willaha Arizona 35.45N 112.15W
110 B4 Willamette R Oregon
110 C6 Willamette, Middle Fork R Oregon
12 G5 Willanora Billabong R New S Wales
110 B3 Willapa R Washington
110 A3 Willapa B Washington
12 G3 Willara New S Wales 29.10S 144.20E
12 F2 Willara,L S Australia
109 G1 Willard Colorado 40.33N 103.30W
115 D3 Willard Mexico 28.58N 110.50W
108 F3 Willard Montana 46.12N 104.22W
109 D7 Willard New Mexico 34.35N 106.03W
104 C5 Willard Ohio 41.03N 82.44W
110 N8 Willard Utah 41.25N 112.03W
104 K8 Willards Maryland 38.23N 75.22W
12 G4 Willaroy New S Wales 30.06S 143.19E
15 L6 Willaumez Pen New Britain
61 E4 Willaupuis Belgium 50.34N 3.36E
111 P9 Willcox Arizona 32.16N 109.50W
63 K9 Willebadessen W Germany 51.38N 9.02E
61 H2 Willebroek Belgium 51.04N 4.22E
69 E2 Willems France 50.38N 3.14E
60 G13 Willemsdorp Netherlands 51.44N 4.38E
60 N8 Willemsoord Overijssel Netherlands 52.50N 6.05E
116 B1 Willemstad Curaçao W I 12.12N 68.56W
60 F13 Willemstad Netherlands 51.41N 4.27E
56 G2 Willenhall W Midlands Eng 52.36N 2.02W
66 F1 Willer France 47.35N 7.19E
57 N5 Willerby Humberside Eng 53.46N 0.27W
13 B3 Willeroo N Terr Australia 15.12S 131.34E
56 E3 Willersley Hereford & Worcs Eng 52.07N 3.00W
61 K7 Willerzie Belgium 49.58N 4.51E
55 E3 Willesden London Eng 51.33N 0.14W
100 C6 Willesden Green Alberta 52.40N 114.35W
60 H11 Willeskop Netherlands 52.02N 4.54E
103 C2 Willet New York 42.27N 75.55W
99 B2 Willet Ontario 50.18N 88.34W
101 T6 William R Saskatchewan
14 B6 Williambury W Australia 23.51S 115.07E
12 D3 William Cr S Australia 28.52S 136.18E
55 G2 William Girling Res London Eng
100 S5 William L Manitoba
12 G6 William,Mt Victoria 37.20S 142.41E
14 B10 William,Mt W Australia 32.58S 115.59E
112 G9 William P. Hobby Airport Houston, Texas
111 M6 Williams Arizona 35.16N 112.10W
111 B2 Williams California 39.09N 122.09W
107 K3 Williams Indiana 38.48N 86.39W
108 R7 Williams Iowa 42.30N 93.32W
108 Q1 Williams Minnesota 48.47N 94.56W
14 B10 Williams W Australia 33.01S 116.45E
13 F5 Williams R Queensland
106 F7 Williams Bay Wisconsin 42.34N 88.34W
103 L6 Williamsbridge New York 40.53N 73.51W
106 B8 Williamsburg Iowa 41.38N 92.01W
107 M5 Williamsburg Kentucky 36.44N 84.10W
103 J2 Williamsburg Massachusetts 42.24N 72.44W
103 K7 Williamsburg New York 40.43N 73.57W
104 A7 Williamsburg Ohio 39.04N 84.04W
99 Q1 Williamsburg Ontario 44.49N 75.16W
104 G6 Williamsburg Pennsylvania 40.28N 78.13W
104 J9 Williamsburg Virginia 37.17N 76.43W
12 K8 Williams Cr New S Wales
116 J2 Williamsfield Jamaica, W I 18.04N 77.28W
99 K8 Williamsford Ontario 44.25N 80.52W
116 E2 Williams I Bahamas 24.39N 78.30W
101 M9 Williams Lake Br Col 52.08N 122.09W
108 R8 Williamson Iowa 41.06N 93.16W
104 H3 Williamson New York 43.14N 77.13W
104 C9 Williamson W Virginia 37.42N 82.16W
123 K5 Williamson Hd Antarctica 69.00S 158.20E
106 G9 Williamsport Indiana 40.18N 87.18W
104 H7 Williamsport Maryland 38.34N 77.50W
98 Q3 Williamsport Newfoundland 50.31N 56.17W
104 H5 Williamsport Pennsylvania 41.16N 77.03W
14 B10 Williams R W Australia
106 K7 Williamston Michigan 42.41N 85.16W
105 K2 Williamston N Carolina 35.53N 77.05W
105 E3 Williamston S Carolina 34.38N 82.29W
107 M3 Williamstown Kentucky 38.39N 84.32W
104 M4 Williamstown Massachusetts 42.42N 73.13W
103 E7 Williamstown New Jersey 39.41N 74.59W
103 A5 Williamstown Pennsylvania 40.35N 76.37W
104 N2 Williamstown Vermont 44.05N 72.33W
104 D7 Williamstown W Virginia 39.24N 81.26W
12 C7 Williamstown dist Melbourne, Victoria
107 F5 Williamsville Missouri 36.58N 90.32W
63 E10 Willich W Germany 51.16N 6.32E
13 G8 Willie's Ra Queensland
116 P4 Willikie's Antigua W I 17.06N 61.42W
103 K3 Willimantic Connecticut 41.43N 72.12W
103 K3 Willimantic R Connecticut
100 E5 Willingdon Alberta 53.50N 112.04W
56 M6 Willingdon E Sussex Eng 50.47N 0.15E
101 P10 Willingdon,Mt Alberta 51.50N 116.20W
64 F1 Willingen W Germany 51.18N 8.37E
56 M3 Willingham Cambs Eng 52.19N 0.04E
101 R3 Willingham Mts N W Terr
57 K3 Willington Durham Eng 54.43N 1.41W
112 M5 Willis Texas 30.25N 95.30W
104 E10 Willis Virginia 36.52N 80.30W
66 H3 Willisau Switzerland 47.07N 7.59E
13 E5 Willis Cr Queensland
13 K3 Willis Grp islds Gt Barrier Reef Australia
121 F8 Willis Is S Georgia
105 E8 Williston Florida 29.23N 82.28W
108 G1 Williston N Dakota 48.09N 103.39W
94 F8 Williston S Africa 31.20S 20.52E
105 F4 Williston S Carolina 33.24N 81.25W
101 M8 Williston Lake Br Col
107 G4 Willisville Illinois 37.59N 89.35W
56 E5 Williton Somerset Eng 51.10N 3.20W
111 A2 Willits California 39.25N 123.21W
108 P4 Willmar Minnesota 45.06N 95.03W
100 P9 Willmar Saskatchewan 49.30N 102.28W
12 E4 Willochra S Australia 32.12S 138.10E
57 O6 Willoughby Lincs Eng 53.14N 0.12E
104 D5 Willoughby Ohio 41.38N 81.22W
12 L6 Willoughby dist Sydney, N S W
12 E6 Willoughby,C S Australia 35.54S 138.04E
104 N2 Willoughby,L Vermont
92 D11 Willoughby's Zimbabwe 19.34S 29.44E
113 M6 Willow Alaska 61.42N 150.08W
103 F2 Willow New York 42.04N 74.15W
109 L6 Willow Oklahoma 35.03N 99.32W
101 M9 Willow R Br Col
112 F9 Willow Bend Houston, Texas 29.38N 95.27W
100 P7 Willowbrook Saskatchewan 51.13N 102.48W
100 M9 Willow Bunch Saskatchewan 49.30N 105.41W
100 M9 Willow Bunch L Saskatchewan 49.25N 105.30W
108 K1 Willow City N Dakota 48.38N 100.18W
100 D8 Willow Cr Alberta
110 E9 Willow Cr California
110 O6 Willow Cr Idaho
110 F4 Willow Cr Oregon
110 H5 Willow Cr Oregon
111 P2 Willow Cr Utah
110 P8 Willow Cr Wyoming
110 B9 Willow Creek California 40.59N 123.37W
100 D8 Willow Creek Prov Park Alberta
103 E3 Willowemoc New York 41.55N 74.38W
103 E3 Willowemoc Cr New York
103 D6 Willow Grove Pennsylvania 40.08N 75.07W
101 O4 Willow L N W Terr
108 N5 Willow Lake S Dakota 44.38N 97.38W
101 N4 Willowlake R N W Terr
95 G9 Willowmore S Africa 33.18S 23.30E
13 C5 Willowra N Terr Australia 21.15S 132.35E
110 E8 Willow Ranch California 41.55N 120.21W
106 E4 Willow Res Wisconsin 45.43N 89.52W
108 S3 Willow River Minnesota 46.18N 92.49W
106 L7 Willow Run Michigan 42.14N 83.32W
111 B2 Willows California 39.32N 122.10W
100 M9 Willows Saskatchewan 49.37N 105.50W
107 E5 Willow Springs Missouri 36.59N 91.59W
103 B7 Willow Street Pennsylvania 39.58N 76.17W
12 K4 Willow Tree New S Wales 31.39S 150.43E
95 M8 Willowvale S Africa 32.16S 28.30E
104 M2 Willsboro New York 44.22N 73.26W
103 B2 Willseyville New York 42.17N 76.22W
14 G5 Wills,L W Australia
112 L3 Wills Point Texas 32.43N 96.01W
12 E6 Willunga S Australia 35.18S 138.33E
123 B5 Wilma Glacier Antarctica
107 H11 Wilmer Alabama 30.50N 88.21W
63 T6 Wilmersdorf E Germany 53.07N 13.55E
63 A2 Wilmersdorf dist W Berlin
106 G7 Wilmette Illinois 42.04N 87.43W
111 D10 Wilmington California 33.47N 118.16W
103 C7 Wilmington Delaware 39.46N 75.31W
56 M6 Wilmington E Sussex Eng 50.49N 0.12E
106 F8 Wilmington Illinois 41.18N 88.08W
55 K4 Wilmington Kent Eng 51.25N 0.12E
105 K3 Wilmington N Carolina 34.14N 77.55W
104 B7 Wilmington Ohio 39.28N 83.50W
12 E5 Wilmington S Australia 32.38S 138.07E
104 N4 Wilmington Vermont 42.52N 72.53W
106 F8 Wilmington South Illinois 41.09N 88.18W
108 P6 Wilmont Minnesota 43.47N 95.50W
109 L4 Wilmore Kansas 37.20N 99.15W
107 M4 Wilmore Kentucky 37.51N 84.49W
107 E8 Wilmot Arkansas 33.02N 91.35W
104 D6 Wilmot Ohio 40.40N 81.41W
11 C11 Wilmot,L New Zealand 44.24S 168.14E
11 B12 Wilmot Pass New Zealand 45.32S 167.14E
57 J6 Wilmslow Cheshire Eng 53.20N 2.15W
60 H11 Wilnis Netherlands 52.12N 4.54E
99 N7 Wilno Ontario 45.31N 77.35W
64 E2 Wilnsdorf W Germany 50.49N 8.06E
60 N11 Wilp Netherlands 52.14N 6.09E
26 Q5 Wilpattu game reserve Sri Lanka
60 O7 Wilp,De Netherlands 53.07N 6.15E
12 E4 Wilpena R S Australia
61 H2 Wilrijk Belgium 51.10N 4.23E
110 P4 Wilsall Montana 45.59N 110.39W
64 Q1 Wilsdruff E Germany 51.03N 13.32E
63 L6 Wilseder Berg mt W Germany 53.10N 9.56E
61 B2 Wilskerke Belgium 51.11N 2.50E
107 F6 Wilson Arkansas 35.34N 90.02W
109 M3 Wilson Kansas 38.50N 98.27W
107 E11 Wilson Louisiana 30.56N 91.08W
105 K2 Wilson N Carolina 35.43N 77.56W
104 G3 Wilson New York 43.18N 78.50W
109 N7 Wilson Oklahoma 34.10N 97.27W
103 D5 Wilson Pennsylvania 40.40N 75.15W
112 F2 Wilson Texas 33.18N 101.45W
110 P6 Wilson Wyoming 43.30N 110.53W
13 G7 Wilson R Queensland
12 A4 Wilson Bluff S Australia
97 L4 Wilson,C N W Terr 67.00N 81.30W
14 F5 Wilson Cliffs hill W Australia 22.00S 126.55E
110 F2 Wilson Cr Washington
13 B4 Wilson Creek N Terr Australia
110 F2 Wilson Creek Washington 47.26N 119.07W
111 K3 Wilson Creek Ra Nevada
107 J7 Wilson Dam Alabama 34.48N 87.38W
123 K5 Wilson Hills Antarctica
109 H3 Wilson Junction Colorado 38.09N 102.37W
107 J7 Wilson L Alabama
12 A2 Wilson,L S Australia 26.03S 129.35E
111 F7 Wilson,Mt California 34.15N 118.04W
109 C4 Wilson,Mt Colorado 37.51N 107.59W
111 K3 Wilson,Mt Nevada 38.18N 114.30W
14 G5 Wilson,Mt W Australia 20.21S 127.44E
14 G3 Wilson,R W Australia
109 M3 Wilson Res Kansas
12 H7 Wilson's Prom Victoria
58 J7 Wilsontown Strathclyde Scotland 55.47N 3.41W
108 K9 Wilsonville Nebraska 40.07N 100.06W
63 K6 Wilstedt W Germany 53.11N 9.05E
63 K5 Wilster W Germany 53.55N 9.23E
60 M9 Wilsum Netherlands 52.32N 5.58E
107 B8 Wilton Arkansas 33.44N 94.10W
103 H4 Wilton Connecticut 41.12N 73.25W
106 C8 Wilton Iowa 41.35N 91.01W
104 P2 Wilton Maine 44.36N 70.14W
108 K2 Wilton N Dakota 47.10N 100.50W
104 O4 Wilton New Hampshire 42.51N 71.46W
Wilton Queensland see Endeavour
56 H5 Wilton Wilts Eng 51.05N 1.52W
106 D6 Wilton Wisconsin 43.49N 90.34W
13 C2 Wilton R N Terr Australia
56 H5 Wiltshire co England
61 O7 Wiltz Luxembourg 49.58N 5.56E
14 D7 Wiluna W Australia 26.37S 120.12E
61 P7 Wilwerwiltz Luxembourg 49.59N 6.00E
64 L8 Wilzhofen W Germany 47.52N 11.11E
100 S3 Wimapedi L Manitoba
105 E10 Wimauma Florida 27.44N 82.17W
55 E4 Wimbledon London England 51.25N 0.13W
108 M2 Wimbledon N Dakota 47.11N 98.28W
11 L7 Wimbledon New Zealand 40.26S 176.30E
56 M2 Wimblington Cambs Eng 52.31N 0.06E
100 D7 Wimborne Alberta 51.55N 113.33W
56 H6 Wimborne Minster Dorset Eng 50.48N 1.59W
69 B2 Wimereux France 50.46N 1.37E
105 B8 Wimico,L Florida
69 B2 Wimille France 50.45N 1.38E
65 K8 Wimitz R Austria
69 N6 Wimmenau France 48.55N 7.25E
12 F6 Wimmera R Victoria
61 M3 Wimmertingen Belgium 50.53N 5.21E
66 G5 Wimmis Switzerland 46.41N 7.38E
90 G8 Wina watercourse Cameroon
100 A3 Winagami L Alberta 55.38N 116.40W
106 H8 Winamac Indiana 41.03N 86.37W
93 F6 Winam Gulf Kenya
Winan see Wannān,Al
12 G4 Winbar New S Wales 30.49S 144.50E
13 G7 Winbin Queensland 26.40S 144.38E
13 G7 Winbin R Queensland
95 L4 Winburg S Africa 28.31S 27.01E
56 G5 Wincanton Somerset Eng 51.04N 2.25W
57 N6 Winceby Lincs Eng 53.12N 0.02W
56 H4 Winchcombe Glos Eng 51.57N 1.58W
112 H4 Winchell Texas 31.28N 99.11W
56 N6 Winchelsea E Sussex Eng 50.55N 0.42E
104 N4 Winchendon Massachusetts 42.41N 72.04W
56 J5 Winchester Hants Eng 51.04N 1.19W
110 J3 Winchester Idaho 46.15N 116.37W
107 F2 Winchester Illinois 39.38N 90.28W
106 K9 Winchester Indiana 40.11N 84.57W
107 M4 Winchester Kentucky 38.00N 84.10W
104 N4 Winchester New Hampshire 42.46N 72.24W
11 F11 Winchester New Zealand 44.11S 171.17E
104 B8 Winchester Ohio 38.56N 83.40W
99 P7 Winchester Ontario 45.04N 75.21W
107 K6 Winchester Tennessee 35.10N 86.09W
112 K5 Winchester Texas 30.02N 97.01W
104 G7 Winchester Virginia 39.11N 78.12W
108 B6 Winchester Wyoming 43.51N 108.10W
104 P8 Winchester dist Boston, Mass
110 A6 Winchester Bay Oregon 43.41N 124.11W
103 H3 Winchester Center Connecticut 41.54N 73.08W
110 R6 Wind R Wyoming
101 F3 Wind R Yukon Terr
12 D4 Windabout,L S Australia 31.21S 137.05E
64 L7 Windach W Germany 48.04N 11.03E
14 D8 Windarra W Australia 28.28S 122.15E
104 G6 Windber Pennsylvania 40.16N 79.51W
108 G6 Wind Cave Nat. Park S Dakota
64 D2 Windeck W Germany 50.49N 7.35E
64 F3 Windecken W Germany 50.13N 8.53E
64 E5 Winden W Germany 49.06N 8.07E
105 D4 Winder Georgia 33.59N 83.43W
13 K7 Windera Queensland 26.04S 151.46E
105 L12 Windermere Bahamas 25.06N 76.08W
57 H4 Windermere Cumbria Eng 54.23N 2.54W
57 H4 Windermere L Cumbria Eng 54.20N 2.57W
99 G5 Windermere L Ontario
60 N10 Windesheim Netherlands 52.27N 6.08E
106 J9 Windfall Indiana 40.22N 85.57W
103 D5 Wind Gap Pennsylvania 40.51N 75.18W
113 V8 Windham Alaska 57.35N 133.20W
103 K3 Windham Connecticut 41.42N 72.10W
110 P2 Windham Montana 47.05N 110.09W
103 F2 Windham New York 42.18N 74.16W
103 B3 Windham Pennsylvania 41.58N 76.18W
103 K3 Windham co Connecticut
103 B3 Windham Center Pennsylvania 41.58N 76.20W
63 K8 Windheim W Germany 52.25N 9.01E
94 D4 Windhoek Namibia 22.34S 17.06E
14 D7 Windich Springs W Australia 25.32S 121.56E
99 R5 Windigo Quebec 47.46N 73.20W
65 M4 Windigsteig Austria 48.47N 15.18E
109 P7 Winding Stair Mts Oklahoma
66 J2 Windisch Switzerland 47.29N 8.14E
64 N4 Windischeschenbach W Germany 49.48N 12.09E
65 K6 Windischgarsten Austria 47.44N 14.20E
123 F2 Windmill Is Antarctica
104 J9 Windmill Pt Virginia 37.37N 76.27W
109 N3 Windom Kansas 38.23N 97.55W
108 P6 Windom Minnesota 43.52N 95.06W
109 C4 Windom Pk Colorado 37.50N 107.33W
13 G7 Windorah Queensland 25.24S 142.37E
64 P6 Windorf W Germany 48.37N 13.15E
106 G7 Wind Pt Wisconsin 42.47N 87.45W
110 R7 Wind River Wyoming 42.59N 108.53W
110 Q6 Wind River Ra Wyoming
56 H4 Windrush,R Glos etc Eng
64 K5 Windsbach W Germany 49.15N 10.51E
Windsheim see Bad Windsheim
56 K5 Windsor Berks Eng 51.29N 0.38W
109 F1 Windsor Colorado 40.28N 104.53W
103 J3 Windsor Connecticut 41.52N 72.38W
107 H2 Windsor Illinois 39.26N 88.38W
103 H2 Windsor Massachusetts 42.30N 73.03W
107 C3 Windsor Missouri 38.32N 93.32W
105 L1 Windsor N Carolina 36.00N 76.59W
98 R5 Windsor Newfoundland 48.58N 55.40W
12 K5 Windsor New S Wales 33.39S 150.50E
103 C2 Windsor New York 42.06N 75.38W
11 E12 Windsor New Zealand 45.00S 170.48E
98 H9 Windsor Nova Scotia 45.00N 64.09W
99 H10 Windsor Ontario 42.18N 83.00W
103 A7 Windsor Pennsylvania 39.55N 76.35W
99 S7 Windsor Quebec 45.35N 72.01W
94 S13 Windsor S Africa 26.08S 27.58E
105 F4 Windsor S Carolina 33.27N 81.31W
104 N3 Windsor Vermont 43.29N 72.25W
104 J10 Windsor Virginia 36.46N 76.45W
13 K1 Windsor dist Brisbane, Qnsld
105 K9 Windsor Airfield New Providence I Bahamas 25.03N 77.28W
56 K5 Windsor Great Park Berks Eng 51.26N 0.38W
104 E6 Windsor Heights W Virginia 40.12N 80.42W
116 H4 Windsor, L Great Inagua Bahamas
103 J3 Windsor Locks Connecticut 41.56N 72.37W
11 A13 Windsor Pt New Zealand 46.13S 166.40E
95 H4 Windsorton S Africa 28.20S 24.43E
100 P8 Windthorst Saskatchewan 50.07N 102.52W
112 J2 Windthorst Texas 33.34N 98.27W
13 F7 Windula R Queensland
11 J13 Windward Is Antipodes Is Pacific Oc
116 P7 Windward Is West Indies
116 G5 Windward Passage Haiti/Cuba
113 N5 Windy Alaska 63.30N 148.50W
113 K5 Windy Fork R Alaska
95 O5 Windy Hill S Africa 29.30S 30.34E
100 P4 Windy L Saskatchewan
101 Q5 Windy Pt Great Slave L, N W Terr 61.18N 115.51W
100 G3 Winefred L Alberta
100 G3 Winefred R Alberta
106 E3 Winegar Wisconsin 46.15N 89.40W
106 K6 Winegars Michigan 43.57N 84.20W
87 A6 Winejpk Sudan 9.01N 27.30E
61 K6 Winenne Belgium 50.06N 4.54E
110 E2 Winesap Washington 47.45N 120.14W
107 J8 Winfield Alabama 33.55N 87.50W
100 C6 Winfield Alberta 52.58N 114.23W
106 C8 Winfield Iowa 41.05N 91.27W
109 O4 Winfield Kansas 37.14N 96.59W
112 M2 Winfield Texas 33.10N 95.07W
56 K4 Wing Bucks Eng 51.54N 0.44W
108 K2 Wing N Dakota 47.10N 100.17W
106 G9 Wingate Indiana 40.10N 87.02W
109 B6 Wingate New Mexico 35.31N 108.33W
13 B2 Wingate Mts N Terr Australia
103 G3 Wingdale New York 41.39N 73.34W
12 K4 Wingen New S Wales 31.43S 150.54E
61 D2 Wingene Belgium 51.04N 3.17E
69 N6 Wingen-sur-Moder France 48.56N 7.22E
12 A8 Wingfield dist Adelaide, S Aust 34.51S 138.33E
56 O5 Wingham Kent Eng 51.17N 1.13E
12 K4 Wingham New S Wales 31.50S 152.20E
99 J9 Wingham Ontario 43.54N 81.19W
107 H5 Wingo Kentucky 36.39N 88.45W
63 K5 Wingst W Germany 53.43N 9.02E
19 D8 Wini Timor Indon 9.13S 124.30E
110 Q2 Winifred Montana 47.34N 109.24W
108 N6 Winifred S Dakota 44.00N 97.23W
121 D6 Winifreda Argentina 36.16S 64.15W
14 E6 Winifred,L W Australia 22.40S 123.33E
97 L6 Winisk Ontario 55.20N 85.15W
97 L7 Winisk R Ontario
97 L7 Winisk L Ontario 53.00N 88.00W
112 D4 Wink Texas 31.44N 103.10W
25 E5 Winkana Burma 15.45N 98.00E
66 F2 Winkel France 47.27N 7.16E
60 H8 Winkel Netherlands 52.45N 4.54E
111 O9 Winkelman Arizona 33.00N 110.48W
66 O2 Winkeln Switzerland 47.24N 9.19E
95 K3 Winkelpos S Africa 27.36S 26.49E
56 K5 Winkfield Berks Eng 51.27N 0.43W
64 O5 Winklarn W Germany 49.25N 12.31E
56 D6 Winkleigh Devon Eng 50.51N 3.56W
100 U9 Winkler Manitoba 49.12N 97.55W
65 G8 Winklern Austria 46.52N 12.53E
65 K7 Winklern Austria 47.13N 14.14E
61 J3 Winksele Belgium 50.54N 4.39E
110 C3 Winlock Washington 46.29N 122.56W
104 R1 Winn Maine 45.28N 68.23W
106 K6 Winn Michigan 43.33N 84.53W
13 B6 Winnalls Ridge N Terr Australia
89 J9 Winneba Ghana 5.22N 0.38W
108 Q6 Winnebago Minnesota 43.46N 94.10W
108 O7 Winnebago Nebraska 42.14N 96.38W
106 F6 Winnebago,L Wisconsin
13 B4 Winnecke Creek N Terr Australia
14 G6 Winnecke Hills N Terr/W Aust
13 B4 Winnecke,Mt N Terr Australia 18.50S 130.19E
14 E6 Winnecke Rock hill W Australia 23.12S 123.55E
106 F5 Winneconne Wisconsin 44.07N 88.43W
110 H9 Winnemucca Nevada 40.58N 117.45W
110 F9 Winnemucca L Nevada 40.10N 119.20W
64 G6 Winnenden W Germany 48.53N 9.25E
108 L6 Winner S Dakota 43.22N 99.51W
106 G7 Winnetka Illinois 42.06N 87.46W
108 N7 Winnetoon Nebraska 42.32N 97.58W
110 R2 Winnett Montana 47.00N 108.21W
107 D10 Winnfield Louisiana 31.56N 92.40W
108 Q2 Winnibigoshish L Minnesota
112 N6 Winnie Texas 29.50N 94.24W
100 F9 Winnifred Alberta 49.55N 111.17W
14 A6 Winning W Australia 23.13S 114.33E
63 O9 Winningen E Germany 51.50N 11.27E
64 C3 Winningen W Germany 50.20N 7.30E
12 E5 Winnininnie S Australia 32.35S 139.40E
100 U9 Winnipeg Manitoba 49.53N 97.10W
100 U8 Winnipeg Beach Manitoba 50.30N 97.00W
100 U6 Winnipeg,L Manitoba
100 S7 Winnipegosis Manitoba 51.40N 99.56W
100 R6 Winnipegosis,L Manitoba
104 O3 Winnipesaukee L New Hampshire
107 E9 Winnsboro Louisiana 32.09N 91.43W
105 F3 Winnsboro S Carolina 34.22N 81.05W
112 M3 Winnsboro Texas 32.58N 95.17W
64 D4 Winnweiler W Germany 49.34N 7.52E
105 E6 Winokur Georgia 31.03N 82.02W
111 N6 Winona Arizona 35.13N 111.21W
109 J2 Winona Kansas 39.03N 101.15W
106 F3 Winona Michigan 46.54N 88.56W
106 C5 Winona Minnesota 44.02N 91.37W
107 G8 Winona Mississippi 33.30N 89.42W
107 E4 Winona Missouri 37.01N 91.20W
112 M3 Winona Texas 32.29N 95.11W
110 H3 Winona Washington 46.57N 117.50W
107 D7 Winona,L Arkansas 34.49N 92.52W
104 M2 Winooski Vermont 44.31N 73.11W
104 N2 Winooski R Vermont
57 F3 Winscales Cumbria Eng 54.38N 3.30W
60 R7 Winschoten Netherlands 53.07N 7.02E
60 P7 Winschoter diep canal Netherlands
61 O7 Winseler Luxembourg 49.58N 5.53E
63 L7 Winsen W Germany 52.41N 9.54E
63 M6 Winsen W Germany 53.22N 10.12E
57 H6 Winsford Cheshire Eng 53.11N 2.31W
56 D5 Winsford Somerset Eng 51.06N 3.34W
108 N7 Winside Nebraska 42.11N 97.11W
111 O6 Winslow Arizona 35.01N 110.43W
107 B6 Winslow Arkansas 35.47N 94.09W
56 K4 Winslow Bucks Eng 51.57N 0.54W
107 J3 Winslow Indiana 38.23N 87.12W
104 Q2 Winslow Maine 44.34N 69.37W
110 C2 Winslow Washington 47.36N 122.30W
10 R2 Winslow Reef Pacific Oc
103 K2 Winsor Dam Massachusetts 42.17N 72.21W
110 N5 Winsper Idaho 44.08N 112.31W
103 H3 Winsted Connecticut 41.55N 73.04W
57 H4 Winster Cumbria Eng 54.20N 2.54W
57 K6 Winster Derbys Eng 53.09N 1.38W
57 K3 Winston Durham Eng 54.33N 1.47W
110 O3 Winston Montana 46.28N 111.38W
109 C8 Winston New Mexico 33.21N 107.40W
105 G1 Winston-Salem N Carolina 36.05N 80.18W
60 P6 Winsum Groningen Netherlands 53.20N 6.31E
60 L7 Winsum Netherlands 53.09N 5.37E
60 K14 Wintelre Netherlands 51.26N 5.20E
100 H6 Winter Saskatchewan 52.38N 109.30W
65 M6 Winterbach Austria 47.57N 15.17E
64 F1 Winterberg W Germany 51.14N 8.32E
95 K8 Winterberge mts S Africa
56 F6 Winterborne Abbas Dorset Eng 50.43N 2.33W
56 G6 Winterborne Whitchurch Dorset Eng 50.48N 2.15W
56 H5 Winterbourne Stoke Wilts Eng 51.10N 1.55W
69 O4 Winterburg W Germany 49.48N 7.35E
63 O7 Winterfeld E Germany 52.45N 11.15E
105 F9 Winter Garden Florida 28.32N 81.35W
97 H3 Winter Harb N W Terr
111 K9 Winterhaven California 32.43N 114.39W
105 F9 Winter Haven Florida 28.01N 81.45W
57 M5 Winteringham Humberside Eng 53.41N 0.35W
100 U3 Wintering L Manitoba
64 G7 Winterlingen W Germany 48.11N 9.08E
109 E2 Winter Park Colorado 39.54N 105.46W
105 F9 Winter Park Florida 28.35N 81.21W
104 R2 Winterport Maine 44.38N 68.53W
111 B3 Winters California 38.30N 122.00W
112 H4 Winters Texas 31.53N 99.59W
111 M8 Wintersburg Arizona 33.27N 112.52W
108 Q8 Winterset Iowa 41.20N 94.01W
61 M3 Wintershoven Belgium 50.51N 5.24E
95 H4 Winter's Rush S Africa 28.27S 24.23E
66 Q2 Winterstaude mt Austria 47.24N 9.59E
103 A7 Winterstown Pennsylvania 39.50N 76.37W
60 P12 Winterswijk Netherlands 51.58N 6.44E
66 L1 Winterthur Switzerland 47.30N 8.45E
57 M5 Winterton Humberside Eng 53.39N 0.35W
98 T6 Winterton Newfoundland 47.59N 53.20W
103 F3 Winterton New York 41.32N 74.28W
56 P2 Winterton Norfolk Eng 52.43N 1.42E
95 N4 Winterton S Africa 28.49S 29.33E
104 Q7 Winterville Maine 46.58N 68.31W
104 Q2 Winthrop Maine 44.18N 70.00W
108 Q5 Winthrop Minnesota 44.32N 94.22W
104 L2 Winthrop New York 44.48N 74.50W
110 E1 Winthrop Washington 48.29N 120.11W
104 R9 Winthrop dist Boston, Mass
106 G7 Winthrop Harbor Illinois 42.27N 87.49W
12 C3 Wintinna S Australia 27.39S 134.05E
12 C3 Wintinna R S Australia
56 H6 Winton Dorset Eng 50.45N 1.54W
108 T2 Winton Minnesota 47.57N 91.48W
105 L1 Winton N Carolina 36.24N 76.57W
105 L9 Winton New Providence I Bahamas 25.03N 77.17W
11 C13 Winton New Zealand 46.10S 168.20E
103 C4 Winton Pennsylvania 41.28N 75.33W
13 G5 Winton Queensland 22.22S 143.00E
95 F3 Winton S Africa 27.28S 22.35E
110 E2 Winton Washington 47.44N 120.45W
57 J4 Winton Westmorland Eng 54.29N 2.20W
110 Q8 Winton Wyoming 41.45N 109.10W
69 N7 Wintzenheim France 48.04N 7.18E
56 L3 Winwick Cambs Eng 52.25N 0.23W
57 H6 Winwick Cheshire Eng 53.26N 2.36W
105 H4 Winyah B S Carolina 33.16N 79.15W
64 P6 Winzer W Germany 48.44N 13.05E
108 Q8 Wiota Iowa 41.25N 94.55W
63 N10 Wipper R E Germany
64 C1 Wipperfürth W Germany 51.07N 7.24E
63 O9 Wippra E Germany 52.35N 11.17E
65 D7 Wipptal V Austria
86 G6 Wirâg, Wâdi el watercourse Egypt
26 S9 Wiraketiya Sri Lanka 6.09N 80.46E
26 T9 Wirawila Sri Lanka 6.16N 81.13E
63 F6 Wirdum W Germany 53.29N 7.13E
11 E3 Wiri New Zealand 36.59S 174.53E
15 B4 Wiriagar R Irian Jaya
87 L6 Wirir Somalia 9.32N 46.12E
57 K6 Wirksworth Derbys Eng 53.05N 1.34W
15 A6 Wirmaf Moluccas Indon 4.47S 131.44E
11 D3 Wiroa I New Zealand 37.01S 174.48E
86 L8 Wirqa, Wâdi watercourse Egypt
12 E5 Wirrabara S Australia 33.03S 138.18E
57 G6 Wirral pen Merseyside/Cheshire Eng
12 D4 Wirraminna S Australia 31.11S 136.04E
12 D4 Wirrapa S Australia 31.28S 137.00E
12 F6 Wirrega S Australia 36.11S 140.37E
12 C3 Wirrida,L S Australia 29.39S 134.40E
Wirriya see Warī'ah,Al
12 C4 Wirrulla S Australia 32.24S 134.33E
95 J2 Wirsing S Africa 26.30S 25.08E
108 R2 Wirt Minnesota 47.44N 93.54W
15 E5 Wiru R Irian Jaya
69 B2 Wirwignes France 50.41N 1.46E
56 M2 Wisbech Cambs Eng 52.40N 0.10E
56 K5 Wisborough Green W Sussex Eng 51.01N 0.31W
104 Q2 Wiscasset Maine 44.01N 69.41W
63 K5 Wischhafen W Germany 53.47N 9.18E
102 H2 Wisconsin state U.S.A.
106 E6 Wisconsin Dells Wisconsin 43.37N 89.48W
106 E6 Wisconsin,L Wisconsin
106 D6 Wisconsin,R Wisconsin
123 G9 Wisconsin Ra Antarctica
106 E5 Wisconsin Rapids Wisconsin 44.24N 89.50W
110 M4 Wisdom Montana 45.38N 113.26W
104 C10 Wise Virginia 37.00N 82.36W
113 M3 Wiseman Alaska 67.25N 150.15W
66 H2 Wisenberg mt Switzerland 47.24N 7.53E
110 N4 Wise River Montana 45.48N 112.58W
100 K7 Wiseton Saskatchewan 51.18N 107.40W
100 O7 Wishart Saskatchewan 51.32N 103.56W
58 J7 Wishaw Strathclyde Scotland 55.47N 3.56W
108 L3 Wishek N Dakota 46.16N 99.32W
110 E4 Wishram Washington 45.40N 120.59W
57 L4 Wiske,R N Yorks Eng
62 L6 Wisła Poland 49.39N 18.50E
62 L2 Wisła R Poland
62 M1 Wislany,Zalew inlet Poland/U.S.S.R.
55 B6 Wisley Surrey Eng 51.20N 0.29W
62 N6 Wisłok R Poland
63 O5 Wismar Rostock E Germany 53.54N 11.28E
63 O4 Wismarbucht B E Germany
107 E10 Wisner Louisiana 31.59N 91.40W
108 O8 Wisner Nebraska 41.59N 96.52W
103 F4 Wisner New York 41.16N 74.19W
15 E6 Wisnumurti,Pk Irian Jaya 4.30S 139.55E
69 B2 Wissant France 50.52N 1.40E
69 O5 Wissembourg France 49.02N 7.57E
64 D2 Wissen W Germany 50.47N 7.45E
60 C2 Wissenkerke Netherlands 51.35N 3.45E
56 N2 Wissey,R Norfolk Eng
63 H8 Wissingen W Germany 52.16N 8.14E
106 C5 Wissota L Wisconsin
101 K9 Wistaria Br Col 53.55N 126.22W
109 Q7 Wister Oklahoma 34.57N 94.44W
109 Q7 Wister Res Oklahoma 34.58N 94.40W
95 N1 Witbank S Africa 25.53S 29.13E
95 L6 Witberge mts S Africa
60 N14 Witbroek Netherlands 51.27N 6.11E
100 V3 Witchai L Manitoba 55.55N 96.98W
14 B10 Witchcliffe W Australia 34.02S 115.06E
100 K5 Witchekan L Saskatchewan
95 H10 Witelsbos S Africa 34.01S 24.06E
56 N4 Witham Essex Eng 51.48N 0.38E
57 N6 Witham, R Lincs Eng
104 M2 Witherbee New York 44.05N 73.32W
56 D6 Witheridge Devon Eng 50.55N 3.42W
57 O6 Withern Lincs Eng 53.19N 0.08E
57 O5 Withernsea Humberside Eng 53.44N 0.02E
13 J6 Withersfield Queensland 23.35S 147.32E
56 M3 Withersfield Suffolk Eng 52.06N 0.25E
113 O6 Witherspoon,Mt Alaska 61.25N 147.11W
109 C8 Withington,Mt New Mexico 33.53N 107.29W
105 D7 Withlacoochee,R Fla/Georgia
105 E9 Withlacoochee,R Florida
56 D6 Withleigh Devon Eng 50.54N 3.33W
86 K8 Withr,Gebel hill Egypt 28.48N 33.15E
110 F2 Withrow Washington 47.44N 119.48W
94 C2 Witklip Namibia 19.52S 14.22E
95 N3 Witkoppies mt S Africa 27.45S 29.20E
62 K3 Witkowo Poland 52.28N 17.45E
98 T6 Witless Bay Newfoundland 47.18N 52.51W
60 K7 Witmarsum Netherlands 53.07N 5.28E
95 J8 Witmos S Africa 32.32S 25.44E
56 J4 Witney Oxon Eng 51.48N 1.29W
95 J2 Witpan S Africa 26.53S 25.15E
95 K3 Witpan salt pan S Africa 27.50S 26.26E
94 K5 Witpoort Transvaal S Africa 25.26S 29.55E
95 K3 Witpoort Transvaal S Africa 27.10S 26.08E
95 H5 Witput S Africa 29.32S 24.16E
61 N7 Witry Belgium 49.52N 5.37E
69 G5 Witry-les-Reims France 49.18N 4.08E
Witsieshoek see Phuthadijhaba
107 G2 Witt Illinois 39.15N 89.21W
63 H3 Wittdün W Germany 54.37N 8.23E
95 D9 Witteberge mts Cape Province S Africa
95 M4 Witteberge mts Orange Free State S Africa
64 L7 Wittelsbach W Germany 48.27N 11.11E
60 T17 Wittem Netherlands 50.48N 5.55E
108 K6 Witten S Dakota 43.26N 100.05W
63 F10 Witten W Germany 51.25N 7.19E
63 R9 Wittenberg E Germany 51.53N 12.39E
106 E5 Wittenberg Wisconsin 44.50N 89.09W
63 P7 Wittenberge E Germany 52.59N 11.45E
63 O5 Wittenburg E Germany 53.31N 11.05E
14 C5 Wittenoom W Australia 22.19S 118.21E
14 G4 Wittenoom,Mt W Australia 18.32S 128.50E
63 L4 Wittensee L W Germany 54.24N 9.46E
56 K6 Witterings,The W Sussex Eng 50.47N 0.54W
66 F1 Wittersdorf France 47.37N 7.16E
56 N5 Wittersham Kent Eng 51.01N 0.43E
64 O2 Wittgensdorf E Germany 50.52N 12.51E
115 N2 Witties,The islds Nicaragua
64 H4 Wittighausen W Germany 49.36N 9.50E
63 N7 Wittingen W Germany 52.43N 10.45E
18 M3 Witti Ra Sabah Malaysia
63 H8 Wittlage W Germany 52.20N 8.22E
64 B4 Wittlich W Germany 49.59N 6.54E
63 K7 Wittlohe W Germany 52.51N 9.21E
111 M8 Wittmann Arizona 33.47N 112.30W
63 G5 Wittmund W Germany 53.34N 7.47E
66 H2 Wittnau Switzerland 47.29N 7.59E
57 K3 Witton Gilbert Durham Eng 54.48N 1.38W
57 K3 Witton le Wear Durham Eng 54.41N 1.46W
63 S3 Wittow pen E Germany 54.39N 13.15E
63 R6 Wittstock E Germany 53.10N 12.30E
93 M8 Witu Kenya 2.24S 40.28E
15 K6 Witu Is Bismarck Arch
94 E4 Witvlei Namibia 22.23S 18.32E
95 L1 Witwatersberg mts S Africa
94 R13 Witwatersrand reg S Africa
64 H1 Witzenhausen W Germany 51.20N 9.51E
56 E5 Wiveliscombe Somerset Eng 51.03N 3.19W
56 N4 Wivenhoe Essex Eng 51.52N 0.58E
100 W2 Wivenhoe Manitoba 56.12N 95.06W
11 J2 Wiwiki,C New Zealand 35.10S 174.09E
56 O4 Wix Essex Eng 51.55N 1.09E
62 O1 Wizajny Poland 54.21N 22.51E
69 C2 Wizernes France 50.42N 2.12E
62 M3 Wkra R Poland
62 L1 Władysławowo Poland 54.48N 18.25E
62 J4 Wleń Poland 51.01N 15.40E
62 L3 Włocławek Poland 52.39N 19.01E
62 O4 Włodawa Poland 51.33N 23.31E
62 M5 Włoszczowa Poland 50.51N 19.58E
63 P6 Wöbbelin E Germany 53.24N 11.30E
87 G6 Woberi Ethiopia 9.39N 39.02E
28 L1 Wobo Xizang Zizhiqu 29.35N 97.32E
93 D5 Wobulenzi Uganda 0.43N 32.33E
56 K4 Woburn Beds Eng 51.59N 0.38W
11 D5 Woburn New Zealand
61 E4 Wodecq Belgium 50.43N 3.45E
12 A6 Woden Valley dist Canberra Australia
87 G6 Wodesha Ethiopia 8.02N 38.19E
14 C5 Wodgina W Australia 21.12S 118.48E
12 H6 Wodonga Victoria 36.08S 146.09E
62 L5 Wodzisław Katowice Poland 50.01N 18.26E
62 M5 Wodzisław Kielce Poland 50.31N 20.08E
60 F14 Woensdrecht Netherlands 51.25N 4.18E
60 H11 Woerden Netherlands 52.06N 4.54E
69 O6 Wœrth France 48.57N 7.45E
60 M11 Woeste Hoeve Netherlands 52.06N 5.57E
61 B3 Woesten Belgium 50.54N 2.47E
69 J5 Wœvre,Forêt de France
69 K5 Woëvres,Les plain France
107 M5 Wofford Kentucky 36.48N 84.09W
60 J9 Wognum Netherlands 52.41N 5.02E
87 K5 Wogr Ra Somalia
66 F4 Wohlen Switzerland 46.59N 7.22E

66 K2 Wohlen Switzerland 47.21N 8.17E
63 O5 Wohlenberg E Germany 53.57N 11.15E
66 F4 Wohlensee *L* Switzerland
66 Q1 Wohmbrechts W Germany 47.39N 9.52E
64 F2 Wohratal W Germany 50.56N 8.47E
63 J4 Wöhrden W Germany 54.11N 9.00E
87 C7 Woi Sudan 7.59N 31.03E
69 J6 Woimbey France 48.59N 5.29E
15 J8 Woitape Papua New Guinea 8.36S 147.15E
99 N7 Woito Ontario 45.41N 77.13W
15 C6 Wokam *isld* Moluccas Indon
21 E4 Woken Heilongjiang China 45.59N 130.28E
21 E4 Woken He *R* Heilongjiang China
101 O8 Woking Alberta 55.36N 118.49W
56 K5 Woking Surrey Eng 51.20N 0.34W
56 K5 Wokingham Berks Eng 51.25N 0.51W
13 G5 Wokingham *R* Queensland
63 S6 Wokuhl E Germany 53.17N 13.13E
108 M8 Wolbach Nebraska 41.26N 98.22W
63 G9 Wolbeck W Germany 51.54N 7.44E
62 M5 Wolbrom Poland 50.24N 19.44E
87 F4 Wolchefit Pass Ethiopia 13.21N 37.54E
109 D2 Wolcott Colorado 39.42N 106.40W
103 J3 Wolcott Connecticut 41.36N 72.57W
104 J3 Wolcott New York 43.14N 76.51W
64 E2 Woldbrunn W Germany 50.32N 8.09E
93 L1 Wolde Ethiopia 4.05N 39.55E
63 T6 Woldegk E Germany 53.27N 13.36E
60 R6 Woldendorp Netherlands 53.17N 7.02E
60 S17 Wolder Netherlands 50.50N 5.39E
17 O10 Woleai *atoll* Caroline Is Pacific Oc 7.24N 143.52E
13 J7 Woleebee Queensland 26.17S 149.20E
91 B3 Woleu *R* Gabon/Equat Guinea
91 B3 Woleu-N'tem *reg* Gabon
107 G11 Wolf *R* Mississippi
107 G6 Wolf *R* Tennessee
101 G5 Wolf *R* Yukon Terr
64 E7 Wolfach W Germany 48.18N 8.14E
64 P6 Wolfachau W Germany 48.34N 13.14E
98 M3 Wolf B Quebec
98 M3 Wolf Bay Quebec 50.14N 60.14W
112 D7 Wolf Cr Texas
107 L5 Wolf Cr. Dam Kentucky 36.52N 85.10W
110 N2 Wolf Creek Montana 47.00N 112.05W
110 B7 Wolf Creek Oregon 42.42N 123.24W
109 D4 Wolf Creek Pass Colorado 37.29N 106.50W
100 J6 Wolfe Saskatchewan 52.20N 108.32W
104 O3 Wolfeboro New Hampshire 43.36N 71.14W
112 L2 Wolfe City Texas 33.24N 96.04W
99 O8 Wolfe Island Ontario 44.11N 76.28W
63 Q9 Wolfen E Germany 51.41N 12.17E
63 N8 Wolfenbüttel W Germany 52.10N 10.33E
66 K4 Wolfenschiessen Switzerland 46.55N 8.24E
10 E11 Wolfe Rock Lord Howe I Pacific Oc 31.34S 159.08E
56 M2 Wolferton Norfolk Eng 52.50N 0.28E
98 Q9 Wolfe's Cove Quebec 46.47N 71.14W
112 E2 Wolfforth Texas 33.30N 102.02W
66 Q4 Wolfgang Switzerland 46.51N 9.52E
64 G1 Wolfhagen W Germany 51.19N 9.10E
66 P2 Wolfhalden Switzerland 47.27N 9.33E
111 L5 Wolf Hole Arizona 36.46N 113.33W
Wolf I *see* Wenman,I
98 L6 Wolf I Madeleine Is, Que 47.35N 61.40W
100 G4 Wolf L Alberta 54.42N 110.55W
101 H5 Wolf L Yukon Terr 60.38N 131.40W
108 C4 Wolf Mts Montana
108 L1 Wolford N Dakota 48.31N 99.41W
108 E1 Wolf Point Montana 48.05N 105.40W
106 F4 Wolf,R Wisconsin
13 B2 Wolfram Hill N Terr Australia 13.56S 132.13E
64 K5 Wolframs-Eschenbach W Germany 49.14N 10.44E
64 L8 Wolfratshausen W Germany 47.55N 11.25E
56 S10 Wolf Rock Lt.Ho English Chan 49.57N 5.49W
65 L8 Wolfsberg Austria 46.50N 14.50E
63 N8 Wolfsburg W Germany 52.27N 10.49E
56 B4 Wolf's Castle Dyfed Wales 51.54N 4.58W
65 J5 Wolfsegg Austria 48.06N 13.42E
64 N2 Wolfsgefärth E Germany 50.49N 12.04E
64 E4 Wolfskehlen W Germany 49.51N 8.30E
64 Q6 Wolfstein Bayern W Germany 48.49N 13.33E
64 D4 Wolfstein Rheinland-Pfalz W Germany 49.34N 7.38E
98 H8 Wolfville Nova Scotia 45.06N 64.22W
119 A5 Wolf, Vol Galápagos Is 0.01N 91.22W
66 H2 Wolfwil Switzerland 47.17N 7.48E
63 T4 Wolgast E Germany 54.03N 13.46E
66 J3 Wolhusen Switzerland 47.04N 8.05E
62 H2 Wolin Poland 53.51N 14.38E
64 L3 Wölkendorf W Germany 50.01N 11.11E
64 P2 Wolkenstein E Germany 50.40N 13.09E
65 P5 Wolkersdorf Austria 48.24N 16.31E
63 N10 Wolkramshausen E Germany 51.26N 10.45E
61 O8 Wolkrange Belgium 49.38N 5.48E
65 J8 Wöllanernock *mt* Austria 46.47N 13.50E
56 K3 Wollaston Northants Eng 52.16N 0.41W
101 P1 Wollaston,C Victoria I, N W Terr 71.09N 117.58W
48 V8 Wollaston Forland Greenland
121 L10 Wollaston,Is Chile
101 W6 Wollaston L Saskatchewan
101 W6 Wollaston Lake Saskatchewan 58.05N 103.38W
101 P1 Wollaston Pen Victoria I, N W Terr
66 G1 Wollbach W Germany 47.40N 7.39E
66 L3 Wollerau Switzerland 47.12N 8.43E
64 B2 Wollersheim W Germany 50.41N 6.34E
63 T6 Wolletz See *L* E Germany
66 N1 Wollmatingen W Germany 47.41N 9.09E
12 K5 Wollongong New S Wales 34.25S 150.52E
64 D4 Wöllstein W Germany 49.49N 7.59E
95 K3 Wolmaransstad S Africa 27.11S 26.00E
63 O9 Wolmirsleben E Germany 51.57N 11.29E
63 P8 Wolmirstedt E Germany 52.16N 11.37E
64 M6 Wolnzach W Germany 48.35N 11.38E
19 B5 Wolo Celebes Indon 3.50S 121.17E
89 E7 Wologisi Mts Liberia
62 N3 Wołomin Poland 52.20N 21.11E
62 K4 Wołow Poland 51.21N 16.40E
19 B8 Wolowaru Indonesia 8.42S 121.56E
60 C2 Wolphaartsdijk Netherlands 51.32N 3.49E
95 C9 Wolseley S Africa 33.25S 19.12E
100 O8 Wolseley Saskatchewan 50.25N 103.16W
12 F6 Wolseley S Australia 36.21S 140.55E
56 H2 Wolseley Bridge Staffs Eng 52.46N 1.57W
108 M5 Wolsey S Dakota 44.26N 98.30W
64 A4 Wolsfeld W Germany 49.55N 6.29E
57 K3 Wolsingham Durham Eng 54.44N 1.52W
97 M5 Wolstenholme,C Quebec 62.30N 77.30W
48 R4 Wolstenholme Fd Greenland
62 J3 Wolsztyn Poland 52.08N 16.08E
63 T8 Woltersdorf E Germany 52.45N 13.28E
60 P6 Woltersum Netherlands 53.16N 6.44E
63 L7 Wolthausen W Germany 52.42N 9.59E
63 M8 Woltorf W Germany 52.18N 10.19E
61 T9 Woluwe-St.-Lambert *dist* Bruxelles Belgium
61 T9 Woluwe-St.-Pierre *dist* Bruxelles Belgium
60 N8 Wolvega Netherlands 52.53N 6.00E
56 G2 Wolverhampton W Midlands Eng 52.36N 2.08W
106 K4 Wolverine Michigan 45.16N 84.37W
101 J1 Wolverine *R* N W Terr
61 H3 Wolvertem Belgium 50.57N 4.19E
56 K3 Wolverton Bucks Eng 52.04N 0.50W
56 J5 Wolverton Hants Eng 51.20N 1.11W
108 O3 Wolverton Minnesota 46.32N 96.43W
56 J3 Wolvey Warwicks Eng 52.29N 1.21W
57 L3 Wolviston Cleveland Eng 54.38N 1.18W
95 D9 Wolwefontein Cape Province S Africa 33.39S 20.58E
95 H9 Wolwefontein Cape Province S Africa 33.18S 24.49E
95 L2 Wolwehoek S Africa 26.55S 27.50E
99 H5 Woman *R* Ontario
99 H5 Woman River Ontario 47.32N 82.40W
87 F7 Wombo,L Ethiopia 7.02N 36.45E
13 F7 Wombunderry *R* Queensland
103 B6 Womelsdorf Pennsylvania 40.22N 76.12W
61 J2 Wommelgem Belgium 51.12N 4.32E
60 L7 Wommels Netherlands 53.07N 5.36E
12 F3 Wompah New S Wales 29.04S 142.05E
13 D4 Wonarah N Terr Australia 19.50S 136.20E
14 E10 Wonberna W Australia 32.36S 123.40E
13 K7 Wondai Queensland 26.19S 151.51E
61 E2 Wondelgem Belgium 51.05N 3.43E
110 B7 Wonder Oregon 42.24N 123.34W
95 N1 Wonderfontein S Africa 25.49S 29.53E
95 L3 Wonderheuwel S Africa 27.11S 27.20E
95 N1 Wonderhoek S Africa 25.40S 29.41E
95 L3 Wonderkop S Africa 27.51S 27.25E
95 L4 Wonderkop *mt* S Africa 28.40S 27.43E
113 M5 Wonder L Alaska 63.30N 151.10W
13 E6 Wonditti,L Queensland 22.45S 138.35E
Wondo *see* Wendo
12 C5 Wondoma,C S Australia 32.42S 134.04E
13 F4 Wondoola Queensland 18.32S 140.54E
15 H7 Wonerara Papua New Guinea 6.46S 145.54E
12 G4 Wongalarroo L New S Wales
13 G5 Wongalee Queensland 20.44S 144.38E
12 G4 Wongallarra L New S Wales 21.34S 144.06E
14 B9 Wongan Hills W Australia 30.55S 116.41E
28 G2 Wong Chu *R* Bhutan
19 B3 Wonggarasi Celebes Indon 0.33N 121.35E
Wong Ma Kok *see* Bluff Pt Hong Kong
21 D9 Wŏnju S Korea 37.24N 127.52E
Wonnerup *see* Capel W. Australia
18 J9 Wonogiri Java Indonesia 7.38S 110.52E
12 F4 Wonominta *R* New S Wales
18 J9 Wonosari Java Indon 7.55S 110.39E
18 H9 Wonosobo Java Indon 7.21S 109.56E
19 E8 Wonreli Indon 8.04S 127.10E
60 K7 Wons Netherlands 53.05N 5.26E
21 D8 Wŏnsan N Korea 39.07N 127.26E
61 D3 Wontergem Belgium 50.58N 3.27E
12 H7 Wonthaggi Victoria 38.38S 145.37E
15 D5 Wonti Irian Jaya 2.16S 136.40E
14 C6 Wonyulgunna,Mt W Australia 24.48S 119.45E
12 D4 Woocalla S Australia 31.44S 137.10E
104 G6 Wood Pennsylvania 40.10N 78.09W
108 K6 Wood S Dakota 43.29N 100.28W
13 D2 Woodah I N Terr Australia
123 J6 Wood B Antarctica
110 L6 Wood, Big *R* Idaho
105 F7 Woodbine Georgia 30.57N 81.46W
108 P8 Woodbine Iowa 41.43N 95.42W
109 O3 Woodbine Kansas 38.47N 96.58W
107 M5 Woodbine Kentucky 36.55N 84.06W
103 E8 Woodbine New Jersey 39.14N 74.49W
103 B7 Woodbine Pennsylvania 39.48N 76.24W
95 K1 Woodbine S Africa 25.34S 26.14E
103 E3 Woodbourne New York 41.46N 74.36W
103 H4 Woodbridge Connecticut 41.22N 73.02W
103 J8 Woodbridge New Jersey 40.33N 74.17W
99 L9 Woodbridge Ontario 43.47N 79.36W
56 O3 Woodbridge Suffolk Eng 52.06N 1.19E
104 H8 Woodbridge Virginia 38.40N 77.17W
56 O4 Woodbridge Haven Essex Eng 51.59N 1.24E
101 Q6 Wood Buffalo Nat.Park Alberta/N W Terr
108 R9 Woodburn Iowa 41.00N 93.35W
107 K5 Woodburn Kentucky 36.48N 86.32W
12 L3 Woodburn New S Wales 29.04S 153.21E
110 C4 Woodburn Oregon 45.09N 122.52W
13 F8 Woodburn Queensland 28.40S 142.13E
103 H3 Woodbury Connecticut 41.32N 73.12W
56 E6 Woodbury Devon Eng 50.41N 3.24W
105 C5 Woodbury Georgia 32.58N 84.35W
103 D7 Woodbury New Jersey 39.50N 75.09W
107 K6 Woodbury Tennessee 35.49N 86.06W
113 Q4 Woodchopper Alaska 65.20N 143.32W
56 N5 Woodchurch Kent Eng 51.05N 0.46E
105 F5 Woodcliff Georgia 32.42N 81.40W
13 C4 Woodcock,Mt N Terr Australia 19.15S 134.03E
12 L3 Wooded Bluff New S Wales
12 L3 Woodenbong New S Wales 28.28S 152.35E
59 K6 Woodenbridge Wicklow Irish Rep 52.50N 6.13W
11 C13 Woodend New Zealand 46.30S 168.22E
101 M11 Woodfibre Br Col 49.36N 123.17W
50 S13 Woodfjorden *inlet* Spitsbergen
59 F5 Woodford Galway Irish Rep 53.03N 8.24W
116 P5 Woodford Grenada, W I 12.07N 61.44W
55 H2 Woodford London England 51.36N 0.02E
119 A6 Woodford, C Galápagos Is 0.47S 90.40W
13 C5 Woodforde *R* N Terr Australia
55 H2 Woodford Green London Eng 51.37N 0.02E
111 E3 Woodfords California 38.47N 119.50W
55 F2 Wood Green London England 51.36N 0.07W
13 C5 Woodgreen N Terr Australia 22.14S 134.12E
57 N6 Woodhall Spa Lincs Eng 53.09N 0.14W
103 L8 Woodhaven New York 40.41N 73.50W
57 K6 Woodhead Derbys Eng 53.30N 1.50W
57 K2 Woodhorn Northumb Eng 55.12N 1.31W
106 D8 Woodhull Illinois 41.10N 90.17W
104 H4 Woodhull New York 42.04N 77.25W
110 C2 Woodinville Washington 47.45N 122.10W
98 K8 Wood Is Prince Edward I 45.57N 62.45W
100 U1 Wood L Manitoba
100 O3 Wood L Saskatchewan
111 E5 Woodlake California 36.26N 119.07W
108 K7 Wood Lake Nebraska 42.39N 100.15W
Woodland *see* Baileyville
111 C3 Woodland California 38.40N 121.50W
57 K3 Woodland Durham Eng 54.38N 1.53W
106 G9 Woodland Illinois 40.43N 87.44W
104 G6 Woodland Pennsylvania 41.00N 78.23W
110 C4 Woodland Washington 45.55N 122.46W
103 A9 Woodland Beach Maryland 38.56N 76.33W
112 N9 Woodland Hills Texas 32.39N 96.51W
109 E3 Woodland Park Colorado 39.00N 105.04W
100 U8 Woodlands Manitoba 50.12N 97.40W
18 H2 Woodlands Singapore 1.27N 103.46E
15 M8 Woodlark I Papua New Guinea
122 F9 Woodlark Ridge Pacific Oc
107 G3 Woodlawn Illinois 38.20N 89.01W
110 L6 Wood, Lit *R* Idaho
14 A3 Woodman Pt W Australia 32.08S 115.45E
55 E6 Woodmansterne Surrey Eng 51.19N 0.10W
100 L9 Wood Mountain Saskatchewan 49.24N 106.23W
101 C5 Wood,Mt Yukon Terr 61.11N 140.31W
100 L9 Wood Mt *ra* Saskatchewan
101 M9 Woodpecker Br Col 53.31N 122.40W
113 O4 Wood,R Alaska
100 F1 Woodridge Manitoba 49.18N 96.08W
103 E3 Woodridge New York 41.43N 74.35W
13 E6 Woodridge,Mt N Terr Australia 23.10S 137.40E
107 F3 Wood River Illinois 38.54N 90.04W
108 M9 Wood River Nebraska 40.50N 98.34W
103 L4 Wood River Junc Rhode I 41.27N 71.42W
13 E5 Woodroffe *R* N Terr/Qnsld
12 B2 Woodroffe,Mt S Australia 26.20S 131.42E
109 G2 Woodrow Colorado 39.58N 103.36W
100 L9 Woodrow Saskatchewan 49.42N 106.22W
112 F2 Woodrow Texas 33.27N 101.51W
111 O7 Woodruff Arizona 34.48N 110.04W
109 L2 Woodruff Kansas 39.59N 99.26W
105 E3 Woodruff S Carolina 34.45N 82.02W
110 O8 Woodruff Utah 41.32N 111.10W
112 K7 Woodsboro Texas 28.15N 97.21W
104 D7 Woodsfield Ohio 39.46N 81.06W
103 N3 Woods Hole Massachusetts 41.32N 70.39W
103 C8 Woodside Delaware 39.04N 75.35W
11 K8 Woodside New Zealand 41.03S 175.22E
111 O2 Woodside Utah 39.15N 110.21W
12 H7 Woodside Victoria 38.31S 146.21E
13 C4 Woods,L N Terr Australia
100 H1 Woods,L.of the Man/Minn/Ont
110 Q4 Woods, Mt Montana 45.18N 109.45W
107 D7 Woodson Arkansas 34.32N 92.12W
107 F2 Woodson Illinois 39.40N 90.14W
112 H2 Woodson Texas 33.01N 99.04W
12 H7 Woods Pt Victoria 37.36S 146.15E
103 L3 Woodstock Connecticut 41.57N 71.58W
106 F7 Woodstock Illinois 42.20N 88.29W
98 E7 Woodstock New Brunswick 46.10N 67.38W
103 F2 Woodstock New York 42.02N 74.08W
99 K9 Woodstock Ontario 43.07N 80.46W
56 J4 Woodstock Oxon Eng 51.52N 1.21W
13 G4 Woodstock Queensland 19.20S 142.42E
13 H4 Woodstock Queensland 19.35S 146.50E
104 N3 Woodstock Vermont 43.37N 72.33W
104 G8 Woodstock Virginia 38.55N 78.31W
94 P11 Woodstock *dist* Cape Town S Africa
109 L2 Woodston Kansas 39.28N 99.07W
103 D7 Woodstown New Jersey 39.39N 75.19W
104 N2 Woodsville New Hampshire 44.08N 72.02W
59 J4 Woodtown Meath Irish Rep 53.49N 6.39W
107 K7 Woodville Alabama 34.37N 86.19W
105 C7 Woodville Florida 30.20N 84.15W
107 E10 Woodville Mississippi 31.05N 91.19W
11 K7 Woodville New Zealand 40.20S 175.54E
104 B5 Woodville Ohio 41.27N 83.23W
99 M8 Woodville Ontario 44.24N 79.00W
112 N5 Woodville Texas 30.47N 94.26W
12 A8 Woodville *dist* Adelaide, S Aust
109 L5 Woodward Oklahoma 36.26N 99.25W
111 D4 Woodward Res California 37.51N 120.54W
98 F9 Woodwards Cove New Brunswick 44.42N 66.45W
58 S11 Woodwick Orkney Scotland 59.06N 3.04W
107 D10 Woodworth Louisiana 31.09N 92.30W
108 L2 Woodworth N Dakota 47.09N 99.18W
56 H6 Woodyates Dorset Eng 50.58N 1.58W
11 J4 Woody Hd New Zealand 37.50S 174.47E
25 M4 Woody I Paracel Islands S China Sea
113 L8 Woody Island Alaska 57.47N 152.23W
98 P4 Woody Pt Newfoundland 49.30N 57.58W
100 Q6 Woody R Manitoba
56 F3 Woofferton Shropshire Eng 52.19N 2.42W
19 E4 Wooi Moluccas Indon 1.40S 127.57E
15 C4 Woöi Yapen I, Irian Jaya 1.40S 135.29E
56 G6 Wool Dorset Eng 50.41N 2.14W
56 C5 Woolacombe Devon Eng 51.10N 4.13W
107 D3 Wooldridge Missouri 38.55N 92.31W
95 L9 Wooldridge S Africa 33.14S 27.15E
13 D1 Woolen *R* N Terr Australia
57 J1 Wooler Northumb Eng 55.33N 2.01W
100 D9 Woolford Prov.Park Alberta 49.12N 113.12W
14 D9 Woolgangie W Australia 31.13S 120.30E
13 G4 Woolgar Queensland 19.47S 143.12E
13 G4 Woolgar *R* Queensland
14 C6 Woolgathara W Australia 24.19S 117.34E
12 L4 Woolgoolga New S Wales 30.07S 153.12E
14 D9 Woolibar W Australia 31.03S 121.45E
13 C5 Woolla Downs N Terr Australia 22.13S 133.53E
12 M7 Woollahra *dist* Sydney, N S W
12 L8 Woolooware B New S Wales
56 N3 Woolpit Suffolk Eng 52.13N 0.54E
110 G9 Woolsey Nevada 40.17N 118.21W
12 B5 Woolshed Creek A.C.Terr Australia
57 K2 Woolsington *airport* Tyne and Wear Eng 55.03N 1.42W
11 M10 Woolston *dist* Christchurch New Zealand
12 E4 Wooltana S Australia 30.28S 139.26E
56 G5 Woolverton Somerset Eng 51.18N 2.19W
55 H4 Woolwich London England 51.29N 0.04E
12 D4 Woomera S Australia 31.11S 136.54E
103 M2 Woonsocket Rhode I 42.00N 71.30W
108 M5 Woonsocket S Dakota 44.04N 98.16W
13 J6 Woorabinda Queensland 24.05S 149.15E
14 A7 Wooramel W Australia 25.42S 114.20E
14 A7 Wooramel R W Australia
57 J7 Woore Shropshire Eng 52.59N 2.24W
12 C3 Woorong *R* S Australia
12 C3 Woorong,L S Australia
104 D6 Wooster Ohio 40.46N 81.57W
56 H4 Wootton Bassett Wilts Eng 51.33N 1.54W
65 O6 Wopfing Austria 47.53N 16.06E
19 F3 Wor *isld* Moluccas Indon 0.38N 128.31E
89 K8 Worawora Ghana 7.33N 0.28E
66 G4 Worb Switzerland 46.56N 7.34E
66 F3 Worben Switzerland 47.06N 7.18E
63 M10 Worbis E Germany 51.25N 10.21E
56 G3 Worcester Hereford & Worcs Eng 52.11N 2.13W
103 L2 Worcester Massachusetts 42.17N 71.48W
104 L4 Worcester New York 42.36N 74.44W
95 C9 Worcester S Africa 33.39S 19.26E
Worcester *co see* Hereford & Worcester *co*
103 K2 Worcester *co* Massachusetts
107 G3 Worden Illinois 38.57N 89.50W
110 R4 Worden Montana 45.59N 108.10W
110 D7 Worden Oregon 42.04N 121.50W
123 F13 Wordie Ice Shelf Antarctica
100 P9 Wordsworth Saskatchewan 49.33N 102.22W
65 F7 Wörgl Austria 47.29N 12.04E
15 C7 Workai *isld* Moluccas Indon
57 F3 Workington Cumbria Eng 54.39N 3.33W
57 L6 Worksop Notts Eng 53.18N 1.07W
60 K8 Workum Netherlands 52.59N 5.26E
108 C5 Worland Wyoming 44.01N 107.58W
26 S8 World's End *mt* Sri Lanka 6.48N 80.47E
92 D12 World's View Zimbabwe 20.30S 28.30E
56 F5 Worle Avon Eng 51.22N 2.57W
63 Q9 Wörlitz E Germany 51.51N 12.26E
61 Q8 Wormeldange Luxembourg 49.37N 6.25E
60 H10 Wormer Netherlands 52.30N 4.50E
60 H10 Wormerveer Netherlands 52.30N 4.47E
69 C2 Wormhoudt France 50.53N 2.28E
58 L6 Wormit Fife Scotland 56.25N 2.58W
56 L4 Wormley Herts Eng 51.45N 0.01W
63 P10 Wormlitz E Germany 51.27N 11.57E
64 E4 Worms W Germany 49.38N 8.23E
56 C4 Worms Hd W Glam Wales 51.34N 4.20W
64 G8 Worndorf W Germany 47.59N 9.00E
64 K6 Wörnitz *R* W Germany
103 J2 Woronoco Massachusetts 42.10N 72.49W
12 K8 Woronora R New S Wales
63 J6 Worpswede W Germany 53.14N 8.57E
64 B1 Worringen Nordrhein-Westfalen W Germany 51.04N 6.52E
64 E4 Wörrstadt W Germany 49.50N 8.08E
65 K6 Wörschach Austria 47.34N 14.10E
11 D6 Worser B Wellington New Zealand
101 O7 Worsley Alberta 56.31N 119.08W
14 E7 Worsnop,Mt W Australia 26.06S 124.48E
61 E3 Wortegem Belgium 50.51N 3.31E
61 K1 Wortel Belgium 51.24N 4.48E
94 D4 Wortel Namibia 23.09S 17.11E
64 G4 Wörth Bayern W Germany 49.48N 9.10E
64 N6 Wörth Bayern W Germany 48.38N 12.22E
64 N7 Wörth Bayern W Germany 48.16N 12.18E
107 B1 Worth Missouri 40.23N 94.28W
64 E5 Wörth Rheinland-Pfalz W Germany 49.03N 8.16E
65 G7 Wörth Salzburg Austria 47.12N 12.58E
65 O7 Wörth Steiermark Austria 47.13N 16.05E
112 L4 Wortham Texas 31.47N 96.30W
64 N6 Wörth an der Donau Bayern W Germany 49.00N 12.26E
56 F2 Worthen Shropshire Eng 52.38N 3.00W
65 K8 Wörther See *L* Austria
116 O6 Worthing Barbados 13.05N 59.35W
56 L6 Worthing W Sussex Eng 50.48N 0.23W
107 J2 Worthington Indiana 39.05N 87.00W
103 J2 Worthington Massachusetts 42.24N 72.56W
108 P6 Worthington Minnesota 43.37N 95.36W
107 D1 Worthington Missouri 40.24N 92.42W
104 B6 Worthington Ohio 40.03N 83.03W
112 L9 Worth,L Texas
64 L7 Wörthsee *L* W Germany 48.03N 11.11E
107 L3 Worthville Kentucky 38.38N 85.05W
103 B8 Worton Maryland 39.17N 76.06W
19 E4 Wosi Halmahera Indon 0.10S 127.57E
100 E5 Wostok Alberta 53.48N 112.26W
19 B5 Wosu Celebes Indonesia 2.20S 121.49E
15 A7 Wotap *isld* Moluccas Indon 7.23S 131.17E
9 B1 Wotho *atoll* Marshall Is Pacific Oc 10.08N 165.55E
9 D2 Wotje *atoll* Marshall Is Pacific Oc 9.30N 170.00E
99 T7 Wotton Quebec 45.44N 71.48W
56 G4 Wotton-under-Edge Glos Eng 51.39N 2.21W
19 B5 Wotu Celebes Indonesia 2.34S 120.46E
61 F3 Woubrechtegem Belgium 50.52N 3.55E
60 G11 Woubrugge Netherlands 52.10N 4.39E
60 K11 Woudenberg Netherlands 52.05N 5.25E
60 J12 Woudrichem Netherlands 51.49N 5.00E
60 L8 Woudsend Netherlands 52.57N 5.38E
61 B3 Woumen Belgium 51.00N 2.52E
108 H6 Wounded Knee S Dakota 43.08N 102.22W
90 G1 Wour Chad 21.20N 15.56E
90 F9 Woutchaba Cameroon 5.12N 13.05E
60 F13 Wouw Netherlands 51.31N 4.23E
60 F14 Wouwse Plantage Netherlands 51.30N 4.24E
13 K6 Wowan Queensland Australia 23.50S 150.12E
15 A7 Wowanda Moluccas Indon 7.53S 131.23E
19 C6 Wowoni *isld* Indonesia 4.10S 123.07E
19 C6 Wowoni,Selat *str* Indonesia
18 B3 Woyla *R* Sumatra Indon
62 L5 Woźniki Poland 50.36N 19.04E
57 N6 Wragby Lincs Eng 53.18N 0.19W
57 L5 Wragby W Yorks Eng 53.39N 1.23W
Wrangel I *see* Vrangelya, Ostrov
113 V8 Wrangell Alaska 56.28N 132.23W
113 L9 Wrangell, C Aleutian Is
113 V8 Wrangell I Alaska 56.20N 132.10W
113 P5 Wrangell Mt Alaska 62.02N 144.05W
113 Q6 Wrangell Mts Alaska
101 G7 Wrangell Narrows Alaska
57 O6 Wrangle Lincs Eng 53.02N 0.07E
58 F1 Wrath,C Highland Scotland 58.37N 5.01W
109 H1 Wray Colorado 40.05N 102.14W
55 A4 Wraysbury Res Bucks/Surrey England
13 G1 Wreck B Gt Barrier Reef Australia
14 B9 Wreck Pt W Australia 31.32S 115.30E
10 M6 Wreck Reef Coral Sea 22.17S 155.25E
122 V9 Wrecks,B.of Christmas I Pacific Oc 1.50N 157.20W
63 R6 Wredenhagen E Germany 53.18N 12.32E
57 K3 Wrekenton Tyne and Wear Eng 54.56N 1.34W
56 F2 Wrekin,The *mt* Shropshire Eng 52.41N 2.32W
63 J5 Wremen W Germany 53.40N 8.30E
110 B5 Wren Oregon 44.36N 123.25W
105 E4 Wrens Georgia 33.13N 82.23W
100 E9 Wrentham Alberta 49.34N 112.11W
103 M2 Wrentham Massachusetts 42.05N 71.20W
56 P3 Wrentham Suffolk Eng 52.23N 1.40E
57 H6 Wrexham Clwyd Wales 53.03N 3.00W
63 U7 Wriezen E Germany 52.43N 14.09E
109 L4 Wright Kansas 37.46N 99.54W
19 M6 Wright Philippines 11.47N 125.02E
99 O6 Wright Quebec 46.03N 76.07W
109 P7 Wright City Oklahoma 34.04N 95.01W
12 A3 Wright,L S Australia
12 F4 Wright,Mt New S Wales 31.11S 142.26E
28 G7 Wrightmyo Andaman Is 11.49N 92.41E
111 O10 Wrightson,Mt Arizona 31.43N 110.52W
103 E6 Wrightstown New Jersey 40.02N 74.37W
105 E5 Wrightsville Georgia 32.44N 82.45W
103 A6 Wrightsville Pennsylvania 40.02N 76.33W
105 K3 Wrightsville Beach N Carolina 34.12N 77.48W
12 H4 Wrightville New S Wales 31.36S 145.53E
99 C8 Wrightville Quebec 45.26N 75.45W
111 G7 Wrightwood California 34.23N 117.36W
101 M4 Wrigley N W Terr 63.16N 123.39W
123 J10 Wrigley G Antarctica
63 L5 Wrist W Germany 53.56N 9.46E
100 F9 Writing-on-Stone Prov.Park Alberta
56 M4 Writtle Essex Eng 51.44N 0.26E
62 K4 Wrocław Poland 51.05N 17.00E
100 V6 Wrong L Manitoba
62 J3 Wronki Poland 52.42N 16.22E
56 M5 Wrotham Kent Eng 51.19N 0.19E
56 M5 Wrotham Heath Kent Eng 51.18N 0.21E
56 F2 Wroxeter Shropshire Eng 52.41N 2.39W
56 O2 Wroxham Norfolk Eng 52.42N 1.24E
56 J3 Wroxton Oxon Eng 52.05N 1.24W
100 Q7 Wroxton Saskatchewan 51.15N 101.51W
62 K3 Września Poland 52.20N 17.32E
62 J4 Wschowa Poland 51.49N 16.15E
22 K8 Wu'an Hebei China 36.45N 114.15E
14 B9 Wubin W Australia 30.09S 116.35E
22 H8 Wubu Shaanxi China 37.34N 110.45E
21 B4 Wuchagou Nei Monggol Zizhiqu China 46.48N 120.20E
21 D5 Wuchang Heilongjiang China 44.53N 127.10E
23 G3 Wuchang Hubei China 30.32N 114.17E
Wu'cheng *see* Sa'ngain
22 K8 Wucheng Shandong China 37.21N 116.01E
22 J8 Wucheng Shanxi China 37.09N 115.50E
Wu-ch'uan *see* Huang-p'o Kwangtung
25 L2 Wuchuan Guangdong China 21.27N 112.47E
23 E4 Wuchuan Guizhou China 28.15N 108.04E
22 J6 Wuchuan Nei Monggol Zizhiqu China 41.10N 111.29E
23 D7 Wucun Guangxi China 23.36N 106.50E
22 G7 Wuda Nei Monggol Zizhiqu China 39.33N 106.40E
21 C3 Wuda Lian Chi *L* Heilongjiang China 48.45N 125.55E
33 M5 Wuḍām 'Alwā Oman 23.49N 57.29E
Wudan *see* Ongniud Qi
23 E2 Wudang Shan *mt* Hubei China
21 B8 Wudao Liaoning China 39.25N 121.22E
21 D2 Wudaogou Heilongjiang China 50.15N 126.29E
21 C6 Wudaogou Jilin China 42.09N 125.57E
24 H8 Wudaoliang Qinghai China 35.13N 93.02E
23 E4 Wudaoshui Hunan China 29.42N 109.50E
33 G8 Wuday'ah Saudi Arabia 16.05N 47.05E
22 L8 Wudi Shandong China 37.47N 117.30E
90 D6 Wudil Nigeria 11.47N 8.51E
23 C6 Wuding Yunnan China 25.26N 102.21E
22 H8 Wuding He *R* Shaanxi China
12 D5 Wudinna S Australia 33.00S 135.22E
23 C2 Wudu Gansu China 33.27N 104.57E
23 C3 Wudu Sichuan China 31.55N 104.45E
23 E3 Wufeng Hubei China 30.13N 110.37E
23 E5 Wugang Hunan China 26.45N 110.37E
23 E1 Wugong Shaanxi China 34.55N 108.06E
23 F5 Wugong Shan *mts* Jiangxi/Hunan China
23 E2 Wuguan Shaanxi China 33.37N 110.39E
22 G7 Wuhai Ningxia China 39.40N 106.40E
23 G3 Wuhan Hubei China 30.35N 114.19E
23 H2 Wuhe Anhui China 33.05N 117.55E
63 J6 Wuhrden *reg* W Germany
23 H3 Wuhu Anhui China 31.23N 118.25E
23 H3 Wuhu Anhui China 31.11N 118.28E
23 G7 Wuhua Guangdong China 23.51N 115.49E
24 C9 Wüjang Xizang Zizhiqu China 33.38N 79.55E
86 O8 Wujeira,El Saudi Arabia 28.58N 35.07E
22 K7 Wuji Hebei China 38.10N 114.57E
23 E8 Wujia Guangxi China 21.46N 109.00E
21 D5 Wujia Heilongjiang China 45.30N 126.20E
22 G6 Wujia He *R* Nei Monggol Zizhiqu China
23 J3 Wujiang Jiangsu China 31.09N 120.38E
23 D5 Wu Jiang *R* Guizhou China
23 D4 Wu Jiang *R* Sichuan China
23 E4 Wu Jiang *R* Sichuan China
21 C5 Wujiazhan Jilin China 44.58N 125.35E
87 E7 Wuka Ethiopia 7.31N 35.48E
23 H3 Wukang Zhejiang China 30.34N 119.59E
90 D8 Wukari Nigeria 7.49N 9.49E
33 J4 Wukayr,Al Qatar, The Gulf 25.06N 51.34E
Wukiao Ling *mts see* Wuchiao Ling
21 E3 Wulaga Heilongjiang China 48.22N 130.09E
21 D5 Wulajie Jilin China 44.08N 126.29E
24 H11 Wulang Xizang Zizhiqu China 30.22N 95.20E
31 H3 Wular L Kashmir
63 P9 Wulfen E Germany 51.50N 11.55E
63 F9 Wulfen W Germany 51.45N 7.00E
63 Q6 Wulfersdorf E Germany 53.15N 12.25E
48 R1 Wulffs Land Greenland
66 L1 Wülflingen Switzerland 47.31N 8.42E
63 F10 Wülfrath W Germany 51.17N 7.03E
63 M6 Wulfsen W Germany 53.18N 10.08E
63 M9 Wulften W Germany 51.40N 10.10E
90 G5 Wulgo Nigeria 12.30N 14.10E
25 K1 Wuli Guangxi China 22.10N 109.14E
24 G8 Wuli Qinghai China 34.21N 92.42E
23 H1 Wulian Shandong China 35.48N 119.12E
23 D3 Wulian Sichuan China 31.55N 105.19E
23 C4 Wulian Feng *mt ra* Guizhou China
23 B7 Wuliang Shan *mts* Yunnan China
15 A7 Wuliaru *isld* Moluccas Indon
23 F2 Wulichuan Henan China 33.47N 111.04E
23 E7 Wuli Jiang *R* Guangxi China
113 F3 Wulik *R* Alaska
21 E5 Wulin Heilongjiang China 44.47N 129.50E
23 E4 Wuling Shan *mt ra* Hunan China
23 E3 Wulingzhen Sichuan China 30.30N 108.17E
Wu-li-ya-ssu-t'ai *see* Dong Ujimqin Qi
65 O6 Wulkaprodersdorf Austria 47.48N 16.29E
23 D4 Wulong Sichuan China 29.22N 107.43E
Wulongji *see* Huaibin
61 A2 Wulpen Belgium 51.06N 2.42E
87 B7 Wulu Sudan 6.27N 29.39E
Wu-lu-k'o-mu-shih Ling *mt see* Muztag
19 F7 Wulur Indon 7.09S 128.39E
61 B3 Wulvergem Belgium 50.46N 2.51E
Wulveringem *see* Beauvoorde
64 L5 Wülzburg W Germany 49.01N 11.01E
90 E8 Wum Cameroon 6.24N 10.04E
12 H5 Wumbulgal New S Wales 34.25S 146.16E
23 C5 Wumeng Shan *mt ra* Guizhou China
23 E7 Wuming Guangxi China 23.12N 108.11E
23 E7 Wuming He *R* Guangxi China
63 K6 Wümme *R* W Germany
29 F7 Wun Maharashtra India 20.03N 79.01E
93 K9 Wundanyi Kenya 3.24S 38.24E
14 C3 Wungang R W Australia
92 F6 Wungu *tribe* Tanzania
23 G4 Wuning Jiangxi China 29.20N 115.09E
12 F5 Wunkar S Australia 34.28S 140.20E
63 J9 Wünnenberg W Germany 51.32N 8.42E
66 F4 Wünnewil Switzerland 46.53N 7.17E
87 B6 Wun Rog Sudan 9.00N 28.20E
63 S8 Wünsdorf E Germany 52.09N 13.27E
87 B6 Wun Shwai Sudan 8.01N 29.36E
64 N3 Wunsiedel W Germany 50.02N 12.01E
63 K8 Wunstorf W Germany 52.26N 9.26E
87 D5 Wuntau Sudan 10.19N 32.25E
25 M9 Wuntho Burma 23.55N 95.41E
111 N6 Wupatki Nat.Mon Arizona 35.34N 111.25E
23 G6 Wuping Fujian China 25.06N 116.10E
23 C4 Wupo Sichuan China 28.09N 103.00E
66 N2 Wuppenau Switzerland 47.30N 9.06E
94 E9 Wuppertal S Africa 32.13S 19.12E
64 C1 Wuppertal W Germany 51.15N 7.10E
33 M5 Wuqbah,Al Oman 23.56N 56.26E
22 H8 Wuqi Shaanxi China 37.04N 108.12E
24 B6 Wuqia Xinjiang Uygur Zizhiqu China 39.40N 74.50E
22 K7 Wuqiang Hebei China 38.00N 116.00E
22 K8 Wuqiao Hebei China 37.40N 116.21E
22 L7 Wuqing Tianjin China 39.20N 117.05E
86 N9 Wuqub, Wādi *watercourse* Saudi Arabia
14 B8 Wurarga W Australia 28.24S 116.29E
95 J5 Wurasoord S Africa 29.37S 26.00E
66 K1 Wurenlingen Switzerland 47.32N 8.16E
66 K2 Würenlos Switzerland 47.27N 8.23E
90 E7 Wurio Nigeria 8.21N 10.33E
87 B5 Wurl,El *watercourse* Sudan
64 O7 Wurmannsquick W Germany 48.20N 12.48E
Würmsee *L see* Starnberger See
90 B5 Wurno Nigeria 13.18N 5.29E
64 A2 Wurselen W Germany 50.49N 6.08E
103 F3 Wurtsboro New York 41.33N 74.29W
15 J7 Wuruf Papua New Guinea 6.44S 146.22E
13 F4 Wurung Queensland 19.00S 140.30E
64 M3 Wurzbach E Germany 50.27N 11.33E
64 H4 Würzburg W Germany 49.48N 9.57E
63 R10 Wurzen E Germany 51.23N 12.45E
87 D4 Wusa'a Sudan 13.04N 32.31E
33 J4 Wusayl,Al Qatar, The Gulf 25.33N 51.32E
33 F2 Wusayṭ,Al Saudi Arabia 28.05N 44.49E
23 C1 Wushan Gansu China 34.35N 105.02E
23 F2 Wushan Hubei China 32.09N 113.05E
23 E3 Wushan Sichuan China 31.07N 109.52E
23 E3 Wu Shan *mts* Hubei China
23 D3 Wusheng Sichuan China 30.17N 106.12E
23 H4 Wusheng Zhejiang China 29.56N 119.24E
23 G3 Wusheng Guan *pass* Hubei/Henan China 31.45N 114.04E
23 E8 Wushi Guangdong China 20.35N 109.48E
24 C5 Wushi Xinjiang Uygur Zizhiqu China 41.10N 79.15E
90 B7 Wushishi Nigeria 9.42N 6.00E
23 E5 Wu Shui *R* Hunan China
23 J3 Wusong Shanghai China 31.23N 121.30E
64 H3 Wüstensachsen W Germany 50.30N 10.00E
63 Q7 Wusterhausen (Dosse) E Germany 52.54N 12.28E
63 R7 Wustermark E Germany 52.33N 12.57E
63 H6 Wüsting W Germany 53.07N 8.21E
63 R7 Wustrau E Germany 52.51N 12.52E
63 O7 Wustrow W Germany 52.55N 11.08E
63 P4 Wustrow *pen* E Germany
21 C1 Wusuli Heilongjiang China 53.30N 123.19E
21 F4 Wusuli Jiang *R* Heilongjiang China
64 E8 Wutach *R* W Germany
22 J7 Wutai Shanxi China 38.42N 113.11E
24 D3 Wutai Xinjiang Uygur Zizhiqu China 44.35N 82.15E
22 J7 Wutai Shan *mts* Shanxi China
Wuthaithiya *see* Uthaythiyah
23 E6 Wutong Guangxi China 25.25N 109.59E
21 E4 Wutong He *R* Heilongjiang China
23 C4 Wutongqiao Sichuan China 29.21N 103.48E
24 H4 Wutongwozi Quan *spring* Xinjiang Uygur Zizhiqu China 42.32N 95.12E
22 F7 Wutuo Jing *well* Nei Monggol Zizhiqu China 39.27N 103.54E
61 J1 Wuustwezel Belgium 51.23N 4.36E
15 G4 Wuvulu I Bismarck Arch 1.44S 142.50E
23 H3 Wuwei Anhui China 31.21N 117.50E
22 F7 Wuwei Gansu China 38.00N 102.54E
23 J3 Wuxi Jiangsu China 31.35N 120.19E
23 E3 Wuxi Sichuan China 31.27N 109.34E
23 E3 Wu Xia *R* Sichuan China
22 J8 Wuxiang Shanxi China 36.50N 112.52E
23 J3 Wuxing Zhejiang China 30.56N 120.04E
23 E7 Wuxuan Guangxi China 23.36N 109.39E
Wuxue *see* Guangji
Wuyang *see* Zhenyuan
23 F2 Wuyang Henan China 33.26N 113.36E
22 J8 Wuyang Shanxi China 36.19N 113.11E
23 H2 Wuyi Anhui China 32.13N 118.26E
22 K8 Wuyi Hebei China 37.52N 115.56E
23 H4 Wuyi Zhejiang China 28.53N 119.50E
21 E3 Wuyiling Heilongjiang China 48.37N 129.21E
21 E3 Wuying Heilongjiang China 48.10N 129.10E
23 G5 Wuyi Shan *mt ra* Jiangxi China
22 H6 Wuyuan Nei Monggol Zizhiqu China 41.05N 108.15E
Wuyuanzhen *see* Haiyan
21 D3 Wuyur He *R* Heilongjiang China
23 H4 Wuyyan Jiangxi China 29.15N 117.53E
87 C3 Wuz, El Sudan 14.59N 30.07E
22 J7 Wuzhai Shanxi China 38.58N 111.46E
21 C2 Wuzhan Heilongjiang China 50.02N 125.20E
21 D5 Wuzhan Heilongjiang China 45.50N 126.13E
23 F3 Wuzhen Hubei China 31.42N 112.00E
22 H8 Wuzhen Shaanxi China 37.50N 109.48E
23 F1 Wuzhi Henan China 35.05N 113.23E
23 E9 Wuzhi Shan *mt pk* Guangdong China 18.59N 109.45E
22 G8 Wuzhong Ningxia China 37.55N 106.11E
23 F7 Wuzhou Guangxi China 23.30N 111.21E
13 F3 Wyaaba Cr Queensland
107 E1 Wyaconda *R* Missouri
14 B9 Wyalkatchem W Australia 31.21S 117.22E
12 H5 Wyalong New S Wales 33.55S 147.17E
103 B3 Wyalusing Pennsylvania 41.40N 76.16W
103 B3 Wyalusing Cr Pennsylvania
106 L7 Wyandotte Michigan 42.12N 83.07W
13 H7 Wyandra Queensland 27.15S 146.00E
12 J5 Wyangala Res New S Wales
13 G8 Wyara *L* Queensland
108 D5 Wyarno Wyoming 44.48N 106.46W
107 G5 Wyatt Missouri 36.54N 89.13W
57 J6 Wybunbury Cheshire Eng 53.03N 2.26W
56 M5 Wych Cross E Sussex Eng 51.04N 0.02E
12 G6 Wycheproof Victoria 36.08S 144.20E
95 D10 Wydgeleë S Africa 34.22S 20.25E
56 N5 Wye Kent Eng 51.11N 0.56E
14 C8 Wyemandoo *mt* W Australia 28.27S 118.31E
103 B9 Wye Mills Maryland 38.56N 76.05W
57 K6 Wye,R Derbys Eng
56 F4 Wye,R Hereford & Worcs etc Eng
106 D5 Wyeville Wisconsin 44.02N 90.25W
66 G1 Wyhlen W Germany 47.33N 7.42E
63 J3 Wyk W Germany 54.42N 8.34E
57 M4 Wykeham N Yorks Eng 54.14N 0.31W
60 M12 Wyler Netherlands 51.48N 5.59E
112 L2 Wylie Texas 33.01N 96.34W
14 B6 Wyloo W Australia 22.39S 115.55E
56 G5 Wylye Wilts Eng 51.08N 2.01W
104 Q1 Wyman Dam Maine 45.05N 69.55W
100 K8 Wymark Saskatchewan 50.07N 107.42W
110 E3 Wymer Washington 46.50N 120.29W
56 J2 Wymeswold Leics Eng 52.49N 1.05W
56 O2 Wymondham Norfolk Eng 52.34N 1.07E
108 O9 Wymore Nebraska 40.06N 96.40W
94 P12 Wynberg Cape Town S Africa 34.00S 18.28E
12 C4 Wynbring S Australia 30.33S 132.32E
11 C13 Wyndham New Zealand 46.21S 168.52E
14 G3 Wyndham W Australia 15.30S 128.09E
14 E3 Wyndham Ra W Australia
108 N3 Wyndmere N Dakota 46.17N 97.10W
56 G3 Wynds Pt Hereford & Worcs Eng 52.04N 2.21W
66 G3 Wynigen Switzerland 47.07N 7.41E
107 F6 Wynne Arkansas 35.14N 90.48W
14 E4 Wynne,Mt W Australia 18.05S 124.29E
109 N7 Wynnewood Oklahoma 34.39N 97.11W
97 H3 Wynniatt B N W Terr
13 L7 Wynnum Queensland 27.29S 153.08E
109 O5 Wynona Oklahoma 36.34N 96.20W
108 N7 Wynot Nebraska 42.45N 97.16W
100 N7 Wynyard Saskatchewan 51.46N 104.10W
12 H8 Wynyard Tasmania 40.59S 145.45E
106 E6 Wyocena Wisconsin 43.30N 89.20W
108 E5 Wyodak Wyoming 44.18N 105.23W
108 C4 Wyola Montana 45.08N 107.22W
12 B3 Wyola L S Australia 29.07S 130.15E
103 C8 Wyoming Delaware 39.07N 75.34W
106 E8 Wyoming Illinois 41.04N 89.46W
108 R4 Wyoming Minnesota 45.20N 93.00W
104 G4 Wyoming New York 42.49N 78.03W
99 H10 Wyoming Ontario 42.57N 82.07W
103 C4 Wyoming Pennsylvania 41.18N 75.50W
103 L3 Wyoming Rhode I 41.32N 71.42W
103 B3 Wyoming *co* Pennsylvania
102 D2 Wyoming *state* U.S.A.
110 P7 Wyoming Pk Wyoming 42.37N 110.37W
110 P6 Wyoming Ra Wyoming
12 K5 Wyong New S Wales 33.17S 151.25E
13 D2 Wyonga *R* N Terr Australia
58 T11 Wyre *isld* Orkney Scotland 59.07N 2.58W
57 H5 Wyre,R Lancs Eng
62 K2 Wyrzysk Poland 53.09N 17.14E
62 O5 Wysokie Poland 50.55N 22.40E
62 N3 Wysokie Mazowieckie Poland 52.55N 22.30E
103 B3 Wysox Pennsylvania 41.46N 76.24W
103 B3 Wysox Cr Pennsylvania
62 N3 Wyszków Poland 52.36N 21.25E
62 M3 Wyszogrod Poland 52.23N 20.09E
57 G3 Wythburn Cumbria Eng 54.31N 3.03W
104 D10 Wytheville Virginia 36.57N 81.07W
26 R16 Wyville-Thomson,Mt Kerguelen Ind Oc 49.31S 70.10E
48 B13 Wyville-Thomson Ridge N Atlantic Oc
21 A3 Xabart Nei Monggol Zizhiqu China 49.47N 119.53E
76 E16 Xabregas Portugal 38.43N 9.07W
24 J10 Xabyaisamba Xizang Zizhiqu China 30.58N 96.15E
91 G8 Xa Cassau Angola 9.05S 20.15E
84 X19 Xaghra Gozo Mediterranean Sea 36.03N 14.16E
24 G10 Xagquka Xizang Zizhiqu China 31.47N 92.46E
24 B7 Xaidulla Xinjiang Uygur Zizhiqu China 36.27N 77.46E
24 F10 Xainza Xizang Zizhiqu China 30.56N 88.40E
24 F11 Xaitongmoin Xizang Zizhiqu China 29.24N 88.07E
115 P7 Xal,Cerro de *pk* Mexico 20.10N 89.25W
115 K9 Xaltianguis Mexico 17.05N 99.46W
91 G12 Xamavera Angola 17.44S 20.10E
Xamba *see* Hanggin Houqi
117 D8 Xambioa Brazil 6.28S 48.38W
91 E8 Xá-Muteba Angola 9.30S 17.48E
22 F6 Xangd Nei Monggol Zizhiqu China 40.15N 103.55E
22 H5 Xangdin Hural Nei Monggol Zizhiqu China 42.50N 110.35E
24 D9 Xangdoring Xizang Zizhiqu China 32.06N 82.02E
115 L9 Xanica Mexico 16.01N 96.13W
63 D9 Xanten W Germany 51.40N 6.27E
83 G3 Xánthi Greece 41.07N 24.56E
36 D6 Xanthus *anc site* Turkey 36.22N 29.20E
118 D10 Xanxerê Brazil 26.53S 52.24W
120 E4 Xapuri Brazil 10.40S 68.30W
120 E4 Xapuri *R* Brazil
22 D8 Xarag Qinghai China 36.25N 98.10E
22 F6 Xar Burd Nei Monggol Zizhiqu China 40.08N 104.48E
22 K4 Xar Hudag Nei Monggol Zizhiqu China 45.08N 114.30E
22 J5 Xar Moron *R* Nei Monggol Zizhiqu China
22 L5 Xar Moron He *R* Nei Monggol Zizhiqu China
22 J5 Xar Moron Sum Nei Monggol Zizhiqu China 42.06N 111.33E
23 B2 Xar'oi Qinghai China 33.45N 100.20E
76 C12 Xarrama *R* Portugal
115 O8 Xascabchén Mexico 19.02N 90.47W
91 F9 Xassengue Angola 10.26S 18.32E
94 F2 Xaudum *watercourse* Botswana
Xauen *see* Chechaouen
94 H3 Xau, L Botswana 21.10S 24.50E
118 E3 Xavantes,Serra dos *mts* Brazil
118 D7 Xavantina Brazil 21.21S 52.46W
24 D5 Xayar Xinjiang Uygur Zizhiqu China 41.16N 82.52E
115 Q7 Xcan Mexico 20.50N 87.39W
Xêgar *see* Tingri
107 H3 Xenia Illinois 38.39N 88.40W
104 B7 Xenia Ohio 39.41N 83.56W
84 C6 Xeniés Greece 37.54N 21.30E
91 F12 Xequessa Angola 16.47S 19.05E
119 H7 Xeriana,R Brazil
119 H8 Xeriuini,R Brazil
84 Q15 Xero *R* Cyprus
84 Q14 Xeros Cyprus 35.08N 32.51E
84 A3 Xerovoúni *mts* Greece
69 L7 Xertigny France 48.03N 6.24E
84 X19 Xewkija Gozo Mediterranean Sea 36.02N 14.16E
61 O4 Xhendelesse Belgium 50.36N 5.47E
61 M4 Xhendremael Belgium 50.42N 5.29E
61 N5 Xhoris Belgium 50.27N 5.36E
95 M7 Xhosa *tribe* Transkei S Africa
94 H3 Xhumo Botswana 21.13S 24.38E
23 H5 Xiabaishi Fujian China 26.48N 119.38E
Xiabancheng *see* Chengde
21 E5 Xiachengzi Heilongjiang China 44.41N 130.30E
23 F1 Xiachuan Shanxi China 35.25N 112.03E

23 F8 **Xiachuan Dao** *isld* Guangdong **China** 21.43N 112.33E
Xiacun *see* **Rushan**
22 C6 **Xiadong** Gansu **China** 40.58N 95.50E
23 B6 **Xiaguan** Yunnan **China** 25.33N 100.09E
23 C1 **Xiaguanying** Gansu **China** 35.55N 104.09E
23 C1 **Xiahe** Gansu **China** 35.12N 102.27E
22 K6 **Xiahuayuan** Hebei **China** 40.30N 115.15E
23 E6 **Xiajiang** Guizhou **China** 25.47N 108.49E
23 G5 **Xiajiang** Jiangxi **China** 27.32N 115.12E
22 K8 **Xiajin** Shandong **China** 37.00N 116.00E
23 H6 **Xiamen** Fujian **China** 24.28N 118.05E
23 E1 **Xi'an** Shaanxi **China** 34.16N 108.54E
23 E4 **Xianfeng** Hubei **China** 29.45N 109.10E
23 F2 **Xiangcheng** Henan **China** 33.51N 113.27E
23 G2 **Xiangcheng** Henan **China** 33.17N 114.40E
23 B4 **Xiangcheng** Sichuan **China** 28.54N 99.40E
23 F5 **Xiangdong** Jiangxi **China** 27.38N 113.41E
23 D7 **Xiangdu** Guangxi **China** 23.14N 106.57E
23 F2 **Xiangfan** Hubei **China** 32.05N 112.03E
23 F1 **Xiangfen** Shanxi **China** 35.57N 111.24E
Xianggang *see* **Hong Kong**
22 L7 **Xianghe** Hebei **China** 39.47N 117.01E
23 E2 **Xianghe** Hubei **China** 33.25N 110.45E
22 J5 **Xianghuang (Hobot Xar) Qi** Nei Monggol Zizhiqu **China** 42.22N 113.57E
23 F5 **Xiang Jiang** *R* Hunan **China**
21 E4 **Xianglan** Heilongjiang **China** 46.39N 129.51E
23 E1 **Xiangning** Shanxi **China** 36.00N 110.51E
24 C10 **Xiangquan He** *R* Qinghai **China**
22 D9 **Xiangride** Qinghai **China** 36.00N 97.52E
23 J4 **Xiangshan** Zhejiang **China** 29.29N 121.51E
23 J4 **Xiangshan Gang** *B* Zhejiang **China**
23 H1 **Xiangshui** Jiangsu **China** 34.12N 119.33E
23 F5 **Xiangtan** Hunan **China** 27.48N 112.55E
23 F5 **Xiangtan** Hunan **China** 27.55N 112.47E
23 F5 **Xiangxiang** Hunan **China** 27.46N 112.26E
21 D5 **Xiangyang** Heilongjiang **China** 44.35N 127.30E
23 F4 **Xiangyin** Hunan **China** 28.43N 112.48E
22 J8 **Xiangyuan** Shanxi **China** 36.25N 113.11E
23 B6 **Xiangyun** Yunnan **China** 25.29N 100.35E
23 E6 **Xiangzhou** Guangxi **China** 24.00N 110.05E
23 B7 **Xianhe** Yunnan **China** 23.51N 101.52E
23 J4 **Xianju** Zhejiang **China** 28.55N 120.44E
23 G4 **Xianning** Jiangxi **China** 29.56N 114.21E
Xiannumiao *see* **Jiangdu**
23 B3 **Xianshui He** *R* Sichuan **China**
Xiantaozhen *see* **Mianyang**
23 H4 **Xianxia Ling** *mt ra* Fujian **China**
22 K7 **Xian Xian** Hebei **China** 38.11N 116.03E
23 E1 **Xianyang** Shaanxi **China** 34.22N 108.42E
23 H6 **Xianyou** Fujian **China** 25.23N 118.40E
Xiaoba *see* **Qingtongxia**
21 D4 **Xiaobai** Heilongjiang **China** 47.00N 128.39E
21 C2 **Xiaobole Shan** *mt pk* Heilongjiang **China** 51.45N 124.10E
21 D5 **Xiaocheng** Jilin **China** 44.16N 127.10E
22 L5 **Xiaochengzi** Nei Monggol Zizhiqu **China** 41.45N 119.02E
22 L6 **Xiaochengzi** Nei Monggol Zizhiqu **China** 41.08N 119.39E
25 K1 **Xiaodong** Guangxi **China** 22.12N 108.34E
21 C3 **Xiao'ergou** Nei Monggol Zizhiqu **China** 49.11N 123.36E
Xiaofan *see* **Wuqiang**
23 F3 **Xiaogan** Hubei **China** 30.58N 113.57E
24 E3 **Xiaoguai** Xinjiang Uygur Zizhiqu **China** 45.10N 85.00E
23 G3 **Xiaohexi** Hubei **China** 31.23N 114.07E
21 D3 **Xiao Hinggan Ling** *mts* Heilongjiang
22 E6 **Xiaohongshan** Nei Monggol Zizhiqu **China** 40.50N 99.10E
21 F4 **Xiaojiahe** Heilongjiang **China** 47.15N 133.45E
Xiaojiang *see* **Pubei**
21 B6 **Xiaojieji** Nei Monggol Zizhiqu **China** 43.52N 121.29E
23 C3 **Xiaojin** Sichuan **China** 31.02N 102.08E
23 C3 **Xiaojin Chuan** *R* Sichuan **China**
24 H8 **Xiaonanchuan** Qinghai **China** 35.46N 94.21E
22 C8 **Xiao Qaidam** Qinghai **China** 37.26N 95.08E
22 C8 **Xiao Qaidam Hu** *L* Qinghai **China**
22 C6 **Xiaoquandong** Gansu **China** 41.10N 95.23E
23 J3 **Xiaoshan** Zhejiang **China** 30.09N 120.14E
23 E1 **Xiao Shan** *mts* Henan **China**
Xiaoshi *see* **Benxi**
23 F6 **Xiao Shui** *R* Hunan **China**
22 H8 **Xiaosuan** Shanxi **China** 37.07N 110.43E
24 J9 **Xiao Surmang** Qinghai **China** 32.20N 96.55E
22 K7 **Xiaowutai Shan** *mt* Hebei **China** 39.59N 115.01E
23 J4 **Xiao Xi** *R* Zhejiang **China**
23 H1 **Xiao Xian** Anhui **China** 34.10N 117.03E
23 C4 **Xiaoxiang Ling** *mts* Sichuan **China**
25 C4 **Xiaoxiang Shan** *mt ra* Sichuan **China**
24 C6 **Xiaoxihaizi Sk** *res* Xinjiang Uygur Zizhiqu **China**
Xiaoxita *see* **Yichang**
21 C2 **Xiaoyangqi** Nei Monggol Zizhiqu **China** 50.54N 124.16E
22 J8 **Xiaoyi** Shanxi **China** 37.04N 111.44E
23 B5 **Xiaozhongdian** Yunnan **China** 27.37N 99.51E
23 H5 **Xiapu** Fujian **China** 26.53N 119.59E
23 B5 **Xiaruo** Yunnan **China** 27.51N 99.20E
23 D6 **Xiashan** Guizhou **China** 25.38N 105.14E
Xiashi *see* **Haining**
115 P8 **Xiatil Mexico** 19.40N 88.29W
23 F1 **Xia Xian** Shanxi **China** 35.12N 111.11E
23 G1 **Xiayi** Henan **China** 34.15N 116.14E
Xiayingpan *see* **Luzhi**
23 B4 **Xibdê** Sichuan **China** 28.46N 99.50E
23 E8 **Xichang** Guangxi **China** 21.37N 108.53E
23 C5 **Xichang** Sichuan **China** 27.52N 102.16E
23 E4 **Xiche** Hunan **China** 29.10N 109.35E
Xicheng *see* **Yangyuan**
23 D3 **Xichong** Sichuan **China** 31.05N 105.52E
23 C7 **Xichou** Yunnan **China** 23.25N 104.42E
115 J7 **Xichú Mexico** 21.26N 100.05W
23 F2 **Xichuan** Henan **China** 33.08N 111.30E
115 K6 **Xicohténcatl Mexico** 22.59N 98.55W
23 C4 **Xide** Sichuan **China** 28.08N 102.19E
84 F6 **Xídheika Greece** 37.30N 23.00E
21 B5 **Xi Dorolj** Nei Monggol Zizhiqu **China** 45.15N 121.13E
Xidu *see* **Hengyang**
Xiedian *see* **Wanrong**
Xiejiaji *see* **Qingyun**
23 F3 **Xiemahe** Hubei **China** 31.40N 111.10E
25 G3 **Xieng Khouang Laos** 19.21N 103.23E
119 F7 **Xié,R Brazil**
23 E1 **Xiexian** Shanxi **China** 34.58N 110.56E
23 E8 **Xieyang Dao** *isld* Guangdong **China** 20.55N 109.12E
23 G2 **Xifei He** *R* Anhui **China**
23 D5 **Xifeng** Guizhou **China** 27.08N 106.42E
21 C6 **Xifeng** Liaoning **China** 42.44N 124.42E
22 L6 **Xifengkou** Hebei **China** 40.26N 118.14E
21 D3 **Xigangzi** Heilongjiang **China** 49.54N 127.18E
24 F11 **Xigazê** Xizang Zizhiqu **China** 29.18N 88.50E
23 B3 **Xi Golog** Sichuan **China** 30.02N 100.45E
23 D1 **Xihe** Gansu **China** 34.01N 105.15E
24 D5 **Xihe** Xinjiang Uygur Zizhiqu **China** 41.32N 82.39E
21 B7 **Xi He** *R* Liaoning **China**
22 E6 **Xi He** *R* Nei Monggol Zizhiqu **China**
23 G2 **Xihua** Henan **China** 33.54N 114.33E
Xihuachi *see* **Heshui**
21 D4 **Xiji** Heilongjiang **China** 46.12N 127.12E
22 G9 **Xiji** Ningxia **China** 35.57N 105.44E
23 F7 **Xi Jiang** *R* Guangdong **China**
24 G8 **Xijir** Qinghai **China** 34.55N 91.50E
23 E4 **Xikou** Hunan **China** 29.15N 110.38E
21 B4 **Xikou** Nei Monggol Zizhiqu **China** 46.46N 120.30E
21 B1 **Xikouzi** Nei Monggol Zizhiqu **China**
22 J5 **Xil** Nei Monggol Zizhiqu **China** 43.30N 112.09E
Xiligou *see* **Ulan**
23 D6 **Xilin** Guangxi **China** 24.34N 105.07E
21 E4 **Xilin** Heilongjiang **China** 47.29N 129.10E
22 K5 **Xilin Gol** *R* Nei Monggol Zizhiqu **China**
21 E5 **Xilinhe** Heilongjiang **China** 44.30N 130.45E
Xilin Hot *see* **Abagnar Qi**
21 B1 **Xilinji** Heilongjiang **China** 53.01N 122.27E
22 J4 **Xilin Qagan Obo** Nei Monggol Zizhiqu **China** 44.18N 111.42E
115 K7 **Xilitla Mexico** 21.28N 99.00W
84 E5 **Xilókastron Greece** 38.04N 22.43E
22 L5 **Xiluga He** *R* Liaoning **China**
23 D5 **Ximahe** Guizhou **China** 26.42N 107.07E
22 M7 **Ximayi Dao** *isld* Liaoning **China**
89 B6 **Xime Guinea-Bissau** 11.59N 14.57W
23 B7 **Ximeng** Yunnan **China** 22.50N 99.27E
22 E6 **Ximiao** Nei Monggol Zizhiqu **China** 41.00N 100.05E
21 B7 **Ximucheng** Liaoning **China** 40.44N 122.55E
23 F1 **Xin'an** Henan **China** 34.50N 112.07E
23 H4 **Xin'anjiang Sk.** *L* Zhejiang **China** 29.40N 119.00E
Xin'anzhen *see* **Guannan**
Xin'anzhen *see* **Xinyi**
Xin'anzhen *see* **Guannan**
Xin'anzhen *see* **Xinyi**
21 C5 **Xin 'anzhen** Jilin **China** 44.04N 123.50E
94 M5 **Xinavane Mozambique** 25.02S 32.47E
22 K2 **Xin Barag Youqi** Nei Monggol Zizhiqu **China** 48.41N 116.45E
22 L2 **Xin Barag Zuoqi** Nei Monggol Zizhiqu **China** 48.12N 118.15E
21 C7 **Xinbin** Liaoning **China** 41.41N 124.55E
Xin Bulag *see* **Xianghuang (Hobot Xar) Qi**
22 L2 **Xin Bulag Dong** Nei Monggol Zizhiqu **China** 48.48N 118.44E
23 G2 **Xincai** Henan **China** 32.47N 114.58E
23 F4 **Xinchang** Hubei **China** 29.53N 112.26E
23 J4 **Xinchang** Zhejiang **China** 29.30N 120.55E
23 C1 **Xincheng** Gansu **China** 34.42N 103.40E
23 E6 **Xincheng** Guangxi **China** 24.10N 108.40E
22 K7 **Xincheng** Hebei **China** 39.20N 115.50E
21 E4 **Xincheng** Heilongjiang **China** 47.12N 131.21E
22 H8 **Xinchengbu** Shaanxi **China** 37.15N 108.38E
21 C6 **Xinchengzi** Liaoning **China** 42.04N 123.30E
23 E9 **Xincun** Guangdong **China** 18.31N 109.55E
Xindeng *see* **Chengyang**
21 D5 **Xindian** Heilongjiang **China** 45.54N 127.54E
23 E3 **Xindianzi** Sichuan **China** 31.22N 109.12E
23 F6 **Xindu** Guangxi **China** 24.03N 111.34E
23 C3 **Xindu** Sichuan **China** 30.50N 104.10E
23 B3 **Xinduqiao** Sichuan **China** 30.01N 101.29E
23 G6 **Xinfeng** Guangdong **China** 24.06N 114.11E
23 G5 **Xinfeng** Jiangxi **China** 27.07N 115.59E
23 G6 **Xinfeng** Jiangxi **China** 25.23N 114.48E
Xing'an *see* **Ankang**
23 E6 **Xing'an** Guangxi **China** 25.38N 110.33E
23 G5 **Xingan** Jiangxi **China** 27.44N 115.23E
22 M6 **Xingcheng** Liaoning **China** 40.38N 120.44E
24 F5 **Xingdi** Xinjiang Uygur Zizhiqu **China** 41.16N 87.52E
91 F8 **Xinge Angola** 9.47S 19.12E
23 G5 **Xingguo** Jiangxi **China** 26.23N 115.04E
22 E9 **Xinghai** Qinghai **China** 35.47N 100.02E
22 J6 **Xinghe** Nei Monggol Zizhiqu **China** 40.47N 113.56E
21 D4 **Xinghua** Heilongjiang **China** 47.03N 126.10E
23 H2 **Xinghua** Jiangsu **China** 32.54N 119.48E
23 H6 **Xinghua Wan** *B* Fujian **China**
22 K7 **Xingji** Hebei **China** 38.26N 116.57E
21 F5 **Xingkai Hu** *L* Heilongjiang **China**
22 L6 **Xinglong** Hebei **China** 40.24N 117.29E
21 C2 **Xinglong** Heilongjiang **China** 51.50N 125.59E
21 D4 **Xinglongzhen** Heilongjiang **China** 46.29N 127.07E
23 G6 **Xingning** Guangdong **China** 24.05N 115.47E
23 E1 **Xingping** Shaanxi **China** 34.20N 108.28E
23 B3 **Xingqêngoin** Sichuan **China** 31.47N 100.18E
23 D5 **Xingren** Guizhou **China** 26.18N 107.48E
23 D6 **Xingren** Guizhou **China** 25.29N 105.14E
22 G8 **Xingrenbu** Ningxia **China** 36.55N 105.16E
23 B1 **Xingsagoinba** Qinghai **China** 34.14N 101.32E
21 C4 **Xingshan** Heilongjiang **China** 46.54N 123.00E
23 E3 **Xingshan** Hubei **China** 31.15N 110.49E
22 K8 **Xingtai** Hebei **China** 37.08N 114.29E
22 K7 **Xingtang** Hebei **China** 38.25N 114.30E
23 H5 **Xingtian** Fujian **China** 27.35N 117.59E
117 C8 **Xingu,R Brazil**
23 D4 **Xingwen** Sichuan **China** 28.22N 104.50E
22 J7 **Xing Xian** Shanxi **China** 38.30N 111.00E
24 H5 **Xingxingxia** Xinjiang Uygur Zizhiqu **China** 41.49N 95.17E
24 J8 **Xingxiu Hai** *salt flat* Qinghai **China**
23 F1 **Xingyang** Henan **China** 34.45N 113.22E
23 C6 **Xingyi** Guizhou **China** 25.05N 105.00E
23 D6 **Xingyi** Guizhou **China** 25.05N 105.00E
23 G4 **Xingzi** Jiangxi **China** 29.25N 116.06E
22 K8 **Xinhe** Hebei **China** 37.35N 115.17E
22 L8 **Xinhe** Shandong **China** 36.55N 119.35E
24 D5 **Xinhe** Xinjiang Uygur Zizhiqu **China** 41.32N 82.39E
Xin Hot *see* **Abag Qi**
23 F5 **Xinhua** Hunan **China** 27.43N 111.22E
23 E5 **Xinhuang Dongzu Zizhixian** Hunan **China** 27.20N 109.10E
Xinhui *see* **Aohan Qi**
23 F7 **Xinhui** Guangdong **China** 22.31N 113.03E
84 D3 **Xinía Greece** 39.02N 22.19E
22 E8 **Xining** Qinghai **China** 36.35N 101.55E
Xinji *see* **Shulu**
23 G4 **Xinjian** Jiangxi **China** 28.37N 115.46E
23 F1 **Xinjiang** Shanxi **China** 35.37N 111.13E
23 G4 **Xin Jiang** *R* Jiangxi **China**
Xinjiangkou *see* **Songzi**
24 D5 **Xinjiang Uygur Zizhiqu** *aut reg* **China**
25 O8 **Xinjie** Yunnan **China** 24.45N 101.40E
21 B8 **Xinjin** Liaoning **China** 39.25N 121.58E
23 C3 **Xinjin** Sichuan **China** 30.27N 103.46E
21 B5 **Xinkai He** *R* Nei Monggol Zizhiqu **China**
22 K7 **Xinle** Hebei **China** 38.25N 114.49E
21 D5 **Xinli** Jilin **China** 44.41N 126.45E
22 L5 **Xinlin** Nei Monggol Zizhiqu **China** 43.57N 117.56E
21 D2 **Xinlitun** Heilongjiang **China** 50.55N 126.44E
21 B6 **Xinlitun** Liaoning **China** 42.00N 122.09E
23 B3 **Xinlong** Sichuan **China** 30.56N 100.14E
23 H2 **Xinmaqiao** Anhui **China** 33.10N 117.22E
21 D3 **Xinmin** Heilongjiang **China** 49.30N 126.18E
21 B7 **Xinmin** Liaoning **China** 42.02N 122.45E
22 D7 **Xinminpu** Gansu **China** 39.52N 97.50E
22 H7 **Xinminzhen** Shaanxi **China** 39.05N 110.44E
23 E5 **Xinning** Hunan **China** 26.34N 110.45E
23 B6 **Xinping** Yunnan **China** 24.04N 101.59E
Xinpu *see* **Lianyungang**
23 F4 **Xinqiang** Hunan **China** 29.07N 113.14E
23 F5 **Xinshao** Hunan **China** 27.20N 111.26E
Xinshiba *see* **Ganluo**
23 C1 **Xinsi** Gansu **China** 34.40N 104.35E
23 H1 **Xintai** Shandong **China** 35.56N 117.49E
23 F3 **Xintankou** Hubei **China** 30.10N 113.53E
23 F6 **Xintian** Hunan **China** 25.56N 112.09E
22 G6 **Xin Us** Nei Monggol Zizhiqu **China** 40.45N 105.21E
23 H1 **Xinwen** Shandong **China** 35.52N 117.40E
23 G3 **Xin Xian** Henan **China** 31.36N 114.44E
22 J7 **Xin Xian** Shanxi **China** 38.25N 112.45E
23 F1 **Xinxiang** Henan **China** 35.16N 113.51E
23 F7 **Xinxing** Guangdong **China** 22.45N 112.14E
23 G2 **Xinyang** Henan **China** 32.10N 114.05E
23 G2 **Xinyang** Henan **China** 32.02N 114.05E
23 J2 **Xinyang Gang** *R* Jiangsu **China**
23 F2 **Xinye** Henan **China** 32.40N 112.10E
23 E7 **Xinyi** Guangdong **China** 22.20N 110.54E
23 H1 **Xinyi** Jiangsu **China** 34.09N 119.25E
23 H1 **Xinyi He** *R* Jiangsu **China**
23 H1 **Xinyi He** *R* Jiangsu **China**
23 G5 **Xinyu** Jiangxi **China** 27.53N 114.56E
Xinyuan *see* **Tianjun**
24 D4 **Xinyuan** Xinjiang Uygur Zizhiqu **China** 43.28N 82.45E
22 L8 **Xinzhai** Shandong **China** 36.25N 118.40E
21 C5 **Xinzhan** Heilongjiang **China** 45.43N 124.26E
21 D6 **Xinzhan** Jilin **China** 43.54N 127.20E
21 B2 **Xinzhangfang** Nei Monggol Zizhiqu **China** 50.09N 121.56E
22 G7 **Xinzhaomiao** Nei Monggol Zizhiqu **China** 39.27N 107.48E
Xin Zhen *see* **Hanggin Qi**
23 F1 **Xinzheng** Henan **China** 34.24N 113.41E
23 G3 **Xinzhou** Hubei **China** 30.56N 114.52E
23 E2 **Xiong'er Shan** *mts* Henan **China**
22 K7 **Xiong Xian** Hebei **China** 38.58N 116.09E
21 B7 **Xiongyuecheng** Liaoning **China** 40.06N 122.08E
120 E4 **Xipamanu** *R* **Brazil/Bolivia**
Xiping *see* **Datong**
23 G2 **Xiping** Henan **China** 33.22N 114.00E
91 H12 **Xipundo Angola** 16.47S 22.10E
23 B1 **Xiqing Shan** *mts* Gansu **China**
118 G2 **Xique Xique Brazil** 10.47S 42.44W
84 D8 **Xirokámbi Greece** 36.57N 22.27E
84 C6 **Xirokhóri Greece** 37.30N 21.39E
84 F5 **Xironomí Greece** 38.15N 23.05E
84 F4 **Xirón Óri** *mt* **Greece**
120 E2 **Xiruá,R Brazil**
Xisha Qundao *see* **Paracel Is**
Xishuanghe *see* **Kenli**
23 D4 **Xishui** Guizhou **China** 28.19N 106.09E
23 G3 **Xishui** Hubei **China** 30.30N 115.19E
22 C8 **Xi Taijnar Hu** *L* Qinghai **China**
22 C8 **Xitieshan** Qinghai **China** 37.20N 95.23E
22 L4 **Xi Ujimqin Qi** Nei Monggol Zizhiqu **China** 44.36N 117.38E
23 H4 **Xiuning** Anhui **China** 29.50N 118.14E
23 E4 **Xiushan** Sichuan **China** 28.25N 109.00E
23 G4 **Xiushui** Jiangxi **China** 29.04N 114.33E
23 G4 **Xiu Shui** *R* Jiangxi **China**
23 D5 **Xiuwen** Guizhou **China** 26.50N 106.34E
23 F1 **Xiuwu** Henan **China** 35.15N 113.23E
21 C7 **Xiuyan** Liaoning **China** 40.18N 123.15E
Xiwanzi *see* **Chongli**
24 J9 **Xiwu** Qinghai **China** 33.13N 97.21E
24 E11 **Xixabangma Feng** *mt pk* Xizang Zizhiqu **China** 28.21N 85.47E
24 E11 **Xixabangma Feng** *mt pk* Xizang Zizhiqu **China** 28.21N 85.47E
23 F2 **Xixia** Henan **China** 33.30N 111.25E
23 G2 **Xi Xian** Henan **China** 32.22N 114.53E
22 H8 **Xi Xian** Shanxi **China** 36.40N 110.58E
23 D2 **Xixiang** Shaanxi **China** 33.00N 107.42E
23 H5 **Xiyang** Fujian **China** 26.22N 118.24E
22 J8 **Xiyang** Shanxi **China** 37.40N 113.39E
23 J5 **Xiyang Dao** *isld* Fujian **China** 26.30N 120.05E
23 D6 **Xiyang Jiang** *R* Yunnan/Guizhou **China**
23 D7 **Xiyangjie** Yunnan **China** 23.55N 105.18E
24 E9 **Xizang Gaoyuan** *plateau* Xizang Zizhiqu **China**
24 D9 **Xizang Zizhiqu** *prov* **China**
22 M7 **Xizhong Dao** *isld* Liaoning **China**
15 D5 **X Keten** *mts* Irian Jaya
115 Q8 **Xoalak Mexico** 18.17N 87.50W
24 H10 **Xobando** Xizang Zizhiqu **China** 30.49N 95.46E
115 K8 **Xochimilco Mexico** 19.08N 99.09W
24 H11 **Xoka** Xizang Zizhiqu **China** 29.56N 93.50E
69 M7 **Xonrupt-Longemer France** 48.05N 6.57E
22 B7 **Xorkol** Qinghai **China** 39.04N 91.05E
24 G6 **Xorkol** Xinjiang Uygur Zizhiqu **China** 39.04N 91.05E
84 Z20 **Xrobb il-Għaġin Malta** 35.51N 14.35E
23 H3 **Xuancheng** Anhui **China** 30.57N 118.43E
23 E3 **Xuan'en** Hubei **China** 30.06N 109.23E
22 G8 **Xuanhepu** Ningxia **China** 37.26N 105.40E
22 K6 **Xuanhua** Hebei **China** 40.36N 115.01E
23 D3 **Xuanhuan** Sichuan **China** 31.25N 107.44E
23 C5 **Xuanwei** Yunnan **China** 26.15N 103.59E
23 F1 **Xuchang** Henan **China** 34.03N 113.48E
23 J4 **Xuedou Shan** *mt* Zhejiang **China** 29.40N 121.05E
23 E5 **Xuefeng Shan** *mt ra* Hunan **China**
23 E1 **Xuejiaying** Henan **China** 34.30N 110.30E
23 B5 **Xue Shan** *mt ra* Yunnan **China**
Xugezhuang *see* **Fengnan**
22 F6 **Xugui** Nei Monggol Zizhiqu **China** 40.17N 103.45E
22 D9 **Xugui** Qinghai **China** 35.44N 95.58E
21 B3 **Xuguit Qi** Nei Monggol Zizhiqu **China** 49.17N 120.48E
23 G5 **Xu Jiang** *R* Jiangxi **China**
21 B7 **Xujiatun** Liaoning **China** 40.00N 122.07E
95 M7 **Xuka Drift S Africa** 31.19S 28.02E
23 A2 **Xümatang** Qinghai **China** 33.52N 97.24E
23 C6 **Xundian** Yunnan **China** 25.33N 103.11E
24 E11 **Xungru** Xizang Zizhiqu **China** 29.13N 84.41E
21 D3 **Xunhe** Heilongjiang **China** 49.21N 128.05E
21 D3 **Xun He** *R* Heilongjiang **China**
23 E2 **Xun He** *R* Shaanxi **China**
23 C1 **Xunhua** Qinghai **China** 35.48N 102.35E
21 D3 **Xunke** Heilongjiang **China** 49.34N 128.25E
23 G6 **Xunwu** Jiangxi **China** 24.57N 115.28E
23 G1 **Xun Xian** Henan **China** 35.39N 114.34E
23 E2 **Xunyang** Shaanxi **China** 32.50N 109.23E
23 E1 **Xunyi** Shaanxi **China** 35.08N 108.21E
23 E5 **Xupu** Hunan **China** 27.55N 110.32E
22 C9 **Xur** Qinghai **China** 35.44N 95.31E
22 K7 **Xushui** Hebei **China** 39.01N 115.38E
23 F4 **Xu Shui** *R* Hunan **China**
23 D2 **Xushui He** *R* Shaanxi **China**
23 G5 **Xuwan** Jiangxi **China** 27.53N 116.30E
23 E8 **Xuwen** Guangdong **China** 20.25N 110.08E
25 J7 **Xuyen Moc Vietnam** 10.33N 107.25E
23 H2 **Xuyi** Jiangsu **China** 33.00N 118.32E
23 D4 **Xuyong** Sichuan **China** 28.17N 105.21E
23 H1 **Xuzhou** Jiangsu **China** 34.17N 117.18E
84 S15 **Xylophagou Cyprus** 34.58N 33.51E
110 K1 **Yaak** Montana 48.49N 115.44W
110 K1 **Yaak** *R* Montana
13 K6 **Yaamba** Queensland 23.07S 150.20E
23 C4 **Ya'an** Sichuan **China** 30.00N 103.02E
12 F6 **Yaapeet** Victoria 35.48S 142.07E
35 D1 **Ya'ara Israel** 33.04N 35.10E
89 H5 **Yaba Upper Volta** 12.59N 2.49W
35 D4 **Ya'bad Jordan** 32.27N 35.10E
Yabanabat *see* **Kızılcahamam**
91 G1 **Yabanyama Zaïre** 4.18N 21.11E
90 D9 **Yabassi Cameroon** 4.30N 9.59E
9 A3 **Yabbenohr** *islet* Marshall Is **Pacific Oc** 9.09N 167.08E
87 G8 **Yabelo Ethiopia** 4.50N 38.10E
35 F4 **Yabis** *R* **Jordan**
35 G9 **Yabis** *watercourse* **Jordan**
115 N2 **Yablis Nicaragua** 14.08N 83.44W
45 L5 **Yablochnoye U.S.S.R.** 51.18N 39.00E
40 J8 **Yablochnyy** Sakhalin **U.S.S.R.** 47.07N 142.02E
39 H2 **Yablon** *R* **U.S.S.R.**
82 J2 **Yablonitse,Pereval** *pass* **U.S.S.R.** 48.19N 24.25E
82 J2 **Yablonov U.S.S.R.** 48.24N 25.00E
45 M4 **Yablonovets U.S.S.R.** 52.28N 40.14E
42 J6 **Yablonovo U.S.S.R.** 51.55N 112.48E
42 J6 **Yablonovyy Khrebet** *mts* **U.S.S.R.**
45 D6 **Yablunovka** Ukraine **U.S.S.R.** 50.27N 32.12E
90 B5 **Yabo Nigeria** 12.40N 5.05E
22 F7 **Yabrai Shan** *mts* Nei Monggol Zizhiqu **China**
22 F7 **Yabrai Yanchang** Nei Monggol Zizhiqu **China** 39.22N 102.54E
33 H5 **Yabrīn** *oasis* **Saudi Arabia**
Yabroûd *see* **Yabrud**
35 D6 **Yabrud Jordan** 31.59N 35.15E
105 K7 **Yabucoa** Puerto Rico 18.02N 65.53W
13 H4 **Yabulu** Queensland 19.12S 145.32E
87 E6 **Yabus, R Ethiopia**
119 D8 **Yabuyanos Peru** 1.10S 73.55W
115 P8 **Yacalobispo Mexico** 18.25N 89.02W
13 H5 **Yacamunda** Queensland 21.20S 147.06E
Yacha *see* **Baisha**
110 A5 **Yachats** Oregon 44.19N 124.05W
23 E9 **Yacheng** Guangdong **China** 18.30N 109.12E
20 D10 **Yachi Japan** 31.55N 130.27E
23 D5 **Yachi He** *R* Guizhou **China**
20 H2 **Yachiyo** Chiba **Japan**
118 C10 **Yaciretá, I Paraguay** 27.25S 56.40W
12 H6 **Yackandandah** Victoria 36.20S 146.21E
120 E7 **Yaco Bolivia** 17.09S 67.20W
110 C4 **Yacolt** Washington 45.53N 122.25W
120 F10 **Yacuiba Bolivia** 22.00S 63.43W
120 E6 **Yacuma,R Bolivia**
119 F5 **Yacurai Venezuela** 4.07N 66.36W
47 L3 **Yada U.S.S.R.** 66.56N 71.31E
28 C2 **Yadgir** Karnataka **India** 16.47N 77.05E
35 D4 **Yad Hanna Israel** 32.20N 35.00E
28 C3 **Yadiki** Andhra Prad **India** 15.04N 77.54E
105 F1 **Yadkin,R** N Carolina
105 G2 **Yadkin,R.,South** N Carolina
105 G1 **Yadkinville** N Carolina 36.07N 80.40W
35 B7 **Yad Mordekhai Israel** 31.35N 34.34E
24 F12 **Yadong** Xizang Zizhiqu **China** 27.28N 88.56E
35 C6 **Yad Rambam Israel** 31.55N 34.54E
25 J6 **Ya Drang** *R* **Cambodia**
45 S1 **Yadrin U.S.S.R.** 55.56N 46.12E
35 G6 **Yaduda,El Jordan** 31.51N 35.54E
35 H3 **Yadudah,El Syria** 32.41N 36.03E
35 A1 **Yad VeShem** *sub* Jerusalem
35 E3 **Yāfā Israel** 32.41N 35.16E
91 H4 **Yafala Zaïre** 1.21S 22.16E
15 F5 **Yafi** Irian Jaya 3.24S 140.58E
Yafia' *see* **Yāfā**
Yafo *see* **Tel Aviv-Yafo**
85 B3 **Yafran Libya** 32.03N 12.29E
89 J6 **Yagaba Ghana** 10.14N 1.17W
20 Q8 **Yagaji-jima** *isld* Okinawa **Japan** 26.40N 128.02E
20 C9 **Yagami** Kyūshū **Japan** 32.47N 129.56E
87 L6 **Yagareh Somalia** 8.44N 46.59E
36 C3 **Yağcılar Turkey** 39.25N 28.22E
83 J5 **Yağcılar Turkey** 39.25N 28.23E
Yağda *see* **Erdemli**
35 C6 **Yagel Israel** 31.59N 34.53E
41 C7 **Yagel'naya U.S.S.R.** 65.60N 76.58E
31 F2 **Yaghurdu** *pass* **Afghanistan** 36.59N 71.21E
42 F4 **Yagi,Khrebet** *mts* **U.S.S.R.**
21 J5 **Yagishiri-tō** *isld* **Japan** 44.27N 141.26E
43 C7 **Yagman** Turkmeniya **U.S.S.R.** 39.46N 54.13E
Yagmish *see* **Yakmish**
37 E5 **Yağmurdere Turkey** 40.33N 39.50E
115 G7 **Yago Mexico** 21.50N 105.04W
45 V3 **Yagodnoye** Kuybyshev **U.S.S.R.** 53.37N 49.00E
39 D3 **Yagodnoye** Magadan **U.S.S.R.** 62.34N 149.33E
47 J6 **Yagodnyy U.S.S.R.** 59.45N 65.00E
12 K8 **Yagoona** *dist* Sydney, N S W
44 B8 **Yagorlytskiy Liman** *lagoon* Ukraine **U.S.S.R.**
45 C6 **Yagotin** Ukraine **U.S.S.R.** 50.15N 31.46E
90 G6 **Yagoua Cameroon** 10.23N 15.13E
24 H8 **Yag Qu** *R* Qinghai **China**
24 D10 **Yagra** Xizang Zizhiqu **China** 31.32N 82.27E
22 C9 **Yagradagzê Shan** *mt pk* Qinghai **China** 35.11N 95.39E
47 F5 **Yagrysh U.S.S.R.** 62.03N 45.01E
41 G7 **Yagtali,Plato** *plat* **U.S.S.R.**
119 B9 **Yaguachi Ecuador** 2.06S 79.43W
116 E3 **Yaguajay Cuba** 22.20N 79.16W
121 G3 **Yaguari** *R* **Uruguay**
121 H4 **Yaguarón** *R* **Uruguay**
120 F6 **Yaguarú Bolivia** 15.19S 63.07W
119 E9 **Yaguas,R Peru**
42 D4 **Yagunovskiy U.S.S.R.** 55.19N 85.59E
35 D3 **Yagur Israel** 32.44N 35.05E
35 D9 **Yagur** *watercourse* **Israel**
18 D2 **Yaha Thailand** 6.27N 101.08E
20 L6 **Yahagi-gawa** *R* **Japan**
87 L6 **Yaheleh Somalia** 8.30N 47.03E
91 H3 **Yahila Zaïre** 1.48N 23.37E
91 J4 **Yahisuli Zaïre** 0.08S 24.04E
101 P11 **Yahk** Br Col 49.05N 116.06W
86 G6 **Yahmûm el Asmar,Gebel** *hill* **Egypt** 29.57N 31.38E
115 H7 **Yahualica Mexico** 21.11N 102.53W
Yahudiya *see* **Yehuda**
86 E4 **Yahûdîya, El Egypt** 30.45N 30.35E
35 F2 **Yahudiye Syria** 32.56N 35.42E
91 H3 **Yahuma Zaïre** 1.06N 23.10E
36 H4 **Yahyalı Turkey** 38.08N 35.23E
31 E5 **Yahya Wana Afghanistan** 31.50N 68.13E
18 B6 **Yai** *R* Pen Malaysia
93 G9 **Yaida Swamp Tanzania**
93 G9 **Yaida Valley Tanzania**
Yai-hsien (Sanya) *see* **Ya Xian**
25 E6 **Yai,Khao** *mt* **Burma/Thailand** 12.19N 99.26E
20 N5 **Yaita Japan** 36.47N 139.56E
96 U8 **Yaiza** Lanzarote **Canary Is** 28.56N 13.47W
20 M7 **Yaizu Japan** 34.52N 138.20E
23 B3 **Yajiang** Sichuan **China** 30.02N 101.03E
35 G5 **Yajuz Jordan** 32.02N 35.55E
90 J9 **Yaka Cent Afr Rep** 4.04N 18.18E
93 L7 **Yaka Kenya** 1.34S 39.24E
37 D3 **Yakacık** *R* **Turkey**
113 Q10 **Yakak,C** Aleutian Is 51.38N 176.59W
91 G2 **Yakala Zaïre** 2.09N 21.59E
26 S5 **Yakalla Sri Lanka** 8.12N 80.42E
15 G5 **Yakamul Papua New Guinea** 3.18S 142.40E
39 K1 **Yakan,Mys** *C* **U.S.S.R.** 69.39N 177.29E
113 Q6 **Yakataga** Alaska 60.06N 142.32W
15 B4 **Yakaturo** Irian Jaya 1.38S 133.08E
31 C4 **Yak Dar Afghanistan** 33.05N 65.30E
Yakeshi *see* **Xuguit Qi**
32 G3 **Yakhab Iran** 34.51N 57.10E
41 B4 **Yakhadyyakha** *R* **U.S.S.R.**
31 C5 **Yakhehal Afghanistan** 31.48N 64.39E
35 B8 **Yakhini Israel** 31.29N 34.36E
45 J1 **Yakhroma U.S.S.R.** 56.16N 37.26E
47 K6 **Yakhtur, Oz** *L* **U.S.S.R.** 59.45N 67.15E
110 E3 **Yakima** Washington 46.37N 120.30W
110 F3 **Yakima** *R* Washington
43 H7 **Yakkabag** Uzbekistan **U.S.S.R.** 38.56N 66.54E
26 R9 **Yakkalamulla Sri Lanka** 6.06N 80.22E
43 M8 **Yakkatu** Tadzhikistan **U.S.S.R.** 40.25N 70.32E
26 T6 **Yakkure Sri Lanka** 7.49N 81.02E
31 B6 **Yakmach Pakistan** 28.44N 63.50E
32 E4 **Yakmish Iran** 32.25N 53.07E
89 H5 **Yako Upper Volta** 12.59N 2.15W
20 E4 **Yakō** *dist* Yokohama **Japan**
Yakobi *see* **Viru-Jaagupi-Lisaku**
113 T8 **Yakobi I** Alaska 58.00N 136.30W
40 C2 **Yakokut U.S.S.R.** 58.59N 125.54E
90 K9 **Yakola Cent Afr Rep** 4.42N 20.21E
91 H1 **Yakoma Zaïre** 4.04N 22.23E
82 H8 **Yakoruda Bulgaria** 42.01N 23.39E
90 L9 **Yakossi Cent Afr Rep** 5.37N 23.19E
45 B2 **Yakovlevichi** Belorussiya **U.S.S.R.** 54.20N 30.32E
41 D5 **Yakovlevka U.S.S.R.** 71.06N 83.13E
45 H6 **Yakovlevo U.S.S.R.** 50.52N 36.27E
40 F9 **Yakovskoye U.S.S.R.** 44.26N 133.28E
Yakow *see* **Ta-ya-k'ou**
89 K6 **Yakrigourou Benin** 10.39N 1.59E
24 D5 **Yakrik** Xinjiang Uygur Zizhiqu **China** 41.34N 81.09E
47 H5 **Yaksha U.S.S.R.** 61.51N 56.59E
46 O1 **Yakshanga U.S.S.R.** 58.24N 46.00E
46 R2 **Yakshur-Bod'ya U.S.S.R.** 57.10N 53.10E
110 L1 **Yakt** Montana 48.02N 115.00W
90 E8 **Yakuba Nigeria** 7.14N 11.38E
21 E12 **Yakujima-kaikyō** *str* **Japan**
20 K2 **Yakumo Japan** 42.14N 140.19E
21 E12 **Yaku-shima** *isld* **Japan**
91 J3 **Yakusu Zaïre** 0.38N 25.00E
Yakut A.S.S.R *see* **Yakutskaya A.S.S.R**
113 S7 **Yakutat** Alaska 59.29N 139.49W
113 R7 **Yakutat B** Alaska
41 N9 **Yakutsk U.S.S.R.** 62.10N 129.50E
38 L2 **Yakutskaya A.S.S.R U.S.S.R.**
39 G2 **Yakuttork U.S.S.R.** 66.00N 160.50E
41 E7 **Yakuty U.S.S.R.** 66.07N 87.58E
93 F5 **Yala Kenya** 0.06N 34.33E
26 U9 **Yala Sri Lanka** 6.22N 81.30E
25 F9 **Yala Thailand** 6.40N 101.10E
91 H3 **Yala Zaïre** 1.12N 22.10E
26 U9 **Yala** *game reserve* **Sri Lanka**
93 F5 **Yala** *R* **Kenya**
37 G2 **Yalak** *R* **Turkey**
37 G2 **Yalakdere Turkey** 40.37N 29.36E
115 L9 **Yalalag,Hidalgo Mexico** 17.12N 96.11W
42 E3 **Yalan' U.S.S.R.** 58.20N 91.50E
88 F10 **Yala,Pen.de Mauritania**
45 T1 **Yal'chiki U.S.S.R.** 55.10N 48.00E
11 L9 **Yaldhurst New Zealand** 43.31S 172.30E
56 M5 **Yalding** Kent **Eng** 51.14N 0.26E
101 N11 **Yale** Br Col 49.31N 121.29W
107 H2 **Yale** Illinois 39.07N 88.01W
108 Q8 **Yale** Iowa 41.48N 94.20W
106 M6 **Yale** Michigan 43.07N 82.47W
109 O5 **Yale** Oklahoma 36.07N 96.43W
108 N5 **Yale** S Dakota 44.27N 97.59W
90 K9 **Yalégo Cent Afr Rep** 5.53N 20.10E
91 J3 **Yaleko Zaïre** 0.02N 24.28E
110 C4 **Yale L** Washington 46.00N 122.18W
91 H3 **Yalemba Zaïre** 1.09N 23.50E
103 J4 **Yalesville** Connecticut 41.30N 72.49W
9 R1 **Yalewa Kalou** *islet* **Fiji** 16.43S 177.50E
14 B8 **Yalgoo** W Australia 28.21S 116.40E
87 C7 **Yali Sudan** 6.41N 30.28E
91 G3 **Yali Zaïre** 0.03N 21.09E
37 F2 **Yalıçiftlık Turkey** 40.22N 28.43E
37 C3 **Yalık Abat Turkey** 40.16N 26.25E
90 L8 **Yalinga Cent Afr Rep** 6.33N 23.14E
115 P7 **Yalkubul,Pta Mexico** 21.32N 88.37W
82 L1 **Yalkushkov U.S.S.R.** 49.00N 27.30E
116 L2 **Yallahs Jamaica, W I** 17.53N 76.36W
116 L2 **Yallahs** *R* **Jamaica, W I**
13 H6 **Yalleroi** Queensland 24.05S 145.46E
14 B10 **Yallingup** W Australia 33.42S 115.04E
12 H7 **Yallourn** Victoria 38.09S 146.22E
37 G4 **Yalnızçam Turkey** 41.03N 42.28E
37 G4 **Yalnızçam Dağları** *mts* **Turkey**
107 F8 **Yalobusha** *R* Mississippi
14 C7 **Yalogínda** W Australia 26.43S 118.25E
90 H9 **Yaloké Cent Afr Rep** 5.20N 17.03E
23 A2 **Yalong Jiang** *R* Sichuan **China**
23 B2 **Yalong Jiang** *R* Sichuan **China**
23 B3 **Yalong Jiang** *R* Sichuan **China**
23 B4 **Yalong Jiang** *R* Sichuan **China**
23 B5 **Yalong Jiang** *R* Sichuan **China**
91 H4 **Yalongwa Zaïre** 0.01S 23.20E
37 G2 **Yalova Turkey** 40.40N 29.17E
37 G2 **Yalovakaplıcaları Turkey** 40.37N 29.11E
45 C4 **Yalovka U.S.S.R.** 52.50N 31.38E
82 M4 **Yalpukh** *R* **U.S.S.R.**
46 G6 **Yalpukh,Oz** *L* Ukraine **U.S.S.R.**
44 C10 **Yalta** Crimea, Ukraine **U.S.S.R.** 44.30N 34.09E
45 J10 **Yalta** Donetsk, Ukraine **U.S.S.R.** 46.56N 37.18E
21 B3 **Yalu** Nei Monggol Zizhiqu **China** 48.30N 122.05E
21 D7 **Yalu** *R* **China/Korea**
21 B4 **Yalu He** *R* Heilongjiang **China**
21 D7 **Yalu Jiang** *R* Jilin **China**
91 H4 **Yalusaka Zaïre** 1.02S 22.55E
47 K7 **Yalutorovsk U.S.S.R.** 56.41N 66.12E
36 E4 **Yalvaç Turkey** 38.16N 31.09E
28 B3 **Yalvigi** Karnataka **India** 15.10N 75.16E
Yal Wahiba *see* **Iyal Wahibah** *tribe*
47 K8 **Yalym U.S.S.R.** 54.47N 65.02E
33 F8 **Yām** *tribe* **Saudi Arabia**
39 E5 **Yama** *R* **U.S.S.R.**
20 M1 **Yamabe Japan** 43.14N 142.23E
20 P2 **Yamada** Honshu **Japan** 39.29N 141.57E
20 D8 **Yamada** Kyūshū **Japan** 33.33N 130.46E
20 P2 **Yamada-wan** *B* **Japan**
20 D8 **Yamaga Japan** 33.02N 130.41E
20 O3 **Yamagata Japan** 38.16N 140.19E
20 N3 **Yamagata** *prefect* **Japan**
20 D10 **Yamagawa Japan** 31.12N 130.38E
20 E7 **Yamaguchi Japan** 34.10N 131.28E
20 E7 **Yamaguchi** *prefect* **Japan**
40 F5 **Yam-Alin',Khrebet** *mts* **U.S.S.R.**
47 K3 **Yamalo-Nenetskiy Nats.Okrug** *dist* **U.S.S.R.**
47 K1 **Yamal,Poluostrov** *pen* **U.S.S.R.**
33 G4 **Yamāmah,Al Saudi Arabia** 24.10N 47.24E
20 M6 **Yamanaka-ko** *L* **Japan**
20 M6 **Yamanashi Japan** 35.44N 138.33E
20 M6 **Yamanashi** *prefect* **Japan**
91 H3 **Yamandjo Zaïre** 1.38N 23.27E
36 C4 **Yamanlar Dağı** *mt* **Turkey** 38.32N 27.13E
33 B8 **Yaman,Ra's al** *C* **Bahrain, The Gulf** 25.51N 50.37E
42 J6 **Yamarovka U.S.S.R.** 50.38N 110.15E
20 H6 **Yamasaki Japan** 35.03N 134.31E
45 V1 **Yamashurma U.S.S.R.** 55.59N 49.37E
99 S6 **Yamaska** Quebec 46.01N 72.55W
32 H7 **Yamāsūr Iran** 26.18N 58.05E
24 D4 **Yamata** Xinjiang Uygur Zizhiqu 43.49N 81.46E
20 C4 **Yamato** Kanagawa **Japan** 35.28N 139.28E
Yamatu *see* **Jamati**
87 E6 **Yamba Ethiopia** 8.18N 35.52E
91 C5 **Yamba Gabon** 2.03S 13.40E
12 L3 **Yamba** New S Wales 29.26S 153.22E
12 F5 **Yamba** S Australia 34.15S 140.54E
12 G7 **Yambacoona** King I, Tasmania 39.44S 143.57E
101 S3 **Yamba L** N W Terr
91 H2 **Yambata Zaïre** 2.25N 22.00E
89 C6 **Yambering Guinea** 11.49N 12.18W
119 E7 **Yambi,Mesa de** *plat* **Colombia**
87 B8 **Yambio Sudan** 4.34N 28.21E
45 O2 **Yambirno U.S.S.R.** 54.07N 42.05E
82 K8 **Yambol Bulgaria** 42.28N 26.30E
120 B1 **Yambrasbamba Peru** 5.45S 77.59W
41 C6 **Yamburg U.S.S.R.** 68.19N 77.09E
47 K2 **Yambuto, Oz** *L* Tyumen **U.S.S.R.** 69.30N 69.00E
47 L1 **Yambuto, Oz** *L* Tyumen **U.S.S.R.** 70.00N 70.50E
41 C5 **Yambuto,Oz** *L* **U.S.S.R.** 71.13N 79.30E
91 J3 **Yambuya Zaïre** 1.17N 24.34E
15 A7 **Yamdena** *isld* Moluccas **Indon**
20 D8 **Yame Japan** 33.14N 130.32E
15 H6 **Yamen Papua New Guinea** 4.23S 144.07E
25 D2 **Yamethin Burma** 20.24N 96.08E
47 J4 **Yamgort U.S.S.R.** 64.58N 64.25E
Yam Hamelah *see* **Dead Sea**
46 H2 **Yami U.S.S.R.** 56.51N 30.11E
19 K1 **Y'ami** *isld* **Philippines** 21.07N 121.58E
90 E5 **Yamia Niger** 13.25N 10.20E
15 G6 **Yaminbot Papua New Guinea** 4.34S 143.56E
20 O5 **Yamizo-san** *mt* **Japan** 36.58N 140.16E
28 B2 **Yamkanmardi** Karnataka **India** 16.07N 74.35E
Yam Kiang *R* *see* **Qin Jiang**
Yam Kinneret *see* **Tiberias** *L*
46 G1 **Yamm U.S.S.R.** 58.28N 27.59E
13 F7 **Yamma Yamma,L** Queensland
86 M3 **Yammit Egypt** 31.16N 34.09E
46 J3 **Yamnaya U.S.S.R.** 54.08N 33.35E
30 B2 **Yamnotri** Uttar Prad **India** 30.57N 78.23E
89 G8 **Yamoussoukro Ivory Coast** 6.49N 5.17W
109 D1 **Yampa** Colorado 40.09N 106.56W
109 B1 **Yampa** *R* Colorado
120 F8 **Yamparaez Bolivia** 19.12S 65.10W
14 E3 **Yampi Sound** W Australia 16.11S 123.40E
45 J8 **Yampol'** Donetsk, Ukraine **U.S.S.R.** 48.55N 37.59E
46 F5 **Yampol'** Kamenets-Podolskiy, Ukraine **U.S.S.R.** 49.59N 26.20E
45 E5 **Yampol'** Sumy, Ukraine **U.S.S.R.** 51.55N 33.50E
46 G5 **Yampol'** Vinnitsa, Ukraine **U.S.S.R.** 48.13N 28.12E
110 D7 **Yamsay Mt** Oregon 42.56N 121.22W
39 E5 **Yamsk U.S.S.R.** 59.34N 154.09E
39 E5 **Yamskaya Guba** *gulf* **U.S.S.R.**
47 F5 **Yamskoye U.S.S.R.** 61.05N 46.57E
15 A4 **Yamtua, Tg** *C* Irian Jaya 1.40S 130.23E
35 D4 **Yamun Jordan** 32.29N 35.14E
30 B2 **Yamuna** *R* Uttar Prad etc **India**
30 A2 **Yamunanagar** Haryana **India** 30.07N 77.17E
15 C5 **Yamur, Danau** *L* Irian Jaya 3.40S 134.55E
43 M2 **Yamyshevo** Kazakhstan **U.S.S.R.** 51.56N 77.21E
24 G11 **Yamzho Yumco** *L* Xizang Zizhiqu **China** 29.00N 90.40E
89 C7 **Yana Sierra Leone** 9.45N 12.22W
39 D5 **Yana** *R* Magadan **U.S.S.R.**
39 A1 **Yana** *R* **U.S.S.R.**
41 P5 **Yana** *R* Yakutsk **U.S.S.R.**
15 L8 **Yanaba I Papua New Guinea** 9.19S 151.55E
12 F6 **Yanac** Victoria 36.09S 141.29E
20 O4 **Yanagawa** Honshu **Japan** 37.51N 140.36E
20 D8 **Yanagawa** Kyūshū **Japan** 33.10N 130.23E
20 C2 **Yanagikubo** Tōkyō **Japan**
20 P8 **Yanaha-jima** *isld* Okinawa **Japan** 26.56N 127.55E
120 B4 **Yanahuanca Peru** 10.15S 76.33W
119 B11 **Yanahuanca,Cerro** *mt* **Peru** 6.10S 79.26W
20 F8 **Yanai Japan** 33.58N 132.09E
28 F2 **Yanam** Andhra Prad **India** 16.45N 82.16E
22 H8 **Yan'an** Shaanxi **China** 36.40N 109.21E
Yanao *see* **Yanam**
120 D6 **Yanaoca Peru** 14.17S 71.25W
46 R2 **Yanaul U.S.S.R.** 56.17N 54.55E
119 C9 **Yanayacu Peru** 3.52S 75.15W
23 B5 **Yanbian** Sichuan **China** 26.50N 101.30E
33 C4 **Yanbu' al Baḩr Saudi Arabia** 24.07N 38.04E
33 C4 **Yanbu' an Nakhl** *oasis* **Saudi Arabia**
12 G4 **Yancannia** New S Wales 30.16S 142.50E
112 H6 **Yancey** Texas 29.09N 99.10W
105 H1 **Yanceyville** N Carolina 36.25N 79.22W
22 H8 **Yanchang** Shaanxi **China** 36.40N 110.04E
Yancheng *see* **Qihe**
23 G2 **Yancheng** Henan **China** 33.38N 114.04E
23 J2 **Yancheng** Jiangsu **China** 33.23N 120.10E
14 B9 **Yanchep** W Australia 31.32S 115.33E
22 G8 **Yanchi** Ningxia **China** 37.49N 107.24E
24 H4 **Yanchi** Xinjiang Uygur Zizhiqu **China** 43.15N 94.10E
22 C7 **Yanchiwan** Gansu **China** 39.10N 95.45E
22 H8 **Yanchuan** Shaanxi **China** 36.54N 110.04E
12 H5 **Yanco** New S Wales 34.35S 146.24E
12 H4 **Yanda** *R* New S Wales
14 D8 **Yandal** W Australia 27.33S 121.05E
12 F3 **Yandama** *R* S Australia
24 F6 **Yandaxkak** Xinjiang Uygur Zizhiqu 39.00N 88.28E
9 A13 **Yandé** *isld* New Caledonia 20.05S 163.48E
90 L8 **Yandia Cent Afr Rep** 7.23N 22.38E
22 H6 **Yandian** Nei Monggol Zizhiqu **China** 40.05N 110.18E
14 C7 **Yandil** W Australia 26.12S 119.45E
13 L7 **Yandina** Queensland 26.36S 152.52E
15 L3 **Yandina** Solomon Is 9.05S 159.15E
91 E4 **Yandja Zaïre** 1.39S 17.46E
91 H2 **Yandonge Zaïre** 2.49N 22.22E
25 C4 **Yandoon Burma** 17.01N 95.38E
9 R5 **Yandua** *isld* **Fiji** 16.50S 178.18E
24 H4 **Yandun** Xinjiang Uygur Zizhiqu **China** 42.24N 94.08E
Yanfa *see* **Renhua**
23 B6 **Yanfeng** Yunnan **China** 25.53N 101.02E
89 F6 **Yanfolila Mali** 11.10N 7.58W
90 J7 **Yanga Chad** 9.30N 19.10E
91 J3 **Yangambi Zaïre** 0.47N 24.24E
24 H10 **Ya'ngamdo** Xizang Zizhiqu **China** 31.15N 94.04E
24 H10 **Ya'ngamdo** Xizang Zizhiqu **China** 31.47N 94.33E
30 E2 **Yangar Nepal** 30.01N 81.36E
93 B3 **Yangarakata Zaïre** 2.59N 30.30E
47 J2 **Yangarey U.S.S.R.** 68.46N 61.29E
24 G10 **Yangbajain** Xizang Zizhiqu **China** 30.05N 90.35E
23 B6 **Yangbi** Yunnan **China** 25.40N 100.00E
23 F1 **Yangcheng** Shanxi **China** 35.30N 112.29E
Yangchuan *see* **Suiyang**
23 F7 **Yangchun** Guangdong **China** 22.07N 111.43E
Yang-chu-yung Hu *L* *see* **Yamdrok Tso** *L*
Yangcun *see* **Wuqing**
23 G7 **Yangcun** Guangdong **China** 23.28N 114.30E
21 C6 **Yangdachengzi** Jilin **China** 43.57N 124.27E
14 A3 **Yangebup L** W Australia 32.07S 115.49E
90 K8 **Yangéré Cent Afr Rep** 7.54N 20.18E
21 F5 **Yanggang** Heilongjiang **China** 45.45N 132.15E
9 R5 **Yangganga** *isld* **Fiji** 16.35S 178.36E
22 J6 **Yanggao** Shanxi **China** 40.22N 113.44E
9 R7 **Yanggeta** *isld* **Fiji** 17.03S 177.17E
22 K8 **Yanggu** Shandong **China** 36.09N 115.48E
21 D8 **Yanggu S Korea** 38.05N 128.00E
Yanghe *see* **Yongning**
23 H2 **Yanghe** Jiangsu **China** 33.46N 118.23E
43 K6 **Yangiabad** Uzbekistan **U.S.S.R.** 41.07N 70.09E
43 F6 **Yangi-Aryk** Uzbekistan **U.S.S.R.** 41.22N 60.33E
43 K6 **Yangibazar** Kirgiziya **U.S.S.R.** 41.38N 70.54E
31 J1 **Yangi Davan** *pass* Kashmir/Xinjiang Uygur Zizhiqu 35.58N 79.25E
32 D3 **Yangi Emām Iran** 35.55N 50.44E
Yangi Hissar *see* **Yengisar**
Yangijeh *see* **Yengejeh**
32 C2 **Yangi Kand Iran** 36.13N 48.02E
43 H6 **Yangikishlak** Uzbekistan **U.S.S.R.** 40.25N 67.10E
43 N7 **Yangikurgan** Uzbekistan **U.S.S.R.** 41.20N 71.40E
Yangi Sudake Oi *see* **Yengisu**
47 K3 **Yangiyegan U.S.S.R.** 66.05N 68.30E
43 J6 **Yangiyer** Uzbekistan **U.S.S.R.** 40.20N 68.46E
43 J6 **Yangiyul'** Uzbekistan **U.S.S.R.** 41.07N 69.02E
23 D2 **Yangjiahe** Shaanxi **China** 32.43N 107.52E
23 F8 **Yangjiang** Guangdong **China** 21.52N 111.52E
22 M6 **Yangjiazhangzi** Liaoning **China** 40.51N 120.35E
22 D8 **Yangkang** Qinghai **China** 37.38N 98.46E
23 H5 **Yangkou** Fujian **China** 26.53N 117.53E
15 K6 **Yangla** Bismarck Arch 5.47S 148.03E
Yang-li *see* **Daxin**
23 C6 **Yanglin** Yunnan **China** 25.12N 103.05E
23 F4 **Yangloudong** Hubei **China** 29.33N 113.42E
23 G1 **Yangmiao** Henan **China** 34.08N 114.54E
23 F5 **Yangming Shan** *mt* Hunan **China**
41 E5 **Yangoda** *R* **U.S.S.R.**
91 H3 **Yangonde Zaïre** 0.03N 22.43E
9 A8 **Yangor** Nauru, Pacific Oc 0.31S 166.54E
15 G5 **Yangoru Papua New Guinea** 3.41S 143.25E
47 D4 **Yangory U.S.S.R.** 62.49N 37.45E
23 F8 **Yangpu Gang** *inlet* Guangdong **China**

23 F4 Yangqiao Hunan China 28.28N 112.58E
22 J7 Yangqu Shanxi China 38.05N 112.37E
23 F5 Yangquan Hunan China 26.17N 112.15E
22 J8 Yangquan Shanxi China 37.52N 113.29E
21 E10 Yangsan S Korea 35.19N 129.05E
23 F6 Yangshan Guangdong China 24.23N 112.34E
23 G1 Yangshan Shandong China 35.19N 116.11E
Yangshe *see* Shazhou
23 E6 Yangshuo Guangxi China 24.40N 110.15E
25 K6 Yang Sin,Chu *mt* Vietnam 12.24N 108.25E
23 H3 Yangtan Anhui China 30.43N 119.10E
23 B6 Yangtouyan Yunnan China 24.17N 101.07E
Yangtze *see* Chang Jiang
Yangtze *R see* Jinsha Jiang
23 D1 Yanguan Gansu China 34.17N 105.27E
75 F3 Yanguas Spain 42.06N 2.20W
41 F4 Yanguda *R* U.S.S.R.
47 K6 Yangutumskiye U.S.S.R. 58.22N 66.40E
25 E6 Yangwa Burma 13.11N 98.58E
23 C7 Yangwu Yunnan China 23.54N 102.10E
23 G4 Yangxin Hubei China 29.52N 115.08E
89 B4 Yang-Yang Senegal 15.31N 15.19W
21 D8 Yangyang S Korea 38.01N 128.50E
Yang Yong *see* Ban Yang Yong
22 K6 Yangyuan Hebei China 40.08N 114.10E
23 H2 Yangzhou Jiangsu China 32.22N 119.22E
23 E4 Yanhe Guizhou China 28.28N 108.42E
22 H8 Yan He *R* Shaanxi China
24 D9 Yanhuqu Xizang Zizhiqu China 32.32N 82.44E
Yanijah Buyuk *see* Büyük Yenija
45 W1 Yanikovo U.S.S.R. 55.35N 50.13E
Yanina *see* Ioánnina
12 D5 Yaninee, L S Australia 32.59S 135.14E
51 P10 Yanis'yarvi, Ozero *L* Karelia U.S.S.R.
21 E6 Yanji Jilin China 42.45N 129.25E
21 E6 Yanji Jilin China 42.52N 129.32E
23 G1 Yanjin Henan China 35.11N 114.17E
23 C4 Yanjin Yunnan China 28.09N 104.15E
23 D4 Yanjing Sichuan China 29.57N 106.20E
23 A4 Yanjing Xizang Zizhiqu China 29.01N 98.38E
110 J1 Yank Br Col 49.06N 116.08W
42 K4 Yankan, Khrebet *mts* U.S.S.R.
12 H6 Yanko *R* New S Wales
12 F4 Yanko Glen New S Wales 31.43S 141.39E
90 D5 Yankwashi Nigeria 12.48N 8.35E
32 C1 Yanlagh Iran 38.01N 48.35E
23 G1 Yanling Henan China 34.08N 114.06E
41 P5 Yano-Indigirskaya Nizmennost' *lowland* U.S.S.R.
91 J3 Yanonge Zaïre 0.37N 24.41E
39 C3 Yano-Oymyakonskoye Nagor'ye *tableland* U.S.S.R.
35 E1 Yânoûh Lebanon 33.16N 35.18E
45 B1 Yanovichi Belorussiya U.S.S.R. 55.20N 30.43E
46 O2 Yanovo U.S.S.R. 55.29N 45.22E
41 D7 Yanov Stan U.S.S.R. 65.58N 84.25E
26 S4 Yan Oya *R* Sri Lanka
24 E4 Yanqi Huizu Zizhixian Xinjiang Uygur Zizhiqu China 42.04N 86.34E
22 K6 Yanqing Beijing China 40.30N 115.58E
33 M5 Yanqul Oman 22.40N 56.30E
39 M3 Yanrakynnot U.S.S.R. 64.53N 172.45W
39 J1 Yanranay U.S.S.R. 69.55N 170.32E
14 A6 Yanrey W Australia 22.33S 114.49E
14 B6 Yanrey,R W Australia
22 L7 Yanshan Hebei China 38.06N 117.13E
23 H4 Yanshan Jiangxi China 28.18N 117.43E
23 C7 Yanshan Yunnan China 23.32N 104.20E
22 L6 Yan Shan *mts* Hebei China
23 F1 Yanshi Henan China 34.46N 112.43E
24 G9 Yanshiping Qinghai China 33.35N 92.04E
21 D5 Yanshou Heilongjiang China 45.30N 128.20E
39 A1 Yanskiy U.S.S.R. 68.30N 134.42E
41 P5 Yanskiye Porogi *falls* U.S.S.R. 70.14N 135.15E
41 O5 Yanskiy Zaliv *B* U.S.S.R.
39 A1 Yanskoye Ploskogor'ye *tableland* U.S.S.R.
12 H3 Yantabulla New S Wales 29.13S 145.01E
21 B9 Yantai Shandong China 37.30N 121.22E
121 A9 Yantales,Cerro *mt* Chile 43.28S 72.52W
12 F3 Yantara L New S Wales 29.52S 142.20E
103 K3 Yantic Connecticut 41.34N 72.07W
23 D3 Yanting Sichuan China 31.16N 105.25E
21 C6 Yantongshan Jilin China 43.20N 125.59E
23 J4 Yantou Zhejiang China 28.21N 120.45E
82 K7 Yantra *R* Bulgaria
15 J7 Yanuf Papua New Guinea 6.04S 147.09E
33 E5 Yanūfi,Jabal al *mts* Saudi Arabia
35 D2 Yanūh Israel 32.59N 35.14E
9 S8 Yanutha *isld* Fiji 18.24S 178.00E
9 U5 Yanutha *isld* Fiji 16.30S 179.43W
35 C4 Yanuv Israel 32.18N 34.57E
9 R7 Yanuya *isld* Fiji 17.35S 177.05E
23 B5 Yanwa Yunnan China 27.40N 98.58E
Yanwu *see* Yuanyang
21 E4 Yanxing Heilongjiang China 47.42N 130.57E
43 H5 Yany-Kurgan Kazakhstan U.S.S.R. 43.49N 67.13E
23 B5 Yanyuan Yizu Zizhixian Sichuan China 27.30N 101.40E
22 E7 Yanzhi Shan *mt* Gansu China 38.24N 100.34E
23 G1 Yanzhou Shandong China 35.35N 116.53E
23 D5 Yanzikou Guizhou China 27.36N 105.24E
90 H5 Yao Chad 12.52N 17.34E
20 J7 Yao Japan 34.36N 135.37E
23 B6 Yao'an Yunnan China 25.31N 101.12E
Yaodu *see* Dongzhi
25 M1 Yaogu Guangdong China 22.53N 112.15E
23 B6 Yaoguan Yunnan China 24.35N 99.15E
22 D7 Yaoquanzi Gansu China 39.58N 97.39E
22 H8 Yaotou Shanxi China 36.16N 110.46E
91 E3 Yaou Congo 1.01N 17.50E
90 E10 Yaoundé Cameroon 3.51N 11.31E
90 E10 Yaoundé *tribe* Cameroon
23 H1 Yaowan Jiangsu China 34.15N 118.09E
23 E1 Yao Xian Shaanxi China 34.55N 109.00E
21 D3 Yaoxiaoling Heilongjiang China 48.04N 127.42E
25 E8 Yao Yai,Ko *isld* Thailand
17 N10 Yap *islds* Caroline Is Pacific Oc 9.30N 138.09E
119 F6 Yapacana, Co *mt* Venezuela 3.44N 66.48W
120 F7 Yapacani,R Bolivia
90 N9 Yapassira Cent Afr Rep 5.04N 26.33E
91 J4 Yapehe Zaïre 0.13S 24.28E
15 C4 Yapen *isld* Irian Jaya
91 H3 Yapere Zaïre 0.34N 22.50E
121 G2 Yapeyu Argentina 29.28S 56.50W
103 J5 Yaphank Long I, N Y 40.50N 72.54W
89 G9 Yapo Ivory Coast 5.47N 4.14W
13 F4 Yappar *R* Queensland
36 G2 Yapraklı Turkey 40.45N 33.46E
122 E7 Yap Ridge Pacific Oc
47 L2 Yaptiksale U.S.S.R. 69.22N 72.30E
122 E7 Yap Trench Pacific Oc
119 J6 Yapukarri Guyana 3.42N 59.22W
Yaqian *see* Yuexi
116 J5 Yaque del Sur *R* Dominican Rep
115 D4 Yaqui Mexico 27.23N 110.08W
115 E3 Yaqui *R* Mexico
110 A5 Yaquina Hd Oregon 44.45N 124.05W
35 C4 Yaqum Israel 32.15N 34.50E
Yāqūq *see* Ḥuqoq
35 F2 Yaqusah,El Syria 32.45N 35.44E
46 Q1 Yar U.S.S.R. 58.13N 52.08E
116 F4 Yara Cuba 20.18N 76.57W
41 D6 Yara *R* U.S.S.R.
119 F2 Yaracal Venezuela 10.59N 68.32W
119 F2 Yaracuy *state* Venezuela
119 F2 Yaracuy,R Venezuela
43 E7 Yaradzha Turkmeniya U.S.S.R. 38.17N 57.13E
13 G6 Yaraka Queensland 24.55S 144.05E
30 H3 Yaral Nepal 27.51N 86.48E
36 G1 Yaralıgöz *mt* Turkey 41.46N 34.04E
Yarangüme *see* Tavas
46 P2 Yaransk U.S.S.R. 57.22N 47.49E
87 G6 Yarar *mt* Ethiopia 8.58N 39.00E
36 D5 Yaraşlı Gölü *L* Turkey
36 D4 Yarbasan Turkey 38.58N 28.46E
56 E6 Yarcombe Devon Eng 50.52N 3.05W
90 J2 Yarda Chad 18.30N 19.03E
12 D4 Yardea S Australia 32.23S 135.32E
35 F3 Yardena Israel 32.34N 35.33E
37 D8 Yardimci Turkey 37.02N 38.59E
103 E6 Yardley Pennsylvania 40.19N 74.50W
56 K3 Yardley Gobion Northants Eng 52.06N 0.54W
56 K3 Yardley Hastings Northants Eng 52.12N 0.45W
103 E6 Yardville New Jersey 40.11N 74.40W
44 J9 Yardymly Azerbaydzhan U.S.S.R. 38.56N 48.15E
46 E5 Yaremcha Ukraine U.S.S.R. 48.26N 24.29E
47 F4 Yarenga U.S.S.R. 62.45N 49.30E
47 F5 Yarenga *R* U.S.S.R.
47 F5 Yarensk U.S.S.R. 62.10N 49.07E
56 O2 Yare,R Norfolk Eng
45 E7 Yares'ki Ukraine U.S.S.R. 49.50N 33.55E
46 G6 Yargora Moldavia U.S.S.R. 46.25N 28.20E
37 G3 Yarhisar Turkey 40.13N 29.43E
35 C5 Yarḥiv Israel 32.09N 34.58E
20 L5 Yariga-dake *pk* Japan 36.21N 137.39E
33 F9 Yarīm Yemen 14.15N 44.26E
Yarımca *see* Cingife
36 E3 Yarımca Turkey 39.56N 30.37E
37 G2 Yarımca Turkey 40.47N 29.44E
35 D1 Yârîne Lebanon 33.06N 35.14E
13 E5 Yaringa *R* Queensland
117 B4 Yaripo Brazil 1.22N 54.54W
119 D8 Yarí,R Colombia
119 E2 Yaritagua Venezuela 10.05N 69.07W
Yarkand *see* Shache
Yarkand Darya *R see* Yarkant He
24 B7 Yarkant He *R* Xinjiang Uygur Zizhiqu China
24 D5 Yarkant He *R* Xinjiang Uygur Zizhiqu China
43 K7 Yarkhichkala Tadzhikistan U.S.S.R. 39.15N 70.54E
31 G2 Yarkhun *R* Pakistan
42 B5 Yarki U.S.S.R. 54.48N 79.45E
45 N5 Yarki U.S.S.R. 51.22N 41.11E
42 F3 Yarkino U.S.S.R. 59.11N 99.27E
47 K7 Yarkovo U.S.S.R. 57.25N 67.01E
12 B4 Yarle Lakes S Australia
28 J1 Yarlung *R* Xizang Zizhiqu China
24 G11 Yarlung Zangbo Jiang *R* Xizang Zizhiqu China
57 L3 Yarm Cleveland Eng 54.30N 1.21W
36 F5 Yarma Turkey 37.48N 32.53E
82 K1 Yarmolintsy U.S.S.R. 49.09N 26.54E
56 J6 Yarmouth I of Wight Eng 50.42N 1.29W
104 P3 Yarmouth Maine 43.48N 70.12W
103 O3 Yarmouth Massachusetts 41.43N 70.13W
98 F10 Yarmouth Nova Scotia 43.50N 66.08W
35 F3 Yarmuk *R* Jordan/Syria/Israel
111 M7 Yarnell Arizona 34.14N 112.45W
45 M4 Yarok U.S.S.R. 52.51N 40.07E
41 P5 Yarok, Ostrov *isld* U.S.S.R.
47 K2 Yarongo U.S.S.R. 68.10N 69.28E
46 L1 Yaroslavl' U.S.S.R. 57.34N 39.52E
44 C3 Yaroslavskaya U.S.S.R. 44.36N 40.27E
46 L1 Yaroslavskaya Oblast *prov* U.S.S.R.
40 F9 Yaroslavskiy U.S.S.R. 44.09N 133.05E
35 E1 Yâroûn Lebanon 33.05N 35.26E
117 C3 Yaroupi *R* Fr Guiana
45 J7 Yarovaya Ukraine U.S.S.R. 49.04N 37.43E
41 D5 Yar-Pan-Ty-Ya U.S.S.R. 70.09N 81.07E
35 F6 Yarqa Jordan 31.58N 35.42E
86 K7 Yarqa, Wâdi *watercourse* Egypt
35 C5 Yarqon *R* Israel
13 G2 Yarraden Queensland 14.17S 143.20E
14 B5 Yarraloola W Australia 21.34S 115.50E
12 A6 Yarralumla *dist* Canberra Australia
12 A6 Yarralumla Creek Canberra Australia
12 H7 Yarram Victoria 38.30S 146.09E
13 K7 Yarraman Queensland 26.50S 151.54E
13 D4 Yarran Ra N Terr Australia
12 H6 Yarrawonga Victoria 36.02S 145.59E
12 H7 Yarra Yarra *R* Victoria
14 B8 Yarra Yarra Lakes W Australia
Yarri *see* Mendleyarri
14 D5 Yarrie W Australia 20.35S 120.16E
13 H7 Yarronvale Queensland 26.50S 145.21E
47 L2 Yarroto U.S.S.R. 68.02N 71.40E
47 L2 Yarroto,Oz *L* U.S.S.R.
13 H5 Yarrowmere Queensland 21.28S 145.50E
57 H1 Yarrow,R Borders Scotland
47 L3 Yar Sale U.S.S.R. 66.50N 70.48E
42 A2 Yarsomovy U.S.S.R. 60.14N 73.35E
28 J1 Yartö Tra La *pass* Xizang Zizhiqu 28.51N 92.05E
42 E2 Yartsevo Krasnoyarsk U.S.S.R. 60.17N 90.02E
45 D1 Yartsevo Smolensk U.S.S.R. 55.06N 32.43E
29 L3 Yaru *R* Xizang Zizhiqu
47 L3 Yarudey *R* U.S.S.R.
119 C4 Yarumal Colombia 6.59N 75.25W
119 B8 Yaruqui Ecuador 0.07S 78.17W
35 F8 Yarut Jordan 31.18N 35.44E
120 D9 Yarvicoya,Cerro *pk* Chile 20.05S 69.00W
47 K2 Yary U.S.S.R. 68.54N 66.30E
39 D4 Yaryga, Gora *mt* U.S.S.R. 61.30N 149.33E
44 G4 Yaryk Aul U.S.S.R. 43.45N 46.00E
44 B9 Yarylgach,Bukhta *bight* Ukraine U.S.S.R.
43 N7 Yarylgan Uzbekistan U.S.S.R. 41.07N 71.41E
82 L2 Yaryshev U.S.S.R. 48.30N 27.39E
23 A4 Yarzhong Xizang Zizhiqu China 29.58N 97.55E
91 E6 Yasa Bandundu Zaïre 4.37S 17.59E
91 G5 Yasa Zaïre 3.50S 21.25E
39 E2 Yasachnaya *R* U.S.S.R.
29 K2 Yasai R W Bengal India
89 G4 Ya Salam Mali 14.39N 5.10W
93 K2 Yasar *water hole* Kenya 2.33N 38.37E
47 N4 Yasashnaya U.S.S.R. 57.56N 61.26E
45 U3 Yasashnaya Tashla U.S.S.R. 53.54N 48.15E
33 J4 Yāsāt,Al *isld* U.A.E. 24.10N 51.59E
47 K2 Yasaveyto,Ozero *L* U.S.S.R.
47 K2 Yasaveyyakha *R* U.S.S.R.
9 R1 Yasawa *I* Fiji
9 R1 Yasawa *island grp* Fiji
10 Q5 Yasawa Trough Pacific Oc
46 F4 Yasel'da *R* Belorussiya U.S.S.R.
46 G3 Yasen Belorussiya U.S.S.R. 53.10N 28.55E
45 K5 Yasenki U.S.S.R. 51.32N 38.14E
46 L6 Yasenskaya U.S.S.R. 46.22N 38.12E
44 B1 Yasenskaya Kosa *sand spit* U.S.S.R.
44 E1 Yashalta U.S.S.R. 46.20N 42.18E
33 G9 Yashbum S Yemen 14.19N 46.53E
90 C5 Yashi Nigeria 12.23N 7.54E
90 A7 Yashikera Nigeria 9.44N 3.29E
43 L7 Yashilkul',Oz *L* Tadzhikistan U.S.S.R.
20 O2 Yashima Japan 39.12N 140.11E
20 F8 Ya-shima *I* Japan 33.44N 132.09E
20 F1 Yashio Saitama Japan
20 F8 Yashiro-jima *isld* Japan 33.55N 132.20E
42 D4 Yashkino Kemerovo U.S.S.R. 55.53N 85.23E
40 G5 Yashkino Khabarovsk U.S.S.R. 52.18N 135.31E
43 C1 Yashkino Orenburg U.S.S.R. 52.41N 53.28E
44 G1 Yashkul' U.S.S.R. 46.10N 45.20E
44 J7 Yashma Azerbaydzhan U.S.S.R. 40.42N 49.27E
35 E4 Yasid Jordan 32.18N 35.17E
31 G2 Yasin Kashmir 36.23N 73.23E
92 J4 Yasini Tanzania 4.40S 39.10E
45 J8 Yasinovataya Ukraine U.S.S.R. 48.06N 37.54E
46 E5 Yasinya Ukraine U.S.S.R. 48.12N 24.20E
43 D7 Yaskha Turkmeniya U.S.S.R. 39.44N 55.33E
40 G9 Yasnaya Polyana Primor'ye U.S.S.R. 45.46N 137.01E
45 J2 Yasnaya Polyana Tula U.S.S.R. 54.04N 37.32E
45 B6 Yasnogorodka Ukraine U.S.S.R. 50.50N 30.25E
46 L3 Yasnogors'k U.S.S.R. 54.28N 37.45E
40 J8 Yasnomorskiy Sakhalin U.S.S.R. 46.44N 141.57E
40 D5 Yasnyy U.S.S.R. 53.14N 128.05E
43 E2 Yasnyy U.S.S.R. 50.56N 60.00E
Ya Soup *see* Ban Ya Soup
12 J5 Yass New S Wales 34.51S 148.55E
12 J5 Yass *R* New S Wales
90 K9 Yassa Cent Afr Rep 5.32N 21.35E
37 F2 Yassi *isld* Turkey 40.52N 28.59E
45 J5 Yastrebovka U.S.S.R. 51.28N 37.38E
20 G8 Yasuda Japan 33.25N 133.58E
35 D5 Yasuf Jordan 32.07N 35.14E
20 G6 Yasugi Japan 35.25N 133.12E
32 D5 Yasuj Iran 30.40N 51.35E
33 J1 Yasuj Iran 30.40N 51.33E
37 D4 Yasun Burun *C* Turkey 41.11N 37.42E
119 C8 Yasuní,R Ecuador
35 D2 Yas'ur Israel 32.54N 35.10E
47 N3 Yas'va U.S.S.R. 58.10N 60.10E
90 F1 Yat Niger 20.28N 13.27E
120 F4 Yata Bolivia 10.30S 65.25W
90 L7 Yata *R* Cent Afr Rep
36 C5 Yatağan Turkey 37.22N 28.08E
89 K4 Yatakala Niger 14.52N 0.22E
120 F4 Yata,R Bolivia
120 F11 Yatasto Argentina 25.38S 65.00W
90 C6 Yatawa Nigeria 11.06N 7.25E
9 C14 Yaté New Caledonia 22.09S 167.00E
89 H5 Yatenga *reg* Upper Volta
89 D5 Yatéra Mali 13.13N 11.10W
109 G5 Yates New Mexico 36.08N 103.55W
101 P6 Yates *R* Alberta
104 F6 Yatesboro Pennsylvania 40.48N 79.21W
109 P4 Yates Center Kansas 37.54N 95.44W
11 B11 Yates Pt New Zealand 44.30S 167.48E
9 U6 Yathata *I* Fiji 17.15S 179.33W
97 K5 Yathkyed L N W Terr 62.35N 98.00W
Yathrib *anc site see* Medina
26 R8 Yatiyantota Sri Lanka 7.03N 80.18E
91 J3 Yatolema Zaïre 0.25N 24.35E
Yatou *see* Rongcheng
77 P2 Yátova Spain 39.23N 0.49W
20 M6 Yatsuga-take *pk* Japan 35.58N 138.22E
20 L5 Yatsuo Japan 36.35N 137.10E
20 D9 Yatsushiro Japan 32.32N 130.35E
20 D9 Yatsushiro-kai *B* Japan
86 O3 Yatta Jordan 31.27N 35.05E
93 J7 Yatta Plat Kenya
35 C8 Yattir *watercourse* Israel
35 D8 Yattir, Hare *hills* Israel
56 F5 Yatton Avon Eng 51.24N 2.49W
13 J6 Yatton Queensland 22.32S 149.00E
56 G5 Yatton Keynell Wilts Eng 51.30N 2.12W
93 N5 Yatu Somalia 0.30N 41.09E
119 F7 Yatua,R Venezuela
28 G2 Yatung Xizang Zizhiqu 27.25N 89.00E
120 C6 Yauca Peru 15.39S 74.35W
120 C6 Yauca,R Peru
105 J7 Yauco Puerto Rico 18.02N 66.51W
105 H4 Yauhannah S Carolina 33.36N 79.13W
120 B4 Yauli Peru 11.45S 76.05W
23 B9 Yau Ma Tei Hong Kong 22.18N 114.09E
119 E8 Yauna Maloca Colombia 0.45S 70.24W
Yaunelgava *see* Jaunjelgava
Yaunpiyebalga *see* Jaunpiebalga
120 D6 Yauri Peru 14.51S 71.24W
120 B5 Yauricocha Peru 12.54S 75.17W
115 K8 Yautepec Mexico 18.52N 99.04W
120 B5 Yauyos Peru 12.19S 75.49W
23 C9 Yau Yue Wan Hong Kong 22.19N 114.16E
115 L3 Yauyupe Honduras 13.45N 87.02W
46 E6 Yauza *R* U.S.S.R.
111 M7 Yava Arizona 34.29N 112.54W
43 J7 Yavan Tadzhikistan U.S.S.R. 38.20N 69.01E
120 C1 Yavari Mirim,R Peru
120 C1 Yavari,R Peru
115 E4 Yavaros Mexico 26.41N 109.32W
29 F7 Yavatmal Maharashtra India 20.22N 78.11E
29 F7 Yavatmal *dist* Maharashtra India
41 C5 Yavay,Poluostrov *pen* U.S.S.R.
120 D5 Yavero *R* Peru
39 G3 Yaveson,Gora *mt* U.S.S.R. 63.00N 164.30E
Yavı *see* Belcik
119 G5 Yaví,Cerro *mt* Venezuela 5.34N 65.59W
115 Q5 Yaviza Panama 8.09N 77.41W
43 J1 Yavlenka Kazakhstan U.S.S.R. 54.20N 68.26E
35 B6 Yavne Israel 31.52N 34.45E
35 F3 Yavneel Israel 32.42N 35.31E
35 F3 Yavneel *R* Israel
35 B6 Yavne, Holot *sand dunes* Israel
46 E5 Yavorov Ukraine U.S.S.R. 49.59N 23.20E
92 C3 Yavoti Zaïre 3.59S 27.32E
51 O3 Yavra *R* U.S.S.R.
36 G4 Yavşantuzlasi Turkey 38.46N 33.07E
37 D5 Yavuzkemal Turkey 40.42N 38.21E
25 C2 Yaw *R* Burma
20 H4 Yawata Chiba Japan
19 M4 Yawata *isld* Truk Is Pacific Oc 7.32N 151.37E
20 F8 Yawatahama Japan 33.27N 132.24E
24 D7 Yawatongguzlangar Xinjiang Uygur Zizhiqu China 37.17N 83.15E
25 D2 Yawng-Hwe Burma 20.35N 96.58E
89 C7 Yawri B Sierra Leone
115 O9 Yaxchilán *ruins* Mexico 16.54N 90.58W
23 D5 Yaxi Guizhou China 27.35N 106.45E
23 E9 Ya Xian Guangdong China 18.25N 109.27E
56 L2 Yaxley Cambs Eng 52.31N 0.16W
42 D4 Yaya U.S.S.R. 56.14N 86.26E
42 D4 Yaya *R* U.S.S.R.
37 F7 Yayla Turkey 38.39N 40.32E
36 J7 Yayladağı Turkey 35.55N 36.00E
37 C2 Yaylâ Dağları *mts* Turkey
Yaylak *see* Baziki
90 H3 Yayo Chad 17.41N 17.12E
43 N8 Yaypan Uzbekistan U.S.S.R. 40.25N 70.50E
Yayrūb *see* Jarūb
47 H6 Yayva U.S.S.R. 59.21N 57.12E
47 H6 Yayva *R* U.S.S.R.
25 L9 Yazagyo Burma 23.32N 94.06E
32 F5 Yazd Iran 31.55N 54.22E
32 E5 Yazd *reg* Iran
32 J4 Yazdān Iran 33.30N 60.55E
32 G5 Yazdānābād Iran 30.52N 56.20E
32 E5 Yazd-e Khvāst Iran 31.32N 52.08E
43 K7 Yazgulemskiy Khrebet *mts* Tadzhikistan U.S.S.R.
33 E7 Yazid,Al Saudi Arabia 18.05N 42.45E
37 D7 Yazıhan Turkey 38.37N 38.10E
43 D1 Yazikovo Bashkir U.S.S.R. 54.41N 55.02E
107 F8 Yazoo *R* Mississippi
107 F9 Yazoo City Mississippi 32.51N 90.26W
47 H5 Yaz'va *R* U.S.S.R.
43 N8 Yaz'yavan Uzbekistan U.S.S.R. 40.29N 71.45E
43 F8 Yazygadzhik Turkmeniya U.S.S.R. 37.27N 60.18E
45 T2 Yazykovo U.S.S.R. 54.19N 47.22E
37 C7 Yazyurdu Turkey 38.48N 36.53E
85 C8 Ybakoura Chad 22.08N 15.48E
90 G1 Ybakoura Chad 22.08N 15.45E
65 M5 Ybbs Austria 48.11N 15.05E
65 M5 Ybbs *R* Austria
65 L6 Ybbsitz Austria 47.57N 14.55E
118 C10 Ybycuí Paraguay 26.00S 57.00W
56 D4 Y Creunant W Glam Wales 51.44N 3.45W
89 H4 Ydaman Mali 15.40N 2.13W
53 A3 Ydby Denmark 56.43N 8.26E
53 G5 Yderby Denmark 55.59N 11.22E
72 J5 Ydes France 45.20N 2.26E
53 D5 Yding Skovhøj *mt* Denmark 56.00N 9.49E
53 S20 Ydstebøhamn Norway 59.08N 5.25E
47 H4 Ydzhid Parma *plat* U.S.S.R.
25 D5 Ye Burma 15.15N 97.50E
89 H5 Ye Upper Volta 12.40N 3.05W
25 D5 Ye *R* Burma
12 H6 Yea Victoria 37.12S 145.25E
55 C3 Yeading Brook London England
57 K5 Yeadon W Yorks Eng 53.52N 1.41W
56 D7 Yealmpton Devon Eng 50.21N 3.59W
56 C7 Yealm,R Devon Eng
Yebaishou *see* Jianping
25 M8 Yebawmi Burma 25.16N 95.49E
90 J1 Yebbi Bou Chad 20.51N 18.04E
90 H1 Yebbi-Souma Chad 21.06N 17.58E
41 K5 Yebe-Khay,Gora *mt* U.S.S.R. 71.40N 114.13E
76 L9 Yébenes,Sierra de *mts* Spain
75 D6 Yebes Spain 40.31N 3.07W
90 H1 Yebigé *watercourse* Chad
70 M2 Yébleron France 49.38N 0.33E
75 K3 Yebra de Basa Spain 42.29N 0.16W
25 E5 Yebyu Burma 14.13N 98.09E
24 B7 Yecheng Xinjiang Uygur Zizhiqu China 37.47N 77.16E
77 O3 Yecla Spain 38.36N 1.07W
76 G7 Yecla de Yeltes Spain 40.57N 6.29W
15 J1 Yecola I Papua New Guinea 4.39S 155.20E
115 E3 Yécora Mexico 28.23N 108.56W
42 G3 Yedarma U.S.S.R. 58.43N 102.35E
25 D3 Yedashe Burma 19.10N 96.20E
28 C4 Yedatore Karnataka India 12.28N 76.22E
93 A4 Yedi Zaïre 2.00N 29.49E
36 D6 Yedi Burun *C* Turkey 36.24N 29.07E
37 D5 Yedigöz Yaylâ *plat* Turkey
37 H3 Yedikule *dist* İstanbul Turkey
57 M4 Yedingham N Yorks Eng 54.12N 0.38W
40 H8 Yedinka U.S.S.R. 47.10N 138.36E
46 F5 Yedintsy Moldavia U.S.S.R. 48.09N 27.18E
47 E4 Yedoma Arkhangel'sk U.S.S.R. 63.50N 44.44E
47 G3 Yedoma Komi U.S.S.R. 65.27N 51.23E
90 H1 Yedri Chad 22.25N 17.30E
90 F6 Yedseram *R* Nigeria
14 E4 Yeeda River W Australia 17.39S 123.39E
12 D5 Yeelanna S Australia 34.06S 135.44E
45 O1 Yefanovo U.S.S.R. 55.43N 42.16E
15 A4 Yef Fam, Kepulauan *islds* Irian Jaya 0.38S 130.16E
47 C6 Yefimovskiy U.S.S.R. 59.32N 34.43E
84 D3 Yéfira Greece 39.17N 22.11E
15 A4 Yeflio Irian Jaya 1.09S 131.16E
45 K3 Yefremov U.S.S.R. 53.08N 38.08E
45 M8 Yefremovo Stepanovka U.S.S.R. 48.42N 40.49E
77 K7 Yegen Spain 36.59N 3.06W
43 M3 Yegendybulak Kazakhstan U.S.S.R. 49.48N 76.23E
90 F1 Yeggueba Niger 19.59N 12.52E
43 J2 Yegindykol' Kazakhstan U.S.S.R. 50.56N 69.25E
44 D1 Yegorlyk *R* U.S.S.R.
44 D1 Yegorlyskskaya U.S.S.R. 46.33N 40.40E
40 G9 Yegorova,Mys *C* U.S.S.R. 44.44N 136.18E
45 G1 Yegorye U.S.S.R. 55.13N 36.00E
40 D6 Yegor'yevka U.S.S.R. 50.40N 127.40E
45 L1 Yegor'yevsk U.S.S.R. 55.21N 39.01E
118 C10 Yegros Paraguay 26.24S 56.28W
112 K5 Yegua Cr Texas
77 H4 Yeguas *R* Spain
77 G6 Yeguas,Sierra de *mts* Spain
121 B5 Yeguas,Vol Chile 36.00S 70.52W
15 J1 Yeharnu I Papua New Guinea 4.47S 155.28E
35 D2 Yeḥi'am Israel 32.59N 35.13E
35 C5 Yehuda Israel 32.02N 34.50E
Yehuda *reg see* Judaea *reg*
93 B1 Yei Sudan 4.05N 30.39E
93 B1 Yei *R* Sudan
15 M9 Yeina I Louisiade Arch 11.22S 153.26E
23 G3 Yeji Anhui China 31.52N 115.58E
89 J7 Yeji Ghana 8.05N 0.37W
Yekabpils *see* Jēkabpils
Yekaterinburg *see* Sverdlovsk
Yekaterinenstadt *see* Marks
47 J5 Yekaterininka U.S.S.R. 60.29N 60.26E
47 L7 Yekaterininskoye U.S.S.R. 56.55N 74.38E
44 F4 Yekaterinogradskaya U.S.S.R. 43.47N 44.15E
Yekaterinoslav *see* Dnepropetrovsk
40 E6 Yekaterinoslavka Amur U.S.S.R. 50.22N 129.05E
47 L8 Yekaterinoslavka Omsk U.S.S.R. 54.24N 72.29E
47 L8 Yekaterinovka Kazakhstan U.S.S.R. 54.40N 70.55E
45 U4 Yekaterinovka Kuybyshev U.S.S.R. 52.42N 48.20E
45 K4 Yekaterinovka Lipetsk U.S.S.R. 52.35N 38.45E
45 Q4 Yekaterinovka Saratov U.S.S.R. 52.04N 44.20E
40 K9 Yekateriny,Proliv *str* Kuril Is U.S.S.R.
Yeke Yulduz *R see* Kaidu (Karaxahar) He
44 G8 Yekhegnadzor Armenia U.S.S.R. 39.44N 45.19E
90 H3 Yékiasahal Chad 16.15N 17.36E
45 E2 Yekimovichi U.S.S.R. 54.07N 33.20E
91 G3 Yekokora *R* Zaïre
91 H4 Yekumbe Zaïre 1.01S 23.27E
47 M3 Yekva U.S.S.R. 57.42N 58.58E
25 B3 Ye Kyun *isld* Burma 18.37N 93.50E
89 E8 Yela Guinea 7.54N 9.18W
46 Q2 Yelabuga U.S.S.R. 55.48N 52.00E
47 M1 Yelagina O *isld* Leningrad U.S.S.R.
15 M9 Yela I Louisiade Arch
47 J6 Yelan' Sverdlovsk U.S.S.R. 57.40N 63.42E
45 P6 Yelan' Volgograd U.S.S.R. 50.58N 43.44E
46 N4 Yelan' *R* Volgograd U.S.S.R.
46 M4 Yelan' *R* Voronezh U.S.S.R.
28 C4 Yelandur Karnataka India 12.03N 77.01E
45 C9 Yelanets Ukraine U.S.S.R. 47.41N 31.53E
45 N5 Yelan'-Kolenovskiy U.S.S.R. 51.09N 41.15E
42 H5 Yelantsy U.S.S.R. 52.50N 106.30E
13 K8 Yelarbon Queensland 28.37S 150.38E
45 N2 Yelat'ma U.S.S.R. 54.57N 41.45E
121 A9 Yelcho *R* Chile
121 A9 Yelcho, L Chile
89 D7 Yele Sierra Leone 8.28N 11.52W
42 J5 Yeleninskiy U.S.S.R. 54.20N 112.20E
45 J9 Yelenovka Ukraine U.S.S.R. 47.49N 37.41E
45 G3 Yelenskiy U.S.S.R. 53.29N 35.23E
45 K4 Yelets U.S.S.R. 52.35N 38.30E
47 J3 Yeletskiy U.S.S.R. 67.04N 64.00E
46 Q1 Yelganskaya U.S.S.R. 57.55N 51.30E
Yelgava *see* Jelgava
15 H7 Yelia, Mt Papua New Guinea 6.59S 145.58E
89 D4 Yelimané Mali 15.09N 10.33W
45 C4 Yelino Ukraine U.S.S.R. 52.02N 31.59E
39 G4 Yelistratova,Poluostrov *pen* U.S.S.R.
47 K5 Yelizarovo U.S.S.R. 61.26N 68.15E
45 D8 Yelizavetgradka Ukraine U.S.S.R. 48.48N 32.25E
43 E2 Yelizavetinka U.S.S.R. 51.41N 59.45E
42 E2 Yelizavetinskiy Krasnoyarsk U.S.S.R. 60.32N 92.43E
42 E3 Yelizavetinskiy Krasnoyarsk U.S.S.R. 58.57N 94.44E
47 M4 Yelizavetinskoye U.S.S.R. 57.48N 59.42E
44 E8 Yelizavetovka Ukraine U.S.S.R. 46.56N 36.25E
40 J4 Yelizavety,Mys *C* Sakhalin U.S.S.R. 54.30N 142.42E
39 F7 Yelizovo U.S.S.R. 53.13N 158.20E
45 W3 Yelkhovka U.S.S.R. 55.52N 50.16E
58 Q8 Yell *isld* Shetland Scotland
91 C6 Yellala Falls Zaïre 5.41S 13.37E
28 E2 Yellandu Andhra Prad India 17.39N 80.23E
28 B3 Yellapur Karnataka India 14.59N 74.46E
28 C1 Yellareddi Andhra Prad India 18.10N 77.59E
74 H9 Yellel Algeria 35.41N 0.19E
37 D6 Yellice Turkey 39.14N 37.48E
107 K11 Yellow *R* Florida/Alabama
15 F5 Yellow *R* Papua New Guinea
100 M6 Yellow Creek Saskatchewan 52.46N 105.16W
14 C9 Yellowdine W Australia 31.19S 119.36E
100 N9 Yellow Grass Saskatchewan 49.49N 104.11W
101 O9 Yellowhead Pass Alberta 52.53N 118.13W
101 Q4 Yellowknife N W Terr 62.30N 114.29W
108 P5 Yellow Medicine *R* Minnesota
12 H4 Yellow Mt New S Wales 32.28S 146.50E
110 K5 Yellow Pine Idaho 44.58N 115.29W
106 D5 Yellow,R Wisconsin
Yellow River *see* Huang He
Yellow Sea *see* Huang Hai
22 M9 Yellow Sea China
17 K5 Yellow Sea China/Korea
104 B7 Yellow Springs Ohio 39.47N 83.54W
108 F2 Yellowstone *R* Montana
110 P5 Yellowstone L Wyoming 44.30N 110.20W
110 P5 Yellowstone Nat.Park Wyoming
58 Q8 Yell Sound Shetland Scotland
107 D5 Yellville Arkansas 36.12N 92.41W
77 L4 Yelmo,El *mt* Spain 38.15N 2.39W
45 P2 Yel'niki U.S.S.R. 54.38N 43.54E
45 E2 Yel'nya U.S.S.R. 54.36N 33.13E
42 D1 Yeloguy U.S.S.R. 62.55N 87.18E
42 D1 Yeloguy *R* U.S.S.R.
47 K7 Yeloshnoye U.S.S.R. 55.28N 66.47E
89 L5 Yélou Niger 12.19N 3.34E
39 D3 Yelou,Gora *mt* U.S.S.R. 64.36N 146.30E
39 G6 Yelovka U.S.S.R. 57.51N 161.01E
39 G6 Yelovka *R* U.S.S.R.
46 R2 Yelovo U.S.S.R. 57.02N 54.58E
46 Q3 Yelshanka Orenburg U.S.S.R. 52.58N 51.55E
45 S5 Yelshanka Saratov U.S.S.R. 51.50N 46.24E
46 G4 Yel'sk Belorussiya U.S.S.R. 51.50N 29.10E
43 O4 Yeltay Kazakhstan U.S.S.R. 46.51N 81.31E
76 G7 Yeltes *R* Spain
42 D5 Yel'tsovka U.S.S.R. 53.15N 86.16E
46 J2 Yel'tsy U.S.S.R. 56.37N 33.52E
88 F11 Yelua Mauritania 21.53N 15.37W
115 M2 Yelucá *pk* Nicaragua 14.20N 84.52W
47 G4 Yelva *R* U.S.S.R.
13 E5 Yelvertoft Queensland 20.08S 138.45E
56 C6 Yelverton Devon Eng 50.30N 4.05W
97 L1 Yelverton B N W Terr
90 D6 Yelwa Kano Nigeria 11.58N 8.18E
90 B6 Yelwa W Central Nigeria 10.48N 4.42E
22 D7 Yema Nanshan *mt ra* Qinghai China
47 M6 Yemanzhelinsk U.S.S.R. 54.50N 61.22E
22 D7 Yema Shan *mts* Gansu China
105 G5 Yemassee S Carolina 32.22N 80.53W
22 D8 Yematan Qinghai China 37.19N 98.22E
23 A1 Yematan Qinghai China 34.40N 98.00E
42 E4 Yemel'yanovo U.S.S.R. 56.11N 92.43E
15 H6 Yemen Papua New Guinea 4.22S 144.11E
27 E6 Yemen *rep* S W Asia
Yemen, Dem Rep of *see* South Yemen
45 A1 Yemenets U.S.S.R. 55.48N 29.57E
84 D5 Yeméni Greece 38.14N 22.07E
Yemen, People's Dem. Rep. of *see* South Yemen
39 H4 Yemet U.S.S.R. 60.36N 168.09E
47 K7 Yemets *R* U.S.S.R.
47 E4 Yemetsk U.S.S.R. 63.28N 41.49E
46 G4 Yemil'chino Ukraine U.S.S.R. 50.58N 27.40E
Yemişenbükü *see* Taşova
47 E4 Yemtsa U.S.S.R. 63.04N 40.30E
47 E4 Yemtsa *R* U.S.S.R.
91 C2 Yen Cameroon 2.19N 12.41E
47 C2 Yena U.S.S.R. 67.30N 31.14E
89 N9 Yenagoa Nigeria 4.58N 6.16E
84 S14 Yenagra Cyprus 35.12N 33.43E
45 K8 Yenakiyevo Ukraine U.S.S.R. 48.14N 38.15E
25 C2 Yenangyat Burma 21.00N 94.55E
25 C2 Yenangyaung Burma 20.28N 94.54E
25 C3 Yenanma Burma 19.47N 94.49E
42 E3 Yenashimskiy Polkan,Gora *mt* U.S.S.R. 59.50N 92.55E
25 H2 Yen Bay Vietnam 21.43N 104.54E
43 O3 Yenbek Kazakhstan U.S.S.R. 47.55N 81.30E
Yenbo *see* Yanbu' al Bahr
25 H2 Yen Chau Vietnam 21.05N 104.18E
15 C5 Yende Irian Jaya 2.24S 134.30E
89 J7 Yendi Ghana 9.30N 0.01W
42 J5 Yendondin U.S.S.R. 53.30N 112.59E
47 K5 Yendra U.S.S.R. 60.44N 67.50E
47 K5 Yendyr' U.S.S.R. 61.25N 66.08E
87 G5 Yeneja Ethiopia 11.40N 39.00E
25 D2 Yengan Burma 21.06N 96.30E
91 G4 Yenge *R* Zaïre
32 B2 Yengejeh Iran 36.53N 47.36E
89 D7 Yengema Sierra Leone 8.40N 10.37W
42 E2 Yengida U.S.S.R. 61.40N 94.45E
24 B6 Yengisar Xinjiang Uygur Zizhiqu China 39.00N 76.09E
24 E5 Yengisar Xinjiang Uygur Zizhiqu China 41.55N 84.34E
24 F5 Yengisu Xinjiang Uygur Zizhiqu China 40.26N 87.47E
42 G6 Yengorboy U.S.S.R. 50.34N 102.59E
51 R6 Yeng Ozero *L* Karelia U.S.S.R. 65.42N 33.20E
91 A2 Yengue Equat Guinea 2.16N 9.45E
23 D2 Yeng Xian Shaanxi China 33.12N 107.30E
89 L5 Yéni Niger 13.31N 3.01E
36 F2 Yeniçağa Turkey 40.45N 32.00E
36 F3 Yenice Ankara Turkey 39.17N 32.40E
37 G3 Yenice Bursa Turkey 40.06N 29.26E
36 C3 Yenice Çanakkale Turkey 39.55N 27.18E
36 H6 Yenice İçel Turkey 36.57N 35.03E
36 F1 Yenice Zonguldak Turkey 41.12N 32.21E
36 H4 Yenice *R* Kayseri/Seyhan Turkey
36 F1 Yenice *R* Zonguldak Turkey
37 C2 Yenicegorice Turkey 40.53N 26.33E
36 J5 Yenicekale Turkey 37.34N 36.35E
37 E2 Yeniceköy Balikesir Turkey 40.24N 28.07E
37 D2 Yeniceköy Tekirdağ Turkey 40.50N 27.16E
36 F4 Yeniceoba Turkey 38.54N 32.44E
Yenidamlar *see* Demirtaş Antalya
36 B4 Yenifoça Turkey 38.43N 26.51E
Yenihan *see* Yıldızeli
37 J2 Yenikapi *dist* İstanbul Turkey 41.00N 28.53E
44 G7 Yenikend Azerbaydzhan U.S.S.R. 40.56N 46.23E
36 C3 Yeniköy Balikesir Turkey 39.47N 27.59E
37 C2 Yeniköy Çanakkale Turkey 40.29N 26.36E
36 J6 Yeniköy Hatay Turkey 36.24N 36.30E
37 F1 Yeniköy İstanbul Turkey 41.08N 29.03E
36 F3 Yenimehmetli Turkey 39.26N 32.10E
62 M1 Yenino U.S.S.R. 54.32N 20.27E
36 C5 Yenipazar Aydın Turkey 37.48N 28.14E
36 E2 Yenipazar Bilecik Turkey 40.10N 30.30E
37 G3 Yenişehir Turkey 40.17N 29.38E
37 J2 Yenişehır *dist* İstanbul Turkey 41.02N 28.56E
38 J3 Yenisey *R* U.S.S.R.
42 E3 Yeniseysk U.S.S.R. 58.27N 92.13E
42 E2 Yeniseyskiy Kryazh *ridge* U.S.S.R.
41 D4 Yeniseyskiy Zaliv *gulf* U.S.S.R.
23 A1 Yeniugou Qinghai China 34.27N 97.55E
Yenıyol *see* Borçka
25 H2 Yen Lap Vietnam 21.21N 105.03E
25 H1 Yen Minh Vietnam 23.07N 105.10E
84 U17 Yennádhi Rhodes 36.01N 27.55E
71 H5 Yenne France 45.42N 5.45E
45 T9 Yenotayevka U.S.S.R. 47.15N 47.01E
47 D2 Yenozero,Oz *L* U.S.S.R.
66 B5 Yens Switzerland 46.32N 6.25E
25 H3 Yen Thanh Vietnam 19.02N 105.30E
113 M5 Yentna *R* Alaska
28 B4 Yenur Karnataka India 13.00N 75.06E
39 E1 Yenzha U.S.S.R. 68.25N 151.51E
14 E8 Yeo Hills W Australia
14 E8 Yeo, L W Australia
29 D7 Yeola Maharashtra India 20.02N 74.31E
56 F5 Yeo,R Somerset Eng
84 R14 Yeorgios B Cyprus 35.22N 33.05E
84 D7 Yeoryítsi Greece 37.11N 22.16E
Yeotmal *see* Yavatmal
12 J5 Yeoval New S Wales 32.47S 148.09E
56 F6 Yeovil Somerset Eng 50.57N 2.39W
Yeo Yeo *R see* Bland *R*
115 E3 Yepachic Mexico 28.27N 108.25W
75 C8 Yepes Spain 39.54N 3.38W
45 K3 Yepifan' U.S.S.R. 53.50N 38.34E
47 L2 Yepoko U.S.S.R. 67.46N 74.42E
13 K6 Yeppoon Queensland 23.05S 150.42E
41 F7 Yerachimo *R* U.S.S.R.
84 A6 Yerakári Greece 37.49N 20.48E
45 N2 Yerakhtur U.S.S.R. 54.43N 41.10E
84 E8 Yeráki Greece 37.00N 22.42E
84 E3 Yerakovoúni *mt* Greece 39.01N 22.43E
44 L4 Yeraliyev Kazakhstan U.S.S.R. 43.12N 51.40E
84 K11 Yeráni Crete 35.21N 24.24E
84 F5 Yerània Óri *mts* Greece
44 G7 Yeranos Armenia U.S.S.R. 40.11N 45.10E
120 F12 Yerba Buena Argentina 26.47S 65.21W
115 J6 Yerbabuena Mexico 23.21N 101.34W
111 B8 Yerba Buena I California 37.50N 122.22W
43 E7 Yerbent Turkmeniya U.S.S.R. 39.23N 58.35E
42 E5 Yerbinskaya U.S.S.R. 54.00N 90.19E
42 H2 Yerbogachen U.S.S.R. 61.18N 108.00E
28 D5 Yercaud Tamil Nadu India 11.46N 78.11E
39 D1 Yercha U.S.S.R. 69.34N 147.30E
12 C4 Yerda S Australia 31.10S 135.00E
70 N2 Yère *R* Seine-Inférieure France
39 D1 Yerekhtenya-Tala U.S.S.R. 67.31N 146.40E
42 H2 Yerema U.S.S.R. 60.25N 107.52E
43 L2 Yerementau, Gory *mts* Kazakhstan U.S.S.R.
69 D6 Yères *R* Seine-et-Marne France
44 F7 Yerevan Armenia U.S.S.R. 40.10N 44.31E
44 J6 Yerfi Azerbaydzhan U.S.S.R. 41.06N 48.30E
75 G3 Yerga *mt* Spain 42.09N 1.59W
42 E5 Yergak-Targak-Tayga, Khrebet *mts* U.S.S.R.
28 C2 Yergara Karnataka India 16.06N 77.23E
42 C4 Yergay U.S.S.R. 57.20N 84.22E
45 Q10 Yergeni *hills* U.S.S.R.
14 D8 Yerilla W Australia 29.26S 121.52E
111 E3 Yerington Nevada 39.00N 119.10W
42 B1 Yerkalnadeypur *R* U.S.S.R.
36 C5 Yerkesik Turkey 37.08N 28.16E
45 C6 Yerkovtsy Ukraine U.S.S.R. 50.07N 31.15E
36 G3 Yerköy Turkey 39.39N 34.28E
47 K2 Yerkutayakha *R* U.S.S.R.
28 B2 Yerla R Maharashtra India
37 C2 Yerlisu Turkey 40.43N 26.43E
39 J3 Yermach-Titkhymveem *R* U.S.S.R.
43 M2 Yermak Kazakhstan U.S.S.R. 52.03N 76.55E
42 H4 Yermaki U.S.S.R. 56.42N 107.55E
40 D5 Yermakovo Amur U.S.S.R. 52.25N 126.19E
41 E7 Yermakovo Krasnoyarsk U.S.S.R. 66.36N 86.11E
42 A2 Yermakovo Tyumen U.S.S.R. 61.49N 74.01E
45 N8 Yermakovskaya U.S.S.R. 48.02N 41.17E
42 E5 Yermakovskoye U.S.S.R. 53.15N 92.23E
43 C1 Yermekeyevo U.S.S.R. 54.08N 53.44E
43 L2 Yermentau Kazakhstan U.S.S.R. 51.35N 73.10E
45 O2 Yermish' U.S.S.R. 54.46N 42.16E
47 G3 Yermitsa U.S.S.R. 66.56N 52.20E
111 H7 Yermo California 34.55N 116.50W
115 G4 Yermo Mexico 26.26N 104.00W
43 D1 Yermolayevo Bashkir U.S.S.R. 52.46N 55.54E
42 E4 Yermolayevo Krasnoyarsk U.S.S.R. 55.14N 92.13E
45 H1 Yermolino U.S.S.R. 55.32N 36.38E
45 S2 Yermolovka U.S.S.R. 54.02N 46.53E
28 E2 Yernagudem Andhra Prad India 17.01N 81.34E
61 M4 Yernée-Fraineux Belgium 50.32N 5.23E
76 G2 Yernes y Tameza Spain 43.15N 6.08W
43 P2 Yerofeyevka Kazakhstan U.S.S.R. 50.03N 83.31E
40 B5 Yerofey-Pavlovich U.S.S.R. 54.00N 121.55E
35 C10 Yeroham Israel 30.59N 34.55E
86 N4 Yeroham Israel 30.59N 34.55E
84 R14 Yerolakkos Cyprus 35.10N 33.16E
84 D4 Yerolékas *mt* Greece 38.37N 22.26E
84 D9 Yerolimín Greece 36.29N 22.24E
13 K2 Yeronga *dist* Brisbane, Qnsld
45 H4 Yeropkino U.S.S.R. 52.45N 36.17E
39 H2 Yeropol U.S.S.R. 65.15N 168.43E
39 H2 Yeropol *R* U.S.S.R.
84 L11 Yeropótamos *R* Crete
84 P15 Yeroskipos Cyprus 34.46N 32.27E
68 G5 Yerres France 48.43N 2.30E
47 G3 Yersa *R* U.S.S.R.
60 E14 Yerseke Netherlands 51.30N 4.03E
45 D3 Yershichi U.S.S.R. 53.39N 32.45E
45 U5 Yershov Saratov U.S.S.R. 51.22N 48.16E
47 K8 Yershovka Kazakhstan U.S.S.R. 54.05N 65.04E
45 Q5 Yershovka U.S.S.R. 51.09N 44.20E
47 F4 Yertom U.S.S.R. 63.31N 47.51E
47 E5 Yertsevo U.S.S.R. 60.47N 40.05E
120 B4 Yerupaja *mt* Peru 10.16S 76.55W
Yerushalayim *see* Jerusalem
45 S6 Yeruslan *R* U.S.S.R.
70 M2 Yerville France 49.40N 0.54E
84 L11 Yéryeri Crete 35.08N 24.56E
75 H2 Yesa Spain 42.37N 1.12W
75 H2 Yesa, Embalse de *res* Spain 42.36N 1.05W
25 C2 Yesagyo Burma 21.35N 95.13E
75 J8 Yesa, La Spain 39.54N 0.59W
23 E3 Yesanguan Hubei China 30.36N 110.19E
47 L5 Yesaulovo Bashkir U.S.S.R. 55.34N 59.29E
42 E4 Yesaulovo Krasnoyarsk U.S.S.R. 56.10N 93.13E
58 S11 Yescanaby Orkney Scotland 59.02N 3.21W
46 J2 Yesenovichi U.S.S.R. 57.16N 34.19E
37 F5 Yeserçöl Dağı *mt* Turkey 40.08N 40.56E
35 A8 Yesha' Israel 31.15N 34.24E
Yeshil Tso *L see* Bangdag Co
43 H2 Yesil' Kazakhstan U.S.S.R. 51.59N 66.20E
36 J1 Yeşil *R* Turkey
36 D3 Yeşil Dağı *mt* Turkey
Yeşildere *see* Ibrala
36 H4 Yeşilhisar Turkey 38.22N 35.08E
37 F2 Yeşilköy Turkey 40.58N 28.49E
Yesilova *see* Sorgun
36 D5 Yeşilova Burdur Turkey 37.32N 29.45E
109 F7 Yeso New Mexico 34.26N 104.37W
35 C6 Yesodot Israel 31.49N 34.52E
75 N3 Yespaguera *mt* Spain 42.11N 1.30E
44 E3 Yessentuki U.S.S.R. 44.03N 42.53E
41 H6 Yessey U.S.S.R. 68.29N 102.15E
41 H6 Yessey, Ozero *L* U.S.S.R.
89 C6 Yessoulou Guinea 10.34N 13.31W
77 M4 Yeste Spain 38.22N 2.19W
56 C6 Yes Tor *mt* Devon Eng 50.42N 4.00W
35 F1 Yesud HaMa'ala Israel 33.04N 35.37E
41 C5 Yesyayakha *R* U.S.S.R.
57 J1 Yetholm Borders Scotland 55.33N 2.17W
90 J8 Yetimandji Cent Afr Rep 7.21N 19.29E
47 M6 Yetkul U.S.S.R. 54.50N 61.35E
42 L2 Yët-Kyuyel' U.S.S.R. 60.58N 120.45E
12 K3 Yetman New S Wales 28.55S 150.49E
42 B1 Yetpur *R* U.S.S.R.
88 J9 Yett *tribe* Mauritania
58 J6 Yetts of Muckart Tayside Scotland 56.12N 3.37W
24 G5 Yetun Bulak *well* Xinjiang Uygur Zizhiqu China 40.57N 90.15E
25 C1 Yeu Burma 22.49N 95.26E
70 F8 Yeu, I.d' France 46.43N 2.20W
41 P1 Yeva-Liv, Ostrov *isld* Franz Josef Land U.S.S.R.
47 L7 Yevgashchino U.S.S.R. 56.25N 74.40E
43 N5 Yevgen'yevka Kazakhstan U.S.S.R. 43.30N 77.32E
44 H7 Yevlakh Azerbaydzhan U.S.S.R. 40.35N 47.08E
45 J4 Yevlanova U.S.S.R. 52.14N 37.23E
45 S3 Yevlashevo U.S.S.R. 53.07N 46.49E
44 C9 Yevpatoriya Ukraine U.S.S.R. 45.12N 33.20E
72 J1 Yèvre *R* France 47.06N 2.18E
39 E5 Yevreinova Mys *C* U.S.S.R. 58.57N 152.54E
40 E7 Yevreyskaya Aut. Oblast *aut prov* U.S.S.R.
42 C5 Yevsino U.S.S.R. 54.32N 83.20E
40 J8 Yevstaf'yovo Sakhalin U.S.S.R. 46.20N 143.31E
45 L6 Yevstratovskiy U.S.S.R. 50.07N 39.45E
45 L7 Yevsug Ukraine U.S.S.R. 49.12N 39.20E
47 J3 Yevsyavan' U.S.S.R. 66.50N 63.00E
90 A8 Yewa *R* Nigeria
23 F2 Ye Xian Henan China 33.37N 113.21E
22 L8 Ye Xian Shandong China 37.10N 119.55E
44 C1 Yeya *R* U.S.S.R.
24 D7 Yeyik Xinjiang Uygur Zizhiqu China 36.44N 83.14E
41 J8 Yeyka *R* U.S.S.R.
34 P3 Yeylāq Kūh *mts* Iran
44 B1 Yeysk U.S.S.R. 46.43N 38.17E
44 B1 Yeyskiy Liman *lagoon* U.S.S.R.
44 B1 Yeyskoye Ukrepleniye U.S.S.R. 46.43N 38.37E
24 E5 Yeyungou Xinjiang Uygur Zizhiqu China 41.59N 84.58E
Yezd *see* Yazd
Yezdanabad *see* Yazdānābād
Yezd-i-Khast *see* Yazd-e Khvāst
45 B1 Yezerishche Belorussiya U.S.S.R. 55.50N 30.00E
46 P1 Yezhikha U.S.S.R. 58.08N 47.42E
47 F4 Yezhuga *R* U.S.S.R.

70 E5 Yffiniac France 48.29N 2.41W
59 C7 Yganavan L Kerry Irish Rep 52.05N 9.53W
72 C8 Ygos St. Saturnin France 43.58N 0.43W
72 K2 Ygrande France 46.34N 2.56E
118 C9 Yguazu, R Paraguay
41 L8 Ygyatta R U.S.S.R.
118 C9 Yhú Paraguay 24.59S 56.00W
83 J8 Yialí isld Greece 36.40N 27.08E
84 Q14 Yialia Cyprus 35.05N 32.31E
86 L5 Yi'allaq Gebel hill Egypt 30.21N 33.31E
84 T13 Yialousa Cyprus 35.31N 34.12E
84 E4 Yiáltra Greece 38.52N 22.59E
21 C4 Yi'an Heilongjiang China 47.54N 125.21E
84 O11 Yianisádhes islds Crete 35.20N 26.10E
84 W22 Yiannádhes Corfu 39.38N 19.45E
83 E4 Yiannitsá Greece 40.46N 22.24E
84 H5 Yiannítsi Greece 38.08N 24.23E
84 D4 Yiannitsoú Greece 39.00N 22.06E
33 M5 Yibal oil field Oman 22.01N 56.12E
23 B7 Yibang Yunnan China 22.15N 101.28E
90 F7 Yibango Nigeria 8.59N 12.20E
33 D7 Yibā, Wādī watercourse Saudi Arabia
Yibei see Minglun
23 C4 Yibin Sichuan China 28.50N 104.35E
23 C4 Yibin Sichuan China 28.42N 104.30E
Yibna see Yavne
93 J1 Yibo, El Kenya 4.09N 37.14E
24 F9 Yibug Caka L Xizang Zizhiqu China
23 F3 Yichang Hubei China 30.43N 111.22E
23 F3 Yichang Hubei China 30.46N 111.20E
23 F3 Yicheng Hubei China 31.46N 112.21E
23 H1 Yicheng Shandong China 35.46N 117.36E
23 F1 Yicheng Shanxi China 35.46N 111.46E
23 C5 Yichexun Yunnan China 26.47N 103.30E
23 F1 Yichuan Henan China 36.04N 110.05E
22 H8 Yichuan Shaanxi China 36.04N 110.05E
21 D4 Yichun Heilongjiang China 47.41N 129.10E
23 G5 Yichun Jiangxi China 27.45N 114.22E
86 A4 Yidma oil well Egypt 30.40N 28.58E
23 F3 Yidu Hubei China 30.24N 111.32E
22 L8 Yidu Shandong China 36.45N 118.24E
23 B3 Yidun Sichuan China 30.13N 99.18E
55 B3 Yiewsley London Eng 51.31N 0.27W
23 G4 Yifeng Jiangxi China 28.22N 114.45E
35 F1 Yiftah Israel 33.08N 35.33E
36 E2 Yığılca Turkey 40.58N 31.27E
36 B3 Yiğitler Turkey 39.52N 26.35E
19 M1 Yigo Guam Pacific Oc 13.33N 144.53E
Yigrong Chu R see Yeh-kung Ch'ü
23 F1 Yi He R Henan China
23 H1 Yi He R Shandong China
Yihe Bogdo see Ih Bogd Uul
Yihe Hid see Ihhet
Yihe Jirgalang see Ihjargalan
Yihe Tamirin see Ihtamir
Yihe Ula see Ih-Uul
Yi Ho R Shandong see I Ho R
Yihsien see I-hsien
23 G5 Yihuang Jiangxi China 27.36N 116.04E
23 E1 Yijun Shaanxi China 35.20N 109.00E
35 D4 Yikkon Israel 32.22N 35.00E
21 C3 Yilaha Heilongjiang China 48.53N 125.10E
21 E4 Yilan Heilongjiang China 46.23N 129.30E
36 E5 Yılanlı Turkey 37.48N 31.02E
36 F2 Yıldırım Dağı mt Turkey
36 F5 Yıldız Dağ mt Turkey 37.07N 31.57E
36 J2 Yıldız Dağı mt Turkey 40.08N 36.55E
36 J3 Yıldızeli Turkey 39.52N 36.37E
37 C2 Yıldız Koyu B Turkey
21 C2 Yilehuli Shan mts Heilongjiang China
23 B3 Yi'lhung Sichuan China 31.52N 99.20E
Yiliang see I-liang
23 C5 Yiliang Yunnan China 27.34N 103.55E
23 C6 Yiliang Yunnan China 24.53N 103.07E
21 B3 Yiliekede Nei Monggol Zizhiqu China 48.50N 121.35E
14 B10 Yilliminning W Australia 32.54S 117.23E
21 C4 Yilong Heilongjiang China 47.31N 125.36E
23 D3 Yilong Sichuan China 31.30N 106.22E
23 G2 Yimen Anhui China 33.48N 116.00E
23 C5 Yimen Sichuan China 26.48N 102.16E
23 C6 Yimen Yunnan China 24.38N 102.00E
21 D5 Yimianpo Heilongjiang China 45.03N 128.04E
22 L2 Yiminhe Nei Monggol Zizhiqu China 48.26N 119.40E
22 L2 Yimin He R Heilongjiang China
21 A3 Yimin He R Nei Monggol Zizhiqu China
84 G5 Yimnón Greece 38.26N 23.53E
84 A3 Yimnótopos Greece 39.17N 20.54E
23 C8 Yim Tin Tsai Hong Kong 22.23N 114.17E
21 B1 Yimuhe Nei Monggol Zizhiqu China 52.46N 120.08E
25 C2 Yin R Burma
23 H1 Yinan Shandong China 35.30N 118.25E
25 D4 Yinbaing Burma 17.24N 97.46E
23 F1 Yincheng Shanxi China 35.55N 113.09E
22 G7 Yinchuan Ningxia China 38.30N 106.19E
Yinchwan see Yin-ch'uan
14 D9 Yindarlgooda, L W Australia
23 F2 Yindian Hubei China 32.05N 113.30E
21 C3 Yingchen Nei Monggol Zizhiqu China 49.36N 124.07E
23 F3 Yingcheng Hubei China 30.55N 113.31E
Yingchow see Fu-yang Anhwei
23 H5 Yingchuan Zhejiang China 27.50N 119.18E
21 F4 Yingchun Heilongjiang China 46.05N 132.51E
23 F6 Yingde Guangdong China 24.12N 113.20E
21 C7 Ying'ebu Jilin China 41.44N 125.35E
13 J7 Yingerbay Queensland 26.26S 148.37E
Yinggen see Qiongzhong
23 G2 Ying He R Anhui China
23 F1 Ying He R Henan China
23 A6 Yingjiang Yunnan China 24.48N 97.52E
23 C4 Yingjing Sichuan China 29.46N 102.44E
21 B7 Yingkou Liaoning China 40.40N 122.17E
21 B7 Yingkou Liaoning China 40.38N 122.30E
23 A6 Yingpanjie Yunnan China 25.40N 98.36E
23 F3 Yingshan Hubei China 31.40N 113.53E
23 G3 Yingshan Hubei China 30.40N 115.40E
23 D3 Yingshan Sichuan China 31.07N 106.31E
23 G2 Yingshang Anhui China 32.42N 116.18E
23 G4 Yingtan Jiangxi China 28.14N 116.58E
90 E9 Yingui Cameroon 4.28N 10.20E
22 J7 Ying Xian Shanxi China 39.32N 113.10E
22 L5 Yin He R Nei Monggol Zizhiqu China
Yin-hsien see Ningbo
24 D4 Yining Xinjiang Uygur Zizhiqu China 44.00N 81.32E
24 D4 Yining Xinjiang Uygur Zizhiqu China 43.50N 81.28E
23 E4 Yinjiang Guizhou China 28.01N 108.33E
12 F5 Yinkanie S Australia 34.21S 140.20E
25 C1 Yinmabin Burma 22.05N 94.57E
21 C5 Yinma He R Jilin China
25 D4 Yinnyein Burma 16.45N 97.22E
22 H6 Yin Shan mt ra Nei Monggol Zizhiqu China
18 J2 Yio Chu Kang Singapore 1.24N 103.50E
84 P15 Yiolou Cyprus 34.55N 32.28E
24 H10 Yi'ong Xizang Zizhiqu China 30.17N 94.50E
24 H10 Yi'ong Zangbo R Xizang Zizhiqu China
83 G5 Yioúra isld Greece 39.23N 24.10E
83 G7 Yioúra isld Greece 37.35N 24.43E
Yipang see I-pang
23 B6 Yipinglang Yunnan China 25.08N 101.55E
Yiquan see Meitan
121 G4 Yí, R Uruguay
87 G7 Yirga 'Alem Ethiopia 6.48N 38.22E
35 D2 Yirkā Israel 32.57N 35.13E
24 F9 Yirna Tso L Xizang Zizhiqu China 32.20N 83.30E
87 C7 Yirol Sudan 6.34N 30.33E
35 E1 Yir'on Israel 33.04N 35.27E
21 A4 Yirshi Nei Monggol Zizhiqu China 47.19N 119.56E
23 E6 Yishan Guangxi China 24.35N 108.35E
22 L8 Yi Shan mt Shandong China 36.12N 118.35E
35 C7 Yish'i Israel 31.44N 34.57E
23 H1 Yishui Shandong China 35.50N 118.39E
Yi Shui R Henan see I Ho R
Yisiang see I-hsiang
84 E8 Yíthion Greece 36.46N 22.34E
22 F8 Yitiaoshan Gansu China 37.12N 104.02E
21 C6 Yitong Jilin China 43.23N 125.19E
21 C5 Yitong He R Jilin China
Yitu see I-tu
21 B2 Yitulihe Nei Monggol Zizhiqu China 50.42N 121.21E
Yiwu see I-wu
24 H4 Yiwu Xinjiang Uygur Zizhiqu China 43.17N 94.44E
23 B8 Yiwu Yunnan China 21.58N 101.27E
23 J4 Yiwu Zhejiang China 29.17N 120.03E
Yixian see Yicheng
23 H4 Yi Xian Anhui China 29.55N 117.57E
22 K7 Yi Xian Hebei China 39.21N 115.21E
21 B7 Yi Xian Liaoning China 41.31N 121.12E
23 B7 Yixiang Yunnan China 23.20N 100.44E
21 C1 Yixiken Heilongjiang China 52.58N 125.39E
23 H3 Yixing Jiangsu China 31.22N 119.45E
22 L6 Yixun He R Hebei China
Yiyang see I-yang
23 F1 Yiyang Henan China 34.28N 112.11E
23 F4 Yiyang Hunan China 28.39N 112.10E
23 H4 Yiyang Jiangxi China 28.21N 117.23E
22 L8 Yiyuan Shandong China 36.11N 118.10E
23 F6 Yizhang Hunan China 25.24N 112.51E
23 H2 Yizheng Jiangsu China 32.12N 119.12E
35 E3 Yizre'el Israel 32.34N 35.20E
35 D3 Yizre'el, 'Emeq V Israel
15 D5 Y Keten mts Irian Jaya
53 U14 Yksnøya isld Norway 62.28N 6.30E
39 B2 Ylagannakh U.S.S.R. 67.11N 135.25E
51 N11 Ylämaa Finland 60.47N 28.00E
51 J11 Yläne Finland 60.54N 22.25E
41 J6 Ylas-Yuryakh U.S.S.R. 68.21N 108.53E
19 L1 Ylig B Guam Pacific Oc
51 K8 Ylihärmä Finland 63.10N 22.45E
51 M6 Ylikiiminki Finland 65.02N 26.10E
51 N5 Yli-Kitka L Finland
51 M6 Yli-li Finland 65.24N 25.50E
51 K9 Ylistaro Finland 62.58N 22.30E
51 K5 Ylitornio Finland 66.19N 23.40E
51 L7 Ylivieska Finland 64.05N 24.30E
51 L4 Ylläsntunturi mt Finland 67.36N 24.14E
51 K10 Ylöjärvi Finland 61.35N 23.35E
48 U6 Ymer Nunatak pk Greenland 77.28N 25.01W
48 U9 Ymers Ø isld Greenland
70 O5 Ymonville France 48.15N 1.46E
40 F5 Yn R U.S.S.R.
47 H5 Yndin U.S.S.R. 61.25N 55.10E
52 K8 Yngaren L Sweden 58.50N 16.35E
53 S17 Ynnesdal Norway 60.57N 5.23E
43 K3 Yntaly Kazakhstan U.S.S.R. 48.56N 70.55E
40 G1 Ynykchanskiy U.S.S.R. 60.11N 137.35E
56 C3 Ynys Lochdyn isld Dyfed Wales 52.11N 4.28W
90 F5 Yo Nigeria 13.32N 13.15E
112 K6 Yoakum Texas 29.18N 97.10W
20 K1 Yobetsu Hokkaido Japan 43.22N 140.24E
15 E4 Yobi Irian Jaya 1.48S 138.04E
15 D4 Yobi Yapen I, Irian Jaya 1.45S 136.23E
87 J5 Yoboki Djibouti 11.29N 42.03E
20 C8 Yobuko Japan 33.32N 129.52E
109 L3 Yocemento Kansas 38.55N 99.26W
107 G7 Yocono R Mississippi
109 F3 Yoder Colorado 38.51N 104.13W
108 F8 Yoder Wyoming 41.56N 104.15W
87 B6 Yodni Sudan 9.22N 29.56E
20 G6 Yodoe Japan 35.30N 133.27E
20 J7 Yodo-gawa R Japan
103 A7 Yoe Pennsylvania 39.55N 76.37W
89 A4 Yoff airport Senegal 14.43N 17.19W
121 F2 Yofre Argentina 29.08S 58.22W
20 D3 Yōga dist Tōkyō Japan
121 K10 Yogan, Cerro pk Chile 54.40S 70.25W
37 E7 Yoğun Turkey 38.03N 39.26E
37 G3 Yoğurtdere Turkey 40.20N 29.28E
18 J9 Yogyakarta Java Indon 7.48S 110.24E
101 P10 Yoho Nat.Park Br Col
72 C7 Yohoux France 44.20N 0.58W
20 K1 Yoichi Japan 43.14N 140.47E
20 K1 Yoichi-dake mt Japan 43.03N 141.01E
115 Q10 Yojoa, L. de Honduras
21 D9 Yŏju S Korea 37.20N 127.35E
20 H6 Yōka Japan 35.25N 134.40E
91 D2 Yokadouma Cameroon 3.26N 15.06E
20 O6 Yōkaichiba Japan 35.40N 140.30E
107 F9 Yokena Mississippi 32.10N 90.58W
20 K7 Yokkaichi Honshu Japan 34.58N 136.38E
90 F9 Yoko Cameroon 5.29N 12.19E
21 D12 Yokoate-shima isld Japan 28.50N 129.00E
20 D5 Yōkōdai Kanagawa Japan
20 F8 Yokogawara Japan 33.47N 133.55E
20 P1 Yokohama Aomori Japan 41.04N 141.15E
20 B3 Yokohama Kanagawa Japan 35.28N 139.38E
91 H4 Yokolo Zaïre 0.40S 23.04E
20 B4 Yokosuka Kanagawa Japan 35.18N 139.39E
20 L7 Yokosuka Shizuoka Japan 34.40N 137.58E
20 G6 Yokota Japan 35.12N 133.04E
20 B2 Yokota Tōkyō Japan
20 O2 Yokote Japan 39.20N 140.31E
20 F4 Yokotsu-dake mt Japan 41.54N 140.45E
87 B8 Yokuluku Zaïre 4.23N 28.49E
20 K3 Yokutsu-dake mt Japan 41.54N 140.49E
29 E1 Yol Himachal Prad India 32.12N 76.26E
90 F7 Yola Nigeria 9.14N 12.32E
115 M4 Yolaina, Cord.de ra Nicaragua
43 F7 Yolbarsli Turkmeniya U.S.S.R. 38.15N 60.03E
37 E7 Yolçatı Turkey 38.34N 39.03E
21 B5 Yolin Mod Nei Monggol Zizhiqu China 44.08N 122.18E
89 H7 Yologo Ivory Coast 9.54N 3.19W
91 H4 Yolombo Zaïre 1.36S 23.13E
115 K9 Yoloxochitl Mexico 16.48N 98.42W
19 E4 Yome Moluccas Indon 1.13S 127.35E
21 J11 Yome-jima isld Ogasawara-Guntō Pacific Oc 27.28N 142.13E
20 P9 Yomitan Airport Okinawa Japan 26.23N 127.43E
37 E5 Yomra Turkey 40.56N 39.51E
28 J2 Yomtam Assam India 27.46N 93.37E
19 L1 Yona Guam Pacific Oc 13.24N 144.47E
20 Q8 Yona Okinawa Japan 26.47N 128.10E
20 P9 Yonabaru Okinawa Japan 26.10N 127.45E
20 G6 Yonago Japan 35.27N 133.20E
23 J6 Yonaguni isld Japan 24.29N 123.00E
20 Q8 Yonaha-dake pk Okinawa Japan 26.43N 128.13E
21 D7 Yŏnam-dong N Korea 41.32N 128.48E
21 D9 Yŏnan N Korea 37.55N 126.11E
35 E8 Yonatan, Har hills Israel 31.17N 35.22E
110 B6 Yoncalla Oregon 43.35N 123.18W
21 E9 Yŏndŏk S Korea 36.28N 129.28E
20 O1 Yoneshiro-gawa R Japan
20 O4 Yonezawa Japan 37.56N 140.06E
41 J8 Yongak, Porog falls U.S.S.R. 63.22N 109.50E
12 E5 Yongala S Australia 33.04S 138.44E
21 D10 Yongam S Korea 34.48N 126.43E
91 J3 Yongama Zaïre 0.02N 24.35E
23 H6 Yong'an Fujian China 25.52N 117.21E
21 E7 Yŏng-an N Korea 41.10N 129.25E
23 F4 Yong'anshi Hunan China 28.13N 113.17E
22 F7 Yongchang Gansu China 38.14N 102.01E
23 G2 Yongcheng Henan China 34.00N 116.20E
21 D9 Yŏngch'ŏn S Korea 36.00N 128.55E
23 D4 Yongchuan Sichuan China 29.24N 105.49E
23 H6 Yongchun Fujian China 25.18N 118.13E
23 E5 Yongcong Guizhou China 26.04N 109.02E
23 B6 Yongde Yunnan China 24.05N 99.25E
22 F8 Yongdeng Gansu China 36.45N 103.16E
23 G6 Yongding Fujian China 24.45N 116.43E
22 K7 Yongding He R Hebei China
21 D9 Yŏngdŭngp'o S Korea 37.31N 126.55E
21 K2 Yongdungp'o-gu dist Seoul S Korea
Yongfeng see Shuangfeng
23 G5 Yongfeng Jiangxi China 27.19N 115.23E
24 F4 Yongfengqu Xinjiang Uygur Zizhiqu China 43.28N 87.09E
23 E6 Yongfu Guangxi China 24.59N 109.50E
21 D10 Yŏnggwang S Korea 35.15N 126.30E
24 H11 Yonggyap pass Xizang Zizhiqu/India 29.17N 95.37E
22 H8 Yonghe Shanxi China 36.50N 110.33E
21 D8 Yŏnghŭng N Korea 39.31N 127.18E
21 D8 Yŏnghŭng-man Bay N Korea
21 D6 Yongji Jilin China 43.40N 126.28E
23 E1 Yongji Shanxi China 34.51N 110.27E
23 J4 Yongjia Zhejiang China 28.10N 120.45E
Yongjing see Xifeng
23 C1 Yongjing Gansu China 35.58N 103.21E
21 D9 Yŏngju S Korea 36.50N 128.40E
25 O9 Yongkang Yunnan China 28.54N 120.02E
23 J4 Yongkang Zhejiang China 28.54N 120.02E
22 K8 Yongnian Hebei China 36.46N 114.29E
Yongning see Xuyong
23 E7 Yongning Guangxi China 22.45N 108.26E
22 G7 Yongning Ningxia China 38.17N 106.19E
23 B5 Yongning Yunnan China 27.43N 100.36E
91 G4 Yongo Zaïre 1.35S 21.53E
90 J9 Yongoro Cent Afr Rep 5.22N 19.08E
18 D9 Yong Peng Pen Malaysia 2.01N 103.03E
23 B6 Yongping Yunnan China 25.25N 99.32E
22 K7 Yongqing Hebei China 39.16N 16.30E
23 B5 Yongren Yunnan China 26.09N 101.40E
21 K2 Yongsan-gu dist Seoul S Korea
21 D10 Yŏngsanp'o S Korea 35.01N 126.42E
21 C8 Yongsap'o N Korea 39.35N 124.40E
23 C4 Yongshan Yunnan China 28.11N 102.32E
23 B5 Yongsheng Yunnan China 26.42N 100.41E
23 E1 Yongshou Shaanxi China 34.55N 108.05E
23 E4 Yongshun Hunan China 29.02N 109.46E
23 H6 Yongtai Fujian China 25.48N 118.54E
23 G5 Yongtai Jiangxi China 27.57N 115.27E
21 D9 Yŏngwŏl S Korea 37.10N 128.26E
23 G5 Yongxin Jiangxi China 27.01N 114.28E
23 F5 Yongxing Hunan China 26.09N 113.06E
23 G4 Yongxiu Jiangxi China 29.09N 115.47E
Yongyang see Weng'an
21 E9 Yŏngyang S Korea 36.40N 129.10E
89 C7 Yonibana Sierra Leone 8.30N 12.14W
91 A3 Yoni, Pta pt Equat Guinea 1.25N 9.27E
100 H6 Yonker Saskatchewan 52.40N 109.40W
103 M5 Yonkers New York 40.57N 73.52W
109 P5 Yonkers Oklahoma 36.03N 95.16W
67 H5 Yonne dept France
69 E7 Yonne R France
89 B4 Yonoféré Senegal 15.10N 14.31W
22 J6 Yonyn Shanxi China 40.07N 112.15E
25 C2 Yonzingyi Burma 21.10N 95.35E
87 K6 Yoobyaboh Somalia 8.26N 45.35E
119 D5 Yopal Colombia 5.20N 72.19W
24 B6 Yopurga Xinjiang Uygur Zizhiqu China 39.16N 76.45E
35 D3 Yoqne'am Israel 32.39N 35.06E
89 K6 Yorgou Upper Volta 11.27N 0.10E
115 L2 Yorito Honduras 15.04N 87.16W
107 H9 York Alabama 32.29N 88.20W
110 O3 York Montana 46.44N 111.46W
108 L1 York N Dakota 48.22N 99.36W
108 N9 York Nebraska 40.52N 97.35W
57 L5 York N Yorks Eng 53.58N 1.05W
99 C10 York Ontario 43.42N 79.27W
103 A7 York Pennsylvania 39.57N 76.44W
95 O5 York S Africa 29.20S 30.29E
105 F3 York S Carolina 34.59N 81.14W
14 B9 York W Australia 31.55S 116.45E
103 A7 Yorkana Pennsylvania 39.58N 76.34W
11 D5 York Bay New Zealand 41.16S 174.54E
13 G1 York, C Queensland 10.42S 142.32E
13 F2 York Downs Queensland 12.40S 142.19E
12 E5 Yorke Pen S Australia
12 E6 Yorketown S Australia 35.02S 137.35E
97 K6 York Factory Manitoba 57.30N 97.30W
98 O4 York Harbour Newfoundland 49.03N 58.23W
103 A6 York Haven Pennsylvania 40.07N 76.44W
48 S4 York, Kap C Greenland 76.00N 66.15W
99 D9 York Mills Ontario 43.45N 79.25W
113 D4 York Mts Alaska
98 R2 York Pt Labrador, Nfld 51.58N 55.54W
98 G5 York R Quebec
104 J9 York R Virginia
14 F2 York Sd W Australia
Yorkshire co see N. Yorks, W. Yorks, S. Yorks, Humberside, Cleveland new counties
57 M4 Yorkshire Moors N Yorks Eng
57 M5 Yorkshire Wolds hills N Yorks/Humberside Eng
104 H6 York Springs Pennsylvania 40.01N 77.07W
100 P7 Yorkton Saskatchewan 51.12N 102.29W
103 D7 Yorktown New Jersey 39.37N 75.18W
112 K7 Yorktown Texas 28.59N 97.31W
104 J9 Yorktown Virginia 37.14N 76.32W
103 G4 Yorktown Heights New York 41.17N 73.47W
57 L5 York, Vale of N Yorks Eng
104 P3 York Village Maine 43.08N 70.38W
106 F8 Yorkville Illinois 41.38N 88.27W
104 K3 Yorkville New York 43.09N 75.17W
90 G4 Yoro Chad 14.30N 14.30E
115 L2 Yoro Honduras 15.08N 87.10W
21 C12 Yoron jima isld Japan 27.04N 128.25E
22 G2 Yöröö Mongolia 49.46N 106.47E
22 G2 Yöröö Gol R Mongolia
89 G5 Yorosso Mali 12.17N 4.55W
37 D2 Yörük Turkey 40.57N 27.04E
37 D1 Yörükler Turkey 41.08N 27.15E
111 E4 Yosemite Falls California 37.45N 119.35W
111 D4 Yosemite L California 37.22N 120.25W
111 E4 Yosemite Lodge California 37.44N 119.36W
111 E3 Yosemite Nat.Park California
20 J2 Yoshida Chiba Japan
20 F7 Yoshida Hiroshima, Honshu Japan 34.41N 132.39E
20 M4 Yoshida Niigata, Honshu Japan 37.42N 138.51E
20 F8 Yoshida Shikoku Japan 33.17N 132.31E
20 P2 Yoshihama-wan B Japan
20 H2 Yoshihashi Chiba Japan
21 F10 Yoshii-gawa R Japan
20 F8 Yoshino Japan 33.13N 132.48E
20 H7 Yoshino-gawa R Japan
20 J7 Yoshino-gawa R Japan
20 K7 Yoshino-Kumano Nat.Park Japan
35 B8 Yoshivya Israel 31.27N 34.37E
46 P2 Yoshkar Ola U.S.S.R. 56.38N 47.52E
20 D8 Yoshu Japan 33.22N 130.46E
Yösönbulag see Altay Govĭaltay Mongolia
110 M8 Yost Utah 41.59N 113.32W
21 D10 Yŏsu S Korea 34.50N 127.30E
Yotala see Villa Oropeza
120 F7 Yotau Bolivia 16.05S 63.02W
20 K2 Yōtei-zan Japan 42.50N 140.40E
Yotsing see Lo-ch'ing
20 P4 Yotsukura Japan 37.08N 141.00E
86 O6 Yotvata Israel 29.53N 35.03E
89 H5 You Upper Volta 13.42N 2.04W
14 C8 Youanmi W Australia 28.39S 118.45E
74 G10 Youb Algeria 34.55N 0.13W
21 D4 Youbao Heilongjiang China 47.52N 128.45E
110 A1 Youbou Vancouver I, Br Col 48.52N 124.12W
90 J1 Youdou Chad 20.29N 18.13E
22 B7 Youdunzi Qinghai China 38.03N 91.53E
59 G8 Youghal Cork Irish Rep 51.57N 7.50W
59 G8 Youghal B Cork Irish Rep
21 D4 Youhao Heilongjiang China 47.57N 128.55E
23 D7 You Jiang R Guangxi China
89 C5 Youkounkoun Guinea 12.35N 13.11W
57 K6 Youlgreave Derbys Eng 53.11N 1.40W
91 E3 Youmba Congo 0.31N 17.54E
111 O7 Young Arizona 34.07N 110.56W
12 J5 Young New S Wales 34.19S 148.20E
100 M7 Young Saskatchewan 51.45N 105.45W
121 F4 Young Uruguay 32.44S 57.36W
11 J10 Young, C Chatham Is Pacific Oc 43.42S 176.36W
12 D4 Younghusband, L S Australia 30.51S 136.05E
12 E6 Younghusband Pen S Australia
123 K5 Young I Antarctica 66.28S 162.30E
13 D3 Young, Mt N Terr Australia 15.09S 135.42E
11 M5 Young Nick's Hd New Zealand 38.45S 177.58E
14 D10 Young, R W Australia
11 D11 Young Ra New Zealand
103 D2 Youngs New York 42.17N 75.17W
92 G7 Young's B Malawi
122 U10 Young's Rock Pitcairn I Pacific Oc 25.03S 130.07W
122 A10 Young's Tooth pk Rarotonga Pacific Oc 21.14S 159.47W
100 F7 Youngstown Alberta 51.32N 111.12W
105 B7 Youngstown Florida 30.22N 85.27W
104 F3 Youngstown New York 43.15N 79.03W
104 E5 Youngstown Ohio 41.05N 80.40W
107 D11 Youngsville Louisiana 30.06N 92.00W
105 J1 Youngsville N Carolina 36.02N 78.29W
109 D5 Youngsville New Mexico 36.12N 106.33W
103 E3 Youngsville New York 41.48N 74.54W
104 F5 Youngsville Pennsylvania 41.52N 79.22W
110 Q6 Younts Pk Wyoming 44.00N 109.53W
111 B3 Yountville California 38.25N 122.22W
22 B7 Youquanzi Qinghai China 38.12N 91.25E
24 G6 Youshashan Qinghai China 38.12N 90.58E
88 J5 Youssoufia Morocco 32.16N 8.33W
23 H5 Youxi Fujian China 26.13N 118.12E
23 F5 You Xian Hunan China 27.08N 113.20E
23 E4 Youyang Sichuan China 28.48N 108.48E
21 E4 Youyi Heilongjiang China 46.45N 131.47E
24 F1 Youyi Feng mt pk Xinjiang Uygur Zizhiqu China 49.12N 87.48E
22 J7 Youyu Shanxi China 40.00N 112.47E
15 J1 Yovo I Papua New Guinea 4.40S 155.25E
13 G8 Yowah R Queensland
14 C7 Yowereena Hill W Australia 25.22S 119.55E
56 H2 Yoxall Staffs Eng 52.46N 1.46W
56 P3 Yoxford Suffolk Eng 52.16N 1.30E
Yoyang see Yüeh-yang
36 H3 Yozgat Turkey 39.50N 34.48E
118 B9 Ypacaraí, L Paraguay 25.15S 57.23W
51 K11 Ypäjä Finland 60.48N 23.15E
118 C8 Ypané, R Paraguay
118 C8 Ypé-Jhú Paraguay 23.55S 55.29W
60 F11 Ypenburg airport Netherlands 52.05N 4.22E
118 B9 Ypoá, L Paraguay 25.50S 57.30W
70 L2 Yport France 49.44N 0.20E
51 L7 Yppäri Finland 64.25N 24.07E
Ypres see Ieper
106 L7 Ypsilanti Michigan 42.15N 83.36W
110 C8 Yreka California 41.44N 122.39W
56 D3 Yrfon, R Powys Wales
53 T20 Yrkje Norway 59.23N 5.41E
53 T20 Yrkjefjord inlet Norway 59.26N 5.49E
15 K5 Ysabel Chan Bismarck Arch
89 J4 Yséyé Mali 14.54N 1.53W
56 D3 Yspytty Ystwyth Dyfed Wales 52.20N 3.51W
71 E6 Yssingeaux France 45.09N 4.07E
52 H11 Ystad Sweden 55.25N 13.50E
56 D4 Ystalyfera W Glam Wales 51.47N 3.47W
95 B9 Ysterfonteinpunt pt S Africa 33.20S 18.10E
95 E10 Ystervarkpunt pt S Africa 34.24S 21.43E
56 D3 Ystradffin Dyfed Wales 52.06N 3.46W
56 D4 Ystradgynlais W Glam Wales 51.47N 3.45W
56 D3 Ystrad Meurig Dyfed Wales 52.18N 3.54W
56 D3 Ystwyth, R Dyfed Wales
40 G2 Yst'-Yudoma U.S.S.R. 59.09N 135.04E
39 C1 Ytbyltakh U.S.S.R. 68.12N 142.59E
58 M4 Ythan, R Grampian Scotland
53 S18 Ytre Arna Norway 60.28N 5.25E
53 R16 Ytre Sula isld Norway 61.03N 4.43E
50 G3 Ytri Bægisá Iceland 65.41N 18.26W
50 K3 Ytri Hágangur mt Iceland 65.52N 15.09W
50 K3 Ytri Hrútá R Iceland
50 E7 Ytri Rangá R Iceland
50 H3 Ytri-Strákur mt Iceland 65.57N 17.47W
52 H4 Ytterhogdal Sweden 62.10N 14.55E
51 B5 Ytterholmen Lt Ho Norway 66.01N 11.40E
52 K7 Ytterjärna Sweden 59.04N 17.48E
52 K3 Ytterlännäs Sweden 63.00N 17.40E
52 F3 Ytterøy Norway 63.47N 11.08E
53 R15 Ytterøyane Lt Ho Norway 61.33N 4.38E
52 M2 Yttersjön Sweden 64.24N 19.40E
40 G2 Ytyga U.S.S.R. 59.30N 137.00E
41 O8 Ytyk-Kyuyel' U.S.S.R. 62.30N 133.45E
40 D3 Ytymdzha R U.S.S.R.
19 F4 Yu isld Moluccas Indon 0.02S 129.38E
23 E3 Yuan'an Hubei China 31.09N 111.32E
23 E6 Yuanbao Shan mt Guangxi China
23 F4 Yuanjiang Hunan China 28.50N 112.15E
23 B7 Yuanjiang Yunnan China 23.35N 101.59E
23 E4 Yuan Jiang R Hunan China
23 B7 Yuan Jiang R Yunnan China
Yuanjiazhuang see Foping
23 J6 Yüan-li Taiwan 24.29N 120.40E
21 B3 Yuanlin Nei Monggol Zizhiqu China 46.09N 126.16E
23 J7 Yüan-lin Taiwan 23.57N 120.33E
23 E4 Yuanling Hunan China 28.30N 110.12E
23 B6 Yuanmou Yunnan China 25.41N 101.54E
22 J7 Yuanping Shanxi China 38.42N 112.45E
23 G2 Yuanqiang Anhui China 33.18N 115.44E
23 F1 Yuanqu Shanxi China 35.12N 111.45E
22 K8 Yuanshi Hebei China 37.47N 114.30E
23 G5 Yuan Shui R Jiangxi China
Yuanwu see Chiu-yüan-wu
23 F1 Yuanyang Henan China 35.04N 113.56E
23 C7 Yuanyang Yunnan China 23.13N 102.49E
23 F5 Yuanyue Hunan China 27.32N 113.10E
20 J7 Yuasa Honshu Japan 34.01N 135.10E
86 O10 Yub'a isld Saudi Arabia
111 C2 Yuba R California
111 C2 Yuba City California 39.09N 121.36W
20 L1 Yūbari Hokkaido Japan 43.04N 141.59E
20 M1 Yūbari-dake mt Hokkaido Japan 43.07N 142.17E
87 E6 Yubdo Ethiopia 8.58N 35.24E
43 K8 Yuben' Tadzhikistan U.S.S.R. 37.16N 72.12E
20 J2 Yūbetsu Japan 44.15N 143.37E
20 N5 Yubiso Honshu Japan 36.45N 139.00E
35 G3 Yubla Jordan 32.41N 35.49E
87 A8 Yubu watercourse Sudan
115 P8 Yucatán pen Mexico
115 P7 Yucatán state Mexico
96 B6 Yucatan Basin Caribbean Sea
102 J6 Yucatan Chan G of Mexico
111 K7 Yucca Arizona 34.52N 114.09W
111 H4 Yucca Flat dry lake Nevada 37.00N 116.03W
109 B4 Yucca House Nat.Mon Colorado 37.14N 108.43W
22 K8 Yucheng Shandong China 36.59N 116.35E
22 J8 Yuci Shanxi China 37.40N 112.44E
21 D7 Yudam-ni N Korea 40.29N 127.10E
22 K5 Yudaokou Hebei China 42.09N 116.54E
Yudino see Petukhovo
45 U1 Yudino U.S.S.R. 55.49N 48.54E
21 B1 Yudi Shan mt pk Nei Monggol Zizhiqu China 52.18N 121.50E
39 C5 Yudman U.S.S.R. 58.58N 141.51E
39 B4 Yudoma R U.S.S.R.
39 B4 Yudoma-Krestovskaya U.S.S.R. 60.04N 139.59E
40 G2 Yudomo-Mayskoye Nagor'ye uplands U.S.S.R.
39 C4 Yudomskiy Khrebet mts U.S.S.R.
23 G6 Yudu Jiangxi China 25.55N 115.13E
23 D3 Yuechi Sichuan China 30.34N 106.25E
24 E3 Yuejin Sk L Xinjiang Uygur Zizhiqu China
23 F3 Yuekou Hubei China 30.27N 113.08E
Yuelai see Huachuan
23 E3 Yuelai Sichuan China 30.11N 108.13E
21 C5 Yueliang Pao L Jilin China
13 B5 Yuendumu Mission N Terr Australia 22.20S 131.45E
23 J4 Yueqing Zhejiang China 28.08N 120.59E
23 J4 Yueqing Wan B Zhejiang China
23 G3 Yuexi Anhui China 30.52N 116.22E
23 C4 Yuexi Sichuan China 28.37N 102.32E
23 C4 Yuexi He R Sichuan China
Yueyang see Gu Xian
23 F4 Yueyang Hunan China 29.23N 113.03E
20 E8 Yufu-dake mt Japan 33.18N 131.23E
47 H6 Yug U.S.S.R. 57.45N 56.08E
47 F5 Yuga R U.S.S.R.
23 G4 Yugan Jiangxi China 28.40N 116.41E
42 A2 Yugan U.S.S.R. 60.50N 73.40E
47 H6 Yugokamskiy U.S.S.R. 57.44N 55.30E
47 M5 Yugo Konevo U.S.S.R. 56.08N 61.16E
44 F5 Yugo-Ostinskaya Aut.Oblast' Georgia U.S.S.R.
47 J2 Yugorskiy Poluostrov pen U.S.S.R.
47 J2 Yugorskiy Shar U.S.S.R. 69.50N 60.55E
47 J2 Yugorskiy Shar, Proliv str U.S.S.R.
49 H8 Yugoslavia rep S Europe
39 E2 Yugo-Tala U.S.S.R. 66.04N 151.03E
43 G8 Yugo-Vostochnyye Karakumy sands Turkmeniya U.S.S.R.
Yugovskoy see Yug
23 J3 Yuhang Zhejiang China 30.30N 120.18E
22 J6 Yu He R Shanxi China
22 H7 Yuhebu Shaanxi China 37.59N 109.51E
23 D6 Yuhong Guangxi China 24.36N 106.32E
23 J4 Yuhuan Zhejiang China 28.10N 121.15E
47 K4 Yuil'sk U.S.S.R. 63.40N 69.40E
14 B8 Yuin W Australia 27.57S 116.03E
23 G4 Yujiang Jiangxi China 28.12N 116.49E
23 E7 Yu Jiang R Guangxi China
23 E4 Yu Jiang R Sichuan China
39 E2 Yukagirskoye Ploskogor'ye tableland U.S.S.R.
46 Q1 Yukamenskoye U.S.S.R. 57.51N 52.14E
37 D3 Yukarı Inoya Turkey 40.06N 27.18E
37 E2 Yukarı Yapıcı Turkey 40.26N 27.53E
Yukarıyırıklar see Kamışlı
43 M7 Yukary-Pangaz Tadzhikistan U.S.S.R. 40.45N 70.17E
36 H1 Yük Dağ mt Turkey
45 V2 Yukhmachi U.S.S.R. 54.38N 49.59E
46 K3 Yukhnov U.S.S.R. 54.42N 35.18E
42 H4 Yukhta U.S.S.R. 55.55N 107.48E
39 E1 Yukhyasen U.S.S.R. 67.41N 154.31E
20 G7 Yuki Hiroshima Japan 34.45N 133.18E
20 N5 Yūki Ibaraki Japan 36.18N 139.52E
91 F5 Yuki Zaïre 3.57S 19.30E
113 J4 Yuki R Alaska
23 B3 Yukog Sichuan China 31.16N 101.08E
105 F7 Yukon Florida 30.13N 81.42W
109 N6 Yukon Oklahoma 35.31N 97.46W
101 D4 Yukon R Yukon Terr
101 E4 Yukon Crossing Yukon Terr 62.20N 136.29W
47 K5 Yukonda R U.S.S.R.
113 E5 Yukon Delta Alaska
113 G5 Yukon River Alaska/Yukon Terr
101 E3 Yukon Territory Canada
42 D4 Yuksa U.S.S.R. 57.08N 85.14E
Yüksekkum see Köyceğiz
37 H8 Yüksekova Turkey 37.35N 44.17E
42 H3 Yukseyeva U.S.S.R. 57.40N 108.00E
41 J8 Yukta U.S.S.R. 63.26N 105.42E
20 D8 Yukuhashi Kyūshū Japan 33.45N 130.59E
24 B6 Yukuriawat Xinjiang Uygur Zizhiqu China 38.56N 77.34E
15 G5 Yula R Papua New Guinea
47 E4 Yula R U.S.S.R.
103 E3 Yulan New York 41.32N 74.56W
43 E2 Yuldybayevo Bashkir U.S.S.R. 52.22N 57.53E
123 K5 Yule B Antarctica
13 J7 Yuleba Queensland 26.37S 149.20E
14 B2 Yule Brook Perth, W Aust
105 F7 Yulee Florida 30.37N 81.38W
15 G9 Yule Entrance Gt Barrier Reef Australia 10.25S 143.58E
15 J8 Yule I Papua New Guinea 8.48S 146.29E
14 C5 Yule R W Australia
24 G5 Yulghun Bulak well Xinjiang Uygur Zizhiqu China 41.40N 90.18E
24 G5 Yulghun Bulak well Xinjiang Uygur Zizhiqu China
90 E7 Yuli Nigeria 9.40N 10.18E
23 J7 Yü-li Taiwan 23.20N 121.20E
24 E5 Yuli Xinjiang Uygur Zizhiqu China 41.19N 86.15E
23 E9 Yulin Guangdong China 18.20N 109.31E
23 E7 Yulin Guangxi China 22.37N 110.08E
22 H7 Yulin Shaanxi China 38.16N 109.29E
22 H8 Yulinqiao Shaanxi China 36.05N 109.25E
23 B5 Yulongxue Shan mt pk Yunnan China 27.08N 100.17E
91 J3 Yulu Rapids Zaïre 1.22N 24.46E
111 K9 Yuma Arizona 32.40N 114.39W
109 H1 Yuma Colorado 40.07N 102.43W
47 C3 Yuma U.S.S.R. 65.03N 33.29E
74 D9 Yumaa el Tolba Morocco 35.06N 5.53W
116 K5 Yuma, B.de Dominican Rep
111 K9 Yuma Desert Arizona
43 D1 Yumaguzino Bashkir U.S.S.R. 52.55N 56.29E
93 C2 Yumbe Uganda 3.27N 31.15E
121 A6 Yumbel Chile 37.05S 72.40W
91 E4 Yumbi Equateur Zaïre 1.53S 16.34E
91 K4 Yumbi Kivu Zaïre 1.20S 26.18E
119 C6 Yumbo Colombia 3.36N 76.29W
22 D7 Yumen Gansu China 39.54N 97.43E
22 D7 Yumen Dong Zhan Gansu China 39.48N 97.52E
22 C6 Yumenguan Gansu China 40.20N 93.50E
22 D6 Yumenzhen Gansu China 40.19N 97.12E
24 D2 Yumin Xinjiang Uygur Zizhiqu China 46.06N 83.00E
87 G8 Yumuda Ethiopia 5.00N 38.42E
42 J5 Yumurchen U.S.S.R. 53.40N 114.00E
37 D2 Yumurta isld Turkey 40.27N 27.06E
36 H6 Yumurtalık Turkey 36.46N 35.45E
14 A8 Yuna W Australia 28.20S 115.00E
116 K5 Yuna R Dominican Rep
36 F4 Yunak Turkey 38.50N 31.42E
45 G5 Yunakovka Ukraine U.S.S.R. 51.08N 35.03E
23 F7 Yunan Guangdong China 23.13N 111.26E
23 E3 Yun'anzhen Sichuan China 31.05N 108.48E
113 T9 Yunaska I Aleutian Is 52.40N 171.00W
120 F9 Yunchara Bolivia 21.48S 65.10W
23 G1 Yuncheng Shandong China 35.37N 115.58E
23 E1 Yuncheng Shanxi China 35.06N 111.02E
75 C7 Yuncos Spain 40.05N 3.53W
14 D8 Yundamindera W Australia 29.14S 122.05E
89 A5 Yundum The Gambia 13.23N 16.42W
41 M8 Yunekit U.S.S.R. 64.01N 121.10E
23 F7 Yunfu Guangdong China 22.57N 112.04E
120 D11 Yungay Antofagasta Chile 24.01S 69.58W
121 A6 Yungay Nuble Chile 37.10S 72.05W
120 B3 Yungay Peru 9.08S 77.43W
Yung-chia see Wenzhou
12 G5 Yungera Victoria 34.48S 143.10E
45 R5 Yungerovka U.S.S.R. 51.36N 45.08E
Yung-hsiu see T'u-chia-pu
Yunghu see Ts'ang-wu
41 F1 Yungshturm, Proliv str U.S.S.R.
23 B10 Yung Shue Ha Hong Kong 22.12N 114.08E
23 B10 Yung Shue Wan Hong Kong 22.13N 114.06E
Yung-shun see Luancheng
120 D7 Yunguyo Peru 16.16S 69.07W
Yunhe see Pei Xian
23 H4 Yunhe Zhejiang China 28.06N 119.33E
Yunjinghong see Jinghong
23 F7 Yunkai Dashan mts Guangdong China
Yün-lin see Tou-lin
23 B6 Yunlong Yunnan China 25.11N 99.24E
23 B6 Yunlong Yunnan China 24.51N 101.45E
Yün-lung see Yunlong
23 F3 Yunmeng Hubei China 31.04N 113.45E
14 D8 Yunndaga W Australia 29.47S 121.04E
20 K3 Yunokawa Japan 41.47N 140.49E
20 E9 Yunomae Japan 32.16N 131.02E
34 P3 Yūnosābād Iran 35.38N 47.18E
20 F6 Yunotsu Japan 35.06N 132.20E
77 G7 Yunquera Spain 36.44N 4.55W
75 D6 Yunquera de Henares Spain 40.45N 3.10W
23 C6 Yunshang Yunnan China 25.34N 104.25E
Yunsiao see Yün-hsiao
12 E5 Yunta S Australia 32.37S 139.34E
75 G6 Yunta,La Spain 40.55N 1.41W
36 C4 Yuntdağ Turkey 38.54N 27.14E
23 C1 Yuntianxiang Gansu China 35.10N 104.40E
Yunting Ho R see Yung-ting Ho
23 E2 Yunxi Hubei China 33.00N 110.20E
23 E2 Yun Xian Hubei China 32.50N 110.50E
23 B6 Yun Xian Yunnan China 24.25N 100.06E
23 H6 Yunxiao Guangdong China 24.01N 117.14E
47 J3 Yun'yakha R U.S.S.R.
23 E3 Yunyang Sichuan China 31.00N 108.52E
22 J7 Yunzhong Shan mts Shanxi China
23 E5 Yuping Guizhou China 27.16N 108.50E
Yupogha see Yopurga
23 D5 Yuqing Guizhou China 27.13N 107.50E
Yuqingsi see Aoxi
40 G2 Yur U.S.S.R. 59.50N 137.41E
120 E9 Yura Bolivia 20.07S 66.10W
120 D7 Yura Peru 16.11S 71.40W
120 E9 Yura R Bolivia
120 B1 Yuracyacu Peru 5.52S 77.15W
20 J6 Yura-gawa R Japan
47 L6 Yurak U.S.S.R. 54.46N 59.19E
20 J2 Yūrappu-dake mt Japan 42.15N 140.01E
20 G6 Yurashuku Japan 35.31N 133.44E
41 C5 Yuratskaya Guba gulf U.S.S.R.
31 D1 Yurchi Uzbekistan U.S.S.R. 38.20N 67.54E
115 H7 Yurécharo Mexico 20.20N 102.15W
42 C4 Yurga U.S.S.R. 55.42N 84.50E
47 J7 Yurgamysh U.S.S.R. 55.25N 64.25E
47 K7 Yurginskoye U.S.S.R. 56.49N 67.19E
41 C5 Yuribey U.S.S.R. 71.02N 77.02E
47 L2 Yuribey R Tyumen U.S.S.R.
41 C5 Yuribey R U.S.S.R.
120 B1 Yurimaguas Peru 5.54S 76.07W
45 S1 Yurino U.S.S.R. 56.18N 46.19E
115 J7 Yuriria Mexico 20.12N 101.10W
44 H3 Yurkovka U.S.S.R. 44.13N 46.42E
47 G6 Yurla U.S.S.R. 59.20N 54.20E
45 M4 Yurlovka U.S.S.R. 52.44N 40.42E
47 M5 Yurma,Gora mt U.S.S.R. 55.30N 60.00E
42 F3 Yurokhta U.S.S.R. 58.58N 99.00E
47 F3 Yuroma U.S.S.R. 65.10N 45.45E
47 K6 Yurovskoye U.S.S.R. 59.30N 69.00E
45 V2 Yurtkul'-Russkiy U.S.S.R. 54.45N 49.21E
42 F4 Yurty Irkutsk U.S.S.R. 56.00N 97.41E
39 G5 Yurty Kamchatka U.S.S.R. 59.50N 161.34E
119 H4 Yuruari,R Venezuela
Yurung Kash Darya R see Yü-lung-k'a-shih Ho
24 C7 Yurungkax He R Xinjiang Uygur Zizhiqu China
45 D2 Yury U.S.S.R. 54.21N 32.07E
47 G3 Yur'yakha R U.S.S.R.
39 C3 Yuryakh-Yurde U.S.S.R. 63.20N 143.10E
46 N2 Yur'yevets U.S.S.R. 57.19N 43.00E
45 H8 Yur'yevka Ukraine U.S.S.R. 48.45N 36.02E
46 L2 Yur'yev Pol'skiy U.S.S.R. 56.28N 39.42E
39 C5 Yur'yevskaya U.S.S.R. 59.40N 142.12E
47 N3 Yur'yevskoye U.S.S.R. 58.28N 60.34E
47 H8 Yuryuzan' U.S.S.R. 54.51N 58.25E
47 H7 Yuryuzan R U.S.S.R.
120 E6 Yusala, L Bolivia 14.06S 67.15W
115 L3 Yuscarán Honduras 13.56N 86.45W
23 H4 Yushan Jiangxi China 28.42N 118.10E
23 J7 Yü-Shan mts Taiwan
44 D7 Yushanly R Ukraine U.S.S.R.
23 E4 Yushanzhen Sichuan China 29.32N 108.20E
22 J8 Yushe Shanxi China 37.00N 113.00E
Yü-shih see Weishi
47 G2 Yushino U.S.S.R. 68.08N 54.15E
47 M5 Yushkovo U.S.S.R. 56.04N 61.22E
47 C4 Yushkozero U.S.S.R. 64.45N 32.03E
21 D5 Yushu Jilin China 44.48N 126.31E
Yü-shu Qinghai China see Yushu
23 A2 Yushu Qinghai China 33.06N 96.48E
21 D5 Yushugou Jilin China 44.08N 127.30E
24 F4 Yushugou Xinjiang Uygur Zizhiqu China 42.12N 87.48E
21 C4 Yushutun Heilongjiang China 47.13N 123.46E
Yushuwan see Huaihua
Yusofabad see Kārīz
45 S9 Yusta U.S.S.R. 47.07N 46.17E
37 F5 Yusufeli Turkey 40.50N 41.31E
20 F8 Yusuhara Japan 33.23N 132.58E
47 G6 Yus'va U.S.S.R. 58.56N 54.59E
23 G1 Yutai Shandong China 35.00N 116.40E
108 O8 Yutan Nebraska 41.15N 96.24W
46 R3 Yutaza U.S.S.R. 54.33N 53.19E
120 G8 Yuti Bolivia 19.00S 62.23W
22 L7 Yutian Hebei China 39.52N 117.44E
24 D7 Yutian Xinjiang Uygur Zizhiqu China 36.50N 81.50E
86 O6 Yutm Wādī el watercourse Jordan
121 D6 Yutuyaco Argentina 37.00S 63.08W
118 C10 Yuty Paraguay 26.31S 56.20W
23 H7 Yü-weng Tao isld Taiwan 23.36N 119.30E
15 G5 Yuwil Papua New Guinea 3.28S 142.15E
Yuxi see Daozhen
23 C6 Yuxi Yunnan China 24.24N 102.29E
22 K7 Yu Xian Hebei China 39.51N 114.30E
23 F1 Yu Xian Henan China 34.13N 113.18E
22 J7 Yu Xian Shanxi China 38.10N 113.15E
23 J3 Yuyao Zhejiang China 30.04N 121.09E
20 D7 Yuya-wan B Japan
47 E6 Yuza R U.S.S.R.
20 O2 Yuzawa Akita Japan 39.11N 140.29E
20 M5 Yuzawa Niigata Japan 36.57N 138.48E
45 O1 Yuzha U.S.S.R. 56.34N 42.01E
47 N4 Yuzhakovo U.S.S.R. 57.38N 61.00E
41 B3 Yuzhnaya Sul'meneva,Guba gulf Novaya Zemlya U.S.S.R.
43 L7 Yuzhno Alichurskiy,Khrebet mts Tadzhikistan U.S.S.R.
42 D7 Yuzhno Chuyskiy,Khrebet mts U.S.S.R.
40 J8 Yuzhno Kamyshovyy Khrebet mts Sakhalin U.S.S.R.
43 H5 Yuzhno-Kazakhstanskaya Oblast' prov Kazakhstan U.S.S.R.
43 G5 Yuzhno-Kazakhstanskiy Kray terr Kazakhstan U.S.S.R.
40 K9 Yuzhno Kuril'sk Kuril Is U.S.S.R. 44.03N 145.48E
42 J4 Yuzhno Muyskiy Khrebet mts U.S.S.R.
43 M1 Yuzhno Podol'skoye U.S.S.R. 54.25N 75.11E
40 J8 Yuzhno-Sakhalinsk Sakhalin U.S.S.R. 46.58N 142.45E
44 G3 Yuzhno-Sukhokumsk U.S.S.R. 44.36N 45.31E
47 J8 Yuzhno-Ural'sk U.S.S.R. 54.26N 61.15E
42 E3 Yuzhno-Yeniseyskiy U.S.S.R. 58.49N 94.33E
45 N9 Yuzhnyy Rostov U.S.S.R. 47.21N 41.51E
42 C5 Yuzhnyy U.S.S.R. 53.15N 83.38E
43 O8 Yuzhnyy Alamyshik Uzbekistan U.S.S.R. 40.46N 72.37E
43 Q3 Yuzhnyy Altay,Khrebet mts Kazakhstan U.S.S.R.
39 G1 Yuzhnyy Anyuyskiy Khrebet mts U.S.S.R.
45 C9 Yuzhnyy Bug R Ukraine U.S.S.R.
43 C7 Yuzhnyy Cheleken,Zaliv B Turkmeniya U.S.S.R.
41 A4 Yuzhnyy Gusinyy Nos,Mys C Novaya Zemlya U.S.S.R. 71.29N 51.59E
43 O8 Yuzhnyy Kanal Uzbekistan U.S.S.R.
39 F5 Yuzhnyy,Mys C Kamchatka U.S.S.R. 57.45N 156.39E
39 H7 Yuzhnyy,Mys C Komandorskiye O-va U.S.S.R. 54.30N 168.09E
41 K3 Yuzhnyy,Ostrov isld U.S.S.R. 76.20N 113.29E
43 E1 Yuzhnyy Ural reg U.S.S.R.
23 C1 Yuzhong Gansu China 35.47N 104.00E
Yuzhou see Chongqing
32 B3 Yūzīdar Iran 35.01N 46.39E
69 B6 Yvelines dept France
66 C4 Yverdon Switzerland 46.47N 6.38E
61 H6 Yves-Gomezée Belgium 50.14N 4.30E
70 M2 Yvetot France 49.37N 0.45E
70 D4 Yvias France 48.43N 3.03W
70 F5 Yvignac France 48.21N 2.11W
61 K5 Yvoir Belgium 50.20N 4.53E
71 J4 Yvoire France 46.21N 6.20E
66 C4 Yvonand Switzerland 46.48N 6.44E
66 D6 Yvorne Switzerland 46.20N 6.57E
70 O6 Yvoy-le-Marron France 47.38N 1.52E
70 L5 Yvre-l'Evèque France 48.01N 0.16E
25 C2 Ywamun Burma 20.34N 95.24E
25 D3 Ywathit Burma 19.08N 97.32E
24 C7 Ywungkax He R Xinjiang Uygur Zizhiqu China
52 J8 Yxviken Sweden 58.45N 15.50E
39 E1 Yyasty U.S.S.R. 67.55N 151.28E

Yygeva see Jõgeva
Yykhvi see Jõhvi
72 C1 Yzernay France 47.02N 0.41W
72 F2 Yzeures-sur-Creuse France 46.48N 0.52E
88 M4 Za R Morocco
95 G9 Zaaimansdal S Africa 33.35S 23.21E
43 K7 Zaalayskiy Khrebet mts U.S.S.R.
43 J7 Zaamin Uzbekistan U.S.S.R. 39.56N 68.25E
60 C3 Zaamslag Netherlands 51.18N 3.55E
60 H10 Zaandijk Netherlands 52.28N 4.48E
60 H10 Zaanstad Netherlands 52.27N 4.49E
77 E10 Zaaroura Morocco 35.14N 5.41W
91 E5 Zaba Zaïre 3.51S 17.54E
82 D8 Zaba mt Yugoslavia 42.58N 17.42E
35 E4 Zababida Jordan 32.23N 35.19E
82 F5 Žabalj Yugoslavia 45.21N 20.05E
32 G3 Zabānābād Iran 35.44N 56.43E
85 N7 Zabâra,Gebel mt Egypt 24.48N 34.40E
82 G6 Žabari Yugoslavia 44.21N 21.12E
35 G6 Zabayir 'Adwan Jordan 31.46N 35.54E
42 K7 Zabaykal'sk U.S.S.R. 49.42N 117.25E
84 Z20 Żabbar Malta 35.52N 14.32E
35 F3 Zabda Jordan 32.34N 35.40E
35 G3 Zabda Jordan 32.32N 35.49E
Zabdani see Zebdāni
Zab e Kūchek see Zab, Little R
32 A2 Zab-e-Kuchele R Iran
89 J6 Zabéré Upper Volta 11.12N 0.32W
34 L2 Zab,Great R Iraq/Turkey
33 E9 Zabīd Yemen 14.10N 43.18E
33 E9 Zabīd,Wādī watercourse Yemen
33 E3 Zabīrah, Az Saudi Arabia 27.59N 43.39E
42 G5 Zabituy U.S.S.R. 53.18N 102.52E
39 E5 Zabiyaka Zaliv B U.S.S.R.
62 K5 Zabkowice Poland 50.36N 16.49E
Zab,Lesser R see Zab,Little R
34 N2 Zab,Little R Iran/Iraq
62 O2 Zabłudów Poland 53.00N 23.19E
88 Q4 Zab,Monts du Algeria
82 C4 Zabok Yugoslavia 46.01N 15.55E
32 J5 Zābol Iran 31.00N 61.32E
32 J7 Zābolī Iran 27.09N 61.37E
82 J2 Zabolotov U.S.S.R. 48.29N 25.19E
46 J1 Zaborov'ye U.S.S.R. 58.50N 33.00E
45 A1 Zabor'ye Belorussiya U.S.S.R. 55.54N 29.18E
45 C1 Zabor'ye U.S.S.R. 55.24N 31.35E
35 E1 Zabqîne Lebanon 33.10N 35.16E
24 F10 Zabqung Xizang Zizhiqu China 31.38N 87.20E
65 P2 Zábřeh Czechoslovakia 49.52N 16.53E
62 L5 Zabrze Poland 50.18N 18.47E
82 G6 Žabugica Yugoslavia 44.13N 21.47E
31 D4 Zabul prov Afghanistan
43 B4 Zaburun'ye Kazakhstan U.S.S.R. 46.45N 50.02E
89 K7 Zabzugu Ghana 9.18N 0.31E
115 P10 Zacapa Guatemala 15.00N 89.30W
115 L8 Zacapoaxtla Mexico 19.51N 97.36W
115 J8 Zacapu Mexico 19.49N 101.48W
118 D2 Zacarias,R Brazil
115 O8 Zacatal Mexico 18.40N 91.52W
115 H6 Zacatecas Mexico 22.48N 102.33W
115 H6 Zacatecas state Mexico
115 P11 Zacatecoluca El Salvador 13.29N 88.51W
115 K8 Zacatelo Mexico 19.16N 98.12W
115 L9 Zacatepec Oaxaca Mexico 16.44N 97.59W
115 K8 Zacatepec Tlaxcala Mexico 18.42N 99.10W
115 L8 Zacatlán Mexico 19.56N 97.58W
107 E11 Zachary Louisiana 30.39N 91.10W
45 G7 Zachepilovka Ukraine U.S.S.R. 49.11N 35.17E
20 P9 Zachimi Okinawa Japan 26.24N 127.44E
63 O5 Zachun E Germany 53.30N 11.21E
115 H7 Zacoalco Mexico 20.14N 103.33W
115 K8 Zacualpán Mexico 18.44N 99.48W
115 K7 Zacualtipán Mexico 20.40N 98.40W
82 C6 Zadar Yugoslavia 44.07N 15.14E
25 E7 Zadetkale Kyun isld Burma
25 E8 Zadetkyi Kyun isld Burma
25 D5 Zadi Burma 14.32N 97.59E
43 N8 Zadiyan Uzbekistan U.S.S.R. 40.25N 71.18E
24 H9 Zadoi Qinghai China 33.06N 95.10E
45 K4 Zadonsk U.S.S.R. 52.23N 38.55E
74 F2 Zadorra R Spain
75 E2 Zadorra, Embalse del res Spain
31 E4 Zadran reg Afghanistan
86 G4 Zafar Egypt 30.59N 31.36E
30 F7 Zafarabad Uttar Prad India 25.42N 82.44E
32 E4 Zafarqand Iran 33.10N 52.25E
77 H7 Zafarraya Spain 36.58N 4.08W
31 H4 Zafarwal Pakistan 32.20N 74.53E
61 F2 Zaffelare Belgium 51.08N 3.52E
81 K8 Zafferana Etnea Sicily 37.42N 15.07E
81 G7 Zafferano,C Sicily 38.07N 13.33E
33 D7 Zafīr, Az Saudi Arabia 19.59N 41.33E
33 E1 Zafīrī, Az Saudi Arabia 30.07N 43.30E
34 L8 Zafīrī, Az ridge Saudi Arabia
83 H8 Zafora isld Greece 36.05N 26.24E
77 D4 Zafra Spain 38.25N 6.25W
75 G7 Zafrilla Spain 40.12N 1.38W
75 G7 Zafrilla, Sierra mts Spain
35 C7 Zafririm Israel 31.40N 34.57E
35 C5 Zafriyya Israel 32.00N 34.51E
88 J7 Zag Morocco 28.10N 9.10W
79 O2 Zaga Yugoslavia 46.18N 13.28E
86 K4 Zagadân hill Egypt 30.48N 33.10E
39 E3 Zagadochnaya,Gora mt U.S.S.R. 63.13N 153.14E
Zagaltum Chai R see Zughaytūn R
62 J4 Zagań Poland 51.37N 15.20E
84 F5 Zagarás mt Greece 38.19N 23.01E
46 E2 Zagare Lithuania U.S.S.R. 56.22N 23.18E
45 T3 Zagarino U.S.S.R. 53.25N 47.15E
80 G5 Zagarolo Italy 41.50N 12.50E
86 G4 Zagazig Egypt 30.35N 31.30E
85 E5 Zaggut Libya 28.29N 19.37E
90 L4 Zaghawa tribe Sudan
32 G3 Zaghdeh Iran 35.50N 56.29E
Zagheh see Zāgheh-ye-Bālā
32 C4 Zāgheh Lorestān Iran 33.28N 48.47E
32 D3 Zāgheh Tehrān Iran 34.35N 50.45E
32 B3 Zāgheh-ye-Bālā Iran 35.43N 47.04E
88 T3 Zaghouan Tunisia 36.24N 10.08E
88 T3 Zaghouan, Jebel mt Tunisia 36.20N 10.05E
86 M8 Zaghra,Wâdi watercourse Egypt
89 L8 Zagnanado Benin 7.18N 2.28E
84 F3 Zagorá Greece 39.27N 23.06E
88 L6 Zagora Morocco 30.22N 5.50W
45 K1 Zagorsk U.S.S.R. 56.20N 38.10E
40 J8 Zagorskiy Sakhalin U.S.S.R. 47.13N 142.35E
77 H6 Zagra Spain 37.15N 4.10W
82 C5 Zagreb Yugoslavia 45.48N 15.58E
Zagros,Kūhhā-ye mts see Zagros Mts
32 B3 Zagros Mts Iran
Zagunao see Li Xian
42 J6 Zagustay U.S.S.R. 52.01N 110.50E
24 F9 Za'gya Zangbo R Xizang Zizhiqu China
35 G3 Zahar Jordan 32.34N 35.46E
77 F7 Zahara Spain 36.51N 5.23W
77 E8 Zahara de los Atunes Spain 36.09N 5.50W
33 J8 Zahawn, Wādī watercourse S Yemen
86 O9 Zahd,Jebel mt Saudi Arabia 28.20N 35.18E
89 F9 Zahebré Ivory Coast 5.18N 6.13W
32 J6 Zāhedān Balūchestān va Sīstān Iran 29.32N 60.54E
32 E6 Zāhedān Fārs Iran 28.46N 53.46E
31 E3 Zahidabad Afghanistan 34.16N 69.06E
77 C4 Zahinos Spain 38.20N 6.56W
33 L5 Zāhirah reg Oman
108 G1 Zahl N Dakota 48.35N 103.42W
Zahlah see Zahle
34 C5 Zahle Lebanon 33.50N 35.55E
63 R9 Zahna E Germany 51.55N 12.47E
65 P5 Záhorská Ves Czechoslovakia 48.23N 16.51E
65 M2 Zahrádka Czechoslovakia 49.38N 15.15E
34 N6 Zahrah R Iraq
33 E8 Zahrān Saudi Arabia 17.40N 43.29E
Zahrān, Az see Dhahran
88 P4 Zahrez Chergui salt L Algeria
88 P4 Zahrez Gharbi salt L Algeria 34.52N 2.51E
88 L5 Zaiane tribe Morocco
Zaidabad see Zeydābād
75 G5 Zaida,L.de Spain 41.01N 1.35W
Zaidan see Cham-e Zeydun
Zaidar see Zeydar
75 L4 Zaidin Spain 41.36N 0.16E
75 L4 Zaidin,Can.de Spain
Zaidiya see Zaydīyah, Az
30 E6 Zaidpur Uttar Prad India 26.50N 81.20E
42 H6 Zaigrayevo U.S.S.R. 51.50N 108.15E
43 M5 Zailyskiy Alatau,Khrebet mts Kazakhstan U.S.S.R.
42 G3 Zaimka U.S.S.R. 58.42N 100.45E
32 E4 Zaindeh R Iran
64 H7 Zainingen W Germany 48.29N 9.33E
33 F6 Zā'in, Jabal mts Saudi Arabia
Zainlha see Xiaojin
46 Q2 Zainsk U.S.S.R. 55.18N 52.00E
91 C7 Zaire dist Angola
91 H3 Zaïre R Cent Africa
73 G6 Zaïre rep Cent Africa
91 C6 Zaïre Central prov Zaïre
91 H2 Zaïre Supérieure prov Zaïre
82 G7 Zaječar Yugoslavia 43.55N 22.16E
65 P4 Zaječi Czechoslovakia 48.54N 16.45E
Zaka see Dona
92 E12 Zaka Zimbabwe 20.20S 31.29E
89 M3 Zakak Niger 17.23N 4.25E
42 G6 Zakamensk U.S.S.R. 50.24N 103.15E
Zakariya see Kefar Zekharya
46 E5 Zakarpatskaya Oblast' prov Ukraine U.S.S.R.
44 H6 Zakataly Azerbaydzhan U.S.S.R. 41.39N 46.40E
84 C6 Zákha Greece 37.33N 21.50E
84 C7 Zakharo Greece 37.29N 21.40E
41 O8 Zakharov U.S.S.R. 64.40N 130.45E
43 K3 Zakharovka Kazakhstan U.S.S.R. 49.45N 71.44E
45 L2 Zakharovo U.S.S.R. 54.23N 39.17E
43 G7 Zakhmet Turkmeniya U.S.S.R. 37.45N 62.30E
34 K1 Zākhō Iraq 37.09N 42.40E
47 D2 Zakhrebetnoye U.S.S.R. 69.02N 36.22E
Zākhū see Zākhō
32 A1 Zaki,Kūh-e mt Iran 38.32N 44.22E
84 A6 Zákinthos Greece 37.47N 20.54E
84 A6 Zákinthos isld Greece
84 B6 Zákinthou,Dhíavlos str Greece
62 N5 Zaklików Poland 50.45N 22.08E
62 M6 Zakopane Poland 49.17N 19.54E
62 M3 Zakroczym Poland 52.27N 20.35E
84 O11 Zákros Crete 35.07N 26.13E
42 G5 Zakuley U.S.S.R. 53.40N 103.05E
42 H4 Zakur'ya U.S.S.R. 56.45N 108.05E
91 D7 Zala Angola 7.55S 14.02E
82 D4 Zala co Hungary
62 K9 Zala R Hungary
65 P8 Zalabaksa Hungary 46.44N 16.34E
65 P8 Zalaegerszeg Hungary 46.53N 16.51E
35 D3 Zalafa Israel 32.33N 35.11E
65 P8 Zalalövö Hungary 46.53N 16.36E
77 E3 Zalamea de la Serena Spain 38.40N 5.39W
77 C5 Zalamea la Real Spain 37.41N 6.40W
Zalantun see Butha Qi
42 G5 Zalari U.S.S.R. 53.33N 102.30E
65 P8 Zalaszentiván Hungary 46.54N 16.56E
82 H3 Zalău Romania 47.10N 23.04E
47 G6 Zalazna U.S.S.R. 58.38N 52.45E
45 H4 Zalegoshch' U.S.S.R. 52.52N 36.53E
46 F5 Zaleshchiki Ukraine U.S.S.R. 48.20N 25.50E
82 K2 Zaleshchiki U.S.S.R. 48.39N 25.44E
104 C7 Zaleski Ohio 39.17N 82.24W
42 C5 Zalesovo U.S.S.R. 53.59N 84.46E
62 N1 Zales'ye U.S.S.R. 54.52N 21.26E
62 M2 Zalewo Poland 53.51N 19.37E
62 H2 Zalew Szczeciński lagoon Poland/E Germany
79 P3 Zali hrb Yugoslavia 45.53N 13.45E
33 E5 Zalim Saudi Arabia 22.43N 42.11E
90 L5 Zalingei Sudan 12.51N 23.29E
75 D1 Zalla Spain 43.12N 3.08W
85 B6 Zallaf watercourse Libya
33 J3 Zallaq,As Bahrain, The Gulf 26.03N 50.30E
107 F4 Zalma Missouri 37.10N 90.05W
33 C3 Zalmā, Jabal az mts Saudi Arabia
64 O3 Zalmanov Czechoslovakia 50.10N 13.00E
60 N9 Zalne Netherlands 52.30N 6.09E
92 D11 Zaloba Zimbabwe 19.12S 29.45E
85 A3 Zaltan Libya 32.59N 11.51E
85 E5 Zaltan, Jabal mts Libya
60 K12 Zaltbommel Netherlands 51.49N 5.15E
46 H1 Zaluch'ye U.S.S.R. 57.43N 31.49E
25 C4 Zalun Burma 17.28N 95.33E
65 L3 Záluží Czechoslovakia 49.15N 14.40E
20 B4 Zama Kanagawa Japan
90 A4 Zama Niger 14.20N 2.49E
20 B4 Zama-Iriya Kanagawa Japan
33 G8 Zamakh S Yemen 16.30N 47.37E
101 O6 Zama L Alberta
86 Q12 Zamâlik Cairo Egypt
30 G7 Zamaniah Uttar Prad India 25.26N 83.34E
36 J4 Zamantı R Turkey
76 H6 Zamayón Spain 41.09N 5.50W
19 K4 Zambales Mts Luzon Philippines
65 O1 Žamberk Czechoslovakia 50.05N 16.27E
92 F9 Zambeze R Mozambique etc
92 A8 Zambezi Zambia 13.33S 23.08E
73 G7 Zambezi R Africa
92 G10 Zambézia dist Mozambique
73 G7 Zambia rep Cent Africa
89 H6 Zambo Upper Volta 10.52N 3.01W
19 L8 Zamboanga Mindanao Philippines 6.55N 122.05E
19 L8 Zamboanga Pen Mindanao Philippines
19 L7 Zamboanguita Philippines 9.09N 123.12E
77 H6 Zambra Spain 37.22N 4.24W
75 E2 Zambrana Spain 42.40N 2.52W
119 D3 Zambrano Colombia 9.45N 74.50W
62 N3 Zambrów Poland 52.59N 22.11E
92 E9 Zambue Mozambique 15.07S 30.50E
76 D14 Zambujal Portugal 37.22N 7.40W
90 B5 Zamfara R Nigeria
121 F5 Zamora Argentina 34.45S 58.25W
111 C3 Zamora California 38.46N 121.53W
119 B10 Zamora Ecuador 4.05S 79.01W
76 H6 Zamora Spain 41.30N 5.45W
74 C3 Zamora prov Spain
119 B10 Zamora Chinchipe prov Ecuador
115 H7 Zamora de Hidalgo Mexico 20.00N 102.18W
115 L2 Zamorano Honduras 14.01N 87.01W
119 B9 Zamora,R Ecuador
62 O5 Zamość Poland 50.43N 23.15E
20 P9 Zampa-misaki C Okinawa Japan 26.26N 127.43E
Zamsar see Yangbajain
119 F2 Zamuro,Pta Venezuela 11.27N 68.51W
119 H5 Zamuro,Sa.del mts Venezuela
44 H1 Zam'yany U.S.S.R. 46.48N 47.40E
85 C4 Zamzam watercourse Libya
42 F4 Zamzor U.S.S.R. 55.20N 98.40E
90 J6 Zan Chad 10.32N 19.08E
120 B8 Zaña Peru 7.00S 79.20W
91 C5 Zanaga Congo 2.50S 13.53E
Zanagun see Zanūghān
36 G5 Zanapa Turkey 37.25N 34.15E
115 M9 Zanatepec Mexico 16.30N 94.20W
66 O4 Zanay Hörner mt Switzerland 46.57N 9.25E
77 K2 Záncara R Spain
44 J10 Zand Iran 37.35N 48.10E
60 H12 Zand Netherlands 51.49N 4.58E
24 C10 Zanda Xizang Zizhiqu China 31.29N 79.50E
94 N5 Zandamela Mozambique 24.47S 34.18E
60 E14 Zandberg Zeeland Netherlands 51.18N 4.06E
61 F3 Zandbergen Belgium 50.48N 3.58E
61 B2 Zande Belgium 51.07N 2.55E
87 A8 Zande tribe Zaïre
117 B2 Zanderij Surinam 5.26N 55.14W
61 J2 Zandhoven Belgium 51.13N 4.40E
91 F6 Zandu Zaïre 5.11S 18.16E
61 H1 Zandvliet Belgium 51.22N 4.19E
61 B2 Zandvoorde Belgium 51.12N 2.59E
61 B3 Zandvoorde Belgium 50.49N 2.59E
60 G10 Zandvoort Netherlands 52.22N 4.31E
113 J3 Zane Hills Alaska
104 C7 Zanesville Ohio 39.55N 82.02W
Zanga R see Razdan R
32 B1 Zangabad Iran 38.27N 46.39E
90 G7 Zangadi Chad 9.00N 14.50E
34 L2 Zanganān Iraq 36.30N 43.45E
Zanganeh see Jowzān
89 G5 Zangasso Mali 12.34N 5.01W
44 H8 Zangelan Azerbaydzhan U.S.S.R. 39.04N 46.37E
44 G8 Zangezurskiy Khrebet mts U.S.S.R.
24 C7 Zangguy Xinjiang Uygur Zizhiqu China 37.23N 78.50E
32 H6 Zangī Aḥmad, Lūt-e des Iran
32 H8 Zangin Iran 25.49N 59.46E
31 J4 Zangla Kashmir 33.40N 77.01E
44 F8 Zangmar R Iran
90 D5 Zango Nigeria 13.02N 8.29E
23 B3 Zango Sichuan China 31.45N 101.02E
23 B4 Zangqênrong Sichuan China 29.06N 99.11E
23 B4 Zangqênrong Sichuan China 29.03N 99.12E
Zanguya see Tsang-kui
37 J7 Zanhireh Iran 38.29N 45.25E
22 K8 Zanhuang Hebei China 37.40N 114.27E
31 E6 Zani Pakistan 29.39N 68.38E
87 C9 Zani Zaïre 2.39N 30.25E
93 B3 Zani Zaïre 2.37N 30.28E
79 G3 Zanica Italy 45.38N 9.41E
32 C2 Zanjān Iran 36.40N 48.30E
32 B2 Zanjān prov Iran
32 C2 Zanjān R Iran
121 C4 Zanjitas Argentina 33.50S 66.28W
121 C3 Zanjón, R Argentina
86 F4 Zankalûn Egypt 30.35N 31.26E
80 H7 Zannone Italy 40.58N 13.04E
35 C7 Zanoaḥ Israel 31.43N 35.00E
Zante isld see Zákinthos I
14 E9 Zanthus W Australia 31.01S 123.32E
32 G4 Zanūghān Iran 33.00N 57.40E
47 F5 Zanul'e U.S.S.R. 60.30N 49.33E
92 J12 Zanzibar Zanzibar 6.10S 39.12E
92 J5 Zanzibar Channel East Africa
92 J5 Zanzibar I Tanzania
45 J2 Zaokskoye U.S.S.R. 54.45N 37.24E
23 G5 Zaolin Jiangxi China 26.22N 114.26E
22 K8 Zaoqiang Hebei China 37.30N 115.40E
75 F6 Zaorejas Spain 40.45N 2.13W
90 H9 Zaorosongou Cent Afr Rep 5.00N 16.13E
20 O3 Zaō-san vol Japan 38.09N 140.26E
88 S9 Zaouatanlaz Algeria 24.52N 8.26E
88 N6 Zaouïac Tahtania Algeria 30.49N 1.59W
88 O7 Zaouïet ed Debarh Algeria 29.39N 0.42E
Zaouiye,Jebel mts see Zāwiye, Jebel ez mts
23 H3 Zaoxi Zhejiang China
23 F2 Zaoyang Hubei China 32.10N 112.45E
23 F2 Zaoyang Zhan Hubei China 32.04N 112.45E
42 E4 Zaozernyy U.S.S.R. 55.58N 94.43E
23 H1 Zaozhuang Shandong China 34.53N 117.38E
108 J2 Zap N Dakota 47.18N 101.54W
37 G8 Zap Turkey 37.23N 43.15E
37 H8 Zap R Turkey
82 F7 Zapadna Morava R Yugoslavia
46 H2 Zapadnaya Dvina U.S.S.R. 56.19N 32.00E
46 F2 Zapadnaya Dvina R U.S.S.R.
47 C2 Zapadnaya Litsa R U.S.S.R.
40 J6 Zapadno Sakhalinskiy Khrebet mts Sakhalin U.S.S.R.
38 F2 Zapadno-Sibirskaya Nizmennost' lowland U.S.S.R.
43 C6 Zapadnyy Chink Ustyurta escarp Kazakhstan U.S.S.R.
41 D4 Zapadnyy Kamennyy,Ostrov isld U.S.S.R.
39 M1 Zapadnyy,Mys C Vrangelya, Ostrov U.S.S.R. 71.04N 178.32E
42 D6 Zapadnyy Sayan mts U.S.S.R.
64 O4 Západočeský Kraj div Czechoslovakia
62 K7 Západoslovenský reg Czechoslovakia
121 B7 Zapala Argentina 38.55S 70.09W
120 E10 Zapaleri,Cerro pk Bolivia/Chile 22.50S 67.10W
121 B4 Zapallar Chile 32.35S 71.30W
76 K6 Zapardiel R Spain
112 H9 Zapata Texas 26.57N 99.17W
116 D3 Zapata,Pen.de Cuba
115 M4 Zapatera, I Nicaragua
119 D4 Zapatoca Colombia 6.52N 73.15W
7 C2 Zapatón R Spain
76 F10 Zapaton R Spain
119 D3 Zapatoza,Ciénaga de marshy L Colombia
64 K3 Zapfendorf W Germany 50.01N 10.57E
121 G4 Zapicán Uruguay 33.31N 54.55W
120 D8 Zapiga Chile 19.40S 79.00W
120 F6 Zapocoz,R Bolivia
42 K6 Zapokrovskiy U.S.S.R. 50.50N 119.15E
47 C2 Zapolyarnyy U.S.S.R. 69.26N 30.50E
45 G9 Zaporozhskaya Oblast prov Ukraine U.S.S.R.
45 G9 Zaporozh'ye Ukraine U.S.S.R. 47.50N 35.10E
119 B8 Zapotal Ecuador 1.23S 79.22W
115 H8 Zapotiltic Mexico 19.40N 103.29W
115 L8 Zapotitlán Salinas Mexico 18.21N 97.30W
115 G7 Zapotlán Mexico 21.08N 104.52W
40 G9 Zapovednik mt U.S.S.R. 45.16N 136.15E
84 D3 Záppion Greece 39.28N 22.27E
80 N6 Zapponeta Italy 41.27N 15.57E
66 N6 Zapporthorn mt Switzerland 46.29N 9.08E
81 J7 Zappulla R Sicily
24 C9 Zapug Xizang Zizhiqu China 33.17N 80.50E
24 H9 Zaqên Qinghai China 33.23N 94.31E
24 H9 Za Qu R Qinghai China
23 A2 Za Qu R Qinghai/Sichuan China
23 A2 Za Qui R Sichuan China
Zara see Zadar
36 H2 Zara Amasya Turkey 40.34N 35.37E
37 D6 Zara Sivas Turkey 39.55N 37.44E
86 K6 Zarâfa,Gebel el hill Egypt 29.56N 33.07E
84 E7 Zarafóna Greece 37.05N 22.38E
43 G6 Zarafshan Uzbekistan U.S.S.R. 41.31N 64.15E
115 F2 Zaragoza Chihuahua Mexico 31.38N 106.20W
115 J3 Zaragoza Coahuila Mexico 28.31N 100.54W
119 D4 Zaragoza Colombia 7.31N 74.57W
75 J4 Zaragoza Spain 41.39N 0.54W
74 G3 Zaragoza prov Spain
Zarakkūh see Zirkūh I
44 F5 Zaramag U.S.S.R. 42.41N 43.59E
92 J5 Zaramu tribe Tanzania
32 G5 Zarand Kermān Iran 30.50N 56.35E
32 D3 Zarand Tehrān Iran 35.16N 50.29E
Zarand Kūhneh see Zarand
82 G4 Zărandului,Munţii mts Romania
31 A5 Zaranj Afghanistan 36.06N 61.53E
89 H8 Zaranou Ivory Coast 6.29N 3.21W
46 F2 Zarasai Lithuania U.S.S.R. 55.40N 26.20E
88 T5 Zarat Tunisia 33.40N 10.18E
76 K5 Zaratán Spain 41.39N 4.48W
121 F5 Zárate Argentina 34.07S 59.00W
75 F1 Zarauz Spain 43.17N 2.10W
45 K2 Zaraysk U.S.S.R. 54.45N 38.54E
119 G3 Zaraza Venezuela 9.23N 65.20W
115 M4 Zarcero Costa Rica 10.10N 84.26W
31 C6 Zard Pakistan 28.41N 64.49E
32 H3 Zardak Iran 34.47N 58.07E
43 K7 Zardaly Kirgiziya U.S.S.R. 39.40N 70.57E
34 M4 Zardāw Iraq 34.34N 44.58E
Zardeh Kūh see Zard Kūh mts
32 C4 Zard Kūh mts Iran
44 H7 Zardob Azerbaydzhan U.S.S.R. 40.12N 47.40E
47 H5 Zarechka U.S.S.R. 60.06N 57.28E
42 F4 Zarechnaya U.S.S.R. 56.03N 97.29E
32 C3 Zāreh Iran 35.07N 49.09E
113 V8 Zarembo I Alaska 56.20N 132.50W
33 D3 Zarghat Saudi Arabia 26.30N 40.29E
31 E4 Zarghun Shahr Afghanistan 32.51N 68.25E
31 D5 Zargun mt Pakistan 30.15N 67.11E
31 D3 Zari Afghanistan 34.40N 66.52E
90 C6 Zaria Nigeria 11.01N 7.44E
32 F5 Zarīgān Iran 31.55N 55.32E
Zarin see Zarrīn
32 H7 Zarīnābād Iran 26.56N 59.57E
32 B2 Zarīneh R Iran
42 C5 Zarinskaya U.S.S.R. 53.42N 84.57E
35 E1 Zar'it Israel 33.06N 35.18E
44 J10 Zarjābād Iran 37.38N 48.03E
43 N7 Zarkent Uzbekistan U.S.S.R. 41.25N 71.41E
84 D2 Zárkon Greece 39.34N 22.08E
84 D2 Zárkon, Óri mts Greece
61 F3 Zarlardinge Belgium 50.46N 3.50E
89 G2 Zarma reg Mali
89 H1 Zarma reg Mali
31 B4 Zarmardan Afghanistan 32.59N 62.42E
32 B4 Zarneh Iran 33.55N 46.08E
82 J5 Zărneşti Romania 45.34N 25.18E
31 C4 Zarni Afghanistan 33.09N 64.19E
62 M4 Żarnów Poland 51.15N 20.10E
84 L11 Zarós Crete 35.08N 24.54E
63 T5 Zarow R E Germany
85 O3 Zarqa Jordan 32.04N 36.06E
35 F5 Zarqa R Jordan
86 G3 Zarqa,El Egypt 31.14N 31.38E
31 C3 Zar Qala Afghanistan 35.41N 65.07E
35 F7 Zarqa Ma'in R Jordan
32 E6 Zarqān Iran 29.46N 52.45E
77 O2 Zarra Spain 39.06N 1.05W
Zarreh see Zāreh
63 N5 Zarrentin E Germany 53.33N 10.56E
61 B2 Zarren-Werken Belgium 51.02N 2.58E
32 F4 Zarrīn Iran 32.46N 54.37E
64 D8 Zarten W Germany 47.59N 7.57E
32 E5 Zarū Iran 31.48N 53.33E
46 J1 Zarubino U.S.S.R. 58.42N 33.30E
119 B9 Zaruma Ecuador 3.46S 79.38W
119 B9 Zarumilla Peru 3.30S 80.20W
62 J4 Żary Poland 51.40N 15.10E
43 D3 Zarya Oktyabrya Kazakhstan U.S.S.R. 48.18N 57.17E
41 F3 Zarya,Poluostrov pen U.S.S.R.
41 P3 Zarya,Proliv str U.S.S.R.
24 A6 Zarya Vostoka mt China/U.S.S.R. 39.28N 73.51E
77 F3 Zarza Capilla Spain 38·49N 5·09W
77 D3 Zarza de Alange Spain 38.49N 6.13W
76 G8 Zarza de Granadilla Spain 40.14N 6.03W
76 G10 Zarza de Montánchez Spain 39.16N 6.03W
77 N5 Zarzadilla de Totana Spain 37.53N 1.43W
88 S7 Zarzaïtine Algeria 28.15N 9.34E
119 C5 Zarzal Colombia 4.24N 76.01W
76 F9 Zarza la Mayor Spain 39.52N 6.51W
88 T5 Zarzis Tunisia 33.34N 11.04E
76 L6 Zarzuela del Pinar Spain 41.15N 4.12W
76 B2 Zas Spain 43.06N 8.55W
64 P1 Zaschwitz E Germany 51.10N 13.03E
44 B7 Zasel'ye Ukraine U.S.S.R. 47.02N 32.25E
43 O2 Zashchita Kazakhstan U.S.S.R. 50.01N 82.30E
47 C3 Zasheyek U.S.S.R. 67.20N 32.30E
62 H4 Zasieki Poland 51.45N 14.40E
31 J4 Zaskar R Kashmir
31 J4 Zaskar reg Kashmir
31 J3 Zaskar Mts Kashmir
46 F3 Zaslavl Belorussiya U.S.S.R. 54.00N 27.15E
65 M2 Zásmuky Czechoslovakia 49.58N 15.03E
45 B4 Zaspa Belorussiya U.S.S.R. 52.15N 30.30E
65 O3 Zastávka Czechoslovakia 49.12N 16.22E
82 K2 Zastavna U.S.S.R. 48.31N 25.50E
95 L6 Zastron S Africa 30.18S 27.05E
45 E6 Zasul'ye Ukraine U.S.S.R. 50.44N 33.31E
34 E7 Zatab ash Shamah mt Saudi Arabia 31.39N 37.56E
35 J5 Zatara watercourse Jordan
64 Q3 Žatec Czechoslovakia 50.20N 13.34E
44 G3 Zaterchnyy U.S.S.R. 44.48N 45.08E
39 F2 Zatish'ye Magadan U.S.S.R. 66.08N 159.01E
45 L2 Zatish'ye Ryazan' U.S.S.R. 54.30N 39.46E
46 G6 Zatish'ye Ukraine U.S.S.R. 47.20N 29.58E
43 G1 Zatobol'sk Kazakhstan U.S.S.R. 53.14N 63.13E
47 K6 Zaton U.S.S.R. 58.18N 68.08E
62 L6 Zator Poland 50.00N 19.23E
44 J1 Zatsarevo U.S.S.R. 46.19N 48.01E
63 R8 Zauche reg E Germany
43 E6 Zaunguzskiye Karakumy des Turkmeniya U.S.S.R.
115 L8 Zautla Mexico 19.42N 97.41W
42 G5 Zaval' U.S.S.R. 54.42N 102.01E
121 E5 Zavalia Argentina 34.55S 61.02W
112 N4 Zavalla Texas 31.11N 94.28W
40 M8 Zavaritskogo caldera Kuril Is U.S.S.R. 46.56N 151.57E
79 F5 Zavattarello Italy 44.52N 9.16E
35 C7 Zavdi'el Israel 31.40N 34.46E
Zâve see Zāyā
Zavelstein see Bad Teinach-Zavelstein
61 H3 Zaventem Belgium 50.53N 4.28E
45 P9 Zavetnoye U.S.S.R. 47.07N 43.54E
40 H7 Zavety Il'icha U.S.S.R. 49.02N 140.20E
82 E6 Zavidovići Yugoslavia 44.27N 18.09E
40 E6 Zavitinsk U.S.S.R. 50.08N 129.24E
84 E7 Závitsa mt Greece 37.27N 22.42E
35 C9 Zavoa, Har hill Israel 31.02N 34.51E
47 K7 Zavodo Petrovskiy U.S.S.R. 56.52N 66.48E
47 K7 Zavodoukovsk U.S.S.R. 56.35N 66.30E
47 K7 Zavodouspenskoye U.S.S.R. 56.54N 65.00E
123 A14 Zavodovski vol S Sandwich Is Atlantic Oc
123 A14 Zavodovski I S Sandwich Is Atlantic Oc 56.17S 27.40W
42 C5 Zavodskoy U.S.S.R. 53.07N 84.27E
46 M2 Zavolzhsk U.S.S.R. 57.30N 42.10E
94 N5 Zavora,Punta C Mozambique 24.25S 35.10E
65 N2 Závratec Czechoslovakia 49.52N 15.35E
39 E5 Zav'yalova,Ostrov isld U.S.S.R.
42 C5 Zav'yalovo Altay U.S.S.R. 52.50N 80.59E
43 O1 Zav'yalovo Altay U.S.S.R. 54.22N 82.18E
42 C5 Zav'yalovo Novosibirsk U.S.S.R. 54.28N 82.30E
24 C7 Zawa Xinjiang Uygur Zizhiqu China 37.12N 79.34E
31 D5 Zawai Afghanistan 31.36N 67.55E
86 F5 Zawâmil,El Egypt 30.21N 31.26E
87 E6 Zawa,Tulu mt Ethiopia 9.29N 34.22E
85 G3 Zaw Ezziat Libya 32.15N 22.40E
25 D2 Zawgyi R Burma
62 L5 Zawiercie Poland 50.30N 19.24E
85 C6 Zawīlah Libya 26.11N 15.06E
35 D5 Zawiya Jordan 32.06N 35.02E
85 B3 Zāwiyah, Az Libya 32.49N 12.43E
85 F4 Zāwiyat Masūs Libya 31.39N 21.01E
34 D3 Zāwiye,Jebel ez mts Syria
33 H3 Zawr,Ra's az C Saudi Arabia 27.26N 49.19E
86 E9 Zâwyet el Amwât Egypt 28.04N 30.50E
86 E8 Zâwyet el Gidâmi Egypt 28.42N 30.54E
86 E5 Zâwyet Razîn Egypt 30.25N 30.51E
86 J4 Zâwyet Shammâs Egypt 31.30N 26.37E
34 M5 Zāyā Iraq 33.34N 44.14E
65 O4 Zaya R Austria
42 G4 Zayarsk U.S.S.R. 56.12N 103.00E
34 M5 Zaydān Iraq 33.15N 44.02E
Zaydī, Wādī az watercourse see Zeidi, Wādī water course
33 E9 Zaydīyah,Az Yemen 15.20N 43.00E
23 A4 Zayii Qu R Xizang Zizhiqu China
33 E9 Zaylah Yemen 15.14N 43.58E
43 P4 Zaysan Kazakhstan U.S.S.R. 47.30N 84.57E
43 P3 Zaysan,Oz res Kazakhstan U.S.S.R.
23 A4 Zayü Xizang Zizhiqu China 27.25N 96.41E
23 A4 Zayü Xizang Zizhiqu China 28.28N 97.05E
44 E4 Zayukovo U.S.S.R. 43.36N 43.17E
Zayul R see Zayu Qu R
23 A4 Zayu Qu R Xizang Zizhiqu China
95 C7 Zazafotsy Madagascar 22.11S 46.21E
88 B5 Zazagawa Nigeria 12.43N 4.24E
88 Q11 Zazir watercourse Algeria
66 G4 Zäziwil Switzerland 46.55N 7.41E
46 F5 Zbarazh Ukraine U.S.S.R. 49.40N 25.49E
62 J3 Zbąszyń Poland 52.16N 15.55E
64 Q4 Zbiroh Czechoslovakia 49.52N 13.46E
64 F5 Zborov Ukraine U.S.S.R. 49.40N 25.09E
65 K2 Zbraslav Czechoslovakia 49.58N 14.24E
65 M2 Zbraslavice Czechoslovakia 49.49N 15.12E
46 F5 Zbruch R Ukraine U.S.S.R.
82 K1 Zbrug R U.S.S.R.
65 O3 Zbýšov Czechoslovakia 49.10N 16.21E
65 J4 Zbytiny Czechoslovakia 48.57N 13.59E
62 N7 Ždaňa Czechoslovakia 48.36N 21.20E
65 Q3 Ždánice Czechoslovakia 49.04N 17.02E
65 O3 Žd'árec Czechoslovakia 49.23N 16.17E
65 N2 Žd'ár nad Sáz Czechoslovakia 49.34N 15.57E
65 J2 Zdice Czechoslovakia 49.56N 13.59E
64 Q5 Zdíkov Czechoslovakia 49.06N 13.43E
65 N2 Zdírec Czechoslovakia 49.42N 15.49E
89 L3 Zdjarat watercourse Mali
46 F4 Zdolbunov Ukraine U.S.S.R. 50.30N 26.10E
62 L4 Zduńska Wola Poland 51.36N 18.55E
42 B5 Zdvinsk U.S.S.R. 54.41N 78.40E
Zealand see Sjælland
100 K7 Zealandia Saskatchewan 51.36N 107.50W
108 R7 Zearing Iowa 42.08N 93.13W
31 F2 Zebak Afghanistan 36.32N 71.21E
101 K11 Zeballos Vancouver I, Br Col 49.58N 126.47W
121 K6 Zeballos pk Argentina 47.00S 71.45W
84 Y20 Żebbieh Malta 35.56N 14.23E
84 X19 Żebbuġ Gozo Mediterranean Sea 36.04N 14.14E
84 Y20 Żebbuġ Malta 35.52N 14.27E
34 D5 Zebdāni Syria 33.44N 36.06E
94 K5 Zebediela S Africa 24.25S 29.12E
85 O8 Zebirget islds Egypt 23.40N 36.08E
95 F9 Zebra S Africa 33.45S 22.18E
65 J2 Žebrák Czechoslovakia 49.53N 13.54E
76 E9 Zébreira Beira Baixa Portugal 39.51N 7.04W
105 J2 Zebulon N Carolina 35.50N 78.19W
63 R6 Zechlin-Dorf E Germany 53.08N 12.47E
63 R6 Zechlin-Flecken E Germany 53.10N 12.46E
79 E2 Zeda,Monte mt Italy 46.03N 8.32E
60 O12 Zeddam Netherlands 51.54N 6.16E
61 C2 Zedelgem Belgium 51.08N 3.09E
65 H7 Zederhaus Austria 47.10N 13.30E
88 H10 Zedness Mt Mauritania 23.45N 10.40W
80 O1 Zedno Yugoslavia 43.30N 16.17E
61 C1 Zeebrugge Belgium 51.20N 3.13E
60 C3 Zeedorp Netherlands 51.23N 3.58E
60 P7 Zeegse Netherlands 53.04N 6.40E
12 H8 Zeehan Tasmania 41.55S 145.21E
95 N1 Zeekoewater S Africa 25.51S 29.15E
106 H7 Zeeland Michigan 42.48N 86.02W
108 L4 Zeeland N Dakota 45.58N 99.50W
60 L13 Zeeland Netherlands 51.42N 5.40E
60 C2 Zeeland prov Netherlands
35 B9 Ze'elim Israel 31.12N 34.32E
86 O3 Ze'elim watercourse Israel
60 K14 Zeelst Netherlands 51.25N 5.25E
60 Q6 Zeerijp Netherlands 53.21N 6.45E
95 K1 Zeerust S Africa 25.33S 26.06E
35 E2 Zefat Israel 32.57N 35.27E
32 E4 Zefreh Iran 32.55N 52.19E
88 L7 Zegdou Algeria 29.48N 4.45W
61 E3 Zegelsem Belgium 50.49N 3.43E
60 G13 Zegge Netherlands 51.33N 4.31E
85 A6 Zegher,Hammādat plat Libya
88 P5 Zegrir watercourse Algeria
60 H11 Zegveld Netherlands 52.07N 4.50E
Zehden see Cedynia
63 S7 Zehdenick E Germany 52.59N 13.20E
63 S8 Zehlendorf W Berlin W Germany 52.26N 13.16E
63 Q5 Zehna E Germany 53.44N 12.09E
103 C4 Zehner Pennsylvania 41.03N 75.50W
103 C5 Zehners Pennsylvania 40.45N 75.58W
65 M2 Zehnšice Czechoslovakia 49.59N 15.25E
64 P1 Zehren E Germany 51.12N 13.25E
Zē i Bādīnān R see Zab,Great R
87 D2 Zeidab,Ez Sudan 17.30N 33.55E
34 D6 Zeidi,Wādī watercourse Syria
33 A4 Zeidun,Wâdi watercourse Egypt
107 G4 Zeigler Illinois 37.54N 89.03W
60 P7 Zeijen Netherlands 53.00N 6.33E
Zē i Kōya R see Zab, Little R
34 L3 Ze i Koya R Iraq
64 K3 Zeil W Germany 50.01N 10.38E
87 J5 Zeila Somalia 11.21N 43.30E
66 H1 Zeiningen Switzerland 47.32N 7.51E
60 K11 Zeist Netherlands 52.05N 5.15E
35 J10 Zeit watercourse Jordan
35 D4 Zeita Jordan 32.23N 35.03E
86 K10 Zeit,Gebel el ra Egypt
63 S10 Zeithain E Germany 51.20N 13.21E
64 O7 Zeitlarn W Germany 48.17N 12.51E
86 R11 Zeitûn, El Cairo Egypt
64 N1 Zeitz E Germany 51.03N 12.08E
35 G3 Zeizun Syria 32.43N 35.56E
84 Z20 Żejtun Malta 35.52N 14.33E
23 B1 Zêkog Qinghai China 35.00N 101.30E
Zēlaf see Zilāf
61 G2 Zele Belgium 51.04N 4.02E
65 L3 Želeč Czechoslovakia 49.20N 14.39E
62 N4 Zelechów Poland 51.49N 21.55E
61 L3 Zelem Belgium 50.58N 5.06E
64 P5 Zelená Lhota Czechoslovakia 49.15N 13.11E
43 M2 Zelenaya Roshcha Kazakhstan U.S.S.R. 52.14N 75.05E
45 M9 Zelenaya Roshcha U.S.S.R. 47.08N 40.15E
44 D4 Zelenchuk R U.S.S.R.
44 D4 Zelenchukskaya U.S.S.R. 43.53N 41.36E
44 J1 Zelenga U.S.S.R. 46.11N 48.37E
45 R7 Zelenkaya Polyana U.S.S.R. 49.33N 45.56E
47 C3 Zelenoborskiy U.S.S.R. 66.50N 32.50E
45 U1 Zelenodol'sk U.S.S.R. 55.50N 48.30E
47 B5 Zelenogorsk U.S.S.R. 60.15N 29.31E
62 M1 Zelenogradsk U.S.S.R. 54.57N 20.28E
44 F3 Zelenokumsk U.S.S.R. 44.25N 43.54E
45 E9 Zelenoye Ukraine U.S.S.R. 47.44N 33.14E
47 E6 Zelentsovo U.S.S.R. 59.51N 44.59E
44 D7 Zelenyy Gay Ukraine U.S.S.R. 47.25N 35.23E
39 G1 Zelenyy Mys C U.S.S.R. 68.49N 161.12E
Zelenyy Ostrov see Shibotsu-jima I
86 M8 Zeleqa, Wâdi watercourse Egypt
65 N3 Želetava Czechoslovakia 49.09N 15.41E
64 P5 Železná Ruda Czechoslovakia 49.10N 13.15E
65 M1 Železné hory mts Czechoslovakia
88 Q5 Zelfana Algeria 32.36N 4.03E
60 O11 Zelham Netherlands 52.00N 6.21E
104 E6 Zelienople Pennsylvania 40.47N 80.08W
62 L7 Želiezovce Czechoslovakia 48.02N 18.40E
90 D2 Zeline Niger 19.50N 8.03E
22 D8 Zelinggou Qinghai China 37.21N 97.49E
84 E4 Zélion Greece 38.39N 22.53E
65 M2 Želiv Czechoslovakia 49.32N 15.14E
65 M2 Želivka R Czechoslovakia
82 F7 Željin mt Yugoslavia 43.29N 20.46E
64 D8 Zell Baden-Württemberg W Germany 47.42N 7.52E
64 E7 Zell Baden-Württemberg W Germany 48.21N 8.04E
64 H4 Zell Bayern W Germany 49.49N 9.53E
64 M3 Zell Bayern W Germany 50.08N 11.50E
64 C3 Zell Rheinland-Pfalz W Germany 50.02N 7.12E
108 M5 Zell S Dakota 44.53N 98.41W
66 H3 Zell Switzerland 47.08N 7.56E
64 K2 Zella-Mehlis E Germany 50.40N 10.41E
65 H6 Zell a Moos Austria 47.54N 13.20E
65 G7 Zell-am-See Austria 47.19N 12.47E
65 E7 Zell-am-Ziller Austria 47.14N 11.53E
65 L5 Zell bei Zellhof Austria 48.22N 14.42E
63 S9 Zellendorf E Germany 51.53N 13.04E
65 N4 Zellerndorf Austria 48.42N 15.58E
65 H6 Zellersee Austria 47.55N 13.18E
65 G7 Zeller See L Austria 47.20N 12.48E
66 M1 Zeller See L W Germany 47.43N 8.58E
61 H3 Zellik Belgium 50.53N 4.16E
64 H4 Zellingen W Germany 49.54N 9.49E
100 M7 Zelma Saskatchewan 51.51N 105.54W
65 J4 Želnava Czechoslovakia 48.49N 13.58E
88 S12 Zeloufiet Niger 19.01N 8.28E
62 L4 Zelów Poland 51.30N 19.10E
85 E5 Zelten Libya 28.51N 19.52E
64 C4 Zeltingen-Rachtig W Germany 49.57N 7.02E
46 H6 Zelts Ukraine U.S.S.R. 46.38N 30.00E
65 L7 Zeltweg Austria 47.12N 14.46E
61 F2 Zelzate Belgium 51.12N 3.49E
46 G3 Zembin Belorussiya U.S.S.R. 54.21N 28.12E
88 T3 Zembra isld Tunisia 37.08N 10.47E
23 B2 Zêmdasam Sichuan China 33.05N 101.32E
84 E5 Zemenón Greece 38.02N 22.36E
45 O3 Zemetchino U.S.S.R. 53.30N 42.37E
87 F6 Zemie Ethiopia 9.57N 37.48E
90 M9 Zemio Cent Afr Rep 5.00N 25.09E
88 S5 Zemlet et Touil reg Tunisia
48 K11 Zemlya Frantsa Iosifa arch U.S.S.R.
45 K5 Zemlyansk U.S.S.R. 51.54N 38.45E
65 E7 Zemm R Austria
88 O4 Zemmora Algeria 35.39N 0.48E
88 G9 Zemmur reg Morocco
44 G6 Zemo Kedi Georgia U.S.S.R. 41.27N 46.25E
90 M8 Zémongo Cent Afr Rep 7.05N 24.58E
88 R6 Zemoul el Akbar,Ez reg Algeria
82 G2 Zempléni-hory mts Hungary
115 M9 Zempoaltepetl pk Mexico 17.11N 95.58W
61 H3 Zemst Belgium 50.59N 4.28E
45 D1 Zemtsy U.S.S.R. 56.15N 32.25E
82 F6 Zemun Yugoslavia 44.50N 20.25E
109 M4 Zenda Kansas 37.27N 98.17W
60 P10 Zenderen Netherlands 52.19N 6.44E
66 H6 Zeneggen Switzerland 46.16N 7.52E
23 F7 Zengcheng Guangdong China 23.18N 113.51E
37 E7 Zengetil Turkey 38.09N 39.47E
110 B9 Zenia California 40.14N 123.31W
82 D6 Zenica Yugoslavia 44.11N 17.53E
86 N5 Zenifim watercourse Israel
Zenjan see Zanjān
45 F6 Zen'kov Ukraine U.S.S.R. 50.11N 34.22E
Zen'kovka see Chkalovskoye
42 D5 Zen'kovo Kemerovo U.S.S.R. 53.50N 86.54E
47 K5 Zen'kovo Tyumen U.S.S.R. 61.12N 69.49E
64 K5 Zenn R W Germany
56 S9 Zennor Cornwall Eng 50.11N 5.35W
34 G3 Zenobia anc site Syria 35.41N 39.51E
80 A2 Zenobito,Pta.del Italy 43.00N 9.52E
100 O5 Zenon Park Saskatchewan 53.03N 103.45W
107 D10 Zenoria Louisiana 31.44N 92.22W
20 G7 Zentsuji Japan 34.14N 133.45E
91 D8 Zenza R Angola
91 D8 Zenza do Itombe Angola 9.20S 14.15E
115 L9 Zenzontepec Mexico 16.31N 97.31W
108 H4 Zeona S Dakota 45.11N 102.55W
82 E6 Žepče Yugoslavia 44.26N 18.03E
63 T7 Zepernick E Germany 52.39N 13.32E
112 J4 Zephyr Texas 31.41N 98.48W
105 E9 Zephyrhills Florida 28.14N 82.11W
14 D8 Zephyr,Mt W Australia 28.21S 121.49E
84 Q15 Zephyros,C Cyprus 34.41N 32.32E
24 B6 Zepu Xinjiang Uygur Zizhiqu China 38.14N 77.18E
87 C7 Zeraf Cuts R Sudan
35 C7 Zeraḥya Israel 31.41N 34.45E
Zera'im see Gid'ona
43 J7 Zeravshan Tadzhikistan U.S.S.R. 39.10N 68.39E
43 H7 Zeravshan R U.S.S.R.
43 H7 Zeravshanskiy Khrebet mts U.S.S.R.
63 Q9 Zerbst E Germany 51.58N 12.06E
43 J1 Zerenda Kazakhstan U.S.S.R. 52.56N 69.09E
64 B4 Zerf W Germany 49.36N 6.41E
88 P5 Zergoun watercourse Algeria
88 M7 Zerhamra Algeria 30.00N 2.28W
88 R4 Zeribet el Oued Algeria 34.42N 6.29E
35 C6 Zerifin Israel 31.57N 34.51E
61 C2 Zerkegem Belgium 51.10N 3.04E
62 K3 Zerków Poland 52.05N 17.32E
66 G7 Zermatt Switzerland 46.01N 7.45E
66 R5 Zernez Switzerland 46.43N 10.06E
63 Q7 Zernitz E Germany 52.53N 12.23E
44 C1 Zernograd U.S.S.R. 46.53N 40.19E
108 E3 Zero Montana 46.40N 105.29W
79 M3 Zero Branco Italy 45.36N 12.10E
88 S4 Zeroud watercourse Tunisia
83 D3 Zerqan Albania 41.30N 20.20E
63 U6 Zerrenthin E Germany 53.29N 14.05E
94 B3 Zerrissenes Mts Namibia
35 B8 Zeru'a Israel 31.28N 34.37E
35 C3 Zerufa Israel 32.39N 34.57E
66 N5 Zervreila-see L Switzerland 46.34N 9.06E
44 E5 Zestafoni Georgia U.S.S.R. 42.07N 43.03E
35 C6 Zetan Israel 31.58N 34.53E
24 G11 Zêtang Xizang Zizhiqu China 29.15N 91.42E
63 G6 Zetel W Germany 53.25N 7.58E
Zetland co see Shetland island area
21 B9 Zetouji Shandong China 37.04N 121.54E
64 M2 Zeulenroda E Germany 50.39N 11.59E
15 J2 Zeune Is Bougainville I Solomon Is
63 T8 Zeuthen E Germany 52.21N 13.38E
61 B2 Zevekote Belgium 51.08N 2.55E
63 K6 Zeven W Germany 53.18N 9.17E
60 N12 Zevenaar Netherlands 51.55N 6.05E
60 G13 Zevenbergen Netherlands 51.39N 4.36E
60 G13 Zevenbergschenhoek Netherlands 51.40N 4.41E
61 F2 Zeveneken Belgium 51.07N 3.54E
60 H11 Zevenhoven Netherlands 52.11N 4.46E
60 O7 Zevenhuizen Groningen Netherlands 53.07N 6.21E
60 G11 Zevenhuizen Zuid Holland Netherlands 52.01N 4.35E
61 E3 Zeveren Belgium 51.00N 3.30E
61 E3 Zevergem Belgium 50.58N 3.42E
84 Q15 Zevgari C Cyprus 34.33N 32.56E
84 D6 Zevgolatío Arkadhía Greece 37.31N 22.26E
84 E6 Zevgolatión Greece 37.56N 22.48E
84 C7 Zevgoletió Messinía Greece 37.15N 21.58E
79 K4 Zévio Italy 45.23N 11.08E
37 D6 Zevker Turkey 39.59N 38.50E
40 D5 Zeya U.S.S.R. 53.48N 127.14E
40 D6 Zeya R U.S.S.R.
32 J8 Zeyarat-e Shamil Iran 25.52N 60.15E
32 F6 Zeydābād Iran 29.38N 55.35E
32 G2 Zeydar Iran 37.50N 57.46E
32 K7 Zeydī Iran 26.38N 62.52E
32 G6 Zeynalābād Iran 29.56N 57.29E
36 G6 Zeyne Turkey 36.27N 33.32E
40 E6 Zeysko Bureinskaya Ravnina plain U.S.S.R.
37 H3 Zeytinburnu Turkey 40.59N 28.47E
36 C4 Zeytindağ Turkey 38.57N 27.04E
Zeytun see Süleymanlı
76 C9 Zêzere R Portugal
89 L3 Zgarat,Vallée de Mali
34 C4 Zghorta Lebanon 34.25N 35.53E
46 C4 Zgierz Poland 51.52N 19.25E
65 N8 Zgornja Duplek Yugoslavia 46.30N 15.44E
65 N8 Zgornja Kungota Yugoslavia 46.38N 15.36E
62 J4 Zgorzelec Poland 51.10N 15.00E
82 L2 Zguritsa U.S.S.R. 48.05N 28.01E
45 C6 Zgurovka Ukraine U.S.S.R. 50.30N 31.46E
Zhabdün see Zhongba
82 J2 Zhabe U.S.S.R. 48.10N 24.46E
45 S3 Zhadovka U.S.S.R. 53.31N 46.57E
Zhaggo see Luhuo
23 A3 Zhag'yab Xizang Zizhiqu China 30.42N 97.30E
23 H5 Zhaili Fujian China 27.41N 117.28E
43 F2 Zhailma Kazakhstan U.S.S.R. 51.37N 61.33E
23 E7 Zhaixu Guangxi China 22.32N 109.38E
46 R5 Zhaksybay R Kazakhstan U.S.S.R.
43 J3 Zhaksykon R Kazakhstan U.S.S.R.
43 F4 Zhaksykylysh,Oz L Kazakhstan U.S.S.R. 46.50N 61.58E
43 L3 Zhaksylyk Kazakhstan U.S.S.R. 47.36N 74.06E
43 K3 Zhaksy Sarysu R Kazakhstan U.S.S.R.
43 N5 Zhalanash Alma-Ata, Kazakhstan U.S.S.R. 43.04N 78.08E
43 H2 Zhalanash Kustanay, Kazakhstan U.S.S.R. 51.09N 65.00E

47 L8 Zhalauly, Oz L Kazakhstan U.S.S.R. 52.55N 74.10E
43 M2 Zhaltyr Kazakhstan U.S.S.R. 51.30N 77.30E
46 Q6 Zhaltyr,Oz L Kazakhstan U.S.S.R.
43 G3 Zhamanakkol',Oz L Kazakhstan U.S.S.R.
45 U8 Zhamankak Kazakhstan U.S.S.R. 48.58N 48.49E
43 C3 Zhamansor Kazakhstan U.S.S.R. 47.48N 53.50E
Zhamo see Bomi
43 L3 Zhamshi Kazakhstan U.S.S.R. 48.00N 74.28E
43 L2 Zhanaaul Kazakhstan U.S.S.R. 51.28N 74.44E
43 J3 Zhanabas Kazakhstan U.S.S.R. 47.39N 68.48E
43 M3 Zhanabek Kazakhstan U.S.S.R. 49.31N 75.52E
43 F4 Zhanakentkala anc site Kazakhstan U.S.S.R. 45.37N 61.53E
43 F4 Zhanakurylys Kazakhstan U.S.S.R. 45.55N 61.15E
43 G5 Zhanala ruins Kazakhstan U.S.S.R. 44.33N 64.04E
24 G11 Zhanang Xizang Zizhiqu China 29.15N 91.20E
43 O2 Zhana-Semey Kazakhstan U.S.S.R. 50.24N 80.14E
43 N5 Zhanatalap Alma-Ata, Kazakhstan U.S.S.R. 43.13N 78.30E
43 G5 Zhanatalap Kzyl-Orda, Kazakhstan U.S.S.R. 44.53N 64.16E
43 J5 Zhanatas Kazakhstan U.S.S.R. 43.35N 69.35E
43 F4 Zhanay Kazakhstan U.S.S.R. 45.29N 61.46E
46 Q6 Zhangaly Kazakhstan U.S.S.R. 47.00N 50.39E
22 K6 Zhangbei Hebei China 41.10N 114.50E
23 F2 Zhangcun Henan China 32.50N 111.56E
Zhangde see Anyang
Zhangdian see Zibo
21 D5 Zhangguangcai Ling mts Jilin China
21 B6 Zhanggutai Liaoning China 42.44N 122.30E
22 K8 Zhang He R Hebei China
23 E7 Zhanghuang Guangxi China 22.02N 109.28E
43 O3 Zhangiz-Tobe Kazakhstan U.S.S.R. 49.15N 81.16E
23 D1 Zhangjiachuan Gansu China 34.55N 106.26E
23 D1 Zhangjiachuan Huizu Zizhixian Gansu China 35.00N 106.11E
22 K6 Zhangjiakou Hebei China 40.51N 114.59E
Zhangjiapan see Jingbian
23 G3 Zhangjiapang Hubei China 30.25N 115.47E
22 C6 Zhangjiaquan Gansu China 40.35N 94.58E
23 G4 Zhangjiashan Jiangxi China 28.02N 115.23E
23 C2 Zhangla Sichuan China 32.50N 103.40E
21 C1 Zhangling Heilongjiang China 52.37N 123.38E
23 E7 Zhangmu Guangxi China 22.33N 109.59E
23 H6 Zhangping Fujian China 25.18N 117.23E
23 H6 Zhangpu Fujian China 24.08N 117.36E
22 L8 Zhangqiu Shandong China 36.47N 117.26E
22 L6 Zhangsanying Hebei China 41.30N 117.36E
23 G6 Zhang Shui R Jiangxi China
Zhangshuzhen see Qingjiang
21 B6 Zhangwu Liaoning China 41.24N 122.30E
23 C1 Zhang Xian Gansu China 34.42N 104.42E
22 E7 Zhangye Gansu China 38.58N 100.30E
23 H6 Zhangzhou Fujian China 24.31N 117.40E
23 F1 Zhangzi Shanxi China 36.05N 112.52E
21 B8 Zhangzi Dao isld Liaoning China
21 D3 Zhanhe Heilongjiang China 48.40N 127.39E
21 D3 Zhan He R Heilongjiang China
22 L8 Zhanhua Shandong China 37.44N 117.45E
23 E8 Zhanjiang Guangdong China 21.10N 110.20E
23 F8 Zhanjiang Gang B Guangdong China
38 P1 Zhannetty,Ostrov isld U.S.S.R.
43 P3 Zhantekets Kazakhstan U.S.S.R. 48.07N 82.50E
43 J3 Zhanteli Kazakhstan U.S.S.R. 49.32N 67.31E
43 C3 Zhanterek Kazakhstan U.S.S.R. 47.56N 54.18E
23 C6 Zhanyi Yunnan China 25.37N 103.50E
21 B5 Zhanyu Jilin China 44.34N 22.38E
23 G7 Zhao'an Guangdong China 23.42N 116.36E
22 J8 Zhaocheng Shanxi China 36.26N 111.44E
23 E2 Zhaochuan Shaanxi China 33.11N 111.43E
21 C4 Zhaodong Heilongjiang China 46.03N 125.58E
Zhaoge see Qi Xian
21 D3 Zhaoguang Heilongjiang China 48.08N 126.49E
23 C4 Zhaojue Sichuan China 28.02N 102.49E
23 E6 Zhaoping Guangxi China 24.06N 110.42E
23 F7 Zhaoqing Guangdong China 23.04N 112.25E
24 D4 Zhaosu Xinjiang Uygur Zizhiqu China 43.07N 81.05E
23 C5 Zhaotong Yunnan China 27.20N 103.39E
22 K8 Zhao Xian Hebei China 37.49N 114.49E
21 E4 Zhaoxing Heilongjiang China 47.41N 131.21E
21 C5 Zhaoyuan Heilongjiang China 45.30N 125.05E
22 M8 Zhaoyuan Shandong China 37.21N 120.22E
Zhaozhen see Jintang
21 C5 Zhaozhou Heilongjiang China 45.42N 125.11E
25 L2 Zhapo Guangdong China 21.33N 111.55E
23 J3 Zhapu Zhejiang China 30.37N 121.05E
43 O4 Zharbulak Kazakhstan U.S.S.R. 46.04N 82.05E
46 H2 Zhari U.S.S.R. 56.37N 30.20E
24 E10 Zhari Namco L Xizang Zizhiqu China 31.00N 85.30E
43 D3 Zharkamys Kazakhstan U.S.S.R. 47.58N 56.30E
42 D3 Zharkova U.S.S.R. 58.02N 87.20E
45 D1 Zharkovskiy U.S.S.R. 55.51N 32.16E
43 N3 Zharlykamys Kazakhstan U.S.S.R. 49.37N 78.45E
43 O3 Zharma Kazakhstan U.S.S.R. 48.50N 80.50E
44 L3 Zharmysh Kazakhstan U.S.S.R. 44.12N 52.28E
43 L3 Zharyk Kazakhstan U.S.S.R. 48.53N 72.55E
46 H5 Zhashkov Ukraine U.S.S.R. 49.12N 30.05E
22 H10 Zhashui Shaanxi China 33.41N 109.04E
23 E2 Zhashui Shaanxi China 33.41N 109.04E
41 N9 Zhatay U.S.S.R. 62.12N 129.55E
Zhaxi see Weixin
24 E9 Zhaxi Co L Xizang Zizhiqu China 32.10N 85.00E
24 C9 Zhaxigang Xizang Zizhiqu China 32.31N 79.33E
24 F11 Zhaxilhünbo Xizang Zizhiqu China 29.12N 88.50E
23 A3 Zhaxizê Xizang Zizhiqu China 30.02N 96.44E
24 J10 Zhaxizê Xizang Zizhiqu China 30.02N 96.44E
42 E5 Zhayma U.S.S.R. 54.53N 93.32E
43 K3 Zhayrem Kazakhstan U.S.S.R. 48.16N 70.14E
46 M2 Zhaysk U.S.S.R. 55.52N 42.22E
44 M5 Zhazgurly,Vpadina depression Kazakhstan U.S.S.R.
41 H5 Zhdanikha U.S.S.R. 72.12N 103.00E
45 J9 Zhdanov Ukraine U.S.S.R. 47.05N 37.34E
44 H8 Zhdanovsk Azerbaydzhan U.S.S.R. 39.46N 47.36E
42 H2 Zhdanovskiy, Porog falls U.S.S.R. 60.18N 107.55E
46 E7 Zhdanoy dist Moscow U.S.S.R.
45 E6 Zhdany Ukraine U.S.S.R. 50.12N 33.14E
82 M5 Zhebriyany U.S.S.R. 45.30N 29.35E
23 G1 Zhecheng Henan China 34.06N 115.30E
23 B3 Zheduo Shan mt ra Sichuan China
23 B3 Zheduo Shankou pass Sichuan China 30.04N 101.50E
23 A6 Zhefang Yunnan China 24.11N 98.50E
45 P2 Zhegalovo U.S.S.R. 54.44N 43.25E
23 H4 Zhejiang prov China
43 M3 Zhekezhal Kazakhstan U.S.S.R. 48.50N 75.08E
43 J3 Zhel'dyadyr Kazakhstan U.S.S.R. 49.25N 67.35E
43 M1 Zhelezinka Kazakhstan U.S.S.R. 53.36N 75.19E
42 G5 Zheleznodorozhnyy U.S.S.R. 57.55N 102.46E
47 G4 Zheleznodorozhnyy U.S.S.R. 62.39N 50.59E
47 J2 Zheleznodorozhnyy U.S.S.R. 67.59N 64.47E
62 N1 Zheleznodorozhnyy U.S.S.R. 54.23N 21.20E
42 G4 Zheleznogorsk U.S.S.R. 56.30N 104.10E
45 G4 Zheleznogorsk U.S.S.R. 52.20N 35.26E
44 E3 Zheleznovodsk U.S.S.R. 44.08N 43.02E
45 P1 Zhelnino U.S.S.R. 56.13N 43.20E
46 G4 Zhelon' R Belorussiya/Ukraine U.S.S.R.
Zhelou see Ceheng
40 H8 Zheltaya U.S.S.R. 47.20N 138.50E
Zheltaya-Reka see Zheltyye Vody
39 E7 Zheltovskaya Sopka vol Kamchatka U.S.S.R. 51.35N 157.19E
45 E8 Zheltoye Ukraine U.S.S.R. 48.28N 33.33E
45 E8 Zheltyye Vody Ukraine U.S.S.R. 48.21N 33.31E
23 E2 Zhen'an Shaanxi China 33.20N 109.05E
23 A6 Zhen'an Yunnan China 24.42N 98.45E
23 D2 Zhenba Shaanxi China 32.40N 107.55E
23 D6 Zhenfeng Guizhou China 25.15N 105.45E
23 D4 Zheng'an Guizhou China 28.25N 107.35E
22 K7 Zhengding Hebei China 38.10N 114.30E
23 H5 Zhenghe Fujian China 27.24N 118.49E
Zhengjiakou see Gucheng
Zhengjiatun see Shuangliao
23 F4 Zhengjiayi Hunan China 28.46N 111.14E
23 E1 Zhengning Shaanxi China 35.25N 108.19E
22 K5 Zhengxiangbai (Xulun Hobot Qagan) Qi Nei Monggol Zizhiqu China 42.24N 115.02E
23 G2 Zhengyang Henan China 32.38N 114.28E
23 G2 Zhengyangguang Anhui China 32.30N 116.35E
23 F1 Zhengzhou Henan China 34.45N 113.38E
23 H6 Zhenhai Fujian China 24.18N 118.06E
23 J4 Zhenhai Zhejiang China 29.56N 121.40E
23 H2 Zhenjiang Jiangsu China 32.08N 119.30E
23 B7 Zhenkang Yunnan China 23.58N 99.00E
21 C5 Zhenlai Jilin China 45.51N 123.12E
22 K5 Zhenlan (Xulun Hoh) Qi Nei Monggol Zizhiqu China 42.15N 116.10E
23 E7 Zhenlong Guangdong China 22.35N 108.41E
23 D5 Zhenning Bouyeizu Miaozu Zizhixian Guizhou China 26.05N 105.45E
23 F2 Zhenping Henan China 33.05N 112.20E
23 E3 Zhenping Shaanxi China 31.59N 109.33E
23 G2 Zhentou He R Henan China
Zhenwudong see Ansai
22 J8 Zhenwu Shan mt Shanxi China 37.47N 111.22E
21 B5 Zhenxi Jilin China 45.50N 122.23E
21 C4 Zhenxiang Heilongjiang China 47.00N 125.44E
23 C5 Zhenxiong Yunnan China 27.30N 104.44E
23 D1 Zhenyuan Gansu China 35.44N 107.41E
23 E5 Zhenyuan Guizhou China 27.05N 108.16E
23 B7 Zhenyuan Yunnan China 23.54N 101.05E
23 E3 Zhenziling Hubei China 31.29N 110.59E
39 F7 Zhepanova,Sopka vol Kamchatka U.S.S.R. 53.35N 159.09E
45 N5 Zherdevka U.S.S.R. 51.51N 41.29E
45 H3 Zherdevo U.S.S.R. 53.06N 36.54E
46 H4 Zherdnoye Belorussiya U.S.S.R. 51.40N 30.11E
40 H6 Zherebtsovo U.S.S.R. 51.15N 138.45E
45 G4 Zhernovets U.S.S.R. 52.32N 35.45E
47 F5 Zheshart U.S.S.R. 62.06N 49.31E
45 V5 Zhestyanka U.S.S.R. 51.36N 49.23E
23 C6 Zhetai Yunnan China 24.18N 104.47E
43 B5 Zhetybay Kazakhstan U.S.S.R. 43.35N 52.05E
45 U8 Zhetybay Kazakhstan U.S.S.R. 48.55N 48.05E
43 F2 Zhety-Kol',Oz L U.S.S.R. 51.00N 60.53E
43 J6 Zhetysay Kazakhstan U.S.S.R. 40.46N 68.17E
23 F3 Zhicheng Hubei China 30.19N 111.30E
23 C7 Zhicun Yunnan China 23.20N 103.33E
46 E5 Zhidachov Ukraine U.S.S.R. 49.20N 24.22E
22 H8 Zhidan Shaanxi China 37.00N 108.42E
23 A2 Zhidoi Qinghai China 32.54N 95.40E
24 H9 Zhidoi Qinghai China 33.54N 95.40E
Zhifang see Wuchang
44 K3 Zhigalgan Kazakhstan U.S.S.R. 44.37N 50.49E
42 H5 Zhigalovo U.S.S.R. 54.48N 105.10E
41 M7 Zhigansk U.S.S.R. 66.48N 123.27E
43 J3 Zhigerli Kazakhstan U.S.S.R. 48.15N 67.57E
25 L2 Zhigong Guangdong China 21.44N 111.34E
45 V3 Zhigulevsk U.S.S.R. 53.26N 49.30E
45 V3 Zhiguli hills U.S.S.R.
24 G10 Zhigung Xizang Zizhiqu China 30.00N 91.47E
23 F3 Zhijiang Hubei China 30.26N 111.45E
23 E5 Zhijiang Hunan China 27.27N 109.39E
23 D5 Zhijin Guizhou China 26.45N 105.50E
45 H7 Zhikhar' Ukraine U.S.S.R. 49.55N 36.15E
23 D8 Zhilang Guangxi China 21.50N 107.07E
43 C4 Zhilaya Kosa Kazakhstan U.S.S.R. 46.49N 53.10E
45 K2 Zhilevo U.S.S.R. 54.58N 38.02E
45 L7 Zhilino U.S.S.R. 49.53N 39.25E
39 F5 Zhilovaya R U.S.S.R.
44 K7 Zhiloy isld Azerbaydzhan U.S.S.R. 40.20N 50.35E
42 H6 Zhipkhegen U.S.S.R. 51.30N 110.10E
Zhi Qu R see Tongtian He
39 F1 Zhirkova U.S.S.R. 67.35N 155.45E
45 Q6 Zhirnovsk U.S.S.R. 51.00N 44.47E
Zhirnovskiy see Zhirnovsk
45 E3 Zhiryatino U.S.S.R. 53.14N 33.45E
23 H4 Zhitan Jiangxi China 29.28N 117.11E
46 G4 Zhitkovichi Belorussiya U.S.S.R. 52.12N 27.49E
45 S8 Zhitkur U.S.S.R. 48.56N 46.16E
46 G4 Zhitomir Ukraine U.S.S.R. 50.18N 28.40E
46 G4 Zhitomirskaya Oblast' prov Ukraine U.S.S.R.
32 B3 Zhīvār Iran 35.15N 46.22E
43 K5 Zhiyembet Kazakhstan U.S.S.R. 43.32N 71.15E
45 F3 Zhizdra U.S.S.R. 53.45N 34.45E
45 G2 Zhizdra R U.S.S.R.
47 D3 Zhizhgin, Ostrov isld U.S.S.R. 65.11N 36.50E
Zhiziluo see Bijiang
46 H3 Zhlobin Belorussiya U.S.S.R. 52.50N 30.00E
46 G5 Zhmerinka Ukraine U.S.S.R. 49.00N 28.02E
31 E5 Zhob dist Pakistan
31 E5 Zhob R Pakistan
41 S3 Zhokhova,Ostrov isld U.S.S.R. 76.06N 152.38E
82 H1 Zholkva Ukraine U.S.S.R. 50.05N 23.56E
43 K2 Zholymbet Kazakhstan U.S.S.R. 51.46N 71.44E
Zhongba see Jiangyou
24 E11 Zhongba Xizang Zizhiqu China 29.40N 84.07E
23 B5 Zhongdian Yunnan China 27.46N 99.45E
23 D7 Zhongdong Guangxi China 22.48N 107.50E
23 E6 Zhongdu Guangxi China 24.40N 109.30E
21 C4 Zhonghe Heilongjiang China 46.49N 125.41E
23 C3 Zhongjiang Sichuan China 31.08N 104.23E
23 G1 Zhongmou Henan China 34.44N 114.01E
22 G8 Zhongning Ningxia China 37.26N 105.40E
23 F7 Zhongshan Guangdong China 22.30N 113.20E
23 F6 Zhongshan Guangxi China 24.31N 111.10E
Zhongsha Qundao see Macclesfield Bank
Zhongshu see Renhuai
23 F1 Zhongtiao Shan mts Shanxi China
22 G8 Zhongwei Ningxia China 37.31N 105.13E
23 E3 Zhong Xian Sichuan China 30.20N 108.00E
23 F3 Zhongxiang Hubei China 31.11N 112.40E
23 G6 Zhongxin Guangdong China 24.13N 114.40E
Zhongxing see Siyang
22 J8 Zhongyang Shanxi China 37.12N 111.14E
21 C2 Zhongyaozhan Heilongjiang China 50.47N 125.50E
25 L3 Zhongyuan Guangdong China 19.08N 110.30E
23 C2 Zhongzhai Gansu China 33.09N 104.31E
65 N3 Zhoř Czechoslovakia 49.27N 15.47E
43 M2 Zhosaly Kazakhstan U.S.S.R. 50.36N 76.07E
22 L8 Zhoucun Shandong China 36.51N 117.51E
23 F4 Zhoujiadian Hunan China 29.15N 111.55E
22 F7 Zhoujiajing Gansu China 38.55N 102.27E
Zhoujiaping see Nanzheng
23 G2 Zhoukouzhen Henan China 33.40N 115.00E
23 H5 Zhouning Fujian 27.12N 119.08E
23 J3 Zhoushan B Zhejiang China
23 J3 Zhoushan Qundao islds Zhejiang China
23 E1 Zhouzhi Shaanxi China 34.12N 108.11E
45 D7 Zhovnino Ukraine U.S.S.R. 49.22N 32.33E
46 E5 Zhovten' Ukraine U.S.S.R. 49.03N 24.44E
46 H6 Zhovten' Ukraine U.S.S.R. 47.12N 30.19E
45 F7 Zhovtnevoye Ukraine U.S.S.R. 49.38N 34.13E
46 H6 Zhovtnevoye Ukraine U.S.S.R. 46.50N 32.00E
21 F3 Zhuaji Heilongjiang China 48.14N 134.34E
21 C8 Zhuanghe Liaoning China 39.30N 123.01E
22 F8 Zhuanglang He R Gansu China
23 A2 Zhubgyügoin Qinghai China 33.27N 96.36E
24 J9 Zhubgyügoin Qinghai China 33.25N 97.17E
23 D5 Zhucang Guizhou China 27.22N 107.25E
23 H1 Zhucheng Shandong China 36.01N 119.28E
23 C2 Zhugqa Gansu China 33.40N 102.15E
23 C2 Zhugqu Gansu China 33.39N 104.12E
23 F7 Zhuhai Guangdong China 22.17N 113.30E
Zhuizishan see Weichang
Zhuji see Shangqiu
23 J4 Zhuji Zhejiang China 29.43N 120.12E
23 J4 Zhujia Jian isld Zhejiang China 29.55N 122.25E
23 G8 Zhujiang Kou inlet Guangdong China
Zhujing see Jinshan
47 J8 Zhukovka Kazakhstan U.S.S.R. 53.30N 63.50E
45 E3 Zhukovka U.S.S.R. 53.32N 33.45E
45 O9 Zhukovskaya U.S.S.R. 47.39N 42.30E
45 K1 Zhukovskiy U.S.S.R. 55.34N 38.10E
22 K7 Zhulong He R Hebei China
22 L6 Zhuluke Liaoning China 41.40N 119.44E
23 G2 Zhumadian Henan China 32.59N 114.01E
22 K6 Zhuolu Hebei China 40.19N 115.05E
22 K7 Zhuo Xian Hebei China 39.30N 116.00E
22 J6 Zhuozi Nei Monggol Zizhiqu China 40.54N 112.36E
22 G7 Zhuozi Shan mt Nei Monggol Zizhiqu China
39 F7 Zhupanova R U.S.S.R.
39 F7 Zhupanovo U.S.S.R. 53.40N 159.52E
39 F7 Zhupanovskiy U.S.S.R. 54.04N 159.58E
22 M8 Zhuqiao Shandong China 37.21N 120.02E
45 B3 Zhuravichi Belorussiya U.S.S.R. 53.14N 30.33E
45 M6 Zhuravka U.S.S.R. 50.03N 40.36E
40 J7 Zhuravleva mt Sakhalin U.S.S.R. 49.20N 142.45E
43 J2 Zhuravlevka Kazakhstan U.S.S.R. 52.00N 69.59E
47 L6 Zhuravlevka Omsk U.S.S.R. 57.30N 72.46E
44 D1 Zhuravlevka Rostov U.S.S.R. 46.51N 41.06E
40 D4 Zhurban U.S.S.R. 54.13N 127.59E
43 L5 Zhusandala,Step' Kazakhstan U.S.S.R.
23 E2 Zhushan Hubei China 32.15N 110.15E
23 G1 Zhushui He R Shandong China
23 F5 Zhuting Hunan China 27.24N 113.00E
22 F7 Zhuwangpu Gansu China 38.13N 102.40E
23 E2 Zhuxi Hubei China 32.18N 109.50E
42 K3 Zhuya R U.S.S.R.
23 E1 Zhuyangzhen Henan China 34.18N 110.42E
23 D2 Zhuyu Sichuan China 32.12N 107.38E
23 C6 Zhuyuan Yunnan China 24.05N 103.25E
43 N4 Zhuzagashskiy Kazakhstan U.S.S.R. 46.53N 79.32E
23 F5 Zhuzhou Hunan China 27.43N 113.10E
23 F5 Zhuzhou Hunan China 27.53N 113.07E
32 C3 Ziā'ābād Iran 36.00N 49.36E
79 L2 Ziano Italy 46.18N 11.35E
32 D2 Ziārān Iran 36.07N 50.30E
31 B4 Ziarat Afghanistan 33.15N 62.58E
32 G2 Ziarat Iran 37.29N 57.46E
31 D5 Ziarat Pakistan 30.25N 67.49E
31 C5 Ziarat Shah Maqsud Afghanistan 31.57N 65.27E
82 E2 Žiar-nad-Hronom Czechoslovakia 48.36N 18.52E
Zib see Tel Akhziv anc site
93 E10 Ziba Tanzania 4.15S 33.24E
34 F8 Zibā salt L Saudi Arabia
88 R4 Zibane reg Algeria
37 H9 Zibār Iraq 36.52N 44.04E
79 H4 Zibello Italy 45.01N 10.08E
22 L8 Zibo Shandong China 36.51N 118.01E
76 B10 Zibreira Ribatejo Portugal 39.29N 8.37W
67 P13 Zicavo Corsica 41.54N 9.07E
22 H8 Zichang Shaanxi China 37.14N 109.30E
61 K3 Zichem Belgium 51.00N 4.59E
61 N3 Zichen-Zussen-Bolder Belgium 50.47N 5.37E
64 Q5 Zichovice Czechoslovakia 49.16N 13.39E
22 L8 Zichuan Shandong China 36.41N 117.51E
115 J8 Zicuirán Mexico 18.50N 101.49W
82 C4 Zidani Most Yugoslavia 46.05N 15.11E
82 L8 Zidarovo Bulgaria 42.20N 27.24E
43 J7 Ziddi Tadzhikistan U.S.S.R. 39.04N 68.22E
63 R5 Ziddorf E Germany 53.42N 12.32E
31 D7 Zidi Pakistan 27.41N 66.50E
31 F3 Zidig Pass Afghan/Pakistan 35.54N 71.06E
45 H7 Zid'ki Ukraine U.S.S.R. 49.40N 36.23E
65 P3 Židlochovice Czechoslovakia 49.02N 16.37E
64 Q3 Zidovice Czechoslovakia 50.29N 13.41E
62 K5 Ziębice Poland 50.37N 17.01E
66 N3 Ziegelbrücke Switzerland 47.08N 9.04E
63 P6 Ziegendorf E Germany 53.19N 11.50E
64 G2 Ziegenhain W Germany 50.55N 9.14E
64 M2 Ziegenrück E Germany 50.36N 11.39E
103 D6 Zieglerville Pennsylvania 40.17N 75.29W
13 B6 Ziel,Mt N Terr Australia 23.30S 132.24E
62 J4 Zielona Góra Poland 51.57N 15.30E
63 K10 Zierenberg W Germany 51.22N 9.16E
60 C2 Zierikzee Netherlands 51.39N 3.55E
65 N4 Ziersdorf Austria 48.33N 15.56E
63 Q8 Ziesar E Germany 52.16N 12.18E
60 P11 Zieuwent Netherlands 52.00N 6.31E
86 F5 Zifeitet Mashtûl Egypt 30.20N 31.21E
Zifreh see Zefreh
86 F4 Zifta Egypt 30.43N 31.14E
25 B2 Zigaing Burma 20.02N 93.31E
43 D1 Zigazinskiy Bashkir U.S.S.R. 53.51N 57.17E
85 F7 Zighan oasis Libya
88 R3 Zighout Youcef Algeria 36.35N 6.45E
25 C3 Zigon Burma 18.20N 95.35E
23 C4 Zigong Sichuan China 29.25N 104.47E
92 H4 Zigua tribe Tanzania
95 L8 Zigudu S Africa 32.11S 27.31E
90 G4 Ziguey Chad 14.40N 15.45E
23 E3 Zigui Hubei China 31.00N 110.42E
89 A5 Ziguinchor Senegal 12.35N 16.20W
46 G2 Zigure Latvia U.S.S.R. 57.20N 27.40E
23 B4 Zihag Sichuan China 29.26N 101.09E
22 L8 Zi He R Shandong China
64 P3 Zihle Czechoslovakia 50.03N 13.23E
66 E3 Zihl Kanal Switzerland
66 O1 Zihlschlacht Switzerland 47.31N 9.16E
86 N5 Zihor watercourse Israel
115 J9 Zihuatanejo Mexico 17.39N 101.33W
60 J12 Zijderveld Netherlands 51.57N 5.08E
23 G7 Zijin Guangdong China 23.36N 115.14E
22 K7 Zijingguan Hebei China 39.25N 115.20E
60 E13 Zijpe Netherlands 51.39N 4.06E
35 C3 Zikhron Ya'aqov Israel 32.34N 34.57E
89 G8 Zikisso Ivory Coast 6.01N 5.39W
34 E6 Zilāf Syria 32.55N 37.20E
43 D2 Zilair Bashkir U.S.S.R. 52.15N 57.30E
37 G6 Zilan R Turkey
36 H2 Zile Turkey 40.18N 35.52E
33 F3 Zilfī,Az Saudi Arabia 26.15N 44.50E
47 H8 Zilim R U.S.S.R.
62 L6 Zilina Czechoslovakia 49.14N 18.40E
85 D5 Zillah Libya 28.30N 17.33E
61 B3 Zillebeke Belgium 50.50N 2.55E
65 E7 Zillertal V Austria
65 E7 Zillertaler Alpen mts Austria
66 O5 Zillis Switzerland 46.38N 9.27E
66 F1 Zillisheim France 47.42N 7.17E
13 K1 Zillmere dist Brisbane, Qnsld
87 E7 Zilmamo Ethiopia 6.01N 35.10E
87 J2 Zilme Yemen 16.24N 43.54E
46 G2 Zilupe Latvia U.S.S.R. 56.26N 28.04E
42 G5 Zima U.S.S.R. 53.58N 102.02E
85 C5 Zimām watercourse Libya
115 K7 Zimapan Mexico 20.54N 99.23W
115 L9 Zimatlán Mexico 16.52N 96.45W
92 E5 Zimba Tanzania 7.52S 31.50E
92 C10 Zimba Zambia 17.20S 26.11E
92 E12 Zimbabwe ruins Zimbabwe 20.16S 30.54E
Zimbabwe-Rhodesia see Zimbabwe
91 K8 Zimbambo, L Zaïre 8.09S 26.51E
32 B3 Zimkan R Iran
88 M9 Zimla Algeria 25.01N 3.15W
108 R4 Zimmerman Minnesota 45.29N 93.36W
64 G1 Zimmersrode W Germany 51.02N 9.15E
89 D8 Zimmi Sierra Leone 7.20N 11.20w
82 J7 Zimnicea Romania 43.39N 25.21E
82 K8 Zimnitsa Bulgaria 42.35N 26.35E
45 F3 Zimnitsy U.S.S.R. 54.00N 34.50E
47 E3 Zimniy Bereg coast U.S.S.R.
42 B3 Zimniye-Kiyevskiye U.S.S.R. 59.50N 79.00E
45 P7 Zimnyatskiy U.S.S.R. 49.44N 43.08E
45 O9 Zimovniki U.S.S.R. 47.09N 42.29E
42 D3 Zimovskoye U.S.S.R. 57.32N 86.53E
92 E11 Zimutu Zimbabwe 19.50S 30.50E
31 E6 Zin Pakistan 29.00N 69.17E
35 C10 Zin watercourse Israel
90 G6 Zina Cameroon 11.19N 14.54E
66 G7 Zinal Switzerland 46.08N 7.38E
66 G7 Zinalrothorn mt Switzerland 46.04N 7.42E
115 J8 Zinapécuaro Mexico 19.50N 100.50W
79 E4 Zinasco Italy 45.07N 9.00E
77 F10 Zinat Morocco 35.29N 5.25W
31 A3 Zindajan Afghanistan 34.19N 61.43E
31 F5 Zindawar Pakistan 31.37N 70.06E
90 D5 Zinder Niger 13.46N 8.58E
90 J10 Zinga Cent Afr Rep 3.49N 18.34E
92 J6 Zinga Tanzania 9.12S 38.49E
91 D6 Zinga Zaïre 4.51S 14.48E
61 E3 Zingem Belgium 50.54N 3.39E
63 R4 Zingst E Germany 54.27N 12.40E
63 R4 Zingst pen E Germany
94 M4 Zinhane Mozambique 22.20S 33.04E
23 G4 Zin Jiang R Jiangxi China
33 F10 Zinjibār S Yemen 13.06N 45.23E
65 L7 Zinken mt Austria 47.21N 14.45E
65 H6 Zinken,Hoher mt Austria 47.40N 13.22E
64 Q5 Zinkovy Czechoslovakia 49.29N 13.30E
60 E7 Zinna Nigeria 9.02N 11.42E
63 T4 Zinnowitz E Germany 54.05N 13.55E
Zinoviyevsk see Kirovograd
89 E7 Zinta Guinea 8.02N 9.30W
85 B4 Zintan Libya 31.55N 12.15E
92 E3 Zinza tribe Tanzania
106 G7 Zion Illinois 42.25N 87.50W
116 P4 Zion Nevis I W I 17.08N 62.32W
111 M4 Zion Canyon gorge Utah
103 B5 Zion Grove Pennsylvania 40.54N 76.13W
111 M4 Zion Nat.Park Utah 37.20N 112.57W
106 H10 Zionsville Indiana 39.57N 86.15W
119 D5 Zipaquirá Colombia 5.03N 74.01W
63 O5 Zippendorf E Germany 53.37N 11.28E
35 E3 Zippori Israel 32.45N 35.17E
35 E2 Zippori anc site Israel 35.45N 35.16E
35 D2 Zippori watercourse Israel
35 B7 Ziqim Israel 31.37N 34.31E
35 F3 Ziqlab R Jordan
24 I9 Zi Qu R Qinghai China
23 A2 Zi Qu R Sichuan China
24 H9 Ziqudukou Qinghai China 33.03N 95.51E
36 F3 Zir Turkey 39.58N 32.30E
Zirab see Istgāh-e Zirab
88 Q6 Zirara watercourse Algeria
86 E7 Zirbi,El Egypt 29.26N 30.56E
65 L7 Zirbitz Kogel mt Austria 47.04N 14.34E
46 S3 Zirgan U.S.S.R. 53.10N 55.50E
89 D1 Ziri Mauritania 21.32N 10.50W
84 E5 Zirikia Greece 38.22N 22.50E
80 N1 Žirje Yugoslavia 43.40N 15.40E
82 C7 Zirje isld Yugoslavia 43.40N 15.40E
109 D1 Zirkel,Mt Colorado 40.50N 106.38W
33 K4 Zirkūh isld The Gulf 24.55N 53.06E
65 D7 Zirl Austria 47.17N 11.16E
64 K5 Zirndorf W Germany 49.27N 10.58E
93 D5 Zirobwe Uganda 0.41N 32.42E
84 O11 Zíros Crete 35.05N 26.08E
82 F9 Žirovnica Yugoslavia 41.40N 20.37E
65 M3 Žirovnice Czechoslovakia 49.16N 15.12E
32 D6 Zīr Rūd Iran 28.06N 51.24E
23 C3 Zishi Sichuan China 30.05N 102.38E
23 F4 Zi Shui R Hunan China
65 P4 Zistersdorf Austria 48.32N 16.45E
115 J8 Zitácuaro Mexico 19.28N 100.21W
117 E7 Zitiua,R Brazil
23 D3 Zitong Sichuan China 31.37N 105.10E
83 D5 Zítsa Greece 39.44N 20.37E
62 H5 Zittau E Germany 50.55N 14.50E
65 A7 Zitterklapfen mt Austria 47.17N 9.59E
113 M4 Zitziana R Alaska
36 F4 Zivarık Turkey 38.19N 32.52E
32 A2 Zīveh Iran 37.13N 44.56E
65 K2 Živohošt Czechoslovakia 49.46N 14.26E
35 G1 Ziwan Syria 33.05N 35.48E
93 J9 Ziwani Kenya 3.23S 37.48E
92 K7 Ziwani Tanzania 10.22S 40.19E
23 H5 Zixi Jiangxi China 27.45N 117.08E
23 F6 Zixing Hunan China 25.57N 113.20E
22 K7 Ziya He R Hebei China
43 D2 Ziyanchurino U.S.S.R. 51.32N 56.52E
23 E2 Ziyang Shaanxi China 32.33N 108.32E
23 C3 Ziyang Sichuan China 30.06N 104.36E
37 F7 Ziyaret Turkey 38.54N 41.17E
23 E5 Ziyuan Guangxi China 26.02N 110.40E
23 D6 Ziyun Guizhou China 25.44N 106.12E
23 H6 Ziyundong Shan mt Fujian China
88 L6 Ziz R Morocco
65 M1 Žiželive Czechoslovakia 50.08N 15.24E
66 P4 Zizers Switzerland 46.57N 9.34E
23 C4 Zizhong Sichuan China 29.46N 104.52E
22 H8 Zizhou Shaanxi China 37.39N 109.46E
91 J1 Zizunga Zaïre 4.41N 25.11E
75 G2 Zizur Spain 42.47N 1.41W
15 D5 Z Keten mts Irian Jaya
80 N1 Zlarin Yugoslavia 43.42N 15.51E
65 K4 Zlatá Koruna Czechoslovakia 48.52N 14.23E
82 K7 Zlataritsa Bulgaria 43.02N 25.55E
62 L7 Zlaté Moravce Czechoslovakia 48.24N 18.20E
82 F7 Zlatibor mts Yugoslavia
82 J8 Zlatitsa Bulgaria 42.41N 24.07E
82 H4 Zlatna Romania 46.08N 23.11E
82 J9 Zlatograd Bulgaria 41.22N 25.07E
45 C8 Zlatopol' Ukraine U.S.S.R. 48.49N 31.39E
47 L5 Zlatoust U.S.S.R. 55.10N 59.38E
40 F5 Zlatoustovsk U.S.S.R. 52.58N 133.35E
44 C1 Zl'buzd R U.S.S.R.
32 K1 Zl'dzhik U.S.S.R. 39.24N 63.00E
65 M2 Žleby Czechoslovakia 49.54N 15.30E
82 G9 Zletovo Yugoslavia 41.59N 22.15E
89 C2 Zli Mauritania 19.29N 12.47W
85 C3 Zlitan Libya 32.32N 14.37E
62 J2 Złocieniec Poland 53.31N 16.01E
62 L4 Złoczew Poland 51.24N 18.33E
47 L5 Zlokazovo U.S.S.R. 55.28N 59.28E
62 H5 Zloniee Czechoslovakia 50.18N 14.04E
82 G6 Zlot Yugoslavia 44.01N 21.59E
62 J4 Złotoryja Poland 51.08N 15.57E
62 K2 Złotów Poland 53.22N 17.01E
64 P3 Žlutice Czechoslovakia 50.05N 13.09E
45 G3 Zlyn' U.S.S.R. 53.17N 35.56E
45 C8 Zlynka Ukraine U.S.S.R. 48.27N 31.32E
45 C4 Zlynka U.S.S.R. 52.24N 31.45E
42 C6 Zmeinogorsk U.S.S.R. 51.11N 82.14E
46 H6 Zmeinyy, Ostrov isld Black Sea 45.15N 30.14E
46 H6 Zmeinyy, Ozero L U.S.S.R. 45.23N 30.06E
45 S5 Zmeyevy Gory hills U.S.S.R.
44 F4 Zmeyskaya U.S.S.R. 43.21N 44.11E
62 K4 Żmigród Poland 51.29N 16.53E
45 H4 Zmiyevka U.S.S.R. 52.40N 36.22E
42 D5 Znamenityy U.S.S.R. 54.30N 89.09E
42 B5 Znamenka Altay U.S.S.R. 53.10N 79.29E
42 G5 Znamenka Irkutsk U.S.S.R. 54.40N 104.42E
43 N2 Znamenka Kazakhstan U.S.S.R. 50.07N 79.32E
42 E5 Znamenka Khakass U.S.S.R. 54.20N 91.08E
45 F2 Znamenka Smolensk U.S.S.R. 54.53N 34.34E
45 N4 Znamenka Tambov U.S.S.R. 52.25N 41.30E
45 D8 Znamenka Oktyabr'skoye Ukraine U.S.S.R. 48.42N 32.40E
45 D8 Znamenka Vtoraya Ukraine U.S.S.R. 48.41N 32.36E
45 G8 Znamenkova Ukraine U.S.S.R. 48.36N 35.28E
62 N1 Znamensk U.S.S.R. 54.37N 21.13E
43 O4 Znamenskoye Kazakhstan U.S.S.R. 47.27N 80.51E
45 L3 Znamenskoye Lipetsk U.S.S.R. 53.18N 39.25E
47 L7 Znamenskoye Omsk U.S.S.R. 57.10N 73.50E
45 G3 Znamenskoye Orël U.S.S.R. 53.16N 35.41E
44 F5 Znauri Georgia U.S.S.R. 42.11N 43.46E
62 K3 Żnin Poland 52.51N 17.41E
45 E4 Znob'-Novgorodskoye Ukraine U.S.S.R. 52.16N 33.38E
65 O4 Znojmo Czechoslovakia 48.52N 16.04E
79 F6 Zoagli Italy 44.20N 9.16E
95 E9 Zoar S Africa 33.30S 21.26E
103 H4 Zoar L Connecticut 41.25N 73.12W
32 B3 Zobeyrī Iran 34.31N 46.43E
91 J2 Zobia Zaïre 2.57N 25.59E
65 B6 Zoblen Austria 47.32N 10.30E
64 P2 Zöblitz E Germany 50.40N 13.15E
79 J6 Zocca Italy 44.21N 10.59E
24 C9 Zoco Xizang Zizhiqu China 32.18N 80.38E
44 G7 Zod Armenia U.S.S.R. 40.13N 45.51E
94 L4 Zoekmekaar S Africa 23.28S 29.56E
60 K12 Zoelen Netherlands 51.55N 5.24E
60 K12 Zoelmond Netherlands 51.56N 5.19E
61 K2 Zoerle-Parwijs Belgium 51.05N 4.52E
61 J1 Zoersel Belgium 51.16N 4.43E
91 B2 Zoétélé Cameroon 3.10N 11.57E
60 F11 Zoetermeer Netherlands 52.04N 4.30E
60 F11 Zoeterwoude-Rijndijk Netherlands 52.08N 4.30E
66 H2 Zofingen Switzerland 47.18N 7.57E
35 C5 Zofit Israel 32.12N 34.54E
Zogainrawar see Huashixia
23 A4 Zogang Xizang Zizhiqu China 29.42N 97.46E
89 L5 Zogirma Nigeria 12.17N 3.59E
79 G3 Zogno Italy 45.47N 9.40E
23 A2 Zogqên Sichuan China 32.19N 98.48E
32 A3 Zōhāb Iran 34.34N 45.54E
35 E9 Zohar watercourse Israel
65 P5 Zohor Czechoslovakia 48.21N 16.59E
Zohra see Zuhrah, Az
32 D5 Zohreh R Iran
89 D8 Zoi Liberia 7.40N 10.34W
23 C2 Zoigê Sichuan China 33.35N 102.55E
92 H4 Zoissa Tanzania 5.44S 36.24E
31 H3 Zoji La pass Kashmir 34.18N 75.31E
Zok see Garzan
93 C2 Zoka Forest Uganda
44 F9 Zola R Iran
61 M2 Zolder Belgium 51.01N 5.19E
79 M2 Zoldo Alto Italy 46.23N 12.08E
79 M2 Zoldo,Val di Italy
105 F10 Zolfo Springs Florida 27.29N 81.48W
64 E3 Zolhaus Rheinland-Pfalz W Germany 50.16N 8.03E
66 G4 Zollbrück Switzerland 46.59N 7.45E
64 F8 Zollhaus-B Baden-Württemberg W Germany 47.50N 8.34E
66 F4 Zollikofen Switzerland 47.00N 7.24E
66 L2 Zollikon Switzerland 47.21N 8.34E
81 R12 Zollino Italy 40.12N 18.15E
45 V3 Zol'noye U.S.S.R. 53.26N 49.45E
45 G6 Zolochev Khar'kov, Ukraine U.S.S.R. 50.18N 36.00E
46 E5 Zolochev L'vov, Ukraine U.S.S.R. 49.48N 24.51E
82 J1 Zolochev U.S.S.R. 49.49N 24.53E
45 R3 Zolotarevka U.S.S.R. 53.04N 45.19E
45 S7 Zolotari U.S.S.R. 49.46N 46.17E
40 D4 Zolotaya Gora U.S.S.R. 54.24N 126.43E
40 C3 Zolotinka U.S.S.R. 56.13N 125.46E
45 N1 Zolotkovo U.S.S.R. 55.30N 41.07E
39 G3 Zolotogorskaya U.S.S.R. 63.40N 160.52E
42 D5 Zolotogorskiy U.S.S.R. 54.41N 88.35E
45 D7 Zolotonosha Ukraine U.S.S.R. 49.39N 32.05E
43 K1 Zolotorunnoye Kazakhstan U.S.S.R. 53.36N 70.47E
45 T5 Zolotovka U.S.S.R. 51.52N 47.10E
39 C5 Zolotoy Khabarovsk U.S.S.R. 59.32N 143.30E
40 L9 Zolotoy Kuril Is U.S.S.R. 45.03N 147.32E
40 G1 Zolotoy U.S.S.R. 60.54N 137.40E
39 B4 Zolotoy Yakutsk U.S.S.R. 60.58N 137.50E
45 K8 Zolotoye Ukraine U.S.S.R. 48.42N 38.33E
45 R6 Zolotoye U.S.S.R. 50.48N 45.53E
39 K3 Zolotoy,Khrebet mts U.S.S.R.
40 H8 Zolotoy,Mys C U.S.S.R. 47.20N 138.55E
45 S9 Zolotukha U.S.S.R. 47.49N 46.46E
45 H4 Zolotukhino U.S.S.R. 52.04N 36.28E
75 J6 Zoma,La Spain 40.47N 0.38W
92 G9 Zomba Malawi 15.22S 35.22E
93 K7 Zombe Kenya 1.27S 38.15E
92 J5 Zombe Tanzania 7.50S 38.19E
93 A2 Zombi Zaïre 3.31N 29.11E
61 E2 Zomergem Belgium 51.07N 3.34E
35 C9 Zon watercourse Israel
56 T9 Zone Pt Cornwall Eng 50.08N 5.00W
Zongga see Gyirong (Zongga)
23 C3 Zonggag Sichuan China 10.220 31.45E
22 D8 Zongjiafangzi Qinghai China 36.18N 97.20E
91 F1 Zongo Zaïre 4.20N 18.35E
36 F1 Zonguldak Turkey 41.26N 31.47E
92 C4 Zongwe Zaïre 5.04S 27.55E
24 G11 Zongxoi Xizang Zizhiqu China 29.54N 91.16E
23 H3 Zongyang Anhui China 30.42N 117.12E
23 B4 Zongza Sichuan China 29.20N 99.17E
22 D7 Zongzhai Gansu China 39.37N 98.41E
61 M3 Zonhoven Belgium 50.59N 5.22E
84 D7 Zóni Greece 37.27N 22.07E
61 B3 Zonnebeke Belgium 50.52N 2.59E
60 C2 Zonnemaire Netherlands 51.43N 3.57E
84 Z20 Zonqor Pt Malta 35.52N 14.35E
64 B1 Zons W Germany 51.07N 6.51E
32 A1 Zonūz Iran 38.32N 45.54E
44 G9 Zonūz R Iran
67 P13 Zonza Corsica 41.46N 9.11E
90 F2 Zoo Baba Niger 18.13N 13.02E
79 N3 Zoppola Italy 45.58N 12.46E
44 J7 Zorat Azerbaydzhan U.S.S.R. 40.58N 49.14E
64 M1 Zorbau E Germany 51.18N 11.47E
63 Q9 Zörbig E Germany 51.38N 12.08E
35 F5 Zōr el Hanāhina Jordan 32.06N 35.31E
63 N9 Zorge W Germany 51.39N 10.38E
63 N10 Zörge R E Germany
89 J5 Zorgo Upper Volta 12.15N 0.37W
Zor Hauran see Zor Ḩawrān
34 H5 Zor Ḩawrān hill Iraq 33.22N 40.54E
76 H10 Zorita Cáceres Spain 39.18N 5.42W
75 E7 Zorita Guadalajara Spain 40.20N 2.54W
31 G2 Zorkul', Ozero L U.S.S.R./Afghan
82 L4 Zorleni Romania 46.14N 27.44E
69 O6 Zorn R France
64 M7 Zorneding W Germany 48.04N 11.50E
115 E9 Zorra, I Panama Canal Zone
119 B9 Zorritos Peru 3.43S 80.42W
110 R2 Zortman Montana 47.55N 108.33W
62 L5 Zory Poland 50.03N 18.40E
89 E8 Zorzor Liberia 7.46N 9.28W
63 Q10 Zöschen E Germany 51.22N 12.07E
63 S8 Zossen E Germany 52.13N 13.27E
45 O6 Zotovskaya U.S.S.R. 50.05N 42.25E
61 F3 Zottegem Belgium 50.52N 3.49E
90 H1 Zouar Chad 20.30N 16.30E
88 G10 Zouerate Mauritania 22.44N 12.21W
89 L6 Zougou Benin 10.42N 3.01E
91 D2 Zoulabot Cameroon 3.16N 14.02E
22 D7 Zoulang Nanshan mt ra Gansu China
90 K4 Zouma Chad 15.14N 20.38E
90 H1 Zoumagar reg Chad
74 D10 Zoumi Morocco 34.48N 5.23W
22 L8 Zouping Shandong China 36.55N 117.40E
22 J8 Zouquan Shanxi China 37.00N 113.29E
90 C2 Zourika Niger 19.16N 7.52E
90 H1 Zourke watercourse Chad
88 N6 Zousfana watercourse Algeria
60 A2 Zoutelande Netherlands 51.30N 3.30E
60 O6 Zoutkamp Netherlands 53.20N 6.18E
61 L3 Zoutleeuw Belgium 50.50N 5.06E
23 H1 Zou Xian Shandong China 35.25N 117.00E
23 E7 Zouxu Guangxi China 23.22N 108.53E
35 D6 Zova Israel 31.47N 35.07E
32 E4 Zovār Iran 33.32N 53.25E
Zowar see Zovār
89 D3 Zrafiét Mauritania 16.35N 10.59W
82 F5 Zrenjanin Yugoslavia 45.22N 10.23E
82 C5 Zrinska Gora mts Yugoslavia
82 C6 Zrmanja R Yugoslavia
82 C1 Zruč Czechoslovakia 49.45N 15.09E
65 M2 Zruč nad Sázava Czechoslovakia 49.45N 15.07E
62 N8 Zsáka Hungary 47.09N 21.26E
63 R9 Zschepplin E Germany 51.30N 12.36E
64 P2 Zschopau E Germany 50.45N 13.05E
64 O1 Zschopau R E Germany
64 O2 Zschorlau E Germany 50.33N 12.40E
31 F2 Zu Afghanistan 36.48N 71.07E
89 J6 Zuarungu Ghana 10.48N 0.46W
119 G3 Zuata Venezuela 8.24N 65.13W
119 G3 Zuata, R Venezuela
75 E2 Zuazo de Cuartango Spain 42.52N 2.53W
Zubair see Zubayr, Az
34 L9 Zubālah, Wādī watercourse Saudi Arabia
34 N6 Zubaydiyah, Az Iraq 32.46N 45.05E
34 P8 Zubayr, Az Iraq 30.24N 47.45E
Zubediya see Zubaydiyah, Az
85 M6 Zubeir, Gebel mt Egypt 27.25N 32.58E
105 E8 Zuber Florida 29.14N 82.11W
39 K3 Zubets, Gora mt U.S.S.R. 62.37N 176.21E
77 J6 Zubia Spain 37.07N 3.34W
75 G1 Zubieta Spain 43.06N 1.45W
Zubīrah, Az see Zabīrah, Az
75 G2 Zubiri Spain 42.55N 1.30W
35 G4 Zubiya Jordan 32.26N 35.45E
45 H3 Zubkovo U.S.S.R. 53.36N 36.10E
45 O2 Zubova Polyana U.S.S.R. 54.04N 42.52E
46 Q3 Zubovka U.S.S.R. 54.18N 51.01E
43 P3 Zubovskiy Kazakhstan U.S.S.R. 49.42N 83.50E
45 F1 Zubtsov U.S.S.R. 56.11N 34.33E
35 D3 Zububa Jordan 32.33N 35.13E
75 K7 Zucaina Spain 40.08N 0.26W
79 D6 Zuccarello Italy 44.07N 8.07E
66 L6 Zucchero, Mt Switzerland 46.22N 8.43E
64 L6 Zuchering W Germany 48.43N 11.25E
65 D8 Zuckerhütl mt Austria 46.58N 11.09E
101 U4 Zucker L N W Terr 62.59N 106.50W
75 F2 Zudaire Spain 42.46N 2.08W
120 F8 Zudañez Bolivia 19.05S 64.45W
63 S4 Zudar E Germany 54.16N 13.21E
89 F8 Zuénoula Ivory Coast 7.34N 6.03W
75 J4 Zuera Spain 41.52N 0.47W
75 J4 Zuera, Montes de Spain
Zuetina see Zuwaytīnah, Az
Zufāf isld see Dhā al Fayf I.
Zufār prov see Dhufar prov
77 D5 Zufre Spain 37.50N 6.20W
88 F11 Zug Mauritania 21.37N 14.10W
66 L3 Zug Switzerland 47.10N 8.31E
66 L3 Zug canton Switzerland
42 J4 Zugdeli U.S.S.R. 55.02N 111.10E
44 D5 Zugdidi Georgia U.S.S.R. 42.30N 41.52E
66 L3 Zuger Berg mt Switzerland 47.08N 8.32E
66 K3 Zuger See L Switzerland
33 F10 Zughaynah S Yemen 13.57N 45.58E
34 M4 Zughaytūn R Iraq
106 M3 Zug Island Detroit, Michigan
65 D7 Zugspitze mt W Germany 47.25N 11.00E
90 B7 Zugurma Nigeria 9.27N 4.52E
75 G1 Zugurramurdi Spain 43.16N 1.32W
34 C10 Zuhd, Jabal az mts Saudi Arabia
77 H5 Zúhéros Spain 37.33N 4.19W
Zuhrabad see Zūrābād
33 E9 Zuhrah, Az Yemen 15.41N 43.00E
Zuhreh R see Zohreh R
37 K3 Zühtüpaşa Turkey 40.59N 29.06E
60 Q8 Zuidbarge Netherlands 52.45N 6.55E
60 F13 Zuid Beijerland Netherlands 51.45N 4.22E
60 C3 Zuid Beveland isld Netherlands
60 D3 Zuid Beveland Kanaal canal Netherlands
60 Q7 Zuidbroek Netherlands 53.10N 6.52E
60 C4 Zuiddorpe Netherlands 51.14N 3.55E
60 K10 Zuidelijk-Flevoland polder Netherlands
Zuider Zee sea see IJsselmeer
60 G11 Zuid Holland prov Netherlands
60 O7 Zuidhorn Netherlands 53.15N 6.25E
60 P7 Zuidlaarder Meer L Netherlands
60 E12 Zuidland Netherlands 51.48N 4.15E
60 P7 Zuidlaren Netherlands 53.06N 6.41E
61 B3 Zuidschote Belgium 50.55N 2.50E
60 N8 Zuidveen Netherlands 52.47N 6.06E
60 Q7 Zuidwending Netherlands 53.06N 6.56E
60 L14 Zuid Willemsvaart Kanaal canal Netherlands
60 O9 Zuidwolde Drenthe Netherlands 52.40N 6.26E
60 P6 Zuidwolde Groningen Netherlands 53.16N 6.35E
60 A3 Zuidzande Netherlands 51.20N 3.27E
60 F13 Zuidzijde Netherlands 51.42N 4.15E
61 C1 Zuienkerke Belgium 51.16N 3.10E
60 J11 Zuilen Netherlands 52.07N 5.05E
60 J12 Zuilichem Netherlands 51.48N 5.07E
Zuitaizi see Kang Xian
Zuitouzhen see Taibai
77 L5 Zujar Spain 37.33N 2.50W
77 F3 Zújar R Spain
77 F3 Zújar, Embalse del res Spain
77 F3 Zújar, Est de Spain 38.35N 5.19W
33 K4 Zukum, Al oil field The Gulf 24.51N 53.42E
87 G6 Zukwala mt Ethiopia 8.32N 38.49E
87 G3 Zula Ethiopia 15.17N 39.40E
87 G3 Zula, G.of Ethiopia
31 A3 Zulfikar Pass Afghan/Iran 35.35N 61.15E
66 G4 Zulg R Switzerland
25 L8 Zulhami Nagaland India 25.50N 94.23E
119 D2 Zulia state Venezuela
119 D3 Zulia, R Colombia
22 F8 Zuli He R Gansu China
23 D1 Zuli He R Gansu China
37 E7 Zulkar R Turkey
64 B2 Zülpich W Germany 50.42N 6.39E
61 D3 Zulte Belgium 50.55N 3.27E
33 H2 Zuluf oil field The Gulf 28.18N 49.09E
95 O9 Zululand hist reg S Africa
35 F1 Zumaghah Syria 33.09N 35.48E
75 F1 Zumárraga Spain 43.05N 2.18W
75 F1 Zumaya Spain 43.18N 2.15W
119 B10 Zumba Ecuador 4.53S 79.10W
118 J8 Zumbi Brazil 22.50S 43.11W
92 E9 Zumbo Mozambique 15.36S 30.30E
108 S5 Zumbro R Minnesota/Wisconsin
108 S5 Zumbro Falls Minnesota 44.19N 92.24W
108 S5 Zumbrota Minnesota 44.19N 92.40W
77 M4 Zumela R Spain
90 F7 Zummu Nigeria 9.51N 12.59E
115 K8 Zumpango Mexico 19.46N 99.05W
115 K9 Zumpango del Río Mexico 17.36N 99.32W
110 J4 Zumwalt Oregon 45.38N 116.58W

113
48
48
48
48
101
100
110
Vancouver
108
Winnipeg
99
98
106
Quebec 98
Montreal 99
Ottawa 99
Toronto 99
104
Detroit 106
Boston 104
111
San Francisco
109
Chicago 106
New York 103
Philadelphia 104
Baltimore 104
Washington 104
103
107
St Louis
Los Angeles
112
115
105
Dallas
Fort Worth 112
Houston 112
New Orleans
116
105
New Providence 105
San Salvador
Mexico City
Puerto Rico
105
St Kitts
Nevis
Antigua
Guadeloupe
116
Jamaica
Martinique
Barbados
115
Grenada
Tobago
Trinidad
Aruba
Curaçao
Panama Canal
116 1:5 500 000 1:5 000 000
107 1:2 500 000
103 1:1 250 000 & larger

North America
Key to map plates